To - Mam.

Oxford Thesaurus of English

From Edward.

2006.

Oxford Thesaurus of English

SECOND EDITION

OXFORD
UNIVERSITY PRESS

Great Clarendon Street, Oxford OX2 6DP

Oxford University Press is a department of the University of Oxford.
It furthers the University's objective of excellence in research, scholarship,
and education by publishing worldwide in

Oxford New York

Auckland Bangkok Buenos Aires Cape Town Chennai
Dar es Salaam Delhi Hong Kong Istanbul Karachi Kolkata
Kuala Lumpur Madrid Melbourne Mexico City Mumbai
Nairobi São Paulo Shanghai Taipei Tokyo Toronto

First edition 2000
Second edition 2004

British Library Cataloguing in Publication Data
Data available

Library of Congress Cataloging in Publication Data
Data available

ISBN-13: 978-0-19-860862-2
ISBN-10: 0-19-860862-4

10 9 8 7 6 5 4 3 2

Typeset in Swift and Arial
by Interactive Sciences Ltd.
Printed in Great Britain by
William Clowes Ltd., Beccles, Suffolk

Contents

Editorial staff

Editor
Maurice Waite

For the first edition

Chief Editor
Patrick Hanks

Maurice Waite
Sara Hawker
Catherine Bailey
Martin Coleman
Chris Cowley
Lucinda Coventry
David Edmonds
Muriel Summersgill
Valerie Fairhurst

Note on trademarks and proprietary status

This thesaurus includes some words which have, or are asserted to have, proprietary status as trademarks or otherwise. Their inclusion does not imply that they have acquired for legal purposes a non-proprietary or general significance, nor any other judgement concerning their legal status. In cases where the editorial staff have some evidence that a word has proprietary status this is indicated in the entry for that word by the label *trademark*, but no judgement concerning the legal status of such words is made or implied thereby.

Preface

The word thesaurus comes from the Greek word *thesauros*, meaning 'storehouse' or 'treasure'. This is an apt description, because a thesaurus is a kind of treasure trove of the language, allowing you to explore its richness and variety. By listing groups of words that have similar meanings to each other, a thesaurus offers a choice of alternative words (synonyms) that can be used in place of one that you already have in mind.

Thus a thesaurus helps you to express yourself more accurately and in more interesting and varied ways. It is an invaluable tool for anyone who writes, whether for memos and reports at work, essays and dissertations at school and college, letters to business contacts, friends, or potential employers, or creative writing for a living or for pleasure. A thesaurus can provide the answer when a word is on the tip of your tongue, or it can expand your vocabulary to help you find new ways of saying what you want to. A thesaurus can also help in solving crossword puzzles and with many other word games.

The *Oxford Thesaurus of English*, first published in 2000 and now appearing in its second edition, contains an unrivalled number of alternative and opposite words: well over 600,000 in total. It is the most comprehensive one-volume thesaurus available, including not only everyday words but also unusual and colourful words, specialist terms, and archaic and obsolete terms. There are more than 16,000 entries, arranged A–Z, which means that you only have to go one place to find what you are looking for, and there is no need for a bulky index. For each of those 16,000 entries, there is an average of 38 alternatives, carefully chosen, sorted, and arranged to help you find the word you need as quickly as possible.

In addition to the standard entries, the *Oxford Thesaurus of English* offers an array of special features designed to enhance the usefulness and accessibility of the book. 'Choose the Right Word' panels explore in detail the differences between close synonyms such as *brusque*, *abrupt*, *curt*, and *terse*; the findings presented here, new to this edition, are the result of sophisticated computational analysis of how these words are used in real English, giving the user the fullest and most accurate account available. Also new to this edition are over 1300 Word Links, at 720 entries, to words which are not synonyms but which have another kind of relation to the headword: for example, at *cat* there are terms for the male and female cat (*tom*, *queen*) as well as the adjective relating to cats (*feline*).

Lastly, there is a new Word List section in the centre of the book, offering hundreds of lists covering everything from types of cheese to species of bird and names of dances. These are cross-referenced from within the main text but can also be used independently, ideal for crossword and word-game enthusiasts.

For a quick tour of the main features of the *Oxford Thesaurus of English*, look at 'How to use this thesaurus' on pp. xi–xii. The Introduction on the next few pages gives more details on the contents and organization of *OTE* and how to get the most out of it.

Introduction

The *Oxford Thesaurus of English* (*OTE*) has been compiled using new evidence in new ways, in order to create an original work of reference that will be most useful to a wide range of users for many different purposes. It is an independent resource in its own right, but it may also be viewed as a companion volume to the *Oxford Dictionary of English*, Oxford's ground-breaking one-volume dictionary which, based on systematic analysis of hundreds of millions of words of real English, presents the most accurate picture of the language available. *OTE* draws on the same data to give sets of words compiled according to their similarity in meaning and checked for actual usage against the evidence in the Oxford English Corpus.

All thesauruses contain lists of words that are linked by having a similar or related meaning, but this thesaurus also contains:

- opposites (e.g. for the different senses of **smart**: *scruffy*, *unfashionable*, *stupid*, *slow*, and *gentle*).
- word links (e.g. words related to **horse**, such as *stallion*, *mare*, and *equine*)
- studies of synonyms with similar meanings, entitled 'Choose the Right Word' (e.g. *brusque*, *abrupt*, *curt*, and *terse*)
- advice on pairs of confusingly similar words (e.g. "**militate or mitigate?**")
- a central reference section of word lists (e.g. **herbs**: *angelica*, *anise*, *basil*, *bay leaf*, *bergamot*, etc.)

For more information on these features, see the relevant sections on p. x.

Selection of entries

The primary purpose of *OTE* is to give synonyms for the common everyday words of English: words with roughly the same meaning as the entry word (headword). Some words, especially those for animals, plants, and physical objects, do not have synonyms, so they do not get entries in a thesaurus. You will not find synonyms of *gerbil* or *geranium*, but there is an entry for *squirrel* because of the phrasal verb *squirrel something away*, which has synonyms such as *save*, *put aside*, and *stash away*.

The words selected as headwords are general words that non-specialists are likely to want to look up. It is the job of a dictionary, not a thesaurus, to explain the meanings of unusual words, such as *supererogatory*, so such words do not get an alphabetical entry here. However, *supererogatory* is given as a synonym at entries for the more familiar words *inessential*, *needless*, and *unnecessary*. A thesaurus can thus lead the user from the familiar to the unfamiliar, improving his or her word power.

Homonyms

Homonyms are words that are written the same but have different and unrelated meanings, such as the *bank* of a river or lake and a *bank* that looks after people's money. Each has its own numbered entry, thus:

bank[1] ... *the banks of Lake Michigan*
bank[2] ... *I paid the money into my bank*

Synonyms

It is sometimes argued that no two words have exactly the same meaning. Even words as similar in meaning as *close* and *shut* may have slightly different nuances. *Closing* a shop implies that the shop is no longer open for business, so no one can come in. On the other hand, *shutting* a shop implies that the shop is being made secure, so that nothing can be taken out. A similar distinction is found between *strong* and *powerful*: *powerful enemies* may threaten from outside, but a *strong defence* on the inside will deter them from attacking. However, these are unusually subtle distinctions. For most practical purposes, *close* and *shut* have the same meaning, as do *strong* and *powerful*. Other synonyms are more distant, or emphasize different aspects of the meaning. For example, another close synonym of *strong* is *muscular*, but it places much more emphasis on physical strength. By contrast, *stalwart* and *staunch* are synonyms that emphasize more abstract aspects of this meaning of *strong*. *Forceful*, *secure*, *durable*, *loud*, *intense*, *bright*, and *alcoholic* are other close synonyms of strong, but all in quite different senses. They are not, of course, synonyms of each other.

In this book, the broadest possible definition of the term 'synonym' has been adopted, as being the one that will be most useful to users. Even words whose meaning is quite distantly related to that of the headword are supplied if they can be used to get the same message across in appropriate contexts or if they are synonymous with a part of the meaning of the headword.

The synonyms in each entry are grouped together in synonym sets. Major synonym sets correspond roughly to different senses of a word in a dictionary, but the divisions are also governed by the matches between headwords and synonyms. Each major synonym set is numbered, and many have finer subdivisions, which are separated by semicolons.

At the start of almost every synonym set is a 'core synonym': the term which is closest in meaning to the headword in that particular sense. Core synonyms are printed in **bold**. If no one synonym is particularly close, there may be no bold core synonym. Some synonym sets have more than one core synonym; for example at *avant-garde* (adjective), both *innovative* and *advanced* are very close in meaning to the headword, so both are given as core synonyms. Two different core synonyms within the same sense group may emphasize slightly different aspects of the meaning of the headword. For example, at *dutiful*, the first core synonym given is *conscientious*, followed by a group of words closely related to this aspect of its meaning. Then, after a semicolon, a second core synonym, *obedient*, is given, with a further group of synonyms related to that aspect.

Synonyms whose usage is restricted in some way, such as regional expressions and informal or very formal words, are placed at the end of each major synonym set and labelled accordingly. See **Register** below.

Illustrative examples

Almost every synonym set in *OTE* is illustrated with a carefully chosen example of the word in use in the relevant sense. These are authentic examples of natural usage taken from the Oxford English Corpus (see **Linguistic evidence** below). The examples can therefore be trusted for guidance on using unfamiliar words in an idiomatic way, but it does not follow that each synonym given can be used in the example, in place of the headword.

Where part of an example is printed in ***bold italic*** type, this indicates that some or all of the synonyms can be substituted for that particular phrase, not just for the headword alone. Thus at *attached*, the example given is:

> *she was very **attached to** her brother*

because the synonyms are equivalent to *attached to*:

> **fond of**, devoted to, full of regard for, full of admiration for; affectionate towards, tender towards, caring towards; *informal* mad about, crazy about, nuts about.

Linguistic evidence

OTE was compiled using the Oxford English Corpus, the collective name for Oxford's holdings of language databases amounting currently to over 300 million words of written and spoken English, which are in machine-readable form and available for computational and lexicographical analysis. The text is drawn from a very diverse range of sources (from scholarly journals to internet chatrooms, via novels and newspapers), either as large portions of continuous text or as short extracts selected for the ever-growing database of the Oxford Reading Programme by its international network of readers.

The Oxford English Corpus allows lexicographers to sort and analyse thousands of examples in context and thereby see more clearly than ever before how words are actually used. For the specific purposes of this thesaurus they have been able to:

- confirm whether a word has senses for which there are suitable synonyms
- check the sense of words being selected as synonyms
- actively find synonyms which have not previously been recorded.

The Corpus is also used to obtain the sentences and phrases given as examples of usage.

Idiomatic phrases and phrasal verbs

English is full of idiomatic expressions—phrases whose meaning is more than the sum of their parts. For example, *a shot in the dark* means 'a guess', while *a shot in the arm* means 'a boost'. Neither of these has very much to do with more literal meanings of *shot*. Phrasal verbs are expressions such as *book in* and *turn out*, consisting of a verb plus a particle. The meaning of a phrasal verb is also often quite idiomatic; for example, the meanings of *take off* are quite distinct from the meanings of *take*. This thesaurus includes a rich selection of both kinds of idiomatic expression, and provides synonyms for each. If a word is used as both a noun and a verb, the idiomatic expressions are entered as subentries under the part of speech in which the word is used. Thus, *by the book* is given under the noun senses of *book*, while *book in* is given under the verb senses.

Register: standard vs. informal and regional English

Informal usage is more prevalent than it was even just a few years ago. People may be heard using slang expressions in quite formal contexts, while the use of swear words and taboo words is on the increase. Taboos generally are weakening, though more so in Australia, where *bastard* is scarcely different from *guy* or *chap*, and less so in southern US States such as Texas. This thesaurus contains a rich selection of informal and vulgar synonyms for more formal expressions. Users who wish to avoid giving offence should treat the *vulgar slang* labels as warning notices.

Most of the synonyms given are, of course, part of standard English; that is, they are in normal use in both speech and writing everywhere in the world, at many different levels of formality, ranging from official documents to casual conversation. These general synonyms are given first in each synonym set. Some words, however, are appropriate only in particular contexts, and these are placed after the standard expressions and labelled accordingly. The technical term for these differences in levels of usage is 'register'. The main register labels used in this thesaurus are the following:

informal: normally used only in contexts such as conversations or letters between friends, e.g. *swig* as a synonym for *drink*.

vulgar slang: informal language that may cause offence, usually because it refers to bodily functions.

formal: normally used only in writing, in contexts such as official documents, e.g. *dwelling* as a synonym for *home*.

technical: normally used only in technical and specialist language, though not necessarily restricted to any specific field, e.g. *littoral* as a synonym for *beach*. Words used in specific fields are given appropriate labels, e.g. *Medicine*, *Christianity*.

literary: found only or mainly in literature written in an 'elevated' style, e.g. *ambrosial* as a synonym for *delicious*.

dated: no longer used by the majority of English speakers, but still encountered occasionally, especially among the older generation, e.g. *measure one's length* as a synonym for *fall down*.

historical: still used today, but only to refer to some practice or article that is no longer part of the modern world, e.g. *ruff*, the type of collar.

humorous: used with the intention of sounding funny or playful, e.g. *terminological inexactitude* as a synonym for *lie*.

archaic: very old-fashioned language, not in ordinary use at all today, but sometimes used to give a deliberately old-fashioned effect, or found in works of the past that are still widely read, e.g. *aliment* as a synonym for *food*.

rare: not in common use, e.g. *acclivitous* as a synonym for *steep*.

World English

It is a truism that English is now a world language. In this thesaurus, particular care has been taken to include synonyms from every variety of English, not just British; and when these are exclusively or very strongly associated with a region of the world they are labelled as such.

The main regional standards are British (abbreviated to *Brit.*), North American (*N. Amer.*), Australian and New Zealand (*Austral./NZ*), South African (*S. African*), Indian (in the sense of the variety of English found throughout the subcontinent), and West Indian (*W. Indian*). If the distinction is very clear, finer labelling may be used, as with *beer parlour*, a Canadian synonym for *bar*.

Scottish, Irish, and Northern English are varieties within the British Isles containing distinctive vocabulary items of their own. The main synonyms found as regional terms of this kind are entered and labelled accordingly.

The term for something found mainly or exclusively in a particular country or region (although it may be mentioned in any variety of English) is identified by an indication such as '(*in the Caribbean*)'. An example is *key* (as a synonym for *island*).

Many regionally restricted terms are informal, rather than being part of the standard language. Writers in the northern hemisphere in search of local colour may be delighted to learn that an Australian synonym for *sordid* is *scungy*, while Australian writers may find it equally useful to be given equivalent British terms, *manky* and *grotty*.

Words that are used in English but still generally regarded is foreign are labelled with their language of origin. For example, among the synonyms for *hotel* are: *French* pension, auberge; *Spanish* posada, parador; *Portuguese* pousada; *Italian* pensione; *German* Gasthaus.

Opposites

Many synonym sets are followed by one or more words that have the opposite meaning from the headword, often called 'antonyms'. There are several different kinds of opposite. *True* and *false* are absolute opposites, with no middle ground. Logically, a statement is either true or false: it cannot be slightly true or rather false. *Hot* and *cold*, on the other hand, are opposites with gradations of meaning: it makes perfectly good sense to say that something is rather hot or very cold, and there are a number of words (*warm*, *tepid*, *cool*) which represent intermediate stages. It makes sense to ask about something "How hot is it?" but that commits the speaker to the notion that it is hot at least to some extent. So *hot* and *cold* are at opposite ends of a continuum, rather than being absolutes.

For many words, such as *senile*, there is no single word that serves as an opposite, but the phrase *in the prime of life* does the job. In this book the broadest possible definition has been adopted, giving the maximum amount of information to the user. In some cases, a phrasal opposite is given for a phrasal subentry, e.g. *bottle things up* as an opposite for *let off steam*.

The antonyms given in this book are not the only possible opposites, but they are usually the furthest in meaning from the headword. By looking up the 'opposite' word as an entry in its own right, the user will generally find a much larger range of opposites to choose from. For example, the entry for *delete* includes:

> OPPOSITES add, insert.

Both *add* and *insert* are entries in their own right and give synonyms such as *include*, *append*, and *interpolate*.

Word links

The 'Word Links' panels at the end of certain entries supply words which are not actual synonyms but which have a different kind of relation to the headword. For example, at *milk*, the adjective relating to milk is given (*lactic*); at *town*, the related adjectives *urban*, *municipal*, and the rarer *oppidan*. Examples of other types of relation include collective nouns (e.g. *school* at *dolphin*, or *charm* at *finch*) and words for the male, female, or young of an animal (e.g. *levret* at *hare*, or *tom*, *queen*, and *kitten* at *cat*), phobias (e.g. *arachnophobia* at *spider*), the study of a particular subject (e.g. *bryology* at *moss*), or a geometric figure with a given number of sides (e.g. *pentagon* at *five*).

Some 'word links' are prefixes or suffixes related to the headword, such as *photo-* at *light*, *cerebro-* at *brain*, and *-metry* at *measurement*; knowledge of prefixes and suffixes helps the user to understand many new or unfamiliar words, such as *photometry* and *cerebrospinal*.

'Choose the Right Word' panels

No two synonyms are exactly the same: they may have subtly different meanings or be used in different contexts. For instance, the words *blunt*, *candid*, *forthright*, *frank*, and *outspoken* are all synonyms of each other because they all have roughly the same meaning, but there are subtle differences. There are 120 'Choose the Right Word' panels devoted to explaining the differences in meaning between groups of close synonyms totalling well over 400. The distinctions are based on careful analysis of actual usage as recorded in the Oxford English Corpus (see **Linguistic Evidence** above). This analysis involved the most up-to-date computational techniques to sift large amounts of data, as well as traditional lexicographical analysis.

Confusables

There are, in addition, 45 panels explaining the difference between pairs of words such as *militate* and *mitigate*, *flaunt* and *flout*, or *principal* and *principle*, that may cause difficulty because they are written or pronounced similarly but have different meanings.

Word lists

The new centre section of *OTE* contains over 400 word lists to supplement the main entries. While the main entry for, say, *sport* gives synonyms for *sport*—*game*, *recreation*, etc.—the list entitled 'Sports' in the centre section gives the names of particular sports—*archery*, *badminton*, *curling*, *dressage*, etc. These lists make *OTE* an invaluable aid to crossword-solving and a fascinating source of encyclopedic information on subjects as diverse as clouds, cocktails, marsupials, and martial arts. There are cross-references to these lists from appropriate words in both the main text and the list section itself.

How to use this thesaurus

headword

part of speech of headword

core synonym

book *See centre pages for list of* **Stories** *(Types of Story and Novel)*
▶ **noun 1** *he published his first book in 1610* **volume**, tome, work, printed work, publication, title, opus, treatise; novel, storybook; manual, handbook, guide, companion, reference book; paperback, hardback, softback; *historical* yellowback.

example of use

2 *he scribbled a few notes in his book* **notepad**, notebook, pad, memo pad, exercise book, binder; ledger, record book, log, logbook, chronicle, journal, diary, daybook; *Brit.* jotter, pocketbook; *N. Amer.* scratch pad; *French* cahier.

form of the headword for which synonyms are given

3 **(books)** *the council had to balance its books* **accounts**, records, archives; account book, record book, ledger, log, balance sheet, financial statement.

noun phrase entered under noun section

□ **by the book** *he does all his police work by the book* **according to the rules**, in accordance with the rules, within the law, abiding by the law, lawfully, legally, legitimately, licitly; honestly, fairly, openly; *informal* on the level, on the up and up, fair and square.

▶ **verb 1** *Steven booked a table at their favourite restaurant* **reserve**, make a reservation for, arrange in advance, prearrange, arrange for, order; charter, hire; *informal* bag; *dated* engage, bespeak.

label indicating currency of following synonyms

2 *we booked a number of events in the Wellington Festival* **arrange**, programme, schedule, timetable, line up, secure, fix up, lay on; *N. Amer.* slate.

phrasal verb entered under verb section

□ **book in** *he booked in at the St Francis Hotel* **register**, check in, enrol, record/log one's arrival.

WORD LINKS

list of books	**bibliography**
book enthusiast	**bibliophile, bibliomane**
relating to rare books	**antiquarian**

article explaining the difference between a confusable pair of words

flaunt or flout?

It is a common error to use **flaunt** as though it meant the same as **flout**. *Flaunt* means 'display ostentatiously', as in *tourists flaunting their wealth*. *Flout*, on the other hand, means 'defy or disobey (a rule)', as in *timber companies are continuing to flout environmental laws*. Saying that someone *flaunts the rules* is an error due to similarity in sound and to the element of ostentation involved in *flouting* a regulation.

homonym number showing that there are other entries for *lead*

pronunciation

lead[2] (rhymes with 'bed') ▶ **noun** *he was removing the lead from the man's chest* **bullet**, pellet, ball, slug; shot, buckshot, ammunition.

WORD LINKS

relating to lead	**plumbic, plumbous**
related prefix	**plumb- (e.g. *plumbate*)**

list of words, in centre section, for different types of rock

Rocks

See also **Gems** **Minerals**

sedimentary

arenite	breccia	coal	flint
argillite	chalk	conglomerate	ironstone
	chert	diatomite	limestone
	claystone	dolomite	marl ...

peculiar ▶ adjective **1** *something even more peculiar began to happen* **strange**, unusual, odd, funny, curious, bizarre, weird, uncanny, queer, unexpected, unfamiliar, abnormal, atypical, anomalous, untypical, different, out of the ordinary, out of the way; exceptional, rare, extraordinary, remarkable; puzzling, mystifying, mysterious, perplexing, baffling, unaccountable, incongruous, uncommon, irregular, singular, deviant, aberrant, freak, freakish; suspicious, dubious, questionable; eerie, unnatural; *Scottish* unco; *French* outré; *informal* fishy, creepy, spooky; *Brit. informal* rum; *N. Amer. informal* bizarro.
OPPOSITES normal, ordinary.
2 *his peculiar behaviour at the airport* **bizarre**, eccentric, strange, odd, weird, queer, funny, unusual, abnormal, idiosyncratic, unconventional, outlandish, offbeat, freakish, quirky, quaint, droll, zany, off-centre; *informal* wacky, freaky, kooky, screwy, kinky, oddball, cranky; *N. Amer. informal* off the wall, wacko; *Austral./NZ informal, dated* dilly.
3 (*informal*) *I still feel a bit peculiar* **unwell**, ill, poorly, bad, out of sorts, indisposed, not oneself, sick, queasy, nauseous, nauseated, peaky, liverish, green about the gills, run down, washed out; *Brit.* off, off colour; *informal* under the weather, below par, not up to par, funny, rough, lousy, rotten, awful, terrible, dreadful, crummy, seedy; *Brit. informal* grotty, ropy; *Scottish informal* wabbit, peely-wally; *Austral./NZ informal* crook; *rare* peaked, peakish.
4 *attitudes and mannerisms* ***peculiar to*** *the islanders* **characteristic of**, typical of, representative of, belonging to, indicative of, symptomatic of, suggestive of, exclusive to, like, in character with.
5 *Elena added her own peculiar contribution* **distinctive**, characteristic, distinct, different, individual, individualistic, distinguishing, typical, special, specific, representative, unique, idiosyncratic, personal, private, essential, natural; identifiable, unmistakable, conspicuous, notable, remarkable; *rare* singular.

semicolon marking subdivision of synonym set

label indicating origin of following synonym

words meaning the opposite of the headword

label indicating informality of following synonyms

label indicating that this sense of *peculiar* is used in informal language

label indicating regional use of following synonyms

rock[2] *See centre pages for lists of* **Gems** **Minerals** **Rocks**
▶ noun **1** *a narrow gully strewn with rocks* **boulder**, stone; *Austral. informal* goolie.
2 *a castle built on a rock* **crag**, cliff, tor, outcrop, outcropping.
3 *he was the rock on which his whole family relied* **foundation**, cornerstone, support, prop, mainstay, backbone; tower of strength, pillar of strength, bulwark, anchor, source of protection, source of security.
4 (*informal*) *she was wearing a massive rock on her fourth finger* **diamond**, precious stone, jewel.
□ **on the rocks** (*informal*) **1** *Sue's marriage was on the rocks* **in difficulty**, in trouble, breaking down, practically over, heading for divorce, heading for the divorce courts; in tatters, in pieces, destroyed, shattered, ruined, beyond repair.
2 *he ordered a Scotch on the rocks* **with ice**, on ice.

cross-reference to lists of words for different types of rock

number for each sense treated separately

words, prefixes, or suffixes with meanings related to that of the headword

WORD LINKS

related prefixes	**litho-** (e.g. ***lithography***), **petro-** (e.g. ***petroleum***)
related suffix	**-lite** (e.g. ***hyalite***)
study of rocks	**lithology, petrology, petrography**

article explaining the differences between a group of close synonyms

CHOOSE THE RIGHT WORD

strange, odd, curious, peculiar

These words are all applied to things that are unusual or unfamiliar; they generally also suggest that something is in some way surprising.

- **Strange** is the most neutral term for something that is not expected or is hard to understand or explain (*this is strange behaviour for a left-wing party | he looked at her with a strange expression*). This is the only word of the four that can be used in the expression *strange to say*, as in *I went to see 'Fallen Angels', which, strange to say, is a hit.*
- **Odd** gives a stronger sense that the speaker or writer is perplexed (*do you think it odd that I pay her bills? | they were an odd family*).
- Describing something as **curious** implies that one finds it not only strange or puzzling but also interesting or appealing (*the church has a curious history | the room is filled with a curious mixture of people*). It rarely has the connotation of deviance that the other words can have.
- Something described as **peculiar** is felt to be very strange, even disturbingly so (*he was struck by the peculiar appearance of a group of birds | whoever thought up that joke has a peculiar sense of humour*).

aback ▶ adverb
□ **take someone aback** *Joanna was taken aback by the violence of his reaction* **surprise**, shock, stun, stagger, astound, astonish, startle, take by surprise; dumbfound, daze, nonplus, stop someone in their tracks, stupefy, take someone's breath away; shake (up), jolt, throw, unnerve, disconcert, disturb, disquiet, unsettle, discompose, bewilder; *informal* flabbergast, knock for six, knock sideways, knock out, floor, strike dumb.

abandon ▶ verb **1** *the party has abandoned policies which made it unelectable* **renounce**, relinquish, dispense with, forswear, disclaim, disown, disavow, discard, wash one's hands of; give up, drop, do away with, jettison; *informal* ditch, scrap, scrub, axe, junk.
OPPOSITES keep, claim.
2 *by that stage, she had abandoned painting* **give up**, stop, cease, drop, forgo, desist from, have done with, abjure, abstain from, discontinue, break off, refrain from, set/lay aside; *informal* cut out, kick, jack in, pack in, quit.
OPPOSITES continue; take up.
3 *he abandoned his wife and children* **desert**, leave, leave high and dry, turn one's back on, cast aside, break (up) with; jilt, strand, leave stranded, leave in the lurch, throw over; *informal* run/walk out on, dump, ditch; *archaic* forsake.
OPPOSITE stick by.
4 *the skipper gave the order to abandon ship* **vacate**, leave, quit, evacuate, withdraw from.
5 *an attempt to persuade businesses not to abandon the area to inner-city deprivation* **relinquish**, surrender, give up, cede, yield, leave.
6 *she abandoned herself to the sensuousness of the music* **indulge in**, give way to, give oneself up to, yield to, lose oneself to/in.
OPPOSITE control oneself.
▶ noun *reckless abandon* **uninhibitedness**, recklessness, lack of restraint, lack of inhibition, unruliness, wildness, impulsiveness, impetuosity, immoderation, wantonness.
OPPOSITE self-control.

abandoned ▶ adjective **1** *an abandoned child* **deserted**, forsaken, cast aside/off; jilted, stranded, rejected; *informal* dumped, ditched.
2 *an abandoned tin mine* **unused**, disused, neglected, idle; deserted, unoccupied, uninhabited, empty.
3 *a wild, abandoned dance* **uninhibited**, reckless, unrestrained, unruly, wild, unbridled, impulsive, impetuous; immoderate, wanton.

abandonment ▶ noun **1** *she will be charged with child abandonment* **desertion**, neglect, stranding; jilting, betrayal.
2 *the buildings were used as rubbish pits after abandonment* **disuse**, evacuation, neglect.
3 *abandonment of the reform plan would probably result in hyperinflation* **renunciation**, relinquishment, rejection, withdrawal, dropping, cessation, discontinuation, termination, stopping, surrender, dispensation.
OPPOSITE adoption.

abase ▶ verb *I watched my colleagues **abasing themselves** before the dean* **humble**, humiliate, belittle, demean, lower, degrade, disgrace, disparage, debase, cheapen, discredit, mortify, bring low, demote, reduce; grovel, kowtow, bow and scrape, toady, fawn; *informal* crawl, suck up to someone, lick someone's boots.

abasement ▶ noun *the dog flattened himself at Mark's feet, tail thumping in abject abasement* **humility**, humbleness, humiliation, belittlement, lowering, degradation, disgrace, mortification.
OPPOSITE pride.

abashed ▶ adjective *the boy looked down, abashed* **embarrassed**, ashamed, shamefaced, remorseful, mortified, conscience-stricken, humiliated, humbled, taken aback, disconcerted, nonplussed, discomfited, discomposed, distressed, chagrined, perturbed, confounded, dismayed, dumbfounded, crestfallen, sheepish, red-faced, blushing, confused, put out of countenance, discountenanced, with one's tail between one's legs; *informal* floored.
OPPOSITES unabashed, undaunted.

abate ▶ verb **1** *thankfully, the storm had abated | the recession showed no signs of abating* **subside**, die down/away/out, drop off/away, lessen, ease (off), let up, decrease, diminish, moderate, decline, fade, dwindle, slacken, recede, cool off, tail off, peter out, taper off, wane, ebb, relent, desist, weaken, become weaker, come to an end; *archaic* remit.
OPPOSITE intensify.
2 *energy efficiency may be the quickest way to abate emissions of carbon dioxide* **decrease**, lessen, diminish, reduce, lower, moderate, ease, soothe, relieve, dampen, calm, tone down, alleviate, mitigate, mollify, allay, assuage, palliate, temper, appease, attenuate.
OPPOSITE increase.

abatement ▶ noun **1** *the storm still rages with no sign of abatement* **subsiding**, dying down/away/out, dropping off/away, lessening, easing (off), decrease, diminishing, moderation, decline, declining, fade, dwindling, cooling off, tailing off, petering out, tapering off, wane, waning, ebb, relenting, desisting, weakening.
OPPOSITE intensification.
2 *as though sensing some abatement of my ferocity, she spoke to me gently* **lessening**, decrease, moderation, easing, softening, soothing, relief, blunting, deadening, alleviation, mitigation, mollification, allaying, assuagement, palliation, tempering, appeasement, attenuation.
OPPOSITE intensification.
3 (*formal*) *the prospective purchaser demanded an abatement on the purchase price* **decrease**, reduction, lowering.
OPPOSITE increase.

abattoir ▶ noun **slaughterhouse**; *Brit.* butchery, knacker's yard; *archaic* shambles, butcher-row.

abbey ▶ noun *there was a Benedictine abbey here in the Middle Ages* **monastery**, **convent**, priory, cloister, friary, nunnery, religious house, religious community; *historical* charterhouse, cell; *rare* coenobium, coenoby.

WORD LINKS
relating to an abbey **abbatial**

abbot ▶ noun

WORD LINKS
relating to an abbot **abbatial**

abbreviate ▶ verb *they called the phenomenon long-term potentiation, soon abbreviated to LTP* **shorten**, reduce, cut, cut short/down, contract, condense, compress, abridge, truncate, clip, crop, pare down, prune, shrink, constrict, telescope, curtail; summarize, abstract, precis, synopsize, digest, edit.
OPPOSITES lengthen, expand, elongate.

CHOOSE THE RIGHT WORD

abbreviate, shorten, abridge, truncate, curtail
See SHORTEN.

abbreviated ▶ adjective *an abbreviated version of the declaration* **shortened**, reduced, cut, cut short/down, contracted, condensed, compressed, abridged, truncated, concise, compendious, compact, succinct, clipped, cropped, pared down, pruned, shrunk, constricted, telescoped; summary, thumbnail, summarized, synoptic, abstracted, edited (down).
OPPOSITES expanded, long.

abbreviation ▶ noun **1** *the abbreviation 'mAh' stands for milliamp hours* **shortened form**, short form, contraction, elision, acronym, initialism, symbol, diminutive.
OPPOSITE full form.

2 *she felt a slight irritation at the abbreviation of her name* **shortening**, reduction, cutting, cutting short/down, contraction, condensation, compression, abridgement, truncation, clipping, cropping, paring down, pruning, shrinking, constricting, telescoping.
OPPOSITE expansion.

abdicate ▶ **verb 1** *in 1936, Edward VIII abdicated in favour of George VI* **resign**, retire, quit, stand down, step down, bow out, renounce the throne; *archaic* demit.
OPPOSITE be crowned.
2 *Napoleon compelled Ferdinand to abdicate the throne* **resign from**, relinquish, renounce, give up, hand over, turn over, deliver up, surrender, vacate, forswear, abjure, cede; *Law* disclaim.
OPPOSITE accede to.
3 *the state virtually abdicated all responsibility for their welfare* **disown**, turn down, spurn, reject, renounce, give up, avoid, refuse, abnegate, relinquish, abjure, repudiate, waive, yield, forgo, abandon, surrender, deliver up, disgorge, cast aside, drop, turn one's back on, wash one's hands of; *informal* shirk; *archaic* forsake.
OPPOSITES accept, take on.

abdication ▶ **noun 1** *the monarchy is facing its biggest crisis since Edward VIII's abdication in 1936* **resignation**, retirement; relinquishment, renunciation, giving up, surrender, abjuration, vacation, ceding, cession; *archaic* demission.
OPPOSITE coronation.
2 *an abdication of responsibility* **disowning**, renunciation, rejection, refusal, avoidance, abnegation, relinquishment, abjuration, repudiation, waiving, yielding, forgoing, abandonment, surrender, disgorgement, casting aside.
OPPOSITE acceptance.

abdomen ▶ **noun** *I woke in the middle of the night with pains in my abdomen* **stomach**, belly, gut, middle, midriff, intestines; *informal* tummy, tum, insides, guts, corporation, maw, breadbasket, pot, paunch; *Austral. informal* bingy.

WORD LINKS
relating to the abdomen **abdominal, ventral, coeliac**
surgical incision of abdomen **laparotomy**

abdominal ▶ **adjective** *abdominal pain can be produced by too much caffeine* **stomach**, gastric, intestinal, stomachic, enteric, duodenal, visceral, coeliac, ventral.

abduct ▶ **verb** *she was abducted by two men and held for 36 hours* **kidnap**, carry off, seize, capture, run away/off with, make off with, spirit away, hold hostage, hold to ransom, hijack; *informal* snatch, shanghai, nobble; *archaic* ravish, rape.

aberrant ▶ **adjective** *Mrs Casper seems to be responsible for Billy's aberrant behaviour* **deviant**, deviating, divergent, abnormal, atypical, anomalous, digressive, irregular; nonconformist, rogue, transgressing; strange, odd, peculiar, uncommon, freakish, eccentric, quirky, exceptional, singular; twisted, warped, perverted.
OPPOSITES normal, typical.

aberration ▶ **noun 1** *economists said the figure was an aberration* **anomaly**, deviation, divergence, abnormality, irregularity, variation, digression, freak, rogue, rarity, quirk, oddity, curiosity, mistake.
2 *it is possible that, in a moment of aberration, the parent may strike the child* **abnormality**, irregularity, eccentricity, deviation, transgression, straying, lapse, aberrancy.
3 *the experience might have been no more than a temporary aberration of an exhausted mind* **disorder**, defect, disease, irregularity, instability, derangement, vagary.

abet ▶ **verb** *several villagers are accused of aiding and abetting the smugglers* **assist**, aid, help, lend a hand, support, back, encourage; cooperate with, collaborate with, work with, connive with, collude with, go along with, be in collusion with, be hand in glove with, side with; second, endorse, boost, favour, champion, sanction, succour; promote, further, expedite, push, give a push to, connive at, participate in.
OPPOSITE hinder.

abeyance ▶ **noun** *the project was left* **in abeyance** *for the time being* **suspension**, a state of suspension, a state of dormancy, a state of latency, a state of uncertainty, suspense, remission, reserve; pending, suspended, deferred, postponed, put off, put to one side, unattended, unfinished, incomplete, unresolved, undetermined, up in the air, betwixt and between; *informal* in cold storage, on ice, on the back burner, hanging fire.
OPPOSITES in hand, under way, continuing.

abhor ▶ **verb** *Walter abhorred sexism in every form* **detest**, hate, loathe, despise, abominate, execrate, regard with disgust, shrink from, recoil from, shudder at, be unable to bear, be unable to abide, feel hostility/aversion to, find intolerable, dislike, disdain, have an aversion to; *archaic* disrelish.
OPPOSITES love, admire, delight in.

abhorrence ▶ **noun** *my husband had an abhorrence of show and pomp* **hatred**, loathing, detestation, execration, revulsion, abomination, disgust, repugnance, horror, antipathy, odium, aversion, hostility, animosity, enmity, dislike, distaste, disdain, contempt; *archaic* disrelish; *rare* repellence, repellency.
OPPOSITES love, admiration, delight.

abhorrent ▶ **adjective** *the rack and thumbscrew are abhorrent to any civilized society* **detestable**, detested, hateful, hated, loathsome, loathed, despicable, despised, abominable, abominated, execrable, execrated, repellent, repugnant, repulsive, revolting, disgusting, distasteful, horrible, horrid, horrifying, awful, heinous, reprehensible, obnoxious, odious, nauseating, offensive, contemptible.
OPPOSITES admirable, loved.

abide ▶ **verb 1** (*informal*) *I cannot abide those Afghan caps everyone is wearing now* **tolerate**, bear, stand, put up with, endure, suffer, accept, cope with, live with, brook, support, take, countenance, face, handle; *informal* stick, swallow, stomach, hack, wear.
2 *at least one memory will abide* **continue**, remain, survive, last, persist, stay, hold on, live on.
OPPOSITES fade, disappear.

□ **abide by** *he expected everybody to abide by the rules* **comply with**, obey, observe, follow, keep to, hold to, conform to, adhere to, stick to, stand by, act in accordance with, uphold, heed, pay attention to, agree to/with, consent to, accede to, accept, acquiesce in, go along with, acknowledge, respect, defer to.
OPPOSITES flout, reject.

abiding ▶ **adjective** *his collections reflect his abiding interest in Italy* **enduring**, lasting, persisting, long-lasting, lifelong, continuing, remaining, surviving, standing, fixed, durable, everlasting, perpetual, eternal, unending, constant, permanent, stable, unchanging, steadfast, immutable.
OPPOSITES short-lived, ephemeral, transitory.

ability ▶ **noun 1** *he was proud of his daughter's ability to read and write* **capacity**, capability, potential, potentiality, power, faculty, aptness, facility, propensity, wherewithal, means, preparedness.
OPPOSITES inability, incapacity.
2 *they are taught French in sets based on their ability | they criticized the president's leadership abilities* **talent**, skill, expertise, expertness, adeptness, aptitude, skilfulness, prowess, mastery, artistry, calibre, accomplishment; competence, competency, proficiency; dexterity, adroitness, deftness, cleverness, smartness, flair, finesse, gift, knack, brilliance, genius; qualification, resources; *French* savoir faire; *informal* know-how.

ab initio ▶ **adverb & adjective** (*Latin*) *the transactions were void ab initio* **from the beginning**, from the start, initially, originally, from first principles, to begin with, to start with, primarily; *Music* da capo; *informal* from scratch, from the word go.

abject ▶ **adjective 1** *many such families are living in abject poverty* **wretched**, miserable, hopeless, pathetic, pitiful, pitiable, piteous, stark, sorry, forlorn, woeful, lamentable, degrading, appalling, atrocious, awful.
2 *an abject sinner* **contemptible**, base, low, vile, worthless, debased, degraded, despicable, ignominious, mean, unworthy, sordid, ignoble, shabby.
OPPOSITES proud, respected.
3 *an abject apology* **obsequious**, grovelling, crawling, creeping, fawning, toadyish, servile, cringing, snivelling, ingratiating, toadying, sycophantic, submissive, craven, humiliating.
OPPOSITE proud.

abjure ▶ **verb** *I have abjured all stimulants* **renounce**, relinquish, reject, dispense with, forgo, forswear, disavow, abandon, deny, gainsay, disclaim, repudiate, give up, spurn, abnegate, wash one's hands of, drop, do away with; eschew, abstain from, refrain from; *informal* kick, jack in, pack in; *Law* disaffirm; *archaic* forsake.

ablaze ▶ **adjective 1** *rioters overturned cars and set them ablaze* **alight**, aflame, on fire, in flames, flaming, burning, blazing, raging, fiery, lit, lighted, ignited; *literary* afire.
OPPOSITE extinguished.
2 *every window was ablaze with light* **lit up**, alight, gleaming, glowing, aglow, illuminated, brilliant, bright, shining, radiant, shimmering, sparkling, flashing, dazzling, luminous, lustrous, incandescent.
OPPOSITE dark.
3 *his piercing eyes were ablaze with fury* **passionate**, impassioned, aroused, excited, stimulated, eager, animated, incensed, intense, heated, ardent, fervent, frenzied, feverish.

CHOOSE THE RIGHT WORD

able, competent, capable, efficient
See COMPETENT.

able ▶ **adjective** *the university attracts able students from across the UK* **intelligent**, clever, brilliant, talented, skilful, skilled, accomplished, gifted, masterly, virtuoso, expert; proficient, apt, good, adroit, adept, qualified, fit, suited, suitable; capable, competent, efficient, effective.
OPPOSITES incompetent, incapable, inept.

□ **able to** *visitors will be able to buy some of the articles on display* **allowed to**, free to, in a position to; capable of, qualified to, competent to, equal to, up to, fit to, prepared to.

able-bodied ▶ adjective *every able-bodied man was required to serve in the armed forces* **healthy**, **fit**, in good health, robust, strong, sound, sturdy, vigorous, hardy, hale and hearty, athletic, muscular, strapping, tough, powerful, mighty, rugged, burly, brawny, stalwart, lusty, staunch; in good shape, in good trim, in tip-top condition, in fine fettle, fighting fit, as fit as a fiddle, as fit as a flea, as strong as an ox; *informal* husky.
OPPOSITES infirm, frail; disabled.

ablutions ▶ plural noun (*formal or humorous*) *she took up water ready for the morning ablutions* **washing**, cleansing, bathing, showering, scrubbing, purification; wash, bath, shower, toilet, soak, dip, douche; *rare* lavage, lavation.

abnegate ▶ verb *he cannot abnegate the responsibility which the choice confers on him* **renounce**, reject, refuse, abandon, spurn, abdicate, give up, relinquish, abjure, repudiate, forswear, disavow, cast aside, drop, turn one's back on, wash one's hands of, eschew; *archaic* forsake.
OPPOSITE accept.

abnegation ▶ noun **1** *to ignore these issues would be a serious abnegation of their responsibilities* **renunciation**, rejection, refusal, abandonment, abdication, surrender, giving up, relinquishment, abjuration, repudiation, denial, eschewal, disavowal, casting aside.
OPPOSITE acceptance.
2 *such people are capable of abnegation and unselfishness* **self-denial**, self-sacrifice, abstinence, temperance, continence, asceticism, abstemiousness, austerity, renunciation, resignation.
OPPOSITE self-indulgence.

abnormal ▶ adjective *the laboratory investigations often yielded abnormal results* **unusual**, uncommon, atypical, untypical, non-typical, unrepresentative, rare, isolated, irregular, anomalous, deviant, deviating, divergent, wayward, aberrant, freak, freakish; **strange**, odd, peculiar, curious, bizarre, weird, queer; eccentric, idiosyncratic, quirky; unexpected, unfamiliar, unconventional, surprising, unorthodox, singular, exceptional, extraordinary, out of the ordinary, out of the way; unnatural, perverse, perverted, twisted, warped, corrupt, unhealthy, distorted, malformed; *Brit.* out of the common; *informal* funny, oddball, off the wall, wacky, wacko, way out, freaky, kinky.
OPPOSITES normal, typical, common.

abnormality ▶ noun **1** *he was born with numerous abnormalities* **malformation**, deformity, irregularity, flaw; oddity, peculiarity, deviation, aberration, divergence, anomaly, idiosyncrasy, singularity, rarity.
2 *if the test shows any abnormality you may need further treatment* **unusualness**, uncommonness, strangeness, waywardness, oddness, unexpectedness, irregularity, singularity, atypicality, anomalousness, deviation, divergence, aberrance, aberration, freakishness, peculiarity, curiousness, eccentricity, idiosyncrasy, quirkiness, unorthodoxy.

abode ▶ noun (*formal*) *you are most welcome to my humble abode* **home**, house, place of residence/habitation, accommodation, habitat, base, seat; quarters, lodgings, rooms; address, location, place, whereabouts; *informal* pad, digs, diggings; *formal* dwelling, dwelling place, residence, habitation.

abolish ▶ verb *a bill to abolish the council tax* **put an end to**, do away with, get rid of, scrap, end, stop, terminate, eradicate, eliminate, exterminate, destroy, annihilate, stamp out, obliterate, wipe out, extinguish, quash, expunge, extirpate, annul, cancel, invalidate, nullify, void, dissolve, erase, delete; rescind, repeal, revoke, overturn; discontinue, remove, withdraw, retract, countermand, excise, drop, jettison, vitiate, abrogate; *informal* axe, ditch, junk, scrub, dump, chop, give something the chop, knock something on the head; *rare* deracinate.
OPPOSITES retain, create.

abolition ▶ noun *the abolition of free eye tests* **scrapping**, ending, stopping, doing away with, termination, eradication, elimination, extermination, destruction, annihilation, obliteration, quashing, extirpation; annulment, cancellation, invalidation, nullification, dissolution; revocation, repeal, rescindment, overturning, discontinuation, removal, withdrawal, retraction, countermanding, excising, vitiation, abrogation; *informal* axing, ditching, junking, scrubbing, dumping, chopping; *rare* deracination, rescission.
OPPOSITES retention; creation.

abominable ▶ adjective *the abominable slave trade* **loathsome**, detestable, hateful, odious, obnoxious, despicable, contemptible, damnable, cursed, accursed, diabolical; disgusting, revolting, repellent, repulsive, offensive, repugnant, abhorrent, reprehensible, atrocious, horrifying, execrable; foul, vile, wretched, base, miserable, horrible, awful, dreadful, appalling, abysmal, brutal, nauseating; horrid, nasty, disagreeable, unpleasant, distasteful; *informal* terrible, shocking, God-awful, beastly; *Brit. informal* chronic.
OPPOSITES good, admirable.

abominably ▶ adverb *I treated her abominably* **reprehensibly**, badly, dreadfully, appallingly, brutally, abysmally, nauseatingly, horridly, nastily; atrociously, horrifyingly, execrably, foully, vilely, wretchedly, miserably, horribly, awfully; disagreeably, unpleasantly, distastefully; hatefully, loathsomely, detestably, odiously; despicably, contemptibly, damnably, diabolically, disgustingly, revoltingly, repellently, repulsively, repugnantly, abhorrently; *informal* terribly, shockingly.
OPPOSITES well, admirably.

abominate ▶ verb *most New Yorkers abominate the countryside* **detest**, loathe, hate, abhor, despise, dislike, execrate, feel aversion/revulsion to, shudder at, recoil from, shrink from, be repelled by, not be able to bear/stand, find intolerable; *informal* be unable to stomach.
OPPOSITES like, love.

abomination ▶ noun **1** *in both wars, internment was an abomination* **atrocity**, disgrace, horror, obscenity, outrage, curse, torment, evil, crime, monstrosity, violation, bugbear, anathema, bane; *French* bête noire.
2 *he had a Calvinist abomination of indulgence* **detestation**, loathing, hatred, aversion, antipathy, revulsion, repugnance, abhorrence, odium, execration, disgust, horror, hostility, disdain, contempt, distaste, dislike.
OPPOSITES liking, love.

aboriginal ▶ adjective *the area's aboriginal inhabitants* **indigenous**, native; original, earliest, first, initial; ancient, primitive, primeval, primordial; *rare* autochthonous, autochthonic.
▶ noun *the social structure of the aboriginals* **native**, indigene, aborigine, local, original inhabitant; *rare* autochthon.

> **CHOOSE THE RIGHT WORD**
>
> **aboriginal, native, indigenous**
>
> *See* NATIVE.

aborigine ▶ noun. *See* ABORIGINAL.

abort ▶ verb **1** *I decided not to abort the pregnancy* **terminate**, end; have an abortion.
2 *this organism infects sheep and can cause pregnant ewes to abort* **miscarry**, have a miscarriage.
3 *the 'escape' key is used to abort the program* **halt**, stop, end, call off, cut short, discontinue, terminate, arrest, suspend, check, nullify; *informal* scrub, axe, pull the plug on.
OPPOSITES continue, complete.
4 *there are times when the mission aborts* **fail**, come to a halt, end, terminate, miscarry, go wrong, not succeed, fall through, break down, be frustrated, collapse, founder, come to grief, fizzle out, flop.
OPPOSITES succeed, complete.

abortion ▶ noun *she had an abortion* **termination**, miscarriage; *rare* feticide.

abortive ▶ adjective *the rebels who led the abortive coup were shot* **failed**, unsuccessful, non-successful, vain, thwarted, futile, useless, worthless, ineffective, ineffectual, to no effect, inefficacious, fruitless, unproductive, unavailing, to no avail, sterile, nugatory; *archaic* bootless.
OPPOSITES successful, fruitful.

abound ▶ verb *omens and prodigies abound in his work* **be plentiful**, be abundant, be numerous, proliferate, superabound, thrive, flourish, be thick on the ground; *informal* grow on trees; *Brit. informal* be two/ten a penny.
OPPOSITE be scarce.

□ **abound in/with** *a beautiful stream which abounded with trout and eels* **be full of**, overflow with, teem with, be packed with, be crowded with, be thronged with, be jammed with; be alive with, be overrun with, swarm with, bristle with, be bristling with, be infested with, be thick with; *informal* be crawling with, be lousy with, be stuffed with, be jam-packed with, be chock-a-block with, be chock-full of; *rare* pullulate with.

abounding ▶ adjective *Ruth had abounding strength and energy* **abundant**, plentiful, superabundant, considerable, copious, ample, lavish, luxuriant, profuse, boundless, munificent, bountiful, prolific, inexhaustible, generous; galore; *literary* plenteous.
OPPOSITES meagre, scanty.

about ▶ preposition **1** *a book about ancient Greece* **regarding**, concerning, with reference to, referring to, with regard to, with respect to, respecting, relating to, on, touching on, dealing with, relevant to, with relevance to, connected with, in connection with, on the subject of, in the matter of, apropos, re; *Scottish* anent.
2 *two hundred people were milling about the room* **around**, round, throughout, over, through, all over, in all parts of, on every side of, encircling, surrounding; here and there, everywhere.
3 *they aren't seen about here very often* **near**, nearby, close to, not far (away) from, a short distance from, in the vicinity of, in the neighbourhood of, within reach of, adjacent to, beside, around, a stone's throw away from; *informal* within spitting distance of, {a hop, skip, and a jump away from}.
4 *while I am about it, I had better apologize for what happened* **occupied with**, concerned with, busy with, taken up with, employed in, involved in, absorbed in, in the process of, in the course of, in the midst of, in the throes of; conducting, pursuing, following, practising.

▫ **about to** *I was about to climb into bed when the bell rang* **going to**, ready to, all set to, preparing to, intending to, soon to; on the point of, on the verge of, on the brink of, within an ace of.

▶ adverb **1** *there were babies crawling about in the grass* **around**, here and there, to and fro, back and forth, from place to place, hither and thither, in every direction, in all directions, abroad.
2 *although I hadn't seen him for two years, I knew he was about somewhere* **near**, nearby, around, about the place, hereabouts, not far off/away, close by, in the vicinity, in the neighbourhood, at hand, within reach, on the doorstep, (just) around the corner.
3 *we think the explosion has caused about £15,000 worth of damage* **approximately**, roughly, around, round about, in the neighbourhood/region of, in the area of, of the order of, something like; or so, or thereabouts, there or thereabouts, more or less, give or take a few, not far off; *Brit.* getting on for; *Latin* circa; *informal* as near as dammit; *N. Amer. informal* in the ballpark of.
OPPOSITES exactly, precisely.
4 *he gave orders to turn about* **in the opposite direction**, in the reverse direction, around, backwards, to face the other way.
5 *there was a lot of flu about* **around**, in circulation, in existence, current, going on, prevailing, prevalent, widespread, pervasive, endemic, happening, in the air, abroad.

about-turn (*Brit.*) ▶ noun **1** *he saluted, did an about-turn, and marched out of the tent* **about-face**, volte-face, turnaround, turnround, turnabout, U-turn; *informal* U-ey, one-eighty.
2 *the government was forced to make an embarrassing about-turn over the bill* **reversal**, retraction, backtracking, swing, shift, swerve, U-turn, volte-face, turnaround, turnround; change of heart, change of mind, sea change.
▶ verb *suddenly he about-turned and saluted again* **about-face**, turn around, turn round, turn about, do a U-turn, reverse.

above ▶ preposition **1** *light filtered through a tiny window above the door* **over**, higher (up) than, overlooking; on top of, atop, on, upon.
OPPOSITES below, under, beneath.
2 *no one above the rank of Colonel was willing to compromise himself* **superior to**, senior to, over, higher than, higher up than, more powerful than, more responsible than, ahead of; in charge of, commanding.
OPPOSITES below, beneath, junior to.
3 *you must be above suspicion of any impropriety* **beyond**, not subject to, insusceptible to, not liable to, not open to, not vulnerable to, not exposed to, not in danger of, superior to, out of reach of, immune to, exempt from.
4 *the Chinese valued pearls above gold* **more than**, over, before, rather than, in preference to, in favour of, instead of, sooner than.
5 *the increase is above the rate of inflation* **greater than**, more than, higher than, exceeding, in excess of, over, over and above, beyond, surpassing, upwards of.
OPPOSITES less than, below.
6 *the river above the bridge* **upstream from**.
7 *they live above the Arctic Circle* **north of**, northward(s) from.

▫ **above all** *the job offered wider horizons, higher status, and, above all, a valuable source of income* **most importantly**, before everything, beyond everything, first of all, most of all, chiefly, primarily, in the first place, first and foremost, mainly, principally, predominantly, especially, essentially, basically, elementally, in essence, at bottom; *informal* at the end of the day, when all is said and done.

▫ **above oneself** *ever since her promotion she'd been getting above herself* **conceited**, proud, arrogant, self-important, haughty, disdainful, snobbish, snobby, supercilious, imperious; *informal* stuck-up, cocky, high and mighty, snooty, uppity, uppish, big-headed, swollen-headed, too big for one's boots.

▶ adverb **1** *in the darkness above, something moved* **overhead**, on/at the top, on/at a higher place, high up, on high, up above, (up) in the sky, high above one's head, aloft, (up) in the heavens.
2 *we will return to some of the issues raised above* **earlier**, previously, before, formerly, further back.

▶ adjective *the above example was chosen to illustrate the underlying problem* **preceding**, precedent, previous, earlier, former, foregoing, prior, antecedent, above-stated; aforementioned, aforesaid; *rare* anterior, prevenient, precursive, supra.

above board ▶ adjective *he had set up a chain of more or less above-board casinos* **honest**, fair, open, frank, straight, overt, candid, forthright, unconcealed, trustworthy, unequivocal; legal, legitimate, lawful, licit; *informal* legit, kosher, pukka, by the book, fair and square, square, on the level, on the up and up, upfront.
OPPOSITES dishonest, shady.
▶ adverb *it's imperative that you play it all above board* **honestly**, fairly, openly, frankly, overtly, candidly, forthrightly, unequivocally; legally, legitimately, lawfully.
OPPOSITES dishonestly, shadily.

ab ovo ▶ adverb (*Latin*) *he was a great man ab ovo* **from the beginning**, from the start, from the first; from the egg; *informal* from the word go.

abracadabra ▶ exclamation hocus-pocus, open sesame; mumbo-jumbo.

abrade ▶ verb *the paintwork had been abraded over the years by the weather* **wear away/down**, wear, erode, scrape away, corrode, eat away at, gnaw away at, bite into, scour, rasp, strip, flay.

abrasion ▶ noun **1** *diamond's extreme resistance to abrasion* **wearing away/down**, wearing, erosion, scraping, corrosion, being eaten away, chafing, rubbing, stripping, flaying, excoriation.
2 *he had abrasions to his forehead* **graze**, scrape, scratch, cut, gash, laceration, tear, rent, slash, injury, contusion; sore, ulcer; *Medicine* trauma, traumatism.

abrasive ▶ adjective **1** *don't use abrasive kitchen cleaners* **grinding**, rubbing, polishing, coarse, caustic, harsh, mordant; corrosive, corroding, erosive, eroding.
2 *she was a tough girl with an abrasive manner* **caustic**, cutting, grating, biting, acerbic, vitriolic; rough, harsh, hard, tough, sharp, curt, brusque, stern, severe; wounding, nasty, cruel, callous, insensitive, unfeeling, unsympathetic, inconsiderate; *N. Amer.* acerb.
OPPOSITES kind, gentle.

abreast ▶ adverb *the roads were full of bicycles, three or more abreast* **in a row**, side by side, alongside, level, abeam, on a level, beside each other, shoulder to shoulder, cheek by jowl.

▫ **abreast of** *it can be a good idea to keep children abreast of current affairs* **up to date with**, up with, in touch with, informed about, familiar with, acquainted with, knowledgeable about, conversant with, au courant with, au fait with.
OPPOSITE out of touch with.

abridge ▶ verb *the editor reserves the right to abridge letters to fit the space available* **shorten**, cut, cut short/down, curtail, truncate, lessen, trim, crop, clip, pare down, prune; abbreviate, condense, contract, compress, reduce, decrease, diminish, shrink; summarize, give a summary of, sum up, abstract, give an abstract of, precis, give a precis of, synopsize, give a synopsis of, digest, give a digest of, outline, give an outline of, sketch, put in a nutshell, edit; *rare* epitomize.
OPPOSITES lengthen, expand on, pad out.

> **CHOOSE THE RIGHT WORD**
>
> **abridge, shorten, abbreviate, truncate, curtail**
>
> *See* SHORTEN.

abridged ▶ adjective *an abridged version of his inaugural lecture* **shortened**, cut, cut short, cut down, concise, condensed, contracted, compressed, abbreviated, reduced, decreased, diminished, curtailed, truncated, lessened, trimmed, cropped, clipped, pared down, pruned, shrunk; summarized, summary, abstracted, precised, synoptic, synopsized, digest, outline, thumbnail, sketch, edited; censored, bowdlerized, expurgated; *informal* potted.
OPPOSITES lengthened, expanded.

abridgement, **abridgment** ▶ noun *an abridgement of a book* **summary**, abstract, synopsis, precis, outline, résumé, sketch, truncation, digest, recapitulation, recap, summing-up, rundown, round-up, review, shortening, shortened version, abridged version, concise version, condensation; *rare* conspectus.
OPPOSITE expansion.

abroad ▶ adverb **1** *a valid passport is essential when travelling abroad* **overseas**, out of the country, to/in foreign parts, to/in a foreign country/land, over the sea, beyond the seas.
2 *rumours of his intention to visit a holy shrine were spread abroad* **widely**, far and wide, everywhere, {here, there, and everywhere}, in all directions; about, around, forth; publicly, extensively; *informal* every which way.
3 *the Christmas spirit was abroad* **at large**, current, in circulation, circulating, in the air, about, afoot, around, astir.

abrogate ▶ verb *the government has formally abrogated the 1977 treaty* **repudiate**, revoke, repeal, rescind, overturn, overrule, override, do away with, annul, cancel, break off, invalidate, nullify, void, negate, dissolve, countermand, veto, declare null and void, discontinue; renege on, go back on, backtrack on, reverse, retract, remove, withdraw, abolish, put an end to, get rid of, suspend, end, stop, quash, scrap; *Law* disaffirm, avoid, vacate, vitiate; *informal* axe, ditch, dump, chop, give something the chop, knock something on the head; *rare* deracinate.
OPPOSITES institute, introduce.

abrogation ▶ noun *the abrogation of the Net Book Agreement* **repudiation**, revocation, repeal, rescinding, rescindment, overturning, overruling, overriding, annulment, cancellation, invalidation, nullification, voiding, negation, dissolution, countermanding, vetoing, discontinuation, reversal, retraction, removal, withdrawal, abolition, suspension, ending, stopping, quashing, scrapping; *Law* rescission, disaffirmation, avoidance, vitiation; *informal* axing, ditching, dumping, chopping; *rare* deracination.
OPPOSITES institution, introduction.

abrupt ▶ adjective **1** *the car came to an abrupt halt | he was grumbling at the abrupt change of weather* **sudden**, immediate, instantaneous, hurried,

hasty, quick, swift, rapid, speedy, precipitate; **unexpected**, surprising, startling, unanticipated, unforeseen, without warning; violent, headlong, breakneck, meteoric.
OPPOSITES gradual, unhurried.
2 *an abrupt manner* **curt**, brusque, blunt, short, sharp, terse, brisk, crisp, gruff, snappish, snappy, unceremonious, offhand, cavalier, rough, harsh; rude, discourteous, uncivil, surly, churlish; bluff, no-nonsense, to the point, laconic; *informal* off.
OPPOSITES friendly, polite, expansive.
3 *he tends to write in abrupt, epigrammatic paragraphs* **jerky**, uneven, irregular, disconnected, discontinuous, broken, rough, inelegant.
OPPOSITES smooth, flowing.
4 *an abrupt slope* **steep**, sheer, precipitous, bluff, sharp, sudden, acute; perpendicular, vertical, dizzy, vertiginous; *rare* declivitous.
OPPOSITES gradual, gentle.

> CHOOSE THE RIGHT WORD
> **abrupt, brusque, curt, terse**
> *See* BRUSQUE.

abscess ▸ noun *a rabbit with a large abscess on its cheek* **ulcer**, ulceration, cyst, boil, blister, sore, pustule, carbuncle, pimple, papule, wen, whitlow, vesication, furuncle, canker; inflammation, infection, eruption.

abscond ▸ verb *he had absconded from a Borstal* **run away**, **escape**, bolt, clear out, flee, make off, take flight, take off, fly, decamp; make a break for it, take to one's heels, make a quick getaway, beat a hasty retreat, show a clean pair of heels, run for it, make a run for it; disappear, vanish, slip away, steal away, sneak away; *informal* do a bunk, do a moonlight flit, cut and run, skedaddle, skip, do a runner, head for the hills, do a disappearing/vanishing act, fly the coop, take French leave, scarper, vamoose; *N. Amer. informal* take a powder, go on the lam.

absence ▸ noun **1** *Derek gave Carol a flimsy excuse for his absence* **non-attendance**, non-appearance, absenteeism; **truancy**, playing truant, truanting; leave, holiday, vacation, sabbatical; *Brit. informal* skiving, bunking off; *N. Amer. informal* playing hookey, goofing off, ditching; *Austral./NZ* playing the wag, wagging.
OPPOSITES presence, attendance.
2 *the absence of a clear candidate was likely to result in civil war* **lack**, want, non-existence, unavailability, deficiency, deprivation, dearth; omission, exclusion, default; need, privation, famine, drought, poverty.
OPPOSITES presence, availability.

absent ▸ adjective (stress on the first syllable) **1** *she was absent from work | an absent parent* **away**, off, out, not present, non-attending, truant; not working, not at work, off duty, on holiday, on leave; gone, missing, lacking, unavailable, non-existent; *Latin* in absentia; *informal* AWOL; *Brit. informal* bunking off, skiving; *Austral./NZ informal* wagging.
OPPOSITE present.
2 *his eyes had an absent, dreaming look* **distracted**, preoccupied, inattentive, vague, absorbed, abstracted, unheeding, oblivious, distrait, absent-minded; daydreaming, dreamy, dreaming, far away, somewhere else, musing, wool-gathering, with one's head in the clouds, in a world of one's own, lost in thought, in a brown study; blank, empty, vacant, vacuous; *informal* miles away, not with us.
OPPOSITES attentive, alert.
▸ verb (stress on the second syllable)
□ **absent oneself** *it might be advisable for Jenny to absent herself during my visit* **stay away**, keep away, be absent, withdraw, retire, take one's leave, remove oneself, slip away, take oneself off, abscond; *informal* slope off.
OPPOSITES attend, be present.

absently ▸ adverb *Hilary absently took the glass he was holding out* **distractedly**, inattentively, abstractedly, unheedingly, carelessly, absent-mindedly, on automatic pilot; dreamily, with one's head in the clouds, in a world of one's own, lost in thought; blankly, vacuously.
OPPOSITE attentively.

absent-minded ▸ adjective *an absent-minded boffin* **forgetful**, **distracted**, preoccupied, inattentive, vague, absorbed, abstracted, unheeding, oblivious, distrait, in a brown study, wool-gathering; lost in thought, pensive, thoughtful, brooding; *informal* scatterbrained, miles away, with a mind/memory like a sieve.
OPPOSITES alert, observant.

absent-mindedness ▸ noun *there are endless stories about his idiosyncrasies and absent-mindedness* **forgetfulness**, amnesia, poor memory, tendency to forget, lapse of memory; **distractedness**, preoccupation, inattentiveness, inattention, vagueness, abstraction, absence, absorption, engrossment, heedlessness, obliviousness; pensiveness, thoughtfulness, musing, brooding; *humorous* blonde moment.
OPPOSITE alertness.

absolute ▸ adjective **1** *there was absolute silence in the house | an absolute disgrace* **complete**, total, utter, out-and-out, outright, entire, perfect, pure, decided; thorough, thoroughgoing, undivided, unqualified, unadulterated, unalloyed, unmodified, unreserved, downright, undiluted, solid, consummate, unmitigated, sheer, arrant, rank, dyed-in-the-wool; plenary; *Law* peremptory.
OPPOSITES partial, qualified.
2 *everything I have told you is the absolute truth* **definite**, certain, positive, unconditional, categorical, unquestionable, undoubted, unequivocal, decisive, conclusive, confirmed, manifest, infallible.
OPPOSITES partial, qualified.
3 *the parliament was only consultative, with absolute power remaining with the king* **unlimited**, unrestricted, unrestrained, unbounded, unbound, boundless, infinite, ultimate, total, supreme, unconditional, full, utter, sovereign, omnipotent.
OPPOSITE conditional.
4 *an absolute monarch* **autocratic**, despotic, dictatorial, tyrannical, tyrannous, authoritarian, arbitrary, imperious, domineering, high-handed, draconian, autonomous, sovereign, autarchic, autarchical.
OPPOSITE constitutional.
5 *absolute moral standards* **universal**, fixed, independent, non-relative, non-variable, absolutist; **rigid**, established, set, settled, definite, decided, irrevocable, unalterable, unquestionable, authoritative, incontrovertible, in black and white.
OPPOSITES relative, flexible.

absolutely ▸ adverb **1** *the honourable gentleman is absolutely right* **completely**, totally, utterly, perfectly, entirely, wholly, fully, quite, thoroughly, unreservedly; definitely, certainly, positively, unconditionally, categorically, unquestionably, no doubt, undoubtedly, without (a) doubt, without question, surely, unequivocally; exactly, precisely, decisively, conclusively, manifestly, in every way/respect, one hundred per cent, every inch, to the hilt; *informal* dead.
OPPOSITE partially.
2 *she ruled absolutely in her own department and dealt summarily with opposition* **autocratically**, despotically, dictatorially, tyrannically, tyrannously, in an authoritarian manner, arbitrarily, imperiously, domineeringly, high-handedly, with draconian powers, autonomously; **unrestrictedly**, supremely, fully, utterly, unconditionally, totally, omnipotently, without challenge, without check, without checks and balances, without let or hindrance.
□ **absolutely no/none** *there was absolutely no room for it* **no ... whatever**, no ... whatsoever, no ... at all; none whatever, none whatsoever, none at all.
▸ exclamation *'Have I made myself clear?' 'Absolutely!'* **certainly**, yes, indeed, of course, definitely, quite, positively, naturally, without (a) doubt, without question, unquestionably; affirmative, by all means.

absolution ▸ noun (*Christianity*) *she had been given absolution for her sins* **forgiveness**, pardoning, exoneration, remission, dispensation, indulgence, purgation, clemency, mercy; pardon, reprieve, discharge, amnesty, delivery, acquittal, clearing; freedom, liberation, deliverance, release; condoning, vindication, exculpation; *informal* let-off, letting off; *archaic* shrift, shriving.
OPPOSITE punishment.

absolve ▸ verb **1** *the fact that a criminal offence occurred a long time ago does not absolve the wrongdoer from guilt* **exonerate**, discharge, acquit, exculpate, vindicate; release, relieve, liberate, free, deliver, clear, spare, exempt; *informal* let off.
OPPOSITES blame, condemn.
2 (*Christianity*) *I absolve you from all your sins* **forgive**, pardon, excuse, give amnesty to, give dispensation to, give indulgence to; reprieve, have mercy on, show mercy to.
OPPOSITE punish.

absorb ▸ verb **1** *when wood gets wet, it absorbs water and expands* **soak up**, suck up, draw up/in, take up/in, blot up, mop up, sponge up, sop up.
OPPOSITES exude, give out.
2 *patience is needed to absorb all this information* **assimilate**, digest, ingest, take in, imbibe, drink in, familiarize oneself with; comprehend, grasp, learn, understand, master.
3 *the company was absorbed into the new concern* **incorporate**, assimilate, integrate, appropriate, take in, subsume, include, co-opt, swallow up.
4 *these roles absorb most of his time and energy* **use (up)**, consume, take up, occupy; waste, squander, go through, deplete, drain, exhaust, swallow up.
5 *the inner lining will absorb some of the sound* **deaden**, soften, cushion; reduce, decrease, lessen; soak up.
OPPOSITES reflect; increase.
6 *she was absorbed in a letter when Mervyn came into the room* **preoccupy**, engross, captivate, occupy, engage; rivet, grip, hold, interest, intrigue, immerse, involve, enthral, spellbind, fascinate, arrest, monopolize; distract, divert, entertain, amuse.

absorbent ▸ adjective *a piece of absorbent cotton wool* **porous**, spongy, sponge-like, permeable, pervious, absorptive, penetrable, assimilative, receptive, soaking, blotting; *technical* spongiform; *rare* sorbefacient.
OPPOSITES impermeable, waterproof.

absorbing ▸ adjective *an absorbing and informative book* **fascinating**,

interesting, captivating, gripping, engrossing, compelling, compulsive, enthralling, riveting, spellbinding, entrancing, preoccupying, overwhelming, intriguing, thrilling, exciting; *informal* unputdownable.
OPPOSITES boring, uninteresting.

absorption ▶ noun **1** *the absorption of water* **soaking up**, sucking up, drawing up/in, taking up/in, blotting up, mopping up, sponging up, sopping up; *technical* osmosis.
2 *by 1543, Scottish fears of absorption by England seemed to have been allayed* **incorporation**, assimilation, integration, appropriation, taking in, subsuming, inclusion, co-opting, swallowing up.
3 *shock absorption* **reduction**, decrease, lessening, softening, deadening, cushioning; soaking up.
4 *she returned to her absorption in the game show on TV* **immersion**, intentness, raptness, involvement, engrossment, occupation, engagement, preoccupation, captivation, monopolization; fascination, enthralment, interest.

abstain ▶ verb **1** *during Lent, Benjamin* ***abstained from*** *wine* **refrain**, desist, hold back, forbear, keep; **renounce**, avoid, shun, eschew, abandon, abjure, forgo, go without, do without; refuse, decline; give up, have done with; *informal* cut out, kick, quit, jack in, pack in.
OPPOSITE indulge in.
2 *our advice is about sensible drinking, not about abstaining* **be teetotal**, be a teetotaller, take the pledge; deny oneself; *informal* be on the wagon.
OPPOSITE drink.
3 *262 voted against, 38 abstained* **not vote**, decline/refuse to vote; *informal* sit on the fence.
OPPOSITE vote.

abstemious ▶ adjective *he seems to have led an abstemious, not to say ascetic life* **temperate**, abstinent, austere, moderate, self-disciplined, self-denying, restrained, self-restrained, non-indulgent, sober, ascetic, puritanical, spartan, strict, severe, self-abnegating, hair-shirt.
OPPOSITES self-indulgent, intemperate.

abstemiousness ▶ noun *the traditional belief in the virtues of abstemiousness* **temperance**, abstinence, austerity, moderation, plain/simple living, self-discipline, self-denial, renunciation, restraint, self-restraint, self-deprivation, sobriety, asceticism, puritanism, severity, self-abnegation, continence.
OPPOSITES self-indulgence, intemperance.

abstention ▶ noun **1** *the election was marked by a high rate of abstention* **refusal to vote**, abstaining, non-voting; *informal* sitting on the fence.
2 *the rights and wrongs of alcohol consumption versus abstention.* See ABSTINENCE.

abstinence ▶ noun **1** *he took a pledge of abstinence* **teetotalism**, temperance, sobriety, abstemiousness, abstention; *rare* nephalism.
2 *only one per cent use abstinence to reduce the risk of unwanted fatherhood* **celibacy**, chastity, singleness, continence, virginity, bachelorhood, spinsterhood, self-restraint, self-denial.
OPPOSITE promiscuity.
3 *a three-day period of* ***abstinence from*** *food and drink* **refraining**, desisting, holding back, forbearing, keeping, withholding; **renunciation of**, refusal of, declining, avoidance of, eschewal of, abjuration of; shunning, forgoing, going without, doing without.

abstract ▶ adjective (stress on the first syllable) **1** *abstract concepts such as love and beauty* **theoretical**, conceptual, notional, intellectual, metaphysical, philosophical, academic; hypothetical, speculative, conjectural, conjectured, suppositional, putative; *rare* suppositious, suppositive, ideational.
OPPOSITES actual, concrete.
2 *abstract art* **non-representational**, non-realistic, non-pictorial, symbolic, impressionistic.
OPPOSITE representational.
▶ verb (stress on the second syllable) **1** *staff who index and abstract material for an online database* **summarize**, write a summary of, precis, abridge, condense, compress, shorten, cut down, abbreviate, synopsize; *rare* epitomize.
2 *they want to abstract water from the river* **extract**, pump, draw (off), tap, suck, withdraw, remove, take out/away; separate, detach, isolate, dissociate.
3 *his pockets contained all he had been able to abstract from the flat* **steal**, purloin, thieve, take, take for oneself, help oneself to, loot, pilfer, abscond with, run off with, appropriate, carry off, shoplift; embezzle, misappropriate; have one's fingers/hand in the till; *informal* walk off/away with, run away/off with, rob, swipe, nab, rip off, lift, 'liberate', 'borrow', filch, snaffle, snitch, souvenir; *Brit. informal* nick, pinch, half-inch, whip, knock off, nobble, bone, scrump, blag; *N. Amer. informal* heist, glom; *Austral. informal* snavel; *W. Indian* tief; *archaic* crib, hook; *rare* peculate, defalcate.
▶ noun (stress on the first syllable) *an abstract of her speech* **summary**, synopsis, precis, résumé, outline, recapitulation, abridgement, condensation, digest, summation; *French* aperçu; *N. Amer.* wrap-up; *archaic* argument; *rare* epitome, conspectus.
OPPOSITES complete version, full text.

abstracted ▶ adjective *she seemed abstracted and unaware of her surroundings* **absent-minded**, distracted, preoccupied, absorbed, engrossed, far away, somewhere else, not there, not with us, in a world of one's own, with one's head in the clouds, daydreaming, dreamy, inattentive, thoughtful, pensive, lost in thought, deep in thought, immersed in thought, wool-gathering, in a brown study, musing, brooding, absent, distrait, heedless, oblivious; *informal* miles away.
OPPOSITE attentive.

abstraction ▶ noun **1** *his style of writing focuses on facts rather than abstractions* **concept**, idea, notion, thought, generality, generalization, theory, theorem, formula, hypothesis, speculation, conjecture, supposition, presumption.
OPPOSITES fact; material consideration.
2 *she sensed his momentary abstraction* **absent-mindedness**, distraction, preoccupation, daydreaming, dreaminess, inattentiveness, inattention, wool-gathering, absence, heedlessness, obliviousness; thoughtfulness, pensiveness, musing, brooding, absorption, engrossment, raptness.
OPPOSITE attention.
3 *the abstraction of metal from ore* **extraction**, removal, separation, detachment.

abstruse ▶ adjective *he was unable to follow the abstruse arguments put forward* **obscure**, arcane, esoteric, little known, recherché, rarefied, recondite, difficult, hard, puzzling, perplexing, enigmatic, inscrutable, cryptic, Delphic, complex, complicated, involved, over/above one's head, incomprehensible, unfathomable, impenetrable, mysterious; *rare* involute, involuted.
OPPOSITES clear, obvious.

> **CHOOSE THE RIGHT WORD**
> **abstruse, obscure, recondite, esoteric, arcane**
> *See* OBSCURE.

absurd ▶ adjective *what an absurd idea!* **preposterous**, ridiculous, ludicrous, farcical, laughable, risible; idiotic, stupid, foolish, silly, inane, imbecilic, insane, hare-brained; unreasonable, irrational, illogical, nonsensical, pointless, senseless; outrageous, shocking, astonishing, monstrous, fantastic, incongruous, grotesque; unbelievable, incredible, unthinkable, implausible; *informal* crazy; *Brit. informal* barmy, daft.
OPPOSITES reasonable, sensible.

absurdity ▶ noun *Duncan laughed at the absurdity of the situation* **preposterousness**, ridiculousness, ludicrousness, absurdness, farcicality, risibility; idiocy, stupidity, foolishness, folly, silliness, inanity, insanity; unreasonableness, irrationality, illogicality, nonsensicality, pointlessness, senselessness, incongruity; *informal* craziness.
OPPOSITES reasonableness, sense.

absurdly ▶ adverb *that is an absurdly optimistic claim* **preposterously**, ridiculously, ludicrously, farcically, laughably, risibly; idiotically, stupidly, foolishly, inanely, insanely, madly, wildly, fantastically, grotesquely; completely, absolutely, entirely, totally, wholly, thoroughly, utterly, quite, altogether, downright, perfectly; unbelievably, incredibly, unthinkably, implausibly; extremely, exceedingly, excessively, exorbitantly, unduly, inordinately, immoderately, unreasonably, irrationally, illogically, impossibly; offensively, unspeakably, intolerably, maddeningly, outrageously, shockingly; *informal* crazily, barmily.
OPPOSITES reasonably, sensibly; somewhat.

abundance ▶ noun *the area is famous for its abundance of wildlife* **profusion**, plentifulness, profuseness, copiousness, amplitude, affluence, lavishness, bountifulness, infinity, opulence, exuberance, luxuriance; host, plenitude, cornucopia, riot; plenty, a lot, mass, quantities, scores, millions, multitude; *informal* sea, ocean(s), wealth, lots, heap(s), mass(es), stack(s), pile(s), load(s), bags, mountain(s), ton(s), oodles; *Brit. informal* shedload; *N. Amer. informal* slew, gobs, scads; *Austral./NZ informal* swag; *vulgar slang* shitload; *rare* nimiety.
OPPOSITES lack, scarcity.

abundant ▶ adjective *there is abundant rainfall during the summer* **plentiful**, copious, ample, profuse, rich, lavish, liberal, generous, bountiful, large, huge, great, bumper, overflowing, superabundant, infinite, inexhaustible, opulent, prolific, teeming; in plenty, in abundance; *informal* a gogo, galore; *S. African informal* lank; *literary* bounteous, plenteous.
OPPOSITES scarce, sparse.
□ **be abundant abound**, be plentiful, be numerous, exist in abundance, proliferate, be thick on the ground; *informal* grow on trees; *Brit. informal* be two/ten a penny.

abundantly ▶ adverb **1** *the plant grows abundantly in the wild* **copiously**, plentifully, amply, profusely, exuberantly, prolifically, luxuriantly, in profusion, in abundance, in great quantity, in large quantities, in plenty, aplenty, in huge numbers, freely, extensively, everywhere, all over the place; *literary* bounteously, plenteously.
OPPOSITE sparsely.
2 *she made her wishes abundantly clear* **extremely**, exceedingly, exceptionally, especially, extraordinarily, extra, tremendously,

immensely, vastly, hugely, singularly, significantly, distinctly, outstandingly, uncommonly, unusually, decidedly, particularly, eminently, supremely, highly, remarkably, really, truly, mightily, thoroughly; all that, to a great extent, most, so; sufficiently, ... enough; Scottish unco; French très; N. English right; informal terrifically, awfully, terribly, devilishly, majorly, seriously, mega, ultra, oh-so, stinking, mucho, damn, damned; Brit. informal ever so, well, dead, bloody, dirty, jolly, fair; N. Amer. informal real, mighty, powerful, awful, plumb, darned, way, bitching; S. African informal lekker; informal, dated devilish, hellish, frightfully; archaic exceeding.
OPPOSITES scarcely; moderately.

abuse ▶ **verb 1** *the judge abused his power by imposing the fines* **misuse**, misapply, misemploy, mishandle; exploit, pervert, take advantage of.
2 *he was accused of abusing children* **mistreat**, maltreat, ill-treat, treat badly, ill-use, misuse; handle/treat roughly, knock about/around, manhandle, mishandle, maul, molest, interfere with, indecently assault, sexually abuse, sexually assault, grope, assault, hit, strike, beat; injure, hurt, harm, damage; wrong, bully, persecute, oppress, torture; informal beat up, rough up, do over.
OPPOSITE look after.
3 *the referee was abused by players from both teams* **insult**, be rude to, swear at, curse, call someone names, taunt, shout at, scold, rebuke, upbraid, reprove, castigate, inveigh against, impugn, slur, revile, smear, vilify, vituperate against, slander, libel, cast aspersions on, offend, slight, disparage, denigrate, defame; Brit. informal slag off; N. Amer. informal trash-talk; archaic miscall.
OPPOSITES compliment, flatter.
▶ **noun 1** *this law is not going to stop the abuse of power* **misuse**, misapplication, misemployment, mishandling; exploitation, perversion.
2 *the abuse of children is a major social problem* **mistreatment**, maltreatment, ill-treatment, ill-use, misuse; rough treatment, manhandling, mishandling, molestation, interference, indecent assault, sexual abuse, sexual assault, assaulting, hitting, striking, beating; injury, hurt, harm, damage; wronging, bullying, persecution, oppression, torture; informal beating up, roughing up, doing over.
OPPOSITE care.
3 *the scheme is open to political control and administrative abuse* **corruption**, injustice, wrongdoing, wrong, misconduct, delinquency, misdeed(s), offence(s), crime, fault, sin.
4 *torrents of abuse* **insults**, curses, jibes, slurs, expletives, swear words; swearing, cursing, name-calling, scolding; rebukes, upbraiding, reproval, invective, castigation, revilement, vilification, vituperation, slander, libel, slights, disparagement, denigration, defamation; informal slanging, a slanging match, mud-slinging, disrespect; Brit. informal verbal(s); N. Amer. informal trash talk; archaic contumely.
OPPOSITES compliments, flattery.

abusive ▶ **adjective** *he was fined for making abusive comments to officials* **insulting**, rude, vulgar, offensive, disparaging, belittling, derogatory, disrespectful, denigratory, uncomplimentary, pejorative, vituperative; disdainful, derisive, scornful, contemptuous; defamatory, slanderous, libellous, scurrilous, blasphemous; scolding, castigatory, reproving, reproachful; informal bitchy; archaic contumelious.

abut ▶ **verb** *one of my pastures abuts your garden* **adjoin**, be adjacent to, border, butt up against/to, be next to, neighbour, verge on, join, touch, meet, reach, impinge on, be contiguous with.

abysmal ▶ **adjective 1** (informal) *some of the teaching was abysmal* **very bad**, dreadful, awful, terrible, frightful, atrocious, disgraceful, deplorable, shameful, woeful, hopeless, lamentable, laughable, substandard, poor, inadequate, inferior, unsatisfactory; informal rotten, appalling, crummy, pathetic, pitiful, useless, lousy, shocking, dire, poxy, the pits; Brit. informal duff, chronic, a load of pants, pants; N. Amer. vulgar slang chickenshit.
OPPOSITE superb.
2 *abysmal ignorance* **profound**, extreme, utter, complete, thorough, deep, endless, immeasurable, boundless, incalculable, unfathomable, bottomless.

abyss ▶ **noun** *a rope led down into the dark abyss* **chasm**, gorge, ravine, canyon, fissure, rift, crevasse, gap, hole, gulf, pit, depth, cavity, void, bottomless pit.

academic ▶ **adjective 1** *an academic institution* **educational**, scholastic, instructional, pedagogical; school, college, collegiate, university.
2 *he has a distinctly academic turn of mind* **scholarly**, studious, literary, well read, intellectual, clever, erudite, learned, educated, cultured, bookish, highbrow, pedantic, donnish, cerebral, serious; informal brainy; dated lettered.
3 *the debate has been largely academic* **theoretical**, conceptual, notional, philosophical, unpragmatic, hypothetical, speculative, conjectural, conjectured, suppositional, putative; indefinite, abstract, vague, general; impractical, unrealistic, ivory-tower, irrelevant, useless; rare suppositious, suppositive, ideational.
OPPOSITE practical.
▶ **noun** *a group of Russian academics is researching this phenomenon* **scholar**, lecturer, don, teacher, educator, instructor, trainer, tutor, professor, fellow, man/woman of letters, highbrow, thinker, bluestocking; informal egghead, bookworm; archaic pedagogue.

academy ▶ **noun educational institution**, training establishment, centre of learning; school, college, university, institute, seminary, conservatory, conservatoire; historical polytechnic.

accede ▶ **verb 1** *the authorities did not accede to the strikers' demands* **agree to**, consent to, accept, assent to, acquiesce in, endorse, comply with, go along with, concur with, allow, recognize, grant, surrender to, yield to, give in to, give way to, defer to; relent, back down.
OPPOSITES refuse, deny.
2 *Elizabeth I acceded to the throne in 1558* **succeed to**, assume, attain, come to, come into, inherit, take over, be elevated to.
OPPOSITES abdicate, renounce.
3 *Albania acceded to the IMF in 1990* **join**, become a member of, become (a) party to, sign up to, enrol in.
OPPOSITES leave, secede.

accelerate ▶ **verb 1** *the car accelerated down the hill* **speed up**, hurry up, get faster, move faster, go faster, drive faster, get a move on, put on a spurt, open it up, gain momentum, increase speed, pick up speed, gather speed; informal step on the gas, step on it, get cracking, get moving; N. Amer. informal get a wiggle on; Austral. informal get a wriggle on.
OPPOSITES decelerate, slow down.
2 *inflation started to accelerate* **increase**, rise, go up, advance, leap, surge, speed up, escalate, spiral, get worse.
OPPOSITES slow down, drop.
3 *the University has accelerated its planning process* **hasten**, expedite, precipitate, speed, speed up, hurry up, make faster, step up, advance, further, forward, promote, boost, give a boost to, stimulate, spur on; aid, assist, help along, facilitate, ease, make easier, simplify; informal crank up.
OPPOSITES delay, slow down.

acceleration ▶ **noun 1** *the car's acceleration is sensational* **speeding up**, increasing speed, increase in speed, gain in momentum, gathering speed, opening up; technical rate of change of velocity.
OPPOSITES deceleration, slowing down.
2 *there was some acceleration of the process* **hastening**, speeding up, quickening, stepping up, advancement, furthering, furtherance, forwarding, promotion, boosting, boost, stimulation, spur, aid, assistance, facilitation, easing, simplification, expedition, precipitation.
3 *an acceleration in the divorce rate* **increase**, rise, advance, leap, surge, escalation, spiralling, worsening.

accent *See centre pages for list of* **Accents**
▶ **noun** (stress on the first syllable) **1** *a Scottish accent* **pronunciation**, intonation, enunciation, elocution, articulation, inflection, tone, modulation, cadence, timbre, utterance, manner of speaking, speech pattern, speech, diction, delivery; brogue, burr, drawl, twang; rare orthoepy.
2 *the accent is on the first syllable* **stress**, emphasis, accentuation, force, prominence; primary stress, secondary stress; beat, rhythm, pulse; technical tone, ictus.
3 *the accent is on comfort* **emphasis**, stress, priority; importance, prominence.
4 *an acute accent* **mark**, diacritic, diacritical mark, accent mark, sign.
▶ **verb** (stress on the second syllable) **1** *both versions of this chant accent the last syllable* **stress**, put/lay/place the stress on, emphasize, put/lay/place the emphasis on, give emphasis to, put the force on, accentuate.
2 *fabrics which accent the background colours in the room* **focus attention on**, bring/call/draw attention to, point up, underline, underscore, accentuate, highlight, spotlight, foreground, feature, give prominence to, make more prominent, make more noticeable, play up, bring to the fore, heighten, stress, emphasize, put/lay emphasis on.
OPPOSITES mask, divert attention from.

accentuate ▶ **verb 1** *the simple outfit accentuated her long legs* **focus attention on**, bring/call/draw attention to, point up, underline, underscore, accent, highlight, spotlight, foreground, feature, give prominence to, make more prominent, make more noticeable, play up, bring to the fore, heighten, stress, emphasize, put/lay emphasis on.
OPPOSITES mask, divert attention from.
2 *that characteristic thump which accentuates the first beat of the bar* **emphasize**, stress, put/lay/place the stress on, put/lay/place the emphasis on, give emphasis to, put the force on, accent.

accept ▶ **verb 1** *he accepted a pen as a present* **receive**, agree to receive, welcome, take, take receipt of, get, gain, obtain, acquire, come by.
OPPOSITES refuse, reject, turn down.
2 *he accepted the job immediately* **take on**, take up, undertake, tackle, take on oneself, shoulder, bear, assume, manage, take responsibility for, be responsible for, engage in, become involved in, take part in, participate in, devote oneself to, concentrate on, address oneself to, go about, set about, approach, handle, get down to, deal with, get to grips with; launch into, enter on, begin, start, embark on, venture on, turn one's hand to; informal get cracking on, have a crack/go/shot/stab at, give something a whirl; formal commence.
3 *she accepted an invitation to lunch* **say yes to**, reply in the affirmative,

agree to, comply with.
4 *she was accepted as one of the family* **welcome**, greet, let in, receive, receive favourably, embrace, offer friendship to, adopt, integrate.
5 *he grudgingly accepted Ellen's explanation* **believe**, trust, give credence to, credit, give credit to, put confidence in, be convinced of, have faith in, count on, rely on, depend on; *informal* go for, buy, fall for, swallow, {swallow something hook, line, and sinker}, take something as gospel.
6 *we have agreed to accept his decision* **go along with**, accede to, agree to, consent to, acquiesce in, concur with, assent to, endorse, comply with, abide by, follow, adhere to, conform to, act in accordance with, defer to, yield to, surrender to, bow to, give in to, submit to, respect, recognize, acknowledge, cooperate with, adopt.
OPPOSITE defy.
7 *she will just have to accept the consequences* **tolerate**, endure, put up with, suffer, bear, take, stand, support, submit to, stomach, undergo, swallow; become reconciled to, reconcile oneself to, become resigned to, get used to, become accustomed to, adjust to, accommodate oneself to, acclimatize oneself to; learn to live with, make the best of; face up to; *Scottish* thole; *Brit. informal* wear.

acceptable ▶ adjective **1** *an acceptable substitute for champagne* **satisfactory**, adequate, reasonable, quite good, fair, decent, good enough, sufficient, sufficiently good, fine, in order, up to scratch, up to the mark, up to standard, up to par, competent, not bad, all right, average, tolerable, passable, middling, moderate; presentable; suitable, convenient; *informal* OK, so-so, fair-to-middling; *N. Amer. & Austral./NZ informal* jake.
OPPOSITES unacceptable, unsatisfactory.
2 *a most acceptable present* **welcome**, appreciated; **pleasing**, agreeable, delightful, desirable, satisfying, gratifying, to one's liking.
OPPOSITES unwelcome, unsuitable, undesirable.
3 *the risk had seemed acceptable at the time* **bearable**, tolerable, allowable, admissible, supportable, sustainable, justifiable, defensible, defendable.
OPPOSITES unacceptable, undesirable.

acceptance ▶ noun **1** *the acceptance of an award* **receipt**, receiving, taking, obtaining, acquiring.
2 *the acceptance of responsibility* **undertaking**, taking on, assumption, tackling.
3 *acceptances to an invitation* **yes**, affirmative reply, affirmation, confirmation, ratification.
4 *she greatly valued her acceptance as one of the family* **welcome**, welcoming, favourable reception, embracing, embrace, approval, adoption, integration.
5 *his instant acceptance of Matilda's explanation | the idea soon gained complete acceptance* **credence (in)**, belief (in), trust (in), confidence (in), faith (in), reliance (on), dependence (on); swallowing.
6 *their acceptance of the decision must be final* **compliance with**, endorsement of, accession to, agreement with, consent to, acquiescence in, concurrence with, assent to, abidance by, adherence to, conformity with, deference to, surrender to, submission to, respect for, recognition of, acknowledgement of, adoption of; *rare* accedence to.
7 *the acceptance of pain* **toleration**, endurance, sufferance, forbearance; putting up with.

accepted ▶ adjective *it is accepted practice | an accepted authority* **recognized**, acknowledged, traditional, orthodox, habitual, confirmed, set, fixed, settled; **usual**, customary, common, normal, general, prevailing, accustomed, familiar, wonted, popular, expected, routine, regular, typical, conventional, established, mainstream, standard, stock.

access ▶ noun **1** *the building has a side access* **entrance**, entry, way in, means of entry, ingress; approach, means of approach.
2 *they were denied access to the stadium* **admission**, admittance, entry, entrée, ingress, right of entry, permission to enter, the opportunity to enter.
3 *students have access to a photocopier* **(the) use of**, the opportunity to use, permission to use.
4 *an access of rage* **fit**, attack, bout, outpouring, eruption, explosion, outburst, burst, outbreak, flare-up, blow-up, blaze, spasm, paroxysm, seizure, rush; gale, flood, storm, hurricane, torrent, surge, upsurge; spurt, effusion, outflow, outflowing, welling up; *informal* splurt; *rare* ebullition, boutade.
▶ verb *the program that is used to access the data* **retrieve**, gain, gain access to, acquire, obtain; read, examine.

accessibility ▶ noun **1** *accessibility to shops is frequently a problem for the handicapped* **ease of access**, availability, approachability, obtainability; nearness, convenience, handiness, readiness; *rare* attainability, reachability.
OPPOSITE inaccessibility.
2 *the accessibility of this type of music* **comprehensibility**, intelligibility, understandability, penetrability, approachability.
OPPOSITE incomprehensibility.
3 *journalists loved his accessibility* **approachability**, availability, easy-going manner, informality, friendliness, hospitable manner, agreeableness, obliging nature, congeniality, affability, cordiality.
OPPOSITE unapproachability.

accessible ▶ adjective **1** *the village is only accessible on foot | the tools should be stored in a place where they are easily accessible* **reachable**, attainable, approachable, within reach, available, on hand, obtainable; nearby, ready, convenient, handy; *informal* get-at-able.
OPPOSITE inaccessible.
2 *he set out to write accessible music* **understandable**, comprehensible, easy to understand, easy to appreciate, intelligible, penetrable, fathomable, graspable, approachable.
OPPOSITE incomprehensible.
3 *he is more accessible than most tycoons* **approachable**, available, easy-going, informal, friendly, welcoming, hospitable, pleasant, agreeable, obliging, congenial, affable, cordial.
OPPOSITE unapproachable.

accession ▶ noun **1** *the Queen's accession to the throne* **succession**, elevation; assumption of, attainment of, inheritance of.
2 *the accession of Spain and Portugal to the EC* **joining**, signing up, enrolment.
3 *accession to the Treaty of Rome was effected in 1971* **assent**, consent, agreement; acceptance of, acquiescence in, endorsement of, compliance with, concurrence with, recognition of.
4 *among recent accessions to the museum are some Victorian watercolours* **addition**, acquisition, new item, gift, purchase, adjunct, add-on, gain.

accessorize ▶ verb *there was no hat to accessorize this dress* **complement**, supplement, add to, augment; enhance, set off, show off; go with, suit; beautify, pretty (up), dress up, decorate, adorn, grace, ornament, embellish, trim, garnish, bedeck, deck (out), festoon; *literary* bedizen, furbelow.

accessory ▶ noun **1** *camera accessories such as tripods and flashguns* **attachment**, extra, addition, add-on, retrofit, adjunct, appendage, appurtenance, (additional) component, fitment, supplement.
2 *Paula wore each suit with perfectly matching accessories* **adornment**, embellishment, finery, trimming, ornament, ornamentation, decoration, complement, fashion detail, frill; trappings; handbag, shoes, gloves, hat, belt, jewellery.
3 *she was charged as an accessory to murder* **accomplice**, partner in crime, abetter, associate, confederate, collaborator, fellow conspirator, henchman, conniver.
▶ adjective *functionally the maxillae are a pair of accessory jaws* **additional**, extra, supplementary, supplemental, auxiliary, ancillary, secondary, subsidiary, supportive, assisting, reserve, complementary, further, more, add-on.

accident ▶ noun **1** *he was involved in an accident at work* **mishap**, misfortune, misadventure, mischance, unfortunate incident, injury, disaster, tragedy, catastrophe, contretemps, calamity, blow, trouble, problem, difficulty; *technical* casualty.
2 *there was an accident on the motorway* **crash**, collision, smash, bump, car crash, car accident, road accident, traffic accident, road traffic accident, RTA, multiple crash, multiple collision; rail accident, derailment; air accident, air crash; *N. Amer.* wreck; *informal* smash-up, pile-up, shunt; *Brit. informal* prang.
3 *it is no accident that there is a similarity between them* **chance**, mere chance, coincidence, twist of fate, freak, hazard; piece of good fortune, (bit of) luck, (bit of) good luck, fluke, happy chance; serendipity, fate, fortuity, fortune, providence; *N. Amer.* happenstance.
□ **by accident** *we met purely by accident* **fortuitously**, accidentally, coincidentally, by chance, by coincidence, by a fluke, unintentionally, inadvertently; unwittingly, unknowingly, unawares, unconsciously; by mistake, mistakenly.
OPPOSITE intentionally.

accidental ▶ adjective **1** *accidental damage | an accidental meeting* **fortuitous**, **chance**, occurring by chance/accident, adventitious, fluky, coincidental, casual, serendipitous, random, aleatory; unexpected, unforeseen, unanticipated, unlooked-for; **unintentional**, unintended, inadvertent, involuntary, unplanned, unpremeditated, unthinking, unmeant; unwitting, unknowing, unconscious, subconscious; mistaken, misguided.
OPPOSITES intentional, planned.
2 *the location is accidental and contributes nothing to the poem* **incidental**, unimportant, by the way, by the by, supplementary, subsidiary, subordinate, secondary, marginal, minor, lesser, accessory, peripheral, tangential, extraneous, extrinsic, parenthetical, irrelevant, immaterial, beside the point, of little account, unnecessary, non-essential, inessential.
OPPOSITES essential, central.

accidentally ▶ adverb *we met accidentally | they accidentally set off a smoke alarm* **fortuitously**, by accident, by chance, by a mere chance, by a twist of fate, adventitiously, as luck would have it, by a fluke, flukily, coincidentally, by coincidence, serendipitously; by a happy chance, by good fortune, by a piece of luck; unexpectedly; **unintentionally**, inadvertently, involuntarily, unpremeditatedly, unthinkingly; unwittingly, unknowingly, unconsciously, subconsciously, unawares; by mistake, mistakenly, misguidedly; *N. Amer.* by happenstance.

acclaim ▶ verb **1** *the booklet has been widely acclaimed by teachers* **praise**, applaud, cheer, commend, express approval of, approve, express admiration for, welcome, pay tribute to, speak highly of, eulogize, compliment, congratulate, celebrate, sing the praises of, praise to the skies, rave about, go into raptures about/over, heap praise on, wax lyrical about, say nice things about, make much of, pat on the back, take one's hat off to, salute, throw bouquets at, lionize, exalt, admire, hail, toast, flatter, adulate, vaunt, extol, glorify, honour, hymn, clap; *informal* crack someone/something up; *N. Amer. informal* ballyhoo; *black English* big someone/something up; *dated* cry someone/something up; *archaic* emblazon; *rare* laud, panegyrize.
OPPOSITE criticize.
2 *Eardwulf was acclaimed king of Northumbria in 796* **proclaim**, announce, declare, pronounce, hail as.
▶ noun *she has won acclaim for her commitment to democracy* **praise**, applause, cheers, ovation, tribute, accolade, acclamation, salutes, plaudits; approval, admiration, approbation, congratulations, commendation, welcome, flattery, kudos, adulation, homage; compliment, a pat on the back, eulogy, encomium, panegyric, bouquets, laurels, testimonial; *rare* extolment, laudation, eulogium.
OPPOSITE criticism.

acclaimed ▶ adjective *an acclaimed public figure* **celebrated**, admired, highly rated, lionized, revered, honoured, esteemed, exalted, lauded, vaunted, much touted, well thought of, well received, acknowledged; eminent, venerable, august, great, renowned, distinguished, prestigious, illustrious, pre-eminent, estimable, of note, noted, notable, of repute, of high standing, considerable.
OPPOSITES criticized; unsung; obscure.

acclamation ▶ noun **1** *the proposal was received with considerable acclamation* **praise**, applause, cheers, ovation, tribute, accolade, acclaim, salutes, plaudits; approval, admiration, approbation, congratulations, commendation, welcome, flattery, kudos, adulation, homage; compliment, a pat on the back, eulogy, encomium, panegyric, bouquets, laurels, testimonial; *rare* extolment, laudation, eulogium.
OPPOSITE criticism.
2 *he was elected* **by acclamation** **shouting**, calling out, oral vote, non-ballot; shouts; without a vote, without a ballot, with overwhelming vocal approval, by popular demand.

acclimatization ▶ noun *you should not rush your acclimatization when you arrive in the Far East* **adjustment**, adaptation, attunement, accommodation, habituation, familiarization, acclimation, acculturation, inurement, hardening, seasoning, conditioning; assimilation, integration, domestication, naturalization.

acclimatize ▶ verb *the need to* **acclimatize to** *life at 3,000 metres | I lowered the bag into the tank to acclimatize the fish* **adjust**, adapt, attune, accustom, get (someone) accustomed, get (someone) used, accommodate, habituate, assimilate, acculturate, become inured, harden, condition, reconcile, become resigned, resign oneself; familiarize someone/oneself with, find one's way around, come to terms with, come to accept, learn to live with; integrate, domesticate; find one's feet, get one's bearings, become naturalized, become seasoned; *N. Amer.* acclimate.

accolade ▶ noun **1** *he received the accolade of knighthood* **honour**, recognition, privilege, award, gift, title; prize, laurels, bays, palm.
2 *his role in the game earned him this accolade from his manager* **tribute**, commendation, acclaim, applause, ovation, acclamation, approval, admiration, approbation, testimonial, praise, welcome, flattery, kudos, adulation, homage, compliment, pat on the back, eulogy, encomium, panegyric; cheers, salutes, plaudits, congratulations, bouquets; *informal* rave; *rare* extolment, laudation, eulogium.
OPPOSITE criticism.

accommodate ▶ verb **1** *the refugees were accommodated in army camps* **lodge**, house, put up, billet, quarter, board, take in, provide shelter for, shelter, give a bed to, give someone a roof over their head, provide a roof over someone's head, harbour, make room for, give accommodation to, provide with accommodation, provide accommodation for.
2 *the cottages accommodate up to six people* **hold**, take, fit, seat, have room for.
3 *the company altered the launch date in order to accommodate a major customer* **help**, fit in with, allow for, assist, aid, lend a hand to, oblige, serve, do someone a service, meet the needs/wants of, do someone a good turn, favour, do someone a favour, cater for, indulge, pander to, humour, gratify, satisfy.
OPPOSITE hinder.
4 *she was desperately trying to* **accommodate herself** *to her new position* **adjust**, adapt, attune, accustom, get (someone) accustomed, get (someone) used, habituate, acclimatize, assimilate, acculturate; familiarize someone/oneself with, find one's way around, come to terms with, come to accept, learn to live with; integrate, domesticate; find one's feet, get one's bearings, become naturalized, become seasoned; *N. Amer.* acclimate.
5 *the bank would be glad to accommodate you with a loan* **provide**, supply, furnish, serve, grant.
OPPOSITES deny, refuse.

accommodating ▶ adjective *we always found our local branch most accommodating* **obliging**, cooperative, helpful, eager to help/please, adaptable, amenable, pliable, compliant, complaisant, indulgent, considerate, unselfish, generous, civil, willing, polite, kindly, hospitable, neighbourly, kind, friendly, pleasant, agreeable; *Brit. informal* decent.
OPPOSITES unobliging, disobliging.

accommodation ▶ noun **1** *they were living in temporary accommodation* **housing**, lodging(s), living quarters, quarters, rooms, chambers; place, place to stay, billet; shelter, board; a roof over one's head; *informal* digs, pad; *formal* abode, residence, place of residence, dwelling, dwelling place, habitation.
2 *there was lifeboat accommodation for 1,178 people* **space**, room, seating; places.
3 *the prime minister was seeking an accommodation with the Social Democrats* **arrangement**, **understanding**, settlement, accord, deal, bargain, compromise.
4 *their capacity for accommodation to novelty is very limited* **adjustment**, adaptation, attunement, fitting in, habituation, acclimatization, acclimation, acculturation, inurement, hardening, seasoning, conditioning, familiarization, assimilation, integration, domestication, naturalization.

accompaniment ▶ noun **1** *a musical accompaniment* **backing**, support, background, soundtrack, comp; ripieno, obbligato, organum.
2 *the wine makes a superb accompaniment to cheese* **complement**, supplement, addition, adjunct, appendage, trimming, companion, accessory.

accompany ▶ verb **1** *his wife accompanied him on overseas trips | the driver accompanied her to the door* **go with**, go along with, travel with, keep someone company, tag along with, partner, escort, chaperone, attend, follow, conduct, lead, take, show, see, guide, steer, usher, pilot, convoy, help, assist, show someone the way; lead the way; *Scottish* chum; *rare* company, bear someone company, companion.
2 *the illness is often accompanied by nausea* **occur with**, co-occur with, coincide with, coexist with, go with, go along with, go together with, go hand in hand with, appear with; be associated with, be connected with, be linked with, attend, be concomitant with, supplement, complement, belong to; be caused by, result from, arise from, follow, be a consequence of.
3 *he accompanied the choir on the piano* **back**, play a musical accompaniment for, play with, play for, support.

accomplice ▶ noun *he was arrested as an accomplice to murder* **abetter**, accessory, partner in crime, associate, confederate, collaborator, fellow conspirator, co-conspirator; henchman; *rare* conniver.

accomplish ▶ verb *the planes accomplished their mission* **fulfil**, achieve, succeed in, realize, attain, manage, bring about, bring off, carry out, carry off, carry through, execute, conduct, effect, fix, engineer, perform, do, perpetrate, discharge, complete, finish, consummate, conclude; *rare* effectuate.
OPPOSITES fail in; give up.

accomplished ▶ adjective *an accomplished pianist* **expert**, skilled, skilful, masterly, virtuoso, master, consummate, proficient, talented, gifted, adept, adroit, deft, dexterous, able, good, competent, capable, efficient, experienced, seasoned, trained, practised, professional, polished, well versed, versed, smart, clever, ingenious, ready, apt, handy, artful; magnificent, brilliant, splendid, marvellous, impressive, excellent, formidable, outstanding, first-class, first-rate, fine; deadly; *informal* great, mean, wicked, nifty, crack, ace, wizard; *Brit. informal* a dab hand at; *N. Amer. informal* crackerjack; *vulgar slang* shit-hot; *archaic or humorous* compleat; *rare* habile.
OPPOSITE incompetent.

accomplishment ▶ noun **1** *the reduction of inflation was a remarkable accomplishment* **achievement**, act, deed, exercise, exploit, performance, attainment, effort, feat, manoeuvre, operation, move, stunt, stratagem, coup, master stroke, stroke of genius, triumph.
2 *typing was another of her accomplishments* **ability**, **talent**, skill, gift, attainment, achievement, aptitude, faculty, capability, proficiency, forte, knack.
3 *a poet of considerable accomplishment* **expertise**, skill, skilfulness, expertness, adeptness, adroitness, deftness, dexterity, ability, prowess, mastery, achievement, competence, competency, capability, proficiency, efficiency, aptitude, artistry, art, finesse, flair, virtuosity, experience, professionalism, talent, cleverness, smartness, ingenuity, versatility; *informal* know-how.

accord ▶ noun **1** *the two countries were about to sign an economic cooperation accord* **pact**, treaty, agreement, settlement, deal, entente, concordat, concord, protocol, compact, contract, convention.
2 *the two sides failed to reach accord* **agreement**, consensus, unanimity, harmony, unison, unity, concord, concert, like-mindedness, rapport, conformity, congruence, settlement.
□ **of one's own accord** *Matthew went to sea of his own accord* **voluntarily**,

of one's own free will, of one's own volition, of one's own choice, of one's own choosing, by choice, by preference; willingly, readily, freely, intentionally, deliberately, on purpose, purposely, spontaneously, without being asked, without being forced, without hesitation, without reluctance; gladly, with pleasure, with good grace, eagerly, enthusiastically.
OPPOSITES reluctantly, under duress.

□ **with one accord** *the association is acting with one accord in this matter* **unanimously**, in complete agreement, with one mind, unitedly, concertedly, without exception, as one, of one voice, to a man.
OPPOSITES separately; in disarray.

▶ **verb 1** *the national assembly accorded the General more power* **give**, grant, tender, present, award, hand, vouchsafe, concede, yield, cede; confer on, bestow on, vest in, put in someone's hands; invest with, endow with, entrust with, favour with.
OPPOSITES withhold; remove.
2 *such an idea appears to accord with the known state of affairs* **correspond**, agree, tally, match up, concur, coincide, be in agreement, be consistent, equate, harmonize, be in harmony, be compatible, be consonant, be congruous, be in tune, dovetail, correlate; conform to; suit, fit, match, parallel; *informal* square; *N. Amer. informal* jibe.
OPPOSITES disagree, contrast.

accordance ▶ **noun** *the accordance of a suitable welcome to a visiting dignitary* **granting**, conferring, bestowal, tendering.
□ **in accordance with** *they had acted in accordance with their orders* **in agreement with**, in conformity with, in line with, commensurate with, in compliance with, true to, in fulfilment of, in obedience to, in the spirit of, following, honouring, heeding, observing.

according ▶ **adjective**
□ **according to 1** *she had had a narrow escape, according to the doctors* **as stated by**, as maintained by, as claimed by, on the authority of, on the report of, in the opinion of.
2 *cook the rice according to the instructions* **as specified by**, as per, in accordance with, in compliance with, in agreement with, in line with, in keeping with, commensurate with, in harmony with, in conformity with, in obedience to, true to, in fulfilment of, following, honouring, heeding, observing.
3 *salary will be fixed according to experience* **in proportion to**, proportional to, commensurate with, in relation to, relative to, corresponding to, dependent on, based on.

accordingly ▶ **adverb 1** *they appreciate the danger and act accordingly* **appropriately**, correspondingly, suitably, fitly, duly, consistently, properly, correctly.
OPPOSITE inappropriately.
2 *they needed each other and accordingly made an effort to conceal their mutual distrust* **therefore**, for that reason, consequently, so, as a result, as a consequence, in consequence, hence, thus, then, that being so, that being the case, on that account; *Latin* ergo; *formal* whence; *archaic* wherefore, thence.

accost ▶ **verb** *the police accosted him in the street* **speak to**, talk to, call to, shout to, hail, initiate a discussion with; address, approach, waylay, take aside, detain, stop, halt, grab, catch, confront, importune, solicit; *informal* buttonhole, collar; *Brit. informal* nobble.

account ▶ **noun 1** *the police officer then gave his account of the incident* **description**, report, version, story, narration, narrative, statement, news, explanation, exposition, interpretation, communiqué, recital, rendition, sketch, delineation, portrayal, tale; chronicle, history, record, archive, annal, minute, transaction, proceeding, transcript, diary, journal, weblog, blog, memoir, review, register, log, relation, rehearsal, side, view, impression; *Military, informal* sitrep.
2 *a sensitive account of the Debussy Sonata* **performance**, interpretation, rendering, rendition, reading, recital, playing, singing, execution.
3 (usually **accounts**) *the firm's accounts are in good order* **financial record**, book, ledger, journal, balance sheet, financial statement, results.
4 *departing guests pay their accounts at the office* **bill**, invoice, statement, list of charges, reckoning, tally; debt, amount due; *N. Amer.* check; *informal* tab; *archaic* score.
5 *he has accounts with several banks* **bank account**; current account, deposit account, savings account.
6 *the casualties they suffer will be of no account* **importance**, import, significance, consequence, moment, momentousness, substance, note, mark, prominence, value, weightiness, weight, concern, interest, gravity, seriousness.
□ **on account of** *they had closed early on account of the snow* **because of**, owing to, due to, as a consequence of, thanks to, through, by reason of, by/in virtue of, on grounds of, in view of; after, following, in the wake of, at a time of.
□ **on no account** *on no account sign any document without reading it* **never**, certainly not, absolutely not, definitely not, not in any event, by no means; not under/in any circumstances, under/in no circumstances, not for any reason, not for a moment; *informal* no way, not on your life, not in a million years, not for love or money; *Brit. informal* not on your nelly.
OPPOSITE definitely.
▶ **verb** *her visit could not be accounted a success* **consider**, regard as, reckon, hold to be, think, think of as, look on as, view as, see as, take for, judge, adjudge, count, deem, rate, gauge, interpret as.
□ **account for 1** *they must account for the delay* **explain**, give an explanation, come up with an explanation, explain away, answer for, give reasons for, rationalize, provide a rationale for, show grounds for, elucidate, illuminate, clear up; defend, vindicate, justify, excuse, make excuses for, make acceptable; *rare* extenuate.
2 *excise duties account for over half the price of Scotch* **constitute**, make up, comprise, form, compose, be responsible for, represent, supply, provide, give.
3 *prompt action has accounted for several terrorist gunmen* **dispose of**, finish off, make an end of, deal with, put paid to, take care of, clear up, mop up, eliminate, kill, destroy, dispatch, put out of action, incapacitate.

accountability ▶ **noun 1** *there must be clear accountability for the expenditure of public money* **responsibility**, liability, answerability.
OPPOSITE unaccountability.
2 *ministers' accountability to parliament* **answerability**, responsibility, reporting, obedience.

accountable ▶ **adjective 1** *the government was held accountable for the food shortage* **responsible**, liable, answerable, chargeable; to blame.
OPPOSITE unaccountable.
2 *ministers are* **accountable to** *parliament* **answerable**, responsible, reporting, subject; under the charge of, bound to obey, obeying, bound by.
3 *the game's popularity is barely accountable* **explicable**, explainable; understandable, comprehensible, intelligible, definable, reasonable, unsurprising.

accoutrements ▶ **plural noun** *all the alarming accoutrements of modern medicine* **paraphernalia**, equipment, stuff, things, apparatus, tackle, kit, implements, tools, utensils, material(s), appliances, rig, outfit, regalia, appurtenances, impedimenta, miscellaneous articles, odds and ends, bits and pieces, bits and bobs, trappings, accessories, trimmings, adornments, ornamentation, furnishings, fittings, appointments; belongings, possessions, effects, personal effects, property, baggage, chattels, movables; *informal* gear, junk, rubbish, the necessary, dunnage, traps; *Brit. informal* clobber, gubbins, odds and sods; *archaic* equipage.

accredit ▶ **verb 1** *he was* **accredited with** *being one of the world's fastest sprinters* **recognize as**, credit with; have something ascribed to one, have something attributed to one, receive the credit for, be given the credit for.
2 *the discovery of distillation is usually* **accredited to** *the Arabs* **ascribe**, attribute, chalk up; lay at the door of.
3 *professional bodies accredit these research degrees* **recognize**, license, authorize, approve, certify, warrant, empower, depute, endorse, sanction, vouch for, put one's seal of approval on, appoint.
OPPOSITE ban.

accredited ▶ **adjective** *the UK accredited representative* **official**, appointed, legal, recognized, licensed, authorized, approved, certified, warranted, empowered, deputed, endorsed, sanctioned, vouched for.

accretion ▶ **noun 1** *the accretion of sediments in coastal mangroves* **accumulation**, collecting, gathering, amassing, cumulation, accrual, growth, formation, enlargement, increase, gain, augmentation, rise, mushrooming, snowballing; *rare* amassment.
2 *the city has a historic core surrounded by recent accretions* **addition**, extension, growth, appendage, add-on, supplement.

accrue ▶ **verb 1** *financial benefits will* **accrue from** *restructuring* **result**, arise, follow, ensue, emanate, stem, spring, flow; be caused by, be brought about by, be produced by, originate in, attend, accompany, be consequent on.
2 *interest is added to the account as it accrues | the funds accrue interest* **accumulate**, collect, gather, build up, mount up, amass, grow, increase, augment, be added.

accumulate ▶ **verb** *he accumulated considerable wealth | the drug accumulates in the heart muscles* **gather**, collect, assemble; amass, stockpile, pile up, heap up, rack up, run up, scrape together, store (up), hoard, cumulate, lay in/up, garner; mass, increase, multiply, accrue, snowball; *Brit.* tot up; *informal* stash (away).
OPPOSITE dissipate.

accumulation ▶ **noun 1** *the accumulation of money* **amassing**, building up, build-up, collection, gathering, assembling, assembly, stockpiling, hoarding, cumulation, accrual; *rare* amassment.
OPPOSITE dissipation.
2 *an accumulation of rubbish* **mass**, build-up, pile, heap, stack, collection, gathering, stock, store, stockpile, reserve, hoard, bank, pool, fund, mine, reservoir, cumulation, accrual, aggregation, accretion, agglomerate, agglomeration.

accuracy ▶ **noun 1** *we have confidence in the accuracy of the statistics* **correctness**, precision, exactness, rightness, perfection, validity, unambiguousness, authority, reliability.

OPPOSITES inaccuracy, inexactness.
2 *the accuracy of his description was remarkable* **factuality**, literalness, correctness, fidelity, faithfulness, exactness, closeness, truth, truthfulness, veracity, authenticity, realism, verisimilitude, fairness; carefulness, strictness, conscientiousness, punctiliousness, thoroughness, scrupulousness, rigour; *rare* veridicality, scrupulosity.
OPPOSITES inaccuracy, looseness.
3 *she hit the ball with great accuracy* **precision**, carefulness, meticulousness.
OPPOSITES inaccuracy, waywardness.

accurate ▶ **adjective 1** *accurate information* **correct**, precise, exact, right, errorless, error-free, without error, faultless, perfect, valid, specific, detailed, minute, explicit, clear-cut, word for word, unambiguous, meticulous, authoritative, reliable, canonical; *Brit. informal* spot on, bang on; *N. Amer. informal* on the money.
OPPOSITES inaccurate, inexact.
2 *an accurate description* **factual**, fact-based, literal, correct, faithful, exact, close, true, truthful, veracious, true to life, telling it like it is, as it really happened, lifelike, authentic, realistic, fair; convincing, careful, word-perfect, strict, conscientious, punctilious, painstaking, thorough, scrupulous, rigorous; *informal* on the mark, on the beam, on the nail, on the button; *Brit. informal* spot on, bang on; *rare* verisimilar, veristic, veridical.
OPPOSITES inaccurate, loose.
3 *an accurate shot* **well aimed**, precise, on target, unerring, deadly, lethal, sure, true, on the mark, careful, meticulous, painstaking, precision; *Brit. informal* spot on, bang on.
OPPOSITES inaccurate, wayward.

CHOOSE THE RIGHT WORD

accurate, precise, exact

All these words apply to information or statements that are correct.

- An **accurate** statement or representation has been put together with great care and corresponds to the facts (*he gave a frighteningly accurate description of her life | an accurate and intelligible technical drawing*). Both *accurate* and *exact* can be used to mean 'providing a faithful representation' (*an accurate description | an exact copy*).
- **Precise** denotes minute attention to detail and implies that something can be measured or quantified. It draws a contrast with something that may be correct (or 'accurate') but is more vague or approximate (*we have no precise figures for possible job losses | he gave her precise directions on the route*). The common idiom *to be precise* is used to narrow the focus of a topic and give more detail (*my parents live abroad—in North Borneo, to be precise*).
- **Exact** emphasizes that something has been definitely identified, with no margin for vagueness or error (*we may never know the exact number of deaths*), and an *exact statement* is one that is both precise and truthful. Unlike *precise*, *exact* is an adjective that cannot generally be modified by an adverb (one cannot say that something is '*very exact*'), which underlines the sense of absoluteness and pinpoint detail. Both *precise* and *exact* are used for emphasis (*at that precise moment | you can show me the exact spot*).

accurately ▶ **adverb 1** *they need to assess the age and numbers of whale stocks accurately* **correctly**, precisely, exactly, right, without error, faultlessly, perfectly, validly, specifically, in detail, minutely, explicitly, word for word, unambiguously, meticulously, authoritatively, reliably; *Brit. informal* spot on, bang on; *N. Amer. informal* on the money.
OPPOSITES inaccurately, inexactly.
2 *the Minister has accurately described the position* **factually**, literally, correctly, faithfully, exactly, closely, truly, truthfully, veraciously, like it is, as it really happened, authentically, realistically, fairly; convincingly, carefully, strictly, conscientiously, punctiliously, painstakingly, thoroughly, scrupulously, rigorously; *rare* veridically.
OPPOSITES inaccurately, loosely.
3 *the gun can shoot accurately at moving targets* **precisely**, with precise aim, on target, unerringly.
OPPOSITES inaccurately, waywardly.

accursed ▶ **adjective 1** (*informal*) *that accursed woman* **hateful**, detestable, loathsome, foul, abominable, damnable, odious, obnoxious, despicable, execrable, horrible, horrid, ghastly, awful, dreadful, terrible; annoying, irritating, infuriating, exasperating; *informal* damned, damn, blasted, beastly, pesky, pestilential, infernal; *archaic* scurvy, loathly.
OPPOSITES pleasant, nice.
2 (*literary*) *he and his line are accursed* **cursed**, under a curse, damned, doomed, condemned, ill-fated, ill-omened, jinxed, wretched, blighted; *rare* anathematized.
OPPOSITE blessed.

accusation ▶ **noun** *the man's lawyer said the accusation was groundless* **allegation**, charge, claim, assertion, asseveration, attribution, incrimination, imputation, denouncement, indictment, arraignment, citation, inculpation, blame, condemnation, criticism, complaint; suit, lawsuit; *Brit.* plaint; *N. Amer.* impeachment, bill of indictment; *N. Amer. informal* beef.

accuse ▶ **verb 1** *four people were accused of assault* **charge with**, indict for, arraign for, take to court for, put on trial for, bring to trial for, prosecute for; summons, cite, make accusations about, lay charges against, file charges against, prefer charges against; *N. Amer.* impeach for; *archaic* inculpate.
OPPOSITES absolve, clear, exonerate.
2 *the companies have been accused of causing job losses* **blame for**, hold responsible for, lay the blame on someone for, hold accountable for, hold answerable for, condemn for, criticize for, denounce for; impute blame to, assign guilt to, attribute liability to, declare guilty; *informal* lay at the door of, point the finger at, stick on, pin on.
OPPOSITES defend, hold blameless.

accustom ▶ **verb** *she could not accustom herself to an altered way of life* **adapt**, adjust, acclimatize, attune, habituate, accommodate, assimilate, acculturate, inure, harden, condition, reconcile, become resigned, resign; get used to, come to terms with, come to accept, learn to live with, make familiar with, become acquainted with; find one's feet, get one's bearings, blend in, fit in; *N. Amer.* acclimate.

accustomed ▶ **adjective 1** *the money would not have kept Nicholas in his accustomed lifestyle* **customary**, usual, normal, habitual, familiar, regular, routine, ordinary, typical, traditional, conventional, established, common, general, standard, prevailing, confirmed, fixed, set, settled, stock; *literary* wonted.
OPPOSITES unusual, unaccustomed.
2 *she is accustomed to being told what to do* **used to**, adapted, adjusted, habituated, hardened, no stranger to; familiar with, acquainted with, at home with, in the habit of, experienced in, versed in, conversant with.
OPPOSITES unfamiliar, unused to.

ace (*informal*) ▶ **noun** *a rowing ace* **expert**, master, genius, virtuoso, maestro, professional, adept, past master, doyen, champion, star, winner; *German* wunderkind; *informal* demon, pro, wizard, hotshot, whizz, wiz; *Brit. informal* dab hand; *N. Amer. informal* maven, crackerjack.
OPPOSITE amateur.
▶ **adjective** *an ace tennis player* **excellent**, very good, first-rate, first-class, marvellous, wonderful, magnificent, outstanding, superlative, formidable, virtuoso, masterly, expert, champion, fine, consummate, skilful, adept; *informal* great, terrific, tremendous, superb, smashing, fantastic, sensational, fabulous, fab, crack, hotshot, A1, mean, demon, awesome, magic, wicked, tip-top, top-notch; *Brit. informal* brilliant, brill; *vulgar slang* shit-hot.
OPPOSITES mediocre, amateurish.

acerbic ▶ **adjective 1** *he was renowned for his abrasive manner and acerbic tongue* **sharp**, sarcastic, sardonic, satirical, scathing, cutting, razor-edged, incisive, penetrating, piercing, biting, stinging, searing, keen, caustic, trenchant, bitter, acrimonious, astringent, harsh, severe, devastating, abrasive, wounding, hurtful, unkind, cruel, vitriolic, virulent, mordant, venomous, waspish, poisonous, spiteful, vicious, malicious; *N. Amer.* acerb; *informal* bitchy, catty; *Brit. informal* sarky; *N. Amer. informal* snarky; *rare* mordacious, acidulous.
OPPOSITES mild, kind.
2 *a yellowy acerbic fluid came out of the tap* **sour**, acid, acidic, acidulated, tart, bitter, unsweetened, sharp, acetic, acetous, vinegary, pungent, acrid; unpleasant, distasteful; *N. Amer.* acerb; *rare* acidulous.
OPPOSITE sweet.

ache ▶ **noun 1** *an extremely bad stomach ache* **pain**, dull pain, pang, twinge, throb; gnawing, stabbing, sting, stinging, spasm, muscular spasm, cramp, convulsion; smarting, soreness, tenderness, irritation, discomfort.
2 *his absence was a constant nagging ache in her heart* **sorrow**, sadness, misery, grief, anguish, suffering, pain, agony, torture, wretchedness, distress, hurt, affliction, woe, mourning.
OPPOSITE joy.
3 *she felt that Christian ache for redemption* **longing**, yearning, craving, desire, pining, hankering, hunger, hungering, thirst, itch, burning; *informal* yen.
OPPOSITE disinclination.
▶ **verb 1** *the box was so heavy that it made his shoulders ache* **hurt**, be sore, be painful, be in pain, throb, pound, twinge; smart, gnaw, burn, tingle, sting, be uncomfortable, be tender, give someone trouble; *informal* play up, give someone gyp.
2 *her heart ached unbearably* **grieve**, sorrow, be sorrowful, be sad, be distressed, be in distress, be miserable, mourn, be mournful, lament, agonize, anguish, be in anguish, suffer, bleed; eat one's heart out, weep and wail.
OPPOSITE rejoice.
3 *the whole world seemed to ache for summer's coming* **long for**, yearn for, hunger for, thirst for, hanker for, hanker after, pine for, pine after, itch for, be desperate for, be unable to wait for; crave, desire, covet; *informal* have a yen for, yen for, be dying for; *archaic* be athirst for, suspire for.

achieve ▶ **verb** *we hope that our goals will be achieved | he achieved distinction*

as an artist **attain**, reach, arrive at; realize, carry off, bring off, pull off, bring about, accomplish, carry through, fulfil, execute, perform, engineer, carry out, bring to fruition, conclude, complete, finish, consummate; earn, win, gain, find, establish, acquire, obtain, procure, come by, get, secure, clinch, seize, wrest, hook, net; *informal* wrap up, polish off, bag, wangle, swing; *rare* effectuate, reify.

achievement ▶ noun **1** *the achievement of a high rate of economic growth* **attainment**, reaching, gaining, winning, acquirement, procurement; realization, accomplishment, fulfilment, fulfilling, carrying out, carrying through, effecting, implementation, execution, performance, engineering; conclusion, concluding, completion, completing, close, closing, finishing, consummation, success, fruition; *informal* winding up; *rare* effectuation, reification.
2 *they felt justifiably proud of their achievement* **accomplishment**, attainment, feat, performance, undertaking, act, action, deed, effort, exploit, manoeuvre, operation, enterprise; work, handiwork, creation; **triumph**, success, positive result, coup, master stroke, stroke of genius.

achiever ▶ noun *he will go down in financial history as a great achiever* **performer**, doer, worker, succeeder, high achiever, activist, man of action, woman of action, entrepreneur; success; *informal* **high-flyer**, go-getter, success story, whizz kid, powerhouse, fireball, human dynamo, wheeler-dealer, live wire, tiger, giant.
OPPOSITES loser; failure.

Achilles heel ▶ noun *the cost of the process may prove to be its Achilles heel* **weak spot**, weak point, weakness, vulnerable spot, soft underbelly, shortcoming, failing, imperfection, flaw, defect, deficiency, fault, foible, chink in one's armour; downfall, undoing, nemesis, Waterloo.
OPPOSITE strength.

aching ▶ adjective **1** *he had a stiff neck and an aching back* **painful**, achy, sore, stiff, hurt, tender, uncomfortable, troublesome; hurting, in pain, throbbing, pounding, twingeing; smarting, gnawing, burning, tingling, stinging, agonizing, searing, feeling tender, feeling uncomfortable, giving someone trouble; *informal* killing, playing someone up, giving someone gyp.
2 *she's nursing an aching heart* **sorrowful**, sad, mournful, miserable, upset, distressed, anguished, heavy with grief, grief-stricken, wretched, heavy; **grieving**, sorrowing, mourning, lamenting, in distress, in anguish, suffering, bleeding.
OPPOSITES cheerful, light.

acid *See centre pages for lists of* **Acids** **Amino Acids**
▶ adjective **1** *a very juicy fruit with a slightly acid flavour* **acidic**, **sour**, tart, bitter, unsweetened, sharp, biting, acrid, pungent, acerbic, vinegary, vinegarish, acetic, acetous; *rare* acidulous, acidulated.
OPPOSITE sweet.
2 *she was prone to making acid remarks* **acerbic**, **sarcastic**, sharp, sardonic, satirical, scathing, cutting, razor-edged; incisive, penetrating, piercing, biting, stinging, searing; keen, caustic, trenchant, mordant, bitter, acrimonious, astringent; harsh, severe, abrasive, wounding, hurtful, unkind, cruel, vitriolic, virulent, venomous, poisonous, waspish, spiteful, vicious, malicious; *N. Amer.* acerb; *informal* bitchy, catty; *Brit. informal* sarky; *N. Amer. informal* snarky; *rare* mordacious, acidulous.
OPPOSITES kind, pleasant, complimentary.

acknowledge ▶ verb **1** *the government acknowledged the need to begin talks* **admit**, accept, grant, allow, concede, confess, own, appreciate, recognize, realize, be aware of, be conscious of; subscribe to, approve (of), agree to, accede to, concur with, acquiesce in, go along with, respect, cooperate with, bow to; *informal* take on board, be wise to; *rare* cognize.
OPPOSITES reject, deny.
2 *he did not acknowledge Colin, but hurried on past* **greet**, salute, address, hail, accost; nod to, wave to, signal to, raise one's hat to, say hello to, smile at; recognize, notice.
OPPOSITE ignore.
3 *few people acknowledged my letters* **answer**, return, reply to, respond to, react to; write back to someone, come back to someone.
OPPOSITE overlook.
4 *Douglas was glad to acknowledge her help* **express gratitude for**, show appreciation for, give thanks for, thank someone for, pay tribute to someone for, salute someone for, toast someone for; honour, celebrate, praise, speak highly of.

acknowledged ▶ adjective *he is the acknowledged leader of the Turkish community* **recognized**, admitted, accepted, approved, accredited, confirmed, declared, proclaimed, confessed, sworn, avowed; undisputed, undoubted, unquestioned, unchallenged; rightful, true, proper, correct, genuine, authorized, sanctioned, just.

acknowledgement ▶ noun **1** *there was* **acknowledgement** *of the need to take new initiatives* **acceptance**, admission, granting, allowing, concession, confession, appreciation, recognition, realization, awareness, cognizance, knowledge; approval of, acquiescence in, agreement with, concurrence with, respect for, cooperation with.
OPPOSITE denial.
2 *Travis gave a smile of acknowledgement* **greeting**, welcome, salutation, saluting, hailing, address, hello, hallo; recognition, notice, heed, consideration.
3 *I sent off the application form but there was no acknowledgement* **answer**, reply, response, reaction; answering; receipt; *informal* comeback.
4 *their land has been exploited without acknowledgement or compensation* **thanks**, gratitude, appreciation, praise, commendation, credit, recognition, regard, respect; expression of appreciation, expression of gratitude, mention, honourable mention; a pat on the back, a round of applause; *informal* bouquets, brownie points; *rare* laudation.
OPPOSITE ingratitude.

acme ▶ noun *she was at the acme of her power* **peak**, pinnacle, zenith, highest point, high point, crown, crest, summit, top, tip, apex, apogee; climax, culmination, height, maximum, optimum, extremity, limit, upper limit, crowning point, prime, flower, flowering, bloom, blooming, highlight; *informal* high noon.
OPPOSITES nadir, bottom, lowest point.

acolyte ▶ noun *he found himself surrounded by eager acolytes* **assistant**, helper, attendant, retainer, servant, minion, underling, lackey, henchman; **follower**, disciple, supporter, votary, satellite, shadow; *informal* sidekick, man/girl Friday, running dog, groupie, hanger-on; *archaic* liegeman, pursuivant; *Hinduism* chela; *rare* janissary.
OPPOSITES leader, master, mistress.

acquaint ▶ verb *it is sensible to* **acquaint** *yourself* **with** *some basic facts | they were getting* **acquainted with** *each other's work* **familiarize**, make familiar, make conversant, get/keep up to date; accustom to, make known to, make aware of, inform of, advise of, apprise of, brief as to, give information about; enlighten, keep posted, let know; prime on, ground in, instruct in, teach in, educate in, school in, indoctrinate in, initiate into; *informal* give the gen about, give the low-down on, give a rundown of, fill in on, gen up on, clue up about, clue in on, put in the picture about, keep up to speed with.

acquaintance ▶ noun **1** *Mr Barnet was no more than a business acquaintance* **contact**, associate, connection, ally, colleague; *French* confrère.
2 *she had prospered from her acquaintance with the sergeant* **association**, relationship, contact, social contact; fellowship, companionship.
3 *the critical reader must have some* **acquaintance with** *poetry already* **familiarity**, conversance, conversancy, contact, acquaintanceship; knowledge of, experience of, awareness of, understanding of, comprehension of, cognizance of, grasp of; proficiency in, skill in, expertise in, insight into; *informal* know-how.

acquainted ▶ adjective **1** *she was well* **acquainted with** *Gothic literature* **familiar**, conversant, at home, up to date, up; well versed in, knowledgeable about, well informed about, cognizant in, apprised of, abreast of, no stranger to; *French* au fait, au courant; *informal* well up on, in the know about, genned up on, clued in on, wise to, hip to.
OPPOSITES unfamiliar; ignorant.
2 *I am not personally* **acquainted with** *him* **known to**; familiar, friendly, on friendly terms, on good terms, on a sociable footing.

acquiesce ▶ verb *he* **acquiesced in** *his sister's marriage with a divorced man* **permit**, consent to, agree to, allow, assent to, give one's consent to, accept, concur with, give one's assent to, give one's blessing to, say yes to, give the nod to, give one's approval to; comply with, conform to, abide by, respect, stand by, cooperate with, tolerate, brook; give in to, bow to, yield to, submit to; *informal* go along with, give the go-ahead to, give the thumbs up to, OK, okay, give the green light to, say the word; *archaic* suffer.
OPPOSITE forbid.

CHOOSE THE RIGHT WORD

acquiesce, agree, consent, assent
See AGREE.

acquiescence ▶ noun *the tsar secured the acquiescence of the nobility* **consent**, agreement, acceptance, accession, concurrence, approval, seal of approval, approbation, assent, leave, permission, blessing, sanction; compliance, conforming, conformity, adherence, respect, accord, accordance; conceding, concession, deference, yielding, bowing, submission, surrender, obedience; *informal* OK, say-so, go-ahead, green light, thumbs up, nod; *archaic* abidance; *rare* permit.
OPPOSITE refusal.

acquiescent ▶ adjective *the masses are generally apolitical and acquiescent* **compliant**, complying, consenting, cooperative, willing, obliging, agreeable, amenable, tractable, persuadable, easily persuaded, pliant, flexible, easy, unprotesting, resigned; **submissive**, servile, subservient, obsequious, ingratiating, toadying, Uriah Heepish, self-effacing, unassertive, yielding, biddable, docile, deferential, respectful; *informal* bootlicking; *rare* obeisant, persuasible, suasible, convincible, susceptive, longanimous, resistless.

acquire ▶ verb *she acquired a collection of fine art prints | I rapidly acquired the confidence of the leadership* **obtain**, come by, come to have, get, receive, gain, earn, win, come into, come in for, take possession of, take receipt of, be given; buy, purchase, procure, possess oneself of, secure; gather, collect, pick up, appropriate, amass, build up, hook, net, land; achieve, attain; *informal* get one's hands on, get one's mitts on, get hold of, grab, bag, score, swing, nab, collar, cop.
OPPOSITES lose; part with.

acquirement ▶ noun **1** *her husband praised her acquirements* **attainment**, achievement, accomplishment, skill, art, talent, capability, qualification; proficiency, mastery.
2 *they lived for the acquirement of money* **acquisition**, acquiring, obtaining, gaining, earning, winning, securing, procuring, procurement; collecting, collection, appropriation, amassing.
OPPOSITE loss.

acquisition ▶ noun **1** *the gallery's Bronze Room will house a new acquisition* **purchase**, **accession**, addition, asset; buy, investment, possession, accretion; property, goods.
2 *the acquisition of funds for the war effort* **obtaining**, acquiring, gaining, gain, procuring, procurement, collecting, collection, attainment, appropriation, amassing.

acquisitive ▶ adjective *he had the acquisitive instinct of a magpie* **greedy**, **hoarding**, covetous, avaricious, possessive, grasping, grabbing, predatory, avid, rapacious, mercenary, materialistic, money-oriented; *informal* money-grubbing, money-grabbing, on the make; *N. Amer. informal* grabby; *Austral. informal* hungry; *rare* quaestuary, Mammonish, Mammonistic.

acquisitiveness ▶ noun *the grasping acquisitiveness of an affluent society* **greed**, greediness, covetousness, cupidity, possessiveness, grasping, graspingness, grabbing, avarice, avidity, predatoriness, rapaciousness, rapacity, voracity, voraciousness, mercenariness, materialism; *informal* money-grubbing, money-grabbing; *N. Amer. informal* grabbiness; *rare* Mammonism.

acquit ▶ verb **1** *the jury acquitted her of attempted arson* **absolve**, clear, exonerate, exculpate, declare innocent, find innocent, pronounce not guilty; discharge, release, liberate, emancipate, free, set free, deliver, spare, exempt, dismiss; vindicate; *informal* let someone off (the hook).
OPPOSITE convict.
2 *the boys **acquitted themselves** exceedingly well* **conduct oneself**, bear oneself; perform, act, behave; *rare* comport oneself, deport oneself.
3 (*archaic*) *they **acquitted** themselves **of** their important duty* **discharge**, execute, perform, do, carry out, effect, implement, bring about, bring off, accomplish, achieve, fulfil, complete; *informal* pull off; *rare* effectuate.

acquittal ▶ noun **1** *we make every effort to secure the acquittal of our clients* **absolution**, clearing, exoneration, exculpation, declaration of innocence; discharge, release, freeing, liberation, deliverance; vindication; *informal* let-off, letting off.
OPPOSITE conviction.
2 (*archaic*) *we received no guidance for the acquittal of these duties* **discharge**, execution, performance, doing, carrying out, effecting, implementation, implementing, bringing off, accomplishment, achievement, fulfilment, fulfilling, completion, completing; *informal* pulling off; *rare* effectuation.

acrid ▶ adjective *the acrid smell of smoke clung about the building* **pungent**, bitter, sharp, sour, tart, harsh, acid, acidic, acidulated, vinegary, acerbic, acetic, acetous; stinging, burning, irritating, nauseating; noxious, strong, malodorous, odorous, burnt, sooty; *literary* mephitic; *rare* acidulous, miasmic, miasmal.
OPPOSITE sweet.

acrimonious ▶ adjective *they had a heated and acrimonious discussion* **bitter**, rancorous, caustic, acerbic, scathing, sarcastic, acid, harsh, sharp, razor-edged, cutting, astringent, trenchant, mordant, virulent; spiteful, vicious, crabbed, vitriolic, savage, hostile, hate-filled, venomous, poisonous, nasty, ill-natured, mean, malign, malicious, malignant, waspish, pernicious, splenetic, irascible, choleric; *informal* bitchy, catty, slashing; *rare* acidulous, mordacious, envenomed, squint-eyed.

acrimony ▶ noun *the meeting ended with acrimony on both sides* **bitterness**, rancour, resentment, ill feeling, ill will, bad blood, animosity, hostility, enmity, antagonism, irascibility, waspishness, spleen; malice, spitefulness, crabbedness, causticity, sarcasm, venom, poison, viciousness, nastiness, harshness, sharpness, acerbity, virulence, astringency; grudge, grievance.
OPPOSITE goodwill.

acrobat ▶ noun *the acrobat performed a back somersault* **tumbler**, gymnast; rope walker, tightrope walker, wire walker, balancer, trapeze artist; stuntman, stuntwoman; *rare* equilibrist, aerialist, funambulist.

acrobatics ▶ plural noun **1** *they performed staggering feats of acrobatics* **gymnastics**, gymnastic feats, gymnastic skills, tumbling, balancing, nimbleness; tightrope walking, rope walking, wire walking; stunts, agility, skill; *rare* funambulism.
2 *the acrobatics required to negotiate major international contracts* **agility**, skill, mental agility, quick thinking, alertness, inventiveness, nimbleness.

across ▶ preposition **1** *I ran across the street* **to the other side of**, from one side of … to the other, over, throughout the width/expanse of, covering, everywhere on, on all parts of.
2 *they lived across the river from us* on the other side of, over, beyond, past.
WORD LINKS
related prefix **trans-** (e.g. ***transfer, transatlantic***)

act ▶ verb **1** *the Government must act to remedy the situation* **take action**, take steps, take measures, take the initiative, move, make a move, react, do something, proceed, go ahead; make progress, make headway, be active, be employed, be busy; *informal* get moving.
OPPOSITE do nothing.
2 *over dinner Alison began to act oddly* **behave**, function, react, perform; conduct oneself, acquit oneself, bear oneself; *rare* comport oneself, deport oneself.
3 *the scents act as a powerful aphrodisiac* **operate**, work, take effect, function, serve, be efficacious.
4 *he acted in a highly successful film* **perform**, play, play a part, take part, be an actor, be an actress, be one of the cast, appear; *informal* tread the boards.
5 *we laughed, but most of us were just acting* **pretend**, play-act, sham, fake, feign, put it on, bluff, pose, posture, masquerade, dissemble, dissimulate; *informal* kid.
□ **act for** *the estate agent was acting for a prospective buyer* **represent**, act on behalf of, speak on behalf of; **stand in for**, fill in for, deputize for, cover for, substitute for, be a substitute for, replace, take the place of, act in place of, do/be a locum for, sit in for, understudy; hold the fort, step into the breach; *informal* sub for, fill someone's shoes/boots; *N. Amer. informal* pinch-hit for.
□ **act on/upon 1** *the drug acted directly on the blood vessels* **affect**, have an effect on, influence, exert influence on, work on, have an impact on, impact on, alter, change, modify, transform, condition, control.
OPPOSITE have no effect on.
2 *he was merely acting on the orders of the party leader* **comply with**, act in accordance with, follow, go along with; **obey**, take heed of, heed, conform to, abide by, adhere to, stick to, stand by, uphold, fulfil, meet, discharge.
OPPOSITE flout.
□ **act up 1** *the pupils are past masters at acting up in class* **misbehave**, give someone trouble, cause someone trouble, act badly, get up to mischief, get up to no good, be bad, be naughty, forget oneself, misconduct oneself; clown about/around, fool about/around, act the clown, act the fool, act the goat, act foolishly; *informal* carry on, mess about/around; *Brit. informal* muck about/around, play up.
2 *the computers are always acting up* **malfunction**, crash, develop a fault, go wrong, break down, give out, stall, be defective, be faulty, fail, cease to function, cease to work, stop working; *informal* conk out, go kaput, go phut, go on the blink, be on the blink; *Brit. informal* pack up, play up.
▶ noun **1** *a life filled with acts of kindness | a criminal act* **deed**, action, gesture, feat, exploit, move, performance, undertaking, manoeuvre, stunt, operation, venture, effort, enterprise, achievement, accomplishment.
2 *the Act raised the tax on tobacco* **law**, decree, statute, bill, Act of Parliament, edict, fiat, dictum, dictate, enactment, resolution, ruling, rule, judgement, canon, ordinance, proclamation, command, commandment, mandate, measure, stipulation, direction, requirement; legislation; (*in Tsarist Russia*) ukase; (*in Spanish-speaking countries*) pronunciamento.
3 *I have written one act of a play* **division**, section, subsection, portion, part, segment, component, bit; passage, episode, chapter.
4 *a marvellous music hall act* **performance**, turn, routine, number, item, piece, sketch, skit, playlet, dance, song; show, production, presentation, entertainment; *informal* gig.
5 *my mother thinks crying is simply putting on an act* **pretence**, false display, show, front, facade, masquerade, charade, guise, posture, pose, affectation, appearance; sham, fake, bluff, hoax; make-believe, play-acting, feigning, shamming, posturing, posing, counterfeit, subterfuge, dissimulation, dissemblance, fabrication, falsification; *informal* a put-on, a put-up job.

acting ▶ noun **1** *she studied the theory and practice of acting* **drama**, the theatre, the stage, the performing arts, dramatic art, dramatics, dramaturgy, stagecraft, theatricals, theatrics, the thespian art, show business; performing, performance, portraying, portrayal, playing a role, appearing on stage; *informal* the boards, treading the boards, show biz; *rare* thespianism, histrionics.
2 *EC law prevents the ministers from acting* **taking action**, taking steps, taking measures, doing something, moving, making a move, reacting, functioning, working, performing.
3 *he looks angry but we know it's all just acting* **pretending**, pretence, play-acting, make-believe, illusion, masquerade, feigning, shamming, hoaxing,

bluffing, posture, posturing, posing, affectation, counterfeit, subterfuge, dissimulation, dissemblance, falsification, humbug; sham, hoax, bluff, show, front, facade, charade, guise, pose; *Brit.* false colours; *informal* a put-on, a put-up job.
▶ **adjective** *the acting governor of the bank* **substitute**, deputy, reserve, fill-in, stand-in, caretaker; **temporary**, short-term, provisional, interim, intervening, pro tem, improvised, surrogate, stopgap, transitional, changeover; *Latin* pro tempore, ad interim; *informal* second-string; *N. Amer. informal* pinch-hitting.
OPPOSITE permanent.

action ▶ **noun 1** *there can be no excuse for their actions* **deed**, act, activity, move, gesture, undertaking, exploit, manoeuvre, achievement, accomplishment, venture, enterprise, endeavour, effort, exertion; work, handiwork, doing, creation, performance, behaviour, conduct; reaction, response.
2 *they recognized the need for local community action* **steps**, measures, activity, movement, work, working, effort, exertion, operation.
3 *he was a patriot and a man of action* **energy**, vitality, vigour, forcefulness, drive, push, ambition, motivation, initiative, spirit, liveliness, vim, pep; activity; *informal* get-up-and-go, punch, zip, pizzazz.
4 *they observed the action of hormones on the pancreas* **effect**, influence, power, working, work; result, consequence.
5 *he missed all the action while he was away* **excitement**, activity, bustle; happenings, occurrences, proceedings, events, incidents, episodes, eventualities, chain of events; *informal* goings-on.
6 *the men saw action in World War II | twenty-nine men died in the action* **fighting**, hostilities, battle, conflict, armed conflict, combat, warfare, war, bloodshed; engagement, clash, encounter, confrontation, skirmish, affray.
7 *he won his action but the damages awarded were nominal* **lawsuit**, legal action, suit, suit at law, case, cause, prosecution, litigation, legal dispute, legal contest; proceedings, legal proceedings, judicial proceedings.

activate ▶ **verb 1** *Mark pressed the button which activated the machine* **operate**, switch on, turn on, start, start off, start up, set going, get going, trigger off, trigger, trip, set in motion, actuate, initiate, initialize, energize, animate.
OPPOSITE switch off.
2 (*rare*) *I think she was activated by an extreme obstinacy* **motivate**, stimulate, actuate, move, drive, rouse, stir, stir up, fire, fire up, arouse, energize, animate; prompt, incite, spark off, influence, impel, spur on, urge, goad.

active ▶ **adjective 1** *they located the area of brain tissue that was active | the active ingredient of tobacco* **operative**, working, functioning, functional, operating, operational, in action, in operation, in force, live; **effective**, effectual, powerful, potent, non-passive, non-inert; *informal* up and running.
OPPOSITES inactive; inert.
2 *despite her illness she remained quite active* **mobile**, **energetic**, agile, sporty, nimble, vigorous, vital, dynamic, sprightly, spry, lively, animated, bouncy, bubbly, perky, frisky, zestful, spirited; busy, bustling, occupied, involved; *informal* on the go, on the move, full of get-up-and-go, full of vim and vigour, full of beans, sparky, zippy, peppy, bright-eyed and bushy-tailed; *N. Amer. informal* go-go.
OPPOSITE listless.
3 *he was an active member of the union* **hard-working**, busy, industrious, diligent, tireless, contributing, enterprising, influential; occupied, engaged, involved; **enthusiastic**, keen, committed, devoted, determined, zealous, militant, radical; *informal* go-getting, go-ahead.
OPPOSITES passive; indifferent.

> **CHOOSE THE RIGHT WORD**
> **active, busy, occupied, engaged**
> *See* BUSY.

activity ▶ **noun 1** *there was a lot of activity around the orchard* **bustle**, hustle and bustle, busyness, action, liveliness, movement, life, stir, animation, commotion, flurry, tumult, hubbub, excitement, agitation, fuss, whirl; happenings, occurrences, proceedings, events, incidents; *informal* toing and froing, comings and goings, to-do; *archaic* hurry scurry, pother.
OPPOSITE calm.
2 *Members of Parliament engage in a wide range of activities* **pursuit**, occupation, venture, undertaking, enterprise, project, scheme, business, job, affair, task, campaign; interest, hobby, pastime, recreation, diversion, entertainment; act, action, deed, doing, exploit, manoeuvre; *informal* thing, lark, caper.
3 *they often experience restricted activity due to illness* **functioning**, effectiveness, mobility, motion, movement; vitality, vigour, energy, strength, potency, dynamism; *informal* get-up-and-go, bounce, oomph, vim, vim and vigour.
OPPOSITE inactivity.

actor, actress *See centre pages for lists of* **Actors** **Roles**
▶ **noun performer**, player, trouper, theatrical, dramatic artist, thespian, member of the cast, artist, artiste; *Indian* filmi; *Brit. informal* luvvy; *archaic* histrionic, stager.
WORD LINKS
relating to actors **histrionic, theatrical, thespian**

actual ▶ **adjective** *they suffered actual physical harm* **real**, true, genuine, authentic, verified, attested, confirmed, definite, hard, plain, clear, clear-cut, undeniable, veritable; existing, existent, manifest, substantial, non-fictional, factual, unquestionable, indisputable; effective, realistic; *Latin* de facto, bona fide; *informal* real live, honest-to-goodness, your actual; *rare* unimaginary.
OPPOSITES notional; non-existent.

actuality ▶ **noun** *dissatisfaction occurs when actuality falls short of expectation* **reality**, fact, truth, the real world, real life, existence, living.
□ **in actuality** *the journey seemed a thousand miles though in actuality it was only five* **really**, in fact, in actual fact, in point of fact, as a matter of fact, in reality, actually, in truth, if truth be told, to tell the truth; *dated* indeed, truly; *archaic* in sooth, verily; *rare* in the concrete.

actually ▶ **adverb 1** *I looked upset but actually I was terribly excited* **really**, in fact, in actual fact, in point of fact, as a matter of fact, in reality, in actuality, in truth, if truth be told, to tell the truth; *dated* indeed, truly; *archaic* in sooth, verily; *rare* in the concrete.
2 *he had actually conspired against his friends* **literally**, to all intents and purposes, in effect; **even**, though it may seem strange, believe it or not, surprisingly, as it happens; *archaic* forsooth.

actuate ▶ **verb 1** *the sprinkler system was actuated by the fire* **activate**, operate, switch on, turn on, start up, set going, get going, start off, trigger off, trigger, trip, set in motion, initiate, initialize, energize, animate.
2 *they proved that the defendant was actuated by malice* **motivate**, stimulate, move, drive, rouse, stir, stir up, fire, fire up, arouse; **prompt**, incite, spark off, influence, impel, spur on, urge, goad; *rare* activate.

acumen ▶ **noun** *a gullible young man with little or no business acumen* **astuteness**, awareness, shrewdness, acuity, sharpness, sharp-wittedness, cleverness, brightness, smartness; judgement, understanding, sense, common sense, canniness, discernment, wisdom, wit, sagacity, perspicacity, ingenuity, insight, intuition, intuitiveness, perception, perspicuity, penetration; capability, enterprise, initiative, resourcefulness, flair, vision; brains, powers of reasoning; *French* savoir faire; *informal* nous, savvy, know-how, horse sense, gumption, grey matter; *Brit. informal* common; *N. Amer. informal* smarts; *rare* sapience, arguteness.
OPPOSITE witlessness.

acute ▶ **adjective 1** *Emily had an acute ear for instrumental sounds* **keen**, sharp, good, penetrating, discerning, perceptive, sensitive, subtle.
OPPOSITE poor.
2 *he has an exceptionally acute mind* **astute**, shrewd, sharp, sharp-witted, razor-sharp, rapier-like, quick, quick-witted, agile, nimble, ingenious, clever, intelligent, bright, brilliant, smart, canny, intuitive, discerning, perceptive, perspicacious, penetrating, insightful, incisive, piercing, discriminating, sagacious, wise, judicious; *informal* on the ball, quick off the mark, quick on the uptake, brainy, streetwise, savvy; *Brit. informal* suss; *Scottish & N. English informal* pawky; *N. Amer. informal* heads-up; *dated, informal* long-headed; *rare* argute, sapient.
OPPOSITE slow-witted.
3 *the acute food shortages of post-war England* **severe**, critical, drastic, dire, dreadful, terrible, awful, grave, bad, serious, profound; urgent, pressing, desperate; all-important, vital, dangerous, hazardous, perilous, precarious; life-threatening, life-and-death; *archaic* parlous; *rare* egregious.
OPPOSITE negligible.
4 *the meal gave us acute pains in our stomachs* **stabbing**, shooting, penetrating, piercing, sharp, keen, racking, searing, burning, consuming; fierce, ferocious; **intense**, severe, extreme, excruciating, agonizing, grievous, hellish, torturous, tormenting, unbearable, insufferable, unendurable, more than one can bear, more than flesh and blood can stand; *literary* exquisite.
OPPOSITES dull; mild.
5 *the patient had acute colitis* **severe**, intense, short-lasting; *Medicine* peracute; *informal* short and sharp.
OPPOSITE chronic.

> **CHOOSE THE RIGHT WORD**
> **acute, keen, penetrating**
> *See* KEEN.

acutely ▶ **adverb** *Lucy looked acutely embarrassed* **extremely**, exceedingly, very, markedly, severely, intensely, in the extreme, deeply, profoundly, keenly, sharply, painfully, desperately, awfully, terribly, tremendously, enormously, thoroughly, heartily; *informal* well, seriously, majorly, oh-so; *informal, dated* jolly, devilish; *N. Amer. informal* mighty, plumb; *S. African informal* lekker.
OPPOSITE slightly.

adage ▶ noun *it is vital for every pilot to remember the old adage 'safety first'* **saying**, maxim, axiom, proverb, aphorism, saw, dictum, precept, epigram, epigraph, motto, truism, platitude, cliché, commonplace; words of wisdom, pearls of wisdom; expression, phrase, formula, slogan, quotation; *rare* apophthegm, gnome.

adamant ▶ adjective *scientists are adamant about the absence of risk* **unshakeable**, immovable, inflexible, unwavering, uncompromising, resolute, resolved, determined, firm, rigid, steadfast; unswerving, stubborn, unrelenting, unyielding, unbending, obdurate, inexorable, intransigent, dead set, iron-willed, strong-willed, steely; *N. Amer.* rock-ribbed; *informal* stiff-necked; *rare* indurate.
OPPOSITE unsure.

adapt ▶ verb **1** *we've adapted the hotels to suit their needs* **modify**, alter, make alterations to, change, adjust, make adjustments to, convert, transform, redesign, restyle, refashion, remodel, reshape, revamp, rework, redo, reconstruct, reorganize; customize, tailor; improve, make improvements to, amend, refine; *informal* tweak.
OPPOSITE preserve.
2 *he has* ***adapted*** *well to his new home* **adjust**, acclimatize, accommodate, attune, habituate, acculturate, conform; familiarize oneself with, habituate oneself to, become habituated to, get used to, orient oneself in, condition oneself to; reconcile oneself to, resign oneself to, become resigned to, come to terms with, find one's way around; become naturalized, become seasoned, get one's bearings, find one's feet, blend in, fit in; *N. Amer.* acclimate.

adaptable ▶ adjective **1** *a conservatory is the most adaptable room in your home* **versatile**, variable, convertible, alterable, modifiable, adjustable, changeable; multi-purpose, all-purpose.
OPPOSITE limited.
2 *an adaptable workforce capable of acquiring new skills* **flexible**, adjustable, pliant, compliant, malleable, versatile, resilient, conformable; easy-going, accommodating, obliging, cooperative, amenable; *informal* easy.
OPPOSITE inflexible.

adaptation ▶ noun **1** *the adaptation of old buildings to new uses* **converting**, conversion, alteration, modification, adjustment, changing, transformation; remodelling, revamping, reshaping, reconstruction; tailoring, customizing.
2 *they studied the adaptation of an ethnic community to British society* **adjustment**, conformity, acclimatization, accommodation, attunement, familiarization, habituation, orientation, conditioning, inurement, hardening, seasoning, acculturation, assimilation, integration, domestication, naturalization; blending in, fitting in, settling in, settling down; *N. Amer.* acclimation.

add ▶ verb **1** *the front porch was added in 1751* **attach**, build on, add on, put on, put in, append, adjoin, join, affix, connect, annex; include.
OPPOSITE remove.
2 *the calculating machine could store and add 23-digit numbers* **add up**, add together, total, count, count up, figure up, compute, calculate, reckon, tally, enumerate, find the sum of; *Brit.* tot up; *dated* cast up.
OPPOSITE subtract.
3 *she added that she had every confidence in Laura* **go on to say**, state further, continue, carry on; *informal* tack on, tag on.
□ **add to** *her decision just added to his woe* **increase**, magnify, amplify, augment, intensify, heighten, deepen, enhance, boost, inflate, escalate; **exacerbate**, aggravate, inflame, worsen, make worse, compound, reinforce; add fuel to the fire/flames, fan the flames, put salt on the wound.
OPPOSITE lessen.
□ **add up 1** *the subsidies* ***added up to*** *£1700* **amount to**, come to, run to, number, make, total, equal, be equal to, be equivalent to, count as; *Brit.* tot up to.
2 *the recent riots* ***add up to*** *a severe and deepening crisis* **amount to**, constitute, comprise, equal, be equivalent to, approximate to; signify, signal, mean, indicate, suggest, denote, point to, be evidence of, be symptomatic of; *informal* spell, spell out; *literary* betoken.
3 *the situation just didn't add up* **make sense**, seem reasonable, seem plausible, stand to reason, stand up, hold up, hold water, bear examination, bear investigation, be verifiable, ring true, be convincing.
□ **add something up** *I added up all the subtotals* **total**, add together, count, count up, figure up, compute, calculate, reckon, tally, enumerate, find the sum of; *Brit.* tot up; *dated* cast up.
OPPOSITE subtract.

addendum ▶ noun *each chapter ends with a short addendum entitled 'Further Reading'* **appendix**, codicil, postscript, afterword, tailpiece, rider, coda, supplement, accompaniment; adjunct, appendage, addition, add-on, attachment, extension; *rare* postlude, subscript, allonge.

addict ▶ noun **1** *her brother was a heroin addict* **abuser**, user; *informal* **junkie**, druggy, druggie, space cadet, -freak, -head, -fiend, tripper, hype, hypo, cokey, pill-popper, metho; *N. Amer. informal* hophead, hoppy, needleman, schmecker, snowbird; *informal, dated* drugger; *N. Amer. informal, dated* dope, dopester, junker, muggler, snifter; *rare* narcotist, morphinist, morphiomaniac, etheromaniac, viper.
2 *the resort is a must for all skiing addicts* **enthusiast**, **fan**, fanatic, lover, devotee, aficionado, master, wizard; adherent, follower, admirer; *informal* buff, freak, nut, fiend, maniac, ace; *N. Amer. informal* geek, jock; *S. African informal* fundi.

addicted ▶ adjective **1** *he was seriously* ***addicted to*** *tranquillizers | he had the occasional bet, but he was never addicted* **dependent on**, given to using, given to abusing, in the habit of using; dependent, obsessive, obsessional; *informal* hooked on.
2 *she became* ***addicted to*** *the theatre* **devoted to**, dedicated to, fond of, partial to, keen on, enthusiastic about, enamoured of, in love with, infatuated with, obsessed with, fixated on, fanatical about; *informal* hooked on, gone on, wild about, nuts about, potty about, dotty about, crazy about.
OPPOSITE indifferent.

WORD LINKS
person addicted to ... **-holic (e.g. *alcoholic, chocoholic*)**

addiction ▶ noun **1** *he blamed Murray for his heroin addiction* **dependency**, dependence, craving, habit, weakness, compulsion, fixation, enslavement; *informal* monkey; *N. Amer. informal* jones.
2 *a slavish* ***addiction to*** *fashion* **devotion**, dedication; obsession with, infatuation with, passion for, love of, fondness for, weakness for, penchant for, predilection for, appetite for, mania for; *informal* thing about, yen for; *rare* appetency for.
OPPOSITE indifference.

addictive ▶ adjective *crack cocaine is highly addictive* **habit-forming**, causing addiction, causing dependency; compelling, compulsive; *Brit. informal* moreish.

addition ▶ noun **1** *the soil is greatly improved by the addition of compost* **inclusion**, adding, adding in, incorporation, introduction, insertion.
2 *an improved machine for the addition of numbers* **adding up**, counting, totalling, computation, calculation, reckoning, tallying, summation; *informal* totting up; *informal, dated* casting up.
3 *he proposes a number of additions to existing taxation* **supplement**, appendage, adjunct, addendum, add-on, extra, accompaniment, extension, rider; increase, increment, augmentation.
□ **in addition 1** *conditions were harsh and in addition some soldiers fell victim to snipers* **additionally**, as well, what's more, besides, furthermore, moreover, also, into the bargain, to boot.
2 *there were eight presidential candidates* ***in addition to*** *the General* **besides**, as well as, on top of, along with, plus, over and above; other than, apart from, excepting, with the exception of, excluding, not including, barring, bar, save (for), omitting, leaving out, not to mention, to say nothing of.

additional ▶ adjective *beach towels are provided without additional charge* **extra**, added, supplementary, supplemental, further, auxiliary, ancillary, subsidiary, secondary, attendant, accessory; more, other, another, new, fresh.

additionally ▶ adverb *the organization relied additionally on a vast network of informers* **also**, in addition, as well, too, besides, on top (of that), moreover, further, furthermore, what's more, over and above that, into the bargain, to boot; *archaic* withal, forbye.

additive ▶ noun *the marmalade is free from any artificial additives* **added ingredient**, addition, extra, add-on, supplement, accompaniment; preservative, flavour enhancer, colouring; *Brit. informal* E-number.

addled ▶ adjective *her brains were irretrievably addled* **muddled**, confused, fuddled, befuddled, bewildered, dazed, dizzy, disoriented, disorientated, stupefied, unbalanced, unhinged, demented, deranged; *informal* discombobulated, woolly, muzzy, woozy, dopey, not with it, bamboozled, fazed.

address ▶ noun **1** *Juliet looked at the scribbled address on the envelope* **inscription**, label, mark, superscription; directions.
2 *she wondered if she had come to the wrong address* **location**, locality, place, situation, whereabouts; house, flat, apartment, home, residence; *formal* dwelling, dwelling place, habitation, abode, domicile.
3 *the president's address received lukewarm applause* **speech**, lecture, talk, monologue, dissertation, discourse, oration, peroration; sermon, homily, lesson; *N. Amer.* salutatory; *informal* spiel; *rare* disquisition, allocution, predication.
▶ verb **1** *I addressed the envelope by hand* **label**, direct, inscribe, superscribe.
2 *the preacher addressed a crowded congregation* **talk to**, give a talk to, give an address to, speak to, make a speech to, lecture, give a lecture to, hold forth to, give a discourse to, give a dissertation to, give an oration to, declaim to; **preach to**, deliver a sermon to, give a sermon to, sermonize; *informal* speechify to, preachify to, spout to, jaw to, sound off to, spiel to, drone on to.
3 *she is always uncertain how to address her boss* **greet**, hail, salute, speak to, write to, talk to, make conversation with, approach; name, call, describe, designate; *formal* denominate.
4 *any correspondence should be addressed to the Banking Ombudsman* **send**, direct, post, mail, communicate, convey, forward, remit.
5 *hold the putter off the ground as you address the ball* **take aim at**, aim at, face.

6 *the minister failed to address the issue of subsidies | he* ***addressed himself to*** *the composition of a letter* **attend to**, tackle, see to, deal with, confront, grapple with, attack, buckle down to, get to grips with, embark on, settle down to, direct one's attention to, turn to, get down to, concentrate on, focus on, apply oneself to, devote oneself to; turn one's hand to, try to deal with, try to sort out, take up, take in hand, undertake, engage in, become involved in; *informal* get stuck into, get cracking on, get weaving on, have a crack at, have a go at, have a shot at, have a stab at.

adduce ▶ **verb** *facts and figures have been adduced to bolster the argument* **cite**, quote, name, mention, instance, specify, identify, give, point out, call attention to, refer to, make reference to; put forward, bring forward, present, offer, advance, propose, proffer, put up, moot, table, suggest, raise, come up with.

adept ▶ **adjective** *the Minoans were adept at sculpting figures from ivory* **expert**, proficient, accomplished, skilful, talented, gifted, masterly, virtuoso, consummate, peerless; adroit, dexterous, deft, nimble-fingered, handy, artful, able, capable, competent; brilliant, very good, splendid, marvellous, formidable, outstanding, first-rate, first-class, excellent, impressive, fine; *informal* great, top-notch, top-drawer, top-hole, tip-top, A1, wizard, magic, ace, fab, smashing, mean, crack, nifty, deadly, slick; *Brit. informal* brill, a dab hand at; *N. Amer. informal* crackerjack; *archaic or humorous* compleat; *rare* habile.
OPPOSITES inept; mediocre.
▶ **noun** *adepts at kung fu and karate can smash through stacks of roofing tiles* **expert**, past master, master, master hand, genius, virtuoso, maestro, doyen, artist, professional, veteran, old hand; grandmaster, champion, star, winner; *German* wunderkind; *informal* wizard, demon, ace, hotshot, pro, whizz, wiz, buff; *Brit. informal* dab hand; *N. Amer. informal* maven, crackerjack.
OPPOSITE amateur.

adequacy ▶ **noun 1** *questions were raised about the adequacy of the firm's audit procedures* **acceptability**, reasonableness, passableness, tolerableness, satisfactoriness, fairness; sufficiency, ampleness; appropriateness, suitability, suitableness, pertinence, appositeness, effectiveness, efficacy, usefulness, helpfulness.
2 *he had deep misgivings about his own adequacy* **capability**, competence, competency, ability, aptitude, skill, skilfulness, adeptness; effectiveness, efficacy, productiveness; qualifications, fitness, suitability; value, worth, merit.

adequate ▶ **adjective 1** *he lacked adequate financial resources* **sufficient**, enough, ample, requisite, apposite, appropriate, suitable.
OPPOSITE insufficient.
2 *the company provides an adequate but not top-notch service* **acceptable**, passable, reasonable, satisfactory, tolerable, fair, fairly good, pretty good, goodish, middle-of-the-road, mediocre, unexceptional, unexceptionable, undistinguished, unremarkable, ordinary, commonplace, indifferent, average, not bad, all right, good enough, so-so, minimal, medium, moderate, run-of-the-mill, forgettable; *informal* OK, okay, fair-to-middling, nothing to write home about, nothing to shout about, no great shakes, (plain) vanilla, bog-standard; *Austral./NZ informal* half-pie.
OPPOSITE inadequate.
3 *the workstations were small but seemed* ***adequate to*** *the task* **equal to**, up to, capable, of, suited to, suitable for, able to do, qualified for, fit for, good enough for, sufficient for; *informal* up to scratch.
OPPOSITE unequal to.

adhere ▶ **verb 1** *a little dollop of cream adhered to her nose* **stick**, stick fast, cling, hold fast, cohere, bond, attach; be stuck, be fixed, be pasted, be glued.
2 *they* ***adhere*** *scrupulously* ***to*** *Judaic law* **abide by**, stick to, hold to, comply with, stand by, be faithful to, act in accordance with, pay attention to, pay regard to, go along with, cooperate with, conform to, submit to; take to heart, bear in mind, be guided by; follow, obey, heed, observe, respect, uphold, fulfil.
OPPOSITES flout, ignore.
3 *most of the county* ***adhered to*** *the episcopal church* **be attached to**, be connected with, be affiliated to, be a member of; follow, support, give support to, cleave to, be loyal to, be faithful to, remain true to; *informal* stick with.

adherent ▶ **noun** *an adherent of the Catholic religion | adherents of the grunge music scene* **follower**, supporter, upholder, defender, advocate, disciple, votary, partisan, member, friend, stalwart; fanatic, zealot; believer, worshipper, attender; **fan**, admirer, enthusiast, devotee, lover, addict, aficionado; *informal* hanger-on, groupie, buff, freak, fiend, nut, maniac; *N. Amer. informal* booster, cohort, rooter; *rare* janissary, sectary.
OPPOSITE opponent.
▶ **adjective** *the colon has an adherent layer of mucus gel* **adhesive**, sticky, sticking, adhering, clinging, tacky, gluey, gummy, gummed, cohesive, viscous, viscid, glutinous, mucilaginous; *Brit.* claggy; *Scottish & N. English* clarty; *informal* gooey, gloopy, cloggy, gungy, icky; *N. Amer. informal* gloppy; *rare* tenacious, viscoid.

adhesion ▶ **noun 1** *pressure will help the adhesion of the gum strip to the paper fibres* **sticking**, adherence, gluing, fixing, fastening, union.
2 *the front tyres were struggling for adhesion* **traction**, grip, purchase, friction, resistance.

adhesive ▶ **noun** *fix the stencil in place with a spray adhesive* **glue**, fixative, gum, paste, cement, bonding, binder, sealer, sealant; superglue, epoxy resin; *N. Amer.* mucilage; *N. Amer. informal* stickum.
▶ **adjective** *a special adhesive mortar suitable for outdoor use* **sticky**, sticking, adhering, adherent, clinging, tacky, gluey, gummy, gummed, cohesive, viscous, viscid, glutinous, mucilaginous; *Brit.* claggy; *Scottish & N. English* clarty; *informal* gooey, gloopy, cloggy, gungy, icky; *N. Amer. informal* gloppy; *rare* tenacious, viscoid.

ad hoc (*Latin*) ▶ **adjective** *discussions were held on an ad hoc basis* **impromptu**, extempore, extemporary, extemporaneous, expedient, emergency, improvised, rough and ready, makeshift, make-do, cobbled together, thrown together; *Nautical* jury-rigged, jury; *informal* quick and dirty.
▶ **adverb** *committees of enquiry can be set up ad hoc* **as the need arises**, when necessary, when needed.

adieu ▶ **noun & exclamation** *I whispered a fond adieu | I bid you adieu, but I will return* **goodbye**, farewell; *French* au revoir; *Italian* ciao; *German* auf Wiedersehen; *Spanish* adios; *Latin* vale; *informal* bye-bye, ta-ta, bye, cheerio, cheers, see you later, see you, so long, toodle-oo.

ad infinitum ▶ **adverb** (*Latin*) *the tradition will be maintained ad infinitum* **forever**, for ever and ever, evermore, always, for all time, till the end of time, in perpetuity; perpetually, eternally, endlessly, interminably, unceasingly, unendingly, everlastingly; *Brit.* for evermore, forever more; *N. Amer.* forevermore; *Latin* in perpetuum; *informal* until the cows come home, until the twelfth of never, until hell freezes over, until doomsday, until kingdom come; *archaic* for aye.

adjacent ▶ **adjective** *a railway museum* ***adjacent to*** *the Moat House Hotel* **adjoining**, neighbouring (on), next door to, abutting, close to, near to, next to, by, close by, by the side of, bordering (on), beside, alongside, abreast of, contiguous with, proximate to, attached to, touching, joining; cheek by jowl with; *rare* conjoining, approximate to, vicinal.
OPPOSITE remote from.

adjoin ▶ **verb** *my office adjoined the doctor's surgery* **be next to**, be adjacent to, border (on), neighbour, verge on, abut, butt up against, butt up to, bound on, be contiguous with, be connected to, communicate with, link up with, extend as far as, extend to; join, conjoin, connect with/to, touch, meet.

adjoining ▶ **adjective** *the two women had adjoining bedrooms* **connecting**, connected, interconnecting, adjacent, abutting, neighbouring, bordering, next-door; contiguous, proximate; attached, joining, touching, meeting; *rare* conjoining, approximate, vicinal.
OPPOSITE remote.

adjourn ▶ **verb 1** *the hearing was adjourned for a week | the opening session adjourned after barely thirty minutes* **suspend**, break off, discontinue, interrupt, postpone, put off, put back, defer, delay, hold over, hold in abeyance, shelve, pigeonhole, stay, prorogue, dissolve, terminate, bring to an end, halt, call a halt to; pause, suspend proceedings, take a break, recess, break up, end, come to an end; *N. Amer.* put over, table, lay on the table, take a recess; *informal* put on ice, put on the back burner, put in cold storage, mothball, take a breather, let up, knock off, take five; *N. Amer. informal* take a rain check; *N. Amer. Law* continue; *rare* remit, respite.
2 *they adjourned to the sitting room for liqueurs and brandy* **withdraw**, retire, retreat, beat a retreat, take oneself, decamp, depart, go out, go off, go away, exit; *formal* repair, remove; *literary* betake oneself; *rare* abstract oneself.

adjournment ▶ **noun** *opposition parties forced the adjournment of the parliament* **suspension**, breaking off, discontinuation, interruption, postponement, rescheduling, deferment, deferral, delay, shelving, stay, pigeonholing, prorogation, dissolution, dissolving, disbandment, termination, halting; break, pause, suspension of proceedings, temporary cessation, recess, rest, time out, stoppage; *N. Amer.* tabling; *informal* let up, breather, mothballing, knocking off, taking five; *Law* moratorium; *N. Amer. Law* continuation; *rare* put-off.

adjudge ▶ **verb** *he was adjudged guilty of the offence of obstruction* **judge**, deem, adjudicate, find, determine, pronounce, proclaim, rule, hold, consider, conclude, think; count, rate, reckon, perceive, regard as, view as, see as, believe to be, suppose.

adjudicate ▶ **verb** *the case was adjudicated in the High Court* **judge**, adjudge, try, hear, examine, arbitrate, decide on, decide, settle, resolve, determine, pronounce on, give a ruling on, sit in judgement on, pass judgement on, give a verdict on, make a ruling on; referee, umpire.

adjudication ▶ **noun** *matters were ultimately settled by adjudication | the jury's verdict is a final adjudication* **arbitration**, refereeing, umpiring; judging, judgement, decision, pronouncement, ruling, settlement, resolution, finding, verdict, conclusion, sentence, decree, order; *Law* determination; *N. Amer.* resolve; *rare* arbitrament.

adjudicator ▶ **noun** *their application for asylum is being considered by an adjudicator* **arbitrator**, arbiter, mediator, referee, umpire, judge.

adjunct ▶ noun *the compound is still used by some practitioners as an adjunct to penicillin therapy* **supplement**, addition, accompaniment, complement, companion, extra, add-on, additive, accessory, appurtenance; attachment, appendage, addendum, affix, auxiliary.

adjust ▶ verb **1** *Kate had adjusted to her new life at boarding school* **adapt**, become accustomed, get used, accommodate, acclimatize, attune, orient oneself, reconcile oneself, habituate oneself, assimilate, conform; come to terms with, familiarize oneself with, acquaint oneself with, blend in with, fit in with, find one's feet in; *N. Amer.* acclimate.
2 *he adjusted the brakes after I found them inefficient* **modify**, alter, regulate, tune, fine-tune, calibrate, balance; adapt, rearrange, change, rejig, rework, revamp, remodel, reshape, convert, transform, tailor, improve, enhance, customize; repair, fix, correct, rectify, make good, put in working order, overhaul, put right, set right, set to rights, standardize, normalize; *informal* jigger, tweak, twiddle, patch up, see to.

adjustable ▶ adjective *the pilots sit on adjustable seats* **modifiable**, alterable, adaptable, convertible, variable, multiway, versatile, accommodating; movable, mobile.
OPPOSITES fixed, immovable.

adjustment ▶ noun **1** *new teachers face a challenging period of adjustment* **adaptation**, adapting, accustoming, accommodation, accommodating, acclimatization, reconciliation, inurement, habituation, habituating, familiarization, acculturation, naturalization, assimilation, assimilating, harmonization; settling in, settling down; *N. Amer.* acclimation.
2 *the car will run on unleaded petrol with no adjustment* **modification**, modifying, alteration, adaptation, regulation, regulating, rearrangement, change, converting, conversion; remodelling, revamping, restyling, reshaping, reconstruction, transformation, variation, customization, tailoring, refinement, refining; fixing, mending, repair, correction, correcting, amendment, amending, rectifying, overhauling, overhaul, improvement; *informal* jiggering, tweaking, twiddling, patching up.

ad lib ▶ verb *I never work from a script—I just ad lib the whole programme* **improvise**, extemporize, speak impromptu, make it up as one goes along, think on one's feet, take it as it comes; *informal* speak off the cuff, speak off the top of one's head, play it by ear, busk it, wing it.
▶ adverb *she spoke ad lib* **impromptu**, extempore, without preparation, without rehearsal, extemporaneously, spontaneously, offhand; *Latin* ad libitum; *informal* off the cuff, off the top of one's head, on the spur of the moment, just like that, at the drop of a hat.
▶ adjective *they gave a live, ad lib commentary as the film was shown* **impromptu**, extempore, extemporaneous, extemporary, improvised, improvisational, improvisatory, improvisatorial, unprepared, unarranged, unplanned, unrehearsed, unscripted, unpremeditated, spontaneous, on-the-spot; *informal* **off-the-cuff**, spur-of-the-moment.
OPPOSITE planned.

administer ▶ verb **1** *the union is administered by a central executive* **manage**, direct, control, operate, regulate, conduct, handle, run, orchestrate, organize, supervise, superintend, oversee, preside over, boss, be the boss of, govern, rule, lead, head, guide, steer, pilot; exercise control over, be in control of, be in charge of, be in command of, take care of, look after, be responsible for, be at the helm of, hold sway over; *informal* head up, call the shots, call the tune, pull the strings, run the show, be in the driving seat, be in the saddle.
2 *the lifeboat crew administered first aid to the fisherman* | *a gym shoe was used to administer punishment* **dispense**, deliver, issue, give, provide, apply, discharge, allot, distribute, apportion, deal, hand out, mete out, measure out, dole out, disburse, bestow; inflict, impose, enforce, deal out, serve out, exact.

administration ▶ noun **1** *the administration of the army was divided between a number of bodies* **management**, managing, direction, directing, command, commanding, control, controlling, charge, conduct, conducting, operation, regulation, regulating, handling, running, leadership, government, governing, superintendence, supervision, supervising, overseeing, oversight, orchestration, orchestrating, guidance, care; *archaic* regiment.
2 *the ministers had also been part of the previous Labour administration* **government**, cabinet, ministry, regime, executive, authority, directorate, council, leadership, management; parliament, congress, senate; rule, term of office, incumbency; *informal* top brass.
3 *the administration of anti-inflammatory drugs* | *a framework for the administration of criminal justice* **dispensation**, dispensing, delivering, issuing, giving, provision, providing, application, applying, discharge, allotment, distribution, apportionment, apportioning, dealing out, handing out, meting out, measuring out, doling out, disbursement, disbursing, bestowal; infliction, inflicting, imposition, imposing, enforcement, enforcing, exacting, execution, exercise, effectuation.

administrative *See centre pages for list of administrative* **Districts**
▶ adjective *he demonstrated his excellent administrative skills* **managerial**, management, directorial, directing, executive, organizational, controlling, governmental, supervisory, regulatory; *rare* gubernatorial.

administrator ▶ noun *he became football's top administrator in 1973* **manager**, director, managing director, executive, chief executive, controller, chair, chairperson, chairman, chairwoman, head, boss, chief, principal, official, leader, governor, premier, president, superintendent, supervisor, employer, proprietor; *informal* gaffer, kingpin, top dog, bigwig, numero uno, Mister Big, honcho, head honcho; *N. Amer. informal* big wheel.

admirable ▶ adjective *the player has done an admirable job for the team* **commendable**, worthy of admiration, worthy of commendation, praiseworthy, laudable, estimable, meritorious, creditable, exemplary, exceptional, notable, honourable, worthy, deserving, respectable, worthwhile; excellent, good, sterling, superb, superlative, brilliant, outstanding, first-rate, first-class, second to none, of the first order, of the highest order, of the first water, supreme, prime, great, fine, masterly, marvellous, wonderful, magnificent; *informal* A1, wicked, super, splendiferous, top-notch, fab, ace, tip-top; *Brit. informal* smashing, brill, top-hole, champion, grand; *N. Amer. informal* bully; *Austral./NZ informal* beaut; *rare* applaudable.
OPPOSITES deplorable, abominable.

admiration ▶ noun **1** *his patience and good nature commanded widespread admiration* **commendation**, acclaim, applause, approbation, approval, appreciation, regard, high regard, respect, praise, esteem, veneration, adulation, extolment; compliments, tributes, accolades, plaudits, pats on the back; *rare* laudation.
OPPOSITE disgust.
2 *their garden was the admiration of the village* **object of admiration**, **pride**, pride and joy, joy, wonder, delight, marvel, sensation.

admire ▶ verb **1** *she was admired for her cheerful efficiency* **applaud**, praise, express admiration for, commend, approve of, express approval for, favour, look on with favour, think highly of, appreciate; **respect**, rate highly, hold in high regard, hold in high esteem, look up to, acclaim; compliment, speak highly of, put on a pedestal.
OPPOSITE disapprove of.
2 *Simon had admired her from afar for a long time* **worship**, adore, love, cherish, dote on, be enamoured of, be infatuated with, be taken with, be attracted to, find attractive; idolize, lionize; *informal* carry a torch for, be mad about, be crazy about, be potty about, be wild about, have a crush on, have a thing about, have a pash on, have the hots for, be soft on, take a shine to; *Brit. informal* fancy.
OPPOSITE loathe.

admirer ▶ noun **1** *he was a great admirer of Churchill* **fan**, enthusiast, devotee, addict, aficionado, supporter, adherent, follower, disciple, votary, fanatic, zealot; *informal* hanger-on, groupie.
2 *a handsome admirer from her Cambridge days* **suitor**, wooer, worshipper, beau, sweetheart, lover, love, beloved, lady love, boyfriend, girlfriend, young man, young lady, man friend, lady friend, escort; catch, conquest; *Italian* inamorato, inamorata; *informal* fancy man, fancy woman, toy boy, sugar daddy; *literary* swain; *archaic* gallant, paramour, leman.

admissible ▶ adjective *an admissible claim for damages* **allowable**, allowed, permissible, permitted, acceptable, passable, tolerable, satisfactory, justifiable, defensible, supportable, well founded, tenable, sound, sensible, reasonable; legitimate, lawful, legal, licit, within the law, above board, valid, recognized, sanctioned; *informal* OK, okay, legit, kosher, pukka, by the book.
OPPOSITE inadmissible.

admission ▶ noun **1** *membership entitles you to free admission* | *they had the necessary ability for admission to grammar school* **admittance**, entry, entrance, right of entry, permission to enter, access, means of entry, ingress, entrée, acceptance.
2 *admission to the fête is fifty pence* **entrance fee**, admission fee, entry charge, ticket.
3 *a written admission of liability for the accident* **acknowledgement**, acceptance, recognition, concession, profession, expression, declaration, confession, revelation, disclosure, divulgence, avowal, claim, unbosoming, owning up; *rare* asseveration, divulgation.

admit ▶ verb **1** *he unlocked the door to admit her* | *he was admitted as a scholar to Winchester College* **let in**, allow entry, permit entry, grant entrance to, give right of entry to, give access to, give admission to, accept, take in, usher in, show in, receive, welcome; take on, enrol, enlist, register, sign up.
OPPOSITES exclude, bar, expel.
2 *he admitted three offences of reckless driving* | *Paul admitted that he was angry with his father* **acknowledge**, confess, reveal, make known, disclose, divulge, make public, avow, declare, profess, own up to, make a clean breast of, bring into the open, bring to light, give away, blurt out, leak; concede, accept, accede, grant, agree, allow, own, concur, assent, recognize, realize, be aware of, be conscious of, appreciate; *informal* get something off one's chest, spill the beans about, tell all about, blow the lid off, squeal about; *Brit. informal* blow the gaff on; *archaic* discover.
OPPOSITES deny, conceal.

admittance ▶ noun *they refused me admittance on the grounds that I wasn't a member* **entry**, right of entry, permission to enter, admission, entrance, access, right of access, ingress, entrée, acceptance.
OPPOSITE exclusion.

admonish ▶ verb **1** *he was severely admonished by his father* **reprimand**, rebuke, scold, reprove, upbraid, chastise, chide, censure, castigate, lambaste, berate, reproach, lecture, criticize, take to task, pull up, read the Riot Act to, give a piece of one's mind to, haul over the coals; *informal* tell off, give someone a telling-off, dress down, give someone a dressing-down, bawl out, pitch into, lay into, lace into, blow up, give someone an earful, give someone a roasting, give someone a rocket, give someone a rollicking, rap over the knuckles, slap someone's wrist, send someone away with a flea in their ear, let someone have it, give someone hell; *Brit. informal* tick off, have a go at, carpet, tear someone off a strip, give someone a mouthful, give someone what for, give someone some stick, give someone a wigging; *N. Amer. informal* chew out, ream out; *Austral. informal* monster; *Brit. vulgar slang* bollock, give someone a bollocking; *dated* trim, rate, give someone a rating; *rare* reprehend, objurgate.
OPPOSITE praise.
2 *she admonished him to drink no more than one glass of wine* **advise**, recommend, urge, caution, warn, counsel, exhort, implore, beseech, entreat, encourage, bid, enjoin, adjure, push, pressure.
OPPOSITE discourage.

admonition ▶ noun **1** *Palmerston sent him a blunt admonition over the mistake* **reprimand**, rebuke, reproof, remonstrance, reproach, admonishment, stricture, lecture, criticism, recrimination, tirade, diatribe, philippic, harangue, attack; scolding, chastisement, castigation, upbraiding, berating, reproval, censure, condemnation; *informal* telling-off, dressing-down, talking-to, tongue-lashing, bashing, blast, rap, rap over the knuckles, slap on the wrist, flea in one's ear, earful, roasting, rollicking, caning, blowing-up; *Brit. informal* rocket, wigging, slating, ticking-off, carpeting; *Austral./NZ informal* serve; *Brit. vulgar slang* bollocking; *dated* rating.
OPPOSITES commendation, pat on the back, praise.
2 *the frequent admonitions of his anxious parents* **exhortation**, warning, caution, caveat, piece of advice, admonishment, recommendation; injunction, monition, enjoinment, instruction, direction, suggestion, lesson, lecture, precept; advice, counsel, guidance, urging, encouragement, persuasion, pressure.

ado ▶ noun *she decided to take matters in hand without further ado* **fuss**, trouble, bother, upset, agitation, commotion, stir, hubbub, confusion, excitement, tumult, disturbance, hurly-burly, uproar, flurry, to-do, palaver, rigmarole, brouhaha, furore; *N. Amer.* fuss and feathers; *Indian* tamasha; *informal* hassle, hoo-ha, ballyhoo, hoopla, rumpus, flap, tizz, tizzy, stew, song and dance, performance, pantomime; *Brit. informal* carry-on, kerfuffle.

adolescence ▶ noun *they spent their adolescence hanging out together* **teenage years**, teens, youth, young adulthood, young days, early life; pubescence, puberty; *rare* juvenescence, juvenility.

adolescent ▶ noun *an awkward adolescent beset with self-doubt* **teenager**, youngster, young person, young adult, young man, young woman, young lady, young one, youth, juvenile, minor; schoolboy, schoolgirl, boy, girl, lad, lass, stripling, fledgling, whippersnapper; *Scottish & N. English* bairn; *informal* teen, teeny-bopper, kid, young 'un, shaver; *archaic* hobbledehoy.
OPPOSITES adult; infant.
▶ adjective **1** *adolescent boys are more likely to join gangs* **teenage**, teenaged, pubescent, youthful, young, juvenile; *informal* teen.
OPPOSITE adult.
2 *his colleagues have to cope with his adolescent mood swings* **immature**, childish, babyish, infantile, juvenile, puerile, jejune, inane, silly, fatuous; undeveloped, unsophisticated, inexperienced, callow.
OPPOSITE mature.

adopt ▶ verb **1** *a republican constitution was adopted in 1971* **embrace**, take on, acquire, affect, espouse, assume, appropriate, arrogate; approve, endorse, agree to, consent to, accede to, accept, ratify, validate, rubber-stamp, sanction, support, back, vote for; *informal* give something the go ahead, give something the green light, give something the thumbs up, OK, okay.
OPPOSITE abandon.
2 *the people adopted him as their patron saint* **choose**, select, pick, pick out, vote for, elect, settle on, decide on, single out, plump for, opt for, name, nominate, designate, appoint.
OPPOSITE reject.

adoption ▶ noun **1** *the consultants recommended the adoption of a new housing policy* **assumption**, assuming, taking on, acquiring, acquisition, affecting, affectation, espousal, advocacy, promotion, appropriation, arrogation; approval, endorsement, acceptance, ratification, validation, rubber-stamping, authorization, sanctioning, support, backing.
OPPOSITE abandonment.
2 *the election campaign will begin with the formal adoption of a candidate* **selection**, choosing, choice, voting in, election, electing, naming, nominating, nomination, designation, designating, appointment, appointing.
OPPOSITE rejection.

adorable ▶ adjective *I have four adorable Siamese cats* **lovable**, appealing, charming, cute, sweet, enchanting, bewitching, captivating, engaging, endearing, dear, darling, precious, delightful, lovely, beautiful, attractive, gorgeous, winsome, winning, fetching, pleasing; chocolate-box; *Scottish & N. English* bonny; *dated* taking.
OPPOSITE hateful.

adoration ▶ noun **1** *they regarded him with an almost breathless adoration* **love**, devotion, care, fondness, warmth, affection; **admiration**, regard, high regard, awe, reverence, idolization, lionization, worship, hero-worship, adulation, deification.
2 *the Mass begins our day of prayer and adoration* **worship**, worshipping, glory, glorification, glorifying, praise, praising, thanksgiving, homage, paying homage, exaltation, exalting, extolment, veneration, venerating, revering, reverence; *rare* laudation, lauding, magnification, magnifying.

adore ▶ verb **1** *the boy had lost the father he adored* **love dearly**, love, be devoted to, dote on, care for, hold dear, cherish, treasure, prize, think the world of, set great store by; **admire**, hold in admiration, hold in high regard, regard highly, have a high opinion of, look up to, stand in awe of, revere, reverence, idolize, lionize, worship, deify; *informal* put on a pedestal.
OPPOSITES hate, loathe, detest.
2 *the people had come to pray and adore God* **worship**, glorify, praise, revere, reverence, exalt, laud, extol, esteem, venerate, pay homage to, pay tribute to; *archaic* magnify.
3 *I adore oysters* **like**, love, have a liking for, be fond of, be keen on, be partial to, have a taste for, have a weakness for, enjoy, delight in, revel in, take pleasure in, relish, savour, rate highly, regard highly; *informal* be crazy about, be wild about, be potty about, have a thing about, get a kick out of, get a charge out of, get a buzz from, get a thrill from, be hooked on, go a bundle on; *N. Amer. informal* be nutso about; *Austral./NZ informal* be shook on.
OPPOSITES hate, loathe, detest.

adorn ▶ verb *the public rooms are adorned with tapestries* **embellish**, decorate, furnish, ornament, add ornament to, enhance; beautify, prettify, grace, enrich, bedeck, deck (out), dress (up), trick out, trim, swathe, wreathe, festoon, garland, array, garnish, emblazon, gild, set off; *informal* get up, do up, do out; *literary* bejewel, bedizen, caparison, furbelow.
OPPOSITES strip; disfigure.

adornment ▶ noun *her drawings needed some adornment* **embellishment**, embellishing, decorating, decoration, ornamentation, ornament, enhancement, enhancing; beautification, beatifying, prettification, prettifying, dressing up, trimming, emblazoning, elaboration, enrichment, garnishing, gilding; frills, accessories, trimmings, finishing touches; *rare* fallalery.

adrift ▶ adjective **1** *the pipe of my breathing apparatus came adrift* **loose**, free, astray; detached, unsecured, unhitched, unfastened, untied, untethered, unknotted, undone.
2 *their empty boat was spotted adrift in the water* **drifting**, unmoored, unanchored.
3 *he was adrift in a strange country* **lost**, off course, off track, off the right track, having lost one's bearings, disorientated, disoriented, confused, bewildered, (all) at sea; unsettled, drifting, rootless, directionless, aimless, purposeless, without purpose, without goal, at a loose end.
4 (*Brit. informal*) *his instincts were not entirely adrift* **wrong**, mistaken, inaccurate, wide of the mark, off target, awry, amiss, astray, off course, off the right track.

adroit ▶ adjective *an adroit shot from a bunker enabled him to finish well | he showed himself to be an adroit politician* **skilful**, adept, dexterous, deft, agile, nimble, nimble-fingered, handy; able, capable, competent, skilled, expert, masterly, masterful, master, practised, polished, slick, proficient, accomplished, gifted, talented, peerless; quick-witted, quick-thinking, quick, clever, intelligent, brilliant, bright, smart, sharp, cunning, artful, wily, resourceful, astute, shrewd, canny, ingenious, inventive; *informal* nifty, nippy, crack, mean, wicked, wizard, demon, ace, A1, on the ball, savvy; *N. Amer. informal* crackerjack; *archaic* compleat, rathe.
OPPOSITES clumsy, incompetent.

adroitness ▶ noun *there in an undeniable adroitness in his economic plan* **skill**, skilfulness, prowess, expertise, expertness, adeptness, handiness, nimbleness, dexterity, dexterousness, deftness; ability, capability, competence, competency, mastery, virtuosity, proficiency, accomplishment, artistry, art, knack, bent, faculty, facility, aptitude, flair, finesse, talent, gift, giftedness; quick-wittedness, cleverness, intelligence, wisdom, brilliance, brightness, sharpness, cunning, artfulness, astuteness, diplomacy, discretion, shrewdness, resourcefulness, ingenuity, inventiveness, imagination, imaginativeness; *French* savoir faire; *informal* niftiness, nippiness, know-how, savvy.
OPPOSITES clumsiness; incompetence.

adulation ▶ noun *he is remarkably unspoilt by all the adulation he has received* **hero-worship**, worship, admiration, admiring, high regard, respect, lionization, lionizing, idolization, idolizing, veneration, awe, devotion, adoration, exaltation, honour, homage, glorification, glory, praise, praising, commendation, flattery, applause; blandishments, compliments, tributes, accolades, plaudits, eulogies, pats on the back; *rare* laudation, eulogiums, magnification, magnifying.

adulatory ▶ adjective *he wrote back to Lewis in adulatory terms* **flattering**, complimentary, highly favourable, commendatory, enthusiastic, glowing, appreciative, praising, worshipping, worshipful, reverential, lionizing, blandishing, acclamatory, rhapsodic, eulogistic, laudatory, fulsome; honeyed, sugary, saccharine, cloying; nauseating, ingratiating, obsequious, unctuous, sycophantic, servile, fawning; *informal* bootlicking, smarmy, rave; *rare* encomiastic, encomiastical.
OPPOSITES disparaging, unflattering.

adult ▶ adjective **1** *the adult population of Great Britain* **mature**, grown-up, fully grown, full-grown, fully developed, fully fledged, of age, having reached one's majority; in one's prime, in full bloom.
OPPOSITES infant, juvenile.
2 *an adult movie* **sexually explicit**, obscene, pornographic, hard-core, soft-core, lewd, smutty, dirty, filthy, vulgar, crude, rude, racy, risqué, ribald, naughty, arousing, earthy, Rabelaisian, erotic, carnal, sensual, sexy, suggestive, titillating, spicy, raw, taboo, off colour, indecent, improper; *informal* porn, porno, blue, raunchy, steamy, X-rated, full-frontal, skin; *Brit. informal* fruity, saucy, near the knuckle, near the bone; *N. Amer. informal* gamy; *rare* rank, ithyphallic, Fescennine, Cyprian.
OPPOSITE family.
▶ noun *the tent is just large enough for three adults* **grown person**, grown man, grown woman, grown-up person, grown-up, mature person, mature man, mature woman, person of mature age; man, woman, gentleman, lady.

adulterate ▶ verb *the brewer was accused of adulterating his beer* **make impure**, degrade, debase, spoil, taint, defile, contaminate, pollute, foul, sully; doctor, tamper with, mix, lace, dilute, water down, thin out, weaken; bastardize, corrupt; *informal* cut, spike, dope; *rare* vitiate.
OPPOSITE refine.

adulterer ▶ noun *an adulterer cheating with someone else's wife* **philanderer**, deceiver, womanizer, ladies' man, playboy, Don Juan, Casanova, Lothario, Romeo, seducer, libertine, rake, reprobate, wanton, profligate, lecher, debauchee, sinner; *informal* cheat, love cheat, love rat, skirt-chaser, ladykiller, lech, goat, wolf, stud; *dated* gay dog, rip, blood; *rare* fornicator, rakehell, dissolute.

adulterous ▶ adjective *British women are the most adulterous in Europe | an adulterous relationship* **unfaithful**, faithless, disloyal, untrue, inconstant, fickle, flighty, unreliable, untrustworthy, false, false-hearted, deceiving, deceitful, treacherous, traitorous; extramarital; *informal* cheating, two-timing.
OPPOSITE faithful.

adultery ▶ noun *she divorced me because of my adultery* **unfaithfulness**, infidelity, falseness, disloyalty, unchastity, cuckoldry, extramarital sex, extramarital relations; affair, liaison, intrigue, amour, entanglement, flirtation; *informal* cheating, two-timing, fooling around, playing around, playing the field, carryings-on, hanky-panky, a bit on the side; *archaic* fornication.
OPPOSITES faithfulness, fidelity.

advance ▶ verb **1** *the battalion advanced on Rawlinson's orders | the tide was advancing* **move forward**, proceed, move along, press on, push on, push forward, make progress, make headway, forge on, forge ahead, gain ground, approach, come closer, move closer, move nearer, draw nearer, near; *dated* draw nigh.
OPPOSITE retreat.
2 *the court may advance the date of the hearing* **bring forward**, put forward, move forward, make earlier.
OPPOSITE postpone.
3 *their firm was to be advanced at the expense of others* **promote**, further, forward, help, aid, assist, facilitate, boost, strengthen, improve, make better, benefit, foster, cultivate, encourage, support, back.
OPPOSITES impede, hinder.
4 *our technology has advanced in the last few years* **progress**, make progress, make headway, develop, improve, become better, thrive, flourish, prosper, mature; evolve, make strides, move forward (in leaps and bounds), move ahead, get ahead; *informal* go places, get somewhere.
5 *they advanced a claim of imperial sovereignty* **put forward**, present, come up with, submit, suggest, propose, introduce, put up, offer, proffer, adduce, moot.
OPPOSITE retract.
6 *he had inadequate funds but a relative advanced him some money* **lend**, loan, credit, pay in advance, supply on credit; pay out, put up, come up with, contribute, give, donate, hand over; *informal* dish out, shell out, fork out, cough up; *Brit. informal* sub.
OPPOSITE borrow.
7 (*dated*) *they apologized for advancing the subscription to one guinea per copy* **increase**, raise, put up, inflate, boost, elevate, escalate, augment; *informal* jack up, hike up, hike.
OPPOSITES reduce, lower.
▶ noun **1** *alarm over the advance of the aggressors was spreading* **progress**, headway, moving forward, forward movement; approach, nearing, coming, arrival.
2 *the treatment would be a significant medical advance | the rapid post-war advance of science* **breakthrough**, **development**, step forward, step in the right direction, leap, quantum leap, find, finding, discovery, invention, success; headway, progress, advancement, evolution, improvement, betterment, furtherance.
3 *the bank was engaged in the task of restraining the pound's advance* **increase**, rise, upturn, upsurge, upswing, growth, boom, boost, elevation, escalation, augmentation; *informal* hike.
4 *the writer is going to be given a huge advance* **down payment**, advance against royalty, deposit, retainer, prepayment, front money, money up front.
5 (usually **advances**) *my tutor made unwelcome sexual advances to me in his office* **sexual approaches**, overtures, moves; a pass, proposal, proposition, offer, suggestion, appeal; *informal* come-on.
□ **in advance** *ski equipment may be hired in advance* **beforehand**, before, ahead of time, earlier, previously, in readiness.
▶ adjective **1** *an advance party of settlers* **preliminary**, leading, forward, foremost, at the fore, sent (on) ahead, first, exploratory, explorative, pilot, vanguard, test, trial.
2 *the new weather monitor gives plenty of advance warning* **early**, previous, prior, beforehand.

advanced ▶ adjective **1** *advanced manufacturing techniques* **state-of-the-art**, new, modern, up to date, up to the minute, the newest, the latest, recently developed, newly discovered, newfangled, ultra-modern, futuristic; **progressive**, forward, highly developed, avant-garde, ahead of the times, pioneering, groundbreaking, trailblazing, revolutionary, innovatory; sophisticated, complex, complicated, elaborate, intricate, ingenious; *informal* flash, snazzy, nifty; *rare* new-fashioned.
OPPOSITES primitive, backward.
2 *there were 14,000 students on advanced courses* **higher-level**, higher, tertiary, third-level.
OPPOSITES foundation, elementary.

advancement ▶ noun **1** *the company has benefited greatly from the advancement of computer technology* **development**, progress, evolution, growth, improvement, advance, furtherance, forwarding, expansion, extension, spread; headway.
2 *employees must be offered appropriate opportunities for advancement* **promotion**, preferment, career development, elevation, upgrading, being upgraded, progress, improvement, betterment, growth, rise, moving up; a step up the ladder, a step up, a move up; aggrandizement; *informal* a kick upstairs.

advantage ▶ noun **1** *the advantages of belonging to a union* **benefit**, value, reward, merit, good point, strong point, asset, plus, bonus, boon, blessing, virtue, privilege, perk, fringe benefit, additional benefit, added extra; attraction, desirability, beauty, usefulness, helpfulness, convenience, advantageousness, expedience, expediency, profit, profitability, advisability; *formal* perquisite.
OPPOSITES disadvantage, drawback, handicap.
2 *they appeared to be gaining the advantage over their opponents* **upper hand**, edge, lead, head, whip hand, trump card; **superiority**, dominance, ascendancy, supremacy, primacy, precedence, power, mastery, control, sway, authority; *N. Amer. informal* the catbird seat; *Austral./NZ informal* the box seat.
3 *they exploit natural resources to their own advantage | there is no advantage to be gained from delaying the process* **benefit**, profit, gain, good, interest, welfare, well-being, enjoyment, satisfaction, comfort, ease, convenience; help, aid, assistance, use, utility, service, purpose, effect, object, reason, worth; *informal* mileage, percentage.
OPPOSITE detriment.

advantageous ▶ adjective **1** *at the end of the war, farmers were in a relatively advantageous position* **superior**, dominant, powerful, important, commanding, excellent, good, fine, fortunate, lucky, privileged, favourable, preferable, preferred, favoured, more desirable, most desirable.
OPPOSITE inferior.
2 *the arrangement is advantageous to both sides* **beneficial**, of benefit, helpful, of assistance, useful, of use, valuable, of value, of service, profitable, fruitful, rewarding, gainful, lucrative; suitable, convenient, expedient, appropriate, fitting, favourable, auspicious, propitious, fortuitous, lucky; in everyone's interests.
OPPOSITES disadvantageous, detrimental.

advent ▶ noun *operative techniques greatly improved with the advent of anaesthesia | the inevitable advent of his death* **arrival**, appearance, emergence, materialization, surfacing, occurrence, dawn, origin, birth, rise, development; approach, coming, looming, nearing, advance.
OPPOSITES departure, disappearance.

adventitious ▶ adjective **1** *he felt that the conversation was not entirely adventitious* **unplanned**, unpremeditated, accidental, unintentional, unintended, unexpected, unforeseen, involuntary, chance, fortuitous, serendipitous, coincidental, casual, random, fluky, unlooked-for, unhoped-for, not bargained for, out of the blue, without warning; *rare* aleatory.

OPPOSITE planned.
2 *some rural parishes recorded high adventitious populations* **foreign**, alien, non-native, outside, external, extraneous, extrinsic.
OPPOSITES native, indigenous.

adventure ▶ noun **1** *stories of astonishing miracles and heroic adventures* **exploit**, escapade, deed, feat, trial, experience, incident, occurrence, event, happening, episode, affair; stunt, caper, romp, antic; quest, crusade, campaign, venture.
2 *they set off in search of adventure* **excitement**, exciting experience, thrill, stimulation; risk, riskiness, danger, dangerousness, hazard, hazardousness, peril, perilousness, uncertainty, precariousness; *informal* a kick, a buzz; *N. Amer. informal* a charge.

adventurer ▶ noun *a tough adventurer who had sailed around the world* **daredevil**, seeker of adventures, hero, heroine, swashbuckler, knight errant, crusader, venturer, traveller, voyager, wanderer; buccaneer, mercenary, soldier of fortune; Argonaut, Ulysses; *French* beau sabreur.

adventurous ▶ adjective **1** *as a child he was always adventurous* **daring**, daredevil, intrepid, venturesome, bold, audacious, fearless, brave, unafraid, unshrinking, undaunted, dauntless, valiant, valorous, heroic, dashing; confident, enterprising; rash, reckless, heedless; *informal* gutsy, spunky, peppy, pushy; *rare* adventuresome, venturous.
OPPOSITES cautious, unadventurous.
2 *they needed someone to finance their more adventurous activities* **risky**, dangerous, perilous, hazardous, precarious, uncertain.
OPPOSITES tame, unadventurous.

adversary ▶ noun *he parried the strokes of his adversary with almost contemptuous ease* **opponent**, rival, enemy, foe, antagonist, combatant, challenger, contender, competitor, opposer, fellow contestant; opposition, competition; *rare* corrival.
OPPOSITES ally, supporter.

adverse ▶ adjective **1** *the plane crashed into a lake in adverse weather conditions* **unfavourable**, disadvantageous, inauspicious, unpropitious, unfortunate, unlucky, untimely, untoward; disagreeable, unpleasant, bad, poor, terrible, dreadful, dire, wretched, nasty, hostile.
OPPOSITE favourable.
2 *the company knew of the drug's adverse side effects* **harmful**, dangerous, injurious, detrimental, hurtful, deleterious, destructive, pernicious, disadvantageous, unfavourable, unfortunate, unhealthy.
OPPOSITE beneficial.
3 *the military feared an adverse response from the American public* **hostile**, **unfavourable**, antagonistic, unfriendly, ill-disposed, negative, opposing, opposed, contrary, dissenting, inimical, antipathetic, at odds.
OPPOSITES positive, friendly.

adversity ▶ noun *they remain steadfast in the face of adversity | it helps to laugh about life's adversities* **misfortune**, ill luck, bad luck, trouble, difficulty, hardship, distress, disaster, misadventure, suffering, affliction, sorrow, misery, heartbreak, heartache, wretchedness, tribulation, woe, pain, trauma, torment, torture; mishap, stroke of ill luck, stroke of bad luck, accident, shock, upset, reverse, reversal, reversal of fortune, setback, crisis, catastrophe, tragedy, calamity, trial, cross, burden, blow, buffet, vicissitude; hard times, dire straits, trials and tribulations; *informal* hell, hell on earth, hassle, stress; *literary* dolour, travails.
OPPOSITE good times.

advertise ▶ verb *the booklets are designed to advertise the hotel* **publicize**, make public, make known, give publicity to, bill, post, announce, broadcast, proclaim, trumpet, shout from the rooftops, give notice of, call attention to, promulgate; promote, market, merchandise, peddle, display, tout, build up, beat/bang the drum for, trail, trailer; *informal* push, plug, hype, hype up, give a plug to, puff, give a puff to, boost, flog; *N. Amer. informal* ballyhoo, flack, huckster, blurb; *Austral./NZ informal* spruik.

advertisement ▶ noun **1** *an advertisement for toothpaste | she placed an advertisement in a Canadian newspaper* **notice**, announcement, bulletin; **commercial**, promotion, blurb, write-up, display; poster, leaflet, pamphlet, flyer, bill, handbill, handout, circular, brochure, sign, placard; *N. Amer.* folder, dodger; *French* affiche; *informal* ad, push, plug, puff, bumf; *Brit. informal* advert.
2 *they showed no desire for advertisement of their intellectual achievements* **publicizing**, publicization, advertising, promotion, touting, broadcasting, declaration, notification, promulgation; *informal* plugging, pushing, puffing; *literary* blazoning.

advice ▶ noun *the charity offers support and advice to people with mental illness* **guidance**, advising, counselling, counsel, help, direction, instruction, information, enlightenment; recommendations, guidelines, suggestions, hints, tips, pointers, ideas, opinions, views, facts, data; *informal* info, gen, dope, the low-down, the inside story.

advisability ▶ noun *the advisability of sticking to a low-fat diet* **preferability**, preferableness, desirability, wisdom, soundness, prudence, sensibleness, sense, appropriateness, aptness, fitness, suitability, judiciousness, expediency, expedience, helpfulness, effectiveness, advantageousness, advantage, benefit, merit, value, profit, profitability, gain.

advisable ▶ adjective *it is advisable to book a table in advance* **wise**, desirable, preferable, well, best, sensible, commonsensical, sound, prudent, proper, appropriate, apt, suitable, fitting, judicious, recommended, recommendable, suggested, expedient, politic, helpful, useful, effective, advantageous, beneficial, valuable, profitable, gainful; in one's (best) interests.
OPPOSITES inadvisable, unwise.

advise ▶ verb **1** *her grandmother advised her about marriage* **counsel**, give counsel, give counselling, give guidance, guide, make recommendations, offer suggestions, offer opinions, give hints, give tips, give pointers, direct, give direction(s), instruct, give instruction, illuminate, educate.
2 *the foreign minister advised negotiations with the Turks* **advocate**, suggest, recommend, commend, urge, admonish, bid, encourage, enjoin, push for, press for, subscribe to, endorse, champion, back, support, speak for, call for, campaign for, argue for, promote, prompt.
3 *club members will be* **advised** *of the outcome of this meeting* **inform**, notify, give notice, apprise, brief, give intelligence, send word, keep posted, warn, forewarn; acquaint with, make familiar with, make known to, let know, enlighten as to, give information about, keep up to date with, update about; *informal* give the gen, give the low-down, give the rundown, fill in on, gen up on, clue up about, clue in on, put in the picture about, put wise about, keep up to speed with.

adviser ▶ noun *he is the president's personal adviser* **counsellor**, mentor, guide, consultant, consultee, confidant, confidante, guide, right hand man, right hand woman, aide, helper; instructor, coach, trainer, teacher, tutor, guru; *Italian* consigliere; *informal* main man; *N. Amer. informal* Dutch uncle.

advisory ▶ adjective *she agreed to serve the central committee in an advisory role* **consultative**, consultatory, consulting, advising, counselling, recommendatory, recommending, assisting, helping, aiding.
OPPOSITE executive.

advocacy ▶ noun *he incurred opprobrium for his* **advocacy** *of contraception* **support for**, argument for, arguing for, calling for, pushing for, pressing for; defence, espousal, espousing, approval, approving, endorsement, endorsing, recommendation, recommending, advising in favour, backing, supporting, favouring, promotion, promoting, championship, championing, sanctioning, acceptance; *N. Amer. informal* boosterism.

advocate ▶ noun **1** *she was a powerful* **advocate** *of children's rights* **champion**, upholder, supporter, backer, promoter, proponent, exponent, protector, patron; spokesman for, spokeswoman for, spokesperson for, speaker for, campaigner for, fighter for, battler for, crusader for; missionary, reformer, pioneer, pleader, propagandist, apostle, apologist; *N. Amer.* booster; *informal* plugger.
OPPOSITE critic.
2 (*Scottish Law*) *he studied law and became an advocate at twenty-one* **barrister**, lawyer, counsel, counsellor, professional pleader, legal practitioner; *N. Amer.* attorney; *N. Amer. & Irish* counsellor-at-law; *informal* brief.
▶ verb *heart disease specialists advocate a diet low in cholesterol* **recommend**, prescribe, commend, advise, favour, approve of, support, back, uphold, subscribe to, champion, campaign on behalf of, stand up for, speak for, argue for, plead for, press for, lobby for, urge, promote, espouse, endorse, sanction, vouch for; *informal* plug, push.
OPPOSITE reject.

aegis ▶ noun *there are many societies run under the aegis of the Students' Union* **patronage**, sponsorship, backing, protection, shelter, umbrella, charge, keeping, care, supervision, guidance, guardianship, trusteeship, support, agency, safeguarding, defence, protectorship, championship, aid, assistance, guaranty; auspices; *archaic* ward.

aeon ▶ noun *the age of piracy was stamped out aeons ago* **age**, epoch, generation, year, time, long period; an eternity, a long time.

aeroplane ▶ noun. *See centre pages for lists of* **Aircraft** **Aircraft Parts**

aesthetic ▶ adjective *the law applies to both functional and aesthetic objects* **decorative**, ornamental, graceful, elegant, exquisite, beautiful, attractive, pleasing, lovely, stylish, artistic, tasteful, in good taste.

affability ▶ noun *a caring doctor blessed with a natural ease and affability* **friendliness**, amiability, geniality, congeniality, cordiality, warmth, warmness, pleasantness, niceness, charm, agreeableness, good humour, good nature, kindliness, kindness, courtesy, courteousness, civility, graciousness, approachability, approachableness, accessibility, amenability, sociability, gregariousness, conviviality, clubbability, neighbourliness, hospitable manner, obliging nature, easy-going manner, informality, lack of reserve, naturalness, relaxedness, ease, easiness; *informal* chumminess, palliness; *N. Amer. informal* clubbiness.
OPPOSITE unfriendliness.

affable ▶ adjective *Murray was in a most affable mood* **friendly**, amiable, genial, congenial, cordial, warm, pleasant, pleasing, nice, likeable, personable, charming, agreeable, sympathetic, benevolent, benign, good-humoured, good-natured, kindly, kind, courteous, civil, gracious,

approachable, accessible, amenable, sociable, outgoing, gregarious, convivial, jovial, clubbable, comradely, neighbourly, welcoming, hospitable, obliging, easy-going, informal, open, communicative, unreserved, uninhibited, natural, relaxed, easy; *informal* chummy, pally; *Brit. informal* matey, decent; *N. Amer. informal* clubby, buddy-buddy; *rare* conversable.
OPPOSITES unfriendly, prickly.

affair ▸ noun **1** *what my mum does in her spare time is her affair* **business**, concern, matter, responsibility, province, preserve, interest; problem, worry, lookout; *informal* pigeon, funeral, headache, baby, bailiwick.
2 (**affairs**) *they aren't worried about their financial affairs* **transactions**, concerns, matters, activities, dealings, undertakings, ventures, proceedings; business, field, sphere; *informal* goings-on, doings.
3 *this is a truly shocking affair* **event**, incident, happening, occurrence, phenomenon, eventuality, episode, interlude, circumstance, set of circumstances, adventure, experience, case, matter, business, thing; proceedings.
4 *I heard there were to be fireworks—it'll be a grand affair* **party**, celebration, function, reception, gathering, soirée, event, social event, occasion, social occasion; *informal* do, rave, bash, get-together, blowout; *Brit. informal* rave-up, thrash, knees-up, beanfeast, beano, bunfight, jolly.
5 *the director and his secretary were having an affair* **relationship**, love affair, romance, fling, flirtation, dalliance, liaison, entanglement, romantic entanglement, involvement, attachment, affair of the heart, intrigue; relations; *French* affaire, affaire de/du cœur, amour; *informal* hanky-panky; *Brit. informal* carry-on.

affect[1] ▸ verb **1** *the climate was likely to be affected by greenhouse gas emissions* **influence**, exert influence on, have an effect on, act on, work on, condition, touch, have an impact on, impact on, take hold of, attack, infect, strike, strike at, hit; change, alter, modify, transform, form, shape, control, govern, determine, decide, guide, sway, bias.
OPPOSITE be unaffected.
2 *she had been deeply affected by her parents' divorce* **upset**, trouble, hit hard, overwhelm, devastate, damage, hurt, pain, grieve, sadden, distress, disturb, perturb, agitate, shake, shake up, stir; move, touch, tug at someone's heartstrings; make an impression on; *informal* knock for six, knock back, bowl over, throw, faze, get to.
OPPOSITES be unaffected, be indifferent to.

affect[2] ▸ verb **1** *he deliberately affected a republican stance* **assume**, put on, take on, adopt, like, have a liking for, embrace, espouse.
2 *she affected a small frown of concentration* **pretend**, feign, fake, counterfeit, sham, simulate, fabricate, give the appearance of, make a show of, make a pretence of, play at, go through the motions of; *informal* put on; *N. Amer. informal* make like.

affect or effect?
Affect and **effect** are quite different in meaning, though frequently confused. *Affect* is primarily a verb meaning either 'make a difference to', as in *their gender need not affect their career*, or 'pretend to have or feel', as in *I affected a supreme unconcern*. *Effect*, on the other hand, is commonly used both as a noun and as a verb, meaning 'something brought about' as a noun (*move the cursor until you get the effect you want*) or 'bring about (a result)' as a verb (*growth in the economy can only be effected by stringent economic controls*).

affectation ▸ noun **1** *she has no affectation | the affectations of a prima donna* **pretension**, pretentiousness, affectedness, artificiality, insincerity, posturing, posing, pretence, ostentation, grandiosity, snobbery, superciliousness; airs, airs and graces, pretensions; *informal* snootiness, uppishness, humbug; *Brit. informal* side.
OPPOSITE naturalness.
2 *nothing would shake his affectation of calm* **facade**, front, show, appearance, false display, pretence, simulation, posture, pose, sham, fake, act, masquerade, charade, mask, cloak, veil, veneer, guise; make-believe, play-acting, feigning, shamming.

affected ▸ adjective *he was talking in the rather affected boom he used with strangers* **pretentious**, high-flown, ostentatious, pompous, grandiose, over-elaborate, overblown, overworked, overdone; contrived, forced, laboured, strained, stiff, posed, stagy, studied, mannered, hollow, insincere, unconvincing; artificial, unnatural, assumed, pretended, feigned, false, fake, faked, counterfeit, sham, simulated, spurious, pseudo, mock, imitation; *informal* la-di-da, hoity-toity, highfalutin, posey, pseud, phoney, pretend, put on; *Brit. informal* poncey, posh, toffee-nosed.
OPPOSITES natural, unpretentious, genuine.

affecting ▸ adjective *their fumbling onstage shyness is oddly affecting* **touching**, moving, emotive, powerful, stirring, impressive, telling, soul-stirring, uplifting, heart-warming; poignant, pathetic, pitiful, piteous, plaintive, emotional, tear-jerking, heart-rending, heartbreaking, disturbing, distressing, upsetting, saddening, sad, painful, agonizing, harrowing, tragic, haunting.
OPPOSITES unaffecting, unmoving.

CHOOSE THE RIGHT WORD
affecting, moving, touching
See MOVING.

affection ▸ noun *they greeted each other with obvious affection* **fondness**, love, liking, endearment, feeling, sentiment, tenderness, warmth, warmness, devotion, care; caring, attentiveness, closeness, attachment, affinity, friendliness, friendship, intimacy, familiarity; amity, favour, regard, respect, admiration; warm feelings.

affectionate ▸ adjective *an affectionate hug | Thomas is such an affectionate child* **loving**, fond, adoring, devoted, caring, doting, tender, warm, warm-hearted, big-hearted, soft-centred, soft-hearted, soft, unselfish, kind, kind-hearted, kindly, comforting; sympathetic, solicitous, supportive, attentive, friendly, demonstrative, cuddly, amicable, cordial, welcoming, good-natured; brotherly, sisterly, motherly, fatherly, maternal, paternal, maternalistic, paternalistic; *informal* touchy-feely, lovey-dovey, chummy, pally; *Brit. informal* matey; *N. Amer. informal* buddy-buddy.
OPPOSITES cold, unfeeling.

affianced ▸ adjective *Edward was affianced to Lady Eleanor* **engaged**, betrothed, espoused, promised, plighted, pledged, contracted, bound; *informal* spoken for.
OPPOSITES unattached, single.

affiliate ▸ verb *the college is* ***affiliated with*** *the University of Wisconsin | the society is not* ***affiliated to*** *any political party* **associate with**, be in league with, unite with, combine with, join with, join up with, join forces with, ally with, form an alliance with, align with, amalgamate with, merge with, coalesce with, federate with, confederate with, form a federation with, form a confederation with, team up with, band together with, cooperate with; **annex to**, attach to, yoke to, incorporate into, integrate into.

affiliated ▸ adjective *the committee comprised two delegates from each affiliated club* **associated**, allied, related, integrated, amalgamated, incorporated, federated, confederated, unified, connected, linked, joined, bound, belonging; in league, in partnership.

affiliation ▸ noun *the Scottish Socialist Party was accepted for affiliation to the Labour Party | an economist with no party political affiliation* **annexing**, attaching, connecting, joining, bonding, uniting, combining, associating, aligning, allying, amalgamation, amalgamating, merging, incorporation, incorporating, integration, integrating, federating, federation, confederating, confederation, coupling, fusion; connection, relationship, fellowship, partnership, association, coalition, union, alliance, alignment, attachment, link, bond, tie, yoke; communication, rapport, sympathy, cooperation, collaboration, belonging; *rare* consociation.

affinity ▸ noun **1** *she has a natural* ***affinity with*** *animals and birds* **empathy**, rapport, sympathy, accord, harmony, like-mindedness; closeness to, fellow feeling for, understanding of; **liking for**, fondness for, inclination towards, partiality for, penchant for, predilection towards, attraction towards; *informal* chemistry.
OPPOSITES dislike, aversion.
2 *there is a semantic affinity between the two words* **similarity**, resemblance, likeness, kinship; correspondence, relationship, association, link, analogy, similitude, agreement, compatibility, congruity, parallelism, consonance; identity, identicalness, uniformity, equivalence.
OPPOSITE dissimilitude.
3 *despite their different backgrounds, an affinity grew and developed* **relationship**, bond, connection, propinquity.
OPPOSITES antipathy; blood relationship.

affirm ▸ verb **1** *he affirmed that they would lend military assistance* **declare**, state, assert, aver, proclaim, pronounce, attest, swear, avow, vow, guarantee, promise, certify, pledge, give one's word, give an undertaking; *rare* asseverate.
OPPOSITE deny.
2 *the charter affirmed the right of national minorities to use their own language* **uphold**, support, defend, maintain, confirm, ratify, endorse, approve (of), agree to, consent to, assent to, sanction.

affirmation ▸ noun **1** *an affirmation of faith* **assertion**, declaration, statement, proclamation, pronouncement, attestation, assurance; oath, vow, swearing, avowal, guarantee, promise, certification, pledge; deposition; *rare* asseveration, averment.
OPPOSITES denial, refutation.
2 *the poem ends with an affirmation of pastoral values* **confirmation**, ratification, endorsement, defence.

affirmative ▸ adjective *an affirmative answer* **positive**, assenting, consenting, agreeing, concurring, corroborative, favourable, approving, encouraging, supportive, in the affirmative.
OPPOSITES dissenting, negative.
▸ noun *Penelope took his grunt as an affirmative* **agreement**, acceptance,

approval, confirmation, assent, ratification, acquiescence, concurrence; OK, yes.
OPPOSITE disagreement.

affix ▶ verb **1** *he affixed a stamp to the envelope* **attach**, stick, fasten, bind, fix, post, secure, join, connect, couple; clip, tack, pin; glue, paste, gum, tape; *trademark* Sellotape.
OPPOSITES detach, remove.
2 (*formal*) *affix your signature to the document* **append**, add, add on, attach.

afflict ▶ verb *he was afflicted with chilblains* **trouble**, bother, burden, distress, cause trouble to, cause suffering to, beset, harass, worry, oppress, annoy, vex, irritate, exasperate, strain, stress, tax; torment, plague, blight, bedevil, pursue, rack, smite, curse, harrow, grip, visit, take; *rare* discommode, ail.
OPPOSITE comfort.

affliction ▶ noun **1** *the herb is reputed to cure a variety of afflictions* **disorder**, disease, malady, complaint, ailment, illness, indisposition, handicap, scourge, plague, trouble, menace, evil, visitation.
2 *he bore his affliction with great dignity* **suffering**, distress, pain, trouble, misery, wretchedness, hardship, misfortune, adversity, sorrow, torment, tribulation, woe, cross to bear, thorn in one's flesh/side; bane, trial, calamity, ordeal; (**afflictions**) ills.

affluence ▶ noun *the affluence of the higher social classes* **wealth**, prosperity, opulence, fortune, richness, luxury, plenty; riches, money, cash, lucre, resources, assets, possessions, property, substance, means.
OPPOSITE poverty.

affluent ▶ adjective *a residence in the affluent part of Montreal* **wealthy**, rich, prosperous, opulent, well off, moneyed, well-to-do, comfortable; propertied, substantial, of means, of substance, with deep pockets, in clover, plutocratic; *N. Amer.* silk-stocking; *informal* well heeled, rolling in it/money, in the money, made of money, filthy rich, stinking rich, loaded, flush, on easy street, quids in, worth a packet/bundle.
OPPOSITES poor, impoverished.

afford ▶ verb **1** *they cannot afford a holiday this year* **pay for**, bear/meet the expense of, spare the price of, have the money for, be rich enough for, have the wherewithal for; run to, stretch to, manage.
2 *we can no longer afford the luxury of complacency* **bear**, sustain, stand, carry; allow oneself.
3 *this highway affords stunning views of California's coastline* **provide**, supply, present, purvey, make available, offer, give, impart, bestow, furnish, render, grant, yield, produce, bear.

affray ▶ noun *his men became involved in a violent affray with a band of archers* **fight**, brawl, battle, engagement, encounter, confrontation, melee, clash, skirmish, scuffle, tussle, fracas, altercation; disturbance, commotion, breach of the peace, riot; *informal* scrap, dust-up, punch-up, set-to, shindy, shindig, free-for-all.

affront ▶ noun *the paintings, in his view, were an affront to public morality* **insult**, offence, indignity, slight, snub, slur, aspersion, provocation, injury, put down, humiliation; outrage, atrocity, scandal, injustice, abuse, desecration, violation; *informal* slap in the face, kick in the teeth.
OPPOSITE compliment.
▶ verb *she was affronted by his familiarity* **insult**, offend, outrage, mortify, provoke, slight, hurt, pique, wound, put out, irk, displease, distress, bother, rankle, needle, vex, gall, scandalize, disgust, disgruntle, put someone's back up, ruffle someone's feathers, make someone's hackles rise, raise someone's hackles.
OPPOSITE compliment.

aficionado ▶ noun *an aficionado of fine wines* **connoisseur**, expert, authority, specialist, pundit, one of the cognoscenti, cognoscente, devotee, appreciator, fan, fanatic, savant; enthusiast, lover, addict; *informal* buff, freak, nut, fiend, maniac, a great one for.

aflame ▶ adjective *most of the city was aflame* **burning**, ablaze, alight, on fire, in flames, flaming, blazing, raging, fiery, red-hot; lit, lighted, ignited.
OPPOSITES extinguished, unlit.

afloat ▶ adverb & adjective *a swimmer fighting to stay afloat* **buoyant**, floating, buoyed up, non-submerged, suspended, drifting, on/above the surface, (keeping one's head) above water.
OPPOSITES sunk, sinking.

afoot ▶ adjective & adverb *evil plans are afoot* **going on**, happening, around, about, abroad, circulating, current, stirring, in circulation, at large, going about, in the air, in the wind; brewing, looming, on the way, in the offing, on the horizon; *informal* on the go, doing the rounds, on the cards, in the pipeline; *literary* astir.

aforesaid ▶ adjective *the insurer undertakes to insure the aforesaid items against all risks* **previously mentioned**, aforementioned, aforenamed, previously described, above, above-stated, foregoing, preceding, precedent, earlier, previous, same, selfsame.
OPPOSITE subsequent.

afraid ▶ adjective **1** *I'm afraid of dogs | they ran away because they were afraid* **frightened**, scared, scared stiff, terrified, fearful, petrified, nervous, scared to death; apprehensive (about), intimidated (by), alarmed (at); uneasy, tense, nervy, worried, panicky, terror-stricken, terror-struck, horror-stricken, horror-struck, frightened/scared out of one's wits, scared witless, beside oneself, frantic, hysterical, with one's heart in one's mouth, shaking in one's shoes, shaking like a leaf; timid, timorous, faint-hearted, cowardly, cowering, cowed, pusillanimous, daunted; *informal* in a (blue) funk, in a cold sweat, in a flap, in a fluster, in a state, in a tizzy/tizz, yellow, chicken, jittery, jumpy; *dialect* frit; *Scottish* feart; *N. Amer. informal* spooked; *vulgar slang* shit scared; *archaic* afeared, affrighted.
OPPOSITES unafraid, brave, confident.
2 *don't be afraid to ask awkward questions* **reluctant**, unwilling, disinclined, loath, slow; hesitant about, chary of, shy of, averse to.
OPPOSITES keen, confident.
3 *I'm afraid that your daughter is ill* **sorry**, sad, distressed, regretful, apologetic, unhappy, remorseful, rueful.

WORD LINKS
afraid of ... **-phobic (e.g. *claustrophobic, oloephobic*)**
person who is afraid of ... **-phobe (e.g. *Anglophobe, technophobe*)**

afresh ▶ adverb *we should go back to the drawing board and start afresh* **anew**, again, over again, once again, once more, a second time, another time.

after ▶ preposition **1** *he made a speech on stage after the performance* **following**, subsequent to, succeeding, at the close/end of, in the wake of, later than; *rare* posterior to.
OPPOSITES before, preceding.
2 *Guy shut the door after them* **behind**, following, in the rear of.
OPPOSITES before, in front of.
3 *after the way he treated my sister I never want to speak to him again* **because of**, as a result of, as a consequence of, in view of, owing to, on account of, on grounds of, by dint of, in the wake of.
4 *he's still going to marry her, after all that's happened?* **despite**, in spite of, regardless of, notwithstanding, in defiance of, in the face of, for all.
5 *the policeman ran after him* **in pursuit of**, in someone's direction, following, on the track of, in the tracks of, in someone's footsteps.
OPPOSITES away from; in front of.
6 *I'm after information, and I'm willing to pay for it* **in search of**, in quest of, on a quest for, in pursuit of, trying to find, looking for, on the lookout for, hunting for.
7 *their next most accessible source after books is television* **next to**, beside, besides, following, nearest to, below, immediately inferior to.
OPPOSITE before.
8 *we asked after Pop and were glad to hear that he was well* **about**, concerning, regarding, with regard to, with respect to, with reference to, referring to, in connection with, on the subject of, in the matter of, apropos, re.
9 *the village is thought to have been named after a Roman officer* **in honour of**, as a tribute to, as a mark of respect to, the same as; *N. Amer.* for.
10 *the exhibition includes some chalk animal studies after Bandinelli* **in the style of**, in the manner of, in imitation of, on the model of, following the pattern of, after the fashion of, along/on the lines of, influenced by; similar to, like, characteristic of.
□ **after all** *I had to come—after all, I am your cousin* **most importantly**, above all, beyond everything, most of all, ultimately, first and foremost, essentially, basically, elementally, at bottom, when you get right down to it; *informal* when all's said and done, at the end of the day, when push comes to shove.
▶ adverb **1** *the week after, we went to Madrid* **later**, following, afterwards, after this/that, subsequently; next, ensuing; *formal* thereafter.
OPPOSITES previously, before.
2 *porters were following on after with their bags* **behind**, in the rear, at the back, in someone's wake, at the end.
OPPOSITES ahead, in front.
▶ adjective (*archaic*) *he treasured this conversation in after years* **later**, succeeding, subsequent, following, ensuing, next.
OPPOSITE previous.

WORD LINKS
related prefix **post- (e.g. *postscript, post-date*)**

after-effect ▶ noun *she was suffering from the after-effects of a hip injury* **repercussion**, aftermath, consequence, spin-off, sequel, follow-up, aftershock, trail, wake, offshoot; *informal* hangover; *Medicine* sequela.

afterlife ▶ noun (**the afterlife**) *they were inspired by their belief in the afterlife* **life after death**, immortality, everlasting life; heaven, paradise, nirvana, the next world, the hereafter; afterworld, world without end.

aftermath ▶ noun *the bleak aftermath of war* **repercussions**, after-effects, by-product, fallout, backwash, trail, wake, corollary; reverberations, consequences, effects, results, fruits; end result, outcome, upshot, issue, end; *informal* follow-up.

afterwards ▶ adverb *we all celebrated afterwards at a little pub near the church* **later**, later on, subsequently, then, after, after this/that, following this/that, at a later time/date, next, eventually, after a period of time, in due course; *formal* thereupon.

again ▶ adverb **1** *her spirits lifted again* **once more**, one more time, another time, a second time, afresh, anew.

2 *a full set of business software can add half as much again to the price of the machine* **extra**, in addition, additionally, over and above, on top, also, too, as well, besides, furthermore, moreover, yet, to boot.
3 *again, evidence was not always consistent* **also**, furthermore, further; **moreover**, besides.
□ **again and again** *I read this book again and again* **repeatedly**, over and over (again), time and (time) again, many times, many a time, on several occasions, often, frequently, recurrently, habitually, continually, persistently, constantly.

against ▸ **preposition 1** *a number of delegates opened by saying that they were against the motion* **opposed to**, in opposition to, hostile to, averse to, antagonistic towards, inimical to, unsympathetic to, resistant to, at odds with, in disagreement with, contra; in defiance of, versus, counter, at cross purposes with, dead set against; *informal* anti, con, agin.
OPPOSITES in favour of, pro.
2 *he was swimming against the tide* **in opposition to**, counter to, contrary to, in the opposite direction to, not in accord with; resisting.
OPPOSITES with, in the same direction as.
3 *his age is against him* **disadvantageous to**, unfavourable to, damaging to, detrimental to, prejudicial to, deleterious to, harmful to, injurious to, hurtful to, inconvenient for, adverse to, unfortunate for, a drawback for.
OPPOSITE advantageous to.
4 *it is advisable to insure all oriental rugs against theft* **in case of**, in/as provision for, in preparation for, in anticipation of, in expectation of.
5 *she had to put up her umbrella against the rain* **to protection oneself from**, in resistance to.
6 *a group of men huddled round a fire, silhouetted against the orange flames* **in contrast to**, as a foil to.
7 *the exchange rate of the dollar against the yen* **in exchange for**, in return for, in compensation for.
8 *she leaned against the wall* **touching**, in contact with, close up to, up against, abutting, on, adjacent to.
WORD LINKS
related prefix **anti-** **(e.g.** ***anti-aircraft, antidote*****)**

age *See centre pages for list of* **Geological Ages**
▸ **noun 1** *he retired at the age of 36 | he has a girlfriend of the same age* **number of years**, lifetime, duration, length of life; stage of life, generation, age group, peer group; years, summers, winters.
2 *her hearing had deteriorated with age* **elderliness**, old age, oldness, seniority, maturity, dotage, senility; one's advancing/advanced years, one's declining years, the winter/autumn of one's life; *formal* senescence; *archaic* eld; *rare* caducity.
OPPOSITES youth, childhood.
3 *the Elizabethan age | an age of computers and fax machines* **era**, epoch, period, time, aeon, span.
4 (*informal*) *you haven't been in touch with me for* **an age** *| I've wanted to do this* **for ages a long time**, a lifetime, an eternity, seemingly forever; hours, days, months, years, aeons, hours/days/months on end, ages and ages, a month of Sundays; *Brit. informal* yonks, donkey's years; *N. Amer. informal, dated* a coon's age.
▸ **verb** *Cabernet Sauvignon ages well, especially in oak | I assume Mother Nature will age me along with everyone else* **mature**, ripen, mellow, become/make mellow, season, condition, soften, sweeten, grow up, come of age; **grow/become/make old**, weather, (cause to) decline, wither, fade.

aged ▸ **adjective** *she treated him with the respect one might give to an aged relative* **elderly**, old, mature, older, senior, ancient, venerable; advanced in years, getting on; in one's dotage, long in the tooth, as old as the hills; grey, grey-haired, grey-bearded, grizzled, hoary; past one's prime, not as young as one was, not as young as one used to be; decrepit, doddering, doddery, not long for this world, senile, superannuated; septuagenarian, octogenarian, nonagenarian, centenarian; *informal* past it, over the hill, no spring chicken; *formal* senescent; *rare* longevous.
OPPOSITE young.

agency ▸ **noun 1** *an advertising agency* **business**, organization, company, firm, office, bureau, concern, service; branch, representative.
2 *there are many diseases in which infection is caused by the agency of insects* **action**, activity, effect, influence, force, power, work; **means**, vehicle, medium, instrument, mechanism, route, channel, mode, technique, expedient.
3 *regional policy was introduced through the agency of the Board of Trade* **intervention**, intercession, involvement, mediation, arbitration, interposing, instrumentality, good offices; auspices, aegis.

agenda ▸ **noun** *a meeting with a fixed agenda* **list of items**, schedule, programme, timetable, line-up, list, listing, to-do list, plan, scheme, syllabus, bill, card, directory, table; *Computing* menu.

agent ▸ **noun 1** *my agent told me that someone wanted to make a film out of my novel* **representative**, negotiator, business manager, emissary, envoy, factor, go-between, proxy, surrogate, trustee, liaison, broker, delegate, spokesperson, spokesman, spokeswoman, mouthpiece; *informal* rep.
2 *a travel agent* **agency**, business, organization, company, firm, office, bureau, concern, service.
3 *a CIA agent* **spy**, secret agent, undercover agent, operative, fifth columnist, Mata Hari; *informal* mole, spook, snooper, G-man; *archaic* intelligencer, beagle, lurcher.
4 *the agents of destruction* **doer**, performer, author, executor, perpetrator, operator, operative, mover, producer; cause, origin, root, source, instrument, catalyst.
5 *a cleansing agent* **medium**, means, instrument, vehicle; power, force.

agglomeration ▸ **noun** *the suburb is an agglomeration of houses, shops, and offices* **collection**, mass, cluster, lump, clump, pile, heap, bunch, stack, bundle, quantity, hoard, store, stockpile; accumulation, aggregate, build-up; miscellany, jumble, hotchpotch; *informal* mixed bag.

aggravate ▸ **verb 1** *according to some, the new law will aggravate the situation* **worsen**, make worse, exacerbate, inflame, compound; intensify, increase, heighten, magnify, add to, amplify, augment; add fuel to the fire/flames, add insult to injury, rub salt in the wound.
OPPOSITES alleviate, improve.
2 (*informal*) *you don't have to aggravate people to get what you want* **annoy**, irritate, exasperate, anger, irk, vex, put out, nettle, provoke, incense, rile, infuriate, antagonize, get on someone's nerves, rub up the wrong way, make someone's blood boil, ruffle someone's feathers, ruffle, try someone's patience, make someone's hackles rise; offend, pique; rankle; *informal* peeve, needle, make someone see red, get someone's back up, get someone's goat, get under someone's skin, get up someone's nose, bug, get someone, miff, hack off; *Brit. informal* wind up, get at, nark, get across, get on someone's wick; *N. Amer. informal* tick off; *vulgar slang* piss off.
OPPOSITES calm, conciliate.

CHOOSE THE RIGHT WORD
aggravate, annoy, irritate, vex, peeve
See ANNOY.

aggravation ▸ **noun 1** *the recession led to the aggravation of unemployment problems* **worsening**, exacerbation, compounding; intensification, increase, heightening, magnification, amplification, augmentation.
OPPOSITE improvement.
2 (*informal*) *she decided that no amount of money is worth the aggravation* **nuisance**, annoyance, irritant, irritation, hassle, pest, grievance, problem, trouble, difficulty, snag, inconvenience, bother, trial, thorn in one's flesh/side, bane of one's life; exasperation, infuriation, vexation; *informal* aggro, headache, pain, pain in the neck/backside; *vulgar slang* pain in the arse/butt.

aggregate ▸ **noun 1** *the specimen is an aggregate of rock and mineral fragments* **collection**, mass, cluster, lump, clump, pile, heap, bundle, quantity; accumulation, build-up, agglomeration, concentration, assemblage; mixture, mix, combination, blend, compound, alloy, amalgam, conjunction, synthesis, marriage; miscellany, jumble, hotchpotch; *informal* mixed bag.
2 *he won with a 90-hole aggregate of 325* **total**, sum total, sum, whole amount, grand total, totality, entirety, summation, gross, result, final figure.
▸ **adjective** *an aggregate score of 3–2* **total**, combined, whole, gross, accumulated, added, entire, complete, full, comprehensive, overall, composite.

aggression ▸ **noun 1** *an act of aggression* **hostility**, aggressiveness, belligerence, bellicosity, antagonism, truculence; pugnacity, pugnaciousness, combativeness, militancy, warmongering, warlikeness, hawkishness, force, violence; attack, assault, encroachment, offence, invasion, infringement.
OPPOSITE meekness.
2 *he played the game with unceasing aggression* **confidence**, self-confidence, boldness, audacity, self-assertion, assertion, assertiveness, self-assertiveness, determination, forcefulness, vigour, energy, dynamism, zeal.
OPPOSITE diffidence.

aggressive ▸ **adjective 1** *an aggressive, grubby schoolkid* **hostile**, belligerent, bellicose, antagonistic, truculent; pugnacious, combative, violent, macho; confrontational, quarrelsome, argumentative.
OPPOSITES meek, friendly.
2 *an aggressive foreign policy* **warmongering**, warlike, warring, hawkish, violent, combative, attacking; jingoistic, militaristic, flag-waving, sabre-rattling; offensive, expansionist, invasive, intrusive; *informal* gung-ho.
OPPOSITE peaceful.
3 *an aggressive promotional drive* **assertive**, forceful, competitive, insistent, vigorous, energetic, dynamic, driving, bold, audacious, enterprising, go-ahead, zealous, pushing; *informal* pushy, in-your-face, feisty.
OPPOSITES submissive, diffident.

aggressor ▸ **noun** *England fought a succession of wars in which she was the aggressor* **attacker**, assaulter, assailant, invader; **instigator**, provoker, initiator, warmonger, offender.
OPPOSITES victim; retaliator.

aggrieved ▸ **adjective 1** *the manager looked aggrieved at the suggestion*

resentful, affronted, indignant, disgruntled, discontented, angry, distressed, unhappy, disturbed, anguished, hurt, pained, upset, offended, piqued, in high dudgeon, riled, nettled, vexed, irked, irritated, annoyed, put out, chagrined; *informal* peeved, miffed, in a huff; *Brit. informal* cheesed off; *N. Amer. informal* sore, steamed; *vulgar slang* pissed off; *N. Amer. vulgar slang* pissed.
OPPOSITE pleased.
2 *the aggrieved party* **wronged**, injured, abused, harmed, mistreated, ill-used, offended, maltreated, ill-treated, maligned.

aghast ▸ adjective *she winced, aghast at his cruelty* **horrified**, appalled, astounded, amazed, dismayed, thunderstruck, stunned, shocked, in shock, flabbergasted, staggered, taken aback, speechless, awestruck, open-mouthed, wide-eyed; *informal* floored, gobsmacked.

agile ▸ adjective **1** *the little girl was as agile as a monkey* **nimble**, lithe, spry, supple, limber, sprightly, acrobatic, dexterous, deft, willowy, graceful, light-footed, nimble-footed, light on one's feet, fleet-footed; active, fit, in good condition; lively, vigorous, quick-moving; *informal* nippy, twinkle-toed; *literary* fleet, lightsome.
OPPOSITES clumsy, stiff.
2 *his agile mind was forever seeking new ways of conserving energy* **alert**, sharp, acute, clever, shrewd, astute, intelligent, quick-witted, perceptive, penetrating, piercing, active, nimble, quick off the mark, finely honed, rapier-like; *informal* smart, on the ball.
OPPOSITES slow, dull.

agitate ▸ verb **1** *I must warn you that any mention of Clare agitates your grandmother* **upset**, perturb, fluster, ruffle, disconcert, unnerve, disquiet, disturb, distress, unsettle, bother, concern, trouble, cause anxiety to, make anxious, alarm, work up, flurry, worry; inflame, incite, provoke, stir up; *informal* rattle, faze, discombobulate.
OPPOSITE calm.
2 *she urged us to agitate for the appointment of more women to cabinet posts* **campaign**, strive, battle, fight, struggle, crusade, push, press; argue, debate, dispute, wrangle.
3 *they were used as stirrers to help to agitate the vast masses of fermenting vegetation* **stir**, whisk, beat, churn, shake, toss, blend, whip (up), fold, roil, jolt, disturb.

agitated ▸ adjective *I could see that he was agitated and edgy* **upset**, perturbed, flustered, ruffled, disconcerted, unnerved, disquieted, disturbed, distressed, unsettled, bothered, concerned, troubled, anxious, alarmed, worked up, worried, harassed; nervous, jittery, jumpy, on edge, tense, overwrought, frantic, keyed up, in a panic; inflamed, stirred up; *informal* rattled, fazed, discombobulated, in a dither, in a flap, in a state, in a lather, in a tizz/tizzy, all of a dither, beside oneself, hot and bothered, hot under the collar; *Brit. informal* having kittens, in a (flat) spin.
OPPOSITES calm, relaxed.

agitation ▸ noun **1** *Freddie gritted his teeth in agitation* **anxiety**, perturbation, disquiet, distress, concern, trouble, alarm, worry, upset; nervous excitement; *rare* disconcertment.
OPPOSITES calmness, relaxation.
2 *there was an upsurge in nationalist agitation* **campaigning**, striving, battling, fighting, struggling, crusading; arguing, argument, wrangling, debate, discussion; rabble-rousing, provocation, stirring up, commotion.
3 *the solutions were prepared by vigorous agitation of the components* **stirring**, whisking, beating, churning, shaking, turbulence, tossing, blending, whipping, folding, rolling, jolting.

agitator ▸ noun *a left-wing agitator* **troublemaker**, rabble-rouser, demagogue, soapbox orator, incendiary; revolutionary, firebrand, rebel, insurgent, revolutionist, subversive; instigator, inciter, provoker, fomenter, dissentient; *French* agent provocateur; *informal* stirrer.

agnostic ▸ noun *he was an agnostic, but his notebooks reveal a kind of religious attitude to the universe* **sceptic**, doubter, questioner, doubting Thomas, challenger, scoffer, cynic; unbeliever, disbeliever, non-believer; rationalist; *rare* nullifidian.
OPPOSITES believer, theist.
▸ adjective *a group of prominent agnostic scientists* **sceptical**, doubting, questioning, unsure, cynical, unbelieving, disbelieving, non-believing, faithless, irreligious; rationalist; *rare* nullifidian.
OPPOSITE theist.

ago ▸ adverb *a few days ago they had a long discussion* **in the past**, before the present, before, earlier, back, in time gone by, since, formerly, previously; *formal* heretofore.

agog ▸ adverb *everyone was agog to hear what on earth he would say* **eager**, excited, impatient, in suspense, on tenterhooks, on the edge of one's seat, on pins and needles, keen, anxious, longing; curious, expectant, enthralled, enthusiastic, avid, breathless, open-mouthed, waiting with bated breath; *informal* itching.
OPPOSITES uninterested, incurious.

agonize ▸ verb *all the way home she* ***agonized about*** *what she should do* **worry**, fret, fuss, upset oneself, rack one's brains, wrestle with oneself, be worried, be anxious, feel uneasy, exercise oneself, brood, muse; mull over, dwell on, contemplate, ruminate, chew over, puzzle over, speculate, weigh up, turn over in one's mind; be indecisive; *informal* stew; *archaic* pore on.

agonizing ▸ adjective *he died after suffering months of agonizing pain* **excruciating**, harrowing, racking, painful, acute, severe, intense, extreme, grievous, hellish, killing, searing, torturous, tormenting, piercing; insufferable, unbearable, unendurable, more than one can bear, more than flesh and blood can stand; *literary* exquisite.

agony ▸ noun *he was screaming in agony* **pain**, hurt, suffering, torture, torment, anguish, affliction, trauma, misery, distress, grief, woe, wretchedness, heartbreak, heartache; pangs, throes; *rare* excruciation.

agrarian ▸ adjective *Brazil is diversifying its agrarian economy* **agricultural**, rural, countryside, farming, rustic, pastoral, bucolic; *literary* georgic, sylvan, Arcadian, agrestic.

agree ▸ verb **1** *I agree with you | officials agreed that it has good potential* **concur**, be of the same mind/opinion, see eye to eye, be in sympathy, sympathize, be united, be as one man, accord; acknowledge, admit, concede, grant, own, confess.
OPPOSITES disagree, differ.
2 *they had* ***agreed to*** *a ceasefire* **consent**, assent, accede; acquiesce in, accept, approve (of), allow, admit, grant, comply with, undertake, go along with, say yes to, give one's approval to, give something the nod, recognize, acknowledge.
OPPOSITE reject.
3 *the plan and the drawing of the church do not agree with each other* **match**, match up, accord, correspond, conform, coincide, fit, tally, harmonize, be in harmony, be in agreement, be consistent, be compatible, be consonant, be congruous, be in tune, equate, be equivalent, dovetail, chime, correlate, be parallel; *informal* square.
OPPOSITES differ, contradict.
4 *they* ***agreed on*** *a price* **settle**, decide, shake hands; arrange, arrive at, negotiate, work out, thrash out, hammer out, reach an agreement on, come to terms about, reach terms on; strike a bargain, make a deal.
5 *she's probably eaten something that didn't agree with her* **be agreeable to**, be good for, be healthy for, be acceptable to, suit.

CHOOSE THE RIGHT WORD

agree, consent, assent, acquiesce

More than one party is needed for an agreement, but the contributions made by each may be different.

- **Agree** is the only word of the four that describes being of one mind with others over something (*we'll have to decide what compromise we can agree on | they agree a currency price and payment terms*), but all of them can be used for giving one's permission. When someone agrees *to* something, the parties to the agreement may be on an equal footing (*the company and the shareholders agreed to a lock-out clause*), but it may depend on the willingness of one party who is in a position of superior power (*the owner has refused to say whether he'll agree to the rescue plan*).
- Someone who **consents** to something proposed to them also has the power to decide on it and typically has some reservations or initial opposition. Many uses are concerned with legal considerations (*the Attorney General has to consent to any prosecution under the Act*). People also consent, for example, to medical *treatment* of various kinds, to *testing* for genetic susceptibility to various disorders, and to *sex*: the phrase *consenting adult* is used exclusively with reference to sexual activity. One can also consent *to do something* (*Loretta was hoping that Koogan would consent to lend them a key*).
- Someone who **assents** to a proposal is generally a person whose approval is required, although they may feel quite indifferent to it. They are free to accept or reject the proposal, but have played no part in working it out: they merely accept what is presented to them (*the inspector assented to the remark with a nod*).
- To **acquiesce** is to accept something by default through failing to resist. Often what is accepted is not something that the person really wants, and their acquiescence is due to exhaustion, attrition, or lack of real bargaining power (*the authorities believed that most refugees would acquiesce and not resist attempts to send them back*). Acquiescence can easily slip into passive connivance in something bad (*the oil company was accused of acquiescing in the pollution of the people's lands*).

agreeable ▸ adjective **1** *a village atmosphere which we find rather agreeable* **pleasant**, pleasing, enjoyable, pleasurable, nice, to one's liking, appealing, engaging, satisfying, fine, charming, delightful.
OPPOSITES disagreeable, unpleasant.
2 *the policeman was an agreeable fellow* **likeable**, charming, amiable, affable, pleasant, nice, friendly, good-natured, sociable, genial, congenial, appealing, sympathetic, benign, benevolent.
OPPOSITES disagreeable, unpleasant.

3 *we should get together for a talk, if you're agreeable* **willing**, amenable, compliant, complying, consenting, assenting, in accord/agreement, disposed, accommodating, acquiescent, tractable, obliging, complaisant.
OPPOSITE unwilling.

agreement ▶ **noun 1** *all heads nodded in agreement* **accord**, concurrence, consensus, harmony, accordance, unity, unison, concord, like-mindedness, rapport, sympathy; **assent**, acceptance, consent, acquiescence, endorsement, confirmation.
OPPOSITE disagreement.
2 *the defence minister signed an agreement on military cooperation* **contract**, compact, treaty, covenant, pact, accord, deal, bargain, settlement, concordat, protocol, entente, arrangement, understanding, pledge, promise, bond.
3 *there is some agreement between my view and that of the author* **correspondence**, consistency, compatibility, conformity, coincidence, harmony, concord, accord, accordance, congruity; similarity, resemblance, likeness, identity, uniformity, relationship, association, similitude.
OPPOSITE discord.

agricultural *See centre pages for list of* **Agricultural Workers**
▶ **adjective 1** *an agricultural labourer* **farm**, farming, agrarian; rural, countryside, country, rustic, pastoral, bucolic; *literary* georgic, sylvan, Arcadian, agrestic.
OPPOSITE urban.
2 *agricultural land* **farmed**, farm, agrarian, cultivated, tilled, productive.
OPPOSITE wild.

agriculture *See centre pages for lists of* **Agricultural Workers** **Farming and Cultivation**
▶ **noun** *the mechanization of agriculture is reducing work opportunities* **farming**, cultivation, tillage, tilling, husbandry, land management, farm management, crofting; agribusiness, agronomics, agronomy.
OPPOSITE industry.

WORD LINKS

related prefixes	**agri-** (e.g. ***agribusiness, agriscience***), **agro-** (e.g. ***agroforestry, agro-industry***)
relating to agriculture	**agrarian**

aground ▶ **adverb & adjective** *a year later, the tanker was still aground* **foundered**, ashore, beached, grounded, stuck, shipwrecked, wrecked, high and dry, on the rocks, on the ground/bottom; marooned, stranded.
OPPOSITE afloat.

ahead ▶ **adverb 1** *he peered ahead, but could see nothing* **forward(s)**, towards the front, frontwards; onwards, on, forth.
OPPOSITE behind.
2 *he had ridden on ahead* **in front**, at the head, in the lead, at the fore, to the fore, in the vanguard, in the van, in advance, at the head of the queue.
OPPOSITES behind, at the back.
3 *she was preparing herself mentally for what lay ahead* **in the future**, in time, in time to come, in the fullness of time, at a later date, after this, henceforth, subsequently, later on, in due course, next, from now on, from this day/time on, from this day forth/forward.
OPPOSITE in the past.
4 *a poll showed them ahead by six points* **leading**, winning, in the lead, (out) in front, to the fore, first, coming first; *informal* up front.
OPPOSITE losing.
□ **ahead of 1** *she stood back to allow Blanche to go ahead of her* **in front of**, before.
OPPOSITE behind.
2 *we have a demanding trip ahead of us* **in store for**, waiting for, in wait for.
3 *the motorway was finished two months ahead of schedule* **in advance of**, before, earlier than, prior to, previous to.
OPPOSITE behind.
4 *in terms of these amenities, Britain was ahead of other European countries* **more advanced than**, further on than, superior to, outdistancing, outstripping, surpassing, exceeding, better than, prevailing over.
OPPOSITES behind; inferior to.

aid ▶ **noun 1** *with the aid of his colleagues he prepared a manifesto* **assistance**, support; help, backing, abettance, encouragement, cooperation, succour; a helping hand.
OPPOSITE hindrance.
2 *we have provided valuable economic and humanitarian aid* **donations**, funding, contributions, subsidies, benefits, welfare, gifts, grants, relief, charity, financial assistance, subvention, alms, offerings, handouts, largesse; patronage, sponsorship, backing; scholarships, bursaries; debt remission; *informal* a leg up, shot in the arm.
3 *a hospital aid* **helper**, assistant; *informal* girl/man Friday.
▶ **verb 1** *he was liable to provide an army to aid the King of England* **help**, assist, abet, come to the aid of, give assistance to, lend a hand to, be of service to; avail, succour, sustain; support, back, back up, second, stand by, uphold.
OPPOSITE hinder.
2 *essences can be added to your bath to aid restful sleep* **facilitate**, promote, encourage, help, speed up, hasten, accelerate, expedite, further, boost, give a boost/lift/push to, spur on, smooth/clear the way for.
OPPOSITES discourage, hinder.

CHOOSE THE RIGHT WORD

aid, help, assist, support
See HELP.

aide ▶ **noun** *a presidential aide* **assistant**, helper, adviser, right-hand man, attaché, adjutant, deputy, second, second in command, acolyte, auxiliary, companion, confidante; subordinate, junior, underling, lackey, flunkey, henchman; *N. Amer.* cohort; *informal* main man, man/girl Friday.

ail ▶ **verb** (archaic) *what ails you, Elizabeth?* **trouble**, afflict, pain, bedevil, beset, rack, curse; distress, bother, worry, sicken, be the matter with.

ailing ▶ **adjective 1** *her husband was away visiting his ailing mother* **ill**, unwell, not well, sick, sickly, poorly, weak, indisposed, in poor/bad health, infirm, debilitated, delicate, off colour; languishing, valetudinarian; dying, at death's door; *informal* under the weather, below par, laid up.
OPPOSITE healthy.
2 *a government programme to rescue the country's ailing economy* **failing**, in poor condition, weak, poor, inadequate, deficient, imperfect, substandard, flawed.
OPPOSITES strong, successful.

ailment ▶ **noun** *the doctor diagnosed a common stomach ailment* **illness**, disease, disorder, sickness, affliction, malady, complaint, infection, upset, condition, infirmity, indisposition, malaise, trouble; *informal* bug, virus; *Brit. informal* lurgy.

aim ▶ **verb 1** *he aimed the rifle* **point**, direct, train, sight, focus, level, line up, position; turn something on someone.
2 *she* ***aimed at*** *the target* **take aim at**, fix on, zero in on, draw a bead on.
3 *undergraduates aiming for a first degree* **work towards**, be after, set one's sights on, try for, strive for, pursue, seek, aspire to, endeavour to achieve, have in view, have designs on, wish for, want; *formal* essay.
4 *this system is* ***aimed at*** *the home entertainment market* **intend for**, mean for, address to, destine for; target at, direct towards, market at, design for, tailor to, orient towards, pitch to/towards.
5 *the course aims to educate children to cope with dangerous situations* **intend**, plan, resolve, propose, purpose, design, mean, have in mind/view.
▶ **noun** *our aim is to develop gymnasts to the top level* **objective**, object, goal, end, target, grail, holy grail, design, desire, desired result, intention, intent, plan, purpose, idea, point, object of the exercise; ambition, aspiration, wish, dream, hope; resolve; *French* raison d'être.

aimless ▶ **adjective 1** *Flavia set out on an aimless walk* **purposeless**, pointless, goalless, undirected, objectless, unfocused, without purpose, without goal; meaningless, senseless, futile, hollow, frivolous, barren, profitless, fruitless.
OPPOSITE purposeful.
2 *the huddles of aimless men standing outside the bars* **unambitious**, purposeless, undirected, apathetic, goalless; drifting, wandering, adrift; unoccupied, idle, at a loose end, with time to kill.
OPPOSITE determined.

air ▶ **noun 1** *hundreds of birds hovered in the air* **sky**, heavens, ether; **atmosphere**, aerosphere, airspace.
2 *I was opening the windows to get some air into the room* **breeze**, draught, wind; breath of air, gust of air, flurry of air, waft of air, puff of wind, whiff of air, blast of air.
3 *he upended his glass with an air of defiance* **expression**, appearance, look, impression, aspect, manner, bearing, mien, countenance; mood, quality, ambience, aura, feeling, flavour, tone; *informal* vibe.
4 (**airs**) *he'd no patience with women putting on airs* **affectations**, pretension, pretentiousness, affectedness, posing, posturing, pretence; **self-importance**, superiority, condescension, ostentation, snobbery, superciliousness, pomposity, arrogance, haughtiness, hauteur, pride, conceit, airs and graces; *informal* swank, snootiness, uppishness, side.
5 *a traditional Scottish air* **tune**, melody, song, theme, strain, refrain, piece, aria; *literary* lay.
▶ **verb 1** *this is a chance for you to air your views* **express**, voice, make public, vent, ventilate, articulate, state, declare, give expression to, give voice to; make known, publicize, publish, disseminate, circulate, communicate, spread, promulgate, broadcast; reveal, announce, proclaim, divulge, submit, raise, moot, propose; discuss, debate; have one's say.
2 *the windows were opened regularly to air the room* **ventilate**, aerate, freshen, refresh, cool, air-condition.
3 *the film was aired nationwide* **broadcast**, transmit, beam, send/put out, televise, show, telecast, relay, put on the air/airwaves, disseminate; *informal* screen.

WORD LINKS

related prefix	**aero-** (e.g. ***aeroplane, aerosol***)
relating to air	**aerial**
study of moving air	**aerodynamics**

A

airborne ▶ adjective *the shuttle was airborne* **flying**, in flight, in the air, on the wing, winging; gliding, hovering, soaring.

aircraft ▶ noun. *See centre pages for lists of* **Aircraft** **Aircraft Parts**

WORD LINKS

related prefix	**aero-** (e.g. ***aerospace, aeromodelling***)
science of aircraft flight	**aeronautics**
commercial operation of aircraft	**aviation**

airily ▶ adverb *the doctor had dismissed his troubles airily* **lightly**, breezily, flippantly, casually, nonchalantly; readily, heedlessly, without consideration, uncaringly, indifferently, unthinkingly; light-heartedly, gaily, blithely, jauntily, cheerfully.
OPPOSITES seriously, thoughtfully.

airing ▶ noun **1** *we should give the place a good airing before we go* **ventilating**, ventilation, aerating, aeration, freshening, refreshing, cooling, air conditioning.
2 *the governess took them out to the park for an airing* **stroll**, walk, saunter, turn, jaunt, amble; outing, excursion, trip, expedition; *formal* promenade; *dated* constitutional.
3 *the media has to be a forum for the airing of different views* **expression**, voicing, venting, ventilation, articulation, statement, declaration; publicizing, publication, dissemination, circulation, communication, spreading, promulgation, broadcast, broadcasting; revelation, announcement, proclamation, divulgence, submission, raising, mooting, proposal; discussion, debate.
4 *I hope the BBC gives the play another airing very soon* **broadcast**, transmission, televising, showing, relaying, telecast, dissemination; *informal* screening.

airless ▶ adjective *a hot, airless room* **stuffy**, close, stifling, suffocating, breathless, sultry, muggy, fuggy, stale, humid, oppressive; unventilated, badly/poorly ventilated; smoky.
OPPOSITES airy, ventilated.

airport ▶ noun airfield, airstrip, landing strip, runway; heliport, helipad; *Military* air station; *Brit.* aerodrome; *N. Amer.* airdrome; *informal, dated* drome.

airtight ▶ adjective **1** *an airtight container* **sealed**, closed, shut tight, tight, impermeable, hermetically sealed; watertight, waterproof.
OPPOSITE leaky.
2 *he had an airtight alibi* **indisputable**, unquestionable, incontrovertible, undeniable, incontestable, irrefutable, unassailable, beyond dispute, beyond question, beyond doubt; foolproof, sound, flawless, watertight, conclusive, without loopholes.
OPPOSITE flawed.

airy ▶ adjective **1** *the conservatory is light and airy* **well ventilated**, fresh; **spacious**, open, uncrowded, uncluttered; light, well lit, bright.
OPPOSITE stuffy.
2 *he rested his face against his airy pillow* **delicate**, soft, fine, feathery, floaty, insubstantial, flimsy, wispy.
OPPOSITES heavy, solid.
3 *'It was obvious,' said Robyn with an airy gesture* **nonchalant**, casual, breezy, flippant, insouciant; heedless, unconsidered, uncaring, indifferent, unthinking, unworried, untroubled; light-hearted, blithe, jaunty, cheerful, unserious, insubstantial.
OPPOSITE serious.

airy-fairy ▶ adjective (*informal*) *an airy-fairy principle of political philosophy* **impractical**, unrealistic, idealistic; unfocused, vague, fanciful, insubstantial, without substance, unconvincing.
OPPOSITES matter of fact, solid.

aisle ▶ noun *she wandered round the aisles, filling up her trolley* **passage**, passageway, corridor, gangway, walkway, path, lane, alley.

ajar ▶ adjective & adverb *a door in the wall stood slightly ajar* **slightly open**, half open, agape; unfastened, unlatched, unlocked, unsecured, off the latch.
OPPOSITES closed; wide open.

akin ▶ adjective *walking through the streets of Hong Kong is an experience* ***akin to*** *a rugby match* **similar**, related, close, near, corresponding, comparable, parallel, equivalent; allied with, connected with, like; alike, matching, analogous, cognate, of a piece.
OPPOSITE unlike.

alacrity ▶ noun *she accepted with alacrity* **eagerness**, willingness, readiness; enthusiasm, ardour, fervour, keenness, joyousness, liveliness, zeal; promptness, haste, briskness, swiftness, dispatch, speed; *dated* address.
OPPOSITE apathy.

alarm ▶ noun **1** *the girl spun round in alarm* **fear**, anxiety, apprehension, trepidation, nervousness, unease, distress, agitation, consternation, disquiet, perturbation, fright, panic, dread, horror, shock, terror.
OPPOSITES calmness, composure.
2 *a smoke alarm* **siren**, warning sound, alarm signal, danger signal, distress signal, alert; warning device, alarm bell, bell, horn, whistle; red light, red flag; *archaic* tocsin.
▶ verb *the news had alarmed her* **frighten**, scare, panic, startle, unnerve, distress, agitate, upset, fluster, ruffle, disconcert, shock, daunt, dismay, disturb, work up, terrify, terrorize, petrify, make someone's blood run cold; *informal* put the wind up someone, rattle, spook, scare the living daylights out of.

alarming ▶ adjective *infant mortality is rising at an alarming rate* **frightening**, startling, unnerving, shocking, hair-raising; distressing, upsetting, disconcerting, perturbing, dismaying, disquieting, daunting, disturbing, harrowing; fearsome, dreadful, monstrous, forbidding, appalling, chilling, terrifying, petrifying; *informal* scary.
OPPOSITE reassuring.

alarmist ▶ noun *this problem is a purely a fabrication by alarmists* **scaremonger**, gloom-monger, doom-monger, voice of doom, doomster, doomsayer, doom merchant, Cassandra; fatalist, pessimist, killjoy, misery; *informal* doom and gloom merchant, wet blanket.
OPPOSITES optimist, Pollyanna.

alchemy ▶ noun *they were involved with the quest for immortality through alchemy* **chemistry**; **magic**, sorcery, witchcraft, enchantment.

alcohol *See centre pages for lists of* **Drinks** **Beers** **Cocktails** **Sherries** **Whiskies** **Wines**
▶ noun *I don't even smoke cigarettes or touch alcohol* **liquor**, intoxicating liquor, alcoholic drink, strong drink, drink, spirits, intoxicants; *informal* booze, hooch, the hard stuff, firewater, gut-rot, rotgut, moonshine, tipple, the demon drink, the bottle, juice, bevvy, grog, Dutch courage, John Barleycorn; *technical* ethyl alcohol, ethanol.

WORD LINKS

addiction to alcohol	**alcoholism, dipsomania**
refusal to drink alcohol	**temperance, teetotalism**

alcoholic ▶ adjective *you should moderate your consumption of alcoholic drinks* **intoxicating**, inebriating, containing alcohol; strong, hard, potent, stiff; brewed, distilled, fermented; *rare* spirituous, vinous.
▶ noun *he took the crucial step of admitting that he was an alcoholic* **dipsomaniac**, drunk, drunkard, heavy/hard/serious drinker, problem drinker, drinker, alcohol-abuser, alcohol addict, person with a drink problem; tippler, sot, toper, inebriate, imbiber; *informal* boozer, lush, alky, dipso, soak, tosspot, wino, sponge, barfly; *Austral./NZ* hophead, metho; *vulgar slang* pisshead, piss artist.

alcove ▶ noun *an old brick fireplace set back in a spacious alcove* **recess**, niche, nook, opening, bay, hollow, cavity, corner, indentation, booth; apse; inglenook.

alert ▶ adjective **1** *police have asked neighbours to be alert after a spate of burglaries in the area* **vigilant**, wide awake, aware, watchful, attentive, observant, circumspect, wary, chary, heedful, canny; on the lookout, on one's guard, on one's toes, all ears, keeping one's eyes open/peeled, keeping a weather eye open, on the qui vive.
OPPOSITE inattentive.
2 *she continued to paint in old age in order to remain mentally alert* **quick-witted**, sharp, bright, quick, keen, perceptive, wide awake, responsive, agile, acute, astute; *informal* on the ball, on one's toes, quick off the mark, quick on the uptake, all there, with it, bright-eyed and bushy-tailed.
OPPOSITE slow.
▶ noun **1** *the army called for a state of alert* **vigilance**, watchfulness, carefulness, attentiveness, guardedness, care, caution, cautiousness, wariness, chariness, alertness, circumspection, prudence, heedfulness, heed, mindfulness.
OPPOSITE carelessness.
2 *a flood alert has been issued* **warning**, caution, notification, notice, exhortation, injunction; siren, alarm, signal, danger signal, distress signal.
▶ verb *police were alerted by a phone call from the house* **warn**, notify, apprise, caution, put on one's guard, forewarn, put on the qui vive, arouse; *informal* tip off, clue in, put in the picture, put wise.

alertness ▶ noun **1** *he had the supernatural alertness of the hunted* **vigilance**, awareness, watchfulness, attentiveness, attention, circumspection, wariness, chariness, heedfulness, canniness, discretion, prudence.
OPPOSITE inattentiveness.
2 *work is unquestionably one of the most important factors in preserving mental alertness and bodily health* **quick-wittedness**, quick thinking, quickness of mind, sharpness, quickness, keenness, perceptiveness, responsiveness, agility, acuteness, acuity, shrewdness, astuteness, intelligence, insight, presence of mind.
OPPOSITE slowness.

alga ▶ noun. *See centre pages for list of* **Algae**

alias ▶ noun *he is known under several aliases by Interpol* **assumed name**, false name, pseudonym, sobriquet, incognito, nickname; pen name, stage name; *French* nom de plume, nom de guerre; *rare* allonym, anonym.
▶ adverb *Cassius Clay, alias Muhammad Ali* **also known as**, aka, also called, otherwise known as, otherwise.

alibi ▶ noun *luckily we've both got a very good alibi for last night* **defence**, defending evidence, plea; justification, explanation, reason, vindication; excuse, pretext; *informal* story, line.

▶ verb (*informal*) *her brother had reluctantly agreed to alibi her* **cover for**, give an alibi to, provide with an alibi, shield, protect.

alien ▶ adjective **1** *the study of alien cultures promotes self-awareness* **foreign**, overseas, non-native, external, distant, remote.
OPPOSITE native.
2 *emerging from the station in the City, they found themselves in an alien landscape* **unfamiliar**, unknown, unheard of, foreign; strange, peculiar, odd, bizarre, outlandish; remote, exotic, novel.
OPPOSITE familiar.
3 *he has been asked to adopt a vicious role* **alien to** *his nature* **incompatible with**, unusual for, opposed to, conflicting with, contrary to, adverse to, in conflict with, at variance with, antagonistic to; unacceptable to, repugnant to, hostile to, inimical to; *rare* oppugnant to.
OPPOSITE familiar.
4 *alien beings have landed on Earth* **extraterrestrial**, other-worldly, unearthly; Martian, Venutian, Jovian.
OPPOSITE earthly.
▶ noun **1** *he was deported as an illegal alien* **foreigner**, non-native, immigrant, emigrant, émigré, incomer, newcomer, visitor, outsider, stranger.
OPPOSITE native.
2 *the alien's spaceship has crashed* **extraterrestrial**, ET; Martian, Venutian, Jovian; *informal* little green man.

alienate ▶ verb **1** *his homosexuality* **alienated** *him* **from** *his conservative father* **estrange**, turn away, set apart, drive apart, isolate, detach, distance, put at a distance; set against, part, separate, cut off, sever, divide, divorce, disunite, set at variance/odds, make hostile to, drive a wedge between, sow dissension.
OPPOSITE unite.
2 *they approached the government for aid in preventing the land from being alienated* **transfer**, convey, pass on, hand over, devolve.

alienation ▶ noun **1** *she shared my deep sense of alienation from our environment* **isolation**, detachment, estrangement, distance, separation, severance, parting, division, divorce, cutting off, turning away, withdrawal; variance, difference, schism.
2 *most leases contain restrictions against alienation* **transfer**, conveyance, passing on, handing over, devolution.

alight[1] ▶ verb **1** *he was the only passenger to* **alight from** *the train* **get off**, step off, get down; dismount, disembark, descend, exit; detrain, deplane; *informal* pile out.
OPPOSITES get on, board.
2 *a swallow alighted on a branch* **land**, come down, come to rest, touch down, light, arrive, descend; settle, perch, roost, sit, rest.
OPPOSITE fly off.

alight[2] ▶ adjective **1** *bales of hay were set alight | he kept the fire alight* **on fire**, ablaze, aflame, in flames, flaming, burning, blazing, raging, fiery, lit, lighted, ignited; *literary* afire.
OPPOSITE extinguished.
2 *her face was suddenly alight with laughter* **lit up**, gleaming, glowing, aglow, ablaze, illuminated, brilliant, bright, shining, radiant, shimmering, sparkling, flashing, dazzling, luminous, incandescent.
OPPOSITE dark.

align ▶ verb **1** *desks are typically aligned in straight rows facing forwards* **line up**, range, arrange in line, put in order, put in rows/columns, straighten (up); marshal, orient, place, position, dispose, situate, set.
2 *he* **aligned himself with** *the workers* **ally**, affiliate, associate, join, side, sympathize, be in league, unite, combine, join (up), join forces, form an alliance, team up, band together, cooperate, collaborate, throw in one's lot, make common cause.

alike ▶ adjective *all the doors looked alike* **similar**, the same, indistinguishable, identical, uniform, interchangeable, undifferentiated, homogeneous, much the same, of a piece, cut from the same cloth; resembling, corresponding, like, parallel, analogous, cognate; *informal* like (two) peas in a pod, much of a muchness, (like) Tweedledum and Tweedledee.
OPPOSITE different.
▶ adverb *great minds think alike* **similarly**, the same, just the same, in the same way/manner/fashion, in like manner, identically, uniformly.
OPPOSITE differently.

alimony ▶ noun (*N. Amer.*) *his ex-wife has been trying to track him down for alimony* **financial support**, maintenance, support, provision, allowance, keep, upkeep, sustenance, livelihood, subsistence, living expenses; child support; *Scottish* aliment.

alive ▶ adjective **1** *he was last seen alive on Boxing Day* **living**, live, having life, not dead; breathing, moving; vital, vigorous, flourishing, dynamic, energetic, functioning; animate, organic, biological, sentient; existing, existent; *informal* in the land of the living, among the living, alive and kicking; *archaic* quick.
OPPOSITES dead; extinct; inanimate.
2 *the synagogue has kept the Jewish faith alive throughout the centuries* **active**, existing, in existence, existent, extant, functioning, in operation, ongoing, going on, continuing, surviving, persisting, remaining, abiding; prevalent, current, contemporary, present; *informal* on the map, on the agenda.
OPPOSITES inactive; obsolete.
3 *the thrills of life that kept him really alive* **animated**, lively, full of life, alert, active, energetic, vigorous, spry, sprightly, vital, vibrant, vivacious, buoyant, exuberant, ebullient, zestful, spirited, enthusiastic, eager, bouncy, bubbly, perky, sparkling; *informal* full of beans, bright-eyed and bushy-tailed, bright and breezy, sparky, chirpy, chipper, peppy, full of vim and vigour, (still) going strong; *N. Amer. informal* peart.
OPPOSITES lethargic, lifeless.
4 *teachers need to be* **alive to** *cultural differences between their pupils' backgrounds* **alert to**, awake to, aware of, sensitive to, conscious of, mindful of, heedful of, watchful of, responsive to; familiar with, cognizant of, apprised of, sensible of; *informal* wise to, hip to.
OPPOSITES unaware, blind.
5 *the place was probably* **alive with** *mice* **teeming**, swarming, thronged, overflowing, overrun, bristling, bustling, rife, infested, thick, crowded, packed; full of, abounding in; *informal* crawling, lousy, hopping, stuffed, jam-packed, chock-a-block, chock-full of, buzzing, jumping; *Scottish* hotching; *rare* pullulating.

all ▶ determiner **1** *all the children went | all creatures need sleep* **each of**, each one of the, every one of the, every single one of the; every, each and every, every single.
OPPOSITE no.
2 *the sun shone all week | did you believe all that?* **the whole of the**, every bit of the, the complete, the entire, the totality of the; in its entirety.
OPPOSITE none of the.
3 *in all honesty | with all speed* **complete**, entire, total, full, utter, perfect, all-out, greatest (possible), maximum.
OPPOSITES no, little.
▶ pronoun **1** *all are welcome* **everyone**, everybody, each/every person, the (whole) lot.
OPPOSITES none, nobody.
2 *all of the cups were broken* **each one**, each thing, the sum, the total, the whole lot.
OPPOSITE none.
3 *they took all of it* **everything**, every part, the whole amount, the total amount, the (whole) lot, the entirety, the sum total, the aggregate.
OPPOSITES none, nothing.
▶ adverb *he was dressed all in black* **completely**, fully, entirely, totally, wholly, absolutely, utterly, outright, thoroughly, altogether, quite, in every respect, in all respects, without reservation, without exception.
OPPOSITES partly; not at all.

WORD LINKS
related prefixes **omni-** (e.g. ***omnivorous, omnipresent***), **pan-** (e.g. ***pan-European, pansexual***), **panto-** (e.g. ***pantograph, pantomime***)

allay ▶ verb *this should help to allay your fears* **reduce**, diminish, decrease, lessen, assuage, alleviate, ease, relieve, soothe, soften, take the edge off, dull, cushion, mollify, moderate, calm, lull, temper, mitigate, palliate, blunt, deaden, abate, tone down; **dispel**, banish, dismiss, dissipate, drive away, drive off, chase away, put to rest, quell, check, eliminate; *rare* lenify.
OPPOSITES increase, intensify.

allegation ▶ noun *he rejected the allegation that he had lied* **claim**, assertion, declaration, statement, proclamation, contention, argument, affirmation, averment, avowal, attestation, testimony, certification, evidence, witness, charge, accusation, suggestion, implication, hint, insinuation, indication, intimation, imputation, plea, pretence, profession; *informal* making out; *technical* deposition, representation; *rare* asseveration.

allege ▶ verb *she alleged that the boy had hit her* **claim**, assert, declare, state, proclaim, maintain, advance, contend, argue, affirm, aver, avow, attest, testify, swear, certify, give evidence, bear witness, charge, accuse, suggest, imply, hint, insinuate, indicate, intimate, impute, plead, pretend, profess; *technical* depose, represent; *informal* make out; *rare* asseverate.

alleged ▶ adjective *the place where the alleged offences were committed* **supposed**, so-called, claimed, professed, purported, ostensible, apparent, putative, unproven, rumoured, reputed, presumed, assumed, reported, declared, stated, avowed, described.

allegedly ▶ adverb *he allegedly stabbed the girl* **reportedly**, supposedly, reputedly, purportedly, ostensibly, apparently, by all accounts, so the story goes, putatively, presumedly, presumably, assumedly, declaredly, avowedly; be accused of being/doing, be alleged to be/have, be said to be/have, be rumoured to be/have.

allegiance ▶ noun *the warriors quickly swore allegiance to the new king* **loyalty**, faithfulness, fidelity, obedience, fealty, adherence, homage, devotion, bond; trueness, true-heartedness; trustiness, trustworthiness; steadfastness, fastness, staunchness, dependability, reliability, duty, constancy, dedication, commitment; patriotism; *archaic* troth.
OPPOSITES disloyalty, treachery.

allegorical ▶ adjective *an allegorical painting* **symbolic**, metaphorical, figurative, representative, emblematic, imagistic, mystical, parabolic, symbolizing; *rare* tropical.
OPPOSITE literal.

allegory ▶ noun *'Pilgrim's Progress' is an allegory of the spiritual journey* **parable**, analogy, metaphor, symbol, emblem; story, tale, myth, legend, saga, fable, apologue.

allergic ▶ adjective **1** *she was allergic to nuts* **hypersensitive**, sensitive, susceptible, sensitized.
2 (*informal*) *boys are allergic to washing* **averse**, opposed, hostile, inimical, antagonistic, antipathetic, resistant, unsympathetic; (dead) set against; *archaic* indisposed.
OPPOSITES receptive, in favour of.

allergy ▶ noun **1** *she developed an allergy to feathers* **hypersensitivity**, sensitivity, susceptibility; allergic reaction.
2 (*informal*) *their allergy to free enterprise* **aversion**, antipathy, opposition, hostility, antagonism; dislike of, hate for, distaste for; *archaic* indisposition.
OPPOSITES affinity, liking.

alleviate ▶ verb *he couldn't prevent her pain, only alleviate it* **reduce**, ease, relieve, take the edge off, deaden, dull, diminish, lessen, weaken, lighten, attenuate, allay, assuage, palliate, damp, soothe, help, soften, temper, control, still, quell, quieten, quiet, tone down, blunt, dilute, moderate, mitigate, modify, abate, lull, pacify, placate, mollify, sweeten; *rare* extenuate.
OPPOSITE aggravate.

alley ▶ noun **passage**, passageway, alleyway, back alley, backstreet, lane, path, pathway, walk; corridor, aisle, arcade; *N. English* ginnel, snicket, twitten; *Scottish* vennel; *Scottish & N. English* wynd; *Indian* gully; *French* allée.

alliance ▶ noun **1** *a defensive alliance between Australia and New Zealand* **association**, union, league, treaty, pact, compact, entente, concordat; bloc, confederation, federation, confederacy, coalition, consortium, combine, syndicate, affiliation, partnership; fraternity, brotherhood, sorority, team, ring, society, club, guild, group, organization.
2 *an alliance between medicine and morality* **relationship**, affinity, association, connection, closeness, kinship, propinquity.
OPPOSITES distance, separation.

allied ▶ adjective **1** *a group of allied nations* **federated**, confederated, federal, associated, in alliance, in league, in partnership, cooperating; unified, united, amalgamated, integrated.
OPPOSITES independent; hostile.
2 *agricultural and allied industries* **associated**, related, connected, interconnected, linked, coupled; similar, like, kindred, comparable, parallel, equivalent, corresponding, cognate, analogous, homologous.
OPPOSITES unrelated, dissimilar.

all-important ▶ adjective *the town's all-important tourist industry* **vital**, essential, indispensable, crucial, key, necessary, needed, required, requisite, important, vitally important, of the utmost importance, of great consequence, of the essence, critical, life-and-death, imperative, mandatory; urgent, pressing, burning, compelling, acute; paramount, pre-eminent, high-priority, significant, consequential.
OPPOSITE inessential.

allocate ▶ verb *the funds will be* **allocated to** *various projects* **allot**, assign, issue, award, grant, administer, devote; **share out**, apportion, portion out, distribute, hand out, deal out, dole out, give out, parcel out, ration out, divide out, divide up, dispense, measure out, mete out; earmark for, designate for, set aside for, appropriate for, budget for; *informal* divvy up, dish out.

allocation ▶ noun **1** *more efficient allocation of resources* **allotment**, assignment, issuing, issuance, awarding, grant, granting, administration; earmarking, designation, setting aside, budgeting; **sharing out**, apportionment, distribution, handing out, dealing out, doling out, giving out, parcelling out, rationing out, dividing out, dividing up, dispensation, measuring out, meting out; *informal* divvying up, dishing out.
2 *the Ministry spent more than its annual allocation of funds* **allowance**, allotment, quota, share, ration, grant, limit, portion, helping, slice, stint, lot, measure, proportion, percentage; *informal* cut, whack.

allot ▶ verb *an extra £3 billion has been* **allotted to** *the health service* **allocate**, assign, issue, award, grant, administer, devote; earmark for, designate for, set aside for, appropriate for, budget for; **share out**, apportion, portion out, distribute, hand out, deal out, dole out, give out, parcel out, ration out, divide out, divide up, dispense, measure out, mete out; *informal* divvy up, dish out.

allotment ▶ noun **1** (*Brit.*) *he grows vegetables on his allotment* rented plot/land/garden.
2 *the allotment of shares by a company* **allocation**, assignment, issuing, issuance, awarding, grant, granting, administration, earmarking, designation, setting aside, budgeting; **sharing out**, apportionment, distribution, handing out, dealing out, doling out, giving out, parcelling out, rationing out, dividing out, dividing up, dispensation, measuring out, meting out; *informal* divvying up, dishing out.
3 *each member received an allotment of new shares* **quota**, share, ration, grant, limit, portion, allocation, allowance, helping, batch, slice, stint, lot, measure, proportion, percentage; *informal* cut, whack.

all out ▶ adverb *I'm working all out to finish my novel* **strenuously**, energetically, vigorously, hard, mightily, with all one's might (and main), heartily, with vigour, with great effort, fiercely, intensely, eagerly, enthusiastically, industriously, diligently, assiduously, conscientiously, sedulously, with application, earnestly, with perseverance, persistently, indefatigably; *informal* like billy-o, like mad, like crazy.
OPPOSITE lackadaisically.
▶ adjective *an all-out attack on the enemy* **strenuous**, energetic, vigorous, powerful, potent, forceful, forcible; spirited, mettlesome, plucky, determined, resolute, aggressive, eager, keen, enthusiastic, zealous, ardent, fervent, vehement, intense, intensive, passionate, fiery; wild, unrestrained, uncontrolled, unbridled; tough, blunt, hard-hitting, pulling no punches; *informal* punchy, in-your-face.
OPPOSITE half-hearted.

allow ▶ verb **1** *the police allowed him to go home* **permit**, let, authorize, give someone permission to, give authorization to, give leave to, sanction, grant, grant someone the right, license, empower, enable, entitle, qualify; **consent to**, assent to, give one's consent/assent to, give one's blessing to, give someone/something the nod, acquiesce in, agree to, accede to, approve of, tolerate, countenance, suffer, brook, admit of; legalize, legitimatize, legitimate; *informal* give the go-ahead to, give the thumbs up to, OK, give the OK to, give the green light to, say the word.
OPPOSITES prevent, forbid.
2 *allow an hour or so for driving* **set aside**, allocate, allot, earmark, designate, spare, devote, give, afford, apportion, assign.
3 *the house was demolished to* **allow for** *road widening* **provide for**, plan for, make plans for, get ready for, cater for, take into consideration, take into account, make provision for, make preparations for, prepare for, accommodate, make allowances for, make concessions for, arrange for; bargain for, reckon with.
OPPOSITE discount.
4 *she allowed that all people had their funny little ways* **admit**, acknowledge, recognize, agree, accept, concede, grant, own, confess, accede.
OPPOSITE deny.

allowable ▶ adjective *the maximum allowable number of users* **permissible**, permitted, allowed, admissible, acceptable, legal, lawful, legitimate, licit, within the law, authorized, sanctioned, sanctionable, approved, above board, within accepted bounds, passable, tolerated, tolerable, proper, all right, in order; excusable, pardonable, venial; *informal* OK, legit, kosher, pukka, by the book.
OPPOSITE forbidden.

allowance ▶ noun **1** *your baggage allowance* **permitted amount/quantity**, allocation, allotment, quota, share, ration, grant, limit, portion, helping, slice, lot.
2 *her father gave her an allowance* **payment**, pocket money, sum of money, remittance, contribution, consideration, handout, grant, subsidy, maintenance, financial support, subsistence, benefit, stipend, pension, annuity, keep, upkeep, expenses.
3 *a tax allowance* **concession**, reduction, decrease, deduction, discount, weighting, rebate, refund, repayment.
□ **make allowance(s) for 1** *you must make allowances for delays* **take into consideration**, take into account, bear in mind, keep in mind, not lose sight of, have regard to, provide for, plan for, make plans for, foresee, anticipate, get ready for, cater for, allow for, make provision for, make preparations for, prepare for, accommodate, make concessions for; bargain for, reckon with, remember.
2 *she made allowances for his faults* **excuse**, make excuses for, forgive, pardon, overlook, pass over, treat leniently, condone; *rare* remit.

alloy *See centre pages for list of* **Alloys**
▶ noun (stress on the first syllable) *bronze is an alloy of copper and tin* **mixture**, mix, amalgam, fusion, meld, blend, compound, combination, admixture, composite, union.
▶ verb (stress on the second syllable) *copper and tin are alloyed to make bronze* **mix**, amalgamate, fuse, meld, blend, compound, combine, unite, intermix, intermingle; *rare* admix.

all-powerful ▶ adjective *an all-powerful ruler* **omnipotent**, almighty, supreme, most high, pre-eminent; dictatorial, despotic, totalitarian, autocratic, autarchic; invincible, unconquerable.
OPPOSITE powerless.

all right ▶ adjective **1** *the tea was all right* **satisfactory**, acceptable, adequate, good enough, fairly good, fine, passable, reasonable, unobjectionable, suitable; *informal* OK, so-so.
OPPOSITE unsatisfactory.
2 *are you sure you're all right?* **unhurt**, uninjured, unscathed, in one piece, undamaged, safe, safe and sound, unharmed, alive and well, well, fine, out of danger, out of the wood(s); *informal* OK.
OPPOSITES hurt, in danger.
3 *it's all right for you to go now* **permissible**, permitted, allowed, allowable, admissible, acceptable; legal, lawful, legitimate, licit, within the law,

authorized, sanctioned, sanctionable, approved, above board, within accepted bounds; passable, tolerated, tolerable, proper, in order; excusable, pardonable, venial; *informal* OK, legit, kosher, pukka.
OPPOSITES forbidden, unacceptable.
▶ **adverb 1** *the system works all right* **satisfactorily**, adequately, well enough, fairly well, fine, passably, acceptably, reasonably, unobjectionably, suitably; *informal* OK.
OPPOSITE unsatisfactorily.
2 *it's him all right* **definitely**, certainly, unquestionably, undoubtedly, positively, without (a) doubt, beyond any doubt, beyond doubt, beyond question, unmistakably, indubitably, undeniably, beyond the shadow of a doubt, surely, assuredly; in truth, truly, really, in reality, actually, in fact; *archaic* forsooth, in sooth, verily.
OPPOSITE possibly.
▶ **exclamation** *all right, I'll go* **very well (then)**, fine, good, right, right then, yes, agreed; *informal* wilco, OK, oke, okey-dokey, okey-doke, roger; *Brit. informal* righto, righty-ho; *Indian informal* acha.
OPPOSITE no.

allude ▶ **verb** *the Vice-Chancellor* ***alluded*** *to the same idea* **refer to**, suggest, hint at, imply, mention, touch on, mention in passing, mention en passant, speak briefly of, make an allusion to, cite; *rare* advert to.

allure ▶ **noun** *the nostalgic allure of Paris in the fifties* **attraction**, lure, draw, pull, appeal, glamour, allurement, enticement, temptation, bewitchment, enchantment, charm, seduction, persuasion, fascination, magnetism.
OPPOSITE repulsion.
▶ **verb** *melody is the element with the most power to allure the listener* **attract**, lure, entice, tempt, appeal to, whet the appetite of, make someone's mouth water, captivate, draw, beguile, bewitch, enchant, win over, charm, seduce, persuade, lead on, tantalize; intrigue, fascinate; *informal* give the come-on to.
OPPOSITE repel.

alluring ▶ **adjective** *the old town offers alluring shops and restaurants* **enticing**, tempting, attractive, appealing, fetching, inviting, glamorous, captivating, seductive; enchanting, beguiling, charming, fascinating, intriguing, tantalizing, magnetic; irresistible; *informal, dated* come-hither.

allusion ▶ **noun** *the bird's name is doubtless an* ***allusion to*** *its raucous call* **reference to**, mention of, comment on, remark about, citation of, quotation of, hint at, intimation of, suggestion of; implication, insinuation.

ally ▶ **noun** *he was forced to dismiss his closest political ally* **associate**, colleague, friend, confederate, partner, supporter, accomplice, helper, accessory, abetter.
OPPOSITES enemy, opponent.
▶ **verb 1** *he allied his racing experience with his father's business acumen* **combine**, marry, couple, merge, amalgamate, join, pool, fuse, weld, knit.
OPPOSITE split.
2 *the Catholic powers in France had allied with Philip II | Bruce once more* ***allied himself*** *with the English* **unite**, join, join up, join forces, band together, go into partnership, team up, combine, collaborate, side, align oneself, league, go into league, affiliate, confederate, form an alliance, throw in one's lot, make common cause.
OPPOSITE split.

almanac ▶ **noun** *a nautical almanac* **yearbook**, calendar, register, annual, manual, handbook, compendium; annal(s), archive(s), chronicle(s).

almighty ▶ **adjective 1** *I swear by almighty God* **all-powerful**, omnipotent, supreme, most high, pre-eminent; invincible, unconquerable.
OPPOSITE powerless.
2 (*informal*) *an almighty explosion* **very great**, huge, enormous, immense, colossal, massive, prodigious, stupendous, tremendous, monumental, mammoth, vast, gigantic, giant, mighty, Herculean, epic, monstrous, titanic, towering, king-sized, king-size; substantial; **very loud**, deafening, ear-splitting, ear-piercing, booming, thundering, thunderous, roaring, resounding, crashing; *informal* whopping, thumping, astronomical, astronomic, mega, monster, humongous, jumbo, hulking, bumper; *Brit. informal* whacking, ginormous.
OPPOSITES insignificant; tiny.

almost ▶ **adverb** *lunch is almost ready* **nearly**, just about, about, more or less, practically, virtually, all but, as good as, next to, close to, near, nigh on, not far from, not far off, to all intents and purposes, approaching, bordering on, verging on, nearing; roughly, approximately; not quite; *informal* pretty nearly, pretty much, pretty well; *literary* well-nigh.

alms ▶ **plural noun** (*historical*) *a beggar held out a hand for alms* **gift(s)**, donation(s), charity, handout(s), bounty, benefaction, subsidy, offering(s), contribution(s), endowment, favour(s), largesse; (*in parts of the Middle & Far East*) baksheesh; *Islam* zakat; *rare* donative.

aloft ▶ **adjective & adverb 1** *he hoisted the Cup aloft* **upwards**, up, high, higher, into the air, into the sky, skyward, on high, heavenward.
OPPOSITE down.
2 *the airships were able to stay aloft for many hours* **in the air**, in the sky, high up, up, high, up above, on high, overhead, above.
OPPOSITE down.

alone ▶ **adjective & adverb 1** *she was alone in the house | he lived alone* **by oneself**, on one's own, all alone, solo, lone, solitary, single, singly; **unescorted**, without an escort, unattended, unchaperoned, partnerless, companionless; *Latin* solus; *Brit. informal* on one's tod, on one's lonesome, on one's jack, on one's Jack Jones; *Austral./NZ informal* on one's pat, on one's Pat Malone.
OPPOSITES accompanied, in company.
2 *he managed alone* **unaided**, unassisted, without help, without assistance, by one's own efforts, under one's own steam, independently, single-handedly, solo, on one's own, all alone, off one's own bat, on one's own initiative.
OPPOSITE with help.
3 *she felt terribly alone* **lonely**, isolated, solitary, deserted, abandoned, forsaken, forlorn, friendless, desolate.
OPPOSITES loved, wanted.
4 *a house standing alone* **apart**, by itself/oneself, separate, detached, isolated, to one side, unconnected.
OPPOSITE among others.
5 *you alone can inspire me* **only**, solely, just, uniquely, exclusively; and no one else, and nothing else, to the exclusion of everyone/everything else, no one but, nothing but.

along ▶ **preposition 1** *she walked along the corridor* **down**, throughout the length of, from one end of … to the other, through, across.
2 *trees grew along the river bank* **beside**, by the side of, on the edge of, alongside, next to, adjacent to, close by, in a line by, one after the other by.
3 *they'll have to stop somewhere along the way* **on**, at a point on, in the middle of; in the course of, during.
▶ **adverb 1** *Maurice moved along past the other exhibits* **onwards**, on, ahead, forward(s), further.
2 *I invited a friend along* **as company**, with one, to accompany one, as a partner, in company.
□ **along with** *he spent three weeks at Etna along with two colleagues* **together with**, accompanying, accompanied by, in company with; at the same time as; as well as, in addition to, plus, coupled with, added to, besides, on top of.

aloof ▶ **adjective** *I used to be aloof because I didn't want people becoming too familiar* **distant**, detached, unresponsive, remote, unapproachable, forbidding, stand-offish, formal, impersonal, stiff, austere, stuffy, withdrawn, reserved, unforthcoming, uncommunicative, indifferent; **unfriendly**, unsympathetic, unsociable, antisocial, cool, cold, chilly, frigid, frosty; haughty, supercilious, disdainful.
OPPOSITES familiar, friendly.

aloud ▶ **adverb** *he read the letter aloud* **audibly**, out loud, for all to hear, clearly, distinctly, plainly, intelligibly.
OPPOSITE silently.

alphabet *See centre pages for list of the names of Greek and Hebrew* **Letters**
▶ **noun** *can you say the alphabet backwards?* **ABC**, letters; symbols, icons, writing system, syllabary; *rare* signary.

already ▶ **adverb 1** *Anna had suffered a great deal already* **by this/that time**, by now/then, thus far, so far, hitherto, before, before now/then, previously, earlier, earlier on, until now/then, up to now/then; *rare* heretofore.
2 *is it 3 o'clock already?* **as early as this/that**, as soon as this/that, so soon, so early, even now/then.

also ▶ **adverb** *he's also very good at sport* **too**, as well, besides, in addition, additionally, furthermore, further, moreover, into the bargain, on top (of that), over and above that, what's more, to boot, else, then, equally; *informal* and all; *archaic* withal, forbye.

alter ▶ **verb 1** *he altered his theories a number of times* **change**, make changes to, make different, make alterations to, adjust, make adjustments to, adapt, amend, improve, modify, convert, revise, recast, reform, reshape, refashion, redesign, restyle, revamp, rework, remake, remodel, remould, redo, reconstruct, reorganize, reorder, refine, reorient, reorientate, vary, transform, transfigure, transmute, evolve; customize, tailor; *informal* tweak; *technical* permute.
OPPOSITE preserve.
2 *the state of affairs has altered* **change**, become different, undergo a change, undergo a sea change, turn, adjust, adapt, convert, vary, transform, metamorphose, evolve, improve.
OPPOSITE stay the same.

alteration ▶ **noun** *he made an alteration to the text* **change**, adjustment, adaptation, modification, variation, conversion, revision, amendment; remodelling, reshaping, remoulding, redoing, reconstruction, rebuilding, recasting, reorganization, rearrangement, reordering, reshuffling, restyling, rejigging, reworking, renewal, renewing, revamping, renovation, remaking; metamorphosis, transformation, transfiguration, translation, evolution, mutation, sea change; *humorous* transmogrification.
OPPOSITE preservation.

altercation ▶ **noun** *I had an altercation with the ticket collector* **argument**, quarrel, squabble, fight, shouting match, contretemps, disagreement,

difference of opinion, dissension, falling-out, dispute, disputation, contention, clash, acrimonious exchange, war of words, wrangle; *Irish, N. Amer., & Austral.* donnybrook; *informal* tiff, set-to, run-in, spat, scrap, dust-up; *Brit. informal* row, barney, slanging match, ding-dong, bust-up, bit of argy-bargy, ruck; *Scottish informal* rammy; *N. Amer. informal* rhubarb; *archaic* broil, miff; *Scottish archaic* threap, collieshangie.

alternate ▶ verb **1** *stands of trees alternate with dense shrubby tundra* **be interspersed**, follow one another, be staggered, take turns, take it in turns, work/act in sequence, occur in turn, occur in rotation; rotate, oscillate, see-saw, yo-yo, chop and change, fluctuate.
2 *we could alternate the groups so that no one felt they had been left out* **give turns to**, take in turn, rotate, take in rotation; intersperse, stagger, swap, exchange, interchange, switch, vary.
▶ adjective **1** *she was asked to attend on alternate days* **every other**, every second.
2 *place the leeks and noodles in alternate layers* **alternating**, in rotation, rotating, occurring in turns, interchanging, following in sequence, sequential.
3 (*N. Amer.*) *an alternate plan of action* **alternative**, other, another, second, different, possible, substitute, replacement, deputy, relief, proxy, surrogate, cover, fill-in, stand-in, standby, emergency, reserve, backup, auxiliary, fallback; *N. Amer. informal* pinch-hitting.

alternative ▶ adjective **1** *an alternative route | an alternative government* **different**, other, another, second, possible, substitute, replacement; deputy, relief, proxy, surrogate, cover, fill-in, stand-in; standby, emergency, reserve, backup, auxiliary, fallback; *N. Amer.* alternate; *N. Amer. informal* pinch-hitting.
2 *alternative medicine | an alternative lifestyle* **unorthodox**, unconventional, non-standard, unusual, uncommon, unwonted, out of the ordinary, radical, revolutionary, nonconformist, unconforming, irregular, offbeat, avant-garde; original, new, novel, fresh; eccentric, exotic, Bohemian, idiosyncratic, abnormal, extreme, divergent, aberrant, anomalous, bizarre, outlandish, perverse; *informal* off the wall, oddball, way-out, cranky, zany; *rare* heteroclite.
▶ noun *we have no alternative but to go | an acceptable alternative to tropical hardwood* **option**, choice, other possibility; substitute, replacement, proxy, reserve, surrogate, stand-in; possible course of action, resort, way out.

alternatively ▶ adverb *alternatively, you can build your own barbecue* **on the other hand**, as an alternative, or, as another option, as a substitute, as a replacement; otherwise, instead, if not, then again, but; *N. Amer.* alternately.

although ▶ conjunction *although the sun was shining it wasn't that warm* **in spite of the fact that**, despite the fact that, notwithstanding the fact that, notwithstanding that, even though, even if, for all that, while, whilst; granted that, even supposing, despite the possibility that, albeit, however, yet, but.

altitude ▶ noun *we are now flying at an altitude of 40,000 feet* **height**, elevation, distance above the sea/ground; loftiness.
OPPOSITE depth.

WORD LINKS
measurement of altitude **altimetry, hypsometry**

altogether ▶ adverb **1** *he wasn't altogether happy* **completely**, totally, entirely, absolutely, wholly, fully, thoroughly, utterly, quite, one hundred per cent, downright, unqualifiedly, in all respects, unconditionally, perfectly, unrestrictedly, consummately, undisputedly, unmitigatedly, wholeheartedly; {lock, stock, and barrel}, in toto; at all, very, terribly.
OPPOSITE partially.
2 *we have five offices altogether* **in all**, all told, in toto, taken together, in sum, counting them all.
3 *altogether it was a great evening* **on the whole**, overall, all in all, all things considered, taking everything into consideration/account, on balance, on average, for the most part, mostly, mainly, in the main, in general, generally, generally speaking, largely, by and large, to a large extent, to a great degree.
OPPOSITE relatively.

altruism ▶ noun *they supported the measures not out of altruism but out of self-interest* **unselfishness**, selflessness, self-sacrifice, self-denial; consideration, compassion, kindness, goodwill, decency, nobility, public-spiritedness; generosity, magnanimity, liberality, open-handedness, free-handedness, big-heartedness, lavishness, benevolence, beneficence, philanthropy, humanitarianism, charity, charitableness; *literary* bounty, bounteousness.
OPPOSITE selfishness.

altruistic ▶ adjective *a wholly altruistic desire to help* **unselfish**, selfless, self-sacrificing, self-denying; considerate, compassionate, kind, decent, noble, public-spirited; generous, magnanimous, ungrudging, unstinting, charitable, benevolent, beneficent, liberal, open-handed, free-handed, philanthropic, humanitarian; *literary* bounteous.
OPPOSITE selfish.

always ▶ adverb **1** *he's always late* **every time**, each time, at all times, all the time, on every occasion, on all occasions, consistently, invariably, without fail, without exception, regularly, repeatedly, habitually, unfailingly, infallibly, inevitably.
OPPOSITES never; seldom; sometimes.
2 *she's always complaining* **continually**, continuously, constantly, forever, repeatedly, perpetually, incessantly, ceaselessly, unceasingly, endlessly, interminably, eternally, the entire time, permanently; *informal* 24-7.
3 *the place will always be dear to me* **forever**, permanently, for always, for good, for good and all, perpetually, ever, (for) evermore, for ever and ever, for all (future) time, until the end of time, eternally, for eternity, in perpetuity, everlastingly, endlessly; *N. Amer.* forevermore; *informal* for keeps, until hell freezes over, until the cows come home, until doomsday; *archaic* for aye.
4 *you can always take it back to the shop* **as a last resort**, whatever the circumstances, no matter what, in any event, in any case, come what may.

amalgam ▶ noun *a curious amalgam of the traditional and the modern* **combination**, union, merger, blend, mixture, mingling, compound, fusion, marriage, weave, coalescence, synthesis, composite, composition, concoction, amalgamation.

amalgamate ▶ verb *the two departments were amalgamated | various companies amalgamated* **combine**, merge, unite, integrate, fuse, blend, mingle, coalesce, consolidate, meld, intermingle, mix, intermix, incorporate, affiliate; join (together), join forces, band (together), club together, get together, link (up), team up, go into partnership, pool resources; unify; *informal* gang up, gang together; *literary* commingle.
OPPOSITE separate.

amalgamation ▶ noun *the Queen's Regiment is an amalgamation of several others* **combination**, union, merger, blend, mixture, mingling, compound, fusion, marriage, weave, coalescence, synthesis, composite, composition, concoction, amalgam.

amass ▶ verb *he amassed a large fortune* **gather**, collect, assemble; accumulate, stockpile, pile up, heap up, rack up, run up, scrape together, store (up), hoard, cumulate, accrue, lay in/up, garner; *informal* stash (away).
OPPOSITE dissipate.

amateur ▶ noun **1** *the crew were all amateurs who had paid £15,000 apiece for the trip* **non-professional**, non-specialist, layman, layperson; dilettante, dabbler, potterer, trifler; enthusiast, devotee, fan, ... lover; *informal* buff, ham.
OPPOSITE professional.
2 *what a bunch of amateurs* **bungler**, blunderer, incompetent, bumbler; *Brit. informal* bodger.
OPPOSITE expert.
▶ adjective **1** *it is still largely an amateur sport* **non-professional**, non-specialist, lay; dilettante; enthusiasts'.
2 *they may scoff at others' amateur efforts* **incompetent**, inept, useless, unskilful, inexpert, clumsy, maladroit, gauche, blundering, bungling, bumbling, amateurish, botched, crude; *Brit. informal* bodged.

amateurish ▶ adjective *he dismissed the tape as an amateurish hoax* **incompetent**, inept, useless, unskilful, inexpert, amateur, clumsy, maladroit, gauche, blundering, bungling, bumbling, botched, crude; *Brit. informal* bodged.
OPPOSITE professional.

amatory ▶ adjective *his amatory exploits* **sexual**, erotic, amorous, romantic, sensual, libidinous, passionate, ardent, hot-blooded, sexy; torrid; *informal* randy, steamy, naughty.
OPPOSITES platonic; frigid.

amaze ▶ verb *it never ceases to amaze me* **astonish**, astound, surprise, bewilder, stun, stagger, flabbergast, nonplus, shock, startle, shake, stop someone in their tracks, stupefy, leave open-mouthed, leave aghast, take someone's breath away, dumbfound, daze, benumb, perplex, confound, dismay, disconcert, shatter, take aback, jolt, shake up; *informal* bowl over, knock for six, floor, blow someone's mind, strike dumb; (**amazed**) thunderstruck, at a loss for words, speechless; *Brit. informal* gobsmacked.

amazement ▶ noun *they stared in amazement* **astonishment**, surprise, bewilderment, shock, stupefaction, dismay, consternation, devastation, confusion, perplexity, incredulity, disbelief, bafflement, speechlessness, awe, wonder, wonderment.

amazing ▶ adjective *yet another amazing coincidence* **astonishing**, astounding, surprising, bewildering, stunning, staggering, shocking, startling, stupefying, breathtaking, perplexing, confounding, dismaying, disconcerting, shattering; awesome, awe-inspiring, sensational, remarkable, spectacular, stupendous, phenomenal, prodigious, extraordinary, incredible, unbelievable; wonderful, marvellous; thrilling, exciting; *informal* mind-blowing, flabbergasting; *literary* wondrous; *rare* dumbfounding.
OPPOSITE everyday.

ambassador ▶ noun **1** *the American ambassador to London* **envoy**, diplomat, ambassador extraordinary, ambassador plenipotentiary, plenipotentiary, consul, attaché, chargé d'affaires, emissary, legate, (papal) nuncio, representative, deputy; *dated* ambassadress.

2 *a great ambassador for the sport* **campaigner**; **representative**, exponent, promoter, proponent, advocate, champion, supporter, backer, upholder, protagonist; *N. Amer.* booster.

ambience ▶ **noun** *the relaxed ambience of the cocktail lounge* **atmosphere**, air, aura, climate, mood, feel, feeling, vibrations, echo, character, quality, complexion, impression, flavour, look, tone, tenor, spirit; **setting**, milieu, background, backdrop, frame, element; environment, conditions, circumstances, situation, context; vicinity, locality, habitat; *informal* vibes.

ambiguity ▶ **noun** *the plot revolves around the ambiguity in the title* **ambivalence**, equivocation; obscurity, vagueness, abstruseness, doubtfulness, uncertainty; puzzle, enigma; *archaic* equivocacy; *rare* dubiety; (**ambiguities**), doublespeak, doubletalk.
OPPOSITES unambiguousness, transparency.

ambiguous ▶ **adjective** *the judge agreed that the law was ambiguous* **equivocal**, ambivalent, open to debate, open to argument, arguable, debatable; Delphic, cryptic, enigmatic, gnomic, paradoxical, misleading; obscure, unclear, vague, abstruse, puzzling, perplexing, riddling, doubtful, dubious, uncertain; double-edged, backhanded.
OPPOSITES unambiguous, clear.

ambit ▶ **noun** *a select committee can review any matter that falls within its ambit* **scope**, extent, bounds, confines, limits, range, breadth, width, reach, sweep, purview, span, stretch, spread, horizon; terms of reference, field of reference, jurisdiction, remit; area, sphere, field, realm, compass, orbit, gamut, competence.

ambition ▶ **noun 1** *young people with ambition* **drive**, determination, desire, enterprise, initiative, eagerness, motivation, enthusiasm, zeal, commitment, a sense of purpose, longing, yearning, hankering; *informal* get-up-and-go.
2 *her ambition was to become a model* **aspiration**, intention, goal, aim, objective, object, purpose, intent, plan, scheme, mission, calling, vocation, desire, wish, design, target, end, dream, hope.

ambitious ▶ **adjective 1** *he was an exceptionally energetic, ambitious, and intelligent politician* **aspiring**, determined, forceful, pushy, enterprising, pioneering, progressive, eager, motivated, enthusiastic, energetic, zealous, committed, go-ahead, go-getting, purposeful, assertive, aggressive, hungry, power-hungry; *informal* on the make.
OPPOSITES unambitious, lazy.
2 *he was ambitious to make it to the top* **eager**, determined, enthusiastic, desirous, anxious, hungry, impatient, striving, yearning, longing, wishing, itching, dying, hoping, avid, hankering; intent on; *informal* raring.
3 *an ambitious task* **difficult**, exacting, demanding, formidable, challenging, hard, arduous, onerous, tough, stiff, strenuous; **bold**, grandiose, extravagant, monumental; *informal* killing, hellish; *Brit. informal* knackering; *archaic* toilsome.
OPPOSITES unambitious, easy; modest.

ambivalence ▶ **noun** *there is ambivalence over whether cars should be encouraged into the countryside* **equivocation**, uncertainty, unsureness, doubt, indecision, inconclusiveness, irresolution, irresoluteness, hesitation, hesitancy, fluctuation, vacillation, shilly-shallying, tentativeness; conflict, contradiction, clash, confusion, dilemma, quandary; muddle, vagueness, haze, haziness, unclearness; *informal* iffiness; *archaic* equivocacy.
OPPOSITES certainty, decisiveness.

ambivalent ▶ **adjective** *the public has a rather ambivalent attitude toward science* **equivocal**, uncertain, unsure, doubtful, indecisive, inconclusive, irresolute, in two minds, undecided, unresolved, in a dilemma, on the horns of a dilemma, in a quandary, on the fence, torn, hesitating, fluctuating, wavering, vacillating, equivocating, mixed; opposing, conflicting, contradictory, clashing; confused, muddled, vague, hazy, unclear; *informal* iffy, blowing hot and cold.
OPPOSITES unequivocal, certain.

amble ▶ **verb** *they ambled along the river bank* **stroll**, saunter, wander, meander, ramble, dawdle, promenade, walk, go for a walk, take a walk, roam, traipse, stretch one's legs, get some exercise, get some air, take the air; *Scottish & Irish* stravaig; *informal* mosey, tootle; *Brit. informal* pootle, mooch, swan; *N. Amer. informal* putter; *rare* perambulate, peregrinate.
OPPOSITE stride.

CHOOSE THE RIGHT WORD

amble, stroll, saunter
See STROLL.

ambush ▶ **noun** *seven members of a patrol were killed in an ambush* **surprise attack**, **trap**, snare, pitfall, lure; *dated* ambuscade.
▶ **verb** *a gang of twenty youths ambushed their patrol car* **attack by surprise**, **trap**, surprise, pounce on, lay a trap for, set an ambush for, lie in wait for, waylay, entrap, ensnare; *N. Amer.* bushwhack; *archaic* ambuscade.

ameliorate ▶ **verb** *any move that ameliorates the situation is welcome* **improve**, make better, better, make improvements to, enhance, help, benefit, boost, raise, amend, refine, reform; relieve, ease, mitigate, retrieve; **rectify**, correct, right, put right, set right, put to rights, sort out, clear up, deal with, remedy, repair, fix, cure, heal, mend, make good, resolve, settle, redress, square; *informal* tweak, patch up.
OPPOSITES worsen; leave alone.

amelioration ▶ **noun** *a decided amelioration in the status of women* **improvement**, change for the better, betterment, enhancement, help, benefit, boost, raising, amendment, refinement, reform; relief, easing, mitigation; **rectification**, correction, righting, putting right, setting right, putting to rights, sorting out, clearing up, remedy, repair, fix, cure, healing, mending, making good, resolution, settlement, redress; *informal* tweaking, patching up.
OPPOSITE worsening.

amenable ▶ **adjective 1** *an easy-going, amenable child* **compliant**, acquiescent, biddable, manageable, controllable, governable, persuadable, tractable, responsive, pliant, flexible, malleable, complaisant, accommodating, docile, submissive, obedient, tame, meek, easily handled; *rare* persuasible.
OPPOSITE uncooperative.
2 *many cancers of this kind are* **amenable to** *treatment* **susceptible**, receptive, responsive, reactive, vulnerable; defenceless against; *rare* susceptive.
OPPOSITE resistant.

amend ▶ **verb** *the government may amend the law* **revise**, alter, change, modify, qualify, adapt, adjust; edit, copy-edit, rewrite, redraft, recast, rephrase, reword, rework, reform, update, revamp; **correct**, remedy, fix, set right, put right, repair, emend, improve, ameliorate, better, enhance, clarify.

amendment ▶ **noun** *Parliament approved an amendment to the Constitution* **revision**, alteration, change, modification, qualification, adaptation, adjustment; edit, editing, rewrite, rewriting, redraft, redrafting, recasting, rephrasing, rewording, reworking, reform; update, revamp, reshaping; **correction**, emendation, improvement, enhancement, clarification.

amends ▶ **plural noun** *I wanted to* **make amends for** *the way I treated his mother* **compensation**, recompense, reparation, restitution, restoration, redress, indemnity, indemnification, atonement, expiation, requital; atone for, make up for, make good, do penance for, expiate, pay the price for; redeem oneself, redress the balance.
□ **make amends to** *we want to make amends to them for the hurt we have caused* **compensate**, recompense, indemnify, make it up to, repay, reimburse, pay back.

amenity ▶ **noun 1** *the older type of housing lacks basic amenities* **facility**, service, convenience, resource, utility, system, appliance, aid, advantage, comfort, benefit, arrangement, opportunity; (**amenities**) equipment, provision, assistance.
2 *gravel working means lorries, dust, noise, and a general loss of amenity* **pleasantness**, agreeableness, pleasurableness, enjoyableness, niceness.

America ▶ **noun.** *See* UNITED STATES OF AMERICA.

amiability ▶ **noun** *she was now all amiability* **friendliness**, affability, cordiality; warmth, warm-heartedness, good nature, niceness, pleasantness, agreeableness, likeability, lovableness, geniality, amicableness, amicability, sociableness; good humour, charm, kindness, kindliness; neighbourliness, hospitality, companionableness, sociability, gregariousness, conviviality, clubbability, clubbableness, personableness; *Scottish* couthiness; *Brit. informal* chumminess, mateyness.
OPPOSITE unfriendliness.

amiable ▶ **adjective** *this amiable young man greeted me enthusiastically* **friendly**, affable, amicable, cordial; warm, warm-hearted, good-natured, nice, pleasant, agreeable, pleasing, likeable, lovable, genial, good-humoured, charming, winning, engaging, delightful, easy to get on/along with, obliging, kind, kindly; neighbourly, hospitable, companionable, sociable, gregarious, convivial, clubbable, personable; *Scottish* couthy; *Brit. informal* chummy, matey; *N. Amer. informal* regular; *rare* conversable.
OPPOSITES unfriendly, disagreeable.

amicable ▶ **adjective** *we have always enjoyed a very amicable relationship* **friendly**, good-natured, cordial, civil, courteous, polite, easy, easy-going, neighbourly, brotherly, fraternal, harmonious, cooperative, civilized; non-hostile, peaceable, peaceful.
OPPOSITES unfriendly, hostile.

amid ▶ **preposition 1** *the jeep was concealed amid pine trees* **in the middle of**, surrounded by, among, amongst, between, in the thick of; *literary* amidst, in the midst of.
OPPOSITE surrounding.
2 *the truce collapsed amid fears of an army revolt* **at a time of**, in an atmosphere of, against a background of, during; as a result of.

amino acid ▶ **noun.** *See centre pages for list of* **Amino Acids**

amiss ▶ **adjective** *an inspection revealed nothing amiss* **wrong**, awry, faulty, out of order, defective, unsatisfactory, incorrect, untoward, adrift, astray, inappropriate, improper, unsuitable.
OPPOSITES right, in order.
□ **not come/go amiss** *an apology wouldn't go amiss* **be welcome**, be appropriate, be useful.

◻ **take something amiss** *they would take it amiss if they were left out* **be offended by**, take offence at, be upset by.

amity ▶ noun *this will bring greater amity between our peoples* **friendship**, friendliness, peace, peacefulness, harmony, harmoniousness, understanding, accord, concord, concurrence, cooperation, amicableness, goodwill, cordiality, warmth, geniality, fellowship, fraternity, brotherhood, brotherliness; *rare* comity.
OPPOSITES animosity, enmity.

ammunition *See centre pages for lists of* **Bombs and Mines** **Bullets and Shot** **Explosives** **Projectiles**
▶ noun **1** *police seized arms and ammunition destined for terrorists* **bullets**, **shells**, projectiles, missiles, rounds, shot, slugs, cartridges, rockets, bombs, stores; munitions, materiel; *informal* ammo.
2 *the report could provide ammunition for legal action* **arguments**, considerations, points, pointers, material, information, evidence, testimony, facts, data, input; fuel, encouragement.

amnesty ▶ noun *an amnesty for political prisoners* **pardon**, pardoning, reprieve; release, discharge, liberty, freedom; absolution, forgiveness, dispensation, remission, indulgence, clemency, mercy; *informal* let-off, letting off.
▶ verb *the guerrillas were amnestied and allowed to return to civilian life* **pardon**, grant an amnesty to, reprieve; release, discharge, liberate, free; forgive, excuse, exempt, spare, deliver; deal leniently with, be lenient on/to, be merciful to, show mercy to, have mercy on; *informal* let off, let off the hook, go easy on.

amok, **amuck** ▶ adverb
◻ **run amok** *the army had run amok in the town, killing and looting* **go berserk**, get out of control, rampage, run riot, riot, rush wildly/madly about, go on the rampage; storm, charge; behave like a maniac, behave wildly, behave uncontrollably; become violent, become destructive; go mad, go crazy, go insane; *informal* steam, raise hell; *N. Amer. informal* go postal.

among, **amongst** ▶ preposition **1** *you're among friends* **surrounded by**, in the company of, amid, in the middle of, between, in the thick of; *literary* amidst, in the midst of.
2 *a child was among the injured* **included in**, one of, some of, in the group of, in the number of, out of.
3 *you'll have to decide among yourselves* **jointly**, with one another, together, mutually, reciprocally; by the joint action of, by all of, by the whole of.
4 *he had to distribute the proceeds among his creditors* **between**, to each of.

amoral ▶ adjective *without society we are amoral beings* **unprincipled**, without standards, without morals; unethical, without scruples, unscrupulous.
OPPOSITES moral, principled.

> **amoral or immoral?**
> **Amoral** means 'not concerned with or affected by morality', so that something described as *amoral* cannot appropriately be criticized for failure to conform to accepted moral standards (*the client pays for the amoral expertise of the lawyer*). **Immoral**, on the other hand, means 'not conforming to accepted standards of morality', and implies condemnation (*they felt it was immoral to accept a loan that they could not hope to repay*).

amorous ▶ adjective *she rejected his amorous advances* **lustful**, sexual, erotic, amatory, ardent; passionate, impassioned; romantic; affectionate, fond, loving, tender, doting; in love, enamoured, lovesick; *informal* lovey-dovey, spoony, kissy, smoochy, goo-goo, hot; *Brit. informal* slap-and-tickle, randy; *archaic* sportive.
OPPOSITES unloving, cold.

amorphous ▶ adjective *an amorphous grey mass which proved to be mashed potato* **shapeless**, formless, unformed, unshaped, structureless, unstructured, indeterminate, indefinite, vague, nebulous.
OPPOSITES shaped; definite.

amount ▶ noun *a substantial amount of money | the same amount of people as last year* **quantity**, **number**, total, aggregate, sum, quota, group, size, mass, weight, volume, bulk, load, consignment; proportion, portion, part, dose, dosage; *technical* quantum.
◻ **the full amount the grand total**, the total, the aggregate; *informal* the whole caboodle, the whole shebang, the full nine yards.
▶ verb
◻ **amount to 1** *the bill amounted to £50* **add up to**, come to, run to, number, be, make, total, equal, be equal to, be equivalent to, represent, count as; *Brit.* tot up to.
2 *the delays amounted to maladministration* **constitute**, comprise, be equivalent to, be tantamount to, approximate to, add up to, come down to, boil down to; signify, signal, mean, indicate, suggest, denote, point to, be evidence of, be symptomatic of; *informal* spell, spell out; *literary* betoken.
3 *her relationships had never amounted to anything significant* **become**, grow into, develop into, mature into, prove to be, turn out to be, progress to, advance to.

amphibian ▶ noun. *See centre pages for list of* **Amphibians**
WORD LINKS
fear of amphibians **batrachophobia**

ample ▶ adjective **1** *there is ample time for discussion* **enough**, sufficient, adequate, plenty of, abundant, more than enough, enough and to spare; suitable, satisfactory, passable, allowable, tolerable; *informal* plenty, decent.
OPPOSITE insufficient.
2 *an ample supply of wine* **plentiful**, abundant, copious, profuse, rich, lavish, liberal, generous, bountiful, large, huge, great, bumper, flush, overflowing, superabundant, infinite, inexhaustible, opulent, prolific, teeming; *informal* a gogo, galore; *S. African informal* lank; *literary* bounteous, plenteous.
OPPOSITE meagre.
3 *he leaned back in his ample chair | his ample tunic* **spacious**, commodious, capacious, roomy, sizeable, substantial, generous, big, large, broad, wide, extensive; voluminous, loose-fitting, baggy, slack, sloppy, full; *rare* spacey.
OPPOSITES cramped; tight-fitting.

amplify ▶ verb **1** *many frogs amplify the sound of their voices* **louden**, make louder, turn up, increase, boost, step up, raise, magnify, intensify, escalate, swell, heighten; add to, augment, supplement.
OPPOSITES reduce, quieten.
2 *the notes amplify information contained in the statement* **expand**, enlarge on, elaborate on, add to, develop, flesh out, add flesh to, add detail to, go into detail about, embroider, supplement, augment, reinforce.
OPPOSITE condense.

amplitude ▶ noun *the amplitude of the output signal* **magnitude**, size, volume, proportions, dimensions; extent, range, scope, compass; breadth, width.

amputate ▶ verb *they had to amputate his leg* **cut off**, sever, remove (surgically), saw off, chop off, lop off, hack off, dock, cleave, hew off, shear off, slice off; separate, part, detach, disconnect; *rare* dissever, abscise.

amulet ▶ noun *they wore amulets to ward off the plague* **lucky charm**, charm, talisman, fetish, mascot, totem, idol, juju, phylactery; *archaic* periapt.

amuse ▶ verb **1** *her annoyance simply amused him* **entertain**, make laugh, delight, divert, gladden, cheer (up), please, charm, tickle, convulse, beguile, enliven, regale; *informal* tickle someone pink, crack someone up, wow, be a hit with; *Brit. informal* crease someone up.
OPPOSITES bore, depress.
2 *he amused himself by writing poetry* **occupy**, engage, busy, employ, distract, absorb, engross, preoccupy, hold, hold someone's attention, immerse, interest, involve, entertain, divert, beguile.

amusement ▶ noun **1** *we looked with amusement at the cartoon* **mirth**, merriment, light-heartedness, hilarity, glee, delight, laughter, levity, gaiety, joviality, fun, jocularity; enjoyment, pleasure, high spirits, mirthfulness, cheerfulness, cheeriness, cheer; *dated* sport.
OPPOSITES boredom, depression.
2 *I read the book for amusement* **entertainment**, pleasure, leisure, relaxation, fun, enjoyment, interest, occupation, refreshment, restoration, distraction, diversion, divertissement, play; *informal* R and R, jollies; *Brit. informal* beer and skittles; *N. Amer. informal* rec; *dated* sport; *archaic* disport.
3 *the camp site offers a wide range of amusements* **activity**, entertainment, diversion, distraction, interest, recreation, game, sport, pastime, hobby.

amusing ▶ adjective *they are very colourful and amusing characters* **entertaining**, funny, comical, humorous, light-hearted, jocular, witty, mirthful, hilarious, ludicrous, laughable, rollicking, facetious, droll, whimsical, novel, interesting, diverting, engaging, beguiling; *informal* wacky, side-splitting, rib-tickling.
OPPOSITES boring, solemn.

anaemic ▶ adjective **1** *his naturally anaemic face became even paler* **colourless**, bloodless, pale, pallid, wan, ashen, white, white as a ghost/sheet, grey, jaundiced, waxen, chalky, chalk-white, milky, pasty, pasty-faced, whey-faced, peaky, sickly, tired-looking, washed out, sallow, drained, drawn, sapped, ghostly, deathly, deathlike, bleached; *rare* etiolated.
OPPOSITE ruddy.
2 *'attraction' was an anaemic description of her feelings* **feeble**, weak, insipid, pallid, pale, wishy-washy, vapid, bland, poor, puny, flat, inadequate; lame, tame, uninspired, unimaginative, lacklustre, spiritless, half-hearted, vigourless, lifeless, powerless, impotent, ineffective, ineffectual, enervated, bloodless; *informal* pathetic; *rare* etiolated.
OPPOSITE punchy.

anaesthetic ▶ noun *the use of chloroform as an anaesthetic* **narcotic**, soporific, stupefacient, painkiller, sedative, anodyne, analgesic, opiate; general, local.
▶ adjective *an anaesthetic drug* **narcotic**, numbing, deadening, dulling, soporific, stupefacient, painkilling, sedative, analgesic, anodyne, opiate.

analgesic ▶ adjective *an analgesic drug* **painkilling**, anodyne, pain-relieving; *rare* palliative.

▶ noun *aspirin is an analgesic* **painkiller**, painkilling drug, anodyne, pain reliever; *rare* palliative.

analogous ▶ adjective *sport is in some ways analogous to life* **comparable**, parallel, similar, like, corresponding, related, kindred, matching, cognate, equivalent, symmetrical, homologous.
OPPOSITES dissimilar, unrelated.

analogy ▶ noun *an analogy between the workings of nature and those of human societies* **similarity**, parallel, parallelism, correspondence, likeness, resemblance, correlation, relation, kinship, equivalence, similitude, symmetry, homology.
OPPOSITE dissimilarity.

analyse ▶ verb **1** *DNA can be analysed by various methods* **break down**, resolve, separate, reduce, decompose, disintegrate, dissect, divide, assay, test; *rare* fractionate.
OPPOSITE synthesize.
2 *the results of the experiment were analysed* **examine**, inspect, survey, scan, study, scrutinize, look over, peruse; search, investigate, explore, probe, research, enquire into, go over, go over with a fine-tooth comb, check, sift, dissect; audit, judge, review, evaluate, interpret; *rare* anatomize.

analysis ▶ noun **1** *analysis of the pottery fragments confirmed their Mediterranean origin* **dissection**, assay, testing; breaking down, separation, reduction, decomposition; *rare* fractionation.
OPPOSITE synthesis.
2 *an analysis of popular culture* **examination**, investigation, inspection, survey, scanning, study, scrutiny, perusal; exploration, probe, research, enquiry, anatomy, audit, review, evaluation, interpretation; *rare* anatomization.

analytical, analytic ▶ adjective *a more analytical approach was needed* **systematic**, logical, scientific, inquisitive, investigative, enquiring, methodical, organized, well organized, ordered, orderly, meticulous, rigorous, searching, critical, interpretative, diagnostic, exact, precise, accurate, mathematical, regulated, controlled, rational.
OPPOSITE unsystematic.

anarchic ▶ adjective *an authority was needed which could restore peace to an anarchic country* **lawless**, without law and order, unruly, in disorder, disordered, disorganized, chaotic, in turmoil, turbulent; rebellious, mutinous.
OPPOSITE ordered.

anarchist ▶ noun *force was used to suppress anarchists and communists* **nihilist**, insurgent, agitator, subversive, guerrilla, terrorist, freedom fighter, resistance fighter, rebel, revolutionary, revolutionist, Bolshevik, mutineer; *rare* insurrectionist; *French rare* frondeur.

anarchy ▶ noun *the country is threatened with anarchy* **lawlessness**, absence of government, nihilism, mobocracy, revolution, insurrection, riot, rebellion, mutiny, disorder, disorganization, misrule, chaos, tumult, turmoil, mayhem, pandemonium.
OPPOSITES government; order.

anathema ▶ noun **1** *racial hatred was anathema to her* **abhorrent**, hateful, odious, repugnant, repellent, offensive; **abomination**, abhorrence, aversion, monstrosity, outrage, evil, disgrace, bane, bugbear, bête noire, pariah.
2 *the Vatican Council expressed their view without an anathema* **curse**, ban, excommunication, damnation, proscription, debarment, denunciation, malediction, execration, imprecation.

anatomy ▶ noun **1** *descriptions of the cat's anatomy and behaviour* | *the anatomy of a town* **structure**, make-up, composition, constitution; construction, layout, organization, arrangement, pattern, plan, mechanisms, framework, form, fabric.
2 *he conducted an anatomy of his society* **analysis**, examination, inspection, survey, study, scrutiny, perusal; investigation, exploration, probe, research, enquiry, dissection, audit, review, evaluation, interpretation; *rare* anatomization.

ancestor ▶ noun **1** *he could trace his ancestors back to King James I* **forebear**, forefather, predecessor, progenitor, antecedent; *rare* primogenitor.
OPPOSITES descendant, successor.
2 *the instrument is an ancestor of the lute* **forerunner**, precursor, predecessor; prototype.

ancestral ▶ adjective *the family's ancestral home* **inherited**, hereditary, familial; *rare* lineal.

ancestry ▶ noun *his Irish ancestry* **ancestors**, forebears, forefathers, progenitors, antecedents; family tree; **lineage**, line, descent, family, parentage, extraction, origin, derivation, genealogy, heredity, pedigree, blood, bloodline, stock, strain, roots; *rare* filiation, stirps.

anchor *See centre pages for list of* **Anchors**
▶ noun **1** *the Liberals are the anchor of the new coalition* **mainstay**, cornerstone, bulwark, chief support, main source of stability/security, foundation, prop, linchpin.
2 *a CBS news anchor* **presenter**, announcer, anchorman, anchorwoman, newsreader, newscaster, broadcaster, reporter.
▶ verb **1** *the ship was anchored in the lee of the island* **moor**, berth, harbour, be at anchor, tie up; cast anchor, drop anchor.
2 *the tail is used as a hook with which the fish anchors itself to the coral* **secure**, fasten, attach, make fast, connect, bind, affix, fix.

anchorage ▶ noun **moorings**, harbour, port, roads; marina; *rare* moorage, harbourage, roadstead.

anchorite ▶ noun **hermit**, recluse, ascetic; *Islam* marabout, santon; *rare* eremite, stylite, coenobite.

ancient ▶ adjective **1** *the ancient civilizations of the Mediterranean* | *ancient history* **of long ago**, earliest, first, early, past, former, bygone; prehistoric, primeval, primordial, primitive; classical; *literary* olden, of yore, foregone.
OPPOSITES recent, contemporary.
2 *an ancient custom* **old**, very old, age-old, antediluvian, time-worn, time-honoured, immemorial, long-lived; atavistic.
OPPOSITES new, recent, modern.
3 *you make me feel positively ancient* **antiquated**, archaic, antediluvian, medieval, obsolete, obsolescent, superannuated, anachronistic, old-fashioned, out of date, outmoded; aged, elderly, venerable, hoary, decrepit; *French* démodé, passé; *informal* fossilized, as old as the hills, cobwebby, in one's dotage, out of the ark, creaky, mouldy; *Brit. informal* past its/one's sell-by date; *N. Amer. informal* mossy, clunky, horse and buggy.
OPPOSITES youthful, up to date.

WORD LINKS
related prefixes **archaeo- (e.g. *archaeology, archaeoastronomy*), palaeo- (e.g. *palaeography, Palaeozoic*)**

ancillary ▶ adjective *ancillary staff* | *ancillary benefits* **additional**, auxiliary, supporting, helping, assisting, extra, supplementary, supplemental, accessory, contributory, attendant; subsidiary, secondary, subordinate; *Medicine* adjuvant; *rare* adminicular.

WORD LINKS
related prefix **para- (e.g. *paramedic, paramilitary*)**

and ▶ conjunction **together with**, along with, with, as well as, in addition to, including, also, too; besides, furthermore, moreover; *informal* plus, what's more.

anecdotal ▶ adjective **1** *the evidence is merely anecdotal* **informal**, unreliable, based on hearsay; **unscientific**.
OPPOSITES experimental, scientific.
2 *her book is anecdotal and chatty* **narrative**, full of stories, packed/crammed with incident.
OPPOSITES abstract, austere.

anecdote ▶ noun **story**, tale, narrative, sketch; urban myth; reminiscence; *informal* yarn, shaggy-dog story.

anew ▶ adverb *tears filled her eyes anew* **again**, once more, once again, a second time, afresh, over again.

angel *See centre pages for list of* **Angels**
▶ noun **1** *God sent an angel to talk to Gideon* **messenger of God**, divine/heavenly messenger, divine being, spirit.
OPPOSITE devil.
2 (*informal*) *she's been an absolute angel* **paragon of virtue**, saint, gem, treasure, nonpareil; darling, dear; *informal* star, brick, one in a million.
3 (*informal*) *a financial angel* **backer**, sponsor, supporter, benefactor, subsidizer, promoter, patron; guarantor, underwriter; *rare* Maecenas.

angelic ▶ adjective **1** *angelic beings* **divine**, heavenly, celestial, holy; seraphic, cherubic, ethereal, spiritual; *rare* empyrean.
OPPOSITES demonic, satanic, infernal.
2 *Sophie's angelic appearance* **innocent**, pure, as pure as the driven snow, virtuous, good, saintly, wholesome, exemplary; **beautiful**, adorable, lovely, lovable, enchanting.

anger ▶ noun *his face darkened with anger* **annoyance**, vexation, exasperation, crossness, irritation, irritability, indignation, pique, displeasure, resentment; **rage**, fury, wrath, outrage, temper, irascibility, ill temper, dyspepsia, spleen, ill humour, tetchiness, testiness, waspishness; *informal* aggravation; *literary* ire, choler, bile.
OPPOSITES pleasure, good humour.
▶ verb *she was angered by his terse reply* **annoy**, irritate, exasperate, irk, vex, put out, provoke, pique, gall, displease; **enrage**, incense, infuriate, madden, inflame, antagonize, make someone's blood boil, make someone's hackles rise, rub up the wrong way, ruffle someone's feathers, ruffle, peeve; *informal* drive mad/crazy, drive up the wall, make someone see red, get someone's back up, get someone's dander up, get someone's goat, get under someone's skin, get up someone's nose, rattle someone's cage; aggravate, get someone, needle, bug, nettle, rile, miff, hack off; *Brit. informal* wind up, get at, nark, get across, get on someone's wick; *N. Amer. informal* tee off, tick off, burn up, gravel; *vulgar slang* piss off; *informal, dated* give someone the pip; *rare* empurple.
OPPOSITES pacify, placate.

angle[1] ▶ noun **1** *the wall is sloping at an angle of 33° to the vertical* **gradient**, slant, inclination; geometrical relation.
2 *the right-hand angle of the goal* **corner**, intersection, point, apex, cusp; nook, niche, recess, crook; projection.

3 *we need to consider the problem from a different angle* **perspective**, way of looking at something, point of view, viewpoint, standpoint, position, side, aspect, slant, direction, approach, outlook, light.
▶ verb 1 *Anna angled her camera towards the tree* **tilt**, slant; point, direct, aim, turn.
2 *angle your answer so that it is relevant to the job for which you are applying* **present**, slant, give a particular slant to, orient; skew, distort, twist, bias.
WORD LINKS
measurement of angles **goniometry**

angle[2] ▶ verb *she smiled, realizing he was* **angling for** *an invitation* **try to get**, seek to obtain, make a bid for, aim for, cast about/around/round for, solicit, hope for, look for; informal fish for, be after.

angler ▶ noun **fisherman**; informal rod; archaic fisher; rare piscator.

angry ▶ adjective 1 *Vivienne got angry and started shouting | she shot him an angry look* **irate**, annoyed, cross, vexed, irritated, exasperated, indignant, aggrieved, irked, piqued, displeased, provoked, galled, resentful; **furious**, enraged, infuriated, in a temper, incensed, raging, incandescent, wrathful, fuming, ranting, raving, seething, frenzied, in a frenzy, beside oneself, outraged, in high dudgeon; irascible, bad-tempered, hot-tempered, choleric, splenetic, dyspeptic, tetchy, testy, crabby, waspish; hostile, antagonistic, black, dark, dirty, filthy; informal mad, hopping mad, wild, livid, as cross as two sticks, boiling, apoplectic, aerated, hot under the collar, riled, on the warpath, up in arms, with all guns blazing, foaming at the mouth, steamed up, in a lather, in a paddy, fit to be tied, aggravated, snappy, snappish; Brit. informal shirty, stroppy, narky, ratty, eggy; N. Amer. informal sore, bent out of shape, soreheaded, teed off, ticked off; Austral./NZ informal ropeable, snaky, crook; W. Indian informal vex; Brit. informal, dated in a bate, waxy; vulgar slang pissed off; N. Amer. vulgar slang pissed; literary ireful, wroth.
OPPOSITES calm; pleased.
2 *an angry debate erupted* **heated**, hot, passionate, furious, fiery, stormy, tempestuous, lively; bad-tempered, ill-tempered, acrimonious, bitter.
OPPOSITES good-humoured, peaceful.
3 *he had an angry spot on the side of his nose* **inflamed**, red, swollen, sore, painful.
□ **get angry lose one's temper**, become enraged, go into a rage, rant and rave, go berserk, fume, seethe, flare up, bristle; informal go/get mad, go crazy, go wild, go bananas, hit the roof, go through the roof, go up the wall, jump up and down, see red, go off the deep end, fly off the handle, blow one's top, blow a fuse/gasket, lose one's rag, go ape, burst a blood vessel, breathe fire, flip, flip one's lid, foam at the mouth, get all steamed up, get worked up, have a fit, explode, have steam coming out of one's ears, gnash one's teeth, go non-linear, go ballistic, go into orbit, go psycho; Brit. informal go spare, go crackers, do one's nut, get one's knickers in a twist, throw a wobbly; N. Amer. informal flip one's wig, blow one's lid/stack, have a cow, go postal, have a conniption fit; vulgar slang go apeshit.

angst ▶ noun **anxiety**, fear, dread, apprehension, worry, perturbation, foreboding, trepidation, malaise, distress, disquiet, disquietude, unease, uneasiness; rare inquietude.

anguish ▶ noun *a cry of anguish* **agony**, pain, torment, torture, suffering, distress, angst, misery, sorrow, grief, heartache, heartbreak, wretchedness, unhappiness, woe, desolation, despair; the dark night of the soul, purgatory, hell on earth; literary dolour.
OPPOSITES happiness, contentment.

anguished ▶ adjective *an anguished cry | her anguished face* **agonized**, tormented, racked with pain/suffering, tortured, harrowed; **miserable**, unhappy, sad, broken-hearted, heartbroken, grief-stricken, wretched, sorrowful, sorrowing, distressed, desolate, devastated, despairing; informal cut up; literary dolorous.
OPPOSITES happy, contented.

angular ▶ adjective 1 *a dark, angular shape* **sharp-cornered**, pointed, V-shaped, Y-shaped; forked, bifurcate.
OPPOSITES rounded, curving.
2 *an angular girl with prominent cheekbones* **bony**, raw-boned, skin-and-bones; **lean**, rangy, spare, thin, lanky, spindly, skinny, gaunt, scrawny, scraggy; informal looking like a bag of bones, anorexic, anorectic; dated spindle-shanked; rare gracile, macilent.
OPPOSITES plump, curvy.

animal *See centre pages for lists of* **Animals—Male and Female Terms** **Amphibians** **Bats** **Bears** **Birds** **Cats** **Cattle** **Chinese Calendar** **Deer and Antelopes** **Dogs** **Fish** **Fowl** **Foxes** **Goats** **Horses and Ponies** **Insects** **Lemurs and Other Prosimians** **Marsupials** **Molluscs** **Monkeys and Apes** **Pigs** **Rabbits and Hares** **Reptiles** **Rodents** **Seals, Sea Lions, and Sea Cows** **Sharks** **Sheep** **Snakes** **Spiders and Other Arachnids** **Squirrels** **Weasels and Similar Animals** **Whales and Dolphins** **Worms** **Young Animals**
▶ noun 1 *rare and endangered animals and plants* **creature**, beast, living thing, being, brute; informal critter; (**animals**) wildlife, fauna.
2 *the man was an animal* **brute**, beast, monster, savage, devil, demon, fiend, villain, sadist, barbarian, ogre; informal swine, bastard, pig.
▶ adjective 1 *the evolution of animal life* **zoological**, animalistic; rare zoic, theriomorphic.
2 *his grunt of animal passion* **carnal**, fleshly, bodily, physical, sensual; instinctive, instinctual; brutish, unrefined, uncultured, coarse, gross, inhuman, subhuman; rare appetitive.
OPPOSITE spiritual.
WORD LINKS

related prefix	**zoo-** (e.g. *zoogeography, zooplankton*)
relating to animals	**faunal, zoological**
study of animals	**zoology**
branch of medicine to do with animals	**veterinary medicine**

animate ▶ verb *a sense of excitement animated the whole school* **enliven**, vitalize, give (new) life to, breathe (new) life into, energize, invigorate, revive, vivify, liven up, light up, cheer up, gladden; encourage, hearten, inspire, exhilarate, thrill, excite, fire, arouse, rouse, stir, stimulate, galvanize, electrify; informal buck up, pep up, give someone a buzz, ginger up; N. Amer. informal light a fire under; rare inspirit.
OPPOSITES depress, inhibit.
▶ adjective *an animate being* **living**, alive, live, breathing, sentient, conscious; organic; archaic quick.
OPPOSITE inanimate.

animated ▶ adjective *an animated discussion | Simon became quite animated* **lively**, spirited, high-spirited, energetic, full of life, excited, enthusiastic, eager, alive, active, vigorous, vibrant, vital, vivacious, buoyant, exuberant, ebullient, effervescent, bouncy, bubbly, perky, sparkling, sprightly, zestful; fiery, passionate, impassioned, heated, dynamic, forceful, fervent, ardent; informal bright-eyed and bushy-tailed, full of beans, bright and breezy, sparky, chirpy, go-go, chipper, peppy, zippy, zappy, full of vim and vigour; N. Amer. informal peart.
OPPOSITES lethargic, apathetic, lifeless.

animation ▶ noun *he had always admired her animation* **liveliness**, spirit, high spirits, spiritedness, high-spiritedness, energy, enthusiasm, eagerness, excitement, vigour, vivacity, vivaciousness, vitality, vibrancy, exuberance, ebullience, buoyancy, bounciness, bounce, perkiness, sprightliness, verve, zest, sparkle, dash, elan, brio; fire, fieriness, passion, dynamism, forcefulness, intensity, ardour, fervour; informal chirpiness, pep, vim, zing, go, get-up-and-go.
OPPOSITES lethargy, sluggishness, inertia.

animosity ▶ noun *there was considerable animosity between him and his brother* **antipathy**, hostility, friction, antagonism, enmity, animus, opposition, aversion, acrimony, bitterness, rancour, resentment, dislike, ill feeling, bad feeling, ill will, bad blood, hatred, hate, loathing, detestation, abhorrence, odium; malice, spite, spitefulness, venom, malevolence, malignity; grudges, grievances; archaic disrelish.
OPPOSITES goodwill, friendship.

annals ▶ plural noun **records**, archives, chronicles, accounts, registers, journals; history; rare muniments.

annex ▶ verb (stress on the second syllable) 1 *the first ten amendments were annexed to the constitution in 1791* **add**, append, attach, join; informal tack on, tag on.
2 *Charlemagne annexed northern Italy, Saxony, and Bavaria* **take over**, take possession of, appropriate, expropriate, arrogate, seize, conquer, occupy, garrison; usurp.
OPPOSITE relinquish.
▶ noun (stress on the first syllable) (also **annexe**) *a school annex* **extension**, supplementary building, addition; wing; N. Amer. informal ell.

annexation ▶ noun *Hitler's annexation of Austria* **seizure**, occupation, invasion, conquest, takeover, appropriation, expropriation, arrogation; usurping.

annihilate ▶ verb *this was an attempt to annihilate an entire people* **destroy**, wipe out, obliterate, wipe off the face of the earth, wipe off the map, kill, slaughter, exterminate, eliminate, liquidate, eradicate, extinguish, finish off, erase, root out, extirpate; informal take out, rub out, snuff out, zap, waste.
OPPOSITES create, build, establish.

anniversary ▶ noun **jubilee**, commemoration.

annotate ▶ verb *the text was annotated with explanatory notes* **comment on**, add notes/footnotes to, gloss; explain, interpret, elucidate, explicate; rare footnote, margin, marginalize.

annotation ▶ noun *Coleridge's marginal annotations* **note**, notation, comment, gloss; footnote; commentary, explanation, interpretation, observation, elucidation, explication, exegesis.

announce ▶ verb 1 *the company's financial results were announced on May 12* **make public**, make known, report, issue a statement about, declare, state, set forth, give out, put out, post, notify, give notice of, publicize, broadcast, publish, advertise, circulate, proclaim, promulgate, trumpet, noise abroad; disclose, reveal, divulge, intimate; informal shout something from the rooftops; literary blazon abroad; rare preconize.
OPPOSITES conceal, suppress.

2 *Victor announced their guests* **introduce**, present, name; usher in.
3 *strains of music announced her arrival in the church* **signal**, indicate, be an indication of, signify, give notice of, herald, proclaim; warn of, foretell, augur, portend; *literary* betoken, harbinger.

announcement ▶ noun **1** *an announcement by the Minister is expected this afternoon* **statement**, report, declaration, proclamation, pronouncement; bulletin, communiqué, dispatch, message; information, word, news; *N. Amer.* advisory; (*in Tsarist Russia*) ukase; (*in Spain & Spanish-speaking countries*) pronunciamento; *Latin* ipse dixit; *rare* rescript, asseveration.
2 *the announcement of the decision* **declaration**, notification, report, reporting, publishing, broadcasting, proclamation, promulgation; disclosure, revelation, intimation, divulging; *archaic* annunciation.

announcer ▶ noun **presenter**, anchorman, anchorwoman, anchor; newsreader, newscaster, broadcaster, reporter, commentator; master of ceremonies, MC, compère, host; *informal* talking head, emcee.

annoy ▶ verb *such remarks never failed to annoy him* **irritate**, vex, make angry, make cross, anger, exasperate, irk, gall, pique, put out, displease, get/put someone's back up, antagonize, get on someone's nerves, rub up the wrong way, ruffle, ruffle someone's feathers, make someone's hackles rise, raise someone's hackles; enrage, infuriate, madden, make someone's blood boil, drive to distraction, goad, provoke; *informal* aggravate, peeve, hassle, miff, rile, nettle, needle, get, get to, bug, hack off, get under someone's skin, get in someone's hair, get up someone's nose, put someone's nose out of joint, get someone's goat, give someone the hump, rattle someone's cage, drive mad/crazy, drive round the bend/twist, drive up the wall, make someone see red; *Brit. informal* wind up, nark, get across, get on someone's wick; *N. Amer. informal* tee off, tick off, burn up, rankle, ride, gravel; *vulgar slang* piss off; *Brit. vulgar slang* get on someone's tits; *informal, dated* give someone the pip, get someone's dander up; *rare* exacerbate, hump, rasp.
OPPOSITES please, gratify.

CHOOSE THE RIGHT WORD

annoy, irritate, aggravate, vex, peeve

- Someone or something that **annoys** a person displeases them and makes them moderately angry (*his tone of joking superiority annoyed me*).
- **Irritate** suggests a trifling but long-lasting cause of annoyance (*nothing irritated him more than to be kept waiting*).
- Some people believe that **aggravate** is properly used to mean only 'make worse', but the sense 'annoy or exasperate' is widespread and represents no greater a departure from an older meaning than many others that have long been accepted without comment. An action that *aggravates* someone else is quite often deliberate or at least easily avoidable (*he hummed under his breath, which aggravated her*).
- **Vex** is a more formal or literary word used of something that irritates or worries someone, especially when they are unable to do anything about it (*I'm vexed at that girl—she ruined Christmas for the family*).
- **Peeve** is an informal word, generally used when someone feels that they have been unfairly treated (*Birkitt was looking distinctly peeved, aware that Banks had upstaged him*). It generally expresses relatively mild annoyance.
- All these words, apart from *peeve*, are widely used as adjectives (*it's so irritating having to constantly stop and put your kagoul on etc.*).

annoyance ▶ noun **1** *much to his annoyance, Louise didn't even notice* **irritation**, exasperation, vexation, indignation, anger, crossness, displeasure, chagrin, pique; *informal* aggravation; *literary* ire.
OPPOSITE pleasure.
2 *the council found him an annoyance* **nuisance**, source of irritation, pest, bother, trial, irritant, inconvenience, menace, thorn in one's flesh; *informal* pain, pain in the neck, bind, bore, headache, hassle; *Scottish informal* nyaff, skelf; *N. Amer. informal* pain in the butt, nudnik, burr in/under someone's saddle; *Austral./NZ informal* nark; *Brit. vulgar slang* pain in the arse.

annoyed ▶ adjective *Maureen was beginning to look annoyed* **irritated**, cross, angry, vexed, exasperated, irked, piqued, displeased, put out, fed up, disgruntled, in a bad mood, in a temper, testy, in high dudgeon, huffy, in a huff, resentful, aggrieved; furious, irate, infuriated, incensed, enraged, wrathful, choleric; *informal* aggravated, peeved, nettled, miffed, miffy, mad, riled, hacked off, peed off, hot under the collar, foaming at the mouth; *Brit. informal* browned off, cheesed off, brassed off, narked, ratty, shirty, eggy; *N. Amer. informal* teed off, ticked off, sore, bent out of shape; *Austral./NZ informal* snaky, crook; *W. Indian informal* vex; *vulgar slang* pissed off; *N. Amer. vulgar slang* pissed; *literary* ireful; *archaic* snuffy, wrath.

annoying ▶ adjective *he really was the most annoying man she'd ever met* **irritating**, infuriating, exasperating, maddening, trying, tiresome, troublesome, bothersome, irksome, vexing, vexatious, galling, provoking, displeasing; awkward, difficult, inconvenient; *informal* aggravating, pesky, cussed, confounded, infernal, pestiferous, plaguy, pestilent.
OPPOSITES pleasant, agreeable.

annual ▶ adjective **1** *an annual report* **yearly**, once-a-year, every twelve months.
2 *an annual subscription* **year-long**, lasting a year, twelve-month.

annually ▶ adverb *subscriptions are payable annually* **yearly**, once a year, each year, by the year, per annum, per year; every year.

annul ▶ verb *the European Court annulled the decision* **declare invalid**, declare null and void, nullify, invalidate, void; **repeal**, reverse, rescind, revoke, set aside, cancel, abolish, undo, abrogate, countermand, dissolve, withdraw, cast aside, quash; *Law* vacate; *rare* disannul, negate, recall.
OPPOSITES restore; enact.

annulment ▶ noun *the annulment of the commission's decision* **invalidation**, nullification, voiding; **repeal**, cancellation, rescinding, reversal, revocation, setting aside, abolition, abrogation, rescindment, withdrawal, countermanding, quashing; *rare* rescission, disannulment, negation, recall.
OPPOSITES restoration, enactment.

anodyne ▶ noun **painkiller**, painkilling drug, analgesic, pain reliever, palliative.
▶ adjective *she tried to keep the conversation as anodyne as possible* **bland**, inoffensive, innocuous, neutral, unobjectionable, unexceptionable, unremarkable, commonplace, dull, tedious, run-of-the-mill.

anoint ▶ verb **1** *during the public baptism, the head of the infant was anointed* **smear with oil**, rub with oil, apply oil to, spread oil over; *archaic* anele.
2 *he was anointed and crowned in Charlemagne's basilica* **consecrate**, sanctify, bless, ordain, hallow.

anomalous ▶ adjective *nuclear weapons testing may have been responsible for the anomalous weather conditions* **abnormal**, atypical, non-typical, irregular, aberrant, exceptional, freak, freakish, odd, bizarre, peculiar, unusual, out of the ordinary, inconsistent, incongruous, deviant, deviating, divergent, eccentric; rare, singular.
OPPOSITES normal, typical, regular.

anomaly ▶ noun *there are a number of anomalies in the present system* **oddity**, peculiarity, abnormality, irregularity, inconsistency, incongruity, deviation, aberration, quirk, freak, exception, departure, divergence, variation; rarity, eccentricity.

anon ▶ adverb (*archaic or informal*) *I'll see you anon* **soon**, shortly, in a little while, in a short time, presently, before long, in the near future; *S. African* just now; *dated* directly; *literary* by and by, ere long.

anonymous ▶ adjective **1** *an anonymous donor* **unnamed**, of unknown name, nameless, incognito, unidentified, unknown, unspecified, undesignated, unacknowledged, mystery; unsung; *rare* innominate.
OPPOSITES known, identified.
2 *an anonymous letter* **unsigned**, unattributed, unattested, uncredited.
OPPOSITE signed.
3 *an anonymous London housing estate* **characterless**, unremarkable, nondescript, impersonal, faceless, colourless, grey.

another ▶ determiner **1** *have another drink | I've got another umbrella* **one more**, a further, an additional, a second; an extra, a spare.
2 *she left him for another man* **a different**, some other, not the same, an alternative.
OPPOSITE the same.

answer ▶ noun **1** *her answer was swift and unequivocal* **reply**, response, rejoinder, return, reaction; acknowledgement; retort, riposte; *informal* comeback.
OPPOSITES question, query.
2 *the answer is 150* **solution**, explanation, resolution; key.
3 *simply increasing the number of troops is not the answer* **solution**, remedy, way of solving the problem, way out; *informal* quick fix.
4 *his answer to the charge* **defence**, plea, refutation, rebuttal; *Law* counterstatement, surrejoinder, rebutter, surrebutter, replication.
▶ verb **1** *Steve was about to answer, but Hazel spoke first | 'Of course I can,' she answered* **reply**, respond, speak/say in response, make a rejoinder, rejoin; retort, come back, fling back, hurl back; acknowledge, write back; *informal* get back to; *rare* riposte.
2 *he has yet to answer the charges made against him* **rebut**, refute, defend oneself against.
3 *the police had a tip-off about a man answering this description* **match**, fit, correspond to, be similar to, conform to, correlate to.
4 *we're looking at new types of programmes to answer the needs of our audience* **satisfy**, meet, fulfil, fill, serve, suit, measure up to, match up to; fit/fill the bill.
5 *I answer to the Assistant Commissioner of Specialist Operations* **report**, be accountable, be answerable, be responsible; work for, work under, be subordinate to, be supervised by, be managed by.
□ **answer someone back respond cheekily to**, be cheeky to, be impertinent to, talk back to; contradict, argue with, disagree with; retaliate, retort, counter; *informal* cheek; *N. Amer. informal* sass, be sassy to.
□ **answer for 1** *no one has been made to answer for the crime* **pay for**, be punished for, suffer the consequences of, suffer for; make amends for,

make reparation for, atone for.
2 *the present government has a lot to answer for* **be accountable for**, be responsible for, be liable for, take the blame for; vouch for; *informal* take the rap for.

answerable ▸ **adjective** *the Attorney General is answerable only to Parliament for his decisions* **accountable**, responsible, liable; subject.

ant ▸ **noun**

WORD LINKS
relating to ants **formic, myrmeco-**
study of ants **myrmecology**

antagonism ▸ **noun** *the overt antagonism between her and Susan* **hostility**, friction, enmity, antipathy, animus, opposition, dissension, rivalry, feud, conflict, discord, contention; acrimony, bitterness, rancour, resentment, aversion, dislike, ill feeling, bad feeling, ill will, bad blood, hatred, hate, loathing, detestation, abhorrence, odium; malice, spite, spitefulness, venom, malevolence, malignity; grudges, grievances; *Brit. informal* needle; *archaic* disrelish.
OPPOSITES rapport, friendship.

antagonist ▸ **noun** **adversary**, opponent, enemy, foe, rival, competitor, contender; (**antagonists**) opposition, competition, the other side; *rare* corrival.
OPPOSITES ally, friend, supporter.

antagonistic ▸ **adjective** **1** *he was increasingly* ***antagonistic to*** *the government's reforms* **hostile**, **opposed**, inimical, antipathetic, unsympathetic, ill-disposed, resistant, averse; against, (dead) set against, at odds with, at variance with, in disagreement with, dissenting from; *informal* anti, agin.
OPPOSITES pro, sympathetic.
2 *an antagonistic group of bystanders* **hostile**, **aggressive**, belligerent, bellicose, pugnacious, combative, contentious, truculent, confrontational, quarrelsome, argumentative; *rare* oppugnant.

antagonize ▸ **verb** *he seemed to be deliberately trying to antagonize her* **arouse hostility in**, alienate, set someone against someone else, estrange, disaffect; **anger**, annoy, provoke, vex, irritate, offend; *informal* aggravate, rile, needle, get someone's back up, make someone's hackles rise, rub up the wrong way, ruffle someone's feathers, rattle someone's cage, get up someone's nose, get in someone's hair, get someone's dander up, get under someone's skin; *Brit. informal* nark, get on someone's wick.
OPPOSITES pacify, placate.

antecedent ▸ **noun** **1** (**antecedents**) *her early life and antecedents have been traced* **ancestors**, ancestry, forefathers, forebears, predecessors, progenitors, family, family tree, stock; descent, genealogy, roots, extraction, birth; history, past, background, record; *rare* filiation, stirps.
OPPOSITE descendant.
2 *music composed for vihuela (the guitar's lute-like antecedent)* **precursor**, forerunner, predecessor.
▸ **adjective** *antecedent events* **previous**, earlier, prior, foregoing, preceding, precursory; pre-existing; *rare* anterior.
OPPOSITES later, subsequent.

antedate ▸ **verb** *a civilization that antedated the Roman Empire* **precede**, predate, come/go before, be earlier than, anticipate.

antediluvian ▸ **adjective** **1** *gigantic bones of antediluvian animals* **before the flood**, **prehistoric**, primeval, primordial, primal, earliest, ancient, early; *rare* primigenial.
2 *his antediluvian attitudes* **out of date**, outdated, outmoded, old-fashioned, ancient, antiquated, archaic, antique, superannuated, anachronistic, outworn, behind the times, primitive, medieval, quaint, old-fangled, obsolescent, obsolete, prehistoric; *French* passé; *informal* out of the ark, fossilized, as old as the hills, old hat, creaky, mouldy; *Brit. informal* past its/one's sell-by date; *N. Amer. informal* horse and buggy, mossy, clunky.
OPPOSITES modern, up to date.

antelope ▸ **noun**. *See centre pages for list of* **Deer and Antelopes**

WORD LINKS
male **buck**
female **doe**
young **calf**

anteroom ▸ **noun** **antechamber**, outer room, vestibule, lobby, waiting room, reception area; foyer; (*in churches*) narthex.

anthem ▸ **noun** *the choir sang two anthems* **hymn**, song, song of praise, chorale, psalm, paean, plainsong, chant, canticle.

anthology ▸ **noun** *an anthology of European poetry* **collection**, selection, compendium, treasury, compilation, miscellany, pot-pourri; *archaic* garland; *rare* analects, collectanea, florilegium.

anticipate ▸ **verb** **1** *the police did not anticipate any trouble* **expect**, foresee, predict, think likely, forecast, prophesy, foretell, contemplate the possibility of, allow for, be prepared for; count on, bank on, look for, bargain on; *informal* reckon on; *N. Amer. informal* figure on; *archaic* apprehend.
2 *Elaine tingled with excitement as she anticipated her meeting with Will* **look forward to**, await, count the days until; *informal* lick one's lips over.
OPPOSITE dread.
3 *warders can't always anticipate the actions of prisoners* **pre-empt**, forestall, intercept; second-guess; *informal* beat someone to it, beat someone to the draw, beat someone to the punch.
4 *she wrote plays for all-women casts, which anticipated her film work* **foreshadow**, precede, antedate, come/go before, be earlier than.

> **CHOOSE THE RIGHT WORD**
>
> **anticipate, expect, foresee**
>
> These words all mean 'regard as probable', but they all have other meanings that can colour the general sense.
>
> - **Anticipate** is used especially when someone takes action or makes plans to prepare for what they think will happen (*the police anticipated trouble and drafted in reinforcements*). It is often used for looking forward to something desirable, and when used as an adjective it is frequently modified by an adverb such as *eagerly* (*it was the most eagerly anticipated show in town*) and, with the same approving sense, *highly* (*one of the year's most highly anticipated video games*). *Anticipate* is less commonly used in a passive construction that the other two words.
> - **Expect** is the most general word (*sales are expected to drop next year | over 20,000 visitors are expected*). *Expect* may also be used of something that is required or demanded, whether or not one thinks it is likely (*the firm expected its employees to be prepared to move*). While all these words can be used with a direct object or a *that*-clause (*I expect that she knew too*), only *expect* can be used with an object and an infinitive (*you expect me to believe you?*).
> - **Foresee** can imply certainty, as its meaning verges on 'prophesy, predict', and the objects with which it is used are typically undesirable (*we foresee enormous problems for local authorities*). Only *foresee* and *anticipate* can be used with a present participle (*Cleo had anticipated having to apologize for him*).

anticipation ▸ **noun** **1** *my anticipation is that we will see a rise in rates on Monday* **expectation**, prediction, forecast; *rare* prolepsis.
2 *her eyes sparkled with anticipation* **expectancy**, expectation, hope, hopefulness; excitement, suspense.
□ **in anticipation of** *they manned the telephones in anticipation of a flood of calls* **in the expectation of**, in preparation for, in case of, ready for, against.

anticlimax ▸ **noun** **let-down**, disappointment, comedown, non-event; disillusionment; bathos; *Brit.* damp squib; *informal* washout, not what it was cracked up to be.
OPPOSITES triumph, climax.

antics ▸ **plural noun** *she laughed, recalling her son's antics* **capers**, amusing behaviour, pranks, larks, escapades, high jinks, skylarking, stunts, tricks, horseplay, romps, frolics; silliness, foolish behaviour, tomfoolery, foolery, clowning, buffoonery; *Brit. informal* monkey tricks; *N. Amer. informal* didoes; *archaic* harlequinades.

antidote ▸ **noun** **1** *there is no known antidote to this poison* **antitoxin**, antiserum; cure, remedy; neutralizer, neutralizing agent, counteragent; *rare* mithridate, antivenin, antivenene, theriac.
2 *laughter is a good antidote to stress* **remedy**, cure, corrective, nostrum, countermeasure, counteragent; solution.

antipathetic ▸ **adjective** *French nationalists became vehemently* ***antipathetic to*** *all things German* **hostile**, opposed, antagonistic, averse, ill-disposed, unsympathetic; against, (dead) set against; *informal* anti, agin, down on.
OPPOSITE pro.

antipathy ▸ **noun** *she felt a violent antipathy to Emily* **hostility**, antagonism, animosity, aversion, animus, opposition, enmity, dislike, distaste, ill will, ill feeling, hatred, hate, abhorrence, loathing, repugnance, odium; grudge; *informal* allergy; *archaic* disrelish.
OPPOSITES liking, affinity, rapport.

antiquated ▸ **adjective** *antiquated attitudes | an antiquated cash register* **outdated**, out of date, outmoded, behind the times, old-fashioned, archaic, anachronistic, superannuated, outworn, ancient, antediluvian, primitive, medieval, quaint, old-fangled, obsolescent, obsolete, prehistoric; *French* passé, démodé, vieux jeu; *informal* out of the ark, fossilized, as old as the hills, creaky, mouldy; *Brit. informal* past its/one's sell-by date; *N. Amer. informal* horse and buggy, mossy, clunky.
OPPOSITES current, modern, up to date.

antique ▸ **noun** *the chair's an antique* **collector's item**, period piece, museum piece, antiquity, object of virtu; heirloom; treasure, relic, curio; *French* objet d'art; *rare* bygone.
▸ **adjective** **1** *antique furniture* **old**, antiquarian, collectable; vintage, classic.
OPPOSITES new, modern, state-of-the-art.
2 *statues of antique gods* **ancient**, of long ago; classical; *literary* of yore.
3 *antique work practices* **out of date**, outdated, outmoded, old-fashioned, archaic, antiquated, anachronistic, ancient, antediluvian, superannuated, outworn, behind the times, primitive, medieval, quaint, old-fangled,

obsolescent, obsolete, prehistoric; *French* passé; *informal* out of the ark, fossilized, as old as the hills, old hat, creaky, mouldy; *Brit. informal* past its/one's sell-by date; *N. Amer. informal* horse and buggy, mossy, clunky.
OPPOSITES current, modern, up to date.

antiquity ▸ noun **1** *the great civilizations of antiquity* **ancient times**, the ancient past, classical times, former times, the distant past, times gone by; *literary* the olden days, days of yore, yesteryear; *archaic* the eld.
2 *a collection of Islamic antiquities* **antique**, period piece, museum piece; treasure, relic, curio; *rare* bygone.
3 *a church of great antiquity* **age**, oldness, elderliness, ancientness.

antiseptic ▸ adjective **1** *an antiseptic substance* **disinfectant**, germicidal, bactericidal; medicated.
2 *antiseptic bandages* **sterile**, aseptic, germ-free, uncontaminated, unpolluted; disinfected, sanitized.
OPPOSITES dirty, contaminated.
3 *the antiseptic surroundings of the conference centre* **characterless**, colourless, soulless, bland, nondescript, uninspiring; clinical, institutional.
OPPOSITE colourful.
▸ noun *a mild antiseptic* **disinfectant**, germicide, bactericide.

antisocial ▸ adjective **1** *antisocial behaviour* **objectionable**, offensive, beyond the pale, unacceptable, unsocial, asocial, distasteful; disruptive, disorderly, lawless, rebellious; sociopathic.
2 *I'm feeling a bit antisocial* **unsociable**, misanthropic, unwilling to mix with other people, unfriendly, uncommunicative, unforthcoming, reserved, withdrawn, retiring, reclusive.
OPPOSITES sociable, gregarious.

antisocial, unsocial, or unsociable?
See **UNSOCIABLE**.

antithesis ▸ noun **1** *love is the antithesis of selfishness* **(direct) opposite**, converse, reverse, reversal, inverse, obverse; the other extreme, the other side of the coin; *informal* the flip side.
2 *the antithesis between sin and grace* **contrast**, opposition.

antithetical ▸ adjective *an administration packed with people holding policy views antithetical to his own* **(directly) opposed to**, contrary to, contradictory to, conflicting with, incompatible with, irreconcilable with, inconsistent with, at variance with, at odds with, contrasting with, different from/to, differing from, divergent from, unlike; opposing, poles apart, polar, obverse; *rare* oppugnant.
OPPOSITES same, identical, like.

anxiety ▸ noun **1** *his anxiety grew as his messages were all left unanswered* **worry**, concern, apprehension, apprehensiveness, consternation, uneasiness, unease, fearfulness, fear, disquiet, disquietude, perturbation, fretfulness, agitation, angst, nervousness, nerves, edginess, tension, tenseness, stress, misgiving, trepidation, foreboding, suspense; *informal* butterflies (in one's stomach), the willies, the heebie-jeebies, the jitters, the shakes, the jumps, the yips, collywobbles, jitteriness, jim-jams, twitchiness; *Brit. informal* the (screaming) abdabs; *Austral. rhyming slang* Joe Blakes; *N. Amer. archaic* worriment.
OPPOSITES calmness, serenity.
2 *her anxiety to please* **eagerness**, keenness, desire, impatience, longing, yearning.

anxious ▸ adjective **1** *I'm very anxious about her welfare | anxious relatives waited for news* **worried**, concerned, apprehensive, fearful, uneasy, ill at ease, perturbed, troubled, disquieted, bothered, disturbed, distressed, fretful, fretting, agitated, in a state of agitation, nervous, in a state of nerves, edgy, on edge, tense, overwrought, worked up, keyed up, strung out, jumpy, afraid, worried sick, with one's stomach in knots, with one's heart in one's mouth, on pins and needles, stressed, under stress, in suspense, flurried; *informal* uptight, a bundle of nerves, on tenterhooks, with butterflies in one's stomach, like a cat on a hot tin roof, jittery, twitchy, in a state, in a stew, all of a dither, in a flap, in a sweat, in a tizz/tizzy, all of a lather, het up, in a twitter; *Brit. informal* strung up, windy, having kittens, in a (flat) spin, like a cat on hot bricks; *N. Amer. informal* antsy, spooky, spooked, squirrelly, in a twit; *Austral./NZ informal* toey; *dated* overstrung, unquiet.
OPPOSITES carefree, unconcerned.
2 *she was anxious for news of him* **eager**, keen, desirous, impatient, itching, longing, yearning, aching, dying.

any ▸ determiner **1** *is there any ginger cake left?* **some**, a piece of, a part of, a bit of.
2 *it doesn't make any difference* **the slightest bit of**, the smallest amount of, a scrap of, a shred of, a particle of, an atom of, an iota of, a jot of, a whit of.
3 *any job will do, to begin with* **whichever**, whichever comes to hand, no matter which, never mind which; *informal* any old.
▸ pronoun **1** *you don't know any of my friends* **a single one**, one, even one.
2 *they ceased payments to any but the aged* **anyone**, anybody.
▸ adverb *is your father any better?* **at all**, in the least, to any extent, to some extent, somewhat, in any degree, to some degree.

anyhow ▸ adverb **1** *anyhow, it doesn't really matter now* **anyway**, in any case, in any event, at any rate, at all events, no matter what, regardless; however, be that as it may; *informal* still and all; *N. Amer. informal* anyways.
2 *her clothes were strewn about anyhow* **haphazardly**, carelessly, heedlessly, negligently, in a muddle, in a disorganized manner; *informal* all over the place, every which way; *Brit. informal* all over the shop; *N. Amer. informal* all over the lot.

apace ▸ adverb (*literary*) *things are moving on apace* **quickly**, fast, swiftly, rapidly, speedily, briskly, without delay, post-haste, expeditiously, at full speed, at full tilt; *Brit. informal* at a rate of knots.
OPPOSITE slowly.

apart ▸ adverb **1** *the villages are only two miles apart* **away from each other**, distant from each other.
2 *Isabel stepped away from Joanna and stood apart* **to one side**, aside, to the side; separately, alone, by oneself/itself; distant, isolated, cut off.
3 *his parents are now living apart* **separately**, not together, independently, on one's own; separated, divorced.
4 *he leapt out of the car just before it was blown apart* **to pieces**, to bits, in pieces; up; in two; *literary* asunder.
□ **apart from** *he was unhurt apart from a huge bump on his head* **except for**, but for, aside from, with the exception of, excepting, excluding, not including, not counting, disregarding, save, bar, barring, besides, other than; *informal* outside of.

apartment ▸ noun **1** *a rented apartment in New York* **flat**; penthouse; *Austral.* home unit; *N. Amer. informal* crib.
2 *the royal apartments* **suite (of rooms)**, set of rooms, rooms, chambers; living quarters, accommodation.

apathetic ▸ adjective *the workforce was described as apathetic and demoralized* **uninterested**, **indifferent**, unconcerned, unmoved, unresponsive, impassive, passive, detached, uninvolved, disinterested, unfeeling, unemotional, emotionless, dispassionate, lukewarm, cool, uncaring, half-hearted, lackadaisical, non-committal; listless, lethargic, languid, phlegmatic, torpid, supine, inert; bored, unmotivated, unambitious; *informal* couldn't-care-less; *Brit. vulgar slang* half-arsed; *rare* Laodicean, poco-curante.
OPPOSITES enthusiastic, eager, passionate.

apathy ▸ noun *there were reports of widespread apathy amongst the electorate* **indifference**, lack of interest, lack of enthusiasm, lack of concern, unconcern, uninterestedness, unresponsiveness, impassivity, passivity, passiveness, detachment, dispassion, dispassionateness, lack of involvement, phlegm, coolness; listlessness, lethargy, languor, lassitude, torpor; boredom, ennui, accidie; *rare* acedia, mopery.
OPPOSITES enthusiasm, interest, passion.

ape *See centre pages for list of* **Monkeys and Apes**
▸ noun **primate**, simian; monkey; *technical* anthropoid.
▸ verb *he aped Barbara's accent* **imitate**, mimic, copy, do an impression of, echo, parrot; take off, mock, parody, caricature; *informal* send up; *archaic* monkey.

WORD LINKS
relating to apes **simian**
collective noun **shrewdness**

aperture ▸ noun **opening**, hole, gap, space, slit, slot, vent, passage, crevice, chink, crack, fissure, perforation, breach, eye, interstice; *technical* orifice, foramen.

apex ▸ noun **1** *the apex of a pyramid* **tip**, peak, summit, pinnacle, top, highest point/part, crest, vertex; *rare* fastigium.
OPPOSITE bottom.
2 *the apex of his career* **climax**, culmination, culminating point, apotheosis; peak, pinnacle, summit, zenith, acme, apogee, high point, highest point, height, crowning moment, high water mark.
OPPOSITE nadir.

WORD LINKS
relating to an apex **apical**

aphorism ▸ noun **saying**, maxim, axiom, adage, precept, epigram, epigraph, dictum, gnome, pearl of wisdom, proverb, saw, tag, motto; expression, phrase, formula; *rare* apophthegm.

aphrodisiac ▸ noun **love potion**, philtre; stimulant.
▸ adjective **erotic**, sexy, sexually arousing, stimulative, stimulant; *rare* venereous.

apiece ▸ adverb *the largest stones weigh over fifty tons apiece* **each**, respectively, per item; individually, separately; *informal* a throw; *formal* severally.

aplenty ▸ adjective *the town has museums and galleries aplenty* **in abundance**, in profusion, galore, in large quantities, in large numbers, by the dozen; everywhere, all over; to spare; *informal* a gogo, by the truckload, by the shedload.

aplomb ▸ noun *he handled the crisis with surprising aplomb* **poise**, self-assurance, assurance, self-possession, self-confidence, calmness,

composure, collectedness, presence of mind, level-headedness, sangfroid, equilibrium, equanimity, nerve, nonchalance; *French* savoir faire, savoir vivre; *informal* cool, unflappability.
OPPOSITE gaucheness.

apocryphal ▸ adjective *an apocryphal story* **fictitious**, made-up, untrue, fabricated, false, spurious; imaginary, mythical, legendary; dubious, doubtful, debatable, questionable, unverified, unauthenticated, unsubstantiated, unsupported.
OPPOSITES authentic, true.

apologetic ▸ adjective *she was very apologetic about the whole incident* **regretful**, full of regret, sorry, contrite, remorseful, penitent, repentant, rueful, deprecatory, self-reproachful; conscience-stricken, red-faced, shamefaced, sheepish, hangdog, ashamed, in sackcloth and ashes; *rare* compunctious.
OPPOSITES unrepentant, impenitent; defiant.

apologia ▸ noun *Norbrook offers a spirited apologia for his methodology* **defence**, justification, vindication, explanation, apology; argument, case; plea.

apologist ▸ noun *an apologist for hard-line government policies* **defender**, supporter, upholder, advocate, proponent, exponent, propagandist, apostle, champion, backer, promoter, campaigner, spokesman, spokeswoman, spokesperson, speaker, arguer, enthusiast.
OPPOSITE critic.

apologize ▸ verb **say sorry**, express regret, be apologetic, make an apology, ask forgiveness, beg (someone's) forgiveness, ask for pardon, beg (someone's) pardon; *informal* eat humble pie, eat one's words.

apology ▸ noun **1** *I owe you an apology* **expression of regret**, one's regrets; *French* amende honorable; *Austral./NZ informal* beg-pardon.
2 *a dire apology for a decent flat* **travesty of**, excuse for, inadequate example of, poor imitation of, poor substitute for, pale shadow of, mockery of, caricature of.
3 *the Acts of the Apostles is in fact an apology for the Church* **defence**, apologia, justification, vindication.

apoplectic ▸ adjective (*informal*) *Mark was apoplectic with rage at the decision* **furious**, enraged, overcome with anger, infuriated, in a temper, incensed, raging; **incandescent**, wrathful, fuming, ranting, raving, seething, frenzied, in a frenzy, beside oneself, outraged, in high dudgeon; *informal* mad, hopping mad, wild, livid, as cross as two sticks, boiling, aerated, with all guns blazing, foaming at the mouth, fit to be tied.

apostasy ▸ noun **renunciation of belief**, abandonment of belief, recantation; treachery, perfidy, faithlessness, disloyalty, betrayal, defection, desertion; heresy; *rare* tergiversation, recreancy.
OPPOSITE loyalty.

apostate ▸ noun *after 50 years as an apostate, he returned to the faith* **dissenter**, heretic, nonconformist; defector, deserter, traitor, turncoat; schismatic; *archaic* recusant, recreant, renegade, tergiversator.
OPPOSITES follower, disciple.

apostle ▸ noun **1** *the 12 apostles of Jesus* **disciple**; follower.
2 *the Christian faith as practised by the apostles of the Slavs, Kiril and Metodije* **missionary**, evangelist, evangelical, proselytizer, spreader of the faith/word, preacher, teacher; reformer.
3 *an apostle of capitalism* **advocate**, apologist, proponent, exponent, promoter, propagandist, spokesperson, spokesman, spokeswoman, supporter, upholder, champion; campaigner, crusader, pioneer; adherent, believer; *N. Amer.* booster.
OPPOSITES opponent, critic.

apotheosis ▸ noun *his appearance as Hamlet was the apotheosis of his career* **culmination**, climax, crowning moment, peak, pinnacle, summit, zenith, apex, acme, apogee, high point, highest point, height, high water mark.
OPPOSITE nadir.

appal ▸ verb *civil-rights activists were appalled by the police brutality* **horrify**, **shock**, dismay, distress greatly, outrage, scandalize, alarm; make someone's blood run cold, make someone's hair stand on end; disgust, repel, revolt, sicken, nauseate, offend.

> **CHOOSE THE RIGHT WORD**
> **appal, dismay, horrify**
> *See* DISMAY.

appalling ▸ adjective **1** *appalling injuries | an appalling crime* **shocking**, **horrific**, horrifying, horrible, terrible, awful, dreadful, ghastly, hideous, horrendous, frightful, atrocious, abominable, abhorrent, outrageous, hateful, loathsome, odious, gruesome, grisly, monstrous, nightmarish, heinous, harrowing, dire, vile, shameful, unspeakable, unforgivable, unpardonable; abject; disgusting, revolting, repellent, repulsive, repugnant, sickening, nauseating; *rare* egregious.
2 (*informal*) *your school work is appalling* **dreadful**, very bad, awful, terrible, frightful, atrocious, disgraceful, deplorable, shameful, hopeless, lamentable, laughable, substandard, poor, inadequate, inferior, unsatisfactory; *informal* rotten, woeful, crummy, pathetic, pitiful, useless, lousy, God-awful, shocking, abysmal, dire, poxy, the pits; *Brit. informal* duff, chronic, pants; *N. Amer. informal* hellacious.
OPPOSITES admirable, excellent.

apparatus ▸ noun **1** *laboratory apparatus | an apparatus for distilling seawater* **equipment**, gear, rig, tackle, gadgetry, paraphernalia; appliance, instrument, tool, utensil, machine, mechanism, device, contraption; hardware, plant, machinery; *informal* things, stuff; *Brit. informal* gubbins.
2 *the apparatus of government* **structure**, system, framework, organization, set-up, network; hierarchy, chain of command.

apparel ▸ noun (*formal*) **clothes**, clothing, garments, dress, attire, wear, garb, wardrobe; outfit, costume; robes, vestments; *informal* gear, get-up, togs, duds; *Brit. informal* clobber, kit, rig-out; *N. Amer. informal* threads; *literary* raiment, habit, habiliments.

apparent ▸ adjective **1** *their relief was all too apparent* **evident**, plain, obvious, clear, manifest, visible, discernible, perceptible, perceivable, noticeable, detectable, recognizable, observable; unmistakable, crystal clear, as clear as crystal, transparent, palpable, patent, distinct, pronounced, marked, striking, conspicuous, overt, blatant, as plain as a pikestaff, staring someone in the face, writ large, written all over someone, as plain as day, beyond (a) doubt, beyond question, self-evident, indisputable; *informal* as plain as the nose on one's face, standing/sticking out like a sore thumb, standing/sticking out a mile.
OPPOSITES unclear, obscure.
2 *his apparent lack of concern* **seeming**, ostensible, outward, superficial, surface, supposed, presumed, so-called, alleged, professed, avowed, declared, claimed, purported, pretended, feigned; *rare* ostensive.
OPPOSITE genuine.

apparently ▸ adverb *apparently he had a mild heart attack | she sipped her tea, apparently content with his answer* **seemingly**, evidently, it seems (that), it would seem (that), it appears (that), it would appear (that), as far as one knows, by all accounts, so it seems; ostensibly, outwardly, on the face of it, to all appearances, to all intents and purposes, on the surface, so the story goes, so I'm told; allegedly, supposedly, reputedly; *rare* ostensively.

apparition ▸ noun **1** *a monstrous apparition* **ghost**, phantom, spectre, spirit, wraith, shadow, presence; vision, hallucination; *Scottish & Irish* bodach; *German* Doppelgänger; *W. Indian* duppy; *informal* spook; *literary* phantasm, shade, revenant, visitant, wight; *rare* eidolon, manes.
2 *he was startled by the apparition of a strange man* **appearance**, manifestation, materialization, emergence; visitation; arrival, advent.

appeal ▸ verb **1** *police are appealing for information* **ask urgently/earnestly**, request urgently/earnestly, make an urgent/earnest request, call, make a plea, plead, beg; sue.
2 *Andrew appealed to me to help them* **implore**, beg, beseech, entreat, call on, plead with, ask, request, petition, pray to, apply to, solicit, exhort, adjure, invoke; lobby; *rare* obtest, obsecrate, impetrate.
3 *the thought of travelling appealed to me* **attract**, be attractive to, interest, be of interest to, please, take someone's fancy, charm, engage, fascinate, intrigue, tempt, entice, allure, beguile, lure, invite, draw, whet someone's appetite; *informal* float someone's boat, tickle someone's fancy.
OPPOSITES bore, leave someone cold.
▸ noun **1** *an emotional appeal for help* **plea**, urgent/earnest request, entreaty, cry, cry from the heart, call, petition, prayer, supplication, solicitation, application, overture, suit; *French* cri de cœur; *Latin* de profundis; *archaic* orison; *rare* imploration, adjuration, obtestation, impetration, obsecration.
2 *the cultural appeal of the island | her lack of sophistication was part of her appeal* **attraction**, attractiveness, interest, allure, charm, enchantment, fascination, beauty, charisma, magnetism, temptation, seductiveness, drawing power, enticement; *informal* pull.
3 *on 13 March 1992, the Court allowed the appeal* **retrial**, reconsideration, re-examination.

appealing ▸ adjective **1** *men found her trim figure and neat little face very appealing* **attractive**, engaging, alluring, enchanting, captivating, bewitching, fascinating, winning, winsome, likeable, lovable, charming, delightful; beautiful, pretty, good-looking, prepossessing, striking, fetching, delectable, desirable; irresistible; *Scottish & N. English* bonny; *Brit. informal* tasty; *dated* taking.
OPPOSITE off-putting.
2 *flying off to the Bahamas was an appealing prospect* **inviting**, attractive, tempting, appetizing, enticing, seductive; agreeable, to one's liking, pleasant, pleasing, pleasurable; interesting, intriguing, irresistible; *informal* juicy, sexy.
OPPOSITES disagreeable, unappealing.

appear ▸ verb **1** *a cloud of dust appeared on the horizon* **become visible**, come into view, come into sight, materialize, take shape; *informal* pop up, bob up.
OPPOSITES disappear, vanish.
2 *by now, fundamental differences between them were beginning to appear* **be revealed**, be seen, emerge, manifest itself, become apparent, become

evident, surface, come to light, arise, crop up, occur, develop, enter into the picture.
3 (*informal*) *by ten o'clock Bill still hadn't appeared* **arrive**, turn up, put in an appearance, make an appearance, come, get here/there, present oneself; *informal* show up, show, show one's face, pitch up, fetch up, roll in, blow in.
4 *he and Charlotte appeared to be completely devoted* **seem**, look, give the impression of being, have the appearance/air of being, come across as being, look as though one is, look to be, strike someone as.
5 *the paperback edition didn't appear for another two years* **become available**, come on the market, go on sale, come out, be published, be produced; come into existence.
6 *he appeared on Broadway | O'Hara* **appeared as** *Captain Hook* **perform**, play, act; take the role of, take the part of.

appearance ▶ noun **1** *she was conscious of her slightly dishevelled appearance* **look(s)**, air, aspect, mien, outward form.
2 *Martha took care to keep up an appearance of respectability* **impression**, air, (outward) show, image; semblance, facade, veneer, guise, pretence, front, illusion.
3 *the sudden appearance of her daughter startled her* **arrival**, advent, coming, coming into view, emergence, materialization, surfacing.
OPPOSITES disappearance, departure.
4 *the appearance of these symptoms* **occurrence**, manifestation, development.

appease ▶ verb **1** *his action was seen as an attempt to appease critics of his regime* **conciliate**, **placate**, pacify, make peace with, propitiate, palliate, allay, reconcile, win over; calm (down), mollify, soothe, quieten down, subdue, soften, content, still, quieten, silence, tranquillize, humour; *informal* sweeten.
OPPOSITES provoke, inflame.
2 *I'd wasted a lot of money to appease my vanity* **satisfy**, fulfil, gratify, meet, fill, serve, provide for, indulge; assuage, relieve, take the edge off, deaden, dull, blunt, quench, slake, sate, diminish.
OPPOSITE frustrate.

appeasement ▶ noun **1** *the National Government's policy of appeasement* **conciliation**, **placation**, pacification, propitiation, palliation, allaying, reconciliation; **acquiescence**, acceding, concession, accommodation, peace offering, peacemaking, peace-mongering, dovishness; calming, mollification, soothing; *informal* sweetening.
OPPOSITES provocation, aggression.
2 *this was a cop-out, designed to provide appeasement for battered male consciences* **satisfaction**, fulfilment, gratification, indulgence, provision; assuagement, relief, deadening, tempering, quenching, slaking, satiation.

appellation ▶ noun (*formal*) *the city fully justifies its appellation 'the Pearl of the Orient'* **name**, **title**, designation, denomination, honorific, tag, epithet, label, sobriquet, byname, nickname; *informal* moniker, handle; *formal* cognomen.

append ▶ verb *the head teacher has the right to append comments to the final report* **add**, attach, affix, adjoin, include, put in/on; *informal* tack on, tag on; *formal* subjoin, conjoin.

appendage ▶ noun **1** *I am a person in my own right, instead of an appendage to the family* **addition**, attachment, adjunct, addendum, appurtenance, accessory, accompaniment, affix, extra, add-on, supplement, accretion, peripheral.
2 *this species has a pair of feathery appendages through which oxygen is absorbed* **protuberance**, projection, extremity, limb, organ; tail, tailpiece, arm, leg; *technical* process; *archaic* member.

appendix ▶ noun *the list was published as an appendix to the report* **supplement**, addendum, postscript, codicil; addition, extension, continuation, adjunct, appendage; coda, epilogue, afterword, rider, sequel, tailpiece, back matter; *rare* postlude.
WORD LINKS
surgical removal of appendix **appendectomy, appendicectomy**

appertain ▶ verb
□ **appertain to** *in those days, the laws appertaining to hygiene were much slacker* **pertain to**, relate to, concern, be concerned with, have to do with; be relevant to, have relevance to, apply to, be pertinent to, have reference to, have a bearing on, bear on, be connected with, be about, affect, involve, cover, deal with, touch; be part of, belong to; *archaic* regard.

appetite ▶ noun **1** *a walk before lunch sharpens the appetite* **hunger**, ravenousness, hungriness, need for food; taste, palate; desire, relish; voracity, greed, gluttony, stomach; *rare* edacity, esurience.
2 *my appetite for learning was insatiable* **craving**, longing, yearning, hankering, hunger, thirst, passion, relish, lust, love, zest, gusto, avidity, ardour; need, demand, urge, addiction, itch, ache; enthusiasm, keenness, eagerness; desire, liking, fancy, inclination, propensity, proclivity, partiality; *informal* yen; *formal* appetency.
OPPOSITE aversion.

appetizer ▶ noun *don't miss the appetizer of fried whitebait* **starter**, canapé, first course, finger food, titbit, savoury, snack; *French* hors d'oeuvre, amuse-gueule; *Italian* antipasto.

appetizing ▶ adjective **1** *an appetizing ploughman's lunch was served* **mouth-watering**, inviting, tempting; **tasty**, succulent, delicious, palatable, delectable, choice, flavoursome, luscious, toothsome; *informal* scrumptious, scrummy, yummy, yum-yum, moreish, lush; *literary* ambrosial, ambrosian.
OPPOSITES bland, off-putting.
2 *party political broadcasts are often regarded by voters as the least appetizing part of election campaigns* **appealing**, attractive, inviting, enticing, alluring, tempting, seductive, enchanting, beguiling.
OPPOSITES unappealing, off-putting.

applaud ▶ verb **1** *the audience applauded* **clap**, cheer, whistle, give a standing ovation to, put one's hands together; hail, acclaim, hurrah, hurray, shout at; show one's appreciation; ask for an encore; *informal* give someone a big hand, bring the house down.
OPPOSITES boo, hiss.
2 *police have applauded members of the public whose information has led to a series of arrests* **praise**, commend, acclaim, salute, extol, laud, admire, welcome, celebrate, express admiration for, express approval of, look on with favour, favour, approve of, sing the praises of, pay tribute to, speak highly of, take one's hat off to, pay homage to, express respect for.
OPPOSITE criticize.

applause ▶ noun **1** *everyone broke out in a massive round of applause* **clapping**, handclapping, cheering, whistling, (standing) ovation, acclamation, cheers, whistles, bravos; curtain calls, encores.
OPPOSITES booing, hissing.
2 *the museum's sloping design won general applause* **praise**, acclaim, acclamation, admiration, commendation, adulation, favour, approbation, approval, éclat, extolment, respect, eulogy; compliments, accolades, plaudits, tributes; *informal* brownie points, kudos; *rare* laudation.
OPPOSITE criticism.

appliance ▶ noun **1** *domestic appliances like microwave ovens* **device**, machine, instrument, gadget, contraption, apparatus, utensil, implement, tool, mechanism, contrivance, labour-saving device, amenity, aid; *informal* gizmo, mod con.
2 *the belief that Utopia is attainable through the appliance of science* **application**, use, exercise, employment, implementation, administration, utilization, practice, applying, discharge, exertion, execution, prosecution, enactment, carrying out, accomplishment, putting into operation/practice; *formal* praxis.

applicable ▶ adjective *there is no consensus on the laws* **applicable to** *the dispute* **relevant**, appropriate, pertinent, apposite, germane, material, felicitous, significant, related, connected; apropos of; fitting, suitable, apt, befitting, to the point, to the purpose, useful, helpful, of use; *formal* ad rem, appurtenant.
OPPOSITES inappropriate, irrelevant.

applicant ▶ noun *admissions tutors vet applicants for places at university* **candidate**, interviewee, competitor, contestant, contender, entrant; claimant, suppliant, supplicant, petitioner, suitor, postulant, prospective student/employee, aspirant, possibility, possible; job-seeker, job-hunter; auditioner.

application ▶ noun **1** *an application for an overdraft* **request**, appeal, petition, entreaty, plea, solicitation, supplication, requisition, suit, approach, enquiry, claim, demand.
2 *the application of anti-inflation policies caused many unforeseen problems* **implementation**, use, exercise, employment, administration, utilization, practice, applying, discharge, exertion, execution, prosecution, enactment, carrying out, accomplishment, putting into operation/practice; *formal* praxis.
3 *the argument is clearest in its application to the theatre* **relevance**, relevancy, bearing, significance, pertinence, aptness, appositeness, germaneness, importance.
4 *her face was scrubbed prior to the application of make-up* **putting on**, rubbing in, spreading, smearing.
5 *an application to relieve muscle pain* **ointment**, lotion, cream, rub, salve, emollient, preparation, liniment, embrocation, balm, poultice, unguent.
6 *a degree shows that you have the intelligence and application needed to hold down a job* **diligence**, industriousness, industry, assiduity, commitment, dedication, devotion, conscientiousness, perseverance, persistence, tenacity, doggedness, sedulousness; concentration, intentness, attention, attentiveness, steadiness, patience, endurance; effort, hard work, labour, striving, endeavour.
7 *a vector graphics application* **program**, software, routine, use.

apply ▶ verb **1** *more than 3,000 people had applied for the jobs* **put in an application**, put in, try, bid, appeal, petition, make an entreaty, sue, register, audition; enquire after, request, seek, solicit, claim, ask for, try to obtain.
2 *the Act did not apply to Scotland* **be relevant**, have relevance to, have a bearing on, bear on, appertain, pertain, relate, concern, be concerned with, have to do with; be pertinent, be significant, be apt, be apposite, be appropriate, be fitting, be germane; affect, involve, cover, deal with, touch.

3 *she applied ointment to the survivors' burns and bruises* **put on**, rub in, spread, smear, cover with, work in.
4 *a firm, steady pressure should be applied* **exert**, administer, implement, use, exercise, employ, utilize, practise, put into practice, execute, prosecute, enact, carry out, put to use, bring into effect/play, bring to bear.
□ **apply oneself** *if he applied himself he could be the best in the world* **be diligent**, be industrious, be assiduous, show commitment, show dedication; work hard, study hard, exert oneself, make an effort, spare no effort, try hard, do one's best, give one's all, buckle down/to, put one's shoulder to the wheel, keep one's nose to the grindstone; strive, endeavour, struggle, labour, toil; pay attention, be attentive, commit oneself, devote oneself; persevere, persist; *informal* put one's back in it, knuckle down, use some elbow grease, get stuck in.

appoint ▸ verb **1** *he was appointed Environment Secretary* **nominate**, name, designate, install as, commission, engage, adopt, co-opt; select, choose, elect, vote in; *Military* detail.
OPPOSITE reject.
2 *the arbitrator shall appoint a date for the preliminary meeting* **specify**, determine, assign, designate, allot, set, fix, arrange, choose, decide on, establish, settle, authorize, ordain, prescribe, decree.

appointed ▸ adjective **1** *I reported to HQ at the appointed time* **scheduled**, arranged, prearranged, specified, decided, agreed, determined, assigned, designated, allotted, set, fixed, chosen, established, settled, preordained, authorized, ordained, prescribed, decreed.
2 *a well appointed room with private facilities* **furnished**, decorated, outfitted, fitted out, rigged out, provided, supplied.

appointment ▸ noun **1** *she failed to keep a six o'clock appointment* **meeting**, engagement, interview, arrangement, consultation, session; date, rendezvous, assignation; commitment, fixture; *literary* tryst.
2 *the appointment of non-executive directors* **nomination**, naming, designation, designating, installation, commissioning, engagement, adoption, co-option; selection, choosing, election, voting in; *Military* detailing.
OPPOSITE rejection.
3 *he held an appointment at the University of Sheffield* **job**, post, position, situation, employment, engagement, place, office, station.

apportion ▸ verb *in many households, domestic work is not apportioned equally between partners* **share out**, divide out, allocate, distribute, allot, assign, dispense; give out, hand out, mete out, deal out, dole out; ration, parcel out, measure out; split, carve up, slice up; *informal* divvy up, dish out.

apportionment ▸ noun *the apportionment of costs* **sharing**, division, allocation, distribution, allotment, assigning, dispensation; ration; splitting, carving up, parcelling out, slicing up; *informal* divvying up.

apposite ▸ adjective *each chapter is prefaced by an apposite quotation* **appropriate**, suitable, fitting, apt, befitting; **relevant**, pertinent, to the point, to the purpose, applicable, germane, material, congruous, felicitous; *Latin* ad rem; *formal* appurtenant.
OPPOSITE inappropriate.

appraisal ▸ noun **1** *my review was an objective appraisal of the book* **assessment**, evaluation, estimation, judgement, rating, gauging, sizing up, summing-up, consideration.
2 *the price of the work leapt from $6,000, an appraisal offered in 1972, to $60,000* **valuation**, pricing, estimate, estimation, quotation, estimated price/value/cost; survey.

appraise ▸ verb **1** *the men stepped back to appraise their handiwork* **assess**, evaluate, estimate, judge, rate, gauge, sum up, review, consider; *informal* size up.
2 *his goods were appraised at £1,800* **value**, price, set a price on, estimate, quote; survey.

appreciable ▸ adjective *tea and coffee both contain appreciable amounts of caffeine* **considerable**, substantial, significant, sizeable, goodly, fair, reasonable, tidy, marked; **perceptible**, noticeable, measurable, detectable, visible.
OPPOSITE negligible.

> **CHOOSE THE RIGHT WORD**
> **appreciable, perceptible, palpable, noticeable**
> See PERCEPTIBLE.

appreciably ▸ adverb *white-collar unionization is appreciably lower in the United States* **considerably**, substantially, significantly, markedly; noticeably, measurably, perceptibly, detectably, visibly, ascertainably; greatly, much, a great deal; sizeably, fairly, reasonably, tidily.
OPPOSITE negligibly.

appreciate ▸ verb **1** *I'd appreciate any advice you can give* **be grateful for**, be thankful for, give thanks for, be obliged for, be indebted for, be beholden for, be in your debt for, be appreciative of.
OPPOSITE disparage.
2 *by this time, the college appreciated me rather more* **value**, respect, prize, cherish, treasure, admire, hold in high regard, hold in esteem, rate highly, think highly of, think much of, have a high opinion of, set (great) store by.
3 *I appreciate the problems of administration that would make this scheme impractical* **acknowledge**, recognize, realize, know; be aware of, be conscious of, be cognizant of; be alive to, be sensitive to, be alert to; sympathize with, understand, comprehend, perceive, discern; *informal* take on board, be wise to.
OPPOSITE be unaware of.
4 *with good advice a couple can buy a home that will appreciate in value* **increase**, gain, grow, build up, rise, go up, mount, inflate, escalate, soar, rocket; improve, enhance.
OPPOSITES depreciate, decrease.

appreciation ▸ noun **1** *he expressed his appreciation for the large amount of work done* **gratitude**, thanks, gratefulness, thankfulness, recognition, sense of obligation; indebtedness, obligation.
OPPOSITE ingratitude.
2 *appreciation of literature comes only from first-hand study of the works of great writers* **valuing**, respect, prizing, cherishing, treasuring, admiration, regard, esteem, high opinion.
3 *he gained an appreciation of the significance of teamwork* **acknowledgement**, recognition, realization, knowledge; awareness, consciousness, cognizance; sensitivity, alertness; sympathy, understanding, comprehension, perception, discernment.
OPPOSITE unawareness.
4 *the appreciation of the franc against the pound* **increase**, gain, growth, rise, mounting, inflation, escalation; improvement, enhancement.
OPPOSITES depreciation, decrease.
5 *an appreciation of the professor's life and work* **review**, critique, criticism, critical analysis, commentary, write-up, notice; assessment, evaluation, judgement, rating, report; praise, acclamation; *Brit. informal* crit.

appreciative ▸ adjective **1** *my colleagues and I are* **appreciative** *of all your efforts* **grateful for**, thankful for, obliged for; indebted for, beholden for; in someone's debt, obligated.
OPPOSITE ungrateful.
2 *they played in front of an appreciative audience* **supportive**, encouraging, sympathetic, responsive, enthusiastic, sensitive.
3 *Harper took a step back and gave Lucille an appreciative smile* **admiring**, approving, complimentary, flattering, praising, congratulatory, laudatory.

> **CHOOSE THE RIGHT WORD**
> **appreciative, grateful, thankful**
> See GRATEFUL.

apprehend ▸ verb **1** *the thieves were quickly apprehended* **arrest**, catch, capture, seize; take prisoner, take into custody, detain, put in jail, throw in jail, put behind bars, imprison, incarcerate; *informal* collar, nab, nail, run in, pinch, bust, pick up, pull in, haul in, do, feel someone's collar; *Brit. informal* nick.
2 *language is the only tool we have at our disposal for apprehending reality* **understand**, comprehend, realize, recognize, appreciate, discern, perceive, fathom, penetrate, catch, follow, grasp, make out, take in; *informal* get the picture, get the drift of, get the hang of, make head or tail of; *Brit. informal* twig, suss (out).

apprehension ▸ noun **1** *he had been filled with apprehension at having to report his failure* **anxiety**, angst, alarm, worry, uneasiness, unease, nervousness, misgiving, disquiet, concern, agitation, restlessness, edginess, fidgetiness, nerves, tension, trepidation, perturbation, consternation, panic, fearfulness, dread, fear, shock, horror, terror; foreboding, presentiment; *informal* butterflies in the stomach, the willies, the heebie-jeebies.
OPPOSITE confidence.
2 *she was popular because of her quick apprehension of the wishes of the people* **understanding**, grasp, comprehension, realization, recognition, appreciation, discernment, perception, awareness, cognizance, consciousness, penetration.
3 *police activity centred around the apprehension of a perpetrator* **arrest**, capture, seizure, catching; detention, imprisonment, incarceration; *informal* collaring, nabbing, nailing, pinching, bust, busting; *Brit. informal* nick.

apprehensive ▸ adjective *many of the pupils were very apprehensive about their first visit to the new school* **anxious**, alarmed, worried, uneasy, nervous, concerned, agitated, restless, edgy, on edge, fidgety, tense, strained, stressed, neurotic, panicky, afraid, scared, frightened, fearful, terrified; *informal* on tenterhooks, trepidatious.
OPPOSITE confident.

apprentice ▸ noun *on leaving school Herbert joined his father as an engineering apprentice* **trainee**, learner, probationer, tyro, novice,

neophyte, raw recruit, fledgling, new boy/girl, novitiate; pupil, student; beginner, starter; *N. Amer. informal* rookie, greenhorn, tenderfoot.
OPPOSITE veteran.

apprenticeship ▶ noun *he served an apprenticeship to a master blacksmith* **traineeship**, training period, studentship, novitiate; initiation, probationary period, trial period; *historical* indentureship.

apprise ▶ verb *he continued to keep them apprised of all that was going on in Salzburg* **inform**, notify, tell, let know, advise, brief, intimate, make aware of, send word to, update, keep posted, keep up to date, keep up to speed, enlighten; *informal* clue in, fill in, put wise, tip off, put in the picture.

approach ▶ verb **1** *she approached the altar with her head bowed* **proceed towards**, come/go towards, advance towards, go near/nearer, come near/nearer, draw near/nearer, come close/closer, go close/closer, draw close/closer, move near/nearer, edge near/nearer, near, draw near; close in on, centre on, focus on, converge on; catch up on, gain on; creep up on, loom; reach, arrive at.
OPPOSITE leave.
2 *the trade deficit is now approaching £20 million* **border on**, approximate, verge on, resemble; be comparable/similar to, compare with; touch, nudge, get on for; near, come near to, come/be close to; *informal* be not a million miles away from.
3 *the publishing tycoon approached him about leaving his job* **speak to**, talk to, make conversation with, engage in conversation; take aside, detain; greet, address, salute, hail, initiate a discussion with; broach the matter to, make advances to, make overtures to, make a proposal to, sound out, proposition, solicit, appeal to, apply to; *informal* buttonhole.
4 *he had approached the whole business in the best way* **set about**, tackle, begin, start, commence, embark on, make a start on, address oneself to, undertake, get down to, launch into, go about, get to grips with; *informal* get cracking on.
▶ noun **1** *the traditional British approach to air pollution control* **attitude**, slant, perspective, point of view, viewpoint, outlook, line of attack, line of action; **method**, procedure, process, technique, MO, style, strategy, stratagem, way, manner, mode, tactic, tack, path, system, means; *Latin* modus operandi.
2 *doctors are considering an approach to the High Court* **proposal**, proposition, submission, motion, offer, application, appeal, plea.
3 (**approaches**) (*dated*) *he found all his approaches repulsed* **advances**, overtures, suggestions, attentions; suit.
4 *at the approach of any intruder, she would raise her wings and screech* **advance**, coming near/nearer, coming, nearing, advent; **arrival**, entrance, appearance.
5 *this department is our nearest approach to a Ministry of Justice* **approximation**, likeness, semblance, correspondence, parallel.
6 *two riders turned in at the approach to the castle* **driveway**, drive, access road, road, avenue, street, passageway.

approachable ▶ adjective **1** *most students said that they found the staff approachable* **friendly**, welcoming, pleasant, agreeable, congenial, affable, cordial, well disposed, obliging, communicative, open, hospitable, helpful; informal, easy-going, accessible, available, easy to get on/along with; *informal* unstuffy.
OPPOSITES aloof, unapproachable.
2 *the south landing is approachable by boat* **accessible**, attainable, reachable, obtainable; *informal* get-at-able, come-at-able.
OPPOSITE inaccessible.

approbation ▶ noun *he yearned for popular approbation* **approval**, acceptance, assent, endorsement, encouragement, recognition, appreciation, support, respect, admiration, commendation, congratulations; **praise**, acclamation, adulation, regard, esteem, veneration, kudos, applause, ovation, accolades, salutes, plaudits; *rare* laudation.
OPPOSITE criticism.

appropriate ▶ adjective *refer to the appropriate page of the atlas | this isn't the appropriate time or place* **suitable**, proper, fitting, apt; **relevant**, connected, pertinent, apposite, applicable, germane, material, significant, right, congruous, to the point, to the purpose; convenient, expedient, favourable, auspicious, propitious, opportune, felicitous, timely, well judged, well timed, seasonable; seemly, befitting, deserved; *Latin* ad rem; *formal* appurtenant; *archaic* meet.
OPPOSITES inappropriate; irrelevant.
▶ verb **1** *he acquired resources by appropriating local church lands* **seize**, commandeer, expropriate, annex, arrogate, sequestrate, sequester, take possession of, take over, assume, secure, acquire, wrest, usurp, claim, lay claim to, hijack.
2 *allegations that he had appropriated DM40,000 had led to his dismissal* **steal**, take, misappropriate; thieve, pilfer, pocket, purloin, make off with; embezzle; *informal* swipe, nab, rip off, lift, filch, snaffle, snitch, bag, walk off/away with, 'abstract', 'borrow', 'liberate'; *Brit. informal* pinch, nick, half-inch, whip, knock off; *rare* peculate, defalcate.
3 *there can be constitutional problems in appropriating funds for these expenses* **allocate**, assign, allot, earmark, set apart/aside, devote, apportion, budget.
4 *his images have been appropriated by advertisers* **plagiarize**, copy, reproduce; poach, steal, 'borrow', bootleg, infringe the copyright of; *informal* pirate, rip off, crib, lift.

CHOOSE THE RIGHT WORD

appropriate, suitable, proper, fitting

- Something that is **appropriate** suits a particular situation (*she searched for an appropriate word | we need care packages appropriate to people's needs*). The word may convey pleasure or satisfaction at the particular relevance of something (*it is appropriate that healing should still be important in the village where the Red Cross was born*), or it can be used if you want to persuade others, by slight subterfuge, to agree with you that something is desirable (*we consider it is now appropriate to consult interested individuals and agencies*). *Appropriate* is often used for something that is socially acceptable (*society seems to think it is appropriate for little girls to shed tears*).
- **Suitable** is a more general word for things that are right for a particular purpose or occasion, and they need not be the only correct or possible ones (*he may be able to find suitable alternative work | the site isn't suitable for residential use*).
- A **proper** person or thing may well be the only correct person or thing for a purpose or a job (*inquiries should be addressed to the proper officer | medium-sized and larger building firms should carry out proper training*). In this sense, *proper* is always used before the noun it qualifies. *Proper* is also used to mean 'socially acceptable' (*her parents' view of what was proper for a well-bred girl*).
- Something that is **fitting** (the least common word of this group) is particularly apposite, and usually desirable (*his election as president of the society was a fitting tribute | it was very fitting that the late Sgt Day's brother and sister were among the guests*).

approval ▶ noun **1** *proposals for the licensing system will now go forward to the ministry for approval* **acceptance**, agreement, consent, assent, acquiescence, compliance, concurrence; blessing, imprimatur, seal/stamp of approval, rubber stamp; sanction, endorsement, ratification, authorization, mandate, licence, validation; confirmation, support, backing; permission, leave; *informal* the go-ahead, the green light, the OK, the thumbs up, the nod, say-so.
OPPOSITE refusal.
2 *Lily looked at him with approval* **approbation**, appreciation, favour, liking, encouragement, support, acceptance; admiration, regard, esteem, respect, commendation, applause, acclaim, acclamation, praise.
OPPOSITE disapproval.
□ **on approval** *we would be happy to send you a selection on approval* **on trial**, under probation; on sale or return; *Brit. informal* on appro.

approve ▶ verb **1** *his boss doesn't approve of his party-boy lifestyle* **agree with**, hold with, endorse, support, back, uphold, subscribe to, recommend, advocate, second, express one's approval of, be in favour of, favour, think well of, like, look on with favour, give one's blessing to, tolerate, appreciate, countenance, take kindly to; be pleased with, admire, hold in regard/esteem, commend, embrace, applaud, acclaim, praise; *informal* go along with.
OPPOSITES condemn, disapprove.
2 *the government has approved proposals for a new waste law* **accept**, agree to, consent to, assent to, acquiesce in, concur in, accede to, give one's blessing to, bless, give one's seal/stamp of approval to, rubber-stamp, say yes to; ratify, sanction, endorse, authorize, mandate, license, warrant, validate, pass; confirm, support, back; give one's permission/leave; *informal* give the go-ahead to, give the green light to, give the OK to, OK, give the thumbs up to, give the nod, say the word, buy.
OPPOSITE refuse.

approving ▶ adjective *Gina paused to pass her approving gaze around the rest of the room* **admiring**, appreciative, appreciating, favourable, respectful, esteeming, commendatory, commending, applauding, acclamatory, acclaiming, praising, flattering, congratulatory, rapturous; *formal* encomiastic, eulogistic, laudatory, panegyrical.
OPPOSITE critical.

approximate ▶ adjective *all measurements are approximate and for guidance only* **estimated**, rough, imprecise, inexact; near, close; indefinite, broad, loose, general, vague, hazy, fuzzy, woolly; *N. Amer. informal* ballpark.
OPPOSITE precise.
▶ verb *research shows that this scenario probably approximates to the truth* **be close to**, be near to, come close to, come near to, approach, border on, verge on, equal roughly; be similar to, resemble, correspond to, compare with, be tantamount to, be not dissimilar to, be not unlike; touch, nudge, get on for.
OPPOSITE be nothing like.

approximately ▶ adverb *approximately £1 million* **roughly**, about,

around, just about, round about, or so, or thereabouts, more or less, in the neighbourhood of, in the region of, in the area of, in the vicinity of, of the order of, something like, or thereabouts, give or take (a few), in round numbers, rounded up/down; near to, close to, nearly, not far off, almost, approaching; *Brit.* getting on for; *Latin* circa; *informal* pushing, as near as dammit; *N. Amer. informal* in the ballpark of; *archaic* nigh.
OPPOSITE precisely.

approximation ▶ noun **1** *a general approximation is that a ten degree rise in temperature doubles the rate of reaction* **estimate**, estimation, guess, conjecture, rough calculation, rough idea, surmise; guesswork; *informal* guesstimate; *N. Amer. informal* ballpark figure.
2 *we can only look for an approximation to the truth about these matters* **semblance**, outward appearance, likeness, resemblance, similarity, correspondence, comparison.

appurtenances ▶ plural noun *the corrupting appurtenances of modern civilization* **accessories**, trappings, appendages, accoutrements, extras, additions, adjuncts, conveniences, incidentals; equipment, paraphernalia, impedimenta, belongings, bits and pieces; *informal* things, stuff.

appurtenant ▶ adjective (*formal*) *the lands appurtenant to his forestership* **pertinent**, belonging, relevant, related, relating, connected, appertaining, appropriate, apposite, applicable, material, germane; *Latin* ad rem.
OPPOSITE unconnected.

April ▶ noun
WORD LINKS
birthstone **diamond**

a priori ▶ adjective *he argued that Conservatism was based on an observation of life, and not a priori reasoning* **theoretical**, deduced, deductive, inferred, scientific; postulated, suppositional, self-evident.
OPPOSITE empirical.
▶ adverb *the words were not necessarily the ones which would have been predicted a priori* **theoretically**, from theory, deductively, scientifically.
OPPOSITE empirically.

apron ▶ noun *a striped butcher's apron* pinafore, overall; *informal* pinny.

apropos ▶ preposition *value judgements apropos of particular works of art | he was asked a question apropos the recent resignation* **with reference to**, with regard to, with respect to, regarding, concerning, respecting, on the subject of, in the matter of, touching on, dealing with, connected with, in connection with, about, re; *Scottish* anent.
□ **apropos of nothing** *suddenly, apropos of nothing, he asked, 'What made you decide your engagement was a mistake?'* **irrelevantly**, arbitrarily, at random, for no reason, illogically.
▶ adjective *the word 'conglomerate' was decidedly apropos* **appropriate**, pertinent, relevant, apposite, apt, applicable, suitable, germane, material, becoming, befitting, significant, to the point/purpose; opportune, felicitous, timely.
OPPOSITE inappropriate.

apt ▶ adjective **1** *this is an apt place to celebrate the end of a great walk* **suitable**, fitting, appropriate, befitting, relevant, felicitous, congruous, fit, applicable, judicious, apposite, apropos, to the purpose, to the point; perfect, ideal, right, just right, made to order, tailor-made; convenient, expedient, useful, timely; *informal* spot on.
OPPOSITE inappropriate.
2 *men left to themselves are apt to get a mite slipshod about meals* **inclined**, given, likely, liable, disposed, predisposed, prone, ready, tending, subject, of a mind, capable.
OPPOSITE unlikely.
3 *an apt pupil* **clever**, quick, bright, sharp, quick to learn, smart, intelligent; able, gifted, talented, adept, proficient, competent, astute.
OPPOSITE slow.

aptitude ▶ noun *he showed an aptitude for skiing* **talent**, gift, flair, bent, skill, knack, facility, finesse, genius; ability, proficiency, competence, capability, potential, capacity, faculty; expertise, expertness, adeptness, prowess, mastery, artistry; propensity, inclination, natural ability, suitability, fitness; head, mind, brain; *informal* know-how.

aptness ▶ noun *he was surprised at the aptness of the comparison* **suitability**, appropriateness, relevance, fitness, felicity, congruity, applicability, pertinence, judiciousness, appositeness, becomingness; convenience, expedience, usefulness, timeliness; correctness, rightness.
OPPOSITE inappropriateness.

aquatic ▶ adjective *aquatic plants* **water**; sea, marine, maritime, saltwater, seawater, oceanic; freshwater, river, fluvial; *rare* pelagic, thalassic.

aqueduct ▶ noun **conduit**, race, channel, watercourse, waterway, sluice, sluiceway, spillway; bridge, viaduct.

aquiline ▶ adjective *he had an aquiline nose* **hooked**, curved, hook-shaped, hook-like, bent, bowed, angular; *technical* falcate, falciform.
OPPOSITE straight.

arable ▶ adjective *acres of arable land* **farmable**, cultivable, cultivatable, ploughable, tillable; fertile, productive, fruitful, fecund, lush.
OPPOSITE infertile.

arachnid ▶ noun. *See centre pages for list of* **Spiders and Other Arachnids**

arbiter ▶ noun **1** *he believed that Britain could play a major role as arbiter between Moscow and Washington. See* ARBITRATOR.
2 *the great arbiter of fashion* **judge**, **authority**, determiner, controller, director, governor, master, expert, pundit, critic.

arbitrary ▶ adjective **1** *an arbitrary decision from the top* **capricious**, whimsical, random, chance, erratic, unpredictable, inconsistent, wild, hit-or-miss, haphazard, casual; **unmotivated**, motiveless, unreasoned, unreasonable, unsupported, irrational, illogical, groundless, unjustifiable, unjustified, wanton; discretionary, personal, subjective; *rare* discretional.
OPPOSITES rational, reasoned.
2 *the arbitrary power of a prince* **despotic**, tyrannical, tyrannous, peremptory, summary, autocratic, dictatorial, authoritarian, draconian, autarchic; oppressive, repressive, undemocratic, illiberal; imperious, domineering, high-handed; absolute, uncontrolled, unlimited, unrestrained.
OPPOSITES democratic, accountable.

arbitrate ▶ verb *James II offered to arbitrate in the dispute* **adjudicate**, judge, adjudge, referee, umpire, sit in judgement, pass judgement, pronounce judgement, give a verdict, make a ruling; **mediate**, negotiate, conciliate, intervene, intercede, interpose, step in, make peace, act as peacemaker; settle, decide, determine, resolve.

arbitration ▶ noun *the council called for arbitration to settle the dispute* **adjudication**, **mediation**, mediatorship, negotiation, conciliation, intervention, interceding, interposition, peacemaking; judgement; *rare* arbitrament.

arbitrator ▶ noun *the facts of the case were put to an independent arbitrator* **adjudicator**, arbiter, judge, referee, umpire; mediator, conciliator, intervenor, intercessor, go-between, negotiator, peacemaker.

arbour ▶ noun *behind the orange blossom was a little arbour with a stone bench* **bower**, alcove, grotto, recess, pergola, gazebo, summer house; shady place, shelter, hideaway, retreat, sanctuary.

arc ▶ noun *the arc of a circle* **curve**, bend, bow, arch; crescent, semicircle, circular section/line, half-moon; curvature, convexity, curling.
▶ verb *I sent the ball arcing out over the river* **curl**, curve, swerve, spin, turn; **soar**, sail, fly, ascend, mount, climb.

arcade ▶ noun **1** *they walked on, past a classical arcade* gallery, colonnade, cloister, loggia, portico, forum, peristyle, stoa.
2 *she went to a cafe in an arcade* **shopping centre**, shopping precinct, shopping complex; *N. Amer.* plaza, mall, strip mall, shopping mall.

arcane ▶ adjective *the arcane world of the legal profession* **mysterious**, secret, hidden, concealed, covert, clandestine, enigmatic, dark; esoteric, obscure, abstruse, recondite, little known, recherché, inscrutable, impenetrable, opaque, incomprehensible, cryptic, occult.
OPPOSITES well known, open.

CHOOSE THE RIGHT WORD
arcane, obscure, abstruse, recondite, esoteric
See OBSCURE.

arch[1] ▶ noun **1** *a stone arch was built at the entrance* **archway**, vault, span, dome; bridge.
2 *the arch of the spine* **curve**, bow, bend, arc, semicircle, sweep; curvature, convexity, curving, curling, bending, flex; hunch, crook.
▶ verb *she arched her eyebrows and shrugged* **curve**, bow, bend, arc, curl.

arch[2] ▶ adjective *'I wonder for how long!' he said in a somewhat arch tone* **knowing**, **playful**, mischievous, puckish, roguish, impish, elfin, devilish, naughty, wicked, cheeky, teasing, saucy, flippant, tongue-in-cheek; artful, sly, cunning, affected; *archaic* frolicsome.

arch- ▶ combining form *archbishop | arch-enemy* **chief**, principal, foremost, leading, main, pre-eminent, cardinal, major, prime, premier, elite, star, outstanding, ultra-, super-; top, highest, greatest, best, first, head; out-and-out, complete, utter, total; *informal* number-one, numero uno.
OPPOSITES minor, pseudo-.

archaic ▶ adjective *an archaic word | archaic conventions* **obsolete**, obsolescent, out of date, anachronistic, old-fashioned, outmoded, behind the times, bygone, antiquated, antique, superannuated, antediluvian, past its prime, having seen better days, olde worlde, old-fangled; **ancient**, very old, aged, prehistoric, primitive, of yore; extinct, defunct, discontinued, discarded, fossilized, dead; *French* passé, démodé; *informal* old hat, out of the ark.
OPPOSITES new, modern.

archbishop ▶ noun
WORD LINKS
relating to an archbishop **archiepiscopal**

arched ▶ adjective *a great arched ceiling* **vaulted**, curved, domed, rounded,

bowed; *formal* embowed.

archer ▶ noun **bowman**.

WORD LINKS
archery **toxophily**

archetypal ▶ adjective *Blackpool is the archetypal British seaside resort* **most typical**, most characteristic, representative, standard, conventional, classic, model, exemplary, quintessential, prime, textbook, copybook; stock, stereotypical, prototypical, paradigmatic, illustrative; average, clichéd, trite, hackneyed.
OPPOSITES atypical, unique.

archetype ▶ noun *an archetype of the old-style football-club chairman* **typification**, type, prototype, representative, stereotype; original, pattern, model, standard, mould; embodiment, exemplar, essence, quintessence, textbook example, paradigm, ideal, idea.

architect ▶ noun **1** *the great Norman architect of Durham Cathedral* **designer**, planner, builder, building consultant, draughtsman.
2 *Aneurin Bevan, architect of the National Health Service* **originator**, author, creator, instigator, founder, father, mother, founding father, prime mover; engineer, designer, deviser, planner, shaper, inventor, maker, producer, contriver, mastermind; cause, agent; *literary* begetter.

architecture *See centre pages for lists of* **Architectural Styles** **Architectural Terms**
▶ noun **1** *schools of architecture and design* **building design**, planning, building, construction; *formal* architectonics.
2 *an example of modern architecture* **building style**, design, structure, construction, framework.
3 *the architecture of a computer system* **structure**, construction, form, formation, shape, composition, organization, layout, design, build, anatomy, make-up, constitution; *informal* set-up.

WORD LINKS
relating to architecture **architectonic**
study of architecture **architectonics**

archive ▶ noun **1** **(archives)** *if you delve into the family archives you'll find that their marriage was a very happy one* **records**, annals, chronicles, registers, accounts; papers, documents, rolls, dossiers, files, deeds, ledgers; history, information, evidence; documentation, paperwork; *formal* muniments.
2 *more and more museums, archives, and libraries are becoming independent* **record office**, registry, repository, museum, chancery.
▶ verb *these videos are archived for future use* **file**, log, catalogue, pigeonhole; **store**, record, register, chronicle, cache; document, put on record, post.

arctic ▶ adjective **1** **(Arctic)** *iceberg movement in Arctic waters* **polar**; **far northern**, northern, northerly; *rare* boreal, hyperborean.
OPPOSITE Antarctic.
2 *February brought arctic conditions* **(bitterly) cold**, intensely cold, frosty, wintry; freezing, frigid, frozen, icy, ice-cold, glacial, sub-zero, polar, Siberian; bitter, biting, piercing, cutting, raw, extreme; *rare* gelid, brumal, rimy, algid.
OPPOSITE tropical.
▶ noun **(the Arctic) the far north**, the North Pole, the Arctic circle.
OPPOSITE the Antarctic.

ardent ▶ adjective *an ardent feminist* **passionate**, avid, impassioned, fervent, fervid, zealous, wholehearted, eager, vehement, intense, fierce, fiery, flaming, emotional, hot-blooded; earnest, sincere; enthusiastic, keen, committed, dedicated, assiduous; *informal* mad keen.
OPPOSITE half-hearted.

ardour ▶ noun *she was unaccustomed to being kissed with such ardour* **passion**, avidity, fervour, zeal, wholeheartedness, eagerness, vehemence, intensity, fierceness, zest, gusto, energy, animation, fire, fieriness, emotion, emotionalism, feeling, hot-bloodedness; earnestness, sincerity; enthusiasm, keenness, dedication, devotion, assiduity, readiness; *archaic* empressement.

arduous ▶ adjective *she was now faced with an arduous journey into a remote country* **onerous**, taxing, difficult, hard, heavy, laborious, burdensome, strenuous, vigorous, back-breaking, stiff, uphill, relentless, Herculean; demanding, trying, tough, challenging, formidable, exacting; exhausting, wearying, fatiguing, tiring, punishing, gruelling, grinding; intolerable, unbearable, murderous, harrowing; *informal* killing, no picnic; *Brit. informal* knackering; *archaic* toilsome; *rare* exigent.
OPPOSITES easy, effortless.

area *See centre pages for lists of* **Districts**
▶ noun **1** *an inner-city area* **district**, region, zone, sector, quarter; locality, locale, neighbourhood, community, domain, realm, sphere, environment, territory; part, section, parish, spot, patch; tract, stretch, sweep, belt; *informal* neck of the woods; *Brit. informal* manor; *N. Amer. informal* turf.
2 *most of these attainments relate to specific areas of scientific knowledge* **domain**, sector, department, province, territory, compartment, line; field, sphere, discipline, realm.
3 *the dining area* **section**, space, sector, part, portion.
4 *he climbed over the area railings* **(sunken) enclosure**, yard.
5 *the area of a circle varies with the square of its radius* **expanse**, extent, size, scope, compass; measurements, dimensions, proportions; square footage, acreage.

WORD LINKS
measurement of area **planimetry**

arena ▶ noun **1** *an ice-hockey arena* **stadium**, amphitheatre, theatre, coliseum; ground, field, ring, rink, pitch, court, stage, platform; (*in ancient Rome*) circus, hippodrome; *N. Amer.* bowl; *informal* park; *rare* cirque.
2 *not all interest groups are able to compete in the political arena* **area**, scene, sphere, realm, province, domain, sector, forum, territory, theatre, stage, world; battleground, battlefield, area/field of conflict, sphere of action/activity, lists.

argot ▶ noun *the argot of CB radio* **jargon**, slang, idiom, cant, dialect, parlance, patter, speech, vernacular, patois, terminology, language, tongue, -speak; *informal* lingo.

arguable ▶ adjective **1** *with hindsight, it is arguable that the relationship should have been more precisely defined* **tenable**, maintainable, assertable, defendable, defensible, supportable, sustainable, able to hold water; reasonable, rational, viable, workable, credible, believable, feasible, conceivable, acceptable, imaginable.
OPPOSITE untenable.
2 *it is arguable whether such conditions existed anyway* **debatable**, disputable, questionable, open to question, controversial, contentious, open to debate, doubtful, open to doubt, dubious, uncertain, unsure, moot.
OPPOSITE certain.

arguably ▶ adverb *these criteria are exceedingly vague and arguably provide too much scope for judicial interpretation* **possibly**, conceivably, feasibly, plausibly, probably, maybe, perhaps, potentially; debatably, contestably, controversially.

argue ▶ verb **1** *critics argued that the government had been to blame for the country's economic problems* **contend**, assert, declare, maintain, state, proclaim, advance, insist, hold, claim, aver, avow, reason, attest, expostulate, testify, swear, certify; propound, submit, posit, postulate, adduce, move, advocate, opine, allege; make a case for, give reasons for, defend, explain, vindicate, justify; *technical* depose, represent; *rare* asseverate.
2 *the children are always arguing* **quarrel**, disagree, row, squabble, bicker, fight, wrangle, dispute, feud, have a row, bandy words, have words, cross swords, lock horns, be at each other's throats; dissent, clash, differ, be at odds; *informal* fall out, scrap, argy-bargy, argufy, spat, go at it hammer and tongs, fight like cat and dog; *archaic* altercate.
3 *it is hard to argue the point* **dispute**, debate, discuss, controvert.
□ **argue someone into something** *it would be better to argue her into going back home* **persuade to**, convince to, prevail on to, coax into; talk someone round.
□ **argue someone out of something** *Vivienne had argued Malcolm out of one of his crazier ideas* **dissuade from**, persuade against, talk out of.

CHOOSE THE RIGHT WORD
argue, quarrel, wrangle, dispute, bicker
See QUARREL.

argument ▶ noun **1** *he had a long argument with Tony* **quarrel**, disagreement, squabble, fight, difference of opinion, dispute, wrangle, clash, altercation, feud, dissension, war of words, contretemps, exchange of views; debate, discussion, discourse, disputation, controversy; *informal* tiff, barney, set-to, dust-up, bust-up, shouting/slanging match, spat, ding-dong, falling-out; *Brit. informal* row; *Scottish informal* rammy.
2 *his arguments for the existence of God* **reasoning**, line of reasoning, logic, case; defence, justification, vindication, apology, explanation, rationalization; evidence, reasons, grounds; argumentation, polemic; assertion, declaration, claim, plea, contention, expostulation, demonstration.
3 (*archaic*) *the argument of the book* **theme**, topic, subject matter; gist, outline, summary, synopsis, abstract, precis; plot, storyline.

argumentative ▶ adjective *he was argumentative, opinionated, and outspoken* **quarrelsome**, disputatious, bickering, wrangling, captious, contrary, cantankerous, contentious, litigious, dissentient, polemical; belligerent, bellicose, combative, antagonistic, aggressive, truculent, pugnacious; *rare* oppugnant.
OPPOSITE compliant.

arid ▶ adjective **1** *an arid landscape* **dry**, dried up, waterless, as dry as a bone, moistureless, parched, scorched, baked, thirsty; dehydrated, desiccated; **barren**, desert, waste, desolate; infertile, non-fertile, unfruitful, unproductive, uncultivatable, sterile; *rare* infecund, droughty, torrefied.
OPPOSITES wet; fertile.
2 *this town has an arid, empty feel* **dreary**, dull, drab, dry, sterile, banal, colourless, monochrome, unstimulating, uninspiring, flat, boring,

uninteresting, monotonous, lifeless, tedious, vapid, jejune, soul-destroying.
OPPOSITES interesting, vibrant.

aright ▶ adverb (*dated*) *I can't believe that I'm hearing you aright* **correctly**, rightly, right, all right; accurately, properly, exactly, precisely, perfectly, unerringly, faultlessly, truly; *informal* OK.

arise ▶ verb **1** *if any problems arise, go to the Citizens' Advice Bureau* **come to light**, become apparent, make an appearance, appear, emerge, crop/turn up, come about, surface, spring up, enter into the picture; **occur**, ensue, set in, transpire, come into being/existence, begin, commence; *literary* befall, come to pass.
2 *manufacturers are liable for all losses* **arising from** *defective products* **result**, proceed, follow, ensue, derive, stem, accrue; originate, emanate, spring, flow; be caused by, be brought about by, be produced by.
3 (*formal*) *the beast stretched his legs and arose* **stand up**, rise, get to one's feet, get up, jump up, leap up, spring up; become erect, straighten up.
OPPOSITES sit down, lie down.

aristocracy ▶ noun (**the aristocracy**) **the nobility**, the peerage, the gentry, the upper class, the ruling class, the privileged class, the elite, high society, the establishment, the patriciate, the haut monde, the beau monde; aristocrats, lords, ladies, peers, peers of the realm, nobles, noblemen, noblewomen, titled men/women/people, patricians; *informal* the upper crust, the jet set, the beautiful people, the crème de la crème, the top drawer, aristos; *Brit. informal* nobs, toffs.
OPPOSITES the working class, the common people, the masses.

aristocrat ▶ noun *a decadent old blue-blooded aristocrat* **nobleman**, noblewoman, lord, lady, peer, peeress, peer of the realm, patrician, grandee, titled man/woman/person; *informal* aristo, top person, member of the upper crust; *Brit. informal* toff, nob, chinless wonder; *rare* optimate.
OPPOSITE commoner.

aristocratic ▶ adjective **1** *an aristocratic family* **noble**, titled, upper-class, blue-blooded, high-born, well born, patrician, elite; grand, distinguished, respectable; born with a silver spoon in one's mouth, silver-spoon; *informal* posh, upper crust, upmarket, top drawer; *archaic* gentle, of gentle birth.
OPPOSITES plebeian, working-class.
2 *he had a stately, aristocratic manner* **well bred**, dignified, courtly; refined, polished, elegant, stylish; decorous, gracious, fine, polite, well mannered, civil, courteous, chivalrous, gallant, gentlemanly, ladylike, urbane, suave, debonair; haughty, proud; *informal* snobbish.
OPPOSITES vulgar, coarse.

arm[1] ▶ noun **1** *she flapped her arms like wings* **upper limb**, forelimb, appendage; *archaic* member.
2 *a jacket with the arms hacked off* **sleeve**.
3 *an arm of the sea* **inlet**, creek, cove, fjord, bay, voe; estuary, firth; branch, strait(s), neck, narrows, sound, channel, passage, stretch of water, waterway.
4 *the political arm of the separatist group* **branch**, section, department, division, subdivision, wing, sector, chapter, lodge, detachment, agency, office, bureau, offshoot, satellite, extension.
5 *the long arm of the law* **reach**, power, force, authority, strength, might, potency.

WORD LINKS
relating to an arm **brachial**

arm[2] ▶ verb **1** *he had armed himself with a revolver* **provide**, supply, equip, furnish, issue, fit out, fit up, outfit, rig out, accoutre, gird, provision, stock.
2 *one has to arm oneself against criticism* **prepare**, forearm, make ready, brace, steel, fortify; *archaic* gird one's loins.

armada ▶ noun *an armada of forty-five warships* **fleet**, flotilla, squadron, navy, naval force, (naval) task force.

armaments ▶ plural noun **arms**, weapons (of war), weaponry, firearms, guns, ordnance, cannon, artillery, munitions, instruments of war, war machines, military supplies, materiel.

armistice ▶ noun *an armistice was concluded between all the warring countries* **truce**, ceasefire, suspension of hostilities, cessation of hostilities, peace; break, respite, lull, moratorium; treaty, peace treaty; *informal* let-up.
OPPOSITES declaration of war; hostilities.

armour *See centre pages for list of parts of a suit of* **Armour**
▶ noun *a suit of armour* **protective covering**, armour plate; covering, protection, sheathing, shield; *historical* chain armour, chain mail, coat of mail, panoply.

armoured ▶ adjective *an armoured vehicle* **armour-plated**, steel-plated, ironclad, mailed; bulletproof, bombproof, mineproof, reinforced, protected, toughened.

armoury ▶ noun **arsenal**, arms depot, arms cache, ordnance depot, magazine, ammunition dump.

arms *See centre pages for lists of* **Bombs and Mines** **Guns** **Projectiles** **Weapons**
▶ plural noun **1** *arms and ammunition* **weapons (of war)**, weaponry, firearms, guns, ordnance, cannon, artillery, armaments, munitions, instruments of war, war machines, military supplies, materiel.
2 *the family arms* **crest**, emblem, heraldic device, coat of arms, armorial bearing, insignia, escutcheon, shield, heraldry, blazonry.

army *See centre pages for lists of* **Ranks** **Soldiers**
▶ noun **1** *the invading army* **armed force**, fighting force, defence force, military force, the military, land force, soldiery, infantry, militia, horde; troops, soldiers, land forces; *informal, dated* thin red line; *archaic* host.
2 *an army of tourists* **crowd**, swarm, multitude, horde, host, mob, gang, throng, stream, mass, body, band, troop, legion, flock, herd, pack, drove, sea, array; *literary* myriad.

WORD LINKS
relating to armies **military, martial**

aroma ▶ noun *the tantalizing aroma of fresh coffee* **smell**, odour, fragrance, scent, perfume, whiff, redolence, tang, savour, bouquet, nose.

aromatic ▶ adjective *an aromatic herb* **fragrant**, scented, sweet-scented, sweet-smelling, perfumed, fragranced, odoriferous; piquant, spicy, savoury, pungent; *literary* redolent; *rare* aromatized, balmy.
OPPOSITE foul-smelling.

around ▶ adverb **1** *there were houses scattered around* **on every side**, on all sides, in all directions, throughout, all over, all over the place, everywhere, about, here and there.
2 *he turned around to face her* **in the opposite direction**, in the reverse direction, to face the other way, backwards, to the rear.
3 *there was no one around* **nearby**, near, about, close by, close, at hand, close at hand, in the vicinity, in the neighbourhood, on the doorstep, (just) round the corner, within (easy) reach, at close range, hard by; accessible, handy, convenient.
▶ preposition **1** *the palazzo is built around a courtyard* **on every side of**, on all sides of, about, circling, encircling, surrounding, encompassing, framing.
2 *they drove around town* **all over**, about, here and there in, everywhere in, in/to all parts of.
3 *around three miles* **approximately**, about, round about, roughly, in the region of, something like, in the area of, in the neighbourhood of, of the order of, or so, or thereabouts, there or thereabouts, more or less, give or take a few, plus or minus a few; nearly, close to, as near as dammit, not far off, approaching; *Brit.* getting on for; *S. African* plus-minus; *Latin* circa; *N. Amer. informal* in the ballpark of.

WORD LINKS
related prefix **amphi- (e.g. *amphitheatre*)**

arouse ▶ verb **1** *they had aroused his hostility and suspicion* **cause**, induce, prompt, set off, trigger, stir up, inspire, call forth, call/bring into being, draw forth, bring out, excite, evoke, pique, whet, stir, engender, generate, kindle, fire, touch off, spark off, provoke, foster, whip up, sow the seeds of; *literary* enkindle.
OPPOSITE allay.
2 *an ability to influence the audience and to arouse the masses* **stir up**, rouse, excite, galvanize, electrify, stimulate, inspire, move, fire up, fire the enthusiasm of, fire the imagination of, get going, whip up, inflame, agitate, goad, provoke, spur on, urge, encourage, animate, incite, egg on; *N. Amer.* light a fire under; *rare* inspirit.
OPPOSITE pacify.
3 *his touch aroused her* **excite**, arouse sexually, stimulate, make feel sexually excited, make feel sexy, titillate; please, attract; *informal* turn on, get going, give someone a thrill, float someone's boat, do it for someone, light someone's fire, tickle someone's fancy.
OPPOSITE turn off.
4 *she was aroused from her sleep by her mother* **wake**, wake up, waken, awaken, bring to, bring around, rouse; *Brit. informal* knock up.
OPPOSITE send to sleep.

arraign ▶ verb **1** *he was arraigned for murder* **indict**, prosecute, put on trial, bring to trial; denounce, sue, take to court, bring an action against, lay charges against, file charges against, prefer charges against, summons, cite; accuse of, charge with; *N. Amer.* impeach; *informal* have the law on, do; *archaic* inculpate.
OPPOSITES clear, acquit.
2 *the soldiers bitterly arraigned the government for failing to keep its word* **criticize**, censure, attack, condemn, castigate, chastise, lambaste, pillory, find fault with, reprimand, rebuke, admonish, remonstrate with, take to task, haul over the coals, berate, reproach, reprove; *informal* knock, slam, hammer, lay into, roast, give someone a roasting, cane, blast, bawl out, dress down, rap over the knuckles, give someone hell; *Brit. informal* carpet, slate, slag off, rollick, give someone a rollicking, give someone a rocket, tear someone off a strip; *N. Amer. informal* chew out, ream out, pummel, cut up; *Austral./NZ informal* bag, monster; *dated* rate; *archaic* slash; *rare* excoriate, objurgate, reprehend.
OPPOSITE praise.

arraignment ▶ noun *he awaited his arraignment in his cell* **indictment**, accusation, denunciation, prosecution, trial, charge, summons, citation; *Brit.* plaint; *N. Amer.* impeachment, bill of indictment; *N. Amer. informal* beef; *archaic* inculpation.
OPPOSITE acquittal.

A

arrange ▸ verb **1** *she had just finished arranging the flowers* **put in order**, order, set out, lay out, spread out, array, present, put out, display, exhibit, group, sort, organize, tidy, position, dispose; marshal, range, align, line up, rank, file; classify, categorize, systematize, methodize.
OPPOSITE disturb.
2 *they hoped to arrange a meeting* **organize**, fix, plan, schedule, pencil in, devise, contrive; make arrangements for, fix up, prepare for, make preparations for; settle on, decide, determine, agree, come to an agreement, come to terms about.
OPPOSITE cancel.
3 *Toscanini arranged the piece for full string orchestra* **adapt**, set, score, orchestrate, instrument, harmonize.

arrangement ▸ noun **1** *the arrangement of the furniture in the room* **positioning**, disposition, marshalling, ranging, ordering; order, array, presentation, display, exhibition, grouping; sorting, organization, system, alignment; filing, classification, categorization.
2 (usually **arrangements**) *how are the arrangements for your trip going?* **preparations**, plans; planning, preparing, groundwork, provision.
3 *we had an arrangement to meet at 10* **agreement**, appointment, engagement, deal, understanding, settlement, bargain, compact, pact, contract, covenant, compromise, gentleman's agreement; *Latin* modus vivendi.
4 *an arrangement of Beethoven's symphonies for piano duet* **adaptation**, setting, scoring, orchestration, instrumentation, reduction, harmonization.

arrant ▸ adjective (*archaic*) *what arrant nonsense!* **utter**, downright, thoroughgoing, absolute, complete, thorough, through and through, total, unmitigated, outright, out-and-out, real, perfect, consummate, surpassing, sheer, rank, pure, unqualified, inveterate, positive, undiluted, unalloyed, unadulterated, in every respect, unconditional; blatant, flagrant, overt, naked, barefaced, brazen; *N. Amer.* full-bore; *informal* deep-dyed; *Brit. informal* right; *Austral./NZ informal* fair; *rare* right-down.

array ▸ noun **1** *a huge array of cars met our eyes* **arrangement**, assembling, assemblage, line-up, formation, ordering, disposition, marshalling, muster, amassing; show, display, exhibition, presentation, exposition, spectacle; agglomeration, collection, aggregation, raft, range, variety, assortment, diversity, mixture, selection.
2 *she arrived in silken array* **dress**, attire, apparel, clothing, garb, finery; garments.
▸ verb **1** *a wonderful buffet was arrayed on the table* **arrange**, assemble, draw up, group, order, range, place, position, set out, set forth, dispose, marshal, muster; **lay out**, display, exhibit, put on show, put on display, put on view, expose to view, unveil, present, uncover, reveal.
2 *the boy was arrayed in a neat grey flannel suit* **dress**, attire, clothe, robe, garb, deck, deck out, drape, accoutre, outfit, fit out, costume, get up, turn out, trick out/up; *informal* doll up; *archaic* apparel, bedizen, caparison, invest, habit, trap out.

arrears ▸ plural noun **1** *council house rent arrears amounted to over £1m* **money owing**, outstanding payment(s), debt(s), liabilities, indebtedness, dues; balance, deficit.
2 *there are huge arrears of work after the holidays* **backlog**, logjam, accumulation, pile-up, reserve, stockpile.
□ **in arrears** *the tenants were in arrears with their rent* **behind**, behindhand, late, overdue, in the red, in default, in debt.
OPPOSITE in credit.

arrest ▸ verb **1** *police arrested him for possession of marijuana* **apprehend**, take into custody, seize, take in, take prisoner, detain, put in jail, throw in jail; *informal* pick up, run in, pull in, haul in, pinch, cop, bust, nab, nail, do, collar, feel someone's collar; *Brit. informal* nick.
OPPOSITE release.
2 *the spread of the disease can be arrested* **stop**, halt, end, bring to a standstill, check, block, hinder, hamper, delay, hold up, hold back, restrict, limit, interrupt, prevent, obstruct, inhibit, impede, interfere with, thwart, baulk, curb, put a brake on, slow, slow down, retard, nip in the bud; *literary* stay.
OPPOSITE start.
3 *she put out a hand to arrest his attention | it was not the mere words which arrested him* **attract**, capture, catch, catch hold of, hold, grip, engage; absorb, occupy, rivet, engross, fascinate, mesmerize, hypnotize, spellbind, bewitch, captivate, entrance, enthral, enrapture.
▸ noun **1** *I have a warrant for your arrest* **detention**, apprehension, seizure, capture, taking into custody.
2 *he suffered a cardiac arrest* **stoppage**, halt, interruption.

arresting ▸ adjective *this is certainly an arresting image* **striking**, eye-catching, conspicuous, noticeable, dramatic, impressive, imposing, spectacular, breathtaking, dazzling, amazing, astounding, astonishing, surprising, staggering, stunning, sensational, awesome, awe-inspiring, engaging; remarkable, notable, noteworthy, distinctive, extraordinary, outstanding, incredible, phenomenal, unusual, rare, uncommon, out of the ordinary.
OPPOSITES inconspicuous, unexceptional.

arrival ▸ noun **1** *they awaited Ruth's arrival* **coming**, advent, appearance, entrance, entry, materialization, approach.
OPPOSITE departure.
2 *hotel staff greeted the late arrivals* **comer**, entrant, newcomer, new boy, new girl, incomer; visitor, caller, guest, immigrant; *archaic* visitant.
3 *the arrival of democracy* **emergence**, (first) appearance, advent, coming, materialization, surfacing, occurrence, dawn, origin, birth, rise, springing up, development, start, onset, inauguration.
OPPOSITE demise.

arrive ▸ verb **1** *more police arrived* **come**, get here/there, reach one's destination, make it, appear, put in an appearance, make an appearance, come on the scene, come up, approach, enter, present oneself, turn up, be along, come along, materialize; *W. Indian* reach; *informal* show up, show, roll in, roll up, blow in, show one's face.
OPPOSITE depart.
2 *we **arrived at** his house* **reach**, get to, get as far as, come to, make, make it to, set foot on, gain, attain; end up at, land up at, fetch up at; *informal* hit, wind up at.
OPPOSITE leave.
3 *they did **arrive at** a tentative agreement* **achieve**, attain, reach, gain, accomplish; work out, draw up, put together, strike, negotiate, thrash out, hammer out; settle on, sign, endorse, ratify, sanction; *informal* clinch.
4 *the moment finally arrived* **happen**, occur, take place, come about, transpire, ensue, present itself, crop up; *literary* come to pass, befall.
OPPOSITE go.
5 *quadraphony had arrived* **emerge**, appear, make an appearance, surface, dawn, be born, come into being, arise, spring up, be developed, start.
6 (*informal*) *their Rolls Royce and gold jewellery proved that they had arrived* **succeed**, achieve success, be successful, be a success, do well, get ahead, reach the top, make good, prosper, flourish, thrive, advance, triumph, be victorious, break through, become famous, achieve recognition; *informal* make it, make the grade, cut it, crack it, make a name for oneself, make one's mark, get somewhere, do all right for oneself, bring home the bacon, find a place in the sun.

arriviste ▸ noun *he regarded trade as a haven for arrivistes* **social climber**, status seeker, would-be, go-getter, self-seeker, adventurer, adventuress; newcomer, upstart, parvenu, parvenue, vulgarian; (**arrivistes**) the nouveau riche, the new rich, new money.

arrogance ▸ noun *to dismiss all the academic work on the subject displays breathtaking arrogance* **haughtiness**, conceit, hubris, self-importance, egotism, sense of superiority; pomposity, high-handedness, swagger, boasting, bumptiousness, bluster, condescension, disdain, contempt, imperiousness; pride, vanity, immodesty; loftiness, lordliness, snobbishness, snobbery, superciliousness, smugness; pretension, pretentiousness, affectation; scorn, mocking, sneering, scoffing; presumption, insolence; *informal* uppitiness, big-headedness.
OPPOSITES humility, modesty.

arrogant ▸ adjective *he's too arrogant to know when he's lost* **haughty**, conceited, hubristic, self-important, opinionated, egotistic, full of oneself, superior; overbearing, pompous, high-handed, swaggering, boastful, bumptious, blustering, patronizing, condescending, disdainful, contemptuous, imperious; proud, vain, immodest; lofty, lordly, snobbish, snobby, overweening, supercilious, smug; pretentious, affected; scornful, mocking, sneering, scoffing; *informal* hoity-toity, high and mighty, uppity, snooty, stuck-up, toffee-nosed, snotty, jumped up, too big for one's boots, big-headed.
OPPOSITES humble, modest.

arrogate ▸ verb *the Church **arrogated to itself** the power to create kings* **assume**, take, take on, take over, secure, acquire, seize, expropriate, take possession of, help oneself to, make free with, appropriate, steal, wrest, usurp, commandeer, hijack, annex, claim, lay claim to.
OPPOSITE renounce.

arrow ▸ noun **1** *he could shoot a bow and arrow* **shaft**, bolt, dart; *literary* reed; *historical* quarrel.
2 *the arrow on the sign pointed to the right* **pointer**, indicator, marker, needle, hand, index.

WORD LINKS
maker or seller of arrows **fletcher**

arsenal ▸ noun **1** *Britain's nuclear arsenal* **weapons**, weaponry, arms, armaments.
2 *the mutineers broke into the arsenal* **armoury**, arms depot, arms cache, ordnance depot, magazine, ammunition dump.
3 *there is an arsenal of penalties for insider trading* **array**, battery, range, line-up, assortment, collection.

arson ▸ noun *the fire is being treated as arson* **incendiarism**, pyromania, firebombing; *Brit.* **fire-raising**.

arsonist ▸ noun *an arsonist is thought to have caused the blaze* **incendiary**, pyromaniac, firebomber; *Brit.* **fire-raiser**; *informal* firebug, pyro; *N. Amer. informal* torch.

art *See centre pages for lists of* **Art Schools and Movements**

Art Techniques and Media Painting Techniques and Methods Painting Types and Forms
▶ noun **1** *he studied art* **fine art**, artwork, creative activity.
2 *the art of writing* **skill**, craft, technique; aptitude, talent, flair, gift, genius, knack, facility, ability, capability, competence; artistry, mastery, dexterity, dexterousness, craftsmanship, expertness, expertise, proficiency, skilfulness, adroitness, adeptness, deftness, cleverness, ingenuity, virtuosity; *informal* know-how.
3 *she knows how to use art to achieve her objectives* **cunning**, artfulness; deceit, deception, wiliness, slyness, craft, craftiness, guile, trickery, duplicity, artifice; wiles.

artery *See centre pages for list of* **Veins and Arteries**
▶ noun **1** *a blocked artery.*
2 *all the arteries taking people out of town are busy* **main/trunk route**, main/trunk road, main/trunk line, high road, highway.
WORD LINKS
surgical incision of artery **arteriotomy**

artful ▶ adjective *an artful political ruse* **sly**, crafty, cunning, wily, scheming, devious, Machiavellian, sneaky, guileful, tricky, conniving, designing, calculating; **shrewd**, astute, sharp-witted, sharp, acute, intelligent, clever, alert, canny; deceitful, deceptive, duplicitous, cheating, dishonest, disingenuous, underhand, untrustworthy, unscrupulous, double-dealing; *informal* dirty, foxy, shifty, smart; *Brit. informal* fly; *Austral./NZ informal* shonky; *S. African informal* slim; *rare* vulpine, carny, subtle.
OPPOSITES ingenuous, honest, dull.

article ▶ noun **1** *small household articles* **object**, thing, item, unit, artefact, piece of merchandise, commodity, product; device, gadget, contrivance, instrument, utensil, tool, implement; *informal* whatsit, what-d'you-call-it, what's-its-name, whatchamacallit, thingummy, thingy, thingamabob, thingamajig, oojamaflip, oojah, gizmo; *Brit. informal* gubbins, doodah, doobry; *N. Amer. informal* doodad, doohickey, doojigger, dingus.
2 *he wrote an article on the subject* **essay**, report, account, story, write-up, feature, item, piece (of writing), composition, column, paper, tract, study, review, commentary, treatise, analysis, disquisition, discourse; *N. Amer.* theme.
3 *the crucial article of the treaty* **clause**, section, subsection, point, item, paragraph, division, subdivision, heading, part, bit, passage, portion, segment; provision, proviso, stipulation.

articulate ▶ adjective *an articulate speaker | an articulate speech* **eloquent**, fluent, communicative, effective, persuasive, coherent, lucid, vivid, expressive, silver-tongued, vocal; cogent, illuminating, intelligible, comprehensible, understandable.
OPPOSITES inarticulate, hesitant, unintelligible.
▶ verb *they were unable to articulate their emotions* **express**, give expression to, voice, give voice to, vocalize, put in words, give utterance to, communicate, declare, state, set forth, bring into the open, make public, assert, divulge, reveal, proclaim, announce, raise, table, air, ventilate, vent, give vent to, pour out, mention, talk of, point out, go into; utter, say, speak, enunciate, pronounce, mouth; *informal* come out with.
OPPOSITE bottle up.

articulated ▶ adjective *an articulated lorry* **hinged**, jointed, segmented; coupled, attached, joined, connected, interlocked; flexible, bending; that bends; *technical* articulate.
OPPOSITE fixed.

articulation ▶ noun *the formal articulation of theories of linguistic knowledge* **expression**, voicing, utterance, uttering, communication, declaration, statement, setting forth, assertion, revelation, proclamation, announcement, raising, tabling, airing, ventilation, venting, mention, talk; enunciation, pronunciation, mouthing; *rare* divulgement, divulgation.

artifice ▶ noun **1** *an industry dominated by artifice* **trickery**, deviousness, deceit, deception, dishonesty, cheating, duplicity, guile, cunning, artfulness, wiliness, craft, craftiness, evasion, slyness, chicanery, intrigue, subterfuge, strategy, bluff, pretence; fraud, fraudulence, sophistry, sharp practice; *informal* monkey business, funny business, hanky-panky, jiggery-pokery, every trick in the book.
2 *the artifice of couching autobiography in the form of a novel did not really work* **device**, **trick**, stratagem, ploy, tactic, ruse, scheme, move, manoeuvre, contrivance, machination, expedient, wile, dodge; swindle, hoax, fraud, confidence trick; *informal* con, con trick, set-up, game, scam, sting, gyp, flimflam; *Brit. informal* wheeze; *N. Amer. informal* bunco, grift; *Austral. informal* lurk, rort; *S. African informal* schlenter; *Brit. informal, dated* flanker; *archaic* shift, fetch, rig.

artificial ▶ adjective **1** *artificial flowers* **synthetic**, fake, false, imitation, mock, simulated, faux, ersatz, substitute; pseudo, sham, bogus, spurious, counterfeit, forged, pretended, so-called; plastic; **man-made**, manufactured, unnatural, fabricated; replica, reproduction, facsimile; *informal* phoney, pretend.
OPPOSITE natural.
2 *an artificial smile* **feigned**, **insincere**, false, affected, mannered, unnatural, stilted, contrived, pretended, put-on, exaggerated, overdone, forced, laboured, strained, hollow, spurious; *informal* pretend, phoney, hammy, ham, campy.
OPPOSITES genuine, sincere.

CHOOSE THE RIGHT WORD

artificial, synthetic, man-made

These words all describe something that does not occur naturally.

- Something **artificial** has been deliberately made by humans; the word is particularly applied to copies or replacements of natural objects, made from some synthetic material such as plastic (*a valve failed in the artificial heart*). By extension, *artificial* is also used of hypocritical displays of emotion (*I thought his smile was artificial*). *Artificial* is the normal word to use with the following: *intelligence*, *insemination*, *light*, *sweetener*, *life*, and replacement body parts such as *retina*, *knee*, and *limb*. Physical objects in the environment, such as *lakes*, *trees*, *islands*, *rocks*, *satellites*, and *reefs*, are described as *artificial* or sometimes *man-made*, but never *synthetic*.
- **Synthetic** materials and substances are produced by humans through chemical processes, rather than grown naturally (*synthetic fabrics can imitate everything from silk to rubber*). The word is from Greek *synthesis* 'putting together'. There is often a hint that the imitation is inferior to its original (*thin cottons, muslins, fine wools—nothing synthetic*). By extension, *synthetic* may be used of emotion and artistic expression that seems contrived and manufactured (*synthetic melodrama*).
- **Man-made** is usually a neutral term, conveying no criticism or disapproval. It emphasizes the fact that something has been brought into being through human intervention, and is applied chiefly to physical objects and materials, but also to certain abstract nouns: *disaster*, *effect*, and *problem*, for example.

artillery ▶ noun **(big) guns**, **ordnance**, cannon(s), cannonry, heavy weapons, heavy weaponry, battery.

artisan ▶ noun *each guild organized the artisans of a particular craft* **craftsman**, craftswoman, craftsperson, skilled worker, mechanic, technician, operative, maker, smith, wright, journeyman; *archaic* artificer; *rare* handicraftsman, handicraftswoman.

artist ▶ noun **1** *their first exhibition devoted to a single artist* **creator**, originator, designer, producer, fine artist; old master; *literary* begetter.
2 *a surgeon who is an artist with the scalpel* **expert**, master, maestro, past master, adept, virtuoso, genius, old hand, skilled person; *informal* pro, ace, whizz, wizard, hotshot; *Brit. informal* dab hand; *N. Amer. informal* maven, crackerjack; *rare* proficient.
OPPOSITES novice, amateur.

artiste *See centre pages for lists of* **Entertainers**
▶ noun *a cabaret artiste* **entertainer**, performer, trouper, showman, artist; player, musician, singer, dancer, actor, actress, Thespian; comic, comedian, comedienne, clown, impressionist, mime artist, conjuror, magician, acrobat; star, superstar; *rare* executant.

artistic ▶ adjective **1** *he's very artistic* **creative**, imaginative, inventive, original; expressive, inspired; poetic, eloquent, aesthetic, cultivated; sensitive, perceptive, discerning.
OPPOSITE unimaginative.
2 *Bali's people are noted for their artistic dances* **aesthetic**, aesthetically pleasing, beautiful, fine, attractive, decorative, ornamental, lovely, moving, emotional, tasteful, graceful, stylish, elegant, subtle, exquisite, expressive.
OPPOSITE inelegant.

artistry ▶ noun *all four perform with innate artistry* **creative skill**, creativity, art, skill, ability, accomplishment, talent, genius, brilliance, expertness, flair, proficiency, virtuosity, finesse, style, touch, expressiveness, perception, sensitivity, inspiration, poetry, eloquence; craftsmanship, workmanship.

artless ▶ adjective *she described her characters with apparently artless sincerity* **natural**, naive, simple, innocent, childlike, pure, ingenuous, guileless, candid, open, honest, sincere, frank, straightforward, unaffected, unpretentious, modest, unassuming; *N. Amer.* on the up and up.
OPPOSITE scheming.

CHOOSE THE RIGHT WORD

artless, naive, ingenuous

See NAIVE.

as ▶ conjunction **1** *she caught a glimpse of him as he disappeared* **while**, just as, even as, at the (same) time that, at the moment that, during the time that, just when; simultaneously.
2 *there were some who felt as Frank did* **in the (same) way that**, the (same) way, in the (same) manner that; *informal* like.

3 *do as you're told* **what**; archaic that which.
4 *the athletes were free to compete again, as the case against them had not been proved* **because**, since, seeing that, seeing as, considering that, on account of the fact that, in view of the fact that, owing to the fact that; informal on account of; literary for; archaic forasmuch.
5 *try as she did, she couldn't laugh* **although**, though, even though/if, in spite of the fact that, despite the fact that, notwithstanding the fact that, notwithstanding that, for all that, while, whilst, albeit, however.
6 *trains compete successfully with the airlines over short distances, as Paris to Lyons* **such as**, like, for instance, for example, e.g., to give an instance, to give an example, by way of illustration, as an illustration.
7 *I'm away a lot, as you know* **which**, a fact which, something which.
□ **as for/as to** *as for composts, he recommends peat-free varieties* **concerning**, respecting, with respect to, on the subject of, as regards, regarding, with reference to, re, in/with regard to, apropos, in the matter of, in connection with; French vis-à-vis; Latin in re.
□ **as it were** *the street plan evolved, as it were, by natural selection* **so to speak**, in a manner of speaking, in a way, in some way or other, to some extent, so to say; informal sort of.
□ **as yet** *there is no sign of them as yet* **so far**, thus far, yet, still, even now, up till now, up to now, until now, up to the present time.
▶ **preposition 1** *he was dressed as a policeman* **in the guise of**, with the appearance of, in the character of, so as to appear to be.
2 *I'm speaking to you as your friend* **in the role of**, being, acting as, functioning as.

ascend ▶ **verb** *she ascended the stairs | the lift ascended to the eighteenth floor* **climb (up)**, come/go/move up, make one's/its way up, come/go/move upwards, rise (up), arise; mount, scale, conquer, clamber up, scramble up, shin up; levitate, fly up, take to the air, take off, soar; slope upwards, loom, tower.
OPPOSITE descend.

ascendancy ▶ **noun** *the ascendancy of good over evil* **dominance**, domination, supremacy, superiority, predominance, pre-eminence, primacy, dominion, hegemony, authority, mastery, control, command, power, sway, rule, sovereignty, lordship, leadership, influence; the upper hand, the whip hand, the edge, advantage; rare predomination, paramountcy, prepotence, prepotency, prepollency.
OPPOSITE subordination.

ascendant ▶ **adjective** *the communist parties of the republics were ascendant* **rising (in power)**, in the ascendant, on the up and up, on the way up, up-and-coming, on the rise, growing, increasing, flourishing, prospering, burgeoning, developing, budding.
OPPOSITE declining.

ascent ▶ **noun 1** *the first ascent of the Matterhorn* **climb**, scaling, conquest, scramble, clamber, trek.
OPPOSITE descent.
2 *a balloon ascent* **rise**, upward movement, take-off, lift-off, launch, blast-off, climb, levitation, soaring; jump, leap; Christianity Ascension.
OPPOSITES descent, drop.
3 *the ascent grew steeper* **(upward) slope**, incline, ramp, rise, bank, tilt, slant, upward gradient, inclination, acclivity.
OPPOSITES descent, drop.

ascertain ▶ **verb** *we ascertained the exact location of the vehicle* **find out**, discover, get/come to know, work out, make out, fathom (out), become aware of, learn, ferret out, dig out/up, establish, fix, determine, settle, decide, verify, make certain of, confirm, deduce, divine, intuit, diagnose, discern, perceive, see, realize, appreciate, identify, pin down, recognize, register, understand, grasp, take in, comprehend; informal figure out, get a fix on, latch on to, cotton on to, catch on to, tumble to, get; Brit. informal twig, suss (out); N. Amer. informal savvy; rare cognize.

ascetic ▶ **adjective** *an ascetic life of prayer, fasting, and manual labour* **austere**, self-denying, abstinent, abstemious, non-indulgent, self-disciplined, frugal, simple, rigorous, strict, severe, hair-shirt, spartan, monastic, monkish, nunlike; reclusive, solitary, cloistered, eremitic, anchoritic, hermitic; celibate, continent, chaste, puritanical, self-abnegating, other-worldly, mortified.
OPPOSITE sybaritic.
▶ **noun** *St Paul the Egyptian was a desert ascetic* **abstainer**, recluse, hermit, solitary, anchorite, anchoress, desert saint, celibate, puritan, nun, monk; Islam fakir, Sufi, dervish; Hinduism yogi, rishi, sannyasi; (in India) sadhu, muni; rare gymnosophist, marabout, santon, self-denier, eremite, stylite, pillar saint, pillar hermit, pillarist, aerialist, coenobite.
OPPOSITE sybarite.

asceticism ▶ **noun** *countless dictators have pointed out the asceticism of their private lives* **austerity**, self-denial, abstinence, abstemiousness, non-indulgence, self-discipline, frugality, simplicity, rigour, strictness, severity; a hair shirt, a spartan life, monasticism, monkishness, reclusiveness, solitude, hermitism, celibacy, continence, chastity, puritanism, self-abnegation, other-worldliness, self-mortification; archaic anchorism.
OPPOSITE sybaritism.

ascribe ▶ **verb** *he ascribed Jane's short temper to her upset stomach* **attribute**, assign, put down, set down, accredit, credit, give the credit for, chalk up, impute; lay on, pin on, blame on, lay at the door of; connect with, associate with.

ash ▶ **noun** *the fire had gone, leaving only ash* **cinders**, ashes, embers, clinker.
WORD LINKS
relating to ash **cinerary**

ashamed ▶ **adjective 1** *she was ashamed of the way she had behaved* **sorry**, shamefaced, abashed, sheepish, guilty, conscience-stricken, guilt-ridden, contrite, remorseful, repentant, penitent, hangdog, regretful, rueful, apologetic; **embarrassed**, mortified, red-faced, chagrined, humiliated, uncomfortable, discomfited, distressed; in sackcloth and ashes; informal with one's tail between one's legs; rare compunctious; (**be ashamed of**) blush to think of.
OPPOSITES proud, unabashed.
2 *he was ashamed to admit it* **reluctant**, loath, unwilling, disinclined, hesitant, indisposed, slow, afraid; averse.
OPPOSITE pleased.

ashen ▶ **adjective** *his ashen face* **pale**, wan, pasty, grey, leaden, colourless, sallow, pallid, white, waxen, ghostly; pale-faced, ashen-faced, grey-faced, anaemic, bloodless; rare etiolated, lymphatic.

ashore ▶ **adverb** *the seals come ashore to breed* **on to (the) land**, on to the shore; towards the shore, shorewards, landwards; on the shore, on the beach, on (the) land, on dry land.

aside ▶ **adverb 1** *they stood aside to let a car pass* **to one side**, to the side; on one side, alongside; apart, away, separately, alone, by oneself/itself, distant, detached, in isolation.
2 *that aside, he seemed a nice man* **apart**, notwithstanding.
□ **aside from** *aside from his London office he has property in several African capitals* **apart from**, besides, in addition to, over and above, beyond, not counting, leaving aside, barring, other than, but (for), excluding, not including, without, with the exception of, except, except for, excepting, omitting, leaving out, short of, save (for).
▶ **noun** *'Both her parents died a couple of years back,' said Mrs Manton in an aside to Betty* **whispered remark**, confidential remark, stage whisper; soliloquy, monologue, apostrophe; casual remark, throwaway line; digression, parenthetic remark, incidental remark, obiter dictum, deviation, departure, red herring, excursus; archaic excursion.

asinine ▶ **adjective** *another asinine bit of advertising* **stupid**, **foolish**, pointless, brainless, mindless, senseless, doltish, idiotic, imbecilic, imbecile, insane, lunatic, ridiculous, ludicrous, absurd, preposterous, nonsensical, fatuous, silly, childish, infantile, puerile, immature, juvenile, inane, witless, half-baked, empty-headed, unintelligent, half-witted, slow-witted, weak-minded; informal crazy, dumb, cretinous, moronic, gormless, damfool; Brit. informal divvy, daft; Scottish & N. English informal glaikit; N. Amer. informal dumb-ass, chowderheaded; S. African informal dof; W. Indian informal dotish.
OPPOSITE intelligent.

ask ▶ **verb 1** *ask her what she did | he asked what time we opened* **enquire (of)**, query, want to know, question, put a question to, interrogate, quiz, cross-question, cross-examine, catechize; informal grill, pump, give the third degree to.
OPPOSITE answer.
2 *they just want to ask a few questions* **put**, put forward, pose, raise, submit, propose, seek/get the answer to.
OPPOSITE answer.
3 *I asked him to call the manager | don't be afraid to ask for advice* **request**, demand, appeal to, apply to, petition, call on, entreat, beg, implore, exhort, urge, enjoin, importune, pray, solicit, beseech, plead with, sue, supplicate; seek, put in for, call for, crave.
4 *let's ask them to dinner* **invite**, bid, have someone over/round, summon; request the pleasure of someone's company.

askance ▶ **adverb 1** *she looked askance at her neighbour* **obliquely**, sideways, indirectly, out of the corner of one's eye.
2 *they look askance at almost anything foreign* **suspiciously**, with suspicion, sceptically, with misgivings, cynically, mistrustfully, distrustfully, with distrust, doubtfully, dubiously, with doubt; **disapprovingly**, with disapproval, with disfavour, contemptuously, scornfully, disdainfully; **suspect**, mistrust, distrust; **disapprove of**, frown on, be hostile towards.
OPPOSITES welcomingly, approvingly.

askew ▶ **adverb & adjective** *her hat was slightly askew | the picture is hanging askew* **crooked(ly)**, lopsided(ly), tilted, angled, at an angle, oblique(ly), at an oblique angle, skew, skewed, slanted, aslant, awry, out of true, out of line, to one side, on one side, uneven(ly), off balance, off centre, asymmetrical(ly), unsymmetrical(ly); Scottish agley, squint, thrawn; informal cock-eyed; Brit. informal skew-whiff, wonky, wonkily, squiffy, squiffily.
OPPOSITES straight, symmetrical(ly).

asleep ▶ **adjective & adverb 1** *she was still asleep in bed* **sleeping**, fast asleep, sound asleep, in a deep sleep, slumbering, napping, catnapping, dozing,

resting, reposing, drowsing, dormant, comatose; *informal* snoozing, dead to the world, flat out, kipping, out like a light, in the land of Nod; *literary* in the arms of Morpheus.
OPPOSITE awake.
2 *my leg's asleep* **numb**, without feeling, numbed, benumbed, dead, deadened, desensitized, insensible, insensate, senseless, unfeeling; anaesthetized; *rare* torpefied.
OPPOSITE sensitive.

aspect ▶ **noun 1** *the photographs depict every aspect of life on a kibbutz* **feature**, facet, side, characteristic, particular, detail, point, ingredient, strand; angle, slant, sense, respect, regard.
2 *the black patch hiding one eye gave his face a sinister aspect* **appearance**, look, air, bearing, cast, manner, mien, demeanour, deportment, expression, countenance, features, semblance, guise, impression, effect; atmosphere, mood, quality, ambience, feeling, flavour.
3 *a summer house with a southern aspect* **outlook**, view, exposure, direction, situation, position, location.
4 *the front aspect of the hotel was unremarkable* **face**, elevation, facade, side.

asperity ▶ **noun** *'How should I know?' he replied with some asperity* **harshness**, sharpness, roughness, abrasiveness, severity, acerbity, astringency, bitterness, acidity, tartness, edge, acrimony, virulence, sarcasm.
OPPOSITE mildness.

aspersions ▶ **plural noun** *he claimed he could prove the aspersions groundless* **vilification**, disparagement, denigration, defamation, defamation of character, abuse, vituperation, condemnation, criticism, censure, castigation, denunciation, flak, deprecation, opprobrium, obloquy, derogation, slander, revilement, reviling, calumny, calumniation, slurs, smears, execration, excoriation, lambasting, upbraiding, bad press, character assassination, attack, invective, libel, insults, slights, curses; *informal* mud-slinging, bad-mouthing, tongue-lashing; *Brit. informal* stick, verbal, slagging off; *archaic* contumely; *rare* animadversion, objurgation.
□ **cast aspersions on** *I don't think anyone is casting aspersions on you* **vilify**, disparage, denigrate, defame, run down, impugn, revile, berate, belittle, abuse, insult, slight, attack, speak badly of, speak ill of, speak evil of, pour scorn on, criticize, censure, condemn, decry, denounce, pillory, lambaste; fulminate against, rail against, inveigh against, malign, slander, libel, conduct a smear campaign against, spread lies about, blacken the name/reputation of, sully the reputation of, give someone a bad name, bring into disrepute, discredit, stigmatize, traduce, calumniate, slur; *informal* bad-mouth, do a hatchet job on, take to pieces, pull apart, throw mud at, drag through the mud, slate, have a go at, hit out at, jump on, lay into, tear into, knock, slam, pan, bash, hammer, roast, skewer, bad-mouth, throw brickbats at; *Brit. informal* rubbish, slag off; *N. Amer. informal* pummel, dump on; *Austral./NZ informal* bag, monster; *archaic* contemn; *rare* derogate, vituperate, asperse, vilipend.

asphyxiate ▶ **verb** *they were asphyxiated by the carbon monoxide fumes* **choke (to death)**, suffocate, smother, stifle; kill; throttle, strangle, strangulate, constrict.

aspiration ▶ **noun** *the jobs created do not match the aspirations of local residents* **desire**, hope, longing, yearning, hankering, urge, wish; **aim**, ambition, expectation, inclination, objective, goal, target, end, object, dream; *informal* yen, itch.

aspire ▶ **verb** *a more prosperous Britain can* ***aspire to*** *excellence in the arts | they* ***aspire to*** *emulate their heroes* **desire (to)**, **aim for/to**, hope for/to, long for/to, yearn for/to, hanker after/for/to, set one's heart on, wish for/to, want (to), expect (to), have the objective of, dream of, hunger for/to, seek (to), pursue, have as one's goal/aim, set one's sights on; be ambitious; *literary* thirst for/after; *archaic* be desirous of.

aspiring ▶ **adjective** *advice to aspiring writers* **would-be**, intending, aspirant, hopeful, optimistic, budding, wishful; potential, possible, prospective, likely, future; ambitious, eager, keen, striving, determined, enterprising, pioneering, progressive, motivated, enthusiastic, energetic, zealous, committed, go-ahead, go-getting, purposeful; *informal* wannabe, on the make; *archaic* expectant.
OPPOSITE feckless.

ass ▶ **noun 1** *he rode on an ass* **donkey**; jackass, jenny; *Scottish* cuddy; *Brit. informal* moke, neddy.

WORD LINKS
collective noun **herd, pace**

2 *don't be a silly ass* **fool**, nincompoop, clown, dolt, simpleton; *informal* idiot, ninny, dope, dimwit, chump, goon, dumbo, dummy, halfwit, dum-dum, loon, jackass, cretin, imbecile, jerk, nerd, fathead, blockhead, numbskull, dunderhead, dunce, dipstick, bonehead, chucklehead, clod, goop, knucklehead, lamebrain, pea-brain, pudding-head, thickhead, wooden-head, pinhead, airhead, birdbrain, dumb-bell, donkey, stupe, noodle; *Brit. informal* nit, nitwit, twit, clot, plonker, berk, prat, pillock, wally, git, wazzock, divvy, nerk, dork, twerp, charlie, mug, muppet; *Scottish informal* nyaff, balloon, sumph, gowk; *Irish informal* gobdaw; *N. Amer. informal* schmuck, bozo, boob, turkey, schlepper, chowderhead, dumbhead, goofball, goof, goofus, galoot, lummox, klutz, putz, schlemiel, sap, meatball, gink, cluck, clunk, ding-dong, dingbat, wiener, weeny, dip, simp, spud, coot, palooka, poop, squarehead, yo-yo, dingleberry; *Austral./NZ informal* drongo, dill, hoon, alec, galah, nong, bogan, poon, boofhead; *S. African informal* mompara; *dated* tomfool, muttonhead, noddy; *archaic* clodpole, loggerhead, spoony, mooncalf.

assail ▶ **verb 1** *the army moved down the slope to assail the enemy* **attack**, assault, make an assault on, launch an attack on, pounce on, set upon, set about, launch oneself at, weigh into, fly at, let fly at, turn on, round on, lash out at, hit out at, beset, belabour, fall on, accost, mug, charge, rush, storm, besiege; *informal* lay into, tear into, lace into, sail into, pitch into, get stuck into, wade into, let someone have it, beat up, jump; *Brit. informal* have a go at; *N. Amer. informal* light into.
2 *she was* ***assailed by*** *doubts* **trouble**, disturb, worry, plague, beset, torture, torment, rack, bedevil, nag, vex, harass, pester, dog; be prey to, be the victim of.
3 *critics assailed the policy* **criticize**, censure, attack, condemn, castigate, chastise, berate, lambaste, lash, pillory, find fault with, abuse, revile, give someone a bad press; *informal* knock, slam, hammer, lay into, give someone a roasting, cane, blast, give someone hell, bite someone's head off, jump down someone's throat; *Brit. informal* slate, slag off; *N. Amer. informal* pummel, cut up; *Austral./NZ informal* bag, monster; *dated* rate; *archaic* slash; *rare* excoriate, objurgate, reprehend.

assailant ▶ **noun** *she escaped from her assailant after kicking him* **attacker**, mugger; *rare* assaulter, assailer.

assassin ▶ **noun** *his presidency was cut short by an assassin's bullet* **murderer**, killer, executioner, gunman, butcher, slaughterer, liquidator, exterminator, terminator; *informal* hit man, contract man, hired gun; *N. Amer. informal* button man; *literary* slayer; *dated* homicide.

assassinate ▶ **verb** *John F. Kennedy was assassinated in 1963* **murder**, kill, execute, slaughter, butcher, liquidate, eliminate, exterminate, terminate; *informal* hit; *literary* slay.

assassination ▶ **noun** *the assassination of John F. Kennedy* **murder**, killing, political execution, slaughter, butchery, homicide, liquidation, elimination, extermination, termination, putting/doing to death, martyrdom; *informal* hit; *literary* slaying.

assault ▶ **verb 1** *he pleaded guilty to assaulting a police officer* **hit**, strike, physically attack, aim blows at, slap, smack, beat, thrash, spank, thump, thwack, punch, cuff, swat, knock, rap; pummel, pound, batter, pelt, welt; cane, lash, whip, club, cudgel, box someone's ears; *informal* clout, wallop, belt, whack, bash, clobber, bop, biff, sock, deck, slug, plug, knock about/around, knock into the middle of next week, lay into, do over, rough up; *Austral./NZ informal* quilt; *literary* smite.
2 *they left their position to assault the hill* **attack**, make an assault on, launch an attack on, assail, pounce on, set upon, launch oneself at, strike at, fall on, swoop on, rush, storm, besiege.
3 *police believe that he first assaulted then murdered her* **rape**, sexually assault, molest, interfere with.
▶ **noun 1** *he was charged with assault* **(physical) violence**, battery, mugging, actual bodily harm, ABH; violent act, physical attack; sexual assault, sexual misconduct, molesting, sexual interference, rape; *Brit.* grievous bodily harm, GBH.
2 *troops began an assault on the city* **attack**, strike, onslaught, offensive, storming, charge, drive, push, thrust, invasion, bombardment, sortie, sally, foray, incursion, raid, act of war, act of aggression, blitz, campaign.

assay ▶ **noun** *new plate was taxed when it was brought for assay* **evaluation**, assessment, analysis, examination, test, trial, check, inspection, appraisal, investigation, scrutiny, probe.
▶ **verb** *silver and gold is assayed to determine its purity* **evaluate**, assess, analyse, examine, test, check, inspect, appraise, investigate, scrutinize, probe.

assemblage ▶ **noun** *the most varied assemblage of plants in the world* **collection**, accumulation, conglomeration, gathering, group, cluster, aggregation, raft, mass, medley, assortment, selection, jumble, series, complete series, batch, number, combination, grouping, arrangement, array.

assemble ▶ **verb 1** *a crowd had assembled* **come together**, get together, gather, collect, meet, muster, rally, congregate, convene, flock together; *rare* foregather.
OPPOSITE disperse.
2 *he assembled the suspects in the lounge* **bring together**, get together, call together, gather, collect, round up, marshal, muster, summon, rally, convene, accumulate, mass, amass; *formal* convoke.
OPPOSITE disperse.
3 *how to assemble the kite* **construct**, build, fabricate, manufacture, erect, set up, join up, fit together, put together, piece together, connect, join, unite, patch up, sew (up).
OPPOSITE dismantle.

assembly ▶ **noun 1** *the Council of Nicaea was the largest assembly of bishops hitherto* **gathering**, meeting, congregation, convention, rally, convocation, congress, council, synod, audience, assemblage, turnout, group, body, crowd, throng, company; *informal* get-together.

2 *the amount of labour needed in assembly is reduced* **construction**, building, fabrication, manufacture, erection, setting up, putting together, fitting together, piecing together, connection, joining.
OPPOSITE dismantling.

assent ▸ noun *a loud murmur of assent* **agreement**, acceptance, approval, approbation, consent, acquiescence, compliance, concurrence; blessing, imprimatur, seal/stamp of approval, rubber stamp; sanction, endorsement, ratification, authorization, mandate, licence, validation; confirmation, support, backing; permission, leave; *informal* the go-ahead, the green light, the OK, the thumbs up, the nod, say-so.
OPPOSITES dissent; refusal.
▸ verb *the Prime Minister* ***assented to*** *the change* **agree to**, accept, approve, consent to, acquiesce in, concur in, accede to, give one's blessing to, bless, give one's seal/stamp of approval to, rubber-stamp, say yes to; ratify, sanction, endorse, authorize, mandate, license, warrant, validate, pass; confirm, support, back; give one's permission/leave; *informal* give the go-ahead to, give the green light to, give the OK to, OK, give the thumbs up to, give the nod, say the word, buy.
OPPOSITES dissent from; refuse.

> CHOOSE THE RIGHT WORD
>
> **assent, agree, consent, acquiesce**
>
> See AGREE.

assert ▸ verb **1** *he asserted that the day of the cottage industry was over* **declare**, maintain, contend, argue, state, claim, propound, submit, posit, postulate, adduce, move, advocate, venture, volunteer, aver, proclaim, announce, pronounce, attest, affirm, protest, profess, swear, insist, avow; *formal* opine; *rare* asseverate.
2 *elderly people find it increasingly difficult to assert their rights* **insist on**, stand up for, uphold, defend, contend, establish, press/push for, stress.
□ **assert oneself** *a large government majority can encourage backbenchers to assert themselves* **behave confidently**, speak confidently, be assertive, put oneself forward, make one's presence felt, exert one's influence, make people sit up and take notice, make people sit up and listen; *informal* put one's foot down.

assertion ▸ noun **1** *I questioned his assertion that little risk is involved* **declaration**, contention, statement, claim, submission, postulation, averment, opinion, proclamation, announcement, pronouncement, assurance, attestation, affirmation, protestation, profession, swearing, insistence, avowal; *rare* maintenance, asseveration.
2 *the demonstration was a principled* ***assertion of*** *the right to march* **defence**, upholding; insistence on.

assertive ▸ adjective *the job may call for assertive behaviour* **confident**, **forceful**, self-confident, positive, bold, decisive, assured, self-assured, self-possessed, believing in oneself, self-assertive, authoritative, strong-willed, insistent, firm, determined, commanding, bullish, dominant, domineering, assaultive; *informal* feisty, not backward in coming forward, pushy; *rare* pushful.
OPPOSITE retiring.

assess ▸ verb **1** *frequent patrols were made to assess the enemy's strength* **evaluate**, judge, gauge, rate, estimate, appraise, form an opinion of, check out, form an impression of, make up one's mind about, get the measure of, determine, weigh up, analyse; *informal* size up.
2 *the damage was assessed at £5 billion* **value**, put a value on, calculate, compute, work out, determine, fix, cost, price, estimate.

assessment ▸ noun **1** *I endorse your assessment of the quality* **evaluation**, judgement, gauging, rating, estimation, appraisal, opinion, analysis.
2 *some assessments valued the estate at between £2 million and £7 million* **valuation**, calculation, computation, costing, pricing, estimate.

asset ▸ noun **1** *his strong sense of humour was a great asset* **benefit**, advantage, blessing, good point, strong point, strength, forte, talent, gift, strong suit, long suit, virtue, recommendation, attraction, attractive feature, selling point, resource, beauty, boon, value, merit, bonus, aid, help; saving grace, redeeming feature, compensating feature; *informal* plus, pro.
OPPOSITES liability, handicap.
2 (usually **assets**) *the company can use its own assets as the security for credit* **property**, resources, estate, holdings, possessions, effects, goods, valuables, belongings, chattels, worldly goods, worldly possessions; capital, funds, wealth, principal, money, riches, means, fortune, finance, reserves, savings, securities.
OPPOSITE liability.

assiduous ▸ adjective *she was assiduous in pointing out every feature* **diligent**, careful, meticulous, thorough, sedulous, attentive, industrious, laborious, hard-working, conscientious, ultra-careful, punctilious, painstaking, demanding, exacting, persevering, unflagging, searching, close, elaborate, minute, accurate, correct, studious, rigorous, particular; religious, strict; pedantic, fussy.

assign ▸ verb **1** *a young physician was assigned the task of solving this problem* **allocate**, allot, give, set; charge with, entrust with.
2 *he was then* ***assigned to*** *another public relations post* **appoint**, promote, delegate, commission, post, nominate, vote, elect, adopt, co-opt; make, create, name, designate, dub; decide on for, select for, choose for, install in, induct in, institute in, invest in, ordain in; *Military* detail for.
3 *managers happily* ***assign*** *large sums of money* ***to*** *travel budgets* **earmark**, appropriate, designate, set aside, set apart, keep, reserve; allot, allocate, apportion; fix, appoint, decide on, determine, specify, stipulate; *rare* hypothecate.
4 *he decided to* ***assign*** *the opinion* ***to*** *the Prince* **ascribe**, attribute, put down, set down, accredit, credit, give the credit for, chalk up, impute; lay on, pin on, blame on, lay at the door of; connect with, associate with.
5 *the depositor may assign the money in his account to a third party* **transfer**, make over, give, pass, hand over, hand down, convey, consign, alienate; *Law* demise, devise, attorn.

assignation ▸ noun *he and Jane arranged a secret assignation in town* **rendezvous**, date, appointment, meeting; *literary* tryst.

assignment ▸ noun **1** *I'm going to finish this assignment tonight* **task**, piece of work, piece of business, job, duty, chore, charge, labour, function, commission, mission, errand, engagement, occupation, undertaking, exercise, business, office, responsibility, detail, endeavour, enterprise; piece of research, project, homework, prep.
2 *the effective assignment of tasks* **allocation**, allotment, issuing, issuance, awarding, grant, granting, administration, earmarking, designation, setting aside, budgeting; **sharing out**, apportionment, distribution, handing out, dealing out, doling out, giving out, dishing out, parcelling out, rationing out, dividing out, dividing up, dispensation, measuring out, meting out; *informal* divvying up.
3 *the assignment of property* **transfer**, making over, giving, passing on, handing down, conveyance, consignment, alienation; *Law* demise, devise, attornment.

assimilate ▸ verb **1** *there are limits to the amount of information he can assimilate | the plants do not assimilate nitrates fast enough* **absorb**, take in, acquire, pick up, grasp, comprehend, understand, learn, master; digest, ingest, imbibe, drink in, soak in; *informal* get the hang of, get.
2 *many tribes disappeared, having been assimilated by the Russian or Turkic peoples* **subsume**, incorporate, integrate, absorb, engulf, swallow up, take over, co-opt, naturalize, adopt, embrace, accept, admit; *rare* acculturate.

assist ▸ verb **1** *I spend much of my time assisting the chef* **help**, aid, abet, lend a (helping) hand to, give assistance to, be of use to, oblige, accommodate, serve, be of service to, do someone a service, do someone a favour, do someone a good turn, bail someone out, come to someone's rescue; cooperate with, collaborate with, work with; succour, encourage, support, back, back up, second, be a tower of strength to; *informal* pitch in with, get someone out of a tight spot, save someone's bacon, save someone's skin, give someone a leg up; *Brit. informal* muck in with, get stuck in with.
OPPOSITE hinder.
2 *the exchange rates assisted the massive expansion of trade* **facilitate**, aid, ease, make easier, expedite, spur, promote, boost, give a boost to, benefit, foster, encourage, stimulate, precipitate, accelerate, advance, further, forward, help along, contribute to, be a factor in, smooth the way for, clear a path for, open the door for, oil the wheels of; *informal* jack up, hike, hike up.
OPPOSITE impede.

> CHOOSE THE RIGHT WORD
>
> **assist, help, aid, support**
>
> See HELP.

assistance ▸ noun *they said that they could manage and did not need assistance* **help**, aid, abettance, support, backing, succour, encouragement, reinforcement, relief, intervention, cooperation, collaboration; a helping hand, a hand, a good turn, a favour, a kindness; ministrations, offices, services; *informal* a break, a leg up; *rare* easement.
OPPOSITE hindrance.

assistant ▸ noun **1** *he spent three years as a photographer's assistant* **subordinate**, deputy, auxiliary, second, second in command, number two, right-hand man, right-hand woman, aide, personal assistant, PA, attendant, mate, apprentice, junior; henchman, underling, hired hand, hired help, servant; **helper**, aider, colleague, associate, partner, confederate, accomplice, collaborator, accessory, abetter, supporter, backer; *informal* vice, man/girl Friday, sidekick, skivvy, running dog, gofer, gopher; *Brit. informal* dogsbody, poodle.
2 *Judy was an assistant in the local shop* **sales assistant**, shop assistant, retail assistant, salesperson, saleswoman, salesman, saleslady, salesgirl, server, checkout girl, checkout person, checkout operator; seller, vendor; *N. Amer.* clerk, sales clerk; *informal* counter-jumper, sales rep, pusher; *dated* shop boy, shop girl, shopman.

WORD LINKS
related prefixes **sub-** (e.g. ***subdirector***), **vice-** (e.g. ***vice-principal***)

associate ▸ verb **1** *elegance was not a concept I associated with nuns* **link**, connect, couple, relate, identify, equate, bracket, think of together; think of in connection with, draw a parallel with, mention in the same breath as, set side by side with.
2 *Simon had been known to associate with anarchist groups* **mix**, keep company, mingle, socialize, get together, go around, rub shoulders, fraternize, consort, have dealings; N. Amer. rub elbows; informal hobnob, run around, hang out, hang around/round, knock about/around, pal up, pal around, chum around, be thick with; Brit. informal hang about.
3 *the firm is associated with a local non-profit-making organization* **affiliate**, align, connect, join, join up, join forces, attach, combine, team up, band together, be in league, ally, form an alliance, syndicate, federate, consolidate, incorporate, conjoin, merge, integrate.
▸ noun *the bank was run by his business associate* **partner**, colleague, co-worker, fellow worker, workmate, compatriot, comrade, friend, ally, supporter, confederate, connection, contact, acquaintance; accomplice, accessory, abetter, partner in crime, collaborator, colluder, fellow conspirator, henchman; French confrère; informal crony, pal, chum, buddy; Brit. informal mate, oppo; Austral./NZ informal offsider; archaic compeer; rare conniver, consociate.

associated ▸ adjective **1** *salaries and associated costs have risen this year* **related**, connected, linked, correlated, analogous, similar, alike, kindred, corresponding; attendant, accompanying, auxiliary, accessory, incidental; formal cognate.
OPPOSITE unrelated.
2 *they share in the results and net assets of their associated company* **affiliated**, allied, integrated, amalgamated, incorporated, federated, confederated, syndicated, unified, connected, interconnected, related, linked, joined, bound; in league, in partnership, in alliance.

association ▸ noun **1** *the industry has established a trade association* **alliance**, consortium, coalition, union, league, guild, syndicate, corporation, federation, confederation, confederacy, conglomerate, cooperative, partnership, amalgamation, merger; body, group, ring, circle, trust, company, organization, affiliation, society, club, band, brotherhood, fraternity, sorority, clique, cartel; rare consociation, sodality.
2 *they study the association between man and environment* **relationship**, relation, interrelation, connection, interconnection, link, bond, tie, attachment, interdependence, union; communication, interchange, contact, affiliation, cooperation; dealings.

assorted ▸ adjective *assorted artefacts were recovered from the site* **mixed**, varied, variegated, varying, various, miscellaneous, diverse, diversified, eclectic, manifold, multifarious, multitudinous, motley, sundry, heterogeneous, disparate, different, differing, dissimilar; literary divers; rare farraginous.
OPPOSITES similar, identical.

assortment ▸ noun *the alcove held an assortment of books* **mixture**, variety, array, mixed bag, mix, miscellany, random selection, motley collection, selection, medley, melange, diversity, mishmash, hotchpotch, hodgepodge, ragbag, pot-pourri, jumble, mess, confusion, conglomeration, farrago, patchwork, hash; rare gallimaufry, omnium gatherum, olio, olla podrida, salmagundi, macédoine, motley.

assuage ▸ verb **1** *an aching pain that could never be assuaged* **relieve**, ease, alleviate, soothe, mitigate, dampen, allay, calm, palliate, abate, lull, temper, suppress, smother, stifle, subdue, tranquillize, mollify, moderate, modify, tone down, attenuate, dilute, lessen, diminish, decrease, reduce, lower; put an end to, put a stop to, take the edge off; informal kill; rare lenify.
OPPOSITE aggravate.
2 *her physical hunger could be quickly assuaged* **satisfy**, fulfil, gratify, appease, indulge, relieve, slake, sate, satiate, quench, quell, overcome, check, keep in check, dull, blunt, allay, take the edge off, diminish.
OPPOSITE intensify.

assume ▸ verb **1** *I assumed he wanted me to keep the book* **presume**, suppose, take it, take for granted, take as read, take it as given, presuppose, conjecture, surmise, conclude, come to the conclusion, deduce, infer, draw the inference, reckon, reason, guess, imagine, think, fancy, suspect, expect, accept, believe, be of the opinion, understand, be given to understand, gather, glean; N. Amer. figure; formal opine; archaic ween.
2 *he had assumed a stage Southern accent* **feign**, fake, put on, simulate, counterfeit, sham, affect, adopt, impersonate.
3 *the disease may assume epidemic proportions* **acquire**, take on, adopt, come to have.
4 *the children are to assume as much responsibility as possible* **accept**, shoulder, bear, undertake, take on, take up, take on oneself, manage, handle, deal with, get to grips with, turn one's hand to.
5 *Edward I used the conflict to assume control of Scotland* **seize**, take, take possession of, take over, take away, appropriate, commandeer, expropriate, confiscate, requisition, hijack, wrest, usurp, pre-empt, arrogate to oneself, help oneself to, claim, lay claim to.

assumed ▸ adjective *he may have travelled under an assumed name* **false**, fictitious, invented, made-up, concocted, feigned, pretended, faked, fake, bogus, sham, spurious, counterfeit, pseudo, make-believe, improvised, affected, adopted; informal pretend, phoney, pseud; Brit. informal, dated cod; rare pseudonymous.
OPPOSITES real, genuine.

assumption ▸ noun **1** *the statistic is only an informed assumption* **supposition**, presupposition, presumption, premise, belief, expectation, conjecture, speculation, surmise, guess, theory, hypothesis, postulation, conclusion, deduction, inference, thought, suspicion, notion, impression, fancy; guesswork, guessing, reckoning; informal guesstimate.
2 *Theresa shrugged with an assumption of ease* **pretence**, simulation, affectation; feigning, faking, shamming, pretending.
3 *there is an early assumption of community obligation in the tribe* **acceptance**, shouldering, handling, managing, tackling, taking on; undertaking, entering on, setting about, embarkation on.
4 *no one had foreseen the assumption of power by the revolutionaries* **seizure**, seizing, taking, taking over, taking away, appropriation, appropriating, commandeering, expropriation, expropriating, confiscation, confiscating, requisition, requisitioning, hijack, hijacking, wresting, usurping, pre-empting, arrogation, claiming.

assurance ▸ noun **1** *nothing could shake her calm assurance* **self-confidence**, confidence, self-assurance, belief in oneself, faith in oneself, positiveness, assertiveness, self-possession, self-reliance, nerve, poise, aplomb, presence of mind, phlegm, level-headedness, cool-headedness; coolness, calmness, composure, collectedness, sangfroid, equilibrium, equanimity, imperturbability, impassivity, nonchalance, serenity, tranquillity, peace of mind; informal cool, unflappability.
OPPOSITES self-doubt; nervousness.
2 *you have my assurance that I shall write to you* **word of honour**, word, guarantee, promise, pledge, vow, avowal, oath, bond, affirmation, undertaking, commitment; archaic troth, parole.
3 *there is no assurance of getting one's money back* **certainty**, guarantee, sureness, certitude, confidence; hope, expectation.
OPPOSITE uncertainty.
4 *they required him to take out life assurance* **insurance**, indemnity, indemnification, protection, security, surety, cover, coverage; guarantee, safeguard, warranty, provision.

assure ▸ verb **1** *we need to assure him of our loyal support | I can assure all our consumers that the water is safe to drink* **reassure**, convince, satisfy, persuade, guarantee, promise, tell; prove to, certify to, attest to, confirm to, affirm to, pledge to, swear to, give one's word to, give one's assurance to, vow to, declare to.
2 *he made some changes in his cabinet to assure a favourable vote* **ensure**, make certain, make sure; **secure**, guarantee, seal, set the seal on, clinch, confirm, establish; informal sew up.
3 *they guarantee to assure your life for £750,000* **insure**, provide insurance for, cover, indemnify, guarantee, warrant.

assured ▸ adjective **1** *the guide spoke in an assured voice* **self-confident**, confident, self-assured, sure of oneself, positive, assertive, self-possessed, self-reliant, poised, filled with aplomb, phlegmatic, level-headed, cool-headed; calm, collected, {cool, calm, and collected}, composed, nonchalant, unperturbed, imperturbable, unruffled, impassive, serene, tranquil, relaxed, at ease; informal unflappable, together, unfazed, laid-back; rare equanimous.
OPPOSITES doubtful; nervous.
2 *the British wanted an assured supply of weapons* **guaranteed**, certain, sure, secure, reliable, dependable, solid, sound, established; infallible, unerring, unfailing, impeccable, faultless; informal sure-fire, in the bag.
OPPOSITE uncertain.

astonish ▸ verb *I was astonished at how much he had learned* **amaze**, astound, stagger, surprise, startle, stun, confound, dumbfound, stupefy, daze, nonplus; throw, shake, unnerve, disconcert, discompose, bewilder; take someone's breath away, take by surprise, take aback, shake up, stop someone in their tracks, strike dumb, leave open-mouthed, leave aghast, catch off balance; informal flabbergast, floor, knock for six, knock sideways, knock out, knock the stuffing out of, bowl over, blow someone's mind, blow away.

astonished ▸ adjective *his tricks attracted crowds of astonished bystanders* **amazed**, filled with astonishment, filled with amazement, astounded, staggered, surprised, startled, stunned, thunderstruck, aghast, taken aback, confounded, dumbfounded, stupefied, dazed, nonplussed, dumbstruck, open-mouthed, agape, lost for words, wide-eyed, awed, filled with awe, filled with wonder, awestruck, wonderstruck; shaken, shaken up, unnerved, disconcerted, discomposed, bewildered, bemused; informal flabbergasted, flummoxed, floored, knocked for six, bowled over, blown away, unable to believe one's eyes/ears; Brit. informal gobsmacked.

astonishing ▸ adjective *she has read an astonishing number of books* **amazing**, astounding, staggering, shocking, surprising, breathtaking, striking, impressive, bewildering, stunning, stupefying; unnerving, unsettling, disturbing, disquieting; awe-inspiring, remarkable, notable, noteworthy, extraordinary, outstanding, incredible, unbelievable, phenomenal, uncommon, unheard of; informal mind-boggling, mind-blowing, hard to swallow.

astonishment ▶ noun *she stared at him in astonishment* **amazement**, surprise, shock, stupefaction, bafflement, bewilderment, confusion, perplexity, incredulity, disbelief, dismay, consternation, speechlessness, awe, wonder, wonderment.

astound ▶ verb *Kate was astounded by his arrogance* **amaze**, astonish, stagger, surprise, startle, stun, confound, dumbfound, stupefy, daze, nonplus; throw, shake, unnerve, disconcert, discompose, bewilder; take someone's breath away, take by surprise, take aback, shake up, stop someone in their tracks, strike dumb, leave open-mouthed, leave aghast, catch off balance; *informal* flabbergast, floor, knock for six, knock someone sideways, knock out, knock the stuffing out of, bowl over, blow someone's mind, blow away.

astounding ▶ adjective *his speed and fitness were astounding* **amazing**, astonishing, staggering, shocking, surprising, breathtaking, striking, impressive, bewildering, stunning, stupefying; unnerving, unsettling, disturbing, disquieting; awe-inspiring, remarkable, notable, noteworthy, extraordinary, outstanding, incredible, unbelievable, phenomenal, uncommon, unheard of; *informal* mind-boggling, mind-blowing, hard to swallow.

astray ▶ adverb **1** *the gunman claimed that the shots had gone astray* **off target**, wide of the mark, wide, awry; **off course**, off track, off the right track, adrift; *informal* off beam.
2 *they were accused of leading young girls astray* **into wrongdoing**, into error, into sin, into iniquity, away from the straight and narrow, away from the path of righteousness; *informal* off the rails.

astringent ▶ adjective **1** *the lotion has a mildly astringent effect on open pores* **constricting**, contracting, constrictive, constringent, styptic.
2 *her godmother's astringent words had the desired effect* **severe**, sharp, stern, harsh, rough, acerbic, austere, caustic, mordant, trenchant; sarcastic, sardonic, scathing, cutting, incisive, penetrating, piercing, stinging, searing; wounding, hurtful, unkind, cruel, spiteful, waspish, poisonous, vicious; *N. Amer.* acerb; *informal* bitchy, catty; *Brit. informal* sarky; *N. Amer. informal* snarky; *rare* acidulous, mordacious.

astrology ▶ noun **horoscopy**, stargazing; horoscopes; *rare* astromancy.

astronaut ▶ noun **spaceman**, **spacewoman**, cosmonaut, space traveller, space pilot, space flyer, space cadet; *N. Amer. informal* jock.

astronomical ▶ adjective **1** *they studied Stonehenge in terms of astronomical alignments* **celestial**, planetary, stellar, astronomic, heavenly.
2 (*informal*) *the sums he has paid out are astronomical* **huge**, enormous, very large, very great, very big, prodigious, tremendous, monumental, mammoth, colossal, vast, gigantic, massive, epic, monstrous, terrific, titanic, towering, king-sized, king-size; substantial, considerable, sizeable, hefty, handsome, kingly, princely, lavish, generous, inordinate; *informal* astronomic, almighty, whopping, whopping great, thumping, thumping great, bumper, mega, monster, jumbo, humongous, serious, dirty great, rip-roaring; *Brit. informal* whacking, whacking great, ginormous.
OPPOSITES insignificant, small.

astronomy ▶ noun
WORD LINKS
Muse **Urania**

astute ▶ adjective *he had a reputation as an astute businessman | an uncomfortably astute remark* **shrewd**, sharp, sharp-witted, razor-sharp, acute, quick, quick-witted, ingenious, clever, intelligent, bright, brilliant, smart, canny, intuitive, discerning, perceptive, perspicacious, penetrating, insightful, incisive, piercing, discriminating, sagacious, wise, judicious; cunning, artful, crafty, wily, calculating; *informal* on the ball, quick off the mark, quick on the uptake, brainy, streetwise, savvy; *Brit. informal* suss; *Scottish & N. English informal* pawky; *N. Amer. informal* heads-up; *dated, informal* long-headed; *rare* argute, sapient.
OPPOSITE stupid.

asunder ▶ adverb (*literary*) *the very fabric of society may be torn asunder* **apart**, up, in two; into pieces, to pieces, to bits, to shreds.

asylum ▶ noun **1** *he appealed to Germany for political asylum | the refugees had to find another asylum* **refuge**, sanctuary, shelter, safety, safe keeping, protection, security, immunity; haven, safe haven, retreat, sanctum, harbour, port in a storm, oasis; safe house, fastness, hideaway, hideout, bolt-hole, foxhole, hiding place, den.
2 *his father went mad and was confined to an asylum* **psychiatric hospital**, mental hospital, mental institution, mental asylum, institution; *informal* madhouse, nuthouse, loony bin, funny farm; *N. Amer. informal* bughouse, booby hatch; *dated* lunatic asylum; *archaic* bedlam.

asymmetrical ▶ adjective *it was an engagingly asymmetrical church | the asymmetrical division of labour* **lopsided**, unsymmetrical, crooked; **uneven**, unbalanced, off-balance, off-centre, to one side, awry, askew, skew, skewed, squint, tilted, tilting, misaligned, sloping, slanted, aslant, out of true, out of line; disproportionate, unequal, misproportioned, ill-proportioned, ill-shaped, misshapen, irregular, distorted, out of shape, malformed, formless; *Scottish* agley, thrawn; *informal* cock-eyed; *Brit. informal* skew-whiff, wonky, squiffy.
OPPOSITE symmetrical.

atheism ▶ noun *atheism is virtually unknown in rural societies* **non-belief**, disbelief, unbelief, scepticism, doubt, agnosticism, irreligion, godlessness, ungodliness, profaneness, impiety, heresy, apostasy, paganism, heathenism, freethinking, nihilism.
OPPOSITES belief, faith.

atheist ▶ noun *he was an intellectually fulfilled atheist* **non-believer**, disbeliever, unbeliever, heretic, sceptic, doubter, doubting Thomas, agnostic, infidel, irreligious person, heathen, pagan, freethinker, libertine, nihilist; *archaic* paynim; *rare* nullifidian.
OPPOSITE believer.

athlete ▶ noun *she is a superbly gifted all-round athlete* **sportswoman**, **sportsman**, sportsperson; runner, racer, player, games player, gymnast, team member; competitor, contestant, contender; *informal* keep-fit buff, keep-fit freak; *N. Amer. informal* jock, jockstrap.

athletic ▶ adjective **1** *his shirt did not hide his athletic physique* **muscular**, muscly, sturdy, strapping, well built, powerfully built, strong, powerful, robust, able-bodied, vigorous, hardy, lusty, hearty, hale and hearty, brawny, burly, broad-shouldered, thickset, Herculean; **fit**, fighting fit, as fit as a fiddle, as fit as a flea, in good shape, in good trim, in trim, in tip-top condition, healthy, in good health, bursting with health, in fine fettle, as strong as an ox, as strong as a horse, as strong as a lion; *Brit.* in rude health; *informal* sporty, husky, hunky, beefy; *dated* stalwart; *literary* thewy, stark; *technical* mesomorphic.
OPPOSITES weak, frail.
2 *they were banned from the athletic events* **sporting**, sports, games, gymnastic; competitive.

athletics *See centre pages for list of* **Athletics Events**
▶ plural noun *he dropped out of athletics after a season without a win* **track and field events**, sporting events, sports, games, organized games, matches, races, contests, competitions; exercises, gymnastics; *archaic* palaestra.

atmosphere *See centre pages for lists of* **Atmosphere Layers** **Cloud Formations** **Weather Phenomena**
▶ noun **1** *ozone-depleting gases are present in the atmosphere* **air**, aerosphere, airspace, sky; *literary* the heavens, the firmament, the vault of heaven, the blue, the wide blue yonder, the azure, the ether, the welkin, the empyrean, the upper regions, the sphere.
2 *the hotel has a friendly and relaxed atmosphere* **ambience**, aura, climate, air, mood, feel, feeling, character, tone, overtone, undertone, tenor, spirit, quality, aspect, element, undercurrent, flavour, colour, colouring, look, impression, suggestion, emanation; environment, milieu, medium, background, backdrop, setting, context; surroundings, environs, conditions, circumstances, vibrations; *informal* vibe, vibes; *rare* subcurrent.
WORD LINKS
study of the atmosphere **meteorology, aerology** (*dated*)
study of the upper atmosphere **aeronomy**

atom ▶ noun *they build tiny circuits atom by atom | there wasn't an atom of truth in the allegations* **particle**, molecule, bit, little bit, tiny bit, tiny piece, fragment, fraction, grain, granule, crumb, morsel, mite, mote, speck, spot, dot; **iota**, jot, whit, scrap, shred, trace, tinge, ounce, modicum, scintilla, vestige; *Irish* stim; *informal* smidgen, smidge, tad; *archaic* scantling, scruple.

atone ▶ verb *what would you have me do to* **atone for** *my sin?* **make amends**, make reparation, make restitution, make recompense, make redress, make up for, compensate, pay, pay the penalty, pay the price, recompense, answer; expiate, make good, offset; do penance, redeem oneself, redress the balance; *formal* requite.

atonement ▶ noun *I was making a pilgrimage in atonement for my sins* **reparation**, compensation, recompense, payment, repayment, redress, restitution, indemnity, indemnification, expiation, penance, redemption; amends; *formal* requital; *rare* solatium.

atrocious ▶ adjective **1** *atrocious cruelties were committed in the name of religion* **brutal**, barbaric, barbarous, brutish, savage, vicious, wicked, cruel, nasty, ruthless, merciless, villainous, murderous, heinous, nefarious, monstrous, base, low, low-down, vile, inhuman, infernal, dark, black, black-hearted, fiendish, hellish, diabolical, ghastly, horrible; abominable, outrageous, offensive, hateful, disgusting, despicable, contemptible, loathsome, odious, revolting, repellent, repugnant, abhorrent, harrowing, nightmarish, gruesome, grisly, sickening, nauseating, horrifying, hideous, unspeakable, unforgivable, intolerable, beyond the pale, scandalous, flagrant, execrable; *informal* horrid, gross, sick-making, sick; *Brit. informal* beastly; *archaic* disgustful, loathly, scurvy; *rare* egregious, flagitious, cacodemonic, facinorous.
OPPOSITES admirable; kindly.
2 *the weather was atrocious* **appalling**, dreadful, terrible, very bad, unpleasant, lamentable, woeful, miserable, poor, inadequate, unsatisfactory; *informal* abysmal, dire, rotten, crummy, lousy, poxy, yucky, God-awful, the pits; *Brit. informal* shocking, duff, beastly, chronic, pants, a load of pants, rubbish, rubbishy, ropy; *vulgar slang* crap, crappy, chickenshit; *archaic* direful.
OPPOSITE superb.

atrocity ▶ noun **1** *press reports detailed a number of atrocities* **act of**

barbarity, act of brutality, act of savagery, act of wickedness, cruelty, abomination, enormity, outrage, horror, monstrosity, obscenity, iniquity, violation, crime, transgression, wrong, wrongdoing, offence, injury, affront, scandal, injustice, abuse; *Law* malfeasance, tort.
2 *he observed conflict and atrocity around the globe* **barbarity**, barbarism, brutality, savagery, inhumanity, cruelty, wickedness, badness, baseness, evil, iniquity, horror, heinousness, villainy, lawlessness, crime, transgression, wrong, wrongdoing, injustice, abuse; *Law* malfeasance; *rare* malefaction.

atrophy ▶ **verb 1** *the body parts which are no longer required gradually atrophy* **waste away**, waste, become emaciated, wither, shrivel, shrivel up, shrink, become shrunken, dry up, decay, wilt; decline, deteriorate, degenerate, grow weak, weaken, become debilitated, become enfeebled.
OPPOSITE strengthen.
2 *in the final few days, the Labour campaign atrophied* **peter out**, taper off, tail off, dwindle, deteriorate, decline, wane, fade, fade away, fade out, give in, give up, give way, crumble, disintegrate, collapse, slump, go downhill, draw to a close, subside; be neglected, be abandoned, be disregarded, be forgotten.
OPPOSITE flourish.
▶ **noun** *they located the gene that causes muscular atrophy* **wasting**, wasting away, emaciation, withering, shrivelling, shrivelling up, shrinking, drying up, wilting, decaying, decay; declining, deteriorating, deterioration, degenerating, degeneration, weakening, debilitation, enfeeblement.
OPPOSITE strengthening.

attach ▶ **verb 1** *his ankles were attached by chains to the wall* **fasten**, fix, affix, join, connect, couple, link, secure, make fast, tie, tie up, bind, fetter, strap, rope, tether, truss, lash, hitch, moor, anchor, yoke, chain; stick, tape, adhere, glue, bond, cement, fuse, weld, solder; pin, peg, screw, bolt, rivet, batten, pinion, clamp, clip; add, append, annex, subjoin.
OPPOSITE detach.
2 *he* **attached** *himself* **to** *the radical section of the Liberal Party* **affiliate with**, associate with, align with, ally with, unite with, combine with, integrate into, join to; join up with, join forces with, band together with, team up with, latch on to, cooperate with, be in league with, form an alliance with, make a pact with; *informal* tag along with.
OPPOSITE break away from.
3 *they* **attached** *great importance* **to** *research* **ascribe**, assign, attribute, accredit, apply, impute; invest with, put on, place on, lay on.
4 *he is the medical officer attached to Brigade Headquarters* **assign**, allot, allocate, detail, appoint; relocate, reassign, transfer, move, send, second, lend.
OPPOSITE separate.
5 (*Law*) *the state attached criminals' property* **seize**, confiscate, commandeer, requisition, appropriate, expropriate, take possession of, take away, take, sequester, sequestrate; *Law* distrain, disseize; *Scottish Law* poind.

attached ▶ **adjective 1** *the young couple are now attached* **married**, wed, wedded, joined in marriage, joined in matrimony, united in wedlock; **engaged**, affianced, pledged, promised, promised in marriage, going out, spoken for, involved; united, bound, contracted; *informal* hitched, spliced, yoked, shackled, going steady, boyfriend and girlfriend; *dated* betrothed; *archaic* espoused, plighted.
OPPOSITES unattached, single.
2 *she was very* **attached to** *her brother* **fond of**, devoted to, full of regard for, full of admiration for; affectionate towards, tender towards, caring towards; *informal* mad about, crazy about, nuts about.

attachment ▶ **noun 1** *he had a strong* **attachment to** *his mother* **bond**, closeness, devotion, loyalty; **fondness for**, love for, liking for, affection for, affinity for, tenderness for, feeling for, sentiment for, regard for, respect for, admiration for, reverence for; relationship with, friendship with, intimacy with.
2 *the shower had a soothing massage attachment* **accessory**, fitting, fitment, extension, supplementary part, supplementary component, extra, extra part, adjunct, addition, add-on, appurtenance, appendage, accoutrement, auxiliary.
3 *all cars have points for the attachment of safety restraints* **fixing**, fastening, affixing, linking, coupling, clamping, connection, connecting; addition, adding, incorporation, introduction, insertion.
4 *he was on attachment from another regiment* **assignment**, detail, appointment, allocation, secondment, transfer, relocation.
5 *he maintained his family's Conservative attachment* **affiliation**, association, alliance, alignment, union, bond, liaison, coalition, partnership, fellowship, belonging; links, ties, connections, sympathies.
6 (*Law*) *the attachment of criminals' property* **seizure**, confiscation, appropriation, expropriation, sequestration, taking away, commandeering; *Law* distrainment, disseizin; *Scottish Law* poinding.

attack ▶ **verb 1** *Christopher had been brutally attacked* **assault**, beat, beat up, batter, thrash, pound, pummel, assail, set upon, fall upon, set about, strike at, let fly at, tear into, lash out at; ambush, mug, pounce on; *informal* jump, paste, do over, work over, knock about/around, rough up, lay into, lace into, sail into, pitch into, get stuck into, beat the living daylights out of, let someone have it; *Brit. informal* have a go at, duff someone up; *N. Amer. informal* beat up on, light into.
2 *by eight o'clock the French had still not attacked* **begin an assault**, charge, pounce, strike, begin hostilities, ambush; bombard, shell, blitz, strafe, fire on/at; rush, storm.
OPPOSITE defend.
3 *the clergy have consistently attacked government policies* **criticize**, censure, condemn, castigate, chastise, lambaste, pillory, savage, find fault with, fulminate against, abuse; berate, reprove, rebuke, reprimand, admonish, remonstrate with, reproach, take to task, haul over the coals, impugn, harangue, blame, revile, vilify, give someone a bad press; *informal* knock, slam, take to pieces, pull apart, crucify, bash, hammer, lay into, tear into, sail into, roast, give someone a roasting, cane, blast, bawl out, dress down, rap over the knuckles, have a go at, give someone hell; *Brit. informal* carpet, slate, slag off, rubbish, rollick, give someone a rollicking, give someone a rocket, tear someone off a strip, tear a strip off someone; *N. Amer. informal* chew out, ream out, pummel, cut up; *Austral./NZ informal* bag, monster; *Brit. vulgar slang* bollock, give someone a bollocking; *dated* rate; *archaic* slash; *rare* excoriate, objurgate, reprehend.
OPPOSITE praise.
4 *they have started to attack the problem of threatened species* **attend to**, address, see to, deal with, grapple with, confront, direct one's attention to, focus on, concentrate on, apply oneself to; buckle down to, get to work on, go to work on, set to work on, set about, get started on, undertake, embark on; *informal* get stuck into, get cracking on, get weaving on, have a crack at, have a go at, have a shot at, have a stab at.
5 *the virus attacks the liver, heart, and lungs* **affect**, have an effect on, strike, strike at, take hold of, infect; **damage**, injure.
OPPOSITE protect.
▶ **noun 1** *they were killed in an attack on their home* **assault**, onslaught, offensive, strike, blitz, raid, sortie, sally, storming, charge, rush, drive, push, thrust, invasion, incursion, inroad; act of aggression; *historical* razzia; *archaic* onset.
2 *she wrote a ferociously hostile attack on him* **criticism**, censure, rebuke, admonition, admonishment, reprimand, reproval; condemnation, denunciation, revilement; invective, vilification; tirade, diatribe, rant, polemic, broadside, harangue, verbal onslaught, stricture; *informal* knocking, telling-off, dressing-down, rap over the knuckles, earful, roasting, rollicking, caning; *Brit. informal* rocket, wigging, slating, ticking-off, carpeting, bashing, blast; *Brit. vulgar slang* bollocking; *dated* rating; *rare* philippic.
OPPOSITES commendation, defence.
3 *she had suffered an acute asthmatic attack* **fit**, seizure, spasm, convulsion, paroxysm, outburst, flare-up; bout, spell, dose; *rare* access.

attacker ▶ **noun** *she was punched in the face by the attacker* **assailant**, assaulter, aggressor, striker; mugger, rapist, killer, murderer; *informal* slasher.

attain ▶ **verb** *they help the child attain his or her full potential* **achieve**, accomplish, reach, arrive at, come by, obtain, gain, procure, secure, get, grasp, hook, net, win, earn, acquire, establish, make; realize, fulfil, succeed in, bring off, bring about, bring to fruition, carry off, carry through, effect; *informal* hit, clinch, bag, wangle, wrap up, polish off; *rare* effectuate, reify.

attainable ▶ **adjective** *a challenging but attainable target* **achievable**, obtainable, accessible, within reach, at hand, reachable, winnable, securable, realizable; practicable, workable, manageable, realistic, reasonable, viable, feasible, possible, within the bounds/realms of possibility, potential, conceivable, imaginable; *informal* doable, get-at-able, up for grabs; *rare* accomplishable.
OPPOSITE unattainable.

attainment ▶ **noun 1** *they are making progress towards the attainment of common goals* **achievement**, accomplishment, realization, realizing, fulfilment, fulfilling, effecting, completion, consummation; success, fruition; securing, gaining, gain, procurement, procuring, acquiring, acquisition; *rare* effectuation, reification.
2 *a low standard of educational attainment* **proficiency**, competence, mastery, accomplishment, achievement, qualification; art, skill, talent, gift, aptitude, faculty, ability, capability.

attempt ▶ **verb** *I attempted to answer the question | he attempted a takeover bid* **try**, strive, aim, venture, endeavour, seek, set out, do one's best, do all one can, do one's utmost, make an effort, make every effort, spare no effort, give one's all, take it on oneself; have a go at, undertake, embark on, try one's hand at, try out; *informal* give it a whirl, give it one's best shot, go all out, pull out all the stops, bend over backwards, knock oneself out, bust a gut, break one's neck, move heaven and earth, have a crack at, have a shot at, have a stab at; *Austral./NZ informal* give it a burl, give it a fly; *formal* essay; *archaic* assay.
▶ **noun** *an attempt to put the economy to rights* **effort**, endeavour, try, bid, venture, trial, experiment; *informal* crack, go, shot, stab, bash, whack; *formal* essay; *archaic* assay.

attend ▶ **verb 1** *they attended a carol service | she attended evening classes* **be**

present at, be at, be there at, sit in on, take part in; appear at, put in an appearance at, make an appearance at, present oneself at, turn up at, visit, pay a visit to, go to; frequent, haunt, patronize; *informal* show up at, pop up at, show one's face at, hang out at, take in, catch.
OPPOSITE miss.
2 *he had not* ***attended*** *sufficiently* ***to*** *the regulations* **pay attention**, pay heed, be attentive, listen, lend an ear; concentrate on, take note of, bear in mind, give thought to, take into consideration, be heedful of, heed, respect, follow, observe, notice, mark; *informal* tune in to, get a load of, check out, be all ears for; *archaic* hearken, give ear, regard.
OPPOSITES disregard, ignore.
3 *the wounded could be* ***attended to*** *at a nearby village* **care for**, look after, take care of, minister to, administer to, keep an eye on, see to; tend, treat, nurse, help, aid, assist, succour, nurture, mind; *informal* doctor.
4 *their father* ***attended to*** *the boy's education* **deal with**, cope with, see to, address, manage, organize, orchestrate, make arrangements for, sort out, handle, take care of, take charge of, take responsibility for, take in hand, take up, undertake, tackle, give one's attention to, apply oneself to.
OPPOSITE neglect.
5 *the queen was attended by a liveried usher* **escort**, accompany, guard, chaperone, squire, convoy, guide, lead, conduct, usher, shepherd, follow, shadow; **assist**, help, serve, wait on.
6 *her giddiness* ***was attended with*** *a fever* **be accompanied by**, be associated with, be connected with, be linked with, go hand in hand with; occur with, co-occur with, coexist with, be produced by, be brought about by, originate from, originate in, stem from, result from, be a result of, arise from, follow on from, be a consequence of.

attendance ▶ noun **1** *you requested the attendance of a doctor* **presence**, appearance, attending, being there; *informal* turning up, showing up, showing.
OPPOSITE absence.
2 *their gig attendances grew at an alarming rate* **audience**, turnout, number present, house, gate; crowd, throng, congregation, assembly, gathering; *Austral./NZ informal* muster.
□ **in attendance** *his wife is in labour with three obstetricians in attendance* **present**, here, there, near, nearby, at hand, by one's side, available; assisting, giving assistance, helping, aiding; supervising, monitoring, on guard.

attendant ▶ noun **1** *a sleeping-car attendant delivered hot-water bottles* **steward**, waiter, waitress, porter, servant, menial, auxiliary, assistant, helper; caretaker, keeper, concierge, warden; *N. Amer.* waitperson, tender; *French* garçon.
2 *he prospered as a royal attendant* **escort**, companion, retainer, aide, assistant, personal assistant, right-hand man, right-hand woman, lady in waiting, equerry, squire, chaperone, guard, bodyguard, minder, custodian; servant, manservant, valet, gentleman's gentleman, maidservant, maid, butler, footman, page, usher, lackey, flunkey; *N. Amer.* houseman; *informal* sidekick, skivvy; *Military, dated* batman.
▶ adjective *we crave new discoveries and the attendant excitement* **accompanying**, associated, related, connected, concomitant, accessory; resultant, resulting, consequent.

attention ▶ noun **1** *the issue clearly needs further attention* **observation**, attentiveness, intentness, notice, concentration, heed, heedfulness, mindfulness, regard, scrutiny; contemplation, consideration, deliberation, thought, thinking, studying, investigation, action.
2 *he was likely to attract the attention of a policeman* **awareness**, notice, observation, consciousness, heed, recognition, regard, scrutiny, surveillance, attentiveness; curiosity, inquisitiveness.
3 *they failed to give adequate medical attention* **care**, treatment, therapy, ministration, succour, relief, support, aid, help, assistance, service.
4 *the parson was effusive in his attentions* **courtesy**, civility, politeness, respect, gallantry, urbanity, deference; compliment, flattery, blandishment; overture, suggestion, approach, suit, pass, wooing, courting.

attentive ▶ adjective **1** *she was a bright and attentive scholar* **alert**, awake, watchful, wide awake, observant, perceptive, percipient, acute, aware, noticing, heeding, heedful, mindful, vigilant, on guard, on one's guard, on one's toes, on the qui vive, on the lookout; concentrating, intent, absorbed, engrossed, focused, committed, studious, diligent, scrupulous, rigorous, earnest, interested; *informal* all ears, beady-eyed, not missing a trick, on the ball; *rare* regardful.
OPPOSITE inattentive.
2 *I haven't been the most attentive of husbands* **conscientious**, considerate, thoughtful, kind, kindly, caring, tender, solicitous, understanding, sympathetic, obliging, accommodating, gallant, chivalrous; polite, well mannered, courteous, gracious, civil, respectful, reverential, dutiful, responsible; *Brit. informal* decent; *dated* mannerly; *rare* regardful.
OPPOSITE inconsiderate.

attenuated ▶ adjective **1** *he rippled his attenuated fingers in the air* **thin**, slender, slim, skinny, spindly, bony, gaunt, skeletal; narrow, thread-like, thinned down, stretched out, drawn out; *rare* extenuated, attenuate.
OPPOSITES plump; broad.
2 *radiation from the sun is attenuated by the earth's atmosphere* **weakened**, reduced, lessened, decreased, diminished, impaired, enervated.
OPPOSITE strengthened.

attest ▶ verb *previous experience is attested by a certificate | I can* ***attest to*** *his tremendous energy* **certify**, corroborate, confirm, verify, substantiate, document, authenticate, give proof of, provide evidence of, evidence, demonstrate, evince, display, exhibit, show, manifest, prove, endorse, back up, support, guarantee; affirm, aver, swear to, testify to, bear witness to, bear out, give credence to, vouch for; *Law* depose to; *informal* stick up for, throw one's weight behind; *rare* asseverate.
OPPOSITE disprove.

attic ▶ noun *a short flight of rickety steps led to the attic* **loft**, roof space, cock loft; garret, mansard, loft conversion; *informal, dated* sky parlour.

attire ▶ noun *Thomas preferred formal attire for dinner* **clothing**, clothes, garments, dress, wear, outfit, turnout, garb, ensemble, costume, array, finery, regalia; wardrobe, accoutrements, trappings; *Brit.* kit, strip; *informal* gear, togs, duds, glad rags, get-up; *Brit. informal* clobber, rig-out; *N. Amer. informal* threads; *formal* apparel; *archaic* raiment, habiliments, habit, vestments.
▶ verb *the widow was correctly attired in black crêpe* **dress**, clothe, dress up, fit out, garb, robe, array, deck, deck out, turn out, trick out, trick up, costume, accoutre; drape, swathe, adorn; *informal* doll up, get up; *Brit. informal* rig out; *formal* apparel; *literary* bedizen, caparison, furbelow; *archaic* invest, habit, trap out.

attired ▶ adjective *he was always impeccably attired* **dressed**, clothed, dressed up, fitted out, garbed, arrayed, decked out, turned out, tricked up, costumed; *informal* dolled up, got up, got out; *Brit. informal* rigged out; *archaic* apparelled, invested, habited, trapped out.

attitude ▶ noun **1** *you seem oddly ambivalent in your attitude* **point of view**, view, viewpoint, vantage point, frame of mind, way of thinking, way of looking at things, school of thought, outlook, angle, slant, perspective, reaction, stance, standpoint, position, inclination, orientation, approach; opinion, ideas, belief, convictions, feelings, sentiments, persuasion, thoughts, thinking, interpretation.
2 *they knelt around her bed in attitudes of prayer* **position**, posture, pose, stance, stand; bearing, deportment, comportment, carriage.

attorney ▶ noun (*N. Amer.*) *the defendant will have trouble finding an attorney* **lawyer**, legal practitioner, legal executive, legal adviser, legal representative, agent, member of the bar, advocate, counsel, counsellor, intercessor, defending counsel, prosecuting counsel; *Brit.* barrister, Queen's Counsel, QC; *N. Amer. & Irish* counsellor-at-law; *informal* brief.

attract ▶ verb **1** *positively charged hydrogen ions are attracted to the negatively charged terminal* **draw**, pull, magnetize.
OPPOSITE repel.
2 *he was immediately attracted by her friendly smile* **entice**, allure, lure, tempt, charm, win over, woo, engage, enchant, entrance, mesmerize, hypnotize, spellbind, captivate, beguile, bewitch, seduce, dazzle, tantalize, inveigle, lead on; interest, fascinate, enthral, absorb, rivet; excite, titillate, arouse, stimulate; *informal* tickle someone's fancy, turn on, light someone's fire, float someone's boat, make someone's mouth water.
OPPOSITE repel.

attraction ▶ noun **1** *the stars are held close together by mutual gravitational attraction* **pull**, draw; magnetism.
OPPOSITE repulsion.
2 *she felt that she had lost whatever attraction she had ever had | he felt the attraction of the literary life* **appeal**, attractiveness, desirability, seductiveness, seduction, allure, allurement, magnetism, animal magnetism, sexual magnetism, charisma, charm, beauty, good looks, glamour, magic, spell; pull, draw, lure, enticement, entrancement, temptation, inducement, interest, fascination, enchantment, captivation; *informal* come-on.
OPPOSITE repulsion.
3 *the fair offers sideshows, stalls, and other attractions* **entertainment**, activity, diversion, interest, feature, crowd-pleaser.

attractive ▶ adjective **1** *they wanted to make military service a more attractive career* **appealing**, agreeable, pleasing, inviting, tempting, interesting, fascinating, irresistible.
OPPOSITES unattractive, uninviting.
2 *I'm sure she has no idea how attractive she is* **good-looking**, nice-looking, beautiful, pretty, as pretty as a picture, handsome, lovely, stunning, striking, arresting, gorgeous, prepossessing, winning, fetching, captivating, bewitching, beguiling, engaging, charming, charismatic, enchanting, appealing, delightful, irresistible; sexy, sexually attractive, sexual, seductive, alluring, tantalizing, ravishing, desirable, sultry, sensuous, sensual, erotic, arousing, luscious, lush, nubile; *Scottish & N. English* bonny; *informal* fanciable, beddable, tasty, hot, smashing, knockout, drop-dead gorgeous, out of this world, easy on the eye, come-hither, come-to-bed; *Brit. informal* fit; *N. Amer. informal* cute, foxy, bootylicious; *Austral./NZ informal* spunky; *literary* beauteous; *dated* taking, well favoured; *archaic*

comely, fair; *rare* sightly, pulchritudinous.
OPPOSITES unattractive, ugly.

attribute ▶ verb (stress on the second syllable) *they **attributed** the success of the expedition entirely **to** one man* **ascribe**, assign, accredit, credit, impute, allot, allocate; put down to, set down to, chalk up to, lay at the door of, hold responsible for, pin something on, lay something on, place something on; connect with, associate with; *informal* stick something on.
▶ noun (stress on the first syllable) **1** *he has all the attributes of a top midfield player* **quality**, feature, characteristic, trait, element, aspect, property, hallmark, mark, distinction, sign, telltale sign, sure sign; idiosyncrasy, peculiarity, quirk.
2 *the hourglass was depicted as the attribute of Father Time* **symbol**, indicator, mark, sign, hallmark, trademark, status symbol.

attrition ▶ noun **1** *the strike developed into a bitter war of attrition* **wearing down**, wearing away, weakening, debilitation, enfeebling, sapping, attenuation; harassment, harrying.
2 *the attrition of the edges of the teeth* **abrasion**, friction, rubbing, chafing, corroding, corrosion, erosion, eating away, grinding, scraping, wearing away, wearing, excoriation, deterioration, damaging; *rare* detrition.

attune ▶ verb *she was **attuned to** the refinements of Cambridge society* **accustom**, adjust, adapt, acclimatize, assimilate, condition, accommodate, tailor; (**be attuned to**) be in tune with, be in harmony with, be in accord with; *N. Amer.* acclimate.

atypical ▶ adjective *a lack of social relationships is atypical* **unusual**, untypical, non-typical, uncommon, unconventional, unorthodox, anomalous, irregular, abnormal, aberrant, deviant, divergent; strange, odd, peculiar, curious, bizarre, weird, queer, freakish, freak, eccentric, quirky, alien; exceptional, singular, rare, unique, isolated, unrepresentative, out of the way, out of the ordinary, extraordinary; *Brit.* out of the common; *informal* funny, oddball, off the wall, wacko, wacky, way out, freaky, kinky, something else; *Brit. informal* rum.
OPPOSITE typical.

auburn ▶ adjective *she had a head of flowing auburn hair* **reddish-brown**, red-brown, dark red, Titian, Titian red, tawny, russet, chestnut, chestnut-coloured, copper, coppery, copper-coloured, rust-coloured, rufous, henna, hennaed; *rare* rufescent.

au courant ▶ adjective (*French*) *he is **au courant with** the twists and turns of all major events* **up to date**, up with, in touch, familiar, at home, acquainted, conversant; abreast of, apprised of, in the know about, well informed about, knowledgeable about, well versed in, enlightened about, aware of, no stranger to; *French* au fait; *informal* clued up about, genned up about, clued up on, well up on, wise to, hip to; *Brit. informal* switched on to; *black English* down.
OPPOSITE out of touch.

audacious ▶ adjective **1** *the audience were left gasping at his audacious exploits* **bold**, daring, fearless, intrepid, brave, unafraid, unflinching, courageous, valiant, valorous, heroic, dashing, plucky, daredevil, devil-may-care, death-or-glory, reckless, wild, madcap; adventurous, venturesome, enterprising, dynamic, spirited, mettlesome; *informal* game, gutsy, spunky, ballsy, have-a-go, go-ahead; *rare* venturous, temerarious.
OPPOSITE timid.
2 *Des made some audacious remark to her* **impudent**, impertinent, insolent, presumptuous, forward, cheeky, irreverent, discourteous, disrespectful, insubordinate, ill-mannered, bad-mannered, unmannerly, rude, crude, brazen, brazen-faced, brash, shameless, pert, defiant, bold, bold as brass, outrageous, shocking, out of line; *informal* brass-necked, cocky, lippy, mouthy, fresh, flip; *Brit. informal* saucy, smart-arsed; *N. Amer. informal* sassy, nervy, smart-assed; *archaic* malapert, contumelious; *rare* tossy, mannerless.
OPPOSITE polite.

> **CHOOSE THE RIGHT WORD**
> **audacious, bold, daring**
> See BOLD.

audacity ▶ noun **1** *he was a traveller of extraordinary audacity* **boldness**, daring, fearlessness, intrepidity, bravery, courage, courageousness, valour, valorousness, heroism, pluck, recklessness; adventurousness, enterprise, dynamism, spirit, mettle, confidence; *informal* guts, gutsiness, spunk, grit; *Brit. informal* bottle, ballsiness; *N. Amer. informal* moxie, cojones, sand; *vulgar slang* balls; *rare* venturousness, temerariousness.
OPPOSITE timidity.
2 *he had the audacity to contradict me* **impudence**, impertinence, insolence, presumption, presumptuousness, forwardness, cheek, cheekiness, impoliteness, unmannerliness, bad manners, rudeness, effrontery, nerve, gall, brazenness, brashness, shamelessness, pertness, defiance, boldness, temerity; *informal* brass, brass neck, neck, face, cockiness; *Brit. informal* sauce; *Scottish informal* snash; *N. Amer. informal* sass, sassiness, nerviness, chutzpah; *informal, dated* hide; *Brit. informal, dated* crust; *archaic* malapertness; *rare* procacity, assumption.
OPPOSITE politeness.

audible ▶ adjective *her voice was weak and barely audible* **perceptible**, discernible, detectable, hearable, able to be heard, recognizable, appreciable; clear, distinct, loud, carrying.
OPPOSITES inaudible, faint.

audience ▶ noun **1** *they performed three sketches which went down well with the audience* **spectators, listeners**, viewers, onlookers, patrons; assembly, gathering, crowd, throng, company, assemblage, congregation, turnout; house, gallery, stalls; *Brit. informal* punters.
2 *the radio station was clearly geared to a teenage audience* **market, public**, following, clientele, patronage, listenership, viewership; followers, fans, devotees, aficionados; *informal* buffs, freaks.
3 *he had an audience with Pope John Paul II* **meeting**, consultation, conference, hearing, reception, interview, question and answer session, exchange, dialogue, discussion.

audit ▶ noun *he announced an immediate audit of the party accounts* **inspection**, examination, survey, scrutiny, probe, vetting, investigation, check, assessment, appraisal, evaluation, review, analysis, study, perusal, dissection; *informal* going-over, once-over, look-see.
▶ verb *we have audited the accounts of the corporation* **inspect**, examine, survey, look over, go over, go through, scrutinize, probe, vet, investigate, look into, enquire into, check, check into, assess, appraise, evaluate, review, analyse, study, pore over, peruse, sift, dissect, go over with a fine-tooth comb, delve into, dig into; *N. Amer.* check out; *informal* give something a/the once-over, give something a going-over.

auditorium ▶ noun *the singer's voice carries through the vast auditorium* **theatre**, hall, concert hall, conference hall, assembly hall, assembly room; chamber, room.

au fait ▶ adjective (*French*) *she was **au fait with** all the latest technology* **familiar**, acquainted, conversant, at home, up to date, up with, in touch; abreast of, apprised of, in the know about, well informed about, knowledgeable about, well versed in, enlightened about, aware of, no stranger to; *French* au courant; *informal* clued up about, genned up about, clued up on, well up on, wise to, hip to; *Brit. informal* switched on to; *black English* down.
OPPOSITE out of touch.

augment ▶ verb *he augmented his meagre income by plying for hire as a ferryman | Aubrey's arrival had augmented their difficulties* **increase**, make larger, make bigger, make greater, add to, supplement, top up, build up, enlarge, expand, extend, raise, multiply, elevate, swell, inflate; magnify, intensify, amplify, heighten, escalate; worsen, make worse, exacerbate, aggravate, inflame, compound, reinforce; improve, make better, boost, ameliorate, enhance, upgrade; *informal* up, jack up, hike up, hike, bump up, crank up, step up.
OPPOSITE decrease.

augur ▶ verb *their recent successes augur well for the future | the happenings augur a neo-Nazi revival* **bode**; **portend**, herald, be a sign of, be an indication of, be a warning of, warn of, forewarn of, be an omen of, be a harbinger of, foreshadow, presage, indicate, signify, signal, point to, promise, threaten, spell, denote; foretell, forecast, predict, prophesy, prognosticate, divine, foresee; *literary* betoken, foretoken, forebode, harbinger; *archaic* foreshow, previse; *Scottish archaic* spae; *rare* vaticinate, auspicate.
▶ noun *the augur's skill consisted in reading the omens correctly* **seer**, soothsayer, fortune teller, crystal-gazer, clairvoyant, psychic, visionary, prognosticator, diviner, prophesier, prophet, prophetess, oracle, sibyl, sage, wise man, wise woman; *Scottish* spaewife, spaeman; *rare* oracler, vaticinator, haruspex.

August ▶ noun
WORD LINKS
birthstone **sardonyx**

august ▶ adjective *she was in august company* **distinguished**, respected, eminent, venerable, hallowed, illustrious, prestigious, renowned, celebrated, honoured, acclaimed, esteemed, exalted, highly regarded, well thought of, of distinction, of repute; great, important, of high standing, lofty, high-ranking, noble, regal, royal, aristocratic; imposing, impressive, awe-inspiring, magnificent, majestic, imperial, stately, lordly, kingly, grand, dignified, solemn, proud.

aura ▶ noun *the Peak District will always retain a magical aura* **atmosphere**, air, quality, aspect, character, ambience, mood, spirit, feeling, feel, flavour, colouring, colour, complexion, climate, tone, overtone, undertone, tenor, impression, suggestion, emanation; vibrations; *informal* vibes, vibe.

auspices ▶ plural noun *the talks were to be held under the auspices of the UN* **patronage**, aegis, umbrella, protection, guidance, support, backing, guardianship, trusteeship, sponsorship, supervision, influence, control, charge, responsibility, keeping, care; *archaic* ward.

auspicious ▶ adjective *an auspicious day was chosen for the wedding*

A

favourable, propitious, promising, full of promise, bright, rosy, good, optimistic, hopeful, encouraging; **opportune**, timely, well timed, lucky, fortunate, providential, felicitous, advantageous, beneficial.
OPPOSITE inauspicious.

> **CHOOSE THE RIGHT WORD**
> **auspicious, opportune, timely**
> *See* OPPORTUNE.

austere ▶ adjective **1** *he was a conscientious and outwardly austere man* **severe**, stern, strict, harsh, unfeeling, stony, steely, flinty, dour, grim, cold, frosty, frigid, icy, chilly, unemotional, unfriendly, formal, stiff, stuffy, reserved, remote, distant, aloof, forbidding, grave, solemn, serious, unsmiling, unsympathetic, unforgiving, uncharitable; hard, rigorous, stringent, unyielding, unbending, unrelenting, inflexible, illiberal, no-nonsense; *informal* hard-boiled, hard-nosed; *Austral./NZ informal* solid.
OPPOSITE genial.
2 *I still enjoy this austere and disciplined life* **strict**, self-denying, self-abnegating, moderate, temperate, sober, simple, frugal, spartan, restrained, self-restrained, self-disciplined, non-indulgent, ascetic, puritanical, self-sacrificing, hair-shirt, abstemious, abstinent, celibate, chaste, continent; moral, upright.
OPPOSITE immoderate.
3 *the buildings around me were understated and austere* **plain**, simple, basic, functional, modest, unadorned, undecorated, unornamented, unembellished, unostentatious, unfurnished, uncluttered, unfussy, without frills, subdued, muted, restrained; **stark**, bleak, bare, bald, clinical, sombre, severe, spartan, ascetic; *informal* no frills.
OPPOSITE ornate.

authentic ▶ adjective **1** *the first authentic Rubens in the museum's collection* | *an authentic document* **genuine**, original, real, actual, pukka, bona fide, true, veritable; sterling; attested, undisputed, rightful, legitimate, lawful, legal, valid; *German* echt; *informal* the real McCoy, the genuine article, the real thing, your actual, kosher, honest-to-goodness; *Austral./NZ informal* dinkum; *rare* simon-pure.
OPPOSITES fake, spurious.
2 *an authentic depiction of the situation* **reliable**, dependable, trustworthy, authoritative, honest, faithful; accurate, exact, factual, true, truthful, veracious, true to life; *informal* straight from the horse's mouth; *rare* veridical.
OPPOSITES unreliable, inaccurate.

authenticate ▶ verb **1** *he must produce evidence which will authenticate his claim* **verify**, validate, prove to be genuine, certify; substantiate, prove, be proof of, give proof of, corroborate, confirm, support, evidence, attest to, bear out, give credence to, back up; document.
2 *a mandate authenticated by an absolute majority of the popular vote* **validate**, ratify, confirm, seal, sanction, endorse, guarantee.

authenticity ▶ noun **1** *the authenticity of the painting* **genuineness**, originality; rightfulness, legitimacy, legality, validity, bona fides.
OPPOSITE spuriousness.
2 *some doubt has been cast on the authenticity of this account* **reliability**, dependability, trustworthiness, truth, veracity, verity, faithfulness, fidelity, authoritativeness, credibility; accuracy, factualness; historicity; *rare* veridicality.
OPPOSITES unreliability, inaccuracy.

author ▶ noun **1** *modern Canadian authors* **writer**, man/woman of letters, wordsmith; novelist, dramatist, playwright, screenwriter, scriptwriter, poet, essayist, biographer; journalist, columnist, reporter, correspondent; librettist, lyricist, songwriter; *French* littérateur; *informal* penman, penwoman, scribe, scribbler, pen-pusher.
2 *the author of the peace plan* **originator**, creator, initiator, instigator, founder, father, prime mover, architect, engineer, designer, deviser, planner, inventor, maker, producer; cause, agent; *literary* begetter.

WORD LINKS
relating to an author **auctorial**

authoritarian ▶ adjective *an authoritarian regime* | *his authoritarian manner* **autocratic**, **dictatorial**, totalitarian, despotic, tyrannical, autarchic, draconian, absolute, arbitrary, oppressive, repressive, illiberal, undemocratic; disciplinarian, domineering, doctrinaire, dogmatic, overweening, overbearing, high-handed, bossy, peremptory, imperious, harsh, strict, severe, rigid, inflexible, unyielding.
OPPOSITES democratic, liberal; lenient, permissive.
▶ noun *the army's high command is dominated by authoritarians* **autocrat**, despot, dictator, tyrant, absolutist; disciplinarian, martinet.
OPPOSITE liberal.

authoritative ▶ adjective **1** *authoritative information* | *an authoritative source* **reliable**, dependable, trustworthy, good, sound, authentic, valid, well founded, attested, certified, verifiable; accurate, factual, from the horse's mouth.
OPPOSITE unreliable.
2 *the authoritative edition* **definitive**, most reliable, best, most scholarly; classic; authorized, accredited, recognized, accepted, approved, sanctioned.
3 *his authoritative manner* **self-assured**, assured, self-confident, confident, sure of oneself; **commanding**, imposing, masterful, magisterial, lordly, assertive, dogmatic, peremptory, arrogant, dominating, domineering, imperious, overbearing, bossy, authoritarian.
OPPOSITES timid, diffident.

authority ▶ noun **1** *he had absolute authority over his subordinates* | *a rebellion against those in authority* **power**, jurisdiction, command, control, mastery, charge, dominance, dominion, rule, sovereignty, ascendancy, supremacy, domination; influence, sway, the upper hand, leverage, hold, grip; *informal* clout, pull, muscle, teeth; *N. Amer. informal* drag.
2 *military forces have the legal authority to arrest drug traffickers* **authorization**, right, power, mandate, prerogative, licence; *French* carte blanche; *Law, historical* droit.
3 *the money was spent without parliamentary authority* **authorization**, permission, consent, leave, sanction, licence, dispensation, assent, acquiescence, agreement, approval, seal of approval, approbation, endorsement, imprimatur, clearance; *informal* the go-ahead, the thumbs up, the OK, the green light, say-so; *rare* permit.
4 (**authorities**) *the plight of the refugees was acknowledged by the authorities* **officials**, officialdom, the people in charge, the government, the administration, the establishment, the bureaucracy, the system; the police; *informal* the powers that be, the (men in) suits, Big Brother.
5 *he was an authority on the stock market* **expert**, specialist, professional, pundit, oracle, past master, master, maestro, doyen, adept; guru, sage, scholar; connoisseur, aficionado, one of the cognoscenti; *informal* walking encyclopedia, bible, buff, boffin, ace, pro, whizz, wizard; *Brit. informal* dab hand; *N. Amer. informal* maven, crackerjack.
6 *the court cited a series of authorities supporting their decision* **source**, reference, piece of documentation; citation, quotation, quote, excerpt, passage.
7 *I have it on good authority that you were there* **evidence**, testimony, witness, attestation, sworn statement, declaration, word, avowal, deposition, profession.

authorization ▶ noun *they will require authorization from the Law Society or another regulator* **permission**, consent, leave, sanction, licence, dispensation, warrant, clearance; assent, acquiescence, agreement, approval, seal of approval, approbation, endorsement, blessing, imprimatur, acceptance, rubber stamp, accreditation; authority, right, power, mandate; *Latin* nihil obstat; *informal* the go-ahead, the thumbs up, the OK, the green light, the nod, say-so; *rare* permit.
OPPOSITES refusal, prohibition.

> **CHOOSE THE RIGHT WORD**
> **authorization, permission, consent, leave**
> *See* PERMISSION.

authorize ▶ verb **1** *the government authorized further aircraft production* **give permission for**, permit, sanction, allow, agree to, approve, give one's consent/assent to, consent to, assent to, accede to, countenance; license, legalize, make legal, legitimize, legitimatize; ratify, endorse, validate, accredit, warrant; *informal* give the green light to, give the go-ahead for, give the OK to, OK, give the thumbs up to; *N. Amer. rare* approbate.
OPPOSITES forbid, veto.
2 *the Commander-in-Chief authorized him to recruit a further six officers* **give someone the authority**, give someone permission, mandate, commission, empower; entitle.

authorized ▶ adjective *authorized financial institutions* | *an authorized biography* **approved**, recognized, sanctioned, commissioned; accredited, licensed, certified, warranted; official, lawful, legal, legitimate, licit.
OPPOSITE unofficial.

autobiography ▶ noun **memoirs**, life story, account of one's life, personal history; diary, journal.

autocracy ▶ noun **absolutism**, absolute power, totalitarianism, dictatorship, despotism, tyranny, monocracy, autarchy; dystopia.
OPPOSITE democracy.

autocrat ▶ noun **absolute ruler**, dictator, despot, tyrant, monocrat; authoritarian, absolutist.

autocratic ▶ adjective *an autocratic government* | *her autocratic management style* **despotic**, tyrannical, oppressive, repressive; **dictatorial**, totalitarian, autarchic, absolute, all-powerful, arbitrary; undemocratic, one-party, monocratic; illiberal, domineering, doctrinaire, dogmatic, draconian, overweening, overbearing, bossy, high-handed, peremptory, imperious, harsh, strict, severe, rigid, inflexible, unyielding; dystopian.

OPPOSITES democratic, liberal.

CHOOSE THE RIGHT WORD

autocratic, despotic, tyrannical

These words are all more or less critical descriptions of someone's exercise of power.

- **Autocratic** is used of a person in sole power (*a traditional, autocratic Chinese patriarch*). It is also typically used to describe a *leader* or *director* or someone's *rule*, *style*, *leadership*, or *management*. *Autocratic* also implies a disregard of the welfare and wishes of the people being ruled and an unwillingness to share power (*autocratic, serf-ridden tsarist Russia*). It is the most technical and objective term of the three and is contrasted with *democratic*, but is also used more commonly than the other two words to describe the character of an ordinary person as well as a political leader (*any second now he would ring the doorbell in his usual autocratic, impatient manner*).
- **Despotic** is an emotionally loaded word, used of someone who not only holds great power but also exercises it cruelly and oppressively (*the cruel, corrupt, and despotic Shah*). The noun that it most commonly qualifies is *regime*, which itself has disapproving connotations.
- **Tyrannical** refers to cruel exercise of power by a group or individual who cannot be called to account (*he had been devastated by the oppression of the tyrannical landowner*). Nouns that it commonly qualifies include *government*, *master*, *regime*, *rule*, and *despot*.

autograph ▶ noun *fans pestered him for his autograph* **signature**; *informal* moniker; *N. Amer. informal* John Hancock.
▶ verb *Jack autographed copies of his book* **sign**, write one's signature on, sign one's name on.

automatic ▶ adjective **1** *automatic garage doors* **mechanized**, mechanical, automated, push-button, preprogrammed, computerized, electronic, robotic, unmanned; self-activating, self-regulating, self-directing, self-executing.
OPPOSITES manual, hand-operated.
2 *an automatic reaction* **instinctive**, involuntary, unconscious, reflex, knee-jerk, reflexive, instinctual, subconscious, unconditioned; **spontaneous**, impulsive, unthinking, unpremeditated, unintentional, unintended, unbidden, unwitting, inadvertent; mechanical; habitual; *informal* gut.
OPPOSITES conscious, intentional, deliberate.
3 *he is the automatic choice for the senior team* **inevitable**, unavoidable, inescapable, necessary, ineluctable; certain, definite, undoubted, assured, obvious; mandatory, compulsory.

autonomous ▶ adjective *an autonomous republic* **self-governing**, **independent**, sovereign, free, self-ruling, self-determining, autarchic; self-sufficient.

autonomy ▶ noun *Tatarstan demanded greater autonomy within the Russian Federation* **self-government**, **independence**, self-rule, home rule, sovereignty, self-determination, freedom, autarchy; self-sufficiency, individualism.

autopsy ▶ noun **post-mortem**, PM, necropsy.

auxiliary ▶ adjective **1** *an auxiliary power source* **additional**, supplementary, supplemental, extra, reserve, backup, emergency, fallback, spare, substitute, other; subsidiary, accessory, adjunct.
2 *auxiliary nursing staff* **ancillary**, assistant, support, supporting, helping, assisting, aiding.
▶ noun *a nursing auxiliary* **assistant**, helper, aide.

WORD LINKS
related prefix **para-** (e.g. *paramedic*)

avail ▶ verb **1** *guests paying by credit card can* **avail themselves** *of the express checkout service* **use**, make use of, take advantage of, utilize, employ; resort to, have recourse to, turn to, look to.
2 *even if his arguments are correct, that cannot avail him in this case* **help**, aid, assist, benefit, be of use to, be useful to, profit, be of advantage to, be of service to.
▶ noun
□ **to no avail** *he searched in several bookshops, but to no avail* **in vain**, without success, unsuccessfully, vainly, with no result, fruitlessly, to no purpose; for nothing; *archaic* bootlessly.
OPPOSITE successfully.

available ▶ adjective **1** *refreshments will be available all afternoon | a few places are still available* **obtainable**, accessible, to be had, ready for use, at hand, to hand, at one's disposal, at one's fingertips, within easy reach, handy, convenient; on sale, on the market, in stock, in season; untaken, unengaged, unused; *informal* up for grabs, yours for the asking, on tap, get-at-able, gettable; *rare* procurable.
OPPOSITE unavailable.
2 *hold the line, and I'll see if he's available* **free**, unoccupied, not busy; present, in attendance; contactable.
OPPOSITES unavailable, busy, engaged.

avalanche ▶ noun **1** **snowslide**, snow-slip; rockslide, icefall; landslide, landslip.
2 *the publication of the book produced an avalanche of press comment* **barrage**, volley; **flood**, deluge, torrent, tide, stream, storm, shower, spate, wave.
OPPOSITE trickle.

avant-garde ▶ adjective *her tastes were too avant-garde for her contemporaries* **innovative**, **advanced**, innovatory, original, experimental, inventive, ahead of the times, new, forward-looking, futuristic, modern, ultra-modern, state-of-the-art, trendsetting, pioneering, progressive, groundbreaking, trailblazing, revolutionary; unfamiliar, unorthodox, unconventional, eccentric, offbeat, bohemian; *N. Amer.* left-field; *informal* go-ahead, way-out; *rare* new-fashioned, neoteric.
OPPOSITES conservative, reactionary.

avarice ▶ noun *he had a reputation for ruthlessness and avarice* **greed**, acquisitiveness, cupidity, covetousness, avariciousness, rapacity, rapaciousness, graspingness, materialism, mercenariness; meanness, miserliness; *informal* money-grubbing, money-grabbing, an itching palm; *N. Amer. informal* grabbiness; *rare* Mammonism, pleonexia.
OPPOSITE generosity.

avaricious ▶ adjective **grasping**, acquisitive, covetous, greedy, rapacious, mercenary, materialistic, mean, miserly; *informal* money-grubbing, money-grabbing; *N. Amer. informal* grabby; *rare* pleonectic, Mammonish, Mammonistic.
OPPOSITE generous.

avenge ▶ verb *his determination to avenge the murder of his brother* **take revenge for**, take vengeance for, exact retribution for, requite; pay someone back for, get even with someone for.

avenue ▶ noun **1** *tree-lined avenues* **road**, street, thoroughfare, boulevard, way, broadway. *See also* **ROAD**.
2 *three possible avenues of research suggested themselves* **line**, path, direction, route; method, approach, course of action.

aver ▶ verb *he averred that he was innocent of the allegations* **declare**, maintain, claim, assert, state, attest, affirm, avow, swear, vow, profess, insist, protest; *archaic* avouch; *rare* asseverate.

average ▶ noun *the price was low compared with the average of the past 25 years* **mean**, median, mode, midpoint, centre; norm, standard, rule, par; the general run.
□ **on average** *on average, I suppose we watch a couple of hours of television a night* **normally**, usually, ordinarily, generally, generally speaking, in general, for the most part, in most cases, as a rule, typically; overall, by and large, on the whole, on balance.
▶ adjective **1** *the average temperature in May was 4°C below normal* **mean**, median, medial, middle.
2 *a woman of average height | the average reader of a newspaper* **ordinary**, standard, usual, normal, typical, regular, unexceptional.
3 *a very average director making very average movies* **mediocre**, second-rate, uninspired, undistinguished, ordinary, commonplace, middle-of-the-road, mainstream, unexceptional, unexciting, unremarkable, unmemorable, indifferent, humdrum, nothing special, everyday, bland, run-of-the-mill, not very good, pedestrian, prosaic, lacklustre, forgettable, amateur, amateurish; acceptable, passable, all right, adequate, fair, middling, moderate, tolerable; *N. Amer.* garden-variety; *informal* OK, so-so, bog-standard, fair-to-middling, (plain) vanilla, nothing to write home about, nothing to get excited about, a dime a dozen, no great shakes, not so hot, not up to much; *Brit. informal* common or garden, not much cop, ten a penny; *N. Amer. informal* bush-league; *N. Amer. & Austral./NZ informal* jake; *NZ informal* half-pie.
OPPOSITES outstanding, exceptional.

averse ▶ adjective *many manufacturing firms remain* **averse to** *innovation and risk-taking* **opposed to**, against, antipathetic to, hostile to, antagonistic to, unfavourably disposed to, ill-disposed to; resistant to; disinclined, unwilling, reluctant, loath; *informal* anti, agin.
OPPOSITE keen.

aversion ▶ noun *their deep-seated* **aversion** *to the use of force* **dislike of**, distaste for, disinclination, abhorrence, hatred, hate, loathing, detestation, odium, antipathy, hostility; disgust, revulsion, repugnance, horror; phobia; resistance, unwillingness, reluctance, avoidance, evasion, shunning; *informal* allergy; *archaic* disrelish.
OPPOSITES liking, inclination, desire.

avert ▶ verb **1** *she averted her head* **turn aside**, turn away, turn to one side.
2 *an attempt to avert political chaos* **prevent**, stop, avoid, nip in the bud; stave off, head off, ward off; forestall, preclude.

aviator ▶ noun (*dated*) **pilot**, airman, airwoman, flyer, aeronaut; aircrew; *dated* aviatrix; *N. Amer. informal* jock, fly boy.

avid ▶ adjective *an avid reader of science fiction* **keen**, eager, enthusiastic,

ardent, passionate, devoted, dedicated, fervent, fervid, zealous, fanatical, voracious, insatiable; wholehearted, earnest; *Brit. informal* as keen as mustard.
OPPOSITES apathetic, half-hearted.

> **CHOOSE THE RIGHT WORD**
>
> **avid, eager, keen, enthusiastic**
>
> *See* EAGER.

avidity ▶ noun **enthusiasm**, keenness, eagerness, avidness, ardour, fervour, passion, zeal, zealousness, fanaticism, voracity, voraciousness; appetite, hunger, thirst; *rare* fervency, ardency, passionateness.
OPPOSITES indifference, apathy.

avoid ▶ verb **1** *I avoid many of the situations that used to stress me* **keep away from**, stay away from, steer clear of, circumvent, give a wide berth to, give something a miss, keep at arm's length, fight shy of.
OPPOSITE confront.
2 *by resigning today, he is trying to avoid responsibility for the political crisis* **evade**, dodge, sidestep, skirt round, bypass; escape, run away from; *informal* duck, wriggle out of, cop out of, get out of; *Brit. informal* funk; *Austral./NZ informal* duck-shove; *archaic* decline.
OPPOSITE face up to.
3 *Guy jerked back to avoid a blow to the head* **duck**, dodge, get out of the way of, body-swerve; *Scottish & N. English* jouk.
4 *you've been avoiding me all evening* **shun**, stay away from, evade, keep one's distance from, hide from, elude; ignore; *informal, dated* give someone the go-by; *archaic* bilk.
OPPOSITE seek out.
5 *women planning to become pregnant should avoid drinking alcohol altogether* **refrain from**, abstain from, desist from, forbear from, eschew.
OPPOSITE indulge.

avoidable ▶ adjective **preventable**, stoppable, avertible; escapable; needless, unnecessary.
OPPOSITES inescapable, inevitable.

avow ▶ verb *he avowed that the president had been fully aware of the situation* **assert**, declare, state, maintain, aver, attest, swear, vow, insist; confess, admit; *rare* asseverate.

avowed ▶ adjective *an avowed Marxist* **declared**, sworn, self-confessed, confessed, self-proclaimed, acknowledged, admitted, open, overt; known.

await ▶ verb **1** *Peter was at home, awaiting news* **wait for**; expect, anticipate, look for, hope for.
2 *many dangers await them* **be in store for**, lie ahead of, lie in wait for, be waiting for.

awake ▶ verb **1** *she awoke late the following morning* **wake (up)**, awaken, stir, come to, come round, bestir oneself, show signs of life, return to the land of the living.
OPPOSITE fall asleep.
2 *the alarm awoke him at 7.30* **wake (up)**, awaken, waken, rouse, arouse; *informal* give someone a shout; *Brit. informal* knock up.
3 *the authorities finally* **awoke to** *the extent of the problem* **realize**, become aware of, become conscious of, become cognizant of, become mindful of; *informal* get wise to; *rare* cognize.
▶ adjective **1** *two hours later she was still awake* **wakeful**, sleepless, wide awake, conscious; tossing and turning, restless, restive; *archaic* watchful; *rare* insomnolent.
OPPOSITE asleep.
2 *too few are* **awake to** *the dangers* **aware of**, conscious of, cognizant of, mindful of, sensible of, alive to, alert to, sensitive to; *archaic* ware of.
OPPOSITES unaware, ignorant, oblivious.

awaken ▶ verb **1** *when she awakened, the sun was streaming through the windows | I was awakened at 2 a.m. by the sergeant* **wake (up)**. *See also* AWAKE.
OPPOSITES go to sleep, put to sleep.
2 *he had awakened strong emotions in her* **arouse**, rouse, call/bring into being, draw/call forth, bring out, engender, generate, evoke, trigger, stir up, inspire, stimulate, excite, kindle, fire, touch off, spark off; revive; *literary* enkindle.
OPPOSITE allay.

awakening ▶ noun *the awakening of her real feelings for him* **arousal**, rousing, triggering off, stirring up, kindling, stimulation, inspiration, birth; revival.

award ▶ verb *a 3.5 per cent pay rise was awarded to staff | the society awarded him a silver medal* **give**, grant; **confer on**, present to, bestow on, gift with, furnish with, endow with, decorate with; accord, assign, apportion, allot, allocate, allow.
▶ noun **1** *the company's annual award for high-quality service* **prize**, trophy, medal; reward, honours, decoration; *informal* gong.
2 *a £200,000 libel award* **payment**, settlement, compensation, damages.
3 *under its Jazz Bursary Scheme, the Arts Council gave him an award of £1,500* **grant**, scholarship; subsidy, subvention, endowment; *Brit.* bursary, bursarship.
4 *the award of an honorary doctorate* **giving**, granting, conferment, conferral, presentation, bestowal.

aware ▶ adjective **1** *most people are* **aware of** *the dangers of sunbathing* **conscious of**, acquainted with, informed of/about, apprised of, cognizant of, mindful of, sensible of, familiar with, conversant with, no stranger to, alive to, awake to, alert to, sensitive to; privy to; *informal* wise to, well up on, up to speed on, in the know about, hip to; *archaic* ware of; *rare* seized of, recognizant of, regardful of.
OPPOSITES unaware, ignorant, oblivious.
2 *everyone needs to become more environmentally aware* **well informed**, knowledgeable, up to date, enlightened; *French* au fait, au courant; *informal* clued up, genned up; *Brit. informal* switched-on; *black English* down.
OPPOSITE ignorant.

awareness ▶ noun *a growing public* **awareness of** *the need to protect the environment* **consciousness**, recognition, realization, cognizance, perception, apprehension, understanding, grasp, appreciation; acknowledgement, knowledge; sensitivity to, sensibility to, insight into; familiarity with, acquaintance with.
OPPOSITE ignorance.

awash ▶ adjective **1** *the road was awash and impassable in places* **flooded**, covered with water, under water; submerged, engulfed, submersed.
2 *the city was* **awash with** *journalists* **inundated**, flooded, deluged, swamped, teeming, heaving, overflowing; overrun by, full of; *informal* knee-deep in.

away ▶ adverb **1** *she began to walk away* **off**, from here, from there.
2 *stay indoors, away from the trouble* **at a distance**, apart, isolated.
3 *Bernice pushed him away* **aside**, off, to one side.
4 *we'll be away for two weeks* **elsewhere**, abroad, not at home, not here, gone, absent; on holiday, on vacation.

WORD LINKS
related prefixes **ab-** (e.g. ***abduct***), **abs-** (e.g. ***abscond***)

awe ▶ noun *the sight filled me with awe* **wonder**, wonderment, amazement, astonishment; admiration, reverence, veneration, respect; dread, terror, fear.
OPPOSITES contempt, indifference.

awed ▶ adjective *he spoke in an awed whisper* **filled with wonder**, wonderstruck, awestruck, amazed, filled with amazement, astonished, filled with astonishment, lost for words, open-mouthed; reverential; terrified, afraid, fearful.

awe-inspiring ▶ adjective *an awe-inspiring sight* **breathtaking**, amazing, stunning, stupendous, astonishing, awesome, extraordinary, incredible; magnificent, wonderful, spectacular, sublime, glorious, magical, dazzling, imposing, stirring, impressive; formidable, terrifying, fearsome; *informal* mind-boggling, mind-blowing, out of this world, sensational; *literary* wondrous; *archaic* awful.
OPPOSITES uninspiring, unimpressive.

awesome ▶ adjective *the scale of the mountains was awesome | an awesome achievement* **breathtaking**, amazing, stunning, astounding, astonishing, awe-inspiring, stupendous, staggering, extraordinary, incredible, unbelievable; magnificent, wonderful, spectacular, remarkable, phenomenal, prodigious, miraculous, sublime; formidable, imposing, impressive; *informal* mind-boggling, mind-blowing, out of this world; *literary* wondrous; *archaic* awful.

awestruck ▶ adjective *Caroline was too awestruck by her surroundings to reply* **awed**, filled with wonder, filled with awe, wonderstruck, amazed, filled with amazement, astonished, filled with astonishment, lost for words, open-mouthed; reverential; terrified, afraid, fearful.

awful ▶ adjective **1** *the place smelled awful* **very unpleasant**, disgusting, nasty, terrible, dreadful, ghastly, horrid, horrible, vile, foul, abominable, appalling, atrocious, horrendous, hideous, offensive, objectionable, obnoxious, frightful, loathsome, revolting, repulsive, repellent, repugnant, odious, sickening, nauseating, nauseous; *informal* gruesome, diabolical, yucky, sick-making, God-awful, gross, from hell, icky; *Brit. informal* grotty, beastly; *N. Amer. informal* hellacious, lousy; *literary* noisome; *archaic* disgustful, loathly.
OPPOSITES lovely, wonderful.
2 *I think it's an awful book* **very bad**, poor, dreadful, terrible, frightful, atrocious, hopeless, inadequate, inferior, unsatisfactory, substandard, laughable, lamentable, execrable; *informal* crummy, pathetic, rotten, useless, woeful, lousy, appalling, abysmal, dire, poxy, God-awful; *Brit. informal* duff, chronic, rubbish, a load of pants; *vulgar slang* crap, shit, chickenshit; *rare* egregious.
OPPOSITES good, excellent.
3 *Ronnie's awful accident at the crossroads* **serious**, grave, bad, terrible, dreadful, alarming, critical.
OPPOSITES slight, minor.
4 *you look awful—you should go and lie down* **ill**, unwell, washed out, peaky; sick, queasy, nauseous, nauseated, green about the gills; faint, dizzy, giddy; *Brit.* off, off colour, poorly; *informal* rough, lousy, rotten, terrible,

dreadful, crummy; *Brit. informal* grotty, ropy; *Scottish informal* wabbit, peely-wally; *Austral./NZ informal* crook; *dated* queer, seedy; *rare* peaked, peakish.
5 *I felt awful for being so angry with him* **remorseful**, conscience-stricken, guilty, guilt-ridden, ashamed, chastened, contrite, sorry, full of regret, regretful, repentant, penitent, shamefaced, self-reproachful, apologetic.
6 (*archaic*) *the awful and majestic sights of nature* **awe-inspiring**, awesome, impressive, amazing; dread, fearful.

awfully ▶ adverb **1** *an awfully nice man* **very**, extremely, really, exceedingly, immensely, thoroughly, decidedly, terribly, frightfully, dreadfully, fearfully, exceptionally, uncommonly, remarkably, eminently, extraordinarily, most, positively, particularly; heartily, profoundly; *N. English* right; *Scottish* unco; *N. Amer.* quite; *French* très; *informal* terrifically, tremendously, desperately, devilishly, ultra, too … for words, mucho, mega, seriously, oh-so, madly, majorly; *Brit. informal* jolly, ever so, dead, well, fair; *N. Amer. informal* real, mighty, awful, plumb, powerful; *S. African informal* lekker; *informal, dated* devilish, hellish; *archaic* exceeding, sore.
2 *we played awfully* **very badly**, atrociously, terribly, dismally, dreadfully, appallingly, execrably, poorly, incompetently, inexpertly; *informal* abysmally, pitifully, crummily, diabolically, rottenly; *rare* egregiously.
3 (*informal, dated*) *thanks awfully for the tea* **very much**, a lot; *informal* a million.

awhile ▶ adverb *stand here awhile* **for a moment**, for a while, for a short time, for a little while; *informal* for a bit.

awkward ▶ adjective **1** *one of the most awkward jobs is painting a ceiling* **difficult**, tricky; *Brit. informal* fiddly.
OPPOSITES easy, straightforward.
2 *the box was heavy and awkward to carry* **cumbersome**, unwieldy, unhandy; *informal* a devil; *vulgar slang* a bugger, a bastard; *rare* cumbrous, lumbersome.
3 *I'm sorry to call at such an awkward time* **inconvenient**, difficult, inappropriate, inopportune, unseasonable, unfortunate.
OPPOSITE convenient.
4 *he had put her in a very awkward position* **embarrassing**, uncomfortable, unpleasant, delicate, ticklish, tricky, sensitive, problematic, problematical, troublesome, perplexing, thorny, vexatious; humiliating, compromising; *informal* sticky, dicey, hairy, cringeworthy, cringe-making; *Brit. informal* dodgy; *N. Amer. informal* gnarly.
5 *she felt awkward alone with him* **embarrassed**, self-conscious, uncomfortable, ill at ease, uneasy, tense, nervous, edgy, unrelaxed, strained; *rare* unquiet.
OPPOSITES relaxed, at ease.
6 *he was long-legged and rather awkward | his awkward movements* **clumsy**, ungainly, uncoordinated, maladroit, graceless, ungraceful, inept, inelegant, unskilful, unhandy, gauche, gawky, gangling, blundering, lumbering, hulking, cloddish; wooden, stiff; coltish; *informal* clodhopping, ham-fisted, ham-handed, with two left feet, cack-handed; *Brit. informal* all thumbs, all fingers and thumbs; *archaic* lubberly.
OPPOSITES graceful, adroit.
7 (*Brit.*) *you're being damned awkward* **unreasonable**, uncooperative, unhelpful, difficult, annoying, obstructive, unaccommodating, refractory, disobliging, contrary, perverse, tiresome, exasperating, trying; stubborn, obstinate; *Scottish* thrawn; *informal* cussed, pesky; *Brit. informal* bloody-minded, bolshie; *N. Amer. informal* balky; *archaic* contumacious, froward; *rare* renitent, pervicacious.
OPPOSITES amenable, cooperative.

awkwardness ▶ noun **1** *the gesture betrayed his momentary awkwardness* **embarrassment**, self-consciousness, discomfort, discomfiture, uneasiness, edginess, tension, nervousness.
2 *the adolescent awkwardness of his angular body* **ungainliness**, clumsiness, lack of coordination, gracelessness, inelegance, ineptness, gaucheness, gawkiness.

awning ▶ noun **canopy**, shade, sunshade, shelter, cover, covering; tarpaulin; *Brit.* blind, sunblind; *technical* velarium.

awry ▶ adjective **1** *I got the impression that something was awry* **amiss**, wrong, not right; *informal* up.
2 *his wig awry, he gasped and coughed for air* **askew**, crooked, lopsided, uneven, asymmetrical, to one side, off-centre, skewed, skew, misaligned; *Scottish* agley, squint, thrawn; *informal* cock-eyed; *Brit. informal* skew-whiff, wonky, squiffy.
OPPOSITES straight, symmetrical.

axe ▶ noun **hatchet**, cleaver; adze; tomahawk; *Brit.* chopper; *historical* battleaxe, poleaxe.
▶ verb **1** *the show was axed last month as a result of poor ratings* **cancel**, withdraw, drop, abandon, end, terminate, put an end to, discontinue; *informal* scrap, cut, junk, ditch, dump, give something the chop, pull the plug on, knock something on the head.
2 *500 staff were axed as part of a rationalization programme* **dismiss**, give someone notice, make redundant, throw out, get rid of, lay off, let go, discharge; *informal* **sack**, fire, kick out, boot out, give someone the sack, give someone the boot, give someone the bullet, give someone the (old) heave-ho, give someone the elbow, give someone the push, give someone their marching orders, show someone the door; *Brit. informal* give someone their cards.

axiom ▶ noun **accepted truth**, general truth, dictum, truism, principle; proposition, postulate; maxim, saying, adage, aphorism; *rare* apophthegm, gnome.

axiomatic ▶ adjective *it was axiomatic that prices and interest rates should be kept down* **self-evident**, unquestionable, undeniable; accepted, understood, given, granted; *rare* apodictic, indemonstrable.

axis ▶ noun **1** *the earth revolves on its axis once every 24 hours* **centre line**, vertical, horizontal.
2 *the Anglo-American axis* **alliance**, coalition, bloc, confederation, confederacy, union, league; agreement, treaty, pact, compact, entente, concordat.

axle ▶ noun **shaft**, spindle, rod, arbor, pin, pivot; mandrel.

azure ▶ adjective **sky-blue**, deep blue, bright blue, blue, ultramarine; *literary* cerulean; *rare* cyanic.

babble ▶ verb **1** *Betty babbled away, oblivious to the look on his face* **prattle**, rattle on, gabble, chatter, jabber, twitter, go on, run on, prate, ramble, burble, blather, blether, blither, maunder, drivel, patter, yap, jibber-jabber; *Scottish & Irish* slabber; *informal* gab, yak, yackety-yak, yabber, yatter, yammer, blabber, jaw, gas, shoot one's mouth off; *Brit. informal* witter, rabbit, chunter, natter, waffle; *N. Amer. informal* run off at the mouth; *Austral./NZ informal* mag; *archaic* twaddle, clack, twattle.
2 *my father babbled out the truth* **blurt out**, blab, reveal, divulge, let slip, let out, give away, come out with; *informal* spill.
3 *just out of sight a brook babbled gently* **burble**, murmur, gurgle, purl, tinkle; *literary* plash.
▶ noun *her soft voice stopped his babble* **prattle**, gabble, chatter, jabber, prating, rambling, blather, blether; gibbering, gibberish, drivel; *informal* gab, yak, yackety-yak, yabbering, yatter, twaddle; *Brit. informal* wittering, waffle, natter, chuntering; *archaic* clack, twattle.

babe ▶ noun **1** (*literary*) *a newborn babe*. See BABY.
2 *just a babe in the world of business* **ingénue**, innocent, babe in arms, greenhorn, novice, tyro, beginner.

babel ▶ noun *the babel of a furious crowd* **clamour**, din, racket, confused noise, tumult, uproar, hubbub; babble, babbling, shouting, yelling, screaming; commotion, chaos, bedlam, pandemonium, confusion; *Scottish & N. English* stramash; *informal* hullabaloo; *Brit. informal* row; *rare* charivari.
OPPOSITE silence.

baby ▶ noun **1** *a newborn baby* **infant**, newborn, child, tot, little one; *Scottish & N. English* bairn; *informal* sprog, tiny; *literary* babe, babe in arms; *technical* neonate.
2 *the baby of the family* **youngest**, junior member; smallest, littlest.
3 (*informal*) *baby, please don't cry* **darling**, sweetheart, dearest, dear; *informal* honey, sweetie, sugar, babe; *archaic* sweeting.
▶ adjective *baby carrots* **miniature**, mini, little, small, small-scale, scaled-down, toy, pocket, midget, dwarf; *Scottish* wee; *N. Amer.* vest-pocket; *informal* teeny, teeny-weeny, teensy, teensy-weensy, weeny, itsy-bitsy, itty-bitty, eensy, eensy-weensy, tiddly, pint-sized, bite-sized; *Brit. informal* titchy; *N. Amer. informal* little-bitty.
OPPOSITE large.
▶ verb *her aunt babied her* **pamper**, mollycoddle, spoil, cosset, coddle, indulge, overindulge, pet, wait on someone hand and foot, feather-bed, wrap in cotton wool, nanny; pander to; *archaic* cocker.

WORD LINKS
relating to babies **infantile**

babyish ▶ adjective **childish**, immature, infantile, juvenile, puerile, adolescent, silly, foolish, inane, jejune, naive.
OPPOSITE mature.

back ▶ noun **1** *they think she's broken her back* **spine**, backbone, spinal column, vertebral column; *technical* dorsum, rachis.
2 *the back of the house* **rear**, rear side, other side; *Nautical* stern.
OPPOSITE front.
3 *the back of the queue* **end**, tail end, rear end, tail, far end; *N. Amer.* tag end.
OPPOSITES front, head.
4 *the back of a postcard* **reverse**, reverse side, other side, underside; verso; *informal* flip side.
OPPOSITES front, face.
□ **behind someone's back secretly**, without someone's knowledge, on the sly, deceitfully, slyly, sneakily, covertly, surreptitiously, furtively.
□ **the back of beyond the middle of nowhere**, the backwoods, the wilds, the hinterland, a backwater; *Austral./NZ* the back country, the backblocks, the booay; *S. African* the backveld, the platteland; *N. Amer. informal* the boondocks, the boonies, the tall timbers; *Austral./NZ informal* Woop Woop, beyond the black stump.
□ **turn one's back on** *in 1973, she turned her back on her career* **abandon**, give up, have done with, throw up; reject, renounce, repudiate; *informal* quit, pack in, jack in.
▶ adverb **1** *she walked away without looking back | he pushed his chair back* **backwards**, behind one, to one's rear, rearwards; away, off.
OPPOSITE forward.
2 *keep back from the roadside* **away**, at a distance.
3 *her husband left her a few months back* **ago**, earlier, previously, before, in the past.
▶ verb **1** *the project was backed by the English Tourist Board* **sponsor**, finance, put up the money for, fund, subsidize, underwrite, promote, lend one's name to, be a patron of, act as guarantor of, support; *informal* foot the bill for, pick up the tab for; *N. Amer. informal* bankroll, stake.
2 *over 97 per cent backed the changes* **support**, endorse, sanction, approve of, give one's blessing to, smile on, favour, advocate, promote, uphold, champion; vote for, ally oneself with, stand behind, side with, be on the side of, defend, take up the cudgels for; second; *informal* throw one's weight behind.
OPPOSITE oppose.
3 *he backed the horse at 33–1* **bet on**, place a bet on, gamble on, stake money on.
4 *he backed slowly out of the garage* **reverse**, move/drive backwards; backtrack, retrace one's steps.
OPPOSITES move forwards, advance.
□ **back away** *he took a step towards her and she hurriedly backed away* **draw back**, step back, move away, back off, retreat, withdraw, pull back, give ground; shrink back, blench, cower, quail, quake.
OPPOSITE move forward.
□ **back down** *the government backed down under pressure from the House of Lords* **give in**, concede defeat, surrender, yield, submit, climb down, concede, reconsider; backtrack, back-pedal.
□ **back out** *Coleman backed out of the deal* **renege on**, go back on, withdraw from, pull out of, retreat from, fail to honour, abandon, default on, repudiate; back-pedal; *informal* get cold feet about, chicken out of.
□ **back something up** *his statement was backed up by evidence from Mr Eric Bartlett* **substantiate**, corroborate, confirm, support, bear out, endorse, bolster, reinforce, lend weight to; prove, verify, validate.
OPPOSITES contradict, undermine.
□ **back someone up** *her husband's bound to back her up* **support**, stand by, give one's support to, side with, be on someone's side, take someone's side, take someone's part; vouch for; help, assist, aid.
▶ adjective **1** *the back garden* **rear**.
OPPOSITE front.
2 *the back row* **end**, hind, hindmost, rearmost.
OPPOSITE front.
3 *the bird's back feathers* **dorsal**, posterior.
OPPOSITE front.
4 *back copies of the journal* **past**, old, previous, earlier, former, out of date.
OPPOSITE future.

WORD LINKS
relating to the back **dorsal, lumbar**
lying on one's back **supine**
further back **posterior**

backbiting ▶ noun *there is a lot of backbiting in the world of television* **malicious talk**, spiteful talk, slander, libel, defamation, abuse, character assassination, scandalmongering, disparagement, denigration, vilification, vituperation, calumny, revilement; insults, slurs, aspersions; *informal* bitching, bitchiness, cattiness, mud-slinging, bad-mouthing; *Brit. informal* slagging off, rubbishing.
OPPOSITE praise.

backbone *See centre pages for list of* **Vertebrae**
▶ noun **1** *an injured backbone* **spine**, spinal column, vertebral column, vertebrae; back; *technical* dorsum, rachis.

B

2 *these firms are the backbone of our industrial sector* **mainstay**, cornerstone, foundation, chief support, buttress, pillar.
3 *he has enough backbone to see us through this difficulty* **strength of character**, strength of will, firmness of purpose, firmness, resolution, resolve, determination, fortitude, mettle, moral fibre, spine, steel, nerve, spirit, pluck, pluckiness, courage, courageousness, bravery, braveness, valour, manliness; *informal* guts, spunk, grit; *Brit. informal* bottle; *vulgar slang* balls.
OPPOSITE weakness.

WORD LINKS
relating to the backbone **spinal, vertebral**

back-breaking ▶ **adjective** *a back-breaking task* **gruelling**, arduous, strenuous, onerous, punishing, murderous, crushing, Herculean, demanding, exacting, taxing, formidable, exhausting, draining, laborious, burdensome, tough, stiff, uphill, heavy; *informal* killing; *Brit. informal* knackering; *archaic* toilsome.
OPPOSITES easy, effortless.

backchat ▶ **noun** (*Brit. informal*) *don't put up with any backchat from them* **impudence**, impertinence, cheek, cheekiness, effrontery, sauciness, pertness, insolence, rudeness, rude retorts; answering back, talking back; *informal* mouth, lip; *Scottish informal* snash; *N. Amer. informal* sassiness, sass, smart mouth, back talk; *rare* malapertness, contumely, procacity.

backer ▶ **noun 1** *£3 million was provided by the project's backers* **sponsor**, investor, subsidizer, underwriter, promoter, financier, patron, benefactor, benefactress, guarantor, supporter, friend; *informal* angel; *rare* Maecenas.
2 *the backers of the proposition* **supporter**, upholder, champion, defender, advocate, promoter, proponent, protagonist; seconder, second; *N. Amer.* booster.

backfire ▶ **verb 1** *the engine backfired* **misfire**.
2 *Bernard's plan* **backfired on** *him* **rebound**, boomerang, come back, have an adverse effect; have unwelcome repercussions for, cause one to be hoist with one's own petard, be self-defeating, be counterproductive; fail, miscarry, go wrong; *informal* blow up in someone's face; *archaic* redound on.

background ▶ **noun 1** *the house stands against a background of sheltering trees* **surrounding(s)**, backdrop, backcloth, framework; scene.
2 *the figures of the saints are shown against a gold background* **setting**, surround, framework.
3 *the airport may be seen* **in the background** **in the distance**, on the horizon.
OPPOSITES foreground, front.
4 *after that evening, she remained* **in the background** **behind the scenes**, out of the public eye, out of the spotlight, out of the limelight, backstage; inconspicuous, unobtrusive, unnoticed.
5 *a mix of students from many different backgrounds* **social circumstances**, family circumstances; environment, class, culture, tradition; upbringing, rearing.
6 *her nursing background* **experience**, record, history, past, training, education, grounding, knowledge; qualifications, credentials; *Latin* curriculum vitae.
7 *the political background* **circumstances**, context, conditions, situation, environment, milieu, scene, scenario, framework, atmosphere; factors, influences; lead-up.

backhanded ▶ **adjective** *a backhanded compliment* **indirect**, ambiguous, oblique, equivocal; **double-edged**, two-edged; tongue-in-cheek, sarcastic, ironic, sardonic.
OPPOSITES direct, straightforward.

backing ▶ **noun 1** *the foreign secretary won the backing of opposition parties* **support**, help, assistance, cooperation, aid; approval, commendation, endorsement, sanction, blessing; promotion, advocacy, championship, espousal.
2 *they had financial backing from local firms* **sponsorship**, funding, financing, promotion, patronage; money, investment, funds, finance; grant, contribution, subsidy.
3 *a mix of slick vocals and sophisticated backing* **musical accompaniment**, orchestration; harmony, obbligato.
4 *the fabric has a special backing for durability* **lining**, interlining, facing, underlay, reinforcement.

backlash ▶ **noun** *the move provoked a furious backlash from union leaders* **adverse reaction/response**, counteraction, counterblast, comeback, recoil; retaliation, reprisal; repercussions, reverberations, fallout, backwash.

backlog ▶ **noun** *a backlog of paperwork* **accumulation**, logjam, pile-up, pile, heap, mountain, excess; arrears.

back-pedal ▶ **verb 1** *although agreeing at first to the peace plan, they soon began to back-pedal* **change one's mind**, change one's opinion, go into reverse, do an about-face, do a U-turn, shift one's ground, sing a different song, have second thoughts, reconsider, climb down; *Brit.* do an about-turn.
2 *the president* **back-pedalled on** *his promises to tax foreign companies heavily* **renege on**, back down on, go back on, back out of, fail to honour, withdraw, backtrack on, take back, abandon, default on.

backslide ▶ **verb 1** *there are many things that can cause slimmers to backslide* **relapse**, lapse, regress, retrogress, revert to one's bad habits, weaken, lose one's resolve, give in to temptation, go astray, leave the straight and narrow, go down the primrose path.
OPPOSITE persevere.
2 *his only worry was that if she left things would backslide* **degenerate**, deteriorate, slip, slide, fall off, revert to a former state, regress, retrogress; *informal* go downhill, go to pot, go to the dogs; *rare* recidivate.
OPPOSITE progress.

backslider ▶ **noun recidivist**, regressor; apostate, defector, deserter, turncoat, renegade, fallen angel.

backup ▶ **noun** *no police backup could be expected* **help**, support, assistance, aid; reinforcements, reserves, additional resources.

backward ▶ **adjective 1** *a backward look | a backward movement* **reverse**; to/towards the rear, rearward, to/towards the back; behind one.
OPPOSITE forward.
2 *the decision was a backward step* **retrograde**, retrogressive, regressive, unprogressive, for the worse, in the wrong direction, downhill, negative.
OPPOSITES progressive, forward-looking.
3 *an economically backward country* **underdeveloped**, undeveloped, unsophisticated; primitive, benighted.
OPPOSITES advanced, sophisticated.
4 *he was not* **backward in** *displaying his talents* **reticent about**, hesitant about, reluctant to, unwilling to, afraid to, loath to, averse to; shy about, diffident about, unconfident about, bashful about, timid about, coy about; *informal* backward in coming forward.
OPPOSITES confident, bold.
▶ **adverb** *the car rolled slowly backward. See* **BACKWARDS**.

WORD LINKS
related prefix **retro-** (e.g. ***retrograde, retrocede***)

backwards ▶ **adverb 1** *Penny glanced backwards | he took a step backwards* **towards the rear**, rearwards, backward, behind one.
OPPOSITE forwards.
2 *count backwards from twenty to ten* **in reverse**, from the highest to lowest, in reverse order.
3 *his campaign is* **going backwards** **deteriorate**, decline, degenerate, worsen, get worse; *informal* go downhill, take a nosedive, go to pot, go to the dogs, hit the skids, go down the toilet, go down the tubes.
OPPOSITE improve.

backwash ▶ **noun 1** *a ship's backwash* **wake**, wash, slipstream, backflow; path, trail.
2 *the backwash of the Cuban missile crisis* **repercussions**, reverberations, after-effects, aftermath, fallout; upshot, consequences, results, effects, by-products.

backwoods ▶ **plural noun the back of beyond**, the middle of nowhere, remote areas, the wilds, the hinterlands, a backwater; *N. Amer.* the backcountry, the backland; *Austral.* the outback, the bush, the backblocks, the booay; *S. African* the backveld, the platteland; *informal* the sticks; *N. Amer. informal* the boondocks, the boonies, the tall timbers; *Austral./NZ informal* Woop Woop, beyond the black stump.

bacteria ▶ **plural noun micro-organisms**, microbes, germs, bacilli, pathogens; aerobes, anaerobes; *informal* bugs.

WORD LINKS

study of bacteria	**bacteriology**
fear of bacteria	**bacteriophobia**
substance that kills bacteria	**bactericide**

bad ▶ **adjective 1** *bad workmanship* **substandard**, poor, inferior, second-rate, second-class, unsatisfactory, inadequate, unacceptable, not up to scratch, not up to par, deficient, imperfect, defective, faulty, shoddy, amateurish, careless, negligent; **dreadful**, awful, terrible, abominable, frightful, atrocious, disgraceful, deplorable, hopeless, worthless, laughable, lamentable, miserable, sorry, third-rate, diabolical, execrable; incompetent, inept, inexpert, ineffectual; *informal* crummy, rotten, pathetic, useless, woeful, bum, lousy, ropy, appalling, abysmal, pitiful, God-awful, dire, poxy, not up to snuff, the pits; *Brit. informal* duff, chronic, rubbish, pants, a load of pants; *vulgar slang* crap, shit, chickenshit; *rare* egregious.
OPPOSITES good, excellent, skilled.
2 *the alcohol is having a bad effect on her health* **harmful**, damaging, detrimental, undesirable, injurious, hurtful, inimical, dangerous, destructive, ruinous, deleterious; unhealthy, unwholesome.
OPPOSITES good, beneficial.
3 *she had heard about him and his dissolute, bad life | the bad guys* **wicked**, sinful, immoral, evil, morally wrong, corrupt, base, black-hearted, reprobate, depraved, degenerate, dissolute, amoral; criminal, villainous, nefarious, iniquitous, dishonest, dishonourable, unscrupulous, unprincipled; *informal* crooked, bent, dirty; *archaic* dastardly.
OPPOSITE virtuous.
4 *Tilda! You bad girl!* **naughty**, badly behaved, disobedient, wayward, wilful, self-willed, defiant, unruly, insubordinate, undisciplined, unmanageable, uncontrollable, ungovernable, unbiddable, disruptive,

rebellious, refractory, recalcitrant; **mischievous**, full of mischief, playful, impish, roguish, puckish, rascally, prankish, tricksy; *informal* brattish, scampish; *Scottish informal* gallus; *archaic* contumacious.
OPPOSITE well behaved.
5 *bad news* **unpleasant**, disagreeable, unwelcome, unfortunate, unfavourable, unlucky, adverse, nasty; terrible, dreadful, awful, grim, distressing, regrettable; *archaic or humorous* parlous.
OPPOSITE good.
6 *a recession is a bad time to try and sell a business* **inauspicious**, disadvantageous, adverse, difficult, inopportune, unpropitious, inappropriate, unsuitable, unfavourable, unfortunate, untoward; *informal* disastrous.
OPPOSITE good.
7 *a bad accident | a bad head injury* **severe**, serious, grave, critical, grievous, acute, dreadful, terrible, awful, ghastly, dire, grim, frightful, shocking; life-threatening; *Medicine* peracute.
OPPOSITES minor, slight.
8 *the meat's gone bad* **rotten**, off, decayed, decomposed, decomposing, putrid, putrefied, putrescent, mouldy, mouldering; sour, rancid, rank, unfit for human consumption; addled; maggoty, worm-eaten, wormy, flyblown; *rare* putrefactive, putrefacient.
OPPOSITE fresh.
9 *if you still feel bad, stay in bed.* See ILL.
10 *a bad knee* **injured**, wounded, diseased; *Brit. informal* gammy, knackered; *Austral./NZ informal* crook; *dated* game.
11 *George always felt bad after shouting at her* **guilty**, conscience-stricken, remorseful, guilt-ridden, ashamed, chastened, contrite, sorry, full of regret, regretful, repentant, penitent, shamefaced, self-reproachful, apologetic.
OPPOSITE unrepentant.
12 *a bad cheque* **invalid**, worthless; counterfeit, fake, false, spurious, fraudulent; *informal* bogus, phoney, dud.
13 *bad language* **offensive**, vulgar, crude, foul, obscene, rude, coarse, smutty, dirty, filthy, indecent, indecorous; blasphemous, profane.
□ **not bad** *the bean casserole wasn't bad* **all right**, quite good, good, adequate, acceptable, good enough, reasonable, fair, decent, average, tolerable, passable, middling, moderate, sufficiently good, fine; *informal* OK, so-so, fair-to-middling; *N. Amer. & Austral./NZ informal* jake.
OPPOSITE outstanding.

WORD LINKS
related prefixes **caco-** (e.g. ***cacophony, cacography***), **dys-** (e.g. ***dyspepsia, dysfunctional***)

badge ▶ noun **1** *a name badge* pin, breastpin, brooch; *N. Amer.* button.
2 *the badge of the Cheshire regiment* **emblem**, crest, insignia, device, shield, escutcheon; trademark, logo.
3 *in places like Dallas, Stetsons have long been considered a badge of success* **sign**, symbol, indication, indicator, signal, mark, token; hallmark, trademark.

badger ▶ verb *let me get on with it, instead of badgering me the whole time* **pester**, harass, bother, plague, torment, hound, nag, chivvy, harry, keep on at, go on at, harp on at, keep after, importune, annoy, trouble; *N. English* mither; *informal* hassle, bug; *Austral. informal* heavy.

WORD LINKS

male	**boar**
female	**sow**
young	**cub**
home	**sett, earth**
collective noun	**cete**

badinage ▶ noun *he engaged in badinage with his guests* **banter**, repartee, witty conversation, bantering, raillery, wit, crosstalk, wordplay, swordplay, cut and thrust; witty remarks, witticisms, ripostes, sallies, quips; joking, jesting; *French* bons mots; *N. Amer. informal* josh; *Austral./NZ informal* borak.

badly ▶ adverb **1** *the job had been badly done* **poorly**, incompetently, ineptly, inexpertly, inefficiently, imperfectly, deficiently, defectively, unsatisfactorily, inadequately, incorrectly, faultily, shoddily, amateurishly, carelessly, negligently; awfully, terribly, dreadfully, abominably, atrociously, frightfully, miserably, wretchedly, lamentably, deplorably, dismally, execrably; *informal* abysmally, appallingly, crummily, diabolically, pitifully, woefully; *rare* egregiously.
OPPOSITE well.
2 *try not to think badly of me* **unfavourably**, ill, critically, with disapproval, with disfavour.
3 *Anna knew she had been behaving badly* **reprehensibly**, naughtily, mischievously.
4 *many of the animals had been badly treated* **cruelly**, wickedly, unkindly, harshly, shamefully; unfairly, unjustly, wrongly, improperly.
5 *it's his own fault it turned out badly* **unsuccessfully**, unfavourably, adversely, unfortunately, unhappily, unluckily.
6 *some of the victims are badly hurt* **severely**, seriously, gravely, greatly, grievously, acutely, critically, dangerously.
OPPOSITE slightly.
7 *the house is badly in need of redecoration* **very much**, greatly, intensely, desperately, exceedingly, painfully, sorely; *informal* seriously.

bad manners ▶ plural noun **rudeness**, discourtesy, discourteousness, impoliteness, incivility, unmannerliness, boorishness, uncouthness, vulgarity, ungentlemanly behaviour, unladylike behaviour, lack of social grace, lack of refinement.

bad-tempered ▶ adjective **irritable**, irascible, tetchy, testy, grumpy, grouchy, crotchety, in a (bad) mood, cantankerous, curmudgeonly, ill-tempered, ill-natured, ill-humoured, peevish, having got out of bed the wrong side, cross, as cross as two sticks; fractious, disagreeable, pettish, crabbed, crabby, waspish, prickly, peppery, touchy, scratchy, crusty, splenetic, shrewish, short-tempered, hot-tempered, quick-tempered, dyspeptic, choleric, bilious, liverish, cross-grained; *informal* snappish, snappy, chippy, on a short fuse, short-fused; *Brit. informal* shirty, stroppy, narky, ratty, eggy, like a bear with a sore head; *N. Amer. informal* cranky, ornery, peckish, soreheaded; *Austral./NZ informal* snaky; *informal, dated* waxy, miffy.
OPPOSITES good-humoured, affable.

baffle ▶ verb **1** *his reaction baffled her* **perplex**, puzzle, bewilder, mystify, bemuse, confuse, confound, nonplus, disconcert, throw, set someone thinking; *informal* flummox, discombobulate, faze, stump, beat, fox, make someone scratch their head, be all Greek to, floor, fog; *N. Amer. informal* buffalo; *rare* wilder, gravel, maze, cause to be at a stand, pose, obfuscate.
OPPOSITE enlighten.
2 *her intention was to baffle their plans* **thwart**, frustrate, foil, baulk, check, block, hinder, obstruct, bar, prevent, deflect, divert.
OPPOSITE further.

CHOOSE THE RIGHT WORD
baffle, puzzle, perplex, mystify
See PUZZLE.

baffling ▶ adjective *I found his explanation baffling* **puzzling**, **bewildering**, perplexing, mystifying, bemusing, confusing, unclear, difficult/hard to understand, beyond one, above one's head; mysterious, enigmatic, obscure, abstruse, unfathomable, inexplicable, incomprehensible, impenetrable, cryptic, opaque; *archaic* wildering.
OPPOSITES clear, comprehensible.

bag ▶ noun **1** *he carried a bag filled with sandwiches* **receptacle**, container; **shopping bag**, string bag, sack; *Brit.* **carrier bag**, carrier; *Scottish* poke; *N. Amer. dated* keister.
2 *I dug around in my bag for my lipstick* **handbag**, shoulder bag, clutch bag, evening bag, pochette; *N. Amer.* pocketbook, purse; *Brit. informal* bumbag; *N. Amer. informal* fanny pack; *historical* reticule, scrip.
3 *she began to unpack her bags* **suitcase**, case, valise, portmanteau, holdall, carryall, grip, overnight bag, overnighter, flight bag, travelling bag, Gladstone bag, carpet bag; backpack, rucksack, knapsack, haversack, kitbag, duffel bag; satchel; (**bags**) luggage, baggage; *Austral./NZ informal* port.
▶ verb **1** *he bagged three pheasants* **catch**, capture, trap, snare, ensnare, land; **kill**, shoot, pick off.
2 *I got there early to bag a seat in the front row | he bagged seven League medals during his career* **get**, secure, obtain, acquire; reserve, commandeer, grab, appropriate, take; win, achieve, attain; *informal* get one's hands on, get one's mitts on, nab, pick up, land, net.
3 *her trousers bagged at the knee* **sag**, hang loosely, bulge, swell, balloon.

baggage ▶ noun **luggage**, suitcases, cases, bags, trunks; things, belongings, possessions, kit, equipment, effects, goods and chattels, impedimenta, paraphernalia, accoutrements, rig, tackle; *informal* gear, stuff, traps, dunnage; *Brit. informal* clobber; *S. African informal* trek.

baggy ▶ adjective *baggy corduroy trousers* **loose-fitting**, loose, roomy, generously cut, full, ample, voluminous, billowing; oversized, shapeless, ill-fitting, tent-like, sack-like, bagging, sagging, saggy, slack, floppy, ballooning.
OPPOSITE tight.

bail ▶ noun *he has been released on bail* **surety**, security, collateral, assurance, indemnity, indemnification; **bond**, guarantee, warranty, pledge; *archaic* gage, earnest.
▶ verb
□ **bail out, bale out 1** *the state will not bail out loss-making industries* **rescue**, save, relieve, deliver, redeem; finance, help (out), assist, aid, come to the aid of, give/lend a helping hand to; *informal* save someone's bacon, save someone's neck, save someone's skin.
2 *he levelled the plane long enough for his crew to bail out* **eject**, parachute to safety.
3 *after the strong run, investors bailed out* **sell up**, sell out, sell; **withdraw**, retreat, beat a retreat, quit, give up.

bait ▶ noun **1** *the fish let go of the bait* **lure**, decoy, fly, troll, jig, plug, teaser.
2 *was she the bait to lure him into a trap?* **enticement**, lure, decoy, snare, trap, siren, carrot, attraction, draw, magnet, incentive, temptation, allurement, incitement, inducement; *informal* come-on.

B

▶ **verb** *the other boys revelled in baiting him* **taunt**, goad, provoke, pick on, torment, torture, persecute, badger, plague, harry, harass, hound, tease, annoy, irritate, get someone's back up; *informal* hassle, needle, give someone a hard time, wind up, nark.

bake ▶ **verb 1** *bake the fish for 15–20 mins* **cook**, oven-bake, dry-roast, roast, spit-roast, pot-roast; *rare* oven.
2 *the surface of the earth has been baked into a crust* **scorch**, burn, sear, parch, dry (up), desiccate, wither, shrivel, fire; *N. Amer.* broil.

balance ▶ **noun 1** *I tripped and lost my balance* **stability**, equilibrium, steadiness, footing.
OPPOSITE instability.
2 *the way to peace and some kind of personal balance* **composure**, assurance, self-assurance, self-control, calmness, coolness, cool head; ease, tranquillity, serenity, imperturbability, impassivity, equanimity, nonchalance, confidence, self-confidence, self-possession, sureness, poise, dignity, aplomb, presence of mind, nerve, sangfroid, countenance, collectedness, suaveness, urbanity, elegance; *informal* cool, unflappability.
OPPOSITE nervousness.
3 *the obligations of political balance in broadcasting* **fairness**, justice, impartiality, egalitarianism, equal opportunity; **parity**, equity, equilibrium, evenness, symmetry, equipoise, correspondence, uniformity, equality, equivalence, similarity, levelness, parallelism, comparability.
OPPOSITE imbalance.
4 *this stylistic development provides a balance to the rest of the work* **counterbalance**, equipoise, counterweight, stabilizer, compensation, recompense, ballast, makeweight; *archaic* countercheck.
5 *a girl was weighing material on a balance* **scale(s)**, weighing machine, weighbridge.
6 *the landlord demanded payment of the balance of the rent* **remainder**, outstanding amount, rest, residue, difference, remaining part/number/quantity.
□ **in the balance** *the aircraft's future is in the balance after this crash* **uncertain**, unknown, undetermined, unsettled, unresolved, unsure, pending, in limbo, up in the air, at a turning point, critical, at a critical stage, at a crisis; debatable, open to question, in doubt; unpredictable, unforeseeable, incalculable, speculative, unreliable, untrustworthy, undependable, risky, chancy; *informal* dicey, hairy, iffy; *Brit. informal* dodgy.
□ **on balance** *their allegation is, on balance, substantially correct* **overall**, all in all, all things considered, taking everything into consideration/account, by and large, on average, for the most part, mostly, mainly, in the main, on the whole, in general, generally, generally speaking, largely, to a large extent, to a great degree.
▶ **verb 1** *she balanced the book on her head* **steady**, stabilize, **poise**, level, prop, position.
2 *he balanced his radical remarks with more familiar declarations* **counterbalance**, balance out, cancel, cancel out, offset, even out/up, counteract, counterpoise, countervail, equalize, neutralize, nullify, compensate for, make up for; *rare* equilibrize.
3 *a country's payments for imports and receipts for exports must balance* **correspond**, agree, tally, match up, concur, coincide, be in agreement, be consistent, equate, be equal, harmonize, be in harmony, be compatible, be consonant, be congruous, be in tune, dovetail, correlate; *informal* square; *N. Amer. informal* jibe.
4 *it is a matter of balancing advantages against disadvantages* **weigh**, weigh up, compare, evaluate, consider, assess, appraise, estimate.

balanced ▶ **adjective 1** *a balanced view of the issues involved* **fair**, equitable, just, unbiased, unprejudiced, objective, impartial, dispassionate, in proportion, that takes everything into account.
OPPOSITE partial.
2 *a balanced diet* **mixed**, varied; **healthy**, sensible, well balanced.
OPPOSITES monotonous, unhealthy.
3 *she would come to terms with her predicament as any balanced individual would do* **level-headed**, well balanced, well adjusted, sensible, practical, realistic, with one's/both feet on the ground, prudent, circumspect, pragmatic, wise, reasonable, rational, mature, stable, sane, even-tempered, commonsensical, full of common sense, judicious, sound, sober, businesslike, reliable, dependable; **calm**, cool, collected, composed, {cool, calm, and collected}, serene, relaxed, at ease, confident, equable, unworried, unmoved, unemotional, cool-headed, imperturbable; *informal* together, laid-back, unflappable.
OPPOSITES neurotic, panicky.

balcony ▶ **noun 1** *the balcony of a villa* veranda, terrace, portico, loggia.
2 *the applause was loudest in the balcony* **gallery**, upper circle; *informal* the gods.

bald ▶ **adjective 1** *he had a bald head* **hairless**, bald-headed, smooth; shaven, depilated; *Scottish & Irish* baldy; *technical* glabrous; *archaic* bald-pated.
OPPOSITE hairy.
2 *the garden contained a few bald bushes* **leafless**, bare, uncovered, stark.
OPPOSITE lush.
3 *such a bald statement requires some elaboration* **plain**, simple, unadorned, unvarnished, unembellished, undisguised, unveiled, stark, severe, austere, brutal, harsh; **blunt**, direct, forthright, plain-spoken, straight, straightforward, candid, honest, truthful, realistic, true to life, frank, outspoken, downright, outright, straight from the shoulder, explicit, unequivocal, unambiguous, unexaggerated, unqualified; *informal* upfront, warts and all.
OPPOSITE exhaustive.

balderdash ▶ **noun** *his story was a load of balderdash* **nonsense**, rubbish, gibberish, claptrap, blather, blether; *informal* rot, tripe, hogwash, baloney, drivel, bilge, bosh, bull, bunk, guff, eyewash, piffle, poppycock, phooey, hooey, malarkey, twaddle, dribble; *Brit. informal* cobblers, codswallop, cock, stuff and nonsense, tosh, cack; *Scottish & N. English informal* havers; *N. Amer. informal* garbage, flapdoodle, blathers, applesauce, wack, bushwa; *informal, dated* bunkum, tommyrot, cod, gammon, toffee; *vulgar slang* shit, bullshit, horseshit, crap, bollocks, balls; *Austral./NZ vulgar slang* bulldust.

balding ▶ **adjective** *a balding man* **losing one's hair**, thinning, with receding hair; *informal* (going) thin on top.

baldness ▶ **noun** *he shaved his head to hide his baldness* **hair loss**, hairlessness; *Medicine* alopecia, madarosis; *archaic* bald-patedness, glabreity.

bale[1] ▶ **noun** *a bale of cotton* **bundle**, truss, bunch, pack, package, parcel, load.

bale[2] ▶ **verb**
□ **bale out**. *See* BAIL OUT.

baleful ▶ **adjective** *she gave him a baleful stare* **menacing**, threatening, unfriendly, hostile, antagonistic, evil, evil-intentioned, wicked, nasty, hate-filled, bitter, acrimonious, malevolent, malicious, malignant, malign, sinister, deadly, harmful, injurious, dangerous, noxious, virulent, pernicious, venomous, poisonous, vitriolic, vindictive; *literary* malefic, maleficent.
OPPOSITES benevolent, friendly.

balk ▶ **verb**. *See* BAULK.

ball[1] *See centre pages for list of* **Ball Games**
▶ **noun 1** *a cricket ball | a ball of wool* **sphere**, globe, orb, globule, spherule, spheroid, ovoid; drop, droplet, bead; *informal* pill.
2 *a musket ball* **bullet**, projectile, shot, pellet, slug, lead.

ball[2] ▶ **noun** *a fancy-dress ball* **dance**, dinner dance, masked ball, masquerade, tea dance; *N. Amer.* hoedown, prom; *French* thé dansant; *informal* hop, disco, bop.
□ **have a ball** (*informal*) **have a good time**, have a great time, have fun, have the time of one's life; enjoy oneself; *informal* let one's hair down, whoop it up, have a fling, make whoopee, push the boat out, paint the town red, live it up.

ballad ▶ **noun** *a ballad sung in the pubs of Ireland* **song**, folk song, shanty, ditty, canzone; poem, tale, saga.

ballet ▶ **noun**. *See centre pages for list of* **Ballet Steps and Positions**

balloon ▶ **noun** hot-air balloon, fire balloon, barrage balloon, weather balloon; airship, dirigible, Zeppelin, Montgolfier; envelope, gasbag; *informal* blimp.
▶ **verb 1** *the slack sail was ballooning in the squall* **swell (out)**, puff out/up, bulge (out), bag, belly (out), fill (out), billow (out); blow up, inflate, distend, expand, dilate.
OPPOSITES sag, flap.
2 *the company's debt has ballooned in the last five years* **increase rapidly**, soar, rocket, shoot up, escalate, mount, surge, spiral, grow rapidly, rise rapidly; *informal* go through the ceiling, go through the roof, skyrocket.
OPPOSITE plummet.

ballot ▶ **noun** *the ballot for the leadership election* **vote**, poll, election, referendum, plebiscite, general election, local election, popular vote, straw poll, show of hands; voting, polling.

ballyhoo ▶ **noun** (*informal*) *after all the ballyhoo, the film was a flop* **publicity**, advertising, promotion, marketing, propaganda, push, puffery, build-up, boosting; **commotion**, fuss, ado, flurry, excitement, ferment, tumult, hurly-burly, hue and cry, bustle, hustle and bustle; *informal* hype, spiel, hoo-ha, hullabaloo, flap, song and dance, splash; *Brit. informal* kerfuffle, carry-on; *NZ informal* bobsy-die.

balm ▶ **noun 1** *a skin balm for use after shaving* **ointment**, lotion, cream, salve, liniment, embrocation, rub, gel, emollient, unguent, balsam, moisturizer; pomade, pomatum; *technical* demulcent, humectant; *archaic* unction.
OPPOSITES astringent; irritant.
2 *the murmur of the water can provide balm for troubled spirits* **relief**, comfort, ease, consolation, cheer, solace; alleviation, mitigation, assuagement, healing.
OPPOSITE exacerbation.

balmy ▶ **adjective** *the balmy days of late summer* **mild**, gentle, temperate, summery, calm, tranquil, clement, fine, pleasant, benign, soothing, soft; fragrant, scented, perfumed.
OPPOSITES harsh, wintry.

bamboozle ▶ **verb** (*informal*) *convicts could bamboozle prison chaplains into believing that they had reformed* **trick**, deceive, delude, hoodwink, mislead, take in, dupe, fool, double-cross; cheat, defraud, swindle, outwit, outmanoeuvre, catch out, gull, hoax, beguile; entrap; *informal* con, bilk, diddle, rook, put one over on, pull a fast one on, pull the wool over someone's eyes, take for a ride, lead up the garden path, spoof, shaft, do, have, gyp, flimflam; *N. Amer. informal* sucker, snooker, goldbrick, give someone a bum steer; *Austral. informal* pull a swifty on; *rare* cozen, chicane, sell, illude.

ban ▶ verb **1** *Norway banned all tobacco advertising in 1975* **prohibit**, forbid, veto, proscribe, disallow, outlaw, make illegal, embargo, place an embargo on, bar, debar, block, stop, put a stop to, put an end to, suppress, interdict; *Law* enjoin, restrain.
OPPOSITE permit.
2 *Gary was banned from the playground* **exclude**, banish, expel, eject, evict, drive out, force out, oust, remove, get rid of, drum out, thrust out, push out, turn out; prohibit from entering; *informal* boot out, kick out, give someone the boot; *Brit. informal* turf out.
OPPOSITE admit.
▶ noun **1** *a total ban on smoking* **prohibition**, veto, proscription, embargo, bar, suppression, stoppage, interdict, interdiction, moratorium, injunction.
OPPOSITE permission.
2 *he faced a possible ban from international football* **exclusion**, banishment, expulsion, ejection, eviction, removal.
OPPOSITE admission.

CHOOSE THE RIGHT WORD

ban, forbid, prohibit
See **FORBID**.

banal ▶ adjective *songs with banal, repeated words* **trite**, hackneyed, clichéd, platitudinous, vapid, commonplace, ordinary, common, stock, conventional, stereotyped, predictable, overused, overdone, overworked, stale, worn out, time-worn, tired, threadbare, hoary, hack, unimaginative, unoriginal, uninspired, prosaic, dull, boring, pedestrian, run-of-the-mill, routine, humdrum; *informal* old hat, corny, played out; *N. Amer. informal* cornball, dime store; *rare* truistic, bromidic.
OPPOSITE original.

banality ▶ noun **1** *the banality of most sitcoms* **triteness**, platitudinousness, vapidity, pedestrianism, conventionality, predictability, staleness, unimaginativeness, lack of originality, lack of inspiration, prosaicness, dullness, ordinariness; *informal* corniness.
OPPOSITE originality.
2 *they exchanged banalities for a couple of minutes* **platitude**, cliché, truism, banal phrase, trite phrase, hackneyed phrase, overworked phrase, stock phrase, commonplace, old chestnut, bromide.
OPPOSITES epigram, witticism.

band¹ ▶ noun **1** *she wore a scarlet band round her waist* **belt**, sash, girdle, strap, tape, ring, hoop, loop, circlet, circle, cord, tie, string, thong, ribbon, fillet, strip; *literary* cincture.
2 *grey socks with a dark red band around their tops* **stripe**, strip, streak, line, bar, belt, swathe, vein, thread, flash; *technical* stria, striation, lane.

band² ▶ noun **1** *a band of robbers* **group**, gang, mob, pack, troop, troupe, company, party, bevy, crew, body, working party, posse; team, side, selection, line-up, array; gathering, crowd, horde, throng, assembly, assemblage; association, society, club, circle, fellowship, partnership, guild, lodge, order, fraternity, confraternity, brotherhood, sisterhood, sorority, union, alliance, affiliation, institution, league, federation, clique, set, coterie; squad, corps, cadre, contingent, detachment, unit, detail, patrol, army, cohort; *informal* bunch, gaggle; *rare* sodality.
2 *he plays the trumpet in a band* **(musical) group**, pop group, ensemble, orchestra; (*in Spain & Spanish-speaking countries*) conjunto; *informal* combo.
▶ verb *local people* **banded together** *to fight the company* **join (up)**, team up, join forces, pool resources, club together, get together, come together; collaborate, cooperate, work together, pull together; amalgamate, unite, form an alliance, form an association, combine, merge, affiliate, federate.
OPPOSITE split up.

bandage ▶ noun *she had a bandage on her foot* **dressing**, covering, gauze, lint, compress, plaster, ligature, tourniquet, swathe, strap, sling; *trademark* Elastoplast, Band-Aid.
▶ verb *she bandaged my knee* **bind**, bind up, dress, cover, wrap, swaddle, swathe, strap (up), plaster, put a plaster on.

bandit ▶ noun *most of the food aid was stolen by bandits* **robber**, raider, mugger; brigand, freebooter, outlaw, desperado, hijacker, plunderer, pillager, looter, marauder, gangster, gunman, criminal, crook, thief; *historical* rustler, highwayman, footpad, reaver, snaphance; *Scottish historical* cateran, mosstrooper.

bandy¹ ▶ adjective *bandy legs* **bowed**, curved, bent, crooked, misshapen, malformed; bow-legged, bandy-legged.
OPPOSITE straight.

bandy² ▶ verb **1** *£40,000 is the figure that has been* **bandied about** **spread (about/around)**, put about, toss about, discuss, rumour; circulate, disseminate, communicate, purvey, diffuse, broadcast, publicize, make public, make known, pass on, propagate, promulgate, announce, give out, repeat; *literary* bruit about/abroad.
2 *I'm not going to bandy words with you* **exchange**, swap, trade, interchange, barter, reciprocate, pass back and forth, give and take.

bane ▶ noun *scurvy was the bane of seamen two centuries ago* **scourge**, ruin, death, plague, ruination, destruction; torment, torture, menace, suffering, pain, distress, hardship, cross to bear, burden, thorn in one's flesh/side, bitter pill, affliction, calamity, despair, trouble, misery, woe, tribulation, misfortune, nuisance, pest, headache, trial, blight, curse, nightmare.

bang ▶ noun **1** *the door slammed with a bang* **sharp noise**, crack, boom, clang, peal, clap, pop, snap, knock, tap, slam, bump, thud, thump, clunk, clonk, clash, crash, smash, smack; stamp, stomp, clump, clomp; report, explosion, detonation, shot; *informal* wham, whump.
2 *a nasty bang on the head* **blow**, hit, punch, knock, thump, rap, bump, thwack, smack, crack, slap, welt, cuff, box; *informal* bash, whack, clobber, clout, clip, wallop, belt, tan, biff, bop, sock, lam, whomp; *Brit. informal* slosh; *N. Amer. informal* boff, bust, slug, whale; *Austral./NZ informal* dong; *dated* buffet.
▶ verb **1** *he began to bang the table with his fist* **hit**, strike, beat, thump, hammer, knock, rap, pound, thud, punch, bump, thwack, smack, crack, slap, slam, welt, cuff, pummel, buffet; *informal* bash, whack, clobber, clout, clip, wallop, belt, tan, biff, bop, sock, lam, whomp; *Brit. informal* slosh; *N. Amer. informal* boff, bust, slug, whale; *Austral./NZ informal* dong.
2 *the door banged* **go bang**, crash, smash, thud.
3 *guns were banging all around them* **explode**, crack, go off with a bang, detonate, burst, blow up.
▶ adverb (*informal*) **1** *bang in the middle of town | the train arrived bang on time* **precisely**, exactly, right, directly, immediately, squarely, just, dead; **promptly**, prompt, dead on, on the stroke of ..., on the dot of ...; sharp, on the dot; *informal* spot on, smack, slap, slap bang, plumb; *N. Amer. informal* on the button, on the nose, smack dab, spang.
2 *the machines will be bang up to date* **completely**, absolutely, totally, entirely, wholly, fully, thoroughly, utterly, quite, altogether, one hundred per cent, downright, unqualifiedly, in all respects, unconditionally, perfectly, unrestrictedly, undisputedly, to the maximum extent; *informal* clean, plumb, dead.
3 *the minute something becomes obsolete, bang, it's gone* **suddenly**, abruptly, immediately, instantaneously, instantly, in an instant, straight away, all of a sudden, at once, all at once, promptly, in a trice, swiftly; **unexpectedly**, without warning, without notice, on the spur of the moment; *informal* straight off, out of the blue, in a flash, like a shot, before you can say Jack Robinson, before you can say knife, in two shakes (of a lamb's tail).

bangle ▶ noun **bracelet**, wristlet, anklet, armlet, slave bangle; *Sikhism* kara.

banish ▶ verb **1** *he was banished for his crime* **exile**, expel, deport, eject, expatriate, extradite, repatriate, transport; cast out, oust, drive away, evict, throw out, exclude, shut out, ban; *Christianity* excommunicate; (*in ancient Greece*) ostracize.
OPPOSITES admit; readmit.
2 *Chris's smile would banish any fear or suspicion* **dispel**, dismiss, disperse, scatter, dissipate, drive away, drive off, chase away, rout, oust, cast out, shut out, get rid of, quell, allay, eliminate, dislodge.
OPPOSITE engender.

banister ▶ noun **handrail**, railing, rail, balustrade, banisters; balusters.

bank¹ ▶ noun **1** *the banks of Lake Michigan* **edge**, side, embankment, levee, border, verge, boundary, margin, rim, fringe, fringes, flank, brink, perimeter, circumference, extremity, periphery, limit, outer limit, limits, bound, bounds; *literary* marge, bourn, skirt.
2 *a grassy bank* **slope**, rise, incline, gradient, ramp, acclivity; mound, ridge, hillock, hummock, knoll, hump, barrow, tumulus, earthwork, parados, berm; elevation, eminence, prominence; bar, reef, shoal, shelf; accumulation, pile, heap, mass, drift; *Welsh & West Midlands* tump.
3 *a bank of switches* **array**, row, line, tier, group, series; panel, console, board.
▶ verb **1** *they* **banked up** *the earth around their hollow | snows have* **banked up** *under the evergreens* **pile (up)**, heap (up), stack (up), make a pile of, make a heap of, make a stack of; accumulate, amass, assemble, put together.
2 *she* **banked up** *the fire* **damp (down)**, smother, stifle.
3 *she taught him how to bank the plane | the aircraft banked gently* **tilt**, **lean**, tip, slant, incline, angle, slope, list, camber, pitch, dip, cant, put/be at an angle.

WORD LINKS
relating to a river bank **riparian, riverine**

bank² ▶ noun **1** *I paid the money into my bank* **financial institution**; commercial bank, merchant bank, savings bank, finance company, finance house, lender, mortgagee; *Brit.* high-street bank, clearing bank, building society; *N. Amer.* savings and loan (association), thrift.
2 *a blood bank* **store**, reserve, accumulation, stock, stockpile, inventory, supply, pool, fund, cache, hoard, deposit; storehouse, reservoir, repository, depository; *rare* amassment.

B

▶ **verb 1** *I banked the cheque* **deposit**, pay in; clear; save, save up, keep, keep in reserve, lay by, put aside, set aside, put by, put by for a rainy day, hoard, cache, garner; *informal* stash (away), salt away, squirrel away.
2 *the family has* **banked with** *Coutts for generations* **have an account at**, deposit one's money with, use, be a customer of, deal with, do business with.

□ **bank on** *the prime minister cannot bank on their support* **rely on, depend on**, count on, place reliance on, bargain on, plan on, reckon on, calculate on, presume on; anticipate, expect, pin one's hopes on, hope for, take for granted, take as read, take on trust; be confident of, have (every) confidence in, place (one's) confidence in, be sure of, pin one's faith on, trust in; *N. Amer. informal* figure on.

banknote ▶ **noun note**; *N. Amer.* **bill**; *N. Amer. informal* greenback; *N. Amer. & historical* Treasury note; (**banknotes**) paper money.
OPPOSITES coin; plastic.

bankrupt ▶ **adjective 1** *the company was declared bankrupt* **insolvent**, bankrupted; failed, ruined, wiped out, gone under; in debt, owing money, in the red, in arrears; *Brit.* in administration, in receivership; *informal* bust, belly up, gone to the wall, on the rocks, broke, flat broke; *informal, dated* smashed; *Brit. informal* skint, stony broke, cleaned out, in Queer Street; *Brit. informal, dated* in Carey Street.
OPPOSITE solvent.
2 *this government is bankrupt of ideas* **completely lacking in**, without, bereft of, exhausted of, devoid of, empty of, depleted of, destitute of, vacant of, bare of, denuded of, deprived of; in need of, wanting; *informal* minus, sans.
OPPOSITE teeming with.

▶ **noun** *he was soon a bankrupt* **insolvent**, bankrupt person; debtor; pauper.

▶ **verb** *the strike nearly bankrupted the union* **ruin**, make bankrupt, cause to go bankrupt, make insolvent, impoverish, reduce to penury/destitution, bring to ruin, bring someone to their knees, wipe out, break, cripple; *rare* pauperize, beggar.

bankruptcy ▶ **noun** *many companies were facing bankruptcy* **insolvency**, liquidation, failure, (financial) ruin, ruination, debt, indebtedness; penury, beggary; *Brit.* administration, receivership; *rare* pauperdom.
OPPOSITE solvency.

banner ▶ **noun 1** *students waved banners and chanted slogans* **placard**, sign, poster, notice.
2 *banners fluttered above the waiting troops* **flag**, standard, ensign, jack, colour(s), pennant, pennon, streamer, banderole; *Brit.* pendant; *Nautical* burgee; (*in ancient Rome*) vexillum; *rare* gonfalon, guidon, labarum.

banquet ▶ **noun** *local caterers were providing a farewell banquet* **feast, dinner**, dinner party, formal meal, celebratory meal, treat; *informal* spread, blowout, binge; *Brit. informal* nosh-up, scoff, slap-up meal, tuck-in.
OPPOSITE snack.

banter ▶ **noun** *a brief exchange of harmless banter* **repartee**, raillery, ripostes, sallies, swordplay, quips, wisecracks, crosstalk, wordplay; badinage, witty conversation, witty remarks, witticism(s), joking, jesting, jocularity, drollery; *French* bons mots; *informal* kidding, ribbing, joshing; *rare* persiflage.

▶ **verb** *a small crowd of sightseers were bantering with the guards* **joke**, jest, pun, sally, quip; *informal* josh, wisecrack.

baptism ▶ **noun 1** *the baptism ceremony* **christening**, naming, immersion, sprinkling; *rare* lustration.
2 *this event constituted his baptism as a politician* **initiation**, debut, introduction, inauguration, launch, beginning, rite of passage; *French* rite de passage; *formal* commencement.

baptize ▶ **verb 1** *he was baptized at the parish church* **christen**, immerse, sprinkle; *rare* lustrate.
2 *he had been baptized into the Roman Catholic Church* **admit**, introduce, initiate, enrol, recruit, convert.
3 *he was baptized with the names John Cyril* **name**, give a name to, call, dub, nickname; label, style, term, describe as, title, entitle, designate; *rare* clepe, denominate.

bar ▶ **noun 1** *an iron bar* **rod**, pole, stake, stick, batten, shaft, shank, rail, pale, paling, spar, strut, support, prop, spoke, crosspiece, girder, beam, boom.
2 *a bar of chocolate* **block**, slab, cake, tablet, brick, loaf, wedge, lump, chunk, hunk, cube, ingot, nugget, piece.
3 *please purchase your drinks from the bar* **counter**, table, buffet, stand.
4 *she went to her favourite bar on West 43rd Street* **hostelry**, tavern, inn, wine bar, taproom; *Brit.* **pub**, public house, free house, tied house; *Scottish* howff; *Canadian* beer parlour; *Austral./NZ* hotel; *Spanish* cantina; *German* Bierkeller, Weinstube; *informal* watering hole; *Brit. informal* local, boozer; *N. Amer. informal* gin mill; *historical* alehouse, pot-house, taphouse, beerhouse; *N. Amer. historical* saloon.
5 *a bar to promotion* **obstacle**, impediment, hindrance, obstruction, check, stop, block, hurdle, barrier, stumbling block, handicap, restriction, limitation.
OPPOSITE aid.
6 (*Brit.*) *members of the Bar* **barristers**, advocates, counsel.
7 *he dredged a channel through the bar across the river mouth* **sandbank**, shoal, bank, shallow, reef, ridge, ledge, shelf.

▶ **verb 1** *they have barred the door* **bolt**, lock, fasten, padlock, secure, latch, deadlock, block, barricade, obstruct; *Scottish & Irish* sneck, snib.
OPPOSITE unbar.
2 *they were barred from entering the country* **prohibit**, debar, preclude, forbid, ban, interdict, inhibit; exclude, keep out; obstruct, hinder, restrain, check, block, impede, stop; *Law* enjoin, estop.
OPPOSITES admit; accept.

▶ **preposition** *all the others, bar one, were killed* **except (for)**, apart from, but (for), other than, besides, aside from, with the exception of, short of, barring, excepting, excluding, omitting, leaving out, save (for), saving; *informal* outside of.
OPPOSITE including.

barb ▶ **noun 1** *the barb on the hook cut his finger badly* **spike**, prong, point, projection, spur, thorn, needle, prickle, spine, quill, bristle, tine; *technical* spicule, spicula, spiculum, spinule.
2 *he ignored the barbs from his critics* **insult**, sneer, jibe, cut, cutting remark, shaft, affront, slap in the face, slight, rebuff, brickbat, slur, scoff, jeer, taunt; (**barbs**) abuse, disparagement, scoffing, scorn, spite, sarcasm, goading, ridiculing, derision, mockery; *informal* dig, put-down.

barbarian ▶ **noun** *the city was besieged by barbarians* **savage**, brute, beast, wild man/woman, troglodyte; ruffian, lout, thug, vandal, hoodlum, hooligan, rowdy; boor, oaf, ignoramus, philistine, vulgarian, yahoo; *informal* clod, clodhopper, roughneck; *Brit. informal* yobbo, yob, lager lout, oik.

▶ **adjective** *the barbarian hordes* **savage**, uncivilized, barbaric, barbarous, primitive, heathen, wild, brutish, Neanderthal; thuggish, loutish, uncouth, coarse, rough, boorish, oafish, vulgar, gross, philistine, uneducated, uncultured, uncultivated, benighted, unsophisticated, unrefined, unpolished, ill-bred, ill-mannered; *informal* yobbish; *archaic* rude.
OPPOSITE civilized.

barbaric ▶ **adjective 1** *the regime's barbaric crimes were exposed after the war was over* **brutal**, barbarous, brutish, bestial, savage, vicious, fierce, ferocious, wicked, cruel, nasty, ruthless, remorseless, merciless, villainous, murderous, heinous, nefarious, monstrous, base, low, low-down, vile, inhuman, infernal, dark, black, black-hearted, fiendish, hellish, diabolical, ghastly, horrible.
OPPOSITE benevolent.
2 *he tore the raw chicken apart with barbaric strength* **savage**, barbarian, barbarous, primitive, heathen, wild, brutish, Neanderthal; thuggish, loutish; uncouth, coarse, rough, boorish, oafish, vulgar; *archaic* rude.
OPPOSITE civilized.

barbarity ▶ **noun 1** *the barbarity of slavery* **brutality**, brutalism, cruelty, bestiality, barbarism, barbarousness, savagery, viciousness, fierceness, ferocity, wickedness, nastiness, ruthlessness, remorselessness, mercilessness, villainy, murderousness, heinousness, nefariousness, monstrousness, baseness, vileness, inhumanity, blackness, fiendishness, black-heartedness, hellishness, ghastliness, horror.
OPPOSITE benevolence.
2 *the barbarities of the last war* **atrocity**, act of brutality, act of savagery, evil, crime, outrage, offence, abomination, obscenity, enormity, wrong.
3 *beyond the empire lay barbarity* **heathendom**, barbarianism, barbarism, barbarousness, primitiveness, wildness; philistinism, benightedness, unsophisticatedness, lack of civilization; *archaic* rudeness.
OPPOSITE civilization.

barbarous ▶ **adjective.** *See* BARBARIC.

barbecue ▶ **noun 1** *there was an evening barbecue* **meal cooked outdoors**, … roast; *N. Amer.* cookout; *S. African* braaivleis; *NZ* hangi; *informal* BBQ; *Austral. informal* barbie.
2 *she bought a barbecue for the garden* rotisserie; *N. Amer.* brazier; (*in Japan*) hibachi.

▶ **verb** *they barbecued some steaks* **cook outdoors**, grill, spit-roast; *N. Amer.* broil, charbroil.

barbed ▶ **adjective 1** *barbed wire* **jagged**, hooked, spiky, spiked, spined, spiny, prickly, thorny, scratchy, bristly, bristled, briary, brambly, sharp, pointed; *technical* spinose, spinous.
2 *a barbed remark* **hurtful**, wounding, cutting, biting, stinging, mean, spiteful, nasty, rude, cruel, vicious, unkind, unfriendly, snide, pointed, hateful, ill-natured, bitter, venomous, poisonous, mordant, acid, acerbic, acrimonious, astringent, caustic, sharp, scathing, hostile, rancorous, malicious, malevolent, evil-intentioned, baleful, vindictive, vengeful, vitriolic, splenetic, malign, malignant, pernicious, bilious; *informal* bitchy, catty; *literary* malefic, maleficent.
OPPOSITES kindly, generous.

bard ▶ **noun** (*archaic or literary*) *the words of the song are by our national bard* **poet**, versifier, verse-maker, rhymester, rhymer, sonneteer, lyricist, lyrist, elegist; laureate; balladeer; *literary* swan; *derogatory* poetaster; *historical* troubadour; *archaic* rhymist, maker; *rare* metricist, ballad-monger, idyllist, Parnassian, poeticule.

bare ▶ **adjective 1** *he was bare from the waist up* **naked**, unclothed,

undressed, uncovered, stripped, with nothing on, in a state of nature, disrobed, unclad, undraped, exposed; nude, in the nude, stark naked; *French* au naturel; *informal* without a stitch on, in one's birthday suit, in the raw, in the altogether, in the buff, as naked as the day one was born, in the nuddy, mother naked; *Brit. informal* starkers; *Scottish informal* in the scud, scuddy; *N. Amer. informal* bare-assed, buck naked; *Austral. informal* bollocky; *Brit. vulgar slang* bollock-naked.
OPPOSITE clothed.
2 *a bare room* **empty**, emptied, unfurnished, vacant, clear, cleared, free, stark, austere, spartan, unadorned, unembellished, unornamented, unfussy, plain.
OPPOSITES furnished, embellished.
3 *bare floorboards* **uncovered**, uncarpeted, unpainted, unvarnished; stripped; polished, sealed.
4 *a cupboard bare of food* **empty of**, emptied of, without, lacking, devoid of, bereft of, wanting, deprived of, destitute of, free from.
OPPOSITE containing.
5 *a bare landscape* **barren**, bleak, exposed, desolate, stark, arid, desert, denuded, lunar; treeless, forestless, without vegetation, defoliated; unsheltered, unprotected, unshielded; *rare* unwooded.
OPPOSITE lush.
6 *Herodotus did not record just the bare facts* **straightforward**, plain, simple, basic, pure, essential, fundamental, stark, bald, cold, hard; truthful, realistic, true to life; brutal, harsh; explicit, unequivocal, unambiguous, unexaggerated, unadorned, unembellished, undisguised, unveiled, unvarnished, unqualified; *informal* warts and all.
7 *the bare minimum | a bare majority* **mere**, no more than, no better than, just a, only a, simple, sheer, very, basic; slim, slight, slender, paltry, skimpy, minimum, trifling.
OPPOSITE comfortable.
▶ **verb** *he bared his arm* **uncover**, strip, lay bare, undress, unclothe, denude, unveil, unmask; expose, expose to view, reveal; display, put on display, put on show, exhibit.
OPPOSITE cover.

CHOOSE THE RIGHT WORD

bare, naked, nude

See NAKED.

barefaced ▶ **adjective** *a barefaced lie* **flagrant**, blatant, glaring, obvious, undisguised, unconcealed, overt, open, transparent, patent, evident, manifest, palpable, unmistakable; **shameless**, unabashed, unashamed, without shame, impudent, insolent, audacious, unembarrassed, unblushing, brazen, brass-necked, brash, bold, unrepentant; *archaic* arrant.

barely ▶ **adverb** *we barely got home in time* **hardly**, scarcely, just, only just, narrowly, by the skin of one's teeth, by a hair's breadth, by a very small margin, by the narrowest of margins, by a nose; almost not; *informal* by a whisker.
OPPOSITE easily.

bargain ▶ **noun 1** *the Government made some kind of bargain with the Opposition* **agreement**, arrangement, understanding, deal; contract, pact, compact, covenant, concordat, treaty, entente, accord, concord, protocol, convention; pledge, promise, engagement; transaction, negotiation.
2 *this binder is a bargain at £1.98* **good buy**, cheap buy; (good) value for money, surprisingly cheap; *informal* snip, steal, giveaway.
OPPOSITE rip-off.
□ **into the bargain** *I'll tell you another thing into the bargain* **also**, as well, in addition, additionally, besides, furthermore, moreover, yet, on top (of that), over and above that, as a bonus, as an extra, to boot, for good measure; *N. Amer.* in the bargain.
▶ **verb** *he bargained with the Council to rent the stadium* **haggle**, barter, negotiate, discuss terms, hold talks, deal, wheel and deal, trade, traffic; *N. Amer.* dicker; *formal* treat; *archaic* chaffer, palter.
□ **bargain for/on** *this was more than we had bargained for* **expect**, anticipate, be prepared for, allow for, plan for, reckon with, take into account/consideration, contemplate, imagine, envisage, foresee, predict, look for, hope for, look to; **count on**, rely on, depend on, bank on, plan on, reckon on, calculate on, be sure of, trust in, take for granted, take as read; *N. Amer. informal* figure on.

barge ▶ **noun** lighter, canal boat, flatboat; *Brit.* narrowboat, wherry; *N. Amer.* scow.
▶ **verb** *he barged his way to the front of the queue* **push**, shove, force, elbow, shoulder, jostle, bludgeon, bulldoze, muscle.
□ **barge in** *I'm sorry for barging in* **burst in**, break in, butt in, cut in, interrupt, intervene, intrude, encroach; gatecrash; *informal* horn in.

bark[1] ▶ **noun** *the bark of a dog* **woof**, yap, yelp, bay; growl, snarl, howl.
▶ **verb 1** *the dog barked* **woof**, yap, yelp, bay; growl, snarl, howl, whine.
2 *'Okay, outside!' he barked* **say/speak brusquely**, say/speak abruptly, say/speak angrily, snap, snarl, growl; **shout**, bawl, cry, yell, roar, bellow, thunder; *N. Amer. informal* holler.

bark[2] ▶ **noun** *the bark of a tree* **rind**, skin, peel, sheath, covering, outer layer, coating, casing, crust; cork; *technical* cortex, integument, bast.
▶ **verb** *he barked his shin on a tree stump* **scrape**, graze, scratch, abrade, scuff, rasp, skin, rub something raw; cut, lacerate, chafe, strip, flay, wound; *technical* excoriate.

WORD LINKS
relating to bark **corticate**

barmy ▶ **adjective** (*Brit. informal*) *I think that's a barmy idea.* See FOOLISH.

barn ▶ **noun** **outbuilding**, shed, outhouse, shelter; stable, mews, stall, pound, sty, coop; Dutch barn, byre; *SW English* linhay; *archaic* grange, garner.

baron ▶ **noun 1** (*historical*) *the French supported the barons against King John* **noble**, nobleman, aristocrat, peer, lord.
2 *a press baron* **magnate**, tycoon, mogul, captain of industry, nabob, grandee, mandarin; industrialist, proprietor, entrepreneur, executive, chief, leader; *informal* big shot, bigwig, honcho; *N. Amer. informal* big wheel; *derogatory* fat cat.
OPPOSITE small fry.

baroque ▶ **adjective 1** *the baroque exuberance of his printed silk shirts* **ornate**, fancy, very elaborate, over-elaborate, curlicued, extravagant, rococo, fussy, busy, ostentatious, showy, wedding-cake, gingerbread.
2 *a baroque prose style* **flowery**, florid, flamboyant, high-flown, high-sounding, magniloquent, grandiloquent, orotund, rhetorical, oratorical, bombastic, laboured, strained, overwrought, overblown, overdone, convoluted, turgid, inflated; *informal* highfalutin, purple; *rare* tumid, pleonastic, euphuistic, aureate, Ossianic, fustian, hyperventilated.
OPPOSITE plain.

barrack ▶ **verb** (*Brit. & Austral./NZ*) *Bob Dylan was barracked for using electric instruments* **jeer**, heckle, taunt, abuse, shout at/down, boo, hiss, interrupt.
OPPOSITES cheer, applaud.

barracks ▶ **plural noun** **garrison**, camp, encampment, depot, billet, quarters, fort, cantonment, guardhouse; *Spanish* cuartel; *Nautical, informal* stone frigate; *archaic, informal* lobster box; *rare* casern.

barrage ▶ **noun 1** *the artillery began to lay down a barrage* **bombardment**, gunfire, cannonade, battery, blast, broadside, salvo, volley, fusillade; storm, hail, shower, cascade, rain, stream, blitz; shelling, wall/curtain/barrier of fire.
2 *a barrage of criticism* **abundance**, mass, superabundance, plethora, profusion; **deluge**, stream, storm, torrent, onslaught, flood, spate, tide, avalanche, hail, burst, blaze; outburst, outpouring.
3 *a barrage across the River Usk* **dam**, weir, barrier, dyke, defence, embankment, wall, obstruction, gate, sluice.

barrel ▶ **noun** **cask**, keg, butt, vat, tun, tub, drum, tank, firkin, hogshead, kilderkin, pin, pipe, barrique; *Spanish* solera; *historical* puncheon, tierce.

barren ▶ **adjective 1** *barren land* **unproductive**, infertile, unfruitful, sterile, arid, desert, waste, desolate, uncultivatable; impoverished.
OPPOSITES fertile, productive.
2 (*archaic*) *a barren woman* **infertile**, sterile, childless; *technical* infecund.
OPPOSITE fertile.
3 *a barren exchange of courtesies* **pointless**, futile, worthless, profitless, valueless, unrewarding, purposeless, useless, vain, aimless; uninteresting, boring, dull, drab, dry, arid, flat, lifeless, uninspiring, unstimulating, stale, prosaic, hollow, empty, vacuous, vapid.
OPPOSITES stimulating, fruitful.

barricade ▶ **noun** *a brick lorry was overturned and used as a barricade* **barrier**, obstacle, blockade, bar, fence, obstruction, roadblock, bulwark, stockade, rampart, palisade, hurdle, protection, defence.
▶ **verb** *they barricaded the building* **blockade**, obstruct, close up, bar, block off, shut off/in, fence in, seal up, defend, protect, fortify, strengthen.

barrier ▶ **noun 1** *police erected barriers to control the crowd* **fence**, railing, barricade, hurdle, bar, blockade, roadblock; fencing.
2 *a barrier to international trade* **obstacle**, obstruction, hurdle, stumbling block, bar, block, impediment, hindrance; snag, catch, drawback, hitch, handicap, deterrent, complication, difficulty, problem, disadvantage, baulk, curb, check, stop; *informal* fly in the ointment, hiccup, facer; *Brit. informal* spanner in the works; *N. Amer. informal* monkey wrench in the works; *literary* trammel; *archaic* cumber.

barring ▶ **preposition** *barring accidents, the whole team should be fit for Saturday* **except for**, with the exception of, excepting, if there is/are no, bar, discounting, short of, apart from, but for, other than, aside from, excluding, omitting, leaving out, save for, saving; *informal* outside of.

barrister ▶ **noun** **advocate**, lawyer, professional pleader, counsel, Queen's Counsel, QC, defending counsel, prosecuting counsel; *N. Amer.* attorney, counselor(-at-law); *informal* brief; *Brit. historical* serjeant-at-law; (**barristers**) *Brit.* the Bar.

barter ▶ **verb 1** *peasants with a surplus of food could barter it for vital equipment* **trade**, **swap**, trade off, exchange, give in exchange, change, traffic, sell.
2 *you can barter for souvenirs in the flea market* **haggle**, bargain, negotiate, discuss terms, hold talks, deal, wheel and deal, trade, traffic; *N. Amer.* dicker; *formal* treat; *archaic* chaffer, palter.

B

▶ **noun** *an economy based on barter* **trading**, trade, exchange, swapping, trafficking, business, commerce, buying and selling, dealing; haggling, negotiation.

base[1] ▶ **noun 1** *the base of the tower* **foundation**, bottom, foot, support, prop, stay, stand, pedestal, plinth, rest, bed, substructure.
OPPOSITE top.
2 *early learning will provide a sound base for what follows* **basis**, bedrock, foundation, core, essence, essential, nitty-gritty, basics, starting point, key component, fundamental, root(s), heart, backbone, theory, principle, rationale; source, origin, spring, well head, fountainhead, fount.
3 *he used the hut as a base for his search* **headquarters**, centre, starting point, camp, site, station, settlement, post.
4 *add a few drops of the aromatic oil to a vegetable oil base* **medium**, vehicle, carrier.
▶ **verb 1** *the legend is based on fact* **found**, build, construct, form, establish, ground, root; use as a basis; rest, hinge; emanate from, derive from, spring from, stem from, originate in, have its origin in, can be traced back to.
2 *the company was based in London* **locate**, station, situate, post, position, place, install, deploy, site, establish, garrison.

base[2] ▶ **adjective** *some of these struggles have been inspired by base motives* **sordid**, improper, low, mean, bad, wrong, evil, wicked, iniquitous, immoral, sinful; unscrupulous, unprincipled, unseemly, unsavoury, shoddy, squalid, vile, foul, vulgar, tawdry, cheap, low-minded, debased, degenerate, depraved, corrupt, reprobate, dissolute, dishonest, dishonourable, disreputable, despicable, discreditable, contemptible, petty, ignominious, ignoble, shameful, wretched, scandalous, infamous, abhorrent, abominable, disgusting.
OPPOSITES good, lofty.

baseless ▶ **adjective** *the accusations were found to be baseless* **groundless**, unfounded, unsubstantiated, unproven, unsupported, uncorroborated, untested, unconfirmed, unverified, unattested, unjustified, unwarranted, foundationless, ill-founded, without basis, without foundation, not backed up by evidence; speculative, conjectural, idle, vain, unsound, unreliable, questionable, misinformed, misguided, spurious, specious, fallacious, erroneous, fabricated, untrue, trumped-up.
OPPOSITES well founded, proven.

basement ▶ **noun** **cellar**, vault, crypt, undercroft, underground room, catacomb; garden flat, sub-basement; *Brit.* lower ground floor; *Scottish* dunny; *Brit. dated* below stairs.

baseness ▶ **noun** *the baseness of which humankind is capable* **meanness**, **sordidness**, evil, wickedness, iniquity, iniquitousness, immorality, sin, wrong; unscrupulousness, unseemliness, unsavouriness, shoddiness, squalidness, vileness, foulness, vulgarity, tawdriness, cheapness, low-mindedness, debasement, degeneracy, depravity, corruption, reprobation, dissolution, dishonesty, dishonour, disreputableness, contemptibility, pettiness, ignominy, wretchedness, infamy; *rare* turpitude.
OPPOSITE nobility.

bash (*informal*) ▶ **verb** *she bashed him across the knuckles with her stick* **strike**, hit, beat, thump, slap, smack, batter, pound, pummel, thrash, rap, buffet, hammer, bang, knock; *informal* wallop, belt, whack, clout, clip, clobber, bop, biff, sock, deck, swipe, lay one on.
□ **bash into** *they bashed into one another* **collide with**, hit, crash into, run into, bang into, smash into, knock into, bump into, meet head-on.
▶ **noun 1** *he got a bash on the head with a golf club* **blow**, rap, hit, knock, bang, slap, crack, thump, tap, clip; *informal* clout, whack, wallop.
2 *Harry's birthday bash.* See PARTY.
3 (*Brit.*) *she'll have a bash at anything.* See ATTEMPT.

bashful ▶ **adjective** *many men are bashful about discussing their feelings* **shy**, reserved, diffident, retiring, self-conscious, coy, demure, reticent, reluctant, shrinking, timid, timorous, meek; hesitant, apprehensive, nervous, insecure, doubting, wary, unconfident, inhibited, faint-hearted; embarrassed, shamefaced, sheepish.
OPPOSITES bold, confident.

> **CHOOSE THE RIGHT WORD**
>
> **bashful, shy, diffident, timid**
>
> *See* SHY.

basic ▶ **adjective 1** *the basic principles of criminal law | basic human rights* **fundamental**, rudimentary, primary, principal, cardinal, chief, elementary, elemental, root; central, pivotal, critical, key, focal, salient, staple; essential, quintessential, vital, necessary, indispensable, foundational, intrinsic, underlying, ingrained.
OPPOSITES secondary, unimportant.
2 *she got a basic salary plus a commission* **lowest**, lowest-level, bottom, starting, ground, undermost; without commission.
3 *all the rooms have basic cooking facilities* **plain**, simple, unsophisticated, straightforward, adequate, unadorned, undecorated, unornamented, without frills; spartan, sparse, stark, severe, austere, limited, meagre, rudimentary, patchy, sketchy, minimal; modest, ordinary, unpretentious, unostentatious, unfussy, homely, homespun; rough, rough and ready, rough-hewn, crude, makeshift; restrained, muted; *informal* bog-standard.
OPPOSITE elaborate.

> **CHOOSE THE RIGHT WORD**
>
> **basic, fundamental**
>
> *Basic* and *fundamental* are synonymous in many contexts and are both used to describe *principles, concepts, understanding, research,* and *rights.*
>
> - Something described as **basic** is seen as a necessary minimum, to which further elaborations may or may not be added. The *basic concept* or *basic design* of something is the essential core of what may be a more complex idea or design, identified for the purpose of better understanding. In examples like *a plain, basic, rock-bottom hatchback* or *teaching basic camera skills, basic* denotes a necessary minimum which can then be improved upon or elaborated upon for purposes of luxury or proficiency. This is illustrated by the fact that *basic*, rather than *fundamental*, is more likely to be used with the following nouns: *necessity, training, information,* and *ingredient.*
> - **Fundamental** derives from Latin *fundamentum* 'foundation'. Something that is *fundamental* to something else is essential to it, determining its nature. So physics might be called a *fundamental* aspect of the curriculum if it influences and shapes some or all of the other topics taught, but *basic* if it merely provides an elementary educational grounding. A *fundamental* flaw, on the other hand, is one which impairs the whole structure; other nouns which are typically used with *fundamental* include: *change, importance,* and *question.*

basically ▶ **adverb** *his disposition is basically peaceful* **fundamentally**, primarily, principally, chiefly, essentially, elementally, firstly, predominantly; above all, first of all, most of all, first and foremost, in essence, at bottom, at heart; mostly, for the most part, in the main, mainly, on the whole, by and large, substantially, in substance; intrinsically, inherently; *French* au fond; *informal* at the end of the day, when all is said and done, when you get right down to it.

basics ▶ **plural noun** (*informal*) *having learnt the basics of dinghy sailing, the next stage is to join a sailing club* **fundamentals**, essentials, rudiments, principles, first principles, foundations, preliminaries, groundwork; essence, basis, core, kernel, nub, marrow, meat, crux, bedrock; facts, hard facts, practicalities, realities; *Latin* sine qua non; *informal* nitty-gritty, brass tacks, nuts and bolts, ABC.

basin ▶ **noun 1** *she poured water into the basin* **bowl**, dish, pan, pot; container, receptacle, vessel.
2 *the loch is cupped in a shallow basin among low hills* **valley**, hollow, gully, gorge, ravine, bed, channel, dip, depression, concavity, trough.

basis ▶ **noun 1** *the factual basis for his criticism* **foundation**, support, base, footing; reasoning, rationale, defence; reason, grounds, justification, rationalization, motive, motivation, cause.
2 *the White Paper formed the basis of the Consumer Credit Act* **starting point**, base, point of departure, beginning, premise; fundamental point/principle, principal constituent, main ingredient, cornerstone, core, heart, thrust, essence, kernel, nub, underpinning, groundwork.
3 *those who are studying on a part-time basis* **footing**, condition, status, position; **arrangement**, system, method, procedure, way.

bask ▶ **verb 1** *I sat on the bank, basking in the warm sunshine* **laze**, lie, lounge, relax, sprawl, loll; sunbathe, sun oneself, warm oneself.
2 *they were still* **basking in** *the glory of success* **revel**, luxuriate, wallow, delight, take pleasure, rejoice, glory, indulge oneself; enjoy, relish, savour, lap up; *informal* get a kick out of, get a thrill out of, get a charge from.

basket ▶ **noun** *a basket of flowers* **receptacle**, container, holder, vessel, box, case; wickerwork box, hamper, creel, pannier, punnet, trug.

bass ▶ **adjective** *a bass drum* **deep-toned**, deep-pitched, deep, low-pitched, low-toned, low, full-toned, resonant, sonorous, powerful, rumbling, booming, resounding; baritone.
OPPOSITE high.

bastard ▶ **noun 1** (*archaic*) *he had fathered a bastard* **illegitimate child**, child born out of wedlock; *dated* love child, by-blow; *archaic* natural child/son/daughter.
2 (*informal*) *the director's an arrogant bastard* **scoundrel**, villain, rogue, rascal, brute, animal, weasel, snake, monster, ogre, wretch, devil, good-for-nothing, reprobate, wrongdoer, evil-doer; *Spanish* picaro; *informal* scumbag, pig, swine, louse, hound, cur, rat, beast, son of a bitch, s.o.b., low life, skunk, nasty piece of work, ratbag, wrong 'un; *Brit. informal* git, toerag; *Scottish informal* scrote; *Irish informal* spalpeen, sleeveen; *N. Amer. informal* fink, rat fink; *W. Indian informal* scamp; *Austral./NZ informal* dingo; *informal, dated* cad, heel, rotter, bounder, bad egg, bad lot, dastard, knave, stinker, blighter; *archaic* blackguard, miscreant, varlet, vagabond, rapscallion, whoreson; *vulgar slang* sod, bugger, shit, fucker; *N. Amer. vulgar slang* fuck,

motherfucker, mofo, mother.
▶ adjective **1** (archaic) *a bastard child* **illegitimate**, born out of wedlock; archaic natural.
2 *a bastard language* **hybrid**, alloyed; adulterated, impure, inferior.

bastardize ▶ verb *he spoke franglais, bastardizing both languages* **adulterate**, corrupt, contaminate, weaken, dilute, spoil, taint, pollute, foul, defile, debase, degrade, devalue, depreciate, distort; formal vitiate.

bastion ▶ noun **1** *he had fortified the stronghold with ditches and bastions* projection, bulwark, rampart, parapet, fortification, buttress, outwork, breastwork, redoubt, barbican, stockade, palisade; rare bartizan.
2 *the last bastion of male-only suffrage in Europe* **stronghold**, bulwark, defender, support, supporter, guard, protection, protector, defence, prop, mainstay.

bat ▶ noun. *See centre pages for list of* **Bats**

batch ▶ noun *a batch of fairy cakes* **group**, quantity, lot, bunch, mass, cluster, raft, set, collection, bundle, series, number; consignment, shipment; pack, crowd, band; accumulation, assemblage, aggregate, aggregation, conglomeration.

bath ▶ noun **1** *the bedrooms have their own bath and shower* **bathtub**, tub, hot tub; hip bath, sitz bath; whirlpool bath, sauna, steam bath, Turkish bath, pool; trademark jacuzzi; archaic slipper bath; (in ancient Greece & Rome) thermae; rare balneal.
2 *she had a quick bath and got dressed* **wash**, soak, dip, shower, douche, soaping, sponging, toilet; formal or humorous ablution.
▶ verb *he would bath the baby and put her to bed* **bathe**, give/have/take a bath, wash, clean, soak, shower, douche, soap, freshen up; literary lave; formal or humorous perform one's ablutions.

WORD LINKS
relating to a bath **balneal, balneary**

bathe ▶ verb **1** *she bathed and went down to dinner. See* BATH.
2 *occasionally I bathed in the local swimming pool* **swim**, go swimming, take a dip, dip, splash around.
3 *his arm was bathed and the wound was lanced* **cleanse**, clean, wash, rinse, wet, moisten; soak, immerse; disinfect.
4 *the room was suddenly bathed in light* **suffuse**, envelop, permeate, cover, pervade, wash, saturate, imbue, fill, load, impregnate, inform, steep, colour; literary mantle.
▶ noun *we would lie together in the sun after a bathe* **swim**, dip, dive, plunge, paddle.

bathetic ▶ adjective *the show begins unpromisingly with a bathetic comedy* **anticlimactic**, disappointing, disillusioning; **mawkish**, sentimental.

bathing costume ▶ noun (Brit.) **swimsuit**, bathing suit, bathing dress, swimming trunks, trunks, swimwear, bikini; Brit. swimming costume; informal swimming togs, cossie; Austral./NZ informal bathers.

bathos ▶ noun *his epic poem has passages of almost embarrassing bathos* **anticlimax**, let-down, disappointment, disillusionment; **mawkishness**, sentimentality; informal comedown.

baton ▶ noun **1** *the conductor stopped the orchestra with a tap of his baton* **stick**, rod, staff, wand, bar.
2 *riot policemen swinging batons* **truncheon**, club, cudgel, bludgeon, stick, bat, mace; N. Amer. nightstick, blackjack; (in Ireland) shillelagh; Brit. informal cosh.

battalion ▶ noun **1** *an infantry battalion* regiment, brigade, force, garrison, division, squadron, squad, company, section, detachment, contingent, legion, corps, troop; unit, group; troops, forces; (in ancient Rome) cohort.
2 *a battalion of women promoting the latest perfumes* **crowd**, army, mob, throng, horde, swarm, multitude, herd, host, mass, drove, large number.

batten[1] ▶ noun *two pieces of hardboard, joined with timber battens* **bar**, bolt, clamp, rail, shaft; board, strip.
▶ verb *Stephen was busy* ***battening down*** *all the shutters with planks of wood* **fasten**, fix, secure, clamp, clasp, bolt, rivet, lash, make fast, nail down, seal, tether.

batten[2] ▶ verb
□ **batten on** *demons who batten on the helpless* **flourish at the expense of**, thrive at the expense of, fatten at the expense of, prosper at the expense of, gain at the expense of, be a parasite on.

batter ▶ verb **1** *he battered his opponent into submission* **pummel**, pound, rain blows on, buffet, belabour, thrash, beat up, abuse; hit, strike, beat, smack, assault, attack, thump, lash, aim blows at; informal whack, clout, wallop, bash, clobber, bop, biff, sock, deck, plug, knock about/around, knock into the middle of next week, beat the living daylights out of, give someone a good hiding, lay into, lace into, do over, rough up.
2 *the storm had severely battered the pier* **damage**, injure, hurt, harm, impair, mar, spoil; destroy, demolish, crush, shatter, smash, ruin; informal total, trash.

battered ▶ adjective **1** *a battered wife* **beaten**, assaulted, thrashed, hit, thumped; **abused**, maltreated, ill-treated, mistreated, misused, victimized, downtrodden, tyrannized.
2 *a battered blue van* **damaged**, **shabby**, run down, worn out, falling to pieces, falling apart, dilapidated, rickety, ramshackle, crumbling, decayed, antiquated, superannuated, the worse for wear, on its last legs.

battery ▶ noun **1** *her car had a flat battery* **cell**, accumulator, power unit.
2 *anti-aircraft missile batteries* **gun emplacement**, artillery unit; (**batteries**) artillery, cannonry, ordnance, heavy weapons, heavy weaponry, guns, cannons.
3 *a battery of equipment to monitor blood pressure* **array**, set, bank, group, row, line, line-up, raft, collection, assortment.
4 *the paediatrician ran a battery of tests* **series**, sequence, range, set, cycle, chain, string, progression, succession.
5 *I'll have the police on you for assault and battery* **violence**, assault, mugging; grievous bodily harm, GBH, actual bodily harm, ABH; **beating**, striking, thumping, thrashing, bashing; aggression.

battle ▶ noun **1** *the battle raged throughout the night* **fight**, conflict, armed conflict, clash, struggle, skirmish, engagement, affray, fray, encounter, confrontation; contest, meeting, collision, duel; tussle, scuffle, melee, fracas; war, campaign, crusade; fighting, warfare, combat, action, hostilities; informal scrap, dogfight, shoot-out.
OPPOSITES truce, peace.
2 *a legal battle to overturn a music licence ban* **conflict**, clash, contest, competition, struggle; disagreement, argument, dispute, controversy, debate; dissension, altercation, strife.
▶ verb **1** *he has been* ***battling against*** *illness* **fight**, combat, contend with; resist, withstand, stand up to, put up a fight against, confront; war, feud; struggle, strive, campaign, work, toil.
OPPOSITES give up, give in.
2 *Mark* ***battled his way*** *back to the bar* **scramble**, struggle, labour; fight, elbow, push.

battleaxe ▶ noun **1** *a severe blow from a battleaxe* **poleaxe**, axe, pike, halberd, tomahawk, war mattock, mace.
2 (informal) *his mother was a right old battleaxe* **harridan**, dragon, crone, witch, hag, gorgon, ogress, hellcat, harpy, tartar, martinet, termagant, virago, fury; shrew, nag; informal old bat, old bag, bitch; archaic scold; rare Xanthippe.

battle cry ▶ noun **1** *the battle cry of the Imperial Army* **war cry**, war whoop, rallying call/cry, cry.
2 *'equal pay for equal work' was a battle cry of the feminist movement* **slogan**, motto, watchword, catchphrase, catchword, byword, shibboleth.

battlefield ▶ noun *the battlefields of the Great War* **battleground**, front, battle front, battle lines, field of operations, field of battle, combat zone, theatre, theatre/arena of war, battle stations; historical lists.

battlement ▶ noun *the castle had seven towers and high battlements* **castellation**, parapet, rampart, balustrade, wall, bulwark, barbican, bastion; fortification, breastwork, crenellation, circumvallation, outwork; (in ancient Rome) vallum; rare bartizan.

batty ▶ adjective (informal) *she has gone completely batty* **mad**, insane, odd, queer, eccentric, deranged, demented, crazed, out of one's mind, not in one's right mind, sick in the head, lunatic, unbalanced, unhinged, unstable; mad as a hatter, mad as a March hare, away with the fairies, foaming at the mouth; foolish, stupid, idiotic, silly; informal crazy, mental, daft, bats, bonkers, nuts, nutty, nutty as a fruitcake, dotty, potty, loony, screwy, off one's head/nut/rocker, round the bend, out to lunch, raving mad, stark staring/raving mad; Brit. informal barmy, crackers, barking (mad), off one's trolley, off the wall, not the full shilling; N. Amer. informal nutsy, whacko.
OPPOSITES sane, rational.

bauble ▶ noun *gift-shop baubles* **trinket**, knick-knack, ornament, toy, novelty, curiosity, gimmick, plaything, trifle, frippery, gewgaw, gimcrack, bagatelle, bibelot, furbelow; informal whatnot; Brit. informal doodah, doobry; N. Amer. informal tchotchke, tsatske; archaic folderol, whim-wham, kickshaw, bijou, gaud.

baulk ▶ verb **1** *sensitive gardeners who* ***baulk at*** *using pesticides* **eschew**, resist, refuse to, be unwilling to, draw the line at, be reluctant to, draw back from, flinch from, shrink from, shy from, recoil from, quail at, demur from, hesitate over, scruple to, take exception to, not like to, hate to, jib at; scorn, disdain.
OPPOSITE accept.
2 *they were baulked by traffic* **impede**, obstruct, thwart, hinder, prevent, check, stop, curb, halt, bar, block, forestall, frustrate, stall, baffle, foil, defeat, beat, counteract, head off.
OPPOSITE assist.

bawd ▶ noun (archaic) *an old bawd procuring a young woman for a besotted admirer* **brothel-keeper**, madam; procurer, procuress, pimp; French souteneur; Brit. informal ponce; Austral. informal hoon; rare pander, panderess, mack, fancy man.

bawdy ▶ adjective *they told bawdy jokes* **ribald**, indecent, risqué, racy, rude, spicy, suggestive, titillating, naughty, improper, indelicate, indecorous, off colour, earthy, broad, locker-room, Rabelaisian; pornographic, obscene, vulgar, crude, coarse, gross, lewd, dirty, filthy, smutty, unseemly, salacious, prurient, lascivious, licentious, X-rated, scatological, near the bone, near the knuckle; erotic, sexy, sexual; informal blue, raunchy, nudge-nudge; euphemistic adult.

B

OPPOSITES clean, innocent.

bawl ▶ verb **1** *'Come on, Simon!' he bawled* **shout**, call out, cry out, cry, yell, roar, bellow, screech, scream, shriek, howl, whoop, bark, growl, snarl, bluster, vociferate, trumpet, thunder; *informal* yammer; *N. Amer. informal* holler.
OPPOSITE whisper.
2 *the children continued to bawl* **cry**, sob, weep, shed tears, wail, blubber, snivel, whimper, whine, howl, squall; *informal* blub; *Scottish informal* greet; *rare* ululate.
▶ noun *he addressed the class in a terrifying bawl* **shout**, yell, cry, roar, bellow, screech, scream, howl, whoop; *N. Amer. informal* holler.
OPPOSITE whisper.
□ **bawl someone out** (*informal*) *the Brigadier had been bawling him out* **reprimand**, rebuke, scold, admonish, reprove, upbraid, chastise, chide, censure, castigate, lambaste, berate, lecture, criticize, take to task, read the Riot Act to, give a piece of one's mind to, haul over the coals; *informal* tell off, give someone a telling-off, dress down, give someone a dressing-down, pitch into, lay into, lace into, blow up at, give someone an earful, give someone a roasting, give someone a rocket, give someone a rollicking; *Brit. informal* have a go at, carpet, tear someone off a strip, give someone what for, let someone have it; *N. Amer. informal* chew out, ream out; *Brit. vulgar slang* bollock, give someone a bollocking.
OPPOSITE compliment.

bay¹ ▶ noun *the ships were anchored in the bay* **cove**, inlet, estuary, indentation, natural harbour, gulf, basin, fjord, ria, sound, arm, bight, firth, anchorage; *Scottish* (sea) loch; *Irish* lough.

bay² ▶ noun *there is a bay in the far wall of the living room* **alcove**, recess, niche, nook, cubbyhole, opening, hollow, cavity, corner, indentation, booth; apse; inglenook.

bay³ ▶ verb **1** *a jackal baying at the moon* **howl**, bark, yelp, yap, cry, growl, bellow, roar, clamour, snarl; *rare* ululate.
2 *the crowd* ***bayed for*** *an encore* **clamour**, shout, call, press, yell, scream, shriek, roar; **demand**, insist on, urge, claim, make a claim for.
▶ noun *the bloodhounds' heavy bay* **baying**, howl, howling, bark, barking, cry, crying, growl, growling, bellow, bellowing, roar, roaring, clamour, clamouring; *rare* ululation.
□ **at bay** *they lit smoky fires to keep the mosquitoes at bay* **at a distance**, away, off, aside, at arm's length.

bayonet ▶ noun *a man armed with a bayonet* sword, knife, blade, spear, lance, pike, javelin, shaft, harpoon.
▶ verb *stragglers were bayoneted where they fell* **stab**, pierce, spear, knife, gore, spike, stick, impale, run through, transfix, prick, puncture, gash, slash.

bazaar ▶ noun **1** *a Turkish bazaar* **market**, market place, mart, exchange; *Arabic* souk.
2 *the church bazaar* **fête**, fair, jumble sale, sale, bring-and-buy sale, car boot sale, carnival; fund-raiser, charity event; *N. Amer.* tag sale; *Dutch* kermis.

be ▶ verb **1** *there was this boy who lived next door* **exist**, have being, have existence; live, be alive, have life, breathe, draw breath, be extant, be viable.
2 *what theatres will there be for them to visit?* **be present**, be around, be available, be near, be nearby, be at hand.
3 *the trial is tomorrow* **occur**, happen, take place, come about, arise, crop up, transpire, fall, materialize, ensue; *literary* come to pass, befall, betide.
4 *Pat was on the sofa in the living room* **be situated**, be located, be found, be present, be set, be positioned, be placed, be installed.
5 *after she'd been there a couple of hours she ordered a drink* **remain**, stay, wait, linger; hold on, hang on; last, continue, survive, endure, persist, prevail, obtain.
6 *I'm at college* **attend**, go to, be present, take part; frequent, haunt, patronize.
7 *tickets are £15* **cost**, be priced at, sell for, be valued at, fetch, come to; *informal* set one back, go for.
8 *one and one is two* **amount to**, come to, add up to, run to, number, make, total, equal, be equal to, be equivalent to, comprise, represent; *Brit.* tot up to.

beach ▶ noun *a fabulous sandy beach* **seaside**, seashore, shore, coast, coastline, coastal region, seaboard, foreshore, water's edge, margin; sands, sand, shingle, (sand) dunes; lido; *dated* plage; *technical* littoral; *literary* strand.
▶ verb **1** *they checked for places where minor craft could beach* **land**, reach the shore, run ashore; ground, be grounded, run aground; shipwreck, wreck, run on the rocks, be high and dry.
OPPOSITES put to sea, depart.
2 *sixty common dolphins have been beached on Cornish shores* **make/become stranded**, make/become beached, strand, ground, get stuck.
3 *he managed to beach a fine trout* **catch**, capture, land, hook, reel in.

beachcomber ▶ noun *anything that came ashore would be snatched up at once by thrifty beachcombers* **scavenger**, scrounger, forager, gatherer, collector, accumulator; tramp, vagrant, wanderer, itinerant, nomad, drifter, transient, homeless person; *N. Amer.* hobo; *informal* bum.

beached ▶ adjective *a beached whale* **stranded**, stuck, marooned, high and dry, helpless; ashore, aground, grounded, stuck fast.

beacon ▶ noun *an uninhabited island supporting a navigational beacon* **warning light/fire**, signal light/fire, bonfire, smoke signal, beam, signal, danger signal, guiding light; rocket, flare, Very light; lighthouse, light-tower, pharos, phare, watchtower.

bead ▶ noun **1** *a long string of beads* ball, pellet, pill, globule, spheroid, spherule, sphere, oval, ovoid, orb, round, pearl; (**beads**) **necklace**, string of beads; *Roman Catholic Church* rosary, chaplet.
2 *beads of sweat* **droplet**, drop, blob, bubble, dot, dewdrop, teardrop; *informal* glob.
□ **draw/get a bead on** *I drew a bead on the nape of his neck* **aim at**, fix on, focus on, zero in on, sight.

beak ▶ noun **1** *a bird with a caterpillar in its beak* **bill**, nib, mandible; *Scottish & N. English* neb.
2 (*informal*) *he blew his beak loudly* **nose**, snout, trunk; *informal* conk, snoot, schnozzle, hooter, sniffer, snitch; *Scottish & N. English* neb; *informal, dated* bracket; *N. Amer. informal, dated* bugle; *rare* proboscis.
3 *the ship's beak* **prow**, bow, bowsprit, stem, rostrum, ram, beak-head.
OPPOSITE stern.
4 (*Brit. informal*) *he got hauled up in front of the local beak* **magistrate**, judge, sheriff.
5 (*Brit. informal*) *an Eton beak* **teacher**, tutor, schoolteacher, schoolmaster, master; *informal* teach.

beaker ▶ noun *she was drinking blackcurrant juice from a plastic beaker* **cup**, tumbler, glass, mug, jug, drinking vessel.

beam ▶ noun **1** *there are very fine oak beams in the oldest part of the house* **joist**, purlin, girder, spar, support, strut, stay, brace, scantling, batten, transom, lintel, stringer, baulk, board, timber, plank, lath, rafter; collar beam, tie beam, summer (tree), hammer beam, cantilever.
2 *a beam of light* **ray**, shaft, stream, streak, pencil, finger; flash, gleam, glow, glimmer, glint, flare, bar; radiation, emission.
3 *seeing the beam on her face was enough to cheer me up* **grin**, smile, bright look.
OPPOSITE frown.
□ **off beam** (*informal*) *you're way off beam on this one* **mistaken**, incorrect, inaccurate, wrong, erroneous, off-target, out, on the wrong track, wide of the mark, awry; *informal* (getting) cold.
OPPOSITES spot on, on the beam.
□ **on the beam** (*informal*) *I've been trying to keep him on the beam* **correct**, right, accurate, true, on the right track, on the right lines; *informal* on the straight and narrow, on the money, on the mark, spot on, (getting) warm.
OPPOSITES wide of the mark, off beam.
▶ verb **1** *satellites for beaming TV to rooftop aerials* **broadcast**, transmit, relay, send/put out, disseminate; direct, aim; televise, show, telecast, put on the air/airwaves.
2 *golden rays beamed down through the clouds* **shine**, radiate, glare, glitter, gleam, shimmer, glimmer, twinkle, flash, flare, streak.
3 *she was beaming from ear to ear* **grin**, smile, dimple, grin like a Cheshire Cat, twinkle, smirk, laugh; *informal* be all smiles.
OPPOSITE frown.

beaming ▶ adjective **1** *his beaming face* **grinning**, smiling, laughing; cheerful, happy, radiant, glowing, sunny, joyful, elated, thrilled, delighted, overjoyed, rapturous, blissful.
OPPOSITE frowning.
2 *he greeted her with a beaming smile* **bright**, **cheery**, sparkling, flashing, brilliant, dazzling, intense, gleaming, radiant.

bean ▶ noun. See centre pages for list of **Beans, Pulses, and Peas**

bear¹ ▶ verb **1** *Bill arrived, bearing a large picnic hamper* **carry**, bring, transport, move, convey, take, fetch, haul, lug, shift; deliver; *informal* tote.
2 *the letter bore the signature of a local councillor* **display**, exhibit, show, present, set forth, be marked with, carry, have.
3 *the track has horizontal concrete slabs, which bear the weight of the vehicle* **support**, carry, hold up, prop up, keep up, bolster up; brace, shore up, underpin, buttress, reinforce.
4 *ratepayers will have to bear the cost of such a move* **sustain**, carry, support, shoulder, uphold, absorb, take on.
5 *the drugs had been planted by someone who bore a grudge against him* **harbour**, foster, entertain, cherish, nurse, nurture, brood over, possess, have, hold (on to), cling to, maintain, retain.
6 *such a solution does not bear close scrutiny* **withstand**, stand up to, stand, put up with, take, cope with, handle, resist, sustain, absorb, accept.
7 *I'm not sure how much longer I can bear the pain* **endure**, tolerate, put up with, stand, suffer, abide, submit to, experience, undergo, go through, countenance, brook, brave, weather, support; *informal* stick, stomach, swallow.
8 *I can't bear being dependent on other people* **tolerate**, stand, put up with, stomach, swallow, brook, undergo, accept, approve of, endorse, allow, admit, permit; *Scottish* thole; *informal* stick, hack, abide; *Brit. informal* wear, be doing with; *archaic* suffer.

9 *at seventeen she bore his daughter* **give birth to**, bring forth, deliver, be delivered of, have, mother, create, produce, spawn; conceive; breed, procreate, reproduce; N. Amer. birth; informal drop; literary beget; archaic engender, be brought to bed of.
10 *the radio bore the news of a policeman shot in Belfast* **communicate**, carry, spread, disclose, tell, disseminate, circulate, diffuse, pass on, make public, make known; transmit, broadcast, publish.
11 *a squash that bears fruit shaped like cucumbers* **produce**, yield, give forth, give, provide, supply, generate, afford, furnish, bestow.
12 *you drive to the end of the street, bear left, and go into the car park* **veer**, curve, swerve, incline, turn, fork, diverge, deviate, bend; go, move; Sailing tack, sheer.
□ **bear oneself** *she bore herself like a queen as she slowly descended the stairs* **conduct oneself**, carry oneself, acquit oneself, act, behave, perform; rare comport oneself, deport oneself.
□ **bear down on** *at a canter they bore down on the mass of men ahead* **advance on**, close in on, move in on, converge on, approach, come/move closer/close to, draw near/nearer to, press on towards; attack, set upon, fall upon, assail, set about, let fly at, tear into.
OPPOSITES retreat from, move away from.
□ **bear fruit** *plans for power-sharing may be about to bear fruit* **yield results**, get results, succeed, meet with success, be successful, be effective, be profitable, work, go as planned; informal pay off, come off, pan out, do the trick, do the business.
OPPOSITE come to nothing.
□ **bear something in mind** *it is important to bear in mind that different countries have different regimes* **take into account**, be mindful, remember, consider, mind, mark, heed, take into consideration, not forget; respect, pay/have regard to, make allowances for, be guided by.
OPPOSITES forget, ignore.
□ **bear on** *there is a long cultural history which bears on the way these writers express themselves* **be relevant to**, appertain to, pertain to, relate to, have a bearing on, have relevance to, apply to, be pertinent to, have reference to, concern, be concerned with, have to do with, be connected with.
OPPOSITE be irrelevant to.
□ **bear something out** *he has conducted experiments that bear out these ideas* **confirm**, corroborate, substantiate, endorse, vindicate, give credence to, support, ratify, warrant, uphold, justify, prove, authenticate, verify.
OPPOSITES contradict, falsify.
□ **bear up** *she looks fantastic and is bearing up remarkably well* **cope**, persevere, manage, endure; muddle through/along, get through, get on, carry on, get along, deal with the situation; grin and bear it, weather the storm; informal make out, get by, hack it.
OPPOSITE go to pieces.
□ **bear with** *bear with me a moment while I make a telephone call* **be patient with**, show forbearance towards, make allowances for, tolerate, put up with, endure, suffer.
□ **bear witness/testimony to** *the great cathedrals bore witness to a towering vision of transcendence* **testify to**, be evidence/proof of, attest to, confirm, evidence, prove, vouch for; demonstrate, show, establish, indicate, reveal, bespeak.

WORD LINKS
...-bearing **-ferous (e.g. *Carboniferous, melliferous*)**

bear² ▸ **noun.** *See centre pages for list of* **Bears**

WORD LINKS

relating to bears	**ursine**
male	**boar**
female	**sow**
young	**cub**
home	**den**
collective noun	**sloth**

bearable ▸ **adjective** *the pain was made more bearable by the fact that their father was in constant touch* **tolerable**, endurable, supportable, sufferable, brookable, sustainable; acceptable, admissible, passable, manageable.
OPPOSITES unbearable, intolerable.

beard *See centre pages for list of* **Beards and Moustaches**
▸ **noun** *he had a black beard* **facial hair**, whiskers, stubble, designer stubble, five o'clock shadow, bristles; full beard, goatee, imperial, Vandyke, Abe Lincoln, side whiskers, sideboards, sideburns, mutton chops; moustache, moustaches; Brit. informal, dated beaver.
▸ **verb** *he was afraid to beard the sultan himself* **confront**, face, challenge, brave, come face to face with, meet head on; defy, oppose, stand up against, square up to, dare, throw down the gauntlet at.

WORD LINKS
fear of beards **pogonophobia**

bearded ▸ **adjective** *a bearded man* **unshaven**, whiskered, whiskery, bewhiskered; stubbly, bristly, hairy, hirsute, bushy, shaggy; Brit. informal, dated beavered.
OPPOSITE clean shaven.

bearer ▸ **noun 1** *they went accompanied by lantern-bearers* **carrier**, porter, conveyor, transporter.
2 *I'm sorry to be the bearer of bad news* **messenger**, agent, conveyor, emissary, carrier, provider; runner, courier.
3 *the bank's promise to pay the bearer on demand* **holder**, possessor, owner, payee, consignee, beneficiary.

WORD LINKS
related suffixes **-fer (e.g. *crucifer, Lucifer*), -phore (e.g. *carpophore, semaphore*)**

bearing ▸ **noun 1** *his greying hair and tanned complexion accentuated his distinguished bearing* **posture**, comportment, carriage, gait, stance; Brit. deportment.
2 *she has a rather regal bearing* **demeanour**, manner, air, aspect, attitude, behaviour, mien, countenance, guise, cast, look, feel, style.
3 *being successful in battle has an important bearing on natural selection* **relevance**, relevancy, significance, pertinence, connection, relation, aptness, appositeness, germaneness, importance, import, application.
4 *the point is on a bearing of 015°* **direction**, orientation, course, trajectory, heading, tack, path, line, run.
5 *his arrogance goaded her beyond bearing* **endurance**, endurability, tolerance, tolerability, acceptance, acceptability, sufferance, manageability.
6 (**bearings**) *I lost my bearings in those country lanes* **orientation**, sense of direction; whereabouts, location, position, situation, track, way.

beast ▸ **noun 1** *the terrible roaring of caged beasts* **animal**, creature, brute; N. Amer. informal critter.
2 *a sex beast* **monster**, brute, savage, barbarian, animal, swine, pig, ogre, fiend, sadist, demon, devil.

beastly ▸ **adjective 1** (Brit. informal) *I think politics is a beastly profession* **awful**, horrible, rotten, nasty, foul, objectionable, unpleasant, disagreeable, offensive, vile, hateful, detestable, loathsome, abominable; informal terrible, shocking, God-awful, yucky; vulgar slang shitty.
OPPOSITE pleasant.
2 (Brit. informal) *Karl had been absolutely beastly to her* **unkind**, malicious, mean, nasty, unpleasant, unfriendly, uncharitable, unfair, spiteful, callous, cruel, vicious, base, low, foul, malevolent, despicable, contemptible, obnoxious; informal horrible, horrid, hateful, rotten, low-down; Brit. informal bitchy, catty.
OPPOSITE kind.

beat ▸ **verb 1** *before running off, the men beat me with pickaxe handles* **hit**, strike, batter, thump, hammer, punch, knock, thrash, pound, pummel, slap, smack, crack, thwack, cuff, buffet, maul, pelt, drub, rain blows on; assault, attack, abuse; flay, whip, lash, cudgel, club, birch; informal wallop, belt, bash, whack, clout, clobber, slug, tan, biff, bop, sock, deck, plug, lay into, do over, knock about/around, rough up, fill in, knock into the middle of next week, beat the living daylights out of, give someone a good hiding; dated chastise.
2 *he could hear a drum being beaten* **bang**, hit, strike, rap, tap, pound, thump, hammer; **play**, sound, perform on, make music on.
3 *the waves beat all along the shore* **lash**, strike, dash, break against; sweep, lap, wash, splash, ripple, roll, splosh, move against; literary plash, lave.
4 *the metal is beaten into a die* **hammer**, forge, form, shape, mould, work, stamp, fashion, model, fabricate, make, cast, frame, sculpt, sculpture.
5 *she could hear her own heart beating* **pulsate**, pulse, palpitate, vibrate, throb, reverberate; pump, pound, thump, thud, hammer, drum; pitter-patter, go pit-a-pat; rare quop.
6 *doves wheel around the rooftops, beating their wings* **flap**, flutter, move up and down, thresh, thrash, wave, shake, swing, agitate, quiver, tremble, vibrate, oscillate.
7 *beat the cream into the mixture* **whisk**, mix, blend, whip, stir, fold.
8 *she beat a path through clumps of bushes* **tread**, tramp, trample, wear, track, groove; crush, flatten, press down, squash.
9 *he played in a team that beat England 2–1 at home* **defeat**, conquer, win against, get the better of, vanquish, trounce, rout, overpower, overcome, overwhelm, overthrow, subdue, quash, crush; informal lick, thrash, whip, wipe the floor with, clobber.
10 *he cleared 2.68m to beat the previous record of 2.67m* **surpass**, outdo, exceed, eclipse, transcend, top, trump, cap, better, outperform, outstrip, outshine, outclass, overshadow, put in the shade, be better than, improve on, go one better than.
□ **beat about the bush** *he never beat about the bush when something was annoying him* **prevaricate**, vacillate, evade/dodge the issue, be non-committal, hedge, hedge one's bets, quibble, parry questions, fudge the issue, mince one's words, stall, shilly-shally, hesitate; Brit. hum and haw; informal pussyfoot around, waffle, flannel, sit on the fence, duck the question; rare tergiversate.
OPPOSITE come to the point.
□ **beat a (hasty) retreat.** *See* RETREAT verb sense 1.
□ **beat it** (informal) *we beat it as fast as we could. See* RUN sense 2.
□ **beat someone/something off** *we beat off the raiders with sticks* **repel**, fight off, repulse, drive away/back, force back, beat back, push back, thrust back, put to flight; hold off, ward off, fend off, stand off, stave off, keep at bay, keep at arm's length.
□ **beat something out** *he beat out the flames* **extinguish**, put out, quench,

B

smother, douse, snuff out, stifle, choke.

□ **beat someone up** **assault**, attack, mug, batter, thrash, pummel, pound; *informal* knock about/around, do over, work over, clobber, rough up, fill in, kick in, jump, paste, lay into, lace into, sail into, pitch into, get stuck into, beat the living daylights out of, let someone have it; *Brit. informal* have a go at, duff someone up; *N. Amer. informal* beat up on.

▶ **noun 1** *this song has a catchy tune and a good beat* **rhythm**, pulse, stress, metre, time, measure, cadence, accent, rhythmical flow/pattern.
2 *the beat of hooves* **pounding**, banging, thumping, thudding, booming, hammering, battering, crashing.
3 *her heart settled to an angry beat* **pulse**, pulsing, pulsating, vibration, vibrating, throb, throbbing, palpitation, palpitating, reverberation, reverberating; beating, pumping, pounding, thumping, thudding, hammering, drumming; pitter-patter, pit-a-pat.
4 *a policeman on his beat* **circuit**, round, course, route, way, path, orbit, tour, turn.

▶ **adjective** (*informal*). See EXHAUSTED.

WORD LINKS
fear of being beaten **mastigophobia**

beaten ▶ **adjective 1** *the beaten team* **defeated**, losing, unsuccessful, conquered, bettered, vanquished, trounced, routed, overcome, overwhelmed, overpowered, overthrown, bested, subdued, quashed, crushed, broken, foiled, hapless, luckless; *informal* licked, thrashed, clobbered.
OPPOSITES victorious, winning.
2 *a beaten dog* **abused**, battered, maltreated, ill-treated, mistreated, misused, downtrodden; **assaulted**, thumped, hit, thrashed, pummelled, smacked, drubbed; *informal* walloped, belted, bashed, whacked, clobbered, knocked about/around, roughed up.
3 *gradually stir in the beaten eggs* **whisked**, whipped, stirred, mixed, blended; frothy, foamy.
4 *a beaten copper coffee table* **hammered**, forged, formed, shaped, moulded, worked, stamped, fashioned, modelled, fabricated, cast, sculpted; dimpled, pockmarked, spotted.
5 *a beaten path* **trodden**, trampled; well trodden, much trodden, well used, much travelled, worn, well worn.

□ **off the beaten track** *we tried to find locations off the beaten track* **unfrequented**, isolated, quiet, private, remote, out of the way, outlying, secluded, hidden, backwoods, in the back of beyond, in the middle of nowhere, in the hinterlands; *informal* in the sticks.
OPPOSITES busy, popular.

beatific ▶ **adjective 1** *he was beaming a beatific smile* **rapturous**, joyful, ecstatic, seraphic, blissful, serene, happy, beaming, glad.
2 *the beatific vision of God* **blessed**, blissful, exalted, sublime, joyful, rapt, heavenly, holy, divine, celestial, paradisical, glorious.

beatify ▶ **verb** *he was beatified by Pope Leo XIII* **canonize**, bless, sanctify, hallow, consecrate, make holy, make sacred; *rare* macarize.

beating ▶ **noun 1** *he received a near fatal beating* **battering**, thrashing, thumping, pounding, pummelling, drubbing, slapping, smacking, hammering, hitting, striking, punching, knocking, thwacking, cuffing, buffeting, boxing, mauling, pelting, lambasting; assault, attack; flaying, whipping, lashing, cudgelling, clubbing, birching; corporal punishment, chastisement; *informal* beating-up, duffing-up, doing-over, belting, bashing, pasting, walloping, whacking, clobbering, slugging, tanning, biffing, bopping, hiding.
2 *she could hear the beating of her heart* **pulsation**, pulsating, pulse, pulsing, palpitating, throb, reverberation, reverberating; pumping, pounding, thumping, thudding, hammering, drumming; pitter-patter, pit-a-pat.
3 *a 5–1 beating at the hands of their rivals* **defeat**, loss, conquest, vanquishing, trouncing, routing, overthrow, downfall; *informal* licking, thrashing, clobbering.

beatitude ▶ **noun** *the everlasting beatitude that follows the second coming* **blessedness**, benediction, grace; bliss, ecstasy, exaltation, supreme happiness, heavenly joy, divine rapture, saintliness, sainthood.

beau ▶ **noun** (*dated*) **1** *she was approached by three potential beaux* **boyfriend**, sweetheart, lover, fiancé, darling, partner, significant other, escort, young man, admirer, suitor, follower; *informal* steady, date, toy boy, fancy man, fella; *literary* swain.
2 *an eighteenth-century beau* **dandy**, fop, gallant, cavalier, man about town; *informal* swell, toff; *archaic* dude, blade, blood, coxcomb, popinjay.

beautiful ▶ **adjective** *a beautiful young woman* **attractive**, pretty, handsome, good-looking, nice-looking, pleasing, alluring, prepossessing, as pretty as a picture; lovely, charming, delightful, appealing, engaging, winsome; ravishing, gorgeous, heavenly, stunning, arresting, glamorous, irresistible, bewitching, beguiling; graceful, elegant, exquisite, aesthetic, artistic, decorative, magnificent; *Scottish & N. English* bonny; *informal* tasty, smashing, divine, knockout, drop-dead gorgeous, fanciable, beddable, easy on the eye; *Brit. informal* fit; *N. Amer. informal* cute, foxy; *Austral./NZ informal* beaut, spunky; *formal* beauteous; *archaic* comely, fair; *rare* sightly, pulchritudinous.
OPPOSITE ugly.

beautify ▶ **verb 1** *he can grow flowers to beautify the garden* **adorn**, embellish, enhance, decorate, ornament, garnish, gild, smarten, prettify, enrich, glamorize, spruce up, deck (out), trick out, grace; *informal* get up, do up, do out, tart up.
OPPOSITES spoil, uglify.
2 *she started to beautify herself* **prettify**, glamorize, prink, primp, preen; apply make-up/cosmetics; *informal* do/doll oneself up.

beauty ▶ **noun 1** *a young woman of great beauty | the raw beauty of the Australian deserts* **attractiveness**, prettiness, good looks, pleasingness, comeliness, allure, allurement; loveliness, charm, appeal, heavenliness, voluptuousness; winsomeness, grace, elegance, exquisiteness; splendour, magnificence, grandeur, impressiveness, picturesqueness, artistry, decorativeness; gorgeousness, glamour, irresistibility; *Scottish & N. English* bonniness; *formal* beauteousness, pulchritude.
OPPOSITE ugliness.
2 *Esther was no beauty* **beautiful woman**, belle, vision, charmer, enchantress, Venus, goddess, beauty queen, English rose, picture, seductress; *French* femme fatale; *informal* looker, good looker, lovely, stunner, knockout, bombshell, dish, cracker, smasher, peach, eyeful, bit of all right.
OPPOSITES ugly woman; hag.
3 *the beauty of the system is that the information can be called up instantaneously* **advantage**, attraction, strength, benefit, asset, draw, lure, pull, strong point, boon, blessing, virtue, merit, selling point, good thing/point, bonus, plus, added extra.
OPPOSITE drawback.

beaver ▶ **verb**

□ **beaver away** (*informal*) *we spent our spare time beavering away in the garage.* See SLOG.

becalmed ▶ **adjective** *the wind never arrived, and the boats were left becalmed* **stranded**, stuck, marooned, motionless, at a halt, still, at a standstill, unmoving.

because ▶ **conjunction** *his classmates liked him because he was very friendly* **since**, as, for the reason that, in view of the fact that, owing to the fact that, seeing that/as.
OPPOSITE despite.

□ **because of** *I thought I could not have children because of my age* **on account of**, as a result of, as a consequence of, owing to, by reason of, on grounds of, by dint of, due to; thanks to, by virtue of, on the strength of; through, after, following, in the wake of.

beckon ▶ **verb 1** *the guard beckoned to Benny* **gesture**, signal, wave, gesticulate, make a gesture, motion, nod, call.
2 *the moorland and miles of coastal path beckon many walkers* **entice**, invite, tempt, coax, lure, charm, attract, draw, pull (in), bring in, call, allure, interest, fascinate, engage, enchant, captivate, persuade, induce, catch the eye of.

become ▶ **verb 1** *she became rich* **come to be**, get to be, turn out to be, grow, get, turn; *literary* wax.
2 *he became Foreign Secretary* **be appointed as**, be assigned as, be nominated, be elected as, be made; be transformed into, be converted into, change into, turn into, transform into.
3 *the dress becomes her* **suit**, flatter, look good on, look right on; set off, show to advantage, enhance, go well with; embellish, ornament, grace; *informal* do something for.
4 *it ill becomes him to preach the gospel* **befit**, behove, suit, be suitable to, be fitting to.

□ **become of** *I asked Harry what had become of the old gang* **happen to**, be the fate of, be the lot of, overtake, be visited on; *literary* befall, betide.

becoming ▶ **adjective** *her soft curls are very becoming* **flattering**, fetching, attractive, lovely, pretty, handsome, stylish, elegant, chic, fashionable, comely, tasteful.
OPPOSITE unbecoming.

bed *See centre pages for list of* **Beds**

▶ **noun 1** *she undressed and climbed into her bed* **couch**, berth, billet; *informal* the sack, the hay; *Brit. informal* one's pit; *Scottish informal* kip.
2 *a flower bed* **patch**, plot, area, lot, space, border, strip, row.
3 *the pavement consists of granite blocks set on a bed of cement* **base**, basis, foundation, support, prop, stay, bottom, core, substructure, substratum; groundwork.
4 *the bed of the stream* **bottom**, floor, ground, depths.

□ **go to bed** **retire**, call it a day; **go to sleep**, get some sleep, sleep, nap, have/take a nap, catnap, doze, have a doze; *informal* hit the sack, hit the hay, turn in, snooze, snatch forty winks, get some shut-eye; *Brit. informal* kip, have a kip, get some kip, hit the pit; *N. Amer. informal* catch some Zs; *literary* slumber.
OPPOSITES get up, rise.

□ **go to bed with someone** **have sex with**, have sexual intercourse with, make love to, sleep with, spend the night with; couple with, mate with; *informal* bed, score with; *euphemistic* have one's (wicked) way with; *formal* copulate with; *archaic* fornicate with.

▶ **verb 1** *the tiles are bedded in mortar* **embed**, set, fix into, insert, inlay, implant, bury, base, plant, settle.

B

2 *I bedded out a few of the house plants in a prominent position in the garden* **plant**, plant out, set in beds/soil, put in the ground, set out, transplant.
□ **bed down**. *See* GO TO BED.

WORD LINKS
fear of beds **clinophobia**

bedaub ▸ verb (*literary*) *their faces were bedaubed with white paint* **smear**, daub, bespatter, stain, spatter, splatter, cover, coat; *literary* befoul, besmirch, begrime.

bedclothes ▸ plural noun **bedding**, sheets, bed linen, linen, bedcovers, covers, blankets.

bedding ▸ noun. *See* BEDCLOTHES.

bedeck ▸ verb *we were in a church bedecked with flowers* **decorate**, adorn, ornament, trim, deck, enhance, beautify, prettify, embellish, furnish, garnish, grace, enrich, dress up, trick out; swathe, wreathe, festoon, array, bespangle; *informal* get up, do up, do out; *literary* furbelow.

bedevil ▸ verb *the party was bedevilled by internal dissensions* **afflict**, torment, beset, assail, beleaguer, plague, blight, harrow, rack, oppress, harry, curse, dog; harass, distress, trouble, worry, torture; frustrate, annoy, vex, irritate, pester, irk, exasperate, strain; *informal* aggravate.

bedlam ▸ noun *there was bedlam in the stadium after he won* **uproar**, pandemonium, commotion, mayhem, confusion, unrest, furore, upheaval, hubbub, hurly-burly, turmoil, riot, ruckus, tumult, disarray, turbulence; disorder, chaos, anarchy, lawlessness; *informal* hullabaloo, ructions, rumpus, snafu.
OPPOSITE calm.

bedraggled ▸ adjective *one by one the men reached the shore, weary and bedraggled* **dishevelled**, disordered, untidy, unkempt, tousled, disarranged, messy, in a mess; dirty, muddy, muddied, soiled, sullied, stained; wet, sodden, soaking, soaking wet, wringing wet, soaked, drenched, saturated, dripping, soggy, splashed; *N. Amer. informal* mussed.
OPPOSITES clean, neat.

bedridden ▸ adjective *her father was bedridden with arthritis* **confined to bed**, housebound, out of action/commission; disabled, incapacitated, crippled, lame, paralysed, immobilized; *informal* laid up, flat on one's back.

bedrock ▸ noun **1** *there was thirty feet of peat on top of the bedrock* **substratum**, substructure, understructure, solid foundation, base, basis, underpinning, bed, rock bed.
2 *Labour's traditional bedrock of support is among the working classes* **core**, basis, base, foundation, root, roots, heart, backbone, essence, nitty-gritty; *informal* nuts and bolts.

bee ▸ noun

WORD LINKS
relating to bees **apian**
home **apiary, hive**
collective noun **swarm, drive, erst**
fear of bees **apiphobia**

beef ▸ noun **1** *the smell of roast beef* steak, beefsteak; red meat.
2 (*informal*) *my girl, you'll have to get a bit of beef on you* **muscle**, muscularity, brawn, bulk, heftiness, burliness, huskiness, physique; strength, powerfulness, robustness, sturdiness, stockiness.
3 (*informal*) *our only beef about this car was the colour* **complaint**, criticism, objection, protestation, cavil, quibble, grievance, grumble, moan, grumbling, carping; *informal* gripe, griping, grouse, grousing, whinge, whingeing, nit-picking.
□ **beef something up** (*informal*) *he noticed that the security was being beefed up* **toughen up**, strengthen, build up, reinforce, substantiate, consolidate, invigorate, improve, flesh out.
OPPOSITE weaken.

beefy ▸ adjective (*informal*) *a beefy tattooed barman* **muscular**, brawny, hefty, burly, hulking, strapping, well built, thickset, solid, strong, powerful, heavy, robust, sturdy, stocky; **fat**, stout, plump, overweight, chubby, obese, flabby, fleshy, rotund, portly, corpulent, paunchy, beer-bellied, dumpy; *informal* hunky, husky, tubby, roly-poly; *Brit. informal* podgy.
OPPOSITES puny, thin.

beer *See centre pages for list of* **Beers**
▸ noun **ale**, beverage, brew; *informal* jar, pint, booze, wallop, sherbet; *Austral./NZ* hop.

beetle ▸ noun **winged insect**; *technical* coleopteran.
▸ verb (*informal*) *I beetled off to the library* **scurry**, scamper, scuttle, bustle, hurry, hasten, rush, race, dash; *informal* scoot, tear, pelt, zip, belt.

WORD LINKS
relating to beetles **coleopteran, coleopterous**

beetling ▸ adjective *Marcus glared at him under beetling brows* **projecting**, protruding, prominent, overhanging, sticking out, jutting out, standing out, bulging, bulbous, pendent.

befall ▸ verb (*literary*) **1** *a catastrophe befell their grandsons* **happen to**, overtake, come upon, fall upon, hit, strike, be visited on.
2 *she was to blame for anything that befell* **happen**, occur, take place, chance to happen, arise, emerge, come about, transpire, materialize, appear, make an appearance, surface, crop up, spring up, present itself; ensue, follow, result, supervene; *N. Amer. informal* go down; *literary* come to pass, betide; *rare* hap, eventuate.

befitting ▸ preposition *the gowns were of good material, befitting the bride's status* **in keeping with**, as befits, fitting, appropriate to, fit for, suitable for, suited to, apt for, proper to, right for, compatible with, consistent with, in character with; *archaic* meet for.
OPPOSITE out of keeping with.

befogged ▸ adjective *her brain is befogged by lack of sleep* **confused**, muddled, fuddled, befuddled, addled, groggy, dizzy, muzzy; *informal* dopey, woozy, not with it.

before ▸ preposition **1** *he locked all the doors before going to bed* **prior to**, previous to, earlier than, preparatory to, in preparation for, preliminary to, in anticipation of, in expectation of; in advance of, ahead of, leading up to, on the eve of; *rare* anterior to.
OPPOSITE after.
2 *he was ordered to appear before Sir Robert* **in front of**, in the presence of, in the sight of; before the very eyes of, under the nose of.
3 *he lived up to the tradition of death before dishonour* **in preference to**, rather than, sooner than, above, over, instead of.
▸ adverb **1** *she had never confided in anyone before* **previously**, before now, before then, until now, until then, up to now, up to then; earlier, formerly, hitherto, in the past, in days gone by; *rare* heretofore.
2 *a small party went on before* **ahead**, in front, in advance, in the lead.

WORD LINKS
related prefixes **pre-** (e.g. ***prewar, precede***), **ante-** (e.g. ***antenatal, ante-post***)

beforehand ▸ adverb *it is important to save any files you have created beforehand* **in advance**, in readiness, ahead of time; before, before now, earlier, earlier on, previously, already, sooner.

befriend ▸ verb *she decided to befriend the new girl* **make friends with**, make a friend of, look after, protect, keep an eye on, support, back, stand by, side with, encourage, sustain, uphold, succour, advise, guide; help, assist, aid, be of service to, lend a helping hand to.
OPPOSITES snub, reject.

befuddled ▸ adjective *his befuddled brain refused to accept that there was a problem* **confused**, muddled, addled, bewildered, disoriented, disorientated, all at sea, mixed up, fazed, perplexed, stunned, dazed, dizzy, stupefied, groggy, foggy, fuzzy, fuddled, benumbed, numbed, numb, vague; *informal* discombobulated, bamboozled, dopey, woolly, woolly-headed, muzzy, woozy, out of it.
OPPOSITE clear.

beg ▸ verb **1** *he scavenged and begged when that was the only way to stay alive* **ask for money**, solicit money, seek charity, seek alms; *informal* sponge, cadge, scrounge, bum, touch someone for money; *Brit. informal* scab; *Scottish informal* sorn on someone; *N. Amer. informal* mooch; *Austral./NZ informal* bludge.
2 *we begged for mercy and he let us live* **ask for**, request, plead for, appeal for, call for, sue for, solicit, seek, look for, press for; *rare* impetrate.
3 *he begged her not to leave him* **beseech**, entreat, implore, adjure, plead with, appeal to, pray to; ask, request, call on, petition, apply to; importune, exhort, enjoin, press; *rare* obsecrate.

beget ▸ verb (*literary*) **1** *he married again and begat Alexander* **father**, sire, engender, generate, spawn, create, give life to, bring into being, bring into the world, have; procreate, reproduce, breed.
2 *we have to make people realize that violence begets more violence* **cause**, give rise to, lead to, result in, bring about, create, produce, generate, engender, spawn, occasion, effect, bring to pass, bring on, precipitate, prompt, provoke, kindle, trigger, spark off, touch off, stir up, whip up, induce, inspire, promote, foster; *literary* enkindle; *rare* effectuate.

beggar ▸ noun **1** *he never turned any beggar from his kitchen door* **tramp**, beggarman, beggarwoman, vagrant, vagabond, down-and-out, homeless person, derelict, mendicant; pauper, poor person; *N. Amer.* hobo; *informal* **scrounger**, sponger, cadger, freeloader, bag lady, have-not, crusty; *Brit. informal* dosser; *N. Amer. informal* bum, moocher, mooch, schnorrer; *Austral./NZ informal* bagman, swagman, bludger; *rare* clochard.
2 (*informal*) *he's been in Bali for three weeks, lucky beggar!* **fellow**, thing, individual, soul, character, creature, wretch; person, man, woman, boy, girl; *informal* guy, fella, devil, bunny, bastard; *Brit. informal* chap, bloke, bugger, sod, bod; *N. Amer. informal* dude, hombre; *informal, dated* body, dog, cove; *archaic* wight.
▸ verb (*rare*) *decades of Communist rule had beggared the vast land* **impoverish**, make poor, reduce to poverty, reduce to penury, reduce to destitution, bankrupt, make bankrupt, make destitute, ruin, wipe out, break, cripple; bring someone to their knees; *rare* pauperize.

beggarly ▸ adjective **1** *a priest's stipend in 1522 was a beggarly 26s 8d* **meagre**, modest, slight, lean, scant, scanty, skimpy, puny, inadequate, insufficient, insubstantial, miserly, paltry, pitiful, derisory, niggardly, ungenerous, miserable, contemptible, despicable; *informal* measly, stingy, lousy, pathetic, piddling, piffling, mingy, poxy; *rare* exiguous.
OPPOSITE considerable.
2 *they lived in the most beggarly part of Bethnal Green* **wretched**, miserable, sordid, squalid, shabby, shoddy, mean, base, vile, foul, despicable,

unpleasant; **poor**, poverty-stricken, impoverished, distressed, beggared, needy, penniless, destitute, indigent, impecunious, penurious; *informal* hard up, on one's uppers.

beggary ▶ noun *there is no unemployment pay to stand between them and beggary* **poverty**, penury, destitution, ruin, ruination, indigence, impecuniousness, impoverishment, need, neediness, privation, want, hardship, distress, difficulties, dire straits, reduced circumstances, straitened circumstances, mendicancy, vagrancy; bankruptcy, insolvency, liquidation, debt, indebtedness, financial ruin; *Brit.* administration, receivership; *Economics* primary poverty; *rare* pauperdom, pauperism, mendicity.

begin ▶ verb **1** *he must begin work first thing in the morning* **start**, set about, go about, embark on, launch into, get down to, take up, turn one's hand to, undertake, tackle; initiate, set in motion, institute, inaugurate, get ahead with; *informal* get cracking on, get going on; *formal* commence.
OPPOSITE cease.
2 *the interviewer began by asking me what my bad points were* **open**, lead off, get under way, get going, get off the ground, start, start off, go ahead; *informal* start the ball rolling, kick off, get the show on the road, get to it, fire away, take the plunge; *formal* commence.
OPPOSITES conclude, finish.
3 *when did the illness actually begin?* **appear**, arise, become apparent, make an appearance, spring up, crop up, turn up, surface, emerge, come into existence, come into being, originate, start, develop, unfold; set in, become established; happen, occur; *formal* commence; *literary* come to pass.
OPPOSITE disappear.

WORD LINKS
relating to a beginning **inceptive, initial**
beginning **incipient, inchoate, embryonic**

beginner ▶ noun *the book guides the beginner through the basics* **novice**, starter, learner, student, pupil, trainee, apprentice, probationer; recruit, raw recruit, newcomer, new boy, new girl, tyro, fledgling, neophyte, initiate, fresher, freshman, cub; *Christianity* postulant, novitiate; *N. Amer.* tenderfoot; *informal* rookie, new kid (on the block), newie, newbie; *N. Amer. informal* greenhorn, probie, punk; *Austral./NZ informal* new chum.
OPPOSITES expert, veteran.

beginning ▶ noun **1** *the events signified the end of capitalism and the beginning of socialism* **dawn**, birth, inception, conception, origination, genesis, emergence, rise, start, starting point, very beginning, launch, onset, outset, unfolding, development, developing, debut; day one; *informal* kick-off; *formal* commencement.
OPPOSITE end.
2 *she read the beginning of the book* **opening**, start, first part, preface, introduction, foreword, preamble, opening statement, opening remarks, prelude, prologue; *formal* commencement; *rare* exordium, proem, prolegomenon.
OPPOSITES conclusion, end.
3 (**beginnings**) *the therapy has its beginnings in China* **origin**, source, starting point, basis, birthplace, cradle, spring, mainspring, embryo, germ; genesis, creation, infancy; roots, seeds, early stages; *Latin* fons et origo; *literary* fountainhead, fount, well spring.

begrime ▶ verb (*literary*) *her face and hands had been begrimed with a black substance* **dirty**, soil, sully, foul, stain, mark, muddy, blacken, black, tarnish, taint; smear, daub, spatter, bespatter, splatter, cover; *informal* make mucky, muck up; *literary* besmirch, smirch, befoul, bedaub.

begrudge ▶ verb **1** *it was plain that she begrudged Brian his affluence* **envy**, grudge, resent; be jealous of, be envious of, be resentful of.
2 *I don't begrudge the support we've given* **resent**, feel aggrieved about, feel bitter about, be annoyed about, be angry about, be displeased about, be resentful of, grudge, mind, object to, take exception to, regret; give unwillingly, give reluctantly, give resentfully, give stintingly, be dissatisfied with.

beguile ▶ verb **1** *he'll beguile you with his famous smile* **charm**, attract, enchant, entrance, win over, woo, captivate, bewitch, spellbind, dazzle, blind, hypnotize, mesmerize, seduce, tempt, lead on, lure, entice, ensnare, entrap; **deceive**, mislead, take in, trick, inveigle, dupe, fool, double-cross, hoodwink, take advantage of; *informal* tickle someone's fancy, float someone's boat, butter up, sweet-talk, soft-soap, bamboozle, con, diddle, shaft, pull a fast one on, put one over on, take for a ride, string along, lead up the garden path, pull the wool over someone's eyes; *N. Amer. informal* sucker, snooker; *Austral./NZ* pull a swifty on.
OPPOSITES repel; be straight with.
2 *the television programme has been beguiling children for years* **entertain**, amuse, delight, please, occupy, absorb, engage, distract, divert, interest, fascinate, enthral, engross, preoccupy, hold the attention of.
OPPOSITE bore.
3 *to beguile some of the time they went to the cinema* **while away**, pass, spend, use up, take up; kill, waste, fritter, dissipate.

beguiling ▶ adjective *he praised her in that soft, beguiling voice* **charming**, attractive, appealing, pleasing, pleasant, lovely, delightful, enchanting, entrancing, charismatic, captivating, bewitching, spellbinding, hypnotizing, mesmerizing, magnetic, alluring, enticing, tempting, inviting, seductive, irresistible; *informal* dreamy, heavenly, gorgeous, come-hither.
OPPOSITE unappealing.

behalf ▶ noun
□ **on behalf of/on someone's behalf 1** *I am writing to you on behalf of my client* **as a representative of**, as a spokesperson for, for, in the name of, with power of attorney for, in place of, on the authority of, at the behest of; appearing for, representing; in the interests of.
2 *she campaigned on behalf of chimpanzees in the wild* **in the interests of**, in support of, for, for the benefit of, for the good of, for the sake of, to the advantage of, to the profit of, on account of.

behave ▶ verb **1** *the children worked hard and behaved themselves* **act correctly**, act properly, conduct oneself well, act in a polite way, show good manners, mind one's manners, mind one's Ps and Qs; be good, be polite, be well behaved.
OPPOSITE misbehave.
2 *she behaved abominably last night* **conduct oneself**, act, acquit oneself, bear oneself, carry oneself; *rare* comport oneself, deport oneself.

behaviour ▶ noun **1** *we are absolutely disgusted with his behaviour* **conduct**, way of behaving, way of acting, deportment, bearing, etiquette; actions, exploits, doings, efforts; manners, ways, habits, practices; *informal* capers; *rare* comportment.
2 *they examined the structure and behaviour of the chromosomes* **functioning**, action, performance, operation, working, running, reaction, response; actions, reactions, responses.

WORD LINKS
science of animal behaviour **ethology**

behead ▶ verb *the axes were used to behead traitors* **decapitate**, cut off the head of, guillotine; execute, put to death, kill.

behest ▶ noun (*literary*) *Mary signed away her kingdom at the behest of Henri II* **instruction**, bidding, request, requirement, wish, desire; command, order, decree, edict, rule, ruling, directive, direction, charge, will, dictate, demand, insistence, injunction, mandate, precept; *informal* say-so; *rare* rescript.

behind ▶ preposition **1** *he slept in a hut behind their house* **at the back of**, at the rear of, beyond, on the other side of, on the far side of, on the further side of; *N. Amer.* in back of.
OPPOSITE in front of.
2 *behind her was a small child* **after**, following, to the rear of, in the wake of, at the back of, close on, hard on the heels of, on the trail of.
3 *you are way behind the rest of the class* **less advanced than**, slower than, weaker than, inferior to.
4 *work on the car is months behind schedule* **later than**, late in relation to, after.
5 *he was believed to have been behind a number of bombings* **responsible for**, at the bottom of, at the back of, the cause of, the source of, the organizer of; to blame for, culpable of, guilty of; causing, instigating, initiating, urging.
6 *the All Blacks have the whole nation behind them* **supporting**, backing, for, on the side of, in agreement with; financing.
□ **put something behind one** *the team have to put this morning's result behind them* **consign something to the past**, put something down to experience, forget about something, pay no heed to something, ignore, regard as water under the bridge.
▶ adverb **1** *each plane took off with a glider following on behind* **after**, afterwards, at the back, in the rear, in the wake, at the end.
OPPOSITES ahead, in front.
2 *'I'm off to dance!' he called behind* **over one's shoulder**, to the rear, to the back, towards the rear, towards the back, backwards.
OPPOSITE ahead.
3 *he stayed behind to sign autographs* **afterwards**, remaining after departure.
4 *we're behind so don't stop* **running late, late**, behind schedule, behindhand, delayed, not on time, behind time.
OPPOSITE ahead.
5 *he was behind with his subscription payments* **in arrears**, overdue, in debt, in the red; **late**, unpunctual, tardy, behindhand, behind target.
OPPOSITE ahead.
▶ noun. *See* BOTTOM *sense* 6.

behindhand ▶ adverb *I'm awfully behindhand with my work* **behind**, behind schedule, behind time, delayed; **late**, belated, dilatory, tardy, unpunctual, slow, remiss; running late, not on time.
OPPOSITE ahead.

behold ▶ verb (*literary*) *the orchids are a sight to behold* **look at**, see, observe, view, watch, survey, gaze at, gaze upon, stare at, scan, witness, regard, contemplate, inspect, eye; catch sight of, glimpse, spot, spy, notice, make out, discern, perceive; take note of, pay attention to, mark, remark, consider, pay heed to; *informal* clap eyes on, lay eyes on, set eyes on, have/take a gander at, have a squint at, get a load of, check out, gawp at, size up; *Brit. informal* have/take a dekko at, have/take a butcher's at, have/take a

shufti at, clock; *N. Amer. informal* eyeball; *literary* espy, descry.
▶ **exclamation** (*archaic*) behold, here I am! **look**, see, lo; *Latin* ecce.

beholden ▶ **adjective** *I don't like to be beholden to anybody* **indebted**, obligated, under an obligation, obliged, bound, duty-bound, honour-bound; owing a debt of gratitude, grateful, thankful, appreciative; in someone's debt, owing someone thanks.

behove ▶ **verb 1** *my brother-in-law is ill and it behoves me to see him* **be incumbent on**, be obligatory for, be required of, be appropriate for, be expected of, be advisable for, be sensible for, be wise for.
2 *it ill behoves our national broadcasting channel to be so underhanded* **befit**, become, suit; be fitting to, be suitable for, be seemly for, be proper for, be decorous for.

beige ▶ **adjective** *David arrived in a beige boiler suit* **fawn**, brownish-yellow, pale brown, buff, sand, sandy, oatmeal, wheaten, biscuit, coffee, coffee-coloured, café au lait, camel, kasha, ecru, taupe, stone, stone-coloured, mushroom, putty, greige; neutral, natural, naturelle.

being ▶ **noun 1** *she finds herself warmed by his very being* **existence**, living, life, animation, animateness, aliveness, reality, actuality, essential nature, lifeblood, vital force, entity; *Philosophy* esse.
OPPOSITE non-existence.
2 *God is alive and working in the being of man* **soul**, spirit, nature, essence, substance, entity, inner being, inner self, psyche; heart, bosom, breast, core, kernel, marrow; *Philosophy* quiddity, pneuma.
3 *I wanted to become an enlightened being* **creature**, life form, living entity, living thing, living soul, soul, individual, person, personage, human being, human, man, woman; life, existence; earthling.

belabour ▶ **verb 1** *Bernard was belabouring Jed with his fists* **beat**, hit, strike, smack, batter, pummel, pound, buffet, rain blows on, thrash, bombard, pelt; beat up, assault, attack, set upon, set about, weigh into; *N. Amer.* beat up on; *informal* wallop, whack, clout, clobber, bop, biff, sock, deck, plug, knock about/around, knock into the middle of next week, beat the living daylights out of, give someone a good hiding, do over, work over, rough up, lay into, tear into, lace into, sail into, get stuck into; *Brit. informal* have a go at; *N. Amer. informal* whale, light into; *archaic* smite.
2 *I have been dreadfully belaboured in the London Magazine* **criticize**, attack, berate, censure, condemn, denounce, denigrate, revile, castigate, pillory, flay, lambaste, savage, tear/pull to pieces, find fault with, run down, abuse; *informal* knock, slam, pan, bash, take apart, crucify, hammer, lay into, roast, skewer, bad-mouth; *Brit. informal* slate, rubbish, slag off; *N. Amer. informal* pummel, cut up; *Austral./NZ informal* bag, monster; *rare* excoriate.
OPPOSITE praise.
3 *there is no need to belabour the point here* **over-elaborate**, labour, discuss at length, dwell on, harp on about, hammer away at, expound on, expand on; overdo, overplay, overdramatize, make too much of, place too much emphasis on; *informal* flog to death, drag out, make a big thing of, blow out of all proportion; *N. Amer. informal* do over.
OPPOSITE understate.

belated ▶ **adjective** *he was given a belated birthday cake* **late**, **overdue**, behindhand, behind time, not on time, behind schedule, delayed, running late, tardy, unpunctual.
OPPOSITE early.

belch ▶ **verb 1** *Laurence belched behind his hand* bring up wind; *Scottish & N. English* rift; *informal* **burp**, gurk; *archaic* bolk, rout, ruck; *rare* eruct, eructate.
2 *the blast furnaces belched flames into the sky* **emit**, issue, vent, gush, discharge, eject, expel, empty, evacuate, give off, give out, pour out, disgorge, spew out, spit out, vomit, cough up, throw up; *rare* disembogue.
▶ **noun** *he gave a loud belch* *informal* **burp**, gurk; *archaic* bolk, ventosity; *Scottish & N. English* rift; *rare* eructation.

beleaguered ▶ **adjective 1** *English forces came to relieve the beleaguered garrison* **besieged**, under siege, blockaded, surrounded, encircled, hemmed in, under attack.
2 *she mobilized popular support behind her beleaguered government* **hard-pressed**, troubled, in difficulties, under pressure, under stress, with one's back to the wall, in a tight corner, in a tight spot; *informal* up against it.

belie ▶ **verb 1** *the expression in his eyes belied his easy manner* **contradict**, be at odds with, call into question, give the lie to, show/prove to be false; disprove, debunk, discredit, explode, knock the bottom out of, drive a coach and horses through; *informal* shoot full of holes, shoot down (in flames); *rare* controvert, confute, negative.
OPPOSITE testify to.
2 *he made a light-hearted speech which belied his deep disappointment* **conceal**, cover, disguise, misrepresent, falsify, distort, warp, put a spin on, colour; give a false idea of, give a false account of.
OPPOSITE reveal.

belief ▶ **noun 1** *she clung to the belief that Diane was innocent* **opinion**, view, viewpoint, point of view, attitude, stance, stand, standpoint, position, perspective, contention, conviction, judgement, thinking, way of thinking, thought, idea, theory, hypothesis, thesis, interpretation, assumption, presumption, supposition, surmise, postulation, conclusion, deduction, inference, notion, impression, sense, feeling, fancy, hunch.
2 *I have no real belief in the power of reason* **faith**, trust, reliance, confidence, credence, freedom from doubt; optimism, hopefulness, hope.
OPPOSITES disbelief, doubt.
3 *he opposed traditional religious beliefs* **ideology**, principle, ideal, ethic, conviction; **doctrine**, teaching, dogma, tenet, canon, article of faith, credence, creed, credo, code of belief.

believable ▶ **adjective** *Dawn's story was not quite believable* **credible**, plausible, likely, convincing, creditable, probable, possible, feasible, tenable, acceptable, reasonable, sound, rational, logical, within the bounds of possibility, able to hold water, with a ring of truth; conceivable, imaginable, thinkable.
OPPOSITE unbelievable.

believe ▶ **verb 1** *I don't believe you* **be convinced by**, trust, have confidence in, consider honest, consider truthful.
OPPOSITE disbelieve.
2 *if you believe that story you will believe anything* **regard as true**, accept as true, accept, be convinced by, give credence to, credit, give credit to, trust, put confidence in, count on, rely on, depend on; *informal* swallow, {swallow something hook, line, and sinker}, fall for, go for, buy, take as gospel.
OPPOSITE disbelieve.
3 *police believe they've identified the smuggler | I believe he worked for you* **think**, be of the opinion that, think it likely that, have an idea that, imagine, feel, have a feeling, hold, maintain, suspect, suppose, assume, presume, conjecture, surmise, postulate that, theorize that, conclude, come to the conclusion that, deduce; understand, be given to understand, take it, gather, fancy, guess, dare say; *N. Amer.* figure; *informal* reckon; *archaic* ween.
OPPOSITE doubt.
□ **believe in 1** *Lucy wasn't sure if she believed in God or not* **be convinced of the existence of**, be sure of the existence of, be persuaded of the existence of, believe in the existence of.
2 *she believed in the benefits of Turkish baths for slimming* **have faith in**, pin one's faith on, trust in, have every confidence in, cling to, set store by, value, swear by, be convinced by, be persuaded by; subscribe to, approve of, back, support, advocate, champion; *informal* rate.

believer ▶ **noun** *she was a believer in the Christian religion* **devotee of**, adherent of, disciple of, follower of, supporter of, upholder of, worshipper in; convert, proselyte, neophyte; *Hinduism* bhakta; *N. Amer.* born-again.
OPPOSITES infidel; sceptic.

belittle ▶ **verb** *the opposition belittled the government's successes* **disparage**, denigrate, run down, deprecate, depreciate, downgrade, play down, trivialize, minimize, make light of, treat lightly, undervalue, underrate, underestimate; **scoff at**, **sneer at**, laugh at, laugh off, mock, ridicule, deride, dismiss, scorn, pour scorn on, cast aspersions on, discredit, vilify, defame, decry, criticize, condemn, censure, abuse, malign, revile; *N. Amer.* slur; *informal* do down, do a hatchet job on, take to pieces, pull apart, pick holes in, drag through the mud, have a go at, hit out at, knock, slam, pan, bash, bad-mouth, pooh-pooh, look down one's nose at; *Brit. informal* rubbish, slate, slag off; *archaic* hold cheap; *rare* asperse, derogate, misprize, minify.
OPPOSITES praise; magnify.

bell ▶ **noun** *the bell rang for the start of school* **chime**, gong, alarm; peal, knell, toll; signal, warning, alert; *archaic* tocsin.
□ **give someone a bell** (*Brit. informal*) *just give me a bell when you need me. See* TELEPHONE.

WORD LINKS
bell-ringing **campanology**

belle ▶ **noun** *a dainty Southern belle from Virginia* **beauty**, beautiful woman, dream, vision, picture, pin-up, goddess, Venus, siren, charmer, enchantress, seductress; *informal* looker, good looker, lovely, sensation, stunner, knockout, bombshell, dish, cracker, smasher, bobby-dazzler, peach, honey, eyeful, sight for sore eyes, bit of all right.

bellicose ▶ **adjective** *the extreme right adopted a bellicose attitude* **belligerent**, aggressive, hostile, threatening, antagonistic, pugnacious, truculent, confrontational, argumentative, quarrelsome, disputatious, contentious, militant, combative; quick-tempered, hot-tempered, ill-tempered, bad-tempered, irascible, captious; *informal* spoiling for a fight; *Brit. informal* stroppy, bolshie; *N. Amer. informal* scrappy; *rare* oppugnant.
OPPOSITE peaceable.

belligerent ▶ **adjective 1** *she stared about her in a belligerent manner* **hostile**, aggressive, threatening, antagonistic, pugnacious, bellicose, truculent, confrontational, argumentative, quarrelsome, disputatious, contentious, militant, combative; quick-tempered, hot-tempered, ill-tempered, bad-tempered, irascible, captious; *informal* spoiling for a fight; *Brit. informal* stroppy, bolshie; *N. Amer. informal* scrappy; *N. Amer. vulgar slang* pissy; *rare* oppugnant.
OPPOSITES friendly, peaceable.
2 *he helped to bring peace between two belligerent states* **warring**, at war, combatant, fighting, battling, contending, conflicting, clashing,

B

quarrelling; militant, militaristic, martial, warlike, warmongering, sabre-rattling, hawkish, gung-ho; *informal* at each other's throats.
OPPOSITES peaceful, neutral.

bellow ▶ **verb** *he cringed as she bellowed in his ear* **roar**, shout, bawl, thunder, trumpet, boom, bark, bay, yawp, yell, yelp, shriek, howl, scream, screech, call, cry, cry out, sing out, whoop, wail, caterwaul; raise one's voice; *N. Amer. informal* holler; *rare* vociferate, ululate.
OPPOSITE whisper.
▶ **noun** *he gave a bellow of pain and rage* **roar**, shout, bawl, bark, bay, yawp, yell, yelp, shriek, howl, scream, screech, call, cry, whoop, wail, caterwaul; *N. Amer. informal* holler; *rare* vociferation, ululation.
OPPOSITE whisper.

belly ▶ **noun 1** *he scratched his hairy belly* **stomach**, abdomen, paunch, middle, midriff, girth; *informal* tummy, tum, gut, guts, insides, pot, bread basket, pot belly, beer belly, beer gut, spare tyre, middle-aged spread; *Scottish informal* kyte; *N. Amer. informal* bay window; *Austral./NZ informal* bingy, bingee; *dated, humorous* corporation.
2 *the aircraft finally came to rest on its belly* **undercarriage**, underbelly, underside, undersurface, underneath, underpart, lower side, bottom.
▶ **verb** *her skirt bellied out in the wind* **billow (out)**, bulge (out), swell (out), balloon (out), bag (out), fill out, puff out; distend.

belong ▶ **verb 1** *the plant probably belongs within this broad group* **have a place**, be located, be situated, be found, lie, stand, be included, be classed, be classified, be categorized.
2 *she is a stranger and doesn't belong here* **fit in**, be suited to, have a rightful place, have a home, be part of; *informal* go, click.
□ **belong to 1** *the house they lived in belonged to a German lady* **be owned by**, be the property of, be the possession of, be in the ownership of, be held by, be at the disposal of, be in the hands of.
2 *I don't belong to a trade union* **be a member of**, be in, be included in, be affiliated to, be allied to, be associated with, be connected to, be linked to, be an adherent of.
3 *the balcony belonged to a room on the first floor* **be part of**, be attached to, be an adjunct of, link up with, go with.

belonging ▶ **noun** *the club helps their members maintain a sense of belonging* **affiliation**, **acceptance**, association, attachment, connection, union, integration, closeness; rapport, fellow feeling, fellowship, kinship, partnership.
OPPOSITE alienation.

belongings ▶ **plural noun** *she carried a canvas bag containing all her belongings* **possessions**, personal possessions, personal effects, effects, goods, worldly goods, chattels, goods and chattels, accoutrements, appurtenances; property, paraphernalia; luggage, baggage; *informal* gear, tackle, kit, things, stuff, junk, rubbish, bits and pieces, bits and bobs; *Brit. informal* clobber, gubbins; *vulgar slang* shit, crap.

beloved ▶ **adjective 1** *she wrote regularly to her beloved brother* **darling**, dear, dearest, precious, adored, loved, much loved, favourite, cherished, treasured, prized, esteemed, worshipped, idolized, lionized.
2 *Tuscany is a region much beloved by artists* **loved**, liked, highly regarded, adored, admired, esteemed, valued, prized, revered, venerated, exalted.
▶ **noun** *he watched his beloved from afar* **sweetheart**, loved one, love, true love, lady love, darling, dearest, dear one, lover, girlfriend, boyfriend, young lady, young man, woman friend, lady friend, man friend, beau, admirer, worshipper, inamorata, inamorato; fiancée, fiancé, betrothed, partner, significant other; the love of one's life, the apple of one's eye, the object of one's affections; *informal* fancy woman, fancy man, flame, steady, baby, angel, honey, pet, bird, fella; *literary* swain; *archaic* gallant, paramour, leman, doxy.

below ▶ **preposition 1** *the overcoat had two side pockets below the hips* **beneath**, under, underneath, further down than, lower than.
OPPOSITES above, over.
2 *they have an income below the national average* **less than**, lower than, under, not as much as, not so much as, smaller than.
OPPOSITES above, more than.
3 *the aristocracy ranked below the monarchy* **lower than**, under, inferior to, subordinate to, secondary to, subservient to; subject to, controlled by, at the mercy of, under the heel of.
OPPOSITE above.
▶ **adverb 1** *the balcony gave a good view of what was happening down below* **further down**, lower down, in a lower position, underneath, beneath, downstairs.
2 *please answer yes or no to the statements below* **underneath**, following, further on, at a later point, in a later place, at the bottom, at the end.

WORD LINKS
related prefixes **hypo-** (e.g. *hypodermic, hypogeum*), **sub-** (e.g. *subterranean, subdominant*)

belt ▶ **noun 1** *she wore a plain raincoat tied with a belt* **girdle**, sash, strap, cummerbund, waistband, band, girth; *Japanese* obi; *archaic* zone; *rare* baldric, cincture, ceinture, cestus, cingulum.
2 *a great wheel driven by a leather belt powered the drill* **band**, loop, hoop, thong; drive belt, fan belt, conveyor belt.
3 *he made a tour of the cotton belt* **region**, area, district, zone, sector, province, quarter, pocket, enclave, territory, neighbourhood, locality; tract, stretch, extent; *informal* neck of the woods, parts; *Brit. informal* patch.
4 *I saw a belt of silver on the horizon* **band**, strip, stripe, swathe, bar, line, streak, flash, vein, thread; *technical* stria, striation.
5 (*informal*) *he gave David a belt across the face* **blow**, punch, smack, crack, slap, bang, thump, knock, rap, thwack, box; *informal* clout, clip, clobber, bash, biff, whack, wallop, sock, swipe, lam, whomp; *Brit. informal* slosh; *N. Amer. informal* boff, bust, slug, whale; *Austral./NZ informal* dong; *dated* buffet.
□ **below the belt** *she thinks what they have done is a bit below the belt* **unfair**, unjust, uncalled for, unjustified, unjustifiable, unacceptable, unreasonable, unsatisfactory, unwarranted, unnecessary, inequitable, off, out of turn; **unethical**, unprincipled, immoral, unscrupulous, treacherous, two-faced, unsporting, sneaky, dishonourable, dishonest, underhand, underhanded; *informal* a bit much, not on, low-down, dirty; *Brit. informal* out of order, a bit thick, not cricket; *Austral./NZ informal* over the fence.
▶ **verb 1** *her trousers are belted at precisely the wrong curve of her hip* **fasten**, tie, bind; **encircle**, gird, encompass, circle.
2 (*informal*) *a guy belted him in the face* **hit**, strike, smack, slap, bang, beat, punch, thump, welt; *informal* clout, bash, biff, whack, thwack, wallop, sock, slog, clobber, bop, lam, larrup; *N. Amer. informal* boff, bust, slug, whale; *archaic* smite.
3 (*informal*) *they watched cars belting around oval tracks. See* SPEED.
□ **belt something out** (*informal*) *she belted out songs from the Fifties* **sing loudly**, carol, trill, yodel; perform, render; *rare* troll.
□ **belt up** (*informal*) *belt up and listen out for your names* **be quiet**, quieten down, be silent, fall silent, hush, stop talking, hold your tongue, keep your lips sealed; *informal* shut up, shut your face, shut your mouth, shut your trap, button your lip, pipe down, cut the cackle, put a sock in it, give it a rest; *Brit. informal* shut your gob, wrap it up, wrap up; *N. Amer. informal* save it.
OPPOSITE speak up.

bemoan ▶ **verb** *they were bemoaning the sad decline of moral standards* **lament**, bewail, deplore, complain about, express regret about; mourn, grieve over, express sorrow about, sorrow for, sigh over, cry over, weep over, shed tears over, wail over, keen over, beat one's breast about; *archaic* plain over.
OPPOSITE applaud.

bemused ▶ **adjective** *they wandered about with bemused expressions* **bewildered**, confused, puzzled, perplexed, baffled, stumped, mystified, stupefied, nonplussed, muddled, befuddled, fuddled, dumbfounded, at sea, at a loss, at sixes and sevens, thrown (off balance), taken aback, disoriented, disconcerted, discomposed, troubled, discomfited, unnerved, shaken, shaken up, dazed, stunned, astonished, astounded; *informal* flummoxed, bamboozled, discombobulated, clueless, fazed, floored, beaten; *Canadian & Austral./NZ informal* bushed; *archaic* wildered, mazed, distracted.

bemusement ▶ **noun** *Rachel shook her head in bemusement* **bewilderment**, confusion, puzzlement, perplexity, bafflement, befuddlement, stupefaction, mystification, incomprehension, disorientation, dumbfoundedness, astonishment; *informal* discombobulation, bamboozlement, cluelessness; *rare* disconcertment.

bench ▶ **noun 1** *he sat on a bench at the front of the hall* **pew**, form, long seat, seat, stall, settle.
2 *in the centre of the laboratory was a huge bench* **workbench**, work table, table, counter, trestle table, board, work surface, worktop, buffet.
3 *the bench began to hear the evidence* **judges**, magistrates, judiciary, judicature; **court**, law court, court of justice, bar, courtroom, tribunal, forum.

benchmark ▶ **noun** *the settlement was used as a benchmark in all further negotiations* **standard**, point of reference, basis, gauge, criterion, specification, canon, convention, guide, guideline, guiding principle, norm, touchstone, yardstick, test, litmus test, barometer, indicator, measure, model, exemplar, classic example, pattern, paradigm, archetype, prototype, ideal.

bend ▶ **verb 1** *copper pipes should not be bent without support* **curve**, crook, make crooked, make curved, flex, angle, hook, bow, arc, arch, buckle, warp, contort, distort, deform; twist, spiral, coil, curl, loop.
OPPOSITE straighten.
2 *the highway bent to the left up ahead* **turn**, curve, incline, swing, veer, swerve, deviate, diverge, fork, change course; twist, snake, wind, meander, zigzag, curl, loop; *rare* divagate, incurvate.
3 *he bent and patted the dog* **stoop**, bow, crouch, squat, kneel, hunch; bend down, bend over, lean down, lean over, hunker down, bob down, duck down.
OPPOSITE straighten up.
4 *they want to bend me to their will* **mould**, shape, manipulate, direct, force, press, influence, incline, sway, bias, warp, impress, compel, persuade; subdue, subjugate.
5 *he bent his mind to the question* **direct**, point, aim, turn, train, steer, set.
□ **bend over backwards** (*informal*) *they have bent over backwards to ensure a*

B

fair trial **try one's hardest**, try as hard as one can, do one's best, do one's utmost, do all one can, give one's all, make every effort; strive, struggle, apply oneself, exert oneself, work hard, endeavour, try; *informal* do one's damnedest, go all out, pull out all the stops, bust a gut, move heaven and earth, give it one's best shot; *Austral./NZ informal* go for the doctor.

▶ **noun** *he came to a bend in the road* **curve**, turn, corner, kink, angle, arc, crescent, twist, crook, deviation, deflection, loop; dog-leg, oxbow, zigzag; *Brit.* hairpin bend, hairpin turn, hairpin; *rare* incurvation.
OPPOSITE straight.

beneath ▶ **preposition 1** *we sat in the shade beneath the trees* **under**, underneath, below, at the foot of, at the bottom of; lower than.
OPPOSITE above.
2 *they seemed to think that you were beneath them* **inferior to**, not so important as, lower in status than, lower than, below; secondary to, subordinate to, subservient to.
OPPOSITE above.
3 *she thought such an attitude was beneath her* **unworthy of**, unbefitting for, inappropriate for, unbecoming to, undignified for, degrading to, below.
OPPOSITE above.

▶ **adverb** *the floor was parquet with concrete beneath* **underneath**, below, further down, lower down, in a lower place.
OPPOSITE above.

benediction ▶ **noun 1** *the preacher asked him to come up and give the benediction* **blessing**, prayer, invocation, dedication; grace, thanksgiving, thanks; *archaic* orison.
2 *those who receive the sacrament may be filled with heavenly benediction* **blessedness**, beatitude, bliss, grace, favour.

benefactor ▶ **noun** *they erected a statue to their most generous benefactor* **patron**, benefactress, supporter, backer, helper, sponsor, promoter, champion; donor, contributor, subscriber, subsidizer; philanthropist, good Samaritan, sympathizer, well-wisher, friend; *informal* angel, fairy godmother; *archaic* almsgiver; *rare* benefactrice, benefactrix, philanthrope, Maecenas.

beneficent ▶ **adjective** *he sees himself as their beneficent saviour* **benevolent**, charitable, altruistic, humane, humanitarian, neighbourly, public-spirited, philanthropic; **generous**, magnanimous, munificent, unselfish, ungrudging, unstinting, open-handed, free-handed, free, liberal, lavish, bountiful, benign, indulgent, kind; *literary* bounteous; *rare* benignant.
OPPOSITES unkind, mean.

beneficial ▶ **adjective** *alcohol taken in moderation can be beneficial to health | their relationship was mutually beneficial* **advantageous**, favourable, helpful, useful, of use, of benefit, of assistance, serviceable, of service, instrumental, valuable, of value, in one's (best) interests, worthwhile, good, positive; **profitable**, rewarding, gainful, fruitful, lucrative, remunerative, productive; propitious, promising.
OPPOSITES disadvantageous, detrimental.

beneficiary ▶ **noun** *she was the major beneficiary of her parents' will* **heir**, heiress, inheritor, legatee; recipient, receiver, payee, donee, assignee; *Law* devisee, grantee, cestui que trust; *Scottish Law* heritor.

benefit ▶ **noun 1** *they improved the station for the benefit of customers* **good**, sake, interest, welfare, well-being, satisfaction, enjoyment, advantage, comfort, ease, convenience; help, aid, assistance, avail, use, utility, service.
OPPOSITE detriment.
2 *the benefits of massage are endless* **advantage**, reward, merit, good point, strong point, strength, asset, plus, plus point, bonus, boon, blessing, virtue; perk, fringe benefit, additional benefit, added extra; usefulness, helpfulness, convenience, advantageousness, value, profit; *formal* perquisite.
OPPOSITES disadvantage, drawback.
3 *there is new hope for those who are dependent on benefit* **social security payments**, social security, state benefit, unemployment benefit, government benefit, benefit payments, public assistance allowance, welfare, insurance money, sick pay, pension; charity, donations, gifts, financial assistance; *informal* the dole; *Scottish informal* the buroo, the broo.

▶ **verb 1** *they came to a compromise that benefited all parties* **be advantageous to**, be beneficial to, be of advantage to, be to the advantage of, profit, do good to, be of service to, serve, be useful to, be of use to, be helpful to, be of help to, help, aid, assist, be of assistance to; better, improve, strengthen, boost, advance, further.
OPPOSITE damage.
2 *she* **benefited from** *a credit and loan scheme* **profit**, gain, reap benefits, reap financial reward, make money; make the most of, exploit, turn to one's advantage, put to good use, do well out of; *informal* cash in, make a killing.

benevolence ▶ **noun** *the hospital depended on the benevolence of local businessmen* **kindness**, kind-heartedness, big-heartedness, goodness, goodwill, benignity, compassion, consideration, thoughtfulness, decency, public-spiritedness, social conscience, charity, charitableness, altruism, humanity, humanitarianism, philanthropism; **generosity**, magnanimity, magnanimousness, munificence, unselfishness, open-handedness, free-handedness, largesse, lavishness, liberality, beneficence, indulgence; *historical* almsgiving; *literary* bounty, bounteousness.
OPPOSITES spite; miserliness.

benevolent ▶ **adjective 1** *they thought him a benevolent and conscientious guardian* **kind**, kindly, kind-hearted, warm-hearted, tender-hearted, big-hearted, good-natured, good, gracious, tolerant, benign, compassionate, caring, sympathetic, considerate, thoughtful, well meaning, obliging, accommodating, helpful, decent, neighbourly, public-spirited, charitable, altruistic, humane, humanitarian, philanthropic; **generous**, magnanimous, munificent, unselfish, ungrudging, unstinting, open-handed, free-handed, free, liberal, lavish, bountiful, beneficent, indulgent; *literary* bounteous; *rare* benignant.
OPPOSITES unkind; tight-fisted.
2 *a benevolent institution for the aged and infirm* **charitable**, non-profit-making, non-profit, not-for-profit; *historical* almsgiving; *rare* eleemosynary.

CHOOSE THE RIGHT WORD

benevolent, kind, kindly

See KIND.

benighted ▶ **adjective** *he knew what was best for the benighted peasant* **ignorant**, unenlightened, uneducated, unschooled, untutored, illiterate, unlettered, unlearned, unscholarly, unread, uninformed, backward, simple; primitive, uncivilized, unsophisticated, unrefined, uncouth, unpolished, uncultured, philistine, barbarian, barbaric, barbarous, savage, crude, coarse, rough, vulgar, gross; *informal* yobbish; *literary* nescient; *archaic* rude.
OPPOSITE enlightened.

benign ▶ **adjective 1** *he adopted a benign grandfatherly role* **kindly**, kind, warm-hearted, good-natured, friendly, warm, affectionate, agreeable, amiable, good-humoured, genial, congenial, cordial, approachable, tender, tender-hearted, soft-hearted, gentle, sympathetic, compassionate, caring, considerate, thoughtful, helpful, well disposed, obliging, accommodating, generous, big-hearted, unselfish, benevolent, gracious, liberal, indulgent; *rare* benignant.
OPPOSITES unfriendly, hostile.
2 *the climate becomes more benign nearer to the Black Sea* **temperate**, mild, gentle, clement, calm, balmy, pleasant, agreeable, soft, soothing, refreshing; healthy, health-giving, wholesome, salubrious.
OPPOSITES harsh; unhealthy.
3 *the lizard has a chance of survival if its environment is benign* **favourable**, advantageous, beneficial; helpful, propitious, auspicious, lucky, opportune, fortunate, providential, encouraging, benevolent, conducive; right, good.
OPPOSITE unfavourable.
4 *he had surgery to remove a benign tumour* **harmless**, non-malignant, non-cancerous, non-dangerous, innocent; curable, remediable, treatable, removable; *technical* benignant.
OPPOSITE malignant.

bent ▶ **adjective 1** *the bucket was dented and had a bent handle* **twisted**, **crooked**, warped, contorted, deformed, misshapen, out of shape, irregular; bowed, arched, curved, angled, hooked, kinked, kinky; *N. Amer. informal* pretzeled.
OPPOSITE straight.
2 (*Brit. informal*) *he hates drug dealers more than he hates bent coppers* **corrupt**, corruptible, bribable, buyable, venal, fraudulent, swindling, grafting, criminal, lawless, villainous; dishonest, underhand, unprincipled, unscrupulous, amoral, dishonourable, untrustworthy, double-dealing, rotten; *Law* malfeasant; *informal* crooked, shady, tricky; *Brit. informal* dodgy; *archaic* hollow-hearted.
OPPOSITE law-abiding.
3 (*Brit. informal*) **homosexual**, gay, lesbian; *informal* queer, camp, swinging the other way, pink, lavender, limp-wristed, homo, lezzy, les, lesbo, butch, dykey; *Brit. informal* poofy; *N. Amer. informal* fruity; *rare* homophile, Uranian, sapphic.
OPPOSITE heterosexual.

□ **bent on** *she's bent on going and nothing will stop her* **intent on**, determined on, set on, insistent on, fixed on, resolved on, hell-bent on, firm about, committed to; single-minded about, obsessive about, obsessed with, fanatical about, fixated on.

▶ **noun** *she has an artistic bent* **inclination**, predisposition, disposition, instinct, orientation, leaning, tendency, penchant, bias, predilection, proclivity, propensity, talent, gift, flair, ability, knack, aptitude, facility, faculty, skill, capability, capacity, forte, genius; mind, brain, head.

benumbed ▶ **adjective** *my benumbed brain was quickened by the bracing air* **numb**, unfeeling, insensible, stupefied, groggy, foggy, muzzy, fuzzy, vague, dazed, dizzy; befuddled, fuddled, disoriented, confused, bewildered, mixed up, all at sea; *informal* woolly, dopey, woolly-headed, woozy, out of it.
OPPOSITE perceptive.

bequeath ▶ **verb 1** *he bequeathed his artworks to the city of Philadelphia*

B

leave, leave in one's will, will, make over, pass on, hand on, hand down, cede, consign, commit, entrust, grant, transfer, convey; **donate**, give, give over, turn over, vouchsafe; bestow on, confer on; *Law* demise, devise.
2 *they bequeathed their expertise to those who built the railways* **hand down**, hand on, pass on, impart, transmit.

bequest ▶ **noun** *they received a bequest of over £300,000* **legacy**, inheritance, endowment, estate, heritage, bestowal, bequeathal, settlement, provision, benefaction, gift, present, contribution, donation; *Law* devise, hereditament.

berate ▶ **verb** *she had to berate Patsy and Betsy for giggling* **rebuke**, reprimand, reproach, reprove, admonish, remonstrate with, chastise, chide, upbraid, take to task, pull up, castigate, lambaste, read someone the Riot Act, give someone a piece of one's mind, go on at, haul over the coals, criticize, censure; *informal* tell off, give someone a talking-to, give someone a telling-off, dress down, give someone a dressing-down, give someone an earful, give someone a roasting, give someone a rocket, give someone a rollicking, rap, rap over the knuckles, slap someone's wrist, let someone have it, send someone away with a flea in their ear, bawl out, give someone hell, come down on, blow up at, pitch into, lay into, lace into, tear into, give someone a caning, put on the mat, slap down, blast, rag, keelhaul; *Brit. informal* tick off, have a go at, carpet, give someone a carpeting, give someone a mouthful, tear someone off a strip, tear a strip off someone, give someone what for, give someone some stick, wig, give someone a wigging, give someone a row, row; *N. Amer. informal* chew out, ream out, take to the woodshed; *Austral. informal* monster; *Brit. vulgar slang* bollock, give someone a bollocking; *N. Amer. vulgar slang* chew someone's ass, ream someone's ass; *dated* call down, rate, give someone a rating, trim; *rare* reprehend, objurgate.
OPPOSITE praise.

bereave ▶ **verb** *she was bereaved of two daughters* **deprive**, dispossess, rob, divest, strip.

bereaved ▶ **adjective** *they sent condolences to the bereaved family* **orphaned**, **widowed**; grieving, sorrowful, lamenting; deprived, dispossessed.

bereavement ▶ **noun 1** *he is slowly getting over his bereavement* **loss**, deprivation, dispossession, privation; grief, sorrow, sadness, suffering, hurt, trauma.
2 *she suffered three bereavements in quick succession* **death in the family**, loss, passing, passing away, passing on, demise, decease, end, expiry, expiration; *rare* quietus.

bereft ▶ **adjective** *the peasantry were* ***bereft of*** *any opportunity for social mobility* **deprived of**, robbed of, stripped of, denuded of; **cut off from**, parted from, devoid of, destitute of, bankrupt of; wanting, in need of, lacking, without, free from; low on, short of, deficient in; *informal* minus, sans, clean out of, fresh out of.

berry ▶ **noun**. *See centre pages for list of* **Fruit**

berserk ▶ **adjective** *he went berserk when he heard his wife had left him* **mad**, crazy, insane, out of one's mind, hysterical, beside oneself, frenzied, crazed, demented, maniacal, manic, frantic, wound up, worked up, raving, wild; **enraged**, raging, out of control, uncontrollable, amok, on the rampage; *informal* off one's head, up the wall, through the roof, off the deep end, ape, bananas, bonkers, mental, barmy, nutty, nuts, bats, batty, hyper; *Brit. informal* spare, crackers; *N. Amer. informal* postal; *Austral./NZ informal* crook; *vulgar slang* apeshit.

berth ▶ **noun 1** *she suffers badly from seasickness and keeps to her berth* **bunk**, bed, bunk bed, cot, couch, hammock; sleeping quarters, sleeping accommodation, cabin, compartment, billet; *informal* sack; *Brit. informal* pit; *Scottish informal* kip.
2 *the vessel left its berth* **docking site**, anchorage, mooring.
3 (*informal*) *he wants to secure one of the remaining berths in the England squad* **place**, position, job, post, situation, appointment, placement; opening, vacancy, opportunity; *Austral./NZ informal* grip; *archaic* employ.
□ **give someone/something a wide berth avoid**, **shun**, keep away from, stay away from, steer clear of, keep at arm's length, fight shy of, have nothing to do with, have no truck with, have no dealings with, have no contact with, give something/someone a miss; eschew, dodge, sidestep, circumvent, skirt round.
▶ **verb 1** *the ship berthed at Wallasey docks* **dock**, moor, land, tie up, make fast.
2 *the boats berthed two or three* **accommodate**, sleep, provide beds for, put up, house, shelter, lodge.

beseech ▶ **verb** (*literary*) *they beseeched him to stay* **implore**, beg, entreat, importune, plead with, appeal to, exhort, ask urgently, petition, call on, supplicate, pray to, adjure; crave, appeal for; *Scottish archaic* prig; *rare* obsecrate, impetrate, obtest.

beset ▶ **verb 1** *the social problems which beset the UK* **plague**, bedevil, attack, assail, beleaguer, afflict, torment, torture, rack, oppress, trouble, worry, bother, harass, hound, harry, dog.
2 *they were beset by enemy forces* **surround**, besiege, hem in, shut in, fence in, box in, encircle, ring round, enclose.

besetting ▶ **adjective** *the besetting sins of greed and sexual immorality* **persistent**, constant, recurrent, recurring; inveterate, habitual, compulsive, obsessive, obsessional, uncontrollable, irresistible.

beside ▶ **preposition 1** *Kate walked beside him* **alongside**, by the side of, at the side of, next to, parallel to, abreast of, at someone's elbow, with, by; **adjacent to**, next door to, cheek by jowl with, hard by; bordering, abutting, neighbouring, close to, near, overlooking; *archaic* aside of.
2 *beside Paula, she always felt clumsy* **compared with**, in comparison with, next to, against, contrasted with, in contrast to/with.
□ **beside oneself** *Ursula was beside herself with worry* **distraught**, overcome, out of one's mind, frantic, desperate, distracted, not knowing what to do with oneself, at one's wits' end, frenzied, in a frenzy; hysterical, unhinged, mad, crazed, berserk, demented; emotional, wound up, worked up, fraught.
□ **beside the point**. *See* POINT[1].
WORD LINKS
related prefix **para-** (e.g. ***parathyroid, parasite***)

besides ▶ **preposition** *who did you ask besides Mary?* **apart from**, other than, aside from, but for, save for, not counting, excluding, not including, except, with the exception of, excepting, bar, barring, leaving aside, beyond; **in addition to**, as well as, over and above, above and beyond; *N. Amer. informal* outside of; *archaic* forbye.
▶ **adverb 1** *I'm capable of doing the work and a lot more besides* **as well**, too, in addition, also, into the bargain, on top of that, to boot; *archaic* therewithal.
2 *besides, it's nothing to do with you* **furthermore**, moreover, further; **anyway**, anyhow, in any case, be that as it may; *informal* what's more; *N. Amer. informal* anyways.

besiege ▶ **verb 1** *in 1560 the English army besieged the town of Leith* **lay siege to**, beleaguer, blockade, surround; shut off, block off; *archaic* invest.
2 *he was besieged by fans* **surround**, mob, crowd round, swarm round, throng round, ring round, encircle; hem in, shut in; set upon, fall upon.
3 *guilt besieged him for many years* **oppress**, torment, torture, rack, plague, afflict, harrow, beset, beleaguer, trouble, bedevil, cause suffering to, prey on, weigh heavily on, lie heavy on, gnaw at, nag at, haunt.
4 *the television station was besieged with calls from worried homeowners* **overwhelm**, inundate, deluge, flood, swamp, snow under; bombard.

besmirch ▶ **verb** *he had besmirched the good name of his family* **sully**, tarnish, blacken, drag through the mud/mire, stain, taint, smear, befoul, soil, contaminate, pollute, disgrace, dishonour, bring discredit to, stigmatize, injure, damage, debase, spoil, ruin; slander, defame; *literary* smirch, besmear; *archaic* breathe on, spot.
OPPOSITES honour, enhance.

besotted ▶ **adjective** *she won't listen to me—she's* ***besotted with*** *him* **infatuated with**, smitten with, in love with, head over heels in love with, hopelessly in love with, obsessed with, passionate about, consumed with desire for, devoted to, doting on, greatly enamoured of, very attracted to, very taken with, charmed by, captivated by, enchanted by, enthralled by, bewitched by, beguiled by, under someone's spell, hypnotized by; *informal* bowled over by, swept off one's feet by, struck on, crazy about, mad about, wild about, potty about, nuts about, very keen on, gone on, really into, hung up on, carrying a torch for; *literary* ensorcelled by.
OPPOSITE indifferent.

bespatter ▶ **verb** *his shoes and trousers were bespattered with mud* **splatter**, spatter, splash, speck, fleck, mark, spot, muddy, dirty, soil, smear, stain, sully, bedaub, begrime, befoul, besmirch; *Scottish & Irish* slabber; *informal* splotch, splodge, splosh.

bespeak ▶ **verb 1** *a room which, without being pretentious, bespoke his new standing in life* **indicate**, be an indication of, be evidence of, be a sign of, testify to, bear witness to, reflect, demonstrate, show, manifest, display, signify, denote, point to, evince, evidence; reveal, betray; imply, intimate; *informal* spell (out); *literary* betoken.
OPPOSITE belie.
2 (*rare*) *Strether accompanied his friend to the room he had bespoken* **order in advance**, reserve, book, make a reservation for, engage in advance, prearrange; commission; requisition; *informal* bag.

best ▶ **adjective 1** *the best hotel in Paris* **finest**, greatest, top, foremost, leading, pre-eminent, premier, prime, first, chief, principal, supreme, of the highest quality, superlative, unrivalled, second to none, without equal, nonpareil, unsurpassed, unsurpassable, peerless, matchless, unparalleled, unbeaten, unbeatable, unexcelled, optimum, optimal, ultimate, surpassing, incomparable, ideal, perfect; highest, record-breaking; *French* par excellence; *informal* star, number-one, one-in-a-million, a cut above the rest, top-drawer; *rare* unexampled.
OPPOSITE worst.
2 *do whatever you think best* **most advantageous**, most suitable, most fitting, most appropriate, most apt; most prudent, most sensible, most advisable, most desirable.
▶ **adverb 1** *the best-dressed man in Britain* **to the highest standard**, in the best way.
OPPOSITE worst.
2 *the food he liked best* **most**, to the highest/greatest degree.

OPPOSITE least.
3 *this is best done at home* **most sensibly**, most prudently, most wisely, most suitably, most fittingly, most advantageously, most usefully; better.
□ **had best** *I'd best be going* **ought to**, should.
▶ **noun 1** *people for whom only the best will do* **finest**, top, cream, choice, choicest, prime, elite, crème de la crème, flower, jewel in the crown, nonpareil; *informal* the tops, the pick of the bunch.
2 *he always tries to see the best in others* **most favourable/pleasant aspect**, best point; advantage, asset, virtue, good point.
3 *she dressed in her best* **best clothes**, finery, Sunday best; *informal* best bib and tucker, glad rags.
4 *give her my best when you see her* **best wishes**, regards, kind/kindest regards, greetings, compliments, compliments of the season, felicitations, respects; love.
□ **at one's best** *Lily was not at her best yesterday* **on top form**, in the pink, in great shape, in the best of health; peak, prime; *Brit. informal* on song; *rare* in fine feather.
□ **do one's best** *Caroline had done her best to help him* **do one's utmost**, try one's hardest, try as hard as one can, make every effort, spare no effort, do all one can, give one's all, be at pains; *informal* bend/fall/lean over backwards, do one's damnedest, go all out, pull out all the stops, bust a gut, break one's neck, move heaven and earth; *N. Amer. informal* do one's darnedest/durnedest; *Austral. informal* go for the doctor.
▶ **verb** (*informal*) *he won't like being bested by a woman* **defeat**, beat, get the better of, gain the advantage over, get the upper hand over, outdo, outwit, outsmart, worst, be more than a match for, prevail over, conquer, vanquish, trounce, triumph over; surpass, outclass, outshine, put someone in the shade, overshadow, eclipse; *informal* lick, get one over on.

bestial ▶ **adjective 1** *Stanley's bestial behaviour* **savage**, brutish, brutal, barbarous, barbaric, cruel, vicious, violent, inhuman, subhuman; **depraved**, degenerate, unnatural, perverted, corrupt, immoral, amoral, warped, vile, gross, sordid; carnal, lustful, lecherous, licentious, lascivious, goatish, libidinous, lubricious, salacious, prurient, lewd, crude.
OPPOSITES civilized, humane.
2 *man's bestial ancestors* **animal**, beast-like, animalistic; *rare* zoic, theriomorphic, theroid.

bestir ▶ **verb**
□ **bestir oneself** *his friends urged him to bestir himself* **exert oneself**, make an effort, rouse oneself, get going, get moving, get on with it; *informal* shake a leg, look lively, get cracking, get weaving, get one's finger out, get off one's backside, get the show on the road; *Brit. informal, dated* stir one's stumps.

bestow ▶ **verb** *the favours bestowed on him by the new king* **confer on**, present to, award to, give, grant, vouchsafe, accord to, afford to; vest in, invest in; bequeath to, donate to; allot to, assign to, consign to, apportion to, distribute to, impart to, entrust to, commit to; lavish on, heap on.

bestride ▶ **verb 1** *he bestrode his horse with the easy grace of a born horseman* **straddle**, bestraddle, sit/stand astride; mount, get on, get astride, hop on to.
2 *the oilfield bestrides the border of the two countries* **extend across**, straddle, lie on both sides of; span, bridge.
3 *he stands alone, a colossus bestriding the entire development of modern art* **dominate**, tower over, be the most important person in.

best-seller ▶ **noun** great success; brand leader; *informal* **blockbuster**, chart topper, chartbuster, hit, smash hit, smash.
OPPOSITES failure, flop.

best-selling ▶ **adjective** *their best-selling album* **very successful**, very popular; *informal* **number-one**, chart-topping, hit, smash.

bet ▶ **verb 1** *most people would bet their life savings on the prospect* **wager**, gamble, stake, risk, venture, hazard, chance, lay down, put, place; lay money, put money, lay bets, speculate, try one's luck; *informal* punt; *Brit. informal* have a flutter, chance one's arm.
2 (*informal*) *I bet it was your idea* **be certain**, be sure, be convinced, be confident; expect, predict; *Brit. informal* put one's shirt on.
▶ **noun 1** *a £20 bet* **wager**, stake, gamble, ante; each-way bet, place bet, ante-post bet, daily double, side bet, Yankee; *Brit.* accumulator, tricast; *N. Amer.* perfecta, quinella, trifecta; *informal* long shot; *Brit. informal* flutter, punt.
2 (*informal*) *my bet is that Liverpool won't win anything* **prediction**, forecast, guess; opinion, belief, feeling, view, theory.
3 (*informal*) *your best bet is to go early* **option**, choice, alternative, course of action, plan.

bête noire ▶ **noun bugbear**, **pet hate**, pet aversion, anathema, abomination, bogey, bugaboo; a thorn in one's flesh/side, the bane of one's life.
OPPOSITE favourite.

betide ▶ **verb** (*literary*) *I waited with beating heart, not knowing what would betide* **happen**, occur, take place, come about, transpire, arise, chance; result, ensue, follow, develop, supervene; *N. Amer. informal* go down; *literary* come to pass, befall, bechance; *rare* hap, arrive, eventuate.

betoken ▶ **verb** (*literary*) **1** *she wondered if his cold, level gaze betokened indifference or anger* **indicate**, be an indication of, signify, be a sign of, be evidence of, evidence, manifest, mean, denote, represent, show, demonstrate, bespeak; *informal* spell.
2 *the falling comet betokened the true end of Merlin's powers* **presage**, portend, augur, be an omen of, be a sign of, be a warning of, warn of, bode, foreshadow, foretell, prophesy, be a harbinger of, herald; *literary* foretoken, forebode, harbinger.

betray ▶ **verb 1** *I trusted them and they betrayed me* **break one's promise to**, **be disloyal to**, be unfaithful to, break faith with, play someone false, fail, let down; double-cross, deceive, cheat; inform on/against, give away, denounce, sell out, stab someone in the back, be a Judas to, give someone a Judas kiss, bite the hand that feeds one; turn traitor, sell the pass; *English Law* turn Queen's/King's evidence; *informal* split on, blow the whistle on, rat on, peach on, stitch up, do the dirty on, sell down the river, squeal on, squeak on; *Brit. informal* grass on, shop, sneak on; *N. Amer. informal* rat out, drop a/the dime on, finger, job; *Austral./NZ informal* dob on, pimp on, pool, shelf, put someone's pot on, point the bone at; *rare* delate.
OPPOSITE be loyal to.
2 *she hoped her face didn't betray her feelings* **reveal**, disclose, divulge, give away, leak, lay bare, make known, uncover, unmask, expose, bring out into the open, tell; let slip, let out, let drop, blurt out; give the game away, let the cat out of the bag; *informal* blab, spill; *archaic* discover.
OPPOSITES conceal, hide.

betrayal ▶ **noun 1** *a cowardly act of betrayal* **disloyalty**, **treachery**, perfidy, perfidiousness, bad faith, faithlessness, falseness; duplicity, deception, double-dealing; breach of faith, breach of trust, stab in the back, Judas kiss; double-cross, sell-out; *French* trahison des clercs; *rare* false-heartedness, Punic faith.
OPPOSITES loyalty, faithfulness.
2 *the betrayal of a secret* **revelation**, disclosure, divulging, giving away, leaking, leak, telling; *rare* divulgation.

betrayer ▶ **noun traitor**, back-stabber, Judas, double-crosser; renegade, quisling, fifth columnist, double agent, collaborator, informer, mole, stool pigeon; turncoat, defector, apostate, deserter; fraternizer, colluder, false friend; *informal* snake in the grass, whistle-blower, grass, supergrass, rat, scab, stoolie, nose; *Brit. informal* nark; *N. Amer. informal* fink; *rare* traditor, renegado, Catilinarian.

betrothal ▶ **noun** (*dated*) **engagement**, betrothment, marriage contract; *French* fiançailles; *archaic* plighting of one's troth, espousal, affiance, affiancing, handfast; *rare* sponsalia, subarrhation.

betrothed ▶ **adjective** (*dated*) *his youngest son is betrothed to the Count's daughter* **engaged (to be married)**, promised, pledged, contracted, bound; *archaic* affianced, plighted, espoused, handfast.
OPPOSITES unattached, single.

better ▶ **adjective 1** *the better player | better facilities* **superior**, finer, of higher quality, greater, in a different class, one step ahead; more acceptable, preferable, recommended; *informal* a cut above, streets ahead, head and shoulders above, ahead of the pack/field.
OPPOSITES worse, inferior.
2 *there couldn't be a better time to take up this job* **more advantageous**, more suitable, more fitting, more appropriate, more useful, more valuable, more desirable.
OPPOSITE worse.
3 *is Emma any better today?* **healthier**, fitter, stronger, less ill; well, cured, healed, recovered; convalescent, recovering, on the road to recovery, making progress, progressing, improving; *informal* on the mend, looking up.
OPPOSITE worse.
▶ **adverb 1** *I played better today* **to a higher standard**, in a superior/finer way.
2 *you may find alternatives that suit you better* **more**, to a greater degree.
3 *the money could be better spent on more urgent cases* **more wisely**, more sensibly, more suitably, more fittingly, more advantageously.
▶ **verb 1** *a record bettered by only one other non-league side* **surpass**, improve on, beat, exceed, excel, top, cap, trump, eclipse, outstrip, outdo, outmatch, go one better than; *informal* best.
2 *refugees who want to better their lot* **improve**, make better, ameliorate, raise, advance, further, lift, upgrade, enhance; reform, rectify; *rare* meliorate.
OPPOSITE worsen.

betterment ▶ **noun** *the betterment of society as a whole* **improvement**, amelioration, advancement, change for the better, furtherance, upgrading, enhancement; reform, rectification.

between ▶ **preposition 1** *Philip stood between his parents* **in the middle of**, with one … on either side; *archaic* betwixt.
2 *the bond between her and her mother* **connecting**, linking, joining; uniting, allying.

WORD LINKS
related prefix **inter-** (e.g. ***international, inter-agency***)

B

bevel ▶ noun **slope**, slant, angle, cant, chamfer, mitre, oblique, diagonal, tilt; *rare* bezel.

beverage *See centre pages for list of* **Drinks**
▶ noun **drink**; liquid refreshment; *archaic* potation; *rare* libation, potable.

bevy ▶ noun *a bevy of beautiful women* **group**, gang, troop, troupe, party, company, band, body, crowd, pack, army, herd, flock, drove, horde, galaxy, assemblage, gathering; knot, cluster, covey; *informal* bunch, gaggle, posse, crew.

bewail ▶ verb *many bewailed the decline of standards* **lament**, bemoan, beat one's breast about, wring one's hands over, rue, express regret about, sigh over, deplore, complain about; mourn, grieve over, sorrow for/over, express woe/sorrow for, cry/weep over, wail/keen over; *archaic* plain over.

beware ▶ verb *there are loose rocks in the area so beware!* **be on your guard**, watch out, look out, mind out, be wary, be careful, be cautious, be on the lookout, be on the alert, keep your eyes open, keep a sharp lookout, be on the qui vive; take care, take heed, have a care, take it slowly, look where you're going, tread carefully, proceed with caution; *informal* watch your step, keep an eye out, keep your eyes peeled/skinned, look before you leap, think twice; *Brit. school slang, dated* cave; *Golf* fore; *Hunting* ware.
OPPOSITE ignore.

bewilder ▶ verb *his words bewildered Sally* **baffle**, mystify, bemuse, perplex, puzzle, confuse, confound, nonplus, disconcert, throw, set someone thinking; *informal* flummox, discombobulate, faze, stump, beat, fox, make someone scratch their head, be all Greek to, make someone's head spin, floor, fog; *N. Amer. informal* buffalo; *archaic* wilder, gravel, maze, cause to be at a stand, distract, pose; *rare* obfuscate.
OPPOSITE enlighten.

bewildered ▶ adjective *Kate looked completely bewildered* **baffled**, mystified, bemused, perplexed, puzzled, confused, nonplussed, at sea, at a loss, thrown off balance, disorientated, taken aback; *informal* flummoxed, bamboozled, discombobulated; *Canadian & Austral./NZ informal* bushed; *archaic* wildered, distracted, mazed.

bewildering ▶ adjective *the bewildering complexity of sectarian politics* **baffling**, difficult to understand, perplexing, puzzling, mystifying, mysterious, confusing, disconcerting; unaccountable, inexplicable, impenetrable, unfathomable, above one's head, beyond one; complex, complicated, involved, intricate, convoluted, labyrinthine, Byzantine, Daedalian, Gordian; *archaic* wildering.
OPPOSITES straightforward, comprehensible.

bewitch ▶ verb **1** *his relatives were convinced that he had been bewitched* **cast a spell on**, put a spell on, enchant; possess, witch, curse; *N. Amer.* hex, hoodoo; *Austral.* point the bone at; (*in S. Africa*) tagati; *literary* entrance.
2 *she was bewitched by her surroundings* **captivate**, enchant, entrance, enrapture, charm, beguile, delight, fascinate, enthral, seduce, ravish, spellbind, hold spellbound, mesmerize, hypnotize, transfix; *rare* rapture.
OPPOSITE repel.

beyond ▶ preposition **1** *farm buildings were visible beyond the trees* **on the far side of**, on the farther side of, on the other side of, further on than, behind, past, after; over; *Scottish* outwith.
2 *nobody ever worked beyond six o'clock* **later than**, past, after.
3 *matters beyond his understanding* **outside the range of**, beyond the power/capacity of, outside the limitations of, surpassing.
4 *inflation beyond 10 per cent* **greater than**, more than, exceeding, in excess of, above, over and above, above and beyond, upwards of.
5 *there was little vegetation beyond scrub and brush growth* **apart from**, except, other than.
▶ adverb *a view of Hobart with Mount Wellington beyond* **further on**, far off, far away, in the distance, afar; *archaic* yonder.
OPPOSITES near, close.

WORD LINKS
related prefixes **extra-** (e.g. ***extraterritorial, extracellular***), **hyper-** (e.g. ***hypersonic, hyperplasia***), **para-** (e.g. ***paranormal, paratyphoid***)

bias ▶ noun **1** *the chairman accused the media of bias | he did not always hide his pro-British bias* **prejudice**, partiality, partisanship, favouritism, unfairness, one-sidedness; bigotry, intolerance, racism, racialism, sexism, heterosexism, homophobia, chauvinism, anti-Semitism, discrimination, a jaundiced eye; predisposition, leaning, tendency, inclination, propensity, proclivity, proneness, predilection; *French* parti pris.
OPPOSITES objectivity, fairness, impartiality.
2 *a dress cut on the bias* **diagonal**, cross, slant, oblique, angle.
▶ verb *witnesses' recollections may be biased by discussions with other people* **prejudice**, influence, colour, sway, weight, predispose; distort, skew, bend, twist, warp; angle, load, slant.

biased ▶ adjective *a biased view of the situation* **prejudiced**, partial, partisan, one-sided, blinkered, subjective; bigoted, intolerant, discriminatory, racist, racialist, sexist, heterosexist, homophobic, chauvinistic, chauvinist, anti-Semitic; jaundiced, distorted, warped, twisted, skewed; *French* parti pris.
OPPOSITES unbiased, impartial, fair.

CHOOSE THE RIGHT WORD

biased, prejudiced, partial

These words all denote a tendency to be unfairly or irrationally opinionated in favour of or against people or groups.

- Someone who is **biased** is predisposed to make judgements in favour of or against someone or something, typically because of some emotional commitment rather than because of any rational consideration. The resulting judgements are generally unfair or inaccurate (*do you think the police in the area are biased against young people? | maybe he was biased, but he thought his daughter was the best player*).
- **Prejudiced** describes someone who brings a ready-made opinion, especially a value judgement, to some question or issue, without consideration of the actual facts. This opinion is likely to affect their other judgements and attitudes, too (*William's grandad was prejudiced against Americans*). It is much more common to be *prejudiced against* someone or something than *prejudiced in favour of* them.
- **Partial** can be used to mean 'unjustly weighted in favour of one side', but often lacks the implication of injustice (*he was partial only in so far as he took a stand against conservatism*). Although *impartial* is a more common word than *unbiased* or *unprejudiced*, *partial* in this sense is relatively uncommon.

Bible *See centre pages for list of Books of the* **Bible**
▶ noun **1** *he read the Bible and prayed* **the (Holy) Scriptures**, Holy Writ, the Good Book, the Book of Books; New English Bible, King James Bible, Authorized Version, Revised Version, Good News Bible, Jerusalem Bible, Geneva Bible; Gideon Bible.
2 (*informal*) *the professional electrician's bible* **handbook**, manual, ABC, companion, guide, primer, essential book, authoritative book; *Latin* vade mecum; *rare* enchiridion.

bibliography ▶ noun **list of references**, book list, list of books, catalogue, record; *rare* bibliotheca.

bibliophile ▶ noun **book lover**; *informal* bookworm; *rare* bibliomaniac, bibliomane, bibliolater, bibliophilist.

bicker ▶ verb *couples who bicker over who gets what from the divorce* **squabble**, argue; **quarrel**, wrangle, fight, fall out, have a disagreement, disagree, dispute, spar, bandy words, have words, be at each other's throats, lock horns; *informal* scrap, argufy, have a tiff, have a spat, spat; *Brit. informal* row, have a row, have a barney; *archaic* altercate, chop logic.
OPPOSITE agree.

CHOOSE THE RIGHT WORD

bicker, quarrel, argue, wrangle, dispute

See QUARREL.

bicycle *See centre pages for list of* **Bicycle Components**
▶ noun **cycle**, two-wheeler, pedal cycle; mountain bike, racing bike, racer, roadster, shopper; tandem, unicycle, tricycle; *informal* **bike**, pushbike; *historical* penny-farthing, velocipede, boneshaker.

bid[1] ▶ verb **1** *a consortium of dealers bid a world record price for the painting* **offer**, make an offer of, put in a bid of, put up, tender, proffer, propose, submit, put forward, advance.
2 *the two forwards are bidding for a place in the England side* **try to obtain**, try to get, make a pitch for, make a bid for.
▶ noun **1** *I put in a bid of £3,000* **offer**, tender, proposal, submission; price, sum, amount; advance, ante.
2 *an investigation carried out in a bid to establish what had happened* **attempt**, effort, endeavour, try; *informal* go, crack, stab.

bid[2] ▶ verb **1** *she turned and bid him farewell* **wish**.
2 (*literary*) *I did as he bade me* **order**, command, tell, instruct, direct, require, enjoin, charge, demand, call upon.
3 (*literary*) *he bade his companions enter* **invite to**, ask to, request to, tell to.

biddable ▶ adjective *a pretty, biddable child* **obedient**, tractable, amenable, pliable, pliant, complaisant, cooperative, malleable, persuadable, like putty in one's hands, manipulable; docile, compliant, dutiful, meek, unresisting, submissive, passive, yielding; *informal, dated* milky; *rare* persuasible.
OPPOSITES disobedient, uncooperative.

CHOOSE THE RIGHT WORD

biddable, obedient, docile, compliant, dutiful

See OBEDIENT.

bidding[1] ▶ noun *she was here at his bidding* **command**, order, instruction, dictate, decree, injunction, demand, mandate, direction, charge, summons, call; wish, desire, will; request, invitation; *literary* behest; *archaic* hest.

bidding² ▶ noun **1** *I opened the bidding at £200* **auction**; making of bids, offering of bids.
2 *the bidding rose to £280,000* **bids**, offers, tenders.

big ▶ adjective **1** *a big garden | big buildings* **large**, sizeable, of considerable size, substantial, considerable, great, huge, immense, enormous, extensive, colossal, massive, mammoth, vast, prodigious, tremendous, gigantic, giant, monumental, mighty, stupendous, gargantuan, elephantine, titanic, epic, mountainous, megalithic, monstrous, Brobdingnagian; towering, tall, high, lofty; outsize, oversized, overgrown, cumbersome, unwieldy; inordinate, unlimited, goodly; capacious, voluminous, commodious, spacious, good-size(d), fair-size(d); king-size(d), man-size, family-size(d), economy-size(d); *informal* jumbo, whopping, whopping great, thumping, thumping great, bumper, mega, humongous, monster, astronomical, almighty, dirty great, socking great, tidy; *Brit. informal* whacking, whacking great, ginormous; *literary* massy.
OPPOSITES small, little.
2 *a big man with a square red face* **well built**, sturdily built, heavily built, sturdy, brawny, burly, broad-shouldered, muscular, muscly, well muscled, robust, rugged, lusty, Herculean, bulky, hulking, strapping, thickset, stocky, solid, hefty, meaty; tall, huge, gigantic; fat, stout, portly, plump, heavy, overweight, oversize, fleshy, paunchy, corpulent, obese, gargantuan, elephantine; *informal* hunky, beefy, husky; *dated* stalwart; *literary* thewy, stark.
OPPOSITES small, slight, short.
3 *you're a big girl now | my big brother* **grown-up**, adult, mature, grown, full grown; elder, older.
4 *it's a big decision, so don't rush it* **important**, significant, major, of great import, of significance, momentous, of moment, weighty, consequential, of consequence, far-reaching, key, vital, critical, crucial, life-and-death, high-priority, serious, grave, solemn; no joke, no laughing matter.
OPPOSITES minor, unimportant, trivial.
5 (*informal*) *a big man in the government* **powerful**, **important**, prominent, influential, high-powered, leading, pre-eminent, of high standing, outstanding, well known, eminent, distinguished, principal, foremost, noteworthy, notable, noted; *N. Amer.* major-league.
OPPOSITES unimportant, obscure.
6 (*informal*) *a small company with big plans* **ambitious**, far-reaching, on a grand scale; grandiose, unrealistic, overambitious.
OPPOSITE modest.
7 *she's got a big heart* **generous**, **kind**, kindly, kind-hearted, caring, compassionate, loving, benevolent, magnanimous, unselfish, altruistic, selfless, philanthropic.
8 (*informal*) *African bands are big in Britain* **popular**, successful, commercially successful, in demand, sought-after, all the rage; *informal* hot, in, cool, trendy, now, hip; *Brit. informal, dated* all the go.
□ **too big for one's boots** (*informal*) **conceited**, full of oneself, cocky, boastful, arrogant, cocksure, above oneself, self-important, immodest, swaggering, strutting; vain, self-satisfied, self-congratulatory, pleased with oneself, self-loving, in love with oneself, self-admiring, self-regarding, smug, complacent; *informal* big-headed, swollen-headed; *literary* vainglorious; *rare* peacockish.
OPPOSITE modest.

big-headed ▶ adjective (*informal*) **conceited**, arrogant, boastful, cocky, cocksure, full of oneself, above oneself, self-important, immodest, swaggering, strutting; vain, self-satisfied, self-congratulatory, pleased with oneself, self-loving, in love with oneself, self-admiring, self-regarding, smug, complacent; *informal* swollen-headed, too big for one's boots; *literary* vainglorious; *rare* peacockish.
OPPOSITES modest, self-effacing.

big-hearted ▶ adjective *thousands of big-hearted readers pledged cash to help the aid effort* **generous**, magnanimous, munificent, open-handed, bountiful, free-handed, generous to a fault, ungrudging, unstinting, charitable, philanthropic, benevolent, beneficent; kind, kindly, kind-hearted, unselfish, altruistic, selfless; *literary* bounteous.
OPPOSITE mean.

bigot ▶ noun **dogmatist**, partisan, sectarian, prejudiced person; racist, racialist, sexist, homophobe, chauvinist, jingoist, anti-Semite; *informal* male chauvinist pig, MCP.

bigoted ▶ adjective *a bigoted group of reactionaries* **prejudiced**, biased, partial, one-sided, sectarian, discriminatory; **intolerant**, narrow-minded, blinkered, illiberal, inflexible, uncompromising, fanatical, dogmatic, opinionated; racist, racialist, sexist, heterosexist, homophobic, chauvinistic, chauvinist, anti-Semitic, jingoistic; jaundiced, warped, twisted, distorted; *French* parti pris.
OPPOSITES tolerant, liberal.

bigotry ▶ noun **prejudice**, bias, partiality, partisanship, sectarianism, discrimination, unfairness, injustice; **intolerance**, narrow-mindedness, fanaticism, dogmatism; racism, racialism, sexism, heterosexism, homophobia, chauvinism, anti-Semitism, jingoism; *US* Jim Crowism.
OPPOSITE tolerance.

bigwig ▶ noun (*informal*) **VIP**, important person, notable, notability, personage, dignitary, grandee, panjandrum; celebrity; magnate, mogul; *informal* somebody, heavyweight, hotshot, big shot, big noise, big gun, big cheese, big fish, biggie, big bug, Big Chief, Big Daddy, honcho; *Brit. informal* brass hat; *N. Amer. informal* big wheel; *Austral./NZ informal* joss.
OPPOSITES nobody, nonentity.

bijou ▶ adjective *a bijou Chelsea flat* **small**, little, compact, snug, cosy; desirable, sought-after; elegant, stylish, chic, fashionable.

bilge ▶ noun (*informal*) *a review dismissed the book as bilge. See* NONSENSE.

bilious ▶ adjective **1** *I woke up feeling bilious and with a raging headache* **nauseous**, sick, queasy, nauseated, green about the gills, liverish; *N. Amer. informal* barfy; *rare* qualmish.
2 *his bilious disposition* **bad-tempered**, irritable, irascible, tetchy, testy, grumpy, grouchy, crotchety, cantankerous, curmudgeonly, ill-tempered, ill-natured, ill-humoured, peevish, fractious, disagreeable, pettish, crabbed, crabby, waspish, prickly, peppery, touchy, scratchy, crusty, splenetic, shrewish, short-tempered, hot-tempered, quick-tempered, dyspeptic, choleric, liverish, cross-grained; *N. Amer. informal* cranky, ornery.
OPPOSITE good-humoured.
3 *a bilious green and pink colour scheme* **lurid**, garish, loud, violent; sickly, nauseating, distasteful, unattractive.
OPPOSITES muted, subtle.

bilk ▶ verb (*informal*) *thousands of investors claimed they had been bilked by his schemes* **swindle**, defraud, cheat, fleece, exploit; deceive, trick; *informal* con, bamboozle, do, diddle, swizzle, sting, rip off, screw, shaft, take for a ride, take to the cleaners, pull a fast one on, put one over on, sell someone a pup, gull, rook, finagle, clip, gyp, skin; *N. Amer. informal* stiff, euchre, bunco, hornswoggle, sucker, snooker; *Austral. informal* pull a swifty on; *archaic* cozen, sharp; *rare* mulct, do someone in the eye.

bill¹ ▶ noun **1** *their bill came to £69* **invoice**, account, statement, list of charges, tally; amount due; *N. Amer.* check; *informal* the damage; *N. Amer. informal* tab; *Brit. informal, dated* shot; *archaic* reckoning, score.
2 *the bill was passed by 189 votes to 108* **draft law**, proposed legislation, proposal, measure; act, Act of Parliament.
3 *she was top of the bill* **programme (of entertainment)**, listing, list, line-up; *N. Amer.* playbill; *dated* bill of fare.
4 (*N. Amer.*) *a ten-dollar bill* **banknote**, note; *N. Amer.* greenback.
5 *he had been hard at work posting bills* **poster**, advertisement, public notice, announcement; flyer, leaflet, circular, handout, handbill; *Brit.* fly-poster; *N. Amer. & Austral.* dodger; *French* affiche; *informal* ad; *Brit. informal* advert.
▶ verb **1** *we shall be billing them for the damage caused* **send an invoice to**, invoice, charge, debit, send a statement to.
2 *Goddard gave assurances that the concert would go ahead as billed* **advertise**, promote, announce, post, give advance notice of, put up in lights; **schedule**, programme, timetable; *N. Amer.* slate.
3 *he was* **billed as** *the new Sean Connery* **describe as**, call, style, label, dub, designate, pronounce; promote as, publicize as, talk up as; *informal* hype as.

bill² ▶ noun **1** *a bird's bill* **beak**; *Scottish & N. English* neb; *technical* mandibles.
2 *a view of Portland Bill* **promontory**, headland, point, head, foreland, cape, peninsula, bluff, ness, naze, horn, spit, tongue; *Scottish* mull.

billet ▶ noun *the troops marched back to their billets* **living quarters**, quarters, rooms; accommodation, lodging, housing; barracks, cantonment; *rare* casern.
▶ verb *the farmhouse in which the men were billeted* **accommodate**, quarter, put up, lodge, house; station, garrison.

billow ▶ noun **1** *billows of smoke* **cloud**, mass.
2 (*archaic*) *the billows that break upon the shore* **wave**, roller, breaker.
▶ verb **1** *her dress* **billowed out** *around her* **puff up/out**, balloon (out), swell, fill out, bulge out, belly out.
2 *smoke was billowing from the chimney* **pour**, flow; swirl, spiral, roll, undulate, rise and fall, eddy.

billowing ▶ adjective *billowing clouds of dust* **rolling**, swirling, undulating, rising and falling, billowy, swelling, rippling; *rare* undulant.

bin ▶ noun *flour storage bins* **container**, receptacle, holder; drum, canister, caddy, box, can, tin, crate; *archaic* reservatory.

bind ▶ verb **1** *bundles of logs bound together with ropes | they bound her hands and feet* **tie**, tie up, fasten (together), hold together, secure, make fast, attach; rope, strap, lash, truss, tether, hitch, chain, fetter, pinion, shackle, hobble; moor.
OPPOSITES untie, release.
2 *Shelley* **bound up** *the wound with a clean dressing* **bandage**, dress, cover, wrap, swathe, swaddle; strap up, tape up.
3 *the experience had* **bound** *them* **together** **unite**, join, bond, knit together, draw together, yoke together.
OPPOSITE separate.
4 *other OPEC members* **bound themselves** *to return to the quotas of 1984* **commit oneself**, undertake, give an undertaking, pledge; vow, promise, swear, give one's word.

5 *clay is made up chiefly of tiny soil particles which bind together tightly* **stick**, cohere.
6 *a frill with the edges bound in a contrasting colour* **trim**, hem, edge, border, fringe, rim, band; finish; *archaic* purfle.
7 *Sarah did not want to be bound by a rigid timetable* **constrain**, restrict, confine, restrain, tie hand and foot, tie down, shackle; hamper, hinder, inhibit, cramp someone's style; *literary* trammel.
▶ **noun** (*informal*) **1** *I know being disturbed on Christmas Day is a bind* **nuisance**, annoyance, inconvenience, bore, bother, source of irritation, irritant, problem, trial; *informal* pain, pain in the neck, pain in the backside, headache, hassle, drag, aggravation, pest; *N. Amer. informal* pain in the butt; *Austral./NZ informal* nark; *Brit. vulgar slang* pain in the arse; *dated* infliction.
2 *he is in a political bind over the abortion issue* **predicament**, awkward situation, quandary, dilemma, plight, difficult situation, cleft stick, mess, quagmire; impasse, double bind; *informal* spot, tight spot, hole.

binding ▶ **adjective** *a legally binding agreement* **irrevocable**, unalterable, unbreakable, indissoluble, permanent; compulsory, obligatory, imperative, mandatory, necessary; conclusive.

binge ▶ **noun** (*informal*) **1** *after a midweek game in London, the two lads went on a two-day binge* **drinking bout**, debauch; *informal* bender, session, sesh, booze-up, beer-up, souse, drunk, blind; *Scottish informal* skite; *N. Amer. informal* jag, toot; *NZ informal* boozeroo; *Brit. vulgar slang* piss-up; *literary* bacchanal, bacchanalia; *archaic* wassail, fuddle, potation.
2 *a shopping binge* **spree**, unrestrained bout, orgy; *informal* splurge.

biography ▶ **noun** **life story**, life history, life, memoir, profile, account; *informal* bio, biog; *rare* prosopography.

bird *See centre pages for lists of* **Birds** **Fowl**
▶ **noun** songbird, warbler, passerine; bird of prey, raptor; fowl; chick, fledgling, nestling; (**birds**) avifauna; *informal* feathered friend, birdie.

WORD LINKS

related prefix	**ornith-**
relating to birds	**avian**
home	**aviary, nest**
collective noun	**flock, flight, pod**
study of birds	**ornithology**
fear of birds	**ornithophobia**

birth ▶ **noun** **1** *the birth of a child* **childbirth**, delivery, nativity, birthing; *informal* the patter of tiny feet; *technical* parturition; *archaic* confinement, accouchement, childbed.
OPPOSITE death.
2 *the birth of Socialist Realism* **beginning(s)**, emergence, genesis, dawn, dawning, rise, start, arrival, advent; origin, source, fountainhead.
OPPOSITES end, demise.
3 *he is of noble birth* **ancestry**, descent, origin(s), parentage, lineage, line, line of descent, heritage, family, stock, blood, bloodline, genealogy, breeding, pedigree, house, extraction, derivation, background; *rare* filiation, stirps.
□ **give birth to** *she gave birth to a son* **have**, bear, produce, be delivered of, bring into the world; *N. Amer.* birth; *informal* drop; *dated* mother; *archaic* be brought to bed of, bring forth.

WORD LINKS

relating to one's birth	**natal**
before birth	**antenatal**
after childbirth	**post-natal**
branch of medicine concerned with birth	**obstetrics**

birthmark ▶ **noun** **naevus**, strawberry mark, port wine stain; mole; blemish, discoloration, patch.

birthright ▶ **noun** **patrimony**, inheritance, heritage; right, due, prerogative, privilege; primogeniture.

birthstone ▶ **noun**. *See centre pages for list of* **Birthstones**

biscuit *See centre pages for list of* **Biscuits**
▶ **noun** (*Brit.*) **cracker**, wafer; *N. Amer.* cookie; *informal* bicky.

bisect ▶ **verb** *bisect the exterior angle* **cut in half**, halve, divide/cut/split in two, split down the middle, cleave, separate into two; cross, intersect.

bisexual ▶ **adjective** **1** (*technical*) **hermaphrodite**, hermaphroditic; androgynous, epicene; *technical* monoclinous, gynandrous, gynandromorphic.
2 *informal* **AC/DC**, bi, swinging both ways, ambidextrous, ambisexual; *N. Amer. informal* switch-hitting.

bishop ▶ **noun** **prelate**, diocesan, metropolitan, suffragan, coadjutor; *Orthodox Church* exarch.

WORD LINKS

relating to a bishop **episcopal**

bishopric ▶ **noun** **diocese**, see; episcopate, episcopacy, primacy.

bit ▶ **noun** **1** *a bit of cake | bits of broken glass | add a bit of salt* **small portion**, small piece, piece, portion, segment, section, part; chunk, lump, hunk, slice; **fragment**, scrap, shred, flake, chip, shaving, paring, crumb, grain, fleck, speck; **spot**, drop, pinch, dash, soupçon, modicum, dollop; morsel, mouthful, spoonful, bite, taste, gobbet, sample; iota, jot, tittle, whit, atom, particle, scintilla, mote, trace, touch, suggestion, hint, tinge; shard, sliver; snippet, snatch, extract, excerpt; *informal* smidgen, smidge, tad; *Austral./NZ informal* skerrick; *N. Amer. rare* smitch.
2 *wait a bit* **moment**, minute, second, little while, short time; *informal* sec, jiffy, jiff; *Brit. informal* mo, tick, two ticks.
□ **a bit** *he came back looking a bit annoyed* **rather**, a little, fairly, slightly, somewhat, relatively, quite, to some degree/extent, comparatively, moderately; *informal* pretty, sort of, kind of, kinda, a tad.
OPPOSITES very, extremely.
□ **bit by bit** *bit by bit the truth started to emerge* **gradually**, little by little, in stages, step by step, slowly, one step at a time; piecemeal.
□ **in a bit** *I'll see you in a bit* **soon**, in a (little) while, in a second, in a minute, in a moment, in a trice, in a flash, shortly, in a short time, in (less than) no time, in no time at all, before you know it, before long, directly; *N. Amer.* momentarily; *informal* in a jiffy, in two shakes, in two shakes of a lamb's tail; *Brit. informal* in a tick, in two ticks, in a mo; *N. Amer. informal* in a snap; *archaic or informal* anon; *literary* ere long.

bitch ▶ **noun** (*informal*) **1** *I was always such a bitch to him* **shrew**, vixen, she-devil, hellcat; *informal* cow, cat; *archaic* grimalkin.
2 *the night shift is a bitch—you're always tired* **nightmare**; *informal* bastard, bummer, ... from hell, swine, pig, stinker; *vulgar slang* bugger, sod.
3 *her number-one bitch is her love life* **complaint**, moan, grumble, gripe, grouse, grouch; *informal* beef, whinge, bellyache.
▶ **verb** *she never* **bitched about** *other members of the team* **be spiteful about**, criticize, find fault with, run down, cast aspersions on, speak ill of, slander, malign; complain, moan, grumble, grouse, grouch, gripe; *informal* whinge, knock, pull to pieces, take apart, do a hatchet job on; *N. Amer. informal* bad-mouth, trash; *Brit. informal* slag off, rubbish.
□ **bitch something up** (*informal*) **make a mess of**, mess up, spoil, ruin, wreck; botch, bungle, mishandle, mismanage; *informal* make a hash of, screw up, louse up, muck up, muff, fluff, foul up; *Brit. informal* make a muck of, make a pig's ear of, cock up, make a Horlicks of; *N. Amer. informal* flub, goof up; *vulgar slang* fuck up, bugger up, balls up.

bitchy ▶ **adjective** (*informal*) *bitchy remarks* **spiteful**, malicious, mean, nasty, cruel, unkind, snide, backbiting, hurtful, wounding, barbed, cutting, hateful, ill-natured, bitter, venomous, vitriolic, poisonous, acid, hostile, rancorous, vindictive, vicious; defamatory, slanderous; *informal* catty; *literary* malefic, maleficent; *rare* squint-eyed.
OPPOSITES charitable, kind.

bite ▶ **verb** **1** *he bit a mouthful from the sandwich* **sink one's teeth into**, chew, munch, crunch, champ, tear at, masticate, eat; nibble at, gnaw at.
2 *the insect does not bite people* **puncture**, prick, pierce, sting, wound.
3 *the acid* **bites into** *the copper plate* **corrode**, eat into, eat away at, wear away, burn (into), etch, erode, dissolve, destroy, consume.
4 *my boots failed to bite* **grip**, hold, get a purchase.
5 *there may be popular unrest as free-market measures begin to bite* **take effect**, have an effect, be effective, be efficacious, work, function, act, have results, take hold; succeed, be successful, work out, go as planned, have the desired effect/result; *informal* come off, pay off, do the trick, do the business; *N. Amer. informal* turn the trick.
6 *a hundred or so retailers are expected to bite* **accept**, go for it, agree, respond; be lured, be enticed, be tempted, be allured; take the bait, rise to the bait.
▶ **noun** **1** *a bite on the ear can be very painful* **nip**, snap, chew, munch, nibble, gnaw.
2 *an insect bite* **puncture**, prick, sting, wound.
3 *Stephen ate a hot dog in three bites* **mouthful**, piece, morsel, bit.
4 *I only have a bite at lunchtime* **snack**, light meal, something to eat, mouthful, soupçon, nibbles, titbit, savoury, appetizer; refreshments; *informal* bite to eat, a little something; *Brit. informal* elevenses.
5 *the appetizer had a fiery bite* **piquancy**, pungency, spice, spiciness, saltiness, pepperiness, flavour, flavouring, savour, taste, tastiness, relish, tang, zest, sharpness, tartness, interest, edge, effect, potency; *informal* kick, punch, oomph, zing.

biting ▶ **adjective** **1** *a biting commentary on contemporary life* **vicious**, harsh, cruel, savage, cutting, sharp, bitter, sarcastic, scathing, incisive, trenchant, caustic, acid, mordant, astringent, acrimonious, acerbic, stinging, blistering, searing, withering; vitriolic, hostile, spiteful, venomous, vindictive, rancorous, abusive, mean, nasty, aggressive, devastating; *informal* bitchy, catty.
OPPOSITE mild.
2 *the biting wind* **bitterly cold**, freezing, icy-cold, arctic, glacial, frigid, frosty, icy, chilly; bitter, piercing, penetrating, nipping, stinging, sharp, raw, harsh, wintry; *informal* nippy; *Brit. informal* parky; *literary* chill.
OPPOSITE balmy.

bitter ▶ **adjective** **1** *very bitter coffee* **sharp**, acid, acidic, pungent, acrid, tart, sour, biting, harsh, unsweetened, vinegary, acetous; *N. Amer.* acerb; *archaic or technical* acerbic.
OPPOSITE sweet.
2 *a bitter old woman* **resentful**, embittered, aggrieved, dissatisfied, disgruntled, discontented, grudge-bearing, grudging, begrudging,

indignant, rancorous, splenetic, spiteful, jaundiced, ill-disposed, sullen, sour, churlish, morose, petulant, peevish, with a chip on one's shoulder.
OPPOSITES magnanimous; content.
3 *today's decision has come as a bitter blow* **painful**, unpleasant, disagreeable, nasty, cruel, awful, distressing, disquieting, disturbing, upsetting, harrowing, heartbreaking, heart-rending, agonizing, unhappy, miserable, wretched, sad, poignant, grievous, traumatic, tragic, chilling, mortifying, galling, vexatious; *rare* distressful.
OPPOSITE welcome.
4 *a bitter north wind* **intensely cold**, bitterly cold, freezing, icy, icy-cold, arctic, glacial, frosty, frigid, chilly; piercing, penetrating, biting, nipping, stinging, sharp, keen, raw, harsh, wintry; *informal* nippy; *Brit. informal* parky; *literary* chill.
OPPOSITES warm, balmy.
5 *a bitter row broke out* **acrimonious**, virulent, angry, rancorous, spiteful, vindictive, vicious, vitriolic, savage, hostile, ferocious, scathing, antagonistic, hate-filled, venomous, poisonous, acrid, bilious, nasty, ill-natured, malign, choleric.
OPPOSITE amicable.

bitterness ▶ noun **1** *the bitterness of the medicine* **sharpness**, acidity, pungency, acridity, tartness, sourness, harshness, vinegariness, acerbity.
OPPOSITE sweetness.
2 *his bitterness against his parents grew* **resentment**, resentfulness, embitteredness, disagreeableness, dissatisfaction, disgruntlement, discontent, grudge, pique, indignation, sourness, rancour, spite, sullenness, churlishness, moroseness, petulance, peevishness, spleen, acrimony.
OPPOSITES magnanimity; contentment.
3 *the bitterness of war* **trauma**, pain, painfulness, agony, grief; unpleasantness, disagreeableness, nastiness, awfulness; upset, heartache, heartbreak, unhappiness, misery, wretchedness, sorrow, sadness, distress, desolation, despair, desperation, poignancy, tragedy.
OPPOSITE delight.
4 *the bitterness of the wind* **intense cold**, bitter cold, iciness, frostiness, chilliness, chill; penetration, intensity, bite, nip, sting, sharpness, keenness, rawness, harshness, wintriness; *Brit. informal* parkiness.
OPPOSITES warmth, balminess.
5 *there was irreconcilable bitterness between strikers and strike-breakers* **acrimony**, hostility, antipathy, antagonism, enmity, animus, friction, virulence, anger, rancour, spite, spitefulness, vindictiveness, viciousness, vitriol, savagery, ferocity, hate, hatred, loathing, detestation, venom, poison, bile, nastiness, ill feeling, ill will, bad blood, malignity, malevolence; *literary or archaic* choler.
OPPOSITE goodwill.

bitty ▶ adjective (*informal*) *the variety of the material leads to the video being rather bitty* **disjointed**, incoherent, fragmented, fragmentary, scrappy, piecemeal; inconsistent, unsystematic, jumbled; variable, varying, irregular, uneven, erratic, fitful, patchy.
OPPOSITE coherent.

bizarre ▶ adjective *his behaviour became more and more bizarre* **strange**, peculiar, odd, funny, curious, offbeat, outlandish, eccentric, unconventional, unorthodox, queer, unexpected, unfamiliar, abnormal, atypical, unusual, out of the ordinary, out of the way, extraordinary; fantastic, remarkable, puzzling, mystifying, mysterious, perplexing, baffling, unaccountable, inexplicable, incongruous, irregular, singular, ludicrous, comical, ridiculous, droll, deviant, aberrant, grotesque, freak, freakish, surreal; *French* outré; *informal* weird, wacky, oddball, way out, freaky, off the wall; *Brit. informal* rum; *N. Amer. informal* wacko, bizarro.
OPPOSITES ordinary, normal.

blab ▶ verb (*informal*) **1** *she blabbed to the press* **talk**, **give the game/show away**, open one's mouth, tell; *informal* let the cat out of the bag, spill the beans; *Brit. informal* blow the gaff, cough.
OPPOSITE keep quiet.
2 *there's no need to blab the whole story* **blurt out**, let slip, let out, tell, reveal, betray, disclose, give away, divulge, leak, take/blow the lid off, blow something wide open; *informal* let on, spill.
OPPOSITE keep something to oneself.

blabber ▶ verb (*informal*) *she blabbered on and on.* See PRATTLE.

blabbermouth ▶ noun (*informal*) *we can't let a blabbermouth loose with information like this.* See CHATTERBOX.

black ▶ adjective **1** *a black horse* **dark**, pitch-black, as black as pitch, pitch-dark, jet-black, inky, coal-black, blackish; *Heraldry* sable; *literary* Stygian; *rare* nigrescent.
OPPOSITE white.
2 *a black night* **unlit**, dark, starless, moonless, unlighted, unilluminated; gloomy, dusky, dim, murky, dingy, shadowy, overcast; *literary* crepuscular, tenebrous; *rare* Stygian, Cimmerian, Tartarean, caliginous.
OPPOSITES clear, bright.
3 *his hands were black from the gardening* **dirty**, filthy, grimy, muddy, mud-caked, grubby, mucky, messy, soiled, stained, smeared, smeary, scummy, slimy, sticky, sooty, dusty, unclean, foul, begrimed, bespattered, befouled, polluted; *informal* cruddy, grungy, yucky, icky, gloopy, crummy; *Brit. informal* manky, gungy, grotty; *Austral./NZ informal* scungy; *literary* besmirched; *rare* feculent.
OPPOSITE clean.
4 *the blackest day of the war* **tragic**, disastrous, calamitous, catastrophic, cataclysmic, ruinous, devastating, fatal, fateful, wretched, woeful, grievous, lamentable, miserable, dire, unfortunate, awful, terrible; *literary* direful.
OPPOSITE joyful.
5 *Mary was in a black mood* **miserable**, unhappy, sad, wretched, broken-hearted, heartbroken, grief-stricken, grieving, sorrowful, sorrowing, mourning, anguished, distressed, desolate, devastated, despairing, inconsolable, disconsolate, downcast, down, downhearted, dejected, crestfallen, cheerless, depressed, pessimistic, melancholy, morose, gloomy, glum, mournful, funereal, doleful, dismal, forlorn, woeful, woebegone, abject, low-spirited, long-faced; *informal* blue, down in the mouth, down in the dumps; *literary* dolorous.
OPPOSITE cheerful.
6 *black humour* **cynical**, sick, macabre, weird, unhealthy, ghoulish, morbid, perverted, gruesome, sadistic, cruel, offensive.
7 *Rory shot her a black look* **angry**, cross, annoyed, irate, vexed, irritated, exasperated, indignant, aggrieved, irked, piqued, displeased, provoked, galled, resentful, irascible, bad-tempered, tetchy, testy, crabby, waspish, dark, dirty, filthy, furious, outraged; **threatening**, menacing, unfriendly, aggressive, belligerent, hostile, antagonistic, evil, evil-intentioned, wicked, nasty, hate-filled, bitter, acrimonious, malevolent, malicious, malignant, malign, venomous, poisonous, vitriolic, vindictive; *Brit. informal* shirty, stroppy, narky, ratty, eggy; *literary* malefic, maleficent.
OPPOSITES pleasant, friendly.
8 (*archaic*) *a black deed* **wicked**, evil, sinful, immoral, wrong, morally wrong, wrongful, bad, iniquitous, corrupt, degenerate, depraved, dissolute, black-hearted; ungodly, unholy, irreligious, unrighteous, sacrilegious, profane, blasphemous, devilish, diabolical, diabolic, fiendish, impious, base, ignoble, mean, vile, irreverent, villainous, nefarious; monstrous, shocking, outrageous, atrocious, abominable, reprehensible, hateful, detestable, despicable, odious, contemptible, horrible, heinous, execrable, godless, vicious, murderous, barbarous, dark, rotten; criminal, illegal, lawless; perverted, reprobate, sordid, dishonourable, unscrupulous; *informal* crooked, bent, warped, low-down, shady; *archaic* dastardly; *rare* peccable, egregious, flagitious.

□ **in the black** *the company's in the black again* **in credit**, in funds, debt-free, out of debt, solvent, financially sound, able to pay one's debts, creditworthy, of good financial standing, solid, secure, profit-making, profitable; *rare* unindebted.
OPPOSITE in debt.

□ **black and white 1** *a black-and-white picture* **monochrome**, greyscale.
OPPOSITE colour.
2 *I wish to see the proposals* **in black and white in print**, printed, written down, set down, on paper, committed to paper, recorded, on record, documented, clearly/plainly/explicitly defined.
OPPOSITE spoken.
3 *they tend to talk around the subject instead of making black-and-white statements* **categorical**, unequivocal, absolute, uncompromising, unconditional, unqualified, unambiguous, clear, clear-cut, positive, straightforward, definite, definitive; simplistic, shallow, pat, glib, jejune, naive.
OPPOSITE equivocal.
4 *children think* **in black and white**, *good and bad* **in absolute terms**, unequivocally, without shades of grey, categorically, uncompromisingly, unconditionally, unambiguously, clearly, positively, straightforwardly, definitely, definitively; simplistically, shallowly, patly, glibly, jejunely, naively.
OPPOSITE equivocally.

▶ verb **1** *the steps of the houses were neatly blacked.* See BLACKEN.
2 *he broke his nose and blacked his eye* **bruise**, contuse; hit, punch, injure; make black, discolour.
3 (*Brit. dated*) *trade union members blacked the work* **boycott**, embargo, put/place an embargo on, blacklist, ban, bar, proscribe.

□ **black out** *the pain hit him and he blacked out* **faint**, lose consciousness, pass out, collapse, keel over; *informal* flake out, conk out, go out; *literary* swoon.

□ **black something out 1** *the city was blacked out as an air-raid precaution* **darken**, make dark/darker, shade, turn off the lights in; keep the light out of.
2 *the report on the incident has over 200 pages blacked out* **censor**, suppress, withhold, cover up, hide, conceal, obscure, veil, draw/pull a veil over, hush up, sweep under the carpet, whitewash.

WORD LINKS
related prefix **melan-** (e.g. ***melanin, Melanesia***)

blackball ▶ verb *her husband was blackballed when he tried to join the Country Club* **reject**, debar, bar, ban, vote against, blacklist, exclude, shut out, leave out in the cold; expel, drum out, oust, cashier, ostracize, repudiate; boycott, snub, shun, spurn, cold-shoulder, give the cold shoulder to; *N. Amer.* disfellowship.

OPPOSITE admit.

blacken ▸ verb **1** *you use it to blacken your hair* **make black**, black, darken, make dark/darker; dirty, make dirty, make sooty, make smoky, stain, grime, begrime, befoul, soil.
OPPOSITES whiten, clean.
2 *the sky blackened* **grow/become black**, **darken**, dim, grow dim, cloud over.
OPPOSITES lighten, brighten.
3 *she won't thank you for blackening her husband's name* **sully**, tarnish, blot, besmirch, drag through the mud/mire, stain, taint, smear, smudge, befoul, soil, contaminate, pollute, disgrace, dishonour, bring discredit to, injure, damage, spoil; slander, defame, traduce; *literary* besmear, smirch; *archaic* spot, breathe on.
OPPOSITES clear, enhance.

blackguard ▸ noun (*archaic*). *See* VILLAIN.

blacklist ▸ verb *workers were blacklisted after being quoted in the newspaper* **boycott**, ostracize, avoid, embargo, put/place an embargo on, consider undesirable, steer clear of, ignore; refuse to employ; *Brit. dated* black.

black magic ▸ noun *they were found guilty of practising black magic* **sorcery**, magic, witchcraft, wizardry, necromancy, enchantment, spell-working, incantation, the supernatural, occultism, the occult, the black arts, devilry; malediction, voodoo, hoodoo, witching, witchery, hex, spell, jinx; *N. Amer.* mojo, orenda; *NZ* makutu; *S. African informal* muti; *rare* sortilege, thaumaturgy, theurgy.

blackmail ▸ noun *troops using narcotics could be susceptible to blackmail* **extortion**, demanding money with menaces, exaction, intimidation; protection racket, bribery; wringing, milking, bleeding, bloodsucking; *informal* hush money; *archaic* chantage.
▸ verb **1** *he was going to blackmail the murderers* **extort money from**, threaten, hold to ransom, milk, bleed; *informal* demand hush money from.
2 *she had tried to blackmail him into marrying her* **coerce**, pressurize, pressure, bring pressure to bear on, bulldoze, force, railroad; *informal* lean on, put the screws on, twist someone's arm.

blackout ▸ noun **1** *a generator would power the computer in the event of a blackout* **power cut**, power failure, electricity failure; trip, blown fuse; brown-out.
2 *the authorities imposed a news blackout* **suppression**, silence, censorship, reporting restrictions, non-communication, cut-off.
3 *he had a blackout on the street* **faint**, fainting fit, loss of consciousness, coma, passing out, period of oblivion, swoon, collapse; *Medicine* syncope.

bladder ▸ noun

WORD LINKS
relating to a bladder **cystic, vesical**

blame ▸ verb **1** *the inquiry blamed the train driver for the accident* **hold responsible**, hold accountable, hold liable, place/lay the blame on; censure, criticize, condemn, accuse of, find/consider guilty of; assign fault/liability/guilt to; *archaic* inculpate.
OPPOSITES absolve; forgive.
2 *they* **blame** *youth crime* **on** *unemployment* **ascribe to**, attribute to, impute to, lay at the door of, put down to, set down to; *informal* pin, stick.
▸ noun *he was cleared of all blame for the incident* **responsibility**, guilt, accountability, liability, onus, blameworthiness, culpability, fault; censure, criticism, condemnation, recrimination; *informal* rap.

blameless ▸ adjective *he led a blameless life* **innocent**, guiltless, above reproach, beyond criticism, above suspicion, irreproachable, unimpeachable, in the clear, not to blame, without fault, faultless, exemplary, perfect, virtuous, pure, moral, upright, impeccable, sinless, unblemished, spotless, stainless, untarnished; *informal* squeaky clean.
OPPOSITES blameworthy, guilty.

CHOOSE THE RIGHT WORD
blameless, innocent, guiltless
See INNOCENT.

blameworthy ▸ adjective *do you consider him blameworthy?* **culpable**, reprehensible, indefensible, inexcusable, guilty, criminal, delinquent, sinful, wicked, wrong, evil, shameful, discreditable; to blame, at fault, blameable, condemnable, censurable, reproachable, responsible, answerable, offending, erring, errant, in the wrong; *rare* reprovable.
OPPOSITES blameless, innocent.

blanch ▸ verb **1** *the moon blanches her hair* **make/turn pale**, whiten, make/turn pallid, lighten, grey, wash out, fade, blench, etiolate, decolorize, bleach, peroxide.
OPPOSITES colour, darken, redden.
2 *his face blanched* **pale**, go/grow/turn/become pale, go/grow/turn/become white, whiten, go/grow/turn/become pallid, lose its colour, lighten, bleach, fade, blench.
OPPOSITES colour, darken, blush.
3 *blanch the spinach leaves in boiling water* **scald**, boil, dunk.

bland ▸ adjective **1** *the peppers give the bland turkey a piquant flavour* **tasteless**, flavourless, insipid, mild, savourless, unflavoured, weak, thin, watery, watered-down, spiceless, unappetizing; *informal* wishy-washy.
OPPOSITE tangy.
2 *a very bland general election campaign* **uninteresting**, dull, boring, tedious, monotonous, dry, drab, dreary, wearisome; unexciting, unimaginative, uninspiring, uninspired, weak, insipid, colourless, lustreless, lacklustre, vapid, flat, stale, trite, vacuous, feeble, pallid, wishy-washy; limp, lame, tired, lifeless, torpid, unanimated, zestless, spiritless, sterile, anaemic, barren, tame, bloodless, antiseptic; middle-of-the-road, run-of-the-mill, commonplace, mediocre, nondescript, characterless, mundane, inoffensive, humdrum, prosaic.
OPPOSITES interesting, stimulating.
3 *bland breezes* **temperate**, mild, soft, calm, balmy, soothing, benign.
OPPOSITES violent, destructive.

blandishments ▸ plural noun *consumers have the capacity to resist the blandishments of advertisers* **flattery**, cajolery, coaxing, wheedling, honeyed words, smooth talk, soft words, blarney; fulsomeness, simpering, fawning, toadying, ingratiating, ingratiation, currying favour, inveiglement; charm offensive; *informal* sweet talk, soft soap, smarm, spiel, ego massage, buttering up, cosying up, cuddling up; *Brit. informal* flannel; *Austral./NZ informal* guyver, smoodging; *rare* glozing, lipsalve, cajolement.

blank ▸ adjective **1** *a blank sheet of paper* **empty**, unfilled, unmarked, unwritten on, unused, clear, free, bare, clean, plain, spotless, white; vacant, void.
OPPOSITE full.
2 *a blank face* **expressionless**, empty, vacant, deadpan, wooden, stony, impassive, inanimate, poker-faced, vacuous, glazed, fixed, lifeless, uninterested, emotionless, unresponsive, inscrutable.
OPPOSITES expressive, mobile.
3 *'What?' said Maxim, looking blank* **baffled**, nonplussed, mystified, stumped, at a loss, stuck, puzzled, perplexed, bewildered, bemused, ignorant, lost, muddled, uncomprehending, befuddled, fuddled, addled, (all) at sea, at sixes and sevens, confused; *informal* clueless, flummoxed, bamboozled, discombobulated, fazed, beaten.
4 *a blank refusal* **outright**, absolute, categorical, unqualified, utter, complete, thorough, flat, straight, positive, certain, explicit, unequivocal, unambiguous, unmistakable, plain, clear, clear-cut.
▸ noun **1** *leave blanks to type in the appropriate names* **space**, gap, blank space, empty space.
2 *that period is a blank to her now* **void**, vacuum, emptiness, vacancy.

blanket ▸ noun **1** *the bed had a red blanket on it* **cover**, covering, rug, afghan, quilt, eiderdown, duvet; bedcover, bedspread, throw-over; bedclothes; *N. Amer.* throw, spread; *S. African* kaross; (*in Latin America*) serape; *archaic* coverlet, counterpane.
2 *a dense grey blanket of cloud* **covering**, layer, cover, coat, coating, film, sheet, carpet, veneer, surface, skin, thickness, overlay, cloak, mantle, veil, pall, shroud, screen, mask, cloud, curtain.
▸ adjective *a blanket ban on tobacco advertising* **wholesale**, across the board, outright, indiscriminate, overall, general, mass, umbrella, inclusive, all-inclusive, all-round, sweeping, total, complete, comprehensive, thorough, extensive, wide-ranging, far-reaching, large-scale, widespread; universal, global, worldwide, international, nationwide, countrywide, coast-to-coast, company-wide.
OPPOSITES partial, piecemeal.
▸ verb **1** *snow blanketed the mountains* **cover**, coat, carpet, overlay, overlie, overspread, extend over, cap, top, crown; conceal, obscure, blot out, hide, mask, cloud, cloak, veil, shroud, swathe, envelop, submerge, surround; *literary* mantle, enshroud.
2 *the double glazing blankets the noise a bit* **muffle**, deaden, soften, mute, silence, quieten, smother, dampen, damp down, tone down, mask, suppress, reduce, abate, kill.
OPPOSITE amplify.

blare ▸ verb *sirens blared across the town* **blast**, sound loudly, trumpet, clamour, boom, roar, thunder, bellow, resound, honk, toot, shriek, screech.
OPPOSITES murmur, waft.
▸ noun *the blare of trumpets* **blast**, blasting, clamour, boom, booming, roar, roaring, thunder, thundering, bellow, bellowing, resounding, honk, honking, shriek, shrieking, screech.
OPPOSITE murmur.

blarney ▸ noun *it took all my Irish blarney to keep us out of court* **blandishments**, honeyed words, smooth talk, soft words, flattery, cajolery, coaxing, wheedling, compliments; fulsomeness, simpering, fawning, toadying, ingratiation, currying favour, inveiglement; charm offensive; *informal* sweet talk, soft soap, smarm, spiel, ego massage, buttering up, cosying up, cuddling up; *Brit. informal* flannel; *Austral./NZ informal* guyver, smoodging; *archaic* glozing, lipsalve; *rare* cajolement.

blasé ▸ adjective *she was becoming quite* **blasé about** *the dangers* **indifferent to**, unconcerned about, uncaring about, casual about, nonchalant about, offhand about, uninterested in, uninvolved in/with, apathetic towards, unimpressed by, bored by, weary of, unmoved by, unresponsive to,

lukewarm about, unenthusiastic about, phlegmatic about; impassive, dispassionate, emotionless, insouciant; jaded, surfeited, glutted, cloyed, satiated; *rare* poco-curante.
OPPOSITES responsive, excited.

blaspheme ▶ verb *how could you blaspheme in church?* **swear**, curse, utter oaths, utter profanities, take the Lord's name in vain; *informal* cuss; *archaic* execrate, imprecate.

blasphemous ▶ adjective *a blasphemous mock communion* **sacrilegious**, profane, irreligious, irreverent, impious, ungodly, godless, unholy, disrespectful; *archaic* execratory, execrative; *rare* desecrative, imprecatory.
OPPOSITE reverent.

blasphemy ▶ noun *he was condemned for his blasphemy* **profanity**, profaneness, sacrilege, irreligiousness, irreverence, taking the Lord's name in vain, swearing, curse, cursing, impiety, impiousness, ungodliness, unholiness, desecration, disrespect; *formal* imprecation; *archaic* execration.
OPPOSITE reverence.

blast ▶ noun **1** *the blast blew in dozens of windows* **shock wave**, pressure wave, bang, crash, crack.
2 *a bomb blast* **explosion**, detonation, discharge, burst, eruption.
3 *a sudden blast of cold air* **gust**, rush, blow, gale, squall, storm, wind, draught, waft, puff, flurry, breeze.
4 *a blast of the ship's siren* **blare**, blaring, honk, bellow, boom, roar, screech, wail.
5 (*informal*) *I braced myself for the inevitable blast* **reprimand**, rebuke, reproof, admonishment, admonition, reproach, reproval, scolding, remonstration, upbraiding, castigation, lambasting, lecture, criticism, censure; *informal* telling-off, rap, rap over the knuckles, slap on the wrist, flea in one's ear, dressing-down, earful, roasting, tongue-lashing, bawling-out, caning, blowing-up; *Brit. informal* ticking-off, carpeting, wigging, rollicking, rocket, row; *Austral./NZ informal* serve; *Brit. vulgar slang* bollocking; *dated* rating.
OPPOSITE commendation.
▶ verb **1** *fighter-bombers were blasting enemy airfields* **blow up**, bomb, blow (to pieces), dynamite, explode; break up, demolish, raze to the ground, destroy, ruin, shatter.
2 *heavy Browning machine guns were blasting away* **fire (away)**, shoot (away), blaze (away), let fly; discharge.
3 *an impatient motorist blasted his horn* **honk**, sound loudly, trumpet, blare, boom, roar.
4 *radios blasting out pop music* **blare**, boom, roar, thunder, bellow, pump, shriek, screech.
5 *Fowler was blasted with an air gun* **shoot (down)**, gun down, mow down, cut down, put a bullet in, pick off, bag, fell, kill; *informal* pot, pump full of lead, plug, zap, let someone have it; *N. Amer. informal* smoke; *literary* slay.
6 (*literary*) *frost blasted the plants* **blight**, kill, destroy, wither, shrivel.
7 *poverty was blasting their hopes* **destroy**, crush, dash, blight, wreck, ruin, spoil, mar, annihilate, disappoint, frustrate.
8 (*informal*) *he blasted the pupils for being late* **reprimand**, rebuke, criticize, upbraid, berate, castigate, reprove, rail at, flay.
□ **blast off** *a rocket blasted off for a rendezvous with the space station* **be launched**, take off, lift off, leave the ground, become airborne, take to the air.
OPPOSITE touch down.

blasted ▶ adjective (*informal*) *make your own blasted coffee!* **damned**, damn, blessed, flaming, precious, confounded, pestilential, rotten, wretched; *Brit. informal* flipping, blinking, blooming, bloody, bleeding, effing, chuffing; *Austral./NZ informal* plurry; *Brit. informal, dated* bally, ruddy, deuced; *vulgar slang* fucking, frigging; *Irish vulgar slang* fecking; *dated* cursed, accursed, damnable.

blast-off ▶ noun *the rocket was ready for blast-off* **launch**, launching, lift-off, take-off, ascent, firing, flight.
OPPOSITE touchdown.

blatant ▶ adjective *a blatant lie* **flagrant**, glaring, obvious, undisguised, unconcealed, overt, open, transparent, patent, evident, manifest, palpable, unmistakable; **shameless**, unabashed, unashamed, without shame, impudent, insolent, audacious, unembarrassed, unblushing, brazen, barefaced, brass-necked, brash, bold, unrepentant; *archaic* arrant.
OPPOSITES inconspicuous, subtle.

blather ▶ verb *he just blathered on and on* **prattle**, babble, chatter, twitter, prate, gabble, jabber, go on, run on, rattle on/away, yap, jibber-jabber, patter, blether, blither, maunder, ramble, drivel; *informal* yak, yackety-yak, yabber, yatter; *Brit. informal* witter, rabbit, chunter, natter, waffle; *Scottish & Irish informal* slabber; *Austral./NZ informal* mag; *archaic* twaddle, clack, twattle.
▶ noun *he has to write about all the blather at the town council* **prattle**, chatter, twitter, babble, talk, prating, gabble, jabber, blether, rambling; **nonsense**, rubbish, balderdash, gibberish, claptrap; *informal* yackety-yak, yabbering, yatter, rot, tripe, twaddle, hogwash, baloney, drivel, bilge, bosh, bull, bunk, guff, eyewash, piffle, poppycock, phooey, hooey, malarkey, dribble; *Brit. informal* wittering, nattering, chuntering, cobblers, codswallop, stuff and nonsense, tosh, cack; *Scottish & N. English informal* havers; *N. Amer. informal* garbage, flapdoodle, blathers, wack, bushwa, applesauce; *informal, dated* bunkum, tommyrot, cod, gammon, toffee; *vulgar slang* shit, bullshit, horseshit, crap, bollocks, balls; *Austral./NZ vulgar slang* bulldust; *archaic* clack, twattle.

blaze ▶ noun **1** *twenty firemen fought the blaze* **fire**, flames, conflagration, inferno, holocaust, firestorm.
2 *the blaze of light from the security lamps* **glare**, gleam, flash, burst, flare, dazzle, streak, radiance, brilliance, beam, glitter.
3 *he left in a blaze of anger* **outburst**, burst, eruption, flare-up, explosion, outbreak, blow-up; blast, attack, fit, spasm, paroxysm, access, rush, gale, flood, storm, hurricane, torrent, outpouring, surge, upsurge, spurt, effusion, outflow, outflowing, welling up; *informal* splurt; *rare* ebullition, boutade.
▶ verb **1** *the fire blazed merrily* **burn**, be ablaze, be alight, be on fire, be in flames, flame, be aflame, flare up; *literary* be afire; *archaic* be ardent.
2 *he drove straight through the crowd, lights blazing* **shine**, beam, flash, flare, glare, gleam, glint, dazzle, glitter, glisten, be radiant, burn brightly.
3 *soldiers blazed away with sub-machine guns* **fire (away)**, shoot (away), blast (away), let fly; discharge.

blazon ▶ verb **1** *the manufacturer's name is blazoned across sporting events* **display**, exhibit, show, put on display, draw attention to, present, spread, emblazon, plaster, flaunt, parade, reveal.
2 *the newspapers blazoned the news* **publicize**, make known, make public, bring to public notice/attention, announce, report, communicate, impart, disclose, reveal, divulge, leak, publish, broadcast, transmit, issue, post, put out, distribute, spread, unfold, disseminate, circulate, air, herald, trumpet, advertise, proclaim, promulgate; *informal* splatter.

bleach ▶ verb **1** *the blinds had been bleached by the sun* **make/turn white**, whiten, make/turn pale, make/turn pallid, blanch, lighten, fade, wash out, decolour, decolorize, peroxide, etiolate.
2 *they saw bones bleaching in the desert* **go/grow/turn/become white**, whiten, go/turn/grow/become pale, pale, go/grow/turn/become pallid, blanch, lose its colour, be washed out, lighten, fade, blench.

bleak ▶ adjective **1** *a bleak landscape* **bare**, exposed, desolate, stark, arid, desert, denuded, lunar, open, empty, windswept; treeless, forestless, without vegetation, defoliated; unsheltered, unprotected, unshielded; *rare* unwooded.
OPPOSITES lush, verdant.
2 *a bleak wind had got up* **cold**, keen, raw, harsh, wintry; piercing, penetrating, biting, nipping, stinging, sharp; freezing, icy, icy-cold, frosty, frigid, chilly; *informal* nippy; *Brit. informal* parky; *literary* chill.
OPPOSITES warm, balmy.
3 *the future looks bleak* **unpromising**, unfavourable, unpropitious, inauspicious, adverse, disadvantageous, uninviting, discouraging, disheartening, depressing, cheerless, joyless, gloomy, sombre, dreary, dismal, wretched, miserable, black, dark, grim, drab, portentous, foreboding, hopeless, ominous.
OPPOSITES promising, hopeful.

bleary ▶ adjective *he tried to focus his bleary eyes* **blurred**, blurry, unfocused; fogged, clouded, cloudy, dim, dull, filmy; muzzy, tired; moist, misty, watery, rheumy; *archaic* blear.
OPPOSITES clear, limpid.

bleat ▶ verb **1** *the sheep were bleating in the field* **baa**, maa, cry, call; *N. Amer. informal* blat.
2 *don't bleat to me about fairness* **complain**, moan, mutter, grumble, grouse, groan, grouch, growl, carp, snivel, make a fuss; *Scottish & Irish* gurn; *informal* gripe, beef, bellyache, bitch, whinge, sound off, go on; *Brit. informal* chunter, create, be on at someone; *N. English informal* mither; *N. Amer. informal* kvetch; *S. African informal* chirp; *Brit. dated* crib, natter.

bleed ▶ verb **1** *his arm was bleeding badly* **lose blood**, haemorrhage.
2 *the doctor bled him* **draw blood from**; *technical* phlebotomize, venesect, exsanguinate.
OPPOSITE transfuse.
3 *one colour bled into another* **flow**, run, ooze, seep, trickle, leak, filter, percolate, escape, leach; permeate, merge with.
4 *sap was bleeding from a cut in the trunk* **flow**, run, ooze, seep, exude, weep, gush, spurt.
5 *the country is being bled dry by poachers* **drain**, exhaust, sap, deplete, deprive, milk, suck dry, empty, reduce.
6 *my heart bleeds for them* **grieve**, ache, sorrow, be sorrowful, be sad, mourn, be mournful, be distressed, be in distress, be miserable, lament, feel, suffer, agonize, anguish, be in anguish; sympathize with, pity; eat one's heart out, weep and wail.

blemish ▶ noun **1** *not a blemish marred her milky skin* **imperfection**, fault, flaw, defect, deformity, discoloration, disfigurement; bruise, scar, pit, pockmark, pock, scratch, dent, chip, notch, nick, line, score, cut, incision, gash; **mark**, streak, spot, fleck, dot, blot, stain, smear, patch, trace, speck, speckle, blotch, smudge, smut, smirch, fingermark, fingerprint, impression, imprint; marking, blaze, stripe; birthmark; *informal* splotch, splodge; *technical* stigma.
OPPOSITE enhancement.
2 *local government is not without blemish* **defect**, fault, failing, flaw, imperfection, frailty, fallibility, foible, vice; shortcoming, weakness, weak spot, weak point, deficiency, limitation; blot, taint, stain, smirch,

B

dishonour, disgrace.
OPPOSITE virtue.

▶ **verb 1** *neither bungalow nor caravan blemished the coast* **mar**, spoil, impair, disfigure, blight, deface, flaw, mark, spot, speckle, blotch, discolour, scar; ruin, destroy, wreck; be a blot on the landscape; *rare* disfeature.
OPPOSITE enhance.
2 *his reign as world champion has been blemished by controversy* **sully**, tarnish, besmirch, blacken, smirch, stain, blot, taint, soil, befoul, spoil, ruin, dirty, disgrace, mar, damage, defame, calumniate, injure, harm, hurt, undermine, debase, degrade, denigrate, dishonour, stigmatize; *informal* drag through the mud; *rare* vitiate.

> **CHOOSE THE RIGHT WORD**
>
> **blemish, imperfection, flaw**
>
> These words all denote a noticeable feature of something that reduces its value or attractiveness.
>
> - A **blemish** is a small mark or injury spoiling the appearance of an otherwise smooth or beautiful surface, especially skin (*your skin hasn't a single blemish*). A blemish may appear unexpectedly on the surface of something that was previously perfect.
> - **Imperfections** are shortcomings which tend to be inherent, unlike *blemishes*, which are generally superficial (*the policy has its imperfections | great art is, like religion, concerned with moral imperfections*).
> - **Flaw** is derived from a Middle English word for 'fragment' or 'splinter'. *Flaws* are inherent cracks or marks on a surface (*most natural crystals have flaws*). A *flaw* may also be a deep imperfection, one that affects and undermines the whole nature of someone or something (*a flaw at the heart of NATO's deterrent strategy*). Nouns commonly described as having flaws include *security, design, strategy, character,* and *system*. The perception that a flaw is more than skin-deep is reflected in the fact that skin may have *imperfections* or *blemishes* but not *flaws*.

blench ▶ **verb** *she blenched at the size of the bill* **flinch**, start, shy (away), recoil, shrink, pull back, back away, draw back, cringe, wince, quiver, shudder, shiver, tremble, quake, shake, quail, cower, waver, falter, hesitate, get cold feet, blanch.

blend ▶ **verb 1** *blend the ingredients until smooth | this allows the flavours to blend together* **mix**, mingle, combine, put together, stir, whisk, fold in, jumble, merge; fuse, unite, unify, join, amalgamate, incorporate; meld, marry, compound, alloy, coalesce, homogenize, intermingle, intermix, interpenetrate; integrate, emulsify, premix; *informal* blunge; *rare* admix, commingle, interflow, commix.
OPPOSITE clash.
2 *the recent buildings* **blend with** *the older ones* **harmonize**, go, go well, go together, fit (in), tone, be in tune, dovetail, coordinate, team, accord, be compatible; match, suit, complement, set off.

▶ **noun** *the chutney is a blend of bananas, raisins, and ginger* **mixture**, mix, combination, admixture, mingling, commingling, amalgamation, amalgam, union, conjunction, marriage, merging, compound, alloy, fusion, meld, composite, concoction, synthesis, homogenization; miscellany, jumble, hotchpotch.

bless ▶ **verb 1** *the chaplain said more prayers and blessed the couple* **ask God's favour for**, ask God's protection for, give a benediction for, invoke happiness on.
OPPOSITE curse.
2 *the Cardinal blessed the memorial plaque* **consecrate**, sanctify, hallow, dedicate (to God), make holy, make sacred, set apart, devote to God; anoint, ordain, canonize, beatify.
OPPOSITE deconsecrate.
3 *let us bless the name of the Lord* **praise**, worship, glorify, honour, exalt, adore, pay tribute to, pay homage to, give thanks to, venerate, reverence, hallow; *archaic* magnify, laud.
4 *the gods have* **blessed us with** *magical voices* **endow**, favour, provide, grace, bestow, furnish, entrust, present; grant, vouchsafe, afford, accord, give, donate; confer on, lavish on; *literary* endue.
OPPOSITE trouble.
5 *I bless the day you came here* **give thanks for**, express gratitude for, be grateful for; thank, appreciate, celebrate.
OPPOSITE rue.
6 *the government refused to bless the undertaking* **sanction**, consent to, give consent for, give assent to, endorse, agree to, concur with, approve, give approval for, give one's blessing to, back, support, be in favour of, smile on; *informal* give the thumbs up to, give the green light to, OK; *N. Amer. rare* approbate.
OPPOSITE oppose.

blessed ▶ **adjective 1** *a blessed place* **holy**, sacred, hallowed, consecrated, sanctified, divine, dedicated, venerated, revered, ordained, canonized, beatified.
OPPOSITE cursed.
2 *blessed are the meek* **favoured**, fortunate, lucky, privileged, select, happy, joyful, joyous, blissful, glad, enviable.
OPPOSITE wretched.
3 *the fresh air made a blessed change from the polluted city atmosphere* **welcome**, pleasant, pleasing, agreeable, refreshing, favourable, cheering, gratifying, heartening, much needed, to one's liking, to one's taste.
OPPOSITE unwelcome.
4 (*informal*) *never mind the blessed television. See* DAMNED *sense 2.*

> **CHOOSE THE RIGHT WORD**
>
> **blessed, sacred, holy, hallowed**
>
> *See* SACRED.

blessing ▶ **noun 1** *may God continue to give us his blessing* **protection**, favour.
OPPOSITE condemnation.
2 *they received a special blessing from a Catholic priest* **benediction**, dedication, consecration, invocation, commendation, prayer for someone, intercession; grace, thanksgiving, thanks; *Jewish* kiddush; *archaic* orison.
OPPOSITE anathema.
3 *he gave the plan his blessing* **sanction**, consent, assent, endorsement, clearance, agreement, concurrence, approval, seal of approval, stamp of approval, imprimatur, backing, support, favour, good wishes; *informal* the go-ahead, the thumbs up, the green light, the OK; *formal* approbation.
4 *it was a blessing that they didn't have very far to go* **advantage**, benefit, help, boon, good thing, godsend, favour, gift, convenience; bonus, plus point, added attraction, additional benefit, extra, added extra; luck, stroke of luck, piece of luck, good fortune, windfall, gain, profit, virtue, bounty; *informal* plus, perk; *literary* benison.
OPPOSITE affliction.

blight ▶ **noun 1** *potato blight* **disease**, canker, infestation, fungus, mildew, mould, rot, decay.
2 *the government are protecting people from the blight of aircraft noise* **affliction**, scourge, bane, curse, plague, menace, evil, misfortune, woe, calamity, trouble, ordeal, thorn in one's flesh/side, trial, tribulation, visitation, nuisance, pest, pollution, contamination, cancer, canker.
OPPOSITE blessing.

▶ **verb 1** *a peach tree blighted by leaf curl* **infect**, wither, shrivel, blast, mildew, nip in the bud, kill, destroy.
2 *the scandal blighted the careers of several leading politicians* **ruin**, wreck, spoil, disrupt, undo, mar, play havoc with, make a mess of, put an end to, end, bring to an end, put a stop to, prevent, frustrate, crush, quell, quash, dash, destroy, scotch, shatter, devastate, demolish, sabotage; *informal* mess up, screw up, louse up, foul up, make a hash of, do in, put paid to, put the lid on, put the kibosh on, stymie, queer, nix, banjax, blow a hole in; *Brit. informal* scupper, dish, throw a spanner in the works of; *N. Amer. informal* throw a monkey wrench in the works of; *Austral. informal* euchre, cruel; *archaic* bring to naught.

blind ▶ **adjective 1** *he has been blind since birth* **sightless**, unsighted, visually impaired, visionless, unseeing, stone blind, eyeless; partially sighted, half blind, purblind; *informal* as blind as a bat; *Austral. informal* boko.
OPPOSITE sighted.
2 *she was ignorant, but not stupid or blind* **imperceptive**, unperceptive, slow, obtuse, stupid, uncomprehending, unimaginative, insensitive, thick-skinned, bovine, stolid, unintelligent; *informal* dense, dim, dim-witted, thick, slow on the uptake, dumb, dopey, not with it; *Brit. informal* dozy; *Scottish & N. English informal* glaikit; *N. Amer. informal* dumb-ass, chowderheaded; *S. African informal* dof.
OPPOSITE perceptive.
3 *you should be* **blind to** *failure at your age* **unmindful of**, mindless of, careless of, heedless of, oblivious to, insensible to, unconcerned about/by, inattentive to, indifferent to; *rare* insensitive of, negligent of.
OPPOSITE mindful.
4 *a blind acceptance of conventional opinions* **uncritical**, unreasoned, unthinking, unconsidered, mindless, injudicious, undiscerning, indiscriminate; airy, insouciant; credulous, naive.
OPPOSITE discerning.
5 *in a blind rage* **impetuous**, impulsive, rash, hasty, reckless, uncontrolled, uncontrollable, uninhibited, unrestrained, immoderate, intemperate, wild, unruly, irrational, frantic, violent, furious, unbridled, uncurbed, unchecked, unrepressed.
OPPOSITE calm.
6 *a blind alley* **without exit**, exitless, blocked, closed, barred, impassable; dead end, no through road, cul-de-sac.
OPPOSITE through.

▶ **verb 1** *he was blinded in a car crash* **make blind**, deprive of sight, deprive of vision, render unsighted, render sightless, put someone's eyes out, gouge someone's eyes out.
2 *the salt water blinded him temporarily* **stop someone seeing**, obscure

someone's vision, block someone's vision, get in someone's line of vision.
3 *Perdita was blinded by sunshine* **dazzle**.
4 *scaffolding blinded the windows* **obscure**, cover, blot out, blanket, mask, shroud, hide, conceal, block, darken, eclipse, obstruct.
OPPOSITE reveal.
5 *he was blinded by his faith* **deprive of understanding**, deprive of perception, deprive of judgement, deprive of reason, deprive of sense.
6 *they try to blind you with science* **overawe**, awe, intimidate, daunt, deter, cow, abash; disquiet, make anxious, make uneasy, perturb, discomfit, disconcert; **confuse**, nonplus, bewilder, confound, perplex, overwhelm; **unsettle**, discompose, unnerve, discourage, subdue, dismay, frighten, alarm, scare, terrify, terrorize, browbeat, bully, trouble, bother, agitate, fluster, ruffle, jolt, shake (up), throw, put off, take aback, unbalance, destabilize, throw off balance, put off one's stroke, pull the rug (out) from under; *informal* rattle, faze, psych out.
▶ **noun 1** *a window blind* **screen**, shade, louvre, awning, canopy, sunshade, curtain, shutter, cover, covering, protection; Venetian blind, Austrian blind, roller blind; *French* jalousie, persienne.
2 *he'd claim that some crook had sent the card as a blind* **deception**, camouflage, screen, smokescreen, front, facade, cover, disguise, cloak, pretext, masquerade, mask, feint; trick, stratagem, ploy, ruse, scheme, device, move, manoeuvre, contrivance, machination, expedient, artifice, wile, dodge.

blindly ▶ **adverb 1** *he continued to stare blindly ahead* **sightlessly**, without sight, without vision, unseeingly.
2 *he ran blindly upstairs* **impetuously**, impulsively, rashly, hastily, recklessly, heedlessly, uncontrolledly, uncontrollably, uninhibitedly, unrestrainedly, wildly, irrationally, frantically, violently, furiously.
OPPOSITE cautiously.
3 *the government has blindly followed US policy* **uncritically**, unthinkingly, mindlessly, injudiciously, indiscriminately; airily, insouciantly; credulously, naively; *rare* undiscerningly.
OPPOSITE critically.

blink ▶ **verb 1** *the man's eyes did not blink* **shut and open**, flutter, flicker, wink, bat; *technical* nictitate, nictate.
2 *several red lights on the control panel had begun to blink* **flash**, flicker, twinkle, waver, wink, scintillate, glint, glimmer, glitter, shine (intermittently).
3 *no one even blinks at the 'waitresses' in drag* **be surprised**, **look twice**, be startled, be shocked; *informal* boggle.

blinkered ▶ **adjective** *blinkered ideological dogma* **narrow-minded**, limited, restricted, inward-looking, conventional, parochial, provincial, insular, small-town, localist, small-minded, petty-minded, petty, close-minded, short-sighted, myopic, hidebound, dyed-in-the-wool, diehard, set, set in one's ways, inflexible, dogmatic, rigid, entrenched, prejudiced, bigoted, biased, partisan, sectarian, discriminatory; *Brit.* parish-pump, blimpish; *French* borné; *N. Amer. informal* jerkwater; *rare* claustral.
OPPOSITE broad-minded.

bliss ▶ **noun 1** *it was sheer bliss to be there* **joy**, pleasure, delight, happiness, gladness, ecstasy, elation, rapture, euphoria, heaven, paradise, seventh heaven, cloud nine, Eden, Utopia, Arcadia; halcyon days; *informal* the top of the world.
OPPOSITE misery.
2 *religions promise perfect bliss after death* **blessedness**, blessing, benediction, glory, heaven, paradise, heavenly joy, divine happiness, supreme happiness, divine rapture, beatitude, saintliness, sainthood.
OPPOSITE hell.

blissful ▶ **adjective** *they spent a blissful week together* **ecstatic**, rapturous, joyful, joyous, elated, beatific, euphoric, enraptured, on cloud nine, in seventh heaven, transported, in transports, in raptures, beside oneself with joy/happiness, rhapsodic, ravished, enchanted, enthusiastic, delighted, thrilled, overjoyed, happy; *informal* over the moon, on top of the world, blissed out; *Austral. informal* wrapped.
OPPOSITE miserable.

blister ▶ **noun 1** *his heels were covered in blisters* bleb, bulla, pustule, vesicle, vesication, blain.
2 *check for cracks and blisters in sheet roofing felt* **bubble**, swelling, bulge, bump, lump, protuberance; cavity, hollow, void.

blistering ▶ **adjective 1** *the blistering heat of the desert* **intense**, extreme, ferocious, fierce, acute, strong, very great; **scorching**, searing, flaming, blazing (hot), baking (hot), burning, fiery, torrid, parching, withering; *informal* boiling, boiling hot, sizzling, roasting, sweltering.
OPPOSITE icy.
2 *a blistering attack on the government's transport policy* **savage**, vicious, fierce, bitter, severe, sharp, harsh, scathing, devastating, mordant, trenchant, caustic, cutting, biting, stinging, searing, withering, virulent, vitriolic.
OPPOSITE mild.
3 *Burke set a blistering pace* **very fast**, breakneck; impressive; *informal* scorching, blinding.
OPPOSITE leisurely.

blithe ▶ **adjective 1** *he drove out with blithe disregard for the rules of the road* **heedless**, uncaring, careless, casual, indifferent, thoughtless, unconcerned, unworried, untroubled; nonchalant, cool, blasé, devil-may-care, irresponsible.
OPPOSITE thoughtful.
2 (*literary*) *his blithe broadly smiling face* **happy**, cheerful, cheery, light-hearted, jolly, merry, sunny, joyous, joyful, blissful, ecstatic, euphoric, elated, beatific, gladsome, mirthful; carefree, easy-going, buoyant, airy, breezy, jaunty, in high spirits, without a care in the world; animated, sprightly, vivacious, spirited, frisky; *literary* blithesome, jocund; *dated* gay.
OPPOSITE sad.

blitz ▶ **noun 1** *the 1940 blitz on London* **bombardment**, battery, bombing, onslaught, barrage, sally; attack, assault, raid, offensive, strike, blitzkrieg; *Italian* razzia.
2 (*informal*) *Katrina and I had a blitz on the cleaning* **all-out effort**, effort, exertion, endeavour, onslaught, attack, push, thrust, set-to.
▶ **verb** *the town was blitzed in the war* **bombard**, attack, pound, blast; bomb, shell, torpedo, strafe; destroy, wipe out, wreck, devastate, ravage, smash.

blizzard ▶ **noun snowstorm**, snow blast, snow squall; white-out.

bloated ▶ **adjective** *his once firm stomach was now bloated from stodgy food* **swollen**, puffed up/out, blown up, distended, inflated, enlarged, expanded, dilated, tumefied, bulging, ballooning (up/out), pumped up/out.
OPPOSITE shrunken.

blob ▶ **noun 1** *a blob of cold gravy* **drop**, droplet, globule, bead, ball, bubble, pellet, pill, pearl; *informal* glob.
2 *a blob of ink* **spot**, dab, splash, daub, blotch, blot, dot, fleck, speck, smudge, smear, streak, mark; *informal* splotch, splodge.
▶ **verb** *the masking fluid is blobbed on very freely* **daub**, dab, spot, smear, bedaub, splash, slap, slop.

bloc ▶ **noun** *a free-trade bloc* **alliance**, **association**, coalition, federation, confederation, league, faction, union, partnership, body, group, grouping; ring, syndicate; concordat, entente, axis; party, camp, lobby, wing, cabal, clique, coterie, caucus.

block ▶ **noun 1** *a block of cheese | a wall of concrete blocks* **chunk**, hunk, brick, slab, lump, piece; bar, cake, cube, wedge, mass, wad, slice; *Brit. informal* wodge.
2 *the convent is likely to be transformed into a block of bedsits* **building**, complex, structure, development.
3 *a block of shares* **batch**, group, cluster, set, section, quantity, series.
4 *a sketching block* **pad**, notebook, jotter, tablet, sketchbook, scratch pad.
5 *imperialism is a block to Third World development* **obstacle**, obstruction, bar, barrier, impediment, hindrance, check, hurdle, stumbling block; difficulty, problem, snag, disadvantage, complication, drawback, hitch, handicap, deterrent.
OPPOSITES assistance, encouragement.
6 *a block in the pipe* **blockage**, obstruction, stoppage, stopping up, clot, occlusion; impediment, hindrance; congestion.
▶ **verb 1** *weeds can block drainage ditches* **clog (up)**, stop up, choke, plug, obstruct, gum up, occlude, dam up, congest, jam, close; *informal* bung up, gunge up.
OPPOSITES unblock, open.
2 *picket lines blocked access to the factory* **hinder**, hamper, obstruct, impede, inhibit, check, arrest, restrict, limit, deter, curb, interrupt; halt, stop, bar, prevent, thwart, baulk, frustrate, foil, scotch, circumvent, stand in the way of; *informal* fetter.
OPPOSITES help, facilitate.
3 *the defender blocked a shot on the goal line* **parry**, stop, defend against, fend off, stave off, turn aside, deflect, hold off, avert, repel, rebuff, repulse, hold/keep at bay.
□ **block something off** *exits from main roads were blocked off* **close up**, bar, obstruct, shut off, barricade, seal.
OPPOSITE open.
□ **block something out 1** *the towering trees blocked out the light* **conceal**, hide, screen, keep out, blot out, exclude; eliminate, obliterate, eradicate, erase, rub out, wipe out, blank out, efface, remove all traces of; halt, stop, deny, suppress, repress.
2 *I would block out an area and then sketch in the detail* **rough (out)**, sketch out, trace out, outline, set out, lay out, delineate, draft.

blockade ▶ **noun 1** *a naval blockade of the island* **siege**, beleaguerment, encirclement; *rare* investment, besiegement.
2 *demonstrators erected blockades in the streets* **barricade**, barrier, roadblock; obstacle, obstruction, impediment, bulwark, block, hindrance, check, deterrent, hurdle.
▶ **verb** *rebels blockaded the capital* **barricade**, close up, block off, shut off, seal, bar; **besiege**, lay siege to, beleaguer, beset, surround; *archaic* invest.

blockage ▶ **noun** *there's a blockage in the drain* **obstruction**, stoppage, block, clot, occlusion; impediment, hindrance; congestion.

blockhead ▶ **noun** (*informal*). See IDIOT.

bloke ▶ **noun** (*Brit. informal*) **man**, boy, male, individual, body; *informal* chap, fellow, geezer, lad, fella, punter, character, customer, sort, cove, bod; *N.*

B

Amer. informal guy, dude, hombre.

blonde ▶ **adjective 1** *her blonde hair tumbled about her face* **fair**, light, light-coloured, light-toned, yellow, flaxen, tow-coloured, strawberry blonde, yellowish, golden, silver, silvery, platinum, ash blonde; bleached, sun-bleached, peroxide, bottle-blonde.
OPPOSITE dark.
2 *a blonde woman* **fair-haired**, light-haired, golden-haired, tow-headed.
OPPOSITE brunette.

blood *See centre pages for list of* **Blood Cells**
▶ **noun 1** *there was blood streaming from a wound in his head* **gore**, lifeblood, vital fluid; *literary* ichor.
2 *a woman of noble blood* **ancestry**, lineage, line, bloodline, descent, parentage, family, house, dynasty, birth, extraction, derivation, origin, genealogy, heritage, breeding, stock, strain, race, pedigree, roots, kinship, consanguinity.
3 *my daughter defies me—my own flesh and blood! | relations by blood or marriage* **kin**, kindred, relation, member of one's family, next of kin; blood relationship, relationship, kinship; *formal* kinsman, kinswoman.
4 (*dated*) *they were young bloods of the smart set* **playboy**, beau, rake, dandy, fop, gallant, cavalier, swashbuckler, man about town, roué; *dated* gay dog, rip, swell, toff; *archaic* rakehell, dude, blade, coxcomb, popinjay.

WORD LINKS

related prefixes	**haem- (e.g. *haemodialysis*), haemat- (e.g. *haematocele*)**
relating to blood	**haemal, haemic, haematic;** *archaic* **sanguineous**
branch of medicine to do with the blood	**haematology**
measurement of blood pressure	**oscillometry, sphygmomanometry**
fear of blood	**haemophobia**

blood-curdling ▶ **adjective** *a blood-curdling scream* **terrifying**, frightening, spine-chilling, hair-raising, chilling, horrifying, petrifying, alarming, shocking, scaring; eerie, sinister, fearsome, horrific, horrible, horrendous, fearful, appalling; *Scottish* eldritch; *informal* spooky, scary, creepy.

bloodless ▶ **adjective 1** *a bloodless revolution* **non-violent**, peaceful, peaceable, pacifistic, strife-free, non-warlike, harmonious; orderly, disciplined.
OPPOSITES bloody, violent.
2 *his face was bloodless* **anaemic**, pale, wan, pallid, ashen, colourless, chalky, chalk-white, milky, waxen, white, grey; pasty, sallow, jaundiced, washed out, sickly, peaked, drained, sapped, drawn, deathly, deathlike, ghostlike, white as a sheet; *informal* peaky; *rare* etiolated.
OPPOSITE ruddy.
3 *a shrewd and bloodless Hollywood mogul* **heartless**, unfeeling, cruel; **ruthless**, merciless, pitiless, cold, hard, stony-hearted, stony, with a heart of stone, cold-blooded, cold-hearted; harsh, callous, severe, unmerciful, unpitying, uncaring, unsympathetic, uncharitable.
OPPOSITES warm-hearted, charitable.
4 *the bloodless flimsiness of modern fiction* **feeble**, spiritless, lifeless, passionless, listless, limp, unanimated, languid, half-hearted, unenthusiastic, lukewarm; bland, vapid, wishy-washy.
OPPOSITE powerful.

bloodshed ▶ **noun** *the president feared bloodshed and disorder if the demands for reform were not met* **slaughter**, slaying, killing, carnage, butchery, massacre, murder, bloodletting, bloodbath, gore, pogrom, genocide; violence, fighting, hostilities, conflict, warfare, war, battle; wounding, injury.
OPPOSITE peace.

bloodthirsty ▶ **adjective** *a bloodthirsty Viking* **murderous**, homicidal, violent, sadistic, warlike, bellicose, bloody; vicious, ruthless, callous, heartless, merciless, barbarous, barbaric, savage, brutal, cut-throat; fierce, ferocious, inhuman; *archaic* sanguinary.
OPPOSITE peaceful.

bloody[1] ▶ **adjective 1** *he wiped his bloody nose* **bleeding**, shedding blood, emitting blood, unstaunched, raw, gaping.
2 *the disposal of bloody medical waste* **bloodstained**, bloodsoaked, blood-spattered, gory; *archaic* sanguinary.
3 *a bloody civil war* **involving bloodshed**, gory, bloodthirsty; vicious, cruel, ferocious, savage, fierce, brutal, murderous; *archaic* sanguinary.

bloody[2] ▶ **adjective** (*informal*) *what a bloody nuisance! See* DAMNED *sense* 2.

bloody-minded ▶ **adjective** (*Brit. informal*) *a truculent, bloody-minded shop steward* **uncooperative**, unreasonable, contrary, unhelpful, awkward, obstructive, truculent, recalcitrant, unaccommodating, unyielding, inflexible, uncompromising, unbending, refractory, disobliging, obstinate, stubborn, perverse, not giving an inch; difficult, exasperating, trying; *Scottish* thrawn; *informal* pig-headed, cussed; *Brit. informal* bolshie, stroppy; *N. Amer. informal* balky.
OPPOSITE compliant.

bloom ▶ **noun 1** *gorgeous orchid-like blooms* **flower**, blossom, floweret; flowering, blossoming, florescence, efflorescence.
2 *a country girl in the bloom of health and youth* **prime**, perfection, acme, zenith, peak, height, heyday, flourishing, strength, vigour; salad days.
OPPOSITES decline, nadir.
3 *your earrings complement the bloom of your skin to perfection* **lustre**, sheen, glow, radiance, freshness, perfection; **blush**, flush, rosiness, pinkness, redness, ruddiness, colour.
▶ **verb 1** *the geraniums had already bloomed* **blossom**, flower, be in blossom/flower, come into flower/blossom, open, open out, bud, sprout, burgeon, mature.
OPPOSITES wither, fade.
2 *the children had bloomed in the soft Devonshire air* **flourish**, thrive, be in good health, get on well, get ahead, prosper, succeed, be successful, progress, make progress, make headway, burgeon; *informal* be in the pink, be fine and dandy, go great guns.

blossom ▶ **noun** *the trees stood flushed with pink blossoms* **flower**, bloom, floweret; blossoming, inflorescence, florescence, efflorescence.
□ **in blossom** *the cherry trees are out in blossom* **in flower**, flowering, blossoming, blooming, in (full) bloom, open, out.
▶ **verb 1** *the snowdrops have blossomed a month early* **bloom**, flower, be in flower, come into flower/blossom, open (out), burgeon, bud, sprout, mature, burst forth, unfold.
2 *the idea has now blossomed into a successful business* **develop**, grow, mature, progress, evolve, burst forth, come to fruition; flourish, thrive, get on well, prosper, succeed, be successful, make headway, bloom, burgeon; *informal* go great guns.
OPPOSITES fade, fail.

blot ▶ **noun 1** *an ink blot* **spot**, dot, mark, speck, fleck, blotch, smudge, patch, dab, smut, splash, smear, streak; *informal* splotch, splodge.
2 *the only blot on an otherwise clean campaign* **blemish**, taint, flaw, fault, defect, stain, tarnishing, imperfection, blight; disgrace, dishonour, stigma, brand, slur.
3 *a blot on the landscape* **eyesore**, monstrosity, carbuncle, atrocity, horror, mess; *informal* sight.
▶ **verb 1** *he used a towel to blot excess water* **soak up**, absorb, take up, suck up, draw up, sponge up, mop up, sop up; dry up, dry out; dab, pat, press.
OPPOSITES exude; moisten.
2 *the writing was messy and blotted* **smudge**, smear, spot, blotch, dot, mark, speckle, bespatter.
3 *he had blotted our name forever by this disgraceful behaviour* **tarnish**, taint, stain, blacken, sully, smear, mar; **dishonour**, disgrace, bring discredit to, calumniate, traduce, drag through the mud/mire; *literary* besmear, besmirch; *archaic* spot, breathe on.
OPPOSITES honour, enhance.
□ **blot something out 1** *Mary blotted out her picture* **erase**, obliterate, delete, efface, rub out, wipe out, blank out, remove all traces of, expunge, eliminate; cancel, cross out, strike out.
2 *clouds were starting to blot out the stars* **conceal**, hide, obscure, exclude, obliterate, erase; darken, dim, shadow, eclipse, cast a shadow over.
OPPOSITE reveal.
3 *he urged her to blot out the memory of what she had seen* **wipe out**, erase, efface, eradicate, obliterate, expunge, destroy, exterminate.

blotch ▶ **noun 1** *huge pink flowers with dark blotches* **patch**, smudge, dot, spot, speck, speckle; blot, stain, smear, streak, dab, daub, splash; *informal* splotch, splodge.
2 *his face was puffy and covered in dark blotches* **rash**, blemish, spot, freckle, birthmark, strawberry mark, port wine stain, eruption; patch, mark, discoloration; *technical* naevus, haemangioma.
▶ **verb** *her face was blotched and swollen with crying* **spot**, mark, speck, speckle, smudge, smear, streak, blemish, cover with blotches.

blotchy ▶ **adjective** *her face had become blotchy* **spotty**, spotted, blemished, blotched, patchy, uneven, smudged, freckled, marked, smeary, streaked, stippled, macular, covered with blotches; reddened, red, inflamed; dappled, mottled, flecked, variegated, particoloured; *informal* splotchy, splodgy.

blow[1] ▶ **verb 1** *the icy wind blew around our ankles* **gust**, puff, flurry, blast, roar, bluster, rush, storm; move, be in motion.
2 *his ship was blown on to the rocks* **sweep**, carry, pull, drag, drive, buffet, move, whisk, toss, waft, whirl.
3 *leaves blew across the concourse* **drift**, flutter, waft, flow, stream, whirl, move, wave, flap, undulate, float, glide, travel, be carried.
4 *he blew a series of smoke rings* **exhale**, breathe out, puff out, emit, expel, discharge, give out, issue, send forth.
5 *Uncle Albert was soon puffing and blowing* **wheeze**, puff, pant, puff and pant, gasp, huff and puff, breathe hard/heavily, fight for breath, catch one's breath.
6 *he blew a trumpet* **sound**, play, blast, toot, pipe, trumpet; make a noise with.
7 *a rear tyre had blown* **burst**, explode, blow out, split, rupture, crack, break, fly open; puncture, get a puncture; get a flat tyre.
8 *the bulb had blown* **fuse**, short-circuit, burn out, expire, break, go.
9 (*informal*) *he blew a lot of his money on gambling* **squander**, waste, misspend, throw away, fritter away, spend freely, run through, go through, lose, lavish, dissipate; make poor use of, be prodigal with,

spend recklessly, spend unwisely, spend like water, throw around like confetti; burn, use up; *informal* splurge, pour/throw down the drain, spend as if it grows on trees, spend as if there were no tomorrow, spend as if it were going out of style; *Brit. informal* splash out, blue.
OPPOSITES save, spend wisely.
10 (*informal*) *if you blow this opportunity you might never get another chance* **spoil**, ruin, bungle, make a mess of, mess up, fudge, muff; **waste**, lose, squander, throw away; *informal* botch, make a hash of, screw up, louse up, foul up, bodge, fluff; *Brit. informal* cock up; *vulgar slang* fuck up, bugger up.
11 *he was a powerful agent before his cover was blown* **expose**, reveal, uncover, disclose, divulge, unveil, betray, leak.
□ **blow hot and cold** (*informal*). See HOT.
□ **blow out 1** *the matches are designed not to blow out in a strong wind* **be extinguished**, go out, be put out, be doused, be quenched, stop burning, fade, die out.
OPPOSITE light.
2 *the front tyre blew out.* See BLOW sense 7.
3 *the observation windows blew out in a shower of glass* **shatter**, rupture, fly into pieces, crack, smash, splinter, disintegrate; burst, explode, blow up, fly apart, break open; *informal* bust, be smashed to smithereens; *rare* shiver.
□ **blow something out** *Rosie blew out the candle* **extinguish**, put out, snuff, douse, quench, smother, stifle, dampen down, choke.
OPPOSITE light.
□ **blow over** *the crisis blew over* **abate**, subside, settle down, drop off/away, lessen, ease (off), let up, diminish, fade, dwindle, slacken, recede, cool off, tail off, peter out, pass away, pass, die down/away/out, be forgotten, fizzle out, sink into oblivion, come to an end; disappear, vanish, cease, terminate; *archaic* remit.
OPPOSITES flare up, get worse.
□ **blow one's top/lid/stack** (*informal*). See BLOW UP sense 2.
□ **blow up 1** *a lorryload of mortars and shells blew up* **explode**, detonate, go off, be set off, ignite, erupt, burst apart, shatter; *informal* go bang, go boom.
2 *he blows up at whoever's in his way when he's in a bad mood* **lose one's temper**, get/become angry, become enraged, become furious, go into a rage/fury, rant and rave, go berserk, flare up, erupt, rage, blow/lose one's cool; *informal* hit the roof, go up the wall, go off the deep end, fly off the handle, go/get mad, go crazy, go wild, go bananas, see red, lose one's rag, go ape, blow a gasket, flip one's lid.
OPPOSITE keep one's temper.
3 *a crisis blew up between the two countries in 1967* **break out**, erupt, flare up, boil over, start/commence/occur suddenly, emerge, arise.
□ **blow something up 1** *they blew the plane up with dynamite* **explode**, bomb, blast, destroy; detonate, blitz.
2 *his party trick was to blow up balloons and make them into little animals* **inflate**, pump up, fill up, swell, enlarge, distend, expand, puff up, balloon, aerate.
OPPOSITES deflate, let down.
3 *these things get blown up out of all proportion* **exaggerate**, overstate, overemphasize, hyperbolize, overstress, overestimate, magnify, amplify; embroider, colour, heighten, expand on, aggrandize, dress up, touch up, embellish, elaborate, gild.
OPPOSITE understate.
4 *I blew the picture up on a colour photocopier* **enlarge**, magnify, expand, extend, increase in size, make larger, make bigger.
OPPOSITE reduce.
▶ **noun 1** *they had lost their storm jib during a severe blow* **gale**, storm, tempest, hurricane, blast; wind, breeze, gust, puff of wind, draught, flurry; turbulence; *literary* zephyr.
2 *a blow on the guard's whistle* **toot**, blare, blast, sound, whistle, shriek.

blow[2] ▶ **noun 1** *death was due to a blow on the head with a blunt instrument* **knock, bang**, hit, punch, thump, smack, crack, thwack, buffet, jolt, stroke, rap, tap, clip; *informal* whack, bash, belt, clout, sock, wallop, battering, lick, slosh, bat.
2 *losing his wife must have been a blow to him* **shock**, surprise, bombshell, bolt from the blue, bolt out of the blue, thunderbolt, jolt, rude awakening; calamity, catastrophe, disaster, upset, misfortune, setback, disturbance, source of distress, disappointment, let-down; *informal* whammy.

blowout ▶ **noun 1** *I always leave plenty of time to get to the airport in case I have a blowout or breakdown* **puncture**, flat tyre, burst tyre; *informal* flat.
2 (*informal*) *this meal may be the last real blowout we have for a while* **party, feast**, banquet, celebration, binge; *informal* shindig, shindy, do; *Brit. informal* beanfeast, beano, bunfight, thrash, nosh-up, scoff, slap-up meal, tuck-in.

blowsy ▶ **adjective** *a blowsy old dame* **untidy**, sloppy, scruffy, messy, dishevelled, slovenly, sluttish, slatternly, tousled, unkempt, frowzy, slipshod, bedraggled, down at heel; coarse-looking; **red-faced**, ruddy, florid, ruddy-complexioned, flushed, raddled, rubicund, rubescent.
OPPOSITES tidy, respectable.

blowy ▶ **adjective** *it was a blowy night* **windy**, windswept, blustery, gusty, breezy, draughty, fresh; wild, stormy, squally, tempestuous, turbulent; *rare* boisterous.
OPPOSITE still.

blubber[1] ▶ **noun 1** *whale blubber* **fat**, fatty tissue.
2 (*informal*) *she wanted to burn off all of her blubber* **fat**, excessive weight, fatness, plumpness, bulk; beer belly, beer gut, paunch; *informal* **flab**, beef.

blubber[2] ▶ **verb** (*informal*) *I was blubbering like a baby* **cry**, sob, weep, shed tears, wail, snivel, whimper, howl, mewl, squall; *informal* blub, boohoo; *Scottish informal* greet; *rare* ululate.

bludgeon ▶ **noun** *they were violently assaulted by hooligans wielding bludgeons* **cudgel**, club, stick, truncheon, baton, bat, heavy weapon, blunt instrument; *N. Amer.* nightstick, blackjack; *Brit. informal* cosh.
▶ **verb 1** *he was waylaid by four of them and bludgeoned to death* **batter**, cudgel, club, strike, hit, beat, beat up, hammer, thrash; *informal* clobber.
2 *there are few things worse than being bludgeoned into reading a book you hate* **coerce**, force, compel, press, pressurize, pressure, drive, bully, browbeat, hector, badger, dragoon, steamroller; oblige, make, prevail on, constrain; *informal* strong-arm, railroad, bulldoze, put the screws on, turn/tighten the screws on.

blue ▶ **adjective 1** *she had bright blue eyes* sky-blue, azure, cobalt (blue), sapphire, cerulean, navy (blue), saxe (blue), Oxford blue, Cambridge blue, ultramarine, lapis lazuli, indigo, aquamarine, turquoise, teal (blue), cyan, of the colour of the sky, of the colour of the sea.
2 (*informal*) *Dad had died that year and Mum was feeling a bit blue* **depressed**, down, sad, saddened, unhappy, melancholy, miserable, sorrowful, gloomy, dejected, downhearted, disheartened, despondent, dispirited, low, in low spirits, low-spirited, heavy-hearted, glum, morose, dismal, downcast, cast down, tearful; *informal* down in the dumps, down in the mouth, fed up.
OPPOSITES happy, cheerful.
3 *a blue movie* **indecent**, dirty, rude, coarse, vulgar, bawdy, lewd, racy, risqué, salacious, naughty, wicked, improper, unseemly, smutty, spicy, raw, off colour, ribald, Rabelaisian; pornographic, filthy, obscene, offensive, prurient, sordid, low, profane, foul, vile; erotic, arousing, sexy, suggestive, titillating, explicit; *informal* near the knuckle/bone, nudge-nudge, porn, porno, X-rated, raunchy, skin; *Brit. informal* fruity, saucy; *euphemistic* adult.
OPPOSITES clean, family.

WORD LINKS
related prefix **cyano-** (e.g. ***cyanic, cyanotype***)

blueprint ▶ **noun 1** *the blueprints of the aircraft and its components* **plan**, design, draft, diagram, drawing, scale drawing, outline, sketch, pattern, map, layout, representation; technical drawing.
2 *the Thai programme provides a blueprint for similar measures in other developing countries* **model**, plan, template, framework, pattern, design, example, exemplar, guide, prototype, paradigm, sample, pilot, recipe.

blues ▶ **plural noun** (*informal*) *a fit of blues bedevilled her* **depression**, sadness, unhappiness, melancholy, misery, sorrow, gloominess, gloom, dejection, downheartedness, despondency, dispiritedness, low spirits, heavy-heartedness, glumness, moroseness, dismalness, despair; the doldrums; *informal* the dumps.
OPPOSITE happiness.

bluff[1] ▶ **noun** *this offer was denounced as a bluff* **deception, subterfuge**, pretence, sham, fake, show, deceit, false show, idle boast, feint, delusion, hoax, fraud, masquerade, charade; trick, stratagem, ruse, manoeuvre, scheme, artifice, machination; humbug, bluster, bombast, bragging; *Irish informal* codology; *informal* put-on, put-up job, kidology.
▶ **verb 1** *the family are simply bluffing to hide their guilt* **pretend**, sham, fake, feign, put on an act, put it on, lie, hoax, pose, posture, masquerade, dissemble, dissimulate; *informal* kid.
2 *I managed to bluff the board into believing that I had a long-term strategy* **deceive**, delude, mislead, trick, fool, hoodwink, dupe, hoax, take in, beguile, humbug, bamboozle, gull, cheat; *informal* con, kid, put one over on, have on, pull the wool over someone's eyes; *vulgar slang* bullshit; *archaic* cozen.

bluff[2] ▶ **adjective** *a bluff, hearty man* **plain-spoken**, straightforward, blunt, direct, no-nonsense, frank, open, candid, outspoken, to the point, forthright, unequivocal, downright, hearty; rough, abrupt, curt, gruff, short, brusque, not afraid to call a spade a spade, speaking as one finds; **genial**, approachable, good-natured, friendly; *informal* straight from the shoulder, upfront.
OPPOSITES diplomatic; evasive.

bluff[3] ▶ **noun** *the villa was set high on a bluff overlooking the sea* **cliff**, ridge, promontory, headland, crag, bank, slope, height, peak, escarpment, scarp, precipice, rock face, overhang; *rare* eminence.

blunder ▶ **noun** *she stopped, finally aware of the terrible blunder she had made* **mistake**, error, gaffe, fault, slip, oversight, inaccuracy, botch; debacle, fiasco; *French* faux pas; *informal* slip-up, clanger, boob, boo-boo, howler, foul-up; *N. Amer. informal* blooper; *Brit. informal, dated* bloomer; *vulgar slang* fuck-up.
▶ **verb 1** *the government admitted that it had blundered in its handling of the affair* **make a mistake**, be mistaken, err, be in error, misjudge, miscalculate, bungle, trip up, be wrong, get something wrong, be wide of the mark;

B

informal slip up, screw up, blow it, foul up, goof, boob, put one's foot in it, make a boo-boo, drop a brick; *vulgar slang* fuck up, bugger up.
2 *I heard her blundering about the flat* **stumble**, lurch, stagger, falter, flounder, muddle, struggle, fumble, grope.

blunt ▶ **adjective 1** *a blunt knife* **not sharp**, unsharpened, dull, dulled, worn (down), edgeless.
OPPOSITE sharp.
2 *the scale is broad with a blunt tip* **rounded**, flat, thick, obtuse, stubby, stubbed, unpointed.
OPPOSITE pointed.
3 *he had a blunt message for the audience* **straightforward**, frank, plain-spoken, candid, direct, bluff, to the point, forthright, unequivocal, point-blank, unceremonious, undiplomatic, indelicate; **brusque**, abrupt, curt, short, sharp, terse, crisp, gruff, bald, brutal, harsh, caustic; stark, bare, simple, unadorned, unembellished, undisguised, unvarnished, unqualified, pulling no punches, hard-hitting, outspoken, speaking one's mind, not mincing one's words, not beating about the bush, calling a spade a spade; *informal* upfront, straight from the shoulder.
OPPOSITES subtle, tactful.
▶ **verb 1** *ebony blunts tools very rapidly* **make less sharp**, make blunt, make dull.
OPPOSITES sharpen, hone.
2 *age hasn't blunted my passion for the good things in life* **dull**, deaden, dampen, soften, numb, weaken, take the edge off; calm, cool, temper, muffle, impair, allay, abate; tone down, dilute, sap, water down, thin, reduce, moderate; assuage, alleviate, mollify, ease, relieve, slake, sate, appease; diminish, decrease, lessen, deplete.
OPPOSITES intensify, sharpen.

blur ▶ **verb 1** *if the ray focus does not fall exactly on the film, the image will be blurred* **make indistinct**, make vague, unfocus, soften; obscure, dim, fade, make hazy, fog, cloud (over); *literary* bedim, befog, becloud; *archaic* blear.
OPPOSITES sharpen, focus.
2 *such 'advertorials' blur the distinction between editorial content and advertising* **make vague**, make unclear, make less distinct; **obscure**, muddy, muddle, mix up, confuse, obfuscate, cloud, befog, garble, lessen, weaken; muddy the waters.
3 *memories of the picnic had blurred* **become dim**, become less sharp, dull, numb, deaden, lessen, decrease, diminish, reduce, mute, tone down.
OPPOSITE sharpen.
▶ **noun** *a blur on the horizon slowly began to take shape* **indistinct shape**, hazy shape, vague shape, something indistinct/hazy/vague, haze, cloud, mist, smear, smudge; haziness, indistinctness, fogginess, murkiness, cloudiness.

blurred ▶ **adjective** *a blurred photograph* **indistinct**, blurry, fuzzy, hazy, misty, foggy, shadowy, smoky, faint; unclear, vague, indefinite, unfocused, obscure, lacking definition, ill-defined, out of focus, nebulous; woolly, muzzy, bleary; *archaic* blear.
OPPOSITES clear, distinct.

blurt ▶ **verb**
□ **blurt something out** *he blurted out his story* **utter suddenly**, exclaim, ejaculate, tell, babble, jabber, call out, cry out, burst out with, come out with; **divulge**, disclose, reveal, betray, leak, let slip, let out, give away, give the game away, bring to light; *informal* blab, gush, let on, spill the beans, spill one's guts, let the cat out of the bag, run off at the mouth, spout.
OPPOSITE keep quiet.

blush ▶ **verb** *Joan blushed at the unexpected compliment* **redden**, turn/go pink, turn/go red, turn/go crimson, turn/go scarlet, flush, colour, crimson, tint, burn up; feel shy, feel embarrassment, feel shame, feel embarrassed, feel ashamed, feel sheepish, feel mortified; *archaic* mantle.
▶ **noun** *a deep blush spread from her head to her neck* **flush**, reddening, high colour, colour, rosiness, pinkness, ruddiness, bloom.

WORD LINKS
fear of blushing **erythrophobia**

bluster ▶ **verb 1** *he's still blustering and saying that he'll never resort to that* **rant**, thunder; boast, brag, swagger, throw one's weight about/around, be overbearing, lord it, vaunt, bray, crow.
2 *in winter the storms bluster in from the Mediterranean* **blow fiercely**, blast, gust, storm, roar, rush.
▶ **noun** *he sought refuge in bluster and bullying* **ranting**, hectoring, thundering, threatening, threats, bullying, domineering; boasting, bragging, swaggering, throwing one's weight around; bombast, bravado, bumptiousness, imperiousness; empty threats, humbug; *literary* braggadocio.

blustery ▶ **adjective** *a wet and blustery night* **stormy**, gusty, gusting, windy, squally, wild, rough, raging, tempestuous, turbulent, violent; howling, roaring; inclement, foul, filthy, dirty, nasty; *informal* blowy.
OPPOSITES calm, still.

board ▶ **noun 1** *a wooden board* **plank**, beam, panel, slat, batten, timber, length of timber, piece of wood, lath.
2 *the board of directors* **committee**, council, panel, directorate, commission, group, delegation, delegates, trustees, panel of trustees, convocation; *Brit.* quango.
3 *your room and board will be free* **food**, meals, daily meals, provisions, sustenance, nourishment, fare, diet, menu, table, bread, daily bread, foodstuffs, refreshments, edibles; keep, maintenance, upkeep; *Scottish* vivas; *informal* grub, nosh, eats, chow, scoff; *formal* comestibles, provender; *archaic* vittles, commons, victuals, viands, aliment.
▶ **verb 1** *he had boarded the aircraft* **get on**, enter, go on board, go aboard, step aboard, climb on, mount, ascend, embark; catch; *informal* hop on, jump on; *formal* emplane, entrain, embus.
OPPOSITES alight, get off.
2 *a number of his students boarded with him and his wife* **lodge**, live, reside, have rooms, be quartered, be housed, be settled, have one's home; *N. Amer.* room; *informal* put up, have digs.
3 *the old system of boarding young trainees on the farm has virtually disappeared* **accommodate**, lodge, take in, put up, house, billet, quarter, harbour, provide shelter for, shelter, give a bed to, give someone a roof over their head, make room for, give accommodation to, receive; keep, feed, cater for, cook for.
□ **board something up/over** *both its windows had been boarded up* **cover up/over**, close up, shut up, seal.

board game ▶ **noun**. *See centre pages for list of* **Board Games**

boast ▶ **verb 1** *his mother had been boasting about how wonderful he was to all her friends* **brag**, crow, swagger, swank, gloat, show off, blow one's own trumpet, sing one's own praises, congratulate oneself, pat oneself on the back; exaggerate, overstate; preen oneself, give oneself airs; *informal* talk big, blow hard, lay it on thick, shoot one's mouth off; *Austral./NZ informal* skite, big-note oneself.
OPPOSITES deprecate, belittle.
2 *the museum boasts a breathtaking collection of glassware* **possess**, have, own, enjoy, pride oneself/itself on, be the proud owner of.
▶ **noun 1** *his proud boast is that he started off without any outside financial backing* **brag**, self-praise; exaggeration, overstatement; bragging, crowing, swaggering; *informal* swank, swanking; *Austral./NZ informal* skite; *literary* fanfaronade; *archaic* vaunt, rodomontade, gasconade.
2 *the hall is the boast of the county* **pride**, pride and joy, joy, wonder, delight, darling, treasure, gem, pearl, apple of someone's eye, valued object, source of satisfaction.

boastful ▶ **adjective** *he always seemed to be rather boastful and above himself* **bragging**, crowing, swaggering, braggart, overweening, overbearing, bumptious, puffed up, vaunting, blowhard, ostentatious, full of oneself; cocky, conceited, proud, arrogant, vain, egotistical; *informal* swanking, swanky, big-mouthed, big-headed, swollen-headed; *formal* vainglorious.
OPPOSITES modest, unassuming.

boat *See centre pages for lists of* **Ships and Boats** **Sailing Ships and Boats**
▶ **noun** *a small rowing boat* **vessel**, craft, watercraft, ship; *literary* keel, barque.
▶ **verb** *he often went boating* **sail**, yacht, go sailing, cruise, travel by boat.

bob ▶ **verb 1** *their yacht bobbed about on the choppy waters* **bounce**, move up and down, float, spring, toss, skip, hop, dance, jump, jounce; quiver, wobble, jiggle, joggle, jolt, jerk, shake, oscillate.
2 *the bookie's head bobbed* **nod**, incline, bow, dip, duck; wag, waggle.
3 *the maid bobbed and left the room* **curtsy**, drop a curtsy, bow, genuflect, prostrate oneself.
▶ **noun 1** *he spoke with a bob of his head* **nod**, inclination, bow, dip, duck; wag, waggle.
2 *the maid scurried away with a bob* **curtsy**, bow, genuflection, obeisance.

bode ▶ **verb** *the look on her face boded ill for anyone who crossed her path* **augur**, presage, portend, foretell, prophesy, predict; forebode, foreshadow, herald, be an omen of, warn of; indicate, signify, be a sign of, purport, point to, threaten, promise, spell, mean; *rare* betoken, foretoken, adumbrate.

bodily ▶ **adjective** *our experience of bodily sensations* **physical**, corporeal, corporal, mortal, carnal, fleshly, sensual; material, concrete, earthly, real, actual, tangible, substantial; *rare* somatic.
OPPOSITES spiritual, mental.
▶ **adverb** *she lifted him bodily out of his seat* **forcefully**, with force, powerfully, forcibly, violently; **wholly**, completely, altogether, entirely, totally.

body *See centre pages for lists:* **Blood Cells** **Bones** **Brain** **Digestive System** **Ear** **Eye** **Glands** **Heart** **Nervous System** **Tooth** **Tooth Types** **Veins and Arteries** **Vertebrae**
▶ **noun 1** *the human body* figure, frame, form, shape, build, physique, framework, anatomy, skeleton, bones, flesh and bones; *informal* bod; *rare* corse, soma.
2 *he was in a critical condition after he was hit in the head and body* **torso**, trunk, chest, stomach, middle.
3 *his body was badly charred in the fire* **corpse**, dead body, cadaver, carcass, skeleton, remains, relics; *informal* stiff.
4 (*archaic*) *Who told you? What body did you hear saying that?* **person**, individual, human being, human, being, man, woman, personage, creature, mortal, soul, living soul; *N. Amer.* hombre; *archaic* wight.

5 *the article would fit equally well into the body of the magazine or the supplement* **main part**, principal part, central part, core, heart, hub, nub, kernel.
6 *the car body* **bodywork**, hull, fuselage, outer casing.
7 *a body of water* **expanse**, mass, area, stretch, region, tract, breadth, sweep, extent, aggregate, accumulation, concretion, accretion.
8 *a growing body of evidence reveals discrimination against the old* **quantity**, amount, volume, collection, proportion, mass, corpus.
9 *the body of parental opinion* **majority**, preponderance, greater part, major part, main part, best part, better part, lion's share, bulk, mass, generality.
10 *the representative body of the employers* **association**, organization, group, grouping, party, band, company, society, club, circle, fellowship, partnership, fraternity, syndicate, guild, federation, confederation, bloc, corporation, contingent, coterie, clique.
11 *the earth is a heavenly body circling a larger heavenly body* **object**, entity, item, piece of matter.
12 *mousse was used to add body and bounce to this feminine style* **fullness**, solidity, density, thickness, firmness, substance, mass; **shape**, structure.
□ **body and soul** *he seemed ready to dedicate himself to them body and soul* **completely**, entirely, totally, utterly, fully, thoroughly, wholeheartedly, unconditionally, unrestrictedly, one hundred per cent, in all respects, to the hilt, all the way.
OPPOSITE half-heartedly.

WORD LINKS

related prefix	**somato-** (e.g. *somatotype, somatotrophin*)
relating to the body	**corporal, corporeal, somatic**
measurement of the human body	**anthropometry**

bodyguard ▶ noun *his bodyguards were watching the door* **minder**, guard, protector, guardian, defender, keeper, escort, companion, chaperone; *informal* heavy, bouncer, hired gun.

boffin ▶ noun (*Brit. informal*) *they wore the white coats of the back-room boffin* **expert**, specialist, authority, genius, mastermind; **scientist**, technician, researcher, inventor; *informal* egghead, brains, Einstein, whizz, wizard; *Brit. informal* brainbox, clever clogs; *N. Amer. informal* maven, rocket scientist, brainiac.

bog ▶ noun *a peat bog* **marsh**, marshland, swamp, swampland, sump, mire, quagmire, quag, morass, slough, fen, fenland, wetland, carr; salt marsh, saltings, salina; *N. Amer.* bayou, moor; *Scottish & N. English* moss.
▶ verb
□ **bog someone/something down** *many great ideas got bogged down in bureaucracy* **mire**, stick, trap, entangle, ensnare, embroil, encumber, catch up; hamper, hinder, obstruct, impede, halt, stop, delay, stall, slow down, detain, hold in check, restrain; swamp, overwhelm, overpower, overburden.

bogey ▶ noun **1** *bogies and other denizens of the night* **evil spirit**, bogle, ghost, spectre, phantom, hobgoblin, ogre, troll, demon, devil, fiend, sprite, witch, warlock, apparition; *informal* spook.
2 *home taping became the record industry's chief bogey* **bugbear**, **pet hate**, bane, anathema, abomination, nightmare, horror, dread, curse, thorn in one's flesh/side, bane of one's life, bugaboo; *French* bête noire; *informal* peeve.

boggle ▶ verb (*informal*) **1** *the proliferation of data makes the mind boggle* **marvel**, wonder, be astonished, be astounded, be amazed, be filled with amazement, be overwhelmed, be shocked, be staggered, be bowled over, be startled; gape, goggle, gawk; *informal* be flabbergasted.
2 *it boggles my mind that everyone thinks that they can pull the wool over the eyes of record companies* **astonish**, astound, amaze, fill with amazement, overwhelm, shock, startle, fill with wonder; *informal* flabbergast, bowl over.
3 *you never* **boggle at** *plain speaking* **demur**, jib, shrink from, flinch from, recoil from, hang back from, waver, falter, dither, baulk, vacillate about, think twice about, be reluctant about, have scruples about, scruple about, have misgivings about, have qualms about, be chary of, hesitate to, be shy about, be coy about, shy away from; *informal* be cagey about, shilly-shally.

boggy ▶ adjective *trudging through boggy ground* **marshy**, swampy, miry, fenny, mucky, muddy, waterlogged, wet, soggy, sodden, squelchy, oozy, slimy; clogged, spongy, heavy, sloughy, soft, yielding; *Scottish & N. English* mossy, clarty; *technical* paludal, uliginose; *archaic* quaggy.
OPPOSITES dry, hard.

bogus ▶ adjective *a bogus insurance claim* **fake**, faked, spurious, false, fraudulent, sham, deceptive, misleading, pretended; **counterfeit**, forged, feigned, simulated; artificial, imitation, mock, make-believe, fictitious, dummy, quasi-, pseudo, ersatz; *informal* phoney, pretend, dud, put-on; *Brit. informal* cod.
OPPOSITES genuine, authentic.

bohemian ▶ noun *he is a real artist and a real bohemian* **nonconformist**, unconventional person, beatnik, hippy, avant-gardist, free spirit, dropout, artistic person; *informal* freak.
OPPOSITES conformist, conservative.
▶ adjective *she lived a bohemian student life in Paris* **unconventional**, nonconformist, unorthodox, avant-garde, offbeat, irregular, original, alternative, experimental, artistic, idiosyncratic, eccentric; *informal* arty, arty-farty, way-out, off the wall, oddball.
OPPOSITES conventional, conservative.

boil[1] ▶ verb **1** *boil the potatoes in salted water* **bring to the boil**, simmer, heat; cook.
OPPOSITE freeze.
2 *the stew is boiling* **simmer**, bubble, seethe, heat, cook, stew.
OPPOSITE freeze.
3 *a huge cliff with the sea boiling below* **be turbulent**, be agitated, froth, foam, churn, seethe, bubble, fizz, effervesce; *literary* roil.
4 *inwardly, she boiled at his lack of consideration* **be angry**, be furious, be indignant, rage, fume, seethe, smoulder; lose one's temper, lose control, rant, rave, storm, fulminate, bluster, explode, flare up, go berserk, throw a tantrum; *informal* blow one's top, fly off the handle, go off the deep end, hit the roof, go up the wall, blow a fuse, see red, get worked up, get steamed up.
OPPOSITE keep calm.
□ **boil something down** *continuing to boil down the syrup produces maple sugar crystals* **condense**, concentrate, reduce, distil, thicken, compress; strengthen.
OPPOSITE dilute.
□ **boil down to** *it all boils down to a personality clash* **come down to**, amount to, be in essence, comprise, add up to.
▶ noun *add the stock and bring it to* **the boil** **boiling point**, 100 degrees Celsius/centigrade.
OPPOSITE freezing point.

boil[2] ▶ noun *a girl with a boil on her nose* **swelling**, **spot**, pimple, blister, pustule, eruption, blemish, carbuncle, wen, cyst, abscess, tumour, ulcer, chilblain, gumboil; *technical* furuncle; *rare* blain.

boiling ▶ adjective **1** *boiling water* **at boiling point**, at 100 degrees Celsius/centigrade; steaming, bubbling, gurgling, evaporating; very hot, piping (hot), red hot, sizzling.
OPPOSITES cold, freezing.
2 (*informal*) *it was a* **boiling hot** *morning* **very hot**, scorching, roasting, baking, blistering, blazing, sweltering, parching, searing, broiling, sultry, torrid, sweaty, oven-like.
OPPOSITES cold, cool.

boisterous ▶ adjective **1** *a boisterous game of handball* **lively**, active, animated, exuberant, spirited, bouncy, frisky, excited, overexcited, in high spirits, high-spirited, ebullient, vibrant, rowdy, unruly, wild, uproarious, unrestrained, undisciplined, uninhibited, uncontrolled, abandoned, rough, romping, rollicking, disorderly, knockabout, riotous, rip-roaring, rumbustious, roistering, tumultuous; noisy, loud, clamorous, clangorous.
OPPOSITES quiet, restrained.
2 *a boisterous wind* **blustery**, gusting, gusty, breezy, windy, stormy, wild, squally, rough, choppy, turbulent, tempestuous, howling, roaring, raging, furious; *informal* blowy.
OPPOSITES calm, quiet.

CHOOSE THE RIGHT WORD

bold, daring, audacious

These words all refer to someone's bravery or courage and are used to describe either a person or an action.

- A **bold** action typically does not involve physical danger and is more likely to be approved of than a *daring* or *audacious* one (*people are looking to their leaders to take bold decisions now*).
- A **daring** action involves adventurousness undeterred by physical danger and does not necessarily describe activities that are approved of (*a daring mission to rescue wounded soldiers | one of the most daring crimes of the century*). Other nouns described as *daring* include *adventure, rescue, robbery, raid,* and *escape. Daring* can also refer to a readiness to shock (*she smoked in the street, which was considered very daring in those days*) and is also used to mean 'provocative' (*the beaded chiffon dress with its daring low back*).
- An **audacious** act is one that goes well beyond the normal boundaries in a readiness to take risks (*ever more audacious and vicious assaults by partisans | he hit the post with an audacious drop goal attempt*). *Audacity* can involve deliberately risking shocking or offending people (*his theatrical roles were funny, audacious, subversive*).

bold ▶ adjective **1** *Derby's manager made another bold move into the transfer market | bold adventurers* **daring**, intrepid, courageous, brave, valiant, fearless, unafraid, undaunted, dauntless, valorous; **audacious**, adventurous, dashing, heroic, gallant, swashbuckling, adventuresome, daredevil, venturesome, plucky, unflinching; spirited, confident, positive, decisive, assured, enterprising; rash, reckless, brash, foolhardy; *informal* gutsy, spunky, ballsy, game, feisty; *literary* temerarious.

B

OPPOSITES timid, unadventurous.
2 (*dated*) *a bold streetwise young girl* **brazen**, shameless, forward, brash, impudent, audacious, cheeky, saucy, cocky, pert, impertinent, insolent, presumptuous, immodest, unabashed, unreserved, barefaced, unshrinking, defiant, brass-necked, bold as brass; *informal* brassy, sassy.
OPPOSITE retiring.
3 *a bold pattern of yellow and black* **striking**, vivid, bright, strong, eye-catching, conspicuous, distinct, pronounced, prominent, obvious, outstanding, well marked, showy, flashy, gaudy, lurid, garish.
OPPOSITE pale.
4 *cross references are printed in bold type* **heavy**, thick, clear, conspicuous, distinct, pronounced, outstanding.
OPPOSITES light, roman.

bolshie ▶ **adjective** (*Brit. informal*) *with your bolshie attitude, you're riding for a fall* **uncooperative**, awkward, contrary, truculent, perverse, difficult, unreasonable, obstructive, disobliging, stubborn, obstinate, unhelpful, recalcitrant, mutinous, refractory, annoying, tiresome, exasperating, trying; *Scottish* thrawn; *informal* bloody-minded, stroppy, cussed, pesky; *N. Amer. informal* balky; *archaic* contumacious, froward.
OPPOSITES helpful, cooperative.

bolster ▶ **noun** *most of them were sitting on the floor which was strewn with cushions, bolsters, and rugs* **pillow**, cushion, pad, support, rest.
▶ **verb** *going away for a few days would bolster her morale* **strengthen**, support, reinforce, make stronger, boost, fortify, give a boost to; prop up, buoy up, shore up, hold up, maintain, buttress, brace, stiffen, uphold; aid, assist, help; supplement, augment, feed, add to, increase; revitalize, invigorate, renew, regenerate.
OPPOSITE undermine.

bolt ▶ **noun 1** *he managed to slip the bolt on the shed door* **bar**, **lock**, catch, latch, fastener, hasp, pin.
2 *nuts and bolts* **rivet**, pin, peg, screw.
3 *I heard the click of a crossbow, and a bolt whirred over my head* **arrow**, quarrel, dart, shaft, missile, projectile; *literary* reed.
4 *the house was struck by a bolt of lightning* **flash**, shaft, streak, burst, discharge, flare, fulmination; *archaic* levin.
5 *Marco made a bolt for the door* **dash**, dart, run, sprint, rush, bound, leap, jump, spring, gallop.
6 *a bolt of cloth* **roll**, reel, spool, bundle, bale, parcel, packet, quantity, amount.
□ **a bolt from the blue/a bolt out of the blue** *it was a bolt out of the blue when Alan resigned* **shock**, surprise, bombshell, jolt, thunderbolt, revelation, source of amazement; *informal* turn-up for the books, shocker, whammy.
▶ **verb 1** *he bolted the door behind us* **lock**, bar, fasten, latch, secure, seal.
OPPOSITES unbolt, open.
2 *the lid was bolted down* **rivet**, pin, clamp, peg, screw, batten, pinion; fasten, fix, secure.
3 *Anna turned and bolted from the room* **dash**, dart, run, sprint, hurtle, rush, hurry, fly, shoot, flash, spring, leap, bound, start; flee, abscond, escape, take flight, make a break/run for it, take to one's heels, beat a (hasty) retreat, clear out; *informal* tear, zoom, skedaddle, scram, beat it, leg it, scoot, make oneself scarce; *Brit. informal* flit, scarper, do a bunk; *N. Amer. informal* hightail (it), take a powder, cut and run.
4 *he* **bolted down** *his breakfast* **gobble**, gulp, wolf, guzzle, devour, gorge (oneself) on, eat greedily/hungrily; *informal* tuck into, put/pack away, demolish, polish off, scoff (down), down, stuff one's face with, pig oneself on, murder, shovel down; *Brit. informal* shift, gollop; *N. Amer. informal* scarf (down/up), snarf (down/up), inhale; *rare* ingurgitate.
▶ **adverb**
□ **bolt upright** *Joanna sat bolt upright on her chair* **straight**, rigidly, stiffly, completely upright.
OPPOSITE slouching.

bomb *See centre pages for lists of* **Bombs and Mines** **Explosives** **Projectiles**
▶ **noun 1** *as they approached they saw bombs bursting on the runway* **explosive**, incendiary device, incendiary, device; missile, projectile, trajectile; *dated* blockbuster, bombshell.
2 (**the bomb**) *for nearly half a century, the world has lived with the bomb* **nuclear weapons**, nuclear bombs, atom bombs, A-bombs.
3 (**a bomb**) (*Brit. informal*) *building a new superstore will take months and cost a bomb* **a fortune**, a small fortune, a king's ransom, a huge amount, a vast sum, a large sum of money, a lot, millions, billions; *informal* a packet, a mint, a bundle, a pile, a wad, a pretty penny, an arm and a leg, a tidy sum, a killing; *Brit. informal* loadsamoney, shedloads; *N. Amer. informal* big bucks, big money, gazillions; *Austral. informal* big bickies.
▶ **verb 1** *their headquarters were bombed in the blitz* **bombard**, drop bombs on, explode, blast; shell, torpedo, blitz, strafe, pound; attack, assault, raid; blow up, blow to bits, blow sky-high, destroy, wipe out, level, raze (to the ground), demolish, flatten, topple, wreck, devastate, pulverize, obliterate, ravage, smash; *archaic* cannonade.
2 (*Brit. informal*) *she bombed across Texas at a hundred miles an hour. See* SPEED.
3 (*informal*) *the film bombed at the box office. See* FAIL.

bombard ▶ **verb 1** *gun batteries bombarded the islands* **shell**, torpedo, pound, blitz, strafe, pepper, fire at/on, bomb; assail, attack, assault, raid, batter, blast, pelt; *archaic* cannonade, fusillade.
2 *we were bombarded with information and statistics* **inundate**, swamp, flood, deluge, snow under; besiege, beset, belabour; bother, pester, plague, harass, badger, hound; *informal* hassle.

bombardment ▶ **noun** *the aerial bombardment of Baghdad* **shelling**, strafing, pounding, pelting, blitz, air raid, strafe, bombing; barrage, strike, attack, assault, onslaught; *archaic* cannonade, fusillade.

bombast ▶ **noun** *the articles lead the text into exaggeration and bombast* **bluster**, **pomposity**, ranting, rant, nonsense, empty talk, humbug, wind, blather, blether, claptrap; turgidity, verbosity, verbiage, periphrasis, euphuism, fustian; pretentiousness, affectedness, ostentation, grandiloquence, magniloquence; *informal* hot air, bunkum, guff, bosh; *literary* braggadocio, rodomontade.
OPPOSITE plain speaking.

bombastic ▶ **adjective** *Howard really was the most bombastic prig* **pompous**, blustering, ranting, blathering; **verbose**, wordy, turgid, periphrastic, euphuistic, orotund, pleonastic, high-flown, high-sounding, highfalutin, lofty, overwrought, convoluted; pretentious, affected, ostentatious, grandiloquent, magniloquent, fustian.
OPPOSITE straightforward.

bona fide ▶ **adjective** *each partner is entitled to an indemnity for all bona fide expenses* **authentic**, genuine, real, true, actual, sterling, sound, legal, legitimate, lawful, valid, non-counterfeit, non-fake, unadulterated, unalloyed, proper, straight, fair and square; *informal* honest-to-goodness, legit, pukka, on the level, the real McCoy.
OPPOSITES fake, bogus.

bonanza ▶ **noun** *the conference will bring in an £11 million bonanza for the city* **windfall**, godsend; stroke/run of luck, boon, bonus, blessing, benefit, advantage; pennies from heaven, manna from heaven; *informal* jackpot; *literary* benison.

bond ▶ **noun 1** *the two women forged a close bond* **friendship**, relationship, fellowship, partnership, association, affiliation, alliance, coalition; attachment, tie, link, connection, union, nexus.
2 (**bonds**) *the prisoner struggled with his bonds* **chains**, fetters, shackles, manacles, irons; ropes, cords, ties, fastenings, restraints; *rare* trammels.
3 *I ran away and I've broken my bond* **promise**, pledge, vow, avowal, oath, word, word of honour, solemn word, guarantee, assurance; agreement, understanding, engagement, commitment, obligation, contract, pact, transaction, bargain, deal, settlement, covenant, compact, treaty, concordat, accord; **bail**, parole; *archaic* troth.
▶ **verb** *the extensions are bonded to small sections of your hair* **join**, connect, fasten, fix, affix, attach, secure, bind, stick, glue, gum, paste, cement, fuse, weld, solder.

bondage ▶ **noun** *the serfs were set free from their bondage* **slavery**, enslavement, servitude, subjugation, subjection, oppression, domination, exploitation, persecution; captivity, imprisonment, incarceration, confinement, detention; bonds, chains, fetters, shackles, restraints, yoke; *literary* thraldom, thrall; *historical* serfdom, vassalage; *archaic* enthralment, duress.
OPPOSITE liberty.

bone *See centre pages for lists of* **Bones** **Fractures** **Vertebrae**

WORD LINKS

relating to bone	**osteo-**
consisting of bone	**osseous**
inflammation of bone	**osteitis**
branch of medicine concerned with bones	**orthopaedics**
study of bones	**osteology**
surgical incision into bone	**osteotomy**
measurement of bones	**osteometry**

bonhomie ▶ **noun** *he radiated an aura of benevolence and bonhomie* **geniality**, congeniality, conviviality, cordiality, affability, amiability, sociability, friendliness, warmth, warm-heartedness, good nature, good humour, joviality, cheerfulness, good cheer, cheeriness, jollity, happiness.
OPPOSITE coldness.

bon mot ▶ **noun** (*French*) *he exchanged bon mots and badinage with his guests* **witticism**, quip, pun, pleasantry, jest, joke, sally; *informal* wisecrack, one-liner; *rare* apophthegm, paronomasia, equivoque, Atticism.

bonny ▶ **adjective** (*Scottish & N. English*) *did you ever see such a bonny baby?* **beautiful**, attractive, handsome, pretty, gorgeous, good-looking, nice-looking, well favoured, fetching, prepossessing, ravishing, stunning; lovely, nice, sweet, cute, appealing, endearing, adorable, lovable, charming, dear, darling, delightful, winsome, winning; blooming, bouncing, healthy, fine; *informal* divine, drop-dead gorgeous, easy on the eye; *Austral./NZ informal* beaut; *literary* beauteous; *archaic* fair, comely, taking.
OPPOSITE unattractive.

bonus ▶ **noun 1** *the work's fun and coming back to Ireland is a real bonus* **benefit**, advantage, boon, blessing, godsend, stroke of luck, asset, attraction, added attraction, fringe benefit, additional benefit, extra, added extra; beauty; *informal* plus, pro, perk; *formal* perquisite.

OPPOSITE disadvantage.
2 *she's on a good salary and she gets a bonus* **extra payment**, gratuity, tip, handout, gift, present, honorarium, reward, prize, commission, dividend, premium, percentage; incentive, inducement; *informal* perk, sweetener, cut; *formal* perquisite; *historical* bounty; *rare* lagniappe.
OPPOSITE penalty.

bon viveur, bon vivant ▶ **noun** (*French*) *he was a bon viveur, savouring his food and especially his wine* **hedonist**, pleasure seeker, pleasure lover, sensualist, sybarite, voluptuary; epicure, epicurean, gourmet, gourmand, gastronome, connoisseur; *informal* foodie.
OPPOSITE puritan.

bony ▶ **adjective** *his pale, bony face was half hidden by hair* **gaunt**, **angular**, hollow-cheeked, skinny, thin, thin as a rake, lean, spare, raw-boned, skin-and-bones, skeletal, cadaverous; underfed, underweight, half-starved, emaciated, fleshless; rangy, gangly, gangling, spindly, scraggy, scrawny; *informal* anorexic, anorectic, like a bag of bones; *dated* spindle-shanked; *rare* gracile, macilent, starveling.
OPPOSITE plump.

booby ▶ **noun** *it wasn't like him to be such a booby* **idiot**, fool, stupid person, simpleton, moron, cretin, imbecile, ignoramus, oaf, dunce, dolt, dullard, nincompoop, duffer, jackass; bungler, blunderer; *informal* dope, chump, clot, clod, nitwit, dimwit, wally, airhead, birdbrain, lamebrain, pea-brain, numbskull, thickhead, fathead, blockhead, bonehead, meathead, dunderhead, chucklehead, knucklehead, pinhead, cloth-head, wooden-head, dipstick, dumb-bell, dumbhead, dumbo, dum-dum, noodle, nerd, ninny, ass, donkey; *Brit. informal* berk, divvy, nit, goat, mug, pillock, prat, silly billy, wazzock, muppet; *Scottish informal* balloon, cuddy, galoot, nyaff; *N. Amer. informal* doofus, goof, goofball, goofus, putz, bozo, boob, chowderhead, meatball, lummox, dummy, turkey, clunk, ding-a-ling, dip, palooka, poop; *Austral./NZ informal* galah, drongo, alec, alick, dingbat, nong; *vulgar slang* arsehole, dick, dildo, fuckwit; *Brit. vulgar slang* arse.

book *See centre pages for list of* **Stories** *(Types of Story and Novel)*
▶ **noun 1** *he published his first book in 1610* **volume**, tome, work, printed work, publication, title, opus, treatise; novel, storybook; manual, handbook, guide, companion, reference book; paperback, hardback, softback; *historical* yellowback.
2 *he scribbled a few notes in his book* **notepad**, notebook, pad, memo pad, exercise book, binder; ledger, record book, log, logbook, chronicle, journal, diary, daybook; *Brit.* jotter, pocketbook; *N. Amer.* scratch pad; *French* cahier.
3 (**books**) *the council had to balance its books* **accounts**, records, archives; account book, record book, ledger, log, balance sheet, financial statement.
□ **by the book** *he does all his police work by the book* **according to the rules**, in accordance with the rules, within the law, abiding by the law, lawfully, legally, legitimately, licitly; honestly, fairly, openly; *informal* on the level, on the up and up, fair and square.
▶ **verb 1** *Steven booked a table at their favourite restaurant* **reserve**, make a reservation for, arrange in advance, prearrange, arrange for, order; charter, hire; *informal* bag; *dated* engage, bespeak.
2 *we booked a number of events in the Wellington Festival* **arrange**, programme, schedule, timetable, line up, secure, fix up, lay on; *N. Amer.* slate.
□ **book in** *he booked in at the St Francis Hotel* **register**, check in, enrol, record/log one's arrival.

WORD LINKS

list of books	**bibliography**
book enthusiast	**bibliophile, bibliomane**
relating to rare books	**antiquarian**

booking ▶ **noun** *he made a provisional booking for Friday afternoon* **reservation**, appointment, date; advance booking, prior arrangement, prearrangement; *dated* engagement.

bookish ▶ **adjective** *he was more bookish than his fellow students* **studious**, scholarly, academic, literary, intellectual, highbrow, erudite, learned, well read, widely read, educated, well educated, well informed, knowledgeable, cultured, accomplished; pedantic, pedagogical, donnish, bluestocking, cerebral, serious, earnest, thoughtful; impractical, ivory-towerish; *informal* brainy, egghead; *dated* lettered; *archaic* clerkly.
OPPOSITE lowbrow.

booklet ▶ **noun** *the information pack includes a free booklet* **pamphlet**, brochure, leaflet, handout, handbill, circular, flyer, notice, tract; *N. Amer.* folder, mailer; *informal* bumf; *N. Amer. & Austral./NZ informal* dodger.

boom ▶ **noun 1** *she heard the boom of the waves on the rocks below* **reverberation**, resonance, resounding; thunder, thundering, roaring, echoing, re-echoing, blasting, crashing, drumming, thrumming, pounding; roar, rumble, bellow, bang, blast, blare, loud noise.
2 *retailers are cashing in on an unprecedented boom* **upturn**, upsurge, upswing, increase, advance, growth spurt, boost; expansion, escalation, augmentation, improvement, progress, development, success.
OPPOSITES recession, slump.
▶ **verb 1** *thunder boomed in the sky overhead* **reverberate**, resound, resonate; rumble, thunder, ring out, sound loudly, blare, echo, fill the air; crack, crash, roll, clap, explode, bang, blast.
2 *a voice boomed at her from a small doorway* **bellow**, roar, thunder, shout, bawl, yell, bark; *N. Amer. informal* holler; *rare* vociferate.
OPPOSITE whisper.
3 *the property market continued to boom* **flourish**, burgeon, thrive, prosper, progress, do well, succeed, be successful, improve, pick up, come on; grow rapidly, develop, expand, balloon, increase, swell, intensify, mushroom, snowball, rocket.
OPPOSITES decline, slump.

boomerang ▶ **verb** *misleading consumers about quality will eventually boomerang on a car maker* **backfire**, recoil, reverse, rebound, come back, bounce back, spring back, return, ricochet; have an adverse effect, have unwelcome repercussions, be self-defeating, cause one to be hoist with one's own petard; *informal* blow up in one's face; *archaic* redound.

booming ▶ **adjective 1** *he had a booming voice that contradicted his physical stature* **resonant**, sonorous, ringing, resounding, reverberating, reverberative, reverberant, reverberatory, carrying, thundering, thunderous, rumbling, roaring; **very loud**, strident, stentorian, strong, powerful, full, full-toned, rich, deep, deep-toned, baritone, bass; *rare* canorous, stentorious.
2 *shops are reporting booming business* **flourishing**, burgeoning, thriving, prospering, prosperous, successful, strong, vigorous, buoyant; productive, profitable, fruitful, lucrative; growing, developing, progressing, improving, expanding, mushrooming, snowballing, ballooning; *informal* going strong.

boon[1] ▶ **noun** *his offer of rent-free accommodation was such a boon* **blessing**, godsend, bonus, good thing, benefit, help, aid, advantage, gain, asset, privilege, luxury; windfall, bonanza, stroke of luck, piece of good fortune; *informal* perk, plus, plus point, pro; *formal* perquisite; *literary* benison.
OPPOSITES curse, disadvantage.

boon[2] ▶ **adjective** *the two girls soon became boon companions* **bosom**, close, intimate, confidential, inseparable, faithful, special, dear; favourite, best; *informal* (as) thick as thieves, pally, matey, chummy, buddy-buddy.

boor ▶ **noun** *he is such a boor when he is intoxicated* **lout**, oaf, ruffian, hooligan, thug, rowdy, bully boy, brawler, rough, churl, lubber, philistine, vulgarian, yahoo, barbarian, Neanderthal, primitive, savage, brute, beast, monster; *Irish* bosthoon; *informal* clodhopper, clod, tough, toughie, roughneck, peasant, pig, bruiser, hard man; *Brit. informal* yobbo, yob, lager lout, oik, lump, ape, gorilla; *N. Amer. informal* lummox.

boorish ▶ **adjective** *they reproached him for his boorish behaviour* **coarse**, uncouth, rude, discourteous, impolite, ungentlemanly, unladylike, ill-bred, ill-mannered, churlish, gruff, uncivilized, uncultured, uncultivated, unsophisticated, unrefined, common, rough, thuggish, loutish; crude, vulgar, crass, tasteless, unsavoury, gross, lumpen, brutish, bearish, barbaric, barbarous, Neanderthal, philistine; *informal* clodhopping, cloddish, slobbish, plebby; *Brit. informal* yobbish; *Austral./NZ informal* ocker.
OPPOSITES refined, sophisticated.

boost ▶ **noun 1** *it's a boost to one's morale to know that people care* **uplift**, lift, spur, encouragement, help, inspiration, stimulus, pick-me-up, fillip; support, bolster; *informal* shot in the arm.
2 *the economy will benefit from a boost in sales* **increase**, expansion, upturn, upsurge, upswing, rise, elevation, escalation, augmentation, improvement, development, advance, growth, boom, spurt; *informal* hike, step up, jack up.
OPPOSITE decrease.
3 *she gave him a boost into the tree* **lift up**, hoist up, push, thrust, shove, heave; *informal* a leg up, a hoick up.
▶ **verb 1** *he phones her regularly to boost her morale* **improve**, raise, uplift, increase, augment, magnify, swell, amplify, enhance, encourage, heighten, help, promote, foster, nurture, arouse, stimulate, invigorate, revitalize, inspire, perk up; support, bolster, buttress, shore up; *informal* buck up, jack up, give a shot in the arm to.
2 *they used radio advertising to boost sales* **increase**, expand, raise, elevate, escalate, augment, add to, improve, strengthen, amplify, enlarge, inflate, push up, promote, advance, develop, further, foster, stimulate; facilitate, help, assist, aid, support, back, shore up; *informal* jack up, hike, hike up, beef up, crank up, bump up, step up.
OPPOSITES decrease, hinder.
3 *he boosted her over the wall and scrambled up behind her* **lift**, raise, hoist, push, thrust, shove, heave, elevate; help, aid, assist; *informal* hoick, give someone a leg up; *rare* upheave.
4 *they employ an agency to boost their products* **publicize**, promote, advertise, write up, praise; *informal* plug, give a plug to.

boot[1] *See centre pages for list of* **Footwear**
▶ **noun 1** *don't come in here in those muddy boots!* **gumboot**, wellington, wader, walking boot, riding boot, field boot, jackboot, thigh boot, half-boot, ankle boot, pixie boot, Chelsea boot, balmoral, desert boot, moon boot, snow boot; galosh, overshoe; football boot; *informal* welly, bovver boot; *Brit. informal* beetle-crusher; *trademark* Doc Martens; *historical* buskin, napoleon, top boot.

B

2 *(informal) he got a boot in the stomach* **kick**, blow, knock.
□ **give someone the boot** *(informal)*. See DISMISS.
▶ **verb 1** *his shot was booted off the line by the goalkeeper* **kick**, punt, bunt, strike with the foot, tap; propel, drive, knock, send; *Scottish* blooter.
2 *the menu is ready as soon as you boot up your computer* **start up**, fire up, prepare, ready, make ready.
□ **boot someone out** *(informal)*. See DISMISS.

boot² ▶ **noun**
□ **to boot** *you're not only a chauvinist, but a voyeur to boot* **as well**, also, too, besides, into the bargain, in addition, additionally, on top (of that), over and above that, what's more, moreover, furthermore; *N. Amer.* in the bargain; *informal* and all; *archaic* withal, forbye.

booth ▶ **noun 1** *the market place was covered with booths for different traders* **stall**, stand, kiosk, trading post; counter, table.
2 *she called headquarters from a phone booth* **cubicle**, kiosk, box, compartment, enclosure, cupboard, carrel, cubbyhole; cabin, hut; alcove, bay, recess.

bootleg ▶ **adjective** *he had a stall selling bootleg cassette tapes* **illegal**, illicit, unlawful, unauthorized, unsanctioned, unlicensed, unofficial, pirated; bootlegged, contraband, smuggled, black-market, under the counter.

bootless ▶ **adjective** *(archaic) remonstrating with him seems to have been a bootless task* **useless**, ineffective, ineffectual, inefficacious, unproductive, fruitless, profitless, unrewarding, unsuccessful, non-successful, without success, abortive, unavailing, to no avail, to no effect, to no purpose, futile, vain, in vain, pointless, worthless, nugatory; *informal* a dead loss; *literary* Sisyphean, for nought; *rare* unfructuous.
OPPOSITE fruitful.

bootlicker ▶ **noun** *(informal) there was a crowd of bootlickers telling him what a star he would be* **sycophant**, obsequious person, toady, fawner, flatterer, creep, crawler, lickspittle, truckler, groveller, doormat, kowtower, spaniel, Uriah Heep; *N. Amer. informal* suck-up, brown-nose, brown-noser; *Brit. vulgar slang* arse-licker, arse-kisser, bum-sucker; *N. Amer. vulgar slang* ass-kisser, suckhole; *archaic* toad-eater.

booty ▶ **noun** *the robbers met up and split the booty* **loot**, plunder, pillage, haul, prize, trophy; **spoils**, stolen goods, gains, ill-gotten gains, profits, pickings, takings, winnings; *informal* swag, boodle, the goods.

booze *(informal)* ▶ **noun** *they had a buffet lunch with loads of booze* **alcohol**, alcoholic drink, liquor, intoxicating liquor, drink, strong drink, spirits, intoxicants; *informal* grog, firewater, gut-rot, rotgut, mother's milk, tipple, the hard stuff, the demon drink, the bottle, Dutch courage, John Barleycorn, hooch, moonshine; *Brit. informal* wallop, bevvy; *N. English & Irish informal* sup; *N. Amer. informal* juice, the sauce.
▶ **verb** *I was boozing with my mates every evening* **drink**, have a drink, drink alcohol, indulge, tipple, imbibe, swill; *informal* hit the bottle, take to the bottle, crack a bottle, knock a few back; *Brit. informal* bevvy; *N. Amer. informal* bend one's elbow; *archaic* wassail, tope.

boozer ▶ **noun 1** *(informal) he is a notorious boozer and womanizer* **drinker**, heavy drinker, problem drinker, drunk, drunkard, alcoholic, dipsomaniac, alcohol-abuser, alcohol addict, person with a drink problem; tippler, imbiber, sot, toper, inebriate; *informal* lush, alky, dipso, soak, tosspot, wino, sponge, barfly; *Austral./NZ informal* hophead, metho; *vulgar slang* pisshead, piss artist.
2 *(Brit. informal) I'm off down the boozer for a bottle of the usual* **bar**, wine bar, inn, tavern, hostelry, roadhouse; *Brit.* **pub**, public house; *Scottish* howff; *N. Amer.* cafe; *Canadian* beer parlour; *Austral./NZ* hotel; *Spanish* cantina; *German* Bierkeller, Weinstube; *informal* watering hole; *Brit. informal* local; *N. Amer. informal* gin mill; *historical* alehouse, pot-house, taphouse, beerhouse; *N. Amer. historical* saloon.

bop *(informal)* ▶ **noun 1** *this is just the sort of music you want when you fancy a bop* **dance**; *informal* boogie, jive.
2 *a college bop* **discotheque**; *informal* disco, hop.
▶ **verb** *they were bopping around the hall to 1970s disco music* **dance**, jig, leap, jump, skip, bounce; *informal* boogie, jive, groove, disco, rock, pogo, mosh, stomp, hoof it; *N. Amer. informal* get down, shake one's booty, cut a/the rug, slam-dance; *dated* step it.

bordello ▶ **noun** *he possessed pornographic pictures taken in a high-class bordello* **brothel**, house of ill repute, house of prostitution; *Law* disorderly house; *French* maison close; *informal* whorehouse, cathouse, drum; *Brit. informal* knocking shop; *N. Amer. informal* creepjoint; *Austral./NZ informal* crib; *euphemistic* massage parlour; *dated* house; *archaic* brothelry, brothel house, bawdy house, house of ill fame, leaping house, bagnio, stew; *archaic, informal* flash house, joy house, hook shop, moll shop, whore shop; *rare* corinth, dress house.

border ▶ **noun 1** *the designs decorating the border of a medieval manuscript* **edge**, **margin**, perimeter, circumference, periphery; rim, fringe, verge; sides, bounds, limits, extremities; *literary* marge, bourn, skirt.
2 *the road runs from Kabul to the Soviet border* **frontier**, boundary, partition, borderline, dividing line, bounding line, perimeter; marches, bounds.
▶ **verb 1** *the fields were bordered by hedges and trees* **surround**, enclose, encircle, circle, edge, skirt, fringe, hem, bound, line, flank.
2 *the shoulder straps are bordered with gold braid* **edge**, fringe, hem; **trim**, pipe, bind, band, decorate, finish.
3 *years ago, Windsor Forest* **bordered on** *Broadmoor* **adjoin**, abut (on), bound on, butt up against, be adjacent to, lie next to, neighbour, be contiguous with, touch, join, connect, meet, reach, extend as far as.
□ **border on** *he looked at her with something that bordered on contempt* **verge on**, approach, come close to, come near to, be near to, be comparable to, approximate to, be tantamount to, be not dissimilar to, be not unlike, be similar to, resemble, look like; *informal* be not a million miles away from.

CHOOSE THE RIGHT WORD

border, boundary, frontier

- **Border** generally denotes a national boundary and, as such, a barrier (*the building of a huge dam on the Thai–Laotian border | a border checkpoint*). It is also used figuratively of the division between concepts (*his mistake in crossing the border between passion and brutality*).
- A **boundary** marks the division between two areas, but the emphasis is less on the existence of a barrier than on simply defining the area (*there were frequent disputes between the two counties as to the exact position of the boundary*). The word *boundary* is commonly used in a figurative sense (*technologies which cut across traditional boundaries between industrial sectors*), and the dividing line is seen as more fluid than a border (*literacy campaigns push back the boundaries of ignorance*).
- A **frontier** is used of national borders, especially borders between hostile powers (*troops had been dispatched to Syria's frontier with Iraq*). *A Europe without frontiers* would be one with no barriers to trade or travel. *Frontier* can also denote the point beyond which no one as yet has gone or can go (*extending the frontiers of knowledge*) and is frequently used in the same context as words such as *new*, *explore*, *last*, *push*, and *science*.

borderline ▶ **noun** *the item is on the borderline between being old and antique* **dividing line**, divide, division, demarcation line, line of demarcation, line, cut-off point; threshold, margin, fringe, limit, border, boundary, periphery.
▶ **adjective** *the moderators discussed student grades and borderline cases* **marginal**, indefinite, uncertain, unsure, unsettled, undecided, up in the air, doubtful, open to doubt, problematic, indeterminate, unclassifiable, ambivalent, equivocal; questionable, open to question, disputable, debatable, arguable, controversial, contentious, moot; *informal* iffy; *Brit. informal* dodgy.

bore¹ ▶ **verb** *you must bore a hole in the ceiling to pass the cable through* **drill**, pierce, perforate, puncture, punch, cut; tunnel, burrow, mine, dig (out), gouge (out), sink; make, create, put, drive.
▶ **noun 1** *a large amount of water had been pumped from the well bore* **borehole**, hole, well, shaft, pit, passage, tunnel.
2 *the canon has a bore of 890 millimetres* **calibre**, diameter, gauge.

bore² ▶ **verb** *the news bored Philip so he didn't watch it* **be tedious to**, pall on, stultify, stupefy, weary, tire, fatigue, send to sleep, exhaust, wear out, leave cold; bore to tears, bore to death, bore out of one's mind, bore stiff, bore rigid, bore stupid; *informal* turn off; *rare* hebetate.
OPPOSITES interest, entertain.
▶ **noun** *the poetry reading turned out to be a great bore | you can be such a bore* **tedious thing**, tiresome thing, nuisance, bother, pest, annoyance, trial, vexation, thorn in one's flesh; tiresome person, tedious person; *informal* drag, pain, pain in the neck, bind, headache, hassle; *N. Amer. informal* pain in the butt, nudnik; *Austral./NZ informal* nark; *Brit. informal, dated* blighter, blister, pill; *Brit. vulgar slang* pain in the arse.

boredom ▶ **noun** *his eyes were glassy with boredom* **weariness**, ennui, lack of enthusiasm, lack of interest, lack of concern, apathy, uninterestedness, unconcern, languor, sluggishness, accidie, malaise, world-weariness; frustration, dissatisfaction, restlessness, restiveness; **tedium**, tediousness, dullness, monotony, repetitiveness, lack of variety, lack of variation, flatness, blandness, sameness, uniformity, routine, humdrum, dreariness, lack of excitement; *informal* deadliness; *Brit. informal* sameyness.
OPPOSITES interest, entertainment.

boring ▶ **adjective** *his letters are really rather boring* **tedious**, dull, monotonous; repetitious, repetitive; unrelieved, lacking variety, lacking variation, lacking excitement, lacking interest, unvaried, unimaginative, uneventful, characterless, featureless, colourless, lifeless, soulless, passionless, spiritless, unspirited, insipid, uninteresting, unexciting, uninspiring, unstimulating, unoriginal, jejune, nondescript, sterile, flat, bland, (plain) vanilla, arid, dry, dry as dust, stale, wishy-washy, grey, anaemic, tired, banal, lame, plodding, ponderous, pedestrian, lacklustre, stodgy, dreary, mechanical, stiff, leaden, wooden; mind-numbing, soul-destroying, wearisome, tiring, tiresome, irksome, trying, frustrating; humdrum, prosaic, mundane, commonplace, workaday, quotidian, unremarkable, routine, run-of-the-mill, normal, usual, ordinary, conventional, suburban; *N. Amer.* garden variety; *informal* deadly, bog-

standard, nothing to write home about, a dime a dozen, no great shakes, not up to much; *Brit. informal* samey, common or garden; *N. Amer. informal* dullsville, ornery.
OPPOSITE interesting.

CHOOSE THE RIGHT WORD

boring, monotonous, tedious, dull

All these words describe uninteresting activities or experiences; all but *monotonous* are also commonly used of people.

- A **boring** person or thing fails to excite or hold your interest. The reason may be unspecified, and the experience can make you feel tired and frustrated (*politics is boring | one of the most boring people in the world*).
- Something **monotonous**, commonly a sound, is uninteresting because it lacks variety (*the monotonous beat of pop music | the statistics that he quotes with monotonous regularity*).
- Something **tedious** is felt to take too long and may arouse irritation as a result (*there was a long, unutterably tedious wait | tedious, repetitive work*). *Tedious* is commonly paired with words like *process, task, chore,* and *job*.
- A **dull** person or thing lacks any exciting or interesting quality or feature (*we've had a dull start to the season | she felt guilty at being dull company*). Of these four words, *dull* implies the least criticism, as is demonstrated by its use in conjunction with the approving adjective *worthy* (*a little sparkle is always welcome among dull but worthy investments*).

borrow ▶ verb **1** *they borrowed a lot of money from the bank* **take as a loan**, ask for the loan of, receive as a loan, use temporarily, have temporarily; lease, hire; *informal* cadge, scrounge, sponge, beg, bum, touch someone for; *Brit. informal* scab; *Scottish informal* sorn on someone for; *N. Amer. informal* mooch; *Austral./NZ informal* bludge.
OPPOSITE lend.
2 (*informal*) *his workmates had 'borrowed' all his tools* **take**, take for oneself, help oneself to, use as one's own, abscond with, carry off, appropriate, commandeer, abstract; steal, purloin, shoplift; *informal* filch, rob, swipe, nab, rip off, lift, 'liberate', snaffle, snitch; *Brit. informal* nick, pinch, half-inch, whip, knock off, nobble, bone, scrump, bag, blag; *N. Amer. informal* heist, glom; *Austral./NZ informal* snavel; *W. Indian informal* tief; *archaic* crib, hook.
3 *adventurous chefs borrow foreign techniques where appropriate* **adopt**, take on, take in, take over, acquire, embrace.

bosom ▶ noun **1** *the gown was set low over her bosom* **bust**, chest; breasts; *technical* mammary glands, mammae; *informal* boobs, boobies, tits, titties, knockers, bazookas, melons, jubblies, bubbies, orbs, globes, jugs; *Brit. informal* bristols, charlies, baps; *N. Amer. informal* bazooms, casabas, chichis, hooters; *Austral. informal* norks; *archaic* dugs, paps, embonpoint.
2 *the family took Gillian into its bosom* **protection**, heart, core, midst, centre, circle, shelter, safety, refuge.
3 *love was kindled within his bosom* **heart**, breast, soul, being, inner being, core, spirit; seat of one's emotions, seat of one's affections.
▶ adjective *the two girls had become bosom friends* **close**, boon, intimate, confidential, inseparable, faithful, constant, devoted, loving; special, dear, good, best, fast, firm, favourite, valued, treasured, cherished; *informal* (as) thick as thieves, pally, matey, chummy.

boss ▶ noun *he is the boss of a large trading company* **head**, head man/woman, top man/woman, chief, principal, director, president, executive, chief executive, chair, chairperson, chairman, chairwoman, manager, manageress, administrator, leader, superintendent, supervisor, foreman, forewoman, overseer, controller, employer, master, owner, proprietor, patron; *informal* boss man, number one, kingpin, top dog, bigwig, big cheese, Mister Big, skipper; *Brit. informal* gaffer, governor, guv'nor; *N. Amer. informal* honcho, head honcho, numero uno, padrone, sachem, big wheel, big kahuna, big white chief, high muckamuck.
▶ verb *you have no right to* **boss** *me* **about** **order about/around**, give orders to, dictate to, impose one's will on, lord it over, bully, push around/about, domineer, dominate, ride roughshod over, trample on, try to control, pressurize, browbeat, use strong-arm tactics on; throw one's weight about/around, call the shots, lay down the law; *informal* bulldoze, walk all over, railroad, lean on.

bossy ▶ adjective *do you treat all your guests in this bossy manner?* **domineering**, dominating, overbearing, imperious, masterful, autocratic, autarchic, officious, high-handed, high and mighty, authoritarian, dictatorial, strict, harsh, severe, iron-handed, controlling, despotic, tyrannical, draconian, oppressive, subjugating, undemocratic; *informal* pushy, cocky, throwing one's weight about.
OPPOSITE submissive.

botch (*informal*) ▶ verb *examiners botched the marking of 1,000 A-Level papers* **bungle**, do badly, do clumsily, make a mess of, mismanage, mishandle, mangle, fumble; *informal* mess up, make a hash of, hash, muff, fluff, foozle, butcher, bodge, make a botch of, foul up, bitch up, screw up, blow, louse up; *Brit. informal* make a muck of, make a pig's ear of, cock up, make a Horlicks of; *N. Amer. informal* flub, goof up, bobble; *vulgar slang* fuck up, bugger up, balls up.
▶ noun *I've probably made a botch of things* **mess**, fiasco, debacle, blunder, failure, wreck; *informal* **hash**, bodge, flop, foul-up, screw-up; *Brit. informal* cock-up, pig's ear; *N. Amer. informal* snafu; *vulgar slang* fuck-up, balls-up.
OPPOSITE success.

both

WORD LINKS
related prefixes **ambi-** (e.g. ***ambidextrous, ambiguous***), **amphi-** (e.g. ***amphibious, amphipathic***)

bother ▶ verb **1** *she had her own life and no one bothered her* **disturb**, trouble, worry, inconvenience, put out, impose on, pester, badger, harass, molest, plague, beset, torment, nag, hound, dog, chivvy, harry, annoy, upset, irritate, vex, provoke, nettle, try someone's patience, make one's hackles rise; *informal* hassle, bug, give someone a hard time, get in someone's hair, get on someone's case, get up someone's nose, rub up the wrong way, drive up the wall; *N. English informal* mither; *N. Amer. informal* ride, devil; *Austral./NZ informal* heavy; *rare* discommode.
2 *the incident was too small to bother about* **concern oneself**, trouble oneself, mind, care, worry oneself, burden oneself, occupy oneself, busy oneself; take the time, make the effort, go to trouble, inconvenience oneself; *informal* give a damn, give a hoot, give a rap, give a hang.
3 *there was something in her voice that bothered him* **worry**, trouble, concern, perturb, disturb, disquiet, disconcert, unnerve, fret, upset, distress, alarm, make anxious, cause someone anxiety, work up, agitate, gnaw at, weigh down, lie heavy on; *informal* rattle, faze, discombobulate.
OPPOSITE comfort.
▶ noun **1** *I don't want to put you to any bother* **trouble**, effort, exertion, strain, inconvenience, fuss, bustle, hustle and bustle, disruption; pains; *informal* hassle.
2 *the food was such a bother to cook* **nuisance**, pest, palaver, rigmarole, job, trial, tribulation, bind, bore, drag, inconvenience, difficulty, trouble, problem, irritation, annoyance, vexation; *informal* hassle, performance, pantomime, song and dance, headache, pain, pain in the neck, pain in the backside; *Scottish informal* nyaff, skelf; *Austral./NZ informal* nark; *vulgar slang* pain in the arse/ass.
3 *he went to sort out a spot of bother in the public bar* **disorder**, fighting, trouble, ado, disturbance, agitation, commotion, uproar, furore, brouhaha, hubbub, hurly burly; *informal* hoo-ha, ballyhoo, hoopla, rumpus, aggro, argy-bargy; *Brit. informal* kerfuffle; *NZ informal* bobsy-die.

bothersome ▶ adjective *I have had a lot of bothersome letters from students* **annoying**, irritating, irking, vexing, vexatious, maddening, exasperating, tedious, wearisome, tiresome; troublesome, trying, taxing, awkward, difficult, tricky, thorny, knotty; *informal* aggravating, pesky, cussed, confounded, infernal, pestiferous, plaguy, pestilent, pestilential.

bottle *See centre pages for list of* **Wine Bottles**
▶ noun **1** *Gareth opened a bottle of whisky* **container**; flask, carafe, decanter, pitcher, flagon, carboy, demijohn.
2 (*Brit. informal*) *no one had the bottle to stand up to McGregor* **courage**, courageousness, bravery, valour, intrepidity, boldness, nerve, confidence, daring, audacity, pluck, pluckiness, spirit, mettle, spine, backbone, steel, fibre, stout-heartedness; *informal* guts, gutsiness, spunk, grit, gumption, gameness; *Brit. informal* ballsiness; *N. Amer. informal* moxie, cojones, sand; *vulgar slang* balls; *rare* temerariousness, venturousness.
OPPOSITE cowardice.
▶ verb
□ **bottle something up** *your feelings have been bottled up for too long* **suppress**, repress, restrain, withhold, keep back, keep in check, keep in, hold in, rein in, bite back, choke back, swallow, fight back, curb, inhibit, smother, stifle, contain, shut in, conceal, hide; *informal* keep a lid on, cork up, button up.
OPPOSITES express, let out.

bottleneck ▶ noun *cars were advised to avoid the bottleneck on Talbot Road* **traffic jam**, jam, congestion, hold-up, gridlock, queue, tailback; constriction, narrowing, restriction, obstruction, block, blockage, stoppage; *informal* snarl-up.

bottom ▶ noun **1** *she reached the bottom of the stairs* **foot**, lowest part, lowest point, base, extremity; **foundation**, basis, support, substructure, substratum, groundwork, underpinning.
OPPOSITE top.
2 *they examined the bottom of the car* **underside**, lower side, underneath, undersurface, undercarriage, underpart, belly, underbelly.
3 *the boat sank to the bottom of Lake Ontario* **floor**, bed, ground, depths.
OPPOSITE surface.
4 *there's a little cottage at the bottom of his garden* **the furthest part**, the farthest point, the far end, the extremity.
OPPOSITE top.
5 *Mark was right at the bottom of his class* **lowest level**, lowest position, least important part, least successful part, least honourable part.
OPPOSITE top.
6 (*Brit.*) *I've got a tattoo on my bottom* **rear**, rump, rear end, backside, seat;

B

buttocks, cheeks, hindquarters, haunches; *French* derrière; *German* Sitzfleisch; *technical* nates; *informal* behind, sit-upon, stern, BTM, tochus; *Brit. informal* bum, botty, prat, jacksie; *N. Amer. informal* butt, fanny, tush, tushie, tail, duff, buns, booty, caboose, heinie, patootie, keister, tuchis; *W. Indian informal* batty; *humorous* fundament, posterior; *black English* rass, rusty dusty; *Brit. vulgar slang* arse; *N. Amer. vulgar slang* ass; *archaic* breech.
7 *Police got to the bottom of a racket in stolen cars* **origin**, cause, root, source, starting point, core, centre, heart, kernel, base, basis, foundation; reality, essence, nitty-gritty, substance; essentials.

□ **from top to bottom** *they had to fumigate the house from top to bottom* **thoroughly**, fully, to the fullest extent, extensively, completely, comprehensively, rigorously, exhaustively, scrupulously, meticulously, conscientiously, minutely, in close detail.

▶ **adjective** *she sat on the bottom step* **lowest**, last, bottommost, undermost, ground; *technical* basal.
OPPOSITE highest.

bottomless ▶ **adjective 1** *you both are doomed to the bottomless pits of hell* **fathomless**, unfathomable, unfathomed, endless, infinite, immeasurable, measureless; deep, profound, yawning.
OPPOSITE shallow.
2 *George's appetite was bottomless* **unlimited**, limitless, boundless, unbounded, inexhaustible, infinite, incalculable, inestimable, immeasurable, indeterminable, endless, never-ending, everlasting; vast, immense, huge, enormous, great, extensive.
OPPOSITE limited.

bough ▶ **noun** *the willows dipped their boughs into the river* **branch**, limb, arm, twig, sprig, offshoot, spur.

boulder ▶ **noun** *she clambered over some boulders at the water's edge* **rock**, stone, boulderstone; *Austral./NZ* gibber, gibber stone.

boulevard ▶ **noun** *they strolled through the parks and boulevards* **avenue**, street, road, main road, high road, drive, row, lane, parade, promenade, way, roadway, thoroughfare; *N. Amer.* strip, highway.

bounce ▶ **verb 1** *the ball hit the ground and bounced* **rebound**, spring back, bob, recoil, ricochet, jounce; *N. Amer.* carom; *rare* resile.
2 *William bounced down the stairs grinning* **bound**, leap, jump, spring, bob, hop, skip, trip, gambol, dance, prance, romp, caper, cavort, frisk, frolic, sport.
3 (*informal*) *the cops bounced me as soon as they found out who I was* **throw out**, eject, remove, expel, oust, get rid of, evict, drive out, force out; *informal* kick out, boot out, show someone the door, send packing; *Brit. informal* turf out; *dated* out.

□ **bounce back** *they haven't knocked out our spirit and we will bounce back* **recover**, revive, rally, make a comeback, take a turn for the better, pick up, be on the mend, be on the road to recovery; perk up, cheer up, brighten up, become livelier, take heart, be heartened, liven up, take on a new lease of life; *informal* buck up.

▶ **noun 1** *he reached the door in a single bounce* **bound**, leap, jump, spring, bob, hop, skip, prance.
2 *the pitch's uneven bounce deceived the batsman* **springiness**, spring; resilience, elasticity, give, rebound, recoil.
3 *she had lost a good deal of her bloom and bounce* **vitality**, vigour, energy, vivacity, liveliness, life, animation, sparkle, effervescence, exuberance, verve, spiritedness, spirit, enthusiasm, dynamism, fire, ardour, zeal, push, drive; cheerfulness, cheeriness, happiness, joy, buoyancy, optimism, high spirits, light-heartedness, merriment, jollity, ebullience; *informal* go, get-up-and-go, pep, oomph, pizzazz, zing, zip, fizz, feistiness.

bouncing ▶ **adjective** *they all have beautiful bouncing babies* **vigorous**, thriving, flourishing, blooming; **healthy**, strong, robust, sturdy, fine, fit, in good health, in good condition, in good shape, in good trim, in fine fettle; *informal* bright-eyed and bushy-tailed, in the pink, fit as a fiddle.

bouncy ▶ **adjective 1** *they crossed a bouncy bridge of wooden planks* **springy**, flexible, resilient; elastic, stretchy, stretchable, spongy, rubbery; *rare* tensible.
2 *the car gives a rather bouncy ride* **bumpy**, jolting, jolty, lurching, jerky, jumpy, jarring, bone-shaking, bone-breaking, turbulent, rough, uncomfortable.
3 *she was always bouncy and rarely lost for words* **lively**, energetic, perky, frisky, jaunty, zestful, dynamic, vital, vigorous, vibrant, animated, spirited, buoyant, bubbly, bubbling, sparkling, effervescent, vivacious, sunny, breezy, bright and breezy, enthusiastic, upbeat; *informal* peppy, zingy, zippy, zesty, chirpy, full of beans; *N. Amer. informal* peart.

bound[1] ▶ **adjective 1** *he raised his bound ankles and kicked the door down* **tied**, tied up, roped, tethered, chained, fettered, shackled, hobbled, secured; in irons, in chains.
2 *she was so far ahead that she seemed bound to win* **certain**, sure, very likely, destined, predestined, fated.
3 *you're bound by the Official Secrets Act to keep this to yourselves* **obligated**, obliged, under obligation, compelled, required, duty-bound, honour-bound, constrained; pledged, committed.
4 *religion and morality are* **bound up with** *one another* **connected with**, linked with, tied up with, united with, allied to, attached to, dependent on, reliant on.

bound[2] ▶ **verb** *the hares bound and skip in the warm sunshine* **leap**, jump, spring, bounce, hop, vault, hurdle; skip, bob, dance, prance, romp, caper, cavort, sport, frisk, frolic, gambol, gallop, hurtle; *rare* curvet, rollick, capriole.

▶ **noun** *he crossed the room with a single bound* **leap**, jump, spring, bounce, hop, vault, hurdle; *rare* curvet, capriole.

bound[3] ▶ **verb 1** *corporate freedom of action is bounded by law* **limit**, restrict, confine, cramp, straiten, restrain, circumscribe, demarcate, delimit, define.
2 *the heath is bounded by a hedge of conifers* **enclose**, surround, encircle, circle, ring, circumscribe, border; hedge in, wall in, fence in, close in, hem in, lock in, cut off.
3 *the garden was bounded on the east by Swan Lane* **border**, adjoin, abut, meet, touch; be next to, be adjacent to, be contiguous with, be connected to.

boundary ▶ **noun 1** *the river Jordan marks the boundary between Israel and Jordan* **border**, frontier, borderline, partition, dividing line, bounding line.
2 *the boundary between art and advertising* **dividing line**, divide, division, borderline, demarcation line, line of demarcation, cut-off point, threshold.
3 *he walked the boundary of his estate* **bounds**, confines, limits, outer limits, extremities, margins, edges, fringes; border, periphery, perimeter, circumference, rim, circuit; *literary* marge, bourn, skirt.
4 (**boundaries**) *the pupils probed the boundaries of accepted behaviour* **limits**, parameters, bounds, outer limits, confines, extremities, barriers, thresholds; ambit, compass.

CHOOSE THE RIGHT WORD

boundary, border, frontier
See BORDER.

boundless ▶ **adjective** *children have boundless curiosity and enthusiasm* **limitless**, without limit, unlimited, illimitable, unbounded, untold, bottomless, immeasurable, measureless, incalculable, inestimable, abundant, abounding, great, inexhaustible, no end of; **endless**, unending, never-ending, without end, infinite, undying, interminable, unfailing, unfading, unceasing, ceaseless, everlasting.
OPPOSITE limited.

bounds ▶ **plural noun 1** *landlords are keeping rents within reasonable bounds* **limits**, confines, restrictions, limitations, demarcations, proportions.
2 *they held land within the forest bounds* **borders**, boundaries, confines, limits, outer limits, extremities, margins, edges, fringes, marches; periphery, perimeter, circumference, compass, precinct, pale.

□ **out of bounds off limits**, restricted, reserved, closed off; **forbidden**, banned, proscribed, vetoed, interdicted, ruled out, not allowed, not permitted, illegal, illicit, unlawful, impermissible, not acceptable, taboo; *German* verboten; *informal* no go; *rare* non licet.

bountiful ▶ **adjective 1** *he was exceedingly bountiful to people in distress* **generous**, magnanimous, munificent, giving, open-handed, free-handed, unselfish, ungrudging, unstinting, unsparing, free, liberal, lavish, indulgent; benevolent, beneficent, charitable, philanthropic, altruistic, kind, kindly; *rare* eleemosynary, benignant.
OPPOSITE mean.
2 *the ocean provided a bountiful supply of fresh food* **abundant**, plentiful, ample, bumper, superabundant, inexhaustible, prolific, profuse, teeming, copious, prodigal, considerable, vast, immense, great, liberal, lavish, generous, princely, handsome, luxuriant, rich; *informal* tidy, whopping; *S. African informal* lank; *literary* plenteous, bounteous, proliferous.
OPPOSITE meagre.

bounty ▶ **noun 1** *the cartel's leader paid a bounty for each policeman killed* **reward**, prize, award, recompense, remuneration, commission, consideration, premium, dividend, bonus, endowment, gratuity, tip, favour, donation, handout; incentive, inducement; purse, winnings, money; *informal* perk, sweetener; *formal* perquisite; *rare* guerdon, meed, lagniappe.
2 (*literary*) *What shall I render to the Lord for all his bounty to me?* **generosity**, magnanimity, munificence, open-handedness, free-handedness, bountifulness, largesse, liberality, lavishness, indulgence; benevolence, beneficence, charity, charitableness, goodwill, big-heartedness, kindness, kindliness, compassion, care; blessings, favours, gifts; *literary* bounteousness; *historical* almsgiving.
OPPOSITE meanness.

bouquet ▶ **noun 1** *she wanted orchids for her bridal bouquet* **bunch of flowers**, posy, nosegay, spray, sprig; wreath, garland, chaplet, corsage, buttonhole; *French* boutonnière; *rare* tussie-mussie.
2 *the Chardonnay has a great depth of flavour and bouquet* **aroma**, nose, smell, fragrance, perfume, scent, odour, redolence, whiff, tang, savour.
3 *bouquets go to Ann for ensuring a well-planned event* **compliment**, commendation, tribute, accolade, eulogy, paean, plaudit, panegyric;

praise, congratulations, applause, homage, acclaim; a pat on the back; *rare* laudation.

bourgeois ▶ adjective **1** *she came from a bourgeois family* **middle-class**, property-owning, propertied, shopkeeping; **conventional**, traditional, conservative, conformist; ordinary, commonplace, provincial, parochial, suburban, small-town, parish-pump.
OPPOSITES proletarian; unconventional.
2 *foreign ideas were denounced as bourgeois decadence* **capitalistic**, materialistic, money-oriented, commercial; *informal, derogatory* yuppie.
OPPOSITE communist.
▶ noun *Liebermann was a self-professed and proud bourgeois* **member of the middle class**, property owner.
OPPOSITE communist.

bout ▶ noun **1** *a short bout of exercise can ease insomnia* **spell**, period, time, stretch, stint, turn, run, session, round, cycle; fit, burst, flurry, spurt, streak; *informal* sesh, spot.
2 *his breathlessness sparked off a coughing bout* **attack**, fit, spasm, paroxysm, convulsion, eruption, outbreak, outburst, burst, spell, dose; *rare* access, boutade.
3 *the bout ended when a fighter was knocked to the ground* **contest**, match, round, heat, competition, tournament, event, meeting, meet, fixture, game; encounter, fight, prizefight, struggle, set-to.

bovine ▶ adjective **1** *she gazed at me with her large, bovine eyes* **cow-like**, cattle-like, calf-like, taurine.
2 *his jaw dropped in an expression of bovine amazement* **stupid**, slow, dim-witted, dull-witted, ignorant, unintelligent, imperceptive, half-baked, vacuous, mindless, witless, obtuse, doltish, blockish, lumpish, wooden; stolid, phlegmatic, placid, somnolent, sluggish, torpid, lifeless, inert, inanimate; *informal* thick, thickheaded, thick as two short planks, dumb, dense, dim, dopey, slow on the uptake, dead from the neck up, boneheaded, blockheaded, lamebrained, chuckleheaded, dunderheaded, wooden-headed, log-headed, muttonheaded, pig-ignorant, birdbrained, pea-brained; *Brit. informal* dozy, divvy, daft, not the full shilling; *Scottish & N. English informal* glaikit; *N. Amer. informal* chowderhead, dumb-ass; *W. Indian informal* dotish; *rare* hebete.
OPPOSITE quick-witted.
▶ noun *the 700-pound bovine bolted back to the herd* **cow**, heifer, bull, bullock, calf, ox; beef; *N. Amer. informal* boss, bossy; *archaic* neat.

bow[1] (rhymes with 'now') ▶ verb **1** *the officers bowed and doffed their caps* **incline the body**, incline the head, make an obeisance, make a bow, nod, curtsy, drop a curtsy, bob, salaam, genuflect, bend the knee, kowtow.
2 *the government reluctantly* **bowed to** *foreign pressure* **give in**, give way, yield, submit, surrender, succumb, capitulate, assent, defer, kowtow, truckle, adhere, conform; acquiesce in, concur with, comply with, act in accordance with, cooperate with, accept, heed, observe.
OPPOSITE defy.
3 *a footman bowed her into the hallway* **usher**, conduct, show, lead, guide, direct, steer, take, escort, accompany, walk, shepherd, chaperone.
□ **bow out** *the player* **bowed out of** *international competition* **withdraw from**, resign from, retire from, step down from, get out of, pull out of, back out of, stop participating in; give up, quit, leave, abandon; *informal* pack in, chuck, chuck in, jack in; call it a day, throw in the towel/sponge; *archaic* forsake, demit.
OPPOSITE engage in.
▶ noun *Webster offered the Prince a perfunctory bow* **inclination**, obeisance, nod, curtsy, bob, **salaam**, salutation; *Indian* **namaskar**; *Chinese, historical* kowtow; *archaic* reverence.

bow[2] (rhymes with 'now') ▶ noun *the bow of the tanker swept by their stern* **prow**, front, forepart, stem, rostrum, ram, nose, head, bowsprit, cutwater; *informal* sharp end; *rare* fore-end, stem-post, beak, beak-head.

bow[3] (rhymes with 'flow') ▶ noun **1** *thread the ribbon through the hole and tie it in a bow* **loop**, knot; lace, ribbon.
2 *he bent the rod into a bow* **arc**, arch, crescent, curve, bend; half-moon, oxbow.
3 *swifter than an arrow from an archer's bow* longbow, crossbow, recurve.
▶ verb *the mast quivered and bowed as Trent climbed up it* **bend**, buckle, stoop, curve, arch, arc, crook, flex, curl, deform.

WORD LINKS
relating to archers' bows **arcuate** (rare)
seller of archers' bows **bowyer**

bowdlerize ▶ verb *he crossed out the expletives in Sheridan and bowdlerized 'Macbeth'* **expurgate**, censor, blue-pencil, cut, edit, redact; make cuts to, delete parts of, make deletions in; purge, purify, sanitize, make presentable, make acceptable, make palatable, water down, emasculate; *informal* clean up.

bowel ▶ noun **1** *he had trouble with his bowels* **intestine(s)**, small intestine, large intestine, colon; entrails, viscera; *informal* guts, insides, innards.
2 (**bowels**) *the skipper emerged from the bowels of the ship* **interior**, inside, core, belly, cavity, pit; depths, recesses; *informal* innards; *rare* penetralia.

bower ▶ noun **1** *the garden had a hidden, rose-scented bower* **arbour**, shady place, leafy shelter, alcove, recess, pergola, grotto, sanctuary; summer house, gazebo, conservatory, pavilion, belvedere; *archaic* kiosk.
2 (*literary*) *the prince looked into the lady's bower* **boudoir**, bedchamber, chamber, bedroom, dressing room, room.

B

bowl[1] ▶ verb **1** *he got a wicket for every thirty balls he bowled* **pitch**, throw, propel, hurl, toss, lob, loft, fling, launch, let fly, shy, cast, project, send, deliver; spin, roll; *informal* chuck, sling, bung, heave, buzz, whang; *N. Amer. informal* peg; *Austral. informal* hoy; *NZ informal* bish.
2 *the car bowled along the country roads* **hurtle**, speed, career, shoot, streak, sweep, hare, fly, wing; drive, motor, move, travel, go, proceed; *informal* belt, pelt, tear, scoot, tool; *Brit. informal* bomb, bucket, shift, go like the clappers; *N. Amer. informal* clip, boogie, hightail, barrel; *archaic* post, hie.
□ **bowl someone over 1** *the explosion bowled us over* **knock down**, knock over, bring down, fell, floor, prostrate; catch off balance.
2 (*informal*) *I have been bowled over by everyone's generosity* **overwhelm**, astound, amaze, astonish, surprise, impress, overawe, dumbfound, stagger, stun, daze, bewilder, nonplus, shock, startle, shake, take aback, leave open-mouthed, leave aghast; take someone's breath away, strike dumb, catch off balance; *informal* knock for six, knock sideways, throw, floor, flabbergast, faze, blow someone's mind, blow away.

bowl[2] ▶ noun **1** *she cracked two eggs into a bowl* **dish**, basin, pan, pot, crock, crucible, mortar; container, vessel, receptacle, repository; pudding bowl, soup bowl, fruit bowl, punchbowl, mixing bowl, sugar bowl, finger bowl, rose bowl; (*in ancient Greece*) crater; *historical* jorum, mazer, porringer, reservatory.
2 *the town lay half a mile away in a shallow bowl* **hollow**, valley, dip, depression, indentation, well, trough, crater, cavity, concavity, sinkhole, hole, pit, excavation; dust bowl; *Brit.* punchbowl.
3 (*N. Amer.*) *they are playing a concert at the Hollywood Bowl next month* **stadium**, arena, amphitheatre, coliseum, colosseum; enclosure, ground; (*in ancient Rome*) circus, hippodrome; *informal* park; *rare* cirque.

box[1] ▶ noun **1** *a box of Havana cigars* **carton**, pack, packet, package; case, crate, chest, trunk, coffer, casket, hamper, canteen; bin, drum, canister; container, receptacle, repository, holder, vessel; *archaic* reservatory.
2 *she left her purse in a telephone box* **booth**, cubicle, kiosk, cabin, hut; enclosure, compartment, carrel, cupboard, cubbyhole, alcove, bay, recess.
▶ verb *Muriel* **boxed up** *Christopher's clothes* **package**, pack, parcel, wrap, bundle, bale, crate; stow, store, put away.
□ **box something/someone in** *he got boxed in by members of the press* **hem in**, fence in, close in, cage in, shut in, coop up, mew up; trap, confine, restrain, constrain, imprison, intern, hold captive; surround, enclose, encircle, circle, ring, encompass; *N. Amer.* corral; *rare* compass.

box[2] ▶ verb **1** *he began boxing professionally before his 15th birthday* **fight**, prizefight, spar; exchange blows, engage in fisticuffs, battle, grapple, brawl; *informal* scrap.
2 *he boxed both my ears and stalked out* **cuff**, strike, hit, thump, slap, smack, crack, swat, punch, jab, knock, thwack, bang, wallop, batter, pummel, buffet; assault, aim blows at; *Scottish & N. English* skelp; *informal* belt, bop, biff, sock, clout, clobber, whack, plug, slug, slam, whop, lam; *Brit. informal* slosh, dot, stick one on; *N. Amer. informal* boff, bust, whale; *Austral./NZ informal* dong, quilt; *literary* smite, swinge.
▶ noun *he sent him away with a box on the ear* **cuff**, hit, thump, slap, smack, crack, swat, punch, fist, jab, hook, knock, thwack, bang, wallop; *Scottish & N. English* skelp; *informal* belt, bop, biff, sock, clout, whack, plug, slug, whop; *Brit. informal* slosh, dot; *N. Amer. informal* boff, bust, whale; *Austral./NZ informal* dong, quilt.

boxer ▶ noun **fighter**, pugilist, ringster, prizefighter, kick-boxer; sparring partner, counterpuncher; *informal* bruiser, scrapper.

boxing ▶ noun *he believes boxing keeps kids on the straight and narrow* **pugilism**, fighting, sparring, fisticuffs; kick-boxing, Thai boxing, prizefighting, bare-knuckle boxing/fighting; the ring, the prize ring; *archaic* the noble art/science (of self defence).

boy ▶ noun *as a boy he had been fascinated by architecture* **lad**, schoolboy, child, little one, young one, youngster, youth, young man, young fellow, young adult, young person, teenager, adolescent, juvenile, minor, junior; stripling, fledgling, whippersnapper; *Scottish & N. English* bairn, wean, laddie; *informal* kid, kiddie, kiddiewink, shaver, nipper, tot, tiny, young 'un, teen, teeny-bopper; *Brit. informal* sprog; *N. Amer. informal* rug rat; *Austral./NZ informal* ankle-biter; *derogatory* brat, chit, urchin, guttersnipe.
OPPOSITE man.

boycott ▶ verb *the main opposition parties boycotted the elections* **spurn**, snub, cold-shoulder, shun, avoid, abstain from, stay away from, steer clear of, give a wide berth to, refuse to take part in, turn one's back on, have nothing to do with, wash one's hands of; ban, bar, reject, veto, embargo, place an embargo on, prohibit, debar, outlaw, proscribe, interdict, blackball, blacklist; *Brit. dated* black.
OPPOSITES support, approve of.
▶ noun *they called for a boycott on the use of tropical timbers* **ban**, bar, veto, embargo, moratorium, prohibition, proscription, interdict, injunction, sanction, restriction, barrier; avoidance, shunning, rejection, refusal; *informal* thumbs down, red light, knock-back.
OPPOSITE approval.

B

boyfriend ▶ **noun** *she carries round a picture of her boyfriend* **lover**, sweetheart, loved one, love, beloved, darling, dearest, young man, man friend, man, escort, suitor, wooer, admirer, worshipper, follower; **partner**, significant other, live-in lover, cohabitee, common-law husband, fiancé; the love of one's life, the apple of one's eye, the object of one's affections; *Italian* inamorato; *S. African* jong; *informal* fella, baby, date, flame, fancy man, toy boy, sugar daddy; *N. Amer. informal* squeeze; *informal, dated* intended; *literary* swain; *dated* beau, steady; *archaic* gallant, paramour, leman.

boyish ▶ **adjective** *his boyish enthusiasm* **youthful**, young, childlike, adolescent, teenage, teenaged, fresh-faced; immature, juvenile, infantile, childish, babyish, callow, green, puerile; *archaic* bread-and-butter.
OPPOSITE manly.

brace ▶ **noun 1** *the saw is best used with a brace* **vice**, clamp, press; clasp, fastener, hasp, coupling.
2 *power drills run at a higher speed than a brace* **drill**, drilling tool, boring tool, rotary tool.
3 *the aquarium is supported by wooden braces* **prop**, beam, joist, batten, rod, post, pole, column, strut, stay, support, truss, reinforcement, buttress, shore, stanchion, bracket; *Mining* sprag.
4 *he has to wear a brace on his right leg* **support**, caliper, truss, surgical appliance.
5 *he killed a brace of partridges* **pair**, couple, duo, twosome; two; *rare* duplet, dyad, duad, doubleton.
6 (*Printing*) *the first term is within braces* **bracket**, parenthesis.
▶ **verb 1** *the plane's wing is braced by a system of rods* **support**, shore up, prop up, hold up, buttress, carry, bear, underpin; strengthen, reinforce, fortify; *archaic* underprop.
2 *he braced his hand on the railing* **steady**, secure, stabilize, fix, make fast, prop, poise; tense, tighten, stiffen, strain.
3 *you'd better brace yourself for disappointment* **prepare**, get ready, make ready, gear up, nerve, steel, galvanize, gird, strengthen, fortify, bolster, buttress; *informal* psych oneself up.

bracelet *See centre pages for list of* **Jewellery**
▶ **noun** *she wore a heavy gold bracelet* **bangle**, band, circlet, armlet, wristlet.

bracing ▶ **adjective** *the sea air is very bracing* **invigorating**, refreshing, stimulating, energizing, exhilarating, enlivening, reviving, restorative, rejuvenating, revitalizing, vitalizing, rousing, fortifying, strengthening, healthy, healthful, health-giving, salubrious, beneficial, tonic, salutary; **fresh**, brisk, crisp, cool, keen; *informal* pick-me-up; *rare* inspiriting.
OPPOSITE tiring.

bracket ▶ **noun 1** *each speaker is fixed on a separate bracket* **support**, prop, stay, batten, joist, buttress; rest, mounting, holder, shelf, rack, frame.
2 *put the words in brackets* **parenthesis**, brace; round bracket, square bracket, angle bracket, curly bracket.
3 *I'm now in a higher tax bracket* **group**, grouping, category, categorization, grade, grading, classification, class, set, section, division, order, batch, cohort, list.
▶ **verb** *women were bracketed with minors for the purpose of wage assessment* **group**, **classify**, class, categorize, grade, list, sort, set, place, assign; couple, pair, twin, yoke, put together, set side by side, regard as the same, regard as identical, liken, compare.

brackish ▶ **adjective** *the fish lay their eggs in brackish water* **slightly salty**, slightly briny, saline, salt, salted; *S. African* brak.
OPPOSITE fresh.

brag ▶ **verb** *she listened to him brag about his connections* **boast**, crow, show off, swagger, swank, bluster, gloat, blow one's own trumpet, sing one's own praises, congratulate oneself, pat oneself on the back, preen oneself, give oneself airs; *informal* talk big, blow hard, lay it on thick, shoot one's mouth off; *N. Amer. informal* shoot the bull, speak for Buncombe; *Austral./NZ informal* skite, big-note oneself; *literary* vaunt, roister, hyperbolize; *archaic* rodomontade, gasconade.

braggart ▶ **noun** *he was a prodigious braggart and a liar* **boaster**, brag, bragger, show-off, blusterer, trumpeter, swaggerer, poser, poseur, poseuse, peacock, egotist, self-publicist; *informal* blowhard, big mouth, big-head, bag of wind, windbag, gasbag, loudmouth, bull-shooter, swank, swanker; *N. Amer. informal* showboat; *Austral./NZ informal* skite; *Brit. informal, dated* swankpot; *vulgar slang* bullshitter; *archaic* blower, bouncer, shaker, puff, rodomont; *rare* braggadocio, gasconader, fanfaronade, attitudinizer.

braid ▶ **noun 1** *the shoulder straps were bordered with gold braid* **cord**, cording, braiding, bullion, thread, twine, yarn, tape, binding, rickrack, ribbon; cordon, torsade, galloon, soutache; *military slang* scrambled egg.
2 *his hair is in braids* **plait**, pigtail, twist; cornrows, dreadlocks.
▶ **verb 1** *she began to braid her long hair* **plait**, entwine, intertwine, interweave, interlace, interthread, criss-cross, weave, knit, lace, twist, twine, wind.
2 *the sleeves are braided in scarlet and lined with ermine* **trim**, edge, border, pipe, hem, fringe, frill; decorate, adorn, ornament, embellish, embroider; *rare* befrill.

brain *See centre pages for list of parts and regions of the human* **Brain**
▶ **noun 1** *the disease attacks certain cells in the brain* cerebrum, cerebral matter; *technical* encephalon.
2 (also **brains**) *success requires brains as well as brawn | she racked her brain for inspiration* **intelligence**, intellect, intellectual capacity, mental capacity, brainpower, cleverness, wit, wits, powers of reasoning, reasoning, wisdom, sagacity, acumen, discernment, shrewdness, judgement, understanding, common sense, sense; mind, head; *informal* nous, grey matter, savvy, braininess, upper storey; *Brit. informal* loaf; *N. Amer. informal* smarts; *S. African informal* kop.
3 (**brains**) (*informal*) *Janice is the brains of the family* **clever person**, intellectual, intellect, bluestocking, thinker, highbrow, mind, scholar, sage; genius, Einstein, polymath, prodigy; mastermind; *informal* egghead, bright spark; *Brit. informal* brainbox, clever clogs, boffin; *N. Amer. informal* brainiac, rocket scientist.
OPPOSITES dunce, idiot.

WORD LINKS

related prefix	**cerebro-** (e.g. ***cerebro-spinal***), **encephalo-** (e.g. ***encephalopathy***)
relating to the brain	**cerebral, encephalic**
inflammation of the brain	**encephalitis**

brainless ▶ **adjective** *they behave as if they are totally brainless* **stupid**, **foolish**, witless, unintelligent, ignorant, mindless, idiotic, imbecilic, imbecile, half-witted, simple-minded, silly, empty-headed, half-baked; *informal* dumb, brain-dead, moronic, cretinous, thick, as thick as two short planks, thickheaded, dopey, dozy, birdbrained, pea-brained, pinheaded, dippy, lamebrained, dunderheaded, wooden-headed; *Brit. informal* divvy; *Scottish & N. English informal* glaikit; *N. Amer. informal* dumb-ass, chowderheaded; *S. African informal* dof; *W. Indian informal* dotish.
OPPOSITES bright, intelligent, clever.

brain-teaser ▶ **noun** (*informal*) **puzzle**, problem, riddle, conundrum, puzzler, poser; *informal* brain-twister.

brainwash ▶ **verb** *women of the nineties have been brainwashed into thinking they should go back to work* **indoctrinate**, condition, re-educate, persuade, propagandize, influence, inculcate, drill; pressurize.

brainy ▶ **adjective** (*informal*) *she was brainy, except for maths* **clever**, intelligent, bright, brilliant, gifted; **intellectual**, erudite, well read, cultured, highbrow, academic, scholarly, cerebral, studious, bookish, bluestocking; *informal* smart; *Brit. informal* swotty.
OPPOSITE stupid.

brake ▶ **noun** *constrained resources will act as a brake on research* **curb**, check, restraint, restriction, constraint, rein, control, damper, impediment, limitation.
▶ **verb** *she braked as a Metro pulled out in front of her* **slow down**, slow, decelerate; reduce speed, put on the brakes, hit the brakes; *Brit. informal* slam on the anchors.
OPPOSITE accelerate.

branch ▶ **noun 1** *the branches of a tree* **bough**, limb, arm, offshoot.
2 *a branch of the river* **tributary**, feeder, side stream.
3 *the judicial branch of government* **division**, subdivision, section, subsection, department, sector, part, side, wing; area, sphere, discipline, field.
4 *the corporation's New York branch* **office**, bureau, agency; affiliate, subsidiary, offshoot, satellite; chapter, lodge.
▶ **verb 1** *when you get to the place where the road branches, bear right* **fork**, bifurcate, divide, subdivide, split, separate, go in different directions; *technical* furcate, divaricate.
2 *several narrow paths* ***branched off*** *the main road* **diverge from**, deviate from, depart from, turn aside from, shoot off from, split off from, go off at a tangent from; fan out from, ray out from, radiate from; *technical* ramify.
□ **branch out** *the company is branching out into Europe* **expand**, spread out, open up, extend; diversify, spread/stretch one's wings, broaden one's horizons.

brand ▶ **noun 1** *a new brand of margarine* **make**, line, label, marque; **type**, kind, sort, variety; trade name, trademark, proprietary name, logo; *Brit. archaic* chop.
2 *her particular brand of humour* **type**, kind, sort, variety, class, category, species, genre, breed, style, stamp, cast, ilk, kidney; *N. Amer. informal* stripe.
3 *the brand on a sheep* **identifying mark**, identification, marker, earmark.
4 *the brand of dipsomania* **stigma**, shame, disgrace; stain, taint, blot, blot on one's escutcheon, blemish, mark, slur; *literary* smirch.
▶ **verb 1** *the letter M was branded on each animal* **mark**, stamp, burn, sear; identify.
2 *the scene was branded on her brain* **fix permanently**, engrave, stamp, etch, imprint, print.
3 *the media was intent on branding us as communists* **stigmatize**, accuse of being, mark out; denounce, discredit, vilify, besmirch; characterize, label, classify, categorize.

brandish ▶ **verb** *an old man approached me, brandishing a stick* **flourish**, wave, shake, wield, raise, hold aloft; swing, twirl, wag, swish, flap; display, flaunt, show off.

brash ▶ **adjective 1** *a brash, noisy man* **self-assertive**, assertive, cocksure, full of oneself, self-confident, arrogant, thrusting, bold, as bold as brass,

audacious, brazen, brazen-faced; forward, impudent, insolent, impertinent, rude, cheeky; *informal* cocky, pushy, brassy.
OPPOSITES meek, diffident.
2 *brash colours* **garish**, gaudy, loud, over-bright, ostentatious, showy, flamboyant, flashy, vulgar, tasteless, tawdry; *informal* tacky; *N. Amer. informal* bling-bling.

brass ▶ noun. *See centre pages for list of* **Brass Instruments**

brassy ▶ adjective **1** (*informal*) *a brassy woman* **brazen**, brazen-faced, forward, bold, as bold as brass, self-assertive, cocksure, brash, shameless, immodest, unashamed, unabashed, impudent, insolent, impertinent, cheeky, pert, saucy; loud, vulgar, flashy, showy, ostentatious; *informal* cocky, pushy.
OPPOSITES demure, modest.
2 *brassy music* **loud**, blaring, noisy, thundering, booming, deafening, ear-splitting; **raucous**, harsh, dissonant, discordant, cacophonous, jangling, grating, jarring, strident, piercing, shrill, tinny.
OPPOSITES soft, dulcet.

brat ▶ noun (*informal*) **badly behaved child**, spoilt child; rascal, wretch, imp, whippersnapper; minx, chit; *informal* monster, horror; *N. Amer. informal* hellion; *archaic* jackanapes.

bravado ▶ noun *despite all his bravado, he was actually a very sensitive man* **boldness**, bold manner, swagger, swaggering, bluster, swashbuckling; machismo; boasting, boastfulness, bragging, bombast; *informal* showing off; *Austral./NZ informal* skite; *rare* braggadocio, rodomontade, fanfaronade, gasconade.
OPPOSITE modesty.

brave ▶ adjective **1** *they put up a brave fight* **courageous**, plucky, fearless, valiant, valorous, intrepid, heroic, lionhearted, manful, macho, bold, daring, daredevil, adventurous, audacious, death-or-glory; undaunted, unflinching, unshrinking, unafraid, dauntless, indomitable, doughty, mettlesome, venturesome, stout-hearted, stout, spirited, gallant, stalwart, resolute, determined; *N. Amer.* rock-ribbed; *informal* game, gutsy, spunky, ballsy, have-a-go; *rare* venturous.
OPPOSITES cowardly, fearful.
2 (*literary*) *his medals made a brave show* **splendid**, magnificent, impressive, fine, handsome, colourful, dramatic, spectacular; ostentatious, showy.
▶ noun (*dated*) *an Indian brave* **warrior**, soldier, fighter, fighting man.
▶ verb *around 400 fans braved freezing temperatures to see them play* **endure**, put up with, bear, withstand, weather, suffer, sustain, go through; face, confront, stand up to, meet head on, face up to, brazen out, defy; *literary* dare.
OPPOSITE get cold feet.

bravery ▶ noun *he received a medal for bravery* **courage**, courageousness, pluck, pluckiness, braveness, valour, fearlessness, intrepidity, intrepidness, nerve, daring, audacity, boldness, dauntlessness, doughtiness, stout-heartedness, hardihood, manfulness, heroism, gallantry; backbone, spine, spirit, spiritedness, mettle, determination, fortitude, resolve, resolution; *informal* guts, grit, spunk, gutsiness, gameness; *Brit. informal* bottle, ballsiness; *N. Amer. informal* moxie, cojones, sand; *vulgar slang* balls.
OPPOSITES cowardice, fear.

bravo ▶ exclamation *people kept on clapping and shouting 'bravo!'* **well done**, good for you, congratulations, take a bow, encore.

bravura ▶ adjective *a bravura performance* **virtuoso**, magnificent, outstanding, exceptional, exceptionally good, excellent, superb, brilliant, dazzling, first-class, masterly, expert; *informal* out of this world, mean, ace, crack, A1; *vulgar slang* shit-hot.

brawl ▶ noun *a drunken brawl* **fight**, fist fight, skirmish, scuffle, tussle, fracas, scrimmage, fray, melee, rumpus, altercation, wrangle, clash, free-for-all, scrum, brouhaha, commotion, uproar; fisticuffs, rough and tumble; *Irish, N. Amer., & Austral.* donnybrook; *Law, dated* affray; *informal* scrap, dust-up, set-to, shindy; *Brit. informal* punch-up, bust-up, ruck, bit of argy-bargy; *Scottish informal* rammy, swedge, square go; *N. Amer. informal* rough house, brannigan; *Austral./NZ informal* stoush; *rare* broil, bagarre.
▶ verb *he ended up brawling with photographers* **fight**, skirmish, scuffle, tussle, exchange blows, come to blows, struggle, grapple, wrestle, scrimmage; *informal* scrap, have a dust-up, have a set-to; *Brit. informal* have a punch-up; *Scottish informal* swedge; *N. Amer. informal* rough-house; *Austral./NZ informal* stoush, go the knuckle.

brawn ▶ noun *commando work requires as much brain as brawn* **physical strength**, muscle, muscles, muscular strength, muscularity, muscliness, brawniness, burliness, huskiness, robustness, toughness, powerfulness, might, mightiness, lustiness; *informal* beef, beefiness; *literary* thew, thewiness.
OPPOSITES weakness, puniness.

brawny ▶ adjective *a big brawny man with tattooed arms* **strong**, as strong as an ox, muscular, well muscled, muscly, muscle-bound, well built, powerfully built, powerful, mighty, Herculean, strapping, burly, robust, sturdy, husky, lusty, sinewy, well knit, rugged; bulky, hefty, meaty, solid, solidly built; *informal* beefy, hunky, hulking; *dated* stalwart; *literary* thewy, stark.
OPPOSITES scrawny, puny, weak.

bray ▶ verb **1** *a donkey brayed* **neigh**, whinny, hee-haw; *rare* hinny.
2 *Billy brayed with laughter* **roar**, bellow, trumpet.

brazen ▶ adjective **1** *brazen defiance* **bold**, **shameless**, as bold as brass, brazen-faced, forward, presumptuous, brash, immodest, unashamed, unabashed, unembarrassed, unblushing; defiant, impudent, insolent, impertinent, cheeky, pert; barefaced, blatant, flagrant, undisguised; *informal* brassy, pushy; *Brit. informal* saucy.
OPPOSITES timid, shy.
2 (*literary*) *brazen objects* **brass**, made of brass, metallic.
▶ verb
□ **brazen it out** *there was nothing to do but brazen it out* **put on a bold front**, put a bold face on it, be defiant, be unrepentant, be impenitent, be unashamed, be unabashed, stand one's ground.

breach ▶ noun **1** *a clear breach of the Race Relations Act* **contravention**, violation, breaking, non-observance, infringement, transgression, neglect, dereliction; failure to observe, non-compliance with; *Law* infraction, delict.
2 *a widening breach between government and Church* **rift**, gulf, chasm, division, difference, schism, disunion, estrangement, alienation, discord, dissension, disaffection; separation, split, break, break-up, parting, parting of the ways, severance, rupture; quarrel, falling-out; *Brit. informal* bust-up; *rare* scission.
3 *a breach in the sea wall* **break**, rupture, split, crack, fracture, rent, rift; opening, gap, hole, fissure, cleft, aperture.
▶ verb **1** *the river breached its bank* **break (through)**, burst (through), rupture, force itself through, split; *informal* bust.
2 *the proposed changes breached trade union rules* **break**, contravene, violate, fail to comply with, infringe, transgress against; defy, disobey, flout, fly in the face of; *Law* infract.

bread *See centre pages for list of* **Bread and Bread Rolls**
▶ noun **1** *bread and jam* the staff of life.
2 (*informal*) *his day job puts bread on the table* **food**, nourishment, sustenance, subsistence, fare, nutriment; provisions, necessities; daily bread, means of keeping body and soul together; *Scottish* vivers; *informal* grub, nosh, eats; *N. Amer. informal* scoff; *archaic* victuals, viands, meat, vittles, commons, aliment.
3 (*informal*) *I hate doing this, but I need the bread. See* MONEY.

breadth ▶ noun **1** *a breadth of about 100 metres* **width**, broadness, wideness, thickness; span, spread; diameter; *Nautical* beam.
2 *the breadth of his knowledge* **range**, extent, scope, width, depth, amplitude, extensiveness, comprehensiveness, all-inclusiveness; spread, sweep, reach, compass, magnitude, scale, degree.
OPPOSITES narrowness, limitedness.

break ▶ verb **1** *the mirror fell to the floor, where it broke into pieces* **shatter**, smash, smash to smithereens, crack, snap, fracture, fragment, splinter; disintegrate, fall to bits, fall to pieces; split, burst, blow out; tear, rend, sever, rupture, separate, divide; *informal* bust; *rare* shiver.
OPPOSITES repair, mend.
2 *she had broken her leg in two places* **fracture**, crack, smash.
3 *the bite had barely broken the skin* **pierce**, puncture, penetrate, perforate; cut, graze, make a flesh wound in.
4 *the machine has broken and they can't fix it until next week* **stop working**, cease to work/function, break down, go wrong, give out, develop a fault, malfunction, be damaged, be unusable; **crash**; *informal* go kaput, go/be on the blink, die, give up the ghost, conk out, go phut, go haywire, have had it; *Brit. informal* pack up.
5 *the council will prosecute traders who break the law* **contravene**, violate, fail to comply with, fail to observe, disobey, infringe, breach, commit a breach of, transgress against; defy, flout, fly in the face of, ignore, disregard; *Law* infract.
OPPOSITES keep, abide by.
6 *his concentration was broken by a sound* **interrupt**, disturb, interfere with.
7 *at mid-morning they broke for coffee* **stop**, pause, take/have a break, have a rest; recess, suspend proceedings; *informal* knock off, take/have a breather, take five.
OPPOSITE resume.
8 *he landed on a pile of carpets which broke his fall* **cushion**, lessen/reduce/soften the impact of, take the edge off, diminish, moderate, mitigate.
9 *the film broke box-office records* **exceed**, surpass, beat, better, cap, top, trump, outdo, outstrip, go beyond, eclipse, put in the shade; *informal* leave standing.
10 *deeply established habits are very difficult to break* **give up**, relinquish, drop, get out of; *informal* kick, shake, pack in, quit.
11 *the strategies used to break the union* **destroy**, crush, smash, quash, defeat, vanquish, overcome, overpower, overwhelm, cripple, bring to one's knees; weaken, enfeeble, sap, suppress, subdue, cow, dispirit, impair, undermine, demoralize, incapacitate, extinguish.
12 *her self-control finally broke* **give way**, collapse, crack, be overcome, give in, cave in, yield, crumple, go to pieces.
13 *four thousand pounds wouldn't break him* **bankrupt**, make bankrupt, ruin, reduce to penury, reduce to nothing, pauperize.

B

14 *he tried to break the news gently* **reveal**, disclose, divulge, let out; announce, tell, impart, make public, make known, release, proclaim.
15 *Krycek managed to break the encryption code* **decipher**, decode, decrypt, unravel, solve, work out; *informal* figure out.
16 *the day broke fair and cloudless* **dawn**, begin, start, come into being, come forth, emerge, appear.
17 *a political scandal broke in mid-1991* **erupt**, burst out, break out.
18 *overnight, the weather broke* **change**, undergo a change, alter, shift, metamorphose.
19 *waves broke against the rocks* **crash**, dash, beat, pound, lash; batter.
20 *her voice broke as she relived the experience* **falter**, quaver, quiver, tremble, shake.

□ **break away 1** *Anna attempted to break away, but he held her tight* **escape**, get away, run away, make a break for it, make a run for it, run for it, make one's getaway, flee, make off; break free, break loose, get out of someone's clutches; *informal* leg it, cut and run, hook it.
2 *a group of intellectuals broke away from the Party to form the Democratic Alliance* **leave**, secede from, break with, split with, split off from, separate (oneself) from, detach oneself from, part company with, disaffiliate from, defect from, desert; form a splinter group.

□ **break down 1** *his van broke down* **stop working**, cease to work/function, go wrong, seize up, give out, develop a fault; *informal* conk out, go kaput, go on the blink, die, give up the ghost, go phut, have had it; *Brit. informal* pack up.
2 *pay negotiations with management broke down* **fail**, collapse, come to nothing, founder, fall through, come to grief, be unsuccessful, not succeed, disintegrate; *informal* fizzle out.
3 *Vicky broke down, sobbing loudly* **burst into tears**, dissolve into tears; **lose control**, be overcome, collapse, go to pieces, come apart at the seams, crumble, disintegrate; *informal* crack up, lose it, lose one's cool.

□ **break something down 1** *they had to get the police to break the door down* **knock down**, kick down, stave in, smash in, pull down, tear down, demolish, destroy; *informal* bust.
2 *break big tasks down into smaller, more manageable parts* **divide**, separate; *rare* fractionate.
3 *graphs show how the information can be broken down* **analyse**, categorize, classify, sort out, itemize, organize; dissect; examine, investigate; *rare* anatomize.

□ **break in 1** *thieves broke in and took her cheque book* **commit burglary**, break and enter; force one's way in, burst in; *Brit. archaic* crack a crib.
2 *'I don't want to interfere,' Mrs Hendry broke in* **interrupt**, butt in, cut in, interject, interpose, intervene, chime in; interfere, put one's oar in, have one's say; *Brit. informal* chip in.

□ **break someone in** *there was no time to break in a new foreign minister* **train**, prepare, prime, initiate, condition; *informal* show someone the ropes.

□ **break into 1** *£1,500 was stolen when thieves broke into a house in Perth Street* **burgle**, rob; force one's way into, burst into.
2 *Phil broke into the discussion* **interrupt**, butt into, cut in on, intervene in; *Brit.* put one's pennyworth in; *N. Amer.* put one's two cents in.
3 *he broke into a song* **begin suddenly**, burst into, launch into.

□ **break off** *the fuselage had broken off just behind the pilot's seat* **snap off**, come off, become detached, become separated, become severed.

□ **break something off 1** *I broke off a branch from one of the trees* **snap off**, pull off, sever, detach, separate; *rare* dissever.
2 *Britain threatened to break off diplomatic relations* **end**, bring to an end, terminate, put an end to, call a halt to, stop, cease, finish, dissolve; **suspend**, discontinue; *informal* pull the plug on; *archaic* sunder.

□ **break out 1** *two suspected terrorists broke out of the detention centre* **escape from**, make one's escape from, break loose from, burst out of, abscond from, flee from; get free.
2 *fighting broke out between rival army units* **flare up**, start/begin suddenly, erupt, burst out, blow up, set in.

□ **break up 1** *after about an hour, the meeting broke up* **come to an end**, end, finish, stop, terminate; adjourn, recess.
2 *the crowd began to break up* **disperse**, scatter, go/move in different directions, go separate ways, disband, separate, part company.
3 *Danny and I broke up last year* **split up**, separate, part, stop living together, part company, reach a parting of the ways, become estranged; divorce, get divorced, get a divorce; *Brit. informal* bust up.
4 (*informal*) *the whole cast broke up* **burst out laughing**, start to laugh, roar with laughter, dissolve into laughter, shake with laughter, laugh uncontrollably, guffaw, be doubled up, split one's sides, hold one's sides; *informal* fall about, be in stitches, crack up, crease up, be creased up, be rolling in the aisles, laugh like a drain.

□ **break something up 1** *police tried to break up a crowd of about 10,000 people* **disperse**, scatter, disband, separate.
2 *I'm not going to let you break up my marriage* **put an end to**, bring to an end, destroy, wreck, ruin.

▶ **noun 1** *the magazine has been published without a break since 1950* **interruption**, interval, gap, hiatus, lapse of time, lacuna; discontinuation, discontinuance, discontinuity, suspension, disruption, cut-off; stop, stoppage, cessation; *Prosody* caesura; *archaic* surcease.
2 *a break in the weather* **change**, alteration, variation.
3 *let's have a break and get something to eat* **rest**, respite, interval, breathing space, lull, recess; stop, pause; tea break, coffee break; intermission, interlude, entr'acte; *informal* breather, let-up, time out, down time; *Austral./NZ informal* smoko.
4 *a weekend break* **holiday**, time off, period of leave; *N. Amer.* vacation; *informal* vac.
5 *a break in diplomatic relations* **rift**, gulf, chasm, division, difference, schism, disunion, estrangement, alienation; separation, split, break-up, parting, parting of the ways, severance, rupture; quarrel, falling-out; *Brit. informal* bust-up; *rare* scission.
6 *a break in the wall* **gap**, opening, space, hole, breach, chink, crack, fissure, cleft, rift, chasm; tear, split, slit, rent, rupture.
7 (*informal*) *she got her first break in 1951, with Broadway's 'Gigi'* **opportunity**, stroke of luck, chance, opening, foot in the door.

CHOOSE THE RIGHT WORD

break, holiday, vacation
See HOLIDAY.

breakable ▶ **adjective** *bubble wrap is used for breakable items* **fragile**, delicate, easily broken, easily damaged, destructible, frangible, frail, flimsy, insubstantial; brittle, crumbly, friable.
OPPOSITES unbreakable, shatterproof.

breakaway ▶ **adjective** *a radical breakaway group* **separatist**, secessionist, splinter; rebel, renegade, dissenting, schismatic, apostate.

breakdown ▶ **noun 1** *the breakdown of the negotiations* **failure**, collapse, disintegration, foundering, falling through; *informal* fizzling out.
2 *since her breakdown, Lily has lost all her self-confidence* **nervous breakdown**, (mental) collapse; *informal* crack-up.
3 *the breakdown of the new computer system* **malfunction**, failure, seizing up; **crash**; *informal* conking out.
4 *a breakdown of the figures* **analysis**, classification, categorization, itemization, dissection; examination, investigation; *rare* anatomization, fractionation.

breaker ▶ **noun** *breakers crashed against the cliffs* **wave**, roller, comber, white horse, white cap; *Austral./NZ* bombora; *informal* boomer; *N. Amer. informal* kahuna; *archaic* billow.

break-in ▶ **noun** *police are investigating a series of break-ins in the area* **burglary**, robbery, theft; raid, breaking and entering, housebreaking, forced entry; *informal* smash-and-grab.

breakneck ▶ **adjective** *the breakneck pace of technological change* **extremely fast**, high-speed, lightning, whirlwind, rapid, speedy; **dangerously fast**, reckless, dangerous, excessive, precipitate, headlong.

□ **at breakneck speed dangerously fast**, at full speed, at full tilt, at full pelt, flat out, as fast as one's legs can carry one; *French* ventre à terre; *informal* hell for leather, at a lick, like the wind, like a bat out of hell, like a bomb, like greased lightning; *Brit. informal* like the clappers, at a rate of knots, like billy-o.

breakthrough ▶ **noun** *a major breakthrough in the fight against Aids* **advance**, development, step forward, leap forward, quantum leap, step in the right direction, success, discovery, find, improvement, innovation, revolution; progress, headway, advancement.
OPPOSITE setback.

break-up ▶ **noun 1** *the break-up of the peace negotiations* **end**, termination, dissolution, splitting up; breakdown, failure, collapse, foundering, disintegration; *Brit. informal* bust-up.
2 *their break-up was very amicable* **separation**, split, split-up, parting, parting of the ways, estrangement, rift, rupture, breach; divorce; *Brit. informal* bust-up.
3 *the break-up of the Soviet Union* **division**, splitting up, partition, breaking up.
OPPOSITE integration.

breakwater ▶ **noun sea wall**, barrier, embankment; jetty, mole, groyne, pier.

breast ▶ **noun 1** *the curve of her breasts* *technical* mammary gland, mamma; (**breasts**) **bosom(s)**, bust, chest; *informal* boobs, knockers, boobies, bazookas, melons, jubblies, bubbies, orbs, globes; *Brit. informal* bristols, charlies, baps; *N. Amer. informal* bazooms, casabas, chichis; *Austral. informal* norks; *vulgar slang* tits, titties, jugs; *N. Amer. vulgar slang* hooters; *archaic* dugs, paps, embonpoint.
2 *wild feelings of frustration were rising up in his breast* **heart**, soul, bosom, seat of one's emotions/feelings, innermost being, core.

WORD LINKS

related prefixes	**mammo- (e.g. *mammogram*), mast- (e.g. *mastitis*)**
surgical removal of a breast	**mastectomy**

breath ▶ **noun 1** *I took a deep breath* **gulp of air**, inhalation, inspiration; exhalation, expiration; sigh; pant, gasp, wheeze; *technical* respiration.
2 *I had barely enough breath left to gasp a reply* wind; *informal* puff.

3 *the night was still, with hardly a breath of wind* **puff**, waft, slight stirring, sigh, faint breeze; *literary* zephyr.
4 *not a breath of scandal was ever associated with his name* **hint**, suggestion, trace, touch, whisper, suspicion, whiff, undertone.
5 (*archaic*) *there was no breath left in him* **life**, life force, animation, vital force.

□ **take someone's breath away astonish**, astound, amaze, surprise greatly, stun, startle, stagger, shock, shatter, take aback, stop someone in their tracks, leave open-mouthed, leave aghast, dumbfound, jolt, shake up; awe, overawe, thrill; *informal* knock for six, knock sideways, floor, flabbergast, blow someone's mind, blow away, knock someone out, bowl over, strike dumb.

WORD LINKS
related prefix **spiro-** (e.g. *spirometer*)
relating to breath **respiratory**

breathe ▸ verb **1** *she breathed deeply* **inhale and exhale**, **respire**, draw breath; puff, pant, blow, gasp, wheeze; *technical* inspire, expire; *literary* suspire.
2 *at least I'm still breathing* **be alive**, be living, live, have life, continue in existence; *informal* be in the land of the living, be alive and kicking.
3 *the Prime Minister would breathe new life into his party* **instil**, infuse, inject, impart, imbue with, transfuse.
4 *'We're together at last,' she breathed* **whisper**, murmur, purr, sigh, say.
5 *the whole room breathed an air of hygienic efficiency* **give an impression of**, suggest, indicate, be indicative of, have all the hallmarks of.
6 (*literary*) *the wind was breathing through the trees* **blow softly**, whisper, murmur, sigh.

breather ▸ noun (*informal*) *reaching the top of the hill, he decided to have a breather* **break**, **rest**, pause, interval, respite, breathing space, lull, recess, time out; stop, halt.

breathless ▸ adjective **1** *Will ran back, arriving flushed and breathless* **out of breath**, panting, puffing, gasping (for breath), huffing and puffing, puffing and blowing, puffed, puffed out, gulping (for breath), wheezing, wheezy, choking, winded; short of breath, short-winded; exhausted, tired out; *informal* out of puff.
2 *the crowd waited, breathless with anticipation* **agog**, all agog, eager, expectant, open-mouthed, waiting with bated breath, on the edge of one's seat, on tenterhooks, in suspense, on pins and needles, on edge, excited, impatient.

breathtaking ▸ adjective *the view over the mountains is breathtaking* **spectacular**, magnificent, wonderful, awe-inspiring, awesome, astounding, astonishing, amazing, stunning, stupendous, incredible; thrilling, exciting; *informal* sensational, out of this world, fabulous, fantastic; *literary* wondrous.
OPPOSITE unimpressive.

breed ▸ verb **1** *Asian elephants breed readily in captivity* **reproduce**, produce offspring, procreate, bear young, multiply, propagate; mate; *literary* beget offspring.
2 *these horses are bred for racing* **rear**, raise, nurture.
3 *she was born and bred in the village* **bring up**, rear, raise, nurture; educate, teach, train.
4 *the political system bred massive discontent* **cause**, bring about, give rise to, lead to, create, produce, generate, spawn, foster, occasion, make for, result in; arouse, stir up; *literary* beget.
▸ noun **1** *a medium-sized breed of cow* **variety**, stock, strain, line, family; type, kind, sort, class.
2 *a new breed of journalist* **type**, kind, sort, variety, class, genre, genus, order, calibre, brand, generation, vintage; *N. Amer. informal* stripe.

breeding ▸ noun **1** *individuals pair late in the season for breeding the following year* **reproduction**, reproducing, procreation, multiplying, propagation; mating.
2 *the breeding of rats and mice for experiment* **rearing**, raising, nurturing.
3 *her aristocratic breeding* **upbringing**, rearing; birth, parentage, family, pedigree, blood, stock, lineage.
4 *people of rank and breeding* **(good) manners**, gentility, refinement, cultivation, culture, polish, civility, urbanity; politeness, courtesy, graciousness; *informal* class.
OPPOSITES bad manners, vulgarity.

breeding ground ▸ noun *Arkansas is a breeding ground for progressive politics* **nursery**, cradle, nest, den; seedbed, hotbed, forcing house.

breeze ▸ noun **1** *a slight breeze ruffled the leaves of the trees* **gentle wind**, breath of wind, puff of air, current of air, flurry of air, gust; *informal* blow; *technical* light air; *literary* zephyr; *rare* cat's paw.
2 (*informal*) *travelling through London was a breeze* **easy task**, easy job, child's play, nothing, five-finger exercise, gift, walkover, sinecure; *informal* doddle, piece of cake, picnic, money for old rope, money for jam, cinch, sitter, kids' stuff, cushy job/number, doss, cakewalk, pushover; *N. Amer. informal* duck soup, snap; *Austral./NZ informal* bludge, snack; *S. African informal* a piece of old tackie; *Brit. vulgar slang* a piece of piss; *dated* snip.
▸ verb (*informal*) *Roger breezed into her office* **saunter**, stroll, sail, cruise, walk casually; glide, drift, float.

breezy ▸ adjective **1** *a bright, breezy day* **windy**, fresh, brisk, airy; blowy, blustery, gusty; *rare* blusterous, boisterous.
OPPOSITES windless, still.
2 *his breezy manner* **jaunty**, **cheerful**, cheery, brisk, airy, carefree, free and easy, easy, easy-going, casual, relaxed, informal, light-hearted, lively, spirited, buoyant, sparkling, animated, vivacious, frisky, sprightly, sunny, full of the joys of spring; nonchalant, insouciant, without a care in the world; *informal* upbeat, bright-eyed and bushy-tailed, sparky; *literary* blithe, blithesome; *dated* gay.
OPPOSITES serious, lifeless.

brevity ▸ noun **1** *the report is notable for its clarity and brevity* **conciseness**, concision, succinctness, economy of language, compendiousness, shortness, briefness, pithiness, pith, incisiveness, crispness, compactness, compression; laconicism, terseness, pointedness, curtness, abruptness; *rare* brachylogy.
OPPOSITES long-windedness, verbosity.
2 *the brevity of human life* **shortness**, briefness, transience, transitoriness, ephemerality, impermanence.

brew ▸ verb **1** *this beer is brewed in Frankfurt* **ferment**, make.
2 *I'll brew some tea* **prepare**, infuse, make.
3 *the tea's brewing* **infuse**, be in preparation; stew; *Brit. informal* mash.
4 *there's trouble brewing* **develop**, gather force, loom, be close, be ominously close, be on the way, be on the horizon, be in the offing, be in the wings, be imminent, be threatening, be impending, impend, be just around the corner.
▸ noun **1** *three pints of his home brew* **beer**, ale.
2 *she took a sip of the hot reviving brew* **drink**; tea, coffee; *formal* beverage.
3 *a dangerous brew of political turmoil and violent conflict* **mixture**, mix, blend, combination, compound, amalgam, concoction, pot-pourri, melange.

bribe ▸ verb *he used his considerable wealth to bribe officials* **buy off**, pay off, suborn, give an inducement to, corrupt; *informal* grease someone's palm, give someone a backhander, give someone a sweetener, keep someone sweet, get at, fix, square; *Brit. informal* nobble.
▸ noun *he accepted bribes from lobbyists* **inducement**, 'incentive'; *N. Amer.* payola; *informal* backhander, pay-off, kickback, sweetener, carrot; *Brit. informal* bung, dropsy; *N. Amer. informal* plugola, schmear; *Austral. informal* sling; *rare* douceur, drop.

bribery ▸ noun *they were charged with bribery and corruption* **corruption**, subornation; *N. Amer.* payola; *informal* palm-greasing, graft, hush money.

bric-a-brac ▸ noun **ornaments**, knick-knacks, trinkets, bibelots, baubles, gewgaws, trumpery, curios, gimcracks; bits and pieces, bits and bobs, odds and ends, miscellanea, sundries, things, stuff; *N. Amer.* kickshaws; *informal* junk; *Brit. informal* odds and sods; *rare* knick-knackery.

brick ▸ noun **1** *bricks and mortar* breeze block, firebrick, engineering brick, stock brick, adobe, clinker; header, stretcher, bondstone; *Brit.* airbrick.
2 *a brick of ice cream* **block**, cube, slab, bar, cake.
3 (*Brit. informal*) *you're a brick—I'll pay you back later* **good person**, the salt of the earth; *informal* star, good sort, pal; *Brit. informal* mate; *informal, dated* trump.

bridal ▸ adjective *her white bridal gown* **nuptial**, wedding, marriage, matrimonial, marital, connubial, conjugal; *literary* hymeneal, epithalamic.

bride ▸ noun **newly-wed**, honeymooner; marriage partner, wife; blushing bride; war bride, GI bride.

bridge *See centre pages for list of* **Bridges**
▸ noun **1** *a bridge over the river* viaduct, aqueduct, flyover, overpass; way over.
2 *a bridge between rival party groups* **link**, connection, means of uniting; bond, tie.
▸ verb **1** *a covered walkway bridged the motorway* **span**, cross, cross over, go over, pass over, extend across, reach across, traverse, arch over.
2 *an attempt to bridge the gap between European and Eastern cultures* **join**, link, connect, unite; straddle; overcome, reconcile.
OPPOSITES divide, separate.

WORD LINKS
relating to bridges **pontine**
fear of bridges **gephyrophobia**

bridle ▸ noun (*archaic*) *put a bridle on her tongue* **curb**, check, restraint, control.
▸ verb **1** *she bridled at his tone* **bristle**, be/become indignant, take offence, take umbrage, be affronted, be offended, get angry, draw oneself up, feel one's hackles rise.
2 *he bridled his indignation* **curb**, restrain, hold back, bite back, control, keep control of, keep in check, check, keep a tight rein on, rein in/back; govern, master, repress, suppress, subdue, stifle; *informal* keep a/the lid on.

brief ▸ adjective **1** *a brief account of what had happened* **concise**, succinct, short, thumbnail, to the point, pithy, incisive, short and sweet, crisp, abridged, condensed, compressed, abbreviated, compact, compendious, potted; epigrammatic, aphoristic; laconic, sparing, terse, pointed, curt, clipped, monosyllabic.
OPPOSITES lengthy, long-winded.
2 *a brief visit* | *a brief smile* **short**, flying, fleeting, hasty, hurried, quick,

B

cursory, perfunctory; temporary, short-lived, momentary, passing, transient, transitory, impermanent, fading, ephemeral, evanescent, fugitive; *informal* quickie; *rare* fugacious.
OPPOSITE long.
3 *a pair of extremely brief black shorts* **skimpy**, scanty, revealing, short; low-cut.
4 *the boss was rather brief with him* **brusque**, abrupt, curt, short, blunt, sharp.
▶ **noun 1** *Kirov had received only a vague brief about his current project* **instructions**, directions, directives, briefing; information, guidelines, guidance; remit, mandate; *informal* gen, rundown, low-down.
2 *a barrister's brief* **summary of the facts**, case, argument, contention; dossier.
3 (*informal*) *it was only his brief's eloquence that saved him from prison* **lawyer**, barrister, counsel, solicitor; *Scottish Law* advocate; *N. Amer.* attorney; *N. Amer. & Irish* counsellor-at-law.
4 *supply them with a brief of our requirements* **outline**, summary, synopsis, abstract, résumé, precis, sketch, abridgement, digest.
▶ **verb** *council employees were* ***briefed about*** *the decision* **inform of**, tell about, bring up to date on, update on, notify of, advise of, acquaint with, apprise of, give information about; prepare, prime, instruct, direct, guide; *informal* give the gen on, give the rundown on, fill in on, gen up on, put in the picture about, clue in on, clue up about, keep up to speed with.

briefing ▶ **noun 1** *the daily press briefing* **press conference**, conference, meeting, question and answer session; *N. Amer.* backgrounder.
2 *this briefing explains the systems, products, and standards* **information**, orientation, preparation, rundown; instructions, directions, guidelines, guidance.

briefly ▶ **adverb 1** *Henry paused briefly* **momentarily**, temporarily, for a few moments, for a few seconds, for a little while; hurriedly, hastily, quickly, fleetingly.
2 *briefly, the plot is as follows* **in short**, in brief, to put it briefly, to cut a long story short, in a word, to sum up, in sum, to come to the point, (to put it) in a nutshell, in essence, in outline.

briefs *See centre pages for list of* **Underwear**
▶ **plural noun underpants**, pants, Y-fronts; knickers, bikini briefs; *informal* panties; *Brit. informal* kecks.

brigade ▶ **noun 1** *a brigade of British soldiers* **unit**, contingent, battalion, regiment, garrison, division, squadron, company, platoon, section, detachment, legion, corps, troop; (*in ancient Rome*) cohort.
2 *it was at this point that the forensic brigade arrived* **squad**, team, group, band, party, body, crew, force, outfit, section; *informal* bunch.

brigand ▶ **noun** *they were robbed by brigands* **bandit**, robber, outlaw, ruffian, desperado, plunderer, marauder, raider, pillager, highwayman, criminal, thug, gangster, pirate, freebooter; *Indian* dacoit; *Scottish historical* cateran, mosstrooper; *archaic* reaver.

bright ▶ **adjective 1** *she stood blinking in the bright sunlight | the bright surface of the metal* **shining**, light, brilliant, vivid, blazing, dazzling, beaming, intense, glaring; sparkling, flashing, glittering, scintillating, gleaming, glowing, aglow, twinkling, flickering, glistening, shimmering; illuminated, lit, lighted, ablaze, luminous, luminescent, radiant, incandescent, phosphorescent, fluorescent; shiny, lustrous, glossy, sheeny, polished, varnished; *literary* irradiant, lucent, effulgent, refulgent, fulgent, lucid, glistering, coruscating, lambent, fulgurant, fulgurating, fulgurous.
OPPOSITES dark, dull.
2 *it had been a cold but bright morning* **sunny**, sunshiny, cloudless, unclouded, clear, fair, fine.
3 *he loved bright colours* **vivid**, brilliant, intense, striking, strong, eye-catching, glowing, bold, rich, flamboyant; gaudy, lurid, garish.
4 *bright flowers* **colourful**, bright-coloured, deep-coloured, vivid, brilliant, rich, vibrant; *dated* gay.
5 *a bright guitar sound* **clear**, vibrant, pellucid; high-pitched, high.
6 *a bright young graduate* **clever**, intelligent, sharp, quick-witted, quick, smart, canny, astute, intuitive, acute, alert, keen, perceptive, ingenious, inventive, resourceful, proficient, accomplished, gifted, brilliant; *informal* brainy.
OPPOSITE stupid.
7 *he felt bright and cheerful | a bright smile* **happy**, genial, cheerful, cheery, jolly, joyful, glad, merry, sunny, light-hearted, blithe, beaming; **vivacious**, animated, lively, spirited, high-spirited, exuberant, ebullient, buoyant, effervescent, bubbly, bouncy, perky, chirpy, chipper, zippy, peppy, fresh, bright-eyed and bushy-tailed, bright and breezy, full of beans; *dated* gay.
8 *she had a bright future* **promising**, rosy, full of promise, optimistic, hopeful, favourable, propitious, auspicious, providential, encouraging, lucky, fortunate, good, excellent, golden.
▶ **adverb** (*literary*) *a full moon shining bright* **brightly**, brilliantly, vividly, intensely.

brighten ▶ **verb 1** *the morning sunshine brightened the room | the sky was brightening* **make/become bright**, make/become brighter, light up, lighten, throw/cast/shed light on, illuminate, illumine, irradiate.
2 *with the right choice of shrubs and plants, you can* ***brighten up*** *the shadiest of corners* **enhance**, embellish, make more attractive, enrich, freshen; dress up, ginger up, add some colour to, prettify, beautify, grace; *informal* jazz up.
3 *Sarah* ***brightened up*** *considerably as she thought of Emily's words* **cheer up**, buoy up, perk up, wake up, rally; gladden, enliven, animate, invigorate, hearten, rejuvenate, uplift, encourage, stimulate, arouse, raise someone's spirits, give someone a lift; *informal* buck up, pep up.

brilliance ▶ **noun 1** *the brilliance of the sunshine* **brightness**, vividness, intensity; sparkle, flash, flashing, glitter, glittering, glow, blaze, beam, dazzle, luminosity, lustre, radiance, resplendence; *rare* effulgence, refulgence.
OPPOSITES darkness, gloom.
2 *a philosopher of great brilliance* **genius**, prowess, mastery, skill, talent, ability, artistry, expertise, adeptness, aptitude, skilfulness, virtuosity, flair, finesse, panache, deftness, excellence, power, greatness, distinction; intelligence, cleverness, wisdom, sagacity, intellect, wit.
OPPOSITE stupidity.
3 *the brilliance and beauty of Paris* **splendour**, splendidness, magnificence, grandeur, glamour, pomp, lustre, resplendence, illustriousness, éclat.

brilliant ▶ **adjective 1** *a brilliant student* **gifted**, talented, virtuoso, genius, accomplished, ingenious, masterly, inventive, creative; intelligent, bright, clever, smart, astute, acute, brainy, intellectual, profound; skilful, able, expert, adept, elite, superior, crack, choice, first-class, first-rate, excellent; educated, scholarly, learned, erudite, cerebral; precocious.
OPPOSITES stupid, untalented.
2 (*Brit. informal*) *we had a brilliant time* **excellent**, marvellous, superb, very good, first-rate, first-class, wonderful, outstanding, exceptional, magnificent, splendid, superlative, matchless, peerless; *informal* great, terrific, tremendous, smashing, fantastic, sensational, fabulous, ace, fab, A1, cool, awesome, magic, wicked, tip-top, top-notch, out of sight, out of this world, way-out, capital; *Brit. informal* brill, top-hole, wizard; *Austral./NZ informal* bonzer; *Brit. informal, dated* spiffing, topping.
OPPOSITE bad.
3 *a shaft of brilliant light* **bright**, shining, blazing, dazzling, light; vivid, intense, ablaze, beaming, gleaming, glaring, luminous, lustrous, luminescent, radiant, incandescent, phosphorescent, scintillating, resplendent; *literary* irradiant, lucent, effulgent, refulgent, fulgent, lucid, glistering, coruscating, lambent, fulgurant, fulgurating, fulgurous.
OPPOSITES dark, gloomy.
4 *a grassy meadow of brilliant green* **vivid**, intense, bright, blazing, dazzling.
OPPOSITES dark, dull.
5 *a brilliant display* **superb**, magnificent, splendid, impressive, remarkable, exceptional, glorious, illustrious.

brim ▶ **noun 1** *the rector fingered the brim of his hat* visor, peak, bill, projecting edge, projection, shield, shade.
2 *the cup was filled to its brim with cocoa* **rim**, lip, brink, edge, margin.
▶ **verb 1** *the pan was brimming with water* **be full**, be filled up, be filled to the top, be full to capacity, be packed with, overflow, run/well over.
2 *the tears brimmed in her eyes* **fill**, fill up, fill to capacity, overflow.

brimful ▶ **adjective** *the reservoir is brimful* **brimming**, **full**, filled, filled up, filled/full to the brim, filled to capacity, overfull, running over; replete, loaded, overloaded, stuffed, chock-full, chock-a-block, bursting, teeming, seething, abounding; *informal* flush, full to the gunwales.
OPPOSITE empty.

brindle, **brindled** ▶ **adjective** *a brindled cat* **tawny**, brownish, brown; **dappled**, streaked, stippled, mottled, speckled, flecked, marbled, pied, piebald, pinto.

bring ▶ **verb 1** *he brought over a tray with coffee on it* **carry**, **fetch**, bear, take; convey, transport; transfer, move, come carrying; lug, haul, shift.
OPPOSITES take, accept.
2 *Philip brought his young bride to his mansion* **conduct**, **escort**, guide, lead, usher, show, show someone the way, lead the way, pilot, accompany; shepherd, herd, drive, convoy; see, help, assist.
OPPOSITE follow.
3 *that evening the wind changed, and brought rain* **cause**, make happen, bring about/on, give rise to, create, produce, result in, wreak, effect, engender, occasion, generate, lead to, precipitate, kindle, trigger (off), spark (off), touch off, stir up, whip up, promote, contribute to; *literary* enkindle, beget; *rare* effectuate.
4 *the police contemplated bringing charges of riot* **put forward**, prefer, propose, present, submit, lay, initiate, introduce, institute, moot.
OPPOSITE drop.
5 *this job brings him a regular salary* **earn**, make, bring in, fetch, yield, net, gross; command, attract, realize, secure, return, produce.
□ **bring something about 1** *the war brought about a large increase in government debt* **cause**, create, produce, give rise to; achieve, result in, lead to, effect, provoke, call forth, occasion, bring to pass; generate, originate, engender, precipitate, wreak, kindle; *rare* effectuate.
2 *he brought the ship about* **turn**, turn round/around, reverse, reverse the direction of, change the direction of.

B

□ **bring something back 1** *the smell brought back memories of when she had been younger* **remind one of**, put one in mind of, bring/call to mind, cause one to recall, make one think of, take one back to, awaken (one's) memories of; conjure up, suggest, evoke, summon up, call up.
2 *the conference renewed its policy to bring back capital punishment* **reintroduce**, re-establish, reinstall, reinstate, relaunch, revive, resuscitate, resurrect, breathe new life into.
OPPOSITE abolish.

□ **bring someone down 1** *he was brought down by a clumsy challenge* **foul**, trip, knock over.
2 *she was in such a good mood that I couldn't bear to bring her down* **depress**, sadden, make sad/unhappy, upset, cast down, get down, make desolate, deject, dispirit, dishearten, discourage, weigh down, dampen the spirits of, oppress.
OPPOSITE cheer up.

□ **bring something down 1** *an attempt to bring down the price of compact discs* **decrease**, reduce, lower, cut, drop, diminish, cause to fall; *informal* slash, knock down.
OPPOSITE increase.
2 *the unrest brought down the government* **overthrow**, depose, oust, unseat, overturn, topple, cause to fall, pull down, lay low.

□ **bring something forward** *we intend to bring forward proposals for new Sunday trading legislation* **propose**, suggest, advance, raise, put forward, table, offer, present, move, submit, prefer, lodge, adduce, come up with; propound, proffer, posit.
OPPOSITE withdraw.

□ **bring someone in** *it was nice of him to bring me in on it* **involve**, include, count in, take in.
OPPOSITE exclude.

□ **bring something in 1** *he brought in a private member's bill* **introduce**, launch, inaugurate, initiate, institute, usher in; **propose**, suggest, submit, present, move, moot, file, lodge.
2 *the event brings in an estimated one million pounds each year. See* BRING *sense 5.*

□ **bring something off** *they knew he could bring off brilliant business coups* **achieve**, accomplish, bring about, succeed in, pull off, carry off, carry through, manage, carry out; execute, realize, perform, discharge, complete, finish, consummate, conclude, attain, engineer; *rare* effectuate.
OPPOSITE fail in/at.

□ **bring something on** *his fatal illness was brought on by severe shock* **cause**, be the cause of, make happen, bring about, give rise to, begin, create, produce, originate, occasion, effect, engender, spawn, lead to, result in, precipitate, provoke, trigger (off), spark (off), touch off, stir up, whip up, induce, foster; *literary* enkindle; *rare* effectuate.

□ **bring something out 1** *they were bringing out a new magazine called 'Teens Today'* **launch**, establish, begin, start, found, set up, open, get going, get under way, initiate, instigate, institute, inaugurate, market; **publish**, print, issue, produce; *informal* churn out, kick off.
2 *the shawl brings out the colour of your eyes* **accentuate**, call attention to, make evident, highlight, emphasize, give prominence to, underline, accent, foreground, throw into relief.
OPPOSITES cover up, play down.

□ **bring someone round 1** *she administered artificial respiration and brought him round* **wake up**, return to consciousness, rouse, arouse, bring to.
OPPOSITE knock out.
2 *we would have brought him round when he got to know the situation a bit better* **persuade**, convince, talk round, win over, sway, influence, coax, entice.

□ **bring oneself to** *he couldn't bring himself to pull the trigger* **force oneself to**, make oneself, bear to.

□ **bring someone up** *she was brought up by her maternal grandparents* **rear**, raise, care for, take care of, look after, nurture, provide for; develop, mother, parent, foster, breed; educate, train, instruct.

□ **bring something up** *later that evening he casually brought the subject up* **mention**, allude to, touch on, raise, broach, introduce; voice, suggest, propose, submit, advance, moot, put forward, bring forward, pose, present, table, propound, air, ventilate.

brink ▶ **noun 1** *the brink of the abyss* **edge**, verge, margin, rim, lip; extremity, border, boundary, fringe; perimeter, circumference, periphery; limit, limits, bound, bounds; *literary* marge, bourn, skirt.
OPPOSITE middle.
2 *border disputes have brought both countries to the brink of war* **verge**, edge, threshold, point, dawn; starting point, start.

brio ▶ **noun** *Britain's early film makers set about the business of film production with some brio* **vigour**, vivacity, vivaciousness, gusto, verve, zest, sparkle, dash, elan, panache, exuberance, ebullience, enthusiasm, eagerness, vitality, dynamism, animation, spirit, energy; *informal* pep, vim, zing, get-up-and-go.
OPPOSITE lethargy.

brisk ▶ **adjective 1** *he set off at a brisk pace* **quick**, rapid, fast, swift, speedy, fleet-footed; hasty, hurried, urgent; **energetic**, lively, vigorous, sharp; agile, nimble, spry, sprightly, spirited; *informal* nippy, snappy; *rare* alacritous.
OPPOSITES sluggish, slow.
2 *the public bar was already doing a brisk trade* **busy**, bustling, lively, active, vibrant, hectic; good.
OPPOSITE quiet.
3 *his tone became brisk and businesslike* **no-nonsense**, decisive, businesslike; **brusque**, abrupt, short, sharp, curt, crisp, blunt, terse, snappy, snappish, gruff; rude, discourteous, uncivil.
4 *there was a brisk breeze* **bracing**, fresh, crisp, invigorating, refreshing, reviving, stimulating, rousing, enlivening, exhilarating, energizing; restorative, tonic, vitalizing, healthful, health-giving; sharp, biting, keen, chilly, cold; *informal* nippy.

bristle ▶ **noun 1** *Curtis smoothed the bristles on his chin* **hair**, whisker; (**bristles**) stubble, designer stubble, five o'clock shadow; *technical* seta.
2 *a hedgehog's bristles* **prickle**, spine, quill, thorn, barb.
▶ **verb 1** *Corbett sensed menace and malevolence, and the hair on the back of his neck bristled* **rise**, stand up, stand on end; *literary* horripilate.
2 *she swivelled round, bristling at his tone* **get angry**, become infuriated, be furious, be maddened, bridle, become indignant, be irritated, get/have one's hackles up, feel one's hackles rise, rear up, draw oneself up, flare up, see red; take offence, take umbrage; be defensive.
3 *the roof bristled with antennae* **abound**, swarm, teem, crawl, overflow, hum, be alive, be packed, be crowded, be thronged, be jammed, be infested, be full, be covered; *informal* be thick, be crawling, be lousy, be stuffed, be jam-packed, be chock-a-block, be chock-full.

bristly ▶ **adjective 1** *the dunes were dotted with bristly little bushes* **prickly**, spiky, spiked, thorny, scratchy, stiff; briary, brambly.
2 *the bristly skin of his cheek* **stubbly**, hairy, scratchy, fuzzy, unshaven; whiskered, whiskery, bewhiskered, bearded, hirsute; rough, coarse, prickly; *technical* hispid.
OPPOSITES smooth, clean-shaven.

Britain ▶ **noun the United Kingdom**, the UK, Great Britain, the British Isles; *Brit. informal* Blighty; *literary* Albion.

brittle ▶ **adjective 1** *glass is a brittle material* **breakable**, splintery, shatterable, fragile, frail, delicate, frangible; **rigid**, hard, crisp.
OPPOSITES flexible; resilient.
2 *she began to speak in a brittle, staccato voice* **harsh**, hard, sharp, strident, grating, rasping.
OPPOSITE soft.
3 *a brittle young woman* **edgy**, on edge, nervous, unstable, nervy, highly strung, anxious, tense, excitable, jumpy, skittish, neurotic, hysterical; sensitive, insecure; *informal* uptight.
OPPOSITES relaxed, cool.

broach ▶ **verb 1** *I thought it over very carefully before broaching the subject to Nigel* **bring up**, raise, introduce, talk about, mention, touch on, open, embark on, enter on, air, ventilate; put forward, propound, propose, suggest, submit.
2 *Jeffrey broached a barrel of beer* **pierce**, puncture, tap; **open**, uncork, start, begin; *informal* crack (open).

broad ▶ **adjective 1** *they descended the broad flight of steps* **wide**, large, big.
OPPOSITE narrow.
2 *the leaves are six inches long and two inches broad* **in breadth**, in width, from side to side, wide, across, thick.
OPPOSITE long.
3 *a broad expanse of grass prairie* **extensive**, vast, immense, great, spacious, expansive, sizeable, sweeping, rambling, rolling, ample, spread out, far reaching, boundless, immeasurable.
4 *they offer a broad range of opportunities for young would-be executives* **comprehensive**, inclusive, extensive, wide, wide-ranging, broad-ranging, encyclopedic, all-embracing; general, universal, catholic, eclectic, unlimited.
OPPOSITE limited.
5 *this report gives only a broad outline of our environmental performance* **general**, non-specific, unspecific, unfocused, rough, approximate, overall, sweeping, basic, loose, indefinite, vague, hazy, fuzzy, woolly; *N. Amer. informal* ballpark.
OPPOSITES detailed; precise.
6 *he dropped a broad hint* **obvious**, direct, plain, clear, unsubtle, explicit, straightforward, bald, clear-cut, manifest, patent, conspicuous, transparent, prominent, unmistakable, undisguised, unconcealed, overt, undeniable.
OPPOSITE subtle.
7 *the broad humour of the campaign has been toned down* **indecent**, improper, coarse, unrefined, indelicate, ribald, risqué, racy, rude, spicy, suggestive, naughty, indecorous, off colour, earthy, smutty, dirty, filthy, vulgar, gross; *informal* blue, near the bone, near the knuckle.
8 *a broad Somerset accent* **noticeable**, strong, thick, heavy, pronounced.
OPPOSITE slight.
9 *he was attacked in broad daylight* **full**, complete, total, clear, bright, plain, undiminished.
▶ **noun** (*N. Amer. informal*) *the broads will go crazy about his looks. See* WOMAN.

WORD LINKS
related prefix **platy-** (e.g. ***platypus, platyhelminth***)

B

broadcast ▶ verb **1** *the show will be broadcast on TV worldwide* **transmit**, relay, air, beam, send/put out, put on the air/airwaves, show, televise, telecast; *informal* screen.
2 *the result of the match was broadcast far and wide* **report**, announce, publicize, publish, make public, make known, advertise, proclaim, declare; spread, circulate, air, pass round, disseminate, promulgate, blazon, trumpet; *informal* shout from the rooftops.
3 *the most common mistake is to broadcast too much seed, resulting in a very heavy crop* **scatter**, sow, disperse, sprinkle, spread, distribute, disseminate, strew, throw, toss, fling; *literary* bestrew.
▶ noun *he communicated with the people via radio and television broadcasts* **programme**, show, production, presentation, performance; transmission, telecast; *informal* screening, prog.

broaden ▶ verb **1** *her smile broadened* **widen**, become/make broader, become/make wider, expand, fill out, stretch (out), draw out, spread out, deepen, thicken.
OPPOSITE narrow.
2 *the government attempted to broaden its political base* **expand**, enlarge, extend, widen, swell; increase, augment, supplement, add to, amplify, fill out; develop, enrich, enhance, intensify, improve, build on, open up.
OPPOSITE diminish.

broadly ▶ adverb **1** *the pattern of mortality is broadly similar for men and women* **in general**, on the whole, as a rule, in the main, mainly, predominantly; loosely, roughly, approximately; chiefly, commonly, usually.
OPPOSITE exactly.
2 *he was smiling broadly now* **widely**, openly.

broad-minded ▶ adjective *I like to think that I'm broad-minded, but his language was beyond the pale* **liberal**, tolerant, open-minded, forbearing, indulgent, receptive, progressive, freethinking, permissive, libertarian, unshockable; unprejudiced, unbiased, unbigoted, impartial, undogmatic, catholic, flexible, dispassionate, just, fair.
OPPOSITES narrow-minded, intolerant.

broadside ▶ noun **1** *the gunners fired broadsides* **salvo**, volley, cannonade, barrage, blast, bombardment, fusillade, hail of bullets.
2 *a broadside against the economic reforms* **criticism**, censure, denunciation, harangue, rant, polemic, diatribe, tirade, philippic; attack, assault, onslaught, abuse, battering; *informal* flak, brickbat; *Brit. informal* slating.

brochure ▶ noun *a travel brochure* **pamphlet**, booklet, prospectus, catalogue, leaflet, handbill, handout, bill, circular, flyer, notice, advertisement; *N. Amer.* mailer, folder.

broil ▶ verb (*N. Amer.*) *he broiled a wedge of sea bass* **grill**, toast, barbecue, cook, fry, bake.

broiling ▶ adjective *the sweaty nights and broiling days* **hot**, scorching, roasting, baking, boiling (hot), blistering, sweltering, parching, searing, blazing, sizzling, burning (hot), sultry, torrid, tropical, like an oven, like a furnace.
OPPOSITES cold, cool.

broke ▶ adjective (*Brit. informal*) *the worst part of being unemployed is having to be always broke* **penniless**, moneyless, bankrupt, insolvent, poor, poverty-stricken, impoverished, impecunious, penurious, indigent, in penury, needy, destitute, ruined, down and out, without a penny to one's name, without two pennies to rub together; *informal* stony broke, flat broke, on one's uppers, cleaned out, strapped (for cash), on one's beam-ends, bust, hard up, without a brass farthing, without a bean, without a sou, as poor as a church mouse; *Brit. informal* skint, without a shot in one's locker; *Brit. rhyming slang* boracic (lint); *N. Amer. informal* stone broke, without a red cent.
OPPOSITE rich.

broken ▶ adjective **1** *a broken bottle* **smashed**, shattered, burst, fragmented, splintered, shivered, crushed, snapped, rent, torn, ruptured, separated, severed, in bits, in pieces; destroyed, wrecked, demolished, disintegrated; cracked, split, chipped; *informal* in smithereens/smithers.
OPPOSITES whole, unbroken.
2 *a broken arm* **fractured**, damaged, injured, maimed, crippled, lame.
3 *his video's broken* **damaged**, faulty, defective, unsound; not working, not functioning, non-functioning, malfunctioning, in disrepair, inoperative, out of order/commission, not in working order, broken-down, out of kilter, down; *informal* on the blink, on its last legs, kaput, bust, busted, conked out, acting/playing up, gone haywire, gone phut, finished, done for, wonky, dud, duff; *Brit. informal* knackered; *Brit. vulgar slang* buggered.
OPPOSITES working, fixed.
4 *never apply a depilatory cream to inflamed or broken skin* **cut**, pierced, punctured, perforated, ruptured.
5 *a broken marriage* **failed**, ended.
6 *his broken promises* **flouted**, violated, infringed, disregarded, ignored, contravened; *informal* infracted.
OPPOSITES kept, obeyed.
7 *it was an enormous humiliation and he was left a broken man* **defeated**, beaten, vanquished, overpowered, overwhelmed, subdued; **demoralized**, dispirited, discouraged, dejected, crushed, humbled, dishonoured, ruined, crippled.
8 *it was a long, noisy night of broken sleep* **interrupted**, disturbed, fitful, disrupted, disconnected, discontinuous, fragmentary, intermittent, unsettled, sporadic, spasmodic, erratic, troubled, incomplete.
OPPOSITE uninterrupted.
9 *he pressed onwards gingerly over the broken ground* **uneven**, rough, irregular, bumpy; jagged, ragged, craggy, rutted, pitted, rutty.
OPPOSITES flat, smooth.
10 *she spoke in broken English* **halting**, hesitating, disjointed, faltering, stumbling, stammering, stuttering, imperfect.
OPPOSITE perfect.

broken-down ▶ adjective **1** *a broken-down hotel* **dilapidated**, ramshackle, rickety, tumbledown, run down, worn out, in disrepair, battered, decayed, crumbling, deteriorated, falling to pieces, gone to rack and ruin; *informal* the worse for wear.
OPPOSITES smart, chic.
2 *a broken-down car* **defective**, broken, damaged, faulty, unsound; not working, not functioning, malfunctioning, in disrepair, inoperative, out of order/commission, not in working order, non-functioning, down; *informal* **kaput**, on the blink, on its last legs, bust, busted, conked out, clapped out, acting/playing up, gone haywire, gone phut, finished, done for, dud; *Brit. informal* knackered, duff.
OPPOSITES working, fixed.

broken-hearted ▶ adjective *the boy was broken-hearted and inconsolable* **heartbroken**, grief-stricken, desolate, despairing, devastated, inconsolable, miserable, depressed, melancholy, wretched, sorrowful, sorrowing, mourning, forlorn, heavy-hearted, woeful, doleful, downcast, bowed down, cast down, crestfallen, woebegone, morose, gloomy, glum, sad, cheerless, down; *informal* down in the mouth, shattered, choked; *literary* dolorous, heartsick.
OPPOSITE happy.

broker ▶ noun *a top City broker* **dealer**, broker-dealer, agent, negotiator, trafficker; middleman, intermediary, mediator; factor, trustee, liaison, representative, go-between; stockbroker, insurance broker; *informal* rep; *historical* scrivener.
▶ verb *an agreement brokered by the Commonwealth Secretariat* **arrange**, organize, orchestrate, work out, thrash out, hammer out, settle, clinch, contract, pull off, bring off/about; negotiate, mediate, arbitrate, act as go-between; *informal* sort out, swing.

bromide ▶ noun (*dated*) **1** *they advised the use of bromide to counteract any stimulation* **sedative**, tranquillizer, calmative, depressant, opiate, neuroleptic, sleeping pill, soporific, drug, narcotic, anodyne; *informal* downer, trank, sleeper; *trademark* Valium, Librium.
OPPOSITE stimulant.
2 *let's set aside the usual bromides about the press* **cliché**, banality, truism, platitude, commonplace, old chestnut, banal phrase, trite phrase, hackneyed phrase, stock phrase, inanity.

bronze ▶ noun *in the relay, Scotland won the bronze* **bronze medal**, third prize.
▶ adjective *the gleam of his bronze skin* **bronze-coloured**, copper-coloured, copper, reddish-brown, chestnut, metallic brown, rust-coloured, rust, henna, tan; tanned, suntanned, sunburned, bronzed, browned.

bronzed ▶ adjective *the firmness of his bronzed skin* **tanned**, suntanned, sunburned, bronze, browned, brown, tan.
OPPOSITE pale.

brooch ▶ noun *an emerald and diamond brooch* **breastpin**, pin, clasp, clip, fastening, badge.

brood ▶ noun **1** *it flew under the bridge to feed its brood* **offspring**, young, progeny, spawn; family, hatch, clutch, nest, litter; *rare* progeniture.
2 (*informal*) *Gillian was the youngest of the brood* **family**, household, ménage, clan, tribe; children, offspring, youngsters, little ones, progeny, descendants, issue; *informal* kids, sprogs.
▶ verb **1** *the male takes over once the eggs are laid and broods them* **incubate**, cover, hatch, sit on.
2 *he slumped in his armchair, brooding on how life had let him down* **worry about**, fret about, agonize over, mope over, moon over, languish over, feel despondent about, grieve over, sulk about, eat one's heart out over; **think about**, ponder, contemplate, pore over, meditate on, muse on, mull over, dwell on, ruminate on/over, chew over, puzzle over, weigh up, turn over in one's mind.

brook[1] ▶ noun *they dozed beside the gurgling brook* **stream**, small river, streamlet, rivulet, rill, brooklet, runnel, runlet, freshet, gill; *N. English* beck; *S. English* bourn; *Austral./NZ* billabong; *Scottish & N. English* burn; *N. Amer. & Austral./NZ* creek.

brook[2] ▶ verb *the authorities would brook no delay* **tolerate**, allow, stand, bear, abide, stomach, swallow, put up with, go along with, endure, suffer, withstand, cope with; accept, permit, admit of, countenance; *Scottish* thole; *informal* stand for, stick, hack.

brothel ▶ noun **bordello**, house of ill repute, house of prostitution; *Law* disorderly house; *French* maison close; *informal* whorehouse, cathouse, drum; *Brit. informal* knocking shop; *N. Amer. informal* creepjoint; *Austral./NZ informal* crib; *euphemistic* massage parlour; *archaic* bawdy house, house of ill fame, bagnio, stew.

brother ▶ noun **1** *she had a younger brother named William* **male sibling**; *informal* bro.
2 *they were brothers in crime* **colleague**, associate, companion, partner, comrade, comrade-in-arms, co-worker, fellow, friend; *French* confrère; *informal* pal, chum; *Brit. informal* mate; *archaic* compeer.
3 *a brother of the Order* **monk**, cleric, friar, religious, regular, monastic, contemplative.

WORD LINKS
relating to a brother **fraternal**
killing of one's brother or sister **fratricide**

brotherhood ▶ noun **1** *we hold the same ideals of justice and brotherhood* **comradeship**, fellowship, brotherliness, fraternalism, kinship; companionship, camaraderie, friendship, amity, rapport; *French* esprit de corps.
2 *a Masonic brotherhood* **society**, association, union, alliance, institution, league, guild, coalition, affiliation, consortium, fraternity, order, body, community, club, syndicate, circle, lodge, clan, set, clique, coterie; *rare* sodality.

brotherly ▶ adjective **1** *brotherly rivalry* **fraternal**, sibling.
2 *he spoke of brotherly love* **friendly**, affectionate, amicable, kind, kindly, devoted, loving, loyal, cordial, sympathetic, comradely; philanthropic, charitable, altruistic; *informal* chummy, pally.

brow ▶ noun **1** *the doctor wiped his brow with his handkerchief* **forehead**, temple; *Zoology* frons.
2 *his eyes were deep set beneath heavy black brows* **eyebrow**.
3 *the beagles tumbled over the brow of the hill* **summit**, peak, top, crest, crown, tip, head, pinnacle, apex, vertex, apogee.
OPPOSITE bottom.

browbeat ▶ verb *the interrogators browbeat a young witness into changing her story* **bully**, hector, intimidate, force, coerce, compel, badger, dragoon, cow, bludgeon, persecute, domineer, oppress, pressure, pressurize, tyrannize, terrorize, menace, subjugate, use strong-arm tactics on; harass, harry, hound, nag, goad, boss about/around; *informal* bulldoze, railroad, lean on.

brown ▶ adjective **1** *brown eyes | a brown coat* hazel, chocolate-coloured, coffee-coloured, cocoa-coloured, nut-brown; brunette, mousy; sepia, mahogany, umber, burnt sienna; beige, buff, tan, fawn, biscuit, camel, café au lait, caramel, mushroom; bay, sorrel, dun, brindle, brindled; auburn, tawny, coppery, chestnut, bronze, russet.
2 *his skin was brown from the wind and the sun* **tanned**, suntanned, sunburned, browned, bronze, bronzed, dark; swarthy, dusky.
3 *brown bread* **unbleached**, wholemeal.
▶ verb *the grill browns food evenly as it turns on the turntable* **singe**, sear, seal, crisp (up); **grill**, toast, barbecue, fry, sauté, bake.

browned off ▶ adjective (*informal*) *it's this bureaucracy that's getting the older staff browned off* **fed up**, irritated, annoyed, exasperated, irked, put out, peeved, piqued, disgruntled; discontented, discouraged, disheartened, depressed; bored, weary, tired; *informal* hacked off, cheesed off, brassed off, narked; *vulgar slang* pissed off.

browse ▶ verb **1** *returning to the main street, I browsed among the many little shops I found there* **look around/round**, have a look, window-shop, peruse.
2 *Stella browsed through the newspaper* **scan**, skim, glance, look, run one's eye over, have a look at, peruse, give something a/the once-over; thumb, leaf, flip, flick, run, dip into; riffle, speed-read.
3 *three cows were browsing at the far end of the meadow* **graze**, feed, eat, nibble, crop, pasture, ruminate.
▶ noun *this brochure is well worth a browse* **scan**, read, skim, leaf, flick through, glance, look.

bruise ▶ noun *she had a bruise across her forehead* **contusion**, lesion, mark, injury, black-and-blue mark, skin discoloration, blackening; swelling, lump, bump, welt; black eye; *informal* shiner; *technical* ecchymosis, trauma.
▶ verb **1** *the right side of her face was badly bruised* **contuse**, injure, mark, make black and blue, discolour, blacken, hurt.
2 *the movement jars the contents, until nearly every apple is bruised* **mark**, discolour, blemish; damage, spoil, impair, mar.
3 *Eric's ego was bruised when the crowd jeered* **upset**, offend, insult, affront, hurt, wound, pain, injure, crush, displease, peeve, vex, distress, grieve.

bruiser ▶ noun (*informal*) *a bruiser standing in the doorway of the pub.* See THUG.

brunette ▶ adjective *a brunette woman* **brown-haired**, dark, dark-haired, darkish.
OPPOSITE blonde.

brunt ▶ noun *her two teenage sons bore the brunt of her bitter and depressed spirit* **full force**, force, impact, shock, burden, pressure, strain, stress, impetus, thrust, weight, violence; effect, repercussions, consequences.

brush[1] ▶ noun **1** *a dustpan and brush | a fine camel-hair brush* **broom**, sweeper, besom, whisk, sweeping brush; hairbrush, clothes brush, scrubbing brush, toothbrush, paintbrush.
2 *he gave the seat a brush with the back of his hand* **clean**, sweep, wipe, dust, mop.
3 *a fox's brush* **tail**, tailpiece; scut, dock.
4 *Luke had said goodbye with no more than the lightest brush of his lips against her cheek* **touch**, stroke, skim, graze, glance, rub, shave, pat, nudge, contact; kiss; *informal* swipe.
5 *a brush with the law* **encounter**, clash, confrontation, collision, conflict; altercation, skirmish, wrangle, scuffle, tussle, fight, battle, engagement, feud, quarrel, incident, to-do; *informal* run-in, scrap, set-to, argy-bargy; *Brit. informal* spot of bother.
▶ verb **1** *he spent most of his day brushing the floors* **sweep**, clean, buff, scrub.
2 *she brushed her long auburn hair* **groom**, comb, neaten, tidy, make neat/tidy, smarten, smooth, arrange, fix, adjust, preen, primp, do, titivate; curry.
3 *she felt his lips lightly brush against her cheek* **touch**, stroke, caress, skim, sweep, graze, shave, glance, contact, flick, scrape; kiss.
4 *she brushed a wisp of hair away from her face* **push**, move, sweep, clear, clean, remove.
□ **brush something aside** *she brushed aside his repeated warnings* **disregard**, ignore, dismiss, shrug off, pass over, put aside, sweep aside, wave aside; overlook, pay no attention to, take no notice of, refuse to acknowledge, neglect, think no more of, forget about, have no time for, shut one's eyes to, turn a blind eye to, turn a deaf ear to; reject, spurn, flout; scoff at, laugh off, make light of, trivialize, belittle, minimize; *informal* play down, pooh-pooh, cock a snook at.
□ **brush someone off** *he scrambled up to help her, but she brushed him off* **rebuff**, dismiss, spurn, reject, repudiate, refuse, disown, slight, deny, scorn, disdain; ignore, disregard, snub, cut, cut dead, turn one's back on, give someone the cold shoulder, cold-shoulder, look right through, freeze out; jilt, cast aside, discard, throw over, send off, send away, send packing, drop, leave; *informal* knock back, give the brush-off, give the heave-ho, give someone their marching orders, give someone their walking papers, tell someone to get lost; *archaic* forsake.
□ **brush up (on)** *I've been brushing up on my Italian* **revise**, read up, go over, refresh one's memory of, relearn, cram, study, learn; improve, sharpen (up), polish up, better, enhance; hone, refine, fine-tune, perfect; *informal* rub up, bone up; *Brit. informal* swot up (on), gen up on.

brush[2] ▶ noun *a haven of open spaces and thick brush* **undergrowth**, underwood, scrub, scrubland, brushwood, bracken, bushes; wood, thicket, copse; *N. Amer.* underbrush, chaparral; *rare* boscage.

brush-off ▶ noun (*informal*) *she gave him a polite brush-off* **rejection**, refusal, rebuff, dismissal, spurning, repudiation, repulse, turndown, discouragement; snub, slight, cut, cold-shouldering; *informal* elbow, knock-back; *N. Amer. informal* kiss-off.
OPPOSITE acceptance.

brusque ▶ adjective *he was disliked because of his brusque manners* **curt**, abrupt, blunt, short, sharp, terse, brisk, crisp, clipped, monosyllabic, peremptory, gruff, bluff; caustic, tart, abrasive; outspoken, plain-spoken, not afraid to call a spade a spade, indelicate, tactless, undiplomatic; discourteous, impolite, rude, uncivil, offhand, snappish, snappy, churlish.
OPPOSITES polite, verbose.

CHOOSE THE RIGHT WORD

brusque, curt, abrupt, terse

All these words apply to remarks that are noticeably short and unadorned, or to the people who make them. Unlike *concise* and *succinct* (see CONCISE), all usually imply criticism, as shown by the other adjectives with which they typically occur: *overbearing, arrogant, impetuous, rude,* and *sharp*.

- **Brusque** remarks are short in an aggressive, dismissive, or off-putting way; the *brusque* person is trying to get a conversation over and move quickly on to something else (*he sounded nicer now he had dropped his brusque, cold manner*).
- A **curt** statement or gesture is excessively businesslike and efficient, having had everything but the absolutely necessary minimum removed (*he led the way with a curt 'Follow me!'*). The absence of any extra polite or friendly remarks may make a *curt* comment or person appear rude.
- Suddenness and unexpectedness are central to the meaning of **abrupt**, which is from a Latin word meaning 'broken off'. An *abrupt* remark has no polite or softening introduction or conclusion; an *abrupt* manner appears rude through the speed with which it deals with and dismisses people (*his abrupt question was laced with impatience | you were rather abrupt with that nice young man*).
- A **terse** statement or expression has had any dispensable words removed—a brevity that is bald at best and verges on the harsh or unfriendly (*Luke's terse reply forbade further talk*).

brutal ▶ adjective **1** *a brutal attack on an elderly man* **savage**, cruel,

B

bloodthirsty, vicious, ferocious, barbaric, barbarous, wicked, murderous, cold-blooded, hard-hearted, harsh; ruthless, callous, heartless, merciless, pitiless, remorseless, sadistic, unfeeling; inhuman, heinous, monstrous, abominable, atrocious, vile, infernal, uncivilized; bestial, brutish, beastly, animal.
OPPOSITES gentle, humane.
2 *he replied with brutal honesty* **unsparing**, unstinting, unadorned, unembellished, unvarnished, bald, naked, stark, blunt, direct, straight, straightforward, frank, outspoken, forthright, plain-spoken; heartless, severe; complete, total, unequivocal, unambiguous.

brutality ▶ noun *the murders were carried out with unbelievable brutality* **savagery**, cruelty, bloodthirstiness, viciousness, ferocity, barbarity, wickedness, murderousness, cold-bloodedness, hard-heartedness, harshness; ruthlessness, callousness, heartlessness, mercilessness, pitilessness, remorselessness, sadism; inhumanity, heinousness, monstrousness, atrocity, vileness; bestiality, brutishness, beastliness.
OPPOSITES gentleness, kindness.

brutalize ▶ verb **1** *the men were brutalized by life in the trenches* **desensitize**, dehumanize, harden, toughen, case-harden, inure, make unfeeling, make callous, degrade.
2 *they were brutalized by the police* **attack**, abuse, assault, beat, thrash, thump, pummel, pound, batter.

brute ▶ noun **1** *he was a callous brute* **savage**, beast, monster, animal, sadist, barbarian, devil, demon, fiend, ogre; thug, lout, boor, oaf, ruffian, yahoo, rowdy, bully boy; *informal* swine, bastard, pig.
2 *the Alsatian, a vicious-looking brute, strained at the leash* **animal**, beast, wild animal, wild beast, creature; *informal* critter.
▶ adjective *by sheer brute strength he almost reached the top of the incline* **physical**, crude, fleshly, bodily, violent.

bubble ▶ noun **1** *he watched the bubbles rise in his glass of mineral water* **globule**, bead, blister, drop; air cavity, air pocket; (**bubbles**) sparkle, fizz, effervescence, froth, head, lather, suds; *informal* glob; *technical* barm.
2 *a great deal of economic activity had been supported by the bubble of housing wealth* **illusion**, delusion, fantasy, dream, pipe dream, daydream, chimera, vanity, castle in the air; transient phenomenon, short-lived phenomenon; *informal* pie in the sky.
▶ verb **1** *two glasses that overflowed with bubbling champagne* **sparkle**, fizz, effervesce, gurgle, foam, froth, spume.
OPPOSITES be flat, be still.
2 *the milk was bubbling above the flame* **boil**, simmer, seethe, gurgle.
3 *she was* **bubbling over** *with enthusiasm* **overflow**, brim over, be filled, run over, gush.

bubbly ▶ adjective **1** *a bubbly wine* **sparkling**, fizzy, carbonated, aerated, effervescent, gassy, frothy, foamy, bubbling; sudsy; *French* (vin) mousseux, pétillant; *Italian* spumante, frizzante; *German* Schaum-, Perl-.
OPPOSITES still, flat.
2 *she was bubbly and full of life* **vivacious**, animated, ebullient, lively, full of life, spirited, high-spirited, scintillating, vibrant, zestful, energetic, dynamic; bubbling, effervescent, sparkling, bouncy, buoyant, carefree, happy-go-lucky; excited, elated, merry, happy, cheerful, cheery, perky, sunny, airy, breezy, bright, bright and breezy, enthusiastic; *informal* upbeat, peppy, zingy, zippy, chirpy, full of beans; *N. Amer. informal* peart.
OPPOSITES dull, listless.
▶ noun (*informal*) *a bottle of bubbly* **champagne**, sparkling wine; *French* mousseux; *Italian* spumante; *Spanish* cava; *S. African* perlé; *informal* champers, fizz, sparkler.

buccaneer ▶ noun *a crew of swashbuckling buccaneers* **pirate**, marauder, raider, sea rover, freebooter, plunderer, cut-throat, privateer, Viking, bandit, robber, desperado; adventurer, swashbuckler; *archaic* corsair.

buck ▶ verb *it takes guts to buck the system* **resist**, oppose, contradict, defy, fight (against), go against, kick against.
□ **buck up** (*informal*) **1** *buck up, for heaven's sake—there's lots of people in the same boat* **cheer up**, perk up, take heart, rally, pick up, bounce back; become more cheerful, become livelier.
2 *buck up or you'll be late* **hurry up**, speed up, make haste, hasten; *informal* get a move on, step on it, shake a leg.
OPPOSITE slow down.
□ **buck someone up** (*informal*) **cheer up**, brighten up, buoy up, ginger up, perk up, rally, animate, invigorate, hearten, uplift, encourage, stimulate, enliven, make someone happier, raise someone's spirits, give someone a lift; *informal* pep up; *rare* inspirit.

bucket ▶ noun *a bucket of cold water* **pail**, scuttle, can, tub, pitcher, vessel.
□ **buckets** (*informal*) *everyone wept buckets* **floods**, gallons, pints, oceans; *Brit. informal* lashings.
▶ verb (*Brit. informal*) **1** *it began to rain again, and soon it was* **bucketing down rain heavily**, rain cats and dogs, rain hard, pour, pelt, lash, teem, stream, tip, beat, sheet.
2 *the car came bucketing out of a side road.* See SPEED.

buckle ▶ noun *his belt buckle* **clasp**, clip, catch, fastener, fastening, hasp.
▶ verb **1** *he buckled the belt round his waist* **fasten**, do up, hook, strap, tie, secure, clasp, catch, clip.
OPPOSITE unfasten.
2 *Harry's front axle buckled | he had buckled the front axle* **warp**, become/make warped, bend, bend out of shape, become/make bent, twist, become/make twisted, curve, become/make curved, distort, become/make distorted, contort, become/make contorted, become/make crooked, deform, become/make deformed, malform, become/make malformed, misshape, become/make misshapen, mangle, become/make mangled, develop a kink/wrinkle/fold, bulge, arc, arch, wrinkle; crumple, collapse, cave in, give way.
OPPOSITE straighten.
□ **buckle down** *I just buckled down and got on with playing as well as I could* **get (down) to work**, set to work, get down to business, roll up one's sleeves, put one's hand to the plough; **work hard**, apply oneself, make an effort, strive, be industrious, be diligent, be assiduous, exert oneself, focus; *informal* get cracking, pull/get one's finger out, get weaving, get off one's backside; *Brit. informal* get stuck in.

bucolic ▶ adjective *the bucolic scene of a farmer ploughing behind a shire horse* **rustic**, rural, pastoral, country, countryside, agricultural, agrarian, outdoor, idyllic, unspoilt; *literary* Arcadian, sylvan; *rare* georgic, agrestic.
OPPOSITE urban.

bud ▶ noun *then comes spring, and fresh buds* **sprout**, shoot, flowerlet, floret; *technical* plumule; *rare* burgeon.
▶ verb *trees began to bud* **sprout**, shoot, form/develop buds, send out shoots, germinate, burgeon, swell, vegetate, mature; *technical* pullulate.
OPPOSITE wither.

budding ▶ adjective *a budding artist* **promising**, up-and-coming, rising, coming, in the making, aspiring, future, prospective, with potential; potential, beginning, fledgling, incipient, embryonic, nascent; developing, growing, burgeoning; *informal* would-be, wannabe.
OPPOSITES veteran, experienced.

budge ▶ verb **1** *they tried to lift the cage, but it wouldn't budge* **move**, shift, change position, stir, give way, go.
2 *I couldn't budge the door* **move**, dislodge, shift, change the position of, remove, relocate, reposition, get/set going.
3 *they might be prepared to budge on the issue* **change one's mind**, give way, give in, yield, acquiesce, compromise, adapt, retract, do a U-turn, eat one's words; *Brit.* do an about-turn.
4 *our customers won't be budged on price alone* **influence**, sway, convince, persuade, prevail on, coax, induce, entice, tempt, lure, cajole, bring round, coerce, alter, change, shift, bend.
□ **budge up/over** (*informal*) **move up/over**, shift up/over, make room, make space.

budget ▶ noun **1** *draw up your own personal budget for a typical week* **financial plan**, financial estimate, financial blueprint, prediction of revenue and expenditure, forecast; **accounts**, statement, spreadsheet.
2 *an announcement of cuts in the defence budget* **allowance**, allocation, allotment, quota, share, ration, helping, lot, slice; grant, award, funds, means, resources, wherewithal, capital.
▶ verb **1** *you will have to budget at least £7,000 for the most basic system* **allocate**, allot, assign, allow, earmark, devote, designate, appropriate, set aside; award, grant.
2 *the repayments will be the same for each month—this will help you budget your finances* **schedule**, plan, cost, cost out, estimate; allocate, ration, apportion.
▶ adjective *a budget hotel* **cheap**, inexpensive, economy, economic, economical, low-cost, low-price, low-budget, reasonable, reasonably priced, cut-price, cut-rate, discount, discounted, bargain, bargain-basement.
OPPOSITE expensive.

buff[1] ▶ adjective *a plain buff envelope* **beige**, straw-coloured, yellowish, yellowish-brown, brownish-yellow, light brown, pale brown, tan, fawn, sand, sandy, oatmeal, wheaten, biscuit, coffee, coffee-coloured, camel, caramel.
▶ verb *Victor buffed the glass until it gleamed* **polish**, burnish, rub up, rub, smooth, shine, wipe, clean.
▶ noun
□ **in the buff** (*informal*). See NAKED.

buff[2] ▶ noun (*informal*) *an opera buff* **enthusiast**, fan, fanatic, devotee, addict, lover, admirer; **expert**, connoisseur, aficionado, authority, pundit, cognoscente, one of the cognoscenti, savant; *informal* freak, nut, fiend, maniac, ham; *N. Amer. informal* maven, geek, nerd; *S. African informal* fundi.

buffer ▶ noun *their agent became a buffer against the business world* **cushion**, bulwark; shield, screen, barrier, guard, safeguard, hedge, shock absorber, armour; **intermediary**, middleman, go-between.
▶ verb *the aromatherapy massage was helping to buffer some of the strain* **cushion**, absorb, soften, lessen, diminish, moderate, mitigate, allay, deaden, muffle, stifle, shield.
OPPOSITE intensify.

buffet[1] (rhymes with 'book day') ▶ noun **1** *a sumptuous buffet was spread out at the restaurant* **cold table**, cold meal, self-service, smorgasbord.
2 *a station buffet* **cafe**, cafeteria, snack bar, canteen, salad bar,

refreshment stall/counter, restaurant.
3 *an old-fashioned built-in buffet in the dining room* **sideboard**, cabinet, china cupboard, counter.

buffet² (rhymes with 'tuffet') ▶ **verb 1** *the car was buffeted by the wind* **batter**, pound, beat/knock/dash against, push against, lash, strike, hit, bang.
2 *he has been buffeted by bad publicity* **afflict**, trouble, harm, distress, burden, bother, beset, harass, worry, oppress, strain, stress, tax, torment, blight, bedevil, harrow, cause trouble to, cause suffering to.
3 (dated) *the infuriated pirates buffeted them in the mouth* **pummel**, thrash, batter, beat, hammer, drub; **strike**, slap, smack, crack, thump, cuff, box someone's ears; informal whack, thwack, clout, wallop, bash, clobber, bop, biff, sock, deck, plug.
▶ **noun 1** (dated) *I began to rain kicks and buffets on the door* **blow**, punch, slap, smack, crack, bang, thump, box, cuff, battering, welt, knock, rap, poke, jab; informal whack, wallop, clout.
2 *all the blows and buffets of this world* **shock**, jolt, jar, upset, setback, crisis, catastrophe, blow; **misfortune**, trouble, problem, difficulty, hardship, adversity, distress, disaster, misadventure; affliction, sorrow, misery, tribulation, woe, pain, tragedy, calamity, vicissitude; trial, cross, burden.

buffoon ▶ **noun 1** (archaic) *Feste the buffoon* **clown**, jester, fool, comic, comedian, wit, wag, merry andrew, droll, harlequin, motley, Pierrot, Punchinello.
2 *he regarded the chaplain as a buffoon* **fool**, idiot, dolt, ass, nincompoop, blockhead, dunce, dunderhead, ignoramus, dullard, moron, simpleton, donkey, jackass; informal chump, numbskull, dope, twit, nitwit, halfwit, clot, bonehead, fathead, birdbrain, twerp, ninny.

bug ▶ **noun 1** *bugs were crawling everywhere* **insect**, flea, mite, midge; informal creepy-crawly, beastie; Brit. informal minibeast.
2 (informal) *he went down with a stomach bug* **illness**, ailment, infection, disease, disorder, sickness, affliction, malady, complaint, upset, condition, infirmity, indisposition, malaise; **bacterium**, germ, virus, bacillus, micro-organism, microbe; Brit. informal lurgy.
3 (informal) *he caught the journalism bug at an early age* **obsession**, enthusiasm, craze, fad, mania, rage, passion, fixation; hobby, interest, pastime; informal thing.
4 *the bug they planted on O'Brien's phone malfunctioned* **listening device**, hidden microphone, receiver, transmitter, wire, wiretap, phone tap, tap; informal bugging device.
5 *the program we used developed a bug* **fault**, error, defect, flaw, imperfection, failing, breakdown; virus; informal glitch, gremlin, snarl-up.
▶ **verb 1** *she fears that her conversations were bugged* **record**, tap, listen in on, eavesdrop on, spy on, overhear; **wiretap**, tap, monitor, phone-tap; informal snoop on.
2 (informal) *if there's one thing that really bugs me, it's trendy, middle-class liberals.* See ANNOY.

bugbear ▶ **noun** *paperwork is our bugbear* **pet hate**, hate, bane, irritant, irritation, dislike, anathema, aversion, vexation, thorn in one's flesh/side, bane of one's life; torment, nightmare, horror, dread, curse, bugaboo, bogey; French bête noire; informal peeve, pain, pain in the neck, hang-up.

build ▶ **verb 1** *a small supermarket had been built* **construct**, erect, put up, assemble, set up, raise.
OPPOSITE demolish.
2 *the kids were building a snowman* **make**, construct, fabricate, form, manufacture, create, fashion, model, mould, shape, forge; informal knock together.
3 *they are building a business strategy for the next decade* **establish**, found, set up, originate, institute, start, begin, inaugurate, initiate, constitute, secure.
□ **build something in/into** *environmental priorities must be built into all economic decision-making* **incorporate in/into**, include in, embody in, absorb into, subsume into, assimilate into.
□ **build on** *a case study will be undertaken to build on existing research* **expand on**, enlarge on, develop, elaborate, flesh out, add flesh to, add detail to, embellish, enhance, amplify; refine, improve, polish, perfect.
□ **build up** *the traffic is steadily building up* **increase**, grow, mount up, intensify, escalate; strengthen, get stronger.
□ **build something up 1** *he built up a huge export business* **establish**, set up, form, found, institute, start, begin, bring into being, create, inaugurate, organize; **develop**, expand, enlarge.
2 *he built up his stamina by playing football* **boost**, strengthen, increase, improve, invigorate, augment, raise, intensify, enhance, escalate, multiply, swell; informal beef up.
3 *over the years I have built up a collection of around 1,700 prints* **accumulate**, accrue, amass, collect, gather, stockpile, heap up, rack up, run up, scrape together, hoard, lay in/up, garner; Brit. tot up.
▶ **noun** *police are looking for a man of slim build* **physique**, frame, body, figure, form, structure, shape, make-up, formation, stature; proportions; informal chassis, vital statistics.

builder ▶ **noun 1** *Thomas Telford was a canal builder and road maker* **designer**, planner, maker, constructor, deviser, contriver, establisher, creator, fabricator, architect, -wright.
2 *by law, builders must finish the job in a proper and workmanlike fashion* **construction worker**, labourer, ganger, craftsman, bricklayer; housebuilder; Brit. dated navvy.

building *See centre pages for lists of* **Architectural Styles** **Architectural Terms** **Bridges** **Towers**
▶ **noun 1** *the church is a plain red brick building* **structure**, construction, edifice, erection, pile; property, premises, establishment, place.
2 *a moratorium on the building of new power stations* **construction**, erection, putting up, raising, establishment, fabrication, production, assembly.

WORD LINKS
relating to building **tectonic**

build-up ▶ **noun 1** *the build-up of military strength* **increase**, growth, expansion, spread, enlargement, escalation, development, accumulation, proliferation, multiplication, snowballing, mushrooming.
OPPOSITE decrease.
2 *the build-up of carbon dioxide in the atmosphere* **accumulation**, building up, accretion, gathering, amassing.
3 *the build-up for the World Cup* **publicity**, promotion, advertising, puff, marketing, propaganda; informal hype, plugging, plug, ballyhoo, hoo-ha.

built-in ▶ **adjective 1** *a built-in cupboard* **fitted**, fixed, integral, integrated, incorporated, permanent.
2 *television has built-in advantages for advertisers* **inherent**, intrinsic, incorporated, inseparable, inbuilt; essential, implicit, basic, fundamental, deep-rooted, rooted, permanent, ingrained, natural, native, radical; rare connatural.

bulb ▶ **noun** *a tulip bulb* **tuber**, corm, rhizome.

bulbous ▶ **adjective** *he had a large bulbous red nose* **bulging**, round, fat, rotund, swollen, spherical, swelling, distended, bloated, protuberant, ovoid, convex, pear-shaped, bulb-shaped, balloon-shaped; rare tumid.

bulge ▶ **noun 1** *the money made a fat bulge in his hip pocket* **swelling**, bump, lump, protuberance, protrusion, prominence, projection, eruption, convexity; rare intumescence.
2 (informal) *there will be a bulge in the prison population* **surge**, upsurge, rise, increase, escalation, jump, leap, boost, intensification, augmentation.
OPPOSITE decrease.
▶ **verb** *his eyes were bulging* **swell**, swell out, puff up/out, stick out, balloon, balloon up/out, fill out, bag, belly; project, protrude, jut (out), stand out, be prominent; expand, inflate, distend, dilate, enlarge, bloat; rare intumesce, tumefy.
OPPOSITE contract.

bulk ▶ **noun 1** *the sheer bulk of the bags* **size**, volume, dimensions, measurements, proportions, mass, substance, scale, magnitude, immensity, hugeness, vastness, massiveness, bulkiness, largeness, bigness, ampleness, amplitude.
2 *the bulk of entrants were British* **majority**, greater quantity/number, larger part/number, best/better part, main part, major part; most, almost all, more than half; (main) body, lion's share, predominance, preponderance, generality.
OPPOSITE minority.
▶ **verb** *some takeaway meals are* **bulked out** *with fat* **make bigger**, make larger, expand, pad out, fill out, eke out, add to, augment, increase.
□ **bulk large** *local factors bulked large in the negotiations* **be important**, loom large, dominate, preponderate, be prominent, be significant, be influential, be of consequence, be of account, be relevant, mean a lot, count, matter, signify, carry weight.
OPPOSITE be insignificant.

bulky ▶ **adjective 1** *bulky items of household refuse* **large**, big, great, huge, of considerable size, sizeable, substantial, voluminous, immense, enormous, colossal, massive, mammoth, vast, goodly, prodigious, tremendous, gigantic, giant, monumental, stupendous, gargantuan, elephantine, titanic, mountainous, monstrous; mighty, epic, inordinate, unlimited, king-size, king-sized, giant-size, giant-sized, man-size, man-sized, outsize, oversized, overgrown, considerable, major, Brobdingnagian; **cumbersome**, unmanageable, unmanoeuvrable, unwieldy, awkward, ponderous, heavy, weighty; informal jumbo, whopping, whopping great, thumping, thumping great, hulking, mega, humongous, monster, astronomical, dirty great; Brit. informal whacking, whacking great, ginormous; dated incommodious.
OPPOSITES small, compact, manageable.
2 *he was a bulky man, not good at climbing* **heavily built**, stocky, thickset, sturdy, sturdily built, well built, burly, strapping, brawny, muscular, solid, heavy, hefty, meaty; **stout**, fat, fattish, plump, chubby, portly, rotund, roly-poly, pot-bellied, round, dumpy, chunky, broad in the beam, overweight, obese, fleshy, paunchy, corpulent; buxom, well upholstered, well covered, well padded, of ample proportions, ample, rounded, well rounded; cobby; informal hulking, tubby, pudgy, beefy, porky, blubbery, poddy; Brit. informal podgy, fubsy; N. Amer. informal zaftig, corn-fed, lard-assed; Austral./NZ nuggety; technical mesomorphic, pyknic; rare squabby, pursy, abdominous.
OPPOSITE slight.

B

bull ▶ **noun**
WORD LINKS
relating to a bull **taurine**

bulldoze ▶ **verb 1** *they are planning to bulldoze the park and build workers' flats* **demolish**, knock down, tear down, pull down, flatten, fell, level, raze, raze to the ground, clear, destroy, lay waste to.
OPPOSITE construct.
2 *the forward bulldozed his way through to score* **force one's way**, push (one's way), shove (one's way), barge (one's way), elbow (one's way), shoulder (one's way), jostle (one's way), muscle, bludgeon one's way, plunge, crash, sweep, bundle, hustle.
OPPOSITE ease.
3 (*informal*) *she believes that to build status you need to bulldoze everyone else* **bully**, hector, browbeat, intimidate, coerce, steamroller, badger, boss about/around, dragoon, cow, bludgeon, persecute, domineer, oppress, pressure, pressurize, tyrannize, terrorize, menace, subjugate, strong-arm, use strong-arm tactics on; *informal* railroad, lean on.

bullet *See centre pages for list of* **Bullets and Shot**
▶ **noun** ball, shot; *informal* slug; (**bullets**) lead.
WORD LINKS
fear of bullets **ballistophobia**

bulletin ▶ **noun 1** *a television news bulletin* **report**, news, news report, newscast, flash, newsflash, headlines, dispatch, piece, story, communiqué, press release, statement, announcement, account, message, communication, notification.
2 *the Society produces a monthly bulletin* **newsletter**, news-sheet, newspaper, journal, proceedings, digest, gazette, magazine, review, periodical, organ.

bullish ▶ **adjective** *individual employers were bullish about the prospects for their own firms* **optimistic**, hopeful, buoyant, positive, disposed to look on the bright side, sanguine, confident, cheerful, cheery, bright, assured, animated, spirited; *informal* upbeat; *archaic* of good cheer.
OPPOSITE pessimistic.

bully ▶ **noun** *you mustn't give in to the village bully* **persecutor**, oppressor, tyrant, tormentor, browbeater, intimidator, coercer, subjugator; scourge, tough, heavy, bully boy, ruffian, thug.
▶ **verb 1** *the other children used to bully him* **persecute**, oppress, tyrannize, torment, browbeat, intimidate, cow, coerce, strong-arm, subjugate, domineer; *informal* push around/about, play the heavy with.
2 *a local man was* **bullied into** *helping them* **coerce**, pressure, pressurize, bring pressure to bear on, use pressure on, put pressure on, constrain, lean on, press, push; force, compel, oblige, put under an obligation; hound, harass, nag, harry, badger, goad, prod, pester, browbeat, brainwash, bludgeon, persuade, prevail on, work on, act on, influence, intimidate, dragoon, twist someone's arm, strong-arm; *N. Amer.* blackjack; *informal* bulldoze, railroad, put the screws/squeeze on; *Brit. informal* bounce; *N. Amer. informal* hustle, fast-talk.

bulwark ▶ **noun 1** *the inner-city ring road follows the line of the ancient bulwarks* **wall**, rampart, fortification, parapet, stockade, palisade, barricade, embankment, earthwork, breastwork, berm; *Latin* vallum; *rare* circumvallation.
2 *a bulwark of liberty* **protector**, protection, guard, defence, defender, support, supporter, prop, buttress, mainstay, bastion, safeguard, stronghold.

bum[1] ▶ **noun** (*Brit. informal*). *See* BOTTOM *sense 6.*

bum[2] (*informal*) ▶ **noun 1** (*N. Amer.*) *bums would wander up and ask for a sandwich. See* TRAMP.
2 *get out of bed, you lazy bum* **idler**, loafer, good-for-nothing, wastrel, drone, scrounger, cadger, ne'er-do-well, do-nothing, layabout, slob, lounger, shirker, sluggard, laggard, slugabed, malingerer; rogue, rascal, scoundrel, villain; *informal* waster, loser, skiver, slacker, lazybones.
▶ **verb 1** *he bummed around Florida for a few months* **loaf**, lounge, idle, laze, languish, moon, stooge, droop, dally, dawdle, amble, potter, wander, drift, meander; *informal* mooch; *N. Amer. informal* lollygag, bat.
2 *they tried to bum money off him* **scrounge**, beg, borrow; *informal* cadge, sponge, touch someone for; *Brit. informal* scab; *Scottish informal* sorn on someone for; *N. Amer. informal* mooch; *Austral./NZ informal* bludge.
▶ **adjective** *they have had a bum deal* **bad**, poor, inferior, second-rate, second-class, unsatisfactory, inadequate, unacceptable, substandard, not up to scratch, not up to par, deficient, imperfect, defective, faulty, shoddy, amateurish, careless, negligent; **dreadful**, awful, terrible, abominable, frightful, atrocious, disgraceful, deplorable, hopeless, worthless, laughable, lamentable, miserable, sorry, third-rate, diabolical, execrable; *informal* crummy, rotten, pathetic, useless, woeful, lousy, ropy, appalling, abysmal, pitiful, God-awful, dire, poxy, not up to snuff, the pits; *Brit. informal* duff, chronic, rubbish; *vulgar slang* crap, shit, chickenshit.
OPPOSITE excellent.

bumble ▶ **verb 1** *they bumbled around the house* **blunder**, lurch, stumble, wobble, lumber, shamble, shuffle, stagger, totter, teeter, reel, weave, pitch, muddle, flounder, falter.
2 *by comparison all the other speakers bumbled* **ramble**, babble, burble, drivel, gibber, blather, mumble, mutter, stumble.

bumbling ▶ **adjective** *Sherlock Holmes' bumbling sidekick Watson* **blundering**, bungling, amateurish, incompetent, inept, unskilful, inexpert, clumsy, maladroit, gauche, awkward, inefficient, muddled, oafish, clodhopping, stumbling, lumbering, foolish, useless; crude, botched; *informal* ham-fisted, ham-handed, cack-handed.
OPPOSITES efficient, expert.

bump ▶ **noun 1** *I landed with a bump* **jolt**, collision, crash, smash, smack, crack, thwack, bang, thud, thump, buffet, knock, rap, tap, impact; *informal* whack, bash, wallop.
2 *I was woken by a bump* **bang**, sharp noise, crack, boom, clang, peal, clap, pop, snap, knock, tap, slam, thud, thump, clunk, clonk, clash, crash, smash, smack; stamp, stomp, clump, clomp; report, explosion, detonation, shot; *informal* wham, whump.
3 *the wheels hit a bump in the road* **hump**, bulge, lump, knob, knot, projection, prominence, eminence, ridge, protuberance.
OPPOSITE pothole.
4 *the police would ask him how he got the bump on his head* **swelling**, lump, bulge, injury, contusion; nodule, node, outgrowth, growth, carbuncle, hunch, excrescence, protuberance, projection; *technical* process, bulla; *rare* tumescence, intumescence, tumefaction.
▶ **verb 1** *all those cars* **bumped into** *each other* **hit**, ram, bang (into), collide with, be in collision with, strike, knock (into), knock against, crash into/against, smash into, slam into, crack into/against, dash against, run into, plough into; *N. Amer.* impact.
OPPOSITE miss.
2 *the cart bumping along the road* **bounce**, jolt, jerk, rattle, shake, jounce.
□ **bump into** (*informal*) *I bumped into an old friend* **meet (by chance)**, encounter, meet up with, run into, come across, run across, chance on, stumble on/across, happen on; *archaic* run against.
□ **bump someone off** (*informal*) *he would try and bump the blackmailer off. See* KILL.

bumper ▶ **adjective** *a bumper crop* **abundant**, rich, heavy, healthy, bountiful, goodly, large, big, huge, immense, massive, exceptional, unusual, good, excellent, fine, magnificent, lovely, vintage, superabundant, prolific, profuse, copious, profitable; *informal* whopping; *S. African informal* lank; *literary* bounteous, plenteous.
OPPOSITES poor, meagre, disastrous.

bumpkin ▶ **noun** *she thought Tom a bit of a country bumpkin* **yokel**, country cousin, rustic, countryman, countrywoman, country dweller, son/daughter of the soil, peasant, provincial; **oaf**, lout, boor, barbarian; *informal* clod, clodhopper, yahoo, yob, yobbo; *Irish informal* culchie, bogman; *N. Amer. informal* hayseed, hillbilly, hick, rube, schlub; *Austral. informal* bushy; *archaic* carl, churl, hind, kern, bucolic.
OPPOSITE sophisticate.

bumptious ▶ **adjective** *you're a bumptious little know-all at times* **self-important**, conceited, arrogant, self-assertive, full of oneself, puffed up, swollen-headed, pompous, overbearing, (self-)opinionated, cocky, swaggering, strutting, presumptuous, forward, imperious, domineering, pontificating, sententious, grandiose, affected, stiff, vain, haughty, overweening, proud, egotistic, egotistical; supercilious, condescending, patronizing; *informal* snooty, uppity, uppish, pushy.
OPPOSITE self-effacing.

bumpy ▶ **adjective 1** *a bumpy road* **uneven**, rough, irregular; holed, potholed, holey, rutted, pitted, rutty; lumpy, knobby, knobbly, gnarled; stony, rocky.
OPPOSITES smooth, level.
2 *a bumpy ride* **bouncy**, rough, uncomfortable, choppy, jolting, jolty, lurching, jerky, jumpy, jarring, bone-shaking, bone-breaking, jouncy, jouncing, turbulent.
OPPOSITES smooth, comfortable.
3 *the season got off to a bumpy start* **inconsistent**, variable, varying, changeable, irregular, fluctuating, intermittent, wavering, erratic, patchy; rocky, unsettled, unstable, roller-coaster, stormy, tumultuous, turbulent, tempestuous, explosive, in turmoil, full of upheavals, full of conflict, full of ups and downs, chaotic.
OPPOSITES consistent, settled.

bunch ▶ **noun 1** *a bunch of flowers* **bouquet**, spray, posy, nosegay, corsage; wreath, garland, chaplet; buttonhole; flower arrangement; *French* boutonnière; *rare* tussie-mussie.
2 *a bunch of keys | a bunch of bananas* **cluster**, clump, knot; group, assemblage, collection.
3 (*informal*) *what a wonderful bunch of people* **group**, set, circle, body, company, troupe, collection, assemblage, gathering, throng, knot, cluster, huddle, multitude, bevy, party, band, horde, pack, drove, flock, swarm, stream, mob; *informal* gang, crowd, load, crew, gaggle.
4 (*N. Amer. informal*) *they did a whole bunch of things. See* LOT.
▶ **verb 1** *he bunched the reins in his hands* **bundle**, clump, cluster, group, arrange, gather, collect, assemble; bind, pack, fasten together, truss.
OPPOSITES spread out, release.
2 *his trousers bunched around his ankles* **gather**, ruffle, pucker, shirr, tuck, fold, pleat.
OPPOSITE spread out.

3 *he halted, forcing the rest of the field to* ***bunch up*** *behind him* **cluster**, huddle, gather, concentrate, congregate, collect, accumulate, amass, group, herd, crowd, flock, mass; pack somewhere, cram somewhere.
OPPOSITE disperse.

bundle ▶ noun *a bundle of clothes* **bunch**, roll, clump, wad, parcel, packet, package, pack, sheaf, bale, bolt, truss, faggot, fascicle; pile, stack, heap, mass, quantity, armful, collection, accumulation, agglomeration, lot, batch; *informal* load, wodge.
▶ verb **1** *she quickly* ***bundled up*** *her clothes* **tie (up)**, tie together, do up, pack (up), pack together, package, parcel (up), packet, wrap (up), roll (up), wind up, fold (up), furl, bind (up), fasten together, bale, truss (up).
OPPOSITE undo.
2 *the figure was bundled in furs* **wrap**, envelop, clothe, cover, muffle, swathe, swaddle, bind, bandage, shroud, drape, wind, enfold, sheathe, enclose, encase; *literary* lap.
3 (*informal*) *he was bundled into a van* **hustle**, jostle, manhandle, frogmarch, sweep, throw, hurry, rush; shove, push, thrust, propel, impel.

WORD LINKS
relating to a bundle **fascicular**

bung ▶ noun *the jar is sealed with a rubber bung* **stopper**, plug, cork, spigot, spile, seal, cap, top, lid, cover; *N. Amer.* stopple.

bungle ▶ verb *the prisoners bungled their escape bid* **mishandle**, mismanage, mess up, make a mess of, botch, spoil, mar, ruin; *informal* make a hash of, muff, fluff, foul up, screw up, louse up, bitch up, blow, foozle; *Brit. informal* make a muck of, make a pig's ear of, cock up, make a Horlicks of; *N. Amer. informal* flub, goof up, bobble; *vulgar slang* fuck up, bugger up, balls up, bollix up.
OPPOSITES succeed in, manage successfully.

bungler ▶ noun *his mistakes have caused him to be branded a bungler* **blunderer**, incompetent, amateur, bumbler, botcher, clown, hopeless case; *informal* mutt, butterfingers; *Brit. informal* bodger, prat; *N. Amer. informal* jackleg, spud; *archaic* lurdan; (**bunglers**) *Brit. informal* shower.
OPPOSITE expert.

bungling ▶ adjective *the work of a bungling amateur* **incompetent**, blundering, amateurish, inept, unskilful, inexpert, clumsy, maladroit, gauche, awkward, inefficient, muddled, oafish, clodhopping, bumbling, stumbling, lumbering, foolish, useless; *informal* ham-fisted, ham-handed, cack-handed.
OPPOSITE expert.

bunk[1] ▶ noun *the skipper slept in a bunk in the forward cabin* **berth**, cot, bunk bed, bed.

bunk[2] (*Brit. informal*) ▶ verb *he* ***bunked off*** *school* **play truant from**, truant from, stay away from, not go to, be absent from, skip, avoid, shirk; *Brit. informal* skive off; *Irish informal* mitch off; *N. Amer. informal* play hookey from, goof off, ditch, cut; *Austral./NZ informal* play the wag from; *rare* bag, hop the wag from.
▶ noun
□ **do a bunk** *he'd done a bunk with all our money* **run off**, run away, make off, take off, take to one's heels, run for it, make a run for it, make a break for it, bolt, beat a (hasty) retreat, make a quick exit, make one's getaway, escape, head for the hills, do a disappearing act; *informal* beat it, clear off, clear out, vamoose, skedaddle, split, cut and run, leg it, show a clean pair of heels, turn tail, scram; *Brit. informal* do a runner, scarper, do a moonlight (flit); *N. Amer. informal* light out, bug out, cut out, peel out, take a powder, skidoo; *Austral. informal* go through, shoot through; *vulgar slang* bugger off; *archaic* fly.

bunk[3] ▶ noun (*informal*) *that idea is just sheer bunk.* See NONSENSE.

bunkum ▶ noun (*informal, dated*) *they talk a lot of bunkum.* See NONSENSE.

buoy ▶ noun *the channel is marked by red and green buoys anchored* **float**, marker, navigation mark, guide, beacon, signal.
▶ verb *the party was buoyed by an election victory* **cheer**, cheer up, brighten up, ginger up, hearten, rally, animate, invigorate, comfort, uplift, lift, encourage, stimulate, raise someone's spirits, give a lift to; support, sustain, give strength to, be a source of strength to, be a tower of strength to, keep someone going, see someone through; *informal* pep up, perk up, buck up; *rare* inspirit.
OPPOSITE depress.

buoyancy ▶ noun **1** *the drum's buoyancy forced it up again* **ability to float**, tendency to float, lightness; *rare* floatability.
2 *the buoyancy of the salt water* **lift**, lifting effect.
3 *the buoyancy of her personality* **cheerfulness**, cheeriness, happiness, light-heartedness, carefreeness, brightness, gladness, merriment, joy, bounce, effervescence, blitheness, sunniness, breeziness, jollity, joviality, animation, liveliness, life, sprightliness, jauntiness, ebullience, high spirits, vivacity, vitality, verve, sparkle, zest; **optimism**, confidence, hope, bullishness, sanguineness, positiveness; *informal* pep, zing, zip.
OPPOSITES depression, pessimism.
4 *the buoyancy of the market* **vigour**, strength, high level of activity, burgeoning, resilience, growth, development, progress, improvement, expansion, mushrooming, snowballing, ballooning.
OPPOSITE depression.

buoyant ▶ adjective **1** *a buoyant substance* **able to float**, light, floating; *rare* floatable.
OPPOSITE heavy.
2 *they dispersed in a buoyant mood* **cheerful**, cheery, happy, light-hearted, carefree, bright, glad, merry, joyful, bubbly, bouncy, effervescent, blithe, sunny, breezy, jolly, jovial, animated, lively, sprightly, jaunty, ebullient, high-spirited, vivacious, vital, sparkling, sparky, zestful, perky; **optimistic**, confident, hopeful, sanguine, bullish, positive; *informal* peppy, zippy, zingy, upbeat; *dated* gay.
OPPOSITES depressed, pessimistic.
3 *car sales were buoyant* **booming**, strong, vigorous, burgeoning, thriving, growing, developing, progressing, improving, expanding, mushrooming, snowballing, ballooning; *informal* going strong.
OPPOSITE depressed.

burble ▶ verb **1** *the exhaust was burbling as only a twin-pipe V8 can burble* **gurgle**, bubble, murmur, purr, purl, tinkle, whirr, drone, rumble, buzz, hum; *literary* plash.
2 *he burbled on about annuities* **prattle**, blather, blether, blither, babble (on), gabble, prate, drivel, rattle on/away, ramble, maunder, go on, run on, talk at length, talk incessantly, talk a lot; chatter, yap, gossip; *Brit.* talk nineteen to the dozen; *Scottish & Irish* slabber on; *informal* jabber, blabber, yatter, jaw, gab, gas, chit-chat, yackety-yak; *Brit. informal* rabbit, witter, waffle, natter, chunter, talk the hind legs off a donkey; *N. Amer. informal* run off at the mouth; *Austral./NZ informal* mag; *archaic* twaddle, twattle, claver, clack.

burden ▶ noun **1** *the porters shouldered their burdens* **load**, cargo, freight, weight; charge, pack, bundle, parcel.
2 *he took on a huge financial burden* **responsibility**, onus, charge, duty, obligation, liability; trouble, care, problem, worry, anxiety, tribulation, affliction, trial, difficulty, misfortune, strain, stress, encumbrance, millstone, cross to bear, albatross; *archaic* cumber.
3 *the burden of his message* **gist**, substance, drift, implication, intention, thrust, meaning, significance, signification, sense, essence, thesis, import, purport, tenor, message, spirit.
▶ verb **1** *he was burdened with a heavy pack* **load**, weight, charge; **weigh down**, encumber, hamper, overload, overburden; (**burdened**) laden; *rare* trammel.
2 *we should avoid burdening parents with too much guilt* **oppress**, trouble, cause trouble to, cause suffering to; worry, beset, bother, harass, disturb, upset, depress, get someone down; distress, grieve, haunt, nag, torment, harrow, afflict, strain, stress, tax, overwhelm, perturb, plague, bedevil.

burdensome ▶ adjective *compliance with the order can be burdensome* **onerous**, oppressive, troublesome, weighty, worrisome, vexatious, irksome, trying, crushing, inconvenient, awkward, a nuisance; harsh, severe, stiff, stringent, formidable, an imposition; arduous, strenuous, rigorous, uphill, difficult, hard, laborious, Herculean, exhausting, tiring, taxing, demanding, punishing, gruelling, back-breaking, exacting, wearing, stressful, wearisome, fatiguing; *rare* toilsome, exigent.
OPPOSITES easy, light.

bureau ▶ noun **1** *a beautiful oak bureau* **desk**, writing desk, writing table, roll-top desk; *Brit.* davenport; *French* secretaire, escritoire.
2 *a marriage bureau* **agency**, service, office, business, company, firm, organization, operation, concern.
3 *the intelligence bureau* **department**, division, branch, section.

bureaucracy ▶ noun **1** *the higher ranks of the bureaucracy* **civil service**, administration, government, directorate, the establishment, the system, the powers that be, corridors of power; ministries, authorities, officials, officialdom; *informal* Big Brother.
2 *the unnecessary bureaucracy in local government* **red tape**, rules and regulations, etiquette, protocol, officialdom, (unnecessary) paperwork; *humorous* bumbledom.

bureaucrat ▶ noun *the faceless bureaucrats who make the rules* **official**, administrator, office-holder, office-bearer, civil servant, public servant, government servant, minister, functionary, appointee, apparatchik, mandarin; *Brit.* jack-in-office.

bureaucratic ▶ adjective **1** *the bureaucratic structure of the Council* **administrative**, official, procedural, red-tape, governmental, ministerial, state, civic, constitutional, political.
2 *the current practice is far too bureaucratic* **rule-bound**, rigid, inflexible, complicated, red-tape-bound; by the book.
OPPOSITES simple, relaxed.

burgeon ▶ verb *tourism has burgeoned over the last ten years* **grow rapidly**, increase rapidly/exponentially, expand, spring up, shoot up, swell, explode, boom, mushroom, proliferate, snowball, multiply, become more numerous, escalate, rocket, skyrocket, run riot, put on a spurt; flourish, thrive, prosper.
OPPOSITE shrink.

burglar ▶ noun *the burglar stole jewellery worth several thousand pounds* **housebreaker**, robber, cat burglar, raider, looter, pilferer, picklock, thief, sneak thief, safe-breaker, safe-blower, safe-cracker; kleptomaniac;

B

intruder, trespasser; *informal* filcher, cracksman; *N. Amer. informal* second-story man/worker, yegg.

burglary ▶ **noun 1** *a two-year sentence for burglary* **housebreaking**, breaking and entering, breaking in, forced entry, theft, thieving, stealing, robbery, robbing, larceny, thievery, pilfering, pilferage, looting; trespassing; *informal* filching.
2 *a series of burglaries* **break-in**, theft, robbery, raid, hold-up; *informal* snatch, smash and grab; *N. Amer. informal* heist, stick-up.

burgle ▶ **verb** *her house was burgled last night* **break into**, force (an) entry into, force one's way into; steal from, rob, loot, plunder, rifle, sack, ransack, pillage; *informal* do.

burial ▶ **noun** *the body was flown home for burial* **burying**, interment, committal, inhumation; entombment; funeral, obsequies, funerary rites; *rare* sepulture, exequies.
OPPOSITE exhumation.
WORD LINKS
relating to burial **funerary, sepulchral**

burial ground ▶ **noun** *in the burial ground will be found the graves of many distinguished men* **cemetery**, graveyard, churchyard, necropolis, burial place, burying place, burying ground, garden of remembrance; *Scottish* kirkyard; *N. Amer.* memorial park; *informal* boneyard; *literary* golgotha; *historical* urnfield; *archaic* God's acre, potter's field.

burlesque ▶ **noun** *the funniest burlesque of music hall there has been* **parody**, caricature, travesty, pastiche, take-off, skit, imitation, satire, lampoon; *informal* send-up, spoof; *Brit. vulgar slang* piss-take; *rare* pasquinade, pasticcio.

burly ▶ **adjective** *two burly bodyguards stood by him* **strapping**, well built, sturdy, sturdily built, powerfully built, broad-shouldered, brawny, strong, muscular, muscly, well muscled, athletic, thickset, big, hefty, bulky, robust, rugged, stocky, lusty, Herculean, vigorous; *informal* hunky, beefy, husky, hulking; *literary* stalwart, thewy, stark; *technical* mesomorphic.
OPPOSITE puny.

burn ▶ **verb 1** *the house was burning* **be on fire**, be alight, be ablaze, blaze, go up, go up in smoke, be in flames, be aflame; smoulder, glow, flare, flash, flicker; *literary* be afire; *archaic* be ardent.
2 *he burned all the letters* **set fire to**, set on fire, set alight, set light to, light, set burning, ignite, touch off, put a match to, kindle, incinerate, reduce to ashes, destroy by fire; *informal* torch; *archaic* fire, inflame.
3 *I forgot to turn off the iron and nearly burned his dress shirt* **scorch**, singe, sear, char, blacken, discolour, brand; scald; *technical* cauterize, calcine; *rare* torrefy.
4 *her face burned with humiliation* **be hot**, be warm, feel hot, be feverish, be fevered, be on fire; **blush**, redden, be red, go red, go pink, turn red, turn crimson, turn scarlet, flush, colour, crimson.
5 *her lip burned where her teeth had pierced it* **smart**, sting, tingle, prick, prickle, be irritated, be sore, hurt, be painful, throb, ache.
6 *Martha was burning with curiosity* **be consumed by/with**, be eaten up by/with, be obsessed by/with, be tormented by/with, be bedevilled by.
7 *he was burning with fury* **seethe**, boil, fume, smoulder, simmer, be boiling over, be beside oneself; *informal* be livid, be wild, jump up and down, froth/foam at the mouth.
8 *Meredith burned to know what the secret was* **yearn**, long, have a longing, ache, be aching, itch, be itching, desire, be consumed with the desire, want, want badly, be unable to wait, be eager, be desperate, hanker, have a hankering, wish, crave, lust, pant, hunger, be hungry, be greedy, thirst, be thirsty; *informal* have a yen, yen, be dying; *archaic* be athirst, be desirous.
9 *people differ considerably in the energy they burn up* **use up**, consume, expend, get through, go through, dissipate, eat up, exhaust.
OPPOSITE conserve.

burning ▶ **adjective 1** *a burning house* **blazing**, flaming, aflame, fiery, flaring, ignited, glowing, red-hot, flickering, smouldering; scorching, raging, roaring, live.
OPPOSITE extinguished.
2 *the burning desert sands* **extremely hot**, red-hot, unbearably hot, baking (hot), blazing (hot), flaming, fiery, blistering, scorching, searing, sweltering, torrid, tropical, like an oven, like a furnace, like a blowtorch; parching, withering; *N. Amer.* broiling; *informal* baking, boiling (hot), roasting, sizzling.
OPPOSITE freezing.
3 *a burning desire to win* **intense**, passionate, deep-seated, profound, wholehearted, strong, powerful, forceful, vigorous, ardent, urgent, fervent, fierce, earnest, eager, keen, enthusiastic, zealous, fanatical, frantic, consuming, extreme, acute, raging, blazing, uncontrollable; *rare* fervid, perfervid, passional.
4 *the burning issues of the day* **important**, crucial, significant, prevalent, pertinent, relevant, topical, current, contemporary, of interest, active, live, controversial, urgent, pressing, compelling, critical, vital, lively, essential, acute, pivotal, climacteric.

burnish ▶ **verb** *marks can be removed by scraping and burnishing the metal* **polish (up)**, shine, brighten, rub up/down, buff (up), smooth, glaze; *archaic* furbish.
OPPOSITE dull.

burp (*informal*) ▶ **verb** *he couldn't help burping* **belch**, bring up wind; *Scottish & N. English* rift; *informal* gurk; *archaic* bolk, rout, ruck; *rare* eruct, eructate.
▶ **noun** *Cranston let out a burp* **belch**; *Scottish & N. English* rift; *informal* gurk; *archaic* bolk; *rare* eructation, ventosity.

burrow ▶ **noun** *the rabbits' burrow* **warren**, tunnel, hole, lair, set, den, earth, retreat, excavation, cave, dugout, hollow, scrape.
▶ **verb** *the mouse can burrow a hiding place* **tunnel**, dig (out), excavate, grub, mine, bore, drill, channel; hollow out, gouge out, scoop out, cut out; *literary* delve.

burst ▶ **verb 1** *one balloon burst | he's burst my balloon* **split open**, burst open, break open, tear open, rupture, crack, fracture, fragment, shatter, shiver, fly open; *literary* tear asunder, rend asunder.
2 *a shell burst a short distance away* **explode**, blow up, detonate, go off, be set off, land; *informal* go bang.
3 *smoke, dust, and heat burst through the hole* **break**, erupt, surge, gush, rush, stream, flow, pour, cascade, spill; sweep, spout, spurt, jet, spew, discharge, roll, whirl.
4 *he burst into the room without knocking* **plunge**, charge, barge, shove, plough, lurch, hurtle, career, rush, dash, tear.
5 *she* **burst into** *tears* **break out in**, launch into, erupt in, have a fit of; suddenly start.
□ **burst out 1** *'Well, I don't care!' she burst out angrily* **exclaim**, blurt out, ejaculate, cry out, call out, shout, yell.
2 *he burst out crying* **suddenly start**.
▶ **noun 1** *damage to tyres by punctures and bursts* **rupture**, breach, split, blowout.
2 *the mortar bursts were further away than before* **explosion**, detonation, blast, discharge, eruption, bang.
3 *a burst of anger | a sudden burst of activity* **outbreak**, outburst, eruption, flare-up, explosion, blow-up, blast, blaze, attack, fit, spasm, paroxysm, access, rush, gale, flood, storm, hurricane, torrent, outpouring, surge, upsurge, spurt, effusion, outflow, outflowing, welling up; *informal* splurt; *rare* ebullition, boutade.
4 *a burst of gunfire* **volley**, salvo, fusillade, barrage, discharge, shower, spray, hail, rain.

bury ▶ **verb 1** *all the crew were buried at Stonefall cemetery* **inter**, lay to rest, consign to the grave, entomb; earth up; *informal* put six feet under, plant; *N. Amer. informal* deep-six; *literary* sepulchre, ensepulchre, inhume, inearth.
OPPOSITE exhume.
2 *she buried her face in her hands* **hide**, conceal, cover, put out of sight, secrete, enfold; submerge, sink, embed, engulf, immerse, enclose, tuck, cup; *literary* enshroud.
OPPOSITES reveal, take out of.
3 *the bullet buried itself in the wood* **embed**, sink, implant, submerge, insert; drive something into.
OPPOSITE extract from.
4 *he buried himself in his work* **absorb**, engross, occupy, engage, busy, employ, distract, preoccupy, immerse, interest, involve.
WORD LINKS
fear of being buried alive **taphephobia**

bush *See centre pages for lists of* **Flowering Plants and Shrubs**, **Trees and Shrubs**
▶ **noun 1** *a rose bush* **shrub**, woody plant; (**bushes**) undergrowth, shrubbery, hedge, thicket.
2 *it is easy to become lost in the bush* **wilds**, remote areas, wilderness; the backwoods, the hinterland(s); *N. Amer.* the backcountry, the backland; *Austral./NZ* the outback, the backblocks, the booay; *S. African* the backveld, the platteland; *N. Amer. informal* the boondocks, the boonies, the tall timbers; *Austral./NZ informal* Woop Woop, beyond the black stump.

bushy ▶ **adjective** *a bushy walrus moustache* **thick**, shaggy, unruly, fuzzy, rough, bristling, bristly, fluffy, woolly, luxuriant, exuberant, spreading; *informal* jungly.
OPPOSITES wispy, straggly.

busily ▶ **adverb** *Sunil was busily getting the machine to work* **actively**, industriously, purposefully, diligently, dutifully, energetically, vigorously, enthusiastically, strenuously, tirelessly, indefatigably; hard.
OPPOSITE idly.

business ▶ **noun 1** *she had to do a lot of smiling in her business* **work**, line of work, line, occupation, profession, career, employment, job, position, pursuit, vocation, calling, field, sphere, walk of life, trade, craft; *Scottish* way; *French* métier; *informal* racket, game; *Austral. informal* grip; *archaic* employ.
2 *who do you do business with in Manila?* **trade**, trading, commerce, buying and selling, dealing, traffic, trafficking, marketing, merchandising, bargaining; dealings, transactions, negotiations, proceedings.
3 *she was running her own business* **firm**, company, concern, enterprise, venture, organization, operation, undertaking, industry, corporation, establishment, house, shop, office, bureau, agency, franchise, practice, partnership, consortium, cooperative, conglomerate, group, combine, syndicate; *informal* outfit, set-up.
4 *that's none of my business | it's our business to know that sort of thing* **concern**, affair, responsibility, province, preserve, duty, function, task, assignment, obligation, problem, worry, lookout; *informal* funeral,

headache, bailiwick; *Brit. informal* pigeon, baby.
5 *the odd business with the keys remained unexplained* **affair**, matter, thing, issue, case, set of circumstances, circumstance, situation, occasion, experience, event, incident, happening, occurrence, phenomenon, eventuality, episode, interlude, adventure.

businesslike ▶ **adjective** *the group was run in a businesslike way* **professional**, efficient, slick, competent, practised, methodical, disciplined, systematic, orderly, organized, well ordered, planned, structured, practical, pragmatic.
OPPOSITES disorganized, inefficient.

businessman, businesswoman ▶ **noun** *he was a shrewd businessman who was also good for the local economy* **entrepreneur**, business person, industrialist, manufacturer, tycoon, magnate, big businessman, employer; dealer, trader, merchant, wholesaler, buyer, seller, buyer and seller, marketeer, merchandiser, broker, agent, distributor, vendor, tradesman, shopkeeper, retailer, purveyor, supplier, trafficker; *French, dated* homme d'affaires.

bust[1] ▶ **noun 1** *a woman with a large bust* **chest**, bosom, breasts; *technical* mammary glands, mammae; *informal* boobs, boobies, tits, titties, knockers, bazookas, melons, jubblies, bubbies, orbs, globes, jugs; *Brit. informal* bristols, charlies, baps; *N. Amer. informal* bazooms, casabas, chichis, hooters; *Austral. informal* norks; *archaic* dugs, paps, embonpoint.
2 *a bust of Julius Caesar* sculpture, carving, effigy, three-dimensional representation; statue, torso, head.

bust[2] (*informal*) ▶ **verb 1** *he had bust the clip that held the lid up* | *the box has bust* **break**, crack, snap, fracture, shatter, smash, smash to smithereens, fragment, splinter; disintegrate, fall to bits, fall to pieces; split, burst, rupture; tear, rend, sever, separate, divide; *rare* shiver.
2 *he promised to bust the mafia* **overthrow**, destroy, bring about the downfall of, topple, bring down, bring low, ruin, break, overturn, overcome, defeat, purge, get rid of, oust, unseat, dislodge, eject, supplant.
OPPOSITES perpetuate; support.
3 *two roadies were busted for drugs*. See ARREST.
4 (*N. Amer.*) *my apartment got busted* **raid**, search, make a search of, swoop on, make a raid on; *informal* do over.
▶ **adjective**
□ **go bust** *his haulage business went bust and he owes £120,000* **fail**, collapse, crash, fold (up), go under, founder, be ruined, cave in; **go bankrupt**, become insolvent, cease trading, go into receivership, go into liquidation, be liquidated, be wound up, be closed (down), be shut (down); *informal* go broke, go bump, go to the wall, go belly up, come a cropper, flop.

bustle ▶ **verb 1** *people clutching clipboards bustled about* **rush**, dash, scurry, scuttle, scamper, scramble, flutter, fuss; hurry, hasten, make haste, race, run, sprint, tear, shoot, charge, chase, career; *Brit.* scutter; *informal* scoot, beetle, whizz, buzz, hare, zoom, zip.
OPPOSITE amble.
2 *she bustled us into the kitchen* **hustle**, bundle, sweep, push, hurry, rush, whisk, whip.
▶ **noun** *the bustle of the market* **activity**, hustle and bustle, animation, commotion, flurry, tumult, hubbub, busyness, action, liveliness, movement, life, stir, excitement, agitation, fuss, whirl; *informal* toing and froing, comings and goings, to-do; *archaic* hurry scurry, pother.
OPPOSITE inactivity.

bustling ▶ **adjective** *the bustling streets of Kowloon* **busy**, crowded, swarming, teeming, full, astir, buzzing, hectic, lively, vibrant, thronging, thronged; energetic, active; *informal* buzzy.
OPPOSITES deserted, inactive.

busy ▶ **adjective 1** *he's always busy with some useful job* | *the team members are busy raising money* **occupied (in)**, engaged in, involved in, employed in, working at, labouring at, toiling at, slaving at, hard at work (on), wrapped up (in/with); rushed off one's feet (with), hard-pressed; at work (on), on the job, absorbed in, engrossed in, immersed in, preoccupied with; active (in), lively, industrious, bustling, energetic, tireless; *informal* busy as a bee, on the go, hard at it; *Brit. informal* on the hop; (**be busy**) have one's hands full.
OPPOSITE idle.
2 *Mr Jenkins is busy at the moment* **unavailable**, otherwise engaged; **engaged**, occupied, in a meeting, working, at work, on duty, on active service, in harness; *informal* tied up; (**be busy**) have a prior/previous engagement.
OPPOSITE free.
3 *I've had a busy day* **strenuous**, hectic, energetic, active, lively, exacting, tiring, full, eventful.
OPPOSITE quiet.
4 *the town centre was unusually busy* **crowded**, bustling, swarming, teeming, astir, buzzing, hectic, full, thronged, thronging, lively, vibrant; *informal* buzzy.
5 *the frame should be fairly plain, to balance the rather busy design* **excessively ornate**, over-ornate, over-elaborate, over-embellished, over-decorated, overblown, overwrought, exaggerated, overdone, florid, fussy, cluttered, contrived, overworked, over-detailed, strained, laboured, baroque, rococo.
OPPOSITES quiet, restrained.
▶ **verb** *a single clerk busied himself with paperwork* **occupy**, involve, engage, concern, employ, absorb, engross, immerse, preoccupy; interest, entertain, distract, divert, amuse, beguile.

B

CHOOSE THE RIGHT WORD

busy, occupied, engaged, active

Each of these words has several meanings, but those applied to people have subtle distinctions.

- Saying that someone is **busy** means that they have a great deal to do (*if I'm busy, my husband does the cooking*) or are occupied with a specified activity (*Bernard was busy with flying lessons*). Either way, they are likely to have no time for further calls on their attention (*I'm too busy to write letters*).
- Someone who is **occupied** has something to do which takes up a good deal of their time or attention. There is a suggestion that this activity is a welcome means of filling empty time, but not unduly onerous (*the children were fully occupied with games and competitions*). In spite of this use of *fully*, neither *occupied* nor *engaged* is often qualified as to degree—someone is either occupied/engaged or they are not, whereas people are frequently described as *very, extremely, really* or *too busy/active*. Both *occupied* and *busy* can be followed by *with* and the relevant activity, as in the examples given.
- **Engaged** emphasizes the fact that someone has no time or attention left for any new activities or demands; in this sense it is somewhat formal (*you'll have to wait to see her, she's engaged at present*). *Occupied* and *engaged* (in this sense) always follow the verb *to be*, rather than being used before a noun.
- To say that someone is **active** is to say that they are doing a great deal (*she has been active in local politics since 1985*). The context or area in which they are active is often expressed by an adverb, such as *sexually, physically*, or *politically*.

busybody ▶ **noun** *others considered him an interfering busybody* **meddler**, interferer, mischief-maker, troublemaker, gossip, scandalmonger, muckraker, eavesdropper, intruder, ghoul, gawker; *informal* nosy parker, snoop, snooper, rubberneck; *Brit. informal* gawper; *N. Amer. informal* buttinsky; *informal, dated* Paul Pry; *rare* pryer, pry.

but ▶ **conjunction 1** *he stumbled but didn't fall* **yet**; **nevertheless**, nonetheless, even so, however, still, notwithstanding, despite that, in spite of that, for all that, all the same, just the same, at the same time, be that as it may; though, although; *informal* still and all; *archaic* withal, natheless, howbeit.
OPPOSITE and.
2 *I am clean but you are dirty* **whereas**; **conversely**, but then, then again, on the other hand, by contrast, in contrast, contrarily, on the contrary.
OPPOSITE and.
3 *one cannot but sympathize* **(do) other than**, otherwise than, except.
▶ **preposition** *everyone but him had gone* **except (for)**, apart from, other than, besides, aside from, with the exception of, short of, bar, barring, excepting, excluding, omitting, leaving out, save (for), saving; *informal* outside of.
OPPOSITE including.
□ **but for** *but for the rain he would have gone* **if it were not for**, were it not for, except for, without, barring, notwithstanding.
▶ **adverb** *he is but a shadow of his former self* **only**, just, simply, merely, no more than, nothing but; a mere; *N. English informal* nobbut.

butch ▶ **adjective** (*informal*) *a butch guardsman* **(aggressively) masculine**, manly, all man, virile, red-blooded, swashbuckling; **mannish**, manlike, unfeminine, unladylike, Amazonian; *informal* macho, dykey; *rare* viraginous, viragoish.
OPPOSITES effeminate, feminine.

butcher ▶ **noun 1** *a butcher's shop* **meat seller**, meat merchant, meat trader; slaughterer, slaughterman; *Scottish archaic* flesher.
2 *a Nazi death camp butcher* **murderer**, mass murderer, slaughterer, killer, assassin, serial killer, homicidal maniac, destroyer, terminator, liquidator; *literary* slayer; *dated* cut-throat, homicide.
▶ **verb 1** *the goat was then butchered and skinned* **slaughter**, cut up, carve up, slice up, joint, prepare, dress.
2 *they rounded up and butchered 150 people* **massacre**, murder, slaughter, kill, put to death, dispatch, dispose of, destroy, exterminate, liquidate, eliminate, terminate, assassinate, put to the sword, cut down, cut to pieces; *literary* slay.
3 *the film was butchered by the studio* **spoil**, ruin, mar, mutilate, mangle, cut about, mess up, make a mess of, wreck; *informal* murder, make a hash of, muck up, screw up, louse up.

butchery ▶ **noun 1** *the butchery trade* **meat selling**, meat retailing.
2 (*Brit.*) *the cattle were taken to the butchery* **abattoir**, slaughterhouse;

B

Brit. knacker's yard; *archaic* shambles, butcher-row.
3 (*Brit.*) *the truck crashed into a butchery and a florist's* **butcher's**, butcher's shop, meat market, meat counter.
4 *the butchery in the trenches in the First World War* **slaughter**, massacre, slaying, murdering, murder, mass murdering, homicide, blood shedding.

butt[1] ▶ **verb** *she butted him in the chest* **ram**, headbutt, bunt; bump, buffet, push, thrust, shove, prod, knock; *N. English* tup.
□ **butt in** *he butted in on our conversation* **interrupt**, break in, cut in, chime in, interject, interpose, intervene; interfere (with), put one's oar in; *informal* poke one's nose in/into; *Brit. informal* chip in.
OPPOSITE keep out (of).

butt[2] ▶ **noun** *she had just been made the butt of a joke* **target**, victim, object, subject, recipient, laughing stock, Aunt Sally.

butt[3] ▶ **noun 1** *the butt of a gun* **stock**, shaft, shank, end, handle, hilt, haft, grip, helve.
2 *a cigarette butt* **stub**, end, tail end, stump, remnant, remains, remainder; *informal* fag end, dog end.
3 (*N. Amer. informal*) *he was just sitting on his butt doing nothing. See* BOTTOM *sense* 6.
▶ **verb** *the shop* **butted up against** *the row of houses* **adjoin**, abut, butt up to, be next to, be adjacent to, border (on), neighbour, verge on, bound on, be contiguous with, be connected to, communicate with, link up with, extend as far as, extend to; join, conjoin, connect with/to, touch, meet.
OPPOSITE be separate from.

butt[4] ▶ **noun** *a butt of brandy* **barrel**, cask, keg, vat, tun, pipe; **tub**, tank, cistern, bin, drum, canister, basin; *rare* kid, kier, keeve.

butter ▶ **verb**
□ **butter someone up** (*informal*) *she was good at buttering up advertisers* **be obsequious towards**, grovel to, be servile towards, be sycophantic towards, kowtow to, abase oneself to, demean oneself to, bow and scrape to, prostrate oneself to, toady to, truckle to, dance attendance on, fawn on, make up to, play up to, ingratiate oneself with, rub up the right way, curry favour with; **wheedle**, flatter, court, persuade, blarney, coax, talk into, get round, prevail on; *informal* suck up to, crawl to, creep to, be all over, lick someone's boots, fall all over, keep someone sweet, sweet-talk, soft-soap; *N. Amer.* brown-nose; *vulgar slang* lick/kiss someone's arse; *archaic* blandish.

butterfly *See centre pages for lists of* **Butterflies** **Butterfly Types** **Moths**
▶ **noun** **lepidopteran**.
WORD LINKS
relating to butterflies **lepidopteran**

buttocks ▶ **plural noun** *stand with you heels, buttocks, and back touching the wall* **backside**, behind, seat, rump, rear, rear end; cheeks, hindquarters, haunches; *Brit.* **bottom**; *French* derrière; *German* Sitzfleisch; *technical* nates; *informal* sit-upon, stern, BTM, tochus; *Brit. informal* bum, botty, prat, jacksie; *N. Amer. informal* butt, fanny, tush, tushie, tail, duff, buns, booty, caboose, heinie, patootie, keister, tuchis; *W. Indian informal* batty; *humorous* fundament, posterior; *black English* rass, rusty dusty; *Brit. vulgar slang* arse; *N. Amer. vulgar slang* ass; *archaic* breech.
WORD LINKS
relating to the buttocks **natal**

button ▶ **noun 1** *he did up his shirt buttons* **fastener**, stud, link, toggle; hook, catch, clasp.
2 *press the appropriate button to record* **knob**, switch, on/off switch, push switch, disc, lever, handle, key, control, controller.

buttonhole ▶ **verb** (*informal*) *in the pub, I buttonholed the team captain. See* ACCOST.

buttress ▶ **noun 1** *the wall was supported by stone buttresses* **prop**, support, abutment, shore, pier, reinforcement, stanchion, stay, strut.
2 *a buttress against social collapse* **safeguard**, defence, defender, protector, protection, guard, support, supporter, prop, mainstay; bulwark, bastion, stronghold.
▶ **verb** *authority was buttressed by religious belief* **strengthen**, reinforce, fortify, support, prop up, bolster up, shore up, underpin, cement, brace, uphold, confirm, defend, maintain, back up, buoy up.

buxom ▶ **adjective** *a buxom young woman* **large-breasted**, big-breasted, full-breasted, heavy-breasted, bosomy, large-bosomed, big-bosomed, full-bosomed; shapely, well covered, well padded, of ample proportions, ample, plump, rounded, well rounded, full-figured, womanly, voluptuous, curvaceous, Junoesque, Rubenesque; *informal* busty, chesty, stacked, well upholstered, well endowed, curvy, pneumatic.
OPPOSITES skinny, petite.

buy ▶ **verb 1** *they bought a new house* **purchase**, make a/the purchase of, acquire, obtain, get, pick up, snap up; take, secure, procure, come by, pay for, shop for; invest in, put money into; *informal* get hold of, get one's hands on, lay one's hands on, get one's mitts on, score.
OPPOSITE sell.
2 *here was a man who could not be bought* **bribe**, buy off, pay off, suborn, give an inducement to, corrupt; *informal* grease someone's palm, give someone a backhander, give someone a sweetener, keep someone sweet, get at, fix, square; *Brit. informal* nobble.
▶ **noun** (*informal*) *salmon trimmings are a good buy for making into mousse* **purchase**, deal, bargain, investment, acquisition, addition, gain, asset, possession, holding.

buyer ▶ **noun** *the typical buyer of this product* **purchaser**, shopper, customer, consumer, client, patron, investor, user; (**buyers**) clientele, patronage, public, trade, market; *Law* vendee; *rare* emptor.
OPPOSITE seller.

buzz ▶ **noun 1** *the buzz of the bees* **hum**, humming, buzzing, murmur, drone, whirr, whirring, fizz, fizzing, fuzz, hiss, singing, whisper; *Brit. informal* zizz; *Medicine* tinnitus; *literary* bombination, bombilation, susurration, susurrus; *rare* sibilation.
2 *there was an insistent buzz from her control panel* **audible warning**, purr, purring, ring, ringing, note, tone, beep, bleep, warble, signal, alarm, alert.
3 (*informal*) *I'll give you a buzz. See* CALL *sense* 3.
4 (*informal*) *the buzz is that he's gone* **rumour**, gossip, story, word, report, whisper, speculation, insinuation, suggestion, hint; *French* on dit; *W. Indian* shu-shu; *Brit. informal* goss; *N. Amer. informal* scuttlebutt; *Austral./NZ informal* furphy; *S. African informal* skinder.
5 (*informal*) *I got a buzz out of seeing the kids' faces* **thrill**, feeling of excitement, feeling of euphoria, stimulation, glow, tingle; delight, joy, pleasure, fun, enjoyment; titillation; *informal* kick; *N. Amer. informal* charge.
▶ **verb 1** *bees buzzed in the clover* **hum**, drone, bumble, whirr, fizz, fuzz, hiss, sing, murmur, whisper; *Brit. informal* zizz; *literary* bombinate, bombilate, susurrate; *rare* sibilate.
2 *the intercom on her desk buzzed* **purr**, sound, reverberate, ring, beep, bleep, warble.
3 (*informal*) *the director buzzed around checking camera angles* **bustle**, scurry, scuttle, scramble, scamper, flutter, fuss; hurry, hasten, make haste, rush, race, dash, run, sprint, tear, shoot, charge, chase, career; *Brit.* scutter; *informal* scoot, beetle, whizz, hare, zoom, zip.
4 *the club is* **buzzing with** *excitement* **have an air of**; be active, be lively, be busy, bustle, be bustling, hum, throb, vibrate, pulse, whirl.

by ▶ **preposition 1** *he was arrested by the police | I broke it by forcing the lid* **through the agency of**, **by means of**, under the aegis of, using, utilizing, employing, with the help of, with the aid of, as a result of, because of, by dint of, by way of, by virtue of, via, through.
2 *please be there by midday* **no later than**, in good time for, at, before.
3 *the house by the lake* **next to**, beside, next door to, alongside, by/at the side of, abreast of, adjacent to, cheek by jowl with, side by side with; near, close to, hard by, nearest to, neighbouring, adjoining, abutting, bordering, overlooking; connected to, connecting with, contiguous with, attached to.
4 *go by the building* **past**, in front of, beyond.
5 *anything you do is all right by me* **according to**, with, as far as … is concerned, concerning.
□ **by oneself 1** *reading by oneself was encouraged only when it was raining* **alone**, all alone, on one's own, in a solitary state, singly, separately, solitarily, unaccompanied, companionless, partnerless, unattended, unescorted, unchaperoned, solo; *informal* by one's lonesome; *Brit. informal* on one's tod, on one's lonesome, on one's jack, on one's Jack Jones.
2 *there is no possibility of creating anything either by oneself or in conjunction with others* **unaided**, unassisted, without help, without assistance, by one's own efforts, under one's own steam, independently, single-handed(ly), solo, on one's own, alone, all alone, off one's own bat, on one's own initiative.
▶ **adverb** *people hurried by* **past**, on, along, beyond ….
□ **by and by** *by and by you will learn the ropes* **eventually**, ultimately, finally, in the end, as time goes on/by, one day, some day, sooner or later, in time, in a while, after a bit, in the long run, in the fullness of time, at a later time, at a later date, at length, at a future time/date, at some point in the future, in the future, in time to come, in due course.

bygone ▶ **adjective** *the values of a bygone age* **past**, former, earlier, one-time, long-ago, gone by, previous, forgotten, lost, finished, completed, of old, ancient, antiquated, obsolete, departed, dead, extinct, defunct, out of date, outmoded, passé; *literary* of yore, olden, foregone; *rare* forepassed.
OPPOSITES present, recent.

by-law ▶ **noun** (*Brit.*) *a by-law banning public drinking in the town centre* **local law**, regulation, rule.

bypass ▶ **noun** *a bypass round the city* **ring road**, detour, diversion, circuitous route, roundabout way, alternative route; *Brit.* relief road; *Brit. informal* rat run.
▶ **verb 1** *bypass the farm and continue to the road* **go round**, go past, make a detour round, pass round; avoid, keep out of, don't go near.
2 *crime surveys attempt to bypass the problems of police statistics* **avoid**, evade, dodge, escape, elude, circumvent, get round, skirt (round), find a way round, give a wide berth to, sidestep, steer clear of, get out of, shirk; *informal* duck.

3 *the unofficial Workers' Combine bypassed the official union structure* **ignore**, pass over, miss out, omit, go over the head of, neglect; *informal* short-circuit.

by-product ▸ **noun** *he saw poverty as the by-product of colonial prosperity* **side effect**, consequence, entailment, corollary, concomitant; ramification, aftermath, after-effect, repercussion, backlash, ripple, shock wave, spin-off, fallout, heritage, fruits; *Brit.* knock-on effect; *technical* externality.

bystander ▸ **noun** *the police had shot dead an innocent bystander* **onlooker**, passer-by, non-participant, observer, spectator, eyewitness, witness, looker-on, sightseer, watcher, viewer, gaper; *informal* gawper, rubberneck; *literary* beholder.
OPPOSITE participant.

byword ▸ **noun 1** *the Court of Chancery had become a* **byword for** *administrative delay* **perfect example of**, classic case of, model of, exemplar of, embodiment of, incarnation of, personification of, epitome of, typification of; synonymous with; *rare* avatar of.
2 *reality was his byword* **slogan**, motto, maxim, axiom, dictum, mantra, catchword, watchword, formula, cry, battle cry, rallying cry; nickname, middle name; *rare* apophthegm.

Cc

cab ▶ **noun 1** *she hailed a cab* **taxi**, taxi cab, minicab, hackney cab; *Brit. formal* hackney carriage; *N. Amer.* hack; *historical* fiacre.
2 *a truck driver's cab* **compartment**, driver's compartment, cabin.

cabal ▶ **noun 1** *a cabal of dissidents* **clique**, faction, coterie, group, set, band, party, camp, gang, ring, cell, sect, caucus, league, confederacy, junta; pressure group; *Brit.* ginger group; *Austral./NZ* push; *historical* junto; *rare* camarilla.
2 (*archaic*) *the cabal against him* **plot**, intrigue, conspiracy, secret plan, secret scheme; machinations; *rare* complot, covin.

cabaret ▶ **noun 1** *the evening's cabaret* **entertainment**, show, floor show, performance.
2 *the dance halls and cabarets of Montreal* **nightclub**, club, boîte, supper club; *N. Amer.* cafe; *informal* nightspot, hot spot, niterie, clip joint; *Brit. informal, dated* drum; *N. Amer. informal* honky-tonk.

cabin ▶ **noun 1** *a first-class cabin on the liner* **berth**, stateroom, compartment, room, deckhouse, sleeping quarters; forecabin, outside cabin; *historical* roundhouse.
2 *an aircraft cabin* **compartment**, passenger area, passenger accommodation.
3 *a cabin by the lake* **hut**, log cabin, shanty, shack, shed; chalet; *Scottish* bothy, shieling, shiel, but and ben; *N. Amer.* cabana; *Canadian* tilt; *Austral.* mia-mia, gunyah, humpy; *NZ* whare; *S. African* hok; *archaic* cot; *N. Amer. archaic* shebang.
4 *the driver's cabin* **cab**, compartment.

cabinet *See centre pages for list of* **Cupboards and Cabinets**
▶ **noun 1** *an inlaid walnut cabinet* **cupboard**; case, container.
2 *the first meeting of the new cabinet* **senior ministers**, ministry, council, counsellors, administration, executive; inner circle; senate.

cable ▶ **noun 1** *a thick cable moored the ship to the dock* **rope**, cord, line, guy, piece of cordage; wire, chain; *Nautical* hawser, stay, bridle, topping lift; *N. Amer.* choker.
2 *electric cables* **wire**, lead, cord; power line; *Brit.* flex.
3 (*dated*) *he immediately sent a cable to the ambassador* **cablegram**, telemessage, telegram, radio-telegraph, radiogram; *informal* wire.
▶ **verb** *the secretariat cabled a reply* **send**, transmit; radio; *informal* wire; *dated* telegraph, radio-telegraph.

cache ▶ **noun 1** *a cache of arms was seized in North London | a cache of gold coins* **hoard**, store, stockpile, stock, supply, collection, accumulation, reserve, fund; arsenal; hidden treasure, treasure; nest egg; *informal* stash; *rare* amassment.
2 *a niche in the rocks that could be used for a cache* **hiding place**, storage place, secret place, hole; hideout; *informal* hidey-hole; *informal, dated* stash.

cachet ▶ **noun** *no other shipping company had quite the cachet of Cunard* **prestige**, prestigiousness, distinction, status, standing, kudos, snob value, stature, prominence, importance, pre-eminence, eminence; street credibility; merit, value; *NZ* mana; *informal* street cred.

cackle ▶ **verb 1** *the geese cackled at him* **squawk**, cluck, clack.
2 *Noel left the room, cackling with glee* **laugh loudly**, laugh uproariously, guffaw, crow, chortle, chuckle, giggle, tee-hee; *informal* laugh like a drain.

cacophonous ▶ **adjective** *cacophonous rock music blared from the speakers* **loud**, noisy, ear-splitting, blaring, booming, thunderous, deafening; **raucous**, discordant, dissonant, inharmonious, unmelodious, unmusical, tuneless, harsh, strident, screeching, screechy, grating, jarring, jangling; *rare* horrisonant, absonant.
OPPOSITES harmonious, sweet.

cacophony ▶ **noun** *despite the cacophony, Rita slept on* **din**, racket, noise, discord, dissonance, discordance, caterwauling, raucousness, screeching, jarring, stridency, grating, rasping.

cactus ▶ **noun.** *See centre pages for list of* **Cactuses**

cad ▶ **noun** (*dated*) *her adulterous cad of a husband. See* SCOUNDREL.

cadaver ▶ **noun corpse**, body, dead body, remains, carcass; *informal* stiff; *archaic* corse.

cadaverous ▶ **adjective** *his cadaverous face | a tall, cadaverous figure* **(deathly) pale**, pallid, white, bloodless, ashen, ashen-faced, ashy, chalky, chalk-white, grey, white-faced, whey-faced, waxen, waxy, corpse-like, deathlike, ghostly; **very thin**, as thin as a rake, bony, skeletal, emaciated, skin-and-bones, scrawny, scraggy, raw-boned, haggard, gaunt, drawn, pinched, hollow-cheeked, hollow-eyed; *informal* like death warmed up, like a bag of bones, anorexic; *dated* spindle-shanked; *rare* livid, etiolated, lymphatic, exsanguinous, starveling, macilent.
OPPOSITES rosy, florid; fat, plump.

cadence ▶ **noun** *there is a biblical cadence in the last words he utters* **rhythm**, tempo, metre, measure, rise and fall, beat, pulse, rhythmical flow/pattern, swing, lilt, cadency; **intonation**, modulation, inflection, speech pattern.

cadge ▶ **verb** (*informal*) *can I cadge £5 off you?* **scrounge**, beg, borrow; *informal* bum, touch someone for, sponge; *Brit. informal* scab; *Scottish informal* sorn on someone for; *N. Amer. informal* mooch; *Austral./NZ informal* bludge.

cadre ▶ **noun** *a cadre of academic specialists* **small group**, body, team, corps; core, nucleus, key group.

cafe, café ▶ **noun snack bar**, cafeteria, buffet; coffee bar, coffee shop, tea room, tea shop; restaurant, bistro, brasserie, wine bar, cafe bar, cybercafe; *Brit.* milk bar; *N. Amer.* diner; *informal* greasy spoon, eatery, noshery; *Brit. informal* caff; *dated* pull-up, pull-in; *rare* estaminet.

cafeteria ▶ **noun self-service restaurant**, canteen, cafe, restaurant, buffet; *N. Amer. dated* automat.

cage ▶ **noun** *people are increasingly uneasy about going to see animals in cages* **enclosure**, pen, pound; coop, hutch, crate; birdcage, aviary, mew; *N. Amer.* corral.
▶ **verb** *many animals are captured and caged in conditions of extreme cruelty* **confine**, shut in/up, pen, lock up, coop up, immure, incarcerate, imprison, impound; mew; *N. Amer.* corral.

cagey ▶ **adjective** (*informal*) *he was rather cagey about his plans* **secretive**, guarded, non-committal, tight-lipped, reticent, cautious, circumspect, chary, wary, careful, evasive, elusive, equivocal; discreet; *informal* playing one's cards close to one's chest.
OPPOSITES frank, open.

cahoots ▶ **plural noun** (*informal*)
□ **in cahoots** *politicians accused of being in cahoots with the Mafia* **in league**, colluding, in collusion, conspiring, conniving, collaborating, hand in glove, allied, in alliance.

cajole ▶ **verb** *he had been cajoled into escorting Nadia to a concert* **persuade**, wheedle, coax, talk into, manoeuvre, get round, prevail on, beguile, blarney, flatter, seduce, lure, entice, tempt, inveigle, woo; *informal* sweet-talk, soft-soap, butter up, twist someone's arm; *archaic* blandish.
OPPOSITE bully.

cajolery ▶ **noun** *it had proved impossible to resist Rose's cajolery* **persuasion**, **wheedling**, coaxing, inveiglement; blandishments, blarney, beguilement, flattery, honeyed words, flattering; *informal* sweet talk, sweet-talking, soft soap, soft-soaping, arm-twisting; *Brit. informal* flannel; *Austral./NZ informal* guyver; *archaic* glozing, lipsalve; *rare* cajolement, suasion.
OPPOSITE bullying.

cake *See centre pages for lists of* **Cakes, Puddings, and Desserts**
▶ **noun 1** *a plate of cream cakes* gateau, kuchen.
2 *a cake of soap* **bar**, tablet; block, slab, lump, cube, loaf, chunk, brick; piece.

▸ **verb 1** *a pair of boots caked with mud* **cover**, coat, encrust, plaster, spread thickly, smother.
2 *the blood under his nose was beginning to cake* **clot**, congeal, coagulate, thicken; solidify, harden, set, dry; *rare* inspissate.
OPPOSITE liquefy.

WORD LINKS
maker or seller of cakes **patissier**
shop selling cakes **patisserie**

calamitous ▸ **adjective** *the consequences of his decision were calamitous* **disastrous**, catastrophic, cataclysmic, devastating, dire, tragic, fatal, ruinous, crippling, awful, dreadful, terrible, woeful, grievous; *literary* direful.
OPPOSITES good, advantageous.

calamity ▸ **noun** *the fire was only the latest calamity to strike the area* **disaster**, catastrophe, tragedy, cataclysm, devastating blow, crisis, adversity, blight, tribulation, woe, affliction, evil; misfortune, misadventure, accident, stroke of bad luck, reverse of fortune, setback, mischance, mishap; *archaic* bale; *Scottish archaic* mishanter.
OPPOSITES godsend, blessing.

calculate ▸ **verb 1** *the interest charged is calculated on a daily basis* **compute**, work out, reckon, figure, enumerate, determine, evaluate, quantify, assess, cost, put a figure on; add up, add together, count up, tally, total, totalize; calibrate, gauge; *Brit.* tot up; *rare* cast.
2 *his last words were calculated to wound her* **intend**, mean, design, plan, aim.
3 *we had calculated on a quiet Sunday* **expect**, anticipate; reckon, bargain, rely, depend, count, bank; take as read; *N. Amer. informal* figure on.

calculated ▸ **adjective** *a vicious and calculated assault | a calculated risk* **deliberate**, **premeditated**, planned, pre-planned, preconceived, intentional, intended, done on purpose, purposeful, purposive, thought out in advance; aforethought; considered, conscious, studied, strategic; *Law, dated* prepense.
OPPOSITES unintentional, spontaneous; reckless.

calculating ▸ **adjective** *a coolly calculating, ruthless man* **cunning**, crafty, wily, shrewd, scheming, devious, designing, conniving, manipulative, Machiavellian, artful, guileful, slippery, slick, sly, disingenuous, unscrupulous; *informal* foxy; *S. African informal* slim; *archaic* subtle.
OPPOSITES ingenuous, artless; thoughtless.

calculation ▸ **noun 1** *by my calculations, that makes £3,500 | the calculation of the overall cost* **computation**, reckoning, adding up, counting up, working out, determining, figuring, estimation, estimate; sum; *Brit.* totting up.
2 *the government's political calculations* **assessment**, judgement; forecast, projection, prediction, expectation.

calendar *See centre pages for list of animals of the* **Chinese Calendar**
▸ **noun 1** almanac; *archaic* ephemeris.
2 *my social calendar's pretty full* **timetable**, schedule, programme, diary.

calibre ▸ **noun 1** *they could ill afford to lose a man of his calibre* **quality**, merit, distinction, character, worth, stature, excellence, superiority, eminence, pre-eminence; **ability**, expertise, talent, capability, capacity, proficiency, competence; gifts, endowments, strengths, qualifications.
2 *if only they could play rugby of this calibre every week* **standard**, level, grade, quality.
3 *the calibre of a gun* **bore**, diameter, gauge; size, measure.

call ▸ **verb 1** *'Wait for me!' she called* **cry out**, cry, shout, yell, sing out, whoop, bellow, roar, halloo, bawl, scream, shriek, screech; exclaim; *informal* holler, yoo-hoo, cooee; *rare* ejaculate, vociferate.
2 *I got so tired, Mum had to call me at least three times every morning* **wake up**, wake, awaken, waken, rouse; *informal* give someone a shout; *Brit. informal* knock up.
3 *I'll call you tomorrow* **phone**, telephone, get on the phone to, get someone on the phone, dial, make/place a call to, get, reach; *Brit.* **ring up**, ring, give someone a ring; *informal* call up, give someone a call, give someone a buzz, buzz; *Brit. informal* give someone a bell, bell, give someone a tinkle, get on the blower to; *N. Amer. informal* get someone on the horn.
4 *you'd better call the doctor | Rose called a taxi* **summon**, send for, ask for; order; page.
5 *he called at Ashgrove Cottage on his way home* **pay a visit to**, pay a brief visit to, visit, pay a call on, call in on, look in on; *informal* drop in on, drop by, stop by, pop into.
6 *the prime minister called a meeting of senior cabinet ministers | there was no alternative but to call a general election* **convene**, summon, call together, order, assemble; **arrange**, arrange a time/date for; announce, declare; *formal* convoke.
7 *they called their daughter Hannah* **name**; christen, baptize; designate, style, term, dub, label, entitle; *archaic* clepe; *rare* denominate; **(be called)** answer to the name of, go by the name of.
8 *he's the only person I would call a friend* **describe as**, **regard as**, look on as, consider to be, judge to be, think of as, class as, categorize as.
□ **call for 1** *desperate times call for desperate measures* **require**, need, necessitate, make necessary, demand; be grounds for, justify, warrant, be a justification/reason for; involve, entail.
2 *I'll call for you around seven* **pick up**, collect, fetch, go/come to get, come for.
□ **call something off** *the proposed tour to Australia was called off* **cancel**, abandon, shelve, scrap, drop, mothball; *informal* axe, scrub, scratch, nix; *N. Amer. informal* redline.
□ **call on 1** *I thought I might call on her later today* **visit**, pay a visit to, pay a call on, go and see, look in on; *N. Amer.* visit with, go see; *informal* look up, drop in on, pop in on.
2 *he called on the government to hold a plebiscite* **appeal to**, ask, request, apply to, petition; urge; beg, implore, entreat, beseech, plead with.
3 *we are able to call on academic staff with a wide variety of expertise* **have recourse to**, avail oneself of, turn to, draw on, look to, make use of, use, utilize, bring into play.
□ **call the shots** *directors call the shots and nothing happens on set without their say-so* **be in charge**, be in control, be in command, be the boss, be at the helm, be in the driving seat, be at the wheel, be in the saddle, pull the strings, hold the purse strings; *informal* run the show, rule the roost; *Brit. informal* wear the trousers.
□ **call to mind 1** *the still lifes call to mind Cézanne's works* **evoke**, put one in mind of, recall, bring to mind, call up, summon up, conjure up; echo, allude to.
2 *I cannot call to mind where I have seen you* **remember**, recall, recollect, think; *Scottish* mind; *archaic* bethink oneself of.
□ **call someone up 1** (*informal*) *Roland called me up at the crack of dawn* **phone**, telephone, call, get on the phone to, get someone on the phone, dial, make/place a call to, get, reach; *Brit.* **ring up**, ring, give someone a ring; *informal* give someone a call, give someone a buzz, buzz; *Brit. informal* give someone a bell, bell, give someone a tinkle, get on the blower to; *N. Amer. informal* get someone on the horn.
2 *they have called up more than 20,000 reservists* **enlist**, recruit, sign up; conscript; *US* draft.
3 *he was called up for England's final Test at the Oval* **select**, pick, choose; *Brit.* cap; *informal* give someone the nod.
▸ **noun 1** *I heard calls of 'Come on Steve' from the auditorium* **cry**, shout, yell, whoop, roar, scream, shriek; exclamation; *informal* holler; *rare* vociferation.
2 *the call of the water rail* **cry**, song, sound.
3 *I'll give you a call tomorrow* **phone call**, telephone call; *Brit.* **ring**; *informal* buzz; *Brit. informal* bell, tinkle.
4 *later that day, he paid a call on Harold Shoesmith* **visit**, social call.
5 *the President issued a call for party unity* **appeal**, request, plea, entreaty; **demand**, order, command.
6 *the last call for passengers on flight BA701* **summons**, request.
7 *there's no call for that kind of language* **need**, necessity, occasion, reason, justification, grounds, excuse, pretext; cause.
8 *there's no call for expensive wine here* **demand**, desire, want, requirement, need; market.
9 *walkers can't resist the call of the Cairngorms* **attraction**, appeal, lure, allure, allurement, fascination, seductiveness; magic, beauty, spell, pull, draw.
□ **on call** *one of the team will be on call around the clock* **on duty**, on standby, standing by, ready, available.

call girl ▸ **noun** **prostitute**, whore, sex worker; *French* fille de joie, demi-mondaine; *Spanish* puta; *N. Amer.* sporting girl/woman/lady; *informal* tart, pro, moll, tail, brass nail, grande horizontale, woman on the game, working girl, member of the oldest profession; *N. Amer. informal* hooker, hustler, chippy; *black English* ho; *euphemistic* model, escort, masseuse; *dated* woman of the streets, lady/woman of the night, scarlet woman, cocotte; *archaic* courtesan, strumpet, harlot, trollop, woman of ill repute, lady of pleasure, Cyprian, doxy, drab, quean, trull, wench; *rare* sing-song girl.

calling ▸ **noun 1** *those who have a special calling to minister to others' needs* **vocation**, mission; call, summons.
2 *he considered engineering one of the highest possible callings* **profession**, occupation, career, work, employment, job, business, trade, craft, line, line of work, pursuit, métier, walk of life, province, field; *archaic* employ.

callous ▸ **adjective** *his callous disregard for the feelings and wishes of others* **heartless**, unfeeling, uncaring, cold, cold-hearted, hard, as hard as nails, hard-hearted, with a heart of stone, stony-hearted, insensitive, lacking compassion, hardbitten, cold-blooded, hardened, case-hardened, harsh, cruel, ruthless, brutal; unsympathetic, uncharitable, indifferent, unconcerned, unsusceptible, insensible, bloodless, soulless; *informal* hard-boiled; *rare* indurate, indurated, marble-hearted.
OPPOSITES kind, compassionate.

callow ▸ **adjective** *a callow youth* **immature**, **inexperienced**, naive, green, as green as grass, born yesterday, raw, unseasoned, untrained, untried; juvenile, adolescent, jejune; innocent, guileless, artless, unworldly, unsophisticated; *informal* wet behind the ears.
OPPOSITES mature, experienced, sophisticated.

calm ▸ **adjective 1** *her voice was steady and she seemed very calm* **serene**, tranquil, relaxed, unruffled, unperturbed, unflustered, undisturbed, unagitated, unmoved, unbothered, untroubled; equable, even-tempered, imperturbable, quiet, steady; **placid**, peaceful, sedate, unexcitable,

impassive, dispassionate, unemotional, phlegmatic, stolid; **composed**, cool, collected, {cool, calm, and collected}, as cool as a cucumber, cool-headed, self-possessed, controlled, self-controlled, poised; *informal* unflappable, unfazed, together, laid-back; *rare* equanimous.
OPPOSITES excited, upset, nervous.
2 *the night was clear and calm* **windless**, still, tranquil, quiet, serene, peaceful, pacific, undisturbed, restful, balmy, halcyon.
OPPOSITES windy, stormy.
3 *the calm waters of the lake* **tranquil**, still, like a millpond, smooth, glassy, flat, motionless, waveless, unagitated, storm-free; *literary* stilly.
OPPOSITES rough, stormy.
▶ **noun 1** *in the centre of the storm, calm prevailed* **tranquillity**, stillness, calmness, quiet, quietness, quietude, peace, peacefulness, serenity, silence, hush; restfulness, repose.
OPPOSITES violence, unrest.
2 *his usual calm deserted him* **composure**, coolness, calmness, self-possession, sangfroid, presence of mind, poise, aplomb, self-control; serenity, tranquillity, equanimity, imperturbability, equability, placidness, placidity, impassiveness, impassivity, dispassion, phlegm, stolidity; *informal* cool, unflappability; *rare* ataraxy, ataraxia.
OPPOSITE anxiety.
▶ **verb 1** *I took him inside and tried to **calm him down** | he went round to the pub to calm his nerves* **soothe**, pacify, placate, mollify, appease, conciliate; hush, lull, gentle, tranquillize; quell, allay, alleviate, assuage; *Brit.* quieten (down); *Austral.* square off; *rare* dulcify.
OPPOSITES excite, upset.
2 *she took a deep breath and forced herself to **calm down*** **compose oneself**, recover/regain one's composure, control oneself, recover/regain one's self-control, pull oneself together, keep one's head, simmer down, cool down, cool off, take it easy; *Brit.* quieten down; *informal* get a grip, keep one's cool, play it cool, keep one's shirt on, wind down, come back down to earth; *N. Amer. informal* chill out, hang loose, stay loose, decompress.
OPPOSITE lose one's temper.

CHOOSE THE RIGHT WORD

calm, serene, tranquil, placid, peaceful

All these words indicate a freedom from disturbance or agitation, and all are used of people, concrete nouns, such as *water*, and abstract nouns, such as *look*.

- Someone who is **calm** remains unperturbed in a worrying or frightening situation (*you were wonderful, coping with all of us and always calm*). *Calm* is often applied to a place where fighting or unrest is normal but is absent or has died down, and is the word most commonly used in connection with weather, to describe the *sea*, *day*, *weather*, or *sky*.
- **Serene** suggests that a person has an inner calm and is used to describe their appearance or behaviour (*the serene beauty of her delicate golden face belied her years | an attitude of serene detachment*). It is also used of places that are relaxed, free from strife, and untouched by human cares (*charming properties of character await—secluded, historic and serene | Cologne is a city of serene parks*).
- **Tranquil** is most commonly used of places that are relaxingly free from noise or disturbance—a *setting*, *scene*, *village*, or *garden*, in particular. It is also used to describe people or their lives (*most people over twenty never have a tranquil moment*).
- Someone with a **placid** nature is not easily worried or upset (*a placid, contented family man | her usually placid temper began to stir*). *Placid* can have critical overtones, suggesting that someone is slow to react and rather dull (*moderate voters of placid and unreflective temperament*). *Placid* is also used to describe animals and children with a quiet, docile nature, as well as areas of calm water, such as a *bay*, *sea*, or *canal*.
- **Peaceful** most commonly refers to an absence of conflict or aggression (*a peaceful solution to the Saharan conflict | 400,000 people participated in a peaceful demonstration*).

calumny ▶ **noun** *a bitter struggle marked by calumny and litigation* **slander**, defamation (of character), character assassination, misrepresentation of character, evil-speaking, calumniation, libel; scandalmongering, malicious gossip, muckraking, smear campaign, disparagement, denigration, derogation, aspersions, vilification, traducement, obloquy, verbal abuse, backbiting, vituperation, revilement, scurrility; lies, slurs, smears, untruths, false accusations, false reports, insults, slights; *informal* mud-slinging; *N. Amer. informal* bad-mouthing; *archaic* contumely.

camaraderie ▶ **noun** *he enjoyed the camaraderie of army life* **friendship**, **comradeship**, fellowship, good fellowship, companionship, brotherliness, brotherhood, sisterhood, closeness, affinity, togetherness, solidarity, mutual support; sociability; team spirit; *French* esprit de corps.

camera ▶ **noun.** *See centre pages for list of* **Cameras**

camouflage ▶ **noun 1** *on the trenches were pieces of turf which served for camouflage* **disguise**, concealment.
2 *an animal may adapt its camouflage to fit into a new environment* **protective colouring**; *technical* cryptic colouring, cryptic coloration, mimicry.
3 *much of my apparent indifference was merely protective camouflage* **facade**, front, false front, smokescreen, cover-up, disguise, mask, cloak, blind, screen, masquerade, concealment, dissimulation, pretence; subterfuge.
▶ **verb** *the caravan was camouflaged with netting and branches* **disguise**, hide, conceal, keep hidden, mask, screen, veil, cloak, cover, cover up, obscure, shroud.

camp[1] ▶ **noun 1** *an army camp | they went back to the camp and lit a fire* **bivouac**, encampment, cantonment, barracks, base; campsite, camping ground; tents; *S. African historical* laager.
2 *both the liberal and conservative camps were annoyed by his high-handed manner* **faction**, wing, side, group, party, lobby, caucus, bloc, clique, coterie, set, sect, cabal.
▶ **verb** *that night they camped in a field* **pitch tents**, set up camp, pitch camp, encamp, bivouac; *S. African* outspan.

camp[2] (*informal*) ▶ **adjective 1** *a heavily made-up and highly camp actor* **effeminate**, effete, foppish, affected, niminy-piminy, mincing, posturing; *informal* campy; *informal, derogatory* poncey, limp-wristed, pansyish, faggy.
OPPOSITES macho, virile.
2 *a film full of camp humour and slapstick* **exaggerated**, theatrical, affected, mannered, flamboyant, extravagant; *informal* over the top, OTT, camped up.
▶ **verb**
□ **camp it up** *he camped it up a bit for the cameras* **posture**, behave theatrically, behave affectedly, overact, overdo it, go overboard; *informal* show off, ham it up; *N. Amer. informal* cop an attitude.

campaign ▶ **noun 1** *Napoleon's Russian campaign | the air campaign* **military operation(s)**, manoeuvre(s); offensive, attack, advance, push, thrust; crusade, war, battle, engagement, action; *Islam* jihad.
2 *the campaign to reduce harmful vehicle emissions | a new campaign against drinking and driving* **crusade**, drive, push, effort, struggle, move, movement; operation, manoeuvre, course of action, strategy, set of tactics, battle plan; battle, war.
▶ **verb 1** *a movement **campaigning for** political reform* **crusade**, fight, battle, work, push, press, strive, struggle, agitate; promote, advocate, champion, speak for, lobby for, propagandize.
2 *she campaigned as a political outsider* **run/stand for office**, throw one's hat in the ring; canvass, electioneer, solicit votes; *N. Amer. informal* stump, take to the stump.

campaigner ▶ **noun** **crusader**, fighter, battler; champion, advocate, promoter, enthusiast; activist, demonstrator, reformer.

can ▶ **noun** *a can of paint | a petrol can* **tin**, canister; jerrycan, oilcan; container, receptacle, vessel.

canal ▶ **noun 1** *brightly painted barges chugged up the canal* **inland waterway**, channel, watercourse, waterway; ship canal.
2 *the ear canal* **duct**, tube, passage, vessel.

cancel ▶ **verb 1** *the match was cancelled due to a frozen pitch* **call off**, abandon, scrap, drop; postpone, mothball; *informal* scrub, scratch, axe, nix; *N. Amer. informal* redline.
2 *his visa had been cancelled | you must inform the bank in writing if you wish to cancel this instruction* **annul**, invalidate, nullify, declare null and void, render null and void, void; **revoke**, rescind, retract, countermand, set aside, take back, withdraw, recall, repeal, overrule, override, abrogate, quash; extinguish, remit, retire; *Law* vacate, discharge; *rare* disannul, negate.
3 *rising unemployment had **cancelled out** the earlier economic gains* **neutralize**, **counterbalance**, counteract, balance (out), countervail; negate, nullify, wipe out; offset, compensate for, make up for; *rare* negative, counterweigh.
4 *there is one paragraph that should be cancelled* **delete**, cross out, strike out, put a line through, blue-pencil, scratch out, obliterate, blot out, cut out, expunge, efface, erase, rub out, eradicate, eliminate; *Brit. trademark* Tippex out; *technical* dele.

cancer ▶ **noun 1** *most skin cancers are curable* **malignant growth**, cancerous growth, malignant tumour, tumour, malignancy; *technical* carcinoma, sarcoma, melanoma, lymphoma, myeloma, neoplasm, metastasis, neurofibroma, teratoma, fibroadenoma, meningioma.
2 *racism is a cancer sweeping across Europe* **evil**, blight, scourge, poison, canker, sickness, disease, pestilence, plague; rot, corruption.

WORD LINKS

related prefix	**carcin-**
relating to cancer	**carcinomatous**
causing cancer	**carcinogenic**
fear of cancer	**carcinophobia**
branch of medicine treating cancer	**oncology**

candid ▶ **adjective 1** *his responses were remarkably candid* **frank**, outspoken, forthright, blunt, open, honest, truthful, sincere, direct, straightforward, plain-spoken, bluff, unreserved, downright, not afraid to call a spade a spade, straight from the shoulder, unvarnished, bald; heart-to-heart,

intimate, personal, man-to-man, woman-to-woman; *informal* upfront, on the level; *N. Amer. informal* on the up and up; *archaic* round, free-spoken.
OPPOSITES secretive, guarded, insincere.
2 *it's better to let the photographer mingle and take candid shots* **unposed**, informal, uncontrived, unstudied, impromptu; **spontaneous**, extemporary, natural.

CHOOSE THE RIGHT WORD

candid, frank, outspoken, forthright, blunt

These words generally show admiration for openness and honesty, although this can be tinged with the feeling that some things are better concealed. They can all describe a person or the things they say or write.

- A **candid** person keeps no secrets and does not gloss over distressing or discreditable facts (*he was candid about the difficulties* | *the head of the information directorate said only that discussions had been candid*). Such total openness is often welcome or unusual, as shown by the frequent accompanying use of *refreshingly*.
- **Frank**, while very close in meaning to *candid*, suggests a greater bluntness and is more often used to describe painful or difficult revelations such as a *confession* or *admission*. It also suggests a down-to-earth openness on matters seen as sensitive or embarrassing (*frank discussion of sexual matters*).
- Someone who is **outspoken** is unusually ready to risk unpopularity or even danger by expressing controversial opinions (*an outspoken critic of the military*). It is much more commonly used than the other four words to describe *critics*, *advocates*, *opponents*, *criticism*, *politicians*, and *leaders*.
- Someone who is **forthright** says what they have to say, without fear or favour and in an uncompromising manner (*a forthright rejection of the idea of electoral pacts*).
- Someone who is **blunt** may even take a perverse delight in mentioning sensitive issues or giving unwelcome news in an abrupt and unadorned way (*to be blunt, a substantial majority of candidates are not fully literate* | *blunt warnings about the dangers of smoking*).

candidate ▶ noun **1** *candidates applying for this position should be computer-literate* **applicant**, job applicant, job-seeker, prospective employee; contender, contestant, nominee, aspirant, possibility, possible; interviewee; postulant, suitor, pretender; *informal* runner.
2 *A-level candidates* **examinee**, entrant.
3 *the most likely candidate for the title of Designer of the Year* **prospect**; *informal* bet.

candle ▶ noun taper, sconce; tallow candle, wax candle, Christmas candle, votary candle, paschal candle; *archaic* wax light, glim, rush candle, rushlight; *rare* bougie, cierge.

WORD LINKS

maker or seller of candles	**chandler**
shop selling candles	**chandlery**

candour ▶ noun *he spoke with a degree of candour unusual in political life* **frankness**, openness, honesty, candidness, truthfulness, sincerity, forthrightness, directness, lack of restraint, straightforwardness, plain-spokenness, plain dealing, plainness, calling a spade a spade, unreservedness, bluffness, bluntness, outspokenness; *informal* telling it like it is.
OPPOSITES guardedness, evasiveness, insincerity.

candy ▶ noun (*N. Amer.*). See CONFECTIONERY.

cane ▶ noun **1** *he carried a silver-topped cane* **walking stick**, stick, staff; alpenstock, malacca, blackthorn, ashplant, rattan; crook; *Austral./NZ* waddy; *historical* ferule.
2 *tie the shoot to a cane if vertical growth is required* **stick**, stake, rod, upright, pole, beanpole.
3 *he told the court he had been beaten with a cane every week* **stick**, rod, birch; *N. Amer. informal* paddle; *historical* ferule.
▶ verb *Matthew was caned for bullying* **beat**, strike, hit, flog, thrash, lash, birch, whip, horsewhip, strap, leather, flagellate, scourge; *N. Amer.* bullwhip; *informal* tan someone's hide, give someone a hiding, take a strap to, larrup; *N. Amer. informal* whale; *rare* yerk, quirt.

canker ▶ noun **1** *a plant which is very susceptible to canker* **fungal disease**, fungal rot, plant rot; blight.
2 *ear cankers in rabbits are caused by a mite* **ulcer**, ulceration, infection, sore, running sore, lesion, abscess, chancre.
3 *racism remains a canker at the heart of the nation* **blight**, evil, scourge, poison, cancer, sickness, disease, pestilence, plague; rot, corruption.

cannabis ▶ noun **marijuana**, hashish, bhang, hemp, kef, kif, charas, ganja, sinsemilla; *informal* dope, hash, grass, pot, blow, draw, stuff, Mary Jane, tea, the weed, gold, green, mezz, skunkweed, skunk, reefer, rope, smoke, gage, boo, charge, jive, mootah, pod; *Brit. informal* wacky backy; *N. Amer. informal* locoweed; *S. African* dagga, zol.

cannibal ▶ noun **maneater**, people-eater; *rare* anthropophagite, anthropophagist.

cannon ▶ noun **mounted gun**, field gun, gun, piece of artillery, piece of ordnance; mortar, howitzer; *informal* big gun; *historical* carronade, bombard, culverin, falconet, long tom, serpentine; *Brit. historical* pom-pom.
▶ verb *the couple behind almost cannoned into us* **collide with**, hit, run into, bang into, crash into, smash into, smack into, crack into, ram into, be in collision with, plough into; *N. Amer.* impact with; *N. Amer. informal* barrel into.

cannonade ▶ noun *the French troops resumed their cannonade* **bombardment**, shelling, gunfire, artillery fire, barrage, battery, attack, pounding; volley, salvo, broadside, fusillade.

canny ▶ adjective *canny investors* **shrewd**, astute, sharp, sharp-witted, discerning, acute, penetrating, discriminating, perceptive, perspicacious, clever, intelligent, wise, sagacious, sensible, judicious, circumspect, careful, prudent, cautious; cunning, crafty, wily, artful, calculating; *informal* on the ball, smart, savvy; *Brit. informal* suss, sussed; *Scottish & N. English informal* pawky; *N. Amer. informal* heads-up, as sharp as a tack; *rare* long-headed, sapient, argute.
OPPOSITES foolish, reckless.

canoe ▶ noun dugout, kayak, outrigger; (*in Alaska*) bidarka; (*in Central America*) pirogue; (*in NZ*) waka.

canon ▶ noun **1** *the appointment violated the canons of fair play and equal opportunity* **principle**, rule, law, tenet, precept, formula; standard, convention, norm, pattern, model, exemplar; criterion, measure, yardstick, benchmark, test.
2 *a set of ecclesiastical canons* **law**, decree, edict, statute, dictate, dictum, ordinance; rule, ruling, regulation; *Roman Catholic Church* decretal.
3 *the Shakespeare canon* **(list of) works**, writings, oeuvre.

canonical *See centre pages for list of* **Canonical Hours**
▶ adjective *the canonical method of comparative linguistics* **recognized**, authoritative, authorized, accepted, sanctioned, approved, received, established, orthodox; standard, normal, usual, ordinary, stock, customary, regular, traditional.
OPPOSITES unorthodox, innovative.

canonize ▶ verb **1** *the last English saint to be canonized* **beatify**, declare to be a saint.
2 *we have canonized freedom of speech as an absolute virtue* **glorify**, acclaim; regard as sacred, deify, idolize, apotheosize; enshrine.

canopy ▶ noun **awning**, shade, sunshade, cover, covering; baldachin, tester, half-tester; *Judaism* chuppah; *technical* velarium.

cant[1] ▶ noun **1** *religious cant* **hypocrisy**, **sanctimoniousness**, sanctimony, humbug, pietism, affected piety, insincerity, sham, lip service, empty talk, pretence; *rare* Pharisaism, Tartufferie.
OPPOSITE sincerity.
2 *thieves' cant* **slang**, jargon, idiom, argot, patter, patois, vernacular, speech, terminology, language; *informal* lingo, -speak, -ese.

cant[2] ▶ verb *the deck canted some twenty degrees* **tilt**, lean, slant, slope, incline, angle, be at an angle; tip, list, bank, heel.
▶ noun *the outward cant of the curving walls* **slope**, slant, tilt, angle, inclination.

cantankerous ▶ adjective *a cantankerous old man* **bad-tempered**, irascible, irritable, grumpy, grouchy, crotchety, tetchy, testy, crusty, curmudgeonly, ill-tempered, ill-natured, ill-humoured, peevish, cross, as cross as two sticks, fractious, disagreeable, pettish, crabbed, crabby, waspish, prickly, peppery, touchy, scratchy, splenetic, shrewish, short-tempered, hot-tempered, quick-tempered, dyspeptic, choleric, bilious, liverish, cross-grained; argumentative, quarrelsome, uncooperative, contrary, perverse, difficult, awkward; *informal* snappish, snappy, chippy, on a short fuse, short-fused; *Brit. informal* shirty, stroppy, narky, ratty, eggy, like a bear with a sore head; *N. Amer. informal* cranky, ornery, peckish, soreheaded; *Austral./NZ informal* snaky; *informal, dated* waxy, miffy.
OPPOSITES good-natured, affable.

canteen ▶ noun **1** *the staff canteen* **restaurant**, cafeteria, refectory, mess hall; *Brit. Military* NAAFI; *N. Amer.* lunchroom; *French* popote; *Russian* stolovaya; *S. African informal* cafe de move-on.
2 *a canteen of water* **container**; flask, bottle, skin; *French* bidon; *S. African* vatje.

canvass ▶ verb **1** *he's canvassing for the Green Party* **campaign**, electioneer, solicit votes, drum up support; *N. Amer.* stump; *Brit. informal* doorstep; *N. Amer. informal* be a ward heeler.
2 *they promised to canvass all member clubs for their views* **poll**, question, ask, survey, interview, sound out, ascertain the opinions of.
3 *they're canvassing support among shareholders* **seek**, try to obtain, go after, make a pitch for.
4 *early retirement was canvassed as a solution to the problem of unemployment* **propose**, suggest, submit, offer, air; **discuss**, debate, consider.

canyon ▶ noun **ravine**, gorge, gully, pass, defile, couloir; chasm, abyss, gulf; *N. Amer.* gulch, coulee, flume; *American Spanish* arroyo, barranca,

C

quebrada; *Indian* nullah, khud; *S. African* sloot, kloof, donga; *rare* khor.

cap *See centre pages for list of* **Hats**

▶ **noun 1** *a small bottle with a white plastic cap* **lid**, top, stopper, cork, bung, spile; ferrule; cover, covering; *N. Amer.* stopple.
2 *school leavers in cap and gown* **mortar board**, academic cap; *dated* trencher, trencher cap, square.
3 *he raised the cap on local authority spending* **limit**, upper limit, ceiling; curb, check.

▶ **verb 1** *mountains capped with snow* **top**, crown; **cover**, coat, blanket, mantle.
2 *his innings capped a great day for the Australians* **round off**, crown, be a fitting climax to, put the finishing touch/touches to, perfect, complete.
3 *they tried to cap each other's stories* **beat**, better, surpass, outdo, outshine, trump, top, upstage; improve on, go one better than; *informal* best.
4 (*Brit.*) *he was capped 22 times for England* **choose**, select, pick, include; *informal* give someone the nod.
5 *council budgets will be capped* **set a limit on**, put a ceiling on, limit, restrict, keep within bounds; curb, control, peg.

capability ▶ **noun** *the company's capability to understand and respond to customer needs | her professional capabilities* **ability**, capacity, power, potential, potentiality; competence, proficiency, accomplishment, adeptness, aptitude, aptness, faculty, experience, skill, skilfulness, talent, flair; cleverness, intelligence; gift, strong point, forte, knack; *informal* know-how.
OPPOSITES inability, incompetence.

capable ▶ **adjective** *a very capable young woman* **competent**, able, efficient, effective, proficient, accomplished, adept, apt, practised, experienced, qualified, skilled, skilful, masterly, talented, gifted; clever, intelligent; *informal* handy, useful; *rare* habile.
OPPOSITES incompetent, inept.

□ **be capable of 1** *I'm quite capable of looking after myself | I don't believe he's capable of murder* **have the ability to**, have the potential to, be equal to (the task of), be up to; be disposed to, be inclined to, be prone to, be liable to, be likely to, be apt to; *informal* have what it takes to.
2 *the strange events are capable of rational explanation* **be open to**, be susceptible of, admit of, allow of.

> **CHOOSE THE RIGHT WORD**
> **capable, competent, efficient, able**
> *See* COMPETENT.

capacious ▶ **adjective** *the car's capacious boot* **roomy**, commodious, spacious, ample, big, large, sizeable, generous, extensive, substantial, vast, huge, immense; voluminous; *rare* spacey.
OPPOSITES cramped, small.

capacity ▶ **noun 1** *the capacity of the freezer is 1.1 cubic feet* **volume**, cubic measure; size, dimensions, measurements, magnitude, proportions, amplitude; room, space; extent, range, scope, compass.
2 *his capacity to inspire trust in others | the task was beyond my intellectual capacities* **ability**, power, potential, potentiality; competence, competency, proficiency, accomplishment, adeptness, aptitude, aptness, faculty, skill, skilfulness, talent, flair; cleverness, intelligence; gift, strong point, forte, knack; experience; *informal* know-how.
OPPOSITE inability.
3 *in his capacity as Commander-in-Chief of the Armed Forces* **position**, post, job, office, appointment; **role**, function.

cape[1] ▶ **noun** *she wore a black cape over a red velvet dress* **cloak**, mantle, shawl, wrap, stole, tippet; *S. American* poncho, serape; *Ecclesiastical* cope, mozzetta, amice; *archaic* mantlet; *rare* pelisse, pelerine.

cape[2] ▶ **noun** *we could just make out the island from the cape* **headland**, promontory, point, head, foreland, neck; bluff, cliff, precipice, prominence, projection, overhang; horn, hook, bill, ness, naze; peninsula; *Scottish* mull; *rare* chersonese.

caper ▶ **verb** *children were capering about the room* **skip**, **dance**, romp, jig, frisk, gambol, cavort, prance, frolic, leap, hop, jump, bound, spring; *rare* curvet, rollick, capriole.

▶ **noun 1** *she did a little caper* **dance**, **skip**, hop, leap, jump; *rare* curvet, gambado, gambade.
2 (*informal*) *I'm too old for this kind of caper* **escapade**, stunt, prank, trick, practical joke, antics, high jinks, mischief, game, sport, fun, jest, jesting, jape; *informal* shenanigans, lark, skylarking; *Brit. informal* monkey tricks, monkey business; *N. Amer. informal* dido.

capital ▶ **noun 1** *Warsaw is the capital of Poland* **first city**, most important city, seat of government, centre of administration; metropolis.
2 *by 1977 he had amassed enough capital to pull off the property deal of the century* **money**, finance(s), funds, the wherewithal, the means, assets, wealth, resources, reserves, stock, principal; working capital, investment capital; *informal* dough, bread, loot, the ready, readies, shekels, moolah, the necessary, wad, boodle, dibs, gelt, ducats, rhino, gravy, scratch, stuff, oof; *Brit. informal* dosh, brass, lolly, spondulicks, wonga, ackers; *N. Amer. informal* dinero, greenbacks, simoleons, bucks, jack, mazuma; *Austral./NZ informal* Oscar; *informal, dated* splosh, green, tin; *Brit. dated* l.s.d.; *N. Amer. informal, dated* kale, rocks, shinplasters; *archaic* pelf.
3 *he wrote the name in capitals* **capital letter**, upper-case letter, block capital; *informal* cap; *technical* uncial, uncial letter, majuscule letter.

▶ **adjective 1** *capital letters* **upper-case**, block; *technical* uncial, majuscule.
2 (*Brit. informal, dated*) *he's a really capital fellow. See* SPLENDID *sense* 3.

capitalism ▶ **noun private enterprise**, free enterprise, private ownership, privatized industries, the free market, individualism; laissez-faire.
OPPOSITE communism.

capitalist ▶ **noun financier**, investor, industrialist; magnate, tycoon, mogul, nabob; plutocrat, money man; *informal* fat cat, yuppie, loadsamoney, moneybags.

capitalize ▶ **verb** *the capacity of mature businesses to capitalize rapidly growing ventures* **finance**, fund, underwrite, provide capital for, back, sponsor; *N. Amer.* bankroll; *N. Amer. informal* stake.

□ **capitalize on** *an attempt by the opposition to capitalize on the government's embarrassment* **take advantage of**, profit from, turn to account, make capital out of, make the most of, exploit, benefit from, put to advantage; maximize; strike while the iron is hot, make hay while the sun shines; *informal* cash in on.

capitulate ▶ **verb** *by the end of the month, the rebels had been forced to capitulate* **surrender**, give in, yield, admit defeat, concede defeat, give up the struggle, submit, back down, climb down, give way, cave in, succumb, crumble, bow to someone/something; relent, acquiesce, accede, come to terms; be beaten, be overcome, be overwhelmed, fall; lay down one's arms, raise/show the white flag; *informal* throw in the towel, throw in the sponge.
OPPOSITES resist, hold out.

capitulation ▶ **noun** *the capitulation of the Republican forces* **surrender**, submission, yielding, giving in, succumbing, acquiescence, laying down of arms; fall, defeat.
OPPOSITE resistance.

caprice ▶ **noun 1** *his wife's caprices and demands made his life impossible* **whim**, whimsy, vagary, fancy, notion, fad, freak, humour, impulse, quirk, eccentricity, foible, crotchet, urge.
2 *the staff tired of his tyranny and his caprice* **fickleness**, changeableness, volatility, inconstancy, capriciousness, fitfulness, unpredictability.
OPPOSITE stability.

capricious ▶ **adjective** *the capricious workings of fate* **fickle**, inconstant, changeable, variable, unstable, mercurial, volatile, erratic, vacillating, irregular, inconsistent, fitful, arbitrary; impulsive, temperamental, wild, ungovernable; whimsical, fanciful, flighty, wayward, quirky, faddish, freakish; unpredictable, random, chance, haphazard.
OPPOSITES stable, consistent.

> **CHOOSE THE RIGHT WORD**
> **capricious, inconstant, changeable, fickle**
> *See* INCONSTANT.

capsize ▶ **verb** *gale force winds capsized their small craft* **overturn**, turn over, turn upside down, upset, upend, knock over, flip over, tip over, topple over, invert, keel over, turn turtle; *Nautical* pitchpole; *archaic* overset.
OPPOSITE right.

capsule ▶ **noun 1** *he placed a capsule under his tongue* **pill**, tablet, lozenge, pastille, pilule, drop, caplet, pellet, bolus, troche; *informal* tab.
2 *the bottle's capsule is lead-free* **cover**, seal, cap, top.
3 *a space capsule* **module**, craft, probe; detachable compartment, section.
4 *sow small pots with two or three capsules* **seed case**, pod, shell, husk, hull, case, sheath; *technical* pericarp, exocarp, legume, integument.

captain ▶ **noun 1** *the ship's captain* **commander**, master, skipper; *informal* old man.
2 *the cup was presented to the winning team's captain* **leader**, head, skipper; representative, figurehead; *informal* boss.
3 *a captain of industry* **magnate**, tycoon, mogul, grandee, baron, nabob, mandarin, industrialist; chief, head, leader, boss, principal; *informal* number one, bigwig, big wheel, big cheese, big shot, big gun, big noise, top dog, fat cat; *N. Amer. informal* honcho, kahuna, top banana, big enchilada, macher.

▶ **verb** *a small vessel captained by a cut-throat* **command**, skipper, run, be in charge of, have charge of, control, have control of, govern, preside over, direct, rule, manage, supervise, superintend.

caption ▶ **noun** *he designed a series of posters with the caption 'No one is innocent'* **title**, heading, wording, head, legend, inscription, explanation, description, rubric, label, motto, slogan.

captious ▶ **adjective** *the losers were glum and captious* **critical**, fault-finding, quibbling, niggling, cavilling, carping, criticizing, disapproving, censorious, judgemental, overcritical, hypercritical, pedantic, hair-splitting, pettifogging; *informal* nit-picking, pernickety.

OPPOSITES forgiving, easy-going.

captivate ▶ verb *his audiences found themselves captivated by his energy and enthusiasm* **enthral**, **charm**, enchant, bewitch, fascinate, beguile, entrance, enrapture, delight, attract, allure, lure; win, ensnare, dazzle, absorb, engross, rivet, grip, hypnotize, mesmerize, spellbind; infatuate, enamour, seduce, woo, ravish.
OPPOSITES repel; bore.

captivating ▶ adjective *a lively and captivating young girl* **charming**, **enchanting**, bewitching, fascinating, beguiling, entrancing, alluring, engaging, interesting, winning, delightful; attractive, beautiful, charismatic; dazzling, engrossing, riveting, gripping, enthralling, spellbinding, seductive.
OPPOSITES repellent; boring.

captive ▶ noun *the policeman put handcuffs on the captive* **prisoner**, convict, detainee, inmate; prisoner of war, POW, internee, hostage; slave, bondsman; informal jailbird, con; Brit. informal (old) lag; N. Amer. informal yardbird.
▶ adjective *she was against keeping wild animals captive* **confined**, caged, incarcerated, locked up, penned up; chained, shackled, fettered, ensnared; restrained, under restraint, restricted, secure; jailed, imprisoned, in prison, interned, detained, in captivity, under lock and key, behind bars, in bondage, taken prisoner; captured.
OPPOSITE free.

captivity ▶ noun *he was weakened by his captivity* **imprisonment**, confinement, internment, incarceration, custody, detention, restraint, constraint, committal, arrest; bondage, slavery, servitude, enslavement, subjugation, subjection; literary thraldom, thrall; archaic duress, durance.
OPPOSITE freedom.

captor ▶ noun *he managed to escape from his captors* **jailer**, guard, incarcerator, custodian, keeper, enslaver; Law detainer.

capture ▶ verb **1** *a spy had been captured in Moscow* **catch**, apprehend, seize, arrest; take prisoner, take captive, take into custody; imprison, detain, put/throw in jail, put behind bars, put under lock and key, incarcerate; lay hold of, abduct, carry off, take; trap, snare, ensnare, net, hook, reel in, land, beach; informal nab, collar, pinch, lift, nail, bust, pick up, bag, run in, haul in, pull in, feel someone's collar; Brit. informal nick.
OPPOSITE free.
2 *guerrillas captured a strategic district* **occupy**, invade, conquer, seize, take, take over, take possession of, annex, subjugate; win, gain, secure.
3 *haunting music captures the atmosphere of a summer morning* **express**, reproduce, represent, show, encapsulate, record.
4 *tales of pirates have captured the imagination of children through the centuries* **engage**, attract, draw, gain, catch, grab, arrest, seize, hold.
▶ noun *he's extremely dangerous and will do anything to evade capture* **arrest**, apprehension, seizure, being trapped, being taken prisoner, being taken captive, being taken into custody, imprisonment, being imprisoned; informal being nabbed, being collared, being pinched, being lifted.
OPPOSITES freedom; escape.

car *See centre pages for lists of* **Cars** **Car Components**
▶ noun **1** *an officer drove up in a car* **motor car**, automobile, motor, machine; informal wheels, heap, crate, (old) banger, jalopy, limo; N. Amer. informal auto; archaic horseless carriage.
2 *they set off up the train to eat in the dining car* **carriage**, coach; Brit. saloon; Indian bogie.

carafe ▶ noun *a carafe of white wine* **flask**, jug, pitcher, decanter, bottle, flagon, container, vessel, ewer, crock, urn.

caravan ▶ noun **1** *they spent a fishing holiday in a caravan* **mobile home**, camper, caravanette; N. Amer. trailer; informal van; Brit. trademark Dormobile.
2 *a gypsy caravan* **wagon**, covered cart, van.
3 *the refugee caravan crossed the border* **convoy**, procession, column, train, cavalcade, fleet, cortège, company, troop, band, group, assemblage.

carbuncle ▶ noun *the carbuncle on his neck* **boil**, blister, sore, abscess, pustule, pimple, wart, papule, wen, whitlow, canker; swelling, lump, growth, outgrowth, eruption, infection, inflammation; technical vesication, furuncle.

carcass ▶ noun **1** *a lamb carcass* **corpse**, cadaver, dead body, body, remains, skeleton, relics; informal stiff; archaic corse.
2 (informal) *shift your carcass from the seat* **body**, person, self; backside; N. Amer. informal butt; Brit. vulgar slang arse; N. Amer. vulgar slang ass.

card *See centre pages for lists of* **Card Games** **Poker Hands** **Suits of Cards**
▶ noun **1** *paste it on a piece of stiff card* **cardboard**, pasteboard, board, stiff paper.
2 *I'll send her some flowers and a card* **greetings card**, postcard, Christmas card, birthday card, good luck card, get well card, sympathy card.
3 *she dug into her bag and produced her card* **identification**, ID, credentials, papers; ID card, identification card, visiting card, business card, calling card.
4 *she paid for the goods with her card* **credit card**, debit card, cash card, swipe card; informal plastic.
5 *the cards were dealt for the last hand* **playing card**; plain card, picture card, tarot card; Brit. court card; N. Amer. face card; (**cards**) pack of cards.
6 (informal, dated) *he laughed at that, and said that she was a card* **eccentric**, character, original, individual, oddity, odd person; **joker**, wit, wag, jester, humorist, comedian, comedienne, clown, jokester; informal one, laugh, scream, hoot, riot, barrel of laughs; informal, dated caution.
□ **give someone their cards** (Brit. informal) *the firm has just given 74,000 workers their cards* **dismiss**, give someone their notice, throw out, get rid of, lay off, make redundant, let someone go, discharge, cashier; informal sack, give someone the sack, fire, kick out, boot out, give someone the boot, give someone their marching orders, give someone the bullet, give someone the (old) heave-ho, give someone the elbow, give someone the push, show someone the door, send packing; Brit. informal turf out; dated out.
OPPOSITES employ, take on.
□ **on the cards** (informal) *a decisive victory was on the cards* **likely**, possible, probable, expected, liable to happen, in the wind, in the air, in the offing, on the horizon, in view, in prospect, in store, to come.
OPPOSITES unlikely, out of the question.

cardinal ▶ adjective **1** *one of the cardinal principles of the law of trusts* **fundamental**, basic, main, chief, primary, prime, principal, premier, first, leading, capital, paramount, pre-eminent; important, major, foremost, top, topmost, greatest, highest, key; essential, vital, crucial, intrinsic, integral, elemental, rudimentary, root, radical.
OPPOSITE unimportant.
2 *a black dress with cardinal trimmings* **scarlet**, red, crimson, vermilion, cinnabar, wine, wine-coloured, claret, claret-red, claret-coloured; literary vermeil.

care ▶ noun **1** *foster-parents had the care of the child* **safe keeping**, **supervision**, custody, charge, protection, keeping, keep, control, management, ministration, guidance, superintendence, tutelage, aegis, responsibility; guardianship, wardship, trusteeship, trust; provision of care, looking after; parenting, mothering, fathering.
OPPOSITE neglect.
2 *these chemicals need to be handled with care* **caution**, carefulness, wariness, awareness, heedfulness, heed, attention, attentiveness, alertness, watchfulness, vigilance, circumspection, prudence, guardedness, observance.
OPPOSITE carelessness.
3 *she chose her words with care* **discretion**, judiciousness, forethought, thought, regard, heed, mindfulness; conscientiousness, painstakingness, pains, effort, meticulousness, punctiliousness, fastidiousness; accuracy, precision.
OPPOSITE carelessness.
4 *a place where you can escape from the cares of the day* **worry**, anxiety, trouble, disquiet, disquietude, bother, unease, upset, distress, concern; sorrow, anguish, grief, sadness, affliction, woe, hardship, tribulation, suffering, pain, torment, misery, angst; responsibility, stress, pressure, strain, perturbation, burdens.
OPPOSITE happiness.
5 *a life of unblemished virtue and constant care for others* **concern**, consideration, attention, attentiveness, thought, regard, mind, notice, heed, solicitude, interest, caringness, sympathy, respect; looking after.
OPPOSITE disregard.
▶ verb *the teachers didn't seem to care about our academic work* **be concerned**, worry (oneself), trouble oneself, bother, mind; concern oneself with, be interested in, interest oneself in, trouble oneself with, have regard for, burden oneself with; informal give a damn, give a hoot, give a rap, give a hang, give a tinker's curse/damn, give a monkey's, lose sleep over, get worked up.
□ **care for 1** *he obviously cares for his children* **love**, be fond of, feel affection for, cherish, hold dear, treasure, prize, adore, dote on, think the world of, worship, idolize, be devoted to; be in love with.
OPPOSITE hate.
2 *would you care for a cup of coffee?* **like**, wish for, want, desire, prefer, fancy, have a fancy for, take a fancy to, feel like; informal have a yen for.
3 *a hospice which cares for the terminally ill* **look after**, take care of, tend, attend to, mind, minister to, take charge of, nurse, provide for, foster, protect, watch, guard; be responsible for, keep safe, keep an eye on; sit with, babysit, childmind.
OPPOSITE neglect.

career ▶ noun **1** *he spent three years training for a business career* **profession**, occupation, vocation, calling, employment, job, line, line of work, walk of life, position, post, sphere; French métier.
2 *these unions had had a chequered career* **existence**, life, progress, course, progression, passage, path.
▶ adjective *a career politician* **professional**, permanent, full-time, committed.
▶ verb *he saw the runaway pram careering down the hill* **rush**, hurtle, streak, shoot, race, bolt, dash, speed, run, gallop, stampede, cannon, careen, whizz, buzz, zoom, flash, blast, charge, hare, fly, wing, pelt, scurry, scud, go like the wind; informal belt, scoot, scorch, tear, skedaddle, zap, zip, whip, burn rubber, go like a bat out of hell; Brit. informal bomb, bucket, shift; N. Amer. informal hightail, clip, boogie.

carefree ▶ adjective *a carefree young woman* **unworried**, untroubled, blithe, airy, nonchalant, insouciant, happy-go-lucky, free and easy, easy-going, blasé, devil-may-care, casual, relaxed, serene; cheerful, cheery, happy, merry, jolly, joyful, gleeful, glad; bright, sunny, buoyant, vivacious, bubbly, bouncy, breezy, jaunty, frisky; *informal* upbeat, laid back.
OPPOSITES anxious, careworn.

careful ▶ adjective **1** *be careful when you go up the stairs* **cautious**, heedful, alert, aware, attentive, watchful, vigilant, wary, on guard, chary, circumspect, prudent, mindful, guarded; unhurried, measured, deliberate; *informal* leery, cagey.
OPPOSITE careless.
2 *Roland was careful of his reputation* **mindful**, heedful, protective, watchful.
OPPOSITE careless.
3 *his mother had always been careful with money* **prudent**, thrifty, economical, economic, economizing, sparing, frugal, scrimping, abstemious, canny, sensible, cautious; mean, miserly, niggardly, penny-pinching, parsimonious; *informal* stingy.
OPPOSITE extravagant.
4 *a careful driver* | *a careful consideration of the facts* **attentive**, conscientious, painstaking, meticulous, diligent, assiduous, sedulous, scrupulous, punctilious, fastidious, methodical, orderly, deliberate, judicious, perfectionist; thorough, exhaustive, rigorous; accurate, precise, correct, particular; fussy, finicky; *informal* pernickety; *archaic* nice, laborious.
OPPOSITE inattentive.

careless ▶ adjective **1** *careless motorists* **inattentive**, incautious, negligent, remiss; forgetful, absent-minded; heedless, irresponsible, impetuous, reckless; *informal* sloppy, couldn't care less, slap-happy.
OPPOSITES careful, attentive.
2 *an unsatisfactory excuse for incomplete or careless work* **shoddy**, slapdash, slipshod, scrappy, slovenly, unconsidered, amateurish, negligent, lax, slack, wild, disorganized; hasty, hurried, perfunctory, cursory, thrown together, sketchy, hit-or-miss; inaccurate, imprecise, inexact, incorrect, wrong, erroneous, error-ridden; *informal* sloppy, slap-happy, scatterbrained; *Brit. vulgar slang* half-arsed.
OPPOSITE meticulous.
3 *a careless remark* **thoughtless**, unthinking, insensitive, indiscreet, unguarded, ill-advised, ill-considered, ill-thought-out, unwise, misguided, incautious, inadvertent, rash, foolhardy; hasty, spur-of-the-moment, hare-brained.
OPPOSITE judicious.
4 *she was very careless of investments and spent too much of her capital* **negligent in**, mindless of, heedless of, improvident about, unconcerned about, indifferent to, oblivious to; reckless about, remiss in, slapdash about, slipshod about, frivolous about; *informal* sloppy in, messy in.
5 *she saw him leaning with careless masculine grace against the wall* **unstudied**, artless, casual, effortless, unconcerned, nonchalant, insouciant, languid, leisurely, informal; *informal* couldn't-care-less.

CHOOSE THE RIGHT WORD

careless, heedless, thoughtless

- Someone who is **careless** is not giving their full attention to what they are doing, typically in a situation where this could result in harm to themselves or to others (*try not to be so careless when you're handling glass* | *a motorist has been charged with causing death by careless driving*). The word may also be used to indicate that someone is relaxed and casual (*she moved with careless grace*), trying to appear so (*she managed to turn the wince into a careless shrug*), or genuinely unconcerned about something (*he was careless of his own safety*).
- **Heedless** indicates that someone is deliberately taking no notice of a factor which might be expected to influence their behaviour, either in their own interests (*she knelt on the floor, heedless of the cold stone*) or in those of others (*she brought him to a halt in the middle of the pavement, heedless of the passers-by*).
- **Thoughtless** is generally used to describe something done by a person who is insensitive, either consciously or unconsciously, to the feelings or convenience of others (*the thoughtless actions of a few loud-mouthed oafs*).

carelessness ▶ noun *the fire was caused through the carelessness of one of the workmen* **inattention**, inattentiveness, heedlessness, thoughtlessness, negligence, improvidence, remissness; forgetfulness, absent-mindedness; irresponsibility, impetuosity, recklessness, rashness; laxity, laxness, slackness; clumsiness, ineptitude; oversight, omission, dereliction; *informal* sloppiness.
OPPOSITE carefulness.

caress ▶ verb *his hands caressed her back* **stroke**, touch, fondle, brush, skim, pet, pat, nuzzle, kiss; cuddle, embrace, hug.
▶ noun *she enjoyed the light caress of his fingers* **stroke**, stroking, touch, touching, fondle, fondling, skim, pat, nuzzle, nuzzling, kiss; cuddle, embrace, hug.

caretaker ▶ noun *he works as a caretaker for a block of flats* **janitor**, warden, attendant, porter, custodian, keeper, watchman, steward, curator, concierge; *N. Amer.* superintendent.
▶ adjective *he has taken over as caretaker manager at Stoke* **temporary**, short-term, provisional, substitute, acting, interim, pro tem, stand-in, fill-in, supply, stopgap, reserve, deputy; transitional, changeover; emergency, impromptu, rough and ready; *Latin* pro tempore, ad interim; *N. Amer. informal* pinch-hitting; *rare* expediential.
OPPOSITE permanent.

careworn ▶ adjective *his old face looked more haggard and careworn than usual* **worried**, anxious, harassed, strained, stressed, under pressure, overburdened; tired, drained, drawn, gaunt, grim, haggard, pinched, exhausted, sapped, spent; *informal* hassled.
OPPOSITE carefree.

cargo ▶ noun *the ship's cargo* **freight**, load, haul, consignment, delivery, shipment, contents, baggage, burden; goods, merchandise; shipload, boatload, lorryload, truckload, containerload; *archaic* lading; *rare* freightage.

caricature ▶ noun *a crude caricature of the Prime Minister* **cartoon**, distorted/exaggerated drawing, distortion; parody, satire, lampoon, burlesque, mimicry, travesty, farce, skit, squib; *informal* send-up, take-off, spoof; *rare* pasquinade.
▶ verb *she has turned her acute eye and pen to caricaturing her fellow actors* **parody**, satirize, lampoon, mimic, ridicule, mock, make fun of, burlesque; distort, exaggerate; *informal* send up, take off.

caring ▶ adjective *a caring, approachable employer* **kind**, kind-hearted, warm-hearted, soft-hearted, tender, feeling; concerned, attentive, thoughtful, solicitous, responsible, considerate; affectionate, loving, doting, fond, warm, benevolent, benign, humane, good-natured, gentle, mild, indulgent, sympathetic, understanding, receptive, compassionate, charitable, gracious; long-suffering, patient.
OPPOSITES uncaring, cruel.

carnage ▶ noun *the carnage and suffering of the trenches* **slaughter**, massacre, mass murder, mass destruction, butchery, bloodbath, indiscriminate bloodshed, bloodletting, annihilation, destruction, decimation, havoc; holocaust, pogrom, ethnic cleansing; *informal* shambles.

carnal ▶ adjective *the carnal desires of the flesh* **sexual**, sensual, erotic, lustful, lascivious, libidinous, lecherous, licentious, lewd, prurient, salacious, coarse, gross, lubricious, venereal; **physical**, bodily, corporeal, fleshly, animal; *informal* sexy.
OPPOSITE spiritual.

carnival ▶ noun **1** *the town's raucous carnival* **festival**, fiesta, fête, gala, jamboree, holiday, celebration, party; parade, procession, march, tattoo.
2 (*N. Amer.*) *he worked at a carnival, climbing Ferris wheels and working 18-hour days* **funfair**, **circus**, fair, amusement show, sideshows.

carnivorous ▶ adjective *a carnivorous lizard* **meat-eating**, predatory, of prey, hunting, raptorial; *rare* creophagous, zoophagous.
OPPOSITES herbivorous; vegetarian.

carol ▶ noun *children came from the village school to sing carols* **Christmas song**, hymn, psalm, canticle; *archaic* noel.
▶ verb *'Yo heave ho,' carolled Boris happily* **sing**, trill, chorus, warble, chirp, pipe, quaver, chant, intone; *archaic* wassail.

carouse ▶ verb *a band of sailors had gone ashore to carouse at the grog stalls* **drink and make merry**, go on a drinking bout, go on a binge, binge, overindulge, drink heavily/freely, go on a pub crawl, go on a spree; have a party, revel, celebrate, feast, enjoy oneself, have a good time, roister, {eat, drink, and be merry}, frolic, romp; *informal* booze, go boozing, go on a bender, paint the town red, bend one's elbow, party, rave, have a ball, raise hell, make whoopee, live it up, whoop it up, have a fling; *Brit. informal* go on the bevvy; *archaic* wassail.

carp ▶ verb *broadcasters always found something to carp about, even after an undoubted success* **complain**, cavil, grumble, moan, grouse, grouch, whine, bleat, quibble, niggle, nag; find fault with, criticize, pick on, censure, denounce, condemn, decry, disparage; *informal* gripe, beef, bellyache, bitch, whinge, nit-pick, pick holes, split hairs, sound off, kick up a fuss, knock; *Brit. informal* chunter, create, be on at someone; *N. English informal* mither; *N. Amer. informal* kvetch.
OPPOSITE praise.

carpenter ▶ noun **woodworker**, joiner, cabinetmaker; *Scottish & N. English* wright; *Brit. informal* chippy, Chips.

carpet *See centre pages for list of* **Carpets and Rugs**
▶ noun **1** *a genuine Turkish carpet* **rug**, mat, matting, floor covering, runner, drugget.
2 *a carpet of wild flowers* **covering**, blanket, layer, cover, coat, coating, sheet, film, overlay, cloak, mantle, canopy, bed, expanse; crust.
▶ verb **1** *the gravel was carpeted in bright green moss* **cover**, coat, overlay, overspread, blanket, overlie, extend over, pave.
2 (*Brit. informal*) *a top fraud officer has been carpeted for leaking information. See* REPRIMAND.

carping ▶ adjective *she has silenced the carping critics with a massively successful*

debut tour **complaining**, cavilling, grumbling, moaning, grousing, grouching, grouchy, whining, bleating, fault-finding, quibbling, niggling, captious, nagging; critical, criticizing, censorious, condemnatory, disparaging, scathing, slighting, reproachful, deprecatory, hypercritical, overcritical, pedantic, hard/difficult/impossible to please; *informal* griping, bellyaching, bitching, whingeing, nit-picking, hair-splitting, picky; *Brit. informal* chuntering; *N. English informal* mithering; *N. Amer. informal* kvetching.
OPPOSITES forgiving; complimentary.

carriage *See centre pages for lists of* **Carriages and Carts** **Trains and Rolling Stock**
▶ **noun 1** *a railway carriage* **coach**; *N. Amer.* car; *Brit.* saloon; *Indian* bogie.
2 *a horse and carriage* **wagon**, hackney, hansom, gig, landau, trap, caravan, car.
3 *the carriage of bikes on trains* **transport**, transportation, conveyance, transfer, transference, delivery, distribution, carrying, transmission, movement, haulage, freight, freightage, portage, cartage, shipment.
4 *she had an erect carriage and a firm step* **posture**, bearing, stance, gait, comportment; attitude, manner, presence, air, demeanour, mien, appearance; behaviour, conduct; *Brit.* deportment.

carrier ▶ **noun** *the carriers of wood and water came and went* **bearer**, conveyor, transporter; porter, runner, courier, delivery man, delivery woman, haulier; *dated* carman.

carry ▶ **verb 1** *she carried the box of food into the kitchen* **convey**, transfer, move, take, bring, bear, shift, switch, fetch, transport; *informal* cart, lug, hump, schlep, tote.
2 *Britain's biggest coach operator carries 12 million passengers a year* **transport**, convey, transmit, move, handle.
3 *satellites were used to carry the signal over the Atlantic* **transmit**, conduct, pass on, relay, communicate, convey, impart, bear, dispatch, beam; disseminate, spread, circulate, diffuse.
4 *the dinghy would carry the weight of the baggage easily enough* **support**, sustain, stand, prop up, shore up, bolster, underpin, buttress.
5 *managers carry as much responsibility as possible* **undertake**, accept, assume, bear, shoulder, support, sustain; take on, take up, take on oneself; manage, handle, deal with, get to grips with, turn one's hand to.
6 *she told him the baby she was carrying was not his* **be pregnant with**, bear, expect; *technical* be gravid with.
7 *she* ***carried herself*** *with a certain assurance* **conduct**, bear, hold; act, behave, perform, acquit; *rare* comport, deport.
8 *a resolution was carried by an overwhelming majority* **approve**, vote for, accept, endorse, ratify, authorize, mandate, support, back, uphold; agree to, consent to, assent to, acquiesce in, concur in, accede to, give one's blessing to, bless, give one's seal/stamp of approval to, rubber-stamp, say yes to; *informal* give the go-ahead to, give the green light to, give the OK to, OK, give the thumbs up to, give the nod to, buy.
OPPOSITE reject.
9 *this argument carried the day* **win**, capture, gain, secure, effect, take, accomplish.
OPPOSITE lose.
10 *I spoke for forty minutes and carried the whole audience* **win over**, sway, prevail on, convince, persuade, influence; affect, have an effect on, have an impact on, impact on, motivate, stimulate, drive, touch, reach.
11 *today's paper carried an article on housing policy* **publish**, print, communicate, give, release, distribute, spread, disseminate; broadcast, transmit.
12 *we carry a wide assortment of hockey sticks* **sell**, **stock**, keep, keep in stock, offer, have for sale, have, retail, market, supply, trade in, deal in, traffic in, peddle, hawk.
13 *most common domestic toxins carry poison warnings* **display**, bear, exhibit, show, present, set forth, be marked with, have.
14 *contempt of court carries a maximum penalty of two years' imprisonment* **entail**, involve, lead to, result in, occasion, have as a consequence, have; require, demand.
15 *his voice carried across the quay* **be audible**, travel, reach, be transmitted.
□ **be/get carried away** *I'm afraid I got a bit carried away* **lose self-control**, get excited, get overexcited, go too far, lose one's sense of proportion, be swept off one's feet; *informal* flip, lose it.
□ **carry someone off** *his elder brother had been carried off by consumption* **kill**, kill off, cause the death of, cause to die, take/end the life of, dispatch, finish off; *informal* polish off, do in.
□ **carry something off 1** *her co-star carried off four awards* **win**, secure, capture, gain, achieve, attain, earn, obtain, acquire, procure, get, collect, pick up, come away with; *informal* land, net, bag, bank, pot, scoop, walk off/away with.
2 *against the odds, he has carried it off* **succeed in**, triumph in, be victorious in, achieve success in, be successful in, be a success in, do well at, make good in; *informal* crack.
□ **carry on 1** *she didn't have the strength to carry on arguing* **continue**, keep on, keep, keep at, go on, push on, press on, persist in, persevere in, not stop, maintain; *informal* stick with/at.
OPPOSITE stop.
2 *it's just not the English way of carrying on* **behave**, act, perform, conduct oneself, acquit oneself, bear oneself, carry oneself; *rare* comport oneself, deport oneself.
3 (*Brit. informal*) *his wife had been carrying on with other men* **have an affair**, commit adultery, philander, dally, be involved; *informal* play around, have a fling, mess about/around, play away; *N. Amer. informal* fool around.
4 *I abused the teachers and was always carrying on* **misbehave**, behave badly, make mischief, get up to mischief, be mischievous, act up, cause trouble, cause a fuss/commotion, get/be up to no good, be bad, be naughty, clown about/around, fool about/around, mess about/around, act the clown, act the fool, act the goat, act foolishly; *informal* create; *Brit. informal* muck about/around, play up.
OPPOSITE behave.
□ **carry something on** *a bank carrying on a bona fide business* **engage in**, conduct, undertake, be involved in, take part in, participate in, carry out, perform, direct.
□ **carry something out 1** *the decision to carry out a Caesarean section* **conduct**, perform, implement, execute, discharge, bring about, bring off, effect; *rare* effectuate.
2 *I carried out my promise to her* **fulfil**, carry through, implement, execute, effect, discharge, perform, honour, redeem, make good; keep, observe, abide by, comply with, obey, respect, conform to, stick to, act in accordance with, act according to, have regard to, heed, follow, pay attention to, defer to, take notice of, be bound by, keep faith with, stand by, adhere to.
OPPOSITE break.

carry-on ▶ **noun** (*Brit. informal*) *he was not going to stand for any of this carry-on* **fuss**, commotion, trouble, bother, upset, agitation, stir, excitement, ado, hurly-burly, palaver, rigmarole; nonsense; *informal* hoo-ha, ballyhoo, song and dance, performance, pantomime, hoopla, rumpus, monkey business, jiggery-pokery; *Brit. informal* carrying-on, kerfuffle.

cart *See centre pages for list of* **Carriages and Carts**
▶ **noun 1** *a horse-drawn cart* **wagon**, carriage; *archaic* wain.
2 *a man with a cart took their luggage* **handcart**, pushcart, trolley, barrow, wheelbarrow.
▶ **verb** *he had the wreckage carted away* **transport**, convey, haul, transfer, move, conduct, transmit, shift, fetch, take, ferry; **carry**, lug, tote, heave, heft, drag; *informal* hump, schlep.

cartilage ▶ **noun**
WORD LINKS
related prefix **chondro- (e.g. *chondrocyte*)**

carton ▶ **noun** *a carton of ice cream* **box**, package, cardboard box, container, case, pack, packet, parcel.

cartoon ▶ **noun 1** *a cartoon of the Prime Minister* **caricature**, parody, lampoon, satire, travesty; distorted/exaggerated drawing, distortion; *informal* take-off, send-up, spoof; *rare* pasquinade.
2 *he could often be found reading cartoons at this time of day* **comic strip**, cartoon strip, comic, graphic novel; *Japanese* manga.
3 *they watched the Saturday morning cartoons on television* **animated film**, animated cartoon, animation; *Japanese* anime.
4 *we have detailed cartoons for the production of another full-size portrait* **sketch**, rough, preliminary drawing, outline, delineation, tracing; *technical* wireframe, underdrawing, maquette, ébauche, esquisse, croquis.

cartridge ▶ **noun 1** *the toner cartridge slots neatly into place* **cassette**, magazine, cylinder, canister, container, capsule, case, pack, packet, package.
2 *a rifle cartridge* **bullet**, round, shell, charge, shot, casing.

carve ▶ **verb 1** *he used to carve horn handles for walking sticks* **sculpt**, sculpture; cut, chisel, hew, whittle, chip, hack, slash; form, shape, fashion.
2 *I carved my initials on the tree* **engrave**, etch, notch, cut in, incise, score, print, mark.
OPPOSITE erase.
3 *he stood carving the roast chicken* **slice**, cut up, chop, dice.
□ **carve something up** *the Empire was carved up into three kingdoms* **divide**, partition, parcel out, apportion, subdivide, split up, break up, separate out, segregate, measure out; share out, dole out; *informal* divvy up.
OPPOSITES unify; reunify.

carving ▶ **noun** *a carving of an elephant* **sculpture**, model, statue, statuette, figure, figurine, effigy; bust, head.
WORD LINKS
relating to carving **glyptic**

cascade ▶ **noun** *a delightful boulder-strewn ravine with a series of cascades* **waterfall**, falls, water chute, cataract, rapids, torrent, flood, deluge, outpouring, white water, fountain, shower, avalanche; *N. English* force; *Scottish archaic* linn.
▶ **verb** *rain cascaded from the veranda roof* **pour**, gush, surge, spill, stream, flow, issue, spurt, jet; tumble, descend, fall, drop, plunge, pitch; overflow.

case[1] ▶ **noun 1** *this moral panic is a classic case of overreaction* **instance**, occurrence, occasion, manifestation, demonstration, exhibition, exposition, expression; **example**, illustration, specimen, sample,

C

exemplification, type, prototype.
2 (**the case**) *he told me that if that was the case I would have to find somebody else* **the situation**, the position, the picture, the state of affairs, the state of play, the lie of the land; plight, predicament; event, contingency; circumstances, conditions, facts; how things stand, what's going on; *informal* kettle of fish, ball game, score, story, set-up.
3 *officers on the case are unable to find a motive* **investigation**, enquiry, examination, exploration, probe, search, scrutiny, scrutinization, study, inspection, inquest, reconnoitring, sounding; **incident**, event, happening, occurrence, episode, proceeding, matter, affair, set of circumstances.
4 *urgent cases were turned away from the hospital* **patient**, sick person, invalid, sufferer, victim; client.
5 *he lost his case and was ordered to pay £1.5 million in damages* **lawsuit**, action, legal action, suit, suit at law, cause, legal cause, trial, proceedings, legal proceeding(s), judicial proceedings, litigation, legal process, legal dispute, indictment.
6 *this book makes a strong case for new research methods* **argument**, contention, reasoning, logic, defence, justification, vindication, apology, polemic; statement, postulation, explanation, exposition, thesis, presentation, proclamation, expounding, claim; plea, appeal, petition.
7 *the genitive case* **inflection**, form, ending; morphology; semantic relationship.

case[2] ▶ **noun 1** *a monogrammed cigarette case* **container**, box, canister, cassette, cartridge, receptacle, holder, vessel, repository; *dated* etui.
2 *a seed case* **casing**, covering, sheath, sheathing, wrapper, wrapping, cover, envelope, sleeve, housing, jacket, capsule, folder; *technical* integument.
3 (*Brit.*) *she hastily threw some clothes into a case* **suitcase**, bag, travelling bag, travel bag, valise, grip, holdall, portmanteau; piece of luggage, item of baggage; briefcase, attaché case, Gladstone bag; trunk, chest; (**cases**) luggage, baggage.
4 *a case of wine* **crate**, box, pack, bin, coffer, casket, chest, basket, hamper.
5 *his art collection sparkled in a glass display case* **cabinet**, cupboard, chiffonier, bureau, sideboard.
▶ **verb 1** *the Lee-Enfield rifle is cased in wood from butt to muzzle* **cover**, surround, coat, encase, sheathe, wrap, envelop.
2 (*informal*) *he went from room to room like a thief casing the joint* **reconnoitre**, inspect, investigate, examine, scrutinize, survey, scout, explore, make an observation of, take stock of; *informal* recce, make a recce of, check out.

cash *See centre pages for lists of* **Coins** **Currency Units**
▶ **noun 1** *a wallet stuffed with cash* **money**, ready money/cash, currency, legal tender, hard cash; notes, bank notes; coins, coinage, coin, coin of the realm, change, silver, copper; *N. Amer.* bills; *informal* dough, bread, loot, the ready, readies, shekels, moolah, wad, boodle, dibs, gelt, ducats, rhino, gravy; *Brit. informal* dosh, brass, lolly, spondulicks, wonga, ackers; *N. Amer. informal* greenbacks, dinero, simoleons, bucks, jack, mazuma; *Austral./NZ informal* Oscar; *informal, dated* splosh, green, tin; *Brit. dated* l.s.d.; *N. Amer. informal, dated* kale, rocks, shinplasters; *formal* specie.
OPPOSITES cheque, credit.
2 *thousands of hospital beds are closing because of a lack of cash* **finance**, resources, funds, money, means, assets, wherewithal, capital, investment capital.
▶ **verb** *the bank cashed her cheque* **exchange**, change, convert into cash/money, turn into cash/money, encash, realize, liquidate; honour, pay, accept, take.
□ **cash in on** *the band is cashing in on merchandising* **take advantage of**, turn to one's advantage, exploit; make money from, profit from, do well out of; milk, bleed, suck dry, squeeze, wring; *informal* make a killing out of.

cashier[1] ▶ **noun** *he hands the day's takings to the cashier* **clerk**, bank clerk, teller, bank teller, banker, treasurer, bursar, purser; accountant, bookkeeper, controller, money man.

cashier[2] ▶ **verb** *he was cashiered from the army on charges of insubordination* **dismiss**, discharge, expel, drum out, throw out, cast out, discard, get rid of; *informal* sack, fire, give someone the boot, boot out, kick out, send packing, give someone their marching orders, give someone the bullet, give someone the push, show someone the door.

casing ▶ **noun** *the hard disk is safe from damage in its casing* **cover**, case, shell, envelope, sheath, sheathing, wrapper, wrapping, sleeve, jacket, housing, capsule, folder; *technical* integument.

casino ▶ **noun** *he enjoyed a flutter at the casino* **gambling house**, gambling club, gaming club, gambling den; *German* kursaal; *dated* gaming house.

cask ▶ **noun** *a cask of cider* **barrel**, keg, butt, tun, vat, drum, tank, vessel, hogshead, firkin, kilderkin, pipe, pin; *archaic* puncheon, tierce.

casket ▶ **noun 1** *a small casket containing four black opals* **box**, chest, case, container, receptacle, coffer, trunk, crate; *rare* pyxis.
2 (*N. Amer.*) *the casket of a soldier who had died fighting* **coffin**, box; *informal* wooden overcoat; *historical* sarcophagus, cist.

casserole ▶ **noun.** *See centre pages for list of* **Stews**

cast ▶ **verb 1** *he cast the stone into the stream* **throw**, toss, fling, pitch, hurl, bowl, dash, shy, lob, launch, flip, let fly, direct, discharge, project, propel, send; *informal* chuck, heave, sling, bung.
2 *fishermen cast their nets into the sea* **spread**, throw, lay out, open out, unroll, fan out, stretch out.
3 *she cast a fearful glance over her shoulder* **direct**, shoot, turn, throw, send, dart, bestow, give.
4 *each adult citizen has the right to cast a vote* **register**, record, enter, file, lodge, post, set down, vote; allot, assign, give.
5 *the fire cast a soft light* **emit**, give off, send out, send forth, shed, radiate, diffuse, spread out.
6 *the figures cast dancing shadows on the carpet* **form**, create, make, produce, cause; project, throw.
7 *the stags' antlers are cast each year* **shed**, discard, slough off, throw off, get rid of, let fall, let drop; moult, peel off; *technical* exuviate.
8 *until the 1880s printing type was cast by hand* **mould**, fashion, form, shape, model; sculpt, sculpture, frame, forge, carve; make, create, build, manufacture.
9 *he gave lectures on astrology and cast horoscopes in his spare time* **calculate**, devise, compute, reckon, determine, assess, work out, formulate, record, write; predict, forecast, foretell, foresee, prophesy.
10 *they were cast as extras in the film* **choose**, select, pick, name, nominate, assign, appoint, give/assign the part to.
□ **cast aside** *he glanced down at a newspaper that had been cast aside* **discard**, reject, cast/throw away, cast/throw out, dispense with, get rid of, dispose of, abandon.
□ **cast away** *he returned home three years after being cast away on the island* **shipwreck**, wreck; strand, leave stranded, maroon, cast ashore, abandon, leave behind, leave; *informal* leave high and dry; *archaic* forsake.
□ **cast down** *she could not bear to see him so miserable and cast down* **depressed**, downcast, unhappy, sad, miserable, gloomy, down, low, blue, melancholy, doleful, mournful; dejected, dispirited, discouraged, disheartened, downhearted, demoralized, daunted, dismayed, desolate, disconsolate, crestfallen, crushed, sapped, shaken, undermined, despondent, weighed down, oppressed, wretched.
▶ **noun 1** *a cast of the writer's hand was taken* **mould**, die, form, matrix, shape, casting, template, pattern, frame; sculpture, model, replica, copy, representation, mock-up, imitation, reproduction, figure.
2 *a cast of the dice* **throw**, toss, fling, pitch, hurl, shy, lob, flip; *informal* chuck, heave, sling, bung, go.
3 *a child with an enquiring, ironical cast of mind* **type**, sort, kind, variety, class, style, stamp, nature, manner, pattern, grain, mould, ilk, kidney, strain, brand, genre; turn, inclination, bent.
4 *he had a pronounced* ***cast in one eye*** **squint**, cross-eyes; *Brit. informal* boss-eye; *technical* strabismus.
5 *he joined the cast of 'The Barber of Seville'* **actors**, performers, players, company, troupe; dramatis personae, characters.

caste ▶ **noun** *prohibitions prevent people from marrying outside their caste* **class**, social class, order, social order, social division, grade, grading, group, grouping, station, stratum, echelon, rank, level, degree, set; place, standing, position, status; *Hinduism* varna; *archaic* estate, sphere.

castigate ▶ **verb** *Leopold castigated his son for leaving the archbishop's service* **reprimand**, rebuke, admonish, chastise, chide, upbraid, reprove, reproach, scold, remonstrate with, berate, take to task, pull up, lambaste, read someone the Riot Act, give someone a piece of one's mind, haul over the coals, lecture, criticize, censure; punish, discipline, chasten; *informal* tell off, give someone a telling-off, give someone a talking-to, give someone an earful, dress down, give someone a dressing-down, give someone a roasting, give someone a rocket, give someone a rollicking, rap, rap someone the knuckles, slap someone's wrist, send someone away with a flea in their ear, let someone have it, bawl out, give someone hell, come down on, blow up at, pitch into, lay into, lace into, give someone a caning, put on the mat, slap down, blast, rag, keelhaul; *Brit. informal* tick off, have a go at, carpet, give someone a mouthful, tear someone off a strip, give someone what for, give someone some stick, wig, give someone a wigging, give someone a row, row; *N. Amer. informal* chew out, ream out; *Austral. informal* monster; *Brit. vulgar slang* bollock, give someone a bollocking; *N. Amer. vulgar slang* chew someone's ass, ream someone's ass; *dated* call down, rate, give someone a rating, trim; *rare* reprehend, objurgate.
OPPOSITES praise, commend.

castle ▶ **noun fortress**, fort, stronghold, fortification, keep, citadel, fastness, tower, peel, palace, chateau, donjon; (*in Spain*) alcazar.

castrate ▶ **verb** *many of these colts are castrated* **neuter**, geld, cut, emasculate, desex, sterilize, unman, remove the testicles of; *N. Amer. & Austral.* alter; *informal* doctor, fix; *rare* evirate, caponize, eunuchize.

casual ▶ **adjective 1** *he has a casual attitude to life* **indifferent**, apathetic, uncaring, uninterested, unconcerned; lackadaisical, blasé, nonchalant, lukewarm, insouciant, offhand, hit-or-miss; easy-going, free and easy, airy, breezy, blithe, carefree; flippant, lax, slack, irresponsible, devil-may-care; *informal* couldn't-care-less, laid-back; *rare* poco-curante.
OPPOSITES careful, concerned.
2 *a casual remark* **offhand**, random, impromptu, spontaneous,

unpremeditated, unthinking, unstudied, unconsidered, parenthetical, passing, throwaway, trivial; ill-considered, ill-judged, unguarded; *informal* off-the-cuff.
OPPOSITE premeditated.
3 *he threw a casual glance over his shoulder* **cursory**, perfunctory, superficial, passing, fleeting, summary, desultory, careless; hasty, hurried, rushed, brief, quick.
OPPOSITES thorough, careful.
4 *she was no more than a casual acquaintance* **slight**, superficial, shallow, vague, faint.
OPPOSITES intimate, close.
5 *he does casual work on farms* **temporary**, part-time, impermanent, freelance; irregular, occasional, intermittent; outside, outsourced.
OPPOSITES permanent; full-time.
6 *casual sex had never been her scene* **promiscuous**, recreational, extramarital; liberated, uninhibited, free; *informal* swinging.
7 *a casual meeting with two students changed his life* **chance**, accidental, random, unintentional, unplanned, unintended, inadvertent, unexpected, unforeseen, unanticipated, unlooked-for, occurring by chance/accident, fortuitous, coincidental, fluky, serendipitous, adventitious, aleatory.
OPPOSITES planned, intentional.
8 *a casual short-sleeved shirt* **informal**, not formal, relaxed, comfortable, sloppy, leisure, sportif, everyday; *Military* undress; *informal* sporty.
OPPOSITES formal, smart.
9 *the inn's casual atmosphere* **relaxed**, friendly, natural, informal, unceremonious, unpretentious, easy-going, free and easy, uninhibited, open; *informal* laid-back.
OPPOSITE formal.
▶ **noun** *we employ eight full-time staff and ten casuals* **temporary worker**, part-timer, freelance, freelancer; *informal* temp.
OPPOSITE full-timer.

casualty ▶ **noun 1** *the shelling caused thousands of casualties* **victim**, fatality, mortality; loss, MIA; (**casualties**) dead and injured/wounded, missing in action, missing.
2 *the corporation was a casualty of the weak economy* **victim**, sufferer, loser, loss.

casuistry ▶ **noun** *the usual teenage casuistry about altruism always being ultimately selfish* **sophistry**, specious reasoning, speciousness, sophism, chicanery, quibbling, equivocation, fallaciousness; *informal* fudging.

cat *See centre pages for list of* **Cats**
▶ **noun** *their pet cat* **feline**; tabby, ginger tom, tortoiseshell, marmalade cat, mouser, wild cat, alley cat; *informal* pussy, pussy cat, puss; *Brit. informal* moggie, mog; *archaic* grimalkin.

WORD LINKS

relating to cats	**feline**
male	**tom, tomcat**
female	**queen**
young	**kitten**
collective noun	**clowder, glaring**
fear of cats	**ailurophobia**

cataclysm ▶ **noun** *their homeland was destroyed by a great cataclysm* **disaster**, catastrophe, calamity, tragedy, act of God, devastation, crisis, holocaust, ruin, ruination, upheaval, convulsion, blow, shock, reverse, trouble, trial, tribulation; misfortune, mishap, accident, mischance, misadventure, woe, affliction, distress; *informal* meltdown, whammy; *archaic* bale; *Scottish archaic* mishanter.
OPPOSITES salvation, godsend.

cataclysmic ▶ **adjective** *the cataclysmic Krakatoa eruption of 1883* **disastrous**, catastrophic, calamitous, tragic, devastating, ruinous, terrible, violent, awful.
OPPOSITES fortunate, beneficial.

catacombs ▶ **plural noun** **underground cemetery**, sepulchre, crypt, vault, mausoleum, tomb, ossuary; tunnels, labyrinth, maze.

catalogue ▶ **noun 1** *a computerized library catalogue* **directory**, register, index, list, listing, record, archive, inventory, roll, table, calendar, classification, roster.
2 *a mail-order catalogue* **brochure**, prospectus, guide, magalogue, mailer; *N. Amer. informal* wish book.
▶ **verb** *it will be some time before the collection is fully catalogued* **classify**, categorize, systematize, systemize, index, list, archive, make an inventory of, inventory, record, register, file, log, enumerate, alphabetize, itemize, pigeonhole, tabulate.

catapult *See centre pages for list of* **Projectiles and Projectile Weapons**
▶ **noun** *a 16-year-old boy fired a catapult at a low-flying helicopter* sling; *N. Amer.* slingshot; *Austral./NZ* shanghai.
▶ **verb** *Sam felt himself being catapulted into the sea* **propel**, launch, hurl, hurtle, fling, send flying, send, let fly, let loose, fire, blast, shoot.

cataract ▶ **noun 1** *the river descends in a succession of spectacular cataracts* **waterfall**, cascade, falls, rapids, white water; torrent; downpour, shower; *N. English* force; *Scottish archaic* linn.
2 *he had cataracts in both eyes* **opacity**, opaqueness.

catastrophe ▶ **noun** *the bush fires were the latest in a growing list of catastrophes* **disaster**, calamity, cataclysm, crisis, holocaust, ruin, ruination, tragedy, blow, shock; adversity, blight, trouble, trial, tribulation, mishap, misfortune, mischance, misadventure, accident, failure, reverse, woe, affliction, distress; *informal* meltdown, whammy; *archaic* bale; *Scottish archaic* mishanter.
OPPOSITES salvation, godsend.

catastrophic ▶ **adjective** *the catastrophic consequences of a major oil spill* **disastrous**, calamitous, cataclysmic, ruinous, tragic, fatal, dire, awful, terrible, dreadful, black, woeful, grievous, lamentable, miserable, unfortunate; *literary* direful.
OPPOSITES fortunate, beneficial.

catcall ▶ **noun** *he walked out of the meeting to jeers and catcalls* **whistle**, **boo**, hiss, jeer, raspberry, hoot, brickbat, taunt, shout of derision; wolf whistle; (**catcalls**) scoffing, abuse, teasing, taunting, derision, ridiculing, mockery; *Brit. informal* the bird.

catch ▶ **verb 1** *he caught the ball* **seize**, grab, snatch, seize/grab/take hold of, lay (one's) hands on, get one's hands on, grasp, grip, clutch, clench, fasten on, pluck, hold, hang on to; receive, acquire, get, come into the possession of, intercept.
OPPOSITE drop.
2 *we've caught a dangerous thief* **capture**, seize; apprehend, take, arrest, lay hold of, take prisoner, take captive, take into custody, haul in; trap, snare, ensnare; net, hook, reel in, land, beach, bag; *informal* nab, collar, run in, pinch, bust, pull in, do, feel someone's collar; *Brit. informal* nick.
OPPOSITE release.
3 *the heel of Gloria's shoe had caught in a hole* **become trapped**, become stuck, stick, become wedged, become entangled, become snarled up, become snagged, snag.
4 *she caught the 7.45 bus* **be in time for**, reach in time, make, get to; **board**, get on, enter, go on board, go aboard, step aboard, mount, ascend, embark; *informal* hop on, jump on; *formal* embus, entrain, emplane.
OPPOSITES miss; alight.
5 *they were caught siphoning petrol from a car* **discover**, detect, find, come upon/across, stumble on, chance on, light on, bring to light, turn up, expose, find out, unmask; surprise, take by surprise, catch unawares, catch off guard, catch red-handed, catch in the act, catch out, burst in on.
6 *it was the business scheme that had caught his imagination* **engage**, capture, attract, draw, gain, grab, arrest, seize, hold, win, absorb, engross, rivet, grip, captivate, bewitch.
7 *she caught a faint trace of discreet aftershave* **perceive**, notice, observe, discern, detect, note, become aware of, make out, spot, see; *Brit. informal* clock.
OPPOSITE miss.
8 *I had to strain my ears to catch what she was saying* **hear**, perceive, recognize, discern, make out; **understand**, comprehend, grasp, take in, fathom, puzzle out, apprehend, get to the bottom of, unravel, decipher; follow, keep up with; *informal* get, get the drift of, get the hang of, catch on to, latch on to, make head or tail of, figure out, get the picture, get the message; *Brit. informal* twig, suss out, suss.
9 *the scenes caught the flavour of London in the sixties* **evoke**, conjure up, suggest, summon up, call to mind, recall, express, reproduce, represent, show, encapsulate, capture, record; film, photograph, draw, paint.
10 *the blow caught her on the side of her face* **hit**, strike, slap, smack, crack, bang, connect with, contact.
OPPOSITE miss.
11 *he served in Macedonia, where he caught malaria* **become infected with**, contract, get, take, become ill/sick with, fall ill/sick with, be taken ill with, show symptoms of, succumb to, develop, go/come down with, sicken for, fall victim to, be struck down with, be stricken with; *Brit.* go down with; *informal* take ill with; *N. Amer. informal* take sick with.
OPPOSITES shake off; escape.
12 *as the kindling caught he added larger pieces of wood* **ignite**, become ignited, burn, start burning, flame, catch/take fire, burst into flames, flame up, kindle.
OPPOSITE go out.
13 *the generator caught immediately* **start**, start running, fire, begin working, go, function, operate.
OPPOSITE stop.
□ **catch it** (*informal*) *I'll catch it if he finds me here* **be reprimanded**, be scolded, be rebuked, be taken to task, be admonished, be chastised, be castigated, get into trouble, be hauled over the coals; *informal* be told off, be for it, be for the high jump, get into hot/deep water, get into shtook, get a dressing-down, get an earful, get a roasting, get a rocket, get a rollicking, get a rap over the knuckles, get a slap on the wrist.
□ **catch on 1** *as radio caught on, politicians became increasingly aware of the medium's power* **become popular**, take off, become fashionable, come into fashion/vogue, boom, flourish, thrive; *informal* become trendy, become all the rage.
2 *it's double Dutch to me at the moment, but I catch on fast* **understand**, comprehend, learn, realize; find out, see the light, see daylight, work out what's going on, get the point; *informal* cotton on, tumble, latch on, get

C

the picture, get the message, get the drift, get wise, understand/see what's what; *Brit. informal* twig.

□ **catch (someone) up** *he stopped and waited for Lily to catch up | you go with Tess and I'll catch you up* **draw level (with)**; get to, come to, reach; gain on, gain.

▶ **noun 1** *he scooped up the net to inspect the catch* **haul**, net, bag, take, yield, booty, prize.
2 (*informal*) *Giles is a good catch for any girl* **eligible man/woman**, marriage prospect, match, suitable husband/wife/spouse.
3 *he put a hand inside the window, trying to slip the catch* **latch**, lock, fastener, fastening, clasp, hasp, hook, bar, clip, bolt; *Scottish* sneck, snib.
4 *the suspicious customer is always looking for the catch* **snag**, disadvantage, drawback, stumbling block, hitch, fly in the ointment, joker in the pack, pitfall, complication, problem, hiccup, hindrance, difficulty, setback, hurdle, downside, minus; trap, trick, snare, wile, dodge; *informal* ploy, con.
5 *there was a catch in her voice* **tremor**, unevenness, shake, shakiness, quiver, quivering, wobble.

catching ▶ **adjective** (*informal*) *Huntington's chorea isn't catching* **infectious**, contagious, communicable, transmittable, transmissible, transferable, spreading; *dated* infective.

catchphrase ▶ **noun** *the movie gave the world the catchphrase 'I'm gonna make him an offer he can't refuse'* **saying**, quotation, quote, sound bite, slogan, catchline, catchword, motto, watchword, mantra; *N. Amer. informal* tag line.

catchword ▶ **noun** *'variety' will be the catchword at the new venue* **motto**, watchword, slogan, byword, catchphrase, formula, refrain, maxim, axiom, mantra, shibboleth; *informal* buzzword.

catchy ▶ **adjective** *a catchy tune* **memorable**, unforgettable; appealing, captivating, snappy, with instant appeal; popular; singable, melodious, melodic, tuneful.
OPPOSITE forgettable.

catechize ▶ **verb** *Mrs Garrowby had catechized her sister about this matter* **interrogate**, question, cross-examine, cross-question, quiz, examine, probe, browbeat, interview, sound out; *informal* grill, pump, give the third degree to, put through the third degree, put the screws on, worm something out of.

categorical ▶ **adjective** *a categorical assurance that the government will not raise VAT* **unqualified**, unconditional, unequivocal, unreserved, absolute, explicit, unambiguous, definite, certain, direct, downright, outright, complete, thorough, thoroughgoing, total, emphatic, positive, express, point-blank, wholehearted, conclusive, undiluted, unalloyed, unadulterated, unstinting, without reservations, out-and-out, one hundred per cent; *formal* apodictic.
OPPOSITES qualified, equivocal.

categorize ▶ **verb** *half the pupils were categorized by their head teachers as casual or persistent truants* **classify**, class, group, grade, rate, designate, label, tag, brand; order, arrange, sort, rank, type, break down; file, catalogue, list, tabulate, index, assign, pigeonhole.

category ▶ **noun** *weedkillers fall into five broad categories* **class**, classification, categorization, group, grouping, bracket, head, heading, list, listing, set; type, sort, kind, variety, species, genre, breed, style, brand, make, model, family, stamp, cast, ilk, kidney; grade, grading, order, rank, status; division, section, department, compartment, pigeonhole.

cater ▶ **verb**

□ **cater for 1** *the hotel is happy to cater for vegetarians* **provide food for**, feed, serve, cook for, wine and dine, regale, provide for, provision; *dated* victual.
2 *a seaside resort catering for older holidaymakers* **serve**, provide for, oblige, meet the needs/wants of, accommodate, entertain, receive; deal with, handle, see to, look after, care for.
3 *he seemed to cater for all tastes in his selection of music* **take into account**, take into consideration, make allowances for, allow for, consider, bear in mind, make provision for, make preparations for, prepare for, make concessions for, have regard for.

□ **cater to** *Britain's vast number of markets and second-hand shops cater to every whim* **satisfy**, indulge, pander to, gratify, please, accommodate, pacify, appease, minister to, give in to, fulfil, satiate, pamper, mollycoddle, feather-bed, spoil.

caterwaul ▶ **verb** **howl**, wail, bawl, cry, yell, scream, screech, yelp, yowl, squall, whine; miaow; *rare* ululate.

caterwauling ▶ **noun** *the caterwauling of an aggressive cat* **howl**, howling, wail, wailing, screech, screeching, shriek, shrieking, scream, screaming, bawl, bawling, cry, crying, yell, yelling, yelp, yelping, yowl, yowling, squall, squalling, whine, whining, ululating; miaowing, miaow.

catharsis ▶ **noun** *there is a view that violent games can exert a positive effect through catharsis* **purging**, purgation, purification, cleansing, release, relief, emotional release, freeing, deliverance, exorcism, ridding; *Psychoanalysis* abreaction; *rare* depuration, lustration.
OPPOSITE repression.

cathartic ▶ **adjective** *writing my first book was a very cathartic experience for me* **purgative**, purging, purifying, cleansing, cleaning, release-bringing, releasing, relieving, freeing, delivering, exorcizing, ridding; *Psychoanalysis* abreactive; *rare* depurative, lustral.
OPPOSITE repressive.

catholic ▶ **adjective** *her musical tastes are pretty catholic* **diverse**, diversified, wide, broad, broad-based, eclectic, indiscriminate; open-minded, broad-minded, liberal, tolerant, undogmatic, flexible, unbigoted, unprejudiced, unsectarian, ecumenical; general, universal, widespread, global, worldwide, comprehensive, all-encompassing all-embracing, all-inclusive, unlimited.
OPPOSITES limited; narrow.

cattle *See centre pages for list of* **Cattle**
▶ **plural noun cows**, bovines, oxen, bulls; stock, livestock; *archaic* neat, kine.

WORD LINKS

relating to cattle	**bovine**
male	**bull**
female	**cow**
young	**calf**
collective noun	**herd, drove**

catty ▶ **adjective** (*informal*) *that was a catty remark—she's not a bad sort* **spiteful**, malicious, mean, nasty, cruel, unkind, snide, backbiting, hurtful, wounding, barbed, cutting, hateful, ill-natured, bitter, venomous, vitriolic, poisonous, acid, hostile, rancorous, vindictive, vicious; defamatory, slanderous; *informal* bitchy; *literary* malefic, maleficent.
OPPOSITES kind, complimentary.

caucus ▶ **noun 1** (*in North America & NZ*) *the Democratic caucus in the House* **parliamentary party**.
2 (*in North America & NZ*) *caucuses will be held in eleven states* **meeting**, assembly, gathering, congress, conference, convention, rally, conclave, congregation, convocation, synod, council, session, parley; *informal* get-together.
3 (*in the UK*) *the right-wing caucus in the Cabinet* **faction**, camp, bloc, group, gang, set, band, ring, party, league, cabal, camarilla, clique, coterie, junta, pressure group; *Brit.* ginger group; *historical* junto.

cause ▶ **noun 1** *the cause of the fire has not been found* **source**, root, origin, beginning(s), starting point, seed, germ, genesis, agency, occasion; mainspring, base, basis, foundation, bottom, seat; originator, author, creator, producer, agent, prime mover, maker; *Latin* fons et origo; *literary* fountainhead, wellspring, fount, begetter; *rare* radix.
OPPOSITES effect; result.
2 *there is no cause for alarm* **reason**, grounds, justification, call, need, necessity, occasion, basis, motive, motivation, inducement, excuse, pretext, purpose, stimulus, provocation.
3 *aid projects must serve the cause of human rights | I am raising money for a good cause* **principle**, ideal, belief (in), conviction, tenet; object, end, aim, objective, purpose, interest; movement, enterprise, undertaking, charity.
4 *he visited Germany to plead his cause with politicians* **case**, suit, lawsuit, action, dispute, contention, point of view.

▶ **verb** *this disease can cause blindness* **bring about**, give rise to, be the cause of, lead to, result in, create, begin, produce, generate, originate, engender, spawn, occasion, effect, bring to pass, bring on, precipitate, prompt, provoke, kindle, trigger, make happen, spark off, touch off, stir up, whip up, induce, inspire, promote, foster; *literary* beget, enkindle; *rare* effectuate.
OPPOSITE result from.

WORD LINKS

suffixes meaning 'causing…'	**-genic (e.g. *carcinogenic, iatrogenic*), -facient (e.g. *abortifacient, liquefacient*)**

caustic ▶ **adjective 1** *a caustic cleaner* **corrosive**, corroding, mordant, acid, alkaline, burning, stinging, acrid, harsh, destructive.
2 *a caustic comment* **sarcastic**, **cutting**, biting, mordant, stinging, sharp, bitter, scathing, derisive, sardonic, ironic, scornful, trenchant, acerbic, vitriolic, tart, acid, pungent, acrimonious, astringent, rapier-like, razor-edged, critical, polemic, virulent, venomous, waspish; *Brit. informal* sarky; *rare* mordacious, acidulous.
OPPOSITE kind.

CHOOSE THE RIGHT WORD

caustic, sarcastic, sardonic, ironic

See SARCASTIC.

cauterize ▶ **verb** (*Medicine*) *the wound needs to be cauterized* **burn**, sear, singe, scorch; disinfect, sterilize, sanitize, clean, cleanse, decontaminate.

caution ▶ **noun 1** *you are advised to proceed with caution* **care**, carefulness, wariness, awareness, heedfulness, heed, attention, attentiveness, alertness, watchfulness, vigilance, circumspection, discretion, prudence, guardedness, chariness, forethought, mindfulness; *informal* caginess.
OPPOSITES incaution, recklessness.
2 *a first offender may receive a caution from the police* **warning**, admonition, admonishment, injunction, monition; **reprimand**, rebuke, reproof,

scolding; exhortation, guidance, caveat, counsel; *informal* telling-off, dressing-down, talking-to; *Brit. informal* ticking-off, carpeting.
3 (*informal, dated*) *her uncle's a caution* **wag**, clown, joker, jester, jokester, comic, comedian, humorist; **oddity**, eccentric, eccentric person, character, original, individual, individualist, odd person, odd fellow, rare bird; *informal* one, laugh, scream, hoot, riot, barrel of laughs, one-off, oddball; *Brit. informal* odd bod, oner; *informal, dated* case, card, yell; *rare* rara avis.
▶ **verb 1** *advisers have cautioned against tax increases* **advise**, **warn**, recommend, counsel, urge, admonish, exhort.
2 *he was cautioned by the police* **warn**, admonish, give an injunction to; **reprimand**, rebuke, reprove, scold; *informal* tell off, give someone a telling-off, give someone a dressing-down, give someone a talking-to; *Brit. informal* give someone a ticking-off, carpet.

cautious ▶ **adjective** *he's a very cautious driver* **careful**, wary, aware, heedful, attentive, alert, watchful, vigilant, circumspect, prudent, guarded, on one's guard, chary, mindful; *informal* cagey.
OPPOSITES incautious; reckless.

cavalcade ▶ **noun** *a royal cavalcade proceeded through the city* **procession**, parade, motorcade, cortège; march, column, troop, file, train, caravan, retinue; *Brit.* march past; *informal* crocodile.

cavalier ▶ **noun 1** (**Cavalier**) (*historical*) *Cavaliers dying for King Charles* **Royalist**, king's man.
OPPOSITES Roundhead, parliamentarian.
2 (*archaic*) *the lady and her latest cavalier* **escort**, beau, gallant, gentleman, partner, courtier.
3 (*archaic*) *foot soldiers and cavaliers* **horseman**, cavalryman, horse soldier, trooper, equestrian, knight, chevalier; dragoon, hussar, lancer, carabineer, cuirassier, sabreur.
▶ **adjective** *a cavalier disregard for the real dangers | a cavalier attitude to other people's problems* **offhand**, indifferent, casual, dismissive, insouciant, uninterested, unconcerned; **supercilious**, patronizing, condescending, haughty, arrogant, lofty, lordly, disdainful, scornful, contemptuous, unceremonious, discourteous, uncivil, insolent, rude, glib, ungracious, perfunctory, cursory, curt, abrupt, terse, brusque; *informal* off, offish, couldn't-care-less, take-it-or-leave-it; *rare* poco-curante.
OPPOSITE thoughtful.

cavalry ▶ **plural noun** *the cavalry charged up the hill* **mounted troops**, cavalrymen, horse soldiers, troopers, horse; dragoons, lancers, hussars, carabineers, cuirassiers, sabreurs.

cave ▶ **noun** *there is a cave at the bottom of the cliff* **cavern**, grotto, hollow, cavity, pothole, underground chamber, gallery, tunnel, dugout.
□ **cave in 1** *the roof caved in* **collapse**, fall in, give, give way, crumble, crumple, disintegrate, subside, fall down, sag, slump.
OPPOSITE hold up.
2 *the manager caved in to their demands* **yield**, surrender, submit, succumb, back down, make concessions, capitulate, give up/in, raise/show the white flag; acquiesce, agree, concur, approve, assent; *informal* throw in the towel, throw in the sponge.
OPPOSITE hold out against.

WORD LINKS
exploration of caves **speleology;** *N. Amer.* **spelunking**
explorer of caves **speleologist, potholer**

caveat ▶ **noun** *he added the caveat that the results still had to be corroborated* **warning**, caution, admonition, monition, red flag, alarm bells; **proviso**, condition, stipulation, provision, clause, rider, qualification, restriction, reservation, limitation, strings.

caveman, **cavewoman** ▶ **noun** **cave-dweller**, troglodyte, primitive man/woman, prehistoric man/woman.
▶ **adjective** (*informal*) *women resent caveman tactics* **primitive**, uncivilized, crude, brutal, savage; masterful, domineering, autocratic.
OPPOSITE sophisticated.

cavern ▶ **noun** *the cave opens up into a fantastic cavern* **large cave**, grotto, hollow, cavity, underground chamber, gallery, tunnel, dugout.

cavernous ▶ **adjective** *the cavernous cargo space* **vast**, huge, large, immense, spacious, roomy, airy, commodious, capacious, voluminous, ample, rambling, extensive, high, deep; hollow, gaping, yawning, unfathomable; dark, gloomy, dismal, sepulchral.
OPPOSITES small, poky.

cavil ▶ **verb** *they cavilled at the cost* **complain**, carp, grumble, moan, grouse, grouch, whine, bleat, find fault with, quibble about, niggle about; criticize, censure, denounce, condemn, decry; *informal* gripe, beef, bellyache, bitch, whinge, nit-pick, pick holes in, split hairs, sound off, kick up a fuss, knock; *Brit. informal* chunter, create; *N. English informal* mither; *N. Amer. informal* kvetch about.

cavity ▶ **noun** *customs officers found a secret cavity in the car* **space**, chamber, hollow, hole, pocket, pouch; orifice, aperture; socket, gap, crater, pit; cutting, concavity; *Anatomy* lacuna, sac, alveolus, ampulla, antrum, archenteron, bulla, bursa, lumen, orbit, sinus, ventricle, vesicle; *Zoology* calyx; *Botany* cyst; *Geology* geode, vug.

cavort ▶ **verb** *two of his companions linked arms and cavorted around him* **skip**, **dance**, romp, jig, caper, cut capers, frisk, gambol, prance, frolic, play, lark; bounce, trip, leap, jump, bound, spring, hop, bob; *dated* sport; *rare* rollick.

cease ▶ **verb 1** *hostilities had ceased* **come to an end**, come to a halt, come to a stop, end, halt, stop, conclude, terminate, finish, wind up, draw to a close, be over, come to a standstill; pause, break off; peter out, fizzle out, abate, fade away, die away.
OPPOSITES start; continue.
2 *they were asked to cease all military activity* **bring to an end**, bring to a halt, bring to a stop, end, halt, stop, conclude, terminate, finish, wind up, discontinue, desist from, refrain from, leave off, quit, shut down, suspend, break off, cut short.
OPPOSITES start; continue.
▶ **noun**
□ **without cease continuously**, incessantly, unendingly, unremittingly, without cessation/stopping/let-up, without a pause/break, on and on, time without end.

ceaseless ▶ **adjective** *they kept up a ceaseless flow of questions* **continual**, constant, continuous; **incessant**, unceasing, unending, endless, never-ending, interminable, non-stop, uninterrupted, unabated, unabating, unremitting, relentless, unrelenting, unrelieved, sustained, persistent, lasting, eternal, perpetual; unfaltering, unflagging, untiring, unwearied, unwavering, unswerving, undeviating, persevering, dogged, tireless, indefatigable.
OPPOSITES intermittent; brief.

CHOOSE THE RIGHT WORD
ceaseless, continual, continuous, constant
See CONTINUAL.

cede ▶ **verb** *Austria ceded the South Tyrol to Italy in 1919* **surrender**, concede, relinquish, yield, part with, give up; **hand over**, deliver up, turn over, give over, make over, transfer, bequeath, grant, remit, renounce, resign, abandon, forgo, sacrifice, waive; *archaic* forsake.
OPPOSITES keep; gain.

ceiling ▶ **noun 1** *the ceiling was painted yellow* **roof**, vault, vaulting; *French* plafond.
OPPOSITE floor.
2 *a ceiling was to be set on prices* **upper limit**, maximum, limitation, highest permissible level/value.
OPPOSITES floor, minimum.

celebrate ▶ **verb 1** *they were celebrating their wedding anniversary* **commemorate**, observe, honour, mark, salute, recognize, acknowledge, remember, memorialize, keep, drink to, toast, drink a toast to.
2 *let's open the champagne and celebrate!* **enjoy oneself**, make merry, have fun, have a good/wild time, rave, party, have a party, {eat, drink, and be merry}, revel, roister, carouse, kill the fatted calf, put the flag(s) out; *N. Amer.* step out; *informal* go out on the town, paint the town red, whoop it up, make whoopee, junket, have a night on the tiles, live it up, have a ball; *Brit. informal* push the boat out; *S. African informal* jol; *dated* spree, go on a spree; *rare* rollick.
3 *the priest celebrated mass* **perform**, observe, officiate at, preside at, solemnize, ceremonialize.
4 *he was celebrated for his achievements* **praise**, laud, extol, glorify, eulogize, reverence, honour, pay tribute to, pay homage to, salute, hymn, sing; *archaic* emblazon.

celebrated ▶ **adjective** *a celebrated amateur artist* **acclaimed**, admired, highly rated, lionized, revered, honoured, esteemed, exalted, lauded, vaunted, much touted, well thought of, well received, acknowledged; eminent, great, distinguished, prestigious, illustrious, pre-eminent, venerable, august, estimable, of note, noted, notable, of repute, of high standing, considerable; famous, renowned, well known.
OPPOSITES criticized; unsung; obscure.

CHOOSE THE RIGHT WORD
celebrated, famous, well known, renowned
See FAMOUS.

celebration ▶ **noun 1** *the school's celebration of its 50th birthday* **commemoration**, observance, honouring, salute to, marking, keeping.
2 *this is a cause for celebration* **jollification**, merrymaking, carousing, carousal, revelry, revels, enjoying oneself, partying, parties, festivity, festivities; roistering, debauchery, frolics; *informal* junketing.
3 *a birthday celebration* **party**, function, gathering, event, affair, occasion, festivities, festival, fête, carnival, gala, jamboree; *W. Indian* jump-up; *Jewish* simcha; *informal* do, bash, get-together, blowout, rave; *Brit. informal* rave-up, thrash, knees-up, jolly, beanfeast, bunfight, beano; *S. African informal* jol.
4 *the celebration of the Eucharist* **observance**, performance, officiation, solemnization.

C

celebrity ▶ noun **1** *his prestige and celebrity grew* **fame**, prominence, renown, eminence, pre-eminence, importance, stardom, popularity, distinction, greatness, note, notability, prestige, stature, standing, position, rank, repute, reputation, illustriousness, glory, acclaim, influence, account, consequence, visibility.
OPPOSITE obscurity.
2 *questions are put to a panel of celebrities* **famous person**, VIP, very important person, personality, name, big name, famous name, household name, star, superstar, leading light, giant, great, master, guru; **dignitary**, luminary, worthy, grandee, lion, public figure, pillar of society, notable, notability, personage, panjandrum; *informal* heavyweight, celeb, somebody, someone, bigwig, biggie, big shot, big noise, big gun, big cheese, big chief, nob, lady muck, lord muck, top brass, honcho, head honcho, top dog, mogul, supremo, megastar, heavy, fat cat; *N. Amer. informal* big wheel, big kahuna, kahuna, top banana, big enchilada, macher, high muckamuck, high muckety-muck.
OPPOSITE nonentity.

celestial ▶ adjective **1** *a celestial body* **(in) space**, heavenly, astronomical, extraterrestrial, stellar, planetary, in the sky, in the heavens; *rare* superterrestrial.
OPPOSITES terrestrial, earthly.
2 *celestial beings* **heavenly**, holy, saintly, divine, godly, godlike, ethereal, paradisical, Elysian, spiritual, empyrean, superlunary; immortal, angelic, seraphic, cherubic, blessed, beatific, blissful, sublime.
OPPOSITES hellish; mundane.

celibacy ▶ noun *a priest who had taken a vow of celibacy* **chastity**, virginity, maidenhood, maidenhead, abstinence, self-denial, self-restraint, abnegation, asceticism; the unmarried state, singleness, bachelorhood, spinsterhood; monkhood, nunhood, monasticism; *rare* single blessedness, continence.
OPPOSITES marriage; sex.

celibate ▶ adjective *a celibate priest* **unmarried**, single, unwed, spouseless, wifeless, husbandless; **chaste**, virginal, virgin, maidenly, maiden, intact, abstinent, self-denying, self-restrained, ascetic; monkish, monklike, nunnish, nunlike, monastic; *rare* continent.
OPPOSITES married; sexually active.

cell *See centre pages for list of* **Blood Cells**
▶ noun **1** *a prison cell* **room**, cubicle, compartment, chamber, stall, enclosure; dungeon, oubliette, lock-up, prison.
2 *each cell of the honeycomb* **compartment**, cavity, hole, hollow, bay, chamber, slot, niche, section.
3 *the weapons may be used to arm terrorist cells* **caucus**, **unit**, faction, arm, section, nucleus, clique, coterie, group, party, clan, wing.

WORD LINKS
related prefix **cyto- (e.g. *cytology, cytotoxic*)**
related suffixes **-cyte (e.g. *phagocyte, lymphocyte*), -blast (e.g. *erythroblast, fibroblast*)**

cellar ▶ noun **basement**, vault, crypt, undercroft, underground room, catacomb; garden flat, sub-basement, lower ground floor; *Brit. dated* below stairs.
OPPOSITE attic.

cement ▶ noun *polystyrene cement* **adhesive**, glue, fixative, gum, paste, bonding, binder, sealer, sealant; superglue, epoxy resin; *N. Amer.* mucilage; *N. Amer. informal* stickum.
▶ verb *he cemented the rock sample to a microscope slide* **stick**, bond, join, connect; **fasten**, fix, affix, attach, secure, bind, glue, gum, paste, fuse, weld, solder.

cemetery ▶ noun **graveyard**, churchyard, burial ground, burial place, burying place, burying ground, garden of remembrance; *Scottish* kirkyard; *N. Amer.* memorial park; *informal* boneyard; *literary* golgotha; *historical* urnfield, potter's field, catacomb, necropolis; *archaic* God's acre.

censor ▶ noun *the film censors* **expurgator**, bowdlerizer; **examiner**, inspector, editor.
▶ verb *letters home from the front line were censored* **cut**, delete, delete parts of, make cuts in, blue-pencil; **examine**, inspect; edit, make changes to; make acceptable, expurgate, bowdlerize, sanitize; *informal* clean up; *rare* redact.

censorious ▶ adjective *the appointment of censorious watchdogs over the broadcasters* **hypercritical**, overcritical, severely critical, disapproving, condemnatory, condemning, castigatory, denunciatory, deprecatory, disparaging, unforgiving, reproachful, reproving, censuring, captious, fault-finding, carping, cavilling, full of reproof, vituperative.
OPPOSITES complimentary, approving.

censure ▶ verb *the commission censured him for his conduct.* See REPRIMAND.
▶ noun *his voice took on a note of censure* **condemnation**, criticism, attack, abuse, revilement; **reprimand**, rebuke, admonishment, admonition, reproof, reproval, upbraiding, castigation, berating, denunciation, disapproval, reproach, scolding, chiding, reprehension, obloquy, vituperation; *rare* excoriation, objurgation.
OPPOSITES approval, commendation.

central ▶ adjective **1** *a Roman basilica always occupied a central position* **middle**, centre, halfway, midway, mid, median, medial, mean, middling, intermediate, intermedial; *Anatomy* mesial.
OPPOSITES side; extreme.
2 *central London* **inner**, innermost, middle, mid, interior, nuclear.
OPPOSITE outer.
3 *their central campaign issue* **main**, chief, principal, primary, leading, foremost, first, most important, predominant, dominant, (most) prominent, key, crucial, vital, essential, basic, fundamental, core, staple, critical, pivotal, salient, prime, focal, premier, paramount, major, ruling, master, supreme, overriding, cardinal, capital, pre-eminent, ultimate, uppermost, highest, utmost, top, topmost, arch-; *informal* number-one.
OPPOSITES subordinate; minor.

centralize ▶ verb *the minister intends to centralize tax collection* **concentrate**, bring under one roof, consolidate, amalgamate, condense, collect, cluster, compact, unify, incorporate, streamline, focus, rationalize.
OPPOSITES disperse, devolve.

centre ▶ noun *the centre of the town | the centre of a circle* **middle**, nucleus, heart, core, hub, pivot, kernel, eye, bosom; middle point, midpoint, halfway point, mean, median; interior; depths, thick, bullseye, focus, focal point, cynosure.
OPPOSITE edge.
▶ verb *the story* **centres on** *an eye surgeon working in Paris* **focus**, concentrate, pivot, hinge, be based; revolve around, have as its starting point.

centrepiece ▶ noun *the tower is the centrepiece of the park* **highlight**, main feature, high point, high spot, best part, climax; focus of attention, focal point, centre of attention/interest, magnet, cynosure; most prominent element, central component, nucleus, heart, core, hub, kernel.

ceramics ▶ noun. *See centre pages for list of* **Pottery**
▶ plural noun **pottery**, pots, china, terracotta.

cereal ▶ noun. *See centre pages for list of* **Cereal Crops**

ceremonial ▶ adjective *a ceremonial occasion* **formal**, official, state, public; ritual, ritualistic, prescribed, set, stately, courtly, solemn, dignified, celebratory, sacramental, liturgical.
OPPOSITES informal, unofficial.
▶ noun *there was great sensitivity over diplomatic ceremonial* **ritual**, ceremony, rite, formality, pomp, solemnity; form, custom, tradition, convention, usage, practice, routine, protocol, office, observance; sacrament, liturgy; *formal* praxis.

ceremonious ▶ adjective *he rose from his desk to take a ceremonious farewell* **dignified**, **majestic**, imposing, impressive, solemn, stately; awe-inspiring, regal, imperial, elegant, grand, glorious, splendid, magnificent, resplendent, important, august, portentous; formal, courtly, punctilious, courteous, civil, deferential, stiff, rigid, affected; slow-moving, measured, deliberate, precise, scrupulous; *informal* starchy, just so.
OPPOSITE unceremonious.

ceremony ▶ noun **1** *a wedding ceremony* **rite**, ritual, ceremonial, observance; **service**, sacrament, liturgy, worship, mystery, office, celebration; performance, act, practice, order, custom, tradition, convention, institution, formality, procedure, usage, habit, form.
2 *the new Queen was proclaimed with due ceremony* **pomp**, protocol, formalities, niceties, decorum, etiquette, good form, propriety, conventionality, punctilio, attention to detail, fuss; *French* politesse.

certain ▶ adjective **1** *I'm certain he's guilty* **sure**, **confident**, positive, convinced, in no doubt, unshaken in one's belief, secure in one's belief, easy in one's mind, satisfied, assured, persuaded; (**be certain**) have no doubt, not question, hold the unwavering view.
OPPOSITE doubtful.
2 *it is certain that more changes are in the offing* **unquestionable**, **sure**, definite, beyond question, not in question, not in doubt, beyond doubt, unequivocal, indubitable, undeniable, irrefutable, indisputable, incontrovertible, incontestable, obvious, patent, manifest, evident, plain, clear, transparent, palpable, unmistakable, conclusive, recognized, confirmed, accepted, acknowledged, undisputed, undoubted, unquestioned, unchallenged, uncontested; there are no two ways about it; *informal* as sure as eggs is eggs.
OPPOSITES unthinkable; doubtful; possible.
3 *they are certain to win* **sure**, **very likely**, bound, destined, predestined, fated, trusted, assured of doing something.
OPPOSITE unlikely.
4 *Pakistan's lead of 380 runs meant certain success* **inevitable**, assured, destined, predestined, fated; reliable, unavoidable, inescapable, automatic, bound to happen, sure to happen, inexorable, ineluctable, predictable, necessary, out of one's hands; *informal* in the bag.
5 *there is no certain cure for this* **reliable**, dependable, trustworthy, sound, foolproof, tested, tried and tested, effective, efficacious, guaranteed, sure, unfailing, infallible, unerring; *informal* sure-fire; *dated* sovereign.
OPPOSITE unreliable.
6 *a certain sum of money is required* **determined**, definite, fixed, established, precise, defined, exact, explicit, express.

OPPOSITE undefined.
7 *a certain lady that you know* **particular**, specific, individual, special, especial.
OPPOSITES nameless; undifferentiated; general.
8 *to a certain extent that is true* **moderate**, modest, medium, middling, unexceptional; tolerable, passable, adequate, fair, decent, acceptable; limited, small.
OPPOSITE great.

CHOOSE THE RIGHT WORD

certain, sure, positive, convinced, definite
See SURE.

certainly ▶ adverb **1** *this is certainly a late work* **unquestionably**, surely, assuredly, definitely, beyond question, without question, beyond doubt, unequivocally, indubitably, undeniably, irrefutably, indisputably, incontrovertibly, incontestably, obviously, patently, manifestly, evidently, plainly, clearly, transparently, palpably, unmistakably, conclusively, undisputedly, undoubtedly; there are no two ways about it; *informal* as sure as eggs is eggs.
OPPOSITE possibly.
2 *our revenues are certainly lower than anticipated* **admittedly**, beyond question, without question, definitely, undoubtedly, without a doubt.
▶ exclamation *'And now, shall we clean the diamonds?' 'Certainly.'* **yes**, definitely, absolutely, sure, by all means, quite, indeed, of course, positively, naturally, without doubt, without question, unquestionably; affirmative; *Brit. dated* rather.
OPPOSITES no; possibly.

certainty ▶ noun **1** *she knew with certainty that he was telling the truth* **confidence**, sureness, positiveness, conviction, certitude, reliability, assuredness, assurance, validity, conclusiveness, authoritativeness, truth, fact, factualness.
OPPOSITES uncertainty; doubt.
2 *he accepted defeat as a certainty | that horse is a certainty for the 2.00 at Newmarket tomorrow* **inevitability**, necessity, foregone conclusion, predictable result, matter of course; certain winner; *informal* sure thing, cert, dead cert, sure-fire winner.
OPPOSITES possibility; impossibility.

certificate ▶ noun *a certificate of motor insurance* **guarantee**, proof, certification, document, authorization, authentication, verification, credentials, accreditation, testimonial, warrant, licence, voucher, diploma.
WORD LINKS
collecting old bond and share certificates **scripophily**

certify ▶ verb **1** *the aircraft was certified as airworthy* **verify**, **guarantee**, attest, validate, ratify, warrant, confirm, corroborate, substantiate, endorse, vouch for, testify to, provide evidence of, authenticate, document; bear witness to, bear out, give proof of, prove, demonstrate, back up, support.
2 *the woman would be taken to a certified hospital for examination* **accredit**, recognize, license, authorize, approve, warrant; empower, qualify, endorse, sanction, vouch for, put one's seal of approval on, appoint, give a certificate to, give a diploma to.

certitude ▶ noun *the question may never be answered with certitude* **certainty**, confidence, sureness, positiveness, conviction, reliability, assuredness, assurance.
OPPOSITE doubt.

cessation ▶ noun *the cessation of hostilities* **end**, ending, termination, stopping, halting, ceasing, finish, finishing, stoppage, closing, closure, close, conclusion, winding up, discontinuation, discontinuance, breaking off, abandonment, interruption, suspension, cutting short; pause, break, respite, let-up.
OPPOSITES start; resumption.

cession ▶ noun *the cession of this province to the Kingdom of Italy* **surrender**, surrendering, ceding, conceding, concession, relinquishment, yielding, giving up, handing over, transfer, transference, transferral, granting, grant, bequest; resignation, abdication, abandonment, forgoing, forsaking, sacrifice, waiving, waiver, renunciation.
OPPOSITE gain.

cetacean ▶ noun. *See centre pages for list of* **Whales and Dolphins**

chafe ▶ verb **1** *the collar chafed his neck* **abrade**, graze, grate, rub against, rub painfully, gall, skin, scrape, scratch, rasp; inflame; *rare* excoriate.
2 *I chafed her feet and wrapped the blanket around her* **rub**, warm, warm up.
3 *material chafed by the rock* **wear away**, wear down, wear out, wear to shreds, fray, tatter, erode, abrade, scour, rasp, scrape away, gnaw away at, bite into.
4 *the bank chafed at the restrictions imposed on it* **be impatient**, be angry, be annoyed, be irritated, be incensed, be exasperated, be frustrated; fume, brood, fuss, upset oneself; *informal* blow one's top, blow a fuse.

chaff[1] ▶ noun **1** *a machine that separated the chaff from the grain* **husks**, hulls, bran, pods, seed cases, shells, capsules, sheaths; *N. Amer.* shucks.
2 *the proposals were characterized as so much chaff* **rubbish**, refuse, waste, garbage, litter, discarded matter, debris, detritus, scrap, dross; flotsam and jetsam, lumber; sweepings, leavings, leftovers, remains, scraps, dregs, offscourings, odds and ends; muck; *N. Amer.* trash; *Austral./NZ* mullock; *informal* dreck, junk; *Brit. informal* grot, gash; *Archaeology* debitage; *rare* draff, raff, raffle, cultch, orts.

chaff[2] ▶ noun *we used to come in for a fair amount of good-natured chaff* **banter**, repartee, raillery, ripostes, sallies, quips, wisecracks, crosstalk, wordplay, teasing, ragging; badinage, witty conversation, witty remarks, witticism(s), joking, jesting, jocularity, drollery; *French* bons mots; *informal* kidding, kidology, ribbing, joshing, wisecracking; *rare* persiflage.
▶ verb *the pleasures of drinking and betting and chaffing your mates* **tease**, make fun of, poke fun at, rag, mock, laugh at, guy; deride, ridicule, scoff at, jeer at, jibe at; taunt, bait, goad, pick on; *informal* take the mickey out of, send up, rib, josh, kid, wind up, have on, pull someone's leg, make a monkey out of; *N. Amer. informal* goof on, rag on, put on, pull someone's chain, razz, fun, shuck; *Austral./NZ informal* poke mullock at, poke borak at, sling off at, chiack; *Brit. vulgar slang* take the piss out of; *archaic* make sport of, twit, quiz, smoke, flout at, rally.

chagrin ▶ noun *to his chagrin, his son chose to become an actor* **annoyance**, irritation, vexation, exasperation, displeasure, pique, spleen, crossness, anger, rage, fury, wrath; dissatisfaction, discontent, indignation, resentment, umbrage, disgruntlement, rankling, smarting, distress, discomposure, discomfiture, disquiet, fretfulness, frustration; embarrassment, mortification, humiliation, shame; *informal* aggravation; *literary* ire.
OPPOSITE delight.

chagrined ▶ adjective *he was chagrined when his friend poured scorn on him.* *See* ANNOYED.

chain ▶ noun **1** *a gold chain* series of links.
2 (**chains**) *he had been held in chains while he was a prisoner* **fetters**, shackles, bonds, irons, leg irons, manacles, handcuffs; *informal* cuffs, bracelets; *archaic* trammels, gyves, darbies, bilboes.
3 *a chain of events* **series**, succession, string, sequence, train, trail, run, pattern, progression, course, set, line, row, concatenation.
4 *a chain of shops* **group**; multiple shop/store, multiple, firm, company.
▶ verb *she chained her bicycle to the railings* **tie**, secure, fasten, tether, hitch, bind, rope, moor; restrain, shackle, fetter, manacle, handcuff, hobble; confine, imprison; *rare* trammel, gyve.

chair *See centre pages for list of* **Chairs and Stools**
▶ noun **1** *he sat down on a chair* **seat**.
2 *he was chair of the union for eight years* **chairperson**, chairman, chairwoman, president, convener, spokesperson, spokesman, spokeswoman, leader, MC, master/mistress of ceremonies; *Brit.* shop steward, father/mother of the chapel.
3 *a university chair* **professorship**.
4 (*N. Amer.*) *he was sent to the chair* **electric chair**; electrocution, execution.
▶ verb *she chairs the economic committee* **preside over**, take the chair of, be in the chair at, officiate at, moderate; lead, direct, conduct, run, manage, control, be in charge of, be in control of, have control of, supervise, superintend, oversee, guide.

chairman, chairwoman ▶ noun *the chairman of the conference* **chair**, chairperson, president, convener; spokesperson, spokesman, spokeswoman, leader, MC, master/mistress of ceremonies; *Brit.* shop steward, father/mother of the chapel.

chalk ▶ verb
□ **chalk something up 1** *he has chalked up another box-office success* **achieve**, attain, accomplish, gain, earn, win, succeed in making, reach, make, get, obtain; score, tally, record, register, enter, mark, log; *informal* clock up, knock up, notch up, turn in, rack up, bag.
2 *I forgot completely—chalk it up to age* **attribute**, assign, ascribe, put down, set down, accredit, credit, give the credit for, impute; lay on, pin on, blame on, lay at the door of; connect with, associate with.
WORD LINKS
chalky **calcareous**

chalky ▶ adjective **1** *Rosaleen's skin was so chalky that her veins showed blue through it* **pale**, bloodless, pallid, colourless, wan, ashen, white; waxen, chalk-white, milky; pasty, pasty-faced, whey-faced, peaky, sickly, anaemic, tired-looking, washed out, sallow, drained, drawn, sapped, ghostly, deathly, deathlike, blanched, bleached; *rare* etiolated.
OPPOSITES rosy; flushed.
2 *there were some chalky bits at the bottom of the glass* **powdery**, floury, mealy, dusty, gritty, crumbly, friable, granulated, granular, ground, crushed, pulverized; *rare* pulverulent, levigated.
OPPOSITE smooth.

challenge ▶ noun **1** *he accepted the challenge* **dare**, provocation; summons.
2 *he successfully resisted a challenge to his leadership* **confrontation with**, **dispute with**, stand against, test of, opposition, disagreement with; questioning of, defiance, ultimatum.
3 *getting ready for the visitors was proving quite a challenge* **problem**, difficult

task, test, trial; trouble, bother, obstacle.
▶ verb **1** *you will need to be able to challenge their statistics in an informed way* **question**, **disagree with**, object to, take exception to, confront, dispute, take issue with, protest against, call into question; demur about/against, dissent from, be a dissenter from.
2 *he challenged one of my men to a duel* **dare**, summon, invite, bid, throw down the gauntlet to, defy someone to do something.
3 *a new way of life that would challenge them* **test**, tax, try; strain, make demands on, weary, wear out, drain, sap; **stretch**, stimulate, arouse, inspire, excite, spur on.

challenging ▶ adjective *an interesting, worthwhile, and challenging job* **demanding**, testing, taxing, exacting, exigent, searching; stretching, exciting, stimulating, inspiring, energizing, inspirational; difficult, tough, hard, heavy, stiff, formidable, onerous, arduous, laborious, burdensome, strenuous, gruelling.
OPPOSITES easy; uninspiring.

chamber ▶ noun **1** *a debating chamber* **room**, hall, assembly room, auditorium.
2 (*archaic*) *we returned to the castle and slept safely in our own chamber* **bedroom**, bedchamber, boudoir, room; *literary* bower.
3 *the lower left chamber of the heart* **compartment**, cavity, hollow, pocket, cell; part; *Anatomy* auricle, ventricle.

champagne ▶ noun sparkling wine; *informal* champers, bubbly.

champion ▶ noun **1** *the world snooker champion* **winner**, title-holder, defending champion, gold medallist; **prizewinner**, cup winner, victor, conqueror; *Latin* victor ludorum; *informal* champ, top dog, number one.
2 *a champion of change* **advocate**, proponent, promoter, proposer, supporter, standard-bearer, torch-bearer, defender, protector, upholder, backer, exponent, patron, sponsor, prime mover; pleader for, campaigner for, propagandist for, lobbyist for, fighter for, battler for, crusader for, apologist for; apostle, evangelist, missionary; *N. Amer.* booster; *informal* plugger.
OPPOSITES opponent, critic.
3 (*historical*) *there was little chance of his defeating the King's Champion* **knight**, man-at-arms, warrior, defender, duellist, paladin, hero.
▶ verb *an organization championing the rights of tribal peoples* **advocate**, promote, plead for, hold a torch for, defend, protect, uphold, support, back, espouse, ally oneself with, stand behind, stand up for, take someone's part, campaign for, lobby for, fight for, battle for, crusade for, take up the cudgels for; propose, sponsor, vouch for, second; *informal* stick up for, throw one's weight behind, plug.
OPPOSITES oppose, criticize.

chance ▶ noun **1** *there was a reasonable chance that he might be released* **possibility**, prospect, probability, odds, likelihood, likeliness, expectation, anticipation, conceivability, feasibility, plausibility; risk, threat, menace, hazard, danger, fear, peril, liability; hope, opportunity, promise.
OPPOSITE unlikelihood.
2 *I gave her a chance to answer* **opportunity**, opening, occasion, turn, time, moment, window (of opportunity), slot; *N. Amer. & Austral./NZ* show; *Canadian* a kick at the can/cat; *informal* break, shot, look-in.
3 *'Test them,' Nigel said, taking an awful chance* **risk**, gamble, hazard, venture, speculation, long shot, leap in the dark, pig in a poke, lottery, pot luck.
OPPOSITE certainty.
4 *it was pure chance that made me notice the writing* **accident**, coincidence, serendipity, fate, a twist of fate, destiny, fortuity, fortune, providence, freak, hazard; a piece of good fortune, (a bit of) luck, (a bit of) good luck, a fluke, a happy chance; *N. Amer.* happenstance.
□ **by chance** *I came across the book by chance* **fortuitously**, by accident, accidentally, coincidentally, serendipitously, unintentionally, inadvertently; unwittingly, unknowingly, unawares, unconsciously.
OPPOSITES intentionally, knowingly.
▶ adjective *a chance discovery* **accidental**, occurring by chance/accident, fortuitous, adventitious, fluky, coincidental, casual, serendipitous, random, aleatory; unexpected, unforeseen, unanticipated, unforeseeable, unlooked-for; unintentional, unintended, inadvertent, involuntary, unplanned, unpremeditated, unthinking, unmeant; unwitting, unknowing, unconscious, subconscious.
OPPOSITES intentional, planned.
▶ verb **1** *I chanced to meet him a year or so later* **happen**.
2 (*informal*) *I waited a few seconds and chanced another look* **risk**, hazard, venture, try, try one's luck with; *formal* essay.
3 (*dated*) *it so chanced that the king was passing through the village* **occur**, happen, come about, transpire, materialize, turn out, arise; *literary* come to pass, befall; *archaic* hap; *rare* eventuate.
□ **chance on/upon** *a passing motorist chanced on the scene* **come across**, run across, run into, happen on, hit on, light on, come upon, stumble on, blunder on, find by chance, meet (by chance); *informal* bump into; *archaic* run against.

chancy ▶ adjective (*informal*) *bookselling is a chancy occupation* **risky**, **unpredictable**, uncertain, speculative, precarious; problematical, unsettled, unsafe, insecure, exposed, touch-and-go, tricky, treacherous, dangerous, fraught with danger, high-risk, hazardous, perilous; *informal* dicey, sticky, hairy; *Brit. informal* dodgy; *N. Amer. informal* gnarly; *archaic or humorous* parlous.
OPPOSITES safe; predictable.

change ▶ verb **1** *this could change the face of Britain | things have changed since my day* **alter**, make different, become different, undergo a change, make alterations to, adjust, make adjustments to, adapt, turn, amend, improve, modify, convert, revise, recast, reform, reshape, refashion, redesign, restyle, revamp, rework, remake, remodel, remould, redo, reconstruct, reorganize, reorder, refine, reorient, reorientate, vary, transform, transfigure, transmute, metamorphose, undergo a sea change, evolve; customize, tailor; *informal* tweak; *technical* permute.
OPPOSITES preserve; stay the same.
2 *he'd changed his job* **swap**, exchange, interchange, substitute, switch, commute, convert, replace, rotate, alternate, transpose; trade, barter; *archaic* truck.
OPPOSITE keep.
▶ noun **1** *there has been a change of plan* **alteration**, modification, variation, conversion, revision, amendment, adjustment, adaptation; remodelling, reshaping, remoulding, redoing, reconstruction, rebuilding, recasting, reorganization, rearrangement, reordering, reshuffling, restyling, rejigging, reworking, renewal, renewing, revamping, renovation, remaking; metamorphosis, transformation, transfiguration, translation, evolution, mutation, sea change; *humorous* transmogrification.
2 *we need a change of government* **swap**, exchange, interchange, substitution, switch, commutation, conversion, replacement, rotation, alternation, transposition; trade, barter, bartering; *archaic* truck.
3 *sorry about the note—I've no change* **coins**, loose change, small change, cash, petty cash, coinage, coin, coin of the realm, hard cash, silver, copper, coppers, gold; *formal* specie.
□ **have a change of heart**. *See* HEART.

WORD LINKS
related prefix **meta- (e.g. *metamorphosis*)**
related suffix **-tropic (e.g. *phototropic, psychotropic*)**

changeable ▶ adjective **1** *the weather will be changeable | she experienced changeable moods and panic attacks* **variable**, inconstant, varying, changing, shifting, fluctuating, irregular, erratic, wavering, vacillating, inconsistent, fluid, floating, unsteady, unfixed, uneven, unstable, unsettled, turbulent, movable, mutable, chameleon-like; fickle, capricious, temperamental, whimsical, ever-changing, kaleidoscopic, volatile, mercurial, fitful, uncertain, unpredictable, undependable, unreliable; *informal* up and down, full of ups and downs, blowing hot and cold; *rare* vicissitudinous, protean, chameleonic, changeful, fluctuant, variational.
OPPOSITES unchanging, constant.
2 *the colours on the screen are instantly changeable* **alterable**, adjustable, modifiable, variable, convertible, mutable, permutable, exchangeable, interchangeable, replaceable, transposable.
OPPOSITES unchangeable; inflexible.

CHOOSE THE RIGHT WORD
changeable, inconstant, capricious, fickle
See INCONSTANT.

changeless ▶ adjective *parents are so utterly changeless in their behaviour* **unchanging**, unvarying, timeless, static, standing, fixed, permanent, constant, unchanged, fast, consistent, uniform, undeviating; stable, steady, unchangeable, unalterable, invariable, immutable; **lasting**, long-lasting, abiding, enduring, persistent, indefinite, continuing, perpetual, everlasting, perennial, unending, endless, never-ending.
OPPOSITES variable; fleeting.

channel ▶ noun **1** *the English Channel* **strait(s)**, sound, neck, arm, narrows, passage, sea passage, stretch of water, waterway.
2 *the clear water from the spring ran down a channel towards the house* **duct**, gutter, groove, furrow, rut, conduit, trough, trench, culvert, cut, sluice, spillway, race, ditch, drain, watercourse, waterway, canal.
3 *it is hard to find the right channel for extraordinary energy* **use**, medium, means/mode of expression, vehicle; release, means of release, release mechanism, safety valve, vent; way of harnessing; **course**, direction, path, route.
4 *a channel of communication* **means**, medium, instrument, mechanism, agency, vehicle, route, avenue, course, method, mode; procedure, technique.
▶ verb **1** *you need to channel out the plaster where the conduit is to go* **hollow out**, gouge (out), cut (out), flute; cut a groove in, make a furrow in.
2 *the arches were put up to channel the waters of an underground river | many countries channel their aid through charities* **convey**, transmit, transport, conduct, direct, guide, bear, carry, relay, pass on, transfer.

chant ▶ noun **1** *a chant of 'Out! Out! Out!' made itself heard* **shout**, cry, slogan, rallying call, war cry, chorus, chanting.

2 *the melodious chant of the monks intoning the psalm* **incantation**, intonation, recitation, singing, song, recitative, mantra; *rare* cantillation.
▶ **verb 1** *protesters were chanting slogans* **shout**, sing, chorus, carol; repeat.
2 *the choir then chanted Psalm 118* **sing**, intone, incant, recite; *rare* cantillate, intonate.

chaos ▶ **noun** *there was complete chaos when she entered the classroom* **disorder**, disarray, disorganization, confusion, mayhem, bedlam, pandemonium, madness, havoc, turmoil, tumult, commotion, disruption, upheaval, furore, frenzy, uproar, hue and cry, babel, hurly-burly; a maelstrom, a muddle, a mess, a shambles, a mare's nest; anarchy, entropy, lawlessness; *W. Indian* bangarang; *informal* hullabaloo, all hell broken loose, a madhouse; *N. Amer. informal* a three-ring circus.
OPPOSITES order, orderliness.

chaotic ▶ **adjective** *their tall Victorian house was like a chaotic museum* **disorderly**, disordered, in disorder, in chaos, in disarray, disorganized, topsy-turvy, haywire, confused, in pandemonium, in turmoil, tumultuous, disrupted; frenzied, in uproar, in a muddle, jumbled, in a mess, messy, in a shambles, anarchic, lawless; *rare* orderless.
OPPOSITE orderly.

chap[1] ▶ **verb** *his skin is very dry and chaps easily* **become raw**, become sore, redden, become inflamed, chafe, crack, roughen.

chap[2] ▶ **noun** *(Brit. informal) some chap gave it to me* **man**, boy, male, individual, body; *informal* fellow, fella, geezer, punter, character, customer, sort, type; *Brit. informal* **bloke**, guy, lad, bod; *N. Amer. informal* dude, hombre; *Brit. informal, dated* cove; *archaic* wight.

chaperone ▶ **noun** *Aunt Millie went with her as chaperone* **companion**, duenna, protectress, escort, governess, 'aunt', nursemaid, carer, keeper, protector, bodyguard, minder.
▶ **verb** *she was chaperoned at the ball by her mother* **accompany**, escort, attend, shepherd, watch over, take care of, keep an eye on, protect, defend, guard, safeguard, shield, keep from harm, mind, screen, shelter, mother, nursemaid, nanny.

chapter ▶ **noun 1** *the first chapter of 'Tom Brown's Schooldays'* **section**, division, part, portion, segment, component, bit; instalment.
2 *it was the start of a new chapter in the country's history* **period**, time, phase, page, stage, episode, epoch, era.
3 *the mistake sparked a chapter of errors* **series**, sequence, succession, string, chain, progression, set, course, cycle; spate, wave, stream, rash, outbreak.
4 *a local chapter of the American Cancer Society* **branch**, division, subdivision, section, department, bureau, agency, lodge, wing, arm, offshoot, subsidiary, satellite.
5 *the cathedral chapter requested consultation with other sees* **governing body**, council, assembly, convocation, convention, synod, consistory.

char ▶ **verb** *the flames charred his clothes* **scorch**, burn, singe, sear; blacken, discolour; *informal* toast; *technical* carbonize, calcine; *rare* torrefy.

character ▶ **noun 1** *Jenny had a forceful character | buildings are important to the character of a town* **personality**, nature, disposition, temperament, temper, mentality, turn of mind, psychology, psyche, constitution, make-up, make, stamp, mould, cast; persona; attributes, features, qualities, properties, traits; **essential quality**, essence, sum and substance, individuality, identity, distinctiveness, uniqueness, spirit, ethos, complexion, key, tone, tenor, ambience, air, aura, feel, feeling, vibrations; *informal* kidney; *archaic* humour, grain.
2 *how could any woman of character live with that man?* **integrity**, honour, moral strength, moral fibre, rectitude, uprightness; fortitude, strength, spine, backbone, toughness, resolve, will power, firmness of purpose; *informal* grit, guts, gutsiness, gumption; *Brit. informal* bottle.
3 *no stain will be on his character* **reputation**, name, good name, standing, stature, position, status, image, credibility, acceptability, prestige, cachet, kudos, eminence; *Indian* izzat; *archaic* report.
4 *(informal) John was a bit of a character* **eccentric**, oddity, odd fellow, madcap, crank, original, individualist, nonconformist, rare bird; square peg in a round hole; *informal* oddball, queer fish, odd fish, one; *Brit. informal* odd bod, oner; *informal, dated* card, caution, case; *rare* rara avis.
5 *(informal) her luncheon companion was a boorish character* **individual**, person, personage, figure, party, being, human being, fellow, man, woman, mortal, soul, creature; *informal* fella, sort, type, thing, customer, punter, cookie, bunny, critter; *Brit. informal* bloke, chap, bod, geezer, gent; *N. Amer. informal* guy, gal, dame, dude, hombre; *informal, dated* body, dog; *Brit. vulgar slang* sod, bugger; *archaic* wight.
6 *the characters develop greatly throughout the novel* **persona**, person, role, part; (**characters**) dramatis personae.
7 *the file name must not exceed thirty characters* **letter**, figure, symbol, sign, mark, type, cipher, device, hieroglyph, rune; *technical* grapheme.

characteristic ▶ **noun** *these men have some interesting characteristics* **attribute**, feature, quality, essential quality, property, trait, aspect, element, facet; mannerism, manner, habit, custom, way, mark, trademark, hallmark, distinction; idiosyncrasy, peculiarity, quirk, oddity, foible; penchant, proclivity, bent.
▶ **adjective** *his characteristic eloquence | poor soils are characteristic of the uplands* **typical**, usual, normal, predictable, habitual, in character; **distinctive**, distinguishing, particular, special, especial, individual, specific, peculiar, idiosyncratic, singular, unique, exclusive, unmistakable; representative, symbolic, symptomatic, indicative, diagnostic.
OPPOSITE unusual.

CHOOSE THE RIGHT WORD

characteristic, typical, distinctive

- A **characteristic** feature or quality is one that is immediately recognizable as an essential part of the nature of someone or something (*he has behaved with characteristic generosity | pinnacles of rock are characteristic of this mountain range*).
- Something that is a **typical** member of a class of things has all the central defining features of the members of that class (*a typical example of 1930s Art Deco style | the printing shop is typical of prison industry*). *Typical* is often used to express annoyance at some regular feature or habit (*he didn't turn up, which was absolutely typical*). Only *characteristic* and *typical* are commonly followed by *of*, as in the examples of each above.
- A **distinctive** feature is not necessarily central or typical but serves to distinguish one item or individual from all others (*the system's most distinctive feature is the transferability of votes | she had a distinctive birthmark on her left knee*).

characterize ▶ **verb 1** *the period was characterized by rapid scientific advancement* **distinguish**, make distinctive, mark, set apart, identify, specify, signalize, indicate, denote, designate, stamp; typify, pervade, permeate, suffuse.
2 *the women are typically characterized as prophets of doom* **portray**, depict, present, represent, describe, outline, delineate, show, draw, sketch; categorize, class, classify, style, brand.

charade ▶ **noun** *the race for the presidential nomination has been a shameless charade* **farce**, pantomime, travesty, mockery, parody, pretence, act, masquerade, sham, fake, false display, show, front, facade; *rare* simulacrum.

charge ▶ **verb 1** *he didn't charge much for her flat* **ask in payment**, ask, fix a charge, fix a price, impose, levy; expect, demand, exact; bill, invoice.
2 *the subscription price will be* **charged to** *your account annually* **bill**, put down, debit from, take from.
OPPOSITE credit to.
3 *two men from London were* **charged with** *affray* **accuse of**, indict for, arraign for; prosecute for, try for, bring to trial for, put on trial for; blame for, hold accountable for, implicate in; *N. Amer.* impeach for; *archaic* inculpate.
OPPOSITE absolve.
4 *they charged him with writing a history of the Ottoman dynasty* **entrust**; **burden**, encumber, hamper, saddle, tax, weigh, weigh down, load.
5 *their mounted cavalry charged the advancing tanks* **attack**, storm, rush, assault, assail, open fire on, fall on, set upon, swoop on, descend on, fly at, make an onslaught on, make a raid on; take by storm, attempt to capture; *informal* lay into, tear into.
6 *riot police charged into the crowd* **rush**, move quickly, storm, stampede, career, tear, push, plough, swoop, dive, lunge, launch oneself, throw oneself, go headlong; *informal* steam; *N. Amer. informal* barrel.
OPPOSITE retreat.
7 *please see to it that your glasses are charged | the guns were charged and primed* **fill**, fill up, fill to the brim, top up, stock; load, load up, pack, plug, arm, prepare to fire.
OPPOSITE empty.
8 *his work was charged with a kind of demonic energy* **suffuse**, pervade, permeate, saturate, infuse, imbue, impregnate, inform, infect, inject, fill, load, instil, inspire, affect.
9 *I charge you to stop this course of action* **order**, command, direct, instruct, tell, exhort, enjoin, adjure, demand, require; *literary* bid.
▶ **noun 1** *customers pay a charge for the water consumed | all bus rides were free of charge* **fee**, price, tariff, amount, sum, figure, fare, rate, payment, toll, levy; **cost**, expense, expenditure, outlay, dues.
2 *his client would be pleading not guilty to the charge* **accusation**, allegation, indictment, arraignment, citation, imputation; blame, incrimination; *N. Amer.* impeachment; *N. Amer. informal* beef; *archaic* inculpation.
3 *Miles mustered the 5th Infantry for a charge* **attack**, assault, offensive, onslaught, offence, drive, push, thrust, onrush, sortie, sally, swoop, foray, raid, invasion, incursion, campaign; storming; *German* blitzkrieg; *Italian* razzia; *archaic* onset.
OPPOSITE retreat.
4 *he put Gabriel in the charge of his daughter* **care**, protection, safe keeping, keeping, supervision, surveillance, control, handling; custody, guardianship, tutelage, wardship, protectorship, patronage, trusteeship, auspices, aegis; hands, lap; *archaic* ward.
5 *his charge was to save the paper from bankruptcy* **duty**, responsibility, task, job, obligation, assignment, mission, business, concern, function,

burden, onus; directive, brief, briefing, instruction; *Brit. informal* pigeon; *dated* office.
6 *I am concerned for the safety of my charge* **ward**, protégé, dependant; pupil, trainee, apprentice; minor.
OPPOSITE guardian.
7 *the judge gave a painstakingly careful charge to the jury* **instruction**, direction, directive, order, command, dictate, injunction, exhortation, mandate.
8 (*N. Amer. informal*) *I get a real charge out of working hard* **thrill**, tingle, glow; excitement, stimulation, fun, enjoyment, amusement, pleasure, gratification; *informal* **kick**, buzz, high.
□ **in charge of** *he was in charge of his father's printing works* **responsible for**, in control of, at the helm of, in the driving seat of, at the wheel of; **managing**, running, administering, directing, supervising, overseeing, controlling, commanding, leading, heading up, looking after, taking care of; *informal* running the show, calling the shots.

charisma ▶ **noun** *some managers acquire authority through their personal charisma* **charm**, presence, aura, personality, force of personality, strength of character, individuality; magnetism, animal magnetism, drawing power, attractiveness, appeal, allure, pull; magic, spell, mystique, glamour.

charismatic ▶ **adjective** *a charismatic leader* **charming**, fascinating, full of personality, strong in character; magnetic, mesmerizing, captivating, bewitching, beguiling, attractive, appealing, alluring, hypnotic; magical, glamorous.

charitable ▶ **adjective 1** *she became involved in local charitable activities* **philanthropic**, humanitarian, humane, altruistic, benevolent, beneficent, welfare, public-spirited, socially concerned, doing good works; non-profit-making, non-profit, not-for-profit; *historical* almsgiving; *rare* eleemosynary.
2 *we were fed by some charitable people* **big-hearted**, giving, generous, liberal, open-handed, free-handed, magnanimous, munificent, bountiful; *literary* bounteous; *rare* benignant.
OPPOSITE mean.
3 *he was charitable in his judgements, never censorious* **magnanimous**, generous, generous to a fault, liberal, tolerant, moderate, easy-going, broad-minded, understanding, considerate, sympathetic, lenient, indulgent, forgiving, kind, kindly, compassionate, kind-hearted, tender-hearted, benign, mild, gracious.
OPPOSITE uncharitable.

charity ▶ **noun 1** *they raised money for an AIDS charity* **non-profit-making organization**, non-profit organization, not-for-profit organization, voluntary organization, charitable institution; fund, trust, foundation, cause, movement.
2 *we may be poor but we don't need charity* **financial assistance**, aid, welfare, relief, financial relief, funding; handouts, gifts, presents, largesse, donations, contributions, grants, endowments, scholarships, bursaries, subsidies; patronage; *historical* alms, almsgiving; *rare* donatives, benefactions.
3 *his actions are rooted in self-interest rather than charity* **philanthropy**, humanitarianism, humanity, altruism, public-spiritedness, social conscience, social concern, benevolence, benignity, beneficence, generosity, magnanimity, munificence, largesse; unselfishness, selflessness, self-sacrifice, self-denial.
OPPOSITE selfishness.
4 *show a bit of charity to those less fortunate than you* **goodwill**, compassion, consideration, concern, kindness, kindliness, kind-heartedness, tenderness, tender-heartedness, warm-heartedness, brotherly love, love, sympathy, understanding, fellow feeling, thoughtfulness, indulgence, tolerance, liberality, decency, nobility, graciousness, lenience, leniency; *literary* bounty, bounteousness; *rare* caritas.
OPPOSITE meanness.

charlatan ▶ **noun** *they denounced him as a corrupt charlatan* **quack**, mountebank, sham, fraud, fake, humbug, impostor, pretender, masquerader, hoodwinker, hoaxer, cheat, deceiver, dissembler, double-dealer, double-crosser, trickster, confidence trickster, cheater, swindler, fraudster, racketeer; rogue, villain, scoundrel; *informal* phoney, sharper, sharp, shark, con man, con artist, hustler, flimflammer, flimflam man; *Brit. informal* twister; *N. Amer. informal* grifter, bunco artist, gold brick, chiseller; *Austral. informal* shicer, magsman, illywhacker; *S. African informal* schlenter; *dated* confidence man/woman; *rare* defalcator, tregetour.

charm ▶ **noun 1** *people were captivated by her charm | she was resistant to his charms* **attractiveness**, beauty, glamour, prettiness, loveliness; appeal, allure, desirability, seductiveness, magnetism, sexual magnetism, animal magnetism, charisma; wiles, blandishments, enticement; *Scottish & N. English* bonniness; *informal* gorgeousness, pulling power, come-on; *formal* beauteousness; *archaic* comeliness.
OPPOSITE unattractiveness.
2 *these traditional stories retain a lot of charm* **appeal**, pull, draw, drawing power, attraction, allure, fascination, captivation, pleasingness, engagingness, delightfulness.
3 *they seek supernatural assistance through magical charms* **spell**, incantation, conjuration, rune, magic formula, magic word, abracadabra, jinx; sorcery, magic, witchcraft, wizardry; *N. Amer.* mojo, hex; *NZ* makutu.
4 *he took the charms from his wife's bracelet* **ornament**, trinket, bauble; *archaic* bijou.
5 *he always carries a lucky charm* **talisman**, fetish, amulet, mascot, totem, idol, juju; *archaic* periapt; *rare* phylactery.
▶ **verb 1** *he charmed thousands with his singing* **delight**, please, win, win over, appeal to, attract, captivate, allure, lure, draw, dazzle, fascinate, bewitch, beguile, enchant, enthral, enrapture, enamour, seduce, ravish, hypnotize, mesmerize, spellbind, transfix, rivet, grip; *rare* rapture.
OPPOSITE repel.
2 *he charmed his mother into letting him have his own way* **coax**, cajole, wheedle; woo; *informal* sweet-talk, soft-soap; *archaic* blandish.

charming ▶ **adjective** *he stayed with a French family and their charming daughter* **delightful**, pleasing, pleasant, agreeable, likeable, endearing, lovely, lovable, adorable, cute, sweet, appealing, attractive, good-looking, prepossessing; striking, alluring, delectable, ravishing, winning, winsome, fetching, captivating, engaging, enchanting, entrancing, fascinating, bewitching, beguiling, spellbinding, hypnotizing, mesmerizing, seductive, desirable, tempting, inviting, irresistible; *informal* dreamy, heavenly, divine, gorgeous, smashing, easy on the eye, as nice as pie; *N. Amer. informal* babelicious, bodacious; *dated* taking; *literary* beauteous; *archaic* fair, comely.
OPPOSITE repulsive.

chart ▶ **noun 1** *check your height and ideal weight on the chart* **graph**, table, tabulation, grid, histogram, diagram, guide, scheme, figure, illustration; bar chart, pie chart, flow chart; map, plan, blueprint; *Computing* graphic.
2 (**charts**) *the song went straight to the top of the pop charts* **hit parade**, top twenty; list, listing, league, catalogue, index.
▶ **verb 1** *the population increase can be charted fairly accurately* **tabulate**, plot, graph, delineate, map, map out, draw up, sketch, draft, document, record, register, represent; make a chart of, make a diagram of.
2 *the book charted his passage through Chicago* **follow**, trace, outline, describe, detail, note, report, record, register, document, chronicle, log, catalogue.

charter ▶ **noun 1** *the company is operating under Royal charter* **authority**, authorization, sanction, covenant, dispensation, consent, permission, sufferance; prerogative, privilege, right; *Law, historical* droit.
2 *they violated the principles of the UN Charter* **constitution**, code, canon, body of law, system of rules; fundamental principles, rules, laws.
3 *there is a fee for the independent charter of yachts* **hire**, hiring, lease, leasing, rent, rental, renting, booking, reservation, reserving; *dated* engaging, engagement; *rare* bespeaking.
4 *Henry II granted him a charter to hold a market* **permit**, licence, warrant, warranty, deed, bond, document, indenture; concession, franchise, privilege.
▶ **verb** *they chartered a train for the trip to Milwaukee* **hire**, lease, rent, pay for the use of, book, reserve; *dated* engage; *rare* bespeak.

chary ▶ **adjective** *he was chary of broaching the subject* **wary**, cautious, circumspect, heedful, careful, on one's guard, guarded, mindful, watchful; distrustful, mistrustful, doubtful, sceptical, suspicious, dubious, hesitant, reluctant, disinclined, loath, averse, shy, nervous, apprehensive, uneasy, afraid; *informal* leery, cagey, iffy, on one's toes.
OPPOSITE heedless.

chase[1] ▶ **verb 1** *the attacker chased Mr Lee into an alley | the dogs chased after the fox* **pursue**, run after, follow, hunt, track, trail; give chase to, be hot on someone's heels; *informal* tail.
OPPOSITE run away from.
2 *Jim had been chasing young girls for years* **court**, woo, pursue, run after, seek the company of, make advances to, make up to, flirt with, romance; *informal* chat up, make (sheep's) eyes at, give the come-on to, come on to, be all over; *Austral. informal* track with, track square with; *dated* set one's cap at, pay addresses to, pay suit to, pay court to, seek the hand of, make love to; *archaic* spark.
3 *she* **chased away** *some donkeys from her garden* **drive away**, drive off, drive out, put to flight, send away, scare off, scatter; *informal* send packing.
4 *she* **chased away** *all thoughts of him* **dispel**, banish, dismiss, drive away, drive off, shut out, put out of one's mind.
OPPOSITE conjure up.
5 *photographers chased on to the runway to photograph him* **rush**, dash, race, speed, streak, shoot, charge, career, scramble, scurry, hurry, make haste, hare, fly, pelt; *informal* scoot, belt, tear, zip, whip, go like a bat out of hell; *N. Amer. informal* boogie, hightail, clip; *N. Amer. vulgar slang* drag/tear/haul ass; *informal, dated* cut along; *archaic* post, hie.
OPPOSITE amble.
□ **chase someone/something up** *his job includes chasing up slow payers* **pester**, harass, harry, nag, plague, hound; seek out, find, go after, follow up; *informal* hassle.
▶ **noun** *the predator finally gave up the chase* **pursuit**, hunt, trail; hunting, coursing, course.

chase[2] ▶ **verb** *figures are chased in low relief on the dish* **engrave**, etch, carve, inscribe, cut, chisel, imprint, impress, print, mark.

chasm ▶ noun **1** *the ground dropped away into an awesome chasm* **gorge**, abyss, canyon, ravine, gully, gulf, pass, defile, couloir, crevasse, cleft, rift, rent; pit, void, crater, cavity, hole, opening, gap, fissure, crevice, hollow; *S. English* chine, bunny; *N. English* clough, gill, thrutch; *Scottish* cleuch, heugh; *N. Amer.* gulch, coulee, flume; *American Spanish* arroyo, barranca, quebrada; *Indian* nullah, khud; *S. African* sloot, kloof, donga; *rare* khor.
2 *the chasm between pluralist and Marxist views* **breach**, gulf, rift; division, schism, split, severance, rupture, break, break-up, parting of the ways; separation, disunion, estrangement, alienation, difference, dissension, discord, argument, quarrel; *rare* scission.

chassis ▶ noun *rubber tyres help to reduce shocks on the chassis* **framework**, frame, skeleton, shell, casing, structure, substructure, bodywork, body; fuselage, hull, keel; anatomy, carcass.

chaste ▶ adjective **1** *the dress gave her a look of chaste girlhood* **virginal**, virgin, intact, maidenly, maiden, unmarried, unwed; celibate, abstinent, self-restrained, self-denying, nunlike; **innocent**, pure, pure as the driven snow, guiltless, sinless, free of sin, uncorrupted, incorrupt, uncontaminated, undefiled, unsullied; virtuous, good, decent, moral, proper, decorous, demure, modest, wholesome, upright; *informal* squeaky clean; *Christianity* immaculate; *literary* vestal; *rare* continent.
OPPOSITES promiscuous, immoral.
2 *he gave her a chaste kiss on the cheek* **non-sexual**, friendly, platonic, innocent.
OPPOSITE passionate.
3 *the dark, chaste interior was lightened by tilework* **plain**, simple, bare, unadorned, undecorated, unornamented, unembellished, restrained, unaffected, unpretentious, unfussy, uncluttered, functional, without frills, spartan, austere, ascetic, monastic; *informal* no-frills.
OPPOSITE ostentatious.

chasten ▶ verb **1** *both men were chastened by the bitter lessons of life* **subdue**, humble, cow, squash, deflate, flatten, bring down, bring low, take down a peg or two, humiliate, mortify; restrain, tame, curb, check; *informal* cut down to size, put down, put someone in their place, settle someone's hash.
2 (*archaic*) *we love the Heaven that chastens us* **discipline**, punish, penalize, castigate, chastise, chide, scold, upbraid, berate, reprimand, reprove, rebuke, take to task, bring to book, teach someone a lesson; *N. Amer. informal* make someone eat crow; *archaic* recompense, visit.

chastise ▶ verb **1** *the staff were chastised for arriving late* **scold**, upbraid, berate, reprimand, reprove, rebuke, admonish, chide, censure, castigate, lambaste, lecture, criticize, pull up, take to task, haul over the coals, bring to book; *informal* tell off, give someone a telling-off, dress down, give someone a dressing-down, bawl out, blow up at, give someone an earful, give someone a caning, give someone a roasting, give someone a rocket, give someone a rollicking, come down on someone like a ton of bricks, have someone's guts for garters, slap someone's wrist, rap over the knuckles, give someone a piece of one's mind, throw the book at, read someone the Riot Act, let someone have it, give someone hell; *Brit. informal* carpet, tear someone off a strip, tick off, have a go at, give someone a mouthful, give someone what for, give someone some stick, give someone a wigging; *N. Amer. informal* chew out, ream out; *Austral. informal* monster; *Brit. vulgar slang* bollock, give someone a bollocking; *dated* trim, rate, give someone a rating; *archaic* chasten, recompense, visit; *rare* reprehend, objurgate.
OPPOSITE praise.
2 (*dated*) *her mistress chastised her with a whip* **punish**, discipline; **beat**, thrash, flog, whip, horsewhip, strap, belt, cane, lash, birch, scourge, flay, flagellate; *informal* wallop, thump, clout, tan, tan someone's hide, beat the living daylights out of someone, give someone a good hiding.

chastity ▶ noun *the Vestals were sworn to a life of chastity* **celibacy**, chasteness, virginity, abstinence, self-restraint, self-denial; singleness, maidenhood, the unmarried state; innocence, purity, virtue, goodness, decency, morality, decorum, modesty, wholesomeness; *Christianity* immaculateness; *rare* continence.
OPPOSITES promiscuity, immorality.

chat ▶ noun *I popped into Gill's house for a chat* **talk**, conversation, gossip, chatter, heart-to-heart, tête-à-tête, powwow, blether, blather; conference, discussion, dialogue, exchange; *Indian* adda; *informal* jaw, gas, confab; *Brit. informal* natter, chinwag, rabbit; *Scottish & N. English informal* crack; *N. Amer. informal* rap, bull session, gabfest; *formal* confabulation; *rare* colloquy.
▶ verb *they sat and chatted with their guests* **talk**, gossip, chatter, speak, converse, have a conversation, engage in conversation, tittle-tattle, prattle, jabber, jibber-jabber, babble, prate, go on, run on; communicate; *Brit.* talk nineteen to the dozen; *Scottish & Irish* slabber; *informal* gas, have a confab, jaw, chew the rag, chew the fat, yap, yak, yackety-yak, yabber, yatter, yammer, powwow; *Brit. informal* natter, witter, rabbit, chunter, waffle, have a chinwag, chinwag; *N. Amer. informal* shoot the breeze, shoot the bull, visit; *Austral./NZ informal* mag; *formal* confabulate; *archaic* twaddle, twattle, clack, claver.
□ **chat someone up** (*informal*) *he cornered her in the canteen and tried to chat her up* **flirt with**, make up to, make advances to, make overtures to, romance; *informal* come on to, give the come-on to, make (sheep's) eyes at, be all over; *dated* make love to, set one's cap at.

chatter ▶ noun *she had often tired him with her chatter* **chat**, talk, gossip, chit-chat, chitter-chatter, patter, jabbering, jabber, prattling, prattle, babbling, babble, tittle-tattle, tattle, blathering, blather, blethering, blether, rambling, gibbering; conversation, dialogue, discourse; *informal* gab, yak, yackety-yak, yabbering, yammering, yattering, yapping, jawing, chewing the fat, chewing the rag, confab; *Brit. informal* chinwagging, nattering, wittering, waffling, waffle, chuntering, rabbiting on; *formal* confabulation; *archaic* clack, claver, twaddle, twattle; *rare* colloquy.
▶ verb *they chattered excitedly throughout the journey.* See CHAT.

chatterbox ▶ noun (*informal*) *Nicola was known as a chatterbox at work* **talker**, chatterer, jabberer, babbler, prattler, blatherer, bletherer, prater; tittle-tattler, tattler, gossip, gossiper, gossipmonger; conversationalist; *N. Amer.* blatherskite; *informal* windbag, gasbag, gabber, big mouth, loudmouth, blabbermouth; *Brit. informal* natterer.

chatty ▶ adjective **1** *he was in an unusually chatty mood* **talkative**, communicative, expansive, forthcoming, open, unreserved, gossipy, gossiping, garrulous, loquacious, voluble, verbose, effusive, gushing, glib; *informal* mouthy, gabby, windy, gassy; *Brit. informal* able to talk the hind legs off a donkey; *rare* multiloquent, multiloquous.
OPPOSITE taciturn.
2 *she received a long chatty letter from Ellen* **conversational**, gossipy, informal, casual, colloquial, familiar, friendly; lively; *informal* newsy.
OPPOSITE formal.

> CHOOSE THE RIGHT WORD
>
> **chatty, talkative, loquacious, garrulous**
>
> *See* TALKATIVE.

chauvinism ▶ noun *they have a tendency towards small-mindedness and chauvinism* **jingoism**, excessive patriotism, blind patriotism, excessive nationalism, sectarianism, isolationism, excessive loyalty, flag-waving, xenophobia, racism, racialism, racial prejudice, ethnocentrism, ethnocentricity; **partisanship**, partiality, prejudice, bias, discrimination, intolerance, bigotry; male chauvinism, sexism, misogyny.

chauvinist ▶ adjective *pamphlets expressing chauvinist and nationalist sentiments* **jingoistic**, chauvinistic, excessively patriotic, excessively nationalistic, sectarian, isolationist, flag-waving, xenophobic, racist, racialist, ethnocentric; **partisan**, partial, prejudiced, biased, discriminating, discriminatory, intolerant, bigoted; **sexist**, male chauvinist, misogynist, woman-hating, anti-feminist, male supremacist; *French* parti pris.
▶ noun *he learned to show women some respect, but he's still a chauvinist* **sexist**, male chauvinist, misogynist, woman-hater, anti-feminist, male supremacist; *informal* male chauvinist pig, MCP.

cheap ▶ adjective **1** *the firm are offering cheap day trips to London* **inexpensive**, low-priced, low-price, low-cost, economical, economic, competitive, affordable, reasonable, reasonably priced, moderately priced, keenly priced, budget, economy, cheap and cheerful, bargain, cut-rate, cut-price, half-price, sale-price, sale, reduced, on special offer, marked down, discounted, discount, rock-bottom, giveaway; *informal* bargain-basement, slashed, going for a song, dirt cheap.
OPPOSITE expensive.
2 *the dashboard is plain without looking cheap* **poor-quality**, second-rate, third-rate, substandard, low-grade, inferior, common, vulgar, shoddy, trashy, rubbishy, tawdry, tinny, brassy, worthless, meretricious, cheap and nasty, cheapjack, gimcrack, Brummagem, pinchbeck; *informal* cheapo, junky, tacky, kitsch, not up to much; *Brit. informal* naff, duff, ropy, grotty, rubbish, twopenny-halfpenny; *N. Amer. informal* a dime a dozen, tinhorn, two-bit, dime-store; *Brit. vulgar slang* crap, crappy; *N. Amer. vulgar slang* chickenshit; *archaic* trumpery.
OPPOSITE high-class.
3 *I disliked this film and its cheap exploitation of suffering* **despicable**, contemptible, low, base, immoral, unscrupulous, unprincipled, unsavoury, distasteful, unpleasant, mean, shabby, sordid, vulgar, tawdry, low-minded, dishonourable, discreditable, ignoble, sorry, shameful; *Brit. informal* beastly; *archaic* scurvy.
OPPOSITE admirable.
4 *he made me feel cheap* **ashamed**, embarrassed, humiliated, mortified, abashed, debased, degraded.
5 (*N. Amer. informal*) *he was so generous he made the other guests look cheap. See* MEAN[2].

cheapen ▶ verb **1** *he needed to cheapen the costs of his raw materials* **reduce**, lower, lower in price, cut, mark down, discount, depreciate, devalue, depress, put down, keep down; *informal* slash, axe.
OPPOSITE raise.
2 *Hetty never compromised or cheapened herself* **demean**, debase, degrade, lower, humble, devalue, drag down, abase, discredit, disgrace, dishonour, shame, humiliate, mortify, betray, prostitute; belittle, diminish, depreciate, denigrate, derogate; sell out, abandon one's principles, be untrue to oneself.

C

cheat ▶ verb **1** *customers were cheated by unscrupulous retailers* **swindle**, defraud, deceive, trick, dupe, hoodwink, double-cross, gull; short-change; exploit, take advantage of, victimize; *informal* do, diddle, rip off, con, bamboozle, rob, fleece, shaft, sting, have, bilk, rook, gyp, finagle, flimflam, put one over on, pull a fast one on, take for a ride, lead up the garden path, sell down the river, pull the wool over someone's eyes; *N. Amer. informal* sucker, snooker, goldbrick, gouge, stiff, give someone a bum steer; *Austral. informal* pull a swifty on; *Brit. informal, dated* rush; *archaic* cozen, chicane, sell; *rare* illude, mulct.
2 *she cheated Ryan out of his fortune* **deprive of**, deny, prevent from gaining, preclude from gaining; rob of, do out of.
3 *a schoolboy cheated death when he was struck by lightning* **avoid**, escape, evade, elude, steer clear of, dodge, duck, miss, sidestep, bypass, skirt, shun, eschew; foil, frustrate, thwart, baulk, defeat.
4 *sixty per cent of husbands have cheated at least once* **commit adultery**, be unfaithful, stray, be untrue, be inconstant, be false; *informal* two-time, play away, play around.
▶ noun **1** *he called the principal witness a liar and a cheat* **swindler**, cheater, fraudster, trickster, confidence trickster, deceiver, hoaxer, hoodwinker, double-dealer, double-crosser, sham, fraud, fake, crook, rogue, charlatan, quack, mountebank, racketeer; *informal* con man, con artist, shark, sharper, phoney, hustler, flimflammer, flimflam man; *Brit. informal* twister; *N. Amer. informal* grifter, bunco artist, gold brick, chiseller; *Austral. informal* shicer, magsman, illywhacker; *S. African informal* schlenter; *dated* confidence man, confidence woman; *rare* defalcator, tregetour.
2 *Is there a sure cheat for generating cash?* **swindle**, fraud, deception, deceit, hoax, sham, trick, ruse, dodge, stratagem, blind, wile, Trojan horse; trickery, imposture, artifice, subterfuge; *informal* con, leg-pull.

check ▶ verb **1** *troops set up a road block and checked all vehicles | I checked up on your background* **examine**, inspect, look at, look over, scrutinize, scan, survey; study, investigate, research, probe, dissect, explore, look into, enquire into, go into, go over with a fine-tooth comb; check out, test, monitor, review; *informal* give something a/the once-over, give something a look-see, give something a going-over.
2 *he checked that the gun was cocked* **make sure**, confirm, verify, corroborate, validate, substantiate.
3 *two successive defeats checked their progress* **halt**, stop, arrest, bring to a standstill, cut short; bar, obstruct, hamper, impede, inhibit, frustrate, foil, thwart, stand in the way of, prevent, curb, block, stall, hold up, interfere with, retard, delay, slow down, brake, put a brake on; stem, staunch; *archaic* stay.
4 *her tears could not be checked* **suppress**, repress, restrain, contain, control, curb, rein in, bridle, smother, muffle, stifle, keep in check, hold back, swallow, choke back, fight back, bite back, bottle up; *informal* nip in the bud, keep a lid on.
OPPOSITE release.
□ **check in** *at the airport they check in at a special desk* **report**, report one's arrival, record one's arrival, book oneself in, book in, enrol, register.
□ **check out** *she checked out of the hotel without saying goodbye* **leave**, vacate, depart from, exit from, take one's leave from; pay the bill, pay up, settle up.
□ **check something out** (*informal*) **1** *the police have checked out dozens of leads* **investigate**, look into, enquire into, probe, research, sound out, examine, go over, go through, vet; assess, weigh up, analyse, evaluate; follow up; *informal* suss out, recce, give something a/the once-over, give something a going-over; *N. Amer. informal* scope out; *rare* anatomize.
2 *she checked herself out in the mirror* **look at**, observe, survey, gaze at, regard, inspect, contemplate; take note of; *informal* have a gander at, have a squint at, get a load of; *Brit. informal* take a dekko at, have a butcher's at, take a shufti at, clock; *N. Amer. informal* eyeball.
▶ noun **1** *they did an official check of the records* **examination**, inspection, scrutiny, scrutinization, check-up, perusal, study, investigation, probe, dissection, analysis, assessment, enquiry; test, trial, assay, monitoring; *informal* once-over, going-over, look-see; *rare* anatomization.
2 *a permanent check on the abuse of authority* **control**, restraint, constraint, break, bridle, curb, deterrent, hindrance, impediment, obstruction, inhibition, limitation.
3 (*N. Amer.*) *the waitress arrived with the check* **bill**, account, invoice, statement, list of charges, tally; amount due; *informal* the damage; *N. Amer. informal* tab; *Brit. informal, dated* shot; *archaic* reckoning, score.
□ **keep something in check** *I strive to keep my temper in check* **curb**, restrain, hold back, keep under control, keep a tight rein on, bridle, rein in, rein back; control, govern, master, repress, suppress, subdue, stifle, smother, tone down; *informal* keep a lid on, nip in the bud.

check-up ▶ noun *you should go to the hospital for a check-up* **examination**, inspection, assessment, evaluation, analysis, survey, scan, scrutinization, scrutiny, observation, exploration, probe, test, appraisal; check, health check; *informal* once-over, going-over, overhaul.

cheek ▶ noun **1** *he kissed her on the cheek* jowl, chop, chap.
2 *he had the cheek to suggest I was too old | less of the cheek, if you don't mind* **impudence**, impertinence, insolence, cheekiness, audacity, temerity, brazenness, presumption, effrontery, nerve, gall, pertness, boldness, shamelessness, impoliteness, disrespect, bad manners, unmannerliness, overfamiliarity; answering back, talking back; *informal* brass, brass neck, neck, face, lip, mouth, cockiness; *Brit. informal* sauce; *Scottish informal* snash; *N. Amer. informal* sass, sassiness, nerviness, chutzpah, back talk; *informal, dated* hide; *Brit. informal, dated* crust, backchat; *archaic* malapertness, contumely; *rare* procacity, assumption.
OPPOSITE politeness.
▶ verb (*informal*) *they were told off for cheeking the dinner lady* **answer back to**, talk back to, be cheeky to, be impertinent to; contradict, argue with, disagree with; *informal* backchat; *N. Amer. informal* sass, be sassy to.

WORD LINKS
relating to the cheek **buccal, malar**

cheeky ▶ adjective *you should have heard the cheeky boy lecturing me* **impudent**, impertinent, insolent, presumptuous, forward, pert, bold, bold as brass, brazen, brazen-faced, shameless, audacious, overfamiliar, irreverent, discourteous, disrespectful, insubordinate, impolite, bad-mannered, ill-mannered, unmannerly, rude, insulting; *informal* brass-necked, cocky, lippy, mouthy, fresh, flip; *Brit. informal* saucy, smart-arsed; *N. Amer. informal* sassy, nervy, smart-assed; *archaic* malapert, contumelious, presumptive, assumptive; *rare* tossy, mannerless.
OPPOSITES respectful, polite.

cheep ▶ verb *the chicks cheeped loudly and paddled for shelter* **chirp**, chirrup, twitter, tweet, peep, chitter, chatter, chirr, trill, warble, sing, pipe.
▶ noun *the bird gave a shrill cheep* **chirp**, chirrup, twitter, tweet, peep, chirr, warble, trill.

cheer ▶ noun **1** *she acknowledged the cheers of the onlookers* **hurrah**, hurray, whoop, bravo, hoot, shout, shriek; hosanna, alleluia; (**cheers**) acclaim, acclamation, shouting, clamour, applause, clapping, ovation; *informal* holler; *rare* laudation; *archaic* huzza.
OPPOSITE boo.
2 *Christmas and New Year are a time of cheer* **happiness**, joy, joyousness, cheerfulness, cheeriness, gladness, merriment, gaiety, hilarity, mirth, glee, blitheness, jubilation, exultation, euphoria, jollity, jolliness, high spirits, joviality, jocularity, conviviality, light-heartedness, buoyancy, optimism, hope, hopefulness; merrymaking, pleasure, enjoyment, rejoicing, revelry, festivity, frolics; *informal* larking about, living it up; *dated* sport.
OPPOSITES sadness, doom and gloom.
3 *the table was groaning with Christmas cheer* **fare**, food, foodstuffs, eatables, provisions, rations, sustenance, meat; drink, beverages; *informal* eats, nibbles, nosh, grub, chow; *Brit. informal* scoff, scran; *N. Amer. informal* chuck; *archaic* viands, victuals, vittles, commons; *rare* comestibles, provender, aliment, commissariat, viaticum.
▶ verb **1** *they'll all be at Lords to cheer their cricket team* **acclaim**, hail, salute, praise, congratulate, toast, hurrah, hurray, applaud, clap, shout for, whistle; honour, glorify; express approval of, express admiration for, show one's appreciation of, put one's hands together for; *informal* root for, holler for, give someone a big hand, bring the house down; *N. Amer. informal* ballyhoo; *black English* big someone/something up; *archaic* emblazon; *rare* laud, panegyrize.
OPPOSITE boo.
2 *the bad weather did little to cheer me* **raise someone's spirits**, brighten, buoy up, enliven, animate, elate, exhilarate, hearten, gladden, uplift, give a lift to, perk up, encourage, comfort, solace, console; *informal* buck up; *rare* inspirit.
OPPOSITE depress.
□ **cheer someone on** *knots of spectators were there to cheer me on* **encourage**, urge on, spur on, drive on, motivate, rally, inspire, fire, fire up; give someone a lift, keep someone going, see someone through; *N. Amer. informal* root for, light a fire under; *rare* inspirit.
OPPOSITE discourage.
□ **cheer up** *once I got inside the house I began to cheer up* **perk up**, brighten (up), become more cheerful, pick up, liven up, become livelier, rally, revive, bounce back, take heart, be heartened, take on a new lease of life; *informal* buck up.
OPPOSITE feel depressed.
□ **cheer someone up** *I asked her out to lunch to cheer her up* **raise someone's spirits**, make happier, make more cheerful, buoy up, perk up, enliven, animate, hearten, gladden, uplift, give a lift to, encourage; comfort, solace, console; *informal* buck up, pep up; *rare* inspirit.
OPPOSITE depress.

cheerful ▶ adjective **1** *he arrived looking relaxed and cheerful* **happy**, jolly, merry, bright, glad, sunny, joyful, joyous, light-hearted, in good spirits, in high spirits, sparkling, bubbly, exuberant, ebullient, cock-a-hoop, elated, gleeful, breezy, airy, cheery, sprightly, jaunty, animated, radiant, smiling, grinning, laughing, mirthful, frolicsome; jovial, genial, good-humoured; happy-go-lucky, carefree, unworried, untroubled, without a care in the world, full of the joys of spring; buoyant, optimistic, hopeful, full of hope, positive; content, contented; *informal* upbeat, chipper, chirpy, peppy, smiley, sparky, zippy, zingy, bright-eyed and bushy-tailed, full of beans, full of vim and vigour; *N. Amer. informal* peart; *dated* gay; *literary* jocund, gladsome, blithe, blithesome; *archaic* of good cheer.
OPPOSITE sad.

2 *primary colours make for a cheerful family room* **pleasant**, attractive, agreeable, cheering, uplifting, bright, sunny, happy, friendly, welcoming, homelike, comfortable; *informal* comfy.
OPPOSITE cheerless.
3 *he supported our scheme with cheerful generosity* **eager**, keen, enthusiastic, happy, glad, ready, willing, obliging, cooperative, compliant, complying, acquiescent, agreeing, assenting, ungrudging; *informal* game.
OPPOSITE unwilling.

cheerio ▶ exclamation (*Brit. informal*) *My car's at the door. Cheerio!* **goodbye**, farewell, adieu; *S. African* check you; *Austral./NZ* hooray; *French* au revoir; *German* auf Wiedersehen; *Italian* ciao; *Spanish* adios; *Japanese* sayonara; *Latin* vale; *informal* bye, bye-bye, so long, see you, see you later, catch you later; *Brit. informal* cheers, ta-ta; *N. English informal* ta-ra; *N. Amer. informal* later, laters; *informal, dated* pip pip, toodle-oo.

cheerless ▶ adjective *his office was grey and cheerless* **gloomy**, dreary, dull, dismal, bleak, drab, grim, sombre, dark, dim, dingy, funereal; austere, stark, bare, desolate, comfortless; miserable, wretched, joyless, unhappy, depressing, disheartening, dispiriting, unwelcoming, uninviting, inhospitable, bland, clinical, institutional, impersonal.
OPPOSITES cheerful, cosy.

cheers ▶ exclamation 1 (*informal*) *he raised his glass and said 'Cheers!'* **here's to you**, good health, your health, here's health, skol, good luck; *Irish* slainte; *German* prost, prosit; *French* salut; *Spanish* salud; *informal* bottoms up, down the hatch; *Brit. informal* here's mud in your eye; *Brit. informal, dated* cheerio, chin-chin, here's how.
2 (*Brit. informal*) *Cheers, Jack, see you in church!* **goodbye**, farewell, adieu; *S. African* check you; *Austral./NZ* hooray; *French* au revoir; *German* auf Wiedersehen; *Italian* ciao; *Spanish* adios; *Japanese* sayonara; *Latin* vale; *informal* bye, bye-bye, so long, see you, see you later, catch you later; *Brit. informal* cheerio, ta-ta; *N. English informal* ta-ra; *N. Amer. informal* later, laters; *informal, dated* pip pip, toodle-oo.
3 (*Brit. informal*) *cheers for listening to me* **thanks**, many thanks, thanks a lot, thank you, thank you kindly, much obliged, much appreciated, bless you; *informal* thanks a million; *Brit. informal* ta.

cheery ▶ adjective *Gareth was a cheery, ever-smiling boy* **jolly**, happy, merry, bright, cheerful, glad, sunny, joyful, joyous, light-hearted, in high spirits, sparkling, bubbly, exuberant, ebullient, cock-a-hoop, elated, blissful, ecstatic, euphoric, gleeful, breezy, airy, sprightly, jaunty, animated, radiant, smiling, grinning, laughing, mirthful, frolicsome; happy-go-lucky, in good spirits, carefree, unworried, untroubled, without a care in the world, full of the joys of spring; buoyant, optimistic, hopeful, full of hope, positive, content; *informal* upbeat, chipper, chirpy, smiley, peppy, sparky, zippy, zingy, bright-eyed and bushy-tailed, full of beans, full of vim and vigour; *N. Amer. informal* peart; *dated* gay; *literary* gladsome, jocund, blithe, blithesome; *archaic* of good cheer.
OPPOSITE gloomy.

cheese ▶ noun. *See centre pages for list of* **Cheeses**

WORD LINKS
relating to cheese **caseous**
seller of cheese **cheesemonger**

chef ▶ noun *he worked as a chef for a catering company* **cook**, cordon bleu cook, food preparer; head chef, sous chef, commis chef, chef de cuisine, chef de partie; pastry cook, saucier; *N. Amer. informal* short-order cook.

chef-d'œuvre ▶ noun (*French*) *his chef-d'œuvre was his biography of George Washington* **masterpiece**, masterwork, best work, finest work, greatest creation, crowning achievement, work of art; treasure, gem, pearl, jewel, jewel in the crown; *Latin* magnum opus; *French* pièce de résistance, tour de force.

chemical ▶ noun. *See centre pages for lists of* **Acids** **Chemicals** **Compounds** **Elements** **Poisonous Substances and Gases** **Sugars** **Vitamins**

chequered ▶ adjective 1 *he wore short chequered breeches* **checked**, multicoloured, many-coloured, harlequin, varicoloured, particoloured.
2 *the corporation has had a chequered history* **varied**, mixed, eventful, full of ups and downs, up and down, with good and bad parts, with its fair share of rough and tumble; unsettled, unstable, irregular, erratic, inconstant, fluctuating, changeful; diverse, diversified, many-faceted; *rare* vicissitudinous.

cherish ▶ verb 1 *he was cherished by a wide circle of friends* **adore**, hold dear, love, care very much for, feel great affection for, dote on, be devoted to, revere, esteem, admire, appreciate; think the world of, set great store by, hold in high esteem; **care for**, look after, tend, protect, preserve, shelter, keep safe, support, nurture, cosset, indulge; *informal* put on a pedestal.
2 *I cherish the letters she wrote* **treasure**, prize, value highly, hold dear.
OPPOSITE neglect.
3 *they cherished dreams of football glory* **harbour**, have, possess, hold (on to), cling to, entertain, retain, maintain, keep in one's mind, foster, nurture, nurse.
OPPOSITE abandon.

cherub ▶ noun 1 *she was borne up to heaven by cherubs* **angel**, seraph.
2 *the picture showed a wistful cherub of 18 months* **baby**, infant, toddler, little one; **pretty child**, lovable child, well behaved child, innocent child; little angel, little dear, little darling; *informal* kid, tot, tiny tot, tiny; *literary* babe, babe in arms.

cherubic ▶ adjective *his cherubic face creased into a wide grin* **angelic**; sweet, cute, attractive, adorable, appealing, lovable, lovely; innocent, seraphic, saintly; *informal* butter-wouldn't-melt.

chest ▶ noun 1 *he had several bullet wounds in his chest* **breast**, upper body, body, torso, trunk; *technical* thorax, sternum.
2 *the matron had a phenomenally large chest* **bust**, bosom; *archaic* embonpoint.
3 *they took logs from a metal-bound oak chest* **box**, case, casket, crate, trunk, coffer, strongbox; container, receptacle.
□ **get something off one's chest** (*informal*) **confess**, disclose, divulge, reveal, make known, make public, own up to, make a clean breast of, bring into the open, tell all about, say what one is thinking; get a load off one's mind, unburden oneself; *informal* spill the beans about, come out with it; *archaic* discover.
OPPOSITE bottle something up.

WORD LINKS
relating to the chest **pectoral, thoracic**
surgical incision of the chest **thoracotomy**

chew ▶ verb *Carolyn chewed a mouthful of toast* **masticate**, munch, champ, chomp, crunch, bite, nibble, gnaw, grind; eat, consume, devour; *technical* manducate, triturate; *rare* chumble.
□ **chew something over** *the doctor chewed over possible responses* **meditate on**, ruminate on, think about, think over, think through, mull over, contemplate, consider, weigh up, ponder on, deliberate on, reflect on, muse on, cogitate about, dwell on, take stock of, give thought to, turn over in one's mind, consider the pros and cons of; brood over, wrestle with, puzzle over, rack one's brains about; *N. Amer.* think on; *informal* kick around/about, bat around/about; *archaic* pore on; *rare* cerebrate.
□ **chew the fat/rag** (*informal*) *he liked drinking with friends and chewing the fat* **chat**, talk, converse, speak to each other, discuss things, have a talk, have a chat, have a tête-à-tête, have a conversation; *informal* have a confab, jaw, rap, yak, yap; *Brit. informal* natter, rabbit, have a chinwag, chinwag; *N. Amer. informal* shoot the breeze, shoot the bull, visit; *Austral./NZ informal* mag; *formal* confabulate.

chic ▶ adjective *she wore a chic black costume and white wrap* **stylish**, smart, elegant, sophisticated, dapper, debonair, dashing, trim, tasteful, understated, attractive, flattering; **fashionable**, high-fashion, modish, voguish, in vogue, up to date, up to the minute, ultra-modern, contemporary; *French* à la mode; *informal* trendy, with it, now, sharp, snappy, snazzy, natty, dressy, swish; *N. Amer. informal* fly, spiffy, sassy, kicky, tony; *archaic* trig.
OPPOSITE unfashionable.

chicanery ▶ noun *political chicanery of all sorts goes on behind closed doors* **trickery**, deception, deceit, deceitfulness, duplicity, dishonesty, unscrupulousness, underhandedness, subterfuge, fraud, fraudulence, legerdemain, sophistry, sharp practice, skulduggery, swindling, cheating, duping, hoodwinking; deviousness, guile, intrigue, craft, craftiness, artfulness, slyness, wiles; misleading talk; *informal* crookedness, monkey business, funny business, hanky-panky, shenanigans, flimflam; *Brit. informal* jiggery-pokery; *N. Amer. informal* monkeyshines; *Irish informal* codology; *archaic* management, knavery.

chicken ▶ noun. *See centre pages for list of* **Fowl**

WORD LINKS
male **cock, rooster**
female **hen**
young **chick**

chide ▶ verb *he was forever being chided for overfamiliarity* **scold**, chastise, upbraid, berate, castigate, lambaste, rebuke, reprimand, reproach, reprove, admonish, remonstrate with, lecture, criticize, censure; call to account, take to task, pull up, go on at, read someone the Riot Act, haul someone over the coals, give someone a piece of one's mind; *informal* tell off, give someone a telling-off, dress down, give someone a dressing-down, give someone an earful, give someone a roasting, give someone a talking-to, give someone a rocket, give someone a rollicking, rap, rap over the knuckles, slap someone's wrist, let someone have it, send someone away with a flea in their ear, bawl out, give someone hell, come down on, blow up at, pitch into, lay into, lace into, tear into, give someone a caning, put on the mat, slap down, blast, rag, keelhaul; *Brit. informal* tick off, have a go at, carpet, give someone a mouthful, tear someone off a strip, give someone what for, give someone some stick, wig, give someone a wigging, give someone a row, row; *N. Amer. informal* chew out, ream out, take to the woodshed; *Austral. informal* monster; *Brit. vulgar slang* bollock, give someone a bollocking; *N. Amer. vulgar slang* chew someone's ass, ream someone's ass; *dated* call down, rate, give someone a rating, trim; *rare* reprehend, objurgate.
OPPOSITE praise.

chief ▶ noun 1 *a Highland chief petitioned her father for her hand* **leader**, chieftain, head, headman, ruler, overlord, master, commander, suzerain, seigneur, liege, liege lord, potentate; (*among American Indians*) sachem.

C

2 *he is the chief of the US central bank* **head**, principal, chief executive, executive, president, chair, chairman, chairwoman, chairperson, governor, director, administrator, manager, manageress, superintendent, foreman, forewoman, controller, overseer; boss, employer, proprietor; *N. Amer.* chief executive officer, CEO; *informal* boss man, kingpin, top dog, big cheese, bigwig, skipper; *Brit. informal* gaffer, guv'nor; *N. Amer. informal* numero uno, Mister Big, honcho, head honcho, padrone, sachem, big white chief, big kahuna, big wheel, high muckamuck; *informal, derogatory* fat cat.

▶ **adjective 1** *he had a meeting with the chief rabbi* **head**, leading, principal, premier, highest, foremost, supreme, grand, superior, arch-; directing, governing; *informal* number-one.
OPPOSITE subordinate.
2 *their chief aim was to remove the invading forces* **main**, principal, most important, uppermost, primary, prime, first, cardinal, central, key, focal, vital, crucial, essential, pivotal, supreme, predominant, pre-eminent, paramount, overriding, leading, major, ruling, dominant, highest; arch; *informal* number-one.
OPPOSITE minor.

chiefly ▶ **adverb** *the theatre was used chiefly for performances of music* **mainly**, in the main, primarily, principally, predominantly, above all, mostly, for the most part, first and foremost, especially, particularly, essentially, substantially; usually, customarily, habitually, typically, commonly, generally, on the whole, largely, by and large, as a rule, in most instances, almost always, almost entirely, to a large extent, to a great degree.

child ▶ **noun** *I've known Kate since she was a child | his wife gave birth to their first child* **youngster**, young one, little one, boy, girl; baby, newborn, infant, toddler; schoolboy, schoolgirl, adolescent, teenager, youth, young man, young woman, young lady, young person, young adult, juvenile, minor, junior; stripling, fledgling, whippersnapper; **son, daughter**, son and heir, scion, descendant; (**children**) offspring, progeny, issue; *technical* neonate; *Scottish & N. English* bairn, wean, laddie, lassie; *informal* kid, kiddie, kiddiewink, nipper, tot, tiny, tiny tot, shaver, young 'un, lad, lass, teen, teeny-bopper; *Brit. informal* sprog; *N. Amer. informal* rug rat; *Austral./NZ informal* ankle-biter; *derogatory* brat, chit, urchin, guttersnipe; *literary* babe, babe in arms; *archaic* hobbledehoy.

WORD LINKS

related prefix	**paedo-**
fear of children	**paedophobia**
branch of medicine dealing with children	**paediatrics**
killing of a young child	**infanticide**

childbirth ▶ **noun** *her mother had major problems during childbirth* **labour**, delivery, giving birth, birthing; *technical* parturition; *literary* travail; *archaic* confinement, lying-in, accouchement, childbed.

WORD LINKS

relating to childbirth	**obstetric**
branch of medicine to do with childbirth	**obstetrics**
fear of childbirth	**tocophobia**

childhood ▶ **noun** *she had been writing poems since her childhood* **youth**, early years, early days, early life, infancy, babyhood, boyhood, girlhood, pre-teens, prepubescence, adolescence, teens, teenage years, young adulthood, immaturity; the springtime of life, one's salad days; *Law* minority; *rare* nonage, juvenility, juniority, juvenescence.
OPPOSITES adulthood, old age.

childish ▶ **adjective 1** *it was childish of her to rip up the picture* **immature**, babyish, infantile, juvenile, puerile; silly, inane, fatuous, jejune, foolish, stupid, irresponsible, naive.
OPPOSITE mature.
2 *she had a round childish face* **childlike**, youthful, young, young-looking, girlish, boyish, children's, child's, adolescent, teenaged, teenage; *archaic* bread-and-butter.
OPPOSITE adult.

childlike ▶ **adjective 1** *my grandmother looked almost childlike in the big white bed* **youthful**, young, young-looking, girlish, boyish, adolescent, teenaged, teenage.
2 *geniuses tend to be rather childlike* **innocent**, artless, guileless, simple, unworldly, unsophisticated, green, inexperienced, naive, ingenuous, trusting, trustful, unsuspicious, unwary, unguarded, credulous, gullible, easily taken in; **unaffected**, without airs, open, frank, uninhibited, natural, spontaneous, down-to-earth; *informal* wet behind the ears.

chill ▶ **noun 1** *there was a distinct chill in the air* **coldness**, chilliness, coolness, iciness, crispness, rawness, bitterness, nip, bite, sting, sharpness, keenness, harshness, wintriness, frigidity; *informal* nippiness; *Brit. informal* parkiness; *rare* gelidity.
OPPOSITE warmth.
2 *he took to his bed with a chill* **cold**, dose of flu, dose of influenza, respiratory infection, viral infection, virus; *archaic* grippe.
3 *he tried to end the chill in his relations with the West* **unfriendliness**, lack of understanding, lack of sympathy, lack of warmth, chilliness, coldness, coolness, frigidity, aloofness, distance, remoteness, unresponsiveness.
OPPOSITE friendliness.

▶ **verb 1** *the dessert is best made ahead and then chilled* **make cold**, make colder, cool, cool down, cool off; refrigerate, freeze, quick-freeze, deep-freeze, ice.
OPPOSITE warm.
2 *his quiet tone chilled Ruth more than if he had shouted* **scare**, frighten, petrify, terrify, alarm, appal, disturb, disquiet, unsettle; make someone's blood run cold, chill someone's blood, chill to the bone, chill to the marrow, make someone's flesh crawl, give someone goose pimples, scare witless, frighten the living daylights out of, fill with fear, strike terror into, put the fear of God into, throw into a panic; *informal* scare the pants off; *Brit. informal* put the wind up, give someone the heebie-jeebies, make someone's hair curl; *Irish informal* scare the bejesus out of; *vulgar slang* scare shitless; *archaic* affright.
OPPOSITES comfort, reassure.

□ **chill out** (*N. Amer. informal*) *the home should be a place to chill out. See* RELAX.

▶ **adjective** (*literary*) *a chill wind came through the open doors* **cold**, chilly, cool, crisp, fresh, brisk; bleak, wintry, snowy, frosty, icy, ice-cold, icy-cold, glacial, polar, arctic, raw, sharp, bitter, bitterly cold, biting, piercing, penetrating, numbing, freezing, frigid; *informal* nippy; *Brit. informal* parky; *rare* gelid, brumal.

chilly ▶ **adjective 1** *the weather had turned chilly* **cold**, cool, crisp, fresh, brisk, bleak, wintry, snowy, frosty, icy, ice-cold, icy-cold, glacial, polar, arctic, raw, sharp, bitter, bitterly cold, biting, piercing, penetrating, freezing, frigid; *informal* nippy; *Brit. informal* parky; *literary* chill; *rare* gelid, brumal.
OPPOSITE warm.
2 *I woke up feeling chilly* **cold**, frozen, frozen stiff, frozen to the marrow/core/bone, freezing, freezing cold, bitterly cold, shivery, numb, numbed, chilled.
3 *her chilly face splintered into a smile* **unfriendly**, unsympathetic, unwelcoming, forbidding, cold, cool, frosty, glacial, frigid; haughty, supercilious, disdainful, aloof, distant, remote; reserved, withdrawn, uncommunicative, unresponsive, unemotional, dispassionate, passionless, wooden, impersonal, formal, stiff, austere; *informal* stand-offish, offish; *rare* gelid.
OPPOSITE friendly.

chime ▶ **verb 1** *at the stroke of nine, the bells began to chime* **ring**, peal, toll, sound; ding, dong, clang, boom, resound, reverberate; tinkle, jingle, jangle; *archaic* knell; *rare* tintinnabulate.
2 *the clock on the mantelpiece chimed eight o'clock* **strike**, sound; indicate, mark.

□ **chime in 1** *'Yes, you do that,' Doreen chimed in eagerly* **interject**, interpose, intervene, interrupt, butt in, cut in, break in, join in, join the conversation; *Brit. informal* chip in, add one's pennyworth.
2 *some of his remarks chimed in with the ideas of Adam Smith* **accord**, correspond, be consistent, be compatible, agree, be in agreement, be in accordance, fit in, be in harmony, harmonize, be in tune, be consonant, be similar; *informal* square.

▶ **noun** *the chimes of the cathedral bells* **peal**, pealing, ringing, carillon, toll, tolling, sound; ding-dong, clanging; angelus; *archaic* knell; *rare* tintinnabulation.

chimera ▶ **noun** *the economic sovereignty she claims to defend is a chimera* **illusion**, fantasy, delusion, dream, fancy, figment of the imagination, will-o'-the-wisp, phantom, mirage; *Latin* ignis fatuus.

chimney ▶ **noun** chimney stack, smokestack, stack; flue, shaft, funnel, vent; *Scottish & N. English* lum; *rare* femerell.

China ▶ **noun.** *See centre pages for list of animals of the* **Chinese Calendar**

WORD LINKS

related prefix	**Sino-** (e.g. *Sino-American*)
study of China	**sinology**

china *See centre pages for list of* **Pottery**

▶ **noun 1** *a china cup* **porcelain**.
2 *a table laid with the best china and crystal glasses* **dishes**, plates, cups and saucers, crockery, dinner service, tea service; tableware, ware; *N. Amer.* dinnerware; *Irish* delph.

chink[1] ▶ **noun** *the sun had found a chink in the clouds | a chink in the wall* **opening**, gap, space, hole, aperture, break, breach, crack, fissure, crevice, cranny, cleft, cut, rift, split, slit, slot.

chink[2] ▶ **verb** *I heard her bracelets chinking as she walked away* **jingle**, jangle, clink, tinkle, rattle, clank.

chip ▶ **noun 1** *wood chips* **fragment**, piece, bit; sliver, splinter, spell, spillikin, shaving, paring; scrap, snippet, flake; shard; *Scottish* skelf; *technical* gallet, spall.
2 *a glass with a chip in the bottom* **nick**, crack, snick, scratch; flaw, fault.
3 *fish and chips* (**chips**) chipped potatoes, potato chips, game chips; *Brit.* French fried potatoes; *N. Amer.* French fries.
4 *gambling chips* **counter**, token, disc, jetton; *N. Amer.* check.

▶ **verb 1** *the teacup was chipped and dirty* **nick**, crack, snick, scratch; damage.
2 *the plaster had chipped and no repairs had been done* **break (off)**, crack, fragment, crumble.
3 *it required a craftsman to chip the blocks of flint to the required shape*

whittle, hew, chisel.

□ **chip in 1** *'He's right,' Gloria chipped in* **interrupt**, cut in, chime in, break in, interject, interpose, butt in.

2 *parents, pupils, and staff chipped in to help raise the cash | the firm chipped in nearly £100,000 in sponsorship* **contribute**, donate, give, make a contribution/donation, hand over, pay; club together; *informal* fork out, shell out, lay out, come across with, cough up; *Brit. informal* stump up, have a whip-round; *N. Amer. informal* kick in, pony up.

chirp ▶ **verb** *a canary chirped from a cage on the veranda* **tweet**, twitter, chirrup, cheep, peep, chitter, chatter, chirr; sing, warble, trill, pipe.

chirpy ▶ **adjective** (*informal*) *Leonard was in a chirpy mood. See* CHEERFUL.

chit-chat ▶ **noun** (*informal*) *Lucenzo didn't indulge in idle chit-chat* **small talk**, chat, chatting, chatter, chitter-chatter, prattling, prattle, gossip, tittle-tattle, tattle; *Brit. informal* nattering, chuntering.

chivalrous ▶ **adjective 1** *he was well known for his chivalrous treatment of women* **gallant**, gentlemanly, honourable, respectful, thoughtful, considerate, protective, attentive; **courteous**, polite, gracious, well mannered, urbane, courtly; *dated* mannerly; *archaic* gentle.

OPPOSITES rude, boorish, unmannerly.

2 *the prince's taste for chivalrous pursuits and warlike deeds* **knightly**, noble, chivalric; brave, courageous, bold, valiant, valorous, heroic, daring, intrepid; honourable, high-minded, just, fair, loyal, constant, true, virtuous.

OPPOSITE cowardly.

chivalry ▶ **noun 1** *small but pleasing acts of chivalry that seemed to come so naturally to him* **gallantry**, gentlemanliness, thoughtfulness, attentiveness, consideration, considerateness; **courtesy**, courteousness, politeness, graciousness, mannerliness, good manners, urbanity, courtliness.

OPPOSITES rudeness, boorishness.

2 *Edward III created a court which exemplified the values of chivalry* **knight errantry**, the knightly code, knighthood, courtly manners, knightliness, courtliness, nobility, magnanimity; bravery, courage, boldness, valour, heroism, daring, intrepidity; honour, integrity, high-mindedness, justice, justness, fairness, loyalty, constancy, trueness, truthfulness, virtuousness.

chivvy ▶ **verb** *she did nothing to help, but constantly chivvied the girls and interfered with their work* **nag**, badger, hound, harass, harry, keep after, keep on at, go on at, pester, plague, torment, persecute, goad, annoy, bother; urge, prod, pressure, pressurize; *informal* hassle, bug, breathe down someone's neck, get on someone's case; *N. English informal* mither; *N. Amer. informal* ride; *Austral. informal* heavy.

choice ▶ **noun 1** *the voters' choice of candidate | an individual's freedom of choice* **selection**, choosing, picking; election, adoption, nomination; decision, say, vote, preference, pick.

2 *you must trust me—you have no other choice* **option**, **alternative**, possibility, possible course of action; solution, answer, way out.

3 *an extensive choice of wines, spirits, and beers* **range**, variety, selection, assortment; array, display.

4 *John would have been the perfect choice* **appointee**; nominee, candidate, selection.

▶ **adjective 1** *choice plums | a choice property in some of the finest country in the state* **superior**, first-class, first-rate, prime, premier, grade A, best, finest, excellent, select, quality, high-quality, top, top-quality, high-grade, of the first water, prize, special, exclusive, hand-picked, carefully chosen, vintage, fine; *French* par excellence; *informal* tip-top, A1, top-notch, plum.

OPPOSITES inferior, mediocre.

2 *she had often rehearsed the choice phrases she would use* **well chosen**, well put, well expressed; appropriate, apposite, apt, fit, felicitous.

3 *a few choice words that he usually saved for the traffic warden* **rude**, abusive, insulting, offensive, unprintable.

OPPOSITE polite.

choir ▶ **noun singers**, chorus, chorale.

WORD LINKS
relating to a choir **choral**

choke ▶ **verb 1** *Christopher gulped and started to choke* **gag**, retch, cough, struggle for air, fight for breath, gasp.

2 *thick clouds of dust choked her* **suffocate**, asphyxiate, smother, stifle; overpower, overcome.

3 *she had been choked to death when her necklace snagged on overhanging branches* **strangle**, throttle; asphyxiate, suffocate; *informal* strangulate.

4 *sections of guttering were choked with leaves and other debris* **clog (up)**, bung up, block, obstruct, stop up, silt up, plug, dam up; congest, jam; *informal* gunge up; *technical* occlude, obturate.

□ **choke something back** *he choked back his tears* **suppress**, hold back, fight back, bite back, gulp back, swallow, check, keep in check, restrain, contain, control, repress, smother, stifle, curb, bridle, rein in; bite one's lip; *informal* keep a/the lid on.

choleric ▶ **adjective** *a choleric, self-important little man* **bad-tempered**, irascible, irritable, grumpy, grouchy, crotchety, tetchy, testy, crusty, cantankerous, curmudgeonly, ill-tempered, ill-natured, ill-humoured, peevish, cross, fractious, disagreeable, pettish, crabbed, crabby, waspish, prickly, peppery, touchy, scratchy, splenetic, shrewish, short-tempered, hot-tempered, quick-tempered, dyspeptic, bilious, liverish, cross-grained; argumentative, quarrelsome, uncooperative, contrary, perverse, difficult, awkward; *informal* snappish, snappy, chippy, short-fused; *Brit. informal* shirty, stroppy, narky, ratty, eggy, like a bear with a sore head; *N. Amer. informal* cranky, ornery, peckish, soreheaded; *Austral./NZ informal* snaky; *informal, dated* waxy, miffy.

OPPOSITES good-natured, affable.

choose ▶ **verb 1** *we chose a quiet country hotel for our honeymoon* **select**, pick, pick out, opt for, plump for, go for, take, settle on, decide on, fix on, come down in favour of, vote for; single out, hand-pick; set, designate, determine, specify, appoint, name, nominate, adopt, espouse; *Brit.* pitch on.

OPPOSITES reject; decline.

2 *you may choose to stay here all night* **wish**, want, desire, prefer, feel/be inclined, please, like, see fit; **decide**, elect, make up one's mind.

choosy ▶ **adjective** (*informal*) *she's become very choosy about the food she'll eat* **fussy**, finicky, over-fastidious, over-particular, faddish, difficult/hard to please, dainty, exacting, demanding; discriminating, discerning, selective; *informal* picky, pernickety; *Brit. informal* faddy; *N. Amer. informal* persnickety; *archaic* nice, overnice; *rare* finical.

OPPOSITES easy to please, indiscriminate.

chop ▶ **verb 1** *chop the potatoes into bite-sized pieces* **cut up**, cut into pieces, chop up; cube, dice, mince; *N. Amer.* hash.

2 *the sound of men chopping wood* **chop up**, cut up, cut into pieces, hew, split, cleave.

3 *all four fingers of his left hand were chopped off* **sever**, cut off, hack off, slice off, lop off, saw off, shear off; remove, take off; *archaic* sunder; *rare* dissever.

4 *the scheme would mean chopping down large areas of rainforest* **cut down**, fell, bring down, hack down, saw down.

5 (*informal*) *their training courses are to be chopped* **reduce drastically**, cut; abolish, scrap; *informal* axe, slash.

□ **the chop** (*Brit. informal*) *hundreds of workers have been given the chop* **notice**, one's marching orders; *informal* **the sack**, the boot, the (old) heave-ho, the elbow, the push, the bullet; *Brit. informal* one's cards.

chopper ▶ **noun** (*Brit.*) **axe**, cleaver, hatchet; butcher's knife.

choppy ▶ **adjective** *the choppy sea* **rough**, full of waves, turbulent, heavy, heaving, storm-tossed, stormy, tempestuous, squally; broken, ruffled, uneven.

OPPOSITES calm, smooth.

chore ▶ **noun** *daily household chores like shopping and cleaning* **task**, job, duty, errand, thing to be done, burden; (**chores**) work, domestic work, drudgery.

CHOOSE THE RIGHT WORD

chore, task, job, duty

See TASK.

chortle ▶ **verb** *pleased with his joke, Robert chortled and slapped his thigh* **chuckle**, laugh, giggle, titter, tee-hee, snigger; guffaw, cackle, crow.

chorus ▶ **noun 1** *the soloists were good and the chorus sang powerfully* **choir**, ensemble, choral group, choristers, vocalists, (group of) singers.

2 *they sang the chorus again* **refrain**, burden, strain; *informal* hook.

3 *the girls of the chorus* **chorus line**, **dance troupe**; dancing girls.

□ **in chorus** *'Good Morning,' we replied in chorus* **in unison**, together, simultaneously, at the same time, as one; in concert, in harmony.

Christ ▶ **noun Jesus**, Jesus Christ, Our Lord, the Messiah, the Saviour, the Son of God, the Lamb of God, the Good Shepherd, the Redeemer, the Prince of Peace, the Nazarene, the Galilean.

christen ▶ **verb 1** *the church in which Jonathan was christened | she was christened Sara* **baptize**; name, give a name to, give the name of, call; *rare* lustrate.

2 *a group who were later christened 'The Magic Circle'* **call**, name, dub, style, term, designate, label, nickname, refer to as, give the name of; *rare* denominate.

3 (*informal*) *Makel christened his new boots with his first goal at the McAlpine Stadium* **begin using**, use for the first time, break in.

Christianity ▶ **noun.** *See centre pages for lists of*

Christian Denominations
Christian Doctrinal Movements and Heresies
Christian Religious Orders
Priests, Religious Officials, and Members of Religious Orders

Christmas ▶ **noun Xmas**, Noel; *Indian* Burra Din; *Brit. informal* Chrimbo, Chrissie; *archaic* Yule, Yuletide.

chronic ▶ **adjective 1** *a chronic illness* **persistent**, long-standing, long-term, constantly recurring; incurable; *rare* immedicable.

OPPOSITE acute.

2 *the chronic shortage of food | chronic economic problems* **constant**, continuing, continual, ceaseless, incessant, unabating, unending, persistent, perennial, long-lasting, lingering; deep-rooted, deep-seated,

C

ineradicable; severe, serious, acute, grave, dire.
OPPOSITES temporary; mild.
3 *a chronic liar* **inveterate**, confirmed, hardened, dyed-in-the-wool, incorrigible, habitual; compulsive, pathological.
OPPOSITE occasional.
4 (*Brit. informal*) *the film was absolutely chronic* **very bad**, appalling, awful, dreadful, terrible, frightful, atrocious, hopeless, abominable, laughable, lamentable, execrable; *informal* crummy, pathetic, rotten, useless, woeful, lousy, abysmal, dire, poxy, God-awful, the pits; *Brit. informal* duff, rubbish, pants, a load of pants; *vulgar slang* crap, shit, chickenshit; *rare* egregious.
OPPOSITES good, excellent.

chronicle ▶ **noun** *a chronicle of the turbulent years of the region's past* **record**, written account, history, annals, archive(s), register; log, diary, journal, calendar, chronology; narrative, description, story.
▶ **verb** *the events that followed have been chronicled by many of those who took part* **record**, put on record, write down, set down, document, register, report, enter; narrate, relate, recount, describe, tell about, retail.

chronicler ▶ **noun** **annalist**, historian, archivist, diarist, recorder, reporter; narrator; scribe; *rare* chronologer, chronologist, chronographer.

chronological ▶ **adjective** *a chronological account of the period | the entries are in chronological order* **sequential**, consecutive, in sequence, in order of time, in order, ordered, progressive, serial; historical.
OPPOSITE random.

chubby ▶ **adjective** *a chubby little man with a red face* **plump**, tubby, roly-poly, rotund, portly, stout, dumpy, chunky, broad in the beam, well upholstered, well covered, well padded, of ample proportions, ample, round, rounded, well rounded; fat, overweight, fleshy, paunchy, pot-bellied, bulky; buxom; *informal* pudgy, beefy, porky, blubbery, poddy; *Brit. informal* podgy, fubsy; *N. Amer. informal* zaftig, corn-fed, lard-assed; *archaic* pursy; *rare* abdominous.
OPPOSITES skinny, slender.

chuck ▶ **verb** (*informal*) **1** *he chucked the letter into the bin* **throw**, toss, fling, hurl, pitch, cast, lob, launch, flip, catapult, shy, dash, project, propel, send, bowl; let fly with; *informal* heave, sling, bung, buzz, whang; *N. Amer. informal* peg; *Austral. informal* hoy; *NZ informal* bish.
2 *I kept the personal bits and pieces and chucked the rest* **throw away**, discard, throw out, dispose of, get rid of, toss out, dump, bin, scrap, jettison; *informal* ditch, junk, get shut of; *Brit. informal* get shot of; *N. Amer. informal* trash.
OPPOSITES keep, retain, hold on to.
3 *I've decided to chuck my job* **give up**, leave, resign from, abandon, relinquish; *informal* quit, pack in, jack in.
4 *Mary chucked him for another guy* **leave**, throw over, drop, finish with, stop going out with, break off one's relationship with, desert, abandon, leave high and dry; *informal* dump, ditch, give someone the elbow, walk out on, run out on, leave flat; *Brit. informal* give someone the push, give someone the big E; *dated* jilt; *archaic* forsake.

chuckle ▶ **verb** *Adam chuckled to himself as he drove away* **chortle**, giggle, titter, laugh quietly, tee-hee, snicker, snigger; crow.

chum ▶ **noun** (*informal*) **friend**, companion, intimate, familiar, confidant, alter ego, second self; playmate, classmate, schoolmate, workmate; *informal* pal, buddy, bosom pal, sidekick, cully, spar, crony, main man; *Brit. informal* mate, oppo, china, mucker, butty; *NE English informal* marrow, marra, marrer; *N. Amer. informal* amigo, compadre, paisan; *N. Amer. & S. African informal* homeboy; *S. African informal* gabba; *archaic* compeer; *rare* fidus Achates.
OPPOSITES enemy; stranger.

chummy ▶ **adjective** (*informal*) *she's become rather chummy with Ted* **friendly**, on good terms, close, familiar, affectionate, intimate; *informal* as thick as thieves, thick, matey, pally, buddy-buddy, palsy-walsy, clubby.

chunk ▶ **noun** *chunks of cheese* **lump**, hunk, wedge, block, slab, square, nugget, nub, brick, cube, bar, cake, loaf; knob, ball; piece, portion, bit; mass; *informal* wodge; *N. Amer. informal* gob.

chunky ▶ **adjective** **1** *a chunky young man* **stocky**, sturdy, thickset, sturdily built, heavily built, well built, burly, bulky, brawny, solid, bull-necked, heavy, hefty, beefy, meaty; short, dumpy, squat, stubby; cobby; *Austral./NZ* nuggety; *Brit. informal* fubsy; *technical* mesomorphic, pyknic.
OPPOSITE slight.
2 *a chunky Aran sweater* **thick**, bulky, heavy-knit, cable-knit.
OPPOSITES light, lightweight.

church *See centre pages for lists of parts of a* **Church** *and* **Places of Worship**
▶ **noun** **1** *a village church* **house of God**, the Lord's house, house of prayer; *Scottish & N. English* kirk.
2 *the Methodist Church* **denomination**, sect, creed; faith.

WORD LINKS
relating to a church **ecclesiastical**
study of churches **ecclesiology**
fear of church **ecclesiophobia**

churchyard ▶ **noun** **graveyard**, cemetery, necropolis, burial ground, burial place, burying place, burying ground, garden of remembrance; *Scottish* kirkyard; *N. Amer.* memorial park; *informal* boneyard; *literary* golgotha; *historical* urnfield; *archaic* God's acre, potter's field.

churlish ▶ **adjective** *it seemed churlish to refuse her invitation* **rude**, ill-mannered, discourteous, impolite, ungracious, unmannerly, uncivil, ungentlemanly, ungallant, unchivalrous; ill-bred, boorish, oafish, loutish; mean-spirited, ill-tempered, unkind, inconsiderate, uncharitable; ill-humoured, surly, sullen; *informal* ignorant.
OPPOSITE polite.

churn ▶ **verb** **1** *village girls churned the milk to make butter* **stir**, agitate; beat, whip, whisk.
2 *beneath the ship the sea churned* **be turbulent**, heave, boil, swirl, toss, seethe, foam, froth; *literary* roil.
3 *the twin propellers churned up the water* **disturb**, stir up, agitate; ruffle; *literary* roil.
□ **churn something out** *the British film industry has churned out many such films in recent years* **produce**, make, turn out; *informal* crank out, bang out.

chute ▶ **noun** **1** *a refuse chute* **channel**, slide, trough, shaft, funnel, conduit; ramp, runway.
2 *magnificent seawater pools with chutes and waterfalls* **water slide**, slide, flume, log flume, hydro-slide.

cigarette ▶ **noun** filter tip, king-size; cigar; *informal* **ciggy**, cig, tab, tube, smoke, cancer stick, coffin nail; *Brit. informal* **fag**, snout, roll-up; *Brit. informal, dated* gasper, burn.

cinch ▶ **noun** (*informal*) **1** *I've done it before—it's a cinch* **easy task**, easy job, child's play, five-finger exercise, gift, walkover, nothing; *informal* doddle, piece of cake, picnic, money for old rope, money for jam, breeze, sitter, kids' stuff, cushy job/number, doss, cakewalk, pushover; *N. Amer. informal* duck soup, snap; *Austral./NZ informal* bludge, snack; *S. African informal* a piece of old tackie; *dated* snip; *Brit. vulgar slang* a piece of piss. *See also* EASY.
OPPOSITE challenge.
2 *he was a cinch to take a prize* **certainty**, sure thing; *informal* cert, dead cert.

cinders ▶ **plural noun** *a cold hearth full of cinders* **ashes**, ash, embers; clinker, charcoal, slag.

cinema *See centre pages for list of* **Film Types, Versions, and Genres**
▶ **noun** **1** *the local cinema* multiplex, cinematheque; *N. Amer.* movie theatre, movie house; *N. Amer. trademark* cineplex; *informal* fleapit; *dated* picture palace, picture theatre; *S. African dated* bioscope; *historical* nickelodeon.
2 *I hardly ever go to the cinema* **the pictures**; *N. Amer.* **the movies**; *informal* the flicks.
3 *one of the giants of British cinema* **films**, pictures; *N. Amer.* movies, motion pictures; *informal* the big screen, the silver screen.

WORD LINKS
relating to the cinema **cinematographic**

cipher ▶ **noun** **1** *the information may be given in cipher* **code**, secret writing; coded message, cryptograph, cryptogram.
2 *he has spent most of his working life as a cipher* **nobody**, nonentity, nothing, non-person, unimportant person, person of no account.
OPPOSITE celebrity.
3 *a row of ciphers* **zero**, nought, nil, 0; *archaic* naught.
4 *Arabic ciphers* **numeral**, number, integer, figure, digit; character, symbol, sign.

circa ▶ **preposition** (*Latin*) *a survey by questionnaire of circa 100 companies* **approximately**, about, around, round about, in the region of, roughly, something like, in the area of, in the neighbourhood of, of the order of, or so, or thereabouts, there or thereabouts, more or less, give or take a few, plus or minus a few; nearly, close to, not far off, approaching; *Brit.* getting on for; *S. African* plus-minus; *informal* as near as dammit; *N. Amer. informal* in the ballpark of.
OPPOSITES exactly, precisely.

circle ▶ **noun** **1** *a circle of gold stars on a background of azure blue | the lamp spread a circle of light* **ring**, round, band, hoop, circlet; halo, disc, wreath; *technical* annulus.
2 *a new circle of friends* **group**, set, ring, company, body, coterie, clique; camp, league, faction; crowd, band, crew; *informal* gang, bunch, pack.
3 *I'm afraid I don't move in such illustrious circles* **sphere**, world, milieu, arena, domain; society.
▶ **verb** **1** *seagulls circled above his head* **wheel**, move round, move round in circles, revolve, rotate, whirl, spiral, gyrate.
2 *Adam circled the building | the satellites circle the earth at tremendous speed* **go round**, walk round, travel round, circumnavigate; **orbit**, revolve round; *rare* circumambulate.
3 *the abbey was circled by a huge wall* **surround**, encircle, ring, ring round, enclose, encompass, bound; hedge in, fence in, hem in; *literary* gird, girdle.

circuit ▶ **noun** **1** *two circuits of the village green* **lap**, turn, tour, round, circle, orbit, revolution, loop; beat.
2 (*Brit.*) *a racing circuit* **track**, racetrack, running track, course.
3 *the judge completed his circuit in a matter of weeks* **tour**, tour of duty, rounds; regular journey; *rare* peregrination.

circuitous ▶ **adjective** **1** *a circuitous route* **roundabout**, indirect, winding, meandering, serpentine, tortuous, twisting; *rare* anfractuous.
OPPOSITES direct, straight.
2 *a circuitous discussion* **indirect**, oblique, roundabout, circumlocutory, periphrastic; meandering, discursive, digressive, long-winded; evasive;

rare circumlocutionary, ambagious.
OPPOSITE to the point.

circular ▶ adjective *a circular window* **round**, disc-shaped, disk-like; ring-shaped, hoop-shaped, hoop-like, annular; *technical* cycloidal, discoid, discoidal.
▶ noun *a circular from a local building society* **leaflet**, pamphlet, handbill; flyer, advertisement, notice; *N. Amer.* mailer, folder; *N. Amer. & Austral.* dodger.

circulate ▶ verb **1** *news of the event was widely circulated* **spread**, spread about/around, pass around, pass on, communicate, disseminate, transmit, make known, air, put about, bandy about; make public, broadcast, publicize, advertise, publish, post, propagate, promulgate, blazon abroad, noise abroad; distribute, give out, issue, purvey; *literary* bruit about/abroad.
2 *rumours of his arrest circulated* **spread**, be passed around, get around, go the rounds.
3 *fresh air circulates freely throughout the house* **flow**, course, move round, go round.
4 *the couple circulated, chatting to their guests* **socialize**, mingle.

circulation ▶ noun **1** *the circulation of fresh air* **flow**, motion, movement, course, passage.
2 *the circulation of the information* **dissemination**, spreading, communication, transmission, making known, putting about; broadcasting, publication, propagation, promulgation; distribution, diffusion, issuance.
3 *the magazine had a large circulation* **distribution**, readership; sales figures.

circumference ▶ noun **1** *the circumference of the pit | the road which acted as the circumference of the downtown area* **perimeter**, border, boundary; edge, rim, verge, margin, outline, fringe; bounds, limits, extremity, confines; *literary* marge, bourn, skirt.
2 *the circumference of his upper arm* **girth**, width.

circumlocution ▶ noun **periphrasis**, circuitousness, indirectness; **tautology**, repetition, repetitiveness, repetitiousness, diffuseness, discursiveness, long-windedness, verbosity, wordiness, prolixity, verbiage, redundancy, superfluity; euphemism; *informal* beating about the bush; *rare* pleonasm, perissology.

circumlocutory ▶ adjective *his circumlocutory language* **periphrastic**, circuitous, indirect, roundabout; **tautological**, repetitive, repetitious, diffuse, discursive, long-winded, prolix, verbose, wordy, rambling, wandering, tortuous; *rare* pleonastic, circumlocutionary, ambagious.

circumscribe ▶ verb *the power of the organization has until recently been severely circumscribed* **restrict**, **limit**, set/impose limits on, keep within bounds, delimit, curb, confine, bound, restrain; regulate, control.

circumspect ▶ adjective *she would have to be very circumspect in her dealings with Catherine* **cautious**, wary, careful, chary, guarded, on one's guard; discreet; watchful, alert, attentive, heedful, vigilant, observant; prudent, judicious, canny, politic; *informal* softly-softly, cagey, leery, playing one's cards close to one's chest.
OPPOSITES unguarded, incautious.

circumspection ▶ noun *circumspection is required in the day-to-day exercise of administrative powers* **caution**, carefulness, care, wariness, chariness, guardedness; discretion; watchfulness, alertness, attentiveness, heed, heedfulness, vigilance; prudence, judiciousness; *informal* caginess; *rare* precaution.

circumstances ▶ plural noun **1** *a combination of favourable political and economic circumstances* **situation**, conditions, set of conditions, state of affairs, things, position; events, turn of events, incidents, occurrences, happenings, episodes; factors, context, background, environment; *informal* circs.
2 *Jane explained* **the circumstances** *to him* **the facts**, the details, the particulars, the picture, how things stand, the lie of the land, how the land lies, the case; *Brit.* the state of play; *N. Amer.* the lay of the land; *informal* what's what, the score, the set-up.
3 *a desire to improve their circumstances* **financial/material position**, financial/material situation, financial/material status, station in life, lot, lifestyle; resources, means, finances, income; plight, predicament.

circumstantial ▶ adjective **1** *the prosecution will have to rely on circumstantial evidence* **indirect**, inferred, inferential, deduced, presumed, conjectural; contingent; inconclusive, unprovable; *technical* presumptive, implicative.
OPPOSITE provable.
2 *the picture was so circumstantial that it began to be convincing* **detailed**, particularized, particular, precise, minute, blow-by-blow; full, comprehensive, thorough, exhaustive; explicit, specific.
OPPOSITE vague.

circumvent ▶ verb *terrorists found the airport checks easy to circumvent* **avoid**, get round, find a way round, evade, get past, bypass, sidestep, dodge; overcome, outwit, outmanoeuvre, foil; *N. Amer.* end-run; *informal* duck.

cistern ▶ noun **tank**, reservoir, container; vat, butt.

citadel ▶ noun **fortress**, fort, stronghold, fortification, castle, burg, keep, tower, donjon, bunker; fastness; (*in Spain*) alcazar; *archaic* hold.

citation ▶ noun **1** *a citation from an eighteenth century text* **quotation**, quote, extract, excerpt, passage, line, piece; *N. Amer.* cite.
2 *he made extensive citations to Baynton v. Morgan* **reference**, allusion.
3 *a citation for gallantry* **commendation**, award, honour; mention, honourable mention.
4 (*N. Amer.*) *a traffic citation* **summons**, subpoena, writ, court order, process; *Latin* subpoena ad testificandum.

cite ▶ verb **1** *I have cited the passage in full* **quote**, reproduce.
2 *he cited the case of Leigh v. Gladstone* **refer to**, make reference to, mention, allude to, adduce, instance, give as an example, point to; specify, name; bring up, advance, invoke, draw attention to.
3 *he has been cited many times for his contributions in this area* **commend**, pay tribute to, praise, recognize, give recognition to.
4 *the writ cited only four of the signatories of the petition* **summon**, summons, serve with a summons, subpoena, serve with a writ, call.

citizen ▶ noun **1** *a British citizen* **subject**, national, passport holder, native; taxpayer, voter.
2 *the citizens of Edinburgh* **inhabitant**, resident, native, townsman, townswoman, householder, local; freeman; *humorous* denizen, burgher; *formal* dweller; *Brit. archaic* burgess; *rare* residentiary, oppidan.

city ▶ noun **town**, municipality, metropolis, megalopolis; **conurbation**, urban area, metropolitan area; *Scottish* burgh; *informal* big smoke; *N. Amer. informal* burg; *archaic* wen.

WORD LINKS
relating to cities **urban, civic, metropolitan**

civic ▶ adjective *civic buildings | the civic life of Swindon* **municipal**, city, town, urban, metropolitan; **public**, civil, community, local, communal; *rare* oppidan.

civil ▶ adjective **1** *a civil marriage ceremony* **secular**, non-religious, lay, non-ecclesiastic; *rare* laic, laical.
OPPOSITE religious.
2 *civil aviation* **non-military**, civilian.
OPPOSITE military.
3 *a civil war | the civil administration* **internal**, domestic, interior, home; national, state, local.
OPPOSITES foreign, international.
4 *a sense of civil duty* **civic**, municipal, public, community, social.
5 *I hope you're going to behave in a civil manner* **polite**, courteous, well mannered, well bred, gentlemanly, chivalrous, gallant, ladylike, gracious, respectful; refined, urbane, polished, cultured, cultivated, civilized, cordial, genial, pleasant, affable, obliging; *Brit. informal* decent; *dated* mannerly.
OPPOSITES rude, discourteous.

CHOOSE THE RIGHT WORD

civil, polite, courteous

See POLITE.

civilian ▶ noun *the slaughter of unarmed civilians* **non-military person**, non-combatant, ordinary citizen, private citizen; *informal* civvy.
▶ adjective *civilian casualties | civilian clothes* **non-military**, non-combatant, civil; *informal* civvy.

civility ▶ noun **1** *he treated me with the utmost civility* **courtesy**, courteousness, politeness, good manners, mannerliness, gentlemanliness, chivalry, gallantry, graciousness, consideration, respect, gentility; urbanity, cordiality, geniality, pleasantness, affability; *French* politesse; *rare* comity.
OPPOSITES discourtesy, rudeness.
2 *she didn't waste time on civilities* **polite remark**, politeness, courtesy; formality.

civilization ▶ noun **1** *a higher stage of civilization* **human development**, advancement, progress, enlightenment, edification, culture, cultivation, refinement, sophistication.
2 *the ancient civilizations of the Mediterranean* **culture**, customs, mores, way of life, attainments, achievements; society, nation, people, community.

civilize ▶ verb *he built roads and attempted to civilize the people* **enlighten**, edify, educate, instruct, refine, cultivate, polish, sophisticate, socialize, humanize; improve, better; *archaic* reclaim; *rare* acculturate.

civilized ▶ adjective *his civilized behaviour | a civilized society* **polite**, courteous, well mannered, good mannered, civil, decorous, gentlemanly, ladylike, gracious; cultured, cultivated, refined, polished, sophisticated, urbane; enlightened, educated, advanced, developed; *informal* couth; *dated* mannerly.
OPPOSITES uncivilized, unsophisticated.

civil servant ▶ noun **public servant**, government official, government worker, civil-service employee; **bureaucrat**, mandarin, official, administrator, office-holder, functionary; *Brit.* jack-in-office.

C

clad ▶ adjective *Verity was clad in a filmy chiffon dress* **dressed**, clothed, attired, got up, garbed, rigged out, costumed; **wearing**, sporting; *informal* dolled up; *literary* caparisoned, accoutred; *archaic* apparelled.

claim ▶ verb **1** *Davies claimed that she was lying* **assert**, declare, profess, maintain, state, hold, affirm, avow, aver, protest, insist, swear, attest; argue, contend, submit, move; allege; *informal* make out; *archaic* avouch; *rare* asseverate, represent.
2 *if no one claims the items, they will become Crown property* **lay claim to**, say that one owns, assert ownership of, formally request; pretend to.
3 *you are entitled to claim compensation* **request**, ask for, apply for, put in for, put in an application for; sue for; demand, exact.
4 *the fire claimed the lives of five people* **take**; cause/result in the loss of.
▶ noun **1** *her claims that she was raped* **assertion**, declaration, profession, affirmation, avowal, averment, protestation, representation; contention, submission, case; allegation; pretence; *rare* asseveration.
2 *a claim for damages* **request**, application; demand, petition, call.
3 *they have first* **claim on** *the assets of the trust* **entitlement to**, title to, right to, rights to.

claimant ▶ noun **applicant**, candidate, supplicant, suppliant, pretender, suitor; petitioner, plaintiff, litigant, appellant; *rare* pretendant.

clairvoyance ▶ noun **second sight**, **psychic powers**, ESP, extrasensory perception, sixth sense; telepathy.

clairvoyant ▶ noun *a woman claiming to be a clairvoyant* **psychic**, fortune teller, forecaster of the future, crystal-gazer, prophet, seer, soothsayer, oracle; medium, spiritualist; telepathist, telepath, mind-reader; palmist, palm-reader, chiromancer; *rare* chirosophist, spiritist, palmister.
▶ adjective *he didn't tell me about it and I'm not clairvoyant* **psychic**, with second sight, with a sixth sense, prophetic, visionary, oracular; telepathic, extrasensory; *rare* second-sighted.

clamber ▶ verb *we* **clambered up** *the hillside* **scramble**, climb, scrabble, move awkwardly, claw one's way; shin; scale, ascend, mount; *N. Amer.* shinny.

clammy ▶ adjective **1** *his clammy hands* **moist**, damp, sweaty, perspiring, sweating, sticky; slimy, slippery, slick.
OPPOSITE dry.
2 *the clammy atmosphere* **damp**, dank, wet, moisture-laden; humid, close, muggy, heavy, steamy.

clamorous ▶ adjective *a crowd of clamorous children* **noisy**, loud, vocal, vociferous, raucous, rowdy, rackety, tumultuous, shouting, shrieking, screaming; importunate, demanding, insistent, vehement.
OPPOSITE quiet.

clamour ▶ noun **1** *her cold, crisp voice rose above the clamour* **din**, racket, loud noise, uproar, tumult, babel, shouting, yelling, screaming, baying, roaring, blaring, clangour; commotion, brouhaha, hue and cry, hubbub, bedlam, pandemonium; *Scottish & N. English* stramash; *informal* hullabaloo, rumpus; *Brit. informal* row; *rare* vociferation, ululation, charivari.
OPPOSITE silence.
2 *the growing clamour for her resignation* **demand(s)**, call(s), urging, insistence.
3 *a smaller trade deficit will still the clamour of protectionists* **protests**, storms of protest, complaints, outcry.
▶ verb **1** *the surging crowds clamoured for attention* **yell**, shout loudly, bay, scream, shriek, roar.
2 *scientists are* **clamouring for** *a ban on all chlorine substances* **demand**, call, bay; press, push, lobby.

clamp ▶ noun **1** *a clamp holds the pieces of wood at right angles* **brace**, vice, press; clasp, fastener, bracket, holdfast; *Music* mute, capo, capo tasto; *Climbing* jumar.
2 *clamps had been fitted to the car's back wheels* **immobilizer**, wheel clamp; *N. Amer.* boot.
▶ verb **1** *the sander is clamped on to the edge of a workbench* **fasten**, secure, fix, clip, attach, make fast; screw, bolt.
2 *an empty pipe was clamped between his teeth* **clench**, grip, hold, press, squeeze; clasp, grasp, clutch.
3 *yesterday, the government clamped a curfew on the city* **impose**, inflict; *informal* clap, slap.
4 *he flew into a rage when he found his car was clamped* **immobilize**, wheel-clamp; *N. Amer.* boot.
□ **clamp down on** *a new initiative to clamp down on software piracy* **suppress**, prevent, stop, put a stop to, put an end to, stamp out; crack down on, come down hard on, limit, restrain, restrict, check, keep in check, control, keep under control.

clampdown ▶ noun (*informal*) *the military regime continued its clampdown on the pro-democracy movement* **suppression**, prevention, stopping, stamping out; crackdown, limitation, restriction, restraint, curb, check.

clan ▶ noun **1** *the Macleod clan* **group of families**, sept, gens; **family**, house, dynasty, tribe, line; *Anthropology* sib, kinship group.
2 *this clan of rich and ambitious art collectors* **group**, set, circle, clique, coterie, in-crowd, fraternity, brotherhood, community, society; crowd, band, ring, crew; faction; *informal* gang, bunch; *rare* sodality, confraternity.

clandestine ▶ adjective *their clandestine meetings* **secret**, covert, furtive, surreptitious, stealthy, cloak-and-dagger, hole-and-corner, hole-in-the-corner, closet, behind-the-scenes, backstairs, back-alley, under-the-table, hugger-mugger, concealed, hidden, private; sly, sneaky, underhand; undercover, underground; *informal* hush-hush.
OPPOSITES open, above board.

clang ▶ noun *the clang of the church bells* **reverberation**, ringing, ring, ding-dong, bong, peal, chime, toll; **clank**, clash, crash, clangour; *informal* boing.
▶ verb *the huge bells clanged* **reverberate**, resound, ring, bong, peal, chime, toll; **clank**, clash, crash; *informal* boing; *rare* tang.

clanger ▶ noun (*Brit. informal*) **mistake**, blunder, gaffe, error, faux pas, slip of the tongue/pen, solecism; misjudgement, miscalculation, indiscretion, impropriety; *informal* slip-up, boo-boo, boner, howler; *Brit. informal* boob; *Brit. informal, dated* bloomer, floater; *N. Amer. informal* goof, blooper, bloop; *Latin* lapsus linguae, lapsus calami.

clank ▶ noun *the clank of rusty chains* **jangling**, clanging, rattling, clinking, jingling, clunking, clattering; clang, jangle, rattle, clangour, clink, jingle, clunk, clatter.
▶ verb *I could hear the chain clanking as the dog moved around* **jangle**, rattle, clink, clang, jingle, clunk, clatter.

clannish ▶ adjective *he was regarded as an outsider in the clannish community* **cliquey**, cliquish, insular, exclusive; unfriendly, unwelcoming; narrow, parochial, provincial.

clap ▶ verb **1** *the crowd clapped and cheered* **applaud**, clap one's hands, give someone a round of applause, put one's hands together; give someone a standing ovation, applaud someone to the echo; *informal* give someone a (big) hand, bring the house down; *N. Amer. informal* give it up.
OPPOSITES boo, jeer.
2 *he clapped Owen on the back* **slap**, strike, hit, smack, crack, bang, thump, cuff; pat; *informal* whack, thwack, wallop.
3 *in the old days, they would have clapped you in jail* **fling**, cast, put, place; *informal* slap, stick.
4 *the dove clapped its wings* **flap**, beat, flutter.
▶ noun **1** *everybody gave him a clap* **round of applause**, hand, handclap; standing ovation.
2 *a clap on the shoulder that almost rattled my teeth* **slap**, blow, smack, crack, thump, cuff; *informal* whack, thwack.
3 *a clap of thunder* **crack**, crash, bang, boom; thunderclap.

claptrap ▶ noun *I've had enough of this sentimental claptrap.* See NONSENSE.

clarification ▶ noun *please advise us if you require further clarification of these matters* **explanation**, elucidation, illumination, simplification; exposition, explication, exegesis.
OPPOSITE obfuscation.

clarify ▶ verb **1** *a meeting was called in order to clarify the situation* **make clear**, shed light on, throw light on, elucidate, illuminate, make plain, make simple, simplify; **explain**, explicate, define, spell out; clear up, sort out, resolve.
OPPOSITES confuse, obscure.
2 *an operation designed to clarify the wine | clarified butter* **purify**, refine; filter, make clear; melt (down), render; *technical* fine.

clarity ▶ noun **1** *the clarity of his account* **lucidity**, lucidness, clearness, perspicuity, intelligibility, comprehensibility, coherence; simplicity, plainness, explicitness, lack of ambiguity, precision.
OPPOSITES obscurity, vagueness.
2 *the clarity of the original image* **sharpness**, clearness, crispness, definition, distinctness, precision.
OPPOSITE blurriness.
3 *the crystal clarity of the water* **limpidity**, limpidness, clearness, transparency, translucence, pellucidity, glassiness; purity; *rare* transpicuousness.
OPPOSITES opacity, murkiness.

clash ▶ noun **1** *eleven people were killed after clashes between armed gangs and security forces* **confrontation**, skirmish, brush, encounter, engagement, collision, incident, conflict, fight, battle; hostilities, fighting, warring; *archaic* rencounter.
2 *a clash between the prime minister and his predecessor* **argument**, **altercation**, confrontation, angry exchange, shouting match, war of words, battle royal, passage of arms; contretemps, quarrel, difference of opinion, disagreement, dispute; *informal* run-in; *Brit. informal* slanging match.
3 *a clash of tweeds and a striped shirt* **mismatch**, discordance, discord, lack of harmony, incompatibility, jarring.
4 *a clash of dates* **coincidence**, concurrence, co-occurrence; conflict.
5 *the clash of cymbals* **striking**, bang, clang, crash, clatter, clank; clangour.
▶ verb **1** *protesters* **clashed with** *police* **fight**, skirmish, contend, come to blows, be in conflict, come into conflict, engage, war, grapple; do battle; confront, attack.
2 *the prime minister clashed with other commonwealth leaders* **disagree**, dissent, differ, wrangle, dispute, cross swords, lock horns, be at odds, be at loggerheads.
3 *her red coat* **clashed** *violently* **with** *her auburn hair* **be incompatible**, not match, not go, be discordant, jar; *informal* scream at.
OPPOSITES match, set off.

4 *the date of this year's conference* **clashed with** *the director's meeting* **conflict**, coincide, occur simultaneously, happen at the same time as.
5 *clashing the cymbals together, he began to walk down the road* **bang**, strike, clang, crash, smash, clank, clatter.

clasp ▶ verb **1** *Ruth clasped his hand* **grasp**, grip, clutch, hold tightly, hang on to, cling to; take hold of, seize, grab.
2 *he clasped Joanne in his arms* **embrace**, hug, enfold, fold, enclose, envelop, wrap; hold, squeeze; *archaic* strain.
▶ noun **1** *a gold bracelet with a turquoise clasp* **fastener**, fastening, catch, clip, pin; hook, hook and eye, buckle, hasp, lock; *Archaeology* fibula.
2 *his tight clasp* **embrace**, hug, cuddle, hold, squeeze; grip, grasp.

class ▶ noun **1** *it was good accommodation for a hotel of this class* **category**, grade, rating, classification, group, grouping, bracket, set, division.
2 *a new class of heart drug* **kind**, sort, type, order, variety, genre, brand; species, genus, family, generation, breed, strain, denomination; stamp, ilk, kidney, style, cast, grain, mould; *N. Amer.* stripe; *technical* phylum.
3 *the middle class | there is no discrimination on the basis of sex, class, or ethnic origin* **social division**, social order, social stratum, rank, level, echelon, group, grouping, set, caste; social status, position/standing in society, social hierarchy, pecking order; *Hinduism* varna; *archaic* estate, sphere, condition, degree.
4 *selected pupils act as representatives for the whole class* **form**, study group, school group, set, stream, band; year; *N. Amer.* grade.
5 *a maths class* **lesson**, period, period of instruction; seminar, tutorial, workshop.
6 (*informal*) *a woman of class | the place had real class* **style**, stylishness, elegance, chic, sophistication, taste, refinement; quality, excellence, distinction, merit, prestige; *French* savoir faire, savoir vivre.
▶ verb *the 12-seater is classed as a commercial vehicle* **classify**, categorize, group, grade, rate, type; order, sort, codify, file, index; bracket, designate, brand, mark down, label, pigeonhole; characterize.
▶ adjective (*informal*) *a class player* **excellent**, very good, first-rate, first-class, marvellous, wonderful, magnificent, outstanding, superlative, superb, formidable, virtuoso, masterly, expert, champion, fine, consummate, skilful, adept; *informal* great, terrific, tremendous, smashing, fantastic, sensational, fabulous, fab, crack, hotshot, A1, mean, demon, awesome, magic, wicked, tip-top, top-notch; *Brit. informal* brilliant, brill; *vulgar slang* shit-hot.

classic ▶ adjective **1** *the classic work on the subject* **definitive**, authoritative; **outstanding**, of the highest quality, first-rate, first-class, best, finest, excellent, superior, masterly, exemplary, consummate; ideal.
2 *a classic example of Norman design* **typical**, archetypal, quintessential, vintage; model, representative, prototypical, paradigmatic; perfect, prime, copybook, textbook; standard, characteristic, stock, true to form.
OPPOSITES atypical, anomalous.
3 *a classic style which never dates* **simple**, **elegant**, understated, uncluttered, restrained; traditional, time-honoured, timeless, ageless, abiding, enduring, immortal.
▶ noun *a classic of the genre* **definitive example**, model, epitome, paradigm, exemplar, prototype; outstanding example, paragon, great work, masterpiece, masterwork; established work, standard; *French* pièce de résistance.

classical ▶ adjective **1** *classical mythology | the birthplace of classical architecture* **ancient Greek**, Grecian, Hellenic, Attic; **Latin**, ancient Roman.
2 *classical ballet | classical music* **traditional**, long-established; serious, highbrow, heavyweight; symphonic, concert; *informal* heavy.
OPPOSITE modern.
3 *a classical style* **simple**, pure, restrained, plain, austere; **well proportioned**, harmonious, balanced, symmetrical, elegant, aesthetic; *Literature* Augustan.

classification ▶ noun **1** *the classification of diseases according to symptoms* **categorization**, categorizing, classifying, classing, grouping, grading, ranking, organization, sorting, codification, systematization, stratification; taxonomy.
2 *a series of classifications into which people are fitted* **category**, class, group, grouping, grade, grading, rating, ranking, bracket; kind, sort, type, variety.

classify ▶ verb *we can classify the students into two distinct groups* **categorize**, class, group, put into sets, grade, rank, rate, order, organize, range, sort, type, codify, bracket, systematize, systemize, stratify, catalogue, tabulate, list, file, index; assign, allocate, consign, place, put; brand, label, pigeonhole; *archaic* assort.

classy ▶ adjective (*informal*) *a classy hotel* **stylish**, high-class, superior, exclusive, chic, elegant, smart, sophisticated, fancy; expensive; *Brit.* upmarket; *N. Amer.* high-toned; *informal* posh, ritzy, plush, plushy, swanky, snazzy; *Brit. informal* swish; *N. Amer. informal* swank, tony; *US black English* dicty.

clatter ▶ verb *an antique fan clattered and whirred in the corner of the office | the coach clattered along the cobbles* **rattle**, clank, clink, clunk, clang, bang; *rare* blatter.

clause ▶ noun *a new clause had been added to the treaty* **section**, paragraph, article, subsection, note, item, point, passage, part, heading; stipulation, condition, proviso, provision, rider; specification, requirement.

claw ▶ noun **1** *a cat's claw | a bird's claw* **nail**, **talon**; *technical* unguis; *rare* pounce.
2 *a crab's claw* **pincer**, nipper; *technical* chela.
▶ verb *her fingers clawed his shoulders* **scratch**, lacerate, tear, rake, rip, slash, scrape, graze, dig into; maul, savage, mutilate; scrabble at.

WORD LINKS
relating to claws **ungual**

clay ▶ noun **1** *his trousers were splattered with wet clay* **earth**, soil, loam; gault, catlinite, pipeclay, pipestone.
2 *lumps of clay awaiting the potter's wheel* argil, china clay, kaolin, adobe, ball clay, bole, pug; slip, barbotine; fireclay.

clean ▶ adjective **1** *he bared his clean, white teeth in a smile | keep the wound clean* **washed**, scrubbed, cleansed, cleaned, polished; spotless, unsoiled, unstained, unspotted, unsullied, unblemished, immaculate, pristine, speckless, dirt-free; hygienic, sanitary, disinfected, sterilized, sterile, aseptic, decontaminated, healthy; pure, white, whiter than white; laundered; *informal* squeaky clean, as clean as a whistle.
OPPOSITE dirty.
2 *a clean sheet of paper* **blank**, empty, bare, clear, plain, white; unused, new, pristine, fresh, unmarked, unfilled, untouched.
OPPOSITE used.
3 *he breathed in the sharp, clean air* **pure**, clear, fresh, crisp, refreshing; unpolluted, uncontaminated, untainted, unmixed, unadulterated; distilled, purified.
OPPOSITE polluted.
4 *Kate had envied her mother her nice clean life* **virtuous**, good, upright, upstanding; honourable, respectable, reputable, decent, righteous, moral, morally correct, ethical, exemplary, honest, just; innocent, pure, chaste, undefiled, guiltless, blameless, irreproachable, unimpeachable, pure as the driven snow, whiter than white; *Christianity* immaculate, impeccable; *informal* squeaky clean.
OPPOSITE immoral.
5 *the investigation demonstrated that the firm is clean* **innocent**, guiltless, blameless, clear, in the clear, not to blame, guilt-free, crime-free, above suspicion, unimpeachable, irreproachable; *informal* squeaky clean.
OPPOSITE guilty.
6 *a good clean fight* **fair**, honest, sporting, sportsmanlike, just, upright, law-abiding, chivalrous, honourable, according to the rules, according to Hoyle; *informal* on the level.
OPPOSITES dirty, unfair.
7 (*informal*) *the staff at the facility gave them counselling and taught them to stay clean* **sober**, teetotal, non-drinking, clear-headed, as sober as a judge; **drug-free**, free of drugs, off drugs; abstinent, self-restrained; *informal* dry, on the wagon, straight.
8 *these secateurs give a clean cut | he took a clean catch* **neat**, smooth, crisp, straight, accurate, precise, slick.
OPPOSITE ragged.
9 *he is making a clean break with the past* **complete**, thorough, total, absolute, entire, thoroughgoing, full, downright, out-and-out; conclusive, decisive, final, ultimate, irrevocable, unalterable, settled; unqualified, unequivocal, categorical.
OPPOSITE partial.
10 *the clean lines of a good design* **simple**, elegant, graceful, uncluttered, trim, shapely, unfussy, uncomplicated; streamlined, smooth, well defined, definite, clean-cut; regular, symmetrical.
OPPOSITES complex, elaborate.
▶ adverb (*informal*) *I clean forgot her birthday* **completely**, entirely, totally, fully, wholly, thoroughly, altogether, quite, utterly, absolutely.
▶ verb **1** *Dad had cleaned the kitchen windows* **wash**, cleanse, wipe, sponge, scrub, mop, rinse, scour, swab, hose down, sluice (down), flush, polish, disinfect; shampoo; floss; *literary* lave.
OPPOSITES dirty, soil.
2 *I would have to get my clothes cleaned* **launder**; dry-clean.
3 *she began to clean the fish* **gut**, eviscerate, remove the innards of, draw, dress.
□ **clean someone out** (*informal*) *the fine cleaned him out* **bankrupt**, ruin, make insolvent, make penniless, wipe out, impoverish, reduce to penury/destitution, bring to ruin, bring to one's knees, break, cripple; *rare* pauperize, beggar.
□ **come clean** (*informal*) *I'll have to come clean: that story is only a rumour* **tell the truth**, be completely honest, tell all, make a clean breast of it; **confess**, own up, admit guilt, admit to one's actions/crimes/sins, accept blame/responsibility, plead guilty; *informal* get something off one's chest, fess up.

cleanse ▶ verb **1** *the wound was then cleansed and redressed aseptically* **clean**, make clean, clean up, wash, bathe, rinse, disinfect, sanitize, decontaminate, purify; *rare* deterge.
2 *a plan to cleanse the environment of traces of lead* **rid**, clear, free, purify, purge, empty, strip, void, relieve.
3 *only God himself can cleanse us from sin* **purify**, purge, absolve, free;

C

deliver; *archaic* shrive; *rare* lustrate.

clear ▸ **adjective 1** *the book gives clear instructions for carrying out various DIY tasks* **understandable**, comprehensible, intelligible, easy to understand, plain, direct, uncomplicated, explicit, lucid, perspicuous, coherent, logical, distinct, simple, straightforward, clearly expressed, unambiguous, clear-cut, crystal clear, accessible, user-friendly; in words of one syllable; *informal* Anglo-Saxon.
OPPOSITES vague, unclear.
2 *he made it clear to the team that he was in charge | a clear case of harassment* **obvious**, evident, plain, apparent, crystal clear, as clear as crystal, transparent; sure, definite, unmistakable, manifest, indisputable, patent, incontrovertible, irrefutable, beyond doubt, beyond question, self-evident; palpable, visible, discernible, noticeable, detectable, recognizable, pronounced, marked, striking, conspicuous, overt, blatant, glaring; as plain as a pikestaff, staring someone in the face, writ large, as plain as day; *informal* as plain as the nose on one's face, standing/sticking out like a sore thumb, standing/sticking out a mile, as clear as day.
OPPOSITES vague, possible.
3 *a beautiful lagoon of clear water* **transparent**, limpid, pellucid, translucent, crystalline, crystal clear, glassy, glass-like; diaphanous, see-through; unclouded, uncloudy; *rare* transpicuous.
OPPOSITES opaque, murky.
4 *a clear blue sky* **bright**, cloudless, unclouded, without a cloud in the sky, fair, fine, light, undimmed; sunny, sunshiny, sunlit, starlit, moonlit.
OPPOSITE cloudy.
5 *her clear complexion* **unblemished**, spot-free; fresh.
OPPOSITES pimply, spotty.
6 *Rosa's clear voice* **distinct**, bell-like, as clear as a bell, clarion, pure; unwavering.
OPPOSITE muffled.
7 *the road was clear | Christina had a clear view of Stephen's face* **unobstructed**, unblocked, passable, unimpeded, open, empty, free, unlimited, unrestricted, unhindered.
OPPOSITES obstructed; limited.
8 *the algae were* **clear of** *toxins* **free**, devoid, empty, vacant, void; rid, relieved; without, unaffected by, no longer affected by.
9 *I left the house with a clear conscience* **untroubled**, undisturbed, unworried, unperturbed, unconcerned, unbothered, with no qualms; peaceful, at peace, tranquil, serene, calm, easy; innocent, guiltless, guilt-free, blameless, clean, sinless, stainless, unimpeachable, irreproachable.
OPPOSITE guilty.
10 *two clear days' notice is required* **whole**, full, entire, complete, total, solid, round, unbroken.
OPPOSITE partial.
▸ **adverb 1** *an indicator told them to stand* **clear** *of the doors* **away from**, apart from, beyond, at a distance from, at a safe distance from, out of contact with.
OPPOSITE close to.
2 *Tommy's voice came loud and clear from the row behind* **distinctly**, clearly, as clear as a bell, plainly, audibly, intelligibly, with clarity.
OPPOSITE indistinctly.
3 *he will have time to get clear away* **completely**, entirely, thoroughly, fully, wholly, totally, utterly, quite, altogether; *informal* clean.
▸ **verb 1** *the sky cleared briefly | the weather was clearing* **brighten** (up), lighten, become light, light up, break, clear up, become bright/brighter/lighter, become fine, become sunny.
OPPOSITE darken.
2 *the drizzle had cleared, leaving the evening fine* **disappear**, go away, melt away, vanish, end; dwindle, peter out, fade, wear off, decrease, lessen, diminish, recede, withdraw, ebb, wane; disperse.
3 *shops have cleared the shelves of anything that could offend the public | together they cleared the table* **empty**, void; free, rid, strip, unload, unburden.
OPPOSITE fill.
4 *plumbers' tools for clearing drains* **unblock**, unclog, unstop.
OPPOSITE block.
5 *he warned the staff to clear the building* **evacuate**, empty, make empty, make vacant; leave.
6 *Karen cleared the dirty plates* **remove**, take away, carry away, move, shift, tidy away/up.
7 *at the moment I'm clearing debts* **pay off**, pay, repay, settle, discharge, square, make good, honour, defray, satisfy, account for, remit, liquidate.
OPPOSITE run up.
8 *I cleared the bar at my first attempt* **go over**, get past, go above, pass over, sail over; jump (over), vault (over), leap (over), hop (over), hurdle, spring over, bound over, skip (over), leapfrog (over).
9 *he was jailed for possessing drugs, but was later cleared by an appeal court* **acquit**, declare innocent, find not guilty; absolve, exonerate, exculpate, vindicate; *informal* let off (the hook).
OPPOSITE convict.
10 *I was cleared to work on the atomic project* **authorize**, give permission, permit, allow, pass, accept, endorse, license, sanction, give approval to, give one's seal of approval to, give consent to; *informal* OK, give the OK, give the thumbs up, give the green light, give the go-ahead.
OPPOSITE veto.
11 *I hoped to clear £50,000 profit from each match* **net**, make a profit of, realize a profit of, take home, pocket; gain, earn, make, get, acquire, secure, reap, bring in, pull in, be paid; *informal* rake in.
OPPOSITE spend.
□ **clear off** (*informal*) *Clear off! You're trespassing!* **go away**, get out, leave; be off with you!, shoo!, make yourself scarce!, on your way!, *informal* beat it, push off, clear out, shove off, scram, scoot, skedaddle, buzz off; *Brit. informal* hop it, sling your hook; *Austral./NZ informal* rack off; *N. Amer. informal* bug off, take a hike; *S. African informal* voetsak, hamba; *vulgar slang* piss off, bugger off; *archaic* begone.
OPPOSITE stay.
□ **clear out** (*informal*) *get everyone to clear out of the building as quickly as possible.* See LEAVE.
□ **clear something out 1** *we had to clear out the junk room to make a nursery for James* **empty**, empty out, void, make vacant; tidy, tidy up, clear up, clean; *informal* dejunk.
2 *clear out the rubbish as you go* **get rid of**, throw out/away, discard, dispose of, dump, bin, scrap, do away with, jettison, eject, eliminate, throw on the scrap heap; *informal* chuck (out/away), ditch, junk, get shut of; *Brit. informal* get shot of; *N. Amer. informal* trash.
□ **clear up** *the weather had cleared up.* See CLEAR *senses 1 & 2.*
□ **clear something up 1** *clear up the garden before you go* **tidy**, tidy up, put in order, straighten up, clean up, put to rights, make shipshape, spruce up.
2 *I'm glad we've cleared up that little problem* **solve**, resolve, straighten out, find an/the answer to, answer, find the key to, decipher, break, get to the bottom of, make head or tail of, piece together, explain, expound; unravel, untangle, elucidate; *informal* crack, figure out, suss out.

clearance ▸ **noun 1** *the dissatisfaction with housing conditions produced schemes for slum clearance* **removal**, clearing, clear-out, demolition; evacuation, eviction, purge, emptying, depopulation, unpeopling.
2 *to become a regular prison visitor you must have Home Office clearance* **authorization**, permission, consent, approval, seal of approval, blessing, acceptance, leave, sanction, licence, dispensation, assent, agreement, concurrence, endorsement, imprimatur; permit; *informal* the green light, the go-ahead, the thumbs up, the OK, the say-so, the nod, the rubber stamp; *rare* nihil obstat.
OPPOSITE veto.
3 *the clearance of a debt* **repayment**, payment, paying, paying off, settling, discharge, squaring, making good, honouring, defrayal, defrayment, defraying, remission, liquidation, reckoning.
4 *adjust the door up or down to ensure equal clearance between door and frame* **space**, gap, room, room to spare, headroom, margin, leeway, allowance, separation, clearing.

clear-cut ▸ **adjective** *we now had a clear-cut objective* **definite**, distinct, clear, well defined, sharply defined, precise, specific, explicit, unambiguous, black and white, hard and fast; unequivocal, straightforward; striking, obvious; marked, decided; sharp, crisp, stark; *informal* cut and dried.
OPPOSITES blurred, indistinct, vague.

clearing ▸ **noun** *at last the trees gave way to a clearing* **glade**, dell, space, gap, opening.

clearly ▸ **adverb 1** *everybody has to be able to write clearly* **intelligibly**, plainly, distinctly, comprehensibly, understandably, perspicuously, with clarity; legibly, readably; audibly.
2 *clearly, substantial changes are needed* **obviously**, evidently, patently, unquestionably, undoubtedly, without doubt, indubitably, plainly, decidedly, surely, assuredly, certainly, definitely, undeniably, incontrovertibly, irrefutably, incontestably, unmistakably, doubtless; visibly, demonstrably, noticeably, manifestly, markedly, transparently, palpably; it goes without saying, needless to say, of course.

cleave[1] ▸ **verb 1** *the axe his father used to cleave wood for the fire* **split**, split open, crack open, lay open, divide, sever, splinter; cut (up), hew, hack, chop up, slice up, halve, bisect, quarter; *literary* rend; *archaic* sunder, rive.
2 *Stan was away, cleaving a path through the traffic* **plough**, drive, bulldoze, cut, carve, make.

cleave[2] ▸ **verb**
□ **cleave to** (*literary*) **1** *her tongue clove to the roof of her mouth* **stick to**, stick fast to, be stuck to, adhere to, cohere to, be attached to, bond to.
2 *a state formerly criticized for cleaving too closely to Moscow's line* **adhere to**, hold to, cling to, stand by, abide by, be loyal to, be faithful to, remain true to.

cleaver ▸ **noun** *a meat cleaver* **chopper**, hatchet, axe, knife; butcher's knife, kitchen knife.

cleft ▸ **noun 1** *a deep cleft in the rocks* **split**, slit, crack, fissure, crevice, chasm, opening, rift, break, fracture, rent, breach, gash; cranny, interstice, furrow, indentation; gap, hole, pit, void, crater.
2 *the cleft in his chin* **dimple**.
▸ **adjective** *the little gull has a cleft tail* **split**, divided, cloven, parted, separated.

clemency ▸ **noun** *the high court commuted his prison term to five years as an*

act of clemency **mercy**, mercifulness, leniency, lenience, mildness, indulgence, forbearance, quarter; compassion, humanity, pity, sympathy, kindness, magnanimity, benignity, charity, grace, humaneness, humanitarianism, soft-heartedness, tenderness.
OPPOSITES ruthlessness, strictness.

clench ▶ verb **1** *she clenched her teeth, fighting waves of nausea | he stood there, clenching and unclenching his hands* **squeeze together**, press together, clamp together, close tightly, shut tightly; grit; make into a fist, make into a ball.
2 *the knuckles on his hand were white where he clenched the back of chair* **grip**, grasp, grab, clutch, clamp, clasp, hold tightly, seize, press, squeeze, lay (one's) hands on, fasten one's hand on, hang on to.
▶ noun *she felt a clench in her stomach* **contraction**, tightening, tensing, tension, constricting, cramp.

clergy *See centre pages for list of* **Priests**
▶ noun **clergymen**, **clergywomen**, churchmen, churchwomen, clerics, priests, ecclesiastics, men/women of God, men/women of the cloth; ministry, priesthood, holy orders, the church, the cloth, first estate.
OPPOSITE laity.

WORD LINKS
relating to clergy **clerical**

clergyman, **clergywoman** *See centre pages for list of* **Priests**
▶ noun **priest**, churchman, churchwoman, man/woman of the cloth, man/woman of God, cleric, minister, preacher, chaplain, father; ecclesiastic, divine, theologian; *Christianity* bishop, pastor, vicar, rector, parson, (assistant) curate, deacon, deaconess; *Judaism* rabbi; *Islam* imam; *Scottish* kirkman; *French* abbé, curé; *N. Amer.* dominie; *informal* reverend, padre, Holy Joe, sky pilot; *Austral. informal* josser; *informal, derogatory* Bible-basher, God botherer.

clerical ▶ adjective **1** *there are a number of clerical jobs to be done in a media department* **office**, desk, back-room; **administrative**, secretarial, writing, typing, keyboarding, filing, bookkeeping; white-collar; *informal* pen-pushing.
2 *a clerical collar* **ecclesiastical**, church, priestly, pastoral, religious, spiritual, prelatic, apostolic, canonical, parsonical; holy, divine; *archaic* vicarial; *rare* sacerdotal, hieratic, rectorial, presbyteral.
OPPOSITE secular.

clerk ▶ noun **office worker**, clerical worker, administrator, administrative officer; bookkeeper, record-keeper, account-keeper; cashier, teller; *Indian* babu; *informal* pen-pusher; *archaic* scrivener.

clever ▶ adjective **1** *an extremely clever and studious young woman* **intelligent**, bright, smart, brilliant; talented, gifted, precocious; capable, able, competent, apt, proficient; educated, learned, erudite, academic, bookish, knowledgeable, wise, sagacious; *informal* brainy.
OPPOSITE stupid.
2 *a clever scheme | he had a cruel, clever face* **shrewd**, astute, sharp, acute, quick, sharp-witted, quick-witted; ingenious, resourceful, canny, cunning, crafty, artful, wily, slick, neat; *informal* foxy, savvy; *Brit. informal* fly; *Scottish & N. English informal* pawky; *N. Amer. informal* as sharp as a tack, cute.
OPPOSITES ill-advised, foolish.
3 *Grandma was clever with her hands* **skilful**, dexterous, adroit, deft, nimble, nimble-fingered, handy, adept; skilled, talented.
4 *a clever remark* **witty**, quick-witted, amusing, droll, humorous, funny, sparkling, entertaining, scintillating.

cleverness ▶ noun **1** *people marvelled at his cleverness* **intelligence**, brilliance, genius, intellect; precocity, precociousness, talent, ability, capability, competence, proficiency; education, learnedness, erudition, bookishness, knowledgeableness, sagacity, wisdom; *informal* braininess, brains; *N. Amer. informal* smarts.
OPPOSITE stupidity.
2 *the cleverness of his strategy* **shrewdness**, astuteness, sharp-wittedness, quick-wittedness, acuteness, acuity; ingenuity, ingeniousness, resourcefulness, canniness, cunning, craftiness, artfulness, wiliness.
OPPOSITE foolishness.

cliché ▶ noun *there is plenty of truth in the cliché that a trouble shared is a trouble halved* **platitude**, hackneyed phrase, commonplace, banality, truism, trite phrase, banal phrase, overworked phrase, stock phrase, bromide; saw, maxim, adage, dictum, saying; tag, aphorism; expression, phrase, formula; *informal* old chestnut; *rare* apophthegm.

click ▶ noun *the door shut with a click* **clink**, clack, chink, snick, snap, pop, tick.
▶ verb **1** *the cameras clicked as the oarsmen prepared for the challenge | he clicked his fingers* **clink**, clack, chink, snick, tick; **snap**, pop.
2 (*informal*) *that night it just clicked that this was what I wanted to do* **become clear**, fall into place, come home to one, make sense, dawn, register, get through, sink in.
3 (*informal*) *we just clicked, and very quickly I found myself falling deeper and deeper in love* **take to each other**, get along/on, warm to each other, be compatible, be in harmony, be like-minded, feel a rapport, see eye to eye; *informal* **hit it off**, get on like a house on fire, be on the same wavelength.
4 (*informal*) *I don't think this issue has clicked with the voters* **go down well**, prove popular, be/make a hit, get an enthusiastic reception, be successful, be a success, succeed.

client ▶ noun *a salesman needs to understand his clients' needs* **customer**, buyer, purchaser, shopper, consumer, user; patient; patron, regular, habitué, frequenter; (**clients**) clientele, patronage, public; market, trade, business; *Brit. informal* punter; *Law* vendee; *rare* emptor.

clientele ▶ noun **clients**. *See* CLIENT.

cliff ▶ noun **precipice**, rock face, face, crag, bluff, ridge, escarpment, scar, scarp, overhang; *S. African* krantz; *Geology* cuesta; *literary* steep; *Scottish archaic* linn.

climactic ▶ adjective *the movie's climactic scene* **final**, culminating, ending, finishing, closing, concluding, ultimate; **exciting**, thrilling, stirring, action-packed, gripping, riveting, dramatic, hair-raising; crucial, decisive, deciding, critical, momentous.
OPPOSITES anticlimactic, bathetic.

climate *See centre pages for lists of* **Climatic Zones** **Weather**
▶ noun **1** *the Channel Islands have an enviably mild climate* **weather pattern**, weather conditions, weather, atmospheric conditions.
2 *they migrate here from colder climates* **region**, area, zone, country, place; *literary* clime.
3 *the political climate of the 1940s* **atmosphere**, mood, temper, spirit, feeling, feel, ambience, aura, tenor, tendency, essence, ethos, attitude, milieu; *informal* vibe(s).

WORD LINKS
study of climate **climatology**

climax ▶ noun **1** *the climax of his career came when he captained Palace to promotion* **peak**, pinnacle, height, high point, highest point, summit, top; acme, zenith, apex, apogee, apotheosis; culmination, crowning point, crown, crest; crescendo, finale, denouement; highlight, high spot, best part, high water mark.
OPPOSITES nadir; anticlimax.
2 **orgasm**, sexual climax; ejaculation.
▶ verb **1** *the event will climax with a gala concert* **culminate**, peak, come to a climax, reach a pinnacle, come to a crescendo; result, end, come to a head.
2 **have an orgasm**, reach/achieve orgasm; ejaculate; *informal* come, feel the earth move, get one's rocks off; *Brit. informal* come off; *literary* die.

climb ▶ verb **1** *we climbed the hill | Auntie slowly* ***climbed up*** *the stairs* **ascend**, mount, scale, scramble up, clamber up, shin up; go up, move up, walk up, make one's way up, swarm up; conquer; *N. Amer.* shinny (up).
OPPOSITE descend.
2 *the plane climbed to eleven thousand feet* **rise**, ascend, fly upwards, gain altitude.
OPPOSITE dive.
3 *the road climbs steeply from the bay* **slope upwards**, rise, go uphill, incline upwards.
OPPOSITE drop.
4 *the shares opened at 47.5p and climbed to 55p* **increase**, rise, go up, mount, escalate, shoot up, leap up, soar, spiral, rocket; *informal* be hiked/jacked up, go through the roof/ceiling.
OPPOSITES fall, decrease.
5 *he's climbed through the ranks to become chairman of the association* **advance**, work one's way up, rise, move up, progress, make progress, make strides, get ahead.
6 *the man climbed out of his car* **clamber**, scramble; scrabble, claw one's way, crawl.
□ **climb down 1** *Sandy climbed down the ladder* **descend**, go down, come down, move down, shin down.
2 *the Government had to climb down over its claim that it was offering the miners a pay increase* **back down**, admit defeat, concede defeat, surrender, capitulate, yield, give in/up, give way, cave in, submit; retreat, backtrack, back-pedal; admit that one is wrong, retract one's words, eat one's words, eat humble pie; do a U-turn, do an about-face, shift one's ground, sing a different song, have second thoughts; *Brit.* do an about-turn; *N. Amer. informal* eat crow.
▶ noun *he was out of breath after his steep climb* **ascent**, clamber; conquest.
OPPOSITE descent.

clinch ▶ verb **1** *a salesman eager to clinch a deal* **secure**, settle, conclude, close, pull off, bring off, complete, confirm, seal, set the seal on, finalize, shake hands on, reach an agreement on; transact; *informal* sew up, wrap up, string, button up.
2 *these findings clinched the matter* **settle**, decide, determine, establish; resolve; *informal* sort out.
3 *his team clinched the title* **win**, be the victor in, be the winner of, be victorious in, come first in, finish first in, take first prize in, triumph in, achieve success in, be successful in, prevail in.
OPPOSITE lose.
4 *they clinch every nail they drive in* **secure**, fasten, make fast, fix, clamp, bolt, rivet, pinion.
5 *there was heavy sparring, then the figures clinched* **grapple**, wrestle,

struggle with each other, scuffle with each other; grasp each other, clutch each other, grip each other.
▶ noun *a passionate clinch* **embrace**, hug, cuddle, squeeze, hold, clasp, bear hug.

cling ▶ verb *shorter rice grains have a tendency to cling together* **stick**, adhere, hold, cohere, bond, bind.
□ **cling (on) to 1** *she clung to him, shuddering with emotion* **hold on to**, clutch, grip, grasp, clasp, attach oneself to, hang on to, hold tightly, clench; embrace, hug, cuddle, entwine oneself around.
2 *some politicians clung to the belief that peace could be maintained* **adhere to**, hold to, stick to, stand by, abide by, remain attached to, remain devoted to, cherish, be loyal to, be faithful to, remain true to, have faith in, swear by; *informal* stick with; *literary* cleave to.

clinic ▶ noun *an orthopaedic clinic* **medical centre**, health centre, outpatients' department, surgery, doctor's, polyclinic.

clinical ▶ adjective **1** *what made it worse was his coldness—he seemed so absolutely serious and clinical* **detached**, impersonal, dispassionate, objective, uninvolved, distant, remote, aloof, removed, cold, indifferent, neutral, unsympathetic, unfeeling, unemotional, non-emotional, unsentimental; scientific, analytic, rational, logical, hard-headed, sober, businesslike.
OPPOSITE emotional.
2 *the room was white and clinical* **plain**, simple, unadorned, unornamented, unembellished, stark, austere, severe, spartan, ascetic, monastic, bleak, bare, chaste, cheerless; clean; functional, basic, institutional, impersonal, characterless, soulless, colourless, antiseptic; *informal* no frills.
OPPOSITE luxurious.

clip[1] ▶ noun **1** *he opened the clip, resting the briefcase on his knee* **fastener**, clasp, hasp, catch, pin, hook, buckle, lock, coupler, link.
2 *a diamanté clip* **brooch**, pin, breastpin; badge.
3 *he pulled the trigger twice, but his clip was empty* **magazine**, cartridge, cylinder.
▶ verb *he clipped the pages together and slipped them into a file* **fasten**, attach, fix, affix, hold, join, connect, secure; pin, staple, tack.

clip[2] ▶ verb **1** *I was clipping the hedges* **trim**, cut, cut short/shorter, snip, prune, shorten, crop, shear, shave, pare; lop, pollard; mow; neaten, shape, tidy up, even up.
2 *simply clip the coupon below* **remove**, cut out, snip out, detach, extract, tear out.
3 *his lorry clipped a van as it overturned* **hit**, strike, make contact with, touch, brush, graze, glance off, tap, run into, bang into, crack into/against.
4 *Maggie clipped his ear, making him yell* **hit**, strike, cuff, smack, slap, thump, punch, knock, rap, box someone's ears; *informal* clout, whack, wallop, belt, clobber, bop, biff, sock; *Scottish & N. English informal* skelp.
▶ noun **1** *I gave him a full clip* **cut**, trim, crop, haircut, shortening; shear, shearing, pruning.
2 *a clip from an old black-and-white film* **extract**, excerpt, snippet, selection, cutting, fragment; scene, moment; trailer.
3 (*informal*) *if he didn't shut up he might get a clip round the ear* **smack**, cuff, slap, thump, punch, box, knock, rap; *informal* clout, whack, wallop, belt, clobbering, bop, biff, sock.
4 (*informal*) *the truck was speeding along at a good clip* **speed**, rate, pace, velocity, tempo, momentum; *informal* lick, fair old rate.
□ **clip someone's wings** *some MPs are eager to clip the Prime Minister's wings* **restrict someone's freedom**, check, curb, set/impose limits on, keep within bounds, keep under control, obstruct, impede, frustrate, thwart, stand in the way of, fetter, hamstring.

clipping ▶ noun *friends are sending us newspaper clippings from the British press* **cutting**, extract, excerpt, snippet, fragment, piece; article, passage, column, paragraph.

clique ▶ noun *his flat became a haven for a clique of young men of similar tastes* **coterie**, circle, inner circle, crowd, in-crowd, set, group; pack, band, ring, mob, crew; club, society, fraternity, sorority, fellowship; camp; cartel, cabal, junta, caucus, cell, lobby; *Austral./NZ* push; *informal* gang, bunch; *rare* camarilla.

cloak *See centre pages for list of* **Coats, Cloaks, and Jackets**
▶ noun **1** *he threw his cloak over his shoulders* **cape**, mantle, robe.
2 *ministers tried to cover up the truth by hiding under a cloak of secrecy* **cover**, screen, mask, blind, front, camouflage, shield, veneer; **veil**, mantle, shroud, blanket; pretext, smokescreen.
▶ verb *the summit was cloaked in thick mist | the brothers were men cloaked in mystery* **conceal**, hide, cover, veil, shroud, screen, mask, cloud; envelop, swathe, surround, cocoon; disguise, camouflage, obscure.

clobber[1] ▶ noun (*Brit. informal*) *the latest designer clobber. See* CLOTHES.

clobber[2] ▶ verb (*informal*) *if he does that I'll clobber him. See* HIT.

clock *See centre pages for list of* **Clocks and Watches**
▶ noun **1** *he glanced at the clock—it was 10.30* **timepiece**, timekeeper, timer; chronometer, chronograph.
2 (*informal*) *the car was three years old and had over 50,000 miles on the clock* **milometer**, odometer, counter; speedometer, taximeter.
▶ verb **1** *he finished second in the 100 metres, clocking 11.8 seconds | the UK clocked up record exports of £4.3 billion in January* **register**, record, log; **achieve**, attain, accomplish, gain, earn, win, make; *informal* do, chalk up, notch up, rack up, bag, turn in, knock up.
2 (*Brit. informal*) *Liz was the first to clock the change in her new neighbour. See* NOTICE.

clod ▶ noun **1** *clods of earth* **lump**, clump, chunk, mass, piece, hunk, slab, wedge; *informal* dollop, wodge.
2 (*informal*) *you're an insensitive clod! See* FOOL.

clog ▶ noun *a pair of wooden clogs* sabot, wooden shoe, wooden-soled shoe.
▶ verb *the drainpipes became clogged with clay and silt* **block**, obstruct, congest, jam, choke, bung up, dam (up), plug, silt up, stop up, seal, fill up, close; *informal* gunge up; *technical* occlude, obturate.
OPPOSITE unblock.

cloister ▶ noun **1** *the shadowed cloisters of the convent* **walkway**, covered walk, corridor, aisle, arcade, loggia, gallery, piazza; *technical* colonnade, ambulatory, stoa.
2 *I was educated in the cloister* **abbey**, monastery, friary, convent, priory, nunnery, religious house, religious community; *historical* charterhouse; *rare* coenobium, coenoby.
▶ verb *the women were all cloistered at home* **confine**, isolate, shut away, sequester, seclude, closet.

cloistered ▶ adjective *his cloistered life was devoted to writing* **secluded**, sheltered, sequestered, shielded, protected; shut-off, isolated, withdrawn, confined, restricted, insulated, reclusive, retiring, unworldly; solitary, monastic, hermitic, hermit-like; *rare* eremitic, anchoritic, cloistral.
OPPOSITES sociable, gregarious.

close[1] (rhymes with 'dose') ▶ adjective **1** *the town is located close to Manchester's airport* **near**, adjacent, in close proximity, close/near at hand; not far from, in the vicinity of, in the neighbourhood of, within reach of, within close range of; neighbouring, hard by, adjoining, abutting, alongside, on the doorstep, within sight, within earshot, a stone's throw away; close by, nearby, at hand, at close quarters, contiguous, proximate; accessible, handy, convenient; *informal* within spitting distance, {a hop, a skip, and a jump away}, within sniffing distance; *archaic* nigh.
OPPOSITES far, distant, remote.
2 *flying in close formation* **dense**, compact, tight, close-packed, tightly packed, packed, solid, condensed, compressed, concentrated; crowded, cramped, crammed, congested, crushed, squeezed, jammed.
OPPOSITE sparse.
3 *I was close to tears in the dressing room* **on the verge of**, near, on the brink of, on the point of, within an ace of, in danger of.
4 *Essex versus Bedfordshire should be a very close match* **evenly matched**, even, well matched; neck and neck, side by side, nose to nose, with nothing to choose between them; hard-fought, sharply contested, nip and tuck; *informal* fifty-fifty, even-steven(s).
OPPOSITE one-sided.
5 *not all elderly people have close relatives they might live with* **immediate**, direct, near.
OPPOSITE distant.
6 *they became close friends* **intimate**, dear, bosom; close-knit, inseparable, attached, loving, devoted, faithful, constant; special, good, best, fast, firm, valued, treasured, cherished; *informal* matey, chummy, pally, (as) thick as thieves; *N. Amer. informal* buddy-buddy, palsy-walsy.
OPPOSITE casual.
7 *he bears a close resemblance to our school janitor* **strong**, marked, distinct, pronounced.
OPPOSITE slight.
8 *a close examination of the language of a text* **careful**, detailed, thorough, minute, painstaking, meticulous, assiduous, diligent, rigorous, scrupulous, conscientious, attentive, focused, intent, concentrated, searching, methodical.
OPPOSITE casual.
9 *we need to keep a close eye on the project* **vigilant**, watchful, keen, alert.
10 *a close translation of a French original* **strict**, faithful, exact, precise, literal; word for word, verbatim.
OPPOSITE loose.
11 *Woolley placed her under close arrest for mutiny* **carefully guarded**, closely guarded, strict, tight.
12 *he's usually pretty close about his clients' deals* **reticent**, quiet, uncommunicative, unforthcoming, private, secretive, tight-lipped, close-mouthed, close-lipped, guarded, evasive; *informal* playing one's cards close to one's chest.
13 *Sylvie was close with money* **mean**, miserly, niggardly, parsimonious, penny-pinching, cheese-paring, ungenerous, illiberal; *informal* tight-fisted, stingy, tight, mingy.
OPPOSITE generous.
14 *the weather was hot and close* **humid**, muggy, stuffy, airless, fuggy, heavy, sticky, steamy, clammy, sultry, oppressive, stifling, suffocating, like a Turkish bath, like a sauna; unventilated.
OPPOSITE fresh.
▶ noun *a small close of semi-detached houses* **street**, road, cul-de-sac; **courtyard**,

quadrangle, enclosure, piazza.

close[2] (rhymes with 'nose') ▶ **verb 1** *she closed the door* **shut**, draw to, pull to, push to, slam; fasten, secure, lock, bolt, bar, latch, padlock; put up the shutter.
OPPOSITES open; unlock.
2 *close the hole with a plug of cotton wool* **block (up/off)**, stop up, plug, seal (up/off), shut up/off, cork, stopper, bung (up); make airtight, make watertight; fill (up), pack, stuff; clog (up), choke, obstruct, occlude; *N. Amer.* stopple.
OPPOSITES open, unblock.
3 *there were a group of aircraft about 130 miles away and closing fast* **catch up**, creep up, near, approach, gain on someone, draw nearer/near, get nearer/near, come nearer/near, draw closer/close, get closer/close, come closer/close.
4 *although unemployment here is still below the national average, the gap is closing* **narrow**, lessen, grow/become/make smaller, dwindle, diminish, reduce, shrink, contract, constrict, get/become/make narrower; *archaic* straiten.
OPPOSITE widen.
5 *his arms closed around her* **come together**, join, connect, come into contact, unite, form a circle.
6 *the chairman hastily closed the meeting* **end**, bring/come to an end, conclude, finish, terminate, wind up, break off, halt, call a halt to, discontinue, dissolve; adjourn, suspend, prorogue, recess.
OPPOSITES open, begin.
7 *the factory is to close within two years* **cease activity**, shut down, close down, cease production, cease operating, come to a halt, cease trading; fail, collapse, go out of business, crash, go under, go bankrupt, become insolvent, go into receivership, go into liquidation, be liquidated, be wound up, be closed (down), be shut (down); *informal* fold, flop, go broke, go bump, go to the wall, go bust.
OPPOSITE open.
8 *it wouldn't be long before he closed a deal with one of the chain stores* **clinch**, settle, secure, seal, set the seal on, confirm, guarantee, establish, transact, pull off, bring off/about; complete, conclude, fix, agree, finalize, shake hands on; *informal* wrap up.
□ **close down** *the company closed down some years later.* See CLOSE sense 7.
▶ **noun** *a statement was issued at the close of the talks* **end**, finish, conclusion, termination, cessation, completion; culmination, finale, resolution, climax, denouement; *informal* wind-up.
OPPOSITE beginning.

closet ▶ **noun** *a clothes closet* **cupboard**, wardrobe, cabinet, locker; storage room, cubicle.
▶ **adjective** *a closet gay* **secret**, covert, unrevealed, undisclosed, private, hidden, concealed, surreptitious, clandestine, underground, furtive.
OPPOSITES out, open.
▶ **verb** *David was closeted in the den with Luther* **shut away**, sequester, seclude, cloister, insulate, confine, isolate.

closure ▶ **noun** *the closure of rural schools* **closing down**, shutting down, shutdown, winding up; termination, discontinuation, discontinuance, cessation, finish, finishing, conclusion, concluding, stoppage, stopping, halting, ceasing; failure; *informal* folding.

clot ▶ **noun 1** *he had two operations to remove blood clots* **lump**, clump, mass, curdling; obstruction; *informal* glob, gob; *Medicine* thrombus, thrombosis, embolus, embolism.
2 (*Brit. informal*) *I felt like a clumsy clot.* See FOOL.
▶ **verb** *such substances make the blood more likely to clot* **coagulate**, set, congeal, cake, curdle, thicken, solidify, harden, dry, stiffen.
OPPOSITES thin, liquefy.

WORD LINKS
surgical removal of a blood clot **embolectomy, thrombectomy**

cloth *See centre pages for list of* **Fabrics and Fibres**
▶ **noun 1** *commodities such as wool and cloth* **fabric**, material, textile, stuff; textiles, dry goods, soft goods.
2 *he fetched a cloth to wipe up the mess* **rag**, dishcloth, floorcloth, wipe, sponge, duster; flannel, facecloth; towel, paper towel, tea towel, tea cloth; tablecloth; *N. Amer.* washcloth, washrag; *Austral.* washer; *UK trademark* J-cloth.
3 (**the cloth**) *a gentleman of the cloth* **the clergy**, the church, the priesthood, the ministry, the first estate; clergymen, clerics, priests, ecclesiastics.

WORD LINKS
seller of cloth **clothier, draper**

clothe ▶ **verb 1** *they were clothed from head to foot in robes of gold* **dress**, attire, outfit, array, rig (out), turn out, fit out, costume, trick out/up, robe, garb, deck out, drape, accoutre; put clothes on; *informal* doll up, get up; *literary* bedizen, caparison; *archaic* apparel, trap out, habit, invest.
OPPOSITE undress.
2 *a long valley clothed in conifers* **cover**, overlay, overspread, cloak, blanket, carpet; envelop, swathe, swaddle, shroud, wrap, surround; *literary* enshroud.
OPPOSITE uncover.

clothes *See centre pages for lists of* **Coats, Cloaks, and Jackets** **Dresses** **Footwear** **Hats and Headgear** **Pullovers** **Shirts** **Skirts** **Ties** **Trousers** **Underwear**
▶ **plural noun** *she took off her clothes and crawled into bed* **clothing**, garments, articles of clothing/dress, attire, garb; dress, wear, wardrobe; outfit, costume, turnout; finery; *informal* gear, togs, duds, get-up, glad rags; *Brit. informal* clobber, kit, rig-out; *N. Amer. informal* threads; *formal* apparel; *literary* raiment, habiliments, habit; *archaic* vestments.

WORD LINKS
relating to clothes **sartorial**
maker or seller of clothes **clothier, outfitter, couturier, tailor**

clothing ▶ **noun** *they were wearing dark clothing.* See CLOTHES.

cloud *See centre pages for list of* **Cloud Formations**
▶ **noun 1** *a cloud of blue exhaust smoke* **mass**, billow, pall, shroud, mantle, blanket, layer, sheet, curtain, canopy.
2 *from the elms rose a cloud of rooks* **swarm**, flock, flight, hive, covey, drove, herd; mass, multitude, host, horde, throng, crowd.
3 *the dark clouds of a recession* **threat**, menace, shadow, spectre, blight; gloom, darkness, chill, pall; trouble, problem, worry.
□ **on cloud nine/seven ecstatic**, rapturous, joyful, elated, blissful, joyous, beatific, euphoric, enraptured, in seventh heaven, transported, in transports, in raptures, beside oneself with joy/happiness, rhapsodic, ravished, enchanted, delighted, thrilled, overjoyed, very happy; *informal* over the moon, on top of the world, walking on air, blissed out; *Austral. informal* wrapped.
OPPOSITE depressed.
▶ **verb 1** *the sky clouded* **become cloudy**, cloud over, become overcast, become gloomy, grow dim, lour, blacken, darken, dim.
OPPOSITE clear.
2 *the bottom of the river is churned up, clouding the water* **make cloudy**, make murky, dirty, darken, blacken; *N. Amer.* roil, rile.
OPPOSITE clear.
3 *anger clouded my professional judgement* **confuse**, muddle; make unclear, obscure, fog, befog, muddy, blur.
OPPOSITE clarify.

WORD LINKS
fear of clouds **nephophobia**

cloudy ▶ **adjective 1** *a cloudy sky* **overcast**, clouded, clouded over, overclouded; dark, darkened, grey, black, leaden, dull, murky; sombre, dismal, dreary, cheerless, heavy, gloomy, dim, louring; sunless, starless; hazy, misty, foggy; threatening, menacing, promising rain.
OPPOSITE bright.
2 *the drinking water looked cloudy* **murky**, muddy, milky, dirty, clouded, dull, opaque, non-transparent, emulsified, opalescent, turbid; *N. Amer.* riled, roily; *literary* roiled.
OPPOSITE clear.
3 *Alexei's eyes grew cloudy* **tearful**, teary, weepy, weeping, lachrymose; moist, misty, watery, rheumy; blurred, blurry, unfocused.
OPPOSITE dry.
4 *it is important to avoid cloudy phrases, in which the real meaning may be obscured* **vague**, blurred, fuzzy, indistinct, imprecise, foggy, hazy, confused, muddled, indefinite, lacking definition, nebulous, obscure, unformed.
OPPOSITES clear, focused.

clout (*informal*) ▶ **noun 1** *I gave him a clout on the ear* **smack**, slap, thump, punch, blow, hit, knock, bang, cuff, box, spanking, spank, tap, clip; *informal* whack, wallop, clobbering, sock.
2 *the negotiating clout of a large business* **influence**, power, pull, weight, sway, leverage, control, say, mastery, dominance, domination, advantage; authority, prestige, standing, stature, rank; *informal* teeth, beef, muscle.
▶ **verb** *he started to clout me around the head* **hit**, strike, punch, smack, slap, cuff, thump, beat, batter, pound, pummel, thrash, rap, spank, buffet, hammer, bang, knock, box someone's ears; *informal* wallop, belt, whack, clobber, sock, clip, bop, biff, swipe, tan, lay one on.

cloven ▶ **adjective** *cloven hooves* **split**, divided, bisected, cleft.

clown ▶ **noun 1** *a circus clown* **comic entertainer**, Pierrot, comedian; *historical* jester, fool, zany, harlequin, merry andrew, Punchinello.
2 *I was always the class clown* **joker**, comedian, comic, humorist, wag, wit, funny man/woman/girl, prankster, jester, jokester, buffoon, character; *informal* case, hoot, scream, laugh, kidder, wisecracker, riot, barrel of laughs; *Austral./NZ informal* hard case; *informal, dated* card, caution.
3 *the department is staffed with bureaucratic clowns* **fool**, idiot, dolt, ass, nincompoop, blockhead, dunce, dunderhead, simpleton, ignoramus, donkey, jackass, dullard; **bungler**, blunderer, incompetent, bumbler, botcher, amateur; *informal* moron, clot, dope, mutt, chump, numbskull, twit, nitwit, halfwit, bonehead, fathead, birdbrain, twerp, berk, ninny; *Brit. informal* bodger, prat.
▶ **verb** *Harvey* **clowned around**, *pretending to be a dog* **fool around/about**, play the fool, act foolishly, act the clown/fool/goat, play about/around, monkey about/around, play tricks, indulge in horseplay, engage in high

jinks; joke, jest; *informal* mess about/around, lark (about/around), horse about/around; *Brit. informal* muck about/around; *N. Amer. informal* cut up; *Brit. vulgar slang* piss about/around, arse about/around, bugger about/around; *dated* play the giddy goat.

cloy ▶ verb *the piece goes on a little too long and the sweetness can tend to cloy* **become sickening**, become nauseating, pall, become distasteful, become tedious, become tiresome; be excessive.

C

cloying ▶ adjective *the romance never becomes cloying* **sickly sweet**, sugary, syrupy, saccharine, honeyed, oversweet; sickening, nauseating, disgusting; mawkish, maudlin, sentimental, over-sentimental; *Brit.* twee; *informal* over the top, OTT, mushy, slushy, sloppy, cutesy, cute, gooey, drippy, treacly, cheesy, corny, icky, sick-making; *N. Amer. informal* cornball, sappy.

club[1] ▶ noun **1** *a youth club | a canoeing club* **society**, association, organization, institution, group; circle, set, clique, coterie, band, body, ring, crew, troupe; affiliation, alliance, league, union, federation, company, coalition, consortium, combine, guild, lodge, order; fraternity, brotherhood, sorority, fellowship; *rare* sodality.
2 *people crowd the island's amazing bars, clubs, and discos* **nightclub**, night spot, disco, discotheque, cabaret club, supper club, bar; *informal* hot spot, nite club, niterie.
3 *the club are struggling at the bottom of the table* **team**, squad, side, group, line-up.
▶ verb
□ **club together** *some friends have clubbed together to buy an old van* **pool resources**, make a kitty, join forces, make a joint contribution, divide/share costs; team up, join up, band together, come together, get together, pull together, collaborate, ally; *informal* have a whip-round, chip in.

club[2] *See centre pages for lists of* **Golf Clubs** **Weapons**
▶ noun *they beat him with a wooden club* **cudgel**, truncheon, bludgeon, baton, stick, mace, staff, bat; *N. Amer.* blackjack, billy, billy club, nightstick; (*in Ireland*) shillelagh; *Indian* lathi, danda; *S. African* kierie, knobkerrie; *Brit. informal* cosh, life preserver.
▶ verb *he was clubbed with an iron bar* **cudgel**, bludgeon, bash, beat/strike with a stick; hit, strike, beat, beat up, batter, belabour; *informal* clout, clobber; *Brit. informal* cosh; *informal, dated* baste.

clue ▶ noun **1** *give me a clue about what's going on | police are still searching for clues* **hint**, indication, sign, signal, pointer, guide, suggestion, intimation, trace, indicator; lead, tip, tip-off, piece of evidence, piece of information.
2 *a long-pondered clue in a half-completed crossword* **question**, problem, puzzle, riddle, poser, conundrum; cryptic clue.
□ **not have a clue** (*informal*) *I didn't have a clue what was happening* **have no idea**, not have any idea, be ignorant, not have an inkling; be puzzled, be perplexed, be bewildered, be baffled, be mystified, be at a loss, be (all) at sea; *informal* be clueless, not have the faintest.
▶ verb
□ **clue someone in** (*informal*) *Stella had clued her in about Peter* **inform**, let know, notify, make aware, give information, prime; familiarize with, make familiar with, acquaint with; keep up to date, keep posted; *informal* tip off, give the gen, give the low-down on, give a rundown on/of, fill in on, gen up on, clue up, put in the picture, put wise, keep up to speed.

clump ▶ noun **1** *a clump of conifers* **cluster**, thicket, group, bunch, collection, assembly, assemblage; tuft, tuffet, tussock, mat, tangle.
2 *a clump of earth* **lump**, clod, mass, gobbet, wad, concentration; agglutination, agglomeration, accumulation, build-up; *informal* glob, gob.
▶ verb **1** *galaxies tend to clump together in clusters* **cluster**, group, bunch, collect, gather, assemble, congregate, mass, lump, bundle, pack, pile.
2 *people were clumping around upstairs* **stamp**, stomp, stump, clomp, tramp, plod, trudge, walk heavily, lumber, stumble; thump, thud, bang; *informal* galumph.

clumsy ▶ adjective **1** *in her haste she was clumsy* **awkward**, uncoordinated, ungainly, graceless, ungraceful, inelegant, gawky, gauche, gangling, hulking, cloddish, blundering, lumbering; bungling, bumbling, fumbling, inept, maladroit, unskilful, inexpert, unhandy, accident-prone, like a bull in a china shop, all fingers and thumbs; *informal* cack-handed, ham-fisted, ham-handed, butterfingered, with two left feet; *N. Amer. informal* klutzy.
OPPOSITE graceful.
2 *a clumsy contraption* **unwieldy**, unmanageable, cumbersome, bulky, hulking, heavy, solid, awkward, unmanoeuvrable.
OPPOSITE elegant.
3 *he said a clumsy farewell* **gauche**, awkward, graceless, unpolished, unsubtle, crude, uncouth, boorish, crass; tactless, insensitive, thoughtless, inconsiderate, undiplomatic, indelicate, impolitic, injudicious, ill-judged.
OPPOSITE tactful.

cluster ▶ noun **1** *clusters of berries | a cluster of buildings* **bunch**, clump, collection, mass, knot, group, clutch, bundle, nest; agglomeration, conglomeration, aggregate; *Botany* raceme, panicle, inflorescence, truss.
2 *a cluster of spectators* **crowd**, group, knot, huddle, bunch, gathering, throng, swarm, flock, pack, troupe, party, band, body, collection, assemblage, congregation; *informal* gang, gaggle.
▶ verb *they clustered around the television set* **congregate**, gather, collect, group, come together, assemble; huddle; crowd, flock, press, pack, mass, swarm.

clutch[1] ▶ verb *he was clutching a pewter tankard* **grip**, grasp, clasp, cling to, hang on to, clench, hold.
□ **clutch at** *she saved herself from falling further by clutching at a branch* **reach for**, snatch at, make a grab for, catch at, claw at; **grab**, seize, lay (one's) hands on, get one's hands on, grab/seize/take hold of.

clutch[2] ▶ noun **1** *a clutch of eggs* **group**, batch, nestful.
2 *a clutch of holiday cottages | the film won a clutch of awards* **group**, collection, set, quantity, raft; handful, fistful, armful; *informal* load, bunch.

clutches ▶ plural noun *we want to rescue the captives from the clutches of the enemy* **power**, control, domination, command, mastery, rule, tyranny; hands, hold, grip, grasp, claws, jaws, evil embrace; custody, possession, keeping.

clutter ▶ noun **1** *a clutter of toys, clothes, and newspapers lay around* **mess**, jumble, litter, heap, tangle, welter, muddle, hotchpotch, hodgepodge, mishmash, farrago, confusion, medley; *rare* gallimaufry.
2 *he liked to work amidst clutter* **disorder**, chaos, disarray, untidiness, mess, muddle, confusion, disorderliness; state of confusion/untidiness; litter, rubbish.
▶ verb *the garden was cluttered with broken appliances and discarded furniture* **litter**, make untidy, make a mess of, mess up, throw into disorder, disarrange, jumble; be strewn about, be scattered about; *informal* make a shambles of; *literary* bestrew.

coach[1] *See centre pages for lists of* **Carriages and Carts** **Vehicles** **Trains and Rolling Stock**
▶ noun **1** *they made their journey by coach* **bus**, minibus, van; *dated* motor coach, omnibus, charabanc; *N. Amer. trademark* greyhound.
2 *a railway coach* **carriage**, wagon, compartment, van, Pullman; *N. Amer.* car.
3 *a coach drawn by two horses* **horse-drawn carriage**, trap, hackney, hansom, gig, landau, brougham, cab.

coach[2] ▶ noun *a football coach* **instructor**, trainer; teacher, tutor, mentor, guru; *Brit.* crammer; *archaic* pedagogue.
▶ verb *Philip coached Richard in his school work* **instruct**, teach, tutor, school, educate, guide, drill, prime, cram, put someone through their paces; train.

coagulate ▶ verb *the heat causes the blood to coagulate* **congeal**, clot, cake, solidify, thicken, harden, gel, curdle, stiffen, set, dry; *rare* inspissate.
OPPOSITE liquefy.

coal ▶ noun
WORD LINKS
coal mine **colliery**
coal miner, coal ship **collier**

coalesce ▶ verb *some of the puddles had coalesced into shallow streams* **unite**, join together, combine, merge, fuse, mingle, meld, blend, intermingle, knit (together), amalgamate, consolidate, integrate, affiliate, link up, homogenize, synthesize, converge; *literary* commingle; *archaic* commix.

coalition ▶ noun *the general election saw no change in the ruling four-party coalition* **alliance**, union, partnership, affiliation, bloc, caucus; federation, league, association, confederacy, confederation, consortium, syndicate, combine, entente, alignment; amalgamation, merger; conjunction, combination, fusion.

coarse ▶ adjective **1** *coarse blankets* **rough**, bristly, scratchy, prickly, hairy, shaggy, wiry.
OPPOSITE soft.
2 *his coarse ugly features contorted with rage* **heavy**, broad, large, rough, rough-hewn, unrefined, inelegant; rugged, craggy.
OPPOSITE delicate.
3 *a coarse, common boy* **oafish**, loutish, boorish, churlish, uncouth, rude, discourteous, impolite, ungentlemanly, unladylike, ill-mannered, uncivil, ill-bred, vulgar, common, rough, uncultured, uncivilized, crass, foul-mouthed; *N. Amer. informal* trailer-park.
OPPOSITES sophisticated, refined.
4 *a coarse innuendo* **vulgar**, crude, rude, off colour, offensive, dirty, filthy, smutty, obscene, indelicate, improper, indecent, indecorous, unseemly, crass, tasteless, lewd, prurient; **bawdy**, earthy, broad, ribald, salty; *informal* blue, raunchy, nudge-nudge, farmyard.
OPPOSITE inoffensive.

coarsen ▶ verb **1** *her hands were coarsened by outside work* **roughen**, thicken, toughen, harden.
OPPOSITE soften.
2 *she felt that I had been coarsened by the army* **desensitize**, harshen, dehumanize; blunt, dull, deaden; *rare* indurate.
OPPOSITES refine, sensitize.

coarseness ▶ noun **1** *the coarseness of her hair* **roughness**, prickliness, wiriness, bristliness, scratchiness; shagginess.
OPPOSITE softness.
2 *he disliked the coarseness of the men around him* **oafishness**, loutishness,

boorishness, churlishness, uncouthness, rudeness, ill manners, discourteousness, ungentlemanliness, vulgarity, roughness, crassness.
OPPOSITES sophistication, refinement.
3 *incapable of coarseness himself, he enjoyed listening to it on the lips of others* **vulgarity**, crudeness, offensiveness, indelicacy, impropriety, indecorousness, unseemliness, crassness, tastelessness, lewdness, prurience; bawdiness, earthiness.

coast ▶ noun *the west coast of Africa* **seaboard**, coastal region, coastline, seashore, shore, shoreline, seaside, beach, sand, sands, foreshore, waterside, water's edge, waterfront; *technical* littoral; *literary* strand.
OPPOSITE interior.
▶ verb *they were coasting down a long hill | Colchester coasted to victory* **freewheel**, cruise, taxi, drift, glide, sail, float, skate, slip, skim.
OPPOSITE struggle.

WORD LINKS
relating to a coast **littoral**

coat *See centre pages for list of* **Coats, Cloaks, and Jackets**
▶ noun **1** *a winter coat* **overcoat**, tunic.
2 *a dog's coat* **fur**, hair, wool, fleece; hide, pelt, skin; *archaic* fell.
3 *a coat of paint* **layer**, covering, overlay, coating, skin, skim, plating, film, wash, glaze, varnish, veneer, lamination, sheet, finish, dusting, blanket, mantle, daub, smear, topping, crust, patina, lustre, deposit, scale, facing, cladding.
▶ verb *the steel tube was coated with a waxy substance* **cover**, overlay, paint, glaze, varnish, wash, surface, veneer, inlay, laminate, plate, blanket, mantle, daub, smear, bedaub, cake, plaster, overspread, encrust, face; *literary* besmear.

coating ▶ noun *a coating of ice* **layer**, covering, overlay, coat, skim, skin, thickness, plating, film, wash, glaze, varnish, veneer, lamination, sheet, finish, dusting, blanket, mantle, daub, smear, topping, crust, patina, lustre, deposit, scale, facing, cladding.

coax ▶ verb *you have to coax some of the children to speak* **persuade**, wheedle, cajole, talk into something, get round, prevail on, beguile, flatter, seduce, lure, entice, tempt, inveigle, woo, manoeuvre; *informal* sweet-talk, soft-soap, butter up, twist someone's arm; *archaic* blandish.

cobble ▶ verb
□ **cobble something together** *she cobbled together a rough draft* **prepare roughly/hastily**, make roughly/hastily, put together roughly/hastily, scribble, improvise, devise, contrive, rig (up), patch together, jerry-build; *informal* throw together, whip up, fix, rustle up; *Brit. informal* knock up.

cock ▶ noun *a cock and two hens* **rooster**, cockerel, male fowl, capon; *literary* chanticleer.
▶ verb **1** *he cocked his head towards the sound* **tilt**, tip, angle, lean, slope, bank, slant, incline, pitch, dip, cant, bevel, camber, heel, careen, put at an angle.
2 *she cocked her little finger when she held a cup* **bend**, flex, crook, angle, curve, kink.
3 *a greyhound cocked its leg against a tree* **lift**, raise, lift up, hold up.

cock-eyed ▶ adjective (*informal*) **1** *he knocked the top slightly cock-eyed* **crooked**, awry, askew, lopsided, uneven, asymmetrical, to one side, off-centre, skewed, skew, misaligned; *Scottish* agley, squint, thrawn; *Brit. informal* skew-whiff, wonky, squiffy.
2 *you expect us to believe a cock-eyed story like that? | some wild, cock-eyed scheme* **absurd**, preposterous, ridiculous, ludicrous, farcical, laughable, risible; idiotic, stupid, foolish, silly, inane, fanciful, imbecilic, insane, wild, hare-brained, impractical, impracticable, unworkable, unfeasible, non-viable, impossible; unreasonable, irrational, illogical, nonsensical, pointless, senseless; outrageous, shocking, astonishing, monstrous, fantastic, incongruous, grotesque; unbelievable, incredible, unthinkable, implausible, improbable; *informal* half-baked, crazy, barmy, daft.

cocksure ▶ adjective *he made a change from the cocksure men she usually met* **arrogant**, **conceited**, overconfident, overweening, cocky, smug, haughty, supercilious, disdainful, lofty, patronizing, proud, vain, vainglorious, self-important, swollen-headed, egotistical, presumptuous, lordly, pompous, blustering, boastful, brash, self-assertive, opinionated, bold, forward, insolent; *informal* high and mighty, throwing one's weight about/around, uppish; *rare* hubristic.
OPPOSITES modest, diffident.

cocktail ▶ noun. *See centre pages for list of* **Cocktails and Mixed Drinks**

cocky ▶ adjective *they appeared cocky even before they went one goal up* **arrogant**, **conceited**, overconfident, overweening, cocksure, smug, haughty, supercilious, disdainful, lofty, patronizing, proud, vain, vainglorious, self-important, swollen-headed, egotistical, presumptuous, lordly, pompous, blustering, boastful, brash, self-assertive, opinionated, bold, forward, insolent; *informal* high and mighty, throwing one's weight about/around, uppish; *rare* hubristic.
OPPOSITES modest, diffident.

cocoon ▶ verb **1** *he cocooned her in a fluffy towel* **wrap**, swathe, bundle up, swaddle, sheathe, muffle, pad, cloak, enfold, envelop, surround, encase, enclose, cover, fold, wind; *literary* lap.
OPPOSITE expose.
2 *this prig was cocooned in a wealthy upper class* **protect**, keep safe, keep from harm, safeguard, shield, defend, shelter, screen, look after, take care of, care for, cushion, insulate, isolate, cloister.

coddle ▶ verb *don't coddle repeat offenders—some of them prefer jail* **pamper**, cosset, mollycoddle, wait on someone hand and foot, cater to someone's every whim; spoil, indulge, overindulge, humour, pander to; spoon-feed, feather-bed, wrap in cotton wool; pet, baby, mother, nanny; *archaic* cocker.
OPPOSITES neglect, treat harshly, be strict with.

code ▶ noun **1** *a message in code* **cipher**, secret language, secret writing, set of symbols, key, hieroglyphics; coded message, cryptogram; *rare* cryptograph.
2 *a strict social code among inmates* **set of principles**, set of standards, set of customs; manners, ethics, morals; morality, convention, accepted behaviour, etiquette, protocol.
3 *the penal code* **law**, laws, body of law, rules, regulations, constitution, system, charter, canon, jurisprudence.

WORD LINKS

study of codes	**cryptology**
writing or cracking of codes	**cryptography**
writer or cracker of codes	**cryptographer**
put into code	**encipher, encode, encrypt**
solve a code	**decipher, decrypt, crack**

codify ▶ verb *the bill codified these standards for the first time* **systematize**, systemize, organize, arrange, order, marshal, set out, chart, structure, tabulate, catalogue, list, sort, dispose, index, classify, class, categorize, compile, group, range, file, log, grade, rate, assort.

coerce ▶ verb *he was coerced into giving evidence* **pressure**, pressurize, bring pressure to bear on, use pressure on, put pressure on, constrain, lean on, press, push; force, compel, oblige, put under an obligation, browbeat, brainwash, bludgeon, bully, threaten, prevail on, work on, act on, influence, intimidate, dragoon, twist someone's arm, strong-arm; *N. Amer.* blackjack; *informal* bulldoze, railroad, squeeze, put the screws/squeeze on; *Brit. informal* bounce; *N. Amer. informal* hustle, fast-talk.
OPPOSITE persuade.

CHOOSE THE RIGHT WORD
coerce, compel, force, oblige
See COMPEL.

coercion ▶ noun *it wasn't slavery because no coercion was used* **force**, compulsion, constraint, duress, oppression, enforcement, harassment, intimidation, threats, insistence, demand, arm-twisting, pressure, pressurization, influence.
OPPOSITE persuasion.

coffee *See centre pages for list of* **Coffee Drinks**
▶ noun *N. Amer.* joe, java.

coffer ▶ noun **1** *the small coffer which had held Herluin's treasury* **strongbox**, money box, cash box, money chest, treasure chest, casket, trunk, box, safe, safety-deposit box, safe-deposit box, repository.
2 (**coffers**) *a huge donation to the Imperial coffers* **fund**, funds, reserves, resources, money, finances, wealth, cash, wherewithal, capital, assets, purse, kitty, pool, bank, treasury, exchequer; *N. Amer.* fisc.

coffin ▶ noun **box**, sarcophagus; *N. Amer.* casket; *humorous* wooden overcoat; *Archaeology* cist.

cogency ▶ noun *the cogency of this argument* **strength**, force, power, potency, weight, plausibility, effectiveness, efficacy, soundness, validity, foundation; impressiveness, eloquence, persuasiveness, credibility, influence, conclusiveness, unanswerability, authoritativeness, authority; **logic**, logicality, reasonableness, rationality, lucidity, coherence, good organization, orderliness, methodicalness, clarity, articulateness, consistency, relevance.
OPPOSITES weakness; illogicality; vagueness.

cogent ▶ adjective *a cogent argument* **convincing**, compelling, strong, forceful, powerful, potent, weighty; **valid**, sound, well founded, plausible, effective, efficacious, telling; impressive, persuasive, irresistible, eloquent, credible, influential, conclusive, unanswerable, authoritative; **logical**, reasoned, well reasoned, rational, reasonable, lucid, coherent, well organized, systematic, orderly, methodical, clear, articulate, consistent, relevant.
OPPOSITES vague; unconvincing; muddled.

CHOOSE THE RIGHT WORD
cogent, valid, sound
See VALID.

cogitate ▶ verb *you were cogitating on some great matter* **think (about)**, contemplate, consider, give thought to, give consideration to, mull over, meditate (on), muse (on), ponder (on/over), reflect (on), deliberate (about/

C

on), ruminate (about/on/over), dwell on, brood (on/over), agonize (over), worry (about), chew over, puzzle (over), speculate about, weigh up, revolve, turn over in one's mind, review, study, be in a brown study; *informal* put on one's thinking cap; *archaic* pore on; *rare* cerebrate.

cogitation ▶ **noun** *Sorry, did I interrupt your cogitation?* **thought**, thinking, contemplation, consideration, mulling over, meditation, study, deliberation, pondering, reflection, rumination, musing, speculation, brooding, agonizing, worrying, puzzling; *rare* cerebration.

cognate ▶ **adjective 1** *the large number of cognate words in English and German* **related**, kindred, akin, with a common ancestor.
OPPOSITE unrelated.
2 *cognate subjects such as physics and chemistry* **associated**, related, connected, allied, interconnected, linked, coupled, correlated; **similar**, like, alike, comparable, parallel, equivalent, corresponding, analogous, homologous.
OPPOSITES unconnected; dissimilar.

cognition ▶ **noun** *a theory of human cognition* **perception**, discernment, awareness, apprehension, learning, understanding, comprehension, enlightenment, insight, intelligence, reason, reasoning, thinking, (conscious) thought.

cognizance ▶ **noun** (*formal*) *he brought the affair to the cognizance of the court* **awareness**, notice, knowledge, consciousness, apprehension, perception, realization, recognition, appreciation.

cognizant ▶ **adjective** (*formal*) *everyone should be fully* ***cognizant of*** *what is happening* **aware**, conscious, apprised, abreast; sensible of/to, alive to, sensitive to, alert to, familiar with, acquainted with, in the know about, au fait with, conversant with, au courant with, up to date (with), up with, well versed in, knowledgeable about, well informed about, no stranger to; *informal* well up on, genned up on, clued in on, wise to, hip to; *archaic* ware of.

cohabit ▶ **verb** *Mary is now* ***cohabiting with*** *Paul* **live together**, live with, live (together) as husband/man and wife, sleep with, sleep together; *informal* shack up with; *informal, dated* live in sin, live over the brush.

cohere ▶ **verb 1** *I wondered how this family had cohered in the past* **stick together**, hold together, be united, bind, cling, fuse, form a whole.
OPPOSITE fall apart.
2 *this view does not cohere with some people's other beliefs* **be consistent**, hang together.

coherence ▶ **noun** *this raises further questions on the coherence of state policy* **consistency**, logicality, good sense, soundness, organization, orderliness, unity; clarity, articulacy; intelligibility, comprehensibility.
OPPOSITE incoherence.

coherent ▶ **adjective** *a coherent argument* **logical**, reasoned, reasonable, well reasoned, rational, sound, cogent; consistent, well organized, systematic, orderly, methodical; clear, lucid, articulate, relevant, intelligible, comprehensible; *informal* joined-up.
OPPOSITES incoherent; muddled.

cohesion ▶ **noun** *rewarding individuals breaks the cohesion in the group* **unity**, togetherness, solidarity, bond, sticking together, continuity, coherence, connection, linkage, interrelatedness.

cohort ▶ **noun 1** *the Roman army was organized into centuries, cohorts, and legions* **unit**, outfit, force; army, group, corps, division, brigade, battalion, regiment, squadron, company, commando, battery, troop, section, patrol, cadre, crew, detachment, contingent, column, squad, detail, band, legion.
2 *52% of the mothers in the 1946 cohort of births had two children* **group**, grouping, category, categorization, grade, grading, classification, class, set, section, division, order, batch, list; age group, generation.

coil ▶ **noun** *Miles found himself in the water, tangled in coils of rope* **loop**, twist, turn, curl, hoop, roll, ring, twirl, gyre, whorl, scroll, curlicue, convolution; spiral, helix, corkscrew; *technical* volute, volution.
▶ **verb** *he coiled a lock of her hair around his finger* **wind**, loop, twist, curl, curve, bend, twine, entwine, snake; spiral, corkscrew, wreathe, meander; *rare* convolute.

coin *See centre pages for lists of* **Coins** **Currency Units**
▶ **noun 1** *a gold coin* **piece**, bit.
2 *large amounts of coin* **coins**, coinage, coin of the realm, (loose) change, small change, silver, copper, coppers, gold; *formal* specie.
▶ **verb 1** *guineas and half-guineas were coined* **mint**, stamp, stamp out, strike, cast, punch, die, mould, forge, make, manufacture, produce.
2 *he coined the term 'desktop publishing'* **invent**, create, make up, devise, conceive, originate, think up, dream up, formulate, fabricate.

WORD LINKS
relating to coins **numismatic**
collector of coins **numismatist**

coincide ▶ **verb 1** *the two events coincided* **occur simultaneously**, happen together, happen at the same time, be concurrent, coexist, concur; clash, conflict.
2 *the interests of employers and employees do not always coincide | his version did not* ***coincide with*** *that of the other witnesses* **tally**, correspond, agree, accord, concur, match, fit, be in agreement, be consistent, conform, equate, harmonize, be in tune, be compatible, dovetail, correlate; be the same as, parallel; *informal* square; *N. Amer. informal* jibe; *archaic* quadrate.
OPPOSITE differ.

coincidence ▶ **noun 1** *the resemblances are too close to be mere coincidence* **accident**, chance, serendipity, fate, a twist of fate, destiny, fortuity, fortune, providence, freak, hazard; a piece of good fortune, (a bit of) luck, (a bit of) good luck, a fluke, a happy chance; *N. Amer.* happenstance.
2 *the coincidence of rising inflation and unemployment* **co-occurrence**, coexistence, conjunction, simultaneity, simultaneousness, contemporaneity, contemporaneousness, concomitance, synchronicity, synchrony; clash, conflict.
3 *a coincidence of interests* **correspondence**, agreement, accord, concurrence, match, fit, consistency, conformity, harmony, compatibility, dovetailing, correlation, parallelism; similarity, likeness.

coincident ▶ **adjective 1** *the rise of the novel was* ***coincident with*** *the decline of storytelling* **concurrent**, coinciding, simultaneous, contemporaneous, concomitant, synchronous, coincidental, coexistent; at the same time (as).
2 *the pursuit of profits and the social interest are therefore coincident* **in agreement**, in harmony, in accord, matching, consonant, consistent, compatible, reconcilable, congruent, in conformity, in step, in tune, in balance, in parallel; the same.
OPPOSITE incompatible.

coincidental ▶ **adjective 1** *a coincidental resemblance* **accidental**, chance, occurring by chance/accident, fortuitous, adventitious, fluky, casual, serendipitous, random, aleatory; unexpected, unforeseen, unanticipated, unforeseeable, unlooked-for; unintentional, unintended, inadvertent, involuntary, unplanned, unpremeditated, unthinking, unmeant.
OPPOSITES intentional, planned.
2 *the coincidental disappearance of some famous jewels and of a young American tourist* **simultaneous**, concurrent, coincident, contemporaneous, concomitant, synchronous, coexistent; at the same time (as).

coitus ▶ **noun** (*formal*). *See* **SEX**.

cold ▶ **adjective 1** *a cold day* **chilly**, cool, freezing, icy, snowy, icy-cold, glacial, wintry, crisp, frosty, frigid, bitter, bitterly cold, biting, piercing, numbing, sharp, raw, polar, arctic, Siberian; *informal* nippy, brass monkeys; *Brit. informal* parky; *literary* chill; *rare* hyperborean, boreal, hibernal, hiemal, gelid, brumal.
OPPOSITE hot.
2 *I'm very cold* **chilly**, chilled, cool, freezing, frozen, frozen stiff, frozen/chilled to the bone/marrow, shivery, numbed, benumbed, suffering from hypothermia, hypothermic, suffering from exposure.
OPPOSITE hot.
3 *Rodrigo met with a cold and scornful reception* **unfriendly**, cool, inhospitable, unwelcoming, unsympathetic, forbidding, stony, frigid, frosty, glacial, lukewarm, haughty, supercilious, disdainful, aloof, distant, remote, indifferent, reserved, withdrawn, uncommunicative, unresponsive, unfeeling, unemotional, dispassionate, passionless, wooden, impersonal, formal, stiff, austere; cold-blooded, cold-hearted, stony-hearted; *informal* stand-offish, offish; *rare* gelid.
OPPOSITES warm; friendly.

WORD LINKS
related prefix **cryo-** (**e.g.** ***cryogenics, cryobiology***)
fear of cold **cheimaphobia**

cold-blooded ▶ **adjective** *a cold-blooded murderer* **cruel**, savage, brutal, callous, barbaric, barbarous, sadistic, inhuman, pitiless, merciless, ruthless, unforgiving, unpitying, inhumane, unfeeling, uncaring, heartless; hard, severe, harsh, austere, cold, cold-hearted, unsympathetic, unemotional, unfriendly, uncharitable, hard-hearted, stony-hearted, with a heart of stone; *informal* hard-boiled, hard-nosed, thick-skinned.

cold-hearted ▶ **adjective** *Tony was unloved by his cold-hearted wife* **unfeeling**, unloving, uncaring, unsympathetic, unemotional, unfriendly, uncharitable, unkind, insensitive, indifferent, detached; hard-hearted, stony-hearted, with a heart of stone, heartless, hard, harsh, austere, cold.
OPPOSITE warm-hearted.

collaborate ▶ **verb 1** *India has collaborated with several nations on space projects* **cooperate**, join (up), join forces, team up, get together, come together, band together, work together, work jointly, participate, unite, combine, merge, link, ally, associate, amalgamate, integrate, form an alliance, pool resources, club together.
2 *they were suspected of having collaborated with the enemy* **fraternize**, conspire, collude, cooperate, consort, sympathize.
OPPOSITE resist.

collaboration ▶ **noun 1** *he wrote on art and architecture in collaboration with John Betjeman* **cooperation**, alliance, partnership, participation, combination, association, concert; teamwork, joint effort, working together, coopetition.
2 *Salengro had been accused of collaboration with the enemy* **fraternizing**, fraternization, colluding, collusion, cooperating, cooperation, consorting, sympathizing, sympathy; conspiring.
OPPOSITE resistance.

collaborator ▶ noun **1** *his collaborator on the book* **co-worker**, fellow worker, associate, colleague, partner, co-partner, confederate, ally, teammate; assistant, helper; *Brit. informal* oppo.
2 *he was a collaborator during the occupation* **quisling**, fraternizer, collaborationist, colluder, (enemy) sympathizer, conspirator; traitor, fifth columnist, renegade, betrayer, turncoat, defector, informer, double agent.

collapse ▶ verb **1** *the roof collapsed* **cave in**, fall in, subside, fall down, sag, slump, settle, give, give way, crumble, crumple, disintegrate, fall to pieces, come apart.
OPPOSITE hold up.
2 *he collapsed from loss of blood* **faint**, pass out, black out, lose consciousness, fall unconscious, keel over; *informal* flake out, conk out, go out; *literary* swoon.
3 *she collapsed in tears* **break down**, go to pieces, lose control, lose one's self-control, be overcome (with emotion), crumble, fall apart; *informal* crack up.
4 *the peace talks collapsed* **break down**, **fail**, fall through, fold, founder, fall flat, miscarry, go wrong, come to nothing, come to grief, be frustrated, be unsuccessful, not succeed, disintegrate; come to a halt, end, terminate; *informal* flop, fizzle out.
OPPOSITE succeed.
▶ noun **1** *the collapse of the roof* **cave-in**, giving way, subsidence, crumbling, disintegration.
2 *she was reported to be 'poorly' after her collapse on stage yesterday* **fainting fit**, blackout, fainting, faint, passing out, loss of consciousness; *informal* flaking out; *literary* swooning, swoon; *Medicine* syncope.
3 *the collapse of the peace talks* **breakdown**, **failure**, disintegration, foundering, miscarriage, lack of success; halt, end, termination.
OPPOSITES outcome; success.
4 *he suffered a collapse from overwork* **breakdown**, attack, seizure, prostration, nervous breakdown, nervous/mental collapse, nervous exhaustion, nervous tension, crisis, personal crisis, psychological trauma; *informal* crack-up.

collar ▶ noun **1** *a shirt collar* **neckband**, choker; *historical* ruff, gorget, bertha, Vandyke; *archaic* rebato.
2 (*technical*) *a small collar can be fitted round the pump rod to limit the length of stroke* **ring**, band, collet, sleeve, pipe, flange, rim, rib.
▶ verb (*informal*) **1** *the cricket star collared a thief who tried to nick his golf clubs* **apprehend**, arrest, catch, capture, seize; take prisoner, take into custody, detain, put in jail, throw in jail, put behind bars, imprison, incarcerate; *informal* nab, nail, run in, pinch, bust, pick up, pull in, haul in, do, feel someone's collar; *Brit. informal* nick.
2 *an elderly chap collared me in the street* **accost**, address, speak to, talk to, call to, shout to, hail, initiate a discussion with; approach, waylay, take aside, detain, stop, halt, grab, catch, confront, importune, solicit; *informal* buttonhole; *Brit. informal* nobble.

collate ▶ verb **1** *the police computer system is being used to collate information from across Britain* **collect**, gather, accumulate, assemble; **combine**, aggregate, put together; **arrange**, organize, order, put in order, sort, categorize, systematize, structure.
OPPOSITE separate.
2 *what follows is based mainly on collating these two sources* **compare**, contrast, set side by side, juxtapose, weigh against, set against, balance, differentiate, discriminate.

collateral ▶ noun *she put up her house as collateral for the bank loan* **security**, surety, guarantee, guaranty, pledge, bond, assurance, insurance, indemnity, indemnification, pawn, backing; bail, hostage; *archaic* gage, earnest.

colleague ▶ noun *one of her colleagues in the lab* **fellow worker**, workmate, teammate, co-worker, associate, partner, co-partner, collaborator, ally, comrade, companion, confederate; *French* confrère; *informal* oppo; *Austral./NZ informal* offsider; *archaic* compeer; *rare* consociate.

collect ▶ verb **1** *he collected the picnic debris | dust and dirt collect so quickly* **gather**, accumulate, assemble; amass, stockpile, pile up, heap up, rack up, run up, scrape together, store (up), hoard, save, cumulate, lay in/up, garner; mass, increase, multiply, accrue, snowball; *Brit.* tot up; *informal* stash (away).
OPPOSITES distribute; squander.
2 *a crowd soon collected* **come together**, get together, gather, assemble, meet, muster, cluster, rally, congregate, convene, converge, flock together; *rare* foregather.
OPPOSITE disperse.
3 *I must collect the children from school* **fetch**, go/come to get, go/come and get, call for, go/come for, meet.
OPPOSITES take, drop off.
4 *they are collecting money for charity* **raise**, appeal for, ask for, ask people to give, solicit, secure, obtain, acquire, gather.
OPPOSITES distribute, give away.
5 *he paused for a moment to collect himself* **recover**, regain one's composure, pull oneself together, take a hold of oneself, steady oneself; *informal* get a grip (on oneself), get one's act together, snap out of it.
6 *she returned to her room to collect her thoughts* **muster**, summon (up), gather (together), get together, rally, call into action, marshal, mobilize, screw up.

collected ▶ adjective *when we found the lady she was very collected* **calm**, cool, {cool, calm, and collected}, as cool as a cucumber, cool-headed, self-possessed, composed, controlled, self-controlled, poised; serene, tranquil, relaxed, unruffled, unperturbed, unflustered, undisturbed, unagitated, unmoved, unbothered, untroubled; equable, even-tempered, imperturbable, placid, quiet, sedate, unexcitable, impassive, dispassionate, unemotional, phlegmatic, stolid; *informal* unflappable, unfazed, together, laid-back; *rare* equanimous.
OPPOSITES excited; hysterical.

collection *See centre pages for list of* **Collective Names for Animals**
▶ noun **1** *police found a collection of stolen items* **hoard**, pile, heap, stack, gathering, stock, store, stockpile; accumulation, mass, build-up, reserve, supply, bank, pool, fund, mine, reservoir; conglomeration, cumulation, accrual, aggregation, accretion, agglomerate, agglomeration; *rare* amassment.
2 *a motley collection of shoppers, festival-goers, and trainspotters* **group**, crowd, body, company, troupe, assembly, assemblage, gathering, throng; knot, cluster, huddle, multitude, bevy, party, number, band, horde, pack, drove, flock, swarm, stream, mob; *informal* gang, load, crew, gaggle.
3 *her collection of Victorian dolls* **set**, series, array, assortment.
4 *a collection of short stories* **anthology**, selection, compendium, treasury, compilation, miscellany, miscellanea, pot-pourri; collected works; *archaic* garland; *rare* analects, collectanea, ana, florilegium, spicilege.
5 *a collection for the poor* **donations**, contributions, gifts, subscription(s), alms; *informal* whip-round.
6 *a church collection* **offering**, offertory, tithe.

collective ▶ adjective *collective ownership of the means of production* **common**, shared, joint, combined, mutual, communal, united, allied, cooperative, collaborative; aggregate, cumulative, undivided, pooled.
OPPOSITES individual; sectional.

college ▶ noun **1** *a college of technology* **educational institution**, training establishment, centre of learning, seat of learning; school, academy, university, institute, seminary, conservatory, conservatoire; *historical* polytechnic.
2 *the College of Heralds* **association**, society, club, group, band, circle, fellowship, body, guild, lodge, order, fraternity, confraternity, brotherhood, sisterhood, sorority, league, union, alliance, affiliation, institution, coterie, federation; *rare* sodality.

collide ▶ verb **1** *she collided with someone | two suburban trains collided* **crash (into)**, come into collision (with), bang (into), slam (into), impact (with); hit, strike, run into, meet head-on, smash into, smack into, cannon into, plough into, bump into, crack into/against, knock into, dash against; *N. Amer. informal* barrel into.
2 *in his work, politics and metaphysics collide* **conflict**, be in conflict, come into conflict, be in opposition, clash, differ, diverge, disagree, be at variance, be at odds, be incompatible.
OPPOSITE coalesce.

collision ▶ noun **1** *a collision on the road to Oxford* **crash**, accident, smash, bump, knock, impact, hit, strike, clash; *Brit.* RTA (road traffic accident); *N. Amer.* wreck; *informal* smash-up, pile-up; *Brit. informal* prang, shunt.
2 *a collision between two mutually inconsistent ideas* **conflict**, clash, opposition, disagreement, variance, incompatibility, contradiction.
OPPOSITE coalescence.

colloquial ▶ adjective *some students have a good grasp of colloquial language* **informal**, conversational, everyday, casual, non-literary; natural, unofficial, unpretentious, familiar, chatty, friendly, idiomatic, slangy; vernacular, popular, demotic.
OPPOSITES literary; formal.

collude ▶ verb *corrupt border officials colluded with the importers of dubious goods* **conspire**, connive, intrigue, be hand in glove, plot, participate in a conspiracy, collaborate, scheme; *informal* be in cahoots; *rare* machinate, cabal, complot.

collusion ▶ noun *there has been collusion between the security forces and paramilitary groups* **conspiracy**, connivance, complicity, intrigue, plotting, secret understanding, collaboration, scheming.

colonist ▶ noun *the first European colonists of North America* **settler**, colonizer, colonial, frontiersman, frontierswoman, pioneer; immigrant, newcomer; *Brit.* incomer; *historical* planter; *N. Amer. historical* homesteader, habitant, redemptioner, squatter.
OPPOSITE native.

colonize ▶ verb *the Germans colonized Tanganyika in 1885* **settle (in)**, establish a colony in, people, populate, pioneer, open up, found; overrun, occupy, take over, seize, capture, take possession of, annex, subjugate.
OPPOSITES leave; grant independence to.

colonnade ▶ noun **row of columns**, peristyle; portico, arcade, loggia, covered walk, gallery, cloisters, stoa.

colony ▶ noun **1** *Belize is a former British colony* **territory**, possession, holding, dependency, province, dominion, protectorate, satellite (state),

C

settlement, outpost; *historical* tributary, fief.
2 *the entire British colony in New York* **population**, community.
3 *an artists' colony* **community**, association, commune, settlement, quarter, district, section, ghetto.

colossal ▶ **adjective** *a colossal building* **huge**, massive, enormous, gigantic, very big, very large, great, giant, mammoth, vast, immense, tremendous, mighty, stupendous, monumental, epic, prodigious, mountainous, monstrous, titanic, towering, elephantine, king-sized, king-size, gargantuan, Herculean, Brobdingnagian; substantial, extensive, hefty, bulky, weighty, heavy, gross; *informal* mega, monster, whopping, whopping great, thumping, thumping great, humongous, jumbo, hulking, bumper, astronomical, astronomic; *Brit. informal* whacking, whacking great, ginormous.
OPPOSITE tiny.

colour *See centre pages for lists of* **Colours** **Dyes** **Horse Colours** **Rainbow**
▶ **noun 1** *the lights flickered and changed colour* **hue**, shade, tint, tone, tinge, cast, tincture.
2 *eight tubes of oil colour* **paint**, pigment, colourant, coloration, dye, stain, tint, wash.
3 *add colour to her cheeks* **redness**, pinkness, rosiness, reddening, ruddiness, blush, flush, high colour, glow, bloom.
OPPOSITE pallor.
4 *people of every colour, creed, and race* **skin colour**, skin colouring, skin tone, complexion, colouring, pigmentation; race, ethnic group, stock.
5 *the anecdotes and examples were chosen to add colour to strictly academic material* **vividness**, life, liveliness, vivacity, vitality, animation, excitement, interest, fascination, richness, zest, verve, spice, spiciness, bite, piquancy, sparkle, impact, vigour, vigorousness, force, forcefulness, point; *informal* oomph, pizzazz, zing, zip, zap, punch, kick; *literary* salt.
6 *woods were unjustifiably disafforested under colour of the Statute of 1327* **the pretext**, the cloak, the mask, the pretence, the outward appearance, the guise, a false show, a show, a front, a facade, a semblance; on the excuse of.
7 (**colours**) *Lynn runs in the colours of the Oxford City club* **strip**, **kit**, uniform, costume, livery, insignia, regalia; badge, ribbon, rosette, emblem.
8 (**colours**) *the regimental colours* **flag**, standard, banner, pennant, pennon, streamer, ensign, banderole; *Brit.* pendant; *Nautical* burgee; (*in ancient Rome*) vexillum; *rare* gonfalon, guidon, labarum.
▶ **verb 1** *the wood was coloured with a penetrating dye* **tint**, dye, tinge, shade, pigment, stain, colour-wash, colour in, paint.
2 *she* **coloured up** *with embarrassment* **blush**, redden, go pink/red, turn red/crimson/scarlet, flush, crimson.
OPPOSITE pale.
3 *the experiences had coloured her whole existence* **influence**, affect, slant, taint, pervert, warp, twist, skew, distort, bias, prejudice, poison.
4 *witnesses might colour evidence to make a story saleable* **exaggerate**, overstate, overdraw, overdo, embroider, embellish, dramatize, enhance, varnish; **falsify**, give a false account of, misrepresent, misreport, disguise, fudge, garble, distort, manipulate, take/quote out of context, bend, put a spin on, massage, strain.

WORD LINKS

relating to colour	**chromatic**
fear of colour	**chromophobia**
measurement of colour	**colorimetry**

colourful ▶ **adjective 1** *a colourful array of fruit* **brightly coloured**, bright-coloured, deep-coloured, brilliant, glowing, radiant, vivid, rich, vibrant; eye-catching, flamboyant, showy, gaudy, glaring, garish, flashy; multicoloured, multicolour, many-coloured, many-hued, rainbow, rainbow-like, varicoloured, variegated, harlequin, motley, prismatic, polychromatic, psychedelic; *informal* jazzy, (looking) like an explosion in a paint factory.
OPPOSITE colourless.
2 *he regaled her with a colourful account of that afternoon's meeting* **vivid**, graphic, lively, animated, dramatic, striking, arresting, picturesque, interesting, stimulating, fascinating, scintillating, rich, evocative, detailed, highly coloured.
OPPOSITE colourless.

colourless ▶ **adjective 1** *a colourless liquid* **uncoloured**, white, bleached, faded, washed out; *literary* achromatic; *technical* achromic.
OPPOSITE coloured.
2 *colourless cheeks* **pale**, pallid, wan, anaemic, bloodless, ashen, white, white as a ghost/sheet, grey, jaundiced, waxen, chalky, chalk-white, milky, pasty, pasty-faced, whey-faced, peaky, sickly, tired-looking, washed out, sallow, drained, drawn, sapped, ghostly, deathly, deathlike, bleached; *rare* etiolated.
OPPOSITE rosy.
3 *a colourless personality* **uninteresting**, dull, boring, tedious, monotonous, dry, drab, dreary, wearisome; unexciting, bland, non-stimulating, unimaginative, uninspiring, uninspired, weak, insipid, lustreless, lacklustre, vapid, flat, stale, trite, vacuous, feeble, pallid, wishy-washy, limp, lame, tired, lifeless, torpid, unanimated, zestless, spiritless, sterile, anaemic, barren, tame, bloodless, antiseptic; middle-of-the-road, run-of-the-mill, commonplace, mediocre, nondescript, characterless, mundane, inoffensive, humdrum, prosaic.
OPPOSITE colourful.

column ▶ **noun 1** *the arches were supported on massive columns* **pillar**, post, pole, support, upright, vertical, baluster, pier, pile, piling, pilaster, stanchion, standard, prop, buttress; rod, shaft, leg, mast, tower, pylon; obelisk, monolith; *technical* newel, caryatid, telamon, herm.
2 *he writes a weekly column in a Sunday paper* **article**, piece (of writing), item, story, report, account, write-up, feature, essay, composition, study, review, criticism, critique, notice, commentary, editorial, leader; *Brit. informal* crit.
3 *we walked in a column* **line**, file, queue, procession, rank, row, string, chain, train, trail, progression, succession, cavalcade, parade, cortège, convoy; *Brit.* march past; *informal* crocodile.

columnist ▶ **noun** *a columnist for the Irish Times* **writer**, feature writer, contributor, journalist, correspondent, newspaperman, newspaperwoman, newsman, newswoman; wordsmith, man/woman of letters, penman; humorist, critic, reviewer, commentator, chronicler; *French* littérateur; *informal* scribbler, scribe, pen-pusher, hack, hackette, journo, talking head; *N. Amer. informal* thumbsucker.

coma ▶ **noun** *the road crash left him in* **a coma** **unconsciousness**, insensibility, stupor, oblivion, inertia; blackout, collapse, torpor, trance; *Medicine* persistent vegetative state, PVS; *rare* sopor.

comatose ▶ **adjective 1** *comatose after the accident* **unconscious**, in a coma, insensible, senseless, blacked out, passed out, insentient, insensate; *rare* soporose, soporous.
2 (*informal*) *a teenager lying comatose in the sun listening to a personal stereo* **inert**, torpid, inactive, lethargic, sluggish, lifeless, listless, languid, lazy, idle, indolent, shiftless, slothful, heavy, stagnant, sleepy, drowsy, somnolent, languorous, apathetic, passive, hibernating, sleeping, dormant, supine.

comb ▶ **verb 1** *she combed her hair* **groom**, untangle, disentangle, smooth out, straighten, arrange, neaten, tidy, dress, rake; curry.
2 *the wool had been cleaned and combed* **separate**, dress, card, tease, hackle, heckle, hatchel.
3 *the police combed the area for the murder weapon* **search**, scour, look around in, explore, sweep, probe, hunt through, look through, scrabble about/around in, root about/around in, ferret (about/around) in, rummage about/around/round in, rummage in/through, forage through, fish about/around in, poke about/around in, dig in, grub about/around in, delve in, go through, sift through, rake, rifle through, ransack, turn over, go through with a fine-tooth comb; turn upside down, turn inside out, leave no stone unturned in; *Brit. informal* rootle around in; *Austral./NZ informal* fossick through; *rare* roust around in.

combat ▶ **noun** *3500 men were killed in combat* **battle**, fighting, action, hostilities, conflict, armed conflict, war, warfare, bloodshed.
▶ **verb** *other cities have tried to combat the disease* **fight**, battle against, do battle with, wage war against, take up arms against, strive against, contend with, tackle, attack, counter, oppose, resist, withstand, stand up to, face up to, make a stand against, put up a fight against, confront, defy; obstruct, impede, hinder, block, thwart, frustrate, inhibit, restrain; stop, halt, put an end to, prevent, check, stem, curb.
OPPOSITE give in to.

combatant ▶ **noun 1** *he was involved in the war, but not as a combatant* **fighter**, fighting man, fighting woman, soldier, serviceman, servicewoman, warrior, trooper.
OPPOSITE civilian.
2 *these are only some of the combatants in a new online war for your custom* **contender**, antagonist, adversary, battler, opponent, contestant, competitor, player, challenger, disputant, rival.
OPPOSITES ally; non-participant.
▶ **adjective** *all the combatant armies went to war with machine guns* **warring**, at war, opposing, contending, belligerent, combating, fighting, battling, conflicting, clashing.
OPPOSITE non-combatant.

combative ▶ **adjective** *Mosley's combative language and stormy oratory* **pugnacious**, aggressive, antagonistic, quarrelsome, argumentative, contentious, hostile, truculent, threatening, belligerent, bellicose, militant, warlike, warmongering, hawkish, militaristic; *informal* spoiling for a fight; *rare* oppugnant.
OPPOSITE conciliatory.

combination ▶ **noun 1** *an elegant combination of ancient and modern* **amalgamation**, amalgam, merger, union, blend, mixture, mix, mingling, meld, fusion, fusing, compound, alloy, marriage, weave, coalescence, coalition, pooling, integration, conjunction, incorporation, synthesis, composite, composition, concoction.
2 *the plaintiff acted in combination with his brother* **cooperation**, collaboration, concert, synergy, association, union, alliance, partnership, coalition, league.

OPPOSITE conflict.

combine ▶ verb **1** *he attempts to combine comedy with more serious themes* **amalgamate**, merge, unite, integrate, incorporate, fuse, blend, meld, mingle, coalesce, compound, alloy, homogenize, synthesize, consolidate, bind, bond, join, marry, put together, unify, pool, intermingle, mix, intermix, affiliate; *literary* commingle.
OPPOSITE separate.
2 *groups of teachers combined to tackle a variety of problems* **cooperate**, collaborate, join forces, pool resources, get together, come together, join (together), band (together), club together, link (up), go into partnership, unite, team up, form an alliance, form an association, league, go into league, throw in one's lot; *informal* gang up.
OPPOSITE split up.

combustible ▶ adjective *they made small piles of combustible material to start the fire* **inflammable**, flammable, incendiary, explosive; *rare* burnable, ignitable.
OPPOSITE incombustible.

combustion ▶ noun *the combustion of fossil fuels* **burning**, firing, kindling, igniting, ignition.

come ▶ verb **1** *do come and listen* **move nearer**, move closer, approach, advance, near, draw nigh, draw close/closer, draw near/nearer; proceed, make progress, make headway, forge.
OPPOSITE go away.
2 *they came last night* **arrive**, get here/there, reach one's destination, make it, appear, put in an appearance, make an appearance, come on the scene, come up, approach, enter, present oneself, turn up, be along, come along, materialize; *W. Indian* reach; *informal* show up, show, roll in, roll up, blow in, show one's face.
OPPOSITE leave.
3 *they came to a stream* **reach**, arrive at, meet, get to, get up to, get as far as, make, make it to, set foot on, gain, attain; come across, run across, run into, happen on, chance on, light on, come upon, stumble on, blunder on, find by chance; end up at, land up at, fetch up at; *informal* hit, wind up at, bump into; *archaic* run against.
4 *the dress comes to her ankles* **extend**, stretch, continue, carry on, spread; reach, come as far as, not stop until.
OPPOSITE stop short of.
5 *she comes from Belgium* **be from**, **be a native of**, have been born in, hail from, originate in, have one's roots in, be ... (by birth); live in, have one's home in, inhabit, be an inhabitant of, be settled in, reside in, be a resident of.
6 *the attacks came without warning* **happen**, occur, take place, come about, transpire, fall, present itself, crop up, materialize, arise, arrive, appear, surface, ensue, follow; *literary* come to pass, befall, betide; *archaic* hap; *rare* eventuate.
7 *the car does not come in red* **be available**, be made, be produced, be for sale, be on offer.
8 (*informal*) **climax**, achieve orgasm, orgasm.

□ **come about** *the change came about in 1989* **happen**, occur, take place, transpire, fall, present itself, crop up, materialize, arise, arrive, appear, surface, ensue, follow; *literary* come to pass, befall, betide; *archaic* hap; *rare* eventuate.

□ **come across 1** *they came across two of his friends | I came across some new evidence* **meet/find by chance**, meet up with, run into, run across, come upon, chance on, stumble on, happen on, light on, hit on; discover, encounter, find, unearth, uncover, locate, bring to light; *informal* bump into, dig up.
2 *this emotion comes across in both books* **be communicated**, be perceived, penetrate, get through, get across, be got across, be clear, be understood, be comprehended, register, be taken in, sink in, be grasped, strike home.
3 *she came across as cool and unemotional* **seem**, appear, look, sound, give the impression of being, have the appearance/air of being, strike someone as, look as though one is, look to be; *Brit.* come over; *N. Amer.* come off.
4 (*informal*) *there was always a chance that she'd* **come across with** *some more information* **hand over**, give, deliver, produce, part with, pay up; *informal* come up with, fork out, shell out, dish out, cough up; *N. Amer. informal* make with, ante up, pony up.

□ **come along 1** *the puppies are coming along nicely* **progress**, make progress, develop, shape up, make headway; come on, turn out, take shape, go; improve, show improvement, get better, pick up, rally, recover, mend.
2 *That's our man, Watson! Come along!* **hurry**, hurry (it) up, be quick (about it), get a move on, come along, look lively, speed up, move faster; *informal* get moving, get cracking, step on it, step on the gas, move it, buck up, shake a leg, make it snappy; *Brit. informal* get your skates on; *Brit. informal, dated* stir your stumps; *N. Amer. informal* get a wiggle on; *Austral./NZ informal* rattle your dags; *S. African informal* put foot; *dated* make haste.
OPPOSITE dawdle.

□ **come apart** *if the straw is too short the bales come apart very easily* **break up**, fall to bits/pieces, come to bits/pieces, disintegrate, splinter, come unstuck, crumble, separate, split, tear, collapse, dissolve.

□ **come back** *he came back from work that evening* **return**, get back, arrive back, arrive home, come home, come again.

□ **come between** *nothing should come between brothers* **alienate**, estrange, separate, divide, split up, break up, disunite, disaffect, set/pit against one another, cause disagreement between, sow dissension between, set at variance/odds.
OPPOSITE unite.

□ **come by** *good medical care was hard to come by* **obtain**, acquire, gain, get, find, pick up, lay hold of, possess oneself of, come to have, procure, secure, get possession of; buy, purchase; *informal* land, get one's hands on, get one's mitts on, get hold of, grab, bag, score, swing, nab, collar, cop.

□ **come down** *the study comes down against kerbside collection* **decide**, conclude, settle, reach a decision; choose, opt, plump.

□ **come down on** *the magistrate came down on him like a ton of bricks. See* REBUKE.

□ **come down to** *either he gives himself up or we arrest him; it comes down to the same thing* **amount to**, add up to, constitute, be tantamount to, approximate to, boil down to, be equivalent to, comprise, count as.

□ **come down with** *many girls came down with minor ailments* **become ill/sick with**, fall ill/sick with, be taken ill with, show symptoms of, become infected with, get, catch, develop, contract, take, sicken for, fall victim to, be struck down with, be stricken with; *Brit.* go down with; *informal* take ill with; *N. Amer. informal* take sick with.
OPPOSITE shake off.

□ **come forward** *a local trader came forward to pay the fines* **volunteer**, step forward, offer one's services, make oneself available.

□ **come in** *a hen came in through the open door* **enter**, gain admission, gain entrance, cross the threshold.
OPPOSITE go out.

□ **come into** *then he came into money and set up his own business* **inherit**, be/become heir to, be left, be willed, be bequeathed; *Law* be devised.

□ **come in for** *he has come in for a lot of criticism* **receive**, experience, sustain, undergo, meet with, encounter, face, go through, be subjected to, be the object of, bear the brunt of, suffer, have to put up with, have to bear, have to endure.

□ **come off 1** *when this fondue comes off it is a very fine dish indeed* **succeed**, be successful, be a success, pan out, work, turn out well, work out, go as planned, produce the desired result, get results; *informal* make it, make the grade, pay off.
OPPOSITE fail.
2 *Anthony always came off worse in an argument* **end up**, finish up.

□ **come on** *the marrows are coming on nicely* **progress**, make progress, develop, shape up, make headway; come along, turn out, take shape; improve, show improvement.

□ **come out 1** *it came out that he'd been to Rome, too* **become known**, become common knowledge, become apparent, come to light, emerge, transpire; get out, be discovered, be uncovered, be made public, be revealed, be divulged, leak out, be disclosed, be reported, be publicized, be released.
OPPOSITE be hushed up.
2 *lots of interesting books are coming out* **be published**, be issued, be released, be brought out, be produced, be printed, appear, go on sale.
3 *the garden looks really nice in the summer when all the flowers come out* **bloom**, come into bloom, flower, appear, open.
OPPOSITE wither.
4 *I expect it will come out all right* **end**, finish, conclude, terminate, develop, result, work out, turn out; *informal* pan out; *rare* eventuate.
5 *if MPs don't come out voluntarily, they risk being outed by a tabloid newspaper* **declare that one is homosexual**, come out of the closet.
6 (*Brit. dated*) *she came out in 1929* **enter society**, be presented, debut, make one's debut in society.

□ **come out with** *she was puzzled that he should come out with this remark* **utter**, say, speak, let out, blurt out, burst out with.

□ **come round 1** *he has just come round from anaesthetic* **regain consciousness**, recover consciousness, come to, come to life, come to one's senses, recover, revive, awake, wake up.
OPPOSITES faint, go under.
2 *he argued at first but came round eventually | I* **came round to** *her point of view* **be converted (to)**, be won over (by), agree (with), change one's mind, be persuaded (by), give way (to), yield (to), relent, concede, grant.
3 *the same combination of number and name only comes round every 260 days* **occur**, take place, happen, come up, crop up, arise; **recur**, happen again, reoccur, occur again, be repeated, repeat (itself); come back (again), return; reappear, appear again.
4 *do come round for a drink* **visit**, call (in/round), pay a call, pay a visit, look in, stop by, drop by/in/round/over, come over; *informal* pop in/round/over.

□ **come through** *his four shops came through the war intact* **survive**, get through, ride out, weather, live through, pull through, outlast, outlive; **withstand**, stand up to, bear up against, stand, endure, rise above, surmount, overcome, resist; *informal* stick out.

□ **come to 1** *their bill came to £17.50* **amount to**, add up to, run to, number, make, total, equal, be equal to, be equivalent to; *Brit.* tot up to.

C

2 *when I came to, I had a splitting headache* **regain consciousness**, recover consciousness, come round, come to life, come to one's senses, recover, revive, awake, wake up.
OPPOSITES faint, go under.

□ **come up** *when the opportunity came up again we didn't hesitate* **arise**, present itself, occur, happen, come about, transpire, emerge, surface, crop up, turn up, pop up.

□ **come up to 1** *she came up to his shoulder* **reach**, come to, come up as far as, be as tall as, extend to, stretch to.
2 *Christmas never really came up to her expectations* **measure up to**, match up to, live up to, reach, satisfy, fulfil, achieve, meet, equal, be equal to, be on a level with, compare with, admit of comparison, bear comparison with; be good enough, fit/fill the bill; *informal* hold a candle to, make the grade.
OPPOSITES exceed; fall short of.

□ **come up with** *I needed to come up with a solution* **produce**, devise, propose, put forward, present, think up, submit, suggest, recommend, advocate, advance, move, introduce, bring forward, put on the table, put up, offer, proffer, tender, adduce, moot.

comeback ▸ **noun 1** *he has made a determined comeback after his defeat in the world championship* **resurgence**, recovery, return, rally, upturn, revival, rebound; *Brit.* fightback.
2 (*informal*) *some of my best comebacks go over people's heads* **retort**, riposte, return, rejoinder, counter, retaliation, sally; answer, reply, response.

comedian ▸ **noun 1** *one of Britain's best-loved comedians* **comic**, funny man, funny woman, comedienne, comedy actor/actress, humorist, gagster, stand-up; *N. Amer.* tummler; *French* farceur.
2 *Dad was a comedian, but unaware of it* **joker**, jester, wit, wag, comic, wisecracker, punner, jokester; prankster, clown, fool, buffoon; *informal* laugh, hoot, case, character, one; *informal, dated* card, caution, sketch, yell; *Austral./NZ informal* hard case.

comedienne ▸ **noun.** See COMEDIAN sense 1.

comedown ▸ **noun** (*informal*) **1** *Patrol duty? Bit of a comedown for a sergeant* **loss of status**, loss of face; **downgrading**, mortification, humiliation, humbling, belittlement, lowering, demotion, reduction, degradation, disgrace.
2 *it's such a comedown after Christmas is over* **anticlimax**, let-down, bathos, disappointment, disillusionment, deflation, decline, setback, reversal; *informal* washout.

comedy ▸ **noun 1** *he excels in comedy | she has appeared in countless comedies* **light entertainment**; **comic play/film**; farce, situation comedy, burlesque, pantomime, slapstick, satire, vaudeville, comic opera; *informal* sitcom.
OPPOSITE tragedy.
2 *advertising people see the comedy in their work* **humour**, fun, funny side, comical aspect, funniness, ludicrousness, absurdity, absurdness, drollness, farce.
OPPOSITE gravity.

WORD LINKS
Muse **Thalia**

comely ▸ **adjective** *a comely young woman* **attractive**, good-looking, nice-looking, beautiful, pretty, handsome, lovely, stunning, striking, arresting, gorgeous, prepossessing, winning, fetching, captivating, bewitching, beguiling, engaging, charming, charismatic, enchanting, appealing, delightful, irresistible; sexy, sexually attractive, sexual, seductive, alluring, tantalizing, ravishing, desirable, sultry, sensuous, sensual, erotic, arousing, luscious, lush, nubile; *Scottish & N. English* bonny; *informal* fanciable, beddable, tasty, hot, smashing, knockout, drop-dead gorgeous, out of this world, easy on the eye, come-hither, come-to-bed; *Brit. informal* fit; *N. Amer. informal* cute, foxy, bootylicious; *Austral./NZ informal* spunky; *literary* beauteous; *dated* taking, well favoured; *archaic* fair; *rare* sightly, pulchritudinous.
OPPOSITE ugly.

come-on ▸ **noun** (*informal*) *the come-on for investors is the potential licensing agreement with a major drug company* **inducement**, attraction, interest, lure, pull, draw, enticement, allure, allurement, appeal, incentive, bait, carrot, temptation, fascination, charm, tantalization.
OPPOSITE turn-off.

comeuppance ▸ **noun** (*informal*) *in those films the villain always got his comeuppance* **just deserts**, deserved fate, due, due reward, just punishment, retribution, requital; *archaic* recompense.

comfort ▸ **noun 1** *they travel in comfort* **ease**, freedom from hardship, repose, relaxation, serenity, tranquillity, contentment, content, well-being, cosiness, enjoyment; **luxury**, affluence, prosperity, prosperousness, wealth, opulence; plenty, sufficiency, welfare; bed of roses; *rare* easefulness.
OPPOSITES discomfort; hardship.
2 *a few words of comfort* **consolation**, solace, condolence, sympathy, fellow feeling, commiseration; help, support, succour, relief, easement, alleviation; reassurance, cheer, gladdening.
OPPOSITE grief.
▸ **verb** *a friend tried to comfort her* **console**, solace, bring comfort to, give solace to, condole with, give condolences to, commiserate with, give sympathy to, sympathize with; help, support, succour, ease; reassure, soothe, assuage, calm, relieve, cheer, hearten, gladden, uplift, give a lift to, encourage; *informal* buck up.
OPPOSITES distress; depress.

comfortable ▸ **adjective 1** *a comfortable lifestyle* **pleasant**, free from hardship, well off, well-to-do, affluent, luxurious, gracious, opulent, elegant.
OPPOSITE hard.
2 *a comfortable room* **cosy**, snug, warm, pleasant, enjoyable, agreeable, congenial, plush, well furnished; sheltered, secure, safe, restful, homelike, homely; *informal* comfy.
OPPOSITE spartan.
3 *comfortable clothes* **loose**, loose-fitting, casual, roomy, soft; *informal* comfy.
OPPOSITES uncomfortable, tight.
4 *a comfortable pace* **leisurely**, unhurried, relaxed, unrushed, easy, easy-going, gentle, sedate, restful, effortless, undemanding, slow, plodding, lazy, dawdling, loitering, lingering; measured, steady; *informal* laid-back.
OPPOSITE frenetic.
5 *they appear very comfortable in each other's company* **at ease**, at one's ease, relaxed, reassured, confident, secure, safe, serene, tranquil, unworried, contented, happy.
OPPOSITES vulnerable, threatened, unsettled; tense.

comforting ▸ **adjective** *Anne gave her a comforting hug* **consoling**, consolatory, condoling, commiserative, sympathetic, understanding, compassionate, solicitous, gentle, tender, warm, protective, caring, loving; helpful, supportive, easing; reassuring, soothing, assuaging, calming, relieving, cheering, heartening, uplifting, encouraging.
OPPOSITE disquieting.

comfortless ▸ **adjective 1** *life in his aunt's colourless, comfortless house was narrow and uninteresting* **gloomy**, dreary, dull, dismal, bleak, drab, grim, sombre, dark, dim, dingy, funereal; miserable, wretched, joyless, cheerless, unhappy, depressing, disheartening, dispiriting, unwelcoming, uninviting, inhospitable; austere, severe, stark, bare, spartan, desolate; clinical, institutional, impersonal.
OPPOSITES bright, welcoming.
2 *he had left her comfortless* **miserable**, broken-hearted, heartbroken, unhappy, sad, grief-stricken, grieving, sorrowful, sorrowing, mourning, anguished, distressed, desolate, devastated, despairing, inconsolable, disconsolate, downcast, down, downhearted, dejected, crestfallen, cheerless, depressed, melancholy, morose, gloomy, glum, mournful, doleful, dismal, forlorn, woeful, woebegone, abject, low-spirited, long-faced; *informal* blue, down in the mouth, down in the dumps; *literary* dolorous; *archaic* chap-fallen.
OPPOSITE buoyant.

comic ▸ **adjective** *the play is so inane as to be comic* **humorous**, funny, droll, amusing, entertaining, diverting, absurd, ridiculous, comical, farcical, silly, slapstick, hilarious, uproarious, hysterical, hysterically funny, zany; witty, jocular, joking, facetious, waggish; *informal* priceless, side-splitting, rib-tickling, killing, killingly funny, screamingly funny, a scream, a hoot, a laugh, a barrel of laughs.
OPPOSITE serious.
▸ **noun 1** *he told jokes in the style of a music hall comic* **comedian**, comedienne, funny man, funny woman, comedy actor, comedy actress, humorist, wit, wag, quipster; joker, jester, prankster, clown; *informal* kidder, wisecracker; *archaic* buffoon.
2 *Tony was reading his comic* **cartoon paper**, comic paper, funny magazine, comic book, graphic novel; *informal* funny.

comical ▸ **adjective 1** *he could be comical while looking as serious as an owl* **funny**, comic, humorous, droll, witty, waggish, facetious, light-hearted, jocular, hilarious, hysterically funny; amusing, diverting, entertaining; *informal* jokey, wacky, side-splitting, rib-tickling, killing, killingly funny, priceless, a scream, a hoot, a laugh; *informal, dated* a card, a caution; *archaic* sportive; *rare* jocose.
OPPOSITE sensible.
2 *don't they look comical in those suits?* **silly**, absurd, ridiculous, laughable, risible, droll, ludicrous, farcical, preposterous, foolish; bizarre, weird, strange, freakish, queer, odd, peculiar, curious, zany; *informal* wacky, freaky, crazy, off the wall; *N. Amer. informal* wacko; *Brit. informal* rum; *rare* derisible.
OPPOSITE normal.

CHOOSE THE RIGHT WORD
comical, humorous, funny, witty
See HUMOROUS.

coming ▸ **adjective** *they wanted to discredit the Government prior to the coming election* **forthcoming**, imminent, impending, approaching, advancing, nearing, near; future, expected, anticipated; close, (close) at hand, in store, in the wind, in the air, in the offing, in the pipeline, on the horizon, on the way, on us, about to happen; *informal* on the cards.

▶ **noun** *primroses are associated with the coming of spring* **approach**, advance, advent, arrival, nearing, looming, appearance, emergence, materialization, surfacing; birth, rise, start, onset.

command ▶ **verb 1** *he commanded his men to retreat* **order**, give orders to, give the order to, tell, direct, instruct, call on, enjoin, adjure, charge, require, prescribe; *literary* bid.
2 *Jones commanded a tank squadron during the Gulf War* **be in charge of**, be in command of, have charge of, have control of, be the leader of, be the boss of, preside over, be in authority over, hold sway over; head, lead, rule, govern, control, direct, guide, manage, supervise, superintend, oversee; be in the driver's seat, be in the saddle, be at the helm, take the chair; *informal* head up, run the show, call the shots, call the tune.
3 *the clergy command great respect from the population* **receive**, be given, get, gain, obtain, secure.
▶ **noun 1** *the officers shouted their commands* **order**, instruction, directive, direction, commandment, injunction, demand, stipulation, requirement, exhortation, bidding, request; decree, dictate, diktat, edict, ruling, resolution, pronouncement, ordinance, mandate, fiat, precept; *literary* behest; *archaic* hest; *rare* rescript.
2 *he had sixteen men under his command* **authority**, control, charge, power, direction, dominion, domination, influence, sway, guidance; leadership, mastery, rule, government, management, supervision, superintendence, administration, jurisdiction.
3 *she had a brilliant* **command of** *English* **knowledge**, mastery, grasp, grip, comprehension, understanding; ability in, fluency in.

commandeer ▶ **verb** *everything surrounding the base was commandeered by the army* **seize**, take, take possession of, take away, requisition, appropriate, expropriate, sequestrate, sequester, confiscate, annex, take over, claim, lay claim to, pre-empt, secure; hijack, arrogate, arrogate to oneself, help oneself to, carry off, loot, grab; *informal* walk off with; *Law* distrain, attach, disseize; *Scottish Law* poind.

commander ▶ **noun** *he was commander of a special force combating drug trafficking* **leader**, head, headman, boss, chief, director, manager, overseer, controller, master; commander-in-chief, C.-in-C., commanding officer, CO, officer, captain; *informal* boss man, skipper, number one, top dog, kingpin, bigwig, Mr Big, big cheese; *Brit. informal* gaffer, guv'nor; *N. Amer. informal* numero uno, sachem, big white chief, big wheel, head honcho, honcho, big kahuna, high muckamuck.

commanding ▶ **adjective 1** *the world champion was in a commanding position* **dominant**, dominating, controlling, superior, powerful, prominent, advantageous, favourable, preferable, more desirable, most desirable; *rare* prepotent, prepollent.
2 *his mother's voice was soft and commanding* **authoritative**, masterful, assertive, confident, firm, emphatic, insistent, imperative, imposing, impressive; bossy, peremptory, autocratic, imperious, magisterial, lordly, high-handed, overbearing, domineering, dictatorial, dominating, bullish, forceful; *informal* pushy, not backward in coming forward; *rare* pushful.

commemorate ▶ **verb** *the event commemorated the courage of the villagers* **celebrate**, pay tribute to, pay homage to, honour, salute, toast; **remember**, recognize, acknowledge, observe, mark, memorialize, immortalize, keep alive the memory of.

commemorative ▶ **adjective** *veterans of the battle will attend commemorative services* **memorial**, remembrance, celebratory, celebrative; in remembrance of ..., in memory of ..., in honour of ....

commence ▶ **verb** (*formal*) *the headmaster commenced his tour of inspection | the meeting commenced at 10am* **begin**, start, start off; get down to business, get the ball rolling, get going, get under way, get off the ground, make a start on, set about, go about, enter on, embark on, launch into, lead off, get down to, set in motion, ring up the curtain on, open, initiate, institute, inaugurate; go ahead; *informal* get cracking on, get stuck into, kick off, get the show on the road; *Brit. informal* get weaving (on).
OPPOSITE conclude.

commencement ▶ **noun** (*formal*) *students shall enrol at the commencement of the academic session* **beginning**, start, starting point, opening, outset, onset, launch, initiation, inception, birth, dawn, origin; day one; *informal* kick-off.
OPPOSITE conclusion.

commend ▶ **verb 1** *we should commend him for his remarkable altruism* **praise**, compliment, congratulate, applaud, clap, cheer, toast, salute, admire, honour, glorify, extol, eulogize, sing the praises of, praise to the skies, heap praise on, go into raptures about, wax lyrical about, speak highly of, look on with favour, pay homage to, pay tribute to, take one's hat off to, pat on the back; *N. Amer. informal* ballyhoo; *black English* big someone up; *dated* cry someone up; *archaic* emblazon; *rare* laud, panegyrize.
OPPOSITE criticize.
2 *she's very hard-working—I commend her to you without reservation* **recommend**, suggest, put forward, propose, advance; approve, endorse, advocate, vouch for, speak for, stand up for, champion, support, back; *informal* plug, push.
3 (*formal*) *I commend my students to your care* **entrust**, trust, deliver, commit, hand over, give, give over, turn over, consign, assign.

commendable ▶ **adjective** *he tackled the tests with commendable zeal* **admirable**, praiseworthy, laudable, estimable, meritorious, creditable, exemplary, exceptional, noteworthy, notable, honourable, worthy, deserving, respectable, sterling, fine, excellent; worthy of commendation, worthy of admiration; *rare* applaudable.
OPPOSITE reprehensible.

commendation ▶ **noun 1** *he received letters of commendation from the chief constable* **praise**, congratulation, appreciation, thanks; acclaim, acclamation, credit, recognition, regard, respect, esteem, admiration, adulation, approval, approbation, homage, tribute; eulogy, encomium, panegyric, paean; *rare* laudation, extolment, eulogium.
OPPOSITE criticism.
2 *he got a commendation for brave conduct* **award**, accolade, prize, honour, honourable mention, mention, citation, recognition; pat on the back, round of applause.
OPPOSITE penalty.

commensurate ▶ **adjective 1** *the clergy had privileges but they had commensurate duties* **equivalent**, equal, corresponding, correspondent, comparable, proportionate, proportional; *rare* commensurable.
OPPOSITE disproportionate.
2 *your initial salary will be* **commensurate with** *your qualifications and experience* **appropriate to**, in keeping with, in line with, consistent with, corresponding to, in accordance with, according to, relative to, in proportion with, proportionate to; dependent on, based on; *rare* commensurable with/to.

comment ▶ **noun 1** *she was upset by their comments on her appearance* **remark**, observation, statement, utterance, pronouncement, judgement, reflection, opinion, view, criticism.
2 *the story excited a great deal of comment* **discussion**, debate, mention, consideration, interest.
3 *a comment had been inserted in the register for 1586* **note**, notation, annotation, footnote, gloss, commentary, explanation, explication, interpretation, elucidation, exposition, exegesis; marginalia; *rare* scholium.
▶ **verb 1** *they* **commented on** *the quality of the water* **remark on**, speak about, talk about, write about, discuss, mention, give a mention to, make mention of, make remarks about, make a comment on, express an opinion on, say something about, touch on, allude to.
2 *'It will soon be night,' he commented* **remark**, observe, reflect, say, state, declare, announce, pronounce, assert, interpose, interject; come out with; *rare* opine.

commentary ▶ **noun 1** *he spent the morning listening to the test match commentary* **narration**, description, account, report, review, analysis.
2 *the second volume contains detailed textual commentary* **explanation**, explication, elucidation, exegesis, examination, interpretation, analysis; **criticism**, critical analysis, critique, assessment, appraisal, opinion; notes, footnotes, comments, weblog, blog; *rare* scholia.

commentator ▶ **noun 1** *he was a BBC television commentator for twenty-five years* **narrator**, commenter, reporter, correspondent, journalist; announcer, presenter, anchor, anchorman, anchorwoman, broadcaster, newscaster, sportscaster; *informal* talking head.
2 *she was the ablest and most devastating political commentator* **critic**, **analyst**, pundit, commenter, monitor, observer, blogger, judge, evaluator, interpreter, exponent, expounder; writer, author, speaker; *rare* scholiast; (**commentators**) the commentariat.

commerce ▶ **noun 1** *Hong Kong was a perfect harbour for eastern commerce* **trade**, trading, buying and selling, business, bargaining, dealing, traffic, trafficking; (financial) transactions, dealings, negotiations; *archaic* merchandising.
2 (*dated*) *the noise and warmth of human commerce* **social relations**, dealings, socializing, communication, intercommunication, association, contact, intercourse, social intercourse; *archaic* traffic.

commercial ▶ **adjective 1** *the vessels were originally built for commercial purposes* **trade**, trading, business, private enterprise, mercantile, merchant, sales; *archaic* merchandising.
2 *they help firms turn good ideas into commercial products* **lucrative**, moneymaking, money-spinning, profitable, profit-making, for-profit, remunerative, financially rewarding, fruitful, gainful, productive; viable, cost-effective, economic, successful, commercially successful.
OPPOSITE loss-making.
3 *public opinion was inward-looking and brashly commercial* **profit-orientated**, money-orientated, commercialized, materialistic, mercenary.
OPPOSITE non-profit-making.
▶ **noun** *she appeared in a TV commercial for a brand of butter* **advertisement**, promotion, display; *informal* ad, push, plug; *Brit. informal* advert.

commercialized ▶ **adjective** *the art world became increasingly commercialized* **profit-orientated**, money-orientated, commercial, materialistic, mercenary.
OPPOSITE uncommercial.

commiserate ▶ **verb** *he commiserated with them for their sufferings* **offer**

sympathy to, be sympathetic to, express sympathy for, send condolences to, offer condolences to, condole with, sympathize with, empathize with, feel pity for, feel sorry for, feel for, be moved by, mourn for, sorrow for, grieve for; comfort, console, solace, give solace to; one's heart goes out to; *archaic* compassion, compassionate.

C

commiseration ▸ noun *the other actors offered him clumsy commiseration | our commiserations to those who didn't win* **condolences**, sympathy, pity, comfort, solace, consolation; compassion, feeling, fellow feeling, understanding, consideration.

commission ▸ noun **1** *the customer is unlikely to know about the dealer's commission* **percentage**, brokerage, share, portion, dividend, premium, fee, consideration, bonus, gratuity, tip, honorarium; *informal* cut, take, whack, rake-off, slice, slice of the cake, piece of the action; *Brit. informal* divvy; *rare* apportionment, quantum, moiety.
2 *he accepted the commission of building a house for the queen* **task**, employment, job, work, piece of work, project, mission, assignment, undertaking, exercise, enterprise, endeavour; duty, charge, responsibility, burden; *dated* office.
3 *the items are made under royal commission* **warrant**, licence, sanction, authority.
4 *their plan requires approval by an independent commission* **committee**, board, board of commissioners, council, panel, directorate, advisory body, advisorate, convocation, delegation.
5 *they did not participate in the commission of any offence* **perpetration**, committing, committal, execution, performance.
□ **in commission** *the company had thirty-six vessels in commission* **in service**, in use, in employment, in action; working, functioning, functional, operative, going, running, up and running, in operation, in working order.
□ **out of commission** *five of the rescue vehicles were out of commission* **not in service**, unavailable for use, not in use, out of action, unserviceable; not working, not functioning, not functional, inoperative, not in operation, not in working order, out of order; down; *Brit. informal* U/S.
▸ verb **1** *he commissioned Van Dyck to paint his portrait* **engage**, contract, charge, employ, hire, recruit, retain, appoint, enlist, co-opt, book, sign up; authorize, empower; *Military* detail.
2 *they decided to commission a sculpture of Molly Malone* **order**, put in an order for, place an order for, contract for, pay for; authorize; *rare* bespeak.

commit ▸ verb **1** *he was on trial for a murder he had not committed* **carry out**, do, perform, perpetrate, engage in, enact, execute, effect, accomplish; be responsible for, be to blame for, be guilty of; *informal* pull off; *rare* effectuate.
2 *she was committed to the care of the local authority* **entrust**, trust, commend, consign, assign, deliver, give, give over, hand over, turn over, give up, relinquish.
3 *local business leaders committed themselves to community projects* **pledge**, devote, apply, give, dedicate, bind, obligate.
4 *the judge committed him to prison for eight months* **consign**, assign, send, deliver, confine.
5 *her husband had her committed after her eccentricity became dangerous* **hospitalize**, **confine**, institutionalize, put away, lock away, lock up; certify.
OPPOSITE release.

commitment ▸ noun **1** *he resigned because of the pressure of other commitments* **responsibility**, obligation, duty, tie, charge, liability, burden, pressure; undertaking, task, engagement, arrangement.
2 *her commitment to her students continued undiminished* **dedication**, devotion, allegiance, loyalty, faithfulness, fidelity, bond, adherence, attentiveness.
3 *he made a commitment to carry on his father's work* **vow**, promise, pledge, oath; covenant, contract, pact, deal, undertaking; decision, resolution, resolve; guarantee, assurance, affirmation.

committed ▸ adjective *they are committed Christians* **devout**, devoted, loyal, dedicated, faithful, staunch, firm, steadfast, resolute, unwavering, sincere, wholehearted, keen, earnest, enthusiastic, zealous, passionate, ardent, fervent, active, sworn, pledged; dutiful, hard-working, diligent, studious, assiduous; *French* engagé; *informal* card-carrying, red-hot, true blue, mad keen, deep-dyed.
OPPOSITE apathetic.

commodious ▸ adjective *she was sitting in a commodious armchair* **roomy**, capacious, spacious, ample, substantial, generous, sizeable, large, big, broad, wide, extensive; *rare* spacey.
OPPOSITE cramped.

commodity ▸ noun *improving productivity will lower the cost of a commodity* **item**, material, type of produce, product, article, object, thing, artefact, piece of merchandise; import, export.

common ▸ adjective **1** *he gained a massive following among the common folk* **ordinary**, normal, typical, average, unexceptional, run-of-the-mill, plain, simple.
2 *this booklet answers the most common questions asked | a very common art form* **usual**, ordinary, customary, habitual, familiar, regular, frequent, repeated, recurrent, routine, everyday, daily, day-to-day, quotidian, standard, typical; conventional, stock, stereotyped, predictable, commonplace, mundane, run-of-the-mill; *literary* wonted.
OPPOSITE unusual.
3 *it is a common belief that elephants have long memories* **widespread**, general, universal, popular, mainstream, prevalent, prevailing, rife, established, well established, conventional, traditional, traditionalist, orthodox, accepted; in circulation, in force, in vogue.
OPPOSITE rare.
4 *they work together for the common good* **collective**, communal, community, public, popular, general; **shared**, joint, combined.
OPPOSITES private, individual.
5 *the fishermen's wives were far too common for my mother* **uncouth**, vulgar, coarse, rough, unsavoury, boorish, rude, impolite, ill-mannered, unladylike, ungentlemanly, ill-bred, uncivilized, unsophisticated, unrefined, philistine, primitive, savage, brutish, oafish, gross; **lowly**, low, low-born, low-ranking, low-class, inferior, humble, ignoble, proletarian, plebeian; *informal* plebby, slobbish, cloddish, clodhopping; *Brit. informal* common as muck; *archaic* baseborn.
OPPOSITES refined; noble.
▸ noun (*Brit. informal*) *use a bit of common!* See COMMON SENSE.

commonly ▸ adverb *shift workers commonly complain of not being able to sleep* **often**, frequently, regularly, repeatedly, recurrently, time and again, time and time again, over and over, all the time, routinely, habitually, customarily; *N. Amer.* oftentimes; *informal* lots; *literary* oft, oft-times.
OPPOSITE rarely.

commonplace ▸ adjective **1** *he had a tame and commonplace style of writing* **ordinary**, run-of-the-mill, middle-of-the-road, mainstream, unremarkable, unexceptional, undistinguished, uninspired, unexciting, unmemorable, forgettable, indifferent, average, so-so, mediocre, pedestrian, prosaic, lacklustre, dull, bland, uninteresting, mundane, everyday, quotidian, humdrum, hackneyed, trite, banal, clichéd, predictable, overused, overdone, overworked, stale, worn out, time-worn, tired, unoriginal; *Brit.* common or garden; *N. Amer.* garden variety; *informal* nothing to write home about, nothing to get excited about, no great shakes, not so hot, not up to much, vanilla, plain vanilla, bog-standard, a dime a dozen, old hat, corny, played out; *Brit. informal* not much cop, ten a penny; *N. Amer. informal* ornery, bush-league, cornball, dime-store; *Austral./NZ informal* half-pie.
OPPOSITES outstanding; original.
2 *business trips abroad are now commonplace occurrences* **common**, normal, usual, ordinary, familiar, routine, standard, everyday, day-to-day, daily, regular, frequent, habitual, conventional, typical, unexceptional, unremarkable.
OPPOSITE unusual.
▸ noun **1** *early death was a commonplace in those days* **everyday thing/event**; routine, nothing out of the ordinary.
2 *he had a great store of commonplaces which he adapted to any subject* **platitude**, cliché, truism, hackneyed/trite/banal/overworked saying, stock phrase, old chestnut, banality, bromide.

common sense ▸ noun *he is quick to praise her professionalism and common sense* **good sense**, sense, sensibleness, native wit, native intelligence, mother wit, wit, judgement, sound judgement, level-headedness, prudence, discernment, acumen, sharpness, sharp-wittedness, canniness, astuteness, shrewdness, judiciousness, wisdom, insight, intuition, intuitiveness, perceptiveness, perspicacity, vision, understanding, intelligence, reason, powers of reasoning; practicality, capability, initiative, resourcefulness, enterprise; *informal* horse sense, gumption, nous, savvy, know-how; *Brit. informal* common; *N. Amer. informal* smarts; *rare* sapience, arguteness.
OPPOSITE folly.

commotion ▸ noun *a commotion broke out in the street behind us* **disturbance**, racket, uproar, tumult, ruckus, clamour, brouhaha, furore, hue and cry, palaver, fuss, stir, to-do, storm, maelstrom, melee; turmoil, disorder, confusion, chaos, mayhem, havoc, pandemonium, upheaval, unrest, fracas, riot, breach of the peace, disruption, agitation, excitement, hurly-burly, hubbub, disquiet, ferment, bother, folderol, bustle, hustle and bustle; *Irish, N. Amer., & Austral.* donnybrook; *Indian* tamasha; *W. Indian* bangarang; *informal* song and dance, pantomime, production, rumpus, ruction, ructions, ballyhoo, hoo-ha, hullabaloo, aggro, argy-bargy; *Brit. informal* carry-on, kerfuffle, row, stink, splash, hoopla; *N. Amer. informal* foofaraw; *NZ informal* bobsy-die; *Law, dated* affray; *archaic* broil.

communal ▸ adjective **1** *the bathrooms and the kitchen were communal* **shared**, joint, common, general, public.
OPPOSITE private.
2 *the villagers farm on a communal basis* **collective**, cooperative, community, communalist, united, combined, pooled, mass.
OPPOSITE individual.

commune ▸ noun (stress on the first syllable) *she was brought up in a commune in Vancouver* **collective**, cooperative, co-op, community, communal settlement, kibbutz, fellowship.
▸ verb (stress on the second syllable) **1** *the purpose of praying is to commune with God* **communicate**, speak, talk, converse, have a tête-à-tête, confer;

be in touch, be in contact, interface.
2 *spare half an hour each day to* ***commune with*** *nature* **empathize**, have a rapport, feel in close touch; feel at one, feel togetherness, identify, relate to, relate spiritually to, feel close to.

communicable ▶ **adjective** *they are concerned about the spread of communicable diseases* **contagious**, **infectious**, transmittable, transmissible, transferable, conveyable, spreadable, spreading; *informal* catching; *dated* infective.

communicate ▶ **verb** **1** *he communicated the bad news to his boss* **convey**, tell, impart, relay, transmit, pass on, hand on, transfer, make known, announce, report, recount, relate, set forth, present, divulge, disclose, mention; spread, disseminate, circulate, promulgate, proclaim, broadcast, make public; *informal* let on about.
OPPOSITES withhold from; keep secret.
2 *parents and teachers should communicate on a daily basis* **liaise**, be in touch, be in contact, be in communication, make contact, have dealings, interface, commune, meet, meet up; talk, speak, converse, chat, have a conversation, have a chat, have a discussion; *N. Amer.* visit; *informal* have a confab, chew the fat, chew the rag, powwow; *Brit. informal* have a chinwag; *N. Amer. informal* shoot the breeze, shoot the bull.
3 *we have to learn how to communicate in an electronic environment* **get one's ideas across**, get one's message across, make oneself understood, explain oneself, get through to someone, have one's say; be articulate, be fluent, be eloquent.
4 *the disease is communicated from one person to another* **transmit**, transfer, spread, carry, pass on, hand on, convey.
5 *each bedroom* ***communicated with*** *a spacious bathroom* **connect with**, be connected to, join up with, link up with, open on to, lead into, give access to.

communication ▶ **noun** **1** *meetings are used for the communication of research results* **transmission**, imparting, conveying, reporting, presenting, passing on, handing on, relay, conveyance, divulgence, divulgation, disclosure; spreading, dissemination, promulgation, broadcasting, circulation, circulating.
2 *there had been no communication between them for years* **contact**, dealings, relations, connection, association, communion, socializing, intercourse, social intercourse, social relations, interface, interchange, correspondence, dialogue, talk, conversation, discussion, speaking, talking, chatting, meeting, getting in touch; *dated* commerce; *archaic* traffic.
3 *there has been no official communication regarding an appeal* **message**, statement, announcement, report, dispatch, communiqué, letter, bulletin, correspondence, news, word, information, intelligence, instruction; *informal* info, gen, low-down, dirt; *literary* tidings.

communications ▶ **plural noun** *the city has excellent road and rail communications* **links**, connections, services, routes.

communicative ▶ **adjective** *she is always very pleasant and communicative* **forthcoming**, expansive, informative, expressive, unreserved, uninhibited, vocal, outgoing, frank, open, candid; **talkative**, conversational, chatty, gossipy, loquacious, garrulous, voluble, verbose, effusive, gushing; *informal* mouthy, gabby, windy, gassy; *rare* multiloquent, multiloquous.
OPPOSITE uncommunicative.

communion ▶ **noun** **1** *we receive a strong sense of communion with others* **affinity**, fellowship, kinship, friendship, fellow feeling, community, togetherness, closeness, sharing, harmony, understanding, rapport, connection, communication, association, empathy, sympathy, agreement, accord, concord, unity.
2 *he believed in Christ's presence among the faithful at Communion* **Eucharist**, Holy Communion, Lord's Supper, Mass.

communiqué ▶ **noun** *the foreign ministry issued a communiqué* **official communication**, press release, bulletin, message, missive, dispatch, statement, report, news flash, notification, announcement, declaration, proclamation, pronouncement; word, news, information; *N. Amer.* advisory; *informal* memo; *literary* tidings.

communism ▶ **noun** *many western governments were highly fearful of communism* **collectivism**, state ownership, socialism, radical socialism; Sovietism, Bolshevism, Marxism, neo-Marxism, Leninism, Marxism–Leninism, Trotskyism, Maoism.

communist ▶ **noun & adjective** *I was very left-wing but I was never a communist | a French communist writer* **collectivist**, leftist, socialist, radical socialist; Soviet, Bolshevik, Bolshevist, Marxist, neo-Marxist, Leninist, Marxist–Leninist, Trotskyist, Trotskyite, Maoist; *informal, derogatory* Commie, Bolshie, red, lefty.

community ▶ **noun** **1** *we can work together for the good of the community* **population**, populace, people, citizenry, public, general public, body politic, collective; society, nation, state, country, realm, commonwealth, homeland, fatherland, motherland; residents, inhabitants, citizens; *humorous* denizens, burghers.
2 *East Durham was very much a mining community* **district**, region, zone, area, local area, locality, locale, neighbourhood; *informal* neck of the woods; *Brit. informal* manor; *N. Amer. informal* hood, nabe, turf.
3 *lesbians and gays are not one homogeneous community* **group**, section, body, company, set, circle, clique, coterie, ring, band, faction; *informal* gang, bunch.
4 *the monastic community at Canterbury* **brotherhood**, sisterhood, fraternity, confraternity, sorority, colony, institution, order, body, circle, association, society, league; *rare* sodality.
5 *they had a harmonious union based on a community of interests* **similarity**, similar nature, likeness, sameness, comparability, correspondence, agreement, alignment, parallel, parallelism, closeness, affinity; *archaic* semblance.
OPPOSITES difference, incompatibility.
6 *the community of goods* **joint ownership**, common ownership, shared possession; joint liability, joint participation.

commute ▶ **verb** **1** *they commute on a stuffy overcrowded train* **travel to and from work**, travel to and fro, travel back and forth, come and go, shuttle.
2 *the death sentence was commuted to life imprisonment* **reduce**, lessen, lighten, shorten, cut, scale down, limit, curtail, attenuate, mitigate, moderate, modify, adjust.
OPPOSITES increase; uphold.
3 *military service was often commuted for a money payment* **exchange**, change, interchange, substitute, swap, trade, barter, switch; *archaic* truck.

commuter ▶ **noun** *a bomb on the line caused widespread delays for commuters* **daily traveller**, traveller, passenger; *informal* straphanger, suburbanite.

compact[1] (stress on the second syllable) ▶ **adjective** **1** *this type of knotting produces extremely compact rugs* **dense**, packed close, close-packed, tightly packed, pressed together; thick, tight, firm, solid.
OPPOSITE loose.
2 *the computer is compact enough to fit in your lap* **small**, little, petite, miniature, mini, small-scale, neat, economic of space; *Scottish* wee; *informal* teeny, teeny-weeny, teensy-weensy; *Brit. informal* dinky; *N. Amer.* little-bitty.
OPPOSITE large.
3 *her tale is compact and readable* **concise**, succinct, condensed, compendious, crisp, terse, brief, pithy, epigrammatic, aphoristic, elliptical; to the point, short and sweet; *informal* snappy; *rare* lapidary.
OPPOSITE rambling.
▶ **verb** *the snow has been compacted by cars* **compress**, condense, pack down, press down, tamp, tamp down, cram down, ram down, flatten.
OPPOSITE loosen.

compact[2] (stress on the first syllable) ▶ **noun** *they signed a compact with the United States* **treaty**, pact, accord, agreement, contract, alliance, bargain, deal, settlement, covenant, indenture, concordat, protocol, entente; arrangement, understanding, pledge, promise, bond; *rare* engagement.

companion ▶ **noun** **1** *Harry and his companion settled down at a table* **associate**, partner, escort, consort, colleague, workmate, co-worker, compatriot, confederate, ally; **friend**, intimate, confidant, confidante, comrade; *French* confrère; *informal* buddy, pal, chum, crony, cully, spar, sidekick; *Brit. informal* mate, oppo, china, mucker; *NE English informal* marrow, marrer, marra; *N. Amer. informal* amigo, compadre, paisan; *N. Amer. & S. African informal* homeboy, homegirl; *S. African informal* gabba; *Austral./NZ informal* offsider; *archaic* compeer; *rare* consociate.
2 *a lady's companion* **attendant**, aide, helper, assistant, personal assistant, valet, equerry, squire, lady in waiting; chaperone, duenna, protector, protectress; carer, minder; *informal* sidekick.
3 *the CD is intended as a companion to their recent hit* **complement**, counterpart, fellow, mate, twin, other half, match; **accompaniment**, supplement, addition, adjunct, appendage, accessory, auxiliary.
4 *The Cottage Gardener's Companion* **handbook**, manual, guide, reference book, instruction book, ABC, primer; *Latin* vade mecum; *informal* bible; *rare* enchiridion.

companionable ▶ **adjective** *he was the most generous and companionable of men* **friendly**, affable, cordial, genial, congenial, amiable, easy-going, approachable, sympathetic, well disposed, good-natured, neighbourly, hospitable, comradely, easy to get along with; sociable, convivial, outgoing, extrovert, extroverted, gregarious, company-loving, hail-fellow-well-met; *informal* chummy, pally; *Brit. informal* matey; *N. Amer. informal* buddy-buddy, clubby, regular.
OPPOSITE unfriendly.

companionship ▶ **noun** *she needed the companionship of like-minded young people* **friendship**, fellowship, closeness, togetherness, amity, intimacy, rapport, camaraderie, comradeship, solidarity, mutual support, mutual affection, brotherhood, sisterhood; company, society, association, social intercourse, social contact, acquaintance; *informal* chumminess, palliness, clubbiness; *Brit. informal* mateyness.

company ▶ **noun** **1** *he works for the world's biggest oil company* **firm**, business, corporation, house, establishment, agency, office, bureau, institution, organization, operation, concern, enterprise, venture, undertaking, practice; conglomerate, consortium, syndicate, group, chain, combine, multiple, multinational; *informal* outfit, set-up.
2 *I was greatly looking forward to the pleasure of his company* **companionship**, presence, friendship, fellowship, closeness, amity,

camaraderie, comradeship; society, association.
3 *I'm expecting company* **guests**, a guest, visitors, a visitor, callers, a caller, people, someone; *archaic* visitants.
4 *he disentangled himself from the surrounding company of poets* **group**, crowd, body, party, band, collection, assembly, assemblage, cluster, flock, herd, horde, troupe, swarm, stream, mob, throng, congregation, gathering, meeting, convention; *informal* bunch, gang, gaggle, posse, crew, pack; *Brit. informal* shower.
5 *he recognized the company of infantry as French* **unit**, section, detachment, troop, corps, squad, squadron, platoon, battalion, division.

WORD LINKS
relating to a company **corporate**

comparable ▸ adjective **1** *he had an income* **comparable to** *that of a king* **similar**, close, near, approximate, akin, equivalent, corresponding, commensurate, proportional, proportionate, parallel, analogous, related; like, matching; bordering on, verging on, approaching; *informal* not a million miles away from; *rare* commensurable.
2 *nobody is* **comparable with** *the British hurdler* **as good as**, equal to, in the same class as, in the same league as, of the same standard as, able to hold a candle to, on a par with, on a level with, on an equal footing with; the equal of, a match for.
OPPOSITE incomparable.

comparative ▸ adjective *they left the city for the comparative cool of the country* **relative**, qualified, modified; in/by comparison.

compare ▸ verb **1** *we compared the data from our present and previous studies* **contrast**, set side by side, juxtapose, collate, differentiate, weigh up, balance, weigh/balance/measure the differences between.
2 *James Dean was constantly being* **compared to** *Brando* **liken**, equate, analogize; draw an analogy between, make an analogy between, mention in the same breath as, class with, bracket with, group with, put together with, set side by side with, regard as the same as, regard as identical to.
OPPOSITE contrast with.
3 *Chelsea porcelain was said to* **compare with** *Dresden's fine china* **be (nearly) as good as**, be comparable to, bear comparison with, be the equal of, match up to, be on a par with, be in the same class as, be in the same league as, be on a level with, compete with, come up to, come near to, come close to, hold a candle to, be not unlike, be not dissimilar to, equal roughly; match, resemble, emulate, rival, approach, approximate, touch, nudge; *informal* be not a million miles from.
□ **beyond compare** *he was a hero beyond compare* **without equal**, without match, without parallel, beyond comparison, second to none, in a class of one's own; peerless, matchless, unmatched, incomparable, inimitable, superlative, supreme, top, outstanding, consummate, unique, singular, rare, perfect; *French* par excellence.

comparison ▸ noun **1** *the table provides a comparison of our performance with last year's results* **contrast**, juxtaposition, collation, differentiation; weighing up, balancing.
2 *there's no comparison between classical music and rap* **resemblance**, likeness, similarity, similitude, correspondence, correlation, parallel, parity, symmetry, equivalence, comparability, analogy.
OPPOSITE difference.

compartment ▸ noun **1** *Benjamin examined the casket for a secret compartment* **section**, part, partition, bay, recess, chamber, cavity, niche, nook, hollow; pocket, pouch, receptacle.
2 *they place magic, science, and religion into separate compartments* **domain**, field, sphere, realm, area, department, sector, section, division, part; category, pigeonhole, bracket, class, group, set.

compartmentalize ▸ verb *we need to compartmentalize the issues we're working on* **categorize**, pigeonhole, sectionalize, bracket, separate, distinguish, group; classify, characterize, stereotype, label, brand, tag, designate, grade, codify, sort, rank, rate.

compass ▸ noun *faith cannot be defined within the compass of human thought* **scope**, range, extent, reach, span, breadth, width, orbit, ambit, stretch, limits, confines, parameters, extremities, bounds, boundary; area, field, sphere, zone, domain.

compassion ▸ noun *she gazed with compassion at the two dejected figures* **pity**, sympathy, feeling, fellow feeling, empathy, understanding, care, concern, solicitude, solicitousness, sensitivity, tender-heartedness, soft-heartedness, warm-heartedness, warmth, love, brotherly love, tenderness, gentleness, mercy, mercifulness, leniency, lenience, tolerance, consideration, kindness, humanity, humaneness, kind-heartedness, charity, benevolence.
OPPOSITES indifference; heartlessness.

compassionate ▸ adjective *they showed a compassionate concern for the victims* **pitying**, sympathetic, empathetic, understanding, caring, concerned, solicitous, sensitive, tender-hearted, soft-hearted, warm-hearted, warm, loving, tender, gentle, merciful, lenient, tolerant, considerate, thoughtful, kind, kindly, kind-hearted, humanitarian, humane, charitable, benevolent, good-natured, well disposed, big-hearted.
OPPOSITES indifferent; heartless.

compatibility ▸ noun *they felt the bond of true compatibility* **like-mindedness**, similarity, agreement, affinity, closeness, fellow feeling, harmony, rapport, empathy, sympathy, friendship, camaraderie, togetherness, communion, concord.
OPPOSITE incompatibility.

compatible ▸ adjective **1** *the two young men were never compatible* **well suited**, suited, well matched, like-minded, of the same mind, in agreement, in tune, in harmony, reconcilable; *archaic* accordant.
OPPOSITE incompatible.
2 *the bruising is compatible with his having had a fall* **consistent**, reconcilable, consonant, congruous, congruent, fitting; in keeping, in accord, in tune, in step.
OPPOSITE inconsistent.

compatriot ▸ noun *Sampras defeated his compatriot Agassi in the final* **fellow countryman**, fellow countrywoman, countryman, countrywoman, fellow citizen, fellow national.

compel ▸ verb **1** *the lords* **compelled** *the peasants* **to** *hand over their harvest* **force**, coerce into, pressurize into, pressure, impel, drive, press, push, urge, prevail on; dragoon into, browbeat into, bully into, bludgeon into, intimidate into, terrorize into; **oblige**, require, put under an obligation, leave someone no option but to; make; *informal* bulldoze, railroad, steamroller, twist someone's arm, strong-arm, lean on, put the screws on; *archaic* constrain.
2 *they can compel compliance by issuing a directive* **exact**, extort, demand, insist on, enforce, force, necessitate; *archaic* constrain.

CHOOSE THE RIGHT WORD

compel, force, coerce, oblige

All these words refer to making someone do something that they would not otherwise choose to do. They are often used in the passive, underlining the sense that the person feels deprived of power or choice. All but *coerce* are used with an infinitive (e.g. *compelled to do something*), as in the examples given.

- Someone who is **compelled** to do something is subjected to pressure that they feel unable to resist. Often, this pressure is applied by someone in authority and takes the form of the threat of penalties if the person fails to comply (*companies are compelled to comply with the regulations* | *the court had powers to compel witnesses to attend*). Adverse circumstances may also compel someone to do something (*he was compelled to retire on grounds of ill health*), or the pressure may be from one's own conscience (*I feel compelled to write this letter of complaint*).
- **Force** is a more general term for using superior power to make someone do what one wants them to. The superior power may be that of uncontrollable circumstances (*the firm has been forced to make nineteen more workers redundant*) or that of someone physically stronger or better equipped (*the raider forced him to open the safe*). People may also *force* themselves to do something, steeling themselves for something necessary but unpleasant (*Lucy forced herself to sound calm*).
- To **coerce** someone into doing something typically involves force or threats (*landlords might try to coerce their tenants into voting for them* | *they claimed that they had been coerced into making their televised confessions*). *Coercion* is nearly always applied by another person, not by circumstances or one's own conscience.
- Typically, if someone is **obliged** to do something, they are legally or morally bound to do it rather than being forced or pressurized (*independent schools are not legally obliged to follow the National Curriculum* | *Stephen felt obliged to sit next to her*).

compelling ▸ adjective **1** *she gave a compelling and intensely dramatic performance* **enthralling**, captivating, gripping, engrossing, riveting, spellbinding, entrancing, transfixing, mesmerizing, hypnotic, mesmeric, absorbing, fascinating, thrilling, irresistible, addictive; *informal* unputdownable.
OPPOSITE boring.
2 *he had no compelling arguments for changing the status quo* **convincing**, persuasive, cogent, irresistible, forceful, powerful, potent, strong, weighty, plausible, credible, effective, efficacious, sound, valid, reasonable, reasoned, well reasoned, rational, well founded, telling, conclusive, irrefutable, unanswerable, authoritative, influential.
OPPOSITE weak.

compendious ▸ adjective *a compendious essay on Italian music* **succinct**, pithy, short and to the point, short and sweet, potted, thumbnail, brief, crisp, compact, concise, condensed, shortened, contracted, compressed, abridged, abbreviated, summarized, summary, abstracted; in a nutshell, in a few well-chosen words; *informal* snappy; *rare* lapidary, epigrammatic, synoptic, aphoristic, gnomic.
OPPOSITES rambling; expanded.

compendium ▸ noun *a compendium of useful information about language* collection, compilation, anthology, treasury, digest; summary, synopsis, precis, résumé, outline, summarization, round-up, summing-up; companion, handbook, manual; Latin vade mecum; rare conspectus, summa, epitome.

compensate ▶ verb **1** *you can never compensate for what you did to me* **make amends**, make up, make restitution, make reparation, make recompense, recompense, atone, requite, pay; expiate, make good, put to rights, rectify, offset, square.
2 *terms were agreed to compensate him for his loss* **recompense**, repay, pay back, reimburse, remunerate, recoup, requite, indemnify; settle up with, settle accounts with.
3 *he had sufficient flair to compensate for his faults* **balance**, balance out, counterbalance, counteract, counterpoise, countervail, make up for, offset, cancel out, neutralize, nullify, even up, square up; rare equilibrize, negative, counterweigh.

compensation ▶ noun *they provide adequate compensation for any costs incurred* **recompense**, repayment, payment, reimbursement, remuneration, requital, indemnification, indemnity, redress, satisfaction; damages, reparations; N. Amer. informal comp; archaic guerdon, meed; rare solatium.

compère ▶ noun *she was the compère of a recent Channel 4 series* **host**, presenter, anchorman, anchorwoman, anchorperson, anchor, master of ceremonies, MC, link person, announcer; informal emcee, talking head.

compete ▶ verb **1** *young footballers are invited to compete in a five-a-side tournament* **take part**, play, be a contestant, be a competitor, participate, be involved, get involved, engage; enter, go in for; informal throw one's hat in the ring, be in the running.
2 *they had to compete with other firms for the contract* **contend**, vie, fight, battle, clash, tussle, grapple, wrestle, wrangle, jockey, wage war, cross swords, lock horns, go head to head; strive against, struggle against, pit oneself against; challenge, take on, try to beat; informal pitch oneself against.
3 *in this sort of form, no one can compete with him* **rival**, challenge, keep up with, keep pace with, compare with, be the equal of, match up to, match, be on a par with, be in the same class as, be in the same league as, come near to, come close to, touch, approach, approximate, emulate; informal hold a candle to.

competence ▶ noun **1** *this area of research is beyond my technical competence* **capability**, ability, competency, capacity, proficiency, accomplishment, adeptness, adroitness, knowledge, expertise, expertness, skill, skilfulness, prowess, mastery, resources, faculties, facilities, talent, bent, aptitude, artistry, virtuosity; informal savvy, know-how.
OPPOSITE incompetence.
2 *doubts arose over the competence of the system* **adequacy**, appropriateness, suitability, fitness; effectiveness, efficacy, productiveness; value, worth, merit.
OPPOSITE inadequacy.
3 *these matters fall within the competence of the church courts* **authority**, power, control, jurisdiction, ambit, scope, remit.

CHOOSE THE RIGHT WORD

competent, capable, efficient, able

These words are all used to express approval of people who are good at what they do.

- Someone described as **competent** has the necessary skill or knowledge to perform a particular task or fulfil a particular role (*a team of competent trainers | he has been pronounced competent to drive*). Alternatively, they may have the general skill and intelligence to cope with any task (*he is the most experienced and competent man around*). When applied to people engaged in an artistic activity, *competent* may convey mere technical proficiency, contrasted with brilliance or genius (*she was never more than a competent actress*).
- Describing someone as **capable** conveys a sense of confidence that any task entrusted to them will be done reliably and well. The word suggests not only competence but also a practicality and organization which ensure that everything that is necessary will be done (*he left the management of their lives largely to his highly capable wife*). It is also used to refer to a specific quality or ability (*I've got players here capable of playing for England*).
- An **efficient** person does whatever they have to do quickly and well and without wasting any effort (*he had a most efficient young secretary | teachers become more efficient at writing objectives the more they practise*).
- Describing someone as **able** emphasizes the intellectual capacity or the talent that makes them good at what they do (*the department attracts able students from across the country*). Like *capable*, *able* can also refer to a more specific capacity (*if anything went wrong I wouldn't be able to cope*).

competent ▶ adjective **1** *he's an extremely competent carpenter* **capable**, able, proficient, adept, adroit, accomplished, skilful, skilled, gifted, talented, masterly, virtuoso, expert, knowledgeable, qualified, trained; **efficient**, good, excellent, brilliant; informal great, mean, wicked, deadly, nifty, crack, ace, wizard, magic; N. Amer. informal crackerjack; vulgar slang shit-hot; archaic or humorous compleat; rare habile.
OPPOSITE incompetent.
2 *she spoke quite competent French* **adequate**, acceptable, satisfactory, reasonable, fair, decent, good enough, sufficiently good, not bad, all right, average, tolerable, passable, moderate, middling; up to scratch, up to the mark, up to par; informal OK, okay, so-so, fair-to-middling, up to snuff.
OPPOSITE inadequate.
3 *the court determined that it was not competent to hear the case* **fit**, fitted, equipped, suitable, suited, appropriate; qualified, empowered, authorized.
OPPOSITE unfit.

competition ▶ noun **1** *Stephanie came second in the competition* **contest**, tournament, match, game, round, heat, fixture, event, meet, encounter; race; bout, fight, prizefight; quiz; trials, stakes.
2 *I'm just not interested in competition* **rivalry**, competitiveness, vying, contesting, opposition, contention, conflict, feuding, battling, fighting, struggling, strife, war; informal keeping up with the Joneses.
3 *they upgraded their services to remain ahead of the competition* **opposition**, opposing side, other side, other team, field, enemy, foe; challengers, opponents, rivals, opposers, adversaries, fellow contenders, fellow competitors; rare corrivals.

competitive ▶ adjective **1** *a very competitive player* **ambitious**, competition-oriented, vying, combative, contentious, aggressive; insistent, driving, pushing, zealous, keen; informal pushy, go-ahead.
OPPOSITE apathetic.
2 *tourism is a highly sophisticated and competitive industry* **ruthless**, merciless, aggressive, fierce; informal dog-eat-dog, cut-throat.
OPPOSITE gentlemanly.
3 *they produce quality merchandise at competitive prices* **reasonable**, moderate, economical, keen; low, inexpensive, cheap, cheap and cheerful, budget, economy, bargain, sale, cut-rate, cut, reduced, marked down, discounted, discount, rock-bottom; informal bargain-basement.
OPPOSITES exorbitant; uncompetitive.

competitor ▶ noun **1** *there were more than forty competitors in the race* **contestant**, contender, challenger, participant, candidate, entrant; runner, racer, player, athlete.
2 *we have to be more efficient than our European competitors* **rival**, challenger, opponent, opposer, adversary, antagonist, combatant, enemy, foe; competition, opposition; rare corrival, vier.
OPPOSITE ally.

compilation ▶ noun *this is the best compilation of American folk tales* **collection**, selection, anthology, treasury, compendium, album, corpus, miscellany, pot-pourri; miscellanea; archaic garland; rare ana, collectanea, analects, florilegium, spicilege.

compile ▶ verb *he compiled a dossier of patients with tropical diseases* **assemble**, put together, make up, collate, compose, marshal, organize, arrange, sort out, systematize, systemize, anthologize; gather, collect, accumulate, amass.

complacency ▶ noun *success brings with it the danger of complacency* **smugness**, self-satisfaction, self-approval, self-approbation, self-admiration, self-congratulation, self-regard; gloating, triumph, pride; satisfaction, contentment; carelessness, slackness, laxity, laxness, laziness; archaic self-content.
OPPOSITE dissatisfaction.

complacent ▶ adjective *no one in industry can afford to stand still and be complacent* **smug**, self-satisfied, pleased with oneself, proud of oneself, self-approving, self-congratulatory, self-admiring, self-regarding; gloating, triumphant, proud; pleased, gratified, satisfied, content, contented; careless, slack, lax, lazy; informal like the cat that got the cream, I'm-all-right-Jack; N. Amer. informal wisenheimer; N. Amer. vulgar slang shit-eating.
OPPOSITES dissatisfied; humble.

complacent or complaisant?
See COMPLAISANT.

complain ▶ verb *the neighbours complained about his singing* **protest**, grumble, moan, whine, bleat, carp, cavil, lodge a complaint, make a complaint, make a fuss; object to, speak out against, rail at, oppose, lament, bewail; criticize, find fault with, run down, inveigh against; informal whinge, kick up a fuss, kick up a stink, bellyache, beef, grouch, grouse, bitch, sound off, go on about, pick holes in; Brit. informal gripe, grizzle, chunter, create, be on at someone; N. English informal mither; N. Amer. informal kvetch; S. African informal chirp; Brit. dated crib, natter; archaic plain over.

C

complaint ▶ noun **1** *they lodged a complaint with the European Commission* **protest**, protestation, objection, remonstrance, statement of dissatisfaction, grievance, charge, accusation, criticism; cavil, quibble, grumble, moan, whine; *informal* beef, gripe, grouse, grouch, whinge; *Law, Brit.* plaint.
2 *there appears to be little cause for complaint* **protesting**, protestation, objection, exception, grievance, grumbling, carping, whining, moaning, muttering, murmuring; criticism, fault-finding, condemnation, disapproval, dissatisfaction, fulmination, outcry, fuss; *informal* beefing, bitching, whingeing, griping, grousing, grouching, bellyaching, nit-picking; *N. English informal* mithering.
3 *the patient has a kidney complaint* **disorder**, disease, infection, affliction, illness, ailment, sickness, malady, malaise, infirmity, indisposition, weakness, condition, problem, upset; trouble; *informal* bug, virus; *Brit. informal* lurgy; *Austral. informal* wog.

complaisant ▶ adjective *he made drunken moves on complaisant chamber maids* **willing**, assenting, acquiescent, agreeable, amenable, cooperative, accommodating, obliging, biddable, compliant, pliant, deferential, docile, obedient, conformable, tractable.
OPPOSITE unwilling.

complaisant or complacent?

Although **complaisant** and **complacent** both come from the Latin *complacere* 'to please', they do not mean the same thing. *Complaisant* means 'willing to please', and is often used to suggest that someone is too ready to do what someone else wants (*it would be impossible in future for the king to prolong the life of a complaisant parliament*). *Complacent*, the more common word, describes someone who is satisfied and confident, often inappropriately so (*we cannot afford to be complacent about what lies ahead | I was too complacent going into the competition*).

complement ▶ noun **1** *local ales provide the perfect complement to the food* **accompaniment**, companion, addition, supplement, accessory, adjunct, trimming, finishing touch, final touch.
OPPOSITE contrast.
2 *the ship had a full complement of lifeboats* **amount**, total, aggregate, contingent, company; capacity, allowance, quota.
▶ verb *this mouth-watering sauce complements the dessert beautifully* **accompany**, go with, round off, set off, suit, harmonize with, be the perfect companion to, be the perfect addition to, add the finishing touch to, add the final touch to, add to, supplement, augment, enhance, complete.
OPPOSITE contrast.

complement or compliment?

Complement and **compliment** (together with their derivative adjectives **complementary** and **complimentary**) are frequently confused but have quite different meanings. As a verb, *complement* means 'add to (something) in a way that enhances, improves, or completes it' (*a classic blazer complements a look that's smart or casual*), while *compliment* means 'congratulate or praise (someone) for something' (*he complimented her on her appearance*). Both are ultimately derived from Latin *complere* 'to fill up, fulfil, or complete'; *compliment*, however, came into English via Italian *complimento* meaning 'a statement that fulfils the requirements of polite behaviour'.

complementary ▶ adjective *neutral tones allow the widest choice of complementary furnishings and decoration* **harmonizing**, harmonious, complementing, supportive, supporting, reciprocal, interdependent, interrelated, compatible, corresponding, matching, twin; completing, finishing, perfecting; *rare* complemental.
OPPOSITES incompatible; contrasting.

complete ▶ adjective **1** *the complete interview will appear in next week's issue* **entire**, whole, full, total, intact, uncut, unshortened, unabridged, comprehensive.
OPPOSITE incomplete.
2 *their research was complete* **finished**, ended, concluded, completed, finalized, accomplished, achieved, fulfilled, discharged, settled, done; *informal* wrapped up, sewn up, polished off, sorted out; *rare* effectuated.
OPPOSITE unfinished.
3 *you're acting like a complete fool* **absolute**, out-and-out, utter, total, real, outright, downright, thoroughgoing, thorough, positive, proper, veritable, prize, perfect, consummate, unqualified, unmitigated, sheer, rank; inveterate, congenital, dyed-in-the-wool, true blue; in every respect; *N. Amer.* full-bore; *informal* deep-dyed; *Brit. informal* right; *Austral./NZ informal* fair; *archaic* arrant; *rare* right-down, apodictic.
OPPOSITE partial.
▶ verb **1** *she advised him to complete his architectural training* **finish**, end, conclude, bring to a conclusion, finalize, wind up, consummate, bring to fruition; crown, cap, set the seal on; *informal* wrap up, sew up, polish off, sort out.
OPPOSITE give up.
2 *the outfit was completed with a delicate veil* **finish off**, round off, top off, make perfect, perfect, crown, cap, complement, add the finishing touch to, add the final touch to.
3 *entrants are required to complete an application form* **fill in**, fill out, fill up, answer.

WORD LINKS
related prefix **holo-** (e.g. ***holocaust, holophytic***)

completely ▶ adverb *he had always been completely honest with her* **totally**, entirely, wholly, thoroughly, fully, utterly, absolutely, perfectly, unreservedly, unconditionally, quite, altogether, downright; in every way, in every respect, in all respects, one hundred per cent, every inch, to the hilt, to the core, all the way; *informal* dead, deadly.
OPPOSITE partially.

completion ▶ noun *the money ran out before the scheme's completion* **realization**, accomplishment, achievement, fulfilment, execution, consummation, finalization, resolution; **finish**, ending, conclusion, close, closing, cessation, termination; fruition, success; *informal* wind-up, winding up, sewing up, polishing off.

complex ▶ adjective **1** *a complex situation | criminal law is an extremely complex subject* **complicated**, involved, intricate, convoluted, tangled, elaborate, serpentine, labyrinthine, tortuous, impenetrable, Byzantine, Daedalian, Gordian; difficult, hard, knotty, tricky, thorny, problematical; *informal* fiddly; *rare* involute, involuted.
OPPOSITES simple, straightforward.
2 *a complex structure* **compound**, composite, compounded, multiplex.
▶ noun **1** *a complex of mountain roads* **network**, system, interconnected system/structure/scheme, nexus, web, tissue; combination, composite, synthesis, fusion, aggregation.
2 (*informal*) *there's no point having a complex about losing your hair* **obsession**, phobia, fixation, preoccupation; neurosis; *French* idée fixe; *informal* hang-up, thing, bee in one's bonnet.

CHOOSE THE RIGHT WORD
complex, complicated, intricate, involved
See COMPLICATED.

complexion ▶ noun **1** *an attractive girl with a pale complexion* **skin**, skin colour, skin colouring, skin tone, skin texture, pigmentation.
2 *this puts an entirely new complexion on things* **perspective**, angle, slant, interpretation; aspect, appearance, light, look, countenance.
3 *successive governments of all complexions* **type**, kind, sort; nature, character, disposition, description, cast, stamp, hue, ilk, kidney, grain, mould.

complexity ▶ noun *the complexities of family life | an issue of great complexity* **complication**, problem, difficulty, twist, turn, convolution, entanglement; intricacy, complicatedness, involvement, convolutedness.
OPPOSITE simplicity.

compliance ▶ noun **1** *the company's **compliance with** international law* **obedience to**, accordance with, observance of, observation of, adherence to, conformity to, respect for; *archaic* abidance by.
OPPOSITES violation, infringement.
2 *he had mistaken her lack of interest for compliance* **acquiescence**, agreement, assent, consent, concession, concurrence, acceptance; complaisance, tractability, malleability, biddableness, pliability, docility, meekness, submissiveness, submission, passivity.
OPPOSITE defiance.

compliant ▶ adjective *her compliant husband* **acquiescent**, amenable, biddable, tractable, complaisant, accommodating, cooperative, adaptable; **obedient**, docile, manageable, malleable, pliable, pliant, flexible, submissive, dutiful, tame, meek, yielding, easily handled, like putty in one's hands, controllable, unresisting, unassertive, passive, governable, persuadable, manipulable; *informal, dated* milky; *rare* persuasible.
OPPOSITES recalcitrant, bloody-minded.

CHOOSE THE RIGHT WORD
compliant, obedient, biddable, docile, dutiful
See OBEDIENT.

complicate ▶ verb *involvement with Adam could only complicate her life* **make (more) difficult**, make complex, make complicated, mix up; confuse, muddle, entangle, embroil; *informal* mess up, snarl up, screw up; *archaic* perplex, embarrass; *rare* ravel.
OPPOSITE simplify.

complicated ▶ adjective *the complicated election rules* **complex**, intricate, involved, convoluted, tangled, elaborate, impenetrable, knotty, tricky, thorny, serpentine, labyrinthine, tortuous, cumbersome, Byzantine,

Daedalian, Gordian; confused, confusing, bewildering, baffling, puzzling, perplexing, difficult to understand, above one's head; *informal* fiddly; *rare* involute, involuted.
OPPOSITES easy, simple, straightforward.

CHOOSE THE RIGHT WORD

complicated, complex, intricate, involved

- Something **complicated** consists of many interrelated parts or strands (*a complicated stereo system*) and may as a result be difficult to understand, deal with, or construct (*a complicated system of voting | robots were getting too complicated*).
- The meaning of **complex** is very similar to that of *complicated* (*highly complex organisms | the organization became more complex*), but complexity may be more deeply seated in the nature of something than complicatedness. *Complex* may also suggest that something is regarded as interesting or intriguing, rather than irritating (*she knew his character to be deep and complex*).
- **Intricate** describes a complex interrelation of small details, calling for very close attention if it is to be appreciated or understood (*they were engaged in intricate political manoeuvres | the roofs are decorated with intricate iron trelliswork*). The word is commonly used of *carvings, designs, jewellery, patterns, embroidery*, and *workmanship* and generally has an approving tone.
- **Involved** suggests a confusing number of details, interrelated in such a way as to make understanding very difficult. It often carries a note of criticism, reinforced by other adjectives applied to the same thing, like *long, cumbersome*, and *messy* (*simple sentences are more likely to be grammatically correct than long, involved ones*).

complication ▶ noun **1** *there is a complication concerning ownership of the site* **difficulty**, problem, obstacle, hurdle, stumbling block, barrier, impediment; drawback, snag, catch, hitch; *informal* fly in the ointment, prob, headache, hiccup, facer; *Brit. informal* spanner in the works; *N. Amer. informal* monkey wrench in the works.
2 *the increasing complication of life in Western society* **complexity**, complicatedness, difficulty, intricacy, convolution, convolutedness, elaboration; confusion, muddle.
OPPOSITES simplicity, straightforwardness.

complicity ▶ noun *they were accused of complicity in the attempt to overthrow the government* **collusion**, involvement, collaboration, connivance, abetment; conspiracy; *informal* being in cahoots.
OPPOSITE ignorance.

compliment ▶ noun **1** *she blushed at the unexpected compliment* **flattering remark**, tribute, accolade, commendation, bouquet, pat on the back, encomium; (**compliments**) praise, acclaim, acclamation, plaudits, admiration, approbation, homage, eulogy; flattery, blandishments, blarney, honeyed words; *N. Amer. informal, dated* trade last; *rare* laudation, eulogium.
OPPOSITES insult; criticism.
2 (**compliments**) *my compliments on your cooking* **congratulations**, praise, commendations.
3 (**compliments**) *Lady Margaret sent her compliments to him* **greetings**, good wishes, best wishes, regards, respects, salutations, felicitations; *archaic* remembrances; *French archaic* devoirs.
▶ verb *critics fell over themselves to compliment his performance* **praise**, sing the praises of, heap praise on, pay tribute to, speak highly/well of, flatter, say nice things about, express admiration for, wax lyrical about, make much of, congratulate, commend, acclaim, pat on the back, take one's hat off to, throw bouquets at, applaud, salute, honour, eulogize, extol; *N. Amer. informal* ballyhoo; *black English* big someone/something up; *dated* cry someone/something up; crack someone/something up, *archaic* emblazon; *rare* laud, panegyrize, felicitate.
OPPOSITES criticize; condemn.

compliment or complement?
See COMPLEMENT.

complimentary ▶ adjective **1** *complimentary remarks* **flattering**, **appreciative**, congratulatory, admiring, approving, commendatory, laudatory, highly favourable, glowing, eulogizing, adulatory; fulsome, honeyed, saccharine, sugary; *informal* rave; *rare* panegyrical, acclamatory, encomiastic, laudative.
OPPOSITES derogatory, scathing.
2 *complimentary tickets* **free**, free of charge, gratis, for nothing; courtesy; *informal* on the house; *N. Amer. informal* comp.

comply ▶ verb *failure to comply with the regulations can result in a £2000 fine | Myra complied with his wishes* **abide by**, act in accordance with, observe, obey, adhere to, conform to, follow, respect; **agree to**, assent to, consent to, concur with/in, fall in with, acquiesce in, go along with, yield to, submit to, bow to, defer to; satisfy, meet, fulfil, measure up to.
OPPOSITES ignore, disobey.

component ▶ noun *the components of electronic devices such as televisions and computers* **part**, piece, bit, constituent, element, ingredient; unit, module, item; section, portion; *rare* integrant.
▶ adjective *the water molecule's component elements* **constituent**, integral; basic, essential, intrinsic; *rare* integrant.

comport ▶ verb (*rare*)
□ **comport oneself** *articulate students who comported themselves well in television interviews* **conduct oneself**, acquit oneself; **behave**, act, perform; *rare* deport oneself.

compose ▶ verb **1** *the first poem composed by Shelley | she also composes music for television and films* **write**, create, devise, make up, think up, frame, formulate, fashion, produce, originate, invent, contrive, concoct; pen, author, draft; *literary* rhyme, sing, verse; *archaic* indite.
2 *Vermeer probably used a camera obscura to help him compose his pictures* **design**, arrange, plan, organize, work out, frame, balance, order, map out, construct, put together, shape, form, concoct.
3 *the National Congress is composed of ten senators* **make up**, constitute, form, comprise.
4 (*archaic*) *the king, with some difficulty, composed this difference* **resolve**, settle, reconcile, find a solution to, sort out, solve, iron out, smooth over, straighten out, put right, set right, set to rights; *informal* patch up, fix.
□ **compose oneself calm down**, settle down, control oneself, regain/recover one's composure, pull oneself together, get control of oneself, collect oneself, steady oneself, keep one's head, simmer down; *informal* get a grip, keep one's cool, keep one's shirt on; *N. Amer. informal* decompress, stay loose.
OPPOSITE get worked up.

composed ▶ adjective *she seemed very composed as she went about her duties* **calm**, collected, {cool, calm, and collected}, cool, as cool as a cucumber, cool-headed, controlled, self-controlled, serene, tranquil, relaxed, at ease, self-possessed, unruffled, unperturbed, unflustered, undisturbed, unmoved, unbothered, untroubled, unagitated; equable, even-tempered, level-headed, imperturbable; *informal* unflappable, unfazed, together, laid-back; *rare* equanimous.
OPPOSITES excited, overwrought.

composer ▶ noun melodist, symphonist, songwriter, singer-songwriter, songster, writer; *informal* tunesmith, songsmith.

composite ▶ adjective *a composite structure* **compound**, complex; combined, blended, mixed, compounded, synthesized.
▶ noun *the English legal system is a composite of legislation and judicial precedent* **amalgamation**, amalgam, combination, compound, fusion, synthesis, mixture, blend, meld, admixture, conglomeration; alloy; pastiche, patchwork, hybrid.

composition ▶ noun **1** *the composition of the new council* **make-up**, constitution, configuration, structure, construction, conformation, formation, form, framework, fabric, anatomy, arrangement, organization, format, layout; *informal* set-up.
2 *Chopin's most romantic compositions | a literary composition* **work of art**, work, creation, literary/musical/artistic work, opus, oeuvre, piece, arrangement; poem, novel, play, drama; symphony, concerto, opera; painting, drawing, picture.
3 *the composition of a poem* **writing**, creation, devising, making up, thinking up, framing, formulation, production, fashioning, origination, invention, concoction, compilation.
4 *a school composition* **essay**, paper, article, text, study, piece of writing; task; *N. Amer.* theme.
5 *the composition of the painting derives from Matteo's 'Madonna and Child'* **arrangement**, disposition, layout, design, organization, construction, proportions, harmony, balance, symmetry.
6 *an adhesive composition* **mixture**, compound, amalgam, blend, mix, admixture.

compost *See centre pages for list of* **Fertilizers**
▶ noun **fertilizer**, plant food, dressing, organic matter, vegetable waste, humus, peat.

composure ▶ noun *Juliet tried desperately to regain some composure* **self-control**, self-possession, self-command, calmness, equanimity, equilibrium, calm, coolness, collectedness, serenity, tranquillity; aplomb, poise, presence of mind, sangfroid, self-assurance, assurance; imperturbability, placidity, placidness, impassiveness, impassivity, dispassion, phlegm, stolidity, unexcitability; *informal* cool, unflappability; *rare* countenance, ataraxy, ataraxia.
OPPOSITES agitation, nervousness, discomposure.

compound *See centre pages for lists of* **Acids** **Amino Acids** **Compounds** **Sugars**
▶ noun (stress on the first syllable) *a compound of two elements | a compound of energy and idealism* **amalgam**, amalgamation, combination, composite, blend, mixture, mix, admixture, meld, fusion, synthesis, consolidation; alloy; hybrid.
▶ adjective (stress on the first syllable) *a compound substance* **composite**,

C

complex; blended, fused, synthesized, compounded, combined.
OPPOSITE simple.
▶ verb (stress on the second syllable) **1** *a smell compounded of dust and mould* **be composed of**, be made up of, be constituted of, be formed from.
2 *detergents consisting of liquid soaps compounded with disinfectant* **mix**, **combine**, blend, put together, amalgamate, alloy, fuse, synthesize, coalesce, mingle, meld, intermingle; *rare* admix, commix, commingle.
3 *the prisoners' lack of contact with the outside world compounds their problems* **aggravate**, **worsen**, make worse, add to, augment, exacerbate, intensify, heighten, increase, magnify; add insult to injury, rub salt in the wound, add fuel to the fire/flames; complicate.
OPPOSITES alleviate, improve.

comprehend ▶ verb **1** *Katie couldn't comprehend what he was saying* **understand**, grasp, take in, see, apprehend, follow, make sense of, fathom, make out, puzzle out, get to the bottom of, penetrate; realize, perceive, discern, divine; unravel, decipher, interpret, piece together; *informal* work out, figure out, make head or tail of, get one's head around, wrap one's mind round, take on board, get a fix on, get the hang of, get the drift of, catch on to, latch on to, tumble to, crack, dig, get, see the light, get the picture; *Brit. informal* twig, suss out, suss; *N. Amer. informal* savvy.
2 (*formal*) *German parties comprehend as many political stances as do the British ones* **comprise**, include, take in, encompass, embrace, involve, contain; cover.
OPPOSITE exclude.

comprehensible ▶ adjective *the information must be accurate and comprehensible* **intelligible**, understandable, easy to understand, digestible, user-friendly, accessible; lucid, coherent, clear, crystal clear, transparent, plain, perspicuous, explicit, unambiguous, straightforward, self-explanatory, penetrable, fathomable, graspable.
OPPOSITES incomprehensible, opaque.

comprehension ▶ noun *matters which seemed beyond her comprehension* **understanding**, ability to understand, grasp, grip, conception, apprehension, cognition, cognizance, ken, knowledge, awareness, perception, discernment; interpretation.
OPPOSITES ignorance, incomprehension.

comprehensive ▶ adjective *a comprehensive review of UK defence policy* **inclusive**, all-inclusive, complete; **thorough**, full, extensive, all-embracing, overarching, umbrella, exhaustive, in-depth, encyclopedic, universal, catholic, eclectic; far-reaching, radical, sweeping, across the board, blanket, wholesale; broad, wide, wide-ranging, broad-ranging; widespread, nationwide, countrywide, coast-to-coast; detailed, compendious; *informal* wall-to-wall.
OPPOSITES partial, selective, limited.

compress ▶ verb **1** *the skirt can be folded and compressed into a relatively small bag* **flatten**; **squeeze**, press, squash, crush, cram, jam, stuff, wedge; tamp, pack, wad, compact; constrict; *informal* scrunch, squidge; *rare* coarct, coarctate.
2 *Polly compressed her lips and sat down* **purse**, press together, squeeze together, pinch, crimp; pucker.
3 *the material has been compressed into 17 pages* **abridge**, shorten, cut, condense, abbreviate, contract, telescope; summarize, synopsize, precis, abstract, digest; truncate; *rare* epitomize.
OPPOSITES expand, pad out.

comprise ▶ verb **1** *the country comprises twenty states* **consist of**, be made up of, be composed of, contain, take in, embrace, encompass, incorporate; include; involve, cover; *formal* comprehend.
2 *this breed comprises 50 per cent of the cattle population* **make up**, constitute, form, compose; account for.

compromise ▶ noun **1** *eventually they reached a compromise* **agreement**, **understanding**, settlement, terms, accommodation; deal, trade-off, bargain; halfway house, middle ground, middle course, happy medium, balance; *Latin* modus vivendi.
2 *the secret of a happy marriage is compromise* **give and take**, concession, cooperation.
OPPOSITE intransigence.
▶ verb **1** *in the end we compromised* **meet each other halfway**, find the middle ground, come to terms, come to an understanding, make a deal, make concessions, find a happy medium, strike a balance; give and take; *informal* split the difference.
2 *his actions could compromise his academic credibility* **undermine**, weaken, be detrimental to, damage, injure, harm, do harm to; prejudice, be prejudicial to, jeopardize, endanger, imperil; bring into disrepute, reflect badly on, put in a bad light, discredit, dishonour, bring shame to, shame, embarrass.

compulsion ▶ noun **1** *he had been under no compulsion to go* **obligation**, constraint, force, coercion, duress, pressure, pressurization, enforcement, oppression, intimidation; *French* force majeure.
2 *he felt an overwhelming compulsion to tell her the truth* **urge**, impulse, need, necessity, desire, longing, motivation, drive; obsession, fixation, addiction; temptation, pull; *US black English* jones.

compulsive ▶ adjective **1** *a compulsive desire* **irresistible**, uncontrollable, compelling, driving, overwhelming, overpowering, urgent, besetting; obsessive, neurotic.
2 *compulsive eating* **obsessive**, obsessional, addictive, uncontrollable, out of control, ungovernable.
3 *a compulsive liar* | *compulsive drinkers* **inveterate**, chronic, incorrigible, incurable, irredeemable, hardened, hopeless, persistent; obsessive, obsessional, addicted, habitual, dependent; *informal* pathological, hooked.
OPPOSITE occasional.
4 *it's compulsive viewing* **fascinating**, compelling, gripping, riveting, engrossing, totally absorbing, enthralling, captivating, spellbinding, mesmerizing, mesmeric, entrancing; *informal* unputdownable.
OPPOSITES dull, tedious.

compulsory ▶ adjective *legislation which made the wearing of seat belts compulsory* **obligatory**, mandatory, required, requisite, necessary, essential, statutory, prescribed; imperative, enforced, demanded, binding, forced, unavoidable, inescapable, incumbent, enforceable; contractual, stipulated, set; *French* de rigueur.
OPPOSITES optional, voluntary.

compunction ▶ noun *she had no compunction about deceiving them* **scruples**, misgivings, qualms, worries, unease, uneasiness, hesitation, hesitancy, doubts, reluctance, reservations; **guilt**, feelings of guilt, guilty conscience, pangs/twinges of conscience, remorse, regret, contrition, contriteness, self-reproach, repentance, penitence.

compute ▶ verb *the hire charge is computed on a daily basis* **calculate**, work out, reckon, figure, enumerate, determine, evaluate, assess, quantify, put a figure on; add up, add together, count up, tally, total, totalize; measure; *Brit.* tot up; *rare* cast.

computer *See centre pages for lists of* **Computer Parts and Peripherals** **Programs**

WORD LINKS
related prefix **cyber-** (e.g. ***cybernetics, cybercafe***)
fear of computers **cyberphobia**

comrade ▶ noun **companion**, friend; **colleague**, associate, partner, co-worker, fellow worker, workmate; fellow soldier; compatriot, confederate, ally; *French* confrère; *informal* pal, buddy, crony; *Brit. informal* mate, chum, oppo; *archaic* compeer; *rare* consociate.

comradeship ▶ noun **camaraderie**, friendship, companionship, fellowship, good fellowship, brotherliness, brotherhood, sisterhood, closeness, affinity, togetherness, solidarity, mutual support; team spirit; *French* esprit de corps.

con (*informal*) ▶ verb *she was jailed for conning her aunt out of £500,000. See* SWINDLE.
▶ noun *a public relations con* **swindle**, deception, trick, racket, bit of sharp practice, fraud; *informal* scam, con trick, sting, gyp, kite, diddle, rip-off, fiddle, swizzle, swizz; *N. Amer. informal* bunco, boondoggle, hustle, grift; *Austral. informal* rort.

concatenation ▶ noun *a concatenation of events which had finally led to the murder* **series**, sequence, succession; **chain**, string, train, course, progression; nexus.

concave ▶ adjective **curved inwards**, hollow, hollowed out, scooped out, depressed, sunken; indented, recessed; *rare* incurved, incurvate.
OPPOSITE convex.

conceal ▶ verb **1** *a leather pouch was concealed under the folds of his kilt* | *a mass of clouds concealed the sun* **hide**, keep out of sight, keep hidden, secrete, tuck away; screen, cover, obscure, block out, blot out, disguise, camouflage, mask, cloak, mantle, shroud; *literary* enshroud.
OPPOSITES reveal, expose.
2 *a cabinet minister with a reputation for concealing information* | *up to now, he'd always managed to conceal his true feelings* **hide**, cover up, disguise, dissemble, mask, veil; **keep secret**, keep quiet about, keep dark, hush up, draw a veil over, sweep under the carpet, gloss over; suppress, repress, bottle up, bury; *informal* keep a/the lid on, keep under one's hat.
OPPOSITES show, disclose, confess.

concealed ▶ adjective *a concealed entrance* | *a concealed weapon* **hidden**, not visible, secret, out of sight, unseen, invisible, screened, covered, disguised, camouflaged, obscured; inconspicuous, unnoticeable; private, privy; secreted, tucked away.

concealment ▶ noun **1** *the concealment of the weapons* **hiding**, secretion.
2 *he darted forwards from the concealment of the bushes* **cover**, shelter, protection, screen, hiding place; privacy, seclusion; secrecy.
3 *the deliberate concealment of material facts* | *the concealment of one's true opinions* **keeping secret**, keeping hidden, hiding, hushing up, covering up, cover-up, suppression; disguise, camouflage; whitewash; *Law, historical* misprision.
OPPOSITES revelation, disclosure.

concede ▶ verb **1** *I had to concede that I'd overreacted* **admit**, acknowledge, accept, allow, grant, recognize, own, confess; agree; *informal* take on board.

OPPOSITE deny.
2 *in 475, the emperor conceded the Auvergne to Euric* **surrender**, yield, give up, relinquish, cede, hand over, turn over, part with, deliver up; forfeit, sacrifice.
OPPOSITES retain, gain.

□ **concede defeat capitulate**, give in, surrender, yield, give up the struggle, cave in, submit, raise/show the white flag, lay down one's arms; back down, climb down; *informal* throw in the towel, throw in the sponge.

conceit ▶ noun **1** *Polly's eyes widened at his extraordinary conceit* **vanity**, narcissism, conceitedness, self-love, self-admiration, self-adulation, self-regard, egotism, egoism, egocentricity, egomania; **pride**, arrogance, hubris, boastfulness, cockiness, self-importance, immodesty; self-satisfaction, smugness, complacency; *French* amour propre; *informal* big-headedness, swollen-headedness, uppishness, uppitiness; *literary* vainglory.
OPPOSITES modesty, humility.
2 *the conceits of Shakespeare's early verse* **image**, imagery, figurative expression, metaphor, simile, trope, figure of speech; **play on words**, pun, quip, witticism.
3 *the conceit of time travel* **idea**, notion, fancy; *archaic* reverie.

conceited ▶ adjective *he's so conceited he'd never believe anyone would turn him down* **vain**, narcissistic, pleased with oneself, self-loving, in love with oneself, self-admiring, self-regarding, self-centred, egotistic, egotistical, egoistic, egocentric, egomaniac; **proud**, arrogant, boastful, cocky, cocksure, full of oneself, above oneself, self-important, immodest, swaggering, strutting; self-satisfied, self-congratulatory, smug, complacent, supercilious, haughty, snobbish; *informal* big-headed, swollen-headed, too big for one's boots, puffed up, stuck-up, snooty, high and mighty, uppity, uppish, snotty, snot-nosed; *Brit. informal* toffee-nosed; *N. Amer. informal* chesty; *literary* vainglorious; *rare* peacockish; (**be conceited**) have an excessively high opinion of oneself, think too highly of oneself, think a lot of oneself, boast, brag, blow one's own trumpet; *informal* think one is the cat's whiskers/pyjamas, think one is God's gift (to women).
OPPOSITES modest, self-effacing.

conceivable ▶ adjective *the only conceivable reason for using nuclear weapons* **imaginable**, possible; plausible, tenable, credible, believable, thinkable, feasible, creditable, admissible; understandable, comprehensible; *informal* mortal; *rare* cogitable.
OPPOSITE inconceivable.

conceive ▶ verb **1** *she was unable to conceive* **get pregnant**, become pregnant, become impregnated, become inseminated, become fertilized.
2 *the project was conceived in 1977* **think up**, think of, come up with, dream up, draw up, devise, form, formulate, design, frame, invent, coin, originate, create, develop, evolve; hatch, cook up, contrive.
3 *I could hardly conceive what it must be like in winter* **imagine**, envisage, visualize, picture, picture in one's mind's eye, conjure up an image of, think, see, perceive, grasp, appreciate, apprehend; *rare* envision, ideate.

concentrate ▶ verb **1** *the government concentrated its efforts on resolving the financial crisis* **focus**, direct, centre, centralize, bring to bear; home in on, zero in on.
OPPOSITE dissipate.
2 *Sabine tried to* **concentrate** *on the film* **focus one's attention on**, focus on, pay attention to, keep one's mind on, apply oneself to, address oneself to, devote oneself to, get down to, put one's mind to; be absorbed in, be engrossed in, be immersed in; think about closely, consider closely, rack one's brains about/over, cudgel one's brains about/over; *informal* get stuck into.
OPPOSITES daydream, let one's mind wander.
3 *troops were concentrating on the western front* **collect**, gather, congregate, draw together, converge, mass, cluster, rally; accumulate, amass; *rare* concentre.
OPPOSITE disperse.
4 *the liquid is filtered and concentrated* **condense**, boil down, reduce, distil, thicken, compress; strengthen.
OPPOSITE dilute.
▶ noun *fruit and berry concentrates* **distillation**, essence, extract; decoction, tincture, elixir, quintessence; *rare* decocture, apozem.

concentrated ▶ adjective **1** *a concentrated effort* **strenuous**, concerted, intensive, intense, vigorous, assiduous; *informal* all-out.
OPPOSITE half-hearted.
2 *a concentrated solution* **condensed**, distilled, reduced, evaporated, thick, thickened, dense; strong, undiluted.
OPPOSITE diluted.

concentration ▶ noun **1** *a task requiring great patience and total concentration* **close attention**, close thought, attentiveness, application, industry, assiduousness, single-mindedness, absorption, engrossment.
OPPOSITES inattention, distraction.
2 *this concentration of effort on field work* **focusing**, centring, centralization, direction.
3 *Islay is famous for its spectacular concentrations of barnacle geese* **gathering**, cluster, mass, flock, congregation, assemblage, assembly, collection; accumulation, aggregation, agglomeration.

concept ▶ noun *the concept of society as an organic entity* | *the Freudian concept of the superego* **idea**, notion, conception, abstraction, conceptualization; theory, hypothesis, postulation; belief, conviction, opinion, view, image, impression, picture.

CHOOSE THE RIGHT WORD

concept, idea, notion
See IDEA.

conception ▶ noun **1** *preparations for pregnancy can begin before conception* **inception of pregnancy**, conceiving, fertilization, impregnation, insemination; *rare* fecundation.
2 *the time between a product's conception and its launch* **inception**, genesis, origination, creation, formation, formulation, invention; beginning, origin.
3 *the original conception involved a shopping complex run by local people* **plan**, scheme, project, proposal, proposition, design, outline; intention, aim, idea.
4 *his conception of democracy* **idea**, concept, notion, conceptualization, understanding, abstraction; theory, hypothesis, postulation; perception, image, impression, picture.
5 *the administration had no* **conception** *of women's problems* **understanding**, ability to understand, ability to imagine, comprehension, appreciation, knowledge, grasp, apprehension; idea, inkling; *informal* clue about.

concern ▶ verb **1** *the report concerns events which took place immediately after the end of the war* **be about**, deal with, cover, treat, have to do with; discuss, tell of, go into, examine, scrutinize, study, review, analyse; relate to, be connected with, pertain to, appertain to; *archaic* regard.
2 *that doesn't concern you, so it's best you don't know* **affect**, be the business of, involve, be relevant to, apply to, pertain to, have a bearing on, bear on, impact on; be of importance to, be important to, interest, be of interest to.
3 *I'm too busy to* **concern myself with** *your affairs* **involve oneself in**, interest oneself in, take an interest in, be interested/involved in, take a hand in, busy oneself with, occupy oneself with, devote one's time to, bother oneself with, notice, take notice of.
4 *the only thing that concerns me is that Tom might be upset* **worry**, disturb, trouble, bother, perturb, unsettle, make anxious, distress, upset, agitate, cause disquiet to, disquiet.
▶ noun **1** *Katie's voice was full of concern* **anxiety**, worry, disquiet, disquietude, apprehension, apprehensiveness, unease, uneasiness, perturbation, consternation, distress, agitation; *N. Amer. archaic* worriment.
OPPOSITES serenity, peace of mind.
2 *part of his attraction is his true concern for others* **solicitude**, consideration, solicitousness, care, sympathy, thought, regard, caringness; *archaic* concernment.
OPPOSITE indifference.
3 *housing is the concern of the Housing Executive* **responsibility**, **business**, affair, charge, duty, job, task, occupation; area of activity, area of interest, province, preserve, department, sphere; problem, worry, lookout; *informal* pigeon, baby, bag, funeral, headache, bailiwick.
4 *the question of how the mass media treats issues that* **are of concern to** *women* **interest**, importance; be relevant to, have relevance for, have a bearing on, be applicable to.
5 *public awareness of Aboriginal concerns* **affair**, issue, matter, question, consideration.
6 *a publishing concern* **company**, business, firm, enterprise, venture, organization, operation, undertaking, industry, corporation, establishment, house, shop, office, bureau, agency, franchise, practice, partnership, consortium, cooperative, conglomerate, group, combine, syndicate; *informal* outfit, set-up.

concerned ▶ adjective **1** *her mother looked concerned* **worried**, anxious, disturbed, perturbed, troubled, bothered, distressed, upset, disquieted, uneasy, ill at ease, apprehensive, agitated; *rare* unquiet.
OPPOSITE unconcerned.
2 *I'm gratified to find that you are so* **concerned about** *my welfare* **solicitous**, caring; attentive to, considerate of.
3 *all concerned parties* **interested**, involved, affected; connected, related, implicated.

concerning ▶ preposition *further revelations concerning his role in the affair* **about**, regarding, on the subject of, relating to, relevant to, with regard to, as regards, to do with, with reference to, referring to, with respect to, respecting, as to, touching on, in the matter of, in connection with, re, apropos of; *Scottish* anent.

concert ▶ noun **1** *a concert at the Albert Hall* **musical performance**, musical entertainment, show, production, presentation; recital; prom, promenade concert; pop concert, rock concert; *informal* gig, jam session.
2 (*rare*) *critics' inability to describe with any precision and concert the characteristics of literature* **agreement**, accord, unanimity, consensus, harmony, like-mindedness, concord, concurrence, concordance, accordance, unity.

C

C

□ **in concert** *we must take stronger action in concert with our European partners* **together**, jointly, in combination, in collaboration, in cooperation, in league, shoulder to shoulder, side by side, cooperatively, concertedly; in unison.
OPPOSITES alone, independently.

concerted ▶ adjective **1** *you must make a concerted effort to curb this behaviour* **strenuous**, vigorous, energetic, active, forceful, forcible, strong, intensive, intense, concentrated; *informal* all-out.
OPPOSITE half-hearted.
2 *there were calls for concerted action* **joint**, united, jointly planned, coordinated, collaborative, collective, combined, cooperative, interactive, synergetic.
OPPOSITES separate, individual.

concession ▶ noun **1** *the government made several concessions over welfare cuts* **compromise**, adjustment, modification; allowance, exception; point conceded, point lost, forfeit, something surrendered; *informal* sop.
2 *a concession of failure* **admission**, acknowledgement, acceptance, recognition, confession.
OPPOSITE denial.
3 *the concession of territory* **surrender**, yielding, giving up, ceding, relinquishment, sacrifice, handover; *rare* cession.
OPPOSITES retention, acquisition.
4 *tax concessions | there are concessions on all party bookings* **reduction**, cut, discount, deduction, decrease; rebate; *N. Amer.* depletion allowance; *informal* tax break.
5 *the granting of new logging concessions* **right**, privilege, favour; licence, permit, franchise, warrant, authorization.

conciliate ▶ verb **1** *concessions were made to conciliate the peasantry* **appease**, placate, pacify, mollify, propitiate, assuage, calm down, soothe, humour, reconcile, disarm, win over, make peace with; *Austral.* square someone off; *informal* sweeten; *rare* disembitter.
OPPOSITE provoke.
2 *he sought to conciliate in the dispute* **mediate**, act as a peacemaker, act as a mediator, arbitrate, make peace, restore harmony, reconcile differences, clear the air; pour oil on troubled waters.

conciliation ▶ noun *he held his hands up in a gesture of conciliation* **appeasement**, pacification, peacemaking, placation, propitiation, mollification, reconciliation.
OPPOSITE provocation.

conciliator ▶ noun **peacemaker**, **mediator**, negotiator, go-between, middleman, intermediary, moderator, broker, honest broker, intervenor, interceder, intercessor, reconciler, pacifier, appeaser; dove.
OPPOSITE troublemaker.

conciliatory ▶ adjective *a conciliatory gesture* **propitiatory**, placatory, appeasing, pacifying, pacific, mollifying, so as to pour oil on troubled waters, peacemaking, reconciliatory; *rare* pacificatory, propitiative, placative, irenic.
OPPOSITE antagonistic.

concise ▶ adjective *a concise account* **succinct**, short, brief, to the point, pithy, incisive, short and sweet, crisp; abridged, condensed, compressed, abbreviated, compact, compendious, potted, thumbnail, in a nutshell; epigrammatic, aphoristic; **terse**, laconic, sparing; *informal* snappy; *rare* lapidary.
OPPOSITES lengthy, discursive, wordy.

CHOOSE THE RIGHT WORD

concise, succinct

These words both refer to brevity in statements or pieces of writing. They are both mainly used approvingly: things described as *concise* or *succinct* are also described as *up-to-date, in-depth, clear, precise*, and *informative*. Compare the use of *brusque, abrupt, curt*, and *terse* (see **BRUSQUE**).

- **Concise** expresses approval of a statement that conveys information briefly. It suggests that by keeping the words used to a minimum, the speaker or writer has achieved clarity as well as brevity (*the instructions were clear and concise*). *Concise* can, however, be more neutral in tone (*the church committee may need a concise report every three or six months*). It is used mainly of written documents, such as *reports, instructions*, and *summaries*.
- **Succinct** language is pithy, made more forceful by its brevity, and is more often praiseworthy (*John McLeish considered this admirably succinct report*). Of the two words, *succinct* is the one more often used of speech or of shorter pieces of writing (*I told him my story in sharp, succinct phrases | each page is introduced by an imaginative, succinct heading*).

conclave ▶ noun *a conclave of American, European, and Japanese business leaders* **(private) meeting**, gathering, assembly, conference, convention, convocation, council, session, summit, forgathering; *informal* parley, powwow, get-together.

conclude ▶ verb **1** *the meeting concluded at 9 o'clock* **finish**, end, come to an end, draw to a close, wind up, be over, stop, terminate, close, cease; culminate.
OPPOSITES start, begin, commence.
2 *he concluded the press conference with another announcement about welfare reform* **bring to an end**, bring to a close, finish, close, wind up, terminate, dissolve; round off; *informal* wrap up; *dated* put a period to.
OPPOSITES start, begin, open.
3 *an attempt to conclude a ceasefire* **negotiate**, reach an agreement on, agree, come to terms on, reach terms on, broker, settle, seal, set the seal on, clinch, finalize, tie up, complete, shake hands on, close, bring about, arrange, effect, engineer, accomplish, establish, resolve, work out, pull off, bring off, thrash out, hammer out; *informal* sew up, swing, button up.
4 *from this letter, one can only conclude that he was a rather unpleasant man* **come to the conclusion**, deduce, infer, draw the inference, gather, judge, decide; assume, presume, suppose, conjecture, surmise; *N. Amer.* figure; *informal* reckon; *archaic* collect.

conclusion ▶ noun **1** *the conclusion of the meeting | the conclusion of his speech* **end**, ending, finish, close, closure, termination, wind-up, cessation; culmination, finale, denouement, coda; peroration, epilogue.
OPPOSITES beginning, start.
2 *the conclusion of a free-trade agreement* **negotiation**, brokering, settlement, settling, clinching, completion, arranging, accomplishment, establishment, resolution.
3 *his original conclusions have been verified by later experiments* **deduction**, inference, interpretation, reasoning; opinion, judgement, decision, diagnosis, verdict, determination; assumption, presumption, supposition, conjecture, surmise.
□ **in conclusion finally**, lastly, in closing, to conclude, last but not least; **to sum up**, in short; *rare* in fine.

conclusive ▶ adjective **1** *conclusive proof* **incontrovertible**, incontestable, irrefutable, unquestionable, undeniable, indisputable, unassailable, beyond dispute, beyond question, beyond doubt, beyond a shadow of a doubt, certain, decisive, convincing, clinching, definitive, definite, positive, final, ultimate, categorical, demonstrative, unequivocal, unarguable, unanswerable, uncontroversial; airtight, watertight.
OPPOSITES inconclusive, unconvincing.
2 *a conclusive 5–0 win* **emphatic**, resounding; *informal* thumping, thundering.
OPPOSITE narrow.

concoct ▶ verb **1** *she began to concoct a dinner likely to appeal to him* **prepare**, make, put together, assemble; cook; *informal* fix, rustle up; *Brit. informal* knock up.
2 *I wonder what story she has concocted to explain her presence* **make up**, think up, dream up, fabricate, invent, contrive, manufacture, trump up; **devise**, create, form, formulate, fashion, forge; hatch, brew, plot, scheme; *informal* cook up.

concoction ▶ noun **1** *a concoction consisting of gin, vodka, and cherry brandy* **mixture**, brew, preparation, creation; potion.
2 *a strange concoction of northern Mannerism and Italian Baroque* **blend**, mixture, mix, combination, composite, compound; hybrid.
3 *her story is an improbable concoction* **fabrication**, piece of fiction, invention, falsification, contrivance; *informal* fairy story, fairy tale.

concomitant ▶ adjective *the rise of urbanism brought a concomitant risk of crime* **attendant**, accompanying, associated, collateral, related, connected, linked; accessory, auxiliary; resultant, resulting, consequent.
OPPOSITE unrelated.

concord ▶ noun **1** *disputatious council meetings which occasionally ended in concord* **agreement**, harmony, accord, consensus, concurrence, unity, unanimity, unison, oneness; *rare* concert.
OPPOSITES disagreement, discord.
2 *a concord was to be drawn up* **treaty**, agreement, accord, concordat, entente, compact, pact, protocol, convention, settlement.

concourse ▶ noun **1** *the station concourse* **entrance**, foyer, lobby, hall; piazza, plaza.
2 (*rare*) *a vast concourse of onlookers* **crowd**, group, gathering, assembly, body, company, throng, flock, horde, mob, mass, multitude.

concrete ▶ adjective **1** *concrete objects* **solid**, material, real, physical, tangible, touchable, tactile, palpable, visible, existing.
OPPOSITES abstract, theoretical, imaginary.
2 *I haven't got any concrete proof | as yet nothing is concrete* **definite**, specific, firm, positive, conclusive, definitive; fixed, decided, set in stone; factual, actual, real, genuine, substantial, material, tangible; *Latin* bona fide.
OPPOSITE vague.

concubine ▶ noun (*archaic*) **mistress**, paramour, kept woman; lover; *informal* fancy woman, bit on the side; *archaic* doxy, courtesan, leman; *historical* odalisque, hetaera, lorette.

concupiscence ▶ noun (*rare*) **sexual desire**, lust, lustfulness, sexual appetite, sexual longing, sexual passion, ardour, desire, passion; libido, sex drive, sexuality, biological urge; **lechery**, lecherousness, lasciviousness, lewdness, wantonness, carnality, licentiousness, salaciousness, prurience; *informal* horniness, raunchiness, the hots; *Brit. informal* randiness, the horn; *rare* salacity, nympholepsy.

concupiscent ▶ adjective (*rare*) *concupiscent dreams* **lustful**, lecherous, lascivious, lewd, libidinous, licentious, lubricious, salacious, goatish; wanton, unchaste, impure, immodest, indecent, prurient; erotic, sexy, passionate; *informal* horny, randy, raunchy, naughty; *rare* lickerish.
OPPOSITES chaste, pure.

concur ▶ verb **1** *there are many who would concur with this view* **agree**, be in agreement, be in accord, be in accordance, accord, go along, fall in, be in harmony, be in sympathy; see eye to eye, be of the same mind, be of the same opinion.
OPPOSITE disagree.
2 *the two events concurred* **coincide**, happen/occur together, happen/occur simultaneously, happen/occur at the same time, be simultaneous, be concurrent, synchronize, coexist; clash.

concurrent ▶ adjective **1** *Moore was sentenced to 17 concurrent life terms* **simultaneous**, coincident, coinciding, contemporaneous, synchronous; parallel, side by side, coexisting, coexistent.
2 *concurrent lines* **convergent**, converging, meeting, joining, uniting, intersecting.
3 (*archaic*) *the results are remarkable and concurrent* **in agreement**, agreeing, in accordance, in accord, coincident, in harmony, harmonious, compatible; of the same mind, as one, at one; *rare* consentient.

concussion ▶ noun **1** *Mr Kirwan suffered concussion together with shoulder and chest injuries* **temporary unconsciousness**, temporary loss of consciousness, bang on the head; *Medicine* mild cranial trauma.
2 *the ground shuddered with the concussion of the blast* **force**, impact, shock; jarring, jolting, jolt, shaking.

condemn ▶ verb **1** *he condemned such players for dragging the name of football through the dirt* **censure**, criticize, castigate, attack, denounce, deplore, decry, revile, inveigh against, blame, chastise, berate, upbraid, reprimand, rebuke, reprove, reprehend, take to task, find fault with, give someone/something a bad press; deprecate, disparage; *informal* slam, hammer, lay into, cane, blast; *Brit. informal* slate, slag off, have a go at; *archaic* slash, reprobate; *rare* excoriate, vituperate, arraign, objurgate, anathematize.
OPPOSITES praise, commend.
2 *the rebels had been condemned to death* **sentence**, pass sentence on; convict, find guilty.
OPPOSITE acquit.
3 *the pool has been condemned as a health hazard* **declare unfit**, declare unsafe; denounce, criticize.
4 *she could see in his eyes that her mistake had condemned her* **incriminate**, prove to be guilty, prove one's guilt, implicate; *archaic* inculpate.
5 *the physical ailments that condemned him to a lonely childhood* **doom**, destine, damn, foredoom, foreordain, mark someone out for; consign, assign; *rare* predoom.

condemnation ▶ noun *a comment which provoked widespread condemnation* **censure**, criticism, castigation, stricture, denunciation, damnation, vilification, opprobrium; reproof, disapproval, disapprobation; *informal* flak, a bad press; *rare* reprobation, arraignment, excoriation, objurgation.
OPPOSITES praise, plaudits.

condemnatory ▶ adjective *a condemnatory press report* **censorious**, critical, damning, damnatory, condemning, censuring, castigatory, fault-finding, denunciatory, vituperative, withering; reproving, reproachful, deprecatory, disapproving, unfavourable; *rare* reprobative, reprobatory.
OPPOSITES complimentary, approving.

condensation ▶ noun **1** *the windows were misty with condensation* **moisture**, water droplets, steam.
2 *the condensation of the vapour* **precipitation**, liquefaction, deliquescence, liquidization; distillation.
3 *a readable condensation of the recent literature* **abridgement**, **summary**, synopsis, precis, abstract, digest, encapsulation.
4 *the condensation of the report* **shortening**, abridgement, abbreviation, cutting, summarization.

condense ▶ verb **1** *the moisture vapour in the air condenses into droplets of water* **precipitate**, liquefy, become liquid, deliquesce, liquidize.
OPPOSITES vaporize, gasify.
2 *he condensed the three plays into a single three-hour drama* **abridge**, **shorten**, cut, abbreviate, compress, compact, contract, telescope; summarize, synopsize, precis, abstract, digest, encapsulate; truncate, curtail; *rare* epitomize.
OPPOSITES lengthen, expand.

condensed ▶ adjective **1** *a condensed version of the book* **abridged**, shortened, cut, cut-down, concise, contracted, compressed, abbreviated, reduced, truncated; summarized, summary, abstracted, precised, synoptic, synopsized, outline, thumbnail; *informal* potted, slimmed down.
2 *condensed soup | condensed milk* **concentrated**, evaporated, thick, thickened, reduced; undiluted.
OPPOSITE diluted.

condescend ▶ verb **1** *take care not to condescend to your reader* **patronize**, treat condescendingly, speak condescendingly to, speak haughtily to, talk down to, look down one's nose at, look down on, put down, be snobbish to.
OPPOSITE respect.
2 *a minor official condescended to see us* **deign**, stoop, descend, lower oneself, humble oneself, demean oneself, debase oneself, vouchsafe, think fit, see fit, deem it worthy of oneself, consent; *informal* come down from one's high horse.

condescending ▶ adjective *she looked us up and down in a condescending manner* **patronizing**, supercilious, superior, snobbish, snobby, scornful, disdainful, lofty, lordly, haughty, imperious; *informal* snooty, snotty, stuck-up; *Brit. informal* toffee-nosed.
OPPOSITE respectful.

condescension ▶ noun *with an air of great condescension he told me that he was 'prepared to give me a try-out'* **superciliousness**, superiority, scorn, disdain, loftiness, airs, lordliness, haughtiness, imperiousness, snobbishness, snobbery; *informal* snootiness, snottiness; *rare* patronization.
OPPOSITE respect.

condition ▶ noun **1** *visually check the condition of your wiring* **state**, shape, order; *Brit. informal* nick.
2 (**conditions**) *refugees were living in appalling conditions* **circumstances**, surroundings; **environment**, situation, state of affairs, set-up, position, context, background, setting, ambience, atmosphere, climate, milieu, habitat, way of life; *informal* circs.
3 *he had the body of an athlete in tip-top condition* **fitness**, physical fitness, health, state of health, form, shape, trim, fettle.
4 *a serious medical condition* **disorder**, problem, defect, disease, illness, complaint, ailment, weakness, infirmity, malady, indisposition, malaise, sickness, affliction, infection, upset; *informal* bug, virus; *Brit. informal* lurgy.
5 *it is a condition of employment that employees should be paid through a bank* **stipulation**, constraint, prerequisite, precondition, requirement, rule, term, specification, provision, proviso, qualification; necessity, essential, demand, restriction.
▶ verb **1** *national choices are conditioned by the international political economy* **constrain**, control, govern, determine, decide; exert influence on, affect, have an effect on, act on, work on, touch, have an impact on, impact on; change, alter, modify, transform, form, shape, guide, sway, bias.
2 *our minds are heavily conditioned by habit* **train**, teach, educate, coach, tutor, guide, groom, drill, accustom, adapt, habituate, mould, inure.
3 *the boards will need to be conditioned with water* **treat**, prepare, make ready, ready, prime, temper, process, acclimatize, acclimate, adapt, adjust, soften, season.
4 *some products contain vitamin E to condition your skin* **improve**, make healthy, build up, nourish, tone, tone up, get something into shape.

conditional ▶ adjective **1** *the supporters' approval is conditional on success* **subject to**, dependent on, depending on, contingent on, hingeing on, resting on, hanging on, based on, determined by, controlled by, tied to, bound up with.
OPPOSITE unconditional.
2 *he was only made a conditional offer of a university place* **contingent**, dependent, qualified, with conditions (attached), with reservations, limited, restrictive, provisional; *rare* stipulatory, provisory.
OPPOSITES unconditional; absolute.

condolences ▶ plural noun *we offer our sincere condolences to his widow* **sympathy**, commiseration(s), solace, comfort, consolation, fellow feeling, understanding, empathy, compassion, pity, solicitude, concern, support.

condom ▶ noun **contraceptive**, sheath; female condom; *N. Amer.* prophylactic; *Brit. trademark* Durex, Femidom; *Brit. informal* johnny, something for the weekend; *N. Amer. informal* rubber, safe, safety, skin; *Brit. informal, dated* French letter, Frenchy; *dated* protective.

condone ▶ verb *we cannot condone such dreadful behaviour* **deliberately ignore**, not take into consideration, disregard, take no notice of, take no account of, accept, allow, make allowances for, let pass, turn a blind eye to, overlook, forget, wink at, blink at, connive at; forgive, pardon, excuse, let someone off with, let go, sink, bury; let bygones be bygones; *informal* let something ride.
OPPOSITES condemn; punish.

> **CHOOSE THE RIGHT WORD**
> **condone, forgive, pardon, excuse**
> See FORGIVE.

conducive ▶ adjective *an environment which is conducive to learning* **good for**, helpful to, instrumental in, calculated to produce, productive of, useful for; favourable, beneficial, valuable, advantageous, opportune, propitious, encouraging, promising, convenient; (**be conducive to**) contribute to, lead to, tend to promote, make for, facilitate, favour, aid, assist, help, benefit, encourage.
OPPOSITE unfavourable.

C

conduct ▶ noun (stress on the first syllable) **1** *townspeople regularly complained about students' conduct* **behaviour**, way of behaving, performance, comportment, demeanour, bearing, deportment; actions, acts, activities, deeds, doings, handiwork, exploits, ways, habits, practices, manners.
2 *the conduct of the elections* **management**, managing, running, direction, control, controlling, overseeing, supervision, regulation, leadership, masterminding, administration, organization, coordination, orchestration, handling, guidance, carrying out, carrying on; *formal* prosecution.
▶ verb (stress on the second syllable) **1** *the election was conducted according to new electoral law* **manage**, direct, run, be in control of, control, oversee, supervise, be in charge of, preside over, regulate, mastermind, administer, organize, coordinate, orchestrate, handle, guide, govern, lead, carry out, carry on.
2 *Lucien was conducted through a maze of corridors* **escort**, guide, lead, usher, pilot, accompany, show, show someone the way; shepherd, herd, drive, convoy; see, bring, take, help, assist.
3 *aluminium, being a metal, readily conducts heat* **transmit**, convey, carry, transfer, pass on, hand on, communicate, impart, channel, bear, relay, dispatch, mediate; disseminate, spread, circulate, diffuse, radiate.
□ **conduct oneself** *I am proud of the way they conducted themselves* **behave**, perform, act, acquit oneself, bear oneself, carry oneself; *rare* comport oneself, deport oneself.

conduit ▶ noun *spring water ran down a conduit into the brewery* **channel**, duct, pipe, tube, gutter, groove, furrow, trough, trench, culvert, cut, sluice, spillway, race, flume, chute, ditch, drain.

confectionery *See centre pages for list of* **Sweets and Confectionery**
▶ noun **sweets**, bonbons; *N. Amer.* candy, sugar candy; *informal* sweeties; *archaic* sweetmeats.

confederacy ▶ noun *the Empire was a loosely organized confederacy of allies* **federation**, confederation, alliance, league, association, coalition, combine, consortium, conglomerate, cooperative, partnership, syndicate, compact, band, group, circle, ring; bloc, axis; society, union, guild, fellowship; *rare* consociation, sodality.

confederate ▶ adjective *some local groups united to form confederate councils* **federal**, confederated, federated, allied, in alliance, in league, cooperating, associated, united, combined, amalgamated.
OPPOSITE split.
▶ noun *he and a confederate shot the miller dead* **associate**, partner, accomplice, abetter, accessory, helper, supporter, assistant, ally, collaborator, colleague; *Brit. informal* oppo; *Austral./NZ informal* offsider.

confederation ▶ noun *a confederation of trade unions* **alliance**, league, confederacy, federation, association, coalition, combine, consortium, affiliation, conglomerate, cooperative, partnership, fellowship, syndicate, compact, band, group, circle, ring; society, union; *rare* consociation, sodality.

confer ▶ verb **1** *the Queen* **conferred** *an honorary knighthood* **on** *him* **bestow on**, present with/to, grant to, award to, decorate with, honour with, give to, give out to, gift with, endow with, vest in, hand out to, extend to, vouchsafe to, accord to.
OPPOSITES withhold; remove.
2 *she broke off to confer with her colleagues* **consult**, have discussions, discuss things, exchange views, talk, have a talk, speak, converse, communicate, have a chat, have a tête-à-tête; negotiate, have negotiations, have talks, parley, palaver; *informal* have a confab, chew the fat/rag, jaw, rap, powwow; *formal* confabulate.

conference ▶ noun **1** *an international conference on the environment* **congress**, meeting, convention, seminar, colloquium, symposium, forum, convocation, summit, synod, conclave, consultation.
2 *he gathered them round the table for a conference* **discussion**, consultation, exchange of views, debate, talk, conversation, dialogue, chat, tête-à-tête; negotiations, talks, parley, palaver; *informal* confab; *formal* confabulation.

confess ▶ verb **1** *he confessed that he had attacked the old man* **admit**, acknowledge, reveal, make known, disclose, divulge, make public, avow, declare, blurt out, profess, own up to, tell all about, bring into the open, bring to light; *informal* blow the lid off; *archaic* discover.
OPPOSITES conceal; deny.
2 *they tried everything they could think of to make him confess* **own up**, admit guilt, plead guilty, accept blame/responsibility, be completely honest, tell the truth, tell all, make a clean breast of it, unbosom oneself; *informal* come clean, fess up, spill the beans, let the cat out of the bag, get something off one's chest, let on; *Brit. informal* cough.
3 *I confess I don't know* **acknowledge**, admit, concede, grant, allow, own, say, declare, affirm, accept, recognize, be aware of/that, realize, be conscious of/that.

confession ▶ noun *the interrogators soon got a confession out of him* **admission**, owning up, acceptance of blame/responsibility, acknowledgement, profession, revelation, disclosure, divulgence, exposure, avowal, unbosoming.
OPPOSITES concealment; denial.

confidant, fem. **confidante** ▶ noun *he was her confidant and business adviser* **close friend**, bosom friend, best friend, close associate, companion, crony, intimate, familiar, second self; mentor, adviser, counsellor; *Latin* alter ego; *Italian* consigliere; *informal* chum, pal, buddy, main man; *Brit. informal* mate, oppo, mucker; *rare* fidus Achates.

confide ▶ verb **1** *he confided his fears to his mother* **reveal**, disclose, divulge, leak, lay bare, make known, betray, impart, pass on, proclaim, announce, report, declare, intimate, uncover, unmask, expose, bring out into the open, unfold, vouchsafe, tell; confess, admit; let slip, let out, let drop, let fall, blurt out, babble, give away; *informal* blab, spill; *archaic* discover.
OPPOSITE keep from.
2 *I really need him to* **confide in** **open one's heart to**, unburden oneself to, unbosom oneself to, confess to, tell all to, tell one's all to, commune with.

confidence ▶ noun **1** *I have little confidence in these figures* **trust**, belief, faith, credence, conviction; reliance, dependence.
OPPOSITES distrust, scepticism.
2 *she's brimming with confidence* **self-assurance**, self-confidence, self-reliance, belief in oneself, faith in oneself, positiveness, assertiveness, self-possession, nerve, poise, aplomb, presence of mind, phlegm, level-headedness, cool-headedness, firmness, courage, boldness, mettle, fortitude.
OPPOSITES doubt; uncertainty.
3 *the girls exchanged confidences about their parents* **secret**, private affair, confidential matter, confidentiality, intimacy.

confident ▶ adjective **1** *we are confident that business will improve* **optimistic**, hopeful, sanguine; **sure**, certain, positive, convinced, in no doubt, unshakeable in one's belief, secure in one's belief, easy in one's mind, satisfied, assured, persuaded; (**be confident**) have no doubt, not question, hold the unwavering view.
2 *she was a confident, outgoing girl* **self-assured**, assured, sure of oneself, self-confident, positive; assertive, self-assertive, self-possessed, believing in oneself, self-reliant, poised, filled with aplomb; cool, cool-headed, calm, collected, {cool, calm, and collected}, phlegmatic, level-headed, composed, nonchalant, unperturbed, imperturbable, unruffled, impassive, serene, tranquil, relaxed, at ease; *informal* unflappable, together, unfazed, laid-back; *rare* equanimous.

> **CHOOSE THE RIGHT WORD**
>
> **confident, sanguine, optimistic, hopeful**
>
> All these words indicate varying degrees of expectation that something is true or will happen.
>
> - If someone is **confident** of something, they are fairly sure of it, or they may be saying they are because they wish to appear so (*I'm fully confident of winning the world title | she was far from confident that she possessed the moral courage*).
> - **Sanguine** is often used when there is a lack of hope (*it is too soon to be sanguine, the board says | we are less sanguine about the prospects for simplifying the current range*). This is the only one of the four words that is not usually followed by *of* or a *that*-clause.
> - Someone who is **optimistic** is moderately sure of something (*Gilroy is optimistic about long-term growth*), but they are chiefly characterized by their attitude towards the future (*pet owners tend to feel happier, healthier, and more optimistic and sociable*). This sense is contrasted with *pessimistic*. Sometimes another person believes that the optimism is misplaced (*a target which some observers dismissed as optimistic*).
> - A **hopeful** person acknowledges the possibility that the event will not happen (*we are hopeful there will be no surcharges levied whatsoever | obviously I'm hopeful of getting to Sweden*).

confidential ▶ adjective **1** *anyone can have a confidential chat with adult education experts* **private**, personal, intimate, privileged, quiet; secret, top secret, sensitive, classified, restricted, non-public, unofficial, off the record, not for publication, not for circulation, not to be made public, not to be disclosed, under wraps, unrevealed, undisclosed, unpublished; *Latin* sub rosa; *informal* hush-hush, mum; *archaic* privy.
OPPOSITES public, on the record.
2 (*dated*) *a confidential friend* **trusted**, trustworthy, trusty, faithful, reliable, dependable, close, bosom, dear, intimate, familiar.

confidentially ▶ adverb *he confidentially approached a number of very senior civil servants* **privately**, in private, in confidence, between ourselves/themselves/yourselves, off the record, quietly, secretly, in secret, behind closed doors, in camera; *Latin* sub rosa; *archaic* privily.

configuration ▶ noun *the poor visibility is a result of the configuration of windows and pillars in the cockpit* **arrangement**, layout, geography, design, organization, order, ordering, array, presentation, grouping, sorting, positioning, disposition, marshalling, ranging, alignment; shape, form, appearance, formation, structure, format; contours, lines, outline, silhouette, profile; cut, pattern, mould.

confine ▶ verb **1** *their cats are confined in the house* **enclose**, incarcerate, imprison, intern, impound, hold captive, trap; shut in/up, keep, pen in/up, cage, lock in/up, coop (up), box up/in, immure, mew up; fence in, hedge in, hurdle, rail in, wall in/up; encircle, surround, ring, encompass, hem in, close in; N. Amer. corral; rare gird, compass.
OPPOSITE release.
2 *he confined his remarks to the job in hand* **restrict**, limit; keep within the limits of, not allow to go beyond.

confined ▶ adjective *she had a fear of confined spaces* **cramped**, constricted, restricted, limited, confining, small, narrow, compact, tight, pinched, squeezed, poky, uncomfortable, inadequate, meagre; archaic strait; rare incommodious, exiguous, incapacious.
OPPOSITES open; roomy.

confinement ▶ noun **1** *he was being held in solitary confinement* **imprisonment**, internment, incarceration, custody, captivity, detention, restraint, arrest, house arrest; literary thraldom, thrall; archaic duress, durance.
OPPOSITE liberty.
2 *prolonged confinement of an animal is prohibited* **penning**, caging, locking up, walling in/up, enclosure, encirclement, surrounding, encompassment; quarantine; N. Amer. corralling; rare immurement.
3 *she was admitted to hospital for her confinement* **labour**, (expected) delivery, giving birth, birthing; birth, childbirth, nativity; technical parturition; archaic lying-in, accouchement, childbed, travail.

confines ▶ plural noun *recorded whale song was used to entice the whales out of the confines of Scapa Flow* **limits**, outer limits, borders, boundaries, margins, extremities, edges, fringes, marches; periphery, perimeter, circumference, compass, precinct, pale.

confirm ▶ verb **1** *written records confirm the archaeological evidence* **corroborate**, bear out, verify, show the truth of, prove, validate, authenticate, substantiate, give substance to, justify, vouch for, vindicate, give credence to, support, uphold, back up.
OPPOSITES contradict; repudiate.
2 *he confirmed that engineers would examine the road* **affirm**, reaffirm, assert, reassert, give an assurance, assure someone, repeat, say again, state again, pledge, promise, guarantee.
OPPOSITE deny.
3 *his appointment as ambassador was confirmed by the President* **ratify**, validate, sanction, endorse, formalize, certify, underwrite, authorize, warrant, accredit, approve, recognize, agree to, consent to, accept.
OPPOSITE revoke.

confirmation ▶ noun **1** *there was no independent confirmation of the reported deaths* **corroboration**, verification, proof, testimony, endorsement, authentication, substantiation, justification, vindication, support, evidence.
2 *confirmation of your appointment is dependent upon satisfactory performance* **ratification**, approval, authorization, validation, sanction, endorsement, formalization, certification, accreditation, recognition, acceptance; agreement to, consent to.

confirmed ▶ adjective *a confirmed bachelor* **established**, long-established, long-standing, firm, committed, dyed-in-the-wool, through and through; seasoned, hardened, settled, set, fixed, rooted; staunch, loyal, faithful, devoted, dedicated, stalwart, steadfast; habitual, compulsive, obsessive, persistent, unapologetic, unashamed, incorrigible, irredeemable, unreformable, impenitent, inveterate, chronic, incurable; informal deep-dyed, card-carrying.

confiscate ▶ verb *the guards confiscated his camera* **impound**, seize, commandeer, requisition, appropriate, expropriate, take possession of, sequester, sequestrate, take away, take over, take, annex; Law distrain, attach, disseize; Scottish Law poind.
OPPOSITE return.

confiscation ▶ noun *laws generally allow the confiscation of the proceeds of crime* **seizure**, impounding, commandeering, requisition, requisitioning, appropriation, expropriation, sequestration, taking away, annexation; forfeiture; Law distraint, distrainment, attachment, disseizin; Scottish Law poind, poinding.
OPPOSITE return.

conflagration ▶ noun *the conflagration spread rapidly through the wooden buildings* **fire**, blaze, flames, inferno, firestorm, holocaust.

conflict ▶ noun (stress on the first syllable) **1** *the industrial conflicts of the 1890s* **dispute**, quarrel, squabble, disagreement, difference of opinion, dissension; discord, friction, strife, antagonism, antipathy, ill will, bad blood, hostility, falling-out, disputation, contention; clash, altercation, shouting match, exchange, war of words; tussle, fracas, affray, wrangle, tangle, passage of/at arms, battle royal, feud, schism.
OPPOSITE agreement.
2 *the Vietnam conflict* **war**, armed conflict, action, military action, campaign, battle, fighting, fight, (armed) confrontation, (armed) clash, engagement, encounter, (armed) struggle, hostilities; warfare, warring, combat, strife; informal set-to, scrap; archaic rencounter.
OPPOSITE peace.
3 *there was a conflict between his business and domestic life* **clash**, incompatibility, incongruity, lack of congruence, friction, opposition, mismatch, variance, difference, divergence, contradiction, inconsistency, discrepancy, divided loyalties.
OPPOSITE harmony.
▶ verb (stress on the second syllable) *parents' and children's interests sometimes conflict* **clash**, be incompatible, be inconsistent, be incongruous, be in opposition, be at variance, vary, be at odds, be in conflict, come into conflict, differ, diverge, disagree, contrast, collide.

C

conflicting ▶ adjective *there are conflicting accounts of what occurred* **contradictory**, incompatible, inconsistent, irreconcilable, incongruous, contrary, opposite, opposing, opposed, antithetical, clashing, discordant, differing, different, divergent, discrepant, varying, disagreeing, contrasting; at odds, in opposition, at variance; rare oppugnant.
OPPOSITE harmonious.

confluence ▶ noun *the confluence of the Rhine and the Mosel* **convergence**, meeting, junction, joining, conflux, watersmeet; Indian sangam.

conform ▶ verb **1** *the kitchen does not conform to hygiene regulations | visitors have to conform to our rules* **comply with**, abide by, obey, observe, follow, keep to, hold to, adhere to; satisfy, match up to, meet, fulfil, be in accordance with; stick to, stand by, act in accordance with, uphold, heed, pay attention to, agree to/with, consent to, accede to, accept, acquiesce in, go along with, fall in with, adapt to, accommodate to, adjust to, acknowledge, respect, defer to.
OPPOSITE flout.
2 *there are penalties for those who refuse to conform* **follow convention**, be conventional, follow tradition, follow custom, fit in, adapt, adjust, follow the crowd, run with the pack, swim with the stream; comply, acquiesce, do what one is told, toe the line, obey the rules, comply with the rules, observe the rules, abide by the rules, adhere to the rules, act in accordance with the rules, follow the rules, keep to the rules, stick to the rules; submit, yield; informal play it by the book, play by the rules, keep in step, go with the flow.
OPPOSITE rebel.
3 *the goods must conform to their description* **match**, fit, suit, answer, agree with, be like, be similar to, coincide with, correspond to, correlate to, be consistent with, be consonant with, be comparable with, measure up to, go with, tally with, square with, accord with, parallel, harmonize with.
OPPOSITE differ from.

conformist ▶ noun *he was too much of a conformist to wear anything but a suit at work* **conventionalist**, **traditionalist**, orthodox person, conservative, bourgeois, (old) fogey, stickler, formalist, diehard, reactionary; crawler, truckler, kowtower, groveller, puppet, spaniel; informal stick-in-the-mud, stuffed shirt, yes-man.
OPPOSITES eccentric; rebel.

conformity ▶ noun **1** *conformity with the law* **compliance with**, adherence to, accordance with, observance of, observation of, obedience to, acquiescence in, respect for, adaptation to, adjustment to, accommodation to; archaic abidance by.
OPPOSITE flouting.
2 *you cannot find more conformity than among young people* **conventionality**, **traditionalism**, orthodoxy, fitting in, following the crowd, running with the pack, swimming with the stream; conservatism, formalism, reaction.
OPPOSITES eccentricity, rebellion.
3 *these changes are intended to ensure conformity between all schemes* **similarity**, likeness, alikeness, resemblance, similitude; **correspondence**, correlation, matching, congruity, congruence, consonance, coincidence, compatibility, concurrence, agreement, harmony, accord, equivalence; comparability, comparableness, comparison, parallelism, mapping, parity, analogy, affinity, closeness, nearness; sameness, identity, identicalness, uniformity, symmetry; archaic semblance.
OPPOSITE dissimilarity.

confound ▶ verb **1** *the inflation figure confounded economic analysts* **amaze**, astonish, dumbfound, stagger, surprise, startle, stun, stupefy, daze, nonplus; throw, shake, unnerve, disconcert, discompose, dismay, bewilder, set someone thinking, baffle, mystify, bemuse, perplex, puzzle, confuse; take someone's breath away, take by surprise, take aback, shake up, stop someone in their tracks, strike dumb, leave open-mouthed, leave aghast, catch off balance; N. Amer. informal buffalo; informal flabbergast, floor, knock for six, knock sideways, knock out, knock the stuffing out of someone, bowl over, blow someone's mind, blow away, flummox, discombobulate, faze, stump, beat, fox, make someone scratch their head, be all Greek to, fog; archaic wilder, gravel, maze, cause to be at a stand, distract, pose; rare obfuscate.
2 *the bad boy of country music has always confounded expectations* **invalidate**, negate, contradict, counter, go against, discredit, give the lie to, drive a coach and horses through; quash, explode, demolish, shoot down, destroy; disprove, prove wrong, prove false, falsify; informal shoot full of holes, blow sky-high; rare controvert, confute, negative.

confront ▶ verb **1** *Jones confronted the alleged burglar* **challenge**, square up

C

to, oppose, resist, defy, beard, tackle, attack, assault; approach, face up to, face, meet, come face to face with, stand up to, brave, detain, accost, waylay, take aside, stop, halt; *informal* collar; *Brit. informal* nobble.
OPPOSITE avoid.
2 *the real problems that confront ordinary citizens* **trouble**, bother, be in someone's way, burden, distress, cause trouble to, cause suffering to, face, beset, harass, worry, oppress, annoy, vex, irritate, exasperate, strain, stress, tax; torment, plague, blight, bedevil, rack, smite, curse, harrow; *rare* discommode.
3 *they've got to learn to confront their own problems* **tackle**, get to grips with, apply oneself to, address oneself to, address, face, set about, go about, get to work at, busy oneself with, set one's hand to, grapple with, approach, take on, attend to, see to, throw oneself into, try to solve, try to deal with, try to cope with, learn to live with, try to sort out; deal with, take measures about, take care of, pursue, handle, manage; *informal* have a crack at, have a go at, have a shot at, get stuck into.
OPPOSITE avoid.
4 *she confronted him with the evidence she had unearthed* **present**, bring face to face, face.
OPPOSITE spare.

confrontation ▶ noun *a peaceful protest turned into a violent confrontation with police* **conflict**, clash, brush, fight, battle, contest, encounter, head-to-head, face-off, engagement, tangle, skirmish, collision, meeting, duel, incident, high noon; hostilities, fighting, warring; *informal* set-to, run-in, dust-up, shindig, shindy, showdown; *archaic* rencounter.

confuse ▶ verb **1** *there was no need to confuse students with too much controversy* **bewilder**, baffle, mystify, bemuse, perplex, puzzle, confound, befog, nonplus, disconcert, throw, set someone thinking; *informal* flummox, discombobulate, faze, stump, beat, fox, make someone scratch their head, floor, fog; *N. Amer. informal* buffalo; *archaic* wilder, gravel, maze, cause to be at a stand, distract, pose; *rare* obfuscate.
OPPOSITE enlighten.
2 *the points made by the authors confuse rather than clarify the issue* **complicate**, **muddle**, jumble, garble, make complex, make (more) difficult, blur, obscure, make unclear, cloud, obfuscate; *archaic* embroil.
OPPOSITE simplify.
3 *a lot of people* confuse *a stroke* with *a heart attack* **mix up**, muddle up, confound; misinterpret as, mistake for, take for.
OPPOSITE distinguish.

confused ▶ adjective **1** *children could be confused about what was going on* **bewildered**, bemused, puzzled, perplexed, baffled, stumped, mystified, stupefied, nonplussed, muddled, befuddled, fuddled, dumbfounded, at sea, at a loss, at sixes and sevens, thrown (off balance), taken aback, disoriented, disconcerted, discomposed, troubled, discomfited, unnerved, shaken, shaken up, dazed, stunned, astonished, astounded; *informal* flummoxed, bamboozled, discombobulated, clueless, fazed, floored, beaten; *Canadian & Austral./NZ informal* bushed; *archaic* wildered, mazed, distracted.
2 *her frail and confused elderly mother* **demented**, bewildered, muddled, addled, befuddled, disoriented, disorientated, (all) at sea, unbalanced, unhinged, senile, with Alzheimer's disease.
OPPOSITE lucid.
3 *the first confused reports of the massacre* **chaotic**, **muddled**, jumbled, unclear, untidy, disordered, disorderly, disarranged, out of order, disorganized, upset, topsy-turvy, at sixes and sevens; *informal* higgledy-piggledy.
OPPOSITE clear.
4 *a confused recollection* **vague**, unclear, indistinct, imprecise, blurred, nebulous, hazy, woolly, foggy, shadowy, dim, imperfect, sketchy, obscure, remote.
OPPOSITE precise.
5 *the bones lay in a confused mass* **disorderly**, disordered, disorganized, disarranged, in disarray, out of order, out of place, untidy, muddled, jumbled, in a jumble, in a mess, mixed up, chaotic, upset, haywire, upside-down, topsy-turvy, at sixes and sevens; *informal* higgledy-piggledy, every which way; *Brit. informal* shambolic, like a dog's dinner/breakfast.
OPPOSITE neat.

confusing ▶ adjective *the instructions are a little confusing* **bewildering**, baffling, difficult (to understand), unclear, perplexing, puzzling, mystifying, mysterious, disconcerting; ambiguous, misleading, inconsistent, contradictory; unaccountable, inexplicable, impenetrable, unfathomable, above one's head, beyond one; complex, complicated, involved, intricate, convoluted, labyrinthine, Byzantine; *archaic* wildering.
OPPOSITE clear.

confusion ▶ noun **1** *there seems to be some confusion about which system does what* **uncertainty**, lack of certainty, unsureness, indecision, hesitation, hesitancy, scepticism, doubt, ignorance; *rare* dubiety, incertitude.
OPPOSITE certainty.
2 *she looked about her in confusion* **bewilderment**, bafflement, perplexity, puzzlement, mystification, stupefaction, disorientation, befuddlement, muddle; discomfiture, discomposure, shock, daze, devastation; wonder, wonderment, astonishment; *informal* bamboozlement, discombobulation; *rare* disconcertment, disconcertion.
3 *your personal life seems to have been thrown into utter confusion* **disorder**, disarray, disorganization, disorderliness, untidiness, chaos, mayhem, bedlam, pandemonium, madness, havoc, turmoil, tumult, commotion, disruption, upheaval, furore, frenzy, uproar, babel, hurly-burly, maelstrom, muddle, mess, shambles; a mare's nest, anarchy, entropy; *informal* hullabaloo, all hell broken loose, a madhouse; *N. Amer. informal* a three-ring circus; *rare* disarrangement.
OPPOSITE order.
4 *a confusion of brown cardboard boxes* **jumble**, muddle, mess, heap, tangle, entanglement, tumble, welter, litter, shambles.

confute ▶ verb (*formal*) *their assertion can certainly be confuted* **disprove**, show/prove to be false, contradict, negate, deny, refute, rebut, gainsay, belie, give the lie to, invalidate, explode, discredit, expose, debunk, quash, knock the bottom out of, drive a coach and horses through; *informal* shoot full of holes, shoot down (in flames); *rare* controvert, negative.
OPPOSITE prove.

congeal ▶ verb *the blood had congealed around the cut* **coagulate**, clot, cake, set, solidify, harden, thicken, stiffen, dry, gel, concentrate; *archaic* fix; *rare* inspissate.
OPPOSITES soften; liquefy.

congenial ▶ adjective **1** *I was working with a bunch of very congenial people* **like-minded**, compatible, kindred, well suited, easy to get along with; **companionable**, sociable, sympathetic, comradely, convivial, neighbourly, hospitable, genial, personable, agreeable, friendly, pleasant, likeable, kindly, pleasing, amiable, nice, good-natured; *French* sympathique; *Italian & Spanish* simpatico.
OPPOSITES disagreeable, incompatible.
2 *Charles found himself in a fairly congenial environment* **pleasant**, pleasing, to one's liking, agreeable, enjoyable, pleasurable, nice, appealing, engaging, satisfying, gratifying, fine, charming, delightful, relaxing, snug, welcome, welcoming, hospitable; suitable, suited, well suited, fit, appropriate, adapted, favourable.
OPPOSITE unpleasant.

congenital ▶ adjective **1** *multiple congenital defects* **inborn**, inherited, hereditary, in the blood, in the family, innate, inbred, constitutional, built-in, inbuilt, ingrown, natural, native, original, inherent, unlearned, instinctual, deep-rooted, deep-seated; *rare* connate, connatural.
OPPOSITE acquired.
2 *he was a congenital liar* **inveterate**, compulsive, persistent, chronic, regular, pathological, established, long-established, long-standing, hardened, confirmed, committed, seasoned, habitual, obsessive, obsessional; incurable, incorrigible, irredeemable, unreformable, hopeless; unashamed, shameless, unrepentant; dyed-in-the-wool, thoroughgoing, thorough, utter, complete.

congested ▶ adjective *more traffic will use the already congested road* **crowded**, overcrowded, full, overfull, overflowing, full to overflowing/bursting, crammed full, cram-full, thronged, packed, jammed, teeming, swarming, overloaded; obstructed, impeded, blocked (up), clogged, choked, plugged, stopped up; *informal* snarled up, gridlocked, jam-packed; *Brit. informal* like Piccadilly Circus.
OPPOSITE clear.

congestion ▶ noun *an attempt to relieve some of the congestion on the roads* **crowding**, overcrowding; obstruction, blockage, stoppage, blocking, clogging, choking, plugging, stuffing; traffic jam, bottleneck; *informal* snarl-up, gridlock.
OPPOSITE flow.

conglomerate ▶ noun **1** *the conglomerate was broken up* **corporation**, combine, group, grouping, consortium, partnership, joint concern, trust, merger, merged firms/companies/businesses; firm, company, business, multinational; *Japanese* zaibatsu.
2 *Austria–Hungary was a conglomerate of disparate peoples* **mixture**, mix, combination, mingling, commingling, amalgamation, amalgam, union, conjunction, marriage, merging, compound, alloy, fusion, meld, composite, concoction, synthesis, homogenization; miscellany, jumble, hotchpotch.
3 (*Geology*) *a rocky conglomerate* **aggregate**, agglomerate.
▶ adjective *a conglomerate mass* **aggregate**, agglomerate, amassed, gathered, clustered, combined.
▶ verb *the debris then conglomerated into planets* **coalesce**, unite, join together, combine, merge, fuse, consolidate, amalgamate, integrate, mingle, meld, blend, intermingle, knit (together), link up, converge, come together; *literary* commingle.
OPPOSITE split up.

conglomeration ▶ noun *an extremely odd conglomeration of church buildings* **collection**, **cluster**, assortment, mix, variety, medley, mixed bag, pot-pourri, miscellany, selection, combination; accumulation, mass, gathering, cumulation, package, aggregation, accretion, agglomerate, agglomeration; *rare* amassment.

congratulate ▶ verb **1** *she took the opportunity to congratulate Nicholas on*

his marriage **give someone one's good wishes**, wish someone good luck, wish someone joy, drink someone's health, toast, drink (a toast) to.
OPPOSITE curse.
2 *all three are to be congratulated for passing with flying colours* **praise**, commend, applaud, salute, honour, eulogize, extol, acclaim, sing the praises of, heap praise on, pay tribute to, speak highly/well of, flatter, compliment, say nice things about, express admiration for, wax lyrical about, make much of, pat on the back, take one's hat off to, throw bouquets at; *informal* crack someone/something up; *N. Amer. informal* ballyhoo; *black English* big someone/something up; *dated* cry someone/something up; *archaic* emblazon; *rare* laud, panegyrize, felicitate.
OPPOSITE criticize.

□ **congratulate oneself** *he congratulated himself on his success* **take pride in**, be/feel proud of, feel proud about, be proud of oneself for, flatter oneself on, preen oneself on, pat oneself on the back for, give oneself a pat on the back for; **find/take satisfaction in**, feel satisfaction at, take delight in, find/take pleasure in, glory in, bask in, delight in, exult in, plume oneself on; *archaic* pique oneself on/in.
OPPOSITE be ashamed of.

congratulations ▶ plural noun **1** *Lily and Stephen accepted Muriel's congratulations on their wedding* **good wishes**, best wishes, greetings, compliments, felicitations.
2 *you all deserve congratulations for ensuring that the visit was such a success* **praise**, commendation, applause, salutes, honour, acclaim, acclamation, tribute, cheers, ovation, accolade, plaudits, felicitations; approval, admiration, approbation, compliments, kudos, adulation, homage; a pat on the back, eulogy, encomium, panegyric, bouquets, laurels, testimonial; *rare* extolment, laudation, eulogium.
OPPOSITE blame.

congregate ▶ verb *some 4000 demonstrators had congregated at a border point* **assemble**, gather, collect, come together, flock together, get together, convene, rally, rendezvous, muster, meet, amass, crowd, cluster, throng, group; *rare* foregather.
OPPOSITE disperse.

congregation ▶ noun **1** *he broke the news to the congregation in the church newsletter* **parishioners**, parish, churchgoers, flock, fold, faithful, following, followers, adherents, believers, loyal members, fellowship, communicants, laity, brethren, brothers and sisters, souls.
2 *such congregations of birds may cause public harm | a large congregation of protesters gathered* **gathering**, assembly, flock, swarm, bevy, herd, pack, group, body, crowd, mass, multitude, horde, host, mob; turnout, throng, company, rally, convocation, congress, council, conclave, synod, assemblage; *informal* get-together; *historical* conventicle.

congress ▶ noun **1** *an international congress of mathematicians* **conference**, convention, seminar, colloquium, symposium, consultation, forum, meeting, assembly, gathering, congregation, rally, convocation, summit, synod, council, conclave; *historical* conventicle.
2 *elections for the new Congress were held on 8 November* **legislature**, legislative assembly, parliament, convocation, diet, council, senate, chamber, chamber of deputies, house; upper house, lower house, upper chamber, lower chamber, second chamber.

congruence ▶ noun *he took care that there should be congruence of meaning and sound in his music* **compatibility**, consistency, conformity, match, balance, consonance, rapport, parallelism, congruity; consilience; agreement, concord, accord, consensus, unanimity, harmony, unison, unity, concert.
OPPOSITE conflict.

conical ▶ adjective *a circular tower with a conical roof* **cone-shaped**, tapered, tapering, pointed, funnel-shaped; *informal* pointy; *technical* infundibular, turbinate, conoid.

conjectural ▶ adjective *comments on inner-city areas are likely to be more conjectural* **speculative**, suppositional, theoretical, hypothetical, putative, academic, notional, abstract; postulated, based on guesswork, inferred, suspected, presumed, assumed, presupposed, tentative; unproven, untested, unfounded, groundless, unsubstantiated; *rare* ideational, suppositious, suppositive, postulational.
OPPOSITE established.

conjecture ▶ noun *we find his conjectures implausible | some of the information is merely conjecture* **guess**, speculation, surmise, fancy, notion, belief, suspicion, presumption, assumption, theory, hypothesis, postulation, supposition; inference, extrapolation, projection; approximation, estimate, rough calculation, rough idea; guesswork, guessing, surmising, imagining, theorizing; *informal* guesstimate, shot in the dark; *N. Amer. informal* ballpark figure.
OPPOSITE fact.
▶ verb *I conjectured that the game was about to end* **guess**, speculate, surmise, infer, fancy, imagine, believe, think, suspect, presume, assume, hypothesize, take as a hypothesis, theorize, form/formulate a theory, suppose.
OPPOSITE know.

conjugal ▶ adjective *the conjugal bond* **marital**, matrimonial, nuptial, marriage, married, wedded, connubial, bridal; *Law* spousal; *literary* hymeneal, epithalamic.

conjunction ▶ noun *the conjunction of low inflation and low unemployment came as a very pleasant surprise* **co-occurrence**, concurrence, coincidence, coexistence, simultaneity, simultaneousness, contemporaneity, contemporaneousness, concomitance, synchronicity, synchrony; combination, juxtaposition.

conjure ▶ verb **1** *he conjured another cigarette out of the air* **make something appear**, produce, materialize, magic, summon, generate; whip up.
2 *the picture that his words* **conjured up** *left her breathless* **bring to mind**, call to mind, put one in mind of, call up, evoke, summon up, recall, recreate; echo, allude to, suggest; rouse (up), stir (up), raise up, awaken.

conjuring ▶ noun *a demonstration of conjuring* **magic**, illusion, sleight of hand, legerdemain, dexterity, deception, hocus-pocus; *formal* prestidigitation.

conjuror ▶ noun *the children were entertained by a local conjuror* **magician**, illusionist; *Brit.* member of the Magic Circle; *formal* prestidigitator.

connect ▶ verb **1** *the electrodes were connected to a recording device* **attach**, join, fasten, fix, affix, couple, link, bridge, secure, make fast, tie, tie up, bind, fetter, strap, rope, tether, truss, lash, hitch, moor, anchor, yoke, chain; stick, tape, adhere, glue, bond, cement, fuse, weld, solder; pin, peg, screw, bolt, rivet, batten, pinion, clamp, clip, hook (up); add, append, annex, subjoin; *technical* concatenate.
OPPOSITE disconnect.
2 *there are lots of customs* **connected with** *Twelfth Night* **associate**, link, couple, identify, equate, bracket, compare; think of something together with, think of something in connection with; relate to, mention in the same breath as, set side by side with; draw a parallel with.
OPPOSITE dissociate.

connection ▶ noun **1** *he does not pursue the connection between commerce and art* **link**, relationship, relation, relatedness, interrelation, interrelatedness, interconnection, interdependence, association, attachment, bond, tie, tie-in, correspondence, parallel, analogy; bearing, relevance.
2 *there's a poor connection in the plug* **attachment**, joint, fastening, coupling.
3 *a politician with all the right connections* **contact**, friend, acquaintance, ally, colleague, associate, sponsor; relation, relative, kindred, kin, kinsman, kinswoman.

□ **in connection with** *a man is being questioned in connection with the murder* **regarding**, concerning, with reference to, referring to, with regard to, with respect to, respecting, relating to, in relation to, on, touching on, dealing with, relevant to, with relevance to, in the context of, connected with, on the subject of, in the matter of, apropos, re; *Scottish* anent; *Latin* in re.

connivance ▶ noun *this infringement of the law had taken place with the connivance of officials* **collusion**, complicity, collaboration, involvement, assistance, abetting; **tacit consent**; conspiracy, plotting, scheming, intrigue, machination, secret understanding; *rare* abetment, condonation.

connive ▶ verb **1** *wardens* **connived at** *offences in return for bribes* **deliberately ignore**, overlook, not take into consideration, disregard, pass over, gloss over, take no notice of, take no account of, make allowances for, turn a blind eye to, close/shut one's eyes to, wink at, blink at, excuse, pardon, forgive, condone, let someone off with, let go, let pass; look the other way; *informal* let something ride.
OPPOSITES condemn; punish.
2 *the government had connived with security forces in permitting murder* **conspire**, collude, be in collusion, collaborate, intrigue, be hand in glove, plot, participate in a conspiracy, scheme; *informal* be in cahoots; *rare* machinate, cabal, complot.

conniving ▶ adjective *a conniving little toady with an eye for the main chance* **scheming**, plotting, colluding, cunning, crafty, calculating, devious, designing, wily, sly, tricky, artful, guileful, slippery, slick; **manipulative**, Machiavellian, unscrupulous, unprincipled, disingenuous; duplicitous, deceitful, underhand, treacherous; *informal* foxy; *S. African informal* slim; *archaic* subtle.

connoisseur ▶ noun *a connoisseur of fine wines* **expert judge (of)**, authority (on), specialist (in); arbiter of taste, pundit, savant, one of the cognoscenti, aesthete; gourmet, epicure, gastronome; *informal* buff; *N. Amer. informal* maven.
OPPOSITE ignoramus.

connotation ▶ noun *the word 'discipline' has unhappy connotations of punishment and repression* **overtone**, undertone, undercurrent, implication, hidden meaning, secondary meaning, nuance, flavour, feeling, aura, atmosphere, colouring, smack, hint, vein, echo, vibrations, association, intimation, suggestion, suspicion, insinuation; *rare* undermeaning, subcurrent.

connote ▶ verb *the British think that crying and showing emotion connote weakness* **imply**, suggest, indicate, signify, have overtones of, have undertones of, hint at, give a feeling of, have an aura of, have an

atmosphere of, give the impression of, smack of, be associated with, allude to.
OPPOSITES denote, mean.

conquer ▶ verb **1** *the Franks conquered the Visigoths in the South of France* **defeat**, beat, vanquish, trounce, annihilate, triumph over, be victorious over, best, get the better of, worst, bring someone to their knees, overcome, overwhelm, overpower, overthrow, subdue, subjugate, put down, quell, quash, crush, repress, rout; *informal* lick, hammer, clobber, thrash, paste, pound, pulverize, demolish, destroy, drub, give someone a drubbing, cane, wipe the floor with, walk all over, give someone a hiding, take to the cleaners, blow someone out of the water, make mincemeat of, murder, massacre, slaughter, flatten, turn inside out, tank; *Brit. informal* stuff; *N. Amer. informal* blow out, cream, shellac, skunk, slam.
OPPOSITE lose to.
2 *Peru had been conquered by Spain* **seize**, take possession of, take control of, take over, appropriate, subjugate, capture, occupy, invade, annex, overrun, win.
OPPOSITES liberate, lose.
3 *the first men to conquer Mount Everest* **climb**, ascend, mount, scale, top, crest.
4 *the only way to conquer fear is to face it* **overcome**, get the better of, control, get control of, master, gain mastery over, get a grip on, deal with, cope with, surmount, rise above, get over; curb, subdue, repress, quell, quash, defeat, vanquish, beat, triumph over, prevail over; *informal* lick.
OPPOSITE yield to.

conqueror ▶ noun *Robert Clive was known as the conqueror of Bengal* **vanquisher**, defeater, subjugator; victor, winner, champion, hero, conquering hero, lord, master; *Spanish* conquistador.
OPPOSITES vanquished; loser.

conquest ▶ noun **1** *the conquest of the Aztecs by the Spanish* **defeat**, beating, conquering, vanquishment, vanquishing, trouncing, annihilation, overpowering, overthrow, subduing, subjugation, rout, mastery, crushing; victory (over), triumph (over); *informal* hammering, clobbering, thrashing, drubbing, caning, murder, massacre.
OPPOSITE victory.
2 *Israel's conquest of the West Bank* **seizure**, seizing, takeover, acquisition, gain, appropriation, subjugation, subjection, capture, occupation, invasion, annexation, overrunning.
OPPOSITE surrender.
3 *the conquest of Everest* **ascent**, climbing, scaling.
4 *he regarded her as someone he could display before his friends as his latest conquest* **catch**, acquisition, captive, prize, slave; admirer, fan, worshipper; lover, love, boyfriend, girlfriend; *informal* fancy man, fancy woman, toy boy, sugar daddy; *literary* swain; *archaic* gallant, paramour, leman.

conscience ▶ noun *her conscience wouldn't allow her to keep silent any longer* **sense of right and wrong**, sense of right, moral sense, still small voice, inner voice, voice within; morals, standards, values, principles, ethics, creed, beliefs; compunction, scruples, qualms.

conscience-stricken ▶ adjective *maybe he is conscience-stricken at having arranged their deaths* **guilt-ridden**, troubled, disturbed, remorseful, ashamed, shamefaced, apologetic, sorry; chastened, contrite, guilty, full of regret, regretful, rueful, repentant, penitent, self-reproachful, abashed, sheepish; *rare* compunctious.
OPPOSITES untroubled, unrepentant.

conscientious ▶ adjective *a conscientious man, he took his duties very seriously* **diligent**, industrious, punctilious, painstaking, sedulous, assiduous, dedicated, careful, meticulous, thorough, attentive, laborious, hard-working, ultra-careful, persevering, unflagging, searching, close, minute, accurate, correct, studious, rigorous, particular; religious, strict.
OPPOSITE casual.

conscious ▶ adjective **1** *the patient was barely conscious* **aware**, **awake**, wide awake, compos mentis, alert, responsive, reactive, feeling, sentient.
OPPOSITE unconscious.
2 *he became conscious of people talking in the hall* **aware of**, alive to, awake to, alert to, sensitive to, cognizant of, mindful of, sensible of; *informal* wise to, in the know about, hip to; *archaic* ware of; *rare* seized of, recognizant of, regardful of.
OPPOSITE unaware.
3 *he made a conscious effort to stop staring* **deliberate**, intentional, intended, done on purpose, purposeful, purposive, willed, knowing, considered, studied, strategic; calculated, wilful, premeditated, planned, pre-planned, preconceived, volitional; aforethought; *Law, dated* prepense.

consciousness ▶ noun **1** *she failed to regain consciousness* **awareness**, wakefulness, alertness, responsiveness, sentience.
OPPOSITE unconsciousness.
2 *her acute consciousness of Luke's presence* **awareness of**, knowledge of the existence of, alertness to, sensitivity to, realization of, cognizance of, mindfulness of, perception of, apprehension of, recognition of.

conscript ▶ verb (stress on the second syllable) *they were conscripted into the army* **call up**, enlist, recruit, mobilize, raise, muster; *US* draft; *historical* press, impress; *archaic* levy.
▶ noun (stress on the first syllable) *an army conscript* impressed man, recruit; *US* draftee, enlisted man.
OPPOSITE volunteer.

consecrate ▶ verb **1** *the Bishop had consecrated two cathedrals in his time* **sanctify**, bless, make holy, make sacred, hallow, set apart, dedicate to God; anoint, ordain, canonize, beatify, lay hands on; *archaic* frock.
OPPOSITE deconsecrate.
2 (*informal*) *the gun room was a male preserve, consecrated to sport* **dedicate**, devote, give (over), set aside, set apart, assign, allot, allocate, reserve, commit, apply, consign, pledge, vow, offer, surrender, sacrifice.

consecutive ▶ adjective *shares prices fell for three consecutive days* **successive**, succeeding, following, in succession, running, in a row, one after the other, back-to-back, continuous, solid, straight, uninterrupted, unbroken; *informal* on the trot.
OPPOSITE separate.

consensus ▶ noun **1** *there was consensus among most delegates* **agreement**, harmony, concord, like-mindedness, concurrence, consent, common consent, accord, unison, unity, unanimity, oneness, solidarity, concert.
OPPOSITE disagreement.
2 *the consensus was that the Government should act now* **general opinion/view**, majority opinion/view, common opinion/view.
OPPOSITE minority view.

consent ▶ noun *a change in the rules requires the consent of all members* **agreement**, assent, concurrence, accord; permission, authorization, sanction, leave, clearance, acquiescence, acceptance, approval, seal of approval, stamp of approval, imprimatur, backing, endorsement, confirmation, support, favour, good wishes; *informal* go-ahead, thumbs up, green light, OK; *formal* approbation.
OPPOSITE dissent.
▶ verb *all the patients consented to surgery* **agree to**, assent to, allow, give permission for, sanction, accept, approve, acquiesce in, go along with, accede to, concede to, yield to, give in to, submit to, comply with, abide by, concur with, conform to.
OPPOSITES dissent; forbid.

> **CHOOSE THE RIGHT WORD**
>
> **consent, permission, authorization, leave**
> *See* PERMISSION.
>
> **consent, agree, assent, acquiesce**
> *See* AGREE.

consequence ▶ noun **1** *inflation is a consequence of a rapid growth in the money supply* **result**, upshot, outcome, out-turn, sequel, effect, reaction, repercussion, reverberations, ramification, end, end result, conclusion, termination, culmination, denouement, corollary, concomitant, aftermath, fruit(s), product, produce, by-product; *Medicine* sequelae; *informal* pay-off; *dated* issue; *archaic* success.
OPPOSITE cause.
2 *the past is of no consequence* **importance**, import, significance, account, moment, momentousness, substance, note, mark, prominence, value, weightiness, weight, concern, interest, gravity, seriousness.

consequent ▶ adjective *this was the best we could do, and we hope that the consequent errors are not too great* **resulting**, resultant, ensuing, consequential; following, subsequent, successive, sequential; attendant, accompanying, concomitant; collateral, associated, related, connected, linked.
OPPOSITES causal; unrelated.

consequential ▶ adjective **1** *the fire can be rapidly controlled and the consequential water and smoke damage reduced* **resulting**, resultant, ensuing, consequent; following, subsequent, successive, sequential; attendant, accompanying, concomitant; collateral, associated, related, connected, linked.
OPPOSITES causal; unrelated.
2 *one of the President's more consequential initiatives* **important**, significant, major, momentous, of moment, weighty, material, meaty, appreciable, memorable, far-reaching, serious; of consequence, of great import, of significance.
OPPOSITES insignificant, minor.

consequently ▶ adverb *many of the subjects available are not taught in school, and consequently may be unfamiliar* **as a result**, as a consequence, in consequence, so, that being so, thus, therefore, accordingly, hence, for this/that reason, because of this/that, on this/that account; inevitably, necessarily; *Latin* ergo.

conservation ▶ noun *the conservation of tropical forests* **preservation**, protection, safeguarding, safe keeping, keeping, guarding, saving, looking after; care, charge, custody, guardianship, husbandry, supervision; upkeep, keeping up, keeping going, keeping alive, maintenance, repair, restoration; ecology, environmentalism.

conservative ▶ adjective **1** *the conservative wing of the party* **right-wing**, reactionary, traditionalist, unprogressive, establishmentarian, blimpish; fundamentalist; (in the UK) Tory; (in the US) Republican; *informal* true blue.
OPPOSITE socialist.
2 *they were held in check by the conservative trade-union movement* **traditionalist**, traditional, conventional, orthodox, stable, old-fashioned, dyed-in-the-wool, unchanging, hidebound; cautious, prudent, careful, safe, timid, unadventurous, unenterprising, set in one's ways; moderate, middle-of-the-road, temperate; *informal* stick in the mud.
OPPOSITE radical.
3 *men should wear a dark conservative suit* **conventional**, sober, quiet, modest, plain, unobtrusive, unostentatious, restrained, reserved, subdued, subtle, low-key, demure; *informal* square, straight.
OPPOSITE ostentatious.
4 *a conservative estimate* **low**, cautious, understated, unexaggerated, moderate, reasonable.
▶ noun *liberals and conservatives are beginning to find common ground on one point* **right-winger**, reactionary, rightist, diehard; (in the UK) Tory; (in the US) Republican.

conservatory ▶ noun **1** *keep plant cuttings in a frost-free conservatory* **greenhouse**, glasshouse, hothouse; **summer house**, gazebo, pavilion, belvedere.
2 *he got a teaching job at the conservatory* **conservatoire**, music school, drama school, academy/institute of music/drama.

conserve ▶ verb *a finite reserve of fossil fuel that should be conserved* **preserve**, protect, maintain, save, safeguard, keep, take care of, care for, look after, sustain, keep intact, prolong, perpetuate; hoard, store up, stockpile, husband, use sparingly, reserve, nurse.
OPPOSITES squander, waste.
▶ noun *cherry conserve* **jam**, preserve, jelly, spread, marmalade, confiture.

consider ▶ verb **1** *Isabel hesitated, considering her choices* **think about**, contemplate, give thought to, reflect on, examine, appraise, review; study, mull over, ponder, deliberate over, cogitate about, chew over, meditate on/over, ruminate over, turn over in one's mind; assess, evaluate, compare, weigh up, judge, consider the pros and cons of, sum up; *informal* size up.
2 *I consider him irresponsible* **regard as**, deem, hold to be, think, think of as, reckon, believe, judge, adjudge, rate, class as, account, count, gauge, look on as, view as, see as, take for, interpret as, suppose, find; esteem.
3 *embarrassed, he considered the ceiling* **look at**, contemplate, observe, regard, survey, view, scrutinize, scan, examine, inspect; *informal* check out, have a gander at, have a squint at, get a load of; *Brit. informal* have a butcher's at, take a dekko at, take a shufti at, clock; *N. Amer. informal* eyeball.
4 *I hope the inquiry will consider all those issues* **take into consideration**, take into account, take account of, make allowances for, respect, bear in mind, be mindful of, have regard to, reckon with, remember, mind, mark, heed, note, not forget, make provision for, take to heart, pay/have regard to, be guided by.
OPPOSITE ignore.

considerable ▶ adjective **1** *he escaped with a considerable amount of money* **sizeable**, substantial, appreciable, significant; goodly, tolerable, fair, reasonable, tidy, hefty, handsome, comfortable, decent, worthwhile, worth having, worth taking into account; ample, plentiful, abundant, superabundant, great, large, lavish, profuse, generous; marked, noticeable; *informal* not to be sneezed at, OK; *literary* plenteous.
OPPOSITE paltry.
2 *he turned professional and met with considerable success* **much**, a lot of, lots of, a great deal of, plenty of, a fair amount of, great.
OPPOSITE minor.
3 *he became a considerable gentleman cricketer* **distinguished**, noteworthy, noted, important, significant, prominent, eminent, influential, illustrious; renowned, celebrated, acclaimed, highly rated, much touted, well thought of, well received, of repute, of high standing, of distinction.
OPPOSITE insignificant.

considerably ▶ adverb *alcoholic drinks vary considerably in strength* **greatly**, much, very much, a great deal, a lot, lots, a fair amount; significantly, substantially, appreciably, markedly, noticeably, materially, signally; *informal* plenty, seriously.
OPPOSITE slightly.

considerate ▶ adjective *we were encouraged to be polite, modest, and considerate towards others* **attentive**, thoughtful, concerned, solicitous, mindful, heedful, obliging, accommodating, helpful, cooperative, patient; kind, kindly, decent, unselfish, compassionate, sympathetic, caring, charitable, altruistic, generous; polite, sensitive, civil, tactful, diplomatic.
OPPOSITE inconsiderate.

consideration ▶ noun **1** *your case needs very careful consideration* **thought**, deliberation, reflection, contemplation, cogitation, rumination, pondering, meditation, musing, mulling, examination, inspection, scrutiny, analysis, review, discussion; attention, heed, notice, regard.
2 *his health has to be the prime consideration* **factor**, issue, point, concern, item, matter, element, detail, aspect, facet, feature, determinant.
3 *it's time for companies to show more consideration for their local communities* **attentiveness**, considerateness, thoughtfulness, concern, care, solicitousness, solicitude, mindfulness; kindness, kindliness, understanding, respect, sensitivity, tact, discretion; unselfishness, compassion, sympathy, charity, generosity, benevolence, friendliness.
OPPOSITES disregard, thoughtlessness.
4 *perhaps, for a consideration, I might be able to arrange something* **payment**, fee, premium, remuneration, compensation, recompense, emolument, perquisite; commission, percentage, share, portion, dividend; *informal* cut, take, whack, slice, slice of the cake, piece of the action.
□ **take into consideration** *the company must take into consideration a number of factors* **consider**, give thought to, take into account, allow for, make allowances for, provide for, plan for, make plans for, foresee, anticipate, make provision for, make preparations for, prepare for, accommodate, make concessions for, arrange for, bargain for, reckon with.
OPPOSITE ignore.

considering ▶ preposition *considering his size he showed an astonishing turn of speed* **bearing in mind**, taking into consideration, taking into account, making allowance(s) for, giving consideration to, keeping in mind, in view of, in the light of.
OPPOSITES apart from, ignoring.
▶ adverb (*informal*) *he'd been lucky, considering* **all things considered**, considering everything, all in all, on the whole, taking everything into consideration/account, at the end of the day, when all's said and done.

consign ▶ verb **1** *he was consigned to a debtor's prison* **send**, deliver, hand over, give over, turn over, sentence; **confine in**, imprison in, incarcerate in, lock up in, jail in, detain in, intern in, immure in; *informal* put away, put behind bars; *Brit. informal* bang up.
2 *the picture was consigned for sale at one of Sotheby's European offices* **assign**, allocate, place, put, entrust, grant, remit, hand down, bequeath; *archaic* commend.
3 *the package was consigned by a company that flies products all over the world* **send**, send off, dispatch, transmit, transfer, convey, post, mail, ship.
4 *I had a clear-out and consigned her picture to the bin* **deposit**, commit, put away, banish, relegate.

consignment ▶ noun *a consignment of goods* **delivery**, shipment, load, containerload, shipload, boatload, lorryload, truckload, cargo; batch, lot, haul, goods.

consist ▶ verb **1** *the exhibition consists of 180 drawings* **be composed**, be made up, be formed; comprise, contain, include, incorporate, embody, involve, embrace.
2 *style consists in the choices that writers make in communicating their thoughts* **exist**, subsist, inhere, be inherent, lie, reside, have its existence/being, be present, be contained; be expressed by, have as its main feature.

consistency ▶ noun **1** *the downward trend in consumption shows a remarkable degree of consistency* **evenness**, steadiness, stability, constancy, regularity, uniformity, equilibrium, unity, orderliness, lack of change, lack of deviation; dependability, reliability.
OPPOSITE inconsistency.
2 *you need a jug of rich cream of pouring consistency* **thickness**, density, firmness, solidity, viscosity, cohesion, heaviness, degree of thickness, degree of density; **texture**.

consistent ▶ adjective **1** *there was consistent opinion-poll evidence that the ALP was likely to lose the next election* **steady**, stable, constant, regular, even, uniform, orderly, unchanging, unvarying, unswerving, undeviating, unwavering, unfluctuating, homogeneous, true to type; dependable, reliable, unfailing, predictable.
OPPOSITES inconsistent, irregular.
2 *her injuries were consistent with an attack with a blunt instrument* **compatible**, congruous, agreeing, accordant, consonant, in harmony, harmonious, in tune, in line, reconcilable, of a piece; corresponding to, conforming to.
OPPOSITES inconsistent, incompatible.

consolation ▶ noun *I murmured some words of consolation* **comfort**, solace; sympathy, compassion, pity, commiseration, fellow feeling; relief, help, aid, support, moral support, cheer, encouragement, reassurance, fortification; soothing, easement, succour, assuagement, alleviation.

console[1] (stress on the second syllable) ▶ verb *his friends tried to console him, but he couldn't help thinking about the money* **comfort**, solace, condole with, give condolences to; sympathize with, express sympathy to, show compassion to, pity, commiserate with, show fellow feeling to; help, aid, support, cheer (up), gladden, hearten, encourage, reassure, fortify; soothe, ease, succour, assuage, alleviate.
OPPOSITES distress, upset.

console[2] (stress on the first syllable) ▶ noun *he bent over the console, pushing buttons at random* **control panel**, instrument panel, dashboard, keyboard, keypad; cabinet; *informal* dash.

consolidate ▶ verb **1** *we have been able to consolidate our position in the market* **strengthen**, make stronger, make secure, secure, make stable,

C

stabilize, reinforce, fortify, tighten, harden, stiffen, cement, enhance.
2 *you must consolidate the results of the audit into an action plan* **combine**, unite, merge, integrate, amalgamate, fuse, blend, mingle, marry, synthesize, bring together; join, affiliate, federate, unify.

consonance ▶ noun *a constitution in consonance with the customs of the people* **agreement**, concord, accord, accordance, harmony, unison, conformity; compatibility, congruity, congruence.

consonant ▶ adjective
□ **consonant with** *these findings are consonant with recent research* **in agreement with**, agreeing with, consistent with, in accordance with, accordant with, consilient with, in harmony with, compatible with, congruous with, in tune with, reconcilable with.
OPPOSITE incompatible with.

consort ▶ noun (stress on the first syllable) *Queen Victoria and her consort, Prince Albert* **partner**, companion, mate, helpmate, helpmeet; spouse, husband, wife.
▶ verb (stress on the second syllable) **1** *my husband never consorted with other women* **associate**, keep company, mix, mingle, go around, spend time, socialize, fraternize, have dealings, rub shoulders; *N. Amer.* rub elbows; *informal* hobnob, run around, hang around/round, hang out, knock about/around, pal around, chum around, be thick; *Brit. informal* hang about.
2 (*archaic*) *it did not consort with his idea of scientific government* **be consistent**, be compatible, accord, be in accord, agree, be consonant, be congruous, go, be in harmony, be in tune.
OPPOSITE contrast.

conspectus ▶ noun (*rare*) *a conspectus of Roman history* **summary**, overview, review, outline, precis, résumé, digest, abstract, summation, summing-up, rundown, round-up, synopsis.

conspicuous ▶ adjective *lots of birds have highly conspicuous plumage | he showed conspicuous bravery* **easily seen**, clear, visible, clearly visible, standing out, noticeable, observable, discernible, perceptible, perceivable, detectable; **obvious**, manifest, evident, apparent, marked, pronounced, prominent, outstanding, patent, crystal clear, as clear as crystal; vivid, striking, dramatic, eye-catching, flagrant, ostentatious, overt, blatant, as plain as a pikestaff, staring one in the face, writ large, as plain as day; distinct, recognizable, distinguishable, unmistakable, inescapable; *informal* as plain as the nose on one's face, standing/sticking out like a sore thumb, standing/sticking out a mile.
OPPOSITE inconspicuous.

conspiracy ▶ noun **1** *the company was involved in a conspiracy with bookmakers to manipulate starting prices* **plot**, scheme, stratagem, plan, machination, cabal; deception, ploy, trick, ruse, dodge, subterfuge, sharp practice; *informal* frame-up, fit-up, racket, put-up job; *rare* complot, covin.
2 *he was due to stand trial for conspiracy to murder* **plotting**, collusion, intrigue, connivance, machination, collaboration; treason.

conspirator ▶ noun *conspirators had planned to seize the state* **conspirer**, **plotter**, schemer, intriguer, colluder, collaborator, conniver, machinator, confederate, cabalist; traitor.

conspire ▶ verb **1** *all six admitted conspiring to steal cars | they were accused of conspiring against the king* **plot**, hatch a plot, form a conspiracy, scheme, plan, lay plans, intrigue, collude, connive, collaborate, consort, machinate, manoeuvre, be/work hand in glove; abet, be an accessory; *informal* be in cahoots; *rare* cabal.
2 *circumstances have conspired to make an immediate share issue an unattractive option* **act together**, work together, combine, join, unite, ally, join forces, cooperate; *informal* gang up; *rare* coact.

constancy ▶ noun **1** *a familiar meditation on the theme of constancy and inconstancy between lovers* **fidelity**, faithfulness, loyalty, trueness, commitment, dedication, devotion; dependability, reliability, trustworthiness.
OPPOSITE fickleness.
2 *there was no doubt about the determination and constancy of Henry VIII* **steadfastness**, resolution, resoluteness, resolve, firmness, fixedness, steadiness; determination, perseverance, tenacity, doggedness, staunchness, dedication, commitment, application, staying power, obstinacy.
OPPOSITE indecision.
3 *this anecdote reminds us of a certain constancy of human motive* **consistency**, permanence, persistence; durability, endurance; uniformity, invariableness, unchangingness, immutability, regularity, evenness, stability, steadiness, lack of change, lack of deviation.
OPPOSITE unpredictableness.

constant ▶ adjective **1** *the constant background noise of the city* **continual**, continuous, persistent, sustained, abiding, round-the-clock; ceaseless, unceasing, perpetual, incessant, never-ending, everlasting, eternal, endless, unending, unabating, non-stop, perennial, unbroken, uninterrupted, unrelieved; interminable, unremitting, relentless, unrelenting, without respite; *literary* sempiternal.
OPPOSITES inconstant, fitful.
2 *the disc revolves at a constant speed* **consistent**, regular, stable, steady, fixed, uniform, even, level, invariable, unvarying, unchanging, changeless, undeviating, unfluctuating, immutable.
OPPOSITES inconstant, variable.
3 *a constant friend* **faithful**, loyal, devoted, true, fast, firm, unswerving, unwavering; steadfast, staunch, stalwart, dependable, trustworthy, trusty, reliable, dedicated, committed; bosom, boon.
OPPOSITES inconstant, fickle.
4 *there is a need for constant vigilance* **steadfast**, steady, resolute, determined, persevering, tenacious, dogged, unwavering, unflagging, unshaken.
▶ noun *dread of cancer has been a constant during the last 100 years* **unchanging factor**, unchanging state of affairs, unchanging situation, given.

CHOOSE THE RIGHT WORD

constant, continual, continuous, ceaseless
See CONTINUAL.

constant, faithful, loyal, true
See FAITHFUL.

constantly ▶ adverb *the English language is constantly in flux* **always**, all the time, the entire time, continually, continuously, persistently, repeatedly, regularly; round the clock, without a break, night and day, day and night, {morning, noon, and night}; endlessly, non-stop, incessantly, unceasingly, ceaselessly, perpetually, eternally, perennially, forever; interminably, unremittingly, relentlessly, unrelentingly; *Scottish* aye; *informal* 24-7; *literary* sempiternally.
OPPOSITES occasionally, sometimes.

consternation ▶ noun *much to the consternation of his detractors, he emerged as a management guru* **dismay**, perturbation, anxiety, distress, disquiet, disquietude, discomposure, angst, trepidation; surprise, amazement, astonishment, stupefaction; alarm, panic, hysteria, fear, fearfulness, fright, shock.
OPPOSITE satisfaction.

constituent ▶ adjective *they are independent but constituent parts of their universities* **component**, integral; elemental, basic, essential, inherent; *rare* integrant.
▶ noun **1** *MPs have a duty to listen to the concerns of their constituents* **voter**, elector, member of the electorate, member of a constituency.
2 *the harmful constituents of tobacco smoke* **component**, component part, ingredient, element; part, piece, bit, integral part, unit, module, fragment, section, segment, portion; *rare* integrant.

constitute ▶ verb **1** *farmers constituted 10 per cent of the population* **amount to**, add up to, account for, form, make up, compose, comprise, represent.
2 *an extract from a book used for the purpose of comment does not constitute a breach of copyright* **be equivalent to**, be the equivalent of, be, embody, be tantamount to, be regarded as, act as, serve as.
3 *the superior courts were constituted in 1875* **inaugurate**, initiate, establish, found, create, set up, start, begin, originate, form, organize, develop, shape; authorize, commission, charter, induct, invest, appoint, name, nominate, install, empower, ordain, decree.

constitution ▶ noun **1** *the constitution guarantees freedom of expression* **charter**, social code, canon, body of law, system of laws/rules; bill of rights; laws, rules, regulations, fundamental principles; *informal* regs.
2 *the chemical constitution of the dye* **composition**, make-up, structure, organization, construction, arrangement, configuration, framework, form, formation, anatomy, shape, design; *informal* set-up.
3 *a woman with the constitution of an ox* **health**, **physique**, state of health, physical condition, physical strength, shape, fettle.

constitutional ▶ adjective **1** *the Amir's constitutional powers* **legal**, lawful, legitimate, licit, authorized, permitted, permissible; sanctioned, ratified, codified, warranted, constituted, statutory, chartered, vested, official; in accordance with the constitution, within the law, by law.
OPPOSITE unconstitutional.
2 *a constitutional weakness* **inherent**, inbred, intrinsic, innate, structural, fundamental, essential; congenital, organic, inborn, ingrained, deep-rooted, built-in.
OPPOSITE cosmetic.
▶ noun *she went out for a constitutional* **walk**, stroll, saunter, turn, wander, amble, breather, airing, ramble, hike; promenade; *N. Amer.* paseo; *Italian* passegiata; *informal* mosey, tootle; *Brit. informal* pootle; *rare* perambulation.

constrain ▶ verb **1** *Ernie felt constrained to explain further* **compel**, force, coerce, drive, impel, oblige, prevail on, require; press, push, pressure, pressurize, urge, bully, dragoon, browbeat; *informal* railroad, bulldoze, steamroller, hustle, twist someone's arm, strong-arm, lean on, out the screws on.
2 *prices were constrained by continuing state controls* **restrict**, limit, curb, check, restrain, regulate, contain, hold back, keep down.
3 *only by acting on the systems which constrain them can women hope to free themselves* **confine**, restrain, restrict, impede, hamstring, baulk, frustrate, stifle, hinder, hamper, check, retard, cramp, rein in; shut in, hem in,

fence in, close in, coop up, chain, lock up, imprison, incarcerate, intern; *literary* trammel.

constrained ▶ adjective *he was acting in an oddly constrained manner* **unnatural**, awkward, self-conscious, mannered, artificial, wooden, stilted, strained, forced, contrived, laboured; inhibited, repressed, uneasy, embarrassed, tongue-tied; restrained, reserved, reticent, guarded, distant, aloof, cold, cool, stand-offish.
OPPOSITE relaxed.

constraint ▶ noun **1** *the availability of water is the main constraint on food production* **restriction**, limitation, curb, check, restraint, control, curtailment, damper, rein; hindrance, impediment, hampering, obstruction, handicap.
2 *on Saturday they would be able to get together, relax, and talk without constraint* **inhibition**, uneasiness, embarrassment; restraint, reservedness, reticence, guardedness, formality, stand-offishness; self-consciousness, awkwardness, forcedness, unnaturalness, woodenness, stiltedness.
OPPOSITE openness.

constrict ▶ verb **1** *fat constricts the blood vessels | Caroline felt her throat constrict* **narrow**, make/become narrower, tighten, compress, contract, make/become smaller, shrink, draw in; squeeze, choke, strangle, strangulate; *archaic* straiten.
OPPOSITES expand, dilate.
2 *scale build-up on shower heads constricts water flow* **impede**, restrict, inhibit, obstruct, limit, interfere with, hinder, hamper, check, curb.
OPPOSITE assist.

constriction ▶ noun *there was a constriction in her throat* **tightening**, narrowing, shrinking, squeezing; tightness, pressure, compression, contraction, cramp; obstruction, blockage, impediment, congestion; choking, strangulation; *Medicine* stricture, stenosis; *archaic* straitening.

construct ▶ verb **1** *the government has plans to construct a hydroelectric dam there* **build**, erect, put up, set up, raise, establish, assemble, manufacture, fabricate, form, fashion, contrive, create, make.
OPPOSITE demolish.
2 *his work aimed to construct a science of public law entirely on empirical foundation* **formulate**, form, put together; create, devise, design, invent, compose, concoct, contrive, work out, hatch; fashion, mould, model, shape, frame; forge, engineer, fabricate, manufacture, hammer out, thrash out.

construction ▶ noun **1** *the construction of a new airport* **building**, erection, putting up, setting up, raising, establishment, assembly, manufacture, fabrication, forming, fashioning, contriving, creation, making.
2 *the central waterway was a spectacular construction* **structure**, building, edifice, assembly, pile, framework.
3 *many candidates have little idea of the basics of sentence construction* **composition**, formation, structure, organization.
4 *I might have known you'd put such a sordid construction on it all* **interpretation**, reading, meaning, explanation, inference, explication, construal, analysis, version, understanding, view, impression; *informal* take.

constructive ▶ adjective *he described the talks as fruitful and constructive* **positive**, **useful**, of use, helpful, encouraging; productive, practical, valuable, profitable, worthwhile, effective, beneficial, advantageous.
OPPOSITES destructive, negative.

construe ▶ verb *his actions could be construed as an admission of guilt* **interpret**, understand, read, see, take, take to mean, parse, render, analyse, explain, elucidate, gloss, decode.

consul ▶ noun *the British consul in Israel* **ambassador**, diplomat, chargé d'affaires, attaché, envoy, emissary, plenipotentiary, consul general; *archaic* legate.

consult ▶ verb **1** *if you consult a solicitor, making a will is a simple procedure* **ask**, seek advice/information from, take counsel from, call on/upon/in, turn to, have recourse to; *informal* pick someone's brains.
2 *there is a growing pressure on managers to consult with employees* **confer**, discuss, talk, talk things over, have a talk, exchange views, have discussions, converse, communicate, parley; deliberate, debate, negotiate; *informal* chew the fat, powwow, have a confab, talk turkey, palaver, put their heads together; *formal* confabulate.
3 *she consulted a large desk diary* **refer to**, turn to, look something up in.
4 *she needed to consult her feelings before acting* **consider**, take into consideration/account, have regard to, respect, have an eye to.

consultant ▶ noun **1** *an education and training consultant* **adviser**, guide, counsellor; **expert**, specialist, authority, pundit; *informal* ace, whizz, wizard, hotshot; *N. Amer. informal* maven.
2 *he's a consultant at the Queen Elizabeth hospital* **senior doctor**, specialist.

consultation ▶ noun **1** *the recommendations include increased consultation with local people* **discussion**, dialogue, discourse, debate, negotiation, conference, deliberation.
2 *if it is a matter of urgency a consultation can be arranged quickly* **meeting**, talk, discussion, interview, conference, audience, hearing, reception, forum; chat, tête-à-tête, parley, heart-to-heart, one-to-one, colloquy; appointment, session, engagement; *informal* powwow, confab; *formal* confabulation.

consume ▶ verb **1** *great plates of cakes were consumed with gusto | he had consumed nine pints of beer* **eat**, eat up, devour, ingest, swallow, gobble, gobble up, wolf down, gorge oneself on, feast on; munch, snack on; **drink**, drink up, guzzle, gulp (down), swill, imbibe, take, sup, sip, lap; *informal* tuck into, scoff (down), put away, stuff down, polish off, dispose of, cram in, stuff one's face with, pig oneself on, graze on, down, neck, sink, kill, get one's laughing gear round; *Brit. informal* gollop, shift; *N. Amer. informal* scarf (down/up), snarf (down/up); *formal* manducate; *rare* ingurgitate.
2 *these factories consumed 600,000 tons of coal a day* **use**, use up, utilize, expend; deplete, exhaust; waste, squander, go through, drain, dissipate, fritter away, swallow up.
3 *the fire consumed fifty houses in four hours* **destroy**, demolish, lay waste, wipe out, annihilate, devastate; raze, gut, ravage, ruin, wreck.
4 *Carolyn was consumed with guilt* **absorb**, preoccupy, engross; eat up, devour, obsess, grip, overwhelm, monopolize, enthral, dominate.

consumer ▶ noun *at the moment the consumer is not prepared to pay higher prices for organically farmed food* **purchaser**, buyer, customer, shopper; user, end-user; client, patron; (**the consumer** or **consumers**) the public, the market, the clientele.

consuming ▶ adjective *his lifetime's consuming interest* **absorbing**, compelling, preoccupying, engrossing, all-consuming, compulsive, besetting; devouring, obsessive, gripping, overwhelming, enthralling, dominating; intense, ardent, strong, powerful, burning, raging, fervid, profound, deep-seated.

consummate ▶ verb *they consummated the deal aboard his yacht* **complete**, conclude, finish, accomplish, achieve; execute, carry out, discharge, perform, put into effect; put the finishing touch to, perfect, crown, cap, set the seal on; *rare* effectuate.
▶ adjective *he conducted his strategy with consummate skill* **perfect**, **exemplary**, supreme, ultimate, faultless, quintessential; superb, superior, accomplished, expert, proficient, skilful, skilled, masterly, master, superlative, first-class; talented, gifted, polished, well versed, well trained, practised; complete, total, utter, absolute, pure, solid, sheer.

consummation ▶ noun *the consummation of a takeover bid* **completion**, accomplishment, achievement, attainment; execution, carrying out, discharge, performance; conclusion, realization, resolution, finalization, finishing, ending, fulfilment, effectuation, fruition, success; crowning, capping, perfecting, perfection.

consumption ▶ noun **1** *the fish were declared unfit for human consumption* **eating**, devouring, ingestion, swallowing, gobbling (up); drinking, imbibing; *formal* manducation.
2 *the consumption of fossil fuels* **using up**, use, utilization, expending, expenditure; depletion, exhaustion; waste, wasting, squander, squandering, draining, dissipation, dissipating.
3 (*archaic*) *his mother had died of consumption* **tuberculosis**, pulmonary tuberculosis, TB, wasting disease, emaciation; *archaic* phthisis.

contact ▶ noun **1** *the disease can be transmitted through direct contact with rats* **touch**, touching; proximity, exposure, contiguity, junction, union, tangency; association, connection, communication, intercourse, relations, dealings; *archaic* traffic.
2 *she was still in contact with her friends* **communication**, connection, correspondence, touch, association.
3 *he had many contacts in Germany* **connection**, acquaintance, associate, liaison, friend.
▶ verb *anyone with any information should contact the police* **get in touch with**, communicate with, make contact with, approach, reach, notify, be in communication with; phone, call, ring up, speak to, talk to, write to; *Brit.* get on to; *informal* get hold of, drop a line to.

contagion ▶ noun *overcrowded and insanitary ships were a breeding ground for every kind of contagion* **contamination**, infection, disease, illness, infirmity, pestilence, plague, blight; *informal* bug, virus.

contagious ▶ adjective *a contagious disease* **infectious**, communicable, transmittable, transmissible, transferable, spreadable; *informal* catching; *technical* epidemic, pandemic, epizootic; *dated* infective.

contain ▶ verb **1** *government often contained men from both sides of the party divide* **include**, comprise, take in, incorporate, involve, encompass, embrace, embody; consist of, be made up, be composed of.
2 *the boat contained four people* **hold**, have room/space/seating/capacity for, carry, accommodate, seat.
3 *he must contain his hatred* **restrain**, curb, rein in, suppress, repress, stifle, subdue, quell, limit, swallow, bottle up, keep under control, keep back, hold in, keep in check; control, master, gain control over, gain mastery over.

container ▶ noun *an airtight container* **receptacle**, vessel, holder, repository, canister, drum, box,case.

contaminate ▶ verb *the water supply was contaminated with manure* **pollute**, adulterate; make impure, defile, debase, corrupt, taint,infect, blight, foul, spoil, soil, mar, impair, stain, befoul, sully, tarnish, poision;

radioactive; *formal* vitiate.
OPPOSITE purify.

contemn ▶ noun (*archaic*) *would he contemn her for forwardness?* **demise**, scorn, treat with contempt, feel contempt for, look down on, disdain, slight, undervalue, disregard, deride, scoff/jeer at, mock, revile, spurn.
OPPOSITE value.

C

contemplate ▶ verb **1** *she contemplated her body in the mirror* **look at**, view, regard, examine, inspect, observe, survey, study, scrutinize, scan, stare at, gaze at, eye, take a good look at; *literary* behold.
2 *she couldn't even contemplate the future* **think about**, meditate on/over, consider, ponder, reflect on/about, mull over, muse on, dwell on, deliberate over, cogitate on/about, ruminate on/about, chew over, brood on/about, puzzle over, turn over in one's mind, weigh up.
3 *she contemplated walking out* **consider**, think about, give thought to; have in mind/view, envisage, aim at, foresee, imagine, visualize; intend, propose, mean to, expect to.

contemplation ▶ noun **1** *the contemplation of beautiful objects* **viewing**, regarding, examination, inspection, observation, survey, study, scrutiny, scanning, staring at, gazing at, eyeing.
2 *the monks sat in quiet contemplation* **thought**, meditation, consideration, pondering, reflection, thinking, musing, rumination, deliberation, cogitation, reverie, concentration, introspection; *informal* brown study; *formal* cerebration.

contemplative ▶ adjective *a peaceful, contemplative mood* **thoughtful**, pensive, reflective, meditative, musing, ruminative, introspective, brooding, intent, rapt, preoccupied, studious, deep/lost in thought; dreamy, daydreaming, with one's head in the clouds; *informal* in a brown study.
OPPOSITE active.

contemporary ▶ adjective **1** *contemporary writing says that the city's walls were formidable* **contemporaneous**, concurrent, coeval, synchronous, synchronic, of the time, of the day, simultaneous; coexisting, coexistent; *rare* coetaneous.
2 *crime and violence in contemporary society* **modern**, present-day, present, current, present-time, immediate, extant; up to date, up to the minute, fashionable, latest, recent, ultra-modern, newfangled, modish, voguish, in vogue; *French* à la mode; *informal* bang up to date, with it.
OPPOSITES old-fashioned, out of date.
▶ noun *the contemporaries of Chaucer* **peer**, fellow; *rare* compeer, coeval.

contempt ▶ noun **1** *she was showing little but contempt for him* **scorn**, disdain, disrespect, deprecation, disparagement, denigration, opprobrium, odium, obloquy, scornfulness; derision, mockery, ridicule; disgust, loathing, detestation, abhorrence, hatred; *archaic* contumely.
OPPOSITE respect.
2 *he is guilty of contempt of court* **disrespect**, disregard, slighting, neglect; *Law* contumacy.
OPPOSITE respect.

contemptible ▶ adjective *that jibe about Alison was mean and contemptible* **despicable**, detestable, hateful, reprehensible, deplorable, loathsome, odious, revolting, execrable, unspeakable, heinous, shocking, offensive; disgraceful, shameful, ignominious, abject, low, mean, cowardly, unworthy, discreditable, pitiful, pitiable, petty, worthless, shabby, cheap, beyond contempt, beyond the pale, sordid, degenerate, base, vile, villainous; *archaic* scurvy.
OPPOSITE admirable.

contemptuous ▶ adjective *he spoke in a coldly contemptuous tone* **scornful**, disdainful, disrespectful, insulting, insolent, full of contempt; derisory, derisive, mocking, sneering, jeering, scoffing, taunting, withering, scathing, snide; condescending, supercilious, arrogant, cavalier, high and mighty, imperious, proud, vain; *informal* sniffy, snotty, on one's high horse; *archaic* contumelious.
OPPOSITE respectful.

contend ▶ verb **1** *none of the groups contending for power is strong enough yet* **compete**, challenge, vie, contest; strive, struggle, tussle, grapple, wrestle, scuffle, squabble, skirmish, battle, combat, fight, war, wage war, join battle, cross swords, lock horns, go head to head; oppose, clash.
2 *the plaintiffs contended that their business plan was confidential* **assert**, maintain, hold, claim, argue, profess, affirm, aver, avow, insist, state, declare, pronounce, allege, plead.
□ **contend with** *the peasants had to contend with lack of food and primitive living conditions* **cope with**, face, grapple with, deal with, take on, pit oneself against; resist, withstand.

content[1] (stress on the second syllable) ▶ adjective *she seemed content with her lot in life* **contented**, satisfied, pleased; gratified, fulfilled; happy, cheerful, cheery, glad, delighted; tranquil, unworried, untroubled, at ease, at peace, comfortable, serene, placid, complacent.
OPPOSITES discontented, dissatisfied.
▶ verb *her reply seemed to content him* **soothe**, pacify, placate, appease, please, mollify, make happy, satisfy, still, quieten, silence.
□ **content oneself** *too confused to argue, she contented herself with a nod* **be content**, be satisfied, satisfy oneself; be fulfilled, be gratified, be pleased, be happy, be glad.
▶ noun *she stood for a moment looking with content at her husband. See* CONTENTMENT.

content[2] (stress on the first syllable) ▶ noun **1** *many restaurant meals are low in fibre content* **amount**, **proportion**, quantity, bulk, total, quota; *rare* quantum.
2 *just as the novel's form is radical, so too is its content* **subject matter**, subject, theme, burden, gist, argument, thesis, message, point, thrust, substance, matter, material, text, ideas.
OPPOSITE style.
3 (**contents**) *she went to examine the contents of the hamper* **things inside**, content, load; *informal* guts, innards.
4 (**contents**) *the book's list of contents | he picked up the letter and scanned its contents* **chapters**, sections, divisions; **subject matter**, subjects, themes, matter, substance, material, text; index; constituents, components, ingredients, elements, items.

contented ▶ adjective *he was contented with his job on the newspaper. See* CONTENT[1].

contention ▶ noun **1** *there were a number of points of contention between the Crown and Parliament* **disagreement**, dispute, disputation, argument, variance; discord, hostility, conflict, friction, acrimony, enmity, strife, dissension, disharmony, quarrelling, feuding.
OPPOSITE agreement.
2 *her contention is that this event was the result of a conspiracy* **argument**, claim, plea, submission, allegation; opinion, stand, position, view, belief, thesis, hypothesis, case, postulation; declaration, assertion, affirmation, pronouncement, announcement, statement.
□ **in contention** *he is in contention for a first-team place* **in competition**, competing, contesting, contending, challenging, vying; striving, struggling, tussling, grappling, battling, fighting, warring.

contentious ▶ adjective **1** *the contentious issue of abortion* **controversial**, disputable, debatable, disputed, contended, open to question/debate, moot, vexed; ambivalent, equivocal, unsure, uncertain, unresolved, undecided, unsettled, borderline; *rare* controvertible.
2 *a contentious debate* **heated**, vehement, fierce, violent, intense, impassioned, committed.
3 *contentious people. See* QUARRELSOME.

contentment ▶ noun *he found contentment in living a basic life* **contentedness**, content, satisfaction, fulfilment; happiness, pleasure, cheerfulness, gladness, gratification; ease, comfort, restfulness, well-being, peace, equanimity, serenity, tranquillity, placidity, placidness, repletion, complacency; *archaic* self-content.

contest ▶ noun (stress on the first syllable) **1** *a boxing contest* **competition**, match, tournament, game, meet; event, trial, bout, heat, fixture, tie, race.
2 *a leadership contest* **struggle**, conflict, confrontation, collision, clash, battle, fight, combat, tussle, skirmish, duel, race.
▶ verb (stress on the second syllable) **1** *he made known his intention to contest the seat* **compete for**, contend for, vie for, challenge for, fight for, fight over, battle for, struggle for, tussle for; try to win, try for, go for, throw one's hat in the ring.
2 *the elections were contested by fifteen parties* **compete in**, contend in, fight in, battle in, enter, take part in, be a competitor in, participate in, put one's name down for, go in for.
3 *we contested the decision vigorously* **oppose**, object to, challenge, dispute, take a stand against, resist, defy, strive/struggle against, take issue with; question, call into question, doubt; litigate.
OPPOSITE agree with.
4 *those conclusions which are not based on published research need to be contested* **debate**, argue about, dispute, quarrel over.

contestant ▶ noun **competitor**, participant, player, contender, candidate, aspirant, entrant; rival, opponent, adversary, antagonist.

context ▶ noun **1** *the historical context out of which the novel arose* **circumstances**, conditions, surroundings, factors, state of affairs; situation, environment, milieu, setting, background, backdrop, scene; climate, atmosphere, ambience, mood, feel.
2 *the quote taken out of context trivializes a dreadful crime* **frame of reference**, contextual relationship; text, subject, theme, topic.

contiguous ▶ adjective *the contiguous states of New Mexico, Arizona, Texas, and California* **adjacent**, neighbouring, adjoining, bordering, next-door; abutting, joining, connecting, meeting, touching, in contact, proximate; near, nearby, close; *rare* conterminous, vicinal.
OPPOSITE distant.

continent[1] ▶ noun *the continent of Europe* **mainland**.
OPPOSITE island.

continent[2] ▶ adjective (*rare*) *sexually continent* **self-restrained**, self-disciplined, abstemious, abstinent, self-denying, ascetic; **chaste**, celibate, monkish, monastic, virtuous, virgin, virginal, pure.
OPPOSITE intemperate.

contingency ▶ noun *a detailed contract which attempts to provide for all*

possible contingencies **eventuality**, (chance) event, incident, happening, occurrence, juncture, possibility, accident, chance, emergency; uncertainty; *rare* fortuity.

contingent ▶ adjective **1** *resolution of the conflict was* **contingent** *on the signing of a ceasefire* **dependent**, conditional; subject to, based on, determined by, hingeing on, resting on, hanging on, controlled by.
2 *contingent events* **chance**, accidental, fortuitous, possible, unforeseen, unforeseeable, unexpected, unpredicted, unpredictable, unanticipated, unlooked-for; random, haphazard.
OPPOSITE predictable.
▶ noun *a contingent of Japanese businessmen | a contingent of 2,000 marines* **group**, party, body, band, set; deputation, delegation, mission; detachment, unit, division, squadron, section, company, corps, cohort; *informal* bunch, gang.

continual ▶ adjective **1** *the service has been disrupted by continual breakdowns* **repeated**, **frequent**, recurrent, recurring, oft repeated, regular; constant, persistent, non-stop; *informal* more … than one can shake a stick at.
OPPOSITES occasional, sporadic.
2 *his son was a continual source of delight to him | she was in continual pain* **constant**, continuous, endless, unending, never-ending, perpetual, perennial, eternal, everlasting; **ceaseless**, incessant, unceasing, sustained, ongoing, uninterrupted, unbroken, round-the-clock, unremitting, unabating, relentless, unrelenting, unrelieved, chronic, interminable.
OPPOSITES temporary, momentary.

CHOOSE THE RIGHT WORD

continual, continuous, constant, ceaseless

These words describe processes or situations which do not stop, but with different emphases.

- **Continual** mainly describes an event that happens repeatedly, on successive occasions (*I regret that we hear continual criticisms of the committee*). However, it can also be used of a process or situation that never actually stops (*he was in continual pain*).
- **Continuous** predominantly describes a non-stop process or situation (*fighting was continuous, both night and day*), but it can also refer to a series of occasions (*the bus service has been interrupted by continuous breakdowns*). It can also describe a physically unbroken object or line (*each farm was separated from its neighbour by a continuous stone wall*).
- **Constant** describes not only something that does not stop (*a welcome relief from the constant travelling*), but also something that does not vary over time (*it is preferable to store samples at a controlled constant temperature*).
- **Ceaseless** is a more literary word describing, typically, something bad that does not stop (*the fort had been subjected to ceaseless bombardment*).
- All these words are used almost interchangeably when it is difficult or unnecessary to say whether something does, technically, happen repeatedly or without stopping at all, as with a *process*, *supply*, or *flow*, or with *change*, *need*, *improvement*, *growth*, or *use*.

continually ▶ adverb **1** *security measures are continually updated and improved* **frequently**, regularly, repeatedly, recurrently, again and again, time and (time) again; constantly.
OPPOSITES occasionally, sporadically.
2 *patients were continually monitored* **constantly**, continuously, round the clock, day and night, night and day, {morning, noon, and night}, without a break, non-stop; all the time, the entire time, always, forever, at every turn, incessantly, ceaselessly, endlessly, perpetually, eternally; *N. Amer. informal* 24-7.

continuance ▶ noun **1** *the continuance of the negotiations* **continuation**, carrying on, prolongation, protraction. *See also* CONTINUATION.
2 *the trademarks shall be used only during the continuance of this agreement* **duration**, period, term.

continuation ▶ noun **1** *the continuation of discussions | the continuation of old traditions* **carrying on**, continuance, prolongation, protraction; maintenance, preservation, keeping up, perpetuation.
OPPOSITES end, cessation.
2 *he was avoiding any prospect of the continuation of the conversation begun that morning* **resumption**, reopening, restart, renewal; *formal* recommencement.
3 *once a separate village, it is now a continuation of the suburbs* **extension**, addition.

continue ▶ verb **1** *the government* **continued with** *its plans to reorganize the country's economy* **carry on with**, go on with, keep on with, proceed with, pursue; **persist in/with**, press on with, persevere in/with, keep up, keep at, push on with, not stop, not give up, stay with; *informal* stick with/at, soldier on with, stick to one's guns.
OPPOSITES stop, discontinue, abandon.
2 *discussions continued throughout the year* **go on**, carry on, extend, run on, drag on; keep up, hold, prevail, subsist.
OPPOSITES stop, cease.
3 *both are keen to continue their business relationship* **maintain**, keep up, sustain, keep going, keep alive, preserve, prolong, extend, protract, perpetuate; retain.
OPPOSITES break off, suspend.
4 *their friendship continued for many years* **last**, endure, go on, be prolonged, live on, survive; abide.
5 *they have indicated their willingness to continue in office* **remain**, stay, carry on, keep going.
6 *we can continue our conversation after supper* **resume**, pick up, take up, carry on with, return to, start/begin again; pick up the threads, pick up where one left off; *formal* recommence.
OPPOSITE end.

continuing ▶ adjective *a background of continuing civil war* **ongoing**, continuous, sustained, persistent, steady, relentless, uninterrupted, unabating, unremitting, unrelieved, unrelenting, unceasing.
OPPOSITE sporadic.

continuity ▶ noun **1** *a breakdown in the continuity of care* **continuousness**, uninterruptedness, flow, progression.
OPPOSITE discontinuity.
2 *the thematic continuity of the texts* **interrelationship**, interrelatedness, intertextuality, interconnectedness, connection, linkage, cohesion, coherence; unity, whole, wholeness.

continuous ▶ adjective *for the past few days there had been continuous rain* **continual**, uninterrupted, unbroken, constant, ceaseless, incessant, steady, sustained, solid, continuing, ongoing, unceasing, without a break, permanent, non-stop, round-the-clock, persistent, unremitting, relentless, unrelenting, unabating, unrelieved, without respite, endless, unending, never-ending, perpetual, without end, everlasting, eternal, interminable; consecutive, running; *informal* with no let-up; *archaic* without surcease.
OPPOSITES intermittent, sporadic.

CHOOSE THE RIGHT WORD

continuous, continual, constant, ceaseless

See CONTINUAL.

contort ▶ verb **1** *her face was contorted with terrible grief* **twist**, screw up, distort; *rare* quirk.
2 *chunks of contorted metal* **twist**, wrench/bend out of shape, misshape, warp, buckle, deform; *N. Amer.* pretzel.

contour ▶ noun *the perfect contours of her body* **outline**, **shape**, form; lines, curves, figure; silhouette, profile; *rare* lineation.

contraband ▶ noun *the salt trade (and contraband in it) were very active in the town* **smuggling**, illegal traffic, black marketeering, trafficking, bootlegging; the black market.
▶ adjective *contraband goods* **smuggled**, black-market, bootleg, bootlegged, under the counter, illegal, illicit, unlawful; prohibited, banned, proscribed, forbidden, interdicted; *informal* hot.

contraceptive ▶ noun. *See centre pages for list of* **Contraceptives**

contract ▶ noun (stress on the first syllable) *a legally binding contract* **agreement**, commitment, arrangement, settlement, undertaking, understanding, compact, covenant, pact, bond; deal, bargain; treaty, concordat, convention, entente; *Commerce* account; *Law* indenture; *rare* engagement.
▶ verb (stress on the second syllable) **1** *glass, like other substances, contracts as it cools | the market for such goods began to contract* **shrink**, get smaller, become smaller; decrease, diminish, reduce, dwindle, decline, shrivel.
OPPOSITES expand; increase.
2 *her stomach muscles contracted | the exercises contract the knee muscles* **tighten**, become/make tighter, tense, flex, constrict, draw in, become/make narrower, narrow.
OPPOSITE relax.
3 *Mrs Thornton contracted her brow* **wrinkle**, knit, crease, corrugate; purse, pucker.
4 *the name 'Jacquenard' was soon contracted to 'Jack' in English* **shorten**, abbreviate, cut, reduce, abridge, truncate.
OPPOSITES expand, lengthen.
5 *the company contracted to purchase 390 acres of forest* **undertake**, pledge, promise, covenant, commit oneself, engage; agree, enter into an agreement, reach an agreement, make a deal, negotiate a deal.
6 *she contracted German measles* **develop**, **catch**, get, pick up, come down with, become infected with, fall ill with, be taken ill with, be struck down with, be stricken with, succumb to; *Brit.* go down with; *informal* take ill with; *N. Amer. informal* take sick with.
7 *he contracted a debt of £3,300* **incur**, become liable to pay, acquire, fall into; run up.
□ **contract out** *if you do not wish to be a member of the pension fund you must*

C

contract out **opt out**, leave, exclude oneself, withdraw, pull out, exit.
□ **contract something out** *local authorities will have to contract out waste management* **subcontract**, outsource, farm out, assign to others.

contraction ▶ **noun 1** *the contraction of industry* **shrinking**, reduction in size, shrinkage; decline, decrease, diminution, dwindling.
OPPOSITES expansion, growth.
2 *neurons control the contraction of muscles | intestinal contractions* **tightening**, tensing, flexing, constricting; spasm, convulsion, clench; *Medicine* myoclonus, hippus.
OPPOSITE relaxation.
3 *her contractions started just after midnight* **labour pains**, labour; Braxton Hicks contractions; cramps; *archaic* travail.
4 *'goodbye' is a contraction of 'God be with you'* **abbreviation**, short form, shortened form, elision; diminutive; *technical* crasis, syneresis.
OPPOSITE expansion.

contradict ▶ **verb 1** *this statement was contradicted by the foreign minister* **deny**, refute, rebut, dispute, counter; say the opposite of; *formal* gainsay; *rare* controvert, confute, negative.
OPPOSITES confirm, verify, agree with.
2 *nobody dared to contradict him* **challenge**, **oppose**, argue against, go against, be at variance with; *formal* gainsay, impugn.
3 *this research contradicts computer models which predict a warmer, wetter world* **conflict with**, be at odds with, be at variance with, disagree with, be inconsistent with, clash with, run counter to, give the lie to, belie; negate; *informal* fly in the face of, make a nonsense of, shoot full of holes, drive a coach and horses through.
OPPOSITES corroborate, support.

contradiction ▶ **noun 1** *the profound contradiction between the economic and the social policies pursued by the government* **conflict**, clash, disagreement, opposition, inconsistency, lack of congruence, incongruity, incongruousness, mismatch, variance; paradox, contradiction in terms; *rare* antinomy, aporia, antilogy.
OPPOSITE agreement.
2 *the second sentence appears to be a flat contradiction of the first* **denial**, refutation, rebuttal, countering, counterstatement, opposite; negation; *formal* gainsaying; *rare* confutation.
OPPOSITES confirmation, reaffirmation.

contradictory ▶ **adjective** *the two attitudes are contradictory* **opposed**, in opposition, opposite, antithetical, contrary, contrasting, conflicting, at variance, at odds, opposing, clashing, divergent, discrepant, different; **inconsistent**, incompatible, irreconcilable, incongruous; paradoxical; *rare* oppugnant, repugnant.
OPPOSITES consistent, compatible.

contraption ▶ **noun** *a newfangled contraption for making coffee* **device**, **gadget**, apparatus, machine, appliance, mechanism, implement, utensil, invention, contrivance; *Brit.* Heath Robinson device; *N. Amer.* Rube Goldberg device; *informal* gizmo, widget, thingamajig, thingamabob, whatsit; *Brit. informal* doodah, doobry, gubbins; *N. Amer. informal* dingus, doodad, doojigger, doohickey; *Austral. informal* bitzer.

contrary ▶ **adjective 1** (stress on the first syllable) *right-wing commentators expressed the contrary view* **opposite**, opposing, opposed, contradictory, clashing, conflicting, antithetical, incompatible, irreconcilable; different, differing, contrasting, inconsistent, incongruous; reverse, counter; *rare* oppugnant, antipathic.
OPPOSITES compatible, same.
2 (stress on the second syllable) *'I don't know why you have to be so contrary,' she snapped* **perverse**, awkward, difficult, uncooperative, unhelpful, obstructive, disobliging, unaccommodating, unreasonable, troublesome, tiresome, annoying, vexatious, disobedient, recalcitrant, refractory, wilful, headstrong, self-willed, capricious, wayward, cross-grained; stubborn, obstinate, obdurate, mulish, pig-headed, bull-headed, intractable; *Scottish* thrawn; *informal* cussed; *Brit. informal* bloody-minded, bolshie, stroppy; *N. Amer. informal* balky; *archaic* froward, contumacious; *rare* renitent, pervicacious, contrarious.
OPPOSITES accommodating, cooperative, obliging.
□ **contrary to** *the court ruled that the restrictions were contrary to the public interest* **in conflict with**, against, at variance with, at odds with, in opposition to, not in accord with, counter to, conflicting with, incompatible with; *rare* repugnant.
▶ **noun** *in fact, the contrary is true* **opposite**, reverse, converse, antithesis; *technical* contrariety.
□ **on the contrary** *there was no malice in her; on the contrary, she was very kind* **conversely**, in contrast, quite/just the opposite, quite/just the reverse; rather, instead.

contrast ▶ **noun** (stress on the first syllable) **1** *the marked contrast between English and Scottish practice* **difference**, dissimilarity, disparity, dissimilitude, distinction, contradistinction, divergence, variance, variation, differentiation; contradiction, incongruity, opposition, polarity; *rare* unlikeness.
OPPOSITES similarity, resemblance.
2 *vivacious and highly intelligent, Jane was a complete contrast to Sarah* **opposite**, antithesis; foil, complement.
□ **by contrast 1** *by contrast, Anderson rejects this view* **conversely**, in contrast, on the other hand; however.
2 *by contrast with Crowe's ruddiness, Anthea looked pale* **compared to/with**, next to, against, beside.
▶ **verb** (stress on the second syllable) **1** *this view* **contrasts with** *his earlier opinion* **differ from**, be at variance with, be contrary to, conflict with, go against, be at odds with, be in opposition to, disagree with, clash with.
OPPOSITES resemble, echo.
2 *a dress of burnt sienna which* **contrasted with** *her pale gold hair* **set off**, complement; clash with; *informal* scream at.
OPPOSITE match.
3 *people* **contrasted** *her* **with** *her sister* **compare**, set side by side, juxtapose; measure against; distinguish from, differentiate from, draw a distinction between.
OPPOSITE liken.

contravene ▶ **verb 1** *certain members of his administration had contravened the law* **break**, breach, fail to comply with, fail to observe, violate, infringe, offend against, transgress against; defy, disobey, flout; *Law* infract.
OPPOSITES uphold, comply with.
2 *the Privy Council held that the prosecution contravened the rights of the individual* **conflict with**, be in conflict with, be at odds with, be at variance with, be in opposition to, clash with, run counter to, be inconsistent with, be contrary to.

contravention ▶ **noun** *a contravention* **of** *EC regulations* **breach**, violation, infringement, non-observance, breaking, transgression, neglect, dereliction; failure to observe, non-compliance with, departure from; *Law* infraction, delict.

contretemps ▶ **noun 1** *her little contretemps with Terry* **argument**, quarrel, squabble, altercation, clash, fight; **disagreement**, difference of opinion, dispute, dissension; *informal* tiff, set-to, run-in, spat; *Brit. informal* row, barney; *Scottish informal* rammy.
2 *there was one last contretemps before the end of the night* **mishap**, misadventure, accident, mischance, unfortunate occurrence, awkward moment; problem, difficulty.

contribute ▶ **verb 1** *the government contributed a million pounds to the fund* **give**, donate, give/make a donation of, put up, come up with, subscribe, hand out, grant, bestow, present, gift, accord; provide, supply, furnish; *informal* chip in, pitch in, fork out, dish out, shell out, cough up; *Brit. informal* stump up; *N. Amer. informal* kick in, ante up, pony up.
2 *the colour scheme contributes a pervading sense of calm and peacefulness to the room* **impart**, lend, add, give, confer.
3 *evidence suggests that a minimum wage would* **contribute to** *economic recovery* **play a part in**, be instrumental in, be a factor in, be partly responsible for, have a hand in, be conducive to, make for, lead to, cause, give rise to; help, promote, advance, further, forward, oil the wheels of, open the door for, add to; *formal* conduce to.
OPPOSITE stand in the way of.

contribution ▶ **noun 1** *the agency is financed mainly from voluntary contributions* **donation**, gift, benefaction, offering, present, handout; subscription; grant, subsidy, allowance; bequest, endowment; *historical* alms; *rare* donative.
2 *local historians requested contributions for a forthcoming book on the area's history* **article**, piece, story, item, chapter, paper, essay, a few paragraphs, a few words; (**contributions**) text, reading matter.
3 *her* **contribution to** *the discussion had been negligible* **input into**, participation in, involvement in; *informal* one's pennyworth.

contributor ▶ **noun 1** *one of the magazine's regular contributors* **writer**, feature writer, columnist, correspondent, reporter, journalist, penman; critic, reviewer; freelancer, freelance; *informal* journo, pen-pusher, hack, hackette, scribbler.
2 *influential campaign contributors* **donor**, benefactor, benefactress, giver, subscriber; supporter, backer, subsidizer, patron, sponsor; philanthropist; *informal* angel; *rare* benefactrice, benefactrix, philanthrope.

contrite ▶ **adjective** *he looked so contrite that she relented* **remorseful**, repentant, penitent, regretful, full of regret, sorry, apologetic, self-reproachful, rueful, sheepish, hangdog; ashamed, chastened, shamefaced, conscience-stricken, guilt-ridden, in sackcloth and ashes; *rare* compunctious.
OPPOSITES unrepentant, defiant.

contrition ▶ **noun** *his eyes were full of contrition* **remorse**, remorsefulness, repentance, penitence, sorrow, sorrowfulness, regret, contriteness, ruefulness, pangs of conscience, prickings of conscience; shame, guilt, self-reproach, self-condemnation, compunction; *archaic* rue; *rare* sorriness.

contrivance ▶ **noun 1** *a mechanical contrivance* **device**, **gadget**, machine, appliance, contraption, apparatus, mechanism, implement, tool, labour-saving device, invention; *informal* gizmo, mod con, widget, thingamajig, thingamabob, whatsit; *Brit. informal* doodah, doobry, gubbins; *N. Amer. informal* dingus, doodad, doojigger, doohickey; *Austral. informal* bitzer.
2 *her matchmaking contrivances* **scheme**, stratagem, tactic, manoeuvre, move, course/line of action, plan, ploy, gambit, device, wile; trick, ruse,

plot, machination, subterfuge, artifice, expedient; *Brit. informal* wheeze; *Austral. informal* lurk; *archaic* shift, fetch.

contrive ▶ verb **1** *his opponents contrived a cabinet crisis | they contrived a plan* **bring about**, engineer, cause to happen, manufacture, orchestrate, stage-manage, create; **devise**, concoct, construct, design, formulate, plan, work out, think up, dream up, come up with, fabricate, plot, hatch; *informal* wangle, set up, cook up; *Law* procure.
2 *Lomax contrived to bump into him as he left the house* **manage**, find a way, engineer a way, arrange; succeed in; *informal* work it, swing it; *archaic* compass.

contrived ▶ adjective *David replied with contrived joviality | the ending of the novel is too contrived to be convincing* **forced**, strained, studied, artificial, affected, put-on, pretended, false, feigned, manufactured, unnatural, non-spontaneous; laboured, overdone, elaborate; far-fetched; *N. Amer. informal* hokey; *rare* voulu.
OPPOSITES natural, spontaneous.

control ▶ noun **1** *China retained control over the region | the whole operation is under the control of a production manager* **jurisdiction**, sway, power, authority, command, dominance, domination, government, mastery, leadership, rule, reign, sovereignty, supremacy, ascendancy, predominance; charge, management, direction, guidance, supervision, superintendence, oversight; influence; *rare* prepotence, prepotency, prepollency.
2 *strict import controls* **restraint**, **constraint**, limitation, restriction, check, curb, brake, rein; regulation.
3 *'How could you?' she yelled, her control slipping* **self-control**, self-restraint, restraint, self-command, self-mastery, self-discipline; self-possession, composure, calmness, coolness; *informal* cool; *rare* countenance.
4 *the volume control | easy-to-use controls* **switch**, **knob**, button, dial, handle, lever; (**controls**) console, instrument panel, dashboard; *informal* dash.
5 *mission control* **headquarters**, HQ, base, centre of operations, command post.
6 *another Petri dish without the DNA solution was used as a control* **standard of comparison**, benchmark, standard, check.
▶ verb **1** *one family had controlled the company since its formation | the entire country was strictly controlled by the Shah* **be in charge of**, **run**, be in control of, manage, direct, administer, head, preside over, have authority over, supervise, superintend, oversee, guide, steer; command, rule, govern, lead, dominate, reign over, hold sway over, be at the helm, be the boss; *informal* head up, call the shots, call the tune, be in the driving seat, be in the saddle, run the show, pull the strings, rule the roost, hold the purse strings, have someone/something in the palm of one's hand, have someone eating out of one's hand; *Brit. informal* wear the trousers; *N. Amer.* have someone in one's hip pocket.
2 *she struggled to control her temper* **restrain**, keep in check, curb, check, contain, hold back, bridle, rein in, keep a tight rein on, subdue, suppress, repress, master, damp down; *informal* keep a/the lid on.
3 *public spending was controlled* **limit**, **restrict**, set/impose limits on, curb, cap, constrain; *informal* put the brakes on.
4 *the extractor fan is controlled by a thermostat | all these processes are controlled by genes* **regulate**, modulate, adjust; affect, determine, govern.

controversial ▶ adjective *controversial issues such as abortion and hanging* **contentious**, disputed, contended, at issue, moot, disputable, debatable, arguable, vexed, open to discussion/question, under discussion; tendentious; emotive, sensitive, delicate, difficult, awkward, problematic; *rare* controvertible.
OPPOSITES uncontroversial, anodyne.

controversy ▶ noun *he refused to be drawn into the political controversy | a major controversy in education* **disagreement**, dispute, argument, debate, dissension, contention, disputation, altercation, wrangle, quarrel, squabble, war of words, storm; wrangling, quarrelling, squabbling, bickering; polemic; *French* cause célèbre; *Brit. informal* row; *rare* velitation.
OPPOSITES agreement, accord.

contumely ▶ noun (*archaic*) **abuse**, insults, slurs, aspersions, derision, invective, slander, defamation, denigration, disparagement, opprobrium, obloquy, vituperation, vilification; **insolence**, rudeness, impertinence, discourtesy; *informal* mud-slinging, bad-mouthing, bitchiness; *archaic* malapertness, billingsgate.
OPPOSITES compliments, flattery.

contusion ▶ noun **bruise**, discoloration, black-and-blue mark, blemish, injury; swelling, bump, lump; *technical* ecchymosis; *rare* mouse.

conundrum ▶ noun **1** *some of the conundrums facing policy-makers in the 1980s* **problem**, difficult question, vexed question, difficulty, quandary, dilemma; puzzle, enigma, mystery; *informal* poser, facer, stumper, cruncher.
2 *Roderick enjoyed conundrums and crosswords* **riddle**, puzzle, word game, anagram; *informal* brain-teaser, brain-twister.

convalesce ▶ verb *he went abroad to convalesce* **recuperate**, get better, recover, get well, regain one's strength/health, get back on one's feet, get over something, get back to normal; be on the road to recovery, be on the mend, improve.
OPPOSITE deteriorate.

convalescence ▶ noun *a long period of convalescence* **recuperation**, recovery, return to health, process of getting better, rehabilitation, improvement, mending, restoration.
OPPOSITE relapse.

convalescent ▶ adjective *you're still convalescent and you need to rest* **recuperating**, recovering, getting better, on the road to recovery, improving, making progress; *informal* on the mend.

convene ▶ verb **1** *he had convened a secret meeting of military personnel* **summon**, call, call together, order; hold; *formal* convoke.
2 *the committee convened for its final session* **assemble**, gather, meet, get together, come together, congregate, collect, muster; *rare* foregather.
OPPOSITE disperse.

convenience ▶ noun **1** *the convenience of this arrangement pleased Paula* **expedience**, expediency, advantageousness, advantage; favourableness, opportuneness, propitiousness, timeliness; suitability, appropriateness, fittingness.
OPPOSITE inconvenience.
2 *it combines the convenience of a portable with the power of a car phone* **ease of use**, usability, usefulness, utility, serviceability, practicality, functionality; advantage, benefit.
OPPOSITES inconvenience; disadvantage.
3 *a shower and toilet were installed for the convenience of swimmers* **benefit**, **use**, good, comfort, ease, enjoyment, satisfaction.
4 *the convenience of the nearby shopping centre* **accessibility**, ease of access, handiness, nearness; *rare* propinquity.
OPPOSITE inaccessibility.
5 *the kitchen is bright and cheerful, with all the modern conveniences* **appliance**, amenity, facility, device, labour-saving device, gadget, machine; *informal* gizmo, gimmick, mod con; *formal* appurtenance.
□ **at your convenience** *please telephone me at your convenience* **at a convenient time**, at a time that suits you, when it suits you, at your leisure, in your own time, when you have a minute, when you can; in due course.
OPPOSITE immediately.

convenient ▶ adjective **1** *try to agree on a mutually convenient time* **suitable**, appropriate, fitting, fit, suited, agreeable; opportune, timely, well timed, favourable, advantageous, seasonable, expedient; *archaic* commodious.
OPPOSITES inconvenient, awkward.
2 *pre-prepared food has become a tempting and convenient option in recent times* **trouble-free**, labour-saving; useful, handy, practical, serviceable; user-oriented.
3 *a friendly, well-run hotel that's* **convenient for** *the beach* **within easy reach of**, near (to), close to, well placed for, well situated for, handy for, just around the corner from, within walking distance of, at close quarters to, not far from; *informal* a stone's throw from, {a hop, skip, and a jump away from}, within spitting distance of.

convent ▶ noun **nunnery**; priory, abbey, religious house, religious community, cloister; *rare* coenobium, coenoby, beguinage.

convention ▶ noun **1** *social conventions | he was an upholder of convention and correct form* **custom**, **usage**, practice, tradition, way, habit, norm; **rule**, code, canon, punctilio; accepted behaviour, conventionality, propriety, etiquette, protocol, formality, ceremonial; *formal* praxis; (**conventions**) mores; *French* moeurs.
2 *a convention signed by the six states bordering on the Black Sea* **agreement**, accord, protocol, compact, pact; treaty, concordat, entente; understanding, arrangement; contract, bargain, deal.
3 *the annual convention of the Institute of Directors* **conference**, meeting, congress, assembly, gathering, summit, council of delegates/representatives, symposium, forum, convocation, synod, conclave, diet, chapter; *informal* con, get-together; *rare* colloquium.

conventional ▶ adjective **1** *the conventional wisdom of the day* **orthodox**, traditional, established, accepted, received, mainstream, prevailing, prevalent, accustomed, customary.
OPPOSITE unorthodox.
2 *a cross between a monorail and a conventional railway* **normal**, standard, regular, ordinary, usual, traditional, typical, common; *Brit.* common or garden; *N. Amer.* garden variety.
3 *Karen was a very conventional woman* **conservative**, traditional, traditionalist, conformist, bourgeois, old-fashioned, of the old school; formal, correct, proper, decorous, staid; small-town, suburban, parochial, narrow-minded; *French* bien pensant, comme il faut; *historical* Biedermeier; *informal* straight, square, strait-laced, stodgy, stuffy, stick-in-the-mud, fuddy-duddy.
OPPOSITES unconventional, radical, bohemian.
4 *an unexciting and rather conventional compilation* **run-of-the-mill**, prosaic, pedestrian, commonplace, unimaginative, uninspired, uninspiring, unadventurous, unremarkable, unexceptional; **unoriginal**, formulaic, predictable, stock, hackneyed, clichéd, stereotypical, stereotyped, trite, platitudinous; *informal* old hat, plain vanilla, bog-standard; *rare* formulistic.
OPPOSITE original.

C

converge ▶ verb **1** *Oxford Circus, a station where three lines converge* **meet, intersect**, cross, come together, connect, link up, coincide; join, unite, merge.
OPPOSITES separate, diverge.
2 *the 90,000 soccer fans* **converging on** *Wembley* **close in on**, bear down on, descend on; approach, draw near/nearer to, come close/closer to, move towards.
OPPOSITES leave, retreat from.

conversant ▶ adjective *the students are* **conversant with** *a wide range mathematical and computing skills* **familiar with**, acquainted with, au fait with, at home with, no stranger to; **well versed in**, well informed about, well up on, knowledgeable about, informed about, abreast of, apprised of, up to date on, au courant with; experienced in, proficient in, practised in, skilled in; *informal* up to speed on, clued up on, genned up on; *formal* cognizant of; *dated* perfect in.
OPPOSITES unfamiliar with; ignorant of.

conversation ▶ noun *he must have overheard her conversation with Victoria* **discussion**, talk, chat, gossip, tête-à-tête, heart-to-heart, head-to-head, exchange, dialogue, parley, consultation, conference; *Indian* adda; *NZ* korero; *informal* confab, jaw, powwow, chit-chat, rap, gas; *Brit. informal* chinwag, natter, rabbit; *Scottish & N. English informal* crack; *N. Amer. informal* bull session, skull session, gabfest, schmooze; *Austral./NZ informal* yarn; *formal* confabulation; *rare* palaver, colloquy, converse.

conversational ▶ adjective **1** *a conversational tone | fluent, conversational English* **informal**, chatty, casual, relaxed, friendly; colloquial, idiomatic.
OPPOSITE formal.
2 *like all dentists, he only became conversational when he had his patient at his mercy* **talkative**, chatty, communicative, forthcoming, expansive, loquacious, garrulous, voluble.
OPPOSITES taciturn, uncommunicative.

converse[1] ▶ verb (stress on the second syllable) *they began to converse amicably* **talk**, speak, chat, have a conversation, have a talk, have a discussion, discourse; confer, parley, consult with each other; chatter, gossip; *informal* chew the fat, chew the rag, gab, jaw, powwow, have a confab; *Brit. informal* natter, rabbit, witter, chunter; *N. Amer. informal* rap, shoot the breeze, shoot the bull; *Austral./NZ informal* mag; *formal* confabulate.
▶ noun (stress on the first syllable) (*rare*) *I had half an hour's converse with him* **conversation**, talk, discourse, discussion; *formal* confabulation.

converse[2] (stress on the first syllable) ▶ noun *the converse is true* **opposite**, reverse, obverse, inverse, contrary, antithesis; other side of the coin; *Italian* per contra; *informal* flip side.
▶ adjective *the converse attitude of many of those on the right of the party* **opposite**, opposing, contrary, counter, antithetical; clashing, incompatible, in disagreement, disagreeing, conflicting, differing; reverse, obverse, inverse.

conversion ▶ noun **1** *the conversion of waste into energy* **change**, changing, transformation, turning, altering, metamorphosis, transfiguration, transmutation, translation, sea change; *humorous* transmogrification.
2 *the conversion of the building* **adaptation**, reconstruction, rebuilding, redevelopment, refashioning, redesign, restyling, revamping; renovation, rehabilitation; alteration, modification, customization.
3 *his religious conversion* **spiritual rebirth**, regeneration, reformation; change of heart; *rare* proselytization.

convert ▶ verb (stress on the second syllable) **1** *plants convert the radiant energy of the sun into chemical energy* **change**, turn, transform, metamorphose, transfigure, transmute, translate; *humorous* transmogrify; *technical* permute.
2 *the sofa* **converts to** *a bed* **change into**, be able to be changed into, adapt to.
3 *we converted the derelict properties into a women's centre* **adapt**, turn, rebuild, reconstruct, redevelop, remake, make over, refashion, redesign, restyle, revamp; renovate, rehabilitate; modify, alter, customize; *N. Amer.* bring up to code; *informal* do up, fix up; *N. Amer. informal* rehab.
4 *a novel which was later converted into a film script* **adapt**, turn, rework, recast, reshape, refashion, remodel, remould; rehash.
5 *that's no way to convert sinners* **proselytize**, evangelize, bring to God, redeem, save, reform, re-educate, cause someone to change their beliefs/mind, make someone see the light; persuade, convince, win over; *N. Amer.* proselyte.
6 *the formula for converting centigrade into Fahrenheit* **change**, turn; exchange for, swap for; switch from.
▶ noun (stress on the first syllable) *Christian converts* **proselyte**, neophyte, new believer; *Christianity* catechumen.

convertible ▶ adjective *assets that are readily convertible into cash* **changeable**, able to be changed, exchangeable; adaptable, adjustable, modifiable.
▶ noun *a black Mercedes convertible* **soft-top**, ragtop, targa; *Brit. dated* drophead.

convex ▶ adjective **curved outwards**, cambered; rounded, bulging, swelling, protuberant; curvilinear; gibbous; *rare* outcurved.
OPPOSITE concave.

convey ▶ verb **1** *a taxi service conveyed guests to Cerrig station | pipes were laid to convey water to the house* **transport**, carry, bring, take, fetch, bear, move, ferry, shuttle, shift, transfer; send, forward, deliver, dispatch; channel, pipe, conduct.
2 *Mr Marr has conveyed the information to me* **communicate**, pass on, make known, impart, relay, transmit, send, hand on; tell, relate, recount, announce, reveal, disclose, divulge.
3 *it's impossible to convey how lost I felt* **express**, communicate, indicate, tell, say, put across/over, get across/over.
4 *he conveys an air of managerial competence* **project**, exude, emit, emanate, send forth.
5 *a deed conveying property to a trustee* **transfer**, give the right/title of, grant, cede, devolve, lease; bequeath, leave, will, pass on; *N. Amer.* deed; *Law* demise, devise.

conveyance ▶ noun **1** *the conveyance of agricultural produce from the Billingsgate area* **transportation**, transport, carriage, carrying, transfer, transference, movement, delivery; haulage, portage, cartage, shipment, freightage.
2 (*formal*) *three-wheeled conveyances* **vehicle**, means/method of transport; car, motor car, bus, coach, van, lorry, truck, carriage, bicycle, motorbike, motorcycle.
3 *the conveyance of meaning* **communication**, imparting, transmission, passing on, conveying; expression.
4 *the conveyance of property* **transfer**, transference, transferral, granting, ceding, devolution; bequest; *Law* demise; *rare* cession.

convict ▶ verb (stress on the second syllable) *her former boyfriend was* **convicted of** *assaulting her* **declare/find/pronounce guilty**; sentence, give someone a sentence; *Brit. informal* send down for.
OPPOSITES acquit, clear.
▶ noun (stress on the first syllable) *two escaped convicts* **prisoner**, inmate; criminal, offender, lawbreaker, felon; trusty; *informal* jailbird, con, (old) lag, lifer, crook; *N. Amer. informal* yardbird; *S. African informal* lighty; *archaic* transport.

conviction ▶ noun **1** *she will appeal against her conviction* **declaration/pronouncement of guilt**, sentence, judgement.
OPPOSITE acquittal.
2 *his deeply held political and religious convictions* **belief**, **opinion**, view, thought, persuasion, idea, position, stance; (article of) faith, credo, creed, tenet, dogma.
3 *she spoke with conviction* **certainty**, certitude, assurance, confidence, sureness, positiveness; no shadow of a doubt.
OPPOSITES uncertainty, doubt.

convince ▶ verb **1** *Wilson convinced me that I was wrong* **persuade**, satisfy, prove to, cause to feel certain; assure, reassure; put/set someone's mind at rest, dispel someone's doubts.
2 *eventually, I convinced her to marry me* **induce**, prevail on, get, talk round, bring around, win over, sway; persuade, cajole, inveigle.

> **CHOOSE THE RIGHT WORD**
>
> **convince, persuade, induce**
>
> All these words refer to causing someone to do something that you wish them to do.
>
> - **Convince** refers primarily to getting someone to believe something by presenting them with arguments or evidence (*he managed to convince the police that his story was true*). The word can also mean 'persuade' (*she convinced my father to branch out on his own*), but this use is disapproved of by some people.
> - **Persuade** refers primarily to getting someone to do something through reasoning or argument, possibly against their better judgement or personal preference (*he persuaded Tom to accompany him | she was persuaded to return to work*). *Persuade* can also be used of causing someone to accept a belief, but *persuading* someone that something is the case may take considerable argument (*he persuaded her that nothing was going on | we need to be persuaded of the case*).
> - **Induce** is used only of getting someone to do something. It is a forceful word, suggesting a good deal of effort or sacrifice on the part of the inducer, and often the use of bribes or threats rather than argument (*we had to give the driver a huge tip to induce him to carry the luggage*).

convincing ▶ adjective **1** *this seemed to me to be a convincing argument* **cogent**, **persuasive**, powerful, potent, strong, forceful, compelling, irresistible, telling, conclusive, incontrovertible, unanswerable, incontestable, unassailable; sound, well founded, plausible, credible, believable, carrying conviction, likely, probable; *rare* suasive, assuasive, verisimilar, colourable.
OPPOSITES unconvincing, improbable, far-fetched.
2 *a convincing 5–0 win* **decisive**, conclusive, impressive, emphatic, resounding.
OPPOSITE narrow.

convivial ▸ adjective *he was always a convivial host | the convivial after-dinner atmosphere* **friendly**, genial, affable, amiable, congenial, agreeable, good-humoured, cordial, warm, sociable, outgoing, gregarious, clubbable, companionable, hail-fellow-well-met; cheerful, jolly, jovial, merry, lively, enjoyable, festive; *Scottish* couthy; *informal* backslapping, chummy, pally; *Brit. informal* matey; *N. Amer.* clubby, buddy-buddy; *rare* conversable.
OPPOSITES unfriendly, unsociable.

conviviality ▸ noun **friendliness**, geniality, affability, amiability, congeniality, good humour, cordiality, warmth, warm-heartedness, good nature, sociability, gregariousness, clubbability, companionability; cheerfulness, cheeriness, good cheer, joviality, jollity, gaiety, liveliness, festivity; *French* bonhomie.
OPPOSITE unfriendliness.

convocation ▸ noun **assembly**, gathering, meeting, conference, convention, congress, rally, council, symposium, forum, conclave, congregation, synod, diet; (*in N. Amer. & NZ*) caucus; *informal* get-together; *rare* colloquium.

convoke ▸ verb (*formal*) *she sent messages convoking a council of ministers* **convene**, summon, call together, call; order.

convoluted ▸ adjective *an extraordinarily convoluted narrative* **complicated**, complex, involved, intricate, elaborate, impenetrable, serpentine, labyrinthine, tortuous, tangled, Byzantine, Daedalian, Gordian; confused, confusing, bewildering, baffling, puzzling, perplexing; *informal* fiddly, plotty; *rare* involute.
OPPOSITES simple, straightforward.

convolution ▸ noun **1** *an elaborate tracery of convolutions and hatching* **twist**, turn, coil, spiral, twirl, curl, helix, whorl, loop, curlicue, kink, sinuosity; *technical* volute, volution, gyrus.
2 *the convolutions of the plot* **complexity**, intricacy, complication, twist, turn, entanglement, contortion; involvement, tortuousness, convolutedness; *rare* involution.

convoy ▸ noun **1** *the convoy of vehicles left at 11.30 p.m.* **group**, fleet, cavalcade, motorcade, cortège, caravan, company, line, train, procession; *Brit. informal* crocodile.
2 (*archaic*) *it was difficult to obtain the convoy of a man of war* **protection**, **escort**, defence, shield.
▸ verb **1** *the 'Trumbull' was to convoy a provision ship to the San Domingo station* **escort**, accompany, attend, flank; protect, guard, defend.
2 *Remington found himself convoying Miss Lawton through the hall* **escort**, accompany, go with, attend, conduct, guide, shepherd, usher.

convulse ▸ verb *his whole body convulsed* **shake uncontrollably/violently**, go into spasms, shudder, jerk, thrash about; suffer a fit.
□ **be convulsed with laughter laugh uproariously**, roar with laughter, hold one's sides, be doubled up with laughter; *informal* split one's sides, be rolling in the aisles, be in stitches, die laughing, laugh like a drain, bust a gut, break up; *Brit. informal* be creased up, fall about laughing.

convulsion ▸ noun **1** *she's started to have convulsions* **fit**, seizure, paroxysm, spasm, attack, muscular contractions; throes; *technical* ictus.
2 (**convulsions**) *the audience collapsed in convulsions* **fits of laughter**, paroxysms of laughter, gales of laughter, peals of laughter, uncontrollable laughter; *informal* hysterics, stitches.
3 *the political convulsions of the mid 20th century* **upheaval**, eruption, turmoil, turbulence, disruption, agitation, disturbance, unrest, disorder, furore, upset, tumult, chaos; earthquake, cataclysm, storm; *German* Sturm und Drang.

convulsive ▸ adjective *convulsive movements* **spasmodic**, jerky, paroxysmal, violent, uncontrollable.

cook *See centre pages for lists of* **Cooking Methods** **Cooking Vessels**
▸ verb **1** *I decided to cook a romantic dinner* **prepare**, make, get, put together; bake; *informal* fix, knock up, rustle up.
2 (*informal*) *he was accused of cooking the books* **falsify**, alter, doctor, tamper with, interfere with, massage, manipulate, rig, misrepresent; forge; *Brit. informal* fiddle.
3 (*informal*) *hey there, Rob, what's cooking?* **happen**, go on, occur, take place; *N. Amer. informal* go down.
□ **cook something up** *he'd already cooked up a little plan to entice Jessica to go with him* **concoct**, devise, put together, create, contrive, fabricate, prepare, trump up, hatch, brew, plot, plan, scheme; invent, make up, think up, dream up.

cooking ▸ noun *authentic Italian cooking* **cuisine**, cookery, baking; food.

WORD LINKS
relating to cooking **culinary**

cool ▸ adjective **1** *a cool, cloudy day | a cool breeze* **chilly**, cold; fresh, crisp, refreshing, invigorating, bracing, brisk; unheated, draughty; *informal* nippy; *Brit. informal* parky; *literary* chill.
OPPOSITES warm, hot.
2 *the proposal met with a cool response | David seemed distinctly cool* **unenthusiastic**, lukewarm, tepid, indifferent, apathetic, half-hearted, negative; **unfriendly**, distant, remote, aloof, cold, chilly, frosty, unwelcoming, inhospitable, unresponsive, uninterested, unconcerned, offhand, detached, impersonal, dispassionate, undemonstrative, uncommunicative, unfeeling, unemotional, emotionless; *informal* standoffish, off, offish, unenthused; *rare* Olympian, gelid.
OPPOSITES enthusiastic; friendly.
3 *no one could doubt his ability to keep cool in a crisis* **calm**, {cool, calm, and collected}, composed, as cool as a cucumber, collected, cool-headed, level-headed, self-possessed, controlled, self-controlled, poised; serene, tranquil, relaxed, unruffled, unperturbed, unflustered, undisturbed, unagitated, unmoved, unbothered, untroubled; equable, even-tempered, imperturbable, placid, quiet, sedate, unexcitable, impassive, dispassionate, unemotional, phlegmatic, stolid; *informal* unflappable, unfazed, together, laid-back; *rare* equanimous.
OPPOSITES panic-stricken, agitated.
4 *a cool lack of morality* **bold**, audacious, nerveless; **brazen**, shameless, unabashed.
5 (*informal*) *she thinks she's so cool* **fashionable**, stylish, chic, up to the minute; sophisticated, cosmopolitan, elegant; *French* le dernier cri; *informal* **trendy**, funky, with it, hip, in, big, happening, now, groovy, sharp, swinging; *N. Amer. informal* kicky, tony, fly; *black English* down.
6 (*informal*) *it's a really cool song—I love it. See* EXCELLENT, SUPERB.
▸ noun **1** *the cool of the evening* **chill**, chilliness, coldness; coolness, freshness, crispness.
OPPOSITE warmth.
2 *Ken finally lost his cool and turned on her* **self-control**, control, composure, self-command, self-possession, calmness, equanimity, equilibrium, calm, collectedness; aplomb, poise, sangfroid, presence of mind.
▸ verb **1** *cool the sauce in the fridge until you are ready to use it* **chill**, refrigerate, make cold/colder.
OPPOSITE heat.
2 *allow the mixture to cool, stirring occasionally* **get cold/colder**, cool down, lose heat.
3 *her reluctance to see him did nothing to cool his interest* **lessen**, moderate, abate, diminish, reduce, dampen, pour cold water on; soothe, take the edge off, assuage, allay, mollify, temper, settle.
OPPOSITES inflame, arouse.
4 *Simpson's ardour had cooled* **subside**, lessen, diminish, decrease, abate, moderate, die down, fade, dwindle, wane.
OPPOSITE intensify.
5 *after I'd cooled off, I realized I was being irrational* **calm down**, recover/regain one's self-control, recover/regain one's composure, compose oneself, control oneself, pull oneself together, simmer down.
OPPOSITE lose one's temper.

coop ▸ noun *she released the hens from the coop* **pen**, run, cage, hutch, enclosure, pound, lock-up; birdcage, aviary, mew; *Scottish* parrock.
▸ verb
□ **coop someone up** *he hates being cooped up at home all day* **confine**, shut in, close in, shut up, mew up, keep, detain, trap; lock up, imprison, incarcerate, immure, intern, impound, hold captive, hold prisoner, put under lock and key; cage, cage in, pen in, fence in, rail in, wall in, hem in, enclose.
OPPOSITE set free.

cooperate ▸ verb **1** *police and social services cooperated in the operation* **collaborate**, work together, work side by side, act together, act jointly, pull together, band together, come together, get together, join forces, team up, unite, combine, merge, amalgamate, pool resources, club together, make common cause, form an alliance; coordinate with each other, liaise with each other; conspire, connive, collude, be in collusion, work hand in glove; *informal* gang up; *rare* coact.
2 *they were more than happy to cooperate* **be of assistance**, assist, help, lend a hand, be of service, give one's support, give one's backing, contribute, chip in, do one's bit, throw in one's lot; participate, take part, join in, get involved, go along; *informal* pitch in, play ball, tag along, get in on the act; *Brit. informal* muck in, get stuck in.

cooperation ▸ noun **1** *there has to be some cooperation between management and workers* **collaboration**, working together, joint action, combined effort, teamwork, mutual support, partnership, coopetition, coordination, liaison, association, synergy, unity, concurrence, concord, accord, understanding, give and take, compromise; dealings, relations; *rare* coaction.
2 *thank you for your cooperation* **assistance**, helpfulness, help, helping hand, aid, abettance, support, backing, contribution, participation; offices, good offices, services, ministrations.

cooperative ▸ adjective **1** *effective organizations depend on cooperative effort* **collaborative**, collective, communal, combined, common, joint, shared, mutual, united, unified, allied, cross-party, pooled, mass, concerted, coordinated, interactive, unanimous, harmonious; *rare* coactive.
OPPOSITE individual.
2 *we have found the staff to be pleasant and cooperative* **helpful**, eager to help, eager to please, glad to be of assistance, obliging, accommodating, indulgent; compliant, complaisant, willing, acquiescent, amenable, persuadable, biddable, tractable, pliable, pliant, adaptable, responsive; *informal* easy, game; *rare* persuasible, suasible.
OPPOSITE uncooperative.

coordinate ▶ verb **1** *the new leadership would coordinate all manufacturing efforts* **harmonize**, correlate, interrelate, synchronize, bring together; fit together, mesh, dovetail; organize, arrange, order, systematize; *rare* concert.
2 *care workers coordinate at a local level* **cooperate**, collaborate, work together, work side by side, act together, act jointly, pull together, band together, come together, get together, join forces, team up, unite, combine, merge, amalgamate, pool resources, club together, make common cause, form an alliance, liaise; conspire, connive, collude, work hand in glove; *informal* gang up; *rare* coact.
3 *she chose floral designs to* **coordinate with** *her decor* **blend**, blend in, fit in, harmonize, go, go well, go together, be compatible, be in tune; **match**, suit, complement, set off.

cop[1] ▶ noun (*informal*) *the cop marched her to the station* **police officer**, policeman, policewoman, officer of the law, law-enforcement officer/agent, officer; *Brit.* constable; *N. Amer.* patrolman, trooper, roundsman, peace officer; *Indian* kotwal; *French* gendarme; *informal* jack; *Brit. informal* copper, bobby, rozzer, busy, bizzy, plod, PC Plod; *N. Amer. informal* bear, uniform; *Austral./NZ informal* walloper, demon; *French informal* flic; *informal, dated* flatfoot, bogey, flattie, woodentop; *informal, derogatory* pig; *archaic* peeler, runner, bluebottle, finger; (**cops**) the police, the police force, the forces of law and order; *Brit.* the constabulary; *black English derogatory* Babylon; *informal* the law, the fuzz, the boys in blue, the long arm of the law; *Brit. informal* the (Old) Bill, the force; *N. Amer. informal* the heat; *informal, derogatory* the filth.

cop[2] ▶ verb
□ **cop out** (*informal*) *he tried to* **cop out of** *his responsibilities* **avoid**, shirk, skip, dodge, sidestep, skirt round, bypass, steer clear of, evade, escape, run away from, shrink from, slide out of, back out of, pull out of, turn one's back on; *informal* duck, duck out of, wriggle out of, get out of; *Brit. informal* skive, skive off, funk; *N. Amer. informal* cut; *Austral./NZ informal* duck-shove; *archaic* decline, bilk.

cope ▶ verb *her elderly parents can no longer cope alone* **manage**, survive, subsist, look after oneself, fend for oneself, shift for oneself, stand on one's own two feet, carry on, get through, get on, get along, get by, muddle through, muddle along, scrape by, bear up, make the grade, come through, hold one's own, keep one's end up, keep one's head above water, keep the wolf from the door, weather the storm; *informal* make out, hack it, paddle one's own canoe; *informal* rub along.
□ **cope with** *the agency helps people to cope with bereavement* **deal with**, handle, manage, address, face, face up to, confront, tackle, sort out, take care of, take in hand, get to grips with, contend with, grapple with, wrestle with, struggle with, tussle with; put up with, get through, weather, endure, withstand, stand up to, bear, brave, accept, come to terms with; master, overcome, surmount, get over, get the better of, beat; *informal* stomach, swallow.

copious ▶ adjective *she listened to me and she took copious notes* **abundant**, superabundant, plentiful, ample, profuse, full, extensive, considerable, substantial, generous, bumper, lavish, fulsome, liberal, bountiful, overflowing, abounding, teeming; in abundance; **many**, numerous, multiple, multifarious, multitudinous, manifold, countless, innumerable; *informal* a gogo, galore; *S. African informal* lank; *literary* bounteous, plenteous; myriad.
OPPOSITE sparse.

cop-out ▶ noun (*informal*) *they sometimes use their kids as a cop-out to retreat from commitment* **excuse**, pretext, ostensible reason, pretence, front, cover, cover-up, subterfuge, fabrication, evasion, escape.

copper ▶ noun
WORD LINKS
related prefixes **cupro-** (e.g. ***cupro-nickel***), **chalco-** (e.g. ***chalcolithic***)
relating to copper **cupric, cuprous**

copse ▶ noun *tall firs form a copse at the back of the house* **thicket**, grove, wood, coppice, stand, clump, brake; *Brit.* spinney; *N. Amer. & Austral./NZ* brush; *archaic* hurst, holt, boscage.

copulate ▶ verb (*formal*) *zebra finches copulate frequently | they believed that witches* **copulated with** *the devil* **mate**, couple, breed; **have sex**, have sexual intercourse, make love, sleep together, go to bed; *informal* do it, do the business, go all the way, make whoopee, have one's way, bed, know someone in the biblical sense, tumble; *Brit. informal* bonk, get one's oats; *N. Amer. informal* boff, get it on; *euphemistic* be intimate; *vulgar slang* **fuck**, screw, bang, lay, get one's leg over, shaft, dick, frig, do, have, hump, poke, shtup, dip one's wick, ride, service, tup; *Brit. vulgar slang* have it away, have it off, shag, knob, get one's end away, knock someone off, give someone one, roger, grind, stuff; *Scottish vulgar slang* podger; *N. Amer. vulgar slang* ball, jump, jump someone's bones, bone, pork, diddle, nail; *Austral./NZ vulgar slang* root; *archaic* lie together, fornicate, possess, swive, know.

copulation ▶ noun (*formal*) *the banned film contained a 15-second sequence of copulation* **sexual intercourse**, sex, intercourse, lovemaking, making love, sexual relations, sexual/vaginal/anal penetration; mating, coupling, breeding; *informal* nooky; *Brit. informal* bonking, rumpy pumpy, a bit of the other, how's your father; *S. African informal* pata-pata; *vulgar slang* screwing, fucking; *Brit. vulgar slang* shagging; *formal* coitus, coition; *archaic* fornication, carnal knowledge, congress, commerce.

copy ▶ noun **1** *copies of his report had been sent to the tribunal* **duplicate**, duplication, reprint, facsimile, photocopy, carbon copy, carbon, mimeograph, mimeo; transcript; *informal* dupe; *trademark* Xerox, photostat.
2 *a copy of a sketch by Leonardo da Vinci* **replica**, reproduction, replication, print, imitation, likeness, lookalike, representation, mock-up, dummy; counterfeit, forgery, fake, sham, bootleg; *informal* pirate, phoney, knock-off, dupe.
3 *I checked my dad's original copy of the book* **edition**, version, impression, imprint, issue; specimen, sample, example.
4 *it is an unfortunate truth that bad news makes good copy* **material**; articles, stories, features.
▶ verb **1** *each form had to be copied and sent to a different editor* **duplicate**, photocopy, xerox, photostat, mimeograph, make a photocopy of, take a photocopy of, run off; transcribe, reproduce, replicate, clone.
2 *the portraits are copied from original paintings by Reynolds* **reproduce**, replicate; forge, fake, falsify, counterfeit, bootleg.
3 *their sound was copied by a lot of jazz players* **imitate**, mimic, ape, emulate, follow, echo, mirror, simulate, parrot, reproduce; plagiarize, poach, steal, 'borrow', infringe the copyright of; *informal* pirate, rip off, crib, lift; *Brit. informal* nick, pinch; *archaic* monkey.

coquettish ▶ adjective *she gave Dan a coquettish glance from beneath her eyelashes* **flirtatious**, flirty, provocative, seductive, inviting, amorous, kittenish, coy, arch, teasing, playful, frisky, flighty, skittish, dallying, philandering; *informal* come-hither, vampish.

cord ▶ noun *her spectacles hung round her neck on a cord | a piece of thin cord* **string**, thread, thong, lace, ribbon, strap, tape, tie, line, rope, cable, wire, ligature; twine, yarn, elastic, braid, cording, braiding; *Falconry* creance; *rare* fillis.

cordial ▶ adjective **1** *he would always receive a cordial welcome at their house* **friendly**, warm, genial, affable, amiable, pleasant, fond, affectionate, warm-hearted, good-natured, gracious, hospitable, welcoming; sincere, earnest, wholehearted, heartfelt, hearty, enthusiastic, eager.
OPPOSITE unfriendly.
2 *I earned his cordial loathing* **intense**, strong, acute, violent, fierce, keen, fervent, ardent, passionate; **heartfelt**, wholehearted, deep, deep-seated, deep-rooted, profound, overwhelming, overpowering; *rare* fervid, perfervid, passional.
OPPOSITE mild.
▶ noun **1** *I often drank water with fruit cordial* **squash**, crush, concentrate.
2 (*N. Amer.*) *ginger wine is a cordial drunk at Christmas time* **liqueur**; alcoholic drink.

cordon ▶ noun **1** *the crowds had broken through the police cordon* **barrier**, line, column, row, file, ranks, chain, ring, circle; picket line; *informal* crocodile.
2 (*rare*) *he untied the rich cordon that fastened his cloak* **braid**, cord, thread, twine, ribbon, riband, sash; braiding, cording, bullion.
▶ verb
□ **cordon something off** *the city centre was cordoned off after a bomb threat* **close off**, seal off, tape off, fence off, rope off, screen off, curtain off, shut off, partition off, separate off, isolate, segregate, quarantine; seal, close, shut, blockade; enclose, encircle, surround.

core ▶ noun **1** *they plan to harness the heat from the earth's core* **centre**, interior, middle, nucleus, bosom; recesses, bowels, depths; *informal* innards; *literary* midst.
2 *this new paper goes to the core of the argument* **heart**, nucleus, nub, hub, kernel, marrow, meat; **essence**, quintessence, crux, gist, pith, substance, sum and substance, body, basis; bedrock, cornerstone, linchpin, mainspring, foundation, root, base, underpinning; fundamentals, essentials, basic principles, main ingredients; heart of the matter; *informal* nitty-gritty, brass tacks, nuts and bolts, ABC, basics.
▶ adjective *the core issue here is that of urban poverty* **central**, key, basic, fundamental, elemental, principal, primary, main, chief, crucial, vital, essential; *informal* number-one.
OPPOSITES peripheral; minor.

cork ▶ noun *Kate pulled the cork from the bottle* **stopper**, stop, plug, bung, peg, spigot, spile, seal; cap, top, lid, cover, covering; *N. Amer.* stopple.
WORD LINKS
like cork **suberose, suberous, subereous**

corn *See centre pages for list of* **Cereal Crops**
▶ noun **1** *the mill was used for grinding corn* **grain**, cereal, cereal crop.
2 *she opened a packet of baby corn* **sweetcorn**, **maize**, corn on the cob, Indian corn; *S. African* mealie.

corner ▶ noun **1** *the cart lurched round the corner* **bend**, curve, arc, kink, dog-leg, crook, deviation, turn, turning, junction, fork, intersection; angle, projection, apex, cusp; *Brit.* hairpin, hairpin bend.
2 *Benjamin hustled me away to a corner* **nook**, cranny, niche, recess, bay, booth, alcove; inglenook, ingle, apse; crevice, cavity, hole, hollow,

indentation; secret place, hideaway, hideout; *informal* hidey-hole.
3 *this corner of Italy is famed for its superb cooking* **district**, region, area, section, quarter, part; *informal* neck of the woods.
4 *society and its rules had trapped him in a corner* **predicament**, plight, tricky situation, ticklish situation, awkward situation, tight corner, tight spot, spot of trouble, bit of bother, difficulty, problem, puzzle, quandary, dilemma, muddle, mess, quagmire, mire, mare's nest, dire straits; with nowhere to turn; *W. Indian* comess; *informal* pickle, jam, stew, fix, hole, scrape, bind, fine kettle of fish, hot water, how-do-you-do.
□ **(just) around the corner 1** *my sister Gillian lives just around the corner* **close by**, nearby, very near, near here, not far away, a short distance away, in the neighbourhood, close at hand, within walking distance, within reach, on the doorstep.
2 *better times are just around the corner* **coming**, coming soon, coming up, approaching, close, imminent, forthcoming, brewing, in prospect, in the offing, in the wings, in the wind, on the way, on the horizon, nearly on us, close at hand, at hand; *informal* on the cards.
▶ **verb 1** *the wolf had cornered his prey and was moving in for the kill* **drive into a corner**, run to earth, run to ground, bring to bay, cut off, block off, trap, hem in, shut in, pen in, close in, enclose, surround; capture, catch, waylay, ambush; *archaic* ambuscade.
2 *crime syndicates have cornered the stolen car market* **gain control of**, gain dominance of, take over, control, dominate, monopolize, capture; *informal* hog, sew up; *archaic* engross.

cornerstone ▶ **noun** *the theory of natural selection is a cornerstone of biological thought* **foundation**, basis, keystone, mainspring, mainstay, linchpin, bedrock, fundament, base, key, fundamental principle, main ingredient, central component, centrepiece, core, heart, centre, focus, crux, prop, backbone, anchor.

corny ▶ **adjective** (*informal*) *the film is quite insubstantial and corny* **banal**, trite, hackneyed, commonplace, clichéd, predictable, stereotyped, platitudinous, inane, fatuous, vapid, jejune, weak, feeble, tired, stale, overworked, overused, well worn; **mawkish**, sentimental, sickly, sickly-sweet, cloying, syrupy, sugary, saccharine, honeyed, oversweet, sickening, nauseating, choking; *Brit.* twee; *informal* old hat, out of the ark, played out, cheesy; mushy, slushy, sloppy, schmaltzy, cutesy, cute, gooey, drippy, treacly, icky, sick-making, toe-curling; *Brit. informal* soppy; *N. Amer. informal* cornball, dime-store, sappy, hokey; *rare* truistic, bromidic.
OPPOSITE original.

corollary ▶ **noun** *the corollary of increased car ownership has been a decline in public transport* **consequence**, result, upshot, outcome, out-turn, effect, repercussion, reverberations, sequel, product, by-product, spin-off, conclusion, end, end result; accompaniment, concomitant, correlate; *technical* externality; *Brit.* knock-on effect.
OPPOSITES cause, origin.

coronation ▶ **noun** *they built a tower to celebrate Victoria's coronation* **crowning**, enthronement, enthroning, accession to the throne, investiture, anointing, inauguration.

coronet ▶ **noun** *the queen put a coronet on the prince's head* **crown**, diadem, tiara, circlet, chaplet, fillet, garland, wreath; *literary* coronal.

corporal ▶ **adjective** *corporal punishment | what seemed corporal melted, as breath into the wind* **bodily**, fleshly, corporeal, carnal, mortal, earthly, worldly, physical, material, real, actual, tangible, substantial; *rare* somatic.
OPPOSITE spiritual.

corporate ▶ **adjective** *he emphasized the corporate responsibility of the congregation* **collective**, shared, common, communal, joint, combined, united, allied, amalgamated, pooled, merged, concerted, collaborative, cooperative; company, business, house.
OPPOSITE individual.

corporation ▶ **noun 1** *he was chairman of the corporation for three years* **company**, firm, business, concern, operation, agency, office, bureau, house, guild, institution, organization, trust, partnership, federation, conglomerate, consortium, syndicate, group, chain, combine, multiple, multinational; *informal* outfit, set-up.
2 (*Brit.*) *the corporation refused two planning applications* **council**, town council, municipal authority, civic authority; authorities.
3 (*dated, humorous*) *that man has a huge corporation* **paunch**, pot belly, beer belly, belly, stomach, middle, girth; *informal* tummy, tum, gut, beer gut, pot, maw, breadbasket, spare tyre, middle-aged spread; *Scottish informal* kyte; *N. Amer. informal* bay window; *Austral. informal* bingy, bingee.

corporeal ▶ **adjective** *they tried to bring Satan into corporeal existence* **bodily**, fleshly, carnal, corporal, human, mortal, earthly; **physical**, material, actual, real, substantial, tangible, concrete.
OPPOSITE incorporeal.

corps ▶ **noun** *she belonged to the local Salvation Army corps | the press corps* **unit**, division, detachment, section, company, troop, contingent, squad, squadron, regiment, garrison, battalion, brigade, platoon, force; **group**, body, band, team, party, troupe, gang, pack; (*in ancient Rome*) cohort; *informal* bunch, crew, gaggle, posse.

corpse ▶ **noun** *she found his corpse at the bottom of the stairs* **dead body**, body, cadaver, carcass, skeleton; remains, relics; *informal* stiff; *archaic* corse.

WORD LINKS
related prefix **necro-** (e.g. ***necropolis***)
fear of corpses **necrophobia**

corpulence ▶ **noun** *he had been called 'Bubbles' because of his corpulence* **obesity**, fatness, plumpness, stoutness, chubbiness, chunkiness, paunchiness, portliness, roundness, rotundity, burliness, heaviness, fleshiness, meatiness; ample proportions, fat, weight, beer belly, paunch; *informal* tubbiness, pudginess, porkiness, beefiness, blubber; *Brit. informal* podginess, fubsiness; *archaic* embonpoint.

corpulent ▶ **adjective** *his corpulent figure seemed to fill the small pulpit* **fat**, fattish, obese, overweight, plump, portly, stout, chubby, paunchy, beer-bellied, thickset, hefty, heavy, heavyset, burly, bulky, chunky, well padded, well covered, well upholstered, meaty, fleshy, rotund, round, well rounded, broad, broad in the beam, of ample proportions, big, large, gargantuan, elephantine; *informal* tubby, pudgy, beefy, porky, roly-poly, blubbery, poddy; *Brit. informal* podgy, fubsy; *N. Amer. informal* zaftig, corn-fed, lard-assed; *Austral./NZ* nuggety; *technical* pyknic; *archaic* squabby, pursy; *rare* abdominous.
OPPOSITE thin.

corpus ▶ **noun** *his work has no parallel in the whole corpus of Renaissance poetry* **collection**, compilation, body, entity, whole, aggregation, mass.

corral (*N. Amer.*) ▶ **noun** *she was galloping a pony round the tiny corral* **enclosure**, pen, fold, compound, pound, stockade, paddock; *Scottish* parrock; *S. African* kraal; (*in S. America*) potrero.
▶ **verb** *the sheep and goats were corralled at night* **enclose**, confine, lock up, shut up, shut in, fence in, pen in, rail in, wall in, cage, cage in, coop up, mew in.

correct ▶ **adjective 1** *the answer he gave was perfectly correct* **right**, accurate, true, veracious, exact, precise, unerring, faithful, strict, faultless, flawless, errorless, error-free, perfect, word-perfect, scrupulous, meticulous; on the right track, along the right lines; *informal* OK, on the mark, on the beam, on the nail, on the button; *Brit. informal* spot on, bang on; *N. Amer. informal* on the money.
OPPOSITES incorrect, wrong.
2 *she wondered whether it was the correct thing to say* **proper**, seemly, decorous, decent, respectable, right, suitable, fit, fitting, befitting, appropriate, apt; conventional, approved, accepted, standard, usual, customary, traditional, orthodox; *French* comme il faut; *informal* OK.
OPPOSITE improper.
▶ **verb 1** *proofread your work and correct any mistakes you find* **rectify**, put right, set right, right, amend, emend, remedy, redress, cure, square, make good, improve, better, ameliorate, repair, revise, alter, edit, rewrite, redraft, reword, rework; sort out, clear up, deal with; *informal* patch up, clean up, iron out.
2 *all homework should be corrected by your teacher* **indicate errors in**, show mistakes in, point out faults in; mark, assess, evaluate, appraise.
3 *it is important that a vitamin deficiency is corrected by good diet* **counteract**, offset, counterbalance, compensate for, make up for, neutralize.
4 *motorists can have their headlights corrected at a reduced price* **adjust**, regulate, fix, set, set right, set to rights, standardize, normalize, calibrate, fine-tune, make good, put in working order, overhaul; *informal* jigger, tweak, twiddle, patch up, see to.
5 *'Courtesy if you please,' he corrected her* **scold**, rebuke, chide, reprimand, reprove, admonish, lecture, berate, chastise, castigate.
OPPOSITE praise.

correction ▶ **noun 1** *the detection and correction of errors is extremely difficult* **rectifying**, rectification, righting, putting right, setting right, putting to rights, amendment, emendation, alteration, altering, adjustment, adjusting, modification, modifying, repair, remedy, resolution, revision, improvement, improving, amelioration, sorting out, clearing up; *informal* patching up, ironing out, tweaking; *archaic* reparation.
2 *he was sentenced to three days in the House of Correction* **punishment**, reform, reformation, discipline; chastisement, castigation, admonition, reproof, reprimand.

corrective ▶ **adjective 1** *he agreed to undergo corrective surgery* **remedial**, therapeutic, restorative, curative, reparatory, reparative, rehabilitative, ameliorative.
2 *he was sentenced to four years in a corrective labour camp* **correctional**, punitive, penal, disciplinary, disciplinarian, castigatory, reformatory; *rare* penitentiary, punitory, castigative.

correctly ▶ **adverb 1** *the message had been sent and received correctly* **accurately**, right, rightly, faithfully, unerringly, precisely, exactly, faultlessly, flawlessly, perfectly, without error, without flaws; *Brit. informal* spot on, bang on; *N. Amer. informal* on the money; *dated* aright.
OPPOSITE incorrectly.
2 *now let's be sensible and behave correctly* **properly**, decorously, with decorum, decently, suitably, fittingly, appropriately, aptly; well, satisfactorily, in a satisfactory manner.
OPPOSITE inappropriately.

C

correlate ▸ verb **1** *inflammation will usually correlate with tissue damage* **correspond**, agree, tally, match up, tie in, be consistent, be in agreement, be compatible, be consonant, be congruous, be in tune, be in harmony, harmonize, coordinate, dovetail; equate to, relate to, conform to; suit, fit, match, parallel; *informal* square; *N. Amer. informal* jibe; *archaic* quadrate.
OPPOSITE contrast.
2 *we can correlate trends in television news content and trends in public perceptions* **connect**, analogize, associate, relate, compare, bring together, set side by side, show a connection between, show a relationship between, show an association between, show a correspondence between, draw an analogy between.

correlation ▸ noun *the correlation between smoking and lung cancer is well known* **connection**, association, link, tie-in, tie-up, relation, relationship, interrelationship, interdependence, interconnection, interaction; correspondence, parallel, equivalence, reciprocity, mutuality, concurrence.

correspond ▸ verb **1** *this ideal model does not correspond to the facts* **correlate with**, agree with, be in agreement with, be consistent with, be compatible with, be consonant with, be congruous with, be in tune with, be in harmony with, accord with, concur with, coincide with, tally with, match up with, tie in with, dovetail with; relate to, equate to, conform to; match, fit, suit, parallel; *informal* square; *N. Amer.* jibe with; *archaic* quadrate.
2 *the German rank of Feldwebel corresponded to the British rank of sergeant* **be equivalent**, be analogous, be comparable, equate, be similar, be akin.
3 *in this diagram the nodes correspond to male members of a family* **represent**, symbolize, stand for, signify, mean, denote, designate, indicate; *literary* betoken.
4 *he met Wordsworth in 1795 and corresponded with him thereafter | Debbie and I corresponded for years* **exchange letters**, communicate, keep in touch, keep in contact; write to, write letters to; *informal* drop someone a line, drop someone a note.

correspondence ▸ noun **1** *there is some correspondence between the two variables* **correlation**, similarity, resemblance, comparability, compatibility, agreement, consistency, congruity, conformity, uniformity, harmony, affinity, accordance, accord, concurrence, coincidence; association, relationship, connection, interaction.
2 *I caught up on some urgent correspondence* **mail**, post, communication, written communication; letters, messages, missives.
3 *he kept up a ceaseless round of correspondence* **letter writing**, writing, written communication.

correspondent ▸ noun **1** *I wrote to Jenny for a while but she wasn't much of a correspondent* **letter-writer**, penfriend, pen pal; communicator.
2 *he joined a Sunday newspaper as a cricket correspondent* **reporter**, journalist, columnist, writer, contributor, newspaperman, newspaperwoman, newsman, newswoman, commentator, chronicler; special correspondent, foreign correspondent; *Brit.* pressman; *N. Amer.* legman, wireman; *Austral.* roundsman; *informal* stringer, news hound, hack, hackette, journo; *N. Amer. informal* newsy.
▸ adjective *the price has been increased without any correspondent improvement in quality* **corresponding**, equivalent, comparable, parallel, matching, related, similar, analogous, commensurate.

corresponding ▸ adjective *a change in money supply brings a corresponding change in expenditure* **commensurate**, relative, proportional, proportionate, correspondent, comparable, equivalent, equal, consistent, parallel, correlated, analogous, complementary, matching; *rare* commensurable.

corridor ▸ noun *the bathroom is at the end of the corridor* **passage**, passageway, aisle, gangway, hall, hallway, gallery, arcade, cloister.

corroborate ▸ verb *Thomas corroborated the boy's account of the attack* **confirm**, verify, endorse, ratify, authenticate, validate, certify; support, back up, back, uphold, stand by, bear out, bear witness to, attest to, testify to, vouch for, give credence to, substantiate, sustain, bolster, reinforce, lend weight to.
OPPOSITE contradict.

corroboration ▸ noun *the paper shouldn't have run the story without corroboration* **confirmation**, verification, attestation, affirmation, ratification, endorsement, accreditation, authentication, validation, certification, documentation, evidence, proof, substantiation; support, backing, bolstering, reinforcement, weight.

corrode ▸ verb **1** *iron objects corrode rapidly in damp conditions* **rust**, become rusty, tarnish; deteriorate, waste away, disintegrate, crumble, fragment, be destroyed, perish, spoil.
2 *bleach at this strength may corrode the container* **wear away**, wear down, eat away (at), gnaw away (at), bite into, burn into, burn through, erode, abrade, consume, dissolve; oxidize, oxidate; rust, tarnish, destroy, spoil.

corrosive ▸ adjective *the workers are exposed to corrosive chemicals* **caustic**, corroding, eroding, erosive, abrasive, biting, mordant, burning, stinging; acid, alkali; destructive, damaging, harmful, harsh; *rare* consumptive.

corrugated ▸ adjective *the roof was made of corrugated iron* **ridged**, fluted, channelled, furrowed, grooved, crimped, folded, crinkled, crinkly, puckered, creased, wrinkled, wrinkly, crumpled, rumpled; *technical* striate, striated.

corrupt ▸ adjective **1** *they alleged that the government was inefficient and corrupt* **dishonest**, dishonourable, unscrupulous, unprincipled, amoral, untrustworthy, underhand, deceitful, double-dealing, disreputable, discreditable, shameful, scandalous; **corruptible**, bribable, buyable, venal, fraudulent, swindling, grafting, criminal, lawless, felonious, villainous, nefarious, iniquitous; *Law* malfeasant; *informal* crooked, shady, tricky, dirty, low-down, rascally, scoundrelly; *Brit. informal* bent, dodgy; *archaic* hollow-hearted.
OPPOSITES honest, law-abiding.
2 *the earth was corrupt in God's sight* **sinful**, ungodly, unholy, irreligious, unrighteous, profane, blasphemous, impious, impure; **immoral**, depraved, degenerate, reprobate, vice-ridden, perverted, debauched, dissolute, dissipated, intemperate, decadent, profligate, wanton, abandoned, immodest, lustful, lascivious, lewd, lecherous, sordid; bad, wicked, evil, base, low; *informal* warped.
OPPOSITE moral.
3 *rural dialects were regarded as corrupt* **impure**, adulterated, bastardized, alloyed, contaminated, debased, tainted, polluted, infected; deviant, distorted.
OPPOSITE pure.
4 (*archaic*) *a corrupt and rotting corpse* **rotten**, rotting, putrid, putrescent, decayed, decaying, decomposed, decomposing.
▸ verb **1** *firms are corrupting politicians in the search for contracts* **bribe**, suborn, buy, buy off, pay off; *informal* grease someone's palm, give someone a backhander, give someone a sweetener, keep someone sweet, get at, fix, square; *Brit. informal* nobble.
OPPOSITE purge.
2 *they argued that pornography did not corrupt its readers* **pervert**, debauch, deprave, warp, subvert, make degenerate, lead astray, debase, degrade, defile, sully, infect, influence; *archaic* demoralize.
OPPOSITE purify.
3 (*archaic*) *his body had corrupted to bone* **rot**, decay, decompose, putrefy.
4 *the apostolic writings had been corrupted by unknown persons* **alter**, **falsify**, manipulate, tamper with, interfere with, tinker with, doctor, distort; adulterate, bastardize, dilute, contaminate, taint; *informal* fiddle with, cook; *rare* vitiate.

corruption ▸ noun **1** *senior officials have been implicated in corruption* **dishonesty**, dishonest dealings, unscrupulousness, deceit, deception, duplicity, double-dealing, fraud, fraudulence, misconduct, lawbreaking, crime, criminality, delinquency, wrongdoing, villainy; bribery, bribing, subornation, venality, graft, extortion, jobbery, profiteering; *N. Amer.* payola; *informal* crookedness, shadiness, sleaze, palm-greasing; *Law* malfeasance, misfeasance; *archaic* knavery; *rare* malversation.
OPPOSITE honesty.
2 *he is aware of his fall into corruption* **sin**, sinfulness, ungodliness, unrighteousness, profanity, impiety, impurity; **immorality**, depravity, vice, iniquity, turpitude, degeneracy, perversion, pervertedness, debauchery, dissolution, dissoluteness, decadence, profligacy, wantonness, indecency, lasciviousness, lewdness, lechery; wickedness, evil, baseness, vileness.
OPPOSITES morality, purity.
3 *these figures have been subject to corruption* **alteration**, **falsification**, doctoring, manipulation, manipulating, fudging, adulteration, debasement, degradation, abuse, subversion, misrepresentation, misapplication; *rare* vitiation.

corsair ▸ noun (*archaic*) *the ships had become game for the corsairs* **pirate**, buccaneer, marauder, raider, plunderer, freebooter, privateer; *archaic* picaroon, filibuster, sea dog, sea rover, rover, reaver, scummer; *rare* marooner, sea thief, sea robber, sea wolf, sea rat, water rat.

corset ▸ noun *she wore a tight corset and bloomers* **girdle**, panty girdle, foundation garment, foundation, support garment, corselette; *Brit.* roll-on; *informal, dated* waspie; *Medicine* truss; *historical* stays.

cortège ▸ noun **1** *the funeral cortège moved solemnly down the road* **procession**, parade, cavalcade, motorcade, convoy, caravan, train, column, file, line, trail, chain, rank, troop; *Brit.* march past; *Brit. informal* crocodile.
2 *the prince had an ever-present cortège* **entourage**, retinue, train, suite, escort, court, company, attendant company; attendants, aides, associates, companions, followers, retainers.

cosmetic ▸ adjective **1** *some cosmetic products have been tested on animals* **make-up**, beauty, beautifying.
2 *she spent large sums on cosmetic surgery* **beautifying**, improving, non-medical; non-essential, inessential, not required, gratuitous, optional.
3 *alterations to the original building have been largely cosmetic* **superficial**, surface, skin-deep, outward, exterior, external.
OPPOSITES fundamental; structural.
▸ noun (**cosmetics**) *their faces were heavily coated with cosmetics* **make-up**, beauty products, beauty aids; *informal* warpaint, face paint, paint, slap; *rare* maquillage.

cosmic ▶ adjective **1** *social development forms part of the process of cosmic evolution* **universal**, worldwide.
2 *the observatory surveyed cosmic X-ray sources* **extraterrestrial**, in space, from space; heavenly, celestial, extramundane, other-worldly.
3 *the drama to be told was an epic of cosmic dimensions* **vast**, huge, immense, enormous, massive, colossal, prodigious, immeasurable, incalculable, unfathomable, fathomless, measureless, infinite, limitless, boundless; *informal* mega, monster, whopping, whopping great, thumping, thumping great, humungous, jumbo, hulking, bumper, astronomical, astronomic; *Brit. informal* whacking, whacking great, ginormous.
OPPOSITE tiny.

cosmonaut ▶ noun **astronaut**, spaceman, spacewoman, space traveller, space pilot, space flyer, space cadet; *N. Amer. informal* jock.

cosmopolitan ▶ adjective **1** *the student body has a cosmopolitan character* **international**, multiracial, worldwide, global, universal.
2 *he had a tolerant, cosmopolitan outlook on the world* **worldly**, worldly-wise, well travelled, knowing, aware, mature, seasoned, experienced, unprovincial, cultivated, cultured, sophisticated, suave, urbane, polished, refined; liberal, broad-minded, unprejudiced; *informal* streetwise, cool.
OPPOSITES provincial; narrow; unsophisticated.

cosset ▶ verb *before her papa died she had been spoiled and cosseted* **pamper**, indulge, overindulge, mollycoddle, coddle, baby, pet, mother, nanny, nursemaid, pander to, spoon-feed, feather-bed, spoil; wrap in cotton wool, wait on someone hand and foot, cater to someone's every whim, kill with kindness; *archaic* cocker.

cost ▶ noun **1** *there was a row over the cost of the equipment* **price**, asking price, market price, selling price, fee, tariff, fare, toll, levy, charge, hire charge, rental; value, face value, valuation, quotation, rate, worth; *informal, humorous* damage.
2 *the human cost of centuries of conflict* **penalty**, **sacrifice**, loss; expense, toll, price; suffering, harm, hurt, injury, damage, detriment, deprivation; disadvantage, downside, drawback, snag, undesirable consequences, adverse effects.
3 (**costs**) *the company is not making enough money to cover its costs* **expenses**, outgoings, disbursements, overheads, running costs, operating costs, fixed costs; expenditure, spending, outlay, money spent, payments.
▶ verb **1** *the chair costs £186* **be priced at**, sell for, be valued at, fetch, come to, amount to, be; *informal* set someone back, go for; *Brit. informal* knock someone back.
2 *the proposal has not yet been costed* **value**, price, put a price on, put a value on, put a figure on, estimate the cost of, estimate the price of, evaluate.
3 *that act of heroism cost him his life* **cause the loss of**, cause the sacrifice of, lead to the end of; destroy, result in harm to, result in damage to, harm, hurt, injure, damage.

costly ▶ adjective **1** *his work was published in small and costly editions* **expensive**, dear, high-cost, high-priced, highly priced, overpriced, exorbitant, extortionate, immoderate, extravagant; lavish, rich, de luxe, choice, fine, exquisite; valuable, priceless, worth its weight in gold, worth a king's ransom; *Brit.* upmarket, over the odds; *informal* steep, pricey.
OPPOSITES cheap, inexpensive.
2 *in those weather conditions any mistakes could be costly* **catastrophic**, ruinous, disastrous, calamitous, cataclysmic, devastating, crippling, crushing, fatal, lethal, damaging, harmful, injurious, deleterious, woeful, grievous, lamentable, dire, awful, terrible, unfortunate; *literary* direful.
OPPOSITE beneficial.

costume ▶ noun **1** *there's a prize for the best costume | the dancers wore Maltese national costume* **outfit**, ensemble, suit; **dress**, clothing, attire, garb, uniform, livery, array, regalia; clothes, garments, robes; *informal* get-up, gear, togs, duds, glad rags; *Brit. informal* clobber, kit, strip, rig-out; *N. Amer. informal* threads; *formal* apparel; *literary* raiment, habiliments; *archaic* vestments, vesture, habit.
2 (*Brit.*) *if you'd like a dip, we can lend you a costume* **swimsuit**, bathing suit, bathing costume, swimming costume, bikini; pair of swimming trunks, pair of trunks; *informal* cossie, swimming togs; *Austral./NZ informal* bathers.

cosy ▶ adjective **1** *she lived in a cosy country cottage | I felt cosy and contented* **snug**, comfortable, warm, restful, homelike, homey, homely, cheerful, welcoming, pleasant, agreeable; safe, sheltered, secure, at ease, mellow; *N. Amer.* down-home, homestyle; *informal* comfy, snug as a bug (in a rug).
OPPOSITE uncomfortable.
2 *she had a cosy chat with an old school friend* **intimate**, relaxed, informal, friendly.

coterie ▶ noun *all prime ministers develop a small coterie of kindred spirits* **clique**, set, circle, inner circle, crowd, in-crowd, gang, band, pack, crew, clan, club, fellowship, brotherhood, fraternity, sorority, sect, camp, community, league, alliance, faction, cabal, junta, caucus, syndicate, nucleus, cell; *Austral./NZ* push.

cottage ▶ noun *she had a cottage in Wales* **small house**, house, bungalow, villa, lodge, chalet, cabin, shack, shanty; holiday home, holiday cottage, retreat; home, residence, place, abode; (*in Scotland*) bothy; (*in Russia*) dacha; (*in France*) gîte; *Scottish* but and ben; *S. African* rondavel; *informal* pad, semi; *N. Amer. informal* crib; *Austral. informal* weekender; *literary* bower; *archaic* cot.

couch ▶ noun *she seated herself on the couch* **settee**, sofa, divan, chaise longue, chesterfield, love seat, settle, ottoman; *Brit.* put-you-up; *N. Amer.* day bed, davenport, studio couch, sectional; *French* canapé, tête-à-tête; *rare* squab.
▶ verb *his reply was couched in deferential terms* **express**, phrase, word, frame, put, formulate, style, render, set forth, put across, convey, communicate, say, state, utter, voice.

cough ▶ noun *the child had a terrible cough* **hack**, rasp, croak, wheeze, tickle in one's throat; *informal* bark, frog in one's throat; *technical* tussis.
▶ verb **1** *the room was heavy with cigarette smoke and she coughed* **hack**, hawk, bark, clear one's throat, hem, croak, wheeze, gasp, choke, struggle for breath, fight for air.
2 (*Brit. informal*) *once he realized the information we had on him, he was ready to cough* **confess**, talk, tell all, tell the truth, blab, open one's mouth, give the game away; *informal* come clean, let on, spill the beans, let the cat out of the bag, get something off one's chest; *Brit. informal* blow the gaff.
□ **cough up** *the tenants refused to cough up the rent | Richard had to cough up for the beer* **pay**, pay up, pay out; come up with, hand over, part with, defray the cost of; foot the bill, settle up; *informal* fork out, shell out, dish out, lay out, come across with; *Brit. informal* stump up; *N. Amer. informal* make with, ante up, pony up.
WORD LINKS
related prefix **tussive**

council ▶ noun **1** *they won an election for their seats on the council* **local authority**, local government, municipal authority, civic authority, legislative body, legislature, administration, executive, chamber, assembly, ministry, governing body, government, parliament, senate, congress, diet, cabinet; *Brit.* corporation.
2 *I took part in a project with the Schools Council* **advisory body**, advisory group, board, board of directors, committee, commission, assembly, panel, trustees, delegates, delegation; synod, convocation, chapter; *rare* advisorate.
3 *the king had been sitting in council* **conference**, conclave, assembly, convocation; meeting, gathering.

council or counsel?

Despite their similarity in pronunciation, **council** and **counsel** have different meanings. A *council* is a formally constituted body of people meeting for administrative or advisory purposes: *he was on the council of the League for Penal Reform. Counsel*, on the other hand, is a rather formal word for advice, as in *the wise counsel of his elder brother.* It can also be used as a verb, meaning 'advise, give advice': *older people counselled prudence.*

counsel ▶ noun **1** *he no longer came to me for counsel* **advice**, guidance, direction, instruction, information, enlightenment; recommendations, suggestions, hints, tips, pointers, guidelines, ideas, opinions, views, facts, data; warning, admonition, caution.
2 *King Richard held counsel with the barons* **conference**, consultation, discussion, deliberation, dialogue, conversation; talks, negotiations; *formal* confabulation.
3 *his counsel told the jury that the charges were false* **barrister**, lawyer, counsellor, legal practitioner; *N. Amer.* attorney; *N. Amer. & Irish* counsellor-at-law; *Scottish Law* advocate; *informal* brief.
▶ verb *he counselled the team to withdraw from the deal* **advise**, guide, direct, recommend, encourage, entreat, urge, warn, admonish, caution; give guidance to, give direction to, give one's opinion to, give one's suggestions to.

counsel or council?

See COUNCIL.

counsellor ▶ noun *they talked through their problems with a trained counsellor | a debt counsellor* **adviser**, consultant, guide, mentor, confidant, confidante; instructor, coach, teacher, tutor, guru, expert, specialist; **therapist**, guidance counsellor, psychologist, psychiatrist, analyst, psychotherapist, mind doctor, head doctor, healer; *informal* shrink, trick cyclist, head shrinker.

count ▶ verb **1** *he was counting a stack of dollar bills* **add up**, add together, find the sum of, sum up, reckon up, figure up, calculate, compute, enumerate, total, tally, add; *Brit.* tot up; *dated* cast up.
2 *you do need to be accurate in counting calories* **keep a tally of**, keep a count of, keep a record of; count up, count off, enumerate, tell, work out.
3 *there were seventy people backstage, not counting the actors* **include**, take into account, take account of, take into consideration, allow for, incorporate.
4 *I count it a privilege to be asked to become chairman* **consider**, think, feel,

regard, look on as, view as, see as, hold to be, judge, adjudge, rate as, deem to be, account, esteem.
5 *I was made to feel that, because I'm not married, my baby and I don't count* **matter**, enter into consideration, be of consequence, be of account, be significant, signify, mean anything, mean a lot, amount to anything, rate, be important, be influential, carry weight, weigh, make an impression; *informal* cut any ice, have any clout.

□ **count on/upon 1** *he could usually be counted on to give lifts* **rely on**, depend on, place reliance on, lean on, bank on, trust, be sure of, trust in, place one's trust in, have (every) confidence in, believe in, put one's faith in, pin one's faith on, swear by, take for granted, take on trust, take as read.
2 *they hadn't counted on Rangers' indomitable spirit* **expect**, reckon on, anticipate, envisage, predict, foresee, forecast, foretell, think likely, contemplate the possibility of, allow for, be prepared for, bargain for, bargain on, bank on, plan on, calculate on; *N. Amer. informal* figure on; *archaic* apprehend.

□ **count someone/something in** *Marie nodded enthusiastically. 'Count me in!'* **include**, involve, bring in, take in, admit, introduce, add, enter, incorporate; take into account, take account of, take note of, allow for; allow to participate, allow to take part, let someone in on something.

□ **count someone/something out** *I think you'd better count me out* **exclude**, omit, leave out, rule out, except, reject, drop, eliminate, cut out, keep out; pass over, disregard, ignore.

▶ **noun 1** *at the last count, the committee had 579 members* **calculation**, enumeration, computation, reckoning, counting, telling, tally, tallying, totting up; poll, census, listing, register.
2 *tests showed she had a raised white blood cell count* **amount**, number, tally, total, total number, sum total, grand total, full amount, aggregate, whole.

□ **out for the count** (*informal*) **unconscious**, comatose, knocked out, inert, insensible, senseless, insensate, insentient; anaesthetized, soundly asleep; *informal* out, out cold, zonked out, dead to the world, kayoed, KO'd; *Brit. informal* spark out; *rare* soporose, soporous.

countenance ▶ **noun 1** *he had a strikingly handsome and sensitive countenance* **face**, features, physiognomy, profile; facial expression, expression, look, appearance, aspect, mien; *informal* mug, clock; *Brit. informal* mush, dial, phizog, phiz; *Brit. rhyming slang* boat race; *Scottish & Irish informal* coupon; *N. Amer. informal* puss, pan; *literary* visage, lineaments; *archaic* front.
2 (*rare*) *he was always in command of his countenance* **composure**, calmness, coolness, poise, balance, equanimity, equilibrium, collectedness, control, presence of mind, dignity, sangfroid, aplomb, assurance, self-assurance, self-possession, self-control, self-command, level-headedness, cool-headedness; *informal* cool, unflappability; *rare* ataraxy, ataraxia.
OPPOSITE nervousness.
3 (*rare*) *the Court did not honour us with their countenance* **support**, backing, encouragement, endorsement, assistance, aid, approval, sanction, approbation, favour, acceptance, adoption, advocacy.

▶ **verb** *they would not countenance any breach of fair play* **tolerate**, permit, allow, admit of, approve (of), agree to, consent to, give one's blessing to, take kindly to, be in favour of, favour, hold with, go along with, put up with, endure, brook, stomach, swallow, bear; *Scottish* thole; *informal* stand for, stick, hack, give the go ahead to, give the green light to, give the thumbs up to, give the okay to; *N. Amer. rare* approbate.

counter[1] ▶ **noun 1** *he left his groceries on the counter* **worktop**, work surface, work table, table, bench, buffet, top, horizontal surface; checkout, bar, stand.
2 *the idea of the game is to collect the most counters* **token**, chip, disc, jetton; piece, man, marker, wafer; *N. Amer.* check.

counter[2] ▶ **verb** *the workers countered accusations of dishonesty with claims of oppression* **parry**, hit back at, answer, respond to, retort to, contradict, negate; ward off, fend off, stave off, deflect, rebuff, rebut, repel, repulse, hold at bay; combat, fight, attack, tackle, confront, stand up to, put up a fight against, oppose, resist, dispute, argue against; counteract; *informal* shoot full of holes, blow sky high; *formal* gainsay; *rare* controvert, confute, negative.
OPPOSITE support.

▶ **adjective** *after years of argument and counter argument there is no conclusive answer* **opposing**, opposed, opposite, contrary, adverse, conflicting, contradictory, contrasting, obverse, different, differing.
OPPOSITE complementary.

▶ **adverb** *the policy would run counter to EC plans* **against**, in opposition to, contrary to, at variance with, in defiance of, in contravention of, contrarily, contrariwise, conversely; against the tide, in the opposite direction, in the reverse direction, in the wrong direction.
OPPOSITE in accordance with.

counteract ▶ **verb 1** *new measures were brought in to counteract counterfeiting* **prevent**, thwart, frustrate, foil, impede, curb, restrain, forestall, hinder, hamper, baulk, oppose, act against, stall, check, resist, withstand, defeat, put a stop to, bring an end to; fend off, ward off, stave off, head off.
OPPOSITE encourage.
2 *studying foreign history counteracts tendencies to insularity* **offset**, counterbalance, balance, balance out, cancel out, even out, counterpoise, countervail, compensate for, make up for, remedy; neutralize, nullify, annul, negate, invalidate; *rare* counterweigh, equilibrize, negative.
OPPOSITES enhance, exacerbate.

counterbalance ▶ **verb** *the risk of failure tends to be counterbalanced by high rewards* **compensate for**, make up for, offset, balance, balance out, even out, equalize, neutralize, nullify, negate, undo, countervail, counterpoise, counteract; *rare* counterweigh, equilibrize, negative.

counterfeit ▶ **adjective** *they were charged with supplying counterfeit cassettes* **fake**, faked, copied, forged, feigned, simulated, sham, spurious, bogus, imitation, substitute, dummy, ersatz; *informal* knock-off, pirate, pirated, phoney, pseud, pseudo; *Brit. informal, dated* cod.
OPPOSITE genuine.

▶ **noun** *the shopkeeper knew the notes to be counterfeits* **fake**, forgery, copy, reproduction, replica, imitation, likeness, lookalike, mock-up, dummy, substitute, fraud, sham; *informal* phoney, pirate, knock-off, rip-off, put-on, dupe.
OPPOSITE original.

▶ **verb** *my signature is extremely hard to counterfeit* **fake**, forge, copy, reproduce, replicate, imitate, simulate, feign, falsify, sham; *informal* pirate.

countermand ▶ **verb** *orders were being issued and then countermanded* **revoke**, rescind, reverse, undo, repeal, retract, withdraw, take back, abrogate, abolish, quash, scrap, override, overturn, overrule, do away with, set aside, cancel, annul, invalidate, nullify, negate, veto, declare null and void; back-pedal on, backtrack on, do a U-turn on; *Law* disaffirm, discharge, avoid, vacate, vitiate; *informal* axe, ditch, dump, knock on the head; *archaic* recall; *rare* disannul.
OPPOSITE uphold.

counterpane ▶ **noun** (*dated*) *the great bed was covered by a gold-tasselled counterpane* **bedspread**, bedcover, cover, coverlet, throw-over, blanket, afghan, quilt; bedclothes; *Brit.* eiderdown; *N. Amer.* throw, spread, comforter; *S. African* kaross.

counterpart ▶ **noun** *the president held talks with his Bangladeshi counterpart* **equivalent**, opposite number, peer, equal, parallel, complement, match, twin, mate, fellow, brother, sister, analogue, correlative; copy, duplicate; *rare* compeer, coequal.

countless ▶ **adjective** *penicillin has relieved the suffering of countless patients* **innumerable**, untold, legion, numberless, unnumbered, numerous, very many, manifold, multitudinous, multifarious; a great number of, incalculable numbers of, immeasurable numbers of, endless numbers of, infinite numbers of, a multitude of, a multiplicity of; more than one can count, too many to be counted; *informal* umpteen, no end of, loads of, stacks of, heaps of, masses of, oodles of, bags of, scads of, zillions of; *N. Amer. informal* a slew of, a bunch of, gazillions of, bazillions of; *S. African informal* lank; *literary* myriad, divers; *rare* innumerous, unnumberable.
OPPOSITE few.

countrified ▶ **adjective** *the countrified ambience was spoilt by the express trains* **rural**, rustic, pastoral, bucolic, countryside, country; idyllic, unspoilt; *literary* Arcadian, sylvan; *rare* georgic, exurban.
OPPOSITE urban.

country ▶ **noun 1** *he became the greatest ruler the country had known* **state**, nation, sovereign state, kingdom, realm, territory, province, principality, palatinate, duchy, empire, commonwealth.
2 *I had a chance of representing my country* **homeland**, native land, native soil, fatherland, motherland, mother country, country of origin, birthplace; the land of one's birth, the land of one's fathers, the old country, one's roots, one's home.
3 *they travelled through thickly forested country* **terrain**, land, territory, parts; landscape, scenery, setting, surroundings, environment.
4 *the president made televised speeches to the country* **people**, public, general public, population, populace, community, citizenry, nation, body politic, collective; inhabitants, residents, citizens, electors, voters, taxpayers, ratepayers, grass roots; *Brit. informal* Joe Public; *rare* indigenes.
5 *in 1700, ninety per cent of the population lived in the country* **countryside**, green belt, great outdoors; provinces, backwoods, wilds, wilderness, hinterland; a rural area, a rural district; farmland, agricultural land; *Austral.* outback, bush, back country, backblocks, booay; *S. African* backveld, platteland; *informal* sticks, back of beyond, middle of nowhere; *N. Amer. informal* boondocks, boonies, tall timbers; *Austral. informal* Woop Woop, beyond the black stump.
OPPOSITE city.

▶ **adjective** *she loved fresh air and country pursuits* **rural**, countryside, outdoor, rustic, pastoral, bucolic; agrarian, agricultural, farming; *literary* sylvan, Arcadian; *rare* georgic, agrestic, exurban.
OPPOSITE urban.

countryman, countrywoman ▶ **noun 1** *she was forced into a betrayal of her countrywoman* **compatriot**, fellow citizen, fellow national, fellow countryman/countrywoman.
2 *the countryman takes a great interest in the weather* **farmer**, farmhand, country dweller, country cousin, son/daughter of the soil; rustic, yokel, bumpkin, peasant, provincial; *French* paysan; *Russian* muzhik, kulak; *Spanish*

campesino, paisano; *Italian* contadino, contadina; *Egyptian* fellah; *Indian* ryot; *Irish informal* culchie, bogman; *N. Amer. informal* hayseed, hick, hillbilly, rube, schlub; *Austral. informal* bushy, ocker; *archaic* swain, hind, kern, carl, churl, cottier; *rare* bucolic.

countryside ▶ **noun 1** *the hotel is set in acres of breathtaking countryside* **landscape**, scenery, surroundings, setting, environment; terrain, land, country, parts.
2 (**the countryside**) *I was brought up in the countryside* **a rural area**, a rural district, farmland, agricultural land, the country, the green belt, the great outdoors; the provinces, the backwoods, the wilds, the wilderness, the hinterland; *Austral.* the outback, the bush, the back country, the booay; *S. African* the backveld, the platteland; *informal* the sticks, the back of beyond, the middle of nowhere; *N. Amer. informal* the boondocks, the boonies, the tall timbers; *Austral. informal* Woop Woop, beyond the black stump.

county ▶ **noun** *the Northern counties of England* **shire**, province, territory, administrative unit, sector, department, state; region, district, area, zone; *archaic* demesne.
▶ **adjective** (*Brit.*) *a county grande dame* **landowning**, landed, upper-class, well born, high-born, noble-born, noble, aristocratic, patrician, titled, blue-blooded, born with a silver spoon in one's mouth; *Brit.* upmarket; *informal* upper-crust, top-drawer, {huntin', shootin', and fishin'}, tweedy, classy, posh; *archaic* gentle, of gentle birth.

coup ▶ **noun 1** *the prime minister was deposed in a coup in 1995* **seizure of power**, overthrow, takeover, ousting, deposition; bloodless coup, palace revolution; **rebellion**, revolt, insurrection, mutiny, revolution, insurgence, insurgency, rising, rioting, riot; *French* coup d'état, jacquerie; *German* putsch.
OPPOSITE election.
2 *securing Springsteen to open the new National Bowl was a coup for the owners* **success**, triumph, feat, successful manoeuvre, stunt, accomplishment, achievement, attainment, stroke, master stroke, stroke of genius; scoop; *French* tour de force.

coup de grâce ▶ **noun** *he administered the coup de grâce with a knife* **death blow**, finishing blow, killing, dispatch; kiss of death; *informal* KO, kayo.

coup d'état ▶ **noun** *the coup d'état which brought the general to power* **seizure of power**, coup, overthrow, takeover, ousting, deposition; bloodless coup, palace revolution; **rebellion**, revolt, insurrection, mutiny, revolution, insurgence, insurgency, rising, rioting, riot; *French* jacquerie; *German* putsch.

couple ▶ **noun 1** *the defenders feed a long pass to either of a couple of strikers* **pair**, duo, twosome, set of two, match; doublets, twins; brace, span, yoke; two, two of a kind; *rare* duplet, dyad, duad, doubleton; *archaic* twain.
2 *a couple whose dream holiday plans have been ruined* **husband and wife**, twosome; newly-weds, partners, lovers, cohabitees; *informal* item.
□ **a couple of** (*informal*) *a couple of drinks* **a few**, two or three, a small number of; *N. Amer.* a couple.
OPPOSITE several.
▶ **verb 1** *the use of weights* **coupled with** *longer exercise periods is very demanding* **combine**, integrate, mix, incorporate, accompany, link, team, associate, connect, ally; add to, join to; *formal* conjoin.
OPPOSITE divorce.
2 *the vans could be coupled together to form a train* **connect**, attach, join, fasten, fix, link, secure, tie, bind, strap, rope, tether, truss, lash, hitch, yoke, chain; stick, tape, glue, bond, cement, fuse, weld, solder; pin, peg, screw, bolt, rivet, clamp, clip, hook (up); add, append, annex, subjoin; *technical* concatenate.
OPPOSITE separate.

coupon ▶ **noun 1** *the bumper membership pack includes money-off coupons* **voucher**, token, ticket, document, certificate, carnet; chit, slip, stub, counterfoil, detachable portion, receipt, docket; *Brit. informal* chitty; *N. Amer. informal* ducat, comp.
2 *for further information, fill in the coupon below* **form**, tear-off slip, entry form, application form.

courage ▶ **noun** *it takes courage to speak out against the tide of opinion* **bravery**, braveness, courageousness, pluck, pluckiness, valour, fearlessness, intrepidity, intrepidness, nerve, daring, audacity, boldness; dauntlessness, doughtiness, stout-heartedness, hardihood, manfulness, heroism, gallantry; backbone, spine, spirit, spiritedness, mettle, determination, fortitude, resolve, resolution; *informal* guts, grit, spunk, gutsiness, gameness; *Brit. informal* bottle, ballsiness; *N. Amer. informal* moxie, cojones, sand; *vulgar slang* balls.
OPPOSITES cowardice; timidity.

courageous ▶ **adjective** *only the children were courageous enough to step out of hiding* **brave**, plucky, fearless, valiant, valorous, intrepid, heroic, lionhearted, manful, bold, daring, daredevil, adventurous, audacious; undaunted, unflinching, unshrinking, unafraid, dauntless, indomitable, doughty, mettlesome, venturesome, stout-hearted, stout, spirited, gallant, stalwart, resolute, determined, death-or-glory; *N. Amer.* rock-ribbed; *informal* game, gutsy, spunky, ballsy, have-a-go; *rare* venturous.
OPPOSITES cowardly, timid.

courier ▶ **noun 1** *the documents were sent by courier* **messenger**, special messenger, dispatch rider, letter carrier, mail carrier, runner, bearer, message bearer, message carrier, delivery man, delivery woman, conveyor, envoy, emissary, harbinger, herald; *historical* pursuivant; *archaic* forerunner, legate, estafette.
2 *he worked as a courier on a package holiday to Majorca* **representative**, guide, tour guide, travel guide, tour company representative; dragoman; *N. Amer.* tour director; *informal* (holiday) rep.

course ▶ **noun 1** *the island was not very far off our course* **route**, way, track, direction, tack, path, line, journey, itinerary, channel, trail, trajectory, flight path, bearing, heading, orbit, circuit, beat, round, run.
2 *a device which changed the course of history* **progression**, development, progress, advance, advancement, evolution, unfolding, flow, movement, continuity, sequence, order, succession, rise, march, furtherance, forwarding, proceeding.
3 *what is the best course to adopt?* **plan (of action)**, course of action, method of working, MO, line of action, process, procedure, practice, approach, technique, style, manner, way, means, mode of behaviour, mode of conduct, methodology, system, policy, strategy, programme, formula, regimen; *Latin* modus operandi; *rare* praxis.
4 *the race is over ten laps of the course* **track**, racetrack, racecourse, circuit, ground, stadium, speedway, velodrome, route, trail; (*in ancient Rome*) circus; *rare* cirque.
5 *the waiter served them their next course* **dish**, menu item.
6 *work flowed in during the course of the day* **duration**, passing, passage, lapse, period, term, span, spell, sweep.
7 *he's taking a course in art history* **programme of study**, course of study, educational programme, set of lectures, curriculum, syllabus, schedule; classes, lectures, studies.
8 *a course of antibiotics* **programme**, series, sequence, system, schedule, regimen.
9 *six courses of bricks were laid* **layer**, thickness, stratum, seam, vein, band, bed.
□ **in due course** *I look forward to hearing from you in due course* **at the appropriate time**, when the time is ripe, in time, in due time, in the fullness of time, in the course of time, at a later time, at a later date, at length, at a future time/date, at some point in the future, in the future, in time to come, as time goes on/by, by and by, one day, some day, sooner or later, in a while, after a bit, eventually.
□ **of course 1** *there are, of course, exceptions to the rule* **naturally**, as might be expected, as you/one would expect, needless to say, not unexpectedly, certainly, to be sure, as was anticipated, as a matter of course; obviously, clearly, it goes without saying; *informal* natch.
2 *'Have you got a minute?' 'Of course.'* **yes**, certainly, definitely, absolutely, by all means, with pleasure; *informal* sure thing.
▶ **verb 1** *she was aware of the blood coursing through her veins* **flow**, pour, race, stream, run, rush, gush, pump, move, cascade, flood, surge, sweep, roll; *Brit. informal* sloosh.
2 *several hares are coursed each week on the estate* **hunt**, chase, pursue, stalk, run down, run after, give chase to, follow, track, trail, shadow, hound, dog; *informal* tail.

court ▶ **noun 1** *the court found him guilty* **court of law**, law court, bench, bar, court of justice, judicature, tribunal, forum, chancery, assizes; courtroom; *French* palais de justice.
2 *a tennis court* **playing area**, enclosure, field, ground, ring, rink, green, alley, stadium, track, arena; *Brit.* close; *informal* park.
3 *walking in the castle court* **yard**, courtyard, quadrangle, square, close, enclosure, precinct, esplanade; (*in Spain*) plaza, patio; (*in Italy*) piazza; cloister, arcade; *S. African* lapa; *informal* quad.
4 *they often put on plays for the Queen's court* **royal household**, establishment, retinue, entourage, train, suite, escort, company, attendant company, staff, personnel, cortège, following, bodyguard; aides, members of court, courtiers, companions, attendants, servants, retainers, associates, followers.
5 *she made her way to Queen Elizabeth's court in England* **royal residence**, palace, castle, manor, hall; (*in France*) château; (*in Italy*) palazzo; (*in German-speaking countries*) schloss; (*in Spain*) alcazar; (*in Turkey, historical*) seraglio.
6 *statesmen came to pay court to the king* **homage**, deference, obedience, suit, courtship, blandishments, respects, attention, addresses; (**pay court to**) **woo**, court, make up to, make advances to, pursue, seek the favour of; **grovel to**, creep to, crawl to, bow and scrape to, toady to, be obsequious to, be servile to, be sycophantic to, abase oneself to, demean oneself to, defer to, ingratiate oneself with, curry favour with, fawn on, flatter, dance attendance on, truckle to, submit to; *informal* suck up to, lick someone's boots, butter up; *N. Amer. informal* brown-nose; *Austral./NZ informal* smoodge to; *vulgar slang* kiss the arse of.
▶ **verb 1** *Western politicians courted the leaders of the newly independent states.* **curry favour with**, make up to, play up to; ingratiate oneself with, cultivate, seek the favour of, try to win over, try to get on the good side of; **be obsequious towards**, grovel to, be servile towards, be sycophantic towards, kowtow to, pander to, abase oneself to, demean oneself to, bow and scrape to, prostrate oneself to, toady to, truckle to, dance attendance

C

on, fawn on/over; *informal* suck up to, crawl to, creep to, be all over, lick someone's boots, fall all over, rub up the right way, keep someone sweet, sweet-talk, soft-soap, butter up; *N. Amer.* brown-nose; *vulgar slang* lick/kiss someone's arse; *archaic* blandish.
2 *he was busily courting public attention* **seek**, try to obtain, pursue, go after, strive for, go for, push towards, work towards, be intent on, aim at/for, have as a goal, have as an objective, aspire to; solicit, ask for.
3 *I knew I was courting disaster climbing without a rope* **risk**, invite, attract, provoke, be likely to cause, bring on oneself; be likely to lead to.
4 (*dated*) *he's courting her sister* **woo**, go out with, be involved with, be romantically linked with, pursue, run after, chase, seek the company of, make advances to, make up to, flirt with; *informal* see, go steady with, date, chat up, make (sheep's) eyes at, give the come-on to, be all over; *Austral. informal* track with, track square with; *dated* set one's cap at, pay addresses to, romance, pay suit to, pay court to, seek the hand of, make love to; *archaic* spark.
5 (*dated*) *we saw the film when we were courting* **go out together**, go out, go with each other, keep company; *informal* date, go steady.

WORD LINKS
relating to law courts **forensic**

courteous ▶ **adjective** *enquiries will be dealt with by our highly skilled, courteous staff* **polite**, well mannered, civil, respectful, deferential, well behaved, well bred; gentlemanly, chivalrous, gallant; ladylike, genteel; cultivated, gracious, obliging, kind, considerate, pleasant, cordial, genial, affable, thoughtful, urbane, well brought up, well spoken; formal, proper, polished, refined, decorous, courtly, civilized, tactful, discreet, diplomatic; *Brit. informal* decent; *dated* mannerly.
OPPOSITES discourteous, rude.

CHOOSE THE RIGHT WORD
courteous, polite, civil
See POLITE.

courtesan ▶ **noun** (*archaic*) *courtesans were invited into the palace to satisfy the Emperor's lust*. *See* PROSTITUTE.

courtesy ▶ **noun 1** *customers deserve to be treated with courtesy* **politeness**, courteousness, good manners, civility, respect, respectfulness, deference, chivalry, gallantry, gallantness, good breeding, gentility, graciousness, kindness, consideration, thought, thoughtfulness, cordiality, geniality, affability, urbanity, polish, refinement, courtliness, decorousness, tact, discretion, diplomacy; *Brit. informal* decency.
OPPOSITES discourtesy, rudeness.
2 *an outing by courtesy of the firm* **benevolence**, kindness, generosity, indulgence, favour, consideration, consent, permission.

courtier ▶ **noun** *the Princess set up her own select circle of trusted courtiers* **attendant**, retainer, companion, adviser, aide, henchman, follower; lady-in-waiting, lady of the bedchamber; cup-bearer, steward, train-bearer; lord, lady, noble, equerry, page, squire; *historical* liegeman.

courtly ▶ **adjective** *he gave a courtly bow* **refined**, polished, cultivated, cultured, civilized, stylish, elegant, sophisticated, urbane, suave, debonair; **polite**, civil, courteous, gracious, well mannered, well bred, chivalrous, gallant, gentlemanly, ladylike, honourable, genteel, aristocratic, dignified, decorous, formal, ceremonious, stately, proper; *informal* couth; *archaic* gentle.
OPPOSITE uncouth.

courtship ▶ **noun 1** *he married his wife after a whirlwind courtship* **romance**, affair, love affair, going out, going steady, dating, engagement, keeping company.
2 *the supposed courtship of Harriet by Mr Elton* **wooing**, courting, suit, pursuit, attentions, advances, blandishments; *archaic* addresses.

courtyard ▶ **noun yard**, court, quadrangle, square, close, enclosure, precinct; (*in Spain*) plaza, patio; (*in Italy*) piazza; cloister, arcade; *S. African* lapa; *informal* quad.

cove[1] ▶ **noun** *the steps carved out of the cliff led down to a small sandy cove* **bay**, inlet, indentation, fjord, natural harbour, anchorage; *Scottish* (sea) loch; *Irish* lough.

cove[2] ▶ **noun** (*informal, dated*) *he's a funny cove* **man**, fellow; *informal* **chap**, bloke, guy.

covenant ▶ **noun** *there is a landlord's covenant to repair the property* **contract**, compact, treaty, pact, accord, deal, bargain, settlement, concordat, protocol, entente, agreement, arrangement, understanding, pledge, promise, bond, indenture, guarantee, warrant; undertaking, commitment.
▶ **verb** *the landlord covenants to repair the property* **undertake**, give an undertaking, pledge, promise, agree, contract, vow, guarantee, warrant, commit oneself, bind oneself, give one's word, enter into an agreement, engage; *archaic* plight (oneself).

cover ▶ **verb 1** *Jack covered the children with the blanket* **put something on top of**, place something over, place under cover; protect, shield, shelter; envelop, enfold, engulf, enclose, tuck, cup, surround, house, sink, embed, bury, submerge, immerse.
OPPOSITE reveal.
2 *his car was covered in mud* **cake**, coat, encrust, plaster, spread thickly, smother, daub, smear, bedaub, overspread; *literary* besmear.
3 *snow covered the fields* **blanket**, overlay, overspread, carpet, overlie, extend over, layer, coat, film, submerge; *literary* mantle, pave.
4 *the scheme covers six local libraries* **include**, involve, take in, deal with, contain, comprise, provide for, embrace, embody, incorporate, subsume, refer to, consider.
5 *the trial was covered by a range of newspapers* **report**, write up, write about, describe, commentate on, tell of, write/give an account of, publish/broadcast details of, investigate, look into, inquire into.
6 *he turned on the radio to cover their conversation* **mask**, disguise, obscure, hide, stop something being overheard, muffle, stifle, smother; camouflage, blot out, cloak, veil, shroud, swathe, secrete, envelop; *literary* enshroud.
7 *if the sergeant wants to know where you are, I'll cover for you* **give an alibi to**, provide with an alibi, shield, protect; *informal* alibi.
OPPOSITE give away.
8 *they could train an extra secretary to* **cover for** *others who are on holiday or sick leave* **stand in for**, fill in for, act as stand-in for, deputize for, act as deputy for, substitute for, act as substitute for, take over from, double for, be a substitute for; replace, relieve, take the place of, act in place of, do duty for, do a locum for, be a locum for, sit in for, understudy; hold the fort, step into the breach; *informal* sub for, fill someone's shoes/boots; *N. Amer. informal* pinch-hit for.
9 *can you make enough to cover your costs?* **offset**, **counterbalance**, balance, cancel out, make up for, pay back, pay, pay for, be enough for, fund, finance, make up, have enough money for, provide for.
10 *your home is covered against damage and loss* **insure**, protect, secure, underwrite, provide insurance for, assure, indemnify.
11 *we covered ten miles each day* **travel**, journey, go, do, put behind one, get under one's belt, travel over, pass over, journey over/across, traverse, cross, go across, make one's way across, range/tramp over.
□ **cover something up** *the government has repeatedly tried to cover up the army's role* **conceal**, hide; keep secret, hush up, keep dark, draw a veil over, suppress, sweep under the carpet, gloss over; *informal* whitewash, keep a/the lid on.
OPPOSITE expose.
▶ **noun 1** *a dust cover for the keyboard* **sleeve**, **wrapping**, wrapper, covering, envelope, sheath, sheathing, housing, jacket, casing, cowling; awning, tarpaulin; lid, top, cap.
2 *a book cover* **binding**, case; boards; jacket, dust jacket, dust cover, wrapper.
3 (**covers**) *she pulled the covers up over her head* **bedclothes**, bedding, sheets, blankets, linen; duvet, quilt, eiderdown; bedspread, counterpane.
4 *a thick cover of snow* **coating**, coat, covering, layer, carpet, blanket, overlay, topping, dusting, cloak, mantle, canopy, film, sheet, veneer, crust, surface, skim, skin, thickness, deposit, veil, pall, shroud.
5 *panicking onlookers ran for cover* **shelter**, protection, refuge, hiding, concealment, housing, sanctuary; shield, defence, haven, hiding place.
6 *there is considerable game cover around the lake* **undergrowth**, vegetation, shrubbery, greenery, ground cover, underwood, copsewood, brushwood, brush, scrub, underscrub; woodland, forest, jungle; bushes, plants; covert, thicket, copse, coppice; *N. Amer.* underbrush, underbush, shin-tangle; *SE English* frith; *archaic* rone; *rare* herbage, verdure.
7 *the company was a cover for an international swindle* **front**, facade, smokescreen, screen, blind, deception, camouflage, disguise, mask, cloak, pretext, masquerade, feint.
8 (*Brit.*) *your policy already provides cover against damage by subsidence* **insurance**, protection, security, assurance, indemnification, indemnity, compensation.
9 *the information you requested is being sent under separate cover* **envelope**, wrapper, package; **wrapping**, packaging.

coverage ▶ **noun** *they praised the newspaper's coverage of sport* **reporting**, reportage, description, treatment, handling, presentation; investigation, exploration, consideration, study, analysis, commentary; reports, accounts, articles, pieces, stories.

covering ▶ **noun 1** *the canvas covering of the back of the wagon* **awning**, tarpaulin, cowling, casing, housing; wrapping, wrapper, cover, envelope, sheath, sheathing, sleeve, jacket, lid, top, cap.
2 *a decent covering of snow on the slopes* **layer**, **coating**, coat, cover, carpet, blanket, overlay, topping, dusting, cloak, mantle, canopy, film, sheet, veneer, crust, surface, skim, skin, thickness, deposit, veil, pall, shroud.
▶ **adjective** *a covering letter* **accompanying**, associated; **explanatory**, expository, introductory, prefatory, descriptive.

coverlet ▶ **noun** *she pulled back the coverlet from the bed* **bedspread**, bedcover, cover, throw, afghan; duvet, quilt; *Brit.* eiderdown; *N. Amer.* spread, comforter; *dated* counterpane.

covert ▶ **adjective** *the Agency was warned to stop all covert aid to terrorist groups* **secret**, furtive, clandestine, surreptitious, stealthy, cloak-and-dagger, hole-and-corner, hole-in-the-corner, closet, behind-the-scenes,

backstairs, back-alley, under-the-table, hugger-mugger, concealed, hidden, private; sly, sneaky, underhand; undercover, underground; *informal* hush-hush.
OPPOSITES overt; above board.

cover-up ▶ **noun** *the other officers charged were mostly implicated in the cover-up rather than the massacre itself* **whitewash**, **concealment**, deception, suppression, false front, facade, veneer, pretext; -gate, camouflage, disguise, mask.
OPPOSITE exposé.

covet ▶ **verb** *people still coveted things which didn't belong to them* **desire**, be consumed with desire for, crave, have one's heart set on; **want**, wish for, long for, yearn for, dream of, aspire to, hanker for, hanker after, hunger after/for, thirst for, ache for, fancy, burn for, pant for.

covetous ▶ **adjective** *the covetous man will never have enough* **grasping**, greedy, rapacious, insatiable, yearning, acquisitive, desirous, possessive, selfish; **jealous**, envious, green with envy, green, green-eyed; grudging, begrudging; *N. Amer. informal* grabby.
OPPOSITE satisfied.

covey ▶ **noun** *a covey of partridges | a covey of young ladies trooped through* **group**, gang, troop, troupe, party, company, band, body, crowd, pack, army, herd, flock, bevy, drove, horde, galaxy, assemblage, gathering; knot, cluster; *informal* bunch, gaggle, posse, crew.

cow[1] ▶ **noun**. *See centre pages for list of* **Cattle**

WORD LINKS
relating to cows **bovine**

cow[2] ▶ **verb** *has he cowed you all with his threats?* **intimidate**, daunt, browbeat, bully, badger, dragoon, bludgeon, tyrannize, overawe, awe, dismay, dishearten, unnerve, subdue, scare, terrorize, frighten, petrify; *informal* psych out, bulldoze, railroad.

coward ▶ **noun** *the cowards turned back as soon as it looked dangerous* **weakling**, milksop, namby-pamby, mouse; *informal* chicken, scaredy-cat, fraidy-cat, yellow-belly, sissy, big baby; *Brit. informal* big girl's blouse; *N. Amer. informal* candy-ass, pussy; *Austral./NZ informal* dingo, sook; *informal, dated* funk; *archaic* poltroon, craven, recreant, caitiff.
OPPOSITE hero.

cowardice ▶ **noun** *he was charged with displaying cowardice in the face of the enemy* **faint-heartedness**, spiritlessness, spinelessness, timidity, timorousness, fearfulness, pusillanimity, weakness, feebleness; *informal* gutlessness, wimpishness, wimpiness, sissiness; *Brit. informal* wetness; *archaic* poltroonery, recreancy, poor-spiritedness; *rare* cravenness.
OPPOSITES bravery, courage.

cowardly ▶ **adjective** *the cowardly little wretches were trying to keep out of his way* **faint-hearted**, lily-livered, chicken-hearted, pigeon-hearted, spiritless, spineless, craven; **timid**, timorous, fearful, trembling, quaking, shrinking, cowering, afraid of one's own shadow, pusillanimous, weak, feeble, soft; *informal* yellow, chicken, weak-kneed, gutless, yellow-bellied, wimpish, wimpy, sissy, sissified; *Brit. informal* wet; *N. Amer. informal* candy-assed; *N. Amer. vulgar slang* chickenshit; *archaic* poltroon, recreant, poor-spirited.
OPPOSITES brave, courageous.

cowboy ▶ **noun** **1** *the cows were separated from the calves by a cowboy on horseback* **cattleman**, cowhand, cowman, cowherd, herder, herdsman, drover, stockman, rancher; (*in Spanish-speaking America*) gaucho, llanero, ranchero, vaquero; *N. Amer. informal* cowpuncher, cowpoke, broncobuster; *N. Amer. dated* buckaroo; *archaic* herd.
2 (*informal*) *the builders we had were complete cowboys* **cheat**, swindler, fraudster, trickster, charlatan, scoundrel, rogue, rascal, unscrupulous operator; **incompetent**, amateur, bungler, blunderer, bumbler; *Brit. informal* bodger.
OPPOSITE professional.

cower ▶ **verb** *children cowered in terror as the shoot-out erupted* **cringe**, shrink, crouch, recoil, flinch, pull back, back away, draw back, shudder, shiver, tremble, shake, quake, grovel, blench, blanch, quail.

coy ▶ **adjective** *she treated him to a coy smile of invitation* **arch**, simpering, coquettish, flirtatious, kittenish, skittish; shy, modest, bashful, reticent, diffident, retiring, backward, self-effacing, shrinking, withdrawn, timid, demure.
OPPOSITE brazen.

coyness ▶ **noun** *she held the scarf across her face in practised coyness* **archness**, simpering, coquettishness, flirtatiousness, kittenishness, skittishness; shyness, modesty, bashfulness, reticence, diffidence, self-effacement, timidity, demureness.
OPPOSITE brazenness.

cozen ▶ **verb** (*archaic*) *you'll not cozen me so. See* TRICK.

crabbed ▶ **adjective** **1** *her handwriting was crabbed and minuscule* **cramped**, bad, shaky, scribbled, spidery, laboured, illegible, unreadable, indecipherable.
OPPOSITES bold; clear.
2 *a crabbed old man. See* CRABBY.

crabby ▶ **adjective** *she was regarded as crabby and reclusive* **irritable**, fractious, fretful, cross, petulant, pettish, crabbed, crotchety, cantankerous, curmudgeonly, disagreeable, miserable, morose, peppery, on edge, edgy, impatient, complaining, querulous; bitter, moody, in a bad mood, grumpy, huffy, scratchy, out of sorts, out of temper, ill-tempered, bad-tempered, ill-natured, ill-humoured, peevish, sullen, surly, sulky, sour, churlish, touchy, testy, tetchy, snappish, waspish, prickly, crusty, bilious, liverish, dyspeptic, splenetic, choleric; *informal* snappy, chippy, grouchy, cranky, whingeing, whingy; *Brit. informal* narky, ratty, eggy, like a bear with a sore head; *N. Amer. informal* sorehead, soreheaded, peckish; *Austral./NZ informal* snaky; *dated* miffy.
OPPOSITES sweet-natured, easy-going, charming.

crack ▶ **noun** **1** *cracks spread from the bullet hole across the window* **split**, fissure, crevice, break, fracture, rupture, breach, rift, cleft, slit, chink, gap, cranny, interstice; *rare* crazing.
2 *the crack of a rifle rang out* **bang**, report, explosion, detonation, clap, pop, snap, crackle, knock, tap, clash, crash, smash, smack; *informal* wham, whump.
3 *he got a crack on the head* **blow**, bang, hit, punch, knock, thump, rap, bump, thwack, smack, slap, welt, cuff, box; *informal* bash, whack, clobber, clout, clip, wallop, belt, tan, biff, bop, sock, lam, whomp; *Brit. informal* slosh; *N. Amer. informal* boff, bust, slug, whale; *Austral./NZ informal* dong; *dated* buffet.
4 (*informal*) *I fancy having a crack at winning a fourth title* **attempt**, try, effort, endeavour, venture; *informal* go, shot, stab, whack, whirl; *formal* essay; *archaic* assay.
5 (*informal*) *it is easy to make cheap cracks about her hair and clothes* **joke**, witticism, funny remark, witty remark, jest, quip, pun, sally, pleasantry, epigram, aphorism; repartee, banter; *French* bon mot; **jibe**, barb, jeer, sneer, taunt, insult, cutting remark, slight, affront, slur, insinuation; *informal* one-liner, gag, wisecrack, funny, dig.

▶ **verb** **1** *take care not to crack the glass* **split**, fracture, fissure, rupture, break, snap, cleave; *rare* craze.
2 *a gun cracked and the bullet fizzed overhead* **go bang**, bang, pop, snap, crackle, crash, thud, thump, boom, ring out, clap; explode, detonate.
3 *she cracked him across the forehead* **hit**, strike, beat, thump, hammer, knock, rap, pound, thud, punch, bump, thwack, smack, slap, slam, welt, cuff, pummel, buffet, box someone's ears; *informal* bash, whack, clobber, clout, clip, wallop, belt, tan, biff, bop, sock, lam, whomp; *Brit. informal* slosh; *N. Amer. informal* boff, bust, slug, whale; *Austral./NZ informal* dong.
4 *the witnesses cracked and the truth came out* **break down**, give way, cave in, crumble, collapse, go to pieces, lose control, yield, succumb, founder; *informal* fall/come apart at the seams.
5 (*informal*) *the naval code proved harder to crack* **solve**, find an/the answer to, find a/the solution to, resolve, work out, puzzle out, fathom, find the key to, decipher, decode, break, clear up, interpret, translate, straighten out, get to the bottom of, make head or tail of, unravel, disentangle, untangle, unfold, piece together, elucidate; *informal* figure out, suss out.

□ **crack down** *a nationwide drive to crack down on crime* **get tough on**, take severe/stern measures against, clamp down on, come down heavily on; eliminate, abolish, eradicate, extinguish, quench, repress, stifle, suppress, put an end to, put a stop to, end, finish, get rid of, crush, put down, weed out, curb, nip in the bud, thwart, frustrate, scotch, squash, quash, quell, subdue, terminate, beat, overcome, defeat, rout, destroy, demolish, annihilate, wipe out, extirpate; limit, restrain, restrict, check, keep in check, control, keep under control; *informal* come down on like a ton of bricks, squelch, put the kibosh on, clobber.

□ **crack up** (*informal*) **1** *I feel I'm cracking up, always on the verge of tears* **break down**, have a breakdown, lose control, be overcome, collapse, go to pieces, go out of one's mind, go mad, crumble, disintegrate; *informal* lose it, lose one's cool, fall/come apart at the seams, go crazy, freak out.
2 *she tried to keep a straight face but kept cracking up* **burst out laughing**, dissolve into laughter, roar with laughter, shake with laughter, laugh uncontrollably, guffaw, be doubled up, split one's sides, hold one's sides; *informal* fall about, be in stitches, break up, crease up, be creased up, be rolling in the aisles, laugh like a drain.

▶ **adjective** *he is a crack shot* **expert**, skilled, skilful, masterly, virtuoso, master, consummate, proficient, accomplished, talented, gifted, adept, adroit, deft, dexterous, able, good, competent, capable, efficient, experienced, seasoned, trained, practised; professional, polished, well versed, versed; magnificent, brilliant, splendid, marvellous, impressive, excellent, formidable, outstanding, first-class, first-rate, fine; deadly; *informal* great, mean, wicked, nifty, ace, wizard; *Brit. informal* a dab hand at; *N. Amer. informal* crackerjack; *vulgar slang* shit-hot; *archaic or humorous* compleat; *rare* habile.
OPPOSITE incompetent.

crackdown ▶ **noun** *a crackdown on car crime* **clampdown**, getting tough, severe/stern measures, repression, suppression, abolition, elimination, eradication, end, stop.

cracked ▶ **adjective** **1** *this cup is cracked* **split**, broken, fissured, fractured, ruptured, splintered, cleft, slit; damaged, defective, flawed, imperfect; *rare* crazed.

C

2 (*informal*) *you're cracked!* See MAD.

crackle ▶ verb *the fire crackled and spat sparks* **sizzle**, frizzle, fizz, hiss, crack, snap, sputter; *technical* decrepitate; *rare* crepitate.

cradle ▶ noun **1** *the baby's cradle* **crib**, bassinet, Moses basket, cot, carrycot.
2 *the cradle of democracy* **birthplace**, fount, fountainhead, source, spring, fountain, origin, place of origin, breeding place, nursery, root, roots, seat, seed, germ; **beginning**, start, origination, genesis, birth, dawning, dawn, emergence, inception, launch, creation, early stages, conception, inauguration, foundation, outset; *Latin* fons et origo; *formal* commencement; *literary* wellspring; *rare* radix.
3 *the lifeboat was displayed on a cradle* **framework**, rack, holder, stand, base, support, mounting, mount, platform, prop, horse, rest, chock, plinth, bottom, trivet, bracket, frame, subframe, structure, substructure, chassis.
▶ verb *she cradled his head in her arms* **hold**, support, prop up, rest, pillow, bolster, cushion, shelter, protect.

craft¹ ▶ noun **1** *the old tailor was proud of his craft* **skill**, skilfulness, facility, ability, capability, competence, art, technique, aptitude, talent, flair, gift, genius, cleverness, knack; artistry, mastery, dexterity, dexterousness, craftsmanship, workmanship, expertness, expertise, proficiency, adroitness, adeptness, deftness, ingenuity, virtuosity; *informal* know-how.
2 *the historian's craft* **activity**, pursuit, occupation, work, line, line of work, profession, job, business, line of business, trade, employment, position, post, situation, career, métier, vocation, calling, skill, field, province, walk of life; *Scottish* way; *informal* racket, game; *Austral. informal* grip; *archaic* employ.
3 *he knew how to win by craft and diplomacy what he could not gain by force* **cunning**, craftiness, guile, wiliness, artfulness, deviousness, slyness, trickery, trickiness; duplicity, dishonesty, cheating, deceitfulness, deceit, deception, sharp practice, chicanery, intrigue, scheming, strategy, subterfuge, evasion; wiles, ploys, schemes, stratagems, tactics, manoeuvres, tricks, ruses; *informal* foxiness, monkey business, funny business, hanky-panky, jiggery-pokery, every trick in the book.
OPPOSITES honesty; naivety.

craft² *See centre pages for lists of* **Ships and Boats** **Sailing Ships and Boats**
▶ noun *the river was teeming with all sorts of craft* **vessel**, ship, boat, watercraft, aircraft, machine, spacecraft, spaceship; *Brit. informal, dated* kite; *literary* keel, barque.

craftsman, craftswoman ▶ noun *the tiles are handmade by craftsmen* **artisan**, craftsperson, tradesman, tradeswoman, tradesperson, mechanic, technician, operative, maker, smith, wright, journeyman; skilled worker, dedicated worker, meticulous worker, master, expert, artist; *archaic* artificer; *rare* handicraftsman, handicraftswoman.

craftsmanship ▶ noun *one of the finest examples of early twentieth-century Russian craftsmanship* **workmanship**, artistry, craft, art, artisanship, handiwork, work; **skill**, skilfulness, technique, expertise, mastery.

crafty ▶ adjective *Mum knew them to be crafty rogues* **cunning**, guileful, wily, artful, devious, sly, tricky, duplicitous, dishonest, underhand, cheating, deceitful, sharp, scheming, calculating, designing, evasive; shrewd, astute, canny; *informal* foxy; *S. African informal* slim; *archaic* subtle.
OPPOSITES honest; naive.

crag ▶ noun *the castle was set on a crag above the village* **cliff**, bluff, ridge, precipice, rock face, overhang; height, peak, tor, pinnacle; promontory, headland; bank, slope, escarpment, scarp; *rare* eminence.

craggy ▶ adjective **1** *the craggy cliffs* **rocky**, rough, ragged, rugged, uneven, bumpy, stony, irregular, pitted, broken up, jagged, precipitous, cragged, rock-bound.
OPPOSITE smooth.
2 *his craggy, lined face* **rugged**, rough-hewn, rough-textured, strong, manly, masculine; weather-beaten, weathered.
OPPOSITE delicate.

cram ▶ verb **1** *the bookcases were crammed with dusty volumes* **stuff**, pack, jam, fill, crowd, throng; overfill, fill up, fill to overflowing, stuff to the gills, fill to the brim, overcrowd, overload.
2 *they all crammed into the car* **crowd**, crush, pack, jam, squash, wedge oneself, shove, push, jostle, throng, force one's way, thrust.
3 *he crammed the sandwiches into his mouth* **force**, ram, thrust, plunge, push, pile, stick, jam, pack, compress, squeeze, wedge, press, tamp, pound, drive, hammer, bang; *informal* shove, stuff.
4 *most of the students are cramming for exams* **study intensively**, revise; *informal* swot, mug up, bone up.

cramp ▶ noun *an attack of cramp* **muscle/muscular spasm**, muscle/muscular contraction, pang, twinge; crick, kink, stitch, stiffness, pain, shooting pain, ache, convulsion, tic, twitch; *Medicine* clonus, hyperkinesis.
▶ verb *tighter rules will cramp economic growth* **hinder**, impede, inhibit, hamper, constrain, hamstring, obstruct, block, thwart, slow, check, arrest, curb, bridle, shackle, encumber, retard, handicap, tie, interfere with; **restrict**, limit, confine, restrain, set/impose limits on, regulate, control, moderate, cut down on; *informal* stymie.

cramped ▶ adjective **1** *the accommodation was cramped and the conditions primitive* **restricted**, confined, constricted; small, tiny, narrow, compact, tight, poky, uncomfortable, minimal, sparse, inadequate; hemmed in, crowded, overfull, packed, jammed, congested; *archaic* strait; *rare* incommodious.
OPPOSITE spacious.
2 *he had very cramped handwriting* **small**, **crabbed**, pinched, tightly packed, close, shaky, scribbled, laboured, illegible, unreadable, indecipherable.
OPPOSITES flowing; bold.

crane ▶ noun *the cargo was put aboard by crane* **derrick**, winch, hoist, davit, windlass, tackle, block and tackle, lifting gear; *Nautical* sheer legs.

cranium ▶ noun **skull**, brain case; brain; head; *informal* brainpan.

crank¹ ▶ verb *you two crank the engine by hand* **start**, turn (over), get going.
□ **crank something up** *they aim to crank up production capacity by the addition of a new factory* **increase**, make larger, make bigger, make greater, add to, augment, build up, enlarge, expand, extend, raise, multiply, elevate, swell, inflate; magnify, intensify, amplify, heighten, escalate; worsen, make worse, exacerbate, aggravate, compound, reinforce; improve, make better, boost, ameliorate, enhance, upgrade; *informal* up, jack up, hike up, hike, bump up, step up.
▶ noun *even light pressure on the crank will turn the shaft* **lever**, arm, bar, pedal.

crank² ▶ noun *I was treated like a crank by the so-called experts* **eccentric**, oddity, odd fellow, unorthodox person, individualist, nonconformist, free spirit, bohemian, maverick, deviant, pervert, misfit, hippy, dropout; madman/madwoman, lunatic, psychotic; **fanatic**, fan, zealot, addict, enthusiast, devotee, aficionado; *informal* oddball, odd/queer fish, freak, character, weirdie, weirdo, crackpot, loony, nut, nutter, nutcase, head case, sicko, perv, fiend, maniac, buff, -head, a great one for; *Brit. informal* one-off, odd bod; *N. Amer. informal* wacko, wack, screwball, kook, geek, jock; *Austral./NZ informal* dingbat; *informal, dated* case.

cranky ▶ adjective **1** *a cranky diet* **eccentric**, **bizarre**, weird, peculiar, odd, quirky, avant-garde, unconventional, strange, outlandish, ridiculous, ludicrous; mad, insane, crazy, absurd; *informal* wacky, screwy, nutty, nuts, crackpot, cracked, oddball, kinky, off the wall, way out, dippy, cuckoo; *Brit. informal* daft; *N. Amer. informal* kooky, wacko, left-field; *Austral./NZ informal, dated* dilly.
2 *the children were getting a bit tired and cranky* **bad-tempered**, irritable, irascible, tetchy, testy, grumpy, grouchy, crotchety, in a (bad) mood, ill-tempered, ill-natured, ill-humoured, peevish; having got out of bed the wrong side, cross, as cross as two sticks, fractious, disagreeable, cantankerous, curmudgeonly, pettish, crabbed, crabby, waspish, prickly, peppery, touchy, scratchy, crusty, splenetic, shrewish, short-tempered, hot-tempered, quick-tempered, dyspeptic, choleric, bilious, liverish, cross-grained; *informal* snappish, snappy, chippy, on a short fuse, short-fused; *Brit. informal* shirty, stroppy, narky, ratty, eggy, like a bear with a sore head; *N. Amer. informal* ornery, peckish, soreheaded; *Austral./NZ informal* snaky; *informal, dated* waxy, miffy.

cranny ▶ noun *every little cranny was filled with drifted snow* **chink**, crack, crevice, slit, split, fissure, rift, cleft, opening, gap, aperture, cavity, hole, hollow, niche, corner, recess, bay, booth, alcove, nook, interstice.

crash ▶ verb **1** *the car crashed into a tree* **smash into**, collide with, be in collision with, come into collision with, hit, strike, ram, smack into, slam into, bang into, cannon into, plough into, meet head-on, run into, drive into, bump into, knock into, crack into/against; dash against; *N. Amer.* impact.
2 *he has crashed his car again* **smash**, wreck, bump; *Brit.* write off; *Brit. informal* prang; *N. Amer. informal* total.
3 *burning timbers crashed to the ground* **fall**, plunge, hurtle, plummet, topple, tumble, overbalance, pitch.
4 *waves **crashed against** the shore* **be hurled**, dash; **batter**, pound, pummel, lash, slam into.
5 *he crashed down the telephone receiver* **slam**, bang, ram, smack.
6 *thunder crashed overhead* **boom**, crack, roll, clap, explode, bang, blast, resound, reverberate, rumble, thunder, ring out, sound loudly, blare, echo, fill the air; clash, clang, clank, clatter, smash.
7 *he used up his fortune repaying creditors after his clothing company crashed* **fail**, collapse, fold (up), go under, founder, be ruined, cave in; go bankrupt, become insolvent, cease trading, go into receivership, go into liquidation, be liquidated, be wound up, be closed (down), be shut (down); *informal* go broke, go bust, go bump, go to the wall, go belly up, come a cropper, flop.
8 (*informal*) *they crashed someone's party* **gatecrash**, come uninvited to, sneak into, slip into, invade, butt in on, intrude on/into; *informal* horn in on.
▶ noun **1** *there was a crash on the main road* **accident**, collision, smash, bump, car crash, car accident, road accident, traffic accident, road traffic accident, RTA, multiple crash, multiple collision; rail accident, derailment; air accident, air crash; *N. Amer.* wreck; *informal* smash-up, pile-up, shunt; *Brit. informal* prang.
2 *I heard the crash when you knocked the statue over* **bang**, smash, smack, crack, boom, bump, thud, thump, slam, clunk, clonk, clash, clang;

report, explosion, detonation, shot; clangour, racket, din; *informal* wham, whump.
3 *the crash of the company meant that 150 jobs would go* **failure**, collapse, foundering, ruin, ruination; **bankruptcy**, insolvency, cessation of trading, receivership, liquidation, winding up, closure, shutting.
▶ **adjective** *a crash course in diesel engine maintenance* **intensive**, concentrated, telescoped, high-pressure, strenuous, vigorous, all-out, thorough, in-depth, all-absorbing, total-immersion, rapid, urgent.
OPPOSITE extensive.

crass ▶ **adjective 1** *the crass assumptions that men make about women* **stupid**, insensitive, blundering, dense, thick, vacuous, mindless, witless, doltish, oafish, boorish, asinine, bovine, coarse, gross; *informal* pig-ignorant.
OPPOSITE intelligent.
2 *you committed an act of crass stupidity* **gross**, utter, sheer, downright, total, out-and-out, outright, very great, complete, absolute, thorough, perfect, blatant, unmitigated, unqualified, glaring, undisguised, naked.

crate ▶ **noun** *the third crate contained the explosives* **case**, packing case, chest, coffer, trunk, box, casket, strongbox, basket, hamper, pack, bin, drum, container, receptacle; *technical* lug.

crater ▶ **noun** *the crater has become a lake* **hollow**, bowl, basin, pan, hole, cavity, pocket; shell hole; *Geology* caldera, maar, solfatara.

crave ▶ **verb** *he craved professional recognition* **long for**, yearn for, hunger for, thirst for, dream of, aspire to, set one's heart on, have as one's aim, have as one's goal, seek, be bent on; desire, want, hope for, hanker after, wish for; sigh for, pant for, pine for; lust after, covet; *informal* have a yen for, itch for, be dying for; *archaic* be athirst for, be desirous of; *rare* desiderate, suspire for.

craven ▶ **adjective** *a craven surrender* **cowardly**, lily-livered, faint-hearted, chicken-hearted, pigeon-hearted, spiritless, spineless, timid, timorous, fearful, trembling, quaking, shrinking, cowering, afraid of one's own shadow, pusillanimous, weak, feeble, soft; *informal* yellow, chicken, weak-kneed, gutless, yellow-bellied, wimpish, wimpy, sissy, sissified; *Brit. informal* wet; *N. Amer. informal* candy-assed; *N. Amer. vulgar slang* chickenshit; *archaic* poltroon, recreant, poor-spirited.
OPPOSITE brave.

craving ▶ **noun** *a craving for chocolate* **longing**, yearning, hankering, hunger, hungering, thirst, pining, desire, want, wish, fancy, urge, need, appetite, greed, lust, ache, burning, addiction, aspiration, aim, goal; *informal* yen, itch; *rare* cacoethes.

crawl ▶ **verb 1** *they crawled from under the table* **creep**, go on all fours, move on hands and knees, inch, drag oneself along, pull oneself along, drag, trail, slither, slink, squirm, wriggle, writhe, scrabble, worm one's way, advance slowly/stealthily, sneak.
2 (*informal*) *let's stop trying to get women to support us by crawling to them* **grovel to**, be obsequious towards, ingratiate oneself with, be servile towards, be sycophantic towards, kowtow to, pander to, abase oneself to, demean oneself to, bow and scrape to, prostrate oneself before, toady to, truckle to, dance attendance on, fawn on/over, curry favour with, cultivate, seek the favour of, try to win over, try to get on the good side of, make up to, play up to; *informal* suck up to, lick someone's boots, creep to, be all over, fall all over, rub up the right way, keep someone sweet, sweet-talk, soft-soap, butter up, twist someone's arm; *N. Amer.* brown-nose; *vulgar slang* lick/kiss someone's arse; *archaic* blandish.
3 *the place was crawling with soldiers* **be full of**, overflow with, teem with, abound in/with, be packed with, be crowded with, be thronged with, be jammed with, be alive with, be overrun with, swarm with, be bristling with, be infested with, be thick with; *informal* be lousy with, be stuffed with, be jam-packed with, be chock-a-block with, be chock-full of; *rare* pullulate with.

craze ▶ **noun** *the latest fitness craze to sweep the country* **fad**, vogue, trend, fashion, enthusiasm, passion, infatuation, love, obsession, mania, compulsion, fixation, fetish, weakness, fancy, taste, novelty, whim, fascination, preoccupation, rage; *informal* thing.

crazed ▶ **adjective** *he took off in pursuit of the crazed murderer* **mad**, insane, out of one's mind, deranged, demented, certifiable, lunatic, wild, raving, distraught, berserk, manic, maniac, frenzied, hysterical, psychopathic; *informal* crazy, mental, off one's head, out of one's head, raving mad.
OPPOSITE sane.

crazy ▶ **adjective** (*informal*) **1** *all the publicity nearly sent her crazy* **mad**, insane, out of one's mind, deranged, demented, not in one's right mind, crazed, lunatic, non compos mentis, unbalanced, unhinged, unstable, disturbed, distracted, mad as a hatter, mad as a March hare, stark mad; *informal* mental, off one's head, out of one's head, off one's nut, nutty, nutty as a fruitcake, off one's rocker, not (quite) right in the head, round the bend, raving mad, stark staring/raving mad, bats, batty, bonkers, cuckoo, loopy, loony, bananas, loco, dippy, screwy, with a screw loose, touched, gaga, doolally, up the pole, not all there, off the wall, out to lunch, not right upstairs, away with the fairies; *Brit. informal* barmy, crackers, barking, barking mad, round the twist, off one's trolley, as daft as a brush, not the full shilling, one sandwich short of a picnic; *N. Amer. informal* buggy, nutsy, nutso, out of one's tree, meshuga, squirrelly, wacko, gonzo; *Canadian & Austral./NZ informal* bushed; *NZ informal* porangi.
OPPOSITE sane.
2 *children get all sorts of crazy ideas* **absurd**, preposterous, ridiculous, ludicrous, farcical, laughable, risible; idiotic, stupid, foolish, foolhardy, unwise, imprudent, ill-conceived, silly, inane, puerile, infantile, fatuous, imbecilic, hare-brained, half-baked; unreasonable, irrational, illogical, nonsensical, pointless, senseless, impracticable, unworkable, unrealistic; outrageous, wild, shocking, astonishing, monstrous; unbelievable, incredible, unthinkable, implausible; peculiar, odd, strange, queer, weird, eccentric, bizarre, fantastic, incongruous, grotesque; *informal* barmy, daft, potty, cock-eyed.
OPPOSITE sensible.
3 *people in Barbados are just crazy about cricket* **very enthusiastic**, passionate, fanatical, excited; very keen on, enamoured of, infatuated with, smitten with, devoted to, fond of; *informal* wild, mad, nutty, nuts, potty, gone on; *informal, dated* sweet on.
OPPOSITES apathetic, indifferent.

creak ▶ **verb** *the floorboards creaked* **squeak**, groan, grate; screech, squeal, grind, jar, rasp, rub, scrape; complain.

cream ▶ **noun 1** *all sorts of creams for the skin* **lotion**, ointment, rub, cosmetic, application, preparation, emollient, moisturizer, paste, gel, salve, unguent, embrocation, balm, liniment, pomade; *archaic* unction.
2 *the cream of the world's photographers* **best**, finest, first class, top, choice, choicest, flower, prize, treasure, pearl, gem, jewel, the jewel in the crown, the crème de la crème; **elite**, elect, nonpareil; *informal* tops, pick of the bunch.
OPPOSITE dregs.
▶ **adjective** *a cream dress* **off-white**, whitish, cream-coloured, creamy, ivory, yellowish-white, pearly.
▶ **verb**
□ **cream something off** *grammar schools creamed off the more academic pupils* **pick and choose**; *informal* cherry-pick.

creamy ▶ **adjective 1** *when mixed with water, the powder forms a creamy paste* **smooth**, thick, whipped, velvety, of an even consistency, rich, buttery.
OPPOSITES lumpy; thin.
2 *the orchids had creamy flowers* **off-white**, whitish, cream-coloured, cream, ivory, yellowish-white, pearly.

crease ▶ **noun 1** *he always has trousers with creases* **fold**, groove, ridge, furrow, line, ruck, pleat, tuck, corrugation; *Brit. rare* ruckle.
2 *she has creases at the corners of her eyes* **wrinkle**, line, crinkle, pucker, laughter line; (**creases**) *informal* crow's feet.
▶ **verb 1** *if I lie on that, I'll crease my clothes* **crumple**, wrinkle, crinkle, scrunch up, rumple, line, pucker, crimp, ruck up, gather, furrow; *Brit. rare* ruckle.
OPPOSITE press.
2 *his trousers were properly creased* **press**, iron, put a crease in, fold; corrugate, pleat, tuck.
OPPOSITE crumple.

create ▶ **verb 1** *the sculpture has been created out of Portland stone* **generate**, produce, design, make, fabricate, fashion, manufacture, build, construct, erect, do, turn out; bring into being, originate, invent, initiate, engender, devise, frame, develop, shape, form, mould, forge, concoct, hatch; *informal* knock together, knock up, knock off.
OPPOSITE dismantle.
2 *regular socializing creates a good working team spirit* **bring about**, result in, cause, be the cause of, give rise to, lead to, breed, generate, engender, produce, make, make for, prompt, promote, foster, sow the seeds of, contribute to, stir up, whip up, inspire; *literary* enkindle.
OPPOSITE destroy.
3 *the governments planned to create a free-trade zone* **establish**, found, institute, constitute, inaugurate, launch, set up, start, lay the foundations of; form, organize, develop, build up; get something going, get something moving, get something working; *informal* kick something off.
4 *she was created a life peer in 1990* **appoint**, make, install as, invest; name, nominate, designate.
5 *sometimes a child is created to replace the loss of another* **conceive**, give birth to, bring into the world, bring into being, bring into existence, give life to, father, sire, spawn, produce; *N. Amer.* birth; *informal* drop; *literary* beget.

creation ▶ **noun 1** *he embarked on the creation of an outstanding garden* **design**, formation, forming, modelling, putting together, setting up, making, construction, constructing, fabrication, fabricating, fashioning, building, erection, erecting; production, generation, origination, devising, invention, initiation, inception, shaping, hatching.
OPPOSITE destruction.
2 *Aten was a universal god of all creation* **the world**, the universe, the cosmos; the living world, the natural world, nature, life, living things.
3 *the Constitution allowed for the creation of a second vice-president* **appointment**, installation, investing, investiture, inauguration; establishment, foundation, institution.
OPPOSITE removal.
4 *there is power associated with the creation and raising of children*

C

C

conception, bringing into the world, bringing into being, bringing into existence, fathering, siring, spawning, giving birth to; genesis, procreation; *N. Amer.* birthing; *informal* dropping; *literary* begetting.
5 *it was hard to distinguish between forgery and original creation* **work**, work of art, achievement, production, opus, oeuvre, invention, handiwork, masterpiece, masterwork; *Latin* magnum opus; *French* chef-d'œuvre, pièce de résistance, tour de force; *informal* brainchild; *rare* opuscule.
6 *she wore a creation by designer Marianne Jessica* **design**, dress, outfit; *informal* number.

WORD LINKS
related suffix **-geny (e.g. *cosmogeny, ontogeny*)**

creative ▶ **adjective** *our pupils are encouraged to be creative | the creative manipulation of language* **inventive**, imaginative, innovative, innovatory, innovational, experimental, original; artistic, expressive, inspired, visionary; productive, prolific, fertile; talented, gifted, resourceful, quick-witted, ingenious, clever, smart; unconventional, unorthodox, unusual, out of the ordinary; *informal* blue-sky.
OPPOSITES unimaginative, conservative.

creativity ▶ **noun** *challenging objectives motivate staff and encourage creativity* **inventiveness**, imagination, imaginativeness, innovation, innovativeness, originality, individuality; artistry, expressiveness, inspiration, vision, creative power, creative talent, creative gift, creative skill, resourcefulness, ingenuity, enterprise.

creator ▶ **noun 1** *the Sabbath is kept to honour the Creator* **God**, the Lord, the Almighty, the Master of the Universe; one's Maker.
2 *he is the creator of several hit musicals* **writer**, author, composer, designer, deviser, maker, inventor, producer, developer; originator, initiator, instigator, generator, engineer, architect, mastermind, prime mover, father, mother; *literary* begetter.

creature ▶ **noun 1** *whales are the largest creatures living on earth* **animal**, beast, brute; **living thing**, living entity, living soul, soul, mortal, being, life form, organism; *informal* critter.
2 *You're such a lazy creature!* **fellow**, individual, character, wretch, beggar, soul; person, personage, human being, human, man, woman, boy, girl; *informal* devil, bunny, cookie, customer, sort, type, thing; *Brit. informal* chap, bloke, geezer, bod, kid, brat; *N. Amer. informal* dude, hombre, guy, gal; *informal, dated* body, dog, cove; *vulgar slang* bastard; *Brit. vulgar slang* sod, bugger; *archaic* wight.
3 *the village teacher was expected to be the creature of his employer* **minion**, lackey, flunkey, hireling, subordinate, servant, retainer, vassal; puppet, pawn, tool, instrument, cat's paw, dupe; *informal* skivvy, stooge, sucker, yes-man; *Brit. informal* poodle, dogsbody; *N. Amer. informal* gofer.

credence ▶ **noun 1** *psychoanalysis finds little credence among laymen* **acceptance**, belief, faith, trust, confidence, reliance.
2 *the messenger gave credence to her tale* **credibility**, credit, reliability, plausibility, believability.

credentials ▶ **plural noun** *the policemen went to check the driver's credentials* **documents**, papers, identity papers, identification papers, bona fides; warrant, licence, permit, pass, ID, card, ID card, identity card, passport, proof of identity, proof of qualifications, certificate, diploma, voucher, documentation; references, testimonial, letter of introduction, letter of recommendation, missive, deed, title.

credibility ▶ **noun 1** *the whole tale lacks credibility* **plausibility**, believability, acceptability, tenability, probability, likelihood, authority, authoritativeness, impressiveness, cogency, weight, validity, soundness; truth, veracity, faithfulness, fidelity, authenticity, accuracy, factualness; *rare* veridicality; *informal* clout.
OPPOSITE implausibility.
2 *the party lacked the moral credibility to govern* **trustworthiness**, reliability, dependability, integrity, character; reputation, standing, status, cachet, kudos, eminence, credit, acceptability.

credible ▶ **adjective 1** *very few people found his story credible* **believable**, plausible, able to hold water, within the bounds of possibility, reasonable, sound, compelling, persuasive; *rare* suasive, assuasive, verisimilar, colourable, cogitable.
OPPOSITE unbelievable.
2 *the existing lists did not form a credible basis for free and fair elections* **acceptable**, trustworthy, reliable, dependable, sure, good, valid; feasible, viable, tenable, sustainable, maintainable.
OPPOSITE untrustworthy.

credit ▶ **noun 1** *the writer got a very good press and a lot of credit* **praise**, commendation, acclaim, approval, approbation, acknowledgement, recognition, kudos, glory, merit, regard, esteem, respect, admiration, adulation, veneration, tributes; thanks, gratitude, appreciation; *informal* bouquets, brownie points; *rare* laudation, extolment, eulogium.
2 *the speech did his credit no good in the House of Commons* **reputation**, repute, character, image, name, good name, prestige, influence, standing, status, regard, esteem, estimation; **credibility**, acceptability; *Indian* izzat; *informal* clout; *N. Amer. informal* rep, rap; *archaic* honour, report; *rare* reputability.
3 *these men are a credit to their country* **source of honour**, source of pride, feather in the cap, asset, proud boast, glory, flower, gem, treasure.
4 *his theory has been given very little credit* **credence**, belief, faith, trust, reliance, confidence.
5 *the shop would be paid whether her credit was good or bad* **financial standing**, financial status, solvency.
□ **on credit** *he purchased £300 worth of goods on credit* **on hire purchase**, on (the) HP, by instalments, by deferred payment, on account; *informal* on tick, on the slate; *Brit. informal* on the never-never.
▶ **verb 1** *the wise will seldom credit all they hear* **believe**, accept, give credence to, have confidence in, trust, have faith in, rely on, depend on, count on; *informal* go for, fall for, buy, swallow, {swallow something hook, line, and sinker}, take something as gospel.
OPPOSITE disbelieve.
2 *the success of the scheme can be* **credited** *to the team's frugality* **ascribe**, attribute, assign, accredit, chalk up, put down, set down, impute; lay at the door of, connect with, associate with; *informal* stick something on.
3 *he* **was credited with** *inventing the lyre* **be accredited with**, be recognized as, be given the credit for, be held responsible for.

creditable ▶ **adjective** *the team worked hard and produced a creditable performance* **commendable**, praiseworthy, laudable, admirable, honourable, estimable, meritorious, exceptional, exemplary, noteworthy, notable, worthy, up to the mark, deserving, respectable, reputable, sterling; good, fine, excellent, outstanding, first-rate, first-class; worthy of commendation, worthy of admiration; *informal* A1, wicked, super, splendiferous, top-notch, fab, ace, tip-top; *Brit. informal* smashing, brill, top-hole, champion, grand; *N. Amer. informal* bully; *Austral./NZ informal* beaut; *rare* applaudable.
OPPOSITE deplorable.

credulity ▶ **noun** *moneylenders prey upon their credulity and inexperience* **gullibility**, gullibleness, credulousness, naivety, naiveness, blind faith, trustfulness, over-trustfulness, lack of suspicion, innocence, ingenuousness, unworldliness, lack of experience, lack of sophistication, guilelessness, greenness, callowness, childlikeness, simpleness, simplicity, ignorance.
OPPOSITES worldliness; suspicion.

credulous ▶ **adjective** *he sold 'miracle' cures to desperate and credulous clients* **gullible**, naive, impressionable, trusting, over-trusting, over-trustful, exploitable, dupable, deceivable, easily deceived, easily taken in, easily led, unsuspicious, unwary, unguarded, unsceptical, uncritical, unquestioning; innocent, ingenuous, unworldly, inexperienced, unsophisticated, artless, guileless, green, as green as grass, callow, raw, immature, childlike, wide-eyed, simple, ignorant; *informal* wet behind the ears, born yesterday; *rare* incognizant, nescient.
OPPOSITES worldly; suspicious.

CHOOSE THE RIGHT WORD

credulous, gullible
See GULLIBLE.

creed ▶ **noun 1** *the godparents will swear that they believe in the creed* **system of belief**, set of principles, statement of beliefs, profession of faith; doctrine, teaching, ideology, ethic, dogma, tenet, catechism, credo; beliefs, principles, canons, articles of faith, maxims, rules, laws.
2 *jobs should be available to all, irrespective of race or creed* **faith**, religion, religious belief(s), religious persuasion, religious conviction, religious group, faith community, church; persuasion, affiliation, denomination, sect, body, following, communion, order, school, fraternity, brotherhood, sisterhood.

creek ▶ **noun 1** (*Brit.*) *they're dredging for oysters in the creek* **tidal inlet**, inlet, arm of the sea, estuary, bay, bight, fjord, gulf, sound; *Scottish* firth, frith; (*in Orkney & Shetland*) voe; *technical* ria; *rare* fleet, armlet.
2 (*N. Amer. & Austral./NZ*) **stream**, rivulet, brook, river, tributary, backwater.

creep ▶ **verb 1** *he saw her creep under the bench* **crawl**, move on all fours, move on hands and knees, pull oneself, inch, edge, slither, slide, squirm, wriggle, writhe, worm, worm one's way, insinuate oneself.
2 *Tim crept out of the house in his pyjamas* **sneak**, steal, slip, slink, sidle, skulk, pad, prowl, tiptoe, pussyfoot, soft-shoe, tread warily, move stealthily, move furtively, move unnoticed, walk quietly.
3 (*informal*) *they're always* **creeping** *to the boss* **grovel**, crawl, toady, fawn, cower, cringe, truckle, kowtow, bow and scrape, prostrate oneself; be servile towards, be sycophantic towards, dance attendance on, ingratiate oneself with, curry favour with; flatter, woo, pay court to, get round; *informal* suck up to, make up to, be all over, fall all over, lick someone's boots, butter up, rub up the right way, keep sweet, sweet-talk, soft-soap; *N. Amer. informal* brown-nose; *archaic* blandish.
▶ **noun 1** *he's just a little creep who's got his sights set on Bella's money* **sycophant**, obsequious person, crawler, groveller, truckler, toady, fawner, flatterer, lickspittle, doormat, kowtower, spaniel, Uriah Heep; *informal* bootlicker, yes-man; *N. Amer. informal* suck-up, brown-nose, brown-noser; *Brit. vulgar slang* arse-licker, bum-sucker; *N. Amer. vulgar slang* ass-kisser, suckhole; *archaic* toad-eater.

2 (*informal*) *some creep had broken into his home* **rogue**, villain, wretch, reprobate; *informal* beast, pig, swine, rat, bastard, louse, snake, snake in the grass, skunk, dog, weasel, lowlife, scumbag, heel, stinker, stinkpot, bad lot, son of a bitch, s.o.b., nasty piece of work; *Scottish informal* scrote; *Irish informal* spalpeen, sleeveen; *N. Amer. informal* rat fink, fink; *Austral. informal* dingo; *informal, dated* hound, bounder, blighter, rotter; *vulgar slang* shit; *dated* cad, scoundrel; *archaic* blackguard, dastard, vagabond, knave, varlet, cur, wastrel.

creeper ▸ noun *the tree trunks were covered with creepers and fungi* **climbing plant**, trailing plant; vine, trailer, climber, rambler.

creeps ▸ plural noun

□ **give someone the creeps** (*informal*) *his slow smile gave her the creeps* **scare**, frighten, terrify, horrify, haunt; **repel**, repulse, revolt, disgust, sicken, nauseate, be repugnant to, be distasteful to, make shudder; make someone's flesh creep, make someone's skin crawl, make someone's blood run cold, make someone's gorge rise, turn someone's stomach; *informal* freak someone out, give someone the heebie-jeebies, make someone want to throw up.

creepy ▸ adjective (*informal*) *that house can be a pretty creepy place* **frightening**, scaring, terrifying, hair-raising, spine-chilling, blood-curdling, chilling, petrifying, alarming, shocking, harrowing, horrifying, horrific, horrible, awful, nightmarish, macabre, ghostly; **disturbing**, eerie, sinister, weird, menacing, ominous, threatening; *Scottish* eldritch; *informal* spooky, freaky, scary, hairy.
OPPOSITES relaxing, pleasant.

crescent ▸ noun *the bay was a small pebbled crescent backed by smooth boulders* **half-moon**, sickle-shape, semicircle; arc, curve, bow, arch, bend, crook; *rare* demilune, lunula.

crest ▸ noun **1** *the bird has a drooping black crest | he wears a gold helmet with a crest* **comb**, plume, tuft, topknot, mane; aigrette, panache, tassel; *technical* caruncle.
2 *they reached the crest of the hill* **summit**, peak, highest point, top, tip, pinnacle, brow, crown, head, cap, brink, apex, vertex, apogee, zenith; ridge, tor; *French* aiguille, serac.
OPPOSITE bottom.
3 *the plate bears the Duke of Wellington's crest* **insignia**, regalia, badge, emblem, ensign, device, heraldic device, coat of arms, arms, armorial bearing, escutcheon, shield; *Heraldry* bearing, charge.

crestfallen ▸ adjective *he came back to his apartment empty-handed and crestfallen* **downhearted**, downcast, despondent, disappointed, disconsolate, disheartened, discouraged, dispirited, dejected, depressed, desolate, heartbroken, broken-hearted, heavy-hearted, low-spirited, in the doldrums, sad, glum, gloomy, dismal, doleful, miserable, unhappy, woebegone, forlorn, long-faced, fed up; abashed, taken aback, dismayed, sheepish, hangdog, abject, defeated; *informal* blue, choked, shattered, down in the mouth, down in the dumps; *Brit. informal* brassed off, cheesed off; *literary* dolorous; *archaic* chap-fallen.
OPPOSITE cheerful.

crevasse ▸ noun *he rescued his climbing partner from a crevasse* **chasm**, abyss, fissure, cleft, crack, split, breach, rift, gap, hole, opening, pit, cavity, crater.

crevice ▸ noun *the termites crawled into a crevice in the ground* **crack**, fissure, cleft, chink, interstice, cranny, nook, vent, slot, slit, split, rift, gash, rent, fracture, rupture, breach, perforation; opening, gap, hole, aperture, orifice, pore, space, groove; *Medicine* hiatus, foramen; *technical* scission.

crew ▸ noun **1** *the captain was much loved by his officers and crew* **sailors**, seamen, mariners, hands; ship's company, ship's complement.
2 *he resigned in front of a local television crew* **team**, company, unit, party, working party, gang, shift, line-up, squad, force, corps, posse; workers, employees, staff.
3 (*informal*) *they're an odd crew, these money men* **crowd**, lot, set, group, circle, band, gang, mob, pack, troop, swarm, herd, posse, company, collection; *informal* bunch, gaggle, tribe.

crib ▸ noun **1** *he made a simple crib for the baby* **cot**, cradle, bassinet, Moses basket, carrycot.
2 *I must fill the oxen's cribs with hay* **manger**, stall, trough, feeding trough, bin, box, rack, fodder rack, bunker; container, receptacle.
3 (*informal*) *an English crib of Caesar's Gallic Wars* **translation**, key, guide.
4 (*informal, dated*) *that's a crib from Walter's work* **copy**, plagiarism, plagiarization, reproduction, replica, duplication, imitation; *informal* pirate, rip-off, knock-off, dupe.
5 (*N. Amer. informal*) *he took the girl back to his crib* **house**, flat, apartment, penthouse, cottage, bungalow; living quarters, quarters, accommodation; home, residence, abode, place; *Austral.* home unit; *informal* pad; *archaic* cot.
▸ verb (*informal, dated*) *she had cribbed the plot from a Shakespeare play* **copy**, reproduce, duplicate, appropriate, plagiarize, poach, steal, 'borrow', bootleg; *informal* pirate, rip off, lift; *Brit. informal* nick, pinch; *archaic* monkey.

crick ▸ noun *he got a crick in the neck from keeping his head down* **cramp**, spasm, muscle spasm, muscular contraction, rick, kink, twinge, pang, pain, shooting pain, ache; stiffness, discomfort, tenderness, soreness.
▸ verb *he cricked his neck during practice* **strain**, sprain, pull, wrench, tear, twist, rick; injure, hurt, damage, impair.

cricket ▸ noun. *See centre pages for list of* **Cricket Roles and Positions**

crier ▸ noun *they heard the voice of a crier in the market place* **announcer**, proclaimer, herald, town crier, messenger, bearer of tidings.

crime ▸ noun **1** *kidnapping is a very serious crime* **offence**, unlawful act, illegal act, breach/violation/infraction of the law, misdemeanour, misdeed, wrong, felony, violation, transgression, fault, injury; *Law* malfeasance, malefaction, tort; *archaic* trespass.
2 *the reduced police presence has brought an increase in crime* **lawbreaking**, delinquency, wrongdoing, transgression, misconduct, criminality, illegality, villainy, felony, corruption; *informal* crookedness, shadiness, dodginess; *Law* malfeasance, malefaction; *archaic* knavery; *rare* malversation.
3 *they condemned apartheid as a crime against humanity* **immoral act**, sin, evil, evil action, wrong, wrongdoing, atrocity, abomination, enormity, disgrace, outrage, monstrosity, violation, abuse, injustice, affront.

WORD LINKS
relating to crime **felonious**
study of crime **criminology**

criminal ▸ noun *she struck up a friendship with a convicted criminal* **lawbreaker**, offender, villain, delinquent, malefactor, culprit, wrongdoer, transgressor, sinner; young offender, juvenile delinquent; felon, thief, robber, armed robber, burglar, housebreaker, shoplifter, mugger, fraudster, swindler, racketeer, gunman, gangster, outlaw, bandit, terrorist, rapist; (*in Japan*) yakuza; *informal* crook, con, jailbird, (old) lag, lifer, baddy; *N. Amer. informal* yardbird, yegg; *Austral. informal* crim; *S. African informal* lighty; *W. Indian informal* tief; *Brit. rhyming slang* tea leaf; *informal, dated* cracksman; *Law* malfeasant, misfeasor, infractor; *archaic* miscreant, trespasser, trusty, transport; *rare* peculator, defalcator.
▸ adjective **1** *they were found guilty of criminal conduct* **unlawful**, illegal, illicit, illegitimate, lawbreaking, lawless, felonious, delinquent, culpable, villainous, nefarious, corrupt, fraudulent; indictable, punishable, actionable, unauthorized, unsanctioned, outlawed, banned, forbidden, interdicted, proscribed; wrong, bad, evil, wicked, iniquitous; *informal* crooked, shady, dirty; *Brit. informal* bent, dodgy; *Law* malfeasant.
OPPOSITE lawful.
2 (*informal*) *closing the railway would be criminal folly* **deplorable**, preposterous, shameful, reprehensible, disgraceful, inexcusable, unforgivable, unpardonable, unacceptable; senseless, foolish, ridiculous, outrageous, monstrous, shocking, scandalous; wicked, sinful, immoral, iniquitous; *rare* egregious.
OPPOSITE commendable.

WORD LINKS
study of crime and criminals **criminology**

crimp ▸ verb **1** *she crimped the edges of her two pies* **flute**, pleat, corrugate, ruffle, furrow, groove, ridge, crease, wrinkle, crinkle, crumple, pucker, gather; pinch, press together, squeeze together; *Brit. rare* ruckle.
2 *her hair had been crimped by the tight ribbons* **curl**, **crinkle**, kink, frizz, frizzle, coil, corkscrew, wave.

cringe ▸ verb **1** *I cringe in terror every time I have to face him* **cower**, shrink, draw back, pull back, recoil, start, shy (away), wince, flinch, blench, blanch, dodge, duck, crouch, shudder, shake, tremble, quiver, quail, quake; get cold feet.
2 *it makes me cringe when I think how stupid I was* **wince**, squirm, blush, flush, go red; feel embarrassed, feel ashamed, feel sheepish, feel mortified, wince with embarrassment.
3 *he was always cringing to the queen* **kowtow**, bow and scrape, grovel, creep, crawl, toady, fawn, truckle, cower; be servile towards, be sycophantic towards, dance attendance on, ingratiate oneself with, curry favour with; flatter, woo, pay court to, get round; *informal* suck up to, make up to, lick someone's boots, be all over, fall all over, sweet-talk, soft-soap; *N. Amer.* brown-nose; *archaic* blandish.

crinkle ▸ verb *the skin around his eyes crinkled as he smiled* **wrinkle**, crease, pucker, furrow, line, corrugate, crimp, crumple, rumple, ruck up, scrunch up; *Brit. rare* ruckle.
▸ noun *the film could be removed and replaced without crinkles* **wrinkle**, crease, fold, pucker, gather, furrow, ridge, line, corrugation, groove, crumple, rumple.

crinkly ▸ adjective *the dress had dried all crinkly* **wrinkled**, wrinkly, crinkled, crumpled, rumpled, creased, crimped, corrugated, fluted, gathered, puckered, furrowed, ridged, grooved, rippled, wavy, kinked, kinky.

cripple ▸ verb **1** *the car crash crippled a young woman for life* **disable**, paralyse, immobilize, make lame, lame, incapacitate, debilitate, handicap; **maim**, impair, damage, injure, hamstring; *rare* torpefy.
2 *sugar producers have been crippled by plummeting prices* **ruin**, destroy, wipe out, crush, break; impair, hamstring, hamper, impede, cramp, spoil, sabotage, scotch, scupper, bring to a standstill, paralyse, enfeeble, weaken, render powerless, put out of action, put out of business, bankrupt, make bankrupt, make insolvent, impoverish, reduce to

C

penury, bring someone to their knees; *informal* clean out, put the kibosh on, do for; *N. Amer. informal* rain on someone's parade; *archaic* bring to naught; *rare* vitiate, beggar, pauperize.
OPPOSITE boost.

crippled ▶ **adjective** *in those days crippled children generally died young* **disabled**, paralysed, lame, incapacitated, debilitated, physically handicapped, physically impaired; immobilized, housebound, bedridden, confined to bed, confined to a wheelchair, wheelchair-bound; **maimed**, injured, damaged, deformed, hunchbacked; *informal* laid up, flat on one's back; *euphemistic* physically challenged; *Medicine* paraplegic, quadriplegic, tetraplegic, monoplegic, hemiplegic, paretic, paraparetic; *dated* palsied; *archaic* halt.
OPPOSITE able-bodied.

C

crisis ▶ **noun 1** *events across the North Sea were building to a crisis* **critical point**, decisive point, turning point, crossroads, critical period, crux, climax, climacteric, culmination, height, head, moment of truth, zero hour, point of no return, Rubicon; *informal* crunch.
2 *the country was in the grip of an economic crisis | the fisheries are in crisis* **catastrophe**, calamity, cataclysm, emergency, disaster; predicament, plight, mess, dilemma, quandary, setback, reverse, reversal, upheaval, drama; **trouble**, dire straits, hard times, hardship, adversity, extremity, distress, difficulty; *informal* fix, pickle, jam, stew, scrape, bind, hole, sticky situation, hot water, hell, hell on earth, hassle, stress; *Brit. informal* spot of bother.

crisp ▶ **adjective 1** *fry the bacon until it is brown and crisp* **crunchy**, crispy, brittle, crumbly, breakable, shatterable, friable, frangible; rigid, hard; well cooked, well done.
OPPOSITE soft.
2 *the grass is looking crisp and healthy* **firm**, fresh, unwilted, unwithered.
OPPOSITE limp.
3 *despite the sunshine it was quite a crisp day* **brisk**, bracing, fresh, refreshing, invigorating, stimulating, energizing, exhilarating, rousing, fortifying, tonic; keen, raw, biting, cool, cold, chilly; *informal* pick-me-up, nippy; *Brit. informal* parky; *literary* chill.
OPPOSITE sultry.
4 *his message was disseminated in crisp language* **terse**, succinct, concise, brief, short, short and sweet, tight, taut, incisive, pithy, epigrammatic, aphoristic, elliptical; laconic, sparing; precise, clear, clear-cut, explicit, unambiguous, straightforward; *informal* snappy; *rare* lapidary, compendious, synoptic, gnomic.
OPPOSITES rambling; ambiguous.
5 *she has a crisp and rather schoolmistressy manner* **brusque**, brisk, vigorous, decisive, businesslike, no-nonsense, curt, blunt, short, sharp, snappy, snappish, abrupt, to the point, frank, plain-spoken, bald, brutal, indelicate, unceremonious, cavalier, offhand, gruff, rough, harsh, caustic, abrasive; pulling no punches, not mincing one's words, not beating about the bush, calling a spade a spade, speaking one's mind; *informal* upfront, straight from the shoulder.
6 *his new suit gave him a very crisp appearance* **smart**, elegant, chic, spruce, dapper, neat, trim, clean-cut, well groomed; *informal* snappy, natty, sharp; *N. Amer. informal* spiffy; *archaic* trig.
OPPOSITE scruffy.

criterion ▶ **noun** *academic ability is not the sole criterion for allocating funds* **basis**, point of reference, standard, norm, yardstick, benchmark, touchstone, test, formula, measure, gauge, scale, barometer, indicator, litmus test; specification, guide, guideline, guiding principle, principle, rule, law, canon, convention.

critic ▶ **noun 1** *he was the foremost literary critic of the 1840s* **commentator**, observer, monitor, pundit, expert, authority, arbiter, interpreter, exponent, expounder; writer, author, speaker; **reviewer**, appraiser, evaluator, analyst, judge; *rare* scholiast, exegete.
2 *he has fewer weaknesses than his critics have claimed* **detractor**, censurer, attacker, fault-finder, carper, backbiter, caviller, reviler, vilifier, traducer, disparager, denigrator, deprecator, belittler; *informal* knocker, nit-picker; *rare* asperser.

critical ▶ **adjective 1** *the safety committee produced a highly critical report* **censorious**, condemnatory, condemning, castigatory, reproving, denunciatory, deprecatory, disparaging, disapproving, scathing, criticizing, fault-finding, judgemental, negative, unfavourable, unsympathetic; hypercritical, ultra-critical, overcritical, pedantic, pettifogging, cavilling, carping, quibbling, niggling; *informal* nit-picking, hair-splitting, pernickety, picky, griping, bitching, bellyaching, whingeing; *rare* reprobatory, reprobative.
OPPOSITE complimentary.
2 *there was critical agreement among Renaissance specialists* **evaluative**, analytic, analytical, interpretative, expository, commentative, explanatory, explicative, elucidative.
3 *the hospital says her condition is critical* **grave**, serious, dangerous, risky, perilous, hazardous, precarious, touch-and-go, in the balance, uncertain, desperate, dire, acute, very bad; life-and-death, life-threatening; *informal* chancy, dicey, hairy, iffy; *Brit. informal* dodgy; *archaic or humorous* parlous; *Medicine* peracute, profound; *rare* egregious.
OPPOSITE safe.
4 *the choice of materials is critical for product safety* **crucial**, vital, essential, of the essence, all-important, important, of the utmost importance, of great consequence, high-priority, paramount, pre-eminent, fundamental, key, pivotal, deciding, decisive, climacteric, momentous; serious, urgent, pressing, compelling, exigent.
OPPOSITE unimportant.

criticism ▶ **noun 1** *in football management you come to expect criticism* **censure**, reproval, condemnation, denunciation, disapproval, disparagement, opprobrium, captiousness, fault-finding, carping, cavilling; chastisement, castigation, upbraiding, berating, abuse, vituperation, scolding, chiding; reproofs, remonstrances, broadsides, strictures, admonishments, recriminations, aspersions, slurs, smears; *informal* nit-picking, knocking, panning, slamming, flak, a bad press, brickbats, knocks, raps, bad notices; *Brit. informal* stick, verbal, slagging off, slating; *archaic* contumely; *rare* animadversion, objurgation, excoriation, reprobation, arraignment.
2 *the book was distributed to people for criticism* **evaluation**, assessment, examination, appreciation, appraisal, analysis, judgement; **comment**, commentary, interpretation, explanation, explication, elucidation, annotation, notation; opinions, views, observations, pronouncements, remarks, notes; *rare* scholia.

criticize ▶ **verb** *they criticized the government's handling of the economy* **find fault with**, censure, denounce, condemn, arraign, attack, lambaste, pillory, disapprove of, carp at, cavil at, rail against, inveigh against, cast aspersions on, pour scorn on, disparage, denigrate, deprecate, malign, vilify, besmirch, run down, give a bad press to; *N. Amer.* slur; *informal* knock, pan, slam, hammer, blast, bad-mouth, nit-pick about, throw brickbats at, give flak to, lay into, lace into, pull to pieces, pull apart, pick holes in, hit out at, maul, savage, roast, skewer, crucify; *Brit. informal* slag off, have a go at, give some stick to, slate, rubbish; *N. Amer. informal* pummel, cut up, trash; *Austral./NZ informal* bag, monster; *dated* rate; *archaic* slash, vituperate against, reprobate; *rare* animadvert on, objurgate, excoriate, asperse, derogate, reprehend.
OPPOSITES praise; approve of.

critique ▶ **noun** *he produced a critique of North American culture* **analysis**, evaluation, assessment, appraisal, appreciation, review, write-up; criticism, critical essay, textual examination, commentary, study, treatise, discourse, exposition, disquisition, account, exegesis; *Brit. informal* crit; *rare* anatomization.

croak ▶ **verb 1** *'You must excuse me,' croaked the old woman* **rasp**, squawk, caw, crow, wheeze, gasp, choke, hack, hawk, bark, cough; speak hoarsely, speak huskily, speak throatily, speak harshly, speak thickly.
2 (*informal*) *the dog finally croaked in 1987.* See DIE.
▶ **noun** *her voice emerged as a dry croak | the croak of a carrion crow* **rasp**, wheeze, gasp, bark, hack, cough; caw, squawk, cackle, clack, cluck.

crock ▶ **noun 1** *she took out bread and a crock of honey* **earthenware pot**, pot, jar, urn, pitcher, jug, ewer; vessel, container, receptacle, repository; *N. Amer.* creamer; *historical* jorum; *archaic* reservatory.
2 (**crocks**) *I washed up the dirty crocks* **crockery**, pots, dishes, plates, bowls, cups; dinner things, tea things; pottery, earthenware, stoneware.
3 (*informal*) *these days I'm a bit of an old crock* **invalid**, infirm person, decrepit person, feeble person; **old person**, senior citizen, senior, pensioner, old-age pensioner, OAP; geriatric, fogey, old fogey, dotard; *informal* crumbly, wrinkly, old stager, old timer, oldie, ancient.

crockery *See centre pages for list of* **Pottery**
▶ **noun** *the waitress dropped a tray of crockery* **dishes**, pots, crocks, plates, bowls, cups, saucers; pottery, china, porcelain, earthenware, stoneware, tableware; dinner service, tea service; *N. Amer.* dinnerware; *Irish* delph.

crony ▶ **noun** (*informal*) *he spent the evening drinking with his cronies* **friend**, best friend, companion, boon companion, intimate, familiar, confidant(e), alter ego, second self; comrade, associate, confederate, compatriot, colleague, workmate, co-worker; *informal* **pal**, chum, bosom chum, buddy, bosom buddy, spar, cully, oppo, main man; *Brit. informal* mate, china, mucker, butty; *N. English informal* marrow, marrer, marra; *N. Amer. informal* amigo, compadre, paisan; *N. Amer. & S. African informal* homeboy, homegirl; *S. African informal* gabba; *Austral./NZ informal* offsider; *archaic* compeer; *rare* fidus Achates, consociate.

crook ▶ **noun 1** (*informal*) *the crook got five years for swindling two families* **criminal**, lawbreaker, offender, villain, delinquent, malefactor, culprit, wrongdoer, transgressor, sinner; young offender, juvenile delinquent; felon, thief, robber, armed robber, burglar, housebreaker, shoplifter, mugger, fraudster, confidence trickster, swindler, racketeer, gunman, gangster, outlaw, bandit, terrorist, rapist; (*in Japan*) yakuza; *informal* con, jailbird, (old) lag, lifer, baddy, shark, con man, con artist, hustler; *N. Amer. informal* yardbird, yegg; *Austral. informal* crim; *S. African informal* lighty; *W. Indian informal* tief; *Brit. rhyming slang* tea leaf; *informal, dated* cracksman; *Law* malfeasant, misfeasor, infractor; *archaic* miscreant, trespasser, trusty, transport; *rare* peculator, defalcator.
OPPOSITE law-abiding citizen.
2 *the leopard sat in the crook of a tree branch* **bend**, curve, curvature, kink, bow, elbow, angle, fork, intersection; *technical* flexure.

▸ **verb** *he crooked his finger and called over the waiter* **cock**, flex, bend, curve, curl, angle, hook, bow.

crooked ▸ **adjective 1** *the village was a maze of crooked streets* **winding**, twisting, zigzag, meandering, deviating, sinuous, tortuous, serpentine, irregular; *rare* anfractuous.
OPPOSITE straight.
2 *the signpost was crooked* **bent**, curved, twisted, contorted, warped, angled, bowed, hooked.
OPPOSITE straight.
3 *the poor boy has a crooked back* **misshapen**, **deformed**, malformed, out of shape, distorted, contorted, wry, gnarled, disfigured, crippled, maimed; hunched, humped, bowed, curved; *Scottish* thrawn.
4 *the picture over the bed looked crooked* **lopsided**, askew, awry, to one side, off-centre, uneven, unsymmetrical, asymmetrical, asymmetric, not straight, out of true, out of line, on one side, tilted, at an angle, angled, slanted, aslant, slanting, sloping, squint; *Scottish* agley, thrawn; *informal* cock-eyed; *Brit. informal* skew-whiff, wonky, squiffy.
5 (*informal*) *his business had almost certainly been crooked | a crooked cop* **criminal**, illegal, unlawful, questionable, dubious, nefarious; **dishonest**, dishonourable, unscrupulous, unprincipled, amoral, untrustworthy, crafty, deceitful, shifty, underhand; corrupt, corruptible, buyable, venal, grafting, swindling, fraudulent; *informal* shady, tricky; *Brit. informal* bent, dodgy; *Law* malfeasant.
OPPOSITES honest, law-abiding.

croon ▸ **verb** *he crooned a few bars | she rocked the baby and began to croon* **sing softly**, hum, lilt, carol, warble, trill, quaver; *rare* troll.

crop ▸ **noun 1** *some farmers lost their entire crop* **harvest**, year's growth, yield, produce, vintage, gathering, reaping, gleaning, garnering; fruits.
2 *this month has brought a bumper crop of mail* **batch**, lot, assortment, selection, collection, supply, intake.
3 *the fruit got wedged in the bird's crop* **craw**, maw, gullet, throat; oesophagus, pharynx; *informal, dated* the red lane; *archaic* throttle, gorge, gula.
4 *the rider picked up his hat and crop* **whip**, lash, scourge, cat, thong, switch, birch, cane, stick; riding crop, hunting crop.
▸ **verb 1** *Sharon chose to crop her long brown hair* **cut short**, cut, clip, trim, snip, shear, shave; pare, prune, fleece, lop, dock, remove, detach; cut off, hack off, chop off, take off; shorten, make shorter, cut shorter, cut into a bob; barber, tonsure.
2 *a flock of sheep were cropping the turf* **graze on**, browse on, feed on, nibble (at), eat; pasture, ruminate.
3 *the hay was cropped several times this summer* **harvest**, reap, mow; gather, collect, pick, pluck; gather in, take in, bring home; *literary* glean, garner, cull.
□ **crop up** *things kept cropping up to delay their work* **happen**, occur, arise, arrive, turn up, spring up, pop up, surface, emerge, materialize, appear, come to light, present itself, make an appearance; *informal* show up; *literary* come to pass, befall; *archaic* hap.

WORD LINKS
science of crop production **agronomy**

cross ▸ **noun 1** *his grave is marked by a bronze cross* **crucifix**, rood.
2 *his wife's illness is a great cross to bear* **burden**, trouble, worry, trial, tribulation, affliction, curse, bane, hardship; vicissitude, misfortune, adversity; millstone, albatross; misery, woe, pain, sorrow, suffering, torment; thorn in one's flesh, thorn in one's side; *informal* hassle, stress, headache; *archaic* cumber.
OPPOSITE blessing.
3 *the animal is a cross between a yak and a cow* **hybrid**, hybridization, cross-breed, mixed breed, half-breed, half-blood, mixture, amalgam, blend, combination, composite, conglomerate; mongrel, cur.
▸ **verb 1** *I warn you not to cross the moors at night* **travel across**, go across, cut across, make one's way across, traverse, range over, tramp over, wander over; negotiate, navigate, cover.
2 *the lake was crossed by a fine stone bridge* **span**, bridge, arch, ford; go across, extend across, stretch across, pass over, arch over, vault over.
3 *they reached the point where the two roads cross* **intersect**, meet, join, connect, criss-cross, interweave, intertwine.
4 *if anybody crossed him he'd raise hell* **oppose**, resist, defy, thwart, frustrate, foil, obstruct, impede, hinder, hamper, block, check, deny, contradict, argue with, quarrel with; stand up to, take a stand against, take issue with, put up a fight against, set one's face against, fly in the face of; *formal* gainsay; *rare* controvert.
OPPOSITE support.
5 *the breed was crossed with the similarly coloured Friesian* **hybridize**, cross-breed, interbreed, cross-fertilize, cross-pollinate, intercross, mix, intermix, blend.
□ **cross something out** *he crossed out several sentences* **delete**, strike out, strike through, ink out, score out, scratch out, block out, blank out, edit out, blue-pencil, cancel, eliminate, obliterate; *technical* dele.
▸ **adjective** *he was exhausted, but he never got cross* **angry**, annoyed, irate, irritated, in a bad mood, peeved, vexed, upset, irked, piqued, out of humour, put out, displeased, galled, resentful; **irritable**, short-tempered, bad-tempered, hot-tempered, ill-humoured, surly, churlish, disagreeable, irascible, touchy, snappy, snappish, impatient, peevish, petulant, fractious, crotchety, grouchy, grumpy, querulous, cantankerous, testy, tetchy, crabby, captious, splenetic, choleric, dyspeptic, waspish; *informal* mad, hopping mad, wild, livid, as cross as two sticks, apoplectic, aerated, hot under the collar, riled, on the warpath, up in arms, foaming at the mouth, steamed up, in a lather, in a paddy, fit to be tied; *Brit. informal* shirty, stroppy, narky, ratty, eggy; *N. English informal* mardy; *N. Amer. informal* sore, steamed, bent out of shape, soreheaded, teed off, ticked off; *Austral./NZ informal* ropeable, snaky, crook; *W. Indian informal* vex; *Brit. informal, dated* in a bate, waxy; *vulgar slang* pissed off; *N. Amer. vulgar slang* pissed; *literary* ireful, wroth.
OPPOSITES pleased; good-humoured.

WORD LINKS
related prefix **cruci- (e.g. *crucify, cruciform*)**

cross-examine ▸ **verb** *the victim did not wish to be cross-examined by the police* **interrogate**, question, cross-question, quiz, catechize; interview, examine, probe, sound out, debrief; put questions to, ask questions of; *informal* grill, pump, give the third degree to, put through the third degree, put through the wringer, put through the mangle, put the screws on.

cross-grained ▸ **adjective** *old people as a group are neither sweet nor cross-grained* **awkward**, difficult, uncooperative, perverse, contrary, unhelpful, obstructive, disobliging, unaccommodating, unreasonable, troublesome, tiresome, annoying, vexatious, disobedient, recalcitrant, refractory, wilful, headstrong, self-willed, capricious, wayward; stubborn, obstinate, obdurate, mulish, pig-headed, bull-headed, intractable; *Scottish* thrawn; *informal* cussed; *Brit. informal* bloody-minded, bolshie, stroppy; *N. Amer. informal* balky; *archaic* froward, contumacious; *rare* renitent, pervicacious, contrarious.
OPPOSITE easy-going.

crossing ▸ **noun 1** *they came to a halt at a busy road crossing* **junction**, crossroads, intersection, interchange; motorway junction, railway junction, level crossing.
2 *the driver failed to notice a child on the crossing* **pedestrian crossing**, street crossing, pelican crossing, zebra crossing; *informal* the green man.
3 *the Mauretania held the Blue Riband for the fastest Atlantic crossing* **traversal**, traverse, passage, voyage, journey; cruise, sail.

crosspatch ▸ **noun** (*informal*) *I'm sorry I've been an old crosspatch sometimes* **shrew**, curmudgeon, discontent, complainer, grumbler, moaner, fault-finder, carper; **misery**, mope, dog in the manger, damper, dampener, spoilsport, pessimist, prophet of doom; *N. Amer.* crank; *informal* sourpuss, grouch, grump, virago, grouser, whinger, wet blanket, party-pooper, doom merchant; *N. Amer. informal* kvetch, sorehead; *rare* jade, melancholiac.

crossways, crosswise ▸ **adverb** *there was just about room to lie crossways in the bed* **diagonally**, obliquely, transversely, aslant, cornerways, cornerwise, on the cross, on the slant, at an angle, on the bias; sideways, athwart; *N. Amer.* cater-cornered, cater-corner, kitty-corner.

crotch ▸ **noun** *she tipped her dinner over his crotch* **groin**; lap.

crotchet ▸ **noun** *the natural crotchets of inveterate bachelors* **whim**, whimsy, fancy, fad, vagary, notion, conceit, caprice, kink, twist, freak, fetish, passion, bent, foible, quirk, eccentricity, idiosyncrasy; *French* idée fixe; *informal* hang-up, thing; *archaic* megrim; *rare* singularity.

crotchety ▸ **adjective** *he was one of those crotchety old people who give ageing a bad name* **bad-tempered**, ill-tempered, ill-natured, ill-humoured, peevish, cross, as cross as two sticks, irritable, irascible, short-tempered, hot-tempered, quick-tempered, touchy, testy, prickly, peppery, fractious, crusty, moody, cantankerous, curmudgeonly, crabbed, crabby, waspish, shrewish, grumpy, grouchy, disagreeable, churlish, surly, awkward, difficult, uncooperative, contrary, perverse, argumentative, quarrelsome; in a mood, in a bad mood, out of sorts, out of temper; *informal* snappish, snappy, chippy, on a short fuse; *Brit. informal* shirty, stroppy, narky, ratty, eggy, like a bear with a sore head; *N. Amer. informal* cranky, ornery, peckish, soreheaded; *Austral./NZ informal* snaky; *informal, dated* waxy, miffy; *rare* iracund, iracundulous.
OPPOSITES good-humoured, sweet-natured.

crouch ▸ **verb** *Ian crouched down and peered under the wagon | we all crouched behind the wall* **squat (down)**, duck (down), hunker down, bob down, hunch over; bend (down), stoop (down), bow (down), kneel (down), cower, cringe, shrink, huddle.

crow ▸ **verb 1** *a cock crowed down in the village* squawk, screech, hoot, cry, caw, croak.
2 *they all crowed about the jolly time they'd had* **boast**, brag, trumpet, show off, bluster, swagger, swank, gloat, be smug, congratulate oneself, preen oneself, pride oneself, pat oneself on the back, sing one's own praises; glory in, exult in, triumph over, parade, flaunt; *informal* talk big, blow hard, rub it in, lay it on thick, shoot one's mouth off, blow one's own trumpet; *Austral./NZ informal* skite; *literary* vaunt, roister; *archaic* rodomontade, gasconade.

WORD LINKS
collective noun **murder**

C

crowd ▶ noun **1** *a crowd of people filled the town square* **throng**, horde, mob, rabble, large number, mass, multitude, host, army, herd, flock, drove, swarm, sea, stream, troupe, pack, press, crush, flood, collection, company, gathering, assembly, assemblage, array, congregation, convention, concourse; *informal* gaggle; *Brit. informal* shower; *archaic* rout.
2 *she wanted to stand out from the crowd* **majority**, multitude, common people, populace, general public, mob, masses, riff-raff, proletariat, rank and file, the commonality, the hoi polloi, the canaille, the great unwashed; *informal* the proles, the plebs.
3 *the theatrical crowd piled into Bernard's Bentley* **set**, group, band, circle, company, fraternity, clique, coterie; camp, league, faction; *informal* lot, gang, bunch, pack, crew, posse, tribe; *rare* sodality, confraternity.
4 *every song received a warm response from the crowd* **audience**, spectators, watchers, listeners, viewers, onlookers, patrons, house, gallery, stalls; turnout, attendance, gate; congregation; *informal* punters.
▶ verb **1** *they ignored the novelist and crowded around the poet* **cluster**, gather, flock, swarm, throng, huddle, assemble, concentrate, congregate, come together, collect, amass, accumulate; *rare* foregather.
2 *the guests all crowded into the dining room* **surge**, push one's way, shove, push, thrust forward, jostle, elbow, elbow one's way, shoulder, nudge, bulldoze; squeeze, pile, pack, jam, cram.
3 *the quayside was crowded with holidaymakers* **throng**, pack, jam, cram, fill, overfill, congest, pervade, occupy all of.
4 *I felt as if he was crowding me* **pressurize**, pressure, lean on, press, goad, prod, bulldoze, browbeat, brainwash, dragoon, strong-arm; harass, harry, hound, nag, badger, pester, torment, plague; *informal* hassle, railroad, put the screws on; *Brit. informal* bounce; *N. Amer. informal* hustle, fast-talk.

WORD LINKS
fear of crowds **demophobia, ochlophobia**

crowded ▶ adjective *we took our places in the crowded cinema* **packed**, congested, crushed, cramped, overcrowded, full, filled to capacity, full to bursting, overfull, overflowing, teeming, swarming, thronged, populous, overpopulated, overpeopled, busy; *N. Amer.* mobbed; *informal* stuffed, jam-packed, chock-a-block, chock-full, bursting at the seams, bulging at the seams, full to the gunwales, wall-to-wall; *Austral./NZ informal* chocker.

crown ▶ noun **1** *he placed the crown on the new monarch's head* **coronet**, diadem, tiara, circlet, chaplet, fillet, wreath, garland, headband; *literary* coronal; (*in India, historical*) taj.
2 *she won the world indoor singles crown* **title**, award, accolade, honour, distinction, glory, kudos; trophy, cup, medal, plate, shield, belt, prize; laurels, bays, palm, wreath, laurel wreath, victor's garland.
3 *his family were loyal servants of the Crown* **monarch**, sovereign, king, queen, emperor, empress, tsar, tsarina, prince, princess, potentate, head of state, leader, chief, ruler, lord, overlord; **monarchy**, sovereignty, royalty; *informal* royals.
4 *she paused at the crown of the hill* **top**, crest, summit, peak, pinnacle, tip, head, brow, cap, brink, highest point, zenith, apex, ridge; *French* aiguille, serac.
OPPOSITE bottom.
▶ verb **1** *David II was crowned at Scone in 1331* **invest**, induct, install, instate, ordain, initiate, inaugurate, enthrone, swear in.
2 *a valuable teaching post at Harvard University crowned his career* **round off**, top off, cap, be the culmination of, be the climax of, be a fitting climax to, add the finishing touch(es) to, perfect, consummate, complete, conclude.
3 *the steeple is crowned by a gilded weathercock* **top**, cap, tip, head, surmount, overtop.
4 (*informal*) *someone crowned him with a poker* **hit over the head**, hit on the head, hit, strike, buffet, bang, knock, thwack, slug, welt, cuff, punch, smash; concuss, stun; *informal* brain, skull, bop, clonk, clout, sock, biff, wallop, bash, plug, lam, deck, floor; *Brit. informal* clock, cosh, slosh, dot, stick one on someone; *N. Amer. informal* bean, conk, ding, boff, bust, whale; *Austral./NZ informal* dong, quilt; *archaic* smite, swinge.

crucial ▶ adjective **1** *a crucial debate on the Maastricht Treaty* **pivotal**, critical, key, climacteric, decisive, deciding, determining, settling, testing, trying, searching; major, significant, influential, momentous, consequential, weighty, big, important, historic, epoch-making, far-reaching, life-and-death.
OPPOSITE minor.
2 *confidentiality is crucial in this case* **very important**, of the utmost importance, of great consequence, of the essence, critical, high-priority, pre-eminent, paramount, all-important, essential, vital, vitally important, indispensable, mandatory, urgent, pressing, compelling, necessary, needed, required, requisite.
OPPOSITE unimportant.

crucify ▶ verb **1** *the imperial authority had crucified Jesus* **nail to a cross**, hang on a cross; **execute**, put to death, kill, martyr.
2 *she had been crucified by Hamish's departure* **devastate**, crush, shatter, hurt deeply, wound, pain, distress, harrow, agonize, mortify, torment, torture; cause agony to, cause suffering to, cause pain to, inflict anguish on.
3 (*informal*) *modern teachers are being crucified for their methods* **condemn**, criticize severely, attack, tear apart, tear to pieces, censure, denounce, arraign, lambaste, pillory, carp at, cavil at, rail against, inveigh against, cast aspersions on, pour scorn on, disparage, denigrate, deprecate, malign, revile, vilify, besmirch, run down, give a bad press to; *N. Amer.* slur; *informal* knock, pan, slam, hammer, blast, bad-mouth, nit-pick about, throw brickbats at, give flak to, lay into, lace into, pull to pieces, pull apart, pick holes in, hit out at, maul, savage, roast, skewer; *Brit. informal* slag off, have a go at, give some stick to, slate, rubbish; *N. Amer. informal* pummel, cut up, trash; *Austral./NZ informal* bag, monster; *dated* rate; *archaic* slash, vituperate against, reprobate; *rare* animadvert on/upon, objurgate, excoriate, asperse, derogate, reprehend.
OPPOSITE praise.
4 (*informal*) *he was crucified by Faldo in the 1990 championship* **trounce**, defeat utterly, beat hollow, annihilate, drub, give a drubbing to, crush, rout; *informal* hammer, clobber, thrash, paste, pound, pulverize, slaughter, massacre, murder, flatten, demolish, destroy, wipe the floor with, take to the cleaners, make mincemeat of, turn inside out; *Brit. informal* stuff, marmalize; *N. Amer. informal* shellac, cream, skunk, blow out.

crude ▶ adjective **1** *they convert crude oil into petroleum* **unrefined**, unpurified, unprocessed, untreated; unmilled, unworked, unpolished, coarse, unprepared; raw, natural, plain.
OPPOSITE refined.
2 *Prussian infantrymen lined the crude barricade* **primitive**, simple, basic, rudimentary, rough, rough and ready, rough-hewn, make-do, makeshift, improvised, cobbled together, thrown together, homespun, unfinished, unpolished, unformed, undeveloped; *dated* rude.
OPPOSITE sophisticated.
3 *he was reprimanded for making crude jokes* **vulgar**, rude, risqué, suggestive, racy, earthy, off colour, colourful, indecent, bawdy, obscene, offensive, lewd, salacious, licentious, ribald, Rabelaisian, boorish, coarse, uncouth, indelicate, crass, tasteless, sordid, smutty, dirty, filthy, pornographic, X-rated, scatological; profane, foul, foul-mouthed, blasphemous, abusive, scurrilous; *informal* naughty, blue, raunchy, sleazy, porno, porn, steamy, spicy, locker-room; *Brit. informal* fruity, saucy, near the knuckle, close to the bone; *N. Amer. informal* gamy; *euphemistic* adult.
OPPOSITES decent, inoffensive.

crudity ▶ noun **1** *we must allow for the crudity of these statistical methods* **primitiveness**, simplicity, oversimplicity, roughness, inaccuracy; lack of refinement, lack of sophistication; *dated* rudeness.
OPPOSITE sophistication.
2 *she shrank from his crudity and teasing* **vulgarity**, rudeness, suggestiveness, raciness, earthiness, bawdiness, blueness, smuttiness, smut, lewdness, salaciousness, licentiousness, ribaldry, seaminess, dirtiness, filthiness, dirt, filth, boorishness, coarseness, uncouthness, indecency, obscenity, indelicacy, indelicateness, crassness, tastelessness, offensiveness; *informal* naughtiness, raunchiness, sleaziness, steaminess, porn; *Brit. informal* fruitiness, sauciness; *N. Amer. informal* gaminess.
OPPOSITE decency.

cruel ▶ adjective **1** *the prisoner was a hard, cruel man | they think fox hunting a cruel practice* **brutal**, savage, inhuman, barbaric, barbarous, brutish, bloodthirsty, murderous, homicidal, cut-throat, vicious, ferocious, fierce; wicked, evil, fiendish, devilish, diabolical, heinous, abominable, monstrous, atrocious, vile, hideous, ghastly, nasty, spiteful, mean; **callous**, sadistic, ruthless, merciless, unmerciful, pitiless, unsparing, unrelenting, remorseless, uncaring, unsympathetic, uncharitable, heartless, stony-hearted, hard-hearted, cold-hearted, cold-blooded, bloodless, unfeeling, unemotional, unkind, inhumane, severe, harsh, stern, inclement, flinty, draconian; *Brit. informal* beastly; *archaic* dastardly, sanguinary.
OPPOSITES compassionate, merciful.
2 *his mother's death was a cruel blow* **harsh**, severe, grim, grievous, hard, tough, bitter, harrowing, heartbreaking, heart-rending, distressing, upsetting, traumatic, painful, agonizing, excruciating; *rare* distressful.
OPPOSITE mild.

cruelty ▶ noun **1** *he treated her with extreme cruelty* **brutality**, savagery, savageness, inhumanity, barbarism, barbarousness, brutishness, bloodthirstiness, murderousness, viciousness, ferocity, ferociousness, fierceness; **callousness**, sadism, ruthlessness, relentlessness, mercilessness, pitilessness, remorselessness, lack of regard, lack of sympathy, lack of charity, heartlessness, cold-heartedness, cold-bloodedness, severity, harshness, inclemency; wickedness, badness, baseness, iniquity, blackness, black-heartedness, evil, fiendishness, devilishness, heinousness, nastiness, unkindness, abuse; *rare* ferity.
OPPOSITES compassion, mercy.
2 *the cruelty of a cold winter night* **harshness**, severity, unkindness, relentlessness, grimness, hardness, toughness, bitterness, painfulness, wretchedness; torment, trauma, pain, distress, misery.
OPPOSITE mildness.

cruise ▶ noun *a cruise up the Thames | they sailed off on a luxury cruise* **boat trip**; **sea trip**, sailing trip, sail; voyage, journey, passage.
▶ verb **1** *she cruised across the Atlantic* **sail**, steam, voyage, journey; travel by boat, take a cruise, take a boat trip, take a sea trip, take a sailing trip, go

sailing, go yachting, go boating.
2 *taxis cruised around the town centre* **coast**, drift, meander, drive slowly, travel slowly, travel aimlessly; *informal* mosey, tootle; *Brit. informal* pootle, swan.

crumb ▶ **noun** *biscuit crumbs | there was only one crumb of comfort* **fragment**, bit, morsel, particle, tiny piece, speck, scrap, shred, sliver, atom, grain, granule, trace, tinge, mite, iota, jot, whit, ounce, scintilla, vestige; *French* soupçon; *Irish* stim; *informal* smidgen, smidge, tad; *archaic* scantling, scruple.

crumble ▶ **verb 1** *the building is crumbling away | his empire began to crumble around him* **disintegrate**, fall down, fall to pieces, fall apart, collapse, break down/up, tumble down, fragment; decay, fall into decay, deteriorate, degenerate, go to rack and ruin, decompose, rot, rot away, come apart at the seams, moulder, perish, come to dust.
2 *she crumbled the dry earth into fine powdery dust* **crush**, grind, break up, pulverize, pound, powder, granulate, fragment; *technical* triturate, comminute; *archaic* levigate, bray, powderize.

crumbly ▶ **adjective** **brittle**, breakable, friable, powdery, granular; short; crisp, crispy; *rare* pulverulent, brashy.
OPPOSITE solid.

crummy ▶ **adjective** *(informal) a crummy little flat in Stoke Newington. See* SECOND-RATE, SUBSTANDARD.

crumple ▶ **verb 1** *she crumpled the note in her fist* **crush**, scrunch up, screw up, squash, squeeze; *Brit.* scrumple.
OPPOSITE smooth out.
2 *his trousers were dirty and crumpled* **crease**, wrinkle, crinkle, rumple, ruck up, tumble; *Brit. rare* ruckle.
OPPOSITE iron.
3 *her lower lip quivered and her face began to crumple* **pucker**, screw up; fall, sag, look sad, look miserable.
4 *her resistance crumpled* **collapse**, give way, cave in, go to pieces, break down, crumble, be overcome.
OPPOSITE hold out.

crunch ▶ **verb 1** *Meryl crunched the biscuit with relish* **munch**, chew noisily, chomp, champ, bite, gnaw, masticate; eat, devour, consume; *rare* chumble.
2 *the bomb had crunched the houses into rubble* **crush**, pulverize, pound, grind, break, smash.
▶ **noun** *(informal) when the crunch comes, she'll be forced to choose* **moment of truth**, critical point, crux, crisis, decision time, zero hour, point of no return; showdown.

crusade ▶ **noun 1** *the medieval crusades* **holy war**; military campaign; *Islam* jihad.
2 *a crusade against crime | a crusade to improve education* **campaign**, drive, push, move, movement, effort, struggle; battle, war, offensive.
▶ **verb** *you know how she likes* ***crusading for*** *the cause of the underdog* **campaign**, fight, do battle, battle, take up arms, take up the cudgels, work, push, press, strive, struggle, agitate, lobby; champion, promote.

crusader ▶ **noun** **campaigner**, fighter, battler; champion, advocate, promoter, enthusiast; reformer.

crush ▶ **verb 1** *essential oils in the leaves are released when the herbs are crushed or heated* **squash**, squeeze, press, compress; pulp, mash, macerate, mangle; flatten, trample on, tread on; *informal* squidge, splat; *N. Amer. informal* smush.
2 *your dress will get crushed* **crease**, crumple, rumple, wrinkle, crinkle, scrunch up, ruck up; *Brit.* scrumple up; *Brit. rare* ruckle.
OPPOSITE smooth out.
3 *crush the biscuits with a rolling pin | crushed stone* **pulverize**, pound, grind, break up, smash, shatter, crumble, crunch, splinter; mill, pestle; *technical* triturate, comminute; *archaic* bray, levigate, powderize; *rare* kibble.
4 *he crushed her in his arms* **hug**, squeeze, hold tight, clutch; embrace, enfold.
5 *the new regime ruthlessly crushed all popular uprisings* **suppress**, put down, quell, quash, squash, stamp out, put an end to, put a stop to, overcome, overpower, defeat, extinguish, vanquish, triumph over, break, bring someone to their knees, repress, subdue.
6 *the England No 1 was crushed 15–7, 15–6, 15–6* **defeat utterly**, beat hollow, win a resounding victory over, drub, rout, give someone a drubbing, overwhelm; *informal* hammer, clobber, thrash, paste, give someone a pasting, whip, pound, pulverize, demolish, destroy, wipe the floor with, take to the cleaners, make mincemeat of, annihilate, slaughter, murder, massacre, crucify, flatten, turn inside out, run rings around; *Brit. informal* stuff, marmalize; *N. Amer. informal* shellac, blow out, cream, skunk.
OPPOSITES lose, be defeated.
7 *Alan was crushed by her words* **mortify**, humiliate, abash, chagrin, deflate, demoralize, flatten, squash; devastate, shatter; *informal* put down, shoot down in flames, take down a peg or two, cut down to size, put someone in their place, make someone eat humble pie, settle someone's hash, knock the stuffing out of; *N. Amer. informal* make someone eat crow.
▶ **noun 1** *we were caught up in the crush of people* **crowd**, throng, horde, swarm, sea, mass, pack, press, multitude, mob; huddle; jam, congestion; *archaic* rout.
2 *(informal) it was just a teenage crush* **infatuation**, obsession, love, passion, passing fancy; *informal* pash, puppy love, calf love; *rare* mash.
3 *lemon crush* **squash**, fruit juice, cordial, drink.

crust *See centre pages for list of layers of the* **Earth's Crust**
▶ **noun 1** *a loaf with a crisp brown crust* **outer layer/part**, outside, exterior; heel, end, remnant.
2 *(informal) I'm just trying to earn an honest crust* **living**, livelihood, means of subsistence, income, daily bread; *informal* bread and butter.
3 *a crust of ice and snow* **covering**, **layer**, coating, cover, coat, sheet, thickness, film, skin; topping, caking; encrustation, scab; *rare* concretion.

crustacean ▶ **noun.** *See centre pages for list of* **Crustaceans**

crusty ▶ **adjective 1** *crusty French bread* **crisp**, crispy, well baked, well done; crumbly, brittle, friable.
OPPOSITES soft, soggy.
2 *a crusty old man* **irritable**, bad-tempered, irascible, grumpy, grouchy, crotchety, tetchy, testy, cantankerous, curmudgeonly, ill-tempered, ill-natured, ill-humoured, peevish, cross, fractious, disagreeable, pettish, crabbed, crabby, waspish, prickly, peppery, touchy, scratchy, splenetic, shrewish, short-tempered, quick-tempered, dyspeptic, choleric, bilious, liverish, cross-grained; argumentative, quarrelsome, captious; *informal* snappish, snappy, chippy, on a short fuse, short-fused; *Brit. informal* shirty, stroppy, narky, ratty, eggy, like a bear with a sore head; *N. Amer. informal* cranky, ornery, peckish, soreheaded; *Austral./NZ informal* snaky.
OPPOSITES good-natured, affable.

crux ▶ **noun** *the crux of the matter* **nub**, heart, essence, most important point, central point, main point, essential part, core, centre, nucleus, kernel; *informal* the bottom line.

cry ▶ **verb 1** *Mandy's face crumpled and she started to cry* **weep**, shed tears, sob, wail, be in tears, cry one's eyes out, cry one's heart out, cry as if one's heart would break, bawl, howl, snivel, whimper, whine, squall, mewl, bleat; lament, grieve, mourn, keen; *Scottish* greet; *informal* boohoo, blub, blubber, turn on the waterworks; *Brit. informal* grizzle; *literary* pule, plain.
OPPOSITE laugh.
2 *'Wait!' he cried | the girl* ***cried out*** *in pain* **call**, shout, exclaim, sing out, yell, shriek, scream, screech, bawl, bellow, roar, whoop; yowl, squeal, yelp, yawp; *informal* holler, yoo-hoo, cooee; *rare* ejaculate, vociferate, ululate.
OPPOSITE whisper.
□ **cry someone/something down** *(dated) they cried down his achievements* **disparage**, run down, belittle, make light of, denigrate, decry, deprecate, depreciate, play down, trivialize, minimize; *archaic* hold cheap; *rare* derogate, misprize, minify.
OPPOSITES acclaim, praise.
□ **cry off** *(informal) he cried off at the last moment* **back out**, pull out, cancel, withdraw, beg off, excuse oneself; change one's mind, go back on one's word, break one's promise; *informal* get cold feet, cop out, wimp out; *N. Amer. informal* crap out.
▶ **noun 1** *Leonora had a good cry | the baby's cries* **sob**, weep, crying fit, fit of crying; (**cries**) weeping, sobbing, wailing, bawling, howling, snivelling, whimpering.
OPPOSITES laugh, laughter.
2 *a cry of despair | his cries of pain* **call**, shout, exclamation, yell, shriek, scream, screech, bawl, bellow, roar, whoop; howl, yowl, squeal, yelp, yawp; ejaculation, interjection; *informal* holler; *rare* vociferation, ululation.
3 *fund-raisers have issued a cry for help* **appeal**, plea, entreaty, urgent request, cry from the heart; *French* cri de cœur.

crypt ▶ **noun** **tomb**, vault, mausoleum, burial chamber, sepulchre, catacomb, ossuary, undercroft; cellar, basement; *Archaeology* mastaba.

cryptic ▶ **adjective** *his cryptic comments taxed her powers of comprehension* **enigmatic**, mysterious, hard to understand, confusing, mystifying, perplexing, puzzling, obscure, abstruse, arcane, oracular, Delphic, ambiguous, elliptical, oblique; *informal* as clear as mud.
OPPOSITES straightforward, clear.

crystallize ▶ **verb 1** *different minerals crystallize at different temperatures* **form crystals**, solidify, harden.
2 *the idea crystallized in her mind* **become clear**, become definite, take shape, emerge, form, materialize; *informal* gel.

cub ▶ **noun 1** *a lioness and her cubs* baby; *archaic* whelp; (**cubs**) **young**, offspring.
2 *as a cub reporter, I was frequently sent out on the least desirable assignments* **trainee**, apprentice, probationer, novice, tyro, new recruit, new boy, new girl, fledgling, learner, beginner; *informal* rookie, new kid (on the block), newie, newbie; *N. Amer. informal* greenhorn, probie, tenderfoot.
OPPOSITES veteran, old hand.

cubbyhole ▶ **noun 1** *the glass-partitioned cubbyhole he called an office* **small room**, booth, cubicle; den, snug; *N. Amer.* cubby.
2 *we went through every drawer and cubbyhole* **compartment**, pigeonhole, niche; slot, recess.

C

cube ▸ noun hexahedron, cuboid, parallelepiped; block, brick, lump, chunk.

cuddle ▸ verb 1 *she sat on the bed, cuddling the baby* **hug**, embrace, clasp, hold tight, hold in one's arms, fold in one's arms.
2 *the pair have been spotted kissing and cuddling* **embrace**, hug, caress, pet, fondle; *informal* canoodle, smooch; *informal, dated* spoon, bill and coo.
3 *I cuddled up to him* **snuggle**, nestle, curl, nuzzle, lie close; burrow against, huddle against; *N. Amer.* snug down.
▸ noun *come and give me a cuddle* **hug**, embrace, bear hug.

cuddly ▸ adjective **huggable**, cuddlesome; plump, curvaceous, rounded, buxom, soft, warm; attractive, endearing, lovable; *N. Amer. informal* zaftig.

cudgel ▸ noun *a thick wooden cudgel* **club**, bludgeon, stick, truncheon, baton, blackthorn, mace, bat; *N. Amer.* blackjack, billy, billy club, nightstick; (*in Ireland*) shillelagh; *Indian* lathi, danda; *S. African* kierie, knobkerrie; *Brit. informal* cosh, life preserver.
▸ verb *she was cudgelled to death* **bludgeon**, club, beat, batter, bash; attack, assault; *Brit. informal* cosh.

cue ▸ noun *he looked at his watch and Sylvie knew it was a cue for her to leave* **signal**, sign, indication, prompt, reminder, prompting; nod, word; hint, suggestion, intimation; *N. Amer. informal* high sign; *Physiology* zeitgeber.

cuff ▸ verb *Cullam grabbed him by the lapels and cuffed him on the head* **hit**, strike, slap, smack, thump, thwack, beat, punch, swat, knock, rap, box someone's ears; *Scottish & N. English* skelp; *informal* clout, wallop, belt, whack, bash, clobber, bop, biff, sock, whop; *Brit. informal* slosh, dot; *N. Amer. informal* boff, slug; *Austral./NZ informal* dong, quilt; *literary* smite.
□ **off the cuff** (*informal*) 1 *an off-the-cuff remark* **impromptu**, extempore, ad lib; unrehearsed, unscripted, unprepared, improvised, spontaneous, unplanned; offhand, casual; *Latin* ad libitum; *rare* extemporaneous.
2 *I spoke off the cuff* **without preparation**, without rehearsal, impromptu, ad lib; spontaneously; *Latin* ad libitum; *informal* off the top of one's head, on the spur of the moment; *rare* extemporaneously.

cuisine ▸ noun **cooking**, cookery, fare, food; *French* haute cuisine, cordon bleu, nouvelle cuisine.

cul-de-sac ▸ noun **no through road**, blind alley, dead end.

cull ▸ verb 1 *anecdotes culled from Greek and Roman history* **select**, choose, pick, take, obtain, get, glean.
2 *he sees culling deer as a necessity* **slaughter**, kill, destroy; reduce the numbers of, thin out the population of.

culminate ▸ verb *nine days of processions and parades* ***culminating in*** *a dramatic fire-walking ceremony* **come to a climax**, come to a crescendo, come to a head, reach a finale, peak, climax, reach a pinnacle; build up to, lead up to; come to an end with, end with, finish with, conclude with, close with, terminate with; *informal* wind up.
OPPOSITES start, begin; peter out.

culmination ▸ noun *the culmination of his career* **climax**, pinnacle, peak, high point, highest point, height, high water mark, top, summit, crest, zenith, crowning moment, apotheosis; apex, apogee, vertex; finale, denouement; consummation, completion, finish, conclusion, close, termination; *informal* high noon.
OPPOSITE nadir.

culpability ▸ noun **guilt**, blame, fault, responsibility, accountability, liability, answerability; guiltiness, blameworthiness.
OPPOSITE innocence.

culpable ▸ adjective *I hold you personally culpable* **to blame**, **guilty**, at fault, in the wrong, blameworthy, blameable, censurable, reproachable, reprovable, found wanting; responsible, answerable, liable, accountable.
OPPOSITES blameless, innocent.

culprit ▸ noun *the police are doing all they can to catch the culprit* **guilty party**, offender, wrongdoer, person responsible; **criminal**, malefactor, lawbreaker, felon, delinquent, reprobate; evil-doer, transgressor, sinner; *informal* baddy, bad guy, wrong 'un, crook, crim; *Law* malfeasant, misfeasor, infractor; *archaic* miscreant.

cult ▸ noun 1 *a religious cult* **sect**, religious group, denomination, religious order, church, faith, faith community, belief, persuasion, affiliation, movement; group, body, faction, clique.
2 *the cult of youth and beauty in Hollywood* **obsession with**, fixation on, mania for, passion for; idolization of, admiration for, devotion to, worship of, veneration of, reverence for.
3 *the series has become a bit of a cult in the UK* **craze**, fashion, fad, vogue; *informal* thing.

cultivate ▸ verb 1 *the peasants who cultivated the land became its owners* **till**, plough, dig, turn, hoe; **farm**, work, prepare; fertilize, mulch.
2 *they were encouraged to cultivate basic food crops* **grow**, raise, rear, bring on, tend; plant, sow.
3 *her father had cultivated Maud's friendship* **try to acquire**, pursue, court; try to develop, work hard at, foster, nurture, encourage.
4 *it helps if you go out of your way to cultivate the local people* **seek the friendship of**, seek the favour of, try to win over, try to get someone on one's side, try to get on someone's good side, woo, court, pay court to, rub up the right way, run after, make advances to, make up to, keep sweet, ingratiate oneself with, curry favour with; associate with, mix with, keep company with; *informal* get in someone's good books, butter up, suck up to; *N. Amer. informal* shine up to; *vulgar slang* brown-nose.
OPPOSITE ignore.
5 *he wants to cultivate his mind—to understand art and literature* **improve**, better, refine, elevate, polish; educate, train, develop, enlighten, enrich, civilize, culture.

cultivated ▸ adjective *a remarkably cultivated man* **cultured**, educated, well read, well informed; civilized, enlightened, discerning, discriminating, refined, polished; sophisticated, urbane, cosmopolitan; courteous, polite, well mannered, mannerly, gracious; *informal* couth.
OPPOSITE ignorant.

cultivation *See centre pages for list of types of* **Farming and Cultivation**
▸ noun 1 *the cultivation of arable crops* **growing**, raising, rearing, farming, culture; planting, sowing.
2 *the reclamation of land for cultivation* **agriculture**, agronomy, horticulture, husbandry; tillage.
3 *the cultivation of the mind* **improvement**, bettering; education, training, development.
4 *Minton could not disguise his underlying seriousness nor the depth of his cultivation* **culture**, culturedness, intellectual/artistic awareness, education, erudition, learning, enlightenment, discrimination, good taste, taste, refinement.

cultural ▸ adjective 1 *cultural differences* **ethnic**, racial, folk; societal, lifestyle.
2 *cultural achievements | cultural events* **aesthetic**, artistic, intellectual; educational, civilizing, enlightening, edifying, enriching.

culture ▸ noun 1 *20th century popular culture* **the arts**, the humanities; **intellectual achievement(s)**, intellectual activity; literature, music, painting, philosophy.
2 *a man of culture* **intellectual/artistic awareness**, education, cultivation, enlightenment, discernment, discrimination, good taste, taste, refinement, polish; sophistication, urbanity, urbaneness; erudition, learning, letters; *French* belles-lettres.
3 *people from many different cultures | Afro-Caribbean culture* **civilization**, society, way of life, lifestyle; customs, traditions, heritage, habits, ways, mores, values.
4 *the culture of crops* **cultivation**, growing, farming; agriculture, husbandry, agronomy.

cultured ▸ adjective *a sensitive, cultured man* **cultivated**, intellectually/artistically aware, artistic, enlightened, civilized, educated, well educated, well read, well informed, learned, knowledgeable, discerning, discriminating, with good taste, refined, polished; sophisticated, urbane; intellectual, highbrow, scholarly, erudite; *informal* arty.
OPPOSITES ignorant, unrefined, unsophisticated.

culvert ▸ noun **channel**, conduit, watercourse, trough; **drain**, gutter.

cumbersome ▸ adjective 1 *a cumbersome rubberized diving suit* **unwieldy**, unmanageable, awkward, clumsy, ungainly, inconvenient, incommodious; **bulky**, large, heavy, hefty, weighty, burdensome; *informal* hulking, clunky; *rare* cumbrous, unhandy, lumbersome.
OPPOSITES manageable, convenient.
2 *cumbersome procedures* **complicated**, complex, involved, inefficient, badly organized, wasteful, unwieldy, slow, slow-moving.
OPPOSITES straightforward, efficient.

cumulative ▸ adjective **increasing**, accumulative, accumulating, growing, progressive, accruing, snowballing, mounting; collective, aggregate, amassed; *Brit.* knock-on.

cunning ▸ adjective *he's been very cunning | a cunning scheme* **crafty**, wily, artful, guileful, devious, sly, knowing, scheming, designing, tricky, slippery, slick, manipulative, Machiavellian, deceitful, deceptive, duplicitous; shrewd, astute, clever, canny, sharp, sharp-witted, skilful, ingenious, resourceful, inventive, imaginative, deft, adroit, dexterous; *informal* foxy, savvy, fiendish, sneaky; *Brit. informal* fly; *Scottish & N. English informal* pawky; *S. African informal* slim; *archaic* subtle; *rare* vulpine, carny.
OPPOSITES honest, guileless, naive.
▸ noun *you have to admire his political cunning* **guile**, craftiness, wiliness, artfulness, deviousness, slyness, trickery, trickiness, duplicity, deceitfulness, deceit, chicanery; shrewdness, astuteness, cleverness, canniness, sharpness, ingenuity, resourcefulness, inventiveness, imagination, deftness, adroitness, dexterity, dexterousness; wiles, ploys, schemes, stratagems, tactics, manoeuvres, subterfuges, tricks, ruses; *informal* foxiness.
OPPOSITES guilelessness, naivety.

cup *See centre pages for list of* **Drinking Vessels**
▸ noun 1 *the winner was presented with a silver cup* **trophy**, chalice; award, prize.
2 *a non-alcoholic fruit cup* **punch**, drink, mixed drink.

cupboard ▸ noun. *See centre pages for list of* **Cupboards and Cabinets**

Cupid ▸ noun 1 *a statue of Cupid* **Eros**, the god of love; *Art* amoretto.

2 *Luigi was delighted to think he was playing Cupid* **matchmaker**, pandar, Pandarus.

cupidity ▶ noun **greed**, avarice, avariciousness, acquisitiveness, covetousness, rapacity, rapaciousness, materialism, mercenariness; meanness, miserliness; *informal* money-grubbing, money-grabbing, an itching palm; *N. Amer. informal* grabbiness; *rare* Mammonism.
OPPOSITE generosity.

cur ▶ noun **1** *a mangy cur* **mongrel**, tyke; half-breed, cross, mixed breed, hybrid; *N. Amer.* yellow dog; *NZ* kuri; *Asian* pye-dog, pariah dog; *informal* mutt; *Austral. informal* mong, bitzer; *technical* bigener.
2 (*informal*) *Neil was beginning to feel even more like a cur. See* SCOUNDREL.

curable ▶ adjective *most skin cancers are curable* **remediable**, treatable, medicable, operable, responsive to treatment.
OPPOSITE incurable.

curative ▶ adjective *the herb's curative properties* **healing**, therapeutic, medicinal, remedial, curing, corrective; restorative, tonic, health-giving, healthful, sanative; *rare* febrifugal, vulnerary, analeptic, iatric.

curator ▶ noun **custodian**, keeper, conservator, guardian, caretaker, steward.

curb ▶ noun *a curb on public spending* **restraint**, restriction, check, brake, rein, control, limitation, limit, constraint, stricture; deterrent, damper, suppressant, retardant; *informal* crackdown, clampdown; *literary* trammel.
▶ verb *he breathed deeply, trying to curb his temper | their failure to curb inflation* **restrain**, hold back, keep back, hold in, repress, suppress, fight back, bite back, keep in check, check, control, keep under control, rein in, keep a tight rein on, contain, discipline, govern, bridle, tame, subdue, stifle, smother, swallow, choke back, muzzle, silence, muffle, strangle, gag; limit, put a limit on, keep within bounds, put the brakes on, slow down, retard, restrict, constrain, deter, impede, inhibit; freeze, peg; *informal* button up, keep a/the lid on; *literary* trammel.
OPPOSITE release.

curdle ▶ verb **clot**, coagulate, congeal, separate into curds/lumps, solidify, thicken, condense; turn, turn sour, sour, ferment.

cure ▶ verb **1** *Casey had been cured, but he needed to convalesce* **heal**, restore to health, make well, make better, restore, rehabilitate, treat successfully; *archaic* cleanse.
2 *the belief that economic equality could cure all social ills* **rectify**, remedy, put right, set right, right, set to rights, fix, mend, repair, heal, make better, ameliorate, alleviate, ease; solve, sort out, be the answer/solution to; eliminate, do away with, end, put an end to, remove, counteract, correct.
OPPOSITES exacerbate, aggravate.
3 *some farmers cured their own bacon* **preserve**, smoke, salt, dry, kipper, pickle.
▶ noun **1** *a cure for cancer* **remedy**, curative, medicine, medication, medicament, restorative, corrective, antidote, antiserum; (course of) treatment, therapy, healing, alleviation; nostrum, panacea, cure-all; *archaic* physic, specific.
2 *he was beyond cure* **healing**, restoration to health.
3 *interest rate cuts are not the cure for the problem* **solution**, answer, antidote, nostrum, panacea, cure-all, magic formula; *informal* quick fix, magic bullet.

cure-all ▶ noun **panacea**, universal cure, cure for all ills, universal remedy, sovereign remedy, heal-all, nostrum, elixir, wonder drug, perfect solution, magic formula, magic bullet; *rare* catholicon, diacatholicon, panpharmacon.

curio ▶ noun **trinket**, knick-knack, bibelot, ornament, bauble, gimcrack, gewgaw; antique, collector's item, object of virtu, rarity, curiosity; *French* objet, objet d'art; *N. Amer.* kickshaw; *informal* whatnot, dingle-dangle; *Brit. informal* doodah, doobry; *N. Amer. informal* tchotchke, tsatske; *archaic* folderol, furbelow, whim-wham, bijou, gaud, bygone.

curiosity ▶ noun **1** *his evasiveness roused my curiosity* **inquisitiveness**, interest, spirit of inquiry; *informal* nosiness.
2 *the coins do have a certain curiosity value* **peculiarity**, oddity, strangeness, oddness, idiosyncrasy, unusualness, novelty.
3 *the shop is a treasure trove of curiosities | geological curiosities* **oddity**, curio, novelty, conversation piece, object of virtu, collector's item; rarity, wonder, marvel, phenomenon.

curious ▶ adjective **1** *she was obviously curious, but too polite to ask questions | the curious stares of her colleagues* **inquisitive**, intrigued, interested, eager to know, dying to know, burning with curiosity, agog; quizzical, inquiring, searching, probing, querying, questioning, interrogative; perplexed, puzzled, baffled, mystified; *informal* nosy, nosy-parker, snoopy.
OPPOSITE uninterested.
2 *her curious behaviour intrigued him* **strange**, odd, peculiar, funny, unusual, bizarre, weird, eccentric, queer, unexpected, unfamiliar, abnormal, out of the ordinary, atypical, anomalous, untypical, different, out of the way, surprising, incongruous, extraordinary, remarkable, puzzling, mystifying, mysterious, perplexing, baffling, unaccountable, inexplicable, irregular, singular, offbeat, unconventional, unorthodox, outlandish, aberrant, freak, freakish, deviant; uncanny, eerie, unnatural; *Brit.* out of the common; *French* outré; *Scottish* unco; *informal* off the wall, wacky; *Brit. informal* rum; *N. Amer. informal* wacko.
OPPOSITE ordinary.

> **CHOOSE THE RIGHT WORD**
> **curious, strange, odd, peculiar**
> See STRANGE.

C

curl ▶ verb **1** *smoke curled up from his cigarette | the road curls round Sibton Park* **spiral**, coil, wreathe, twirl, swirl, furl; **wind**, curve, bend, twist, twist and turn, loop, meander, snake, corkscrew, zigzag.
2 *Ruth curled her arms around his neck* **wind**, twine, entwine, wrap.
3 *she washed and curled my hair* **crimp**, wave, tong; **perm**.
4 *the rain had made his hair curl even more* **go curly**, go frizzy, frizz out, frizzle, crinkle.
5 *they curled up together on the sofa* **nestle**, snuggle, cuddle; huddle; *N. Amer.* snug down.
□ **make someone's hair curl** (*informal*) *I could tell you things about him that would make your hair curl* **shock**, stun, horrify, appal, scandalize, make someone's blood run cold; *informal* make someone's hair stand on end.
▶ noun **1** *her blonde hair was a mass of tangled curls* **ringlet**, corkscrew, coil, kink, wave; kiss-curl.
2 *a curl of smoke* **spiral**, coil, wreath, twirl, swirl, furl, twist, corkscrew, curlicue, whorl, helix, gyre.

curly ▶ adjective *thick, curly hair* **wavy**, curling, curled, crimped, permed, frizzy, frizzed, kinked, kinky, crinkly, fuzzy, corkscrew; wiry; *rare* ringletty, ringletted.
OPPOSITE straight.

curmudgeon ▶ noun **bad-tempered person**; *N. Amer.* crank; *informal* crosspatch, sourpuss, old trout; *Brit. informal* a bear with a sore head; *N. Amer. informal* kvetch, sorehead.

currency *See centre pages for lists of* **Coins** **Currency Units**
▶ noun **1** *foreign currency* **money**, legal tender, medium of exchange, cash, banknotes, notes, paper money, coins, coinage; *N. Amer.* bills; *formal* specie. *See also* MONEY.
2 *since the war, the term has gained new currency* **prevalence**, circulation, dissemination, publicity, exposure; acceptance, popularity, fashionableness, voguishness.

current ▶ adjective **1** *current events | current fashions* **contemporary**, present-day, present, contemporaneous, ongoing; topical, in the news, live, alive, happening, burning; modern, latest, popular, fashionable, in fashion, in vogue, up to date, up to the minute; *French* de nos jours; *informal* trendy, now, in.
OPPOSITE past.
2 *the idea is still current in some quarters* **prevalent**, prevailing, common, in general use, accepted, in circulation, circulating, going around, doing/making the rounds, popular, widespread, rife, about; talked of, on everyone's lips, bruited about.
OPPOSITE obsolete.
3 *a current driving licence* **valid**, usable, up to date.
OPPOSITES old, out of date.
4 *the current prime minister* **incumbent**, present, in office, in power; reigning.
OPPOSITES past; former.
▶ noun **1** *a current of air | ocean currents* **steady flow**, stream, backdraught, slipstream; airstream, thermal, updraught, draught; undercurrent, undertow, tide.
2 *the current of human life* **course**, progress, progression, flow, tide, movement.
3 *the current of opinion* **trend**, drift, direction, tendency, swing, tenor.

WORD LINKS
instrument for measuring electric currents **galvanometer**

curriculum ▶ noun **syllabus**, course of study/studies, programme of study/studies, educational programme, subjects, modules; timetable, schedule.

curse ▶ noun **1** *she'd put a curse on him* **malediction**, the evil eye, imprecation, execration, voodoo, hoodoo; anathema, excommunication; *N. Amer.* hex; *Irish* cess; *informal* jinx; *archaic* malison, ban.
2 *those who seek to overcome the curse of racism* **evil**, blight, scourge, plague, cancer, canker, poison.
3 *the curse of unemployment* **affliction**, burden, cross to bear, bane, bitter pill, misfortune, misery, ordeal, trial, tribulation, torment, trouble, problem.
OPPOSITES blessing, advantage.
4 *I heard the sound of breaking glass and muffled curses* **swear word**, expletive, oath, profanity, four-letter word, dirty word, obscenity, imprecation, blasphemy, vulgarism, vulgarity; swearing, bad/foul language, strong language; *informal* cuss, cuss word.
▶ verb **1** *it seemed as if the family had been cursed* **put a curse on**, put the evil

C

eye on, execrate, imprecate, hoodoo; anathematize, excommunicate, damn; *N. Amer.* hex; *informal* put a jinx on, jinx; *rare* accurse.
2 *Miss Lewis was cursed with self-consciousness and feelings of inadequacy* **be afflicted with**, be troubled by, be plagued with, suffer from, be burdened with, be blighted with, be bedevilled by.
OPPOSITE be blessed with.
3 *drivers were cursing and sounding their horns* **swear**, utter profanities, utter oaths, use bad/foul language, be foul-mouthed, blaspheme, be blasphemous, take the Lord's name in vain, swear like a trooper, damn; *informal* cuss, turn the air blue, eff and blind; *archaic* execrate.

cursed ▶ adjective **1** *the cursed city of Anlec* **under a curse**, damned, doomed, ill-fated, ill-starred, star-crossed; anathematized, excommunicated, excommunicate; *Scottish* fey; *informal* jinxed.
2 (*informal, dated*) *those cursed children* **annoying**, irritating, infuriating, exasperating, maddening, trying, tiresome, troublesome, bothersome, irksome, vexing, vexatious, galling, provoking; *informal* **damned**, blasted, confounded, cussed, flaming, infernal, damn, damnable, wretched, dratted, aggravating, pesky, pestiferous, plaguy, pestilent; *Brit. informal* bloody, blinking, bleeding, flipping, blooming, effing, chuffing; *Austral./NZ informal* plurry; *Brit. informal, dated* bally, ruddy, deuced, dashed; *vulgar slang* fucking, frigging; *Irish vulgar slang* fecking.
OPPOSITES pleasant, agreeable.

cursory ▶ adjective *a cursory inspection* **perfunctory**, desultory, casual, superficial, token, uninterested, half-hearted, inattentive, unthinking, offhand, mechanical, automatic, routine; **hasty**, quick, hurried, rapid, brief, passing, fleeting, summary, sketchy, careless, slapdash.
OPPOSITES thorough, painstaking.

curt ▶ adjective *'No,' was his curt reply* **terse**, brusque, abrupt, clipped, blunt, short, monosyllabic, summary, snappy, snappish, sharp, crisp, tart; gruff, offhand, unceremonious, ungracious, rude, impolite, discourteous, uncivil; laconic, brief, succinct, compact, pithy, to the point, economical; *informal* snippy; *Brit. rare* dusty.
OPPOSITES polite, expansive.

> **CHOOSE THE RIGHT WORD**
> **curt, brusque, abrupt, terse**
> *See* BRUSQUE.

curtail ▶ verb *economic policies designed to curtail spending | his visit was curtailed* **reduce**, cut, cut down, cut back, decrease, lessen, diminish, slim down, tighten up, retrench, pare down, trim, dock, lop, shrink; **shorten**, cut short, break off, truncate; restrict, put a restriction on, limit, put a limit on, curb, put the brakes on, rein in, rein back; *informal* chop.
OPPOSITES increase; lengthen.

> **CHOOSE THE RIGHT WORD**
> **curtail, shorten, abbreviate, abridge, truncate**
> *See* SHORTEN.

curtailment ▶ noun *the curtailment of the government's public expenditure plans* **reduction**, cut, cutback, decrease, lessening, diminution, retrenchment, shrinkage; shortening, truncation, guillotine; restriction, limitation.
OPPOSITES increase, expansion.

curtain ▶ noun **1** *Colin closed the window and drew the curtains* **window hanging**, hanging, screen, blind; net curtain, cafe curtain, portière, blackout; drop curtain, drop scene, tableau curtain, safety curtain; *N. Amer.* drape; (*in Muslim & Hindu societies*) purdah.
2 *the curtain of falling snow* **screen**, cover, shield, cloak, veil, pall.
▶ verb *the bed was* **curtained off** *from the rest of the room | her unbound hair curtained her face* **screen**, separate, isolate; **conceal**, hide, shield, mask, veil, shroud.

curtsy ▶ verb bend one's knee, drop a curtsy, bob, genuflect.
▶ noun bob, genuflection; *archaic* courtesy, obeisance.

curvaceous ▶ adjective *a curvaceous young woman* **shapely**, voluptuous, sexy, full-figured, rounded, buxom, full-bosomed, bosomy, Junoesque, Rubensesque, opulent; cuddly; *informal* curvy, well endowed, pneumatic, stacked, well upholstered, busty, chesty; *archaic* comely.
OPPOSITES skinny, boyish.

curve *See centre pages for lists of* **Curves** **Lens Shapes** **Patterns**
▶ noun *the serpentine curves of the river* **bend**, turn, loop, curl, twist, hook; arch, bow, half-moon; corner, dog-leg, oxbow; bulge, swell, curvature, camber; undulation, meander; *Brit.* hairpin bend, hairpin turn; *technical* flexure, trajectory, inflection; *rare* incurvation.
▶ verb *the road dipped steeply and then curved back on itself* **bend**, turn, loop, wind, meander, undulate, snake, spiral, twist, coil, curl; arc, arch, bow; bulge, swell; *technical* inflect; *rare* incurve.

curved ▶ adjective **bent**, arched, bowed, crescent, curving, wavy, twisted, twisty, sinuous, serpentine, meandering, undulating, curvilinear, curvy; vaulted, rounded, concave, convex, domed, humped; hooked, aquiline; *technical* arcuate, falcate, falciform, circumflex, flexural; *literary* embowed; *rare* curviform.
OPPOSITE straight.

cushion ▶ noun **1** *she leaned back against the cushions* pillow, bolster, headrest; scatter cushion, floor cushion, beanbag, booster cushion, squab; hassock, kneeler, mat; *historical* pillion; *rare* zabuton.
2 *a cushion against fluctuations in demand* **protection**, buffer, shield, defence, bulwark.
▶ verb **1** *he stared out of the window, his chin cushioned on one hand* **support**, cradle, prop (up), rest; pillow.
2 *George told me the news, trying hard to cushion the blow* **soften**, lessen, diminish, decrease, mitigate, temper, allay, alleviate, reduce the effect of, take the edge off, dull, blunt, deaden, absorb, muffle, stifle.
OPPOSITES intensify, exacerbate.
3 *residents are cushioned from the outside world* **protect**, shield, shelter, cocoon.
OPPOSITE expose.

cushy ▶ adjective (*informal*) *a cushy job* **easy**, undemanding, untaxing; comfortable, secure; *Brit. informal* jammy.
OPPOSITES difficult, demanding.

custodian ▶ noun *the custodian of the archives | the acknowledged custodians of academic standards* **curator**, keeper, conservator, guardian, overseer, superintendent; caretaker, steward, warden, warder, attendant; watchdog, protector, defender.

custody ▶ noun **1** *the parent who has custody of the child | the property was placed in the custody of a trustee* **care**, **guardianship**, charge, keeping, safe keeping, wardship, ward, responsibility, protection, guidance, tutelage; custodianship, trusteeship, trust, keep, possession, hands; supervision, superintendence, surveillance, control, aegis, auspices; *Law* escrow.
2 *he has been in custody for 12 months* **imprisonment**, detention, confinement, incarceration, internment, captivity; remand; *archaic* duress, durance.

custom ▶ noun **1** *he was unfamiliar with the local customs and culture* **tradition**, practice, usage, observance, way, convention, procedure, ceremony, ritual, ordinance, form, formality, fashion, mode, manner; shibboleth, sacred cow, unwritten rule; mores, way of doing things; *Scottish* consuetude; *formal* praxis.
2 *it is our custom to visit the Lake District in October* **habit**, **practice**, routine, way, wont; policy, rule; *rare* habitude.
3 (*Brit.*) *special offers to attract custom away from competitors* **customers**, shoppers, buyers, purchasers, consumers; clientele; market share; *Brit. informal* punters; *Law* vendees; *rare* emptors.
4 (*Brit.*) *if you keep me waiting I will take my custom elsewhere* **business**, patronage, trade, support.

customarily ▶ adverb *these discussions customarily take place in the early evening* **usually**, traditionally, normally, as a rule, conventionally, generally, in the ordinary way, ordinarily, commonly; habitually, routinely.
OPPOSITE occasionally.

customary ▶ adjective **1** *it is customary to mark such an occasion with a toast | customary social practices* **usual**, traditional, normal, conventional; familiar, accepted, prevailing, routine, fixed, set, established, confirmed, everyday, ordinary, common, stock, well worn, time-honoured.
OPPOSITES unusual, exceptional, rare.
2 *she responded with her customary good sense* **usual**, accustomed, habitual, wonted, regular.
OPPOSITES unusual, unaccustomed.

customer ▶ noun **1** *businesses need to think up new ways of attracting customers* **shopper**, consumer, buyer, purchaser; **patron**, client; regular, frequenter, habitué; (**customers**) clientele, patronage, business, trade; *Brit. informal* punter; *Law* vendee; *rare* emptor.
OPPOSITE seller.
2 (*informal*) *he's a tough customer—a man to be reckoned with* **person**, individual, creature, fellow, man, woman; *informal* sort, type, fella, cookie, bunny, critter; *Brit. informal* bloke, chap, bod, geezer, gent; *N. Amer. informal* guy, gal, dame, dude, hombre; *informal, dated* dog; *Brit. vulgar slang* sod, bugger; *archaic* wight.

customs ▶ plural noun **import taxes**; duties, levies, dues, tolls, tariffs, imposts.

cut ▶ verb **1** *the knife slipped and cut his finger* **gash**, slash, lacerate, slit, pierce, penetrate, wound, injure; scratch, graze, nick, snick, notch, incise, score; lance.
2 *cut the red pepper into small pieces* **chop**, cut up, slice, dice, cube, mince; carve; divide; *N. Amer.* hash.
3 *they cut the rope before he choked | he has cut his ties with the church* **sever**, cleave, cut in two; *literary* rend; *archaic* sunder; *rare* dissever.
4 *she's had her hair cut | cut back the new growth to about half its length* **trim**, snip, clip, crop, bob, barber, shear, shave; pare; prune, pollard, poll, lop, dock; mow.
5 *I went out into the garden to cut some flowers* **pick**, pluck, gather; harvest,

reap; *literary* garner, cull.
6 *she gazed at the lettering cut into the stonework* **carve**, engrave, incise, etch, score; chisel, whittle.
7 *the government is likely to cut public expenditure | prices were cut by up to 15 per cent* **reduce**, cut back/down on, decrease, lessen, retrench, diminish, trim, prune, slim down, ease up on; rationalize, downsize, slenderize, economize on; mark down, discount, lower; *informal* slash, axe.
OPPOSITE increase.
8 *the text has been substantially cut* **shorten**, abridge, condense, abbreviate, truncate, pare down; edit; precis, summarize, synopsize; bowdlerize, expurgate; *rare* epitomize.
OPPOSITES lengthen, expand.
9 *you need to cut at least ten lines per page* **delete**, remove, take out, edit out, excise, blue-pencil.
OPPOSITE add.
10 *oil supplies to the area had been cut* **discontinue**, break off, suspend, interrupt; stop, end, put an end to.
OPPOSITE restore.
11 *he brought the car to a halt and cut the engine* **turn off**, switch off, shut off, deactivate; *informal* kill.
OPPOSITE turn on.
12 *the point where the line cuts the vertical axis* **cross**, intersect, bisect; meet, join; *technical* decussate.
OPPOSITE diverge.
13 (*dated*) *even Mrs Blenkinsop, the banker's wife, cut her at church* **snub**, ignore, shun, give someone the cold shoulder, cold-shoulder, turn one's back on, cut dead, look right through, pretend not to see; rebuff, spurn, ostracize; *Brit.* send to Coventry; *informal* give someone the brush-off, freeze out, stiff-arm; *N. Amer. informal* give someone the bum's rush, give someone the brush; *Austral. informal* snout; *informal, dated* give someone the go-by.
14 *he realized the remark had cut her* **hurt someone's feelings**, hurt, wound, upset, distress, make unhappy, grieve, pain, sting, cut to the quick.
15 *the demos which he cut for the recording company* **record**, make a recording of, put on disc/tape, make a tape of, tape-record; *informal* lay down.
□ **be cut out** *I don't think I'm cut out for this sort of work* **be suited**, be suitable, be right, be designed, be equipped; be qualified.
□ **cut across** *a movement which cut across class barriers* **transcend**, go beyond, rise above.
□ **cut back** *some companies* **cut back on** *foreign investment | we're going to have to cut back* **reduce**, cut, cut down, decrease, lessen, retrench, trim, prune, slim down, scale down; rationalize, downsize, economize on; pull/draw in one's horns, tighten one's belt; *informal* slash, axe.
□ **cut someone/something down 1** *24 hectares of trees were cut down* **fell**, chop down, hack down, saw down, hew.
2 *Barker had been cut down by a sniper's bullet* **kill**, slaughter, dispatch; shoot down, mow down, gun down; cut someone off in their prime; *informal* take out, blow away, snuff out; *literary* slay.
□ **cut and dried** *there were agreements which needed to be cut and dried* **definite**, decided, settled, explicit, specific, precise, unambiguous, clear-cut, unequivocal, black and white, hard and fast.
OPPOSITE vague.
□ **cut in** *'It's urgent,' Raoul cut in* **interrupt**, butt in, break in, interject, interpose, chime in; *Brit. informal* chip in.
□ **cut someone/something off 1** *they cut off his finger* **sever**, chop off, hack off; amputate.
2 *Moscow threatened to cut off oil and gas supplies to Lithuania* **discontinue**, break off, disconnect, interrupt, suspend; stop, end, bring to an end.
OPPOSITE restore.
3 *a community cut off from the mainland by the surging flood waters* **isolate**, separate, keep apart, keep away; seclude, closet, cloister, sequester.
4 *Gabrielle's family cut her off without a penny* **disinherit**, disown, repudiate, reject, have nothing more to do with, have done with, wash one's hands of.
□ **cut out** *both the lifeboat's engines cut out* **stop working**, cease to function, stop, fail, give out; break down, malfunction; *informal* die, give up the ghost, conk out, go on the blink, go kaput; *Brit. informal* pack up.
□ **cut someone/something out 1** *I cut his photograph out of the paper | you need to cut out the diseased wood* **remove**, take out, excise, extract; snip out, clip out.
2 *it's best to cut out alcohol altogether when you're pregnant* **give up**, refrain from, abstain from, go without, stop drinking/eating; *informal* quit, leave off, pack in, lay off, knock off.
3 *his mother cut him out of her will* **exclude**, leave out, omit, eliminate.
OPPOSITE include.
□ **cut something short** *they decided to cut short their holiday* **break off**, bring to a premature end, leave unfinished, shorten, truncate, curtail, terminate, end, stop, abort, bring to an untimely end.
OPPOSITE extend.
□ **cut someone short** *Peter cut him short* **interrupt**, cut off, butt in on, break in on.
▶ **noun 1** *blood ran from a cut on his jaw* **gash**, slash, laceration, incision, slit, wound, injury; scratch, graze, nick, snick.
2 *a cut of beef* **joint**, piece, section, bit.
3 (*informal*) *there wasn't much left after his agents took their cut* **share**, portion, bit, quota, percentage; commission, dividend; *informal* whack, slice of the cake, rake-off, piece of the action.
4 *his hair was in need of a cut* **haircut**, trim, clip, crop.
5 *a smart cut of the whip* **blow**, slash, stroke; *informal* swipe.
6 *he followed this with the unkindest cut of all* **insult**, slight, affront, slap in the face, jibe, barb, cutting remark, shaft; *informal* put-down, dig, brush-off.
7 *a 20 per cent pay cut | a cut in interest rates* **reduction**, cutback, decrease, retrenchment, lessening, curtailment; *N. Amer.* rollback; *informal* slash.
OPPOSITE increase.
8 *fortunately the cut happened at night, and power was quickly restored* **power cut**, loss of supply, interruption of supply, breakdown; blackout.
9 *the elegant cut of his dinner jacket* **style**, design; tailoring, lines, fit.
□ **a cut above** (*informal*) *he considered himself to be a cut above the rest* **superior to**, much better than; *informal* streets ahead of, way ahead of the field/pack.

C

WORD LINKS
related suffixes **-tomy** (e.g. ***gastrotomy, anatomy***), **-ectomy** (e.g. ***hysterectomy, appendectomy***)

cutback ▶ **noun** *cutbacks in defence spending* **reduction**, cut, decrease, retrenchment, trimming; economy, saving; *N. Amer.* rollback; *informal* slash.
OPPOSITE increase.

cute ▶ **adjective** *a picture of a cute kitten* **endearing**, adorable, lovable, sweet, lovely, appealing, engaging, delightful, dear, darling, winning, winsome, charming, enchanting; attractive, pretty, as pretty as a picture; chocolate-box; *Scottish & N. English* bonny; *informal* cutesy, dinky, twee, pretty-pretty.
OPPOSITES unattractive, unappealing.

cut-price ▶ **adjective** **cheap**, marked down, reduced (in price), on (special) offer, discount, discounted, bargain (price), sale-price, sale, half-price; *N. Amer.* cut-rate; *informal* bargain-basement, cheapo.
OPPOSITE expensive.

cut-throat ▶ **noun** (*dated*) *a band of robbers and cut-throats* **murderer**, killer, assassin, butcher, liquidator, executioner, thug, bravo; *informal* hit man; *N. Amer. informal* button man; *literary* slayer; *dated* homicide.
▶ **adjective 1** (*dated*) *cut-throat robbers* **murderous**, homicidal, death-dealing, savage, brutal, violent, bloody, bloodthirsty, fierce, ferocious, vicious, barbarous, cruel.
2 *advertising is a cut-throat business* **ruthless**, merciless, pitiless, unfeeling, relentless, aggressive; dog-eat-dog, fiercely competitive, intensely competitive.

cutting ▶ **noun 1** *a newspaper cutting* **clipping**, clip, snippet, extract, excerpt; article, piece, passage, column, paragraph.
2 *plant cuttings* **scion**, slip; graft.
3 *fabric cuttings* **piece**, bit, fragment, part; trimming.
▶ **adjective 1** *a cutting remark* **hurtful**, wounding, barbed, pointed, scathing, acerbic, mordant, trenchant, caustic, acid, abrasive, sarcastic, sardonic, snide, spiteful, malicious, mean, nasty, cruel, unkind, vicious, venomous, poisonous, vitriolic; *N. Amer.* acerb; *informal* bitchy, catty; *Brit. informal* sarky; *N. Amer. informal* snarky; *rare* acidulous, mordacious, squint-eyed.
OPPOSITES friendly, pleasant.
2 *cutting winter winds* **icy**, bitterly cold, icy-cold, freezing, arctic, Siberian, glacial, bitter, chilling, chilly; **biting**, piercing, penetrating, raw, keen, sharp, stinging, harsh; *literary* chill; *rare* gelid.
OPPOSITES warm, balmy.

cut up ▶ **adjective** (*informal*) *he's pretty cut up about it* **upset**, distressed, miserable, unhappy, sad, troubled, dismayed, saddened, grieved, hurt, devastated, traumatized; *informal* in a state, in a bad way.
OPPOSITES unaffected, phlegmatic.

cycle ▶ **noun 1** *a myth embodying the cycle of birth, death, and rebirth* **round**, rotation, revolution; circle, pattern, rhythm.
2 *the painting is one of a cycle of seven* **series**, sequence, succession, run; set.
3 *cycles may be hired from the station. See* BICYCLE.

cyclical ▶ **adjective** *the cyclical fluctuations in demand* **recurrent**, recurring, happening at regular intervals, regular, repeated, repetitive; **periodic**, seasonal, circular.

cyclone ▶ **noun** **hurricane**, typhoon, tropical storm, storm, tornado, windstorm, whirlwind, tempest; *Austral./NZ informal* willy-willy; *N. Amer. informal* twister.

cynic ▶ **noun** **sceptic**, doubter, doubting Thomas, scoffer; **pessimist**, prophet of doom, doom merchant, doom and gloom merchant, doomster, doomsayer, doom-monger, doomwatcher, Cassandra.
OPPOSITES idealist; optimist.

cynical ▶ **adjective** **sceptical**, doubtful, distrustful, suspicious, disbelieving, unbelieving, scoffing, doubting, incredulous; **pessimistic**, negative, hardbitten, hardened, hard, world-weary, disillusioned, disenchanted, jaundiced, sardonic, black, bleak; *informal* hard-boiled.

C

OPPOSITES optimistic; credulous.

cynicism ▶ noun **scepticism**, doubt, distrust, mistrust, doubtfulness, suspicion, disbelief, incredulity, unbelief, scoffing; **pessimism**, negative thinking, negativity, world-weariness, disillusion, disenchantment; *rare* dubiety, sardonicism.

OPPOSITE optimism.

cynosure ▶ noun *Araminta remained the cynosure of all eyes* **focus of attention**, centre of attention, focus, focal point.

cyst ▶ noun **growth**, abscess, boil, blister, bleb, wen, carbuncle; *technical* vesicle, vesication, hydatid, oocyst, saccule, steatoma.

dab ▶ verb *he dabbed his mouth with a napkin | she dabbed disinfectant on the cut* **pat**, press, touch, blot, mop, swab, smudge; spread, daub, bedaub, apply, wipe, stroke, stipple.

▶ noun **1** *the screw can be held in place with a tiny dab of superglue* **drop**, dash, spot, smear, dribble, trickle, splash, sprinkle, speck, taste, lick, trace, touch, hint, suggestion, soupçon, particle, bit, modicum; little; *informal* smidgen, tad.

2 *apply concealer with light dabs* **pat**, press, touch, blot, mop, wipe, smudge, smear.

dabble ▶ verb **1** *they dabbled their feet in the rock pools* **splash**, dip, paddle, wet, moisten, dampen, immerse, trail.

2 *he dabbled in politics* **toy with**, dip into, scratch the surface of, flirt with, tinker with, potter about/around/round with, trifle with, play with, fiddle with, dally with, have a smattering of.

dabbler ▶ noun *he was a dabbler in psychology* **amateur**, dilettante, non-professional, layman, layperson, tinkerer, potterer, trifler, dallier.

OPPOSITES expert, professional.

daemon ▶ noun **inspiring force**, genius, numen, demon; tutelary spirit, familiar spirit, attendant spirit; *Latin* genius loci.

daft ▶ adjective (*Brit. informal*) **1** *that's a daft idea* **absurd**, preposterous, ridiculous, ludicrous, farcical, laughable, risible; idiotic, stupid, foolish, foolhardy, unwise, imprudent, ill-conceived, silly, inane, puerile, infantile, fatuous, imbecilic, hare-brained, half-baked; unreasonable, irrational, illogical, nonsensical, pointless, senseless, impracticable, unworkable, unrealistic; peculiar, odd, strange, queer, weird, eccentric, bizarre, fantastic, incongruous, grotesque; *informal* crazy, barmy, potty, cock-eyed.

OPPOSITE sensible.

2 *are you daft or something?* **simple-minded**, simple, stupid, idiotic, moronic, imbecilic, dull-witted, dull, dim-witted, slow-witted, slow, witless, half-witted, feeble-minded, dunce-like, cretinous, empty-headed, vacuous, vapid; deranged, unhinged, insane, mad; *informal* touched, thick, thick as two short planks, dim, dopey, dumb, dozy, birdbrained, pea-brained, pig-ignorant, bovine, slow on the uptake, soft in the head, brain-dead, boneheaded, lamebrained, chuckleheaded, dunderheaded, wooden-headed, fat-headed, muttonheaded, not all there, not quite right, crazy, mental, nuts, nutty, crackers, cracked, potty, barmy, batty, cuckoo, bonkers, dotty, dippy; *Brit. informal* not the full shilling; *N. Amer. informal* dumb-ass.

3 *she's **daft about** him* **infatuated with**, enamoured of, obsessed by, smitten with, besotted by, doting on, very fond of; *informal* crazy, wild, mad, nutty, nuts, potty, gone on; *informal, dated* sweet on.

dagger ▶ noun. *See centre pages for list of* **Knives and Daggers**

daily ▶ adjective *a daily event* **occurring/done/produced every day**, everyday, day-to-day, quotidian; *rare* diurnal, circadian.

▶ adverb *the museum is open daily* **every day**, seven days a week; once a day, day after day, day by day, per diem; *rare* diurnally.

dainty ▶ adjective **1** *a dainty china cup | her dainty body* **delicate**, neat, refined, tasteful, fine, elegant, exquisite; graceful, petite, slight, slim, trim, pretty; *Brit. informal* dinky.

OPPOSITE unwieldy.

2 *a dainty morsel* **tasty**, delicious, choice, palatable, luscious, mouth-watering, delectable, toothsome, succulent, juicy; appetizing, inviting, tempting; *informal* scrumptious, yummy, scrummy, finger-licking, moreish; *literary* ambrosial.

OPPOSITES tasteless; unpalatable.

3 *a dainty eater* **fastidious**, fussy, hard to please, finicky, finical, faddish, squeamish; refined, particular, discriminating, discerning, critical, exacting, demanding, scrupulous, meticulous, careful, cautious; *informal* choosy, pernickety, picky; *Brit. informal* faddy; *archaic* nice.

OPPOSITES easy to please; undiscriminating.

▶ noun *home-made breads, jams, and dainties* **delicacy**, tasty morsel, titbit, fancy, luxury, treat, nibble, savoury, appetizer, bonne bouche, confection, bonbon; *N. Amer.* tidbit; *informal* goody; *archaic* sweetmeat.

dais ▶ noun **platform**, stage, podium, rostrum, stand, grandstand, staging, apron, soapbox, stump; lectern, pulpit, box, dock; *Indian* mandapam; *rare* tribune.

dale ▶ noun **valley**, vale; hollow, hole, basin, gully, gorge, ravine; *Brit.* dene, combe, slade; *N. English* clough; *Scottish* glen, strath; *literary* dell, dingle.

dally ▶ verb **1** *there's no time to dally on the way to work* **dawdle**, delay, loiter, linger, waste time, kill time, take one's time, while away time; lag, trail, straggle, fall behind; amble, plod, trudge, meander, drift; *informal* dilly-dally; *literary* tarry.

OPPOSITE hurry.

2 *he should stop dallying with film stars* **trifle**, toy, play, amuse oneself, flirt, play fast and loose, tinker, philander, womanize, carry on; *informal* play around, mess about/around.

dam ▶ noun *the dam burst after torrential rain* **barrage**, barrier, wall, embankment, levee, barricade, obstruction, hindrance, blockage.

▶ verb *the river was dammed to create a lake* **block (up)**, obstruct, choke, clog (up), bung up, close; *technical* occlude.

damage ▶ noun **1** *did the thieves do any damage?* **harm**, injury, destruction, vandalization, vandalism; impairment, defilement, desecration, defacement, disfigurement, scarring, mutilation, vitiation, detriment; ruin, havoc, devastation; wear and tear, battering, friction, erosion, attrition, corrosion, abrasion, deterioration, degeneration; *rare* detrition.

2 (*informal*) *what's the damage?* **cost**, price, expense, charge, bill, account, total.

3 (**damages**) *she won £4,300 damages in the county court* **compensation**, recompense, restitution, redress, reparation(s); repayment, reimbursement, remuneration, requital, indemnification, indemnity, satisfaction; *N. Amer. informal* comp; *archaic* guerdon, meed; *rare* solatium.

▶ verb *the parcel had been damaged by rough handling* **harm**, do damage to, injure, mar, deface, mutilate, mangle, impair, blemish, disfigure, vandalize, blight, spoil, defile, desecrate; tamper with, sabotage, disrupt, play havoc with, vitiate; ruin, devastate, destroy, wreck, cripple; *N. Amer. informal* trash; *rare* disfeature.

OPPOSITES repair; improve.

damaging ▶ adjective *pesticides have had a damaging effect on a lot of wildlife* **harmful**, detrimental, injurious, hurtful, inimical, dangerous, destructive, ruinous, calamitous, disastrous, deleterious, pernicious, ill, bad, evil, baleful, malign, corrupting, malignant, adverse, undesirable, prejudicial, unfavourable, unfortunate, counterproductive; unhealthy, unwholesome, poisonous, cancerous, noxious; *literary* malefic, maleficent; *rare* prejudicious.

OPPOSITES benign; beneficial.

damn ▶ verb **1** *the voices all around me were damning Menzies* **curse**, put a curse on, put the evil eye on, execrate, imprecate, hoodoo; anathematize, excommunicate; *N. Amer.* hex; *informal* put a jinx on, jinx; *rare* accurse.

OPPOSITE bless.

2 *we are certainly not going to damn a product just because it is non-traditional* **condemn**, censure, criticize, attack, denounce, deplore, decry, revile, inveigh against; blame, chastise, castigate, berate, upbraid, reprimand, rebuke, reprove, reprehend, take to task, find fault with, give someone/something a bad press; deprecate, disparage; *informal* slam, hammer, lay into, cane, blast; *Brit. informal* slate, slag off, have a go at; *archaic* slash, reprobate; *rare* excoriate, vituperate, arraign, objurgate, anathematize.

OPPOSITES acclaim; praise.

▶ noun (*informal*) *your evidence isn't worth a damn | I don't care a damn* **jot**, whit, iota, rap, scrap, bit; one bit, even a little bit, the smallest amount, the tiniest bit; *informal* hoot, two hoots, tinker's cuss/curse, brass farthing.

damnable ▶ adjective **1** (*dated*) *a damnable nuisance* **unpleasant**, disagreeable, objectionable, offensive, execrable, horrible, horrid, ghastly, awful, nasty, dreadful, terrible; annoying, irritating, infuriating, maddening, exasperating; hateful, detestable, loathsome, foul, abominable, odious, obnoxious; *informal* beastly, pestilential; *archaic* scurvy.
OPPOSITE pleasant.
2 *we must keep this damnable magic from our shores* **accursed**, cursed, under a curse, damned, diabolical, devilish, demonic, demoniac, fiendish, Mephistophelian, hellish, infernal, execrable, base, wicked, evil, sinful, iniquitous, heinous; *rare* anathematized.
OPPOSITE holy.

D

damnation ▶ noun *sins that risk eternal damnation* **condemnation to hell**, eternal punishment, perdition, doom, hellfire; curse, execration, imprecation, excommunication, anathema, anathematization, malediction; *N. Amer.* hex; *archaic* malison.

damned ▶ adjective **1** *each of the damned souls was guarded by a demon* **cursed**, accursed, doomed, lost, condemned to hell, execrated; anathematized, excommunicated; *informal* jinxed.
2 (*informal*) *this damned car won't start* **blasted**, damn, flaming, precious, confounded, pestilential, rotten, wretched; *Brit. informal* blessed, flipping, blinking, blooming, bloody, bleeding, effing, chuffing; *Austral./NZ informal* plurry; *Brit. informal, dated* bally, ruddy, deuced; *vulgar slang* fucking, frigging, sodding; *Irish vulgar slang* fecking; *dated* cursed, accursed, damnable.

damning ▶ adjective *in the face of such damning evidence Jakobs had little defence* **incriminating**, condemnatory, condemning, damnatory; damaging, derogatory; conclusive, strong; *rare* implicatory.
OPPOSITES vindicatory; inconclusive.

damp ▶ adjective *her hair was still damp from the shower* **moist**, moistened, wettish, dampened, dampish; humid, steamy, muggy, clammy, sweaty, sticky, dank, moisture-laden, wet, wetted, rainy, drizzly, showery, misty, foggy, vaporous, dewy.
OPPOSITE dry.
▶ noun *you could feel the damp in the air* **moisture**, dampness, humidity, wetness, wet, water, liquid, condensation, steam, vapour, clamminess, mugginess, dankness, wateriness; rain, raininess, dew, drizzle, precipitation, spray; perspiration, sweat.
OPPOSITE dryness.
▶ verb *gradually sweat damped the edges of his hair | this did nothing to damp my enthusiasm.* See DAMPEN.

WORD LINKS
related prefix **hygro- (e.g. *hygrometer, hygroscopic*)**
fear of damp **hygrophobia**

dampen ▶ verb **1** *the fine rain dampened her face* **moisten**, damp, wet, dew, water, irrigate, humidify; *literary* bedew; *rare* sparge, humify, humect.
OPPOSITES dry; drench.
2 *nothing could dampen her enthusiasm* **lessen**, decrease, diminish, reduce, lower, moderate, damp, damp down, put a damper on, throw cold water on, calm, cool, chill, dull, blunt, tone down, deaden, temper, discourage; **suppress**, extinguish, quench, stamp out, smother, stifle, muffle, blanket, mute, silence, quieten, overcome, curb, limit, check, still, restrain, inhibit, deter.
OPPOSITE heighten.

damper ▶ noun *this will put a damper on the liberal agenda for the next couple of years* **curb**, check, restraint, restriction, limit, limitation, constraint, stricture, rein, brake, control, impediment, obstacle, hindrance; discouragement, depressant, depression, chill, pall, gloom, cloud.

dampness ▶ noun *dampness within the building encourages insects and fungi* **moisture**, damp, humidity, wetness, wet, water, liquid, condensation, steam, vapour, clamminess, mugginess, dankness, wateriness; rain, raininess, dew, drizzle, precipitation, spray; perspiration, sweat.

damsel ▶ noun (*literary*) *a damsel in distress.* See GIRL sense 2.

dance *See centre pages for lists of* **Ballet Steps and Positions** **Dances and Types of Dancing**
▶ verb **1** *he danced with her at the party* sway, trip, spin, whirl, twirl, pirouette, gyrate; *informal* bop, disco, rock, shake a leg, hoof it, cut a rug, trip the light fantastic; *N. Amer. informal* get down, step it; *archaic* foot it, tread a measure.
2 *a dozen sweet-faced little girls danced round me chanting* **caper**, cavort, frisk, frolic, skip, prance, romp, gambol, jig, bound, leap, jump, spring, bob, hop, trip, bounce; *rare* rollick.
3 *she could see flames dancing in the fireplace* **flicker**, sparkle, twinkle, shimmer, leap, ripple, dart, play, flick, flit, quiver, jiggle, joggle, oscillate.
▶ noun *they were going to a dance* **ball**, discotheque; tea dance, dinner dance, masked ball, masquerade; *N. Amer.* prom, hoedown; *French* thé dansant; *informal* disco, hop, bop.

WORD LINKS
Muse **Terpsichore**

dancer ▶ noun *French* danseur, danseuse; *informal* bopper, hoofer; *formal* terpsichorean.

dandle ▶ verb *he dandled his two-year-old son on his knee* **bounce**, jiggle, ride, dance, toss, pet, rock; hug, cradle, fondle, cuddle, caress.

dandy ▶ noun *I even smartened myself up, becoming something of a dandy* **fop**, beau, man about town, bright young thing, glamour boy, rake; *French* boulevardier, petit-maître; *informal* swell, toff, dude, sharp dresser, snappy dresser, natty dresser, trendy, pretty boy; *archaic* blade, blood, buck, coxcomb, masher, peacock, popinjay, dapperling.
▶ adjective (*N. Amer. informal*) *our trip to Spain was dandy.* See FINE[1].

danger ▶ noun **1** *there is an element of danger in the show* **peril**, hazard, risk, jeopardy, endangerment, imperilment, insecurity; perilousness, riskiness, precariousness, uncertainty, instability.
OPPOSITE safety.
2 *such people are a danger to society* **menace**, hazard, threat, risk, peril; source of apprehension, source of dread, source of fright, source of fear, source of terror.
3 *there is a serious danger of fire* **possibility**, chance, risk, probability, likelihood, fear, prospect.

CHOOSE THE RIGHT WORD

danger, peril, hazard, risk

- **Danger** is the most general word for a possibility of suffering harm or injury (*they were in great danger*). It can also refer to a likely cause of harm or injury (*he is a danger to himself and others*) or, in the plural, to the quality of potentially causing harm (*the dangers of smoking*). *Danger* can have connotations of excitement (*the Prince has always enjoyed flirting with danger*).
- **Peril** is a more formal or literary word (*the self-government of this country is in peril | the immediate peril confronting the world in the early 1940s*), and is normally used in the plural when referring to a quality of something (*the perils of drink-driving*). *Peril* can refer to a possibility of harm that a person may knowingly undergo (*we ignore these warnings at our peril*).
- **Hazard** is principally used to describe an actual source of danger (*lead pipes are a serious hazard to health*), as well as the dangers inherent in something named (*cuts and grazes are a hazard of life*). It is used in the plural when referring to the dangerous quality of something (*increased official recognition of the hazards of asbestos*).
- **Risk** denotes a more predictable possibility of harm arising from an action or a situation, or from an action or object that increases the likelihood of harm (*ozone depletion may increase the risk of skin cancer | going on holiday without insurance is always a risk*). A *risk* may often be a danger that someone chooses to incur because it is outweighed by some other consideration (*you're taking a risk by meeting me*).

dangerous ▶ adjective **1** *a dangerous wild animal* **menacing**, threatening, treacherous; **savage**, wild, vicious, murderous, desperate; *rare* minacious.
OPPOSITE harmless.
2 *overloading a power socket is dangerous* **hazardous**, perilous, risky, high-risk, fraught with danger, unsafe, uncertain, unpredictable, precarious, insecure, exposed, vulnerable, touch-and-go, chancy, tricky, treacherous; breakneck, reckless, daredevil; *Scottish* unchancy; *informal* warm, dicey, sticky, hairy; *Brit. informal* dodgy; *N. Amer. informal* gnarly.
OPPOSITE safe.

dangle ▶ verb **1** *a long chain dangled from his belt* **hang (down)**, droop, sag, swing, sway, wave, trail, stream; *archaic* depend.
2 *he dangled the speedboat's keys enticingly* **wave**, swing, flap, jiggle, brandish, flourish, flaunt.
3 *the prince* **dangled** *money* **in front of** *the local chief* **offer**, hold out; entice someone with, lure someone with, tempt someone with, tantalize someone with, seduce someone with.

dangling ▶ adjective *she had long, dangling earrings* **hanging**, drooping, droopy, suspended, supported from above, pendulous, pendent, swinging, swaying, trailing, flowing, falling, tumbling; *rare* pensile.

dank ▶ adjective *he shivered as he entered the dank cellar* **damp**, musty, chilly, clammy, wet, moist, unaired, moisture-laden, humid.
OPPOSITE dry.

dapper ▶ adjective *Pablo looked very dapper in his best clothes* **smart**, spruce, trim, debonair, neat, tidy, neat and tidy, crisp, well dressed, besuited, well groomed, well turned out, smartly dressed, elegant, chic, dashing; *French* soigné; *informal* snazzy, snappy, natty, sharp, nifty; *N. Amer. informal* sassy, spiffy, fly, kicky; *dated* as if one had just stepped out of a bandbox; *Brit. informal, dated* swagger; *archaic* trig.
OPPOSITE scruffy.

dapple ▶ verb *fine rays of sunlight dappled the surface of a lake* **dot**, spot, mark, fleck, streak, speck, speckle, bespeckle, mottle, stipple, marble.

dappled ▶ adjective *the dappled purple carpet of flowers* **speckled**, blotched, blotchy, spotted, spotty, dotted, streaked, streaky, mottled, marbled, flecked, freckled, stippled, piebald, skewbald, pied, brindled, brindle, tabby, marled; patchy, variegated, multicoloured, particoloured; *N. Amer.* pinto; *informal* splotchy, splodgy; *rare* jaspé.

dare ▶ verb **1** *nobody dared to say a word* **be brave enough**, have the courage, pluck up courage, take the risk; **venture**, have the nerve, have the temerity, make so bold as, be so bold as, have the effrontery, have the audacity, presume, go so far as; risk doing, hazard doing, take the liberty of doing; *informal* stick one's neck out, go out on a limb; *N. Amer. informal* take a flyer; *archaic* make bold to.
2 *she dared him to go* **challenge**, provoke, goad, taunt, defy, summon, invite, bid; throw down the gauntlet to.
▶ noun *she didn't quite know why she accepted the dare* **challenge**, provocation, goad, taunt; gauntlet, invitation, ultimatum, summons.

daredevil ▶ noun *spectators watched in horror as the nineteen-year-old daredevil smashed into the ground* **madcap**, hothead, adventurer, exhibitionist, swashbuckler; **stuntman**; *Brit.* tearaway; *informal* show-off, showboat; *dated* desperado.
OPPOSITE coward.
▶ adjective *a daredevil skydiver* **daring**, bold, adventurous, madcap, hot-headed, audacious, courageous, brave, intrepid, fearless, death-or-glory, undaunted, dauntless, heedless; **reckless**, rash, hasty, impulsive, precipitous, impetuous, wild, desperate, foolhardy, incautious, imprudent, ill-advised, hare-brained; *Brit.* tearaway; *informal* harum-scarum, bull-in-a-china-shop.
OPPOSITES cowardly; cautious.

daring ▶ adjective *a lone torpedo-bomber attempted a daring attack on the battleship* **bold**, audacious, adventurous, intrepid, venturesome, fearless, brave, unafraid, unshrinking, undaunted, dauntless, valiant, valorous, heroic, dashing; confident, enterprising; madcap, rash, reckless, heedless; *informal* gutsy, spunky, peppy, pushy; *rare* adventuresome, venturous.
OPPOSITES cowardly; cautious.
▶ noun *this recording eclipses the others by its sheer daring* **boldness**, audacity, temerity, audaciousness, fearlessness, intrepidity, bravery, courage, courageousness, valour, valorousness, heroism, pluck; **recklessness**, rashness, foolhardiness; adventurousness, enterprise, dynamism, spirit, mettle, confidence; *informal* nerve, guts, gutsiness, spunk, grit; *Brit. informal* bottle, ballsiness; *N. Amer. informal* moxie, cojones, sand; *vulgar slang* balls; *rare* venturousness, temerariousness.
OPPOSITES cowardice; caution.

CHOOSE THE RIGHT WORD

daring, bold, audacious

See BOLD.

dark ▶ adjective **1** *a dark night* **black**, pitch-black, pitch-dark, inky, jet-black, unlit, unlighted, unilluminated, ill-lit, poorly lit; starless, moonless, dim, dingy, gloomy, dusky, indistinct, shadowy, shady; leaden, overcast, sunless; *literary* crepuscular, tenebrous; *rare* Stygian, Cimmerian, Tartarean, caliginous.
OPPOSITE bright.
2 *keep it dark | a dark secret* **mysterious**, **secret**, hidden, concealed, veiled, unrevealed, covert, clandestine; enigmatic, arcane, esoteric, obscure, abstruse, recondite, recherché, inscrutable, impenetrable, opaque, incomprehensible, cryptic.
3 *dark hair* **brunette**, dark brown, auburn, tawny, copper-coloured, coppery, chestnut, chestnut-coloured, jet-black, sable, ebony; dark-haired.
OPPOSITE blonde.
4 *dark skin* **swarthy**, sallow, olive, dusky, black, ebony; tanned, bronzed, suntanned, sunburned; dark-skinned.
OPPOSITE pale.
5 *the dark days of the war* **tragic**, **disastrous**, calamitous, catastrophic, cataclysmic, ruinous, devastating; **dire**, ghastly, awful, unfortunate, dreadful, horrible, terrible, horrific, hideous, horrendous, frightful, atrocious, abominable, abhorrent, gruesome, grisly, monstrous, nightmarish, heinous, harrowing; wretched, woeful; *literary* direful.
OPPOSITE happy.
6 *my mind is full of dark thoughts* **gloomy**, dismal, pessimistic, negative, defeatist, downbeat, gloom-ridden, cynical, bleak, grim, fatalistic, black, sombre, drab, dreary; **despairing**, despondent, depressed, dejected, demoralized, hopeless, cheerless, joyless, melancholy, glum, lugubrious, Eeyorish, grave, funereal, morose, mournful, doleful, suspicious, distrustful, doubting, alarmist.
OPPOSITE optimistic.
7 *Matthew flashed a dark look at her* **moody**, brooding, sullen, dour, glum, morose, sulky, frowning, scowling, glowering, angry, forbidding, threatening, ominous.
OPPOSITE kindly.
8 *so many dark deeds had been committed | a dark secret* **evil**, wicked, sinful, immoral, wrong, morally wrong, wrongful, bad, iniquitous; ungodly, unholy, irreligious, unrighteous, sacrilegious, profane, blasphemous, impious, godless, base, mean, vile; **shameful**, discreditable, unspeakable, foul, monstrous, shocking, outrageous, atrocious, abominable, reprehensible, hateful, detestable, despicable, odious, contemptible, horrible, heinous, execrable, diabolical, diabolic, fiendish, vicious, murderous, barbarous, black, rotten, perverted, reprobate, sordid, degenerate, depraved, dissolute, dishonourable, dishonest, unscrupulous, unprincipled; *informal* crooked, bent, warped, low-down, stinking, dirty, shady; *Law* malfeasant; *rare* dastardly, peccable, egregious, flagitious.
OPPOSITES good, virtuous.
▶ noun **1** *he's afraid of the dark* **darkness**, blackness, absence of light, gloom, gloominess, dimness, dullness, murk, murkiness, shadowiness, shadow, shade, shadiness, dusk, twilight, gloaming; *rare* tenebrosity.
OPPOSITE light.
2 *as dark fell, the street lights went on | she only went out after dark* **night**, night-time, darkness, hours of darkness; **nightfall**, evening, twilight, sunset.
OPPOSITES day; dawn.
□ **in the dark** (*informal*) *we're being kept **in the dark about** what is happening* **unaware of**, ignorant of, in ignorance of, oblivious to, uninformed about, unenlightened about, unacquainted with, unconversant with; *rare* nescient of.
OPPOSITE aware.

darken ▶ verb **1** *the sky darkened* **grow dark/darker**, blacken, grow black/blacker, dim, grow dim, cloud over, lour.
OPPOSITE lighten.
2 *fixative can darken the colours in a picture* **make dark/darker**, blacken, make black/blacker, make dim, shade, eclipse, fog, obscure.
3 *the misery that darkened his later life | his mood darkened* **make/become gloomy**, make/become angry, make/become unhappy, make/become annoyed, make/become depressed, cast down, become cast down, deject, become dejected, weigh down, oppress, dampen the spirits of, make/become dispirited, make/become troubled, cast a pall over, blacken, look black, sadden; spoil, mar, detract from.

darkness ▶ noun **1** *lights shone in the darkness* **dark**, blackness, absence of light, gloom, gloominess, dimness, dullness, murk, murkiness, shadowiness, shadow, shade, shadiness, dusk, twilight, gloaming; *rare* tenebrosity.
OPPOSITE light.
2 *the sun went down, and darkness fell* **night**, night-time, dark, hours of darkness.
OPPOSITE day.
3 *the forces of darkness* **evil**, wickedness, corruption, sin, sinfulness, iniquity, immorality, devilry, the Devil, hell.
OPPOSITE good.

WORD LINKS
fear of darkness **scotophobia**

darling ▶ noun **1** *good night, darling* **dear**, dearest, dear one, love, lover, sweetheart, beloved, sweet; *informal* honey, angel, pet, sweetie, sugar, babe, baby, doll, poppet, treasure; *archaic* sweeting.
2 *the darling of the media* **favourite**, pet, apple of one's eye, celebrity, idol, hero, heroine; *informal* blue-eyed boy/girl; *N. Amer. informal* fair-haired boy/girl.
▶ adjective **1** *his darling wife* **dear**, dearest, precious, adored, loved, beloved, much loved, favourite, cherished, treasured, prized, esteemed, worshipped, idolized, lionized.
2 (*informal, dated*) *a darling little hat* **adorable**, lovable, precious, appealing, charming, cute, sweet, enchanting, bewitching, captivating, alluring, engaging, endearing, dear, delightful, lovely, beautiful, attractive, gorgeous, winsome, winning, fetching, pleasing; chocolate-box; *Scottish & N. English* bonny; *dated* taking.

darn ▶ verb *Michael was darning his socks* **mend**, repair, reinforce; sew up, stitch; cobble, botch, patch; *informal* vamp; *archaic* clout.
▶ noun *a sweater with darns in the elbows* **patch**, repair, reinforcement, stitch, mend.

dart ▶ noun **1** *he was killed by a poisoned dart* **small arrow**, flechette, bolt, shaft; missile, projectile; *literary* reed; *historical* quarrel.
2 *the cat made a dart for the door as he came in* **dash**, rush, run, bolt, break, charge, race, sprint, bound, spring, leap, jump, lunge, pounce, dive, swoop, gallop, scurry, scamper, stampede, scramble, start, flight.
▶ verb **1** *Karl darted across the road* **dash**, rush, tear, run, bolt, fly, flash, shoot, charge, race, sprint, bound, spring, leap, jump, lunge, dive, swoop, gallop, scurry, scamper, stampede, scramble, break, start; *informal* scoot.
2 *Tam darted a terrified glance over his shoulder* **direct**, cast, throw, shoot, send, fling, toss, flash, bestow, give.

dash ▶ verb **1** *he dashed straight home to see his father* **rush**, race, run, sprint, bolt, dart, gallop, career, charge, shoot, hurtle, hare, bound, fly, speed, streak, zoom, plunge, dive, whisk, scurry, scuttle, scamper, scramble; *informal* tear, belt, pelt, scoot, zap, zip, whip, step on it, get a move on, hotfoot it, leg it, go hell for leather, steam, put on some speed, go like a bat out of hell, burn rubber; *Brit. informal* bomb, go like the clappers, bucket, put one's foot down; *Scottish informal* wheech; *N. Amer. informal* boogie, hightail it, clip, barrel, get the lead out; *informal, dated* cut

D

along; *N. Amer. vulgar slang* drag/tear/haul ass; *literary* fleet; *archaic* post, hie, haste.
OPPOSITE dawdle.
2 *he picked up the glass case and dashed it to the ground* **hurl**, smash, crash, slam, throw, toss, fling, pitch, cast, lob, launch, flip, catapult, shy, aim, direct, project, propel, send, bowl; *informal* chuck, heave, sling, buzz, whang, bung; *N. Amer. informal* peg; *Austral. informal* hoy; *NZ informal* bish.
3 *the wind and rain* **dashed against** *the thick stone walls* **be hurled**, crash, smash; batter, strike, beat, pound, pummel, lash, slam into.
4 *it was a 15-year-old newcomer who dashed her hopes for a third title* **shatter**, destroy, wreck, ruin, crush, devastate, demolish, wreak havoc with, blast, blight, wipe out, overturn, torpedo, scotch, spoil, frustrate, thwart, baulk, check; burst someone's bubble; *informal* put the kibosh on, banjax, do for, blow a hole in, nix, put paid to, queer; *Brit. informal* scupper, dish; *archaic* bring to naught.
OPPOSITE raise.
▸ **noun 1** *they made a dash for the door* **rush**, race, run, sprint, bolt, dart, leap, charge, plunge, dive, bound, break, scamper, scramble; stampede.
2 *the soup needs a dash of salt* **small amount**, touch, sprinkle, pinch, taste, lick, spot, drop, dab, speck, smack, smattering, sprinkling, splash, dribble, trickle, grain, soupçon, trace, bit, modicum, little, suggestion, suspicion, hint, scintilla, tinge, tincture, whiff, whisper, overtone, undertone, nuance, colouring; *informal* smidgen, tad.
OPPOSITE lashings.
3 *he led the raids with such skill and dash* **verve**, **style**, stylishness, flamboyance, gusto, zest, confidence, self-assurance, elan, flair, flourish, vigour, vivacity, vivaciousness, sparkle, brio, panache, éclat, exuberance, ebullience, enthusiasm, eagerness, vitality, dynamism, animation, liveliness, spirit, energy; *informal* pizzazz, pep, oomph, vim, zing, get-up-and-go.
OPPOSITES ineptitude; apathy.

dashing ▸ **adjective 1** *she met and married a dashing test pilot* **debonair**, jaunty, devil-may-care, breezy, raffish, sporty, stylish, dazzling, romantic, attractive, spirited, lively, buoyant, energetic, animated, exuberant, flamboyant, dynamic, gallant, bold, intrepid, daring, adventurous, venturesome, plucky, swashbuckling; *informal* peppy.
OPPOSITES boring, unadventurous.
2 *he was exceptionally dashing in his polo clothes | dashing suits for bridegrooms* **stylish**, smart, elegant, chic, crisp, dapper, spruce, trim, debonair, well dressed, well groomed, well turned out, smartly dressed; tasteful, understated, attractive, flattering, fancy; **fashionable**, high-fashion, modish, voguish, in vogue, modern, up to date, up to the minute, ultramodern, contemporary, designer; *French* à la mode, soigné; *informal* trendy, in, with it, bang up to date, now, hip, sharp, snappy, snazzy, classy, natty, nifty, dressy, swish; *N. Amer. informal* fly, spiffy, sassy, kicky, tony; *dated* as if one had just stepped out of a bandbox; *Brit. informal, dated* swagger; *archaic* trig.
OPPOSITES dowdy, unfashionable.

dastardly ▸ **adjective** (*archaic or humorous*) *a dastardly plan was hatched to kidnap him* **wicked**, evil, iniquitous, heinous, villainous, diabolical, diabolic, fiendish, vicious, murderous, barbarous, cruel, black, dark, rotten, nefarious, vile, foul, monstrous, shocking, outrageous, atrocious, abominable, reprehensible, despicable, execrable, corrupt, degenerate, reprobate, sordid, depraved, dissolute, bad, base, mean, low, dishonourable, dishonest, unscrupulous, unprincipled, underhand, roguish; *informal* crooked, low-down, stinking, dirty, shady, rascally, scoundrelly; *Brit. informal* beastly, not cricket; *Law* malfeasant; *rare* egregious, flagitious.
OPPOSITES noble, praiseworthy.

data ▸ **noun** *there is a lack of data on the drug's effect on humans* **facts**, figures, statistics, details, particulars, specifics, features; **information**, evidence, intelligence, material, background, input; proof, fuel, ammunition; statement, report, return, dossier, file, documentation, archive(s); *informal* info, gen, dope, low-down.

date ▸ **noun 1** *the only dates he can remember are his birthday and 1066* **day**, day of the month, occasion, year, anniversary, time.
2 *a later date than the 15th century is suggested for this bridge* **age**, time, period, era, epoch, century, decade, year, stage.
3 *we have a lunch date* **appointment**, meeting, engagement, rendezvous, assignation; commitment, fixture; *literary* tryst.
4 (*informal*) *have you got a date for tonight?* **partner**, escort, girlfriend, boyfriend, young lady, young man, woman friend, lady friend, man friend, man, boy, girl; *informal* steady, bird, fella.
□ **to date** *this is his best book to date* **so far**, thus far, yet, as yet, up to now/then, till now/then, until now/then, as of now, up to the present (time), up to this/that point, hitherto; *rare* thitherto.
OPPOSITES since then; to come.
▸ **verb 1** *this piece of sculpture can be dated very accurately* **assign a date to**, establish/determine/ascertain the date of, put a date on/to, establish/determine/ascertain the age of.
2 *the present building* **dates from** *the early 16th century | this law* **dates back to** *the Middle Ages* **was made in**, was built in, was created in, came into being in, bears the date of, originates in, comes from, belongs to, goes back to, has existed since.
3 *the very best films just don't date* **become old-fashioned**, become outmoded, become obsolete, become dated, show its age.
4 (*informal*) *he's dating the girl next door* **go out with**, take out, go around with, go with, be involved with, be romantically linked with, see, court, woo; *informal* go steady with; *N. Amer. informal* step out with; *Austral. informal* track square with.

WORD LINKS
relating to dates **chronological**

dated ▸ **adjective** *the graphics are looking a little dated* **old-fashioned**, out of fashion, out of date, outdated, outmoded, out of style, behind the times, last year's, superseded, archaic, obsolete, antiquated; unfashionable, unpopular, unstylish; bygone, old-fangled, crusty, olde worlde, prehistoric, antediluvian; *French* passé, démodé; *informal* old hat, out, square, out of the ark.
OPPOSITES modern, up to date.

daub ▸ **verb** *he daubed a rock with paint | they daubed blood on the walls* **bedaub**, **smear**, plaster, bespatter, splash, stain, spatter, splatter, cake, cover thickly, smother, coat, deface; slap; *literary* besmear, befoul, besmirch, begrime.
▸ **noun** *these modernistic painters who just splash on daubs of paint* **smear**, smudge, splash, blot, spot, patch, blotch, stain, mark; *informal* splodge.

daughter ▸ **noun** **female child**, girl; *informal* lass.

WORD LINKS
relating to a daughter or son **filial**
killing of one's daughter or son **filicide**

daunt ▸ **verb** *it will take more than December sleet and gales to daunt the crews* **intimidate**, abash, take aback, shake, ruffle, throw, demoralize, discourage; **deter**, put off, dishearten, dispirit, deject, sap, cow, overawe, awe, frighten, scare, alarm, unman, dismay, distress, disconcert, discompose, perturb, upset, discomfit, unsettle, unnerve, disquiet, subdue; throw off balance, put someone off their stroke, cause someone to lose their composure, confound, panic, stupefy, stun; *informal* rattle, faze, put into a flap, throw into a tizz, discombobulate, shake up, psych; *Brit. informal* put the wind up.
OPPOSITES encourage; hearten.

dauntless ▸ **adjective** *an ambitious and dauntless woman, who truckled to no man* **fearless**, determined, resolute, indomitable, intrepid, doughty, plucky, spirited, game, mettlesome, gritty, steely, confident, undaunted, undismayed, unalarmed, unflinching, unshrinking, unabashed, unfaltering, unflagging, bold, audacious, valiant, brave, stout-hearted, lionhearted, gallant, courageous, heroic, daring, daredevil; *informal* gutsy, spunky, ballsy, feisty.

dawdle ▸ **verb 1** *holidaymakers were dawdling over breakfast* **linger**, dally, take one's time, drag one's feet, be slow, waste time, kill time, fritter time away, idle; delay, procrastinate, stall, hang fire, mark time, potter about/around/round; *informal* dilly-dally, let the grass grow under one's feet; *dated* tarry.
OPPOSITE hurry.
2 *Ruth dawdled back through the wood* **amble**, stroll, go/walk slowly, loiter (along), move at a snail's pace, not keep pace, hold back, lag behind, fall behind, trail behind; *informal* mosey, tootle; *Brit. informal* pootle, mooch, swan; *N. Amer. informal* putter.
OPPOSITE speed.

CHOOSE THE RIGHT WORD

dawdle, linger, loiter
See LINGER.

dawn ▸ **noun 1** *we got up at dawn* **daybreak**, break of day, crack of dawn, sunrise, first light, daylight, first thing in the morning, early morning, cockcrow; *N. Amer.* sunup; *literary* dawning, peep of day, aurora, dayspring.
OPPOSITE dusk.
2 *the dawn of civilization* **beginning**, start, birth, inception, conception, origination, genesis, emergence, advent, coming, appearance, debut, arrival, dawning, rise, starting point, origin, launch, institution, inauguration, opening, initiation, onset, outset, unfolding, development, infancy; day one; *informal* kick-off, the word go; *formal* commencement.
OPPOSITE end.
▸ **verb 1** *Thursday dawned crisp and sunny* **begin**, open, break, arrive, emerge, grow light, lighten, brighten.
OPPOSITE end.
2 *a bright new future has dawned* **begin**, start, come into being, be born, come into existence, appear, arrive, come forth, emerge, erupt, burst out; arise, rise, originate, break, unfold, develop, crop up, first see the light of day; *formal* commence.
OPPOSITE end.
3 *she became calmer as realization dawned | it* **dawned on** *him that he was not*

alone **occur to**, come to, come to mind, spring to mind, enter someone's mind/head, come into someone's head/mind, strike, hit, register with, enter someone's consciousness, flash across someone's mind, pass through someone's mind, cross someone's mind, suggest itself.

WORD LINKS
fear of dawn **eosophobia**

day ▶ **noun 1** *the festival lasts five days* **twenty-four-hour period**, full day, twenty-four hours, working day; *technical* solar day, sidereal day.
2 *you could gamble at night and enjoy the beaches during the day* **daytime**, daylight, daylight hours, hours of light, hours of sunlight, broad daylight, waking hours, the waking day.
OPPOSITE night.
3 *he was the leading architect of the day* **period**, time, point in time, age, era, epoch, generation.
4 *in his day he exercised tremendous influence* **heyday**, prime, hour, time, best days, best years, maturity; peak, pinnacle, height, zenith, ascendancy; youth, vigour, springtime, salad days, full flowering, bloom.
OPPOSITES decline, nadir.

□ **day after day** *day after day, we learn of new allegations* **repeatedly**, again and again, over and over (again), time and (time) again, frequently, often, many times, many a time, time after time, on many occasions, many times over; {year in, year out}, {week in, week out}, {day in, day out}, night and day, all the time; persistently, recurrently, constantly, continuously, without a break, ceaselessly, relentlessly, continually, regularly, habitually, unfailingly, always; *N. Amer.* oftentimes; *Latin* ad nauseam; *informal* 24-7; *literary* many a time and oft, oft, oft-times.

□ **day by day 1** *day by day they were being forced to retreat* **gradually**, bit by bit, by degrees, by stages, inchmeal, inch by inch, little by little, step by step, slowly, slowly but surely, steadily, progressively.
OPPOSITE all at once.
2 *the sort of life they led day by day in their homes* **daily**, every day, day after day, a day at a time; *rare* diurnally.

□ **day in, day out** *they mechanically pursue the same routine, day in, day out* **repeatedly**, again and again, over and over (again), time and (time) again, frequently, often, many times, many a time, time after time, day after day, on many occasions, many times over; {year in, year out}, {week in, week out}, night and day, all the time; persistently, recurrently, constantly, continuously, without a break, ceaselessly, relentlessly, continually, regularly, habitually, unfailingly, always; *N. Amer.* oftentimes; *Latin* ad nauseam; *informal* 24-7; *literary* many a time and oft, oft, oft-times.

WORD LINKS
relating to the day **diurnal**

daybreak ▶ **noun** *they rested for the night and journeyed on at daybreak* **dawn**, break of day, crack of dawn, sunrise, daylight, first light, first thing in the morning, early morning, cockcrow; *N. Amer.* sunup; *literary* dawning, peep of day, aurora, dayspring.
OPPOSITE nightfall.

daydream ▶ **noun 1** *she was lost in a daydream* **reverie**, trance, fantasy, vision, fancy, hallucination, musing, brown study, imagining; inattention, inattentiveness, wool-gathering, preoccupation, brooding, obliviousness, engrossment, absorption, self-absorption, absent-mindedness, absence of mind, staring into space, abstraction, lack of concentration, lack of application; *Scottish* dwam; *humorous* blonde moment.
OPPOSITE concentration.
2 *the thought of living in a mews cottage had been one of her daydreams* **dream**, pipe dream, fantasy, figment of the imagination, unrealizable dream, castle in the air, castle in Spain; wishful thinking; fond hopes, wishes; *informal* pie in the sky.
▶ **verb** *stop daydreaming and pay attention* **dream**, muse, be lost in thought, be in a brown study, stare into space, hallucinate; fantasize, indulge in fantasy, indulge in fancy, indulge in wool-gathering, be in cloud cuckoo land, be unrealistic, build castles in the air, build castles in Spain.
OPPOSITES concentrate, focus.

daydreamer ▶ **noun** *David was sacked from his very first job because he was a daydreamer* **dreamer**, fantasist, fantasizer, romantic, romancer, wishful thinker, pipe-dreamer, castle-builder, Walter Mitty, idealist, impractical person, unrealistic person; visionary, theorizer, utopian, Don Quixote; *rare* fantast, reverist.

daylight ▶ **noun 1** *do the test in daylight for maximum accuracy of colour matching* **natural light**, sunlight, light of day.
OPPOSITE darkness.
2 *not many people go near it in daylight, never mind after dark* **daytime**, daylight hours, day, hours of sunlight; broad daylight.
OPPOSITE night-time.
3 *police moved in at daylight to make arrests* **dawn**, daybreak, break of day, crack of dawn, sunrise, first light, first thing in the morning, early morning, cockcrow; *N. Amer.* sunup; *literary* dawning, peep of day, aurora, dayspring.
OPPOSITE nightfall.

□ **see daylight 1** *Sam saw daylight. 'You think he might be your father?'* **understand**, comprehend, realize, find out, see the light, work out what's going on, get the point; *informal* cotton on, catch on, tumble, latch on, get the picture, get the message, get the drift, get it, get wise, see what's what, savvy; *Brit. informal* twig.
2 *his project never saw daylight* **be completed**, be accomplished, see (the) light of day; **be published**, be issued, come to public attention.

day-to-day ▶ **adjective** *day-to-day expenditure such as food, household goods, and petrol or bus fares* **regular**, routine, habitual, everyday, daily, frequent, normal, standard, usual, familiar, typical.

daze ▶ **verb 1** *he was dazed from being flung out of the car* **stun**, stupefy, knock senseless, knock unconscious, knock out, lay out; *informal* knock for six, knock the stuffing out of.
2 *she was still dazed by the revelations of the past half hour* **astound**, amaze, astonish, startle, take someone's breath away, dumbfound, stupefy, overwhelm, overcome, overpower, devastate, dismay, disconcert, stagger, shock, confound, bewilder, take aback, nonplus, shake up; *informal* flabbergast, knock for six, knock sideways, knock the stuffing out of, hit like a ton of bricks, bowl over, floor, blow away.
▶ **noun** *he was walking around in a daze* **stupor**, state of stupefaction, state of shock, trance-like state, haze, confused state, spin, whirl, muddle, jumble; confusion, bewilderment, distraction, numbness; *Scottish* dwam.

dazzle ▶ **verb 1** *she was dazzled by the headlights* **blind temporarily**, deprive of sight.
2 *I was dazzled by the beauty and breadth of the exhibition* **overpower**, overcome, overwhelm, impress, bedazzle, strike, move, stir, affect, touch, sweep someone off their feet, awe, overawe, leave speechless, take someone's breath away, spellbind, hypnotize, fascinate, take aback, daze, stagger, floor, amaze, astonish; *informal* bowl over, blow away, knock out.
▶ **noun 1** *dazzle can be a problem to sensitive eyes* **glare**, flare, blaze, brightness, brilliance, gleam, flash, shimmer, radiance, shine.
2 *he happily endured the dazzle of the limelight* **sparkle**, glitter, showiness, flashiness, brilliance, glory; splendour, magnificence, glamour, attraction, lure, allure, draw, drawing power, fascination, captivation, appeal; *informal* razzle-dazzle, razzmatazz, pizzazz, pull.

dazzling ▶ **adjective 1** *the sunlight was dazzling* **extremely bright**, blinding, glaring, brilliant, gleaming, shining.
2 *they turned in yet another dazzling performance* **impressive**, remarkable, extraordinary, outstanding, exceptional, staggering, incredible, amazing, astonishing, phenomenal, imposing, breathtaking, thrilling; **excellent**, wonderful, magnificent, splendid, marvellous, superb, very good, first-rate, first-class, awe-inspiring, superlative, matchless, peerless; *informal* mind-boggling, mind-blowing, out of this world, fabulous, fab, super, fantastic, tremendous, great, terrific, sensational, smashing, ace, A1, cool, awesome, magic, wicked, tip-top, top-notch, out of sight, way-out; *Brit. informal* brill, top-hole, wizard; *Austral./NZ informal* bonzer; *Brit. informal, dated*, capital, spiffing, topping; *literary* wondrous.

deacon ▶ **noun**

WORD LINKS
relating to a deacon **diaconal**

dead ▶ **adjective 1** *my parents are dead* **deceased**, expired, departed, gone, no more, passed on, passed away; late, lost, lamented; perished, fallen, slain, slaughtered, killed, murdered; lifeless, not breathing, having breathed one's last, defunct, extinct, inanimate, insentient, insensate, inert; *informal* (as) dead as a doornail, six feet under, pushing up daisies, under the sod; *euphemistic* with God, asleep, at peace; *rare* demised, exanimate.
OPPOSITES alive, living.
2 *there are patches of dead ground on both sides of the plain* **barren**, lifeless, bare, empty, desolate, sterile; without life, without living things.
OPPOSITES fertile, lush.
3 *he is fluent in ancient Hebrew and other dead languages* **obsolete**, extinct, defunct, discontinued, no longer in use, disused, fallen into disuse, lapsed, abandoned, discarded, superseded, vanished, forgotten; archaic, antiquated, fossilized, ancient, very old; *literary* of yore.
OPPOSITES current, modern.
4 *there was no dialling tone—the phone was dead* **not working**, out of order, out of commission, inoperative, inactive, ineffective, in (a state of) disrepair, broken, broken-down, malfunctioning, defective; *informal* kaput, conked out, on the blink, bust, busted, gone phut, finished, done for, dud; *Brit. informal* knackered, duff; *Brit. vulgar slang* buggered.
OPPOSITE in working order.
5 *I gave him a dead leg* **numb**, benumbed, deadened, desensitized, insensible, insensate, unfeeling; paralysed, crippled, incapacitated, immobilized, frozen, useless.
6 *his voice was dead and cold | she has dead eyes* **emotionless**, unemotional, unfeeling, impassive, unresponsive, insensitive, indifferent, dispassionate, inexpressive, wooden, stony, cold, frigid, inert; deadpan, flat, toneless, hollow; blank, vacant, glazed, glassy.
OPPOSITE passionate.
7 *his old affection for Alison was not quite dead* **extinguished**, quenched, quashed, quelled, suppressed, smothered, stifled; finished, terminated, over, gone, no more; a thing of the past, ancient history.

D

8 *this is such a dead town* **uneventful**, uninteresting, unexciting, uninspiring, dull, boring, flat, quiet, sleepy, slow, stale, humdrum, tame, pedestrian, lacklustre, lifeless; tedious, tiresome, wearisome; backward, backwoods, behind the times; *informal* one-horse, dead-and-alive; *N. Amer. informal* dullsville.
OPPOSITE lively.
9 *there was dead silence in the room* **complete**, absolute, total, entire, outright, utter, downright, out-and-out, thorough, unqualified, unmitigated.
OPPOSITE partial.
10 *Bill is a dead shot with a rifle or revolver* **unerring**, unfailing, impeccable, sure, true, correct, accurate, exact, precise, direct; deadly, lethal; *Brit. informal* spot on, bang on.
OPPOSITE poor.
▶ **adverb 1** *he was dead serious in his accusations* **completely**, absolutely, totally, utterly, deadly, perfectly, entirely, wholly, fully, quite, thoroughly, unreservedly; definitely, certainly, positively, unconditionally, categorically, unquestionably, no doubt, undoubtedly, without a doubt, without question, surely, unequivocally; exactly, precisely, decisively, conclusively, manifestly, in every way, in every respect, one hundred per cent, every inch, to the hilt.
OPPOSITE partially.
2 *red flares were seen dead ahead* **directly**, exactly, precisely, immediately, right, straight, plumb, due, squarely; *informal* bang, slap bang, smack.
3 (*Brit. informal*) *the windows are dead easy to open* **very**, extremely, exceedingly, exceptionally, tremendously, immensely, hugely; extraordinarily, extra, inordinately, unusually, uncommonly, distinctly, decidedly, particularly, especially, remarkably, really, truly; most, so; *French* très; *N. English* right; *informal* awfully, terribly, mega, ultra, oh-so, damn, damned; *Brit. informal* ever so, well, jolly, bloody; *N. Amer.* real, mighty, awful, plumb, darned, way; *S. African informal* lekker; *informal, dated* frightfully, devilishly; *archaic* exceeding.

deadbeat ▶ **noun** (*informal*) *there's no room for deadbeats in the navy* **layabout**, loafer, lounger, idler, waster, wastrel, good-for-nothing, cadger, parasite, useless article; *informal* bum, scrounger, sponger, sponge, freeloader; *Brit. informal* skiver.

deaden ▶ **verb 1** *surgeons used ether to deaden the pain* **numb**, stifle, dull, blunt, suppress; **alleviate**, mitigate, moderate, weaken, diminish, reduce, decrease, lessen, palliate, abate, ease, soothe, relieve, assuage, subdue, take the edge off, get rid of, put an end to.
OPPOSITE intensify.
2 *the wood panelling deadened any noise from outside* **muffle**, mute, smother, stifle, dull, damp, damp down, tone down, hush, silence, quieten, soften, cushion, blanket, buffer, absorb.
OPPOSITE amplify.
3 *laughing at the joke might deaden us to the moral issue* **desensitize**, render insensitive, make insensitive, numb, benumb, anaesthetize; harden, toughen, harden someone's heart.
OPPOSITE sensitize.

deadline ▶ **noun** *they stipulated a deadline for the army's withdrawal* **time limit**, limit, finishing date, finishing time, target date, target time, cut-off point.

deadlock ▶ **noun 1** *the strike appeared to have reached a deadlock* **stalemate**, **impasse**, checkmate, stand-off; standstill, halt, stop, stoppage, cessation, full stop, dead end.
2 *the game ended in a 1–1 deadlock* **tie**, draw, dead heat.
3 *the deadlock can only be opened with a key* **bolt**, lock, latch, catch, fastening, fastener; *Scottish* sneck, snib.

deadly ▶ **adjective 1** *certain mixtures of drugs can be deadly | a deadly disease* **fatal**, lethal, mortal, death-dealing, life-threatening; dangerous, destructive, injurious, harmful, pernicious, detrimental, deleterious, unhealthy; noxious, toxic, poisonous; terminal, incurable, untreatable, malignant; *literary* deathly, nocuous, mephitic; *archaic* baneful.
OPPOSITES harmless; beneficial.
2 *the two men rapidly became deadly enemies* **mortal**, irreconcilable, implacable, remorseless, relentless, unrelenting, unappeasable, unforgiving, merciless, pitiless; **bitter**, hostile, antagonistic, murderous, fierce, grim, savage; *informal* at each other's throats.
3 *I noted their deadly seriousness* **intense**, great, marked, extreme, excessive, immoderate, inordinate.
OPPOSITE mild.
4 *he was deadly pale and too weak to speak* **deathly**, deathlike, ashen, ghostly, white, pallid, wan, pale, ghastly.
5 *his aim is deadly* **unerring**, unfailing, impeccable, perfect, flawless, faultless, assured, sure, true, precise, accurate, correct, exact, direct, on target, on the mark; *Brit. informal* spot on, bang on; *vulgar slang* shit hot.
OPPOSITES poor, inaccurate.
6 (*informal*) *life in a small village can be deadly* **boring**, dull, dull as ditchwater, dreary, uninteresting, unexciting, uneventful, uninspiring, unstimulating, humdrum, lacklustre, dry, dry as dust, arid, flat, bland, monotonous, unrelieved, lacking variety, lacking variation, tedious, tiresome, tiring, wearisome, irksome, trying, frustrating, mind-numbing, soul-destroying; *informal* no great shakes, not up to much, nothing to write home about; *Brit. informal* samey; *N. Amer. informal* dullsville, ornery.
OPPOSITE exciting.
▶ **adverb** *her voice was deadly calm* **completely**, absolutely, totally, utterly, perfectly, entirely, wholly, fully, quite, dead, thoroughly; in every way, in every respect, in all respects, one hundred per cent, every inch, to the hilt, to the core.

deadpan ▶ **adjective** *he cracked jokes with a deadpan expression on his face* **blank**, expressionless, unexpressive, inexpressive, impassive, inscrutable, poker-faced, straight-faced, dispassionate, unresponsive, stony, wooden, empty, vacant, glazed, fixed, lifeless.
OPPOSITES expressive; comical.

deaf ▶ **adjective 1** *she is deaf and blind but fiercely independent* **hard of hearing**, unhearing, stone deaf, with impaired hearing, deafened, profoundly deaf; *informal* deaf as a post.
2 *how could she be so deaf to their pleading?* **unmoved by**, untouched by, unaffected by, dispassionate about, indifferent to, heedless of, unresponsive to, unconcerned with, unmindful of, unaware of, unconscious of, oblivious to, insensible to, impervious to.
OPPOSITES heedful, attentive.

deafen ▶ **verb** *they were deafened by the explosion of a shell* **make deaf**, make temporarily deaf, cause to be hard of hearing, deprive of hearing, impair someone's hearing, burst someone's eardrums.

deafening ▶ **adjective** *the guns started up with a deafening roar* **very loud**, extremely noisy, ear-splitting, ear-piercing, ear-shattering; booming, thundering, thunderous, tumultuous, roaring, blaring, resounding, resonant, reverberating, reverberant, echoing, ringing, dinning, carrying; overpowering, overwhelming, almighty, mighty, tremendous.
OPPOSITE quiet.

deal ▶ **noun** *it may be some weeks before completion of the deal* **agreement**, understanding, pact, compact, bargain, covenant, contract, treaty, protocol, concordat, entente, accord, arrangement, accommodation, compromise, settlement, negotiation; terms; transaction, sale; *Commerce* account; *Law* indenture; *rare* engagement.
□ **a great deal/a good deal** *the team have achieved a great deal | she is under a good deal of pressure* **a lot**, a great amount, a large amount, a fair amount, much, plenty; *informal* lots, loads, heaps, bags, masses, piles, stacks, tons; *Brit. informal* a shedload; *vulgar slang* a shitload.
OPPOSITE very little.
▶ **verb 1** *they got advice on how to* **deal with** *difficult children* **cope with**, handle, manage, attend to, see to, take care of, take charge of, take in hand, sort out, tackle, take on; control, master, influence, manipulate.
2 *the article* **deals with** *recent advances in chemistry* **concern**, be about, be concerned with, concern itself with, have to do with, discuss, consider, cover, treat of, pertain to, appertain to; tackle, study, explore, investigate, examine, go into, review, analyse, weigh up; *archaic* regard.
3 *the security forces* **deal** *firmly* **with** *demonstrators* **treat**, handle, serve, use; act towards, behave towards, conduct oneself towards.
4 *the company* **deals in** *high-tech goods* **trade in**, buy and sell, be concerned with trading, be engaged in trading, do business in; sell, vend, purvey, supply, stock, offer, offer for sale, have for sale, peddle, market, merchandise; traffic in, smuggle, run, rustle; *informal* push; *Brit. informal* flog.
5 *the cards were dealt for the last hand* **distribute**, give out, share out, divide out, divide up, hand out, pass out, pass round, dole out, mete out, dispense, allocate, allot, assign, apportion, bestow; *informal* divvy up.
6 *the appeal court dealt a blow to government reforms* **deliver**, administer, dispense, inflict, give, impose; direct, aim.

dealer ▶ **noun 1** *he set up in business as an antique dealer* **trader**, tradesman, tradesperson, merchant, salesman, saleswoman, salesperson, seller, buyer, buyer and seller, marketeer, merchandiser, distributor, supplier, vendor, shopkeeper, retailer, wholesaler, purveyor, marketer, trafficker; *Brit.* stockist; *N. Amer.* storekeeper; *informal* pusher, runner, fence; *dated* pedlar, chandler, hawker, shopman; *archaic* chapman.
2 *she is a dealer with a Japanese bank* **stockbroker**, broker-dealer, broker, agent, negotiator; *historical* jobber.

dealing ▶ **noun 1** *her husband took to drink and dishonest dealing* **business methods**, business practices, business, commerce, trading, trafficking, marketing, merchandising, transactions, financial transactions; **behaviour**, conduct, actions, policy.
2 (**dealings**) *the UK was unnecessarily cautious in its dealings with China* **relations**, relationship, association, connections, contact, intercourse, interchange, communication, negotiations, bargaining, operations, transactions, proceedings; **trade**, trading, business, commerce, traffic, trafficking; *informal* truck, doings.

dean ▶ **noun** *student admission targets must be agreed with the dean* **faculty head**, department head, head of faculty, head of department, college head, provost, university official; head, chief, director, leader, principal, president, governor.

dear ▶ **adjective 1** *my dear sister was talking about you only today | he is a dear friend* **beloved**, loved, much loved, darling, adored, cherished, precious; esteemed, respected, worshipped; close, intimate, confidential, bosom,

boon, favourite, best.
OPPOSITE hated.
2 *her belongings were too dear to entrust to sea transport* **precious**, treasured, valued, prized, cherished, special, favourite, favoured.
3 *your father was such a dear man* **endearing**, adorable, lovable, appealing, engaging, charming, enchanting, captivating, winsome, winning, attractive, lovely, nice, pleasant, delightful, angelic, sweet, darling; *N. Amer.* cunning; *Italian & Spanish* simpatico; *French* sympathique; *German* sympatisch; *dated* taking.
OPPOSITE disagreeable.
4 *the dining car served rather dear meals* **expensive**, costly, high-cost, high-priced, highly priced, overpriced, exorbitant, extortionate; immoderate, extravagant, lavish, valuable; *Brit.* upmarket, over the odds; *informal* pricey, steep, stiff.
OPPOSITE inexpensive.
▶ **noun 1** *there's no need to worry, my dear* **darling**, dearest, love, beloved, loved one, sweetheart, sweet, precious, treasure; *informal* sweetie, sugar, honey, baby, babe, pet, sunshine, poppet; *archaic* sweeting.
2 *Philip's such a dear* **lovable person**, adorable person, endearing person; darling, sweetheart, pet, angel, gem, treasure; *informal* star.
▶ **adverb** *they buy property cheaply and sell dear* **at a high price**, at an excessive price, at an exorbitant price, at high cost, at great cost.

dearly ▶ **adverb 1** *she dearly wanted to see her family | I love my son dearly* **very much**, a great deal, greatly, deeply, profoundly, extremely; **fondly**, affectionately, devotedly, tenderly.
2 *our freedom has been bought dearly* **at great cost**, at a high cost, at a high price, with great loss, with much loss, with much suffering, with much sacrifice.

dearth ▶ **noun** *there is a dearth of properly trained specialists* **lack**, scarcity, scarceness, shortage, shortfall, want, deficiency, insufficiency, inadequacy, paucity, sparseness, meagreness, scantiness, rareness, infrequency, uncommonness, destitution, privation; famine, drought, poverty; absence, non-existence; *rare* exiguity, exiguousness.
OPPOSITES abundance; surfeit.

death ▶ **noun 1** *she broke down when she learnt of her father's death* **demise**, dying, end, passing, passing away, passing on, loss of life, expiry, expiration, departure from life, final exit, eternal rest; murder, killing, assassination, execution, dispatch, slaying, slaughter, massacre; *informal* snuffing, curtains, kicking the bucket; *Law* decease; *rare* quietus.
OPPOSITE life.
2 *their liberation was also the death of their dream* **end**, finish, cessation, termination, extinction, extinguishing, collapse, ruin, ruination, destruction, extermination, eradication, annihilation, obliteration, extirpation.
OPPOSITE birth.
3 *Death gestured towards an open grave* **the Grim Reaper**, the Dark Angel, the Angel of Death.
□ **put someone to death** *the rebels were captured and put to death* **execute**, hang, send to the gibbet/gallows, behead, guillotine, decapitate, electrocute, send to the electric chair, send to the chair, shoot, put before a firing squad, send to the gas chamber, gas, crucify, stone, stone to death; **kill**, murder, assassinate, do to death, do away with, take the life of, eliminate, terminate, exterminate, destroy; *informal* string up, bump off, polish off, do in, knock off, top, wipe out, take out, croak, stiff, blow away; *N. Amer. informal* ice, rub out, waste, whack, scrag, smoke; *literary* slay.

WORD LINKS

related prefix	**necr-** (e.g. ***necromancy***)
related suffix	**-thanasia** (e.g. ***euthanasia***)
ancient cemetery	**necropolis**
fear of death	**thanatophobia**
study of death	**thanatology**

deathless ▶ **adjective** *the notion that animals have immaterial and deathless souls | his compositions are deathless* **immortal**, undying, imperishable, inextinguishable, indestructible, unfading, enduring, everlasting, perpetual, eternal; timeless, ageless, memorable; *rare* sempiternal, perdurable.
OPPOSITES mortal; ephemeral.

deathly ▶ **adjective 1** *the wounded soldiers had a deathly pallor* **deathlike**, corpse-like, cadaverous, ghostly, ghostlike, ghastly, grim, haggard; ashen, chalky, chalk-white, white, pale, pallid, bloodless, colourless, wan, anaemic, pasty, sickly, drained, sapped; *informal* like death warmed up, peaky; *rare* etiolated.
2 (*literary*) *the eagle carried a snake in its deathly grasp* **deadly**, fatal, lethal, mortal, death-dealing; terrible, baleful, harmful, injurious, dangerous, perilous; *archaic* baneful.

debacle, débâcle ▶ **noun** *the coup attempt resulted in an embarrassing debacle* **fiasco**, failure, catastrophe, disaster, disintegration, mess, wreck, ruin; downfall, collapse, defeat, rout, overthrow, conquest, trouncing; *informal* foul-up, screw-up, hash, botch, washout; *Brit. informal* cock-up, pig's ear; *N. Amer. informal* snafu; *vulgar slang* fuck-up, balls-up.

debar ▶ **verb 1** *women were no longer debarred from the club* **exclude**, ban, bar, disqualify, disentitle, declare ineligible, preclude, rule out, shut out, lock out, keep out, reject, blackball; say no to, leave out in the cold, give the cold shoulder to, stand in the way of, refuse entrance to; *N. Amer.* disfellowship.
OPPOSITE admit.
2 *the unions were debarred from holding a strike ballot* **prevent**, prohibit, proscribe, disallow, ban, interdict, block, stop, curb, restrict, restrain, obstruct, hinder; forbid to; *Law* enjoin, estop; *archaic* let.
OPPOSITE allow.

debase ▶ **verb 1** *the code of chivalry has been debased and sentimentalized* **degrade**, devalue, demean, lower the status of, reduce the status of, cheapen, prostitute, discredit, drag down, drag through the mud, tarnish, blacken, blemish; disgrace, dishonour, shame, bring shame to, humble, humiliate; damage, harm, undermine.
OPPOSITE enhance.
2 *copper hardens the coin without significantly debasing the silver* **reduce in value**, reduce in quality; contaminate, adulterate, pollute, taint, defile, spoil, foul, sully, depreciate, corrupt, bastardize; dilute, alloy; *rare* vitiate.

debased ▶ **adjective 1** *their moral downfall was the result of their debased amusements* **immoral**, **debauched**, dissolute, abandoned, perverted, degenerate, profligate, degraded, wicked, sinful, vile, base, iniquitous, corrupt, corrupted, criminal, vicious, brutal, lewd, licentious, lascivious, lecherous, prurient, obscene, indecent, libertine.
OPPOSITE honourable.
2 *the myth lives on in a debased form* **corrupt**, corrupted, bastardized, adulterated, diluted, polluted, tainted, sullied, spoiled, spoilt; *rare* vitiated.
OPPOSITES original; pure.

debatable ▶ **adjective** *the extent to which personality is inherited is debatable* **arguable**, disputable, questionable, open to question, open to debate, subject to debate, controversial, contentious, doubtful, open to doubt, in doubt, dubious, uncertain, unsure, unclear, vague, borderline, inconclusive, moot, unsettled, unresolved, unconfirmed, undetermined, undecided, unknown, up in the air, not yet established; problematical, puzzling, perplexing, riddling; a controversial subject, a live issue, a moot point, a matter of opinion; *informal* iffy, on the back burner, on ice; *rare* controvertible, unestablished.
OPPOSITE indisputable.

debate ▶ **noun** *I would welcome a debate on the reforms | there is renewed debate about NATO's defence role* **discussion**, exchange of views, discourse, parley; argument, dispute, wrangle, altercation, war of words; arguing, argumentation, wrangling, sparring, disputation, dissension, disagreement, controversy, contention, conflict, disharmony; negotiations, talks; dialogue, comment, interest; *informal* confab, powwow, rap session; *rare* velitation, contestation.
▶ **verb 1** *MPs will debate the future of the railways* **discuss**, confer about, talk over, talk through, talk about, exchange views on, exchange views about, thrash out, argue, argue about, argue the pros and cons of, dispute, wrangle over, bandy words concerning, contend over, contest, controvert, moot; *informal* kick around/about, bat around/about; *archaic* altercate.
2 *he debated whether to telephone Charlotte* **consider**, give some thought to, think over, think about, chew over, mull over, turn over in one's mind, weigh up, ponder, deliberate, reflect, contemplate, muse, meditate, cogitate; *archaic* pore on; *rare* cerebrate.

debauch ▶ **verb** *he had debauched sixteen schoolgirls* **corrupt**, deprave, warp, pervert, subvert, lead astray, make degenerate, ruin; **seduce**, ravish, deflower, defile, sully, violate, abuse, brutalize; *informal* take someone's cherry; *archaic* demoralize; *rare* vitiate.

debauched ▶ **adjective** *our fleet is commanded by debauched young men* **dissolute**, dissipated, degenerate, corrupt, depraved, louche, rakish, shameless, sinful, unprincipled, immoral, impure, unchaste, lascivious, lecherous, libertine, lewd, lustful, libidinous, licentious, promiscuous, loose, wanton, abandoned, unrestrained, fast, decadent, profligate, intemperate, sybaritic, voluptuary, pleasure-seeking, indulgent, self-indulgent; *informal* easy, swinging; *archaic* light; *rare* concupiscent.
OPPOSITES wholesome, clean-living.

debauchery ▶ **noun** *he was reviled for his playboy lifestyle and debauchery* **dissipation**, dissoluteness, degeneracy, corruption, vice, turpitude, depravity, loucheness, rakishness, libertinism, immodesty, indecency, perversion, shamelessness, iniquity, wickedness, sinfulness, sinning, impropriety, lack of morals, lack of principles, immorality, impurity, unchastity, lasciviousness, salaciousness, lechery, lecherousness, lewdness, bawdiness, lust, lustfulness, libidinousness, licentiousness, promiscuity, wantonness, abandonment, abandon, profligacy, decadence, immoderateness, intemperance, lack of restraint, indulgence, self-indulgence, pleasure-seeking, hedonism, sybaritism; *rare* voluptuousness, concupiscence, lubricity, salacity.
OPPOSITES morality, clean living.

debilitate ▶ **verb** *she was severely debilitated by a stomach upset* **weaken**, make weak, make feeble, enfeeble, enervate, devitalize, sap, drain, exhaust, weary, tire, fatigue, wear out, prostrate; undermine, impair, render infirm, indispose, incapacitate, cripple, disable, paralyse,

D

D

immobilize, lay low, put out of action, confine to bed, confine to a wheelchair; informal knock out, do in, knacker, shatter; rare torpefy.
OPPOSITES strengthen, invigorate.

debilitating ▶ adjective *he was suffering the debilitating effects of flu* **weakening**, enfeebling, enervating, enervative, devitalizing, draining, sapping, wearing, exhausting, tiring; impairing, crippling, paralysing.
OPPOSITE restorative.

debility ▶ noun *his chronic debility made it hard to do even the basic things* **frailty**, weakness, feebleness, enfeeblement, enervation, devitalization, lack of energy, lack of vitality, lassitude, exhaustion, weariness, tiredness, overtiredness, fatigue, prostration; incapacity, impairment, indisposition, infirmity, illness, sickness, sickliness, decrepitude, malaise; informal weediness; Medicine asthenia.

debonair ▶ adjective *a debonair young man* **suave**, urbane, sophisticated, cultured, self-possessed, self-assured, confident, charming, gracious, well mannered, civil, courteous, gallant, chivalrous, gentlemanly, refined, polished, well bred, genteel, dignified, courtly; well dressed, well groomed, well turned out, elegant, stylish, smart, dashing, dapper, spruce, trim, attractive; French soigné; informal smooth, swish, swanky, snappy, sharp, cool; N. Amer. informal spiffy, fly; dated mannerly; archaic trig, gentle.
OPPOSITE unsophisticated.

debrief ▶ verb *Soviet scientists were debriefed by the KGB* **question**, quiz, interview, examine, cross-examine, interrogate, probe, sound out; put questions to, ask questions of; informal grill, pump, give the third degree to, put through the third degree, put through the wringer, put through the mangle, put the screws on.

debris ▶ noun *the irrigation channels were blocked with debris* **detritus**, refuse, rubbish, waste, waste matter, discarded matter, litter, scrap, dross, chaff, flotsam and jetsam, lumber, rubble, wreckage, spoilage; remains, remnants, fragments, scraps, dregs, offscourings, odds and ends; slag; N. Amer. trash, garbage; Austral./NZ mullock; informal dreck, junk; Brit. informal grot, gash, odds and sods, gubbins; vulgar slang shit, crap; Archaeology debitage; rare draff, raffle, raff, cultch, orts.

debt ▶ noun **1** *the company was unable to pay its debts* **bill**, account, tally, financial obligation, outstanding payment, amount due, money owing; dues, arrears, debits, charges; N. Amer. check; informal tab; archaic score.
2 *he wanted to acknowledge his debt to the author* **indebtedness**, obligation, liability; gratitude, appreciation, thanks.
□ **in debt** *he was forever short of money and frequently in debt* **owing money**, in arrears, behind with payments, late with payments, overdue with payments, overdrawn; insolvent, bankrupt, bankrupted, ruined, in the hands of the receivers; Brit. in liquidation; informal in the red, in Queer Street, on the rocks, gone to the wall, bust; Brit. informal, dated in Carey Street.
OPPOSITE in credit.
□ **in someone's debt** *after what Clive had done, Chris would be forever in his debt* **indebted to**, beholden to, obliged to, duty-bound to, honour-bound to, obligated to, under an obligation to, owing someone a debt of gratitude, owing someone thanks; grateful, thankful, appreciative.

debtor ▶ noun *the summons gave the debtor fourteen days to pay* **borrower**, mortgagor; bankrupt, bankrupt person, insolvent, defaulter.
OPPOSITE creditor.

debunk ▶ verb *he debunked the myth that savants rely on photographic memories* **explode**, deflate, puncture, quash, knock the bottom out of, drive a coach and horses through, expose, show in its true light, discredit, disprove, contradict, controvert, confute, invalidate, negate, give the lie to, prove to be false, challenge, call into question; informal shoot full of holes, shoot down in flames, blow sky-high.
OPPOSITE confirm.

debut ▶ noun *the new car made its debut at the German Grand Prix* **first appearance**, first showing, first performance, launch, launching, coming out, entrance, premiere, beginning, introduction, inception, inauguration; informal kick-off; formal commencement.
OPPOSITE swansong.

decadence ▶ noun **1** *he attacked the decadence of modern society* **dissipation**, dissoluteness, degeneracy, debauchery, corruption, depravity, loucheness, vice, sinfulness, perversion, moral decay, immorality, lack of morals, lack of principles, lack of restraint, lack of control, lack of self-control, immoderateness, intemperance, licentiousness, wantonness, self-indulgence, hedonism, epicureanism; rare sybaritism, voluptuousness.
OPPOSITE morality.
2 (dated) *political errors cause the decadence of nations* **decline**, fall, decay, wane, degeneration, deterioration, debasement, degradation, retrogression.

decadent ▶ adjective **1** *he turned his back on decadent city life* **dissolute**, dissipated, degenerate, corrupt, depraved, louche, rakish, shameless, sinful, unprincipled, immoral, licentious, wanton, abandoned, unrestrained, profligate, intemperate; sybaritic, voluptuary, epicurean, hedonistic, pleasure-seeking, indulgent, self-indulgent.
OPPOSITE moral.
2 (dated) *there were demands for the regeneration of the decadent empire* **declining**, decaying, waning, ebbing, degenerating, deteriorating, debased, degraded; on the wane.
OPPOSITES burgeoning, resurgent.

decamp ▶ verb **1** *he sold their paintings and decamped with the proceeds* **abscond**, make off, run off, run away, flee, bolt, take off, take flight, disappear, vanish, slip away, steal away, sneak away, beat a hasty retreat, escape, make a run for it, make one's getaway, leave, depart, make oneself scarce; informal split, scram, skedaddle, vamoose, skip, cut and run, make tracks, push off, shove off, clear off, hightail it, hotfoot it, show a clean pair of heels, do a bunk, do a runner, do a moonlight flit, do a disappearing act, head for the hills, fly the coop, take French leave, go AWOL; Brit. informal scarper; N. Amer. informal take a powder, go on the lam, light out, bug out, peel out, cut out; Brit. informal, dated hook it.
OPPOSITE return.
2 (archaic) *the armies of both chiefs had decamped* **strike one's tents**, break camp, move on.
OPPOSITE encamp.

decant ▶ verb *the wine was decanted into a clean flask* **pour out**, pour off, draw off, siphon off, drain, tap, tip, discharge, transfer.

decapitate ▶ verb *he was found guilty of high treason and decapitated* **behead**, cut off the head of, guillotine, put on the block; archaic decollate.

decay ▶ verb **1** *the flesh of the corpses had decayed* **decompose**, rot, putrefy, go bad, go off, spoil, fester, perish, deteriorate; degrade, break down, break up, moulder, shrivel, shrivel up, wither; technical mortify, necrotize, sphacelate; archaic corrupt.
2 *the inner cities in Britain continue to decay* **deteriorate**, degenerate, decline, go downhill, slump, slip, slide, go to rack and ruin, go to seed, run to seed, worsen, crumble, disintegrate, fall to pieces, come apart at the seams, fall into disrepair, become dilapidated; fail, wane, ebb, dwindle, collapse; informal go to pot, go to the dogs, hit the skids, go down the tubes, go down the toilet; Austral./NZ informal go to the pack.
OPPOSITE improve.
▶ noun **1** *the fish showed no signs of decay* **decomposition**, rotting, going bad, putrefaction, putrescence, putridity, festering, spoilage, perishing, withering, shrivelling; rot, mould, mildew, fungus; archaic corruption.
2 *consumption of sugar can lead to tooth decay* **rot**, rotting, corrosion, corroding, decomposition; **caries**, cavities, holes; rare cariosity.
3 *they blame TV for the decay of American values* **deterioration**, degeneration, debasement, degradation, decline, slipping, waning, ebb, shrinking, withering, weakening, atrophy, crumbling, disintegration, collapse, lapse, fall, failure; formal devolution; dated decadence.
OPPOSITE improvement.

WORD LINKS
related prefix **sapro-** (e.g. *saprophagous*)

decayed ▶ adjective *she discovered his decayed body* **decomposed**, decomposing, rotten, rotting, putrescent, putrid, bad, off, spoiled, spoilt, perished; mouldy, mouldering, mildewy, festering, fetid, stinking, smelly, rancid, rank; maggoty, worm-eaten, wormy, flyblown.

decaying ▶ adjective **1** *the decaying bodies of fish filled the pond* **decomposing**, decomposed, rotting, rotten, putrescent, putrid, bad, off, spoiled, spoilt, perished; mouldy, mouldering, festering, fetid, stinking, smelly, rancid, rank; maggoty, worm-eaten, wormy, flyblown.
2 *Liverpool was a visibly decaying city* **declining**, degenerating, dying, waning, crumbling, collapsing; run down, broken-down, tumbledown, ramshackle, shabby, battered, decrepit; in decline, on the decline, in ruins, in (a state of) disrepair, falling apart, falling to pieces; informal on its last legs, on the way out.

decease ▶ noun (Law) *her decease was imminent* **death**, dying, demise, end, passing, passing away, passing on, loss of life, departure from life, expiry, expiration, final exit, eternal rest; informal snuffing, curtains, kicking the bucket, croaking; rare quietus.
▶ verb (archaic) *he deceased at his palace of Croydon.* See DIE.

deceased ▶ adjective *they removed the body of the deceased ambassador* **dead**, expired, departed, gone, no more, passed on, passed away; late, lost, lamented; perished, fallen, slain, slaughtered, killed, murdered; lifeless, not breathing, having breathed one's last, defunct, extinct, inanimate, insentient, insensate, inert; informal (as) dead as a doornail, six feet under, pushing up daisies, under the sod; euphemistic with God, asleep, at peace; rare demised, exanimate.

deceit ▶ noun **1** *we are caught in an endless round of lies and deceit* **deception**, deceitfulness, duplicity, double-dealing, fraud, fraudulence, cheating, trickery, duping, hoodwinking, chicanery, underhandedness, deviousness, slyness, cunning, craftiness, craft, wiliness, artfulness, guile, dissimulation, dissembling, bluff, bluffing, lying, pretence, artifice, treachery; informal crookedness, monkey business, funny business, hanky-panky, jiggery-pokery; N. Amer. informal monkeyshines; Irish informal codology; archaic management, knavery.
OPPOSITE honesty.
2 *their life is all a deceit* **sham**, fraud, pretence, imposture, hoax, fake,

misrepresentation, blind, wile, artifice, Trojan horse; trick, stratagem, device, ruse, scheme, dodge, manoeuvre, contrivance, machination, deception, subterfuge, cheat, swindle, confidence trick; *informal* con, con trick, set-up, game, scam, sting, gyp, leg-pull, flimflam; *Brit. informal* wheeze; *N. Amer. informal* bunco, grift; *Austral. informal* lurk, rort; *S. African informal* schlenter; *Brit. informal, dated* flanker; *archaic* shift, fetch, rig.

deceitful ▶ adjective **1** *he was surrounded by foolish and deceitful women* **dishonest**, untruthful, lying, mendacious, insincere, false, deceiving, dissembling, disingenuous, untrustworthy, unscrupulous, unprincipled, two-faced, duplicitous, double-dealing, cheating, underhand, crafty, cunning, sly, guileful, scheming, calculating, conniving, designing, hypocritical, perfidious, treacherous, Machiavellian; *informal* sneaky, tricky, foxy, crooked, sharp, shady, shifty, slippery; *Brit. informal* bent; *S. African informal* slim; *archaic* subtle, hollow-hearted; *rare* false-hearted, double-faced, truthless, Punic.
OPPOSITE honest.
2 *they dismissed the allegations as deceitful* **fraudulent**, counterfeit, fabricated, invented, concocted, made up, trumped up, untrue, hollow, false, sham, bogus, fake, illusory, spurious, specious, fallacious, deceptive, misleading, misguided, distorted; *humorous* economical with the truth.
OPPOSITE true.

deceive ▶ verb **1** *she had been deceived by a clever confidence trickster* **swindle**, defraud, cheat, trick, hoodwink, hoax, dupe, take in, mislead, delude, fool, outwit, misguide, lead on, inveigle, seduce, ensnare, entrap, beguile, double-cross, gull; *informal* con, bamboozle, do, sting, gyp, diddle, fiddle, swizzle, rip off, shaft, bilk, rook, pull a fast one on, pull someone's leg, take for a ride, pull the wool over someone's eyes, throw dust in someone's eyes, put one over on, sell a pup to, take to the cleaners; *N. Amer. informal* sucker, snooker, stiff, euchre, bunco, hornswoggle; *Austral. informal* pull a swifty on; *archaic* cozen, sharp; *rare* mulct.
2 *he had deceived her with another woman* **be unfaithful to**, be disloyal to, be untrue to, be inconstant to, cheat on, cheat, betray, break one's promise to, play someone false, fail, let down; *informal* two-time.

decelerate ▶ verb *there is a whine coming from the gearbox every time I decelerate* **slow down**, slow up, slow, go slower, ease up, slack up, reduce speed, lessen one's speed, brake, put the brakes on, hit the brakes; *Brit. informal* slam on the anchors.
OPPOSITE accelerate.

December ▶ noun
WORD LINKS
birthstone **turquoise**

decency ▶ noun **1** *TV companies need to maintain standards of taste and decency* **propriety**, decorum, seemliness, good taste, respectability, dignity, correctness, good form, etiquette, appropriateness, fitness, suitability; morality, virtue, modesty, purity, delicacy, demureness, wholesomeness.
OPPOSITE indecency.
2 *he didn't have the decency to tell me he couldn't come* **courtesy**, politeness, good manners, civility, respect, respectfulness; consideration, thought, thoughtfulness, tact, diplomacy.
OPPOSITE rudeness.

decent ▶ adjective **1** *I'd like them to have a decent Christian burial* **proper**, correct, appropriate, apt, apposite, fitting, fit, befitting, right, suitable, respectable, dignified, becoming, decorous, seemly, modest, nice, tasteful, in good taste, refined, genteel; conventional, accepted, approved, standard, traditional, orthodox; *French* comme il faut; *informal* pukka.
OPPOSITE indecent.
2 (*Brit. informal*) *he was a devoted husband and a very decent chap* **honourable**, honest, trustworthy, dependable, worthy, respectable, upright, clean-living, incorrupt, virtuous, good, ethical, moral; obliging, helpful, accommodating, indulgent, unselfish, altruistic, generous, kind, kindly, thoughtful, considerate, courteous, civil, polite, well mannered, neighbourly, hospitable, pleasant, agreeable, amiable; *informal* squeaky clean; *dated* mannerly; *rare* regardful.
OPPOSITES disobliging; dishonest.
3 *she's trying to find a job with decent pay* **satisfactory**, reasonable, fair, acceptable, adequate, sufficient, sufficiently good, good enough, ample, up to scratch, up to the mark, up to standard, up to par, competent, not bad, all right, average, tolerable, passable, suitable; *informal* OK, okay, up to snuff.
OPPOSITE unsatisfactory.

deception ▶ noun **1** *the court found that they had obtained money by deception* **deceit**, deceitfulness, duplicity, double-dealing, fraud, fraudulence, cheating, trickery, duping, hoodwinking, chicanery, underhandedness, deviousness, slyness, cunning, craft, craftiness, wiliness, artfulness, guile, dissimulation, dissembling, bluff, bluffing, lying, pretence, artifice, treachery; *informal* crookedness, monkey business, funny business, hanky-panky, jiggery-pokery, kidology; *N. Amer. informal* monkeyshines; *Irish informal* codology; *archaic* management, knavery.
2 *she had proof that this was a deception* **trick**, stratagem, device, ruse, scheme, dodge, manoeuvre, contrivance, machination, subterfuge, cheat, swindle, confidence trick; sham, fraud, pretence, imposture, hoax, fake, misrepresentation, blind, wile, artifice, Trojan horse; *informal* con, con trick, set-up, game, scam, sting, gyp, leg-pull, flimflam; *Brit. informal* wheeze; *N. Amer. informal* bunco, grift; *Austral. informal* lurk, rort; *S. African informal* schlenter; *Brit. informal, dated* flanker; *archaic* shift, fetch, rig.

deceptive ▶ adjective **1** *distances over water are very deceptive* **misleading**, illusory, illusive, illusionary, ambiguous, deceiving, delusive, distorted, specious.
2 *deceptive practices account for at least half of the offences* **deceitful**, duplicitous, fraudulent, counterfeit, sham, bogus, cheating, underhand, cunning, crafty, sly, guileful, scheming, perfidious, treacherous, Machiavellian, dissembling, disingenuous, untrustworthy, unscrupulous, unprincipled, dishonest, untruthful, lying, mendacious, insincere, false; *informal* crooked, sharp, shady, slippery, sneaky, tricky, foxy; *Brit. informal* bent; *S. African informal* slim; *archaic* subtle, hollow-hearted; *rare* false-hearted, double-faced, truthless, Punic.
OPPOSITE honest.

decide ▶ verb **1** *they took no time at all to decide | she decided to become a writer* **resolve**, determine, make up one's mind, make a decision, come to a decision, reach a decision, come to a conclusion, reach a conclusion, settle on a plan of action; elect, choose, opt, plan, aim, commit oneself, have the intention, have in mind, set one's sights on.
OPPOSITE dither.
2 *further research is needed to decide a variety of questions* **settle**, resolve, bring to a conclusion, determine, work out, answer, clinch, confirm; *informal* sort out, figure out.
3 *the court declined to decide the case* **adjudicate**, arbitrate, adjudge, judge, umpire, referee; hear, try, examine; make a judgement on, pass judgement on, sit in judgement on, pronounce judgement on, pronounce on, give a verdict on, make a ruling on, rule on; *informal* ref.

CHOOSE THE RIGHT WORD

decide, determine, resolve

All these words denote the settling of a question in one's mind as to one's future action.

- To **decide** is to make up one's mind, often after having to choose between competing possibilities (*I decided it was the moment for me to change my life | they have decided to go to Italy*).
- Decisively influencing something is the primary sense of **determine** (*the quality of the grapes is determined by their position in the vineyard*). Using *determine* to refer to someone's reaching a decision suggests that they have given careful consideration to the options and come to a firm conclusion (*she determined to tackle Stephen the next day*). This sense of an unwavering firmness of purpose is continued in the adjective *determined* (*I was determined to cash in on my success*).
- **Resolve** emphasizes the act of will involved in making a decision (*she must, she resolved, keep Robert firmly at a distance | I resolved to return and face the problem*).

decided ▶ adjective **1** *public officials have a decided advantage in the matter* **distinct**, clear, clear-cut, marked, pronounced, obvious, striking, noticeable, unmistakable, patent, manifest, express, definite, certain, positive, absolute, emphatic, categorical, unambiguous, undeniable, unequivocal, indisputable, undisputed, unquestionable, assured, guaranteed; *archaic* sensible.
OPPOSITE possible.
2 *you could never talk him round—he was very decided* **determined**, resolute, firm, strong-minded, strong-willed, dogged, purposeful, forceful, emphatic, dead set, unhesitating, unwavering, unswerving, unfaltering, unyielding, unbending, inflexible, unmalleable, unshakeable, unrelenting, obdurate, obstinate, stubborn, intransigent; *N. Amer.* rock-ribbed; *rare* indurate.
OPPOSITE indecisive.
3 *the future of the tribe is decided* **settled**, established, resolved, determined, worked out, concluded, clinched, agreed, designated, allotted, chosen, ordained, prescribed, decreed; set, fixed, concrete, set in stone; *informal* sewn up, wrapped up.
OPPOSITE undecided.

decidedly ▶ adverb *they were decidedly hostile to one another* **distinctly**, clearly, markedly, obviously, noticeably, unmistakably, patently, manifestly, expressly, emphatically, definitely, certainly, positively, absolutely, downright, undeniably, unquestionably, indisputably; extremely, exceedingly, exceptionally, uncommonly, unusually, singularly, particularly, especially; *N. English* right; *Scottish* unco; *French* très; *informal* terrifically, tremendously, desperately, devilishly, ultra, mucho, mega, majorly; *Brit. informal* jolly, ever so, dead, well, fair; *N. Amer. informal* real, mighty, awful, plumb, powerful; *S. African informal* lekker; *informal, dated*

D

devilish, hellish; *archaic* exceeding, sore.

deciding ▶ adjective *the deciding factor may be the size of your budget* **determining**, decisive, conclusive, final, settling, key, pivotal, crucial, critical, most influential, significant, major, chief, principal, prime, paramount.

decipher ▶ verb **1** *he was the only one who could decipher the code* **decode**, decrypt, break, work out, solve, interpret, translate, construe, explain; make sense of, make head or tail of, get to the bottom of, unravel, find the key to, find the answer to, throw light on; *informal* crack, figure out; *Brit. informal* twig, suss, suss out.
OPPOSITE encode.
2 *the writing was rather wobbly and hard to decipher* **make out**, discern, perceive, see, read, follow, fathom, penetrate, make sense of, interpret, understand, comprehend, apprehend, grasp; untangle, disentangle, sort out, piece together.

decision ▶ noun **1** *a number of factors led me to this decision* **resolution**, conclusion, settlement, commitment, resolve, determination; choice, option, selection.
2 *they're delighted with the judge's decision* **verdict**, finding, ruling, recommendation, judgement, pronouncement, adjudgement, adjudication, arbitration; sentence, decree, order, rule, injunction; findings, results; *Law* determination; *N. Amer.* resolve; *rare* arbitrament.
3 *his executive order had a ring of decision* **decisiveness**, determination, resolution, resoluteness, resolve, firmness; strong-mindedness, single-mindedness, doggedness, strength of mind, strength of will, firmness of purpose, fixity of purpose, purpose, purposefulness.

decisive ▶ adjective **1** *Crane was a very decisive man* **resolute**, firm, strong-minded, strong-willed, determined; dogged, purposeful, forceful, emphatic, dead set, unhesitating, unwavering, unswerving, unfaltering, unyielding, unbending, inflexible, unmalleable, unshakeable, unrelenting, obdurate, obstinate, stubborn, intransigent; *N. Amer.* rock-ribbed; *rare* indurate.
OPPOSITE indecisive.
2 *your qualifications are unlikely to be the decisive factor* **deciding**, **conclusive**, determining, final, settling, key; pivotal, critical, crucial, momentous, significant, influential, important, major, chief, principal, prime, paramount.
OPPOSITE insignificant.

deck ▶ verb **1** *the cottage was decked with red, white, and blue bunting* **decorate**, bedeck, adorn, ornament, trim, trick out, garnish, cover, hang, festoon, garland, swathe, wreathe; embellish, beautify, prettify, enhance, grace, set off; *informal* get up, do up, do out, tart up; *literary* bejewel, bedizen, caparison, furbelow.
2 *Ingrid was* **decked out** *in her Sunday best* **dress up**, dress, clothe, attire, array, garb, robe, drape, accoutre, turn out, fit out, rig out, trick out, trick up, outfit, costume; *informal* doll up, get up, do up, tog up, tart up; *archaic* apparel, bedizen, caparison, invest, habit, trap out.

declaim ▶ verb **1** *he spoke like a preacher declaiming from the pulpit* **make a speech**, give an address, give a talk, give a lecture, make an oration, deliver a sermon, give a sermon; speak, hold forth, orate, pronounce, preach, lecture, sermonize, moralize; *informal* sound off, mouth off, spiel, spout, speechify, preachify, jaw; *rare* perorate.
2 *they loved to hear him declaim poetry* **recite**, say aloud, read aloud, read out loud, read out; quote, deliver, render; *informal* spout; *rare* bespout.
3 *he* **declaimed against** *the evils of society* **speak out**, protest strongly, make a protest, make a stand, rail, inveigh, fulminate, rage, thunder; rant about, expostulate about, make a fuss about, express disapproval of; **condemn**, criticize, castigate, attack, decry, disparage; *informal* mouth off about, kick up a stink about, go on about; *rare* vociferate.

declamation ▶ noun *he delivered a passionate declamation* **speech**, address, lecture, sermon, homily, discourse, delivery, oration, recitation, disquisition, monologue; harangue, tirade, diatribe, broadside, rant; *informal* spiel; *N. Amer. informal* stump speech; *rare* peroration, allocution, predication.

declamatory ▶ adjective *his speech-making was quiet and factual, very different from Clark's declamatory style* **rhetorical**, oratorical, elaborate, ornate, bold, extravagant, flowery, florid, dramatic, theatrical, lofty, high-flown, high-sounding, bombastic, magniloquent, grandiloquent, overblown, overdone, overwrought, affected, orotund, inflated, overinflated, pompous, pretentious; *informal* highfalutin, purple; *rare* fustian, tumid, euphuistic, aureate, Ossianic.

declaration ▶ noun **1** *they issued a declaration at the close of the talks* **announcement**, statement, communication, pronouncement, proclamation, memorandum, bulletin, communiqué, dispatch, report, edict, manifesto; *N. Amer.* advisory; (*in Spanish-speaking countries*) pronunciamento; *Latin* ipse dixit; *informal* memo; *rare* rescript.
2 *Parliament arranged the declaration of war* **proclamation**, notification, announcement, revelation, disclosure, broadcasting, promulgation; *archaic* annunciation; *rare* asseveration.
3 *her words were taken as a declaration of faith* **assertion**, profession, affirmation, acknowledgement, revelation, disclosure, manifestation, confirmation, proof, testimony, validation, certification, attestation; pledge, avowal, vow, oath, guarantee, protestation; *rare* asseveration, averment, maintenance.
OPPOSITE denial.

declare ▶ verb **1** *she loses no opportunity to declare her political principles* **proclaim**, announce, make known, state, communicate, reveal, divulge, mention, talk about, raise, moot, air, bring into the open, voice, articulate, pronounce, express, vent, set forth, make public, publicize, disseminate, circulate, publish, broadcast, promulgate, trumpet, blazon; *informal* come out with, shout from the rooftops; *literary* noise abroad, blazon abroad; *rare* preconize.
2 *he declared that the defendants were guilty* **assert**, maintain, state, aver, affirm, contend, argue, insist, hold, profess, move, claim, allege, avow, vow, swear, attest, testify, certify; *informal* make out; *technical* depose, represent; *formal* opine; *archaic* avouch; *rare* asseverate.
3 *his speech and bearing declared him a gentleman* **show to be**, reveal as, confirm as, prove to be, validate as, certify to someone's being, attest to someone's being.

decline ▶ verb **1** *she declined all invitations | he offered me a cigarette but I declined* **turn down**, **reject**, brush aside, refuse, rebuff, spurn, disdain, look down one's nose at, repulse, repudiate, dismiss, forgo, deny oneself, pass up, refuse to take advantage of, turn one's back on; abstain (from), say no (to), shake one's head, send one's regrets; *informal* give the thumbs down (to), give the red light (to), give something a miss, give someone the brush-off; *Brit. informal* knock back; *Austral. informal* snout.
OPPOSITE accept.
2 *the number of small local traders has declined* **decrease**, reduce, get smaller, grow smaller, lessen, get less, diminish, wane, dwindle, contract, shrink, fall off, taper off, tail off, peter out; drop, fall, go down, sink, slump, plummet, plunge; *informal* nosedive, take a nosedive, take a header, go into a tailspin, crash.
OPPOSITE increase.
3 *standards of craftsmanship steadily declined* **deteriorate**, degenerate, decay, crumble, collapse, fail, fall, sink, slump, slip, slide, go downhill, worsen, get worse, go to rack and ruin, stagnate, atrophy, wither, weaken, fade, fade away, wane, ebb; be abandoned, be neglected, be disregarded, be forgotten; *informal* go to pot, go to the dogs, hit the skids, go down the toilet, go down the tubes; *Austral./NZ informal* go to the pack; *rare* retrograde.
OPPOSITE flourish.
4 (*rare*) *the garden declined towards the street* **descend**, **slope down**, slant, slant down, dip, sink, fall away.
OPPOSITE rise.
▶ noun **1** *the company suffered a decline in profits* **reduction**, decrease, downturn, downswing, lowering, devaluation, depreciation, lessening, diminishing, diminution, slackening, waning, dwindling, fading, ebb, falling off, abatement, drop, slump, plunge, tumble; *informal* nosedive, crash, let-up.
OPPOSITE increase.
2 *there is a link between pollution and forest decline* **deterioration**, degeneration, degradation, shrinkage, shrinking, withering, atrophy, weakening, enfeeblement, fall, failure, death, decay, decaying; *dated* decadence; *rare* devolution.
□ **in decline** *the prosperity of the Mediterranean world was in decline* **waning**, declining, on the decline, decaying, crumbling, collapsing, atrophying, failing, disappearing, dying, moribund, past its prime, obsolescent; *informal* on its last legs, on the way out.

CHOOSE THE RIGHT WORD

decline, refuse, reject, spurn
See REFUSE.

decode ▶ verb *battle plans sent out on Germany's Enigma machine were quickly decoded* **decipher**, decrypt, unravel, untangle, work out, sort out, piece together, solve, interpret, translate, construe, explain, understand, comprehend, apprehend, grasp; make sense of, get to the bottom of, find the key to, find the answer to, throw light on; *informal* crack, figure out; *Brit. informal* twig, suss, suss out.

decompose ▶ verb **1** *the chemical prevents corpses from decomposing* **decay**, rot, putrefy, go bad, go off, spoil, fester, perish, deteriorate, degrade, break down, break up, moulder; *technical* mortify, necrotize, sphacelate; *archaic* corrupt.
2 *some minerals decompose very rapidly* **break up**, break apart, fall apart, fragment, disintegrate, crumble, dissolve; **break down**, decay.
3 *semantic markers decompose the meanings of words into more primitive elements* **separate**, divide, break down, dissect, atomize, dissolve, resolve, reduce; *rare* fractionate.

decomposition ▶ noun **1** *the body is in an advanced state of decomposition* **decay**, rotting, going bad, putrefaction, putrescence, putridity, festering, spoilage, perishing; *archaic* corruption.
2 *china clay is formed by the decomposition of granite* **breaking up**, breaking apart, fragmenting, disintegration, crumbling, dissolution, dissolving;

breaking down, decay, decaying.
3 *they presented a tree-like decomposition of a sentence into its parts* **separation**, division, breakdown, break-up; **dissection**, atomization, dissolution, resolution, analysis, reduction; *rare* fractionation.

decontaminate ▶ verb **sanitize**, sterilize, disinfect, clean, cleanse, purify; fumigate; *rare* depurate.

decor ▶ noun *inside, the decor is elegant and traditional* **decoration**, furnishing, furbishing, ornamentation; look, colour scheme.

decorate ▶ verb **1** *the door was decorated with a lion's head knocker* **ornament**, adorn, trim, embellish, garnish, furnish, accessorize, enhance, grace, enrich; festoon, garland, trick out, bedeck, beautify, prettify; *literary* furbelow.
2 *a house painter called to decorate his home* **paint**, **wallpaper**, paper, furbish, smarten up; renovate, refurbish, redecorate, retouch; *informal* do up, spruce up, do out, do over, fix up, tart up, give something a facelift, titivate.
3 *he was decorated for courage on the battlefields* **give a medal to**, pin a medal on, honour, confer an award on; cite, mention in dispatches, reward.

decoration ▶ noun **1** *a vaulted ceiling with rich decoration* **ornamentation**, adornment, trimming, embellishment, garnishing, gilding; beautification, prettification; enhancements, enrichments, frills, accessories, trimmings, finery, frippery.
2 *the carriages were built with simple but attractive internal decoration. See* DECOR.
3 *a Christmas tree decoration* **ornament**, trinket, bauble, knick-knack, gimcrack, spangle, doodah, gewgaw, folderol, fandangle; trimming, tinsel.
4 *a decoration won on the field of battle* **medal**, award, badge, star, ribbon, laurel, wreath, trophy, prize; colours, insignia; *military slang* fruit salad; *Brit. informal* gong.

decorative ▶ adjective *mirrors were used as decorative features* **ornamental**, adorning, embellishing, garnishing, beautifying, prettifying, enhancing, non-functional; fancy, ornate, attractive, pretty, showy, for show, flashy.
OPPOSITES functional; plain.

decorous ▶ adjective *he always behaved towards her in a decorous way* **proper**, seemly, decent, becoming, befitting, tasteful, in good taste; tactful, correct, appropriate, suitable, fitting, fit; polite, well mannered, well behaved, genteel, refined, polished, well bred, dignified, respectable, courtly, civilized; formal, reserved, modest, demure, sedate, staid, gentlemanly, ladylike; *French* comme il faut; *dated* mannerly; *humorous* couth.
OPPOSITES indecorous; unseemly; immodest.

decorum ▶ noun **1** *he had acted with the utmost decorum* **propriety**, properness, seemliness, decency, decorousness, good taste, correctness, appropriateness; politeness, courtesy, good manners; refinement, breeding, deportment, dignity, respectability, modesty, demureness.
OPPOSITE impropriety.
2 *a breach of decorum* **etiquette**, protocol, customary behaviour, good form, custom, convention, conformity, conventionality, usage, ritual; formalities, niceties, punctilios, politeness; *French* politesse; *informal* the thing to do.

decoy ▶ noun (stress on the first syllable) *we need a decoy to distract their attention* **lure**, bait, red herring; enticement, inducement, temptation, attraction, allurement, draw, carrot, ensnarement, entrapment; snare, trap, pitfall, ambush.
▶ verb (stress on the second syllable) *he was decoyed to the mainland by his enemies* **lure**, entice, induce, inveigle, ensnare; tempt, seduce; entrap, snare, trap.

decrease ▶ verb (stress on the second syllable) **1** *pollution levels had been gradually decreasing* **lessen**, grow/become less, grow/become smaller, reduce, drop, diminish, decline, dwindle, contract, shrink, fall off, die down; abate, subside, let up, tail off, ebb, wane, taper off, peter out, lighten; sink, slump, plummet, plunge.
OPPOSITE increase.
2 *you could exercise to decrease the amount of fat in your body* **reduce**, lessen, make less/fewer, lower, cut down/back (on), cut, curtail, contract, diminish, narrow, pare down, slim down, tone down, temper, weaken, deplete, minimize; *informal* slash.
▶ noun (stress on the first syllable) *a decrease in crime* **reduction**, drop, lessening, lowering, decline, falling off; letting up, slackening, downturn, cut, cutback, curtailment, diminution, contraction, shrinkage, ebb, wane, de-escalation; dying down, abatement.
OPPOSITE increase.

decree ▶ noun **1** *an emergency presidential decree* **order**, edict, command, commandment, mandate, proclamation, dictum, fiat, promulgation, precept; law, statute, act, bill, ordinance, regulation, rule, injunction, enactment, manifesto; (*in Tsarist Russia*) ukase; (*in Spanish-speaking countries*) pronunciamento; *rare* firman, decretal, irade, rescript.
2 *the council succeeded in obtaining a court decree against him* **judgement**, verdict, adjudication, ruling, rule, resolution, arbitration, decision, conclusion; findings.
▶ verb *the government decreed that a new national stadium should be built* **order**, command, rule, dictate, lay down, prescribe, pronounce, proclaim, ordain; enact, adjudge, enjoin, direct, decide, determine.

decrepit ▶ adjective **1** *a decrepit old man* **feeble**, enfeebled, infirm, weak, weakened, weakly, frail, debilitated, disabled, incapacitated, crippled, wasted, doddering, tottering, out of shape, in bad shape; **old**, elderly, aged, ancient, in one's dotage, long in the tooth, senile; superannuated, senescent; *informal* past it, over the hill, no spring chicken.
OPPOSITES strong, fit.
2 *a decrepit house* **dilapidated**, rickety, run down, broken-down, tumbledown, ramshackle, worn out, derelict, in ruins, ruined, falling apart, falling to pieces, in (a state of) disrepair, creaky, creaking, gone to rack and ruin, on its last legs; battered, decayed, decaying, crumbling, deteriorated, deteriorating, antiquated, superannuated, the worse for wear.
OPPOSITE sound.

decrepitude ▶ noun **1** *over the years she fell into a state of decrepitude* **feebleness**, enfeeblement, infirmity, weakness, frailty, debilitation, debility, sickliness, incapacitation, malaise; old age, agedness, elderliness, dotage, senility; superannuation, senescence.
OPPOSITES strength, fitness.
2 *the house had an air of decrepitude* **dilapidation**, ricketiness, dereliction, ruin, disrepair, rack and ruin, decay, deterioration.
OPPOSITES soundness, good repair.

decry ▶ verb *she decried sexists' double standards* **denounce**, condemn, criticize, censure, damn, attack, fulminate against, rail against, inveigh against, blame, carp at, cavil at, run down, pillory, rap, lambaste, deplore, disapprove of, vilify, execrate, revile; disparage, deprecate, discredit, derogate, cast aspersions on; *informal* slam, slate, blast, knock, snipe at, do a hatchet job on, hold forth against, come down on, pull to pieces, tear to shreds; *formal* excoriate, animadvert; *rare* asperse.
OPPOSITES praise; overrate.

dedicate ▶ verb **1** *she had dedicated her life to helping people and animals* **devote**, commit, pledge, bind, obligate, give, give over, surrender, set aside, allot, allocate, consign, sacrifice.
2 *each book was dedicated to a noblewoman* **inscribe**, address, name; assign, offer.
3 *the chapel was dedicated to the Virgin Mary* **devote**, assign; bless, consecrate, sanctify, hallow, make holy, make sacred.

dedicated ▶ adjective **1** *a dedicated socialist | a dedicated musician* **committed**, devoted, staunch, stalwart, firm, steadfast, resolute, unwavering, loyal, faithful, true, dyed-in-the-wool, through and through; wholehearted, single-minded, enthusiastic, eager, keen, earnest, zealous, ardent, passionate, fervent, fervid, fanatical; hard-working, dutiful, diligent, assiduous, studious; sworn, pledged; *informal* card-carrying, deep-dyed, as keen as mustard, mad keen.
OPPOSITES indifferent, apathetic.
2 *the data can be accessed by a dedicated machine or an ordinary personal computer* **exclusive**, allocated, assigned, custom built, customized.

dedication ▶ noun **1** *success in sport requires tremendous dedication* **commitment**, wholeheartedness, single-mindedness, enthusiasm, zeal, application, diligence, industry, assiduity, resolve, resoluteness, purposefulness, conscientiousness, perseverance, persistence, tenacity, doggedness, drive, staying power, backbone, sedulousness; hard work, effort, labour, striving.
OPPOSITES apathy, laziness.
2 *her superiors could not fault her dedication to the job* **devotion**, devotedness, commitment, loyalty, faithfulness, adherence, allegiance, constancy, staunchness.
OPPOSITE indifference.
3 *the hardback edition contains a dedication to his wife* **inscription**, address, message.
4 *the dedication of the church* **blessing**, consecration, sanctification, hallowing, benediction.
OPPOSITE deconsecration.

deduce ▶ verb *from the observation of fossils, he deduced that the whole Earth had once been covered by water* **conclude**, come to the conclusion, reason, work out, gather, infer, draw the inference; extrapolate, glean, divine, intuit, come to understand, understand, assume, presume, conjecture, surmise, reckon, dare say; *N. Amer.* figure; *informal* suss out.

deduct ▶ verb *any tax due will be deducted from the pension* **subtract**, take away, take from, take off, withdraw, abstract, remove, debit, dock, discount; *informal* knock off, minus.
OPPOSITE add.

deduction ▶ noun **1** *the deduction of tax* **subtraction**, taking away, taking off, withdrawal, abstraction, removal, debit, docking, discounting; *informal* knocking off.
OPPOSITE addition.

D

D

2 *NI contributions are worked out on gross pay, before all deductions* **stoppage**, subtraction.
3 *she had been right in her deduction that he was in love with someone else* **conclusion**, inference, supposition, hypothesis, thesis, assumption, presumption, suspicion, conviction, belief; reasoning; results, findings.

deed ▶ noun **1** *tales of knightly deeds* **act**, action, activity; **feat**, exploit, performance, achievement, accomplishment, attainment, endeavour, effort; undertaking, enterprise.
2 *working-class unity must be established in deed and not only in words* **fact**, reality, truth, actuality.
3 *mortgage deeds* **legal document**, contract, legal agreement, indenture, instrument; title deed, deed of covenant.

deem ▶ verb *many of these campaigns have been deemed successful* **regard as**, consider, judge, adjudge, hold to be, look on as, view as, see as, take to be, take for, class as, estimate as, count, rate, find, esteem, calculate to be, gauge, suppose, reckon, account, interpret as; think, believe to be, feel to be, imagine to be, conceive to be.

deep ▶ adjective **1** *a deep ravine* **extending far down**; cavernous, yawning, gaping, huge, big, great, extensive, profound, unplumbed; bottomless, immeasurable, fathomless, unfathomable; *rare* chasmic.
OPPOSITE shallow.
2 *a deep shelf* **extending far back/in**, extending a long way back, extensive.
OPPOSITE shallow.
3 *a puddle about two inches deep* **in depth**, downwards, inwards, from top to bottom, from the surface, in vertical extent.
4 *I have a deep affection for you | he was viewed with deep suspicion* **intense**, heartfelt, deeply felt, fervent, ardent, impassioned, wholehearted, deep-seated, deep-rooted, thorough, thoroughgoing, serious; sincere, honest, genuine, unfeigned; earnest, enthusiastic, keen, great; grave, abject.
OPPOSITES superficial, insincere.
5 *Laura drifted into a deep sleep* **sound**, heavy, profound, intense.
6 *Helen was a deep thinker* **clever**, intelligent, intellectual; **knowledgeable**, learned, wise, sagacious, sage, scholarly; discerning, penetrating, perspicacious, perceptive, percipient, insightful, keen, sharp, sharp-witted, quick-witted; **profound**, philosophical, complex, weighty, serious, difficult, abstruse, esoteric, recondite, impenetrable, unfathomable, mysterious, obscure.
OPPOSITE straightforward.
7 *he was deep in concentration* **rapt**, absorbed, engrossed, preoccupied, immersed, steeped, lost, captivated, spellbound, riveted, gripped, enthralled, intent, engaged.
8 *a deep mystery* **obscure**, mysterious, hidden, secret, unfathomable, fathomless, opaque, abstruse, recondite, esoteric, enigmatic, arcane, Delphic; puzzling, perplexing, baffling, mystifying, inexplicable; *informal* as clear as mud.
9 *his deep voice* **low-pitched**, low, bass, full-toned, rich, powerful, resonant, rumbling, booming, resounding, sonorous.
OPPOSITE high.
10 *a deep reddish-brown colour* **dark**; **intense**, vivid, rich, strong, brilliant, glowing, vibrant, bold, warm, flamboyant, eye-catching.
OPPOSITES light; thin.
▶ noun (**the deep**) **1** (*literary*) *the strange creatures of the deep* **the sea**, the ocean; the high seas; *informal* the drink, the briny; *literary* the waves, the main, the foam, the profound.
2 *in the deep of night* **the middle**, the midst, the mid point, the central point; the depths, the thick, the dead, the heart, the kernel, the interior.
▶ adverb **1** *I dug deep* **far down**, far in, deep down, way down, to a great depth.
2 *he brought them deep into thick woodland* **far**, a long way, a great distance, a good way.

deepen ▶ verb **1** *the recession continues to deepen | his love for his wife had been deepened by the way she had stood by him* **grow**, increase, intensify, strengthen, escalate, mushroom, snowball; add to, heighten, reinforce, enhance, boost, magnify, amplify, augment, enrich, promote, encourage; exacerbate, aggravate, inflame, worsen, make/become worse; *informal* hot up, step up.
2 *the archaeologists deepened and widened the hole* **dig out**, make deeper, dig deeper, scoop out, scrape out, hollow out, excavate.

deeply ▶ adverb *she was deeply affected by the story* **greatly**, enormously, extremely, very much, to a great extent/degree; strongly, powerfully, profoundly, intensely, keenly, sharply, acutely; thoroughly, completely, entirely; severely, awfully, terribly, painfully, desperately; *informal* well, seriously, majorly, jolly, oh-so; *N. Amer. informal* mighty, plumb.

deep-rooted ▶ adjective *a fear of deep-rooted taboos* **deep-seated**, deep, profound, fundamental, basic; well established, established, settled, firm, ingrained, entrenched, unshakeable, irremovable, ineradicable, dyed-in-the-wool, inveterate, built-in, inbuilt, radical, secure; persistent, long-lasting, abiding, lingering.
OPPOSITES superficial, temporary.

deep-seated ▶ adjective *a deep-seated concern that values are in decline*. See DEEP-ROOTED.

deer ▶ noun. *See centre pages for list of* **Deer and Antelopes**

WORD LINKS

relating to deer	**cervine**
male	**stag**
female	**doe**
collective noun	**herd, mob**

deface ▶ verb *a graffiti artist who defaced buildings and motorway bridges* **vandalize**, disfigure, mar, spoil, ruin, deform, sully, tarnish, damage; injure, uglify, blight, blemish, impair; *informal* tag, trash.
OPPOSITE beautify.

de facto ▶ adverb *the republic has been de facto divided into two states* **in practice**, in effect, in fact, in reality, really, actually, in actuality.
OPPOSITES in theory; de jure.
▶ adjective *they took de facto control of the land* **actual**, existing, existent, real, effective.
OPPOSITES theoretical; de jure.

defamation ▶ noun *he sued the newspaper for defamation* **libel**, **slander**, character assassination, defamation of character, calumny, vilification, traducement, obloquy, scandal, scandalmongering, malicious gossip, tittle-tattle, backbiting, aspersions, muckraking, abuse, malediction; disparagement, denigration, detraction, derogation, opprobrium, censure, criticism; smear, slur, lie, false report, smear campaign, rumour, insult; *informal* mud-slinging, slagging-off, knocking, bitching; *N. Amer. informal* bad-mouthing; *archaic* contumely.
OPPOSITE commendation.

defamatory ▶ adjective *there were defamatory statements in the book* **libellous**, **slanderous**, defaming, calumnious, calumniatory, vilifying, traducing, scandalous, scandalmongering, malicious, vicious, backbiting, muckraking, abusive, maledictory, maledictive; disparaging, denigratory, detracting, derogatory, censorious, critical; insulting, slurring, injurious; *informal* mud-slinging, bitchy, catty; *archaic* contumelious.
OPPOSITE complimentary.

defame ▶ verb *he had been defamed by an article in a tabloid newspaper* **libel**, **slander**, malign, cast aspersions on, smear, traduce, blacken the name/character of, give someone a bad name, defame someone's character, sully someone's reputation, run down, speak ill/evil of, back-bite, run a smear campaign against, calumniate, vilify, besmirch, tarnish, stigmatize, disparage, denigrate, discredit, decry, insult, lie about, tell lies about; *informal* do a hatchet job on, sling/fling/throw mud at, drag through the mud/mire; *N. Amer.* slur; *Brit. informal* slag off; *N. Amer. informal* bad-mouth; *rare* asperse, derogate, vilipend.

CHOOSE THE RIGHT WORD

defame, malign, slander, libel, traduce
See MALIGN.

default ▶ noun **1** *the recession has been accompanied by a rise in the incidence of defaults on loans* **non-payment**, failure to pay, non-remittance; *informal* welshing, bilking; *Brit. archaic* levant.
OPPOSITE repayment.
2 *I became a TV presenter by default, rather than by design | in default of evidence* **failure to act/appear**, inaction, omission, lapse, lack, exclusion, neglect, negligence, disregard; want, deficiency, delinquency, dereliction, absence, non-appearance.
▶ verb **1** *the dealer can repossess the goods if the customer defaults* **fail to pay**, not pay, renege, fail to honour, back out, backtrack, backslide; break one's promise/word, go back on one's word; *informal* welsh, bilk.
OPPOSITE repay.
2 *when you start a fresh letter, the program will default to its own style* **revert**; select automatically.

defaulter ▶ noun **1** *a mortgage defaulter* **non-payer**, debt-dodger; tax-dodger; *informal* welsher, bilker; *N. Amer.* delinquent; *Brit. archaic* levanter.
2 (*Military*) *he was confined to the defaulters' room* **minor offender**, wrongdoer, felon, delinquent, malefactor, culprit; *archaic* miscreant.

defeat ▶ verb **1** *the victorious army which defeated the Scots at Halidon Hill* **beat**, conquer, win against, win a victory over, triumph over, prevail over, get the better of, best, worst, vanquish; rout, trounce, overcome, overpower, overthrow, overwhelm, crush, quash, bring someone to their knees; quell, subjugate, subdue, repulse; *informal* lick, thrash, hammer, whip, wipe the floor with, walk all over, give someone a hiding, take to the cleaners, blow out of the water, run rings round/around, make mincemeat of, clobber, paste, pound, pulverize, crucify, murder, massacre, slaughter, demolish, drub, give someone a drubbing, cane, zap, flatten, turn inside out, tank; *Brit. informal* stuff, marmalize; *N. Amer. informal* blow out, cream, shellac, skunk, slam.
OPPOSITE lose to.
2 *budgets should not be so complex that they defeat their purpose* **thwart**, block, frustrate, prevent, foil, baulk, ruin, put a stop to, scotch, obviate, forestall, debar, snooker, derail; obstruct, impede, hinder, hamper, deter, discomfit; *informal* put the kibosh on, nip in the bud, put paid to, put the

stopper on, do for, stymie; *Brit. informal* scupper, put the mockers on, nobble.
OPPOSITES advance, assist.
3 *the motion was defeated* **reject**, overthrow, throw out, dismiss, outvote, spurn, rebuff, turn down; *informal* give the thumbs down.
OPPOSITE pass.
4 *I managed to fit to the machine, but how to make it work defeats me* **baffle**, puzzle, perplex, bewilder, mystify, bemuse, confuse, confound, frustrate, nonplus, throw; *informal* beat, flummox, discombobulate, faze, stump, fox, be all Greek to.
▶ **noun 1** *a crippling defeat for the government* **loss**, beating, conquest, conquering, besting, worsting, vanquishing, vanquishment; rout, trouncing, overpowering, subjugation, subduing; **reverse**, debacle, downfall; *informal* thrashing, hiding, drubbing, licking, hammering, whipping, clobbering, pasting, pounding, pulverizing, massacre, slaughter, demolition, caning, flattening.
OPPOSITE victory.
2 *the defeat of his plans* **failure**, downfall, breakdown, collapse, ruin, lack of success, discomfiture, rejection, frustration, foundering, misfiring, overthrow, abortion, miscarriage; undoing, reverse; disappointment, setback.
OPPOSITE success.

defeatist ▶ **adjective** *they were criticized for their defeatist attitude* **pessimistic**, fatalistic, negative, resigned, cynical, discouraged, despondent, despairing, hopeless, bleak, gloomy, gloom-ridden, looking on the dark/black side.
OPPOSITES optimistic, positive.
▶ **noun pessimist**, fatalist, yielder, cynic, prophet of doom, doomwatcher; misery, killjoy, worrier, Job's comforter; *informal* quitter, doom and gloom merchant, doomster, wet blanket.
OPPOSITE optimist.

defecate ▶ **verb excrete**, pass/discharge/excrete faeces, have a bowel movement, have a BM, evacuate one's bowels, open one's bowels, void excrement, relieve oneself, go to the lavatory; *informal* do number two, do a pooh, do a whoopsie; *vulgar slang* crap, have a crap, shit, have a shit, dump, have a dump.

defecation ▶ **noun excretion**, passing/discharging/excreting faeces, evacuation of one's bowels, opening one's bowels, going to the lavatory; bowel movement, BM; *informal* number twos, poohing, whoopsies; *vulgar slang* crapping, crap, shitting, shit, dump.

defect[1] (stress on the first syllable) ▶ **noun** *a defect in the software* **fault**, flaw, imperfection, deficiency, weakness, weak spot/point, inadequacy, shortcoming, limitation, failing, obstruction; snag, kink, deformity, blemish, taint, crack, break, tear, split, scratch, chip, fracture, spot; mistake, error; *Computing* bug, virus; *informal* glitch, gremlin.

defect[2] (stress on the second syllable) ▶ **verb** *their ruthlessness discouraged army officers from defecting | one MP* **defected from** *the party* **desert**, go over to the enemy, change sides/loyalties/allegiances, turn traitor, rebel, renege, abscond, go AWOL, quit, escape; shift ground, break faith, be apostate, apostatize; abandon, renounce, repudiate, secede from, revolt against; *informal* rat on; *archaic* forsake; *rare* tergiversate.

defection ▶ **noun** *his defection to the United States* **desertion**, absconding, decamping, flight; changing sides/allegiances, apostasy, recantation, secession; treason, betrayal, disloyalty, rebellion, mutiny, perfidy; *rare* tergiversation, recreancy.

defective ▶ **adjective 1** *a defective seat belt* **faulty**, flawed, imperfect, shoddy, inoperative, not working, not functioning, non-functioning, malfunctioning, out of order, unsound; weak, deficient, incomplete; in disrepair, broken, cracked, torn, scratched, deformed, warped, buckled; *informal* gone wrong, on the blink; *Brit. informal* knackered, duff.
OPPOSITES working, perfect.
2 *these methods are defective in strength and durability* **lacking**, wanting, deficient, inadequate, insufficient, short, low, scant.
3 (*dated*) *a mentally defective child* **impaired**, retarded, backward, slow, simple, deficient, subnormal, educationally subnormal, ESN.
OPPOSITES bright, intelligent.

defector ▶ **noun deserter**, turncoat, traitor, rebel, renegade, tergiversator, apostate, recreant, Judas, quisling; *informal* rat.

defence ▶ **noun 1** *the defence of fortresses against enemies* **protection**, shielding, safeguarding, guarding; security, fortification, cover, shelter, screen, resistance, deterrent.
2 *the enemy's defences were sited all along the ridge* **barricade**, fortification, bulwark, buttress, fortress, fastness, keep, rampart, outpost, bastion.
3 *he planned to speak in defence of his old chief* **vindication**, justification, support, advocacy, approval, endorsement, promotion; apology, apologia, explanation, explication, excuse, extenuation, exoneration, palliation.
4 *they urged lower spending on defence* **armaments**, weapons, weaponry, arms, military resources/measures; the military, the army, the navy, the air force; deterrence.
5 *the prisoner was unable to speak for pain, so his defence was never heard* **rebuttal**, denial; **vindication**, explanation, mitigation, justification, rationalization, excuse, alibi, reason; plea, pleading; testimony, declaration, case.

defenceless ▶ **adjective 1** *it is a disgrace that these thugs terrorized defenceless animals* **vulnerable**, **helpless**, powerless, impotent, weak, frail; susceptible, easily hurt/wounded/damaged; *rare* impuissant, resistless.
OPPOSITES well protected, resilient.
2 *scrapping the weapons would leave the country wholly defenceless* **undefended**, unprotected, unguarded, unfortified, unshielded, unarmed, without arms, without defences; vulnerable, assailable, open to attack, wide open, open, exposed, endangered, in danger, in peril, in jeopardy, at risk, insecure; *rare* pregnable.
OPPOSITE well protected.

defend ▶ **verb 1** *a tower built to defend Ireland from Napoleon's threatened invasion | we will defend freedom of speech* **protect**, guard, safeguard, keep from harm, preserve, secure, shield, shelter, screen; fortify, garrison, barricade; fight for, uphold, support, be on the side of, take up cudgels for; watch over, be the defender of.
OPPOSITE attack.
2 *he defended his policy of charging high interest rates* **justify**, vindicate, argue/speak for, speak on behalf of, support, speak in support of, give an apologia for, make a case for, plead for, make excuses for, excuse, exonerate, palliate; explain, give reasons for, give the rationale behind.
OPPOSITES attack, criticize.
3 *the manager defended his players* **support**, speak in support of, back, stand by, stick up for, stand up for, argue for, champion, endorse, uphold, come to the defence of, sustain, bolster; *informal* throw one's weight behind.
OPPOSITE criticize.

defendant ▶ **noun** *the defendant was charged with murder* **accused**, prisoner at the bar; appellant, litigant, respondent; suspect, suspected person.
OPPOSITE plaintiff.

defender ▶ **noun 1** *the defenders of the rural environment* **protector**, guard, guardian, preserver, bodyguard; custodian, watchdog, keeper, overseer, superintendent, caretaker, steward, trustee.
2 *a defender of colonialism* **supporter**, upholder, backer, champion, advocate, endorser, sustainer, bolsterer, apologist, proponent, exponent, promoter, apostle, standard-bearer, torch-bearer, adherent, believer.
OPPOSITES attacker, critic.
3 *he burst between two defenders and cracked a shot at the bar* **fullback**, back, sweeper; (**defenders**) back four.
OPPOSITES attacker, striker.

defensible ▶ **adjective 1** *this is a perfectly defensible attitude* **justifiable**, arguable, tenable, defendable, maintainable, sustainable, supportable, plausible, well founded, sound, sensible, reasonable, rational, logical, able to hold water; acceptable, satisfactory, valid, legitimate, warrantable, permissible, excusable, pardonable, understandable, condonable, vindicable.
OPPOSITES indefensible, untenable.
2 *a defensible patch of territory* **secure**, safe, fortified, protectable, able to be protected, holdable; invulnerable, impregnable, impenetrable, unattackable, unassailable.
OPPOSITE vulnerable.

defensive ▶ **adjective 1** *troops in defensive positions* **defending**, **guarding**, safeguarding, protecting, protective, shielding, screening; wary, watchful; averting, withstanding, opposing.
OPPOSITE attacking.
2 *my innocent inquiry had provoked a defensive, almost hostile response* **self-justifying**, oversensitive, thin-skinned, easily offended, prickly, paranoid, neurotic; *informal* uptight, twitchy; *rare* umbrageous.
OPPOSITE confident.

defer[1] ▶ **verb** *he deferred the final decision till a later meeting* **postpone**, put off, adjourn, delay, hold over/off, put back, carry over; shelve, suspend, stay, hold in abeyance, prorogue, pigeonhole, mothball; *N. Amer.* put over, table, lay on the table, take a rain check on; *N. Amer. Law* continue; *informal* put on ice, put on the back burner, put in cold storage; *rare* remit, respite.

defer[2] ▶ **verb** *he readily* **deferred to** *his parents and to his eldest sister* **yield**, submit, give way, give in, surrender, accede, bow, capitulate, acquiesce, knuckle under; comply with, agree with, respect, honour, truckle.
OPPOSITES stand up to, disobey.

deference ▶ **noun** *his writings show excessive deference to the gentry* **respect**, respectfulness, regard, esteem; consideration, attentiveness, attention, thoughtfulness; courteousness, courtesy, politeness, civility, dutifulness, reverence, veneration, awe, homage; **submissiveness**, submission, obedience, yielding, surrender, accession, capitulation, acquiescence, complaisance, obeisance.
OPPOSITE disrespect.

deferential ▶ **adjective** *a deferential batman* **obsequious**, humble, respectful, considerate, attentive, thoughtful; courteous, courteous, polite, civil, dutiful, reverent, reverential, awed; obedient, submissive, subservient,

fawning, toadying, yielding, acquiescent, complaisant, compliant, pliant, tractable, biddable, manageable, docile, slavish; *dated* mannerly; *rare* regardful, obeisant.
OPPOSITES arrogant; impolite.

deferment ▶ noun *they allowed deferment of the repayments* **postponement**, deferral, suspension, putting off/back, adjournment, delay, shelving, rescheduling, interruption, arrest, pause; respite, stay, moratorium, reprieve, grace; *N. Amer.* tabling; *N. Amer. Law* continuation; *rare* put-off.

defiance ▶ noun *he wasn't used to such outspoken defiance* **resistance**, opposition, confrontation; non-compliance, disobedience, insubordination, dissent, recalcitrance, subversion, subversiveness; rebelliousness, mutinousness, provocation, daring, boldness, temerity, audacity, bravado, aggression; contempt, disregard, scorn, insolence, truculence, contumacy.
OPPOSITES submission, obedience.

defiant ▶ adjective *he is defiant in the face of critics* **intransigent**, resistant, obstinate, uncooperative, non-compliant, recalcitrant, confrontational, challenging; aggressive, belligerent, pugnacious, bellicose, combative, ready for a fight, antagonistic, hostile; obstreperous, truculent, dissenting, argumentative, quarrelsome, contentious, disobedient, insubordinate, subversive, rebellious, mutinous; *informal* feisty, spoiling for a fight; *Brit. informal* stroppy, bolshie; *N. Amer. informal* scrappy; *archaic or Law* contumacious.
OPPOSITES apologetic; cooperative.

deficiency ▶ noun **1** *she has a vitamin deficiency in her diet* **insufficiency**, lack, shortage, want, dearth, inadequacy, deficit, shortfall; scarcity, scarceness, scantiness, paucity, absence, undersupply, sparseness, deprivation, meagreness, shortness; *rare* exiguity, exiguousness.
OPPOSITE surplus.
2 *the team's big deficiency was in the front five* **defect**, fault, flaw, imperfection, weakness, weak spot/point, inadequacy, shortcoming, limitation, failing.
OPPOSITE strength.

deficient ▶ adjective **1** *his diet is* **deficient in** *vitamin A* **lacking**, wanting, defective, inadequate, insufficient, limited, poor, scant; short of/on, low on, with an insufficiency of, with too little/few ...; *informal* strapped for, pushed for.
OPPOSITE excessive.
2 *on all levels, this is deficient leadership* **defective**, faulty, flawed, inadequate, imperfect, impaired, shoddy, scrappy, sketchy, weak, inferior, unsound, substandard, second-rate, poor, shabby, incomplete, leaving much to be desired; *informal* duff.
OPPOSITE perfect.

deficit ▶ noun *there was a large, continuing deficit in the federal budget* **shortfall**, deficiency, shortage, undersupply, slippage; indebtedness, debt, arrears; minus amount, negative amount, loss.
OPPOSITES surplus, profit.

defile ▶ verb **1** *she was afraid that her very capacity for love had been defiled* **spoil**, sully, mar, impair, debase, degrade; pollute, poison, corrupt, taint, tarnish, infect; foul, befoul, dirty, soil, stain; destroy, ruin.
OPPOSITE purify.
2 *the sacred bones had been defiled* **desecrate**, profane, violate, treat sacrilegiously; make impure, contaminate, pollute, debase, degrade, dishonour, vitiate.
OPPOSITE sanctify.
3 (*archaic*) *she was defiled by a married man* **rape**, ravish, deflower, violate, molest.

defilement ▶ noun **1** *I cannot accept this town's continued defilement* **degradation**, debasement, spoiling, sullying, impairment; pollution, poisoning, corruption, tainting, tarnishing.
OPPOSITE purification.
2 *any defilement disqualified priests from contact with holy things* **desecration**, profanation, profanity, violation, sacrilege; impurity, contamination, pollution, debasement, degradation, dishonour, vitiation.
OPPOSITE sanctification.

definable ▶ adjective *Aunt Emily wasn't ill, at least she had no definable complaint* **determinable**, ascertainable, known, definite, clear-cut, precise, exact, specific.
OPPOSITE indefinable.

define ▶ verb **1** *the dictionary defines it as a type of pasture* **explain**, expound, interpret, elucidate, explicate, describe, clarify; give the meaning of, state precisely, spell out, put into words, express in words.
2 *the difficulty lay in defining the upper and lower limits of the middle class* **determine**, establish, fix, specify, designate, decide, stipulate, settle, set out, mark out, mark off; **demarcate**, bound, delimit, delineate, circumscribe, set the boundaries/limits of.
3 *he could see the farm buildings defined against the fields beyond* **outline**, delineate, silhouette; trace, pencil.

definite ▶ adjective **1** *I need a definite answer* **explicit**, specific, express, precise, exact, defined, well defined, clear-cut; determined, fixed, established, confirmed, direct; concrete, hard, plain, outright.
OPPOSITES vague, indefinite.
2 *there is definite evidence of decreasing per capita incomes* **certain**, sure, positive, absolute, conclusive, decisive, firm, concrete, final, unambiguous, unequivocal, unquestionable, unarguable, clear, manifest, obvious, patent, unmistakable, proven; black and white, hard and fast, as plain as the nose on your face, as plain as daylight; guaranteed, settled, decided, assured; *informal* cut and dried.
OPPOSITES uncertain, ambiguous.
3 *she had a definite dislike for Robert's wife* **unmistakable**, irrefutable, unequivocal, unambiguous, certain, undisputed, decided, marked, distinct, unquestioned, not in question, not in doubt.
OPPOSITES vague, slight.
4 *some organizations occupy a definite geographical area* **fixed**, marked, demarcated, delimited, stipulated, particular, circumscribed.
OPPOSITE indeterminate.

CHOOSE THE RIGHT WORD

definite, sure, certain, positive, convinced

See SURE.

definitely ▶ adverb *it was definitely a case of exploiting child labour* **certainly**, surely, for sure, unquestionably, without/beyond doubt, without/beyond question, beyond any doubt, undoubtedly, indubitably, assuredly, positively, absolutely; undeniably, irrefutably, incontrovertibly, incontestably, unmistakably; plainly, clearly, obviously, patently, palpably, transparently, categorically, decidedly, unequivocally; easily, far and away, by a mile, without fail, there are no two ways about it, there's no denying it, needless to say; *informal* as sure as eggs is eggs.
OPPOSITE possibly.

definition ▶ noun **1** *there is no agreed definition of 'intelligence'* **meaning**, denotation, sense; **interpretation**, explanation, elucidation, explication, description, clarification, exposition, expounding, illustration; deciphering, decoding; statement/outline of meaning.
2 *the definition of the picture can be aided by using computer graphics* **clarity**, clearness, visibility, precision, sharpness, crispness, acuteness, distinctness; resolution, focus, contrast.
OPPOSITES blurriness, fuzziness.

definitive ▶ adjective **1** *a definitive decision* **conclusive**, final, ultimate; **decisive**, unconditional, unqualified, absolute, categorical, positive, definite.
OPPOSITE provisional.
2 *the definitive guide to the movies* **authoritative**, exhaustive, most reliable, most complete, most perfect, most scholarly, best, finest, consummate; classic, standard, recognized, accepted, approved, official, established.

deflate ▶ verb **1** *he deflated one of the tyres* **let down**, empty the air out of, collapse, flatten, void; puncture.
OPPOSITES inflate; blow up.
2 *the balloon deflated* **go down**, collapse, shrink, contract, flatten.
OPPOSITES inflate; expand.
3 *the news had deflated the old man* **subdue**, humble, cow, humiliate, mortify, chasten, chagrin, dispirit, dismay, discourage, dishearten; squash, crush, flatten, bring down, bring low, take down a peg or two, take the wind out of someone's sails; *informal* cut down to size, knock the stuffing out of, put down.
OPPOSITE aggrandize.
4 *the budget deflated the economy* **reduce**, slow down, make less active, diminish, lessen, lower; devalue, depreciate, depress.
OPPOSITE inflate.

deflect ▶ verb **1** *the bullet was deflected sideways | she was anxious to deflect attention from herself* **turn aside/away**, divert, avert, sidetrack; distract, draw away; block, parry, stop, fend off, stave off.
2 *the ball deflected off the centre half* **bounce**, glance, ricochet; turn aside/away, turn, alter course, change course/direction, diverge, deviate; veer, swerve, slew, drift, bend, swing, twist, curve.

deflection ▶ noun *the deflection of a missile away from its target* **turning aside/away**, turning, diversion, drawing away; deviation, divergence, declination, aberration, turn, veer, swerve, slew, drift, straying, bend, swing, twist, curve; *rare* divarication, divagation.

deform ▶ verb *broad shoes that will not cramp or deform the toes* **make misshapen**, distort the shape of, disfigure, bend out of shape, misshape, contort, buckle, twist, warp, damage, impair, maim, injure, cripple.

deformation ▶ noun *a deformation of the visual cortex* **distortion**, malformation, contortion, buckling, twisting, warping, bending, wrenching, misshaping; twist, warp, bend, buckle, curve.

deformed ▶ adjective *a deformed skeleton* **misshapen**, distorted, malformed, contorted, out of shape; twisted, crooked, curved, warped, buckled, gnarled; crippled, maimed, injured, damaged, humpbacked, hunchbacked, disfigured; ugly, unsightly, grotesque, monstrous; marred, mutilated, mangled.

deformity ▶ noun *the frame can be used to correct bone deformities* **malformation**, misshapenness, disproportion, distortion, crookedness; imperfection, abnormality, irregularity; ugliness, unsightliness, defacement, disfigurement; defect, flaw, blemish.

defraud ▶ verb *the men were alleged to have defrauded thousands of investors* **swindle**, cheat, rob, deceive, dupe, hoodwink, double-cross, fool, trick; *informal* con, bamboozle, do, sting, diddle, fiddle, swizzle, rip off, shaft, bilk, rook, take for a ride, pull a fast one on, pull the wool over someone's eyes, put one over on, sell a pup to, take to the cleaners, gyp, gull, finagle, milk; *N. Amer. informal* sucker, snooker, stiff, euchre, bunco, hornswoggle; *Austral. informal* pull a swifty on; *archaic* cozen, sharp; *rare* mulct, do someone in the eye.

defray ▶ verb *the rest of the money was used to* **defray the costs of** *restoring the house* **pay (for)**, cover, meet, square, settle, clear, discharge, liquidate; foot the bill for; *N. Amer. informal* pick up the tab/check for.

deft ▶ adjective *a deft piece of footwork | his deft handling of the situation* **skilful**, adept, adroit, dexterous, agile, nimble, neat, nimble-fingered, handy, able, capable, skilled, proficient, accomplished, expert, experienced, practised, polished, efficient, slick, professional, masterful, masterly, impressive, finely judged, delicate; clever, shrewd, astute, canny, sharp, artful; *informal* nifty, nippy, mean, wicked, ace, wizard, crack; *rare* habile.
OPPOSITES clumsy, awkward, inept.

defunct ▶ adjective **1** *the now defunct local paper mill* **disused**, no longer in use, unused, inoperative, non-functioning, unusable, obsolete; no longer in existence, discontinued; extinct, fossilized.
OPPOSITES working, extant.
2 *his defunct parents* **dead**, deceased, expired, departed, gone; late; *rare* demised.
OPPOSITES alive, living.

defuse ▶ verb **1** *explosives specialists tried to defuse the grenade* **deactivate**, disarm, disable, make safe.
OPPOSITE activate.
2 *an attempt to defuse the situation* **reduce**, lessen, diminish, lighten, relieve, ease, alleviate, allay, moderate, mitigate, take the edge off; clear the air.
OPPOSITES heighten, intensify.

defuse or diffuse?
See DIFFUSE.

defy ▶ verb **1** *61 rebel MPs defied the prime minister and voted against the bill | he had defied European and French laws* **disobey**, refuse to obey, go against, rebel against, flout, fly in the face of, thumb one's nose at, disregard, ignore, set one's face against, kick against; break, violate, contravene, breach, infringe; *informal* cock a snook at; *archaic* set at naught.
OPPOSITE obey.
2 *about 150 settlers defied Sant'Anna's army of 5,000* **resist**, withstand, take a stand against, hold out against, stand up to, confront, face, meet head-on, take on, square up to, beard, brave, outface.
OPPOSITE surrender.
3 *the logic of this defied her | his actions defy belief* **elude**, escape, defeat; foil, frustrate, thwart, baffle.
4 *he glowered at her, defying her to mock him* **challenge**, dare; throw down the gauntlet.

degeneracy ▶ noun *an attack on the sexual degeneracy and intellectual deterioration of the time* **corruption**, corruptness, decadence, moral decay, dissipation, dissoluteness, dissolution, profligacy, depravity, perversion, pervertedness, vice, immorality, lack of morals, lack of principles, baseness, turpitude, wickedness, evil, sin, sinfulness, ungodliness; debauchery, lewdness, lechery, lecherousness, lasciviousness, licentiousness, libidinousness, promiscuity, wantonness, libertinism, intemperance.
OPPOSITES morality, purity.

degenerate ▶ adjective **1** *a degenerate form of High Renaissance classicism* **debased**, degraded, corrupt, corrupted, vitiated, bastard, impure.
OPPOSITE pure.
2 *her degenerate brother* **corrupt**, decadent, dissolute, dissipated, debauched, rakish, reprobate, profligate, depraved, perverted, despicable, base, vice-ridden, wicked, sinful, ungodly; immoral, unprincipled, amoral, dishonourable, disreputable, unsavoury, sordid, low, mean, ignoble; lewd, lecherous, lascivious, licentious, libidinous, loose, promiscuous, wanton, libertine, intemperate; *informal* pervy.
OPPOSITE moral.
▶ noun *a group of drunkards and degenerates* **reprobate**, debauchee, rake, profligate, libertine, roué, loose-liver; pervert, deviant, deviate; *informal* perv; *rare* retrograde, dissolute.
▶ verb **1** *certain areas of the city have degenerated into slums | their quality of life had degenerated* **deteriorate**, decline, sink, slip, slide, worsen, get/grow worse, take a turn for the worse, lapse, fail, fall off, slump, go downhill, regress, retrogress; decay, rot, go to rack and ruin; *informal* go to pot, go to the dogs, hit the skids, go down the tubes, go down the toilet; *Austral./NZ informal* go to the pack; *rare* retrograde, devolve.
OPPOSITE improve.
2 *the muscles started to degenerate* **waste away**, waste, atrophy, weaken, become debilitated.

degeneration ▶ noun *the social degeneration of the area* **deterioration**, decline, decay, debasement, degradation, slide, sinking, descent, drop, regression, retrogression, lapse; atrophy; *rare* devolution.
OPPOSITE improvement.

degradation ▶ noun **1** *such poverty brings with it degradation, starvation, and the loss of human life* **humiliation**, shame, loss of dignity, loss of self-respect, loss of pride, abasement, mortification, indignity, ignominy.
2 *the degradation of women* **demeaning**, debasement, cheapening, devaluing, discrediting, dishonouring.
3 *the degradation of the tissues in rheumatoid arthritis* **deterioration**, degeneration, atrophy, decay, wasting away; breakdown.

degrade ▶ verb **1** *many supposedly erotic pictures simply degrade women | British prisons should not degrade prisoners* **demean**, debase, cheapen, devalue, prostitute, lower the status of, reduce, shame, humiliate, bring shame to, humble, mortify, abase, disgrace, dishonour; desensitize, dehumanize, brutalize.
OPPOSITES dignify, ennoble.
2 *the product, called a biopolymer, will not degrade until attacked by micro-organisms* **break down**, deteriorate, degenerate, decay, atrophy.
3 (*archaic*) *he was degraded from his high estate* **demote**, downgrade, reduce/lower in rank, reduce to the ranks, strip someone of their rank; unseat, dethrone; *Military* cashier.
OPPOSITE promote.

degraded ▶ adjective **1** *you made me feel so degraded* **humiliated**, demeaned, debased, cheapened, cheap, ashamed, abased; used.
OPPOSITES proud, dignified.
2 *he had revealed more of his degraded sensibilities than he realized* **degenerate**, corrupt, corrupted, depraved, perverted, decadent, dissolute, dissipated, debauched, immoral, base, sordid.
OPPOSITES moral, pure.

degrading ▶ adjective *claiming benefit can be a degrading experience* **humiliating**, demeaning, shaming, shameful, bringing shame, mortifying, abject, lowering, ignominious, undignified, inglorious, discrediting, wretched; menial; *informal* infra dig.
OPPOSITE ennobling.

degree ▶ noun **1** *those who have achieved a considerable degree of economic stability | the high degree of risk involved* **level**, stage, point, rung, standard, grade, gradation, mark; amount, extent, measure, magnitude, intensity, strength; proportion, ratio.
2 (*archaic*) *persons of unequal degree* **social class**, social status, rank, standing/position in society; *dated* station; *archaic* estate, condition.
□ **by degrees** *rivalries and prejudice were by degrees fading out* **gradually**, little by little, bit by bit, inch by inch, by stages, step by step, day by day, slowly, slowly but surely; piecemeal; *rare* inchmeal, gradatim.
OPPOSITES suddenly, all at once.
□ **to a degree** *to a degree, it is possible to educate oneself* **to some extent**, to a certain extent, up to a point, to a limited extent.

dehydrate ▶ verb **1** *alcohol and coffee dehydrate the skin* **dry**, dry up, dry out, desiccate, make dry, dehumidify, remove the moisture from; parch, sear; *technical* effloresce; *rare* exsiccate.
OPPOSITE hydrate.
2 *amphibians' skins must be kept moist or they will dehydrate and die* **dry up**, dry out, lose water, become dry; become thirsty.

deify ▶ verb **1** *she was deified by the early Romans as a fertility goddess* **worship**, revere, venerate, reverence, hold sacred, pay homage to, extol, exalt, adore; immortalize; *rare* divinize.
2 *he was deified by his colleagues and the press* **idolize**, apotheosize, lionize, hero-worship; idealize, glorify, aggrandize; *informal* put on a pedestal.
OPPOSITE demonize.

deign ▶ verb *I'm not going to hang around here waiting until you deign to come back to me* **condescend**, stoop, lower oneself, descend, think fit, see fit, deem it worthy of oneself, consent, vouchsafe; demean oneself, humble oneself; *informal* come down from one's high horse.

deity ▶ noun **god**, **goddess**, divine being, celestial being, supreme being, divinity, immortal; creator, demiurge; godhead; daemon, numen; *Hinduism* avatar.

dejected ▶ adjective *he looked so dejected that Alice began to have second thoughts* **downcast**, downhearted, despondent, disconsolate, dispirited, crestfallen, cast down, depressed, disappointed, disheartened, discouraged, demoralized, crushed, desolate, heartbroken, broken-hearted, heavy-hearted, low-spirited, in the doldrums, sad, unhappy, doleful, melancholy, miserable, woebegone, forlorn, long-faced, fed up, wretched, glum, gloomy, dismal; shamefaced, hangdog; *informal* blue, choked, down, down in the mouth, down in the dumps; *Brit. informal* brassed off, cheesed off, looking as if one had lost a pound and found a penny; *literary* dolorous; *archaic* chap-fallen.

D

OPPOSITES cheerful, happy.

dejection ▶ noun *he wandered around in a state of utter dejection* **despondency**, depression, downheartedness, dispiritedness, disconsolateness, disappointment, discouragement, desolation, despair, heavy-heartedness, unhappiness, sadness, sorrowfulness, sorrow, dolefulness, melancholy, misery, forlornness, wretchedness, glumness, gloom, gloominess, low spirits; *informal* the blues, the dumps; *rare* mopery.
OPPOSITE happiness.

de jure ▶ adverb & adjective **by right**, rightfully, legally, according to the law; rightful, legal.
OPPOSITE de facto.

D

delay ▶ verb **1** *a few guests were delayed by rush-hour traffic* **detain**, hold up, make late, retard, keep (back), slow up, slow down, set back, bog down; hinder, hamper, impede, obstruct.
2 *time being of the essence, they delayed no longer* **linger**, dally, take one's time, drag one's feet, be slow, hold back, lag/fall behind, dawdle, loiter, not keep pace, waste time; procrastinate, stall, play for time, buy time, hang fire, mark time, temporize, hesitate, dither, shilly-shally; stonewall, filibuster; *informal* dilly-dally, let the grass grow under one's feet; *dated* tarry.
OPPOSITE hurry.
3 *he may decide to delay the next cut in interest rates* **postpone**, put off, defer, hold over, shelve, suspend, stay, hold in abeyance, pigeonhole; reschedule, adjourn; *N. Amer.* put over, table, lay on the table; *N. Amer. Law* continue; *informal* put on ice, put on the back burner, put in cold storage; *rare* remit, respite.
OPPOSITES advance, bring forward.
▶ noun **1** *drivers heading for the capital are certain to face lengthy delays | the delay between the exchange of contracts and completion* **hold-up**, wait, waiting period, detainment; hindrance, impediment, obstruction, setback; interval, gap, interlude.
2 *the delay of his trial* **postponement**, deferral, deferment, putting off, stay, respite; rescheduling, adjournment; *N. Amer. Law* continuation; *rare* put-off.
3 *I set off without delay* **lingering**, dallying, dawdling, loitering; **procrastination**, stalling, hesitation, dithering, shilly-shallying; *informal* dilly-dallying; *dated* tarrying; *rare* cunctation.

delectable ▶ adjective **1** *a delectable meal* **delicious**, mouth-watering, appetizing, flavoursome, flavourful, toothsome, inviting, very enjoyable, very palatable; succulent, luscious, rich, sweet; tasty, savoury, piquant; *informal* scrumptious, delish, scrummy, yummy, yum-yum; *Brit. informal* moreish; *N. Amer. informal* finger-licking, nummy; *literary* ambrosial; *rare* ambrosian, nectareous, nectarean, flavorous, sapid.
OPPOSITES inedible, unpalatable.
2 *the delectable Ms Davis* **delightful**, lovely, adorable, captivating, charming, enchanting, winning, engaging, appealing, beguiling; **beautiful**, ravishing, gorgeous, stunning, pretty, extremely attractive, alluring, enticing, sexy, seductive, desirable, luscious; *Scottish & N. English* bonny; *informal* divine, heavenly, dreamy, sensational, knockout, drop-dead; *Brit. informal* tasty; *N. Amer. informal* babelicious, bodacious, bootylicious; *archaic* fair, comely; *rare* pulchritudinous.
OPPOSITES ugly, unattractive.

delectation ▶ noun *they had all manner of goodies for our delectation* **enjoyment**, gratification, delight, pleasure, happiness, satisfaction, relish; entertainment, amusement, diversion; titillation.

delegate ▶ noun *delegates from the UN | trade union delegates* **representative**, envoy, emissary, commissioner, agent, deputy, commissary; spokesperson, spokesman, spokeswoman; ambassador, plenipotentiary; messenger, go-between, proxy; *Scottish* depute; *Roman Catholic Church* nuncio; *archaic* legate.
▶ verb **1** *she must learn to delegate routine tasks to others* **assign**, **entrust**, give, pass on, hand on/over, turn over, consign, devolve, depute, transfer.
2 *members of the Council delegated to negotiate with the Baltic States* **authorize**, commission, depute, appoint, nominate, name, mandate, empower, charge, choose, select, designate, elect; *Military* detail.

delegation ▶ noun **1** *a delegation from the South African government* **deputation**, delegacy, legation, (diplomatic) mission, commission; delegates, representatives, envoys, emissaries, deputies; contingent, group, party, body.
2 *the delegation of tasks to others* **assignment**, entrusting, giving, committal, devolution, deputation, transference.

delete ▶ verb *the offending paragraph was deleted from the letter* **remove**, cut out, take out, edit out, expunge, excise, eradicate, cancel; **cross out**, strike out, put a line through, blue-pencil, ink out, score out, scratch out, obliterate, white out; rub out, erase, efface, wipe out, blot out; *Computing, informal* kill; *Printing* dele; *Brit. trademark* Tippex out.
OPPOSITES add, insert.

deleterious ▶ adjective *these policies are having a deleterious effect on British industry* **harmful**, damaging, detrimental, injurious, inimical, hurtful, bad, adverse, disadvantageous, unfavourable, unfortunate, undesirable; destructive, pernicious, ruinous.
OPPOSITES beneficial, advantageous.

deliberate ▶ adjective **1** *a deliberate attempt to provoke conflict* **intentional**, calculated, conscious, done on purpose, intended, planned, meant, considered, studied, knowing, wilful, wanton, purposeful, purposive, premeditated, pre-planned, thought out in advance, prearranged, preconceived, predetermined; aforethought; voluntary, volitional; *Law, dated* prepense.
OPPOSITES accidental, unintentional.
2 *she took a couple of small, deliberate steps towards him* **careful**, cautious, unhurried, measured, regular, even, steady; leisurely; laborious, ponderous.
OPPOSITE hasty.
3 *a careful and deliberate worker* **methodical**, systematic, careful, painstaking, meticulous, thorough.
OPPOSITE careless.
▶ verb *there was a long painful silence while she* **deliberated on** *his words | they sat and deliberated what to do with him* **think about**, think over, ponder, consider, contemplate, reflect on, muse on, meditate on, ruminate on, mull over, chew over, turn over in one's mind, give thought to, cogitate about; brood over, dwell on; put on one's thinking cap, be in a brown study; discuss, debate, weigh up; *N. Amer.* think on; *archaic* pore on; *rare* excogitate, cerebrate.

deliberately ▶ adverb **1** *he deliberately tried to hurt me* **intentionally**, on purpose, purposely, by design, knowingly, wittingly, consciously, purposefully; premeditatedly, calculatedly, in cold blood, wilfully, wantonly; with malice aforethought.
OPPOSITES by mistake, accidentally.
2 *he rose and walked deliberately down the aisle* **carefully**, unhurriedly, steadily, evenly, measuredly; cautiously, slowly, laboriously, ponderously.
OPPOSITE hastily.

deliberation ▶ noun **1** *after much deliberation, I decided to accept* **thought**, thinking, consideration, reflection, contemplation, cogitation, pondering, weighing up, musing, meditation, rumination, brooding; discussion, debate, consultation, conferring; *rare* excogitation, cerebration.
2 *he replaced the glass on the table with deliberation* **care**, carefulness, lack of haste, steadiness; caution, slowness, laboriousness, ponderousness.
OPPOSITE haste.

delicacy ▶ noun **1** *miniature pearls of exquisite delicacy | the fabric's delicacy* **fineness**, exquisiteness, delicateness, intricacy, daintiness, airiness, elegance, gracefulness, grace; flimsiness, gauziness, floatiness, silkiness.
OPPOSITES crudeness, coarseness.
2 *the children's delicacy was apparently inherited from their mother* **sickliness**, poor/ill health, valetudinarianism, frailty, frailness, fragility, feebleness, weakness, debility; infirmity.
OPPOSITE robustness.
3 *the delicacy of the situation* **difficulty**, trickiness; **sensitivity**, sensitiveness, ticklishness, awkwardness, touchiness, controversiality.
4 *I have to treat this matter with the utmost delicacy* **care**, sensitivity, tact, discretion, diplomacy, finesse, subtlety, consideration, considerateness, sensibility.
OPPOSITES clumsiness, ineptness, insensitivity.
5 *his delicacy of touch* **deftness**, dexterousness, skill, skilfulness, adeptness, adroitness, expertise.
OPPOSITES clumsiness, ineptness.
6 *the delicacy of the mechanism* **sensitivity**, precision, accuracy, exactness.
7 *the crabs are an Australian delicacy* **choice food**, gourmet food, dainty, treat, luxury, titbit, bonne bouche; speciality; *N. Amer.* tidbit; *archaic* cate.

delicate ▶ adjective **1** *delicate embroidery | delicate fabrics* **fine**, exquisite, intricate, dainty, airy, elegant, graceful; **flimsy**, gauzy, filmy, floaty, gossamer, diaphanous, chiffony, silky, wispy, thin, insubstantial, papery.
OPPOSITES crude; coarse.
2 *a delicate shade of blue* **subtle**, soft, subdued, muted; **pastel**, pale, light.
OPPOSITES bold, vibrant; lurid.
3 *delicate bone-china cups* **fragile**, breakable, easily broken/damaged, frail, frangible; eggshell.
OPPOSITES strong, durable.
4 *his wife is delicate* **sickly**, in poor health, unhealthy, valetudinarian, frail, feeble, weak, weakly, debilitated; unwell, infirm, ailing, poorly; *N. English informal* nesh.
OPPOSITES healthy, strong, robust.
5 *a delicate issue* **difficult**, tricky, sensitive, ticklish, awkward, problematic, problematical, touchy, prickly, controversial, emotive, embarrassing; *informal* sticky, dicey.
OPPOSITE uncontroversial.
6 *the matter required delicate handling* **careful**, considerate, sensitive; **tactful**, diplomatic, discreet, gentle, kid-glove, softly-softly.
OPPOSITES inept, clumsy, insensitive.
7 *his delicate ball-playing skills* **deft**, dexterous, skilled, skilful, expert, finely judged, adept, adroit, neat, slick; *informal* nifty.
OPPOSITES clumsy, inept.
8 *Faustina's delicate palate* **discriminating**, discerning; **fastidious**, fussy,

finicky, dainty, hard to please; *informal* picky, choosy, pernickety, faddy, faddish.
9 *a delicate mechanism* **sensitive**, precision, precise, accurate, exact.

delicious ▶ **adjective 1** *a delicious meal* **mouth-watering**, appetizing, tasty, flavoursome, flavourful, delectable, toothsome, inviting, very enjoyable, very palatable; succulent, luscious, rich, sweet; savoury, piquant; *informal* scrumptious, delish, scrummy, yummy, yum-yum; *Brit. informal* moreish; *N. Amer. informal* finger-licking, nummy; *literary* ambrosial; *rare* ambrosian, nectareous, nectarean, flavorous, sapid.
OPPOSITES inedible, unpalatable.
2 *a delicious languor was stealing over her* **delightful**, exquisite, delectable, lovely, pleasurable, extremely pleasant/enjoyable; *informal* glorious, heavenly, divine.
OPPOSITES unpleasant, horrible.

delight ▶ **verb 1** *her lack of reserve delighted him* **please greatly**, charm, enchant, captivate, entrance, bewitch, thrill, excite, take someone's breath away; gladden, gratify, appeal to, do someone's heart good, entertain, amuse, divert; *informal* send, tickle, give someone a buzz, give someone a kick, tickle pink, bowl over.
OPPOSITES dismay, displease; disgust.
2 *Fabia* **delighted in** *his touch* **take great pleasure**, find great pleasure, glory, revel, luxuriate, wallow; adore, love, relish, savour, enjoy greatly, lap up; *informal* get a kick out of, have a thing about, get a buzz out of, get a thrill out of, get a charge out of, get off on, dig; *N. Amer. informal* get a bang out of.
OPPOSITES dislike, loathe.
▶ **noun** *she squealed with delight* **pleasure**, happiness, joy, joyfulness, glee, gladness, gratification, relish, excitement, amusement; bliss, rapture, ecstasy, elation, euphoria; transports of delight; *humorous* delectation; *rare* jouissance.
OPPOSITES displeasure, pain.

delighted ▶ **adjective** *a delighted smile | we're delighted to have him back* **very pleased**, glad, happy, joyful, thrilled, overjoyed, ecstatic, euphoric, elated, blissful, enraptured, on cloud nine/seven, walking on air, in seventh heaven, in transports of delight, jumping for joy, beside oneself with happiness, excited; enchanted, charmed, entertained, gratified, amused, diverted, like a child with a new toy; gleeful, triumphant, cock-a-hoop; *French* enchanté; *informal* over the moon, tickled pink, like a dog with two tails, as pleased as Punch, on top of the world, on a high, as happy as Larry, blissed out, sent; *Brit. informal* chuffed; *N. English informal* made up; *N. Amer. informal* as happy as a clam; *Austral. informal* wrapped.
OPPOSITES dismayed, disappointed.

delightful ▶ **adjective 1** *a delightful evening* **very pleasant**, lovely, greatly to one's liking, very agreeable, very pleasurable; enjoyable, congenial, amusing, entertaining, diverting, gratifying, satisfying; marvellous, wonderful, magnificent, splendid, magical, exciting, thrilling, sublime; *informal* great, super, fantastic, fabulous, fab, terrific, heavenly, divine, glorious, grand, magic, out of this world, cool; *Brit. informal* brilliant, brill, smashing; *N. Amer. informal* peachy, neat, ducky; *Austral./NZ informal* beaut, bonzer; *Brit. informal, dated* capital, wizard, corking, spiffing, ripping, cracking, top-hole, topping, champion, beezer; *N. Amer. informal, dated* swell; *rare* frabjous.
OPPOSITES unpleasant, disagreeable.
2 *the delightful Sally Drayton* **charming**, enchanting, captivating, bewitching, entrancing, engaging, appealing, winning, fetching, sweet, endearing, cute; **lovely**, adorable, delectable, delicious, gorgeous, ravishing, beautiful, pretty, very attractive; *Scottish & N. English* bonny, couthy; *informal* dreamy, divine; *Brit. informal* tasty.
OPPOSITES unattractive, unappealing.

delimit ▶ **verb** *their responsibilities will be more strictly delimited* **determine**, establish, set, fix, mark (out/off), demarcate, bound, define, delineate.

delineate ▶ **verb 1** *the initial aims of the study as delineated by the deputy head* **describe**, set forth, set out, present, outline, depict, portray, represent, characterize; map out, chart; define, detail, specify, identify, particularize; *literary* limn.
2 *a section on the map delineated in red marker pen* **outline**, trace, draw the lines of, draw, sketch, block in, mark (out/off), delimit, mark the boundaries/limits of.

delineation ▶ **noun** *the accurate delineation of social problems in the area* **portrayal**, description, presentation, depiction, representation, picture, portrait, account.

delinquency ▶ **noun 1** *the social causes of teenage delinquency* **crime**, wrongdoing, criminality, lawbreaking, lawlessness, misconduct, misbehaviour; misdemeanours, offences, misdeeds.
2 (*formal*) *he relayed this in such a manner as to imply grave delinquency on the host's part* **negligence**, dereliction of duty, remissness, neglectfulness, irresponsibility.

delinquent ▶ **adjective 1** *delinquent teenagers* **lawless**, lawbreaking, criminal, offending; errant, badly behaved, troublesome, difficult, unmanageable, unruly, disobedient, uncontrollable, out of control.
OPPOSITES well behaved; conformist.
2 (*formal*) *delinquent parents need to face tougher penalties* **negligent**, neglectful, remiss, careless of one's duty, irresponsible, lax, slack; *N. Amer.* derelict; *rare* disregardful, inadvertent, oscitant.
OPPOSITE dutiful.
▶ **noun** *teenage delinquents* **offender**, wrongdoer, malefactor, lawbreaker, culprit, criminal; hooligan, vandal, ruffian, hoodlum; juvenile delinquent, young offender; *informal* juvie, tearaway; *Brit. informal* yob, yobbo; *archaic* miscreant.

delirious ▶ **adjective 1** *for much of the time she was delirious, but there were lucid intervals* **incoherent**, raving, babbling, irrational, hysterical, wild, feverish, frenzied; **deranged**, demented, unhinged, mad, insane, crazed, out of one's mind.
OPPOSITES lucid, coherent.
2 *there was a great roar from the delirious crowd* **ecstatic**, euphoric, elated, thrilled, overjoyed, beside oneself, walking on air, on cloud nine/seven, in seventh heaven, jumping for joy, in transports of delight, carried away, transported, rapturous, in raptures, exultant, jubilant, in a frenzy of delight, hysterical, wild with excitement, frenzied; *informal* blissed out, over the moon, on a high; *N. Amer. informal* wigged out; *rare* corybantic.
OPPOSITES disappointed, depressed.

delirium ▶ **noun 1** *before she died she had fits of delirium* **derangement**, dementia, dementedness, temporary madness/insanity; **incoherence**, raving, irrationality, hysteria, wildness, feverishness, frenzy, hallucination; *rare* calenture.
OPPOSITES lucidity, coherence.
2 *in the delirium of desire, she muttered his name over and over* **ecstasy**, rapture, transports, wild emotion, passion, wildness, excitement, frenzy, feverishness, fever; euphoria, elation.

deliver ▶ **verb 1** *the parcel was delivered to his house yesterday* **bring**, take, take round, convey, carry, transport, distribute, drop-ship; send, dispatch, remit.
OPPOSITE collect.
2 *the money should have been* **delivered up** *to the official receiver* **hand over**, turn over, transfer, make over, sign over; surrender, give up, yield, relinquish, cede, render up; consign, commit, entrust, trust, commend.
3 *he was delivered from his enemies* **save**, rescue, set free, free, liberate, release, set at liberty, set loose, extricate, discharge, emancipate, redeem, ransom; *literary* disenthral; *historical* manumit.
4 *the President delivered a six-minute radio address | the court was due to deliver its verdict* **utter**, give, make, read, recite, broadcast, give voice to, voice, speak, declaim; **pronounce**, announce, declare, proclaim, hand down, bring in, return, render, set forth.
5 *Paul delivered a two-handed blow to the back of his head* **administer**, deal, inflict, give, direct, aim; *informal* land.
6 *as he delivered the first ball of his third over, he stumbled* **bowl**, pitch, hurl, throw, cast, launch, lob; discharge, fire off; *Brit. Sport* flight.
7 *the trip delivered everything she had wanted* **provide**, supply, furnish.
8 *we have taken significant action to* **deliver on** *our commitments* **fulfil**, live up to, carry out, carry through, implement, make good; achieve; *informal* come up with, deliver the goods, come across.
9 *she returned to Madras to deliver her child* **give birth to**, bear, be delivered of, have, bring into the world, bring forth; *N. Amer.* birth; *informal* drop; *archaic* be brought to bed of.

deliverance ▶ **noun 1** *their deliverance from prison* **liberation**, release, freeing, rescue, delivery, discharge, ransom, emancipation; salvation, redemption; *historical* manumission.
2 *the tone he adopted for such deliverances* **utterance**, statement, announcement, pronouncement, declaration, proclamation; lecture, sermon, speech, oration, disquisition, peroration.

delivery ▶ **noun 1** *the delivery of the goods* **conveyance**, carriage, transportation, transporting, transport, distribution; dispatch, remittance; freightage, haulage, portage, shipment.
OPPOSITE collection.
2 *we are receiving several deliveries a day* **consignment**, load, batch; shipment, container load, boatload, shipload, lorryload, truckload.
3 *practically all deliveries take place in hospital* **birth**, childbirth; *technical* parturition; *archaic* confinement, accouchement.
4 *he reached 59 runs off only 42 deliveries* **ball bowled**, throw, bowl, lob, pitch.
5 *her delivery was stilted* **manner of speaking**, speech, pronunciation, enunciation, articulation, intonation, elocution; utterance, expression, presentation, recitation, recital, performance, execution; *French* façon de parler.

delude ▶ **verb** *you're lying—why do you persist in trying to delude me?* **mislead**, deceive, fool, take in, trick, dupe, hoodwink, double-cross, gull, beguile, lead on; cheat, defraud, swindle; *informal* con, bamboozle, pull the wool over someone's eyes, pull a fast one on, lead up the garden path, take for a ride, put one over on; *N. Amer. informal* sucker, snooker, hornswoggle; *Austral. informal* pull a swifty on; *literary* cozen, illude.

deluge ▶ **noun 1** *many homes were swept away by the deluge* **flood**, flash flood, torrent; *Brit.* spate.
2 *yesterday's deluge had turned the pitch into a muddy swamp* **downpour**, torrential rain, torrent of rain; thunderstorm, rainstorm, cloudburst.

D

D

OPPOSITE drizzle.
3 *a deluge of complaints* **barrage**, volley; **flood**, torrent, avalanche, stream, storm, shower, cascade, spate, wave, rush, outpouring.
OPPOSITE trickle.
▶ **verb 1** *caravans were deluged by the heavy rains* **flood**, inundate, engulf, submerge, swamp, drown.
2 *we have been deluged with calls for information* **inundate**, overwhelm, overload, overrun, flood, swamp, snow under, engulf; shower, bombard.

delusion ▶ **noun 1** *the male delusion that attractive young women are harbouring romantic thoughts about them* **misapprehension**, mistaken impression, false impression, mistaken belief, misconception, misunderstanding, mistake, error, misinterpretation, misconstruction, misbelief; fallacy, illusion, figment of the imagination, fantasy, chimera; fool's paradise, self-deception.
2 *a web of delusion* **deception**, misleading, deluding, fooling, tricking, trickery, duping.

delusive ▶ **adjective** *events showed that such hope was delusive* **misleading**, deceptive; misconceived, mistaken, false, in error, illusory, chimerical, insubstantial; *rare* delusory, illusive.
OPPOSITES well founded, genuine.

de luxe ▶ **adjective** *a de luxe hotel* **luxurious**, luxury, sumptuous, palatial, opulent, splendid, magnificent, lavish, grand, rich, superior, high-class, quality, exclusive, choice, select, elegant, well appointed, fancy; expensive, costly; *Brit.* upmarket; *informal* plush, plushy, posh, classy, ritzy, swanky, pricey; *Brit. informal* swish; *N. Amer. informal* swank, loaded; *rare* palatian, Lucullan.
OPPOSITES basic, cheap, downmarket.

delve ▶ **verb 1** *she delved in her pocket* **rummage (about/around/round) in**, search (through), hunt through, scrabble about/around in, root about/around in, ferret (about/around) in, fish about/around in, poke about/around in, dig in, grub about/around in, go through, burrow in; rifle through, scour, ransack, turn upside down, turn inside out; *Brit. informal* rootle around in; *Austral./NZ informal* fossick through; *rare* roust around in.
2 *the society is determined to* **delve** *deeper* **into** *the matter* **investigate**, conduct investigations into, make enquiries into, enquire into, probe, examine, explore, research, study, look into, go into; try to get to the bottom of.

demagogue ▶ **noun** **rabble-rouser**, political agitator, agitator, soapbox orator, firebrand; troublemaker, incendiary; *informal* tub-thumper.

demand ▶ **noun 1** *his demands for electoral reform | I finally gave in to her demands* **request**, call; command, order, dictate, ultimatum, stipulation; (**demands**) insistence, pressure, clamour, importunity, urging; *Austral./NZ informal* a big ask; *archaic* behest, hest.
2 *a job that fits in with the demands of a young family* **requirement**, need, desire, wish, want; claim, imposition, exigency.
3 *the big* **demand** *for such toys* **market**, call, appetite, desire; run on, rush on.
□ **in demand** *his work is much in demand by magazines who like such candid portraiture* **sought-after**, desired, coveted, wanted, requested, required; marketable, desirable, popular, in vogue, fashionable, all the rage, at a premium, like gold dust; *informal* big, trendy, hot, to die for; *Brit. informal, dated* all the go.
OPPOSITE unpopular.
▶ **verb 1** *workers demanded wage increases* **call for**, ask for, request, press for, push for, hold out for, clamour for, bay for; **insist on**, lay claim to, claim, requisition.
2 *Harvey* **demanded that** *I tell him the truth* **order to**, command to, tell to, call on to, enjoin to, urge to; *literary* bid.
3 *'Where is she?' he demanded* **ask**, inquire, question, interrogate; challenge.
4 *a complex activity demanding detailed knowledge* **require**, need, necessitate, call for, take, involve, entail; cry out for, want.
5 *most of those who contacted us demanded complete anonymity* **insist on**, stipulate, make a condition of, exact, impose; expect, look for.

demanding ▶ **adjective 1** *a demanding task* **difficult**, **challenging**, testing, taxing, exacting, tough, hard, onerous, burdensome, stressful, formidable; arduous, tiring, wearing, exhausting, wearying, wearisome, draining, uphill, rigorous, gruelling, back-breaking, Herculean, punishing; *informal* a tall order; *Brit. informal* knackering; *archaic* toilsome.
OPPOSITES easy, effortless.
2 *a demanding child | her demanding behaviour* **nagging**, clamorous, importunate, insistent; possessive; trying, tiresome, hard to please; *rare* exigent.
OPPOSITE easy-going.

demarcate ▶ **verb** *plots of land demarcated by barbed wire* **separate**, divide, mark (out/off), delimit, distinguish, differentiate, delineate; bound.

demarcation ▶ **noun 1** *a clear demarcation of function between administrative and judicial business* **separation**, distinction, differentiation, division; delimitation, marking off, definition.
2 *territorial demarcations* **boundary**, border, borderline, frontier, bound, limit; dividing line, line, divide.

demean ▶ **verb** *his actions only served to demean him in the eyes of the public* **discredit**, lower, lower someone's dignity, lower someone's status, degrade, debase, devalue, demote; **cheapen**, abase, humble, humiliate, disgrace, dishonour; (**demean oneself**) condescend, deign, stoop, descend.
OPPOSITES dignify, exalt.

demeaning ▶ **adjective** *a demeaning experience | demeaning work* **degrading**, humiliating, shaming, shameful, bringing shame, mortifying, abject, lowering, ignominious, undignified, inglorious, discrediting; menial; *informal* infra dig.
OPPOSITE ennobling.

demeanour ▶ **noun** *his normally calm demeanour* **manner**, air, attitude, appearance, look, aspect, mien, cast; **bearing**, carriage, way of carrying oneself; **behaviour**, conduct, way of behaving, comportment; *Brit.* deportment.

demented ▶ **adjective** *the ravings of a demented old man* **mad**, insane, deranged, out of one's mind, not in one's right mind, crazed, lunatic, unbalanced, unhinged, unstable, disturbed, distracted, as mad as a hatter, as mad as a March hare, stark mad; *Latin* non compos mentis; *informal* crazy, mental, off one's head, out of one's head, off one's nut, nutty, nutty as a fruitcake, off one's rocker, not (quite) right in the head, round the bend, raving mad, stark staring/raving mad, bats, batty, bonkers, cuckoo, loopy, loony, bananas, loco, dippy, screwy, with a screw loose, touched, gaga, doolally, up the pole, not all there, out to lunch, off the wall, not right upstairs, away with the fairies; *Brit. informal* barmy, crackers, barking, barking mad, round the twist, off one's trolley, as daft as a brush, not the full shilling, one sandwich short of a picnic; *N. Amer. informal* buggy, nutsy, nutso, out of one's tree, meshuga, squirrelly, wacko, gonzo; *Canadian & Austral./NZ informal* bushed; *NZ informal* porangi.
OPPOSITE sane.

dementia ▶ **noun** **mental illness**, madness, insanity, derangement, lunacy; senile dementia, Alzheimer's disease, Alzheimer's; *informal* softening of the brain.
OPPOSITE sanity.

demise ▶ **noun 1** *her tragic demise* **death**, dying, passing, passing away, passing on, loss of life, expiry, expiration, end, departure from life, final exit; *Law* decease; *rare* quietus.
OPPOSITE birth.
2 *the demise of the Ottoman empire* **end**, break-up, disintegration, fall, downfall, ruin; failure, collapse, foundering.
OPPOSITE start.

demobilize ▶ **verb** *the militia were demobilized* **disband**, decommission, discharge; *Brit. informal* demob.
OPPOSITE conscript.

democracy ▶ **noun** **representative government**, elective government, constitutional government, popular government; self-government, government by the people, autonomy; republic, commonwealth.
OPPOSITES tyranny; dictatorship.

democratic ▶ **adjective** *a democratic government | democratic countries* **elected**, representative, parliamentary, popular, of the people, populist; egalitarian, classless; self-governing, autonomous, republican.
OPPOSITES totalitarian, despotic.

demolish ▶ **verb 1** *the explosion demolished a block of flats* **knock down**, pull down, tear down, bring down, destroy, flatten, raze, raze to the ground, level, reduce to ruins, bulldoze, break up, topple; blow up, blow to bits/pieces, obliterate, annihilate, wipe off the face of the earth, wipe off the map; dismantle, disassemble; *N. Amer. informal* total; *dated* throw down; *rare* unbuild.
OPPOSITES build, construct.
2 *they have demolished her credibility* **destroy**, ruin, wreck, put an end to, smash, crush, squelch, squash; refute, disprove, prove wrong, discredit, overturn, explode, give the lie to, drive a coach and horses through; *informal* shoot full of holes, blow sky-high, blow out of the water, do for.
OPPOSITES confirm, strengthen.
3 (*informal*) *Arsenal demolished Coventry City 3–0* **defeat utterly**, beat hollow, win a resounding victory over, crush, drub, rout, give someone a drubbing, overwhelm; *informal* hammer, clobber, thrash, paste, give someone a pasting, whip, pound, pulverize, destroy, annihilate, wipe the floor with, take to the cleaners, make mincemeat of, slaughter, murder, massacre, crucify, flatten, turn inside out, run rings around; *Brit. informal* stuff; *N. Amer. informal* shellac, blow out, cream, skunk.
OPPOSITES lose, be defeated.
4 (*informal*) *Brown was busy demolishing a sausage roll* **devour**, eat (up), consume, guzzle, gobble, wolf down, polish off, finish off, gulp down, bolt; *informal* put away, nosh, get outside of, pack away, shovel down, scoff (down), stuff one's face with, stuff oneself with, pig oneself on, pig out on, sink, get one's laughing gear round; *Brit. informal* gollop, shift; *N. Amer. informal* scarf (down/up), snarf (down/up), inhale; *rare* ingurgitate.

demolition ▶ **noun 1** *the demolition of the building* **destruction**, knocking down, pulling down, tearing down, flattening, razing, levelling,

bulldozing, clearance; obliteration, annihilation.
OPPOSITE construction.
2 *the demolition of this theory* **destruction**, wrecking; **refutation**, disproval, disproving.
OPPOSITE confirmation.
3 (*informal*) *New Zealand's demolition of England* **defeat**, conquest, vanquishing, trouncing, routing, rout; *informal* massacre, annihilation, slaughter, licking, thrashing, clobbering, hammering.

demon ▶ noun **1** *the demons from hell* **devil**, fiend, evil spirit, fallen angel, cacodemon; incubus, succubus; hellhound; *Arabian & Muslim mythology* afreet; *Hindu mythology* rakshasa.
OPPOSITE angel.
2 *the man was a demon and he had hurt her to the depths of her being* **monster**, ogre, fiend, devil, villain, brute, savage, beast, barbarian, animal.
OPPOSITE saint.
3 *Surrey's fast-bowling demon | a demon tennis player* **genius**, wizard, expert, master, adept, virtuoso, maestro, past master, marvel, prodigy; star; *German* wunderkind; *informal* hotshot, wiz, whizz, whizz-kid, buff, old hand, pro, ace, something else, something to shout about, something to write home about; *Brit. informal* dab hand; *N. Amer. informal* maven, crackerjack; *rare* proficient.
OPPOSITE amateur.
4 *the demon of creativity. See* DAEMON.

WORD LINKS
study of demons **demonology**

demonic, demoniac, demoniacal ▶ adjective **1** *demonic powers* **devilish**, diabolic, diabolical, fiendish, satanic, Mephistophelian, hellish, infernal, evil, wicked, ungodly, unholy; *rare* cacodemonic.
OPPOSITE angelic.
2 *the demonic intensity of his playing* **wild**, **frenzied**, feverish, frenetic, hectic, frantic, furious, hysterical; **maniacal**, manic, like one possessed.

demonstrable ▶ adjective *there are demonstrable links between French and American art* **verifiable**, provable, attestable, evincible; verified, proven, confirmed; obvious, clear, clear-cut, plain, evident, apparent, manifest, patent, conspicuous, prominent, transparent, striking, distinct, noticeable, perceptible, observable, unmistakable, undeniable, self-evident.
OPPOSITE unverifiable.

demonstrate ▶ verb **1** *his findings demonstrate that boys commit more offences than girls* **show**, show beyond doubt, indicate, determine, establish, prove, validate, confirm, verify, corroborate, substantiate, constitute evidence, constitute proof.
2 *she was asked to demonstrate quilting to the Women's Institute* **give a demonstration of**, show how something is done, show how something works; exhibit, display, show, illustrate, exemplify, give an idea of.
3 *his work demonstrated an analytical ability* **reveal**, bespeak, indicate, signify, signal, denote, show, display, exhibit, express, manifest, evince, evidence, be evidence of, be an indication of, bear witness to, testify to; imply, intimate, give away; *informal* spell; *literary* betoken.
OPPOSITE hide.
4 *students demonstrated against the Government* **protest**, rally, hold a rally, march, parade; sit in, stage a sit-in, picket, form a picket line, strike, go on strike, walk out; mutiny, rebel.

demonstration ▶ noun **1** *there can be no valid demonstration of God's existence* **proof**, substantiation, confirmation, affirmation, corroboration, verification, validation; evidence, indication, witness, testament.
2 *there will be a talk on woodcarving followed by a demonstration* **exhibition**, **presentation**, display, illustration, exposition, teach-in; *informal* demo, expo, taster.
3 *his paintings are a powerful demonstration of his talents* **manifestation**, **indication**, revelation, sign, mark, token, embodiment, record; expression; *rare* evincement.
4 *he travelled to Paris to join an anti-racism demonstration* **protest**, protest march, march, parade, rally, lobby, sit-in, sit-down, sleep-in, stoppage, strike, walkout, picket, picket line, blockade; *Indian* morcha, gherao, hartal; *informal* demo, get-together.

demonstrative ▶ adjective **1** *we were a very demonstrative family* **expressive**, open, forthcoming, emotional, communicative, responsive, unreserved, unrestrained, effusive, expansive, gushing, non-reticent, affectionate, cuddly, loving, warm, friendly, approachable; *informal* touchy-feely, lovey-dovey.
OPPOSITES undemonstrative, reserved.
2 *these military successes are demonstrative of their skill* **indicative**, indicatory, suggestive, illustrative, evincive, expository.
3 *he presented demonstrative evidence of his theorem* **convincing**, definite, positive, telling, conclusive, certain, decisive, material, airtight, watertight; incontrovertible, incontestable, irrefutable, unquestionable, undeniable, indisputable, unassailable.
OPPOSITE inconclusive.

demoralize ▶ verb **1** *they kept wages low, which demoralized the staff* **dishearten**, dispirit, deject, cast down, depress, dismay, daunt, discourage, unman, unnerve, crush, sap, shake, throw, cow, subdue, undermine, devitalize, weaken, enfeeble, enervate; break someone's spirit, bring someone low; *informal* knock the stuffing out of, knock for six, knock sideways.
OPPOSITES encourage, hearten.
2 (*archaic*) *she feared that her daughter might be demoralized by the free manners of the English* **lead astray**, corrupt, deprave, debauch, warp, pervert, subvert, make degenerate, debase, ruin, contaminate, sully, defile, infect, influence; *rare* vitiate.

demoralized ▶ adjective *the king's demoralized army broke and fled* **dispirited**, disheartened, downhearted, dejected, cast down, downcast, low, depressed, despairing; disconsolate, crestfallen, disappointed, dismayed, daunted, discouraged, unmanned, unnerved; crushed, humbled, cowed, subdued; sapped, drained, shaken, thrown, undermined, devitalized; *informal* fed up; *Brit. informal* brassed off, cheesed off; *vulgar slang* pissed off.

demote ▶ verb *she was demoted after a rift with her boss* **downgrade**, relegate, declass, move down, lower in rank, reduce in rank, strip of rank, reduce to the ranks; depose, unseat, dethrone, displace, oust, drum out, remove from office; *Military* cashier, disrate; *N. Amer.* bust.
OPPOSITE promote.

demotic ▶ adjective *in trade journals he would adopt a more demotic style* **popular**; **vernacular**, colloquial, idiomatic, vulgar, common; informal, everyday, non-literary, unofficial, slangy; *rare* enchorial.
OPPOSITE formal.

demur ▶ verb *Mr Steed demurred when the suggestion was put to him* **raise objections**, object, take exception, take issue, protest, lodge a protest, cavil, dissent; raise doubts, express doubt, express reluctance, express reservations, express misgivings, be unwilling, be reluctant, baulk, hesitate, think twice, hang back, drag one's heels, refuse; *informal* be cagey, boggle, kick up a fuss, kick up a stink.
▶ noun *they accepted the ruling without demur* **objection**, protest, protestation, complaint, dispute, dissent, carping, cavilling, recalcitrance, opposition, resistance; reservation, hesitation, reluctance, unwillingness, disinclination, lack of enthusiasm; doubts, qualms, misgivings, second thoughts; a murmur, a peep, a word, a sound; *informal* niggling, griping, grousing, boggling; *Law* demurrers; *rare* demurral.

demure ▶ adjective *the painting shows a demure Victorian miss* **modest**, unassuming, meek, mild, reserved, retiring, quiet, shy, bashful, diffident, reticent, timid, timorous, shrinking; coy; decorous, decent, seemly, ladylike, respectable, proper, virtuous, pure, innocent, maidenly, virginal, chaste; sober, sedate, staid, prim, prim and proper, priggish, prissy, prudish, goody-goody, strait-laced, puritanical, old-maidish; *informal* straight, starchy, uptight, square, butter-wouldn't-melt; *archaic* retired.
OPPOSITES brazen; shameless.

den ▶ noun **1** *the mink left its den* **lair**, sett, earth, drey, lodge, burrow, hole, tunnel, cave, dugout, hollow, covert, shelter, hiding place, hideout; *informal* hidey-hole.
2 *the club was a notorious drinking den* **haunt**, site, patch, hotbed, cradle, nest, pit, hole; place of crime, place of vice; *informal* joint, dive, dump.
3 *the poet was scribbling in his den* **study**, studio, library; **sanctum**, retreat, sanctuary, hideaway, snuggery, snug, cubbyhole; *N. Amer.* cubby; *informal* hidey-hole; *humorous* sanctum sanctorum.

denial ▶ noun **1** *reports of a revolt met with a denial from field commanders* **contradiction**, counterstatement, refutation, rebuttal, repudiation, disclaimer, retraction, abjuration; negation, dissent; *Law* disaffirmation; *rare* confutation, retractation.
OPPOSITE confirmation.
2 *the denial of insurance to people with certain medical conditions* **refusal**, withholding, withdrawal; rejection, dismissal, rebuff, repulse, declination, veto, turndown; *informal* thumbs down, red light, knock-back.
OPPOSITE acceptance.
3 *the denial of all worldly values* **renunciation**, renouncement, forsaking, eschewal, repudiation, disavowal, disowning, rejection, casting aside, casting off, abandonment, surrender, giving up, relinquishment; *rare* abjuration.
OPPOSITE embracing.

denigrate ▶ verb *it amused him to denigrate his guests* **disparage**, belittle, diminish, deprecate, cast aspersions on, decry, criticize unfairly, attack, speak ill of, speak badly of, blacken the character of, blacken the name of, give someone a bad name, sully the reputation of, spread lies about, defame, slander, libel, calumniate, besmirch, run down, abuse, insult, slight, revile, malign, vilify; *N. Amer.* slur; *informal* bad-mouth, slate, do a hatchet job on, pull to pieces, pull apart, sling mud at, throw mud at, drag through the mud; *Brit. informal* rubbish, slag off, have a go at; *rare* asperse, derogate, vilipend, vituperate.
OPPOSITE extol.

denizen ▶ noun *the denizens of Bolton were hungry for answers* **inhabitant**, resident, townsman, townswoman, native, local; occupier, occupant, dweller; *informal, derogatory* local yokel; *historical* burgher, burgess; *rare* habitant, residentiary, oppidan, indweller.

D

denominate ▶ verb *this baking process is technically denominated 'setting the sponge'* **call**, name, term, designate, style, dub, label, entitle; christen, baptize; *archaic* clepe.

denomination *See centre pages for list of* **Christian Denominations**
▶ noun **1** *he was associated with a Christian denomination known as the Collegians* **religious group**, **sect**, Church, cult, movement, faith community, body, persuasion, religious persuasion, communion, order, fraternity, brotherhood, sisterhood, school; faith, creed, belief, religious belief, religion; *rare* sodality.
2 *the banknotes come in a number of denominations* **value**, unit, grade, size, measure.
3 (*formal*) *they called the computer 'XT', a denomination that still stands today* **name**, title, term, designation, epithet, label, tag, style, sobriquet, nickname, byname; *informal* handle, moniker; *formal* appellation, cognomen; *rare* agnomen, allonym, anonym, appellative.

denote ▶ verb **1** *the elaborate headdresses denoted accomplished warriors* **designate**, **indicate**, be a sign of, be a mark of, signify, signal, symbolize, represent, stand for, mean; typify, characterize, distinguish, mark, identify; *literary* bespeak, betoken.
2 *he had an air about him that denoted an inner strength* **suggest**, point to, be evidence of, smack of, conjure up, bring to mind, indicate, show, reveal, demonstrate, intimate, imply, connote, convey, give away, betray; *informal* spell; *literary* bespeak.

denouement, **dénouement** ▶ noun **1** *the film's denouement was unsatisfying and ambiguous* **finale**, final scene, final act, last act, epilogue, coda, end, ending, finish, close; **culmination**, climax, conclusion, resolution, solution, clarification, unravelling; *informal* wind-up.
OPPOSITE beginning.
2 *the debate had an unexpected denouement* **outcome**, upshot, consequence, result, end result, end, ending, termination, culmination, climax; *informal* pay-off; *dated* issue; *archaic* success.
OPPOSITE origin.

denounce ▶ verb **1** *the pope denounced abortion and the use of contraceptives* **condemn**, criticize, attack, censure, castigate, decry, revile, vilify, besmirch, discredit, damn, reject, proscribe; find fault with, cast aspersions on, malign, pour scorn on, rail against, inveigh against, fulminate against, declaim against, give something a bad press, run something down; *N. Amer.* slur; *informal* bad-mouth, knock, pan, slam, hammer, blast, hit out at, lay into, lace into, pull to pieces, pull apart, savage, maul; *Brit. informal* slate, slag off, have a go at, give some stick to; *archaic* rate, slash, reprobate; *rare* vituperate, excoriate, arraign, objurgate, asperse, anathematize, animadvert on, denunciate.
OPPOSITE praise.
2 *he feared he would be denounced as a traitor* **expose**, betray, inform against, inform on; incriminate, implicate, cite, name, accuse; *informal* do; *archaic* inculpate.

dense ▶ adjective **1** *she stumbled through a dense birch forest* **close-packed**, closely packed, tightly packed, closely set, thick, packed, crowded, crammed, jammed together, compressed, compacted, compact, solid, tight; overgrown, jungle-like, jungly, impenetrable, impassable; *archaic* thickset.
OPPOSITE sparse.
2 *a fire can fill your home with dense smoke* **thick**, heavy, opaque, soupy, murky, smoggy, impenetrable; concentrated, condensed, of high density.
OPPOSITES thin; light.
3 (*informal*) *they were dense enough to believe me* **stupid**, unintelligent, ignorant, brainless, mindless, foolish, slow, slow-witted, dull-witted, witless, doltish, blockish, dunce-like, simple-minded, empty-headed, vacuous, vapid, half-witted, idiotic, moronic, imbecilic, obtuse, bovine, lumpish; gullible, naive; *informal* thick, dim, dumb, dopey, dippy, dozy, cretinous, as thick as two short planks, thickheaded, chuckleheaded, dunderheaded, wooden-headed, fat-headed, thick-skulled, muttonheaded, boneheaded, lamebrained, birdbrained, pea-brained, pig-ignorant, slow on the uptake, soft in the head, brain-dead, dead from the neck up; *Brit. informal* daft, not the full shilling; *S. African informal* dof; *W. Indian informal* dotish; *N. Amer. vulgar slang* dumb-ass.
OPPOSITE clever.

density ▶ noun *vitamin D deficiency causes a loss of bone density* **solidity**, solidness, denseness, thickness, substance, bulk, weight, mass; compactness, tightness, hardness.

WORD LINKS
measurement of density of liquids **hydrometry**

dent ▶ noun **1** *her hat had a dent at the crown | I made a dent in his car* **indentation**, dint, dimple, dip, depression, hollow, crater, pit, trough; *rare* concavity.
2 *lawyers' fees will make a nasty dent in their finances* **reduction**, depletion, deduction, cut, hole.
OPPOSITE increase.
▶ verb **1** *he grumbled that Jamie had dented his bike* **make a dent in**, make an indentation in, dint, indent, mark.
2 *the experience did not dent her confidence* **diminish**, reduce, lessen, shrink, weaken, erode, undermine, sap, shake, break, crush, cripple, destroy, damage, impair; *informal* put the kibosh on.
OPPOSITE increase.

dentist ▶ noun. *See centre pages for list of* **Doctors and Dentists**

denude ▶ verb *the island had been denuded of trees | the pines were denuded by a recent fire* **divest**, strip, clear, deprive, bereave, rob; **lay bare**, make bare, bare, uncover, expose; deforest, defoliate; *literary* despoil.
OPPOSITE cover.

deny ▶ verb **1** *the report was denied by several witnesses* **contradict**, repudiate, gainsay, declare untrue, dissent from, disagree with, challenge, contest, oppose; retract, take back, back-pedal; disprove, debunk, explode, discredit, refute, rebut, invalidate, negate, nullify, quash; *informal* shoot full of holes, shoot down (in flames); *Law* disaffirm; *rare* controvert, confute, negative.
OPPOSITE confirm.
2 *he found it difficult to deny the request* **refuse**, turn down, reject, rebuff, repulse, decline, veto, dismiss; *informal* knock back, give the thumbs down to, give the red light to, give the brush-off to.
OPPOSITE accept.
3 *she was told that she must deny her father and mother* **renounce**, turn one's back on, forswear, eschew, repudiate, disavow, disown, wash one's hands of, reject, discard, cast aside, cast off, abandon, surrender, give up, relinquish; *archaic* forsake; *rare* abjure, abnegate.
OPPOSITE embrace.

deny or refute?
See REFUTE.

deodorant ▶ noun **1** *she uses an underarm deodorant* **antiperspirant**, body spray, perfume, scent.
2 *in some cinemas they sprayed the auditorium with perfumed deodorant* **air-freshener**, deodorizer, fumigant.

deodorize ▶ verb *the sewage waters were deodorized without chemicals* **freshen**, sweeten, purify, disinfect, sanitize, sterilize; fumigate, aerate, air, ventilate; *rare* depollute.

depart ▶ verb **1** *James departed soon after lunch* **leave**, go, go away, go off, take one's leave, take oneself off, withdraw, absent oneself, say one's goodbyes, quit, make an exit, exit, break camp, decamp, retreat, beat a retreat, retire; make off, clear out, make oneself scarce, run off, run away, flee, fly, bolt; set off, set out, start out, get going, get under way, be on one's way; *informal* make tracks, up sticks, pack one's bags, shove off, push off, clear off, take off, skedaddle, scram, split, scoot, flit; *Brit. informal* sling one's hook; *N. Amer. informal* vamoose, hightail it, cut out; *formal* repair, remove; *literary* betake oneself; *rare* abstract oneself.
OPPOSITE arrive.
2 *the budget announcement departed from the trend of recent years* **deviate**, diverge, digress, drift, stray, slew, veer, swerve, turn away, turn aside, branch off, differ, vary, be different; be at variance with, run counter to, contrast with, contravene, contradict; *rare* divagate.

departed ▶ adjective *he saw the ghost of his departed wife* **dead**, deceased, late, lost, lamented; gone, no more, passed away, passed on, perished, expired, extinct; *informal* (as) dead as a doornail; *euphemistic* with God, asleep, at peace; *rare* demised.
OPPOSITE living.

department ▶ noun **1** *Percy worked in the public health department* **division**, section, sector, subsection, subdivision, unit, branch, arm, wing, segment, compartment; office, bureau, agency, ministry.
2 *the turnout was low in rural departments* **district**, administrative district, canton, province, territory, state, county, shire, parish; region, area, zone, sector, division; *archaic* demesne.
3 *don't ask me about the food—that's Kay's department* **domain**, territory, realm, province, preserve, jurisdiction, sphere, sphere of activity, area, area of interest, field, line, speciality, specialism; area of responsibility, responsibility, duty, function, business, affair, charge, task, occupation, job, concern; *informal* pigeon, baby, bag, thing, bailiwick, turf.

departure ▶ noun **1** *he thought of a ploy to delay her departure* **leaving**, going, going away, going off, leave-taking, withdrawal, exit, egress, quitting, decamping, retreat, retirement, retiral; flight, fleeing, running away, desertion; setting off, setting out, starting out.
OPPOSITE arrival.
2 *a departure from normality* **deviation**, divergence, digression, shift, variation, change.
3 *the film represents an exciting departure for feminist film-makers* **change of direction**, change, difference of emphasis, innovation, novelty, rarity.

depend ▶ verb **1** *their career progression depends on getting a good reference* **be contingent on**, be conditional on, be dependent on, turn on, pivot on, hinge on, hang on, rest on, be based on, rely on; be subject to, be controlled by, be determined by, be influenced by, be decided by, be resultant from, relate to.
2 *my employees and their families depend on me* **rely on**, place reliance on, lean on, cling to, be supported by, be sustained by, be unable to manage

without; count on, bank on, trust, trust in, put one's trust in, put one's faith in, have faith in, have (every) confidence in, believe in, swear by, be sure of, pin one's hope on.

dependable ▸ adjective *he was a solid and dependable person* **reliable**, trustworthy, honourable, true, faithful, loyal, constant, unswerving, unwavering, unfailing, sure, steadfast, steady, stable, trusty; **sensible**, responsible, conscientious, competent; *Brit. informal* copper-bottomed. OPPOSITE unreliable.

dependant ▸ noun *he wanted to provide for his dependants after his death* **child**, minor; ward, charge, protégé; relative, family member; hanger-on, parasite; (**dependants**) offspring, progeny; *archaic* fosterling.

dependence ▸ noun **1** *she cast off her **dependence on** her brother* **reliance on**, need for, seeking support from, leaning on, clinging to; trust in, faith in, confidence in, belief in.
2 *they help patients to cope with enforced dependence* **helplessness**, weakness, defencelessness, vulnerability; subservience, subordination. OPPOSITE independence.
3 *the figure show a rise in drug dependence* **addiction**, dependency, over-reliance, reliance; craving, compulsion, fixation, obsession; abuse.

dependency ▸ noun **1** *he saw no problem in a wife's **dependency on** her husband* **dependence**, reliance; need for, seeking support from, leaning on, clinging to.
2 *the automatic association of retirement with dependency* **helplessness**, dependence, weakness, defencelessness, vulnerability; subservience, subordination, inferiority. OPPOSITE independence.
3 *taking tranquillizers in large doses can lead to dependency* **addiction**, dependence, over-reliance, reliance; craving, compulsion, fixation, obsession; abuse.
4 *the army invaded a British dependency* **colony**, **protectorate**, province, dominion, outpost, satellite, satellite state; holding, possession; *historical* tributary, fief; *archaic* demesne.
5 *they work for a dependency of the parent firm* **subsidiary**, subordinate company, peripheral unit, adjunct, appendage, offshoot, auxiliary, attachment, satellite, derivative; *archaic* tributary.

dependent ▸ adjective **1** *your placement will be **dependent on** the decision of a third party* **conditional on**, contingent on, based on, depending on, resting on, hanging on, hingeing on; subject to, determined by, controlled by, influenced by, swayed by, resultant from.
2 *the army was still **dependent on** voluntary enlistment* **reliant on**, relying on, counting on, leaning on; supported by, sustained by.
3 *these people are **dependent on** drugs* **addicted to**, reliant on, over-reliant on, fixated on; given to using, given to abusing; *informal* hooked on.
4 *it's hard caring for someone who is ill and dependent* **reliant**, needy; **helpless**, weak, feeble, infirm, invalid, impotent, incapable, debilitated, disabled; defenceless, vulnerable; *informal* laid up.
5 *the island is a United Kingdom dependent territory* **subsidiary**, subject, subservient; satellite, ancillary; puppet; *historical* tributary. OPPOSITE independent.

depict ▸ verb **1** *the painting depicts Christ and the Virgin Mary* **portray**, represent, picture, illustrate, delineate, outline, reproduce, render; draw, paint, sketch, draft; *literary* limn.
2 *evolution is not the haphazard process depicted by Darwin's theory* **describe**, detail, relate, narrate, recount, unfold; present, set forth, set out, outline, delineate, sketch, paint; represent, portray, characterize; record, chronicle.

depiction ▸ noun **1** *a mirror with a depiction of Aphrodite on the reverse* **picture**, painting, portrait, drawing, sketch, study, illustration, portrayal, representation, image, likeness.
2 *he was criticized for his depiction of black women* **portrayal**, representation, presentation, description, delineation, characterization.

deplete ▸ verb *clan warfare has severely depleted the food supply* **exhaust**, use up, consume, expend, spend, drain, empty, sap, milk, suck dry, evacuate; reduce, decrease, diminish, lessen, lower, attenuate; slim down, pare down, cut back; *informal* bleed, slash. OPPOSITES augment; increase.

depletion ▸ noun *they enquired into the depletion of fish stocks* **exhaustion**, using up, use, consumption, expending, expenditure; draining, emptying, sapping, milking; reduction, decrease, dwindling, diminution, lessening, lowering, attenuation, impoverishment; *informal* bleeding. OPPOSITE augmentation.

deplorable ▸ adjective **1** *the conduct of the workers is deplorable* **disgraceful**, shameful, dishonourable, disreputable, discreditable, unworthy, shabby, inexcusable, unpardonable, unforgivable; reprehensible, despicable, abominable, base, sordid, vile, hateful, contemptible, loathsome, offensive, execrable, heinous, odious, revolting, unspeakable, beyond contempt, beyond the pale; *rare* egregious, flagitious. OPPOSITE admirable.
2 *the back garden is in a deplorable state* **lamentable**, regrettable, grievous, unfortunate, wretched, dire, atrocious, abysmal, very bad, awful, terrible, dreadful, diabolical; miserable, pitiable, pathetic, sorry, unhappy, sad, woeful; substandard, poor, inadequate, inferior, unsatisfactory, unacceptable; *informal* appalling, rotten, crummy, lousy, God-awful; *Brit. informal* chronic; *dated* frightful. OPPOSITE excellent.

deplore ▸ verb **1** *we deplore all use of violence and provocation* **abhor**, be shocked by, be offended by, be scandalized by, find unacceptable, be against, frown on; **disapprove of**, take a dim view of, look askance at, take exception to, detest, despise, execrate; **condemn**, denounce, decry, deprecate, censure, damn. OPPOSITE admire.
2 *he deplored the lack of flair in the England squad* **regret**, express regret about, lament, mourn, rue, bemoan, bewail, complain about, grieve over, express sorrow about, sorrow over, sigh over, cry over, weep over, shed tears over, beat one's breast about, wring one's hands over; *archaic* plain over. OPPOSITE applaud.

deploy ▸ verb **1** *paramilitary forces were deployed at strategic locations* **position**, station, post, place, install, locate, situate, site, establish; base, garrison; **distribute**, arrange, range, dispose, redistribute, spread out, extend, put into position; *informal* plant, park; *rare* posit. OPPOSITE concentrate.
2 *the Empress deployed all her social skills* **use**, utilize, employ, make use of, avail oneself of, turn to account, take advantage of, exploit; bring into service, bring into play, bring into action; have recourse to, call on, turn to, resort to.

deport ▸ verb **1** *immigrants without work permits were fined and deported* **expel**, banish, exile, transport, expatriate, extradite, repatriate; evict, oust, cast out, throw out, turn out, drive out, drum out; *informal* kick out, boot out, chuck out, give someone the boot, send packing, give someone their marching orders, throw someone out on their ear; *Brit. informal* turf out; *N. Amer. informal* give someone the bum's rush; *dated* out; (*in ancient Greece*) ostracize. OPPOSITE admit.
2 (*rare*) *he has **deported himself** with great dignity* **behave**, act, perform, conduct oneself, acquit oneself; bear oneself, carry oneself, hold oneself; *rare* comport oneself.

deportation ▸ noun *they called for the deportation of illegal immigrants* **expulsion**, expelling, banishment, banishing, exile, exiling, transportation, transporting, extradition, extraditing, expatriation, expatriating, repatriation, repatriating; eviction, evicting, ejection, ejecting, ousting, throwing out, casting out, turning out, driving out, drumming out; *informal* kicking out, booting out; *Brit. informal* turfing out; *dated* outing; (*in ancient Greece*) ostracism. OPPOSITE admission.

deportment ▸ noun **1** (*Brit.*) *poise is directly concerned with good deportment* **gait**, **posture**, carriage, comportment, bearing, stance, way of standing, way of holding oneself, way of carrying oneself, way of bearing oneself; attitude, demeanour, mien, air, appearance, aspect, style, manner.
2 (*N. Amer.*) *she reprimanded him for unprofessional deportment* **behaviour**, conduct, performance, way of behaving, way of acting, way of conducting oneself; etiquette, manners, ways, habits, practices; actions, acts, activities, exploits; *informal* capers.

depose ▸ verb **1** *the president was deposed by a right-wing junta* **overthrow**, overturn, topple, bring down, remove from office, remove, unseat, dethrone, supplant, displace; dismiss, discharge, oust, drum out, throw out, force out, drive out, expel, eject; strip of rank, demote; *Military* cashier; *informal* sack, fire, axe, chuck out, boot out, get rid of, give someone the push, give someone the boot, give someone their marching orders, show someone the door; *Brit. informal* turf out.
2 (*Law*) *an independent witness deposed that he had seen the accused* **swear**, testify, attest, undertake, assert, declare, profess, aver, submit, claim; swear on the Bible, swear under oath, state on oath, make a deposition, give an undertaking, solemnly promise; *rare* asseverate, represent.

deposit ▸ noun **1** *the floor was covered by a thick deposit of ash* **accumulation**, sediment, sublimate; layer, covering, coating, dusting, blanket.
2 *they discovered a new copper deposit* **seam**, vein, lode, layer, stratum, bed, accumulation.
3 *they made the booking and paid a deposit* **down payment**, part payment, advance payment, prepayment, instalment, security, retainer, pledge, stake; front money, money up front.
▸ verb **1** *she deposited a pile of school books on the table* **put (down)**, place, lay (down), set (down), unload, rest, settle, sit; drop, let fall, throw down, fling down; *informal* dump, stick, park, plonk, pop, shove; *Brit. informal* bung; *N. Amer. informal* plunk; *archaic* unlade; *rare* posit. OPPOSITE pick up.
2 *the silt was deposited by flood water* **leave behind**, leave, set down, let settle, precipitate, dump; wash up, cast up.
3 *the gold had been deposited at the Bank of England* **lodge**, bank, house,

store, stow, put away, hoard, lay in; entrust, consign, commit; *informal* stash, squirrel away, salt away, put aside for a rainy day; *rare* reposit.

deposition ▶ noun **1** *a commissioner is to take depositions from witnesses* **statement**, sworn statement, affidavit, attestation, affirmation, assertion; allegation, submission, declaration, pronouncement, profession; testimony, evidence; *rare* asseveration, averment, representation.
2 *the pebbles are formed by the deposition of calcium* **depositing**, settling; accumulation, build-up; *informal* dumping; *technical* precipitation.
3 *the barons plotted the King's deposition* **overthrow**, overturning, toppling, downfall, removal from office, removal, unseating, dethronement, supplanting, displacement, dismissal, discharge, ousting, drumming out, throwing out, forcing out, driving out, expulsion, expelling, ejection, ejecting; demotion; *N. Amer.* ouster; *informal* sacking, firing; *Brit. informal* turfing out; *rare* deposal.

D

depository ▶ noun *the burial chamber was used as a depository for a coin hoard* **repository**, cache, store, storage place, storeroom, storehouse, warehouse, depot; vault, strongroom, safe, safe deposit, safety deposit, bank, treasure house, treasury; container, receptacle; (*in the Far East*) godown; *informal* lock-up; *archaic* garner.

depot ▶ noun **1** *the bus pulled into the depot* **terminal**, terminus, station, garage; bus station, coach station, railway station, train station; headquarters, base.
2 *he was killed in an explosion at an arms depot* **storehouse**, warehouse, store, storage place, storing place, repository, depository, cache; arsenal, magazine, armoury, ammunition dump, ordnance depot; *archaic* garner.

deprave ▶ verb *they have been depraved by pornography* **corrupt**, lead astray, warp, subvert, pervert, debauch, debase, degrade, make degenerate, defile, sully, pollute, poison, contaminate, infect; *archaic* demoralize; *rare* vitiate.
OPPOSITE purify.

depraved ▶ adjective *a depraved father abused his two young daughters* **corrupt**, corrupted, perverted, deviant, degenerate, debased, degraded, immoral, unprincipled, reprobate; **debauched**, dissolute, profligate, lewd, licentious, lascivious, lecherous, lustful, prurient, obscene, indecent, libertine, sordid; wicked, sinful, vile, base, iniquitous, nefarious, criminal, vicious, brutal; *informal* warped, twisted, pervy, sick, sicko.
OPPOSITES virtuous, moral.

depravity ▶ noun *she viewed her ex-husband as a monster of depravity* **corruption**, corruptness, vice, perversion, pervertedness, deviance, degeneracy, degradation, immorality, shamelessness, debauchery, dissipation, dissoluteness, turpitude, loucheness, profligacy, licentiousness, lewdness, lasciviousness, salaciousness, lechery, lecherousness, prurience, obscenity, indecency, libertinism, sordidness; wickedness, sinfulness, vileness, baseness, iniquity, nefariousness, criminality, viciousness, brutality, brutishness; *informal* perviness; *rare* vitiation.
OPPOSITE morality.

deprecate ▶ verb **1** *the school deprecates the social mixing of older and younger boys* **disapprove of**, deplore, abhor, find unacceptable, be against, frown on, take a dim view of, look askance at, take exception to, detest, despise, execrate; criticize, censure, condemn, denounce, protest against, inveigh against, rail against; *informal* knock, slam, hammer, cane, blast, bad-mouth, pull to pieces, pull apart, hit out at; *Brit. informal* slate, slag off, rubbish; *archaic* slash, vituperate against, reprobate; *rare* animadvert on, asperse, derogate.
OPPOSITE praise.
2 *he deprecates the value of children's television* **belittle**, **disparage**, denigrate, run down, discredit, decry, cry down, play down, make little of, trivialize, underrate, undervalue, underestimate, diminish, depreciate, deflate; think little of, treat lightly, scoff at, sneer at, scorn, disdain; *informal* sell short, knock, pooh-pooh; *archaic* hold cheap; *rare* derogate, misprize, minify.
OPPOSITES emphasize; overrate.

deprecate or depreciate?

Although they are very similar in spelling and meaning, **deprecate** and **depreciate** are not identical. *Deprecate* means 'express disapproval of', as in *I deprecate his rather ungracious words*, while *depreciate* means 'disparage or belittle', as in *we should not depreciate the importance of art in education*.

deprecatory ▶ adjective **1** *he made deprecatory remarks about the opposition* **disapproving**, censorious, censuring, critical, scathing, damning, damnatory, condemnatory, condemning, denunciatory; castigatory, reproachful, reproving, upbraiding, admonishing; *informal* slating, knocking; *rare* reprobative, reprobatory.
2 *Greene was deprecatory about his own writing* **disparaging**, belittling, denigratory, derogatory, discrediting, diminishing, detracting, deflating, negative, unflattering, slighting; disdainful, derisive, snide, sneering, mocking, jibing.
3 *she gave a deprecatory smile at her mistake* **apologetic**, regretful, full of regret, sorry, remorseful, contrite, penitent, repentant, rueful, appeasing; conscience-stricken, red-faced, shamefaced, sheepish, hangdog; *rare* propitiatory, compunctious.
OPPOSITE unrepentant.

depreciate ▶ verb **1** *these cars will depreciate heavily in the first year* **decrease in value**, lose value, decline in price, drop in price, fall in price, cheapen, devalue.
OPPOSITE appreciate.
2 *the decision to depreciate land and property is good news for buyers* **devalue**, cheapen, reduce, lower in value, lower in price, mark down, cut, discount; *informal* slash.
OPPOSITE raise.
3 *they depreciate the importance of art in education* **belittle**, **disparage**, denigrate, decry, deprecate, make light of, treat lightly, discredit, underrate, undervalue, underestimate, deflate, detract from, diminish, minimize, trivialize, run down, traduce, defame; disdain, ridicule, deride, sneer at, scoff at, mock, scorn, pour scorn on; *informal* knock, slam, pan, bad-mouth, sell short, put down, pooh-pooh, look down one's nose at, do down, do a hatchet job on, take to pieces, pull apart, pick holes in, drag through the mud, have a go at, hit out at; *Brit. informal* rubbish, slate, slag off; *dated* cry down; *archaic* hold cheap; *rare* derogate, misprize, minify.
OPPOSITE appreciate.

depreciate or deprecate?

See DEPRECATE.

depreciation ▶ noun *we are concerned about the depreciation of house prices* **devaluation**, devaluing, decrease in value, lowering in value, reduction in value, cheapening, markdown, reduction, decline, downturn, downswing, drop, slump, plunge, tumble; *informal* nosedive, crash.
OPPOSITE rise.

depredation ▶ noun *few survived the depredation of the barbarian invasion* **plundering**, plunder, looting, pillaging, robbing, robbery, raiding, ravaging, sacking, sack, ransacking, devastation, laying waste, wreckage, destruction, damage; ravages, raids, acts of destruction; *literary* despoiling, despoliation, rape, rapine, ravin; *archaic* spoliation, reaving.

depress ▶ verb **1** *the news from the doctor depressed him* **make sad**, sadden, make unhappy, cast down, get down, make gloomy, make despondent, dispirit; dampen someone's spirits, break someone's spirit, dash someone's hopes, dishearten, demoralize, discourage, daunt, crush, shake, desolate, make desolate, weigh down, weigh heavily on, hang over, oppress; upset, distress, grieve, haunt, harrow, cause suffering to, break someone's heart, make someone's heart bleed, bring tears to someone's eyes; *informal* give someone the blues, make someone fed up, knock the stuffing out of, knock for six, knock sideways; *archaic* deject.
OPPOSITE cheer up.
2 *the government's economic policies depressed sales* **slow down**, slow up, reduce, lower, weaken, sap, devitalize, impair, deflate; limit, check, curb, bridle, inhibit, restrict.
OPPOSITE encourage.
3 *the increase in EC imports will depress farm prices* **reduce**, lower, cut, cheapen, put down, keep down, mark down, discount, deflate, depreciate, devalue, diminish, downgrade; *informal* slash, axe.
OPPOSITE raise.
4 *you have to depress each key in turn* **push (down)**, press (down), exert pressure on, lower, hold down; thumb, tap; operate, activate, actuate.
OPPOSITE lift.

depressant ▶ noun *the drug is a stimulant rather than a depressant* **sedative**, tranquillizer, calmative, sleeping pill, soporific, opiate, hypnotic; *informal* downer, trank, sleeper, dope; *technical* neuroleptic, stupefacient; *literary* nepenthes; *dated* bromide, sleeping draught.
OPPOSITE stimulant.

depressed ▶ adjective **1** *he turned to whisky because he felt lonely and depressed* **sad**, saddened, unhappy, gloomy, glum, melancholy, miserable, sorrowful, dejected, disconsolate, downhearted, downcast, cast down, down, crestfallen, woebegone, despondent, dispirited, low, low in spirits, low-spirited, heavy-hearted, morose, dismal, desolate, weighed down, oppressed; tearful, upset, broken-hearted; disheartened, discouraged, daunted, pessimistic; *informal* blue, down in the dumps, down in the mouth, fed up, moody; *literary* dolorous, heartsick, heartsore; *archaic* chap-fallen.
OPPOSITE cheerful.
2 *there is a relationship between crime and a depressed economy* **weak**, weakened, enervated, debilitated, devitalized, impaired; inactive, flat, quiet, slow, slow-moving, slack, sluggish, static, stagnant, dull.
OPPOSITE strong.
3 *he snapped up property at depressed prices* **reduced**, lowered, cut,

cheapened, cheap, devalued, marked down, discounted, discount; *informal* slashed.
OPPOSITE inflated.
4 *a depressed Lancashire cotton town* **poverty-stricken**, poor, destitute, disadvantaged, deprived, needy, distressed; down at heel, run down, seedy, shabby; *informal* slummy.
OPPOSITE prosperous.
5 *a depressed fracture of the skull* **sunken**, hollow, concave, indented, dented, pushed in, caved in, recessed, set back; *rare* incurved, incurvate.
OPPOSITE raised.

depressing ▶ adjective **1** *she wanted to get rid of her depressing thoughts* **upsetting**, distressing, painful, heartbreaking, heart-rending, dispiriting, disheartening, discouraging, demoralizing; dismal, bleak, black, sombre, gloomy, grave, unhappy, melancholy, sad, saddening; wretched, doleful; daunting, disenchanting, unfavourable; *informal* morbid, blue; *archaic* dejecting; *rare* distressful, lachrymose.
2 *it was such a depressing room* **gloomy**, bleak, dreary, grim, drab, sombre, dark, dingy, funereal, miserable, cheerless, joyless, comfortless, uninviting; *literary* drear.

depression ▶ noun **1** *she ate to ease her depression* **melancholy**, misery, sadness, unhappiness, sorrow, woe, gloom, gloominess, dejection, downheartedness, despondency, dispiritedness, low spirits, heavy-heartedness, moroseness, discouragement, despair, desolation, dolefulness, moodiness, pessimism, hopelessness; the slough of despond; upset, tearfulness; *informal* the dumps, the doldrums, the blues, one's black dog, a low; *N. Amer. informal* the blahs, a funk, a blue funk; *informal, dated* the mopes; *technical* clinical depression, endogenous depression, reactive depression, post-natal depression, dysthymia, melancholia; *literary* dolour; *archaic* the megrims; *rare* mopery, disconsolateness, disconsolation.
OPPOSITE cheerfulness.
2 *the country was in the grip of an economic depression* **recession**, slump, decline, downturn, slowdown, standstill; paralysis, inactivity, stagnation; hard times, bad times; *technical* stagflation.
OPPOSITE boom.
3 *the car slid into a depression in the ground* **hollow**, indentation, dent, dint, cavity, concavity, dip, pit, hole, pothole, sink, sinkhole, excavation, trough, crater; valley, basin, bowl; *Anatomy* fossa, lacuna.
OPPOSITE protuberance.

deprivation ▶ noun **1** *the cause of the rioting was unemployment and deprivation* **poverty**, impoverishment, penury, privation, hardship, destitution, need, neediness, want, distress, financial distress, indigence, pauperdom, beggary, ruin; reduced circumstances, straitened circumstances, hand-to-mouth existence; *rare* pauperism, pauperization, impecuniousness, impecuniosity.
OPPOSITE wealth.
2 *he was sentenced to one year's deprivation of political rights* **dispossession**, withholding, withdrawal, removal, taking away, stripping, divestment, divestiture, wresting away, expropriation, seizure, confiscation, robbing, appropriation; denial, forfeiture, loss; absence, lack, unavailability, deficiency, dearth.
OPPOSITE possession.

deprive ▶ verb *she was **deprived of** her royal privileges* **dispossess**, strip, divest, relieve, bereave; rob of, cheat out of, trick out of, do out of; deny, prevent from having, prevent from using; *informal* diddle out of.

deprived ▶ adjective *the most deprived sections of society* **disadvantaged**, underprivileged, poverty-stricken, impoverished, poor, destitute, needy, in need, in want, badly off, unable to make ends meet, in reduced circumstances, unable to keep the wolf from the door; depressed, distressed, forlorn; *Brit.* on the bread line; *formal* penurious, impecunious; *rare* necessitous.
OPPOSITES fortunate; wealthy.

depth ▶ noun **1** *he wondered about the depth of the caves* **deepness**, distance downwards, distance inwards, distance from the outside; drop, vertical drop, vertical extent, profundity.
OPPOSITE shallowness.
2 *Bill tested the depth of his knowledge* **extent**, range, scope, breadth, width, extensiveness, comprehensiveness; compass, magnitude, scale, degree.
3 *they made remarks about the girls' lack of depth* **profoundness**, profundity, deepness, wisdom, understanding, intelligence, sagacity, discernment, perceptiveness, penetration, perspicuity, insight, awareness, intuition, astuteness, acumen, shrewdness, acuity; learning, erudition, knowledgeability; *rare* sapience.
OPPOSITE shallowness.
4 *this book is a work of great depth* **complexity**, intricacy, profoundness, profundity, gravity, seriousness, weight, importance, moment, solemnity.
OPPOSITE triviality.
5 *the vase has incredible depth of colour* **intensity**, richness, deepness, darkness, vividness, strength, brilliance.
6 (**depths**) *they studied life in the depths of the sea* **deepest part**, remotest area, bottom, floor, bed, abyss, back, pit; bowels.
OPPOSITE surface.
□ **in depth** *the student concentrates on one or two subjects in depth* **thoroughly**, extensively, comprehensively, well, rigorously, exhaustively, completely, fully; meticulously, scrupulously, assiduously, painstakingly, methodically.
OPPOSITE superficially.

WORD LINKS
measurement of depth of seas and lakes **bathymetry**
fear of depth **bathophobia**

deputation ▶ noun *the prime minister agreed to receive a suffrage deputation* **delegation**, delegacy, legation, commission, committee, (diplomatic) mission; contingent, group, party, body, band, set; delegates, representatives, envoys, emissaries, legates; *historical* embassy; *archaic* embassage.

depute ▶ verb **1** *he was deputed to handle negotiations in Baldwin's absence* **appoint**, designate, nominate, assign, commission, charge, choose, select, elect, co-opt; empower, authorize, mandate; *Military* detail.
2 *the judge deputed the examination of lesser cases to others* **delegate**, transfer, turn over, hand over, hand on, pass on, consign, assign, entrust, give, devolve.

deputize ▶ verb *the assistant's task is to **deputize for** the account executive* **stand in for**, sit in for, fill in for, cover for, substitute for, replace, take the place of, understudy, be a locum for, relieve, take over from; hold the fort, step into the breach; **act for**, act on behalf of, speak on behalf of, represent; *informal* sub for; *N. Amer. informal* pinch-hit for.

deputy ▶ noun *he handed over his duties to his deputy* **second in command**, second, number two, subordinate, junior, auxiliary, adjutant, lieutenant, subaltern, assistant, personal assistant, PA, aide, helper, right-hand man, henchman, underling; substitute, stand-in, fill-in, relief, understudy, supply; representative, surrogate, proxy, delegate, agent, spokesperson, ambassador, legate; *Scottish* depute; *Latin* locum tenens; *informal* vice, man/girl Friday, sidekick, locum, temp.
▶ adjective *she brought in an old friend as deputy editor* **assistant**; substitute, stand-in, acting, reserve, fill-in, caretaker, temporary, short-term, provisional, stopgap, surrogate, proxy, representative; *Latin* pro tempore, ad interim; *informal* second-string; *N. Amer. informal* pinch-hitting; *rare* expediential.

deranged ▶ adjective *five schoolchildren were shot by a deranged gunman* **insane**, mad, of unsound mind, out of one's mind, not in one's right mind, disturbed, unbalanced, unhinged, unstable, crazed, demented, irrational, berserk, frenzied, maniac, lunatic, psychopathic, certifiable, raving, raving mad; *Latin* non compos mentis; *informal* touched, crazy, cracked, mental; *Brit. informal* barmy, barking, barking mad, round the twist.
OPPOSITES sane; rational.

derelict ▶ adjective **1** *a derelict old building* **dilapidated**, ramshackle, run down, broken-down, worn out, tumbledown, in (a state of) disrepair, in ruins, ruined, falling to pieces, falling apart; rickety, creaky, creaking, decrepit, deteriorating, crumbling, deteriorated; neglected, untended, unmaintained, gone to rack and ruin, gone to seed, on its last legs, the worse for wear.
OPPOSITE in good repair.
2 *a vast, derelict airfield* **disused**, abandoned, deserted, discarded, rejected, forsaken, cast off, relinquished, ownerless.
OPPOSITE in use.
3 (*N. Amer.*) *he was derelict in his duty to his country* **negligent**, neglectful, remiss, lax, careless, sloppy, slipshod, slack, irresponsible, delinquent.
OPPOSITES dutiful, punctilious.
▶ noun *the community of derelicts who survive on the capital's streets* **tramp**, vagrant, vagabond, down and out, homeless person, drifter, person of no fixed address/abode, knight of the road; beggar, mendicant; outcast, pariah, ne'er do well, good-for-nothing, wastrel; *informal* dosser, bag lady; *N. Amer. informal* hobo, bum; *Austral./NZ informal* derro.

dereliction ▶ noun **1** *more buildings were reclaimed from dereliction* **dilapidation**, disrepair, decrepitude, deterioration, ruin, rack and ruin; **abandonment**, neglect, disuse, desertion, rejection, forsaking.
2 *he could have been shot for **dereliction of duty*** **negligence**, neglect, neglectfulness, delinquency, failure, non-performance; carelessness, remissness, lack of care, laxity, laxness, sloppiness, slackness, irresponsibility, oversight, omission; misconduct, unprofessionalism; *informal* slip-up.
OPPOSITE fulfilment.

deride ▶ verb *the decision was derided by environmentalists* **ridicule**, mock, jeer at, scoff at, jibe at, make fun of, poke fun at, laugh at, hold up to ridicule, pillory; disdain, disparage, denigrate, pooh-pooh, dismiss, slight, detract from; sneer at, scorn, pour/heap scorn on, taunt, insult, torment; treat with contempt, vilify; lampoon, satirize; *informal* knock, take the mickey out of; *Austral./NZ informal* poke mullock at; *vulgar slang* take the piss out of; *archaic* contemn, flout at.
OPPOSITES respect, praise.

de rigueur ▶ adjective **1** *a straight brown bob and invisible make-up were de rigueur* **fashionable**, in fashion, voguish, in vogue, modish, up to date, up to the minute, all the rage, trendsetting, latest; smart, chic, elegant,

D

natty; *informal* trendy, with it, ritzy.
OPPOSITE unfashionable.
2 *an email address is considered de rigueur for business cards today* **customary**, standard, conventional, normal, orthodox, usual, ubiquitous; compulsory; *French* comme il faut; *informal* done.

derision ▶ noun *my stories were greeted with disbelief and derision* **mockery**, ridicule, jeering, jeers, sneers, scoffing, jibing, taunts; disdain, disparagement, denigration, disrespect, pooh-poohing; sneering, scorn, scornfulness, taunting, insults; contempt, vilification, obloquy; lampooning, satire; ragging, teasing, chaffing, raillery; *archaic* contumely.
OPPOSITES respect, praise.

D

CHOOSE THE RIGHT WORD

derision, mockery, ridicule
See MOCKERY.

derisive ▶ adjective *he gave a harsh, derisive laugh* **mocking**, ridiculing, jeering, scoffing, jibing, pillorying, teasing, derisory, snide; disdainful, disparaging, denigratory, dismissive, slighting, detracting, contemptuous; sneering, scornful, taunting, insulting; caustic, scathing, sarcastic; satirical, lampooning; *informal* snidey; *Brit. informal* sarky; *rare* contumelious.
OPPOSITES respectful, praising.

derisive or derisory?
See DERISORY.

derisory ▶ adjective **1** *it was sold at auction for a derisory sum* **inadequate**, insufficient, tiny, small, minimal, trifling, paltry, pitiful; miserly, miserable; negligible, token, nominal; **ridiculous**, laughable, ludicrous, risible, preposterous, absurd; insulting, contemptible, outrageous; *informal* measly, stingy, lousy, pathetic, piddling, piffling, mingy, poxy; *N. Amer. informal* nickel-and-dime.
2 *there were derisory calls from the crowd. See* DERISIVE.

derisory or derisive?
Derisory and **derisive** are both derived from Latin *deridere* 'mock, scoff', but their meanings are connected with mockery in different ways. *Derisory* usually means 'ridiculously small or inadequate', as in *a derisory pay offer. Derisive*, on the other hand, means 'showing contempt', as in *he gave a derisive laugh.*

derivation ▶ noun **1** *the derivation of universal laws from empirical observation* **deriving**, **induction**, deduction, deducing, inferring, inference, gathering, gleaning, drawing out, extraction, eliciting; *rare* eduction.
2 *the derivation of the word 'toff'* **origin**, **etymology**; source, root, etymon, provenance; fountainhead, wellspring, origination, beginning, foundation, basis, cause; ancestry, descent, genealogy, development, evolution, extraction.

derivative ▶ adjective *her poetry was mannered and derivative* **imitative**, unoriginal, uninventive, non-innovative, unimaginative, uninspired; copied, plagiarized, plagiaristic, second-hand, secondary, echoic; trite, hackneyed, clichéd, stale, tired, worn out, flat, rehashed, warmed-up, stock, banal; *informal* copycat, cribbed, old hat.
OPPOSITE original.
▶ noun **1** *laudanum is a derivative of opium* **by-product**, spin-off, offshoot, subsidiary product.
2 *the word 'samurai' is a derivative of a verb meaning 'to serve'* **derived word**, descendant.

derive ▶ verb **1** *he hated the work, only deriving consolation from his reading of poetry* **obtain**, get, take, gain, acquire, procure, extract, attain, glean.
2 *'coffee' **derives from** the Turkish 'kahveh'* **originate in**, have its origins in, have as a source, arise in; stem, descend, spring, be taken, be got.
OPPOSITE give rise to.
3 *his fortune **derives from** international property and finance* **originate in**, have its origin in, be rooted in, be traceable to; stem, proceed, flow, pour, spring, emanate, issue, ensue, descend, come.

derogate ▶ verb **1** *his contribution has been underestimated and derogated by his critics* **disparage**, denigrate, belittle, diminish, deprecate, downplay, detract from, deflate, decry, discredit, cast aspersions on, downgrade, slight, run down, criticize, defame, vilify, abuse, insult, attack, speak ill of, speak evil of, pour scorn on; *informal* bad-mouth, do a hatchet job on, take to pieces, pull apart, throw mud at, drag through the mud, slate, have a go at, hit out at, lay into, tear into, knock, slam, pan, bash, hammer, roast, skewer, bad-mouth, throw brickbats at; *Brit. informal* rubbish, slag off; *N. Amer. informal* pummel, dump on; *Austral./NZ informal* bag, monster; *archaic* contemn; *rare* vituperate, asperse, vilipend.
OPPOSITE praise.
2 *agreeing to swear such an oath would certainly have derogated the majesty of the king* **detract from**, devalue, diminish; reduce, lessen, lower, depreciate, take away from; demean, cheapen, defame.
OPPOSITES improve, increase.
3 *there is no person who can make rules which override or **derogate from** an Act of Parliament* **deviate**, diverge, depart, take away, digress, veer, swerve, drift, stray; differ, vary; change; conflict with, be incompatible with.

derogatory ▶ adjective *a derogatory remark* **disparaging**, denigratory, belittling, diminishing, slighting, deprecatory, depreciatory, depreciative, detracting, deflating; disrespectful, demeaning, discrediting, dishonouring; critical, pejorative, negative, unfavourable, disapproving, uncomplimentary, unflattering, insulting; **offensive**, personal, abusive, vituperative, rude, spiteful, nasty, mean; hurtful, damaging, injurious; defamatory, slanderous, libellous, scurrilous, calumnious, calumniatory, vilifying, traducing; *informal* mud-slinging, bitchy, catty; *archaic* contumelious.
OPPOSITES complimentary, flattering.

CHOOSE THE RIGHT WORD

derogatory, offensive, insulting
See OFFENSIVE.

descend ▶ verb **1** *the plane started descending towards the runway* **go down**, come down; drop, fall, sink, subside; dive, plummet, plunge, nosedive, pitch, tumble, slump.
OPPOSITES ascend, climb.
2 *she descended the stairs* **climb down**, go down, come down, move down, pass down, walk down; shin down.
OPPOSITES ascend, climb.
3 *the road descends to a village situated on the shore* **slope**, dip, slant, decline, go down, sink, fall away.
4 *she saw Leo **descend from** the local bus* **alight**, disembark, get down; get off, dismount; detrain, deplane, debus; *informal* pile out.
OPPOSITE board.
5 *if they had right on their side they would not need to **descend to** such mean tricks* **condescend**, **stoop**, lower oneself, abase oneself, humble oneself, demean oneself, debase oneself, deign; **resort**, be reduced, go as far as; *informal* come down from one's high horse.
6 *the army had descended into chaos* **degenerate**, deteriorate, decline, sink, slide, fall, drop; go downhill, decay, worsen, get/grow worse, take a turn for the worse, go to rack and ruin; *informal* go to pot, go to the dogs, go to seed, hit the skids, go down the tubes, go down the toilet.
OPPOSITE improve.
7 *groups of visiting supporters **descended on** a local pub* **come in force**, arrive in hordes, attack, assail, assault, storm, invade, pounce on, raid, swoop on, charge.
8 *he **is descended from** a Flemish family* **be a descendant of**, originate from, issue from, spring from, have as an ancestor, derive from.
9 *his estates **descended to** his son* **be handed down**, be passed down, pass by heredity, be transferred by inheritance; be inherited by.
OPPOSITE bequeath to.

descendant ▶ noun *a descendant of Charles Darwin* **successor**, scion; offshoot, heir; (**descendants**) **offspring**, progeny, issue, family, lineage, line; *archaic* posterity, seed, fruit, fruit of someone's loins.
OPPOSITE ancestor.

descent ▶ noun **1** *the plane began its descent to Brussels* **going down**, coming down; drop, fall, sinking, subsiding; dive, pitch, slump.
OPPOSITES ascent, climb.
2 *they started their descent of the mountain* **downward climb**, descending.
OPPOSITES ascent, climb.
3 *a steep, badly eroded descent* **slope**, incline, dip, drop, gradient, declivity, declination, slant, downslope, hill.
4 *he began his calamitous descent into alcoholism* **degeneration**, degeneracy, deterioration, decline, sinking, slide, fall, drop, regression, retrogression, debasement, degradation, comedown.
5 *his mother was of Italian descent* **ancestry**, parentage, ancestors, family; lineage, line, line of descent; extraction, origin, derivation, birth; genealogy, heredity, succession; stock, pedigree, blood, bloodline, strain; roots, origins, forefathers, antecedents; *rare* filiation, stirps.
6 *the descent of property can sometimes be traced over several generations through archives* **inheritance**, passing down/on, succession.
7 *the sudden descent of the cavalry* **attack**, assault, raid, onslaught, charge, thrust, push, drive, incursion, foray, sortie, sally, storming, assailing.

describe ▶ verb **1** *he described his experiences in a letter to his parents* **report**, **narrate**, recount, relate, tell of, set out, chronicle; express, put into words, give a description/account of, give details of, detail, represent; evoke, conjure up; catalogue, give a rundown of, paint a word picture of, paint in words; explain, expound, elucidate, illustrate, discuss, comment on.
2 *a lawyer **described** him **as** a pathetic figure* **designate**, pronounce, call,

label, style, dub; characterize, classify, class, categorize, portray, depict, brand, hail, paint.
3 *the tip of the light pen described a circle* **delineate**, mark out, outline, trace, draw, sketch.

description ▶ noun **1** *Darwin's description of the theory of sexual selection | the court demanded a written description of the missing animals* **account**, explanation, elucidation, illustration, representation, interpretation; chronicle, report, narration, narrative, story, recounting, rendition, relation, commentary, version, portrayal, portrait, word picture, evocation; details.
2 *the picturesque description of coal as 'bottled sunshine'* **designation**, styling, calling, labelling, naming, dubbing, pronouncement; **characterization**, classification, classing, categorization, branding; portrayal, depiction, hailing, painting.
3 *the roads were jammed with vehicles of every description* **sort**, variety, kind, style, type, category, order, breed, species, class, designation, specification, genre, genus, brand, make, character, ilk, kidney, grain, stamp, mould; *N. Amer.* stripe.

descriptive ▶ adjective *his style uses colourful descriptive language* **illustrative**, expressive, pictorial, depictive, graphic, picturesque, vivid, striking; explanatory, elucidatory, explicative, exegetic, expository; detailed, lively, circumstantial.

descry ▶ verb (*literary*) *she descried two figures* **spot**, **notice**, catch sight of, see, make out, glimpse, sight, discern, perceive, observe, detect, distinguish, pick out, spy out, recognize, identify, mark, remark; *Brit. informal* clock; *literary* espy, behold.

desecrate ▶ verb *invaders desecrated the temple* **violate**, profane, treat sacrilegiously, treat with disrespect; pollute, contaminate, infect, befoul; defile, debase, degrade, dishonour, blaspheme against; vandalize, damage, destroy, deface.
OPPOSITES venerate; sanctify.

desecration ▶ noun *the desecration of the church* **violation**, profanation, sacrilege; pollution, contamination, infection, befouling; defilement, debasement, degradation, degrading, dishonour, dishonouring, blasphemy; vandalism, damaging, destruction, defacement.
OPPOSITES veneration; sanctification.

desert[1] (stress on the second syllable) ▶ verb **1** *his wife had deserted him* **abandon**, leave, give up, cast off, turn one's back on; throw over, betray, jilt, break (up) with; neglect, shun; leave high and dry, leave in the lurch, leave behind, strand, leave stranded, maroon; relinquish, renounce; *informal* walk/run out on, rat on, drop, dump, ditch; *archaic* forsake.
OPPOSITE stand by.
2 *his allies were quite capable of deserting the cause when it suited them* **renounce**, renege on, repudiate, forswear, relinquish, wash one's hands of, have no more truck with, have done with, abjure, disavow; abandon, turn one's back on, betray; apostatize, recant; *archaic* forsake; *rare* disprofess.
3 *soldiers deserted in droves* **abscond**, defect, run away, make off, decamp, flee, fly, bolt, turn tail, go absent without leave, take French leave, depart, quit, escape; *informal* go AWOL.
OPPOSITE stay.

desert[2] (stress on the first syllable) ▶ noun **1** *the desert of the Sinai peninsula* **wasteland**, waste, wilderness, wilds, dust bowl, barren land.
2 *a cultural desert* **uninteresting place/period**, unproductive place/period, wasteland.
▶ adjective **1** *animals have overgrazed the area, creating desert conditions* **arid**, dry, moistureless, dried up, parched, scorched, burnt, hot, burning, torrid; barren, bare, stark; uncultivatable, infertile, non-fertile, unproductive, unfruitful, dehydrated, sterile.
OPPOSITE fertile.
2 *a desert island* **uninhabited**, empty, solitary, lonely, desolate, bleak, dismal, waste; wild, uncultivated, untended, untilled.

deserted ▶ adjective **1** *a deserted wife* **abandoned**, forsaken, cast off/aside, thrown over, betrayed, jilted; shunned, neglected; stranded, marooned; relinquished, renounced; forlorn, bereft; *informal* dumped, ditched, dropped.
2 *a deserted village* **empty**, uninhabited, unoccupied, unpeopled, abandoned, evacuated, vacant, vacated; untenanted, tenantless, unfrequented, neglected; secluded, isolated, desolate, lonely, solitary, godforsaken, forlorn.
OPPOSITES crowded; populous.

deserter ▶ noun *a deserter from the Foreign Legion* **absconder**, runaway, renegade, fugitive, truant, escapee; defector, turncoat, traitor, betrayer, apostate; *informal* rat.

desertion ▶ noun **1** *he petitioned for divorce on the grounds of his wife's desertion* **abandonment**, leaving, forsaking; betrayal, neglect, shunning; stranding, jilting; relinquishment, renunciation.
2 *the desertion of the president's closest colleagues* **defection**, reneging, betrayal; renunciation, repudiation, forswearing, relinquishment, abjuration; apostasy.
3 *soldiers were executed for desertion* **absconding**, running away, decamping, flight, fleeing, flying, bolting, turning tail, truancy, going absent without leave, taking French leave, departure, escape, dereliction; defection, treason, betrayal, cowardice; *informal* going AWOL.

deserve ▶ verb *everyone involved with this book deserves the greatest praise* **merit**, **earn**, warrant, rate, justify, be worthy of, be entitled to, have a right to, have a claim on, be qualified for, be good enough for.
OPPOSITE be unworthy of.

> **CHOOSE THE RIGHT WORD**
> **deserve, earn, merit**
> *See* EARN.

deserved ▶ adjective *they clinched a deserved victory* **well earned**, well deserved, earned, merited, warranted, justified, justifiable; rightful, due, right, just, fair, fitting, appropriate, suitable, proper, reasonable, apt; *formal* condign; *archaic* meet.
OPPOSITE undeserved.

deservedly ▶ adverb *a deservedly popular restaurant* **justifiably**, **rightfully**, rightly, by rights, justly, fairly, appropriately, fittingly, suitably, aptly, according to one's due, duly; *formal* condignly.
OPPOSITE undeservedly.

deserving ▶ adjective **1** *the deserving poor* **worthy**, meritorious, commendable, praiseworthy, laudable, excellent, fine, admirable, estimable, exemplary, creditable; respectable, decent, honourable, virtuous, righteous, upright, good.
OPPOSITE undeserving.
2 *a moral lapse deserving of punishment* **meriting**, warranting, justifying, qualified for, suiting, suitable for, worthy.

desiccated ▶ adjective *desiccated coconut* **dried**, dried up, dry, dehydrated, powdered.
OPPOSITE moist.

desideratum ▶ noun *integrity was a desideratum* **requirement**, prerequisite, need, indispensable thing, desired thing, needed thing, essential, requisite, necessary; lack, want, missing thing; dream, ideal, hope, wish; *Latin* sine qua non.

design ▶ noun **1** *an architect submitted a design for the offices* **plan**, blueprint, drawing, scale drawing, sketch, outline, map, plot, diagram, delineation, draft, depiction, representation, scheme, model, prototype, proposal.
2 *tableware with a sophisticated black and gold design* **pattern**, motif, device; style, arrangement, composition, make-up, layout, constitution, configuration, organization, construction, shape, form, formation, figure.
3 *he was determined to carry out his design of reaching the top* **intention**, aim, purpose, plan, intent, objective, object, goal, end, target, point, hope, desire, wish, dream, aspiration, ambition, idea.
□ **by design** *as much as by accident as by design, the group found themselves in a strong position* **deliberately**, intentionally, on purpose, purposefully; knowingly, wittingly, consciously, premeditatedly, calculatedly.
OPPOSITES by accident, accidentally.
▶ verb **1** *this simple church was designed by John Hicks in 1869* **plan**, draw plans of, draw, sketch, outline, map out, plot, block out, delineate, draft, depict.
2 *they designed a new kind of motor* **invent**, originate, create, think up, come up with, devise, form, formulate, conceive; make, produce, develop, fashion, fabricate, forge, hatch, coin; *informal* dream up.
3 *this paper is designed to provoke discussion | a low-price laser printer designed for home use* **intend**, aim; devise, contrive, purpose, plan; tailor, fashion, make fitting, adjust, adapt, fit, gear, equip; mean, destine, orient.

designate ▶ verb **1** *some organizations designate a press officer within the PR office* **appoint**, nominate, depute, delegate; select, choose, pick, decide on, settle on; elect, name, identify, assign, allot, co-opt, ordain, induct; *informal* plump for.
2 *a few of the rivers are designated 'Sites of Special Scientific Interest'* **classify**, class, pronounce, label, tag; name, call, entitle, term, christen, dub, style, brand; *formal* denominate.
3 *try designating the same time every week to catch up on paperwork* **allot**, appoint, specify, define; **earmark**, set aside, devote, stipulate, state, particularize, pinpoint.

designation ▶ noun **1** *the designation of a leader* **appointment**, nomination, selection, choice, choosing, picking, election, naming, identifying; co-opting, induction.
2 *one of its roles is the designation of nature reserves* **classification**, classing, labelling, specification, definition, defining, earmarking, stipulation, particularization, pinpointing.
3 *he added to his existing titles the designation 'Generalissimo'* **title**, denomination, honorific, label; name, epithet, tag, style, form of address; nickname, byname, sobriquet; rank, status, office, position; *informal* moniker, handle; *formal* cognomen, appellation.

designedly ▶ adverb *the atmosphere here is designedly old-fashioned* **deliberately**, by design, on purpose, purposefully, intentionally;

D

consciously, wilfully, intendedly.
OPPOSITE unintentionally.

designer ▶ noun **1** *he developed a reputation as a designer of farmhouses* **creator**, deviser, producer, inventor, originator, planner, author, artificer, fabricator; maker, fashioner; architect, engineer, builder.
2 *she picked two young designers to make the wedding dress* **couturier**, fashion designer, tailor, costumier, dressmaker.

designing ▶ adjective *Bob had fallen into the hands of this designing woman* **scheming**, calculating, conniving, plotting, intriguing, conspiring; cunning, crafty, artful, wily, devious, guileful, canny, shrewd, astute, sharp, insidious, manipulative; treacherous, sly, underhand, deceitful, dishonest, Machiavellian, double-dealing, tricky; *informal* crooked, foxy.
OPPOSITE ingenuous.

desirability ▶ noun **1** *the desirability of the property* **appeal**, attractiveness, allure; agreeableness, worth, eligibility, excellence.
OPPOSITE undesirability.
2 *the desirability of a more laissez-faire type of economy* **advisability**, preferableness, advantage, expedience, benefit, merit, value, profit, profitability; *rare* advantageousness.
OPPOSITES undesirability, disadvantage.
3 *it was humiliating to have her desirability called into question* **sexual attractiveness**, sexual attraction, attractiveness, beauty, handsomeness, good looks; charm, seductiveness, eroticism, fascination; *informal* sexiness.

desirable ▶ adjective **1** *hospitals are often sited in very desirable locations* **attractive**, sought-after, in demand, popular, looked-for, longed-for, desired; eligible, appealing, agreeable, pleasant; valuable, good, excellent; covetable, enviable; *informal* to die for.
OPPOSITE undesirable.
2 *it is desirable that they should meet and get to know each other* **advantageous**, advisable, wise, sensible, prudent, recommendable; helpful, useful, beneficial, worthwhile, profitable, preferable, expedient, in everyone's interests.
OPPOSITE disadvantageous.
3 *you're a very desirable woman* **sexually attractive**, attractive, beautiful, pretty, handsome, appealing; seductive, alluring, enchanting, engaging, erotic, fetching, fascinating, beguiling, captivating, bewitching, irresistible; *informal* sexy, beddable.
OPPOSITES unattractive, ugly.

desire ▶ noun **1** *I had a desire to see the world* **wish**, want; fancy, inclination, aspiration, impulse, preference; **yearning**, longing, craving, hankering, pining, ache, hunger, thirst, itch, burning, need; eagerness, enthusiasm, determination; predilection, proclivity, predisposition; *informal* yen.
2 *he gazed at her, his eyes glittering with desire* **lust**, lustfulness, sexual appetite, sexual attraction, passion, carnal passion, libido, sensuality, sexuality; lasciviousness, lechery, lecherousness, salaciousness, libidinousness, lewdness, licentiousness, prurience, wantonness, carnality; *informal* the hots, raunchiness, horniness; *Brit. informal* randiness; *rare* concupiscence.
▶ verb **1** *they earnestly desired peace* **wish for**, **want**, long for, yearn for, crave, set one's heart on, hanker after/for, pine for/after, thirst for, itch for, be desperate for, be bent on, have a need for, covet, aspire to; have a fancy for, fancy, feel like, feel in need of; *informal* have a yen for, yen for, be dying for.
2 *she knew he wanted her as much as she desired him* **be attracted to**, lust after, burn for, be captivated by, be infatuated by; *informal* fancy, lech after/over, have the hots for, have a crush on, be wild/mad about, go for.

desired ▶ adjective **1** *the cloth is then cut to the desired length* **required**, necessary, proper, right, correct; appropriate, fitting, suitable, called for; preferred, chosen, selected, expected.
2 *the ruling party is able to manipulate the economy for the desired results on election day* **wished for**, wanted; sought-after, longed for, yearned for, craved, pined for, needed, coveted.
OPPOSITE unwanted.

desirous ▶ adjective *he became restless and* **desirous of** *change* **eager for**, desiring, wishing for, hoping for, anxious for, keen on/for, avid for, craving for, yearning for, itching for, longing for, thirsty for, hungry for, ravening for, greedy for; ambitious for, aspiring to; covetous, envious; *informal* dying for.
OPPOSITE averse to.

desist ▶ verb *we must* **desist from** *any industrial action that may disturb national unity* **abstain**, refrain, forbear, hold back, keep; **stop**, cease, discontinue, suspend, give up, quit, break off, leave off, conclude, call a halt/stop to, forgo, drop, dispense with, eschew, have done with, wash one's hands of; *informal* lay off, give over, pack in, pack up; *nautical slang* belay.
OPPOSITES continue, persist in.

desk *See centre pages for list of* **Tables and Desks**
▶ noun *he sat at his desk reading reports* **table**, work surface, bureau, writing desk, writing table, roll-top desk, lectern; counter; *Brit.* davenport; *French* escritoire, secretaire.

desolate ▶ adjective **1** *the loch was bounded by desolate moorlands* **barren**, bleak, stark, bare, dismal, grim; desert, waste, arid, sterile; wild, windswept, inhospitable, exposed.
OPPOSITE fertile.
2 *a desolate building on a lonely island* **deserted**, uninhabited, unoccupied, depopulated, forsaken, godforsaken, abandoned, unpeopled, untenanted, evacuated; empty, vacated, vacant; unfrequented, unvisited, solitary, lonely, secluded, isolated, remote.
OPPOSITE populous.
3 *she is desolate because she had to disappoint you* **miserable**, sad, unhappy, melancholy, gloomy, glum, despondent, comfortless, depressed, mournful, disconsolate; broken-hearted, heavy-hearted, grief-stricken; wretched, downcast, cast down, dejected, downhearted, dispirited, devastated, despairing, inconsolable, anguished, crushed, forlorn, crestfallen, upset, distressed, grieving, woebegone, bereft, in low spirits; *informal* blue, down, cut up.
OPPOSITE joyful.
▶ verb **1** *the droughts that desolated the dry plains* **devastate**, ravage, ruin, make/leave desolate, leave in ruins, destroy, wreck, lay waste to, wreak havoc on; level, raze, demolish, wipe out, obliterate, annihilate, gut; depopulate, empty; *rare* depredate, spoliate.
2 *she was desolated by the sudden loss of her husband* **dishearten**, dispirit, daunt, distress, depress, make sad/unhappy, sadden, cast down, deject, make miserable, make gloomy/despondent, weigh down, oppress; *informal* shatter, floor.
OPPOSITE cheer.

desolation ▶ noun **1** *the arid, stony desolation of the Gobi desert* **barrenness**, bleakness, starkness, bareness, dismalness, grimness; aridity, sterility; wildness; isolation, solitude, solitariness, loneliness, remoteness.
OPPOSITE fertility.
2 *she was racked by a feeling of utter desolation* **misery**, sadness, unhappiness, melancholy, gloom, gloominess, glumness, despondency, sorrow, comfortlessness, depression, grief, mournfulness, woe; broken-heartedness, heavy-heartedness, wretchedness, dejection, downheartedness, discouragement, devastation, despair, anguish, distress, low spirits.
OPPOSITE joy.

despair ▶ noun *many parents feel pain and despair about their teenage children* **hopelessness**, desperation, distress, anguish, pain, unhappiness; dejection, depression, despondency, disconsolateness, gloom, melancholy, melancholia, misery, wretchedness; disheartenment, discouragement, resignedness, forlornness, defeatism, pessimism.
OPPOSITES hope; joy.
□ **be the despair of** *my handwriting was the despair of my teachers* **be the bane of**, be the scourge of, be a burden on, be a trial to, be a thorn in the flesh/side of, be a bother to, be the ruin of, be the death of.
▶ verb *don't despair if you didn't win this time* **lose hope**, give up hope, abandon hope, give up, lose heart, be discouraged, be despondent, be demoralized, resign oneself, throw in the towel/sponge, quit, surrender; be pessimistic, look on the black side; *archaic* despond.

despairing ▶ adjective *her mother gave me a despairing look* **hopeless**, desperate, anguished, distressed, broken-hearted, heartbroken, grief-stricken, inconsolable, sorrowing, suicidal, in despair; dejected, depressed, despondent, disconsolate, gloomy, melancholy, miserable, wretched, desolate, forlorn; disheartened, discouraged, demoralized, devastated, downcast, resigned, defeatist, pessimistic; *literary* dolorous.
OPPOSITES cheerful, optimistic.

despatch ▶ verb & noun. See DISPATCH.

desperado ▶ noun *a gun-toting desperado* **bandit**, criminal, outlaw, renegade, marauder, raider, robber, lawbreaker, villain; thug, ruffian, tough, hooligan, cut-throat; gangster, pirate, swashbuckler, terrorist, gunman, hoodlum.

desperate ▶ adjective **1** *he gave me a desperate look* **despairing**, hopeless; **anguished**, distressed, in despair, suicidal; miserable, wretched, desolate; forlorn, disheartened, discouraged, demoralized, devastated, downcast, resigned, defeatist, pessimistic; distraught, fraught, overcome, out of one's mind, at one's wits' end, beside oneself, at the end of one's tether; *literary* dolorous.
OPPOSITES cheerful; composed.
2 *a desperate attempt to escape* **last-ditch**, last-chance, last-resort, last-minute, last-gasp, eleventh-hour, all-out, do-or-die, final; **frantic**, frenzied, wild, straining; futile, hopeless, doomed, lost.
3 *his finances were in a desperate state* **grave**, serious, dangerous, risky, perilous, hazardous, precarious, critical, acute; **dire**, very bad, calamitous, appalling, awful, terrible, frightful, dreadful, outrageous, intolerable, deplorable, lamentable, sorry, poor; hopeless, irretrievable; *informal* lousy, chronic; *archaic or humorous* parlous.
4 *the church is in desperate need of repair* **urgent**, pressing, compelling, crying; acute, critical, crucial, vital, drastic, serious, grave, dire, extreme, great; *formal* exigent.
5 *they were* **desperate for** *food* | *she is* **desperate to** *get back to work* **in great**

need of, urgently requiring, craving, in want of, lacking, wanting; **eager**, aching, longing, yearning, hungry, thirsty, thirsting, itching, crying out, desirous; *informal* dying.
6 *armed bands of desperate men* | *a desperate act* **violent**, dangerous, lawless; reckless, rash, hasty, impetuous, foolhardy, incautious; death-or-glory, do-or-die, hazardous, risky.

desperately ▸ **adverb 1** *he screamed desperately for help* **in desperation**, in despair, despairingly, in anguish, in distress; miserably, wretchedly, hopelessly, desolately; forlornly, resignedly, defeatedly, pessimistically.
2 *many of them will become desperately ill* **seriously**, gravely, severely, critically, acutely, dangerously, perilously, hazardously, precariously; very, extremely, awfully, terribly, tremendously, frightfully, dreadfully; hopelessly, irretrievably; *informal* chronically; *archaic or humorous* parlously.
OPPOSITE slightly.
3 *he desperately wanted to talk to me* **urgently**, pressingly, intensely, with urgency, eagerly.

desperation ▸ **noun 1** *he became a thief out of sheer desperation* **hopelessness**, despair, distress; anguish, pain, agony, torment, torture, misery, wretchedness; disheartenment, discouragement, resignedness, forlornness, defeatism, pessimism.
2 *an act of desperation* **recklessness**, rashness, impetuosity, foolhardiness, riskiness, audacity, boldness, wildness, imprudence, injudiciousness.

despicable ▸ **adjective** *these were particularly despicable crimes* **contemptible**, loathsome, hateful, detestable, reprehensible, abhorrent, abominable, awful, heinous, beyond the pale; odious, execrable, repellent, repugnant, repulsive, revolting, disgusting, horrible, horrid, horrifying, obnoxious, nauseating, offensive, distasteful, beneath/below contempt; vile, base, low, mean, abject, shameful, degrading, ignominious, cheap, shabby, miserable, wretched, sorry, scurvy; infamous, villainous, ignoble, disreputable, discreditable, unworthy, unscrupulous, unprincipled, unsavoury; *informal* dirty, filthy, dirty rotten, rotten, low-down, no-good, beastly, lousy; *archaic* caitiff.
OPPOSITES admirable; noble.

despise ▸ **verb** *he despised weakness in any form* **detest**, hate, loathe, abhor, abominate, execrate, regard with contempt, feel contempt for, shrink from, be repelled by, not be able to bear/stand/stomach, find intolerable, deplore, dislike; **scorn**, disdain, slight, look down on, pour/heap scorn on, deride, scoff at, jeer at, sneer at, mock, revile; spurn, shun; *archaic* contemn, disrelish.
OPPOSITES like, respect.

despite ▸ **preposition** *he was forced to step down as mayor despite his popularity with voters* **in spite of**, notwithstanding, regardless of, in defiance of, without being affected by, in the face of, for all, even with, undeterred by.
OPPOSITE because of.

despoil ▸ **verb** (*literary*) **1** *a Cornish village that was despoiled by invaders* **plunder**, pillage, rob, ravage, harry, maraud, ravish, rape, raid, ransack, loot, sack, rifle; devastate, lay waste, wreak havoc on, vandalize, destroy, ruin, wreck, raze, level, annihilate, gut; *rare* depredate; *archaic* reave.
2 *the robbers despoiled him of all he had* **rob**, strip, deprive, dispossess, denude, divest, relieve, clean out; *archaic* reave.

despoliation ▸ **noun** *the despoliation of the countryside by the advance of civilization* **devastation**, destruction, ruin, ruination, ravaging, vandalism, depredation, despoilment; plunder, plundering, looting, pillage, harrying, marauding, ransacking, raiding, ravishing, rape, raping, sacking; *archaic* reaving.

despondency ▸ **noun** *the mood became one of gloom and despondency* **disheartenment**, discouragement, dispiritedness, downheartedness, low spirits, hopelessness, despair, wretchedness; melancholy, gloom, gloominess, glumness, melancholia, misery, depression, desolation, disappointment, dolefulness, dejection, sorrow, sadness, grief, distress, unhappiness; defeatism, pessimism; the doldrums; *informal* the blues, heartache.
OPPOSITES cheerfulness, hopefulness.

despondent ▸ **adjective** *they were tired and despondent* **disheartened**, discouraged, dispirited, downhearted, low-spirited, in low spirits, hopeless, downcast, cast down, crestfallen, down, low, disconsolate, in despair, despairing, wretched, oppressed; melancholy, gloomy, glum, morose, Eeyorish, doleful, dismal, woebegone, miserable, depressed, dejected, distressed, sorrowful, sad; defeatist, pessimistic; *informal* blue, down in the mouth, down in the dumps, as sick as a parrot.
OPPOSITES hopeful; cheerful.

despot ▸ **noun** *we must not support such despots by arming them* **tyrant**, dictator, absolute ruler, totalitarian, authoritarian, autocrat, oppressor, autarch, monocrat.
OPPOSITE democrat.

despotic ▸ **adjective** *a despotic regime* **autocratic**, dictatorial, totalitarian, authoritarian, absolute, absolutist, arbitrary, unconstitutional, undemocratic, uncontrolled, unaccountable, summary; one-party, single-party, autarchic, monocratic; **tyrannical**, oppressive, tyrannous, repressive, harsh, ruthless, merciless, draconian, illiberal; domineering, imperious, arrogant, high-handed.
OPPOSITES democratic, accountable.

> **CHOOSE THE RIGHT WORD**
>
> **despotic, autocratic, tyrannical**
>
> *See* AUTOCRATIC.

despotism ▸ **noun tyranny**, dictatorship, totalitarianism, authoritarianism, absolute rule, absolutism; oppression, repression, suppression; autocracy, monocracy, autarchy.
OPPOSITE democracy.

dessert *See centre pages for list of* **Cakes, Puddings, and Desserts**
▸ **noun pudding**, sweet, sweet course/dish, second course, last course; *Brit. informal* afters, pud.

destabilize ▸ **verb** *the tsar's isolation helped to destabilize the regime* **undermine**, weaken, impair, damage, subvert, sabotage, unsettle, upset, disrupt, wreck, ruin.
OPPOSITES strengthen, shore up.

destination ▸ **noun** *at around 1pm we arrived at our destination* **journey's end**, end of the line, landing place, point of disembarkation; terminus, station, stop, stopping place, port of call; goal, target, objective, end, purpose.

destined ▸ **adjective 1** *he seemed* **destined for** *a military career* | *he is* **destined** *to lead a troubled life* **fated**, ordained, preordained, foreordained, predestined, predetermined, certain; sure, bound, assured, guaranteed, very likely; doomed, foredoomed, meant; written in the cards, in the wind/air.
2 *a consignment of computers* **destined for** *Pakistan* **heading**, bound, en route, scheduled; directed to, routed to; **intended**, meant, designed, set; set apart, designated, appointed, allotted, booked, reserved.

destiny ▸ **noun 1** *man is master of his own destiny* **future**, fate, fortune, doom; lot, portion, due; nemesis; *literary* dole.
2 *the girl who found him that day was sent by destiny* **fate**, providence; predestination; divine decree, God's will, kismet, the stars; luck, fortune, chance; *Hinduism & Buddhism* karma; *Greek & Roman Mythology* the Fates; *Greek Mythology* Moirai; *Roman Mythology* Parcae; *Norse Mythology* the Norns.

destitute ▸ **adjective 1** *her parents died and she was left destitute* **penniless**, impoverished, poverty-stricken, poor, impecunious, indigent, down and out, pauperized, without a penny to one's name, without two farthings/pennies to rub together; insolvent, ruined; needy, in need, in want, hard up, on the breadline, hard-pressed, in reduced/straitened circumstances, deprived, disadvantaged, distressed, badly off; beggarly, beggared; *informal* on one's uppers, up against it, broke, flat broke, strapped (for cash), without a brass farthing, without a bean, without a sou, as poor as a church mouse, on [illegible]-ends; *Brit. informal* stony broke, skint, boracic (lint); *N. Amer. informal* ston[illegible]out a red cent, on skid row; *formal* penurious.
OPPOSITE rich.
2 *we were* **destitute of** *clothing* **devoid**, bereft, deprived, in need; bankrupt, empty, drained, exhausted, depleted, bare, denuded; lacking, without, deficient in, wanting; *informal* sans.
OPPOSITE well provided with.

destitution ▸ **noun** *he died leaving a wife and child in destitution* **dire poverty**, extreme poverty, poverty, impoverishment, insolvency, penury, pennilessness, impecuniousness, privation, indigence, ruin, ruination, pauperdom; hardship, neediness, need, want, reduced/straitened circumstances, dire straits, deprivation, disadvantage, distress, financial distress, difficulties; life on the breadline; beggary, mendicancy, vagrancy.
OPPOSITE wealth.

destroy ▸ **verb 1** *their offices were completely destroyed by bombing* **demolish**, knock down, pull down, tear down, level, raze (to the ground), fell, dismantle, break up, wreck, ruin, smash, shatter, crash, blast, blow up, blow to bits/pieces, dynamite, explode, bomb, torpedo.
OPPOSITES build; reconstruct.
2 *the increased traffic would destroy the adjoining conservation area* **spoil**, ruin, wreck, disfigure, blight, mar, blemish, impair, flaw, deface, scar, injure, harm, devastate, damage, lay waste, ravage, wreak havoc on; *literary* waste; *rare* disfeature.
OPPOSITES preserve; restore.
3 *his illness destroyed his hopes of going to university* **wreck**, ruin, spoil, disrupt, undo, upset, play havoc with, make a mess of, put an end to, end, bring to an end, put a stop to, terminate, prevent, frustrate, blight, crush, quell, quash, dash, scotch, shatter, vitiate, blast, devastate, demolish, sabotage, torpedo; upset someone's apple cart, cook someone's goose; *informal* mess up, muck up, screw up, louse up, foul up, make a hash of, do in, put paid to, put the lid on, put the kibosh on, do for, scupper, dish, stymie, queer, nix, banjax, blow a hole in; *Brit. informal* throw a spanner in the works of; *N. Amer. informal* throw a monkey wrench

in the works of; *Austral. informal* euchre, cruel; *vulgar slang* bugger up, fuck up, balls up; *archaic* bring to naught.
OPPOSITE raise.
4 *the horse broke its leg and had to be destroyed* **kill**, kill off, put down, put to sleep, slaughter, terminate, exterminate.
5 *the brigade's mission was to destroy the enemy* **annihilate**, wipe out, obliterate, wipe off the face of the earth, wipe off the map, eliminate, eradicate, liquidate, extinguish, finish off, erase, root out, extirpate; kill, slaughter, massacre, butcher, exterminate, decimate; *informal* take out, rub out, snuff out, zap; *N. Amer. informal* waste.
OPPOSITE spare.
6 *Rangers last night destroyed Leeds 4–0* **defeat utterly**, beat hollow, win a resounding victory over, annihilate, vanquish, drub, trounce, rout, crush, give someone a drubbing, overwhelm; *informal* lick, thrash, hammer, clobber, paste, give someone a pasting, whip, pound, pulverize, demolish, wipe the floor with, take to the cleaners, make mincemeat of, slaughter, murder, massacre, crucify, flatten, turn inside out, run rings around; *Brit. informal* stuff, marmalize; *N. Amer. informal* shellac, blow out, cream, skunk.
OPPOSITE lose to.

D

destruction ▸ noun **1** *journalists reported considerable destruction within the town by allied bombers* **demolition**, knocking down, pulling down, tearing down, levelling, razing (to the ground), felling, dismantling, breaking up, wrecking, ruination, smashing, shattering, blasting, blowing up, dynamiting, bombing, torpedoing.
2 *the continuing destruction of the countryside* **spoliation**, devastation, spoiling, ruination, wrecking, blighting, marring, disfigurement, impairment, defacing, scarring, injury, harm, laying waste, desolation, ravaging; *literary* wasting.
3 *the destruction of BSE-infected cattle* **killing**, killing off, putting down, putting to sleep, slaughter, slaughtering, extermination, termination.
4 *the careful and strategic destruction of the enemies' forces* **annihilation**, wiping out, obliteration, elimination, eradication, liquidation, extinction, finishing off, rooting out, extirpation; killing, slaughter, slaughtering, massacre, massacring, butchery, butchering, extermination, decimation; *informal* taking out, rubbing out, snuffing out, zapping; *N. Amer. informal* wasting.

destructive ▸ adjective **1** *the most destructive war the world has seen* **devastating**, ruinous, disastrous, catastrophic, calamitous, cataclysmic; pernicious, noxious, harmful, damaging, injurious, hurtful, wounding, violent, detrimental, deleterious, disadvantageous, ravaging, crippling, savage, fierce, brutal, dangerous, fatal, deadly, lethal, death-dealing.
OPPOSITES non-violent; creative.
2 *he takes a savage pleasure in destructive rather than constructive criticism* **negative**, hostile, antagonistic; unhelpful, disobliging, obstructive, vexatious, vicious, unfriendly, discouraging.
OPPOSITE constructive.

desultory ▸ adjective *the Commission took only a desultory interest in humane slaughter methods* **casual**, half-hearted, lukewarm, cursory, superficial, token, perfunctory, passing, incidental, sketchy, haphazard, random, aimless, rambling, erratic, unmethodical, unsystematic, automatic, unthinking, capricious, mechanical, offhand, chaotic, inconsistent, irregular, intermittent, occasional, sporadic, inconstant, fitful.
OPPOSITES keen; systematic; lasting.

detach ▸ verb **1** *he detached the front lamp from its bracket* **unfasten**, disconnect, disengage, part, separate, uncouple, remove, loose, loosen, untie, unhitch, undo, unhook, unbutton, unzip, free, sever, pull off, cut off, clip off, hack off, chop off, prune off, nip off, tear off, break off, strip off, disunite; *rare* disjoin.
OPPOSITE attach.
2 *a policeman* ***detached himself from*** *the crowd* **free**, separate, segregate; **move away**, walk away, move off, split off; leave, abandon.
OPPOSITE join.
3 *he has completely* ***detached himself from*** *the group whose principles he rejects* **dissociate**, divorce, alienate, separate, segregate, isolate, cut off, delink; break away, become estranged, disaffiliate, defect; leave, quit, withdraw from, secede from, break with, part company with, sever connections with, break off relations with; reach a parting of the ways; *Brit. informal* bust up.
OPPOSITES associate; join.

detached ▸ adjective **1** *a detached collar* **unfastened**, disconnected, disengaged, parted, separated, separate, uncoupled, removed, loosed, loosened, untied, unhitched, undone, unhooked, unbuttoned, unzipped, free, severed, cut off, hacked off, torn off, broken off.
OPPOSITE connected.
2 *she remained a detached observer of these events* **dispassionate**, disinterested, indifferent, objective, uninvolved, aloof, outside, remote, distant, impersonal, open-minded, neutral, unbiased, unprejudiced, impartial, non-partisan, with no axe to grind, fair, fair-minded, just, equitable, even-handed, unselfish.
OPPOSITES biased; involved.
3 *a detached house* **standing alone**, separate, unconnected, not attached.
OPPOSITES semi-detached; terraced.

detachment ▸ noun **1** *as an anthropologist you look on everything with detachment* **objectivity**, **dispassion**, dispassionateness, disinterest, indifference, aloofness, remoteness, distance, open-mindedness, neutrality, lack of bias, lack of prejudice, impartiality, fairness, fair-mindedness, equitability, even-handedness, unselfishness.
OPPOSITES bias; involvement.
2 *a detachment of soldiers* **unit**, detail, squad, troop, contingent, outfit, task force, crew, patrol, section, formation; squadron, flight, division, platoon, company, corps, regiment, brigade, battalion, force, garrison, legion.
3 *moisture coming through the plaster accounted for the detachment of the wallpaper* **loosening**, disconnection, unfastening, disengagement, parting, separation, uncoupling, removal, loosing, untying, unhitching, undoing, unhooking, unbuttoning, unzipping, freeing, severing, pulling off, cutting off, hacking off, chopping off, pruning, breaking off, disuniting.
OPPOSITE attachment.

detail ▸ noun **1** *he had made a replica of the uniform, correct in every detail* **particular**, feature, characteristic, respect, ingredient, attribute, item, specific, fact, piece of information, point, factor, element, circumstance, consideration, aspect, facet, side, part, unit, component, constituent, member, accessory.
OPPOSITES outline; overview.
2 *never mind—that's just a detail* **unimportant point**, insignificant item, trivial fact, nicety, subtlety; **triviality**, technicality, minor detail, petty detail, mere detail, matter/thing of no importance, matter/thing of no consequence, trifle, fine point, incidental, non-essential, inessential, nothing; (**details**) trivia, minutiae.
OPPOSITE salient point.
3 *some clubs maintain their records with a considerable degree of detail* **precision**, exactness, accuracy, rigour, strictness, thoroughness, carefulness, scrupulousness, meticulousness, particularity.
4 *the sergeant major was inspecting a guard detail* **unit**, detachment, squad, troop, contingent, outfit, task force, crew, patrol, section, formation.
5 *I didn't often get the toilet detail* **task**, job, duty, chore, charge, labour, piece of work, piece of business, assignment, function, commission, secondment, mission, engagement, occupation, undertaking, exercise, business, office, responsibility, errand.
□ **in detail** *this assumption will be examined in detail in Chapter 3* **thoroughly**, in depth, exhaustively, from top to bottom, minutely, closely, point by point, item by item, blow by blow, meticulously, rigorously, scrupulously, assiduously, conscientiously, painstakingly, methodically, carefully, sedulously, completely, comprehensively, fully, to the fullest extent, intensively, extensively.
▸ verb **1** *the report details a series of objections to the plan* **present**, describe, set out, set forth, draw up, delineate, frame; explain, expound, relate, give an account of, recount, narrate, recite, rehearse, catalogue, list, spell out, point out, itemize, enumerate, tabulate, particularize; **identify**, specify, define, state, declare, announce, cite, quote, instance, mention, name, designate, be specific about; *rare* individuate.
OPPOSITE outline.
2 *troops were detailed to prevent the feared rescue attempt* **assign**, allocate, appoint, delegate, commission, ordain, charge, send, post, nominate, vote, elect, adopt, co-opt, select, choose.

detailed ▸ adjective *he was able to give the police a detailed description of his attacker* **comprehensive**, full, complete, circumstantial, thorough, exhaustive, all-inclusive; elaborate, minute, intricate; explicit, specific, precise, exact, accurate, meticulous, painstaking; itemized, particularized, particular, blow-by-blow.
OPPOSITES general; brief.

detain ▸ verb **1** *they were detained for questioning* **hold**, take into custody, put into custody, place in custody, remand in custody, hold in custody, keep in custody, take (in), seize, confine, imprison, lock up, put in jail, put behind bars, incarcerate, impound, intern, restrain, arrest, apprehend; *informal* pick up, run in, pull in, haul in, cop, bust, nab, nail, do, collar, feel someone's collar; *Brit. informal* nick, pinch.
OPPOSITE release.
2 *don't let me detain you* **delay**, hold up, make late, retard, keep (back), slow up, slow down, set back, get bogged down; hinder, hamper, impede, obstruct.

detect ▸ verb **1** *because of the extractor fans, no one had detected the smell of diesel* **notice**, become aware of, perceive, note, discern, make out, observe, spot, become conscious of, recognize, distinguish, mark, remark, identify, diagnose; catch, decry, sense, see, catch sight of, smell, scent, taste; *Brit. informal* clock; *literary* behold, descry, espy.
2 *the directors are responsible for preventing and detecting fraud* **discover**, uncover, find, find out, turn up, unearth, dig up, dredge up, root out, hunt out, nose out, ferret out, expose, reveal, bring to light, bring into the open; come across, stumble on, chance on, hit on, encounter.
3 *police are still hoping to detect this crime* **solve**, clear up, get to the bottom of, find the perpetrator of, find the person behind; *informal* figure out, crack.
4 *hackers can make huge sums of money before being detected* **catch**, hunt

down, find, expose, reveal, unmask, smoke out, ferret out, track down, apprehend, arrest; *informal* nail.

detection ▸ noun **1** *the detection of methane and ammonia in the atmosphere in the 1930s* **observation**, noticing, noting, discernment, perception, spotting, awareness, recognition, distinguishing, identification, diagnosis; sensing, sight, smelling, tasting.
2 *the detection of insider dealing has increased* **discovery**, uncovering, unearthing, rooting out, exposure, revelation.
3 *the detection rate for burglary in dwellings is now less than 20%* **solving**, clear-up.
4 *somehow he managed to escape detection* **capture**, identification, exposure, unmasking, tracking down, apprehension, arrest.

detective *See centre pages for list of* **Police Officers and Forces**
▸ noun **investigator**, private detective, private investigator, operative; *Brit.* enquiry agent, CID officer, detective constable, DC, detective sergeant, DS, detective inspector, DI, detective chief inspector, DCI, detective superintendent, detective chief superintendent; *informal* private eye, PI, sleuth, sleuth-hound, jack, snoop, snooper; *N. Amer. informal* peeper, shamus, gumshoe; *informal, dated* dick, private dick, tec, bogey, hawkshaw, sherlock; *N. Amer. dated* Pinkerton.

detention ▸ noun *she was released after spending over a year in police detention* **custody**, imprisonment, confinement, incarceration, internment, captivity, restraint, arrest, house arrest, remand, committal; quarantine; *archaic* duress, durance; *rare* detainment.

deter ▸ verb **1** *the high cost has deterred many from attending* **put off**, discourage, dissuade, scare off; warn, caution; dishearten, demoralize, daunt, make worried/nervous/anxious, frighten, unnerve, intimidate.
OPPOSITE encourage.
2 *the presence of a caretaker deters crime* **prevent**, stop, put a stop to, avert, nip in the bud, fend off, turn aside, stave off, ward off, head off, shut out, block, intercept, halt, arrest, check, stay, keep, hinder, impede, hamper, obstruct, baulk, foil, thwart, obviate, frustrate, forestall, counteract, inhibit, hold back, curb, restrain, preclude, pre-empt, save, help; *archaic* let.
OPPOSITE encourage.

> CHOOSE THE RIGHT WORD
> **deter, discourage, dissuade**
> *See* DISCOURAGE.

detergent ▸ noun *use ordinary washing detergent* **cleaner**, cleanser; washing powder, washing-up liquid; soap powder, soap flakes.
▸ adjective *staining that resists detergent action* **cleaning**, cleansing; *technical* abstergent, surface-active.

deteriorate ▸ verb **1** *his condition has deteriorated in the intensive care unit* **worsen**, get worse, decline, be in decline, degenerate, decay; collapse, fail, fall, drop, sink, slump, slip, slide, go downhill, go backwards, go to rack and ruin, stagnate, wane, ebb; *informal* go to pot, go to the dogs, hit the skids, go down the toilet, go down the tubes; *Austral./NZ informal* go to the pack; *rare* retrograde.
OPPOSITE improve.
2 *many of these materials deteriorate badly if stored in damp conditions* **decay**, degrade, degenerate, break down, decompose, rot, putrefy, go bad, go off, spoil, perish; wither, atrophy, weaken, fade, break up, disintegrate, become dilapidated, crumble, fall down, collapse, fall apart, fall to pieces; *archaic* corrupt.

deterioration ▸ noun **1** *a sharp deterioration in law and order* **worsening**, decline, decay, collapse, failure, fall, drop, downturn, slump, slip, slide, stagnation, waning, ebb, retrogression.
OPPOSITE improvement.
2 *condensation in lofts can cause deterioration of the roof structure* **decay**, degradation, degeneration, breakdown, decomposition, rot, putrefaction, spoliation, perishing; withering, atrophy, weakening, fading, break-up, disintegration, dilapidation, crumbling, collapse, falling down, falling apart, falling to pieces; *archaic* corruption.

determinate ▸ adjective *a determinate hierarchy of authority* **fixed**, settled, specified, quantified, established, defined, explicit, known, determined, definitive, conclusive, express, precise, final, ultimate, absolute, categorical, positive, definite.
OPPOSITE indeterminate.

determination ▸ noun **1** *it took all her determination to stand her ground* **resolution**, resolve, resoluteness; **will power**, strength of will, strength of character, single-mindedness, sense of purpose, firmness of purpose, fixity of purpose, purposefulness; intentness, decision, decidedness; steadfastness, staunchness, perseverance, persistence, indefatigability, tenacity, tenaciousness, staying power, strong-mindedness, backbone, the bulldog spirit, pertinacity, pertinaciousness; stubbornness, doggedness, obstinacy, obdurateness, obduracy, inflexibility; spiritedness, braveness, bravery, boldness, courage, courageousness, pluck, pluckiness, stout-heartedness; *German* sitzfleisch; *informal* guts, spunk, grit, stickability; *N. Amer. informal* stick-to-it-iveness; *archaic* intension; *rare* perseveration.
OPPOSITES weak-mindedness, pusillanimity.
2 *provision should be made for determination of the rent* **setting**, fixing, specification, a decision about, settlement, designation, allotment, arrangement, choice, naming, nomination, appointment, establishment, authorization, prescription.
3 *the first determination of the speed of light* **calculation**, discovery, ascertainment, establishment, fixing, deduction, divination, diagnosis, discernment, check, verification, confirmation.

determine ▸ verb **1** *it is this last pair of chromosomes which determines the sex of the embryo* **control**, decide, regulate, direct, rule, dictate, govern, condition, form, shape; affect, have an effect on, influence, exert influence on, sway, act on, work on, mould, modify, alter, touch, have an impact on, impact on.
2 *he determined to sell up and go abroad* **resolve**, decide, come to a decision, make a decision, reach a decision, make up one's mind, choose, elect, opt; *formal* purpose.
3 *the rent shall be determined by a qualified accountant* **specify**, set, fix, decide on, come to a decision about, settle, assign, designate, allot, arrange, choose, name, appoint, establish, authorize, ordain, prescribe, decree.
4 *the first step is to determine the composition of the raw materials* **find out**, discover, ascertain, learn, establish, fix, settle, decide, calculate, work out, make out, fathom (out), get/come to know, ferret out, deduce, divine, intuit, diagnose, discern, check, verify, confirm, make certain of, certify; *informal* figure out, get a fix on.
5 *I am not sure what determined her to write to me* **prompt**, impel, induce, influence, sway, lead, move, cause, motivate, stimulate, prod, spur on, provoke, incite, dispose, incline, persuade, encourage, urge, inspire; make.

> CHOOSE THE RIGHT WORD
> **determine, decide, resolve**
> *See* DECIDE.

determined ▸ adjective **1** *he was determined to have his way | she was absolutely determined on going* **intent on**, bent on, set on, dead set on, insistent on, fixed on, resolved on/to, firm about, committed to, hell-bent on; single-minded about, obsessive about, obsessed with, fanatical about, fixated on.
2 *he sounds a very determined man* **resolute**, full of determination, purposeful, purposive, resolved, decided, adamant, single-minded, firm, unswerving, unswervable, unwavering, undaunted, fixed, set, intent, insistent; steadfast, staunch, stalwart, earnest, manful, deliberate, unfaltering, unhesitating, unflinching, persevering, persistent, pertinacious, indefatigable, tenacious, bulldog, strong-minded, strong-willed, unshakeable, unshaken, steely, four-square, dedicated, committed; stubborn, dogged, obstinate, obdurate, inflexible, relentless, intransigent, implacable, unyielding, unbending, immovable, unrelenting; spirited, brave, bold, courageous, plucky, stout, stout-hearted, mettlesome, indomitable, strenuous, vigorous, gritty, stiff; *N. Amer.* rock-ribbed; *informal* gutsy, spunky; *rare* perseverant, indurate.
OPPOSITES irresolute; weak-willed, pusillanimous.

determining ▸ adjective *the size of your house may be the determining factor* **deciding**, decisive, conclusive, final, settling, definitive, key, pivotal, crucial, critical, most influential, significant, major, chief, principal, prime, paramount.

deterrent ▸ noun *complications of this nature are a deterrent to investors* **disincentive**, discouragement, dissuasion, damper, brake, curb, check, restraint; obstacle, hindrance, impediment, obstruction, block, barrier, inhibition.
OPPOSITES incentive; encouragement.

detest ▸ verb *I do detest social climbers* **abhor**, hate, loathe, despise, abominate, execrate, regard with disgust, feel disgust for, feel repugnance towards, feel distaste for, shrink from, recoil from, shudder at, be unable to bear, be unable to abide, feel hostility to, feel aversion to, feel animosity to, find intolerable, dislike, disdain, have an aversion to; *archaic* disrelish.
OPPOSITES love, admire.

detestable ▸ adjective *all terrorist crime is detestable* **abhorrent**, detested, hateful, hated, loathsome, loathed, despicable, despised, abominable, abominated, execrable, execrated, repellent, repugnant, repulsive, revolting, disgusting, distasteful, horrible, horrid, horrifying, awful, heinous, reprehensible, obnoxious, odious, nauseating, offensive, contemptible.
OPPOSITES lovable, admirable.

detestation ▸ noun *her detestation of socialism* **hatred**, loathing, abhorrence, execration, revulsion, abomination, disgust, repugnance, horror, antipathy, odium, aversion, hostility, animosity, enmity, dislike, distaste, disdain, contempt; *archaic* disrelish; *rare* repellence, repellency.
OPPOSITE love.

D

dethrone ▸ verb *he had hoped to dethrone the king* **depose**, oust, uncrown, topple, overthrow, bring down, unseat, remove from office, dislodge, discharge, displace, supplant, usurp, overturn, dismiss, eject; *informal* drum out; *archaic* unthrone.
OPPOSITES enthrone, crown.

detonate ▸ verb **1** *the depth charge detonated directly under the engine compartment* **explode**, go off, be set off, blow up, burst apart, shatter, erupt; ignite; bang, blast, boom, go bang, go boom.
2 *they detonated the bomb by remote control* **set off**, explode, discharge, let off, touch off, trigger; ignite, kindle, light, spark.

detonation ▸ noun *the detonation of the first atomic bomb* **explosion**, discharge, blowing up, ignition, blast, burst, crack, bang, report.

detour ▸ noun *visiting Bagley meant a detour of only a mile or so* **roundabout route**, indirect route, circuitous route, scenic route, tourist route, diversion, bypass, ring road, alternative route, digression, deviation, byway, bypath; *Brit.* relief road; *Brit. informal* rat run.
OPPOSITE direct route.

detract ▸ verb **1** *the few reservations I have expressed are not intended to detract from the book's excellence* **belittle**, take away from, diminish, reduce, lessen, minimize, lower, make light of, play down, discount, soft-pedal, brush aside, gloss over, trivialize, decry, depreciate, denigrate, devalue, devaluate, deprecate; *informal* pooh-pooh; *archaic* hold cheap; *rare* derogate, misprize, minify.
OPPOSITE enhance.
2 *if too many patterns are used together, they will detract attention from each other* **divert**, distract, turn away, turn aside, draw away, head off, deflect, avert, shift.
OPPOSITE attract.

detractor ▸ noun *detractors complained about the display's confused nature* **critic**, disparager, denigrator, deprecator, belittler, attacker, censurer, fault-finder, carper, backbiter, caviller, reviler, vilifier, slanderer, libeller, calumniator, defamer, traducer; *informal* mud-slinger, knocker, nit-picker; *rare* asperser.

detriment ▸ noun *some light industry can generally be carried out in a residential area without detriment to its amenities* **harm**, damage, injury, hurt, impairment, loss, prejudice, disadvantage, disservice, ill, wrong, mischief.
OPPOSITES benefit, good.

detrimental ▸ adjective *the erosion will have a detrimental effect on water quality* **harmful**, damaging, injurious, hurtful, inimical, deleterious, dangerous, destructive, ruinous, calamitous, disastrous, pernicious, ill, bad, evil, baleful, malign, corrupting, malignant, adverse, undesirable, prejudicial, unfavourable, unfortunate, counterproductive; unhealthy, unwholesome, poisonous, cancerous, noxious, deadly, lethal, fatal; *literary* malefic, maleficent; *rare* prejudicious.
OPPOSITES benign; beneficial.

detritus ▸ noun *large areas of land are now littered with military detritus* **debris**, waste, waste matter, discarded matter, refuse, rubbish, litter, scrap, flotsam and jetsam, lumber, rubble, wreckage; remains, remnants, fragments, scraps, spoilage, dregs, leavings, sweepings, dross, scum, chaff, offscourings, swill, slag; *N. Amer.* trash, garbage; *Austral./NZ* mullock; *informal* dreck, junk; *Brit. informal* grot, gash; *vulgar slang* shit, crap; *Archaeology* debitage; *rare* draff, raffle, raff, cultch, orts.

devalue ▸ verb *our culture devalues the reasons for getting married* **belittle**, depreciate, disparage, denigrate, decry, deprecate, make light of, treat lightly, discredit, underrate, undervalue, underestimate, deflate, detract from, diminish, minimize, trivialize, run down, traduce, defame; *informal* knock, slam, pan, bad-mouth, sell short, put down, pooh-pooh, look down one's nose at, do down, do a hatchet job on, take to pieces, pull apart, pick holes in, drag through the mud, have a go at, hit out at; *Brit. informal* rubbish, slate, slag off; *archaic* cry down, hold cheap; *rare* derogate, misprize, minify.

devastate ▸ verb **1** *the city was devastated by a huge earthquake* **destroy**, ruin, leave in ruins, wreck, lay waste, wreak havoc on, ravage, ransack, leave desolate, demolish, raze (to the ground), level, flatten, annihilate.
2 *he was devastated by the news* **shatter**, shock, stun, daze, dumbfound, traumatize, crush, overwhelm, overcome, greatly upset, distress; *informal* knock for six, knock sideways, knock the stuffing out of.

devastating ▸ adjective **1** *a devastating cyclone struck Bangladesh in April* **destructive**, ruinous, disastrous, catastrophic, calamitous, cataclysmic; pernicious, noxious, harmful, damaging, injurious, hurtful, wounding, violent, detrimental, deleterious, disadvantageous, ravaging, crippling, savage, fierce, brutal, dangerous, fatal, deadly, lethal, death-dealing.
2 *a bereavement can be a devastating blow* **shattering**, shocking, traumatic, overwhelming, crushing, extremely upsetting, distressing, severe, savage, terrible, very great; *informal* gut-wrenching.
3 (*informal*) *he could look utterly devastating when he wanted to* **gorgeous**, stunning, glamorous, dazzling, ravishing, striking, beautiful, lovely, captivating, bewitching, beguiling, engaging, charming, charismatic, enchanting, appealing, arresting, delightful, irresistible, desirable, luscious, sexy, sexually attractive, seductive, alluring; *informal* fanciable, beddable, tasty, hot, smashing, knockout, drop-dead gorgeous, out of this world, easy on the eye; *Brit. informal* fit; *N. Amer. informal* cute, foxy; *Austral./NZ informal* spunky; *literary* beauteous; *archaic* taking, well favoured, comely, fair; *rare* sightly, pulchritudinous.
4 (*informal*) *he presented devastating arguments against the plan* **incisive**, highly effective, penetrating, cutting, mordant, trenchant; withering, blistering, searing, scathing, scorching, fierce, ferocious, savage, severe, stinging, biting, virulent, caustic, vitriolic, scornful, sharp, bitter, acid, harsh, unsparing; *rare* mordacious.

devastation ▸ noun **1** *the hurricane passed, leaving a trail of devastation in its wake* **destruction**, ruin, desolation, depredation, waste, havoc, wreckage; ruins, ravages.
2 *the devastation of East Prussia by Russian troops in 1758* **laying waste**, destruction, wrecking, ruination, despoliation, ransacking, ravaging; demolition, razing, levelling, flattening, annihilation; *literary* rape.
3 *the devastation you have caused the families of your victims* **shock**, trauma, upheaval, distress, stress, strain, pain, anguish, suffering, upset, agony, misery, sorrow, grief, heartache, heartbreak, torture, traumatization.

develop ▸ verb **1** *France's space industry developed rapidly after 1973* **grow**, evolve, mature, expand, enlarge, spread, advance, progress, prosper, succeed, thrive, get on well, flourish, blossom, bloom, burgeon, make headway, be successful; *informal* go great guns.
2 *a plan was developed to restore the company to profitability* **initiate**, instigate, set in motion, institute, inaugurate, originate, invent, form, establish, fashion, generate; undertake, embark on.
3 *education allows people to develop their talents to the full* **expand**, enlarge, add to, flesh out, supplement, reinforce, augment, extend, broaden, fill out, embellish, enhance, elaborate, amplify, refine, improve, polish, perfect.
4 *a row developed* **come into being**, come about, start, begin, be born, come into existence, appear, arrive, come forth, emerge, erupt, burst out, arise, originate, break, unfold, crop up, follow, happen, result, ensue, break out; *formal* commence.
5 *he developed the disease at age 67* **fall ill with**, be taken ill with, be struck down with, be stricken with, succumb to; contract, catch, get, pick up, come down with, become infected with; *Brit.* go down with; *informal* take ill with; *N. Amer. informal* take sick with.

development ▸ noun **1** *the next stage in the development of this form of transport* **evolution**, growth, maturing, expansion, enlargement, spread, buildout, progress, success, blossoming, blooming, burgeoning, headway.
2 *the development of the idea of a nation* **forming**, establishment, institution, initiation, instigation, inauguration, origination, invention, generation.
3 *have there been any developments?* **event**, turn of events, occurrence, happening, circumstance, incident, phenomenon, situation, issue, outcome, upshot.
4 *a housing development* **estate**, complex, site, conglomeration.

deviant ▸ adjective *deviant behaviour* **aberrant**, deviating, divergent, abnormal, atypical, untypical, non-typical, anomalous, digressive, irregular, non-standard; nonconformist, rogue, perverse, transgressing, wayward; strange, odd, peculiar, uncommon, unusual, freak, freakish, curious, bizarre, eccentric, idiosyncratic, unorthodox, exceptional, singular, unrepresentative; distorted, twisted, warped, perverted; *informal* bent, kinky, quirky.
OPPOSITES normal; orthodox.
▸ noun *lone parents are likely to be treated as deviants* **nonconformist**, eccentric, maverick, individualist, exception, outsider, misfit, fish out of water, square peg in a round hole, round peg in a square hole; *informal* oddball, odd fish, weirdo, weirdie, freak; *N. Amer. informal* screwball, kook.

deviate ▸ verb *you must not deviate from the agreed route* **diverge**, digress, drift, stray, slew, veer, swerve, turn away, turn aside, get sidetracked, branch off, differ, vary, change, depart, be different; be at variance with, run counter to, contrast with, contravene, contradict; *rare* divagate.

deviation ▸ noun *the slightest deviation from approved procedures could prove disastrous* **divergence**, digression, turning aside, departure, deflection, difference, variation, variance, alteration, veering, straying, fluctuation, aberration, abnormality, irregularity, anomaly, inconsistency, discrepancy, variableness, oddness, freakishness; change, shift, veer, swerve, bend, drift.

device ▸ noun **1** *a device for measuring rapid pressure fluctuations* **implement**, gadget, utensil, tool, appliance, piece of equipment, apparatus, piece of apparatus, piece of hardware, instrument, machine, mechanism, contrivance, contraption, invention, convenience, amenity, aid; *informal* gizmo, widget, mod con.
2 *he found an ingenious legal device to avoid facing prosecution* **ploy**, plan, cunning plan, tactic, move, means, stratagem, scheme, plot, trick, ruse, gambit, manoeuvre, machination, intrigue, contrivance, expedient, dodge, artifice, subterfuge, game, wile; *Brit. informal* wheeze; *archaic* shift.
3 *their shields bear the device of the Blazing Sun* **emblem**, symbol, logo, badge, stamp, trademark, crest, insignia, coat of arms, escutcheon, seal, mark, figure, design, rune, logotype, logogram, monogram, hallmark, tag, motto, token, motif, colophon, ideogram.

devil ▸ noun **1** *they perform the ritual of driving out the devils from their bodies* **evil spirit**, demon, fiend, imp, bogie, ghost, spectre; *informal* spook; *archaic* bugbear; *rare* cacodemon.
2 *look what the cruel devil has done to me* **brute**, beast, monster, savage, demon, fiend; villain, sadist, barbarian, terror, ogre; *informal* swine, bastard, pig; *vulgar slang* shit.
3 (*informal*) *he is four and a naughty little devil* **rascal**, rogue, imp, demon, fiend, monkey, wretch, scamp, mischief-maker, troublemaker, badly behaved child; *informal* mischief, monster, horror, holy terror; *Brit. informal* perisher; *Irish informal* spalpeen; *N. English informal* tyke, scally; *N. Amer. informal* varmint, hellion; *archaic* scapegrace, rapscallion, jackanapes.
4 (*informal*) *the poor devils looked as though they could do with some refreshment* **wretch**, unfortunate, creature, soul, person, fellow; *informal* thing, beggar, bastard; *Brit. vulgar slang* sod, bugger.

WORD LINKS
relating to the Devil **diabolical, diabolic**

devilish ▸ adjective **1** *he gave a wide, devilish grin* **diabolical**, diabolic, fiendish, satanic, demonic, demoniac, demoniacal, Mephistophelian; hellish, infernal, Hadean.
2 *what devilish torture had they dreamed up?* **wicked**, evil, accursed, sinful, iniquitous, nefarious, vile, foul, abominable, unspeakable, loathsome, monstrous, atrocious, heinous, hideous, odious, horrible, horrifying, shocking, appalling, dreadful, awful, terrible, ghastly, abhorrent, despicable, damnable, villainous, shameful, depraved, perverted, ungodly, dark, black, black-hearted, immoral, amoral; vicious, cruel, savage, brutish, bestial, barbaric, barbarous; *rare* cacodemonic, egregious, flagitious, facinorous.
3 *it turned out to be a devilish job* **difficult**, tricky, ticklish, troublesome, thorny, awkward, problematic, problem, impossible, messy; *informal* a bitch of a, the (very) devil of a; *archaic* kittle.
▸ adverb (*informal, dated*) *a devilish clever plan*. See EXTREMELY.

devil-may-care ▸ adjective *those devil-may-care young pilots* **reckless**, rash, incautious, heedless, unheeding, hasty, overhasty, precipitate, precipitous, impetuous, impulsive, daredevil, hot-headed; **irresponsible**, wild, foolhardy, headlong, over-adventurous, over-venturesome, audacious, death-or-glory, hare-brained, madcap, imprudent, unwise, unthinking; **nonchalant**, casual, airy, breezy, flippant, swaggering, insouciant, indifferent, happy-go-lucky, easy-going; unworried, untroubled, unconcerned; *Brit.* tearaway; *informal* harum-scarum; *rare* temerarious.
OPPOSITES solemn, serious.

devilment ▸ noun *we got up to all kinds of devilment*. See DEVILRY *sense 2*.

devilry, **deviltry** ▸ noun **1** *some devilry was afoot* **wickedness**, evil, evil-doing, evilness, sin, sinfulness, iniquity, iniquitousness, vileness, foulness, baseness, badness, wrong, wrongdoing, dishonesty, unscrupulousness, roguery, villainy, rascality, delinquency, viciousness, devilishness, fiendishness, heinousness; *informal* crookedness, shadiness; *Law* malfeasance; *archaic* knavery.
2 *a perverse sense of devilry urged her to lead him on* **mischief**, naughtiness, badness, bad behaviour, misbehaviour, mischievousness, troublemaking, misconduct, misdemeanour, perversity, disobedience, pranks, impishness, tricks, larks, capers, nonsense, roguery, rascality, devilment, funny business; *French* diablerie; *informal* monkey tricks, monkey business, shenanigans, goings-on, hanky-panky; *Brit. informal* carry-on, carryings-on, jiggery-pokery.
3 *they dabbled in devilry* **black magic**, sorcery, magic, witchcraft, wizardry, necromancy, enchantment, spell-working, incantation, the supernatural, occultism, the occult, the black arts, divination, malediction, voodoo, hoodoo, sympathetic magic, witching, witchery; charms, hexes, spells, jinxes; *N. Amer.* mojo, orenda; *NZ* makutu; *S. African informal* muti; *rare* sortilege, thaumaturgy, theurgy.

devious ▸ adjective **1** *he exposed the many devious ways in which governments bent the rules in their favour* **underhand**, underhanded, deceitful, dishonest, dishonourable, disreputable, unethical, unprincipled, immoral, unscrupulous, fraudulent, cheating, dubious, dirty, unfair, treacherous, duplicitous, double-dealing, below the belt, two-timing, two-faced, unsporting, unsportsmanlike; crafty, cunning, calculating, artful, conniving, scheming, designing, sly, wily, guileful, tricky; sneaky, sneaking, furtive, secret, secretive, clandestine, surreptitious, covert, veiled, shrouded, cloak-and-dagger, hugger-mugger, hole-and-corner, hidden, back-alley, backstairs, under the table, conspiratorial; *N. Amer.* snide, snidey; *informal* crooked, shady, bent, low-down, murky, fishy; *Brit. informal* dodgy; *Austral./NZ informal* shonky; *S. African informal* slim.
OPPOSITE above board.
2 *the A832 is a devious route around the coastal fringes* **circuitous**, roundabout, indirect, meandering, winding, serpentine, tortuous, rambling; *rare* anfractuous.
OPPOSITE direct.

devise ▸ verb *scientists have devised a method of recycling oil contaminated with PCBs* **conceive**, think up, come up with, dream up, draw up, work out, form, formulate, concoct, design, frame, invent, coin, originate, compose, construct, fabricate, create, produce, put together, make up, develop, evolve; discover, hit on; hatch, cook up, contrive.

devitalize ▸ verb *her spirit had not been devitalized by the city* **weaken**, make weak, make feeble, enfeeble, debilitate, enervate, sap, drain, tax, overtax, wash out, overtire, exhaust, weary, tire, tire out, fatigue, jade, wear out, prostrate, undermine, impair, render infirm, indispose, incapacitate, cripple, disable, paralyse, immobilize, lay low, put out of action; *informal* knock out, do in, knacker, shatter, whack, bush, frazzle, wear to a frazzle, poop, take it out of, fag out; *rare* torpefy.
OPPOSITES strengthen, reinforce.

devoid ▸ adjective *the moorland is* **devoid of** *interest except to grazing sheep* **lacking**, without, free from/of, empty of, vacant of, void of, bare of, barren of, bereft of, drained of, denuded of, deprived of, depleted of, destitute of, bankrupt of; wanting, in need of; *informal* minus, sans.

D

devolution ▸ noun *the devolution of power to the regions* **decentralization**, delegation, dispersal, distribution, transfer, surrender, relinquishment.
OPPOSITE centralization.

devolve ▸ verb *the move would devolve responsibility to local units* **delegate**, pass (down/on), hand down/over/on, depute, transfer, transmit, commit, assign, consign, convey, entrust, turn over, make over, sign over, give, part with, let go of, leave, cede, surrender, relinquish, deliver; bestow, grant; offload, dump, get rid of, palm off, foist, fob off.
OPPOSITES centralize; retain.

devote ▸ verb *they need to devote considerable time to career planning* **allocate**, assign, allot, commit, give, give over, afford, apportion, surrender, consign, sacrifice, pledge, dedicate, consecrate; set aside, earmark, reserve, designate, spare.

devoted ▸ adjective *a devoted follower* **loyal**, faithful, true, true blue, staunch, steadfast, constant, committed, dedicated, devout; fond, loving, admiring, affectionate, caring, attentive, warm, ardent.
OPPOSITES disloyal; unfaithful; indifferent.

devotee ▸ noun **1** *a devotee of rock music* **enthusiast**, fan, fanatic, addict, lover, aficionado, admirer; *informal* buff, freak, nut, fiend, maniac, a great one for; *N. Amer. informal* geek, jock; *S. African informal* fundi.
2 *devotees thronged the temple* **follower**, adherent, supporter, upholder, defender, advocate, champion, disciple, votary, partisan, member, friend, stalwart, fanatic, zealot; believer, worshipper, attender; *informal* hanger-on, groupie; *N. Amer. informal* booster, cohort, rooter; *rare* janissary, sectary.

devotion ▸ noun **1** *Eleanor's devotion to her husband* **loyalty**, faithfulness, fidelity, trueness, staunchness, steadfastness, constancy, commitment, adherence, allegiance, dedication, devoutness; fondness, love, admiration, affection, attentiveness, care, caring, warmness, closeness.
OPPOSITES disloyalty; indifference; hatred.
2 *the order's aim was to live a life of devotion* **devoutness**, piety, religiousness, spirituality, godliness, holiness, sanctity, saintliness.
3 (**devotions**) *morning devotions* **religious worship**, worship, religious observance; prayers, vespers, matins; prayer meeting, church service.

devotional ▸ adjective *the devotional paintings of the period* **religious**, sacred, spiritual, divine, church, churchly, ecclesiastical.
OPPOSITE secular.

devour ▸ verb **1** *she watched him as he devoured his meal* **eat hungrily**, eat quickly, eat greedily, eat heartily, eat up, swallow, gobble (up/down), guzzle (down), gulp (down), bolt (down), cram down, gorge oneself on, wolf (down), feast on, consume; *informal* scoff (down), pack away, demolish, dispose of, make short work of, polish off, shovel down, stuff one's face with, stuff oneself with, stuff (down), pig oneself on, pig out on, sink, put away, tuck away, get outside of, get one's laughing gear round; *Brit. informal* gollop, shift; *N. Amer. informal* scarf (down/up), snarf (down/up), inhale; *rare* ingurgitate.
2 *we watched in dismay as the flames devoured the old house* **destroy**, consume, engulf, envelop, demolish, lay waste, wipe out, annihilate, devastate; raze, gut, ravage, ruin, wreck.
3 *he was devoured by remorse* **afflict**, torture, plague, bedevil, trouble, harrow, rack; consume, swallow up, engulf, swamp, overcome, overwhelm.

devout ▸ adjective **1** *a devout Christian* **pious**, religious, devoted, dedicated, reverent, God-fearing, believing, spiritual, prayerful, holy, godly, saintly, faithful, dutiful, righteous, churchgoing, orthodox.
OPPOSITES insincere; lapsed.
2 *a devout soccer fan* **dedicated**, devoted, committed, loyal, faithful, staunch, genuine, firm, steadfast, resolute, unwavering, sincere, wholehearted, keen, earnest, enthusiastic, zealous, passionate, ardent, fervent, intense, vehement, active, sworn, pledged; *French* engagé; *informal* card-carrying, red-hot, true blue, mad keen, deep-dyed.
OPPOSITE apathetic.

CHOOSE THE RIGHT WORD

devout, religious, pious
See RELIGIOUS.

dexterity ▸ noun **1** *the hand-decorating of china demanded great dexterity*

deftness, adeptness, adroitness, agility, nimbleness, handiness, ability, capability, talent, skilfulness, skill, proficiency, accomplishment, expertise, experience, efficiency, effortlessness, slickness, mastery, delicacy, knack, facility, artistry, sleight of hand, craft, finesse, felicity; *informal* niftiness, wizardry.
OPPOSITE clumsiness.
2 *his political dexterity* **shrewdness**, astuteness, sharp-wittedness, sharpness, acuteness, acumen, acuity, intelligence; ingenuity, inventiveness, cleverness, smartness; sensitivity, alertness, wit, canniness, common sense, discernment, insight, understanding, penetration, perception, perceptiveness, perspicacity, perspicaciousness, discrimination, sagacity, sageness; cunning, artfulness, craftiness, wiliness, calculation, calculatedness; *informal* nous, horse sense, savvy; *rare* sapience, arguteness.
OPPOSITES stupidity; insensitivity.

D

dexterous ▶ adjective **1** *a dexterous flick of the wrist* **deft**, adept, adroit, agile, nimble, neat, nimble-fingered, handy, able, capable, talented, skilful, skilled, proficient, accomplished, expert, experienced, practised, polished, efficient, effortless, slick, professional, masterful, masterly, impressive, finely judged, delicate; *informal* nifty, nippy, mean, wicked, ace, wizard, crack; *rare* habile.
OPPOSITE clumsy.
2 *Klein had achieved notoriety for his dexterous accounting abilities* **shrewd**, ingenious, inventive, clever, intelligent, bright, brilliant, smart, sharp, sharp-witted, razor-sharp, acute, quick, quick-witted, astute, canny, intuitive, discerning, perceptive, perspicacious, insightful, incisive, sagacious, wise, judicious; cunning, artful, crafty, wily, calculating; *informal* on the ball, quick off the mark, quick on the uptake, brainy, streetwise, savvy; *Brit. informal* suss; *N. Amer. informal* heads-up; *dated, informal* long-headed; *rare* argute, sapient.
OPPOSITE stupid.

diabolic ▶ adjective *diabolic rituals had taken place. See* DIABOLICAL.

diabolical ▶ adjective **1** *his diabolical skill* **devilish**, fiendish, satanic, Mephistophelian, demonic, demoniacal, hellish, infernal, evil, wicked, ungodly, unholy; *rare* cacodemonic.
2 (*informal*) *the team manager was sacked after that diabolical performance* **very bad**, poor, dreadful, awful, terrible, frightful, disgraceful, shameful, lamentable, deplorable, appalling, atrocious; inferior, substandard, mediocre, unsatisfactory, inadequate, second-rate, third-rate, shoddy, inept, bungling, hopeless; *informal* crummy, dire, dismal, God-awful, shocking, abysmal, bum, rotten, pathetic, woeful, pitiful, lousy, useless, poxy, the pits; *Brit. informal* duff, rubbish, ropy, chronic, a load of pants; *vulgar slang* crap, crappy, shitty; *N. Amer. vulgar slang* chickenshit, hellacious; *archaic* direful; *rare* egregious.
3 (*informal*) *a diabolical liberty* **very great**, extreme, excessive, undue, inordinate, immoderate, unconscionable, outrageous; uncalled for, unprovoked, intolerable, unacceptable, unreasonable, unjustifiable, unwarrantable, without justification, indefensible, inexcusable, unforgivable, unpardonable.

diacritic ▶ noun. *See centre pages for list of* **Accents**

diadem ▶ noun *the queen wore a jewelled diadem* **crown**, coronet, tiara, circlet, chaplet, headpiece, headband, fillet, wreath, garland; *literary* coronal; (*in India, historical*) taj.

diagnose ▶ verb *the neurologist diagnosed a possible brain haemorrhage* **identify**, determine, distinguish, recognize, discover, spot, detect, pinpoint; pronounce, confirm, verify.

diagnosis ▶ noun **1** *the correct diagnosis of appendicitis depends on clinical acumen* **identification**, recognition, discovery, detection, pinpointing, reading, determination; confirmation, verification.
2 *the experts could offer no diagnosis* **opinion**, **prognosis**, judgement, verdict, pronouncement, conclusion, interpretation; solution, result.

diagonal ▶ adjective *he drew a diagonal line across the page* **crossways**, crosswise, from corner to corner, slanting, slanted, aslant, slant, slantwise, sloping, oblique, inclined, inclining, tilted, tilting, angled, at an angle, cornerways, cornerwise; *Scottish* squint; *N. Amer.* cater-cornered, cater-corner, catty-cornered, kitty-cornered.

diagonally ▶ adverb *she cut the cake in half diagonally* **obliquely**, at an angle, crossways, crosswise, on the cross, on the slant, slantwise, aslant, cornerwise, on the bias; *N. Amer.* cater-cornered, cater-corner, catty-cornered, kitty-cornered.

diagram ▶ noun *a diagram of the alimentary canal* **drawing**, line drawing, illustration, picture; **schematic representation**, representation, scale drawing, technical drawing, plan, figure, sketch, draft, outline, delineation, exploded view, cutaway, layout; *Computing* graphic; *rare* schema.

diagrammatic ▶ adjective *the information is presented in diagrammatic form* **graphic**, graphical, tabular, pictorial, delineative, illustrative, representational, representative, schematic.

dial ▶ verb *he grabbed the telephone and dialled 999 | she dialled her parents* **telephone**, phone, phone up, call, call up; place a call to, make a call to, give someone a call, get on the phone to, get someone on the phone; *Brit.* ring, ring up, give someone a ring; *informal* buzz, give someone a buzz; *Brit. informal* give someone a bell, give someone a tinkle, get on the blower to; *N. Amer. informal* get someone on the horn.

dialect ▶ noun *Hilary found it hard to understand the moorland dialect* **regional language**, local language, local tongue, local speech, local parlance, variety of language; **vernacular**, patois, non-standard language, idiom; regionalisms, localisms, provincialisms; *informal* lingo, local lingo, -ese, -speak; *Linguistics* acrolect, basilect, sociolect, idiolect.

dialectic ▶ noun *feminism has contributed a good deal to this dialectic* **reasoning**, argumentation, contention, logic; **discussion**, debate, dialogue, logical argument; *rare* ratiocination.
▶ adjective *Japanese negotiation is different from the Western dialectic habit* **rational**, rationalistic, logical, analytical; **disputatious**, dialectical, argumentative, contentious.

dialogue ▶ noun **1** *he studied dialogue among kindergarten children* **conversation**, talk, communication, interchange, discourse, argument; chat, chatter, chit-chat, chitter-chatter, gossip; *informal* jawing, gassing, gabbing; *Brit. informal* nattering, chinwagging; *formal* confabulation; *archaic* converse; *rare* interlocution, duologue, colloquy.
2 *they called for a serious political dialogue* **discussion**, exchange, debate, discourse, exchange of views, head-to-head, tête-à-tête, consultation, conference, parley, interview, question and answer session; talks, negotiations; *informal* powwow, rap session, confab; *N. Amer. informal* skull session, rap; *formal* confabulation.
3 *the actors learnt the dialogue by heart* **script**, text, screenplay, speech; lines, words, parts, spoken parts.

diameter ▶ noun *the mill wheel is eight feet in diameter | the pipe has a diameter of 14mm* **breadth**, width, depth, thickness; calibre, bore, gauge; size, extent.

diametrical, **diametric** ▶ adjective *they set themselves in diametrical opposition to their society* **direct**, absolute, complete, exact, extreme.

diametrically ▶ adverb *their views are diametrically opposed* **directly**, absolutely, completely, utterly.

diamond ▶ noun

WORD LINKS
relating to diamonds **diamantine**

diaphanous ▶ adjective *she wore a diaphanous dress of pale gold* **sheer**, fine, ultra-fine, delicate, light, lightweight, thin, insubstantial, floaty, flimsy, filmy, silken, chiffony, gossamer, gossamery, gossamer-thin, gossamer-like, gauzy, gauzelike, cobwebby, feathery; translucent, transparent, see-through; *rare* transpicuous, translucid.
OPPOSITES thick; opaque.

diarrhoea ▶ noun loose motions, looseness of the bowels; *informal* the skitters, the runs, the trots, gippy tummy, holiday tummy, Spanish tummy, Delhi belly, Montezuma's revenge, Aztec revenge, Aztec two-step; *Brit. informal* the squits; *N. Amer. informal* turista; *Medicine* dysentery, lientery; *archaic* the flux, lax.
OPPOSITE constipation.

diary ▶ noun **1** (*Brit.*) *that trip on the 4th should be pencilled into your diary* **appointment book**, engagement book, organizer, personal organizer, calendar, agenda; schedule, timetable, programme; *trademark* Filofax.
2 *she kept a diary during the war* **journal**, memoir, chronicle, log, logbook, weblog, blog, day-by-day account, daily record, history, annal, record; *N. Amer.* daybook.

diatribe ▶ noun *he launched into a diatribe against the Catholic Church* **tirade**, harangue, verbal onslaught, verbal attack, stream of abuse, denunciation, broadside, fulmination, condemnation, criticism, stricture, reproof, reproval, reprimand, rebuke, admonishment, admonition; invective, upbraiding, vituperation, abuse, castigation; *informal* tongue-lashing, knocking, slamming, panning, bashing, blast, flak; *Brit. informal* slating; *rare* philippic, obloquy.

dicey ▶ adjective (*informal*) *refuelling at sea is a bit dicey in bad weather* **risky**, uncertain, unpredictable, touch-and-go, precarious, unsafe, dangerous, perilous, high-risk, hazardous, fraught with danger; tricky, ticklish, delicate, difficult, awkward, thorny, problematical, problematic; *Scottish* unchancy; *informal* chancy, hairy, sticky, iffy; *Brit. informal* dodgy; *N. Amer. informal* gnarly; *archaic or humorous* parlous.
OPPOSITES safe; simple.

dichotomy ▶ noun *there is a great dichotomy between social theory and practice* **division**, separation, divorce, split, gulf, chasm; **difference**, contrast, disjunction, polarity, lack of consistency, contradiction, antagonism, conflict; *rare* contrariety.

dicky ▶ adjective (*Brit. informal*) *he was rejected for military service because of his dicky heart* **unsound**, unsteady, unreliable; **weak**, frail, infirm, unhealthy, ailing, poorly, sickly, sick; shaky, fluttery, fluttering, trembling; *informal* iffy; *Brit. informal* dodgy.
OPPOSITE robust.

dictate ▶ verb (stress on the second syllable) **1** *he sent for his secretary and dictated a letter* **say aloud**, utter, speak, read out, read aloud, recite.
OPPOSITE write.

2 *the government's official position is dictated by the prime minister* **prescribe**, **lay down**, impose, set down, set out; order, command, decree, ordain, direct, pronounce, enjoin, promulgate; **determine**, decide, influence, affect, choose, control, govern.
3 *my daughter is always* **dictating to** *her friends* **give orders to**, order about/around, boss (about/around), impose one's will on, lord it over, bully, domineer, dominate, tyrannize, oppress, ride roughshod over, control, pressurize, browbeat; lay down the law, act the tin god; *informal* push around/about, bulldoze, walk all over; call the shots, throw one's weight about/around.
▶ **noun** (stress on the first syllable) **1** *he showed blind obedience to the dictates of his superior* **order**, command, decree, edict, rule, ruling, ordinance, dictum, directive, direction, instruction, pronouncement, mandate, requirement, stipulation, injunction, ultimatum, demand, exhortation; (**dictates**) bidding, request, charge, promulgation; (*in Tsarist Russia*) ukase; (*in Spanish-speaking countries*) pronunciamento; *informal* say-so; *literary* behest; *archaic* hest; *rare* rescript.
2 *the dictates of fashion* **principle**, guiding principle, code, canon, law, rule, regulation, precept, dictum, axiom, maxim.

dictator ▶ **noun** *the country was ruled by a right-wing dictator* **autocrat**, monocrat, absolute ruler; **tyrant**, despot, oppressor, absolutist, totalitarian, authoritarian; *informal* supremo, Big Brother; *rare* autarch.

dictatorial ▶ **adjective 1** *he wanted to retain dictatorial leadership* **autocratic**, monocratic, undemocratic, totalitarian, authoritarian; **despotic**, tyrannical, tyrannous; **absolute**, unrestricted, unlimited, unaccountable, arbitrary, omnipotent, all-powerful, supreme; *rare* autarchic, autarchical.
OPPOSITE democratic.
2 *she became irritated by his dictatorial manner* **tyrannical**, **domineering**, despotic, oppressive, draconian, iron-handed, iron-fisted, imperious, lordly, magisterial, officious, overweening, overbearing, bossy, repressive, peremptory, high-handed, authoritarian, autocratic, dogmatic, high and mighty; harsh, strict, severe, rigid, inflexible, unyielding; *informal* pushy, cocky; *rare* Neronian.
OPPOSITE liberal.

dictatorship ▶ **noun 1** *the party was seeking to establish a dictatorship* **totalitarian state**, autocracy, autarchy, monocracy; dystopia.
OPPOSITE democracy.
2 *an entire generation grew up in the shadow of dictatorship* **absolute rule**, undemocratic rule, despotism, autocracy; **tyranny**, authoritarianism, totalitarianism, absolutism, Fascism; oppression, suppression, repression, subjugation, domination.
OPPOSITE democracy.

diction ▶ **noun 1** *a dialogue coach was employed to improve the actors' diction* **enunciation**, articulation, elocution, locution, pronunciation, speech, speech pattern, manner of speaking, intonation, inflection; delivery, utterance, speech-making, public speaking, declamation, oratory; fluency.
2 *he recognized the need for contemporary diction in poetry* **phraseology**, phrasing, turn of phrase, choice of words, wording, language, parlance, usage, vocabulary, terminology, expression, idiom, style, locution; *informal* lingo; *rare* idiolect.

dictionary ▶ **noun** *half of the words in his text were not in the dictionary* **lexicon**, wordbook, glossary, vocabulary list, vocabulary, word list, wordfinder.

WORD LINKS
relating to dictionaries **lexicographic**
writing of dictionaries **lexicography**
writer of dictionaries **lexicographer**

dictum ▶ **noun 1** *he received the head's dictum with evident reluctance* **pronouncement**, proclamation, direction, injunction, assertion, statement; **dictate**, command, commandment, mandate, order, decree, edict, fiat, promulgation, precept, requirement, stipulation, instruction; law, ordinance, rule, regulation; (*in Tsarist Russia*) ukase; (*in Spanish-speaking countries*) pronunciamento; *rare* rescript, firman, decretal, irade.
2 *'live well with all creatures' is an apt dictum for today* **saying**, maxim, axiom, proverb, adage, aphorism, saw, precept, epigram, epigraph, motto, truism, platitude, commonplace; words of wisdom, pearls of wisdom; expression, phrase, formula, slogan, quotation, quote; *rare* apophthegm, gnome.

didactic ▶ **adjective** *the inmates preferred social rather than didactic activities* **instructive**, instructional, educational, educative, informative, informational, doctrinal, preceptive, teaching, pedagogic, academic, scholastic, tuitional; edifying, improving, enlightening, illuminating, heuristic; pedantic, moralistic, homiletic; *rare* propaedeutic.

die ▶ **verb 1** *he was eighteen when his mother died* **pass away**, pass on, lose one's life, depart this life, expire, breathe one's last, draw one's last breath, meet one's end, meet one's death, lay down one's life, be no more, perish, be lost, go the way of the flesh, go the way of all flesh, go to glory, go to one's last resting place, go to meet one's maker, cross the great divide, cross the Styx; *informal* give up the ghost, kick the bucket, bite the dust, croak, conk out, buy it, turn up one's toes, cash in one's chips, go belly up, shuffle off this mortal coil, go the way of the dinosaurs; push up the daisies, be six feet under; *Brit. informal* snuff it, peg out, pop one's clogs, hop the twig/stick; *N. Amer. informal* bite the big one, buy the farm, check out, hand in one's dinner pail; *Austral./NZ informal* go bung; *literary* exit; *archaic* decease.
OPPOSITES live, survive.
2 *the last hope that there had been some mistake died* **fade**, fall away, dwindle, melt away, dissolve, subside, decline, sink, lapse, ebb, wane, wilt, wither, evanesce, come to an end, end, vanish, disappear.
OPPOSITE exist.
3 (*informal*) *the car gave a stutter and the engine died* **fail**, cut out, give out, stop, halt, break down, stop working, cease to function; peter out, fizzle out, run down, fade away, lose power; *informal* conk out, go kaput, give up the ghost, go phut; *Brit. informal* pack up.
OPPOSITE start.
4 (*informal*) *I'm going to* **die of** *boredom in this place* **be overcome with**, be overwhelmed by, be overpowered by, collapse with, succumb to.
5 (*informal*) *she's just dying to meet you* **be very eager**, be very keen, be desperate, long, yearn, burn, ache, itch; *informal* have a yen, yen.
OPPOSITE be reluctant.
□ **die away** *the sound of hoofbeats died away* **fade (away)**, fall away, dwindle, melt away, subside, ebb, wane, come to an end.
□ **die down** *we sheltered until the wind had died down* **abate**, subside, drop, drop off, drop away, fall away, lessen, ease (off), let up, decrease, diminish, moderate, decline, fade, dwindle, slacken, recede, tail off, peter out, taper off, wane, ebb, relent, become weaker, weaken, come to an end; *archaic* remit.
□ **die out** *the trout population could die out completely | the ceremony has died out in many areas* **become extinct**, **vanish**, disappear, cease to be, cease to exist, be no more, perish, pass into oblivion; become less common, become rarer, dwindle, peter out.

diehard ▶ **adjective** *the committee was full of diehard Stalinists* **hard-line**, hard-core, reactionary, ultra-conservative, conservative, traditionalist, unprogressive, dyed-in-the-wool, deep-dyed, long-standing, staunch, steadfast, intransigent, inflexible, immovable, unchanging, uncompromising, unyielding, indomitable, adamant, rigid, entrenched, set in one's ways; *informal* blimpish.
▶ **noun** *some of the diehards are refusing to reach an agreement* **hardliner**, reactionary, ultra-conservative, conservative, traditionalist, intransigent; fanatic, zealot; *informal* stick-in-the-mud, blimp.
OPPOSITE modernizer.

diet[1] *See centre pages for list of* **Dietary Habits**
▶ **noun 1** *your health problems could be related to your diet* **selection of food**, food and drink, food, foodstuffs, provisions, edibles, fare; menu, table, meals; nourishment, nutriment, sustenance; *informal* grub, nosh, eats, chow, scoff; *formal* comestibles, provender; *archaic* aliment, victuals, vittles, viands, commons.
2 *they aim to become slimmer by following a diet* **dietary regime**, dietary regimen, dietary programme, restricted diet, crash diet; fast, period of fasting, abstinence.
OPPOSITE binge.
▶ **verb** *she had dieted for most of her life* **follow a diet**, be on a diet, eat sparingly, eat selectively, abstain, fast; slim, lose weight, watch one's weight; *N. Amer.* reduce; *informal* weight-watch; *N. Amer. informal* slenderize.
OPPOSITES overindulge, binge.

diet[2] ▶ **noun** *the budget was passed by the diet's lower house* **legislative assembly**, legislature, parliament, congress, senate, synod, council; assembly, committee, convocation, conclave.

differ ▶ **verb 1** *child-rearing patterns differ across cultural groups* **vary**, be different, be unlike, be dissimilar, be distinguishable, diverge.
OPPOSITE coincide.
2 *their beliefs* **differed from** *those of other religious parties* **deviate from**, depart from, run counter to, contradict, contrast with, conflict with, be incompatible with, be at odds with, be in opposition to, go against.
OPPOSITE resemble.
3 *lawyers differ about the best interpretation of the legislation* **disagree**, fail to agree, dissent, be at variance, be in dispute, be in opposition, take issue, conflict, clash, cross swords, lock horns, be at each other's throats; quarrel, argue, wrangle, quibble, squabble; *informal* fall out, scrap, argy-bargy, spat; *archaic* altercate.
OPPOSITE agree.

difference ▶ **noun 1** *there is no difference between the two accounts* **dissimilarity**, contrast, distinction, distinctness, differentiation; **variance**, variation, variability, divergence, deviation, polarity, gulf, breach, gap, split, disparity, imbalance, unevenness, incongruity, contradiction, contradistinction, nonconformity; *rare* unlikeness, contrariety, dissimilitude.
OPPOSITE similarity.
2 *the couple are patching up their differences* **disagreement**, difference of opinion, misunderstanding, dispute, disputation, argument, debate, quarrel, wrangle, altercation, contretemps, clash, controversy, dissension;

informal tiff, set-to, run-in, spat, ruction; *Brit. informal* row, barney, bit of argy-bargy.
3 *you pay a reduced amount and the bank makes up the difference* **balance**, outstanding amount, remaining amount, remainder, rest, residue, excess, extra; *technical* residuum.

different ▶ adjective **1** *the plots of the two books are very different* **dissimilar**, unalike, unlike, non-identical, contrasting, divergent, disparate, poles apart; incompatible, mismatched, inconsistent, opposed, at variance, at odds, clashing, conflicting, contradictory, contrary; *informal* like chalk and cheese; *rare* contrastive.
OPPOSITE similar.
2 *suddenly everything in her life was different* **changed**, altered, modified, transformed, metamorphosed, other, new, unfamiliar, unknown, strange.
OPPOSITE the same.
3 *Gareth had tried fifteen different occupations* **distinct**, separate, individual, discrete, non-identical, unrelated, unconnected, unassociated, independent; disparate.
OPPOSITES related, similar.
4 *the Bible was interpreted differently by different groups of reformers* **various**, several, sundry, assorted, varied, varying, miscellaneous, diverse, diversified, manifold, multifarious; *informal* a mixed bag; *literary* divers.
5 *he wanted to try something different* **unusual**, out of the ordinary, uncommon, unfamiliar, rare, unique, novel, new, fresh, original, unprecedented, unconventional, unorthodox, atypical, out of the way; special, singular, remarkable, noteworthy, exceptional, extraordinary, outrageous, outlandish, exotic; *Brit.* out of the common; *informal* way out, offbeat, off the wall.
OPPOSITES ordinary, conventional.

WORD LINKS
related prefixes **hetero-** (e.g. ***heterogeneous, heterosexual***), **allo-** (e.g. ***allopathy, allotrope***)

differential ▶ adjective *differential treatment is accorded to working- and middle-class crime* **distinctive**, different, dissimilar, contrasting, divergent, disparate, contrastive; distinguishing, discriminating, discriminatory.
OPPOSITES similar, the same.
▶ noun *the cost differential is rapidly diminishing* **difference**, gap, gulf, divergence, disparity, discrepancy, imbalance, inequality, contrast, distinction.
OPPOSITE uniformity.

differentiate ▶ verb **1** *he is no longer able to differentiate between fantasy and reality | birds can differentiate colours* **distinguish**, discriminate, make a distinction, draw a distinction, see a difference, discern a difference, tell the difference; discern, tell apart, recognize, identify, pick out, determine, contrast.
2 *they understand what differentiates their business from all other booksellers* **make different**, distinguish, set apart, single out, separate, segregate, mark off, characterize, individualize, individuate.
3 *the cells differentiate into a wide variety of types* **transform**, metamorphose, evolve, convert, change, become different, modify, alter, adapt.

differentiation ▶ noun *there is not enough differentiation between the two types of investment* **distinction**, distinctness, disparity, polarity, contrast, difference, divergence, separation, demarcation, delimitation.
OPPOSITE association.

difficult ▶ adjective **1** *digging through the snow was becoming increasingly difficult* **hard**, strenuous, arduous, laborious, heavy, tough, onerous, burdensome, demanding, punishing, gruelling, grinding, back-breaking, painful; exhausting, tiring, fatiguing, wearing, wearying, wearisome; *informal* hellish, killing; *Brit. informal* knackering; *archaic* toilsome; *rare* exigent.
OPPOSITE easy.
2 *she found maths very difficult* **problematic**, hard, puzzling, baffling, perplexing, confusing, mystifying, mysterious; **complicated**, complex, involved, intricate, knotty, thorny, ticklish; obscure, abstract, abstruse, recondite, enigmatic, impenetrable, unfathomable, over one's head, above one's head, beyond one; *informal* fiddly, sticky, no picnic; *N. Amer. informal* gnarly; *archaic* wildering; *rare* involute, involuted.
OPPOSITES straightforward, simple.
3 *the office manager was a difficult man* **troublesome**, tiresome, trying, exasperating, demanding, unmanageable, intractable, perverse, contrary, recalcitrant, obstreperous, refractory, fractious; **unaccommodating**, unhelpful, uncooperative, unamenable, unreasonable, disobliging, stubborn, obstinate, bull-headed, pig-headed; **hard to please**, hard to satisfy, fussy, particular, over-particular, fastidious, perfectionist, critical, hypercritical, finicky; *Brit.* awkward; *Scottish* thrawn; *informal* cussed; choosy, picky; *Brit. informal* bloody-minded, bolshie, stroppy; *N. Amer. informal* balky; *archaic* contumacious, froward; *rare* contrarious, finical.
OPPOSITE accommodating.
4 *you've come at a difficult time* **inconvenient**, awkward, unfavourable, unfortunate, inappropriate, unsuitable, untimely, ill-timed, inopportune, inexpedient, unseasonable, disadvantageous.
OPPOSITE convenient.
5 *the family have been through very difficult times* **bad**, tough, grim, terrible, awful, dreadful, nightmarish, dark, black, hard, adverse, unpleasant, unwelcome, disagreeable, distressing, harrowing; straitened, hard-pressed; *literary* direful; *archaic or humorous* parlous.
OPPOSITE happy.

difficulty ▶ noun **1** *her note had been penned with obvious difficulty* **strain**, struggling, awkwardness, trouble, toil, labour, laboriousness, strenuousness, arduousness; pains, problems, trials and tribulations; *informal* hassle, stress; *literary* dolour, travails.
OPPOSITE ease.
2 *the questions are arranged in order of difficulty* **complexity**, complicatedness, intricacy, perplexity, knottiness, awkwardness; difficultness, trickiness, hardness; obscurity, abstruseness.
OPPOSITE simplicity.
3 *the cost of the journey was not an insurmountable difficulty* **problem**, complication, disadvantage, snag, hitch, drawback, pitfall, handicap, impediment, hindrance, obstacle, hurdle, stumbling block, obstruction, barrier; *informal* fly in the ointment, prob, headache, hiccup, facer; *Brit. informal* spanner in the works; *N. Amer. informal* monkey wrench in the works; *dated* cumber; *literary* trammel.
4 *they felt unable to ask for help when they were in difficulty* **trouble**, distress, crisis, hardship; **adversity**, extremity, need; hard times, dire straits; predicament, quandary, dilemma, plight; *informal* hot water, deep water, a fix, a jam, a spot, a scrape, a stew, a hole, a pickle.

diffidence ▶ noun *he regretted his diffidence and awkwardness in large groups* **shyness**, bashfulness, unassertiveness, modesty, modestness, self-effacement, humility, humbleness, meekness, timidity, timidness, timorousness, reserve, reticence, introversion; **insecurity**, self-doubt, apprehension, uncertainty, hesitancy, nervousness, reluctance, restraint, inhibition, unease, uneasiness; self-consciousness, shame, embarrassment, sheepishness.
OPPOSITE confidence.

diffident ▶ adjective *underneath his diffident exterior there was a passionate temperament* **shy**, bashful, modest, self-effacing, unassuming, unpresuming, humble, meek, unconfident, unassertive, timid, timorous, shrinking, reserved, withdrawn, introverted, inhibited; **insecure**, self-doubting, doubtful, wary, unsure, apprehensive, uncertain, hesitant, nervous, reluctant, fearful; self-conscious, ill at ease, ashamed, abashed, embarrassed, shamefaced, sheepish; *Scottish* mim; *informal* mousy.
OPPOSITES confident; conceited.

CHOOSE THE RIGHT WORD
diffident, shy, bashful, timid
See SHY.

diffuse ▶ verb *the light of the moon was diffused by cloud | such ideas were diffused widely in the 1970s* **spread**, spread out, spread around, send out, scatter, disperse; disseminate, distribute, dispense, put about, circulate, communicate, impart, purvey, propagate, transmit, broadcast, promulgate; *literary* bruit abroad.
OPPOSITES concentrate; collect.
▶ adjective **1** *skylights give a diffuse illumination through the rooms* **spread out**, diffused, scattered, dispersed, not concentrated.
OPPOSITE concentrated.
2 *Tania's narrative is rather diffuse* **verbose**, wordy, prolix, long-winded, overlong, long-drawn-out, protracted, discursive, rambling, wandering, meandering, maundering, digressive, circuitous, roundabout, circumlocutory, periphrastic; loose, vague; *informal* windy, gassy; *Brit. informal* waffling; *rare* pleonastic, circumlocutionary, ambagious, logorrhoeic.
OPPOSITE succinct.

diffuse or defuse?
The verbs **diffuse** and **defuse** are quite different in meaning, though they are sometimes confused on account of their similarity in sound. *Diffuse* means 'scatter, spread widely' (*power is diffused and decentralized*). *Defuse*, on the other hand, means 'reduce the danger or tension in' (*the agreement was designed to defuse a dangerous rivalry*).

diffusion ▶ noun *he studies smoke diffusion in the atmosphere | the diffusion of Marxist ideas* **spreading**, scattering, dispersal, dispersing; dissemination, disseminating, distribution, distributing, circulation, circulating, putting about, propagation, transmission, broadcasting, broadcast, promulgation, issuance; *archaic* bruiting.

dig ▶ verb **1** *they dug my garden for me | he grabbed a shovel and began to dig* **cultivate**, till, harrow, plough, turn over, work, break up, spade; delve, break up soil, break up earth, break up ground, move soil/earth.
2 *they tried to dig a tunnel under the house* **excavate**, dig out, quarry, hollow out, scoop out, gouge out, cut, bore, tunnel, burrow, mine, channel.
3 *there were no cows to milk and no vegetables to dig* **unearth**, dig up, pull up, grub up, root up, root out, bring to the surface, extract from the ground; harvest, gather, collect.
4 *Winnie dug her elbow into his ribs* **poke**, prod, jab, stab, shove, ram, push,

thrust, drive, nudge.
5 *they asked questions and dug into my past* **delve**, **probe**, search, inquire, look; investigate, research, examine, scrutinize, check up on, vet; *N. Amer.* check out.
6 (*informal, dated*) *he's great and I dig talking with him* **like**, love, adore, take great pleasure in, delight in, enjoy, appreciate, be keen on; *informal* get a kick out of, get a buzz out of, go a bundle on.
OPPOSITE dislike.
7 (*informal, dated*) *this art is symbolic—do you dig me?* **understand**, comprehend, follow; grasp, make out; *informal* get, get someone's drift, get the picture, see the light.
□ **dig something up 1** *the bodies were hastily dug up* **exhume**, disinter, unearth, bring to the surface, bring out of the ground; *rare* disentomb, unbury.
2 *they dug up scandalous facts about top businessmen* **uncover**, unearth, dredge up, root out, hunt out, ferret out, nose out, sniff out, track down, extricate, find (out), turn up, come across, discover, detect, reveal, bring to light, bring into the open, expose.
▶ **noun 1** *Emma gave me a dig in the ribs* **poke**, prod, jab, stab, shove, push, nudge, elbow.
2 (*informal*) *they're always making digs at one another* **snide remark**, cutting remark, jibe, jeer, taunt, sneer, insult, barb, slur, slight, affront, insinuation; *informal* wisecrack, crack, put-down.

digest ▶ **verb** (stress on the second syllable) **1** *babies take longer to digest formula milk* **break down**, dissolve, assimilate, absorb, take in, take up.
2 *they take ages to digest even simple facts* **assimilate**, absorb, take in, understand, comprehend, grasp, master, learn, familiarize oneself with; consider, think about, contemplate, mull over, chew over, weigh up, reflect on, ponder, meditate on, study; *informal* get, get the hang of, pick up, get clued up about, get the point of.
3 *the source material needs to be digested* **classify**, catalogue, tabulate, codify, arrange, order, dispose, systematize, methodize; **condense**, compress, compact, telescope, summarize, precis, abstract; *rare* epitomize.
▶ **noun** (stress on the first syllable) *a digest of current world news is published monthly* **summary**, synopsis, abstract, precis, résumé, outline, sketch, (quick) rundown, round-up, abridgement, summation, review, compendium; *N. Amer.* wrap-up; *archaic* argument; *rare* epitome, summa, conspectus.

digestion *See centre pages for list of parts of the* **Digestive System**
▶ **noun** *ineffective chewing prevents the proper digestion of food* **breaking down**, maceration, dissolution; assimilation, absorption, taking in, taking up, ingestion; *rare* eupepsia.

digit ▶ **noun 1** *we wanted to warm our frozen digits* **finger**, thumb, toe; extremity.
2 *the door code has ten digits* **numeral**, number, figure, integer; numerical symbol; *rare* cipher.

dignified ▶ **adjective** *the butler was dignified and courteous* **stately**, noble, courtly, majestic, kingly; **distinguished**, proud, august, lofty, exalted, regal, lordly, imposing, impressive, grand; solemn, serious, grave, formal, proper, ceremonious, decorous, reserved, composed, sedate, staid; *informal* couth, just so, starchy.
OPPOSITE undignified.

dignify ▶ **verb** *they dignified their departure with a ceremony* **distinguish**, add distinction to, add dignity to, honour, bestow honour on, grace, adorn, exalt, enhance, add lustre to, magnify, ennoble, glorify, elevate, make lofty, aggrandize, upgrade.

dignitary ▶ **noun** *there are many foreign dignitaries attending today's ceremony* **grandee**, important person, VIP, very important person, notable, notability, worthy, personage, luminary, public figure, pillar of society, leading light, leader, panjandrum; famous person, distinguished person, eminent person, eminence, celebrity, personality, name, big name, household name, star, superstar; *informal* heavyweight, bigwig, biggie, top brass, top dog, Mr Big, big gun, big shot, big noise, big fish, big cheese, big chief, supremo, somebody, someone, celeb, Lord Muck, Lady Muck; *Brit. informal* nob; *N. Amer. informal* big wheel, kahuna, big kahuna, big enchilada, top banana, macher, high muckamuck, high muckety-muck.
OPPOSITE nonentity.

dignity ▶ **noun 1** *he is careful to uphold the dignity of the Crown* **stateliness**, nobleness, nobility, majesty, regalness, regality, royalness, courtliness, augustness, loftiness, exaltedness, lordliness, impressiveness, grandeur, magnificence; ceremoniousness, formality, decorum, propriety, correctness, righteousness, respectability, worthiness, honourability, integrity; solemnity, gravity, gravitas, reserve, sobriety, sedateness, composure.
OPPOSITE informality.
2 *the prisoners were treated with little regard for human dignity* **self-esteem**, self-worth, self-respect, pride, morale; decency, modesty, delicacy; feelings, sensibilities; *French* amour propre.
3 *Cnut promised dignities and favour to the noblemen* **high rank**, high standing, high station, status, elevation, eminence, honour, glory, greatness, importance, prominence, prestige.
OPPOSITES dishonour; low rank.

digress ▶ **verb** *I have digressed a little from my original plan* **deviate**, go off at a tangent, diverge, turn aside, turn away, depart, drift, stray, ramble, wander, meander, maunder; get off the subject, stray from the subject, stray from the point, deviate from the topic, get sidetracked, lose the thread; *rare* divagate.

digression ▶ **noun** *her book is full of long digressions | Victorian novelists had a tendency toward verbosity and digression* **deviation**, detour, diversion, departure, excursus; **aside**, incidental remark, footnote, parenthesis; deviation from the subject, straying from the topic, straying from the point, going off at a tangent, getting sidetracked, losing one's thread; divergence, straying, drifting, rambling, wandering, meandering, maundering; *Latin* obiter dictum; *archaic* excursion; *rare* apostrophe, divagation.

digs ▶ **plural noun** (*Brit. informal*) *he had just been thrown out of his digs* **lodgings**, living quarters, quarters, rooms; accommodation, billet; lodging place, bedsit, flat, apartment, house, home; *informal* pad, place; *formal* abode, dwelling, dwelling place, residence, domicile, habitation.

dilapidated ▶ **adjective** *a terrace of dilapidated Edwardian houses* **run down**, tumbledown, ramshackle, broken-down, in disrepair, shabby, battered, rickety, shaky, unsound, crumbling, in ruins, ruined, decayed, decaying, deteriorating, deteriorated, decrepit, worn out; neglected, uncared-for, untended, unmaintained, badly maintained; the worse for wear, falling to pieces, falling apart, gone to rack and ruin, gone to seed; *informal* shambly, slummy; *N. Amer. informal* shacky.
OPPOSITES smart; intact.

dilate ▶ **verb 1** *she took a deep breath and her nostrils dilated* **enlarge**, become larger, widen, become wider, expand, distend, swell.
OPPOSITE contract.
2 *he would dilate on any subject that took his fancy* **expatiate**, expound, expand, enlarge, elaborate, speak at length, write at length, talk in detail.

dilatory ▶ **adjective 1** *they were dilatory in providing the researchers with information* **slow**, unhurried, tardy, unpunctual, lax, slack, sluggish, sluggardly, snail-like, tortoise-like, lazy, idle, indolent, slothful; *N. Amer. informal* lollygagging.
OPPOSITES fast; prompt.
2 *they resorted to dilatory procedural tactics* **delaying**, stalling, temporizing, procrastinating, postponing, deferring, putting off, tabling, shelving; **time-wasting**, dallying, dilly-dallying, loitering, lingering, dawdling, tarrying; *rare* Fabian.

dilemma ▶ **noun** *a discussion with a colleague resolved her dilemma* **quandary**, predicament, difficulty, problem, puzzle, conundrum, awkward situation, tricky situation, difficult situation, difficult choice, catch-22, vicious circle, plight, mess, muddle; trouble, perplexity, confusion, conflict, uncertainty, indecision; *informal* no-win situation, sticky situation, pickle, fix, spot, tight spot, tight corner, poser, facer; *Brit. informal* sticky wicket.
□ **on the horns of a dilemma between the devil and the deep blue sea**, between Scylla and Charybdis; *informal* in a no-win situation, between a rock and a hard place.

dilettante ▶ **noun 1** *there is no room for the dilettante in this business* **dabbler**, potterer, tinkerer, trifler, dallier; **amateur**, non-professional, non-specialist, layman, layperson.
OPPOSITE professional.
2 (*archaic*) *heaven forbid that the dilettantes should all turn painters* **art lover**, lover of the arts, connoisseur, aesthete, member of the cognoscenti, arbiter elegantiae, arbiter elegantiarum.
OPPOSITE philistine.

diligence ▶ **noun** *they set about their assigned jobs with diligence* **conscientiousness**, **assiduousness**, assiduity, industriousness, rigour, rigorousness, punctiliousness, meticulousness, carefulness, thoroughness, sedulousness, attentiveness, heedfulness, earnestness, intentness, studiousness; constancy, perseverance, persistence, tenacity, pertinacity, zeal, zealousness, dedication, commitment; tirelessness, indefatigability, doggedness; industry, hard work, application, effort, concentration, care, attention; *archaic* laboriousness, continuance; *rare* perseveration.
OPPOSITES laziness; carelessness.

> **CHOOSE THE RIGHT WORD**
>
> **diligent, hard-working, industrious**
> *See* **HARD-WORKING**.

diligent ▶ **adjective** *their drive to achieve makes them extremely diligent workers* **industrious**, hard-working, assiduous; **conscientious**, particular, punctilious, meticulous, painstaking, rigorous, exacting, careful, thorough, sedulous, attentive, heedful, intent, earnest, studious; constant, persevering, persistent, tenacious, pertinacious, zealous, dedicated, committed, active, busy; unflagging, untiring, tireless, indefatigable, dogged, plodding, slogging; *archaic* laborious.

D

OPPOSITES lazy; casual.

dilly-dally ▶ verb (*informal*) *the board can't afford to dilly-dally over this issue* **waste time**, dally, dawdle, loiter, linger, take one's time, delay, mark time, kill time, while away time, potter, trifle, temporize, stall, procrastinate, drag one's feet, play a waiting game; dither, hesitate, falter, vacillate, waver, fluctuate; *Brit.* haver, hum and haw; *Scottish* swither; *informal* shilly-shally, blow hot and cold, let the grass grow under one's feet, pussyfoot around; *dated* tarry.
OPPOSITE hurry.

dilute ▶ verb **1** *strong bleach can be diluted with water* **make weaker**, weaken; **thin out**, thin, make thinner, water down, add water to; mix, doctor, lace, adulterate; *informal* cut.
OPPOSITE concentrate.
2 *I trust I have been able to dilute your misgivings* **diminish**, reduce, decrease, lessen, attenuate, make weaker, weaken, mitigate, temper, quell, quieten, allay, assuage, alleviate, palliate, moderate, modify, tone down; *rare* lenify.
OPPOSITE intensify.
▶ adjective *the metal is etched with a dilute acid* **weak**, diluted, thin, thinned out, watered down, watery; adulterated; *informal* cut.

diluted ▶ adjective *wash the brushes in diluted bleach* **weak**, dilute, thin, thinned out, watered down, watery; adulterated.
OPPOSITE concentrated.

dim ▶ adjective **1** *the stage lighting was extremely dim* **faint**, weak, feeble, soft, pale, dull, dingy, subdued, muted, flat, lustreless; *informal* wishy-washy.
OPPOSITE bright.
2 *it was a dim, grey day | he left her in a dim room* **dark**, darkish, sombre, dingy, dismal, gloomy, dusky, murky; grey, overcast, leaden, cloudy, misty, foggy; badly lit, poorly lit, ill-lit, unlit, unilluminated; *literary* crepuscular, tenebrous; *rare* Stygian, Cimmerian, caliginous.
OPPOSITE bright.
3 *he glimpsed dim shapes through the foliage* **indistinct**, ill-defined, unclear, vague, shadowy, imperceptible, nebulous, obscured, blurred, blurry, fuzzy, bleary; *rare* obfuscated.
OPPOSITE distinct.
4 *he had only dim memories of his late father* **vague**, unclear, indistinct, imprecise, imperfect, confused, sketchy, hazy, blurred, shadowy, foggy, obscure, remote.
OPPOSITE clear.
5 (*informal*) *I expect you think I'm awfully dim.* See STUPID.
6 *their prospects for the future looked fairly dim* **gloomy**, sombre, unpromising, unfavourable, discouraging, disheartening, depressing, dispiriting.
OPPOSITE encouraging.
▶ verb **1** *she insisted the lights be dimmed* **turn down**, lower, dip; make dim, make faint, make less bright, make less intense, soften, subdue, mute; *literary* bedim.
OPPOSITE turn up.
2 *wait until the gas lamps dim* **grow faint**, grow feeble, grow dim, fade, dull.
3 *the skies dimmed* **grow dark**, darken, blacken, cloud over, become overcast, grow leaden, lour, become gloomy.
OPPOSITE brighten.
4 *my memories have not dimmed with the passage of time* **fade**, become vague, become indistinct, grow dim, blur, become blurred, become shadowy, become confused; dull, numb, fail, disappear.
OPPOSITE sharpen.
5 *the fighting dimmed hopes of peace* **diminish**, reduce, lessen, weaken, fade, make faint, undermine, impair.
OPPOSITE increase.

dimension ▶ noun **1** (usually **dimensions**) *the approximate dimensions of the master bedroom* **proportions**, measurements, extent, size; length, width, breadth, depth, area, volume, capacity; footage, acreage.
2 *we underestimated the dimension of the problem* **size**, scale, extent, scope, range, measure, magnitude, largeness; greatness, importance, significance, value.
3 *water can add a new dimension to your garden* **aspect**, feature, element, facet, side.

diminish ▶ verb **1** *the number of books published has not diminished* **decrease**, decline, reduce, lessen, shrink, contract, grow smaller, fall off, drop off, slacken off; fall, drop, sink, slump, plummet, plunge; *informal* hit the floor, go through the floor, go downhill.
OPPOSITE increase.
2 *new legislation diminished the authority of the courts* **reduce**, curtail, cut, cut down, cut back, prune, pare down, lessen, lower, decrease, shrink, contract, narrow, constrict, restrict, limit, curb, check, blunt; weaken, make weaker, erode, undermine, sap.
OPPOSITE increase.
3 *they returned to their homes as the fighting diminished* **subside**, wane, abate, dwindle, fade, decline, slacken, moderate, ebb, recede, die away, die down, die out, peter out, tail off, cool off, let up, fizzle out, settle down, come to an end; *archaic* remit.
OPPOSITES flare up, get worse.
4 *she lost no opportunity to diminish him in her daughter's presence* **belittle**, disparage, denigrate, deprecate, depreciate, devalue, demean, decry, cast aspersions on, speak ill of, speak badly of, run down, abuse, insult, revile, malign, vilify; *N. Amer.* slur; *informal* bad-mouth, pull to pieces, pull apart, sling mud at, do a hatchet job on; *Brit. informal* rubbish, slate, slag off, have a go at; *rare* asperse, derogate, vilipend, vituperate.
OPPOSITE boost.

diminution ▶ noun **1** *any diminution of freedom reduces the quality of life* **curtailment**, curtailing, cutting back, cutback, cut, attenuation, reduction, lessening, lowering, decrease, contraction, constriction, restriction, limitation, limiting, curbing; weakening, undermining, sapping.
OPPOSITES increase, expansion.
2 *a gradual diminution in mental faculties* **decline**, decrease, reduction, dwindling, shrinking, fading, failing, weakening, slackening, ebb, receding, wane, falling off; loss, erosion, depletion, impoverishment.
OPPOSITES increase, growth.

diminutive ▶ adjective *a diminutive breed of parrot* **tiny**, small, little, petite, minute, miniature, mini, minuscule, microscopic, small-scale, compact, pocket, toy, midget, undersized, short, stubby, elfin, dwarfish, dwarf, pygmy, bantam, homuncular, Lilliputian; *Scottish* wee; *informal* teeny, weeny, teeny-weeny, teensy-weensy, itty-bitty, itsy-bitsy, tiddly, dinky, baby, pint-sized, half-pint, sawn-off, knee-high to a grasshopper; *Brit. informal* titchy, ickle; *N. Amer. informal* little-bitty, vest-pocket.
OPPOSITE enormous.

dimple ▶ noun *she smiles, and two dimples appear in her cheeks* **indentation**, concavity, depression, hollow, cleft, dent, dint, dip, pit.

dimwit ▶ noun (*informal*) *he's the biggest dimwit in the class.* See FOOL.

dim-witted ▶ adjective (*informal*) *a dim-witted muscleman.* See STUPID.

din ▶ noun *he could not be heard above the din* **uproar**, racket, loud noise, confused noise, commotion, cacophony, babel, hubbub, tumult, fracas, clangour, crash, clatter, clash; shouting, yelling, screaming, caterwauling, babble, babbling, clamour, outcry; brouhaha, fuss, disturbance, ado; pandemonium, bedlam, chaos, confusion; *Scottish & N. English* stramash; *informal* hullabaloo, rumpus, ruction; *Brit. informal* row; *rare* vociferation, ululation, charivari.
OPPOSITES silence; quiet.
▶ verb **1** *since she was a child she had had the evils of drink **dinned into** her* **instil**, drive, drum, hammer, drill, implant, ingrain, inculcate; teach over and over again, indoctrinate, brainwash.
2 *the sound dinning in my ears was the phone ringing* **blare**, blast, clang, clatter, crash, clamour.

dine ▶ verb *they are dining at a downtown restaurant | they* **dined on** *lobster* **have dinner**, have supper; eat, feed, feast, banquet; consume, take, partake of, devour; *informal* nosh, tuck into; *Brit. informal* scoff; *dated* sup, break bread.

dingle ▶ noun (*literary*) **valley**, dale, vale, hollow, gully; *Brit.* dene, combe, slade, nook; *N. English* clough; *Scottish* glen, strath; *literary* dell.

dingy ▶ adjective *a dingy bed-sitting room* **gloomy**, drab, dark, dull, badly/poorly lit, dim; dismal, sombre, grim, dreary, cheerless; dirty, discoloured, grimy, soiled; faded, shabby, dowdy, worn, seedy, run down, tacky; *literary* tenebrous.
OPPOSITES bright; clean.

dinky ▶ adjective (*Brit. informal*) *a dinky toy rabbit* **small**, little, petite, dainty, diminutive, mini, miniature; cute, neat, trim, dear, adorable; *Scottish* wee; *informal* teeny, teeny weeny, teensy-weensy; *N. Amer. informal* little-bitty.

dinner ▶ noun *a five-course dinner was served* **evening meal**, supper, main meal, repast; lunch; feast, banquet, dinner party; *Brit.* tea; *informal* blowout, binge, feed; *Brit. informal* nosh-up, scoff, slap-up meal, spread, tuck-in; *formal* refection, collation.

WORD LINKS
relating to dinner **prandial**

dinosaur ▶ noun. *See centre pages for lists of* **Dinosaurs** **Fossils**

dint ▶ noun *the dints and holes were the work of arrows* **dent**, indentation, depression, dip, dimple, cleft, hollow, crater, pit; notch, nick, chip, mark, cut, gouge, gash.
□ **by dint of** *our premier position is maintained by dint of sheer hard work* **by means of**, by use of, by virtue of, on account of, as a result of, as a consequence of, owing to, by reason of, on grounds of, on the strength of, due to, thanks to, by, via.

diocese ▶ noun **bishopric**, see, parish.

dip ▶ verb **1** *he dipped a rag in the water* **immerse**, submerge, plunge, duck, dunk, lower, sink; douse, soak, drench, souse, steep, saturate, bathe, rinse.
2 *the sun had dipped below the horizon* **sink**, set, drop, go/drop down, fall, descend; fade, disappear, subside, vanish, be engulfed.
OPPOSITE rise.
3 *the news sent the stock dipping 5p to 663p* **decrease**, fall, go down, drop, fall off, drop off, decline, diminish, dwindle, depreciate, deteriorate,

slump, plummet, plunge; *informal* hit the floor.
OPPOSITE increase.
4 *the road dipped and we picked up speed* **slope down**, slope, slant down, descend, go down, drop away, fall away, fall, sink, decline, be at an angle; droop, sag.
OPPOSITE rise.
5 *the flag was dipped* **lower**, move downwards/down, let fall, let sink.
OPPOSITE raise.
6 *he dipped his headlights* **dim**, **lower**, turn down, darken, make less intense.
OPPOSITES brighten, raise.
□ **dip into 1** *she dipped into her handbag* **reach into**, put one's hand into.
2 *if an emergency arises, you might have to dip into your savings* **draw on**, spend part of, touch, use, make use of, have recourse to, employ.
3 *it is an interesting book to dip into* **browse through**, skim through, scan, look through, flick through, flip through, leaf through, riffle through, run through, glance at, peruse, read quickly, have a quick look at, run one's eye over, give something a/the once-over.
▶ **noun 1** *the pool is ideal for a relaxing dip* **swim**, bathe, dive, plunge, splash, paddle.
2 *the best remedy is to give the fish a ten-minute dip in a salt bath* **immersion**, plunge, ducking, dunking; sousing, dousing, soaking, drenching, steeping, saturation, bath, rinse, splash.
3 *the disposal of used sheep dip is tightly controlled* **disinfectant**, parasiticide, germicide, bactericide, preservative; liquid preparation/mixture, solution.
4 *chicken satay with peanut dip* **sauce**, dressing, relish, creamy mixture.
5 *there's a big hedge at the bottom of the dip* **slope**, incline, decline, slant, descent, cant; **hollow**, concavity, depression, basin, indentation, dimple, trough.
6 *there was a dip in sales* **decrease**, fall, drop, downturn, decline, falling off, dropping off, slump, reduction, lessening, diminution, lowering, slackening, ebb.
OPPOSITE increase.

diplomacy ▶ **noun 1** *diplomacy has failed to win them independence* **statesmanship**, statecraft; **negotiation(s)**, discussion(s), talks, consultation, conference, dialogue; international relations/politics, foreign affairs.
2 *she was uncertain of how to combine honesty and diplomacy in her answer* **tact**, tactfulness, sensitivity, discretion, subtlety, finesse, delicacy; judiciousness, discernment, prudence, cleverness, skill; politeness, thoughtfulness, understanding, care; *French* savoir faire.
OPPOSITE tactlessness.

diplomat ▶ **noun 1** *a British diplomat working in our consulate in Germany* **ambassador**, envoy, emissary, consul, attaché, plenipotentiary, chargé d'affaires, official; *archaic* legate.
2 *'Gentlemen, please,' said Norman, ever the diplomat* **tactful person**, conciliator, reconciler, peacemaker; mediator, negotiator, arbitrator, intermediary, moderator, go-between, middleman.

diplomatic ▶ **adjective 1** *a month of hectic diplomatic activity* **ambassadorial**, consular, foreign-policy, political; *Brit.* Foreign-Office.
2 *he tried his best to be diplomatic* **tactful**, sensitive, subtle, delicate, discreet; judicious, discerning, prudent, politic, clever, skilful; polite, thoughtful, understanding, careful.
OPPOSITES indiscreet, tactless.

dire ▶ **adjective 1** *the dire economic situation* **terrible**, dreadful, appalling, frightful, awful, horrible, atrocious, grim, unspeakable, distressing, harrowing, alarming, shocking, outrageous; grave, serious, grievous, disastrous, ruinous, calamitous, catastrophic, cataclysmic, devastating, crippling; miserable, wretched, woeful; hopeless, irretrievable; *informal* lousy, chronic; *literary* direful; *archaic or humorous* parlous.
OPPOSITE good.
2 *he was in dire need of help* **urgent**, desperate, pressing, crying, sore, grave, serious, extreme, acute, drastic; critical, crucial, vital.
OPPOSITE mild.
3 *dire warnings of fuel shortages* **ominous**, portentous, gloomy, doom and gloom, sinister; grim, dreadful, dismal; unpropitious, inauspicious, unfavourable, pessimistic.
OPPOSITE encouraging.

direct ▶ **adjective 1** *this was the most direct route* **straight**, undeviating, unswerving, uncircuitous; shortest, quickest.
OPPOSITE indirect.
2 *he took a direct flight to Cyprus* **non-stop**, unbroken, uninterrupted, straight through, through.
3 *he is very direct and honest* **frank**, straightforward, honest, candid, open, sincere, straight, straight to the point, blunt, plain-spoken, outspoken, forthright, downright, uninhibited, unreserved, point blank, no-nonsense, matter-of-fact, bluff, undiplomatic, tactless; not afraid to call a spade a spade, not beating around the bush, speaking as one finds; explicit, clear, plain, unequivocal, unambiguous, unqualified, categorical; *informal* straight from the shoulder, upfront.
OPPOSITE evasive.
4 *he preferred to rely on direct contact with the leaders* **face to face**, personal, unmediated, head-on, immediate, first-hand; *French* tête-à-tête; *informal* from the horse's mouth.
5 *a direct quotation* **verbatim**, word for word, letter for letter, to the letter, faithful, undeviating, strict, exact, precise; unadulterated, unabridged, unvarnished, unembellished; accurate, correct.
OPPOSITE loose.
6 *Martin is his direct opposite* **exact**, absolute, complete, diametrical, downright, thorough, extreme.
▶ **adverb** *accommodation can be booked direct from the hotel* **directly**, straight, in person, without an intermediary; *French* tête-à-tête.
▶ **verb 1** *the elders directed the affairs of the tribe* **administer**, manage, run, control, govern, conduct, handle; be in charge of, be in control of, be in command of, be the boss of, lead, head, command, rule, preside over, exercise control over, be responsible for, be at the helm of; supervise, superintend, oversee, guide, regulate, orchestrate, coordinate, engineer, mastermind; *informal* run the show, call the shots, call the tune, pull the strings, be in the driving seat, be in the saddle.
2 *Jennifer was unsure if this comment was **directed at** her* **aim**, point, level; **address to**, intend for, mean for, destine for; focus on, train on, turn on, fix on.
3 *most of these books are **directed at** teenage girls* **target**, market; orient towards, pitch to/towards; design for, tailor to.
4 *a man in uniform directed them to the hall* **give directions to**, show/point/indicate the way; guide, steer, lead; conduct, accompany, usher, escort, navigate, pilot.
5 *put all the documents in one package and direct it to me* **address**, label, superscribe; post, send, mail, dispatch.
6 *the judge directed the jury to return a not guilty verdict* **instruct**, tell, command, order, give orders to, charge, call on, require, dictate; adjure, enjoin; *literary* bid.

direction ▶ **noun 1** *the village is over the moor in a northerly direction* **way**, **route**, course, line, run, bearing, orientation.
2 *there's uncertainty over the political direction the newspaper might adopt* **orientation**, inclination, leaning, tendency; bent, bias, preference, disposition; drift, aim, tack, attitude, tone, tenor, mood, feel, style, flavour, vein; current, trend.
3 *the department is under the direction of a senior executive* **administration**, management, supervision, superintendence, government, regulation, orchestration; control, command, rule; conduct, handling, running, overseeing, masterminding; leadership, guidance.
4 *the ward sister gave explicit directions about nursing care* **instruction**, command, order, bidding, charge, injunction, dictate, decree, edict, enjoinment, prescription, rule, regulation, requirement; guideline, recommendation, suggestion; (**directions**) guidance, information, briefing.

directive ▶ **noun** *an EC directive on drinking water* **instruction**, direction, command, order, charge, injunction, enjoinment, prescription, demand; **rule**, ruling, regulation, law, dictate, decree, dictum, edict, notice, ordinance, mandate, fiat, diktat.

directly ▶ **adverb 1** *the hijacker ordered the crew to fly directly to New York* **straight**, right, in a straight line, as the crow flies, by a direct route, without deviation, in a beeline, by the shortest route.
2 *she'll be down here directly* **immediately**, at once, instantly, right away, straight away, now, instantaneously, post-haste, without delay, without hesitation, forthwith; quickly, speedily, promptly; **soon**, as soon as possible, shortly, in a little while, in a second, in a moment, in a trice, in a flash, in (less than) no time, in no time at all, before you know it; *informal* pronto, double quick, p.d.q. (pretty damn quick), before you can say Jack Robinson, in a bit, in a jiffy, in two shakes (of a lamb's tail); *Brit. informal* in a tick, in two ticks, in a mo; *archaic or informal* anon.
3 *he'd never spoken directly to his lordship* **face to face**, personally, in person, without an intermediary, at first hand, head on, direct, man to man; *French* tête-à-tête.
4 *they sat down directly opposite him* **exactly**, immediately, precisely, right, squarely, just, dead; diametrically; *informal* bang.
5 *we didn't talk directly about sex* **frankly**, bluntly, straightforwardly, openly, candidly, outspokenly, forthrightly, without beating around the bush, point-blank, matter-of-factly, without prevarication; explicitly, clearly, plainly, unequivocally, unambiguously, categorically; sincerely, truthfully.
OPPOSITES equivocally, euphemistically.
▶ **conjunction** (*Brit.*) *directly he had finished praying he looked up* **as soon as**, the moment, the instant, the second, once, when, immediately after.

director ▶ **noun 1** *the director of a major British museum* **administrator**, manager, chairman, chairwoman, chairperson, chair, head, chief, boss, principal, leader, governor, president, premier; managing director, MD, chief executive, CEO; superintendent, supervisor, controller, overseer, organizer; member of the board; *informal* kingpin, top dog, gaffer, bigwig, big cheese; *N. Amer. informal* honcho, head honcho, numero uno, Mister Big, big wheel.
2 *an Oscar-winning director* auteur, supervisor, controller; choreographer; regisseur.

D

D

directory ▸ noun *the London phone directory* **index**, list, listing, register, catalogue, record, archive, inventory.

dirge ▸ noun *he wrote dirges for funerals* **elegy**, lament, funeral song/chant, burial hymn, requiem, dead march; *Irish & Scottish* keen, coronach; *rare* threnody, threnode, monody.

dirt ▸ noun **1** *his face was streaked with dirt* **grime**, dust, soot, smut; muck, mud, filth, mire, sludge, slime, ooze, dross, scum, pollution, waste; smudges, stains; *informal* crud, yuck, grot, gunge, grunge.
2 *the packed dirt of the road* **earth**, soil, loam, clay, silt; turf, clod, sod; ground.
3 (*informal*) *a lawn covered in dog dirt* **excrement**, excreta, droppings, faeces, dung, manure, ordure; muck, mess; *informal* poo; *N. Amer. informal* poop; *vulgar slang* crap, shit.
4 (*informal*) *they tried to dig up dirt on the President* **scandal**, gossip, talk, revelations, rumour(s), tittle-tattle, tattle; slander, libel, calumny; smears; *informal* low-down, gen, dope; *N. Amer. informal* poop.
5 *we object to the dirt that television projects into homes* **obscenity**, indecency, smut, smuttiness, filth, pornography, sordidness, coarseness, bawdiness, earthiness, suggestiveness, vulgarity, ribaldry, salaciousness, salacity, lewdness; *informal* sleaze, porn, sleaziness, naughtiness, raunchiness, steaminess, spiciness.

WORD LINKS
fear of dirt **mysophobia**

dirty ▸ adjective **1** *a dirty sweatshirt | dirty water* **soiled**, grimy, grubby, filthy, mucky, stained, unwashed, greasy, smeared, smeary, spotted, smudged, cloudy, muddy, dusty, sooty; unclean, sullied, impure, tarnished, polluted, contaminated, defiled, foul, unhygienic, insanitary, unsanitary; *informal* cruddy, yucky, icky; *Brit. informal* manky, gungy, grotty; *literary* befouled, besmirched, begrimed; *rare* feculent.
OPPOSITE clean.
2 *the deer was a dirty grey in colour* **dull**, **cloudy**, muddy, dingy, dark, not clear, not pure, not bright.
OPPOSITE bright.
3 *a dirty joke* **indecent**, obscene, rude, vulgar, smutty, coarse, crude, filthy, bawdy, suggestive, ribald, racy, salacious, risqué, prurient, offensive, lewd, lascivious, licentious, pornographic, explicit, X-rated; *N. Amer.* off colour; *informal* naughty, blue; *euphemistic* adult.
OPPOSITE clean.
4 *firms are resorting to dirty tricks to keep ahead of rivals | you dirty cheat!* **unfair**, dishonest, deceitful, unscrupulous, dishonourable, unsporting, ungentlemanly, below the belt, unethical, unprincipled, immoral; crooked, illegal, fraudulent; rotten, corrupt, double-dealing, treacherous, underhand, sly, crafty, cunning, wily, devious, Machiavellian, sneaky, guileful, conniving, designing, calculating; nasty, unpleasant, mean, base, low, vile, contemptible, despicable, cowardly, shameful, ignominious, sordid, beggarly, squalid; *informal* low-down; *Brit. informal* out of order, not cricket.
OPPOSITES honest; decent.
5 *she gave her brother a dirty look* **malevolent**, smouldering, resentful, full of dislike/hate, hostile, black, dark, bitter; angry, indignant, annoyed, peeved, offended.
6 *dirty weather* **unpleasant**, nasty, foul, inclement, rough, bad; stormy, squally, gusty, windy, blowy, rainy; misty, gloomy, murky, overcast, louring.
OPPOSITE fair.
7 *how dare you come here throwing around such dirty lies?* **scandalous**, defamatory, slanderous, libellous.
▸ verb *she didn't like him dirtying her nice clean towels* **soil**, stain, muddy, blacken, mess up, spoil, tarnish, taint, make dirty; mark, spatter, bespatter, smudge, smear, daub, spot, splash, splatter; sully, pollute, foul, defile; *literary* befoul, besmirch, begrime.
OPPOSITE clean.

disability ▸ noun *my disability makes getting into bed rather a slow process* **handicap**, disablement, incapacity, impairment, infirmity, defect, abnormality; condition, disorder, affliction, ailment, complaint, illness, malady, disease.

disable ▸ verb **1** *the gunfire could kill or disable the pilot* **incapacitate**, impair, damage, put out of action, render/make powerless, weaken, enfeeble, debilitate, indispose, make unfit, render infirm; cripple, lame, handicap, maim, injure, wound; immobilize, hamstring, paralyse, prostrate; *rare* torpefy.
2 *the bomb squad disabled the device* **deactivate**, defuse, disarm, render inoperative, make ineffective, put out of action, make harmless.
OPPOSITES set, repair.
3 *after the Restoration he was disabled from holding public office* **disqualify**, prevent, invalidate, declare incapable, rule out, preclude, debar, prohibit, disentitle; *rare* disenable.
OPPOSITE allow.

disabled ▸ adjective *they design computer aids for disabled people* **handicapped**, physically handicapped, physically impaired, impaired, incapacitated; debilitated, infirm, weak, weakened, enfeebled, out of action; paralysed, immobilized; bedridden, confined to bed; wheelchair-using, wheelchair-bound, confined to a wheelchair; crippled, lame; *euphemistic* physically challenged, differently abled; *Medicine* paraplegic, quadriplegic, tetraplegic, monoplegic, hemiplegic, paretic, paraparetic.
OPPOSITE able-bodied.

disabuse ▸ verb *he had thought he was good enough to become a professional, and Dinah had disabused him* **disillusion**, undeceive, correct, set right/straight, open the eyes of, enlighten, reveal the truth to, wake up, disenchant, shatter the illusions of, make sadder and wiser.

disadvantage ▸ noun **1** *price is probably the biggest disadvantage of rail travel* **drawback**, snag, downside, stumbling block, catch, pitfall, fly in the ointment; weak spot/point, weakness, flaw, defect, fault; handicap, limitation, trouble, difficulty, problem, complication, liability, nuisance; hindrance, obstacle, impediment; *informal* minus, hiccup; *Brit. informal* spanner in the works; *N. Amer. informal* monkey wrench in the works.
OPPOSITES advantage, benefit.
2 *she could think of nothing to his disadvantage* **detriment**, prejudice, disservice, harm, damage; loss, injury, hurt, mischief.
OPPOSITE advantage.
▸ verb *policies which unfairly disadvantage certain groups* **treat unfavourably**, put at a disadvantage, treat harshly/unfairly, put in an unfavourable position, handicap, inflict a handicap on, do a disservice to, be unfair to, wrong.

disadvantaged ▸ adjective *a disadvantaged rural area* **deprived**, **underprivileged**, depressed, in need, needy, in want, in distress; destitute, poor, poverty-stricken; discriminated against; *Brit.* on the bread line; *rare* necessitous.
OPPOSITE privileged.

disadvantageous ▸ adjective *a very disadvantageous position* **unfavourable**, adverse, inauspicious, unpropitious, unfortunate, unlucky, bad; detrimental, prejudicial, deleterious, harmful, damaging, injurious, hurtful, destructive; inopportune, ill-timed, untimely, inexpedient.
OPPOSITE advantageous.

disaffected ▸ adjective *a plot by disaffected elements in the army* **dissatisfied**, disgruntled, discontented, malcontent, restless, frustrated, fed up; alienated, estranged; disloyal, rebellious, insubordinate, mutinous, seditious, renegade, insurgent, insurrectionary, dissident, up in arms; hostile, antagonistic, unfriendly.
OPPOSITES contented, loyal.

disaffection ▸ noun *the government's oppressive policies heightened popular disaffection* **dissatisfaction**, disgruntlement, discontent, restlessness, frustration; alienation, estrangement; disloyalty, rebellion, insubordination, mutiny, sedition, insurgence, insurrection, dissidence; hostility, antagonism, animosity, discord, dissension.
OPPOSITES contentment, loyalty.

disagree ▸ verb **1** *no one was willing to **disagree with** him* **fail to agree**, be in dispute/contention, be at variance/odds, not see eye to eye, differ from, dissent from, diverge from; contradict, gainsay, challenge, oppose; argue, debate, quarrel, bicker, wrangle, squabble, spar, dispute, take issue, row, altercate, clash, be at loggerheads, cross swords, lock horns; *informal* fall out, have words, scrap; *archaic* disaccord.
OPPOSITE agree.
2 *they **disagreed with** American policy* **disapprove of**, oppose, dissent from, think wrong, be against, demur about/against, not believe in, not support.
OPPOSITE agree.
3 *their accounts disagree on details* **differ**, be dissimilar, be unlike, be different, vary; contradict each other, conflict, clash, contrast, diverge, not correspond, not accord, be discordant.
OPPOSITE agree.
4 *the North Sea crossing seemed to have **disagreed with** her* **make ill**, make unwell, nauseate, sicken, upset, cause illness to, cause discomfort to, be injurious to, have an adverse effect on.

disagreeable ▸ adjective **1** *a disagreeable smell* **unpleasant**, displeasing, nasty, horrible, dreadful, horrid, frightful, abominable, odious, offensive, obnoxious, objectionable, repugnant, repulsive, repellent, revolting, disgusting, foul, vile, nauseating, sickening, hateful, detestable, distasteful, unsavoury, unpalatable.
OPPOSITE pleasant.
2 *he was a very disagreeable character* **bad-tempered**, ill-tempered, ill-natured, ill-humoured, curmudgeonly, cross, crabbed, irritable, grumpy, peevish, snappish, petulant, sulky, sullen, prickly; **unfriendly**, unpleasant, nasty, mean, mean-spirited; rude, surly, discourteous, impolite, brusque, abrupt, difficult, contrary, churlish, disobliging; cruel, vicious, spiteful; *informal* grouchy.
OPPOSITES likeable, pleasant.

disagreement ▸ noun **1** *at the conference there was disagreement over possible solutions* **dissent**, lack of agreement, difference of opinion, dispute; variance, controversy, disaccord, discord, contention, divisions.
OPPOSITES consensus, agreement.
2 *a heated disagreement over politics* **argument**, debate, quarrel, wrangle,

squabble, altercation, dispute, disputation, war of words, contretemps, misunderstanding; discord, strife, conflict; bickering, sparring, contention, dissension, disharmony; *informal* falling-out, tiff, barney, set-to, shouting/slanging match, spat, ding-dong; *Brit. informal* row; *Scottish informal* rammy.
3 *there was disagreement between the results of the two assessments* **difference**, dissimilarity, variation, variance, discrepancy, disparity, dissimilitude, unlikeness; incompatibility, incongruity, contradiction, conflict, clash, contrast; divergence, deviation, nonconformity.
OPPOSITES agreement, correspondence.

disallow ▸ verb *if the registration officer disallows your application he will let you know | Derby had two goals disallowed* **reject**, refuse, dismiss, say no to; ban, bar, block, stop, debar, forbid, prohibit, blackball; cancel, declare null and void, invalidate, overrule, quash, overturn, countermand, reverse, throw out, set aside; veto, embargo, proscribe; *informal* give the thumbs down to, squash.
OPPOSITE allow.

disappear ▸ verb **1** *they disappeared through the gates of the house | most symptoms should disappear in six months* **vanish**, pass from sight, cease to be visible, vanish from sight, recede from view, be lost to view/sight, fade, fade/melt away; withdraw, depart, retire, retreat; go, pass, ebb, wane, dissipate, be dispelled, dematerialize, evaporate; *literary* evanesce.
OPPOSITES appear; reappear.
2 *this way of life has disappeared* **die out**, die, become extinct, cease to be/exist, be no more, come to an end, end, pass away, pass into oblivion, expire, perish, wither away, peter out, fizzle out, leave no trace.
OPPOSITES survive, live on.
3 *we had to change the locks after the keys disappeared* **get lost**, go missing, be mislaid, be forgotten, be left behind; be stolen, be taken.

disappearance ▸ noun **1** *the sun's disappearance at night* **vanishing**, fading, fading/melting away, passing from sight, receding from view; withdrawal, departure, retirement, retreat; going, passing, exit; ebb, wane, dissipation, dematerialization, dissolution, evaporation; *literary* evanescence.
OPPOSITES appearance, reappearance.
2 *the disappearance of the last big predators from Western Europe* **dying out**, dying, death, extinction, coming to an end, ending, passing away, passing into oblivion, expiry, vanishing, perishing, withering away, petering out, fizzling out.
3 *the disappearance of the money* **loss**; **theft**, robbery, stealing, thieving, robbing, pilfering, pilferage, purloining.
OPPOSITE recovery.

disappoint ▸ verb **1** *he disappointed the home crowd by losing in the semi-finals* **let down**, fail, dash the hopes of; dishearten, dispirit, discourage, upset, dismay, depress, sadden, dampen the spirits of, disenchant, disillusion, shatter the illusions of, dissatisfy, disgruntle, chagrin; fall short (of expectations).
OPPOSITES cheer; satisfy.
2 *his hopes were disappointed by the death of his patron* **thwart**, frustrate, baulk, foil, dash, defeat, baffle, put a/the damper on, nip in the bud; hinder, obstruct, hamper, impede, interfere with; *informal* stymie, throw cold water on.
OPPOSITE fulfil.

disappointed ▸ adjective **1** *I was disappointed that my mother wasn't there* **saddened**, upset, let down, disheartened, downhearted, cast down, downcast, depressed, dispirited, discouraged, despondent, dismayed, crestfallen, distressed, chagrined; disenchanted, disillusioned; displeased, discontented, dissatisfied, frustrated, disgruntled; *informal* choked, miffed, cut up; *Brit. informal* gutted, as sick as a parrot.
OPPOSITES pleased, satisfied.
2 *a bitter tale of disappointed hopes* **thwarted**, frustrated, baulked, foiled, dashed, defeated, failed, baffled; *informal* stymied.
OPPOSITE fulfilled.

disappointing ▸ adjective **1** *the predominance of white, middle-class characters is disappointing* **saddening**, disheartening, dispiriting, discouraging, upsetting, dismaying, depressing, distressing; disenchanting, disillusioning, dissatisfying; regrettable, unfortunate.
OPPOSITES encouraging, cheering.
2 *Derry made a disappointing start* **unsatisfactory**, inadequate, insufficient, unworthy, substandard, not good enough; poor, inferior, deficient, second-rate, pathetic, lame, pitiful; anticlimactic; *informal* below par, not up to scratch, not up to snuff, sorry, not all it's cracked up to be; *Brit. informal* underwhelming, duff, ropy, rubbish.
OPPOSITES encouraging, satisfactory.

disappointment ▸ noun **1** *members expressed disappointment at the decision* **sadness**, regret, dismay, sorrow; dispiritedness, despondency, heavy-heartedness, depression; distress, mortification, chagrin; disenchantment, disillusionment; displeasure, discontent, dissatisfaction, disgruntlement.
OPPOSITES satisfaction, happiness.
2 *he agreed that the recent defeats against Norway and the USA had been bitter disappointments* **failure**, let-down, non-event, anticlimax; misfortune, setback, blow, reversal, stroke of bad luck, body blow, one in the eye; fiasco, disaster, catastrophe, mess, debacle; *Brit.* damp squib; *informal* flop, dud, washout, non-starter, lead balloon.
OPPOSITE success.
3 *the disappointment of the high hopes invested in reform* **frustration**, thwarting, baulking, foiling, dashing, baffling; defeat, failure, lack of success.
OPPOSITE fulfilment.

disapprobation ▸ noun *she had braved her mother's disapprobation and slipped out to enjoy herself. See* DISAPPROVAL.

disapproval ▸ noun *they expressed their strong disapproval of the law* **disapprobation**, dislike; dissatisfaction, disfavour, displeasure, distaste, odium, objection, demurral, exception; dissent, disagreement; criticism, censure, condemnation, denunciation, opprobrium; blame, reproach, rebuke, reproof, remonstration; disparagement, deprecation; *informal* the thumbs down; *rare* animadversion.
OPPOSITE approval.

disapprove ▸ verb **1** *he disapproves of gamblers* **have/express a poor opinion of**, dislike, be against, object to, find unacceptable, think wrong, take exception to, not believe in, not support, frown on, take a dim view of, look askance at; be dissatisfied with, be displeased with, be hostile towards; detest, deplore, despise, loathe; criticize, censure, blame, condemn, denounce, decry, reproach, rebuke, reprove, remonstrate against; disparage, deprecate; *informal* look down one's nose at, knock; *rare* animadvert.
OPPOSITE approve.
2 *the board disapproved the bank's plan* **reject**, refuse, turn down, veto, disallow, set aside, throw out, dismiss, say 'no' to, rule against, rule out; *informal* give the thumbs down to.
OPPOSITES approve, accept.

disapproving ▸ adjective *he cast a disapproving glance at Bridget* **reproachful**, reproving, full of reproof; **critical**, criticizing, censorious, condemnatory, condemning, denouncing, scathing, damning; disparaging, deprecatory, unfavourable, pejorative, derogatory; dissatisfied, displeased, hostile; *informal* knocking, slating.
OPPOSITE approving.

disarm ▸ verb **1** *the UN must disarm the country and arrest the warlords* **deprive of arms**, take weapons from, render defenceless, make powerless; **demilitarize**, demobilize.
OPPOSITES arm, militarize.
2 *the militia had refused government demands to disarm* **lay down arms/weapons**, demilitarize, turn over weapons, decommission arms/weapons, become unarmed; *literary* sheathe the sword, turn swords into ploughshares.
OPPOSITE arm.
3 *police disarmed a parcel bomb* **defuse**, disable, deactivate, remove the fuse from, put out of action; make safe, make harmless.
OPPOSITES arm, set.
4 *the warmth in his voice disarmed her* **win over**, charm, undermine someone's resistance, sweeten; persuade, convert; mollify, appease, placate, pacify, conciliate, humour, propitiate.
OPPOSITE antagonize.

disarmament ▸ noun *the public wanted peace and disarmament* **demilitarization**, demobilization, deactivation of arms/weapons, decommissioning (of arms/weapons), laying down of arms/weapons; arms/weapons reduction, arms/weapons limitation, arms/weapons control, de-escalation.

disarming ▸ adjective *a disarming smile* **winning**, charming, likeable, enchanting, beguiling; persuasive, irresistible; conciliatory, mollifying, placating, pacifying, propitiating.

disarrange ▸ verb *it's amazing how quickly my few possessions become disarranged* **disorder**, bring/throw into disorder, put out of place, throw into disarray, make disorderly, disorganize, disturb, displace; make untidy, mess up, make a mess of; confuse, throw into confusion, jumble, mix up, muddle, turn upside-down, derange, scatter; dishevel, tousle, rumple; *informal* turn topsy-turvy, make a shambles of; *N. Amer. informal* muss up.
OPPOSITES arrange, tidy.

disarray ▸ noun **1** *the room was in disarray* **disorder**, confusion, chaos; untidiness, dishevelment; mess, muddle, clutter, jumble, mix-up, tangle, hotchpotch, shambles.
OPPOSITE tidiness.
2 *the political disarray which followed the death of Offa* **disorganization**, lack of order, discomposure, disunity; indiscipline, unruliness.
OPPOSITE orderliness.
▸ verb *her clothes were disarrayed* **disarrange**, make untidy, bring/throw into disarray, bring/throw into disorder, disorganize, throw into a state of disorganization, turn upside-down, unsettle; dishevel, tousle, rumple.
OPPOSITES tidy, organize.

disassemble ▸ verb *the furniture was disassembled for transport* **dismantle**, take apart, take to pieces, pull apart, pull to pieces, take/pull to bits,

deconstruct, break up, strip down.
OPPOSITES assemble, put together.

disaster ▶ noun **1** *a railway disaster* **catastrophe**, calamity, cataclysm, tragedy, act of God, holocaust; accident, mishap, misadventure, mischance; setback, reversal, reverse of fortune, contretemps, stroke of ill luck, problem, difficulty, heavy blow, shock, buffet; adversity, trouble, misfortune, ruin, ruination, tribulation, woe, distress; *technical* casualty; *archaic* bale; *Scottish archaic* mishanter.
OPPOSITE blessing.
2 *my personal life had been a disaster* **failure**, fiasco, catastrophe, mess, debacle; *Brit.* damp squib; *informal* flop, dud, washout, dead loss, dead duck, non-starter, no-hoper.
OPPOSITE success.

disastrous ▶ adjective *a disastrous fire | a disastrous decision* **catastrophic**, calamitous, cataclysmic, tragic; devastating, ravaging, ruinous, harmful, injurious, detrimental, adverse; dire, terrible, awful, shocking, appalling, dreadful, grievous, horrible, black, dark, bad; unfortunate, unlucky, ill-fated, ill-starred, inauspicious, unfavourable.
OPPOSITES fortunate, successful, beneficial.

disavow ▶ verb *the chairman publicly disavowed the press release* **deny**, disclaim, disown, wash one's hands of; reject, repudiate; contradict, rebut, abjure, renounce, forswear, eschew.

disavowal ▶ noun *it's a complete disavowal of responsibility* **denial**, disowning, disclaimer; rejection, repudiation, contradiction, rebuttal; renunciation, eschewal, casting off/aside, abandonment.

disband ▶ verb *the unit was scheduled to disband* **break up**, disperse, demobilize, dissolve, scatter, separate, go separate ways, part company.
OPPOSITE assemble.

disbelief ▶ noun **1** *she stared at him in disbelief* **incredulity**, incredulousness, lack of belief, lack of credence, lack of conviction, scepticism, doubt, doubtfulness, dubiety, dubiousness, questioning, cynicism, suspicion, distrust, mistrust, wariness, chariness; bewilderment, bafflement, surprise, shock, stupefaction, confusion, perplexity.
OPPOSITES belief, credence.
2 *I'll burn in hell for disbelief* **atheism**, unbelief, godlessness, ungodliness, impiety, irreligion, agnosticism, nihilism.
OPPOSITE faith.

disbelieve ▶ verb *he totally disbelieved her | he had come to* **disbelieve in** *his own assertions* **not believe**, not credit, give no credence to, discredit, discount, doubt, distrust, mistrust, be suspicious of, have no confidence/faith in, be incredulous of, be unconvinced about; not accept, reject, repudiate, question, challenge, contradict; *informal* take with a pinch of salt.
OPPOSITE believe.

disbeliever ▶ noun *as a disbeliever I can still read the Bible for the beauty of its prose* **unbeliever**, non-believer, atheist, irreligionist, nihilist; rationalist; sceptic, doubter, agnostic, doubting Thomas, questioner, challenger; cynic, scoffer; *rare* nullifidian.
OPPOSITE believer.

disbelieving ▶ adjective *he gave a disbelieving laugh* **incredulous**, unbelieving, doubtful, dubious, unconvinced; distrustful, mistrustful, suspicious, lacking trust, cynical, sceptical.
OPPOSITE believing.

disburden ▶ verb *I decided to disburden myself of the task* **relieve**, free, liberate, unburden, disencumber, discharge, ease, unload; excuse from, absolve from.
OPPOSITE burden.

disburse ▶ verb *the officers disbursed some £1.8 million on behalf of the fund* **pay out**, lay out, spend, expend, dole out, hand out, part with, donate, give; *informal* fork out, shell out, dish out, lash out, cough up, splurge, blow; *Brit. informal* stump up; *N. Amer. informal* ante up, pony up.
OPPOSITE claim.

disbursement ▶ noun *the commission decided to delay the disbursement of funds* **payment**, disbursal, paying out, laying out, spending, expending, expenditure, disposal, outlay, doling out, handing out, parting with, donation, giving.

disc, disk ▶ noun **1** *the sun was a huge scarlet disc* **circle**, round, saucer, discus, ring.
2 *the module comes with a manual and software on disk* **diskette**, floppy disk, floppy; hard disk; CD-ROM.
3 *this is one of the best of this conductor's discs* **record**, album, LP, gramophone record, vinyl; **compact disc**, CD.

discard ▶ verb *his old suit had been discarded* **dispose of**, throw away, throw out, get rid of, toss out; reject, jettison, scrap, dispense with, cast aside/off, repudiate, abandon, relinquish, drop, have done with, shed, slough off, shrug off, throw on the scrap heap; *informal* chuck (away/out), fling away, dump, ditch, axe, bin, junk, get shut of; *Brit. informal* get shot of; *N. Amer. informal* trash; *archaic* forsake.
OPPOSITES keep; acquire.

discern ▶ verb *in the dim light he could discern a handful of ghostly figures* **perceive**, make out, pick out, detect, recognize, notice, observe, see, spot; identify, determine, distinguish, differentiate, discriminate, tell apart; become cognizant of, become aware of, become conscious of; *literary* descry, espy.
OPPOSITES overlook; miss.

discernible ▶ adjective *the figure was scarcely discernible in the pale moonlight* **visible**, detectable, noticeable, perceptible, observable, perceivable, distinguishable, recognizable, identifiable; apparent, obvious, clear, manifest, conspicuous, patent, plain, evident, distinct, appreciable.
OPPOSITE imperceptible.

discerning ▶ adjective *we have some real treasures for the discerning collector* **discriminating**, selective, judicious, tasteful, refined, cultivated, cultured, sophisticated, enlightened, sensitive, subtle, critical; perceptive, insightful, percipient, perspicacious, penetrating; astute, shrewd, ingenious, clever, intelligent, sharp, wise, erudite, aware, knowing, sagacious; *rare* sapient.
OPPOSITES undiscerning, indiscriminate.

discernment ▶ noun *each object in the room spoke of his taste and discernment* **judgement**, taste, discrimination, refinement, cultivation, sophistication, enlightenment, sensitivity, subtlety; insight, perceptiveness, perception, perspicacity; astuteness, acumen, shrewdness, ingeniousness, cleverness, intelligence, sharpness, wisdom, erudition, awareness, sagacity; *rare* sapience.

discharge ▶ verb **1** *he was discharged from the RAF* **dismiss**, remove, eject, expel, deprive of office, get rid of, throw out, oust; let go, give someone notice, lay off, make/declare redundant; *Military* cashier; *informal* sack, give someone the sack, fire, axe, send packing, give someone the boot, boot out, turf out, give someone their cards, give someone their marching orders, give someone the heave-ho, give someone the push, give someone the bullet, show someone the door.
OPPOSITES recruit, engage.
2 *he was discharged from prison* **release**, liberate, free, set free, let go, let out, allow to leave, set/let/turn loose; acquit, clear, absolve, pardon, exonerate, reprieve, exculpate; deliver, spare, exempt; emancipate; *informal* let off (the hook); *historical* manumit.
OPPOSITE imprison.
3 *oil is routinely discharged from ships* **send out**, **pour**, release, eject, emit, let out, void, issue, dispense, give off, exude, excrete, ooze, leak, gush, jet; *Medicine* extravasate; *literary* disembogue.
OPPOSITE absorb.
4 *he accidentally discharged a pistol* **fire**, shoot, let off, set off, loose off, trigger, explode, detonate.
5 *there is an elevator for discharging grain from ships* **unload**, offload, empty, unburden, disburden, remove, relieve; deliver, deposit, put off; *rare* unlade.
OPPOSITE load.
6 *the bank had failed to discharge its supervisory duties* **carry out**, perform, conduct, do; complete, accomplish, achieve, fulfil, execute, implement, dispatch, bring off, bring about, effect; observe, abide by, stand by; *rare* effectuate.
7 *the executor must discharge the funeral expenses* **pay**, pay off, pay in full, settle (up), clear, honour, meet, liquidate, satisfy, defray, make good; *informal* square.
▶ noun **1** *his discharge from the service* **dismissal**, release, removal, ejection, ousting, expulsion, congé; *Military* cashiering; *informal* the sack, firing, axing, the axe, the boot, one's marching orders, the heave-ho, the push, the bullet.
OPPOSITE recruitment.
2 *she was given an absolute discharge by the magistrates* **release**, liberation; **acquittal**, clearance, clearing; absolution, pardon, exoneration, reprieve, amnesty, exculpation; *informal* let-off, letting off; *historical* manumission.
OPPOSITE conviction.
3 *there was a discharge of diesel oil into the river* **leak**, leaking, emission, release, exuding, oozing, excretion, ejection; emptying, voiding, voidance; *literary* disemboguing.
4 *symptoms include a watery discharge from the eyes* **emission**, secretion, excretion, exudate, effusion; flow, ooze, seepage, suppuration; pus, matter.
5 *he killed eight birds with a single discharge of his gun* **shot**, shooting, firing, discharging, explosion, detonation; blast, crack, bang, pop, report; burst, volley, salvo, fusillade, barrage; (**discharges**) gunfire.
6 *we have two hundred passengers and freight for discharge* **unloading**, offloading, unburdening, disburdening, removal, removing, relieving; emptying; delivering, deposit; *rare* unlading.
OPPOSITE loading.
7 *the teachers appeared somewhat lax in the discharge of their duties* **carrying out**, performance, performing, conduct, doing; completion, accomplishment, achievement, fulfilment, execution, implementation,

dispatch, effectuation; observance.
8 *the residue of the estate after the discharge of all debts* **payment**, repayment, paying (off), settlement, settling (up), clearance, clearing, honouring, meeting, liquidation, defraying, making good; *informal* squaring.

WORD LINKS
related suffix **-rrhoea (e.g. *diarrhoea, logorrhoea*)**

disciple ▶ **noun 1** *the disciples of Jesus* **apostle**; follower.
2 *a disciple of Rousseau* **follower**, adherent, believer, admirer, devotee, acolyte, votary; pupil, student, protégé, learner; upholder, supporter, advocate, proponent, apologist; *Hinduism* chela, bhakta.
OPPOSITES critic, opponent.

disciplinarian ▶ **noun martinet**, hard taskmaster, authoritarian, stickler for discipline; tyrant, despot; *N. Amer.* ramrod; *informal* slave-driver.

discipline ▶ **noun 1** *discipline in the camp was strict* **control**, regulation, direction, order, authority, rule, strictness, a firm hand; routine, regimen; training, teaching, instruction, drill, drilling, exercise; use of punishment.
2 *it may take courage and discipline to do this, but it is worth the effort* **self-control**, self-discipline, self-government, control, controlled behaviour, self-restraint; good behaviour, orderliness, obedience.
3 *sociology is a fairly new discipline* **field (of study)**, branch of knowledge, course of study, subject, area; specialist subject, speciality, specialty.
▶ **verb 1** *these families have different ways of disciplining their children | you must discipline yourself into adopting regular working methods* **train**, drill, teach, school, coach, educate, regiment, indoctrinate; lay down the law to someone, bring into line.
2 *she had learned to discipline her emotions* **control**, bring/keep under control, restrain, regulate, govern, keep in check, check, curb, keep a tight rein on, rein in, bridle, tame.
OPPOSITE give free rein to.
3 *a member of staff was to be disciplined by the management* **punish**, penalize, take disciplinary action against, bring to book; **reprimand**, rebuke, reprove, chastise, castigate, upbraid, remonstrate with; *informal* dress down, give someone a dressing-down, rap over the knuckles, give someone a roasting, give someone a rocket, put on the mat; *Brit. informal* carpet, put on the carpet; *archaic* chasten.

disclaim ▶ **verb 1** *the school disclaimed any responsibility for his death* **deny**, refuse to accept, refuse to acknowledge, reject, wash one's hands of.
OPPOSITES acknowledge, accept.
2 (*Law*) *the earl disclaimed his title* **renounce**, relinquish, resign, give up, abandon; repudiate, disown, cast off, discard, abjure, forswear, disavow; *Law* disaffirm.
OPPOSITE claim.

disclaimer ▶ **noun 1** *the disclaimer of responsibility set out in the memorandum* **denial**, refusal, rejection.
OPPOSITES acceptance, acknowledgement.
2 (*Law*) *a deed of disclaimer* **renunciation**, relinquishment, resignation, abdication; repudiation, abjuration, disavowal, disaffirmation.

disclose ▶ **verb 1** *the information is confidential and must not be disclosed to anyone* **reveal**, make known, divulge, tell, impart, communicate, pass on, vouchsafe, unfold; release, make public, broadcast, publish, report, unveil, go public with; leak, betray, let slip, let drop, blurt out, give away; admit, confess; *informal* let on, blab, spill the beans about, spill, let the cat out of the bag about, blow the lid off, squeal about; *Brit. informal* blow the gaff; *archaic* discover, unbosom.
OPPOSITES conceal; hide.
2 *exploratory surgery disclosed an aneurysm* **uncover**, expose to view, allow to be seen, reveal, show, exhibit, lay bare, bring to light; *rare* unclose.

disclosure ▶ **noun 1** *she was acutely embarrassed by this unexpected disclosure* **revelation**, surprising fact, divulgence, declaration, announcement, news, report; exposé, leak; admission, confession.
2 *the unauthorized disclosure of official information* **publishing**, broadcasting; revelation, revealing, making known, communication, divulging, divulgence; release, uncovering, unveiling, exposure; leakage; *Law* discovery; *rare* divulgation.
OPPOSITE concealment.

discoloration ▶ **noun** *a brown discoloration on the skin* **stain**, mark, patch, soiling, streak, spot, blotch, tarnishing; blemish, flaw, defect, disfigurement, bruise, contusion; birthmark; liver spot, age spot; *informal* splodge, splotch; *technical* ecchymosis, naevus.

discolour ▶ **verb** *smoke from the coal fire had discoloured the original paintwork* **stain**, mark, soil, dirty, make dirty, streak, smear, spot, tarnish, sully, spoil, mar, disfigure, blemish; blacken, char; fade, bleach, wash out; rust, weather.

discoloured ▶ **adjective** *the shaft of the sword was twisted and discoloured* **stained**, marked, spotted, dirty, soiled, tarnished, blackened; bleached, faded, yellowed; rusted, rusty, oxidized, weathered.
OPPOSITES shiny, clean.

discomfit ▶ **verb** *she kissed Sir John on the cheek, which discomfited him even more* **embarrass**, make uncomfortable, make uneasy, abash, disconcert, nonplus, discompose, discomfort, take aback, unsettle, unnerve, put someone off their stroke, ruffle, confuse, fluster, agitate, disorientate, upset, disturb, perturb, distress; chagrin, mortify; *informal* faze, rattle, discombobulate, set someone back on their heels, make someone laugh on the other side of their face; *N. Amer. informal* make someone laugh out of the other side of their mouth.
OPPOSITE reassure.

discomfiture ▶ **noun** *Sweetman laughed at her obvious discomfiture* **embarrassment**, unease, uneasiness, awkwardness, discomfort, discomposure, abashment, confusion, agitation, nervousness, flusteredness, disorientation, perturbation, distress; chagrin, mortification, shame, humiliation; *informal* discombobulation; *rare* disconcertment, disconcertion, nonplus.

discomfort ▶ **noun 1** *he complained of increasing abdominal discomfort* **pain**, aches and pains, soreness, tenderness, irritation, stiffness, malaise; ache, twinge, pang, throb, cramp, hurt; *Brit. informal* gyp.
2 *the discomforts of life at sea* **inconvenience**, difficulty, bother, nuisance, vexation, drawback, disadvantage, trouble, problem, trial, tribulation; lack of comfort, unpleasantness, hardship, distress; *informal* hassle.
OPPOSITES comfort, luxury.
3 *Ruth flushed and Thomas noticed her discomfort* **embarrassment**, discomfiture, unease, uneasiness, abashment, awkwardness, discomposure, confusion, agitation, nervousness, flusteredness, perturbation, distress, anxiety; chagrin, mortification, shame, humiliation; *rare* disconcertment, disconcertion.
▶ **verb** *his purpose was to discomfort the Prime Minister* **discomfit**, make uneasy, make uncomfortable, embarrass, abash, disconcert, nonplus, discompose, take aback, unsettle, unnerve, put someone off their stroke, upset, ruffle, fluster, perturb, disturb; chagrin, mortify; *informal* rattle, discombobulate, faze, set someone back on their heels.
OPPOSITE reassure.

discomposure ▶ **noun** *she laughed to cover her discomposure* **agitation**, discomfiture, discomfort, uneasiness, unease, confusion, disorientation, perturbation, distress, nervousness, flusteredness; anxiety, worry, consternation, disquiet, disquietude; embarrassment, abashment, chagrin, loss of face; *informal* discombobulation; *rare* disconcertment, disconcertion, inquietude.
OPPOSITE composure.

disconcert ▶ **verb** *the abrupt change of subject disconcerted her* **unsettle**, nonplus, discomfit, throw/catch off balance, take aback, unnerve, disorient, perturb, disturb, perplex, confuse, bewilder, baffle, fluster, ruffle, shake, upset, agitate, worry, dismay, put out of countenance, discountenance, discompose; surprise, take by surprise, startle, stop someone in their tracks, put someone off (their stroke/stride), distract; embarrass, abash; *informal* throw, faze, make someone scratch their head, discombobulate, rattle, set someone back on their heels, psych out; *archaic* cause to be at a stand, gravel.
OPPOSITE reassure.

disconcerting ▶ **adjective** *it was disconcerting to be subjected to such intense scrutiny* **unsettling**, unnerving, discomfiting, disturbing, perturbing, troubling, upsetting, worrying, alarming, embarrassing, awkward, bothersome, distracting; confusing, bewildering, perplexing; *informal* off-putting, anxious-making.
OPPOSITE reassuring.

disconnect ▶ **verb 1** *the trucks will be disconnected from the train at various stopping places* **detach**, disengage, uncouple, decouple, unhook, unhitch, unlink, undo, unfasten, unyoke, disarticulate; *rare* disjoin, disunite.
OPPOSITES attach, connect.
2 *take all the violence out of television drama and you disconnect it from reality* **separate**, cut off, divorce, sever, isolate, divide, part, disengage, delink, dissociate, remove; *rare* dissever.
3 *by law, if your appliance is dangerous, the engineer has to disconnect it* **deactivate**, shut off, turn off, switch off, unplug, de-energize, detach from a power supply.
OPPOSITE connect.
4 *the electricity board had disconnected the power supply* **cut off**, stop.
OPPOSITE restore.
5 *her call was disconnected* **terminate**, stop, discontinue, break off; **interrupt**, suspend.
OPPOSITE put through.

disconnected ▶ **adjective 1** *I drove away feeling disconnected from the real world* **detached**, separate, separated, divorced, cut off, isolated, dissociated, disengaged, removed, unconnected, unattached; apart.
2 *a disconnected narrative* **disjointed**, **incoherent**, garbled, confused, jumbled, mixed up, unintelligible, rambling, wandering, disorganized, uncoordinated, ill-thought-out, illogical, irrational; haphazard, random.
OPPOSITE coherent.

disconsolate ▶ **adjective** *Giles was looking increasingly disconsolate* **sad**, unhappy, doleful, woebegone, dejected, downcast, downhearted, despondent, dispirited, crestfallen, cast down, depressed, fed up, disappointed, disheartened, discouraged, demoralized, crushed, desolate, heartbroken, broken-hearted, inconsolable, heavy-hearted, low-spirited, forlorn, in the doldrums, melancholy, miserable, long-faced, wretched,

D

glum, gloomy, dismal; *informal* blue, choked, down, down in the mouth, down in the dumps; *Brit. informal* brassed off, cheesed off, as sick as a parrot, looking as if one had lost a pound and found a penny; *literary* dolorous; *archaic* chap-fallen, heartsick, heartsore.
OPPOSITES cheerful, happy.

discontent ▶ noun *there were reports of growing discontent among the military* **dissatisfaction**, disaffection, discontentment, discontentedness, disgruntlement, grievances, unhappiness, displeasure, bad feelings, resentment, envy; restlessness, unrest, uneasiness, unease, disquiet, fretfulness, frustration, impatience, irritation, chagrin, annoyance, pique; *informal* a chip on one's shoulder.
OPPOSITES contentment, satisfaction.

discontented ▶ adjective *his education only made him discontented with his lot in life* **dissatisfied**, disgruntled, fed up, disaffected, discontent, malcontent, unhappy, aggrieved, displeased, resentful, envious; restless, impatient, querulous, fretful, complaining, frustrated, irritated, chagrined, annoyed, peeved, piqued; *informal* fed up to the (back) teeth, with a chip on one's shoulder, sick to death, sick and tired; *Brit. informal* browned off, cheesed off, brassed off, hacked off; *N. Amer. informal* teed off, ticked off; *vulgar slang* pissed off, peed off; *N. Amer. vulgar slang* pissed.
OPPOSITES contented, satisfied.

discontinue ▶ verb *the ferry service was discontinued | he discontinued his studies* **stop**, end, terminate, bring to an end, put an end to, put a stop to, wind up, finish, bring to a halt, call a halt to, cancel, drop, dispense with, do away with, get rid of, abolish; suspend, interrupt, break off, phase out, withdraw; abandon, give up, cease, refrain from; *informal* cut, pull the plug on, axe, scrap, give something the chop, knock something on the head, leave off, pack in; *N. Amer. informal* quit; *rare* intermit.
OPPOSITE continue.

discontinued ▶ adjective *a discontinued product* **no longer available**, no longer produced, no longer manufactured; obsolete, no longer in existence.
OPPOSITE new.

discontinuity ▶ noun *the discontinuity of policy frustrated industrialists and investors* **disconnectedness**, disconnection, break, lack of unity, disruption, interruption, lack of coherence, disjointedness.
OPPOSITE continuity.

discontinuous ▶ adjective *a person with a discontinuous employment record* **intermittent**, sporadic, broken, fitful, interrupted, on and off, disrupted, erratic, disconnected.
OPPOSITE continuous.

discord ▶ noun **1** *stress resulting from financial difficulties or family discord* **strife**, conflict, friction, hostility; **disagreement**, lack of agreement, dissension, dispute, difference of opinion, discordance, disunity, division, incompatibility, variance; antagonism, antipathy, enmity, opposition, bad feeling, ill feeling, bad blood, argument, quarrelling, squabbling, bickering, wrangling, feuding, contention, clashing, falling-out, war, vendetta; *archaic* jar; *rare* disaccord.
OPPOSITES agreement, accord, harmony.
2 *the music faded in discord* **dissonance**, discordance, lack of harmony, disharmony, cacophony, jarring, jangling.
OPPOSITE harmony.

discordant ▶ adjective **1** *the messages from Washington and London were discordant* **in disagreement**, at variance, at odds, disagreeing, differing, divergent, discrepant, contradictory, contrary, in conflict, conflicting, opposite, opposed, opposing, clashing; incompatible, inconsistent, irreconcilable, inconsonant, incongruous; *rare* oppugnant.
OPPOSITES in agreement, harmonious, compatible.
2 *discordant sounds* **inharmonious**, unharmonious, unmelodic, unmusical, tuneless, off-key, dissonant, harsh, jarring, grating, jangling, jangly, strident, shrill, screeching, screechy, cacophonous; sharp, flat; *rare* absonant, horrisonant.
OPPOSITES harmonious, dulcet.

discount ▶ noun (stress on the first syllable) *many rail commuters will get a discount on next year's season tickets* **reduction**, deduction, markdown, price cut, cut, lower price, cut price, concession, concessionary price; rebate.
▶ verb (stress on the second syllable) **1** *I'd heard rumours, but discounted them* **disregard**, pay no attention to, take no notice of, take no account of, pass over, overlook, dismiss, ignore, brush off, gloss over; disbelieve, give no credence to, reject, pooh-pooh; *informal* take with a pinch of salt.
OPPOSITE believe.
2 *top Paris hotels discounted 20 per cent off published room rates* **deduct**, take off, rebate; *informal* knock off, slash.
OPPOSITE add.
3 *a recommended retail price of £82.95, but you'll find it discounted in many stores* **reduce**, mark down, cut, lower, lessen; *informal* knock down.
OPPOSITES put up, increase.
4 *many titles are discounted by up to 40 per cent on the publishers' price* **mark down**, reduce, put on sale.
OPPOSITE mark up.

discountenance ▶ verb **1** *Amanda was not discountenanced by the accusation* **disconcert**, discomfit, unsettle, nonplus, throw/catch off balance, take aback, unnerve, disorient, perturb, disturb, perplex, confuse, bewilder, baffle, fluster, ruffle, shake, upset, agitate, worry, dismay, put out of countenance, discompose; put someone off their stroke/stride, distract; embarrass, abash; *informal* throw, faze, make someone scratch their head, discombobulate, rattle, set someone back on their heels, psych out; *archaic* cause to be at a stand, gravel.
2 *in some parts of the Puritan country, kissing was discountenanced at weddings* **disapprove of**, frown on, take a dim view of, be against, not believe in, object to, find unacceptable, think wrong.

discourage ▶ verb **1** *we want to discourage children from smoking* **deter**, dissuade, disincline, turn aside; put off, talk out of, scare off, warn off, advise against, urge against; *rare* dehort.
OPPOSITES encourage, persuade.
2 *Nicky was discouraged by his hostile tone* **dishearten**, dispirit, demoralize, make despondent, make downhearted, cast down, depress, disappoint, dampen someone's hopes, dash someone's hopes, cause to lose heart; put off, unnerve, daunt, intimidate, cow, unman, crush; *archaic* deject.
OPPOSITES encourage, hearten.
3 *he looked the other way to discourage further conversation* **prevent**, stop, put a stop to, avert, fend off, stave off, ward off; **inhibit**, hinder, check, curb, obstruct, suppress, put a damper on, throw cold water on.
OPPOSITE encourage.

CHOOSE THE RIGHT WORD

discourage, deter, dissuade

Someone who lacks the authority to order another person not to do something may have to adopt other means of preventing them.

- To **discourage** someone from doing something is to make them more reluctant to do or continue with it by undermining their confidence or optimism about their chances of success or about the desirability of what they are aiming to achieve (*her father discouraged her from going into the legal profession*). Circumstances, as well as a person, may have this effect (*their work experience has discouraged them from a career in engineering*), and the object of the verb can be an action rather than a person (*inflation discourages investment*). *Discourage* can also be used to express official disapproval that stops short of an actual order (*the Hospital discourages smoking*).
- To **deter** someone from doing something involves creating, constituting, or pointing out a serious obstacle that will confront them if they go ahead with their plans (*high fees deter some patients from visiting a consultant*). The object of *deter* can also be an action (*the main aim of cruise missiles is to deter an attack*). The word is often associated with preventing crime and military aggression (*even an unwired alarm box is often sufficient to deter a burglar*), and this sense is continued in the noun *deterrent* (*NATO's nuclear deterrent*).
- To **dissuade** someone is to use rational arguments that make them see the difficulty or undesirable nature of their proposed course of action (*we tried to dissuade Steven from marrying*). The object of *dissuade* is always a person (or body of people), not an action or event.

discouraged ▶ adjective *Doug must be feeling pretty discouraged* **disheartened**, dispirited, demoralized, deflated, disappointed, let down, disconsolate, despondent, fed up, dejected, cast down, downcast, depressed, crestfallen, dismayed, low-spirited, gloomy, glum, pessimistic, unenthusiastic, having lost heart, lacking in enthusiasm, lacking in confidence, unconfident; put off, daunted, intimidated, cowed, crushed; *informal* down in the mouth, down in the dumps, unenthused, with cold feet; *literary* heartsick, heartsore; *archaic* chap-fallen.
OPPOSITES encouraged, optimistic.

discouragement ▶ noun **1** *his discouragement was partly caused by the failure to raise sufficient funds* **dispiritedness**, downheartedness, dejection, depression, demoralization, disappointment, despondency, hopelessness, lack of enthusiasm, lack of confidence, pessimism, despair, gloom, gloominess, low spirits; *informal* cold feet.
OPPOSITE optimism.
2 *a discouragement to crime* **deterrent**, disincentive; hindrance, obstacle, impediment, barrier, curb, check, damper, restraint, constraint, restriction; dissuasion; *informal* put-down; *archaic* damp.
OPPOSITES incentive, stimulus.

discouraging ▶ adjective *most news reports from the area are discouraging* **depressing**, demoralizing, disheartening, dispiriting, disappointing, gloomy, off-putting; unfavourable, unpromising, not hopeful, not encouraging, unpropitious, inauspicious; *archaic* dejecting.
OPPOSITES encouraging, promising.

discourse ▶ noun (stress on the first syllable) **1** *a small group of women had chosen to prolong their discourse outside the door* **discussion**, conversation, talk, dialogue, communication, conference, debate,

consultation, verbal exchange; parley, powwow, chat; *Indian* adda; *NZ* korero; *informal* confab, chit-chat; *formal* confabulation; *rare* palaver, colloquy, converse, interlocution.
2 *a discourse on critical theory* **essay**, treatise, dissertation, paper, study, critique, monograph, disquisition, tract; **lecture**, address, speech, oration, peroration; sermon, homily.
▶ **verb** (stress on the second syllable) **1** *she could discourse at great length on the history of Europe* **hold forth**, expatiate, pontificate; talk, give a talk, give an address, give a speech, lecture, sermonize, preach, orate; write learnedly, write at length; *informal* spout, spiel, speechify, preachify, sound off; *archaic* perorate, lucubrate; *rare* dissertate.
2 *he spent an hour discoursing with his supporters* **converse**, talk, speak, have a discussion, discuss matters, debate, confer, consult, parley, chat; *informal* have a confab, chew the fat, rap; *formal* confabulate.

discourteous ▶ **adjective** *it would be discourteous to ignore her* **rude**, impolite, ill-mannered, bad-mannered, disrespectful, uncivil, unmannerly, unchivalrous, ungallant, ungentlemanly, unladylike, ill-bred, churlish, boorish, crass, ungracious, graceless, uncouth; insolent, impudent, cheeky, audacious, presumptuous; curt, brusque, blunt, offhand, unceremonious, short, sharp, uncomplimentary, offensive, insulting, derogatory, disparaging; *informal* ignorant; *archaic* malapert, contumelious; *rare* underbred, mannerless.
OPPOSITES polite, courteous.

discourtesy ▶ **noun** **rudeness**, impoliteness, ill manners, lack of manners, bad manners, ill-manneredness, lack of civility, incivility, disrespect, disrespectfulness, unmannerliness, ungentlemanly behaviour, ungraciousness, churlishness, boorishness, ill breeding, uncouthness, crassness; insolence, impudence, impertinence; curtness, brusqueness, abruptness.
OPPOSITES politeness, courtesy.

discover ▶ **verb** **1** *two guards discovered her hiding in the back of the minivan* **find**, locate, come across, come upon, stumble on, chance on, light on, bring to light, uncover, unearth, turn up, track down; run down, run to earth, run to ground, smoke out.
OPPOSITE hide.
2 *I discovered that she had been lying | he was anxious to discover the truth* **find out**, come to know, learn, realize, recognize, see, ascertain, work out, fathom out, detect, determine, spot, notice, perceive; dig up/out, ferret out, root out, nose out, dredge up; reveal, disclose; *informal* get wise to the fact, get wind of the fact, figure out, sniff out, rumble, tumble to; *Brit. informal* twig, suss out; *N. Amer. informal* dope out.
OPPOSITES conceal, hide.
3 *scientists have discovered a new way of dating fossil crustaceans* **hit on**, come up with, invent, originate, devise, design, contrive, conceive of; pioneer, develop.

discoverer ▶ **noun** **1** *the annals of the famous European discoverers* **explorer**, pioneer.
2 *the Bach flower remedies are named after their discoverer, Dr Edward Bach* **originator**, inventor, creator, deviser, designer; pioneer, introducer.

discovery ▶ **noun** **1** *the discovery of the body* **finding**, locating, location, uncovering, unearthing.
OPPOSITE concealment.
2 *the discovery that she was pregnant* **finding out**, learning, realization, recognition, detection, determination; revelation, disclosure.
3 *the discovery of new drugs* **invention**, origination, devising; pioneering, introduction.
4 *he failed to take out a patent on his discoveries* **find**, finding; invention, breakthrough, innovation, advance, lucky strike.
5 *a voyage of discovery* **exploration**, pioneering, research.

discredit ▶ **verb** **1** *I've been offered a lot of money for information which might discredit him* **disgrace**, dishonour, bring into disrepute, damage someone's reputation, blacken someone's name, destroy someone's credibility, drag through the mud/mire, put/show in a bad light, reflect badly on, compromise, give someone a bad name, bring into disfavour; stigmatize, detract from, disparage, denigrate, devalue, diminish, demean, belittle; defame, slander, cast aspersions on, malign, vilify, calumniate, smear, tarnish, besmirch, soil; *N. Amer.* slur; *informal* do a hatchet job on; *literary* smirch, besmear.
OPPOSITE do credit to.
2 *that theory has since been discredited* **disprove**, prove false, prove wrong, invalidate, explode, drive a coach and horses through, give the lie to, refute, reject, deny; challenge, dispute, raise doubts about, shake one's faith in; *informal* debunk, shoot full of holes, shoot down (in flames), blow sky-high, blow out of the water; *rare* controvert, confute, negative.
OPPOSITES prove, confirm.
▶ **noun** **1** *they committed crimes which brought discredit on the administration* **dishonour**, disrepute, ill repute, loss of reputation, loss of respect, disgrace, shame, humiliation, ignominy, infamy, notoriety; censure, blame, reproach, odium, opprobrium; stigma, harm, damage, scandal; *rare* disesteem.
OPPOSITES honour, glory.
2 *the ships were a* **discredit to** *the country* **disgrace**, source of disgrace, source of shame, reproach; bad reflection on, blot on the escutcheon of.
OPPOSITE credit.

discreditable ▶ **adjective** *his discreditable conduct* **dishonourable**, **reprehensible**, shameful, deplorable, disgraceful, disreputable, blameworthy, culpable, wrong, bad, ignoble, shabby, objectionable, regrettable, unfortunate, indefensible, unjustifiable, unacceptable, unworthy, remiss; *rare* exceptionable.
OPPOSITES creditable, praiseworthy, good.

discreet ▶ **adjective** **1** *I'll make some discreet inquiries | we can rely on him to be discreet* **careful**, circumspect, cautious, wary, chary, guarded, close-lipped, close-mouthed; **tactful**, diplomatic, considerate, politic, prudent, judicious, strategic, wise, sensible; delicate, kid-glove; *informal* softly-softly.
OPPOSITES indiscreet, rash.
2 *the discreet lighting* **unobtrusive**, inconspicuous; **subtle**, low-key, understated, subdued, muted, soft, restrained, unostentatious, downbeat, low-profile.
OPPOSITE obtrusive.

discreet or discrete?
The words **discreet** and **discrete** sound the same, and both derive from Latin *discretus* 'separate'; but in English they have quite different meanings. *Discreet* means 'careful to avoid being noticed or giving offence' (*we made discreet inquiries*). *Discrete*, on the other hand, means 'separate, distinct' (*research tends to focus on discrete areas*).

discrepancy ▶ **noun** *the discrepancy between the two sets of figures* **inconsistency**, **difference**, disparity, variance, variation, deviation, divergence, disagreement, dissimilarity, dissimilitude, mismatch, lack of similarity, contrariety, contradictoriness, disaccord, discordance, incongruity, lack of congruence, incompatibility, irreconcilability, conflict, opposition.
OPPOSITES similarity, correspondence.

discrete ▶ **adjective** *speech sounds are produced as a continuous signal rather than discrete units* **separate**, distinct, individual, detached, unattached, disconnected, discontinuous, disjunct, disjoined.
OPPOSITE connected.

discrete or discreet?
See DISCREET.

discretion ▶ **noun** **1** *the negotiations have been carried out with the utmost discretion* **circumspection**, care, carefulness, caution, wariness, chariness, guardedness; **tact**, tactfulness, diplomacy, delicacy, sensitivity, subtlety, consideration, prudence, judiciousness, judgement, discrimination, sense, good sense, common sense; kid gloves.
OPPOSITES indiscretion, rashness.
2 *honorary fellowships may be awarded at the discretion of the council* **choice**, option, judgement, preference, disposition, volition; pleasure, liking, wish, will, inclination, desire.

discretionary ▶ **adjective** *a 12.5 per cent discretionary service charge* **optional**, non-compulsory, voluntary, at one's discretion, up to the individual, non-mandatory, elective, open to choice; open, unrestricted; *Law* permissive; *rare* discretional.
OPPOSITES compulsory, obligatory.

discriminate ▶ **verb** **1** *at birth, a baby cannot* **discriminate between** *foreground and background in its visual field* **differentiate**, distinguish, draw/recognize a distinction, tell the difference, discern a difference; separate, tell apart; separate the sheep from the goats, separate the wheat from the chaff.
2 *existing employment policies* **discriminate against** *women* **be biased**, show prejudice, be prejudiced; treat differently, treat as inferior, treat unfairly, put at a disadvantage, disfavour, be intolerant towards; victimize.

discriminating ▶ **adjective** *a discriminating collector and patron of the arts* **discerning**, perceptive, astute, shrewd, judicious, perspicacious, insightful; **selective**, with good taste, particular, fastidious, critical, keen, tasteful, refined, sensitive, cultivated, cultured, artistic, aesthetic; *archaic* nice; *rare* discriminative.
OPPOSITE indiscriminate.

discrimination ▶ **noun** **1** *victims of racial discrimination* **prejudice**, bias, bigotry, intolerance, narrow-mindedness, unfairness, inequity, favouritism, one-sidedness, partisanship; sexism, chauvinism, racism, racialism, anti-Semitism, heterosexism, ageism, classism; positive discrimination, reverse discrimination, ableism; (*in S. Africa, historical*) apartheid.
OPPOSITE impartiality.
2 *the discrimination between right and wrong* **differentiation**, distinction, telling the difference.
3 *those who could afford to buy showed little taste or discrimination* **discernment**, judgement, perception, perceptiveness, perspicacity,

acumen, astuteness, shrewdness, judiciousness, insight, subtlety; **selectivity**, (good) taste, fastidiousness, refinement, sensitivity, cultivation, culture, culturedness, connoisseurship, aestheticism.

discriminatory ▶ adjective *discriminatory employment practices* **prejudicial**, biased, prejudiced, preferential, unfair, unjust, invidious, inequitable, weighted, one-sided, partisan; sexist, chauvinistic, chauvinist, racist, racialist, anti-Semitic, ageist, disablist, classist.
OPPOSITES impartial, fair.

discursive ▶ adjective **1** *dull, discursive prose* **rambling**, digressive, meandering, wandering, maundering, diffuse, long, lengthy; circuitous, roundabout, circumlocutory, periphrastic; verbose, long-winded, prolix; *informal* wordy; *Brit. informal* waffly; *rare* pleonastic, logorrhoeic, ambagious.
OPPOSITE concise.
2 *an elegant piece of work combining sound judgement with an excellent discursive style* **fluent**, flowing, fluid, eloquent, articulate, elegant, expansive.
OPPOSITE terse.

D

discuss ▶ verb **1** *I discussed the matter with my wife* **talk over**, talk about, talk through, converse about, debate, confer about, put your heads together about, deliberate about, chew over, consider, exchange views on/about, weigh up, consider the pros and cons of, thrash out, argue, dispute; moot, air, ventilate; *Brit.* canvass; *informal* kick around/about, bat around/about.
2 *chapter three discusses this topic in more detail* **examine**, explore, study, analyse, go into, scrutinize, review; **deal with**, treat, consider, concern itself with, write about, tackle.

discussion ▶ noun **1** *after a long discussion with her husband, she came to a decision* **conversation**, talk, dialogue, discourse, conference, debate, exchange of views, consultation, deliberation; powwow, chat, tête-à-tête, heart-to-heart; seminar, symposium; talks, negotiations, parley; argument, dispute; *Indian* adda; *NZ* korero; *informal* confab, chit-chat, rap; *N. Amer. informal* skull session, bull session; *formal* confabulation; *rare* palaver, colloquy, converse, interlocution.
2 *the book's candid discussion of sexual matters* **examination**, exploration, analysis, study, review, scrutiny; **treatment**, consideration.

disdain ▶ noun *she looked at him with open disdain* **contempt**, scorn, scornfulness, contemptuousness, derision, disrespect; disparagement, condescension, superciliousness, hauteur, haughtiness, arrogance, lordliness, snobbishness, aloofness, indifference, dismissiveness; distaste, dislike, disgust; *archaic* despite, contumely.
OPPOSITES admiration, respect.
▶ verb **1** *she disdained such vulgar exhibitionism* **scorn**, deride, pour scorn on, regard with contempt, show contempt for, be contemptuous about, sneer at, sniff at, curl one's lip at, pooh-pooh, look down on, belittle, undervalue, slight; despise; *informal* look down one's nose at, turn up one's nose at, thumb one's nose at; *archaic* contemn; *rare* misprize.
OPPOSITES respect, value.
2 *she pointedly disdained his invitation to sit down* **spurn**, reject, refuse, rebuff, disregard, ignore, snub; decline, turn down, brush aside.
OPPOSITE accept.

disdainful ▶ adjective *she gave him a disdainful look* **contemptuous**, scornful, full of contempt, derisive, sneering, withering, slighting, disparaging, disrespectful, condescending, patronizing, supercilious, haughty, superior, arrogant, proud, snobbish, lordly, aloof, indifferent, dismissive; mocking, jeering, insolent, insulting; *informal* high and mighty, hoity-toity, sniffy, snotty, on one's high horse, uppish; *archaic* contumelious.
OPPOSITES admiring, respectful.

disease *See centre pages for lists of* **Illnesses**
▶ noun **illness**, sickness, ill health; infection, ailment, malady, disorder, complaint, affliction, condition, indisposition, upset, problem, trouble, infirmity, disability, defect, abnormality; pestilence, plague, cancer, canker, blight; *informal* bug, virus; *Brit. informal* lurgy; *Austral. informal* wog; *dated* contagion.
OPPOSITE health.

WORD LINKS

related prefixes	**patho-** (e.g. ***pathogenic***), **noso-** (e.g. ***nosography***)
related suffix	**-pathy** (e.g. ***neuropathy***)
relating to disease	**pathological**
branches of medicine to do with diseases	**epidemiology, pathology, therapeutics**
fear of disease	**pathophobia, nosophobia**

diseased ▶ adjective *the dogs were painfully thin and many were diseased* | *diseased organs* **unhealthy**, **ill**, sick, unwell, ailing, infirm, sickly, unsound, unwholesome, infected, septic, contaminated, blighted, rotten, bad, abnormal; *Austral. informal* crook; *archaic* peccant.
OPPOSITES healthy, well.

disembark ▶ verb *we disembarked from the ferry at Dun Laoghaire* **get off**, step off, leave; go ashore, debark, detrain; land, arrive; *Brit.* alight from; *N. Amer.* deplane; *informal* pile out.
OPPOSITE embark.

disembodied ▶ adjective *a disembodied spirit* **bodiless**, incorporeal, spiritual, intangible, insubstantial, impalpable; ghostly, spectral, phantom, wraithlike; *rare* immaterial, discarnate, disincarnate, unbodied, phantasmal, phantasmic.

disembowel ▶ verb **eviscerate**, gut, draw, remove the innards from; *rare* embowel, disbowel, exenterate, gralloch, paunch.

disenchanted ▶ adjective *disenchanted with politics, he retired from the foreign service* **disillusioned**, disappointed, let down, fed up, dissatisfied, discontented, disabused, undeceived, set straight; cynical, soured, jaundiced, sick, out of love, indifferent.

disenchantment ▶ noun **disillusionment**, disappointment, dissatisfaction, discontent, discontentedness, rude awakening; cynicism, disillusion.

disengage ▶ verb **1** *I disengaged his hand from mine* **remove**, detach, disentangle, extricate, separate, release, loosen, loose, disconnect, unfasten, unclasp, uncouple, decouple, undo, unhook, unloose, unhitch, untie, unyoke, disentwine; free, set free, liberate; *rare* disjoin, disunite, disarticulate.
OPPOSITES attach, connect.
2 *the only means by which the Americans could* **disengage** *gradually* **from** *Korea* **withdraw**, leave, pull out of, move out of, quit, retreat from, retire from, delink from.
OPPOSITE enter.

disengagement ▶ noun **1** *his disengagement from the provisional government* **withdrawal**, departure, retirement, retreat.
2 *the mechanism prevents accidental disengagement* **disconnection**, detachment, separation, unfastening, uncoupling.
OPPOSITES attachment, connection.

disentangle ▶ verb **1** *Allen was on his knees disentangling a coil of rope* **untangle**, unravel, remove the knots from, unknot, unsnarl, untwist, unwind, undo, untie, straighten out, smooth out; comb; card.
2 *he disentangled his fingers from her hair* **extricate**, extract, free, remove, disengage, untwine, disentwine, release, liberate, loosen, unloose, detach, unfasten, unclasp, disconnect.

disfavour ▶ noun **1** *the headmaster regarded her with disfavour* **disapproval**, disapprobation, lack of favour; **dislike**, displeasure, distaste, dissatisfaction, low opinion, low esteem; *archaic* disesteem, disrelish.
OPPOSITE approval.
2 (*archaic*) *she did me a disfavour* **disservice**, bad turn, ill deed, discourtesy.
OPPOSITE favour.
□ **fall into disfavour** *he fell into disfavour with the king* **become unpopular**, become disliked, get on the wrong side of someone; *informal* be/get in someone's bad books, be/get in someone's black books, be in the doghouse; *NZ informal* be in the dogbox.
OPPOSITE be in favour.

disfigure ▶ verb *disused quarries remain to disfigure the landscape* **mar**, spoil, deface, make ugly/unattractive, impair, scar, blemish, flaw; damage, injure, blight, mutilate, deform, maim, ruin; vandalize; *rare* uglify, disfeature.
OPPOSITES beautify, adorn, enhance.

disfigurement ▶ noun **1** *the disfigurement of Victorian and Edwardian buildings* **defacement**, spoiling, scarring, mutilation, damage, damaging, vandalizing, ruin; *rare* uglification.
OPPOSITE beautification.
2 *a permanent facial disfigurement* **blemish**, flaw, defect, imperfection, discoloration, blotch; scar, pockmark; deformity, malformation, misshapenness, misproportion, irregularity, abnormality, injury, wound; ugliness, unsightliness; *technical* stigma.

disgorge ▶ verb **1** *the combine disgorged a steady stream of grain* **pour out**, discharge, eject, emit, expel, evacuate, empty, spit out, spew out, belch forth, spout; vomit, regurgitate, throw up; *archaic* regorge.
2 *any firm that infringes the rules will be required to disgorge its profits* **surrender**, relinquish, hand over, give up, turn over, yield, cede, part with; renounce, resign, abandon.
OPPOSITE retain.

disgrace ▶ noun **1** *if he'd married her it would have brought disgrace on the family* **dishonour**, **shame**, ignominy, discredit, degradation, disrepute, ill-repute, infamy, scandal, stigma, odium, opprobrium, obloquy, condemnation, vilification, contempt, disrespect, disapproval, disfavour, disapprobation; humiliation, embarrassment, loss of face; *Austral.* strife; *rare* disesteem, reprobation, derogation.
OPPOSITES honour, glory.
2 *the unemployment figures are a disgrace* | *the system is a* **disgrace to** *British justice* **scandal**, outrage, source of shame; **discredit**, reproach, affront, insult; bad reflection on, stain on, blemish on, blot on, blot on the escutcheon of, black mark on; stigma, brand; black sheep; *informal* crime, sin; *literary* smirch on.
OPPOSITE credit.
□ **in disgrace out of favour**, unpopular, in bad odour; *informal* in someone's bad/black books, in the doghouse; *NZ informal* in the dogbox.

OPPOSITE in favour.

▶ **verb 1** *you have disgraced the family name* **bring shame on**, shame, dishonour, discredit, bring into disrepute, degrade, debase, defame, stigmatize, taint, sully, tarnish, besmirch, stain, blacken, drag through the mud/mire, give a bad name to, put in a bad light, reflect badly on; *literary* smirch, besmear; *archaic* spot.
OPPOSITES honour, do credit to.
2 *he has been publicly disgraced for offences of which he was not guilty* **discredit**, dishonour, defame, disparage, stigmatize, reproach, censure, blame; **humiliate**, mortify, embarrass, cause to lose face, chasten, humble, demean, put someone in their place, take down a peg or two, cut down to size, show up; *N. Amer. informal* make someone eat crow.
OPPOSITE honour.

CHOOSE THE RIGHT WORD

disgrace, dishonour, shame, ignominy

- A person in **disgrace** has incurred general disapproval as a result of behaviour considered to be unacceptable (*Nixon had resigned in disgrace*). There is a suggestion of outrage and scandal. A person or thing can also be described as *a disgrace*, meaning that they deserve disapproval or condemnation (*you're an absolute disgrace | what went on at Westminster on Wednesday was a disgrace to Parliament*).
- **Dishonour** is a less common word, perhaps because the notion of honour that it involves has itself become unfashionable. Typically it denotes a situation in which someone is considered to have behaved in a cowardly or dishonest way (*feelings which induce a man to prefer death to dishonour*).
- **Shame** is frequently used in the same context as *guilt*, *embarrassment*, and *humiliation*. While a person who is in disgrace is disapproved of, someone who suffers shame feels intense distress as a result of this disapproval and their awareness of having done wrong (*she hung her head in shame*). *Shame* also describes a loss of repect in the eyes of other people (*the incident brought shame on his family*). A state of affairs seen as regrettable or unfortnuate can be called *a shame* (*it is just a shame we don't treat our fellow human beings so well | what a shame Ellie won't be here to meet you*).
- **Ignominy** is a literary word deriving from a Latin expression for the loss of one's 'good name'. It denotes great public humiliation (*he was not spared the ignominy of a public trial*).

disgraced ▶ **adjective** *the disgraced city financier* **discredited**, shamed, humiliated, in disgrace, under a cloud, brought into disrepute.
OPPOSITES honoured, respected.

disgraceful ▶ **adjective** *she intended to tell him exactly what she thought of his disgraceful conduct* **shameful**, shocking, scandalous, deplorable, despicable, contemptible, beyond contempt, beyond the pale, dishonourable, discreditable, reprehensible, objectionable, base, mean, low, blameworthy, unworthy, ignoble, shabby, inglorious, infamous, unprincipled, outrageous, abominable, atrocious, appalling, dreadful, terrible, disgusting, shameless, vile, odious, monstrous, heinous, iniquitous, unspeakable, loathsome, sordid, bad, wicked, immoral, nefarious, indefensible, inexcusable, unforgivable, intolerable; embarrassing, humiliating, degrading; *informal* low-down, hateful, diabolical, criminal; *archaic* knavish, dastardly, scurvy; *rare* egregious, flagitious, exceptionable.
OPPOSITES admirable, honourable.

disgruntled ▶ **adjective** *he faced tough questioning from disgruntled shareholders* **dissatisfied**, discontented, aggrieved, resentful, fed up, displeased, unhappy, disappointed, disaffected, malcontent; angry, irate, annoyed, cross, exasperated, indignant, vexed, irritated, piqued, irked, put out, out of temper; sulky, sullen, petulant, peevish, grumpy, churlish, testy; *informal* peeved, miffed, aggravated, hacked off, riled, peed off, hot under the collar, in a huff; *Brit. informal* cheesed off, browned off, narked, eggy; *N. Amer. informal* sore, teed off, ticked off; *W. Indian informal* vex; *vulgar slang* pissed off; *N. Amer. vulgar slang* pissed; *archaic* snuffy.
OPPOSITES pleased, contented.

disguise ▶ **verb** *she tried to disguise the bruises with make-up | Stephen's controlled voice disguised his true feelings* **camouflage**, conceal, hide, cover up, make inconspicuous, mask, screen, shroud, veil, cloak; dissemble, dissimulate, gloss over, varnish over, paper over; put up a smokescreen, misrepresent, falsify, give a false picture of.
OPPOSITES reveal, expose.
□ **disguise oneself as** *Eleanor disguised herself as a man* **dress oneself up as**, pass oneself of as, pretend to be, impersonate, pose as; *rare* personate.
▶ **noun 1** *his bizarre disguise drew stares from fellow shoppers* **false appearance**, camouflage, concealment; outfit, costume; *informal* get-up.
2 *a counsellor hopes gradually to strip away the disguises and help partners to understand each other* **facade**, front, false front, cover-up, masquerade, veneer, mask, veil; smokescreen, dissimulation, pretence, deception.

disguised ▶ **adjective** *a disguised police officer* **in disguise**, camouflaged, incognito, under cover; unrecognizable; sailing under false colours.

disgust ▶ **noun 1** *he reached into the bin with a look of disgust on his face* **revulsion**, repugnance, aversion, distaste, abhorrence, loathing, detestation, odium, execration, horror; nausea; *archaic* disrelish; *rare* repellence, repellency.
OPPOSITE relish.
2 *the bowler hurled his cap to the ground in disgust* **annoyance**, exasperation, anger, fury, outrage, indignation, contempt, disapproval, disapprobation, displeasure, dissatisfaction, disgruntlement, discontent, discontentment.
▶ **verb 1** *the hospital food disgusted me* **revolt**, repel, repulse, sicken, nauseate, cause to feel nauseous, make shudder, turn someone's stomach, make someone's gorge rise; be repugnant to, be repulsive to, be distasteful to; *informal* turn off, make someone want to throw up; *N. Amer. informal* gross out.
OPPOSITE attract.
2 *he is disgusted by Clare's easy morals* **outrage**, shock, horrify, appal, scandalize, offend, affront, dismay, displease, dissatisfy; annoy, anger; nauseate, sicken.
OPPOSITE please.

disgusting ▶ **adjective 1** *Kirsty complained that the food was disgusting* **revolting**, repellent, repulsive, sickening, nauseating, nauseous, stomach-churning, stomach-turning, off-putting, unpalatable, unappetizing, uninviting, unsavoury, distasteful, foul, nasty, obnoxious, odious; *N. Amer.* vomitous; *informal* yucky, icky, gross, sick-making, gut-churning; *Brit. informal*, grotty; *archaic* disgustful.
OPPOSITE delicious.
2 *I find your racism absolutely disgusting* **offensive**, **appalling**, outrageous, objectionable, displeasing, shocking, horrifying, scandalous, monstrous, unspeakable, shameless, shameful, vulgar, gross, vile, wicked, odious, heinous, abhorrent, loathsome, obnoxious, detestable, hateful, sickening, contemptible, despicable, deplorable, abominable, execrable; unforgivable, unpardonable, inexcusable, intolerable, insupportable, beyond the pale; *informal* horrid, ghastly, sick, God-awful; *Brit. informal* beastly; *archaic* disgustful, loathly, scurvy; *rare* egregious, exceptionable.
OPPOSITES charming; commendable.

dish ▶ **noun 1** *place the ravioli on a dish and cover with sauce* **bowl**, **plate**, soup plate, platter, salver; serving dish, oven dish; container, receptacle, vessel, repository; *Scottish & N. English* ashet; *archaic* trencher, charger, porringer; *rare* paten.
2 *she tried a new vegetarian dish* **recipe**, item of food, course; special, dish of the day; food, fare; *French* plat du jour.
3 (*informal*) *she's quite a dish* **beauty**, belle, goddess, Venus, siren, dream, vision, picture, sensation, joy to behold; *informal* stunner, knockout, looker, good-looker, cracker, smasher, peach, honey, lovely, eyeful, eye-catcher, sight for sore eyes.
▶ **verb**
□ **dish something out** *the waitress was dishing out free glasses of wine* **distribute**, dispense, issue, disburse, hand out, give out, pass out, pass round; deal out, dole out, mete out, share out, allocate, allot, apportion.
OPPOSITES collect, reserve.
□ **dish something up 1** *Mrs Mackay dished up the porridge* **serve (up)**, spoon out, ladle out, scoop out.
2 *they dish up remixes of their old hits* **present**, offer, produce, prepare.

disharmony ▶ **noun** *they hope he will heal the racial disharmony in their city* **discord**, **friction**, strife, conflict, hostility, acrimony, bad blood, bad feeling, enmity, dissension, disagreement; feuding, quarrelling; disunity, division, divisiveness; *informal* falling-out; *rare* disaccord, discordance.
OPPOSITE harmony.

dishearten ▶ **verb** *I thought the weather would dishearten him, but he kept going* **discourage**, dispirit, demoralize, depress, dismay, daunt, deter, unman, unnerve, sap, shake, throw, crush, cast down, desolate, make dispirited, make dejected, make crestfallen, make downhearted, disappoint, sadden, weigh down, weigh heavily on, put a damper on, cow, subdue, undermine, enervate, weaken; *informal* give someone the blues, make someone fed up, knock the stuffing out of, knock for six, knock sideways; *archaic* deject.
OPPOSITES hearten, encourage.

disheartened ▶ **adjective** *the weather got worse and he felt cold and disheartened* **downhearted**, dispirited, low-spirited, demoralized, despondent, depressed, disconsolate, dejected, dismayed, disappointed, daunted, discouraged, deterred, unmanned, unnerved, sapped, shaken, thrown, crushed, cast down, low, down, crestfallen, saddened, weighed down; *informal* blue, down in the mouth, down in the dumps.
OPPOSITE heartened.

dishevelled ▶ **adjective** *the young man's hair was long and dishevelled | a dishevelled old woman* **untidy**, unkempt, scruffy, messy, in a mess, disordered, disarranged, rumpled, bedraggled; uncombed, ungroomed, tousled, tangled, tangly, knotted, knotty, matted, shaggy, straggly, windswept, windblown, wild; slovenly, sluttish, slatternly, blowsy, frowzy; *informal* ratty; *N. Amer. informal* mussed (up); *archaic* draggle-tailed.

OPPOSITES tidy; neat.

dishonest ▸ adjective *he is accused of dishonest business practices | a dishonest account of events* **fraudulent**, corrupt, swindling, cheating, double-dealing; underhand, crafty, cunning, devious, designing, treacherous, perfidious, unfair, unjust, disreputable, rascally, roguish, dirty, unethical, immoral, dishonourable, unscrupulous, unprincipled, amoral; criminal, illegal, unlawful; **false**, untruthful, deceitful, deceiving, deceptive, lying, mendacious, untrustworthy; *informal* crooked, shady, tricky, sharp, shifty; *Brit. informal* bent, dodgy; *Austral./NZ informal* shonky; *S. African informal* slim; *Law* malfeasant; *archaic* knavish, subtle, hollow-hearted; *rare* false-hearted, double-faced, truthless.
OPPOSITE honest.

D

dishonesty ▸ noun *he lost money as a result of his solicitor's dishonesty* **deceit**, deception, duplicity, lying, falseness, falsity, falsehood, untruthfulness; **fraud**, fraudulence, sharp practice, cheating, chicanery, craft, cunning, trickery, artifice, artfulness, wiliness, guile, double-dealing, underhandedness, subterfuge, skulduggery, treachery, perfidy, unfairness, unjustness, improbity, rascality, untrustworthiness, dishonour, unscrupulousness, corruption, criminality, lawlessness, lawbreaking, misconduct; *informal* crookedness, shadiness, foxiness, dirty tricks, kidology, shenanigans, monkey business, funny business, hanky-panky; *Brit. informal* jiggery-pokery; *N. Amer. informal* monkeyshines; *Irish informal* codology; *Law* malfeasance; *archaic* management, knavery, knavishness.
OPPOSITE probity.

dishonour ▸ noun *the incident brought dishonour upon the police profession* **disgrace**, shame, discredit, humiliation, degradation, ignominy, scandal, infamy, disrepute, ill repute, loss of face, disfavour, ill favour, unpopularity, ill fame, notoriety, debasement, abasement, odium, opprobrium, obloquy; stigma; *rare* disesteem, reprobation, vitiation.
OPPOSITE honour.
▸ verb **1** *you have betrayed our master and dishonoured the banner* **disgrace**, bring dishonour to, bring discredit to, bring shame to, shame, embarrass, humiliate, discredit, degrade, debase, lower, cheapen, drag down, drag through the mud, blacken the name of, give a bad name to, show in a bad light; sully, stain, taint, smear, mar, blot, stigmatize.
OPPOSITE honour.
2 (*archaic*) *some girls burned themselves to death after being dishonoured* **rape**, violate, seduce, debauch; assault, sexually assault, sexually abuse; *euphemistic* take advantage of, take away someone's innocence; *literary* ravish, deflower, defile, ruin; *rare* vitiate.

CHOOSE THE RIGHT WORD

dishonour, disgrace, shame, ignominy
See DISGRACE.

dishonourable ▸ adjective *he is accused of dishonourable conduct* **disgraceful**, shameful, shameless, shaming, disreputable, discreditable, degrading, debasing, ignominious, ignoble, blameworthy, contemptible, despicable, reprehensible, shabby, shoddy, sordid, sorry, base, low, improper, unseemly, unworthy; unprincipled, unscrupulous, corrupt, untrustworthy, treacherous, perfidious, traitorous, villainous; *informal* shady, crooked, low-down, dirty, rotten, rascally, scoundrelly; *Brit. informal* beastly; *archaic* scurvy, knavish.
OPPOSITE honourable.

disillusion ▸ verb *if they think we have a magic formula, don't disillusion them* **disabuse**, undeceive, enlighten, set straight, open someone's eyes; **disenchant**, shatter someone's illusions, disappoint, make sadder and wiser; *informal* throw cold water on.
OPPOSITES deceive, fool.
▸ noun *the future held almost certain disillusion* **disenchantment**, disillusionment, disappointment, disaffection, dissatisfaction; a rude awakening.
OPPOSITES promise, enchantment.

disillusioned ▸ adjective *his experience at the club left him disillusioned* **disenchanted**, disappointed, let down, cast down, downcast, discouraged; disabused, undeceived; cynical, sour, negative, world-weary.
OPPOSITES trusting, enthusiastic.

disincentive ▸ noun *high interest rates are a disincentive to investment* **deterrent**, discouragement, dissuasion, damper, brake, curb, check, restraint, inhibition; obstacle, impediment, hindrance, obstruction, block, barrier.
OPPOSITE incentive.

disinclination ▸ noun *they show a disinclination to face up to these issues* **reluctance**, unwillingness, lack of enthusiasm, indisposition, slowness, hesitancy, hesitance, diffidence; loathness, aversion, dislike, distaste; objection, demur, resistance, opposition, recalcitrance; *archaic* disrelish; *rare* nolition, sweerness.
OPPOSITES inclination, enthusiasm.

disinclined ▸ adjective *she was disinclined to abandon the old ways* **reluctant**, unwilling, unenthusiastic, unprepared, indisposed, ill-disposed, not disposed, not in the mood, slow, hesitant, nervous, afraid; loath, averse, antipathetic, resistant, opposed, recalcitrant.
OPPOSITES inclined, willing.

disinfect ▸ verb *use bleach to disinfect your kitchen surfaces* **sterilize**, sanitize, clean, cleanse, purify, decontaminate; fumigate; pasteurize; *technical* autoclave; *rare* deterge, depollute, depurate.
OPPOSITES infect, contaminate.

disinfectant ▸ noun *I swabbed the table with disinfectant* **bactericide**, germicide, antiseptic, sterilizer, sanitizer, cleaning agent, cleansing agent, cleanser, decontaminant; fumigant.

disingenuous ▸ adjective *it would be disingenuous of us to pretend ignorance of our book's impact* **dishonest**, deceitful, underhand, underhanded, duplicitous, double-dealing, two-faced, dissembling, insincere, false, lying, untruthful, mendacious; not candid, not frank, not entirely truthful; artful, cunning, crafty, wily, sly, sneaky, tricky, scheming, calculating, designing, devious, unscrupulous; *informal* shifty, foxy; *humorous* economical with the truth, terminologically inexact; *archaic* subtle, hollow-hearted; *rare* false-hearted, double-faced, truthless, unveracious.
OPPOSITES ingenuous, frank.

disingenuous or ingenuous?
See INGENUOUS.

disinherit ▸ verb *the Duke is seeking to disinherit his eldest son* **cut someone out of one's will**, cut off, dispossess, impoverish; disown, repudiate, renounce, reject, oust, cast off, cast aside, wash one's hands of, have nothing more to do with, turn one's back on; *informal* cut off without a penny.

disintegrate ▸ verb **1** *the plane caught fire and disintegrated in the air | his empire quickly disintegrated* **break up**, break apart, fall apart, fall to pieces, fall to bits, fragment, fracture, shatter, splinter; rupture, explode, blow up, blow apart, fly apart; crumble, dissolve, collapse, founder, fail, decline, go downhill, go to rack and ruin, degenerate, deteriorate; *informal* bust, be smashed to smithereens; *rare* shiver.
2 *some plastics will take over 400 years to disintegrate* **break down**, decompose, decay, rot, moulder, perish, corrode, deteriorate.

WORD LINKS
related suffix **-lysis (e.g. *hydrolysis, autolysis*)**

disinter ▸ verb *his corpse was disinterred and reburied in another grave* **exhume**, unearth, dig up, bring out of the ground, bring to the surface; *rare* disentomb, unbury, ungrave.

disinterest ▸ noun **1** *I do not pretend any scholarly disinterest with this book* **impartiality**, neutrality, objectivity, detachment, disinterestedness, lack of bias, lack of prejudice; open-mindedness, fairness, fair-mindedness, equitability, equity, balance, even-handedness, unselfishness, selflessness.
OPPOSITE bias.
2 (*informal*) *he looked at us with complete disinterest* **indifference**, lack of interest, lack of curiosity, lack of concern, lack of care, lack of enthusiasm, dispassionateness, dispassion, impassivity; boredom, apathy, nonchalance.
OPPOSITE interest.

disinterested ▸ adjective **1** *she is offering disinterested advice* **unbiased**, unprejudiced, impartial, neutral, non-partisan, non-discriminatory, detached, uninvolved, objective, dispassionate, impersonal, clinical; open-minded, fair, just, equitable, balanced, even-handed, unselfish, selfless; free from discrimination, with no axe to grind, without fear or favour.
OPPOSITE biased.
2 (*informal*) *he looked at her with disinterested eyes* **uninterested**, indifferent, incurious, unconcerned, unmoved, unresponsive, impassive, passive, detached, unfeeling, uncaring, unenthusiastic, lukewarm, bored, apathetic, blasé, nonchalant; *informal* couldn't-care-less.
OPPOSITE interested.

disinterested or uninterested?
Disinterested is frequently used as a synonym of **uninterested**, meaning 'having or showing no interest in something'. The traditional meaning of *disinterested*, however, is 'not biased; impartial', as in *bankers are under an obligation to give disinterested advice*. *Uninterested* is the preferred word used to mean 'having no interest', as in *he was totally uninterested in politics*.

disjointed ▸ adjective **1** *a disjointed series of impressions in her mind* **unconnected**, disconnected, without unity, disunited, discontinuous, fragmented, fragmentary, disorganized, disordered, muddled, mixed up, jumbled, garbled, incoherent, confused, fitful, erratic, spasmodic, patchy,

scrappy, bitty, piecemeal; rambling, wandering, aimless, directionless.
2 *the blast left him a twisted assembly of disjointed limbs* **dislocated**, displaced, dismembered, disconnected, severed, separated, disarticulated, torn apart.

disk ▶ **noun**. *See* DISC.

dislike ▶ **verb** *I cannot defend a policy I candidly dislike* **hate**, detest, loathe, abominate, abhor, despise, scorn, shun, execrate; **be averse to**, have an aversion to, hold in disfavour, have no liking for, disapprove of, object to, oppose, disagree with, take exception to, find distasteful, regard with distaste, regard with disgust, be unable to tolerate, find intolerable, be unable to bear, be unable to stand, be unable to abide, shrink from, shudder at, find repellent; *informal* be unable to stomach; *rare* antipathize, disrelish, disfavour.
OPPOSITE like.
▶ **noun** *she viewed the other woman with dislike* **aversion**, distaste, disfavour, disapproval, disapprobation, disesteem, enmity, animosity, hostility, animus, antipathy, antagonism; hate, hatred, detestation, loathing, disgust, repugnance, revulsion, abhorrence, abomination, odium, disdain, contempt; *rare* disrelish, repellence, repellency.
OPPOSITE liking.

dislocate ▶ **verb 1** *Georgina dislocated her hip* **put out of joint**, put out of place, displace, disjoint, disconnect, disengage; *informal* put out; *Medicine* luxate, subluxate; *dated* slip; *rare* unjoint.
2 *trade was dislocated by a famine* **disrupt**, disturb, throw into disorder, throw into disarray, throw into confusion, confuse, disorganize, disorder, disarrange, derange, turn upside-down; *informal* mess up.

dislodge ▶ **verb** *replace any stones you dislodge | economic sanctions failed to dislodge the dictator* **remove**, move, shift, displace, knock out of place, knock out of position, knock over, upset; force out, drive out, oust, eject, get rid of, evict, unseat, depose, topple, overturn, bring down, bring low, bring about the downfall of; *informal* drum out, kick out, boot out; *Brit. informal* turf out.

disloyal ▶ **adjective** *many of her colleagues judged her disloyal* **unfaithful**, faithless, false, false-hearted, untrue, inconstant, untrustworthy; treacherous, perfidious, traitorous, subversive, seditious, unpatriotic, two-faced, double-dealing, double-crossing, deceitful; dissident, renegade; adulterous; *informal* back-stabbing, two-timing; *archaic* recreant; *rare* hollow-hearted, double-faced, Punic, Janus-faced.
OPPOSITE loyal.

disloyalty ▶ **noun** *they accused him of disloyalty and a lack of solidarity with other leaders* **unfaithfulness**, infidelity, inconstancy, faithlessness, fickleness, unreliability, untrustworthiness, breach of trust, breach of faith, betrayal, falseness, false-heartedness, falsity; duplicity, double-dealing, treachery, perfidy, perfidiousness, treason, subversion, sedition, dissidence; adultery; *informal* back-stabbing, two-timing; *rare* hollow-heartedness, Punic faith, recreancy.
OPPOSITE loyalty.

dismal ▶ **adjective 1** *he had a dismal look in his eyes* **gloomy**, glum, mournful, melancholy, morose, doleful, woeful, woebegone, forlorn, abject, dejected, depressed, dispirited, downcast, crestfallen, despondent, disconsolate, miserable, sad, unhappy, sorrowful, sorrowing, desolate, wretched, lugubrious; *informal* blue, fed up, down in the dumps, down in the mouth, as sick as a parrot; *literary* dolorous; *archaic* chap-fallen.
OPPOSITE cheerful.
2 *she led them into a dismal cavernous hall* **dingy**, dim, dark, gloomy, sombre, dreary, drab, dull, desolate, bleak, cheerless, comfortless, depressing, grim, funereal, inhospitable, uninviting, unwelcoming.
OPPOSITES bright, cheerful.
3 (*informal*) *the team have produced a string of dismal performances* **bad**, poor, dreadful, awful, terrible, pitiful, disgraceful, lamentable, deplorable; inferior, mediocre, unsatisfactory, inadequate, second-rate, third-rate, shoddy, inept, bungling; *informal* crummy, dire, diabolical, bum, rotten, pathetic, lousy, poxy; *Brit. informal* duff, rubbish, ropy, chronic, pants, a load of pants; *vulgar slang* crap, crappy, shitty; *N. Amer. vulgar slang* chickenshit; *archaic* direful; *rare* egregious.
OPPOSITE excellent.

dismantle ▶ **verb** *he began to dismantle the revolver | the old opera house was dismantled* **take apart**, take to pieces, take to bits, pull apart, pull to pieces, deconstruct, disassemble, break up, strip (down); knock down, pull down, tear down, demolish, fell, destroy, flatten, level, raze (to the ground), bulldoze; *rare* unbuild.
OPPOSITES assemble, build.

dismay ▶ **verb** *he was dismayed by the change in his old friend* **appal**, horrify, shock, shake, shake up; **disconcert**, take aback, confound, surprise, startle, alarm, frighten, scare, daunt, discomfit, unnerve, unman, unsettle, throw off balance, discompose, discountenance; **trouble**, bother, concern, perturb, disturb, upset, distress, sadden, dishearten, dispirit; *informal* rattle, spook, faze, psych, knock sideways, knock for six; *archaic* pother.
OPPOSITES encourage, please.
▶ **noun** *they greeted his decision with great dismay* **alarm**, shock, surprise, consternation, concern, perturbation, disquiet, disquietude, discomposure, distress, upset, anxiety, trepidation, fear.
OPPOSITES pleasure, relief.

CHOOSE THE RIGHT WORD

dismay, appal, horrify

These words all describe someone's reaction to bad news or adverse circumstances.

- Something that **dismays** someone causes them concern and distress, ranging from the fairly mild (*Mark stopped, dismayed at finding himself breaking into rhyme*) to the intense (*she was dismayed to see that the damage was greater than she had expected*).
- **Appal** suggests a response of extreme horror at something almost unbelievable (*we have waited 22 months for justice to be done and are appalled at the verdict*). In its adjectival form, *appalling*, it has a wide range of meaning (*guilty of appalling crimes against humanity | the appalling pile of rubbish strewn around the University campus*).
- To **horrify** someone is to shock them deeply (*the surgeon was horrified by her injuries*) or cause them intense fear (*as Bernice watched, horrified, Bishop produced a large handgun*).

dismember ▶ **verb** *a stag carcass was in the process of being dismembered* **disjoint**, joint, cut off the limbs of; pull apart, cut up, chop up, break up, dissect, divide, segment; mutilate, hack up, butcher, tear limb from limb; *rare* limb.

dismiss ▶ **verb 1** *the president dismissed five of his ministers* **give someone their notice**, throw out, get rid of, discharge; lay off, make redundant; oust, expel; *informal* **sack**, give someone the sack, fire, send packing, kick out, boot out, give someone the boot, give someone the elbow, give someone the (old) heave-ho, give someone their marching orders, give someone the push, give someone the bullet, show someone the door; *Brit. informal* give someone their cards, turf out; *Military* cashier.
OPPOSITE engage.
2 *the guards reported to HQ and were dismissed* **send away**, let go, release, free; **disband**, disperse, dissolve, discharge, demobilize.
OPPOSITES form, assemble.
3 *he dismissed all morbid thoughts | they dismissed any suggestion of a rift* **banish**, put away, set aside, lay aside, abandon, have done with, drop, disregard, brush off, shrug off, forget, think no more of, pay no heed to, put out of one's mind; **reject**, deny, repudiate, spurn, scoff at, sneer at; *informal* pooh-pooh.
OPPOSITE entertain.

dismissal ▶ **noun 1** *the firm ultimately sanctions poor performance with dismissal* **one's notice**, discharge; redundancy; expulsion, ousting; *informal* **the sack**, sacking, firing, laying off, the push, the boot, the axe, the elbow, the (old) heave-ho, one's marching orders; *Brit. informal* turfing out, one's cards, the chop; *Military* cashiering.
OPPOSITE recruitment.
2 *a condescending dismissal of ancient systems of thought* **rejection**, repudiation, refusal, repulse, non-acceptance; snub, slight; *informal* pooh-poohing, brush-off, knock-back.
OPPOSITE acceptance.

dismissive ▶ **adjective** *she often talked of him in dismissive terms* **contemptuous**, disdainful, scornful, sneering, snide, scathing, disparaging, negative, unenthusiastic, offhand, perfunctory; *informal* sniffy, snotty; *rare* dismissory.
OPPOSITES admiring; interested.

dismount ▶ **verb 1** *the postman slowed his bicycle and dismounted* **alight**, get off, get down.
OPPOSITE mount.
2 *the horse had dismounted the trooper* **unseat**, dislodge, throw, spill, upset, unhorse.

disobedience ▶ **noun** *he was scolded for his disobedience* **insubordination**, unruliness, waywardness, indiscipline, bad behaviour, misbehaviour, misconduct, delinquency, disruptiveness, troublemaking, rebellion, defiance, mutiny, revolt, recalcitrance, lack of cooperation, non-compliance, wilfulness, intractability, awkwardness, perversity, perverseness, contrariness; naughtiness, mischievousness, mischief, roguery, impishness; *informal* carryings-on, acting-up; *archaic or Law* contumacy, infraction.
OPPOSITE obedience.

disobedient ▶ **adjective** *the slave masters punished anyone who became disobedient* **insubordinate**, unruly, wayward, errant, badly behaved, disorderly, delinquent, disruptive, troublesome, rebellious, defiant, mutinous, recalcitrant, refractory, uncooperative, non-compliant, wilful, unbiddable, intractable, obstreperous, awkward, difficult, perverse, contrary; naughty, mischievous, impish, roguish, rascally; *Brit. informal* bolshie; *archaic or Law* contumacious.
OPPOSITE obedient.

D

disobey ▸ verb *the king severely chastised those who disobeyed his orders* **defy**, go against, flout, contravene, infringe, overstep, transgress, violate, fail to comply with, resist, oppose, rebel against, fly in the face of; disregard, ignore, pay no heed to, fail to observe; informal cock a snook at; Law infract; archaic set at naught.
OPPOSITE obey.

disobliging ▸ adjective *we have such disobliging neighbours | a disobliging remark* **unhelpful**, uncooperative, unaccommodating, unamenable, unyielding, inflexible, uncompromising, unreasonable, awkward, difficult, obstructive, contrary, perverse; discourteous, uncivil, unfriendly, unsympathetic.
OPPOSITES helpful; civil.

disorder ▸ noun **1** *he hates disorder in his house* **untidiness**, disorderliness, mess, disarray, disorganization, chaos, confusion; clutter, jumble; a muddle, a mess, a shambles, a mare's nest; Brit. informal a dog's dinner, a dog's breakfast.
OPPOSITE order.
2 *4,000 people were arrested in incidents of public disorder* **unrest**, disturbance, disruption, upheaval, tumult, turmoil, mayhem, pandemonium; violence, fighting; rioting, insurrection, rebellion, mutiny, lawlessness, anarchy; breach of the peace, riot, fracas, rumpus, brouhaha, melee, hubbub, furore, affray; informal hoo-ha, aggro, argy-bargy, snafu; N. Amer. informal wilding.
OPPOSITES order, peace.
3 *she nearly died of pneumonia and a blood disorder* **disease**, infection, complaint, problem, condition, affliction, malady, sickness, illness, ailment, infirmity; defect, irregularity; informal bug, virus; Brit. informal lurgy.

disordered ▸ adjective **1** *Dorothy looked tired and her grey hair was disordered | a disordered pile of documents* **untidy**, unkempt, messy, in a mess, disarranged, uncombed, unbrushed, ungroomed, tousled, tangled, tangly, knotted, knotty, matted, shaggy, straggly, windswept, windblown, wild; disorganized, chaotic, confused, jumbled, muddled, unsystematic, out of order, out of place; informal ratty; N. Amer. informal mussed (up), all over the place; Brit. informal shambolic; archaic draggle-tailed.
2 *a disordered digestive system* **dysfunctional**, disturbed, unsettled, unbalanced, unstable, unsound, upset, poorly, sick, diseased; informal screwed up.

disorderly ▸ adjective **1** *a disorderly desk* **untidy**, disorganized, messy, chaotic, cluttered, littered, jumbled, muddled, confused, unsystematic, irregular; out of order, out of place, in disarray, in a mess, in a jumble, in a muddle, upside-down, at sixes and sevens, haywire, haphazard; informal all over the place, like a bomb's hit it, higgledy-piggledy; Brit. informal shambolic.
OPPOSITE tidy.
2 *he was arrested for disorderly behaviour* **unruly**, boisterous, rough, rowdy, wild, turbulent, tumultuous; disruptive, troublesome, antisocial, disobedient, undisciplined, lawless, unmanageable, uncontrollable, ungovernable, out of hand, out of control; obstreperous, refractory, rebellious, mutinous, insurrectionary, insurgent, seditious, anarchic, riotous, rioting.
OPPOSITE peaceful.

disorganized ▸ adjective **1** *a disorganized tool box* **disorderly**, disordered, unorganized, mixed up, jumbled, muddled, untidy, messy, cluttered, chaotic, confused, topsy-turvy, haphazard, random; in disorder, in disarray, out of order, in a mess, in a muddle, in a shambles; informal all over the place, like a bomb's hit it, higgledy-piggledy; Brit. informal shambolic, all over the shop; N. Amer. informal all over the map, all over the lot; rare orderless.
OPPOSITE orderly.
2 *my boss decided that I was unproductive and disorganized* **unmethodical**, unsystematic, undisciplined, unorganized, badly organized, unprepared, inefficient, ineffective, ineffectual, incapable; erratic, haphazard, indiscriminate, remiss, careless, slapdash, slipshod, slovenly, lax; informal sloppy, hit-or-miss; Brit. vulgar slang not capable of organizing a piss-up in a brewery.
OPPOSITE organized.

disorientated, disoriented ▸ adjective *when he emerged into the street he was completely disorientated* **confused**, bewildered, perplexed, nonplussed, at a loss, (all) at sea, in a state of confusion, in a muddle; **lost**, adrift, astray, off-course, off-track, having lost one's bearings, going round in circles; informal all over the place, not knowing whether one is coming or going; archaic wildered, mazed.

disown ▸ verb *he has been disowned by his parents* **reject**, cast off, cast aside, abandon, repudiate, renounce, deny; turn one's back on, wash one's hands of, have nothing more to do with, end relations with; disinherit, cut off (without a penny); informal ditch, drop, send packing; archaic forsake.
OPPOSITE acknowledge.

disparage ▸ verb *it has become fashionable to disparage Lawrence and his achievements* **belittle**, denigrate, deprecate, depreciate, downgrade, play down, deflate, trivialize, minimize, make light of, treat lightly, undervalue, underrate, underestimate; disdain, dismiss, ridicule, deride, mock, scorn, pour scorn on, scoff at, sneer at, laugh at, laugh off; **run down**, defame, decry, discredit, slander, libel, malign, speak ill of, speak badly of, cast aspersions on, impugn, vilify, traduce, revile, criticize, condemn; N. Amer. slur; informal do down, do a hatchet job on, take to pieces, pull apart, pull to pieces, pick holes in, drag through the mud, hit out at, knock, slam, pan, bash, bad-mouth, pooh-pooh, look down one's nose at; Brit. informal rubbish, slate, slag off, have a go at; dated cry down; archaic hold cheap; rare misprize, minify, asperse, derogate, calumniate, vilipend, vituperate.
OPPOSITES praise; overrate.

disparaging ▸ adjective *people walked past him making disparaging comments* **derogatory**, deprecating, deprecatory, denigratory, belittling, slighting, insulting, abusive; critical, scathing, negative, unfavourable, uncomplimentary, uncharitable, unsympathetic; contemptuous, scornful, snide, derisive, disdainful, sneering; informal bitchy, catty; archaic contumelious.
OPPOSITE complimentary.

disparate ▸ adjective *the document is made up from several disparate chunks* **contrasting**, different, differing, dissimilar, unlike, unalike, poles apart; varying, various, diverse, diversified, heterogeneous, unrelated, unconnected, distinct, separate, divergent; literary divers, myriad; rare contrastive.
OPPOSITE homogeneous.

disparity ▸ noun *there was a disparity between the two sets of figures* **discrepancy**, inconsistency, imbalance, inequality, incongruity, unevenness, disproportion; **variance**, variation, divergence, polarity, gap, gulf, breach; difference, dissimilarity, contrast, distinction, differential; rare unlikeness, dissimilitude, contrariety.
OPPOSITES parity, similarity.

dispassionate ▸ adjective **1** *she dealt with life's disasters in a dispassionate way* **unemotional**, non-emotional, unsentimental, emotionless, impassive, nonchalant, cool, collected, calm, {cool, calm, and collected}, unruffled, unperturbed, composed, self-possessed, level-headed, self-controlled, temperate, sober, placid, equable, tranquil, serene, unexcitable, unflappable; clinical, cold, indifferent, unmoved, unfeeling, uncaring, unsympathetic; informal laid-back.
OPPOSITE emotional.
2 *a dispassionate analysis of the issues* **objective**, detached, neutral, disinterested, uninvolved, impersonal, impartial, non-partisan, non-discriminatory, unbiased, unprejudiced, open-minded, fair, fair-minded, just, equitable, balanced, even-handed, unselfish; scientific, analytical, rational, logical, businesslike; free from discrimination, without fear or favour.
OPPOSITE biased.

dispatch, despatch ▸ verb **1** *the press releases have all been dispatched* **send**, send off, post, mail, ship, freight; forward, transmit, consign, remit, convey.
2 *all serious business was dispatched in the morning* **deal with**, finish, dispose of, conclude, settle, sort out, discharge, execute, perform; expedite, push through, accelerate, hasten, speed up, hurry on; informal make short work of.
3 *in such films the good guy must always dispatch a host of vicious villains* **kill**, put to death, do to death, do away with, put an end to, finish off, take the life of, end the life of; slaughter, butcher, massacre, wipe out, mow down, shoot down, cut down, destroy, exterminate, eliminate, eradicate, annihilate; murder, assassinate, execute; informal bump off, knock off, polish off, do in, top, take out, snuff out, erase, croak, stiff, zap, blow away, blow someone's brains out, give someone the works; N. Amer. informal ice, off, rub out, waste, whack, smoke, scrag; N. Amer. euphemistic terminate with extreme prejudice; literary slay.
▸ noun **1** *we have 125 cases of wine ready for dispatch* **sending**, posting, mailing, shipping, transmittal, consignment.
2 *he carries out his duties with efficiency and dispatch* **promptness**, speed, speediness, swiftness, rapidity, quickness, briskness, haste, hastiness, hurriedness, urgency; literary fleetness, celerity; rare expedition, expeditiousness, promptitude.
3 *she read out the latest dispatch from the front* **communication**, communiqué, bulletin, release, report, account, announcement, statement, missive, letter, epistle, message, instruction; news, intelligence; informal memo, info, low-down, dope; literary tidings.
4 *the hound was used for the capture and dispatch of the wolf* **killing**, slaughter, massacre, destruction, extermination, elimination, liquidation; murder, assassination, execution; literary slaying.

dispel ▸ verb *the sunshine did nothing to dispel her feelings of dejection* **banish**, eliminate, dismiss, chase away, drive away, drive off, get rid of, dissipate, disperse, scatter, disseminate; relieve, allay, ease, calm, quell, check, put to rest.
OPPOSITE engender.

dispensable ▸ adjective *he regards all of his lieutenants as highly dispensable* **expendable**, disposable, replaceable, inessential, unessential, non-

essential; unnecessary, unneeded, needless, not required, redundant, superfluous, surplus to requirements, gratuitous, uncalled for.
OPPOSITE indispensable.

dispensation ▶ noun **1** *regulations control the dispensation of supplies* **distribution**, provision, providing, supply, supplying, issue, issuing, passing round, passing out, giving out, handing out, dealing out, doling out, sharing out, dividing out, parcelling out; division, allocation, allotment, apportionment, assignment, bestowal, conferment, disbursement; *informal* dishing out.
2 *the dispensation of justice* **administration**, administering, delivery, delivering, discharge, bestowal, dealing out, doling out, meting out; carrying out, execution, implementation, application, effectuation, operation, direction; imposition, enforcement.
3 *they were given dispensation from National Insurance contributions* **exemption**, immunity, exception, exclusion, exoneration, freedom, release, relief, reprieve, remission, relaxation, absolution; impunity; *informal* a let-off.
4 *minorities have a special voice in the new constitutional dispensation* **system**, order, scheme, plan, arrangement, organization.

dispense ▶ verb **1** *the servants are ready to dispense the drinks* **distribute**, pass round, pass out, hand out, deal out, dole out, share out, divide out, parcel out, allocate, allot, apportion, assign, bestow, confer, supply, disburse; *informal* dish out.
OPPOSITE collect.
2 *the soldiers dispensed a form of summary justice* **administer**, deliver, issue, discharge, deal, bestow, dole out, mete out; carry out, execute, implement, apply, operate, direct; inflict, impose, enforce, exact; *rare* effectuate.
OPPOSITE receive.
3 *the pharmacists dispense only licensed medicines* **prepare**, make up, mix; **supply**, provide, sell.
4 *the pope nominated him as bishop, dispensing him from his impediment* **exempt**, excuse, except, release, relieve, reprieve, absolve; grant someone a dispensation, grant someone an exemption; *informal* let off.
□ **dispense with 1** *I think we can dispense with the formalities* **waive**, omit, drop, leave out, forgo, give up, relinquish, renounce; ignore, disregard, pass over, brush aside; do away with, put a stop to, put an end to; *informal* cut out, give something a miss, knock something on the head.
OPPOSITE include.
2 *he was able to dispense with his crutches* **get rid of**, throw away, throw out, cast aside, do away with, dispose of, discard, shed; manage without, do without, cope without; *informal* ditch, scrap, axe, junk, dump, chuck out, chuck away, get shut of; *Brit. informal* get shot of; *N. Amer. informal* trash.
OPPOSITE keep.

disperse ▶ verb **1** *the crowd began to disperse | police used tear gas to disperse the demonstrators* **break up**, split up, disband, separate, scatter, leave, go their separate ways, go in different directions; dispel, drive away, drive off, chase away, put to flight, banish, get rid of; *rare* disunite.
OPPOSITE assemble.
2 *the blanket of fog finally dispersed* **dissipate**, be dispelled, thin out, dissolve, melt away, fade away, vanish, disappear, clear, lift, rise.
3 *some plants rely on birds to disperse their seeds* **scatter**, disseminate, distribute, spread, broadcast, diffuse, strew, sow, sprinkle, pepper; *literary* bestrew, besprinkle.
OPPOSITE gather.

> **CHOOSE THE RIGHT WORD**
>
> **disperse, dissipate, scatter**
> See SCATTER.

dispirit ▶ verb *the army was dispirited by the uncomfortable winter conditions* **dishearten**, discourage, demoralize, cast down, make dejected, make downhearted, depress, dismay, disappoint, daunt, deter, unman, unnerve, crush, sap, shake, throw, cow, subdue, undermine; dampen someone's spirits, bring low; *informal* knock sideways, knock the stuffing out of, knock for six, give someone the blues; *archaic* deject.
OPPOSITE hearten.

dispirited ▶ adjective *she was tired and dispirited after her long journey* **disheartened**, discouraged, demoralized, cast down, downcast, low, low-spirited, dejected, downhearted, depressed, disconsolate; crushed, shattered, sapped, shaken, thrown, cowed, subdued; *informal* blue, fed up; *Brit. informal* brassed off, cheesed off.

dispiriting ▶ adjective *the article gives a dispiriting view of the future* **disheartening**, depressing, discouraging, disappointing, daunting, disenchanting, demoralizing; unfavourable, inauspicious, off-putting, pessimistic, hopeless, grim, dismal, gloomy, sombre, cheerless, black; *informal* morbid; *archaic* dejecting.

displace ▶ verb **1** *roof tiles are commonly displaced by gales* **dislodge**, dislocate, upset, unsettle, move, shift, relocate, reposition; put out of place, move out of place, knock out of place, knock out of position, disarrange, derange, discompose, mess up, disorder, throw into disorder, throw into disarray; scatter, disperse.
OPPOSITES replace, put back; leave in place.
2 *they struggled to displace the ruling class* **depose**, dislodge, unseat, dethrone, remove from office, remove, dismiss, eject, oust, expel, force out, throw out, drive out, drum out; overthrow, overturn, topple, bring down; *informal* sack, fire, boot out, give someone the boot, show someone the door; *Brit. informal* turf out; *Military* cashier; *dated* out.
OPPOSITE reinstate.
3 *fuel crops must not displace food crops* **replace**, take the place of, take over from, supplant, oust, supersede, succeed, override; *informal* crowd out.

display ▶ noun **1** *a display of dolls and puppets | planned events include a motorcycle display* **exhibition**, exposition, exhibit, array, arrangement, presentation, demonstration; **spectacle**, show, parade, pageant, extravaganza; *informal* expo, demo.
2 *every clansman was determined to outdo the Campbells in display* **ostentation**, ostentatiousness, showiness, show, pomp, extravagance, ornateness, flamboyance, lavishness, resplendence, splendour, splendidness; *informal* swank, swankiness, pizzazz, razzle-dazzle, flashiness, glitz, glitziness, splashiness.
OPPOSITE modesty.
3 *any display of outrage or temperament was frowned upon* **manifestation**, expression, show, showing, indication, evidence, betrayal, revelation, disclosure.
OPPOSITE concealment.
▶ verb **1** *the Crown Jewels displayed are only copies* **exhibit**, show, put on show, put on view, expose to view, present, unveil, set forth; arrange, dispose, array, lay out, set out.
2 *he uses the play to display his many theatrical talents* **show off**, parade, flaunt, flourish, reveal; publicize, make public, make known, give publicity to, call attention to, draw attention to; *informal* flash, push, plug, hype, boost.
OPPOSITE hide.
3 *every so often she would display a vein of sharp humour* **manifest**, show evidence of, evince, betray, give away, reveal, disclose; demonstrate, show.
OPPOSITE conceal.

displease ▶ verb *he was plainly displeased by Jenny's decision* **annoy**, irritate, infuriate, incense, anger, irk, vex, provoke, pique, peeve, gall, nettle, exasperate, madden; **dissatisfy**, disgruntle, dismay, put out, affront, offend, insult, mortify, outrage, scandalize, disgust; bother, trouble, upset, perturb, disturb, discompose; *informal* aggravate, needle, bug, rile, rattle, miff, hack off; *Brit. informal* nark, wind up, get at; *N. Amer. informal* tee off, tick off, gravel; *vulgar slang* piss off.
OPPOSITE please.

displeasure ▶ noun *the scowl on his face indicated displeasure* **annoyance**, irritation, crossness, infuriation, anger, vexation, wrath, pique, chagrin, rancour, resentment, indignation, exasperation; **dissatisfaction**, discontent, discontentment, discontentedness, disgruntlement, disfavour, disapproval, disapprobation, disgust, distaste, offence; perturbation, disturbance, discomposure, upset, dismay; *informal* aggravation; *literary* ire, choler.
OPPOSITES pleasure, satisfaction.

disposable ▶ adjective **1** *we ate off disposable plates* **throwaway**, expendable, one-use, non-returnable, replaceable; paper, plastic; biodegradable, photodegradable.
2 *the family had little disposable income* **available**, usable, accessible, obtainable, spendable.

disposal ▶ noun **1** *the ageing planes are earmarked for disposal* **throwing away**, getting rid of, discarding, jettisoning, ejection, scrapping, destruction; *informal* dumping, ditching, chucking, chucking out, chucking away.
2 *we have twenty copies of this promotional album for disposal* **distribution**, handing out, giving out, giving away, allotment, allocation, donation, transfer, transference, making over, conveyance, bestowal, bequest; sale.
3 *the disposal of the troops in two lines* **arrangement**, arranging, ordering, positioning, placement, lining up, setting up, organization, disposition; marshalling, mustering, grouping, gathering; *Military* dressing.
4 *they may appeal against the decision of the Panel in the disposal of a case* **settlement**, determination, deciding, conclusion.
□ **at someone's disposal** *Sir Henry placed £15,000 at the club's disposal* **for use by**, in reserve for, in the hands of, in the possession of, within the reach of, within easy reach of, at someone's fingertips.

dispose ▶ verb **1** *the chief disposed his attendants in a circle* **arrange**, order, place, put, position, orient, array, spread out, range, set up, form, organize, seat, stand; marshal, muster, gather, group, assemble; *informal* park, plant, pop, stick; *rare* posit.
2 *she hoped the trip might dispose her husband to be more charitable* **incline**, encourage, persuade, predispose, make willing, make, move, prompt, lead, induce, inspire, tempt, motivate, actuate; bias, sway, influence, determine, direct.
□ **dispose of 1** *industrial waste was disposed of in official sites* **throw away**, throw out, cast out, get rid of, do away with, discard, jettison, abandon,

eject, unload; scrap, destroy; *informal* dump, ditch, chuck, chuck out, chuck away, junk, get shut of; *Brit. informal* get shot of; *N. Amer.* trash.
OPPOSITE retain.
2 *he had disposed of all his costumes, props, and scenery* **part with, give away**, make over, hand over, deliver up, bestow, transfer; sell, auction; unload, palm off, fob off; *informal* get shut of, see the back of; *Brit. informal* get shot of.
OPPOSITES acquire; keep.
3 (*informal*) *she disposed of a fourth cake.* See CONSUME.
4 (*informal*) *he robbed her and then disposed of her.* See KILL.
5 *she disposed of her errand and went home* **deal with**, discharge, execute, perform, do, sort out, settle, finish, conclude, end, dispatch.

D

disposed ▶ adjective **1** *for reasons of religious belief they are philanthropically disposed* **inclined**, predisposed, minded.
2 *we are not disposed to argue with their recommendations* **willing**, inclined, prepared, ready, minded, of a mind, in the mood; keen, eager; *informal* game.
3 *he was disposed to be cruel and self-centred* **liable**, apt, inclined, likely, predisposed, given, prone, tending, subject; capable of, in danger of.

disposition ▶ noun **1** *the book is not recommended to readers of a nervous disposition* **temperament**, nature, character, constitution, make-up, grain, humour, temper, mentality, turn of mind; *informal* kidney.
2 *he admired the Chief Justice because of his disposition to clemency* **inclination**, tendency, proneness, propensity, proclivity, leaning, orientation, bias, bent, predilection.
OPPOSITE disinclination.
3 *the disposition and control of the armed forces* **arrangement**, arranging, disposal, ordering, positioning, placement, lining up, setting up, organization, configuration; set-up, line-up, layout, array; marshalling, mustering, grouping, gathering; *Military* dressing.
4 (*Law*) *the court controls the disposition of the company's property* **distribution**, disposal, allocation, transfer, transference, conveyance, making over, bestowal, bequest; sale, auction.
□ **at someone's disposition** *our wealth is at the disposition of the state* **at the disposal of**, for use by, in reserve for, in the hands of, in the possession of, within the reach of, within easy reach of, at someone's fingertips.

dispossess ▶ verb **1** *the peasants have been dispossessed of their land* **divest**, strip, rob, cheat out of, do out of, deprive, relieve, bereave; *informal* diddle out of; *archaic* reave.
2 *the rebels appear to have dispossessed the aristocrats* **dislodge**, oust, eject, expel, drive out, evict, turn out, cast out, throw out, throw someone out on their ear, put out in the street, show someone the door; banish, exile; *informal* chuck out, kick out, boot out, heave out, bounce; *Brit. informal* turf out; *N. Amer. informal* give someone the bum's rush; *dated* out.

disproportionate ▶ adjective *the sentences are disproportionate to the offences they have committed | they obtained a disproportionate share of NHS resources* **out of proportion to**, not in proportion to, not appropriate to, not commensurate with, relatively too large for, relatively too small for; **inordinate**, unreasonable, excessive, uncalled for, undue, unfair, unbalanced, uneven, unequal, irregular.
OPPOSITE proportional.

disprove ▶ verb *new forensic evidence disproved the allegations* **refute**, prove false, show to be false, give the lie to, rebut, deny, falsify, debunk, negate, invalidate, contradict, confound, be at odds with, demolish, discredit; challenge, call into question; *informal* shoot full of holes, shoot down (in flames), blow sky-high, blow out of the water; *formal* confute, gainsay; *rare* controvert, negative.
OPPOSITE prove.

disputable ▶ adjective *some of these figures are disputable and some are out of date* **debatable**, open to debate, open to discussion, arguable, contestable, moot, open to question, questionable, doubtful, dubious; controversial, contentious, disputed, contended, unconfirmed, unsettled, unsound; *informal* iffy; *Brit. informal* dodgy; *rare* controvertible.

disputation ▶ noun *we'll have no politics and no religious disputation in this house* **debate**, discussion, dispute, argument, arguing, argumentation, altercation, wrangling, sparring, dissension, disagreement, disharmony, conflict, contention, controversy; polemics; *rare* contestation, velitation.

dispute ▶ noun **1** *the extent of the king's powers was the subject of constant dispute* **debate**, discussion, discourse, disputation, argument, controversy, contention, disagreement, altercation, falling-out, quarrelling, variance, dissension, conflict, friction, strife, discord, antagonism; *rare* velitation, contestation.
OPPOSITE agreement.
2 *the police were called to resolve their dispute* **quarrel**, argument, altercation, squabble, falling-out, shouting match, disagreement, difference of opinion, clash, wrangle, feud, fight, fracas, brawl; *Irish, N. Amer., & Austral.* donnybrook; *informal* tiff, spat, scrap, run-in; *Brit. informal* row, barney, slanging match, ding-dong, bust-up; *Scottish informal* rammy; *N. Amer. informal* rhubarb; *archaic* broil, miff.
OPPOSITE agreement.
▶ verb **1** *George visited him and disputed with him* **debate**, discuss, exchange views; **quarrel**, argue, disagree, have a disagreement, have an altercation, clash, wrangle, bicker, squabble, bandy words, cross swords, lock horns; *informal* fall out, have words, argufy, scrap, have a tiff, have a spat; *archaic* altercate.
2 *there might be good reason to dispute his proposals* **challenge**, contest, deny, doubt, question, call into question, impugn, quibble over, contradict, argue about, object to, oppose, disagree with, take issue with, protest against; *formal* gainsay; *rare* controvert.
OPPOSITES accept, agree with.

CHOOSE THE RIGHT WORD

dispute, quarrel, argue, wrangle, bicker
See QUARREL.

disqualified ▶ adjective *he admitted driving while disqualified* **banned**, barred, disbarred, debarred; eliminated, precluded, disentitled; ineligible, unfit, unqualified; *informal* out of the running, ruled out, knocked out.
OPPOSITE allowed.

disqualify ▶ verb *he'd been disqualified from driving* **ban**, bar, debar, prohibit, forbid, interdict, block; exclude, declare ineligible, rule out, preclude, disentitle; *archaic* unfit.
OPPOSITE allow.

disquiet ▶ noun *there has been grave disquiet about the state of the prisons* **unease**, uneasiness, worry, anxiety, anxiousness, distress, concern; unrest, disquietude, inquietude; perturbation, consternation, upset, malaise; alarm, anguish, fear, fright, dread, panic, angst; nervousness, agitation, restlessness, fretfulness, jitteriness; foreboding, trepidation.
OPPOSITE calm.
▶ verb *I was so disquieted by the book that I finished it that evening* **perturb**, agitate, upset, disturb, unnerve, unsettle, discompose, disconcert, ruffle, startle; make uneasy, worry, make anxious; trouble, bother, concern, distress, alarm, appal, frighten, panic, make fretful, make restless, vex.
OPPOSITE calm.

disquisition ▶ noun *his memoirs include disquisitions on film and football* **essay**, dissertation, treatise, paper, discourse, tract, monograph, study, article; **discussion**, lecture, address, presentation, speech, talk, monologue; analysis, commentary, review, critique.

disregard ▶ verb *Annie disregarded the remark* **ignore**, take no notice of, take no account of, pay no attention/heed to, refuse to acknowledge; discount, set aside, forget, overlook, dismiss; turn a blind eye to, turn a deaf ear to, shut one's eyes to, pass over, gloss over, brush off/aside, shrug off, look the other way; laugh off, make light of, thumb one's nose at, write off; *Brit. informal* blank.
OPPOSITES heed, pay attention to.
▶ noun *he drove with blithe disregard for the rules of the road* **indifference**, non-observance; **inattention**, heedlessness, carelessness, neglect, lack of attention, lack of notice, lack of heed, negligence.
OPPOSITES heed, attention.

disrepair ▶ noun *a building in a state of disrepair* **dilapidation**, decrepitude, shabbiness, ruin, ruination, rack and ruin, ricketiness; deterioration, decay, degeneration, collapse; abandonment, neglect, disuse.

disreputable ▶ adjective **1** *he fell into disreputable company* **scandalous**, of bad reputation, infamous, notorious, louche; dishonourable, dishonest, villainous, rascally, ignominious, corrupt, unscrupulous, unprincipled, immoral, untrustworthy, discreditable; contemptible, reprehensible, despicable, disgraceful, shameful, shocking, outrageous; unworthy, base, low, mean; questionable, suspect, suspicious, dubious, unsavoury, slippery; seedy, sleazy, seamy, unwholesome; *informal* crooked, shady, shifty, fishy; *Brit. informal* dodgy.
OPPOSITES reputable, respectable.
2 *they looked so filthy and disreputable that a woman stopped to stare at them* **scruffy**, shabby, slovenly, down at heel, seedy, untidy, unkempt, dishevelled, disordered, bedraggled, dilapidated, threadbare, tattered, sloppy.
OPPOSITE smart.

disrepute ▶ noun *Beth had shamed herself and brought the family name into disrepute* **disgrace**, shame, dishonour, infamy, notoriety, ignominy, stigma, scandal, bad reputation, lack of respectability; degradation, humiliation, odium, opprobrium, obloquy; discredit, ill repute, disesteem, low esteem, loss of face; unpopularity, disfavour, ill favour.
OPPOSITE honour.

disrespect ▶ noun **1** *there is growing disrespect for authority* **contempt**, lack of respect, scorn, disregard, disdain, opprobrium; derision, mockery, ridicule.
OPPOSITES respect, esteem.
2 *he said it on the spur of the moment, he meant no disrespect to anybody* **discourtesy**, rudeness, impoliteness, incivility, unmannerliness, lack of respect, lack of civility, ungraciousness, irreverence, lack of consideration, ill/bad manners; insolence, impudence, impertinence,

cheek, flippancy, churlishness; *informal* lip, nerve.
OPPOSITES respect, esteem.

disrespectful ▶ adjective *he was cheeky and disrespectful towards his parents* **discourteous**, rude, impolite, uncivil, unmannerly, ill-mannered, bad-mannered, ungracious, irreverent, inconsiderate; insolent, impudent, impertinent, cheeky, flippant, insubordinate, churlish; contemptuous, disdainful, derisive, scornful, disparaging, insulting, abusive; *informal* fresh.
OPPOSITES respectful, polite.

disrobe ▶ verb *she began to disrobe* **undress**, strip, strip naked, take off one's clothes, remove one's clothes, doff one's clothes, shed one's clothes, denude, uncover oneself; *informal* peel off; *dated* divest oneself of one's clothes.

disrupt ▶ verb **1** *a 24-hour strike disrupted public transport* **throw into confusion**, throw into disorder, throw into disarray, cause confusion/turmoil in, play havoc with, derange, turn upside-down, make a mess of; **disturb**, disorder, disorganize, disarrange, interfere with, upset, unsettle, convulse; interrupt, suspend, discontinue; obstruct, impede, hamper; hold up, delay, retard, slow (down); *Brit. informal* throw a spanner in the works of; *N. Amer. informal* throw a monkey wrench in the works of.
2 *the explosion would disrupt the walls of the crater* **distort**, damage, buckle, warp; break open/apart, shatter, split, sever, cleave, split asunder; *literary* rend; *archaic* sunder, rive.
OPPOSITES organize; arrange.

disruption ▶ noun *he was exasperated at this disruption of his plans* **disturbance**, disordering, disarrangement, disarranging, interference, upset, upsetting, unsettling, confusion, confusing; disorderliness, disorganization, turmoil, disarray; interruption, suspension, discontinuation, stoppage; obstruction, impeding, hampering, spoiling, ruining, wrecking, undermining; holding up, delaying, delay, retardation.

disruptive ▶ adjective *a very disruptive child* **troublemaking**, troublesome, unruly, rowdy, disorderly, undisciplined, riotous, wild, turbulent; unmanageable, uncontrollable, out of control/hand, unrestrained, obstreperous, truculent, fractious, divisive; badly behaved, misbehaving, errant, uncooperative, rebellious; disturbing, distracting, unsettling, upsetting, noisy, raucous; *formal* refractory.
OPPOSITES well behaved, manageable.

dissatisfaction ▶ noun *polls revealed widespread dissatisfaction with the new law* **discontent**, discontentment, disappointment, disaffection, disquiet, unhappiness, malaise, disgruntlement, frustration, vexation, annoyance, irritation, anger, exasperation, resentment; restlessness, restiveness; disapproval, disapprobation, disfavour, displeasure, grievance, disregard, disgust; regret, chagrin, dismay; *German* Weltschmerz.
OPPOSITE satisfaction.

dissatisfied ▶ adjective *the radical wing was dissatisfied with these policies | a dissatisfied customer* **discontented**, malcontent, unsatisfied, disappointed, disaffected, disquieted, unhappy; disgruntled, aggrieved, frustrated, vexed, annoyed, irritated, angry, angered, exasperated, fed up, resentful; restless, restive, disapproving, displeased, unfulfilled, regretful; *informal* cheesed off, brassed off, browned off; *vulgar slang* pissed off.
OPPOSITES satisfied, contented.

dissatisfy ▶ verb *what is it about this wording that dissatisfies you?* **displease**, fail to satisfy, give cause for complaint, not be good enough; disappoint, let down; disquiet, disgruntle, aggrieve, frustrate, vex, annoy, irritate, put out, anger, exasperate.
OPPOSITE satisfy.

dissect ▶ verb **1** *the body was dissected in the infirmary* **anatomize**, cut up, cut/lay open, dismember; vivisect.
2 *as the text of the gospels was dissected, some parts came to look earlier than others* **analyse**, examine, study, inspect, scrutinize, probe, explore, pore over, investigate, sift, delve into, go over with a fine-tooth comb; break down, take apart, deconstruct.

dissection ▶ noun **1** *the dissection of corpses* **cutting up**, cutting open, dismemberment; autopsy, post-mortem, necropsy, anatomy, vivisection, zootomy.
2 *a thorough dissection of the government's industrial policies* **analysis**, examination, study, inspection, scrutiny, scrutinization, probe, probing, exploration, investigation, enquiry; evaluation, assessment, criticism; breakdown, deconstruction.

dissemble ▶ verb *she is an honest, sincere person who has no need to dissemble* **dissimulate**, pretend, deceive, feign, act, masquerade, sham, fake, bluff, counterfeit, pose, posture, hide one's feelings, be dishonest, put on a false front, lie; cover up, conceal, disguise, hide, mask, veil, shroud.

dissembler ▶ noun *he was a born showman and dissembler* **liar**, dissimulator, deceiver, deluder; humbug, bluffer, fraud, hoodwinker, impostor, actor, faker, hoaxer, charlatan, cheat, cheater.

disseminate ▶ verb *health authorities should foster good practice by disseminating information* **spread**, circulate, distribute, disperse, diffuse, proclaim, promulgate, propagate, publicize, communicate, pass on, make known, put about; dissipate, scatter; broadcast, put on the air/airwaves, publish; herald, trumpet; *literary* bruit abroad/about.

dissemination ▶ noun *the collection and dissemination of information* **spreading**, circulation, distribution, dispersal, diffusion; proclamation, promulgation, propagation, publicizing, communication, passing on, making known, putting about; dissipation, scattering; broadcasting, relaying, transmission, putting on the air/airwaves, publishing, publication.

dissension ▶ noun *there was dissension within the Cabinet over these policies* **disagreement**, difference of opinion, dispute, dissent, variance, conflict, friction, strife, discord, discordance, discordancy, disunion, disaffection, rivalry, antagonism; argument, debate, controversy, disputation, contention, quarrelling, wrangling, bickering, squabbling, falling-out.
OPPOSITES agreement; harmony.

dissent ▶ verb *we do not* **dissent from** *the points that have been made* **differ**, demur, diverge; **disagree with**, fail to agree with, express disagreement with, be at variance/odds with, argue with, take issue with; decline/refuse to support, not ratify, protest against, object to, dispute, challenge, quibble over; reject, repudiate, renounce, abjure.
OPPOSITES assent, agree, accept.
▶ noun *there were murmurs of dissent from the opposition benches* **disagreement**, lack of agreement, difference of opinion, argument, dispute, demur; disapproval, objection, protest, opposition, defiance, insubordination; conflict, friction, strife; arguing, quarrelling, wrangling, bickering.
OPPOSITES agreement, acceptance.

dissenter ▶ noun **1** *there was a chorus of criticism from dissenters within the party* **dissident**, dissentient, objector, protester, disputant; rebel, revolutionary, renegade, maverick, independent; apostate, heretic.
2 (**Dissenter**) *liberty of conscience for Dissenters* **Nonconformist**, Protestant, freethinker, recusant; Puritan; Baptist, Methodist, Quaker, Calvinist, Lutheran; *N. Amer.* Mennonite; *historical* Anabaptist.

dissentient ▶ adjective *there were some dissentient voices* **dissenting**, dissident, disagreeing, differing, discordant, contradicting, contrary, negative, anti-; opposing, opposed, objecting, protesting, complaining, rebellious, rebelling, revolutionary; **nonconformist**, non-compliant, unorthodox, recusant, heterodox, heretical; *formal* gainsaying.
▶ noun. *See* DISSENTER.

dissertation ▶ noun *a dissertation on the novels of the Brontë sisters* **essay**, thesis, treatise, paper, study, composition, discourse, disquisition, tract, monograph; critique, exposition, criticism, appraisal, assessment, discussion.

disservice ▶ noun *not checking your headlines does your readers a disservice* **unkindness**, bad turn, ill turn, disfavour, mischief; **injury**, harm, hurt, damage, offence; wrong, injustice; *informal* kick in the teeth.
OPPOSITE favour.

dissidence ▶ noun *the chairman was faced by dissidence within his own party* **disagreement**, dissent, disaccord, discord, discontent, disapproval; **opposition**, resistance, protest, insurrection, rebellion, sedition.
OPPOSITES agreement, acceptance.

dissident ▶ noun *a dissident who had been jailed by the regime* **dissenter**, objector, protester, disputant; freethinker, nonconformist, independent thinker; rebel, revolutionary, recusant, renegade; subversive, agitator, insurgent, insurrectionist, insurrectionary, mutineer; *informal* refusenik.
OPPOSITE conformist.
▶ adjective *a demonstration coordinated by dissident intellectuals and workers* **dissentient**, dissenting, disagreeing; opposing, opposed, opposition, objecting, protesting, complaining; rebellious, rebelling, revolutionary, recusant; nonconformist, non-compliant.
OPPOSITE conforming.

dissimilar ▶ adjective *contact between dissimilar cultures* **different**, differing, unlike, unalike, varying, variant, various, diverse, heterogeneous, disparate, unrelated, distinct, contrasting, contradictory, poles apart; divergent, mismatched, inconsistent; *informal* like chalk and cheese; *literary* divers, myriad; *rare* contrastive.
OPPOSITE similar.

dissimilarity ▶ noun *the enzymes' structural dissimilarity* **difference(s)**, dissimilitude, variance, variation, diversity, heterogeneity, disparateness, disparity, distinctness, distinction, contrast, non-uniformity, incomparability, incongruity, polarity; divergence, deviation; unrelatedness, inconsistency, discrepancy; *rare* unlikeness.
OPPOSITE similarity.

dissimilitude ▶ noun *people are often drawn together by their very dissimilitude. See* DISSIMILARITY.

dissimulate ▶ verb *now they have power, they no longer need to dissimulate* **pretend**, deceive, feign, act, dissemble, masquerade, pose, posture, sham, fake, bluff, counterfeit, go through the motions, hide one's feelings, be dishonest, put on a false front, lie.

dissimulation ▶ noun *he was capable of great dissimulation and hypocrisy* **pretence**, dissembling, misrepresentation, deceit, dishonesty, duplicity, lying, guile, subterfuge, feigning, falsification, shamming, faking, bluff, bluffing, counterfeiting, posturing, hypocrisy, double-dealing; concealment, concealing, masking, disguising, hiding, veiling, shrouding; *Irish informal* codology; *informal* kidology.

D

dissipate ▶ verb **1** *his anger had dissipated | the queue dissipated* **disappear**, **vanish**, evaporate, dissolve, melt away, melt into thin air, be dispelled, dematerialize; disperse, scatter; drive away, dispel, banish; quell, allay, check; *literary* evanesce.
OPPOSITES grow, develop.
2 *he had dissipated his fortune* **squander**, fritter (away), misspend, waste, throw away, make poor use of, be prodigal with; spend recklessly/freely, lavish, expend, spend like water, throw around like confetti; exhaust, drain, deplete, burn (up), use up, consume, run through, go through, lose; *informal* blow, splurge, pour/throw down the drain, spend money as if it grows on trees, spend money as if there were no tomorrow, spend money as if it were going out of style/fashion; *Brit. informal* blue; *vulgar slang* piss away.
OPPOSITE save.

CHOOSE THE RIGHT WORD
dissipate, disperse, scatter
See SCATTER.

dissipated ▶ adjective *the new heir was a dissipated youth* **dissolute**, **debauched**, decadent, intemperate, immoderate, profligate, abandoned, self-indulgent, wild, unrestrained; depraved, degenerate, corrupt, sinful, immoral, impure; rakish, louche; licentious, promiscuous, lecherous, libertine, wanton, lustful, libidinous, lewd, unchaste, loose; drunken.
OPPOSITE ascetic.

dissipation ▶ noun **1** *a day of drunken dissipation* **debauchery**, decadence, dissoluteness, dissolution, intemperance, immoderation, excess, profligacy, abandonment, self-indulgence, wildness; depravity, degeneracy, corruption, sinfulness, immorality, vice, impurity; rakishness; licentiousness, promiscuity, lecherousness, lechery, libertinism, libertinage, wantonness, lustfulness, libidinousness, lewdness; drunkenness.
OPPOSITES asceticism, restraint.
2 *concern was expressed about the dissipation of the country's mineral wealth* **squandering**, frittering (away), waste, misspending; expenditure, wild spending, draining, depletion, losing, loss.
OPPOSITES saving, preservation.

dissociate ▶ verb *the word 'spiritual' has become dissociated from religion* **separate**, detach, disconnect, sever, cut off, divorce, set apart, segregate, distinguish; isolate, alienate.
OPPOSITES relate, connect.
□ **dissociate oneself from 1** *he dissociated himself from the Church of England* **break away from**, break off relations with, end relations with, sever connections with; withdraw from, delink from, quit, leave, disaffiliate from, resign from, pull out of, drop out of, have nothing more to do with, part company with, defect, desert, secede from, take one's leave of, become estranged from.
OPPOSITE join.
2 *the French president dissociated himself from the statement* **denounce**, disown, reject, condemn, disagree with, wash one's hands of, distance oneself from.
OPPOSITES endorse, support.

dissociation ▶ noun *there can be a dissociation of behaviour from consciousness* **separation**, disconnection, detachment, severance, divorce, uncoupling, split, setting apart; segregation, distinction, division; isolation, alienation, distancing; *literary* sundering; *rare* disseverment.
OPPOSITES association, union.

dissolute ▶ adjective *a dissolute, disreputable rogue* **dissipated**, debauched, decadent, intemperate, profligate, abandoned, self-indulgent, rakish, louche, licentious, promiscuous, lecherous, libertine, wanton, lustful, libidinous, lewd, unchaste, loose; wild, unrestrained, depraved, degenerate, corrupt, sinful, immoral, impure; drunken.
OPPOSITE ascetic.

dissolution ▶ noun **1** *the dissolution of parliament | he called for the dissolution of the secret police* **cessation**, conclusion, end, ending, finish, termination, break-up, split-up, winding up/down, discontinuation, suspension; **disbandment**, disbanding, disestablishment, disunion, separation, dispersal, scattering; prorogation, recess.
2 (*technical*) *the dissolution of a polymer in a solvent* **dissolving**, liquefaction, melting, deliquescence; breaking up, separation, resolution, decomposition, disintegration.
3 *the slow dissolution of the Ottoman empire* **disintegration**, breaking up, fragmenting; decay, collapse, death, demise, extinction; destruction, ruin, overthrow.
4 *the corruption and dissolution of this moribund society. See* DISSIPATION.

dissolve ▶ verb **1** *heat the water until the sugar dissolves* **go into solution**, become a solution, break down; liquefy, melt, deliquesce; disintegrate, diffuse; *technical* solvate.
OPPOSITE condense.
2 *his hopes dissolved* **disappear**, vanish, melt away, evaporate, disperse, dissipate, disintegrate; dwindle, fade (away), fall away, subside, ebb, wane, peter out, fizzle out, crumble, decompose, wilt, wither; perish, die, be destroyed, cease to exist, come to an end, pass away, evanesce.
OPPOSITE appear.
3 *the crowd had dissolved* **disperse**, disband, break up, split up, separate, scatter, go their separate ways, go in different directions, disjoin.
OPPOSITE join together.
4 *the National Assembly was dissolved after a coup* **disband**, disestablish, dismiss; **bring to an end**, end, terminate, finish, cease, conclude, discontinue, break up, split up, close down, wind up/down, suspend; prorogue, adjourn; scrap, abolish, do away with, get rid of.
OPPOSITE establish.
5 *the marriage was dissolved in 1985* **annul**, nullify, void; cancel, invalidate, overturn, repeal, rescind, revoke; divorce.
□ **dissolve into/in** *a timid child who was always the first to dissolve into tears* **burst into**, break into, collapse into, break down into; be overcome with; *informal* crack up.

dissonance ▶ noun **1** *there is hardly any dissonance on this album* **inharmoniousness**, discordance, unmelodiousness, atonality, cacophony; harshness, stridency, grating, jarring.
OPPOSITE harmony.
2 *there is dissonance between the form and content* **incongruity**, disparity, discrepancy, disagreement, tension; difference, dissimilarity, variance, inconsistency; contradiction, clash.
OPPOSITES harmony; similarity.

dissonant ▶ adjective **1** *dissonant sounds* **inharmonious**, disharmonious, discordant, unmelodious, atonal, tuneless, off-key, cacophonous; harsh, strident, grating, jarring.
OPPOSITE harmonious.
2 *Jackson employs both harmonious and dissonant colour choices* **incongruous**, anomalous, irreconcilable, discrepant, disagreeing, clashing; disparate, different, dissimilar, inconsistent, incompatible, contradictory.
OPPOSITES harmonious, similar.

dissuade ▶ verb *I tried to dissuade him from telling that story* **discourage**, deter, prevent, disincline, turn aside, divert, sidetrack; talk out of, persuade against, persuade not to, argue out of, put off, stop, scare off, warn off; advise against, urge against, advise/urge not to, caution against, expostulate against; *rare* dehort.
OPPOSITES persuade, encourage.

CHOOSE THE RIGHT WORD
dissuade, discourage, deter
See DISCOURAGE.

distance ▶ noun **1** *they measured the distance between Hartwell and Roade Station* **interval**, space, span, gap, separation, interspace, stretch, extent; length, width, breadth, depth; range, reach.
2 *binocular vision gives us a perception of distance* **remoteness**, farness; closeness.
3 *a mix of warmth and distance makes a good neighbour* **aloofness**, remoteness, detachment, stand-offishness, unfriendliness, unapproachableness, haughtiness, hauteur, coolness, coldness, frigidity; reserve, reticence, restraint, stiffness, formality, unresponsiveness.
OPPOSITE friendliness.
□ **in the distance** *he could see them in the distance* **far away**, far off, afar; yonder, just in view; on the horizon, in the background.
OPPOSITE close to.
▶ verb *he had distanced himself from her emotionally* **withdraw**, detach, separate, dissociate, remove, isolate, put at a distance, keep at arm's length, set apart, place far off.
OPPOSITE draw closer.
WORD LINKS
to or at a distance **tele-** (e.g. ***telephone, telekinesis***)

distant ▶ adjective **1** *distant parts of the world* **faraway**, far-off, far; **remote**, out of the way, outlying, abroad, far-flung, obscure; isolated, cut off, off the beaten track.
OPPOSITE near.
2 *the distant past* **long ago**, bygone; ancient, prehistoric, antediluvian, immemorial; *literary* olden, of yore.
OPPOSITE recent.
3 *the town lay half a mile distant* **away**, off, apart, separated.
4 *a distant memory* **vague**, faint, dim, faded, feeble; **indistinct**, obscure, unclear, uncertain, indefinite, indeterminate; confused, sketchy, hazy, rough.
OPPOSITES strong, intense.
5 *there is a distant family connection* **remote**, indirect, slight.
OPPOSITE close.
6 *my father was always very distant with me* **aloof**, reserved, remote, detached, unapproachable, stand-offish, keeping people at arm's length; withdrawn, restrained, reticent, taciturn, uncommunicative, undemonstrative, unforthcoming; cool, cold, frigid, chilly, icy, frosty; formal, stiff, stuffy, ceremonious, unresponsive, unfriendly, haughty,

forbidding, austere.
OPPOSITE friendly.
7 *he had a distant look in his eyes* **distracted**, **absent-minded**, absent, faraway, detached, distrait, vague.
OPPOSITE attentive.

> **CHOOSE THE RIGHT WORD**
>
> **distant, remote, faraway, far-off**
>
> These words all describe something that is a long way away in space or time.
>
> - **Distant** is the most general and neutral word for something that is a long way away (*fine views stretch to the distant mountains | the dim and distant past*).
> - **Remote** suggests isolation and inaccessibility rather just distance (*they went into hiding in a remote fishing village | areas remote from the coast*).
> - **Faraway** may emphasize the difficulty of getting somewhere, but often it also suggests an exotic and romantic quality (*I dream of faraway exotic places*). It is always used before a noun in this sense.
> - A **far-off** place or time is often very different from one with which it is tacitly compared (*an adventure story set in a far-off mystical land*).

distaste ▶ **noun** *she has shown a distaste for politics* **dislike**, disfavour, disdain; **repugnance**, disgust, revulsion, contempt, antipathy, odium, hatred, loathing, detestation, execration, abomination, horror; disinclination towards, aversion to, disapproval of, disapprobation of, displeasure with, dissatisfaction with, discontent with; *rare* disrelish, repellence, repellency.
OPPOSITE liking.

distasteful ▶ **adjective** **1** *his behaviour has been distasteful* **unpleasant**, disagreeable, displeasing, unpleasing, undesirable; off-putting, uninviting; objectionable, offensive, unsavoury, unpalatable, obnoxious, odious; disgusting, repellent, repulsive, revolting, repugnant, abhorrent, loathsome, detestable, obscene, foul, nasty, vile.
OPPOSITE agreeable.
2 *certain sea urchins make their eggs distasteful to predators* **unpalatable**, unsavoury, unappetizing, inedible, disgusting, sickening, nauseating, nauseous, horrible, horrid.
OPPOSITE tasty.

distend ▶ **verb** *the pressure acts to distend blood vessels* **swell**, bloat, bulge, puff out/up, blow up/out, expand, dilate, inflate, enlarge; *rare* tumefy, intumesce.
OPPOSITES shrink, contract.

distended ▶ **adjective** *a grossly distended belly* **swollen**, bloated, tumescent, dilated, engorged, enlarged, inflated, stretched, blown up, pumped up/out; expanded, extended, ballooning, puffy, puffed up; bulbous, bulging, protuberant, prominent, sticking out; *technical* turgescent, ventricose; *rare* tumid.
OPPOSITES shrunken, deflated.

distil ▶ **verb** **1** *all the water used was distilled and deionized* **purify**, refine, filter, treat, process; vaporize/evaporate and condense, sublime, sublimate; *rare* fractionate.
2 *oil distilled from marjoram* **extract**, press out, squeeze out, express, draw out, take out.
3 *most Scotch whiskies are distilled from barley malt cured with peat* **brew**, ferment, make.
4 *the solvent is distilled to leave the oil as a solid material* **boil down**, reduce, concentrate, thicken, compress, condense; purify, refine, separate, rectify.
5 (*literary*) *she drew back from the dank breath that distilled out of the earth* **emanate**, exude, drip, leak, trickle, dribble, flow.

distillation ▶ **noun** **1** *a way of making fresh water from seawater by distillation* **distilling**, **purification**, refining, filtering, filtration, treatment, processing; sublimation; *rare* fractionation.
2 *the flowers were ready to gather for distillation* **pressing**, squeezing; extraction, extracting, drawing out; concentration, condensation, reduction.

distinct ▶ **adjective** **1** *any employee would fall into one of two distinct categories* **discrete**, **separate**, individual, different, unconnected, unassociated, detached; precise, specific, distinctive, dissimilar, unalike, contrasting, disparate, unique; *Latin* sui generis.
OPPOSITES indistinct; overlapping; approximate.
2 *the tail has distinct black tips* **clear**, clear-cut, definite, well defined, sharp, marked, decided, unmistakable, easily distinguishable; recognizable, visible, perceptible, noticeable, obvious, plain, plain as day, evident, apparent, manifest, patent, palpable, unambiguous, unequivocal, pronounced, prominent, striking.
OPPOSITES indistinct; fuzzy; indefinite.

distinction ▶ **noun** **1** *the distinction between academic and vocational qualifications* **difference**, contrast, dissimilarity, dissimilitude, divergence, variance, variation; division, separation, differentiation, contradistinction, discrimination, segregation, dividing line, gulf, gap, chasm.
OPPOSITE similarity.
2 *a painter of distinction* **importance**, significance, note, consequence, account; **renown**, fame, celebrity, prominence, eminence, pre-eminence, repute, reputation, honour, prestige, status, high standing, illustriousness, name, mark, rank; merit, worth, greatness, excellence, glory, quality, superiority.
OPPOSITE mediocrity.
3 *he had served with distinction in the Great War* **honour**, **credit**, excellence, merit.

distinctive ▶ **adjective** *each subculture developed a distinctive dress style* **distinguishing**, characteristic, typical, individual, particular, peculiar, idiosyncratic, differentiating, unique, exclusive, special, especial; remarkable, unusual, singular, noteworthy, different, uncommon, extraordinary, original.
OPPOSITE common.

> **CHOOSE THE RIGHT WORD**
>
> **distinctive, characteristic, typical**
>
> *See* CHARACTERISTIC.

distinctly ▶ **adverb** **1** *there's something distinctly odd about him* **decidedly**, markedly, definitely, emphatically; clearly, noticeably, obviously, plainly, evidently, unmistakably, manifestly, patently, palpably; blatantly, glaringly, conspicuously, pointedly; unquestionably, undeniably, indisputably; *Brit. informal* dead.
OPPOSITES vaguely, possibly.
2 *'No!' Laura said quite distinctly* **clearly**, plainly, intelligibly, audibly, unambiguously, loud and clear, with clarity, precisely.
OPPOSITE indistinctly.

distinguish ▶ **verb** **1** *a food allergy may be difficult to distinguish from a viral infection* **differentiate**, tell apart, discriminate, discern, determine, pick out; tell the difference between, decide between, make/draw a distinction between.
2 *he was able to distinguish the shapes of the trees in the dark* **discern**, see, perceive, make out; observe, notice, spot, glimpse, catch sight of; detect, recognize, identify, pick out; *formal* apprehend; *literary* descry, espy.
3 *this is what distinguishes history from other disciplines* **separate**, set apart, make distinctive, make different; **single out**, mark off, demarcate, delimit, delineate; characterize, individualize, individuate, identify, designate, categorize, classify.
□ **distinguish oneself** *he had distinguished himself during his university days* **attain distinction**, be successful, bring fame/honour to oneself, become famous, dignify oneself, glorify oneself, excel oneself, win acclaim for oneself, ennoble oneself, become lionized, become immortalized, elevate oneself.

distinguishable ▶ **adjective** *chapels on this pattern were barely distinguishable from parish churches of the same period* **discernible**, recognizable, identifiable, detectable; divisible, separable.
OPPOSITE indistinguishable.

distinguished ▶ **adjective** *a distinguished physicist* **eminent**, famous, famed, renowned, prominent, well known; esteemed, respected, illustrious, august, venerable, honoured, acclaimed, celebrated, legendary, great; noted, notable, important, significant, influential.
OPPOSITES unknown; obscure.

distinguishing ▶ **adjective** *a distinguishing feature of British society* **distinctive**, differentiating, discriminating, determining; individualistic, particular, peculiar, singular, idiosyncratic, unique, noteworthy, different, uncommon, extraordinary, original; characteristic, typical.
OPPOSITES unremarkable, common.

distort ▶ **verb** **1** *his face was distorted with anger* **twist**, warp, contort, bend, buckle, deform, malform, misshape, disfigure; mangle, wrench, wring, wrest.
2 *he oversimplified and distorted the truth* **misrepresent**, pervert, twist, falsify, misreport, misstate, prejudice, manipulate, garble, take/quote out of context; slant, bias, skew, colour, put a spin on, spin; tamper with, tinker with, doctor, alter, change.

distorted ▶ **adjective** **1** *a distorted face* **twisted**, warped, contorted, bent, buckled, deformed, malformed, misshapen, disfigured, crooked, irregular, awry, wry, out of shape; mangled, wrenched, gnarled.
OPPOSITE straight.
2 *a distorted version of Freud's ideas* **misrepresented**, perverted, twisted, falsified, misreported, misstated; **garbled**, inaccurate; biased, prejudiced, slanted, coloured, loaded, weighted; tampered with, tinkered with, doctored, altered, changed.
OPPOSITE accurate.

distortion ▶ **noun** **1** *strain on the muscles of the eye leading to a distortion in*

D

D

shape or structure **warp**, twist, contortion, bend, buckle, deformation, deformity, curve, curvature, malformation, disfigurement, crookedness; gnarl, knot.
2 *a gross distortion of the facts* **misrepresentation**, perversion, twisting, falsification, misreporting, misstatement, manipulation; **garbling**, travesty; slant, bias, skew, colouring, prejudice, imbalance, spin; tampering, tinkering, doctoring, alteration, change.

distract ▶ **verb** *don't let me distract you from what you were saying | he was distracted by a ringing sound* **divert**, deflect, sidetrack, turn aside/away, draw away; disturb, put off, cause to lose concentration.

distracted ▶ **adjective** *he glanced at me with a distracted smile* **preoccupied**, diverted, inattentive, vague, absorbed, engrossed, abstracted, distrait, distant, absent, absent-minded, faraway; bemused, confused, bewildered, perplexed, puzzled, agitated, flustered, ruffled, disconcerted, discomposed, nonplussed, befuddled, mystified; troubled, pestered, harassed, worried, tormented; *informal* miles away, in a world of one's own, not with it, fazed, hassled, in a flap.
OPPOSITE attentive.

distracting ▶ **adjective** *some people find even the slightest noise distracting* **disturbing**, unsettling, intrusive, disconcerting, bothersome, confusing; *informal* off-putting.

distraction ▶ **noun 1** *he called these stories a distraction from the real issues* **diversion**, interruption, disturbance, intrusion, interference, obstruction, hindrance.
2 *the frivolous distractions of student life* **amusement**, entertainment, diversion, activity, pastime, recreation, interest, hobby, game, leisure pursuit, occupation, divertissement.
3 *he had been driven to distraction when his daughter would not settle down* **frenzy**, hysteria, mental distress, madness, insanity, wildness, mania, derangement, delirium; bewilderment, befuddlement, perplexity, confusion, disturbance, agitation, perturbation, harassment; *archaic* crazedness.

distrait, fem. **distraite** ▶ **adjective** *he was unusually distrait as he ate his breakfast* **distracted**, preoccupied, absorbed, engrossed, abstracted, distant, faraway; **absent-minded**, absent, forgetful, vague, inattentive, oblivious, heedless, in a brown study, wool-gathering, with one's head in the clouds, in a world of one's own; *informal* scatterbrained, miles away.
OPPOSITES alert, concentrating.

distraught ▶ **adjective** *the poor child was distraught* **worried**, **upset**, distressed, fraught, devastated, shattered; overcome, overwrought, beside oneself, out of one's mind, desperate, at one's wits' end; hysterical, frenzied, raving, deranged; *informal* in a state, worked up.

distress ▶ **noun 1** *she was trying to conceal her distress* **anguish**, suffering, pain, agony, ache, affliction, torment, torture, discomfort, heartache, heartbreak; misery, wretchedness, sorrow, grief, woe, sadness, unhappiness, desolation, despair; trouble, worry, anxiety, perturbation, uneasiness, disquiet, angst.
OPPOSITES happiness, comfort.
2 *a ship in distress* **danger**, peril, difficulty, trouble, jeopardy, risk, hazard, endangerment, imperilment; insecurity, instability, precariousness.
OPPOSITE safety.
3 *the poor were helped in their distress* **hardship**, adversity, tribulation, misfortune, ill/bad luck, trouble, calamity; poverty, deprivation, privation, destitution, indigence, impoverishment, penury, need, want, lack, beggary, dire straits.
OPPOSITES prosperity, comfort.
▶ **verb 1** *he's been distressed by the trial* **cause anguish to**, cause suffering to, pain, upset, make miserable, make wretched; grieve, sadden; trouble, worry, bother, arouse anxiety in, perturb, disturb, disquiet, agitate, vex, harrow, torment, torture, afflict, rack, curse, oppress, plague, dog; *informal* cut up.
OPPOSITES calm, soothe; please.
2 (*technical*) *the fireplaces were distressed* **age**, season, condition, mellow, weather, simulate age in; damage, spoil, dent, scratch, chip, batter.
OPPOSITE restore.

distressing ▶ **adjective** *it was distressing to hear her talking like that* **upsetting**, worrying, affecting, painful, traumatic, agonizing, harrowing, tormenting; sad, saddening, pitiful, heartbreaking, heart-rending, tragic, haunting; disturbing, unsettling, disquieting; shocking, alarming; *informal* gut-wrenching; *rare* distressful.
OPPOSITE comforting.

distribute ▶ **verb 1** *his property was sold and the proceeds distributed among his creditors* **give out**, deal out, hand out/round, issue, dispense, administer, pass round, dole out, dispose of; **allocate**, allot, apportion, assign, share out, divide out/up, measure out, mete out, parcel out, ration out; *informal* divvy up, dish out.
OPPOSITE collect.
2 *the newsletter is distributed free to all staff* **circulate**, issue; hand out, deliver, convey, transmit.
3 *the cuckoo family is very large, with a hundred and thirty different species distributed worldwide* **disperse**, diffuse, disseminate, scatter, spread, strew.

distribution ▶ **noun 1** *the distribution of charity* **giving out**, dealing out, handing out/round, issue, issuing, issuance, dispensation, administering, administration, passing round, doling out; allocation, allotment, apportioning, apportionment, assigning, assignment, sharing out, dividing up/out, division, measuring out, meting out, parcelling out, rationing out.
OPPOSITE collection.
2 *the geographical distribution of plants* **dispersal**, diffusion, dissemination, scattering, spread; placement, position, location, disposition, arrangement, organization; grouping, classification, assortment.
3 *the towns were the centres of food distribution* **supply**, supplying, delivery, transport, transportation, conveyance, dispatch, handling, mailing.
4 *this approach could involve studying the statistical distribution of the problem* **frequency**, probability, prevalence, incidence, commonness, weighting.

district *See centre pages for lists of administrative* **Districts** *and* **Districts of a City**
▶ **noun** *the business district of Manila* **neighbourhood**, area, region, place, locality, locale, community, quarter, sector, vicinity, zone, territory, block, part, spot, patch, domain; administrative division, ward, parish, constituency, department; *informal* neck of the woods; *Brit. informal* manor; *N. Amer. informal* turf.

distrust ▶ **noun** *the general distrust of authority amongst drug users* **mistrust**, **suspicion**, wariness, chariness, lack of trust, lack of confidence, lack of faith; scepticism, doubt, doubtfulness, dubiety, cynicism; misgivings, questioning, qualms; disbelief, unbelief, incredulity, incredulousness, discredit; *informal* leeriness.
OPPOSITE trust.
▶ **verb** *for some reason Aunt Louise distrusted him* **mistrust**, be suspicious of, be wary/chary of, regard with suspicion, suspect, look askance at, have no confidence/faith in; be sceptical of, have doubts about, doubt, be unsure of/about, be unconvinced about, take with a pinch/grain of salt; have misgivings about, wonder about, question; disbelieve (in), not believe, discredit, discount, be incredulous of; *informal* be leery of, smell a rat.
OPPOSITE trust.

distrustful ▶ **adjective** *he was distrustful of local politicians* **mistrustful**, **suspicious**, chary, apprehensive, lacking trust, lacking confidence, lacking faith; sceptical, unsure, doubtful, dubious, cynical; cautious, circumspect, careful, wary, uneasy; questioning, disbelieving, unbelieving, incredulous; *informal* leery, cagey.
OPPOSITE trusting.

disturb ▶ **verb 1** *we need somewhere where we won't be disturbed while we have our chat* **interrupt**, intrude on, butt in on, barge in on; **distract**, interfere with, disrupt, bother, trouble, pester, plague, harass, molest; *informal* horn in on, hassle.
2 *he does not want his books and papers disturbed* **disarrange**, **muddle**, rearrange, disorganize, disorder, mix up, interfere with; confuse, throw into disorder/confusion, derange, get into a tangle; unsettle, convulse, turn upside down, make a mess of.
3 *the surface waters are constantly disturbed by winds* **agitate**, churn up, stir up, whisk, beat, convulse, ruffle; *literary* roil.
4 *he wasn't disturbed by all the allegations* **perturb**, trouble, concern, worry, upset; agitate, fluster, discomfit, disconcert, dismay, distress, discompose, unsettle, ruffle, stir up; alarm, frighten, startle, shake; confuse, bewilder, perplex, confound, daze, excite.
5 *his mother had told him not to disturb himself* **inconvenience**, put out, put to trouble, discommode.

disturbance ▶ **noun 1** *we oppose the new filling station because we are concerned about disturbance to local residents* **disruption**, distraction, interference, bother, trouble, inconvenience, upset, annoyance, irritation; interruption, intrusion; harassment, molestation; *informal* hassle.
2 *the Tsar's policies gave rise to disturbances among the peasantry* **riot**, fracas, affray, upheaval, brawl, street fight, melee, free-for-all; uproar, commotion, row, ruckus, furore, tumult, turmoil; *W. Indian* bangarang; *informal* ruction, hullabaloo, rumpus.
3 *the seal disappeared underwater, leaving ripples of disturbance* **agitation**, churning (up), stirring (up), whisking, beating, convulsion, ruffling; *literary* roiling.
OPPOSITE stillness.
4 *poor educational performance is related to emotional disturbance* **trouble**, perturbation, distress, concern, worry, upset; **agitation**, discomposure, discomfiture, dismay, fluster, alarm; **neurosis**, illness, sickness, disorder, complaint; bewilderment, perplexity; *rare* disconcertion, disconcertment.
OPPOSITE stability.

disturbed ▶ **adjective 1** *he woke early after a disturbed sleep* **disrupted**, interrupted, fitful, disconnected, discontinuous, intermittent, fragmentary, broken.
OPPOSITE undisturbed.
2 *a home for disturbed children* **troubled**, distressed, unsettled, upset, distraught; unbalanced, unstable, disordered, dysfunctional, maladjusted, ill-adjusted; **neurotic**, emotionally confused, unhinged; *informal* screwed up, mixed up, messed up, hung up.
OPPOSITE well adjusted.

disturbing ▶ adjective *this is disturbing news* **worrying**, perturbing, troubling, upsetting; distressing, agitating, discomfiting, disconcerting, disquieting, unsettling, off-putting, dismaying, discomposing; alarming, frightening, threatening, startling, devastating; *informal* gut-wrenching.

disunion ▶ noun *his rejection of disunion was consistent with his nationalism* **breaking up**, dismantling, separation, dissolution, partition; splitting, parting, severance, schism.
OPPOSITE federation.

disunite ▶ verb *these nations are never to be disunited* **break up**, separate, divide, split up, partition, segregate, part, dismantle; sever, disjoin, disperse; *archaic* sunder, rive.
OPPOSITES unite, unify.

disunity ▶ noun *there was disunity within the administration* **disagreement**, dissent, dissension, argument, arguing, quarrelling, difference of opinion, feuding; conflict, strife, friction, discord, division, disharmony, acrimony, disaffection, disaccord, discordance.
OPPOSITE unity.

disuse ▶ noun *many of the mills fell into disuse* **non-use**, non-employment, lack of use; **neglect**, abandonment, desertion; cessation, discontinuance, obsolescence; *formal* desuetude.
OPPOSITES use, employment.

disused ▶ adjective *a disused building* **unused**, no longer in use, fallen into disuse, unemployed, idle; neglected, abandoned, deserted, vacated, evacuated, unoccupied, uninhabited, empty; discontinued, obsolete, defunct, superannuated, moribund.
OPPOSITE in use.

ditch ▶ noun *she rescued an animal from a ditch* **trench**, trough, channel, dyke, drain, gutter, gully, moat, duct, watercourse, conduit; ha-ha; *technical* fosse; *historical* sap; *rare* fleet.
▶ verb **1** *they started draining and ditching the coastal areas* **dig a ditch in**, provide with ditches, trench, excavate, drain.
2 (*informal*) *she decided to ditch her old curtains | the plans were ditched following a public inquiry* **throw out**, throw away, discard, get rid of, dispose of, do away with, shed; abandon, drop, shelve, scrap, jettison, throw on the scrap heap; *informal* dump, junk, scrub, axe, get shut of, chuck (away/out), pull the plug on, knock on the head; *Brit. informal* get shot of; *N. Amer. informal* trash.
OPPOSITE keep.
3 (*informal*) *she ditched her husband to marry the window cleaner* **break up with**, jilt, cast aside, throw over, finish with; leave, desert, abandon, turn one's back on, leave high and dry, leave in the lurch; *informal* dump, drop, chuck, run out on, walk out on, give someone the elbow, give someone the heave-ho, leave someone holding the baby; *Brit. informal* give someone the push, give someone the big E; *archaic* forsake.

dither ▶ verb *they wasted several minutes while she dithered* **hesitate**, falter, waver, teeter, vacillate, oscillate, fluctuate, change one's mind, be in two minds, be ambivalent, be indecisive, be unsure, be undecided; procrastinate, hang back, delay, stall, temporize, drag one's feet, dawdle, dally; *Brit.* hum and haw, haver; *Scottish* swither; *informal* shilly-shally, dilly-dally, blow hot and cold, pussyfoot around, sit on the fence.

diurnal ▶ adjective **1** *the patient's mood is determined by diurnal events* **daily**, everyday, day-to-day, quotidian; occurring every day, occurring each day; *technical* circadian.
2 *flight demands good eyesight, so birds tend to be diurnal | a diurnal predator* **active during the day**, non-nocturnal; daytime.

divan ▶ noun *Zoe curled up on a divan* **day bed**, sofa bed, settee, sofa, couch; *Brit.* put-you-up; *N. Amer.* davenport, studio couch.

dive ▶ verb **1** *they strip off and dive into the clear water | the plane was diving towards the ground* **plunge**, plummet, nosedive, descend, jump, fall, drop, swoop, pitch, bellyflop.
2 *the islanders dive for oysters* **swim under water**, go under water, submerge, sink; snorkel, scuba dive.
3 *he opened fire, forcing them to dive for cover* **leap**, jump, lunge, launch oneself, throw oneself, go headlong, bolt, dart, dash, rush, scurry; duck, dodge.
▶ noun **1** *he made daredevil dives into the pool* **plunge**, plummet, nosedive, descent, jump, fall, drop, swoop, pitch, bellyflop; *archaic* plump.
2 *she made a sideways dive between a couple of stalls* **lunge**, spring, jump, leap, bolt, dart, dash, dodge.
3 (*informal*) *John got into a fight in some dive* **sleazy bar**, sleazy nightclub, drinking den; *informal* drinking joint, seedy joint, dump, hole.

diverge ▶ verb **1** *the two roads diverged* **separate**, part, disunite, fork, branch off, divide, subdivide, split, go in different directions, go separate ways; *technical* bifurcate, divaricate, ramify.
OPPOSITE converge.
2 *there are inevitably areas where our views diverge* **differ**, be different, be unlike, be dissimilar; disagree, be at variance, be at odds, be incompatible, come into conflict, conflict, clash.
OPPOSITE agree.
3 *suddenly he diverged from his text* **deviate**, digress, depart, veer, swerve, turn away, turn aside, branch off, drift, stray; ramble, wander, meander, maunder; get sidetracked, stray from the point, get off the subject; *rare* divagate.

divergence ▶ noun **1** *the divergence of the human and great ape lineages* **separation**, dividing, parting, forking, branching; fork, division; *technical* bifurcation.
2 *there is a marked political divergence between them* **difference**, dissimilarity, variance, polarity, disparity, contrast; disagreement, discrepancy, incompatibility, mismatch, conflict, clash; *rare* unlikeness, dissimilitude.
OPPOSITE similarity.
3 *they record any divergence from standard behaviour* **deviation**, digression, departure, shift, drift, drifting, straying, deflection, wandering, moving away; variation, change, alteration; *rare* divagation.

divergent ▶ adjective **1** *they adopted divergent approaches to almost every issue* **differing**, varying, different, dissimilar, unlike, unalike, disparate, contrasting, contrastive, antithetical; opposed, disagreeing, conflicting, clashing, incompatible, contradictory; at odds, at variance, in opposition.
OPPOSITE similar.
2 *divergent statistical results* **separating**, divagating, deviating, digressing, abnormal, aberrant.

divers ▶ adjective (*literary*) *he stood accused of divers abuses and misdemeanours* **several**, many, numerous, a number of, multiple, manifold, multifarious, multitudinous; sundry, miscellaneous, assorted, various, a variety of, varying, different; *informal* a mixed bag of; *literary* myriad, legion.

diverse ▶ adjective *the company has to manage data from diverse databases* **various**, many and various, sundry, manifold, multiple; varied, varying, miscellaneous, assorted, mixed, diversified, divergent, variegated, heterogeneous; different, differing, distinct, unlike, dissimilar, distinctive, contrasting, conflicting; *informal* a mixed bag of; *literary* divers, myriad, legion; *rare* contrastive.
OPPOSITES similar, uniform.

diversify ▶ verb **1** *farmers were forced to look for ways to diversify* **branch out**, vary output, expand, enlarge operations, extend operations, spread one's wings, broaden one's horizons.
2 *the government launched a plan aimed at diversifying the economy* **vary**, bring variety to, variegate, mix; modify, alter, change, transform; expand, enlarge, widen; *rare* permutate.

diversion ▶ noun **1** *the development requires the diversion of 19 rivers* **re-routing**, redirection, turning aside, deflection, digression, deviation, divergence.
2 *there are traffic diversions along roads into Wales* **detour**, deviation, alternative route, bypass.
3 *the bomb threats were intended to create a diversion* **distraction**, disturbance, smokescreen.
4 *London is a city full of diversions | she was desperate for a little diversion* **entertainment**, amusement, recreation, pastime, game, hobby; fun, relaxation, rest and relaxation, relief, play, pleasure, delight, merriment, enjoyment, beguilement; *informal* jollies, R and R; *N. Amer. informal* rec; *dated* sport; *rare* divertissement.

diversity ▶ noun *a diversity of abstract design styles | a land of astonishing geographical diversity* **variety**, miscellany, assortment, mixture, mix, melange, range, array, medley, multiplicity; variation, variance, diverseness, diversification, variegation, heterogeneity, difference, unlikeness, dissimilarity, dissimilitude, distinctiveness, contrast.
OPPOSITE uniformity.

divert ▶ verb **1** *they planned to divert Siberia's rivers to desert areas* **re-route**, redirect, change the course of, draw away, turn aside, head off, deflect, avert, transfer, channel.
2 *he diverted her from her studies* **distract**, detract, sidetrack, lead away, draw away, be a distraction, put off, disturb someone's concentration.
OPPOSITE focus.
3 *only a richly variegated story can divert them* **amuse**, entertain, distract, titillate, delight, give pleasure to, beguile, enchant, interest, fascinate, occupy, absorb, engross, rivet, grip, hold the attention of; *informal* tickle someone's fancy, tickle pink, bowl over, be a hit with; *archaic* recreate.
OPPOSITE bore.

diverting ▶ adjective *a diverting comedy about two New York kids* **entertaining**, amusing, fun, enjoyable, pleasurable, pleasing, pleasant, agreeable, delightful, appealing, beguiling, captivating, engaging, interesting, fascinating, intriguing, absorbing, riveting, compelling; humorous, funny, witty, droll, comical, hilarious.
OPPOSITE boring.

divest ▶ verb **1** *he intends to divest you of all your power* **deprive**, strip, dispossess, relieve; rob, cheat out of, trick out of, do out of; *informal* diddle out of; *literary* despoil; *archaic* reave.
2 (*dated*) *she divested him of his coat* **strip**, relieve, denude; remove, take off, pull off, peel off, shed; unclothe, undress, disrobe; *dated* doff.

divide ▶ verb **1** *he divided his kingdom into four* **split**, cut up, cleave, carve up, slice up, chop up, split up; dissect, bisect, halve, quarter; *archaic* sunder, rive; *rare* fractionate, disjoin.
OPPOSITES unify, join.
2 *a curtain divided her cabin from the galley* **separate**, segregate, partition,

detach, disconnect, screen off, section off, split off, demarcate, distinguish; sever, rend.
OPPOSITES unify, join.
3 *the stairs divide at the mezzanine* **diverge**, separate, part, branch, branch off, fork, split, split in two, go in different directions, go separate ways; *technical* divaricate, bifurcate, furcate, ramify.
OPPOSITE converge.
4 *the time came to divide Aunt Bessie's property | Jack* **divided up** *the rest of the cash* **share out**, allocate, allot, apportion, portion out, ration out, measure out, mete out, parcel out, deal out, dole out, hand out, distribute, dispense; split, carve up, slice up, break up; *informal* divvy up, dish out; *rare* admeasure.
5 *he aimed to divide and defeat his party's opponents* **disunite**, drive apart, break up, split up; detach, divorce, separate, isolate, estrange, alienate, disaffect; set against one another, pit against one another, cause disagreement among, sow dissension among, drive a wedge between, set at variance, set at odds, come between; *archaic* sunder, tear asunder; *rare* dichotomize, factionalize, dissever.
OPPOSITE unite.
6 *biologists divide living things into three broad categories* **classify**, sort, sort out, categorize, order, group, pigeonhole, grade, rank; organize, arrange, dispose; separate, segregate, partition.
OPPOSITE combine.
▶ **noun** *the school system reinforces the sectarian divide* **breach**, gulf, gap, split, divergence, differentiation; borderline, boundary, dividing line.

dividend ▶ **noun 1** *the shareholder receives a substantial annual dividend* **share**, portion, percentage, premium, return, payback, gain, surplus, profit; *informal* cut, take, rake-off, divvy, whack, slice of the cake, piece of the action, pickings.
2 *the research will produce dividends for future heart patients* **benefit**, advantage, gain, bonus, extra, added extra, plus, fringe benefit, additional benefit; *informal* perk; *formal* perquisite.
OPPOSITE disadvantage.

divination ▶ **noun** *she looked to divination for guidance when important decisions loomed* **fortune telling**, divining, foretelling the future, forecasting the future, prophecy, prediction, soothsaying, augury; **clairvoyance**, second sight; magic, sorcery, witchcraft, spell-working; *rare* vaticination, sortilege, auspication, witchery.
WORD LINKS
relating to divination **mantic, -mancy, (e.g.** ***geomancy, necromancy*****)**

divine[1] ▶ **adjective 1** *Jesus is one person in both divine and human natures | he asked for divine guidance* **godly**, godlike, angelic, seraphic, saintly, beatific; spiritual, heavenly, celestial, holy; *rare* empyrean, deiform, deific.
OPPOSITE mortal.
2 *he could not be persuaded to attend divine worship* **religious**, holy, sacred, sanctified, consecrated, blessed, devotional, devoted to God, dedicated to God.
3 *(informal) don't you think he looks rather divine? | we ate the most divine food* **lovely**, handsome, beautiful, good-looking, prepossessing, charming, delightful, appealing, engaging, winsome, ravishing, gorgeous, bewitching, beguiling; wonderful, glorious, marvellous, excellent, superlative, perfect; delicious, mouth-watering, delectable; *Scottish & N. English* bonny; *informal* heavenly, sublime, dreamy, sensational, knockout, stunning, super, great, tasty, fanciable, easy on the eye, a sight for sore eyes, as nice as pie; *Brit. informal* brilliant, brill, smashing; *N. Amer. informal* cute; *Austral./NZ informal* beaut; *formal* beauteous; *dated* taking; *archaic* comely, fair; *rare* sightly.
OPPOSITES mundane; dreadful.
▶ **noun** *puritan divines were concentrated on the salvation of the human soul* **theologian**, clergyman, member of the clergy, churchman, churchwoman, cleric, ecclesiastic, man of the cloth, man of God, holy man, holy woman, preacher, priest; *Scottish* kirkman; *informal* reverend, Holy Joe, sky pilot; *Austral. informal* josser.

divine[2] ▶ **verb 1** *Fergus had divined how afraid she was* **guess**, surmise, conjecture, suspect, suppose, assume, presume, deduce, infer, work out, theorize, hypothesize; **discern**, intuit, perceive, recognize, see, realize, appreciate, understand, grasp, apprehend, comprehend; *N. Amer.* figure; *informal* figure out, latch on to, cotton on to, catch on to, tumble to, get, get the picture; *Brit. informal* twig, suss; *N. Amer. informal* savvy; *rare* cognize.
2 *they had divined through omens that this was an auspicious day* **foretell**, predict, prophesy, forecast, foresee, prognosticate; forewarn, forebode; *archaic* previse, presage, foreshow, croak; *Scottish archaic* spae; *rare* vaticinate, auspicate.
3 *he divined water supplies for desert troops* **dowse**, find by dowsing.

diviner ▶ **noun** *she asked a diviner about her son's prospects* **fortune teller**, **clairvoyant**, crystal-gazer, visionary, psychic, seer, soothsayer, prognosticator, prophesier, prophet, prophetess, oracle, sibyl, sage, wise man, wise woman; *Scottish* spaewife, spaeman; *rare* oracler, vaticinator, haruspex.

divinity ▶ **noun 1** *they attacked the doctrine of the trinity and denied Christ's divinity* **divine nature**, divineness, godliness, deity, godhead, holiness, sanctity, sanctitude, sacredness, blessedness.
2 *they persuaded him to read mathematics, not divinity* **theology**, religious studies, religion, scripture.
3 *the ancient religions worshipped a female divinity* **deity**, god, goddess, mother goddess, divine being, celestial being, supreme being; creator, demiurge; godhead; daemon, numen, power; *Hinduism* avatar.

division *See centre pages for lists of administrative* **Districts** *and* **Districts of a City**
▶ **noun 1** *they protested against the division of the island | a special kind of cell division* **dividing**, dividing up, breaking up, break-up, cutting up, carving up, severance, splitting, dissection, bisection, cleaving; **partitioning**, separation, segregation, disconnection, detachment.
2 *she supervised the division of his estates* **sharing out**, dividing up, parcelling out, allocation, allotment, apportionment, distribution, dispensation, disbursement; splitting up, carving up, slicing up; *informal* divvying up, dishing out.
OPPOSITE integration.
3 *the division between nomadic and urban cultures* **dividing line**, divide, boundary, boundary line, borderline, border, partition, margin, demarcation line, line of demarcation, cut-off point.
4 *each of these classes is divided into nine divisions* **section**, subsection, subdivision, part, portion, piece, bit, segment, slice, fragment, chunk, component, share; compartment, category, class, group, grouping, set, order, batch, family.
5 *an independent division of the Health and Safety Executive* **department**, branch, arm, wing, sector, section, subsection, subdivision, subsidiary, detachment, office, bureau, offshoot, satellite, extension.
6 *the causes of social division were analysed* **disunity**, disunion, conflict, discord, disagreement, dissension, disaffection, estrangement, alienation, isolation, detachment; variance, difference; difference of opinion, feud, breach, rupture, split, chasm; *informal* falling-out; *rare* scission.
OPPOSITE unity.
WORD LINKS
related prefix **schizo- (e.g.** ***schizocarp*****)**

divisive ▶ **adjective** *they declared outrage at the divisive effects of government policy* **alienating**, estranging, isolating, schismatic; discordant, disharmonious, inharmonious.
OPPOSITE unifying.

divorce ▶ **noun 1** *his wife announced that she wanted a divorce | the church did not permit divorce* **dissolution**, annulment, official separation, judicial separation, separation, disunion, break-up, split, split-up, severance, rupture, breach, parting; *(in Islamic law)* khula, talaq.
OPPOSITE marriage.
2 *there was a growing divorce between the church and people* **separation**, division, severance, split, partition, disunity, disunion, distance, estrangement, alienation; variance, difference, schism, gulf, chasm.
OPPOSITE unity.
▶ **verb 1** *she was a young child when her parents divorced | Rebecca divorced her husband* **split up (with)**, end one's marriage (to), get a divorce (from), separate (from), part (from), split (from), break up (with), part company (with), dissolve one's marriage (to), annul one's marriage (to); repudiate; *Brit. informal* bust up (with).
OPPOSITE marry.
2 *what is learnt in school cannot be divorced from what happens outside* **separate**, disconnect, divide, disunite, sever, disjoin, split, dissociate, detach, isolate, alienate, set apart, keep apart, cut off; *archaic* sunder; *rare* dissever.
OPPOSITE unite.

divulge ▶ **verb** *he refused to divulge Father O'Neill's whereabouts* **disclose**, reveal, make known, tell, impart, communicate, pass on, publish, broadcast, proclaim, promulgate, declare; expose, uncover, make public, go public with, bring into the open, give away, let slip, let drop, blurt out, leak, confess, betray, admit, come out with; *informal* spill the beans about, let the cat out of the bag about, let on about, tell all about, blow the lid off, squeal about; *Brit. informal* blow the gaff on; *archaic* discover, unbosom.
OPPOSITE conceal.

dizzy ▶ **adjective 1** *she loved spinning in circles and making herself dizzy* **giddy**, light-headed, faint, weak, weak at the knees, unsteady, shaky, wobbly, off-balance; reeling, staggering, tottering, teetering; *informal* woozy, with legs like jelly, with rubbery legs; *rare* vertiginous.
2 *she was still dizzy from her long sleep* **dazed**, confused, muddled, befuddled, bewildered, disoriented, disorientated, stupefied, groggy; *informal* woozy, muzzy, dopey, woolly, woolly-headed, not with it, discombobulated.
OPPOSITE clear-headed.
3 *the gondola cable car will take you to dizzy heights* **giddy-making**, dizzy-making, causing dizziness, causing giddiness; *rare* vertiginous.
4 *(informal) she's not as dizzy as she sounds* **silly**, foolish, giddy, light-headed, scatty, scatterbrained, feather-brained, hare-brained, empty-headed, vacuous, stupid, brainless; skittish, flighty, fickle, capricious, whimsical, inconstant; *informal* dippy, dopey, batty, dotty, nutty; *N. Amer. informal* ditzy.
OPPOSITES sensible; intelligent.

D

do ▶ verb **1** *she is expected to do most of the manual work* **carry out**, undertake, discharge, execute, perpetrate, perform, accomplish, implement, achieve, complete, finish, conclude; bring about, engineer, effect, realize; *informal* pull off; *rare* effectuate.
2 *they are free to do as they please* **act**, behave, conduct oneself, acquit oneself; *rare* comport oneself, deport oneself.
3 *if you can't get espresso, regular coffee will do* **suffice**, be adequate, be satisfactory, be acceptable, be good enough, be of use, fill the bill, fit the bill, answer the purpose, serve the purpose, meet one's needs, pass muster; be enough, be sufficient; *informal* make the grade, cut the mustard, be up to snuff.
4 *the boys will do the dinner when they get home* **prepare**, make, get ready, fix, produce, see to, arrange, organize, be responsible for, be in charge of, look after, take on.
5 *he noticed a portrait I had been doing | the company have done a small range of V-neck tops* **paint**, draw, sketch; **make**, create, produce, turn out, fashion, design, fabricate, manufacture; *informal* knock up, knock together, knock off.
6 *each room was done in a different colour* **decorate**, furnish, adorn, ornament, embellish; deck out, trick out, trim; *informal* do up; *Brit. informal* tart up.
7 *her maid would dress her and then do her hair* **style**, arrange, adjust, groom, preen, primp, prink; brush, comb, wash, dry, cut; *informal* fix.
8 *I was doing a show to raise money for our local scouts* **put on**, present, produce, give; perform in, act in, play in, take part in, participate in, be involved in, be engaged in.
9 *thanks—you've done me a favour* **grant**, pay, render, afford, give, bestow.
10 *I'm doing the VAT on a multiple dispatch | show me how these equations should be done* **work out**, figure out, calculate, add up; solve, resolve, puzzle out, decipher; *Brit.* tot up.
11 *she's doing archaeology at university* **study**, read, learn, take a course in, take classes in, be taught.
12 *what does he do?* **do for a living**, work at, be employed as, earn a living as/at; what is ...'s job?
13 *he was doing well at college* **get on**, get along, progress, fare, make out, get by, manage, cope, survive; succeed, prosper.
14 *he was caught doing 80mph in a 50mph area* **drive at**, travel at, go at, proceed at, move at.
15 *the cyclists do 30 to 40 miles per day* **travel**, journey, go, cover, travel over, pass over, journey over, traverse, cross, range over, put behind one, get under one's belt, attain, achieve, log; *informal* chalk up, notch up.
16 (*informal*) *we're doing Scotland this summer* **visit**, tour, sightsee in, look around/round, take in the sights of.

□ **do away with 1** *they want to do away with the old customs* **abolish**, quash, get rid of, discard, remove, eliminate, discontinue, cancel, stop, end, terminate, put an end to, put a stop to, call a halt to, dispense with, drop, abandon, give up; *informal* bin, scrap, ditch, dump, axe, cut out, pack in, get shut of, pull the plug on, knock something on the head, give something the chop; *Brit. informal* get shot of.
OPPOSITE uphold.
2 *she tried to do away with her husband* **kill**, put to death, do to death, put an end to, finish off, take the life of, end the life of, murder, assassinate, execute, slaughter, butcher, wipe out, mow down, shoot down, cut down; dispatch, liquidate, exterminate, eliminate, eradicate, destroy; *informal* do in, bump off, knock off, polish off, top, take out, snuff out, snuff, erase, croak, stiff, zap, blow away, blow someone's brains out, give someone the works; *N. Amer. informal* ice, off, rub out, waste, whack, scrag, smoke; *N. Amer. euphemistic* terminate with extreme prejudice; *literary* slay.

□ **do someone/something down** (*informal*) *he loves an opportunity to do down his colleagues* **belittle**, disparage, denigrate, run down, deprecate, depreciate, cast aspersions on, discredit, vilify, defame, decry, criticize, abuse, insult, malign; *N. Amer.* slur; *informal* do a hatchet job on, take to pieces, take apart, pull apart, pick holes in, drag through the mud, have a go at, hit out at, knock, slam, pan, bash, bad-mouth, look down one's nose at; *Brit. informal* rubbish, slate, slag off; *rare* asperse, derogate, minify.

□ **do someone/something in** (*informal*) **1** *the poor devil's been done in* **kill**, put to death, do to death, put an end to, finish off, take the life of, end the life of, murder, assassinate, execute, slaughter, butcher, wipe out, mow down, shoot down, cut down; dispatch, liquidate, exterminate, eliminate, eradicate, destroy; *informal* do away with, bump off, knock off, polish off, top, take out, snuff out, snuff, erase, croak, stiff, zap, blow away, blow someone's brains out, give someone the works; *N. Amer. informal* ice, off, rub out, waste, whack, scrag, smoke; *N. Amer. euphemistic* terminate with extreme prejudice; *literary* slay.
2 *the long walk home did me in* **wear out**, tire out, exhaust, fatigue, weary, overtire, drain, prostrate, enervate, devitalize; *informal* fag out, shatter, whack, poop, take it out of.
3 *I did my back in and I can't work any more* **injure**, hurt, damage, maim, cripple, disable, paralyse; *Brit. informal* knacker.

□ **do something out** (*Brit. informal*) *the basement is done out in limed oak* **decorate**, furnish, adorn, ornament, embellish; deck out, trick out, trim; *informal* do up; *Brit. informal* tart up.

□ **do someone out of something** *he tried to do them out of their livestock profits* **swindle out of**, cheat out of, trick out of, prevent from having, prevent from gaining, deprive of, dispossess of, rob of, strip of, relieve of; *informal* con out of, diddle out of.

□ **do something up 1** *she stopped to do her bootlace up* **fasten**, tie, tie up, lace, knot, make a knot in, tie a bow in; make fast, secure, bind, tighten.
OPPOSITE undo.
2 (*informal*) *he's had his house done up* **renovate**, refurbish, refit, restore, redecorate, decorate, revamp, make over, modernize, improve, spruce up, smarten up, brighten up, prettify, enhance; *informal* fix up, vamp up, give something a facelift; *Brit. informal* tart up, posh up; *N. Amer. informal* rehab.

□ **do without** *they were forced to do without certain bodily comforts* **forgo**, dispense with, abstain from, refrain from, eschew, give up, renounce, forswear, swear off, keep off, keep away from, manage without; *informal* lay off, cut out, quit, give something a miss.

▶ noun (*Brit. informal*) *he invited us to this do in his mansion* **party**, reception, gathering, celebration, function, affair, event, social event, social occasion, social function, social; *French* soirée; *W. Indian* jump-up; *Jewish* simcha; *N. Amer.* levee; *informal* bash, blowout, rave, shindig, shindy, shebang, junket; *Brit. informal* rave-up, thrash, knees-up, jolly, beanfeast, bunfight, beano; *Austral./NZ informal* shivoo, rage, jollo; *S. African informal* jol; *informal, dated* ding-dong.

docile ▶ adjective *Alex was of a docile nature and readily deferred to his parents* **compliant**, obedient, pliant, dutiful, willing, passive, submissive, deferential, tame, meek, mild, lamblike, unassertive, unresisting, yielding, cooperative, amenable, accommodating, biddable, persuadable, ductile, manageable, controllable, tractable, malleable, manipulable, easily manipulated, easily handled, like putty in one's hands; *informal, dated* milky; *rare* persuasible.
OPPOSITES disobedient; wilful.

> **CHOOSE THE RIGHT WORD**
>
> **docile, obedient, biddable, compliant, dutiful**
>
> *See* OBEDIENT.

dock[1] ▶ noun *his boat was moored at the end of the dock* **harbour**, marina, waterfront, port, anchorage; wharf, quay, pier, jetty, landing stage; dockyard, boatyard; *archaic* hithe; *rare* moorage, harbourage.
▶ verb *the ship docked and began debarking troops* **moor**, berth, land, beach, anchor, drop anchor, put in, tie up.
OPPOSITE put to sea.

dock[2] ▶ verb **1** *they enforce payment by docking money from the father's salary* **deduct**, subtract, remove, debit, discount, take off, take away; *informal* knock off, minus.
OPPOSITE add.
2 *workers had their pay docked by three quarters* **reduce**, cut, cut back, decrease, lessen, diminish.
OPPOSITE increase.
3 *the dog's tail is docked close to the body* **cut off**, cut short, shorten, crop, lop, prune, truncate; remove, amputate, detach, disconnect, sever, hack off, chop off, take off; *rare* dissever.

docket (*Brit.*) ▶ noun *they write out an individual docket for every transaction* **document**, chit, coupon, voucher, certificate, counterfoil, bill, receipt, sales slip, proof of purchase; label, tag, ticket, tab; documentation, paperwork; *Brit. informal* chitty; *Law, dated* acquittance.
▶ verb *neatly docketed bundles* **document**, record, register, log; label, tag, tab, mark, ticket.

doctor *See centre pages for list of* **Doctors and Dentists**
▶ noun *Tim isn't well but he refuses to see a doctor* **physician**, medical practitioner, medical man, medical woman, clinician, doctor of medicine, MD; *Navy* surgeon; *informal* doc, medic, medico, quack; *archaic* leech, sawbones.
▶ verb **1** (*informal*) *he doctored the horses' wounds with some strong-smelling salve* **treat**, medicate, dose, soothe, cure, heal; tend, attend to, minister to, administer to, care for, take care of, nurse.
2 *he denied doctoring Stephen's drinks* **adulterate**, contaminate, taint, tamper with, lace, mix, dilute, water down, thin out, weaken; *informal* spike, dope, cut, slip a Mickey Finn into; *rare* vitiate.
3 *the reports are bland and could have been doctored* **falsify**, tamper with, tinker with, interfere with, manipulate, massage, rig, alter, change; forge, fake, trump up; fudge, pervert, distort; *informal* cook, juggle; *Brit. informal* fiddle (with).

WORD LINKS
related prefix iatro- (e.g. ***iatrogenic***)

doctrinaire ▶ adjective *democratic socialism was feared by doctrinaire Marxists* **dogmatic**, rigid, inflexible, uncompromising, unyielding, holding fixed views, adamant, insistent, pontifical; authoritarian, domineering, opinionated, intolerant, biased, prejudiced, fanatical, zealous, extreme.
OPPOSITES liberal; flexible.

doctrine ▶ noun *they rejected the doctrine of the Trinity* **creed**, credo, dogma, belief, set of beliefs, code of belief, conviction, teaching; tenet, maxim, article of faith, canon; principle, precept, notion, idea, ideology, theory, thesis.

document ▶ noun *their solicitor drew up a document* **official paper**, legal paper, paper, form, certificate, deed, charter, contract, legal agreement; record, report; *Law* instrument, indenture, acquittance; (**documents**) paperwork, documentation; *informal* treeware.

▶ verb *many aspects of school life have been documented* **record**, register, report, log, chronicle, file, archive, catalogue, put on record, commit to paper, set down, take down, write down, set down in writing, set down in black and white, write about; detail, note, describe, cite, instance; tabulate, chart; *rare* diarize.

D

documentary ▶ adjective **1** *there is documentary evidence that a corn mill stood here in the 14th century* **recorded**, documented, registered, written, chronicled, archived, archive, on record, in writing, on paper; tabulated, charted.
2 *the event will be the subject of a documentary film* **factual**, non-fictional, real-life, true to life, fact-based.
OPPOSITE fictional.

▶ noun *the BBC showed a documentary about life in rural England* **factual programme**, factual film; programme, film, report, presentation, broadcast, transmission.

dodder ▶ verb *the old couple doddered out of the hotel lounge* **totter**, teeter, toddle, hobble, shuffle, shamble, falter, walk haltingly, walk with difficulty, move falteringly, stumble, stagger, sway, lurch, reel; wobble, shake, tremble, quiver; *Scottish & N. English* hirple; *rare* doddle.

doddering ▶ adjective *a doddering old man with an ear trumpet* **tottering**, tottery, teetering, doddery, staggering, shuffling, shambling, faltering, shaking, shaky, unsteady, wobbly, wobbling, trembling, trembly, quivering; feeble, frail, weak, weakly, infirm, decrepit; aged, old, elderly, long in the tooth, in one's dotage, senile.
OPPOSITE sprightly.

doddery ▶ adjective *a doddery old lady. See* DODDERING.

dodge ▶ verb **1** *she dodged into a telephone booth* **dart**, bolt, duck, dive, swerve, body-swerve, sidestep, veer, lunge, jump, leap, spring.
2 *he could easily dodge the two coppers in the car* **elude**, evade, avoid, stay away from, steer clear of, escape, run away from, break away from, lose, leave behind, shake, shake off, fend off, keep at arm's length, give someone a wide berth, keep one's distance from; deceive, trick, cheat; *N. Amer.* end-run; *informal* ditch, give someone the slip.
3 *the Secretary of State may try to dodge the debate* **avoid**, evade, shun, get out of, slide out of, back out of, steer clear of, sidestep, circumvent, skirt round, bypass, give something a miss, find a way out of; *informal* duck, wriggle out of, cop out of; *Brit. informal* funk, skive, skive off; *N. Amer. informal* cut; *Austral./NZ informal* duck-shove; *archaic* decline, bilk.
OPPOSITES face up to, tackle.

▶ noun **1** *he made a dodge to the right* **dart**, bolt, duck, dive, swerve, jump, leap, spring.
2 *a clever dodge for covering up the car's real origins | a tax dodge* **ruse**, ploy, scheme, tactic, stratagem, subterfuge, trick, hoax, wile, cheat, deception, blind, pretext, manoeuvre, device, machination, contrivance, artifice, expedient; swindle, fraud, loophole; *informal* scam, con, con trick, set-up, wangle; *Brit. informal* wheeze; *N. Amer. informal* bunco, grift; *Austral. informal* lurk, rort; *Brit. informal, dated* flanker; *archaic* shift.

dodgy ▶ adjective (*Brit. informal*) **1** *a dodgy second-hand car salesman. See* DISHONEST.
2 *the champagne was decidedly dodgy* **second-rate**, third-rate, substandard, low-grade, low-quality, cheap; of low quality, of poor quality, not up to scratch, not up to par; awful, terrible, dreadful, woeful, dire, deplorable, unacceptable, unsatisfactory; *Brit.* cheap and nasty; *N. Amer.* cheapjack; *informal* cheapo, tenth-rate, not up to much; *Brit. informal* ropy, grotty, duff.

doer ▶ noun **1** *she is the doer of unspeakable deeds* **performer**, perpetrator, executor, accomplisher, effectuator, operator, operative, agent, author.
2 *Daniel is a thinker more than a doer* **worker**, organizer, activist, man of action, achiever, high achiever, succeeder, hustler, entrepreneur; *informal* mover and shaker, busy bee, eager beaver, live wire, go-getter, high-flyer, whizz kid, powerhouse, fireball, human dynamo, wheeler-dealer, success story.

doff ▶ verb (*dated*) *he doffed his cap as we walked past | they doffed their tuxedos* **take off**, remove, raise, lift, touch, tip; divest oneself of, shed, strip off, pull off, peel off, climb out of, slip out of, shrug off, throw off, cast off, fling off, fling aside, discard.
OPPOSITE don.

dog *See centre pages for lists of* **Dogs** **Foxes**

▶ noun **1** *she went for long walks with her dog* **hound**, canine, mongrel, cur, tyke; **male dog**; bitch, pup, puppy, whelp; *informal* doggy, pooch, mutt; *Austral. informal* mong, bitzer.
2 (*informal*) *you black-hearted dog!* **scoundrel**, rogue, villain, cur, wretch, reprobate, good-for-nothing; *informal* beast, pig, swine, rat, creep, louse, snake, snake in the grass, skunk, weasel, lowlife, scumbag, heel, stinker, stinkpot, bad lot, nasty piece of work; *Scottish informal* scrote; *Irish informal* spalpeen; *N. Amer. informal* rat fink, fink; *informal, dated* rotter, bounder, blighter; *vulgar slang* bastard, son of a bitch, s.o.b., shit; *dated* cad; *archaic* blackguard, dastard, knave, varlet, vagabond.
3 (*informal, dated*) *George, you're a lucky dog* **fellow**, thing, individual, soul, character, creature, wretch, beggar; person, man, woman; *informal* fella, guy, devil, bunny, bastard, critter; *Brit. informal* chap, bloke, bod; *N. Amer. informal* dude, hombre, gal, dame; *informal, dated* body, cove; *vulgar slang* bugger, sod; *archaic* wight.

▶ verb *they dogged him the length and breadth of the country | the scheme was dogged by bad weather* **pursue**, follow, stalk, track, trail, shadow, hound; plague, beset, bedevil, assail, beleaguer, blight, trouble, torment, haunt; *informal* tail.

WORD LINKS

relating to dogs	**canine**
male	**dog**
female	**bitch**
young	**pup, puppy**
collective noun	**pack**
fear of dogs	**cynophobia**

dogged ▶ adjective *he was a fine player and a dogged opening batsman* **tenacious**, determined, resolute, resolved, purposeful, persistent, persevering, pertinacious, relentless, intent, dead set, single-minded, focused, dedicated, committed, undeviating, unshakeable, unflagging, indefatigable, untiring, never-tiring, tireless, unfailing, unfaltering, unwavering, unyielding, unbending, immovable, obdurate, strong-willed, firm, steadfast, steady, staunch, stout-hearted; *archaic* laborious; *rare* perseverant, indurate.
OPPOSITES hesitant; half-hearted.

dogma ▶ noun **1** *a dogma of the Sikh religion* **teaching**, belief, conviction, tenet, principle, ethic, precept, maxim, article of faith, canon, law, rule; creed, credo, code of belief, set of beliefs, set of principles, doctrine, ideology, orthodoxy.
2 *they were urged to emancipate their minds from the fetters of dogma* **blind faith**, unquestioning belief, certainty, invincible conviction, unchallengeable conviction, arrogant conviction.
OPPOSITES doubt; open-mindedness.

dogmatic ▶ adjective *he criticized the prime minister's strident, dogmatic style* **opinionated**, **peremptory**, assertive, imperative, insistent, emphatic, adamant, doctrinaire, authoritarian, authoritative, domineering, imperious, high-handed, pontifical, arrogant, overbearing, dictatorial, uncompromising, unyielding, unbending, inflexible, rigid, entrenched, unquestionable, unchallengeable; intolerant, narrow-minded, small-minded.
OPPOSITES low-key, tentative; open-minded.

dogmatism ▶ noun *he avoided dogmatism and presented his subject as one open to debate* **opinionatedness**, **peremptoriness**, assertiveness, imperativeness, doctrinairism, authoritarianism, imperiousness, high-handedness, arrogance, dictatorialness; inflexibility, rigidity, entrenchment, intolerance, narrow-mindedness, small-mindedness, bigotry.

dogsbody ▶ noun (*Brit. informal*) *she spent a year as a dogsbody in a Norwich theatre* **drudge**, menial, menial worker, factotum, man of all work, maid of all work, servant, slave, galley slave, lackey, underling, minion; hewer of wood and drawer of water; *informal* gofer, running dog, runner, man/girl Friday; *Brit. informal* skivvy; *N. Amer. informal* peon; *archaic* scullion, servitor.

doing ▶ noun **1** *the doing of the act constitutes the offence* **performance**, performing, carrying out, effecting, execution, implementation, implementing, bringing off, discharge, discharging, achievement, accomplishment, realization, completion, completing; *informal* pulling off; *archaic* acquittal; *rare* effectuation.
2 *he gave a brief account of his doings in Paris* **exploit**, activity, act, action, undertaking, deed, feat, endeavour, work, venture, enterprise, achievement, accomplishment; (**doings**) performance, behaviour, conduct; handiwork; *informal* caper.
3 *it would take some doing to diffuse the situation* **effort**, exertion, work, hard work, application, labour, toil, struggle, strain; pains; *informal* elbow grease; *literary* travail.
4 (**doings**) (*Brit. informal*) *he looked into the drawer where he kept the doings* **thing**, whatever it is (called); *informal* **whatsit**, whatnot, doofer, thingummy, thingamajig, thingamabob, what's-its-name, what-d'you-call-it, oojamaflip, oojah, gizmo; *Brit. informal* doobry, doodah, gubbins; *N. Amer. informal* doodad, doohickey, doojigger, dingus, hootenanny.

doldrums ▶ plural noun *a fit of the winter doldrums* **depression**, melancholy, gloom, gloominess, glumness, downheartedness, dejection, despondency, dispiritedness, heavy-heartedness, heartache, unhappiness, sadness, misery, woe, dismalness, despair, pessimism, hopelessness; inertia, apathy, listlessness, malaise, boredom, tedium, ennui; low spirits; *informal* blues; *N. Amer. informal* blahs.
OPPOSITE happiness.

□ **in the doldrums** *the property market is in the doldrums* **inactive**, quiet, slow, slack, sluggish, subdued, stagnant, static, inert, flat, dull.
OPPOSITES busy, lively.

dole ▶ noun **1** (*dated*) *the customary dole was a tumblerful of rice* **handout**, alms, charity; gift, donation, allowance, grant, portion.
2 (**the dole**) (*Brit. informal*) *he was out of work and on the dole* **unemployment benefit**, state benefit, government benefit, benefit, benefit payments, social security, social security payments, public assistance allowance, allowance, welfare, insurance money, grant; financial assistance; *Scottish* the buroo, the broo.
▶ verb
□ **dole something out** *Dad began to dole out the porridge* **deal out**, share out, mete out, divide up, allocate, allot, apportion, assign, distribute, dispense, hand out, give out, pass out, pass round, issue, disburse; *informal* dish out, dish up, divvy up.

doleful ▶ adjective *she regarded him with doleful eyes* **mournful**, woeful, sorrowful, sad, unhappy, depressed, dismal, gloomy, morose, melancholy, miserable, forlorn, wretched, woebegone, despondent, dejected, disconsolate, downcast, crestfallen, downhearted, heartbroken, heavy-hearted, despairing, desolate, grief-stricken; tearful, teary, lachrymose; *informal* blue, down, down in the mouth, down in the dumps, weepy; *literary* dolorous; *archaic* heartsick, heartsore.
OPPOSITE cheerful.

doll ▶ noun **1** *the child was sitting hugging a doll* **puppet**, marionette, figure, figurine, model; **toy**, plaything; *informal* dolly.
2 (*informal*) *she was quite a doll, with good teeth and nice skin* **beauty**, beautiful woman, attractive woman, belle, vision, Venus, goddess, beauty queen, English rose, picture; *informal* looker, good looker, stunner, lovely, knockout, bombshell, dish, cracker, smasher, peach, eyeful, sight for sore eyes, bit of alright.
▶ verb
□ **doll someone up** (*informal*) *she dolled herself up before he came round to dinner* **dress up**, dress smartly, dress attractively; *informal* get up, do up, tog up, dress up to the nines, put on one's glad rags; *Brit. informal* tart up.
OPPOSITE dress down.

dollop ▶ noun (*informal*) *she had a little dollop of cream on her nose* **blob**, glob, gobbet, lump, clump, ball, mound; *Brit. informal* gob, wodge.

dolorous ▶ adjective (*literary*) *a dolorous sigh.* See DOLEFUL.

dolour ▶ noun (*literary*) *the illness had long been a source of dolour to his brother.* See SORROW.

dolphin ▶ noun. *See centre pages for list of* **Whales and Dolphins**

WORD LINKS
collective noun **school**

dolt ▶ noun *he makes me feel like a dolt* **idiot**, fool, dunce, numbskull, dullard, ignoramus, ass, bonehead, nincompoop, simpleton, clown, booby; *informal* blockhead, thickhead, fathead, dunderhead, airhead, chump, dope, dimwit, goon, dumbo, dummy, nerd, halfwit, cretin, imbecile, dork; *Brit. informal* nit, nitwit, twit, clot, plonker, pillock, wally, berk, prat, wazzock, twerp, charlie, mug; *Austral./NZ informal* dingbat.

doltish ▶ adjective *the yokels are doltish but harmless* **stupid**, idiotic, moronic, imbecilic, foolish, ignorant, simple, simple-minded, dense, brainless, mindless, dull-witted, dull, slow-witted, witless, half-witted, dunce-like, slow, cretinous, empty-headed, vacuous, vapid; gullible, naive; *informal* thick, thick as two short planks, dim, dopey, dumb, dozy, birdbrained, pea-brained, pig-ignorant, bovine, slow on the uptake, soft in the head, brain-dead, boneheaded, lamebrained, chuckleheaded, dunderheaded, wooden-headed, fat-headed, muttonheaded; *Brit. informal* daft, not the full shilling; *N. Amer. informal* dumb-ass.

domain ▶ noun **1** *they extended their domain by raiding neighbouring peoples | the garden was his domain* **realm**, kingdom, empire, dominion, province, estate, territory, land, lands, dominions; state, country; **preserve**, zone, sphere, area, place; *informal* turf, spot, patch, stamping ground; *Brit. informal* manor.
2 *the report was very significant in the arts education domain* **field**, area, arena, sphere, discipline, sector, section, region, province, world.

dome ▶ noun *the dome of St Paul's Cathedral* **cupola**, vault, rotunda, arched roof, arched ceiling; mound, hemisphere.

domestic ▶ adjective **1** *her domestic commitments prevented her from returning to employment* **family**, home, private; **household**, domiciliary.
OPPOSITE public.
2 *she was not at all domestic* **housewifely**, domesticated, stay-at-home, home-loving, homely.
3 *I only treat small domestic animals* **domesticated**, tame, pet, household, trained, not wild; *Brit.* house-trained; *N. Amer.* housebroken.
OPPOSITE wild.
4 *the domestic car manufacturing industry* **national**, state, home, local, internal, interior, not foreign, not international.
OPPOSITES foreign, international.
5 *the flower garden housed domestic and exotic blooms* **native**, indigenous, home-grown, home-bred, aboriginal; *technical* autochthonous.
▶ noun *all of the cleaning was undertaken by domestics* **servant**, domestic servant, domestic worker, domestic help, hired help, home help, daily help, maid, housemaid, maid-of-all-work, cleaner, menial, housekeeper; *Brit. dated* charwoman, charlady, char; *Brit. informal* daily, daily woman, skivvy, Mrs Mop; *archaic* scullion.

domesticate ▶ verb **1** *the wild cat would have been troublesome for early man to domesticate* **tame**, train, break in, gentle; master, subdue, subjugate, bring to heel; *Brit.* house-train.
2 *maize was first domesticated in Mexico* **cultivate**, raise, rear; **naturalize**, establish, acclimatize, habituate, assimilate; *N. Amer.* acclimate.

domesticated ▶ adjective **1** *pollution harms wildlife and also domesticated animals* **tame**, tamed, pet, domestic, broken-in; *Brit.* house-trained; *N. Amer.* housebroken.
OPPOSITE wild.
2 *the researchers are studying domesticated crops* **naturalized**, acclimatized, habituated; cultivated.
OPPOSITES foreign; wild.
3 (*humorous*) *I like housework—I'm quite domesticated really* **housewifely**, stay-at-home, home-loving, homely; *Brit. informal* house-trained; *N. Amer. informal* housebroken.

domicile (*formal*) ▶ noun *military service brings about frequent changes of domicile* **residence**, **home**, house, address, residency, lodging, lodging place, accommodation, quarters, billet; *informal* pad; *Brit. informal* digs; *formal* dwelling, dwelling place, abode, habitation.
▶ verb (**be domiciled**) *born in the UK, he is now domiciled in Australia* **settle**, establish oneself, live, make one's home, set up home, set up house, take up residence, put down roots, have one's domicile; go to live in, move to, emigrate to; *N. Amer.* set up housekeeping.

dominance ▶ noun *he is in a position of political dominance* **supremacy**, superiority, ascendancy, pre-eminence, predominance, domination, dominion, mastery, power, authority, rule, command, control, sway, leverage, influence; *literary* puissance; *rare* predomination, paramountcy, prepotence, prepotency, prepollency.
OPPOSITES subservience, subjugation.

dominant ▶ adjective **1** *the dominant classes* **presiding**, ruling, governing, controlling, commanding, ascendant, supreme, authoritative, most influential, most powerful, superior; *rare* prepotent, prepollent.
OPPOSITE subservient.
2 *he has a dominant personality* **assertive**, self-assured, self-possessed, authoritative, forceful, domineering, commanding, controlling, bullish; *informal* feisty, not backward in coming forward, pushy; *rare* pushful.
OPPOSITE submissive.
3 *we will discuss the dominant issues in psychology* **main**, principal, prime, premier, chief, cardinal, foremost, uppermost, leading, primary, predominant, most important, most prominent, paramount, pre-eminent, outstanding, prominent, prevailing; central, key, crucial, core, salient; *informal* number-one.
OPPOSITE secondary.

dominate ▶ verb **1** *the British and the Russians dominated Iran in the nineteenth century* **control**, influence, exercise control over, be in control of, command, be in command of, be in charge of, rule, govern, direct, be the boss of, preside over, have ascendancy over, have mastery over, master, have the upper hand over; domineer, tyrannize, oppress, bully, intimidate, have the whip hand over, push around/about, boss (about/around), ride roughshod over, trample on, have under one's thumb; *informal* head up, call the shots, call the tune, be in the driver's seat, be in the saddle, be at the helm, rule the roost, lay down the law, walk all over; *Brit. informal* wear the trousers; *N. Amer. informal* have someone in one's hip pocket; *literary* sway.
2 *the Puritan work ethic still dominates* **predominate**, prevail, reign, be prevalent, be paramount, be pre-eminent, be most important, be influential, be significant, be of consequence, be of account, count, matter, signify, carry weight, bulk large.
3 *the village is dominated by the railway viaduct* **overlook**, command, tower above, tower over, stand over, project over, jut over, hang over, loom over, dwarf, overtop, overshadow, overhang; bestride, span, straddle, extend across.

domination ▶ noun *they believed that Communists were aiming for world domination* **rule**, government, sovereignty, control, command, authority, power, dominion, dominance, mastery, supremacy, superiority, ascendancy, sway, influence; tyranny, intimidation, oppression, suppression, subjugation, dictatorship; the upper hand, the whip hand, the edge; *rare* paramountcy, prepotence, prepotency, prepollency.

domineer ▶ verb *all her life she was domineered by Granny* **browbeat**, **bully**, intimidate, pressurize, menace, hector, boss (about/around), push around/about, order about/around, give orders to, lord it over, tyrannize, terrorize, persecute, oppress, dictate to, be overbearing, ride roughshod over, trample on, have under one's thumb, rule with an iron hand, rule with a rod of iron, use strong-arm tactics on, impose one's will on, bend to one's will, subjugate; *informal* bulldoze, walk all over, railroad, lean on, put the screws on, strong-arm, squeeze.

domineering ▶ adjective *he was brought up by a cold, domineering father* **overbearing**, authoritarian, imperious, high-handed, high and mighty, autocratic, autarchic; officious, peremptory, bossy, arrogant, haughty, masterful, forceful, coercive, bullish, dictatorial, tyrannical, draconian,

D

despotic, controlling, oppressive, subjugating, iron-fisted, iron-handed, strict, harsh, severe; *informal* throwing one's weight about; *rare* pushful.
OPPOSITE meek.

dominion ▶ noun **1** *France then decided to establish dominion over Laos and Cambodia* **supremacy**, ascendancy, dominance, domination, superiority, predominance, pre-eminence, primacy, hegemony, authority, mastery, control, command, direction, power, sway, rule, government, jurisdiction, sovereignty, suzerainty, lordship, overlordship; leadership, influence; the upper hand, the whip hand, the edge, advantage, hold, grasp; *archaic* empire; *rare* predomination, paramountcy, prepotence, prepotency, prepollency.
2 *the country was a British dominion for over eighty years* **dependency**, colony, protectorate, territory, province, outpost, satellite, satellite state; holding, possession; *historical* tributary, fief; *archaic* demesne; (**dominions**) realm, kingdom, empire, domain, country, nation, land.

don[1] ▶ noun *he had been a don at Oxford* **university teacher**, (university) lecturer, fellow, professor, reader, lector, college tutor, academic, scholar; *informal* egghead; (**dons**) *Brit.* senior common room.

don[2] ▶ verb *he donned a heavy overcoat* **put on**, get dressed in, dress (oneself) in, pull on, climb into, get into, fling on, throw on, slip into, slip on, change into, rig oneself out in, clothe oneself in, array oneself in, deck oneself out in, accoutre oneself in, put round one's shoulders, put on one's head; *informal* tog oneself up/out in, doll oneself up in, pour oneself into.
OPPOSITE take off.

donate ▶ verb *he donated his fee to charity* **give**, give/make a donation of, make a gift of, contribute, make a contribution of, present, gift, subscribe, hand out, grant, bestow, pledge, put oneself down for, put up, come up with, accord; provide, supply, furnish; endow someone with, confer on someone; *informal* chip in, pitch in, fork out, dish out, shell out, cough up; *Brit. informal* stump up; *N. Amer. informal* kick in, ante up, pony up.
OPPOSITES keep; receive.

donation ▶ noun *his employer also made a donation to the fund* **gift**, contribution, subscription, present, handout, grant, offering, gratuity, endowment; bestowal, giving; charity, benefaction, largesse; *historical* alms; *rare* donative.
OPPOSITE receipt.

done ▶ adjective **1** *a few days later the job was done* **finished**, ended, concluded, terminated, complete, completed, finalized, accomplished, achieved, realized, fulfilled, perfected, consummated, discharged, settled, executed; *informal* wrapped up, sewn up, polished off, sorted out; *rare* effectuated.
OPPOSITE incomplete.
2 *is the meat done?* **cooked**, ready, cooked through, tender, crisp, browned.
OPPOSITES underdone; raw.
3 *those days are done* **over**, at an end, finished, ended, concluded, terminated, no more, extinct, dead, run, gone, dead and gone, dead and buried, forgotten, over and done with, a thing of the past, in the past, ancient history.
OPPOSITES ongoing; to come.
4 (*informal*) *I can't do that—it's just not done* **proper**, seemly, decorous, decent, respectable, right, correct, in order, suitable, fit, fitting, befitting, appropriate, apt; conventional, approved, accepted, acceptable, standard, usual, customary, traditional, orthodox; the done thing; *French* comme il faut; *informal* OK.

□ **be done with** *she was done with him* **be/have finished with**, have done with, be through with, want no more to do with, have no further dealings with, turn one's back on, be no longer involved with/in, end relations with, give up, wash one's hands of, have no more truck with.

□ **done for** (*informal*) *if you're caught you will be done for* **ruined**, finished, destroyed, broken, wrecked, undone, doomed, lost, defeated, beaten, foiled, frustrated, thwarted; *informal* washed-up.
OPPOSITES safe; saved.

□ **done in** *you look done in* **worn out**, exhausted, fatigued, tired, tired out, weary, wearied, strained, drained, worn, sapped, spent, washed out, on one's last legs; *informal* worn to a frazzle, done, all in, dog-tired, dead on one's feet, dead beat, fit to drop, played out, fagged out, shattered, bushed; *Brit. informal* knackered, whacked; *N. Amer. informal* pooped, tuckered out.
OPPOSITE fresh.

□ **have done with** *when I put something behind me I have done with it* **be/have finished with**, be done with, be through with, want no more to do with, have no further dealings with, turn one's back on, be no longer involved with/in, end relations with, give up, wash one's hands of, have no more truck with.

▶ exclamation *'I'll lay three to one he's sane.' 'Done!'* **agreed**, settled, all right, very well, that's a bargain, accepted, right; *informal* you're on, OK, okay, oke, okey-dokey, okey-doke; *Brit. informal* righto, righty-ho.

Don Juan ▶ noun **womanizer**, philanderer, Casanova, Romeo, Lothario, flirt, ladies' man, playboy, seducer, rake, roué, libertine, debauchee, lecher; *informal* skirt-chaser, ladykiller, wolf, goat, lech; *informal, dated* gay dog.
OPPOSITE celibate.

donkey ▶ noun **1** *the cart was drawn by a donkey* **ass**; jackass, jenny; mule, hinny; *Spanish* burro; *Brit. informal* moke, neddy; *Scottish dated* cuddy.
2 (*informal*) *you silly donkey! See* FOOL.

WORD LINKS

relating to donkeys	**asinine**
male	**jackass**
female	**jennyass**

donnish ▶ adjective *you can never tell with these quiet, donnish types* **scholarly**, studious, academic, scholastic, bookish, book-loving, intellectual, erudite, educated, learned, serious, earnest, thoughtful, cerebral, highbrow; pedantic; impractical, ivory-towerish; *informal* brainy, egghead; *Brit. informal* swotty; *dated* lettered; *archaic* clerkly.

donor ▶ noun *the cost has been met by a generous donor* **giver**, contributor, benefactor, benefactress, subscriber, donator; supporter, backer, subsidizer, patron, sponsor; philanthropist; *informal* angel; *rare* benefactrice, benefactrix, philanthrope.
OPPOSITE recipient.

doom ▶ noun **1** *John may have anticipated his impending doom* **destruction**, downfall, grim/terrible fate, ruin, ruination, rack and ruin, catastrophe, disaster; extinction, annihilation, death, end, termination; *rare* quietus.
2 (*archaic*) *the day of doom* **Judgement Day**, the Last Judgement, doomsday, Armageddon, the end of the world, the last trump.

▶ verb *we were doomed to wait for ever | such attempts are usually doomed to failure* **destine**, fate, predestine, ordain, preordain, foredoom, mean, foreordain, consign; condemn, sentence; (**doomed**) certain, sure, bound, guaranteed, assured, very likely.

doomed ▶ adjective *a doomed friendship* **ill-fated**, ill-starred, ill-omened, star-crossed, under a curse, cursed, jinxed, foredoomed, hapless, damned, bedevilled, luckless, unlucky; *Scottish* fey.
OPPOSITES happy, lucky, promising.

door ▶ noun *she disappeared through a door* **doorway**, portal, opening, hatch, entrance, entry, exit, egress.

□ **out of doors** *food tastes even better out of doors* **outside**, outdoors, out, in/into the open air, alfresco, out of the house.

doorkeeper ▶ noun **doorman**, door attendant, commissionaire, gatekeeper; caretaker, janitor, custodian, concierge; *Freemasonry* tiler.

dope ▶ noun **1** (*informal*) *he was caught smuggling dope* **drugs**, narcotics, addictive drugs, recreational drugs, illegal drugs; cannabis, heroin.
2 (*informal*) *what a dope she must have looked. See* FOOL.
3 (*informal*) *the government had plenty of dope on Mr Dixon. See* INFORMATION.

▶ verb **1** *the horse was doped before the race* **drug**, administer drugs/opiates/narcotics to; tamper with, interfere with; disable, stupefy, sedate, befuddle, inebriate, intoxicate, narcotize, incapacitate, weaken; knock out, anaesthetize, give an anaesthetic to, make/render unconscious; *Brit. informal* nobble.
2 *they may have doped his drink at the club* **add drugs to**, tamper with, adulterate, contaminate; *informal* lace, spike, slip a Mickey Finn into, doctor, cut.

dopey ▶ adjective (*informal*) *he became dopey and fell into a deep sleep* **dazed**, confused, muddled, befuddled, bewildered, disoriented, disorientated, stupefied, groggy, dizzy; *informal* woozy, muzzy, woolly, woolly-headed, not with it, discombobulated.
OPPOSITE alert.

dormant ▶ adjective *the bacteria may lie dormant in the bird | a dormant company is entitled to exemption from auditing* **asleep**, sleeping, slumbering, resting, reposing, drowsing, comatose, supine; **inactive**, passive, inert, latent, fallow, quiescent, inoperative, stagnant, sluggish, lethargic, torpid, motionless, immobile; *Zoology* aestivating.
OPPOSITES awake, active.

dose ▶ noun **1** *a dose of cough mixture* **amount**, quantity, measure, portion, dosage, drench, draught; overdose, lethal dose; *informal* hit.
2 *we all got a dose of diarrhoea* **bout**, attack, outbreak, flare-up, fit, eruption, spell, burst.

dossier ▶ noun *I've built up a dossier on his drug and arms deals* **file**, report, case history, case study, casebook; account, notes, document(s), documentation, data, information, evidence; annal(s), archive(s), chronicle(s), diary, journal, memoir, register, log, logbook; inventory, list, catalogue; *rare* muniments.

dot ▶ noun *the photograph is made up of tiny dots* **spot**, speck, fleck, speckle, point, pinpoint, pinprick, mark, dab; bit, particle, atom, molecule, iota, jot, mote, mite; full stop, decimal point; *rare* macule, macula.

□ **on the dot** (*informal*) *at six o'clock on the dot | will they be here on the dot?* **precisely**, exactly, sharp, prompt, to the minute, on the nail; dead on, on the stroke of …; **promptly**, punctually, on time; *informal* bang on, spot on; *N. Amer. informal* on the button, on the nose; *Austral./NZ informal* on the knocker.

▶ verb **1** *spots of rain began to dot his shirt* **spot**, fleck, bespeckle, mark, dab,

stipple, pock, freckle, sprinkle, dust; *literary* befleck, bestrew, besprinkle.
2 *North Africa was once dotted with freshwater lakes | restaurants are dotted around the site* **scatter**, pepper, sprinkle, strew, litter; punctuate, stud, cover; spread, disperse, intersperse, distribute.

dotage ▶ noun *Uncle Henry was in his dotage* **declining years**, winter/autumn of one's life; advanced years, old age, elderliness, agedness, oldness, senescence, senility, superannuation, decrepitude, second childhood; *literary* eld; *rare* caducity.
OPPOSITE childhood.

dote ▶ verb
□ **dote on** *she doted on the boy* **adore**, love dearly, be devoted to, idolize, treasure, cherish, lavish affection on, worship, think very highly of, appreciate greatly, admire, hold dear, prize; indulge, spoil, pamper.
OPPOSITES hate; neglect.

doting ▶ adjective *all her doting admirers* **adoring**, loving, amorous, besotted, infatuated, lovesick, passionate; affectionate, fond, devoted, solicitous, caring, tender, warm, warm-hearted; overindulgent, indulgent; *informal* lovey-dovey, touchy-feely.
OPPOSITE stony.

dotty ▶ adjective (*informal*) *it was enough to drive you dotty.* See MAD.

double ▶ adjective **1** *a double garage | double yellow lines* **dual**, duplex, twin, binary, duplicate, matched, matching, paired, in pairs, complementary, coupled, twofold; *Botany* binate; *rare* binal.
OPPOSITE single.
2 *a double helping* **twice the usual size**, doubled, twofold.
3 *he thought there was a double meaning in her words* **ambiguous**, equivocal, dual, two-edged, ambivalent, open to debate, open to argument, arguable, debatable; Delphic, cryptic, enigmatic, gnomic, paradoxical, misleading; double-edged.
OPPOSITE unambiguous.
4 *he led a double life* **deceitful**, double-dealing, two-faced, dual; hypocritical, back-stabbing, false, duplicitous, insincere, deceiving, dissembling, dishonest; disloyal, treacherous, perfidious, faithless; lying, untruthful, mendacious; *rare* Janus-faced.
OPPOSITES simple; honest.
▶ adverb *we had to pay double* **twice**, twice over, twice the amount, doubly.
▶ noun **1** *if it's not her, it's her double* **lookalike**, twin, clone, duplicate, perfect likeness, exact likeness, replica, copy, facsimile, imitation, picture, image, living image, mirror image, counterpart, match, mate, fellow; *German* Doppelgänger; *informal* spitting image, dead ringer, ringer, (very) spit, dead spit, spit and image.
2 *she used a double for the stunts* **stand-in**, body double, understudy, substitute.
□ **at the double** *Charlie disappeared across the parade ground at the double* **very quickly**, as fast as one's legs can carry one, at a run, at a gallop, hotfoot, on the double, fast, swiftly, rapidly, briskly, speedily, at high speed, with all speed, at (full) speed, at the speed of light, at full tilt, express, post-haste, as fast as possible, with all possible haste, like a whirlwind, like an arrow from a bow, at breakneck speed, expeditiously, madly, with dispatch; *informal* double quick, in double quick time, p.d.q. (pretty damn quick), nippily, like (greased) lightning, hell for leather, like mad, like crazy, like blazes, like the wind, like a bomb, like nobody's business, like a scalded cat, like the deuce, a mile a minute, like a bat out of hell; *Brit. informal* like the clappers, at a rate of knots, like billy-o; *N. Amer. informal* lickety-split; *literary* apace.
▶ verb **1** *they offered to double his salary* **multiply by two**, increase twofold, enlarge, magnify, repeat.
2 *the bottom sheet had been* ***doubled up*** *halfway down the bed* **fold (back/up/down/over/under)**, turn back/up/down/over/under, tuck back/up/down/under, bend back/over, crease.
3 *the kitchen doubles as a dining room* **function**, do, (also) serve; have/serve a dual purpose, have a dual role.
4 *the Customs officer was* ***doubling for*** *Immigration* **stand in for**, fill in for, act as stand-in for, deputize for, act as deputy, substitute for, act as substitute for, take the place of, take over from, be a substitute for, cover for, replace, relieve, act in place of, do duty for, do a locum for, be a locum for, sit in for, understudy; hold the fort, step into the breach; *informal* sub for, fill someone's shoes/boots; *N. Amer. informal* pinch-hit for.

WORD LINKS
related prefixes **di-** (e.g. ***dihedral, dichromatic***), **diplo-** (e.g. ***diplopod, diplococcus***), **zygo-** (e.g. ***zygodactyl, zygopteran***)

double-cross ▶ verb *he was double-crossing his family behind their backs* **betray**, **cheat**, defraud, trick, hoodwink, mislead, deceive, swindle, break one's promise to, be disloyal to, be unfaithful to, break faith with, play false, fail, let down; *informal* two-time, stitch up, do the dirty on, sell down the river.
OPPOSITES be loyal; play it straight.

double-dealing ▶ noun *one day his double-dealing would be discovered* **duplicity**, treachery, betrayal, double-crossing, faithlessness, unfaithfulness, untrustworthiness, infidelity, bad faith, disloyalty, perfidy, perfidiousness, treason, breach of trust, fraud, fraudulence, underhandedness, cheating, dishonesty, deceit, deceitfulness, deception, falseness, stab in the back, back-stabbing, lying, mendacity, trickery, two-facedness; *informal* crookedness, two-timing; *rare* Punic faith.
OPPOSITES honesty, straightforwardness, trustworthiness.

double entendre ▶ noun *he was unable to resist a smutty double entendre* **ambiguity**, double meaning, suggested meaning, suggestiveness, innuendo, play on words, wordplay, pun.

doubly ▶ adverb *we have to be doubly careful* **twice as**, as ... again, in double measure, in two ways, for two; even more, especially, extra.

doubt ▶ noun **1** *there was some doubt as to the caller's identity* **uncertainty**, lack of certainty, unsureness, indecision, hesitation, hesitancy, dubiousness, suspicion, confusion; question mark, queries, questions; *rare* dubiety, incertitude.
OPPOSITE certainty.
2 *a weak, indecisive leader racked by doubt* **indecision**, hesitation, diffidence, uncertainty, insecurity, inhibition, unease, uneasiness, apprehension; hesitancy, wavering, vacillation, irresolution, lack of conviction, demurral.
OPPOSITES conviction, confidence.
3 *there is doubt about the motive behind this move* **scepticism**, distrust, mistrust, lack of trust, doubtfulness, suspicion, cynicism, disbelief, incredulity, unbelief, misbelief, lack of confidence/conviction, uneasiness, apprehension, wariness, chariness, questioning; reservations, misgivings, suspicions, qualms; *informal* leeriness; *rare* dubiety.
OPPOSITE trust.
□ **in doubt 1** *the issue was never in doubt* **doubtful**, uncertain, open to question, unsure, unconfirmed, unknown, unsettled, undecided, moot, unresolved, debatable, open to debate, in the balance, pending, in limbo, up in the air, confused, problematic, ambiguous; *informal* iffy.
OPPOSITE settled.
2 *if you are in doubt, ask for advice* **irresolute**, hesitant, tentative, vacillating, dithering, wavering, teetering, fluctuating, faltering, ambivalent, divided; doubtful, unsure, uncertain, in two minds, shilly-shallying, undecided, indefinite, unresolved, undetermined; in a quandary/dilemma; *informal* sitting on the fence.
OPPOSITES sure, confident.
□ **no doubt** *it was all necessary, no doubt* **doubtless**, undoubtedly, indubitably, doubtlessly, without (a) doubt, beyond (a) doubt, beyond the shadow of a doubt; unquestionably, beyond question, indisputably, undeniably, incontrovertibly, irrefutably; unequivocally, clearly, plainly, obviously, patently, positively, absolutely, certainly, with certainty; decidedly, definitely, surely, assuredly, of course, indeed.
OPPOSITE possibly.
▶ verb **1** *they did not doubt my story* **disbelieve**, distrust, mistrust, suspect, lack confidence in, have doubts about, be suspicious of, have suspicions about, have misgivings about, feel uneasy about, feel apprehensive about, call into question, cast doubt on, query, question, challenge, dispute, have reservations about; *archaic* misdoubt.
OPPOSITE trust.
2 *I doubt whether he will come* **think something unlikely**, have (one's) doubts about, question, query, be dubious, lack conviction, have reservations about.
OPPOSITE be confident.
3 *stop doubting and believe more firmly!* **be undecided**, have doubts, be irresolute, be hesitant, be tentative, be ambivalent, be divided, be doubtful, be unsure, be uncertain, be in two minds, hesitate, shilly-shally, waver, falter, vacillate, dither, demur; *informal* sit on the fence.
OPPOSITE believe.

doubter ▶ noun *this is his chance to confound the doubters* **sceptic**, doubting Thomas, non-believer, unbeliever, disbeliever, cynic, scoffer, questioner, challenger, nihilist, dissenter; irreligionist, atheist, agnostic, freethinker; infidel, pagan, heathen; *archaic* paynim; *rare* Pyrrhonist, nullifidian.
OPPOSITE believer.

doubtful ▶ adjective **1** *at first I was doubtful about going* **irresolute**, hesitant, tentative, vacillating, dithering, wavering, teetering, fluctuating, faltering, ambivalent, divided, in doubt, unsure, uncertain, in two minds, shilly-shallying, undecided, indefinite, unresolved, in a quandary/dilemma, undetermined; *informal* iffy, blowing hot and cold, sitting on the fence.
OPPOSITES confident, decisive.
2 *it is doubtful whether he will come* **in doubt**, dubious, uncertain, open to question, questionable, unsure, unconfirmed, not definite, unknown, unsettled, undecided, unresolved, debatable, open to debate, moot, in the balance, pending, in limbo, up in the air; confused, problematic, ambiguous; *informal* iffy.
OPPOSITE certain.
3 *the whole trip is looking rather doubtful* **unlikely**, improbable, not likely, dubious, unthinkable, implausible, impossible, far-fetched, inconceivable, unimaginable, remote, beyond the bounds of possibility.
OPPOSITE probable.
4 *they are doubtful of the methods used* **distrustful**, mistrustful, suspicious, cautious, circumspect, careful, wary, uneasy, chary, apprehensive, lacking

D

trust, lacking confidence, lacking faith; sceptical, unsure, ambivalent, dubious, cynical; questioning, disbelieving, unbelieving, incredulous; (**be doubtful**) have reservations, have misgivings; *informal* leery, cagey.
OPPOSITE trusting.
5 *this decision is of doubtful validity* **questionable**, arguable, disputable, debatable, open to question, open to debate, subject to debate, controversial, contentious, open to doubt, in doubt, dubious, borderline; *rare* controvertible, unestablished; *informal* iffy; *Brit. informal* dodgy.
OPPOSITE sound.

D

doubtless ▶ **adverb** *Henry was doubtless glad of the opportunity* **undoubtedly**, indubitably, doubtlessly, no doubt, without (a) doubt, beyond (a) doubt, beyond the shadow of a doubt; unquestionably, beyond question, indisputably, undeniably, incontrovertibly, irrefutably; unequivocally, clearly, plainly, obviously, patently, positively, absolutely, certainly, with certainty; decidedly, definitely, surely, assuredly, of course, indeed.
OPPOSITE possibly.

doughty ▶ **adjective** *a doughty fighter for democracy* **fearless**, dauntless, determined, resolute, indomitable, intrepid, plucky, spirited, game, mettlesome, gritty, steely, confident, undaunted, undismayed, unalarmed, unflinching, unshrinking, unabashed, unfaltering, unflagging, bold, audacious, valiant, brave, stout-hearted, lionhearted, gallant, courageous, heroic, daring, daredevil; *informal* gutsy, spunky, ballsy, feisty.
OPPOSITE timid.

dour ▶ **adjective** *they were barely acknowledged by the dour receptionist* **stern**, unsmiling, unfriendly, frowning, poker-faced, severe, forbidding, morose, sour, gruff, surly, uncommunicative, grim, gloomy, dismal, sullen, sombre, grave, sober, serious, solemn, austere, stony, unsympathetic, disapproving.
OPPOSITES cheerful; friendly.

douse, dowse ▶ **verb 1** *a mob doused the thieves with petrol* **drench**, soak, souse, saturate, drown, flood, inundate, deluge, wet, splash, slosh, hose down.
2 *a guard doused the flames with a fire extinguisher* **extinguish**, put out, quench, stamp out, smother, beat out, dampen down; blow out, snuff out; *Scottish* dout.

dovetail ▶ **verb 1** *the ends of the logs were cut and dovetailed* **joint**, join, fit together, link, interlock, splice, mortise, tenon.
2 *this company will dovetail well with the division's existing activities* **fit in**, go together, be consistent, agree, accord, concur, coincide, match, fit, be in agreement, conform, equate, harmonize, fall in, be in tune, correlate, correspond, tally; *informal* square; *N. Amer. informal* jibe; *archaic* quadrate.

dowdy ▶ **adjective** *she had serviceable but dowdy clothes* **unfashionable**, frumpish, frumpy, drab, dull, old-fashioned, outmoded, out of style, not smart, inelegant, badly dressed, ill-dressed, shabby, scruffy, faded, untidy, dingy, frowzy; *informal* sad, tacky; *Brit. informal* mumsy; *Austral./NZ informal* daggy.
OPPOSITE fashionable.

down[1] ▶ **adverb 1** *they went down in the lift* **towards a lower position**, downwards, downstairs, towards the bottom, from top to bottom.
OPPOSITE up.
2 *they're down in the hall* **in a lower position**, downstairs, at the bottom.
3 *she fell down* **to the ground**, to the floor, over.
▶ **preposition 1** *the lift plunged down the shaft* **lower in/on**, to the bottom of.
OPPOSITE up.
2 *I walked down the street* **along**, throughout the length of, to the other end of, from one end of ... to the other, through, across, by way of, via.
3 *we have done him many favours down the years* **throughout**, through, during, in.
▶ **adjective 1** *I'm feeling a bit down* **depressed**, sad, saddened, unhappy, melancholy, miserable, wretched, sorrowful, gloomy, dejected, downhearted, disheartened, despondent, dispirited, low, in low spirits, low-spirited, heavy-hearted, glum, morose, dismal, downcast, cast down, tearful; *informal* blue, down in the dumps, down in the mouth, fed up.
OPPOSITE elated.
2 *the computer is down* **not working**, not functioning, not functional, not in working order, not in operation, inoperative, malfunctioning, out of order, broken, broken-down, acting up, unserviceable, faulty, defective, in disrepair; **not in service**, unavailable for use, not in use, out of action, out of commission; *informal* conked out, bust, (gone) kaput, gone phut, on the blink, gone haywire, shot; *Brit. informal* knackered, jiggered, wonky; *N. Amer. informal* on the fritz, out of whack; *Brit. vulgar slang* buggered.
OPPOSITE working.
▶ **verb** (*informal*) **1** *he struck Slater on the face, downing him* **knock down**, knock over, knock to the ground, throw to the ground, bring down, bring to the ground, fell, topple, prostrate, tackle, trip up; *informal* deck, floor, flatten.
2 *he downed his pint of beer* **drink (up/down)**, gulp (down), guzzle, quaff, drain, imbibe, sup, slurp, suck, sip, swallow, finish off, polish off; *informal* sink, swig, swill (down), toss off, slug, knock back, put away, kill; *N. Amer. informal* scarf (down/up), snarf (down/up); *rare* ingurgitate.
▶ **noun 1** (**downs**) *the ups and downs of running a business* **setbacks**, upsets, reverses, reversals, reversals of fortune, downturns, mishaps, strokes of ill luck, strokes of bad luck, accidents, shocks, vicissitudes, crises, catastrophes, tragedies, calamities, trials, crosses, knocks, burdens, blows, buffets; *informal* glitches, (double) whammies, knock-backs; *archaic* foils.
OPPOSITE ups.
2 *he's having a bit of a down at the moment* **fit of depression**, period of despondency; *informal* the blues, the dumps, one's black dog, a low; *N. Amer. informal* the blahs, a funk, a blue funk; *informal, dated* the mopes; *literary* dolour; *archaic* the megrims.
OPPOSITE high.
□ **have a down on** (*informal*) *poor Fairfax, I think they had a down on him* **disapprove of**, be against, be prejudiced against, be set against, bear a grudge towards, show antagonism to, be hostile to, show/feel ill will towards; **persecute**, pick on, push around/about, lean on, bully, abuse, discriminate against, ill-treat, mistreat, maltreat, harass, hound, torment, terrorize, torture, punish unfairly; *informal* get at, have it in for, be down on, give someone a hard time, hassle, needle, get on someone's back, make things hot for someone.

down[2] ▶ **noun** *the young puffin stopped preening tufts of grey down from its feathers* **soft feathers**, fluff, fuzz, floss, lint, bloom, fine hair, nap, pile.

down and out ▶ **adjective** *a novel about being down and out on the streets of London* **destitute**, poverty-stricken, impoverished, indigent, penniless, insolvent, impecunious, ruined, pauperized, without a penny to one's name, without two farthings/pennies to rub together; needy, in need, in want, hard up, on the breadline, hard-pressed, in reduced/straitened circumstances, deprived, disadvantaged, distressed, badly off; beggarly, beggared; **homeless**, without a roof over one's head, on the streets, of no fixed abode/address, vagrant, sleeping rough, living rough; **unemployed**, jobless, out of a job, workless, redundant, laid off, idle, between jobs; *informal* on one's uppers, up against it, broke, flat broke, strapped (for cash), without a brass farthing, without a bean, without a sou, as poor as a church mouse, on one's beam-ends; *Brit. informal* stony broke, skint, boracic (lint), on the dole, signing on, 'resting'; *N. Amer. informal* stone broke, without a red cent, on skid row; *Austral. informal* on the wallaby track; *formal* penurious.
OPPOSITES wealthy, well heeled.
▶ **noun** (**down-and-out**) *he gave his packed lunch to a hungry down-and-out* **poor person**, pauper, indigent, bankrupt, insolvent; beggar, mendicant; **homeless person**, vagrant, tramp, drifter, derelict, vagabond, person of no fixed address/abode, knight of the road, bird of passage, rolling stone; **unemployed person**, job-seeker; *N. Amer.* hobo; *Austral.* bagman, knockabout, overlander, sundowner, whaler; *informal* have-not, dosser, bag lady; *N. Amer. informal* bum, bindlestiff; *Austral./NZ informal* derro; *S. African informal* outie; (**down-and-outs**) the poor, the destitute, the needy, the homeless, the unemployed.

down at heel ▶ **adjective 1** *the whole resort now looks down at heel* **run down**, dilapidated, in disrepair, neglected, uncared-for, unmaintained, depressed; **seedy**, insalubrious, squalid, sleazy, slummy, seamy, sordid, dingy, mean, wretched; *informal* crummy, scruffy, scuzzy, grungy; *Brit. informal* grotty; *N. Amer. informal* shacky, skanky.
2 *a down-at-heel English journalist lived nearby* **scruffy**, shabby, shabbily dressed, poorly dressed, shoddy, ragged, out at elbows, tattered, mangy, sorry, disreputable; **unkempt**, bedraggled, messy, dishevelled, ungroomed, ill-groomed, sleazy, seedy, slatternly, untidy, slovenly; **dirty**, squalid, filthy; *informal* tatty, the worse for wear, scuzzy, grungy, yucky; *Brit. informal* grotty; *N. Amer. informal* raggedy.
OPPOSITES smart, stylish.

downbeat ▶ **adjective 1** *the overall mood is decidedly downbeat* **pessimistic**, gloomy, negative, defeatist, gloom-ridden, cynical, bleak, fatalistic, dark, black, despairing, despondent, depressed, dejected, demoralized, hopeless, melancholy, glum, lugubrious, suspicious, distrustful, doubting, alarmist; *informal* given to looking on the black side.
OPPOSITE upbeat.
2 *the songs are full of downbeat joviality* **relaxed**, easy-going, equable, free and easy, easy, at ease, casual, informal, nonchalant, insouciant, understated, inconspicuous, low-key, subdued, discreet, muted, subtle, played down, toned down, unostentatious, blasé, cool; *informal* laid-back, unflappable, together.

downcast ▶ **adjective** *Morgan was understandably downcast following Scotland's defeat* **despondent**, disheartened, discouraged, dispirited, downhearted, low-spirited, in low spirits, hopeless, cast down, crestfallen, down, low, disconsolate, in despair, despairing, wretched, oppressed; **sad**, melancholy, gloomy, glum, morose, doleful, dismal, woebegone, miserable, depressed, dejected, distressed, sorrowful; defeatist, pessimistic; *informal* blue, down in the mouth, down in the dumps, as sick as a parrot.
OPPOSITE elated.

downfall ▶ **noun** *their book predicted the downfall of communism* **undoing**, ruin, ruination, loss of power/prosperity/status; defeat, conquest, vanquishing, toppling, deposition, ousting, unseating, overthrow,

nemesis, destruction, annihilation, elimination, end, collapse, fall, crash, failure, debasement, degradation, disgrace; Waterloo; *rare* labefaction.
OPPOSITES rise; salvation; survival.

downgrade ▸ verb **1** *there were plans to make six staff redundant and to downgrade three others* **demote**, lower, lower in status, reduce/lower in rank, reduce in importance; relegate; *N. Amer. informal* bust; *archaic* degrade.
OPPOSITES upgrade, promote.
2 *I have no wish to downgrade their achievement* **disparage**, denigrate, detract from, run down, decry, belittle, make light of, minimize, defame; *N. Amer. informal* bad-mouth.
OPPOSITES praise; talk up.

downhearted ▸ adjective *Stirling was obviously downhearted, but he did not show it* **despondent**, disheartened, discouraged, dispirited, downcast, low-spirited, in low spirits, hopeless, cast down, crestfallen, down, low, disconsolate, in despair, despairing, wretched, oppressed; melancholy, gloomy, glum, morose, doleful, dismal, woebegone, miserable, depressed, dejected, distressed, sorrowful, sad; defeatist, pessimistic; *informal* blue, down in the mouth, down in the dumps, as sick as a parrot.
OPPOSITE elated.

downmarket ▸ adjective *the quality papers and the downmarket tabloids* **cheap**, cheap and nasty, inferior, rubbishy; low-class, lowbrow, uncultured, unsophisticated, rough, poor, insalubrious, unfashionable, disreputable; *informal* tacky, dumbed down.
OPPOSITES upmarket, smart.

downpour ▸ noun *the drizzle was becoming a downpour* **rainstorm**, cloudburst, torrent of rain, deluge; thunderstorm; torrential/pouring rain.

downright ▸ adjective **1** *smears, half-truths, and downright lies* **complete**, total, absolute, utter, thorough, perfect, out-and-out, outright, thoroughgoing, all-out, sheer, positive, rank, pure, dyed-in-the-wool, deep-dyed, real, veritable, consummate, categorical, unmitigated, unqualified, unadulterated, unalloyed, unconditional, unequivocal; *Brit. informal* right, proper; *archaic* arrant.
OPPOSITES partial; anything but.
2 *a true downright character who did not care a damn for her* **frank**, direct, straightforward, straight, straight to the point, blunt, plain-spoken, outspoken, forthright, uninhibited, unreserved, point blank, no-nonsense, matter-of-fact, bluff, undiplomatic, tactless; explicit, clear, plain, unequivocal, unambiguous, unqualified, categorical; honest, candid, open, sincere; not afraid to call a spade a spade, no beating around the bush, speaking as one finds; *informal* straight from the shoulder, upfront.
OPPOSITE devious.
▸ adverb *suppressing emotions is downright dangerous* **thoroughly**, utterly, positively, simply, profoundly, really, absolutely, completely, totally, entirely, perfectly, properly, consummately, surpassingly, unconditionally, unreservedly, categorically, incontrovertibly, unquestionably, undeniably, in every respect, through and through, outright; *informal* plain, clean.
OPPOSITES slightly; not at all.

downside ▸ noun *the downside is that getting a patent costs big money* **snag**, drawback, disadvantage, stumbling block, catch, pitfall, fly in the ointment; handicap, limitation, trouble, difficulty, problem, complication, liability, nuisance; hindrance, obstacle, impediment; weak spot/point, weakness, flaw, defect, fault; *informal* minus, flip side, hiccup; *Brit. informal* spanner in the works; *N. Amer. informal* monkey wrench in the works.
OPPOSITES benefit, advantage.

down-to-earth ▸ adjective *she seemed a good, down-to-earth type* **practical**, sensible, realistic, matter-of-fact, responsible, full of common sense, reasonable, rational, logical, sound, balanced, sober, no-nonsense, pragmatic, level-headed, serious-minded, businesslike, commonsensical, hard-headed, sane, mundane, unromantic, unidealistic.
OPPOSITES idealistic; dreamy.

downtrodden ▸ adjective *they kept alive the spirit of a downtrodden nation during centuries of foreign occupation* **oppressed**, subjugated, persecuted, subdued, repressed, tyrannized, ground down, crushed, enslaved, burdened, weighed down, exploited, disadvantaged, underprivileged, victimized, bullied, browbeaten, under the heel, powerless, helpless, prostrate; abused, misused, maltreated, ill-treated.

downward ▸ adjective *the downward flow of water* **descending**, downhill, falling, sinking, going down, moving down, sliding, slipping, dipping, earthbound, earthward.
OPPOSITE upward.

WORD LINKS
related prefix **cata-** (e.g. ***catastrophe, catadromous***)

downy ▸ adjective *I stroked the downy hair on my tiny son's head* **soft**, velvety, smooth, fleecy, fluffy, fuzzy, feathery, furry, woolly, silky, silken, satiny.
OPPOSITES rough; wiry.

dowry ▸ noun (*historical*) **marriage settlement**, (marriage) portion; *Scottish & N. English* tocher; *archaic* dot.

dowse ▸ verb. *See* DOUSE.

doze ▸ verb *he dozed but woke with a start* **catnap**, nap, take a nap, take a siesta, sleep lightly, drowse, rest; *informal* snooze, have a snooze, snatch forty winks, get some shut-eye; *Brit. informal* kip, have a kip, get some kip, zizz, have a zizz, get some zizz; *N. Amer. informal* catch some Zs, catch a few Zs; *literary* slumber.
OPPOSITE be awake.
□ **doze off** *he dozed off in front of the fire* **fall asleep**, go to sleep, drop off, get to sleep; *informal* nod off, go off, drift off, crash out, go out like a light, flake out, conk out; *N. Amer. informal* sack out, zone out.
OPPOSITES wake up; stay awake.
▸ noun *she had a short doze before work* **catnap**, nap, siesta, light sleep, drowse, rest; *informal* snooze, forty winks; *Brit. informal* kip, zizz; *literary* slumber.

dozy ▸ adjective *the guard on night duty would be too dozy to spot anything* **drowsy**, sleepy, half asleep, heavy-eyed, somnolent; **lethargic**, listless, lacking in energy, unenergetic, enervated, inactive, slow, torpid, languid, weary, tired, fatigued; lazy, idle, indolent, slothful, sluggardly; *Medicine* asthenic, neurasthenic; *informal* dopey, yawny; *N. Amer. informal* logy; *archaic* lymphatic.

drab ▸ adjective **1** *blocks of drab council flats* **colourless**, grey, greyish, dull, dull-coloured, washed out, neutral, pale, muted, lacklustre, lustreless, muddy, watery; lightish brown, brownish, brownish-grey, mousy, dun-coloured; dingy, dreary, dismal, cheerless, gloomy, sombre, depressing.
OPPOSITES bright; cheerful.
2 *a drab suburban existence* **uninteresting**, dull, boring, tedious, monotonous, dry, dreary, wearisome; unexciting, bland, non-stimulating, unimaginative, uninspiring, uninspired, insipid, lustreless, lacklustre, vapid, flat, stale, trite, vacuous, feeble, pallid, wishy-washy, colourless, limp, lame, tired, lifeless, zestless, spiritless, sterile, anaemic, barren, tame, bloodless, antiseptic; middle-of-the-road, run-of-the-mill, commonplace, mediocre, nondescript, characterless, mundane, unexceptional, unremarkable, humdrum, prosaic.
OPPOSITE interesting.

draconian ▸ adjective *collaborators suffered draconian reprisals* **harsh**, severe, strict, extreme, drastic, stringent, tough, swingeing, cruel, brutal, oppressive, ruthless, relentless, summary, punitive, authoritarian, despotic, tyrannical, arbitrary, repressive, iron-fisted; *rare* suppressive.
OPPOSITE mild.

draft ▸ noun **1** *the draft of his speech* **preliminary version**, rough sketch, outline, plan, blueprint, skeleton, abstract; main points, bones, bare bones.
OPPOSITE final version.
2 *a draft of the building to be erected* **plan**, blueprint, design, diagram, drawing, scale drawing, outline, sketch, pattern, map, layout, representation.
3 *payment should be made by a banker's draft* **cheque**, order, banker's order, money order, bill of exchange, postal order; *technical* negotiable instrument.

drag ▸ verb **1** *she dragged the heavy chair nearer to the bed* **haul**, pull, draw, tug, heave, trail, trawl, tow; *Irish* streel; *informal* yank, lug; *archaic* hale.
2 *the day dragged for Anne* **become tedious**, appear to pass slowly, go slowly, move slowly, creep along, limp along, crawl, hang heavy, go at a snail's pace, wear on, go on too long, go on and on.
□ **drag on** *the war dragged on* **persist**, continue, go on, carry on, extend, run on, be protracted, linger, endure, keep up, hold, prevail, subsist.
□ **drag something out** *that procedure was bound to drag out the negotiations* **prolong**, protract, draw out, stretch out, spin out, string out, make something go on and on, extend, extend the duration of, lengthen, carry on, keep going, keep alive, continue; *archaic* wire-draw.
▸ noun **1** *the drag of the air brakes causes more rapid deceleration* **pull**, tug, tow, heave, yank; resistance, braking, retardation.
2 (*informal*) *working nine to five can be a drag* **bore**, tedious thing, tiresome thing, nuisance, bother, trouble, pest, annoyance, source of annoyance, trial, vexation, thorn in one's flesh; tiresome person, tedious person; *informal* pain, pain in the neck, bind, headache, hassle; *N. Amer. informal* pain in the butt, nudnik; *Austral./NZ informal* nark; *Brit. informal, dated* blighter, blister, pill; *Brit. vulgar slang* pain in the arse.

dragoon ▸ noun (*historical*) *the dragoons charged our left flank* **cavalryman**, mounted soldier, horse soldier, cavalier, knight, chevalier; carabineer, hussar, lancer, cuirassier, sabreur.
▸ verb *he dragooned his friends into amateur dramatics* **coerce**, pressure, pressurize, bring pressure to bear on, use pressure on, put pressure on, constrain, lean on, press, push; force, compel, impel, oblige, put under an obligation, squeeze, hound, harass, nag, harry, badger, goad, drive, prod, pester, browbeat, brainwash, bludgeon, bully, threaten, tyrannize, prevail on, work on, act on, influence, intimidate, twist someone's arm, strong-arm; *N. Amer.* blackjack; *informal* bulldoze, railroad, put the screws/squeeze on; *Brit. informal* bounce; *N. Amer. informal* hustle, fast-talk.

D

drain ▶ verb **1** *there is a valve for draining the tank* **empty (out)**, remove the contents of, void, clear (out), unload, evacuate.
OPPOSITE fill.
2 *then drain any surplus liquid* **draw off**, extract, withdraw, remove, pump off, siphon off, milk, bleed, tap, void, filter, pour out, pour off, tip, discharge, transfer.
3 *the water drained away to the sea* **flow**, pour, escape, leak, trickle, empty, well, ooze, seep, exude, drip, dribble, issue, filter, percolate, bleed, sweat, leach; stream, run, rush, gush, roll, cascade, flood, surge, sweep.
4 *jailing more people would just drain resources* **use up**, exhaust, deplete, consume, expend, swallow up, absorb, get through, go through, run through, take up, occupy, empty, sap, strain, tax, bleed.
5 *he drained what was left in his glass* **drink (up/down)**, gulp (down), guzzle, quaff, down, imbibe, sup, slurp, suck, sip, swallow, finish off, polish off; *informal* sink, swig, swill (down), toss off, slug, knock back, put away, kill, get one's laughing gear round; *N. Amer. informal* scarf (down/up), snarf (down/up); *rare* ingurgitate.
▶ noun **1** *a flash storm filled the drain with water* **sewer**, channel, conduit, ditch, culvert, duct, pipe, tube, gutter, groove, furrow, trough, trench, cut, sluice, spillway, race, flume, chute.
2 *a significant drain on the camcorder's battery* **strain**, demand, pressure, burden, load, imposition, tax; outflow, sapping, depletion.

dram ▶ noun *Menzies offered the man a dram from his flask* **drink**, nip, tot, sip, thimbleful, mouthful, drop, finger, splash, little, spot, taste, small amount; *Scottish informal* scoosh; *rare* toothful.

drama *See centre pages for list of* **Plays** *(Types of Play and Drama)*
▶ noun **1** *a television drama* **play**, show, piece, theatrical work, spectacle, dramatization; screenplay.
2 *he is studying drama* **acting**, the theatre, the stage, the performing arts, dramatic art, dramatics, dramaturgy, stagecraft, theatricals, theatrics, the thespian art, show business; performing, performance, playing a role, appearing on stage; *informal* the boards, treading the boards, show biz; *rare* thespianism, histrionics.
3 *nothing could stop Granny when she wanted to create a drama* **incident**, scene, spectacle, crisis; excitement, thrill, sensation, adventure, affair, business, occasion, circumstance; disturbance, row, commotion, turmoil, fracas; dramatics, theatrics, histrionics.

dramatic ▶ adjective **1** *dramatic art* **theatrical**, stage, dramaturgical, thespian; show-business; *informal* showbiz; *rare* histrionic, theatric.
2 *a dramatic increase in speed* **considerable**, substantial, sizeable, goodly, fair, reasonable, tidy, marked, pronounced; **noticeable**, measurable, perceptible, conspicuous, obvious, detectable, visible, appreciable; significant, striking, signal, notable, noteworthy, worthy of attention, remarkable, outstanding, extraordinary, exceptional, phenomenal; important, of importance, of consequence, consequential.
OPPOSITE insignificant.
3 *there were dramatic scenes in the capital's central square* **exciting**, stirring, action-packed, sensational, spectacular, startling, unexpected, tense, suspenseful, rip-roaring, gripping, riveting, fascinating, thrilling, hair-raising, rousing, lively, animated, spirited, electrifying, impassioned, emotive, emotional, emotion-charged, moving, soul-stirring, powerful, heady; *N. Amer. informal* stem-winding; *rare* inspiriting, anthemic.
OPPOSITE boring.
4 *dramatic rocky headlands* **striking**, eye-catching, impressive, imposing, spectacular, breathtaking, dazzling, vivid, amazing, astounding, astonishing, surprising, staggering, stunning, sensational, awesome, awe-inspiring, remarkable, notable, noteworthy, distinctive, graphic, extraordinary, outstanding, incredible, phenomenal, unusual, rare, uncommon, out of the ordinary.
OPPOSITE unimpressive.
5 *he flung out his arms in a dramatic gesture* **exaggerated**, theatrical, ostentatious, actressy, stagy, showy, melodramatic, overacted, overdone, histrionic, affected, mannered, artificial, stilted, unreal, forced; *informal* hammy, ham, campy.
OPPOSITES natural, unaffected.

dramatist ▶ noun **playwright**, writer, tragedian; scriptwriter, screenwriter, scenarist; *rare* dramaturge, dramaturgist, comedist.

dramatize ▶ verb **1** *the novel was dramatized in six episodes for television* **turn into a play/film**, adapt for the stage/screen, base a screenplay on, put into dramatic form, present as a play/film.
2 *the tabloids sought to dramatize an already dramatic event* **exaggerate**, overdo, overstate, overemphasize, overplay, hyperbolize, overstress, magnify, amplify, inflate; sensationalize, embroider, colour, heighten, expand on, aggrandize, dress up, touch up, embellish, elaborate, gild; *informal* make a big thing out of, blow up (out of all proportion), lay it on thick, ham up.
OPPOSITE understate.

drape ▶ verb **1** *she draped a shawl round her shoulders* **wrap**, arrange, wind, swathe, sling, hang, let fall in folds.
2 *the chair was draped with blankets* **cover**, envelop, swathe, shroud, decorate, adorn, array, deck, bedeck, festoon, bundle up, muffle up, blanket, overlay, cloak, veil, wind, enfold, sheathe.
3 *the youth draped one leg over the arm of his chair* **dangle**, hang, suspend, let fall, droop, drop, place loosely, lean.

drastic ▶ adjective *drastic measures were necessary* **extreme**, serious, forceful, desperate, dire, radical, far-reaching, momentous, substantial; heavy, sharp, severe, harsh, rigorous, swingeing, punishing, excessive, oppressive, draconian.
OPPOSITES mild, moderate.

draught ▶ noun **1** *the draught made Robyn shiver* **current of air**, rush of air, breath, whiff, waft, wind, breeze, gust, puff, blast, gale; *informal* blow; *literary* zephyr.
2 *he took another deep draught of his beer* **gulp**, drink, swallow, mouthful; *informal* swig, swill, slug.

draw ▶ verb **1** *he drew the house in his notebook* **sketch**, make a drawing (of), make a diagram (of), pencil; portray, depict, delineate, outline, draft, rough out, illustrate, render, represent, trace, map out, mark out, plot, chart, design; do drawings; *literary* limn.
2 *she drew her chair in to the table* **pull**, haul, drag, tug, heave, trail, trawl, tow; *Irish* streel; *informal* yank, lug; *archaic* hale.
OPPOSITE push.
3 *the train drew into Victoria Station* **move**, go, come, walk, proceed, progress, travel, continue, advance, get, make it, make one's way, pass, make a move, drive; crawl, creep, inch, roll, glide, cruise, drift, nose; sneak, steal, slip, slink, sidle; bear, press, blow, forge, sweep, lurch, be carried; back; budge, stir, shift, change position; *rare* locomote.
4 *the nurse drew the curtains* **close**, shut, pull together, pull shut, pull to, draw to, lower; **open**, part, pull back, pull open, fling open, raise.
5 *he drew some fluid off the knee joint* **drain**, extract, withdraw, remove, suck, pump, siphon, milk, bleed, tap, void, filter, pour, tip, discharge, transfer.
6 *he drew his gun and fired* **pull out**, take out, bring out, draw out, produce, fish out, extract, withdraw; unsheathe.
OPPOSITES put away; put up.
7 *I drew £50 out of the bank* **withdraw**, take out.
OPPOSITE deposit.
8 *while I draw breath* **breathe in**, inhale, suck in, inspire, respire.
9 *she was drawing huge audiences | he drew the attention of millions of viewers* **attract**, interest, win, capture, catch the eye of, catch, catch hold of, hold, grip, engage, allure, lure, entice, invite; absorb, occupy, rivet, engross, fascinate, mesmerize, hypnotize, spellbind, bewitch, captivate, entrance, enthral, enrapture.
10 *what conclusion can we draw?* **deduce**, infer, conclude, derive, gather, glean; *formal* educe.
□ **draw lots**. *See* LOT.
□ **draw on** *we can draw on centuries of experience* **call on**, have recourse to, avail oneself of, turn to, look to, fall back on, rely on, make use of, exploit, use, employ, utilize, bring into play.
□ **draw something out 1** *he drew out a gun* **pull out**. *See* DRAW *sense* 6.
2 *they always drew their parting out* **prolong**, protract, drag out, stretch out, spin out, string out, make something go on and on, extend, extend the duration of, lengthen, carry on, keep going, keep alive, continue; *archaic* wire-draw.
□ **draw someone out** *show an interest in other people, draw them out with questions* **get/persuade/encourage someone to talk**, put someone at their ease.
□ **draw up** *a car drew up beside us* **stop**, pull up, come to a stop/halt, halt, come to a standstill, brake, park, arrive.
□ **draw something up 1** *the police drew up a list of five or six suspects* **compose**, formulate, frame, write out, write down, put in writing, put down (on paper), draft, prepare, think up, devise, work out, map out, plan, conceive, create, invent, originate, coin, design.
2 *he drew up his forces in battle array* **arrange**, marshal, muster, assemble, group, order, range, rank, line up, parade, place, dispose, position, put into position, set out, array, set forth.
▶ noun **1** *she won first prize in the Christmas draw* **raffle**, lottery, sweepstake, sweep, tombola, ballot; *Brit. trademark* Instants; *N. Amer.* lotto, numbers game/pool/racket; *Austral./NZ* tote, pakapoo.
2 *the match ended in a draw* **tie**, dead heat, stalemate.
3 *the draw of central London is considerable* **attraction**, lure, allure, pull, appeal, glamour, allurement, enticement, temptation, bewitchment, enchantment, charm, seduction, persuasion, fascination, magnetism; *informal* come-on.

drawback ▶ noun *the major drawback to this method is that it can be very time-consuming* **disadvantage**, snag, downside, stumbling block, catch, hitch, pitfall, fly in the ointment; weak spot/point, weakness, flaw, defect, imperfection, fault; handicap, limitation, trouble, difficulty, problem, complication, liability, nuisance; hindrance, obstacle, hurdle, impediment, obstruction, inconvenience, barrier, curb, check, discouragement, deterrent, damper; *informal* minus, hiccup; *Brit. informal* spanner in the works; *N. Amer. informal* monkey wrench in the works.
OPPOSITES benefit, advantage.

drawing ▸ noun *he did a pencil drawing of the house* **sketch**, picture, illustration, representation, portrayal, delineation, depiction, composition, study, diagram, outline, design, plan; tracing.

WORD LINKS
relating to drawing **graphic**

drawl ▸ verb *'Can't do that,' he drawled lazily* **say slowly**, speak slowly; draw out one's vowels, drone.
OPPOSITE gabble.

drawn ▸ adjective *she looked pale and drawn* **worn**, pinched, haggard, gaunt, drained, wan, hollow-cheeked; fatigued, tired, exhausted, sapped, spent; **tense**, stressed, strained, under pressure, overburdened, worried, anxious, harassed, fraught; *informal* hassled.

dread ▸ verb *I used to dread going home at night* **fear**, be afraid of, worry about, be anxious about, have forebodings about, feel apprehensive about; be terrified by, cower at, tremble/shudder at, cringe from, shrink from, quail from, flinch from; *informal* have cold feet about, be in a blue funk about.
OPPOSITE look forward to.
▸ noun *she was filled with dread* **fear**, fearfulness, apprehension, trepidation, anxiety, worry, concern, foreboding, disquiet, disquietude, unease, uneasiness, angst; fright, panic, alarm; terror, horror, trembling, shuddering, flinching; *informal* the jitters, a blue funk, the heebie-jeebies.
OPPOSITE confidence.
▸ adjective *a dread secret* **awful**, feared, frightening, alarming, terrifying, frightful, terrible, horrible, dreadful, dire; dreaded, awesome.

dreadful ▸ adjective **1** *a dreadful accident* **terrible**, frightful, horrible, grim, awful, dire; frightening, terrifying, horrifying, alarming; distressing, shocking, appalling, harrowing; ghastly, fearful, hideous, horrendous, monstrous, unspeakable, gruesome, tragic, calamitous, grievous, grisly.
OPPOSITE mild.
2 *that dreadful woman | a dreadful brandy* **unpleasant**, disagreeable, nasty; frightful, shocking, awful, abysmal, atrocious, disgraceful, deplorable, wretched, very bad, lamentable, repugnant, odious; poor, inadequate, inferior, unsatisfactory, distasteful; *informal* hopeless, pathetic, useless, woeful, crummy, rotten, sorry, third-rate, lousy, ropy, God-awful, poxy, not up to snuff, the pits, from hell; *Brit. informal* duff, chronic, rubbish, pants, a load of pants.
OPPOSITES pleasant, agreeable.
3 *you're a dreadful flirt* **outrageous**, shocking; inordinate, immoderate, unrestrained; great, tremendous.

dreadfully ▸ adverb **1** *I'm dreadfully hungry* **extremely**, very, really, frightfully, fearfully, exceedingly, immensely, terribly, exceptionally, uncommonly, remarkably, extraordinarily; decidedly, most, positively, particularly; *N. English* right; *Scottish* unco; *N. Amer.* quite; *informal* terrifically, tremendously, desperately, awfully, devilishly, ultra, too ... for words, mucho, mega, seriously, majorly, oh-so; *Brit. informal* jolly, ever so, dead, well, fair; *N. Amer. informal* real, mighty, awful, plumb, powerful; *S. African informal* lekker; *informal, dated* devilish, hellish; *archaic* exceeding, sore.
OPPOSITE slightly.
2 *she was missing James dreadfully* **very much**, intensely, desperately, a great deal, a good deal, to a great extent, much, a lot, lots.
OPPOSITE slightly.
3 *the company has performed dreadfully* **terribly**, awfully, very badly, atrociously, dismally, appallingly, abominably, execrably, poorly; *informal* abysmally, pitifully, crummily, diabolically, rottenly; *rare* egregiously.
OPPOSITE well.

dream ▸ noun **1** *I awoke from turbulent dreams* dream sequence; nightmare; vision, fantasy, hallucination.
2 *Leonora went around in a dream the following week* **daydream**, reverie, trance, daze, stupor, haze, hypnotic state, half-conscious state, state of unreality; *Scottish* dwam.
3 *he realized his childhood dream of running the estate* **ambition**, aspiration, hope; goal, design, plan, aim, object, objective, grail, holy grail, target, intention, intent; desire, wish, notion, yearning; daydream, fantasy; illusion, delusion, pipe dream, chimera; (**dreams**) castles in the air, castles in Spain; *informal* pie in the sky.
4 *he's an absolute dream* **delight**, joy, marvel, wonder, gem, treasure, pleasure; beauty, vision, vision of loveliness, pleasure to behold.
▸ verb **1** *she dreamed that she had been present at her own funeral* **have a dream**, have dreams, have a nightmare, have nightmares.
2 *I dreamed of making the Olympic team* **fantasize about**, daydream about; **wish for**, hope for, long for, yearn for, hunger for, hanker after, set one's heart on; aspire to, desire to, wish to; aim for, seek to, have as one's goal/aim, set one's sights on; *literary* thirst for/after.
3 *she's always dreaming—I think she lives in a world of her own* **daydream**, be in a reverie, be in a trance, be lost in thought, be preoccupied, be abstracted, let one's thoughts wander, stare into space, indulge in wool-gathering, be in a brown study, be in cloud cuckoo land; muse, wonder.
4 *I wouldn't dream of being late for Aunt Louise* **think**, consider, contemplate, conceive, entertain the thought of, visualize.
□ **dream something up** *I dreamed up some new excuse* **think up**, invent, concoct, devise, hatch, contrive, create, fabricate, work out, come up with, conjure up; *informal* cook up, brew.
▸ adjective *he bought his Californian dream home for $3,000,000* **ideal**, perfect, flawless, exemplary; fantasy.

WORD LINKS
relating to dreams **oneiric**
interpretation of dreams **oneiromancy**
fear of dreams **oneirophobia**

dreamer ▸ noun *you're just a bunch of naive dreamers* **fantasist**, fantasizer, daydreamer; romantic, sentimentalist, romancer; **idealist**, impractical/unrealistic person, wishful thinker, pipe-dreamer, castle-builder, Utopian, Don Quixote, Walter Mitty; visionary; *rare* reverist; *archaic* fantast.
OPPOSITE realist.

dreamland ▸ noun **1** *I can't drift off to dreamland while she's pacing around the flat* **sleep**, slumber, land of Nod.
2 *they must be living in dreamland if they thought their standards had risen to match those of Australia* **the land of make-believe**, never-never land, fairyland, world of fantasy, cloud cuckoo land; paradise, (the Garden of) Eden, Utopia, heaven, seventh heaven, Shangri-La.
OPPOSITE the real world.

dreamlike ▸ adjective *the gardens have a special dreamlike quality* **unreal**, unsubstantial, illusive, illusory, illusionary, imaginary, chimerical, ethereal, phantasmagorical, trance-like; surreal, psychedelic; nightmarish, Kafkaesque, ghostly, ghostlike; vague, dim, hazy, shadowy, misty, faint, indistinct, unclear.
OPPOSITES real, tangible.

dreamy ▸ adjective **1** *his eyes took on a dreamy expression* **daydreaming**, dreaming; **pensive**, thoughtful, reflective, meditative, musing, ruminative, speculative, lost in thought; preoccupied, distracted, abstracted, rapt, inattentive, wool-gathering, vague, absorbed, distrait, absent-minded, with one's head in the clouds, in a world of one's own, far away, in a brown study; *informal* miles away.
OPPOSITES attentive, alert.
2 *Paul was impractical and dreamy* **idealistic**, romantic, starry-eyed, impractical, unrealistic, Utopian, quixotic, out of touch with reality; **fanciful**, fantasizing, daydreaming, head-in-the-clouds; visionary, far-sighted, prophetic; *Brit. informal* airy-fairy.
OPPOSITES realistic, practical.
3 *a dreamy recollection* **dreamlike**, vague, dim, hazy, shadowy, misty, faint, indistinct, unclear.
OPPOSITES clear, sharp.
4 *dreamy guitar pop* **gentle**, tranquil, peaceful, relaxing, soothing, calming, lulling, romantic.
OPPOSITE harsh.
5 (*informal*) *I bet the prince was really dreamy* **wonderful**, marvellous, terrific, fabulous, lovely, delightful; attractive, appealing; *informal* heavenly, divine, gorgeous.
OPPOSITES unpleasant, unattractive.

dreary ▸ adjective **1** *another dreary day at school* **dull**, drab, uninteresting, flat, dry, banal, bland, insipid, colourless, lifeless, sterile, tedious, wearisome, boring, unexciting, unstimulating, uninspiring, desolate, vapid, jejune, bloodless, soul-destroying, as dry as dust; humdrum, routine, monotonous, uneventful, run-of-the-mill, prosaic, pedestrian, commonplace, everyday, unexceptional, unremarkable, quotidian, unvaried, repetitive, featureless, ho-hum.
OPPOSITE exciting.
2 *she shouldn't be thinking of dreary things like funerals* **sad**, miserable, depressing, grim, gloomy, glum, sombre, grave, doleful, mournful, melancholic, joyless, cheerless, wretched.
OPPOSITE cheerful.
3 *it was a dark, dreary day* **gloomy**, dismal, bleak, dull, dark, dingy, murky, overcast, depressing, sombre.
OPPOSITE bright.

dregs ▸ plural noun **1** *the dregs from a bottle of wine* **sediment**, deposit, residue, remains, accumulation; slops, sludge; scum, debris, dross, detritus, refuse; lees, grounds, scourings; *technical* precipitate, sublimate, residuum, settlings, alluvium; *literary* draff; *archaic* grouts.
2 *the dregs of humanity* **scum**, refuse; rabble, vermin; down-and-outs, good-for-nothings, outcasts, deadbeats, tramps, vagrants; the underclass, the untouchables, the lowest of the low, the great unwashed, the hoi polloi, the ragtag (and bobtail), the canaille; *informal* riff-raff, trash, dossers.

drench ▸ verb *rain was falling fast, drenching the countryside* **soak**, saturate, wet through, wet thoroughly, permeate, drown, swamp, submerge, inundate, flood; douse, souse, swill down, sluice down, slosh; steep, bathe; rinse, wash.
OPPOSITE dry.

dress *See centre pages for list of* **Dresses**
▸ verb **1** *he dressed quickly and ran out of the house* **put on clothes**, don clothes, slip into clothes, clothe oneself, get dressed.
OPPOSITES undress, strip.
2 *he was dressed in an expensive grey suit* **clothe**, attire, garb, fit out, turn out, deck, deck out, trick out/up, costume, array, robe, accoutre; *informal* get up, doll up; *literary* bedizen; *archaic* apparel.

D

3 *they used to dress for dinner every day* **wear formal clothes**, put on evening dress, dress up; change (one's clothes).
OPPOSITES dress informally, dress down.
4 *she'd enjoyed dressing the tree and singing carols* **decorate**, adorn, ornament, trim, deck, bedeck, embellish, beautify, prettify, array, festoon, garland, rig, drape; garnish, furbish, enhance, grace, enrich; *informal* trick out, tart up; *literary* furbelow.
5 *they took him in and dressed his wounds* **bandage**, cover, bind (up), wrap, swaddle, swathe, plaster, put a plaster on.
6 *she still had the chickens to dress* **prepare**, get ready, make ready; clean.
7 *the field was dressed with unrotted farmyard manure* **fertilize**, add fertilizer to, feed, enrich, manure, mulch, compost, top-dress.
8 *it takes two days to dress a pair of millstones* **smooth**, polish, gloss, level, face.
9 *Patrick dressed Michelle's hair in a sculptured style* **style**, groom, arrange, comb, brush, do, put in order, straighten, adjust, preen, primp; *informal* fix.
10 *the battalion dressed its ranks with precision* **line up**, put in line, align, straighten, arrange, put into order, dispose, set out, get into rows/columns; fall in.
□ **dress down** *she was dressed down in a T shirt and torn jeans* **dress informally**, dress casually, be untidy; *informal* slob around.
OPPOSITES dress up, dress smartly.
□ **dress someone down** (*informal*) *the president dressed down the media during the press conference.* See REPRIMAND.
□ **dress up 1** *Angela loved dressing up* **dress smartly**, dress formally, wear evening dress; *informal* doll oneself up, dress to the nines, put on one's glad rags.
OPPOSITES dress casually, dress down.
2 *Hugh was dressed up as Santa Claus* **disguise oneself**, dress; put on fancy dress, wear a costume, put on a disguise, wear disguise.
□ **dress something up** *tabloids make their money by dressing up the prejudices of their readers as informed opinion* **present**, represent, portray, depict, characterize; embellish, enhance, touch up, embroider, gloss, adorn; ginger up; *informal* jazz up.
▶ **noun 1** *she had on a long blue dress* **frock**, gown, robe, shift.
2 *at ten o'clock Morton put on full evening dress* **clothes**, clothing, garments, attire, costume, outfit, ensemble, garb, turnout; finery, regalia; *informal* gear, get-up, togs, duds, glad rags, schmutter; *Brit. informal* clobber, kit, rig-out; *N. Amer. informal* threads; *formal* apparel, habiliment, raiment; *archaic* vestments.
WORD LINKS
relating to dress **sartorial**

dressing *See centre pages for list of salad* **Dressings**
▶ **noun 1** *spoon the dressing over the salad* **sauce**, relish, condiment, dip, flavouring.
2 *they put fresh dressings on her burns* **bandage**, covering, plaster, gauze, lint, compress, ligature, swathe, poultice, salve; *Medicine* spica; *trademark* Elastoplast, Band-Aid.
3 *a dressing of farmyard manure* **fertilizer**, mulch; manure, compost, dung, bonemeal, {blood, fish, and bone}, fishmeal, guano; humus, peat; top-dressing.

dressmaker ▶ **noun** **garment-maker**, seamstress, needlewoman, tailoress; tailor, outfitter, costumier, clothier; couturier, designer; *dated* modiste.

dressy ▶ **adjective** (*informal*) *nobody changes into anything dressy for dinner* **smart**, formal, elaborate, ornate; stylish, elegant, dashing, sophisticated, chic, fashionable, modish; *French* à la mode; *informal* sharp, snappy, snazzy, natty, ritzy, classy, swish, trendy, with it.
OPPOSITE casual.

dribble ▶ **verb 1** *the cat started to retch and dribble* **drool**, slaver, slobber, salivate, drivel, water at the mouth; *Scottish* slabber.
2 *rainwater dribbled down her temples* **trickle**, drip, fall in drops, drop, drizzle; leak, ooze, exude, seep.
▶ **noun 1** *there was dribble down his chin* **saliva**, spittle, spit, slaver, slobber, drool.
2 *there was a dribble of sweat on her forehead* **trickle**, drip, driblet, small stream, drizzle; drop, dash, spot, smear, splash, speck, lick.

dried ▶ **adjective** *dried fruit* **dehydrated**, desiccated, dry, dried up, moistureless.
OPPOSITE fresh.

drift ▶ **verb 1** *his life raft drifted back over the horizon* **be carried**, be carried (away/along), be borne, be wafted; float, bob, move slowly, go with the current, coast, meander.
2 *the guests drifted away from the centre of the room* **wander**, wander aimlessly, roam, rove, meander, stray, coast; potter, dawdle, dally; *Brit. informal* mooch.
3 *don't allow your attention to drift* **stray**, digress, depart, diverge, veer, swerve, deviate, get sidetracked; *rare* divagate.
4 *snow had drifted deep over the path* **pile up**, bank up, heap up, accumulate, gather, form heaps/drifts, amass.
▶ **noun 1** *there was a drift from the country to the urban areas* **movement**, shift, flow, transfer, transferral, relocation, gravitation.
2 *the pilot had not noticed any appreciable drift* **deviation**, digression, veering, straying.
3 *he caught the drift of her thoughts* **gist**, essence, core, meaning, sense, thesis, substance, significance, signification; thrust, import, purport, tenor, vein, spirit; implication, intention, direction, course, tendency, trend.
4 *a drift of deep snow* **pile**, heap, bank, mound, mass, accumulation, dune, ridge.

drifter ▶ **noun** **wanderer**, traveller, transient, roamer, tramp, vagabond, vagrant, person of no fixed abode; *N. Amer.* hobo; *Austral./NZ informal* derro.

drill ▶ **noun 1** *a hydraulic drill* **drilling tool**, boring tool, rotary tool, auger, (brace and) bit, gimlet, awl, bradawl.
2 *he used military discipline and drill to train the boys* **training**, instruction, coaching, teaching, grounding; (physical) exercises, workout; discipline; *informal* square-bashing.
3 *Estelle seemed to know the drill* **procedure**, routine, practice, pattern, regimen, programme, schedule, method, system, custom, order.
▶ **verb 1** *drill the end of the piece of wood* **bore a hole in**, make a hole in, cut a hole in, drill a hole in; **bore**, pierce, puncture, penetrate, perforate, sink.
OPPOSITES punch, gouge.
2 *a sergeant drilling new recruits* **train**, instruct, coach, teach, ground, inculcate, discipline, exercise, make fit, rehearse, put someone through their paces.
3 *his mother had always* **drilled into** *him the need to pay for one's sins* **instil**, hammer, drive, drum, din, bang, knock, implant, ingrain; teach, indoctrinate, inculcate, brainwash.

drink *See centre pages for lists of* **Beers** **Cocktails and Mixed Drinks** **Coffee Drinks** **Drinking Vessels** **Drinks** **Sherries** **Teas** **Whiskies** **Wines**
▶ **verb 1** *she drank her coffee* **swallow**, gulp down, quaff, swill, guzzle, sup; imbibe, partake of, sip, consume, take; drain, toss off; *informal* swig, down, knock back, put away, neck, sink, kill, slug, inhale, wet one's whistle; *N. Amer. informal* scarf (down/up), snarf (down/up); *rare* ingurgitate.
2 *a churchgoing man who never drank* **drink alcohol**, take alcohol, tipple, indulge; be a serious/heavy/hard drinker, be an alcoholic; carouse, go drinking; *informal* take a drop, hit the bottle, take to the bottle, booze, knock a few back, have a few, have one over the eight, tank up, get tanked up, drink like a fish, go on a binge/bender; *Brit. informal* bevvy; *N. Amer. informal* bend one's elbow, lush; *archaic* wassail, tope.
OPPOSITES be teetotal, be on the wagon.
3 *let's* **drink to** *the success of our venture* **toast**, propose a toast to, wish success/luck/health to, salute.
□ **drink something in** *he drank in the details of the crime* **absorb**, assimilate, digest, ingest, take in, be absorbed in, be immersed in, be rapt in, be lost in, be fascinated by, pay close attention to.
▶ **noun 1** *he took another sip of his drink* **beverage**, drinkable/potable liquid, liquid refreshment, thirst-quencher; dram, bracer, nightcap, nip, tot, spot; *N. Amer.* eye-opener; *Scottish & Irish* deoch an doris; *Brit. informal* cuppa, pint; *rare* potation, libation.
2 *he sought refuge in drink because of his loneliness* **alcohol**, liquor, intoxicating liquor, alcoholic drink, strong drink, intoxicants; *informal* booze, hooch, the hard stuff, firewater, gut-rot, rotgut, moonshine, tipple, the demon drink, the bottle, juice, the sauce, grog, Dutch courage, John Barleycorn; *Brit. informal* wallop, bevvy.
3 *she took a drink of her wine* **swallow**, gulp, sip, draught, swill; *informal* swig, slug.
4 *she asked if she could have a drink of orange juice* **glass**, cup, mug.
5 (**the drink**) (*informal*) *he heaved the outboard motor into the drink* **the sea**, the ocean, the water; *informal* the briny, Davy Jones's locker; *literary* the deep.
WORD LINKS
fear of drink **potophobia**

drinkable ▶ **adjective** *the well water is drinkable* **fit to drink**, potable, palatable; pure, fresh, clean, safe, unpolluted, untainted, unadulterated, uncontaminated.
OPPOSITE undrinkable.

drinker ▶ **noun** *he was a notorious drinker and womanizer* **drunkard**, drunk, inebriate, imbiber, tippler, sot, heavy drinker, hard drinker, serious drinker, problem drinker; alcoholic, dipsomaniac, chronic alcoholic, alcohol-abuser, alcohol addict, person with a drink problem; *informal* boozer, soak, lush, wino, alky, sponge, elbow-bender, barfly, tosspot; *Austral./NZ informal* hophead, metho; *archaic* toper; *vulgar slang* pisshead, piss artist.
OPPOSITE teetotaller.

drip ▶ **verb 1** *there was a tap dripping in the kitchen* **dribble**, drop, leak.
OPPOSITE gush.
2 *the sweat was dripping from his chin* **drop**, dribble, trickle, drizzle, run, splash, sprinkle, plop, fall in drops; leak, ooze, seep, exude, be discharged, emanate, issue.
▶ **noun 1** *a bucket to catch drips from the leak in the ceiling* **drop**, dribble, bead,

spot, trickle, splash, plop.
2 (*informal*) *I hope that drip from Oxford isn't still after you* **weakling**, ninny, milksop, Milquetoast, namby-pamby, crybaby, pushover, softie, doormat, ineffective person; bore, tiresome person; *informal* **wimp**, weed, sissy, pansy, nebbish; *Brit. informal* wet, wally, big girl's blouse, chinless wonder; *N. Amer. informal* candy-ass, pantywaist, pussy, wuss.

drive ▶ verb **1** *you can't drive a car without a speedometer* **operate**, pilot, steer, handle, manage; guide, direct, navigate.
2 *he drove to the police station* **travel by car**, go by car, motor; *informal* travel on wheels, tool along, bowl along, spin.
OPPOSITE walk.
3 *I'll drive you to the airport* **chauffeur**, run, give someone a lift, take, bring, ferry, transport, convey, carry.
4 *a two-litre engine drives the front wheels* **power**, propel, move, push.
5 *he drove a nail into the sole of the boot* **hammer**, screw, ram, bang, pound, sink, plunge, thrust, stab, propel, knock, send.
6 *I was allowed to drive cattle to market* **impel**, urge, press, move, get going; **herd**, round-up, shepherd.
7 *a desperate mother driven to crime* **force**, compel, constrain, impel, press, prompt, precipitate, catapult; oblige, coerce, make, pressure, goad, spur, prod.
8 *he drove himself and his staff extremely hard* **work**, exert, push, tax; overwork, overtax, overburden.
□ **drive at** *I can see what you're driving at, but you're quite wrong* **suggest**, imply, hint at, allude to, intimate, insinuate, indicate, have in mind; refer to, mean, intend; *informal* get at.
▶ noun **1** *a family out for a Sunday afternoon drive* **excursion**, outing, trip, jaunt, tour, turn; ride, run, journey; *Scottish* hurl; *informal* spin, joyride.
2 *the house is approached by a long drive* **driveway**, approach, access road; road, roadway, avenue.
3 *a low level of sexual drive* **urge**, appetite, desire, need; impulse, instinct.
4 *she lacked the drive to start on a new career* **motivation**, **ambition**, push, single-mindedness, will power, dedication, doggedness, tenacity, enterprise, initiative, enthusiasm, zeal, commitment, aggression, aggressiveness, forcefulness, spirit; energy, vigour, verve, vitality, liveliness, vim, pep; *informal* get-up-and-go, zip, pizzazz, punch.
OPPOSITE inertia.
5 *an anti-corruption drive* **campaign**, crusade, movement, effort, push, surge, appeal.
6 (*Brit.*) *a whist drive* **tournament**, competition, contest, event, match.

drivel ▶ noun *Walter was talking complete drivel* **nonsense**, twaddle, claptrap, balderdash, gibberish, rubbish, mumbo-jumbo; *informal* rot, tommyrot, poppycock, phooey, hot air, eyewash, piffle, garbage, tripe, waffle, bosh, bull, bunk, blah, hogwash, baloney; *Brit. informal* cobblers, codswallop, cock, stuff and nonsense, tosh, double Dutch; *N. Amer. informal* flapdoodle, blathers, wack, bushwa, applesauce; *informal, dated* bunkum; *vulgar slang* crap, bullshit, bollocks, balls; *Austral./NZ vulgar slang* bulldust.
OPPOSITE sense.
▶ verb *you always* **drivel on** *like this* **talk nonsense**, talk rubbish, babble, ramble, gibber, burble, blather, blether, prate, prattle, gabble, chatter, twitter, maunder; *informal* waffle, witter on, gab, talk through one's hat; *vulgar slang* bullshit.

driver ▶ noun **motorist**; chauffeur; pilot, operator, engineer.
OPPOSITE passenger.

drizzle ▶ noun **1** *they shivered in the cold drizzle* **fine rain**, Scotch mist, sprinkle of rain, light shower, spray; *N. English* mizzle.
2 *top with a drizzle of sour cream* **trickle**, dribble, drip, drop, droplet, stream, rivulet, runnel; topping, covering, sprinkle, sprinkling.
▶ verb **1** *it's beginning to drizzle* **rain lightly**, shower, spot, spit; *N. English* mizzle; *N. Amer.* sprinkle.
2 *leave the jelly to cool and drizzle over the cream* **trickle**, sprinkle, drip, dribble, pour, splash, spill.

droll ▶ adjective **1** *a droll comment* **funny**, humorous, amusing, comic, comical, mirthful, hilarious, rollicking; clownish, farcical, zany, quirky, eccentric, preposterous; ridiculous, ludicrous, risible, laughable; jocular, light-hearted, facetious, waggish, witty, whimsical, wry, sportive, tongue-in-cheek; entertaining, diverting, engaging, sparkling; *informal* wacky, side-splitting, rib-tickling.
OPPOSITE serious.
2 *a droll little girl* **quaint**, odd, strange, queer, eccentric, outlandish, bizarre, whimsical.

drone ▶ verb **1** *we heard a plane droning overhead* **hum**, buzz, whirr, vibrate, murmur, rumble, purr, hiss, whisper, sigh.
2 *the president* **droned on** *about right and wrong* **speak boringly**, speak monotonously, go on and on, talk interminably; intone, pontificate; *informal* spout, sound off, jaw, spiel, speechify, preachify.
▶ noun **1** *the drone of aircraft taking off* **hum**, buzz, whirr, whirring, vibration, murmur, murmuring, purr, purring, hiss, hissing, whisper, whispering, sigh.
2 *students came to be regarded as drones supported by taxpayers' money* **hanger-on**, parasite, leech, passenger; **idler**, loafer, layabout, lounger, good-for-nothing, do-nothing, sluggard, laggard; *informal* lazybones, scrounger, sponger, cadger, freeloader, bloodsucker, waster, skiver, slacker.

drool ▶ verb *his mouth was open and drooling* **salivate**, dribble, slaver, slobber, drivel, water at the mouth; *Scottish* slabber.
▶ noun *a fine trickle of drool leaked from the corner of his mouth* **saliva**, spit, spittle, dribble, slaver, slobber.

droop ▶ verb **1** *the horse had his tail drooping* **hang down**, hang, dangle, bend, bow, stoop, sag, sink, slump, fall down, drop, flop, wilt, become limp, become flaccid, drape.
OPPOSITE be upright.
2 *Danny's eyelids were drooping* **close**, shut, fall.
OPPOSITE open.
3 *he had to break some news to her that made her droop still more* **be despondent**, lose heart, give up hope, become dispirited, become dejected, despond; flag, fade, languish, falter, weaken, wilt, go into a decline, waste away.
OPPOSITE cheer.
▶ noun *the lustreless droop of her hair* **drooping**, sag, sagging, sinking, slump, slumping; bend, bow, bowing, stoop, stooping.

droopy ▶ adjective *a droopy moustache* **hanging down**, drooping, hanging, dangling, falling, dropping, draped; bending, bent, bowed, bowing, stooping; sagging, sinking, slumping, flopping, wilting, becoming limp, becoming flaccid.
OPPOSITE upright.

drop ▶ verb **1** *Eric dropped a tea chest full of crockery* **let fall**, let go (of), fail to hold, lose one's grip on; release, unhand, relinquish.
OPPOSITES hold on to; lift.
2 *stalactites are formed when water drops from a cave roof* **drip**, fall in drops, fall, dribble, trickle, drizzle, flow, run, plop, leak.
3 *an aeroplane had dropped out of the sky* **fall**, come/go down, descend, sink; plunge, plummet, dive, nosedive, tumble, pitch, slump.
OPPOSITE rise.
4 *she dropped to her knees* **fall**, sink, collapse, descend, go down, slide, stumble, tumble.
OPPOSITE rise.
5 (*informal*) *I was dropping with exhaustion* **collapse**, faint, pass out, black out, swoon, lose consciousness, fall unconscious, keel over, fall/sink down; *informal* flake out, conk out, go out.
6 *the track separated as it dropped from the ridge* **slope downwards**, slope, slant downwards, descend, go down, decline, fall away, sink, dip.
OPPOSITE rise.
7 *they decided to drop the price | the exchange rate dropped* **decrease**, lessen, make less, reduce, diminish, depreciate; fall, decline, become less, dwindle, sink, slump, slacken off, plunge, plummet.
OPPOSITE increase.
8 *pupils will be allowed to drop history or geography at 14* **give up**, finish with, withdraw from, retire from, cancel; discontinue, end, stop, cease, halt, terminate; abandon, forgo, relinquish, dispense with, have done with, throw up; *informal* pack in, quit, cry off.
OPPOSITES take up; continue.
9 *he was dropped from the team* **exclude**, discard, expel, oust, throw out, leave out, get rid of; dismiss, discharge, let go; *informal* boot out, kick out, chuck out, turf out.
OPPOSITE pick.
10 *he was determined to drop his more unsuitable friends* **abandon**, desert, throw over; repudiate, renounce, disown, disclaim, disavow, turn one's back on, wash one's hands of; discard, reject, give up, cast off; neglect, shun; *archaic* forsake.
OPPOSITES keep, retain.
11 *he tried to look working-class and dropped his aitches | he dropped all reference to 'compensation'* **omit**, leave out, leave off, eliminate, take out, miss out, delete, cut, erase; elide, contract, slur.
OPPOSITE pronounce.
12 *he* **dropped** *the tapes* **off** *| the taxi* **dropped** *her* **off** **deliver**, bring, take, convey, carry, transport; leave, put off, unload; allow to alight.
OPPOSITE pick up.
13 *drop the gun on the floor* **put**, place, rest, deposit, set, set down, lay, leave, settle, shove, stick, position, station; *informal* pop, plonk.
OPPOSITE pick up.
14 *she dropped the names of her most prestigious clients* **mention**, refer to, speak of, hint at; bring up, raise, broach, introduce; show off.
15 *the club has yet to drop a point in the second division* **lose**, fail to win, concede, miss out on, give away, let slip.
OPPOSITE win.
□ **drop back/behind** *she dropped back unnoticed by the others* **fall back/behind**, get left behind, lag behind, straggle, linger, dawdle, dally, hang back, loiter, bring/take up the rear; *informal* dilly-dally; *dated* tarry.
OPPOSITES go ahead, keep up.
□ **drop off 1** *trade between the two countries dropped off sharply.* *See* DROP *sense* 7.
2 *insomnia can mean dropping off in the day* **fall asleep**, go to sleep, get to sleep, doze (off), have a nap, catnap, drowse; *informal* nod off, go off, drift

D

D

off, snooze, take forty winks, get some shut-eye, crash out, go out like a light, flake out, conk out; *N. Amer. informal* sack out, zone out.
OPPOSITE wake up.
□ **drop out** *he had dropped out of his studies.* See **DROP** *sense 8.*
▶ **noun 1** *a drop of water* **droplet**, blob, globule, bead, bubble, tear, dot, spheroid, oval; *informal* glob.
2 *it just needs a drop of oil* **small amount**, little, bit, dash, spot, soupçon; dribble, driblet, sprinkle, trickle, splash, scintilla; lick, taste, dram, sip, trace, whiff, whisper, nuance, murmur, breath; pinch, dab, speck, grain, smattering, sprinkling; particle, modicum; *informal* smidgen, tad.
OPPOSITES large amount, great deal.
3 *an acid drop* **sweet**, lozenge, pastille, piece of confectionery; chocolate, bonbon, fondant, toffee; *N. Amer.* candy.
4 *a small drop in profits* **decrease**, reduction, decline, lowering, lessening, falling off, fall-off, downturn, slump; cut, cutback, curtailment, diminution; depreciation, devaluation.
OPPOSITES rise, increase.
5 *I walked over to the edge of the drop* **cliff**, abyss, chasm, gorge, gully, precipice; slope, descent, incline, declivity, downslope, ramp.
6 (**the drop**) (*informal*) *they only just avoided the drop last season* **relegation**, demotion, lowering, reduction, downgrading.
OPPOSITE promotion.
7 (**the drop**) *he walked around her like a hangman measuring her for the drop* **hanging**, gibbeting; execution, capital punishment, death sentence/penalty; *informal* stringing up.

dropout ▶ **noun** *long hair was the trademark of the dropout* **beatnik**, hippy, bohemian, nonconformist, free spirit, avant-gardist, rebel, misfit, outsider, loner, eccentric; idler, layabout, loafer, lounger, good-for-nothing; *informal* freak, oddball, deadbeat, waster, bum.

droppings ▶ **plural noun** *rat droppings* **excrement**, excreta, faeces, stools, dung, ordure, manure; *informal* poo, doo-doo; *vulgar slang* shit, crap, turds.

dross ▶ **noun** *sometimes it's possible to find a little gem amongst the mass-produced dross* **rubbish**, junk, debris, chaff, draff, detritus, flotsam and jetsam; *N. Amer.* trash, garbage; *informal* dreck; *Brit. informal* grot.

drought ▶ **noun** **dry spell**, dry period, lack of rain, shortage of water; *Scottish* drouth.

drove ▶ **noun 1** *a drove of cattle* **herd**, flock, pack, fold.
2 *they came down the street in droves* **crowd**, swarm, horde, multitude, mob, throng, host, mass, army; collection, gathering, assembly, company; rabble, herd, crush, press, stream, sea.

drown ▶ **verb 1** *he was shipwrecked, and very nearly drowned* **suffocate in water**, inhale water; go under; go to a watery grave; *informal* go to Davy Jones's locker.
2 *when the ice melted, the valleys were drowned* **flood**, submerge, immerse, inundate, deluge, swamp, engulf, drench, soak, cover, saturate.
OPPOSITE drain.
3 *his voice was drowned by the clatter of footsteps* **make inaudible**, drown out, be louder than, overpower, overwhelm, overcome, override, engulf, swallow up, devour, bury; muffle, deaden, stifle, wipe out, extinguish, silence.
OPPOSITE augment.
4 *she had spent every waking hour working, trying to drown her private pain* **suppress**, deaden, stifle, restrain, smother, bottle up, hold back, keep back, check, keep in check, curb, contain, bridle, put a lid on; extinguish, quash, quench, obliterate, wipe out, get rid of.

drowse ▶ **verb** *they were content to drowse in the sun* **doze**, sleep (lightly), nap, take a nap, catnap, take a siesta, rest; *informal* snooze, have a snooze, snatch/get forty winks, get some shut-eye; *Brit. informal* kip, have a kip, get some kip; *N. Amer. informal* catch some Zs, catch a few Zs; *literary* slumber.
OPPOSITE be awake.
▶ **noun** *she had been alerted from her drowse* **doze**, light sleep, nap, catnap, siesta, lie-down, rest; *informal* snooze, forty winks, shut-eye; *Brit. informal* kip, zizz; *literary* slumber.
OPPOSITE wakefulness.

drowsiness ▶ **noun** *these tablets often cause drowsiness* **sleepiness**, somnolence, tiredness, fatigue, weariness, exhaustion; sluggishness, lethargy, listlessness, torpor, enervation, lifelessness, laziness, indolence, inertia, lassitude, apathy, debility; *informal* doziness, dopiness, grogginess.
OPPOSITES wakefulness; energy.

drowsy ▶ **adjective 1** *the stove warmed the tent up and we became drowsy* **sleepy**, half asleep, dozy, dozing, heavy, heavy-eyed, yawning, nodding, groggy, somnolent, ready for bed, hardly able to keep one's eyes open; tired, weary, fatigued, exhausted; lethargic, sluggish, torpid, lifeless, listless, languid, languorous, comatose, dazed, drugged; *informal* snoozy, dopey, yawny, dead beat, all in, done in, dog-tired; *Brit. informal* knackered; *literary* slumberous.
OPPOSITES wakeful, alert.
2 *a warm, drowsy afternoon* **soporific**, sleep-inducing, sleepy, somniferous, narcotic, sedative, calmative, tranquillizing; lulling, soothing; dreamy; *rare* somnific.
OPPOSITE invigorating.

drubbing ▶ **noun 1** *I decided to give her fancy man a good drubbing* **beating**, thrashing, walloping, thumping, battering, pounding, pummelling, slapping, smacking, punching, bludgeoning, thwacking, cuffing, buffeting, mauling, pelting, lambasting; whipping, flogging, flaying, birching, cudgelling, clubbing; *informal* hammering, licking, clobbering, belting, bashing, pasting, whacking, slugging, tanning, biffing, bopping, hiding, beating-up, duffing-up, doing-over, working-over, kicking.
2 *Scotland's 3-0 drubbing by France* **defeat**, beating, trouncing, rout, loss, vanquishing, crushing; *informal* licking, thrashing, clobbering.
OPPOSITE win.

drudge ▶ **noun** *her family reduced her to a household drudge* **menial**, menial worker, slave, toiler, lackey; servant, labourer, hack, worker, maid/man of all work, houseboy, factotum, hewer of wood and drawer of water; *informal* skivvy, dogsbody, gofer, running dog, runner; *N. Amer.* peon; *Brit. dated* charwoman, charlady, char; *archaic* scullion, servitor.
▶ **verb** (*archaic*) *he was drudging in the fields as a day labourer.* See **TOIL**.

drudgery ▶ **noun** *the housewives were left alone with their drudgery* **hard work**, menial work, donkey work, toil, toiling, labour, hard/sweated labour, chores, plodding; slavery; *informal* skivvying, grind, slog; *Brit. informal* graft; *Austral./NZ informal* (hard) yakka; *archaic* travail, moil.
OPPOSITE relaxation.

drug *See centre pages for lists of* **Drugs** **Medication**
▶ **noun 1** *drugs prescribed by doctors can be extremely hazardous if misused* **medicine**, medical drug, medication, medicament; remedy, cure, antidote; cure-all, panacea; nostrum; potion, elixir; *informal* magic bullet; *archaic* physic.
2 *she was obviously under the influence of drugs or booze* **narcotic**, **stimulant**, hallucinogen, addictive drug, recreational drug, illegal drug, substance; *informal* dope, junk, gear, stuff, downer, upper; *vulgar slang* shit.
▶ **verb 1** *he was drugged and bundled into the boot of a car* **anaesthetize**, give an anaesthetic to, narcotize, give drugs to, give narcotics to, give opiates to, poison; knock out, make/render unconscious, make/render insensible, stupefy, befuddle; *informal* dope.
2 *she had drugged his coffee* **add drugs to**, tamper with, adulterate, contaminate, poison; *informal* dope, spike, lace, slip a Mickey Finn into, doctor.

WORD LINKS

related prefixes	**pharmaco-, narco- (e.g. *narcoterrorism*)**
relating to drugs	**pharmaceutical**
branch of medicine to do with drugs	**pharmacology**
fear of drugs	**pharmacophobia**
shop selling drugs	*Brit.* **pharmacy, chemist's;** *N. Amer.* **drugstore**
seller of drugs	*Brit.* **pharmacist, chemist;** *N. Amer.* **druggist**

drug addict ▶ **noun.** *See* **ADDICT**.

drugged ▶ **adjective** *he was obviously drunk or drugged when he wrote it* **stupefied**, insensible, befuddled; delirious, hallucinating, narcotized; anaesthetized, knocked out, comatose; *informal* **stoned**, high, doped, dopey, on a trip, tripping, spaced out, zonked, wasted, wrecked, high as a kite, off one's head, out of one's mind, flying, turned on, hyped up, freaked out, charged up; *Brit. informal* loved-up.
OPPOSITE sober.

drum *See centre pages for list of* **Percussion Instruments**
▶ **noun 1** *the steady drum of raindrops* **beat**, rhythm, patter, tap, chatter, pounding, thump, thumping, thud, thudding, rattle, rattling, pitter-patter, rat-a-tat, pit-a-pat, thrum, tattoo, vibration, throb, throbbing, pulsation; *archaic* bicker, clacket.
2 *a drum of radioactive waste* **canister**, barrel, cylinder, tank, bin, can; container, receptacle, holder, vessel, repository.
▶ **verb 1** *she drummed her fingers on the desktop* **tap**, beat, rap, knock, strike, thud, thump, hit; tattoo, thrum.
2 *an unwritten law which was drummed into us at school* **instil**, drive, drive home, din, hammer, drill, drub, implant, ingrain, inculcate; teach over and over again, indoctrinate, brainwash.
□ **drum someone out** *he was drummed out of office* **expel from**, dismiss from, discharge from, throw out of, oust from; drive out of, get rid of, thrust out of, push out of; exclude from, banish from; *Military* cashier; *informal* give someone the boot, boot out, kick out, give someone their marching orders, give someone the bullet, give someone the push, show someone the door, send packing.
□ **drum something up** *he was drumming up business for his new investment company* **round up**, gather, collect; summon, obtain, get, attract; canvass, solicit, petition, bid for.

WORD LINKS
player of drums **drummer, timpanist, percussionist**

drunk ▶ **adjective** *they went to a pub and got drunk* **intoxicated**, inebriated, drunken, befuddled, incapable, tipsy, the worse for drink, under the influence, maudlin; blind drunk, dead drunk, rolling drunk, roaring drunk, (as) drunk as a lord, (as) drunk as a skunk; sottish, tippling, toping, gin-soaked; *informal* tight, merry, the worse for wear, woozy, pie-

eyed, two/three sheets to the wind, under the table, plastered, smashed, wrecked, sloshed, soused, well oiled, sozzled, blotto, blitzed, canned, stewed, pickled, tanked (up), soaked, bombed, hammered, blasted, off one's face, out of/off one's head, out of one's skull, wasted, wired, in one's cups, reeling, cock-eyed, zonked, guttered, fuddled, stinko, ratted; *Brit. informal* legless, steaming, bevvied, paralytic, Brahms and Liszt, half cut, out of it, having had a skinful, bladdered, trolleyed, well away, squiffy, tiddly, out of one's box, having had one over the eight, cut, steamed; *Brit. vulgar slang* pissed, as pissed as a newt/fart, rat-arsed; *Scottish informal* fou; *N. Amer. informal* loaded, trashed, crock, juiced, sauced, squiffed, swacked, strung out, liquored up, out of one's gourd, in the bag, zoned; *N. Amer. & Austral./NZ informal* shickered, shot; *Austral. informal* full, as full as a goog, inked; *S. African informal* lekker; *euphemistic* tired and emotional; *informal, dated* stoned, lit up, as tight as a tick; *Brit. informal, dated* half seas over, pixilated; *archaic* sotted, besotted, foxed, screwed; *rare* crapulent, crapulous, inebriate, bibulous, ebrious, ebriose, ebriate.
OPPOSITE sober.
▶ **noun** *a drunk lay slumped against a wall* **drunkard**, inebriate, drinker, imbiber, tippler, sot; heavy drinker, hard drinker, serious drinker, problem drinker; alcoholic, dipsomaniac, chronic alcoholic, alcohol-abuser, alcohol addict, person with a drink problem; *informal* boozer, soak, lush, wino, alky, sponge, elbow-bender, barfly, tosspot; *Austral./NZ informal* hophead, metho; *archaic* toper; *vulgar slang* pisshead, piss artist.
OPPOSITE teetotaller.

drunken ▶ **adjective 1** *a drunken driver. See* DRUNK.
2 *a drunken all-night party* **debauched**, dissipated, riotous, carousing, revelling, roistering, uproarious, unruly, intemperate, unrestrained, uninhibited, abandoned; orgiastic, bacchanalian, Bacchic, wassailing, Dionysian, saturnalian; *informal* boozy.
OPPOSITE restrained.

drunkenness ▶ **noun** *he was prone to bouts of drunkenness* **intoxication**, inebriation, insobriety, tipsiness; intemperance, overindulgence, debauchery; hard drinking, serious drinking, heavy drinking, alcoholism, alcohol abuse, dipsomania; *rare* inebriety, sottishness, crapulence, bibulousness.
OPPOSITE sobriety.

dry ▶ **adjective 1** *the dry desert lay behind* **arid**, parched, scorched, baked, burned, dried up/out, torrid, hot, sizzling, burning; waterless, moistureless, rainless; dehydrated, desiccated; thirsty; as dry as a bone, bone dry, as dry as dust; *rare* droughty, torrefied.
OPPOSITE wet.
2 *the crackle of dry leaves* **parched**, dried, withered, shrivelled, wilted, wizened; crisp, crispy, brittle; dehydrated, desiccated, sun-baked; sapless, juiceless.
OPPOSITE fresh.
3 *the hamburgers were dry* **hard**, hardened, dried out, stale, old, past its best, past its sell-by date, off.
OPPOSITES fresh; moist.
4 *the river is dry | a dry well* **waterless**, dried out, empty.
5 *I brought a few beers in case you got dry* **thirsty**, dehydrated, longing for a drink; *informal* parched, gasping.
6 *it was dry work* **thirst-making**, thirst-provoking, thirsty, hot, strenuous, arduous, heavy, tiring, exhausting.
7 *a piece of dry toast* **unbuttered**, plain, butterless.
8 *the story brings the dry facts to life* **bare**, simple, basic, fundamental, stark, naked, bald, cold, hard, straightforward; unadorned, unembellished.
OPPOSITE embellished.
9 *a dry debate on science policy* **dull**, uninteresting, boring, unexciting, tedious, tiresome, wearisome, dreary, monotonous, dry as dust, arid; unimaginative, sterile, flat, bland, insipid, lacklustre, stodgy, colourless, lifeless, prosaic, run-of-the-mill, humdrum, mundane, commonplace, workaday, quotidian, routine, vapid; stiff, leaden, wooden; *informal* deadly; *Brit. informal* samey; *Scottish informal* dreich.
OPPOSITES interesting, lively.
10 *he's got a dry sense of humour* **wry**, subtle, low-key, laconic, sly, sharp; deadpan, straight-faced, poker-faced; ironic, sardonic, sarcastic, cynical, mordant, biting; satirical, mocking, scoffing, droll, waggish; *Brit. informal* sarky.
11 *he was nonplussed by this dry response to his cordial advance* **unemotional**, indifferent, undemonstrative, impassive, cool, cold, clinical, passionless, emotionless; aloof, reserved, remote, distant, restrained, impersonal, formal, stiff, rigid, wooden, starchy.
OPPOSITES emotional, expressive.
12 *sorry, this is a dry state | she has been dry for almost a year* **Prohibitionist**; **teetotal**, alcohol-free, non-drinking, abstinent; clean, sober; *informal* on the wagon, straight.
13 *dry white wine* **crisp**, sharp, piquant, not sweet, tart, bitter.
OPPOSITE sweet.
14 (*Brit.*) *they deliberately selected dry candidates* **monetarist**; **arch-conservative**, right-wing, reactionary; *Economics* supply-side; *informal* true-blue.
OPPOSITES wet; left-wing.
▶ **verb 1** *the hot sun had dried the ground again* **make dry**, dry out/up, parch, scorch, sear, bake; dehydrate, desiccate, dehumidify.
OPPOSITE moisten.
2 *dry the leaves and break them into small pieces* **dry up**, dehydrate, desiccate; wither, shrivel, wilt, wizen, mummify.
OPPOSITE moisten.
3 *I saw you drying your hair | he dried the dishes* **dry off**, towel, rub; mop up, blot up, soak up, absorb, sop up, clean up; drain.
4 *she dried her eyes* **wipe**, wipe tears from, rub, dab.
5 *there are various methods of drying meat* **desiccate**, dehydrate, remove the moisture from; preserve, cure, smoke.
□ **dry out** *he has spent periods drying out in a clinic* **give up drinking**, **give up alcohol**, become teetotal, overcome alcoholism, take the pledge; *informal* go on the wagon.
□ **dry up 1** (*informal*) *then he dried up, and Phil couldn't get another word out of him* **stop speaking/talking**, fall silent, say no more, shut up; forget one's lines/words; *informal* belt up, put a sock in it.
2 *foreign investment may dry up* **dwindle**, wane, disappear, fail, vanish, subside, peter out, fade (away), die away/out/off, taper off, trail away/off, ebb, melt away, evaporate, come to nothing, come to a halt/an end, run out, give out; become unproductive, grow barren/sterile, cease to yield.
OPPOSITE continue.
▶ **noun** *on economic policy he is a dry* **monetarist**; **arch-conservative**, right-winger, reactionary; *Economics* supply-sider.
OPPOSITES wet; left-winger.

WORD LINKS
related prefix **xero-** (e.g. ***xeroderma, xerography***)

dual ▶ **adjective** *a small flap fulfils a dual purpose as cupboard door and table* **double**, twofold, binary; duplicate, duplex, twin, matched, matching, paired, in pairs, coupled; *rare* binate.
OPPOSITE single.

duality ▶ **noun** *there was a duality in her feelings towards Johnny* **doubleness**, dualism, duplexity, ambivalence; dichotomy, polarity, separation, opposition, difference.

dub ▶ **verb 1** *he was dubbed 'the world's sexiest man'* **nickname**, call, name, give a name, label, christen, term, tag, entitle, style; **describe as**, designate, classify, class, categorize, characterize, denominate, nominate.
2 *this was followed by the dubbing of twenty four new knights* **knight**, confer/bestow a knighthood on, invest with a knighthood.

dubiety ▶ **noun** (*rare*) *anxiety had been excited by the dubiety of his fate* **doubtfulness**, uncertainty, lack of certainty, unsureness, incertitude; ambiguity, ambivalence, confusion; indecision, hesitancy, doubt; *rare* dubiosity.
OPPOSITE certainty.

dubious ▶ **adjective 1** *I was rather dubious about the whole idea* **doubtful**, uncertain, unsure, in doubt, hesitant; undecided, unsettled, unconfirmed, undetermined, indefinite, unresolved, up in the air; wavering, vacillating, irresolute, in a quandary, in a dilemma, on the horns of a dilemma; sceptical, suspicious; *informal* iffy.
OPPOSITES certain, definite.
2 *a dubious businessman* **suspicious**, suspect, under suspicion, untrustworthy, unreliable, undependable, questionable; *informal* shady, fishy, funny, not kosher; *Brit. informal* dodgy.
OPPOSITE trustworthy.
3 *she gave him a dubious reply* **equivocal**, ambiguous, indeterminate, indefinite, unclear, vague, imprecise, hazy, puzzling, enigmatic, cryptic; open to question, debatable, questionable.
OPPOSITES decisive, clear, definite.

dubitable ▶ **adjective** (*rare*) *these beliefs are certainly dubitable* **debatable**, disputable, questionable, open to question, open to debate, arguable; controversial, contentious; *informal* iffy.
OPPOSITE certain.

duck[1] ▶ **noun.** *See centre pages for list of* **Fowl**

WORD LINKS
male **drake**
female **duck**
young **duckling**

duck[2] ▶ **verb 1** *the ball passed over the batsman as he ducked | he ducked behind the wall* **bob down**, bend (down), bow down, stoop (down), crouch (down), squat (down), hunch down, hunker down, sit on one's haunches; cower, cringe, shrink, huddle.
OPPOSITES straighten up; stand.
2 *she was ducked in the river* **dip**, dunk, plunge, immerse, submerge, lower, sink.
3 (*informal*) *he* ***ducked out of*** *history lessons | they cannot duck the issue much longer* **shirk**, dodge, evade, avoid, steer clear of, run away from, elude, escape, find a way out of, back out of, pull out of, shun, eschew, miss; sidestep, bypass, skirt round, circumvent, give a wide berth to, find a way round, turn one's back on; *informal* cop out of, get out of, wriggle out of, worm one's way out of; *Brit. informal* skive, skive off, funk; *N. Amer. informal* cut; *Austral./NZ informal* duck-shove; *archaic* decline, bilk.

OPPOSITES take part in; face up to.

duct ▶ noun *the glands drain into a common duct | a ventilation duct* **tube**, channel, passage, canal, vessel; conduit, culvert; pipe, pipeline, outlet, inlet, flue, shaft, vent, airway; *Anatomy* ductus, ductule, vas, trachea.

ductile ▶ adjective **1** *ductile metals are often used to make machinery* **pliable**, pliant, flexible, supple, plastic, tensile, tractile; soft, malleable, workable, shapable, mouldable, bendable; *informal* bendy; *rare* fictile.
OPPOSITE brittle.
2 *the government found new ways to make the people ductile* **docile**, obedient, submissive, subservient, meek, mild, lamblike, willing, accommodating, amenable, cooperative, complaisant, compliant, pliant, pliable, malleable, tractable, biddable, persuadable, manipulable, easily manipulated, easily controlled, controllable, easily handled, like putty in someone's hands; gullible; *informal, dated* milky; *rare* persuasible, suasible.
OPPOSITE intransigent.

D

dud (*informal*) ▶ noun *their new product turned out to be a complete dud* **failure**, flop, let-down, disappointment; *Brit.* damp squib; *informal* washout, lemon, loser, no-hoper, non-starter, dead loss, dead duck, lead balloon; *N. Amer. informal* clinker.
OPPOSITE success.
▶ adjective **1** *a dud typewriter ribbon* **defective**, faulty, unsound, inoperative, broken, broken-down, not working, not in working order, not functioning, malfunctioning, failed; *informal* bust, busted, kaput, on its last legs, conked out, done for; *Brit. informal* duff, knackered; *Brit. vulgar slang* buggered.
OPPOSITE in working order.
2 *he payed with a dud £50 note* **counterfeit**, fraudulent, forged, fake, faked, false, bogus, spurious; bad, invalid, worthless; *informal* phoney.
OPPOSITE genuine.

dudgeon ▶ noun
□ **in high dudgeon** *Kirsty swept out of the room in high dudgeon* **indignantly**, resentfully, angrily, furiously, wrathfully; in a temper, in indignation, in anger, with resentment, with displeasure, having taken offence, having taken umbrage; *informal* in a huff, in a lather, in a paddy, foaming at the mouth, fit to be tied, as cross as two sticks, seeing red; *Brit. informal, dated* in a bate, in a wax.

due ▶ adjective **1** *she reminded them that their fees were due* **owing**, owed, to be paid, payable, payable now, payable immediately, receivable immediately; outstanding, overdue, unpaid, unsettled, undischarged; *N. Amer.* delinquent, past due.
OPPOSITE paid.
2 *the chancellor's Autumn statement is due today* **expected**, required, awaited, anticipated, scheduled for.
3 *he was treated with the respect* **due to** *a great artist* **deserved by**, merited by, earned by, warranted by; appropriate to, fit for, fitting for, suitable for, right for, proper to; *archaic* meet for.
OPPOSITE undeserved by.
4 *he drove without due care and attention* **proper**, right and proper, correct, rightful, fitting, suitable, appropriate, apt, adequate, sufficient, enough, ample, satisfactory, requisite; *formal* condign; *archaic* meet.
OPPOSITE unsuitable.
□ **due to 1** *her death was due to an infection of the abdominal wall* **attributable to**, caused by, ascribed to, ascribable to, assignable to, because of, put down to.
2 *the train was cancelled due to staff shortages* **because of**, owing to, on account of, as a consequence of, as a result of, thanks to, by reason of, on grounds of, in view of.
▶ noun **1** *he attracts more criticism than is his due* **rightful treatment**, fair treatment, deserved fate, just punishment; right, entitlement; rights, just deserts, deserts; *informal* comeuppance; *archaic* recompense.
2 (**dues**) *union members have already paid their dues* **fee**, membership fee, subscription, charge, toll, levy; payment, contribution.
▶ adverb *he hiked due north and arrived back at his base* **directly**, straight, exactly, precisely, without deviating, undeviatingly, dead, plumb, squarely.

duel ▶ noun **1** *the Baron was killed in a duel* **affair of honour**, mano-a-mano, single combat; fight, battle, clash, encounter, confrontation, head-to-head; *informal* face-off, shoot-out; *archaic* field meeting, duello, judicial duel, rencounter, meeting, meeting for satisfaction of honour; *rare* monomachy.
2 *the snooker duel got under way in earnest* **contest**, competition, match, game, event, fixture, meet; battle, fight, clash, encounter, engagement.
▶ verb *they duelled with swords* **fight a duel**; fight, clash, battle, combat, contend; *archaic* go out.

duff ▶ adjective (*Brit. informal*) *he's made some really duff films.* See BAD.

duffer ▶ noun (*informal*) *he's such a duffer—we shouldn't have hired him* **bungler**, blunderer, incompetent, oaf, dunce, dolt, dunderhead, fool, idiot, booby, stupid person, moron, cretin, imbecile; *informal* chump, clot, clod, nitwit, dimwit, airhead, birdbrain, lamebrain, pea-brain, numbskull, thickhead, fathead, blockhead, bonehead, meathead, chucklehead, knucklehead, pinhead, wooden-head, dipstick, dumb-bell, dumbhead, dumbo, dum-dum, noodle, donkey, ass, nerd; *Brit. informal* berk, divvy, wally, wazzock, nit, mug, prat, pillock, muppet; *Scottish informal* balloon, galoot, cuddy, nyaff; *N. Amer. informal* doofus, goofball, goof, putz, bozo, boob, chowderhead, meatball, lummox, dummy, turkey, clunk, ding-a-ling, palooka; *Austral./NZ informal* galah, drongo, alec, dingbat.

dulcet ▶ adjective *the Grand Duchess Anna spoke in dulcet tones* **sweet**, sweet-sounding, mellifluous, euphonious, soothing, mellow, honeyed, pleasant, agreeable; melodious, melodic, tuneful, musical, lilting, lyrical, harmonious, silvery, silver-toned, bell-like, golden; *informal* easy on the ear; *rare* mellifluent.
OPPOSITE harsh.

dull ▶ adjective **1** *he is the author of several dull novels* **uninteresting**, boring, tedious, tiresome, wearisome, dry, dry as dust, flat, bland, characterless, featureless, colourless, monotonous, unexciting, uninspiring, unstimulating, lacking variety, lacking variation, lacking excitement, lacking interest, unimaginative, uneventful, lifeless, soulless, insipid; unoriginal, commonplace, prosaic, run-of-the-mill, humdrum, unremarkable, banal, lame, plodding, ponderous, pedestrian; *informal* dull as dishwater, deadly, no great shakes, not up to much; *Scottish informal* dreich; *N. Amer. informal* dullsville, ornery.
OPPOSITE interesting.
2 *it was a miserably dull Saturday morning* **overcast**, cloudy, gloomy, dark, dim, dismal, dreary, bleak, sombre, grey, leaden, murky, sunless, louring; *literary* subfusc.
OPPOSITES sunny, bright.
3 *the window frames were painted in dull colours* **drab**, dreary, sombre, dark, subdued, muted, toned down, lacklustre, lustreless, colourless, faded, washed out, muddy, watery, pale; *literary* subfusc.
OPPOSITE bright.
4 *he heard a dull sound outside his door* **muffled**, muted, quiet, soft, softened, faint, indistinct; stifled, smothered, suppressed.
OPPOSITES loud; resonant.
5 *the edge of the chisel soon became dull* **blunt**, blunted, not sharp, unkeen, unsharpened, dulled, edgeless, worn down.
OPPOSITE sharp.
6 *an otherwise dull stock market was enlivened by merger plans* **slack**, sluggish, flat, slow, slow-moving, quiet, inactive, static, stagnant, depressed.
OPPOSITE brisk.
7 *the teacher was talking slowly to a rather dull child* **unintelligent**, stupid, slow, dull-witted, slow-witted, witless, doltish, dunce-like, stolid, vacuous, empty-headed, brainless, mindless, foolish, half-witted, idiotic, moronic, imbecilic, cretinous, obtuse; *informal* dense, dim, dim-witted, thick, thick as two short planks, dumb, dopey, dozy, lamebrained, pig-ignorant, bovine, slow on the uptake, soft in the head, brain-dead, boneheaded, chuckleheaded, dunderheaded, wooden-headed, fat-headed, muttonheaded; *Brit. informal* daft, not the full shilling; *N. Amer. vulgar slang* dumb-ass.
OPPOSITE clever.
8 *her cold made her feel dull* **sluggish**, lethargic, enervated, unenergetic, listless, languid, torpid, inactive, inert, slow, slow-moving, sleepy, somnolent, drowsy, weary, tired, fatigued, heavy, apathetic; *informal* dozy, dopey, yawny; *N. Amer. informal* logy; *Medicine* asthenic, neurasthenic; *archaic* lymphatic.
OPPOSITE lively.
▶ verb **1** *the pain was temporarily dulled by drugs* **lessen**, decrease, diminish, reduce, dampen, depress, take the edge off, blunt, deaden, mute, soften, tone down, allay, ease, soothe, assuage, alleviate, palliate, moderate, mitigate.
OPPOSITE intensify.
2 *sleep had dulled her mind* **numb**, benumb, deaden, desensitize, render insensitive, stupefy, daze, stun; drug, sedate, tranquillize, narcotize; *rare* torpefy, obtund.
OPPOSITE enliven.
3 *the leaves are dulled by powdery mildew* **fade**, pale, bleach, wash out, decolorize, decolour, dim, etiolate.
OPPOSITES enhance; brighten.
4 *the rain came in flurries, dulling the sky* **darken**, blacken, dim, blur, veil, obscure, shadow, fog; *literary* bedim.
OPPOSITE brighten.
5 *the sombre atmosphere of that place dulled her spirit* **dampen**, put a damper on, cast a pall over, cast down, lower, depress, crush, shake, sap, suppress, extinguish, smother, stifle.
OPPOSITE raise.

CHOOSE THE RIGHT WORD

dull, boring, monotonous, tedious
See BORING.

dullard ▶ noun *the MP was caricatured as a dupe and a dullard* **idiot**, fool, stupid person, simpleton, ignoramus, oaf, dunce, dolt, moron, cretin, imbecile; *informal* duffer, nincompoop, booby, dope, chump, nitwit, dimwit, airhead, birdbrain, lamebrain, pea-brain, numbskull, thickhead, fathead, blockhead, bonehead, dunderhead, meathead, muttonhead, wooden-head, dipstick, dumb-bell, noodle, dumbo, dum-dum, ass, donkey, jerk; *Brit. informal* wally, berk, divvy, nit, mug, pillock, prat, wazzock, silly billy; *N. Amer. informal* doofus, goof, goofball, putz, bozo, boob, lummox, dummy, turkey; *Austral./NZ informal* galah, dingbat, drongo.

duly ▶ adverb **1** *the document was duly signed and authorized* **properly**, correctly, in due manner, rightly, fittingly, fitly, aptly, appropriately, suitably.
OPPOSITE improperly.
2 *the footman duly arrived to collect Alice* **at the proper time**, at the right time, in due time, on time, punctually.

dumb ▶ adjective **1** *he was born deaf and dumb | she stood dumb while he poured out a stream of abuse* **mute**, unable to speak, without the power of speech; **speechless**, tongue-tied, wordless, silent, at a loss for words, voiceless, inarticulate, taciturn, uncommunicative, untalkative, tight-lipped, close-mouthed, saying nothing; *informal* mum; *technical* aphasic, aphonic.
2 (*informal*) *he is not as dumb as he wants people to believe* **stupid**, unintelligent, ignorant, dense, brainless, mindless, foolish, slow-witted, slow, dull, dull-witted, witless, half-witted, blockish, doltish, dunce-like, simple, simple-minded, empty-headed, vacuous, vapid, idiotic, moronic, imbecilic, cretinous, obtuse, bovine, lumpish; *informal* thick, dim, dopey, dippy, dozy, half-baked, slow on the uptake, soft in the head, as thick as two short planks, thickheaded, chuckleheaded, dunderheaded, wooden-headed, fat-headed, thick-skulled, muttonheaded, boneheaded, lamebrained, birdbrained, pea-brained, brain-dead, dead from the neck up; *Brit. informal* daft, not the full shilling; *S. African informal* dof; *W. Indian informal* dotish; *N. Amer. vulgar slang* dumb-ass.
OPPOSITE clever.

dumbfound ▶ verb *she was dumbfounded by Bruce's actions* **astonish**, astound, amaze, stagger, surprise, startle, stun, confound, stupefy, daze, nonplus; throw, shake, unnerve, disconcert, discompose, bewilder; take someone's breath away, take by surprise, take aback, shake up, stop someone in their tracks, strike dumb, leave open-mouthed, leave aghast, catch off balance; *informal* flabbergast, floor, knock for six, knock sideways, knock out, knock the stuffing out of, bowl over, blow someone's mind, blow away.

dumbfounded ▶ adjective *when you told me I had won I was dumbfounded* **astonished**, astounded, amazed, staggered, surprised, startled, stunned, confounded, nonplussed, stupefied, dazed, dumbstruck, open-mouthed, agape, speechless, at a loss for words, thunderstruck, goggle-eyed, wide-eyed; taken aback, thrown, shaken, unnerved, disconcerted, discomposed, bewildered; *informal* flabbergasted, floored, flummoxed, knocked for six, knocked sideways, knocked out, bowled over, blown away, unable to believe one's eyes/ears; *Brit. informal* gobsmacked.

dummy ▶ noun **1** *a shop-window dummy dressed in a military uniform* **mannequin**, manikin, lifelike model, figure, lay figure.
2 *the book is just a dummy* **mock-up**, imitation, likeness, lookalike, representation, substitute, sample, copy, replica, reproduction; counterfeit, sham, fake, forgery; *informal* dupe.
3 (*informal*) *if you still don't get it, you're a dummy. See* IDIOT.
▶ adjective *we were to mount a dummy attack on the airfield | a dummy bomb* **simulated**, feigned, pretended, practice, trial, mock, make-believe; **fake**, artificial, false, bogus, sham, imitation, reproduction, replica; *informal* pretend, phoney.
OPPOSITE real.

dump ▶ noun **1** *it's time to take the rubbish to the dump* **rubbish tip**, rubbish dump, refuse dump, rubbish heap, refuse heap, tip, dumping ground, dustheap, slag heap, midden, dunghill, dung heap; *Brit.* scrapyard; *N. Amer.* junkyard, nuisance grounds.
2 (*informal*) *the house is a dump, but the rent is cheap* **hovel**, shack, slum, shanty, mess; *informal* hole, pigsty.
▶ verb **1** *he dumped a bag of groceries on the table* **put down**, lay down, set down, deposit, place, put, unload; drop, let fall, throw down, fling down; *informal* stick, park, plonk, shove, pop; *Brit. informal* bung; *N. Amer. informal* plunk; *archaic* unlade; *rare* posit.
2 *they gained permission to dump asbestos at the site* **dispose of**, get rid of, throw away, throw out, discard, scrap, bin, jettison, cast aside, cast out, fling out, toss out; *informal* ditch, junk, get shut of; *Brit. informal* get shot of; *N. Amer. informal* trash.
3 *pumps are used to dump effluent from the tanks* **discharge**, empty out, pour out, tip out, unload, jettison, eject, spew out, throw out, force out.
4 (*informal*) *he dumped her and ran off with a richer woman* **abandon**, desert, leave, leave in the lurch, leave high and dry, turn one's back on, jilt, break up with, finish with, cast aside, throw over; *informal* walk out on, run out on, rat on, drop, ditch, chuck, give someone the elbow, give someone the old heave-ho, leave someone holding the baby; *Brit. informal* give someone the push, give someone the big E; *archaic* forsake.

dumps ▶ plural noun
□ **down in the dumps** (*informal*) **unhappy**, sad, depressed, gloomy, glum, melancholy, melancholic, miserable, sorrowful, dejected, despondent, dispirited, disconsolate, downhearted, downcast, cast down, down, crestfallen, woebegone, low, low in spirits, low-spirited, heavy-hearted, morose, dismal, desolate, weighed down, oppressed; tearful, upset, broken-hearted; *informal* blue, down in the mouth, fed up, moody; *literary* dolorous, heartsick, heartsore; *archaic* chap-fallen.
OPPOSITE cheerful.

dumpy ▶ adjective *that skirt makes you look dumpy and middle-aged* **short**, squat, stubby; **plump**, stout, chubby, chunky, portly, paunchy, corpulent, fat, bulky, broad, broad in the beam, well covered, well padded, well rounded; *informal* tubby, roly-poly, pudgy, porky; *Brit. informal* podgy, fubsy; *N. Amer. informal* zaftig; *archaic* pursy.
OPPOSITES tall; slender.

D

dun[1] ▶ adjective *the typical dun coat of a wild horse* **greyish-brown**, brownish, dun-coloured, mud-coloured, mouse-coloured, mousy, muddy, khaki, umber.

dun[2] ▶ verb *he was constantly being dunned for the rent* **importune**, solicit, petition, press, pressurize, plague, pester, nag, harass, hound, badger, beset; *N. English* mither; *informal* hassle, bug.

dunce ▶ noun *they all called him a dunce at school* **fool**, idiot, stupid person, simpleton, halfwit, ignoramus, oaf, dolt, dullard, moron, imbecile, cretin; *informal* dummy, dumbo, dumb-bell, dum-dum, clot, thickhead, nitwit, dimwit, dope, duffer, booby, chump, numbskull, nincompoop, bonehead, blockhead, fathead, meathead, airhead, birdbrain, pea-brain, lamebrain, jerk, ninny, ass, donkey; *Brit. informal* wally, berk, divvy, nit, mug, pillock, wazzock, silly billy; *N. Amer. informal* doofus, goof, goofball, schmuck, putz, bozo, boob, lummox, turkey; *Austral./NZ informal* galah, drongo, dingbat.
OPPOSITE genius.

dune ▶ noun *high sand dunes fringe the beach* **bank**, mound, hillock, hummock, rise, knoll, ridge, heap, drift, accumulation.

dung ▶ noun *they use cow dung as fertilizer* **manure**, muck, animal excrement; faeces, droppings, ordure, cowpats; *Indian* gobar; *N. Amer. informal* cow chips, horse apples; *vulgar slang* shit, crap.

WORD LINKS

study of fossilized dung	**scatology**
dung-eating	**copraphagous**

dungeon ▶ noun *the king imprisoned him in the castle dungeon* **underground cell**, underground prison, oubliette; cell, prison, jail, lock-up, black hole; *archaic* hole, thieves' hole, bocardo.

dupe ▶ verb *her daughters were duped by a handsome Lothario* **deceive**, trick, hoodwink, hoax, swindle, defraud, cheat, double-cross, gull, mislead, take in, fool, delude, misguide, lead on, inveigle, seduce, ensnare, entrap, beguile; *informal* con, do, sting, gyp, rip off, diddle, swizzle, shaft, bilk, rook, bamboozle, finagle, pull the wool over someone's eyes, pull someone's leg, pull a fast one on, put one over on, sell a pup to, take to the cleaners; *N. Amer. informal* sucker, snooker, stiff, euchre, bunco, hornswoggle; *Austral. informal* pull a swifty on; *archaic* cozen, sharp; *rare* mulct.
▶ noun *you were an innocent dupe in Caroline's little game* **victim**, gull, pawn, puppet, instrument; fool, simpleton, innocent; *informal* sucker, stooge, sitting duck, sitting target, soft touch, pushover, chump, muggins, charlie, fall guy; *Brit. informal* mug; *N. Amer. informal* pigeon, patsy, sap, schlemiel, mark; *Austral./NZ informal* dill; *Brit. informal, dated* juggins.
OPPOSITES swindler, con man.

duplicate ▶ noun *he made a duplicate of the invoice* **copy**, carbon copy, carbon, photocopy, facsimile, mimeo, mimeograph, reprint; replica, reproduction, exact likeness, close likeness, twin, double, clone, match, mate, fellow, counterpart; *informal* dupe; *trademark* Xerox, photostat.
OPPOSITE original.
▶ adjective *she kept a duplicate copy of the parchment | duplicate keys* **matching**, identical, twin, corresponding, equivalent; matched, paired, twofold, coupled.
OPPOSITE different.
▶ verb **1** *he urged readers to duplicate and circulate the newsletter* **copy**, photocopy, photostat, xerox, mimeograph, make a photocopy of, take a photocopy of, make a carbon copy of, make a carbon of, make a facsimile of, reproduce, replicate, reprint, run off.
2 *a feat that will be difficult to duplicate* **repeat**, do over again, do again, redo, perform again, replicate.

duplication ▶ noun *the new system will reduce the need for duplication of documents* **copying**, duplicating, replicating, replication; photocopying, xeroxing, photostatting, reprinting.

duplicity ▶ noun *his conscience would not allow him to enter into duplicity* **deceitfulness**, deceit, deception, deviousness, two-facedness, double-dealing, underhandedness, dishonesty, falseness, falsity, fraud, fraudulence, sharp practice, swindling, cheating, chicanery, trickery, craft, guile, artifice, subterfuge, skulduggery, treachery, unfairness, unjustness, perfidy, improbity; *informal* crookedness, shadiness, foxiness, dirty tricks, shenanigans, monkey business, funny business, hanky-

panky; *Brit. informal* jiggery-pokery; *N. Amer. informal* monkeyshines; *Irish informal* codology; *archaic* knavery, knavishness, management.
OPPOSITE honesty.

durability ▶ noun *man-made fibres give the fabric extra durability* **imperishability**, permanence, longevity, ability to last, lastingness, resilience, strength, sturdiness, toughness, robustness, soundness; *rare* durableness.
OPPOSITE fragility.

durable ▶ adjective **1** *they make highly durable carpets for hotels* **long-lasting**, **hard-wearing**, heavy-duty, tough, resistant, strong, sturdy, stout, sound, substantial, imperishable, indestructible, made to last, well made, strongly made.
OPPOSITES flimsy, delicate.
2 *a durable peace can be established* **lasting**, long-lasting, long-lived, long-term, enduring, persisting, persistent, abiding, continuing; constant, stable, secure, fast, firm, fixed, deep-rooted, permanent, unfading, undying, everlasting.
OPPOSITE short-lived.

D

duration ▶ noun *the student's fees will be paid for the duration of their course* **full length**, length of time, time, time span, time scale, period, term, span, spell, stretch, fullness, length, extent, continuation, continuance, perpetuation, prolongation.

duress ▶ noun **1** *their confessions were extracted under duress* **coercion**, compulsion, force, pressure, pressurization, intimidation, threats, constraint, enforcement, exaction; *informal* arm-twisting.
OPPOSITE free will.
2 (*archaic*) *some of the missionaries had been four year in duress* **imprisonment**, confinement, incarceration, internment, detention, custody, captivity, restraint, constraint, bondage; *informal* porridge; *archaic* enthralment, durance; *rare* detainment.
OPPOSITE liberty.

during ▶ preposition *the exhibit attracted 5,000 visitors during January* **throughout**, through, in, in the course of, throughout the time of, for the time of, in the time of.

dusk ▶ noun *he arrived just before dusk | lighted windows shone through the dusk* **twilight**, nightfall, sunset, sundown, evening, close of day; dark, darkness, semi-darkness, gathering darkness, gloom, gloominess, murk, murkiness, shades of evening; *literary* gloaming, eventide, eve, even, evenfall; *rare* tenebrosity, owl light, crepuscule.
OPPOSITES dawn; daylight.

dusky ▶ adjective **1** *she looked out into the dusky countryside* **shadowy**, dark, darkish, dim, gloomy, murky, shady, cloudy, misty, hazy, foggy; unlit, unlighted, unilluminated, sunless, moonless; *literary* crepuscular, tenebrous; *rare* Stygian, Cimmerian, Tartarean, caliginous.
OPPOSITE bright.
2 (*dated*) *a dusky Moorish maiden* **dark-skinned**, dark-complexioned, dark, dark-coloured, olive-skinned, swarthy; tanned, bronzed, brown, ebony, black; *rare* swart.
OPPOSITE fair.

dust ▶ noun **1** *all of the furniture was covered in dust* **fine powder**, fine particles; **dirt**, grime, filth, smut, soot.
2 *they rolled in the dust, fighting* **earth**, soil, dirt, clay; ground, sod.
□ **kick up a dust** (*informal*) **make a fuss**, kick up a fuss, cause a row, cause a commotion, cause a disturbance, cause uproar, cause a fracas, cause a rumpus, make a racket.
▶ verb **1** *she dusted her mantelpiece* **wipe**, clean, buff, brush, sweep, mop.
2 *dust the cake with icing sugar* **sprinkle**, scatter, powder, dredge, sift, spray, cover, spread, strew; dot, fleck, freckle, dab; *literary* befleck, bestrew, besprinkle.

WORD LINKS
fear of dust **koniophobia**

dust-up ▶ noun (*informal*) *they had a dust-up over money. See* SCRAP².

dusty ▶ adjective **1** *the shop was dark and dusty* **dirty**, grimy, grubby, unclean, soiled, begrimed, befouled, mucky, sooty, stained, smudged, spotty; dust-covered, dust-filled, undusted; *informal* grungy, cruddy; *Brit. informal* manky, grotty, gungy; *Austral./NZ informal* scungy; *literary* besmirched.
OPPOSITES clean; dust-free.
2 *the walls are made of dusty brown sandstone* **powdery**, crumbly, chalky, friable; granulated, granular, gritty, sandy.
3 *her eiderdown is a dusty pink* **muted**, dull, flat, faded, pale, pastel, subtle, restrained; greyish, darkish, dirty.
OPPOSITE bright.
4 (*Brit. informal*) *I complained and they gave me a very dusty answer* **curt**, abrupt, terse, brusque, blunt, short, clipped, snappy, snappish, sharp, crisp, tart, gruff, offhand, ungracious, rude, impolite, discourteous, bad-tempered; unhelpful, uncooperative, disobliging; *informal* snippy.
OPPOSITES expansive; helpful.

dutiful ▶ adjective *she helped out, as a dutiful daughter should* **conscientious**, responsible, dedicated, devoted, faithful, loyal, attentive; **obedient**, compliant, pliant, docile, submissive, biddable, deferential, reverent, reverential, respectful, good, well disciplined, well trained; *Brit. informal* decent; *rare* regardful.
OPPOSITES remiss; disrespectful.

CHOOSE THE RIGHT WORD
dutiful, obedient, biddable, docile, compliant
See OBEDIENT.

duty ▶ noun **1** *she was free of any binding love or duty* **responsibility**, obligation, commitment, obedience, allegiance, loyalty, faithfulness, fidelity, respect, deference, reverence, homage; *historical* fealty.
2 *it was his duty to attend the king* **job**, task, chore, assignment, commission, mission, function, charge, part, place, role, concern, requirement, responsibility, obligation; work, burden, onus; *Brit. informal* pigeon; *dated* office.
3 *the duty was raised on alcohol and tobacco* **tax**, levy, tariff, excise, toll, fee, imposition, impost, exaction, tithe, payment, rate; customs, dues; *rare* mulct.
□ **off duty** *he helped at the hospital even when he was off duty* **not working**, at leisure, on holiday, on leave, off, off work, free.
□ **on duty** *the night security man was on duty* **working**, at work, busy, occupied, engaged; on call, on standby; *informal* on the job, tied up.

CHOOSE THE RIGHT WORD
duty, task, job, chore
See TASK.

dwarf ▶ noun **1** person of restricted growth, small person, short person; midget, pygmy, Tom Thumb, Lilliputian, manikin.
2 *the wizard captured the dwarf* **gnome**, goblin, hobgoblin, troll, imp, elf, brownie, kelpie, leprechaun, fairy, pixie, sprite.
OPPOSITE giant.
▶ adjective *the driveway was flanked by dwarf conifers* **miniature**, small, little, tiny, minute, toy, pocket, diminutive, baby, pygmy, stunted, undersized, undersize, small-scale, scaled-down; *Scottish* wee; *N. Amer.* vest-pocket; *informal* mini, teeny, teeny-weeny, teensy-weensy, itsy-bitsy, tiddly, pint-sized, half-pint, sawn-off, knee-high to a grasshopper; *Brit. informal* titchy, ickle; *N. Amer. informal* little-bitty.
OPPOSITE giant.
▶ verb **1** *the buildings will dwarf the countryside for miles around* **dominate**, tower above, tower over, loom over, overlook, overshadow, overtop.
2 *her progress was dwarfed by the achievements of her sister* **overshadow**, outshine, put in the shade, surpass, exceed, outclass, outstrip, outdo, top, cap, trump, transcend; shame, put to shame, diminish, minimize; *archaic* extinguish, outrival.

dwell ▶ verb (*formal*) *groups of gypsies still dwell in these amazing caves* **reside**, live, have one's home, have one's residence, be settled, be housed, lodge, stay; *informal* hang out, hang one's hat, put up; *formal* abide, be domiciled, sojourn; *archaic* bide.
□ **dwell on** *she had no time to dwell on her disappointment* **linger over**, mull over, muse on, brood about, brood over, think about, spend time thinking about, be preoccupied by, be obsessed by, eat one's heart out over; harp on about, discuss at length, expatiate on, elaborate on, expound on, keep talking about.

dwelling *See centre pages for list of* **Homes**
▶ noun (*formal*) *she had been invited to his dwelling* **residence**, place of residence, place of habitation, home, house, accommodation, lodging place, billet; lodgings, quarters, rooms; *informal* place, pad; *Brit. informal* digs; *formal* dwelling place, dwelling house, abode, domicile, habitation.

dwindle ▶ verb **1** *the porpoise population has dwindled* **diminish**, decrease, reduce, get smaller, become smaller, grow smaller, become less, grow less, lessen, wane, contract, shrink, fall off, taper off, tail off, drop, fall, go down, sink, slump, plummet; disappear, vanish, die out; *informal* nosedive, take a nosedive.
OPPOSITE increase.
2 *her career dwindled over the years* **decline**, degenerate, deteriorate, fail, ebb, wane, sink, slip, slide, go downhill, go to rack and ruin, decay, wither, fade, fade away; *informal* peter out, go to pot, go to the dogs, hit the skids, go down the toilet, go down the tubes; *Austral./NZ informal* go to the pack.
OPPOSITE flourish.

dye *See centre pages for lists of* **Colours** **Dyes**
▶ noun *the cloth had been soaked in blue dye* **colourant**, colouring agent, colouring, colour, dyestuff, pigment, tint, stain, wash.
▶ verb *the gloves were dyed to match the dress* **colour**, tint, pigment, stain, wash, colour-wash, tinge, shade.

dyed-in-the-wool ▶ adjective *she's a dyed-in-the-wool Conservative* **inveterate**, confirmed, entrenched, established, long-established, long-standing, deep-rooted, diehard, complete, absolute, utter, thorough, thoroughgoing, out-and-out, true blue, through and through; firm, unshakeable, staunch, steadfast, committed, devoted, dedicated, loyal, faithful, unswerving, unwavering, unfaltering; unashamed, unapologetic, unrepentant, incurable, incorrigible; *N. Amer.* full-bore; *informal* deep-dyed, card-carrying, mad keen, keen as mustard; *archaic* arrant; *rare* right-down.

dying ▶ adjective **1** *he went to visit his dying aunt* **terminally ill**, at death's door, on one's deathbed, in the jaws of death, on the point of death, near death, passing away, fading fast, sinking fast, expiring, moribund, breathing one's last, not long for this world; *Latin* in extremis; *informal* on one's last legs, with one foot in the grave, giving up the ghost.
2 *ballet is a dying art form* **declining**, vanishing, fading, passing, ebbing, waning; in decline; *informal* on the way out, on its last legs.
OPPOSITE thriving.
3 *he strained to catch her dying words* **final**, last, departing; deathbed.
OPPOSITE first.
▶ noun *there were no unhappy memories to taunt her in her dying* **death**, demise, passing, passing away, passing on, expiry, expiration, departure from life, final exit, eternal rest; *Law* decease; *rare* quietus.

dynamic ▶ adjective *he was eclipsed by his more dynamic colleagues* **energetic**, spirited, active, lively, zestful, vital, vigorous, strong, forceful, powerful, potent, positive, effective, effectual, high-powered, aggressive, driving, pushing, bold, enterprising; electric, magnetic, flamboyant, passionate, fiery; *informal* go-getting, zippy, peppy, sparky, high-octane, full of get-up-and-go, full of vim and vigour, full of beans, gutsy, spunky, ballsy, feisty, have-a-go, go-ahead; *N. Amer. informal* go-go.
OPPOSITES half-hearted; lethargic.

dynamism ▶ noun *there's real dynamism in his performance on the pitch* **energy**, spirit, liveliness, zestfulness, vitality, vigour, vigorousness, strength, forcefulness, power, powerfulness, potency, positiveness, positivity, effectiveness, efficacy; aggression, aggressiveness, boldness, drive, push, ambition, enterprise; magnetism, flamboyance, passion, fire; *informal* go-getting, zip, pep, spark, get-up-and-go, vim and vigour, guts, balls, have-a-go attitude; *N. Amer. informal* feistiness.

dynasty ▶ noun *he was the fourth king of the Shang dynasty* **bloodline**, line, ancestral line, lineage, house, family, ancestry, descent, extraction, succession, genealogy, family tree; regime, rule, reign, dominion, empire, sovereignty, ascendancy, government, authority, administration, jurisdiction.

dyspeptic ▶ adjective *a rather dyspeptic senator put the blame on his European counterpart* **bad-tempered**, short-tempered, irritable, snappish, testy, tetchy, touchy, crabbed, crabby, crotchety, grouchy, cantankerous, peevish, cross, fractious, disagreeable, pettish, waspish, prickly, peppery, cross-grained; bilious, liverish; *informal* snappy, chippy, on a short fuse, short-fused; *Brit. informal* shirty, stroppy, narky, ratty, eggy, like a bear with a sore head; *N. Amer. informal* cranky, ornery, peckish, soreheaded; *Austral./NZ informal* snaky; *informal, dated* waxy, miffy.

Ee

each ▸ pronoun *there are five thousand books and each must be individually cleaned* **every one**, each one, each and every one, one and all, all, the whole lot.
▸ determiner *he visited her each month* **every**, each and every, every single.
▸ adverb *they contributed a tenner each* **apiece**, per person, per capita, to each, for each, from each, individually, respectively; *formal* severally.

eager ▸ adjective **1** *small eager faces looked up and listened* **keen**, enthusiastic, avid, fervent, ardent, zealous, passionate, motivated, wholehearted, dedicated, committed, earnest, diligent; *informal* bright-eyed and bushy-tailed, mad keen, (as) keen as mustard; *rare* fervid, perfervid, passional.
OPPOSITE apathetic.
2 *her friends were* **eager for** *news* **anxious**, impatient, waiting with bated breath, longing, yearning, aching, wishing, hoping, hopeful, thirsty, hungry, greedy; desirous of, hankering after, intent on, bent on, set on; on the edge of one's seat, on pins and needles, on tenterhooks; *informal* hot, itching, gagging, dying.
OPPOSITE uninterested.

CHOOSE THE RIGHT WORD

eager, keen, enthusiastic, avid

- Someone who is **eager** wants to do or have something very much and feels excited pleasure at the prospect of it (*small eager faces looked up and listened* | *he seemed eager to talk to her*).
- **Keen** also suggests intense interest and enjoyment, but without the connotations of bubbly anticipation. A *keen* person's interest in what they do results in commitment and concentration (*he is a keen rugby player*). *Keen* can also be used to indicate that someone is anxious to do something, typically because they think it will be advantageous (*Laughton is keen to add Davies to his squad*). To be *keen on* something can just mean to like or approve of it (*I'm not that keen on the food here*).
- Someone who is **enthusiastic** about something shows great enjoyment of or approval for it (*make it clear that you are enthusiastic about the project*). An *enthusiastic* person does things with energy, gusto, and dedication (*an enthusiastic supporter of music from Africa*).
- **Avid** derives from a Latin word meaning 'greedy, hungry'. Someone described as *avid* enjoys something so much that they can never have enough of it (*I am an avid reader of your magazine* | *she was avid for information about the murder inquiry*).

eagerness ▸ noun *they underestimated the eagerness of potential buyers* **keenness**, enthusiasm, avidity, fervour, ardour, zest, zeal, passion, wholeheartedness, earnestness, commitment, dedication; impatience, desire, longing, yearning, wishing, thirst, hunger, greed, voracity, voraciousness, appetite, ambition; *informal* yen; *rare* appetency, fervency, ardency, passionateness.
OPPOSITES apathy, indifference.

eagle ▸ noun. *See centre pages for list of* **Birds**

WORD LINKS

young	**eaglet**
nest	**eyrie**

ear *See centre pages for list of parts of the human* **Ear**
▸ noun **1** *Helen had an infection of the ear* inner ear, middle ear, external ear, outer ear; cauliflower ear; *Scottish & N. English or informal* lug; *informal* earhole; *Brit. informal* lughole, shell-like.
2 *he had the ear of President Roosevelt* **attention**, attentiveness, notice, heed, regard, consideration.
3 *he has an ear for a good song* **appreciation**, discrimination, perception, musical taste.
□ **play it by ear** *he had no special game plan and said he would play it by ear* **improvise**, extemporize, ad lib; make it up as one goes along, take it as it comes, think on one's feet; *Latin* ad libitum; *informal* busk it, wing it.

WORD LINKS

relating to the ear	**aural, auricular, otic**
relating to hearing	**auditory**
relating to both ears	**binaural**
branch of medicine concerning the ear	**audiology, otology**
branch of medicine concerning the ear and throat	**otolaryngology**
branch of medicine concerning the ear, nose, and throat	**otorhinolaryngology**
inflammation of the ear	**otitis**
surgery to repair an ear	**otoplasty**

early ▸ adjective **1** *early copies of the book are now ready* **advance**, forward, prior; initial, preliminary, first, primary; pilot, test, trial.
OPPOSITE late.
2 *an early death* **untimely**, premature, unseasonable; too soon, too early, before time.
3 *bronze was used widely by early man* **primitive**, ancient, prehistoric, antediluvian, primeval, primordial; of long ago; *literary* of yore; *rare* primigenial, pristine.
OPPOSITE modern.
4 *he produced an early official statement* **prompt**, timely, quick, speedy, rapid, fast, without delay, expeditious; *archaic* rathe.
OPPOSITE overdue.
▸ adverb **1** *Rachel has to get up early* **early in the day**, in the early morning; at dawn, at daybreak, at cockcrow, with the lark.
OPPOSITE late.
2 *they hoped to leave school early* **before the usual time**, before the appointed time; prematurely, too soon; ahead of time, ahead of schedule, in good time; *literary* betimes.

earmark ▸ verb *the cash had been* **earmarked for** *a big expansion of the firm* **set aside**, lay aside, set apart, keep back, appropriate, reserve, keep; designate, assign, label, tag, mark; allocate to, allot to, devote to, pledge to, commit to, give over to; *rare* hypothecate.
▸ noun *he had all the earmarks of a big leaguer* **characteristic**, attribute, feature, quality, essential quality, property, mark, trademark, hallmark; mannerism, way, tendency; *literary* lineament.

earn ▸ verb **1** *they earn £20,000 per year* **be paid**, receive a salary of, take home, take home earnings of, gross; receive, get, make, obtain, draw, clear, collect, bring in; *informal* pocket, bank, rake in, pull in, haul in, net, bag.
OPPOSITE pay out.
2 *he has earned their trust over the years* **deserve**, merit, warrant, justify, be entitled to, be worthy of, be deserving of, have a right to; **gain**, win, attain, achieve, secure, establish, obtain, procure, get, acquire, come to have, find; *informal* clinch, bag, net, land.
OPPOSITE lose.

CHOOSE THE RIGHT WORD

earn, deserve, merit

- To **earn** something is to receive it as the appropriate result of what you have done (*his first foray into film earned him an Oscar nomination*).
- Someone who **deserves** something ought to receive it for what they have done or by virtue of personal qualities, but they may not do so (*Middlesbrough deserved their win* | *he is a lovely man who deserves to be loved*).
- **Merit** is a more formal term for deserving something (*the whole of the evidence merited consideration by a fresh jury*).

earnest[1] ▶ adjective **1** *he had a reputation for being dreadfully earnest* **serious**, serious-minded, solemn, grave, sober, humourless, staid, steady, intense; committed, dedicated, assiduous, keen, diligent, zealous, industrious, hard-working; studious, thoughtful, cerebral, deep, profound, bookish, donnish.
OPPOSITES frivolous; apathetic.
2 *they were engaged in earnest prayer* **devout**, heartfelt, wholehearted, sincere, impassioned, deeply felt, from the heart, fervent, ardent, passionate, intense, burning, urgent; *rare* full-hearted, passional, perfervid, fervid.
OPPOSITE half-hearted.
▶ noun
□ **in earnest 1** *we are in earnest about stopping burglaries* **serious**, not joking, sincere, wholehearted, genuine; **committed**, firm, resolute, resolved, determined, insistent.
OPPOSITE joking.
2 *he started writing in earnest after the war* **zealously**, purposefully, determinedly, resolutely, with enthusiasm, with dedication, with commitment; ardently, fervently, fervidly, passionately, wholeheartedly.
OPPOSITE half-heartedly.

earnest[2] ▶ noun (*archaic*) *early man saw the solstice as an earnest for the promise of a good harvest* **token**, security, surety, deposit, down payment; guarantee, pledge, bond, assurance; *archaic* gage.

earnestly ▶ adverb *he took my hand and looked at me earnestly* **seriously**, solemnly, gravely, soberly, sincerely, intently, resolutely, firmly; **ardently**, fervently, warmly, keenly, eagerly, intensely, zealously.

earnings ▶ plural noun *they lived off his wife's earnings* **income**, wages, salary, stipend, pay, take-home pay, gross pay, net pay; revenue, yield, profit, takings, proceeds, dividends, gain, return, remuneration, emolument; payment, fees, honoraria, fringe benefits; *informal* pickings, perks.

earth *See centre pages for list of layers of the* **Earth's Crust**
▶ noun **1** *the moon moves in its orbit around the earth* **world**, globe, planet, sphere, orb.
2 *he felt an infinitesimal trembling of the earth* **land**, ground, dry land, solid ground, terra firma; floor.
3 *the blades ploughed gently into the soft earth* **soil**, topsoil, loam, clay, silt, dirt, sod, clod, turf; ground, terrain.
4 *the fox ran back to its earth* **den**, lair, sett, burrow, warren, tunnel, hole, cave; retreat, shelter, hideout, hideaway, hiding place; habitation; *informal* hidey-hole.

WORD LINKS

related prefix	**geo-**
relating to the earth	**terrestrial, telluric**
study of the earth	**geography, geology, geochemistry, geomorphology**

earthenware *See centre pages for list of* **Pottery and Porcelain**
▶ noun *the Wedgwood potteries produced cream-coloured earthenware* **pottery**, crockery, stoneware; china, porcelain; pots, crocks.

earthly ▶ adjective **1** *the mobile and metamorphosing earthly environment* **terrestrial**, telluric, tellurian; *rare* terrene, subastral.
OPPOSITE extraterrestrial.
2 *they were seduced by the promise of earthly delights* **worldly**, temporal, secular, mortal, human, mundane, material, non-spiritual, materialistic; carnal, fleshly, bodily, physical, corporal, corporeal, sensual; gross, base, sordid, vile, profane; *rare* somatic, sublunary, terrene.
OPPOSITES heavenly; spiritual.
3 (*informal*) *there can be no earthly explanation for his behaviour* **feasible**, possible, likely, conceivable, imaginable, perceivable.

earthquake ▶ noun *many homes were destroyed in the earthquake* **earth tremor**, tremor, convulsion, shock, foreshock, aftershock; *informal* quake, shake, trembler; *technical* microseism.

WORD LINKS

relating to earthquakes	**seismic**
study of earthquakes	**seismology**

earthy ▶ adjective **1** *the cellar had an earthy smell* **soil-like**, dirt-like.
2 *preaching in the earthy Calvinistic tradition* **down-to-earth**, unsophisticated, unrefined, homely, simple, plain, unpretentious, natural, uninhibited, rough, robust.
3 *she was shocked by Emma's earthy language* **bawdy**, ribald, off colour, racy, rude, vulgar, lewd, crude, foul, coarse, uncouth, rough, dirty, filthy, smutty, unseemly, indelicate, indecent, indecorous, obscene; *informal* blue, raunchy, locker-room, X-rated; *Brit. informal* fruity, saucy, near the knuckle, close to the bone; *N. Amer. informal* gamy; *euphemistic* adult.
OPPOSITES decorous, proper, prim.

ease ▶ noun **1** *the 15-year old beat all the adult players with ease* **effortlessness**, no difficulty, no trouble, no bother, facility, facileness, simplicity; deftness, adroitness, dexterity, proficiency, mastery.
OPPOSITE difficulty.
2 *friends recall his ease of manner with children* **naturalness**, casualness, informality, unceremoniousness, lack of reserve, lack of constraint, relaxedness, amiability, affability; unconcern, composure, aplomb, nonchalance, insouciance.
OPPOSITES formality, stiffness.
3 *only in his sleep could he find any ease* **peace**, peacefulness, calmness, tranquillity, composure, serenity, repose, restfulness, quiet, contentment, security, comfort.
OPPOSITES trouble, disturbance.
4 *a life of ease* **affluence**, wealth, prosperity, prosperousness, luxury, opulence, plenty, sufficiency; **comfort**, cosiness, contentment, content, enjoyment, well-being, freedom from hardship, freedom from troubles; *rare* easefulness.
OPPOSITES hardship; poverty.
□ **at ease/at one's ease** *when he woke he felt wonderfully at ease* **relaxed**, calm, serene, tranquil, unworried, contented, content, happy; comfortable, secure, safe.
OPPOSITES tense; uncomfortable.
▶ verb **1** *he hoped the alcohol would ease his pain* **relieve**, alleviate, mitigate, assuage, allay, soothe, soften, palliate, ameliorate, mollify, moderate, tone down, blunt, dull, deaden, numb, take the edge off; lessen, reduce, lighten, diminish.
OPPOSITE aggravate.
2 *it was dawn before the rain* ***eased off*** **abate**, subside, die down, die away, die out, drop off, let up, slacken off, diminish, quieten, lessen, grow less, tail off, peter out, taper off, wane, ebb, relent, weaken, become weaker, come to an end; *archaic* remit.
OPPOSITE worsen.
3 *concentrating on work helped to ease her mind* **calm**, quieten, pacify, soothe, comfort, bring comfort to, give solace to, solace, console; hearten, gladden, uplift, encourage.
4 *we want to ease our employees' adjustment to the new policy* **facilitate**, make easy, make easier, expedite, speed up, assist, help, aid, advance, further, forward, smooth the way for, clear the way for, simplify.
OPPOSITE hinder.
5 *he eased out the champagne cork with his thumbs* **guide**, manoeuvre, inch, edge, steer, slide, slip, squeeze.

easily ▶ adverb **1** *I overcame this problem quite easily in the end* **effortlessly**, comfortably, simply, straightforwardly; with ease, without effort, with no trouble, with no bother, without difficulty, without a hitch, smoothly; skilfully, deftly, nimbly, smartly, very well; *informal* no sweat.
OPPOSITE laboriously.
2 *he's easily the best military brain in the country* **undoubtedly**, doubtlessly, without doubt, without question, indubitably, indisputably, undeniably, definitely, certainly, assuredly, positively, absolutely, clearly, obviously, patently, simply, surely, by far, far and away, by a mile, beyond the shadow of a doubt; *informal* as sure as eggs is eggs.

east ▶ noun (**the East**) **the Orient**.
OPPOSITE the West.
▶ adjective *the cathedral's east face | a biting east wind* **eastern**, easterly, eastwardly, oriental.
OPPOSITE west.
▶ adverb *traffic wishing to go east on the North Circular* **to the east**, eastward, eastwards, eastwardly.
OPPOSITE west.

easy ▶ adjective **1** *Wilf's task was very easy* **uncomplicated**, not difficult, undemanding, unexacting, unchallenging, effortless, painless, trouble-free, facile, simple, straightforward, elementary, idiot-proof, plain sailing; *informal* easy-peasy, easy as pie, as easy as falling off a log, as easy as ABC, a piece of cake, child's play, kids' stuff, a cinch, no sweat, a doddle, a breeze, a pushover, money for old rope, money for jam; *N. Amer. informal* duck soup, a snap; *Austral./NZ informal* a bludge; *S. African informal* a piece of old tackle; *Brit. vulgar slang* a piece of piss; *dated* a snip.
OPPOSITE difficult.
2 *some parents have easy babies and amenable children* **docile**, manageable, amenable, biddable, tractable, compliant, pliant, yielding, acquiescent, accommodating, obliging, cooperative, easy-going, flexible.
OPPOSITES difficult; demanding.
3 *the thug thought he had picked an easy target* **vulnerable**, susceptible, exploitable, defenceless, naive, gullible, trusting, credulous, impressionable.
OPPOSITE streetwise.
4 *Vic's easy manner made everyone feel at home* **natural**, casual, informal, unceremonious, unreserved, uninhibited, unconstrained, unforced, unaffected, free and easy, easy-going, familiar, amiable, affable, genial, congenial, agreeable, good-humoured; carefree, nonchalant, unconcerned, composed, insouciant, urbane, suave; *informal* laid-back, unflappable, together.
OPPOSITE formal.
5 *they are hoping for an easy life* **calm**, tranquil, serene, quiet, peaceful, trouble-free, untroubled, undisturbed, unworried, contented, relaxed, comfortable, secure, safe; *informal* cushy.
OPPOSITE uneasy.
6 *the walkers set off at an easy pace* **leisurely**, leisured, unhurried, unrushed, comfortable, unexacting, undemanding, easy-going, gentle, sedate, moderate, steady, regular, even; *informal* laid-back.

E

OPPOSITE demanding.
7 (*informal*) *she had a reputation at school for being easy* **promiscuous**, sexually indiscriminate, free with one's favours, of easy virtue, unchaste, loose, wanton, abandoned, licentious, dissolute, dissipated, debauched; *informal* swinging, sluttish, whorish, tarty, slaggy; *N. Amer. informal* roundheeled; *W. Indian informal* slack; *archaic* light; *rare* concupiscent, riggish.
OPPOSITE chaste.

easy-going ▶ adjective *Fred was easy-going and a pleasure to work with* **relaxed**, even-tempered, equable, placid, mellow, mild, happy-go-lucky, serene, blithe, carefree, free and easy, nonchalant, insouciant, unruffled, unworried, untroubled, imperturbable, unexcitable; amiable, considerate, undemanding, forbearing, patient, tolerant, lenient, liberal, broad-minded, open-minded, understanding, generous, indulgent; good-natured, good-humoured, pleasant, agreeable, cordial; *informal* laid-back, together, unflappable, unfazed.
OPPOSITES tense; intolerant.

E

eat ▶ verb 1 *we ate a hearty breakfast and then set off* **consume**, devour, ingest, partake of, gobble (up/down), gulp (down), bolt (down), wolf (down), cram down, finish (off); swallow, chew, munch, chomp, champ; *informal* guzzle, nosh, put away, pack away, tuck into, tuck away, scoff (down), demolish, dispose of, make short work of, polish off, shovel down, get stuck into, stuff one's face with, stuff down, pig out on, sink, get outside of, get one's laughing gear round; *Brit. informal* gollop, shift; *N. Amer. informal* scarf (down/up), snarf (down/up), inhale; *rare* ingurgitate.
OPPOSITES starve; fast.
2 *we ate at a local restaurant* **have a meal**, partake of food, take food, consume food, feed; breakfast, lunch, dine, have breakfast, have lunch, have dinner, have supper; feast, banquet; *informal* snack, graze, nosh; *dated* sup, break bread.
3 *acidic water can* ***eat away at*** *concrete pipes* **erode**, corrode, abrade, wear away (at), wear down, wear through, gnaw away (at), bite into, burn into, burn through, consume, dissolve, disintegrate, crumble, waste away, rot, decay; damage, destroy, spoil.
□ **eat one's heart out**. *See* HEART.

WORD LINKS
related suffixes **-phagous (e.g. *anthropophagous*), -vorous (e.g. *carnivorous*)**

eatable ▶ adjective *the soufflé's not perfect, but it is eatable* **edible**, palatable, digestible; fit to eat, fit for consumption, fit to be consumed; *rare* comestible.
OPPOSITE inedible.

eats ▶ plural noun (*informal*) *we had to pay for our own booze and eats* **food**, sustenance, nourishment, nutriment, fare; eatables, snacks, titbits; meals, rations, provisions, supplies; *informal* nosh, grub, chow; *Brit. informal* scoff, tuck; *N. Amer. informal* chuck; *archaic* victuals, vittles, viands, commons, meat; *rare* comestibles, provender, aliment, viaticum.

eavesdrop ▶ verb *we tried to* ***eavesdrop on*** *his telephone conversation* **listen in**, spy, intrude; monitor, tap, wiretap, record, overhear; *informal* snoop, bug; *Austral./NZ informal* stickybeak.

ebb ▶ verb 1 *the tide ebbed in the afternoon* **recede**, **go out**, retreat, flow back, draw back, fall back, fall away, abate, subside; *rare* retrocede.
OPPOSITE come in.
2 *his courage began to ebb* **diminish**, dwindle, wane, fade away, melt away, peter out, decline, die away, die down, die out, flag, let up, lessen, decrease, weaken, dissolve, disappear, come to an end; deteriorate, decay, degenerate; *archaic* remit.
OPPOSITES increase, intensify.
▶ noun 1 *the rocks were revealed by the ebb of the tide* **receding**, going out, flowing back, retreat, retreating, drawing back, abating, subsiding; *rare* retrocession.
2 *they welcomed the ebb of the fighting* **abatement**, subsiding, easing, waning, dwindling, petering out, dying away, dying down, dying out, fading away, de-escalation, decrease, decline, diminution, diminishing, lessening.
OPPOSITE intensification.

ebony ▶ adjective *he stared at her with his ebony eyes* **black**, jet-black, pitch-black, coal-black, ink-black, black as night, black as pitch, sable, inky, sooty, raven, dark; *literary* ebon.
OPPOSITE ivory.

ebullience ▶ noun *the director's ebullience is a fantastic morale booster for the cast* **exuberance**, buoyancy, cheerfulness, joy, joyfulness, gladness, cheeriness, merriment, jollity, sunniness, breeziness, jauntiness, light-heartedness, high spirits, high-spiritedness, exhilaration, elation, euphoria, jubilation, animation, sparkle, effervescence, vivacity, enthusiasm, zest, irrepressibility, perkiness; *informal* bubbliness, chirpiness, bounciness, pep, zing, zip, fizz; *archaic* good cheer.
OPPOSITE depression.

ebullient ▶ adjective *the superb weather put him in an ebullient mood* **exuberant**, buoyant, cheerful, joyful, cheery, merry, sunny, breezy, jaunty, light-hearted, in high spirits, high-spirited, exhilarated, elated, euphoric, jubilant, animated, sparkling, effervescent, vivacious, enthusiastic, irrepressible; *informal* bubbly, bouncy, peppy, zingy, upbeat, chipper, chirpy, smiley, sparky, full of beans; *N. Amer. informal* peart; *literary* gladsome, blithe, blithesome; *dated* gay; *archaic* as merry as a grig, of good cheer.
OPPOSITE depressed.

eccentric ▶ adjective *they were worried by his eccentric behaviour* **unconventional**, uncommon, abnormal, irregular, aberrant, anomalous, odd, queer, strange, peculiar, weird, bizarre, outlandish, freakish, extraordinary; **idiosyncratic**, quirky, singular, nonconformist, capricious, whimsical; *French* outré, avant garde; *informal* way out, far out, offbeat, dotty, nutty, screwy, freaky, oddball, wacky, cranky, off the wall, madcap, zany; *Brit. informal* rum; *N. Amer. informal* kooky, wacko, bizarro, in left field.
OPPOSITES ordinary; conventional.
▶ noun *like all princes he was something of an eccentric* **oddity**, odd fellow, unorthodox person, character, individualist, individual, free spirit, misfit; *informal* oddball, queer fish, weirdo, weirdie, freak, nut, nutter, nutcase, case, head case, crank, crackpot, loony, loon; *Brit. informal* one-off, odd bod; *N. Amer. informal* wacko, wack, screwball, kook; *Austral./NZ informal* dingbat.

CHOOSE THE RIGHT WORD

eccentric, unconventional, idiosyncratic, quirky

These words all describe unusual people or things and express varying degrees of disapproval, interest, or curiosity.

- Someone referred to as **eccentric** behaves in an usual or unexpected way. The description suggests a strange mental state, possibly even insanity (*an eccentric millionaire has built his own UFO landing pad | a bachelor of somewhat eccentric habits*).
- **Unconventional** is less strong. It describes behaviour that is not bound by generally accepted rules or ways of doing things. *Unconventional* expresses interest rather than suspicion or disapproval (*inspiring and unconventional teaching | he was one of the most unconventional men she had ever met*). An *unconventional* person deliberately cultivates an independent-minded approach to life.
- **Idiosyncratic** is used to describe actions or attributes more often than people themselves. It emphasizes the fact that someone's ideas or behaviour are unique to them (*Brayne also held idiosyncratic views on the hereafter*).
- **Quirky** suggests an unusual, distinctive, and surprising or unpredictable quality, which may cause amusement or curiosity (*his quirky and award-winning composition | a quirky sense of humour*).

eccentricity ▶ noun *a charming example of English eccentricity* **unconventionality**, unorthodoxy, singularity, oddness, queerness, strangeness, weirdness, bizarreness, quirkiness, freakishness, extraordinariness; peculiarity, irregularity, abnormality, anomaly, foible, idiosyncrasy, caprice, whimsy, quirk; *informal* nuttiness, dottiness, screwiness, freakiness, wackiness, crankiness, zaniness; *N. Amer. informal* kookiness.
OPPOSITE conventionality.

ecclesiastic *See centre pages for list of* **Priests**
▶ noun *the consecration could only be performed by a high ecclesiastic* **clergyman**, clergywoman, priest, churchman, churchwoman, man/woman of the cloth, man/woman of God, cleric, minister, preacher, chaplain, father; divine, theologian; bishop, pastor, vicar, rector, parson, (assistant) curate, deacon, deaconess; *Scottish* kirkman; *French* abbé, curé; *N. Amer.* dominie; *informal* reverend, padre, Holy Joe, sky pilot; *Austral. informal* josser; *informal, derogatory* Bible-basher, God botherer.
▶ adjective. *See* ECCLESIASTICAL.

ecclesiastical ▶ adjective *his ecclesiastical duties* **priestly**, ministerial, clerical, ecclesiastic, prelatic, canonical, parsonical, pastoral; **church**, churchly, religious, spiritual, non-secular, non-temporal, holy, divine; *informal* churchy; *rare* sacerdotal.

echelon ▶ noun *he reached the upper echelons of government* **level**, rank, grade, step, rung, tier, stratum, plane, position, order, division, sector.

echo ▶ noun 1 *the hills sent back a faint echo of my shout* **reverberation**, reverberating, reflection, resounding, ringing, repetition, repeat, reiteration, answer.
2 *the scene she described was an echo of the one Lisa had always imagined* **duplicate**, copy, replica, facsimile, reproduction, imitation, exact/close likeness, mirror image, twin, double, clone, match, mate, fellow, counterpart, parallel; *informal* lookalike, spitting image, ringer, dead ringer.
3 *was there even the slightest echo of the love they had known?* **trace**, vestige, remains, remnant, relic, survival, ghost, memory, evocation, recollection, remembrance, reminiscence, reminder, souvenir, sign, mark, indication, token, suggestion, hint, evidence, clue, allusion, intimation; overtones, reminiscences.
▶ verb 1 *his laughter echoed round the room* **reverberate**, re-echo, resonate, resound, reflect, ring, pulsate, vibrate, be repeated.
2 *Bill echoed Rex's words in a sarcastic sing-song* **repeat**, say again, restate, reiterate, copy, imitate, parrot, parody, mimic; reproduce, iterate, recite,

quote, rehearse, recapitulate, regurgitate; *informal* recap, trot out; *rare* reprise, ingeminate.

éclat ▶ noun *he finished his recital with great éclat* **style**, stylishness, flamboyance, confidence, self-assurance, elan, dash, flair, flourish, vigour, vivacity, vivaciousness, gusto, verve, zest, sparkle, brio, panache, exuberance, ebullience, enthusiasm, eagerness, vitality, dynamism, animation, liveliness, spirit, energy; *informal* pizzazz, pep, oomph, vim, zing, get-up-and-go.
OPPOSITE lethargy.

eclectic ▶ adjective **1** *they played an eclectic mix of party music* **wide-ranging**, wide, broad, broad-ranging, broad-based, extensive, comprehensive, encyclopedic, general, universal, varied, diverse, diversified, catholic, liberal, all-embracing, non-exclusive, inclusive, indiscriminate, many-sided, multifaceted, multifarious, heterogeneous, miscellaneous, assorted.
OPPOSITE narrow.
2 *an eclectic approach to teaching the curriculum* **selective**, selecting, choosing, picking and choosing; discriminating, discerning, critical.
OPPOSITE dogmatic.

eclipse ▶ noun **1** *the eclipse of the sun* **blotting out**, blocking, covering, obscuring, hiding, concealing, veiling, shrouding, darkening; *Astronomy* occultation.
2 *the eclipse of the empire* **decline**, fall, failure, decay, deterioration, degeneration, weakening, ebb, waning, withering, descent, sinking, slide, tumble, regression, lapse, collapse, comedown, crash.
OPPOSITE rise.
3 *the eclipse of his rival* **outshining**, overshadowing, surpassing, excelling, outclassing, outstripping, outdistancing, outdoing, transcending, dwarfing, upstaging, shaming.
▶ verb **1** *the last piece of the sun was eclipsed by the moon* **blot out**, block, cover, obscure, veil, shroud, hide, conceal, obliterate, darken, dim; shade, cast a shadow over; *Astronomy* occult.
2 *the use of procaine was eclipsed by the discovery of cortisone* **outshine**, overshadow, put in the shade, surpass, exceed, excel, be superior to, outclass, outstrip, outdistance, outdo, top, cap, trump, transcend, tower above/over, dwarf, upstage, shame, put to shame; *informal* be head and shoulders above, be a cut above; *archaic* extinguish, outrival.

economic ▶ adjective **1** *the government's commitment to economic reform* **financial**, monetary, pecuniary, budgetary, fiscal, commercial, trade, mercantile.
2 *many organizations must become larger if they are to remain economic* **profitable**, profit-making, moneymaking, money-spinning, lucrative, remunerative, financially rewarding, fruitful, gainful, productive; **solvent**, viable, cost-effective, successful, commercial, commercially successful.
OPPOSITE unprofitable.
3 *rugs or matting are a practical and economic alternative to fitted carpets* **cost-effective**, effective, efficient, worthwhile, valuable, advantageous, cheap, inexpensive, low-cost, low-price, low-budget, budget, economy, reasonable, reasonably priced, cut-price.
OPPOSITE extravagant.

economic or economical?

These two words are related to different senses of *economy* and hence have different meanings. **Economic** means 'relating to a country's wealth and resources' (*the government's economic policy*), 'justifiable in terms of profitability' (*if prices remained high, it could become economic to develop cobalt deposits in other parts of the world*), or 'requiring fewer resources' (*this type of construction provided an economic solution to the problem*). **Economical**, on the other hand, relates to *economy* in the sense 'careful managing of resources' and means 'costing little to run' (*a safe and economical heating system*) or 'taking care not to be extravagant' (*he was economical in all areas of life*).

economical ▶ adjective **1** *it is a very economical little car* **cheap**, inexpensive, low-cost, low-price, low-budget, budget, economy, reasonable, reasonably priced, cut-price, cut-rate, discount, discounted, bargain, bargain-basement.
OPPOSITE expensive.
2 *my friend is a very economical shopper with a keen eye for a bargain* **thrifty**, careful (with money), provident, prudent, canny, sensible, frugal, sparing, scrimping, economizing, abstemious; *N. Amer.* forehanded.
OPPOSITE spendthrift.

economize ▶ verb *they economized by growing their own vegetables* **save (money)**, cut expenditure, cut costs; **cut back**, make cutbacks, make cuts, retrench, husband one's resources, budget, be (more) economical, make economies, be thrifty, be sparing, be frugal, buy (more) cheaply, use less, reduce/decrease wastage, scrimp, scrimp and save, scrimp and scrape, cut corners, tighten one's belt, draw in one's horns, count the/your pennies, watch the/your pennies; *N. Amer.* pinch the/your pennies; *black English* rake and scrape.
OPPOSITES spend, be extravagant.

economy ▶ noun **1** *the nation's economy* **wealth**, (financial) resources; **financial system**, financial state, financial management.
2 *Mrs Beeton attempted to combine good living with economy* **thrift**, **providence**, prudence, thriftiness, canniness, carefulness, care, good management, good husbandry, careful budgeting, economizing, saving, scrimping and saving, scrimping, restraint, frugality, abstemiousness; meanness, penny-pinching, miserliness, niggardliness, parsimony; *N. Amer.* forehandedness; *informal* stinginess; *rare* sparingness, frugalness.
OPPOSITE extravagance.

ecstasy ▶ noun *the ecstasy of loving him* **rapture**, bliss, elation, euphoria, cloud nine, seventh heaven, transports, rhapsodies; joy, joyousness, jubilation, exultation, heaven, paradise, delight; *informal* the top of the world.
OPPOSITE misery.

ecstatic ▶ adjective *she was sometimes ecstatic with love* **enraptured**, elated, transported, in transports, in raptures, euphoric; rapturous, joyful, joyous, overjoyed, blissful, beatific; on cloud nine, in seventh heaven, delirious (with happiness), beside oneself with joy/happiness, jumping for joy, rhapsodic, ravished, enchanted, enthusiastic, delighted, thrilled, jubilant, exultant, happy; *informal* over the moon, on top of the world, blissed out; orgasmic; *Austral. informal* wrapped.
OPPOSITE miserable.

ecumenical ▶ adjective *an ecumenical church service* **non-denominational**, non-sectarian, universal, catholic, all-embracing, all-inclusive.
OPPOSITE denominational.

eddy ▶ noun *the river was smooth apart from the small eddies at the edge* **swirl**, whirlpool, vortex, maelstrom; countercurrent, counterflow; *N. Amer. informal* suckhole; *literary* Charybdis.
▶ verb *cold air eddied around her* **swirl**, whirl, spiral, wind, churn, swish, circulate, revolve, spin, twist; flow, ripple, stream, surge, seethe, billow, foam, froth, boil, ferment.

edge ▶ noun **1** *the edge of the lake* **border**, boundary, extremity, fringe; margin, side, lip, rim, brim, brink, verge; perimeter, circumference, periphery, contour, outline; limit, limits, outer limit, bound, bounds; *literary* marge, bourn, skirt.
OPPOSITE middle.
2 *'What do you mean?' I asked, with an edge in my voice* **sharpness**, severity, bite, sting, pointedness, asperity, pungency, mordancy, acerbity, acidity, tartness, trenchancy; **sarcasm**, acrimony, malice, spite, venom; *rare* causticity, mordacity.
OPPOSITE kindness.
3 *they have an edge over their rivals* **advantage**, lead, head, head start, trump card, the whip hand; **superiority**, the upper hand, dominance, ascendancy, supremacy, primacy, precedence, power, mastery, control, sway, authority; *N. Amer. informal* the catbird seat; *Austral./NZ informal* the box seat.
OPPOSITE disadvantage.
□ **on edge** *she felt on edge and wanted to get moving* **tense**, **nervous**, edgy, highly strung, anxious, apprehensive, uneasy, ill at ease, unsettled, unstable; excitable, twitchy, jumpy, nervy, keyed up, fidgety, restive, skittish, neurotic, brittle, hysterical; sensitive, insecure; **irritable**, touchy, tetchy, testy, crotchety, irascible, peevish, querulous, bad-tempered, short-tempered, hot-tempered, quick-tempered, temperamental, snappy, captious, crabbed, prickly; *informal* uptight, wired.
OPPOSITE calm.
▶ verb **1** *the tall poplars that edged the orchard* **border**, fringe, rim, verge, skirt, be alongside; **surround**, enclose, encircle, circle, encompass, bound, line, flank.
2 *a white party frock edged with lace* **trim**, pipe, band, decorate, finish; border, fringe; bind, hem.
3 *he edged closer to the fire | he* **edged his way** *carefully out along the branch* **creep**, inch (one's way), worm (one's way), work (one's way), pick one's way, nose (one's way), ease (oneself), ease (one's way), advance slowly; advance stealthily, sidle, steal, slink.

edgy ▶ adjective *she felt edgy, dreading tomorrow* **tense**, **nervous**, on edge, highly strung, anxious, apprehensive, uneasy, ill at ease, unsettled, unstable; excitable, twitchy, jumpy, nervy, keyed up, fidgety, restive, skittish, neurotic, brittle, hysterical; sensitive, insecure; **irritable**, touchy, tetchy, testy, crotchety, irascible, peevish, querulous, bad-tempered, short-tempered, hot-tempered, quick-tempered, temperamental, snappy, captious, crabbed, prickly; *informal* uptight, wired.
OPPOSITE calm.

edible ▶ adjective *are these edible mushrooms?* **safe to eat**, fit to eat, fit to be eaten, fit for human consumption, wholesome, good to eat, consumable, digestible, palatable, comestible.
OPPOSITE inedible.

edict ▶ noun *oil exploration is prohibited by government edict* **decree**, order, command, commandment, mandate, proclamation, pronouncement, dictum, dictate, fiat, promulgation, precept; law, statute, act, enactment, bill, ordinance, regulation, rule, ruling, injunction, manifesto; (*in Tsarist Russia*) ukase; (*in Spanish-speaking countries*) pronunciamento; *rare* firman, decretal, irade, rescript.

edification ▶ **noun** (*formal*) *museum administrators are tempted to place profit above edification* **education**, instruction, tuition, teaching, schooling, tutoring, coaching, training, tutelage, guidance; **enlightenment**, cultivation, development, information, inculcation, indoctrination, improvement, bettering, uplifting, elevation.

edifice ▶ **noun** (*formal*) **building**, structure, construction, erection, pile, complex, assembly; property, development, premises, establishment, place.

E

edify ▶ **verb** (*formal*) *no doubt Hamish will edify us on the subject* **educate**, instruct, teach, school, tutor, coach, train, guide; **enlighten**, inform, cultivate, develop, inculcate, indoctrinate, improve, better, uplift, elevate.

edit ▶ **verb 1** *she has expertly edited the text to avoid anything that would jar in an English context* **correct**, **check**, copy-edit; **improve**, revise, emend, polish, modify, adapt, rewrite, reword, rework, redraft, rephrase; assemble, prepare for publication; shorten, condense, cut, abridge; approve, censor; *informal* clean up, iron out; *rare* redact.
2 *this volume of essays and interviews was edited by a consultant psychotherapist* **select**, choose, assemble, organize, put together, arrange, rearrange.
3 *he edited The Times for many years* **be the editor of**, control the content of, control, direct, run, manage, be in charge of, be responsible for, be at the helm of, be chief of, head, lead, supervise, superintend, oversee, preside over, be the boss of; *informal* head up.

edition ▶ **noun** *the early editions of tomorrow's papers* **issue**, number, volume; printing, impression, publication; version, recension, redaction, revision.

educate ▶ **verb** *they decided to educate Edward at home* **teach**, school, tutor, instruct, coach, train, drill, prime, prepare, guide, inform, enlighten, edify, cultivate, develop, inculcate, indoctrinate, improve, better, uplift, elevate.

educated ▶ **adjective** *an educated workforce learns how to exploit new technology* **informed**, literate, schooled, tutored, well informed, well read, learned, knowledgeable, intellectually aware, enlightened, discerning, discriminating; intellectual, academic, erudite, scholarly, studious, bookish, highbrow, literary, cultivated, cultured, refined; *informal* cerebral; *dated* lettered.
OPPOSITE uneducated.

education ▶ **noun 1** *the education of children with special needs* **teaching**, schooling, tuition, tutoring, instruction, coaching, training, tutelage, drilling, preparation, guidance, indoctrination, inculcation, enlightenment, edification, cultivation, development, improvement, bettering.
2 *a young woman of some education* **learning**, knowledge, literacy, schooling, scholarship, enlightenment, cultivation, culture, refinement; *archaic* letters.
OPPOSITE ignorance.

WORD LINKS
relating to education **pedagogic**

educational ▶ **adjective 1** *an educational establishment* **academic**, scholastic, school, for study, learning, teaching, pedagogic, tuitional, instructional.
2 *it was a very educational experience* **instructive**, instructional, educative, informative, informational, illuminating, pedagogic, doctrinal, preceptive, enlightening, edifying, improving, didactic, heuristic; pedantic, moralistic, homiletic; *rare* propaedeutic.

educative ▶ **adjective** *the educative value of broadcasting* **educational**, instructive, instructional, informative, informational, illuminating, pedagogic, doctrinal, preceptive, enlightening, edifying, improving, didactic, heuristic; pedantic, moralistic, homiletic; *rare* propaedeutic.

educator ▶ **noun teacher**, tutor, instructor, pedagogue, schoolteacher, schoolmaster, schoolmistress, master, mistress; educationalist, educationist; supply teacher; coach, trainer; lecturer, professor, don, fellow, reader, academic; guide, mentor, guru, counsellor; *Scottish* dominie; *Indian* pandit; *N. Amer. informal* schoolmarm; *Brit. informal* beak; *Austral./NZ informal* chalkie, schoolie; *archaic* doctor, schoolman, usher; *rare* preceptor.
OPPOSITE pupil.

eel ▶ **noun**

WORD LINKS
young **elver**
eel-shaped **anguilliform**

eerie ▶ **adjective** *an eerie silence descended over the house* **uncanny**, sinister, ghostly, spectral, unnatural, unearthly, preternatural, supernatural, other-worldly, unreal, mysterious, strange, abnormal, odd, curious, queer, weird, bizarre, freakish; **frightening**, spine-chilling, hair-raising, blood-curdling, scaring, terrifying, petrifying, chilling; *Scottish* eldritch; *informal* creepy, scary, spooky, freaky; *Brit. informal* rum.
OPPOSITES normal, reassuring.

efface ▶ **verb 1** *the young ladies have made an impression on my mind which will not easily be effaced* **erase**, eradicate, expunge, blot out, rub out, wipe out, remove, eliminate, excise; delete, cancel, cross out, strike out, ink out, score out, obliterate, blank out, block out, cover over, conceal.
OPPOSITE preserve.
2 *he retired to the largest chair and attempted to efface himself* **make oneself inconspicuous**, keep out of sight, keep oneself to oneself, keep quiet, keep out of the public eye, avoid publicity, keep out of the limelight, lie low, keep a low profile, regard/treat oneself as unimportant, be modest/diffident/retiring, withdraw.
OPPOSITE make one's presence felt.

effect ▶ **noun 1** *the effect of these changes is hard to assess* **result**, consequence, upshot, outcome, out-turn, sequel, reaction, repercussions, reverberations, ramifications; end result, conclusion, termination, culmination, denouement, corollary, concomitant, aftermath, fruit(s), product, by-product; *Medicine* sequelae; *informal* pay-off; *dated* issue; *archaic* success.
OPPOSITE cause.
2 *the effect of this drug can be long-lasting* **impact**, action, effectiveness, efficacy, efficaciousness, influence; power, potency, strength, usefulness, success.
3 *with effect from tomorrow* **force**, operation, enforcement, implementation, execution, action, effectiveness; validity, lawfulness, legality, legitimacy, authenticity, legal acceptability.
4 *he said 'See you later', or words to that effect* **sense**, meaning, theme, drift, thread, import, purport, intent, intention, burden, thrust, tenor, significance, message; gist, essence, substance, spirit; mood, character, vein, flavour; *archaic* strain.
5 (**effects**) *they went through the dead man's effects* **belongings**, possessions, personal possessions, personal effects, goods, worldly goods, chattels, goods and chattels, accoutrements, appurtenances; property, paraphernalia; luggage, baggage; *informal* gear, tackle, kit, things, stuff, junk, rubbish, bits and pieces, bits and bobs; *Brit. informal* clobber, gubbins; *vulgar slang* shit, crap.

□ **in effect** *the battle had, in effect, already been won* **really**, in reality, in truth, in fact, in actual fact, effectively, essentially, in essence, virtually, practically, in practical terms, for all practical purposes, to all intents and purposes, in all but name, all but, as good as, more or less, as near as dammit, almost, nearly, well nigh, nigh on, just about; *S. African* plus-minus; *informal* pretty much, pretty nearly, pretty well.

□ **take effect 1** *these measures will take effect on 23rd November* **come into force**, come into operation, come into being, begin, become operative, become valid, become law, apply, be applied.
OPPOSITE lapse.
2 *the drug started to take effect* **work**, act, be effective, produce results, have the desired effect, be efficacious.
OPPOSITE wear off.

▶ **verb** *the government effected a good many changes* **achieve**, accomplish, carry out, succeed in, realize, attain, manage, bring off, carry off, carry through, execute, conduct, fix, engineer, perform, do, perpetrate, discharge, fulfil, complete, finish, consummate, conclude; **cause**, bring about, cause to happen/occur, create, produce, make, give rise to; provoke, call forth, occasion, bring to pass; generate, originate, engender, precipitate, actuate, initiate, wreak, kindle; *rare* effectuate.

effect or affect?
See AFFECT.

effective or efficient?
Both these words express approval of the way in which someone or something works; but their meanings are different. **Effective** describes something which successfully produces an intended result, without reference to morality, economy of effort, or efficient use of resources (*the drug is more effective in treating ulcers than its predecessors | the trap was hideously unpleasant and equally hideously effective*). **Efficient**, on the other hand, applies to someone or something able to produce results with the minimum expense or effort, as a result of good organization or good design and making the best use of available resources (*staff offer efficient and unobtrusive service*).

effective ▶ **adjective 1** *there is no effective treatment for this condition* **successful**, effectual, efficacious, productive, constructive, fruitful, functional, potent, powerful; worthwhile, helpful, of help, of assistance, beneficial, advantageous, valuable, useful, of use.
OPPOSITES ineffective; incompetent; weak.
2 *a more effective argument can be constructed in support of the opposite point of view* **convincing**, compelling, strong, forceful, forcible, powerful, potent, weighty, plausible, efficacious, sound, valid, well founded, telling;

impressive, persuasive, irresistible, credible, influential, conclusive, unanswerable, authoritative; **logical**, reasoned, reasonable, well reasoned, rational, lucid, coherent, cogent, eloquent, clear, articulate.
OPPOSITE weak.
3 *the new law will become effective three months from now* **operative**, in force, in effect, in operation, valid, official, signed and sealed; lawful, legal, licit, legitimate, legally binding, binding; Law effectual.
OPPOSITE invalid.
4 *Korea was then under effective Japanese control* **virtual**, practical, essential, operative, actual, implied, implicit, unacknowledged, tacit.
OPPOSITE theoretical.

effectiveness ▶ **noun** *pupils' progress is a far better measure of a school's effectiveness* **success**, successfulness, efficacy, productiveness, fruitfulness, potency, power; benefit, advantage, value, virtue, use, usefulness; rare effectuality, constructiveness.
OPPOSITE ineffectiveness.

effectual ▶ **adjective 1** *effectual political action* **effective**, successful, efficacious, productive, constructive, fruitful, potent, powerful; worthwhile, helpful, of help, of assistance, beneficial, advantageous, valuable, useful, of use.
OPPOSITE ineffectual.
2 (Law) *an effectual document* **valid**, authentic, legally acceptable, proper, bona fide, genuine, official, signed and sealed; lawful, legal, licit, legitimate, (legally) binding, contractual; in force, in effect, effective.

effeminate ▶ **adjective** *as his manicured fingers played with the gold medallion around his neck, he looked very effeminate* **womanish**, unmanly, effete, foppish, affected, niminy-piminy, mincing, posturing; informal campy; informal, derogatory poncey, limp-wristed, pansyish, faggy.
OPPOSITE manly.

effervesce ▶ **verb 1** *heat the mixture until it effervesces* **fizz**, sparkle, bubble, froth, foam, spume.
2 *managers are supposed to effervesce with praise and encouragement* **sparkle**, be vivacious, be lively, be animated, be ebullient, be exuberant, be bubbly, be effervescent, be sparkling, be witty, be brilliant, be enthusiastic, be full of life.

effervescence ▶ **noun 1** *sparkling wines of uniform effervescence and taste* **fizz**, fizziness, sparkle, gassiness, bubbles, carbonation, aeration, bubbliness, frothiness, froth, foam, head, spume.
2 *the youngsters' cheeky effervescence* **vivacity**, liveliness, animation, life, spirit, spiritedness, high spirits, ebullience, exuberance, buoyancy, sparkle, light-heartedness, gaiety, jollity, joy, fun, the joys of spring, cheeriness, cheerfulness, perkiness, sunniness, airiness, breeziness, brightness, enthusiasm, irrepressibility, vibrancy, vividness, vitality, zest, energy, dynamism, vigour, vim, lustiness; informal pep, zing, zip, bounce, chirpiness; N. Amer. informal peartness.
OPPOSITE depression.

effervescent ▶ **adjective 1** *an effervescent drink* **fizzy**, sparkling, carbonated, aerated, gassy, bubbly, bubbling, fizzing, foaming, frothy; French mousseux, pétillant; Italian spumante, frizzante; German Schaum-, Perl-.
OPPOSITES still, flat.
2 *thousands of effervescent young people* **vivacious**, lively, animated, full of life, spirited, high-spirited, bubbling, bubbly, ebullient, buoyant, sparkling, scintillating, light-hearted, carefree, happy-go-lucky, jaunty, merry, happy, jolly, joyful, full of fun, full of the joys of spring, cheery, cheerful, perky, sunny, airy, breezy, bright, enthusiastic, irrepressible, vibrant, vivid, vital, zestful, energetic, dynamic, vigorous, full of vim and vigour, lusty; informal bright-eyed and bushy-tailed, bright and breezy, peppy, zingy, zippy, bouncy, upbeat, chirpy, full of beans, chipper; N. Amer. informal peart; dated gay.
OPPOSITE depressed.

effete ▶ **adjective 1** *effete trendies from art colleges* **affected**, over-refined, ineffectual, artificial, studied, pretentious, precious, chichi, flowery, mannered; informal twee, la-di-da, pseud; Brit. informal poncey, toffee-nosed; rare alembicated.
OPPOSITE unpretentious.
2 *I distrusted the effete young man* **effeminate**, unmasculine, unmanly; womanish, girlish, feminine, **weak**, soft, timid, timorous, fearful, cowardly, lily-livered, limp-wristed, spineless, craven, milksoppish, pusillanimous, chicken-hearted, weak-kneed; informal sissy, wimpish, wimpy, pansy-like.
OPPOSITE manly.
3 *the whole fabric of society is becoming effete* **weakened**, enfeebled, enervated, worn out, exhausted, finished, burnt out, played out, drained, spent, powerless.
OPPOSITE powerful.

efficacious ▶ **adjective** *a change in diet may be as efficacious as treatment with steroids* **effective**, successful, effectual, productive, constructive, fruitful, potent, powerful; worthwhile, helpful, of help, of assistance, beneficial, advantageous, valuable, useful, of use.
OPPOSITE inefficacious.

efficacy ▶ **noun** *information on the safety and efficacy of drugs* **effectiveness**, success, successfulness, productiveness, fruitfulness, potency, power; benefit, advantage, value, virtue, use, usefulness; rare effectuality, constructiveness.
OPPOSITE inefficacy.

efficiency ▶ **noun 1** *there was a need to reform local government to bring greater efficiency* **organization**, order, orderliness, planning, regulation, logicality, coherence, productivity, effectiveness, cost-effectiveness.
OPPOSITE inefficiency.
2 *I must compliment you all on your efficiency and your bravery* **competence**, capability, ability, proficiency, adeptness, deftness, expertise, professionalism, skilfulness, skill, effectiveness, productivity, organization.
OPPOSITE incompetence.

efficient ▶ **adjective 1** *efficient managerial techniques* **well organized**, methodical, systematic, structured, well planned, logical, coherent, well regulated, well run, well ordered, orderly, businesslike, systematized, streamlined, productive, effective, labour-saving, cost-effective.
OPPOSITES inefficient; disorganized.
2 *a most efficient young secretary* **competent**, capable, able, proficient, adept, deft, expert, professional, skilful, skilled, effective, productive, organized, workmanlike, businesslike; French rangé.
OPPOSITES inefficient; incompetent.

efficient or effective?
See EFFECTIVE.

CHOOSE THE RIGHT WORD
efficient, competent, capable, able
See COMPETENT.

effigy ▶ **noun** *they venerate an effigy of the saint* **statue**, statuette, carving, sculpture, graven image, model, dummy, figure, figurine, guy; likeness, representation, image; bust, head.

effluent ▶ **noun** *the effluent from papermaking contains many contaminants* **(liquid) waste**, sewage, effluvium, outflow, discharge, emission; pollutant, pollution.

effort ▶ **noun 1** *they made an effort to reach a settlement* **attempt**, try, endeavour; informal crack, go, shot, stab, bash, whack; formal essay; archaic assay.
2 *Guy's score of 68 was a fine effort* **achievement**, accomplishment, performance, attainment, result, feat, deed, exploit, undertaking, enterprise; work, handiwork, creation, production, opus; **triumph**, success, positive result, coup, master stroke, stroke of genius.
3 *it requires little effort to operate the handle* **exertion**, force, power, energy, work, muscle, application, labour, the sweat of one's brow, striving, endeavour, toil, struggle, slog, strain, stress, trouble, bother; informal sweat, elbow grease; Brit. informal graft; Austral./NZ informal (hard) yakka; archaic travail, moil.

effortless ▶ **adjective** *Alexei rose to his feet in a single effortless movement* **easy**, undemanding, unexacting, unchallenging, painless, trouble-free; leisurely, simple, uncomplicated, straightforward, elementary; **flowing**, fluid, fluent, smooth, graceful, elegant, natural; informal easy-peasy, as easy as pie, as easy as falling off a log, as easy as ABC, a piece of cake, child's play, kids' stuff, a cinch, no sweat, a doddle, a breeze, a pushover, money for old rope, money for jam; N. Amer. informal duck soup, a snap; Austral./NZ informal a bludge.
OPPOSITES difficult; awkward.

effrontery ▶ **noun** *one of the jurors had the effrontery to challenge the coroner's authority* **impudence**, impertinence, cheek, insolence, cheekiness, audacity, temerity, brazenness, forwardness, front, presumption, nerve, gall, pertness, boldness, shamelessness, impoliteness, disrespect, bad manners, unmannerliness, overfamiliarity; answering back, talking back; informal brass, brass neck, neck, face, lip, mouth, cockiness; Brit. informal sauce; Scottish informal snash; N. Amer. informal sass, sassiness, nerviness, chutzpah, back talk; informal, dated hide; Brit. informal, dated crust, backchat; rare malapertness, contumely, procacity, assumption.
OPPOSITE timidity.

effusion ▶ **noun 1** *a massive effusion of poisonous gas from a volcanic lake* **outflow**, outpouring, outflowing, outrush, rush, current, flood, deluge, emission, discharge, issue; spurt, surge, jet, fountain, cascade, spout, stream, torrent, gush, outburst, flow, flux, welling, leakage, escape, voidance, drain, drainage, outflux, emanation, effluence, exudation; technical efflux.
2 (usually **effusions**) *newspaper reporters' flamboyant effusions* **outburst**, outpouring, gush, stream of words, flow of speech; utterance, wordiness, speech, address, talk, words, writing(s); informal spiel, verbiage.

effusive ▶ **adjective** *a barrage of effusive compliments* **gushing**, gushy, unrestrained, unreserved, extravagant, fulsome, demonstrative, lavish,

enthusiastic, rhapsodic, lyrical, exuberant, ebullient; expansive, wordy, verbose, long-winded, profuse; *informal* over the top, OTT, all over someone.
OPPOSITE restrained.

egg ▶ noun **ovum**, gamete, germ cell, zygote; *informal* nit; *Austral. informal* goog; (**eggs**) clutch, roe, spawn, seed, flyblow.
▶ verb
□ **egg someone on** *'Teach him a lesson,' shouted the boys, egging their friend on* **urge**, goad, incite, provoke, prick, sting, propel, push, drive, prod, prompt, induce, impel, spur on, cheer on; encourage, exhort, stimulate, motivate, galvanize, act as a stimulus to, act as an incentive to, inspire, stir; *N. Amer. informal* root on, light a fire under; *rare* incentivize.

WORD LINKS

egg-shaped	**ovate, ovoid, oviform**
batch of eggs	**clutch**

E

egghead ▶ noun (*informal*) *in spite of her love of reading Eva denies being an egghead* **intellectual**, intellect, bluestocking, thinker, academic, scholar, sage; bookworm, bookish person, highbrow; expert, genius, Einstein, polymath, prodigy, mastermind; *informal* brains, bright spark, whizz, wizard, walking encyclopedia; *Brit. informal* brainbox, clever clogs, boffin; *N. Amer. informal* brainiac, rocket scientist, maven.
OPPOSITE dunce.

ego ▶ noun *he needed a boost to his ego* **self-esteem**, self-importance, self-worth, self-respect, self-conceit, self-image, self-confidence; *French* amour propre.

egocentric ▶ adjective *most children are unshakeably egocentric up to the age of seven* **self-centred**, egomaniacal, self-interested, selfish, self-seeking, self-regarding, self-absorbed, self-obsessed, self-loving, narcissistic, vain, conceited, proud, self-important.
OPPOSITE altruistic.

egotism, **egoism** ▶ noun *in his arrogance and egotism, he underestimated Gill* **self-centredness**, egocentricity, egomania, self-interest, selfishness, self-seeking, self-serving, self-regard, self-absorption, self-obsession, self-love, narcissism, self-admiration, self-adulation, vanity, conceit, conceitedness, self-conceit, pride, self-esteem, self-importance; **boastfulness**, boasting, bragging, blowing one's own trumpet; *French* amour propre; *informal* looking after number one; *rare* braggadocio.
OPPOSITES altruism; modesty.

egotist, **egoist** ▶ noun *boxing is a sport that breeds egotists and exhibitionists* **self-seeker**, egocentric, egomaniac, self-admirer, narcissist; **boaster**, brag, bragger, braggart, show-off; *informal* blowhard, swank, big-head; *N. Amer. informal* showboat; *Austral./NZ informal* skite; *Brit. informal, dated* swankpot.
OPPOSITE altruist.

egotistic, **egoistic** ▶ adjective *an egotistic lifestyle is a very bad sign indeed* **self-centred**, selfish, egocentric, egomaniacal, self-interested, self-seeking, self-regarding, self-absorbed, self-obsessed, self-loving, narcissistic, vain, conceited, proud, self-important; **boastful**, bragging.
OPPOSITES altruistic; modest.

egregious ▶ adjective *an egregious error of judgement* **shocking**, appalling, horrific, horrifying, horrible, terrible, awful, dreadful, grievous, gross, ghastly, hideous, horrendous, frightful, atrocious, abominable, abhorrent, outrageous; monstrous, nightmarish, heinous, harrowing, dire, unspeakable, shameful; flagrant, glaring, blatant, scandalous, unforgivable, unpardonable, intolerable.
OPPOSITE marvellous.

egress ▶ noun **1** *the egress from the gallery was blocked* **exit**, way out, out door, escape route; outlet, vent.
OPPOSITE entrance.
2 *a means of egress for the crowds* **departure**, leaving, exit, withdrawal, retreat, pull-out, exodus, issue; emergence, flowing out, escape, emanation, debouchment; vacation of a place.
OPPOSITE entry.

eight ▶ cardinal number **octet**, eightsome, octuplets; *Poetry* octrain, octameter; *Music* octuplet, octave; *technical* octad; *rare* ogdoad, octarchy.

WORD LINKS

related prefixes	**octo-, octa-,**
relating to eight	**octonary**
eight-sided figure	**octagon**
relating to eight years	**octennial**

ejaculate ▶ verb **1** **emit semen**; climax, have an orgasm, orgasm; *informal* come, shoot one's load.
2 *the sperm is ejaculated* **emit**, eject, discharge, release, expel, excrete, disgorge, exude, spout, shoot out, squirt out, spew out, spurt out.
3 *'What?' he ejaculated* **exclaim**, cry out, call out, yell, sing out, utter suddenly, blurt out; burst out with, come out with.

ejaculation ▶ noun **1** *the ejaculation of fluid* **emission**, ejection, discharge, release, expulsion, exudation, excretion, disgorgement.
2 *he suffers from premature ejaculation* **emission of semen**; climax, orgasm; night emission; *informal* coming, wet dream.
3 *the usual chorus of ejaculations of welcome* **exclamation**, interjection, cry, call, shout, yell, utterance.

eject ▶ verb **1** *the volcano ejected ash at a phenomenal rate* **emit**, spew out, pour out, discharge, give off, give out, send out, belch, vent; exude, excrete, expel, cast out, release, disgorge, spout, vomit, throw up, spit out, cough up; *rare* disembogue.
OPPOSITE take in.
2 *the pilot had time to eject* **bail out**, escape, leave the aircraft, get out, parachute to safety.
3 *his opponents were ejected from the hall* **expel**, throw out, turn out, put out, cast out, remove, oust; put out in the street, evict, dispossess, banish, deport, exile; *informal* chuck out, kick out, turf out, boot out, heave out, bounce.
OPPOSITE admit.
4 *he was swiftly ejected from his first job* **dismiss**, remove, discharge, oust, expel, deprive of office, get rid of, throw out, turn out, fling out, force out, drive out; let someone go, give notice to, lay off, make/declare redundant; *Military* cashier; *informal* sack, give the sack to, fire, axe, send packing, give someone the boot, boot out, chuck out, kick out, give someone their marching orders, give someone the push, give someone the (old) heave-ho, throw someone out on their ear, give someone the bullet, show someone the door; *Brit. informal* give someone their cards, give someone the chop, turf out; *N. Amer. informal* give someone the bum's rush.
OPPOSITE appoint.

ejection ▶ noun **1** *the ejection of an electron from an atom* **emission**, discharge, expulsion, release, exudation, excretion, elimination, disgorgement.
OPPOSITE absorption.
2 *fans were angry at their ejection from the ground* **expulsion**, throwing out, removal, ousting; eviction, dispossession, banishment, deportation, exile.
OPPOSITE admission.
3 *the crowd called for his ejection from office* **dismissal**, removal, discharge, ousting, expulsion, lay-off, redundancy, notice; *Military* cashiering; *informal* sacking, the sack, firing, axing, the boot, the push, the (old) heave-ho, the bullet; *Brit. informal* turfing out, one's cards, the chop; *N. Amer. informal* the bum's rush.
OPPOSITE appointment.

eke ▶ verb
□ **eke something out 1** *she eked out a living as a washerwoman* **scrape**, scratch, scrimp; **survive**, live, stay alive, exist, support oneself, cope, manage, fare, get along, get by, get through, make (both) ends meet, keep body and soul together; *informal* keep the wolf from the door, keep one's head above water, make out.
2 *people would eke out their supplies through the winter* **economize on**, skimp on, be (more) economical with, make economies with, scrimp and scrape, save; **be thrifty with**, be frugal with, be sparing with, cut back on, make cutbacks in, budget, husband; *informal* go easy on.
OPPOSITE squander.
3 *the emergency rations need to be eked out with other food to maintain health* **augment**, add to, increase, supplement; enlarge, expand, amplify, make bigger, pad out, fill out, bulk out, stretch out.

elaborate ▶ adjective **1** *an elaborate political system* **complicated**, detailed, intricate, complex, involved, tortuous, convoluted, serpentine, tangled, knotty, confusing, bewildering, baffling; painstaking, careful; inextricable, entangled, impenetrable, Byzantine, Daedalian, Gordian; *rare* involute, involuted.
OPPOSITE simple.
2 *an elaborate plasterwork ceiling* **ornate**, decorated, embellished, adorned, ornamented, fancy, over-elaborate, fussy, busy, ostentatious, extravagant, showy, baroque, rococo, florid, wedding-cake, gingerbread; *informal* flash, flashy.
OPPOSITE plain.
▶ verb *both sides refused to elaborate on their reasons* **expand on**, enlarge on, add to, flesh out, add flesh to, put flesh on the bones of, add detail to, expatiate on; supplement, reinforce, augment, extend, broaden, develop, fill out, embellish, enhance, amplify, refine, improve.

elan, **élan** ▶ noun *they performed with uncommon elan* **flair**, stylishness, smartness, elegance, grace, gracefulness, poise, polish, suaveness, sophistication, urbanity, chic, finesse, panache, flourish, taste; **vigour**, energy, pep, dynamism, forcefulness, force, strength, determination, motivation, push, vehemence, fanaticism, go, vitality, vivacity, buoyancy, liveliness, animation, sprightliness, zest, sparkle, effervescence, fizz, verve, spirit, spiritedness, ebullience, life, dash, brio; **enthusiasm**, eagerness, keenness, passion, zeal, fervour, relish, gusto, feeling, ardour, fire, fieriness, drive; *French* esprit; *informal* class, pizzazz, ritziness, zing, zip, vim, punch, get-up-and-go, oomph, feistiness.
OPPOSITE clumsiness.

elapse ▶ verb *a month elapsed before the appeal hearing began* **pass**, go by/past, proceed, progress, advance, wear on, march on, slip by/away/past, roll by/past, glide by/past, slide by/past, steal by/past, tick by/past; fly by/past; creep by/past, crawl by/past.

elastic ▶ adjective **1** *the elastic waist fits most people* **stretchy**, elasticated, stretchable, springy, flexible, pliant, pliable, supple, yielding, rubbery,

plastic, rebounding, recoiling, resilient, bouncy; *rare* tensible.
OPPOSITE rigid.
2 *this option is probably the most elastic way of working* **adaptable**, flexible, adjustable, pliant, compliant, accommodating, malleable, variable, fluid, versatile, conformable; *informal* easy.

elasticity ▶ noun **1** *the skin's natural elasticity* **stretchiness**, flexibility, pliancy, suppleness, rubberiness, plasticity, resilience, springiness; *informal* give.
OPPOSITE rigidity.
2 *there may be elasticity in a government with a very narrow majority* **adaptability**, flexibility, adjustability, fluidity, accommodation, versatility, variability, malleability, conformability.
OPPOSITE dogmatism.

elated ▶ adjective *she was elated at having pocketed some £400,000* **thrilled**, exhilarated, happy, delighted, overjoyed, joyous, gleeful, excited, animated, jubilant, beside oneself with happiness, exultant, ecstatic, euphoric, rapturous, in raptures, enraptured, rapt; walking on air, on cloud nine/seven, in seventh heaven, jumping for joy, in transports of delight, transported, carried away, in a frenzy of delight, delirious (with happiness), hysterical, wild with excitement, frenzied; *informal* blissed out, over the moon, on a high; *N. Amer. informal* wigged out; *rare* corybantic.
OPPOSITE miserable.

elation ▶ noun *we shared the general mood of elation at the success* **happiness**, exhilaration, joy, joyousness, delight, glee; excitement, animation, jubilation, exultation, ecstasy, euphoria, bliss, rapture, rhapsody, rhapsodies, transport(s), cloud nine, heaven, paradise, seventh heaven; *informal* the top of the world.
OPPOSITE misery.

elbow ▶ noun **1** *leaning on one's elbow* **arm joint**, bend of the arm.
2 *you need to fit a 15mm elbow to the end of the pipe* **bend**, joint, curve, corner, (right) angle, crook; *technical* flexure.
▶ verb *she elbowed him out of the way | he elbowed his way through the crowd* **push (one's way)**, shove (one's way), force (one's way), shoulder (one's way), jostle (one's way), nudge, muscle, bulldoze, bludgeon one's way.

elbow room ▶ noun *the province wants a little more elbow room within the federation* **room to manoeuvre**, room, space, breathing space, scope, freedom, play, free rein, licence, latitude, leeway, margin, clearance; *German* Lebensraum.

elder ▶ adjective *he has an elder brother* **older**, senior, first, firstborn, more grown up, big.
OPPOSITES younger; little.
▶ noun **1** *he longed for the approval of his elders* **senior**, old/older person, geriatric.
2 *the church elders* **leader**, senior figure, official, patriarch, father, guiding light, guru.

elderly ▶ adjective *she has an elderly mother in a nursing home* **aged**, old, mature, older, senior, ancient, venerable; advanced in years, getting on, ageing; in one's dotage, long in the tooth, as old as the hills; grey, grey-haired, grey-bearded, grizzled, hoary; past one's prime, not as young as one was, not as young as one used to be; decrepit, doddering, doddery, not long for this world, senile, superannuated; septuagenarian, octogenarian, nonagenarian, centenarian; *informal* past it, over the hill, no spring chicken; *formal* senescent; *rare* longevous.
OPPOSITE young.
▶ noun (**the elderly**) *purpose-built accommodation for the elderly* **old people**, older people, elderly people, elders, geriatrics, senior citizens, (old-age) pensioners, OAPs, retired people; *N. Amer.* seniors, retirees, golden agers; *informal* (golden) oldies, wrinklies; *N. Amer. informal* oldsters, woopies.
OPPOSITE the young.

eldest ▶ adjective *my eldest son* **oldest**, first, firstborn, most grown up, big, biggest.
OPPOSITES youngest, littlest.

elect ▶ verb *they have just elected a new president* **vote (for)**, **vote in**, choose (by ballot), cast one's vote for; pick, select, return, appoint, put in, put in power, opt for, decide on, settle on, fix on, plump for.
OPPOSITE vote out.
▶ adjective *the president elect* **future**, -to-be, soon-to-be, designate, chosen, elected, coming, next, appointed, presumptive.
▶ noun (**the elect**) *those who are numbered among the elect* **the chosen**, the elite, the select, the favoured; the crème de la crème.

election ▶ noun **1** *he was defeated in the 1992 election* **ballot**, vote, poll, referendum, plebiscite, general election, local election, popular vote, straw vote/poll, show of hands.
2 *the election of a new leader* **voting (in)**, choosing, picking, selection, choice, appointment.
OPPOSITE voting out.

WORD LINKS
study of elections **psephology**

electioneer ▶ verb *he accused the opposition of electioneering by raising the issue* **campaign**, canvass, go on the hustings, doorstep; *Brit. informal* go out on the knocker.

elector ▶ noun *each elector has one vote* **voter**, member of the electorate, enfranchised person, constituent, member of a constituency, selector.

electric ▶ adjective **1** *electric power* **generated by electricity**, galvanic, voltaic.
2 *an electric kettle* **electric-powered**, powered by electricity, electrically operated, electrically powered, mains-operated, battery-operated, electrically charged.
3 *the atmosphere was electric* **tense**, charged, electrifying; **exciting**, dramatic, exhilarating, intoxicating, dynamic, thrilling, stimulating, galvanizing, invigorating, animating, energizing, rousing, stirring, heady, moving, jolting, shocking, startling, knife-edge, explosive, volatile, cliffhanging; *informal* buzzy.
OPPOSITE lifeless.

electricity ▶ noun **power**, electric power, energy, current, static, power supply; *Brit.* mains; *Canadian* hydro; *Brit. informal* leccy; *historical* galvanism.

WORD LINKS
fear of electricity **electrophobia**

electrify ▶ verb **1** **convert to electricity**, wire up, install electric wiring in.
2 *both lecturers have for several years electrified students at Columbia University* **excite**, thrill, stimulate, arouse, rouse, inspire, stir (up), exhilarate, intoxicate, galvanize, move, motivate, fire (with enthusiasm), fire someone's imagination, invigorate, animate, get someone going; startle, jolt, shock; *N. Amer.* light a fire under; *informal* give someone a buzz, give someone a kick; *N. Amer. informal* give someone a charge.
OPPOSITE bore.

elegance ▶ noun **1** *the elegance of their suave escorts* **style**, stylishness, grace, gracefulness, smoothness; taste, tastefulness, discernment, refinement, sophistication, dignity, distinction, propriety, poise, finesse; fashion, culture, beauty; charm, polish, suaveness, urbanity, panache, flair, dash; luxury, sumptuousness, opulence, grandeur, plushness, exquisiteness; *informal* swankiness.
OPPOSITES inelegance, gaucheness.
2 *they liked the elegance of the idea* **neatness**, simplicity; **ingenuity**, cleverness, deftness, intelligence, inventiveness.
OPPOSITE messiness.

elegant ▶ adjective **1** *she was dressed in an elegant black outfit* **stylish**, graceful, tasteful, discerning, refined, sophisticated, dignified, cultivated, distinguished, classic, smart, fashionable, modish, decorous, beautiful, artistic, aesthetic, lovely; charming, polished, suave, urbane, cultured, dashing, debonair; luxurious, sumptuous, opulent, grand, plush, high-class, exquisite; *informal* swanky.
OPPOSITES inelegant, gauche.
2 *an elegant solution* **neat**, simple, effective; **ingenious**, clever, deft, intelligent, inventive.
OPPOSITE messy.

elegiac ▶ adjective *a movingly elegiac piece for small orchestra* **mournful**, melancholic, melancholy, plaintive, sorrowful, sad, lamenting, doleful; funereal, dirgelike; touching, moving, poignant; *literary* dolorous; *rare* threnodic, threnodial.
OPPOSITE cheerful.

elegy ▶ noun *I wrote an elegy for my father* **funeral poem/song**, burial hymn, lament, dirge, plaint, requiem, keening; *Irish & Scottish* keen, coronach; *rare* threnody, threnode.

element *See centre pages for list of chemical* **Elements**
▶ noun **1** *village shops are an essential element of the local community* **component**, constituent, part, section, portion, piece, segment, bit; factor, feature, facet, ingredient, strand, detail, point; member, unit, module, item; essential; *rare* integrand.
2 *there is an element of truth in this stereotype* **trace**, touch, hint, smattering, suspicion, soupçon.
3 (**elements**) *it is assumed that the reader is familiar with the elements of thermodynamics* **basics**, essentials, principles, first principles; foundations, fundamentals, rudiments; *informal* nuts and bolts, ABC.
4 *Graham was in his element building a fire and cooking the steaks* **natural environment**, favoured environment, familiar territory, territory, habitat, medium, milieu, sphere, field, domain, realm, circle, resort, haunt.
5 (**the elements**) *having come prepared with an umbrella, I braved the elements* **the weather**, the climate, meteorological conditions, atmospheric conditions/forces; the wind, the rain, storms.

elemental ▶ adjective **1** *the elemental principles of accountancy* **basic**, primary, principal, fundamental, essential, elementary, radical, root, underlying; rudimentary, primitive, primordial.
2 *a thunderstorm is the inevitable outcome of battling elemental forces* **natural**, atmospheric, meteorological, environmental.

elementary ▶ adjective **1** *an elementary astronomy course | the elementary principles of accountancy* **basic**, rudimentary, fundamental, basal; primary, preparatory, introductory, initiatory, early; essential, radical, underlying; *rare* rudimental.
OPPOSITE advanced.

E

2 *playing the blues really is elementary* **easy**, simple, straightforward, uncomplicated, undemanding, unexacting, effortless, painless, uninvolved, child's play, plain sailing; rudimentary, facile, simplistic; *informal* as easy as falling off a log, as easy as pie, as easy as ABC, a piece of cake, easy-peasy, no sweat, kids' stuff.
OPPOSITES difficult, complicated.

elephantine ▶ adjective *a ring of elephantine boulders* **enormous**, huge, great, massive, giant, immense, tremendous, colossal, mammoth, gargantuan, vast, prodigious, gigantic, monumental, stupendous, titanic, monstrous, very big, very large; hulking, bulky; heavy, weighty; ponderous, lumbering, clumsy, laborious; *informal* jumbo, whopping, whopping great, thumping, thumping great, humongous, monster, almighty, dirty great, socking great; *Brit. informal* whacking, whacking great, ginormous.
OPPOSITE small.

E

elevate ▶ verb **1** *we have to rely on a breeze to elevate the kite* **raise**, lift (up), raise up/aloft, buoy up, upraise, bear aloft; hoist, hike up, haul up, heft up, boost.
OPPOSITE lower.
2 *in the 1920s he was elevated to Secretary of State* **promote**, give promotion, upgrade, improve the position/status of, give a higher rank, advance, move up, raise, give advancement, prefer; ennoble, exalt, aggrandize, dignify; *informal* kick upstairs, move up the ladder.
OPPOSITE demote.

elevated ▶ adjective **1** *an elevated motorway* **raised**, upraised, uplifted, lifted up, high up, aloft, aerial, overhead, hoisted.
2 *he told the story with the elevated language of an old Roman* **lofty**, exalted, high, grand, fine, sublime; inflated, pompous, bombastic, orotund; *rare* fustian.
OPPOSITES lowly, base.
3 *the parish gentry were conscious of their elevated status* **dignified**, grand, lofty, noble, eminent, exalted, revered, august, great, high, higher, high/higher up, superior; magnificent, sublime, inflated.
OPPOSITE humble.

elevation ▶ noun **1** *his elevation to the peerage* **promotion**, upgrading, advancement, advance, preferment, aggrandizement, move up, step up; ennoblement; *informal* step up the ladder, kick upstairs, leg-up.
OPPOSITE demotion.
2 *as the road gains elevation, the maples begin to appear* **altitude**, height, distance above the sea/ground; loftiness.
3 *most early plantation development was at the higher elevations* **height**, hill, mound, mountain, mount, eminence, rise; high ground, raised ground, rising ground; *formal* acclivity.
OPPOSITE depth.
4 *houses with plastered elevations and tiled roofs* **side**, face, facade, aspect.
5 *elevation of thought* **grandeur**, greatness, nobility, magnificence, loftiness, majesty, grandioseness, sublimity.

elf ▶ noun *birthmarks were thought to be bruises left by elves* **pixie**, fairy, sprite, imp, brownie; dwarf, gnome, goblin, hobgoblin; leprechaun, puck, troll; *Irish* Sidhe; *rare* nix, nixie.

elfin ▶ adjective *her short hair accentuated her elfin face* **elflike**, elfish, elvish, pixie-like; puckish, impish, playful, mischievous; **dainty**, delicate, small, petite, slight, little, tiny, diminutive.

elicit ▶ verb *the police claimed that his fingerprints had been found in order to elicit admissions from him* **obtain**, bring out, draw out, extract, evoke, bring about, bring forth, induce, excite, give rise to, call forth, prompt, generate, engender, spark off, trigger, kindle; extort, exact, wrest, derive, provoke, wring, screw, squeeze; *informal* worm out.

eligible ▶ adjective **1** *she had paid sufficient contributions to be eligible to receive unemployment benefit* **entitled**, permitted, allowed, qualified; **acceptable**, suitable, appropriate, fit, fitting, worthy, competent.
OPPOSITE ineligible.
2 *an eligible bachelor* **desirable**; **available**, single, unmarried, unattached, unwed.

eliminate ▶ verb **1** *the cause of the disease has been eliminated* **remove**, get rid of, abolish, put an end to, do away with, banish; end, stop, terminate, eradicate, destroy, annihilate, stamp out, obliterate, wipe out, extinguish, quash, finish off; *informal* give something the chop, knock something on the head.
2 *he was eliminated from the title race* **knock out**, beat, get rid of; rule out, disqualify.

elite ▶ noun *the party attracted the elite of London society* **best**, pick, cream, flower, nonpareil, elect; aristocracy, nobility, gentry, upper class, privileged class, first class, establishment; high society, jet set, beautiful people; *Indian* bhadralok; *French* beau monde, haut monde, crème de la crème; *N. Amer. informal* four hundred.
OPPOSITE dregs.

elixir ▶ noun **1** *an elixir guaranteed to induce love* **potion**, concoction, brew, philtre, decoction; medicine, tincture, tonic; *literary* draught; *archaic* potation.
2 *a cough elixir* **mixture**, solution, potion, tincture; extract, essence, concentrate, distillate, distillation.

elliptical ▶ adjective **1** *an elliptical orbit* **oval**, egg-shaped, elliptic, ovate, ovoid, oviform, ellipsoidal; *technical* obovate.
2 *the elliptical phraseology of the law* **terse**, concise, succinct, compact, economic, brief, laconic, sparing, pithy, curt, clipped; abstruse, cryptic, ambiguous, obscure, incomprehensible, unfathomable, oblique, recondite, Delphic.
OPPOSITES clear, direct.

elocution ▶ noun *she had lessons in singing and elocution* **pronunciation**, enunciation, articulation, diction, speech, voice production, intonation, voicing, vocalization, modulation; phrasing, delivery, utterance, fluency; public speaking, oratory, speech-making, declamation.

elongate ▶ verb **1** *the door had been elongated so that the wheelchair could go in* **lengthen**, stretch out, make longer, extend, broaden, widen, enlarge.
OPPOSITE shorten.
2 *he elongated and emphasized the word* **prolong**, protract, draw out, string out, drag out, continue, sustain.
OPPOSITE shorten.

elope ▶ verb **1** *perhaps they'll elope to Gretna Green* **run away to marry**, run off/away together, slip away, sneak off, steal away; run off/away with a lover.
2 (*archaic*) *he eloped with all the cash and movables he could lay his hands on* **run away**, flee, fly, abscond, bolt, decamp, escape, make one's escape, make one's getaway; *informal* do a runner/bunk, vamoose, skedaddle, hightail it, fly the coop.

eloquence ▶ noun **1** *he was known for the eloquence of his sermons* **oratory**, rhetoric, grandiloquence, magniloquence; expressiveness, articulacy, articulateness, fluency, facility, persuasiveness; diction, enunciation, locution; command of language, power of speech; *informal* gift of the gab, way with words, blarney.
OPPOSITE inarticulacy.
2 *the quality and eloquence of the string playing* **expressiveness**, sensitivity, meaningfulness, significance, suggestiveness.

eloquent ▶ adjective **1** *an eloquent and well-informed speech* **persuasive**, expressive, articulate, fluent; strong, forceful, powerful, potent; well spoken, silver-tongued, smooth-tongued, well expressed, graceful, lucid, vivid, effective, graphic; glib.
OPPOSITE inarticulate.
2 *her dark eloquent eyes lifted up* **expressive**, sensitive, meaningful, suggestive, revealing, telling, significant, indicative.

elsewhere ▶ adverb *the negatives are stored in one place, and the prints are stored elsewhere* **somewhere else**, in/at/to another place, in/at/to a different place; not here, not present, absent, away, abroad, not at home, gone, out, hence.
OPPOSITES here, in the same place.

elucidate ▶ verb *collections of letters can elucidate what was uppermost in an artist's mind* **explain**, make clear, make plain, illuminate, throw/shed light on, clarify; comment on, interpret, explicate, expound on, gloss, annotate, spell out; clear up, sort out, resolve, straighten up/out, unravel, untangle.
OPPOSITES confuse, obscure.

elucidation ▶ noun *his elucidation of the finer points of horse racing is excellent* **explanation**, clarification, illumination; commentary, interpretation, explication, gloss, annotation, account, report, setting out, exegesis; comment, exposition.

elude ▶ verb *the murderer managed to elude the police for several weeks* **evade**, avoid, get away from, dodge, flee, escape (from), run (away) from; lose, duck, shake off, give the slip to, slip away from, throw off the scent; *informal* slip through someone's fingers, slip through the net; *archaic* circumvent, bilk.
OPPOSITE be caught by.

elusive ▶ adjective **1** *he tried to reach her by telephone, but she continued to be elusive* **difficult to catch/find**, difficult to track down; evasive, slippery, shifty; *informal* always on the move, cagey.
2 *the notion of meaning is exceedingly elusive and complex* **subtle**, indistinct, indefinite, ambiguous, indefinable, intangible, impalpable, unanalysable, fugitive, deceptive, baffling.
OPPOSITE clear.
3 *as usual she gave an elusive answer* **ambiguous**, baffling, puzzling, misleading, evasive, equivocal, deceptive; *rare* elusory.

Elysian ▶ adjective *an Elysian vision* **heavenly**, paradisal, paradisiacal, celestial, empyrean, superlunary, divine.
OPPOSITES hellish; mundane.

Elysium ▶ noun (*Greek Mythology*) *a chariot ready to convey the human soul to Elysium* **heaven**, paradise, the Elysian fields, empyrean, Arcadia, Arcady, Shangri-La; eternity, kingdom come, the next life, the afterlife, the next world, the hereafter; bliss; *Scandinavian Mythology* Valhalla; *Classical Mythology* the islands of the blessed; *Arthurian Legend* Avalon.

emaciated ▶ adjective *the captives were sick and emaciated men* **thin**, skeletal, bony, wasted, thin as a rake; scrawny, skinny, scraggy, skin and

bones, raw-boned, angular, stick-like; starved, underfed, undernourished, underweight, half-starved; cadaverous, shrivelled, shrunken, withered; gaunt, haggard, drawn, pinched, wizened, attenuated, atrophied; *informal* anorexic, looking like a bag of bones; *archaic* phthisical.
OPPOSITE fat.

emaciation ▸ noun *animal rescue workers took away goats suffering from emaciation* **thinness**, boniness, scrawniness, skinniness, scragginess; **starvation**, underfeeding, undernourishment; cadaverousness, shrunkenness, gauntness, haggardness, attenuation, atrophy; *informal* anorexia; *archaic* phthisis.
OPPOSITE obesity.

emanate ▸ verb **1** *policy statements which emanate from government departments* **emerge**, flow, pour, proceed, issue, ensue, come out, come forth, spread out, come; be uttered, be emitted, be transmitted; arise, originate, stem, derive, spring, start.
2 *the delicious aura of perfume which the women emanated* **exude**, give off, give out, send out, send forth, pour out, throw out, spread, discharge, disgorge, emit, exhale, radiate; *literary* distil.

emanation ▸ noun **1** *we can look at what is on the page as an emanation of its time and place* **product**, consequence, result, fruit; corollary, concomitant, by-product, side effect.
2 *the risk of radon gas emanation* **discharge**, emission, radiation, diffusion, effusion, exhalation, exudation, outflow, outpouring, flow, secretion, leak; effluent, effluvium; *technical* efflux.

emancipate ▸ verb *the serfs privately owned by members of the nobility were emancipated* **free**, liberate, set free, release, let loose/out, set loose/free, discharge; unchain, unfetter, unshackle, untie, unyoke, uncage, unbridle; give rights to, free from restriction/restraint; *historical* manumit; *rare* disenthral.
OPPOSITE enslave.

emancipated ▸ adjective *an emancipated woman of the twenty-first century* **liberated**, independent, unconstrained, unrepressed, uninhibited, free and easy, free.

emancipation ▸ noun *the emancipation of the serfs* **freeing**, liberation, liberating, setting free, release, releasing, letting loose/out, setting loose/free, discharge; unchaining, unfettering, unshackling, untying, unyoking, uncaging, unbridling; freedom, liberty; *historical* manumission; *rare* disenthralment.
OPPOSITES enslavement, slavery.

emasculate ▸ verb **1** *the Parliament Act of 1911 which emasculated the House of Lords* **weaken**, make feeble/feebler, debilitate, enfeeble, enervate, dilute, erode, undermine, impoverish, cripple, reduce the powers of; remove the sting from, pull the teeth of; *informal* water down.
OPPOSITE strengthen.
2 *young cocks should be emasculated at three months old* **castrate**, neuter, geld, cut, desex, asexualize, sterilize, remove the testicles of; unman; *N. Amer. & Austral.* alter; *informal* doctor, fix; *rare* evirate, caponize, eunuchize.

embalm ▸ verb **1** *the Egyptians used citrus juices for embalming their dead* **preserve**, mummify, lay out, anoint.
2 *the poem ought to embalm his memory* **conserve**, preserve, immortalize, enshrine; cherish, treasure, store, consecrate.
3 (*archaic*) *the buxom air, embalm'd with odours* **perfume**, make fragrant, scent, aromatize.

embankment ▸ noun *a steep grassy embankment* **bank**, mound, ridge, earthwork, causeway, barrier, levee, dam, dyke; slope, verge.

embargo ▸ noun *an embargo on oil sales* **ban**, bar, prohibition, stoppage, interdict, proscription, veto, moratorium; restriction, restraint, blockage, check, barrier, impediment, obstruction, hindrance; boycott.
▸ verb *arms sales were embargoed* **ban**, bar, prohibit, stop, interdict, debar, proscribe, outlaw, make illegal; restrict, restrain, block, check, impede, obstruct, hinder; boycott, blacklist, ostracize.
OPPOSITE allow.

embark ▸ verb **1** *he stood on the pier to watch me embark* **board ship**, go on board, go aboard, climb aboard, step aboard, take ship; take off; *informal* hop on, jump on.
OPPOSITES disembark; land.
2 *he was about to* **embark on** *a career in the family's department store chain* **begin**, start, commence, undertake, set about, enter on, go into, take up; venture into, launch into, plunge into, turn one's hand to, engage in, settle down to; institute, initiate, tackle; *informal* have a go/crack/shot at.

embarrass ▸ verb *he was embarrassed by a front-page story which alleged that he had had an affair* **shame**, humiliate, make ashamed, demean, abash; mortify, horrify, appal, crush; make uncomfortable, make awkward, make self-conscious, make uneasy; upset, disconcert, discomfit, discompose, confuse, fluster, agitate, nonplus, discountenance, distress, chagrin; discredit, dishonour; *informal* show up, faze, rattle, discombobulate.

embarrassed ▸ adjective *she felt embarrassed at having been so frank before a servant* **awkward**, **self-conscious**, uneasy, uncomfortable, unsettled, sheepish, red-faced, blushing, shy; shamed, ashamed, shamefaced, humiliated, humbled, demeaned, abashed; mortified, horrified, appalled, crushed; upset, disconcerted, discomfited, discomposed, confused, flustered, agitated, nonplussed, discountenanced, distressed, chastened, chagrined; discredited, dishonoured; *informal* with egg on one's face, wishing the earth would swallow one up.
OPPOSITE unabashed.

embarrassing ▸ adjective **1** *he was frightened of making an embarrassing mistake* **shaming**, shameful, humiliating, mortifying, demeaning, degrading, ignominious; upsetting, disconcerting, discomfiting, discomposing, confusing, flustering, agitating, discountenancing, distressing; discreditable, dishonouring, disgraceful; *informal* blush-making.
2 *there may be some embarrassing questions at the shareholders' meeting* **awkward**, uncomfortable, difficult, tricky, delicate, sensitive, problematic, troublesome, thorny, knotty, vexatious, ticklish; compromising, humiliating; *informal* sticky, dicey, hairy, cringeworthy, cringe-making; *Brit. informal* dodgy.

embarrassment ▸ noun **1** *Louise's heightened colour betrayed her embarrassment* **awkwardness**, **self-consciousness**, unease, uneasiness, discomfort, discomfiture, edginess; shame, humiliation, mortification, ignominy; sheepishness, shyness, bashfulness; discomposure, flusteredness, perturbation, confusion, agitation, distress, chagrin.
OPPOSITE confidence.
2 *his current financial embarrassment* **difficulty**, predicament, plight, problem, mess, entanglement, imbroglio; dilemma, quandary; *informal* bind, jam, pickle, fix, scrape.
3 *an embarrassment of riches* **surplus**, excess, overabundance, superabundance, profusion, glut, surfeit, superfluity, more than enough, too many, too much, enough and to spare; avalanche, deluge, flood, abundance, plethora.
OPPOSITE dearth.

embassy ▸ noun **1** *the Italian embassy* consulate, legation, ministry.
2 (*historical*) *Charles sent an embassy to the Lombards* **envoy**, representative, legate, delegate, emissary; **delegation**, deputation, delegacy, legation, (diplomatic) mission; *archaic* embassage.

embed, **imbed** ▸ verb *the plaque was embedded in a wall at the rear of the house* **implant**, plant, set, fix, lodge, root, insert, place; sink, submerge, immerse; drive in, hammer in, ram in.

embellish ▸ verb **1** *weapons were often embellished with precious metal* **decorate**, adorn, ornament, dress, dress up, furnish; beautify, enhance, enrich, grace; trim, garnish, gild, varnish; brighten up, ginger up; deck, bedeck, festoon, emblazon, bespangle; *informal* do up, do out, jazz up; *Brit. informal* tart up; *literary* bejewel, bedizen, caparison, furbelow, befrill.
2 *the legend was embellished further by a visiting American academic* **elaborate**, embroider, colour, expand on, exaggerate, dress up, touch up, gild.
OPPOSITE simplify.

embellishment ▸ noun **1** *the embellishments in medieval manuscripts* **decoration**, ornamentation, adornment; beautification, enhancement, trimming, trim, garnishing, gilding, frill, enrichment; varnishing, embroidery; decorating, embellishing, bedecking, festooning, emblazoning.
2 *stripped of her embellishments, the core of hard facts was disappointingly small* **elaboration**, addition, exaggeration; digression, deviation.

ember ▸ noun *the fire's dying embers* **glowing coal**, live coal; cinder; (**embers**) ashes, residue, clinker, charcoal.

embezzle ▸ verb *he was charged with embezzling more than £3,000 from a country club* **misappropriate**, steal, rob, thieve, pilfer, appropriate, abstract, defraud someone of, siphon off, pocket, take, take for oneself, help oneself to, line one's pockets/purse with; put one's hand in the till, dip into the public purse, commit white-collar crime, commit fraud; *informal* rip off, filch, swipe, lift, skim, snaffle; *Brit. informal* pinch, nick, half-inch, whip, nobble; *formal* peculate, defalcate, purloin.

embezzlement ▸ noun *the embezzlement of public funds* **misappropriation**, theft, stealing, robbing, robbery, thieving, pilfering, pilferage, appropriation, abstraction, swindling; white-collar crime, fraud, larceny, misuse of funds; *informal* ripping off, filching, swiping, lifting, skimming, snaffling, monkey business; *Brit. informal* pinching, nicking, half-inching, whipping, nobbling; *formal* peculation, defalcation, purloining.

embitter ▸ verb *Hugh was embittered by William's failure to keep his word* **make bitter**, make resentful, sour, anger, poison, envenom, make rancorous, jaundice, antagonize, vex, frustrate, alienate; disillusion, disaffect, dissatisfy, discourage; *N. Amer.* rankle.

emblazon ▸ verb **1** *each shirt was emblazoned with the company name* **adorn**, decorate, ornament, embellish, illuminate; colour, paint.
2 *a flag with a hammer and sickle emblazoned on it* **display**, depict, exhibit, show, present.
3 (*archaic*) *their success was emblazoned* **extol**, proclaim, publicize, publish, trumpet; acclaim, celebrate, glorify, praise, laud.

emblem ▸ noun *the white rose was the emblem of the Yorkist side* **symbol**, representation, token, image, figure, mark, sign; **crest**, badge, device, insignia, stamp, seal, design, heraldic device, coat of arms, shield; logo, trademark.

emblematic, **emblematical** ▶ adjective **1** *the experience of these writers was seen as emblematic of the social mobility of post-war writers* **symbolic**, representative, demonstrative, suggestive, symptomatic, indicative, typical, characteristic.
2 *emblematic works of art* **allegorical**, symbolic, symbolizing, metaphorical, parabolic, evocative, figurative.
OPPOSITES representational, realistic.

embodiment ▶ noun *she was the living embodiment of '80s values* **personification**, incarnation, incorporation, realization, manifestation, expression, representation, actualization, concretization, symbol, symbolization; paradigm, epitome, paragon, soul, model; type, typification, essence, quintessence, exemplification, example, exemplar, ideal, idea, textbook example; *formal* reification.

E

embody ▶ verb **1** *he embodies what everybody takes to be typical of the skinhead movement* **personify**, incorporate, give human form/shape to, realize, manifest, express, concretize, symbolize, represent, epitomize, stand for, encapsulate, typify, exemplify; *formal* reify; *rare* incarnate, image.
2 *the proposals were eventually embodied in legislation* **incorporate**, include, contain, take in, consolidate, encompass, assimilate, integrate, concentrate; organize, systematize; combine, bring together, gather together, collect.

embolden ▶ verb *emboldened by the brandy, he walked over to her table* **give courage**, make brave/braver, encourage, hearten, strengthen, fortify, stiffen the resolve of, lift the morale of; rouse, stir, stimulate, cheer, rally, give confidence, brace; fire, inflame, animate, motivate, invigorate, vitalize; *informal* buck up; *rare* inspirit.
OPPOSITES dishearten, discourage.

embrace ▶ verb **1** *he ran to meet Jacob and embraced him* **hug**, take/hold in one's arms, hold, cuddle, clasp to one's bosom, clasp, squeeze, clutch, seize, grab; nuzzle, caress; enfold, enclasp, encircle, enclose, envelop, entwine oneself around; *informal* canoodle, smooch; *literary* embosom.
2 *many women are turning their backs on careers and embracing family life* **welcome**, accept, receive enthusiastically/wholeheartedly, take up, take to one's heart, welcome/receive with open arms, adopt; support, be in favour of, back, champion; *formal* espouse.
OPPOSITE reject.
3 *the faculty embraces a wide range of departments* **include**, take in, cover, involve, take into account, contain, comprise, incorporate, encompass, encapsulate, embody, subsume, comprehend.
OPPOSITE exclude.
▶ noun *they were locked in an embrace* **hug**, cuddle, squeeze, clasp, hold, clutch, clinch, nuzzle, caress; bear hug; *informal* necking session.

embrocation ▶ noun *a rub with embrocation* **ointment**, lotion, cream, rub, salve, emollient, preparation, application, liniment, balm, poultice, unguent.

embroider ▶ verb **1** *the cushion was embroidered with a pattern of golden keys* **decorate**, adorn, ornament, embellish; **sew**, stitch.
2 *she embroidered her stories with colourful detail* **elaborate**, embellish, colour, enlarge on, exaggerate; add detail to, go into detail about, flesh out, add flesh to; touch up, dress up, gild, ginger up; *informal* jazz up.
OPPOSITE simplify.

embroidery *See centre pages for list of* **Sewing Techniques and Stitches**
▶ noun **1** *my mother decided I should learn embroidery* **needlework**, needlepoint, needlecraft, sewing, cross stitch, tatting, crochet, crewel work; tapestry, sampler.
2 *fanciful embroidery of the facts* **elaboration**, embellishment, adornment, ornamentation, colouring, enhancement; exaggeration, overstatement, hyperbole; touching up, dressing up, gilding, varnishing, gingering up; *informal* jazzing up.
OPPOSITE simplification.

embroil ▶ verb *she became embroiled in a dispute between the two women* **involve**, entangle, ensnare, enmesh, catch up, mix up, bog down, mire.

embryo ▶ noun **1** *the development of the embryo in the uterus* **fetus**, fertilized egg, unborn child/baby.
2 *the building is used as the embryo of a university for the island* **rudimentary version**, germ, nucleus, seed, root, source; rudiments, basics; beginning, start, basis, mainspring.

WORD LINKS
branch of medicine concerning embryos **embryology**

embryonic ▶ adjective **1** *an embryonic chick* **fetal**, unborn, unhatched.
OPPOSITE mature.
2 *an embryonic pro-democracy movement* **rudimentary**, undeveloped, unformed, immature, incomplete, incipient, inchoate, just beginning; fledgling, budding, beginning, potential, nascent, emerging, developing; early, primary, elementary, germinal.
OPPOSITES mature, developed.

emend ▶ verb *the journalistic practice of emending quotations in the areas of grammar and syntax* **correct**, rectify, repair, fix; improve, enhance, polish, refine, clarify; edit, alter, rewrite, revise, copy-edit, subedit, amend, change, modify; redraft, recast, rephrase, reword, rework; expurgate, censor, bowdlerize; *rare* redact.

emendation ▶ noun *different editors applied rival principles of textual emendation* **correction**, rectification; improvement, improving, enhancement, enhancing, polishing, refinement, refining, clarification; editing, alteration, rewriting, revision, copy-editing, subediting, amendment, modification; redrafting, recasting, rephrasing, rewording, reworking; expurgation, censorship, censoring, bowdlerization; *rare* redaction.

emerge ▶ verb **1** *a policeman emerged from the alley* **come out**, appear, come into view, become visible, make an appearance; turn up, spring up, come up, surface, crop up, pop up; materialize, manifest oneself, arise, proceed, issue, come forth, emanate.
OPPOSITE disappear.
2 *the results were collected and several unexpected facts emerged* **become known**, become apparent, become evident, be revealed, come to light, come out, transpire, come to the fore, enter the picture, unfold, turn out, prove to be the case; become common knowledge, get around.

emergence ▶ noun **1** *we are witnessing the emergence of a new generation of managers* **appearance**, arrival, coming; turning up, springing up, surfacing, cropping up, popping up; advent, inception, dawn, birth, origination, start; development, rise, blossoming, blooming; materializing, materialization, arising, issue, emanation.
OPPOSITE disappearance.
2 *the emergence of the facts* **disclosure**, becoming known, coming to light, exposure, unfolding, publication, publicizing, publishing, broadcasting.

emergency ▶ noun *your quick response in an emergency could be a lifesaver* **crisis**, urgent situation, extremity, exigency; accident, disaster, catastrophe, calamity; difficulty, plight, predicament, tight spot, tight corner, mess; quandary, dilemma; unforeseen circumstances, dire/desperate straits, danger; *informal* scrape, jam, fix, pickle, spot, hole, hot water, crunch, panic stations.
▶ adjective **1** *an emergency meeting* **urgent**, crisis; impromptu, extraordinary.
2 *an emergency exit* **alternative**, substitute, replacement, spare, extra, standby, auxiliary, reserve, backup, fill-in, fallback, in reserve.
OPPOSITES main, primary.

emergent ▶ adjective *their methods suited the needs of the emergent recording industry* **emerging**, beginning, coming out, arising, dawning; developing, budding, burgeoning, embryonic, infant, fledgling, nascent, incipient; rising, promising, potential, up-and-coming.
OPPOSITES declining; mature.

emigrate ▶ verb **move abroad**, move overseas, leave one's country, migrate; relocate, resettle, start a new life; defect.
OPPOSITE immigrate.

emigration ▶ noun *the major financial reason for emigration was higher salaries* **moving abroad**, moving overseas, expatriation, departure, withdrawal, migration, evacuation; exodus, diaspora; relocation, resettling; defection.
OPPOSITE immigration.

eminence ▶ noun **1** *his eminence as a scientist is well known* **illustriousness**, distinction, renown, pre-eminence, notability, greatness, calibre, prestige, importance, reputation, repute, note; fame, celebrity, prominence; stature, standing, rank, station.
2 *her first-class mind made her an eminence in the British establishment* **important person**, influential person, distinguished person, dignitary, luminary, worthy, grandee, notable, notability, personage, leading light, VIP; *informal* somebody, someone, bigwig, big shot, big noise, big gun, big cheese, nob, lady muck, heavyweight; *N. Amer. informal* big wheel, big kahuna, top banana, big enchilada.
3 (*formal*) *the hotel dominated Scarborough from its eminence above the sea* **elevation**, rise, rising/raised ground, height, hill, bank, mound.

eminent ▶ adjective **1** *an eminent man of letters* **illustrious**, distinguished, renowned, esteemed, pre-eminent, notable, noteworthy, great, prestigious, important, significant, influential, outstanding, noted, of note; famous, celebrated, prominent, well known, lionized, acclaimed; superior, of high standing, high-ranking, exalted, revered, elevated, august, grand, lofty, venerable, foremost, leading, paramount, legendary; *informal* big-time, big/major league.
OPPOSITES unimportant; unknown.
2 *the eminent reasonableness of their wage claims* **obvious**, clear, conspicuous, marked, singular, signal, outstanding; total, complete, utter, absolute, thorough, perfect, downright, sheer.

eminently ▶ adverb *this car is eminently suitable for town driving* **very**, most, greatly, highly, exceedingly, extremely, particularly, positively, exceptionally, supremely, remarkably, uniquely; **obviously**, clearly, conspicuously, markedly, singularly, signally, outstandingly, strikingly, notably, prominently, surpassingly; totally, completely, utterly, absolutely, thoroughly, perfectly, downright; *French* par excellence.

emissary ▶ noun *he sent an emissary to Constantinople for bilateral talks* **envoy**, ambassador, diplomat, delegate, attaché, legate, consul, plenipotentiary, minister; agent, representative, deputy, factor, proxy, surrogate, liaison, messenger, courier, herald; *informal* go-between; *Roman*

Catholic Church nuncio.

emission ▶ noun *targets for reducing carbon dioxide emissions* **discharge**, release, outpouring, outflow, outrush, leak, excretion, secretion, ejection; emanation, radiation, exhalation, exudation, exuding, venting, effusion, ejaculation, disgorgement, issuance, issue; oozing, leaking.

emit ▶ verb **1** *hydrocarbons are emitted from vehicle exhausts* **discharge**, release, give out/off, pour out, send forth, throw out, void, effuse, vent, give vent to, issue; leak, ooze, shed, excrete, disgorge, secrete, eject; spout, belch, spew out; emanate, radiate, exhale, ejaculate, exude; *rare* eruct.
OPPOSITE absorb.
2 *suddenly he emitted a loud cry* **utter**, voice, let out, produce, give vent to, issue, come out with, pronounce, express; declare, articulate, vocalize.

emollient ▶ adjective **1** *a rich emollient shampoo* **moisturizing**, palliative, balsamic; soothing, softening; *technical* humectant.
OPPOSITE irritating.
2 *he gave a confidently emollient response* **conciliatory**, conciliating, appeasing, soothing, calming, pacifying, assuaging, placating, mollifying, relaxing, propitiatory.
OPPOSITE aggravating.
▶ noun *always moisturize exposed skin with an effective emollient* **moisturizer**, cream, oil, ointment, rub, lotion, salve, unguent, balsam; *technical* humectant; *dated* pomade.
OPPOSITE irritant.

emolument ▶ noun (*formal*) *the emoluments of the director* **payment**, fee, charge, consideration; salary, pay, wage(s), earnings, allowance, stipend, honorarium; income, revenue, return, profit, gain, proceeds; reward, compensation, premium, recompense; *informal* perks, pickings; *formal* perquisites.

emotion ▶ noun **1** *she was good at hiding her emotions* **feeling**, sentiment, sensation; reaction, response.
2 *overcome by emotion, she turned away* **passion**, intensity, warmth, ardour, fervour, vehemence, fire, fieriness, excitement, spirit, soul.
OPPOSITES coldness, indifference.
3 *we are not basing our views on emotion, but on pure business considerations* **instinct**, intuition, gut feeling, inclination; sentiment, sentimentality, the heart; tenderness, softness, soft-heartedness, tender-heartedness.
OPPOSITE intellect.

emotional ▶ adjective **1** *their emotional needs are often ignored* **spiritual**, inner, psychic, psychological, of the heart.
OPPOSITE material.
2 *an emotional young man* **passionate**, feeling, hot-blooded, warm, ardent, fervent, excitable, temperamental, melodramatic, tempestuous, overcharged, responsive; demonstrative, tender, loving, sentimental, sensitive.
OPPOSITES apathetic, cold.
3 *he paid an emotional tribute to his wife* **poignant**, moving, touching, affecting, powerful, stirring, emotive, heart-rending, heartbreaking, heart-warming, soul-stirring, uplifting, impassioned, dramatic; harrowing, tragic, haunting, pathetic; sentimental, over-sentimental, mawkish, cloying, sugary, syrupy, saccharine, lachrymose; *informal* tear-jerking, soppy, mushy, schmaltzy, weepy, cutesy, lovey-dovey, gooey, drippy; *N. Amer. informal* cornball, sappy, hokey, three-hankie.
OPPOSITES dry, unfeeling, emotionless.
4 *an emotional issue* **emotive**, sensitive, delicate, difficult, problematic; controversial, contentious, subjective.

emotionless ▶ adjective *a flat, emotionless voice* **unemotional**, unfeeling, dispassionate, passionless; unexpressive, cool, cold, cold-blooded, impassive; reserved, controlled, restrained, self-controlled, {cool, calm, and collected}, indifferent, detached, remote, aloof; toneless, flat, dead, expressionless, bland, blank, wooden, stony, deadpan, hollow, vacant, undemonstrative, imperturbable, frigid, phlegmatic, glacial.
OPPOSITE emotional.

emotive ▶ adjective *fox-hunting is another emotive issue* **inflammatory**, controversial, contentious, emotional; sensitive, delicate, difficult, problematic, touchy, awkward.

empathize ▶ verb *counsellors need to be able to* **empathize with** *people* **identify**, be in tune, have a rapport, feel togetherness, feel at one, commune, sympathize, be in sympathy; be on the same wavelength as, talk the same language as; understand, relate to, feel for, have insight into; *informal* put oneself in the shoes of.

emperor ▶ noun *the Emperor of Austria* **ruler**, sovereign, king, monarch, potentate, lord, overlord; (*formerly, in certain Muslim countries*) khan; *Russian, historical* tsar; *German, historical* kaiser; *Japanese, historical* mikado; (*in ancient Rome*) imperator; *rare* ethnarch, autarch.
WORD LINKS
relating to an emperor **imperial**

emphasis ▶ noun **1** *the curriculum for 16-year-olds gave more emphasis to reading and writing* **prominence**, importance, significance; stress, weight, attention, priority, urgency, force, forcibleness, insistence, underlining, underscoring, intensity; import, power, moment, mark, pre-eminence.
2 *the emphasis is on the word 'little'* **stress**, accent, accentuation, weight, force, prominence; beat; *Prosody* ictus.

emphasize ▶ verb **1** *the prime minister emphasized his commitment to reform* **bring/call/draw attention to**, focus attention on, highlight, point up, spotlight, foreground, play up, make a point of; stress, weight, put/lay stress on, give an emphasis to, give prominence to, bring to the fore; dwell on, harp on, insist on, belabour; accent, accentuate, underline, intensify, strengthen, heighten, deepen, italicize, underscore, prioritize; *informal* press home, rub it in.
OPPOSITES understate, play down.
2 *'It's only a bachelor pad' I said, emphasizing the word 'bachelor'* **stress**, put the stress/accent/force on, accent, accentuate, weight.

emphatic ▶ adjective **1** *he was emphatic that athletes would not be paid to take part* | *an emphatic denial* **vehement**, firm, wholehearted, forceful, forcible, energetic, vigorous, ardent, assertive, insistent; certain, direct, definite, out-and-out, one hundred per cent; decided, determined, earnest; categorical, unqualified, unconditional, unequivocal, unambiguous, absolute, explicit, downright, outright, clear.
OPPOSITES hesitant, tentative.
2 *an emphatic victory* **conclusive**, decisive, marked, pronounced, decided, unmistakable, positive, definite, strong, powerful, striking, distinctive; resounding, telling, momentous; *informal* thumping, thundering.
OPPOSITE narrow.

empire ▶ noun **1** *the Ottoman Empire* **kingdom**, realm, domain, territory, province; commonwealth, federation, confederation; power, world power, superpower; jurisdiction; *Latin* res publica.
2 *a worldwide shipping empire* **organization**, corporation, multinational, conglomerate, consortium, company, business, firm, operation, institution, establishment, body.
3 (*archaic*) *her empire over his spirit was complete* **power**, command, rule, control, mastery, authority, ascendancy, supremacy, dominance, domination, sway; government, sovereignty, dominion.
WORD LINKS
relating to an empire **imperial**

empirical ▶ adjective *many of these predictions have received empirical confirmation* **observed**, seen, factual, actual, real, verifiable, first-hand; **experimental**, experiential; practical, pragmatic, hands-on, applied; *technical* heuristic; *rare* empiric.
OPPOSITE theoretical.

employ ▶ verb **1** *Mary bought a Daimler and employed a chauffeur* **hire**, engage, recruit, take on, take into employment, secure the services of, sign up, sign, put on the payroll, enrol, appoint, commission, enlist; retain, have in employment, have on the payroll; indenture, apprentice; *informal* take on board.
OPPOSITE dismiss.
2 *Sam was employed in carving a stone figure* **occupy**, engage, involve, keep busy, tie up; absorb, engross, immerse.
3 *the reactors employ carbon dioxide gas as a coolant* | *the team employed subtle psychological tactics* **use**, utilize, make use of, avail oneself of, put into service; implement, apply, exercise, practise, put into practice, exert, bring into play, bring into action, bring to bear; draw on, resort to, turn to, have recourse to, take advantage of.

employed ▶ adjective *employed married women tend to delay their childbearing* **working**, in work, in employment, with a job, holding down a job, with a career; professional, career; earning, waged, in gainful employment, earning one's living, breadwinning.
OPPOSITE unemployed.

employee ▶ noun *the firm supports employees who show ambition* **worker**, member of staff, member of the workforce; blue-collar worker, white-collar worker, workman, labourer, artisan, hand, hired hand, hired man, hired person, hired help, hireling; wage-earner, breadwinner; (**employees**) personnel, staff, workforce.

employer ▶ noun **1** *his employer gave him a glowing reference* **boss**, manager, manageress, patron, proprietor, director, managing director, chief executive, principal, president, head man, head woman; *informal* boss man, skipper; *Brit. informal* gaffer, governor, guv'nor; *N. Amer. informal* padrone, sachem.
2 *the largest private sector employer in Sheffield* **firm**, company, business, organization, manufacturer.

employment ▶ noun **1** *Christine found employment as a clerk* **job**, post, position, situation, occupation, profession, trade, livelihood, career, business, line, line of work, calling, vocation, craft, pursuit; **work**, labour, service; *French* métier; *informal* racket, game; *archaic* employ.
2 *they forbid the employment of children under ten years old* **hiring**, hire, engagement, engaging, taking on, signing up, enrolment, enrolling, commissioning, enlisting; apprenticing.
3 *the employment of nuclear weapons* **use**, utilization, implementation, application, exercise; putting into operation.

emporium ▶ noun **1** *he was working at a boot and shoe emporium* **shop**, store, boutique, outlet, retail outlet; department store, chain store,

supermarket, hypermarket, superstore, megastore; establishment, place of business.
2 (archaic) *the labyrinthine layout of the emporium* **market**, bazaar, fair, mart, marketplace, shopping quarter, shopping centre, shopping mall, retail centre; *Arabic* souk; *historical* agora.

empower ▶ verb **1** *the act empowered Henry to punish heretics* **authorize**, license, entitle, permit, allow, sanction, warrant, commission, delegate, certify, accredit, qualify; give someone the authority, give someone permission; enable, equip, give the power to, give the means to; *informal* give the go-ahead to, give the green light to, OK, give the OK to, give the thumbs up to.
OPPOSITE forbid.
2 *movements to empower the poor* **emancipate**, unyoke, unfetter, unshackle, unchain, set free, give freedom to; *historical* enfranchise.
OPPOSITE enslave.

E

empress ▶ noun *the Empress of Austria* **ruler**, sovereign, monarch, potentate; *Russian, historical* tsarina; *rare* imperatrix, autarch, ethnarch.

emptiness ▶ noun **1** *the peaceful emptiness of her mother's sitting room* **vacantness**, bareness, blankness, clearness, barrenness, desolation; lack of contents, lack of adornment; *rare* voidness.
OPPOSITES crowdedness; fullness.
2 *the emptiness of his boasting* **meaninglessness**, hollowness, idleness, ineffectiveness, ineffectuality, uselessness, futility, worthlessness, fruitlessness, insubstantiality.
OPPOSITE meaningfulness.
3 *she was suffering from a sense of utter emptiness* **futility**, purposelessness, pointlessness, aimlessness, meaninglessness, worthlessness, valuelessness, hollowness, barrenness, senselessness, banality, triviality, insignificance, unimportance; *archaic* bootlessness.
OPPOSITE worth.
4 *Sarah had filled an emptiness in his life* **void**, vacuum, vacuity, empty space, blank space, gap, vacancy, hiatus, hole, hollow, cavity, chasm, abyss, gulf.
5 *she was shocked by the emptiness in his eyes* **blankness**, expressionlessness, vacancy, vacantness, vacuousness, glaze, fixedness, woodenness, stoniness, impassivity, emotionlessness, unresponsiveness, inscrutability; lack of life, lack of animation.
OPPOSITE expressiveness.

empty ▶ adjective **1** *an empty house* **vacant**, unoccupied, uninhabited, untenanted, clear, free, bare, desolate, deserted, abandoned.
OPPOSITE full.
2 *the aspirin bottle was empty* **containing nothing**, unfilled, not filled, void, emptied.
OPPOSITE full.
3 *my teacher did not issue empty threats* **meaningless**, aimless, worthless, useless, idle, vain, insubstantial, ineffective, ineffectual.
OPPOSITE meaningful.
4 *without her my life is empty* **futile**, pointless, purposeless, motiveless, worthless, meaningless, valueless, of no value, useless, of no use, senseless, hollow, barren, unsatisfactory, unimportant, insignificant, inconsequential, trivial, trifling, nugatory.
OPPOSITE worthwhile.
5 *his face was grey and his eyes were empty* **blank**, expressionless, vacant, deadpan, wooden, stony, impassive, inanimate, vacuous, absent, glazed, fixed, lifeless, emotionless, unresponsive, inscrutable.
OPPOSITE expressive.
▶ verb **1** *he was emptying the dishwasher* **unload**, unpack, unburden, disburden, clear, make vacant, vacate, evacuate, void; *rare* unlade.
OPPOSITES fill; load.
2 *the wine had been secretly opened and emptied* **drain**, discharge, draw off, extract, withdraw, remove, siphon off, pump out, pour out, tap, milk, bleed; **deplete**, exhaust, use up, sap, consume.

empty-headed ▶ adjective *certain types of men treat me like some empty-headed bimbo* **stupid**, unintelligent, idiotic, foolish, silly, brainless, half-witted, witless, vacuous, vapid, hare-brained, feather-brained, birdbrained, pea-brained, scatterbrained, scatty, giddy, skittish, flighty, frivolous, thoughtless; *informal* dumb, dense, dim, airheaded, brain-dead, dippy, dizzy, dopey, dozy, batty, dotty, screwy, soft in the head, slow on the uptake; *Brit. informal* daft, not the full shilling; *N. Amer. informal* ditzy, dumb-ass.
OPPOSITE intelligent.

empyrean (literary) ▶ adjective *the empyrean regions* **heavenly**, celestial, ethereal; aerial, upper; *rare* empyreal.
▶ noun (**the empyrean**) **heaven**, the heavens, the sky, the upper regions, the upper atmosphere, the stratosphere; *literary* the ether, the azure, the blue, the wide blue yonder, the firmament, the sphere, the vault (of heaven), the welkin.

emulate ▶ verb *they tried to emulate Lucy's glowing performance* **imitate**, copy, reproduce, mimic, mirror, echo, follow, model oneself on, take as a model, take as an example; **match**, equal, parallel, be the equal of, be on a par with, be in the same league as, come near to, come close to, approximate; compete with, contend with, rival, vie with, surpass; *informal* take a leaf out of someone's book.

enable ▶ verb **1** *the act enabled ordinary citizens to operate radio stations* **authorize**, sanction, warrant, license, qualify, allow, permit, entitle, empower, accredit, legalize, validate; commission, delegate; *informal* OK, give the OK to, give the green light to, give the thumbs up to.
OPPOSITE forbid.
2 *these scholarships have enabled graduates to pursue diverse studies* **allow**, permit, let, give the means to, give the resources to, equip, prepare, facilitate, capacitate, fit.
OPPOSITE prevent.

enact ▶ verb **1** *the government enacted an environmental protection bill* **make law**, pass, approve, ratify, validate, sanction, authorize, accept, give the seal of approval to; order, decree, ordain, legislate, legalize, rule; impose, lay down, implement, bring into effect, bring to bear, put into practice; *informal* give the go-ahead to, give the green light to, give the thumbs up to, OK, give the OK to.
OPPOSITE repeal.
2 *members of the church are to enact a nativity play* **act out**, act, perform, play, appear in, stage, mount, put on, present, do; represent.

enactment ▶ noun **1** *the enactment of a bill of rights* **passing**, making law, ratification, ratifying, validation, validating, sanction, sanctioning, approval, approving, endorsement, adoption; decreeing, ordaining, legislating; application, appliance, implementation.
OPPOSITE repeal.
2 *parliamentary enactments covering food safety* **bill**, act, law, by-law, order, decree, resolution, ruling, rule, regulation, statute, edict, measure, motion, command, commandment, pronouncement, proclamation, dictate, dictum, diktat, fiat; (**enactments**) legislation; *N. Amer.* ordinance.
3 *the enactment of the play | a classic enactment of the character* **acting**, playing, performing, performance, staging, appearance; portrayal, depiction, representation, personification; *formal* personation.

enamoured ▶ adjective *she was secretly* **enamoured** *of the prince* **in love with**, infatuated with, besotted with, smitten with, captivated by, charmed by, enchanted by, fascinated by, bewitched by, beguiled by, enthralled by, entranced by, enraptured by, keen on, taken with, head over heels for, under the spell of, consumed with desire for; *informal* mad about, crazy about, wild about, nuts about, potty about, dotty about, bowled over by, hot for, gone on, hooked on, stuck on, struck on, sweet on, soft on, hung up on, carrying a torch for; *Brit. informal* daft about; *literary* ensorcelled by.
OPPOSITE indifferent to.

encampment ▶ noun *they planned an attack on the enemy's encampment* **camp**, military camp, bivouac, cantonment, barracks, base, station, post; campsite, camping ground; tents; *S. African historical* laager.

encapsulate ▶ verb **1** *their conclusions are encapsulated in one brief sentence* **summarize**, sum up, give a summary of, precis, abridge, digest, abbreviate, condense, compress, compact, contract, telescope; capture, express, record, sketch, give the gist of, give the main points of, put in a nutshell; *rare* epitomize, capsulize.
2 *the adult worms are encapsulated in a cyst* **enclose**, encase, contain, confine, envelop, enfold, sheath, cocoon, surround.

enchant ▶ verb *the play continued to enchant all who watched it* **captivate**, charm, delight, dazzle, enrapture, entrance, enthral, beguile, bewitch, spellbind, ensnare, fascinate, hypnotize, mesmerize; divert, absorb, engross, rivet, grip, transfix; *informal* tickle someone pink, bowl someone over, get under someone's skin; *rare* rapture.
OPPOSITES repel; bore.

enchanter ▶ noun *they have been trapped by an evil enchanter* **wizard**, witch, sorcerer, warlock, magician, necromancer, spellbinder, magus, conjuror; hypnotist, mesmerist; witch doctor, medicine man, shaman, voodooist, occultist; *Irish* pishogue; *N. Amer. & W. Indian* conjure man/woman; *rare* thaumaturge, thaumaturgist, theurgist, spell-caster, mage, magian. *See also* ENCHANTRESS.

enchanting ▶ adjective *Erica smiled an enchanting smile* **captivating**, charming, delightful, attractive, appealing, engaging, winning, dazzling, bewitching, beguiling, alluring, tantalizing, seductive, ravishing, disarming, irresistible, spellbinding, entrancing, enthralling, fetching, dreamy; *Scottish & N. English* bonny; *dated* taking.
OPPOSITE repulsive.

enchantment ▶ noun **1** *the horses had been turned to wood by enchantment* **magic**, witchcraft, sorcery, wizardry, necromancy, conjuration; hypnotism, mesmerism; occultism, voodoo, the black arts; charms, spells, incantations; *N. Amer.* mojo; *rare* spell-working, sortilege, thaumaturgy, theurgy.
2 *to look through one of these shop windows is instant enchantment | the enchantment of the garden by moonlight* **captivation**, entrancement, bewitchment, fascination, attraction, temptation, seduction, allure, enticement; **delight**, charm, beauty, attractiveness, appeal, irresistibility, magnetism, pull, draw, lure.
OPPOSITE repulsion.
3 *being with him was sheer enchantment* **bliss**, ecstasy, heaven, rapture, joy.

OPPOSITE misery.

enchantress ▶ noun *she was under the spell of an enchantress* **witch**, sorceress, magician, fairy, fairy godmother; *N. Amer.* hex, conjure woman; (*Greek Mythology*) Circe, siren; *rare* spell-caster, thaumaturge, thaumaturgist, Wiccan, pythoness. *See also* ENCHANTER.

encircle ▶ verb *medieval walls encircle the town* **surround**, enclose, circle, ring, encompass, circumscribe, border, bound, edge, skirt, fringe, form a ring around, form a barrier round; close in, shut in, fence in, wall in, hem in, lock in, cut off, confine; *literary* gird, girdle, engird.

enclose ▶ verb **1** *tall trees enclosed the garden | he bought new fences to enclose his sheep* **surround**, circle, ring, encompass, encircle, circumscribe, border, bound, edge, skirt, fringe, hem, line, flank; **confine**, close in, shut in, fence in, wall in, hedge in, hem in, lock in, lock up, cut off; *literary* gird, girdle, engird.
2 *please enclose a stamped addressed envelope with your order* **include**, insert, put in, enfold; send.

WORD LINKS
fear of enclosed spaces **claustrophobia**

enclosure ▶ noun **1** *they drove the donkeys into the enclosure* **paddock**, fold, pen, compound, stockade, ring, yard, pound; sty, coop, cage; *Scottish* parrock; *N. Amer.* corral; *S. African* kraal; (*in S. America*) potrero; *rare* circumvallation.
2 *she watched the race from the royal enclosure* **area**, special area, assigned area, compound, arena; box, compartment.
3 *her cheque arrived and the only other enclosure was a compliments slip* **insertion**, inclusion, addition; thing enclosed.

encomium ▶ noun *the poet produced an appropriate encomium after the king's death* **eulogy**, speech of praise, panegyric, paean, accolade, tribute, testimonial, compliment; praise, acclaim, acclamation, homage, extolment; *rare* laudation, eulogium.

encompass ▶ verb **1** *the ancient monument is encompassed by Hunsbury Country Park* **surround**, enclose, ring, encircle, circumscribe, skirt, bound, border, fringe; close in, shut in, fence in, wall in, hedge in, hem in, confine; *literary* gird, girdle, engird; *rare* compass, environ.
2 *the debates encompassed a vast range of subjects* **cover**, embrace, include, incorporate, take in, contain, comprise, involve, deal with; *formal* comprehend.

encore ▶ noun *the audience roared approval and demanded an encore* **repeat performance**, extra performance, additional performance, replay, repeat, repetition; curtain call.

encounter ▶ verb **1** *I encountered a girl I used to know* **meet**, meet by chance, run into, run across, come across, come upon, stumble across, stumble on, chance on, happen on; *informal* bump into; *archaic* run against.
2 *the guides will help if you encounter any problems* **experience**, come into contact with, run into, come across, come up against, face, be faced with, confront, be forced to contend with.
3 *the soldiers encountered a large crowd of demonstrators* **confront**, accost, oppose, meet head-on; clash with, come into conflict with, engage with, struggle with, contend with, fight, do battle with, skirmish with.
▶ noun **1** *I told them of my encounter with the priest* **meeting**, chance meeting, brush, rendezvous; contact.
2 *the monument is thought to commemorate a Viking encounter* **battle**, fight, clash, conflict, confrontation, engagement, skirmish, brush; *informal* run-in, set-to, dust-up, scrap; *archaic* rencounter.

encourage ▶ verb **1** *the players were encouraged by the crowd's response* **hearten**, cheer, buoy up, uplift, inspire, motivate, egg on, spur on, stir, stir up, whip up, fire up, stimulate, animate, invigorate, vitalize, revitalize, embolden, fortify, rally, incite; lift the spirits of, raise the morale of, stiffen the resolve of; *informal* buck up, pep up, give a shot in the arm to; *N. Amer. informal* light a fire under; *rare* inspirit, spirit someone up, fillip, incentivize.
OPPOSITE discourage.
2 *he would never encourage Joan to leave her husband* **persuade**, coax, urge, press, push, pressure, pressurize, exhort, spur, prod, goad, egg on, prompt, influence, sway; *informal* put the heat on, put the screws on, twist someone's arm.
OPPOSITE dissuade.
3 *the Government was keen to encourage local businesses* **support**, back, endorse, champion, advocate, recommend, promote, further, advance, forward, foster, strengthen, enrich; help, assist, aid, abet, boost, fuel, favour.
OPPOSITE hinder.

encouragement ▶ noun **1** *she needed a bit of encouragement* **heartening**, cheering, cheering up, buoying up, pepping up, uplifting, inspiration, rallying, motivation, incitement, stimulation, animation, invigoration, invigorating, emboldening, fortification; morale-boosting; *informal* bucking up, a shot in the arm; *rare* spiriting up, inspiriting.
OPPOSITE discouragement.
2 *they required no encouragement to get back to work* **persuasion**, coaxing, urging, pushing, pressure, pressurization, exhortation, prodding, egging on, prompting; spur, goad, inducement, incentive, bait, lure, motive; *informal* arm-twisting, carrot, kick up the backside.
OPPOSITE dissuasion.
3 *the encouragement of foreign investment* **supporting**, support, backing, endorsement, championship, championing, sponsoring, advocacy, promotion, furtherance, furthering, advance, advancing, forwarding, fostering, strengthening, nurture, cultivation; help, assistance, boosting, fuelling, favouring; *N. Amer. informal* boosterism.
OPPOSITE hindering.

encouraging ▶ adjective **1** *the Scottish team made an encouraging start* **promising**, hopeful, auspicious, propitious, favourable, bright, rosy, cheerful, full of promise; heartening, reassuring, stimulating, inspiring, uplifting, cheering, comforting, welcome, pleasing, gratifying.
OPPOSITE discouraging.
2 *my parents were very encouraging* **supportive**, reassuring, affirmative, sympathetic, sensitive, understanding, helpful; positive, responsive, enthusiastic, appreciative.
OPPOSITE unsupportive.

encroach ▶ verb *she didn't want to encroach on his privacy* **intrude**, trespass, impinge, butt in, barge in, cut in, obtrude, impose oneself; invade, infiltrate, interrupt, infringe, violate, interfere with, disturb, disrupt; tread on someone's toes, step on someone's toes; *informal* gatecrash, horn in on, muscle in on, invade someone's space; *archaic* entrench on.

encroachment ▶ noun *I resisted even the slightest encroachment on my territory* **intrusion into**, trespass on, invasion of, infiltration of, incursion into, obtrusion into, overrunning of, usurping of, appropriation of; infringement of, impingement on, impinging on.

encumber ▶ verb **1** *her movements were encumbered by her heavy skirts* **hamper**, hinder, obstruct, impede, check, cramp, inhibit, restrict, limit, constrain, restrain, bog down, retard, slow, slow down, stall, delay; inconvenience, disadvantage, handicap.
OPPOSITES aid, facilitate.
2 *they are heavily encumbered with debt* **burden**, load, weigh down, saddle; tax, overtax, stress, strain, overwhelm, overload, overburden; *Brit. informal* lumber; *literary* trammel.

encumbrance ▶ noun **1** *he found the equipment a great encumbrance* **hindrance**, obstruction, obstacle, impediment, restraint, constraint, handicap, inconvenience, nuisance, disadvantage, drawback; *archaic* cumber.
OPPOSITES help; asset.
2 *I am twenty-nine and without encumbrances of any kind* **responsibility**, obligation, liability; imposition, burden, weight, load, tax, stress, strain, pressure, trouble, worry; millstone, albatross, cross to bear; *literary* trammel; *archaic* cumber.

encyclopedic ▶ adjective *he has an encyclopedic knowledge of food* **comprehensive**, complete, thorough, thoroughgoing, full, exhaustive, in-depth, wide-ranging, broad-ranging, broad-based, all-inclusive, all-embracing, all-encompassing, universal, vast, compendious; across the board; *informal* wall-to-wall.

end ▶ noun **1** *Laura's house was at the end of the row* **extremity**, furthermost part, limit, margin, edge, border, boundary, periphery; point, tip, tail end; *N. Amer.* tag end.
OPPOSITES beginning; middle.
2 *I never plan the end of the novel I'm writing* **conclusion**, termination, ending, finish, close, resolution, climax, finale, culmination, denouement; epilogue, coda, peroration; *informal* wind-up.
OPPOSITES beginning, start.
3 *he jabbed a cigarette end into the ashtray* **butt**, stub, stump, remnant, fragment, vestige; (**ends**) leftovers, remains, remainder; *informal* fag end, dog end.
4 *to her, wealth is a means and not an end in itself* **aim**, goal, purpose, objective, object, grail, holy grail, target, mission; intention, intent, design, motive; aspiration, wish, desire, ambition; *French* raison d'être.
5 *the commercial end of the music business* **aspect**, side, section, area, field, part, share, portion, segment, province.
6 *he knew that his end might come at any time* **death**, dying, demise, passing, passing on, passing away, expiration, expiry; doom, extinction, annihilation, extermination, destruction; downfall, ruin, ruination, Waterloo; *informal* curtains, croaking, snuffing; *Law* decease; *rare* quietus.
OPPOSITE birth.
▶ verb **1** *the show ended with a wedding scene* **finish**, conclude, terminate, come to an end, draw to a close, close, stop, cease; culminate, climax, build up to, lead up to, reach a finale, come to a head; *informal* wind up.
OPPOSITES begin, start.
2 *she attempted to end the relationship* **break off**, call off, bring to an end, put an end to, call a halt to, halt, stop, drop, finish, terminate, discontinue, dissolve, cancel, annul; *informal* nip something in the bud, wind something up, knock something on the head, give something the chop, pull the plug on, axe, scrap, pack in, get shut of; *Brit. informal* get shot of; *archaic* sunder.
OPPOSITE begin.
3 *the young artist chose to end his life* **destroy**, put an end to, extinguish,

snuff out, do away with, wipe out, take.

endanger ▶ verb *river pollution is likely to endanger fish* **imperil**, jeopardize, risk, put at risk, put in danger, expose to danger, put in jeopardy, leave vulnerable, put someone's life on the line; **threaten**, pose a threat to, be a danger to, be detrimental to, damage, injure, harm, do harm to; *archaic* peril.

CHOOSE THE RIGHT WORD

endanger, imperil, jeopardize, risk

- **Endanger** is the most general term for putting someone or something in a position where they might be harmed (*the company admitted endangering workers by failing to maintain safety standards*). The past participle *endangered* is used particularly of plants and animals that are threatened with extinction (*sea turtles are an endangered species*).
- **Imperil** is a more literary word, used to emphasize the serious nature of a danger (*troops moved from their positions on the Somme to bolster their imperilled comrades at Verdun*).
- **Jeopardize** is generally used with an abstract object which is likely to be adversely affected by a certain course of action (*a devaluation of the dollar would jeopardize New York's position as a financial centre*).
- **Risk** is most often used of consciously exposing someone or something to harm, generally oneself or one's possessions, as the price of something regarded as more important (*a father risked his life to save his children from a fire*).

endearing ▶ adjective *hedgehogs are endearing creatures* **lovable**, adorable, cute, sweet, dear, delightful, lovely, charming, appealing, attractive, engaging, winning, captivating, enchanting, beguiling, winsome; *Scottish & N. English* bonny; *dated* taking.

endearment ▶ noun **1** (usually **endearments**) *between kisses she murmured endearments* **sweet nothings**, sweet words, sweet talk, affectionate talk, soft words; term of affection, term of endearment, pet name, affectionate name; *rare* hypocoristic, hypocorism.
2 *he spoke to her formally and without endearment* **affection**, fondness, tenderness, feeling, sentiment, warmth, love, liking, care, regard, attachment.

endeavour ▶ verb *the company* **endeavoured to** *expand its activities* **try**, attempt, venture, undertake, aspire, aim, seek, set out; strive, struggle, labour, toil, work hard, try hard, exert oneself, apply oneself, do one's best, do one's utmost, give one's all, be at pains; work at, try one's hand at; *informal* slog away, give something a whirl, have a go at, have a shot at, have a stab at, give something one's best shot, do one's damnedest, go all out, bend over backwards, break one's neck, bust a gut, move heaven and earth; *formal* essay.
▶ noun **1** *an endeavour to build a more buoyant economy* **attempt**, try, bid, effort, trial, venture; *informal* go, crack, shot, stab, bash, whack, whirl.
2 *after several days of endeavour he completed the task* **striving**, struggling, labouring, struggle, labour, hard work, hard slog, effort, exertion, application, industry; pains; *informal* sweat, {blood, sweat, and tears}, elbow grease; *Brit. informal* graft; *Austral./NZ informal* (hard) yakka; *archaic* travail, moil.
3 *what you are proposing is an extremely unwise endeavour* **undertaking**, enterprise, venture, pursuit, exercise, activity, exploit, deed, act, action, move; scheme, plan, project; *informal* caper.

ending ▶ noun *the story has a happy ending | the ending of the Cold War* **end**, finish, close, closing, conclusion, resolution, summing-up, denouement, finale, final scene, last act; cessation, stopping, termination, discontinuation, breaking off; *informal* wind-up, winding up.
OPPOSITE beginning.

endless ▶ adjective **1** *she was a caring woman with endless energy* **unlimited**, limitless, infinite, inexhaustible, boundless, unbounded, untold, immeasurable, measureless, incalculable, inestimable; abundant, abounding, great; **ceaseless**, unceasing, unending, without end, everlasting, constant, continuous, continual, interminable, unfading, unfailing, perpetual, eternal, enduring, lasting, round-the-clock; *informal* loads of, stacks of, heaps of, masses of, oodles of, bags of.
OPPOSITES limited; transient.
2 *as children we played endless games* **countless**, innumerable, untold, legion, numberless, unnumbered, numerous, very many, manifold, multitudinous, multifarious; a great number of, countless numbers of, infinite numbers of, a multitude of, a multiplicity of, more than one can count, too many to be counted; *informal* umpteen, no end of, loads of, stacks of, heaps of, masses of, oodles of, scads of, zillions of; *N. Amer. informal* gazillions of, bazillions of; *literary* myriad, divers; *rare* innumerous, unnumberable.
OPPOSITE few.
3 *the tobacco moves through the machine on an endless belt* **continuous**, unbroken, uninterrupted, never-ending, without end, non-stop.

endorse ▶ verb **1** *they fully endorse a general trade agreement* **support**, back, approve (of), be in agreement with, favour; recommend, advocate, champion; subscribe to, uphold, affirm, confirm, authorize, authenticate, ratify, sanction, warrant; *informal* throw one's weight behind, stick up for.
OPPOSITE oppose.
2 *the cheque should be endorsed and sent to the third party* **countersign**, sign on the back, initial, autograph, put one's mark on, inscribe, superscribe; witness, validate; *archaic* underwrite, side-sign; *rare* chirographate.

endorsement ▶ noun **1** *the proposal received their overwhelming endorsement* **support**, backing, approval, seal of approval, agreement, acceptance, recommendation, advocacy, championship, patronage; affirmation, confirmation, authorization, authentication, ratification, sanction, warrant, validation, licence; rubber stamp; *informal* the nod, the thumbs up, the OK.
OPPOSITE opposition.
2 *several cheques required endorsement* **countersigning**, signing on the back, autographing, initialling, inscribing, superscribing; witnessing, validation; *archaic* underwriting, side-signing.

endow ▶ verb **1** *Henry II endowed a hospital for poor pilgrims* **finance**, fund, pay for, donate money for, give money towards, provide capital for, subsidize, support financially; bequeath money for, leave money for, settle money on; establish, set up, institute, initiate, start, create, bring into being; *informal* fork out for, shell out for, cough up for, chip in for, pitch in for; *Brit. informal* stump up for; *N. Amer. informal* ante up for, kick in for, pony up for.
2 *nature endowed the human race with intelligence* **provide**, supply, furnish, equip, invest, give, present, favour, bless, grace, award, gift, confer, bestow, enrich, arm; *literary* endue.

endowment ▶ noun **1** *the endowment of a chair of botany* **funding**, financing, subsidizing; donation of money for, provision of capital for, bequest of money for; establishment, establishing, foundation, institution, setting up, inauguration.
2 *a generous endowment from the will of the late professor* **bequest**, bequeathal, legacy, inheritance; **gift**, present, benefaction, bestowal, grant, award, donation, contribution, subsidy, settlement, provision; *Law* devise, hereditament; *historical* alms; *rare* donative.
3 *his taste and inquiring mind were natural endowments* **quality**, characteristic, feature, attribute, facility, faculty, ability, talent, gift, strength, aptitude, capability, capacity.

endurable ▶ adjective *his confinement had gradually become endurable* **bearable**, tolerable, supportable, manageable, sufferable, sustainable; *rare* brookable.
OPPOSITE unbearable.

endurance ▶ noun **1** *she had pushed him beyond the limit of his endurance* **toleration**, **bearing**, tolerance, sufferance, fortitude, forbearance, patience, acceptance, resignation, stoicism.
2 *the race is a test of endurance* **stamina**, **staying power**, fortitude, perseverance, persistence, tenacity, pertinacity, doggedness, indefatigability, tirelessness, resoluteness, resolution, determination; *informal* stickability, guts, grit, spunk; *Brit. informal* bottle.
3 *Edward III had a vested interest in the endurance of Balliol's rule* **continuance**, continuity, continuation, lasting power, durability, permanence, longevity; constancy, stability, changelessness, immutability; *rare* lastingness, everlastingness.

endure ▶ verb **1** *he had to endure a great deal of suffering* **undergo**, go through, live through, experience, meet, encounter; cope with, deal with, face, face up to, handle, suffer, tolerate, put up with, brave, bear, withstand, sustain, weather; become reconciled to, reconcile oneself to, become resigned to, get used to, become accustomed to, learn to live with, make the best of; *Scottish* thole.
2 *she would not endure a marriage that was a travesty* **tolerate**, **bear**, put up with, go along with, suffer, submit to, countenance, accept, give one's blessing to, brook, support, take; *informal* stick, hack, stand for, stomach, swallow, abide, hold with, be doing with; *Brit. informal* wear.
3 *God's love will endure for ever* **last**, live, live on, go on, hold on, abide, continue, persist, remain, stay, survive; *literary* bide, tarry.
OPPOSITE fade.

enduring ▶ adjective *an enduring commitment to democracy and human rights* **lasting**, long-lasting, durable, continuing, remaining, persisting, prevailing, abiding, eternal, perennial, permanent, unending, everlasting; constant, stable, steady, steadfast, fixed, firm, unwavering, unfaltering, unchanging, changeless, long-standing, long-established, long-running, long-term; *rare* perdurable, sempiternal.
OPPOSITE short-lived.

enemy ▶ noun *he aimed the gun at his enemy* **foe**, adversary, opponent, rival, antagonist, combatant, challenger, competitor, opposer, hostile party; (**the enemy**) the opposition, the competition, the other side, the opposing side; *rare* corrival, vier.
OPPOSITES friend, ally.

energetic ▶ adjective **1** *a skinny, energetic young man* **active**, lively, dynamic, zestful, spirited, animated, vital, vibrant, sparkling, bouncy,

bubbly, perky, bright and breezy, frisky, sprightly, tireless, indefatigable, enthusiastic, zealous, fiery, passionate; *informal* peppy, zippy, sparky, full of get-up-and-go, full of vim and vigour, full of beans, full of the joys of spring, bright-eyed and bushy-tailed; *N. Amer. informal* go-go, peart.
OPPOSITES inactive, lethargic.
2 *energetic exercises* **vigorous**, strenuous, brisk, lively; rigorous, hard, arduous, demanding, taxing, tough.
OPPOSITE gentle.
3 *an energetic advertising campaign* **forceful**, aggressive, vigorous, high-powered, all-out, determined, zealous, fiery, impassioned, emphatic, bold, pushing, driving, effective, effectual, powerful, potent; intense, intensive, hard-hitting, pulling no punches; *informal* pushy, punchy, gutsy, in-your-face, go-ahead, high-octane, feisty.
OPPOSITE half-hearted.

energize ▶ verb **1** *people are energized by his ideas* **enliven**, liven up, animate, vitalize, invigorate, perk up, excite, electrify, dynamize, stimulate, stir up, fire up, rouse, motivate, move, move to action, drive, spur on, encourage, embolden, galvanize; *informal* pep up, buck up, give a shot in the arm to; *rare* activate, inspirit.
OPPOSITE demotivate.
2 *a bell sounds when the distress frequency is energized* **activate**, trigger, trigger off, trip, operate, actuate, switch on, turn on, start, start up, get going, set going; power, supply power to, supply energy to.
OPPOSITE deactivate.

energy *See centre pages for list of* **Energy and Fuels**
▶ noun **1** *she set out feeling full of energy* **vitality**, vigour, life, liveliness, animation, vivacity, spirit, spiritedness, fire, passion, ardour, zeal, verve, enthusiasm, zest, vibrancy, spark, sparkle, effervescence, exuberance, buoyancy, perkiness, sprightliness; strength, stamina, forcefulness, power, might, potency, dynamism, drive, push; *informal* zip, zing, pep, pizzazz, punch, bounce, fizz, oomph, go, get-up-and-go, vim and vigour; *N. Amer. informal* feistiness.
2 *the panels turn solar energy into electricity* **power**.

enervate ▶ verb *the scorching sun enervated her* **exhaust**, tire, fatigue, weary, wear out, devitalize, drain, sap, weaken, make weak, make feeble, enfeeble, debilitate, incapacitate, indispose, prostrate, immobilize, lay low, put out of action; *informal* knock out, do in, take it out of one, shatter, poop, frazzle, wear to a frazzle, fag out; *Brit. informal* knacker; *rare* torpefy.
OPPOSITE invigorate.

enervation ▶ noun *his enervation is due to his lingering illness* **fatigue**, exhaustion, tiredness, overtiredness, weariness, lassitude, lack of energy, lack of vitality, devitalization, weakness, feebleness, impotence, enfeebled state, debilitation, incapacitation, indisposition, prostration, immobility; *informal* weediness; *Medicine* asthenia.

enfeeble ▶ verb *the animal was enfeebled by lack of nutrition* **weaken**, make weak, make feeble, debilitate, incapacitate, indispose, prostrate, immobilize, lay low, disable, handicap, cripple, paralyse; drain, sap, exhaust, tire, fatigue, devitalize; *informal* knock out, do in, shatter; *Brit. informal* knacker; *rare* torpefy.
OPPOSITE strengthen.

enfold ▶ verb **1** *the summit was enfolded in white cloud* **envelop**, engulf, sheathe, swathe, swaddle, cocoon, shroud, veil, cloak, drape, cover, conceal, mask; surround, encircle, circle, enclose, encase; *literary* enshroud, mantle, pall, pave, lap; *rare* obnubilate.
2 *he enfolded her in his arms* **clasp**, hold, fold, wrap, squeeze, clutch, take, gather; embrace, hug, cuddle, cradle; *literary* embosom; *archaic* strain.

enforce ▶ verb **1** *the sheriff enforced the law and judged local disputes* **impose**, apply, carry out, administer, implement, bring to bear, discharge, fulfil, execute, prosecute; *rare* effectuate.
2 *they cannot enforce cooperation between the parties* **force**, compel, exact, extort, demand, insist on, require, necessitate; *archaic* constrain.

enforced ▶ adjective *an enforced break from work* **compulsory**, obligatory, mandatory, involuntary, forced, exacted, coerced, imposed, demanded, required, requisite, stipulated, contractual, binding, necessitated, necessary, unavoidable, inescapable, obliged, impelled, constrained, dictated, ordained, prescribed; *French* de rigueur.
OPPOSITE voluntary.

enforcement ▶ noun **1** *they were responsible for the enforcement of the law* **imposition**, implementation, application, carrying out, administration, administering, discharge, fulfilment, execution, prosecution, pursuance; *rare* effectuation.
2 *the enforcement of school attendance* **forcing**, compelling, exacting, exactment, extorting, extortion, demanding, requiring; *archaic* constraint.

enfranchise ▶ verb **1** *women over thirty were enfranchised in 1918* **give voting rights to**, give the vote to, give suffrage to, grant suffrage to, grant franchise to.
OPPOSITE disenfranchise.
2 (*historical*) *he is said to have enfranchised his slaves* **emancipate**, liberate, free, set free, release, empower; unchain, unyoke, unfetter, unshackle; naturalize, grant citizenship to, confer citizenship on; *historical* manumit; *rare* affranchise, disenthral, citizenize.
OPPOSITE enslave.

engage ▶ verb **1** *the tasks must engage the children's interest* **capture**, catch, arrest, grab, seize, draw, attract, gain, win, captivate, hold, grip, engross, absorb, occupy.
OPPOSITE lose.
2 *he engaged a nursemaid to look after them* **employ**, hire, recruit, take on, take into employment, secure the services of, put on the payroll, enrol, appoint, commission, enlist; retain, have in employment, have on the payroll; *informal* take on board.
OPPOSITE dismiss.
3 (*dated*) *she engaged a room in the boarding house* **book**, reserve, make a reservation for, prearrange, arrange in advance, arrange for; rent, hire, charter, lease; *informal* bag; *rare* bespeak.
4 *he engaged to pay them £10,000* **contract**, promise, agree, pledge, vow, covenant, commit oneself, bind oneself, undertake, enter into an agreement, reach an agreement, negotiate a deal.
5 *they like to engage in active sports | Turkey will not* **engage in** *a ground war* **participate in**, take part in, join in, become involved in, go in for, partake in/of, occupy oneself with, throw oneself into; share in, play a part in, play a role in, be a participant in, be associated with, have a hand in, be a party to, enter into, undertake, embark on, set about, launch into.
6 *they were sent to engage enemy aircraft* **do battle with**, fight with, enter into combat with, wage war on, wage war against, take up arms against, attack, mount an attack on, take on, set upon, clash with, skirmish with, grapple with, wrest with; encounter, meet; *informal* scrap with.
7 *he engaged the gears with a crash* **interlock**, interconnect, mesh, intermesh, fit together, join together, join, unite, connect, yoke, mate, couple.
OPPOSITE disengage.

engaged ▶ adjective **1** *the phone lines are constantly engaged* **busy**, unavailable, occupied; in use, active; *informal* tied up; (**be engaged**) have a prior engagement.
OPPOSITES free; unoccupied.
2 *many engaged couples had to postpone their weddings* **betrothed**, affianced, promised in marriage; attached, involved; *informal* spoken for; *archaic* plighted, espoused.
OPPOSITE unattached.

> **CHOOSE THE RIGHT WORD**
>
> **engaged, busy, occupied, active**
> *See* BUSY.

engagement ▶ noun **1** *they broke off their engagement* **betrothal**, betrothment, marriage contract; *French* fiançailles; *archaic* plighting of one's troth, espousal, affiance, affiancing, handfast; *rare* sponsalia, subarrhation.
2 *he had a business engagement that morning* **appointment**, arrangement, commitment, meeting, interview, consultation, session; date, assignation, rendezvous; *literary* tryst.
3 *some 80,000 workers were on more than a three-year engagement* **contract**, agreement, bond, pact, compact, covenant, pledge, promise, obligation, stipulation.
4 *Britain's continued engagement in open trading* **participation**, participating, taking part, sharing, partaking, involvement, association.
5 *his engagement as a curate* **employment**, appointment, work, job, post, situation; hiring, hire, enrolment, enrolling, enlisting; apprenticing.
6 (*dated*) *the engagement of a boat to take them to the island* **hire**, booking, advance booking, reserving, reservation, prearrangement, arrangement; rent, charter, lease; *dated* engaging.
7 *all of his men were killed in an engagement at sea* **battle**, fight, clash, confrontation, encounter, conflict, struggle, skirmish, affray, attack, assault, offensive; warfare, action, combat; hostilities; *informal* dogfight, shoot-out, scrap.

engaging ▶ adjective *she had such an engaging smile* **charming**, appealing, attractive, pretty, delightful, lovely, pleasing, pleasant, agreeable, likeable, lovable, sweet, winning, winsome, fetching, dazzling, arresting, captivating, enchanting, bewitching, alluring, irresistible, dreamy, heavenly, divine, gorgeous; *Scottish & N. English* bonny; *Brit. informal* smashing; *dated* taking; *archaic* comely, fair.
OPPOSITE unappealing.

engender ▶ verb **1** *his works engendered considerable controversy* **cause**, be the cause of, give rise to, bring about, lead to, result in, produce, create, generate, arouse, rouse, provoke, incite, kindle, trigger, spark off, touch off, stir up, whip up, induce, inspire, instigate, foment, effect, occasion, promote, foster; *literary* beget, enkindle; *rare* effectuate.
2 (*archaic*) *he engendered a child by the Empress Judith* **father**, sire, generate, spawn, create, conceive, have, give life to, bring into being, bring into the world, bring forth; procreate, reproduce, breed; *literary* beget.

engine *See centre pages for lists of* **Engines** **Trains and Rolling Stock**

E

▸ noun **1** *a car engine* **motor**, mechanism, machine, power source, drive.
2 *industrialization was the main engine of change* **cause**, agent, instrument, driver, originator, initiator, generator.
3 *siege towers and other engines of war* **device**, contraption, gadget, apparatus, machine, appliance, mechanism, implement, instrument, tool, utensil, aid, invention, contrivance; machinery, means.

engineer ▸ noun **1** *the structural engineer's drawings* **designer**, planner, builder, architect, producer, fabricator, developer, creator; inventor, originator, deviser, contriver, mastermind.
2 *the ship's engineer rarely came up to the bridge* **engineering officer**, controller, handler, driver; **operator**, mechanic, machinist, technician, fitter; *Military* artificer; *informal* mech.
▸ verb *he engineered the overthrow of the Conservative majority* **bring about**, cause, arrange, pull off, bring off, fix, set up, plot, scheme, contrive, plan, put together, devise, manoeuvre, manipulate, negotiate, organize, orchestrate, choreograph, mobilize, mount, stage, put on, mastermind, originate, manage, stage-manage, coordinate, control, superintend, direct, conduct, handle, concoct; *informal* wangle; *rare* concert.

E

engineering ▸ noun. *See centre pages for list of branches of* **Engineering**

England ▸ noun *Brit. informal* Blighty; *Austral./NZ informal* Old Dart; *literary* Albion.

WORD LINKS

related prefix	**Anglo-**
mania for English things	**Anglomania**
hatred or fear of English people and things	**Anglophobia**

engrain ▸ verb. *See* INGRAIN.

engrained ▸ adjective. *See* INGRAINED.

engrave ▸ verb **1** *the stone was engraved with his name* **carve**, inscribe, cut (in), incise, chisel, chase, score, etch, imprint, impress, print, mark.
2 *the picture she had just seen was engraved in her mind* **fix**, set, imprint, stamp, brand, impress, embed, etch, ingrain, lodge, register, record.

engraving ▸ noun **1** *an engraving of a Georgian coffee house* **etching**, print, impression, block, plate, dry point, cut, woodcut, linocut, vignette.
2 *he was skilled at drawing and engraving* **etching**, inscribing, inscription, cutting, incising, incision, chiselling, chasing, scoring, notching, imprinting, impressing.

engross ▸ verb **1** *the notes on the staves totally engrossed him* **preoccupy**, absorb, engage; rivet, grip, hold, interest, catch, captivate, enthral, charm, spellbind, bewitch, fascinate, entrance, beguile, intrigue, arrest, immerse, involve, envelop, engulf, fixate, hypnotize, mesmerize.
OPPOSITE bore.
2 (*Law*) *the solicitors will submit a draft conveyance and engross the same after approval* **copy**, reproduce, type (out); print out the final version of, rewrite/reproduce in larger/final form.

engrossed ▸ adjective *he was* **engrossed in** *his book* **absorbed**, involved, immersed, caught up, rapt, interested; preoccupied by, engaged in/with, riveted by, gripped by, intent on, captivated by, beguiled by, intrigued by, fixated by, hypnotized by, mesmerized by.
OPPOSITE inattentive.

engrossing ▸ adjective *a taut, engrossing thriller* **absorbing**, involving, engaging, riveting, gripping, captivating, compelling, compulsive, irresistible, arresting, interesting, fascinating, intriguing, enthralling, spellbinding, entrancing, bewitching, beguiling, hypnotic, mesmeric; *informal* unputdownable.

engulf ▸ verb *their new home was engulfed by stinking brown flood water* **inundate**, flood, deluge, immerse, swamp, wash out, swallow up, submerge; bury, envelop, snow under, overtake, overwhelm, overrun.

enhance ▸ verb *his dramatic appearance enhanced his reputation* **increase**, add to, intensify, magnify, amplify, inflate, strengthen, build up, supplement, augment, boost, upgrade, raise, lift, escalate, elevate, exalt, aggrandize, swell; **improve**, enrich, complement, heighten, deepen, stress, reinforce, underline, emphasize; *informal* jack up, hike.
OPPOSITES diminish; mar.

enhancement ▸ noun *the enhancement of the school's reputation* **improvement**, intensification, magnification, amplification, increase, strengthening, inflation, augmenting, augmentation; boost, rise, increment, lift; escalation, elevation, exaltation, aggrandizement, swelling, heightening, emphasis, stress, reinforcement, enrichment; *informal* jacking up, hike.
OPPOSITE diminution.

enigma ▸ noun *how it works is a complete enigma to me* **mystery**, puzzle, riddle, conundrum, paradox, problem, unsolved problem, question, question mark, quandary, a closed book; *informal* poser, teaser, brain-teaser, stumper.

enigmatic ▸ adjective *she smiled that enigmatic smile again* **mysterious**, puzzling, hard to understand, mystifying, inexplicable, baffling, perplexing, bewildering, confusing, impenetrable, inscrutable, incomprehensible, unexplainable, unfathomable, indecipherable, Delphic, oracular; ambiguous, equivocal, paradoxical, sibylline, unaccountable, insoluble, obscure, elliptical, oblique; arcane, abstruse, recondite, secret, esoteric, occult, cryptic; *informal* as clear as mud.
OPPOSITE straightforward.

enjoin ▸ verb **1** *the Code enjoined members to trade fairly and responsibly* **urge**, encourage, try to persuade, adjure, admonish, press, prompt, prod, goad, egg on, spur, push, pressure, put pressure on, use pressure on, pressurize, lean on; **instruct**, order, command, direct, give the order to, give the command to, tell, require, call on, demand, charge, warn; entreat, exhort, implore, appeal to, beg, beseech, plead with, nag; *informal* put the heat on, put the screws on, twist someone's arm, railroad into, bulldoze into; *literary* bid.
2 (*Law*) *the company was* **enjoined from** *making any further assertions* **prohibit**, ban, bar, prevent, inhibit, interdict; forbid to; *Law* restrain.
OPPOSITE compel.

enjoy ▸ verb **1** *he enjoys playing the piano* **like**, love, be fond of, be entertained by, be amused by, be pleased by, find/take pleasure in, be keen on, delight in, appreciate, rejoice in, relish, revel in, adore, lap up, savour, luxuriate in, bask in, wallow in, glory in; *informal* fancy, get a kick out of, get a thrill out of, get a buzz out of, go a bundle on.
OPPOSITES dislike; hate.
2 *they enjoyed considerable legal protection* **benefit from**, have the benefit of, reap the benefits of, have the advantage, have the use of, have available, avail oneself of, be blessed with, be favoured with, be endowed with, be born with, be possessed of; have, possess, own, boast; *archaic* participate of.
OPPOSITE lack.
□ **enjoy oneself** *she travels purely to enjoy herself* **have fun**, have a good time, enjoy life, be happy, live, live life to the full, have the time of one's life; party, make merry, celebrate, revel, roister; *informal* have a ball, have a whale of a time, groove, make whoopee, whoop it up, let one's hair down.
OPPOSITE be miserable.

enjoyable ▸ adjective *a most enjoyable film* **entertaining**, amusing, delightful, nice, to one's liking, pleasant, congenial, lovely, fine, good, great, agreeable, pleasurable, delicious, delectable, diverting, satisfying, gratifying; marvellous, wonderful, magnificent, splendid, magical, exciting, thrilling, sublime; *informal* super, fantastic, fabulous, fab, terrific, glorious, grand, magic, out of this world, cool; *Brit. informal* brilliant, brill, smashing; *N. Amer. informal* peachy, neat, ducky; *Austral./NZ informal* beaut, bonzer; *Brit. informal, dated* capital, wizard, corking, spiffing, ripping, cracking, top-hole, topping, champion, beezer; *N. Amer. informal, dated* swell; *rare* frabjous.
OPPOSITE disagreeable.

enjoyment ▸ noun **1** *he has brought enjoyment and happiness to millions | Rupert devoured his sandwich with enjoyment* **pleasure**, entertainment, amusement, diversion, recreation, relaxation; comfort, relief, delight, happiness, merriment, gladness, joy, fun, gaiety, jollity, satisfaction, gratification; liking, zeal, relish, gusto; *N. Amer. informal* rec; *humorous* delectation; *dated* sport; *rare* beguilement.
OPPOSITE displeasure.
2 *the enjoyment of one's rights* **benefit**, advantage, use, possession, ownership, blessing, favour, exercise, endowment, availability.
OPPOSITE lack.

enlarge ▸ verb **1** *they've enlarged their house | the pressure causes the eyeball to enlarge* **make/become bigger**, make/become larger, make/become greater, increase in size, grow, expand; extend, amplify, augment, top up, build up, add to, supplement; magnify, intensify, multiply; stretch, swell, distend, bloat, bulge, dilate, snowball, mushroom, blow up, puff up, fatten, fill out, balloon; widen, make/become wider, broaden, make/become broader, lengthen, elongate, make/become longer, deepen, make/become deeper, thicken, make/become thicker; *informal* jumboize; *literary* wax; *rare* tumefy, intumesce, protuberate.
OPPOSITES dwindle, reduce.
2 *he didn't choose to* **enlarge on** *his remark* **elaborate on**, expand on, add to, build on, flesh out, add flesh to, put flesh on the bones of, add detail to, expatiate on; supplement, reinforce, augment, extend, broaden, develop, fill out, embellish, embroider, enhance, amplify, refine, improve, polish, perfect.

enlargement ▸ noun **1** *the modernization and enlargement of the factory* **expansion**, growth, increase in size, extension, amplification, augmentation, topping up, building up, addition, supplementing; magnification, intensification, multiplication; stretching, swelling, distension, dilatation, blowing up, puffing up, fattening, filling out, ballooning; widening, broadening, lengthening, elongation, deepening, thickening; *literary* waxing; *rare* tumefaction, intumescence.
OPPOSITES reduction; diminution.
2 *a photographic enlargement* **blow-up**, magnification, large print; *Brit.* enprint.
OPPOSITE reduction.

enlighten ▸ verb **1** *will you kindly enlighten me as to what this is?* **inform**, make aware, notify, tell, advise, let know, illuminate, open someone's eyes, apprise; explain the situation to, explain the circumstances to, describe the state of affairs to, brief, update, give details to, give

information to, bring up to date; *informal* clue in, fill in, put wise, tip off, put in the picture, bring up to speed.
OPPOSITE keep in the dark.
2 *museums were built to enlighten the people* **civilize**, bring civilization to, bring culture to; sophisticate, socialize, humanize; improve, better; edify, educate, instruct, teach, tutor, indoctrinate; *rare* acculturate.
OPPOSITE stultify.

enlightened ▶ **adjective** *without an informed and free press there cannot be an enlightened people* **informed**, aware, educated, knowledgeable, learned, wise, literate, intellectual, tutored, illuminated, apprised; civilized, refined, cultured, cultivated, sophisticated, advanced, developed, liberal, open-minded, broad-minded.
OPPOSITES ignorant; benighted.

enlightenment ▶ **noun** *the reader will be hoping for enlightenment from the text* **understanding**, insight, education, learning, knowledge, awareness, information, erudition, wisdom, instruction, teaching; illumination, light, edification, awakening; culture, refinement, cultivation, civilization, sophistication, advancement, development, liberalism, open-mindedness, broad-mindedness.
OPPOSITES ignorance; benightedness.

enlist ▶ **verb 1** *he had enlisted in the Royal Engineers* **join up**; join, enrol in, sign up for, volunteer for; *Brit. archaic* take the King's shilling.
OPPOSITE leave.
2 *he was enlisted in the army* **recruit**, call up, enrol, sign up; mobilize, raise, muster, rally, hire, employ, take on, engage, conscript; *N. Amer.* draft, induct; *historical* press, press-gang; *archaic* levy, list.
OPPOSITE discharge.
3 *he has enlisted the help of a friend* **obtain**, engage, win, get, procure, secure.
OPPOSITE spurn.

enliven ▶ **verb 1** *several attractive illustrations enliven the text* **brighten up**, make more interesting, make more exciting, liven up, put some spirit into, add colour to, wake up, give a lift/boost to, ginger up; improve, enhance, season, leaven, add spice to, spice up, revitalize, vitalize; *informal* perk up, jazz up, pep up.
OPPOSITE detract from.
2 *her visit had clearly enlivened my mother* **cheer up**, brighten up, liven up, raise someone's spirits, uplift, gladden, ginger up, buoy up, make lively, waken/wake up; hearten, stimulate, galvanize, fire, light a fire under, boost, rejuvenate, animate, give life to, vivify, vitalize, exhilarate, invigorate, restore, revive, rouse, refresh; *informal* perk up, buck up, pep up.
OPPOSITE subdue.

en masse ▶ **adverb** (*French*) *the Cabinet immediately resigned en masse* **(all) together**, as a group, in a body, as one, as a whole, in a mass, wholesale; simultaneously, all at once, at the same time, at one and the same time, at the same instant, at the same moment, contemporaneously; in unison, in concert, in chorus; *French* en bloc, ensemble; *rare* synchronously.
OPPOSITE singly.

enmesh ▶ **verb** *the party became increasingly enmeshed in the parliamentary system* **entangle**, ensnare, snare, trap, entrap, ensnarl, embroil, involve, catch up, mix up, bog down, mire; *rare* trammel.

enmity ▶ **noun** *a world free from enmity between nations and races* **hostility**, animosity, antagonism, friction, antipathy, animus, opposition, dissension, rivalry, feud, conflict, discord, contention, acrimony, bitterness, rancour, resentment, aversion, dislike, ill feeling, bad feeling, ill will, bad blood, hatred, hate, loathing, detestation, abhorrence, odium; malice, spite, spitefulness, venom, malevolence, malignity; grudges, grievances; *Brit. informal* needle.
OPPOSITES friendship; goodwill.

ennoble ▶ **verb 1** *he was ennobled by the Emperor in 1875* **elevate to the nobility/peerage**, raise to the nobility/peerage, make/create someone a noble; *Brit.* send to the House of Lords; *informal* kick upstairs; *archaic* nobilitate.
2 *choreography tended to ennoble rustic figures* **dignify**, honour, bestow honour on, exalt, elevate, raise, enhance, add distinction to, add dignity to, distinguish, add lustre to; magnify, glorify, lionize, make lofty, aggrandize, upgrade.
OPPOSITES demean, disennoble.

ennui ▶ **noun** (*French*) *an ennui bred of long familiarity* **boredom**, tedium, listlessness, lethargy, lassitude, languor, restlessness, weariness, sluggishness, enervation; **malaise**, dissatisfaction, unhappiness, uneasiness, unease, melancholy, depression, despondency, dejection, disquiet; *German* Weltschmerz.
OPPOSITES animation; contentment.

enormity ▶ **noun 1** *they were aware of the enormity of the task* **immensity**, vastness, massiveness, hugeness; size, extent, magnitude, expanse, greatness, largeness, bigness; *rare* enormousness.
OPPOSITES triviality, smallness.
2 *there must be a severe penalty for the enormity of what you have done* **wickedness**, evilness, vileness, baseness, blackness, depravity; outrageousness, monstrousness, hideousness, dreadfulness, heinousness, awfulness, nastiness, horror, atrocity; villainy, cruelty, inhumanity, mercilessness, brutality, brutalism, bestiality, barbarism, barbarousness, savagery, viciousness; *rare* nefariousness.
OPPOSITE goodness.
3 *the enormities of the Hitler regime* **outrage**, horror, evil, villainy, atrocity, barbarity, act of brutality, act of savagery, act of wickedness, act of cruelty, abomination, monstrosity, obscenity, iniquity; violation, crime, transgression, wrong, wrongdoing, offence, injury, affront, disgrace, scandal, injustice, abuse; *Law* malfeasance, tort.

enormous ▶ **adjective** *enormous waves batter the archipelago's western shores* **huge**, vast, extensive, expansive, broad, wide; boundless, immeasurable, limitless, infinite, gigantic, very big, very large, great, giant, massive, colossal, mammoth, immense, tremendous, mighty, stupendous, monumental, epic, prodigious, mountainous, monstrous, titanic, towering, elephantine, king-sized, king-size, gargantuan, Herculean, Brobdingnagian, substantial; hefty, bulky, weighty, heavy, gross; *informal* mega, monster, whopping, whopping great, thumping, thumping great, humongous, jumbo, hulking, bumper, astronomical, astronomic; *Brit. informal* whacking, whacking great, ginormous.
OPPOSITE tiny.

enormously ▶ **adverb 1** *an enormously important factor* **very**, extremely, exceedingly, exceptionally, especially, tremendously, immensely, vastly, hugely; extraordinarily, extra, excessively, overly, over, abundantly, inordinately, singularly, significantly, distinctly, outstandingly, uncommonly, unusually, decidedly, particularly, eminently, supremely, highly, remarkably, really, truly, mightily, thoroughly; all that, to a great extent, most, so, too; *Scottish* unco; *French* très; *N. English* right; *informal* terrifically, awfully, terribly, devilishly, madly, majorly, seriously, desperately, mega, ultra, oh-so, too-too, stinking, mucho, damn, damned, too ... for words; *informal, dated* devilish, hellish, frightfully; *Brit. informal* ever so, well, dead, bloody, dirty, jolly, fair; *N. Amer. informal* real, mighty, powerful, awful, plumb, darned, way, bitching; *S. African informal* lekker; *archaic* exceeding, sore.
OPPOSITE moderately.
2 *prices vary enormously* **considerably**, greatly, much, very much, a great deal, a lot, lots, a fair amount; significantly, substantially, appreciably, markedly, noticeably, materially, signally; *informal* plenty, seriously.
OPPOSITES slightly; not at all.

enough ▶ **determiner** *have we enough food?* **sufficient**, adequate, ample, abundant, as much ... as necessary, the necessary; *informal* plenty of.
OPPOSITE insufficient.
▶ **pronoun** *there's enough for everyone* **sufficient**, plenty (of), a sufficient amount (of), an adequate amount (of), as much as necessary; a sufficiency, an adequacy, an ample supply, a satisfactory amount, a passable amount, a tolerable amount, an acceptable amount, an abundance, an amplitude; full measure.
OPPOSITE insufficient.
▶ **adverb** *in large enough numbers* **sufficiently**, adequately, amply, satisfactorily, passably, tolerably, reasonably, fairly.
OPPOSITE insufficiently.

en passant ▶ **adverb** (*French*) *the report mentions, en passant, certain features of the Danish system* **in passing**, incidentally, by the way, parenthetically, while on the subject, apropos.

enquire, inquire ▶ **verb 1** *I enquired about part-time training courses* **ask**, make enquiries, ask questions, pose a question, request information; want to know, look to someone for answers.
2 *the commission is to* **enquire into** *alleged illegal payments* **conduct an enquiry**, make enquiries, probe, look; **investigate**, research, examine, explore, scan, sift, delve, dig, search, scrutinize, study, inspect, survey, analyse, consider, appraise; subject to an examination; *informal* check out, suss out, snoop.

enquiring, inquiring ▶ **adjective** *youngsters with enquiring minds* **inquisitive**, curious, interested, questioning, probing, investigative, analytical, analytic, exploring, searching, scrutinizing; burning with curiosity, dying to know.

enquiry, inquiry ▶ **noun 1** *telephone enquiries* **question**, query.
2 *there is to be an enquiry into alleged security leaks* **investigation**, examination, exploration, probe, search, scrutiny, scrutinization, study, inspection; inquest, hearing.

enrage ▶ **verb** *the scheme is bound to enrage farmers* **anger**, incense, infuriate, madden, inflame, incite, antagonize, provoke, rub up the wrong way, ruffle someone's feathers, exasperate; *informal* hack off, drive mad/crazy, drive up the wall, make someone see red, make someone's blood boil, make someone's hackles rise, get someone's back up, get someone's dander up, get someone's goat, get under someone's skin, get up someone's nose, rattle someone's cage; *Brit. informal* wind up, get on someone's wick, nark; *N. Amer. informal* burn up, tee off, tick off, gravel; *vulgar slang* piss off; *Brit. vulgar slang* get on someone's tits; *rare* empurple.
OPPOSITES placate; please.

E

enraged ▸ adjective *an enraged mob screamed abuse and hurled missiles* **very angry**, irate, furious, infuriated, angered, in a temper, incensed, raging, incandescent, fuming, ranting, raving, seething, frenzied, in a frenzy, beside oneself, outraged, in high dudgeon; hostile, antagonistic, black, dark; *informal* mad, hopping mad, wild, livid, as cross as two sticks, boiling, apoplectic, aerated, hot under the collar, on the warpath, up in arms, with all guns blazing, foaming at the mouth, steamed up, in a lather, in a paddy, in a filthy temper, fit to be tied; *Brit. informal* shirty, stroppy; *N. Amer. informal* sore, bent out of shape, soreheaded, teed off, ticked off; *Austral./NZ informal* ropeable, snaky, crook; *W. Indian informal* vex; *Brit. informal, dated* in a bate, waxy; *vulgar slang* pissed off; *N. Amer. vulgar slang* pissed; *literary* wrathful, ireful, wroth.
OPPOSITES calm, good-humoured.

enrapture ▸ verb *all of us in the theatre were enraptured by the music* **delight**, give great pleasure to, give joy to, please greatly, charm, enchant, captivate, enthral, entrance, bewitch, beguile, transport, ravish, thrill, excite, exhilarate, intoxicate, take someone's breath away; gladden, gratify, appeal to, do one's heart good, entertain, amuse, divert; *informal* give someone a buzz, give someone a kick, tickle someone pink, bowl someone over, turn someone on, send; *N. Amer. informal* give someone a charge.
OPPOSITE repel.

enrich ▸ verb **1** *the fine arts can certainly enrich our society* **enhance**, make richer, improve, add to, augment, supplement, complement, boost, upgrade, reinforce; raise, lift, refine, polish, heighten, deepen, elevate, aggrandize, intensify, exalt.
OPPOSITES spoil, devalue.
2 *many convenience foods are enriched with minerals and vitamins* **make more nutritious**, improve, vitaminize.
3 *ants enrich, drain, and air the soil* **fertilize**, add fertilizer to, make more fertile, improve; compost, dung, manure, mulch, dress.
OPPOSITE impoverish.

enrol ▸ verb **1** *they both* **enrolled** *for the course* **register**, sign on, sign up, apply, volunteer, put one's name down, matriculate; go in for, enter, join, become a member of, take up.
OPPOSITE leave.
2 *280 new members were enrolled this year* **accept**, admit, take on, register, sign on, sign up, matriculate, recruit, engage.
OPPOSITES expel; reject.

en route ▸ adverb (*French*) *he was en route from Paris to Bordeaux* **on the way**, in transit, on the journey, during the journey, during transport, along/on the road, on the move, in motion; coming, going, proceeding, journeying, travelling.

ensconce ▸ verb *Agnes* **ensconced herself** *in their bedroom* **settle**, install, establish, park, shut, plant, lodge, position, seat, entrench, shelter, screen; nestle, curl up, snuggle up; *informal* dig in.

ensemble ▸ noun **1** *the ensemble includes two flutes* **group**, band, orchestra, combo; company, troupe, cast, chorus, corps, circle, association; duo, trio, quartet, quintet, sextet, septet, octet, nonet.
2 *the buildings in the square present a charming provincial ensemble* **whole**, whole thing, entity, unit, unity, body, piece, object, discrete item; collection, set, combination, package, accumulation, conglomeration, sum, total, totality, entirety, assemblage, aggregate, composite; *informal* whole caboodle.
3 *she wore a pink and black ensemble* **outfit**, costume, suit, coordinates, matching separates, set of clothes; *informal* get-up, rig-out.

enshrine ▸ verb *the following rights should be enshrined in the treaty* **set down**, set out, spell out, express, lay down, set in stone, embody, realize, manifest, incorporate, represent, contain, include, preserve, treasure, immortalize, cherish.

enshroud ▸ verb (*literary*) *grey clouds enshrouded the city* **envelop**, shroud, swathe, veil, cloak, cloud, submerge, enfold, enwrap, surround, bury; cover, coat, carpet, blanket, overlay, overlie, overspread, extend over, cap, top, crown; conceal, obscure, blot out, hide, mask; *literary* mantle, pall, pave.
OPPOSITE reveal.

ensign ▸ noun *the ship flew a British ensign* **flag**, standard, colour(s), jack, banner, pennant, pennon, streamer, banderole; *Brit.* pendant; *Nautical* burgee; (*in ancient Rome*) vexillum; *rare* gonfalon, guidon, labarum.

enslave ▸ verb *there were few natives left to enslave* **sell into slavery**, condemn to slavery, take away someone's human rights, disenfranchise, condemn to servitude; subject to forced labour; **subjugate**, suppress, tyrannize, oppress, dominate, exploit, persecute; *rare* enthral, bind, yoke.
OPPOSITES liberate; emancipate.

enslavement ▸ noun *the enslavement of Africans continued for most of the nineteenth century* **subjugation**, disenfranchisement, suppression, tyranny, subjection, oppression, domination, exploitation, persecution; **slavery**, servitude, bondage, forced labour; bonds, chains, fetters, shackles, restraints, yoke; *Biology* dulosis; *literary* thraldom, thrall; *historical* serfdom, vassalage, helotage, helotry, helotism; *archaic* enthralment, duress.
OPPOSITES liberation; emancipation.

ensnare ▸ verb *the larvae construct pits to ensnare their prey* **capture**, catch, seize, trap, entrap, snare, entangle, enmesh, net, bag, ambush, ensnarl; *rare* springe.
OPPOSITE release.

ensue ▸ verb *a fierce argument* **ensued from** *his remark* **result**, follow, develop, stem, spring, arise, derive, evolve, proceed, emerge, emanate, issue, flow; occur, happen, take place, surface, crop up, spring up, present itself, come next, come about, transpire, supervene; be caused by, be brought about by, be produced by, originate in, accompany, be attended by, be consequent on, come after; *Philosophy* supervene on; *literary* come to pass, befall, betide; *archaic* hap; *rare* eventuate.

ensure ▸ verb **1** *ensure that the surface to be painted is completely clean* | *we will ensure equal opportunities for all* **make sure**, make certain, see to it; secure, guarantee, warrant, certify, set the seal on, clinch; confirm, check, verify, corroborate, establish; *informal* sew up.
2 *the project has been set up to ensure the future of small woodlands* **safeguard**, protect, guard, shield, shelter, fortify, make invulnerable; **assure**, secure, make safe, watch over, look after, take care of.

> **ensure or insure?**
> In both British and American English the primary meaning of **insure** is the commercial one of providing financial compensation for loss or damage. **Ensure** is not used at all in this sense; it means 'take care, and take action if necessary, to make certain that something is the case' (*the client must ensure that accurate records are kept*).

entail ▸ verb *this proposal will entail additional expenditure* **necessitate**, make necessary, require, need, demand, call for; presuppose, assume, warrant, be grounds for; involve, mean, imply; cause, bring about, produce, result in, end in, culminate in, finish in, terminate in, lead to, give rise to, occasion, engender, generate, prompt, effect, evoke, elicit, precipitate, trigger, spark off, provoke.

entangle ▸ verb **1** *all four bodies were entangled in a heap* **intertwine**, entwine, tangle, intertwist, twist, ravel, snarl, knot, coil, mat, jumble, muddle.
OPPOSITE disentangle.
2 *the thread entangles the insect and brings it down* **catch**, capture, trap, snare, ensnare, entrap, enmesh, ensnarl.
OPPOSITES disentangle; release.
3 *he felt no call to entangle himself in the political questions of his day* **involve**, implicate, embroil, mix up, catch up, bog down, mire.
OPPOSITE steer clear of.

entanglement ▸ noun **1** *he would not contemplate foreign entanglements whose outcome was unpredictable* **involvement**, complication, mix-up, adventure, undertaking.
2 *his entanglements with the opposite sex* **affair**, relationship, love affair, romance, fling, flirtation, dalliance, liaison, involvement, attachment, affair of the heart, intrigue; relations; *French* affaire, affaire de/du cœur, amour; *informal* hanky-panky; *Brit. informal* carry-on.

entente ▸ noun *the Foreign Office was reluctant to upset the entente with France* **understanding**, agreement, arrangement, entente cordiale, covenant, settlement; deal, alliance, treaty, pact, accord, compact, concordat, protocol, convention.

enter ▸ verb **1** *police entered the house* | *knock and enter* **go in/into**, come in/into, get in/into, set foot in, cross the threshold of, pass into, move into, gain access to, be admitted to, make/effect an entrance into, break into, burst into, irrupt into, intrude into, invade, infiltrate.
OPPOSITE leave.
2 *a bullet entered his chest* **penetrate**, pierce, puncture, perforate, make a hole in, make a wound in; impale, stick, spike, stab, spear, skewer, run through, transfix; *rare* transpierce.
OPPOSITE leave.
3 *America entered the war* | *she rarely entered into the conversation* **join (in)**, get involved in, go in for, throw oneself into, engage in, embark on, venture into/on, launch into, plunge into, undertake, take up; **participate in**, take part in, share in, play a part in, play a role in, be a participant in, partake in, contribute to, be associated with, associate oneself with, have a hand in, have something to do with, be (a) party to; cooperate in, help with, assist with, lend a hand with; *informal* get in on the act, pitch in with.
OPPOSITE leave.
4 *the planning entered a new phase* **begin**, start, move into, go into, enter on; *informal* kick off; *formal* commence.
OPPOSITE finish.
5 *both boys entered the Army at eighteen* **join**, become a member of, enrol in/for, enlist in, volunteer for, sign up for, take up, become connected/associated with, commit oneself to.
OPPOSITE leave.
6 *Mum entered a national cookery competition* **go in for**, put one's name down for, register for, enrol for, sign on/up for, become a competitor in, become a contestant in, obtain/gain entrance to; compete in, take part

in, participate in, be a competitor in, be a contestant in, play in; *informal* throw one's hat in the ring, be in the running.
OPPOSITE scratch.
7 *the cashier entered the details in a ledger* **record**, write down, set down, put in writing, put down, take down, note, make a note of, jot down, put down on paper, commit to paper; **document**, put on record, minute, register, chronicle, file, put on file, chart, docket, log; list, catalogue, make an inventory of; *rare* diarize.
OPPOSITE erase.
8 (*Law*) *he entered a plea of guilty* **submit**, register, lodge, put on record, record, table, file, put forward, place, advance, lay, present, press, prefer, tender, offer, proffer.
OPPOSITE withdraw.

enterprise ▶ **noun 1** *approaching such an aggressive and powerful creature is a dangerous enterprise* **undertaking**, endeavour, venture, pursuit, exercise, activity, operation, exploit, mission, deed, act, action, move, measure, task, business, affair, proceeding; scheme, plan, plan of action, programme, campaign; project, proposal, proposition, suggestion, idea, conception; *informal* caper; *Brit. informal* wheeze.
2 *the school showed enterprise in its attempt to attract pupils* **initiative**, resourcefulness, resource, imagination, imaginativeness, ingenuity, inventiveness, originality, creativity; quick-wittedness, cleverness, native wit, talent, ability, capability; spirit, spiritedness, enthusiasm, dynamism, leadership, drive, zest, dash, ambition, ambitiousness, energy, verve, vigour, vitality; boldness, daring, spirit of adventure, audacity, courage, intrepidity; *informal* gumption, get-up-and-go, go, push, oomph, pizzazz, pep, zip, vim.
OPPOSITES unimaginativeness; fecklessness.
3 *a fan club should be a service rather than a profit-making enterprise* **business**, company, firm, (commercial) undertaking, venture, organization, operation, concern, industry, corporation, establishment, house, shop, office, bureau, agency, franchise, practice, partnership, consortium, cooperative, conglomerate, group, combine, syndicate; *informal* outfit, set-up.

enterprising ▶ **adjective** *an enterprising farmer is now charging visitors £1 each to park in her field* **resourceful**, imaginative, ingenious, inventive, original, creative; quick-witted, clever, bright, sharp, talented, gifted, able, capable; spirited, enthusiastic, dynamic, ambitious, energetic, entrepreneurial, vigorous; bold, daring, audacious, courageous, intrepid, adventurous; *informal* go-ahead.
OPPOSITES unimaginative; feckless.

entertain ▶ **verb 1** *he wrote his first stories to entertain his children* **amuse**, divert, distract, delight, please, charm, cheer, beguile, interest, fascinate, enthral, engage, involve, occupy, absorb, immerse, engross, preoccupy, hold the attention of.
OPPOSITE bore.
2 *he often entertains foreign visitors at home* **receive**, play host/hostess to, show hospitality to, invite to a meal/party, invite (round/over), ask (round/over), have (round/over), give someone a meal, throw a party for; dine, wine and dine, feast, cater for, serve, feed, treat, welcome, host, fête.
3 *I expect you entertain a lot* **receive guests**, have guests, play host/hostess, provide hospitality, have people round/over, have company, hold/throw a party, keep open house, have a dinner/lunch party.
4 *would you entertain the possibility of undertaking such a venture again?* **consider**, give consideration to, take into consideration, think about, contemplate, give thought to, bear in mind; countenance, tolerate, brook, suffer, agree to, approve of, support.
OPPOSITE reject.
5 *he entertained the suspicion that he was being swindled* **harbour**, nurture, foster, nurse, cherish, hold, have, bear, hold (on to), possess, cling to, retain, maintain, brood over, hide, conceal.
OPPOSITE eschew.

entertainer *See centre pages for lists of* **Actors** **Entertainers** **Musicians** **Singers**
▶ **noun** *one of Hollywood's highest-paid entertainers* **performer**, artiste, artist; *rare* executant.

entertaining ▶ **adjective** *she found him a charming and entertaining companion | a very entertaining play* **delightful**, **enjoyable**, diverting, amusing, pleasurable, pleasing, pleasant, agreeable, nice, to one's liking, congenial, charming, appealing, beguiling, enchanting, captivating, engaging, interesting, fascinating, intriguing, absorbing, riveting, compelling; humorous, funny, witty, droll, comical, hilarious; *informal* fun.
OPPOSITES boring; uninteresting.

entertainment ▶ **noun 1** *he read the books purely for entertainment* **amusement**, pleasure, leisure, relaxation, fun, enjoyment, interest, occupation, refreshment, restoration, distraction, diversion, divertissement, play; *informal* R and R, jollies; *Brit. informal* beer and skittles; *N. Amer. informal* rec; *dated* sport; *archaic* disport.
2 *a theatre company is to present an entertainment for the Emperor* **show**, performance, presentation, production, staging, spectacle, extravaganza.

enthral ▶ **verb** *last night he enthralled fans from six to sixty* **captivate**, charm, enchant, bewitch, fascinate, beguile, entrance, enrapture, delight, attract, allure, lure; win, ensnare, dazzle, absorb, engross, rivet, grip, transfix, root someone to the spot, transport, carry away, hypnotize, mesmerize, intrigue, spellbind, hold spellbound; *informal* get under someone's skin.
OPPOSITES bore; repel.

enthralling ▶ **adjective** *wildlife programmes on television are enthralling viewing* **fascinating**, entrancing, enchanting, bewitching, captivating, charming, beguiling, enrapturing; **delightful**, attractive, alluring, winning, dazzling, absorbing, engrossing, memorable, compelling, riveting, readable, gripping, exciting, transfixing, transporting, hypnotic, mesmerizing, intriguing, spellbinding; *informal* unputdownable.
OPPOSITES boring, dull.

enthuse ▶ **verb 1** *I immediately enthused about the idea* **rave**, be enthusiastic, gush, wax lyrical, bubble over, effervesce, be effusive, rhapsodize, go into raptures; praise to the skies, heap praise on, make much of, throw bouquets at, eulogize, extol, acclaim; *informal* go wild/mad/crazy, get all worked up, go over the top; *N. Amer. informal* ballyhoo; *black English* big someone/something up; *dated* cry someone/something up; *rare* laud, panegyrize.
2 *He is a brilliant producer. He enthuses people.* **motivate**, inspire, stimulate, encourage, spur (on), galvanize, arouse, rouse, excite, stir (up), fire, fire with enthusiasm, make enthusiastic, fire the imagination of; *rare* inspirit, incentivize.

enthusiasm ▶ **noun 1** *Watkins worked quickly and with enthusiasm* **eagerness**, keenness, ardour, fervour, warmth, passion, zeal, zealousness, zest, gusto, brio, pep, go, sap, liveliness, vivacity, vivaciousness, energy, verve, vigour, dynamism, vehemence, fire, excitement, exuberance, ebullience, spirit, avidity, avidness; wholeheartedness, commitment, willingness, readiness, devotion, devotedness, fanaticism, earnestness; *informal* oomph, zing, zip, zap, vim, get-up-and-go; *rare* fervency, ardency, passionateness.
OPPOSITE apathy.
2 *they can put their skills and enthusiasms to good use* **interest**, passion, obsession, fad, craze, mania, rage; inclination, preference, penchant, predilection, fancy, impulse; pastime, hobby, recreation, (leisure) pursuit, leisure activity, entertainment; *informal* bug, thing.

enthusiast ▶ **noun** *a good present for a railway enthusiast* **fan**, fanatic, devotee, aficionado, addict, lover, admirer, supporter, follower; **expert**, wizard, connoisseur, authority, pundit, cognoscente, one of the cognoscenti, savant; *informal* buff, freak, nut, fiend, maniac, ham, a great one for; *N. Amer. informal* maven, geek, jock, nerd; *S. African informal* fundi.

enthusiastic ▶ **adjective** *an enthusiastic supporter of Scottish rugby* **eager**, keen, avid, ardent, fervent, warm, passionate, zealous, lively, vivacious, energetic, vigorous, dynamic, vehement, fiery, excited, exuberant, ebullient, spirited, hearty, wholehearted, committed, willing, ready, devoted, fanatical, earnest.
OPPOSITE apathetic.

> **CHOOSE THE RIGHT WORD**
> **enthusiastic, eager, keen, avid**
> *See* EAGER.

entice ▶ **verb** *the show should entice a new audience into the theatre* **tempt**, allure, lure, attract, dangle a carrot in front of, appeal to, invite, persuade, convince, inveigle, induce, beguile, cajole, wheedle, coax, woo; seduce, lead astray, lead on, decoy; *informal* sweet-talk, smooth-talk.

> **CHOOSE THE RIGHT WORD**
> **entice, lure, tempt**
> *See* TEMPT.

enticement ▶ **noun** *the enticement of power* **lure**, temptation, allure, attraction, desirability, bait, draw, pull, call, appeal; glamour, allurement, bewitchment, enchantment, charm, seduction, persuasion, fascination, captivation, magnetism; *informal* come-on.

enticing ▶ **adjective** *we caught enticing glimpses of tables laden with food* **tempting**, alluring, attractive, appealing, fetching, inviting, glamorous, captivating, seductive; enchanting, beguiling, charming, fascinating, intriguing, tantalizing, magnetic; irresistible; *informal, dated* come-hither.

entire ▶ **adjective 1** *I have devoted my entire adult life to the pursuit of my ideals* **whole**, complete, total, full; continuous, unbroken, uninterrupted, undivided.
OPPOSITE partial.
2 *the arch of one of the gates is entire* **intact**, unbroken, undamaged, unharmed, unimpaired, unflawed, unscathed, unspoilt, unmutilated, unblemished, unmarked, perfect, inviolate, in one piece; sound, solid.
OPPOSITES broken, partial.
3 *an ideological system with which he is in entire agreement* **absolute**, total,

utter, out-and-out, thorough, thoroughgoing, wholehearted; unqualified, unreserved, unmitigated, unmodified, unmixed, unalloyed, unrestricted, perfect, outright, pure, sheer.
OPPOSITES partial, qualified.

WORD LINKS
related prefix **pan- (e.g. *pan-African, panacea*)**

entirely ▶ adverb **1** *his solution was entirely out of the question* **absolutely**, completely, totally, fully, wholly; altogether, utterly, quite, in every respect, in every way, in all respects, {lock, stock, and barrel}; unreservedly, without reservation, without exception, thoroughly, perfectly, downright, one hundred per cent, every inch; to the hilt, to the core, all the way; *informal* bang, dead.
OPPOSITES partially, slightly.
2 *the gift was entirely for charitable purposes* **solely**, only, exclusively, purely, merely, simply, just, alone.
OPPOSITE partially.

E

entirety ▶ noun *in the 1920s, cheap production constituted almost the entirety of British film-making* **whole**, sum, total, aggregate, totality, gross, sum total, grand total.
OPPOSITE part.
□ **in its entirety** *the scheme was approved in its entirety* **completely**, entirely, totally, fully, wholly; in every respect, in every way, in all respects, {lock, stock, and barrel}, one hundred per cent, from beginning to end, alpha and omega, all the way, every inch, to the hilt, to the core.
OPPOSITE in part.

entitle ▶ verb **1** *this pass entitles you to free entrance to the museum* **qualify**, make eligible, authorize, sanction, allow, permit, grant, grant/give the right, give permission; enable, empower, accredit; enfranchise, capacitate.
2 *the concluding chapter was entitled 'Comedy and Tragedy'* **title**, name, call, give the title of, label, term, designate, dub; baptize, christen; *rare* denominate.

entitlement ▶ noun **1** *their entitlement to social-security benefits* **right**, prerogative, claim, title, licence; permission, dispensation, privilege, liberty.
2 *your annual holiday entitlement* **allowance**, allocation, allotment, quota, ration, grant, limit.

entity ▶ noun **1** *a single biological entity* **being**, body, creature, individual, organism, life form; person; object, article, thing, piece of matter, real thing; substance, quantity, existence; *Philosophy* ens.
2 *the subsidiary company is a distinct entity* **organization**, institution, establishment, body, operation; structure, system, unit, whole; *informal* set-up, outfit.
3 *the distinction between entity and nonentity* **existence**, being; life, living, animation, animateness, vital force; substance, essence, reality, actuality; essential nature, quintessence; *Philosophy* quiddity, esse.
OPPOSITES nonentity, non-existence.

entomb ▶ verb *mummified bodies were entombed in the pyramids* **inter**, place in a tomb, lay to rest, bury, consign to the grave; *informal* place six feet under, plant; *literary* inhume, sepulchre.

entombment ▶ noun *the ritual entombment of the pharaoh* **interment**, laying to rest, burial, burying, consignment to the grave, committal, inhumation; funeral, obsequies; *rare* exequies.

entourage ▶ noun *the king's entourage* **retinue**, escort, company, cortège, train, suite, court, staff, bodyguard; attendants, companions, followers, retainers, members of court, camp followers, associates, hangers-on; *informal* groupies.

entrails ▶ plural noun *the embalmers removed the entrails* **intestines**, internal organs, bowels, guts, vital organs, viscera; offal; *informal* insides, innards; *Brit. archaic* numbles.

entrance[1] (stress on the first syllable) ▶ noun **1** *the main entrance to the site* **entry**, way in, means of entry/access, ingress, access, approach; door, doorway, portal, gate, gateway; opening, mouth; drive, driveway, passageway, gangway; entrance hall, foyer, lobby, porch, concourse, threshold; *N. Amer.* entryway.
OPPOSITE exit.
2 *they were interrupted by the entrance of Mrs Little* **appearance**, arrival, entry, ingress, coming, coming/going in, materialization, approach, introduction.
OPPOSITES departure, exit.
3 *he was refused entrance until somebody arrived who could vouch for him* **admission**, admittance, entry, access, ingress, entrée, permission to enter, right of entry, the opportunity to enter.

entrance[2] (stress on the second syllable) ▶ verb **1** *I was entranced by the bird's beauty* **enchant**, bewitch, beguile, enrapture, captivate, capture, mesmerize, hypnotize, spellbind, hold spellbound, send into transports/raptures; enthral, grip, engage, rivet, engross, absorb, fascinate, carry away; stun, overpower, take someone's breath away; charm, delight; thrill, excite, electrify; *informal* bowl over, knock out; *literary* ravish.
OPPOSITE bore.
2 (*literary*) *Orpheus entranced the wild beasts* **cast a spell on**, put a spell on, put under a spell, put in a trance, bewitch, witch, hex, spellbind, hypnotize, mesmerize; *literary* trance.

entrant ▶ noun **1** *the majority of our entrants are school-leavers from the United Kingdom* **new member**, new arrival, beginner, newcomer, fresher, freshman, recruit, new boy/girl; novice, trainee, apprentice, probationer, tyro, initiate, neophyte; *N. Amer.* tenderfoot, hire; *informal* rookie, greenhorn, new kid, newbie, cub.
OPPOSITE veteran.
2 *the prize will be awarded to the entrant who wins the tiebreak* **competitor**, contestant, contender, challenger, participant, player, candidate, applicant.

entrap ▶ verb **1** *discarded fishing lines can entrap wildlife* **trap**, snare, ensnare, entangle, enmesh; catch, capture, net, bag, hook, land.
OPPOSITE release.
2 *his client had been entrapped by an undercover police officer* **entice**, lure, tempt, inveigle; bait, decoy, lay a trap for, trap; lead on, seduce; **trick**, deceive, dupe, gull, hoodwink, delude; *informal* **set up**, frame; *Brit. informal* fit up.

entreat ▶ verb *my lord, I entreat you to believe what you find in this letter* **implore**, beseech, beg, plead with, supplicate, pray, ask, request; bid, enjoin, appeal to, call on, petition, solicit; exhort, urge, importune; *dated* crave; *rare* impetrate, obtest, obsecrate.

entreaty ▶ noun *he ignored her entreaties* **plea**, appeal, request, petition, cry from the heart; suit, application, claim; beseeching, pleading, begging, solicitation, importuning, supplication; bidding, exhortation, urge, demand, enjoinment; prayer; *French* cri de cœur; *rare* impetration, obtestation, obsecration, imploration.

entrée ▶ noun **1** *there is a choice of half a dozen entrées on the menu* **main course**, main dish, main meal.
OPPOSITES starter; dessert.
2 *university dramatic societies were an excellent entrée into the acting profession* **means of entry**, entrance, entry, ingress, opportunity to enter; route, path, avenue, way, key, passport; access, admission, admittance, acceptance, right of entry.

entrench, **intrench** ▶ verb **1** *this country is entrenched in a litigation mentality* **establish**, settle, ensconce, lodge, set, root, install, plant, embed, anchor, seat, station; *informal* dig in.
OPPOSITE dislodge.
2 (*archaic*) *concessions which* **entrenched on** *the dignity of the Crown* **encroach**, impinge, intrude, trespass; **infringe**, violate, interfere with, infiltrate, invade.

entrenched, **intrenched** ▶ adjective *officials tended to cling to entrenched attitudes* **ingrained**, established, well established, long-established; confirmed, fixed, set firm, firm; deep-seated, deep-rooted, rooted, deep-set; unshakeable, irremovable, indelible, ineradicable, inveterate, immutable, inexorable, dyed-in-the-wool.
OPPOSITE superficial.

entre nous ▶ adverb (*French*) *entre nous, the old man's a bit of a case* **between ourselves**, between us, between you and me, in (strict) confidence, confidentially, in private, privately, off the record; *informal* between you and me and the bedpost/gatepost/wall; *Latin* sub rosa; *archaic* under the rose.

entrepreneur ▶ noun *an entrepreneur who had set up his own firms* **businessman**, **businesswoman**, business person, business executive, enterpriser, speculator, tycoon, magnate; dealer, trader, buyer and seller, merchant; commercial intermediary, intermediary, middleman, promoter, impresario; *informal* **wheeler-dealer**, mogul, big shot, bigwig, whizz-kid, mover and shaker, go-getter, high-flyer, hustler.

entrust ▶ verb **1** *he was entrusted with the task of liaising with fellow intellectuals* **give responsibility for**, charge, invest, endow; burden, encumber, saddle, tax.
2 *there are a great many powers* **entrusted to** *the Home Secretary* **assign**, confer on, bestow on, vest in, consign; delegate, depute, devolve; put into the hands of, give into the charge/care/custody of, turn over, hand over, give, grant, vouchsafe.
3 *she was afraid to entrust the children to the hospital* **hand over**, give custody of, make over, turn over, commit, assign, consign, deliver; *formal* commend.

entry ▶ noun **1** *my moment of entry was masked by smoke* **appearance**, arrival, entrance, ingress, coming, coming/going in, approach, introduction, materialization.
OPPOSITE departure.
2 *the entry to a block of flats* **entrance**, way in, means of entry/access, ingress, access, approach; door, doorway, portal, gate, gateway; drive, driveway, passageway, gangway; entrance hall, foyer, lobby, porch, concourse, threshold; *N. Amer.* entryway.
OPPOSITE exit.
3 *he was refused entry to the meeting* **admission**, admittance, entrance, access, ingress, entrée, permission to enter, right of entry, the opportunity to enter.
4 *the entries in the cash book* **item**, record, statement, note, listing, jotting;

memo, memorandum; account, description.
5 *pull-down menus make data entry a snap* **recording**, noting, filing, registering, archiving, logging, taking down, setting down, documenting, documentation, capture.
6 *the judges had the difficult task of choosing a winner from the 340 entries* **contestant**, competitor, contender, challenger, entrant, participant, player, candidate, applicant; **submission**, attempt, try, effort, turn; entry form, application; *informal* go.

entwine ▶ **verb** *her hair was entwined with ropes of pearls* **wind round**, twist round, coil round, wrap round, weave, intertwine, interlink, interlace, interweave, interthread, criss-cross, entangle, tangle; twine, link, lace, braid, plait, knit, wreathe; *literary* pleach.
OPPOSITES unravel, disentangle.

enumerate ▶ **verb 1** *he enumerated four objectives for the company* **list**, itemize, catalogue, set out, set forth, give; cite, name, mention, specify, identify, spell out, detail, particularize; summarize, recount, recite, rehearse, recapitulate, quote, relate; run through, reel off, rattle off, tick/check off.
2 *research projects have attempted to enumerate hospital readmission rates* **calculate**, compute, count, add up, sum up, tally, total, number, put a figure on, quantify; reckon, figure up, work out; *Brit.* tot up; *archaic* tell.

enunciate ▶ **verb 1** *she enunciated each word slowly and carefully* **pronounce**, articulate; say, speak, utter, express, voice, vocalize, sound, mouth; *informal* get one's tongue round; *rare* enounce.
2 *in the speech I enunciated a belief which I still hold to* **express**, utter, state, give voice/expression to, put into words, give utterance to, declare, profess, set forth, assert, affirm; put forward, raise, table, air, ventilate; propound, proclaim, promulgate, publish, broadcast, preach; *informal* come out with.

envelop ▶ **verb** *the gases of the atmosphere that envelop the Earth* **surround**, cover, enfold, enwrap, blanket, swathe, swaddle, wrap (up), engulf, encircle, encompass, cocoon, sheathe, encase, enclose; cloak, conceal, hide, obscure, cover (up), screen, shield, mask, veil, shroud; *literary* mantle, enshroud; *rare* obnubilate.

envelope ▶ **noun** *she tore open the envelope* **wrapper**, wrapping, wrap, sleeve, cover, covering; casing, case.

envenom ▶ **verb 1** *the arrows are envenomed with asp drool* **poison**, add poison to, spike, lace, contaminate.
2 *incidents like this can envenom international relations* **embitter**, make bitter, sour, poison, make rancorous, jaundice, colour, taint; anger, aggravate, antagonize.
OPPOSITE sweeten.

enviable ▶ **adjective** *this hotel has an enviable position on the main square* **desirable**, **attractive**, sought-after, desired, admirable, fortunate, lucky, favoured, blessed, worth having, excellent; covetable, exciting envy, tempting; *informal* to die for.
OPPOSITE unenviable.

envious ▶ **adjective** *she felt envious of her friend's beauty* **jealous**, covetous, desirous; grudging, begrudging, resentful; jaundiced, bitter, malicious, spiteful; green with envy, green, green-eyed; *formal* emulous.
OPPOSITE generous.

environ ▶ **verb** *at home I am environed by pets* **surround**, encircle, enclose, ring, envelop; blanket, swathe, swaddle, wrap, cloak.

environment ▶ **noun 1** *birds and mammals from a wide range of environments* **habitat**, territory, domain, home, abode; surroundings, conditions, environs, circumstances.
2 *potential hazards in the hospital environment are numerous* **situation**, **setting**, milieu, medium, background, backdrop, scene, scenario, location, locale, context, framework; sphere, world, realm; preserve, province; ambience, atmosphere, climate, mood, air, aura.
3 (**the environment**) *the impact of pesticides on the environment* **the natural world**, nature, the living world, the world, the earth, the ecosystem, the biosphere, Mother Nature, Gaia; wildlife, flora and fauna, the countryside, the landscape.

WORD LINKS
study of the environment **ecology**
destruction of the environment **ecocide**

environmentalist ▶ **noun** *environmentalists are pressing for a ban on logging* **conservationist**, preservationist, ecologist, green, nature-lover, eco-activist; *informal, derogatory* econut, ecofreak, tree hugger.

environs ▶ **plural noun** *the environs of London* **surroundings**, surrounding area, vicinity; locality, neighbourhood, district, region; outskirts, suburbs, suburbia, precincts, borders, periphery, purlieus; *N. Amer.* vicinage.

envisage ▶ **verb 1** *it was envisaged that such hospitals would be opened in all the principal towns* **foresee**, predict, forecast, foretell, anticipate, expect, think likely, envision; **intend**, propose, mean.
2 *I cannot envisage what the circumstances will be in twenty years time* **imagine**, contemplate, visualize, envision, picture, see in one's mind's eye; conceive of, think of, understand, grasp, appreciate, apprehend; *rare* ideate.

envision ▶ **verb** *we now have the chance to build the world envisioned by the founders of the UN* **visualize**, **imagine**, envisage, picture, see in one's mind's eye, conjure up an image of; intend, propose, mean; conceive of, think of, see; *rare* ideate.

envoy ▶ **noun 1** *he served as an envoy to France* **ambassador**, emissary, diplomat, legate, consul, attaché, chargé d'affaires, plenipotentiary; *Roman Catholic Church* nuncio.
2 *a visit by the president's personal envoy* **representative**, delegate, deputy, agent, intermediary, mediator, negotiator, proxy, surrogate, liaison, broker, accredited messenger, courier, spokesperson, spokesman, spokeswoman, mouthpiece, stand-in; *informal* go-between; *archaic* factor.

envy ▶ **noun 1** *Carla felt a sharp pang of envy* **jealousy**, enviousness, covetousness, desire; resentment, resentfulness, bitterness, discontent, spite; the green-eyed monster.
OPPOSITE generosity.
2 *France has a film industry that is the envy of Europe* **object**/**source of envy**; **best**, finest, pride, top, cream, pick, choice, elite, prize, jewel, jewel in the crown, flower, paragon, leading light, glory, the crème de la crème.
OPPOSITES shame; dregs.
▶ **verb 1** *I admired and envied her* **be envious of**, be jealous of; begrudge, grudge, be resentful of.
OPPOSITE be glad for.
2 *most girls would have envied her lifestyle* **covet**, be covetous of; desire, aspire to, wish for, want, long for, yearn for, hanker after/for, be consumed with desire for, crave, have one's heart set on; *informal* have the hots for.

ephemeral ▶ **adjective** *fashions are ephemeral* **transitory**, transient, fleeting, passing, short-lived, momentary, brief, short, cursory, temporary, impermanent, short-term; fading, evanescent, fugitive, fly-by-night; *literary* fugacious.
OPPOSITES long-lived, permanent.

WORD LINKS
collector of ephemeral things **ephemerist**

CHOOSE THE RIGHT WORD
ephemeral, transient, transitory, fleeting
See TRANSIENT.

epic ▶ **noun 1** *the epics of Homer* **heroic poem** long poem, long story; **saga**, legend, romance, lay, history, chronicle, myth, fable, folk tale, folk story.
2 *a big Hollywood epic* **epic film**, long film; *informal* **blockbuster**.
▶ **adjective 1** *a traditional epic poem* **heroic**, **long**, grand, monumental, vast, Homeric, Miltonian; lofty, grandiloquent, high-flown, high-sounding, extravagant, bombastic.
OPPOSITE understated.
2 *their epic journey through the mountains* **ambitious**, heroic, grand, arduous, extraordinary, Herculean; very long, very great, very large, huge, monumental.

epicene ▶ **adjective 1** *the epicene shape resolved into that of a cloaked female* **sexless**, asexual, neuter, unsexed; bisexual, androgynous, hermaphrodite; *technical* monoclinous, gynandrous, gynandromorphic, parthenogenetic; *rare* androgyne.
2 *he gave an epicene titter* **effeminate**, womanish, unmanly, unmasculine, girlish; effete, weak, namby-pamby; *informal* sissy, girly, camp, limp-wristed, nancy, pansified.
OPPOSITES masculine, macho.

epicure ▶ **noun** *as an epicure, he is entranced by their new range of speciality foods* **gourmet**, gastronome, gourmand, connoisseur; glutton, sensualist, hedonist; *French* bon viveur, bon vivant; *informal* foodie.

epicurean ▶ **noun** *a generous, life-loving epicurean* **hedonist**, sensualist, pleasure seeker, pleasure lover, sybarite, voluptuary; epicure, gourmet, gastronome, connoisseur, gourmand, glutton; *French* bon viveur, bon vivant.
OPPOSITE puritan.
▶ **adjective 1** *their careers have been undone by epicurean excess* **hedonistic**, sensualist, pleasure-seeking, self-indulgent, indulgent, libertine, sybaritic, voluptuary, lotus-eating; dissolute, decadent, louche, licentious, sinful, shameless, depraved; wanton, abandoned, unrestrained, profligate, extravagant, intemperate, immoderate; sensual, carnal; Dionysiac, Bacchanalian, saturnalian; gluttonous, gourmandizing, greedy.
OPPOSITE puritanical.
2 *an epicurean feast* **gourmet**, gastronomic.

epidemic ▶ **noun 1** *an epidemic of typhoid* **outbreak**, plague, scourge, infestation; widespread illness/disease; *Medicine* pandemic, epizootic; *formal* recrudescence, boutade.
2 *he's a victim of the county's joyriding epidemic* **spate**, rash, wave, explosion, eruption, outbreak, outburst, flare-up, craze; flood, torrent, burst, blaze, flurry; upsurge, upswing, upturn, increase, growth, rise, mushrooming; *rare* ebullition, boutade.
▶ **adjective** *the obsession with the motor car is now epidemic* **rife**, rampant,

widespread, wide-ranging, extensive, sweeping, penetrating, pervading; global, universal, inescapable, ubiquitous; prevalent, predominant; *Medicine* endemic, pandemic, epizootic.
OPPOSITES limited, local.

epigram ▶ noun **1** *a witty epigram* **quip**, witticism, gem, play on words, jest, pun, sally, nice turn of phrase; *French* bon mot, double entendre, jeu d'esprit; *informal* one-liner, gag, crack, wisecrack; *rare* paronomasia, equivoque.
2 *a collection of ancient epigrams* **proverb**, saying, maxim, adage, axiom, aphorism, saw, gnome, dictum, precept, epigraph, motto, catchphrase; cliché, truism, commonplace; words of wisdom, pearls of wisdom; *informal* (old) chestnut; *rare* apophthegm.

epigrammatic ▶ adjective *her short, epigrammatic verses* **concise**, succinct, terse, pithy, aphoristic, compact, condensed, compressed, short, brief; laconic, sparing, clipped, elliptical; tight, crisp, incisive, pointed, to the point, short and sweet; witty, clever, amusing, quick-witted, piquant, ingenious; sharp, trenchant, well tuned, finely honed, in well-chosen words; *informal* snappy; *rare* lapidary, compendious, synoptic, gnomic, apophthegmatic.
OPPOSITES expansive, rambling.

epilogue ▶ noun *the body of the book is summarized in the epilogue* **afterword**, postscript, PS, coda, codicil, appendix, tailpiece, supplement, addendum, postlude, rider, back matter; conclusion, concluding speech, denouement, swan song, peroration; *rare* postlude.
OPPOSITE prologue.

episode ▶ noun **1** *the most hair-raising episode of his career* **incident**, event, occurrence, happening, occasion, interlude, chapter, experience, adventure, exploit; matter, affair, business, circumstance, set of circumstances, thing; ordeal, trial.
2 *the final episode of the series* **instalment**, section, chapter, scene, act, passage; part, division, portion, subsection, segment, component; programme, show.
3 *an episode of childhood illness* **period**, spell, bout, fit, attack, interval, phase; *informal* dose.

episodic ▶ adjective **1** *episodic wheezing* **intermittent**, irregular, sporadic, periodic, fitful, spasmodic, occasional; uneven, scattered, patchy, on and off, on again and off again, in fits and starts.
OPPOSITE continuous.
2 *the film is an episodic account of how a group of people had been affected by the war* **in episodes**, in instalments, in sections, in parts.

epistle ▶ noun (*formal*) **letter**, missive, communication, written message, written communication, dispatch, report, bulletin, note, line; correspondence, news, information, intelligence, word; *Roman Catholic Church* encyclical.

epitaph ▶ noun *an epitaph on a tombstone* **elegy**, commemoration, obituary, funeral oration; **inscription**, engraving, etching, legend.

epithet ▶ noun **1** *these works earned him the epithet 'the Spanish Heretic'* **sobriquet**, nickname, byname, title, name, label, tag; **description**, descriptive word/expression/phrase, designation, denomination, characterization, identification; *informal* moniker, handle; *formal* appellation, cognomen, anonym.
2 *he felt the urge to hurl epithets in his face* **obscenity**, expletive, swear word, term of abuse, oath, curse, four-letter word, exclamation; *informal* dirty word; *N. Amer. informal* cuss word.

epitome ▶ noun **1** *he was the epitome of conservative respectability* **personification**, embodiment, incarnation, paragon; essence, quintessence, archetype, paradigm, typification, type; exemplar, definitive example, prototype; representation, model, soul, example, byword, classic example/case; acme, ultimate, zenith, height; *rare* avatar.
2 *an epitome of a larger work* **summary**, abstract, synopsis, precis, résumé, outline, digest, recapitulation, summation, compendium, potted version; abridgement, abbreviation, condensation; *N. Amer.* wrap-up; *archaic* argument, summa; *rare* conspectus.
OPPOSITES complete version, full text.

epitomize ▶ verb **1** *the railway station epitomizes the spirit of the nineteenth century* **embody**, give form/shape to, incorporate; typify, exemplify, represent, be representative of, encapsulate, manifest, symbolize, stand for, illustrate, sum up; personify; *formal* reify; *rare* incarnate.
2 (*rare*) *for the benefit of our readers, we will epitomize the pamphlet* **summarize**, abstract, synopsize, precis, make a résumé/outline of, digest, encapsulate, recapitulate, sum up, put in a nutshell; abridge, condense, shorten, reduce, cut, cut short/down, abbreviate; *rare* capsulize.
OPPOSITES expand on, elaborate.

epoch *See centre pages for list of* **Geological Ages**
▶ noun *the Tudor epoch* **era**, age, period, time, aeon, span; stage, point in history; date.

eponym ▶ noun. *See centre pages for list of* **Eponyms**

equable ▶ adjective **1** *he was in a remarkably equable mood* **even-tempered**, calm, composed, collected, self-possessed, cool, {cool, calm, and collected}, relaxed, easy-going, at ease, as cool as a cucumber; nonchalant, insouciant, blithe, mellow, mild; serene, tranquil, placid, steady, stable, quiet, level-headed; imperturbable, unexcitable, unruffled, unperturbed, unflustered, undisturbed, unagitated, untroubled, well balanced; *informal* unflappable, unfazed, together, laid-back; *rare* equanimous.
OPPOSITES temperamental, excitable.
2 *the island enjoys an equable climate* **stable**, constant, steady, even, uniform, regular, unvarying, consistent, unchanging, changeless; moderate, temperate, non-extreme, fair.
OPPOSITES uneven, extreme.

equal ▶ adjective **1** *two lines of equal length* **identical**, uniform, alike, like, the same, one and the same, equivalent, indistinguishable; matching, twin; comparable, similar, corresponding, correspondent, commensurate.
OPPOSITES unequal, different.
2 *fares were equal to a fortnight's wages for a skilled craftsman* **equivalent**, identical, amounting; proportionate, tantamount; the same as, commensurate with, on a par with.
OPPOSITES unequal; more than; less than.
3 *the right to equal treatment before the law* **unbiased**, impartial, non-partisan, fair, fair-minded, just, even-handed, equitable; unprejudiced, unbigoted, non-discriminatory, free from discrimination, egalitarian; neutral, objective, disinterested, without fear or favour.
OPPOSITES unequal; discriminatory.
4 *a fair and equal contest* **evenly matched**, evenly balanced, even, balanced, level, evenly proportioned, well matched, on a par, on an equal footing; *informal* fifty-fifty, level pegging, neck and neck.
OPPOSITES uneven, unequal.
□ **equal to** *Patricia was equal to the task* **capable of**, fit for, up to, good/strong enough for, adequate for, sufficient for, ready for; suitable for, suited to, appropriate for; *informal* up to scratch, having what it takes.
▶ noun *they did not treat him as their equal* **equivalent**, **peer**, fellow, coequal, like; mate, twin, alter ego, counterpart, match, parallel; *rare* compeer.
OPPOSITES superior; inferior.
▶ verb **1** *thirty six divided by two equals eighteen* **be equal to**, be equivalent to, be the same as, correspond to; come to, amount to, make, total, add up to; *Brit.* tot up to.
2 *he equalled the world record* **match**, reach, parallel, come up to, be level with, measure up to, achieve.
3 *the fable equals that of any other poet* **be as good as**, be equal/even/level with, be a match for, match, measure up to, come up to, equate with, be in the same league as, be in the same category as, be tantamount to; rival, compete with, contend with, vie with.
OPPOSITES lose to; beat.

WORD LINKS
related prefix **iso-** (e.g. ***isobar, isochronous***)

equality ▶ noun **1** *the union's efforts to promote equality for women* **fairness**, justness, equitability, impartiality, even-handedness, egalitarianism, equal rights, equal opportunities, non-discrimination; justice, freedom, emancipation; *rare* coequality.
OPPOSITE inequality.
2 *equality between the demand for, and supply of, money* **parity**, sameness, identicalness, identity, equalness; likeness, alikeness, similarity, comparability, resemblance; uniformity, evenness, levelness, balance, equilibrium, correspondence, consistency, agreement, concord, congruence, parallelism, symmetry; *rare* coequality.
OPPOSITE difference.

equalize ▶ verb **1** *attempts to equalize men and women's earnings* **make equal**, make even, even out/up/off, make level, level (up/off), make uniform, make the same, make consistent, regularize, standardize, bring into line, balance, square, match.
2 *Northampton equalized ten minutes into the second half* **level the score**, even up the score, draw.

equanimity ▶ noun *she was able to confront the daily crises with equanimity* **composure**, calmness, calm, level-headedness, self-possession, self-control, even-temperedness, coolness, cool-headedness, presence of mind; serenity, placidity, tranquillity, phlegm, impassivity, imperturbability, unexcitability, equilibrium; poise, self-assurance, assurance, self-confidence, aplomb, sangfroid, nerve; *informal* cool, unflappability; *rare* ataraxy.
OPPOSITE anxiety.

equate ▶ verb **1** *his single-mindedness led him to equate criticism with treachery* **regard as the same as**, regard as identical to; **identify**, liken to, compare; bracket, class, associate, connect, pair, link, relate, ally, think of together, set side by side.
2 *the rent equates to £24 per square foot* **correspond**, be equivalent, amount; equal, be the same as.
3 *the price moved to equate supply and demand* **equalize**, balance, even out/up/off, level up/off, square, tally, match; make equal, make even, make level, make equivalent, make identical, make the same, make uniform.

equation ▶ noun **1** *a boy was solving a quadratic equation* **mathematical problem**, sum, calculation, question; equality.
2 *the equation of success with material rewards* **equating**, equalization, identification, association, connection, likening, matching; equivalence,

likeness, identity, correspondence, agreement, comparison, balance, balancing.
3 (**the equation**) *other factors also came into the equation* **the situation**, the problem, the case, the question, the quandary, the predicament.

equatorial ▶ adjective *the equatorial regions* **tropical**, hot, torrid, sweltering; humid, sultry, steamy, sticky, oppressive; jungle-like.
OPPOSITES polar; temperate.

equestrian *See centre pages for list of* **Equestrian Sports**
▶ adjective *an equestrian statue* **on horseback**, mounted, riding, in the saddle.
▶ noun *a network of tracks for equestrians* **horseman**, **horsewoman**, rider, horse rider, jockey; cavalryman, trooper; *archaic* hussar, cavalier.

equilibrium ▶ noun **1** *the equilibrium of the economy* **balance**, symmetry, equipoise, parity, equality, evenness; stability, steadiness; *archaic* counterpoise, equipollence.
OPPOSITE imbalance.
2 *he was hardly ever shaken from his equilibrium by the excesses of criminals* **composure**, calmness, calm, equanimity, collectedness, sangfroid, coolness; steadiness, stability, level-headedness, cool-headedness, imperturbability, poise, presence of mind; self-possession, self-control, self-command; impassiveness, impassivity, unexcitability, placidity, placidness, tranquillity, serenity; *informal* cool, unflappability; *rare* ataraxy, ataraxia.
OPPOSITES agitation, nervousness.

equip ▶ verb **1** *each was equipped with a flare gun* **provide**, furnish, supply, issue, fit out, kit out, rig out, deck out, stock, provision, arm; array, attire, dress, outfit, accoutre; *informal* fix up.
2 *the course will equip graduates for careers in software development* **prepare**, qualify, suit, endow; enable, facilitate.

equipment ▶ noun *the museum has a collection of early sound-recording equipment* **apparatus**, paraphernalia, articles, appliances, impedimenta; tools, utensils, implements, instruments, hardware, gadgets, gadgetry; stuff, things; kit, rig, tackle, outfit; resources, amenities, supplies; furniture, furnishings, fittings; odds and ends, bits and pieces, bits and bobs; trappings, appurtenances, accoutrements, regalia; *Military* materiel, baggage; *informal* gear, box of tricks; *Brit. informal* clobber, gubbins, odds and sods; *archaic* equipage.

equipoise ▶ noun **1** *this wine represents a marvellous equipoise of power and elegance* **equilibrium**, balance, evenness, symmetry, parity, equality, equity; stability, steadiness, poise; *archaic* counterpoise, equipollence.
OPPOSITE imbalance.
2 *capital flow acts as an equipoise to international imbalances in savings* **counterweight**, counterbalance, counterpoise, balance; ballast, stabilizer, makeweight; compensation, recompense; *archaic* countercheck.

equitable ▶ adjective *Parliament is to distribute the burden of tax in an equitable way* **fair**, just; impartial, even-handed, fair-minded, unbiased, unprejudiced, non-discriminatory, unbigoted, egalitarian, with no axe to grind, without fear or favour; honest, right, rightful, proper, decent, good, honourable, upright, scrupulous, conscientious, above board; reasonable, sensible; disinterested, objective, neutral, uncoloured, dispassionate, non-partisan, balanced, open-minded; *informal* fair and square, upfront, on the level; *N. Amer. informal* on the up and up.
OPPOSITES inequitable, unfair.

> **CHOOSE THE RIGHT WORD**
>
> **equitable, fair, just**
>
> *See* FAIR.

equity ▶ noun **1** *the equity of Finnish society* **fairness**, fair-mindedness, justness, justice, equitableness, fair play; impartiality, even-handedness, lack of discrimination/bias/prejudice/bigotry, egalitarianism; honesty, integrity, rightness, rightfulness, rectitude, uprightness, righteousness, properness, decency, goodness, honourableness, scrupulousness, conscientiousness; reasonableness, sensibleness; disinterest, disinterestedness, neutrality, objectivity, balance, open-mindedness.
OPPOSITES inequity, imbalance.
2 *the builder owns 25% of the equity in the property* **value**, worth, valuation; ownership, rights, proprietorship, right of possession.

equivalence ▶ noun *equivalence of birth and death rates is rare in human populations* **equality**, equalness, sameness, identicalness, identity, interchangeability, indistinguishability, uniformity, agreement; similarity, likeness, resemblance, comparability, correspondence, commensurateness, parallelism, closeness, nearness, affinity; *rare* coequality.

equivalent ▶ adjective *a sound quality* **equivalent** *to that of CDs | you must have a degree or equivalent qualification* **equal**, identical; similar, parallel, analogous, comparable, corresponding, correspondent, interchangeable; like, commensurate with, the same as, synonymous with, much the same as; amounting, tantamount, approximate, near, close; of a kind, of a piece; *rare* coequal.
OPPOSITES different; dissimilar.
▶ noun *the campaign was backed by Denmark's equivalent of the Daily Mirror* **counterpart**, parallel, alternative, match, complement, analogue, double, twin, opposite number; equal, peer, rival; answer; *rare* coequal.

equivocal ▶ adjective *an equivocal statement* **ambiguous**, indefinite, non-committal, vague, indeterminate, imprecise, inexact, indistinct, inexplicit, blurry, hazy, foggy, nebulous, borderline; obscure, unclear, cryptic, enigmatic, puzzling, perplexing, gnomic, Delphic; ambivalent, uncertain, unsure, indecisive, inconclusive, doubtful; roundabout, oblique, circumlocutory, circuitous, periphrastic; misleading, evasive, elusive, duplicitous, equivocating, prevaricating; contradictory, confusing, two-edged, double-edged, paradoxical, confused, muddled.
OPPOSITES unequivocal; definite.

equivocate ▶ verb *the government have equivocated too often in the past* **prevaricate**, be evasive, be non-committal, be vague, be ambiguous, evade/dodge the issue, beat about the bush, hedge, hedge one's bets, fudge the issue; fence, parry questions; vacillate, shilly-shally, cavil, waver, quibble; temporize, hesitate, stall (for time), shuffle about; *Brit.* hum and haw; *informal* pussyfoot around, waffle, flannel, sit on the fence, duck the issue/question; *archaic* palter; *rare* tergiversate.

equivocation ▶ noun *these attacks must be condemned without equivocation* **prevarication**, vagueness, qualification, ambiguity, uncertainty, ambivalence, indecision, doubt; beating about the bush, evasion, dodging, hedging, fudging, doublespeak; fencing, parrying; vacillation, shilly-shallying, cavilling, wavering, quibbling, quibble; temporizing, hesitation, stalling (for time), shuffling; *Brit.* humming and hawing; *informal* pussyfooting (around), waffle, waffling, flannel, weasel words; *archaic* paltering; *rare* tergiversation.
OPPOSITE directness.

era *See centre pages for list of* **Geological Ages**
▶ noun *the Stalinist era* **epoch**, age, period, time, aeon, span; generation; stage, point in history, date; times, days, years.

eradicate ▶ verb *make sure that the lice have all been eradicated* **get rid of**, eliminate, do away with, remove, suppress; **exterminate**, destroy, annihilate, extirpate, obliterate, kill, wipe out, liquidate, decimate, finish off; abolish, stamp out, extinguish, quash, wipe off the face of the earth, wipe off the map; erase, efface, excise, expunge; root out, uproot, weed out; *informal* zap; *rare* deracinate.

eradication ▶ noun *the eradication of smallpox* **elimination**, removal, suppression; **extermination**, destruction, annihilation, extirpation, obliteration, killing, liquidation, decimation, wiping out, extinction; abolition, extinguishing, quashing; erasure, effacement, excision, expunction, expunging, blotting out, rubbing out; *rare* deracination.

erasable ▶ adjective *erasable ink* **removable**, eradicable, washable, deletable, non-permanent.
OPPOSITE permanent.

erase ▶ verb **1** *they erased his name from all street signs and monuments* **delete**, rub out, wipe out/off; cross out, strike out, score out, blot out, blank out, scratch out, scrape off, cancel, put a line through; efface, expunge, excise, remove, obliterate, eliminate, remove all traces of; censor, blue-pencil, bowdlerize; *technical* dele.
2 *the old national differences in styles of play are being gradually erased by the globalization of football* **destroy**, wipe out, obliterate, eradicate, abolish, stamp out, quash, do away with, get rid of, remove, dissolve.

erasure ▶ noun *the erasure of files from the hard disk* **deletion**, rubbing out, wiping out/off; crossing out, striking out, scoring out, blotting out, blanking out, scratching out, cancelling, cancellation; effacement, expunction, expunging, excision, removal, obliteration, elimination; censorship, censoring, bowdlerization; *rare* erasement.

erect ▶ adjective **1** *she held her body erect* **upright**, bolt upright, straight, vertical, perpendicular, plumb, standing up; *Heraldry* rampant.
OPPOSITES bent; flaccid.
2 *an erect penis* **engorged**, enlarged, swollen, tumescent; hard, rigid, stiff, firm.
OPPOSITE limp.
3 *the hairs stood erect around his neck* **bristling**, standing up (on end), upright.
OPPOSITE flat.
▶ verb **1** *the bridge was erected as a temporary measure* **build**, construct, put up; assemble, put together, fabricate, form, manufacture.
OPPOSITE demolish.
2 *it took three minutes to erect the inner tent* **assemble**, put up, set up, set upright, fit together, put together, piece together; pitch, position, fix in position, place, locate.
OPPOSITE dismantle.
3 *someone had erected a red flag* **put up**, raise, elevate, mount.
OPPOSITE lower.
4 *the party that erected the welfare state* **establish**, form, set up, found, institute, initiate, formulate, devise, create, organize, frame.
OPPOSITE break up.

erection ▶ noun **1** *the erection of a house* **construction**, building, putting up; assembly, putting together, fitting together, fabrication, forming,

E

manufacture, production; raising, elevation.
OPPOSITE demolition.
2 *the cafe was a bleak concrete erection* **building**, structure, edifice, construction, pile.
3 *men who cannot get an erection* **phallus**, erect penis; **tumescence**, tumidity, turgescence, hardness, rigidity, stiffness, firmness; *vulgar slang* hard-on, stiffy, boner, ramrod; *Brit. vulgar slang* horn.

eremite ▶ noun **hermit**, recluse, solitary, ascetic, coenobite; *historical* anchorite, anchoress, stylite; *rare* solitudinarian.

ergo ▶ adverb (Latin) *I'm a writer, ergo I write* **therefore**, consequently, so, as a result, as a consequence, hence, thus, accordingly, for that reason, this/that being so, this/that being the case, on this/that account; *formal* whence, wherefore, thence.

E

erode ▶ verb *the soil has been eroded by the rainwater | a world whose moral base has been eroded* **wear away/down**, abrade, scrape away, grind down, crumble, dissolve, weather; eat (away at), gnaw (away at), chip away at, corrode, consume, devour; waste away, rot, decay; undermine, weaken, sap, disintegrate, deteriorate, destroy, spoil.

erosion ▶ noun *the erosion of the cliffs | the erosion of democratic freedoms* **wearing away**, abrasion, scraping away, grinding down, crumbling, wear and tear, weathering, dissolving, dissolution; eating away, gnawing away, chipping away, corrosion, corroding, attrition; wasting away, rotting, decay; undermining, weakening, sapping, deterioration, disintegration, destruction, spoiling; *rare* detrition.

erotic ▶ adjective *erotic literature* **sexually arousing**, sexually exciting, sexually stimulating; **titillating**, salacious, prurient, lubricious, suggestive; pornographic, sexually explicit, lewd, smutty, hard-core, soft-core, dirty, off colour, indecent, improper, filthy, vulgar, crude; libidinous, lustful, lascivious, lecherous, licentious; sexual, sexy, sensual, carnal, venereal, amatory; seductive, alluring, tantalizing, desirable, aphrodisiac; racy, risqué, ribald, naughty, bawdy, earthy, spicy, Rabelaisian; erogenous, erotogenic; *informal* blue, X-rated, steamy, raunchy, randy, horny; *euphemistic* adult; *formal* concupiscent; *rare* venereous, anacreontic.

err ▶ verb **1** *the Court of Appeal ruled that the judge had erred in not allowing new evidence* **make a mistake**, **be wrong**, be in error, be mistaken, mistake, make a blunder, blunder, be incorrect, be inaccurate, misjudge, miscalculate, get things/something/it wrong, bark up the wrong tree, get the wrong end of the stick, be wide of the mark; *informal* slip up, screw up, blow it, foul up, goof, boob, fluff something, make a hash of something, put one's foot in it, make a boo-boo, make a bloomer, drop a brick; *vulgar slang* fuck something up, bugger something up.
OPPOSITE be right.
2 *she struck their fingers with a ruler when they erred* **misbehave**, **do wrong**, go wrong, behave badly, misconduct oneself, be bad, be naughty, get up to mischief, get up to no good, act up, act badly, give someone trouble, cause someone trouble; sin, go astray, transgress, trespass, fall from grace, lapse, degenerate; clown about/around, fool about/around, act the clown, act the fool, act the goat, act foolishly, forget oneself; *informal* mess about/around; *Brit. informal* muck about/around, play up.

errand ▶ noun *he ran errands for local shopkeepers* **task**, job, chore, assignment; collection, delivery, shopping; trip, run, journey; mission, expedition; operation, undertaking, commission, business; *Scottish* message.

errant ▶ adjective **1** *financial penalties were imposed on errant local authorities* **offending**, guilty, culpable, misbehaving, delinquent, lawless, lawbreaking, criminal, transgressing, aberrant, deviant, erring, sinning; mischievous, badly behaved, troublesome, difficult, unmanageable, unruly, disobedient, uncontrollable, out of control.
OPPOSITES innocent; well behaved.
2 (archaic) *a knight errant* **travelling**, wandering, itinerant, journeying, rambling, roaming, roving, drifting, floating, wayfaring, voyaging, touring; peripatetic, unsettled, rootless, restless, on the move, on the go, on the wing; nomadic, vagabond, vagrant, migrant, migratory, migrating, transient, displaced; globetrotting, jet-setting.
OPPOSITE sedentary.

erratic ▶ adjective *can you explain his swings of mood, his erratic behaviour?* **unpredictable**, inconsistent, changeable, variable, inconstant, uncertain, irregular, unstable, turbulent, unsteady, unsettled, unreliable, undependable, changing, ever-changing, volatile, varying, shifting, fluctuating, fluid, mutable, protean, fitful, wavering, full of ups and downs; mercurial, capricious, whimsical, fickle, flighty, giddy, impulsive, wayward, temperamental, highly strung, excitable, moody; *informal* blowing hot and cold; *technical* labile; *rare* fluctuant, changeful.
OPPOSITES predictable; consistent.

erring ▶ adjective *the court case resulted in a heavy fine for the erring skipper* **offending**, guilty, culpable, misbehaving, delinquent, lawless, lawbreaking, criminal, transgressing, aberrant, deviant, errant, sinning.
OPPOSITES innocent, well behaved.

erroneous ▶ adjective *the report was based on an erroneous assumption* **wrong**, incorrect, mistaken, in error, inaccurate, not accurate, inexact, not exact, imprecise, invalid, untrue, false, fallacious, wide of the mark, off target; misleading, illogical, unsound, specious, unfounded, without foundation, faulty, flawed, spurious; *informal* off beam, bogus, phoney, out, way out, full of holes, dicey, iffy; *Brit. informal* dodgy; *archaic* abroad.
OPPOSITES right; correct.

error ▶ noun *the common error of calling schizophrenia a split personality* **mistake**, fallacy, misconception, delusion; inaccuracy, miscalculation, misreckoning; blunder, fault, flaw, oversight; misprint, literal, erratum, misinterpretation, misreading; *informal* slip-up, bloomer, boob, boo-boo, howler, boner.

□ **in error** *£86 million of tax was collected in error* **wrongly**, by mistake, mistakenly, incorrectly, inappropriately, misguidedly; **accidentally**, by accident, inadvertently, unintentionally, unwittingly, unknowingly, unconsciously, by chance.
OPPOSITES correctly; intentionally.

ersatz ▶ adjective *ersatz coffee* **artificial**, substitute, imitation, synthetic, fake, false, faux, mock, simulated; pseudo, sham, bogus, spurious, counterfeit, forged, pretended, so-called, plastic; manufactured, man-made, unnatural, fabricated; replica, reproduction, facsimile; **inferior**, low-quality, poor-quality, low-grade, shoddy, substandard, unsatisfactory, adulterated; *informal* phoney.
OPPOSITE genuine.

erstwhile ▶ adjective *written in memory of the composer's erstwhile teacher* **former**, old, past, one-time, sometime, ex-, late, then; previous, prior, foregoing; *formal* quondam; *archaic* whilom.
OPPOSITES present; future.

erudite ▶ adjective *he was so erudite that only men who were his equals in scholarship could understand him | erudite editions of minor classical writers* **learned**, scholarly, well educated, knowledgeable, well read, widely read, well versed, well informed, lettered, cultured, cultivated, civilized, intellectual; intelligent, clever, academic, literary, bookish, highbrow, studious, sage, wise, sagacious, discerning, donnish, cerebral, enlightened, illuminated, sophisticated, pedantic; esoteric, obscure, recondite; *informal* brainy; *rare* sapient.
OPPOSITES ignorant; ill-educated.

erudition ▶ noun *a man of immense talent and massive erudition* **learning**, scholarship, knowledge, education, culture, intellect, academic attainment, attainments, acquirements, enlightenment, illumination, edification, book learning, insight, information, understanding, sageness, wisdom, sophistication, training; letters.
OPPOSITE ignorance.

erupt ▶ verb **1** *the volcano erupted* **emit lava**, belch lava, become active, flare up, eject/vent material, explode.
OPPOSITE lie dormant.
2 *lava was erupted close to the summit* **emit**, discharge, eject, expel, spew out, belch (out), pour (out), disgorge, give off/out; gush, spout, spurt, stream, flow, issue.
3 *fighting erupted in the streets* **break out**, flare up, blow up, boil over, start suddenly; ensue, arise, happen.
OPPOSITE die down.
4 *a boil had erupted on her temple* **appear**, break out, flare up, come to a head, burst forth, make an appearance, pop up, emerge, become visible.
OPPOSITE heal.

eruption ▶ noun **1** *a volcanic eruption* **discharge**, venting, ejection, emission, explosion.
2 *a sudden eruption of street violence* **outbreak**, flare-up, upsurge, outburst, epidemic, breakout, sudden appearance, start, rash, wave, spate, flood, explosion, burst, blaze, flurry; *rare* recrudescence, ebullition, boutade.
3 *a skin eruption* **rash**, outbreak, inflammation.

escalate ▶ verb **1** *in three years' time prices will have escalated* **increase rapidly**, soar, rocket, shoot up, mount, surge, spiral, grow rapidly, rise rapidly, climb, go up; *informal* be jacked up, go through the ceiling, go through the roof, skyrocket, balloon.
OPPOSITE plunge.
2 *the dispute escalated into a sit-in* **grow**, develop, mushroom, increase, be increased, be stepped up, build up, heighten, strengthen, intensify, accelerate, be extended, be enlarged, be magnified, be amplified.
OPPOSITE shrink.

escalation ▶ noun **1** *an escalation in oil prices* **rapid increase**, rise, hike, advance, growth, leap, upsurge, upturn, upswing, climb, jump, spiralling.
OPPOSITE plunge.
2 *a drastic escalation of the conflict* **intensification**, aggravation, exacerbation, compounding, increase, enlargement, magnification, mushrooming, amplification, augmentation; expansion, stepping-up, build-up, buildout, heightening, widening, worsening; deterioration.
OPPOSITE relaxation.

escapade ▶ noun *he is a paragliding fanatic famous for his flying escapades* **exploit**, stunt, caper, skylarking, mischief, romp, antic(s), fling, spree, prank, jape, game, trick; adventure, venture, mission; deed, feat, trial, experience, incident, occurrence, event, happening, episode, affair;

informal lark, scrape, fooling around, shenanigans; *rare* frolic.

escape ▶ **verb 1** *he had escaped from prison* **get away**, get out, run away, run off, break out, break free, get free, break loose, make a break for it, bolt, clear out, flee, fly, take flight, make off, take off, decamp, abscond, take to one's heels, make a/one's escape, make good one's escape, make a/one's getaway, beat a (hasty) retreat, show a clean pair of heels, run for it, make a run for it; disappear, vanish, slip away, steal away, sneak away; get out of someone's clutches; *informal* bust, do a bunk, do a moonlight flit, cut and run, skedaddle, skip, head for the hills, do a disappearing/vanishing act, fly the coop, take French leave, scarper, vamoose, hightail it, leg it; *Brit. informal* do a runner, hook it; *N. Amer. informal* take a powder, go on the lam.
OPPOSITES be captured; be imprisoned.
2 *he escaped his pursuers* **get away from**, escape from, elude, avoid, dodge, leave behind, shake off, fend off, keep at arm's length, keep out of someone's way, steer clear of, give someone a wide berth; *informal* give someone the slip; *archaic* bilk.
OPPOSITE be caught by.
3 *all three drivers escaped injury | I came in here to escape the washing-up* **avoid**, evade, dodge, elude, miss, cheat, trick, sidestep, circumvent, skirt, keep out of the way of, bypass, shun, steer clear of, shirk; *informal* duck.
OPPOSITE suffer.
4 *a lethal gas escaped from a pesticide factory* **leak (out)**, spill (out), seep (out), ooze (out), exude, discharge, emanate, issue, flow (out), pour (out), gush (out), drip, drain, bleed; stream, spurt, spout, squirt, spew, jet.
▶ **noun 1** *he had been at large since his escape from prison* **getaway**, breakout, bolt for freedom, running away, flight, bolting, absconding, decamping, fleeing, flit; disappearance, vanishing act; *informal, dated* springing.
OPPOSITES capture; imprisonment.
2 *a narrow escape from death* **avoidance of**, evasion of, dodging of, eluding of, circumvention of; *informal* ducking of; *rare* elusion of.
3 *a gas escape* **leak**, leakage, spill, seepage, drip, dribble, discharge, emanation, issue, flow, outflow, outpouring, gush; stream, spurt, spout, squirt, jet; *technical* efflux.
4 *boarding school seemed to me an escape from boredom* **distraction**, diversion, interruption.

escapee ▶ **noun runaway**, escaper, jailbreaker, fugitive, absconder, truant, deserter, defector; refugee, displaced person, DP, asylum seeker; *archaic* runagate.

escapism ▶ **noun** *musicals always do well in a recession because people want escapism* **fantasy**, fantasizing, dreaming, daydreaming, daydreams, reverie, romance, illusion(s), fancy, imagination, flight(s) of fancy, pipe dreams, castles in the air, castles in Spain, wishful thinking, wool-gathering; *informal* pie in the sky.
OPPOSITE realism.

eschew ▶ **verb** *he firmly eschewed political involvement* **abstain from**, refrain from, give up, forgo, forswear, shun, renounce, swear off, abjure, steer clear of, have nothing to do with, give a wide berth to, fight shy of, relinquish, reject, dispense with, disavow, abandon, deny, gainsay, disclaim, repudiate, renege on, spurn, abnegate, abdicate, wash one's hands of, drop; *informal* kick, jack in, pack in; *Law* disaffirm; *archaic* forsake.
OPPOSITE indulge in.

escort ▶ **noun** (stress on the first syllable) **1** *they were given a police escort* **guard**, bodyguard, protector, safeguard, defender, minder, custodian; attendant, guide, chaperone, retainer, aide, assistant, personal assistant, right-hand man, right-hand woman, lady in waiting, 'aunt', duenna, equerry, squire; entourage, retinue, suite, train, cortège, attendant company, caravan; protection, defence, convoy.
2 *she didn't like going to clubs by herself and Graham was a great escort* **companion**, partner, beau, attendant; *informal* date.
3 *we offer a wide selection of young, good-looking, fun escorts* **paid companion**, hostess; male escort, gigolo; (*in Japan*) geisha (girl); (*in China*) sing-song girl; *archaic* courtesan.
▶ **verb** (stress on the second syllable) **1** *Father Barnes was escorted home by police officers* **conduct**, accompany, guide, convoy, lead, usher, shepherd, take, direct, steer; guard, protect, safeguard, defend.
2 *he escorted her in to dinner* **accompany**, partner, take, bring, come with, go with, take out, go out with.

esoteric ▶ **adjective** *the question is dominated by esoteric debate* **abstruse**, obscure, arcane, recherché, rarefied, recondite, abstract, difficult, hard, puzzling, perplexing, enigmatic, inscrutable, cryptic, Delphic; complex, complicated, involved, over/above one's head, incomprehensible, opaque, unfathomable, impenetrable, mysterious, occult, little known, hidden, secret, private, mystic, magical, cabbalistic; *rare* involuted.
OPPOSITES simple; familiar.

> **CHOOSE THE RIGHT WORD**
>
> **esoteric, obscure, abstruse, recondite, arcane**
>
> *See* **OBSCURE**.

especial ▶ **adjective 1** *especial care is required* **exceptional**, particular, special, extra special, extraordinary, outstanding, superior, unusual, marked, singular, signal; out of the ordinary, uncommon, rare, unwonted, notable, noteworthy, surprising, remarkable, striking, unique.
OPPOSITE standard.
2 *her own especial brand of charm* **distinctive**, individual, special, particular, distinct, peculiar, personal, own, unique, singular, exclusive, specific, private.
OPPOSITES common, general.

especially ▶ **adverb 1** *work continued to pour in, especially from South Africa* **mainly**, mostly, chiefly, principally, for the most part, in the main, on the whole, largely, by and large, to a large extent, to a great degree, predominantly, above all, first and foremost, basically, substantially, overall, in general, particularly, in particular, primarily, generally, usually, typically, commonly, as a rule.
2 *a committee formed especially for the purpose* **expressly**, specially, specifically, exclusively, just, particularly, uniquely, precisely, explicitly, purposefully, on purpose; with someone/something in mind.
3 *especially talented* **exceptionally**, particularly, specially, very, extremely, singularly, peculiarly, distinctly, unusually, extraordinarily, extra, uncommonly, uniquely, remarkably, strikingly, outstandingly, amazingly, incredibly, awfully, terribly, really, unwontedly, notably, markedly, decidedly, surprisingly, conspicuously, signally; *N. English* powerful, right; *informal* seriously, majorly, mucho; *Brit. informal* jolly, dead, well; *informal, dated* devilish, frightfully.

espionage ▶ **noun** *the shadowy world of espionage* **spying**, undercover work, cloak-and-dagger activities, surveillance, reconnaissance, intelligence, eavesdropping, infiltration, counter espionage, counter-intelligence; (*in Japan*) ninjutsu; *informal* bugging, wiretapping, recon.

espousal ▶ **noun** *they began to retreat from their espousal of populist causes* **adoption**, embracing, taking up, taking to, taking to one's heart, enthusiastic/wholehearted reception, acceptance, welcome; **support**, backing, championship, help, assistance, aid, siding with, favouring, preferring, abetting, aiding and abetting, encouragement; defence; sponsorship, vouching for, promotion, furtherance, endorsement, advocacy, sanctioning, approval.
OPPOSITES rejection; opposition.

espouse ▶ **verb** *the government espoused the concept of sustainable economic development* **adopt**, embrace, take up, take to, take to one's heart, receive enthusiastically/wholeheartedly, accept, welcome; **support**, back, champion, give help to, help, assist, aid, be on the side of, side with, be in favour of, favour, prefer, abet, aid and abet, encourage; vote for, ally oneself with, stand behind, fall in with, stand up for, defend, take someone's part, take up the cudgels for; sponsor, vouch for, promote, further, endorse, advocate, sanction, approve of, give one's blessing to, smile on; *informal* stick up for, throw one's weight behind.
OPPOSITES reject; oppose.

espy ▶ **verb** (*literary*) *he espied a niche up in the rocks* **catch sight of**, glimpse, catch/get a glimpse of, see, spot, spy, notice, observe, make out, discern, perceive, pick out, sight, detect, have sight of; *informal* clap/lay/set eyes on; *literary* behold, descry.
OPPOSITE lose sight of.

essay ▶ **noun** (stress on the first syllable) **1** *he wrote an essay on overpopulation* **article**, piece of writing, composition, study, paper, dissertation, assignment, thesis, discourse, treatise, text, tract, disquisition, monograph; leader, commentary, critique, criticism, exposition, appraisal, assessment, discussion, *N. Amer.* theme; *informal* piece.
2 (*formal*) *the device was Alexander Graham Bell's first essay in telecommunications* **attempt**, effort, endeavour, try, venture, trial, experiment, undertaking; *informal* crack, go, shot, stab, bash, whack.
▶ **verb** (stress on the second syllable) (*formal*) *many essayed to travel that way* **attempt**, make an attempt at, try, strive, aim, venture, endeavour, seek, set out, do one's best, do all one can, do one's utmost, make an effort, make every effort, spare no effort, give one's all, take it on oneself; have a go at, undertake, embark on, try one's hand at, try out, take on; *informal* give it a whirl, give it one's best shot, go all out, pull out all the stops, bend over backwards, knock oneself out, bust a gut, break one's neck, move heaven and earth, have a crack at, have a shot at, have a stab at.

essence ▶ **noun 1** *uncertainty is part of the very essence of economic activity* **quintessence**, soul, spirit, ethos, nature, life, lifeblood, core, heart, centre, crux, nub, nucleus, kernel, marrow, meat, pith, gist, substance, principle, central part, fundamental quality, basic quality, essential part, intrinsic nature, sum and substance, reality, actuality; *Philosophy* quiddity, esse; *informal* nitty-gritty.
2 *essence of ginger* **extract**, concentrate, concentration, quintessence, distillate, elixir, abstraction, decoction, juice, tincture, solution, suspension, dilution; scent, perfume.
□ **in essence** *for them society was in essence a collection of discrete individuals* **basically**, fundamentally, elementally, essentially, at bottom, at heart, primarily, principally, chiefly, firstly, predominantly, substantially, in substance, materially; above all, first of all, most of all, first and foremost; effectively, in effect, virtually, to all intents and purposes, intrinsically, inherently; *French* au fond; *informal* at the end of the day,

when all is said and done, when you get right down to it.

□ **of the essence** *approval can take months when speed is not of the essence* **vital**, essential, indispensable, crucial, key, necessary, needed, required, called for, requisite, important, all-important, vitally important, of the utmost importance, of great consequence, critical, life-and-death, imperative, mandatory, compulsory, obligatory, urgent, pressing, burning, compelling, acute, paramount, pre-eminent, high-priority, significant, consequential.
OPPOSITE inessential.

essential ▶ adjective **1** *it is essential to remove all the old plaster* **crucial**, necessary, key, vital, indispensable, needed, required, called for, requisite, important, all-important, vitally important, of the utmost importance, of great consequence, of the essence, critical, life-and-death, imperative, mandatory, compulsory, obligatory, compelling, urgent, pressing, burning, acute, paramount, pre-eminent, high-priority, significant, consequential.
OPPOSITES inessential, unimportant, optional.
2 *the essential simplicity of his style* **basic**, inherent, fundamental, quintessential, intrinsic, underlying, characteristic, innate, rudimentary, primary, principal, cardinal, chief, elementary, elemental; central, pivotal, critical, key, focal, salient, staple, vital, necessary, indispensable, foundational, ingrained.
OPPOSITE secondary.
3 *he is the essential English gentleman* **ideal**, absolute, complete, perfect, quintessential.
▶ noun **1** *the gift of the gab was an essential for an up-and-coming broadcaster* **necessity**, necessary/essential item, prerequisite, requisite, requirement, need; condition, precondition, specification, stipulation; qualification; *Latin* desideratum, sine qua non; *informal* must.
OPPOSITE inessential.
2 (**essentials**) *they were taught the essentials of the job in three days* **fundamentals**, basics, rudiments, principles, first principles, foundations, preliminaries, groundwork; essence, basis, core, kernel, nub, marrow, meat, crux, bedrock; facts, hard facts, practicalities, realities; *Latin* sine qua non; *informal* nitty-gritty, brass tacks, nuts and bolts, ABC.
OPPOSITE minutiae.

> **CHOOSE THE RIGHT WORD**
>
> **essential, necessary, requisite, indispensable**
> *See* NECESSARY.
>
> **essential, inherent, intrinsic, innate**
> *See* INHERENT.

establish ▶ verb **1** *the company is hoping to establish an office in Moscow* **set up**, start, begin, get going, initiate, institute, form, found, create, bring into being, inaugurate, organize, lay the foundations of, build, construct, install, plant.
OPPOSITES disband; demolish.
2 *there was sufficient evidence to establish his guilt* **prove**, demonstrate, show, show to be true, show beyond doubt, indicate, signify, signal, display, exhibit, manifest, denote, attest to, evidence, determine, validate, confirm, verify, certify, ratify, corroborate, substantiate, evince, bespeak, constitute evidence of, constitute proof of.
OPPOSITE disprove.

established ▶ adjective **1** *this approach flies in the face of established practice* **accepted**, traditional, orthodox, habitual, confirmed, entrenched, set, fixed, official, settled, dyed-in-the-wool, inveterate; **usual**, customary, common, normal, general, prevailing, accustomed, familiar, wonted, popular, expected, routine, regular, typical, conventional, mainstream, standard, stock.
OPPOSITE unfamiliar.
2 *he is an established composer of international repute* **well known**, recognized, acclaimed, esteemed, acknowledged; respected, respectable, famous, prominent, noted, renowned.
OPPOSITE unknown.

establishment ▶ noun **1** *the establishment of a democratic constitution* **setting up**, start, getting going, initiation, institution, formation, founding, foundation, inception, creation, inauguration, organization, building, construction, installation.
OPPOSITES disbandment; demolition.
2 *her house was turned into a dressmaking establishment* **business**, place of business, premises, firm, company, concern, enterprise, venture, organization, operation, undertaking, industry; factory, plant, house, shop, store, emporium, office, bureau, agency, franchise, practice, partnership, consortium, cooperative, corporation, conglomerate, group, combine, syndicate; *informal* outfit, set-up.
3 *graduates of higher educational establishments* **institution**, place, premises, foundation, institute.
4 (**the Establishment**) *an irreverent comedy series that dared to poke fun at the Establishment* **the powers that be**, the authorities, the system, the ruling class, the regime, bureaucracy, officialdom; the status quo, the prevailing political/social order; *informal* Big Brother; *archaic* the regimen.

estate ▶ noun **1** *she had a house on the Balmoral estate* **property**, grounds, garden(s), park, parkland, land(s), piece of land, tract, landholding, manor, domain, territory; *archaic* demesne.
2 *a housing estate* **area**, site, development, complex, piece of land, land, region, tract.
3 *a large coffee estate* **plantation**, farm, holding; forest, vineyard; *N. Amer.* ranch; (*in Spanish-speaking countries*) hacienda; (*in the W. Indies*) pen; (*in E. Africa*) shamba; (*in the Indian subcontinent*) tope.
4 *he left an estate worth £610,000* **assets**, capital, wealth, riches, holdings, fortune, property, worth, resources, effects, possessions, belongings, things, goods, worldly goods, stuff, chattels, valuables; legacy, bequest; *Law* personalty, goods and chattels; *informal* gear; *S. African informal* trek.
5 (*archaic*) *attention is directed to all estates of society* **class**, social group, socio-economic group, political group, level, order, social order, social division, stratum, grade, grading, rank, station, echelon, degree; standing, status, position, caste; *archaic* sphere.
6 (*archaic*) *the estate of matrimony* **state**, condition, situation, position, circumstance, lot, fate.

estate agent ▶ noun **property agent**; *Brit.* house agent; *N. Amer.* realtor, real estate agent.

estate car ▶ noun (*Brit.*) *N. Amer.* station wagon; *Brit. informal* estate; *N. Amer. informal* wagon; *Brit. dated* shooting brake, traveller.
OPPOSITES saloon; hatchback.

esteem ▶ noun *she was held in high esteem by colleagues* **respect**, **admiration**, (high) regard, (high/good) opinion, estimation, acclaim, approbation, approval, appreciation, favour, popularity, recognition, veneration, awe, reverence, deference, honour, praise, adulation, extolment, homage; *rare* laudation.
OPPOSITE disrespect.
▶ verb **1** *contemporary Japanese ceramics are highly esteemed* **respect**, **admire**, value, regard, hold in (high) regard, think (highly) of, acclaim, approve of, appreciate, like, prize, treasure, favour, recognize, venerate, hold in awe, look up to, revere, reverence, honour, praise, adulate, extol, pay homage to.
OPPOSITE disparage.
2 (*formal*) *I would esteem it a favour if you could speak to him* **consider**, regard as, deem, hold to be, think, think of as, reckon, count, account, believe, judge, adjudge, rate, class as, gauge, look on as, view as, see as, interpret as.

estimate ▶ verb **1** *the first thing to do is to estimate the cost* **roughly calculate**, approximate, make an estimate of, guess, evaluate, judge, gauge, reckon, rate, appraise, form an opinion of, form an impression of, get the measure of, determine, weigh up; *informal* size up, guesstimate.
2 *we **estimate** the carpet **to be** worth about £50,000* **consider**, believe, guess, reckon, deem, hold, judge, adjudge, surmise, rate, gauge, take, suppose; regard as being, view as being, see as being, class as being, think of as being, look on as being; be of the opinion, conjecture; *formal* opine.
▶ noun **1** *an estimate of the repair cost* **rough calculation**, approximation, estimation, educated/informed guess, rough guess; approximate price/cost/value, estimated price/cost/value; costing, quotation, pricing, valuation, evaluation, assessment, appraisal; *informal* guesstimate.
2 *his estimate of Paul's integrity dropped a few notches* **evaluation**, estimation, judgement, gauging, rating, appraisal, opinion, view, analysis.

estimation ▶ noun **1** *the Treasury first makes an estimation of economic growth* **estimate**, rough calculation, approximation, educated/informed guess, rough guess, evaluation, assessment, appraisal; *informal* guesstimate.
2 *his hard bargaining raised him even higher in Chapman's estimation* **assessment**, evaluation, judgement, gauging, rating, appraisal, esteem, opinion, view, analysis.

estrange ▶ verb *she realized that she had estranged her favourite uncle* **alienate**, antagonize, disaffect, make hostile/unfriendly, destroy the affections of, turn away, drive away, distance, put at a distance; sever connections between, set against, set at variance, set at odds with, make hostile to, drive a wedge between, cause antagonism between, sow dissension between.
OPPOSITES attract, unite.

estrangement ▶ noun *there had been a definite estrangement between her and her daughter-in-law* **alienation**, turning away, antagonism, antipathy, disaffection, hostility, unfriendliness, embitteredness, isolation, variance, difference; parting, separation, division, divorce, disunity, distance, break-up, split, breach, severance, schism.
OPPOSITES unity; reconciliation.

estuary ▶ noun **(river) mouth**, firth; delta; *archaic* embouchure, debouchure, debouchment, discharge, disemboguement; *Scottish archaic* beal, inver, water mouth.

et cetera, **etcetera** ▶ adverb *you need wellingtons, raincoats, umbrella, et cetera* **and so on**, and so forth, and so on and so forth, and the rest, and/

or the like, and/or suchlike, and/or more of the same, and/or similar things, et cetera et cetera, and others, among others, et al., etc.; *informal* and what have you, and whatnot.

etch ▶ verb **1** *the metal is etched with a dilute acid* **corrode**, bite into, eat into/away, burn into.
2 *a Pictish stone etched with mysterious designs* **engrave**, carve, inscribe, cut (in), incise, chisel, chase, score, notch, imprint, impress, stamp, print, mark.

etching ▶ noun *the gallery contains drawings, etchings, and watercolours* **engraving**, print, impression, block, plate, dry point, cut, woodcut, linocut, vignette.

eternal ▶ adjective **1** *the hope of eternal happiness* **everlasting**, never-ending, endless, without end, perpetual, undying, immortal, deathless, indestructible, imperishable, immutable, abiding, permanent, enduring, infinite, boundless, timeless; *rare* sempiternal, perdurable.
OPPOSITE transient.
2 *the price of freedom is eternal vigilance* **constant**, continual, continuous, perpetual, persistent, sustained, unremitting, relentless, unrelenting, unrelieved, uninterrupted, unbroken, unabating, interminable, never-ending, non-stop, round-the-clock, incessant, endless, ceaseless.
OPPOSITE intermittent.

eternally ▶ adverb **1** *I shall be eternally grateful* **forever**, permanently, for always, for good, for good and all, perpetually, (for) evermore, for ever and ever, for all (future) time, until/to the end of time, world without end, endlessly, timelessly, for eternity, in perpetuity, everlastingly, enduringly; *Scottish* aye; *N. Amer.* forevermore; *informal* for keeps, until hell freezes over, until doomsday, until the cows come home; *archaic* for aye; *rare* immortally, deathlessly, imperishably, abidingly, sempiternally, perdurably.
OPPOSITE temporarily.
2 *he was eternally squabbling with the referee* **constantly**, continually, continuously, always, all the time, the entire time, persistently, repeatedly, regularly; round-the-clock, without a break, night and day, day and night, {morning, noon, and night}; endlessly, non-stop, incessantly, unceasingly, ceaselessly, perpetually, perennially, forever; interminably, unremittingly, relentlessly, unrelentingly; *informal* 24-7.
OPPOSITE never.

eternity ▶ noun **1** *his reply will ring in my ears for eternity* **ever**, all time, perpetuity.
2 *eventually we shall all be in eternity* **the afterlife**, everlasting life, life after death, the life to come, the life hereafter, the hereafter, the world hereafter, the afterworld, the next world, the beyond; heaven, paradise, nirvana, immortality.
OPPOSITES limbo; hell.
3 (*informal*) *I waited* ***an eternity*** *for a bus* **a long time**, an age, ages (and ages), a time, a lifetime; hours, days, months, years, aeons, hours/days/months on end, a month of Sundays, the duration; (seemingly) forever; *Brit. informal* yonks, donkey's years.
OPPOSITE instant.

ethereal ▶ adjective **1** *melodic phrases of ethereal beauty* **delicate**, exquisite, dainty, elegant, graceful, beautiful, lovely; fragile, airy, gossamer, gossamery, light, fine, diaphanous, thin, tenuous, subtle, insubstantial, shadowy.
OPPOSITES tangible, substantial.
2 *theologians may discuss abstract and ethereal ideas* **celestial**, heavenly, spiritual, unearthly, other-worldly, paradisical, Elysian, sublime, divine, holy; *rare* empyrean, superlunary.
OPPOSITE earthly.

ethical ▶ adjective **1** *there is an ethical dilemma to be faced* **moral**; social, behavioural; having to do with right and wrong.
2 *an ethical investment policy* **morally correct**, right-minded, right-thinking, principled, irreproachable, unimpeachable, blameless, guiltless; righteous, upright, upstanding, high-minded, virtuous, good, moral; exemplary, clean, law-abiding, lawful; just, honest, honourable, unbribable, incorruptible; scrupulous, reputable, decent, respectable, noble, lofty, elevated, worthy, trustworthy, meritorious, praiseworthy, commendable, admirable, laudable; pure, pure as the driven snow, whiter than white, sinless, saintly, saintlike, godly, angelic; *Christianity* immaculate, impeccable; *informal* squeaky clean.
OPPOSITE unethical.

ethics ▶ plural noun *the ethics of journalism* **moral code**, morals, morality, moral stand, moral principles, moral values, rights and wrongs, principles, ideals, creed, credo, ethos, rules of conduct, standards (of behaviour), virtues, dictates of conscience.

ethnic ▶ adjective *a wide spectrum of ethnic groups* **racial**, race-related, ethnological, genetic, inherited; cultural, national, tribal, ancestral, traditional, folk; native, indigenous, aboriginal; *rare* autochthonous.

ethos ▶ noun *the governing body has responsibility for the ethos of the school* **spirit**, character, atmosphere, climate, prevailing tendency, mood, feeling, temper, tenor, flavour, essence, quintessence; **animating principle**, dominating characteristic, motivating force, disposition, rationale, code, morality, moral code, attitudes, beliefs, principles, standards, ethics.

etiquette ▶ noun *the club's brochure includes advice on etiquette* **protocol**, polite behaviour, good manners, manners, acceptable behaviour, accepted behaviour, proper behaviour, code of behaviour, rules of conduct/behaviour, decorum, form, good form; courtesy, politeness, civility, propriety, formalities, niceties, punctilios; custom, customary behaviour, convention, conformity, conventionality; *French* politesse; *informal* the thing to do.

etymology ▶ noun **derivation**, word history, development, origin, source.

eulogize ▶ verb *the police eulogized the positive effect of speed cameras* **praise enthusiastically**, go into raptures about/over, wax lyrical about, sing the praises of, praise to the skies, heap praise on, rhapsodize about/over, rave about/over, enthuse about/over, gush about/over, throw bouquets at, express delight over, acclaim, extol; *informal* go wild about, be mad about, go on about; *N. Amer. informal* ballyhoo; *black English* big someone/something up; *dated* cry someone/something up; *rare* laud, panegyrize.
OPPOSITE criticize.

eulogy ▶ noun *his lifelong collaborator delivered a graveside eulogy* **accolade**, speech of praise, panegyric, paean, encomium, tribute, testimonial, compliment, commendation; praise, acclaim, acclamation, raving, homage, plaudits, bouquets; *rare* extolment, laudation, eulogium.
OPPOSITE attack.

euphemism ▶ noun *'professional foul' is just a euphemism for cheating* **polite term**, substitute, mild alternative, indirect term, understatement, underplaying, softening, politeness, genteelism, coy term.
OPPOSITES dysphemism, calling a spade a spade.

euphemistic ▶ adjective *euphemistic expressions for sacking someone, such as 'letting them go'* **polite**, substitute, mild, understated, softened, indirect, neutral, evasive, diplomatic, coded, newspeak, vague, inoffensive, genteel.
OPPOSITE dysphemistic.

euphonious ▶ adjective *the great woodrush's euphonious scientific name, Luzula sylvatica* **pleasant-sounding**, sweet-sounding, mellow, mellifluous, dulcet, sweet, honeyed, lyrical, silvery, silver-toned, golden, bell-like, rhythmical, lilting, pleasant, agreeable, soothing; harmonious, melodious, melodic, tuneful, musical, symphonious; *informal* easy on the ear; *rare* mellifluent, canorous.
OPPOSITE cacophonous.

euphoria ▶ noun *they were swept up in the euphoria of victory* **elation**, happiness, joy, joyousness, delight, glee, excitement, exhilaration, animation, jubilation, exultation; ecstasy, bliss, rapture, rhapsody, rhapsodies, intoxication, transport(s), cloud nine, heaven, paradise, seventh heaven; *informal* the top of the world.
OPPOSITES misery; depression.

euphoric ▶ adjective *the liberators received a euphoric welcome* **elated**, happy, joyful, joyous, delighted, gleeful, excited, exhilarated, animated, jubilant, exultant, ecstatic, blissful, enraptured, rapturous, rhapsodic, in rhapsodies, intoxicated, transported, on cloud nine, in heaven, in paradise, in seventh heaven; *informal* on top of the world, over the moon, on a high.
OPPOSITE miserable.

euthanasia ▶ noun **mercy killing**, assisted suicide, physician-assisted suicide; merciful release, happy release; *rare* quietus.

evacuate ▶ verb **1** *200 residents were evacuated while an unexploded bomb was made safe* **remove**, clear, move out, shift, take away, turn out, expel, evict.
2 *people evacuated the bombed town* **leave**, vacate, abandon, desert, move out of, get out of, exit from, quit, withdraw from, go away from, be gone from, retreat from, retire from, decamp from, disappear from, take oneself off from, flee, depart from, escape from, pull out of; *archaic* forsake.
OPPOSITE return to.
3 *police cordoned off and evacuated the area* **clear**, ask/force people to leave, make people leave, make people get out, empty, depopulate; *rare* unpeople.
4 *patients had difficulty evacuating their bowels* **empty (out)**, void, open, move, purge, drain; defecate.
5 *he suddenly doubled over to evacuate the contents of his stomach* **expel**, eject, discharge, excrete, pass, eliminate, void, empty (out), drain; *rare* egest.
OPPOSITE retain.

evacuation ▶ noun **1** *the evacuation of civilians* **removal**, clearance, shifting, expulsion, eviction, deportation.
2 *the evacuation of military bases* **clearance**, emptying, depopulation; abandonment, quitting, vacation, desertion, leaving, forsaking; departure from, withdrawal from, retreat from, pull-out from, disappearance from, exodus from, flight from; *rare* unpeopling.
3 *terror and stress can cause involuntary evacuation of the bowels* **emptying (out)**, voidance, voiding, opening, purging, drainage; (bowel) movement, defecation, urination, vomiting.

4 *the evacuation of waste products from the body* **expulsion**, ejection, discharge, excretion, passing, elimination, voidance, voiding, emptying (out), purging, emptying, draining; *rare* egestion.
OPPOSITE retention.
5 *dysenteric evacuations frequently contain blood* **bowel movement/motion**, stools, excrement, excreta, faeces, bodily waste, droppings, dung; urine, vomit; *rare* feculence, egesta.

evade ▶ **verb 1** *they split up to evade the border guards* **elude**, avoid, dodge, escape (from), stay away from, steer clear of, run away from, break away from, lose, leave behind, shake, shake off, keep at arm's length, keep out of someone's way, give someone a wide berth, sidestep, keep one's distance from; deceive, trick, cheat; *N. Amer.* end-run; *informal* ditch, give someone the slip; *archaic* bilk.
OPPOSITES confront; run into.
2 *he evaded the question* **avoid**, not give a straight answer to, dodge, sidestep, bypass, hedge, fence, fend off, parry, skirt round, fudge, quibble about, be equivocal about, be evasive about; get out of, find a way round; not pay; *informal* duck, cop out of.
OPPOSITE face.

E

evaluate ▶ **verb** *it is important to evaluate the results of surgery* **assess**, assess the worth of, put a value/price on; judge, gauge, rate, estimate, appraise, form an opinion of, check something out, form an impression of, make up one's mind about, get the measure of, weigh up, analyse; *informal* size up.

evaluation ▶ **noun** *proper evaluation of results is crucial* **assessment**, appraisal, judgement, gauging, rating, estimation, ranking, weighing up, summing up, consideration, assay, analysis, opinion; *informal* sizing up.

evanescent ▶ **adjective 1** *they were operating on an evanescent budget* **vanishing**, fading, evaporating, melting away, disappearing, diminishing, dwindling, shrinking, fugitive; *rare* fugacious.
OPPOSITE unlimited.
2 *this has only an evanescent effect on the rate of inflation* **ephemeral**, fleeting, short-lived, short-term, passing, transitory, transient, fugitive, momentary, temporary, brief, here today and gone tomorrow; *rare* fugacious.
OPPOSITE permanent.

evangelical ▶ **adjective 1** *evangelical Christianity* **scriptural**, biblical, Bible-believing, fundamentalist, orthodox.
2 *an evangelical preacher* **evangelistic**, evangelizing, missionary, crusading, propagandist, propagandizing, converting, proselytizing, televangelical; *informal* Bible-bashing, Bible-thumping, Bible-punching.

evangelist ▶ **noun** *people flocked to hear evangelists preach about Jesus* **preacher**, missionary, gospeller, proselytizer, converter, crusader, propagandist, campaigner, televangelist.

evangelistic ▶ **adjective** *the evangelistic work of Billy Graham* **missionary**, preaching, evangelical, evangelizing, revivalist, crusading, propagandist, campaigning, converting, proselytizing, televangelical.

evangelize ▶ **verb** *some small groups have been evangelized by Protestant missionaries* **convert**, proselytize, bring to God/Christ/Jesus, bring into the fold, redeem, save, make someone change their beliefs/mind, make someone see the light, spread the gospel/faith/word (to), preach (to), seek/make converts (among), act as a missionary; crusade, campaign; win over, recruit; *N. Amer.* proselyte.

evaporate ▶ **verb 1** *most of the water soon evaporated* **vaporize**, become vapour, volatilize.
OPPOSITE condense.
2 *a stream of hot air is used to evaporate the water* **dry up**, vaporize.
OPPOSITE condense.
3 *rock salt is mined, then washed and evaporated before being left to crystallize* **dry out**, remove moisture from, dehydrate, desiccate, dehumidify.
OPPOSITE wet.
4 *the feeling has evaporated* **end**, come to an end, cease to exist/be, pass away, pass, die out, be no more, fizzle out, peter out, wear off; vanish, fade, disappear, melt away, dissolve, disperse; *rare* evanesce.
OPPOSITE materialize.

evasion ▶ **noun 1** *the alleged evasion of immigration control* **avoidance**, dodging, eluding, elusion, sidestepping, bypassing, circumvention, shunning, shirking; getting out of, finding a way round; *informal* ducking, the go-by; *archaic* bilking.
OPPOSITE confrontation.
2 *she grew tired of all the evasion* **prevarication**, evasiveness, beating about the bush, hedging, fencing, shilly-shallying, shuffling, dodging the issue, dodging, sidestepping the issue, sidestepping, pussyfooting, equivocation, vagueness, quibbling, cavilling, temporization, stalling, stalling for time; *Brit.* humming and hawing; *informal* ducking, ducking the issue; *rare* tergiversation.
OPPOSITE directness.

evasive ▶ **adjective 1** *they picked the missile up on the radar and had to take evasive action* **avoiding**, dodging, escaping, eluding, sidestepping.
OPPOSITE direct.
2 *she was undeterred by evasive replies* **prevaricating**, elusive, ambiguous, equivocal, equivocating, indefinite, non-committal, vague, indeterminate, imprecise, inexact, indistinct, inexplicit; cryptic, enigmatic, obscure, unclear, puzzling, perplexing, gnomic, Delphic; roundabout, indirect, oblique, circumlocutory, circuitous, periphrastic; *informal* cagey.
OPPOSITE frank.

eve ▶ **noun 1** *on the eve of the election* **day before**, evening before, night before; period before, the run-up to.
OPPOSITE day after.
2 (*literary*) *a summer eve* **evening**, night, late afternoon, end of day, close of day; twilight, dusk, nightfall, sunset, sundown; *literary* even, eventide, evenfall, gloaming.
OPPOSITE morning.

even ▶ **adjective 1** *it is easier to print on an even surface* **flat**, smooth, uniform, featureless, unbroken, undamaged, unwrinkled; level, levelled, plane, flush, true; *informal* (as) flat as a pancake; *technical* planar; *rare* homaloidal.
OPPOSITES uneven, bumpy.
2 *electric fan ovens have a more even temperature than gas* **uniform**, constant, steady, stable, consistent, changeless, unvarying, unchanging, unwavering, unfluctuating, unaltering, regular.
OPPOSITES variable, irregular.
3 *all participants are given an even chance* **equal**, the same, much the same, identical, like, alike, similar, to the same degree, comparable, commensurate, corresponding, parallel, on a par, on an equal footing, evenly matched; *informal* even-steven(s).
OPPOSITE unequal.
4 *he played a perfect ball to keep the score even* **level**, drawn, tied, all square, balanced, on a par, on an equal footing; neck and neck, nip and tuck, with nothing to choose between them; *Brit.* level pegging; *informal* even-steven(s).
OPPOSITES unequal, uneven.
5 *the child was of an even disposition* **even-tempered**, well balanced, stable, equable, placid, serene, calm, composed, poised, tranquil, cool, {cool, calm, and collected}, cool-headed, relaxed, easy, imperturbable, unexcitable, unruffled, unflustered, unagitated, unworried, untroubled, unbothered; *informal* together, laid-back, unflappable, unfazed; *rare* equanimous.
OPPOSITES moody; excitable.
□ **get even** *he has been wronged and he has sworn to get even* **have one's revenge**, take one's revenge, be revenged, revenge oneself, avenge oneself, take vengeance, even the score, settle accounts, settle the score, hit back, give as good as one gets, return tit for tat, return like for like, pay someone back, repay someone, reciprocate, retaliate, take reprisals, exact retribution, demand an eye for an eye and a tooth for a tooth; give someone their just deserts, let someone see how it feels; *informal* get back at someone, get one's own back, give someone a taste of their own medicine, give someone their comeuppance, fix someone, sort someone out, settle someone's hash, cook someone's goose.
▶ **verb 1** *the canal bottom was* **evened out** **flatten**, make flat, make level, level, level off, level out, smooth, smooth out, smooth off, make flush, plane, make uniform, make regular.
2 *the union wants to* **even up** *the differences in wages* **equalize**, make equal, make even, make level, level up, make the same, balance, square; make uniform, make comparable, standardize, regularize; *rare* equilibrize.
▶ **adverb 1** *the weather became even colder* **still**, yet, more so, all the more, all the greater, to a greater extent.
2 *even the best hitters missed the ball* **surprisingly**, unexpectedly, paradoxically, though it may seem strange, believe it or not, as it happens.
3 *she is too afraid, even ashamed, to ask for help* **indeed**, you could say, possibly, more precisely, veritably, in truth, actually, or rather, nay.
4 *she couldn't even afford the essentials* **so much as**, hardly, barely, scarcely.
□ **even as** *we laugh even as we empathize with his discomfort* **while**, whilst, as, at the (same) time that, just as, at the very time that, at the very moment that, exactly when, during the time that.
□ **even so** *I feel better, but the doubts persist even so* **nevertheless**, nonetheless, all the same, just the same, anyway, anyhow, still, yet, however, notwithstanding, despite that, in spite of that, for all that, be that as it may, in any event, at any rate; *informal* still and all; *archaic* withal, natheless, howbeit.

even-handed ▶ **adjective** *teachers must have an even-handed approach towards both sexes* **fair**, just, equitable, impartial, unbiased, unprejudiced, non-partisan, non-discriminatory; disinterested, dispassionate, detached, uninvolved, objective, neutral, impersonal, fair-minded, open-minded, with no axe to grind.
OPPOSITES unfair; biased.

evening ▶ **noun 1** *he came over to see me one evening* **night**, late afternoon, end of day, close of day; twilight, dusk, nightfall, sunset, sundown; *literary* eve, even, eventide, evenfall, gloaming.
OPPOSITE morning.
2 *the evening of her life* **latter part**, last part, latter stage, close, end, later years, declining years; autumn.

OPPOSITE springtime.

event ▸ noun **1** *the school trip was an annual event* **occurrence**, happening, proceeding, episode, incident, affair, circumstance, occasion, business, matter, experience, eventuality, phenomenon; function, gathering, get-together, jamboree; *informal* bash, do, jolly, shindig, shindy.
2 *the British team lost the event* **competition**, contest, tournament, round, heat, game, match, fixture, meet, meeting, encounter; race, bout, fight; play-off, replay, rematch; *Canadian & Scottish* playdown; *N. Amer.* split; *informal, dated* mill; *archaic* tourney.

□ **in any event/at all events** *he is going to prison in any event, guilty plea or not* **regardless**, regardless of what happens, whatever happens, come what may, no matter what, at any rate, in any case, anyhow, anyway, even so, still, nevertheless, nonetheless; *informal* still and all; *N. Amer. informal* anyways; *archaic* howbeit, natheless.

□ **in the event** *in the event, they squabbled and the plan fell through* **as it turned out**, as it happened, in the end; as the outcome, as a result, as a consequence, as an effect.

even-tempered ▸ adjective *Russell was a gentle and even-tempered man* **serene**, calm, composed, poised, tranquil, relaxed, easy-going, mild, mellow, unworried, untroubled, unbothered, unruffled, unflustered, unexcitable, imperturbable, placid, equable, stable, well balanced, level-headed; *informal* unflappable, together, laid-back, unfazed; *rare* equanimous.
OPPOSITES excitable, unstable.

eventful ▸ adjective *it had been a long and eventful day* **busy**, event-filled, action-packed, full, lively, active, hectic, strenuous; **momentous**, significant, noteworthy, notable, remarkable, outstanding, important, crucial, critical, historic, consequential, fateful, decisive.
OPPOSITES dull, uneventful.

eventual ▸ adjective *the eventual outcome of the competition* **final**, ultimate, concluding, closing, endmost, end, terminal; resulting, ensuing, consequent, subsequent.

eventuality ▸ noun *it is impossible to anticipate every eventuality* **event**, incident, occurrence, happening, development, phenomenon, thing, situation, circumstance, case, contingency, chance, likelihood, possibility, probability; **outcome**, result, upshot; *rare* fortuity.

eventually ▸ adverb *eventually we arrived at a small town | the offender will be allowed out eventually* **in the end**, in due course, by and by, in time, after some time, after a period of time, after a long time, after a bit, finally, at last, at long last; **ultimately**, in the long run, in the fullness of time, at some point in the future, at a future date, at the end of the day, one day, one of these fine days, some day, sometime, in time to come, sooner or later, when all is said and done.
OPPOSITES immediately; never.

eventuate ▸ verb (*rare*) **1** *you never know what might eventuate* **happen**, occur, take place, chance to happen, arise, emerge, come about, transpire, materialize, appear, surface, crop up, spring up, present itself; **ensue**, follow, result, develop, supervene, be the result, be the consequence; *N. Amer. informal* go down; *literary* come to pass, befall, betide, bechance; *archaic* hap, arrive.
2 *the fight* **eventuated in** *the death of Mr Gonzales* **result in**, end in, have as a result, have as a consequence, lead to, give rise to, bring about, cause.

ever ▸ adverb **1** *it's the best thing I've ever done* **at any time**, at any point, on any occasion, under any circumstances, on any account; up till now, until now.
2 *ever the optimist, he was intent on winning* **always**, forever, at all times, eternally, until the end of time; *informal* until the twelfth of never, until the cows come home, until hell freezes over, until doomsday.
OPPOSITE never.
3 *the statistics show an ever increasing rate of crime* **continually**, constantly, always, at all times, endlessly, perpetually, incessantly, unceasingly, unremittingly, repeatedly, recurrently.
4 *will she ever learn?* **at all**, in any way, on earth.

□ **ever so** (*Brit. informal*) *she's ever so happy* **very**, extremely, exceedingly, exceptionally, especially, tremendously, immensely; extra, excessively, distinctly, uncommonly, unusually, decidedly, particularly, remarkably, really, truly, most, so; to a great extent, to a great degree; *Scottish* unco; *French* très; *N. English* right; *informal* terrifically, awfully, terribly, majorly, seriously, desperately, mega, ultra, oh-so, too-too, mucho, damned, too … for words; *Brit. informal* well, dead, jolly; *N. Amer. informal* real, mighty, awful, darned; *S. African informal* lekker; *informal, dated* devilish, hellish, frightfully; *archaic* exceeding.

everlasting ▸ adjective **1** *gold is the symbol of everlasting love* **eternal**, never-ending, endless, without end, perpetual, undying, immortal, deathless, indestructible, immutable, abiding, enduring, infinite, boundless, timeless; *rare* sempiternal, perdurable.
OPPOSITE transient.
2 *they got tired of my everlasting complaints* **constant**, continual, continuous, persistent, sustained, unremitting, relentless, unrelenting, unrelieved, uninterrupted, unbroken, unabating, endless, interminable, never-ending, non-stop, round-the-clock, incessant, ceaseless.
OPPOSITE occasional.

evermore ▸ adverb *we pray that we may evermore dwell in Him* **always**, forever, for ever and ever, ever, for always, for all time, until the end of time, eternally, in perpetuity; endlessly, without end, ceaselessly, unceasingly, constantly; ever after, henceforth; *Brit.* for evermore, forever more; *N. Amer.* forevermore; *Latin* in perpetuum, ad infinitum; *informal* until the cows come home, until the twelfth of never, until hell freezes over; *formal* hereafter; *archaic* for aye.

every ▸ determiner **1** *he exercised his hounds every day* **each**, each and every, every single.
2 *the firm will make every effort to satisfy its clients* **all possible**, all probable, the utmost, as much as possible, as great as possible.
OPPOSITE no.

everybody ▸ pronoun *everybody complains about taxes these days* **everyone**, every person, each person, each one, each and every one, all, one and all, all and sundry, the whole world, the world at large, the public, the general public, people everywhere; *informal* {every Tom, Dick, and Harry}, every man jack, every mother's son.

everyday ▸ adjective **1** *the everyday demands of a baby* **daily**, day-to-day, quotidian; *rare* diurnal, circadian.
2 *everyday drugs like aspirin* **commonplace**, ordinary, common, usual, regular, familiar, conventional, run-of-the-mill, typical, standard, stock, plain, workaday; household, domestic, family; unexceptional, unremarkable; *Brit.* common or garden; *N. Amer.* garden variety; *informal* bog-standard, a dime a dozen.
OPPOSITE unusual.

everyone ▸ pronoun *she didn't want everyone to know her business* **everybody**, every person, each person, each one, each and every one, all, one and all, all and sundry, the whole world, the world at large, the public, the general public, people everywhere; *informal* {every Tom, Dick, and Harry}, every man jack, every mother's son.

everything ▸ pronoun *the guards searched through everything* **each item**, each thing, every article, every single thing, the lot, the whole lot, the entirety, the total, the aggregate; all; *informal* the whole (kit and) caboodle, the whole shooting match, the whole shebang, everything but the kitchen sink; *Brit. informal* the full monty; *N. Amer. informal* the whole ball of wax, the whole nine yards.
OPPOSITE nothing.

WORD LINKS
fear of everything **panphobia, panophobia, pantophobia**

everywhere ▸ adverb *he searched everywhere for his horse* **all over**, all around, in all places, in every place, in every spot, in every part, in every nook and cranny, in each place, far and wide, near and far, high and low, here and there, {here, there, and everywhere}, throughout the land, the world over, worldwide; widely, extensively, exhaustively, thoroughly; *informal* all over the place; *Brit. informal* all over the shop; *N. Amer. informal* all over the map.
OPPOSITE nowhere.

evict ▸ verb *the police moved in and evicted the squatters* **expel**, eject, oust, remove, dislodge, turn out, put out, force out, throw out, throw out on the streets, throw out on one's ear, drum out, drive out; dispossess, expropriate; *informal* chuck out, kick out, boot out, heave out, bounce, give someone the (old) heave-ho, throw someone out on their ear, show someone the door; *Brit. informal* turf out; *N. Amer. informal* give someone the bum's rush; *dated* out.
OPPOSITE admit.

eviction ▸ noun *the eviction of workers from company houses* **expulsion**, ejection, ousting, throwing out, drumming out, driving out, banishing, banishment, removal, dislodgement, displacement, clearance; dispossession, expropriation; *informal* booting out, chucking out, kicking out, bouncing; *Brit. informal* turfing out; *humorous* defenestration; *Law* ouster; *dated* outing.
OPPOSITE admission.

evidence ▸ noun **1** *they found evidence of his participation in the burglary* **proof**, confirmation, verification, substantiation, corroboration, affirmation, authentication, attestation, documentation; support for, backing for, reinforcement for, grounds for.
2 *the court refused to accept Mr Scott's evidence* **testimony**, statement, sworn statement, attestation, declaration, avowal, plea, submission, claim, contention, charge, allegation; *Law* deposition, representation, affidavit; *rare* asseveration, averment.
3 *the room showed evidence of a struggle* **signs**, indications, pointers, marks, traces, suggestions, hints; manifestation.

□ **in evidence** *team spirit was much in evidence* **noticeable**, conspicuous, obvious, perceptible, perceivable, visible, on view, on display, easily seen, easily noticed, plain to see; palpable, tangible, unmistakable, undisguised, unconcealed, prominent, striking, glaring, writ large; *informal* as plain as the nose on your face, as plain as a pikestaff, standing/sticking out like a sore thumb, standing/sticking out a mile, right under one's nose, staring someone in the face, written all over someone; *archaic* sensible.

▸ verb *the rise of racism is evidenced by the increase in racial attacks* **indicate**,

show, reveal, be evidence of, display, exhibit, manifest, denote, evince, signify; testify to, attest to, verify, confirm, prove, substantiate, endorse, back up, support, bear out, give credence to.
OPPOSITE disprove.

evident ▶ adjective *he regarded her with evident interest* **obvious**, apparent, noticeable, conspicuous, perceptible, perceivable, visible, observable, discernible, transparent, clear, crystal clear, clear-cut, writ large, plain, manifest, patent, palpable, tangible, distinct, pronounced, marked, striking, glaring, blatant; unmistakable, indisputable, undoubted, incontrovertible, incontestable; *informal* as plain as the nose on your face, as plain as a pikestaff, standing/sticking out like a sore thumb, standing/sticking out a mile, written all over someone, as clear as day; *archaic* sensible.
OPPOSITE unnoticeable.

E

evidently ▶ adverb **1** *he was evidently dismayed by what he saw* **obviously**, clearly, plainly, perceptibly, visibly, discernibly, transparently, manifestly, patently, palpably, distinctly, markedly, blatantly; unmistakably, indisputably, undeniably, undoubtedly, incontrovertibly, without question, without doubt; *informal* as sure as eggs is eggs.
2 *evidently, she believed herself to be unobserved* **seemingly**, apparently, so it seems, as far as one can tell, from all appearances, on the face of it, to all intents and purposes, on the surface, outwardly, ostensibly; it seems (that), it would seem (that), it appears (that), it would appear (that); *rare* ostensively.

evil ▶ adjective **1** *an evil deed | the most evil man he had ever met* **wicked**, bad, wrong, morally wrong, wrongful, immoral, sinful, ungodly, unholy, foul, vile, base, ignoble, dishonourable, corrupt, iniquitous, depraved, degenerate, villainous, nefarious, sinister, vicious, malicious, malevolent, demonic, devilish, diabolic, diabolical, fiendish, dark, black-hearted; monstrous, shocking, despicable, atrocious, heinous, odious, contemptible, horrible, execrable; *informal* low-down, stinking, dirty, shady, warped, bent, crooked; *archaic* dastardly, black; *rare* egregious, flagitious, peccable.
OPPOSITES good, virtuous.
2 *the evil influence of society | an evil spirit* **harmful**, hurtful, injurious, detrimental, deleterious, inimical, bad, mischievous, pernicious, malignant, malign, baleful, venomous, noxious, poisonous; corrupting, subversive; calamitous, disastrous, destructive, ruinous; *literary* malefic, maleficent; *rare* prejudicious.
OPPOSITES good, beneficial.
3 *his army suffered in the evil weather* **unpleasant**, disagreeable, nasty, horrible, foul, filthy, vile; inclement, wet, rainy, stormy, squally, blustery, cold, freezing, foggy.
OPPOSITES pleasant; fine.
4 *she helped those who had fallen on evil times* **unlucky**, unfortunate, unfavourable, adverse, unhappy, disastrous, catastrophic, ruinous, calamitous, unpropitious, inauspicious, dire, woeful.
▶ noun **1** *I sense the evil in our midst* **wickedness**, bad, badness, wrong, wrongdoing, sin, sinfulness, ungodliness, immorality, vice, iniquity, turpitude, degeneracy, vileness, baseness, perversion, corruption, depravity, villainy, nefariousness, atrocity, malevolence, devilishness; *informal* shadiness, crookedness; *rare* peccability, peccancy.
OPPOSITE goodness.
2 *nothing but evil would come out of such a meeting* **harm**, pain, hurt, misery, sorrow, suffering, trauma, trouble, disaster, detriment, destruction, loss, misfortune, catastrophe, calamity, affliction, woe, ruin, hardship; ills.
OPPOSITE benefit.
3 *the evils of war* **abomination**, atrocity, obscenity, outrage, enormity, crime, monstrosity, barbarity, barbarism; torment, curse, bane.
OPPOSITE blessing.

evil-doer ▶ noun *they exacted vengeance on the evil-doers* **wrongdoer**, transgressor, criminal, delinquent, offender, villain, malefactor, reprobate, scoundrel, rogue, sinner, sinful person, wicked person, evil person, bad person; *informal* baddy, bad guy, crook, crim, wrong 'un, ne'er-do-well, nasty piece of work, ratbag, scumbag, bad egg; *Law* malfeasant, misfeasor, infractor; *archaic* miscreant, knave, blackguard, varlet, trespasser.

evil-doing ▶ noun *a fiend bent on evil-doing* **wrongdoing**, wrong, badness, bad, evil, sin, sinfulness, immorality, iniquity, turpitude, vileness, baseness, corruption, depravity, villainy, nefariousness, atrocity, malevolence, devilishness; *informal* shadiness, crookedness; *Law* malfeasance; *archaic* knavery, trespassing; *rare* peccability, peccancy.

evince ▶ verb *his letters evince the excitement he felt* **reveal**, show, make clear, make plain, make obvious, make manifest, manifest, indicate, display, exhibit, demonstrate, be evidence of, evidence, attest to, testify to, bear witness to; convey, communicate, proclaim, impart, bespeak; disclose, divulge, betray, give away, expose, lay bare.
OPPOSITE conceal.

eviscerate ▶ verb *the goat had been skinned and eviscerated* **disembowel**, gut, remove the innards from, draw, dress; *rare* embowel, disbowel, exenterate, gralloch, paunch.

evocative ▶ adjective *dark interiors are highly evocative of past centuries | evocative lyrics* **reminiscent**, suggestive, redolent; resonant with; **expressive**, vivid, graphic, powerful, haunting, moving, poignant; *rare* remindful of.

evoke ▶ verb *the poems evoke a sense of desolate emptiness* **bring to mind**, call to mind, put one in mind of, call up, conjure up, summon up, summon, invoke, give rise to, bring forth, elicit, induce, kindle, stimulate, stir up, awaken, arouse, excite, raise, suggest; recall, echo, reproduce, encapsulate, capture, express; *formal* educe.

evolution ▶ noun **1** *the evolution of Bolshevik thinking* **development**, advancement, growth, rise, progress, progression, expansion, extension, unfolding; transformation, adaptation, modification, revision, reworking, reconstruction, recasting, change; *humorous* transmogrification; *rare* evolvement.
2 *early ecologists were not interested in evolution* **Darwinism**, natural selection.

evolve ▶ verb **1** *the economies of all four nations evolved in different ways* **develop**, progress, make progress, advance, move forward, make headway, mature, grow, open out, unfold, unroll, expand, enlarge, spread, extend; alter, change, transform, adapt, metamorphose, differentiate; *humorous* transmogrify.
2 (*Chemistry*) *on reacting the two acids, a gas is evolved* **emit**, yield, give off, discharge, release, produce.

exacerbate ▶ verb *political changes have exacerbated the conflict* **aggravate**, make worse, worsen, inflame, compound; intensify, increase, heighten, magnify, add to, amplify, augment; make matters worse, compound the problem; *informal* add fuel to the fire/flames, fan the flames, rub salt in the wounds, add insult to injury.
OPPOSITES calm; reduce.

exacerbate or exasperate?
See EXASPERATE.

exact ▶ adjective **1** *write an exact description of everything you see* **precise**, accurate, correct, faithful, close, true, veracious, literal, strict, unerring, faultless, errorless, error-free, perfect, impeccable; explicit, detailed, minute, meticulous, thorough, blow-by-blow; *informal* on the nail, on the mark, on the beam, on the button; *Brit. informal* spot on, bang on; *N. Amer. informal* on the money.
OPPOSITES inexact, inaccurate.
2 *he didn't approve of sloppiness and liked to be exact* **careful**, meticulous, painstaking, precise, punctilious, conscientious, rigorous, scrupulous, exacting; methodical, systematic, well organized, ordered, orderly, controlled.
OPPOSITE careless.
▶ verb **1** *she exacted high standards of cleanliness from them* **demand**, require, insist on, command, call for, impose, request, ask for, expect, look for; extract, compel, force, wring, wrest, squeeze, obtain; *archaic* constrain.
2 *they exacted a terrible vengeance on the helpless tribe* **inflict**, impose, deliver, administer, issue, apply.

CHOOSE THE RIGHT WORD
exact, accurate, precise
See ACCURATE.

exacting ▶ adjective **1** *he set himself an exacting training routine* **demanding**, hard, tough, stringent, testing, challenging, difficult, onerous, arduous, laborious, tiring, taxing, gruelling, punishing, back-breaking, burdensome, Herculean; *archaic* toilsome; *rare* exigent.
OPPOSITE easy.
2 *a highly efficient but exacting boss* **strict**, stern, firm, demanding, rigorous, tough, hard, harsh, rigid, inflexible, uncompromising, unyielding, unbending, unsparing, imperious; hard to please; *Austral./NZ informal* solid.
OPPOSITE easy-going.

exactly ▶ adverb **1** *the room's exactly as I expected it to be* **precisely**, entirely, absolutely, completely, totally, just, quite, in every way, in every respect, one hundred per cent, every inch, to the hilt; *informal* on the nail, bang on, spot on, to a T; *N. Amer. informal* on the money.
OPPOSITE not at all.
2 *mention your source and write the quotation out exactly* **accurately**, precisely, correctly, without error, without flaws, without mistakes, unerringly, faultlessly, perfectly; **verbatim**, word for word, letter for letter, to the letter, literally, closely, faithfully, in every detail, with strict attention to detail; *rare* veridically.
OPPOSITES inaccurately, inexactly.
□ **not exactly** *I'm not exactly a spring chicken any more* **by no means**, not by any means, not, not at all, in no way, certainly not; not really.
▶ exclamation *'You mean she escaped?' 'Exactly.'* **precisely**, yes, right, that's right, just so, quite so, quite, indeed, absolutely, truly, certainly, definitely, assuredly, undoubtedly, indubitably, without a doubt; *informal*

you bet, you got it, I'll say.

exactness, exactitude ▶ noun *in this job, detail and exactness are essential* **precision**, accuracy, accurateness, correctness, veracity, faithfulness, fidelity, closeness; care, carefulness, meticulousness, scrupulousness, punctiliousness, conscientiousness, rigour, rigorousness, thoroughness, strictness; *rare* veridicality, scrupulosity.
OPPOSITES inaccuracy; negligence.

exaggerate ▶ verb *the conflict was exaggerated by the media | they often exaggerate for dramatic effect* **overstate**, overemphasize, overstress, overestimate, overvalue, magnify, amplify, aggrandize, inflate; embellish, embroider, colour, elaborate, over-elaborate, oversell, overdraw, overplay, dramatize; hyperbolize, add colour, stretch the truth; *Brit.* overpitch; *informal* pile it on, lay it on thick, lay it on with a trowel/shovel, make a mountain out of a molehill, blow something out of all proportion, make a drama out of a crisis, make a big thing of; *Brit. informal* shoot a line; *archaic* draw the longbow.
OPPOSITES play down; understate.

exaggerated ▶ adjective *I gave her an exaggerated account of my exploits* **overstated**, overemphasized, inflated, magnified, amplified, aggrandized, excessive, hyperbolic, over-elaborate, overdone, overplayed, overdramatized, theatrical, dramatic, highly coloured, extravagant, melodramatic, sensational, sensationalist, sensationalistic; *informal* over the top, OTT, tall.
OPPOSITE understated.

exaggeration ▶ noun *the debate is characterized by confusion and exaggeration* **overstatement**, overemphasis, magnification, amplification, aggrandizement, overplaying, dramatization, overdramatization, enhancement, elaboration, over-elaboration, embellishment, over-embellishment, embroidery, hyperbole, overkill, gilding the lily; *informal* purple prose, puffery.

exalt ▶ verb **1** *they exalted their hero* **glorify**, extol, praise, acclaim, pay homage to, pay tribute to, revere, reverence, venerate, worship, hero-worship, lionize, idolize, deify, esteem, hold in high regard, hold in high esteem, hold in awe, look up to; *informal* put on a pedestal; *rare* laud, magnify.
OPPOSITES disparage; despise.
2 *this power exalts the peasant above his brethren* **elevate**, promote, raise, advance, boost, upgrade, ennoble, dignify, aggrandize; improve the status of, improve the standing of, give someone a higher rank.
OPPOSITE lower.
3 *the works of Milton and Wordsworth exalted me* **uplift**, elevate, inspire, excite, stimulate, animate, enliven, exhilarate, elate, delight, transport.
OPPOSITE depress.

exaltation ▶ noun **1** *her heart was full of exaltation* **elation**, exultation, joy, joyfulness, joyousness, rapture, ecstasy, bliss, happiness, delight, gladness, glee, exuberance, exhilaration, excitement; transports.
OPPOSITE sadness.
2 *their exaltation of Shakespeare* **praise**, praising, extolment, acclamation, glory, glorification, glorifying, reverence, revering, veneration, venerating, worship, worshipping, hero-worship, hero-worshipping, adoration, idolization, idolizing, lionization, lionizing, deification, deifying; homage, tribute, high regard, high esteem; *rare* laudation, lauding, magnification, magnifying.
OPPOSITE disparagement.
3 *the exaltation of Jesus to the Father's right hand* **elevation**, raising, rise, promotion, advancement, upgrading, ennoblement, aggrandizement.
OPPOSITE lowering.

exalted ▶ adjective **1** *he is no longer fit to retain his exalted office* **high**, high-ranking, elevated, prominent, superior, lofty, grand, noble, dignified, eminent, prestigious, august, illustrious, distinguished, esteemed, venerable; influential, important, powerful.
OPPOSITE low.
2 *their hearts were stirred by his exalted aims* **noble**, lofty, high-minded, elevated, intellectual, ideal, sublime; inflated, pretentious.
OPPOSITE base.
3 *she felt tired but spiritually exalted* **elated**, exultant, jubilant, joyful, joyous, triumphant, rapturous, rhapsodic, ecstatic, blissful, transported, delighted, happy, gleeful, exuberant, exhilarated; *informal* high, up.
OPPOSITES depressed, low.

exam ▶ noun *she prepared for her biology exam* **test**, examination, paper, question paper, oral, practical, assessment; set of questions, set of exercises; *Brit.* viva, viva voce; *N. Amer.* quiz.

examination ▶ noun **1** *the artefacts were spread on a table for examination* **scrutiny**, inspection, perusal, study, scanning, vetting, investigation, exploration, consideration, analysis, appraisal, evaluation.
2 *employees are required to undergo a medical examination* **inspection**, check, check-up, assessment, review, appraisal; exploration, probe, test, scan; *informal* going-over, once-over, overhaul.
3 *there was an examination at the end of the course* **test**, exam, paper, question paper, oral, practical, assessment; set of questions, set of exercises; *Brit.* viva, viva voce; *N. Amer.* quiz.
4 (*Law*) *the examination of witnesses in open court* **questioning**, **interrogation**, cross-questioning, cross-examination, inquisition; the third degree; *informal* pumping, grilling.

WORD LINKS
related suffix **-scopy (e.g. *microscopy, endoscopy*)**

examine ▶ verb **1** *fraud squad officers wanted to examine the bank records* **inspect**, survey, scrutinize, look at, look into, inquire into, study, investigate, scan, sift, delve into, dig into, explore, probe, check out, consider, appraise, weigh, weigh up, analyse, review, vet; subject to an examination.
2 *students were examined after nine months' instruction* **test**, quiz, question, set an examination for; assess, appraise.
3 *they must name in advance all the witnesses to be examined* **interrogate**, put questions to, ask questions of, quiz, question, cross-examine, cross-question; catechize, give the third degree to, probe, sound out; *informal* grill, pump, put through the wringer, put through the mangle.

examiner ▶ noun *a university examiner | the accounts are checked by an independent examiner* **tester**, questioner, interviewer, assessor, marker, inspector; auditor, analyst, appraiser, reviewer; arbiter, adjudicator, judge, scrutineer, scrutinizer; *rare* examinant, scrutinator.

example ▶ noun **1** *a fine example of a 16th-century longhouse* **specimen**, sample, exemplar, exemplification, instance, case, representative case, typical case, case in point, illustration.
2 *we ought to follow their example* **precedent**, lead, guide, model, pattern, blueprint, template, paradigm, exemplar, ideal, standard; parallel case; role model.
3 *he was found guilty as an example to would-be burglars* **warning**, caution, lesson, deterrent, admonition; sign, signal message, moral.
□ **for example** *their teeth resemble those of many mammals, for example, bears* **for instance**, e.g., to give an example, to give an instance, by way of illustration, as an illustration, to illustrate, such as, as, like; in particular, namely, viz.

exasperate ▶ verb *Smith's erratic behaviour exasperated him* **infuriate**, incense, anger, annoy, irritate, madden, enrage, send into a rage, inflame, antagonize, provoke, irk, vex, gall, pique, try someone's patience, get on someone's nerves, make someone's blood boil, make someone's hackles rise, make someone see red, get someone's back up, rub up the wrong way, ruffle someone's feathers, drive to distraction; *informal* aggravate, drive mad, drive crazy, bug, needle, rile, miff, hack off, get to, get at, get up someone's nose, get under someone's skin, put someone's nose out of joint, get someone's goat, give someone the hump, rattle someone's cage, get someone's dander up; *Brit. informal* nark, wind up, get on someone's wick; *N. Amer. informal* tee off, tick off, burn up, rankle, ride, gravel; *rare* exacerbate, hump, rasp.
OPPOSITES please, delight.

exasperate or exacerbate?
These words may be confused on account of their similar sound; but their meanings are different. **Exasperate** means 'irritate intensely' (*his colleague's erratic behaviour exasperated him*). **Exacerbate**, on the other hand, means 'make (an existing problem) worse' (*anaemia may be exacerbated by some medicines*). Someone's late arrival may *exasperate* his colleagues, and this in turn may *exacerbate* the tension between them.

exasperating ▶ adjective *he has such exasperating habits* **infuriating**, annoying, irritating, maddening, antagonizing, provoking, irking, irksome, vexing, vexatious, galling, trying, troublesome, bothersome, displeasing; *informal* aggravating, cussed, pesky, confounded, infernal, plaguy, pestilent.
OPPOSITES pleasing, delightful.

exasperation ▶ noun *she provoked exasperation among her colleagues* **irritation**, annoyance, chagrin, vexation, anger, fury, rage, wrath, spleen, ill humour, crossness, tetchiness, testiness, pique, indignation, resentment, disgruntlement, disgust, discontent, displeasure; *informal* aggravation, crabbiness; *Brit. informal* stroppiness; *literary* ire, choler, bile.
OPPOSITES pleasure, delight.

excavate ▶ verb **1** *the animal has excavated a narrow tunnel* **dig**, dig out, hollow out, scoop out, gouge, cut out, bore, burrow, tunnel, sink; quarry, mine.
2 *numerous artefacts have been excavated* **unearth**, dig up, bring out of the ground, bring to the surface, uncover, reveal; disinter, exhume; *rare* unbury.

excavation ▶ noun **1** *the excavation of a medieval grave* **unearthing**, digging up, uncovering, revealing; disinterment, exhumation.
2 *the excavation of an extra moat* **digging**, digging out, hollowing out, scooping out, gouging, boring, channelling, sinking; quarrying, mining.

E

3 *a number of agricultural implements were found in the excavations* **hole**, hollow, cavity, pit, crater, cutting, trench, trough; **archaeological site**.

exceed ▶ verb **1** *the total cost will exceed £400* **be more than**, be greater than, be over, run over, go over, go beyond, overshoot, overreach, pass, top.
OPPOSITE fall short of.
2 *Brazil far exceeds America in available fertile land* **surpass**, outdo, outstrip, outshine, outclass, transcend, top, cap, beat, be greater than, be superior to, be better than, go one better than, better, pass, eclipse, overshadow, put in the shade, put to shame; *informal* best, leave standing, be head and shoulders above, be a cut above; *archaic* extinguish, outrival, outvie.

exceeding (*archaic*) ▶ adjective *she spoke warmly of his exceeding kindness* **great**, very great, considerable, exceptional, marked, distinct, tremendous, immense, extreme, supreme, outstanding.
▶ adverb *the Lord has been exceeding gracious* **very**, exceedingly, extremely, exceptionally, especially, tremendously, immensely, supremely, really, truly, most, distinctly, decidedly; *Scottish* unco; *French* très; *N. English* right; *informal* terribly, awfully, devilishly, majorly, seriously, mega, ultra, oh-so, damn, damned; *Brit. informal* ever so, well, dead, jolly; *N. Amer. informal* real, mighty, awful, darned.

exceedingly ▶ adverb *an exceedingly comfortable home* **extremely**, exceptionally, especially, tremendously, immensely, supremely, very, really, truly, most, distinctly, decidedly; *Scottish* unco; *French* très; *N. English* right; *informal* terribly, awfully, devilishly, majorly, seriously, mega, ultra, oh-so, damn, damned; *Brit. informal* ever so, well, dead, jolly; *N. Amer. informal* real, mighty, awful, darned; *archaic* exceeding.

WORD LINKS
related prefix **ultra-** (e.g. ***ultra-modern, ultramicroscopic***)

excel ▶ verb **1** *he excelled at football* **shine**, be very good, be excellent, be brilliant, be outstanding, be skilful, be talented, be proficient, be expert, be pre-eminent, reign supreme, wear the crown, stand out, be the best, be unrivalled, be unparalleled, be unequalled, be without equal, be second to none, be unsurpassed; *rare* be unexampled.
2 *she excelled him in her command of the language* **surpass**, outdo, outshine, outclass, outstrip, beat, beat hollow, top, cap, transcend, be better than, be superior to, go one better than, better, pass, eclipse, overshadow, put in the shade, put to shame; *informal* best, leave standing, be head and shoulders above, be a cut above; *archaic* extinguish, outrival, outvie.

CHOOSE THE RIGHT WORD

excel, surpass, outdo

All these words denote superiority or pre-eminence.

- **Excel** is most often used without a direct object, emphasizing someone's outstanding ability (*he excelled at maths and won a scholarship to Cambridge | it was not enough to excel in the swimming and running*). The most common transitive use is to *excel oneself*, which is to do better than one has ever done before (*Miss Lodsworth, who organized the flower rota, had excelled herself*). It is comparatively rare to *excel someone else*.
- **Surpass** literally means 'go beyond'. It indicates that someone has passed a previous limit, proving themselves greater or better (*he won five races and surpassed the all-time record*). It is also quite common to *surpass someone* (*he was never surpassed by recent comedians*); its reflexive use, to *surpass oneself*, has the same sense as *excel oneself* (*he surpassed himself once more in the 1991 Ryder Cup*).
- **Outdo** indicates that someone is more successful or goes to greater lengths than their competitors (*they tried to outdo each other in generosity | she could not hope to outdo the big contractors*). The note of competition with others is strongest in this word (*everybody was trying to outdo each other with stories of how exciting their holidays had been | not to be outdone, Pentos also produced its own fully-illustrated catalogue*). It is unusual to *outdo oneself*.

excellence ▶ noun *the children's hospital is a centre of medical excellence* **distinction**, quality, high quality, superiority, brilliance, greatness, merit, calibre, eminence, pre-eminence, supremacy, peerlessness, transcendence, value, worth; skill, talent, genius, virtuosity, accomplishment, expertness, mastery, prowess, ability; *rare* supereminence.
OPPOSITES inferiority, mediocrity.

excellent ▶ adjective *the wine was good and the meal excellent* **very good**, superb, outstanding, magnificent, of high quality, of the highest quality, of the highest standard, exceptional, marvellous, wonderful, sublime, perfect, eminent, pre-eminent, matchless, peerless, supreme, first-rate, first-class, superior, superlative, splendid, admirable, worthy, sterling, fine; *informal* A1, ace, great, terrific, tremendous, fantastic, fab, top-notch, tip-top, class, awesome, magic, wicked, cool, out of this world, too good to be true, mind-blowing; *Brit. informal* brilliant, brill, smashing, champion; *Austral. informal* beaut, bonzer; *Brit. informal, dated* spiffing, ripping, topping, top hole, wizard, capital; *N. Amer. informal, dated* swell; *vulgar slang* shit hot; *rare* applaudable.
OPPOSITES poor, inferior.

except ▶ preposition *the shop is open every day except Monday | there was no sound* ***except for*** *the rain* **excluding**, not including, excepting, omitting, leaving out, not counting, but, besides, barring, bar, other than, exclusive of, saving, save, apart from, aside from; with the exception of, with the omission of, with the exclusion of; *informal* outside of; *archaic* forbye.
OPPOSITE including.
▶ verb *you're all crooks, present company excepted* **exclude**, omit, leave out, rule out, count out, disregard, pass over, bar.
OPPOSITE include.

exception ▶ noun *an unexpected outcome was more the rule than the exception* **anomaly**, irregularity, deviation, special case, departure, inconsistency, quirk, peculiarity, abnormality, oddity; misfit; *informal* freak.
□ **take exception** *they took exception to the story we printed* **object**, raise an objection, express objections; be offended by, take offence at, take umbrage at, resent, demur at, disagree with, cavil at, argue against, protest against, lodge a protest against, take a stand against, oppose, complain about; *informal* kick up a fuss about, kick up a stink about, beef about, gripe about.
OPPOSITE approve of.
□ **with the exception of** *everyone shook their heads with the exception of Alice* **except**, except for, excepting, excluding, not including, omitting, leaving out, not counting, but, besides, barring, bar, other than, exclusive of, saving, save, apart from, aside from; with the omission of, with the exclusion of; *informal* outside of; *archaic* forbye.
OPPOSITE including.

exceptionable ▶ adjective (*rare*) *this passage is the most exceptionable in the whole poem* **objectionable**, offensive, disagreeable, obnoxious, repugnant, disgusting, abhorrent, unpleasant, distasteful, displeasing, unacceptable, deplorable, reprehensible, contemptible, insufferable, intolerable, insupportable, beyond the pale, out of line; *informal* out of order; *archaic* disgustful, loathly.
OPPOSITES agreeable; acceptable.

exceptional ▶ adjective **1** *meteorologists described the drought as exceptional* **unusual**, uncommon, abnormal, atypical, extraordinary, out of the ordinary, out of the way, rare, singular, unprecedented, unexpected, surprising; strange, odd, queer, bizarre, freakish, anomalous, peculiar, inconsistent, deviant, divergent, aberrant, unheard of; *Brit.* out of the common; *informal* weird, way out, freaky, something else; *dated* seldom; *rare* unexampled.
OPPOSITES usual, normal.
2 *we were taught by men of quite exceptional ability* **outstanding**, extraordinary, remarkable, unusually good, special, especial, excellent, phenomenal, prodigious; unequalled, unparalleled, unrivalled, unsurpassed, unsurpassable, unexcelled, peerless, matchless, second to none, in a league of their own, first-rate, first-class, of the first order, of the first water; *informal* A1, top-notch, tip-top.
OPPOSITE average.

exceptionally ▶ adverb **1** *that winter was exceptionally cold* **unusually**, uncommonly, abnormally, atypically, extraordinarily, unexpectedly, surprisingly; strangely, oddly, freakishly; *informal* weirdly, freakily.
2 *she had an exceptionally acute mind* **outstandingly**, extraordinarily, remarkably, exceedingly, especially, specially, phenomenally, prodigiously.

excerpt ▶ noun *he read an excerpt from his book* **extract**, part, section, piece, portion, fragment, snippet, clip, bit, selection, reading; citation, quotation, quote, line, paragraph, passage, scene, verse, stanza, canto; *N. Amer.* cite; *rare* pericope.

excess ▶ noun **1** *an excess of calcium in the bloodstream* **surplus**, surfeit, overabundance, superabundance, superfluity, oversufficiency, profusion, plethora, glut; too much, more than enough, enough and to spare; *informal* more … than one can shake a stick at; *rare* nimiety.
OPPOSITES dearth; lack.
2 *we eat more than we need, so the excess is turned into fat* **remainder**, rest, residue, remaining quantity, overflow, overspill; leftovers, remnants, leavings; surplus, extra, difference; *technical* residuum.
3 *he lived a life of excess* **overindulgence**, intemperance, intemperateness, immoderation, profligacy, lack of restraint, prodigality, lavishness, excessiveness, extravagance, decadence, self-indulgence, self-gratification, debauchery, dissipation, dissolution, dissoluteness.
OPPOSITES moderation, restraint.
□ **in excess of** *the book sold in excess of 10,000 copies* **more than**, over, above, over and above, upwards of, beyond.
OPPOSITES fewer than, less than.
▶ adjective *cleansing gets rid of excess skin oils* **surplus**, superfluous, spare, redundant, unwanted, unneeded, unused, excessive, leftover; extra, additional, reserve.

excessive ▶ adjective **1** *his excessive alcohol consumption* **immoderate**,

intemperate, imprudent, overindulgent, unrestrained, unrestricted, uncontrolled, uncurbed, unbridled, lavish, extravagant; superfluous, superabundant.
2 *the cost is excessive* **exorbitant**, extortionate, unreasonable, outrageous, undue, uncalled for, extreme, inordinate, unwarranted, unnecessary, needless, disproportionate, too much; *informal* over the top, OTT, a bit much.

excessively ▶ **adverb** *her father had excessively high standards | he drank excessively* **inordinately**, unduly, unnecessarily, unreasonably, absurdly, ridiculously, overly, to too great a degree, extra, very, extremely, exceedingly, exceptionally, unusually, impossibly, illogically, irrationally; **immoderately**, intemperately, too much, overmuch, without restraint, without control, without reserve; *informal* too-too.

WORD LINKS
related prefix **hyper-** (e.g. ***hypercritical, hyperventilate***)

exchange ▶ **noun 1** *they aim to promote the open exchange of ideas* **interchange**, trade, trading, trade-off, swapping, barter, giving and taking, traffic, trafficking, bandying, reciprocity; *archaic* truck.
2 *he became a broker on the exchange* **stock exchange**, money market, bourse.
3 *they had a brief and acrimonious exchange* **conversation**, dialogue, chat, talk, word, discussion, meeting, conference; debate, argument, altercation, war of words; *Brit. informal* confab, row, barney, slanging match; *formal* confabulation; *rare* colloquy.
▶ **verb** *we exchanged shirts* **trade**, swap, switch, barter, change, interchange; reciprocate; *archaic* truck.
□ **exchange blows** *they exchanged blows with men from a nearby village* **fight**, brawl, grapple, scuffle, tussle, box, come to blows, engage in fisticuffs; hit each other; *informal* scrap, have a set-to, have a ding-dong; *Brit. informal* have a punch-up; *Scottish informal* swedge; *N. Amer. informal* rough-house; *Austral./NZ informal* stoush, go the knuckle.
□ **exchange words** *the two exchanged words and a fight ensued* **argue**, disagree, quarrel, squabble, clash, have an argument, have a disagreement, have a quarrel, have a squabble; *Brit. informal* have a slanging match.

excise[1] (stress on the first syllable) ▶ **noun** *measures to generate further revenue included higher excise* **duty**, tax, levy, tariff, toll, tithe; customs, customs duties; *rare* mulct.

excise[2] (stress on the second syllable) ▶ **verb 1** *the tumours were excised immediately* **cut out**, cut off, cut away, snip out, take out, extract, remove, eradicate, extirpate; *technical* resect.
OPPOSITES replace; insert.
2 *all unnecessary detail should be excised* **delete**, cross out, cross through, strike out, score out, scratch out, cancel, put a line through, blue-pencil, ink out, edit out, blank out; erase, efface, take out, remove, cut out, cut, expunge, eliminate; expurgate, bowdlerize; *informal* axe, scrub, scrap, give something the chop; *Computing, informal* kill; *Printing* dele.
OPPOSITE add.

excitable ▶ **adjective** *the horses were very excitable* **temperamental**, mercurial, volatile, emotional, sensitive, highly strung, easily upset, easily agitated, easily frightened, unstable, nervous, tense, brittle, edgy, jumpy, twitchy, skittish, unsettled, uneasy, neurotic; tempestuous, hot-tempered, quick-tempered, hot-headed, passionate, fiery, irascible, testy, moody, touchy, snappy; *informal* uptight, wired, blowing hot and cold.
OPPOSITE placid.

excite ▶ **verb 1** *the prospect of a holiday excited me* **thrill**, exhilarate, animate, enliven, rouse, stir, move, stimulate, galvanize, electrify, fire the imagination of, fire the enthusiasm of; delight, enrapture, intoxicate; *informal* send, tickle, tickle someone pink, buck up, pep up, ginger up, give someone a buzz, give someone a kick, get someone going; *N. Amer. informal* light a fire under, give someone a charge; *rare* inspirit.
OPPOSITES bore, depress.
2 *she wore a chiffon nightgown to excite him* **arouse**, arouse sexually, make someone feel sexually excited, stimulate, titillate, inflame; please, attract, entice; *informal* turn someone on, give someone a thrill, get someone going, float someone's boat, do it for someone, light someone's fire, tickle someone's fancy.
OPPOSITE turn off.
3 *his clothes excited envy and admiration* **provoke**, stir up, elicit, rouse, arouse, stimulate, kindle, trigger (off), touch off, spark off, awaken, incite, instigate, foment, bring out, cause, bring about; *literary* enkindle.

excited ▶ **adjective 1** *Louise felt excited and proud of her achievement* **thrilled**, exhilarated, elevated, animated, enlivened, electrified, stirred, moved; delighted, exuberant, enraptured, intoxicated, feverish, enthusiastic, eager; *informal* high, high as a kite, fired up, tickled, tickled pink, full of beans, bright-eyed and bushy-tailed, peppy, sparky.
OPPOSITES indifferent; depressed.
2 aroused, sexually aroused, stimulated, titillated, inflamed, impassioned; attracted; *informal* turned on, on fire, hot, horny, sexed up; *Brit. informal* randy; *N. Amer. informal* squirrelly; *rare* concupiscent.
OPPOSITE turned off.

excitement ▶ **noun 1** *the excitement of seeing a leopard in the wild* **thrill**, thrilling sensation, exciting sensation, adventure, treat; pleasure, delight, joy; *informal* kick, buzz, high; *N. Amer. informal* charge.
2 *he saw the excitement in her eyes* **exhilaration**, elation, animation, enthusiasm, eagerness, anticipation, feverishness, fever, delirium, agitation, emotion, fire, fieriness, intensity, zeal, zest; *informal* pep, vim, zing, spark.
OPPOSITES boredom, indifference.
3 arousal, sexual arousal, passion, fire, glow; stimulation, titillation, attraction; *informal* turning on.

exciting ▶ **adjective 1** *I think your stories are really exciting* **thrilling**, exhilarating, stirring, rousing, stimulating, intoxicating, electrifying, invigorating, moving, inspiring; gripping, compelling, sensational, powerful, dramatic, shocking, startling, hair-raising, explosive, knife-edge, cliffhanging; *informal* mind-blowing; *N. Amer. informal* stem-winding.
OPPOSITE boring.
2 *the intimacy had been both frightening and exciting* **arousing**, sexually arousing, stimulating, sexually stimulating, titillating, tantalizing, provocative, erotic, sexual, sexy; *informal* raunchy, steamy.
OPPOSITE off-putting.

exclaim ▶ **verb** *'Well, I never!' she exclaimed* **cry out**, cry, declare, come out with, burst out with, blurt out, utter suddenly; call, call out, shout, sing out, yell, shriek, scream, screech, roar, bellow; *rare* ejaculate, vociferate, ululate.
OPPOSITES mutter, whisper.

exclamation ▶ **noun** *an exclamation of amazement* **cry**, call, shout, yell, shriek, roar, bellow, interjection, sudden utterance; expletive; *rare* ejaculation.

exclude ▶ **verb 1** *women had been excluded from many scientific societies | she was trying to exclude David from the conversation* **keep out**, deny access to, shut out, debar, disbar, bar, ban, prohibit, put an embargo on, embargo; reject, blackball, ostracize, banish; cut out, freeze out; *Brit.* send to Coventry.
OPPOSITES accept, admit.
2 *clauses designed to exclude any possibility of judicial review* **eliminate**, rule out, factor out; preclude, prevent the occurrence of; *formal* except.
OPPOSITE allow for.
3 *the price excludes postage and packing* **be exclusive of**, not include, not be inclusive of.
OPPOSITE include.
4 *I was surprised to see that he excluded his own name from the list* **leave out**, omit, miss out, fail to include.
OPPOSITE include.

exclusion ▶ **noun 1** *the exclusion of women from the society* **barring**, keeping out, debarment, debarring, disbarring, banning, ban, prohibition, embargo; rejection, ostracism, banishment.
OPPOSITES acceptance, admission.
2 *the exclusion of other factors* **elimination**, ruling out, factoring out; precluding.
OPPOSITE inclusion.
3 *the exclusion of pupils from the school* **expulsion**, removal, ejection, throwing out; suspension.
OPPOSITE admission.

exclusive ▶ **adjective 1** *one of Britain's most exclusive clubs* **select**, chic, high-class, elite, fashionable, stylish, elegant, choice, special, premier, grade A; expensive; restrictive, restricted, limited, private, closed, cliquish, cliquey, clannish, snobbish; *Brit.* upmarket; *N. Amer.* high-toned; *informal* posh, ritzy, classy, upper-crust, top-drawer, top-people's; *Brit. informal* swish; *N. Amer. informal* swank, tony; *rare* discriminative.
OPPOSITE open.
2 *his exclusive concern with himself* **complete**, full, entire, whole, total, absolute; to the exclusion of everything else.
OPPOSITE partial.
3 *I have reserved a room for your exclusive use* **sole**, undivided, unshared, unique, only, individual, personal, private, single, especial; dedicated.
4 *prices are exclusive of VAT and delivery* **not including**, excluding, leaving out, omitting, excepting, with the omission/exception of, except for, not counting, leaving aside, barring.
OPPOSITE inclusive of.
5 *mutually exclusive alternatives* **incompatible**, irreconcilable.
▶ **noun** *the magazine's six-page exclusive* **scoop**, exposé, revelation, special, inside story; coup.

excommunicate ▶ **verb** *Martin Luther was excommunicated by the Pope* cast out of the church, exclude from participating in the sacraments; *rare* unchurch. *See also* EXCLUDE, DEBAR.

excoriate ▶ **verb 1** (*technical*) *the surrounding skin had been excoriated* **abrade**, rub away, rub off, rub raw, scrape, scratch, chafe, damage; strip away, peel away, skin; *technical* decorticate.
2 (*rare*) *he was excoriated in the press for covering up the truth. See* CRITICIZE.

E

excrement ▶ noun **faeces**, excreta, stools, droppings; waste matter, ordure, dung, manure, mess, muck; sewage, black water; *informal* poo, doo-doo, doings; *Brit. informal* cack, whoopsies, jobbies; *N. Amer. informal* poop; *vulgar slang* shit, crap, turds; *archaic* night soil, sullage; *rare* egesta.

WORD LINKS

related prefixes	**copro-, scato-**
medical study of excrement	**scatology**
fear of excrement	**coprophobia**
excrement-eating	**coprophagous**

excrescence ▶ noun **1** *a large excrescence on his leg* **growth**, lump, swelling, protuberance, protrusion, knob, nodule, outgrowth; wart, boil, pustule, carbuncle, tumour.
2 *the new buildings around the cathedral were an excrescence* **eyesore**, blot on the landscape, monstrosity, disfigurement; *informal* sight.

E

excrete ▶ verb *the process by which waste products are excreted from the body* **expel**, pass, void, discharge, eject, evacuate, eliminate; exude, emit; defecate, urinate; *rare* egest.
OPPOSITES absorb, ingest.

excruciating ▶ adjective *an excruciating pain in her head* **agonizing**, extremely painful, severe, acute, intense, extreme, savage, violent, racking, searing, piercing, stabbing, raging, harrowing, tormenting, grievous; dreadful, awful, terrible, unbearable, unendurable, more than one can bear, more than flesh and blood can bear; *informal* splitting, thumping, pounding, killing; *literary* exquisite.
OPPOSITES slight, mild.

excursion ▶ noun *an excursion to Blackpool* **trip**, outing, jaunt, expedition, journey, tour; day trip, day out, drive, run, ride; *informal* junket, spin, hop; *Scottish informal* hurl.

excusable ▶ adjective *an excusable mistake under the circumstances* **forgivable**, pardonable, defensible, justifiable, condonable, understandable, explainable; venial.
OPPOSITES inexcusable, unforgivable.

excuse ▶ verb **1** *eventually she excused him, as she always did* **forgive**, pardon, absolve, exonerate, acquit; make allowances for; *informal* let someone off (the hook); *rare* exculpate.
OPPOSITES punish, blame.
2 *such conduct can never be excused* **justify**, defend, make excuses for, make a case for, explain (away), rationalize, condone, vindicate, warrant; mitigate, palliate; apologize for; forgive, overlook, disregard, ignore, pass over, turn a blind eye to, turn a deaf ear to, wink at, blink at, indulge, tolerate, sanction; *rare* extenuate.
OPPOSITE condemn.
3 *she has been* ***excused from*** *her duties for now* **let off**, release, relieve, exempt, spare, absolve, free, liberate; *rare* dispense.
OPPOSITE hold to.
▶ noun **1** *that's no excuse for stealing* **justification**, defence, reason, explanation, mitigating circumstances, mitigation, extenuation, palliation, vindication; grounds, cause, basis, call; argument, apology, apologia, plea.
2 *he needed an excuse to get away from his family* **pretext**, ostensible reason, pretence, front, cover-up, fabrication, evasion; *informal* story, alibi, line, cop-out; *Brit. informal* get-out.
3 (*informal*) *that pathetic* ***excuse for*** *a man!* **travesty of**, apology for, poor specimen of, pitiful example of, mockery of; pale shadow of, poor imitation of.

CHOOSE THE RIGHT WORD

excuse, forgive, pardon, condone
See FORGIVE.

execrable ▶ adjective *an execrable piece of work* **appalling**, awful, dreadful, terrible, frightful, atrocious, very bad, lamentable; disgusting, deplorable, disgraceful, reprehensible, shameful, abominable, abhorrent, loathsome, odious, heinous, hateful, detestable, despicable, foul, vile, scandalous, contemptible, repugnant, repellent, revolting, unspeakable, wretched; *informal* abysmal, diabolical, shocking, rotten, woeful, lousy, dire, the pits, God-awful, tenth-rate; *Brit. informal* chronic, pants, a load of pants; *vulgar slang* crap, shit; *rare* egregious.
OPPOSITES good, admirable.

execrate ▶ verb **1** *the men were execrated as dangerous and corrupt* **revile**, denounce, decry, condemn, vilify; **detest**, loathe, hate, abhor, abominate, despise, regard with disgust, feel disgust for, feel aversion/revulsion to; *rare* excoriate, anathematize, vilipend.
OPPOSITES praise; adore.
2 (*archaic*) *he longed to execrate aloud* **swear**, **curse**, blaspheme, utter profanities, utter oaths, be foul-mouthed, use bad/foul language, be blasphemous, take the Lord's name in vain, swear like a trooper, damn; *informal* cuss.

execration ▶ noun (*archaic*) *Oswald howled execrations* **expletive**, **oath**, curse, swear word, imprecation, profanity, obscenity, four-letter word, dirty word; *informal* cuss, cuss word.

execute ▶ verb **1** *he was convicted of treason and executed* **put to death**, carry out a sentence of death on, kill; hang, send to the gibbet, behead, guillotine, decapitate, electrocute, shoot, put before a firing squad, send to the gas chamber, garrotte, crucify, stone to death; lynch; *N. Amer.* send to the electric chair, send to the chair; *informal* string up; *N. Amer. informal* fry; *in Turkey, historical* bowstring.
2 *the corporation executed a series of financial deals* **carry out**, accomplish, perform, implement, effect, bring off, bring about, achieve, carry off, carry through, complete, enact, enforce, put into effect, put into practice, do, discharge, prosecute, engineer, administer, attain, realize, fulfil; perpetrate; *informal* pull off, swing, cut; *archaic* acquit oneself of; *rare* effectuate.
3 *a variety act which is cleverly conceived and fairly well executed* **perform**, present, render; stage, put on.

execution ▶ noun **1** *the execution of the plan* **implementation**, carrying out, accomplishment, performance, effecting, bringing off, bringing about, achievement, carrying off, carrying through, completion, enactment, enforcement, discharge, prosecution, engineering, attainment, realization, fulfilment; perpetration.
2 *the execution of the play* **performance**, presentation, rendition, rendering, staging; delivery, technique, style.
3 *thousands were sentenced to execution or imprisonment* **capital punishment**, the death penalty, being put to death, killing; the gibbet, the gallows, the noose, the rope, the scaffold, the guillotine, the firing squad; *N. Amer.* the (electric) chair; *informal* the drop; *N. Amer. informal* necktie party; *historical* noyade.

executioner ▶ noun **hangman**, official killer; firing squad; *historical* headsman, Jack Ketch.

executive ▶ adjective *a district assembly with executive powers* **administrative**, decision-making, directorial, directing, controlling, managerial; law-making, regulating; professional, white-collar.
▶ noun **1** *a top-level meeting of executives at the investment bank* **chief**, head, principal, senior official, senior manager, senior administrator; director, managing director, MD, CEO, chief executive officer, president, chairman, chairwoman, controller; *Brit.* director general; *informal* boss, boss man, top dog, bigwig, big wheel, big Daddy, big Chief, exec, suit; *Brit. informal* guv'nor; *N. Amer. informal* numero uno, Mister Big, (head) honcho, big kahuna, big white chief, sachem, padrone; *derogatory* fat cat.
2 *the executive has increased in number* **administration**, leadership, management, directorate, directors; government, legislative body; *informal* top brass.

exegesis ▶ noun *the exegesis of ancient texts* **interpretation**, explanation, exposition, explication, elucidation, clarification; gloss, annotation.

exemplar ▶ noun *he was regarded as an exemplar of rationality and decorum* **epitome**, perfect example, shining example, model, paragon, ideal, type, exemplification, definitive example, textbook example, embodiment, essence, quintessence; paradigm, archetype, prototype, pattern, blueprint, standard, criterion, benchmark, yardstick; byword; *rare* avatar.

exemplary ▶ adjective **1** *her exemplary behaviour* **perfect**, ideal, model, faultless, without fault, copybook, flawless, impeccable, consummate; excellent, outstanding, exceptional, admirable, fine, very good, commendable, laudable, praiseworthy, meritorious, honourable, estimable, above/beyond reproach, blameless, irreproachable, unimpeachable; *rare* applaudable.
OPPOSITES deplorable, unworthy.
2 *exemplary jail sentences* **serving as a deterrent**, example-setting, lesson-teaching; **cautionary**, warning, admonitory; *rare* monitory.
3 *her works are exemplary of certain feminist arguments* **typical**, characteristic, representative, illustrative; archetypal, paradigmatic; *rare* epitomic.
OPPOSITES unrepresentative, atypical.

exemplify ▶ verb **1** *a case study of a police operation which exemplifies current trends* **typify**, epitomize, be a typical example of, serve as a typical example of, represent, be representative of, symbolize; personify, embody, be the embodiment of; demonstrate, show.
2 *he exemplified his point with an anecdote* **illustrate**, give an example of, give an instance of, demonstrate, instance; *rare* instantiate.

exempt ▶ adjective *these patients are exempt from all charges* **free from**, not liable to, not subject to; exempted, spared, excepted, excused, absolved, released, discharged; immune.
OPPOSITES liable to, subject to.
▶ verb *he had been* ***exempted from*** *military service* **excuse**, free, release, exclude, give/grant immunity, spare; let off, relieve of, make an exception of/for; liberate, absolve, discharge; *informal* let off the hook; *N. Amer. informal* grandfather; *rare* dispense.

exemption ▶ noun *exemption from the payment of road tax* **immunity**, exception, dispensation, indemnity, exclusion, freedom, release, relief, absolution, exoneration; special treatment, privilege, favouritism; impunity; *informal* let-off; *rare* derogation.
OPPOSITE liability.

exercise ▶ noun **1** *exercise improves your heart and lung power* **physical activity**, movement, exertion, effort, work; a workout, working-out, training, drilling; gymnastics, sports, games, PE (physical education), PT (physical training), aerobics, step aerobics, jogging, running, circuit training, aquarobics, callisthenics, isometrics, eurhythmics, keep-fit, dancercise, bodybuilding; *informal* physical jerks; *informal, dated* one's daily dozen; *trademark* Boxercise.
2 *translation exercises from and into French* **task**, piece of work, problem, assignment, piece of school work, piece of homework; *Music* étude.
3 *the exercise of professional skill* **use**, utilization, employment; **practice**, putting into practice, application, operation, exertion, performance, implementation, discharge, accomplishment.
4 (**exercises**) *military exercises* **manoeuvres**, operations; war games, field day.
▶ verb **1** *she still exercised every day* **work out**, do exercises, keep fit, train, drill, engage in physical activity; *informal* pump iron.
2 *he must learn to exercise patience* **use**, employ, make use of, utilize, avail oneself of, put to use; **practise**, apply, bring to bear, bring into play, implement, exert, wield.
3 *the problem continued to exercise him* **worry**, trouble, concern, make anxious, bother, disturb, perturb, perplex, puzzle, distress, occupy someone's thoughts, preoccupy, prey on someone's mind, gnaw at, lie heavy on, burden, make uneasy, agitate; *informal* bug, make someone scratch their head, do someone's head in; *archaic* pother.

exert ▶ verb **1** *he exerted considerable emotional pressure on me* **bring to bear**, apply, bring into play, exercise, employ, use, make use of, utilize, deploy; wield; expend, spend.
2 *he had been exerting himself to make a good impression on her* **make an effort**, try hard, strive, endeavour, apply oneself, do one's best, do all one can, do one's utmost, give one's all, make every effort, spare no effort, be at pains, put oneself out; struggle, labour, toil, strain, push oneself, drive oneself, work hard, work like a Trojan; rack/cudgel one's brains; *informal* give it one's best shot, go all out, pull out all the stops, bend/lean over backwards, put one's back into it, knock oneself out, do one's damnedest, move heaven and earth, beaver away, slog away, keep one's nose to the grindstone, work one's socks off, break sweat; *N. Amer. informal* do one's darnedest/durnedest, bust one's chops; *Austral. informal* go for the doctor.

exertion ▶ noun **1** *she was panting with the exertion* **effort**, strain, struggle, toil, endeavour, hard work, labour, industry, {blood, sweat, and tears}; pains, assiduity, assiduousness; exercise, activity; *informal* elbow grease, sweat; *Brit. informal* graft; *Austral./NZ informal* yakka; *literary* travail, moil.
2 *the exertion of pressure* **use**, application, appliance, bringing to bear, exercise, employment, utilization; expenditure.

exhalation ▶ noun **1** *a long exhalation of relief* **breath**, breathing out; sigh; *technical* expiration.
OPPOSITE inhalation.
2 *the exhalation of gases | noxious exhalations* **emission**, giving off, emanation, discharge; fume, vapour, effluvium, effluent; *rare* exsufflation.

exhale ▶ verb **1** *he exhaled a cloud of cigarette smoke* **breathe out**, blow out, puff out; *technical* expire.
OPPOSITE inhale.
2 *the jungle exhaled mists of early morning* **give off**, emanate, send forth, emit, discharge; *rare* exsufflate.

exhaust ▶ verb **1** *the effort had exhausted him* **tire out**, wear out, overtire, overtax, fatigue, weary, tire, drain, run someone into the ground, run someone ragged, enervate, sap, debilitate, prostrate, enfeeble; wear oneself to a shadow; *informal* do in, take it out of one, wipe out, fag out, knock out, shatter, wear oneself to a frazzle, frazzle, nearly kill; *Brit. informal* knacker; *N. Amer. informal* poop, tucker out; *Austral./NZ & Irish informal* root.
OPPOSITES invigorate, refresh.
2 *the country has exhausted its treasury reserves* **use up**, run through, go through, consume, finish, deplete, expend, spend, dissipate, waste, squander, fritter away; empty, milk, drain, suck dry, impoverish; *informal* blow, bleed.
OPPOSITES replenish, restock.
3 *I think we've exhausted the subject* **say all there is to say about**, leave nothing left to say about, do to death; treat thoroughly, develop completely, expound in great detail about, study in great detail, research completely, leave no stone left unturned, go over with a fine-tooth comb.
OPPOSITE touch on.

exhausted ▶ adjective **1** *I must go to bed—I'm exhausted* **tired out**, worn out, weary, dog-tired, bone-tired, bone-weary, ready to drop, on one's last legs, asleep on one's feet, drained, fatigued, enervated, debilitated, spent; jet-lagged; out of breath, breathless, panting, puffing, puffed, puffed out, puffing and blowing, gasping (for breath); *informal* done in, all in, dead on one's feet, beat, dead beat, shattered, bushed, fagged out, knocked out, wiped out, running on empty, zonked out, worn to a frazzle, frazzled, bushwhacked; *Brit. informal* knackered, whacked (out), shagged out, jiggered; *Scottish informal* wabbit; *N. Amer. informal* pooped, tuckered out, fried, whipped; *Austral./NZ informal* stonkered; *Brit. vulgar slang* buggered; *Austral./NZ vulgar slang* rooted; *archaic* toilworn; *rare* fordone.
OPPOSITES fresh as a daisy, raring to go.
2 *the treasury's exhausted reserves* **used up**, at an end, consumed, finished, spent, depleted; empty, drained, impoverished, bankrupt.
OPPOSITES replenished, restocked.

exhausting ▶ adjective *a long and exhausting journey* **tiring**, wearying, taxing, fatiguing, wearing, enervating, draining, sapping, debilitating; arduous, strenuous, uphill, onerous, punishing, demanding, exacting, burdensome, gruelling, back-breaking, crushing, crippling; *informal* killing, murderous, hellish; *Brit. informal* knackering; *rare* exigent.
OPPOSITES invigorating, refreshing.

exhaustion ▶ noun **1** *sheer exhaustion forced Paul to give up* **extreme tiredness**, overtiredness, fatigue, weariness, lack of energy, enervation, debilitation, debility, faintness, prostration, enfeeblement, lassitude; jet lag; *Medicine* inanition, asthenia.
OPPOSITE vigour.
2 *the rapid exhaustion of fossil fuel reserves* **consumption**, depletion, using up, expenditure; draining, emptying, sapping.
OPPOSITE replenishment.

exhaustive ▶ adjective *an exhaustive study of the subject* **comprehensive**, all-inclusive, complete, full, full-scale, all-embracing, all-encompassing, encyclopedic, thorough, in-depth, thoroughgoing, extensive, intensive, all-out, profound, far-reaching, sweeping, umbrella; definitive; detailed, minute, meticulous, painstaking, careful; *informal* wall-to-wall.
OPPOSITES perfunctory, incomplete.

exhibit ▶ verb **1** *a selection of the paintings were exhibited at Sotheby's* **put on display**, put on show, display, show, show to the public, put on public view, present, unveil, model, parade, showcase; set out, lay out, array, arrange; hang.
2 *Luke had begun to exhibit signs of jealousy* **show**, reveal, display, manifest, evince, betray, give away, disclose; express, indicate, demonstrate, present, make clear, make plain, evidence; parade, flaunt.
OPPOSITES conceal, hide.
▶ noun **1** *it is now an exhibit at the British Museum* **object on display**, item, piece.
2 (*N. Amer.*) *people flocked to the exhibit.* See EXHIBITION.

exhibition ▶ noun **1** *an exhibition of French sculpture* **(public) display**, show, showing, presentation, demonstration, showcase, mounting, spectacle; retrospective, biennale; exposition, Expo, fair, trade fair, world fair; *N. Amer.* exhibit; *informal* demo.
2 *a false but convincing exhibition of concern* **display**, show, demonstration, manifestation, expression, indication; revelation, betrayal, disclosure; parade.

exhibitionist ▶ noun **show-off**, posturer, poser, self-publicist; extrovert; *N. Amer. informal* showboat; *Austral./NZ informal* lair; *rare* attitudinizer.
OPPOSITE shrinking violet.

exhilarate ▶ verb *he was exhilarated by the boat's speed* **thrill**, excite, intoxicate; **elate**, make someone's spirits soar, make very happy, give someone great pleasure, delight, gladden, brighten, cheer up, enliven, animate, invigorate, energize, lift, stimulate, raise someone's spirits, revitalize, refresh; *informal* give someone a kick, give someone a thrill, give someone a buzz, turn someone on; *N. Amer. informal* give someone a charge; *rare* inspirit.
OPPOSITE depress.

exhilarating ▶ adjective *an exhilarating experience* **thrilling**, exciting, intoxicating, heady, stimulating, invigorating, electrifying, energizing, uplifting, enlivening, revitalizing, vitalizing, stirring, breathtaking; refreshing, bracing; *informal* mind-blowing.
OPPOSITES boring, depressing.

exhilaration ▶ noun *a feeling of exhilaration swept through her* **elation**, euphoria, exultation, exaltation, joy, happiness, delight, joyousness, jubilation, rapture, ecstasy, bliss, rhapsody; excitement, intoxication, invigoration, ebullience, high spirits, glee, gleefulness, gaiety, animation, revitalization.
OPPOSITES dejection, depression.

exhort ▶ verb *he exhorted delegates to fight corruption and bureaucracy* **urge**, encourage, call on, enjoin, adjure, charge, try to persuade, press, pressure, put pressure on, use pressure on, pressurize, lean on, push; egg on, spur, incite, goad; bid, appeal to, entreat, implore, beseech; advise, counsel, admonish, warn.
OPPOSITE discourage.

exhortation ▶ noun **1** *no amount of exhortation had any effect* **urging**, encouragement, persuasion, pressure, pressurization, pushing, insistence; incitement, goading, egging on; beseeching; admonishment, warning; *rare* paraenesis.
OPPOSITE discouragement.
2 *the government's exhortations to the electorate* **enjoinder**, call, charge, injunction; **entreaty**, appeal; admonition, warning, sermon, lecture, harangue; *rare* obtestation, protreptic.

exhume ▶ verb *four years later his body was exhumed* **disinter**, dig up, unearth, bring out of the ground; *rare* disentomb, unbury, ungrave.

OPPOSITE bury.

exigency ▶ noun (*rare*) **1** *the exigencies of the continuing war* **need**, demand, requirement, want; necessity, essential, requisite.
2 *financial exigency dictated that the government adopt a peace policy* **urgency**, emergency, extremity, crisis, difficulty, pressure.

exiguous ▶ adjective (*rare*) *the exiguous post-war sugar ration* **meagre**, inadequate, insufficient, small, scant, scanty, paltry, negligible, limited, restricted, modest, sparse, spare, deficient, skimpy, short, little, miserable, pitiful, puny, miserly, niggardly, beggarly; *informal* measly, stingy, pathetic, piddling.
OPPOSITES ample, generous.

exile ▶ noun **1** *his exile from the land of his birth* **banishment**, expulsion, expatriation, deportation, eviction; uprooting, separation; extradition; *historical* transportation; (*in ancient Greece*) ostracism.
OPPOSITE return.
2 *political exiles* **émigré**, expatriate; displaced person, refugee, deportee; outcast, pariah; *informal* DP, expat.
▶ verb *a corrupt dictator who had been exiled from his country* **expel**, **banish**, expatriate, deport, ban, bar; drive out, throw out, cast out, eject, oust, outlaw; uproot, separate; extradite; *Christianity* excommunicate; *historical* transport, displace; (*in ancient Greece*) ostracize.

exist ▶ verb **1** *animals which existed at some time in the distant past* **live**, be alive, be living, have life, breathe, draw breath; be, have being, have existence, be extant.
2 *the liberal climate that existed during his presidency* **prevail**, **occur**, be found, be met with, be in existence; remain, obtain, continue, last, endure; be the case.
3 *she had to exist on an average income of £50 a week* **survive**, subsist, live, stay alive, support oneself, eke out a living, eke out an existence; manage, make do, keep going, struggle along, scrape by, keep one's head above water, make ends meet; *informal* get by, keep the wolf from the door.

existence ▶ noun **1** *a crisis that threatened the industry's continued existence* **actuality**, **being**, existing, reality, fact; survival, continuance, continuation, subsistence, living; *Philosophy* quiddity, esse.
OPPOSITE non-existence.
2 *her drab suburban existence* **way of life**, way of living, manner of living, life, lifestyle, circumstances, situation.
3 (*archaic*) *the malevolent existences of the night* **being**, entity, creation.
□ **in existence 1** *scientists believe there are several million unidentified species in existence* **alive**, existing, extant, existent.
OPPOSITE extinct.
2 *the only copy of the book still in existence* **surviving**, remaining, undestroyed, lasting, continuing, enduring; about, around, in circulation.
OPPOSITES destroyed, lost.

existent ▶ adjective *species that are no longer existent* **in existence**, alive, existing, living, extant, surviving, remaining, undestroyed, enduring, lasting; around, about in circulation; prevailing, current.
OPPOSITE non-existent.

exit ▶ noun **1** *the fire exit* **way out**, door, egress, passage out, escape route; doorway, gate, gateway, portal; outlet, vent.
OPPOSITE entrance.
2 *take the second exit on the left* **turning**, turn-off, turn, side road; *N. Amer.* turnout.
3 *his sudden exit from America* **departure**, leaving, withdrawal, retirement, going, decamping, retreat, pull-out, evacuation; leave-taking, farewell, adieu; flight, exodus, escape; *informal* quitting.
OPPOSITE arrival.
▶ verb *the doorway through which the doctor had just exited* **leave**, go (out), depart, take one's leave, make one's departure, make an exit; withdraw, retreat, retire; *informal* quit.
OPPOSITE enter.

exodus ▶ noun *the exodus of refugees from Albania* **mass departure**, withdrawal, evacuation, leaving, exit; migration, emigration, hegira, diaspora; flight, escape, retreat, fleeing; *S. African informal* chicken run.
OPPOSITE arrival.

exonerate ▶ verb **1** *the inquiry exonerated Lewis and his company* **absolve**, clear, acquit, declare innocent, find innocent, pronounce not guilty, discharge; vindicate; *rare* exculpate.
OPPOSITES charge, convict.
2 *Pope Clement V exonerated the king from his oath to the barons* **release**, discharge, relieve, free, liberate; excuse, exempt, except; *informal* let off; *rare* dispense.
OPPOSITE hold to.

exoneration ▶ noun **1** *despite his exoneration, he resigned* **vindication**, freeing from blame, absolution, acquittal, discharge; *rare* exculpation.
OPPOSITES conviction, blaming.
2 *we should not seek exoneration from the consequences of our acts* **immunity**, exemption, indemnity, dispensation; release, freedom; *informal* let-off; *rare* derogation.
OPPOSITE liability.

exorbitant ▶ adjective *the fees charged by the consultants were exorbitant* **extortionate**, excessively high, extremely high, excessive, sky-high, prohibitive, outrageous, unreasonable, preposterous, inordinate, immoderate, inflated, monstrous, unwarranted, unconscionable, huge, enormous, disproportionate; punitive, ruinous; expensive, extravagant; *Brit.* over the odds; *informal* criminal, steep, stiff, over the top, OTT, costing an arm and a leg, costing a bomb, costing the earth, daylight robbery, a rip-off.
OPPOSITES reasonable, competitive.

exorcism ▶ noun **1** *the exorcism of evil spirits* **driving out**, casting out, expulsion; *rare* insufflation.
2 *returning to the scene of the crime would be a kind of exorcism for them both* **catharsis**, cleansing, purification, purgation, release, deliverance; *rare* lustration.

exorcize ▶ verb **1** *an attempt to exorcize a spirit* **drive out**, cast out, expel.
2 *Jesuit priests were called in to exorcize the house of the demon* **rid**, deliver, free, purify, cleanse, purge; *rare* lustrate.

exordium ▶ noun (*rare*) *his eloquent exordium* **introduction**, opening, beginning, preface, prelude, foreword, preamble, prologue, preliminary/opening remarks; *informal* intro; *rare* prolegomenon, proem, prolusion, prodrome.
OPPOSITE conclusion.

exotic ▶ adjective **1** *exotic birds* **foreign**, non-native, tropical; alien, imported, introduced, non-naturalized, unnaturalized.
OPPOSITE native.
2 *exotic places like Indonesia and Thailand* **foreign**, faraway, far-off, far-flung, unfamiliar; distant, remote.
OPPOSITES familiar, nearby.
3 *Linda's exotic appearance* **striking**, colourful, eye-catching; **unusual**, unconventional, out of the ordinary, extravagant, remarkable, sensational, astonishing, strange, outlandish, bizarre, fantastic, peculiar, weird, outrageous, curious, different, unfamiliar; Bohemian, alternative, avant-garde, foreign-looking; attractive, glamorous, romantic, fascinating; *Brit.* out of the common; *informal* offbeat, off the wall.
OPPOSITES unremarkable, conventional.
4 *exotic dancers* **erotic**, sexy, provocative, go-go, striptease, titillating, risqué; *informal* raunchy.

expand ▶ verb **1** *metals expand when heated* **increase in size**, become larger, enlarge; swell, become distended, dilate, inflate, balloon, puff out/up; lengthen, stretch; thicken, fatten, fill out; *rare* intumesce, tumefy.
OPPOSITES shrink, contract, condense.
2 *the company is expanding | an excellent opportunity for him to expand his business* **grow**, become/make larger, become/make bigger, increase in size/scope; extend, augment, broaden, widen, develop, diversify, multiply, add to, build up, scale up; branch out, broaden one's horizons, extend one's operations; spread, proliferate, mushroom.
OPPOSITES shrink, scale down.
3 *the young leaves began to expand* **open out**, unfold, unfurl, spread out, unroll.
4 *the minister* **expanded on** *the government's proposals* **elaborate on**, enlarge on, add detail to, go into detail about, flesh out, put flesh on the bones of, develop, supplement, amplify, expatiate on; embellish, embroider, pad out, fill out.
OPPOSITE touch on.
5 *she was made to feel witty and entertained—she expanded and flourished* **relax**, unbend, become relaxed, grow friendlier, become less reserved, become more sociable; *informal* loosen up; *N. Amer. informal* hang loose.
OPPOSITES tense up, clam up.

expanse ▶ noun *this wide expanse of grass and heather* **area**, stretch, sweep, tract, swathe, plain, field, belt, region; sea, carpet, blanket, sheet; breadth, range, spread, reach, space, extent, vastness.
OPPOSITES confined space, enclosure.

expansion ▶ noun **1** *the expansion and contraction of blood vessels* **enlargement**, increase in size, swelling, distension, dilation; lengthening, elongation, stretching, thickening; *Medicine* dilatation.
OPPOSITE contraction.
2 *the expansion of the company* **growth**, increase in size, enlargement, extension, augmentation, development, evolution; diversification, build-up, buildout, scaling up, aggrandizement; spread, proliferation, mushrooming, multiplication; *rare* evolvement.
OPPOSITE reduction in size.
3 *the book is an expansion of a lecture given last year* **elaboration**, enlargement, amplification, development; embellishment.
OPPOSITES summary, abridgement.

expansive ▶ adjective **1** *fine views of the expansive moorland* **extensive**, sweeping, rolling; spacious.
2 *chapters which are expansive in their historical coverage* **wide-ranging**, extensive, broad, wide, all-embracing, comprehensive, thorough, inclusive.
OPPOSITES limited, restricted.
3 *after a glass or two of wine, Cara became engagingly expansive*

communicative, forthcoming, sociable, friendly, outgoing, unreserved, uninhibited, open, affable, amiable, genial, chatty, talkative, conversational, garrulous, loquacious, voluble, effusive, demonstrative, extrovert, extroverted; discursive.
OPPOSITES uncommunicative, reserved, taciturn.

expatiate ▶ verb *she expatiated* ***on*** *the subject at some length* **hold forth about**, speak/write at length about, pontificate about, discourse on, expound, go into detail about, go on about, dwell on; expand on, enlarge on, elaborate on, amplify, embellish; *informal* spout about, sound off about; *rare* perorate on, dilate on, dissertate on.

expatriate ▶ noun *the level of salary paid to expatriates working overseas* **emigrant**, non-native, émigré, migrant, economic migrant, guest worker; displaced person, refugee, exile; *German* Gastarbeiter; *informal* expat, DP.
OPPOSITE national.
▶ adjective *expatriate workers* **emigrant**, living abroad, working abroad, non-native, émigré; displaced, refugee, exiled; *informal* expat.
OPPOSITES native, indigenous.
▶ verb 1 *he never visited Europe—still less was he tempted to* ***expatriate himself*** **settle abroad**, live abroad, relocate abroad.
2 *he was expatriated for the term of his natural life* **exile**, deport, banish, expel; *historical* displace, transport.
OPPOSITE repatriate.

expect ▶ verb 1 *I expect she'll be late* **suppose**, presume, think it likely, think, believe, imagine, assume, conjecture, surmise, calculate, judge; trust; *informal* guess, reckon; *N. Amer. informal* figure.
2 *I'm expecting a letter from him | a 10 per cent rise in profits was expected* **anticipate**, await, look for, hope for, watch for, look forward to, look ahead to, have in prospect; contemplate, bargain for/on, bank on, be prepared for, plan for; predict, forecast, foresee, prophesy, envisage, envision.
3 *we expect total discretion and loyalty* **require**, ask for, call for, look for, wish, want, hope for; count on, rely on; insist on, demand.

> CHOOSE THE RIGHT WORD
> **expect, anticipate, foresee**
> *See* ANTICIPATE.

expectancy ▶ noun 1 *an atmosphere of feverish expectancy* **anticipation**, expectation, eagerness, hope, hopefulness; excitement, suspense.
2 *a life expectancy of 77.6 years* **likelihood**, probability, outlook, prospect.

expectant ▶ adjective 1 *hundreds of expectant fans* **eager**, **excited**, agog, waiting with bated breath, breathless, waiting, anticipatory, hopeful; in suspense, on tenterhooks, on the edge of one's seat, keyed up, on pins and needles, anxious.
OPPOSITE uninterested.
2 *an expectant mother* **pregnant**, having a baby, having a child, carrying a child; *French* enceinte; *informal* expecting, in the family way, expecting a happy event, eating for two, preggers, preggy, with a bun in the oven, with one in the oven; *Brit. informal* up the duff, in the club, in the pudding club, up the spout, up the stick; *N. Amer. informal* knocked up; *Austral. informal* preggo, clucky; *informal, dated* in trouble, in pod; *technical* gravid, parturient; *archaic* with child, heavy/big with child, in a delicate condition, in an interesting condition, childing, on the way; *rare* impregnate.

expectation ▶ noun 1 *her expectations were unrealistic* **supposition**, assumption, belief, presupposition, presumption, conjecture, surmise, reckoning, calculation, prediction, forecast, projection; assurance, confidence, trust.
2 *his body grew tense with expectation* **anticipation**, expectancy, eagerness, hope, hopefulness; excitement, suspense.
3 (*archaic*) *a young man of expensive habits and no expectations* **prospects**, prospects of inheritance, hopes, outlook, lookout.

expecting ▶ adjective (*informal*) *his wife's expecting again* **pregnant**, expecting a baby, having a baby, having a child, carrying a child; *French* enceinte; *informal* in the family way, expecting a happy event, eating for two, preggers, preggy, with a bun in the oven, with one in the oven; *Brit. informal* in the club, in the pudding club, up the duff, up the spout, up the stick; *N. Amer. informal* knocked up; *Austral. informal* preggo, clucky; *informal, dated* in trouble, in pod; *technical* gravid, parturient; *archaic* with child, heavy/big with child, in a delicate condition, in an interesting condition, childing, on the way; *rare* impregnate.

expediency, **expedience** ▶ noun *he has abandoned his principles for the sake of political expediency* **convenience**, **advantage**, advantageousness, usefulness, utility, benefit, profitability, profit, gain, gainfulness, effectiveness; practicality, pragmatism; prudence, judiciousness, desirability, suitability, advisability, appropriateness, aptness, fitness, timeliness, opportunism, propitiousness.
OPPOSITE disadvantage.

expedient ▶ adjective *a politically expedient strategy* **convenient**, **advantageous**, in one's own interests, to one's own advantage, useful, of use, of service, beneficial, of benefit, profitable, gainful, effective, helpful; practical, pragmatic, strategic, tactical; politic, prudent, wise, judicious, sensible, desirable, suitable, advisable, appropriate, apt, fit, timely, opportune, propitious.
OPPOSITES inexpedient, ill-advised.
▶ noun *a temporary expedient adopted for the purpose of settling the financial crisis* **measure**, means, method, stratagem, scheme, plan, course of action, move, tactic, manoeuvre, recourse, resource, device, tool, contrivance, ploy, plot, machination, trick, ruse, artifice, invention; stopgap; *informal* dodge; *Austral. informal* lurk; *archaic* shift, fetch.

expedite ▶ verb *the court has the power to expedite the decree absolute* **speed up**, accelerate, hurry, hasten, step up, quicken, precipitate, rush; advance, facilitate, ease, make easier, further, promote, aid, push through, push, give a push to, press, urge on, forward, boost, give a boost to, stimulate, spur on, help along, oil the wheels for, smooth the way for, clear a path for; finish/accomplish/achieve quickly, dispatch; *informal* dash off, make short work of.
OPPOSITES delay; hinder.

expedition ▶ noun 1 *Captain Scott's expedition to the South Pole* **journey**, voyage, tour, odyssey; undertaking, enterprise, mission, project, quest, operation, commission, assignment, exploit; exploration, safari, trek, hike, survey; *archaic* peregrination.
2 (*informal*) *a shopping expedition* **trip**, excursion, outing, journey, jaunt, run; *informal* junket, hop.
3 *Gould was the only member of the expedition satisfied with its outcome* **group**, team, party, company, crew, band, troop, squad, crowd.
4 (*formal*) *he was told to use all expedition possible* **speed**, haste, hastiness, hurriedness, promptness, speediness, swiftness, quickness, rapidity, briskness, promptitude, velocity; alacrity, urgency, readiness, dispatch; *rare* expeditiousness; *literary* fleetness, celerity.

expeditious ▶ adjective *an expeditious system for examining claims for refugee status* **speedy**, swift, quick, rapid, fast; prompt, punctual, immediate, instant, sudden; high-speed, fast-track, whistle-stop, lightning, meteoric, whirlwind; brisk, nimble; efficient, diligent; hasty, summary, abrupt; *literary* fleet, rathe.
OPPOSITE slow.

expel ▶ verb 1 *the opposition leader was expelled from her party* **throw out**, bar, ban, debar, drum out, thrust out, push out, turn out, oust, remove, get rid of; reject, dismiss; blackball, blacklist; *Military* cashier; *informal* chuck out, sling out, fling out, kick/boot out, heave out, send packing; *Brit. informal* turf out; *N. Amer. informal* give someone the bum's rush; *dated* out.
OPPOSITES admit; welcome.
2 *he was released and expelled from the country* **banish**, exile, deport, evict, expatriate, dismiss, displace; oust, drive out, throw out, cast out, purge, proscribe, outlaw; (*in ancient Greece*) ostracize.
3 *Dolly expelled a hiss* **let out**, discharge, eject, force out, issue, send forth; excrete, evacuate, ejaculate, belch, disgorge, eliminate, void, spew out, spit out, vomit.

expend ▶ verb 1 *they had already expended $75,000 in legal costs* **spend**, pay out, lay out, disburse, dole out, get through, go through; lavish, squander, waste, fritter (away), dissipate, spend like water, throw around like confetti; *informal* fork out, shell out, dish out, cough up, blow, splurge, pour/throw down the drain, spend money as if it grows on trees, spend money as if there were no tomorrow, spend money as if it were going out of style/fashion; *Brit. informal* splash out, stump up, blue; *N. Amer. informal* ante up, pony up.
OPPOSITES save, conserve.
2 *pushing heavy crates expends a lot of energy* **use up**, use, utilize, make use of, consume, eat up, deplete, drain, sap; exhaust, empty, get through, go through, finish off.
OPPOSITE conserve.

expendable ▶ adjective 1 *he was tossed out of work when an accountant decided he was expendable* **dispensable**, able to be sacrificed, replaceable; non-essential, inessential, not essential, unimportant, unnecessary, unneeded, not required; superfluous, extraneous; disposable.
OPPOSITES indispensable; important.
2 *an expendable satellite launcher* **disposable**, throwaway, one use, single-use, replaceable.

expenditure ▶ noun 1 *the expenditure of funds* **spending**, paying out, outlay, disbursement, doling out; lavishing, squandering, waste, wasting, frittering (away), dissipation, dissipating.
OPPOSITES saving; conservation.
2 *the government is anxious to reduce public expenditure* **outgoings**, costs, payments, expenses, overheads, dues, money spent; spending, outlay.
OPPOSITE income.

expense ▶ noun 1 *Nigel resented the expense of entertaining* **cost**, price; charge, outlay, fee, tariff, toll, levy, payment, amount, rate, figure; *informal, humorous* damage.
2 *most regular expenses can be paid by standing order* **outgoing**, payment, outlay, disbursement, expenditure, charge, bill, overhead; (**expenses**) incidentals.
3 *the imposition of stringent pollution controls will come at the expense of jobs*

E

sacrifice, cost, loss.

expensive ▶ adjective *an expensive restaurant* **costly**, dear, high-priced, high-cost, exorbitant, extortionate, overpriced; immoderate, extravagant, lavish; valuable, precious, priceless, worth its weight in gold, worth a king's ransom; *Brit.* over the odds; *informal* steep, pricey, sky-high, costing an arm and a leg, costing the earth, costing a bomb, daylight robbery.
OPPOSITES cheap; economical.

experience ▶ noun **1** *salary will be commensurate with qualifications and experience* **skill**, **practical knowledge**, practice; training, learning, education, grounding, knowledge, understanding, wisdom, professionalism; background, record, history, past; maturity, worldliness, sophistication, suaveness; *French* savoir faire; *informal* know-how.
2 *an enjoyable experience* **incident**, occurrence, event, happening, affair, episode, encounter; adventure, exploit, escapade; circumstance, case; test, trial, ordeal.
3 *David gained his first* **experience** *of business with his father and brothers* **involvement in**, participation in; **contact with**, acquaintance with, exposure to; observation of, awareness of; familiarity with, conversance with, understanding of, impression of, insight into.
▶ verb *policemen can experience harassment and distress* **undergo**, encounter, meet, have experience of, come into contact with, run into, come across, come up against, face, be faced with, confront, be forced to contend with; feel, know, become familiar with; live/go through, sustain, suffer, endure, tolerate; participate in, taste, try.

experienced ▶ adjective **1** *an experienced pilot* **knowledgeable**, skilful, skilled, expert, accomplished, adept, adroit, master, consummate, professional; proficient, trained, competent, capable, qualified, well trained, well versed; seasoned, with experience, practised, mature, veteran, long-serving, time-served, hardened, battle-scarred; *informal* crack, ace, mean, wizard.
OPPOSITES inexperienced, novice.
2 *she was naive, but deluded herself that she was experienced* **worldly wise**, sophisticated, suave, urbane, polished, refined, mature, cultivated, cultured, knowing, initiated; worldly, well travelled, unprovincial; *informal* having been around, streetwise.
OPPOSITE naive.

experiment ▶ noun **1** *she carried out experiments in the breeding of silkworms* **test**, investigation, trial, enquiry, demonstration; examination, observation; assessment, evaluation, appraisal, inspection, analysis, scrutiny, study, probe; trial run, try-out, pilot study, dummy run, dry run.
2 *these results have been established by experiment* **research**, experimentation, observation, trial and error, analysis, testing.
OPPOSITE theory.
▶ verb *in 1809 he experimented with a glider capable of lifting a man* **conduct experiments**, carry out trials/tests, conduct research; test, trial, put to the test, do tests on, try out, carry out trials on, assess, appraise, evaluate; investigate, examine, explore, observe, verify.

WORD LINKS
relating to experiment **empirical**

experimental ▶ adjective **1** *interactive computing was still at an experimental stage* **exploratory**, investigational, probing, fact-finding, trial and error; trial, test, pilot; speculative, conjectural, hypothetical, tentative; preliminary, probationary, prototype, under review, under the microscope, on the drawing board, empirical, observational; untested, untried.
OPPOSITES finished; theoretical.
2 *he started making music that was far more experimental* **innovative**, innovatory, new, original, inventive, radical, avant-garde, alternative, fringe; unfamiliar, unorthodox, unconventional, eccentric, offbeat, bohemian; *N. Amer.* left-field; *informal* go-ahead, way-out.
OPPOSITES stale, hackneyed.

expert ▶ noun *he is an expert in kendo* **specialist**, authority, pundit, oracle; adept, maestro, virtuoso, master, past master, professional, genius, wizard; connoisseur, aficionado, one of the cognoscenti, cognoscente, doyen, savant; *informal* ace, buff, pro, whizz, hotshot, old hand; *Brit. informal* dab hand; *N. Amer. informal* maven, crackerjack; *rare* proficient.
OPPOSITES inexpert, amateur.
▶ adjective *an expert chess player* **skilful**, skilled, adept, accomplished, talented, fine; master, masterly, brilliant, virtuoso, bravura, magnificent, marvellous, wonderful, outstanding, great, exceptional, superlative, formidable, excellent, dazzling, first-class, first-rate, elite, superb; proficient, good, able, apt, capable, competent, clever; experienced, practised, qualified, knowledgeable, well versed; specialist, professional; deft, dexterous, adroit; *French* au fait; *informal* wizard, ace, class, crack, top-notch, out of this world, mean, A1, demon; *vulgar slang* shit hot.
OPPOSITES inexpert, incompetent.

expertise ▶ noun *GPs will require a high level of expertise in psychiatry* **skill**, skilfulness, expertness, prowess, proficiency, competence; knowledge, command, mastery, virtuosity; ability, aptitude, facility, knack, capability, gift; deftness, dexterity, adroitness; calibre, professionalism; *informal* know-how.
OPPOSITE incompetence.

expiate ▶ verb *an attempt to expiate his sins* **atone for**, make amends for, make up for, do penance for, pay for, redress, redeem, offset, square, make good, make redress for, make reparation for, make recompense for, make restitution for, purge.

expiation ▶ noun *a great drama of revenge and expiation* **atonement**, redemption, redress, reparation, restitution, recompense, requital, purgation, penance; amends.

expire ▶ verb **1** *my contract expires at the end of the season* **run out**, become invalid, become void, be no longer valid, lapse, cease, become obsolete; **end**, finish, stop, come to an end, conclude, terminate, be over, be at an end.
OPPOSITE begin.
2 *a plaque marks the spot where he expired* **die**, pass away/on, decease, perish, depart this life, be no more, breathe one's last, draw one's last breath, meet one's end, meet one's death, meet one's Maker, give up the ghost, go to the great beyond, cross the great divide, shuffle off this mortal coil, go the way of the/all flesh, go to one's last resting place; *informal* kick the bucket, bite the dust, croak, conk out, buy it, turn up one's toes, cash in one's chips, go belly up; *Brit. informal* snuff it, peg out, pop one's clogs.
3 (*technical*) *afterwards the breath is expired* **breathe out**, exhale, puff out, blow out, expel, emit.
OPPOSITES inhale, inspire.

expiry ▶ noun **1** *the expiry of the lease* **lapse**, expiration, invalidity.
2 *the expiry of his term of office* **end**, finish, termination, conclusion, discontinuation, cessation.
OPPOSITE beginning.
3 (*archaic*) *the sad expiry of their friend* **death**, demise, passing (away/on), dying; *Law* decease; *rare* quietus.
OPPOSITE birth.

explain ▶ verb **1** *a technician explained the procedure* **describe**, give an explanation of, make clear/plain/intelligible, spell out, put into words, express in words; elucidate, expound, explicate, delineate; clarify, unfold, throw light on, clear up, simplify; gloss, interpret, decipher, decode, translate; demonstrate, show, teach, illustrate; unravel, untangle, resolve, solve; *informal* get across, get over.
OPPOSITE obscure.
2 *there was nothing in his file to explain his new-found wealth* **account for**, give an explanation for, give a reason for; justify, give a justification for, give an excuse/alibi/apologia for, make excuses for, explain away, rationalize, give a rationale for; defend, vindicate, legitimize, mitigate; *rare* extenuate.

explanation ▶ noun **1** *an explanation of the ideas contained in the essay* **clarification**, simplification; description, report, version, statement; elucidation, exposition, expounding, explication, delineation; gloss, interpretation, deciphering, decoding, translation, commentary, exegesis; demonstration, illustration; resolution, solution; *informal* the why and wherefore.
2 *I suppose I owe you an explanation about Louise* **account**, reason; justification, excuse, alibi, apologia, rationalization, rationale; defence, vindication, mitigation; *rare* extenuation.

explanatory ▶ adjective *an explanatory leaflet* **explaining**, descriptive, describing, illustrative, illuminative, elucidative, elucidatory, explicative, evaluative, interpretive, expository, revelatory, by way of explanation; prefatory; *rare* exegetic, hermeneutic.

expletive ▶ noun **1** *she let out an expletive and slammed the phone down* **swear word**, oath, curse, obscenity, profanity, epithet, imprecation, four-letter word, exclamation; (**expletives**) bad language, foul language, strong language, swearing; *informal* dirty word; *N. Amer. informal* cuss word, cuss.
2 (*technical*) *expletives are employed for the sake of the metre, not the sense* **filler**, fill-in, stopgap, meaningless word/phrase, redundant word/phrase, superfluous word/phrase, unnecessary word/phrase.

explicable ▶ adjective *the success of the revolution is explicable in terms of the weakness of the king* **explainable**, interpretable, definable; understandable, comprehensible, accountable, intelligible; *rare* exponible.
OPPOSITE inexplicable.

explicate ▶ verb *scholars who have been devoted to explicating these stories* **explain**, explain in detail, make explicit, clarify, make plain/clear, spell out; interpret, elucidate, expound, comment on, develop, work out; illuminate, throw light on, unfold, untangle, clear up, put into plain English; criticize, appraise.

explicit ▶ adjective **1** *Cara's instructions had been quite explicit* **clear**, direct, plain, obvious, straightforward, clear-cut, crystal clear, clearly expressed, easily understandable, blunt; **precise**, exact, definite, distinct, express, emphatic, absolute, specific, positive, unequivocal, unambiguous, unmistakable, overt, manifest; detailed, minute, comprehensive, exhaustive, categorical.
OPPOSITE vague.
2 *sexually explicit material* **uncensored**, unrestrained, unreserved, unrestricted, uninhibited, graphic; open, candid, frank, forthright, direct,

plain-spoken, outspoken, point-blank, straight from the shoulder; full-frontal, no holds barred.
OPPOSITES suggestive, implicit.

explode ▶ verb **1** *a bomb exploded at the university* **blow up**, detonate, blow, burst (apart), fly apart, fly into pieces, shatter, go off, erupt; bang, crack, boom; *informal* go bang; *literary* fulminate.
2 *the first British atomic device was exploded in the Monte Bello islands* **detonate**, set off, let off, discharge, touch off, trigger (off), fire off, let fly.
OPPOSITE disarm.
3 *he exploded in a torrent of foul language* **lose one's temper**, give vent to one's feelings, blow up, rage, rant and rave, storm, bluster, get angry, become enraged, go into a rage, go berserk; *informal* fly off the handle, hit the roof, go through the roof, go up the wall, blow one's cool/top, blow a fuse/gasket, flip one's lid, freak out, go wild, go bananas, see red, go off the deep end, lose one's rag, go ape, burst a blood vessel; *Brit. informal* go spare, go crackers, do one's nut, get one's knickers in a twist, throw a wobbly; *N. Amer. informal* blow one's lid/stack.
4 *the city's exploding pet population* **increase suddenly**, increase rapidly, increase dramatically, mushroom, snowball, escalate, multiply, burgeon, rocket, shoot up, accelerate, heighten.
5 *this report explodes the myth that men are the bed-hopping rogues* **disprove**, refute, deny, rebut, invalidate, gainsay, negate, repudiate, discredit, debunk, belie, give the lie to, expose, deflate, puncture, quash, contradict, ridicule; blow up, blow sky-high, knock the bottom out of, drive a coach and horses through, cut down to size, pick holes in; *informal* shoot full of holes, shoot down (in flames), blow out of the water; *rare* controvert, confute, negative.
OPPOSITE confirm.

exploit ▶ verb (stress on the second syllable) **1** *platinum was originally exploited by the Indians of Colombia and Ecuador* **utilize**, **make use of**, put to use, use, use to good advantage, turn/put to good use, make the most of, capitalize on, benefit from, turn to account, draw on; profit from/by, make capital out of; *informal* cash in on, milk.
2 *a ruling class which exploited workers* **take advantage of**, make use of, abuse, impose on, prey on, play on, misuse, ill-treat, bleed, suck dry, squeeze, wring, enslave, treat unfairly, withhold rights from; manipulate, cheat, swindle, fleece, victimize, live off the backs of; *informal* walk (all) over, take for a ride, put one over on, cash in on, rip off.
OPPOSITE treat fairly.
▶ noun (stress on the first syllable) *his exploits brought him fame and notoriety* **feat**, deed, act, adventure, stunt, escapade, manoeuvre, enterprise, undertaking, move; achievement, accomplishment, attainment, triumph; (**exploits**) handiwork; *informal* lark, caper.

exploitation ▶ noun **1** *the exploitation of mineral resources* **utilization**, utilizing, use, making use of, putting to use, making the most of, capitalization on; *informal* cashing in on, milking.
2 *the exploitation of the poor by the wealthy* **taking advantage**, making use, abuse of, misuse, ill-treatment, unfair treatment, bleeding dry, sucking dry, squeezing, wringing; manipulation, cheating, swindling, fleecing, victimization; enslavement, slavery, oppression; imposing on, preying on, playing on.

exploration ▶ noun **1** *the exploration of space* **investigation**, study, survey, research, search, inspection, probe, examination, inquiry, scrutiny, observation; consideration, analysis, review, anatomy.
2 *a base for explorations into the mountains* **expedition**, trip, tour, journey, voyage, odyssey, safari, trek, hike; (**explorations**) travels; *archaic* peregrination.

exploratory ▶ adjective *an oil company has started exploratory drilling in the region* **investigative**, investigational, explorative, probing, fact-finding, analytic, searching; experimental, trial, test, pilot, preliminary, provisional, tentative.

explore ▶ verb **1** *they wanted to explore the possibility of achieving a longer-term solution* **investigate**, look into/over, enquire into, consider, check out; examine, research, survey, scrutinize, scan, study, review, probe, dissect, take stock of, go into, go over with a fine-tooth comb.
2 *an opportunity to explore the stunning scenery all around them* **travel over**, tour, traverse, range over; survey, take a look at, inspect, investigate, scout, reconnoitre, search, prospect; *informal* recce, give something a/the once-over, give something a look-see, give something a going-over.

explorer ▶ noun **traveller**, discoverer, voyager, rambler, globetrotter, rover; tourer, surveyor, scout, reconnoitrer, prospector; **adventurer**, pioneer; *informal* gallivanter.

explosion ▶ noun **1** *Edward was in the car when he heard the explosion* **detonation**, discharge, eruption, blowing up, ignition; **bang**, blast, boom, rumble, crash, crack, report, thunder, roll, clap, pop; *informal* wham, whump; *literary* fulmination.
2 *an explosion of anger* **outburst**, flare-up, blow-up, outbreak, eruption, storm, rush, spate, surge, rash, wave, access, effusion; fit, paroxysm, spasm, attack, spell; *informal* paddy; *rare* ebullition, boutade.
3 *the explosion of human populations in the last hundred years* **sudden increase**, rapid increase, dramatic increase, mushrooming, snowballing, escalation, multiplication, burgeoning, rocketing, shooting up.

explosive *See centre pages for lists of* **Bombs and Mines** **Explosives**
▶ adjective **1** *the danger of explosive gases* **volatile**, inflammable, flammable, combustible, incendiary, eruptive, unstable.
2 *Marco's explosive temper* **fiery**, stormy, violent, volatile, volcanic, angry, fierce, impassioned, passionate, intense, vehement, tempestuous, turbulent, touchy, irritable, irascible, hot-headed, short-tempered, quick-tempered.
3 *he had been able to defuse an explosive situation* **tense**, charged, highly charged, overwrought; critical, serious, dangerous, perilous, hazardous, knife-edge, touch-and-go; sensitive, delicate, unstable, volatile, inflammable, volcanic, ugly, nasty; *informal* iffy, dicey.
4 *pressure on the land was increased by explosive population growth* **sudden**, dramatic, rapid, abrupt, meteoric; mushrooming, snowballing, escalating, rocketing, accelerating.
▶ noun *stocks of explosives* **bomb**, incendiary device, incendiary, device.

E

exponent ▶ noun **1** *an exponent of free-trade policies* **advocate**, supporter, proponent, upholder, backer, defender, champion; promoter, propagandist, spokesperson, spokesman, spokeswoman, speaker; campaigner, fighter, battler, crusader, missionary, evangelist, pioneer, apostle; enthusiast, apologist, arguer, expounder.
OPPOSITES critic; opponent.
2 *a female karate exponent* **practitioner**, performer, player; interpreter, presenter; *rare* executant.

export ▶ verb **1** *most hard currency comes from exporting raw materials* **sell overseas/abroad**, market overseas/abroad, send overseas/abroad, trade internationally, transport.
OPPOSITE import.
2 *he is trying to export his gastronomic ideas to America* **transmit**, spread, disseminate, circulate, communicate, pass on, put about, convey; *literary* bruit about/abroad.

expose ▶ verb **1** *the gold covering was flaking away, exposing the white plaster* **reveal**, uncover, lay bare, bare, leave unprotected.
OPPOSITE cover.
2 *he was* **exposed to** *asbestos at his workplace* **make vulnerable**, make subject, subject, lay open; **put at risk of**, put in jeopardy of, leave unprotected from; endanger by, imperil by, jeopardize by.
OPPOSITE protect from.
3 *the colony had been* **exposed to** *new liberal ideas* **introduce**; **bring into contact with**, present with, make familiar/conversant/acquainted with, familiarize with, acquaint with, make aware of.
OPPOSITES keep away from, keep free of.
4 *he has been exposed as a liar and a traitor* **uncover**, reveal, show, display, exhibit, disclose, manifest, unveil, unmask; discover, bring to light, bring into the open, make known, unearth, let out, divulge, make obvious; denounce, condemn; detect, find out, catch out, smoke out; betray, give away; *informal* spill the beans on, blow the whistle on, pull the plug on.
□ **expose oneself** *police are hunting a man who exposed himself to a young woman*: *informal* flash.

exposé ▶ noun *a TV exposé on chart hyping* **revelation**, disclosure, exposure, uncovering, divulgence; **report**, feature, piece, column; scandal; *informal* scoop.
OPPOSITE cover-up.

exposed ▶ adjective *the farm is on an exposed hillside* **unprotected**, open, wide open, without shelter/protection, unsheltered, open to the elements/weather; barren, bare, windswept; vulnerable, defenceless, undefended, unshielded, susceptible; *rare* pregnable.
OPPOSITES sheltered, protected.

exposition ▶ noun **1** *a lucid exposition of educational theories* **explanation**, description, elucidation, explication, interpretation, illustration; account, commentary, study, article, essay, thesis, paper, treatise, dissertation, disquisition; critique, criticism, appraisal, assessment, discussion, discourse; *formal* exegesis.
2 *the exposition will feature exhibits by 165 companies* **exhibition**, fair, trade fair, display, show, presentation, demonstration; *N. Amer.* exhibit; *informal* expo, demo.

expository ▶ adjective *the film suffers from too obviously expository dialogue* **explanatory**, descriptive, describing, elucidatory, elucidative, explicatory, explicative, interpretative, illustrative, illuminating; *rare* exegetic, hermeneutic.

expostulate ▶ verb *one of the prisoners* **expostulated with** *him* **remonstrate**, disagree, argue, take issue, reason, express disagreement; make a protest to, protest to, raise objections to, object to, complain to.

exposure ▶ noun **1** *the exposure of the lizard's vivid blue tongue alarms the attacker* **revealing**, revelation, uncovering, presentation; baring, laying bare, stripping, denudation.
2 *injuries resulting from exposure to harmful chemicals* **subjection**, submission, vulnerability, laying open.
OPPOSITE protection from.
3 *the only survivor was suffering from exposure* **frostbite**, cold, hypothermia.
4 *exposure to great literature* **introduction**, presentation; **experience of**,

contact with, familiarity with, conversance/conversancy with, acquaintance with, awareness of, insight into.
5 *the exposure of a banking scandal* **uncovering**, revelation, showing, display, exhibition, disclosure, manifestation, unveiling, unmasking; discovery, unearthing, rooting out, divulgence; denunciation, condemnation; detection, betrayal; exposé, publication, publishing.
6 *we're getting a lot of exposure for our new act* **publicity**, publicizing, advertising, advertisement; public attention, public notice, public interest, the public eye, media interest/attention, the limelight; dissemination, broadcasting, airing; *informal* hype.
7 *the exposure is perfect—a gentle slope to the south-west* **outlook**, aspect, view, frontage, direction; position, setting, location.

E

expound ▶ verb **1** *he expounded his theories on the cultural state of the nation* **present**, put forward, set forth, proffer, offer, advance, propose, propound, frame, give an account of, recount; **explain**, give an explanation of, detail, spell out, describe, discuss, explicate, delineate, elucidate.
2 *a detailed treatise expounding Paul's teachings* **explain**, interpret, explicate, elucidate; comment on, give a commentary on, annotate, gloss, illustrate.
□ **expound on** *he expounded on the virtues of books and learning* **elaborate on**, expand on, expatiate on, dwell on, harp on, discuss at length.

express[1] ▶ verb **1** *community leaders expressed anger over the result of the referendum* **communicate**, convey, indicate, show, demonstrate, reveal, intimate, manifest, make manifest, exhibit, evidence, put across/over, get across/over; **articulate**, put into words, utter, voice, give voice to, give expression to, enunciate, pronounce, verbalize, word, phrase, render, frame, couch; state, assert, proclaim, profess, air, make public, give vent to, vent; say, tell, speak, mouth, point out; denote, illustrate, symbolize, signify, embody; *rare* evince, asseverate.
2 *the grapes are trodden until all the juice is expressed* **squeeze out**, press out, wring out, force out, extract, expel.
□ **express oneself** *he had difficulty expressing himself* **communicate one's thoughts/opinions/views**, put thoughts into words, speak one's mind, say one's piece, say what's on one's mind.

express[2] ▶ adjective *an express bus* **rapid**, swift, fast, quick, speedy, high-speed, brisk, flying, prompt, expeditious; non-stop, direct, uninterrupted, undeviating, unswerving, uncircuitous; *informal* nippy.
OPPOSITES slow; indirect.
▶ noun *we travelled on an overnight express* **express train**, fast train, direct train.

express[3] ▶ adjective **1** *the letter made express reference to the confidential nature of the information* **explicit**, clear, direct, plain, distinct, unambiguous, unequivocal, unmistakable, obvious; specific, precise, clear-cut, crystal clear, straightforward, certain, categorical, positive, conclusive, pointed; well defined, exact, manifest, outright, emphatic.
OPPOSITES vague; implied.
2 *they bought the land with the express purpose of giving it to the trust* **sole**, specific, particular, special, especial, singular, exclusive, specified, fixed, purposeful.

expression ▶ noun **1** *the government refused to allow the free expression of opposition views* **utterance**, uttering, voicing, pronouncement, declaration, articulation, verbalization, statement, proclamation, assertion, announcement, setting forth, venting, mouthing; dissemination, broadcast, circulation, communication, spreading, promulgation, publicizing, publication; *rare* asseveration.
2 *he raised his eyebrows in an expression of sympathy* **indication**, intimation, demonstration, show, exhibition, manifestation, token; conveyance, communication, illustration, revelation, disclosure, embodiment.
3 *Blanche invariably wore an expression of harassed fatigue* **look**, **appearance**, air, manner, bearing, countenance, guise, cast, aspect, impression; *formal* mien.
4 *the old expression 'curiosity killed the cat'* **idiom**, phrase, idiomatic expression, set phrase; proverb, saying, adage, maxim, axiom, aphorism, saw, motto, platitude, cliché, quotation, quote, formula; term, word; *informal* old chestnut; *formal* locution.
5 *the height of poetic expression* **diction**, style, choice of words, turn of phrase, wording, phrasing, phraseology, language; delivery, execution; speech, intonation.
6 *these pieces are very different from one another, both in choice of instruments and expression* **emotion**, feeling, passion, intensity, poignancy; **style**, intonation, tone, nuance; artistry, depth, spirit, imagination; vividness, ardour, power, force.
7 *essential oils obtained by distillation or expression* **squeezing**, pressing, wringing, forcing out, extraction, extracting.

expressionless ▶ adjective **1** *his face was expressionless, giving nothing away* **inscrutable**, unreadable, deadpan, poker-faced; blank, empty, vacant, emotionless, unemotional, unexpressive, inexpressive; glazed, fixed, lifeless, stony, wooden, impassive, inanimate, unresponsive.
OPPOSITE expressive.
2 *he spoke in a flat, expressionless tone* **dull**, dry, toneless, monotonous, drab, boring, tedious, flat, static, wooden, unmodulated, unvarying, undemonstrative, devoid of feeling/emotion; apathetic, unimpassioned, uninspiring, weak.
OPPOSITES interesting, lively.

expressive ▶ adjective **1** *he gave an expressive shrug* **eloquent**, meaningful, telling, revealing, demonstrative, suggestive.
OPPOSITE expressionless.
2 *a haunted and expressive song* **emotional**, full of emotion/feeling, indicating emotion/feeling, passionate, intense, deeply felt, poignant, moving, stirring, striking, evocative, artistic; vivid, graphic, descriptive, ardent, powerful, charged, imaginative, inspired, visionary.
OPPOSITES inexpressive; unemotional.
3 *his diction is very expressive of his Englishness* **indicative**, demonstrative, demonstrating, showing, suggesting, revealing, underlining.

expressly ▶ adverb **1** *he was expressly forbidden to discuss the matter* **explicitly**, clearly, directly, plainly, distinctly, unambiguously, unequivocally, unmistakably, obviously, absolutely; precisely, specifically, straightforwardly, certainly, categorically, positively, conclusively, pointedly, markedly, exactly, manifestly, patently, emphatically.
2 *a machine expressly built for spraying paint* **solely**, specifically, particularly, specially, especially, singularly, exclusively, purposefully, just, only, explicitly, with something/someone in mind.

expropriate ▶ verb *legislation to expropriate land from absentee landlords* **seize**, take away, take over, take, appropriate, take possession of, requisition, commandeer, claim, make claim to, assume, acquire, sequestrate, wrest; impound, confiscate; misappropriate, usurp, arrogate, hijack; *Law* distrain, disseize, attach; *Scottish Law* poind.

expulsion ▶ noun **1** *they faced expulsion from the party* **removal**, debarment, dismissal, exclusion, discharge, ejection, rejection, blackballing, blacklisting; suspension; banishment, exile, deportation, eviction, expatriation, repatriation, purging, displacement, transportation; *informal* sacking, drumming out, the bounce.
OPPOSITE admission.
2 *the expulsion of bodily wastes* **discharge**, ejection, excretion, voiding, voidance, evacuation, ejaculation, disgorgement, elimination, emptying out, passing, draining.

expunge ▶ verb *that moment can never be expunged from his memory* **erase**, remove, delete, rub out, wipe out, efface; cross out, strike out, blot out, blank out; cancel, annul, destroy, obliterate, eradicate, extinguish, eliminate, abolish, annihilate, extirpate.

expurgate ▶ verb *a book which had been expurgated for use in schools* **censor**, bowdlerize, blue-pencil, cut, edit; clean up, purge, purify, sanitize, make acceptable, make palatable, make presentable, water down, emasculate.

exquisite ▶ adjective **1** *a piece of exquisite antique glass* **beautiful**, lovely, elegant, graceful; magnificent, superb, superlative, excellent, wonderful, well-crafted, well-made, well-executed, perfect; delicate, fragile, dainty, subtle; intricate, tasteful, fine, choice.
OPPOSITE crude.
2 *the garden was tended with exquisite taste* **discriminating**, discerning, sensitive, selective, fastidious; refined, cultivated, cultured, educated, appreciative; impeccable, polished, consummate.
3 *an exquisite agony* **intense**, acute, keen, piercing, sharp, severe, racking, excruciating, agonizing, harrowing, torturous, tormenting, searing; unbearable, insufferable, unendurable, more than one can bear, more than flesh and blood can stand.
▶ noun *even among these snappy dressers, he was an exquisite* **dandy**, fop, beau, man about town, bright young thing, glamour boy, rake; dilettante, aesthete; *informal* swell, dude, sharp dresser, snappy dresser, natty dresser; *archaic* blade, blood.

extant ▶ adjective *only one copy of Cavendish's book is extant* **still existing**, in existence, surviving, remaining, abiding, enduring, undestroyed, present, existent; living, alive.
OPPOSITES no longer existing, non-existent, dead.

extemporary, **extemporaneous** ▶ adjective *a member of the audience made notes of his extemporaneous address* **extempore**, impromptu, spontaneous, unscripted, ad lib, on-the-spot; improvised, improvisatory, unrehearsed, unplanned, unprepared, unarranged, unpremeditated; makeshift, thrown together, cobbled together; *informal* off-the-cuff, spur-of-the-moment, off the top of one's head.
OPPOSITES rehearsed, planned.

extempore ▶ adjective *an extempore speech* **impromptu**, spontaneous, unscripted, ad lib; on-the-spot, extemporary, extemporaneous; improvised, improvisatory, unrehearsed, unplanned, unprepared, unarranged, unpremeditated; makeshift, thrown together, cobbled together, rough and ready; *Latin* ad libitum; *informal* off-the-cuff, spur-of-the-moment, off the top of one's head.
OPPOSITES rehearsed, planned.
▶ adverb *he was speaking extempore* **spontaneously**, extemporaneously, ad lib; on the spot, unpremeditatedly, without preparation, without rehearsal, without planning; *Latin* ad libitum; *informal* off the cuff, on the spur of the moment, off the top of one's head, just like that, at the drop of a hat.
OPPOSITES from notes, with preparation.

extemporize ▶ verb *in modern jazz, players extemporize in a very free manner* **improvise**, ad lib, play it by ear, think on one's feet, throw/cobble something together, make it up as one goes along, take it as it comes; *informal* busk it, wing it, do something off the cuff, do something off the top of one's head, do something on the spur of the moment.

extend ▶ verb **1** *in 1712 he attempted to extend his dominions* **expand**, enlarge, increase, make larger, make bigger, make greater; lengthen, widen, broaden; stretch, stretch out, draw out, elongate.
OPPOSITES reduce, shrink.
2 *the garden extends down to the road* **continue**, carry on, run on, last, stretch (out), spread, range, reach, lead; unroll, unfurl.
3 *we have continued to extend our range of services* **widen**, expand, broaden; augment, supplement, increase, add to, enhance, amplify, develop, top up, build up, diversify.
OPPOSITE narrow.
4 *a bill to extend the life of parliament* **prolong**, lengthen, increase, continue, run on, keep going, perpetuate, sustain; stretch out, protract, spin out, string out, drag out; postpone, defer, delay, put back, put off.
OPPOSITE shorten.
5 *lie flat on the floor with your arms and legs extended* **stretch out**, spread out, reach out, straighten out, open out; unroll, unfurl.
6 *he extended a hand in greeting* **hold out**, put out, stick out, hold forth, put forth, reach out; offer, give, outstretch, proffer.
7 *the society wishes to extend their sincere thanks to Mr Bayes* **offer**, proffer, hold out, advance; give, grant, bestow, accord, present, confer, impart.
□ **extend to** *her tolerance did not always extend to her staff* **include**, go/extend as far as, take in, incorporate, encompass, comprise, comprehend, subsume, be applicable to.

extended ▶ adjective **1** *an extended legal battle* **prolonged**, protracted, long-lasting, long-drawn-out, drawn out, spun out, dragged out, strung out; extensive, lengthy, long; lengthened, increased, stretched out; elongated, enlarged, widened.
OPPOSITES shortened; short.
2 *an extended family* inclusive, comprehensive, expanded, enlarged, widened, broad, far-reaching.
OPPOSITES immediate; nuclear.

extension ▶ noun **1** *they plan an extension at the hospital to create a new outpatients' department* **addition**, add-on, adjunct, addendum, augmentation, supplement, appendage, appendix; annexe, wing, supplementary building; *N. Amer.* ell.
2 *scientific method has led to a marvellous extension of knowledge* **expansion**, increase, enlargement; widening, broadening, deepening, diversification, heightening; augmentation, enhancement, amplification; development, growth, continuation; elongation, lengthening, stretching, drawing out.
OPPOSITES shrinking, contraction.
3 *an extension of opening hours* **prolongation**, lengthening, increase, protraction, continuation, perpetuation.
OPPOSITE shortening.
4 *I need an extension for my assessed essay* **postponement**, deferral, delay; longer period, more/extra time, increased time, additional time.

extensive ▶ adjective **1** *a mansion with extensive grounds* **large**, large-scale, sizeable, substantial, considerable, ample, great, huge, vast, immense, boundless, immeasurable; spacious, capacious, commodious, voluminous, roomy; broad, expansive, sweeping.
OPPOSITE small.
2 *his extensive knowledge of antiques made the shop popular* **comprehensive**, thorough, complete, exhaustive, profound, boundless; broad, wide, vast, wide-ranging, all-inclusive, all-embracing, all-encompassing, sweeping, wholesale, catholic, universal, across the board.
OPPOSITES small; limited.

extent ▶ noun **1** *the garden was about two acres in extent* **area**, size, expanse, length, stretch, range, scope, compass; proportions, dimensions.
2 *she kept the full extent of her father's illness from her cousin* **degree**, scale, level, magnitude, scope, extensiveness, amount, size; coverage, breadth, width, reach, range, compass, comprehensiveness, thoroughness, completeness, all-inclusiveness.

extenuate ▶ verb (*rare*) *I've no wish to extenuate his transgressions* **excuse**, mitigate, palliate, make allowances for, make excuses for, defend, vindicate, justify, explain, explain away, give an explanation for, come up with an explanation for, make a case for; diminish, lessen, moderate, qualify, soften, play down, reduce, temper, weaken.
OPPOSITE aggravate.

extenuating ▶ adjective *there were extenuating circumstances* **mitigating**, excusing, exonerative, palliating, palliative, justifying, justificatory, vindicating, exculpatory; moderating, qualifying, softening, tempering, diminishing, lessening.
OPPOSITE aggravating.

exterior ▶ adjective *the exterior walls are bare brick* **outer**, outside, outermost, outward, external, surface, superficial, extrinsic, visible.
OPPOSITE interior.
▶ noun *the exterior of the building* **outside**, outside surface, outer surface, external surface, outward appearance, outward aspect, externals, facade, front; shell, skin, covering, coating, finish.
OPPOSITE interior.

WORD LINKS
related prefixes **ecto-** (e.g. ***ectoderm***), **exo-** (e.g. ***exoskeleton***), **extra-** (e.g. ***extraterritorial***)

exterminate ▶ verb *the invaders intended simply to exterminate any natives they found* **kill**, put to death, do to death, do away with, put an end to, finish off, take the life of, end the life of, get rid of, dispatch; slaughter, butcher, massacre, wipe out, mow down, shoot down, cut down, put to the sword, send to the gas chambers, ethnically cleanse, destroy, eliminate, eradicate, annihilate, extirpate; murder, assassinate, execute; *informal* bump off, knock off, polish off, do in, top, take out, snuff out, erase, croak, stiff, zap, blow away, blow someone's brains out, give someone the works; *N. Amer. informal* ice, off, rub out, waste, whack, smoke, scrag; *N. Amer. euphemistic* terminate with extreme prejudice; *literary* slay.

extermination ▶ noun *such feuds could be settled only by the extermination of an entire family* **killing**, murder, assassination, putting to death, doing to death, execution, dispatch, slaughter, massacre, genocide; taking of someone's life, homicide, manslaughter, liquidation, elimination, destruction, eradication, annihilation, wiping out, extinction; *literary* slaying.

external ▶ adjective **1** *an external wall* **outer**, outside, outermost, outward, exterior, surface, superficial; visible, extrinsic, extraneous.
OPPOSITE internal.
2 *the exam scripts then have to be sent to an external examiner* **outside**, non-resident, visiting, from elsewhere, extramural, independent, consultant, consulting, advisory.
OPPOSITES local; resident; in-house.

WORD LINKS
related prefixes **ecto-** (e.g. ***ectoderm***), **exo-** (e.g. ***exoskeleton***), **extra-** (e.g. ***extraterritorial***)

extinct ▶ adjective **1** *an extinct species* **vanished**, lost, died out, dead, defunct, no longer existing, no longer extant, wiped out, destroyed, exterminated, gone.
OPPOSITES extant; living.
2 *an extinct volcano* **inactive**, old, former, no longer active.
OPPOSITES active; dormant.

extinction ▶ noun *the sudden extinction of the mammoths* **dying out**, disappearance, vanishing, death; extermination, destruction, elimination, eradication, annihilation.

extinguish ▶ verb **1** *the fire had to be extinguished* **douse**, put out, quench, stamp out, smother, beat out, dampen down; blow out, snuff out; *Scottish* dout.
OPPOSITE light.
2 *the Liberal majority was extinguished by 1910* **destroy**, **end**, finish off, put an end to, put a stop to, bring to an end, terminate, remove, annihilate, wipe out, wipe off the face of the earth, wipe off the map, erase, eliminate, eradicate, obliterate, liquidate, expunge, abolish, exterminate, kill, extirpate, obscure, suppress, disrupt, undo, upset; *informal* take out, rub out, snuff out.
OPPOSITE start up.

extirpate ▶ verb *those who tried to extirpate Christianity* **weed out**, destroy, eradicate, stamp out, root out, eliminate, suppress, crush, put down, put an end to, put a stop to, do away with, get rid of, wipe out, abolish, extinguish, quash, squash.
OPPOSITES found; support.

extol ▶ verb *nutritionists have long extolled the virtues of rice* **praise enthusiastically**, go into raptures about/over, wax lyrical about, sing the praises of, praise to the skies, heap praise on, eulogize, rhapsodize over, rave about, enthuse about/over, gush about/over, throw bouquets at, express delight over, acclaim; *informal* go wild about, be mad about, go on about; *N. Amer. informal* ballyhoo; *black English* big someone/something up; *dated* cry someone/something up; *rare* laud, panegyrize.
OPPOSITE criticize.

extort ▶ verb *he was convicted of extorting money from local residents* **force**, obtain by force, obtain by threat(s), blackmail someone for, extract, exact, coerce, wring, wrest, screw, squeeze, milk, worm something out of someone; *N. Amer. & Austral. informal* put the bite on someone for; *archaic* rack.

extortion ▶ noun *he was arrested on a charge of extortion* **demanding money with menaces**, exaction, extraction, blackmail; *N. Amer.* shakedown.

extortionate ▶ adjective **1** *extortionate prices* **exorbitant**, excessively high, excessive, sky-high, outrageous, preposterous, immoderate, unreasonable, inordinate, prohibitive, ruinous, punitive, inflated, more than one can afford; *Brit.* over the odds; *informal* criminal, steep, stiff, over the top, OTT.
OPPOSITE reasonable.

E

2 *an unreasonable and extortionate clause in the contract* **grasping**, bloodsucking, avaricious, greedy, rapacious, predatory, usurious, exacting, harsh, severe, rigorous, hard, oppressive; *informal* money-grubbing; *N. Amer. informal* grabby.

extortionist ▶ **noun** *he was once a big-time kidnapper and extortionist* **racketeer**, extortioner, extorter, profiteer, exploiter, blackmailer, black marketeer; (*in Japan*) yakuza; *informal* bloodsucker; *Austral. informal* urger; *dated* rack-renter.

extra ▶ **adjective** *a potential source of extra income* **additional**, more, added, supplementary, supplemental, further, auxiliary, ancillary, subsidiary, secondary, attendant, accessory; other, another, new, fresh.
OPPOSITE normal.

▶ **adverb 1** *we have to work extra hard tonight* **exceptionally**, particularly, specially, especially, very, extremely, singularly, peculiarly, distinctly; **unusually**, extraordinarily, uncommonly, uniquely, remarkably, strikingly, outstandingly, amazingly, incredibly, awfully, terribly, really, unwontedly, notably, markedly, decidedly, surprisingly, conspicuously, signally; *informal* seriously, majorly, mucho; *Brit. informal* jolly, dead, well; *informal, dated* devilish, frightfully; *N. English* powerful, right.
2 *postage has to be charged extra* **in addition**, additionally, as well, also, too, besides, over and above that, on top (of that), further, into the bargain, to boot; then, again, furthermore; *archaic* withal, forbye.
OPPOSITE included.

▶ **noun 1** *an optional extra* **addition**, supplement, adjunct, addendum, add-on, bonus, accompaniment, complement, companion, additive, extension, appendage, accessory, attachment, retrofit; *Computing* peripheral.
OPPOSITES standard item; necessity, essential.
2 *a film extra* **walk-on**, supernumerary, spear carrier; walk-on part, minor role, non-speaking role, bit part.

extract ▶ **verb** (stress on the second syllable) **1** *he switched off the recorder and extracted the cassette* **take out**, draw out, bring out, pull out, remove, withdraw, pluck out, fish out, prize out, extricate; wrench out, tear out, uproot, unsheathe; produce; free, release; *rare* deracinate.
OPPOSITE insert.
2 *the Crown was adept at extracting money from its subjects* **wrest**, exact, wring, screw, squeeze, milk, force, coerce, obtain by force, obtain by threat(s), extort, blackmail someone for, worm something out of someone; *N. Amer. & Austral. informal* put the bite on someone for; *archaic* rack.
3 *the roots are crushed to extract the sugary juice* **squeeze out**, express, separate, press out, obtain, distil.
OPPOSITE add.
4 *the table is extracted from the report* **excerpt**, select, choose, reproduce, repeat, copy, quote, cite, cull, take, abstract.
OPPOSITE insert.
5 *the following ideas are extracted from a variety of theories* **derive**, develop, evolve, deduce, infer, conclude, gather, elicit, obtain, get, take, gain, acquire, procure, attain, glean; *formal* educe.

▶ **noun** (stress on the first syllable) **1** *an extract from his article* **excerpt**, passage, abstract, citation, selection, quotation, cutting, clipping, snippet, fragment, piece; (**excerpts**) *rare* analects.
2 *an extract of the ginseng root* **decoction**, distillation, distillate, abstraction, concentrate, essence, juice, solution, tincture, elixir, quintessence; *rare* decocture, apozem.

extraction ▶ **noun 1** *the extraction of gall bladder stones* **removal**, taking out, drawing out, pulling out, extrication, wrenching out, tearing out, uprooting, withdrawal, unsheathing; production; freeing, release; *rare* deracination.
OPPOSITE insertion.
2 *the extraction of rights has been a constant struggle* **exaction**, exacting, wresting, coercion, extortion.
OPPOSITE relinquishment.
3 *the extraction of grape juice* **squeezing**, expressing, separation, pressing, obtaining, distillation.
4 *a man of Irish extraction* **descent**, ancestry, parentage, ancestors, family; lineage, line, line of descent; race, origin, derivation, birth; genealogy, heredity, succession; stock, pedigree, blood, bloodline, strain; roots, origins, forefathers, antecedents; *rare* filiation, stirps.

extradite ▶ **verb 1** *the Russian government announced that it would extradite him to Germany* **deport**, hand over, send back, send home, repatriate, expel, banish.
2 *the British government attempted to extradite terrorist suspects from Belgium and the Netherlands* **have someone deported**, request the extradition of, have someone handed over, have someone sent back, have someone sent home, bring back.

extradition ▶ **noun** *they are in Pentonville Prison, fighting extradition to Hong Kong on fraud charges* **deportation**, handover, repatriation, expulsion, banishment.

extraneous ▶ **adjective 1** *do not allow extraneous considerations to influence your judgement* **irrelevant**, immaterial, beside the point, not to the point, neither here nor there, nothing to do with it, not pertinent, not germane, not to the purpose, off the subject, unrelated, unconnected, inapposite, inappropriate, inapplicable, inconsequential, incidental, pointless, out of place, wide of the mark, peripheral, tangential.
OPPOSITE material.
2 *extraneous influences came to bear* **external**, outside, exterior, extrinsic, outward, adventitious, alien, foreign.
OPPOSITE intrinsic.

extraordinary ▶ **adjective 1** *an extraordinary coincidence* **remarkable**, exceptional, amazing, astonishing, astounding, marvellous, wonderful, sensational, stunning, incredible, unbelievable, miraculous, phenomenal, prodigious, spectacular; **striking**, outstanding, momentous, impressive, singular, signal, pre-eminent, memorable, unforgettable, never to be forgotten, unique, arresting, eye-catching, conspicuous, noteworthy, notable, great; out of the ordinary, unusual, uncommon, rare, surprising, curious, strange, odd, peculiar, uncanny; *Scottish* unco; *informal* fantastic, terrific, tremendous, stupendous, awesome, out of this world, unreal; *literary* wondrous.
OPPOSITE ordinary.
2 *moving with extraordinary speed* **very great**, considerable, tremendous, huge, enormous, immense, colossal, massive, prodigious, stupendous, monumental, mammoth, vast, gigantic, giant, mighty, epic, monstrous, substantial; *informal* astronomical, almighty.
OPPOSITE negligible.

extravagance ▶ **noun 1** *the sumptuous sofa had been bought in a fit of extravagance* **profligacy**, lack of thrift, unthriftiness, thriftlessness, improvidence, wastefulness, waste, overspending, prodigality, squandering, lavishness; immoderation, excess, recklessness, lack of restraint, irresponsibility; spendthrift behaviour, free-spending ways.
OPPOSITE thrift.
2 *the costliest brands are an extravagance* **luxury**, indulgence, self-indulgence, comfort, treat, extra, non-essential, frill, refinement.
OPPOSITE necessity.
3 *the extravagance of the decor* **ornateness**, elaborateness, decoration, embellishment, adornment, ornamentation, showiness; overstatement, ostentation, exaggeration, over-elaborateness.
OPPOSITE plainness.
4 *the extravagance of his compliments* **excessiveness**, exaggeration, exaggeratedness, unreservedness, outrageousness, immoderation; preposterousness, absurdity, irrationality, recklessness, wildness; excess, overkill, lack of restraint/reserve.

extravagant ▶ **adjective 1** *he siphoned off money to fund his extravagant lifestyle* **spendthrift**, profligate, unthrifty, thriftless, improvident, wasteful, free-spending, prodigal, squandering, lavish; immoderate, excessive, imprudent, reckless, irresponsible.
OPPOSITE thrifty.
2 *extravagant gifts like computer games* **expensive**, costly, dear, high-priced, high-cost, exorbitant, extortionate, overpriced; immoderate, lavish; valuable, precious, priceless, worth its weight in gold, worth a king's ransom; *Brit.* over the odds; *informal* pricey, costing an arm and a leg, costing the earth, costing a bomb, daylight robbery.
OPPOSITE cheap.
3 *extravagant prices* **exorbitant**, extortionate, excessive, high, unreasonable, outrageous, undue, uncalled for, extreme, inordinate, unwarranted, unnecessary, needless, disproportionate, too much; *informal* sky-high, over the top, OTT, a bit much.
OPPOSITES reasonable, low.
4 *he was touched by the extravagant praise heaped on him* **excessive**, immoderate, exaggerated, gushing, gushy, unrestrained, unreserved, effusive, fulsome; outrageous, preposterous, absurd, irrational, reckless, wild; *informal* steep, over the top, OTT.
OPPOSITE moderate.
5 *mirror frames which are decorated in an extravagant style* **ornate**, elaborate, decorated, embellished, adorned, ornamented, fancy; over-elaborate, fussy, busy, ostentatious, exaggerated, overstated, showy, baroque, rococo, florid, wedding-cake, gingerbread; *informal* flash, flashy.
OPPOSITE plain.

extravaganza ▶ **noun** *a live extravaganza featuring a host of stars* **spectacular**, display, spectacle, exhibition, performance, presentation, show, pageant.

extreme ▶ **adjective 1** *they were in extreme danger* **utmost**, uttermost, very great, greatest, greatest possible, maximum, maximal, highest, ultimate, supreme, paramount, great, acute, major, intense, enormous, severe, high, superlative, exceptional, extraordinary.
OPPOSITE slight.
2 *such an appalling situation calls for extreme measures* **drastic**, serious, forceful, desperate, dire, radical, far-reaching, momentous, consequential, substantial; unrelenting, unbending, unyielding, remorseless, uncompromising, unmitigated; heavy, sharp, severe, austere, stern, harsh, tough, strict, rigorous, swingeing, punishing, punitive, excessive, oppressive, draconian, ferocious.
OPPOSITE mild.
3 *a person of extreme views* **radical**, **extremist**, immoderate, exaggerated, intemperate, outrageous, unreasonable; fanatical, diehard, overzealous,

revolutionary, rebel, rebellious, subversive, militant, combative; *informal* over the top, OTT.
OPPOSITE moderate.
4 *extreme sports* **dangerous**, hazardous, risky, high-risk; reckless, foolhardy, daredevil, breakneck, daring, adventurous.
OPPOSITES safe; tame.
5 *the extreme tip of a narrow peninsula* **furthest**, farthest, furthermost, farthermost, furthest/farthest away, very, utmost, outermost, most distant, aftermost, endmost, ultimate, final, last, terminal, remotest; *rare* outmost.
OPPOSITE near.
▶ **noun 1** *the two extremes of standardized and non-standardized interviews* **opposite**, antithesis, (other) side of the coin, (opposite) pole, contrary, (exclusive) alternative; opposing pair; *rare* antipode.
OPPOSITE medium.
2 *this attitude is taken to its extreme in the following quote* **limit**, extremity, highest/greatest degree, maximum, height, high, low; ceiling, top, zenith, pinnacle, peak, apex, climax, ultimate, optimum, acme, epitome.
OPPOSITE minimum.
□ **in the extreme** *David was generous in the extreme.* See EXTREMELY.

WORD LINKS
related prefix **ultra-** (e.g. ***ultra-cautious***)

extremely ▶ **adverb** *we are all extremely worried* **very**, exceedingly, exceptionally, especially, extraordinarily, to a fault, in the extreme, extra, tremendously, immensely, vastly, hugely, abundantly, intensely, acutely, singularly, significantly, distinctly, outstandingly, uncommonly, unusually, decidedly, particularly, eminently, supremely, highly, remarkably, really, truly, mightily, thoroughly; all that, to a great extent, most, so; *Scottish* unco; *French* très; *N. English* right; *informal* terrifically, awfully, fearfully, terribly, devilishly, majorly, seriously, mega, ultra, oh-so, stinking, mucho, damn, damned; *informal, dated* devilish, hellish, frightfully; *Brit. informal* ever so, well, bloody, dead, dirty, jolly, fair; *N. Amer. informal* real, mighty, powerful, awful, plumb, darned, way, bitching; *S. African informal* lekker; *archaic* exceeding.
OPPOSITES moderately; slightly; by no means.

extremism ▶ **noun** *the dangers of political extremism* **fanaticism**, radicalism, zealotry, zeal, fundamentalism, dogmatism, bigotry, militancy, activism; sectarianism, chauvinism, partisanship.
OPPOSITE moderation.

extremist ▶ **noun** *the attack was carried out by a group of right-wing extremists* **fanatic**, **radical**, zealot, fundamentalist, hardliner, dogmatist, bigot, diehard, militant, activist; sectarian, chauvinist, partisan; *informal* ultra, maniac, crank.
OPPOSITE moderate.

extremity ▶ **noun 1** *the eastern extremity of the county* **limit**, end, edge, side, farthest point, boundary, border, frontier, boundary line, bound, bounding line, partition line, demarcation line, end point, cut-off point, termination; perimeter, circumference, outside, outline, confine, periphery, outskirts, margin, brink, rim, lip, fringe, verge, threshold, compass; *literary* bourn, marge, skirt; *rare* ambit.
OPPOSITE middle.
2 (**extremities**) *she began to regain some feeling in her extremities* **hands and feet**, fingers and toes, limbs.
3 *the extremity of the violence concerns us greatly* **intensity**, high degree, magnitude, acuteness, ferocity, vehemence, fierceness, violence, severity, seriousness, strength, power, powerfulness, potency, vigour, force, forcefulness, gravity, graveness, severeness, grievousness.
4 *he has promised that in extremity he will send for her* **dire straits**, trouble, difficulty, hard times, hardship, adversity, misfortune, distress; **crisis**, emergency, disaster, catastrophe, calamity, cataclysm; predicament, plight, mess, dilemma; setback, reverse, reversal; destitution, indigence, exigency; *informal* fix, pickle, jam, spot, bind, stew, scrape, hole, sticky situation, hot water, deep water, hell, hell on earth; *Brit. informal* spot of bother.

extricate ▶ **verb** *Deborah managed to extricate herself from the melee* **extract**, free, release, disentangle, get out, remove, withdraw, let loose, loosen, unloose, detach, disengage, disencumber, untwine, disentwine, unfasten, unclasp, disconnect; liberate, rescue, save, deliver; *informal* get someone/oneself off the hook.
OPPOSITES entangle; involve.

extrinsic ▶ **adjective** *the animal population is influenced by extrinsic factors like food supply and predation* **external**, extraneous, exterior, outside, outward, alien, foreign, adventitious, superficial, surface.
OPPOSITE intrinsic.

extrovert ▶ **noun** *like most extroverts he was a good dancer* **outgoing person**, sociable person, life and soul of the party, socializer, mixer, mingler, social butterfly, socialite.
OPPOSITE introvert.
▶ **adjective** *his extrovert personality made him the ideal host* **outgoing**, hail-fellow-well-met, extroverted, sociable, gregarious, socializing, social, genial, cordial, affable, friendly, people-oriented, lively, exuberant, uninhibited, unreserved, demonstrative.
OPPOSITE introverted.

extrude ▶ **verb** *lava that has been extruded under water* **force out**, thrust out, squeeze out, express, press out, eject, expel, release, give off, emit, void, exude, excrete.
OPPOSITE suck in.

exuberance ▶ **noun 1** *the wild exuberance of the dance* **ebullience**, buoyancy, cheerfulness, sunniness, breeziness, jauntiness, light-heartedness, high spirits, exhilaration, excitement, elation, exultation, euphoria, joy, joyfulness, cheeriness, gaiety, jubilation, sparkle, effervescence, vivacity, enthusiasm, irrepressibility, energy, animation, life, liveliness, vigour, zest; *informal* bubble, bounce, pep, zing, chirpiness; *N. Amer. informal* peartness; *literary* gladsomeness, blitheness, blithesomeness; *archaic* good cheer.
OPPOSITE gloom.
2 *the exuberance of the bougainvillea flowers* **luxuriance**, lushness, richness, abundance, superabundance, profusion, proliferation, copiousness, riotousness, vigour; denseness, thickness; jungle; *rare* plentifulness, prolificness, rankness, rampancy.
OPPOSITE meagreness.

exuberant ▶ **adjective 1** *exuberant groups of guests were dancing on the terrace* **ebullient**, buoyant, cheerful, sunny, breezy, jaunty, light-hearted, in high spirits, high-spirited, exhilarated, excited, elated, exultant, euphoric, joyful, cheery, merry, jubilant, sparkling, effervescent, vivacious, enthusiastic, irrepressible, energetic, animated, full of life, lively, vigorous, zestful; *informal* bubbly, bouncy, peppy, zingy, upbeat, chipper, chirpy, smiley, sparky, full of beans; *N. Amer. informal* peart; *dated* gay; *literary* gladsome, blithe, blithesome; *archaic* as merry as a grig, of good cheer.
OPPOSITE gloomy.
2 *an exuberant coating of mosses* **luxuriant**, lush, rich, abundant, abounding, superabundant, profuse, copious, plentiful, riotous, prolific, teeming, flourishing, thriving, vigorous; dense, thick, rank, rampant, overgrown, jungle-like; verdant, green; *informal* jungly.
OPPOSITES meagre, stunted.
3 *she flung her arms wide apart in exuberant welcome* **effusive**, lavish, extravagant, fulsome, expansive, gushing, gushy, demonstrative, exaggerated, unreserved, unrestrained, unlimited, wholehearted, generous; excessive, superfluous, prodigal; *informal* over the top, OTT.
OPPOSITE restrained.

exude ▶ **verb 1** *milkweed exudes a milky sap* **give off/out**, discharge, release, send out, send forth, emit, issue, emanate; ooze, weep, leak, leach, secrete, excrete; *Medicine* extravasate.
OPPOSITES absorb, take up.
2 *slime exudes from the fungus* **ooze**, seep, trickle, issue, filter, percolate, escape, discharge, flow, well, drip, dribble, leak, leach, drain, bleed, sweat; *Medicine* extravasate; *rare* filtrate, transude, exudate.
3 *a charismatic character who exuded self-confidence* **emanate**, radiate, ooze, give out, give forth, send out, issue, emit; display, show, exhibit, manifest, demonstrate, transmit, breathe, embody, be a/the picture of.

exult ▶ **verb 1** *her opponents exulted when she left* **rejoice**, be joyful, be happy, be pleased, be glad, be delighted, be elated, be ecstatic, be euphoric, be overjoyed, be as pleased as Punch, be cock-a-hoop, be jubilant, be rapturous, be in raptures, be transported, be beside oneself with joy, be delirious, be thrilled, jump for joy, be on cloud nine, be walking/treading on air, be in seventh heaven, glory, triumph, be triumphant; celebrate, cheer, revel, make merry; *informal* be over the moon, be on top of the world, be blissed out, whoop it up; *Austral. informal* be wrapped; *rare* joy, jubilate.
OPPOSITE sorrow.
2 *he* ***exulted in*** *the triumph of the new order* **rejoice at/in**, take delight in, find/take pleasure in, find/take satisfaction in, feel satisfaction at, find joy in, enjoy, appreciate, revel in, glory in, bask in, delight in, relish, savour, luxuriate in, wallow in; **be/feel proud of**, feel proud about, be proud of oneself for, congratulate oneself on, flatter oneself on, preen oneself on, pat oneself on the back for, give oneself a pat on the back for; **crow about**, feel self-satisfied about, vaunt, boast about, brag about, gloat over; *archaic* pique oneself on/in.
OPPOSITE sorrow.

exultant ▶ **adjective** *the exultant winners waved to the crowd* **jubilant**, thrilled, triumphant, delighted, exhilarated, happy, overjoyed, joyous, joyful, gleeful, cock-a-hoop, excited, animated, exulting, rejoicing, beside oneself with happiness, ecstatic, euphoric, elated, rapturous, in raptures, enraptured, rapt, walking on air, on cloud nine/seven, in seventh heaven, jumping for joy, in transports of delight, transported, carried away, in a frenzy of delight, delirious (with happiness), hysterical, wild with excitement, frenzied; **crowing**, gloating, boastful, swaggering; *informal* blissed out, over the moon, on a high; *N. Amer. informal* wigged out; *rare* corybantic.
OPPOSITES sorrowing, gloomy.

exultation ▶ **noun** *to have won the first prize filled me with exultation* **jubilation**, rejoicing, happiness, pleasure, joy, gladness, delight, glee, elation, cheer, euphoria, exhilaration, delirium, ecstasy, rapture,

transports (of delight), exuberance, glory, triumph; celebration, revelry, merrymaking, festivity, feasting; **crowing**, gloating, boasting.
OPPOSITES gloom, depression.

eye *See centre pages for list of parts of the human* **Eye**
▶ **noun 1** *he rubbed his eyes wearily* **organ of sight**, eyeball; *informal* peeper; *literary* orb; *archaic or humorous* optic; *rare* globe.
2 (**eyes**) *his sharp eyes had missed nothing* **eyesight**, vision, sight, power of sight, faculty of sight, ability to see, power of seeing, powers of observation, observation, perception, visual perception.
3 *shoppers with an eye for a bargain* **appreciation**, awareness, alertness, perception, discernment, discrimination, taste, judgement, recognition, consciousness, knowledge, understanding, comprehension, cognizance, feeling, sensitivity, instinct, intuition, nose.
4 *her nervous movement did not escape his watchful eye* **watch**, observance, lookout, gaze, stare, regard; observation, surveillance, vigilance, view, notice, contemplation, examination, inspection, study, scrutiny.
5 (also **eyes**) *to desert was despicable in their eyes | the picture quality is, to my eye, excellent* **opinion**, thinking, way of thinking, mind, view, viewpoint, point of view, attitude, stance, stand, standpoint, position, perspective, belief, contention, conviction, judgement, assessment, analysis, evaluation, gauging, rating, appraisal, estimation, estimate.
6 *the eye of a needle* **hole**, opening, aperture, eyelet, gap, slit, slot, crevice, chink, crack, perforation, interstice.
7 *the eye of the storm* **centre**, middle, nucleus, heart, core, hub, pivot, kernel, bosom, interior, depths, thick.
OPPOSITE edge.
□ **clap/lay/set eyes on** (*informal*) *I have never clapped eyes on him before* **see**, observe, notice, spot, sight, have sight of, spy, catch sight of, glimpse, catch/get a glimpse of, make out, discern, perceive, pick out, detect; *literary* behold, espy, descry.
□ **see eye to eye** *we don't always see eye to eye about things* **agree**, concur, be in agreement, be of the same mind/opinion, be in accord, be in sympathy, sympathize, be united, think as one; be on the same wavelength, get on, get along, feel a rapport.
OPPOSITE disagree.
□ **up to one's eyes** *not now, I'm afraid, I'm up to my eyes this morning* **very busy**, fully occupied; overwhelmed, inundated, overloaded, overburdened, overworked, overtaxed, under pressure, hard-pressed, harassed, rushed/run off one's feet, with one's back to the wall; *informal* pushed, up against it, up to here.
▶ **verb 1** *he eyed the stranger suspiciously* **look at**, see, observe, view, gaze at, gaze upon, stare at, scan, regard, contemplate, survey, inspect, examine, scrutinize, study, consider, glance at, take a glance at; **watch**, keep an eye on, keep under observation, keep watch on, keep under scrutiny, keep under surveillance, monitor, watch like a hawk, keep a weather eye on; spy on; *informal* have/take a gander at, have a squint at, get a load of, give someone/something a once-over, check out, gawp at, size up, keep a beady eye on, keep tabs on, keep a tab on; *Brit. informal* have/take a butcher's at, have/take a dekko at, have/take a shufti at, clock; *N. Amer. informal* eyeball; *literary* behold; *rare* twig, surveil.
OPPOSITE ignore.
2 *sometimes he would eye young women in the street* **ogle**, leer at, stare at, gaze at, make eyes at, make sheep's eyes at; *informal* eye up, give someone the glad eye, give someone a/the once-over, lech after/over, undress with one's eyes, give someone the come-on; *Brit. informal* gawp at, gawk at; *Austral./NZ informal* perv on.

WORD LINKS

relating to the eye	**ocular, ophthalmic, optic**
inflammation of the eye	**ophthalmitis**
branch of medicine concerning the eye	**ophthalmology**
measurement of the eye	**ophthalmometry**

eyebrow ▶ **noun** brow, monobrow.

eye-catching ▶ **adjective** *each pot is decorated with eye-catching designs* **striking**, arresting, conspicuous, noticeable, dramatic, impressive, imposing, spectacular, breathtaking, dazzling, amazing, astounding, astonishing, surprising, staggering, stunning, sensational, awesome, awe-inspiring, engaging, remarkable, notable, noteworthy, distinctive, extraordinary, outstanding, incredible, phenomenal, unusual, rare, uncommon, out of the ordinary.
OPPOSITES inconspicuous; unexceptional.

eyeful ▶ **noun** (*informal*) **1** *did you get an eyeful of that?* **look at**, peep at, peek at, glimpse of, view of, stare at, gaze at, gape at, ogle at, glance at; examination of, inspection of, scan of, survey of, study of; sight of; *informal* gander at, load of, squint at; *Brit. informal* dekko at, shufti at, butcher's at; *Austral./NZ informal* geek at, squiz at.
2 *even now, in middle age, she was still quite an eyeful* **beautiful sight**, vision, joy to behold, picture, dream, sensation, beauty, dazzler; belle, beauty queen, goddess, Venus; *informal* stunner, looker, knockout, sight for sore eyes, bombshell, dish, cracker, smasher, lovely, good-looker, peach, honey, eye-catcher, bit of all right; *Brit. informal, dated* bobby-dazzler.
OPPOSITE eyesore.

eyelash ▶ **noun** lash; *technical* cilium.

WORD LINKS

relating to eyelashes	**ciliary**

eyelid ▶ **noun** lid; *technical* palpebra, nictitating membrane.

WORD LINKS

relating to the eyelids	**palpebral, ciliary**
inflammation of the eyelid	**blepharitis**
surgery to repair eyelids	**blepharoplasty**

eyesight ▶ **noun** *he has poor eyesight* **sight**, vision, power of sight, faculty of sight, ability to see, power of seeing, powers of observation, observation, perception, visual perception.

WORD LINKS

measurement of eyesight	**optometry**

eyesore ▶ **noun** *the rubbish tip is an eyesore* **ugly sight**, blot (on the landscape), mess, scar, blight, disfigurement, blemish, defacement, defect, monstrosity, horror, carbuncle, excrescence, atrocity, disgrace, ugliness; *informal* sight, fright.
OPPOSITE vision.

eyewitness ▶ **noun** *eyewitnesses stated that one plane crashed in the harbour* **observer**, onlooker, witness, looker-on, bystander, spectator, watcher, viewer, passer-by; *informal* rubberneck; *literary* beholder.

fable ▶ noun **1** *the fable of the sick lion and the wary fox* **moral tale**, parable, apologue, allegory, bestiary.
2 *the fables of ancient Greece* **myth**, legend, saga, epic, folk tale, folk story, traditional story, tale, story, fairy tale, narrative, romance; folklore, lore, mythology, fantasy, oral history, tradition, folk tradition, old wives' tales; *technical* mythos, mythus; *informal* yarn.
3 *it's a fable that I have a taste for fancy restaurants* **falsehood**, fib, fabrication, deception, made-up story, trumped-up story, invention, concoction, piece of fiction, fiction, falsification, falsity, fairy story/tale, cock and bull story; lie, untruth, barefaced lie; (little) white lie, half-truth, exaggeration, prevarication, departure from the truth; yarn, story, red herring, rumour, myth, flight of fancy, figment of the imagination; pretence, pretext, sham, ruse, wile, trickery, stratagem; *informal* tall story, tall tale, whopper; *Brit. informal* porky, pork pie, porky pie; *humorous* terminological inexactitude; *vulgar slang* bullshit; *Austral./NZ vulgar slang* bulldust.

fabled ▶ adjective **1** *a fabled god-giant of Irish myth* **legendary**, mythical, mythic, mythological, fabulous, folkloric, fairy-tale, heroic, traditional; fictitious, imaginary, imagined, made up, unreal, hypothetical, fantastic, proverbial, apocryphal; allegorical, symbolic, parabolic.
OPPOSITES real, historical.
2 *the fabled high quality of French cabinetmaking* **celebrated**, renowned, famed, famous, well known, (rightly) prized, much publicized, noted, notable, distinguished, acclaimed, illustrious, pre-eminent, prominent, great, esteemed, prestigious, well thought of, of note, of consequence, of repute, of high standing.
OPPOSITES unknown; unsung; derided.

fabric *See centre pages for list of* **Fabrics and Fibres**
▶ noun **1** *they weave silks into the finest fabric* **cloth**, material, textile, stuff, tissue, web.
2 *the fabric of the building has deteriorated* **structure**, framework, frame, form, make-up, constitution, composition, construction, organization, infrastructure, foundations, mechanisms, anatomy, essence.

WORD LINKS
seller of fabrics **clothier, draper**

fabricate ▶ verb **1** *he was found to have fabricated research data* **forge**, falsify, fake, counterfeit, make up, invent.
2 *he is guilty of fabricating a pack of lies* **concoct**, make up, contrive, think up, dream up, invent, manufacture, trump up; *informal* cook up.
3 *you will have to fabricate an exhaust system* **make**, create, manufacture, produce; construct, build, assemble, put together, cobble together, form, fashion, contrive, model, shape, forge; erect, put up, set up, raise, elevate.
OPPOSITES destroy, dismantle.

fabrication ▶ noun **1** *the story was a complete fabrication* **invention**, concoction, piece of fiction, fiction, falsification, falsity, lie, untruth, falsehood, fib, deception, made-up story, trumped-up story, fairy story/tale, cock and bull story, barefaced lie; (little) white lie, half-truth, exaggeration, prevarication, departure from the truth; yarn, story, red herring, rumour, myth, flight of fancy, figment of the imagination; pretence, pretext, sham, ruse, wile, trickery, stratagem; *informal* tall story, tall tale, whopper; ; *Brit. informal* porky, pork pie, porky pie; *humorous* terminological inexactitude; *vulgar slang* bullshit; *Austral./NZ vulgar slang* bulldust.
2 *the lintels are galvanized after fabrication* **manufacture**, making, creation, production; construction, building, assembly, putting together, forming, fashioning, contriving, modelling, shaping, forging; erection, putting up, setting up, raising, elevation.

fabulous ▶ adjective **1** *they are paid fabulous salaries* **tremendous**, stupendous, prodigious, phenomenal; extraordinary, remarkable, exceptional; astounding, amazing, astonishing, fantastic, breathtaking, overwhelming, staggering, unthinkable, inconceivable, unimaginable, incredible, unbelievable, unheard of, unthought of, unspeakable, unutterable, untold, ineffable, implausible, improbable, unlikely, impossible, undreamed of, beyond one's wildest dreams, beyond the realm of reason; *informal* mind-boggling, mind-blowing.
OPPOSITES ordinary; tiny.
2 (*informal*) *we had a fabulous time* **excellent**, marvellous, superb, very good, first-rate, first-class, wonderful, outstanding, exceptional, magnificent, splendid, superlative, matchless, peerless; *informal* great, super, terrific, tremendous, smashing, fantastic, sensational, ace, fab, A1, cool, awesome, magic, wicked, tip-top, top-notch, out of sight, out of this world, way-out, capital; *Brit. informal* brill, top-hole, wizard; *Austral./NZ informal* bonzer; *Brit. informal, dated* spiffing, topping; *humorous* super-duper.
OPPOSITES bad; boring.
3 *a fabulous horse-like beast with a female human head* **mythical**, legendary, mythic, mythological, fabled, folkloric, fairy-tale, heroic, traditional; fictitious, imaginary, imagined, made up, unreal, hypothetical, fantastic, proverbial, apocryphal; allegorical, symbolic, symbolical.

facade, façade ▶ noun **1** *the house has a half-timbered facade* **front**, frontage, face, aspect, elevation, exterior, outside.
2 *a facade of laughing bonhomie* **show**, front, appearance, false display, pretence, simulation, affectation, semblance, illusion, posture, pose, sham, fake, act, masquerade, charade, guise, mask, cloak, veil, veneer.

face ▶ noun **1** *she has a beautiful face* **countenance**, physiognomy, profile, features; *informal* mug, kisser, clock; *Brit. informal* mush, dial, phizog, phiz; *Brit. rhyming slang* boat race; *Scottish & Irish informal* coupon; *N. Amer. informal* puss, pan; *literary* visage, lineaments; *archaic* front.
2 *her face grew sad again* **expression**, facial expression, look, appearance, air, manner, bearing, countenance, guise, cast, aspect, impression; *formal* mien.
3 *he made a face at the sourness of the drink* **grimace**, scowl, wry face, wince, frown, glower, smirk, pout, moue.
4 *a cube has six faces* **side**, aspect, flank, vertical, surface, plane, facet, wall, elevation; front, frontage, facade; slope.
5 *the face of a watch* **dial**, display.
6 *a number of dramatic events changed the face of the industry* **(outward) appearance**, aspect, air, nature, image.
7 *he put on a brave face for his audience* **front**, show, display, act, appearance, false front, facade, exterior, guise, mask, masquerade, pretence, charade, pose, illusion, smokescreen, veneer, camouflage.
8 *criticism, if it is to be constructive, should never cause the recipient to lose face* **respect**, honour, esteem, regard, admiration, approbation, acclaim, approval, favour, appreciation, popularity, estimation, veneration, awe, reverence, deference, recognition, prestige, standing, status, dignity, glory, kudos, cachet, image; self-respect, self-esteem, self-image.
9 (*informal*) *they had the face to upbraid others* **effrontery**, audacity, nerve, gall, brazenness, brashness, shamelessness; defiance, boldness, temerity, impudence, impertinence, insolence, presumption, presumptuousness, forwardness, cheek, cheekiness; impoliteness, unmannerliness, bad manners, rudeness; *informal* brass, brass neck, neck, cockiness; *Brit. informal* sauce; *Scottish informal* snash; *N. Amer. informal* sass, sassiness, chutzpah; *informal, dated* hide; *Brit. informal, dated* crust.
□ **face to face** *the two men stood face to face* **facing (each other)**, confronting (each other), opposite (each other), across from each other, opposing (each other); *informal* eyeball to eyeball (with).
□ **on the face of it** *on the face of it, the government's decision is the height of folly* **ostensibly**, to the casual eye, at face value, to all appearances, from appearances, to go/judge by appearances, to all intents and purposes, at first glance, on the surface, superficially; **apparently**, seemingly, evidently, outwardly, it seems (that), it would seem (that), it appears (that), it would appear (that), as far as one knows, as far as one can see/tell, by all accounts, so it seems; so the story goes, so I'm told, so it

appears/seems, so it would appear/seem; allegedly, supposedly, reputedly.
▶ **verb 1** *the hotel faces the sea* **look out on**, front on to, look towards, be facing, have/afford/command a view of, look over/across, open out over, look on to, overlook, give on to, give over, be opposite (to).
OPPOSITE back on to.
2 *you'll just have to face facts | we should be strong enough to* **face up to** *the situation* **accept**, come to accept, become reconciled to, reconcile oneself to, reach an acceptance (of), get used to, become accustomed to, adjust to, accommodate oneself to, acclimatize oneself to; learn to live with, cope with, deal with, come to terms with, get to grips with, become resigned to, make the best of; confront, meet head-on.
OPPOSITE dodge.
3 *he is likely to face a humiliating rejection* **be confronted by**, be faced with, encounter, experience, come into contact with, run into, come across, meet, come up against, be forced to contend with.
4 *those are the problems that face our police force* **beset**, worry, distress, cause trouble to, trouble, bother, confront, burden; harass, oppress, vex, irritate, exasperate, strain, stress, tax; torment, plague, blight, bedevil, rack, smite, curse, harrow; *rare* discommode.
5 *though unprepared for such a challenge, he faced it boldly* **brave**, face up to, encounter, meet, meet head-on, confront, dare, defy, oppose, resist, withstand.
OPPOSITE succumb to.
6 (usually **be faced with**) *a low, curving wall faced with flint* **cover**, clad, veneer, skin, overlay, surface, dress, pave, put a facing on, laminate, inlay, plate, coat, line.

facelift ▶ **noun 1** *she's planning to have a facelift when she gets older* **cosmetic surgery**, plastic surgery; *technical* rhytidectomy.
2 (*informal*) *the theatre is reopening after a £200,000 facelift* **renovation**, redecoration, refurbishment, revamp, revamping, makeover, rehabilitation, reconditioning, overhauling, modernization, restoration, repair, redevelopment, rebuilding, reconstruction, remodelling, updating, improvement; gentrification, upgrading; refit.

facet ▶ **noun 1** *a larger number of small facets preserves the size of the gem* **surface**, face, side, plane, angle, slant.
2 *she'd also seen other facets of his character* **aspect**, feature, side, dimension, particular, characteristic, detail, point, ingredient, strand, factor; component, constituent, element, part, section, portion, piece, bit; angle, slant, sense, respect, regard, way, viewpoint, standpoint.

facetious ▶ **adjective** *no facetious remarks, please* **flippant**, flip, glib, frivolous, tongue-in-cheek, waggish, whimsical, joking, jokey, jesting, jocular, playful, roguish, impish, teasing, arch, mischievous, puckish; in fun, in jest, witty, amusing, funny, droll, comic, comical, light-hearted, high-spirited, bantering; *archaic* frolicsome, sportive; *rare* jocose.
OPPOSITE serious.

facile ▶ **adjective 1** *that's too facile an explanation* **simplistic**, superficial, oversimple, oversimplified, schematic, black and white; shallow, pat, glib, slick, jejune, naive; *N. Amer. informal* dime-store, bubblegum.
OPPOSITES thorough, profound.
2 *he achieved a facile six-lengths victory* **effortless**, easy, undemanding, unexacting, painless, trouble-free, unchallenged; leisurely, simple, uncomplicated, straightforward, elementary; *informal* easy-peasy, as easy as pie, as easy as falling off a log, as easy as ABC, a piece of cake, child's play, kids' stuff, a cinch, no sweat, a doddle, a breeze, a pushover, money for old rope, money for jam; *N. Amer. informal* duck soup, a snap; *Austral./NZ informal* a bludge.
OPPOSITE hard-won.

facilitate ▶ **verb** *working in pairs appears to facilitate learning* **make easy/easier**, ease, make possible, make smooth/smoother, smooth, smooth the path of, smooth the way for, clear the way for, open the door for; enable, assist, help, help along, aid, oil, oil the wheels of, lubricate, expedite, speed up, accelerate, forward, advance, promote, further, encourage; simplify.
OPPOSITE impede.

facility ▶ **noun 1** (**facilities**) *many shopping centres include car-parking facilities* **provision**, space, means, potential, prerequisite, equipment.
2 *the camera has a zoom facility* **possibility**, opportunity, feature.
3 *there is a wealth of local facilities* **amenity**, resource, service, advantage, convenience, benefit.
4 *a medical facility deep in the jungle* **establishment**, centre, installation, place, depot, station, location, premises, site, post, base, camp; *informal* joint, outfit, set-up.
5 *his facility for drawing* **aptitude**, **talent**, gift, flair, bent, skill, knack, finesse, genius; ability, proficiency, competence, capability, potential, capacity, faculty; expertise, expertness, adeptness, prowess, mastery, artistry; propensity, inclination, natural ability, suitability, fitness; head, mind, brain; *informal* know-how.
6 *I was turning out poetry with facility* **ease**, effortlessness, no difficulty, no trouble, no bother, facileness, simplicity; deftness, adroitness, dexterity, proficiency, mastery.

facing ▶ **noun 1** *a tartan smoking jacket with green velvet facings* **covering**, trimming, lining, interfacing, reinforcement, backing.
2 *the bricks were used as a facing on a concrete core* **cladding**, veneer, skin, protective/decorative layer, surface, facade, front, fronting, false front, coating, covering, dressing, overlay, revetment, paving, lamination, inlay, plating; *N. Amer.* siding.

facsimile ▶ **noun 1** *a facsimile of the manuscript* **copy**, reproduction, duplicate, photocopy, mimeograph, mimeo, replica, likeness, carbon, carbon copy, print, reprint, offprint, image; fax, telefax; clone; *N. Amer.* telecopy; *Printing* autotype; *trademark* Xerox, photostat.
OPPOSITE original.
2 *somewhere out there a facsimile of Jenny roamed* **double**, lookalike, twin, clone, duplicate, perfect likeness, exact likeness, echo, replica, copy, imitation, picture, image, living image, mirror-image; *German* Doppelgänger; *informal* spitting image, dead ringer, ringer, (very) spit, dead spit, spit and image.

fact ▶ **noun 1** *it is a fact that the water supply is seriously polluted* **reality**, actuality, certainty, factuality, certitude; truth, naked truth, verity, gospel.
OPPOSITES lie; fiction.
2 *every fact in the report was double-checked* **detail**, piece of information, particular, item, specific, element, point, factor, feature, characteristic, respect, ingredient, attribute, circumstance, consideration, aspect, facet; (**facts**) information, itemized information, whole story; *informal* info, gen, low-down, score, dope.
3 *he was charged with being an accessory after the fact* **event**, happening, occurrence, incident, act, deed.
□ **in fact** *he said that he was going home, but in fact he went to the pub* **actually**, in actuality, in actual fact, really, in reality, in point of fact, as a matter of fact, in truth, if truth be told, to tell the truth, the truth is/was; *dated* indeed, truly; *archaic* in sooth, verily; *rare* in the concrete.

faction ▶ **noun 1** *he was supported by a faction of the Liberal Party* **clique**, coterie, caucus, cabal, bloc, camp, group, grouping, side, sector, section, wing, arm, branch, division, contingent, set, ring, lobby; ginger group, pressure group, splinter group, fringe movement, minority group.
2 *the council was increasingly split by faction* **infighting**, dissension, dissent, dispute, discord, strife, contention, conflict, friction, argument, difference of opinion, disagreement, controversy, quarrelling, wrangling, bickering, squabbling, disputation, falling-out, debate, division, divisiveness, clashing, disharmony, disunity, variance, rupture, tumult, turbulence, upheaval, dissidence, rebellion, insurrection, sedition, mutiny, schism.
OPPOSITE harmony.

factious ▶ **adjective** *he had transformed a fragmented, factious resistance movement into a monolithic one* **divided**, split, sectarian, schismatic, dissenting, contentious, discordant, conflicting, argumentative, disagreeing, disputatious, quarrelling, quarrelsome, clashing, warring, at variance, at loggerheads, at odds, disharmonious, tumultuous, turbulent, dissident, rebellious, insurrectionary, seditious, mutinous.
OPPOSITE harmonious.

factitious ▶ **adjective** *the outcry was, to a certain extent, factitious* **bogus**, fake, not genuine, specious, false, counterfeit, fraudulent, spurious, trumped-up, sham, mock, feigned, affected, pretended, contrived, unnatural, fabricated, manufactured, engineered; artificial, imitation, simulated, ersatz; *informal* phoney, pseudo, pretend; *Brit. informal* cod; *rare* adulterine.
OPPOSITE genuine.

factor ▶ **noun 1** *this had been a key factor in his decision to withdraw* **element**, part, component, ingredient, strand, constituent, point, detail, item, feature, facet, aspect, characteristic, consideration, influence, circumstance, thing, determinant.
2 (*Scottish*) *he worked as a factor in Perthshire* **agent**, representative, deputy, middleman, intermediary, go-between; **estate manager**, land agent, land steward, reeve.

factory *See centre pages for list of* **Factories and Workshops**
▶ **noun works**, plant, manufacturing complex/facility, yard, mill, industrial unit; workshop, shop; shop floor; *archaic* manufactory.

factotum ▶ **noun** *in former times he might have been a nobleman's factotum* **odd-job man**, (general) handyman, general employee, man of all work, maid of all work, jack of all trades, personal assistant; *Brit.* PA; *Austral.* knockabout; *informal* (Mr) Fixit, man/girl Friday.

factual ▶ **adjective** *a factual account of events* **truthful**, true, accurate, authentic, historical, genuine, fact-based, realistic, real; true-to-life, lifelike, telling it like it is, as it really happened, correct, circumstantial, sure, veritable, exact, precise, honest, fair, faithful, literal, matter-of-fact, verbatim, word for word, unbiased, objective, unprejudiced, unvarnished, unadorned, unadulterated, unexaggerated; *rare* verisimilar, veristic, veridical.
OPPOSITE fictitious.

faculty ▶ **noun 1** *the faculty of speech* **power**, capability, capacity, facility, potential, potentiality, propensity, wherewithal, means, preparedness; (**faculties**) senses, wits, reason, intelligence.

2 *he had a quite unusual faculty for unearthing contributors* **ability**, proficiency, competence, capability, potential, capacity, facility, readiness; **aptitude**, talent, gift, flair, bent, skill, knack, finesse, genius; expertise, expertness, adeptness, adroitness, dexterity, prowess, mastery, artistry, accomplishment; propensity, inclination, natural ability, suitability, fitness; head, mind, brain; *informal* know-how.
3 *the arts faculty* **department**, school, division, section.
4 *the vicar introduced certain ornaments without the necessary faculty to do so* **authorization**, authority, power, right, permission, consent, leave, sanction, licence, dispensation, assent, acquiescence, agreement, approval, seal of approval, approbation, endorsement, imprimatur, clearance; *informal* the go-ahead, the thumbs up, the OK, the green light, say-so; *rare* permit.

fad ▶ **noun** *there is a general fad for see-through products* **craze**, vogue, trend, fashion, mode, enthusiasm, passion, infatuation, love, obsession, mania, rage, compulsion, fixation, fetish, weakness, fancy, taste, novelty, whim, fascination, preoccupation; *informal* thing, latest.

faddy ▶ **adjective** (*Brit. informal*) *offering a varied diet can be difficult when a child is faddy* **fussy**, finicky, difficult/hard to please, over-particular, faddish, over-fastidious, dainty, exacting, demanding, selective; *informal* choosy, picky, pernickety; *N. Amer. informal* persnickety; *archaic* nice, overnice; *rare* finical.

fade ▶ **verb 1** *the paintwork has faded and peeled* **become pale**, grow pale, pale, become bleached, become washed out, lose colour, decolour, decolorize, discolour; dull, dim, grow dull, grow dim, lose lustre.
OPPOSITE brighten.
2 *sunlight had faded the picture* **bleach**, wash out, make pale, decolour, decolorize, blanch, whiten; dull, discolour, dim, etiolate.
OPPOSITES enhance; brighten.
3 *remove the flower heads as they fade* **wither**, wilt, droop, shrivel, decay, die, perish; *technical* become marcescent; *rare* etiolate.
4 *the afternoon light began to fade | the noise* ***faded away*** **dim**, grow dim, grow faint, grow feeble, fail, dwindle, grow less, die away, wane, disappear, vanish, decline, dissolve, peter out, melt away, evanesce.
OPPOSITE increase.
5 *the Communist movement was* ***fading away*** **decline**, die out, diminish, deteriorate, degenerate, decay, crumble, collapse, fail, fall, sink, slump, slip, slide, go downhill, go to rack and ruin; *informal* go to pot, go to the dogs, go down the toilet, go down the tubes, hit the skids; *Austral./NZ informal* go to the pack; *rare* retrograde.
OPPOSITE thrive.

faeces ▶ **plural noun** **excrement**, bodily waste, waste matter, ordure, dung, manure, scat; excreta, stools, droppings; dirt, filth, muck, mess; *informal* poo, doo-doo, doings, turds; *Brit. informal* cack, whoopsies, jobbies; *N. Amer. informal* poop; *vulgar slang* crap, shit; *archaic* night soil; *rare* egesta, feculence.

WORD LINKS

related prefixes	**scato-, copro-** (e.g. ***coprolite***)
medical study of faeces	**scatology**
fear of faeces	**coprophobia**
faeces-eating	**scatophagous, coprophagous**

fag[1] (*Brit. informal*) ▶ **noun** *it's too much of a fag to drive all the way there and back* **chore**, slog, grind, drudgery, exertion, trouble, bother, pain, hardship, bore; *informal* sweat.
▶ **verb** *he had to* ***fag away*** *in the lab all day* **toil**, slave, labour, grind; work hard, work one's fingers to the bone, work like a Trojan, work like a dog, keep one's nose to the grindstone, exert oneself; *informal* slog, plug, work one's guts out, work one's socks off, kill oneself, sweat blood, knock oneself out; *Brit. informal* graft; *Austral./NZ informal* bullock; *N. Amer. vulgar slang* work one's ass/butt off; *archaic* travail, moil.
OPPOSITE relax.
□ **fag someone out** *I've been fagged out by my run* **exhaust**, tire, tire out, wear out, fatigue, overtire, overtax, weary, drain, run someone into the ground, run someone ragged; enervate, sap, debilitate, enfeeble, prostrate; *informal* do in, wipe out, knock out, shatter, frazzle, wear to a frazzle, take it out of someone; *Brit. informal* knacker; *N. Amer. informal* poop, tucker out; *Austral./NZ & Irish informal* root.

fag[2] ▶ **noun** (*Brit. informal*) *he had a fag clamped between his teeth.* See CIGARETTE.

fagged ▶ **adjective** *I'm off to bed now—I'm absolutely* ***fagged out*** **exhausted**, tired, tired out, worn out, fatigued, weary, wearied, drained, sapped, spent, washed out, on one's last legs; *informal* done in, all in, dog tired, dead beat, dead on one's feet, fit to drop, shattered, bushed, frazzled, worn to a frazzle; *Brit. informal* knackered; *N. Amer. informal* tuckered, pooped.

fail ▶ **verb 1** *they could not explain why the enterprise had failed* **be unsuccessful**, not succeed, lack success, fall through, fall flat, break down, abort, miscarry, be defeated, suffer defeat, be in vain, be frustrated, collapse, founder, misfire, backfire, not come up to scratch, meet with disaster, come to grief, come to nothing, come to naught, miss the mark, run aground, go astray; *informal* flop, fizzle out, come a cropper, bite the dust, bomb, blow up in someone's face, go down like a lead balloon.
OPPOSITE succeed.
2 *he failed all his examinations* **be unsuccessful in**, not pass; be found wanting, be found deficient, not make the grade, not pass muster, not come up to scratch, be rejected; *informal* flunk.
OPPOSITE pass.
3 *he felt that his friends had failed him* **let down**, disappoint, break one's promise to, dash someone's hopes, fall short of someone's expectations; neglect, desert, abandon; betray, be disloyal to, be unfaithful to, break faith with, play someone false; *informal* do the dirty on; *N. Amer. informal* bail on; *archaic* forsake.
OPPOSITE support.
4 *the crops failed* **be deficient**, be wanting, be lacking, fall short, be insufficient, be inadequate; not come to ripeness, wither.
OPPOSITE thrive.
5 *they went to bed when the daylight failed* **fade**, grow less, grow dim, dim, die away, dwindle, wane, disappear, vanish, peter out, dissolve.
6 *the ventilation system failed* **break down**, break, stop working, cease to function, cut out, stop, stall, crash, give out; malfunction, act up, go wrong, develop a fault, be faulty, be defective; *informal* conk out, go kaput, go phut, give up the ghost, go on the blink, be on the blink; *Brit. informal* pack up, play up.
OPPOSITES work, be in working order.
7 *Ceri's health was failing* **deteriorate**, degenerate, decline, go into decline, fade, diminish, dwindle, wane, ebb, sink, collapse, decay.
OPPOSITE improve.
8 *there are 900 businesses failing a week* **collapse**, crash, go under, go bankrupt, become insolvent, go into receivership, be in the hands of the receivers, go into liquidation, cease trading, cease production, be closed, be shut down, close down, be wound up; *informal* fold, flop, go bust, go broke, go bump, go to the wall, go belly up.
OPPOSITE thrive.
▶ **noun**
□ **without fail** *she went to Mass every Sunday without fail* **without exception**, unfailingly, constantly, regularly, invariably, dependably, conscientiously, reliably, faithfully, predictably, punctually, religiously, whatever happened, always; *informal* like clockwork.

failing ▶ **noun** *Jeanne accepted him despite his failings* **fault**, shortcoming, weakness, weak point, weak spot, imperfection, defect, flaw, blemish, frailty, infirmity, foible, quirk, idiosyncrasy, vice; deficiency, inadequacy, limitation; *informal* hang-up.
OPPOSITE strength.
▶ **preposition** *failing further financial assistance, you should declare yourself bankrupt* **in the absence of**, in default of, lacking, wanting, notwithstanding.

failure ▶ **noun 1** *the failure of the assassination attempt* **lack of success**, non-success, non-fulfilment, abortion, miscarriage, defeat, frustration, collapse, foundering, misfiring, coming to nothing, falling through; *informal* fizzling out.
OPPOSITE success.
2 *every one of his schemes had been a failure* **fiasco**, debacle, catastrophe, disaster, blunder, vain attempt, abortion, defeat; *Brit.* damp squib; *informal* flop, botch, hash, foul-up, screw-up, washout, let-down, dead loss, dead duck, lead balloon, lemon; *Brit. informal* cock-up, pig's ear; *N. Amer. informal* snafu, clinker; *vulgar slang* fuck-up, balls-up.
OPPOSITE success.
3 *I was regarded by everyone as a failure* **loser**, born loser, incompetent, nonachiever, underachiever, ne'er-do-well, disappointment, write-off; no one, nobody; *informal* no-hoper, flop, dud, non-starter, washout, dead loss, lemon.
OPPOSITE success.
4 *he felt guilty for what seemed like a failure in duty* **negligence**, remissness, non-observance, non-performance, dereliction; omission, neglect, oversight.
5 *any crop failure could affect a farming business* **inadequacy**, insufficiency, deficiency, lack, dearth, scarcity, shortfall.
6 *he was puzzled by the failure of the camera* **breaking down**, breakdown, non-function, cutting out, seizing up; **malfunction**, faultiness; crash; *informal* conking out; *Brit. informal* playing up.
7 *the failure of several state-owned companies* **collapse**, crash, going under, bankruptcy, insolvency, liquidation, close-down, closure, closing, shutting down, winding up, termination; decline, failing, foundering, sinking, ruin, ruination; *informal* folding, flop.
OPPOSITE success.

WORD LINKS

fear of failure	**kakorrhaphiaphobia**

faint ▶ **adjective 1** *her skirt had a faint mark or two* **indistinct**, vague, unclear, indefinite, ill-defined, obscure, imperceptible, hardly noticeable, hardly detectable, unobtrusive; pale, light, faded, bleached.
OPPOSITE clear.
2 *the baby gave a faint cry* **quiet**, muted, muffled, stifled, subdued; **feeble**, weak, thin, whispered, murmured, indistinct, scarcely audible, scarcely

perceptible, hard to hear, hard to make out, vague; low, soft, gentle.
OPPOSITE loud.
3 *the faint possibility of his returning* **slight**, slender, slim, small, tiny, minimal, negligible, remote, distant, vague, unlikely, improbable, doubtful, dubious, far-fetched; poor, outside; *informal* minuscule; *rare* exiguous.
OPPOSITE great.
4 *only faint praise was offered to the management team* **unenthusiastic**, half-hearted, weak, feeble, low-key; *informal* wishy-washy.
OPPOSITE strong.
5 *I suddenly felt hot and faint* **dizzy**, giddy, light-headed, muzzy, weak, weak at the knees, unsteady, shaky, wobbly, off-balance, reeling; *informal* woozy, woolly, woolly-headed, dopey, trembly, all of a quiver; *rare* vertiginous.
▶ **verb** *he was so pale she thought he would faint* **pass out**, lose consciousness, fall unconscious, black out, collapse; *informal* flake out, keel over, conk out, zonk out, drop, go out, go out like a light; *literary* swoon.
▶ **noun** *she collapsed to the floor in a dead faint* **blackout**, fainting fit, loss of consciousness, collapse; coma; *literary* swoon; *Medicine* syncope.

F

faint-hearted ▶ **adjective** *the more faint-hearted tenants left after the raid* **timid**, timorous, nervous, nervy, easily scared, easily frightened, scared, fearful, afraid, trembling, quaking, cowering, daunted; **cowardly**, craven, spiritless, spineless, pusillanimous, weak, weak-willed, unmanly, lily-livered, pigeon-hearted, weak-kneed, weakling; *Scottish* feart; *informal* soft, jumpy, jittery, chicken, chicken-hearted, chicken-livered, yellow, yellow-bellied, gutless, sissy, wimpy, wimpish; *Brit. informal* wet; *N. Amer. informal* spooked, candy-assed; *N. Amer. vulgar slang* chickenshit; *archaic* recreant, poor-spirited; *archaic, informal* funky.
OPPOSITES bold; brave.

faintly ▶ **adverb 1** *Maria called his name faintly* **indistinctly**, softly, gently, weakly, feebly; in a whisper, in a murmur, in a low voice, in subdued tones.
OPPOSITES brightly; loudly.
2 *the newcomer looked faintly bewildered* **slightly**, vaguely, somewhat, quite, fairly, rather, a little, a bit, a little bit, a touch, a shade; to some extent, to a certain extent, to some degree; *informal* sort of, kind of, kinda.
OPPOSITE extremely.

fair[1] ▶ **adjective 1** *the courts were generally regarded as fair* **just**, equitable, fair-minded, open-minded, honest, upright, honourable, trustworthy; impartial, unbiased, unprejudiced, non-partisan, non-discriminatory, objective, neutral, even-handed, dispassionate, disinterested, detached; above board, lawful, legal, legitimate, proper, good; *informal* legit, kosher, pukka, on the level, square; *N. Amer. informal* on the up and up.
OPPOSITE unfair.
2 *I am hoping for fair weather for next week's trip* **fine**, dry, bright, clear, sunny, sunshiny, sunlit, cloudless, without a cloud in the sky; warm, balmy, summery, clement, benign, agreeable, pleasant, good.
OPPOSITE inclement.
3 *their voyage was helped by fair winds and calm seas* **favourable**, advantageous, helpful, benign, beneficial; opportune, timely; on one's side, in one's favour.
OPPOSITE unfavourable.
4 *she had fair curling hair* **blond(e)**, yellow, yellowish, golden, flaxen, light, light brown, light-coloured, strawberry blonde, tow-coloured, platinum, ash blonde, bleached, bleached-blonde, sun-bleached, peroxide, bottle-blonde; fair-haired, light-haired, golden-haired, flaxen-haired, tow-headed.
OPPOSITES dark; brunette.
5 *Belinda's skin was very fair* **pale**, light, light-coloured, white, cream-coloured, creamy, peaches and cream.
OPPOSITE dark.
6 (*archaic*) *he won the fair maiden's heart* **beautiful**, pretty, lovely, attractive, good-looking, nice-looking, gorgeous, stunning, striking, arresting, captivating, prepossessing, winning, enchanting, appealing, ravishing, desirable, luscious, nubile; *Scottish & N. English* bonny; *informal* drop-dead gorgeous, smashing, knockout, out of this world, easy on the eye, tasty, hot, fanciable, beddable; *N. Amer. informal* cute; *literary* beauteous; *dated* taking, well favoured; *archaic* comely.
OPPOSITE ugly.
7 *scoring twenty points was a fair achievement* **reasonable**, passable, tolerable, satisfactory, acceptable, respectable, decent, all right, good enough, goodish, pretty good, not bad, moderate, average, middling, ample, adequate, sufficient; *informal* OK, okay, so-so, fair-to-middling.
□ **fair and square** *I won the race fair and square* **honestly**, fairly, without cheating, without foul play, by the book, according to the rules, in accordance with the rules; lawfully, legally, licitly, legitimately; *informal* on the level; *N. Amer. informal* on the up and up.

fair[2] ▶ **noun 1** *an English country fair* **fête**, gala, festival, carnival, funfair.
2 *a local antiques fair* **market**, bazaar, mart, exchange, sale; open-air market, indoor market, flea market; *archaic* emporium.
3 *Manchester is to host a new British art fair* **exhibition**, display, show, showing, presentation, demonstration, exposition, spectacle, extravaganza; *N. Amer.* exhibit; *informal* expo, demo.

> **CHOOSE THE RIGHT WORD**
>
> **fair, just, equitable**
>
> These words express judgements springing from a belief that everyone should get what they are entitled to.
>
> - **Fair** is the most general term and means 'treating people equally, without favouritism or discrimination'. It is an emotive word, expressing a deep-seated sense of what is basically right, and appeals to one's sense of balance and good conduct (*consumers will receive a fair share of the resulting benefit* | *a free and fair election*). *Fair* is used not only to judge people and their behaviour but also to complain about impersonal bad luck (*life's just not fair*).
> - **Just** derives from Latin *ius* 'law' and suggests that there is an objective standard of what is right and fair, against which someone's behaviour can be measured. The standard may be either a legal one or a moral one (*he would continue to battle for a just settlement* | *those responsible have received their just deserts* | *a just war*).
> - **Equitable** is a rarer, more formal term deriving ultimately from Latin *aequus* 'equal'. It suggests an unbiased outcome reached through scrupulous consideration of competing interests and rights. It is typically used in connection with sharing (*a more equitable distribution of wealth* | *his reforms will make the NHS more equitable as well as more efficient*). Unlike *fair* and *just*, it is not used to describe people, only actions.

fairly ▶ **adverb 1** *all pupils were treated fairly* **justly**, equitably, impartially, without bias, without prejudice, without fear or favour, with an open mind, open-mindedly, even-handedly, objectively, neutrally, disinterestedly; properly, lawfully, legally, legitimately, licitly, by the book, in accordance with the rules, according to the rules; equally, the same; *informal* fairly and squarely.
OPPOSITE unfairly.
2 *the pipes are in fairly good condition* **reasonably**, passably, tolerably, satisfactorily, sufficiently, adequately, moderately, quite, rather, somewhat, relatively, comparatively; *informal* pretty, kind of, sort of, kinda.
OPPOSITES insufficiently; extremely.
3 *he fairly hauled her along the street* **positively**, really, veritably, simply, actually, absolutely, decidedly; practically, almost, nearly, all but, to all intents and purposes; *informal* plain, plumb.

fair-minded ▶ **adjective** *he was respected as a fair-minded chief* **fair**, just, even-handed, equitable, egalitarian, impartial, non-partisan, non-discriminatory, unbiased, unprejudiced, open-minded, objective, dispassionate, unselfish, with no axe to grind; honest, honourable, trustworthy, upright, decent; *informal* on the level; *N. Amer. informal* on the up and up.

fairy ▶ **noun** *all of the children believed in fairies* **sprite**, pixie, elf, imp, brownie, puck; dwarf, gnome, goblin, hobgoblin, troll; *Scottish Folklore* kelpie; *Irish Folklore* leprechaun, pishogue, Sidhe; *S. African Folklore* tokoloshe; *Persian Mythology* peri; *literary* faerie, fay; *rare* nix, nixie, hob, elfin.

fairy tale, fairy story ▶ **noun 1** *the film was inspired by a fairy tale* **folk tale**, folk story, traditional story, myth, legend, romance, fantasy, fable, fiction; *informal* yarn.
2 (*informal*) *she accused him of telling fairy tales* **lie**, white lie, fib, half-truth, untruth, falsity, falsehood, story, tall story, tall tale, made-up story, trumped-up story, fabrication, invention, piece of fiction, falsification; *informal* whopper, cock and bull story, angler's tale; *Brit. informal* porky, porky pie, pork pie; *humorous* terminological inexactitude.

faith ▶ **noun 1** *he completely justified his boss's faith in him* **trust**, belief, confidence, conviction, credence, reliance, dependence; optimism, hopefulness, hope, expectation.
OPPOSITE mistrust.
2 *she gave her life for her faith* **religion**, church, sect, denomination, persuasion, religious persuasion, religious belief, belief, code of belief, ideology, creed, teaching, dogma, doctrine.
□ **break faith with be disloyal to**, be unfaithful to, be untrue to, betray, play someone false, break one's promise to, fail, let down, disappoint; double-cross, deceive, cheat, stab in the back, be a Judas to, give away; *informal* do the dirty on, stitch up, rat on, sell down the river.
□ **keep faith with be loyal to**, be faithful to, be true to, stand by, stick by, keep one's promise to, make good one's promise to.

faithful ▶ **adjective 1** *she stayed faithful all her married life* | *his faithful assistant* **loyal**, constant, true, devoted, true-blue, true-hearted, unswerving, unwavering, staunch, steadfast, dedicated, committed; trusted, trusty, trustworthy, dependable, reliable, obedient, dutiful.
OPPOSITE unfaithful.
2 *a faithful copy of a famous painting* **accurate**, precise, exact, errorless, error-free, unerring, without error, faultless, true, close, strict; realistic, authentic, convincing; *informal* on the button, on the mark, on the beam, on the nail; *Brit. informal* spot on, bang on; *N. Amer. informal* on the money; *rare* verisimilar.

OPPOSITE inaccurate.
▶ **noun** (**the faithful**) *he read the sacred scriptures to the faithful* **believers**, communicants; adherents, followers, loyal followers, loyal members; congregation, brethren, flock.

CHOOSE THE RIGHT WORD

faithful, loyal, constant, true

All these words are used to describe an unwavering commitment to someone or something.

- Someone who is **faithful** shows unchanging affection or support for a person or cause, often in the face of difficulty or some temptation to desert. It can refer to marital fidelity (*he has been faithful to his wife for 42 years*) or religious faith (*faithful Jews were required to make the pilgrimage to Jerusalem three times a year*) and is used informally of inanimate objects regarded as absolutely reliable (*he drove his faithful Toyota overland from Saudi Arabia*).
- **Loyal** typically refers to allegiance to a superior or employer (*he proved to be a loyal subject of the king | a loyal workforce*) or support for a business or other organization (*we look forward to providing our loyal customers with a first-class service*). A *loyal friend* will show unwavering support, particularly in standing by one in the face of criticism or hostility from others.
- **Constant** is a rather literary term for unchanging and utterly reliable fidelity (*they are constant and dependable, consistently dispensing happiness*).
- **True** has a rather archaic ring when used to convey fidelity (*she is as true to me as the day is long*), since the sense tends to merge with the sense 'real' (*a true friend*). It is also used in the phrase *true to* (*true to his word, he schooled her in horsemanship*).

faithfulness ▶ **noun 1** *she never doubted her husband's faithfulness* **fidelity**, loyalty, constancy, devotion, trueness, true-heartedness, dedication, commitment, allegiance, adherence; dependability, reliability, trustworthiness, staunchness, steadfastness; *historical* fealty.
OPPOSITE unfaithfulness.
2 *the faithfulness of the description* **accuracy**, precision, exactness, closeness, strictness, fairness, justness, factuality, truth, truthfulness, veracity, authenticity, reliability, dependability; *rare* veridicality.
OPPOSITE inaccuracy.

faithless ▶ **adjective 1** *she left her faithless lover* **unfaithful**, disloyal, inconstant, false, false-hearted, untrue, adulterous, traitorous, treacherous, perfidious, fickle, flighty, untrustworthy, unreliable, undependable, deceitful, deceiving, two-faced, double-dealing, double-crossing; *informal* cheating, two-timing, back-stabbing; *rare* double-faced, Janus-faced.
OPPOSITE faithful.
2 *the natives were ungodly and faithless* **unbelieving**, non-believing, irreligious, without religious faith, disbelieving, doubting, sceptical, agnostic, atheistic; pagan, heathen; *rare* nullifidian.

fake ▶ **noun 1** *one of the sculptures was found to be a fake* **forgery**, counterfeit, copy, sham, fraud, hoax, imitation, mock-up, dummy, reproduction, lookalike, likeness; *informal* phoney, pirate, knock-off, rip-off, dupe.
2 *that doctor is a fake* **charlatan**, quack, mountebank, sham, fraud, humbug, impostor, pretender, masquerader, hoodwinker, hoaxer, cheat, cheater, deceiver, dissembler, trickster, confidence trickster, fraudster; *informal* phoney, con man, con artist; *dated* confidence man.
▶ **adjective 1** *he gave his wife fake banknotes* **counterfeit**, forged, fraudulent, sham, imitation, false, bogus, spurious, pseudo; worthless, invalid; *informal* phoney, dud.
OPPOSITE genuine.
2 *they adorn themselves with fake diamonds* **imitation**, artificial, synthetic, simulated, reproduction, replica, ersatz, plastic, man-made, dummy, false, mock, sham, bogus, so-called; *informal* pretend, phoney, pseudo.
OPPOSITE genuine.
3 *she adopted a fake accent* **feigned**, faked, put-on, assumed, improvised, invented, affected, pseudo, insincere, unconvincing, artificial, imitation, mock, sham; *informal* phoney, pseud, pretend; *Brit. informal* cod.
OPPOSITE authentic.
▶ **verb 1** *her death certificate was faked* **forge**, counterfeit, falsify, sham, feign, mock up, copy, reproduce, replicate; doctor, alter, tamper with, tinker with; *informal* pirate; *Brit. informal* fiddle (with).
2 *he faked a yawn* **feign**, pretend, simulate, sham, put on, make-believe, affect; give the appearance of, make a show of, make a pretence of, go through the motions of.

fall ▶ **verb 1** *bombers screamed above and bombs began to fall* **drop**, drop down, plummet, descend, come down, go down, plunge, sink, dive, nosedive, tumble, pitch; cascade; *technical* gravitate.
OPPOSITE rise.
2 *he lost his balance and fell* **topple over**, tumble over, keel over, fall down, fall over, go head over heels, go end over end, fall headlong, go headlong, collapse, fall in a heap, take a spill, pitch forward; trip, trip over, stumble, stagger, slip, slide; *informal* come a cropper, go for six; *dated* measure one's length.
OPPOSITE get up.
3 *little by little, the river began to fall* **subside**, recede, ebb, fall back, flow back, fall away, go down, get lower, sink; abate, settle; *rare* retrocede.
OPPOSITES rise; flood.
4 *inflation is expected to fall* **decrease**, decline, diminish, fall off, drop off, go down, grow less, lessen, dwindle; plummet, plunge, slump, sink; depreciate, decrease in value, lose value, decline in price, cheapen, devalue; *informal* hit the floor, go through the floor, nosedive, take a nosedive, take a header, go into a tailspin, crash.
OPPOSITES rise, increase.
5 *the Mogul empire fell several centuries later* **decline**, deteriorate, degenerate, go downhill, go to rack and ruin; die, decay, atrophy, wither, fade, fail; *informal* go to the dogs, go to pot, hit the skids, go down the toilet, go down the tubes; *Austral./NZ informal* go to the pack; *rare* retrograde.
OPPOSITE flourish.
6 *a monument to those who fell in the Civil War* **die**, be killed, be slain, be a casualty, be a fatality, be lost, lose one's life, perish, drop dead, meet one's end, meet one's death; *informal* bite the dust, croak, buy it; *Brit. informal* snuff it, peg out; *N. Amer. informal* bite the big one; *archaic* decease.
7 *the town fell to the barbarians* **surrender**, yield, submit, give in, give up, give way, capitulate, succumb; be overthrown by, be taken by, be defeated by, be conquered by, be overcome by, be overwhelmed by, lose one's position to, pass into the hands of, fall victim to.
OPPOSITE resist.
8 *Easter falls on 23rd April* **occur**, take place, happen, come about, come to pass.
9 *he waited for night to fall* **come**, arrive, appear, occur, arise, materialize.
10 *my grandmother fell ill* **become**, come/get to be, grow, get, turn.
11 *more of the domestic tasks may **fall to him*** **be the responsibility of**, be the duty of, be borne by, be one's job, be one's task; come someone's way.
12 (*archaic*) *it is their husbands' fault if wives do fall* **sin**, do wrong, transgress, err, yield to temptation, commit a sin, commit an offence, fall from grace, stray, go astray, stray from the straight and narrow, lapse, backslide, misbehave; *archaic* trespass.
OPPOSITE do good.

□ **fall apart 1** *my boots fell apart* **fall to pieces**, come to pieces, fall to bits, come to bits, come apart (at the seams); **disintegrate**, fragment, break up, break apart, crumble, dissolve, degenerate, decay, moulder, perish; go downhill, go to rack and ruin; *informal* bust.
OPPOSITE remain intact.
2 *I was gentle with him when he fell apart* **break down**, have a breakdown, go to pieces, fall to pieces, lose control, lose one's self-control, crumble; *informal* crack up, freak, freak out.

□ **fall asleep** *Claire tried not to fall asleep* **doze off**, drop off, go to sleep; *informal* nod off, go off, drift off, crash, crash out, flake out, conk out, go out like a light; *N. Amer. informal* sack out, zone out.
OPPOSITES stay awake; wake up.

□ **fall away** *the ground fell away abruptly* **slope down**, slope, slant down, go down, incline downwards, tilt downwards, drop away, drop, descend, dip, sink, plunge; *rare* decline.
OPPOSITE rise.

□ **fall back** *the force of her blow caused him to fall back* **retreat**, withdraw, back off, draw back, pull back, pull away, move away, retire, pull out; turn tail, flee, take flight, beat a (hasty) retreat.
OPPOSITE advance.

□ **fall back on** *you can always fall back on the support of relatives* **resort to**, turn to, look to, call on, call into play, call into action, call into service, press into service, have recourse to, make use of, use, employ; rely on, depend on, lean on.

□ **fall behind 1** *she walked so fast that the others soon fell behind* **lag**, lag behind, trail, trail behind, be left behind, fall back, drop back, not keep up, lose one's place, not keep pace, bring up the rear; straggle, dally, dawdle, hang back, drag one's feet, take one's time.
OPPOSITE overtake.
2 *customers **fell behind** on their payments* **get into debt**, get into arrears, default, be in the red, be late, be overdue; not keep up with.
OPPOSITE be up to date.

□ **fall down 1** *I spin round and round till I fall down* **fall over**, fall, topple over, tumble down, keel over, collapse, fall in a heap, trip, take a spill, stumble, stagger; *informal* come a cropper, go for six; *dated* measure one's length.
2 *the federation fell down in some areas* **fail**, be unsuccessful, not succeed, lack success, not make the grade, not come up to expectations, fall short, fall flat, disappoint; miss the mark, run aground, go astray, suffer defeat; *informal* come a cropper, flop.
OPPOSITES come through, succeed.

□ **fall for 1** *she fell for a younger man* **fall in love with**, become infatuated with, lose one's heart to, take a liking to, take a fancy to, be smitten by,

be attracted to, desire; *informal* fancy, be turned on by, have the hots for.
2 *Jenkins is far too astute to fall for that trick* **be deceived by**, be duped by, be fooled by, be taken in by, accept, believe, trust, be convinced by, have confidence in; *informal* go for, buy, swallow, {swallow something hook, line, and sinker}, take something as gospel.

□ **fall in 1** *the roof of our house fell in* **collapse**, cave in, come down about one's ears, crash in, fall down; subside, sag, slump, sink inwards; give way, crumple, crumble, disintegrate, fall to pieces.
OPPOSITE hold up.
2 *he ordered his troops to fall in* **get in formation**, get in line, line up, take one's position, get in order, get into rows/columns; *Military* dress; *Brit. informal* form a crocodile.
OPPOSITE fall out.

□ **fall in with 1** *he fell in with a bad crowd* **get involved with**, take up with, join up with, go around with, string along with, become friendly with, make friends with, strike up a friendship with, start seeing, make the acquaintance of; *informal* hang out with, hang about with, knock about/around with.
2 *he refused to fall in with their demands* **comply with**, go along with, support, back, give one's backing to, cooperate with, act in accordance with, obey, yield to, submit to, bow to, defer to, adhere to, conform to; agree to, agree with, accept, assent to, concur with.
OPPOSITE disobey.

□ **fall off** *the amount of container shipping has fallen off* **decrease**, decline, diminish, drop off, go down, go downhill, grow less, lessen, dwindle, plummet, plunge, slump, sink; *informal* hit the floor, go through the floor, nosedive, take a nosedive, take a header, go into a tailspin, crash.
OPPOSITE increase.

□ **fall on 1** *the army fell on the besiegers* **attack**, assail, assault, make an assault on, fly at, let fly at, launch oneself at, set about, set upon, pounce upon, ambush, surprise, accost, rush, storm, charge; *informal* jump, lay into, lace into, tear into, sail into, pitch into, get stuck into, let someone have it, beat someone up; *Brit. informal* have a go at; *N. Amer. informal* light into.
2 *the cost should not fall on the students* **be borne by**, be carried by, be the responsibility of, be paid by.

□ **fall out 1** *let's not fall out over silly things* **quarrel**, argue, row, fight, have a row, have a fight, squabble, bicker, have words, disagree, differ, have a difference of opinion, have a disagreement, be at odds, clash, wrangle, get into conflict, get into a dispute, cross swords, lock horns, be at loggerheads, be at each other's throats; *informal* scrap, argufy, go at it hammer and tongs, argy-bargy; *archaic* altercate, chop logic; *Scottish archaic* threap.
OPPOSITE make up.
2 *the soldier fell out without permission* **move out of formation**, move out of line, get out of line, get out of formation; stand at ease.
OPPOSITE fall in.
3 *it fell out that we lost* **happen**, occur, come about, take place, turn out, chance, arise, befall, result.

□ **fall short** *the results fall short of what was expected* **fail to meet**, fail to reach, fail to live up to; **be deficient**, be inadequate, be insufficient, be wanting, be lacking, disappoint, fail, fail to live up to one's expectations; *informal* not come up to scratch.
OPPOSITE measure up (to).

□ **fall through** *unfortunately the deal fell through* **fail**, be unsuccessful, come to nothing, come to naught, fail to happen, miscarry, abort, go awry, be frustrated, collapse, founder, come to grief; come to a halt, grind to a halt, end, terminate; *informal* fizzle out, flop, fold, come a cropper, blow up in someone's face, go down like a lead balloon.
OPPOSITE succeed.

□ **fall to** *(dated) you must take off your coats and fall to* **start**, commence, begin, set to, set about; get working, set to work, set the ball rolling, put one's shoulder to the wheel, put one's hand to the plough, roll up one's sleeves, get things moving, get moving, get the show on the road; *informal* get cracking, get weaving, pull one's finger out, get off one's backside; *Brit. informal* get stuck in; *dated* buckle to.
OPPOSITE stop.

▶ **noun 1** *he had an accidental fall* **tumble**, trip, spill, topple, stumble, slip; collapse; *informal* nosedive, header, cropper.
2 *September's reports showed a fall in sales* **decline**, fall-off, drop, dropping off, decrease, cut, lessening, lowering, dip, diminishing, dwindling, reduction, plummet, plunge, slump, deterioration, downswing; *informal* nosedive, crash, let-up.
OPPOSITE increase.
3 *the fall of the Roman Empire* **downfall**, ruin, ruination, collapse, failure, decline, deterioration, degeneration, destruction, overthrow, demise.
OPPOSITE rise.
4 *the fall of the city to the enemy* **surrender**, surrendering, capitulation, yielding, giving in, submission, acquiescence, succumbing, resignation, laying down of arms; defeat.
5 *there is a fall of some fifty feet down to the ocean* **descent**, declivity, slope, downward slope, downward slant, incline; *N. Amer.* downgrade.
OPPOSITE ascent.
6 *(Christianity) the Fall of Man* **sin**, sinning, wrongdoing, transgression, error, yielding to temptation, offence, lapse, fall from grace, backsliding; original sin.
7 (**falls**) *they went on rafting trips below the falls* **waterfall**, cascade, cataract, chute, torrent; rapids, white water; *N. English* force; *Scottish archaic* linn.

fallacious ▶ **adjective** *the fallacious assumption underlying this reasoning* **erroneous**, **false**, untrue, wrong, incorrect, faulty, flawed, inaccurate, inexact, imprecise, mistaken, misinformed, misguided, misleading, deceptive, delusive, delusory, illusory, sophistic, specious, fictitious, spurious, fabricated, distorted, made up, trumped up; baseless, groundless, unfounded, foundationless, unsubstantiated, unproven, unsupported, uncorroborated, ill-founded, without basis, without foundation; *informal* bogus, phoney, iffy, dicey, full of holes, (way) off beam; *Brit. informal* dodgy.
OPPOSITES true, correct.

fallacy ▶ **noun** *the fallacy that we all work from nine to five* **misconception**, mistaken belief, misbelief, delusion, false notion, mistaken impression, misapprehension, misjudgement, miscalculation, misinterpretation, misconstruction, error, mistake, untruth, inconsistency, illusion, myth, fantasy, deceit, deception, sophism; sophistry, casuistry, faulty reasoning, unsound argument.

fallen ▶ **adjective 1** *he attended a mass for his fallen comrades* **dead**, killed, murdered, slain, slaughtered, perished, expired, deceased; lost, late, lamented, departed, gone; *rare* demised.
OPPOSITE surviving.
2 *(dated) they encouraged the moral reform of fallen women* **immoral**, loose, promiscuous, unchaste, sinful, depraved, degenerate, impure, sullied, tainted, dishonoured, disgraced, ruined, shamed.
OPPOSITES chaste; pure.

fallible ▶ **adjective** *all human beings are fallible* **error-prone**, erring, errant, liable to err, prone to err, open to error; imperfect, flawed, frail, weak.
OPPOSITE infallible.

fallow ▶ **adjective 1** *fallow farmland* **uncultivated**, unploughed, untilled, unplanted, unsown, unseeded, unused, undeveloped, dormant, resting, empty, bare, virgin; neglected, untended, unmaintained, unmanaged.
OPPOSITE cultivated.
2 *trading is set to emerge from a fallow period* **inactive**, dormant, quiet, slack, slow, slow-moving, flat, idle, inert, static, stagnant, depressed; barren, unproductive, unfruitful.
OPPOSITE busy.

false ▶ **adjective 1** *he gave a false account of his movements* **incorrect**, untrue, wrong, erroneous, fallacious, faulty, flawed, distorted, inaccurate, inexact, imprecise, invalid, unfounded; untruthful, fictitious, concocted, fabricated, invented, made up, trumped up, unreal, counterfeit, forged, fraudulent, spurious, misleading, deceptive.
OPPOSITES correct; truthful.
2 *Briggs proved himself a false friend* **faithless**, unfaithful, disloyal, untrue, inconstant, false-hearted, treacherous, traitorous, perfidious, two-faced, double-dealing, double-crossing, deceitful, deceiving, deceptive, dishonourable, dishonest, duplicitous, hypocritical, untrustworthy, unreliable; untruthful, lying, mendacious; *informal* cheating, two-timing, back-stabbing; *rare* hollow-hearted, double-faced, Janus-faced.
OPPOSITE faithful.
3 *she would never wear false pearls* **fake**, artificial, imitation, synthetic, simulated, reproduction, replica, ersatz, faux, plastic, man-made, dummy, mock, sham, bogus, so-called; counterfeit, feigned, forged; *informal* phoney, pretend, pseudo.
OPPOSITE genuine.

falsehood ▶ **noun 1** *this is an exaggeration if not a downright falsehood* **lie**, fib, untruth, false statement, falsification, fabrication, invention, piece of fiction, fiction, story, yarn, made-up story, trumped-up story, cock and bull story, flight of fancy, figment of the imagination; barefaced lie, (little) white lie, half truth, departure from the truth, red herring; *informal* tall story, tall tale, fairy story, fairy tale, whopper; *Brit. informal* porky, porky pie, pork pie; *humorous* terminological inexactitude.
OPPOSITE truth.
2 *no one has accused me of falsehood before* **lying**, mendacity, untruthfulness, fibbing, fabrication, invention, perjury, perfidy, perfidiousness, lack of veracity, telling stories, misrepresentation, prevarication, equivocation; deceit, deception, deceitfulness, pretence, artifice, falseness, two-facedness, double-dealing, double-crossing, dissimulation, treachery; *Irish informal* codology; *informal* kidology.
OPPOSITES truthfulness, honesty.

falsetto ▶ **noun** *he sang in a piercing falsetto* **high voice**, high-pitched voice, high-pitched tone, shrill tone, piercing tone, ear-piercing tone.

falsification ▶ **noun** *the illegal falsification of records* **forgery**, counterfeiting, fabrication, invention, alteration, changing, doctoring, distortion, manipulation, manipulating, tampering, fudging, adulteration, debasement, perversion, corruption, misrepresentation, misapplication; *rare* vitiation.

falsify ▸ verb **1** *she falsified the accounts* **forge**, fake, counterfeit, fabricate, invent, alter, change, doctor, tamper with, fudge, manipulate, massage, adulterate, pervert, corrupt, debase, misrepresent, misreport, distort, warp, embellish, embroider, colour, put a spin on; *rare* vitiate.
2 *the theory is falsified by the evidence* **disprove**, show to be false, prove unsound, refute, rebut, deny, debunk, negate, invalidate, contradict, confound, be at odds with, demolish, discredit; *informal* shoot full of holes, shoot down (in flames), blow sky-high, blow out of the water; *formal* confute, gainsay; *rare* controvert, negative.

falsity ▸ noun *he was compelled to reveal the falsity of his assertions* **untruthfulness**, untruth, fallaciousness, falseness, falsehood, fictitiousness, fiction, inaccuracy, inexactness, hollowness; mendacity, fabrication, dishonesty, deceitfulness, deceit, hypocrisy; *rare* unveracity.

falter ▸ verb **1** *when war seemed imminent the government faltered* **hesitate**, delay, drag one's feet, stall, think twice, get cold feet, change one's mind, waver, oscillate, fluctuate, vacillate, be undecided, be indecisive, be irresolute, see-saw, yo-yo; *Brit.* haver, hum and haw; *informal* sit on the fence, dilly-dally, shilly-shally, pussyfoot around, blow hot and cold; *rare* tergiversate.
2 *she faltered over his name* **stammer**, stutter, stumble, speak haltingly, hesitate, pause, halt, splutter, flounder, blunder, fumble.

fame ▸ noun *she is a designer of international fame* **renown**, celebrity, stardom, popularity, notability, note, distinction, prominence, esteem, importance, account, consequence, greatness, eminence, pre-eminence, glory, honour, illustriousness, prestige, stature, standing, reputation, repute; notoriety, infamy; *rare* supereminence.
OPPOSITES obscurity; disgrace.

famed ▸ adjective *he is famed for his grace and artistry* **famous**, celebrated, well known, prominent, noted, notable, renowned, distinguished, esteemed, respected, acclaimed, honoured, exalted, remarkable, legendary, lionized, much publicized; notorious, infamous.

familiar ▸ adjective **1** *I see a lot of familiar faces | a familiar task* **well known**, known, recognized, accustomed; common, everyday, day-to-day, ordinary, commonplace, frequent, habitual, usual, customary, repeated, routine, standard, stock, mundane, run-of-the-mill, conventional; household, domestic; *Brit.* common or garden; *N. Amer.* garden variety; *informal* bog-standard; *literary* wonted.
OPPOSITE unfamiliar.
2 *she was an old and familiar friend* **close**, intimate, dear, near, confidential, bosom; friendly, neighbourly, sociable, amicable, easy; *informal* pally, chummy, matey, buddy-buddy, palsy-walsy, thick, thick as thieves.
3 *he enjoyed the familiar atmosphere in their house* **informal**, non-formal, casual, relaxed, comfortable, easy, free, free and easy, at ease, at home, friendly, unceremonious, unrestrained, unconstrained, unreserved, open, natural, simple, unpretentious.
OPPOSITE formal.
4 *they object to him **being familiar with** the staff* **overfamiliar**, unduly familiar, over-free, presumptuous, disrespectful, forward, bold, impudent, impertinent, intrusive; making passes at, chatting up, making advances towards; *informal* pushy.
OPPOSITE formal.
□ **familiar with** *are you familiar with the subject?* **acquainted with**, conversant with, versed in, informed about, knowledgeable about, well informed about, instructed in, skilled in, proficient in; at home with, no stranger to, au fait with, au courant with, apprised of, abreast of, up to date with, in touch with; *informal* well up on, in the know about, genned up on, clued in on, clued up on; *Brit. informal* switched on to; *archaic* ware of.
OPPOSITE unfamiliar with.

familiarity ▸ noun **1** *he wants to gain greater **familiarity with** European politics* **acquaintance with**, acquaintanceship with, awareness of, experience of, insight into, conversancy with, conversance with; knowledge of, understanding of, comprehension of, cognizance of, grasp of, mastery of, skill with, skill in, proficiency in, expertise in.
2 *the reassuring familiarity of his parents' home* **ordinariness**, customariness, normality, conventionality.
3 *they feel comfortable with you because of your familiarity* **informality**, casualness, ease, comfortableness, friendliness, lack of ceremony, lack of restraint, lack of reserve, naturalness, simplicity.
4 *she was affronted by his familiarity* **overfamiliarity**, presumption, presumptuousness, forwardness, boldness, audacity, cheek, impudence, impertinence, intrusiveness, disrespect, disrespectfulness; liberties; *informal* sauce, cockiness; *archaic* assumption.
5 *our familiarity allows us to give each other nicknames* **closeness**, intimacy, attachment, affinity, friendliness, friendship, amity; *informal* chumminess, palliness; *Brit. informal* mateyness.

familiarize ▸ verb **1** *I aim to **familiarize** pupils **with** the creation and use of a database* **make conversant**, make familiar, acquaint, get up to date, keep up to date; accustom to, habituate to, instruct in, coach in, train in, teach in, educate in, school in, prime in, indoctrinate in, initiate into, introduce to; *informal* gen up on, clue in on, clue up on, put in the picture about, put wise to, keep up to speed with, give the gen about, give the low-down on, give a rundown of, fill in on.
2 *the exercises help to familiarize the terms used* **make known**, make better known, make familiar, bring to notice, bring to public attention.

family *See centre pages for list of* **Relatives**
▸ noun **1** *growing up in the bosom of one's family* household, ménage; nuclear family; *informal* brood.
2 *I wanted to meet his family* **relatives**, relations, blood relations, family members, kin, next of kin, kinsfolk, kinsmen, kinswomen, kindred, one's (own) flesh and blood, connections; extended family; clan, tribe; *informal* folks, nearest and dearest; *dated* people.
3 *a prospective husband must come from the right kind of family* **ancestry**, parentage, birth, pedigree, genealogy, background, family tree, descent, lineage, line, line of descent, bloodline, blood, extraction, derivation, race, strain, stock, breed; dynasty, house; forebears, forefathers, antecedents, progenitors, roots, origins; *rare* filiation, stirps.
4 *she is married with a family* **children**, little ones, youngsters; offspring, progeny, descendants, scions, heirs; brood; *informal* kids, kiddies, kiddiewinks, tots, sprogs, quiverful; *Law* issue.
5 *a member of the weaver bird family* **taxonomic group**, group, order, class, subclass, genus, species; stock, strain, line; *technical* taxon, phylum.

F

family tree ▸ noun *I traced my own family tree* **ancestry**, genealogy, descent, lineage, line, line of descent, bloodline, blood, parentage, pedigree, background, extraction, derivation, race, strain, stock, breed; family, dynasty, house; forebears, forefathers, antecedents, roots, origins; *rare* filiation, stirps.

famine ▸ noun **1** *the nation is threatened by famine* **scarcity of food**, food shortages; deprivation, want.
OPPOSITE plenty.
2 *the cotton famine of the 1860s* **shortage**, scarcity, lack, dearth, want, deficiency, insufficiency, shortfall, undersupply, scantiness, rareness, paucity, poverty, drought, unavailability; *rare* exiguity, exiguousness.
3 (*archaic*) *the king was dying of famine* **hunger**, hungriness, starvation, food deprivation, lack of food, emptiness, ravenousness; malnutrition, malnourishment, undernourishment, poor diet, inadequate diet, anorexia; *rare* inanition, famishment.

famished ▸ adjective *the troops were exhausted and famished* **very hungry**, **ravenous**, starving, starving to death, starved, dying of hunger, faint from lack of food, deprived of food, empty; undernourished, malnourished, half-starved, unfed; *informal* peckish; *rare* sharp-set, esurient.
OPPOSITES well fed; full up.

famous ▸ adjective *a famous pop star* **well known**, celebrated, prominent, famed, popular, having made a name for oneself; **renowned**, noted, notable, eminent, pre-eminent, leading, distinguished, esteemed, respected, venerable, august, of high standing, of distinction, of repute; illustrious, acclaimed, honoured, exalted, great, glorious, remarkable, signal, legendary, lionized, much publicized; notorious, infamous.
OPPOSITES unknown; obscure.

CHOOSE THE RIGHT WORD

famous, well known, celebrated, renowned

- Someone or something **famous** is known by large numbers of people and typically much admired (*Turner's famous painting 'Rain, Steam, and Speed'*). *A famous landmark*, however, may be widely recognized but little admired.
- **Well known** conveys the idea of being recognized by a large number of people but generally without the glamorous connotations of *famous* (*many well-known companies built ships*). Someone may be *well known* without being admired, although the adjective itself (unlike *notorious*) does not carry any bad connotations.
- **Celebrated** suggests that someone or something is highly thought of (*a portrait of a celebrated actress | one of Rodin's most celebrated works*). Something *celebrated* is not necessarily also famous—*the celebrated book 'Pedagogy of the Oppressed'* is highly regarded but is not known by a large group of people.
- **Renowned** means widely known and, in almost all cases, admired, and is a slightly more formal word than *famous* (*the nation and its people were renowned for fair play | many internationally renowned chefs*). It is typically applied to a person, and when not directly to a person, then it often relates to something for which a person is professionally responsible and deserves credit (*Burgundy is renowned for its beef, poultry and wine*).

fan[1] ▸ noun *his living room had a couple of ceiling fans* **air-cooler**, air conditioner, ventilator, blower, aerator; *Indian* punkah.
▸ verb **1** *she lifted a hand to fan her hot cheeks* **cool**, **air**, aerate, blow, ventilate; freshen, refresh.
2 *the article fanned the public's fear of nuclear radiation* **intensify**, increase, agitate, inflame, exacerbate; stimulate, stir up, work up, whip up, incite,

fuel, animate; ignite, kindle, trigger, spark, instigate, arouse, excite, provoke, foment.
3 *the police squad fanned out with their weapons at the ready* **spread**, open, branch, stretch; outspread, unfurl, unfold.

fan² ▶ **noun** *a fan of classical violin music | an Arsenal fan* **enthusiast**, devotee, admirer, lover, addict; **supporter**, follower, disciple, adherent, backer, zealot, champion, votary; expert, connoisseur, aficionado; *informal* buff, fiend, freak, bug, nut, maniac, groupie, junkie; *N. Amer. informal* jock.

fanatic ▶ **noun 1** *a religious fanatic* **zealot**, extremist, militant, dogmatist, devotee, sectarian, bigot, chauvinist, partisan, radical, diehard, ultra, activist, apologist, adherent; visionary; *informal* maniac, crank, freak.
OPPOSITE moderate.
2 (*informal*) *a keep-fit fanatic* **enthusiast**, fan, devotee, lover, addict; *informal* nut, maniac, fiend, freak, junkie, bug, crank, buff, …head, a great one for; *N. Amer. informal* geek, jock.

fanatical ▶ **adjective 1** *they are fanatical about their faith* **zealous**, **extremist**, extreme, militant, dogmatic, sectarian, bigoted, rabid, maniacal, radical, diehard, activist; prejudiced, chauvinistic, intolerant, narrow-minded, single-minded, partisan, blinkered, illiberal, inflexible, uncompromising.
OPPOSITES moderate; open-minded.
2 (*informal*) *the band gained a fanatical following* **enthusiastic**, eager, keen, fervent, ardent, fervid, passionate, devoted, dedicated; over-enthusiastic, obsessive, obsessed, infatuated, fixated, compulsive, immoderate, frenzied, frenetic; *informal* wild, gung-ho, nuts, potty, dotty, crazy, hooked.
OPPOSITE indifferent.

fanaticism ▶ **noun 1** *ethnic hatred and religious fanaticism are tearing apart the human family* **zealotry**, zeal, extremism, militancy, sectarianism, fundamentalism, bigotry, dogmatism, chauvinism, radicalism, immoderation.
OPPOSITE moderation.
2 (*informal*) *his love of James Dean verged on fanaticism* **obsessiveness**, over-enthusiasm, addiction, fixation, madness, monomania, immoderation, passion, infatuation; enthusiasm, dedication, devotion, single-mindedness; *informal* fandom; *rare* fervency, ardency, passionateness.
OPPOSITE indifference.

fancier ▶ **noun** *a keen pigeon fancier* **enthusiast**, devotee, hobbyist, lover, addict, fan, fanatic; expert, connoisseur, aficionado; breeder; *informal* buff, fiend, freak, bug, nut, maniac, junkie.

fanciful ▶ **adjective 1** *Maria is a fanciful girl* **imaginative**, inventive; **whimsical**, impractical, capricious, flighty, dreamy, daydreaming, quixotic, chimerical, head in the clouds, out of touch with reality, in a world of one's own; *archaic* visionary.
OPPOSITE down-to-earth.
2 *some of these stories were pretty fanciful* **fantastic**, extravagant, far-fetched, romantic, unbelievable, ridiculous, absurd, preposterous; **imaginary**, fancied, unreal, illusory, made-up, make-believe; mythical, fabulous, legendary, fairy tale; *informal* far out, tall, crackpot, cock and bull, hard to swallow/take.
OPPOSITE literal.
3 *the fanciful cornices and turrets of an imperial palace* **ornate**, exotic, imaginative, creative, fancy; curious, odd, bizarre, strange, eccentric, unusual, original; extravagant, fantastic, grotesque, gothic, baroque.
OPPOSITE practical.

fancy ▶ **verb 1** (*Brit. informal*) *I fancied a change of scene* **wish for**, want, desire; long for, yearn for, crave, have a yearning/craving for, hanker after, hunger for, thirst for, sigh for, pine for, dream of, covet; *informal* have a yen for, itch for; *archaic* be desirous of; *rare* desiderate.
2 *she'd fancied him for ages* **be attracted to**, find attractive, be captivated by, be infatuated with, be taken with, desire; lust after, burn for; *informal* have taken a shine to, have a crush on, have the hots for, be wild/mad/crazy about, have a thing about, have a pash on, have a soft spot for, be soft on, have eyes for, carry a torch for, go for, lech after/over.
3 *I fancied that I could see lights to the south* **think**, imagine, guess, believe, have an idea, suppose; gather, surmise, suspect, conjecture, be of the opinion, be of the view, be under the impression, think it likely/conceivable; *informal* reckon.
□ **fancy oneself** *a couple of lads who fancy themselves* **have a high opinion of oneself**, be confident of one's abilities; *informal* think one is the cat's whiskers/pyjamas, think one is God's gift (to women); *Brit. informal* reckon oneself.
OPPOSITE be modest.
▶ **adjective** *he is too hard up to buy fancy clothes* **elaborate**, ornate, ornamented, ornamental, decorated, decorative, adorned, embellished, intricate, baroque, rococo, fussy, busy; **ostentatious**, showy, flamboyant, gaudy; luxurious, sumptuous, lavish, extravagant, expensive, de luxe, select, superior, high-class, quality, prime; *informal* flash, flashy, jazzy, ritzy, glitzy, snazzy, posh, classy, over the top, OTT; *Brit. informal* swish.
OPPOSITES plain, unobtrusive.
▶ **noun 1** *he was able to indulge his fancy to own a farm* **desire**, urge, wish, want; inclination, bent; **whim**, impulse, caprice, notion, whimsy, eccentricity, peculiarity, quirk, kink; preference, fondness, liking, partiality, predilection, predisposition, taste, relish, love, humour, penchant; yearning, longing, hankering, craving, pining, ache, hunger, thirst, need; *informal* yen, itch.
2 *they appeal to our wildest fancy rather than our judgement* **imagination**, imaginative faculty/power, creativity, creative faculty/power, conception, fancifulness, inventiveness, invention, originality, ingenuity, cleverness, wit, artistry; images, mental images, visualizations.
OPPOSITE intellect.
3 *they had a vague fancy that it was cruel to leave the dolls in the dark* **idea**, notion, thought, supposition, opinion, belief, impression, image, understanding, conceptualization; feeling, suspicion, sneaking suspicion, hunch, inkling, intimation; illusion, fantasy, dream.

fanfare ▶ **noun 1** *a fanfare announced the arrival of the duchess* **peal of trumpets**, flourish, fanfaronade, trumpet call, trumpet blare; *archaic* trump, tucket.
2 *the laying of the foundation stone was greeted with great fanfare* **fuss**, commotion, stir, show, showiness, display, ostentation, flashiness, publicity, sensationalism, pageantry, splendour, hubbub, brouhaha; *informal* ballyhoo, hullabaloo, hype, to-do, pizzazz, razzle-dazzle, glitz, ritziness.

fang ▶ **noun** *the creature bared its fangs and charged* **large tooth**, tusk; *informal* gnasher; *rare* tush.

fantasize ▶ **verb** *I fantasized about London and what I'd do when I lived there* **daydream**, dream, muse, indulge in fantasy, indulge in fancy, make-believe, play-act, pretend, imagine, give free rein to one's imagination, build castles in the air, build castles in Spain, live in a dream world, indulge in wool-gathering.

fantastic ▶ **adjective 1** *it's a fantastic notion, but it would explain everything* **fanciful**, extravagant, extraordinary, irrational, wild, mad, absurd, far-fetched, nonsensical, incredible, unbelievable, unthinkable, implausible, improbable, unlikely, doubtful, dubious; strange, peculiar, odd, queer, weird, eccentric, insane, whimsical, capricious; imaginary, visionary, romantic, unreal, illusory, make-believe; *informal* crazy, barmy, potty, daft, cock-eyed, oddball, off the wall.
OPPOSITE rational.
2 *a memory of fantastic accuracy* **tremendous**, remarkable, great, terrific, enormous, huge, striking, impressive, outstanding, phenomenal, monumental, overwhelming.
3 *the mountains assumed weird and fantastic shapes* **strange**, weird, bizarre, outlandish, queer, peculiar, eccentric, grotesque, freakish, surreal, exotic; whimsical, fanciful, quaint, imaginative, elaborate, ornate, intricate, rococo, baroque, phantasmagoric, Kafkaesque.
OPPOSITES ordinary, unremarkable.
4 (*informal*) *a fantastic new car* **marvellous**, wonderful, sensational, magnificent, outstanding, superb, superlative, excellent, very good, first-rate, first-class, dazzling, out of this world, breathtaking; *informal* great, terrific, tremendous, smashing, fabulous, fab, mega, super, ace, magic, A1, cracking, cool, wicked, awesome, way-out, def; *Brit. informal* brilliant, brill; *Austral./NZ informal* bonzer; *Brit. informal, dated* spiffing, topping, tip-top, top-notch, capital.
OPPOSITES ordinary, poor.

fantasy ▶ **noun 1** *the movie is ambitious in its mix of fantasy and realism* **imagination**, creativity, fancy, invention, originality, vision, speculation, make-believe, daydreaming, reverie.
OPPOSITES truth, realism.
2 *his fantasy about appearing on television* **dream**, daydream, pipe dream, flight of fancy, fanciful notion, wish, wishful thinking; fond hope, chimera, delusion, illusion, figment of the imagination, castle in the air, castle in Spain; *informal* pie in the sky, cloud cuckoo land.
3 *fantasy was considered a subset of science fiction for a long time* **myth**, legend, fable, fairy tale, romance; science fiction, sci-fi, horror; sword and sorcery; escapism.
OPPOSITE realism.

far ▶ **adverb 1** *not far from the palace a fine garden was built* **a long way**, a great distance, a good way, afar.
OPPOSITE near.
2 *the liveliness of the production far outweighs any flaws* **much**, very much, considerably, markedly, immeasurably, decidedly, greatly, significantly, substantially, appreciably, noticeably, materially, signally; to a great extent/degree, by much, by a great amount, by a great deal, by a long way, by far, by a mile, easily.
OPPOSITE slightly.
□ **by far** *this would be by far the best solution* **by a great amount**, by a good deal, by a long way/chalk/shot, by a mile, far and away; undoubtedly, doubtlessly, without doubt, without question, decidedly, markedly, positively, absolutely, easily, immeasurably; significantly, substantially, appreciably, noticeably, materially, beyond the shadow of a doubt, much; *informal* as sure as eggs is eggs.
□ **far and away** *they were far and away the most powerful union. See* BY FAR.
□ **far and near** *guests had travelled from far and near to be there* **everywhere**, {here, there, and everywhere}, all over, all around, all over the world, throughout the land, worldwide; *informal* all over the place; *Brit. informal* all

over the shop; *N. Amer. informal* all over the map.

□ **far and wide** *he was known far and wide* **everywhere**, in all places, all over, all around, {here, there, and everywhere}, extensively, widely, broadly, worldwide.

□ **far from** *staff were far from happy with the outcome* **not**, not at all, nowhere near, a long way from, the opposite of.

□ **go far** *she was a girl who would go far* **be successful**, succeed, prosper, flourish, thrive, get on, get on in the world, make good, make one's way in the world, make headway/progress, gain advancement, climb the ladder of success, rise in the world, set the world/Thames on fire; *informal* make a name for oneself, make one's mark, go places, make it, make the grade, cut it, get somewhere, do all right for oneself, arrive, find a place in the sun, be someone.
OPPOSITE fail.

□ **go too far** *they locked him up because he went too far* **go over the top**, go to extremes, go overboard, not know when to stop.

□ **so far 1** *nobody had taken any notice of me so far* **until now**, up till/to now, up to this point, as yet, thus far, hitherto, up to the present, until/till the present, to date, by this time; *rare* heretofore, thitherto.
2 *his liberalism only extends so far* **to a certain extent**, to a limited extent, up to a point, to a degree, to some extent, within reason, within limits.

▸ **adjective 1** *he'd travelled to far places in the war* **distant**, faraway, far off, remote, out of the way, far flung, far removed, outlying, obscure, isolated, cut-off, inaccessible, off the beaten track, in the back of beyond, godforsaken.
OPPOSITES near; neighbouring.
2 *a building on the far side of the campus* **further**, more distant; opposite.
OPPOSITE near.

faraway ▸ **adjective 1** *flying to exotic faraway places* **distant**, far off, far, remote, out of the way, far flung, far removed, outlying, obscure, isolated, secluded, cut off, off the beaten track, in the back of beyond, in the middle of nowhere.
OPPOSITES nearby; neighbouring.
2 *Noreen had that faraway look in her eyes* **dreamy**, daydreaming, abstracted, absent-minded, distracted, preoccupied, absorbed, engrossed, vague, lost in thought, somewhere else, not there, not with us, in a world of one's own, with one's head in the clouds; *informal* miles away.
OPPOSITE alert.

> **CHOOSE THE RIGHT WORD**
>
> **faraway, far-off, distant, remote**
>
> *See* DISTANT.

farce ▸ **noun 1** *at one or two points the stories approach bedroom farce* **slapstick comedy**, broad comedy, slapstick, burlesque, vaudeville, travesty, buffoonery; skit, squib; *rare* pasquinade.
OPPOSITE tragedy.
2 *he denounced the trial as a farce* **absurdity**, mockery, travesty, sham, pretence, masquerade, charade, piece of futility, joke, waste of time, laughing stock; apology, excuse, poor substitute; *informal* shambles.

farcical ▸ **adjective 1** *he considered the whole idea farcical* **ridiculous**, preposterous, ludicrous, absurd, laughable, risible, nonsensical; futile, senseless, pointless, useless, vain, in vain, to no avail, ineffectual; silly, foolish, idiotic, stupid, imbecilic, asinine, hare-brained; *informal* crazy, barmy, daft.
2 *the farcical goings-on in a witty comedy of manners* **madcap**, zany, slapstick, comic, comical, clownish, light-hearted, humorous, amusing, droll, witty, entertaining; hilarious, uproarious, hysterical, hysterically funny; *informal* wacky, side-splitting, rib-tickling, killing, priceless.

fare ▸ **noun 1** *we can't afford the air fare* **ticket price**, transport cost, price, cost, charge, fee, payment, toll, tariff, levy.
2 *the taxi driver was anxious to pick up a fare* **passenger**, traveller, fare payer, ticket buyer, customer; commuter; *informal* pickup, punter.
3 *when they eat at home they prefer simple fare* **food**, meals, board, sustenance, nourishment, nutriment, foodstuffs, refreshments, eatables, provisions, daily bread; cooking, cuisine; menu, diet, table; *Scottish* vivers; *informal* grub, nosh, eats, chow; *Brit. informal* scoff, scran; *formal* comestibles, provender; *archaic* vittles, commons, victuals, viands, aliment.

▸ **verb** *they went to see how their old friend was faring* **get on**, proceed, get along, progress, make out, do, manage, muddle through/along, cope, survive; succeed, prosper.

farewell ▸ **exclamation** *farewell, Patrick!* **goodbye**, so long, adieu; *Austral./NZ* hooray; *S. African* check you; *French* au revoir; *Italian* ciao; *German* auf Wiedersehen; *Spanish* adios; *Japanese* sayonara; *Latin* vale; *informal* bye, bye-bye, cheerio, see you, see you later, cheers, toodle-oo, toodle-pip; *Brit. informal* ta-ta; *N. Amer. informal* later, laters.

▸ **noun** *an emotional farewell* **valediction**, **goodbye**, adieu; leave-taking, parting, departure, departing, going away; send-off.

far-fetched ▸ **adjective** *the storyline was too far-fetched* **improbable**, unlikely, implausible, scarcely credible, difficult to believe, dubious, doubtful, unconvincing, incredible, unbelievable, unthinkable, beyond the bounds of possibility; **contrived**, strained, laboured, forced, elaborate, overdone; fanciful, unrealistic, ridiculous, absurd, preposterous; *informal* hard to swallow/take, fishy; *N. Amer. informal* hokey.
OPPOSITES credible, likely.

farm ▸ **noun** *a farm of 100 acres* **smallholding**, holding, farmstead, steading, grange, plantation, estate; farmland, land, acreage, acres; vineyard; *Scottish* croft; *N. Amer.* ranch; *Austral./NZ* station; (*in the W. Indies*) pen; (*in East Africa*) shamba; (*in the Indian subcontinent*) tope.

▸ **verb 1** *his dad farmed near Marlborough* **be a farmer**, practise farming, cultivate/till/work the land, till the soil, rear livestock, do agricultural work.
2 *the marshes are being drained in order to farm the land* **cultivate**, bring under cultivation, till, work, plough, dig, plant.
3 *the family has been farming cranberries for generations* **grow**, cultivate, raise, plant, tend, bring on, harvest; breed, rear, keep.

□ **farm someone out** *he had farmed the child out* **have fostered**, have cared for, send to a childminder, put in care.

□ **farm something out** *the job of building the models was farmed out to the Shawcraft firm* **contract out**, outsource, assign to others, subcontract, delegate.

F

farmer *See centre pages for list of* **Agricultural Workers**

▸ **noun agriculturalist**, agronomist, smallholder, grazier, farmhand, countryman, son/daughter of the soil; *Scottish* crofter; *N. Amer.* rancher; *Austral./NZ informal* cocky; *archaic* yeoman, husbandman.

farming *See centre pages for list of types of* **Farming and Cultivation**

▸ **noun agriculture**, cultivation, tilling, tillage, husbandry, land management, farm management; agriscience, agronomy; breeding, keeping, raising, rearing, tending; culture, planting, sowing; *rare* geoponics.
OPPOSITE industry.

WORD LINKS
relating to agriculture **agrarian**
related prefixes **agri- (e.g. *agribusiness*), agro- (e.g. *agrochemical*)**

far out ▸ **adjective** (*informal*) *some club owners thought our music was too far out* **unconventional**, unorthodox, unusual, nonconformist, individual, individualistic, idiosyncratic, quirky, out of the ordinary; weird, bizarre, outlandish, freakish; avant-garde, innovative, groundbreaking, radical, bohemian, extreme, esoteric; *French* outré; *informal* way out, offbeat, left-field, oddball, wacky, off the wall.
OPPOSITE conventional.

farrago ▸ **noun** *academics exposed the whole business as a farrago of fantasies and errors* **hotchpotch**, hodgepodge, mishmash, ragbag, pot-pourri, jumble, mess, confusion, patchwork, melange, hash, random collection, motley collection, chaos, assortment, miscellany, mixture, conglomeration, medley; *informal* dog's dinner/breakfast; *rare* gallimaufry, olio, olla podrida, mingle-mangle, omnium gatherum, salmagundi, macédoine.

far-reaching ▸ **adjective** *a far-reaching change in the law* **extensive**, wide-ranging, radical, profound, comprehensive, widespread, all-embracing, overarching, across the board, sweeping, blanket, wholesale; important, significant, major, of great import, of significance, ambitious, momentous, of moment, weighty, consequential, of consequence.
OPPOSITES limited, insignificant.

far-sighted ▸ **adjective** *his far-sighted management brought great prosperity* **prudent**, prescient, foresighted, discerning, judicious, shrewd, percipient, provident, forearmed, politic, canny; cautious, careful, watchful; wise, sagacious, visionary.
OPPOSITES short-sighted, short-termist.

farther ▸ **adverb & adjective.** *See* FURTHER.

farthest ▸ **adjective & adverb.** *See* FURTHEST.

fascinate ▸ **verb** *he was fascinated by Laura's stories* **engross**, captivate, absorb, interest, enchant, beguile, bewitch, enthral, enrapture, entrance, hold spellbound, transfix, rivet, mesmerize, hypnotize, spellbind, occupy, engage, compel; allure, lure, tempt, entice, draw, tantalize; charm, attract, intrigue, delight, divert, entertain, amuse.
OPPOSITES bore; repel.

fascinating ▸ **adjective** *a fascinating story* **engrossing**, captivating, absorbing, interesting, enchanting, beguiling, bewitching, enthralling, enrapturing, entrancing, spellbinding, transfixing, riveting, mesmerizing, hypnotizing, engaging, compelling, compulsive, gripping, thrilling; alluring, tempting, enticing, irresistible, tantalizing, seductive; charming, attractive, intriguing, delightful, diverting, entertaining, amusing; *informal* unputdownable.
OPPOSITES boring; dull.

fascination ▸ **noun** *crime and criminals are topics of endless fascination* **interest**, preoccupation, passion, obsession, compulsion, captivation, enchantment; allure, lure, allurement; charm, attraction, intrigue, attractiveness, appeal, magnetism, pull, draw.

OPPOSITE boredom.

fascism ▶ noun **authoritarianism**, totalitarianism, dictatorship, despotism, autocracy, absolute rule, Nazism, rightism, militarism; nationalism, xenophobia, racism, anti-Semitism, chauvinism, jingoism, isolationism; neo-fascism, neo-Nazism; corporativism, corporatism; German, historical Hitlerism; Spanish, historical Francoism, Falangism.
OPPOSITES democracy; liberalism.

fascist ▶ noun *he was branded a fascist and an anti-Semite* **authoritarian**, totalitarian, autocrat, Nazi, extreme/far right-winger, rightist, blackshirt, militarist; nationalist, xenophobe, racist, anti-Semite, chauvinist, jingoist, isolationist; neo-fascist, neo-Nazi; corporativist, corporatist; Brit. historical Mosleyite; German, historical Hitlerite; Spanish, historical Francoist, Falangist.
OPPOSITES democrat; liberal.
▶ adjective *the fascist regimes in Europe* **authoritarian**, totalitarian, dictatorial, despotic, draconian, autocratic, Nazi, undemocratic, illiberal, extreme/far right-wing, rightist, militarist; nationalist, nationalistic, xenophobic, racist, anti-Semitic, chauvinist, jingoistic, isolationist; neo-fascist, neo-Nazi; corporativist, corporatist; Brit. historical Mosleyite; German, historical Hitlerite; Spanish, historical Francoist, Falangist.
OPPOSITES democratic, liberal.

F

fashion ▶ noun 1 *the fashion for figure-hugging clothes* **vogue**, trend, craze, rage, mania, mode, fad, fancy, passing fancy; current/latest style, latest thing, latest taste; style, look; general tendency, convention, custom, practice, usage; informal thing.
2 *she was always interested in fashion* **clothes**, the clothes industry, clothes design, couture; glamour; informal the rag trade.
3 *a Victorian lady of fashion* **fashionable society**, high society, society, social elite, the beautiful people, the beau monde, the A-list; informal the jet set.
4 *it needs to be run in a sensible and organized fashion* **manner**, way, style, method, mode; system, approach.
5 *they built a boat of some fashion* **type**, kind, sort, make, design, description.
□ **after a fashion** *the arrangement worked after a fashion* **to a certain extent**, in a way, in a rough way, somehow or other, somehow, in an approximate manner, in a manner of speaking, in its way.
□ **in fashion** *the Sixties look is in fashion again* **fashionable**, in vogue, up to date, up to the minute, all the rage, bang up to date; smart, chic, elegant; French de rigueur, à la mode; informal trendy, with it, cool, in, the in thing, hot, big, hip, happening, now, sharp, groovy, mod, swinging; N. Amer. kicking, tony, fly; Brit. informal, dated all the go.
OPPOSITE out of fashion.
□ **out of fashion** *such gallantry is out of fashion* **unfashionable**, out of style, no longer fashionable, old-fashioned, out of date, outdated, dated, outmoded, behind the times, last year's, superseded; unstylish, unpopular; French passé, démodé; informal old hat, out, square, out of the ark, old school.
OPPOSITE in fashion.
▶ verb *the head section was fashioned from a separate sheet of lead* **construct**, build, manufacture, make, create, fabricate, contrive; cast, frame, shape, form, mould, sculpt; forge, hew, carve, whittle, hammer, chisel.

fashionable ▶ adjective *a fashionable wine bar* **in fashion**, in vogue, voguish, popular, (bang) up to date, up to the minute, modern, all the rage, modish, trendsetting; stylish, smart, chic, glamorous, elegant, classy, high-class, high-toned; French à la mode, de rigueur; informal trendy, with it, cool, in, the in thing, hot, big, massive, hip, happening, now, sharp, groovy, mod, swinging, snazzy; N. Amer. informal kicking, tony, fly; Brit. informal, dated all the go.
OPPOSITES unfashionable; old-fashioned.

fast[1] ▶ adjective 1 *a fast sports car | the game is played at a fast pace* **speedy**, quick, swift, rapid; brisk, nimble, sprightly, lively; fast-moving, high-speed, turbo, sporty, accelerated, express, flying; whirlwind, blistering, breakneck, pell-mell, meteoric, smart; hasty, hurried; unhesitating, expeditious; fleet-footed; informal nippy, zippy, spanking, scorching, blinding, supersonic; Brit. informal cracking; literary fleet; rare tantivy, alacritous, volant.
OPPOSITE slow.
2 *his hand slammed against the door, holding it fast* **secure**, secured, fastened, tight, firmly fixed; stuck, jammed, immovable, unbudgeable, stiff; closed, shut, to.
OPPOSITE loose.
3 *the dyes are boiled with yarn to produce a fast colour* **indelible**, lasting, permanent, stable.
OPPOSITE temporary.
4 *they remained fast friends* **loyal**, devoted, faithful, firm, steadfast, staunch, true, boon, bosom, inseparable; constant, lasting, unchanging, unwavering, enduring, unswerving; informal as thick as thieves.
5 *a fast woman* **promiscuous**, licentious, dissolute, impure, unchaste, wanton, abandoned, of easy virtue; informal easy; N. Amer. informal roundheeled; W. Indian informal slack; derogatory sluttish, whorish, tarty, slaggy; dated loose; archaic light.
OPPOSITE chaste.
6 *the fast life she led in London* **wild**, dissipated, dissolute, debauched, intemperate, immoderate, louche, rakish, decadent, unrestrained, reckless, profligate, self-indulgent, shameless, sinful, immoral, extravagant; informal swinging.
OPPOSITE sedate.
▶ adverb 1 *she drove fast towards the gates* **quickly**, rapidly, swiftly, speedily, briskly, at speed, at full speed, at full tilt; energetically; hastily, with all haste, in haste, hurriedly, in a hurry, post-haste, pell-mell; without delay, expeditiously, with dispatch, like a shot, like a flash, in a flash, in the blink of an eye, in a wink, in a trice, in no time (at all), on the double, at the speed of light, like an arrow from a bow; informal double quick, in double quick time, p.d.q. (pretty damn quick), nippily, like (greased) lightning, hell for leather, like mad, like crazy, like the wind, like a bomb, like nobody's business, like a scalded cat, like the deuce, a mile a minute, like a bat out of hell; Brit. informal like the clappers, at a rate of knots, like billy-o; N. Amer. informal lickety-split; literary apace.
OPPOSITE slowly.
2 *his wheels were stuck fast* **securely**, tightly, immovably, fixedly, firmly.
3 *Richard's fast asleep* **deeply**, sound, completely.
4 *she lived fast and dangerously* **wildly**, dissolutely, intemperately, immoderately, rakishly, recklessly, self-indulgently, extravagantly.

WORD LINKS
related prefix **tachy-** (e.g. ***tachycardia*** | ***tachygraphy***)

fast[2] ▶ verb *the ministry instructed people to fast, pray, and read scripture* **abstain from food**, refrain from eating, deny oneself food, go without food, go hungry, eat nothing, starve oneself; go on hunger strike.
OPPOSITES eat; indulge oneself.
▶ noun *a five-day fast* **period of fasting**, period of abstinence; hunger strike; diet.
OPPOSITE feast.

fasten ▶ verb 1 *he fastened the door behind him* **bolt**, lock, secure, make secure, make fast, chain, seal.
OPPOSITES unfasten, unlock.
2 *they fastened splints to his leg* **attach**, fix, affix, clip, pin, tack; stick, bond.
OPPOSITES unfasten, remove.
3 *the belt was fastened with an enormous silver buckle* **buckle**, join, do up, connect, couple, close, unite, link; lace (up), knot; button (up); zip (up).
OPPOSITES unfasten, open.
4 *he fastened his horse to a sapling on the bank of the river* **tie**, tie up, bind, tether, truss, fetter, lash, hitch, anchor, strap, rope.
OPPOSITES unfasten, untie.
5 *the dress fastens at the front with ten small buttons* **become closed**, close, do up; button (up), zip (up).
OPPOSITES unfasten, undo.
6 *his gaze **fastened on** me* **focus**, fix, be riveted, concentrate, zero in, zoom in, be brought to bear; direct at, aim at, point at.
7 *blame had been **fastened on** some unknown nutter* **ascribe to**, attribute to, assign to, chalk up to, impute to; lay on, pin on, lay at the door of.
8 *the critics **fastened upon** two sections of the report* **single out**, concentrate on, focus on, select, pick out, fix on, seize on.

fastidious ▶ adjective *he was fastidious about personal hygiene* **scrupulous**, punctilious, painstaking, meticulous, assiduous, sedulous, perfectionist, fussy, finicky, dainty, over-particular; critical, overcritical, hypercritical, hard/difficult/impossible to please; pedantic, precise, exact, hair-splitting, exacting, demanding; informal pernickety, nit-picking, choosy, picky; N. Amer. informal persnickety; archaic nice, overnice.
OPPOSITES easy-going; sloppy.

fat ▶ adjective 1 *a fat man walked in* **plump**, stout, overweight, heavy, large, solid, chubby, portly, rotund, flabby, paunchy, pot-bellied, beer-bellied, dumpy, meaty, broad in the beam, of ample proportions, Falstaffian; buxom; obese, corpulent, bloated, gross, gargantuan, elephantine; fleshy; informal tubby, roly-poly, beefy, porky, blubbery, poddy, chunky, well padded, well covered, well upholstered; Brit. informal podgy, fubsy; N. Amer. informal lard-assed; Scottish literary sonsy; rare pursy, abdominous.
OPPOSITES thin, skinny.
2 *fat bacon* **fatty**, greasy, oily, oleaginous, unctuous; formal pinguid, adipose, sebaceous.
OPPOSITE lean.
3 *those fat books you're always reading* **thick**, big, chunky, substantial, extended, long.
OPPOSITE thin.
4 (informal) *a fat salary* **large**, substantial, considerable, sizeable; generous, handsome, ample; excellent, good, competitive.
OPPOSITE small.
5 (informal) *fat chance she had of influencing Guy* **very little**, not much, minimal, hardly any.
OPPOSITE good.
▶ noun 1 *whales insulate themselves with layers of fat* **fatty tissue**, fat cells, blubber, adipose tissue.
2 *he was tall and running to fat* **fatness**, **plumpness**, stoutness, heaviness, chubbiness, tubbiness, portliness, rotundity, podginess, flabbiness, bulk, excessive weight; obesity, corpulence, grossness; paunch, pot belly, beer

belly, beer gut; *informal* flab, blubber, beef.
OPPOSITE thinness.
3 *fried bread in sizzling fat* **cooking oil**, animal fat, vegetable fat, grease; lard, suet, butter, margarine.

WORD LINKS
relating to fat **lipoid**
related prefix **lipo- (e.g. *liposuction, lipoprotein*)**

fatal ▶ **adjective 1** *a fatal disease* **deadly**, lethal, mortal, causing death, death dealing, killing; final, terminal, incurable, untreatable, inoperable, malignant; tragic; *literary* deathly; *archaic* baneful.
OPPOSITES harmless; superficial.
2 *don't make the fatal mistake of assuming others think as you do* **disastrous**, devastating, ruinous, catastrophic, calamitous, cataclysmic, destructive, grievous, dire, crippling, crushing, injurious, harmful, costly; *literary* direful.
OPPOSITES harmless; beneficial.

fatalism ▶ **noun** *he experienced a sense of fatalism that kept his fear at bay* **passive acceptance**, resignation, acceptance, acceptance of the inevitable, stoicism; defeatism, pessimism, negativism, negative thinking, gloominess, doom and gloom, gloom; predeterminism, predestinarianism, necessitarianism, fate, fatedness.

fatality ▶ **noun 1** *there were hundreds of fatalities from radiation contamination* **death**, casualty, mortality, victim, loss, dead person; (**fatalities**) dead.
2 *the programme is a recipe for increased fatalities on our roads* **fatal accident**, tragedy, disaster, catastrophe, calamity.

fate ▶ **noun 1** *I was ready for whatever fate had in store for me* **destiny**, providence, God's will, nemesis, kismet, astral influence, the stars, what is written in the stars, one's lot in life; predestination, predetermination; chance, luck, serendipity, fortuity, fortune, hazard, Lady Luck, Dame Fortune; *Hinduism & Buddhism* karma; *archaic* dole, cup, heritage.
2 *I didn't want to put my fate in someone else's hands* **future**, destiny, outcome, issue, upshot, end, lot, due; *archaic* doom, dole.
3 *the authorities warned that a similar fate would befall other convicted killers* **death**, demise, end, destruction, doom; ruin, downfall, undoing, finish, disaster, catastrophe; retribution, sentence.
4 (**the Fates**) *the Fates might decide that it was his time to die* the weird sisters; *Roman Mythology* the Parcae; *Greek Mythology* the Moirai; *Scandinavian Mythology* the Norns.
▶ **verb** (**be fated**) *his daughter was fated to face the same problem* **be predestined**, be preordained, be foreordained, be destined, be meant, be doomed, be foredoomed, be cursed, be damned; be sure, be certain, be bound, be guaranteed; be inevitable, be inescapable, be ineluctable.

fateful ▶ **adjective 1** *that fateful day when she met him* **decisive**, determining, critical, crucial, pivotal; momentous, important, of great importance, all-important, key, significant, far-reaching; historic, weighty, consequential, of great consequence, epoch-making, portentous, apocalyptic; *informal* earth-shattering, world-shattering, earth-shaking, world-shaking.
OPPOSITES trivial, unimportant.
2 *the fateful defeat of 1402* **disastrous**, ruinous, calamitous, cataclysmic, devastating, destructive, tragic, awful, terrible, harmful, fatal, deadly.

father ▶ **noun 1** *he went home to see his mother and father* **male parent**, begetter, patriarch, paterfamilias; birth/biological father; adoptive father, foster father, stepfather; *informal* dad, daddy, pop, poppa, pa, old boy, old man; *Brit. informal, dated* pater.
OPPOSITE child.
2 (usually **fathers**) (*literary*) *let me be free to follow the religion of my fathers* **ancestor**, forefather, forebear, progenitor, predecessor, antecedent, forerunner, precursor; *rare* primogenitor.
OPPOSITE descendant.
3 *he was the father of democracy* **originator**, initiator, founder, founding father, inventor, creator, maker, author, prime mover, instigator, architect, engineer, designer, deviser, planner, contriver, mastermind; *literary* begetter.
4 *the city fathers* **leader**, elder, senior figure, patriarch, senator, guiding light, official.
5 (**Father**) *our heavenly Father* **God**, Lord, Lord God, Deity.
6 (usually **Father**) *the Father joined the other priests* **priest**, pastor, parson, clergyman, father confessor, churchman, man of the cloth, man of God, cleric, minister, preacher; (*in French-speaking countries*) abbé, curé; *informal* reverend, padre.
▶ **verb 1** *he fathered six children* **be the father of**, sire, engender, generate, bring into being, bring into the world, give life to, spawn; procreate, reproduce, breed; *literary* beget.
2 *he fathered a strand of applied economics* **establish**, institute, originate, initiate, invent, found, create, generate, conceive.

WORD LINKS
relating to a father **paternal**
related prefix **patri- (e.g. *patriarch, patrilineal*)**
killing of one's father **patricide**

fatherland ▶ **noun** *they were considered to be traitors to the fatherland* **native land**, native country, homeland, home, mother country, motherland, native soil, native heath, land of one's birth, land of one's fathers, the old country.

fatherly ▶ **adjective** *his son needs some fatherly advice* **paternal**, fatherlike, avuncular; protective, supportive, encouraging, vigilant; kindly, kind, warm, affectionate, tender, caring, compassionate, benevolent, sympathetic, understanding, indulgent; patriarchal.
OPPOSITE hostile.

fathom ▶ **verb 1** *Charlie tried to fathom the expression on his friend's face* **understand**, comprehend, work out, fathom out, make sense of, grasp, catch, follow, perceive, make out, penetrate, divine, search out, ferret out, puzzle out, take in, assimilate, absorb, get to the bottom of; interpret, decipher, decode, disentangle, untangle, unravel, piece together; *informal* make head or tail of, take on board, get a fix on, get/catch the drift of, tumble to, crack, dig, get, get the picture, get the message, see what's what; *Brit. informal* twig, suss (out); *N. Amer. informal* savvy; *rare* cognize.
2 *an attempt to fathom the ocean* **measure the depth of**, sound, plumb, probe; gauge, estimate.

fathomless ▶ **adjective 1** *her serene, fathomless eyes* **enigmatic**, mysterious, impenetrable, incomprehensible, unfathomable, opaque, profound, deep.
2 *a fathomless well* **bottomless**, unfathomable, unfathomed, unsounded, immeasurable, endless, infinite, measureless; very deep, unplumbed, profound, yawning, cavernous, gaping; *literary* abysmal; *rare* chasmic.
OPPOSITE shallow.

fatigue ▶ **noun 1** *his face was grey with fatigue* **tiredness**, weariness, exhaustion, overtiredness; drowsiness, somnolence; lethargy, sluggishness, lassitude, debility, enervation, listlessness, prostration, lack of energy, lack of vitality.
OPPOSITES energy, vigour.
2 (**fatigues**) (*Military*) *right, Private, it's kitchen fatigues for you* **menial work**, drudgery, chores, donkey work; *informal* dirty work, skivvying.
3 (**fatigues**) (*Military*) *a conscript dressed in battle fatigues* **khakis**, camouflage clothing/gear, *informal* camo clothing/gear.
▶ **verb** *the troops were fatigued by nine days of marching* **tire**, tire out, exhaust, wear out, drain, make weary, weary, wash out, tax, overtax, overtire, jade, make sleepy; prostrate, enervate; *informal* knock out, take it out of, do in, fag out, whack, poop, shatter, bush, frazzle, wear to a frazzle; *Brit. informal* knacker; *Brit. vulgar slang* shag out.
OPPOSITES invigorate, refresh.

WORD LINKS
fear of fatigue **kopophobia**

fatness ▶ **noun** *his fatness was the result of good living* **plumpness**, stoutness, heaviness, largeness, chubbiness, portliness, rotundity, flabbiness, paunchiness, dumpiness, meatiness; obesity, corpulence, bloatedness, grossness; fleshiness; excessive weight, bulk; paunch, pot belly, beer belly, beer gut; *informal* tubbiness, beefiness, porkiness, chunkiness, podginess.
OPPOSITE thinness.

fatten ▶ **verb 1** *a farm where livestock are fattened* **make fat/fatter**, feed up, feed, build up; overfeed, bloat.
2 *we're sending her home to her parents to fatten up* **put on weight**, gain weight, get heavier, grow fat/fatter, get fat, flesh out, fill out; thicken, widen, broaden, expand, spread out.
OPPOSITE lose weight.

fatty ▶ **adjective** *fatty foods* **greasy**, oily, fat, oleaginous, unctuous; *formal* pinguid, adipose, sebaceous.
OPPOSITE lean.

fatuous ▶ **adjective** *she was irritated by a fatuous question* **silly**, foolish, stupid, inane, nonsensical, childish, puerile, infantile, idiotic, brainless, mindless, vacuous, imbecilic, asinine, witless, empty-headed, hare-brained; pointless, senseless; ridiculous, ludicrous, absurd, preposterous, laughable, risible; *informal* daft, moronic, cretinous, dumb, gormless.
OPPOSITES intelligent, sensible.

fault ▶ **noun 1** *he has his faults, but he's a good man* **defect**, failing, imperfection, flaw, blemish, shortcoming, weakness, weak point, weak spot, frailty, foible, vice, limitation, lack, deficiency, Achilles heel, chink in one's armour.
OPPOSITES merit, strength.
2 *engineers have still not located the fault* **defect**, flaw, imperfection, snag; error, mistake, inaccuracy, oversight, blunder, gaffe, slip; *Computing* bug; *informal* glitch, gremlin, slip-up, boob, boo-boo, clanger, howler, foul-up, snarl-up; *Brit. informal* cock-up.
3 *it was my fault for being late* **responsibility**, liability, culpability, blameworthiness, guilt; accountability, answerability; *informal* rap.
4 *don't blame one child for another's faults* **misdeed**, wrongdoing, offence, misdemeanour, misconduct, sin, vice, lapse, indiscretion, peccadillo, transgression, trespass.
□ **at fault** *police say the driver was not at fault* **to blame**, blameworthy, blameable, censurable, reproachable; culpable, accountable, answerable; responsible, guilty, in the wrong, offending, erring, errant.
OPPOSITE innocent.

F

F

□ **to a fault** *Barry's generous to a fault* **excessively**, unduly, immoderately, overly, in the extreme, out of all proportion, overmuch, needlessly; *informal* over the top, OTT.

▶ **verb** *you couldn't fault any of the players* **find fault with**, find lacking; criticize, attack, censure, condemn, impugn, reproach, reprove, run down, take to task, haul over the coals; complain about, quibble about, carp about, moan about, grouse about, grouch about, whine about, arraign; *informal* knock, slam, hammer, lay into, gripe about, beef about, bellyache about, bitch about, whinge about, nit-pick over, pick holes in, sound off about; *Brit. informal* slag off, have a go at, give some stick to, slate, rubbish.

fault-finding ▶ **noun** *the manager tries to get results by fault-finding and nagging* **criticism**, captiousness, cavilling, quibbling, niggling, pedantry, hair-splitting; complaining, grumbling, carping, moaning, whining, bleating; *informal* nit-picking, griping, grousing, grouching, bellyaching; *archaic* overnice.
OPPOSITE praise.
▶ **adjective** *a fault-finding spectator* **critical**, **censorious**, carping, captious, cavilling, quibbling, niggling; overcritical, hypercritical, pedantic, over-precise, over-exact, over-rigorous, over-strict, hair-splitting, hard/difficult/impossible to please, pettifogging; *informal* nit-picking, pernickety.

faultless ▶ **adjective 1** *he replied in faultless English* **perfect**, flawless, without fault, error-free, without blemish, unblemished, impeccable, accurate, precise, exact, correct, unerring; exemplary, model, ideal, copybook, scrupulous, meticulous, just so; *Brit. informal* spot on, bang on, on the mark, on the nail, on the button.
OPPOSITES flawed, faulty.
2 *the wife of the prisoner was faultless* **guiltless**, without guilt, innocent, blameless, above reproach, irreproachable, sinless, pure, unsullied.
OPPOSITE guilty.

faulty ▶ **adjective 1** *a faulty electric blanket* **malfunctioning**, broken, damaged, defective, not working, not functioning, in disrepair, out of order, out of commission, inoperative, unsound, unusable, useless; *informal* on the blink, on its last legs, kaput, bust, busted, conked out, acting/playing up, gone haywire, gone phut, done for, wonky, dud; *Brit. informal* knackered, duff; *informal* on the fritz.
OPPOSITES working, functioning.
2 *her logic is faulty* **defective**, flawed, unsound, distorted, inaccurate, incorrect, erroneous, imprecise, fallacious, wrong; impaired, weak, invalid.
OPPOSITE sound.

WORD LINKS
related prefix **dys-** (e.g. ***dysfunction, dysphasia***)

faux pas ▶ **noun** *I committed a faux pas which they never let me forget* **gaffe**, blunder, mistake; indiscretion, impropriety, breach/lapse of etiquette, solecism, gaucherie, peccadillo; *informal* boob, boo-boo, slip-up, clanger, howler, boner; *N. Amer. informal* blooper; *Brit. informal, dated* bloomer.

favour ▶ **noun 1** *will you do me a favour?* **good turn**, service, kind act, good deed, act of kindness, kindness, courtesy, indulgence; benefit, boon.
OPPOSITE disservice.
2 *she looked on him with favour* **approval**, approbation, commendation, esteem, goodwill, kindness, benevolence, friendliness.
OPPOSITES disfavour; disapproval.
3 *they accused you of showing favour to one of the players* **favouritism**, bias, partiality, unfair preference, prejudice, partisanship, one-sidedness.
4 *serve the king well and you shall receive his favour* **patronage**, backing, support, aid, assistance, championship, aegis; auspices.
5 (*archaic*) *I am your lady and you shall wear my favours* **ribbon**, rosette, badge; token, token of affection, token of esteem; keepsake, souvenir, memento; *archaic* remembrancer.

□ **in favour of** *two thirds of them were in favour of a strike* **on the side of**, pro, for, all for, giving support to, giving backing to, right behind, encouraging of, approving of, sympathetic to.
OPPOSITE against.

▶ **verb 1** *the party favours reform of the electoral system* **advocate**, recommend, advise, subscribe to, approve of, look on with favour, be in favour of, support, back, champion; campaign for, stand up for, argue for, press for, lobby for, urge, promote, espouse, endorse, sanction, vouch for; *informal* plug, push.
OPPOSITE oppose.
2 *Robyn favours loose dark clothes* **prefer**, go in for, go for, choose, opt for, select, pick, plump for, single out, incline towards, lean towards, be partial to, like; *informal* fancy.
OPPOSITE dislike.
3 *he was angry that his father always favoured George* **show favouritism towards**, have a bias towards, treat with partiality, have as a favourite, think more highly of, hold in higher regard; indulge, pamper, spoil.
4 *the conditions favoured the other team* **benefit**, be to the advantage of, be advantageous to, oblige, help, assist, aid, lend a hand to, advance, abet, succour, serve, be of service to, do someone a favour, meet the needs of.
OPPOSITE hinder.
5 *he favoured Lucy with a smile* **oblige**, accommodate, gratify, satisfy, humour, indulge, pander to, put oneself out for; honour.
6 (*informal*) *Travis favours our father in colouring* **resemble**, look like, be like, be similar to, bear a resemblance to, remind one of, put one in mind of, take after, have the look of; *informal* be the spit of, be the spitting image of, be a dead ringer for; *archaic* bear semblance to.
OPPOSITE differ from.

favourable ▶ **adjective 1** *a favourable assessment of his ability* **approving**, commendatory, commending, praising, complimentary, flattering, glowing, appreciative, enthusiastic; good, pleasing, agreeable, successful, positive; *informal* rave.
OPPOSITES unfavourable; critical.
2 *the birds nest where conditions are favourable* **advantageous**, beneficial, of benefit, in one's favour, on one's side, helpful, good, right, conducive, convenient, suitable, fit, fitting, appropriate; **propitious**, auspicious, hopeful, promising, fair, encouraging.
OPPOSITE disadvantageous.
3 *he hoped for a favourable reply to his request* **positive**, affirmative, assenting, agreeing, concurring, approving, in the affirmative; encouraging, reassuring, supportive, in one's favour.
OPPOSITE negative.

favourably ▶ **adverb** *they were desperate to be judged favourably by their superiors* **positively**, approvingly, well, sympathetically, agreeably, enthusiastically, appreciatively, admiringly.
OPPOSITE unfavourably.

favoured ▶ **adjective** *he is the president's favoured candidate for prime minister* **preferred**, favourite, recommended, chosen, choice, selected, most-liked, ideal, particular, special, pet; *informal* blue-eyed.

favourite ▶ **adjective** *Laura was his favourite aunt* **best-loved**, most-liked, favoured, dearest, treasured, pet, special, closest to one's heart; preferred, chosen, choice, ideal; of choice.
OPPOSITE least-liked.
▶ **noun 1** *Brutus was always Caesar's favourite* **first choice**, choice, pick, preference, pet, beloved, darling; idol, hero, god, goddess, gem, jewel, jewel in the crown; *informal* blue-eyed boy, golden boy, teacher's pet, the apple of one's eye; *N. Amer. informal* fair-haired boy.
OPPOSITE bête noire.
2 *the favourite fell at the very first fence* **expected winner**, probable winner, front runner.
OPPOSITE underdog.

favouritism ▶ **noun** *we want one rule for everyone and no favouritism* **partiality**, partisanship, unfair preference, preferential treatment, special treatment, preference, favour, one-sidedness, prejudice, bias, inequality, unfairness, inequity, discrimination, positive discrimination, reverse discrimination; nepotism, keeping it in the family, looking after one's own; *Brit.* jobs for the boys.

fawn[1] ▶ **adjective** *a thick fawn carpet* **beige**, yellowish-brown, pale brown, buff, sand, sandy, oatmeal, wheaten, biscuit, café au lait, camel, kasha, ecru, taupe, stone, stone-coloured, greige, greyish-brown, mushroom, putty; neutral, natural, naturelle.

fawn[2] ▶ **verb** *congressmen fawn over him whenever he comes to town* **be obsequious to**, be sycophantic to, be servile to, curry favour with, pay court to, play up to, crawl to, creep to, ingratiate oneself with, dance attendance on, fall over oneself for, kowtow to, toady to, truckle to, bow and scrape before, grovel before, cringe before, abase oneself before; **flatter**, praise, sing the praises of, praise to the skies, praise to excess, eulogize; *informal* sweet-talk, soft-soap, suck up to, make up to, smarm around, be all over, fall all over, butter up, lick someone's boots, rub up the right way, lay it on thick, lay it on with a trowel; *Austral./NZ informal* smoodge to; *vulgar slang* kiss someone's arse.

fawning ▶ **adjective** *a circle of fawning civil servants* **obsequious**, servile, sycophantic, flattering, ingratiating, unctuous, oleaginous, oily, toadyish, slavish, bowing and scraping, grovelling, abject, crawling, creeping, cringing, prostrate, over-deferential, Uriah Heepish; *informal* bootlicking, smarmy, slimy, sucky, soapy; *N. Amer. informal* brown-nosing; *Brit. vulgar slang* arse-kissing, bum-sucking; *N. Amer. vulgar slang* kiss-ass, ass-kissing, suckholing; *rare* saponaceous.

fear *See centre pages for list of* **Phobias**
▶ **noun 1** *she felt fear at entering the house* **terror**, fright, fearfulness, horror, alarm, panic, agitation, trepidation, dread, consternation, dismay, distress; **anxiety**, worry, angst, unease, uneasiness, apprehension, apprehensiveness, nervousness, nerves, timidity, disquiet, disquietude, discomposure, unrest, perturbation, foreboding, misgiving, doubt, suspicion; *informal* the creeps, the willies, the heebie-jeebies, the shakes, the collywobbles, jitteriness, twitchiness, butterflies (in the stomach); *Brit. informal* funk, blue funk, the (screaming) abdabs; *Austral. rhyming slang* the Joe Blakes; *N. Amer. archaic* worriment; *rare* inquietude.
OPPOSITES calmness; confidence.
2 *she sought help to overcome her fears* **phobia**, aversion, antipathy, dread, bugbear, bogey, nightmare, horror, terror; anxiety, neurosis, complex, mania; abnormal fear, irrational fear, obsessive fear; *French* bête noire; *informal* hang-up.

3 (archaic) *they taught their children the love and fear of God* **awe**, wonder, wonderment, amazement; reverence, veneration, respect; **dread**.
OPPOSITE indifference.
4 *there's no fear of me leaving you alone* **likelihood**, likeliness, prospect, possibility, chance, odds, probability, expectation, conceivability, feasibility, plausibility; risk, danger.
▶ **verb 1** *she feared her husband* **be afraid of**, be fearful of, be scared of, be apprehensive of, dread, live in fear of, go in terror of, be terrified of, be terrified by, cower before, tremble before, cringe from, shrink from, flinch from; be anxious about, worry about, panic about, feel consternation about, have forebodings about, feel apprehensive about; *Brit. informal* be in a blue funk about.
2 *he fears heights and open spaces* **have a phobia about**, have a horror of, have a dread of, shudder at, take fright at.
3 *he feared to let them know he was awake* **be too afraid**, be too scared, be too apprehensive, hesitate; dare not; *informal* have cold feet about.
4 *they all feared for his health* **worry about**, feel anxious/concerned about, have anxieties about, have qualms about, feel disquiet for, be solicitous for.
5 (archaic) *blessed are all who fear the Lord* **stand in awe of**, regard with awe, revere, reverence, venerate, respect; **dread**, be intimidated by.
6 *I fear that you may be right* **suspect**, have a (sneaking) suspicion, have a (sneaking) feeling, feel, be inclined to think, be afraid, have a foreboding, have a hunch, think it likely, be of the opinion, suppose, reckon.

WORD LINKS
fear of … **-phobia (e.g. *claustrophobia*)**
fear of fear **phobophobia**

fearful ▶ **adjective 1** *they are fearful of being overheard by the enemy* **afraid**, frightened, scared, scared stiff, scared to death, terrified, petrified; alarmed, panicky, nervy, nervous, tense, apprehensive, uneasy, hesitant, disquieted, worried, worried sick, anxious; *informal* jittery, jumpy, in a (blue) funk; *Brit. informal* strung up; *dialect* frit; *archaic* afeared, affrighted.
2 *the guards were ill trained and fearful* **nervous**, trembling, quaking, quivering, shrinking, cowering, cowed, daunted; **timid**, timorous, diffident, faint-hearted, cowardly, pusillanimous; *Brit.* nervy; *informal* jittery, jumpy, twitchy, keyed up, yellow, chicken, in a cold sweat, a bundle of nerves, like a cat on a hot tin roof, frightened of one's own shadow; *Brit. informal* having kittens, like a cat on hot bricks, windy; *N. Amer. informal* spooked, spooky, antsy; *dated* overstrung, unquiet.
3 *there has been a fearful accident* **terrible**, dreadful, awful, appalling, frightful, ghastly, horrific, horrible, horrifying, horrendous, very bad, terribly bad, shocking, atrocious, abominable, hideous, monstrous, dire, grim, unspeakable, gruesome, grievous, lamentable, distressing, harrowing, alarming.
OPPOSITE minor.
4 (informal) *he was in a fearful hurry* **very great**, great, extreme, real, dreadful; *informal* terrible, impossible; *Brit. informal* right, proper.

fearfully ▶ **adverb 1** *she opened the door fearfully* **apprehensively**, uneasily, nervously, timidly, timorously, diffidently, hesitantly; with apprehension/trepidation, with bated breath, with one's heart in one's mouth.
2 (informal) *Stephanie looked fearfully glamorous* **extremely**, exceedingly, exceptionally, remarkably, uncommonly, extraordinarily, incredibly, most, very, really, immensely, thoroughly, positively, decidedly, downright; *Scottish* unco; *N. Amer.* quite; *informal* tremendously, awfully, terribly, frightfully, dreadfully, terrifically, desperately, seriously, devilishly, hugely, fantastically, madly, ultra, too … for words, mucho, mega, majorly, oh-so; *Brit. informal* jolly, ever so, dead, well, fair, right; *N. Amer. informal* real, mighty, awful, plumb, powerful, way; *S. African informal* lekker; *informal, dated* devilish, hellish, frightfully; *archaic* exceeding.

fearless ▶ **adjective** *the most fearless man I've ever seen in battle* **bold**, brave, courageous, intrepid, valiant, valorous, gallant, plucky, lionhearted, stout-hearted, heroic, daring, dynamic, spirited, mettlesome, confident, audacious, indomitable, doughty; unafraid, undaunted, unflinching, unshrinking, unblenching, unabashed; *informal* game, gutsy, spunky, ballsy, go-ahead, have-a-go, feisty; *rare* venturous.
OPPOSITES timid; cowardly.

fearsome ▶ **adjective** *the crocodile's teeth are a fearsome sight* **frightening**, horrifying, terrifying, menacing, chilling, spine-chilling, hair-raising, alarming, startling, unnerving, daunting, formidable, forbidding, dismaying, disquieting, disturbing, harrowing; appalling, dreadful, monstrous, horrendous; awe-inspiring, awesome, impressive, imposing, tremendous; *informal* scary, hairy.

feasibility ▶ **noun** *they will consider the feasibility of an aid programme* **practicability**, practicality, workability, workableness, viability, achievability, attainability, reasonableness, sensibleness; usefulness, suitability, expedience, helpfulness, constructiveness, use, utility, value; possibility, likelihood, likeliness, chance, conceivability; *informal* doability.
OPPOSITE impracticability.

feasible ▶ **adjective** *there is only one feasible solution* **practicable**, practical, workable, achievable, attainable, realizable, viable, realistic, sensible, reasonable, within reason, within the bounds of possibility; useful, suitable, expedient, helpful, constructive; possible, likely, conceivable, imaginable; *informal* doable, earthly; *rare* accomplishable.
OPPOSITES impractical; impossible.

feast *See centre pages for list of* **Festivals**
▶ **noun 1** *the occasion was celebrated with a great feast* **banquet**, celebration meal, lavish dinner, sumptuous repast, large meal, formal meal, formal dinner; treat, entertainment, jollification; revels, festivities; *informal* blowout, feed, junket, spread, binge, bash, do; *Brit. informal* nosh-up, beanfeast, bunfight, beano, scoff, slap-up meal, tuck-in.
OPPOSITES snack; fast.
2 *the feast of St Stephen* **festival**, religious festival, feast day, saint's day, holy day, holiday, fête, festivity, celebration.
3 *the decorations are a feast for the eyes* **treat**, delight, joy, pleasure, gratification.
▶ **verb 1** *they feasted on lobster and beef* **gorge on**, dine on, eat one's fill of, indulge in, overindulge in; eat, devour, consume, partake of; banquet; *informal* binge on, stuff one's face with, stuff oneself with, stuff down, shovel down, wolf down, pig oneself on, pig out on, make a pig of oneself on, cram in, tuck into, put away, pack away, make short work of, get outside of, get one's laughing gear round; *Brit. informal* gollop, shift; *N. Amer. informal* snarf; *rare* gourmandize.
2 *they feasted the deputation* **hold a banquet for**, throw a feast for, wine and dine, ply with food and drink, give someone a meal, feed, cater for; entertain lavishly, regale, treat, fête, throw a party for, play host to.

feat ▶ **noun** *the mounting of the expedition was a remarkable feat* **achievement**, accomplishment, attainment, coup, master stroke, triumph; **undertaking**, enterprise, venture, operation, exercise, endeavour, effort, performance; deed, act, action, manoeuvre, move, exploit, stunt; **(feats)** doings; *informal* caper.

feather ▶ **noun** *the bird preened its feathers* **plume**, quill, contour feather, flight feather, tail feather, primary feather, secondary feather, scapular feather, pin feather; **(feathers) plumage**, feathering, down, eider (down), hackles, crest, tuft, topknot, pinion; *technical* covert, quill covert, tail covert, wing covert, remex, rectrix, plumule, semi-plume; vibrissae; *archaic* flag, pen feather.

WORD LINKS
fear of feathers **pteronophobia**

feathery ▶ **adjective 1** *the feathery grey bodies of the geese* **feathered**, plumed, plumy; downy, fluffy, fuzzy, fleecy; *technical* plumose, plumate.
OPPOSITE bald.
2 *she wore a feathery nightdress* **flimsy**, delicate, diaphanous, fine, thin, sheer, gossamer, gossamer-like, gossamer-thin, gossamery, gauzelike, gauzy, wispy, floaty, insubstantial, unsubstantial, ethereal, incorporeal, vaporous, airy; light, lightweight, feather-like, light as a feather.

feature ▶ **noun 1** *a typical feature of French music* **characteristic**, attribute, quality, property, trait, mark, hallmark, trademark; aspect, facet, side, point, detail, factor, ingredient, component, constituent, element, theme; peculiarity, idiosyncrasy, quirk, oddity.
2 **(features)** *his eyes swept over her delicate features* **face**, countenance, physiognomy, profile; *informal* mug, kisser, clock, *Brit. informal* mush, phiz, phizog, dial; *Brit. rhyming slang* boat race; *Scottish & Irish informal* coupon; *N. Amer. informal* puss, pan; *literary* visage, lineaments; *archaic* front.
3 *she made a feature of her garden sculptures* **centrepiece**, **special attraction**, attraction, highlight, focal point, focus, focus of attention, centre of interest, draw, crowd-pleaser, cynosure; selling point; *informal* crowd-puller.
4 *the journal contains a series of short features* **article**, piece, item, report, story, column, review, commentary, criticism, analysis, write-up, exposé; *N. Amer.* theme.
▶ **verb 1** *Radio Ulster intends to feature a week of live concerts* **present**, promote, make a feature of, give prominence to, focus attention on, call attention to, spotlight, highlight, accent.
2 *she is to feature in a major advertising campaign* **star**, appear, participate, play a part, have a place, have prominence.

febrile ▶ **adjective** *the patient was febrile and had abdominal pain* **feverish**, fevered, hot, burning, burning up, fiery, flushed, sweating, in a cold sweat; shivering; delirious; *informal* with a temperature; *rare* pyretic.

February ▶ **noun**

WORD LINKS
birthstone **amethyst**

feckless ▶ **adjective** *a feckless lot of layabouts* **useless**, worthless, incompetent, inefficient, inept, good-for-nothing, ne'er-do-well; lazy, idle, slothful, indolent, shiftless, spiritless, apathetic, aimless, unambitious, unenterprising; *informal* no-good, no-account, lousy.

fecund ▶ **adjective** *a lush and fecund garden* **fertile**, fruitful, productive, high-yielding, prolific, proliferating, propagative, generative; rich, lush, flourishing, thriving; *rare* fructuous.
OPPOSITE barren.

federal ▶ **adjective** *an assembly consisting of delegations from the federal states* **confederate**, federated, federative; **combined**, allied, united, amalgamated, integrated, linked, associated, cooperating, in alliance, in league, in partnership, banded together.

federate ▶ verb *the organizations will be federated at national level* **confederate**, **combine**, ally, unite, unify, merge, amalgamate, integrate, fuse, marry, link, join, join up, align, associate, band together, team up.

federation ▶ noun *a world federation of Protestant denominations* **confederation**, confederacy, federacy, league; **combination**, combine, alliance, coalition, union, syndicate, guild, consortium, partnership, co-partnership, cooperative, association, amalgamation, entente, alignment; *German* Bund; *rare* consociation, sodality.

fee ▶ noun *he delivered the parcels for a very modest fee* **payment**, emolument, wage, salary, allowance, stipend, handout; **price**, cost, charge, tariff, toll, rate, amount, sum, figure, percentage, commission, consideration, honorarium; (**fees**) remuneration, dues, earnings, pay.

feeble ▶ adjective **1** *he was very old and feeble* **weak**, weakly, weakened, puny, wasted, frail, infirm, delicate, sickly, ailing, unwell, poorly, failing, helpless, powerless, impotent, enfeebled, enervated, debilitated, incapacitated, effete; decrepit, doddering, doddery, tottering, tottery, shaky, trembling, trembly; *Scottish* shilpit; *rare* etiolated.
OPPOSITE strong.
2 *this is a transparently feeble argument* **ineffective**, ineffectual, unsuccessful, inadequate, unconvincing, implausible, unsatisfactory, poor, weak, inept, tame, paltry, shallow, thin, flimsy, insubstantial; futile, useless, profitless, fruitless.
OPPOSITE effective.
3 *he's too feeble to stand up to his boss* **cowardly**, craven, faint-hearted, spineless, spiritless, lily-livered, chicken-livered, pigeon-hearted; timid, timorous, fearful, unassertive, soft, weak, ineffective, ineffectual, inefficient, incompetent, inadequate, indecisive; *informal* wishy-washy, wimpy, sissy, sissified, gutless, weak-kneed, yellow, yellow-bellied, chicken; *Brit. informal* wet; *N. Amer. informal* candy-assed; *N. Amer. vulgar slang* chickenshit; *archaic* poor-spirited.
OPPOSITES brave; forceful.
4 *the lamp shed a feeble light* **faint**, dim, weak, pale, soft, subdued, muted, indistinct, unclear, vague; *informal* wishy-washy.
OPPOSITE strong.

feeble-minded ▶ adjective **1** *don't be so feeble-minded* **stupid**, idiotic, moronic, imbecilic, foolish, half-baked, half-witted, dim-witted, witless, dunce-like, doltish, cretinous, empty-headed, vacuous, vapid; *informal* daft, dumb, dim, dopey, dozy, birdbrained, pea-brained, fat-headed, lamebrained, chuckleheaded, dunderheaded, wooden-headed, muttonheaded, boneheaded, crazy, mental, nuts, nutty, crackers, cracked, potty, barmy, batty, cuckoo, bonkers, dotty, dippy; *N. Amer. informal* dumb-ass.
OPPOSITE clever.
2 (*dated*) *they advocated the segregation of those who were feeble-minded* **with learning difficulties**, with a learning disability, with special (educational) needs; *informal* mental; *euphemistic* special; *dated* backward, simple, simple-minded, slow, slow-witted, dull-witted, subnormal, ESN (educationally subnormal), mentally handicapped, mentally disabled, retarded, mentally retarded, mentally defective.
OPPOSITE gifted.

feed ▶ verb **1** *I have a large family to feed* **give food to**, provide food for, provide for, cater for, prepare food for, cook for, make a meal for, wine and dine; nourish, sustain; suckle, breastfeed, bottle-feed; *dated* victual.
2 *the baby spends all day sleeping and feeding* **eat**, take nourishment, partake of food, consume food, devour food, have a meal; *informal* snack, graze; *Brit. informal* nosh; *dated* sup.
3 *there are too many cows feeding in a small area* **graze**, browse, crop, pasture, ruminate; eat.
4 *the birds feed on a varied diet of fish* **live on**, live off, exist on, subsist on, rely for nourishment on, depend on, thrive on; eat, consume, take in, have as food.
5 *we all have ways of feeding our self-esteem* **strengthen**, fortify, support, bolster, reinforce, boost, augment, supplement, add to, add fuel to, fuel, encourage, gratify, minister to.
OPPOSITE undermine.
6 *she fed secrets to the Russians* **supply**, provide, give, deliver, present, furnish, issue, impart, sell.
▶ noun **1** *he provides feed for his goats and sheep* **fodder**, food, foodstuff, forage, pasturage, herbage, silage; *formal* comestibles, provender.
2 (*informal*) *the hikers had decided to halt for their feed* **meal**, lunch, dinner, supper, repast; feast, banquet; *Brit.* tea; *informal* spread, blowout, binge; *Brit. informal* nosh, nosh-up, scoff, tuck-in; *formal* refection, collation.

feel ▶ verb **1** *she encourages her customers to feel the fabrics* **touch**, stroke, caress, fondle, finger, thumb, handle, manipulate, fiddle with, play with, toy with, maul; put one's hand on, lay a finger on; *informal* paw.
2 *she felt a steady breeze on her back* **perceive**, sense, detect, discern, make out, notice, observe, identify; be sensible of, have a sensation of, be aware of, be conscious of.
3 *the patient does not feel pain during the procedure* **experience**, undergo, go through, bear, endure, suffer, be forced to contend with; know, have.
4 *he began to feel his way towards the door* **grope**, fumble, scrabble, pick, poke, explore.
5 *feel the temperature of the water* **test**, try, try out, assess.
6 *he feels that he should go to the meeting* **believe**, think, consider it right, consider, fancy, be of the opinion, hold, maintain, judge, deem; suspect, suppose, assume, presume, conclude, come to the conclusion that; *N. Amer.* figure; *informal* reckon.
OPPOSITE doubt.
7 *I feel that he is only biding his time* **sense**, have a feeling, get the impression, feel in one's bones, have a hunch, have a funny feeling, just know, intuit.
8 *the air feels damp* **seem**, appear, strike one as.
□ **feel for** *the press persecuted John and I felt for him* **sympathize with**, be sorry for, pity, feel pity for, feel sympathy for, feel compassion for, empathize with, identify with, be moved by, weep for, grieve for, sorrow for; commiserate with, condole with; *archaic* compassion.
□ **feel like** *I feel like an ice cream* **want**, would like, wish for, desire, fancy, feel in need of, feel the need for, long for, crave, hanker after, pine for, thirst for, be desperate for, be bent on; *informal* have a yen for, yen for, be dying for.
▶ noun **1** *in murky water the divers work by feel* **touch**, sense of touch, tactile sense, tactility, feeling, feeling one's way, contact; texture.
2 *he liked the feel of the paper* **texture**, surface, finish, grain, nap; weight, thickness, consistency; quality, character.
3 *lighting can radically alter the feel of a room* **atmosphere**, ambience, aura, mood, feeling, air, impression, climate, character, overtone, undertone, tenor, spirit, quality, flavour, colour; *informal* vibrations, vibes, vibe; *rare* subcurrent.
4 *he has a real feel for the language* **aptitude**, knack, flair, bent, talent, gift, art, trick, faculty, ability, propensity, inclination; head, mind, brain; *informal* know-how.

feeler ▶ noun **1** *the fish has two feelers at the front of the head* **antenna**, tentacle, horn; whisker, hair, barb; tactile organ, sensory organ; *technical* palp, palpus, pedipalp, antennule, tactor.
2 (usually **feelers**) *the prime minister put out feelers to members of other parties* **tentative enquiry**, tentative proposal, tentative suggestion; advance, approach, overture, appeal; probe, trial balloon; *French* ballon d'essai.

feeling ▶ noun **1** *it's important to assess the fabric by feeling* **touch**, feel, sense of touch, tactile sense, tactility, contact, using one's hands.
2 *she was overcome by a feeling of nausea* **sensation**, sense; awareness, consciousness, perception, impression.
3 *I had a feeling that I would win* **suspicion**, sneaking suspicion, notion, inkling, hunch, fancy, apprehension, presentiment, premonition, foreboding; idea, vague idea, impression; *informal* gut feeling, feeling in one's bones, funny feeling, sixth sense.
4 *he was amazed at the strength of her feeling* **love**, care, affection, fondness, tenderness, warmth, warmness, emotion, sentiment; passion, ardour, desire, lust, infatuation; adulation, adoration, reverence, devotion.
5 *the government is out of touch with public feeling* **sentiment**, emotion, emotional state; **opinion**, attitude, belief; ideas, views.
6 *Emma felt a rush of feeling for the poor child* **compassion**, sympathy, empathy, fellow feeling, understanding, care, concern, solicitude, solicitousness, tender-heartedness, tenderness, love, brotherly love; pity, sorrow, commiseration, condolences.
7 (**feelings**) *he hadn't meant to hurt her feelings* **sensibilities**, sensitivities, self-esteem, ego, pride; emotions, passions, sentiments.
8 *my feeling is that his claim is true* **opinion**, belief, view, impression, intuition, instinct, hunch, estimation, guess, theory, hypothesis, thought, way of thinking, point of view.
9 *a feeling of peace prevailed in the quiet street* **atmosphere**, ambience, aura, air, feel, mood, impression, climate, character, overtone, undertone, tenor, spirit, quality, flavour, colour; *informal* vibrations, vibes, vibe; *rare* subcurrent.
10 *he has a remarkable feeling for language* **aptitude**, knack, flair, bent, talent, gift, skill, art, trick, faculty, ability, propensity, inclination; head, mind, brain; *informal* know-how.
▶ adjective *he considers himself to be a feeling man* **sensitive**, warm, warm-hearted, tender, tender-hearted, caring, soft-hearted, sympathetic, compassionate, understanding, empathetic, responsive, receptive, intuitive, thoughtful; emotional, demonstrative, passionate, fiery; *archaic* sensible.

feign ▶ verb **1** *she lay still and feigned sleep* **simulate**, fake, sham, affect, give the appearance of, make a show of, make a pretence of, play at, go through the motions of; *informal* put on.
2 *he's not really ill, he's only feigning* **pretend**, put it on, fake, sham, bluff, pose, posture, masquerade, make believe, act, play-act, go through the motions, put on a false display; malinger; *informal* kid; *Brit. informal* mess.

feigned ▶ adjective *he accepted the invitation with feigned enthusiasm* **pretended**, simulated, assumed, affected, artificial, insincere, put-on, fake, faked, false, sham; apparent, ostensible, seeming, surface, avowed, professed; *informal* pretend, pseudo, phoney; *Brit. informal* cod.

OPPOSITE sincere.

feint ▸ **noun** *the attack on the main gate was merely a feint* **bluff**, blind, ruse, deception, subterfuge, hoax, trick, ploy, device, wile, sham, pretence, artifice, cover, smokescreen, distraction, expedient, contrivance, machination; *informal* dodge, put-on, put-up job, red herring.

felicitations ▸ **plural noun** *I extend my felicitations to you on the occasion of your marriage* **congratulations**, good wishes, best wishes, kind regards, regards, love, blessings, compliments, respects; greetings, salutations.

felicitous ▸ **adjective 1** *his nickname was particularly felicitous* **apt**, well chosen, well expressed, well put, choice, fitting, suitable, appropriate, apposite, pertinent, germane, to the point, relevant, congruous, apropos; *informal* spot on.
OPPOSITE inappropriate.
2 *the view is the room's only felicitous feature* **fortunate**, advantageous, good, favourable, lucky, happy, pleasing, encouraging.
OPPOSITE unfortunate.

felicity ▸ **noun 1** *a scene of domestic felicity* **happiness**, joy, joyfulness, joyousness, rapture, bliss, euphoria, delight, cheer, cheerfulness, gaiety; contentedness, satisfaction, pleasure, fulfilment; transports.
OPPOSITE unhappiness.
2 *David expressed his feelings with his customary felicity* **eloquence**, aptness, appropriateness, suitability, suitableness, applicability, fitness, relevance, pertinence, correctness, rightness.
OPPOSITE inappropriateness.

feline ▸ **adjective** *she moved with feline grace* **catlike**, leonine; graceful, sleek, sinuous, slinky, sensual; stealthy.
▸ **noun** *she gave a silly name to her pet feline* **cat**, domestic cat, wild cat, alley cat, kitten; tabby, tomcat, tom, queen, mouser; *informal* puss, pussy, pussy cat; *Brit. informal* moggie, mog; *archaic* grimalkin.

fell[1] ▸ **verb 1** *all the dead sycamores had to be felled* **cut down**, chop down, hack down, saw down, knock down, hew, demolish, tear down, bring down, raze, level, clear.
2 *she felled him with one punch | he was felled by a sniper's bullet* **knock down**, knock over, knock to the ground, bowl over, strike down, bring down, bring to the ground, topple, ground, prostrate, catch off balance; knock out, knock unconscious; kill, cut down, mow down, pick off, shoot down, gun down, blast; *informal* deck, floor, flatten, down, knock for six, knock into the middle of next week, lay out, KO.

fell[2] ▸ **adjective** (*archaic*) *the men had a fell intent* **murderous**, savage, violent, vicious, fierce, ferocious, barbarous, barbaric, brutish, monstrous, cruel, ruthless, grim, bloody; terrible, dreadful, awful, atrocious, heinous; deadly, lethal, destructive; *Brit. informal* beastly; *archaic* sanguinary.
□ **at/in one fell swoop** *she solved all her problems in one fell swoop* **all at once**, together, at the same time, in one go, with one move, outright.

fellow ▸ **noun 1** (*informal*) *he's a decent sort of fellow* **man**, boy; person, individual, soul; *informal* guy, lad, fella, codger, sort, character, customer, punter, devil, bunny, bastard; *Brit. informal* chap, bloke, gent, geezer, bod; *Scottish & Irish informal* bodach; *N. Amer. informal* dude, hombre; *Austral./NZ informal* digger; *S. African informal* ou, oke; *Indian informal* admi; *informal, dated* body, dog, cove; *Scottish archaic* carl.
2 (*informal*) *she longed to be like ordinary girls and have a fellow* **boyfriend**, lover; *informal* fella.
3 *he exchanged relieved glances with his fellows* **companion**, friend, crony, comrade, partner, associate, co-worker, colleague; *informal* chum, pal, buddy; *Brit. informal* mate, oppo.
4 *some peasants were wealthier than their fellows* **peer**, equal, contemporary, brother; *French* confrère; *archaic* compeer; *rare* coeval, coequal.
5 *the fellow to the absent key lay on the table* **counterpart**, mate, partner, match, twin, brother, double; copy, duplicate.
□ **fellow feeling** *she felt a rush of fellow feeling for the unfortunate woman* **sympathy**, **empathy**, feeling, compassion, care, concern, solicitude, solicitousness, warmth, tenderness, brotherly love; pity, sorrow, commiseration, condolences; affinity, rapport, harmony, understanding, fellowship, closeness, togetherness, connection, communion; *rare* caritas.

fellowship ▸ **noun 1** *a community bound together in fellowship* **companionship**, companionability, sociability, comradeship, fraternization, camaraderie, friendship, mutual support, mutual respect, mutual liking; amiability, amity, affability, geniality, kindliness, cordiality, intimacy; social intercourse, social contact, association, closeness, togetherness, solidarity; *informal* chumminess, palliness, clubbiness; *Brit. informal* mateyness.
2 *a new member of the church fellowship* **association**, society, club, league, union, guild, lodge, affiliation, alliance, order, fraternity, brotherhood, sorority; band, group, circle, ring, clan, set, coterie; *rare* consociation, sodality.

female See centre pages for list of male and female **Animals**
▸ **adjective** *typical female attributes* **feminine**, womanly, womanlike, ladylike; she-, to do with women; pretty, graceful, delicate, gentle; *archaic* feminal.
OPPOSITE male.
▸ **noun** *the author was a female.* See WOMAN.

feminine ▸ **adjective 1** *a very feminine young woman* **womanly**, womanlike, ladylike, girlish, female; soft, delicate, gentle, tender, graceful, refined, modest; *informal* girly; *archaic* feminal.
OPPOSITE masculine.
2 *his friends thought him slightly feminine* **effeminate**, womanish, unmanly, unmasculine, effete, weak, soft, milksoppish; *informal* sissy, sissyish, wimpy, wimpish, limp-wristed, pansy-like.
OPPOSITES manly; butch.

femininity ▸ **noun** *she had always delighted in her femininity* **womanliness**, feminineness, womanhood, womanly qualities, feminine qualities.
OPPOSITE masculinity.

feminism ▸ **noun** *she was a great pioneer of feminism* **the women's movement**, the feminist movement, women's liberation, female emancipation, women's rights; post-feminism, womanism; *informal* women's lib.

femme fatale ▸ **noun** *a femme fatale who plays men off against each other* **seductress**, temptress, siren, enchantress, sorceress, charmer; Delilah, Circe, Lorelei, Mata Hari; *informal* mantrap; *N. Amer. informal* vamp.

F

fen ▸ **noun** *they opposed the drainage of the fen* **marsh**, marshland, salt marsh, fenland, wetland, bog, peat bog, bogland, swamp, swampland; *Scottish & N. English* moss, carr; *Irish* corcass; *N. Amer.* bayou, moor, pocosin, salina; *archaic* marish.

fence ▸ **noun 1** *she crept through a gap in the fence* **barrier**, paling, railing, rail, bar, hurdle, enclosure; wall, hedge, hedgerow, windbreak, groyne, partition; barricade, stockade, palisade, rampart, protection, defence; *rare* circumvallation.
2 (*informal*) *he was an accomplished fence, dealing mainly in jewellery* **receiver of stolen goods**, dealer in stolen goods; receiver, dealer, trafficker; *informal* pusher.
□ **(sitting) on the fence** (*informal*) *they were on the fence about the whole issue* **undecided**, uncommitted, uncertain, unsure, vacillating, wavering, dithering, hesitant, tentative, doubtful, irresolute, ambivalent, torn, in two minds, in a dilemma, on the horns of a dilemma, in a quandary; abstaining; neutral, impartial, non-aligned, non-partisan, unbiased, open-minded; *Brit.* humming and hawing; *informal* iffy, blowing hot and cold.
▸ **verb 1** *they intend to fence off many acres of wild land* **enclose**, surround, circumscribe, encircle, circle, encompass, bound, form a barrier around, form a ring round; divide up, section off, separate off, partition off, cut off, cordon off, close off, isolate, segregate, seal, close; *literary* gird, girdle, engird; *rare* compass.
2 *he needed more wire to fence in his chickens* **confine**, pen in, coop up, rail in, box in, wall in, hedge in, hem in, close in, shut in, shut up, mew up, immure, lock in, shut off, separate off, cut off; intern, impound, hold captive, keep under lock and key; enclose, surround; secure, protect, defend; *N. Amer.* corral.
3 *the man fenced but Jim persisted with his questions* **be evasive**, be vague, be ambiguous, be non-committal, equivocate, prevaricate, stall, vacillate, quibble, hedge, beat about the bush, dodge the issue, sidestep the issue, parry questions, fudge the issue, mince one's words; *informal* pussyfoot around, duck the question, duck the issue, waffle, flannel, shilly-shally; *rare* palter, tergiversate.
4 (*informal*) *these fellows fenced for a band of grave robbers* **receive stolen goods**, deal in stolen goods.

fend ▸ **verb** *they were unable to fend off a Viking invasion | Mary tried to fend off his questions* **ward off**, head off, stave off, hold off, keep off, repel, repulse, resist, forestall, pre-empt, fight off, defend oneself against, guard against, discourage, prevent, stop, put a stop to, block, intercept, halt, arrest, check, curb, hold back, baulk, foil, thwart, keep at bay, keep at arm's length; parry, turn aside, divert, deflect, avert; skirt round, dodge, duck, escape, evade.
OPPOSITE encourage.
□ **fend for oneself** *how could any mother leave a child to fend for itself?* **take care of oneself**, look after oneself, provide for oneself, shift for oneself, manage by oneself, get by alone, get by without help, cope alone, cope unaided, stand on one's own two feet, hold one's own, make it on one's own; *informal* paddle one's own canoe.

feral ▸ **adjective 1** *a pack of feral dogs* **wild**, untamed, undomesticated, untrained, unused to humans; unbroken, not broken in; *Brit.* not house-trained; *N. Amer.* not housebroken.
OPPOSITES tame; pet.
2 *he gave a feral snarl* **fierce**, ferocious, vicious, savage, aggressive, tigerish, wolfish, predatory, menacing, threatening, bloodthirsty.

ferment ▸ **verb** (stress on the second syllable) **1** *the beer continues to ferment in the cask* **undergo fermentation**, brew; **effervesce**, fizz, foam, froth, bubble, seethe, boil; rise.
2 *the mixture is fermented by the addition of yeast* **brew**; **subject to fermentation**, cause to ferment, cause to effervesce.
3 *the brutalizing environment that ferments prison disorder* **cause**, bring on, bring about, give rise to, lead to, result in, generate, engender, spawn, instigate, prompt, provoke, incite, excite, arouse, stir up, whip up, foment, kindle, trigger off, spark off, touch off; *literary* beget, enkindle; *rare* effectuate.
▸ **noun** (stress on the first syllable) **1** *a ferment of revolutionary upheaval* **fever**,

furore, frenzy, tumult, storm, flurry, bustle, hubbub, brouhaha, stir, fuss, stew, ruckus, clamour; **turmoil**, upheaval, unrest, disquiet, uproar, agitation, turbulence, hurly-burly, excitement, disruption, confusion, disorder, chaos, mayhem; *informal* hoo-ha, to-do, rumpus; *Brit. informal* kerfuffle, carry-on, aggro, argy-bargy, hoopla; *archaic* moil, coil.
2 (*archaic*) *the protein is produced through the action of a ferment* **fermenting agent**, fermenting substance, fermentation agent, enzyme; yeast, mould, bacteria, leaven, leavening; *archaic* barm.

WORD LINKS
science of fermentation **zymology**

fern ▸ **noun** (**ferns**) **bracken**; *archaic* brake.

WORD LINKS
study of ferns **pteridology**

ferocious ▸ **adjective 1** *bears are ferocious animals* **fierce**, savage, wild, feral, untamed; predatory, rapacious, ravening, aggressive, dangerous.
OPPOSITES tame; gentle.
2 *a ferocious attack on a policeman* **brutal**, brutish, vicious, violent, bloody, barbarous, barbaric, savage, sadistic, ruthless, remorseless, cruel, pitiless, merciless, heartless, bloodthirsty, murderous, tigerish, wolfish; wicked, inhuman, monstrous, abominable, fiendish, hellish, diabolical; *Brit. informal* beastly; *literary* fell; *archaic* sanguinary.
OPPOSITE gentle.
3 *the ferocious midday sun | a ferocious headache* **intense**, extreme, strong, powerful, fierce, burning, searing; severe, acute, unbearable, insufferable, hellish, diabolical.
OPPOSITE mild.

ferocity ▸ **noun** *detectives were shocked by the ferocity of the attack* **savagery**, brutality, brutishness, barbarity, fierceness, violence, aggression, bloodthirstiness, murderousness; ruthlessness, cruelty, pitilessness, mercilessness, heartlessness, inhumanity, sadism; intensity, severity, extremity, force, strength; *rare* ferity.
OPPOSITE gentleness.

ferret ▸ **verb 1** *she ferreted in her handbag* **rummage**, search about, scrabble around, feel around, grope around, forage around, fish about/around, poke about/around, scratch about/around, delve, dig, hunt; search through, hunt through, rifle through, sift through, go through, scour, ransack, explore; *Brit. informal* rootle around; *Austral./NZ informal* fossick through; *rare* roust around.
2 *our headmistress was good at* **ferreting out** *misdemeanors* **unearth**, uncover, discover, detect, search out, elicit, bring to light, bring into the open, reveal, get at, run to earth, track down, turn up, dig up, dig out, root out, hunt out, fish out, nose out, sniff out; *informal* get wind of, get wise to, rumble; *rare* uncloak.

WORD LINKS
male **jack**
female **jill**
young **kit**
collective noun **busyness**

ferry ▸ **noun** *I took the ferry from Dover to Calais* **passenger boat**, passenger ship, ferry boat, packet boat, packet, shuttle; car ferry, train ferry, drive-on ferry, roll-on/roll-off ferry; ship, boat, vessel; *S. African* pont; (*in Venice*) traghetto.
▸ **verb 1** *the ship will ferry passengers to and from the Continent* **transport**, convey, carry, bear, ship, run, chauffeur, take, bring, shuttle.
2 *the boat ferried hourly across the river* **go back and forth**, shuttle, come and go, run.

fertile ▸ **adjective 1** *the soil is moist and fertile* **fecund**, fruitful, productive, high-yielding, prolific, proliferating, propagative, generative; rich, lush; *rare* fructuous.
OPPOSITE infertile.
2 *even couples who are fertile may adopt a child* **able to conceive**, able to have children, fecund, potent, generative, reproductive.
OPPOSITE barren.
3 *he has a particularly fertile brain* **imaginative**, inventive, innovative, innovational, creative, visionary, original, ingenious, resourceful, constructive; productive, prolific.
OPPOSITE unimaginative.

fertility ▸ **noun 1** *he uses compost to maintain the fertility of his land* **fecundity**, fruitfulness, productiveness, prolificacy, propagativeness, generativeness; richness, lushness.
2 *happiness has an effect on one's fertility* **ability to conceive**, ability to have children, virility, fecundity, potency, reproductiveness.

fertilization ▸ **noun** *the sex of the embryo is determined at fertilization* **conception**, impregnation, insemination, implantation, inception of pregnancy; pollination, propagation; *rare* fecundation.

fertilize ▸ **verb 1** *the field is ploughed up and fertilized* **add fertilizer to**, enrich with fertilizer, feed, mulch, compost, manure, dung, dress, top-dress; make more fertile; *rare* fecundate, fructify.
2 *the eggs were fertilized during the breeding season* **impregnate**, inseminate; *rare* fecundate.
3 *these orchids are fertilized by insects* **pollinate**, cross-pollinate, cross-fertilize, make fruitful; *rare* fecundate, fructify.

fertilizer *See centre pages for list of* **Fertilizers**
▸ **noun** *farmers rely on fertilizer to expand output* **plant food**, dressing.

fervent ▸ **adjective** *Annie uttered a fervent prayer | a fervent rugby supporter* **impassioned**, passionate, intense, vehement, ardent, sincere, feeling, profound, deep-seated, heartfelt, deeply felt, emotional, animated, spirited; enthusiastic, zealous, fanatical, wholehearted, avid, eager, earnest, keen, committed, dedicated, devout; *informal* mad keen, card-carrying, true blue; *Brit. informal* keen as mustard; *rare* fervid, perfervid, passional.
OPPOSITE apathetic.

fervid ▸ **adjective** (*rare*) *fervid protestations of love* **fervent**, ardent, passionate, impassioned, intense, vehement, heated, wholehearted, heartfelt, deeply felt, deep-seated, deep-rooted, profound, emotional, sincere, earnest, eager, avid, enthusiastic; *rare* perfervid, passional, full-hearted.
OPPOSITE half-hearted.

fervour ▸ **noun** *he preached and laboured with tremendous fervour* **passion**, ardour, intensity, zeal, vehemence, vehemency, emotion, warmth, sincerity, earnestness, avidness, avidity, eagerness, keenness, enthusiasm, excitement, animation, vigour, energy, fire, fieriness, heat, spirit, zest, appetite, hunger, urgency; dedication, devoutness, assiduity, commitment, committedness; *rare* fervency, ardency, passionateness.
OPPOSITE apathy.

fester ▸ **verb 1** *the deep wound in his neck festered* **suppurate**, become septic, form pus, secrete pus, discharge, run, weep, ooze; come to a head; *technical* maturate, be purulent; *rare* rankle, apostemate.
2 *rubbish festered in the crowded streets* **rot**, moulder, decay, decompose, putrefy, go bad, go off, perish, spoil, deteriorate, disintegrate, degrade, break down, break up; *technical* mortify, necrotize; *archaic* corrupt.
3 *we must not allow our resentment to fester* **rankle**, chafe, gnaw (at one's mind), eat away at one's mind, ferment, brew, smoulder; cause bitterness, cause resentment, cause vexation, cause annoyance.

festival *See centre pages for list of religious* **Festivals**
▸ **noun 1** *we took part in the town's autumn festival* **fête**, fair, gala day, gala, carnival, fiesta, jamboree, pageant; celebrations, festivities; arts festival, festival of music and drama, musical festival, festival of music, science festival; *Welsh* eisteddfod.
2 *forty days' fasting precede the festival* **holy day**, feast day, saint's day, holiday; anniversary, commemoration, day of observance; rite, ritual, ceremony.

festive ▸ **adjective** *everyone was in a festive mood despite the recession* **jolly**, merry, joyous, joyful, happy, jovial, light-hearted, cheerful, cheery, jubilant, convivial, good-time, high-spirited, gleeful, mirthful, uproarious, rollicking, backslapping, hilarious; celebratory, holiday, carnival; Christmassy; *informal* chirpy; *dated* gay; *archaic* festal, frolicsome, sportive.
OPPOSITE miserable.

festivity ▸ **noun 1** (**festivities**) *food plays an important part in the festivities* **celebration**, festival, festive event, festive occasion, entertainment, party, jamboree; merrymaking, feasting, revelry, carousal, carousing, jollification; revels, fun and games, frolics, celebrations, festive proceedings; *informal* bash, shindig, shindy; *Brit. informal* rave-up, thrash, knees-up, jolly, beanfeast, bunfight, beano.
2 *the festivity of the Last Night of the Proms* **jollity**, jolliness, merriment, gaiety, cheerfulness, cheeriness, cheer, joyfulness, euphoria, jubilance, conviviality, gleefulness, glee, high spirits, jocularity, revelry; *dated* sport; *archaic* sportiveness.

festoon ▸ **noun** *the streets are hung with festoons of paper flowers* **garland**, chain, lei, swathe, swag, wreath, chaplet, loop.
▸ **verb** *the room was festooned with streamers* **decorate**, adorn, ornament, trim, dress up, array, deck (out), hang, loop, thread, cover, drape, swathe, garland, wreathe, bedeck, beribbon, bespangle; *informal* do up, do out, get up, tart up, trick out; *literary* bedizen, furbelow, caparison, befrill, bejewel.

fetch ▸ **verb 1** *he went to fetch a doctor from the village* **get**, go and get, go for, call for, summon, pick up, collect, bring, carry, deliver, convey, ferry, transport; escort, conduct, lead, usher in.
2 *the land could fetch a million pounds* **sell for**, bring in, raise, realize, yield, make, earn, command, cost, be priced at, come to, amount to; *informal* go for, set one back, pull in, rake in; *Brit. informal* knock someone back.
□ **fetch up** (*informal*) *the boat somehow fetched up on a remote Pacific island* **end up**, finish up, turn up, arrive, appear, pop up, materialize, find itself; land, beach, wash up; *informal* wind up, pitch up, show up.

fetching ▸ **adjective** *she looked rather fetching in her nurse's uniform* **attractive**, appealing, adorable, sweet, winsome, pretty, lovely, delightful, charming, prepossessing, captivating, enchanting; sexy, alluring, seductive, ravishing, desirable, irresistible; *Scottish & N. English* bonny; *informal* divine, heavenly, smashing, tasty, hot, fanciable, easy on the eye; *Brit. informal* fit; *N. Amer. informal* cute, foxy; *dated* taking; *archaic* comely, fair.

fête ▸ **noun** (*Brit.*) *the village fête was held on the green* **gala**, gala day, garden party, bazaar, fair, feast, festival, fiesta, jubilee, pageant, carnival, funfair; fund-raiser, charity event; *Dutch & N. Amer.* kermis.

fetid, **foetid** ▶ adjective *the air was heavy and fetid* **stinking**, smelly, foul-smelling, evil-smelling, malodorous, stinking to high heaven, reeking, pungent, acrid, high, rank, foul, unpleasant, nasty, noxious; W. Indian fresh; informal stinky, reeky; Brit. informal niffing, niffy, pongy, whiffy, humming; N. Amer. informal funky; literary noisome, mephitic; rare miasmic, miasmal, olid.
OPPOSITE fragrant.

fetish ▶ noun **1** *he developed a rubber fetish* **fixation**, sexual fixation, obsession, compulsion, mania; weakness, fancy, taste, fascination, craze, fad; French idée fixe; informal thing, hang-up.
2 *he worshipped an African fetish* **juju**, talisman, charm, amulet; totem, icon, idol, image, effigy, doll, statue, figure, figurine; archaic periapt.

fetter ▶ verb **1** *the captive was branded and fettered* **shackle**, manacle, handcuff, clap in irons, put in chains, chain (up), bind, tie (up), tether, rope, hobble; secure, restrain; informal cuff; rare enfetter, gyve.
2 *these obligations do not fetter the company's powers* **restrict**, restrain, constrain, confine, limit; hinder, hamper, impede, obstruct, handicap, hamstring, encumber, inhibit, check, curb, tie down; tie someone's hands, cramp someone's style; literary trammel.

fetters ▶ plural noun *the prisoner lay bound with fetters of iron* **shackles**, manacles, handcuffs, irons, leg irons, chains, bonds; tethers, ropes, restraints; informal cuffs, bracelets; archaic trammels, gyves, darbies, bilboes.

fettle ▶ noun *his best players were in fine fettle* **shape**, trim, fitness, physical fitness, health, state of health; **condition**, form, repair, state of repair, state, order, working order, way; informal kilter; Brit. informal nick.

fetus, **foetus** ▶ noun *antibodies are passed via the placenta to the fetus* **embryo**, fertilized egg, unborn baby, unborn child.

WORD LINKS
killing of a fetus **feticide**

feud ▶ noun *a region riven by tribal feuds* **vendetta**, conflict, war; rivalry, hostility, enmity, strife, discord, bad blood, animosity, antagonism, grudge, estrangement, schism; quarrel, argument, bickering, falling-out; archaic broil.
▶ verb *he feuded with management and teammates* **quarrel**, fight, argue, bicker, squabble, dispute, clash, differ, be at odds, be at daggers drawn; wage war, take up arms; informal scrap, fall out, go at it hammer and tongs, fight like cat and dog.

fever ▶ noun **1** *he subsequently developed fever* **feverishness**, high temperature, febricity, febrility; shivering; delirium; Medicine pyrexia; informal temperature, temp; rare calenture.
2 *Terry was in a fever of excitement* **ferment**, frenzy, furore, ecstasy, rapture, hubbub, hurly-burly.
3 *World Cup football fever* **excitement**, frenzy, agitation, turmoil, restlessness, unrest, passion.

WORD LINKS
relating to fever **febrile**
fear of fever **febriphobia**
medicine for fever **febrifuge**

fevered ▶ adjective **1** *Fernando soothed her fevered brow* **feverish**, febrile, hot, burning, sweating; rare pyretic.
2 *a lunatic with a fevered imagination* **excited**, agitated, energetic, frenzied, overwrought, frantic, worked up, fervid.

feverish ▶ adjective **1** *she's really sick and feverish* **febrile**, fevered, with a high temperature, hot, burning, sweating; shivering; delirious; informal with a temperature; rare pyretic.
2 *he was thrown into a state of feverish excitement* **frenzied**, frenetic, hectic, agitated, excited, restless, nervous, worked up, overwrought, frantic, furious, distracted, hysterical, wild, manic, maniacal, like one possessed; uncontrolled, unrestrained; informal in a tizzy.
OPPOSITE calm.

few ▶ determiner *police are revealing few details about the victim* **not many**, hardly any, scarcely any; a small number of, a small amount of, a small quantity of, one or two, a handful of, a sprinkling of; little; informal a couple of.
OPPOSITE many.
▶ adjective *though the car parks are few, they are strategically placed* **scarce**, scant, scanty, meagre, insufficient, negligible, in short supply; thin on the ground, scattered, seldom met with, few and far between, infrequent, uncommon, rare, sporadic.
OPPOSITES many, plentiful.
▶ pronoun
□ **a few** *to a few, overcoming their fear of flying becomes a challenge* **a small number**, a handful, a sprinkling, one or two, a couple, two or three; not many, hardly any.
OPPOSITE a lot.

WORD LINKS
related prefix **oligo- (e.g. *oligarch, oligosaccharide*)**

fiancée, masc. **fiancé** ▶ noun *he went back to the valley to marry his fiancée* **betrothed**, wife-to-be, husband-to-be, bride-to-be, future wife/husband, prospective wife/husband, prospective spouse; informal, dated intended.

fiasco ▶ noun *the whole thing was a total fiasco* **failure**, disaster, catastrophe, debacle, shambles, farce, mess, wreck, ruin, ruination, blunder, botch, abortion; informal flop, washout, dud, hash, lead balloon, foul-up, screw-up; Brit. informal pig's ear, cock-up; N. Amer. informal snafu; Austral./NZ informal fizzer; vulgar slang fuck-up, balls-up.
OPPOSITE success.

fiat ▶ noun *a political union was imposed through imperial fiat* **decree**, edict, order, command, commandment, injunction, proclamation, mandate, dictum, diktat, promulgation, precept; (in Tsarist Russia) ukase; (in Spanish-speaking countries) pronunciamento; rare rescript, firman, decretal, irade.

fib ▶ noun *you're telling a fib* **lie**, untruth, falsehood, made-up story, trumped-up story, invention, fabrication, deception, piece of fiction, fiction, falsification, fairy story/tale, cock and bull story; (little) white lie, half-truth, exaggeration, departure from the truth; informal tall story, tall tale, whopper; Brit. rhyming slang pork pie, porky pie, porky; humorous terminological inexactitude.
OPPOSITES truth, fact.
▶ verb *she had bunked off school, fibbing about a sore throat* **lie**, tell a fib, tell a lie, invent a story, make up a story, dissemble, dissimulate, pretend, depart from the truth; exaggerate, stretch the truth; pull the wool over someone's eyes, pull someone's leg; informal lie through one's teeth, con, kid; humorous be economical with the truth, tell a terminological inexactitude; vulgar slang bullshit.
OPPOSITE tell the truth.

fibre *See centre pages for list of* **Fabrics and Fibres**
▶ noun **1** *fibres from the murderer's jumper were found on the victim's body* **thread**, strand, tendril, filament; technical fibril.
2 *designer clothing in natural fibres* **material**, substance, cloth, fabric, stuff.
3 *a man with no fibre. See* MORAL FIBRE.
4 *a lack of fibre in his diet* **roughage**, bulk, fibrous material.

fickle ▶ adjective *today's fickle fans demand instant success* **capricious**, changeable, variable, volatile, mercurial, vacillating, fitful, irregular; inconstant, disloyal, undependable, unstable, unsteady, unfaithful, faithless; irresolute, flighty, giddy, skittish, erratic, impulsive; unpredictable, random; informal blowing hot and cold; technical labile; literary mutable.
OPPOSITES constant; stable.

CHOOSE THE RIGHT WORD
fickle, inconstant, changeable, capricious
See INCONSTANT.

fickleness ▶ noun *the fickleness of public taste* **capriciousness**, changeability, variability, volatility, vacillation, fitfulness, irregularity, tendency to blow hot and cold; disloyalty, undependability, inconstancy, instability, unsteadiness, infidelity, unfaithfulness, faithlessness; irresolution, flightiness, giddiness, skittishness, impulsiveness; unpredictability, unpredictableness, randomness; technical lability; literary mutability.
OPPOSITES constancy, stability.

fiction ▶ noun **1** *the traditions of British fiction* **novels**, stories, creative writing, imaginative writing, works of the imagination, prose literature, narration, story telling; romance, fable.
OPPOSITE non-fiction.
2 *the president dismissed the allegation as absolute fiction* **fabrication**, invention, lies, fibs, concoction, untruth, falsehood, fantasy, fancy, illusion, sham, nonsense; vulgar slang bullshit; Austral./NZ vulgar slang bulldust.
OPPOSITES fact; truth.

fictional ▶ adjective *a fictional character* **fictitious**, **invented**, imaginary, imagined, made up, make-believe, unreal, fabricated, concocted, devised, mythical, storybook, the product of someone's imagination.
OPPOSITES real; actual.

fictitious ▶ adjective **1** *police said the name was fictitious* **false**, fake, counterfeit, fabricated, sham; untrue, bogus, spurious, assumed, affected, adopted, feigned, invented, made up, concocted, improvised; informal pretend, phoney; Brit. informal, dated cod.
OPPOSITE genuine.
2 *a fictitious character* **fictional**, imaginary, imagined, invented, made up, make-believe, unreal, non-existent, mythical, storybook, apocryphal; fabricated, concocted, devised; the product of someone's imagination, a figment of someone's imagination.
OPPOSITE factual.

fiddle (informal) ▶ noun **1** *their feet moved in time with the fiddle* **violin**, viola, cello, double bass; historical kit.
2 *the men were involved in a major VAT fiddle* **fraud**, swindle, fix, wangle, confidence trick, ruse, wile, piece of deception, bit of sharp practice; informal racket, con trick, flimflam, sting.
▶ verb **1** *he fiddled with a beer mat* **fidget**, play, toy, twiddle, fuss, fool about/around, trifle; finger, thumb, handle, feel, touch; waste time, act aimlessly; informal mess about/around, paw.

F

2 *he fiddled with some dials and buttons* **tinker**, play about/around, tamper, meddle, interfere, monkey; adjust.
3 *the government is trying to fiddle the figures* **falsify**, manipulate, massage, rig, distort, pervert, misrepresent, juggle, doctor, alter, tamper with, interfere with; *informal* cook, fix, diddle, finagle, flimflam, cook the books.

fiddling ▶ adjective *fiddling little details* **trivial**, petty, trifling, insignificant, unimportant, inconsequential, inconsiderable, negligible, paltry, footling, minor, small, slight, incidental, of little/no account; *informal* piddling, piffling, penny-ante; *Brit. informal* twopenny-halfpenny; *N. Amer. informal* nickel-and-dime, picayune; *N. Amer. vulgar slang* chickenshit.
OPPOSITES important; large.

fidelity ▶ noun **1** *she was never tempted to stray from fidelity to her husband* **faithfulness**, loyalty, constancy; devotedness, devotion, commitment, adherence; true-heartedness, trustworthiness, trustiness, honesty, dependability, reliability; monogamy; *archaic* troth.
OPPOSITES disloyalty; infidelity.
2 *fidelity to your king* **loyalty**, allegiance, obedience, constancy, fealty, homage; staunchness, fastness.
3 *the fidelity of the reproduction* **accuracy**, exactness, exactitude, precision, preciseness, correctness, scrupulousness; strictness, closeness, faithfulness, correspondence, literalness, conformity; realism, verisimilitude, veracity, authenticity, naturalism.
OPPOSITE inaccuracy.

fidget ▶ verb **1** *the audience had begun to fidget | she fidgeted with her scarf* **move restlessly**, wriggle, squirm, twitch, jiggle, writhe, twist, shuffle, be jittery, be anxious, be agitated; play, fuss, toy, twiddle, fool about/around, trifle; *informal* fiddle, mess about/around, have ants in one's pants.
OPPOSITES sit still, be at ease.
2 *she seemed to fidget him* **make uneasy**, worry, agitate, bother, upset, ruffle.
▶ noun **1** *he disturbed other people with convulsive fidgets* **twitch**, wriggle, squirm, jiggle, shuffle, tic, spasm, shudder.
2 *what a fidget you are!* **restless person**, bundle of nerves; *informal* cat on hot bricks, cat on a hot tin roof.
3 (**the fidgets**) *that woman gives me the fidgets* **restlessness**, nervousness, fidgetiness, unease, uneasiness; *informal* the jitters, twitchiness.

fidgety ▶ adjective *I get a bit fidgety around females* **restless**, restive, on edge, uneasy, nervous, nervy, keyed up, anxious, agitated, discomposed; jumpy, shaky, quivering; *informal* jittery, like a cat on hot bricks, twitchy.
OPPOSITES calm; still.

field ▶ noun **1** *a large ploughed field* **meadow**, pasture, paddock, green, pen, grassland, pastureland, sward; park; *N. Amer.* corral; *Irish & Canadian* bawn; *literary* glebe, lea, mead, greensward.
2 *a football field* **pitch**, ground, sports field, playing field, recreation ground, arena; stadium; *Brit. informal* park.
3 *a pioneer in the field of biotechnology* **area**, **sphere**, area of activity, discipline, province, department, domain, sector, line, branch, subject, speciality, specialty, specialization, specialism; *French* métier, forte; *informal* scene, bailiwick, pigeon.
4 *you can't see events out of your field of vision* **scope**, range, sweep, reach, extent, purview; limits, confines, parameters, bounds, horizons.
5 *her superb technique means she is head and shoulders ahead of the field* **competitors**, entrants, competition, runners; applicants, candidates, possibles, possibilities, hopefuls.
▶ verb **1** *she could field a ball with the best of the boys* **catch**, stop, retrieve; **return**, throw back.
2 *they should have been kicked out of the competition for fielding an ineligible player* **put in the team**, send out, play, put up.
3 *they can field an army of about one million* **deploy**, position, post, station, range, dispose.
4 *he fielded a battery of awkward questions* **deal with**, handle, cope with, answer, reply to, respond to, react to; parry, deflect, turn aside, evade, sidestep, avoid, dodge, answer evasively, fend off; *informal* duck.
▶ adjective **1** *he has field experience in educational research* **practical**, hands-on, applied, actual, active, experiential, empirical, in the field, non-theoretical; *rare* empiric.
OPPOSITE theoretical.
2 *field artillery* **mobile**, portable, transportable, movable, manoeuvrable, light, lightweight; *rare* portative.
OPPOSITE heavy.

fiend ▶ noun **1** *a fiend had taken possession of him* **demon**, devil, evil spirit, imp, bogie; incubus, succubus; hellhound; *informal* spook; *rare* cacodemon.
2 *a fiend bent on global evil-doing* **brute**, beast, villain, barbarian, monster, ogre, sadist, evil-doer; *informal* baddy, swine; *archaic* blackguard.
3 (*informal*) *a drug fiend* **addict**, abuser, user; *informal* junkie, …head/freak.
4 (*informal*) *I'm a fiend for Mexican food* **enthusiast**, fanatic, maniac, addict; devotee, fan, lover, follower; aficionado, connoisseur, appreciator; *informal* buff, freak, nut, ham, sucker, great one.

fiendish ▶ adjective **1** *a fiendish torturer* **wicked**, cruel, vicious, evil, nefarious, unspeakable; brutal, brutish, savage, barbaric, barbarous, beastly, inhuman, murderous, bloodthirsty, ferocious; ruthless, heartless, pitiless, merciless, black-hearted, unfeeling; malevolent, malicious, villainous, malignant, devilish, diabolical, hellish, demonic, satanic, Mephistophelian, ungodly; odious, base; *archaic or humorous* dastardly.
2 *a fiendish plot* **cunning**, clever, ingenious, artful, crafty, canny, wily, guileful, devious, scheming, shrewd, astute, sharp, sharp-witted, imaginative; *informal* foxy, savvy, sneaky, cute; *Scottish & N. English informal* pawky; *S. African informal* slim; *rare* vulpine, carny.
3 *a fiendish puzzle* **difficult**, complex, complicated, intricate, involved, knotty, thorny, ticklish, abstruse, impenetrable, unfathomable; challenging, puzzling, baffling, perplexing, bemusing; frustrating.

fierce ▶ adjective **1** *a fierce black mastiff* **ferocious**, savage, vicious; wild, feral, untamed, undomesticated; aggressive, bloodthirsty, dangerous; cruel, brutal, murderous; menacing, threatening, terrible, grim.
OPPOSITES gentle; tame.
2 *they are facing fierce competition from American firms* **aggressive**, cut-throat, competitive; keen, intense, strong, relentless.
OPPOSITE mild.
3 *a fierce, murderous jealousy lanced through Meredith* **intense**, powerful, vehement, passionate, impassioned, fervent, fervid, fiery, flaming, ardent, uncontrolled, immoderate, intemperate, inordinate.
OPPOSITE mild.
4 *a fierce wind coming in off the sea* **powerful**, strong, violent, forceful, bitter; stormy, blustery, gusty, boisterous, tempestuous, raging, furious, turbulent, tumultuous, cyclonic, typhonic; destructive, devastating.
5 *a fierce pain shot between his eyes* **severe**, extreme, intense, acute, grave, very bad, awful, dreadful, grievous; excruciating, agonizing, torturous, tormenting, piercing, penetrating, harrowing.
OPPOSITE mild.

fiery ▶ adjective **1** *the fiery breath of dragons* **burning**, blazing, flaming, raging; on fire, ablaze, afire, lighted, lit; incandescent, red-hot, scorching.
2 *she had blushed a fiery red* **bright**, brilliant, vivid, vibrant, intense, deep, rich, strong, bold.
3 *her fiery spirit* **passionate**, impassioned, ardent, fervent, fervid, lively, zealous, spirited; uncontrollable, ungovernable; quick-tempered, ill-tempered, bad-tempered, volatile, explosive, angry, heated, aggressive, determined, resolute.
OPPOSITES bland, indifferent.

fiesta ▶ noun *a five-day fiesta* **festival**, carnival, holiday, celebration, party.

fight ▶ verb **1** *he saw two men fighting* **brawl**, come to blows, exchange blows, attack/assault each other, hit/punch each other; box; struggle, grapple, wrestle, scrimmage; do battle, engage in conflict, contend; spar, joust, tilt, cross swords, lock horns, lock antlers; *informal* scrap, have a dust-up, have a set-to; *Brit. informal* have a punch-up; *Scottish informal* swedge; *N. Amer. informal* rough-house; *Austral./NZ informal* stoush, go the knuckle.
2 *Edward went to fight in the First World War* **battle**, do battle, give battle, wage war, go to war, make war, take up arms; attack, mount an attack; combat, engage, meet, clash, skirmish; be a soldier, fight for Queen/King and country; crusade.
3 *a war fought for freedom* **engage in**, wage, conduct, prosecute, carry on, pursue, undertake, practise, proceed with, go on with.
4 *she and her sister are always fighting* **quarrel**, argue, row, bicker, squabble, have a row/fight, wrangle, dispute, be at odds, disagree, fail to agree, differ, be at variance, have words, bandy words, be at each other's throats, be at loggerheads; battle, feud; *informal* fall out, scrap, go at it hammer and tongs, fight like cat and dog, argufy; *archaic* altercate, chop logic; *Scottish archaic* threap.
5 *the firemen fought the blaze* **try to extinguish**, try to put out.
6 *textile workers fought against further wage reductions* **campaign**, strive, battle, struggle, contend, grapple, war, crusade, agitate; speak, lobby; work, push, press.
7 *party leaders warned that they would fight the decision* **oppose**, contest, contend with, confront, challenge, combat, dispute, object to, quarrel with, argue against/with; withstand, resist, defy, fly in the face of; strive/struggle against, take a stand against, put up a fight against, stand up and be counted against, take issue with, question; *rare* controvert.
OPPOSITES accept, support.
8 *Donaldson fought the urge to put his tongue out* **repress**, restrain, suppress, stifle, smother, hold back, keep back, fight back, keep in check, check, curb, contain, control, keep under control, rein in, silence, muffle, bottle up, choke back, swallow, strangle, gag; *informal* button up, keep the lid on, cork up.
OPPOSITE give in to.

□ **fight back 1** *use your pent-up anger to fight back* **retaliate**, counterattack, strike back, hit back, reply, respond, react, reciprocate, return fire, give tit for tat, give as good as one gets, return the compliment, defend oneself, put up a fight, return like for like, get back at someone, give someone a dose/taste of their own medicine; *formal* requite something; *archaic* serve someone out, give someone a Roland for an Oliver.
OPPOSITE turn the other cheek.
2 *she had to fight back tears of frustration* **repress**, restrain, suppress, stifle, smother, hold back, keep back, keep in check, check, curb, contain, control, keep under control, rein in, silence, muffle, bottle up, choke back, swallow, strangle, gag; *informal* button up, keep the lid on, cork up.

OPPOSITES give in to, let out.

□ **fight someone/something off** *he fought off a bull terrier that attacked his dog* **repel**, repulse, beat off, stave off, ward off, hold off, fend off, keep/hold at bay, drive away/back, force back, beat back, push back, resist.

□ **fight shy of** *some people fight shy of taking out a personal loan* **flinch from**, demur from, recoil from, hang back from; have scruples about, scruple about, have misgivings about, have qualms about, be averse to, be chary of, not be in favour of, be against, be opposed to, be diffident about, be bashful about, be shy about, be coy about; be loath to, scruple to, be reluctant to, be unwilling to, be disinclined to, not be in the mood to, be indisposed to, be slow to, be hesitant to, be afraid to, hesitate to, hate to, not like to, not have the heart to, drag one's feet/heels over, waver about, vacillate about, think twice about, baulk at, quail at, mind doing something; *informal* be cagey about, boggle at; *archaic* disrelish.

▶ **noun 1** *he'd got into a fight outside a club* **brawl**, fracas, melee, row, rumpus, confrontation, skirmish, sparring match, exchange, struggle, tussle, scuffle, altercation, wrangle, scrum, clash, disturbance; fisticuffs, rough and tumble; *Irish, N. Amer., & Austral.* donnybrook; *informal* scrap, dust-up, set-to, shindy, shindig, free-for-all; *Brit. informal* punch-up, bust-up, ruck, bit of argy-bargy, barney; *Scottish informal* rammy, swedge, square go; *N. Amer. informal* rough house, brannigan; *Austral./NZ informal* stoush; *Law, dated* affray; *rare* broil, bagarre.
2 *a heavyweight championship fight* **boxing match**, bout, match, meeting, fixture, game, encounter.
3 *Britain might have given up her fight against Germany* **battle**, engagement, clash, conflict, contest, encounter; skirmish, scuffle, tussle, struggle, brush, exchange; war, campaign, crusade, warfare, combat, action, hostilities.
4 *I just had a fight with my girlfriend* **argument**, quarrel, squabble, row, wrangle, disagreement, difference of opinion, falling-out, contretemps, tangle, altercation, fracas; dispute, disputation, contention; feud; *informal* tiff, set-to, shindig, shindy, stand-up, run-in, spat, scrap, ruction; *Brit. informal* slanging match, barney, bunfight, ding-dong, bust-up, ruck.
5 *their fight for control of the company* **struggle**, battle, campaign, endeavour, drive, push, effort, movement, move.
6 *she had no fight left in her* **will to resist**, power to resist, resistance, morale, spirit, courage, pluck, pluckiness, gameness, will to win, strength, backbone, spine, mettle, stout-heartedness, determination, firmness of purpose, resolution, resolve, resoluteness, confidence; **aggression**, aggressiveness, belligerence, militancy, boldness, audacity, forcefulness; *informal* guts, grit, spunk; *Brit. informal* bottle; *N. Amer. informal* sand, moxie.

fightback ▶ **noun** (*Brit.*) *Hibs mounted a spirited fightback* **counterattack**, counteroffensive; rally, recovery, recuperation, resurgence, revival, rebound; *informal* comeback.

fighter *See centre pages for list of types of* **Soldier**

▶ **noun 1** *a guerrilla fighter* **soldier**, fighting man, fighting woman, warrior, combatant, serviceman, servicewoman, trooper; (*in the US*) GI, enlisted man; *Brit. informal* squaddie; *archaic* man-at-arms.
2 *the bout ends when a fighter is knocked to the ground* **boxer**, pugilist, prizefighter; wrestler, grappler; contestant, contender, competitor; *informal* champ, bruiser, scrapper, pug.
3 *he was shot down by enemy fighters* **warplane**, armed aircraft.

fighting ▶ **adjective** *Hugh was a fighting man* **violent**, combative, aggressive, pugnacious, truculent, belligerent, bellicose, disputatious, antagonistic, argumentative, hawkish.
OPPOSITE peaceful.

▶ **noun** *more than 200 were injured in the fighting* **violence**, hostilities, conflict, combat; warfare, war, battles, skirmishing, affray, rioting; bloodshed, slaughter, slaying, killing, carnage, butchery, massacre, murder, bloodletting; *informal* action.
OPPOSITE peace.

figment ▶ **noun** *all this nonsense about ghosts is just a* ***figment of her imagination*** **invention**, production, creation, concoction, fabrication; hallucination, illusion, delusion, mirage, apparition, chimera, fancy, fiction, fable, falsehood, imagining, vision.

figurative ▶ **adjective** *a figurative expression* **metaphorical**, non-literal, symbolic, allegorical, representative, emblematic; imaginative, fanciful, poetic, ornate, literary, flowery, florid; *rare* tropical, parabolic.
OPPOSITE literal.

figure ▶ **noun 1** *the production figure is down 27 per cent* **statistic**, number, integer, quantity, amount, level, total, sum; (**figures**) data, information, particulars.
2 *the second figure was a nine* **digit**, numeral, numerical symbol, character; *rare* cipher.
3 *he can't put a figure on how much this is going to cost* **price**, cost, amount, quantity, value, valuation, quotation, quote, rate; total, sum, aggregate; *informal, humorous* damage.
4 (**figures**) *I'm good at figures* **arithmetic**, mathematics, sums, calculations, reckoning, computation, numbers, statistics, counting; *Brit. informal* maths; *N. Amer. informal* math.
5 *her petite, curvaceous figure* **physique**, build, frame, body, proportions, torso, shape, form, stature; *informal* vital statistics, chassis, bod.
6 *a dark figure emerged from the shadows* **silhouette**, outline, shape, form, profile, shadow.
7 *a figure of authority* **person**, personage, individual, man, woman, character, personality, presence; representative, embodiment, personification, epitome, symbol, representation, exemplification, exemplar.
8 *the show features life-size figures* **human representation**, image of a person, effigy; likeness.
9 *the figure that is formed when a smaller square is cut out of a large square* **shape**, pattern, design, motif, device, depiction.
10 *this structure is shown in figure 4* **diagram**, illustration, drawing, picture, plate, graphic, sketch, chart, plan, map.

▶ **verb 1** *an awesome beast who figured in Egyptian legend* **feature**, appear, be featured/mentioned, be referred to; participate, play a part, play a role, be conspicuous, have prominence, have a place; star.
2 *a way to figure the values* **calculate**, work out, total, sum, reckon, compute, enumerate, determine, evaluate, quantify, assess, count, add up, put a figure on, tally, totalize, gauge; *Brit.* tot up; *rare* cast.
3 (*N. Amer. informal*) *I figured that I didn't have much of a chance* **suppose**, think, believe, fancy, consider, expect, take it, suspect, have a sneaking suspicion, sense; assume, dare say, conclude, take it as read, presume, be of the opinion, trust; deduce, infer, gather, glean, divine; *N. Amer.* guess.
4 (*N. Amer. informal*) *'Rosemary's away.' 'That figures.'* **make sense**, be understandable, seem reasonable, stand to reason, be to be expected, be logical, follow, add up, stand up, hold up; ring true, be convincing; be likely/probable, go without saying.

□ **figure on** (*N. Amer. informal*) *I figured on starting the day with a good breakfast* **plan on**, calculate on, count on, rely on, bank on, bargain on, depend on, pin one's hopes on; anticipate, expect to, take for granted, take as read.

□ **figure something out** (*informal*) *he tried to figure out how to switch on the lamp* **work out**, make out, fathom, reason, puzzle out, decipher, solve, ascertain, make sense of, think out, think through, get to the bottom of, find an answer/solution to, unravel, untangle; understand, comprehend, see, grasp, get the hang of, get the drift of; calculate, compute, reckon, assess; *informal* make head or tail of, twig, crack; *Brit. informal* suss out.

figurehead ▶ **noun 1** *the president was just a figurehead* **titular head**, nominal leader, leader in name only, front man, cipher, token, mouthpiece, puppet, instrument, man of straw.
2 *the figurehead on the Cutty Sark* **carving**, bust, sculpture, image, statue.

figure of speech ▶ **noun.** *See centre pages for list of* **Rhetorical Devices and Figures of Speech**

filament ▶ **noun** *a network of lace-like filaments* **fibre**, thread, strand, tendril; string, wire, cable, cord; *technical* fibril, cilium.

filch ▶ **verb** (*informal*) *she had filched a bottle of claret* **pilfer**, steal, thieve, rob, take, purloin, snatch, abstract, misappropriate, embezzle, shoplift; *informal* **pinch**, nick, swipe, nab, whip, rip off, lift, 'liberate', 'borrow', walk off/away with, run off/away with, snaffle, snitch; *Brit. informal* knock off, nobble, blag; *Brit. rhyming slang* half-inch; *N. Amer. informal* glom, heist; *Austral. informal* snavel; *W. Indian informal* tief; *formal* peculate; *archaic* crib, hook.

file[1] ▶ **noun 1** *he opened the file and began to read* **folder**, portfolio, binder, box, document case; filing cabinet.
2 *we maintain files on all the major companies* **dossier**, document, record, report, case history, case study; (**files**) data, information, particulars, case notes, documentation, annals, archives.
3 *when saving a file the summary information menu may be displayed* **batch of data**, document, text; program.

▶ **verb 1** *make sure that this material is filed in such a way that it is easy to find* **categorize**, classify, organize, put in place, put in order, order, arrange, catalogue, tabulate, index, pigeonhole; put on record, record, enter, store, log, archive.
2 *Debbie has filed for divorce* **apply**, put in, register, sign up, ask.
3 *two women have filed a civil suit against him* **bring**, press, lodge, place, lay, prefer, put forward, present, submit.

file[2] ▶ **noun** *a file of boys in football kit making their way along the path* **line**, column, row, string, chain, queue, procession, train, convoy, caravan; *Brit. informal* crocodile.

▶ **verb** *we filed out into the car park* **walk in a line**, proceed in a line, march, parade, troop, pass in formation.

file[3] ▶ **verb** *when I have nothing else to do I file my nails* **smooth**, buff, rub, rub down, polish, burnish, furbish; shape, refine; scrape, abrade, rasp, sandpaper.

filial ▶ **adjective** *a display of filial affection* **dutiful**, devoted, loyal, faithful, compliant, respectful, dedicated, affectionate, loving; **befitting a son or daughter**, familial.

filibuster ▶ **noun** *many hours in committee characterized by filibuster and slow progress* **delaying tactics**, stonewalling, procrastination, obstruction, delaying, blocking, hold-up; *informal* speechifying, speechification.

▶ **verb** *it is an abuse of the house for the opposition to filibuster* **waste time**, stall, play for time, stonewall, procrastinate, buy time, employ delaying tactics; obstruct, delay, block; speak/talk at length, speak/talk on and on; *informal* speechify.

filigree ▶ noun *a bench decorated with gold filigree* **wirework**, fretwork, fret, latticework, lattice, grillwork, scrollwork, lacework, lace, tracery.

fill ▶ verb **1** *he filled a bowl with breakfast cereal | his eyes filled* **make/become full**, fill up, fill to the brim, fill to overflowing, top up, charge, load (up), pack.
OPPOSITE empty.
2 *guests filled the parlour* **crowd**, throng, pack (into), jam, occupy all of, press into, squeeze into, cram (into); overcrowd, congest, overfill.
3 *he began filling his shelves with a selection of beers* **stock**, pack, load; supply, furnish, provide, replenish, restock, refill.
4 *fill all the holes with a wood-repair compound* **block up**, bung up, stop (up), plug, seal, caulk, close, clog (up), choke, obstruct, occlude, dam up.
OPPOSITES unblock, open.
5 *the perfume filled the room* **pervade**, spread throughout/through, permeate, suffuse, be diffused through, diffuse through, imbue, penetrate, pass through, infuse, perfuse, extend throughout, be disseminated through, flow through, run through, saturate, impregnate.
6 *he was going to fill a government post* **occupy**, hold, take up, be in, have; *informal* hold down.
7 *we filled a big order for a Yorkshire company* **carry out**, complete, fulfil, execute, perform, implement, discharge, bring about; *rare* effectuate.

□ **fill in** *I'm going to fill in for Jim on the project* **substitute**, deputize, stand in, cover, provide cover, take over, act, act as deputy, act as stand-in, sit in, act as understudy, understudy, be a proxy, act as locum tenens; take the place of; *informal* sub, fill someone's shoes/boots, step into someone's shoes/boots; *N. Amer. informal* pinch-hit.

□ **fill someone in** *Iain filled me in on the essential details* **inform of**, advise of, tell about, notify of, acquaint with, apprise of, brief on, enlighten about, update with, bring up to date about, make conversant with, report to about; *informal* put wise about, put in the picture about, clue in about, bring up to speed on, tip off about.

□ **fill something in** (*Brit.*) *he filled in all the forms* **complete**, answer, fill up; *N. Amer.* fill out.

□ **fill out** *she had filled out a little since Sarah had last seen her* **grow fatter**, become plumper, become rounder, flesh out, put on weight, gain weight, get heavier.

□ **fill something out 1** *this account needs to be filled out by detailed evidence from local studies* **expand**, enlarge, add to, round out, elaborate, add substance/detail to, flesh out, add flesh to, put flesh on the bones of; supplement, reinforce, extend, broaden, develop, amplify.
2 (*N. Amer.*) *he filled out the requisite forms. See* FILL SOMETHING IN.

▶ noun

□ **one's fill** *I've eaten my fill* **enough**, sufficient, plenty, ample, as much as necessary, all one wants, a sufficiency, an abundance, as much as one can take, more than enough.

filling ▶ noun *filling for cushions and mattresses* **stuffing**, padding, wadding, filler, quilting, cushioning, lining, packing.
▶ adjective *a cheap but filling meal* **substantial**, hearty, ample, abundant, solid, nutritious, nourishing, satisfying, square; heavy, stodgy, starchy, leaden.

fillip ▶ noun *they are reducing their lending rates to give a fillip to the housing market* **stimulus**, stimulation, stimulant, boost, encouragement, incitement, incentive, impetus, inducement, motivation; tonic, uplift, lift, reviver, spur, goad, prod, push, prompt, aid, help; *informal* shot in the arm, pick-me-up.
OPPOSITE curb.

film *See centre pages for list of* **Film Types, Versions, and Genres**
▶ noun **1** *there was a film of sweat on his face* **layer**, coat, coating, covering, cover, surface, sheet, patina, blanket, dusting, skin, overlay, screen, mask, wash, glaze, varnish, veneer, veil.
2 *Emma was watching a film* **movie**, picture, feature, feature film; programme, broadcast, transmission; *N. Amer.* motion picture; *dated* moving picture; *informal* flick, pic, vid; *dated, informal* talkie.
3 *she would like to work in film* **cinema**, movies, the pictures.
▶ verb **1** *he immediately filmed the next scene* **record on film**, shoot, record, take pictures of, make a film of, capture on film, video, photograph.
2 *the book was filmed in 1983* **adapt for film**, make into a film.
3 *his eyes had* **filmed over cloud**, mist, fog, haze; become blurred, blur, dull; *archaic* blear.

WORD LINKS
relating to film **cinematographic**

film star ▶ noun *a Hollywood film star* **actor**, **actress**, film actor/actress, leading man, leading woman, leading lady, lead, principal, performer, starlet; **celebrity**, star, famous actor/actress, personality, household name, superstar; *N. Amer.* movie star; *informal* celeb; *dated* matinee idol; *Brit. informal* luvvie.

filmy ▶ adjective *a filmy black blouse* **diaphanous**, transparent, see-through, translucent, sheer, gauzelike, gauzy, gossamer, gossamery, cobwebby, shimmering; delicate, fine, ultra-fine, light, thin, airy, floaty, wispy, silky; fragile, flimsy, unsubstantial, insubstantial.
OPPOSITES thick, coarse, opaque.

filter ▶ noun *pass the water through a carbon filter* **strainer**, sifter; sieve, riddle, colander; gauze, netting.
▶ verb **1** *the farmers filter the water* **sieve**, strain, sift, filtrate, riddle; clarify, purify, clear, clean, make pure, refine, treat, process, decontaminate.
2 *the rain had succeeded in filtering through her jacket* **seep**, percolate, leak, trickle, ooze, dribble, bleed, flow; drain, well, exude, escape, leach.

filth ▶ noun **1** *he grew up among the filth of the coal mines and steel mills* **dirt**, muck, grime, mud, mire, sludge, slime, ooze, foul matter; excrement, excreta, dung, manure, ordure, sewage; rubbish, refuse, garbage, trash, dross, scum; pollution, contamination, defilement, decay, putrefaction, putrescence; squalor, squalidness, sordidness, shabbiness, sleaziness, filthiness, uncleanness, foulness, nastiness; *informal* crud, grot, gunge, grunge, yuck.
2 *I felt sick to my stomach after reading that filth* **pornography**, pornographic literature/films/videos, dirty books, smut, vice; obscenity, indecency, corruption, lewdness, rudeness, vulgarity, coarseness, crudeness, grossness, vileness, nastiness, immorality; *informal* porn, hard porn, soft porn, porno, raunchiness.

filthy ▶ adjective **1** *the room was filthy* **dirty**, mucky, grimy, muddy, murky, slimy, unclean; foul, squalid, sordid, shabby, sleazy, nasty, soiled, sullied, scummy; polluted, contaminated, unhygienic, unsanitary; rotten, defiled, decaying, putrid, putrefied, smelly, fetid, faecal; *informal* cruddy, grungy, yucky; *Brit. informal* grotty; *literary* befouled, besmirched, begrimed; *rare* feculent.
OPPOSITE clean.
2 *his face was filthy* **unwashed**, unclean, dirty, grimy, dirt-encrusted, smeared, smeary, grubby, muddy, mucky, black, blackened, begrimed, stained, unkempt.
OPPOSITES clean, scrubbed.
3 *she told filthy jokes* **obscene**, indecent, dirty, smutty, rude, improper, corrupt, coarse, bawdy, unrefined, indelicate, vulgar, lewd, racy, raw, off colour, earthy, ribald, risqué, licentious, 'adult'; vile, depraved, foul, impure, offensive, prurient, salacious, pornographic, explicit, foul-mouthed; *informal* blue, raunchy, near the knuckle/bone, nudge-nudge, porn, porno, X-rated.
OPPOSITES clean, polite.
4 *you filthy brute!* **despicable**, contemptible, nasty, low, base, mean, vile, disgusting, unpleasant, obnoxious, wretched, shabby, sordid; *informal* dirty, dirty rotten, low-down, no-good, beastly, lousy.
5 *he was in a filthy mood* **bad**, foul, unpleasant, bad-tempered, ill-tempered, irritable, grumpy, grouchy, cantankerous, curmudgeonly, aggressive, cross, fractious, peevish, short-tempered, hot-tempered, quick-tempered; *informal* snappish, snappy, chippy, on a short fuse, short-fused; *Brit. informal* shirty, stroppy, narky, ratty; *N. Amer. informal* cranky, ornery, peckish, soreheaded; *informal, dated* waxy, miffy.
OPPOSITE good.
▶ adverb *he wants to be filthy rich* **very**, extremely, tremendously, immensely, vastly, hugely, remarkably; disgustingly, excessively, exceedingly, abominably, revoltingly; *informal* stinking, terrifically, awfully, terribly, madly, seriously, mega, ultra, damn, damned, too … for words.

final ▶ adjective **1** *their final year of study* **last**, closing, concluding, finishing, end, ending, terminating, terminal, culminating, ultimate, eventual, endmost.
OPPOSITES first, initial.
2 *the experts' decisions are final* **irrevocable**, unalterable, absolute, conclusive, irrefutable, incontrovertible, indisputable, unappealable, unchallengeable, binding; decisive, definitive, definite, settled, determinate, ultimate.
OPPOSITE provisional.
▶ noun *the FA Cup final* **decider**, final game/match.
OPPOSITE qualifier.

finale ▶ noun *the work ends with an elaborate finale* **climax**, culmination; end, ending, finish, close, conclusion, termination, resolution; denouement, last act, final scene, final curtain, epilogue, coda, peroration; *informal* wind-up.
OPPOSITE beginning.

finality ▶ noun *'No,' she said with finality* **conclusiveness**, decisiveness, decision, definiteness, definitiveness, absoluteness, completeness; irrevocability, irrefutability, incontrovertibility, unalterableness; certainty, certitude, sureness, fixedness.
OPPOSITE indecision.

finalize ▶ verb *the two countries had yet to finalize a peace treaty* **conclude**, complete, bring to a conclusion, clinch, settle, establish, work out, resolve, decide, secure, tie up, wrap up, put the finishing touches to, set the seal on, seal, confirm; negotiate, broker, reach (an) agreement on, agree on, come to terms on, reach terms on, shake hands on; *informal* sew up, wind up, polish off, put the icing on the cake, thrash out, hammer out.

finally ▶ adverb **1** *she finally got her man to the altar* **eventually**, ultimately, in the end, by and by, at length, after a long time, after some time; at last, at long last, in the long run, when all was said and done, in the

fullness of time; *Brit. informal* at the end of the day.
OPPOSITE immediately.
2 *finally, wrap the ribbon round the edge of the board* **lastly**, last, in conclusion, to conclude, in closing, to end, last but not least.
OPPOSITES firstly, initially.
3 *this should finally dispel the belief that the auditors are clients of the company* **conclusively**, irrevocably, decisively, definitively, definitely, absolutely, for ever, for good, for all time, once and for all, permanently.
OPPOSITE temporarily.

finance ▶ noun **1** *the job taught him a great deal about finance* **financial affairs, money matters**, pecuniary matters, fiscal matters, economics, money management, commerce, business, investment, banking, accounting.
2 *companies seeking short-term finance* **funds**, assets, money, capital, resources, cash, wealth, reserves, wherewithal, revenue, income, stock; funding, backing, subsidy, sponsorship; (**finances**) financial condition/state, cash flow, budget.
▶ verb *the project was financed by grants* **fund**, pay for, back, capitalize, provide capital/security for, endow, subsidize, invest in; underwrite, guarantee, furnish credit for, sponsor, act as guarantor of, support; *informal* foot the bill for, pick up the tab for; *N. Amer.* bankroll.

WORD LINKS
relating to finance **fiscal**

financial ▶ adjective *a major financial institution* **monetary**, money, economic, pecuniary, banking, commercial, business, investment, accounting, fiscal, budgetary.

financier ▶ noun *a corporate financier* **investor**, speculator, banker, capitalist, industrialist, tycoon, magnate, business person, businessman, businesswoman, stockbroker; *informal* money man.

find ▶ verb **1** *I went to the library and found a book called 'Christian Words'* **locate**, spot, pinpoint, unearth, obtain, detect, put one's finger on; search out, nose out, track down, dig up, hunt out, root out, sniff out, smell out; **come across**, chance on, light on, happen on, stumble on, hit on, encounter, run across, run into, come upon; *informal* bump into; *literary* espy, descry.
2 *he claims to have found a cure for rabies* **discover**, think of, invent, come up with, hit on, turn up, bring to light, uncover, unearth, ferret out.
3 *the police found her purse* **retrieve**, recover, get back, regain, repossess, recoup, recuperate, reclaim.
OPPOSITE lose.
4 *I hope you find peace* **obtain**, acquire, get, procure, come by, secure, gain, earn, achieve, attain, lay hold of, come to have, win; *informal* bag, wangle, swing, land, get one's hands/mitts on, get hold of.
5 *I found the courage to speak* **summon (up)**, gather, muster (up), screw up, command, call up, rally.
6 (**be found**) *caffeine is found in coffee and tea* **be present**, occur, exist, be met with, be existent, appear, show itself, manifest itself, be; *rare* obtain.
7 *you'll find that many lively towns are but a short drive away* **discover**, become aware, realize, observe, notice, note, perceive, learn, detect.
8 *I respect their decision, but I find it strange* **consider**, think, believe to be, hold to be, feel to be, look on as, view as, see as, take to be, take for, judge, deem, gauge, rate, regard as, reckon, suppose, account, interpret as, esteem.
9 *he was found guilty of driving without due care and attention* **judge**, adjudge, adjudicate, deem, rule, hold, consider, count, rate, reckon, see as; declare, determine, pronounce.
10 *she knew the barb had found its mark* **arrive at**, reach, attain, gain, achieve, hit, strike.
□ **find something out** *I found out that my husband was having an affair | he found out the truth* **discover**, become aware, learn, detect, discern, perceive, observe, notice, note, get/come to know, work out, deduce, fathom out, realize; bring to light, reveal, expose, unearth, disclose, lay bare, unmask, ferret out, dig out/up; establish, determine, make certain of, pin down, grasp; *informal* figure out, get a fix on, latch on to, cotton on to, catch on to, tumble to, rumble, get the picture, get the message, get the drift, get wise; *Brit. informal* twig, suss; *N. Amer. informal* savvy; *rare* cognize.
▶ noun **1** *this exciting find dates from the second century* **discovery**, acquisition, asset; unearthing, uncovering.
2 *this table is a real find for anyone who's short of space* **good buy**, bargain; godsend, boon, windfall.

finding ▶ noun **1** *the finding of the leak* **discovery**, location, locating, detection, detecting, uncovering, unearthing.
2 (often **findings**) *he appealed against the tribunal's findings* **conclusion**, result; **decision**, verdict, pronouncement, judgement, ruling, rule, decree, order, recommendation, resolution; *Law* determination; *N. Amer.* resolve.

fine[1] ▶ adjective **1** *fine wines | a fine collection of furniture* **excellent**, first-class, first-rate, great, exceptional, outstanding, admirable, quality, superior, splendid, magnificent, beautiful, exquisite, choice, select, prime, supreme, superb, wonderful, sublime, superlative, very good, of high quality, of a high standard, second to none, top, rare; *informal* A1, top-notch, top-hole, splendiferous; *N. Amer. informal* dandy.
OPPOSITE poor.
2 *he proposed marriage to a fine lady* **worthy**, admirable, praiseworthy, laudable, estimable, upright, upstanding, respectable, seemly, ladylike, gentlemanly; attractive, good-looking, handsome, lovely, pretty, striking, stunning, delightful, well favoured; *Scottish & N. English* bonny; *archaic* comely, fair.
3 *the advertising initiative is fine, but it's not enough on its own* **all right**, acceptable, suitable, good, good enough, agreeable, fair, passable, satisfactory, adequate, reasonable, up to scratch, up to the mark, up to standard, up to par, average, tolerable; *informal* OK, tickety-boo.
OPPOSITE unsatisfactory.
4 *I feel fine* **in good health**, well, healthy, all right, fit, fighting fit, as fit as a fiddle, as fit as a flea, robust, strong, vigorous, blooming, thriving, in good shape, in good condition, in fine fettle; *informal* OK, in the pink, up to snuff.
OPPOSITE ill.
5 *it was a fine day* **fair**, dry, bright, clear, sunny, sunshiny, cloudless, unclouded, without a cloud in the sky, warm, balmy, summery, clement, agreeable, pleasant, nice, benign.
OPPOSITE inclement.
6 *a fine old eighteenth-century house* **impressive**, imposing, dignified, striking, splendid, grand, majestic, magnificent, august, lofty, stately.
7 *she went out to show off her fine clothes* **elegant**, stylish, graceful, expensive, smart, chic, fashionable, modish, high fashion; fancy, luxurious, sumptuous, lavish, opulent, grand, plush, exquisite; *informal* flashy, flash, snazzy, snappy, swanky, ritzy, sharp.
8 *he has a fine mind* **keen**, **quick**, alert, acute, sharp, bright, brilliant, astute, clever, intelligent, perspicacious, finely honed, penetrating.
OPPOSITE slow.
9 *a fine china tea service* **delicate**, fragile, frail, breakable, dainty, insubstantial; *formal* frangible.
OPPOSITE coarse.
10 *her fine golden hair* **thin**, light, delicate, wispy, floaty, flyaway, feathery.
OPPOSITE thick.
11 *she sharpened her pencil to a fine point* **sharp**, keen, acute, sharpened, honed, razor-sharp, razor-like, whetted; narrow, slender, slim, thin.
OPPOSITES blunt, thick.
12 *the fine material of her nightdress* **sheer**, light, lightweight, thin, flimsy, ultra-fine, insubstantial; diaphanous, filmy, chiffony, gossamer, gossamery, wispy, silky, gauzelike, gauzy, cobwebby, shimmering, transparent, translucent, see-through, airy, ethereal.
OPPOSITES coarse, thick.
13 *a fine gold chain* **pure**, sterling, solid, refined, unadulterated, unalloyed, unmixed, unblended, unpolluted, uncontaminated, one hundred per cent, flawless, perfect.
OPPOSITES plated, alloyed.
14 *a beach of fine sand* **fine-grained**, powdery, dusty, chalky, floury, powdered, ground, granulated, crushed, pulverized; *technical* comminuted, triturated; *archaic* pulverulent, levigated.
OPPOSITE coarse.
15 *for fine detailed work you could use a smaller brush* **intricate**, delicate, detailed, minute, elaborate, ornate, dainty, meticulous, painstaking.
16 *there is a fine distinction between the two* **subtle**, fine-drawn, ultra-fine, precise, minute, nice, narrow, tenuous; hair-splitting, elusive, abstruse, overnice.
17 *you have no respect for people's finer feelings* **elevated**, lofty, exalted, high, grand, sublime; **refined**, cultivated, cultured, civilized, distinguished, sophisticated.
OPPOSITE base.
18 *there's no better gift you could choose to show your fine taste* **discerning**, discriminating, tasteful, refined, sensitive, cultivated, cultured, fastidious, particular, critical, intelligent, stylish; *rare* discriminative.
OPPOSITE vulgar.
▶ adverb (*informal*) *you're doing fine* **well**, all right, not badly, satisfactorily, in a satisfactory manner/way, adequately, nicely, tolerably, suitably, aptly, appropriately; *informal* OK, good.
OPPOSITE badly.
▶ verb **1** *it can be fined right down to the required shape* **thin**, make/become thin, make/become thinner, narrow, taper, attenuate, constrict; *archaic* straiten.
2 (*technical*) *we don't use synthetic additives for fining our wine* **clarify**, clear, make/become clear, purify, refine, filter.

fine[2] ▶ noun *if convicted they face heavy fines* **financial penalty**, punishment, forfeit, forfeiture, sanction, punitive action, penalty, fee, charge, penance; (**fines**) damages; *formal* mulct; *Brit. historical* amercement.
▶ verb *they were fined for breaking environmental laws* **penalize**, punish by fining, impose a fine on, exact a penalty from, charge; *informal* sting; *formal* mulct; *Brit. historical* amerce.

finery ▶ noun *she was in all her bridal finery* **regalia**, elaborate/best clothes, garb, best, Sunday best; splendour, showiness, gaudiness, trumpery, frippery, adornment, trappings, decorations; *informal* glad rags, best gear, best bib and tucker, clobber; *formal* apparel; *rare* fallalery.
OPPOSITE rags.

F

F

finesse ▶ noun **1** *the comedy is performed with masterly finesse* **skill**, subtlety, expertise, flair, knack, panache, dash, flourish, elan, polish, adroitness, skilfulness, adeptness, artistry, art, artfulness, virtuosity, mastery, genius; *informal* know-how.
2 *these decisions call for a little delicacy and a modicum of finesse* **tact**, tactfulness, discretion, diplomacy, delicacy, sensitivity, discernment, perceptiveness, prudence, judgement, consideration; refinement, grace, elegance, sophistication, wisdom, worldly wisdom; *French* savoir faire.
3 *he won by a clever finesse* **winning move**, trick, stratagem, ruse, manoeuvre, scheme, artifice, machination, bluff, wile; *informal* dodge.
▶ verb *he could hardly finesse his way out of a serious downturn* **bluff**, manoeuvre, cheat, evade, trick, feign.

finger ▶ noun **1** *he wagged his finger at her* **digit**; thumb, index finger, forefinger, first finger, middle finger, ring finger, little finger; *N. Amer.* pinkie.
2 *a dark finger of land* **strip**, rectangle, sliver, streak, pencil.
▶ verb **1** *she fingered her brooch uneasily* **touch**, feel, handle, manipulate, stroke, rub, caress, fondle, toy with, play (about/around) with, fiddle with, twiddle with, maul, meddle with, manhandle, pull, grab; put one's hands on, lay a finger on; *informal* paw, mess.
2 (*N. Amer. informal*) *any seasoned thriller addict will immediately finger the culprit* **identify**, recognize, single out, pick out, spot, choose, select, point out; inform on, denounce; *informal* point the finger at, grass on, rat on, squeal on, tell tales about, tell on, blow the whistle on, spill the beans about, sell down the river, snitch on, peach.

WORD LINKS
relating to fingers **digital**

finicky ▶ adjective *these intellectuals with their fancy words and finicky manners* **fussy**, fastidious, punctilious, over-particular, hard to please, overcritical, difficult, awkward, exacting, demanding, perfectionist; *informal* picky, choosy, pernickety; *N. Amer. informal* persnickety; *archaic* nice.

finish ▶ verb **1** *Mrs Porter had just finished the task* **complete**, end, conclude, close, bring to a conclusion, bring to an end, bring to a close, consummate, finalize, bring to fruition; crown, cap, set the seal on, round off, put the finishing touches to; stop, cease, terminate; accomplish, execute, discharge, carry out, deal with, do, get done, fulfil; *informal* wind up, wrap up, sew up, polish off, knock off.
OPPOSITES start; leave unfinished.
2 *Sarah finished school last year* **leave**, abandon, give up, drop, dispense with, break off; stop, cease, discontinue, have done with, complete, suspend; *informal* pack in, leave off; *N. Amer.* quit.
OPPOSITES begin; continue.
3 *Hitch finished his dinner and got up* **consume**, eat, devour, drink, finish off, polish off, gulp (down), guzzle, quaff; use, use up, exhaust, empty, deplete, drain, expend, dispatch, dispose of, get through, go through, run through; *informal* down.
OPPOSITES start; leave unfinished.
4 *when the programme has finished it displays the 'Press any key' message* **end**, come to an end, stop, conclude, come to a conclusion/end/close, cease, terminate; *informal* wind up.
OPPOSITES start, begin.
5 *some items were finished in a black lacquer* **varnish**, lacquer, veneer, coat, stain, wax, shellac, enamel, put a finish on, glaze, give a shine to, gloss, polish, burnish, smooth off.
6 *she went to Switzerland to finish her education* **perfect**, polish, refine, put the final/finishing touches to, crown.
□ **finish someone/something off 1** *the executioners finished them off with bayonets* **kill**, cause the death of, take/end the life of, destroy, execute, annihilate, exterminate, liquidate, put an end to, do away with, dispose of, get rid of, eradicate, deliver the coup de grâce to; *informal* wipe out, do in, bump off, polish off, knock off, top, take out, croak, stiff, blow away; *N. Amer. informal* ice, off, rub out, waste, whack.
2 *financial difficulties finished off the business* **overpower**, overwhelm, overcome, defeat, get the better of, best, worst, rout, conquer, bring down; *informal* drive to the wall.
▶ noun **1** *a party to celebrate the finish of filming* **end**, ending, completion, conclusion, close, closing, cessation, finalization, termination; final part, final stage, final act, finale, denouement, last stages; accomplishment, execution, fulfilment, realization, achievement, consummation, resolution, fruition; *informal* winding up, wind-up, sewing up, polishing off.
OPPOSITES start; beginning.
2 *it was a real gallop to the finish* **finishing line**, finishing post, tape, end point.
3 *this furniture has a mellow antiquated paint finish* **veneer**, lacquer, lamination, coating, covering, coat; **surface**, texture, grain; glaze, lustre, gloss, polish, shine, patina.

finished ▶ adjective **1** *he looked approvingly at the finished job* **completed**, concluded, consummated, finalized, terminated, over and done with, over, in the past, at an end; accomplished, executed, discharged, done with, done, fulfilled, settled; achieved, attained, realized; *informal* wound up, wrapped up, sewn up, polished off, knocked off; *rare* effectuated.
OPPOSITES unfinished, incomplete.
2 *a finished performance* **accomplished**, polished, flawless, faultless, perfect; expert, proficient, masterly, impeccable, classic, virtuoso, consummate, skilful, skilled, dexterous, adroit, professional, talented, gifted, elegant, graceful.
OPPOSITE crude.
3 *he was old and almost finished* **ruined**, doomed, lost, bankrupt, wrecked, broken, defeated, beaten, thwarted; at an end, gone, gone to the wall, over with; *informal* washed up, over the hill, past it, played out, through.

finite ▶ adjective *there is a finite amount of water in the system* **limited**, not infinite, subject to limitations, restricted; definable, defined, determinate, fixed; bounded, terminable; delimited, demarcated.
OPPOSITE infinite.

fire ▶ noun **1** *a fire broke out in the kitchen* **blaze**, conflagration, inferno, holocaust, firestorm; flames, burning, combustion.
2 *he turned on the electric fire* **heater**, radiator, convector.
3 *he lacked fire and animation* **dynamism**, energy, vigour, animation, vitality, vibrancy, exuberance, ebullience, zest, elan; passion, ardour, impetuosity, intensity, zeal, spirit, life, liveliness, verve, vivacity, vivaciousness; sparkle, scintillation, dash; enthusiasm, eagerness, gusto; fervour, fervency, force, potency, vehemence; inspiration, imagination, creativity, inventiveness, flair; *informal* pep, vim, zing, go, get-up-and-go, oomph, pizzazz.
4 *rapid machine-gun fire* **gunfire**, firing, sniping, flak, bombardment; fusillade, volley, barrage, salvo, cannonade.
5 *journalists would be better off directing their fire at the prime minister* **criticism**, censure, condemnation, castigation, denunciation, opprobrium, admonishments, vituperation, scolding, chiding; disapproval, hostility, antagonism, animosity, ill will, enmity; *informal* flak, brickbats, knocks, raps.
□ **catch fire** *the driver got out before the car caught fire* **ignite**, catch light, burst into flames, go up in flames, begin to burn.
□ **on fire 1** *the restaurant was on fire* **burning**, ablaze, blazing, aflame, in flames, flaming, raging, fiery; alight, lit, lighted, ignited; *literary* afire.
2 *she was on fire with passion* **ardent**, passionate, fervent, intense, excited, aflutter; eager, enthusiastic.
▶ verb **1** *howitzers that fired shells in a high arc* **launch**, shoot, discharge, eject, hurl, throw, send flying, let fly with, loose off, shy, send; *N. Amer. informal* pop.
2 *someone fired a gun at me* **shoot**, discharge, let off, trigger, set off, blast; let fly with.
3 (*informal*) *he was fired for serious misconduct* **dismiss**, discharge, give someone their notice, make redundant, lay off, let go, throw out, get rid of, oust, depose; *Military* cashier; *informal* sack, give the sack to, axe, kick out, boot out, give someone the boot, give someone the bullet, give someone the (old) heave-ho, give someone the elbow, give someone the push, give someone their marching orders, show someone the door; *Brit. informal* give someone their cards.
4 *the engine fired and she put her foot down* **ignite**, start, catch, get started, get going.
5 (*archaic*) *I fired the straw* **light**, ignite, kindle, set fire to, set on fire, set alight, set ablaze, put a match to, touch off, spark off, incinerate; *informal* torch; *literary* enkindle, inflame.
OPPOSITE put out.
6 *she fired my imagination with her tales of warfare and terror* **stimulate**, stir up, excite, enliven, awaken, arouse, rouse, draw/call forth, bring out, engender, evoke, inflame, put/breathe life into, animate; inspire, motivate, quicken, incite, drive, impel, spur on, galvanize, electrify, trigger, impassion.
OPPOSITE deaden.

WORD LINKS
related prefix **pyro- (e.g. *pyroclastic*)**
fear of fire **pyrophobia**
obsession with fire **pyromania**

firearm *See centre pages for list of* **Guns**
▶ noun **gun**, weapon; *informal* shooter, cannon; *N. Amer. informal* heater, piece, gat, rod, roscoe, shooting iron.

WORD LINKS
seller of firearms **gunsmith**

firebrand ▶ noun *a political firebrand* **radical**, revolutionary; **troublemaker**, agitator, rabble-rouser, demagogue, soapbox orator, incendiary, subversive; *informal* tub-thumper.

fireproof ▶ adjective *he wore fireproof overalls* **non-flammable**, non-inflammable, incombustible, unburnable, fire resistant, flame resistant, flame retardant, heatproof.
OPPOSITES flammable, inflammable.

fireworks *See centre pages for list of* **Fireworks**
▶ plural noun **1** *many people watch fireworks at organized displays* **pyrotechnics**, explosions, illuminations; *French* feu d'artifice.
2 *there have been times when his stubbornness has produced some fireworks* **uproar**, trouble, mayhem, fuss; tantrums, hysterics, paroxysms; rage, fit,

outburst, frenzy, row.

firm[1] ▶ adjective **1** *the ground is fairly firm* **hard**, solid, unyielding, resistant; solidified, hardened; compacted, compressed, condensed, dense, close-grained; stiff, rigid, inflexible, inelastic; congealed, frozen, set, gelled; stony, steely; *literary* adamantine.
OPPOSITES soft, yielding.
2 *no building can stand without firm foundations* **secure**, secured, stable, steady, strong, sturdy, fixed, fast, set, taut, established, tight; immovable, irremovable, unshakeable; stationary, motionless; anchored, moored, rooted, embedded; riveted, braced, cemented, nailed, tied.
OPPOSITE unstable.
3 *a firm handshake* **strong**, vigorous, sturdy, robust, forceful.
OPPOSITE limp.
4 *I was very firm about what I wanted to do | he was a firm supporter of the National Democratic Party* **resolute**, determined, decided, resolved, steadfast; adamant, assertive, emphatic, insistent, single-minded, in earnest, whole-hearted; unfaltering, unwavering, unflinching, unswerving, unyielding, unbending, inflexible, obdurate, obstinate, stubborn, intransigent; implacable, relentless, unrelenting, hard-line, strict, unmalleable; strong-willed, dominant, domineering; committed, dyed-in-the-wool, through-and-through, seasoned, hardened.
OPPOSITE irresolute.
5 *she became a firm friend of the couple* **close**, good, boon, intimate, confidential, inseparable, dear, special, fast, valued, treasured, cherished; **constant**, enduring, abiding, devoted, loving, faithful, durable, reliable, deep-rooted, long-standing, long-lasting, steady, steadfast, stable, staunch.
OPPOSITE distant.
6 *she had no firm plans for the next day* **definite**, fixed, settled, decided, established, confirmed, agreed, exact, clear-cut, concrete, hard and fast; unalterable, unchangeable, irreversible, writ in stone.
OPPOSITE indefinite.

firm[2] ▶ noun *a law firm* **company**, business, concern, enterprise, venture, undertaking, house, establishment, organization, corporation, conglomerate, franchise, cooperative, office, bureau, service, agency, practice, partnership, consortium, syndicate; *informal* outfit, set-up, shop.

firmament ▶ noun **(the firmament)** (*literary*) **the sky**, heaven, the blue, the wide blue yonder, the azure, the heavens, the skies; *literary* the vault (of heaven), the celestial sphere, the empyrean, the welkin.

first ▶ adjective **1** *the first chapter of Genesis* **earliest**, initial, opening, introductory, original.
OPPOSITES last, closing.
2 *the management decided to start from first principles* **fundamental**, basic, rudimentary, primary, beginning, elemental, underlying, basal, foundation; key, cardinal, central, chief, vital, essential.
OPPOSITE developed.
3 *his first priority would be law and order* **foremost**, principal, highest, greatest, paramount, top, topmost, utmost, uppermost, prime, chief, leading, main, major; pre-eminent, overriding, outstanding, supreme, premier, predominant, prevailing, most important, of greatest importance, of prime importance; vital, key, essential, crucial, central, core, focal, pivotal, dominant; ruling, head; *informal* number-one.
OPPOSITE last.
4 *he is hoping to win the £3,000 first prize* **top**, best, prime, premier, superlative; winner's, winning, champion.
▶ adverb **1** *they went back to the room they had first entered* **at first**, to begin with, at the beginning/start, first of all, at the outset, initially.
2 *she would eat first, she decided* **before anything else**, first and foremost, firstly, in the first place; without further ado, now.
OPPOSITE last.
3 *she longed to go abroad, but not at this man's expense—she'd die first!* **in preference**, more willingly, sooner, rather.
▶ noun **1** *from the first, surrealism was theatrical* **the beginning**, the very beginning, the start, the outset, the commencement; *informal* the word go, square one, the off.
OPPOSITE the end.
2 (*informal*) *we travelled by air, a first for both of us* **novelty**, new experience, first experience, first occurrence, unusual event; *informal* a turn-up for the books.

WORD LINKS
related prefixes **proto- (e.g.** ***prototype, protohuman*****), ur- (e.g.** ***urtext*****)**

first-class ▶ adjective *a first-class hotel* **superior**, first-rate, high-quality, top-quality, top, quality, high-grade, five-star, fine; prime, premier, premium, grade A, best, finest, select, of the first water; exclusive, elite, special; excellent, exceptional, exemplary, superlative, superb; *French* par excellence; *informal* tip-top, A1, top-notch, plum.
OPPOSITE poor.

first-hand ▶ adjective *they have first-hand experience of bringing up children* **direct**, immediate, personal, unmediated, hands-on, experiential, empirical, from the original source.
OPPOSITES vicarious, indirect.
▶ adverb *an event she witnessed first-hand* **directly**, immediately, personally, at first hand, from the original source, with one's own eyes/ears.
OPPOSITES vicariously, indirectly.

first name ▶ noun *my first name's Gordon* **forename**, Christian name, given name, baptismal name.
OPPOSITE surname.

first-rate ▶ adjective *they have done a first-rate job* **top quality**, high quality, top grade, first class, second to none, top, five star, premier, premium, fine, grade A; superlative, excellent, superb, outstanding, exceptional, exemplary, marvellous, magnificent, admirable, very good, splendid; matchless, peerless, unparalleled; *informal* tip-top, top-notch, ace, A1, super, crack, great, terrific, tremendous, smashing, fantastic, sensational, fabulous, fab, out of this world, capital; *Brit. informal* brill, top-hole, wizard; *Brit. informal, dated* spiffing, topping.

fiscal ▶ adjective *the government's fiscal policies* **tax**, budgetary, revenue; financial, economic, monetary, money, pecuniary, capital.

fish *See centre pages for lists of* **Fish** **Fish Types** **Sharks**
▶ verb **1** *some people were fishing in the lake* **go fishing**, angle, cast, trawl.
2 *she opened her handbag and fished for her purse* **search**, delve, look, hunt, cast about/around/round; grope, ferret (about/around), root about/around, rummage (about/around/round), scrabble, fumble; seek, look high and low.
3 *I'm not fishing for compliments* **try to get**, seek to obtain, solicit; make a bid, angle, aim, cast about/around/round, hope, look; *informal* be after.
□ **fish something out** *they fished him out of the water* **pull out**, haul out, take out, bring out; remove, extricate, extract, retrieve; rescue from, save from.

WORD LINKS
related prefixes **ichthyo-, pisci-**
young **fry**
collective noun **school, run**
study of fish **ichthyology**
fish farming **pisciculture, mariculture**
fish-eating **piscivorous**
fear of fish **ichthyophobia**

fisherman ▶ noun **angler**; *informal* rod; *archaic* fisher; *rare* piscator, piscatorian.

fishing ▶ noun *they went to sea for a day's fishing* **angling**, trawling, catching fish.

WORD LINKS
relating to fishing **halieutic**

fishy ▶ adjective **1** *a fishy smell* **fishlike**, piscine, of fish.
2 *she had round fishy eyes* **expressionless**, inexpressive, vacant, deadpan; dull, lacklustre, wooden, glassy, glassy-eyed.
3 (*informal*) *there was something fishy about the whole set-up* **suspicious**, questionable, dubious, doubtful, suspect; odd, queer, peculiar, strange, not quite right; mysterious, murky, dark, shifty, disreputable, underhand; *informal* funny, shady, crooked, bent, not kosher, off; *Brit. informal* dodgy; *Austral./NZ informal* shonky.
OPPOSITES honest, open.

fission ▶ noun *the fission of uranium atoms* **splitting**, parting, division, dividing, cleaving, rupture, breaking, severance, separation, disjuncture; *technical* scission.
OPPOSITE fusion.

fissure ▶ noun *fissures in the ocean floor* **opening**, crevice, crack, cleft, cranny, chink, slit, groove, gap, hole, breach, aperture, vent, interstice; crevasse, chasm, ravine, crater; break, fracture, fault, rift, rupture, split, rent, gash; *technical* scission, grike.

fist ▶ noun **clenched hand**; *informal* duke, meat hook, paw, mitt; *Brit. informal* bunch of fives; *Scottish & N. English* nieve.

fit[1] ▶ adjective **1** *the house is fit for human habitation | he is a fit subject for such a book* **suitable**, good enough; relevant, pertinent, apt, appropriate, suited, apposite, apropos, -worthy; fitting, befitting, proper, due, seemly, decorous, decent, right, correct; *French* comme il faut; *archaic* meet.
OPPOSITES unfit, inappropriate.
2 *do you think you're fit to look after a child?* **competent**, **able**, capable; adequate, good enough, satisfactory, proficient; ready, prepared, qualified, trained, equipped, eligible, worthy; *informal* up to scratch.
OPPOSITES unfit, incapable.
3 (*informal*) *you look fit to commit murder!* **ready**, prepared, on the point of, set, all set, in a fit state, primed, disposed, likely, about; *informal* up for, geared up, psyched up.
4 *he looked tanned and fit* **healthy**, well, in good health; **in good shape**, in shape, in good trim, in trim, in good condition, in tip-top condition, in fine fettle, fighting fit, as fit as a fiddle, as fit as a flea, as strong as an ox; strong, robust, hale and hearty, sturdy, hardy, stalwart, lusty, vigorous, sound; athletic, muscular, strapping, tough, powerful, rugged; *informal* right as rain, husky.

OPPOSITES unfit, unwell.

▶ **verb 1** *my overcoat should fit you | a gown that did not fit* **be the right/correct size (for)**, be big/small enough (for), be the right shape (for); *informal* fit like a glove.
OPPOSITE be too big/small (for).
2 *it makes sense to have your carpet fitted professionally* **lay**, put in place/position, position, place, fix, insert; arrange, adjust, shape.
3 *some cameras are fitted with a backlight button* **equip**, provide, supply, fit out, rig out, furnish, outfit, endow.
4 *concrete slabs were fitted together | I could not see how to fit the various pieces of evidence together* **join**, connect, put together, piece together, attach, unite, link, splice, fuse, weld.
5 *a sentence that fits his crimes* **be appropriate to**, suit, correspond to; agree with, tally with, go with, be in agreement with, accord with, correlate to, be congruous with, be congruent with, concur with, dovetail with, conform to, be consonant with, match.
6 *an MSc fits the student for a professional career* **qualify**, prepare, make ready, make suitable, prime, condition, train, coach, groom, tailor.

F

□ **fit in** *he made the effort to fit in with the locals* **conform**, be in harmony, belong, blend in; accord, agree, concur, be in line; be assimilated into; match, square with; *informal* click.

□ **fit someone/something out/up** *the carriage was fitted out with everything they would need* **equip**, provide, supply, furnish, kit out, rig out, outfit, accoutre, array, stock.

□ **fit someone up** (*Brit. informal*) *the security forces are trying to fit me up* **falsely incriminate**, entrap, fabricate charges/evidence against; *informal* **frame**, set up.

▶ **noun** *the degree of fit between a school's philosophy and its classroom practice* **correlation**, correspondence, agreement, consistency, equivalence, match, similarity, resemblance, comparability, compatibility, affinity, concurrence.

fit² ▶ **noun 1** *an epileptic fit* **convulsion**, spasm, paroxysm, seizure, attack; (**fits**) throes; *Medicine* ictus.
2 *a fit of the giggles | she had a coughing fit* **outbreak**, outburst, burst, attack, bout, spell, eruption, explosion, flare-up, blow-up; *rare* access.
3 *my mother would have a fit if she heard that* **tantrum**, fit of temper, outburst of anger, outburst of rage, frenzy, fury; *informal* paddy, state, stress; *N. Amer. informal* blowout, hissy fit; *rare* ebullition, boutade.
4 *she went walking when the fit took her* **mood**, whim, fancy, impulse, caprice, urge, notion, whimsy; desire, wish, inclination, bent.

□ **in/by fits and starts** *he spoke in fits and starts* **spasmodically**, intermittently, sporadically, erratically, irregularly, interruptedly, fitfully, haphazardly, on and off, off and on, now and then, now and again.
OPPOSITES steadily, regularly.

fitful ▶ **adjective** *I drifted off into a brief and fitful sleep* **intermittent**, sporadic, spasmodic, broken, disturbed, disrupted, patchy, irregular; variable, uneven, unsettled, disconnected, unsteady, on and off, off and on; restless, sleepless, wakeful, insomniac, tossing and turning.
OPPOSITE constant.

fitfully ▶ **adverb** *I slept fitfully that night* **intermittently**, sporadically, spasmodically, irregularly, patchily, discontinuously, erratically, in/by fits and starts, in snatches; variably, unevenly, disconnectedly, unsteadily, on and off, off and on.

fitness ▶ **noun 1** *polo requires tremendous fitness* **health**, strength, robustness, sturdiness, hardiness, vigour, lustiness, stalwartness; athleticism, toughness, ruggedness, physical fitness, muscularity, tone; **good health**, good condition, good shape, well-being; state of health, condition, shape, trim, fettle; *informal* huskiness; *Brit. informal* nick.
OPPOSITE unfitness.
2 *he was called before medical boards to assess his fitness for active service* **suitability**, capability, competence, competency, proficiency, ability, aptitude; readiness, preparedness, qualification, eligibility, worthiness, appropriateness; adequacy.
OPPOSITES unfitness, unsuitability.

fitted ▶ **adjective 1** *a fitted sheet* **shaped**, contoured, fitting tightly/well; *N. Amer.* contour.
2 *a fitted wardrobe* **built-in**, integral, integrated, incorporated; fixed, permanent.
3 *I don't think he was fitted for the job* **suited**, well suited, right, suitable, ideal; equipped, fit, appropriate; *informal* cut out.
OPPOSITE unsuited.

fitting ▶ **noun 1** *the centre light fitting* **attachment**, connection, installation; part, piece, component, accessory.
2 (**fittings**) *a manufacturer of bathroom fittings* **furnishings**, furniture, units, fixtures, fitments, equipment, appointments, accoutrements, appurtenances.
3 *the fitting of catalytic converters to vehicles* **installation**, installing, putting in, fixing, placing, situating.

▶ **adjective** *his story provides a fitting conclusion for this book* **apt**, **appropriate**, suitable, apposite; fit, proper, due, right, seemly, correct, becoming; convenient, expedient, opportune, felicitous, timely; *French* comme il faut; *archaic* meet.
OPPOSITE unsuitable.

> **CHOOSE THE RIGHT WORD**
>
> **fitting, appropriate, suitable, proper**
>
> *See* APPROPRIATE.

five ▶ **cardinal number quintet**, quintuplets; *Poetry* pentameter, cinquain; *technical* pentad; *archaic* quintain; *rare* quintuple, fivesome.

WORD LINKS

related prefixes	**quin- (e.g. *quintuple*), quinque- (e.g. *quinquereme*), penta- (e.g. *pentameter*)**
relating to five	**quinary**
five-sided figure	**pentagon**
relating to five years	**quinquennial**
five-hundredth anniversary	**quincentenary**

fix ▶ **verb 1** *twenty-five signs were fixed to lamp posts* **fasten**, attach, affix, secure; make fast, join, connect, couple, link; install, implant, plant, embed, anchor; stick, glue, bond, cement; pin, nail, screw, bolt, clamp, clip; bind, tie, lash; establish, position, station, situate.
OPPOSITE remove.
2 *the words have remained fixed in my memory* **stick**, lodge, implant, embed, anchor.
3 *Ben nodded, his eyes fixed on the ground* **focus**, direct, level, point, rivet, train, turn; converge, zero in.
4 *modern television techniques of fixing human attention* **attract**, draw; **hold**, grip, engage, captivate, absorb, rivet.
OPPOSITE lose.
5 *he fixed my washing machine* **repair**, mend, patch up, put right, put to rights, set right, get working, make as good as new, see to; restore, restore to working order, remedy, rectify, put back together; overhaul, service, renovate, recondition, rehabilitate, rebuild, reconstruct, refit, adjust; *N. English* fettle.
OPPOSITES break, damage.
6 *James fixed it for his parents to watch the show from the wings* **arrange**, organize, contrive, sort out, see to, see about; manage, engineer, orchestrate, find a way; *informal* swing, wangle, pull strings.
7 (*informal*) *Laura was fixing her hair* **neaten**, arrange, put in order, adjust; style, groom, comb, brush, preen, primp, dress; *informal* do.
8 *Chris will fix supper* **prepare**, cook, make, make ready, put together, get; *informal* rustle up, knock up.
9 *the committee will fix a date for a special meeting* **decide on**, select, choose, resolve on; determine, arrive at, settle, set, finalize, arrange, prearrange, establish, allot, prescribe; designate, define, name, ordain, appoint, specify, stipulate.
10 *chemicals must be used to fix the dye* **make permanent**, make fast, set.
11 (*informal*) *the fight was fixed* **rig**, arrange fraudulently, prearrange/predetermine the result of; tamper with, manipulate, manoeuvre, twist, influence; *informal* fiddle, set up.
12 (*informal*) *don't tell anybody what I said, or I'll fix you!* **revenge oneself on**, get one's revenge on, be revenged on, avenge oneself on, wreak vengeance on, take retribution on, get even with, give someone their just deserts, hit back at, get back at, settle the/a score with, settle accounts with, take reprisals against, punish, deal with; *informal* get one's own back on, pay someone back/out, give someone their comeuppance, sort someone out, settle someone's hash, cook someone's goose.
13 (*informal*) *two junkies looking for a place where they could fix* **inject drugs**, take drugs; *informal* shoot up, mainline, get one's fix.
14 *the cat has been taken to the vet to be fixed* **castrate**, neuter, geld, cut, emasculate; **spay**; desex, sterilize; *N. Amer. & Austral.* alter; *informal* doctor; *rare* evirate, caponize, eunuchize.

□ **fix someone up** *we need to get Dolly fixed up with a job* **provide**, supply, furnish, accommodate, equip, endow.

□ **fix something up** *he fixed up a holiday in St Tropez* **organize**, arrange, make arrangements for, plan, fix, sort out, see to, put together, see about; mastermind, choreograph, orchestrate.

▶ **noun** (*informal*) **1** *they got themselves into a bit of a fix* **predicament**, plight, difficulty, difficult situation, awkward situation, spot of trouble, bit of bother, corner, ticklish/tricky situation, tight spot; muddle, mess, mare's nest; quandary, dilemma; dire straits; *informal* pickle, jam, hole, spot, scrape, bind, pinch, sticky situation, hot water, the soup.
2 *he needed his fix* **dose**; *informal* hit, rush.
3 *I don't believe that there is a quick fix for the coal industry* **solution**, answer, resolution, way out; remedy, antidote, cure, nostrum, panacea; *informal* magic bullet.
4 *the quiz was a complete fix* **fraud**, swindle, pretence, hoax, trick, charade, sham; *informal* set-up, scam, con trick, fiddle, sting.

fixated ▶ **adjective** *she has for some time been fixated on photography* **obsessed with**, preoccupied with/by, obsessive about, single-minded

about, possessed by, gripped by, in the grip of; engrossed in, immersed in, taken up with, wrapped up in; devoted to, dedicated to; enthusiastic about, fanatical about; infatuated with, besotted with; focused, keen, hell-bent; *informal* hung up on, hooked on, gone on, wild on, nuts about, potty about, dotty about, crazy about.
OPPOSITE uninterested.

fixation ▸ noun *the modern fixation on fitness* **obsession with**, preoccupation with, mania for; monomania, fetish, addiction, complex, neurosis, compulsion; *French* idée fixe; *informal* hang-up, thing, yen, rage, bug, craze, fad, bee in one's bonnet.

fixed ▸ adjective **1** *there are fixed ropes on the rock face* **fastened**, secure, fast, firm, stable; rooted, riveted, moored, anchored, permanent.
OPPOSITE temporary.
2 *a contract for a fixed period of time* **predetermined**, set, established, allotted, settled, prearranged, arranged, specified, decided, agreed, determined, confirmed, prescribed, decreed; definite, defined, explicit, express, precise, exact; not subject to change, inflexible, unalterable, unchangeable, irreversible, rigid, hard and fast, writ in stone.
OPPOSITE flexible.
3 *he stood watching with a fixed grin* **insincere**, false, fake, vacuous; **emotionless**, lifeless, motionless.
OPPOSITE sincere.

fixture ▸ noun **1** *the hotel retains many of the original fixtures and fittings* **fixed appliance**, attachment, installation, unit.
OPPOSITE movable.
2 (*Brit.*) *their first fixture of the season* **match**, **race**, game, competition, contest, meet, meeting, encounter, sporting event.

fizz ▸ verb **1** *the mixture fizzed like mad* **effervesce**, sparkle, bubble, froth, foam, seethe; *literary* roil, spume.
2 *all the screens were fizzing* **crackle**, sputter, buzz, hiss, fizzle, crack.
▸ noun **1** *this process puts the fizz in champagne* **effervescence**, sparkle, fizziness, bubbles, bubbliness, gassiness, carbonation, aeration; froth, foam, lather, suds, head.
2 (*informal*) *they all had another glass of fizz* **sparkling wine**, champagne; *informal* bubbly, champers, sparkler.
3 (*informal*) *their set is a little lacking in fizz* **ebullience**, exuberance, liveliness, life, vivacity, animation, vigour, brio, energy, verve, dash, spirit, sparkle, enthusiasm, buoyancy, jauntiness, zest; *informal* pizzazz, pep, zing, zip, go, get-up-and-go, oomph.
4 *the fizz of the static* **crackle**, crackling, buzz, buzzing, hiss, hissing, sizzle, sizzling, crack, sputter, white noise; *Brit. informal* zizz; *literary* bombination, susurration, susurrus; *rare* sibilation.

fizzle ▸ verb *the loudspeaker fizzled again* **crackle**, sputter, buzz, hiss, crack; *rare* sibilate, crepitate.
□ **fizzle out** *their romance will just fizzle out* **peter out**, die off, blow over, ease off, cool off, let up; tail off, taper off, trail away/off, wither away, grind to a halt; ebb, wane, wilt; come to nothing, fall through, come to grief; *informal* flop, fold; *archaic* remit.
OPPOSITE flourish.
▸ noun **1** *the electric fizzle of the waves* **hiss**, hissing, buzz, buzzing, crackle, crackling, sputter, sputtering, crack, cracking, white noise; *Brit. informal* zizz; *literary* bombination, susurration, susurrus; *rare* sibilation.
2 (*informal*) *we'll look ridiculous if the whole thing turns out to be a fizzle* **failure**, fiasco, debacle, catastrophe, disaster, blunder; *Brit.* damp squib; *informal* flop, washout, let-down, botch, hash, foul-up, screw-up, dead loss, dead duck, lead balloon, lemon; *Brit. informal* cock-up, pig's ear; *N. Amer. informal* snafu, clinker; *vulgar slang* fuck-up, balls-up.
OPPOSITE success.

fizzy ▸ adjective *a fizzy drink* **effervescent**, sparkling, carbonated, gassy, aerated, bubbly, bubbling, frothy, foaming; *French* mousseux, pétillant; *Italian* spumante, frizzante; *German* Schaum-, Perl-.
OPPOSITES still, flat.

flab ▸ noun (*informal*) *fight the flab with aerobic dance* **fat**, fatty tissue, excessive weight, fatness, plumpness, bulk, fleshiness, flesh; paunch, pot belly, beer belly, beer gut; *informal* beef.

flabbergast ▸ verb (*informal*) *we were flabbergasted when we found out* **astonish**, astound, amaze, surprise, startle, shock, take aback, take by surprise; dumbfound, strike dumb, render speechless, stun, stagger, stop someone in their tracks, take someone's breath away, confound, daze, overcome, overwhelm, nonplus, stupefy, disconcert, unsettle, bewilder; *informal* bowl over, knock for six, knock sideways, knock the stuffing out of, floor; *Brit. informal* gobsmack.

flabbiness ▸ noun (*informal*) *there was a little flabbiness in her lower belly* **fat**, fatness, fleshiness, plumpness, chubbiness, portliness, rotundity, meatiness, obesity, corpulence, bloatedness, grossness; **softness**, looseness, flaccidity, slack, laxity, droopiness, sag, limpness; *informal* flab, blubber, tubbiness, beefiness, porkiness.
OPPOSITES leanness; firmness.

flabby ▸ adjective **1** *his flabby stomach* **soft**, loose, flaccid, unfirm, yielding, slack, lax, out of tone, drooping, droopy, sagging, saggy, pendulous, limp.
OPPOSITES firm, taut.
2 *she was a flabby woman* **fat**, fleshy, overweight, plump, chubby, portly, rotund, meaty, broad in the beam, of ample proportions, obese, corpulent, bloated, gross; *informal* blubbery, out of shape, tubby, roly-poly, beefy, porky, well padded, well covered, well upholstered; *N. Amer. informal* lard-assed.
OPPOSITES thin, lean.

flaccid ▸ adjective **1** *your muscles are sagging, they're flaccid* **soft**, loose, flabby, unfirm, yielding, slack, lax, out of tone, toneless; drooping, droopy, sagging, saggy, pendulous, limp, floppy, wilting.
OPPOSITES firm, taut.
2 *his play seemed flaccid and lifeless* **lacklustre**, ineffective, ineffectual, lifeless, listless, muted, spiritless, lustreless, uninspiring, apathetic, unanimated, tame; worthless, futile, fruitless.
OPPOSITE spirited.

flag[1] ▸ noun *the Irish flag* **banner**, standard, ensign, pennant, pennon, banderole, streamer, jack; bunting; colours; symbol, emblem, representation, figure, image; *Brit.* pendant; *Nautical* burgee; (*in ancient Rome*) vexillum; *rare* gonfalon, guidon, labarum.
▸ verb *spelling checkers can flag words that are not in a dictionary* **indicate**, identify, pick out, point out; mark, mark out, label, tab, tag, tick.
□ **flag someone/something down** *she flagged down a police car* **hail**, wave down, signal to stop, gesture to stop, motion to stop, make a sign to; stop, halt, summon.

WORD LINKS
relating to flags **vexillary**
study of flags **vexillology**

flag[2] ▸ noun *the stone flags beneath his feet.* See FLAGSTONE.

flag[3] ▸ verb **1** *they were flagging as the finish came into sight* **tire**, become fatigued, grow tired/weary, weaken, grow weak, lose (one's) strength/energy, falter, languish, wilt, droop, sag.
OPPOSITE revive.
2 *one's mental energy flags in the afternoon* **fade**, fail, decline, deteriorate, wane, ebb, diminish, decrease, lessen, abate, dwindle, erode, recede, sink, slump, taper off; wither, melt away, peter out, die away, die down, die out, die off; *informal* go downhill.
OPPOSITE increase.

flagellate ▸ verb *he was constantly flagellating pupils* **flog**, whip, beat, scourge, lash, birch, switch, tan, strap, belt, cane, thrash, leather, flail, flay, welt, horsewhip, tan/whip someone's hide, give someone a hiding, strike, hit, spank; *informal* beat the living daylights out of.

flagellation ▸ noun *the use of flagellation for discipline and pleasure* **flogging**, whipping, beating, scourging, lashing, birching, switching, tanning, strapping, belting, caning, thrashing, flailing, flaying, welting, horsewhipping, spanking; sadomasochism (S & M, SM), algolagnia.

flagon ▸ noun *a flagon of mead* **jug**, vessel, container, bottle, carafe, flask, decanter, mug, tankard, ewer, pitcher, crock, demijohn; *dated* seidel.

flagrant ▸ adjective *a flagrant disregard for human rights* **blatant**, glaring, obvious, overt, evident, conspicuous; naked, barefaced, shameless, brazen, audacious, brass-necked; undisguised, unconcealed, patent, transparent, manifest, palpable; out and out, utter, complete; outrageous, scandalous, shocking, disgraceful, reprehensible, dreadful, terrible; gross, enormous, heinous, atrocious, monstrous, wicked, iniquitous, villainous; *archaic* arrant.
OPPOSITES unobtrusive; slight.

flagstone ▸ noun **paving slab**, paving stone, stone block, slab, flag, sett.

flail ▸ verb **1** *he fell headlong, his arms flailing* **wave**, swing, thrash about, flap about, beat about, windmill, move erratically.
2 *I was flailing about in the water* **flounder**, struggle, thrash, thresh, squirm, wriggle, writhe, twist, splash, stumble, blunder, fumble, wiggle, twitch.
3 *he flailed their shoulders with his cane* **thrash**, beat, strike, batter, drub, flog, whip, lash, scourge, flay, flagellate, strap, switch, tan, cane, tan/whip someone's hide, give someone a hiding, beat the living daylights out of, clout, welt, belabour; *informal* wallop, whack, lam, give someone a (good) hiding, larrup.

flair ▸ noun **1** *an activist with a flair for publicity* **aptitude**, talent, gift, knack, instinct, natural ability, ability, capability, capacity, faculty, facility, skill, bent, feel, genius.
OPPOSITE inability.
2 *she dressed with flair* **style**, stylishness, panache, verve, dash, elan, finesse, poise, elegance, sparkle, brio; inventiveness, creativity; taste, good taste, discernment, discrimination; *informal* class, pizzazz.

flak ▸ noun **1** *my aircraft had been damaged by flak* **anti-aircraft fire**, shelling, gunfire; bombardment, barrage, salvo, volley, cannonade, fusillade; *informal* ack-ack.
2 *he has come in for a lot of flak from the press* **criticism**, censure, disapproval, disapprobation, hostility, complaints; castigation, condemnation, denunciation; opprobrium, obloquy, calumny, calumniation, execration, excoriation, vilification, abuse, revilement, lambasting; *informal* brickbats, knocking, panning, slamming, tongue-lashing, a bad press; *Brit. informal* stick, verbal, slagging off.

F

flake[1] ▶ noun *flakes of pastry | soap flakes* **sliver**, wafer, shaving, paring, peeling; chip, shard, scale, crumb, grain, speck, spillikin; fragment, scrap, shred, bit, particle; *Scottish* skelf; *technical* spall, lamina.
▶ verb *the paint on the door was flaking* **peel off**, peel, chip, scale off, blister, come off, come off in layers; *technical* desquamate, exfoliate.

flake[2] ▶ verb
□ **flake out** (*informal*) *he flaked out on my bed* **fall asleep**, go to sleep, drop off; collapse, drop, keel over; faint, pass out, lose consciousness, black out; *informal* conk out, go out, go out like a light, nod off; *N. Amer. informal* sack out, zone out; *literary* swoon.

flaky ▶ adjective *the door was covered with flaky green paint* **flaking**, peeling, cracking, scaly, blistering; scabrous; *technical* desquamative, exfoliative, furfuraceous.

flamboyant ▶ adjective **1** *she was famed for her flamboyant personality* **ostentatious**, exuberant, confident, lively, buoyant, animated, energetic, vibrant, vivacious, extravagant, theatrical, showy, swashbuckling, dashing, rakish; *informal* over the top (OTT).
OPPOSITES modest, restrained.
2 *a flamboyant cravat* **colourful**, brilliantly coloured, brightly coloured, bright, rich, vibrant, vivid; exciting, dazzling, eye-catching, bold, splendid, resplendent, glamorous; showy, gaudy, garish, lurid, loud, flashy, brash, ostentatious; *informal* jazzy; *dated* gay.
OPPOSITES dull, restrained.
3 *a flamboyant architectural style* **elaborate**, ornate, fancy; baroque, rococo, arabesque.
OPPOSITE simple.

flame ▶ noun **1** *they could see flames shooting up into the air* glow, gleam, spark, brightness, brilliant light; (**flames**) fire, blaze, conflagration, inferno, holocaust, firestorm.
2 *the flames of her anger* **passion**, passionateness, warmth, ardour, fervour, fervency, fire, intensity, keenness; excitement, eagerness, enthusiasm.
3 (*informal*) *an old flame* **sweetheart**, boyfriend, girlfriend, lover, love, partner, beloved, beau, darling, escort, suitor; *Italian* inamorato, inamorata; *informal* steady.
□ **in flames** *two ships are in flames* **on fire**, burning, alight, flaming, blazing, raging, fiery, lit, lighted, ignited; *literary* afire.
OPPOSITE extinguished.
▶ verb **1** *logs crackled and flamed* **burn**, blaze, be ablaze, be alight, be on fire, be in flames, be aflame; burst into flame, catch fire.
2 *pour the whisky over the lobster and flame it* **ignite**, light, set light to, set fire to, set on fire, set alight, kindle, inflame, burn, touch off; *informal* set/put a match to.
OPPOSITE extinguish.
3 *the log flamed orange and pink behind the trees* **glow**, shine, flash, beam, glare, sparkle.
4 *Erica's cheeks flamed* **become red**, go red, blush, flush, redden, grow pink/crimson/scarlet, colour, glow, be suffused with colour.

flameproof ▶ adjective *flameproof gloves* **non-flammable**, non-inflammable, flame-resistant, fire-resistant, flame-retardant, incombustible, uninflammable, unburnable.
OPPOSITE flammable.

flaming ▶ adjective **1** *a flaming bonfire* **blazing**, ablaze, burning, on fire, afire, in flames, aflame; ignited, lit, lighted; fiery, red-hot, raging, flaring; glowing, flickering, smouldering.
OPPOSITE extinguished.
2 *she had green eyes and flaming hair* **bright**, brilliant, vivid, flamboyant; **red**, reddish-orange, scarlet, crimson, ginger.
OPPOSITE dull.
3 *we had a flaming row* **furious**, violent, vehement, frenzied, angry, incensed, passionate, raging.
OPPOSITE mild.
4 *a girl in a flaming temper* **furious**, enraged, fuming, seething, incensed, infuriated, mad, angry, raging, wrathful, irate; *informal* livid, wild; *Brit. informal, dated* waxy.
OPPOSITE placid.
5 (*informal*) *where's that flaming ambulance?* **wretched**, unspeakable, rotten, hellish, cursed, accursed; *informal* **damned**, damnable, blasted, blessed, precious, confounded, infernal; *Brit. informal* flipping, blinking, blooming, bleeding, effing, chuffing; *Brit. informal, dated* bally, ruddy, deuced.

flammable ▶ adjective *hazardous commodities such as flammable liquids* **inflammable**, burnable, combustible, incendiary, unstable; *rare* ignitable, deflagrable.
OPPOSITE non-flammable.

flank ▶ noun **1** *he touched the horse's flanks* **side**, haunch, loin, quarter, thigh.
2 *the southern flank of the Eighth Army* **side**, wing; face, aspect, facet.
▶ verb *the garden is flanked by two great rivers* **edge**, bound, line, border, fringe, skirt, be situated along; surround, circle, ring, circumscribe.

flannel ▶ noun **1** (*Brit.*) *she dabbed her face with a cold flannel* **facecloth**, cloth; *N. Amer.* washcloth, washrag; *Austral.* washer.
2 (*Brit. informal*) *don't accept any flannel from salespeople* **smooth talk**, flattery, blarney, blandishments, honeyed words; prevarication, hedging, equivocation, evasion, doubletalk, doublespeak; nonsense, rubbish; *informal* **spiel**, soft soap, sweet talk, buttering up, weasel words, baloney, rot, waffle, hot air, poppycock, tripe, bosh, bunk; *Irish informal* codology; *Austral./NZ informal* guyver, smoodging.
OPPOSITE straight-talking.
▶ verb (*Brit. informal*) *she can tell if you're flannelling* **use flattery**, talk blarney, flatter, pull the wool over someone's eyes; prevaricate, hedge, equivocate, be evasive, vacillate, blather, evade/dodge the issue, stall; *Brit.* hum and haw; *informal* waffle, shilly-shally, soft-soap, sweet-talk, butter someone up, pussyfoot around; *N. Amer. informal* fast-talk; *rare* tergiversate.

flap ▶ verb **1** *the mallards flapped their wings angrily* **beat**, flutter, move up and down, agitate, wave, wag, waggle, shake, swing, twitch; thresh, thrash, flail; vibrate, quiver, tremble, oscillate.
2 *his shirt tails flapped in the breeze* **flutter**, swing, sway, ripple, undulate, stir, shake, quiver, shiver, tremble, fly, blow.
3 (*informal*) *it was a deliberate ploy to make us flap* **panic**, go into a panic, become flustered, be agitated, fuss; *informal* press the panic button, be in a state, be in a tizzy, be in a dither, be in a twitter.
▶ noun **1** *large pockets with buttoned flaps* **fold**, overhang, overlap, covering; lappet, lap, tab.
2 *the surviving bird made a few final despairing flaps* **flutter**, fluttering, beat, beating, waving, shaking, flailing.
3 *I'm in a frightful flap about leaving* **panic**, fluster, state of panic/agitation; *informal* state, dither, twitter, blue funk, stew, tizz, tizzy, tiz-woz; *N. Amer. informal* twit.
4 (*informal*) *she created a flap when she came out with her controversial statement* **fuss**, agitation, commotion, stir, hubbub, excitement, tumult, ado, storm, uproar, flurry; controversy, to-do, palaver, brouhaha, furore; *informal* ballyhoo, hoopla, hoo-ha, song and dance; *Brit. informal* carry-on, kerfuffle.

flare ▶ noun **1** *the flare of the match lit up his face* **blaze**, flash, dazzle, glare, burst; unsteady flame, flicker, glimmer, shimmer, gleam.
2 *a helicopter spotted a flare set off by the crew* **distress signal**, **rocket**, Very light, beacon, light, flashlight, signal.
3 *Kelly felt a flare of anger within her* **burst**, rush, attack, eruption, explosion, bout, spasm; *rare* access.
4 *a skirt with a flare* gradual widening, outward spread.
▶ verb **1** *a match flared as he lit a cigarette* **blaze**, flash, flare up, flame, burn unsteadily, burn violently, burn up; gleam, glow, glisten, sparkle, glitter, flicker, glimmer, scintillate.
2 *her nostrils flared* **spread**, broaden, widen, get wider, expand, splay; dilate.
□ **flare up 1** *the wooden houses flared up like matchsticks.* **burn**, blaze, be ablaze, be alight, be on fire, be in flames, flame, be aflame; blaze up, burn up, go up, go up in flames; *literary* be afire; *archaic* be ardent.
2 *the injury flared up again at the end of the year* **recur**, reoccur, reappear; **break out**, burst out, start suddenly, burst forth, erupt.
3 *I flared up at him right off* **lose one's temper**, lose control, become enraged, go into a rage, fly into a temper/passion, boil over, boil over with rage, fire up, go berserk, throw a tantrum, explode; *informal* blow one's top, fly off the handle, lose one's cool, get mad, go crazy, go wild, go bananas, hit the roof, go through the roof, go up the wall, see red, go off the deep end, blow a fuse/gasket, lose one's rag, go ape, burst a blood vessel, flip, flip one's lid, foam at the mouth, get all steamed up, get worked up, have a fit; *Brit. informal* go spare, go crackers, do one's nut, get one's knickers in a twist, throw a wobbly; *N. Amer. informal* flip one's wig, blow one's lid/stack, have a cow, go postal, have a conniption fit; *vulgar slang* go apeshit.
OPPOSITES keep one's temper, remain calm.

flash ▶ verb **1** *a torch flashed* **light up**, shine, flare, blaze, glare, beam, gleam, glint, sparkle, spark, burn, fluoresce; **blink**, wink, flicker, shimmer, twinkle, glimmer, glisten, scintillate; *literary* glister, coruscate, fulgurate, effulge.
2 *the computer flashed the result on the scoreboard* **display**, show, present, set forth, unveil.
3 (*informal*) *he was flashing all this money about in the pub* **show off**, flaunt, flourish, display, exhibit, parade, brag about, exult in.
4 (*informal*) *he opened his coat and flashed at me* **expose oneself**, show/display/reveal one's genitals, commit indecent exposure.
5 *racing cars flashed past* **zoom**, streak, tear, shoot, dash, dart, fly, whistle, hurtle, rush, hurry, bolt, race, bound, speed, career, charge, hare, whizz, whoosh, buzz; *informal* scoot, skedaddle, belt, zap, zip, scorch; *Brit. informal* bomb, bucket, burn rubber, go like the clappers; *N. Amer. informal* barrel, lay rubber.
▶ noun **1** *a flash of light* **flare**, blaze, burst, glare, pulse, blast; gleam, glint, sparkle, flicker, shimmer, twinkle, glimmer; beam, shaft, ray, streak, bar, finger, stream.
2 *a basic uniform with no flashes* **emblem**, insignia, badge, marking; patch, bright patch, streak, stripe, bar, chevron.
3 *a sudden flash of inspiration* **burst**, outbreak, outburst, wave, rush, surge, stab, flush, blaze; sudden show, brief display/exhibition.
□ **in/like a flash** *it was all over in a flash* **instantly**, suddenly, abruptly,

immediately, instantaneously, all of a sudden; quickly, rapidly, swiftly, speedily, without delay; in an instant, in a moment, in a (split) second, in a minute, in a trice, like a shot, straight away, in a wink, in the blink of an eye, in the twinkling of an eye, in two shakes (of a lamb's tail), before you know it, on the double, at the speed of light, like an arrow from a bow; *informal* in a jiffy, before you can say Jack Robinson, double quick, in double quick time, p.d.q. (pretty damn quick), like (greased) lightning.
OPPOSITES eventually, slowly.
▶ adjective (*informal*) *a flash sports car.* See FLASHY.

flashy ▶ adjective *a flashy car* **ostentatious**, showy, bold, flamboyant, conspicuous, obtrusive, extravagant, expensive, pretentious; vulgar, tasteless, in bad/poor taste, tawdry, brash, lurid, garish, loud, gaudy, crude, trashy; *informal* snazzy, nifty, fancy, swanky, flash, jazzy, glitzy, ritzy, tacky, naff, kitsch, Brummagem; *N. Amer. informal* bling-bling.
OPPOSITES understated, tasteful.

flask ▶ noun *a flask of whisky* **bottle**, container, vessel; hip flask, vacuum flask; *trademark* Thermos.

flat[1] ▶ adjective **1** *a flat surface* **level**, horizontal, levelled; smooth, even, uniform, consistent, featureless, flush, plumb, regular, unvarying, continuous, unbroken, plane.
OPPOSITES vertical; bumpy.
2 *the sea was flat* **calm**, still, tranquil, pacific, undisturbed, without waves, like a millpond; glassy, motionless, waveless, unagitated; *literary* stilly.
OPPOSITE choppy.
3 *a flat wooden box* **shallow**, not deep, wide.
OPPOSITE deep.
4 *she put on some flat sandals* **low**, low-heeled, heelless, without heels.
OPPOSITE high-heeled.
5 *his voice was flat and without expression* **monotonous**, toneless, droning, boring, dull, tedious, uninteresting, unexciting, soporific; bland, vapid, vacant, insipid, prosaic, dreary, colourless, featureless, jejune; emotionless, unfeeling, unexcited, unexpressive, expressionless, lifeless, spiritless, lacklustre, dead; *informal* deadly.
OPPOSITES exciting; emotional.
6 *he felt flat, used-up, weary* **depressed**, dejected, dispirited, despondent, downhearted, disheartened, discouraged, low, low-spirited, down, gloomy, glum, unhappy, blue, desolate, weighed down, oppressed; without energy, enervated, sapped, weary, tired out, worn out, exhausted, devitalized, drained; *informal* down in the mouth, down in the dumps.
OPPOSITES cheerful, full of beans.
7 *the market was flat* **slow**, inactive, sluggish, slow-moving, slack, quiet, not busy, depressed, stagnant, static, dead, unproductive.
OPPOSITE busy.
8 *flat champagne* **still**, dead, no longer effervescent.
OPPOSITE sparkling.
9 (*Brit.*) *a flat battery* **expired**, dead, finished, used up, run out; *informal* kaput, dud; *Brit. informal* duff.
OPPOSITES fresh; working.
10 *a flat tyre* **deflated**, punctured, burst, collapsed, blown out, ruptured, pierced, empty of air, decompressed, depressurized.
OPPOSITE inflated.
11 *I charge a flat £30 fee* **fixed**, set, regular, established, unchanging, unvarying, invariable, unfluctuating, consistent, constant, uniform, straight, hard and fast.
12 *a flat denial of any impropriety* **outright**, direct, point blank, out and out, downright, absolute, definite, positive, straight, stark, all out; plain, explicit; firm, resolute, adamant, assertive, emphatic, insistent, final, conclusive; complete, utter, categorical, unconditional, sheer, thorough, thoroughgoing; unqualified, unmodified, unequivocal, unquestionable, unrestricted, unmitigated.
▶ adverb **1** *I lay down flat on the floor* **stretched out**, outstretched, spreadeagled, prone, reclining, sprawling, supine, prostrate, recumbent; on one's back, on one's stomach/front, (flat) on one's face; *rare* procumbent.
2 (*informal*) *I thought you'd turn me down flat* **outright**, directly, absolutely; plainly, explicitly; firmly, resolutely, adamantly, assertively, emphatically, insistently, finally, conclusively; completely, utterly, categorically, unconditionally, thoroughly, definitely; unequivocally, unquestionably.
□ **flat out** *I'd been working flat out* **hard**, as hard as possible, for all one's worth, vigorously, with a vengeance, to the utmost, to the full, to the limit, all out; **at full speed**, as fast as possible, post-haste, at full tilt, at breakneck speed, full steam ahead; *informal* hell for leather, hammer and tongs, like crazy, like mad, like a bat out of hell, at a lick, like the wind, like a bomb, like greased lightning; *Brit. informal* like billy-o, like the clappers, at a rate of knots.
OPPOSITE moderately.

flat[2] ▶ noun *a two-bedroom flat* **apartment**, set of rooms, penthouse, home, residence, accommodation; rooms, living quarters, quarters; *Austral.* home unit; *informal* pad, digs; *N. Amer. informal* crib.

flatten ▶ verb **1** *Tom flattened the crumpled paper | my stomach has flattened* **make/become flat**, make/become even, make/become smooth, smooth (out/off), level (out/off), even out; iron, steamroller.
OPPOSITES roughen, make uneven.
2 *he had trampled around and flattened the grass* **compress**, press down, crush, squash, compact; trample, tread, tramp, wear.
3 *tornadoes can flatten buildings in seconds* **demolish**, raze, raze to the ground, level, tear down, knock down, destroy, wipe out, topple, wreck, reduce to ruins, devastate, annihilate, pulverize, obliterate, ravage, smash, wipe off the face of the earth, wipe off the map; *N. Amer. informal* total; *rare* unbuild.
4 (*informal*) *Flynn flattened him with a single punch* **knock down**, knock over, knock to the ground, knock off one's feet, fell, topple, prostrate; *informal* lay out, floor, deck, knock for six, knock into the middle of next week.
5 *I flattened a drunken heckler with a couple of speedy put-downs* **humiliate**, **crush**, quash, squash, deflate, subdue, humble, cow, chasten, bring down/low, take down a peg or two, mortify; *informal* put down, floor, cut down to size, put someone in their place, settle someone's hash.

flatter ▶ verb **1** *it amused him to flirt with her and flatter her* **compliment**, praise, commend, admire, express admiration for, pay tribute to, say nice things about; pay court to, pay blandishments to, fawn on, wax lyrical about, make much of; cajole, humour, flannel, blarney; *informal* sweet-talk, soft-soap, butter up, lay it on thick, lay it on with a trowel, play up to, suck up to, crawl to, creep to, be all over, fall all over; *archaic* blandish; *rare* laud, panegyrize.
OPPOSITE insult.
2 *I was flattered to be asked to join them* **honour**, gratify, please, give pleasure to, make someone pleased/glad, delight, gladden; *informal* tickle pink.
OPPOSITE offend.
3 *a hairstyle that flattered her small features* **suit**, become, set off, show to advantage, enhance, look good on, look right on, be appropriate to, go well with, embellish, ornament, grace, befit; *informal* do something for.
OPPOSITE clash with.

F

flatterer ▶ noun *the prince is surrounded by flatterers* **sycophant**, groveller, fawner, lackey, obsequious person, kowtower, time server; *informal* crawler, creep, toady, bootlicker, yes man, lickspittle, doormat, truckler; *N. Amer. informal* suck-up, brown-nose; *Brit. vulgar slang* arse-licker, arse-kisser; *formal* encomiast; *archaic* toad-eater.
OPPOSITE critic.

flattering ▶ adjective **1** *these are very flattering remarks* **complimentary**, praising, favourable, commending, admiring, applauding, appreciative; honeyed, sugary, cajoling, flannelling, blarneying, silver-tongued, honey-tongued; fawning, obsequious, ingratiating, servile, sycophantic, unctuous, oleaginous, oily; *informal* sweet-talking, soft-soaping, crawling, creeping, bootlicking, smarmy; *rare* encomiastic, encomiastical.
OPPOSITES unflattering, insulting.
2 *Mr Crosbie said it was very flattering to be nominated* **pleasing**, gratifying, honouring, gladdening.
OPPOSITE offensive.
3 *she had worn her most flattering dress* **becoming**, enhancing, appropriate, embellishing, ornamenting, gracing, befitting.
OPPOSITES unflattering, unbecoming.

flattery ▶ noun *the old man sounded mollified by the flattery* **praise**, adulation, compliments, blandishments, admiration, honeyed words, pats on the back; fawning, simpering, puffery, blarney, cajolery, wheedling; *informal* sweet talk, soft soap, spiel, buttering up, cosying up, toadying, currying favour, weasel words; *Brit. informal* flannel; *Brit. vulgar slang* arse-kissing, arse-licking; *N. Amer. vulgar slang* brown-nosing, ass-kissing, ass-licking; *rare* laudation.
OPPOSITE criticism.

flatulence ▶ noun **1** *medications that help with flatulence* **intestinal gas**, wind, gas; *informal* farting; *formal* flatus, borborygmus.
2 *the flatulence of his latest recordings* **pomposity**, pompousness, pretension, pretentiousness, posing, posturing, grandiosity, grandness, grandiloquence, bombast, turgidity, hot air.

flaunt ▶ verb *he hated the way the rich flaunted their possessions* **show off**, display ostentatiously, draw attention to, make a (great) show of, put on show, put on display, parade, exhibit; flourish, brandish, wave, dangle; exult in, brag about, crow about, vaunt; *informal* flash.
OPPOSITES be modest about, hide.

flaunt or flout?

It is a common error to use **flaunt** as though it meant the same as **flout**. *Flaunt* means 'display ostentatiously', as in *tourists flaunting their wealth*. *Flout*, on the other hand, means 'defy or disobey (a rule)', as in *timber companies are continuing to flout environmental laws*. Saying that someone *flaunts the rules* is an error due to similarity in sound and to the element of ostentation involved in *flouting* a regulation.

flavour ▶ noun **1** *the slightly sweet flavour of prosciutto* **taste**, savour, tang, relish, palate; *rare* sapor.

2 *salami can give extra flavour to spaghetti sauces* **flavouring**, seasoning, tastiness, tang, tanginess, relish, bite, piquancy, pungency, savour, smack, spice, spiciness, sharpness, zest, raciness, edge, interest; *informal* zing, zip, punch.
OPPOSITE blandness.
3 *the tournament had a strong international flavour* **character**, quality, feel, feeling, ambience, atmosphere, aura, air, mood, aspect, tone, tenor, complexion, style, stamp, property; element, vein, strand, streak; spirit, essence, soul, nature, heart; *informal* vibe.
4 *this excerpt will give a flavour of the report* **impression**, indication, suggestion, hint, taste, nuance.
□ **flavour of the month** (*informal*) *he's flavour of the month in Tinseltown* **all the rage**, the latest thing, the fashion, the trend, in vogue, in (great) demand; a flash in the pan, a one-hit wonder; *informal* hot, in, cool; *Brit. informal, dated* all the go.
▶ **verb** *many cuisines use spices to flavour their foods* **add flavour to**, add flavouring to, season, spice (up), add seasoning/herbs/spices to, add piquancy to, ginger up, enrich, enliven, liven up; *informal* spike, pep up.

F

flavouring ▶ **noun 1** *this cheese is often combined with other cheeses or flavourings* **seasoning**, spice, herb, additive, added flavour; condiment, dressing, relish, sauce, dip.
2 *vanilla flavouring* **essence**, extract, tincture, concentrate, concentration, distillate.

flaw ▶ **noun** *the type of reactor used at Chernobyl had a design flaw | he had two small flaws in his character* **defect**, blemish, fault, imperfection, deficiency, weakness, weak spot/point, inadequacy, shortcoming, limitation, failing, foible; shortfall, insufficiency, lack, want, omission; snag, kink, deformity, taint, crack, fissure, break, tear, split, scratch, chip, fracture, spot; mistake, error; *Computing* bug, virus; *informal* glitch, gremlin.
OPPOSITE strength.

CHOOSE THE RIGHT WORD

flaw, blemish, imperfection
See BLEMISH.

flawed ▶ **adjective 1** *a flawed mirror blurred the Hubble telescope's vision* **faulty**, defective, imperfect, shoddy; broken, cracked, torn, scratched, deformed, distorted, warped, buckled; malfunctioning, inoperative, not working, not functioning, non-functioning, out of order, in disrepair, unsound; weak, deficient, incomplete; *informal* gone wrong, on the blink; *Brit. informal* duff, knackered.
OPPOSITE flawless.
2 *the Commission's findings were fundamentally flawed* **unsound**, defective, faulty, distorted, inaccurate, incorrect, erroneous, imprecise, fallacious, wrong; impaired, weak, invalid.
OPPOSITE sound.

flawless ▶ **adjective** *her smooth, flawless skin* **perfect**, without blemish, unblemished, unmarked, unimpaired; whole, intact, sound, unbroken, undamaged, as sound as a bell, mint, as good as new, pristine; stainless, spotless, pure, impeccable, immaculate, consummate, superb, superlative, masterly, accurate, correct, faultless, without fault, error-free, unerring; exemplary, model, ideal, copybook, just so; *Brit. informal* tip-top, A1.
OPPOSITE flawed.

flay ▶ **verb 1** *one shoulder had been flayed to reveal the muscles* **skin**, strip the skin off; *technical* excoriate.
2 *he flayed the government for not moving fast enough on economic reform* **criticize**, attack, berate, censure, condemn, denounce, denigrate, revile, castigate, pillory, belabour, lambaste, savage, tear/pull to pieces, find fault with, run down, abuse; *informal* knock, slam, pan, bash, take apart, crucify, hammer, lay into, roast, skewer, bad-mouth; *Brit. informal* slate, rubbish, slag off; *N. Amer. informal* pummel, cut up; *Austral./NZ informal* bag, monster; *rare* excoriate.

flea bite ▶ **noun** *the proposed energy tax amounted to little more than a flea bite* **very small sum**, pittance, trifle, trifling sum, drop in the ocean, insignificant sum, derisory sum, paltry sum; small change, pence; next to nothing, hardly anything; *informal* peanuts, chicken feed, piddling amount, shoestring; *N. Amer. informal* chump change; *S. African informal* tickey; *archaic* driblet.
OPPOSITE fortune.

fleck ▶ **noun** *a dusty grey colour interspersed with flecks of pale blue* **spot**, mark, patch, dot, speck, speckle, freckle, smudge, smear, streak, stain, blotch, blot, splash, dab, daub; *technical* petechia; *informal* splotch, splosh, splodge; *rare* macule, macula.
▶ **verb** *the deer's red flanks were flecked with white* **spot**, mark, stain, dot, speckle, bespeckle, freckle, stipple, stud, bestud, blotch, mottle, smudge, streak, splash, spatter, bespatter, scatter, sprinkle; dirty, soil; *informal* splotch, splosh, splodge; *Scottish & Irish informal* slabber; *literary* besmirch, smirch.

fledgling ▶ **noun** *the bird had been ringed as a fledgling* **chick**, baby bird, nestling.
▶ **adjective** *fledgling industries in the developing world* **emerging**, emergent, arising, sunrise, dawning, beginning; developing, in the making, budding, rising, burgeoning, growing, embryonic, infant, nascent, incipient; promising, potential, up-and-coming.
OPPOSITES declining; mature.

flee ▶ **verb 1** *she fled to her room and hid* **run**, run away, run off, make a run for it, run for it, take flight, be gone, make off, take off, take to one's heels, make a break for it, bolt, beat a (hasty) retreat, make a quick exit, make one's getaway, escape, absent oneself, make oneself scarce, abscond, head for the hills, do a disappearing act; *informal* beat it, clear off, clear out, vamoose, skedaddle, split, cut and run, leg it, show a clean pair of heels, turn tail, scram; *Brit. informal* do a runner, scarper, do a bunk; *N. Amer. informal* light out, bug out, cut out, peel out, take a powder, skidoo; *Austral. informal* go through, shoot through; *vulgar slang* bugger off; *archaic* fly.
2 *they fled the country* **run away from**, leave hastily/abruptly, fly, escape from; *informal* skip.

fleece ▶ **noun** *a sheep's fleece* **wool**, coat, hair, fur, pelt.
▶ **verb** (*informal*) *the traders are notorious for fleecing tourists* **swindle**, cheat, defraud, deceive, trick, dupe, hoodwink, double-cross, gull; short-change; exploit, take advantage of, victimize; *informal* do, diddle, rip off, con, bamboozle, rob, shaft, sting, have, bilk, rook, gyp, finagle, flimflam, put one over on, pull a fast one on, take for a ride, lead up the garden path, sell down the river, pull the wool over someone's eyes; *N. Amer. informal* sucker, snooker, goldbrick, gouge, stiff, give someone a bum steer; *Austral. informal* pull a swifty on; *Brit. informal, dated* rush; *archaic* cozen, chicane, sell; *rare* illude, mulct.

fleecy ▶ **adjective** *a fleecy tracksuit* **fluffy**, woolly, downy, fuzzy, feathery, furry, velvety, shaggy; soft, smooth, silky, silken, satiny, cushiony; *technical* floccose, lanate, pilose; *rare* lanose.
OPPOSITE coarse.

fleet[1] ▶ **noun** *the fleet set sail* **navy**, naval force, (naval) task force, armada, flotilla, squadron, convoy, column.

fleet[2] ▶ **adjective** (*literary*) *the horse was strong but fleet, built for speed* **nimble**, agile, deft, lithe, limber, lissom, acrobatic, supple, light-footed, nimble-footed, light, light of foot, light on one's feet, spry, sprightly, lively, active; quick, quick-moving, fast, fast-moving, swift, swift-footed, rapid, speedy, brisk, smart; *informal* nippy, zippy, twinkle-toed; *literary* fleet-footed, fleet of foot, lightsome.
OPPOSITE lumbering.

fleeting ▶ **adjective** *we only had a fleeting glimpse of the sun* **brief**, transient, short-lived, short, momentary, sudden, cursory, transitory, ephemeral, fugitive, evanescent, fading, vanishing, flying, fly-by-night, passing, flitting, here today and gone tomorrow, temporary, impermanent, short-term, rapid, quick, swift, rushed; *literary* fugacious.
OPPOSITE lasting.

CHOOSE THE RIGHT WORD

fleeting, transient, transitory, ephemeral
See TRANSIENT.

flesh ▶ **noun 1** *you're as thin as a rake—you need a sight more flesh on your bones* **muscle**, tissue, muscle tissue, meat, brawn; *informal* beef.
2 *the villagers used to eat turtle eggs and flesh* **meat**.
3 *Mrs Barnet carried too much flesh on her small frame* **fat**, weight, obesity, corpulence; *Anatomy* adipose tissue; *informal* blubber, flab.
4 *cut the melon in half and scoop out the flesh* **pulp**, soft part, fleshy part, marrow, meat.
5 (**the flesh**) *a fierce inner struggle against the pleasures of the flesh* **the body**, the human body, human nature, man's physical nature, physicality, corporeality, carnality, animality; sensuality, sensualism, sexuality.
□ **one's (own) flesh and blood** *the child was after all their own flesh and blood* **family**, relative(s), relation(s), blood relation(s), family member(s), kin, next of kin, kinsfolk, kinsman, kinsmen, kinswoman, kinswomen, kindred, connection(s); *informal* folks, nearest and dearest; *dated* people.
□ **in the flesh** *he seems just as charming in the flesh as on television* **in person**, before one's eyes, in front of one, before one's very eyes, in one's presence; in real life, in actual life, live; physically, bodily, in bodily/human form, incarnate.
OPPOSITE on screen.
□ **put flesh on the bones of** *Parliament will soon put flesh on the bones of the principle by drafting a law. See* FLESH SOMETHING OUT.
▶ **verb**
□ **flesh out** *the once lean physique had fleshed out* **put on weight**, gain weight, get heavier, grow fat/fatter, fatten up, get fat, fill out; thicken, widen, broaden, expand, spread out.
OPPOSITE slim.
□ **flesh something out** *the shadow chancellor tried to flesh out his party's economic philosophy* **expand (on)**, elaborate on, add to, build on, add flesh

to, put flesh on (the bones of), add detail to, expatiate on, supplement, reinforce, augment, extend, broaden, develop, fill out, enlarge on, embellish, embroider, enhance, amplify, refine, improve, polish, perfect.
OPPOSITE condense.

WORD LINKS
related prefixes **carn-** (e.g. *carnivore, carnosaur*), **sarc-** (e.g. *sarcoma, sarcophagus*)
flesh-eating **carnivorous**
fear of flesh **selaphobia**

fleshly ▸ adjective **1** *he urged the audience to abstain from fleshly lusts* **carnal**, sexual, sensual, erotic, lustful, lascivious, libidinous, lecherous, licentious, lewd, prurient, salacious, coarse, physical, animal, bestial, gross, lubricious, venereal.
OPPOSITES spiritual; noble.
2 *those film stars were fleshly analogues of the American cars of the time* **physical**, bodily, corporeal, corporal, mortal; material, concrete, earthly, worldly, mundane, of this world, real, actual, tangible, substantial; *rare* somatic.

fleshy ▸ adjective *Rufus had curiously sharp features for so fleshy a man* **plump**, chubby, portly, fat, fattish, obese, overweight, stout, corpulent, paunchy, beer-bellied, thickset, hefty, heavy, heavyset, burly, bulky, chunky, well padded, well covered, well upholstered, meaty, rotund, round, well rounded, of ample proportions, big, large; *informal* tubby, pudgy, beefy, porky, roly-poly, blubbery, poddy; *Brit. informal* podgy, fubsy; *N. Amer. informal* zaftig, corn-fed, lard-assed; *Austral./NZ* nuggety; *technical* pyknic; *rare* squabby, pursy, abdominous.
OPPOSITE thin.

flex[1] ▸ verb **1** *he would flex his knees and then spring up* **bend**, curve, crook, hook, cock, angle, kink, buckle, double up.
OPPOSITE straighten.
2 *Rachel stood up and flexed her cramped muscles* **tighten**, tauten, make taut, tense (up), tension, contract, stiffen, brace, knot.
OPPOSITE relax.

flex[2] ▸ noun (*Brit.*) *an electric flex* **cable**, wire, lead, extension; *N. Amer.* cord.

flexibility ▸ noun **1** *the boat's very short timbers are designed to give flexibility* **pliability**, suppleness, pliancy, malleability, mouldability, stretchability, workability, limberness, ductility, plasticity; elasticity, stretch, stretchiness, whippiness, springiness, spring, resilience, give, bounce, bounciness; *informal* bendiness; *rare* flexility, tensility.
OPPOSITE rigidity.
2 *he likes the flexibility of his endowment loan* **adaptability**, adjustability, open-endedness, openness, openness to change, changeability, freedom, latitude, mobility, variability, fluidity, versatility.
OPPOSITE inflexibility.
3 *the panel will normally show some flexibility over this deadline* **willingness to compromise**, accommodation, adaptability, amenability, cooperation, tolerance, forgivingness.
OPPOSITE intransigence.

flexible ▸ adjective **1** *the shoe is comfortable and flexible* **pliable**, supple, easily bent, bendable, pliant, malleable, mouldable, stretchable, workable, limber, ductile, tensile, plastic; **elastic**, whippy, springy, resilient; *informal* bendy; *rare* flexile.
OPPOSITE rigid.
2 *job sharing and other flexible arrangements* **adaptable**, adjustable, open-ended, open, open to change, changeable, variable, fluid, versatile.
OPPOSITE inflexible.
3 *they have accepted the need to be flexible towards tenants* **accommodating**, adaptable, amenable, biddable, willing to compromise, cooperative, tolerant, forgiving, long-suffering, easy-going.
OPPOSITE intransigent.

flick ▸ noun *a flick of the wrist* **jerk**, snap, flip, stroke, brush, sweep, swipe, whisk, dab, jab, click, touch.
▸ verb **1** *he flicked the switch on his intercom* **click**, snap, flip, jerk; pull, tug, tweak; *informal* yank.
2 *the horse flicked its tail* **swish**, twitch, wave, wag, waggle, shake, whip, twirl, swing, brandish.
□ **flick through** *Christina flicked through her diary* **thumb (through)**, leaf through, flip through, run through, skim through, scan, look through, riffle through, browse through, dip into, glance at/through, peruse, read quickly, have a quick look at, run one's eye over, give something a/the once-over.
OPPOSITE pore over.

flicker ▸ verb **1** *the gas lamp flickered in the wind* **glimmer**, glint, gleam, flare, shine, dance, gutter; **twinkle**, sparkle, blink, wink, flash, scintillate, glisten, shimmer, glitter; *literary* glister; *rare* coruscate, fulgurate, effulge.
OPPOSITE burn steadily.
2 *his eyelids flickered in his sleep* **flutter**, quiver, vibrate, tremble, wobble, shiver, shudder, spasm, jerk, twitch, bat, flap, wink, blink, open and shut; *technical* nictitate, nictate.

flight ▸ noun **1** *the machine was modelled on the flight of a bird* **flying**, soaring, gliding.
2 *the history of flight* **aviation**, flying, air transport, aerial navigation, aeronautics.
3 *did you have a good flight?* **plane trip**, trip by air, air trip, journey by air, air journey.
4 *Newton's theories allow us to predict the flight of a cricket ball* **trajectory**, track, flight path, orbit, glide path, approach.
5 *a noisy flight of birds went over* **flock**, flying group; skein, bevy, covey; swarm, cloud, knot, cluster.
6 *chroniclers recorded his flight from England after Cnut's death* **escape**, getaway, fleeing, running away, absconding, retreat, departure, hasty departure, exit, exodus, decamping, disappearance, vanishing.
7 *she ran up a **flight of stairs*** **staircase**, set of steps/stairs.
□ **put someone to flight** *the Scots were put to flight with heavy casualties* **chase away**, chase off, drive back/away, drive off, drive out, send away, scare off, scatter, scatter to the four winds, disperse, stampede, rout; *Brit.* see off; *informal* send packing.
□ **take flight** *many took flight at the air-raid warning* **flee**, run, run away, run off, make a run for it, run for it, be gone, make off, take off, take to one's heels, make a break for it, bolt, beat a (hasty) retreat, make a quick exit, make one's getaway, escape, absent oneself, make oneself scarce, abscond, head for the hills, do a disappearing act; *informal* beat it, clear off, clear out, vamoose, skedaddle, split, cut and run, leg it, show a clean pair of heels, turn tail, scram; *Brit. informal* do a runner, scarper, do a bunk; *N. Amer. informal* light out, bug out, cut out, peel out, take a powder, skidoo; *Austral. informal* go through, shoot through; *vulgar slang* bugger off; *archaic* fly.
OPPOSITE remain.

flighty ▸ adjective *you may be seen as too flighty for such responsibility* **fickle**, erratic, changeable, inconstant, irresolute, mercurial, skittish, whimsical, capricious, volatile, unsteady, unstable, unbalanced, impulsive; **irresponsible**, flippant, giddy, silly, frivolous, light-minded, feather-brained, scatterbrained, scatty, reckless, wild, careless, thoughtless, heedless, carefree, insouciant; *informal* dippy, dopey, batty, dotty, nutty; *N. Amer. informal* ditzy.
OPPOSITES steady; responsible.

flimsy ▸ adjective **1** *a succession of great waves had carried away all the flimsy wooden buildings* **insubstantial**, slight, light, fragile, breakable, frail, shaky, unstable, wobbly, tottery, rickety, ramshackle, makeshift; **jerry-built**, badly built, thrown together, cheap, shoddy, gimcrack.
OPPOSITE sturdy.
2 *the flimsy material of her dress* **thin**, light, lightweight, fine, ultra-fine, diaphanous, sheer, delicate, insubstantial, floaty, filmy, silken, chiffony, gossamer, gossamer-thin, gossamer-like, gossamery, gauzy, gauzelike, cobwebby, feathery; translucent, transparent, see-through; *rare* transpicuous, translucid.
OPPOSITE thick.
3 *this is very flimsy evidence on which to base any such assessment* **weak**, feeble, poor, inadequate, insufficient, thin, unsubstantial, unconvincing, implausible, unsatisfactory, paltry, trifling, trivial, shallow.
OPPOSITE sound.

flinch ▸ verb **1** *Curtis flinched as the passenger window imploded* **wince**, start, shy (away), recoil, shrink, pull back, back away, shy away, draw back, withdraw, blench, cringe, squirm, quiver, shudder, shiver, tremble, quake, shake, quail, cower, waver, falter, hesitate, get cold feet, blanch.
OPPOSITE stand firm.
2 *he has never **flinched from** the job in hand* **shrink**, recoil, shy away, turn away, swerve, hang back, demur; dodge, evade, avoid, duck, baulk at, jib at, quail at, fight shy of; *informal* boggle at.

fling ▸ verb *he flung the axe into the river* **throw**, toss, sling, hurl, cast, pitch, lob, bowl, launch, flip, shy, send, propel, project, aim, direct, catapult, fire, send flying, let fly with; *informal* chuck, heave, bung, buzz, whang; *N. Amer. informal* peg; *Austral. informal* hoy; *NZ informal* bish.
▸ noun **1** *it was his birthday, so he decided he was entitled to a fling* **good time**, binge, spree, bit of fun, bit of amusement, night on the town; fun and games, enjoyment, entertainment, recreation, revelry, skylarking, larks.
2 *Eva's husband left her when she had her fling with Androulis* **affair**, love affair, relationship, romance, flirtation, dalliance, liaison, entanglement, romantic entanglement, involvement, attachment, affair of the heart, intrigue; relations; *French* affaire, affaire de/du cœur, amour; *informal* hanky-panky; *Brit. informal* carry-on.

flip ▸ verb **1** *he saw a car **flip over** and land upside down | their upturned catamaran had been flipped by a huge wave* **overturn**, turn over, tip over, roll over, upturn, capsize, turn topsy-turvy; keel over, topple over, turn turtle; throw over, overthrow, upend, invert, knock over; *Nautical* pitchpole; *informal* roll; *archaic* overset.
2 *he flipped the key through the air to McGowan* **throw**, flick, toss, fling, sling, pitch, cast, spin, twist, hurl, shy, lob, propel, launch, project, send, dash, bowl; *informal* chuck, bung.
3 *I flipped the transmitter switch* **flick**, click, snap, jerk, pull, tug, tweak; *informal* yank.
□ **flip through** *he flipped through his address book* **thumb (through)**, leaf

through, flick through, run through, skim through, scan, look through, riffle through, browse through, dip into, glance at/through, peruse, read quickly, have a quick look at, run one's eye over, give something a/the once-over.
OPPOSITE pore over.

flippancy ▶ noun *as someone bereaved through the disease, I was upset by the flippancy with which you dealt with it* **frivolousness**, levity, superficiality, shallowness, glibness, thoughtlessness, carefreeness, irresponsibility, insouciance, offhandedness; **disrespect**, irreverence, facetiousness, cheek, cheekiness, pertness, overfamiliarity; *Brit. informal* sauciness; *N. Amer. informal* sassiness.
OPPOSITES seriousness; respect.

flippant ▶ adjective *a flippant remark* **frivolous**, superficial, shallow, glib, thoughtless, carefree, irresponsible, insouciant, offhand; **disrespectful**, irreverent, facetious, cheeky, pert, overfamiliar, impudent, impertinent; *informal* flip; *Brit. informal* saucy; *N. Amer. informal* sassy.
OPPOSITES serious; respectful.

F

flirt ▶ verb **1** *she's always flirting with the boys* **trifle with**, toy with, tease, lead on, philander with, dally with, make romantic advances to, court, woo, vamp; *informal* pull, chat up, make eyes at, make sheep's eyes at, give the come-on to, come on to, be all over; *dated* set one's cap at.
2 *those conservatives who flirted with fascism* **dabble in**, toy with, trifle with, amuse oneself with, play with, entertain the idea/possibility of, consider, give thought to, potter about/around/round with, tinker with, dip into, scratch the surface of.
3 *the Prince has always enjoyed flirting with danger* **dice with**, court, risk, not be afraid of, treat frivolously, make light of.
▶ noun *Anna was quite a flirt in those days* **tease**, trifler, philanderer, coquette, heartbreaker; *informal* puss, ladies' man; *vulgar slang* cock-teaser, prick-teaser; *archaic* fizgig, gallant.

flirtation ▶ noun *she always engaged in a bit of mild flirtation at parties* **coquetry**, teasing, trifling, toying, dalliance, philandering, romantic advances; *informal* chat-up, come-on.

flirtatious ▶ adjective *he observed Doreen's blatantly flirtatious manner towards the men* **coquettish**, flirty, provocative, seductive, inviting, amorous, kittenish, coy, arch, teasing, playful, frisky, flighty, skittish, dallying, philandering; *informal* come-hither, vampish.

flit ▶ verb *butterflies flitted among the tall grasses* **dart**, dance, skip, play, dash, trip, flick, skim, flutter, bob, bounce, spring, scoot, hop, gambol, caper, cavort, prance, frisk, scamper; *informal* beetle.

float ▶ verb **1** *oil floats on water* **stay afloat**, stay on the surface, be buoyant, be buoyed up.
OPPOSITE sink.
2 *the huge craft floated above the surface of the planet* **hover**, levitate, be suspended, hang, defy gravity.
3 *a dark cloud floated across the moon* **drift**, glide, sail, slip, slide, waft, flow, stream, move, travel, be carried.
OPPOSITE rush.
4 *the Chancellor floated the idea of offering dual citizenship* **suggest**, put forward, come up with, submit, raise, moot, propose, advance, offer, proffer, posit, present, table, test the popularity of; *informal* run something up the flagpole (to see who salutes).
OPPOSITE withdraw.
5 *the company was floated on the Stock Exchange* **launch**, get going, get off the ground, offer, sell, introduce, establish, set up, institute, promote.
OPPOSITES wind up; buy back.

floating ▶ adjective **1** *a floating piece of seaweed* **buoyant**, buoyed up, non-submerged, on the surface, above water, afloat, drifting.
OPPOSITE sunken.
2 *floating gas balloons* **hovering**, levitating, suspended, hanging, defying gravity.
OPPOSITE grounded.
3 *floating voters* **uncommitted**, undecided, in two minds, torn, split, uncertain, unsure, wavering, vacillating, indecisive, in a quandary, in a dilemma, in doubt; **non-partisan**, non-aligned, unaffiliated, unattached, neutral, impartial, independent, undeclared; *informal* iffy, blowing hot and cold, sitting on the fence.
OPPOSITE committed.
4 *a floating population* **unsettled**, not settled, not fixed, transient, temporary, variable, fluctuating; migrant, wandering, nomadic, moving, on the move, migratory, travelling, drifting, roving, roaming, itinerant, gypsy, vagrant, vagabond.
OPPOSITE settled.
5 *a floating currency exchange rate* **variable**, changeable, changing, fluid, fluctuating, free, not fixed; *informal* up and down.
OPPOSITE fixed.

flock ▶ noun **1** *a flock of sheep* **herd**, drove, fold.
2 *a flock of birds* **group**, flight, congregation.
3 (**flocks**) *flocks of people* **crowd**, throng, horde, mob, rabble, large number, mass, multitude, host, army, pack, swarm, sea, stream, troupe, press, crush, flood, collection, company, gathering, assembly, assemblage; *informal* gaggle; *Brit. informal* shower; *archaic* rout.
▶ verb **1** *people flocked around Jesus* **gather**, collect, congregate, assemble, come together, get together, converge, convene, rally, rendezvous, muster, meet, mass, amass, crowd, throng, cluster, herd, group, bunch, swarm, huddle, mill; *rare* foregather.
2 *collectors flocked to the tiny village* **stream**, go in large numbers, swarm, surge, seethe, spill, crowd, herd, troop.

flog ▶ verb **1** *the Romans used to flog their victims* **whip**, **scourge**, flagellate, lash, birch, switch, tan, strap, belt, cane, thrash, beat, leather, tan/whip someone's hide, give someone a hiding, beat the living daylights out of.
2 *they were flogging themselves to finish the project on schedule* **try one's hardest**, try as hard as one can, do one's best, do one's utmost, do all one can, give one's all, make every effort; strive, struggle, strain, drive, push, apply oneself, exert oneself, work hard, endeavour, try; *informal* do one's damnedest, bend over backwards, go all out, kill oneself, pull out all the stops, bust a gut, move heaven and earth, give it one's best shot; *Austral./NZ informal* go for the doctor.
3 (*Brit. informal*) *insurance brokers flogging life policies* **sell**, put on sale, put up for sale, offer for sale, vend, retail, trade in, deal in, traffic in, peddle, hawk, advertise; *informal* push.

flood ▶ noun **1** *several villages were cut off by the flood* **inundation**, swamping, deluge; torrent, overflow, flash flood, freshet; downpour, cloudburst; *Brit.* spate.
2 *she came home in a flood of tears* **outpouring**, torrent, rush, stream, gush, surge, cascade, flow.
3 *a flood of complaints* **succession**, series, string, chain; barrage, volley, battery; avalanche, torrent, stream, tide, spate, storm, shower, cascade, wave, rush, outpouring.
OPPOSITE trickle.
▶ verb **1** *the dam burst, flooding a small town* **inundate**, swamp, deluge, immerse, submerge, drown, engulf.
2 *the major river in the area has already flooded* **overflow**, burst its banks, brim over, run over; *rare* overbrim, disembogue.
3 *imports were allowed to flood the domestic market* **glut**, swamp, saturate, oversupply, overfill, overload, overwhelm.
4 *congratulatory messages flooded in* **pour**, stream, surge, swarm, pile, crowd, throng.
OPPOSITE trickle.

WORD LINKS
relating to floods **diluvial**
fear of floods **antlophobia**

floor ▶ noun **1** *he put the parcel down on the floor* ground, flooring.
2 *they live on the second floor* **storey**, level, tier, deck; piano nobile, mezzanine, entresol.
▶ verb **1** (*informal*) *he threw a punch which floored the other man* **knock down**, knock over, bring down, fell, prostrate; catch off balance; *informal* lay out.
2 *that question had always floored him* **baffle**, defeat, perplex, puzzle, nonplus, mystify, confound, bewilder, bemuse, dumbfound, confuse, discomfit, disconcert, throw; *informal* beat, flummox, discombobulate, faze, stump, fox, fog, make someone scratch their head, be all Greek to; *N. Amer. informal* buffalo; *archaic* wilder, gravel, maze, cause to be at a stand, pose; *rare* obfuscate.

flop ▶ verb **1** *he flopped into a chair* **collapse**, slump, crumple, subside, sink, drop, fall, tumble.
2 *his blonde hair flopped over his eyes* **hang (down)**, drop, hang loosely/limply, dangle, droop, sag, flap, loll.
3 (*informal*) *the play flopped* **be unsuccessful**, fail, not work, fall flat, founder, misfire, backfire, be a disappointment, do badly, lose money, be a disaster, meet with disaster, come to grief, miss the mark, run aground; *informal* bomb, bellyflop, fold, go to the wall, come a cropper, go down like a lead balloon, bite the dust, blow up in someone's face; *N. Amer. informal* tank.
OPPOSITE be successful.
▶ noun (*informal*) *the play was a flop* **failure**, disaster, debacle, catastrophe, loser; *Brit.* damp squib; *informal* flopperoo, washout, also-ran, bellyflop, dud, dog, lemon, lead balloon, no-hoper, no-go, non-starter; *N. Amer.* clinker.
OPPOSITE success.

floppy ▶ adjective *the bloodhound's floppy ears* **limp**, flaccid, slack, flabby, relaxed; drooping, droopy, sagging, saggy, hanging, dangling, pendulous; loose, flowing.
OPPOSITES erect; stiff.

floral ▶ adjective **1** *a floral arrangement* **flower**, (made) of flowers.
2 *a floral dress* **flower-patterned**, flower-pattern, flower-covered, flowery; *rare* florid.

florid ▶ adjective **1** *a florid complexion* **ruddy**, red, red-faced, reddish, rosy, rosy-cheeked, pink, pinkish, roseate, rubicund; healthy-looking, glowing, fresh; flushed, blushing, high-coloured, blowsy; *archaic* sanguine; *rare* erubescent, rubescent.
OPPOSITE pale.
2 *the florid plasterwork of the ceilings* **ornate**, fancy, very elaborate, over-elaborate, embellished, curlicued, extravagant, flamboyant, baroque, rococo, fussy, busy, ostentatious, showy, wedding-cake, gingerbread.

OPPOSITE plain.
3 *endearments in florid English* **flowery**, flamboyant, high-flown, high-sounding, magniloquent, grandiloquent, ornate, fancy, baroque, orotund, rhetorical, oratorical, bombastic, laboured, strained, overwrought, elaborate, over-elaborate, overblown, overdone, convoluted, turgid, inflated; *informal* highfalutin, purple; *rare* tumid, pleonastic, euphuistic, aureate, Ossianic, fustian, hyperventilated.
OPPOSITE plain.

flotsam ▶ **noun 1** *we were still finding interesting pieces of flotsam on the beach* **wreckage**, lost cargo, floating remains.
2 *the room was cleared of boxes and other flotsam* **rubbish**, debris, detritus, waste, waste matter, discarded matter, dross, refuse, remains, scrap, lumber, odds and ends; *N. Amer.* trash, garbage; *Austral./NZ* mullock; *informal* dreck, junk; *Brit. informal* grot, gash; *vulgar slang* shit, crap; *Archaeology* debitage; *rare* draff, raffle, raff, cultch, orts.

flounce[1] ▶ **verb** *she rose from the table in a fury and flounced out* **storm**, stride angrily, sweep, stomp, stamp, march, strut, stalk.
OPPOSITE slink.

flounce[2] ▶ **noun** *a black suit with a little white flounce at the neckline* **frill**, ruffle, ruff, peplum, jabot, furbelow, ruche, ruching, gather, tuck, fringe; *archaic* purfle.

flounder ▶ **verb 1** *the dragoons were floundering in the boggy ground* **struggle**, thrash, thresh, flail, toss and turn, twist and turn, pitch, splash, stagger, stumble, falter, lurch, blunder, fumble, grope, squirm, writhe.
OPPOSITE make good progress.
2 *you may find yourself floundering as you try to answer a question you have not really understood* **struggle mentally**, be out of one's depth, be in the dark, have difficulty, be confounded, be confused, be dumbfounded; *informal* scratch one's head, be flummoxed, be clueless, be foxed, be fazed, be floored, be beaten.
3 *more firms are floundering* **struggle financially**, be in dire straits, face financial ruin, be in difficulties, face bankruptcy/insolvency.
OPPOSITE prosper.

flourish ▶ **verb 1** *rainforests flourish because of the heat and the rain* **grow**, **thrive**, prosper, grow/do well, develop, burgeon, increase, multiply, proliferate; spring up, shoot up, bloom, blossom, bear fruit, burst forth, run riot; put on a spurt, boom, mushroom.
OPPOSITES die; wither.
2 *the arts flourished in this period* **thrive**, prosper, bloom, be in good shape, be in good health, be well, be strong, be vigorous, be in its heyday; **progress**, make progress, advance, make headway, develop, improve, become better, mature; evolve, make strides, move forward (in leaps and bounds), move ahead, get ahead, expand; *informal* be in the pink, go places, go great guns, get somewhere.
OPPOSITE decline.
3 *he flourished the sword at them in a mocking salute* **brandish**, wave, shake, wield, raise, hold aloft; swing, twirl, wag, swish, flap; display, exhibit, flaunt, vaunt, parade, show off.

CHOOSE THE RIGHT WORD

flourish, thrive, prosper

All three words denote a healthy or successful state.

- **Flourish** and **thrive** both mean 'grow healthily' or 'be successful, active, or widespread', and is used especially of plants, but also of people (either physically or emotionally), animals, businesses, activities, and abstract things such as ideas and movements (*only algae will thrive in such an environment | Macedonian religious and cultural life continued to flourish under the Byzantines*). Both are often found in their adjectival forms, *flourishing* and *thriving*, which predominantly have a financial sense (*he joined his father's thriving business*).
- **Thrive** is also used with *on* in a sense tending towards 'enjoy' (*the kind of plants that thrive on heat and dust | he is the kind of person who thrives on arguments*).
- **Prosper** is used of people and groups of people and refers mainly to material or financial success (*the company has grown and prospered*). Although the adjective *prosperous* is an everyday word, *to prosper* can have a slightly archaic ring.

flourishing ▶ **adjective** *a flourishing economy* **thriving**, prosperous, prospering, booming, burgeoning, successful, strong, vigorous, buoyant; productive, profitable, fruitful, lucrative; growing, developing, progressing, improving, expanding, mushrooming, snowballing, ballooning; *informal* going strong.
OPPOSITE moribund.

flout ▶ **verb** *retailers have been flouting the law by selling tobacco to under-16s* **defy**, refuse to obey, go against, rebel against, scorn, disdain, show contempt for, fly in the face of, thumb one's nose at, make a fool of, poke fun at; disobey, break, violate, fail to comply with, fail to observe, contravene, infringe, breach, commit a breach of, transgress against; ignore, disregard, set one's face against, kick against; *informal* cock a snook at; *Law* infract; *archaic* set at naught.
OPPOSITE observe.

flout or flaunt?
See FLAUNT.

flow ▶ **verb 1** *the water flowed down the channel she had dug* **run**, move, go along, course, pass, proceed, glide, slide, drift, circulate, trickle, dribble, drizzle, spill, gurgle, babble, ripple; stream, swirl, surge, sweep, gush, cascade, pour, roll, rush, whirl, well, spurt, spout, squirt, spew, jet; leak, seep, ooze, percolate, drip.
2 *many questions flow from today's announcement* **result**, proceed, arise, follow, ensue, derive, stem, accrue; originate, emanate, spring, emerge; be caused by, be brought about by, be produced by, originate in.
▶ **noun** *the pump produces a good flow of water* **movement**, motion, course, passage, current, flux, drift, circulation; **stream**, swirl, surge, sweep, gush, roll, rush, welling, spate, tide, spurt, squirt, jet, outpouring, outflow; trickle, leak, seepage, ooze, percolation, drip.

WORD LINKS
related prefix **rheo- (e.g. *rheostat, rheology*)**
related suffixes **-rrhoea (e.g. *diarrhoea, logorrhoea*), -rrhagia (e.g. *menorrhagia*)**

flower *See centre pages for lists of* **Flowering Plants and Shrubs** **Flower Parts**
▶ **noun 1** *the shrub produces blue flowers in early summer* **bloom**, blossom, floweret, floret.
2 *a man in the flower of his strength* **prime**, peak, pinnacle, zenith, acme, height, ascendancy, climax, culmination, crowning point, perfection, heyday, springtime, bloom, flowering, salad days.
3 *the flower of the nation's youth* **best**, finest, top, pick, choice, choicest, prime, cream, prize, treasure, pearl, gem, jewel, the jewel in the crown, the crème de la crème, first class, elite, elect; *informal* the tops.
OPPOSITE dregs.

WORD LINKS
relating to flowers **floral**
related prefixes **flor- (e.g. *floriated*), antho- (e.g. *anthophilous*)**
fear of flowers **anthophobia**
seller of flowers **florist**

flowery ▶ **adjective 1** *flowery patterns* **floral**, flower-covered, flower-patterned.
2 *his flowery language made no impression* **florid**, flamboyant, high-flown, high-sounding, magniloquent, grandiloquent, ornate, fancy, baroque, orotund, rhetorical, oratorical, bombastic, laboured, strained, overwrought, elaborate, over-elaborate, overblown, overdone, convoluted, turgid, inflated; *informal* highfalutin, purple; *rare* tumid, pleonastic, euphuistic, aureate, Ossianic, fustian, hyperventilated.
OPPOSITE plain.

flowing ▶ **adjective 1** *she pushed back her long flowing hair* **loose**, hanging loose/free, unconfined; limp, flaccid, floppy.
OPPOSITES stiff; curly.
2 *the new model will have soft, flowing lines and no hard edges* **sleek**, streamlined, trim, aerodynamic, smooth, clean, uncluttered, unfussy; elegant, graceful; *technical* faired.
OPPOSITE jagged.
3 *he writes in an easy, flowing style* **fluent**, fluid, free-flowing, effortless, easy, natural, smooth, unbroken, uninterrupted, continuous, graceful, elegant.
OPPOSITES stilted; halting.

fluctuate ▶ **verb 1** *the size of harvest fluctuates from year to year* **vary**, differ, shift, change, alter, waver, swing, oscillate, alternate, rise and fall, go up and down, see-saw, yo-yo, be unstable, be unsteady.
OPPOSITE be steady.
2 *she fluctuates between wanting to go and being afraid of going* **vacillate**, hesitate, waver, falter, veer, swing, sway, oscillate, alternate, teeter, totter, hover, see-saw, yo-yo, go from one extreme to the other, vary, change one's mind, be in two minds, be ambivalent, be indecisive, be unsure, be undecided; *Brit.* hum and haw, haver; *Scottish* swither; *informal* shilly-shally, dilly-dally, blow hot and cold, pussyfoot around, sit on the fence, wobble.

fluctuation ▶ **noun** *a natural fluctuation in the earth's temperature* **variation**, shift, change, alteration, swing, movement, oscillation, undulation, alternation, rise and fall, rising and falling, see-sawing, yo-yoing, instability, unsteadiness.
OPPOSITE stability.

flue ▶ **noun duct**, tube, passage, channel, canal, conduit, shaft, air passage, airway, vent, well; funnel, chimney, chimney stack, smokestack; pipe, pipeline, outlet, inlet.

fluency ▶ **noun 1** *a job that calls for verbal fluency* **eloquence**, articulacy,

articulateness, expressiveness, communicativeness, coherence, cogency, intelligibility, comprehensibility, lucidity, vividness, persuasiveness, glibness, volubility.
OPPOSITE inarticulacy.
2 *fluency in Japanese will be a major asset* **articulacy**, facility, ability to speak or write ... easily and accurately; command of.
3 *his walk had a feline kind of fluency to it* **fluidity**, flow, smoothness, effortlessness, ease, naturalness; grace, gracefulness, elegance; regularity, rhythm, rhythmicity; *rare* flowingness.
OPPOSITE jerkiness.

fluent ▶ **adjective 1** *a fluent introductory speech* **articulate**, eloquent, expressive, communicative, coherent, cogent, illuminating; vivid, silver-tongued, persuasive, glib, voluble.
OPPOSITE inarticulate.
2 *he soon became fluent in Welsh* **articulate**, able to speak or write ... easily and accurately; (**be fluent in**) have a (good) command of.
3 *he has a very fluent running style* **free-flowing**, smooth, effortless, easy, natural, fluid, unbroken, uninterrupted, continuous; graceful, elegant; regular, rhythmic.
OPPOSITE jerky.

F

fluff ▶ **noun 1** *there was fluff all over my coat* **fuzz**, lint, dust; *N. Amer.* dustballs, dust bunnies; *Scottish* ooze.
2 *on his head was a fluff of pale downy hair* **down**, soft/fine hair, soft fur, soft feathers, downiness, fuzz, floss, nap, pile.
3 (*informal*) *commentary should be free of fluffs such as mispronounced words or hesitations* **mistake**, error, gaffe, blunder, fault, slip, slip of the tongue, solecism, indiscretion, oversight, inaccuracy, botch; *French* faux pas; *Latin* lapsus linguae, lapsus calami; *informal* slip-up, clanger, boner, boo-boo, howler; *Brit. informal* boob; *N. Amer. informal* goof, blooper, bloop; *Brit. informal, dated* bloomer, floater.
▶ **verb 1** (*informal*) *the out-takes show him hopelessly fluffing his lines* **bungle**, deliver badly, muddle up, make a mess of; forget; *informal* mess up, foul up, screw up, cock up.
OPPOSITE get right.
2 (*informal*) *he fluffed his tee shot on the fourteenth hole* **bungle**, fumble, miss; *informal* mess up, make a mess of, make a hash of, hash, muff, foozle, butcher, make a botch of, foul up, bitch up, screw up, blow, louse up; *Brit. informal* make a muck of, make a pig's ear of, cock up, make a Horlicks of; *N. Amer. informal* flub, goof up, bobble; *vulgar slang* fuck up, bugger up, balls up, bollix up.
OPPOSITES succeed in, make a good job of.

fluffy ▶ **adjective** *a fluffy toy rabbit* **fleecy**, woolly, fuzzy, shaggy, hairy, feathery, downy, furry, velvety, cushiony; soft; *rare* floccose, flocculent, lanate, lanose.
OPPOSITE rough.

fluid ▶ **noun** *he designed instruments to measure the flow of fluids* **flowing substance**; liquid, watery substance, moisture, solution, juice, sap; gas, gaseous substance, vapour.
OPPOSITE solid.
▶ **adjective 1** *in fluid magmas, these gas bubbles can expand freely* **flowing**, able to flow easily; liquid, liquefied, melted, molten, uncongealed, running; gaseous, gassy; *technical* fluxional.
OPPOSITE solid.
2 *at this stage his plans were still fluid* **adaptable**, flexible, adjustable, open-ended, open, open to change, changeable, not fixed, not settled, variable, versatile.
OPPOSITE firm.
3 *the fluid state of affairs in the Far East* **fluctuating**, changeable, subject/likely to change, unsteady, (ever-)shifting, mobile, inconstant; **unstable**, unsettled, turbulent, volatile, mercurial, protean, kaleidoscopic, knife-edge, explosive.
OPPOSITE static.
4 *he stood up in one fluid movement* **free-flowing**, flowing, fluent, smooth, effortless, easy, natural, unbroken, uninterrupted, continuous; graceful, elegant; regular, rhythmic.
OPPOSITE jerky.

> **CHOOSE THE RIGHT WORD**
>
> **fluid, liquid**
>
> *See* LIQUID.

fluke ▶ **noun** *by a fluke I had a cancellation* **chance**, coincidence, accident, a twist of fate; **piece/stroke of luck**, piece/stroke of good luck, piece/stroke of good fortune, lucky stroke, happy/lucky chance, lucky break.

fluky ▶ **adjective** *we didn't deserve to win—our goals were a bit fluky* **lucky**, fortunate, providential, timely, opportune, serendipitous, expedient, heaven-sent, auspicious, propitious, felicitous, convenient, apt; chance, fortuitous, accidental; unexpected, unanticipated, unforeseen, unlooked-for, coincidental, haphazard, inadvertent, random, unintended; *Brit. informal* jammy.
OPPOSITE planned.

flummox ▶ **verb** *Linear B script had flummoxed generations of academics* **baffle**, bewilder, mystify, bemuse, perplex, puzzle, confuse, confound, nonplus, disconcert, throw, throw off balance, disorientate, take aback, set thinking; *informal* bamboozle, discombobulate, faze, stump, beat, fox, make someone scratch their head, be all Greek to, make someone's head spin, floor, fog; *N. Amer. informal* buffalo; *archaic* wilder, gravel, maze, cause to be at a stand, distract, pose; *rare* obfuscate.

flummoxed ▶ **adjective** *I was flummoxed until I remembered something* **baffled**, bewildered, mystified, bemused, perplexed, puzzled, confused, confounded, nonplussed, disconcerted, thrown, thrown off balance, at sea, at a loss, disorientated, taken aback; *informal* bamboozled, discombobulated, fazed, stumped, beat, foxed, floored; *Canadian & Austral./NZ informal* bushed; *archaic* wildered, distracted, mazed.

flunkey ▶ **noun 1** *a flunkey brought us a bottle of champagne* **liveried manservant**, liveried servant, lackey, steward, butler, footman, valet, retainer, attendant, factotum, houseboy, page.
2 *government flunkeys searched his offices* **minion**, lackey, hireling, subordinate, underling, servant, retainer, vassal; puppet, spaniel, pawn, tool, creature, instrument, cat's paw; *informal* skivvy, stooge, sucker, yes-man; *Brit. informal* poodle, dogsbody; *N. Amer. informal* gopher.

flurried ▶ **adjective** *I was so flurried that I broke the cork* **agitated**, flustered, ruffled, in a panic, worked up, beside oneself, overwrought, perturbed, frantic; *informal* in a flap, in a state, in a twitter, in a fluster, in a dither, all of a dither, all of a lather, in a tizz/tizzy, in a tiz-woz; *Brit. informal* in a (flat) spin, having kittens; *N. Amer. informal* in a twit.
OPPOSITE calm.

flurry ▶ **noun 1** *he opened the door and a flurry of snow blew in* **swirl**, whirl, eddy, billow, shower, gust, rush, burst, gale, squall, storm.
2 *there was a renewed flurry of activity outside* **burst**, outbreak, spurt, fit, spell, bout, rash, blaze, eruption; *informal* spot.
3 *his account of the deliberations caused a* **flurry of excitement** *in the press* **fluster**, fuss, bustle, whirl, stir, ferment, hubbub, commotion, hustle, tumult; agitation, disturbance, furore, perturbation, state of anxiety, panic; *informal* to-do, flap; *archaic* pother.
4 *there was a flurry of imports* **spate**, wave, flood, deluge, torrent, stream, tide, avalanche, storm, shower, cascade; series, succession, string; barrage, volley, battery; outbreak, rash, explosion, run, rush.
OPPOSITES dearth; trickle.
▶ **verb** *gusts of snow flurried through the door* **swirl**, whirl, eddy, billow, gust, blast, blow, rush, wind, churn, swish, spin, twist, spurt, surge, seethe, stream, flow, puff, squall, squirt, boil.

flush[1] ▶ **verb 1** *he kissed her cheek and she flushed in embarrassment* **blush**, redden, turn/go pink, turn/go red, turn/go crimson, turn/go scarlet, colour (up), change colour, crimson, tint, burn up; *archaic* mantle.
OPPOSITE pale.
2 *fruit helps to flush toxins from the body* **rinse (out)**, wash (out/down), sluice, swill, cleanse, clean, hose (down), swab; *Brit. informal* sloosh (down).
3 *one of the beaters was flushing birds from their hiding places* **drive**, send up, chase, force, dislodge, expel, frighten, scare.
▶ **noun 1** *a flush crept over her face* **blush**, reddening, high colour, colour, rosiness, pinkness, ruddiness, bloom.
OPPOSITE paleness.
2 *in the first flush of manhood* **bloom**, glow, freshness, radiance, vigour, rush.

flush[2] ▶ **adjective** (*informal*) **1** *the company was flush with cash* **well supplied with**, replete with, overflowing with, bursting with, brimful with, brimming with, loaded with, overloaded with, abounding in, well provided with, well stocked with, rich in, abundant in, rife with; crammed with, crowded with, packed with, jammed with, stuffed with, teeming with, swarming with, thick with, solid with, charged with, fraught with; *informal* jam-packed with, chock-a-block with, chock-full of, awash with; *Austral./NZ informal* chocker with.
OPPOSITES bereft of; low on.
2 *the years when cash was flush* **plentiful**, **abundant**, copious, ample, profuse, superabundant, infinite, inexhaustible, opulent, prolific, teeming, in abundance; *informal* a gogo, galore; *S. African informal* lank; *literary* bounteous, plenteous.
OPPOSITES lacking; low.

flushed ▶ **adjective 1** *the children's happy, flushed faces* **red**, pink, ruddy, glowing, reddish, pinkish, florid, high-coloured, healthy-looking, aglow, burning, flaming, feverish, rubicund, roseate, rosy; blushing, red-faced, blowsy, embarrassed, shamefaced; *archaic* sanguine; *rare* erubescent, rubescent.
OPPOSITE pale.
2 *flushed with success, he was now getting into his stride* **elated**, thrilled, exhilarated, happy, delighted, overjoyed, joyous, gleeful, excited, animated, jubilant, exultant, ecstatic, euphoric, rapturous, in raptures, enraptured, intoxicated, beside oneself, transported, carried away, impassioned, in a frenzy, delirious, hysterical, wild, frenzied; *informal* blissed out, over the moon, high, on a high; *N. Amer. informal* wigged out; *rare* corybantic.

OPPOSITE dismayed.

fluster ▶ verb *what could have flustered the normally imperturbable Robert?* **unsettle**, make nervous, unnerve, agitate, ruffle, upset, bother, put on edge, discompose, disquiet, disturb, worry, alarm, panic, perturb, disconcert, confuse, throw off balance, confound, nonplus; *informal* hassle, rattle, faze, discombobulate, put into a flap, throw into a tizz; *Brit. informal* send into a spin.
OPPOSITE calm.
▶ noun *his appearance put the household into quite a fluster* **state of agitation**, state of anxiety, nervous state, flutter, panic, frenzy, fever, fret, upset, turmoil, commotion; *informal* dither, flap, tizz, tizzy, tiz-woz, twitter, state, sweat, stew; *N. Amer. informal* twit.
OPPOSITE state of calm.

fluted ▶ adjective *the roof is supported by fluted columns* **grooved**, channelled, furrowed, ribbed, corrugated, ridged.
OPPOSITES smooth; plain.

flutter ▶ verb **1** *a couple of butterflies fluttered around the garden* **flit**, hover, flitter, dance.
2 *a small white tern was fluttering its wings* **flap**, move up and down, beat, quiver, agitate, vibrate, twitch, shake, wag, waggle, swing, oscillate, thresh, thrash, flail.
3 *she fluttered her eyelashes* **flicker**, bat.
4 *flags fluttered from every mast* **flap**, wave, ripple, undulate, stir, shake, quiver, shiver, tremble; fly, blow.
5 *her heart fluttered when she found that his eyes were still on her* **beat weakly/irregularly**, palpitate, miss/skip a beat, quiver, go pit-a-pat; *Medicine* exhibit arrhythmia; *rare* quop.
▶ noun **1** *the flutter of the birds' wings* **agitation**, beating, flapping, quivering, vibrating, twitching, shaking, wagging, oscillation, threshing, thrashing, flailing.
2 *a flutter of dark eyelashes* **flicker**, bat.
3 *the flutter of the flags in the breeze* **flapping**, waving, rippling.
4 *a flutter of nervousness started up inside her* **tremor**, wave, rush, surge, flash, stab, flush, tremble, quiver, shake, shaking, shakiness, shiver, frisson, chill, thrill, tingle, vibration, quaver, quake, shudder, palpitation, pulsation, throb, oscillation, fluctuation, waver, ripple, flicker.
5 *she was in a flutter at the unexpected news* **fluster**, flurry, bustle, panic, state of panic/agitation; *informal* state, dither, twitter, blue funk, stew, tizz, tizzy, tiz-woz; *N. Amer. informal* twit.
6 (*Brit. informal*) *he enjoys a flutter on the horses* **bet**, wager, gamble; *Brit. informal* punt.

flux ▶ noun **1** *the flux of water vapour along the tube* **flow**, movement, motion, transfer, course, passage, current, drift, circulation, trickle, stream, swirl, surge, sweep, gush, roll, rush, welling, spate, tide.
2 *prices are in a state of flux* **continuous change**, changeability, changeableness, variability, inconstancy, fluidity, instability, unsteadiness, unpredictability, irregularity, fitfulness, unreliability, fickleness; fluctuation, variation, shift, alteration, swing, movement, oscillation, alternation, rise and fall, rising and falling, see-sawing, yo-yoing.
OPPOSITE stability.

fly[1] ▶ verb **1** *a bird flew overhead* **travel through the air**, wing its way, wing, glide, soar, wheel; flutter, flit; hover, hang; take wing, take to the air, mount.
2 *they flew to Paris* **travel/go by air**, travel/go by plane, jet.
3 *military planes flew in food supplies* **transport by air/plane**, airlift, lift, jet.
4 *he would pretend not to know how to fly the plane* **pilot**, operate, control, manoeuvre, steer, guide, direct, navigate.
5 *the ship was flying a quarantine flag* **display**, show, exhibit; have hoisted, have run up.
6 *the British flag flew proudly from the roof* **flutter**, flap, wave, blow, waft, float, stream.
7 *doesn't time fly when you're having fun?* **go quickly**, fly by/past, pass swiftly, slip past, rush past.
8 *the runners flew by* **race**, hurry, hasten, flash, dash, dart, rush, shoot, speed, hurtle, streak, really move, spank along, whirl, whizz, go like lightning, go hell for leather, whoosh, buzz, zoom, swoop, blast, charge; stampede, gallop, chase, career, bustle, sweep, hare, wing, scurry, scud, scutter; *informal* belt, scoot, scorch, tear, zap, zip, whip (along), get cracking, get a move on, step on it, burn rubber, go like a bat out of hell; *Brit. informal* bomb, bucket, shift, put one's foot down; *N. Amer. informal* clip, boogie, hightail, barrel, lay rubber; *N. Amer. vulgar slang* drag/tear/haul ass; *literary* fleet; *archaic* post, hie.
9 (*archaic*) *the beaten army had to fly* **flee**, run, run away, run off, make a run for it, run for it, take flight, be gone, make off, take off, take to one's heels, make a break for it, bolt, beat a (hasty) retreat, make a quick exit, make one's getaway, escape, absent oneself, make oneself scarce, abscond, head for the hills, do a disappearing act; *informal* beat it, clear off, clear out, vamoose, skedaddle, split, cut and run, leg it, show a clean pair of heels, turn tail, scram; *Brit. informal* do a runner, scarper, do a bunk; *N. Amer. informal* light out, bug out, cut out, peel out, take a powder, skidoo; *Austral. informal* go through, shoot through; *vulgar slang* bugger off; *archaic* levant.
10 (*dated*) *he was forced to fly the country* **run away from**, leave hastily/abruptly, flee, escape from; *informal* skip.
□ **fly at** *Robbie flew at him, fists clenched* **attack**, assault, make an assault on, launch an attack on, pounce on, set upon, set about, launch oneself at, weigh into, let fly at, turn on, round on, lash out at, hit out at, strike out at, beset, belabour, fall on, accost, mug, charge, rush, storm; *informal* lay into, tear into, lace into, sail into, pitch into, get stuck into, wade into, let someone have it, beat up, jump; *Brit. informal* have a go at; *N. Amer. informal* light into.
□ **let fly**. *See* LET.

fly[2] ▶ noun. *See centre pages for list of* **Insects**

fly[3] ▶ adjective (*Brit. informal*) *she's fly enough not to get done out of it* **shrewd**, sharp, astute, acute, canny, worldly-wise, knowing, clever, sharp-witted, quick-witted, nimble-witted, wily; *informal* streetwise, not born yesterday, smart, savvy, downy, having been around, on the ball, quick on the uptake, with all one's wits about one, not missing a trick, no fool, nobody's fool; *Brit. informal* suss, knowing how many beans make five; *Scottish & N. English informal* pawky.
OPPOSITE naive.

fly-by-night ▶ adjective *sometimes these fly-by-night contractors take off without paying us at all* **unreliable**, undependable, irresponsible, untrustworthy; **dishonest**, deceitful, not to be trusted, dubious, double-dealing, treacherous, traitorous, two-faced, unfaithful, duplicitous, dishonourable, unprincipled, unscrupulous, corrupt, underhand; *informal* iffy, shady, shifty, slippery, crooked; *Brit. informal* dodgy, bent; *Austral./NZ informal* shonky.
OPPOSITE reputable.

flyer, flier ▶ noun **1** *we have increased the privileges and awards for our most frequent flyers* **air traveller**, air passenger, airline customer.
2 *the memorial was for flyers killed in a raid* **aviator**, airman/airwoman, pilot, co-pilot, aeronaut, wingman; *N. Amer. informal* jock.
3 *he was handing out flyers promoting a new sandwich bar* **handbill**, bill, handout, leaflet, circular, bulletin, pamphlet, brochure, advertisement, announcement, poster, public notice; *Brit.* fly-poster; *N. Amer. & Austral.* dodger; *French* affiche; *informal* ad; *Brit. informal* advert.

flying ▶ adjective **1** *a flying beetle* **airborne**, in the air, in flight; fluttering, flitting, flapping, hovering, floating, gliding, wind-borne, soaring, winging, wheeling; winged; *rare* volitant.
2 *a flying visit* **brief**, short, whistle-stop, lightning, fleeting, hasty, rushed, hurried, quick, cursory, perfunctory; momentary; *informal* quickie; *rare* fugacious.
OPPOSITE long.

foal ▶ noun **young horse/donkey/pony/mule**; colt, filly.

foam ▶ noun *the white foam on the huge breaking waves* **froth**, spume, surf, spindrift, spray; fizz, effervescence, bubbles, head; lather, suds.
▶ verb *the water churned and foamed* **froth**, froth up, cream, bubble, fizz, effervesce, spume, lather, ferment, rise, boil, seethe, simmer.

foamy ▶ adjective *leave the yeast mixture until it is foamy* **frothy**, foaming, spumy, bubbly, aerated, bubbling; sudsy; whipped, whisked; *rare* spumous, spumescent.

fob ▶ verb
□ **fob someone off** *I wasn't going to be fobbed off with excuses* **put off**, stall, give someone the runaround, deceive; placate, appease; deter, discourage, daunt, scare off, intimidate, unnerve.
□ **fob something off on** *he fobbed off the chairmanship on Clifford* **impose**, palm off, unload, dump, get rid of, foist, offload, inflict, thrust; saddle someone with something, land someone with something, lumber someone with something, burden someone with something.

focus ▶ noun **1** *schools are a focus of community life* **centre**, focal point, central point, centre of attention, hub, pivot, nucleus, heart, cornerstone, linchpin, kingpin, bedrock, basis, anchor, backbone, cynosure.
2 *the focus of this criticism is on helping people find solutions* **emphasis**, accent, priority, attention, concentration.
3 *the main focus of this chapter is elected local government* **subject**, theme, concern, subject matter, topic, issue, question, text, thesis, content, point, motif, thread; substance, essence, gist, matter.
4 *the resulting light beams are brought to a focus at the eyepiece* **focal point**, point of convergence.
□ **in focus** *colour snaps will do as long as they are in focus* **sharp**, crisp, distinct, clear-cut, clear, well defined, well focused.
OPPOSITE out of focus.
□ **out of focus** *why are some of the shots out of focus?* **blurred**, unfocused, indistinct, blurry, fuzzy, hazy, misty, cloudy, foggy, fogged, shadowy, smoky, faint; unclear, vague, indefinite, obscure, lacking definition, ill-defined, nebulous; woolly, muzzy, bleary; *archaic* blear.
OPPOSITE in focus.
▶ verb **1** *he focused his binoculars on the distant tower* **bring into focus**, bring to a focus; aim, point, turn.

2 *the investigation will **focus on** areas of social need* **concentrate**, fix, centre, pivot, zero in, zoom in; address itself to, pay attention to, pinpoint, spotlight, revolve around, have as its starting point.

foe ▶ **noun** *these horsemen were a well-armed foe* **enemy**, adversary, opponent, rival, antagonist, combatant, challenger, competitor, opposer, hostile party; (**the foe**) the opposition, the competition, the other side, the opposing side; *rare* corrival, vier.
OPPOSITE friend.

fog ▶ **noun 1** *he lost his way in the fog* **mist**, mistiness, fogginess, haar, smog, murk, murkiness, haze, haziness, gloom, gloominess; *N. English* (sea) fret; *informal* pea-souper; *literary* brume, fume.
2 *I was in such a fog that I couldn't write my name* **daze**, stupor, trance, haze, muddle; state of bewilderment, state of confusion, state of disorientation.
▶ **verb 1** *the windscreen **fogged up** | his breath fogged the glass* **steam up**, mist over, cloud over, film over, become misty, become blurred, become covered in condensation; make hazy, make cloudy, obscure, shade, veil; *literary* befog, becloud.
OPPOSITE clear.
2 *his brain was fogged with sleep* **muddle**, daze, stupefy, fuddle, befuddle, bewilder, confuse, perplex, baffle, obscure; *literary* bedim, becloud; *rare* obfuscate.

WORD LINKS
fear of fog **homichlophobia**

foggy ▶ **adjective 1** *the weather was wet and foggy* **misty**, smoggy, hazy, overcast, murky, gloomy, grey, dark, dim, dingy, dull; smoky, steamy; *informal* soupy; *Brit. informal* fuggy.
OPPOSITE clear.
2 *the foggy recesses of her mind* **muddled**, fuddled, befuddled, confused, bewildered, dazed, stupefied, numb, numbed, benumbed, groggy, fuzzy, bleary; dark, dim, hazy, shadowy, cloudy, clouded, blurred, obscure, remote, vague, indistinct, unclear; *informal* dopey, woolly, muzzy, woozy, out of it; *archaic* blear.
OPPOSITE clear.

foible ▶ **noun** *we have to tolerate each other's little foibles* **weakness**, weak point, weak spot, failing, shortcoming, flaw, imperfection, blemish, fault, defect, frailty, infirmity, inadequacy, limitation; quirk, kink, idiosyncrasy, eccentricity, peculiarity, abnormality; Achilles heel, chink in one's armour; *informal* hang-up.
OPPOSITE strength.

foil[1] ▶ **verb** *his attempts to escape were constantly foiled* **thwart**, frustrate, counter, oppose, baulk, disappoint, impede, obstruct, hamper, hinder, snooker, cripple, scotch, derail, smash, dash; stop, check, block, prevent, defeat, nip in the bud; *informal* mess up, screw up, do for, put paid to, stymie, cook someone's goose; *Brit. informal* scupper, nobble, queer, put the mockers on; *Austral./NZ & Irish vulgar slang* root; *archaic* traverse.
OPPOSITE assist.

foil[2] ▶ **noun** *the black gown was the perfect foil for her colouring* **contrast**, background, setting, relief, antithesis; **complement**.

foist ▶ **verb 1** *poor-quality lagers are being **foisted on** unsuspecting drinkers* **impose**, force, thrust, offload, unload, dump, palm off, fob off; shift on to; pass off, get rid of; (**foist something on to someone**) saddle someone with, land someone with, burden someone with, lumber someone with.
2 *he attempted to foist a new minister into the conference* **sneak**, insinuate, interpolate, insert, introduce, squeeze, edge; *informal* stick.

fold[1] ▶ **verb 1** *I helped him fold his sheets* **double**, double over, double up, crease, turn under, turn up, turn over, bend, overlap; tuck, gather, pleat, crimp, bunch.
2 *fold the cream into the chocolate mixture* **mix**, blend, stir gently; envelop, introduce, spoon.
3 *he folded her in his arms* **enfold**, wrap, wrap up, envelop; take, gather, clasp, squeeze, clutch; embrace, hug, cuddle, cradle; *literary* embosom; *archaic* strain.
4 *the firm finally folded in the mid '70s* **fail**, collapse, crash, founder, be ruined, cave in; **go bankrupt**, become insolvent, cease trading, go into receivership, go into liquidation, be liquidated, be wound up, be closed (down), be shut (down); *informal* go bust, go broke, go bump, go under, go to the wall, go belly up, come a cropper, flop.
▶ **noun** *the curtain falls in soft folds* **pleat**, gather, ruffle, bunch, turn, folded portion, double thickness, overlap, layer; crease, knife-edge; wrinkle, crinkle, pucker, furrow.

fold[2] ▶ **noun 1** *the sheep were pushing into the fold* **enclosure**, pen, paddock, pound, compound, ring, stall; sty, coop; *Scottish* parrock; *N. Amer.* corral; *S. African* kraal; (*in S. America*) potrero.
2 *he urged them to return to the Roman Catholic fold* **community**, company, group, body, mass, throng, congregation, assembly; Church, church membership, brethren, parishioners, churchgoers; *informal* flock.

folder ▶ **noun** *he tucked the notes into a folder* **file**, binder, ring binder, portfolio, document case; envelope, sleeve, jacket, wrapper, wallet.

foliage ▶ **noun** *a garden full of green and gold foliage* **leaves**, leafage, greenery, vegetation; *rare* herbage, verdure.

folk ▶ **noun 1** *he doesn't work the same hours as ordinary folk | the folk of East Anglia* **people**, humans, persons, individuals, (living) souls, mortals; citizenry, inhabitants, residents, populace, population, public, {men, women, and children}; *informal* peeps; *rare* denizens.
2 (**folks**) (*informal*) *my folks came from the north* **relatives**, relations, blood relations, family, family members, kinsfolk, kinsmen, kinswomen, kin, kindred, next of kin, flesh and blood; *informal* nearest and dearest; *dated* people.

folklore ▶ **noun** *he studied the local customs and folklore* **mythology**, lore, oral history, tradition, folk tradition; **legends**, fables, myths, folk tales, folk stories, old wives' tales; *technical* mythus, mythos.

follow ▶ **verb 1** *I'll go with you and we'll let the others follow* **come behind**, come after, go behind, go after, walk behind, tread on the heels of.
OPPOSITE lead.
2 *he was expected to follow his father in the business* **take the place of**, replace, succeed, take over from, supersede, supplant; *informal* step into someone's shoes, fill someone's shoes/boots.
3 *loads of people used to **follow** the band **around*** **accompany**, go along with, go around with, travel with, escort, attend, trail around with; *informal* tag along with, string along with.
OPPOSITE lead.
4 *the KGB man followed her everywhere* **shadow**, trail, pursue, chase, stalk, hunt, track, dog, hound, course; give chase to, be hot on someone's heels; *informal* tail.
5 *always follow the manufacturer's guidelines* **act in accordance with**, abide by, adhere to, stick to, keep to, comply with, conform to, obey, observe, heed, pay attention to, note, have regard to, mind, bear in mind, take to heart, be guided by, accept, yield to, defer to, respect.
OPPOSITE flout.
6 *a new way of life **followed from** contact with Europeans* **result**, arise, develop, ensue, emanate, issue, proceed, spring, flow, originate, stem; be a consequence of, be caused by, be brought about by, be produced by, be a result of, come after.
OPPOSITE lead to.
7 *he said something complicated and I couldn't follow it* **understand**, comprehend, apprehend, take in, grasp, fathom, appreciate, keep up with, see; *informal* make head or tail of, latch on to, catch on to, tumble to, get, get the hang of, figure out, get one's head around, get one's mind around, take on board, get the picture, get the drift, get the message, see the light; *Brit. informal* suss out; *N. Amer. informal* savvy; *rare* cognize.
OPPOSITE misunderstand.
8 *Rembrandt's last pupil followed the style of his master* **imitate**, copy, mimic, ape, reproduce, mirror, echo; **emulate**, take as a pattern, take as an example, take as a model, adopt the style of, style oneself on, model oneself on; *informal* take a leaf out of someone's book.
9 *he follows Manchester United* **be a fan of**, be a supporter of, support, be a follower of, be an admirer of, be a devotee of, be devoted to; be interested in, cultivate an interest in.
OPPOSITE dislike.
□ **follow something through** *they lack the resources to follow the project through* **complete**, bring to completion, bring to a finish, continue to the end, see something through; continue with, carry on with, keep on with, keep going with, stay with; *informal* stick something out.
OPPOSITE abandon.
□ **follow something up** *I've had one of my hunches and I'm going to follow it up* **investigate**, research, find out about, look into, dig into, delve into, make enquiries into, enquire about, ask questions about, pursue, chase up; *informal* check out; *N. Amer. informal* scope out.

follower ▶ **noun 1** *the president summoned his closest followers* **acolyte**, assistant, attendant, satellite, companion, retainer, henchman, minion, lackey, toady, servant, page, squire; *informal* hanger-on, camp follower, sidekick; *archaic* liegeman, pursuivant.
OPPOSITE leader.
2 *the picture was painted by a follower of Caravaggio* **imitator**, emulator, copier, copyist, mimic, ape; pupil, tutee, trainee, disciple; *informal* copycat.
3 *a follower of Christ* **disciple**, apostle, supporter, defender, champion; believer, worshipper, votary.
OPPOSITE opponent.
4 *she's a follower of the Rolling Stones* **fan**, enthusiast, admirer, devotee, lover, supporter, adherent; *informal* groupie, camp follower, hanger-on; *N. Amer. informal* rooter, booster.

following ▶ **noun** *the Jacobite cause retained a substantial following* **body of support**, backing, patronage; public, audience, circle, coterie; retinue, train; supporters, backers, admirers, fans, adherents, devotees, advocates, patrons; *informal* groupies.
▶ **adjective 1** *he sent a reply the following day* **next**, ensuing, succeeding, subsequent, successive; *archaic* after.

OPPOSITE preceding.
2 *candidates must satisfy the following criteria* **upcoming**, about to be mentioned, about to be specified, further on, below, underneath, at the end; *formal* hereunder, hereinafter.
OPPOSITE aforementioned.

folly ▸ **noun** *he cursed himself for his folly* **foolishness**, foolhardiness, stupidity, idiocy, imbecility, silliness, inanity, lunacy, madness, rashness, recklessness, imprudence, injudiciousness, lack of caution, lack of foresight, lack of sense, irrationality, illogicality, irresponsibility, thoughtlessness, indiscretion; *informal* craziness; *Brit. informal* daftness.
OPPOSITES wisdom; good sense.

foment ▸ **verb** *they were accused of fomenting civil unrest* **instigate**, incite, provoke, agitate, excite, stir up, whip up, arouse, inspire, encourage, urge, actuate, initiate, generate, cause, prompt, start, bring about, kindle, spark off, trigger off, touch off, fan the flames of; *rare* enkindle, effectuate.

fond ▸ **adjective 1** *she was fond of dancing | I'm very fond of Chris* **keen on**, partial to, addicted to, enthusiastic about, passionate about; attached to, attracted to, enamoured of, in love with, with a soft spot for; *informal* into, hooked on, gone on, wild about, nuts about, potty about, dotty about, crazy about, sweet on, struck on.
OPPOSITE indifferent to.
2 *his fond father plied him with cakes* **adoring**, devoted, doting, loving, caring, affectionate, warm, tender, kind, attentive, solicitous; indulgent, overindulgent, overfond.
OPPOSITE unfeeling.
3 *fond hopes of success* **unrealistic**, **naive**, foolish, foolishly optimistic, over-optimistic, deluded, delusory, absurd, empty, vain; *rare* Panglossian.
OPPOSITE realistic.

fondle ▸ **verb** *he fondled the Labrador's ears* **caress**, stroke, pat, pet, pull, finger, touch, tickle, twiddle, play with, massage, knead; maul, molest; *informal* paw, grope, feel up, touch up, cop a feel of.

fondness ▸ **noun 1** *they look at each other with such fondness* **affection**, love, liking, warmth, tenderness, kindness, devotion, care, endearment, feeling, sentiment, attachment, closeness, friendliness, familiarity, intimacy; regard, respect, admiration, adoration, worship, reverence.
OPPOSITE hatred.
2 *he has a fondness for spicy food* **liking**, love, taste, partiality, preference, keenness, inclination, penchant, predilection, fancy, relish, passion, proclivity, appetite; weakness, soft spot, susceptibility, addiction; *informal* thing, yen; *rare* appetency.
OPPOSITE dislike.

food *See centre pages for lists of* **Beans, Pulses, and Peas** **Biscuits** **Bread and Bread Rolls** **Cakes, Puddings, and Desserts** **Cereal Crops** **Cheeses** **Dietary Habits** **Fish** **Fruit** **Fungi, Mushrooms, and Toadstools** **Herbs** **Meals** **Meat** **Nuts** **Pasta** **Pies** **Sauces and Dips** **Sausages** **Soups** **Spices** **Stews** **Sugar** **Sweets and Confectionery** **Vegetables** **Vitamins**
▸ **noun 1** *he went three days without food* **nourishment**, sustenance, nutriment, subsistence, fare, bread, daily bread; cooking, baking, cuisine; **foodstuffs**, edibles, refreshments, meals, provisions, rations, stores, supplies; solids; *Scottish* vivers; *informal* eats, eatables, nosh, grub, chow, nibbles; *Brit. informal* scoff, tuck; *N. Amer. informal* chuck; *archaic* victuals, vittles, viands, commons, meat; *rare* comestibles, provender, aliment, commissariat, viaticum.
2 *food for the cattle and horses* **fodder**, feed, forage, herbage, pasturage, silage; *rare* comestibles, provender.
□ **food for thought mental stimulation**, mental nourishment, something to think about, something to be seriously considered.

WORD LINKS
relating to food **alimentary, culinary**
related suffix **-trophic (e.g. *oligotrophic, mycotrophic*)**
fear of food **cibophobia, sitophobia**

foodie ▸ **noun** (*informal*) *he is an avid foodie and successful restaurateur. See* **EPICURE**.

fool ▸ **noun 1** *you've acted like a complete fool* **idiot**, ass, halfwit, nincompoop, blockhead, dunce, dolt, ignoramus, cretin, imbecile, dullard, moron, simpleton, clod; *informal* dope, ninny, chump, dimwit, goon, dumbo, dummy, dum-dum, dumb-bell, loon, jackass, bonehead, fathead, numbskull, dunderhead, chucklehead, knucklehead, muttonhead, pudding-head, thickhead, wooden-head, airhead, pinhead, lamebrain, pea-brain, birdbrain, zombie, jerk, nerd, dipstick, donkey, noodle; *Brit. informal* nit, nitwit, twit, clot, goat, plonker, berk, prat, pillock, wally, git, wazzock, divvy, nerk, dork, twerp, charlie, mug, muppet; *Scottish informal* nyaff, balloon, sumph, gowk; *Irish informal* gobdaw; *N. Amer. informal* schmuck, bozo, boob, turkey, schlepper, chowderhead, dumbhead, goofball, goof, goofus, galoot, lummox, klutz, putz, schlemiel, sap, meatball, gink, cluck, clunk, ding-dong, dingbat, wiener, weeny, dip, simp, spud, coot, palooka, poop, squarehead, yo-yo, dingleberry; *Austral./NZ informal* drongo, dill, hoon, alec, galah, nong, bogan, poon, boofhead; *S. African informal* mompara; *archaic* tomfool, noddy, clodpole, loggerhead, spoony, mooncalf.
2 *she always makes a fool of him* **laughing stock**, dupe, butt, gull, pushover, easy mark, tool, cat's paw; *informal* stooge, sucker, mug, fall guy; *N. Amer. informal* sap.
3 (*historical*) *the fool in King James's court* **jester**, court jester, clown, buffoon, comic, joker, jokester, zany, merry andrew; wearer of the motley, harlequin, Pierrot, Punchinello, Pantaloon.
▸ **verb 1** *he found he'd been fooled by a schoolboy* **deceive**, trick, play a trick on, hoax, dupe, take in, mislead, delude, hoodwink, bluff, beguile, gull, make a fool of, outwit; swindle, defraud, cheat, double-cross; *informal* con, bamboozle, pull a fast one on, pull someone's leg, take for a ride, pull the wool over someone's eyes, throw dust in someone's eyes, put one over on, have on, diddle, fiddle, swizzle, rip off, do, sting, gyp, shaft; *Brit. informal* sell a pup to; *N. Amer. informal* sucker, snooker, stiff, euchre, bunco, hornswoggle; *Austral. informal* pull a swifty on; *rare* cozen, sharp, mulct.
2 *she screamed but they thought she was fooling* **pretend**, make believe, feign, put on an act, act, sham, fake, counterfeit; tease, joke, jest, play tricks, clown about/around, play the fool; *informal* kid, mess about/around; *Brit. informal* wind someone up, have someone on, muck someone about/around.
3 *she fooled around with a bunch of keys while she spoke* **fiddle**, play (about/around), toy, trifle, meddle, tamper, interfere, monkey about/around; *informal* mess about/around; *Brit. informal* muck about/around.
4 (*informal*) *my husband's been fooling around behind my back* **philander**, womanize, flirt, have an affair, commit adultery; *informal* play around, mess about/around, carry on, play the field, play away, sleep around, swing; *vulgar slang* screw around; *rare* coquet.

foolery ▸ **noun** *we had to endure his foolery all afternoon* **clowning**, fooling, tomfoolery, hoaxing, mischief, buffoonery, silliness, silly behaviour, skylarking, horseplay; antics, capers, practical jokes, pranks; foolishness, stupidity, idiocy; *informal* larking around, larks, shenanigans; *Brit. informal* monkey tricks; *N. Amer. informal* didoes; *archaic* harlequinade.

foolhardy ▸ **adjective** *he'd been stupid and foolhardy* **reckless**, rash, incautious, careless, heedless, unheeding, thoughtless, unwise, imprudent, irresponsible, injudicious, impulsive, hot-headed, impetuous, daredevil, devil-may-care, death-or-glory, madcap, hare-brained, precipitate, precipitous, desperate, hasty, overhasty, over-adventurous, over-venturesome; *literary* temerarious.
OPPOSITE wise.

CHOOSE THE RIGHT WORD
foolhardy, rash, reckless
See **RASH**.

foolish ▸ **adjective** *her desperation led her to do something foolish* **stupid**, silly, idiotic, half-witted, witless, brainless, mindless, thoughtless, imprudent, incautious, irresponsible, injudicious, indiscreet, unwise, unintelligent, unreasonable; ill-advised, ill-considered, impolitic, rash, reckless, foolhardy, lunatic; absurd, senseless, pointless, nonsensical, inane, fatuous, ridiculous, laughable, risible, derisible; *informal* dumb, dim, dim-witted, dopey, gormless, damfool, half-baked, hare-brained, crackbrained, pea-brained, wooden-headed, thickheaded, nutty, mad, crazy, dotty, batty, dippy, cuckoo, screwy, wacky; *Brit. informal* barmy, daft, *Scottish & N. English informal* glaikit; *N. Amer. informal* dumb-ass, chowderheaded; *W. Indian informal* dotish.
OPPOSITES sensible; wise.

foolishly ▸ **adverb** *he'd be very cross with me if I acted foolishly* **stupidly**, idiotically, ineptly, inanely, senselessly, unwisely, ill-advisedly, incautiously, indiscreetly, short-sightedly; without thinking, without forethought; fatuously, absurdly; *informal* crazily; *Brit. informal* barmily.

foolishness ▸ **noun** *I regretted my foolishness over the matter* **folly**, foolhardiness, stupidity, idiocy, imbecility, silliness, inanity, lunacy, madness, rashness, recklessness, imprudence, injudiciousness, lack of caution/foresight/sense, irrationality, illogicality, irresponsibility, thoughtlessness, indiscretion; *informal* craziness; *Brit. informal* daftness.
OPPOSITES wisdom; sense.

foolproof ▸ **adjective** *we need a foolproof security system* **infallible**, never failing, unfailing, unerring, dependable, reliable, trustworthy, certain, sure, guaranteed, safe, sound, effective, efficacious, tried and tested; watertight, airtight, flawless, perfect; *informal* sure-fire.
OPPOSITE flawed.

foot ▸ **noun 1** *he trod on someone's foot informal* tootsie, trotter; (**feet**) *rhyming slang* plates of meat; *N. Amer. informal* dogs.
2 *a four-footed animal* paw, forepaw, hind paw, hoof, trotter, pad; *technical* tarsus, ungula; *rare* slot, dewclaw.
3 *she lived at the foot of the hill* **bottom**, base, toe, edge, end, lowest part, lowest point, lower limits; foundation.

F

▶ verb
□ **foot the bill** (*informal*) *ministers expected the taxpayer to foot the bill* **pay**, pay up, pay out, pay the bill, settle up; bail someone out; *informal* pick up the tab, cough up, fork out, shell out, come across, chip in; *Brit. informal* stump up; *N. Amer. informal* ante up, pony up, pick up the check.

WORD LINKS

related prefix	**ped-** (e.g. ***pedal, pedometer***)
related suffix	**-pod(e)** (e.g. ***gastropod, megapode***)
medical treatment of the feet	**chiropody**

footing ▶ noun **1** *Jenny lost her footing and plunged into the river* **foothold**, toehold, hold, grip, anchorage, purchase, secure position, firm contact, support; steadiness, stability, balance, equilibrium.
2 *the business was put on a solid financial footing* **basis**, base, foundation, underpinning, support, cornerstone.
3 *female clerks should be on an equal footing with male clerks* **standing**, status, state, station, position, rank, grade; condition, arrangement, basis, foundation; relationship, relations, terms.

footling ▶ adjective *she insisted on some footling changes to the text* **trivial**, trifling, petty, insignificant, unimportant, minor, silly, pointless, immaterial, irrelevant, inessential, non-essential, time-wasting, fiddling, hair-splitting, paltry, nugatory, worthless; of little account, not worth bothering about, not worth mentioning; *informal* piddling, piffling, penny-ante; *Brit. informal* twopenny-halfpenny; *N. Amer. informal* nickel-and-dime, small-bore, picayune.
OPPOSITES important; major.

footnote ▶ noun *the journal has discreet and informative footnotes* **note**, marginal note, annotation, comment, gloss; aside, incidental remark, digression, parenthesis; (**footnotes**) notation, marginalia, commentary; *rare* scholium.

footprint ▶ noun *the walkway was covered with footprints* **footmark**, footstep, track, print, mark, spoor, trace, impression.

footslog ▶ verb *they footslogged around two villages* **trudge**, traipse, slog, hike, trek, tramp, plod, troop, walk, march, pace, stride; toil, labour, drag oneself; *Brit. informal* yomp, trog; *N. Amer. informal* schlep.
▶ noun *the eighteen-mile footslog raised £600 for charity* **hike**, trek, slog, traipse, trudge, tramp, walk, march, route march, long haul; *Brit. informal* yomp; *N. Amer. informal* schlep.

footstep ▶ noun **1** *her footsteps echoed down the bare corridor* **footfall**, step, stride, tread, pace, stomp, stamp.
2 *they left their footsteps in the sand* **footprint**, footmark, track, print, mark, spoor, trace, impression.

footwear ▶ noun. *See centre pages for list of* **Footwear**

fop ▶ noun *a flamboyant bunch of young fops* **dandy**, beau, poseur, glamour boy, man about town, bright young thing, rake; *French* boulevardier, petit-maître; *informal* swell, toff, snappy dresser, sharp dresser, natty dresser, trendy, pretty boy; *archaic* coxcomb, popinjay, peacock, buck.

foppish ▶ adjective *the clothes were less foppish than his usual attire* **dandyish**, dandified, dapper, dressy, spruce; affected, dainty, preening, vain; **effeminate**, effete, girly, niminy-piminy, mincing, posturing; *informal* la-di-da, natty, sissy, camp, campy; *informal, derogatory* poncey, pansyish.

forage ▶ verb *villagers were forced to forage for food* **hunt**, hunt around, search, look about/around/round, cast about/around/round, rummage (about/around/round), ferret (about/around), root about/around, scratch about/around, nose around/about/round, scour, look high and low; seek, look, explore; *informal* scrounge around; *Brit. informal* rootle around.
▶ noun **1** *there was little forage for the horses* **fodder**, feed, food, foodstuff, herbage, pasturage; silage, hay, straw; *formal* comestibles, provender.
2 *a nightly forage for food* **scavenge**, hunt, search, look, exploration, quest, scout, probe.

foray ▶ noun *the garrison made a foray against Richard's camp* **raid**, attack, assault, incursion, swoop, strike, charge, sortie, sally, rush, onrush, push, thrust, onslaught, offensive, bombardment; act of aggression, act of war, blitz, campaign; *archaic* onset.

forbear ▶ verb *the boy forebore from touching anything* **refrain**, abstain, desist, keep, restrain oneself, stop oneself, hold back, withhold; resist the temptation to, steer clear of, give a wide berth to, fight shy of; eschew, avoid, shun, decline to; cease, give up, break off; *informal* lay off, leave off, swear off; *Brit. informal* give over, jack in; *nautical slang* belay.
OPPOSITE persist in.

forbearance ▶ noun *her unfailing courtesy and forbearance under provocation* **tolerance**, toleration, patience, resignation, endurance, fortitude, stoicism, long-sufferingness, leniency, lenity, clemency, indulgence; **restraint**, self-restraint, self-control, moderation, temperance, mildness.

forbearing ▶ adjective *he was tactful and forbearing when I got angry* **patient**, tolerant, easy-going, forgiving, merciful, understanding, accommodating, indulgent, kind; uncomplaining, long-suffering, resigned, stoical, stoic; **restrained**, self-restrained, self-controlled, moderate, mild, easy, calm; *informal* unflappable, cool; *rare* longanimous.
OPPOSITES impatient, intolerant.

forbid ▶ verb *the act forbade discrimination on the grounds of sex* **prohibit**, ban, outlaw, make illegal, veto, proscribe, disallow, preclude, exclude, rule out, bar, debar, block, stop, put a stop to, put an end to, declare taboo; *informal* give the red light to, give the thumbs down to, put the kibosh on; *N. Amer.* interdict; *Law* enjoin, restrain.
OPPOSITE permit.

CHOOSE THE RIGHT WORD

forbid, ban, prohibit

These words refer to the issuing of orders by people in a position of authority, to prevent something from happening or to exclude someone from somewhere.

- To **forbid** is to order someone not to do something or to say that something may not be done, typically in matters of custom, religion, or personal conduct (*her father forbade her to see Philip again | the code of business ethics forbids bribery*).
- **Ban** denotes an official order, often a law or rule, and often applies to abolishing an existing practice or item (*the government pledged itself to ban hunting*). It can be followed by *from* and either an activity (*he was banned from driving for a year*) or a place (*a proposal to ban tankers from Venice*).
- To **prohibit** something is usually done by means of a law or regulation (*legislation prohibiting late abortions | vehicles will be prohibited from entering High Row*). *Prohibit* can also mean 'make impossible' (*severe physical problems prohibited these children from entering regular school*).

forbidden ▶ adjective *smoking is now forbidden in certain areas* **prohibited**, banned, debarred, vetoed, proscribed, ruled out, not allowed, disallowed, taboo, impermissible, not acceptable, unauthorized, unsanctioned; outlawed, illegal, unlawful, illicit, illegitimate, criminal; *N. Amer.* interdicted; *German* verboten; *Islam* haram; *NZ* tapu; *informal* no go, not on, out; *rare* non licet.
OPPOSITES permitted; legal.

forbidding ▶ adjective **1** *he had a rather forbidding manner* **hostile**, unwelcoming, unfriendly, unsympathetic, unapproachable, harsh, grim, stern, hard, tough, cool, cold, chilly, frosty; disagreeable, nasty, mean, abhorrent, repellent; *informal* off-putting.
OPPOSITE friendly.
2 *the dark castle looked forbidding* **threatening**, ominous, menacing, sinister, brooding, daunting, fearsome, frightening, chilling, disturbing, disquieting; hostile, unwelcoming, uninviting, unfriendly; foreboding, unpromising, inauspicious, evil-looking, suggestive of evil; *informal* spooky, scary, creepy; *archaic* direful, bodeful.
OPPOSITE inviting.

force ▶ noun **1** *Eddie delivered a blow with all his force* **strength**, power, energy, might, potency, vigour, muscle, stamina, effort, exertion, impact, pressure, weight, impetus; *informal* punch.
OPPOSITE weakness.
2 *they used force to achieve their aims* **coercion**, compulsion, constraint, duress, oppression, enforcement, harassment, intimidation, threats, pressure, pressurization, influence; **violence**; *French* force majeure; *informal* arm-twisting.
3 *they couldn't deny the force of the argument* **cogency**, weight, effectiveness, efficacy, efficaciousness, soundness, validity, strength, might, power, significance, influence, authority, impressiveness, eloquence, persuasiveness, credibility, conclusiveness; logic, logicality, foundation, reasonableness, coherence; *informal* bite, punch.
OPPOSITE weakness.
4 *he gave a performance of staggering expressive force* **intensity**, feeling, passion, vigour, vigorousness, vehemence, drive, fierceness; vividness, impact; *informal* pizzazz, oomph, zing, zip, zap, punch.
OPPOSITE shallowness.
5 *they see male lust as a corrupting force* **agency**, power, influence, instrument, vehicle, means, cause, effect.
6 *the government sent in a peacekeeping force* **body**, body of people, group, outfit, party, team; **corps**, detachment, unit, squad, squadron, company, battalion, division, patrol, regiment, army; (*in ancient Rome*) cohort; *informal* bunch.
□ **in force 1** *the state of emergency remained in force* **effective**, in operation, operative, operational, in action, valid, on the statute book, current, live, active; binding; *informal* up and running.
2 *her fans were out in force* **in great numbers**, in great quantities, in hordes, in full strength.
▶ verb **1** *the raiders forced him to open the safe* **compel**, coerce, make, constrain, oblige, impel, drive, necessitate, pressurize, pressure, press, push; exert force on, use force on, urge by force, use duress on, bring pressure to bear on, press-gang, browbeat, steamroller, bully, dragoon, bludgeon, terrorize, menace; *informal* put the squeeze on, put the bite on, put the screws on, tighten the screws on, lean on, twist someone's arm, use strong-arm tactics on, strong-arm, railroad, bulldoze.
2 *the doors had to be forced* **break open**, force open, burst open, prise

open, kick in, knock down, blast; crack.
3 *water was forced through a hole in the pipe* **propel**, push, thrust, shove, drive, press, pump, expel.
4 *they forced a confession out of the kids* **extract**, elicit, exact, extort, wrest, wring, wrench, drag, screw, squeeze, milk; *informal* bleed.

CHOOSE THE RIGHT WORD

force, compel, coerce, oblige
See COMPEL.

forced ▸ **adjective 1** *a programme of forced industrialization* **enforced**, compulsory, obligatory, mandatory, involuntary, exacted, coerced, imposed, demanded, compelled, required, requisite, stipulated, dictated, ordained, prescribed; necessitated, unavoidable, inescapable; *French* de rigueur.
OPPOSITE voluntary.
2 *her vivacity seemed a little bit forced* **strained**, laboured, unnatural, artificial, false, feigned, simulated, contrived, stilted, wooden, stiff, studied, mannered, self-conscious, overdone, overworked, affected, unconvincing, insincere, hollow; *informal* phoney, pretend, pseudo, put on.
OPPOSITE natural.

forceful ▸ **adjective 1** *she had a forceful personality* **dynamic**, energetic, assertive, authoritative, vigorous, powerful, potent, strong, strong-willed, pushing, driving, determined, insistent, commanding, bullish, dominant, domineering; bold, confident, self-confident, self-assured, self-possessed, audacious, enterprising, competitive, go-ahead, zealous; *informal* pushy, bossy, in-your-face, not backward in coming forward, feisty.
OPPOSITES weak; submissive.
2 *the board was persuaded by his forceful arguments* **cogent**, convincing, compelling, strong, powerful, potent, weighty, plausible, effective, efficacious, sound, valid, well founded, telling; impressive, persuasive, irresistible, eloquent, credible, influential, conclusive, unanswerable, authoritative; **logical**, reasoned, reasonable, rational, lucid, coherent.
OPPOSITES weak; unconvincing.

forcible ▸ **adjective 1** *they checked the doors for signs of forcible entry* **forced**, violent; by force, using force, with force.
2 *the forcible conversion of the Saxons to Christianity* **compulsory**, forced, enforced, obligatory, mandatory, involuntary, imposed, exacted, coerced, demanded, compelled, required, stipulated, dictated, ordained, prescribed; unavoidable, inescapable.
3 *a forcible demonstration of his changed attitude* **forceful**, cogent, convincing, compelling, strong, powerful, potent, weighty, plausible, effective, efficacious, valid, telling; impressive, persuasive, eloquent, credible, influential, conclusive, unanswerable.

forcibly ▸ **adverb 1** *he was thrown out of the club forcibly* **by force**, against one's will, under protest, compulsorily, under compulsion, under coercion, of necessity; with force, with violence, violently, roughly, unceremoniously, willy-nilly; bodily.
2 *they made their point forcibly* **forcefully**, vigorously, powerfully, potently, dynamically, energetically, assertively, heartily, eagerly, zealously, strenuously, aggressively; **cogently**, effectively, persuasively, convincingly, authoritatively, tellingly, movingly, impressively.

ford ▸ **noun** *a ford across the Tweed* **crossing place**, crossing, causeway; shallow place; *S. African* drift.
▸ **verb** *if I could find the river, I could ford it somehow* **cross**, traverse; wade across, walk across, drive across, travel across, make it across, make one's way across.

forebear ▸ **noun** *she speaks the language of her forebears* **ancestor**, forefather, predecessor, progenitor, father, grandfather, parent, grandparent; antecedent, forerunner, precursor; *rare* primogenitor.
OPPOSITE descendant.

forebode ▸ **verb** (*literary*) *this lull foreboded some new assault upon him* **presage**, augur, portend, prognosticate, foreshadow, foreshow, foretell, forecast, predict, prophesy, forewarn, warn of, be a warning of, herald, be an omen of, be a harbinger of; signify, mean, indicate, add up to, point to, announce, promise; *informal* spell; *literary* foretoken, betoken, harbinger; *rare* prefigure.

foreboding ▸ **noun 1** *she was seized with a feeling of foreboding* **apprehension**, apprehensiveness, anxiety, perturbation, trepidation, disquiet, disquietude, unease, uneasiness, misgiving, suspicion, worry, fear, fearfulness, dread, alarm; *informal* butterflies (in the stomach), the willies, the heebie-jeebies, the jitters, jitteriness, twitchiness; *rare* inquietude.
OPPOSITE calm.
2 *in the end their forebodings proved justified* **premonition**, presentiment, intuition, feeling, vague feeling, suspicion, inkling, hunch; warning, omen, portent, sign, token; prediction, augury, prophecy, presage, prognostication, forecast; *informal* gut feeling, feeling in one's bones, funny feeling, sixth sense.

forecast ▸ **verb** *they forecast that shares in the company will start trading at a profit soon* **predict**, prophesy, prognosticate, augur, divine, foretell, foresee, forewarn; guess, hazard a guess, conjecture, speculate, estimate, calculate, reckon, expect; *Scottish archaic* spae; *rare* presage, previse, vaticinate, auspicate.
▸ **noun** *a gloomy forecast of the impact of global warming* **prediction**, prophecy, forewarning, prognostication, augury, divination, prognosis, projection, calculation; guess, estimate, conjecture, speculation; warning, signal, sign, token; *informal* guesstimate; *literary* foretoken; *rare* prognostic, vaticination, auspication.

forefather ▸ **noun** *they gave up the wicked customs of their forefathers* **forebear**, ancestor, predecessor, progenitor, father, grandfather, parent, grandparent; antecedent, forerunner, precursor; *rare* primogenitor.
OPPOSITE descendant.

forefront ▸ **noun** *a cabinet post thrust him to the forefront of British politics* **vanguard**, van, spearhead, head, lead, fore, front, front line, cutting edge, foreground, foremost/leading position, position of prominence.
OPPOSITES rear, background.

forego ▸ **verb**. *See* FORGO.

foregoing ▸ **adjective** *despite the foregoing criticisms, we welcome the changes* **preceding**, aforesaid, aforementioned, previously mentioned, earlier, above, above-stated; antecedent, previous, prior; *rare* anterior, prevenient, precedent, precursive, supra.
OPPOSITE following.

foregone ▸ **adjective** (*literary*) *the ghosts of foregone dreams* **past**, former, earlier, previous, prior, bygone, old, of old, ancient, long-ago; forgotten; *literary* of yore; *rare* forepassed.
□ **a foregone conclusion** *they accepted an interest rate rise as a foregone conclusion* **certainty**, predictable result, predictable outcome, inevitability, matter of course; *informal* sure thing, cert, dead cert.
OPPOSITE possibility.

foreground ▸ **noun 1** *she repainted the figures in the foreground* **front**, fore, forefront, forepart, foremost part, nearest part, closest part.
2 *he was in the foreground of the political drama* **forefront**, vanguard, van, spearhead, head, lead, fore, front, front line, cutting edge, foremost position, leading position, position of prominence.

forehead ▸ **noun** *she brushed a lock of hair from her forehead* **brow**, temple; *Zoology* frons.

WORD LINKS
relating to the forehead **frontal**

foreign ▸ **adjective 1** *foreign branches of UK banks* **overseas**, distant, remote, far off, far flung, external, outside; alien, non-native, adventitious.
OPPOSITES domestic; native.
2 *the concept is very foreign to us Westerners* **unfamiliar**, unknown, unheard of, strange, alien, exotic, outlandish, odd, peculiar, curious, bizarre, weird, queer, funny; novel, new.
OPPOSITE familiar.
3 (*formal*) *this matter is altogether* **foreign to** *the affair in hand* **irrelevant**, not pertinent, inappropriate, inapposite, extraneous, unrelated, unconnected; outside, distant from, remote from, disconnected from, different from; *rare* extrinsic.
OPPOSITE relevant.

foreigner ▸ **noun** *the country was ruled by a foreigner* **alien**, non-native, immigrant, settler, newcomer, stranger, outsider; visitor, tourist; *Brit.* incomer; *N. English* offcomer; *SE Asian* gweilo.
OPPOSITE native.

WORD LINKS
fear of foreigners **xenophobia**

foreman, forewoman ▸ **noun** *the foreman was left in charge of the printing works* **supervisor**, overseer, superintendent, manager, manageress, boss, team leader, line manager, controller; foreperson; *Brit.* chargehand, captain, ganger; *Scottish* grieve; *S. African* induna; (*in the Indian subcontinent*) maistry; *informal* chief, head honcho, governor, super; *Brit. informal* gaffer, guv'nor; *N. Amer. informal* ramrod, straw boss; *Austral. informal* pannikin boss; *Mining* overman.

foremost ▸ **adjective** *one of the foremost Spanish Renaissance artists* **leading**, principal, premier, prime, elite, top, top-level, first-rate, greatest, best, supreme, pre-eminent, major, most important, most prominent, most influential, most skilled, most illustrious, outstanding, notable, noteworthy, of note; first, primary, main, paramount, chief, key, central; *N. Amer.* ranking; *informal* number-one, top-notch.
OPPOSITE minor.

foreordained ▸ **adjective** *the outcome of the matter was foreordained* **predetermined**, **preordained**, ordained, predestined, destined, fated; *rare* predestinated.

forerunner ▸ **noun 1** *archosaurs were the forerunners of dinosaurs* **predecessor**, precursor, antecedent, ancestor, forebear; prototype; *rare* primogenitor.
OPPOSITE descendant.
2 *the pain was feared as a forerunner of something worse* **herald**, harbinger, usher, advance guard; precursor, prelude; sign, signal, warning, token,

F

portent, omen, augury.

foresee ▶ verb *Harry foresaw further problems for them* **anticipate**, predict, forecast, expect, envisage, envision, see, think likely; foretell, prophesy, divine, prognosticate, augur; *literary* foreknow, forebode; *Scottish archaic* spae; *rare* vaticinate, auspicate.

CHOOSE THE RIGHT WORD

foresee, anticipate, expect

See ANTICIPATE.

foreshadow ▶ verb *the city's decline was foreshadowed by earlier events* **augur**, presage, portend, prognosticate, foreshow, foretell, indicate, suggest, signal, herald, forewarn, warn of, promise, point to, anticipate; *literary* forebode, foretoken, betoken, harbinger; *rare* prefigure.

foresight ▶ noun *a little foresight might have saved them a lot of money* **forethought**, anticipation, planning, forward planning, provision, prescience, circumspection, watchfulness, attentiveness, vigilance, prudence, care, caution, precaution, readiness, preparedness; **far-sightedness**, discernment, presence of mind, judiciousness, discrimination, perspicacity, vision, awareness, penetration; *N. Amer.* forehandedness.
OPPOSITE hindsight.

F

forest *See centre pages for list of* **Forests**
▶ noun *they came to a clearing in the forest* **wood(s)**, woodland, trees, tree plantation, plantation; jungle; *archaic* greenwood, holt.
WORD LINKS
relating to forests **sylvan**

forestall ▶ verb *they will resign to forestall a vote of no confidence* **pre-empt**, get in before, get ahead of, steal a march on, anticipate, second-guess, nip in the bud, thwart, frustrate, foil, stave off, ward off, fend off, avert, preclude, obviate, prevent, intercept, check, block, hinder, impede, obstruct; *informal* beat someone to it, beat someone to the draw/punch.

forestry ▶ noun **forest management**, forest planting, forest cultivation, tree growing, forestation, afforestation, agroforestry; woodcraft, woodsmanship; *technical* arboriculture, silviculture, dendrology.

foretaste ▶ noun *the opening parade gives a foretaste of the spectacle to come* **sample**, taster, taste, preview, trailer, appetizer, tester, specimen, example; indication, suggestion, hint, whiff; warning, forewarning, advance warning, omen; *informal* tip-off, try-out.

foretell ▶ verb **1** *it all happened as she had foretold* **predict**, forecast, foresee, anticipate, envisage, envision, see, prophesy, prognosticate, augur, divine; warn, forewarn; *archaic* foreshow, croak; *Scottish archaic* spae; *rare* vaticinate, auspicate.
2 *the shootings foretold more terrible violence* **augur**, presage, portend, foreshadow, indicate, signal, point to, add up to, be an omen of, be a warning of, be a harbinger of; *literary* forebode, foretoken, betoken, harbinger; *rare* prefigure.

forethought ▶ noun *forethought is needed before you embark on such a project* **anticipation**, planning, forward planning, provision, precaution, prescience, circumspection, prudence, care, caution; foresight, far-sightedness, discernment, presence of mind, judiciousness, perspicacity, vision, awareness, penetration; *N. Amer.* forehandedness.

foretoken ▶ verb (*literary*) *a shiver in the night air foretokens December* **signal**, be a sign of, be a warning of, be an omen of, be a harbinger of, foretell, herald, announce, point to, add up to, spell, promise, indicate the coming of, be evidence of, be symptomatic of; *literary* betoken, forebode, harbinger.

forever ▶ adverb **1** *their love would last forever* **for always**, evermore, for ever and ever, for good, for good and all, for all time, until the end of time, eternally, undyingly, perpetually, in perpetuity; *Brit.* for evermore; *N. Amer.* forevermore; *informal* for keeps, until the cows come home, until hell freezes over, until the twelfth of never, until doomsday, until kingdom come; *archaic* for aye.
2 *he was forever banging into things* **continually**, continuously, constantly, perpetually, incessantly, endlessly, persistently, repeatedly, regularly; always, all the time, the entire time, non-stop, day and night, {morning, noon, and night}; *Scottish* aye; *informal* 24-7.
OPPOSITES occasionally; never.

forewarn ▶ verb *he had been forewarned of a coup plot* **warn**, prewarn, warn in advance, give advance warning, give fair warning, give notice, advise, apprise, inform; put on one's guard about, alert about, caution about; *informal* tip off about, put wise to, put in the picture about, clue in about; *Brit. informal* tip someone the wink about; *rare* premonish.
OPPOSITE take by surprise.

forewarning ▶ noun *when dogs howled at night it was a forewarning of death* **harbinger**, omen, augury, sign, signal, herald, indication, presage, portent, promise, prediction, forecast, premonition; warning, advance warning, prior warning; *informal* tip-off; *literary* foretoken.

foreword ▶ noun *he wrote the foreword to one of her books* **preface**, introduction, prologue, preamble, opening remarks, opening statement, preliminary matter, front matter, forward matter; *informal* intro, prelims; *rare* prolegomenon, proem, prooemium, exordium, prolusion.

forfeit ▶ verb *they had to forfeit benefits for the period of the strike* **surrender**, relinquish, hand over, deliver up, part with, yield, sacrifice, give up, renounce, be stripped of/deprived of, lose; *informal* pass up, lose out on.
OPPOSITE retain.
▶ noun *if they fail to obey they are liable to a forfeit* **penalty**, financial penalty, fine, fee, charge, sanction, punitive action, penance; damages; confiscation, loss, relinquishment, forfeiture; *Law* sequestration; *English Law, historical* amercement; *rare* mulct.

forfeiture ▶ noun *non-compliance may lead to forfeiture of the lease* **confiscation**, sequestration, loss, losing, denial; relinquishment, giving up, surrender, surrendering, sacrifice, sacrificing, yielding, ceding; *historical* attainder.

forge[1] ▶ verb **1** *the smith forged swords and knives* **hammer out**, beat into shape, found, cast, mould, model; **fashion**, form, shape, make, manufacture, produce, turn out; *informal* knock together, knock up, knock off.
2 *they forged a partnership with city government* **build**, build up, construct, form, create, establish, set up, put together.
3 *it took great skill to forge the signature* **fake**, falsify, counterfeit, copy fraudulently, copy, imitate, reproduce, replicate, simulate; *informal* pirate.

forge[2] ▶ verb *he forged through the busy side streets* **advance steadily**, advance gradually, press on, push on, soldier on, march on, push forward, move forward, move along, proceed, progress, make progress/headway.
□ **forge ahead** *Jack's horse forged ahead and took the lead* **advance rapidly**, progress quickly, make swift progress, increase speed, put a spurt on.

forged ▶ adjective *he was charged with passing forged banknotes* **fake**, faked, false, counterfeit, imitation, reproduction, replica, copied; sham, bogus, dummy, ersatz, invalid; *informal* phoney, dud, pretend, crooked.
OPPOSITE genuine.

forger ▶ noun *the painting was the work of a forger* **counterfeiter**, falsifier, faker, copyist, imitator; *archaic* coiner.

forgery ▶ noun **1** *the defendant was found guilty of forgery* **counterfeiting**, fraudulent copying, fraudulent imitation; falsification, faking, fabrication; *archaic* coining.
2 *the painting was discovered to be a forgery* **fake**, counterfeit, sham, fraud, imitation, dummy, mock-up, reproduction, replica, copy, print, lookalike, likeness; *informal* phoney, pirate, bootleg, knock-off, rip-off, dupe.

forget ▶ verb **1** *he forgot where he had parked his car* **fail to remember**, fail to recall, fail to think of, let slip.
OPPOSITE remember.
2 *how could you forget your notes?* **leave behind**, omit to take, overlook, lose track of, mislay, misplace, lose.
3 *I forgot to close the door* **neglect**, fail, omit, not remember; *archaic* pretermit.
4 *the rich world would love to forget Africa* **stop thinking about**, think no more of, cease to think of, cease to remember, put out of one's mind, shut out, blank out, pay no heed to, not worry about, ignore, overlook, never mind, take no notice of, banish from one's thoughts, put away, get over, set aside, lay aside, pass over, abandon, have done with, drop, disregard, brush off, shrug off.
□ **forget oneself** *I'm sorry about that—I forgot myself* **act improperly**, misbehave, do wrong, go wrong, behave badly, be misbehaved, misconduct oneself, be bad, be naughty, get up to mischief, get up to no good, act up, give/cause someone trouble; sin, go astray, transgress, trespass, fall from grace, lapse, degenerate; *Brit. informal* muck about, play up.

forgetful ▶ adjective **1** *those forgetful members who have not renewed their membership* **absent-minded**, apt to forget, amnesic, amnesiac, vague, abstracted; *informal* scatterbrained, with a mind/memory like a sieve.
OPPOSITE reliable.
2 *she was forgetful of the time* **heedless**, neglectful, careless, unmindful, disregardful; inattentive to, negligent about, oblivious to, lax about, indifferent to, remiss in/about.
OPPOSITE heedful.

forgetfulness ▶ noun **1** *loss of function of some brain cells can result in forgetfulness* **absent-mindedness**, amnesia, poor memory, a lapse of memory, vagueness, abstraction.
OPPOSITES a good memory; reliability.
2 *concentration on things material meant a forgetfulness of God* **neglect**, negligence, heedlessness, carelessness, disregard; inattention to, obliviousness to, indifference to; *rare* unmindfulness.
OPPOSITE heed.

forgivable ▶ adjective *I reckon the odd lapse is forgivable* **pardonable**, excusable, condonable, understandable, tolerable, permissible, allowable, justifiable; all right, within accepted bounds; minor, petty, slight, unimportant, insignificant, trivial, venial, not serious.
OPPOSITE unforgivable.

forgive ▸ verb **1** *she would not forgive him for deceiving her* **pardon**, excuse, exonerate, absolve, acquit, let off, grant an amnesty to, amnesty; make allowances for, stop feeling resentful towards, feel no resentment towards, stop feeling malice towards, feel no malice towards, harbour no grudge against, bury the hatchet with; let bygones be bygones; *informal* let someone off the hook, go easy on; *rare* exculpate.
OPPOSITES blame; convict; resent.
2 *you must forgive his rude conduct* **excuse**, overlook, disregard, ignore, pass over, make allowances for, allow; **condone**, let go, let pass, sanction, turn a blind eye to, turn a deaf ear to, wink at, connive at, blink at, indulge, tolerate; *rare* extenuate.
OPPOSITE punish.

CHOOSE THE RIGHT WORD

forgive, pardon, excuse, condone

- **Forgive** is the standard word used when someone to whom a wrong has been done makes a deliberate decision to put aside the feelings of anger and blame occasioned by that wrong (*he forgave the bomber who killed his daughter | she could never forgive her friend's betrayal*). It is also used informally in the sense of 'excuse', especially in the passive, to indicate that an error is understandable (*you could be forgiven for thinking that our basic foods haven't changed for years*).
- **Pardon** is used mainly to refer to the official remission of a punishment to which an offender has been sentenced (*the President pardoned nine prisoners with heavy sentences*). When used as a synonym for *forgive*, it has a rather old-fashioned or mannered tone (*you have pardoned all their wrongs*).
- A circumstance that **excuses** an action provides reasons for seeing it as less blameworthy than it would otherwise be (*nothing can excuse a teacher who fails to draw attention to these facts | his friend's betrayal could be excused as a simple error of judgement*). *Excuse* implies that wrongdoing is merely being overlooked, rather than that the wrongdoer is absolved.
- **Condone** is a more critical term than the other three and is used only of relatively serious misdemeanours. It suggests that someone who does not condemn behaviour that is morally wrong is in turn wrong to be so forgiving, so is often used in the negative. The object is always an action, not a person (*union leaders cannot condone the use of violence*).

forgiveness ▸ noun *we beg your forgiveness for keeping you waiting* **pardon**, absolution, exoneration, remission, dispensation, indulgence, understanding, tolerance, purgation, clemency, mercy, pity, lenience, leniency, quarter; reprieve, discharge, amnesty, delivery, acquittal, clearing, pardoning, condoning, condonation, vindication, exculpation; *informal* let-off, letting off; *archaic* shrift, shriving.
OPPOSITES mercilessness; punishment.

forgiving ▸ adjective *Oliver Cromwell was not renowned for his forgiving nature* **merciful**, lenient, compassionate, pitying, magnanimous, humane, clement, mild, soft-hearted, forbearing, tolerant, easy-going, indulgent, accommodating, understanding, placable.
OPPOSITES merciless; vindictive.

forgo, forego ▸ verb *no one else on the team was prepared to forgo his lunch hour* **do without**, go without, give up, waive, renounce, surrender, disavow, relinquish, part with, drop, sacrifice, forswear, abjure, swear off, steer clear of, abandon, cede, yield, abstain from, refrain from, eschew, cut out; decline, refuse, repudiate, spurn.
OPPOSITE keep.

forgotten ▸ adjective *Vivaldi's operas are largely forgotten* **unremembered**, out of mind, gone clean out of someone's mind, past recollection, beyond/past recall, consigned to oblivion, obliterated, blotted out, buried, left behind, bygone, past, gone, lost, irrecoverable, irretrievable; neglected, overlooked, ignored, disregarded, unappreciated, unrecognized, of no interest.
OPPOSITE remembered.

fork ▸ verb *where the road forks, bear left* **branch**, split, divide, subdivide, separate, part, diverge, go in different directions, go separate ways, bifurcate, split in two; branch off; *technical* furcate, divaricate, ramify.

forked ▸ adjective *the red kite has a forked tail* **branching**, branched, diverging, Y-shaped, V-shaped, pronged, divided, split, separated; *technical* bifurcate, divaricate.
OPPOSITE straight.

forlorn ▸ adjective **1** *she looked so forlorn that Maggie's heart lurched* **unhappy**, sad, miserable, sorrowful, dejected, despondent, disconsolate, wretched, abject, morose, regretful, broken-hearted, heartbroken, down, downcast, dispirited, downhearted, heavy-hearted, crestfallen, depressed, melancholy, blue, gloomy, glum, mournful, despairing, doleful, woebegone, woeful, tearful, long-faced, joyless, cheerless, out of sorts; pitiful, pitiable, heart-rending, piteous, pathetic, uncared-for; *informal* down in the mouth, down in the dumps, fed up; *rare* lachrymose.
OPPOSITE happy.
2 *Brooke End signal box was left to stand forlorn* **desolate**, deserted, abandoned, forsaken, forgotten, neglected.
3 *his voice rose in a forlorn attempt to drown the racket* **hopeless**, with no chance of success, beyond hope; useless, futile, pointless, purposeless, vain, unavailing, nugatory; unsuccessful, failed; *archaic* bootless.

form ▸ noun **1** *the general form of the landscape was well established before the glaciations* **shape**, configuration, formation, conformation, structure, construction, arrangement, disposition, appearance, outward form/appearance, exterior; contours, lines, outline, silhouette, profile; design, format; cut, pattern, mould.
2 *the human form* **body**, shape, figure, silhouette, proportions, stature, build, frame, physique, anatomy; *informal* vital statistics, chassis, bod.
3 *as a dramatist he was a perfectionist about the form of his work* **structure**, arrangement, construction, framework, format, layout, design, organization, system, planning, order, orderliness, symmetry, proportion.
OPPOSITE content.
4 *many of these diseases take the form of persistent infections* **manifestation**, appearance, embodiment, incarnation, semblance, shape, guise, character, description, expression.
5 *sponsorship is a form of advertising* **kind**, sort, type, order, class, classification, category, variety, genre, brand, style; species, genus, family, generation, breed, strain, denomination; *technical* phylum.
6 *put the mixture into a form* **mould**, cast, shape, matrix, die, pattern.
7 *Are fish knives passé? What is the correct form?* **etiquette**, social practice, custom, usage, use, habit, wont, protocol, procedure, rules, convention, tradition, fashion, style, routine, ritual, pattern, regimen, policy, method, system, way, rule, formula, set formula; *Latin* modus operandi; *formal* praxis.
8 *they handed her a form to fill in* **questionnaire**, document, coupon, tear-off slip, sheet of paper, paper; application (form), entry form, report, return, record.
9 *what form is your daughter in?* **class**, year, school group, tutor group, set, stream, band; *N. Amer.* grade.
10 *he has been working hard to get into top form for the Olympics* **fitness**, physical fitness, condition, fettle, shape, trim, health, state of health; *Brit. informal* nick.
11 (*Brit. informal*) *he must have form—I'd swear he's been in prison* **a criminal record**, a police record, previous convictions, a history of crime; *informal* previous.
12 (*Brit.*) *people sat on forms by wooden tables* **bench**, long seat, pew, settle, stall.
□ **good form** *it is not good form to leave visitors on their own* **good manners**, manners, polite behaviour, correct behaviour, acceptable conduct, convention, etiquette, protocol; *informal* the done thing.
OPPOSITE bad form.
▸ verb **1** *the urns were formed from unbaked clay* **make**, fashion, shape, model, mould, forge, found, cast, sculpt, hew, carve; construct, build, manufacture, fabricate, assemble, put together; create, produce, concoct, devise, contrive, frame.
2 *he formed a plan to write about the period* **formulate**, devise, conceive, work out, think up, prepare, make ready, get ready, work up, lay, draw up, put together, produce, fashion, concoct, construct, frame, forge, hatch, develop, organize; *informal* dream up.
3 *they plan to form a new company* **set up**, devise, establish, found, launch, float, create, bring into being, organize, institute, start, begin, get going, initiate, bring about, inaugurate, lay the foundations of.
OPPOSITES abolish; dissolve.
4 *a mist was forming in the valley* **materialize**, come into being/existence, crystallize, emerge, spring up, develop; **take shape**, appear, loom, show up, become visible, come into view, present itself, reveal itself, show itself.
OPPOSITE disappear.
5 *the horse may form bad habits which are destructive to itself* **acquire**, develop, get, pick up, contract, grow into, slip into, get into.
OPPOSITES avoid; get out of.
6 *his men formed themselves into an arrowhead* **arrange**, draw up, line up, assemble, organize, sort, order, range, array, dispose, marshal, deploy, gather, group, place, position, rank, grade.
7 *they assume that the parts of society form an integrated whole* **comprise**, make, make up, constitute, compose, add up to, account for, represent.
8 *the city formed a natural meeting point for traders and adventurers* **constitute**, serve as, act as, function as, perform the function of, do duty for, make, embody, compose, comprise.
9 *natural objects are most important in forming the mind of the child* **develop**, mould, shape, train, teach, instruct, educate, school, tutor, coach, groom, drill, discipline, prime, prepare, guide, direct, inform, verse, enlighten, inculcate, indoctrinate, edify, cultivate, improve, better, uplift, elevate.

WORD LINKS
related prefix **morpho-** (e.g. ***morphology, morphometry***)
related suffix **-morph** (e.g. ***polymorph, ectomorph***)

F

formal ▶ adjective **1** *a formal dinner* **ceremonial**, ceremonious, ritualistic, ritual, conventional, traditional, orthodox, prescribed, fixed, set; stately, courtly, solemn, dignified; elaborate, ornate, dressy.
OPPOSITE informal.
2 *he has a very formal manner* **aloof**, reserved, remote, detached, unapproachable, stand-offish, keeping people at arm's length; stiff, prim, stuffy, staid, ceremonious, correct, proper, decorous, conventional, precise, exact, punctilious, unbending, inflexible, strait-laced; unresponsive, unfriendly, unsympathetic, haughty, forbidding, austere; withdrawn, restrained, reticent, taciturn, uncommunicative, undemonstrative, unforthcoming; unsocial, antisocial.
OPPOSITES informal; casual.
3 *in the US 'autumn' is a formal alternative to 'fall'* **literary**, scholarly, learned, intellectual, erudite, bookish, highbrow, academic, cultivated.
OPPOSITES informal; colloquial.
4 *a formal garden* **symmetrical**, regular, orderly, arranged, methodical, systematic, in straight lines, regimented.
OPPOSITE informal.
5 *formal permission is required to demolish a listed building* **official**, legal, authorized, approved, validated, certified, endorsed, documented, sanctioned, licensed, recognized, authoritative, accepted, verified, legitimate, lawful, valid, bona fide, proper, prescribed, pro forma.
OPPOSITES informal; unofficial.
6 *she had had no formal education* **conventional**, mainstream, rigid; school, institutional.
OPPOSITE informal.

formality ▶ noun **1** *he disliked the formality of the occasion* **ceremony**, ceremoniousness, ritual, conventionality, red tape, protocol, decorum; stateliness, courtliness, solemnity, etiquette.
OPPOSITE informality.
2 *the book tells of Pétain's formality as a colonel* **aloofness**, reserve, remoteness, detachment, unapproachability, stand-offishness; stiffness, primness, stuffiness, staidness, correctness, decorum, punctiliousness, inflexibility; reticence, taciturnity; antisocial nature.
OPPOSITE informality.
3 (**formalities**) *when you apply for a loan, we keep the formalities to a minimum* **official procedure**, rule, regulation, convention, ritual, custom, matter of form, formal gesture; bureaucracy, red tape, paperwork, form, punctilio, protocol.
4 *the medical examination is just* ***a formality*** **routine**, routine practice, normal procedure.
OPPOSITE exceptional measure.
5 *politicians were confident that Cabinet approval would be a formality* **matter of course**, foregone conclusion, inevitability, certainty; *informal* sure thing.
OPPOSITES possibility; unlikely possibility.

format ▶ noun *the journal has been well received in its new format* **design**, style, presentation, appearance, look; form, shape, size; arrangement, plan, scheme, composition, make-up, configuration, structure, set-up.

formation ▶ noun **1** *they are trying to date the formation of the island's sand ridges* **emergence**, coming into being, genesis, development, evolution, origination, shaping, generation.
OPPOSITES destruction; disappearance.
2 *the formation of a new government* **establishment**, setting up, start, getting going, initiation, institution, founding, foundation, inception, creation, inauguration, organization, building, construction, installation, planting.
OPPOSITE dissolution.
3 *the aircraft were flying in tight formation* **configuration**, arrangement, pattern, array, alignment, positioning, disposition, order, ordering, organization, design, marshalling, grouping, layout, format.

formative ▶ adjective **1** *schooling is not the only significant element in a child's formative years* **developmental**, developing, growing, mouldable, malleable, impressionable, susceptible.
2 *the early Fabians had a formative influence on the social history of the United Kingdom* **determining**, controlling, influential, guiding, decisive, forming, shaping, moulding, determinative.

former ▶ adjective **1** *the former Bishop of London* **one-time**, erstwhile, sometime, late; **previous**, foregoing, preceding, old, earlier, prior, precursory, antecedent, ex-, past, last; *French* ci-devant; *rare* quondam, whilom, anterior, precedent.
OPPOSITES future; next.
2 *in former times* **earlier**, old, past, bygone, long-ago, forgotten, immemorial, remote; ancient, primeval, primordial, prehistoric, antediluvian; gone by, long ago, long departed, long gone, long past, of old; *literary* of yore, olden, foregone; *rare* primigenial, pristine.
OPPOSITES present; future.
3 *those who take the former view* **first-mentioned**, first.
OPPOSITE latter.

formerly ▶ adverb *he was formerly the head of a large comprehensive school* **previously**, earlier, earlier on, before, until now/then, hitherto, née, once, once upon a time, at one time, at an earlier time, in the past, in days gone by, back in the day, in years gone by, in times gone by, in bygone days, in times past, in former times, in earlier times, time was when; back, ago; *formal* heretofore.

formidable ▶ adjective **1** *every man wore a formidable curved dagger* **intimidating**, forbidding, redoubtable, daunting, alarming, frightening, terrifying, petrifying, horrifying, chilling, disturbing, disquieting, dreadful, brooding, awesome, fearsome, ominous, foreboding, sinister, menacing, threatening, dangerous; *informal* spooky, scary, creepy; *archaic* direful, bodeful.
OPPOSITES pleasant-looking; comforting.
2 *they face a formidable task* **onerous**, arduous, taxing, difficult, hard, heavy, laborious, burdensome, strenuous, vigorous, back-breaking, stiff, uphill, relentless, Herculean, monumental, colossal; demanding, trying, tough, challenging, exacting, overwhelming; exhausting, wearying, fatiguing, tiring, punishing, gruelling, grinding; *informal* killing, no picnic; *Brit. informal* knackering; *rare* toilsome, exigent.
OPPOSITE easy.
3 *a formidable opponent* **capable**, able, proficient, adept, adroit, accomplished; **impressive**, strong, powerful, mighty, terrific, tremendous, great, redoubtable, indomitable, invincible; seasoned, skilful, skilled, gifted, talented, masterly, virtuoso, expert, knowledgeable, qualified, trained; efficient, good, excellent, brilliant, outstanding, first-class, first-rate; *informal* mean, wicked, deadly, nifty, crack, ace, wizard, magic; *N. Amer. informal* crackerjack; *vulgar slang* shit-hot; *archaic or humorous* compleat; *rare* habile.
OPPOSITE weak.

formless ▶ adjective *the tremor turned several houses into a formless heap of rubble* **shapeless**, amorphous, unformed, unshaped; nebulous, vague, hazy, misty, shadowy, ill-defined, indistinct, obscure, blurred, blurry, indefinite, indeterminate; structureless, unstructured, ill-organized.
OPPOSITES shaped; definite.

formula ▶ noun **1** *a legal formula* **form of words**, set expression, phrase, saying, aphorism; code, set of words, set of symbols; *rare* formulary.
2 *the four foreign ministers failed to agree on a formula* **recipe**, prescription, blueprint, plan, method, procedure, technique, system; rules, principles, precepts; modus operandi, mechanism, convention, ritual.
3 *a formula for removing grease from clothing* **preparation**, concoction, mixture, compound, creation, substance; cream, lotion, liquid, solution, potion, application, paste.

formulate ▶ verb **1** *the miners formulated a plan to keep the mines open* **draw up**, put together, work out, map out, plan, prepare, get ready, compose, produce, construct, make, develop, contrive, hatch, devise, think up, conceive, create, frame, lay, invent, originate, coin, design; write out, write down, put in writing, put down (on paper), draft.
2 *there is a problem with the way you have formulated this question* **express**, articulate, put into words, utter, state, say, verbalize, word, phrase, render, frame, couch, voice, give voice to, give form to, give expression to; convey, communicate, put across/over, get across/over; specify, define, particularize, itemize, detail, indicate, designate, systematize.

fornication ▶ noun (*archaic*) *the punishment for fornication was flogging* **extramarital sex**, extramarital relations, adultery, infidelity, unfaithfulness, cuckoldry; affair, liaison, sexual intercourse, sex, intercourse, sexual relations, coupling; *informal* hanky-panky, a bit on the side, bonking, rumpy pumpy, a bit of the other, how's your father; *S. African informal* pata-pata; *archaic* carnal knowledge, congress, commerce.

forsake ▶ verb **1** (*archaic*) *she forsook her child, giving him up for adoption | he forsook his wife* **abandon**, desert, leave, quit, depart from, leave behind, leave high and dry, turn one's back on, cast aside, give up, reject, disown; break (up) with, jilt, strand, leave stranded, leave flat, leave in the lurch, throw over, cast aside/off, betray; *informal* run/walk out on, rat on, drop, dump, ditch, chuck; *N. Amer. informal* give someone the air.
OPPOSITES stay with; return to.
2 *it was never expected that voters would forsake their loyalties* **renounce**, give up, relinquish, dispense with, forgo, desist from, forswear, disclaim, disown, disavow, discard, set aside, wash one's hands of, turn one's back on, repudiate, have done with; withdraw, drop, do away with, jettison; betray, renege on; *informal* ditch, scrap, scrub, axe, junk.
OPPOSITE keep.

forsaken ▶ adjective **1** *when the bride failed to appear the forsaken groom fled to the men's room* **abandoned**, deserted, jilted, stranded, discarded, shunned, renounced, betrayed, rejected, disowned; *informal* dropped, dumped, ditched.
2 *what brought those poor unfortunates to this forsaken place?* **desolate**, bleak, godforsaken, remote, isolated, sequestered, lonely, solitary, deserted, derelict, dreary, forlorn, uninviting, cheerless, depressing, sad.

forswear ▶ verb *we are formally forswearing the use of chemical weapons* **renounce**, swear off, forgo, abjure, reject, relinquish, abstain from, refrain from, shun, avoid, eschew, do without, go without, steer clear of, give a wide berth to, have nothing to do with, decline, refuse, repudiate, spurn; **give up**, dispense with, stop, cease, finish, discontinue, break off, drop, cut out; *informal* kick, quit, jack in.
OPPOSITES adhere to; persist with.

fort ▸ noun **fortress**, castle, citadel, blockhouse, burg, keep, tower, donjon, turret; stronghold, redoubt, fortification, bastion; fastness; (*in Spain*) alcazar; *rare* hold, fortalice.

forte ▸ noun *acting had always been her forte* **strength**, strong point, speciality, long suit, strong suit, talent, special ability, skill, bent, gift, claim to fame, department; *French* métier, pièce de résistance; *informal* bag, thing, cup of tea.
OPPOSITE weakness.

forth ▸ adverb **1** *smoke billowed forth when the air was still* **out**, outside, away, off, ahead, forward, away from home, abroad; into view, into the open, out of hiding; into existence.
2 *from that day forth* **onward**, onwards, on, forward, forwards; for ever, into eternity; until now.

forthcoming ▸ adjective **1** *forthcoming events* **imminent**, impending, coming, approaching, advancing, nearing, near; future, expected, anticipated, prospective; close, (close) at hand, in store, in the wind, in the air, in the offing, in the pipeline, on the horizon, on the way, on us, about to happen; *informal* on the cards.
OPPOSITES past; current.
2 *no reply was forthcoming* **available**, made available, ready, at hand, accessible, obtainable, at someone's disposal, on offer; obtained, given, vouchsafed to someone; *informal* up for grabs, on tap.
OPPOSITE unavailable.
3 *most viewers voiced no opinions, but some were more forthcoming* **communicative**, expansive, informative, expressive, unreserved, uninhibited, outgoing, frank, open, candid; **talkative**, conversational, chatty, gossipy, loquacious, garrulous, voluble, verbose, effusive, gushing; *informal* mouthy, gabby, windy, gassy; *rare* multiloquent, multiloquous.
OPPOSITE uncommunicative.

forthright ▸ adjective *he was forthright in speaking out against human rights abuses* **frank**, direct, straightforward, honest, candid, open, sincere, straight, straight to the point, blunt, plain-spoken, outspoken, downright, uninhibited, unreserved, point blank, no-nonsense, matter-of-fact, bluff, undiplomatic, tactless; not afraid to call a spade a spade, not beating around the bush, speaking as one finds; explicit, clear, plain, unequivocal, unambiguous, unqualified, categorical; *informal* straight from the shoulder, upfront.
OPPOSITES secretive; dishonest.

forthwith ▸ adverb *the government insisted that all the hostages be released forthwith* **immediately**, at once, instantly, directly, right away, straight away, now, this/that (very) minute, this/that instant, then and there, there and then, here and now, in/like a flash, instantaneously, by return, post-haste, without delay, without further/more ado, without hesitation, unhesitatingly; quickly, as quickly as possible, fast, speedily, with all speed, promptly, as soon as possible, a.s.a.p., expeditiously; *N. Amer.* momentarily, in short order; *French* tout de suite; *informal* straight off, toot sweet, pronto, double quick, p.d.q. (pretty damn quick), in double quick time; *Indian informal* ekdam; *archaic* straightway, instanter, forthright.
OPPOSITE sometime.

fortification ▸ noun **1** *to demolish enemy fortifications, heavy guns had been developed* **rampart**, defensive wall, defences, bulwark, palisade, stockade, redoubt, earthwork, outwork, bastion, parapet, battlement, blockhouse, barricade, buttress, stronghold; *rare* fieldwork, ravelin, fortalice.
2 *forced labour was used in the fortification of ports and harbours* **strengthening**, reinforcement, consolidation, shoring up, bracing, boosting, buttressing, toughening; *informal* beefing up.
3 *the fortification of Madeira with brandy began in the mid-eighteenth century* **strengthening**, reinforcement, bolstering, stiffening, supplementing, augmenting; *informal* beefing up.
OPPOSITE adulteration.

fortify ▸ verb **1** *the knights fortified their citadel as a defence against raids* **build defences round**, strengthen with defensive works, secure, protect, surround; *rare* embattle, rampart, mound.
2 *such a timber enclosure may have been fortified by a masonry wall* **strengthen**, reinforce, toughen, consolidate, bolster, shore up, brace, buttress, stiffen, support, hold up.
OPPOSITE weaken.
3 *he fortified himself with a large tot of rum* **invigorate**, strengthen, energize, enliven, liven up, animate, vitalize, rejuvenate, restore, revive, refresh; galvanize, dynamize, fire up, rouse, motivate, boost, perk up, stimulate, inspire, pick up, embolden, give courage to, encourage, cheer, hearten, buoy up, reassure, make confident, brace, sustain; *informal* pep up, buck up, give a shot in the arm to; *rare* activate, inspirit.
OPPOSITES sedate; subdue.
4 *fortified wine* **add spirits/alcohol to**, strengthen.
OPPOSITE dilute.
5 *breakfast cereals are fortified with vitamins* **add vitamins/minerals to**, boost, improve; *informal* beef up.

fortitude ▸ noun *he accepted his increasing illness with fortitude* **courage**, bravery, strength of mind, strength of character, moral strength, toughness of spirit, firmness of purpose, strong-mindedness, resilience, backbone, spine, mettle, spirit, nerve, pluck, pluckiness, doughtiness, fearlessness, valour, intrepidity, stout-heartedness, endurance; stoicism, steadfastness, patience, long-suffering, forbearance, tenacity, pertinacity, perseverance, resolve, resolution, resoluteness, determination; *informal* guts, grit, spunk.
OPPOSITE faint-heartedness.

fortress ▸ noun **fort**, castle, citadel, blockhouse, burg, keep, tower, donjon, turret, bunker; stronghold, redoubt, fortification, bastion; fastness; (*in Spain*) alcazar; *rare* hold, fortalice.

fortuitous ▸ adjective **1** *his success depended on entirely fortuitous events* **chance**, unexpected, unanticipated, unpredictable, unforeseen, unlooked-for, serendipitous, casual, incidental, coincidental, haphazard, random, accidental, inadvertent, unintentional, unintended, unplanned, unpremeditated.
OPPOSITE predictable.
2 *United were saved by a fortuitous penalty* **lucky**, fortunate, providential, advantageous, timely, opportune, serendipitous, expedient, heaven-sent, auspicious, propitious, felicitous, convenient, apt; *informal* fluky; *Brit. informal* jammy.

fortunate ▸ adjective **1** *he was fortunate that the punishment was so slight* **lucky**, favoured, blessed, blessed with good luck, in luck, born with a silver spoon in one's mouth, born under a lucky star, having a charmed life, charmed, happy; *informal* sitting pretty; *Brit. informal* jammy.
OPPOSITE unfortunate.
2 *in a fortunate position* **favourable**, advantageous, providential, auspicious, welcome, heaven-sent, beneficial, propitious, fortuitous, promising, encouraging, fruitful, opportune, happy, felicitous, profitable, gainful, rewarding, helpful, useful, valuable, timely, well timed, convenient, expedient; *archaic* seasonable.
OPPOSITE unfavourable.
3 *we have to raise money in more fortunate areas like Oxfordshire* **wealthy**, rich, affluent, opulent, prosperous, well off, moneyed, well-to-do, well heeled, comfortable; favoured, privileged, advantaged, socially advantaged, enviable; successful, flourishing.
OPPOSITE underprivileged.

fortunately ▸ adverb *fortunately, the church was in very sound structural order* **luckily**, happily, providentially, opportunely, by good luck, by good fortune, as luck would have it, propitiously; mercifully, thankfully; thank goodness, thank God, thank heavens, thank the stars.

fortune ▸ noun **1** *some malicious act of fortune keeps them separate | fortune smiled on them* **chance**, accident, coincidence, serendipity, twist of fate, destiny, fortuity, providence, freak, hazard; **fate**, Lady Luck, Dame Fortune; *N. Amer.* happenstance.
2 *the company has enjoyed two drastic changes of fortune over the past twenty years* **luck**, fate, destiny, predestination, the stars, fortuity, serendipity, karma, kismet, lot, what is written in the stars.
3 (**fortunes**) *there should be an upswing in Sheffield's fortunes* **circumstances**, state of affairs, condition, financial/material position, financial/material situation, financial/material status; resources, means, finances, income; plight, predicament; station in life, lot, lifestyle; future, prospects.
4 *he made his fortune in wholesale grocery* **wealth**, riches, substance, property, assets, resources, means, possessions, treasure, estate; affluence, prosperity.
5 (**a fortune**) (*informal*) *this place costs a fortune to run* **a huge amount**, a small fortune, a king's ransom, a vast sum, a large sum of money, a lot, millions, billions; *informal* a packet, a mint, a bundle, a pile, a wad, a pretty penny, an arm and a leg, a tidy sum, a killing; *Brit. informal* a bomb, loadsamoney, shedloads; *N. Amer. informal* big bucks, big money, gazillions; *Austral. informal* big bickies.

fortune teller ▸ noun **clairvoyant**, crystal-gazer, psychic, prophet, forecaster of the future, seer, oracle, soothsayer, prognosticator, prophesier, augur, diviner, sibyl; medium, spiritualist; telepathist, telepath, mind-reader; palmist, palm-reader, chiromancer; astrologer; *Scottish* spaewife, spaeman; *rare* haruspex, vaticinator, oracler, chirosophist, spiritist, palmister.

forum ▸ noun **1** *forums were held for staff to air grievances and make suggestions* **meeting**, assembly, gathering, conference, seminar, convention, colloquy, convocation, congress, rally, council, symposium, conclave, congregation, synod, diet; (*in N. Amer. & NZ*) caucus; *informal* get-together; *rare* colloquium.
2 *the UN could provide a valuable forum for discussions* **setting**, place, scene, context, stage, framework, backdrop; medium, means, agency, channel, avenue, vehicle, mechanism, apparatus, auspices.
3 *every Roman town of any size had a forum and a temple* **public meeting place**, public square, marketplace; (*in Greece*) agora.

forward ▸ adverb **1** *the traffic moved slowly forward* **ahead**, forwards, onwards, onward, on, further.
2 *police asked witnesses to come forward* **towards the front**, frontwards, out, forth, into view, into the open, into public notice, into prominence.
3 *from that day forward* **onward**, onwards, on, forth, forwards; for ever, into eternity; until now.
▸ adjective **1** *in a forward direction* **moving forwards**, moving ahead, onward,

F

advancing, progressing, progressive.
OPPOSITE backward.
2 *the fortress served as the Austrian army's forward base against the Russians* **front**, advance, foremost, head, leading, frontal.
OPPOSITE rear.
3 *forward planning* **future**, forward-looking, for the future, prospective.
4 *the girls seemed very forward to a middle-class boy like him* **bold**, **brazen**, brazen-faced, barefaced, brash, shameless, immodest, audacious, daring, presumptuous, presuming, assuming, familiar, overfamiliar; irreverent, over-assertive, overconfident, overweening, aggressive, thrusting, pert, impudent, impertinent, cheeky, insolent, unabashed; *informal* brass-necked, cocky, fresh.
OPPOSITE shy.
5 *I never saw the trees so forward as they are this year* **advanced**, well advanced, early, premature; precocious.
OPPOSITE late.
▸ **verb 1** *my mother forwarded me your letter the day she received it* **send on**, post on, redirect, readdress, pass on.
2 *the goods were forwarded by sea* **send**, dispatch, transmit, carry, convey, deliver, remit, post, mail, ship, freight.
3 *my five months in England were used to forward my plans* **advance**, further, hasten, hurry along, expedite, accelerate, speed up, step up, aid, assist, help, foster, encourage, contribute to, promote, favour, support, back, give backing to, facilitate.

forward-looking ▸ **adjective** *meanwhile, the forward-looking countries of Europe forged ahead* **progressive**, enlightened, go-ahead, dynamic, pushing, bold, modern, enterprising, ambitious, pioneering, progressivist, positive, reforming, radical, liberal; *informal* go-getting.
OPPOSITE backward-looking.

forwardness ▸ **noun** *Constance was so appalled at his forwardness that she burst out, 'Don't be cheeky!'* **boldness**, brashness, brazenness, barefacedness, shamelessness, immodesty, audacity, effrontery, daring, presumption, familiarity, overfamiliarity, irreverence, over-assertiveness, overconfidence, overweening nature; aggressiveness, aggression, pertness, impudence, impertinence, cheek, insolence; *informal* neck, brass neck, face, cockiness, freshness.
OPPOSITE shyness.

forwards ▸ **adverb.** *See* FORWARD.
OPPOSITE backwards.

fossil *See centre pages for lists of* **Dinosaurs** **Fossils** **Humans**
▸ **noun** *fossils of eels have been found in rocks a hundred million years old* **petrified remains**, petrified impression, cast, impression, mould, remnant, relic; *Geology* reliquiae.

WORD LINKS
study of fossil animals and plants **palaeontology, palaeobiology**
study of fossil plants **palaeobotany**

fossilized ▸ **adjective 1** *the fossilized remains of extinct animals* petrified, ossified; *rare* lapidified.
2 *a traditional pattern of etiquette was the fossilized norm in the royal court* **archaic**, antiquated, antediluvian, old-fashioned, quaint, outdated, outmoded, behind the times, anachronistic, stuck in time; *informal* prehistoric.

foster ▸ **verb 1** *a ruler known for fostering the arts* **encourage**, promote, further, stimulate, advance, forward, cultivate, nurture, strengthen, enrich, help, aid, abet, assist, contribute to, support, endorse, champion, speak for, proselytize, sponsor, espouse, uphold, back, boost, give backing to, facilitate.
OPPOSITES neglect; suppress; destroy.
2 *they have fostered a succession of children* **bring up**, rear, raise, care for, take care of, look after, nurture, provide for; mother, parent.

foul ▸ **adjective 1** *the skunk produces a foul stench* **disgusting**, revolting, repellent, repulsive, repugnant, abhorrent, loathsome, offensive, detestable, awful, dreadful, horrible, terrible, horrendous, hideous, appalling, atrocious, vile, abominable, frightful, sickening, nauseating, nauseous, stomach-churning, stomach-turning, off-putting, uninviting, unpalatable, unappetizing, unsavoury, distasteful, nasty, obnoxious, objectionable, odious; noxious, evil-smelling, foul-smelling, smelly, stinking, high, rank, rancid, fetid, malodorous; *N. Amer.* vomitous; *informal* ghastly, horrid, gruesome, God-awful, gross, diabolical, putrid, yucky, icky, grotty, sick-making, gut-churning; *Brit. informal* beastly, whiffy, pongy, niffy; *N. Amer. informal* lousy, skanky, funky; *Austral. informal* on the nose; *literary* noisome, mephitic; *archaic* disgustful, loathly; *rare* miasmic, miasmal, olid.
OPPOSITE fragrant.
2 *get your foul clothes out of my bedroom* **dirty**, filthy, mucky, grimy, grubby, stained, dirt-encrusted, muddy, muddied, unclean, unwashed; squalid, sordid, shabby, sleazy, nasty, soiled, sullied, scummy; rotten, defiled, decaying, putrid, putrefied, smelly, fetid; *informal* cruddy, yucky, icky; *Brit. informal* manky, gungy, grotty; *literary* befouled, besmirched, begrimed; *rare* feculent.
3 *she's been foul to poor Adam* **unkind**, unfriendly, disagreeable, inconsiderate, uncharitable, rude, churlish, spiteful, malicious, mean, mean-spirited, ill-tempered, ill-natured, ill-humoured, bad-tempered, hostile, vicious, malevolent, evil-minded, surly, obnoxious, poisonous, venomous, vindictive, malign, malignant, cantankerous, hateful, hurtful, cruel, wounding, abusive; *informal* bitchy, catty; *vulgar slang* shitty.
OPPOSITE kind.
4 *foul weather* **inclement**, unpleasant, disagreeable, dirty, nasty, rough, bad; stormy, squally, gusty, windy, blustery, blowy, wild, rainy, wet; foggy, misty, gloomy, murky, overcast, louring.
OPPOSITE fair.
5 *foul drinking water was blamed for the outbreak* **contaminated**, polluted, adulterated, infected, tainted, defiled, impure, filthy, dirty, unclean; *rare* feculent.
OPPOSITE clean.
6 *the foul fiend | these foul deeds cannot be ignored* **evil**, wicked, sinful, immoral, wrong, morally wrong, wrongful, bad, iniquitous, corrupt, black-hearted, ungodly, unholy, irreligious, unrighteous, sacrilegious, profane, blasphemous, impious, base, mean, vile; villainous, nefarious, erring, fallen, impure, sullied, tainted, monstrous, shocking, outrageous, atrocious, abominable, reprehensible, hateful, detestable, despicable, odious, contemptible, horrible, heinous, execrable, godless, diabolical, diabolic, fiendish, vicious, murderous, barbarous, black, dark; perverted, reprobate, sordid, depraved, degenerate, dissolute, dishonourable, dishonest, unscrupulous, unprincipled, underhand, roguish; criminal, illicit, unlawful, illegal, illegitimate, lawless; *informal* crooked, bent, warped, low-down, stinking, dirty, shady, rascally, scoundrelly; *Brit. informal* beastly, not cricket; *Law* malfeasant; *archaic* dastardly; *rare* peccable, egregious, flagitious.
OPPOSITE righteous.
7 *she had been subjected to abuse and foul language* **vulgar**, obscene, profane, blasphemous, gross, coarse, crude, filthy, dirty, indecent, indelicate, suggestive, smutty, off colour, low, lewd, ribald, salacious, scatological, offensive, abusive; *informal* blue.
OPPOSITE mild.
8 *he was booked for a foul tackle in the 67th minute* **unfair**, against the rules, illegal, unsporting, unsportsmanlike, below the belt, dirty, dishonourable, dishonest, underhand, unscrupulous, unjust, unprincipled, immoral, crooked, fraudulent; *informal* shady.
OPPOSITE fair.
▸ **verb 1** *every stream was being fouled with chemical waste* **dirty**, soil, stain, blacken, muddy, begrime, splash, spatter, smear, befoul, besmirch, blight, defile, make filthy, infect, pollute, contaminate, poison, taint, adulterate, sully; *literary* besmear.
2 *the vessel had fouled her nets* **tangle up**, entangle, snarl, catch, entwine, enmesh, twist, tangle.
3 *the rivers have been fouled by silt* **clog**, choke, block, jam, obstruct, congest, bung up, dam (up), plug, silt up, stop up, seal, fill up, close; *informal* gunge up; *technical* occlude, obturate.

foul-mouthed ▸ **adjective** *a drunken, foul-mouthed yob | foul-mouthed racist abuse* **vulgar**, crude, coarse; **obscene**, rude, smutty, dirty, filthy, indecent, indelicate, offensive, distasteful, obnoxious, risqué, suggestive, racy, earthy, off colour, colourful, ribald, Rabelaisian, bawdy, lewd, salacious, vile, depraved, sordid, X-rated, scatological; profane, foul, blasphemous, abusive, scurrilous; *informal* blue.

foul play ▸ **noun** *he died of a head wound, but foul play is not suspected* **criminal activity**, crime, a criminal offence, villainy, murder, criminal violence, criminality; *informal* dirty deeds.

found ▸ **verb 1** *he founded his company in 1989* **establish**, set up, start, begin, get going, initiate, institute, form, create, bring into being, launch, float, originate, develop, inaugurate, constitute, endow.
OPPOSITES dissolve; liquidate.
2 *they abandoned Attica and founded a new city* **build**, construct, erect, put up, elevate; plan, lay plans for; start to build, lay the foundations of.
OPPOSITES abandon; demolish.
3 *the British parliamentary system* **is founded** *on debate and opposition* **base**, build, construct, establish; ground in, root in; rest, hinge, depend.

foundation ▸ **noun 1** (often **foundations**) *the weight of the roof is transmitted through the walls down to the foundations* **footing**, foot, base, substructure, understructure, underpinning; bottom, bedrock, substratum.
2 *keeping records is the foundation of any personnel system* **basis**, starting point, base, point of departure, beginning, premise; fundamental point/principle, principal constituent, main ingredient; principles, fundamentals, rudiments; cornerstone, core, heart, thrust, essence, kernel, nub, underpinning, groundwork.
3 *there was no foundation for the claim* **justification**, grounds, defence, reason, cause, mitigating circumstances, mitigation, extenuation, explanation, occasion, basis, motive, motivation, excuse, call, pretext, provocation.
4 *soon after the foundation of the company* **founding**, establishing, setting up, starting, initiation, institution, forming, creation, launch, flotation, origination, development, inauguration, constitution, endowment.
OPPOSITES dissolution; liquidation.
5 *in his will he set up an educational foundation* **endowed institution**,

institution, charitable body, funding agency, source of funds.

founder[1], **foundress** ▶ noun *Thomas Bodley, the founder of Oxford's Bodleian Library* **originator**, creator, initiator, institutor, instigator, organizer, father, founding father, prime mover, architect, engineer, designer, deviser, developer, pioneer, author, planner, framer, inventor, mastermind, maker, producer, builder, constructor; literary begetter; rare establisher.

founder[2] ▶ verb **1** *the ship foundered on a voyage to Holland* **sink**, go to the bottom, go down, be lost at sea, submerge, capsize, run aground, be swamped; informal go to Davy Jones's locker.
2 *the scheme foundered due to lack of organizational backing* **fail**, be unsuccessful, not succeed, lack success, fall through, fall flat, break down, abort, miscarry, be defeated, suffer defeat, be in vain, be frustrated, collapse, misfire, backfire, not come up to scratch, meet with disaster, come to grief, come to nothing, come to naught, miss the mark, run aground, go wrong, go awry, go astray; informal flop, fizzle out, come a cropper, bite the dust, blow up in someone's face, go down like a lead balloon.
OPPOSITE succeed.
3 *some of their horses foundered in the river bed* **stumble**, trip, trip up, lose one's balance, lose/miss one's footing, slip, pitch, stagger, lurch, totter, fall, fall down, fall over, fall headlong, tumble, topple, sprawl, go lame, collapse.

foundling ▶ noun *the foster family was seen as the best place for foundlings* **abandoned infant**, waif, stray, orphan, outcast; French enfant trouvé; archaic wastrel.

fountain ▶ noun **1** *a fountain sprayed cool water into the air* **jet**, spray, spout, spurt, well, fount, cascade.
2 *the head porter needs to be a fountain of knowledge* **source**, fount, fountainhead, well head, wellspring, well; reservoir, fund, mass, mine, repository; informal walking encyclopedia.

four ▶ cardinal number **quartet**, foursome, tetralogy, quadruplets; Poetry quatrain, tetrastich; Music quadruplet; technical quaternion, tetrad; rare quaternary, quadrumvirate.

WORD LINKS

related prefixes	**quadr-** (e.g. ***quadraphonic***), **tetra-** (e.g. ***tetralogy***)
relating to four	**quaternary**
four-sided plane figure	**quadrilateral**
four-sided solid figure	**tetrahedron**
relating to four years	**quadrennial**

four-square ▶ adjective *a four-square and formidable hero* **resolute**, determined, full of determination, purposeful, purposive, resolved, decided, adamant, single-minded, firm, unswerving, unswervable, unwavering, undaunted, fixed, set, intent, insistent; steadfast, staunch, stalwart, earnest, manful, deliberate, unfaltering, unhesitating, unflinching, persevering, persistent, pertinacious, indefatigable, tenacious, bulldog, strong-minded, strong-willed, unshakeable, unshaken, steely, dedicated, committed, constant; stubborn, dogged, obstinate, obdurate, inflexible, relentless, intransigent, implacable, unyielding, unbending, immovable, unrelenting; spirited, brave, bold, courageous, plucky, stout, stout-hearted, mettlesome, indomitable, strenuous, vigorous, gritty, stiff; N. Amer. rock-ribbed; informal gutsy, spunky; rare perseverant, indurate.

fowl *See centre pages for list of* **Fowl**
▶ noun **poultry**; domestic fowl.

fox *See centre pages for list of* **Foxes**
▶ noun literary Reynard.

WORD LINKS

relating to foxes	**vulpine**
male	**fox**
female	**vixen**
young	**cub**
collective noun	**skulk**
home	**earth, hole, burrow**

foxy ▶ adjective (informal) *Alexis was a clever, foxy woman* **cunning**, crafty, wily, artful, guileful, devious, sly, knowing, scheming, designing, tricky, slippery, slick, manipulative, Machiavellian, deceitful, deceptive, duplicitous; shrewd, astute, clever, canny, sharp, sharp-witted, skilful, ingenious, resourceful, inventive, imaginative, deft, adroit, dexterous; informal savvy, fiendish, sneaky; Brit. informal fly; Scottish & N. English informal pawky; S. African informal slim; archaic subtle; rare vulpine, carny.

foyer ▶ noun *I'll meet you in the hotel foyer* **entrance hall**, hall, hallway, entrance, entry, porch, portico, reception area, atrium, concourse, lobby, vestibule, anteroom, antechamber, outer room, waiting room; N. Amer. entryway.

fracas ▶ noun *two officers were kicked and punched in a fracas earlier this week* **disturbance**, quarrel, scuffle, brawl, affray, tussle, melee, free-for-all, fight, clash, skirmish, brouhaha, riot, uproar, commotion; **argument**, altercation, angry exchange, war of words, shouting match, tiff, dispute, disagreement, row, wrangle, squabble, rumpus; Scottish stooshie; Irish, N. Amer., & Austral. donnybrook; W. Indian bangarang; informal falling-out, set-to, run-in, shindig, shindy, dust-up, punch-up, scrap, spat, ruckus, argy-bargy, ruction, fisticuffs; Brit. informal barney, bunfight, ding-dong, bust-up, ruck, slanging match; Scottish informal rammy; N. Amer. informal rhubarb; archaic broil, miff.

fraction ▶ noun **1** *a fraction of the population* **part**, subdivision, division, portion, segment, section, sector; proportion, percentage, ratio; share, ration, allotment, apportionment, helping, slice, lot, measure, quota, allocation; bit, piece; element, constituent, unit, module, ingredient; informal cut, whack.
OPPOSITE whole.
2 *these are only a fraction of the collection* **tiny part**, small part, fragment, snippet, snatch, smattering, selection.
3 *he moved a fraction closer to her* **tiny amount**, little, bit, touch, hint, soupçon, trifle, mite, scrap, dash, spot, modicum, shade, jot; informal smidgen, smidge, tad.

fractious ▶ adjective **1** *they fight and squabble like fractious children* **grumpy**, grouchy, crotchety, in a (bad) mood, cantankerous, bad-tempered, ill-tempered, ill-natured, ill-humoured, peevish, having got out of bed the wrong side, cross, as cross as two sticks, disagreeable, pettish; **irritable**, irascible, tetchy, testy, curmudgeonly; crabbed, crabby, waspish, prickly, peppery, touchy, scratchy, crusty, splenetic, shrewish, short-tempered, hot-tempered, quick-tempered, dyspeptic, choleric, bilious, liverish, cross-grained; informal snappish, snappy, chippy, on a short fuse, short-fused; Brit. informal shirty, stroppy, narky, ratty, eggy, like a bear with a sore head; N. Amer. informal cranky, ornery, peckish, soreheaded; Austral./NZ informal snaky; informal, dated waxy, miffy.
OPPOSITES contented; affable.
2 *the National Olympic Committee has to hold its fractious members together* **wayward**, unruly, uncontrollable, unmanageable, out of hand, obstreperous, difficult, headstrong, refractory, recalcitrant, intractable; disobedient, insubordinate, disruptive, disorderly, undisciplined, troublemaking, rebellious, mutinous, anarchic; defiant, stubborn, obstinate, contrary, wilful; archaic contumacious.
OPPOSITE dutiful.

fracture *See centre pages for list of* **Fractures of Human Bones**
▶ noun **1** *fracture will probably occur at the stress point* **breaking**, breakage, cracking, cleavage, rupture, shattering, fragmentation, splintering, splitting, separation, bursting, disintegration.
2 *she sustained two fractures to her leg* **break**, breakage, crack, split.
3 *crystals grow in the pores of the rock, causing tiny fractures* **crack**, split, fissure, crevice, break, rupture, breach, rift, cleft, slit, chink, gap, cranny, interstice, opening, aperture, rent; crazing.
▶ verb *she had fallen and fractured her skull | second-hand glass may fracture under pressure* **break**, snap, crack, cleave, rupture, shatter, smash, smash to smithereens, fragment, splinter, split, separate, burst, blow out; sever, divide, tear, rend; disintegrate, fall to bits, fall to pieces; informal bust; rare shiver.

fragile ▶ adjective **1** *she was anxious about her fragile porcelain* **breakable**, easily broken, brittle, frangible, smashable, splintery, flimsy, weak, frail, insubstantial, delicate, dainty, fine; eggshell.
OPPOSITE robust.
2 *moves were made to consolidate the fragile ceasefire* **tenuous**, easily broken, easily destroyed, easily threatened, vulnerable, perilous, flimsy, shaky, rocky, risky, unreliable, suspect, nebulous, unsound, insecure; informal iffy, dicey; Brit. informal dodgy.
OPPOSITES sound; durable.
3 *she is still very fragile after her ordeal* **weak**, delicate, frail, debilitated, tottery, shaky, trembly, ill, unwell, ailing, poorly, sickly, infirm, feeble, enfeebled, unsound; Brit. informal dicky.
OPPOSITE strong.

fragility ▶ noun **1** *they were worried by the fragility of the bridge* **frailty**, flimsiness, weakness, delicacy, daintiness, fineness, brittleness; rare frangibility.
OPPOSITE robustness.
2 *this is a movie about the fragility of relationships* **tenuousness**, vulnerability, flimsiness, shakiness, rockiness, riskiness, unreliability, nebulosity, unsoundness, insecurity; informal iffiness; Brit. informal dodginess.

fragment ▶ noun (stress on the first syllable) **1** *more than 5000 meteorite fragments* **piece**, bit, particle, speck; chip, shard, sliver, splinter; shaving, paring, snippet, scrap, offcut, flake, shred, tatter, wisp, morsel, shiver, spillikin; (**fragments**) smithereens; Scottish skelf; technical spall.
2 *I overheard a fragment of conversation* **snatch**, snippet, scrap, bit, smattering, extract, excerpt; part, section, chapter, movement.
▶ verb (stress on the second syllable) *frequent explosions caused the chalk to fragment | the dangers of fragmenting the health service* **break up**, break, break into pieces, crack open/apart, shatter, splinter, fracture, burst apart, explode, blow apart, implode; disintegrate, come to pieces, fall to pieces, fall apart, collapse, break down, tumble down; smash, smash to smithereens; informal bust; technical spall; rare shiver.

fragmentary ▶ adjective *fragmentary evidence* **incomplete**, fragmental, fragmented, disconnected, disjointed, broken, discontinuous, piecemeal, in pieces; incoherent, inconsistent, scrappy, bitty, sketchy, uneven,

patchy, deficient, untidy, unsystematic, jumbled, inconclusive.
OPPOSITES extensive; complete.

fragrance ▶ noun **1** *sweet williams add fragrance to a herbaceous border* **sweet smell**, scent, perfume, bouquet, aroma, odour, redolence, nose, balm, balminess.
OPPOSITE stench.
2 *a bottle of fragrance* **perfume**, scent, eau de toilette, toilet water; eau de cologne, cologne; aftershave; informal scoosh.

fragrant ▶ adjective *fragrant herbs play a great part in aromatherapy* **sweet-scented**, sweet-smelling, scented, perfumed, aromatic, sweet; literary redolent; rare fragranced, aromatized, perfumy.
OPPOSITE smelly.

frail ▶ adjective **1** *her elderly parents had become frail* **infirm**, weak, weakened, feeble, enfeebled, debilitated, incapacitated, crippled, wasted; delicate, slight, slender, puny; ill, ailing, unwell, sickly, poorly, in poor health; decrepit, doddering, tottering, shaky; informal weedy.
OPPOSITES strong; fit.
2 *some houses are frail structures of cardboard and plywood* **fragile**, breakable, easily broken, easily damaged, delicate, flimsy, insubstantial; unsteady, unstable, rickety, ramshackle; informal teetery, jerry-built; Brit. informal wonky, dicky, dodgy; rare frangible.
OPPOSITE robust.
3 *the workers were frail creatures enslaved by the machines* **weak**, easily led/tempted, susceptible, impressionable, malleable, vulnerable, defenceless, impotent; fallible, errant, erring, flawed, imperfect; rare resistless.
OPPOSITE strong.

F

frailty ▶ noun **1** *I hated my elders for their frailty* **infirmity**, infirmness, weakness, weakliness, feebleness, enfeeblement, debility, incapacity, impairment, indisposition; fragility, delicacy, slightness, puniness; illness, sickness, sickliness, ill health; decrepitude, dodderiness, shakiness; informal weediness.
OPPOSITES strength; healthiness.
2 *human beings are full of frailties* **weakness**, susceptibility, impressionability, vulnerability, fallibility; foible, weak point, flaw, blemish, imperfection, defect, failing, fault, shortcoming, deficiency, inadequacy, limitation; informal hang-up, chink in one's armour.
OPPOSITE strength.

frame ▶ noun **1** *the plane is based on a wooden frame* **framework**, structure, substructure, skeleton, chassis, shell, casing, body, bodywork; support, scaffolding, foundation.
2 *his clothes clung to his tall, slender frame* **body**, figure, form, shape, physique, build, size, proportions; skeleton, bones, framework, structure; informal bod, chassis.
3 *the photograph hung in a polished frame* **setting**, mount, mounting, surround, fixture, support, stand.
4 *an appropriate frame through which to explore dramatic situations* **structure**, framework, context; scheme, system, plan, order, form, fabric, constitution, organization.
□ **frame of mind** *she was in a relaxed and receptive frame of mind* **mood**, state of mind, emotional state, humour, temper, spirit, vein, attitude, perspective, condition, persuasion.
▶ verb **1** *the picture was painted and framed by a local artist* **mount**, set in a frame; surround, enclose, encase.
2 *the legislators who frame the regulations* **formulate**, draw up, plan, draft, map out, sketch out, work out, shape, compose, put together, arrange, form, devise, create, establish, conceive, think up, hatch, originate, orchestrate, engineer, organize, coordinate; informal dream up, cook up.
3 (informal) *he didn't kill those blokes—he was framed* **falsely incriminate**, fabricate charges against, fabricate evidence against, entrap; informal fit up, set up.

frame-up ▶ noun (informal) *he was allegedly the victim of a police frame-up* **conspiracy**, plot, scheme, collusion; trick, trap, deception, entrapment; false charge, trumped-up charge; informal put-up job, fit-up, set-up.

framework ▶ noun **1** *the mannequins were made of plastic on a metal framework* **frame**, **substructure**, structure, skeleton, chassis, shell, body, bodywork; support, scaffolding, foundation.
2 *the changing framework of society* **structure**, shape, fabric, frame, order, scheme, system, organization, construction, configuration, composition, constitution, architecture, anatomy; informal set-up, make-up.

France ▶ noun

WORD LINKS

related prefixes	**Franco-, Gallo-**
hatred or fear of French people and things	**Francophobia, Gallophobia**
lover of French people and things	**Francophile**

franchise ▶ noun **1** *the working class had to struggle for the franchise* **suffrage**, the vote, the right to vote, voting rights, enfranchisement; a voice, one's say.
OPPOSITE disenfranchisement.
2 *the company lost its TV franchise* **warrant**, charter, licence, permit, authorization, permission, sanction; concession, privilege, prerogative; seal of approval.

frank[1] ▶ adjective **1** *he is disarmingly frank about his attitudes* **candid**, direct, forthright, plain, plain-spoken, straight, straightforward, straight from the shoulder, explicit, unequivocal, unambiguous, unvarnished, bald, to the point, no-nonsense, matter-of-fact; open, honest, truthful, sincere, guileless, artless; outspoken, bluff, blunt, brutal, unsparing, not afraid to call a spade a spade; informal upfront, warts and all, on the level; N. Amer. informal on the up and up; archaic round, free-spoken.
OPPOSITES secretive; dishonest.
2 *she looked at Sam with frank admiration* **open**, undisguised, unconcealed, naked, unmistakable, clear, obvious, transparent, patent, manifest, evident, noticeable, visible, perceptible, palpable; blatant, barefaced, flagrant, glaring, bold, stark.
OPPOSITE hidden.

frank[2] ▶ verb *he franked the letter and sent it off* **stamp**, postmark, imprint, print, mark.
▶ noun *an envelope with a first class frank* **stamp**, postmark, imprint, mark, official mark.

CHOOSE THE RIGHT WORD

frank, candid, outspoken, forthright, blunt
See CANDID.

frankly ▶ adverb **1** *frankly, I'm not very interested* **to be frank**, to be honest, to tell you the truth, to be truthful, in all honesty, in all sincerity, as it happens.
2 *he stated the case quite frankly* **candidly**, directly, straightforwardly, straight from the shoulder, forthrightly, openly, honestly, truthfully, without dissembling, without beating about the bush, without mincing one's words, without prevarication, point-blank, matter-of-factly, unequivocally, unambiguously, categorically, plainly, explicitly, clearly; bluntly, baldly, starkly, outspokenly, with no holds barred.
OPPOSITE evasively.

frantic ▶ adjective *her mother is frantic about her safety | a frantic attempt to break free* **panic-stricken**, panic-struck, panicky, beside oneself, at one's wits' end, berserk, distraught, overwrought, worked up, agitated, distressed; **frenzied**, wild, frenetic, fraught, fevered, feverish, hysterical, mad, crazed, out of control, uncontrolled, unhinged, out of one's mind, maniacal, demented, desperate; informal in a state, in a tizzy/tizz, wound up, het up, in a flap, in a cold sweat, tearing one's hair out; Brit. informal having kittens, in a flat spin.
OPPOSITE calm.

fraternity ▶ noun **1** *the meeting engendered a spirit of fraternity* **brotherhood**, fellowship, kinship, friendship, companionship, support, mutual support, solidarity, community, union, togetherness; sisterhood.
2 *the dedicated enthusiasts among the teaching fraternity* **profession**, body of workers; band, group, set, circle.
3 (N. Amer.) *we belonged to the same college fraternity* **society**, club, association, guild, lodge, union, organization, alliance, brotherhood; group, set, circle, clique, coterie, clan; sorority, sisterhood; rare sodality, confraternity.

fraternize ▶ verb *she forbade her musicians to fraternize with the dancers* **associate**, mix, mingle, consort, socialize, go around, keep company, rub shoulders; N. Amer. rub elbows; informal hang around/round, hang out, run around, knock about/around, hobnob, pal up, pal around, chum around, be thick with; Brit. informal hang about.

fraud ▶ noun **1** *his business partner was arrested for fraud* **fraudulence**, sharp practice, cheating, swindling, trickery, artifice, deceit, deception, double-dealing, duplicity, treachery, chicanery, skulduggery, imposture, embezzlement; informal monkey business, funny business, crookedness, hanky-panky, shenanigans, flimflam; Brit. informal jiggery-pokery; N. Amer. informal monkeyshines; archaic management, knavery.
2 *they were accomplices in a fraud* **deception**, trick, cheat, hoax, subterfuge, stratagem, wile, ruse, artifice, swindle, racket; informal scam, con, con trick, rip-off, leg-pull, sting, gyp, kite, diddle, fiddle, swizzle; N. Amer. informal bunco, boondoggle, hustle, grift; Austral. informal rort.
3 *they exposed him as a fraud* **impostor**, fake, sham, pretender, hoodwinker, masquerader, charlatan, quack, mountebank; **swindler**, fraudster, racketeer, cheat, cheater, double-dealer, trickster, confidence trickster; informal phoney, con man, con artist; dated confidence man.
4 *the report is a fraud* **sham**, hoax, imitation, copy, dummy, mock-up; **fake**, forgery, counterfeit; informal phoney, dupe.

fraudulent ▶ adjective *he was convicted of fraudulent share dealing* **dishonest**, cheating, swindling, corrupt, criminal, illegal, unlawful, illicit; deceitful, double-dealing, duplicitous, dishonourable, unscrupulous, unfair, unjust, unethical, unprincipled; informal crooked, sharp, shady, tricky, shifty, dirty; Brit. informal bent, dodgy; Austral./NZ informal shonky.
OPPOSITES honest, above board.

fraught ▶ adjective **1** *their world is fraught with danger* **full of**, filled with, swarming with, rife with, thick with, bristling with, charged with,

loaded with, brimful of, brimming with; attended by, accompanied by.
2 *she scanned the platform with a fraught expression* **anxious**, worried, upset, distraught, overwrought, agitated, distressed, distracted, desperate, frantic, panic-stricken, panic-struck, panicky; beside oneself, at one's wits' end, at the end of one's tether, out of one's mind; *informal* stressed, hassled, wound up, worked up, in a state, in a flap, in a cold sweat, tearing one's hair out; *Brit. informal* having kittens, in a flat spin.
OPPOSITE calm.

fray[1] ▶ verb **1** *cheap fabric soon frays* **unravel**, wear, wear thin, wear out, wear away, wear through, become worn, become threadbare, become tattered, become ragged, go into holes, go through.
2 *despite the situation, remarkably few nerves were frayed* **strain**, tax, overtax, irritate, put on edge, make edgy, make tense.

fray[2] ▶ noun *the swordsman launched himself into the fray* **battle**, engagement, conflict, armed conflict, fight, clash, skirmish, altercation, tussle, struggle, scuffle, melee, brawl, riot, commotion, disturbance; contest, competition; *informal* scrap, dust-up, set-to, free-for-all; *Brit. informal* punch-up, bust-up, ruck; *Scottish informal* rammy, swedge; *Law, dated* affray.

frayed ▶ adjective **1** *the shirt had frayed cuffs* **unravelling**, unravelled, worn, well worn, threadbare, tattered, ragged, holey, moth-eaten, shabby; torn, ripped, split; worn out, worn through, worn thin, in holes, in tatters, falling to pieces, the worse for wear; *informal* tatty, ratty; *N. Amer. informal* raggedy.
2 *his frayed nerves couldn't take much more* **strained**, taxed, overtaxed, irritated, edgy, tense, nervy, stressed, fraught.

freak ▶ noun **1** *the mouse was a genetically engineered freak* **aberration**, abnormality, irregularity, oddity, monster, monstrosity, malformation, mutant; freak of nature.
2 *they were dismissed as a bunch of freaks* **oddity**, eccentric, eccentric person, peculiar person, strange person, unorthodox person, individualist, free spirit, maverick, misfit; crank, lunatic; *informal* queer fish, oddball, weirdo, weirdie, nutcase, nut, nutter; *Brit. informal* odd bod; *N. Amer. informal* wacko, screwball, kook; *informal, dated* case.
3 *the accident was a complete freak* **fluke**, anomaly, aberration, rogue, rarity, quirk, oddity, unusual occurrence, peculiar turn of events, twist of fate; chance, coincidence, hazard, accident, mistake.
4 (*informal*) *he's a radio ham and an electronics freak* **enthusiast**, fan, fanatic, addict, devotee, lover; master, wizard, expert, aficionado; *informal* buff, fiend, nut, maniac, ace; *N. Amer. informal* maven, geek, jock; *S. African informal* fundi.
5 (*archaic*) *we wonder what they will think of our freaks and follies* **whim**, whimsy, caprice, vagary, fad, fancy, quirk, foible, eccentricity, crotchet, notion, humour, impulse, urge; *informal* hang-up; *rare* singularity.
▶ adjective *the flood was caused by a freak storm* **unusual**, anomalous, atypical, untypical, unrepresentative, abnormal, aberrant, irregular, fluky, exceptional, unparalleled, unaccountable, bizarre, queer, peculiar, odd, freakish; unpredictable, unforeseeable, unexpected, unanticipated, surprise, surprising; rare, singular, isolated.
OPPOSITE normal.
▶ verb (*informal*) *he freaked out and started smashing the place up* **go crazy**, go mad, go out of one's mind, go to pieces, crack, snap, lose control, lose one's self-control, lose control of the situation, act wildly; panic, get worked up, get hysterical; *informal* lose it, crack up, lose one's cool, go bananas, blow one's top, fly off the handle; *Brit. informal* go crackers, throw a wobbly; *N. Amer. informal* blow one's stack.
OPPOSITE calm down.

freakish ▶ adjective *his behaviour had been so freakish*. See FREAKY.

freaky ▶ adjective (*informal*) *the freaky characters in his films* **strange**, peculiar, odd, bizarre, queer, curious, funny, eccentric, outlandish, offbeat; unusual, abnormal, atypical, untypical, anomalous, out of the ordinary, out of the way, extraordinary, irregular, deviant, aberrant, freakish; surreal, eerie, unnatural, perverse; unexpected, surprising; *French* outré; *Scottish* unco; *informal* screwy, way out, wacky, oddball, fishy, creepy, spooky; *Brit. informal* rum; *N. Amer. informal* wacko, bizarro.

free ▶ adjective **1** *elementary education should be free* **without charge**, free of charge, for nothing, complimentary, gratis, gratuitous, at no cost; *informal* for free, on the house.
OPPOSITES paid for; expensive.
2 *she was free of any pressures* **unencumbered by**, unaffected by, clear of, without, devoid of, lacking in; exempt from, not liable to, safe from, immune to, relieved of, released from, excused of, exempted from; rid of; *informal* sans, minus.
OPPOSITE encumbered by.
3 *he will be free at the weekend* **unoccupied**, not at work, not working, not busy, not tied up, between appointments, off duty, off work, off, on holiday, on leave; idle, at leisure, with time on one's hands, with time to spare; available, contactable.
OPPOSITES occupied; unavailable.
4 *he found a free seat on the bus* **vacant**, empty, available, spare, unoccupied, untaken, unfilled, unused, not in use; uninhabited, tenantless; *informal* up for grabs.
OPPOSITES occupied, engaged, taken.
5 *a citizen of a proud free nation* **independent**, self-governing, self-governed, self-ruling, self-legislating, self-determining, self-directing, non-aligned, sovereign, autonomous, autarkic, democratic, emancipated, enfranchised; self-sufficient; *historical* manumitted.
OPPOSITE dependent.
6 *a known child killer is still free* **on the loose**, at liberty, at large; loose, unconfined, unbound, untied, unchained, untethered, unshackled, unfettered, unrestrained, unsecured.
OPPOSITE captive.
7 *people are free to choose where they wish to live* **able to**, in a position to, capable of; **allowed**, permitted, unrestricted.
OPPOSITE unable.
8 *the free flow of water between adjoining tanks* **unobstructed**, unimpeded, unrestricted, unhampered, unlimited, clear, open, unblocked.
OPPOSITE obstructed.
9 *she caught the free end of the rope* **unattached**, unfastened, unsecured, unhitched, untied, uncoupled, not fixed, detached, loose.
OPPOSITE attached.
10 *she was always free with her money* **generous**, lavish, liberal, open-handed, unstinting, giving, munificent, bountiful, bounteous, charitable, extravagant, prodigal.
OPPOSITE mean.
11 *he was known for his free and hearty manner* **easy-going**, free and easy, tolerant, liberal, permissive, indulgent, relaxed, casual, informal, unceremonious, unforced, natural, open, frank, spontaneous, uninhibited, artless, ingenuous; good-humoured, affable, friendly; *informal* laid-back, unflappable.
OPPOSITES strained; formal.
12 *the children were rather too free with us* **impudent**, impertinent, disrespectful; familiar, overfamiliar, over-free, presumptuous, forward, bold, assertive; *informal* cheeky, cocky, pushy.
OPPOSITE polite.
□ **free and easy** *the restaurant has a free and easy atmosphere* **easy-going**, relaxed, casual, informal, unceremonious, unforced, natural, open, spontaneous, uninhibited, friendly; breezy, airy, jaunty, carefree; *informal* laid-back, upbeat.
OPPOSITE formal.
□ **a free hand** *he was allowed a free hand in appointing new staff* **free rein**, freedom, licence, latitude, leeway, scope, flexibility; liberty, independence; *French* carte blanche.
□ **make free with** *he was unhappy about her making free with his belongings* **help oneself to**, take, take possession of, take over, hijack, appropriate, 'borrow', steal; use without asking, treat without respect; *informal* walk off with; *Brit. informal* nick, pinch.
▶ verb **1** *the government freed all political prisoners* **release**, liberate, discharge, emancipate, set free, let go, set at liberty, set loose, let loose, turn loose, deliver; untie, unchain, unfetter, unshackle, unmanacle, uncage, unleash; spare, pardon, reprieve, clear; *informal* let off, let off the hook; *literary* disenthral; *historical* manumit.
OPPOSITES confine, lock up.
2 *earthquake victims had to be freed by firefighters* **extricate**, extract, disentangle, disentwine, disengage, disencumber, loosen, release, remove, get out, pull out, pull free, get loose, get free; **rescue**, set free.
OPPOSITE trap.
3 *they wish to be freed from all legal ties* **exempt**, make exempt, except, excuse, absolve; relieve of, absolve of, unburden of, disburden of; strip of; *rare* dispense from.

freebooter ▶ noun *the islands offered sanctuary to freebooters* **pirate**, marauder, raider, plunderer, bandit, robber; adventurer, swashbuckler; *historical* buccaneer, privateer; *rare* picaroon, filibuster, sea thief, sea robber, water thief, sea wolf, water rat, marooner, corsair, rover, sea rover.

freedom ▶ noun **1** *the prisoners made a desperate bid for freedom* **liberty**, liberation, release, emancipation, deliverance, delivery, discharge, non-confinement, extrication; amnesty, pardoning; *historical* manumission; *rare* disenthralment.
OPPOSITE captivity.
2 *a national revolution was the only path to freedom* **independence**, self-government, self-determination, self-legislation, self rule, home rule, sovereignty, autonomy, autarky, democracy; self-sufficiency, individualism, separation, non-alignment; emancipation, enfranchisement; *historical* manumission.
OPPOSITE dependence.
3 *they want freedom from local political accountability* **exemption**, immunity, dispensation, exception, exclusion, release, relief, reprieve, absolution, exoneration; impunity; *informal* letting off, a let-off; *rare* derogation.
OPPOSITE liability.
4 *the law interfered with their freedom of expression* **right to**, entitlement to; privilege, prerogative, due.
5 *patients have more freedom to choose who treats them* **scope**, latitude, leeway, margin, flexibility, facility, space, breathing space, room, elbow room; licence, leave, free rein, a free hand; leisure; *French* carte blanche.
OPPOSITE restriction.
6 *I admire her freedom of manner* **naturalness**, openness, lack of reserve/

inhibition, casualness, informality, lack of ceremony, spontaneity, ingenuousness.
7 *he treats her with too much freedom* **impudence**; familiarity, overfamiliarity, presumption, forwardness; *informal* cheek.

WORD LINKS
fear of freedom **eleutherophobia**

CHOOSE THE RIGHT WORD
freedom, liberty, independence
See LIBERTY.

free-for-all ▶ noun *prompt action by staff prevented a violent free-for-all* **brawl**, fight, scuffle, tussle, struggle, battle, confrontation, clash, altercation, fray, fracas, melee, rumpus, riot, commotion, disturbance; breach of the peace; *Scottish* rammy, swedge; *Irish, N. Amer., & Austral.* donnybrook; *informal* dust-up, scrap, set-to, shindy, shindig; *Brit. informal* punch-up, bust-up, ruck, barney; *N. Amer. informal* brannigan; *Austral./NZ informal* stoush; *Law, dated* affray; *rare* broil, bagarre.

freely ▶ adverb **1** *he felt a reluctance to talk freely* **openly**, candidly, frankly, plainly, matter-of-factly, straightforwardly, directly, explicitly, bluntly, outspokenly, unreservedly, without constraint, without inhibition; truthfully, honestly, without beating about the bush, without mincing one's words, without prevarication.
OPPOSITE evasively.
2 *these workers gave their time and labour freely* **voluntarily**, willingly, readily; of one's own volition, of one's own accord, of one's own free will, without being asked, without being forced, without reluctance.
OPPOSITE under duress.

freethinker ▶ noun **nonconformist**, individualist, independent, maverick, dissenter, heretic; **libertine**, agnostic, atheist, non-believer, unbeliever, disbeliever, sceptic, doubter, doubting Thomas, apostate, humanist; pagan, heathen, infidel; *archaic* paynim, renegade; *rare* nullifidian.
OPPOSITES conformist; believer.

freewheel ▶ verb *she freewheeled downhill on her bicycle* **coast**, cruise, drift, glide, sail, skim, float.
OPPOSITE pedal.

free will ▶ noun *God has blessed us with free will* **volition**, independence, self-determination, self-sufficiency, autonomy, spontaneity; freedom, liberty.
□ **of one's own free will** *she left of her own free will* **voluntarily**, willingly, readily, freely, spontaneously, without reluctance, without being forced, without being asked, without being encouraged; of one's own accord, of one's own volition, of one's own choosing, by one's own preference.
OPPOSITE under duress.

freeze ▶ verb **1** *it was so cold that the river Thames froze* **turn into ice**, ice over, ice up, solidify, harden; *archaic* glaciate.
OPPOSITES thaw, melt.
2 *they freeze the fish as soon as they catch them* **deep-freeze**, quick-freeze, freeze-dry, put in the freezer, pack in ice, put on ice, ice; store at a low temperature, chill, cool, refrigerate; preserve.
OPPOSITES thaw; warm up.
3 *the campers stifled in summer and froze in winter* **feel very cold**, go numb with cold, turn blue with cold, shiver, shiver with cold, get chilled, get chilled to the bone/marrow; *informal* feel Jack Frost's fingers.
OPPOSITE overheat.
4 *when under attack the animals freeze* **stop dead**, stop in one's tracks, stop, stand (stock) still, go rigid, become motionless, become paralysed.
OPPOSITE run away.
5 *the prices of basic foodstuffs were frozen* **fix**, suspend, hold, peg, set; limit, restrict, curb, check, cap, confine, control, regulate; hold/keep down.
OPPOSITE change.
□ **freeze someone out** (*informal*) *she was frozen out by her husband's relatives* **exclude**, leave out, shut out, cut out, neglect, ignore, ostracize, reject, disown, spurn, slight, snub, shun, cut, cut dead, turn one's back on, cold-shoulder, give someone the cold shoulder, leave out in the cold; *Brit.* send to Coventry; *informal* knock back, brush off, give someone the brush-off, stiff-arm, hand someone the frozen mitt; *Brit. informal* blank; *N. Amer. informal* give someone the brush; *Austral. informal* snout; *informal, dated* give someone the go-by; *Christianity* excommunicate.
OPPOSITES include; welcome.
▶ noun **1** *only three race meetings have escaped the big freeze* **cold snap**, spell of cold weather, freeze-up, frost.
OPPOSITE heatwave.
2 *a two-year wage freeze* **fix**, suspension, hold.

WORD LINKS
related prefix **cryo-** (e.g. ***cryonic, cryolite***)

freezing ▶ adjective **1** *a freezing wind blew across the moor* **bitterly cold**, cold, chill, chilling, frosty, frozen, glacial, wintry, sub-zero; raw, biting, piercing, penetrating, cutting, stinging, numbing; arctic, polar, Siberian; *rare* gelid, brumal, rimy, algid, circumpolar.
OPPOSITE balmy.
2 *come inside—you must be freezing* **frozen**, extremely cold, painfully cold, numb with cold, very chilly, chilled through, chilled to the bone/marrow, frozen to the core, frozen stiff, shivery, shivering; frostbitten; *informal* frozen to death.
OPPOSITE hot.

freight ▶ noun **1** *the Panama Canal has lost importance because of air freight* **transportation**, transport, conveyance, freightage, carriage, carrying, portage, haulage, distribution, delivery; traffic.
2 *the freight is unloaded here* **cargo**, load, haul, consignment, delivery, shipment; merchandise, goods; *rare* lading, freightage.
▶ verb *the goods were freighted to Kansas City* **transport**, transport in bulk, convey, carry, ship, drive; send, send off, dispatch.

French ▶ adjective **Gallic**.

frenetic ▶ adjective *the frenetic bustle of the metropolis* **frantic**, wild, frenzied, hectic, fraught, feverish, fevered, mad, manic, hyperactive, energetic, intense, fast and furious, turbulent, tumultuous, confused, confusing; exciting, excited.
OPPOSITE calm.

frenzied ▶ adjective *the workrooms were a hive of frenzied activity* **frantic**, wild, frenetic, hectic, fraught, feverish, fevered, mad, crazed, manic, hyperactive, energetic, intense, furious, fast and furious, turbulent, tumultuous, confused, confusing; panic-stricken, panic-struck, panicky, hysterical, desperate.
OPPOSITE calm.

frenzy ▶ noun **1** *the crowd worked themselves into a state of frenzy* **hysteria**, madness, mania, insanity, derangement, dementedness, delirium, feverishness, fever, wildness, distraction, agitation, turmoil, tumult; wild excitement, euphoria, elation, ecstasy; *informal* craziness; *rare* deliration.
2 *he contorted his face in a frenzy of anger* **fit**, seizure, paroxysm, spasm, bout, outburst; ferment, fever, storm.

frequency ▶ noun *the frequency of errors* **rate of occurrence**, commonness, frequentness, prevalence, incidence, amount; rate of repetition, recurrence, repetition, persistence, regularity; *Statistics* distribution.

frequent ▶ adjective (stress on the first syllable) **1** *he has frequent bouts of chest infection* **recurrent**, recurring, repeated, persistent, periodic, perennial, chronic, continuing, occurring often, continual, constant, incessant, non-stop, endless; many, very many, a great many, numerous, countless, quite a few, quite a lot of, lots of, several; *informal* eternal, loads of, masses of, heaps of, dozens of, hundreds of, thousands of, millions of, more ... than one can shake a stick at.
OPPOSITES infrequent; few.
2 *she's a frequent business traveller* **habitual**, customary, regular, common, everyday, daily, routine; continual, constant, incessant; *literary* wonted.
OPPOSITES infrequent; rare.
▶ verb (stress on the second syllable) *he frequented the most chic supper clubs* **visit**, visit often, be a regular visitor to, be a regular client of, go to regularly, go to repeatedly, attend, attend frequently; haunt, patronize, spend time in, spend all of one's time in, loiter in, linger in; *informal* hang out at, hang around at, show up often at.

frequenter ▶ noun *he was known as a frequenter of public houses* **regular visitor to**, regular customer of, regular client of, regular patron of, regular of, habitué of, familiar face at, haunter of; *Brit. informal* regular punter at.

frequently ▶ adverb *he frequently attended church* **regularly**, often, very often, all the time, habitually, customarily, routinely, usually, normally, commonly; again and again, time and again, over and over again, repeatedly, recurrently, continually, constantly; many times, many a time, lots of times, on several occasions; *N. Amer.* oftentimes; *literary* oft, oft-times.

fresh ▶ adjective **1** *salads made with fresh, wholesome ingredients* **newly harvested**, garden-fresh, not stale, crisp, firm, unwilted, unfaded; raw, natural, unprocessed, unpreserved, undried, uncured, unsmoked, without additives, without preservatives.
OPPOSITES stale; processed.
2 *she drew on a fresh sheet of paper* **clean**, blank, empty, bare, clear, plain, white; unused, new, pristine, unmarked, unfilled, untouched.
OPPOSITE used.
3 *a fresh approach to studying* **new**, brand new, recent, latest, up to date, modern, modernistic, ultra-modern, newfangled; **original**, novel, different, innovative, unusual, uncommon, unwonted, out of the ordinary, unconventional, unorthodox, offbeat, radical, revolutionary; *Brit.* out of the common.
OPPOSITES old, well-worn.
4 *the general knew fresh forces were coming* **additional**, further, extra, added, supplementary, supplemental, auxiliary; more, other, new.
5 *a row of fresh recruits* **young**, youthful, juvenile, adolescent, boyish, girlish, new, newly arrived; **inexperienced**, untrained, unqualified, untried, raw, callow, green, immature, artless, ingenuous, naive; *informal*

wet behind the ears.
OPPOSITE experienced.
6 *I must be fresh for work in the morning* **refreshed**, rested, restored, revived, like a new person; fresh as a daisy, energetic, vigorous, invigorated, full of vim and vigour, vital, lively, vibrant, spry, sprightly, bright, alert, bouncing, perky; *informal* full of beans, raring to go, bright-eyed and bushy-tailed, chirpy, chipper.
OPPOSITE tired.
7 *she had the fresh complexion of a true Celt* **healthy**, healthy-looking, clear, bright, youthful, youthful-looking, wholesome, blooming, glowing, unblemished; fair, rosy, rosy-cheeked, pink, pinkish, reddish, ruddy, flushed, blushing.
OPPOSITE unhealthy.
8 *the morning was clear and fresh* **cool**, crisp, refreshing, invigorating, tonic; pure, clean, clear, unpolluted, uncontaminated, untainted.
9 *a fresh wind had sprung up from the east* **chilly**, cool, cold, brisk, bracing, invigorating; bleak, wintry, snowy, frosty, icy, ice-cold, icy-cold, glacial, polar, arctic, raw, bitter, bitterly cold, biting; *informal* nippy; *Brit. informal* parky; *literary* chill; *rare* gelid, brumal.
OPPOSITES warm, sultry.
10 (*informal*) *that young man has been getting a little too fresh* **impudent**, impertinent, insolent, presumptuous, audacious, forward, cheeky, irreverent, discourteous, disrespectful, insubordinate, rude, crude, brazen, brazen-faced, brash, shameless, pert, defiant, bold, (as) bold as brass, outrageous, shocking, out of line; *informal* brass-necked, cocky, lippy, mouthy, flip; *Brit. informal* saucy, smart-arsed; *N. Amer. informal* sassy, nervy, smart-assed; *rare* malapert, contumelious, tossy, mannerless.
OPPOSITE polite.

CHOOSE THE RIGHT WORD

fresh, new, novel, original, newfangled
See NEW.

freshen ▸ verb **1** *the water chilled his face and freshened him* **refresh**, revitalize, restore, revive, reinvigorate, reanimate, wake up, rouse, enliven, liven up, energize, stimulate, brace, fortify, invigorate; *informal* buck up, pep up, blow away the cobwebs; *rare* inspirit.
OPPOSITE tire.
2 *he opened a window to freshen the room* **ventilate**, air, aerate, fan, oxygenate, deodorize, purify, cleanse; refresh, cool; *rare* depollute.
3 *she went to* **freshen up** *before dinner* **have a wash**, wash oneself, bathe, shower; tidy oneself (up), spruce oneself up, smarten up, groom oneself, preen oneself, primp oneself, prink oneself; *N. Amer.* wash up; *informal* titivate oneself, do oneself up, doll oneself up; *Brit. informal* tart oneself up; *literary* lave; *formal or humorous* perform one's ablutions; *archaic* plume oneself, trig oneself, make one's toilet.
4 (*N. Amer.*) *the waitress freshened their coffee* **refill**, top up, fill up, replenish, recharge, reload, resupply; *Scottish* plenish.
OPPOSITE empty.
5 *it was getting dark and the wind had freshened* **become stronger**, strengthen; **become colder**, become more bracing, cool, cool off.

freshman, freshwoman ▸ noun *a freshman at Miami University* **first-year student**, undergraduate; newcomer, new recruit, starter, probationer, fledgling; beginner, learner, novice; *N. Amer.* tenderfoot; *informal* undergrad; *Brit. informal* fresher; *N. Amer. informal* greenhorn, rookie, frosh.

fret ▸ verb **1** *the workers fretted about being displaced by machines* **worry**, be anxious, feel uneasy, be distressed, be upset, upset oneself, concern oneself, feel unhappy; agonize, anguish, sorrow, sigh, pine, brood, mope; fuss, make a fuss, complain, grumble, whine, eat one's heart out; *informal* stew, feel peeved.
2 *his absence began to fret her* **trouble**, bother, concern, perturb, disturb, disquiet, disconcert, make anxious, cause anxiety, distress, upset, torment, alarm, panic, cause to panic, agitate; *informal* rattle, eat away at; *archaic* pother.
OPPOSITE comfort.

fretful ▸ adjective *the heat was making the child fretful* **distressed**, upset, miserable, unsettled, uneasy, ill at ease, uncomfortable, agitated, distraught, overwrought, wrought up, worked up, tense, stressed, restive, fidgety; **irritable**, cross, crabbed, fractious, peevish, petulant, out of sorts, bad-tempered, ill-natured, edgy, irascible, grumpy, crotchety, touchy, captious, testy, tetchy; querulous, complaining, grumbling, whining; *N. Amer.* cranky; *informal* het up, uptight, twitchy, rattled, crabby; *dated* overstrung, unquiet.

friable ▸ adjective *the soil was dark and friable* **crumbly**, easily crumbled, powdery, dusty, chalky, soft; dry, crisp, brittle; *rare* pulverulent, levigated, brashy.

friar *See centre pages for list of* **Christian Religious Orders**
▸ noun **monk**, brother, male member of a religious order, religious, contemplative; prior, abbot; Dominican, Black Friar, Carmelite, White Friar, Franciscan, Friar Minor, Grey Friar, Minorite, Augustinian, Augustine, Austin Friar, Crutched Friar, Capuchin, Servite; *historical* mendicant; *rare* coenobite, cloisterer, religioner, religieux.

friction ▸ noun **1** *the friction of the rope on the winding sheave* **abrasion**, abrading, rubbing, chafing, grating, rasping, scraping, excoriation, grinding, gnawing, eating away, wearing away/down; resistance, drag, adhesion, traction, grip, purchase; *rare* attrition, fretting, detrition.
2 *there was considerable friction between father and son* **discord**, disharmony, disunity, strife, conflict, disagreement, dissension, dissent, opposition, variance, clashing, contention, dispute, disputation, arguing, argument, quarrelling, bickering, squabbling, wrangling, fighting, feuding, rivalry; hostility, animosity, antipathy, enmity, antagonism, resentment, acrimony, bitterness, bad feeling, ill feeling, ill will, bad blood; grudges, grievances; *informal* falling-out; *rare* jar, disaccord, discordance.
OPPOSITE harmony.

WORD LINKS
related prefix **tribo-** (e.g. ***triboelectricity***)
study of friction **tribology**

friend ▸ noun **1** *she went to stay with her friend in the next town* **companion**, boon companion, bosom friend, best friend, close friend, intimate, confidante, confidant, familiar, soul mate, alter ego, second self, shadow, playmate, playfellow, classmate, schoolmate, workmate, ally, comrade, associate; sister, brother; *informal* pal, bosom pal, buddy, bosom buddy, chum, spar, sidekick, cully, crony, main man; *Brit. informal* mate, oppo, china, mucker, butty; *N. English informal* marrow, marrer, marra; *N. Amer. informal* amigo, compadre, paisan, homie; *N. Amer. & S. African informal* homeboy, homegirl; *S. African informal* gabba; *Austral./NZ informal* offsider; *archaic* compeer; *rare* fidus Achates.
OPPOSITE enemy.
2 *a meeting of the friends of the Royal Botanic Garden* **patron**, backer, supporter, benefactor, benefactress, sponsor; well-wisher, defender, champion; *informal* angel; *rare* benefactrice, benefactrix, Maecenas.
OPPOSITE opponent.

friendless ▸ adjective *she cared for those who were poor and friendless* **alone**, all alone, by oneself, solitary, with no ties, unattached, single, lone, isolated; without friends, companionless, unbefriended, unpopular, unwanted, unloved, uncared-for, abandoned, deserted, rejected, forsaken, outcast, shunned, spurned; lonely, with no one to turn to, forlorn, desolate; *N. Amer.* lonesome.
OPPOSITE popular.

friendliness ▸ noun *she appreciated her host's friendliness* **affability**, amiability, geniality, congeniality, cordiality, good nature, good humour, warmth, affection, affectionateness, demonstrativeness, conviviality, joviality, companionability, companionableness, sociability, gregariousness, clubbability, comradeship, neighbourliness, hospitableness, approachability, accessibility, easy-going manner, communicativeness, openness, lack of reservation, lack of inhibition, good-naturedness, kindness, kindliness, sympathy, amenability, benevolence; *French* bonhomie; *informal* chumminess, palliness, clubbiness; *Brit. informal* mateyness, decency.
OPPOSITE unfriendliness.

friendly ▸ adjective **1** *she is a naturally friendly child* **affectionate**, **affable**, amiable, genial, congenial, cordial, warm, demonstrative, convivial, companionable, company-loving, sociable, gregarious, outgoing, clubbable, comradely, neighbourly, hospitable, approachable, easy to get along with, accessible, communicative, open, unreserved, easy-going, good-natured, kindly, benign, amenable, agreeable, obliging, sympathetic, well disposed, benevolent; *Scottish* couthy; *informal* chummy, pally, clubby; *Brit. informal* matey, decent; *N. Amer. informal* buddy-buddy; *rare* conversable.
OPPOSITE unfriendly.
2 *she drew him into friendly conversation* **amicable**, congenial, cordial, pleasant, good-natured, easy, casual, informal, unceremonious, comradely, confidential, close, intimate, familiar; peaceable, peaceful, conciliatory, harmonious, non-hostile.
OPPOSITE hostile.
3 *a friendly wind swept the boat to the shore* **favourable**, advantageous, beneficial, benevolent, helpful, well disposed, good; lucky, providential.
OPPOSITE unfavourable.

friendship ▸ noun *their friendship was based on mutual liking and respect* **relationship**, friendly relationship, close relationship, attachment, mutual attachment, alliance, association, close association, bond, tie, link, union; **amity**, camaraderie, friendliness, comradeship, companionship, fellowship, fellow feeling, closeness, affinity, rapport, understanding, harmony, unity; intimacy, mutual affection; cordial relations.
OPPOSITE enmity.

fright ▸ noun **1** *Amanda was paralysed with fright* **fear**, fearfulness, terror, horror, alarm, panic, dread, trepidation, uneasiness, nervousness, apprehension, apprehensiveness, consternation, dismay, perturbation, disquiet, discomposure; *informal* jitteriness, twitchiness.
2 *the experience gave everyone a bit of a fright* **scare**, shock, surprise, turn, jolt, start; the shivers, the shakes; *informal* the jitters, the heebie-jeebies, the willies, the creeps, the collywobbles, a cold sweat; *Brit. informal* the

(screaming) abdabs, butterflies (in one's stomach).
3 (*informal*) *she didn't want to look a fright on her wedding day* **ugly sight**, horrible sight, grotesque sight, eyesore, monstrosity, horror, frightful spectacle; *informal* mess, sight, state, blot on the landscape.
OPPOSITE beauty.

frighten ▶ **verb** *she was frightened by the strange sounds outside* **scare**, startle, alarm, terrify, petrify, shock, chill, appal, agitate, panic, throw into panic, fluster, ruffle, shake, disturb, disconcert, unnerve, unman, intimidate, terrorize, cow, daunt, dismay; fill someone with fear, strike terror into, put the fear of God into, chill someone's blood, chill someone to the bone, chill someone to the marrow, make someone's blood run cold, freeze someone's blood, make someone's flesh crawl, give someone goose pimples; *informal* scare the living daylights out of, scare stiff, scare someone out of their wits, scare witless, scare someone (half) to death, scare the pants off, rattle, spook, make someone's hair stand on end, throw into a blue funk, make someone jump out of their skin; *Brit. informal* put the wind up, give someone the heebie-jeebies, make someone's hair curl; *Irish informal* scare the bejesus out of; *vulgar slang* scare shitless; *archaic* affright.
OPPOSITES reassure, comfort.

F

CHOOSE THE RIGHT WORD

frighten, scare, startle

These three words can all describe the generation of fear.

- **Frighten** is the most general word (*he only meant to frighten his victim, not to kill him*). The fear may be of immediate harm (typically physical) or of longer-term misfortune or suffering (*I was uncertain what would happen and frightened about the future*).
- **Scare** is a less formal word, especially when applied to fear of something other than an immediate physical threat. Saying that someone is *scared* may imply that they lack courage or strength of character (*I was scared of meeting people*).
- **Startle** denotes a sudden, momentary feeling of fear on being surprised by something (*a sudden sound in the doorway startled her*).

frightening ▶ **adjective** *she had many vivid and frightening dreams* **terrifying**, horrifying, alarming, startling, shocking, chilling, spine-chilling, hair-raising, blood-curdling, appalling, disturbing, disconcerting, unnerving, intimidating, daunting, dismaying, upsetting, harrowing, traumatic; eerie, sinister, fearsome, dreadful, horrible, awful, nightmarish, monstrous, grim, gruesome, macabre, menacing; *Scottish* eldritch; *informal* scary, spooky, creepy, hairy.
OPPOSITE comforting.

frightful ▶ **adjective 1** *he had some frightful wounds* **horrible**, gruesome, grisly, ghastly, hideous, grim, revolting, repulsive, disgusting, horrendous, grievous, dreadful, terrible, nasty, dire, unspeakable; alarming, shocking, terrifying, harrowing, appalling, daunting, unnerving, fearful, fearsome; *informal* horrid, beastly; *archaic or humorous* parlous.
OPPOSITE mild.
2 (*informal*) *the children were making a frightful racket* **awful**, very bad, terrible, dreadful, appalling, ghastly, nasty, abominable; unpleasant, disagreeable, lamentable, deplorable, insufferable, unbearable, annoying, irritating; *informal* beastly, God-awful.
OPPOSITE pleasant.

frigid ▶ **adjective 1** *the frigid climate of the north* **very cold**, bitterly cold, bitter, freezing, frozen, frosty, icy, icy-cold, ice-cold, chilly, wintry, bleak, sub-zero, arctic, Siberian, polar, glacial; *informal* nippy; *Brit. informal* parky; *literary* chill; *rare* Hyperborean, hibernal, boreal, hiemal, gelid, algid, brumal, rimy.
OPPOSITES hot; tropical.
2 *she addressed him with frigid politeness* **stiff**, formal, stony, steely, flinty, wooden, impersonal, indifferent, unresponsive, unemotional, unfeeling, unsmiling, unenthusiastic, austere, distant, aloof, remote, reserved, unapproachable; frosty, cold, icy, cool, lukewarm, forbidding, unfriendly, unwelcoming, hostile; *informal* offish, stand-offish.
OPPOSITE friendly.
3 *he said that his wife was frigid* **sexually unresponsive**, unresponsive, undemonstrative, unaffectionate, cold, cold-blooded, cold-hearted, passionless, unfeeling, unemotional, unloving, uncaring.
OPPOSITE passionate.

frill ▶ **noun 1** *a full skirt with a wide frill* **ruffle**, flounce, ruff, furbelow, jabot, peplum, flute, ruche, ruching, gather, tuck, fringe; *archaic* purfle.
2 (**frills**) *a comfortable flat with no frills* **ostentation**, ornamentation, decoration, embellishment, fanciness, fuss, chichi, garnishing, garnishment, gilding, excess; trimmings, affectations, extras, additions, non-essentials, luxuries, extravagances, superfluities; *informal* jazz, jazziness, flashiness, fandangle; *rare* folderols, fallalery.

frilly ▶ **adjective** *she wore a mob cap and frilly apron* **ruffled**, flounced, frilled, crimped, gathered, pleated, ruched, tucked, trimmed, lacy, frothy; fancy, ornate.

fringe ▶ **noun 1** *he lived on the city's northern fringe* **perimeter**, periphery, border, borderline, margin, rim, outer edge, edge, extremity, limit; outer limits, limits, borders, bounds, outskirts, marches; *literary* marge, bourn, skirt; *rare* ambit.
OPPOSITE middle.
2 *the curtains are blue with a honey-coloured fringe* **edging**, edge, border, hem, trimming, frill, flounce, ruffle; tassels; *archaic* purfle.
▶ **adjective** *he played small parts in fringe theatre* **unconventional**, unorthodox, offbeat, alternative, avant-garde, experimental, innovative, innovatory, radical, extreme; peripheral, unofficial; *N. Amer.* left-field, off Broadway; *informal* way out.
OPPOSITE mainstream.
▶ **verb 1** *she fringed the edges of the cloak with black velvet* **trim**, hem, edge, border, rim, bind, braid; tassel; decorate, adorn, ornament, embellish, finish; *archaic* purfle; *rare* befringe, befrill.
2 *the lake is fringed by a belt of trees* **border**, edge, bound, skirt, line, hem, flank, verge, surround, enclose, encircle, circle, encompass, ring, circumscribe; *literary* gird, girdle, engird; *rare* compass, environ.

fringe benefit ▶ **noun** *they were attracted to the deal by the fringe benefits* **added extra**, additional benefit, privilege; *informal* plus, plus point, perk; *formal* perquisite.

frippery ▶ **noun 1** *a functional building with not a hint of frippery* **ostentation**, showiness, embellishment, ornamentation, ornament, adornment, decoration, trimming, garnishing, garnishment, gilding, beautification, prettification, gingerbread; finery, luxury; *informal* flashiness, glitz, glitziness, bells and whistles; *archaic* trumpery.
2 (usually **fripperies**) *one of those shops that sells charming fripperies* **trinket**, bauble, knick-knack, gewgaw, gimcrack, bibelot, furbelow, ornament, novelty, curiosity, gimmick, trifle, bagatelle; *informal* whatnot; *Brit. informal* doodah, doobry; *archaic* folderol, fallalery, whim-wham, kickshaw, bijou, gaud.

frisk ▶ **verb 1** *the spaniels frisked around my ankles* **frolic**, gambol, cavort, caper, cut capers, sport, scamper, skip, dance, romp, trip, prance, leap, spring, hop, jump, bounce, bob; *rare* curvet, rollick, capriole.
2 *he raised his arms to allow the officer to frisk him* **search**, body-search, check, inspect, examine; *informal* give someone the once-over; *N. Amer. informal* shake down.

frisky ▶ **adjective** *the donkey was quite frisky and pranced around the field* **lively**, bouncy, bubbly, perky, active, energetic, animated, zestful, full of vim and vigour; playful, full of fun, coltish, skittish, spirited, high-spirited, in high spirits, exuberant; *informal* high, frolicky, full of beans, full of get-up-and-go, sparky, zippy, peppy, bright-eyed and bushy-tailed; *archaic* frolicsome, gamesome, sportive, frolic, wanton; *rare* ludic.

fritter ▶ **verb** *he frittered away the money his father left him* **squander**, waste, misuse, misspend, spend unwisely, throw away, dissipate, make poor use of; overspend, spend like water, throw around like confetti, be prodigal with, be wastefully extravagant with, run through, get through, lose, let money slip through one's fingers; *informal* blow, splurge, pour/chuck something down the drain, spend money as if it grew on trees, spend money as if there were no tomorrow, spend money as if it were going out of style; *Brit. informal, dated* blue; *vulgar slang* piss away.
OPPOSITES save; spend wisely.

frivolity ▶ **noun** *he avoided the realities of life by resorting to frivolity* **light-heartedness**, levity, joking, jocularity, gaiety, fun, frivolousness, silliness, foolishness, zaniness, giddiness, flightiness, skittishness; flippancy, facetiousness, inanity, superficiality, shallowness, vacuity, empty-headedness; *informal* dizziness, dippiness; *Brit. informal* daftness; *N. Amer. informal* ditziness.
OPPOSITE seriousness.

frivolous ▶ **adjective 1** *all of the girls were indolent and frivolous* **giddy**, silly, foolish, facetious, zany, light-hearted, merry, superficial, shallow, lacking seriousness, non-serious, light-minded, whimsical, skittish, flighty, irresponsible, thoughtless, lacking in sense, feather-brained, empty-headed, pea-brained, birdbrained, vacuous, vapid; *informal* dizzy, dippy, dopey, batty, dotty, nutty; *N. Amer. informal* ditzy.
OPPOSITES sensible, serious.
2 *they never indulged in frivolous remarks* **flippant**, glib, waggish, joking, jokey, light-hearted, facetious, fatuous, inane, shallow, superficial, senseless, thoughtless, ill-considered, non-serious; *informal* flip; *Brit. informal* daft; *archaic* frolicsome, sportive, jocose.
OPPOSITE serious.
3 *her face was thickly painted and her clothes were frivolous* **impractical**, frothy, flimsy, insubstantial.
OPPOSITE practical.
4 *new rules to stop frivolous lawsuits* **time-wasting**, trivial, trifling, minor, petty, lightweight, insignificant, unimportant, worthless, valueless, pointless, paltry, niggling, peripheral.
OPPOSITE important.

frizzle[1] ▶ **verb** *a hamburger frizzled in the frying pan* **sizzle**, crackle, fizz, hiss, spit, sputter, crack, snap; fry, cook; *technical* decrepitate; *rare* crepitate.

frizzle[2] ▶ verb *their hair was powdered and frizzled* **curl**, coil, crimp, crinkle, kink, wave, frizz.
OPPOSITE straighten.

frizzy ▶ adjective *she had frizzy blonde hair* **curly**, curled, corkscrew, crimped, crinkled, crinkly, kinked, kinky, waved, frizzed, corrugated; permed; *rare* ringletty, ringletted.
OPPOSITE straight.

frock *See centre pages for list of* **Dresses**
▶ noun *she looked demure in a cream silk frock* **dress**, gown, robe, shift; garment, costume.

frog ▶ noun. *See centre pages for list of* **Amphibians**

WORD LINKS
young **tadpole**
relating to frogs **batrachian, anuran**

frolic ▶ verb *the children frolicked on the sand* **frisk**, gambol, cavort, caper, cut capers, sport, scamper, skip, dance, romp, trip, prance, leap, spring, hop, jump, bounce, bob; *rare* curvet, rollick, capriole.
▶ noun *the youngsters enjoyed their frolic* **antic**, caper, game, romp, stunt, escapade, exploit, revel, spree, sport, fling; prank, jape; giggle, laugh; (**frolics**) fun (and games), merrymaking, amusement; *informal* lark, skylark.

frolicsome ▶ adjective (*archaic*) *he met a group of frolicsome girls* **playful**, frisky, fun-loving, jolly, merry, gleeful, light-hearted, exuberant, high-spirited, spirited, lively, perky, skittish, coltish, kittenish; mischievous, impish, roguish, prankish, waggish, jokey; *informal* peppy, zippy, full of beans, frolicky; *archaic* gamesome, sportive, frolic, wanton.

front ▶ noun **1** *a little deck at the front of the boat* **forepart**, fore, foremost part, anterior, forefront, nose, head; bow, prow; foreground, nearest part, closest part; *informal* sharp end; *rare* fore-end.
OPPOSITES rear, back.
2 *the car swerved and crashed into a shop front* **frontage**, face, facing, facade; window.
3 *the battlefield surgeons who work at the front* **front line**, vanguard, van, first line, firing line, battlefield, battleground, field of battle, combat zone; trenches; *historical* lists.
4 *she pushed her way to the front of the queue* **head**, beginning, start, top, lead; forefront.
OPPOSITE back.
5 *she kept up a brave front for most of the week* **appearance**, look, expression, face, manner, air, countenance, demeanour, bearing, posture, pose, mien, aspect, exterior, veneer, (outward) show, false display, act, pretence, affectation.
6 *he kept a shop as a front for dealing in stolen goods* **cover**, cover-up, pretext, false front, blind, disguise, facade, mask, cloak, screen, smokescreen, camouflage.
7 (*informal*) *he's got a bit of talent and a lot of front* **self-confidence**, boldness, forwardness, audacity, audaciousness, temerity, brazenness, presumption, presumptuousness; rashness, daring; *informal* cockiness, pushiness, nerve, face, neck, brass neck; *archaic* assumption.
OPPOSITE shyness.
□ **in front** *she could hardly see the runners in front* **ahead**, to the fore, at the fore, at the head, up ahead, in the vanguard, in the van, in the lead, leading, coming first; at the head of the queue; *informal* up front.
OPPOSITE behind.
□ **in front of 1** *he stepped out in front of me* **ahead of**, before, preceding.
OPPOSITE behind.
2 *she sat in front of the mirror* **facing**, before.
3 *I won't embarrass him in front of his new friends* **in the presence of**, before, before the very eyes of, in the sight of, under the nose of.
□ **up front** *they didn't have the cash to pay me up front* **in advance**, beforehand, ahead of time, in readiness.
▶ adjective **1** *he opened the front door* **at the front**, foremost.
OPPOSITE back.
2 *the front runners headed towards the finish* **leading**, lead, first, foremost; in first place.
OPPOSITE last.
▶ verb *the houses fronted on a reservoir* **overlook**, look on to, look out on, look out over, look towards, face (towards), lie opposite (to); have a view of, command a view of.
OPPOSITE back on to.

frontier ▶ noun *the lakes sit astride the US–Canadian frontier* **border**, boundary, partition, borderline, dividing line, bounding line, demarcation line; perimeter, limit, edge, rim; marches, bounds.

CHOOSE THE RIGHT WORD

frontier, border, boundary
See BORDER.

frost ▶ noun **1** *the hedges and trees were covered with frost* **ice crystals**, ice, rime, rime ice, verglas; rime frost, white frost, black frost, hoar frost, ground frost; *informal* Jack Frost; *archaic* hoar.
2 *there had been a frost overnight* **cold snap**, period of cold weather; hoar frost, ground frost; *informal* freeze, freeze-up.
OPPOSITE heatwave.
3 *there was frost in his tone* **coldness**, coolness, frostiness, ice, iciness, glaciality, frigidity; hostility, unfriendliness, stiffness, stand-offishness.
OPPOSITE friendliness.

frosty ▶ adjective **1** *a frosty autumn morning* **freezing**, frigid, glacial, arctic, wintry, bitter, bitterly cold, cold, ice-cold, icy-cold, cool, chilly, crisp, bleak; frozen, rimy, icy; *informal* nippy; *Brit. informal* parky; *literary* frore, chill; *rare* gelid, brumal.
2 *Mary fixed a frosty gaze on him* **unfriendly**, unsympathetic, inhospitable, unwelcoming, forbidding, hostile, disdainful, haughty, stony, stern, hard, fierce; icy, glacial, frigid, cold, cool.

froth ▶ noun **1** *the froth on top of stout* **foam**, lather, head, suds; bubbles, frothiness, fizz, effervescence; scum; *literary* spume.
2 *the froth of party politics* **trivia**, trifles, irrelevancies, nonsense, rubbish, trash, pap; *Brit.* candyfloss; *informal* drivel, twaddle, hot air, gas.
OPPOSITE nitty-gritty.
▶ verb *the beer frothed up* **bubble**, fizz, foam, cream, lather; effervesce, aerate; churn, seethe; *literary* roil, spume.

frothy ▶ adjective **1** *the beer was sharp and frothy* **foaming**, foamy, bubbling, bubbly, fizzy, sparkling, effervescent, gassy, carbonated, aerated; creamy, yeasty, sudsy; *literary* spumy, spumous.
OPPOSITES flat, still.
2 *a frothy pink evening dress* **frilly**, flouncy, insubstantial.
OPPOSITE plain.
3 *a frothy love song* **insubstantial**, light, lightweight, lacking substance, superficial, shallow, slight, empty; trivial, trifling, frivolous, petty, paltry, insignificant, worthless, of no account, of no merit, of no value.
OPPOSITE deep.

frown ▶ verb *the old lady frowned at him* **scowl**, glower, glare, lour, look sullen, make a face, look daggers; give someone black looks; knit/furrow one's brows; *informal* give someone dirty looks.
OPPOSITE smile.
□ **frown on** *drink-driving was frowned on by the interviewees* **disapprove of**, view with dislike/disfavour, show/indicate disapproval of, dislike, discourage, look askance at, not take kindly to, not think much of, take a dim view of, find unacceptable, be against, take exception to, object to, think wrong, discountenance, have a low opinion of.
OPPOSITES smile on, approve of.
▶ noun *I put the phone down with a frown* **scowl**, glower, glare, black look, dirty look; knitted brows, furrowed brows.
OPPOSITE smile.

frowsty ▶ adjective (*Brit.*) *a frowsty room* **stuffy**, musty, airless, unventilated, fusty, close, muggy, stifling, suffocating, oppressive; stale, stagnant, smelly; *N. Amer.* funky; *rare* mucid.
OPPOSITES airy, ventilated.

frowzy ▶ adjective **1** *a frowzy old biddy* **scruffy**, unkempt, untidy, sloppy, messy, dishevelled, slovenly, slatternly, bedraggled, down at heel, ill-dressed, badly dressed, dowdy; *N. Amer. informal* raggedy.
OPPOSITE tidy.
2 *the frowzy room above the saloon* **dingy**, gloomy, dull, drab, dark, badly/poorly lit, dim, **stuffy**, close, musty, stale, stagnant, stifling, suffocating, unfresh; shabby, seedy, run down, tacky; *Brit.* frowsty, fuggy.

frozen ▶ adjective **1** *the frozen ground* **ice-cold**, ice-covered, icy, ice-bound, frosted; hard, solid, hard as iron; *literary* rimy.
2 *frozen fish* **chilled**, iced, preserved.
3 *the frozen countryside* **bitterly cold**, wintry, frosty, icy, glacial, frigid, arctic, sub-zero, Siberian, polar, raw, extreme; *rare* gelid, algid.
4 *his hands were frozen* **freezing**, very cold, chilled, chilled to the bone/marrow/core, numb with cold, numb, numbed, frozen stiff; shivering; *informal* frozen to death.
OPPOSITE boiling.

frugal ▶ adjective **1** *she lives a frugal life* **thrifty**, sparing, economical, saving; careful, cautious, prudent, provident, unwasteful, sensible, canny; abstemious, abstinent, austere, self-denying, ascetic, non-indulgent, self-disciplined, spartan, puritanical, nunlike, monastic, monkish; miserly, parsimonious, niggardly, scrimping, cheese-paring, penny-pinching, close-fisted, ungenerous, grasping; *N. Amer.* forehanded; *informal* tight-fisted, tight, mingy, stingy; *N. Amer. informal* cheap.
OPPOSITE extravagant.
2 *the boys finished their frugal breakfast* **meagre**, scanty, scant, paltry, skimpy, insufficient; plain, simple, moderate, temperate, austere, ascetic, spartan, restrained; inexpensive, cheap, economical.
OPPOSITE lavish.

frugality ▶ noun *he was known for his frugality and modesty* **thriftiness**, carefulness, scrimping and saving, conservation, good management; caution, prudence, providence, canniness; abstemiousness, abstinence,

F

austerity, asceticism, self-discipline, restraint, moderation, puritanism, monasticism, monkishness; miserliness, meanness, parsimoniousness, niggardliness, close-fistedness; *informal* tight-fistedness, tightness, stinginess; *rare* sparingness.
OPPOSITE extravagance.

fruit *See centre pages for list of* **Fruit**
▶ **noun** (also **fruits**) *the fruit of victory | the fruits of their labours* **reward**, benefit, advantages; product, produce, profit, return, yield, legacy, issue, deserts; outcome, upshot, result, results, consequences, effect, effects.
▶ **verb** *the strawberries should fruit in May* **produce fruit**, bear fruit.

WORD LINKS

related prefixes	**fruct- (e.g. *fructification*), frug-, carp-, pom-**
study of fruit and seeds	**carpology**
seller of fruit	**fruiterer;**
	(*Brit.*) **greengrocer;**
	(*Brit. dated*) **costermonger**
fruit-growing	**pomiculture, orcharding, citriculture**
science of fruit-growing	**pomology**
fruit-eating	**frugivorous**

F

fruitful ▶ **adjective 1** *a fruitful tree* **fruit-bearing**, fructiferous, fruiting; **fertile**, fecund, high-yielding, lush, abundant, profuse, prolific, bounteous; generative, progenitive; *rare* fructuous.
OPPOSITE infertile.
2 *the two days of talks had been fruitful* **productive**, constructive, useful, of use, worthwhile, helpful, of help, of assistance, beneficial, valuable, rewarding, profitable, advantageous, gainful, successful, effective, effectual, well spent.
OPPOSITES fruitless, futile.

fruition ▶ **noun** *scientific projects need a great deal of time to come to fruition* **fulfilment**, realization, actualization, materialization; achievement, attainment, accomplishment, resolution; success, completion, consummation, conclusion, close, finish, perfection; maturity, maturation, ripening, ripeness; effecting, implementation, execution, performance; *informal* winding up, sewing up, polishing off; *rare* effectuation, reification.
OPPOSITE inception.

fruitless ▶ **adjective** *the search proved fruitless* **futile**, vain, in vain, to no avail, to no effect, idle; pointless, useless, worthless, needless, wasted, hollow; ineffectual, ineffective, inefficacious; unproductive, unrewarding, profitless, unsuccessful, unavailing, barren, for naught; abortive; *archaic* bootless.
OPPOSITES fruitful, productive.

CHOOSE THE RIGHT WORD

fruitless, futile, vain, pointless
See FUTILE.

fruity ▶ **adjective 1** *fruity jam* **tasting of fruit**, containing fruit.
2 *he had a wonderfully fruity voice* **resonant**, deep, rich, full, full-toned, full-bodied; mellow, smooth; clear, strong, vibrant, loud, booming.
OPPOSITE thin.
3 (*Brit. informal*) *a fruity story* **smutty**, bawdy, naughty, spicy, earthy, broad, wicked; racy, risqué, juicy, ribald, Rabelaisian, raw; indecent, improper, dirty, rude, indelicate, vulgar, coarse, lewd, sordid, off colour, filthy, profane, obscene, scatological, offensive; sexy, suggestive, titillating, salacious, prurient; *N. Amer.* gamy; *euphemistic* adult; *informal* blue, near the knuckle, nudge-nudge, raunchy, locker-room; *Brit. informal* saucy.
OPPOSITE clean.

frumpy ▶ **adjective** *her mother's frumpy clothes* **dowdy**, frumpish, unfashionable, old-fashioned; drab, dull, shabby, scruffy; *Brit. informal* mumsy; *Austral./NZ informal* daggy.
OPPOSITE fashionable.

frustrate ▶ **verb 1** *the settlers' attempts at agriculture were frustrated by the climate* **thwart**, defeat, foil, block, stop, put a stop to, counter, spoil, check, baulk, circumvent, disappoint, forestall, bar, dash, scotch, quash, crush, derail, nip in the bud, baffle, nullify, snooker; obstruct, impede, hamper, hinder, stifle, fetter, hamstring, cripple, put a brake on, stand in the way of, spike someone's guns; *informal* stymie, foul up, screw up, put the kibosh on, put the lid on, banjax, do for; *Brit. informal* scupper.
OPPOSITES help, facilitate.
2 *the objections of his colleagues clearly frustrated him* **exasperate**, infuriate, annoy, anger, madden, vex, irritate, irk, embitter, sour, get someone's back up, try someone's patience; **discourage**, dishearten, dispirit, depress, dissatisfy, make discontented; *informal* aggravate, drive mad, drive crazy, bug, miff, hack off, get to, get under someone's skin, give someone the hump; *Brit. informal* wind up, get on someone's wick, nark.
OPPOSITE please.

frustration ▶ **noun 1** *he clenched his fists in frustration* **exasperation**, annoyance, anger, vexation, irritation, bitterness, resentment; disappointment, discouragement, disheartenment, dispiritedness, depression, dissatisfaction, discontentment, discontent; *informal* aggravation.
OPPOSITE satisfaction.
2 *the repeated frustration of his attempts to introduce changes* **thwarting**, defeat, foiling, blocking, stopping, countering, spoiling, checking, baulking, circumvention, forestalling, dashing, scotching, quashing, crushing; disappointment, derailment, baffling, snookering; obstruction, hampering, hindering, stifling, crippling; failure, collapse, foundering, lack of success, non-success; *Brit. informal* scuppering.
OPPOSITES success; promotion.

fuddled ▶ **adjective** *she forced her weary fuddled brain to work* **stupefied**, addled, befuddled, confused, muddled, bewildered, dumbfounded, dazed, stunned, dizzy, muzzy, groggy, foggy, fuzzy, vague, disorientated, disoriented, all at sea, mixed up, at a loss, at sixes and sevens; *informal* dopey, woozy, woolly-minded, discombobulated, fazed, not with it.
OPPOSITES clear, sharp.

fuddy-duddy ▶ **noun** (*informal*) *he called me an old fuddy-duddy* **fogy**, conservative, traditionalist, conformist; museum piece, fossil, dinosaur, troglodyte; *informal* stick-in-the-mud, square, stuffed shirt, back number, dodo; *N. Amer. informal* sobersides.

fudge ▶ **noun 1** *she helped herself to a square of fudge* **chewy sweet**, toffee.
2 *the latest proposals are a fudge* **compromise**, **cover-up**, halfway house; equivocation, spin, casuistry, sophistry, speciousness; *informal* cop-out.
OPPOSITE straightforwardness.
▶ **verb 1** *I am sure a no-nonsense chap like you will not fudge the issue* **evade**, dodge, skirt, avoid, duck, shift ground about; hedge, prevaricate, vacillate, be non-committal, shuffle, parry questions, stall, shilly-shally, beat about the bush, mince (one's) words; *Brit.* hum and haw; *informal* waffle, cop out, flannel, sit on the fence; *rare* tergiversate.
OPPOSITE be forthright about.
2 *the government has been fudging figures* **falsify**, fake, distort, manipulate, misrepresent, misreport, bend, spin, put a spin on, massage, tamper with, tinker with, interfere with, change, doctor, juggle; embellish, embroider, warp, colour; *informal* cook, fiddle with.

fuel *See centre pages for list of* **Energy and Fuels**
▶ **noun 1** *one aircraft ran out of fuel and had to ditch* **power source**, combustible, propellant; petrol, diesel oil; *N. Amer.* gasoline, gas.
2 *she got up to add more fuel to the fire* **firewood**, wood, kindling, logs; coal, coke, anthracite; charcoal; oil, paraffin, kerosene; heat source.
3 *we all need fuel to keep our bodies going* **nourishment**, sustenance, nutriment, nutrition, food, fodder.
4 *his antics added fuel to the Republican cause* **encouragement**, incentive, ammunition, incitement, stimulus; provocation, goading.
▶ **verb 1** *power stations fuelled by low-grade coal* **power**, charge, fire, stoke up, supply with fuel.
2 *pictures of the two of them together fuelled rumours* **stimulate**, boost, encourage, intensify, fortify, support, nurture; incite, inflame, exacerbate, animate, vitalize, fan, feed, whip up; provoke, goad.
OPPOSITE dampen.

fug ▶ **noun** (*Brit. informal*) *the fug of the bar* **stuffiness**, fustiness, frowstiness, staleness, stuffy atmosphere.
OPPOSITE airiness.

fuggy ▶ **adjective** *a fuggy little room* **stuffy**, smoky, close, muggy, stale, fusty, unventilated, airless, suffocating, stifling, oppressive; heavy.
OPPOSITE airy.

fugitive ▶ **noun** *he is a hunted fugitive* **escapee**, escaper, runaway, deserter, refugee, renegade, absconder; *archaic* runagate.
▶ **adjective 1** *a fugitive criminal* **escaped**, escaping, runaway, fleeing, deserting; on the loose, at large, wanted; *informal* AWOL, on the run; *N. Amer. informal* on the lam.
2 *ours is a fugitive life* **fleeting**, transient, transitory, ephemeral, evanescent, flitting, flying, fading, momentary, short-lived, short, brief, passing, impermanent, fly-by-night, here today and gone tomorrow; *literary* fugacious.
OPPOSITES permanent, long-lasting.

fulfil ▶ **verb 1** *I knew I could fulfil my ambition to be a millionaire before I was thirty* **succeed in**, attain, realize, consummate, satisfy, manage, bring off, bring about, carry off, carry out, carry through, bring to fruition, deliver; *informal* pull something off, clinch.
OPPOSITE fail in.
2 *some officials were dismissed because they could not fulfil their duties* **carry out**, accomplish, achieve, execute, perform, discharge, implement, effect, effectuate, conduct; complete, bring to completion, finish, conclude, perfect; honour, be true to, keep faith with, make good, observe.
OPPOSITE neglect.
3 *they fulfilled the criteria for entry into the programme* **comply with**, satisfy, conform to, fill, answer, meet, obey, adhere to, respond to.
OPPOSITE fail.

fulfilled ▶ **adjective** *I am confident in this role, and feel fulfilled* **satisfied**, content, contented, happy, pleased, gratified, comfortable, serene, placid, untroubled, at ease, at peace.

OPPOSITES unfulfilled, discontented.

full ▶ adjective **1** *her glass was full* **filled**, filled up, filled to capacity, filled to the brim, brimming, brimful, topped up; overflowing, running over.
OPPOSITE empty.
2 *the bus was quite full* **crowded**, packed, crammed, cramped, congested, crushed, solid (with people), full of people, full to capacity, full to bursting, overfull, teeming, swarming, overcrowded, thronged; *N. Amer.* mobbed; *informal* jam-packed, wall-to-wall, stuffed, chock-a-block, chock-full, bursting at the seams, bulging at the seams, packed to the gunwales.
OPPOSITE empty.
3 *all the seats were full* **occupied**, taken, in use, engaged, unavailable.
OPPOSITE empty.
4 *the shelves are full* **well stocked**, well supplied, filled, loaded, packed, burdened, stuffed, crammed, stacked.
OPPOSITE empty.
5 *he was too full to protest when the waiter took his plate away* **replete**, satisfied, well fed, sated, satiated, full up, full to bursting, having had enough; gorged, glutted, cloyed; *informal* stuffed; *archaic* satiate, surfeited.
OPPOSITE hungry.
6 *he was full of mirth* **abounding in**, bursting with, brimming with, rich in, possessed by; *informal* awash with.
OPPOSITE free of.
7 *she'd had a full life* **eventful**, interesting, exciting, lively, action-packed, noteworthy; busy, strenuous, hectic, frantic, energetic, active.
OPPOSITES uneventful, limited.
8 *we can provide a full list of sailing clubs* **comprehensive**, thorough, exhaustive, all-inclusive, all-encompassing, all-embracing, in depth; complete, entire, whole, unabridged, uncut; extensive, long.
OPPOSITES incomplete, selective.
9 *the prospectus contains full details of the degree courses offered* **abundant**, plentiful, ample, copious, profuse, rich, lavish, liberal; detailed, in detail, specific, precise, exact, accurate, minute, particular; sufficient, satisfying; broad-ranging, complete.
OPPOSITES partial; vague.
10 *a fire engine driven at full speed* **maximum**, top, greatest, highest.
OPPOSITE low.
11 *she had a full figure* **well rounded**, rounded, round, plump, buxom, shapely, ample, curvaceous, voluptuous, womanly, Junoesque, Rubensesque; *informal* busty, chesty, curvy, well upholstered, well endowed; *N. Amer. informal* zaftig.
OPPOSITE thin.
12 *the dress had a full skirt* **loose-fitting**, loose, baggy, easy-fitting, generously cut, roomy, voluminous, capacious, billowing.
OPPOSITE tight.
13 *this song relies on his full and husky voice* **resonant**, rich, sonorous, deep, full-bodied, vibrant, fruity, clear, loud, strong.
OPPOSITE thin.
14 *the full flavour of a Bordeaux* **rich**, intense, deep, heavy, vivid, strong, vibrant, bold, warm.
OPPOSITES thin, watery.
▶ adverb **1** *she looked full into his face* **directly**, right, straight, squarely, square, just, dead, point-blank; *informal* smack (bang), bang, slap, plumb.
OPPOSITE indirectly.
2 *he knows full well that four out of five investments will be lost* **very**, perfectly, quite, extremely, entirely; *informal* darn, damn, damned; *Brit. informal* jolly, bloody; *N. Amer. informal* darned; *archaic or N. English* right.
□ **full out** *he was working full out to supply the demand* **to the maximum**, flat out; at full speed, at maximum speed, as fast as possible, with maximum power, at full tilt, at full pelt, at breakneck speed; *informal* hell for leather, hammer and tongs, like crazy, like mad, like a bat out of hell; *Brit. informal* like the clappers, like billy-o.
▶ noun
□ **in full** *my letter was published in full* **in its entirety**, in total, without omission/abridgement, unabridged, uncut, fully; *Latin* in toto.
OPPOSITES in part, partially.
□ **to the full** *do your best to live life to the full* **fully**, thoroughly, completely, to the utmost, to capacity, to the limit, to the maximum, for all one's worth, with a vengeance, will all the stops out.

full-blooded ▶ adjective *a full-blooded price war* **all out**, complete, total, uncompromising, committed, out and out, thorough, thoroughgoing, vigorous, strenuous, intense; unrestrained, uncontrolled, unbridled, hard-hitting, pulling no punches.
OPPOSITE half-hearted.

full-blown ▶ adjective *this problem could flare up into a full-blown crisis* **fully developed**, full-scale, full-blooded, fully fledged, complete, total, thorough, entire, full, advanced.
OPPOSITE partial.

full-bodied ▶ adjective *a full-bodied claret* **full-flavoured**, flavourful, flavoursome, full of flavour, rich, intense, fruity, deep, heavy, strong, robust, bold, warm, mellow, redolent, well-matured.
OPPOSITE tasteless.

full-grown ▶ adjective *a full-grown woman* **adult**, mature, grown-up, of age, having reached one's majority; fully grown, fully developed, fully fledged, in full bloom, ripe, in one's prime.
OPPOSITES infant; immature.

fullness ▶ noun **1** *the honesty and fullness of the information they provide* **completeness**, comprehensiveness, thoroughness, exhaustiveness, all-inclusiveness, extensiveness, length, depth.
OPPOSITE incompleteness.
2 *the fullness of her body* **roundedness**, roundness, plumpness, buxomness, shapeliness, ampleness, curvaceousness, voluptuousness, womanliness; *informal* bustiness, chestiness, curviness.
OPPOSITE thinness.
3 *the recording has a fullness and warmth* **resonance**, richness, depth, vibrancy, fruitiness, clarity, intensity, loudness, strength.
OPPOSITES weakness, thinness.
□ **in the fullness of time** *I hoped my ploy would get results in the fullness of time* **in due course**, when the time is ripe, eventually, in time, in time to come, at a later date, one day, some day, sooner or later, in a while, after a while, after a bit, ultimately, finally, in the end; *Brit. informal* at the end of the day.
OPPOSITES immediately; never.

full-scale ▶ adjective **1** *a full-scale model* **full-size**, unreduced, actual size.
OPPOSITES scale, scaled down.
2 *a full-scale public inquiry* **thorough**, comprehensive, extensive, exhaustive, complete, all-encompassing, all-inclusive, all-embracing, thoroughgoing, wide-ranging, sweeping, major, in-depth, profound, far-reaching.
OPPOSITE partial.

fully ▶ adverb **1** *the panel are fully aware of the law* **completely**, entirely, wholly, totally, thoroughly, quite, utterly, perfectly, altogether, exhaustively, extensively, intimately, in all respects, in every respect, without reservation, without exception, {lock, stock, and barrel}, from first to last, to the hilt.
OPPOSITE partially.
2 *fully two minutes must have passed* **at least**, without exaggeration, easily, quite; *informal* without a word of a lie.
OPPOSITE nearly.

fully fledged ▶ adjective *her ambition to become a fully fledged teacher* **trained**, qualified, proficient; experienced, time-served; mature, fully developed, full grown, full scale, full blown.
OPPOSITE novice.

fulminate ▶ verb **1** *ministers and preachers fulminated against the new curriculum* **protest**, rail, rage, rant, thunder, storm, declaim, inveigh, speak out, make/take a stand; denounce, decry, condemn, criticize, censure, disparage, attack, execrate, arraign; *informal* mouth off about, kick up a fuss/stink about, go on about; *rare* animadvert, excoriate, vociferate about, vituperate.
2 (*literary*) *thunder fulminated around the house* **explode**, flash, crack, detonate, blow up, go off; rumble.

fulmination ▶ noun **1** *the fulminations of media moralists* **protest**, objection, complaint, rant; denunciation, condemnation, criticism, censure, disparagement, attack, broadside; (**fulminations**) decrying, railing, invective, tirade, diatribe, harangue, philippic, obloquy, execration, arraignment; *informal* brickbat, tongue-lashing, bashing, blast; *Brit. informal* slating; *formal* excoriation, vociferation, vituperation.
2 (*literary*) *the echo of the previous fulminations faded away* **explosion**, flash, crack, crash, bang, report, detonation, eruption, blowing up; rumbling.

fulsome ▶ adjective *he paid fulsome tribute to his secretary* **enthusiastic**, ample, profuse, extensive, generous, liberal, lavish, glowing, gushing, gushy; **excessive**, extravagant, overdone, immoderate, inordinate, over-appreciative; fawning, ingratiating; adulatory, laudatory, acclamatory, eulogistic, rapturous, flattering, complimentary, effusive, cloying, unctuous, saccharine, sugary, honeyed; *informal* over the top, OTT, buttery; *formal* encomiastic.

fumble ▶ verb **1** *he fumbled for his keys* **grope**, feel about, search blindly, scrabble around, muddle around; fish, delve, cast about/around/round for; *archaic* grabble for.
2 *he fumbled about in the dark but could not find her* **stumble**, blunder, flounder, lumber, bumble, stagger, totter, lurch, move clumsily, move awkwardly; feel one's way, grope one's way.
3 *the keeper fumbled the ball* **fail to catch**, miss, drop, mishandle, handle awkwardly; misfield.
4 *he had fumbled the initiative* **botch**, bungle, mismanage, mishandle, spoil; blunder, make a mistake; *informal* make a mess of, make a hash of, fluff, muff, screw up, foul up, blow, louse up; *Brit. informal* make a pig's ear of, make a muck of, cock up; *N. Amer. informal* flub.
▶ noun **1** *a fumble from the goalkeeper* **slip**, miss, drop, mishandling; misfielding; mistake, error, gaffe, fault, botch; *informal* slip-up, clanger, boob, boo-boo, howler, foul-up; *Brit. informal* cock-up.
2 (*informal*) *a kiss and a fumble* **fondle**, grope, caress, hug, embrace, cuddle; *informal* feel-up.

F

fume ▸ verb **1** *a liquid which fumes in moist air* **emit smoke**, emit gas, smoke; *archaic* reek.
2 *I am absolutely fuming that our young people are missing out again* **be furious**, be enraged, be angry, seethe, smoulder, simmer, boil, be livid, be incensed, bristle, be beside oneself, spit, chafe; rage, rant and rave, lose one's temper, lose control, explode, flare up, go berserk, bluster; *informal* be up in arms, be hot under the collar, be at boiling point, be all steamed up, get steamed up, get worked up, fly off the handle, foam at the mouth, raise the roof, flip one's lid, blow one's top, hit the roof, go up the wall, blow a fuse, see red.
▸ noun (**fumes**) **1** *a fire giving off toxic fumes* **smoke**, vapour, gas, exhalation, exhaust, effluvium, pollution; *archaic* miasma.
2 *her perfume overpowered the tobacco fumes* **smell**, stink, reek, stench, odour; *Brit. informal* pong, niff, whiff, hum; *Scottish informal* guff; *N. Amer. informal* funk; *rare* fetor, malodour, mephitis.

fumigate ▸ verb *we got sulphur candles to fumigate the house* **disinfect**, purify, sterilize, sanitize, sanitate, decontaminate, cleanse, clean out; smoke out; *rare* depollute, depurate, deterge.

fun ▸ noun **1** *I joined in with the fun* **pleasure**, entertainment, enjoyment, amusement, excitement, gratification; jollification, merrymaking; leisure, relaxation, relief, respite, rest, refreshment; recreation, diversion, distraction; good time, great time; *informal* R and R (rest and recreation), living it up, junketing, a ball, whoopee, beer and skittles.
OPPOSITE boredom.
2 *he plays the role with an infectious sense of fun* **merriment**, cheerfulness, cheeriness, cheer, joy, jollity, joviality, jocularity, high spirits, gaiety, mirth, mirthfulness, laughter, hilarity, glee, gladness, light-heartedness, levity; vivacity, liveliness, exuberance, ebullience, buoyancy, perkiness, zest, sunniness, brightness, enthusiasm, vibrancy, vividness, vitality, energy, vigour, vim; *dated* sport.
OPPOSITE misery.
3 *he became a figure of fun in the music press* **ridicule**, derision, mockery, laughter, scorn, scoffing, contempt; joking, jokes, jesting, jeering, sneering, jibing, teasing, taunting, ragging, lampooning.
OPPOSITE respect.
□ **fun and games cavorting**, clowning about/around, fooling around, horseplay, play, playfulness, tomfoolery, buffoonery, mischief; revels, frolics, revelry, larks, antics, high jinks; *informal* skylarking.
□ **in fun** *the teasing was all in fun* **playful**, in jest, joking, jokey, as a joke, tongue in cheek, light-hearted, high-spirited, unserious, facetious, flippant, flip, glib, frivolous, for a laugh; to tease, teasing, bantering, whimsical; *archaic* frolicsome, sportive; *rare* jocose.
OPPOSITES in earnest, serious.
□ **make fun of** *he was making fun of her.* See MAKE.
▸ adjective (*informal*) **1** *a fun evening out* **enjoyable**, amusing, diverting, pleasurable, pleasing, agreeable, interesting.
OPPOSITE boring.
2 *a smart, fun girl* **entertaining**, lively, amusing, fun-loving, witty, convivial, clubbable.
OPPOSITE serious.

function ▸ noun **1** *the main function of the machine* **purpose**, task, use, role; reason, basis, justification.
2 *the committee's function is to arrange social activities* **responsibility**, duty, concern, province, aim, activity, assignment, obligation, charge; task, chore, job, role, errand, mission, detail, undertaking, commission; capacity, post, situation, office, occupation, employment, business, operation; *French* raison d'être; *informal* thing, bag, line of country, pigeon.
3 *casualties are a function of war* **consequence**, result, outcome, ramification, corollary, concomitant; *dated* issue.
OPPOSITE cause.
4 *he was obliged to attend political functions* **social event**, party, occasion, social occasion, affair, gathering, reception, soirée, celebration, jamboree, gala; *N. Amer.* levee; *informal* do, bash, shindig, shindy, blowout; *Brit. informal* rave-up, thrash, knees-up, jolly, beanfeast, bunfight, beano, lig.
▸ verb **1** *if we unplug a TV set, it ceases to function* **work**, go, run, be in working/running order, operate, perform, be in action, be operative.
OPPOSITE malfunction.
2 *the museum intends to* **function as** *an educational and study centre* **serve**, act, operate, perform, work, behave; have/do the job of, play the role of, act the part of, perform the function of, do duty as, constitute, form.

functional ▸ adjective **1** *an ugly functional concrete building* **practical**, useful, utilitarian, utility, workaday, serviceable; minimalist, plain, simple, basic; severe, spartan, ascetic, bare, modest, unadorned, undecorated, unornamented, unembellished, unostentatious, uncluttered, unfussy, without frills; impersonal, characterless, soulless, colourless, institutional, antiseptic, clinical; *informal* no frills.
OPPOSITES ornate; impractical.
2 *the air vent needs clearing to keep it fully functional* **working**, in working order, functioning, effective, usable, in service, in use; going, running, operative, operating, in operation, in commission, in action; *informal* up and running.
OPPOSITES out of order, malfunctioning.

functionary ▸ noun *a Whitehall functionary* **official**, office-bearer, office-holder, public servant, civil servant, bureaucrat, administrator, apparatchik; *Brit.* jack-in-office.

fund ▸ noun **1** *an emergency fund for refugees* **collection**, kitty, reserve, pool, purse; endowment, foundation, trust, charity, grant; investment, capital; savings, nest egg; *informal* stash.
2 (**funds**) *I was very short of funds* **money**, cash, hard cash, ready money; wealth, means, assets, resources, savings, capital, reserves, the wherewithal; *informal* dough, bread, loot, dosh, green, the ready, folding money; *Brit. informal* lolly, spondulicks.
3 *his fund of stories seems inexhaustible* **stock**, store, supply, accumulation, mass, collection, cumulation, bank, pool; mine, reservoir, storehouse, treasury, treasure house, hoard, repository.
▸ verb *the agency was funded by the Treasury* **finance**, pay for, back, capitalize, sponsor, provide finance/capital for, put up the money for, subsidize, underwrite, endow, support, be a patron of, float, maintain; *informal* foot the bill for, pick up the tab for; *N. Amer. informal* bankroll, stake.

fundamental ▸ adjective *a fundamental political principle* **basic**, foundational, rudimentary, elemental, elementary, underlying, basal, radical, root; primary, cardinal, initial, original, prime, first, primitive, primordial; principal, chief, capital, key, central; structural, organic, constitutional, inherent, intrinsic, ingrained; vital, essential, important, indispensable, necessary, crucial, pivotal, critical.
OPPOSITES secondary, unimportant.

> **CHOOSE THE RIGHT WORD**
>
> **fundamental, basic**
>
> *See* BASIC.

fundamentally ▸ adverb **1** *they were of fundamentally different temperaments* **basically**, elementally, radically; structurally, organically, constitutionally, inherently, intrinsically, materially; vitally, essentially; crucially, centrally, critically.
OPPOSITE superficially.
2 *she was, fundamentally, a good person* **essentially**, in essence, basically, at heart, at bottom, deep down, principally, predominantly, above all, first of all, most of all, first and foremost, on the whole, by and large, substantially; *French* au fond; *informal* at the end of the day, when all is said and done, when you get right down to it.
OPPOSITE ostensibly.

fundamentals ▸ plural noun *he taught me the fundamentals of the job* **basics**, essentials, rudiments, foundations, basic principles, first principles, preliminaries; crux, essence, core, nucleus, heart, base, bedrock, groundwork, crux of the matter, heart of the matter; *Latin* sine qua non; *informal* nuts and bolts, nitty-gritty, brass tacks, ABC.
OPPOSITE advanced principles.

funeral ▸ noun **1** *he'd attended a funeral* **burial**, burying, interment, entombment, committal, inhumation, laying to rest, consignment to the grave; cremation; funeral rites, obsequies, last offices; wake, vigil; *rare* sepulture, exequies.
OPPOSITE exhumation.
2 (*informal*) *remember, it was you who asked—it's your funeral* **responsibility**, problem, worry, concern, business, affair; *informal* headache; *Brit. informal* lookout, pigeon.

funereal ▸ adjective **1** *the funereal atmosphere of the place* **solemn**, sombre, grave, serious; gloomy, dismal, doleful, dreary, sad, cheerless, joyless, bleak, melancholy, miserable, morose, sorrowful, morbid, maudlin, dark, depressing, woeful, lugubrious, sepulchral; *literary* dolorous; *rare* exequial, funebrial.
OPPOSITES cheerful, lively.
2 *funereal colours* **dark**, black, drab.

fungus *See centre pages for lists of* **Fungi, Mushrooms, and Toadstools** **Poisonous Plants and Fungi**
▸ noun **mushroom**, toadstool; mould, mildew, rust, fungal disease, rot, decay; *technical* mycelium, saprophyte.

WORD LINKS

related prefix	**myco-** (e.g. *mycoprotein*), **fungi-**
science of fungi	**mycology**
fungus-eating	**fungivorous**
chemical that destroys fungus	**fungicide**

funk (*informal*) ▸ noun **1** (*Brit.*) *he put us all into a funk* **panic**, state of fear, fluster; *informal* cold sweat, flap, state, tizzy, tizz, tiz-woz, dither, stew; *Brit. informal* blue funk; *N. Amer. informal* twit.
2 (*N. Amer.*) *he was in a deep funk because his wife had left him* **depression**; *informal* the dumps, the doldrums, low; *N. Amer. informal* blue funk.
▸ verb (*Brit.*) *I'm certain he funked it* **avoid**, evade, dodge, escape from, run away from, baulk at, flinch from; *informal* chicken out of, duck, wriggle out of, cop out of, get out of.

funnel ▸ noun **1** *fluid was being poured through the funnel* **tube**, pipe, channel, conduit.

2 *smoke was pouring from the funnel* **chimney**, flue, vent, shaft; Scottish & N. English lum.
▸ **verb** *some of the money was funnelled through secret bank accounts* **channel**, guide, feed, direct, convey, move, pass; pour, filter, siphon.
OPPOSITES scatter, splurge.

funny ▸ **adjective 1** *a book with many funny episodes* **amusing**, humorous, comic, comical, droll, laughable; hilarious, hysterical, riotous, uproarious; witty, quick-witted, waggish, facetious, jolly, jocular, light-hearted; entertaining, diverting, sparkling, scintillating; silly, absurd, ridiculous, ludicrous, risible, farcical, preposterous, slapstick; informal side-splitting, rib-tickling, laugh-a-minute, wacky, zany, off the wall, daft, killing, a scream, rich, priceless.
OPPOSITES serious; tragic.
2 *a funny coincidence* **strange**, **peculiar**, odd, queer, weird, bizarre, curious, freakish, freak, quirky; mysterious, mystifying, puzzling, perplexing; unusual, uncommon, anomalous, irregular, abnormal, exceptional, singular, rare, unique, out of the ordinary, extraordinary, outlandish; Brit. out of the common; Scottish unco; Brit. informal, dated rum.
OPPOSITES obvious, straightforward.
3 *make sure there are no funny characters hanging around outside* **suspicious**, suspect, dubious, untrustworthy, questionable; informal shady, fishy, not kosher; Brit. informal dodgy; Austral./NZ shonky.
OPPOSITE trustworthy.

CHOOSE THE RIGHT WORD

funny, humorous, witty, comical
See HUMOROUS.

fur ▸ **noun** *a layer of fur* **hair**, wool; coat, mane, fleece, pelt; technical pelage; archaic fell.
WORD LINKS
fear of fur **doraphobia**

furbish ▸ **verb** *the kitchen was furbished with every kind of modern gadget* **supply**, furnish, provide, equip, kit out, rig out, fit, appoint.

furious ▸ **adjective 1** *he was furious when he learned about it* **enraged**, raging, infuriated, very angry, inflamed, incandescent, fuming, boiling, seething, incensed, irate, frenzied, in a frenzy, raving mad, mad, maddened, ranting, raving, wrathful, in a temper, beside oneself; in high dudgeon, indignant, outraged; informal livid, hot under the collar, hopping mad, wild, as cross as two sticks, apoplectic, riled, aerated, on the warpath, up in arms, foaming at the mouth, steamed up, in a lather, in a paddy, fit to be tied, up the wall; N. Amer. informal sore, bent out of shape, soreheaded; Austral./NZ informal ropeable, snaky, crook; W. Indian informal vex; Brit. informal, dated in a bate; literary ireful, wroth.
OPPOSITES calm, placid.
2 *a furious argument* **fierce**, wild, violent; intense, vehement, unrestrained; heated, hot, passionate, fiery, 'lively'; tumultuous, turbulent, tempestuous, stormy, boisterous; blustery, gusty, gusting, windy, squally, rough, raging, howling, roaring, foul, filthy, dirty, nasty.
OPPOSITES mild, calm.

furnish ▸ **verb 1** *the bedrooms are elegantly furnished* **provide with furniture**, fit out, rig out, kit out, appoint, outfit, embellish, enhance.
2 *grooms furnished us with horses for our journey* **supply**, equip, provide, provision, issue, kit out, fix up, grant, present; give, offer, make available, serve, confer, afford, purvey, bestow, endow.
OPPOSITE divest.

furniture *See centre pages for lists of* **Beds Chairs and Stools Cupboards and Cabinets Furniture Types and Styles Tables and Desks**
▸ **noun** **furnishings**, house fittings, fittings, fitments, movables, fixtures, appointments, appliances, effects, chattels, amenities, units, equipment, paraphernalia; informal stuff, things.

furore ▸ **noun 1** *the letter caused a furore in Britain* **commotion**, uproar, outcry, disturbance, hubbub, hurly-burly, fuss, upset, tumult, brouhaha, palaver, to-do, pother, turmoil, tempest, agitation, pandemonium, confusion; stir, excitement; scandal, sensation; informal song and dance, hoo-ha, hullabaloo, ballyhoo, hoopla, rumpus, flap, tizz, tizzy, tizz-woz, stink, performance, pantomime, scene; Brit. informal carry-on, kerfuffle; N. Amer. informal snafu.
2 (archaic) *they excited a furore among stamp collectors* **craze**, enthusiasm, mania, passion, fad, obsession, compulsion, preoccupation.

furrow ▸ **noun 1** *regular furrows in a ploughed fields* **groove**, trench, rut, trough, ditch, channel, seam, gutter, gouge, hollow, fissure, gash, track.
2 *the furrows on either side of her mouth* **wrinkle**, line, crease, crinkle, crow's foot, cleft, indentation, corrugation; scar; technical sulcus.
▸ **verb** *his brow furrowed* **wrinkle**, crease, line, crinkle, pucker, crumple, screw up, scrunch up, corrugate.
OPPOSITE smooth.

furry ▸ **adjective** *a small furry animal* **covered with fur**, hairy, long-haired, downy, fleecy, soft, fluffy, fuzzy, woolly.

further ▸ **adverb 1** *Orkney is further from the mainland than the Western Isles* **at a greater distance**, more distant, farther.
OPPOSITE closer.
2 *nothing could be further from the truth* **more unlike**, less like; farther.
OPPOSITE closer.
3 *this theme will be developed further in Chapter 6* **additionally**, more, to a greater extent.
4 *further, firms' employment practices may be discriminatory when they appear not to be* **furthermore**, moreover, what's more, also, additionally, in addition, besides, as well, too, to boot, on top of that, over and above that, into the bargain, by the same token; archaic withal, forbye.
▸ **adjective 1** *the further side of the field* **more distant**, more remote, remoter, more advanced, more extreme, further away/off, farther; far, other, opposite.
OPPOSITES nearer; near.
2 *the further reaches of the valley* **remote**, distant, far away/off/removed.
OPPOSITE near.
3 *for further information please contact the Visitors' Office* **additional**, more, extra, supplementary, supplemental, other; new, fresh.
▸ **verb** *he decided to further his career in politics* **promote**, advance, forward, develop, stimulate; facilitate, aid, assist, help, help along, lend a hand to, abet; expedite, hasten, speed up, accelerate, step up, spur on, oil the wheels of, push, give a push to, boost, encourage, cultivate, nurture, succour; back, contribute to, foster, champion.
OPPOSITE impede.

furtherance ▸ **noun** *he was acting in the furtherance of his business interests* **promotion**, furthering, advancement, forwarding, improvement, development, betterment, stimulation; facilitating, aiding, assisting, helping, abetting; expediting, hastening, speeding up, acceleration, pushing, boosting, encouragement, cultivation, nurturing, succouring, backing, fostering, championing, endorsement, patronage.
OPPOSITE hindrance.

furthermore ▸ **adverb** *This program is simple to use. Furthermore, it can be used as a powerful document transmission system* **moreover**, further, what's more, also, additionally, in addition, besides, as well, too, to boot, on top of that, over and above that, into the bargain, by the same token; archaic withal, forbye.

furthest ▸ **adjective** *the furthest limits of the universe* **most distant**, most remote, remotest, furthest/farthest away, farthest, furthermost, farthermost; outlying, outer, outermost, extreme, uttermost, ultimate, very; rare outmost.
OPPOSITE nearest.

furtive ▸ **adjective** *they cast furtive glances at one another* **secretive**, secret, surreptitious; sly, sneaky, wily, underhand, under the table; clandestine, hidden, covert, cloaked, conspiratorial, underground, cloak and dagger, hole and corner, hugger-mugger; stealthy, sneaking, skulking, slinking; sidelong, sideways, oblique, indirect; informal hush-hush, shifty.
OPPOSITES open; above board.

fury ▸ **noun 1** *she exploded with fury* **rage**, anger, wrath, passion, outrage, spleen, temper, savagery, frenzy, madness; crossness, indignation, umbrage, annoyance, exasperation; literary ire, choler, bile.
OPPOSITES good humour; calmness.
2 *the fury of the storm* **fierceness**, ferocity, violence, turbulence, tempestuousness, savagery; severity, intensity, vehemence, force, forcefulness, power, potency, strength; rare ferity.
OPPOSITE mildness.
3 *she turned on Mother like a fury* **virago**, hellcat, termagant, spitfire, vixen, shrew, hag, harridan, dragon, gorgon, ogress, harpy, tartar, fishwife; (**Furies**) Greek Mythology Eumenides.

fuse ▸ **verb 1** *they found a wider audience by fusing rap with rock* **combine**, amalgamate, put together, blend, merge, meld, mingle, intermix, intermingle, synthesize; coalesce, compound, alloy, agglutinate; unite, marry; rare admix, commingle, commix, interflow.
OPPOSITE separate.
2 *when fired in a kiln the film of metal fuses on to the pot* **bond**, stick, join, attach, bind, integrate, weld, solder; **melt**, smelt, dissolve, liquefy.
OPPOSITE disconnect.
3 (Brit.) *a light had fused* **short-circuit**, burn out, stop working, trip, break; informal go, blow.
▸ **noun** *a plug fitted with a fuse* **circuit-breaker**, trip switch, residual current device.

fusillade ▸ **noun** *a fusillade of missiles* **salvo**, volley, barrage, bombardment, cannonade, battery, burst, blast, hail, shower, rain, stream, broadside, blitz, discharge.

fusion ▸ **noun 1** *the fetus originates from the fusion of two sex cells* **blend**, blending, combination, amalgamation, joining, bonding, binding, merging, melding, mingling, integration, intermixture, intermingling, synthesis; coalescence, compounding, agglutination; uniting, marrying, alliance, unification; rare commingling, commixture, interflow.
OPPOSITE separation.
2 *the fusion of resin and glass fibre in the moulding process* **melting**, smelting, dissolving, dissolution, liquefaction.

F

F

fuss ▶ noun **1** *there was all that fuss over his marriage breaking up* **ado**, excitement, agitation, uproar, to-do, stir, commotion, confusion, disturbance, tumult, hubbub, rigmarole, folderol, brouhaha, furore, storm in a teacup, much ado about nothing; upset, worry, bother, row; fluster, flurry, bustle; *informal* palaver, hoo-ha, ballyhoo, flap, tizzy, stew, song and dance, performance, pantomime; *Brit. informal* carry-on, kerfuffle; *N. Amer. informal* fuss and feathers; *literary* pother.
2 *she liked to cook with a minimum of fuss* **bother**, trouble, inconvenience, effort, exertion, labour; *informal* hassle.
OPPOSITE convenience.
3 *children make a fuss when limits are set down* **protest**, complaint, objection; grumble, whine; tantrum, outburst, hysterics; commotion, trouble; *informal* grouse, gripe.
▶ verb **1** *he has a tendency to fuss over detail* **worry**, fret, be agitated, be worried, take pains, make a big thing out of; make a mountain out of a molehill; *informal* get worked up, be in a flap, flap, be in a tizzy, be in a stew, make a meal of, make a (big) thing of.
OPPOSITE get into perspective.
2 *he fussed about like an old hen* **bustle**, dash, rush, scurry, charge, fly; tear around, buzz around, run round in circles.
3 (*Brit.*) *oh for heaven's sake, don't fuss me* **pester**, disturb, harass; irritate, annoy, vex, bother, nag; *informal* hassle.

fusspot ▶ noun (*informal*) **fussy person**, worrier, perfectionist, stickler, grumbler; *informal* nit-picker, old woman; *N. Amer. informal* fussbudget.

fussy ▶ adjective **1** *she's very fussy about the wine she drinks* **finicky**, particular, over-particular, fastidious, discriminating, selective, dainty, punctilious; hard to please, difficult, exacting, demanding; faddish, faddy; *informal* pernickety, choosy, picky, nit-picking, old womanish, old maidish; *N. Amer. informal* persnickety; *archaic* nice, overnice; *rare* finical.
OPPOSITES easy to please, indiscriminate.
2 *a fussy, frilly bridal gown* **over-elaborate**, over-embellished, over-decorated, over-ornate, overdone, overworked, busy, cluttered, laboured, strained, florid; ornate, fancy.
OPPOSITE understated.

fusty ▶ adjective **1** *a fusty drawing room* **stuffy**, musty, stale, stagnant, airless, unventilated, close, suffocating, oppressive, mouldering; damp, mildewed, mildewy; *Brit.* frowsty.
OPPOSITES airy, ventilated.
2 *a fusty conservative* **old-fashioned**, out of date, outdated, behind the times, antediluvian, backward-looking, past it; crusty, fogeyish; *informal* square, out of the ark, creaky, mouldy.
OPPOSITES modern, up-to-date.

futile ▶ adjective *I wore my cape in a futile attempt to keep dry* **fruitless**, vain, pointless; **useless**, worthless, ineffectual, ineffective, inefficacious, to no effect, of no use, in vain, to no avail, unavailing; unsuccessful, failed, thwarted; unproductive, barren, unprofitable, abortive; impotent, hollow, empty, forlorn, idle, sterile, nugatory, valueless; hopeless, doomed, lost; *Austral./NZ informal* no good to gundy; *archaic* bootless.
OPPOSITES useful; fruitful.

futility ▶ noun *he could see the futility of his actions* **fruitlessness**, vanity, pointlessness; **uselessness**, worthlessness, ineffectuality, ineffectiveness, inefficacy; failure, unproductiveness, barrenness, unprofitability, abortiveness; impotence, hollowness, emptiness, meaningless, forlornness, hopelessness, sterility, valuelessness; *archaic* bootlessness.
OPPOSITES usefulness, fruitfulness.

CHOOSE THE RIGHT WORD

futile, fruitless, vain, pointless

These words all describe unsuccessful undertakings, but some refer to the prospects of success, some to the outcome, and some can refer to either.

- A **futile** undertaking has no chance of success, which may or may not be recognized by the person embarking on it (*it would be futile to argue | the Bank of England threw away £10 billion in a futile attempt to prop up sterling*).
- **Fruitless** is most commonly used to describe an undertaking that turns out unsuccessfully (*an aerial search of the area proved fruitless, and the men were presumed dead | talks collapsed after months of fruitless negotiation*).
- **Vain** is a more literary word, which can refer either to the prospects of success (*I pulled the blankets over my head in a vain attempt to shut out the ugly visions*) or the result, usually in the phrase *in vain* (*after I had waited in vain for six months, I lost hope*).
- **Pointless** describes something that serves no useful purpose (*pointless committee meetings*), so is used to convey the lack of any prospect of success, which should be obvious to the person contemplating the action (*I knew it would be pointless expecting him to change his mind*).

future ▶ noun **1** *Mike's plans for **the future*** **time to come**, time ahead; what lay/lies ahead, coming times; the fullness of time; *formal* hereafter.
OPPOSITE past.
2 *she knew that her future lay in acting* **destiny**, fate, fortune, doom; prospects, expectations, chances, likely success/advancement/ improvement.
□ **in future** *I modified the program so that in future it would keep accessible records* **from now on**, after this, in the future, from this day forth/ forward, from this day/time on, hence, henceforward, subsequently, in time to come; *formal* hereafter, hereinafter.
▶ adjective **1** *customers guarantee repayment at a future date* **later**, following, ensuing, succeeding, subsequent, upcoming, to come, coming.
OPPOSITE past.
2 *it was here that he met his future wife* **destined**, **intended**, planned, to be, prospective, expected, anticipated.

fuzz[1] ▶ noun **1** *his face is covered with white fuzz* **hair**, **fluff**, fur, down, floss, fine hair.
2 *there was plenty of fuzz from the guitars* **distortion**, buzz, hiss, fizz, buzzing, hissing, fizzing, white noise.

fuzz[2] ▶ noun (*informal*) *the fuzz came in with a warrant.* See POLICE.

fuzzy ▶ adjective **1** *I stroked the baby's fuzzy head* **downy**, down-covered, frizzy, woolly, velvety, silky, silken, satiny, linty, napped, soft; *technical* floccose, lanate.
2 *a fuzzy picture* **blurry**, blurred, indistinct; unclear, bleary, misty, distorted, out of focus, unfocused, lacking definition, low resolution, nebulous; **ill-defined**, indefinite, vague, hazy, imprecise, inexact, loose, woolly.
OPPOSITES clear, sharp.
3 *my mind was so fuzzy* **confused**, muddled, addled, fuddled, befuddled, groggy, disoriented, disorientated, mixed up, fazed, perplexed, dizzy, stupefied, benumbed; foggy, misty, shadowy, blurred.
OPPOSITE clear.

Gg

gab (*informal*) ▶ **verb** *they were all gabbing away like crazy* **chatter**, chitter-chatter, chat, talk, gossip, gabble, babble, prattle, jabber, blather, blab; *informal* yak, yackety-yak, yabber, yatter, yammer, blabber, blah, blah-blah, jaw, gas, shoot one's mouth off; *Brit. informal* witter, rabbit, chunter, natter, waffle; *N. Amer. informal* run off at the mouth; *Austral./NZ informal* mag; *archaic* twaddle, clack, twattle.

▶ **noun** *their meetings turn into marathons of gab* **chatter**, chat, talk, gossip, blather, blether, gibberish, drivel; chattering, chatting, talking, gossiping, jabbering, babbling, gabbling, prating, rambling; *informal* flannel, yak, yackety-yak, yabbering, yatter, twaddle, blah, blah-blah; *Brit. informal* wittering, waffle, natter, chuntering; *archaic* clack, twattle.

□ **the gift of the gab** *you'd make a good lawyer—you've got the gift of the gab* **eloquence**, fluency, clarity of speech, expressiveness, articulateness, articulacy, good command of the language; persuasiveness; *informal* a way with words, blarney.
OPPOSITE inarticulacy.

gabble ▶ **verb** *the hysterical child just gabbled at me* **jabber**, babble, prattle, rattle, blabber, gibber, cackle, blab, drivel, twitter, splutter; talk rapidly, talk incoherently, talk unintelligibly; *Brit. informal* waffle, chunter, witter.

▶ **noun** *the boozy gabble of the crowd* **jabbering**, babbling, chattering, gibbering, babble, chatter, rambling; gibberish, drivel, twaddle, nonsense; *informal* flannel, blah, mumbo-jumbo; *Brit. informal* waffle, waffling, chuntering, double Dutch.

gabby ▶ **adjective** (*informal*) *we are an incurably gabby lot.* See TALKATIVE.

gad ▶ **verb** *she looked worn out and must have been* **gadding about** *too much* **gallivant**, jaunt around, flit around, run around, travel around, roam (around); wander, rove, ramble, traipse, meander, stray.

gadabout ▶ **noun** *she was an inveterate gadabout* **gallivanter**, pleasure-seeker; **wanderer**, rover, rambler, drifter, bird of passage; traveller, journeyer, explorer, globetrotter.

gadget ▶ **noun** *the kitchen had every kind of modern gadget* **appliance**, apparatus, instrument, implement, tool, utensil, contrivance, contraption, machine, mechanism, device, labour-saving device, convenience, invention, thing; Heath Robinson device; *N. Amer.* Rube Goldberg device; *informal* widget, gismo, thingummy, gimmick, mod con; *Brit. informal* doobry, doodah.

gaffe ▶ **noun** *I made some real gaffes at work* **blunder**, mistake, error, slip; indiscretion, impropriety, breach of etiquette, miscalculation, gaucherie, solecism; *French* faux pas; *Latin* lapsus linguae, lapsus calami; *informal* slip-up, howler, boo-boo, boner, botch, fluff; *Brit. informal* boob, bloomer, clanger; *N. Amer. informal* blooper, bloop, goof; *Brit. informal, dated* floater; *vulgar slang* fuck-up.

gaffer ▶ **noun 1** (*Brit. informal*) *being the gaffer's gone to her head* **boss**, manager, manageress, foreman, forewoman, overseer, controller, supervisor, superintendent; *Brit.* ganger; *informal* bossman, number one, kingpin, top dog, bigwig, big cheese, Mr Big, skipper; *Brit. informal* governor, guv'nor; *N. Amer. informal* honcho, head honcho, numero uno, padrone, sachem, big wheel, big kahuna, big white chief, high muckamuck.
2 (*informal*) *old gaffers tottering past on sticks* **old man**, elderly man, senior citizen, pensioner, OAP, grandfather; *Scottish & Irish* bodach; *informal* old bloke, old boy, old guy, old codger, old geezer, old-timer, greybeard, grandad, wrinkly; *Brit. informal* buffer, josser; *N. Amer. informal* old coot; *archaic* grandsire, ancient; *rare* senex.

gag[1] ▶ **verb 1** *a dirty rag was used to gag her mouth* **stop up**, block, plug, clog, stifle, smother, muffle; put a gag on, silence, hush, quiet.
2 *the press is gagged by more and more complex rules* **silence**, muzzle, mute, muffle, stifle, smother, strangle, subdue, suppress, repress; censor, curb, check, restrain, fetter, shackle, restrict, limit.
OPPOSITES encourage; give a voice to.
3 *the stench grew worse, making her gag* **retch**, heave, dry-heave, convulse, almost vomit, feel nauseous; choke, gasp, struggle for breath, fight for air; *informal* keck.

▶ **noun** *his scream was muffled by the gag* **muzzle**, tie, restraint.

gag[2] ▶ **noun** (*informal*) *even the worst of gags will amuse someone somewhere* **joke**, jest, witticism, quip, pun, play on words, double entendre, funny remark, witty remark; flash of wit, rejoinder, sally; *French* bon mot, *informal* crack, wisecrack, one-liner, funny, comeback.

gaiety ▶ **noun 1** *there was unusual gaiety in her manner* **cheerfulness**, cheer, light-heartedness, merriment, glee, gladness, happiness, joy, joyfulness, joyousness, delight, pleasure, high spirits, good spirits, good humour, jollity, jolliness, hilarity, mirth, joviality, exuberance, elation, exultation, euphoria, jubilation; liveliness, vivacity, animation, effervescence, levity, buoyancy, sprightliness, zest, zestfulness; *French* joie de vivre; *informal* chirpiness, bounce, pep, zing; *literary* gladsomeness, blitheness, blithesomeness; *rare* gayness.
OPPOSITE misery.
2 *the hotel restaurant was a scene of gaiety* **merrymaking**, festivity, fun, fun and games, frolics, revels, revelry, jollification, celebration, rejoicing, pleasure; *informal* living it up, larking about; *dated* sport.

gaily ▶ **adverb 1** *she skipped gaily along the path* **merrily**, cheerfully, cheerily, happily, joyfully, joyously, light-heartedly, blithely, jauntily, gleefully, with pleasure.
OPPOSITE miserably.
2 *a harbour full of gaily painted boats* **brightly**, brilliantly, colourfully, flamboyantly.
OPPOSITE sombrely.
3 *pedestrians skipped gaily into the fast-moving traffic* **heedlessly**, unthinkingly, thoughtlessly, without thinking, without care, without consideration; **casually**, nonchalantly, airily, breezily, lightly, uncaringly.
OPPOSITE anxiously.

gain ▶ **verb 1** *he gained an entrance scholarship to the college* **obtain**, get, acquire, come by, procure, secure, attain, achieve, earn, win, capture, clinch, pick up, carry off, reap, gather; receive, be given, be awarded, come away with; *informal* land, net, bag, pot, scoop, wangle, swing, score, nab, collar, cop, hook, get one's hands on, get one's mitts on, get hold of, walk away with, walk off with.
OPPOSITE lose.
2 *the workers gain high salaries* **earn**, bring in, make, get, get paid, pocket, clear, gross, net, realize; *informal* rake in, haul in, bag.
3 *they stood to* **gain from** *the deal* **profit**, make money, reap financial reward, reap benefits, benefit; do well out of, make capital out of; *informal* make a killing, milk, cash in on.
OPPOSITE lose.
4 *all four patients recovered and gained weight* **increase in**, put on, add on, build up; acquire more of something.
OPPOSITE lose.
5 *we were in the lead but the others were* **gaining on** *us* **catch up with**, catch up on, catch someone up, catch, narrow the gap between, get nearer to, draw nearer to, close in on, creep up on, come up to, approach, near.
6 *it took a while to gain the high ridge* **reach**, arrive at, get to, come to, get as far as, make, make it to, attain, set foot on; end up at, land up at, fetch up at; *informal* hit, wind up at.

□ **gain time** *the government was using the negotiations to gain time* **play for time**, stall, procrastinate, delay, use delaying tactics, temporize, hold back, hang back, hang fire, dally, drag one's feet, use dilatory tactics; *informal* put something on the back burner.

▶ **noun 1** *his gain from the deal was negligible* **profit**, earnings, income, advantage, benefit, reward, emolument, yield, return, winnings, receipts, proceeds, dividend, interest, percentage, takings; *informal* pickings, cut, take, rake-off, divvy, whack, slice of the cake; *Brit. informal* bunce.
OPPOSITE loss.
2 *the effect of overeating is weight gain* **increase**, augmentation, addition,

rise, increment, accretion, accumulation.
OPPOSITE decrease.
3 *he made the biggest gain in the last leg of the race* **advance**, advancement, progress, forward movement, headway, improvement, step forward.

gainful ▶ adjective *they see no prospect of finding gainful employment* **profitable**, paid, well paid, remunerative, lucrative, moneymaking, financially rewarding; rewarding, fruitful, worthwhile, useful, productive, constructive, beneficial, advantageous, valuable; *rare* fructuous.

gainsay ▶ verb (*formal*) *it was difficult to gainsay his claim* **deny**, dispute, disagree with, argue with, dissent from, contradict, repudiate, declare untrue, challenge, oppose, contest, counter, fly in the face of; disprove, debunk, explode, discredit, refute, rebut, brush aside; *informal* shoot full of holes, shoot down (in flames); *Law* disaffirm; *rare* controvert, confute.
OPPOSITE confirm.

gait ▶ noun *he had the gait of a professional soldier* **walk**, step, stride, pace, tread, manner of walking, way of walking; bearing, carriage, comportment, way of holding oneself, way of carrying oneself; *Brit.* deportment.

G

gala ▶ noun *the village is holding its annual summer gala* **fête**, gala day, fair, feast, festival, carnival, pageant, jubilee, jamboree, party, garden party, celebration; festivities; fund-raiser, charity event, charity show; *Dutch & N. Amer.* kermis.
▶ adjective *his concerts have been gala occasions for some years* **festive**, celebratory, merry, joyous, joyful; diverting, entertaining, enjoyable, spectacular, showy; *dated* gay.

galaxy ▶ noun **1** *he focused his telescope on the galaxy* **star system**, solar system, constellation, cluster, nebula; spiral galaxy, Seyfert galaxy; stars, heavens.
2 *a galaxy of the rock world's biggest stars* **brilliant gathering**, dazzling assemblage, illustrious group; host, multitude, array, mass, bevy, horde, company, army, flock, group.

gale ▶ noun **1** *the church spire was blown down during a gale* **storm**, tempest, squall, hurricane, tornado, cyclone, typhoon, whirlwind; strong wind, high wind; *N. Amer.* windstorm; *informal* burster, buster; *literary* flaw.
2 *she collapsed in gales of laughter* **outburst**, burst, eruption, explosion, effusion, attack, fit, paroxysm; peal, howl, hoot, shriek, scream, shout, roar.

gall[1] ▶ noun **1** *Melanie had the gall to ask Nick for money* **impudence**, insolence, impertinence, cheek, cheekiness, nerve, audacity, brazenness, effrontery, temerity, presumption, presumptuousness, brashness, shamelessness, pertness, boldness; bad manners, rudeness, impoliteness; *informal* brass neck, brass, neck, face, chutzpah, cockiness; *Brit. informal* sauce, sauciness; *Scottish informal* snash; *N. Amer. informal* sass, sassiness, nerviness; *informal, dated* hide; *Brit. informal, dated* crust; *rare* malapertness, procacity, assumption.
2 *scholarly gall was poured forth upon this work* **acrimony**, resentment, rancour, sourness, acerbity, asperity; bitterness, bile, spleen, malice, spite, spitefulness, malignity, venom, vitriol, poison, malevolence, virulence, nastiness, animosity, antipathy, hostility, enmity, bad blood, ill feeling, ill will, animus; *literary* choler.

gall[2] ▶ noun **1** *this was a gall that she frequently had to endure* **irritation**, irritant, annoyance, vexation, pest, nuisance, provocation, bother, torment, plague, source of vexation, source of irritation, source of annoyance, thorn in one's side/flesh; *informal* aggravation, peeve, pain, pain in one's neck, bind, bore, headache, hassle; *Scottish informal* nyaff, skelf; *N. Amer. informal* pain in the butt, nudnik, burr under someone's saddle; *Austral./NZ informal* nark.
2 *a bay horse with a gall on its side* **sore**, ulcer, ulceration, canker; abrasion, scrape, scratch, graze, chafe.
▶ verb **1** *it galled him to have to sit impotently in silence* **irritate**, annoy, vex, make angry, make cross, anger, exasperate, irk, pique, put out, displease, get/put someone's back up, antagonize, get on someone's nerves, rub up the wrong way, ruffle, ruffle someone's feathers, make someone's hackles rise, raise someone's hackles; infuriate, madden, drive to distraction, goad, provoke; *informal* aggravate, peeve, hassle, miff, rile, nettle, needle, get, get to, bug, hack off, get under someone's skin, get in someone's hair, get up someone's nose, put someone's nose out of joint, get someone's goat, rattle someone's cage, get someone's dander up, drive mad/crazy, drive round the bend/twist, drive up the wall, make someone see red; *Brit. informal* wind up, nark, get across, get on someone's wick, give someone the hump; *N. Amer. informal* tee off, tick off, burn up, rankle, ride, gravel; *informal, dated* give someone the pip; *rare* exacerbate, hump, rasp.
2 *the straps galled their shoulders* **chafe**, abrade, rub (against), rub painfully, rub raw, scrape, graze, skin, scratch, rasp, bark, fret; *rare* excoriate.

gallant ▶ adjective **1** *a gallant band of British officers* **brave**, courageous, valiant, valorous, bold, plucky, daring, fearless, intrepid, heroic, lionhearted, stout-hearted, doughty, mettlesome, great-spirited; honourable, noble, manly, manful, macho, dashing, daredevil, death-or-glory, undaunted, unflinching, unshrinking, unafraid, dauntless, indomitable; *informal* gutsy, spunky, ballsy, have-a-go; *rare* venturous.
OPPOSITE cowardly.
2 *he made a gallant remark to a self-conscious girl* **chivalrous**, gentlemanly, courtly, courteous, respectful, polite, attentive, gracious, considerate, thoughtful, obliging; *dated* mannerly; *archaic* gentle.
OPPOSITES discourteous, rude.
3 (*archaic*) *they made a gallant array as they set off next morning* **fine**, splendid, elegant, magnificent, majestic, imposing, glorious, regal, august, great, dignified, stately, noble.
OPPOSITE unimposing.
▶ noun (*archaic*) **1** *a young gallant resplendent in red and white silks* **fine gentleman**, man about town, man of fashion, dandy, fop, beau, cavalier, swashbuckler; playboy, man of the world, ladies' man; *informal* swell, toff, ladykiller; *archaic* gay dog, rip, dude, blade, blood, coxcomb.
2 *she was delighted to see her amorous gallant* **suitor**, wooer, admirer, worshipper; beau, sweetheart, lover, love, beloved, boyfriend, young man, man friend, escort, partner; *informal* fancy man, flame, fella; *literary* swain; *archaic* paramour.

gallantry ▶ noun **1** *he received medals for gallantry* **bravery**, braveness, courage, courageousness, valour, pluck, pluckiness, nerve, daring, boldness, fearlessness, dauntlessness, intrepidity, intrepidness, manliness, heroism, doughtiness, stout-heartedness, backbone, spine, spirit, spiritedness, mettle, determination, fortitude; *informal* guts, grit, spunk, gutsiness, gameness; *Brit. informal* bottle, ballsiness; *N. Amer. informal* moxie, cojones, sand; *vulgar slang* balls.
OPPOSITE cowardice.
2 *she acknowledged his selfless gallantry* **chivalry**, chivalrousness, gentlemanliness, courtliness, graciousness, respectfulness, respect, courtesy, courteousness, politeness, good manners, mannerliness, attentiveness, consideration, considerateness, thoughtfulness.
OPPOSITE rudeness.

gallery ▶ noun **1** *his paintings were bought by a London gallery* **exhibition room**, display room, art gallery, museum.
2 *they sat up in the gallery* **balcony**, circle, upper circle; *informal* gods.
3 *a long gallery with doors along each side* **passage**, passageway, corridor, hall, hallway, walkway, arcade.

galling ▶ adjective *his display of hypocrisy was extremely galling* **annoying**, irritating, vexing, vexatious, infuriating, maddening, irksome, provoking, exasperating, trying, tiresome, troublesome, bothersome, displeasing, disagreeable; *informal* aggravating.
OPPOSITE pleasing.

gallivant ▶ verb *he goes gallivanting about looking for excitement* **gad**, flit, jaunt, run, roam, wander, travel, range, rove, ramble, traipse, stray.

gallop ▶ verb *the horse galloped away* **race**, **canter**, run, rush, dash, tear, sprint, bolt, fly, shoot, dart, hurry, hasten, speed, streak, hurtle, career, hare, scamper, scurry, scud, go like lighting, go like the wind; lope, prance, frisk; *informal* zoom, pelt, scoot, hotfoot it, leg it, belt, zip, whip, go like a bat out of hell; *Brit. informal* bomb.
OPPOSITE amble.

gallows ▶ plural noun **1** *the felon had been hanged on the gallows* **gibbet**, scaffold; *archaic* gallow-tree, Gregorian tree, derrick, three-legged mare, nubbing cheat, nub; *archaic, informal* leafless tree, triple tree, Tyburn tree.
2 (**the gallows**) *they were condemned to the gallows* **hanging**, being hanged, the noose, the rope, the gibbet, the scaffold; the death penalty, execution, being executed; *informal* the drop, being strung up.

galore ▶ adjective *the shop contained fine furniture and paintings galore* **aplenty**, in abundance, in profusion, in great quantity, in large numbers, by the dozen; to spare; everywhere, all over (the place); *informal* a gogo, by the truckload, by the shedload.
OPPOSITE in short supply.

galvanize ▶ verb *the letter managed to galvanize him into action* **jolt**, shock, startle, impel, stir, spur, prod, urge, motivate, stimulate, electrify, excite, rouse, arouse, awaken, invigorate, fire, fuel, animate, vitalize, energize, exhilarate, thrill, dynamize, inspire; get someone going; *informal* light a fire under, give someone a shot in the arm, give someone a kick; *rare* inspirit, incentivize.
OPPOSITE demotivate.

gambit ▶ noun *the most ambitious financial gambit in history* **stratagem**, machination, scheme, plan, tactic, manoeuvre, move, course of action, line of action, device, operation; ruse, trick, ploy, artifice; *Brit. informal* wheeze, wangle.

gamble ▶ verb **1** *I go to the races when I want to gamble* **bet**, wager, place a bet, lay a bet, stake money on something, back the horses, try one's luck on the horses; *informal* play the ponies; *Brit. informal* punt, chance one's arm, have a flutter; *rare* game.
2 *we gambled today and we were fortunate to get away with it* **take a chance**, take a risk, take a leap in the dark, leave things to chance, speculate, venture, buy a pig in a poke; *N. Amer.* take a flyer; *informal* stick one's neck out, go out on a limb; *Brit. informal* chance one's arm.
3 *he* **gambled on** *finding someone to give him a lift* **act in the hope of**, trust in, take a chance on, bank on.

▶ **noun 1** *his grandfather enjoyed a gamble* **bet**, wager, speculation; game of chance; *Brit. informal* flutter, punt.
2 *I took a gamble and it paid off* **risk**, chance, hazard, speculation, venture, random shot, leap in the dark; pig in a poke, pot luck, blind bargain; lottery.

gambler ▶ **noun** *he was a daring and fortunate gambler* **backer**, staker, speculator, risk-taker, better; *N. Amer.* bettor; *informal* plunger; *Brit. informal* **punter**; *N. Amer. informal* high roller, piker; *Austral./NZ informal* spieler, dasher.

gambol ▶ **verb** *the foal gambolled beside its mother* **frolic**, frisk, cavort, caper, skip, dance, romp, prance, leap, hop, jump, spring, bound, bounce; play; *dated* sport; *rare* rollick, curvet, capriole.

game *See centre pages for lists of* **Ball Games** **Board Games** **Card Games** **Games** **Sports** *and* **Birds**
▶ **noun 1** *the children invented a new game* **pastime**, diversion, entertainment, amusement, distraction, divertissement, recreation, sport, activity, leisure activity; frolic, romp, source of fun.
2 *he broke his leg two weeks before the big game* **match**, contest, tournament, meeting, sports meeting, meet, event, athletic event, fixture, tie, cup tie, test match, final, cup final, play-off; *Canadian & Scottish* playdown; *N. Amer.* split; *archaic* tourney.
3 *we were only playing a game on him* **practical joke**, **prank**, jest, trick, hoax; *informal* lark.
4 *he's in the banking game* **business**, profession, occupation, trade, industry, line (of work), line of business, field, province, area; *informal* racket.
5 *I spoiled his little game* **scheme**, plot, ploy, stratagem, strategy, gambit, cunning plan, master plan, grand design, crafty designs, tactics; trick, artifice, device, manoeuvre, wile, dodge, ruse, machination, contrivance, subterfuge; *informal* con, set-up, scam; *Brit. informal* wheeze; *archaic* shift.
6 *he spent his time shooting game in the parks* **wild animals**, wild fowl, big game; quarry, prey.
□ **on the game** (*Brit. informal*) *she says she's an 'escort', but actually she's on the game* **working as a prostitute**, involved in prostitution, whoring, prostituting oneself, selling oneself, selling one's body, walking the streets, on the streets, practising the oldest profession, working in the sex industry; a prostitute, a whore, a call girl.
▶ **adjective 1** *they weren't game enough to join in* **brave**, courageous, valiant, plucky, bold, intrepid, stout-hearted, lionhearted, unafraid, daring, dashing, spirited, mettlesome; fearless, dauntless, undaunted, unblenching, unflinching; *informal* gutsy, spunky, ballsy; *rare* venturous.
OPPOSITE timid.
2 *I need a bit of help—are you game?* **willing**, favourably inclined, prepared, disposed, in the mood, of a mind, desirous, eager, keen, interested, enthusiastic, ready.
OPPOSITE unwilling.
▶ **verb** (*rare*) *they were drinking and gaming all evening* **gamble**, bet, place bets, lay bets, wager, stake money; *Brit. informal* have a flutter, punt.

gamin, fem. **gamine** ▶ **noun** (*dated*) *a crowd of gamins playing in the gutter* **urchin**, street urchin, ragamuffin, guttersnipe, waif, stray, outcast; orphan; *informal* scarecrow; *archaic* mudlark, scapegrace, street Arab, tatterdemalion.

gamut ▶ **noun** *the complete gamut of human emotion* **range**, spectrum, span, sweep, compass, scope, area, breadth, width, reach, extent, catalogue, scale, sequence, series; variety.

gang ▶ **noun 1** *a gang of teenagers* **band**, group, crowd, pack, horde, throng, mob, herd, swarm, multitude, mass, body, troop, drove, cluster; company, gathering, assemblage, assembly; *informal* posse, bunch, gaggle, load.
2 (*informal*) *John was one of our gang* **circle**, social circle, social set, group of friends, clique, in-crowd, coterie, lot, ring, clan, club, league, faction, cabal; fraternity, sorority, brotherhood, sisterhood; *informal* crew, posse; *rare* sodality, confraternity.
3 *a work gang hammering cobbles into the highway* **squad**, team, troop, shift, detachment, posse, troupe; working party.
▶ **verb**
□ **gang up** *they all ganged up to put me down* **conspire**, cooperate, work together, act together, combine, join up, join forces, team up, club together, get together, unite, ally; *rare* coact.

gangling, **gangly** ▶ **adjective** *a gangling teenager in jeans* **lanky**, rangy, wiry, stringy, bony, angular, skinny, skin-and-bones, spindly, spindling, scrawny, thin, spare, gaunt, skeletal; loosely built, loosely jointed; awkward, uncoordinated, ungainly, gawky, inelegant, graceless, ungraceful; *informal* like a bag of bones; *dated* spindle-shanked.
OPPOSITE squat.

gangster ▶ **noun** *they were held up at gunpoint by gangsters* **hoodlum**, racketeer, bandit, robber, ruffian, thug, tough, desperado, outlaw, villain, lawbreaker, criminal; gunman, murderer, assassin, terrorist; gang member, member of a criminal gang, member of the Mafia, Mafioso; (*in Japan*) yakuza; *informal* mobster, crook, hit man, hatchet man, heavy; *N. Amer. informal* hood; *literary* brigand.

gaol ▶ **noun** (*Brit. dated*). See JAIL.

gaoler ▶ **noun** (*Brit. dated*). See JAILER.

gap ▶ **noun 1** *she peered through a gap in the shutters* **opening**, aperture, space, breach, chink, slit, slot, vent, crack, crevice, cranny, cavity, hole, orifice, interstice, perforation, break, fracture, rift, rent, fissure, cleft, divide, discontinuity; *technical* scission, grike.
2 *a gap between meetings* **pause**, intermission, interval, interlude, delay, break, breathing space, breather, respite, hiatus; *N. Amer.* recess.
3 *there appears to be a gap in our records* **omission**, blank, blank space, empty space, lacuna, hiatus, void, vacuity.
4 *the gap between the rich and the poor* **chasm**, gulf, rift, polarity, split, separation, breach; contrast, difference, disparity, divergence, variation, variance, imbalance, unevenness.

gape ▶ **verb 1** *she gaped at him in astonishment* **stare**, stare open-mouthed, stare in wonder, gawk, goggle, gaze, ogle, look fixedly, look vacantly; *informal* rubberneck; *Brit. informal* gawp.
2 *he wore a leather jerkin which gaped at every seam* **open wide**, open up, yawn; part, crack, split.

gaping ▶ **adjective** *the volcano collapsed to form a gaping crater* **cavernous**, yawning, wide, broad; vast, huge, enormous, immense, extensive.

garage ▶ **noun 1** *he let them park in his garage* **car port**, lock-up.
2 *she called at the garage for petrol* **petrol station**, service station; *Austral. informal* servo.
3 *a new bus garage was to be built* **depot**, terminus, terminal, base, headquarters; bus station, coach station.

garb ▶ **noun** *he was dressed in the garb of a Catholic priest* **clothes**, clothing, garments, attire, dress, costume, outfit, wear, uniform, turnout, array; livery, regalia, trappings, finery; *informal* gear, get-up, togs, rig-out, duds, glad rags; *Brit. informal* clobber; *N. Amer. informal* threads; *formal* apparel; *literary* raiment, habiliment, habit, vestments.
▶ **verb** *both men were garbed in black* **dress**, clothe, attire, fit out, turn out, deck (out), trick out/up, kit out, costume, array, robe, accoutre, cover; *informal* get up, doll up; *Brit. informal* tart up; *rare* bedizen, apparel.

garbage ▶ **noun 1** *the garbage is taken to landfill sites* **rubbish**, refuse, domestic refuse, waste, waste material, debris, detritus, litter, junk, scrap, discarded matter; filth, swill, muck, dross; scraps, scourings, leftovers, remains, slops; *N. Amer.* trash; *Austral./NZ* mullock; *informal* drek, dreck; *Brit. informal* grot, gash; *Archaeology* debitage; *rare* draff, raffle, raff, cultch, orts.
2 *most of what they write will be garbage* **drivel**, gibberish, rubbish, nonsense, balderdash, dross, claptrap, twaddle, blarney, blather, blether, moonshine, foolishness; *informal* hogwash, baloney, tripe, bilge, bull, bunk, poppycock, rot, bosh, piffle, hot air, eyewash, phooey, hooey, guff, gobbledegook; *Brit. informal* tosh, codswallop, cobblers, stuff and nonsense, taradiddle, cack; *Scottish & N. English informal* havers; *N. Amer. informal* flapdoodle, blathers, wack, bushwa, applesauce; *informal, dated* tommyrot, bunkum, cod, gammon, toffee; *vulgar slang* crap, shit, bullshit, horseshit, balls; *Austral./NZ vulgar slang* bulldust.
OPPOSITE sense.

garble ▶ **verb** *the message was garbled in transmission* **mix up**, muddle, jumble, confuse, blur, slur, obscure, distort, twist, twist around, warp, misstate, misquote, misreport, misrepresent, mistranslate, misinterpret, misconstrue; tamper with, tinker with, change, alter, doctor, falsify, pervert, corrupt, adulterate; *rare* misarticulate, misrender.

garden *See centre pages for list of* **Gardens**
▶ **noun** *she longed for a house with a garden* **piece of land**, plot; lawn; park, estate, grounds; *N. Amer.* yard; *archaic* garth.
□ **lead someone up the garden path** (*informal*) **deceive**, mislead, lead on, delude, hoodwink, dupe, trick, ensnare, entrap, tempt, entice, allure, lure, beguile, tantalize, tease, frustrate, flirt with, inveigle, seduce, take in, fool, pull the wool over someone's eyes, gull; *informal* string along, take for a ride, put one over on.

WORD LINKS
relating to gardens **horticultural**

gargantuan ▶ **adjective** *a gargantuan wedding cake* **enormous**, extremely big, extremely large, massive, huge, colossal, vast, immense, tremendous, gigantic, giant, monstrous, towering, mammoth, prodigious, elephantine, mountainous, mighty, monumental, epic, king-size, king-sized, titanic, Herculean, Brobdingnagian, substantial, hefty, weighty, bulky; *informal* whopping, whopping great, thumping, thumping great, humongous, mega, monster, jumbo, hulking, bumper; *Brit. informal* whacking, whacking great, ginormous.
OPPOSITE tiny.

garish ▶ **adjective** *they wore silly hats in garish colours* **gaudy**, lurid, loud, over-bright, harsh, glaring, violent, flashy, showy, glittering, brassy, brash; tasteless, in bad taste, vulgar, distasteful, unattractive, nauseating, bilious, sickly; *informal* flash, tacky.
OPPOSITES drab; tasteful.

garland ▶ **noun** *she wore a garland of flowers* **festoon**, lei, wreath, chain, loop, ring, circle, swathe, swag; coronet, crown, coronal, chaplet, fillet, headband.
▶ **verb** *the gardens were garlanded with coloured lights* **festoon**, wreathe,

G

swathe, hang, loop, thread, drape, cover; adorn, ornament, embellish, decorate, deck, trim, dress, array, bedeck, bespangle; *informal* do up, do out, get up, trick out; *literary* bedizen, furbelow, caparison.

garlic ▸ noun

WORD LINKS

relating to garlic **alliaceous**

garment ▸ noun *she wore a shapeless black garment* **item of clothing**, article of clothing, item of dress; costume, outfit, habit, robe, shift; cover, covering; (**garments**) clothes, clothing, dress, garb, attire; *informal* get-up, rig-out, gear, togs, rags, duds.

garner ▸ verb *Edward garnered ideas and experience from his travels* **gather**, collect, accumulate, amass, assemble; store, lay up, lay by, put away, stow away, hoard, stockpile, reserve, save, preserve; *informal* stash away.
▸ noun (*archaic*) *all of the malt went into a garner* **granary**, silo, storehouse, store, storeroom, storage place, depository, warehouse; vault, treasure house.

garnish ▸ verb *garnish the dish with chopped parsley* **decorate**, adorn, trim, dress, ornament, embellish, enhance, grace, beautify, prettify, brighten up, set off, add the finishing touch to; *informal* jazz up.
▸ noun *a cucumber garnish for the lobster salad* **decoration**, adornment, trim, trimming, ornament, ornamentation, embellishment, enhancement, beautification, finishing touch; *rare* garniture.

garret ▸ noun *the innkeeper gave them a bed in the garret* **attic**, loft, roof space, cock loft; mansard, loft conversion, attic room; *informal, dated* sky parlour.

garrison ▸ noun **1** *the rebels attacked the English garrison in their barracks* **armed force**, force, military detachment, military unit, unit, platoon, brigade, regiment, squadron, battalion, company, legion, corps; troops, militia, soldiers.
2 *the bombardment left gaping holes in the garrison* **fortress**, fort, fortification, stronghold, blockhouse, citadel, camp, encampment, cantonment, command post, base, station; barracks, billet, quarters; *rare* casern.
▸ verb **1** *the French infantry garrisoned the town* **defend**, guard, protect, preserve, fortify, barricade, shield, secure; man, occupy, supply with troops.
2 *the troops are garrisoned in various regions* **station**, post, put on duty, assign, billet, deploy, install; base, site, place, position, locate, situate.

garrulity ▸ noun *they were irritated by his ungovernable garrulity* **talkativeness**, garrulousness, loquacity, loquaciousness, volubility, verbosity, verboseness, long-windedness, wordiness, chattiness, effusiveness, profuseness, communicativeness, expansiveness; *informal* mouthiness, gabbiness, windiness, gassiness, yakking, big mouth, gift of the gab; *Brit. informal* wittering; *rare* logorrhoea, multiloquence.
OPPOSITE taciturnity.

garrulous ▸ adjective **1** *a garrulous old man who chattered like a magpie* **talkative**, loquacious, voluble, verbose, long-winded, chatty, chattery, chattering, gossipy, gossiping, babbling, blathering, prattling, prating, jabbering, gushing, effusive, expansive, forthcoming, conversational, communicative; *informal* mouthy, gabby, gassy, windy, yacking, big-mouthed, with the gift of the gab, having kissed the Blarney Stone; *Brit. informal* wittering, able to talk the hind legs off a donkey; *rare* multiloquent, multiloquous.
OPPOSITES taciturn; reticent.
2 *his garrulous and unreliable reminiscences* **long-winded**, wordy, verbose, prolix, lengthy, prolonged; rambling, wandering, maundering, meandering, digressive, diffuse, discursive, periphrastic; gossipy, chatty; *informal* windy, gassy.
OPPOSITE concise.

CHOOSE THE RIGHT WORD

garrulous, talkative, chatty, loquacious

See TALKATIVE.

gas ▸ noun. *See centre pages for lists of* **Gases**
Poisonous Substances and Gases

gash ▸ noun *there was blood running from a gash on his forehead* **laceration**, cut, slash, tear, gouge, puncture, score, incision, slit, split, rip, rent, nick, cleft; scratch, scrape, graze, abrasion; wound, injury, lesion, contusion; *Medicine* trauma, traumatism.
▸ verb *Frank gashed his hand on some broken glass* **lacerate**, cut (open), slash, tear (apart), gouge, puncture, incise, score, slit, split, rend, nick, snick, notch, cleave; scratch, scrape, graze, abrade; wound, injure, hurt, damage, maim.

gasp ▸ verb *the ice cold water made him gasp* **pant**, puff, puff and pant, blow, heave, wheeze, breathe hard, breathe heavily, catch one's breath, draw in one's breath, gulp, choke, fight for breath, struggle for air.
▸ noun *a gasp of pain* **pant**, puff, blow, breath, inhalation, inspiration, drawing in of breath, choke, gulp (of air); exclamation, ejaculation.

gastric ▸ adjective *he suffers from excessive gastric acid* **stomach**, **intestinal**, enteric, duodenal, coeliac, abdominal, ventral; *technical* gastrocolic; *rare* stomachic, stomachical.

gate ▸ noun **1** *the horse vaulted over the gate* **barrier**, wicket, wicket gate, lychgate, five-barred gate, turnstile; *Brit.* kissing gate; *Scottish* port; (*in China*) moon gate; (*in ancient Egypt*) pylon.
2 *a small girl came out of the gate* **gateway**, doorway, entrance, exit, egress, opening; door, portal; *N. Amer.* entryway.

gather ▸ verb **1** *we gathered in the hotel lobby* **congregate**, convene, assemble, meet, collect, come/get together, muster, rally, converge; cluster together, crowd, mass, flock together; *rare* foregather.
OPPOSITE scatter.
2 *he gathered a coterie of followers | he paused to gather his thoughts* **summon**, summon up, call together, bring together, assemble, convene, rally, round up; collect, muster, marshal, organize; *formal* convoke.
OPPOSITE disperse.
3 *badgers gather bedding throughout the year* **collect**, get together, put together, accumulate, amass, assemble, garner; store, stockpile, heap up, pile up, stack up, hoard, put by, put away, lay by, lay in, set aside; *informal* stash away, squirrel away.
4 *the people gather fruits, berries, and roots* **harvest**, collect, reap, pick, pluck, garner, crop, glean.
5 *the show soon gathered a fanatical following* **attract**, draw, pull, pull in, collect, pick up, whip up, raise.
6 *I gather he's a keen footballer* **understand**, be given to understand, believe, be led to believe, think, conclude, come to the conclusion, deduce, infer, draw the inference, assume, surmise, fancy; take it, hear, hear tell, be informed, notice, see, learn, discover.
7 *he gathered her to his chest* **clasp**, clutch, take, pull, embrace, enfold, hold, hug, cuddle, squeeze; *literary* embosom; *archaic* strain.
8 *his tunic was gathered at the waist* **pleat**, shirr, pucker, tuck, fold, corrugate, ruffle, crimp, crease, scrunch up.
9 (*archaic*) *the boil on his leg gathered and burst* **come to a head**, suppurate, fester, become septic, form pus, secrete pus; swell up; *technical* maturate, be purulent; *rare* rankle, apostemate.

gathering ▸ noun **1** *she rose to address the gathering* **assembly**, meeting, meet, convention, rally, turnout, congress, convocation, conclave, council, synod, symposium, forum, muster; assemblage, collection, company, congregation, audience, crowd, throng, mass, multitude, group, party, band, knot, flock, mob, horde, pack; *informal* get-together; *formal* concourse; *historical* conventicle.
2 *the gathering of data for a future book* **collecting**, collection, garnering, amassing, accumulation, accrual, cumulation, assembly, assembling; stockpiling, hoarding, building up, build-up; *rare* amassment.
3 (*archaic*) *I have a gathering on my thimble finger* **pustule**, boil, abscess, carbuncle, pimple, spot, sore, ulcer, ulceration, blister, cyst, gumboil, wen; *N. Amer.* canker sore; *informal* zit; *technical* aphtha, chancre, furuncle, vesication, noma; *archaic* fester, impostume.

gauche ▸ adjective *she grew from a gauche teenager into a poised young woman* **awkward**, gawky, inelegant, graceless, ungraceful, ungainly, bumbling, maladroit, inept; socially awkward, socially inept, lacking in social grace(s), unpolished, unsophisticated, uncultured, uncultivated, unrefined, raw, inexperienced, uneducated, unworldly.
OPPOSITES elegant; sophisticated.

gaudy ▸ adjective *he wears cheap, gaudy clothes* **garish**, lurid, loud, over-bright, glaring, harsh, violent, flashy, showy, glittering, brassy, ostentatious; tasteless, in bad taste, vulgar, distasteful, unattractive, nauseating, bilious, sickly; *informal* flash, tacky; *N. Amer. informal* bling-bling.
OPPOSITES drab; tasteful.

gauge ▸ noun **1** *she checked the temperature gauge* **measuring instrument**, measuring device, meter, measure; indicator, dial, scale, index, display.
2 *exports are an important gauge of economic activity* **measure**, indicator, barometer, basis, standard, point of reference, guide, guideline, touchstone, yardstick, benchmark, criterion, example, model, pattern, formula, exemplar, sample, test, litmus test.
3 *the railway has a track gauge of two feet* **size**, measure, extent, degree, scope, capacity, magnitude; width, breadth, area, thickness, span, depth, height; bore, calibre, diameter.
▸ verb **1** *astronomers can gauge the star's intrinsic brightness* **measure**, calculate, compute, work out, determine, ascertain; count, weigh, quantify, put a figure on.
2 *it is difficult to gauge how effective the ban was* **assess**, evaluate, appraise, analyse, weigh up, get the measure of, judge, adjudge, rate, reckon, determine, estimate, guess; form an opinion of, form an impression of, make up one's mind about; *informal* guesstimate, size up.

gaunt ▸ adjective **1** *a gaunt, greying man with thick spectacles* **haggard**, drawn, cadaverous, skeletal, emaciated, skin-and-bones, skinny, spindly, thin, over-thin, spare, bony, angular, lank, lean, raw-boned, pinched, hollow-cheeked, hollow-eyed, lantern-jawed, scrawny, scraggy, shrivelled, wasted, withered, raddled; as thin as a rake, as thin as a reed, without an ounce of fat; *informal* looking like death warmed up, looking like a bag of bones; *dated* spindle-shanked; *archaic* starveling.

OPPOSITE plump.
2 *the gaunt ruin of Pendragon Castle* **bleak**, stark, barren, bare, drab, desolate, dreary, dismal, gloomy, sombre, forlorn, grim, stern, harsh, forbidding, uninviting, unwelcoming, cheerless.
OPPOSITE cheerful.

gauzy ▶ adjective *she wore a loose gauzy nightdress* **translucent**, transparent, sheer, see-through, gauzelike, fine, ultra-fine, delicate, flimsy, filmy, gossamer, gossamer-like, diaphanous, chiffony, wispy, thin, light, airy, insubstantial; *Brit.* floaty.
OPPOSITES thick; coarse.

gawk ▶ verb *he gawked unashamedly at the beautiful girl* **gape**, goggle, gaze, ogle, stare, stare stupidly, stare open-mouthed, stare in wonder, look fixedly, look vacantly; *informal* rubberneck; *Brit. informal* gawp.

gawky ▶ adjective *she had been a thin, gawky adolescent* **awkward**, ungainly, inelegant, graceless, ungraceful, gauche, maladroit, inept, bumbling, blundering, lumbering; socially awkward, socially unsure, unpolished, unsophisticated, uncultured, uncultivated, unworldly; nervous, nervy, shy, bashful.
OPPOSITES graceful; adroit.

gay ▶ adjective **1** *an organization for gay youngsters* **homosexual**, lesbian, sapphic; *informal* queer, camp, pink, lavender, limp-wristed, swinging the other way, homo, lezzy, les, lesbo, butch, dykey; *Brit. informal* bent, poofy; *N. Amer. informal* fruity; *rare* homophile, Uranian.
OPPOSITE heterosexual.
2 (*dated*) *her children all looked chubby and gay* **cheerful**, cheery, merry, jolly, light-hearted, mirthful, jovial, glad, happy, bright, in good spirits, in high spirits, joyful, elated, exuberant, animated, lively, sprightly, vivacious, buoyant, bouncy, bubbly, perky, effervescent, playful, frolicsome; *informal* chirpy, on top of the world, as happy as a sandboy; *N. Amer. informal* as happy as a clam.
OPPOSITE gloomy.
3 (*dated*) *they were having a gay old time* **jolly**, merry, convivial, hilarious, amusing, uproarious, rollicking, entertaining, enjoyable; festive.
OPPOSITE dull.
4 (*dated*) *the windows sported gay checked curtains* **bright**, brightly coloured, vivid, brilliant, rich, vibrant; richly coloured, many-coloured, multicoloured; flamboyant, gaudy.
OPPOSITE drab.
▶ noun *in Denmark gays can marry in church* **homosexual**, lesbian; *W. Indian* zami; *informal* queer, homo, queen, friend of Dorothy, pansy, nancy, nelly, dyke, les, lesbo, lezzie, butch, femme; *Brit. informal* poof, poofter, ponce, jessie, woofter; *N. Amer. informal* cupcake, swish, twinkie; *Austral. informal* wonk; *S. African informal* moffie; *W. Indian informal* batty boy, batty man; *rare* tribade.
OPPOSITE heterosexual.

gaze ▶ verb *he gazed at the photograph* **stare**, look fixedly, look vacantly, look, take a good look, gape, goggle, peer, leer; ogle, eye, contemplate, survey, scan, study; *informal* gawk at, rubberneck at, give something the once-over, get a load of, check out; *Brit. informal* gawp at; *N. Amer. informal* eyeball; *literary* behold.
▶ noun *she raised her head and met his piercing gaze* **stare**, fixed look, intent look, gape, eye; regard, watch, observance, inspection, scrutiny.

gazebo ▶ noun *a little gazebo in front of the house* **summer house**, pavilion, belvedere; arbour, bower; shelter, hut, shed; *archaic, (in Turkey & Iran)* kiosk.

gazette ▶ noun *she put a notice in the local gazette* **newspaper**, paper, tabloid, broadsheet, journal, periodical, weekly, organ, news-sheet, newsletter, bulletin; digest, review; *informal* rag, scandal sheet; *N. Amer. informal* tab; *Indian informal* eveninger; *dated* extra.

gear ▶ noun **1** *he dropped out of the race with damaged gears* **gearwheel**, toothed wheel, cog, cogwheel.
2 *my bike has five gears* **gear ratio**, speed.
3 *the steering gear of a boat* **mechanism**, gears, machinery, works.
4 (*informal*) *he stowed the fishing gear in the aft locker* **equipment**, apparatus, paraphernalia, articles, appliances, impedimenta; tools, utensils, implements, instruments, hardware, gadgets, gadgetry; stuff, things; kit, rig, tackle, outfit; resources, amenities, supplies; furniture, furnishings, fittings; odds and ends, bits and pieces, bits and bobs; trappings, appurtenances, accoutrements, regalia; *Military* materiel, baggage; *informal* box of tricks; *Brit. informal* clobber, gubbins, odds and sods; *archaic* equipage.
5 (*informal*) *I'll go back to my hotel and pick up my gear* **belongings**, possessions, effects, personal effects, property, baggage, chattels, movables, paraphernalia, appurtenances, impedimenta, miscellaneous articles, odds and ends, bits and pieces, bits and bobs, trappings, accessories; *informal* things, stuff, kit, junk, rubbish, dunnage, traps; *Brit. informal* clobber, gubbins, odds and sods.
6 (*informal*) *the best designer gear* **clothes**, clothing, garments, articles of clothing/dress, attire, garb; dress, wear, wardrobe; outfit, costume, turnout; finery; *informal* togs, duds, get-up, glad rags; *Brit. informal* clobber, kit, rig-out; *N. Amer. informal* threads; *formal* apparel; *literary* raiment, habiliments, habit; *archaic* vestments.

gel, jell ▶ verb **1** *the meat and broth are put into moulds to gel* **set**, stiffen, solidify, thicken, harden; cake, congeal, coagulate, clot; *rare* gelatinize.
OPPOSITES melt; liquefy.
2 *they got the team they wanted and things started to gel* **take shape**, come together, fall into place, happen, take form, form, emerge, crystallize, materialize, become definite.
OPPOSITE fall apart.

gelatinous ▶ adjective *the grain is cooked until it becomes gelatinous* **jelly-like**, glutinous, ropy, gummy, sticky, gluey, slimy, thick, viscous; *technical* mucilaginous, colloidal, viscid; *informal* gooey, gunky, gloopy, cloggy, icky; *N. Amer. informal* gloppy; *rare* viscoid.
OPPOSITE runny.

geld ▶ verb *it is best to geld a colt before he is one year old* **castrate**, neuter, cut, desex, remove the testicles of; *N. Amer. & Austral.* alter; *informal* doctor, fix; *rare* caponize, emasculate, eunuchize, evirate.

gelid ▶ adjective *the gelid green spikes of the glacier* **frozen**, freezing, icy, ice-cold, arctic, glacial, polar, frosty, wintry, snowy, bitterly cold, sub-zero, chilly, Siberian, hyperborean, hyperboreal; *rare* algid.
OPPOSITE hot.

gem *See centre pages for lists of* **Gems** **Minerals** **Rocks**
▶ noun **1** *diamonds, rubies, and other gems* **jewel**, precious stone, semi-precious stone, stone, solitaire, brilliant, baguette, cabochon; *archaic* bijou.
2 *the gem of the collection is the tyrannosaurus skeleton* **best**, finest, pride, prize, treasure, glory, wonder, flower, pearl, jewel, the jewel in the crown, masterpiece, chef-d'œuvre, leading light, pick, choice, paragon, prime, cream, the crème de la crème, elite, elect; outstanding example, shining example, perfect example of its kind, model, epitome, archetype, ideal, exemplar, nonpareil, paradigm, embodiment, personification, quintessence, standard, prototype, apotheosis, acme; *informal* one in a million, the bee's knees, something else, the tops.
OPPOSITE dregs.

genealogy ▶ noun *a lengthy genealogy of the kings of France* **pedigree**, ancestry, descent, lineage, line, line of descent, family tree, extraction, derivation, origin, heritage, parentage, paternity, birth, family, dynasty, house, race, strain, stock, breed, blood, bloodline, history, background, roots; *rare* stirps, filiation, stemma.

general ▶ adjective **1** *they are moderately priced and suitable for general use* **widespread**, common, extensive, universal, wide, popular, public, mainstream, prevalent, prevailing, rife, established, well established, conventional, traditional, traditionalist, orthodox, accepted; in circulation, in force, in vogue.
OPPOSITE restricted.
2 *a general pay increase* **comprehensive**, overall, across the board, blanket, umbrella, mass, total, complete, wholesale, sweeping, panoramic, broad, broad-ranging, extended, inclusive, all-inclusive, all-round, generic, outright, encyclopedic, indiscriminate, catholic; universal, global, worldwide, international, nationwide, countrywide, coast-to-coast, company-wide.
OPPOSITE localized.
3 *a general store | general knowledge* **miscellaneous**, mixed, assorted, variegated, diversified, composite, heterogeneous.
OPPOSITE specialist.
4 *it is the general practice for players to receive all the prize money* **usual**, customary, habitual, traditional, normal, conventional, typical, standard, regular; familiar, accepted, prevailing, routine, run-of-the-mill, fixed, set, established, confirmed, everyday, ordinary, common, stock, well worn, time-honoured; popular, favourite.
OPPOSITE exceptional.
5 *most guidebooks give only a general description of the island* **broad**, imprecise, inexact, rough, sweeping, overall, loose, basic, approximate, non-specific, unspecific, vague, hazy, fuzzy, woolly, ill-defined, indefinite, unfocused; *N. Amer. informal* ballpark; *rare* undetailed.
OPPOSITE detailed.

generality ▶ noun **1** *the debate has moved from generalities to specifics* **generalization**, general statement, general principle, general truth, non-specific statement, loose/vague statement, indefinite statement, sweeping statement, abstraction, extrapolation.
OPPOSITE specific.
2 *there were exceptions to the generality of this principle* **universality**, comprehensiveness, all-inclusiveness, extensiveness, broadness, catholicity.
3 *the generality of people are kind* **majority**, larger part/number, greater part/number, best/better part, main part; bulk, mass, weight, (main) body, preponderance, predominance, lion's share; most, almost all, more than half.
OPPOSITE minority.

generally ▶ adverb **1** *the summers were generally fairly good* **normally, in general**, as a (general) rule, in the general run of things, by and large, more often than not, almost always, in the main, mainly, mostly, for the most part, in most cases, most of the time, predominantly, on the whole; usually, habitually, customarily, standardly, routinely, regularly, typically,

ordinarily, commonly, conventionally, traditionally, historically.
OPPOSITE occasionally.
2 *France was moving generally to the left* **overall**, in general terms, in a general sense, generally speaking, altogether, all in all, broadly, on average, principally, basically, substantially, effectively.
3 *it is too early to say whether the method will be generally accepted* **widely**, commonly, extensively, comprehensively, universally, popularly.
OPPOSITE sporadically.

generate ▶ verb **1** *the move should generate extra business* **cause**, give rise to, lead to, result in, bring about, bring into being, create, make, produce, initiate, engender, spawn, sow the seeds of, occasion, effect, originate, bring to pass, bring on, precipitate, prompt, provoke, kindle, trigger, spark off, touch off, stir up, whip up, induce, inspire, promote, foster, conjure; *literary* beget, enkindle; *rare* effectuate.
OPPOSITE destroy.
2 *many factors determine which male is most likely to generate offspring* **procreate**, breed, father, sire, engender, spawn, create, produce, give life to, give birth to, bring into being, bring into the world, bring forth, have; reproduce, propagate; *literary* beget.

generation ▶ noun **1** *people of the same generation* **age**, age group, peer group, cohort, stage of life.
2 (**generations**) *generations ago* **ages**, an age, years, aeons, an aeon, a long time, an eternity; *Brit. informal* donkey's years, yonks.
3 *the next generation of computers* **crop**, batch, wave, type, range.
4 *creativity is the generation of novel ideas* **creation**, causing, causation, making, engendering, spawning, production, initiation, origination, inception, occasioning, prompting, kindling, triggering, inspiration.
OPPOSITE destruction.
5 *the male role in human generation* **procreation**, reproduction, propagation, breeding, fathering, siring, engendering, spawning, creation; *literary* begetting.

generic ▶ adjective **1** *'assault' is used as a generic term for the separate offences of assault and battery* **general**, common, collective, non-specific, inclusive, all-inclusive, all-encompassing, broad, comprehensive, blanket, umbrella, sweeping, universal.
OPPOSITE specific.
2 *generic drugs are generally cheaper than branded drugs* **unbranded**, untrademarked, non-proprietary.
OPPOSITE branded.

generosity ▶ noun **1** *the generosity of our host* **liberality**, lavishness, magnanimity, magnanimousness, munificence, open-handedness, free-handedness, bounty, unselfishness, indulgence, prodigality, princeliness; *literary* bounteousness; *rare* benignancy, liberalness.
OPPOSITE meanness.
2 *with her generosity of spirit, she always forgave me* **magnanimity**, kindness, kindliness, benevolence, beneficence, altruism, charity, philanthropism, nobility, nobleness, loftiness, high-mindedness, big-heartedness, honourableness, honour, goodness, unselfishness, self-sacrifice, lack of prejudice, disinterest.
3 *diners certainly cannot complain about the generosity of portions* **abundance**, plentifulness, copiousness, amplitude, profuseness, richness, lavishness, liberality, munificence, largeness, superabundance, infinity, inexhaustibility, opulence; *literary* bounteousness, plenteousness.

generous ▶ adjective **1** *generous with money* **liberal**, lavish, magnanimous, munificent, giving, open-handed, free-handed, bountiful, unselfish, ungrudging, unstinting, unsparing, free, indulgent, prodigal, princely; *literary* bounteous, plenteous; *rare* eleemosynary, benignant.
OPPOSITES mean; selfish.
2 *he was generous in spirit, often refusing to hurt an opponent in trouble* **magnanimous**, kind, kindly, benevolent, beneficent, altruistic, charitable, philanthropic, noble, lofty, high-minded, big-hearted, honourable, good, unselfish, self-sacrificing, unprejudiced, disinterested.
OPPOSITE mean.
3 *you will need a generous amount of fabric* **lavish**, plentiful, copious, ample, liberal, munificent, bountiful, large, huge, great, abundant, profuse, rich, bumper, flush, overflowing, superabundant, infinite, inexhaustible, opulent, prolific, teeming; in plenty, in abundance; *informal* a gogo, galore; *S. African informal* lank; *literary* bounteous, plenteous.
OPPOSITE meagre.

genesis ▶ noun **1** *the hatred had its genesis in something darker* **origin**, source, root, beginning, commencement, start, outset.
2 *the influence of a childhood trauma on the subsequent genesis of neurosis* **formation**, emergence, development, evolution, coming into being, inception, origination, birth, creation, shaping, formulation, invention, engendering, generation, propagation.

genial ▶ adjective *Fred is genial and well liked* **friendly**, affable, cordial, congenial, amiable, warm, easy-going, approachable, sympathetic, well disposed, good-natured, good-humoured, cheerful, cheery, neighbourly, hospitable, companionable, comradely, bluff, easy to get along with; sociable, convivial, outgoing, extrovert, extroverted, gregarious, company-loving, hail-fellow-well-met; *informal* chummy, pally; *Brit. informal* matey; *N. Amer. informal* buddy-buddy, clubby, regular.
OPPOSITES unfriendly; morose.

geniality ▶ noun *his geniality made him the centre of a circle of faithful friends* **friendliness**, affability, cordiality, congeniality, amiability, warmth, easy-going nature, approachability, sympathetic nature, good nature, good humour, cheerfulness, cheeriness, neighbourliness, hospitality, companionableness, bluffness; sociability, conviviality, gregariousness; *informal* chumminess, palliness; *Brit. informal* mateyness.
OPPOSITE unfriendliness.

genitals ▶ plural noun **private parts**, genitalia, sexual organs, reproductive organs, pudenda, nether regions, crotch, groin; *informal* privates, bits, naughty bits, dangly bits.

genius ▶ noun **1** *the world had already heard of Hawking's genius* **brilliance**, great intelligence, great intellect, great ability, cleverness, brains, erudition, wisdom, sagacity, fine mind, wit, artistry, flair, creative power, precocity, precociousness.
OPPOSITE stupidity.
2 *that woman has a genius for organization* **talent**, gift, flair, aptitude, facility, knack, technique, touch, bent, ability, expertise, capacity, power, faculty; endowment, strength, strong point, forte, brilliance; dexterity, adroitness, skill, cleverness, virtuosity, artistry.
3 *the boy is an absolute genius* **brilliant person**, mental giant, mastermind, Einstein, intellectual, intellect, brain, highbrow, expert, master, artist, polymath; prodigy, gifted child; *French* idiot savant; *informal* egghead, brains, bright spark, whizz, wizard, walking encyclopedia; *Brit. informal* brainbox, clever clogs, boffin; *N. Amer. informal* brainiac, rocket scientist, maven.
OPPOSITE dunce.

genocide ▶ noun *the killing of native Americans was the biggest genocide in world history* **racial killing**, massacre, wholesale slaughter, mass slaughter, wholesale killing, indiscriminate killing; mass murder, mass homicide, mass destruction, annihilation, extermination, elimination, liquidation, eradication, decimation, butchery, bloodbath, bloodletting; pogrom, ethnic cleansing, holocaust, Shoah; *literary* slaying; *rare* battue, hecatomb.

genre ▶ noun *a whole new genre of novels* **category**, class, classification, categorization, group, grouping, bracket, head, heading, list, listing, set; type, sort, kind, variety, species, breed, style, brand, make, model, family, school, stamp, cast, ilk, kidney; division, section, department, compartment.

genteel ▶ adjective *an extremely genteel couple who have fallen on hard times* **refined**, respectable, polished, decorous, proper, polite, correct, seemly, well mannered, well bred, cultivated, cultured, sophisticated, courteous, ladylike, gentlemanly, civil, elegant, stylish, urbane, civilized, courtly, dignified, gracious, punctilious; affected; *Brit. informal* posh; *dated* mannerly.
OPPOSITE uncouth.

gentility ▶ noun **1** *her grandmother's pretensions to gentility* **social superiority**, respectability, refinement, pre-eminence, pride of place, distinction, ascendancy; *Brit. informal* poshness.
OPPOSITE vulgarity.
2 *an aura of elegance and gentility* **respectability**, refinement, polish, decorousness, correctness, seemliness, politeness, good manners, culture, breeding, cultivation, sophistication, courtesy, ladylikeness, gentlemanliness, civility, elegance, style, stylishness, urbanity, civilization, courtliness, dignity, grace, graciousness, punctiliousness; affectedness, affectation, ostentation, ostentatiousness; *dated* mannerliness.

gentle ▶ adjective **1** *he was powerful, though his manner was gentle* **kind**, kindly, tender, benign, humane, lenient, merciful, forgiving, forbearing, sympathetic, considerate, understanding, clement, compassionate, benevolent, kind-hearted, tender-hearted, good-natured, sweet-tempered, loving; **mild**, soft, quiet, shy, demure, modest, humble, retiring, unassuming, still, tranquil, peaceful, peaceable, pacific, placid, serene, reposeful, reverent, meek, docile, lamblike, dovelike.
OPPOSITES unkind; brutal.
2 *a gentle breeze* **light**, soft, zephyr-like, moderate, pleasant.
OPPOSITE strong.
3 *a gentle slope* **gradual**, slight, easy, imperceptible.
OPPOSITE steep.
4 (archaic) *a woman of gentle birth* **aristocratic**, noble, titled, upper-class, blue-blooded, high-born, well born, patrician, elite; born with a silver spoon in one's mouth, silver-spoon; *informal* posh, upper-crust, upmarket, top-drawer.
OPPOSITE low.

gentlemanly ▶ adjective *the girls declined his gentlemanly offer to allow them to go first* **chivalrous**, gallant, honourable, noble, courtly, courteous, civil, respectful, polite, well mannered, well bred, well behaved, attentive, gracious; considerate, thoughtful, obliging, accommodating; cultivated, cultured, civilized, polished, refined, suave, urbane; *dated* mannerly; *archaic* gentle.

OPPOSITES rude; unbecoming.

gentleness ▶ noun *Jack treated these outbursts with firmness as well as gentleness* **kindness**, kindliness, tenderness, benignity, humaneness, humanity; leniency, mercy, clemency, forgiveness, forbearance; sympathy, considerateness, consideration, understanding, compassion, benevolence, kind-heartedness, tender-heartedness, good nature, love; **mildness**, softness, quietness, shyness, demureness, modesty, humility, stillness, tranquillity, peacefulness, peaceableness, placidness, serenity, repose, reverence, meekness, docility.
OPPOSITES unkindness; brutality.

gentry ▶ noun (**the gentry**) **the upper classes**, **the upper middle class**, the privileged classes, the wealthy, the elite, high society, the establishment, the haut monde, the county set, the smart set; *Indian* bhadralok; *informal* the upper crust, the jet set, the beautiful people, the crème de la crème, the top drawer; *Brit. informal* nobs, toffs; *informal, dated* swells.

genuine ▶ adjective **1** *is that a genuine Picasso?* **authentic**, real, actual, original, pukka, bona fide, true, veritable, unfeigned, unadulterated, unalloyed; sterling; attested, undisputed, rightful, legitimate, lawful, legal, valid, sound; *German* echt; *informal* the real McCoy, the genuine article, the real thing, your actual, kosher, honest-to-goodness; *Austral./NZ informal* dinkum; *rare* simon-pure.
OPPOSITE bogus.
2 *she's a very genuine person* **sincere**, honest, truthful, unhypocritical, meaning what one says, straightforward, direct, frank, candid, open; artless, natural, unaffected, guileless, ingenuous; *informal* straight, upfront, on the level; *N. Amer. informal* on the up and up; *Austral./NZ informal* dinkum.
OPPOSITES fake; bogus; insincere.

> **CHOOSE THE RIGHT WORD**
> **genuine, sincere, unfeigned, unaffected**
> *See* SINCERE.

genus ▶ noun **1** (*Biology*) *the largest genus of plants with fleshy fruits* subdivision, group, subfamily.
2 *he had created a new genus of music* **type**, sort, kind, genre, style, variety, category, class; species, breed, brand, make, model, family, stamp, cast, ilk, kidney; division, subdivision, section, department, compartment.

geography ▶ noun. *See centre pages for list of branches of* **Geography**

geology ▶ noun. *See centre pages for list of* **Geological Ages**

germ ▶ noun **1** *the powerful cleansing action kills germs as well* **microbe**, micro-organism, bacillus, bacterium, virus; *informal* bug.
2 *a fertilized germ* **embryo**, bud, nucleus, seed, spore, egg, ovum; *technical* ovule.
3 *he had the germ of a brilliant idea* **start**, beginning(s), commencement, starting point, genesis, inception, seed, embryo, bud, root, rudiment, origin, source, fountain, potential (for); **core**, nucleus, heart, kernel, nub, essence; *Latin* fons et origo; *literary* fountainhead, wellspring, fount.

WORD LINKS
substance that destroys germs **germicide**

germane ▶ adjective *those factors are not germane to the present discussion* **relevant**, pertinent, applicable, apposite, material; apropos, to the point, to the purpose, admissible; appropriate, apt, fitting, suitable, suited, proper, felicitous; connected, related, linked, akin, allied, analogous; *Latin* ad rem; *rare* appurtenant.
OPPOSITE irrelevant.

Germany ▶ noun

WORD LINKS

related prefixes	**Germano-, Teuto-**
relating to Germany	**Germanic, Teutonic**
fear of German people and things	**Germanophobia, Teutophobia**

germinate ▶ verb **1** *the grain is allowed to germinate* **sprout**, put forth shoots, shoot, shoot up, bud, put forth buds, form/develop buds; develop, grow, spring up, swell; *rare* burgeon, vegetate, pullulate.
2 *the idea of a songwriting partnership began to germinate in his mind* **develop**, take root, grow, spring up, arise, emerge, evolve, mature, expand, enlarge, spread, advance, progress.

gestation ▶ noun **1** *tree shrews give birth after a gestation of thirty days* **pregnancy**, development, incubation, maturation, ripening; *rare* gravidity, parturiency.
2 *the law underwent a long period of gestation* **development**, origination, drafting, formation, evolution, emergence, coming into being, materializing.

gesticulate ▶ verb *they were gesticulating wildly and pointing at the tyres* **gesture**, make gestures, signal, make signals, sign, motion, wave.

gesticulation ▶ noun *the rudder had stuck, hence the pilot's gesticulation towards the tail!* **gesturing**, gesture, hand movement, signalling, signals, signing, signs, motioning, waving, wave, indication; body language.

gesture ▶ noun **1** *he threw out both hands in a gesture of surrender* **signal**, signalling, sign, signing, motion, motioning, wave, indication, gesticulation.
2 *they burned the flag as a symbolic gesture* **action**, deed, act, move.
▶ verb *he gestured to her to remain where she was* **signal**, make a gesture, make a sign, give a sign, sign, motion, wave, indicate, gesticulate.

get ▶ verb **1** *I got the impression he didn't like me | where did you get that hat?* **acquire**, **obtain**, come by, come to have, come into possession of, receive, gain, earn, win, come into, come in for, take possession of, take receipt of, be given; buy, purchase, procure, possess oneself of, secure; gather, collect, pick up, appropriate, amass, build up, hook, net, land; achieve, attain; *informal* get one's hands on, get one's mitts on, get hold of, grab, bag, score, swing, nab, collar, cop.
OPPOSITE give.
2 *I was glad to get your letter* **receive**, be sent, be in receipt of, accept delivery of, be given.
OPPOSITE send.
3 *your tea's getting cold* **become**, grow, turn, go, come to be, get to be; *literary* wax.
4 *I'll get the children from school* **fetch**, collect, go for, call for, pick up, bring, carry, deliver, convey, ferry, transport; escort, conduct, lead, usher.
OPPOSITES take; leave.
5 *the chairman gets £650,000 a year* **earn**, be paid, receive a salary of, take home, take home earnings of, bring in, make, receive, collect, clear, gross; *informal* pocket, bank, rake in, pull in, haul in, net, bag.
6 *have the police got their man?* **apprehend**, catch, arrest, capture, seize, take; take prisoner, take captive, take into custody, detain, put in jail, throw in jail, put behind bars, imprison, incarcerate; *informal* collar, grab, nab, nail, run in, pinch, bust, pick up, pull in, haul in, do, feel someone's collar; *Brit. informal* nick.
7 *I got a taxi in the end* **travel by/on/in**, journey by/on/in; take, catch, use, make use of, utilize.
8 *one winter she got flu* **succumb to**, develop, go/come down with, sicken for, fall victim to, be struck down with, be stricken with, be afflicted by/with, be smitten by/with; become infected with/by, catch, contract, become ill/sick with, fall ill/sick with, be taken ill with, show symptoms of; *Brit.* go down with; *informal* take ill with; *N. Amer. informal* take sick with.
9 *I got a sharp pain in my right arm* **experience**, suffer, be afflicted with, undergo, sustain, feel, have.
10 *I could get him on the radio and ask* **contact**, get in touch with, communicate with, make contact with, reach, be in communication with; phone, call, ring up, radio, speak to, talk to; *Brit.* get on to; *informal* get hold of.
11 *I didn't get what he said* **hear**, recognize, discern, distinguish, make out, pick out, perceive, follow, keep up with, take in.
12 *sorry, I don't get the joke* **understand**, comprehend, grasp, see, take in, fathom, follow, puzzle out, work out, perceive, apprehend, get to the bottom of, unravel, decipher; *informal* get the drift of, catch on to, latch on to, make head or tail of, figure out, get the picture, get the message; *Brit. informal* twig, suss out, suss.
13 *we got there early* **arrive**, reach, come, make it, turn up, appear, put in an appearance, make an appearance, come on the scene, come up, approach, enter, present oneself, be along, come along, materialize; *informal* show up, show, roll in, roll up, blow in, show one's face.
14 *we got her to go* **persuade**, induce, prevail on, influence, talk round; wheedle into, talk into, cajole into, inveigle into; win over, bring around, sway.
15 *I'd like to get to meet him sometime* **contrive**, arrange, find a way, engineer a way, manage; succeed in, organize; *informal* work it, fix it; *archaic* compass.
16 *I'll get supper if you wash up afterwards* **prepare**, get ready, cook, make, put together, assemble, muster, dish up, concoct; *informal* fix, rustle up; *Brit. informal* knock up.
17 (*informal*) *I'll get him for that* **take revenge on**, be revenged on, exact/wreak revenge on, get one's revenge on, avenge oneself on, take vengeance on, get even with, settle a/the score with, pay back, pay out, retaliate on/against, get back at, take reprisals against, exact retribution on, give someone their just deserts, give someone a dose/taste of their own medicine; give/return like for like, give tit for tat, take an eye for an eye (and a tooth for a tooth); *informal* give someone their comeuppance; *Brit. informal* get one's own back on.
18 *He scratched his head. 'You've got me there.'* **baffle**, nonplus, perplex, puzzle, bewilder, mystify, bemuse, confuse, confound, disconcert, throw, set someone thinking; *informal* flummox, discombobulate, faze, stump, beat, fox, make someone scratch their head, floor, fog; *archaic* wilder, gravel, maze, cause to be at a stand, pose.
19 *what gets me is how neurotic she is* **annoy**, irritate, exasperate, anger, irk, vex, inflame, put out, nettle, needle, provoke, incense, infuriate, madden, rub up the wrong way, try someone's patience, make someone's blood boil, ruffle someone's feathers, make someone's hackles rise, get someone's hackles up, rattle someone's cage; *informal* aggravate, peeve,

G

miff, rile, get to, hack off, get someone's back up, get on someone's nerves, get up someone's nose, get under someone's skin, get someone's goat, give someone the hump, get someone's dander up, get in someone's hair, be a thorn in someone's flesh, drive mad, drive crazy, drive nuts, make someone see red; *Brit. informal* wind up, nark, get across, get someone's wick; *N. Amer. informal* tee off, tick off, eat, burn up; *vulgar slang* piss off; *Brit. vulgar slang* get on someone's tits.

□ **get about** *he has to rely on a wheelchair to get about* **move about**, move around, travel.

□ **get something across** *a photo will help to get the message across* **communicate**, get over, put over, impart, convey, transmit, make understood, make clear, express.

□ **get ahead** *people with ideas and the desire to get ahead* **prosper**, flourish, thrive, do well, get on well; succeed, be successful, make it, do all right for oneself, progress, make progress, make headway, advance, get on in the world, rise in the world, go up in the world, fly high, make one's mark, make good, become rich, strike gold/oil, be in clover; *informal* go places, get somewhere, go great guns, make the big time.

□ **get along 1** *does he get along with his family?* **be friendly**, be on friendly terms, be in harmony, be compatible, get on, feel a rapport; agree, see eye to eye, concur, be in agreement, be in accord, be in sympathy; be of the same mind/opinion (as); *informal* hit it off, be on the same wavelength (as).
2 *he was getting along well at school* **fare**, manage, progress, advance, get on, do, cope, survive, muddle through/along; succeed, prosper, flourish; *informal* get by, make out.

G

□ **get around 1** *she certainly gets around* **travel**, circulate, socialize, make the rounds.
2 *See* GET ROUND.

□ **get at 1** *it's difficult to get at the timbers once you have insulated* **access**, gain access to, get to, reach, touch.
2 *he had been got at by government officials* **corrupt**, suborn, influence, bribe, buy off, pay off; *informal* give someone a backhander, give someone a sweetener, grease someone's palm, fix, square; *Brit. informal* nobble.
3 (*informal*) *what are you getting at?* **imply**, suggest, intimate, insinuate, hint, mean, intend, lead up to, drive at, allude to.
4 (*Brit. informal*) *I don't like being got at* **criticize**, pick on, find fault with, carp at, nag; **bully**, victimize, attack, tyrannize, torment, persecute, punish repeatedly and unfairly, discriminate against; *informal* have it in for, have a down on, be down on; *Brit. informal* be on at.

□ **get away** *the prisoners got away* **escape**, run away, run off, get out, break out, break/get free, break loose, make a break for it, bolt, flee, fly, take flight, make off, take off, decamp, abscond, take to one's heels, make a/one's escape, make good one's escape, make a/one's getaway, beat a hasty retreat, show a clean pair of heels, run for it, make a run for it; disappear, vanish, slip away, steal away, sneak away; get out of someone's clutches; *informal* do a bunk, do a moonlight flit, cut and run, skedaddle, skip, head for the hills, do a disappearing/vanishing act, fly the coop, take French leave, scarper, vamoose, hightail it, leg it; *Brit. informal* do a runner, hook it; *N. Amer. informal* take a powder, go on the lam.

□ **get away with** *it's not our policy to let kidnappers get away with their crimes* **escape blame for**, escape punishment for.

□ **get back** *they should get back at dawn* **return**, come home, come back, arrive home, arrive back, come again.
OPPOSITE set out.

□ **get something back** *she got her gloves back from the lost property office* **retrieve**, regain (possession of), win back, recover, take back, recoup, reclaim, repossess, recapture, retake, redeem; find (again), track down, trace; claw back; *Law* replevin, replevy.
OPPOSITE lose.

□ **get back at** *she made the story up to get back at the teacher for punishing her* **take revenge on**, be revenged on, exact/wreak revenge on, get one's revenge on, avenge oneself on, take vengeance on, get even with, settle a/the score with, pay back, pay out, retaliate on/against, take reprisals against, exact retribution on, let someone see how it feels, give someone their just deserts, give someone a dose/taste of their own medicine, give as good as one gets; give/return like for like, give tit for tat, take an eye for an eye (and a tooth for a tooth); *informal* get, give someone their comeuppance; *Brit. informal* get one's own back on.
OPPOSITE forgive.

□ **get someone down** *sometimes I can laugh it off but inside it gets me down* **depress**, make sad, sadden, make unhappy, cast down, make gloomy, make despondent, dispirit; dampen/break someone's spirit, dash someone's hopes, dishearten, demoralize, discourage, daunt, crush, shake, desolate, weigh down, weigh heavily on, hang over, oppress; upset, distress, grieve, haunt, harrow, cause suffering to, break someone's heart, make one's heart bleed, bring tears to one's eyes; *informal* give someone the blues, make someone fed up, knock the stuffing out of, knock for six, knock sideways.
OPPOSITE cheer someone up.

□ **get by** *he had just enough money to get by* **manage**, cope, survive, exist, subsist, muddle through/along, scrape by/along/through, make ends meet, get along, make do, barely/scarcely have enough to live on, keep the wolf from the door, keep one's head above water, scrimp, scrape a living; *informal* make out.

□ **get off 1** *Sally got off the bus outside her house* **alight (from)**, step off, climb off, dismount (from), get down (from), descend (from), disembark (from), leave, exit; *formal* deplane (from), detrain (from), debus.
OPPOSITE get on.
2 (*informal*) *he was charged with fraud but got off* **escape punishment**, **be acquitted**, be absolved, be cleared, be exonerated, be exculpated, be declared/found innocent, be vindicated.

□ **get on 1** *we got on the train at Kinshasa* **board**, enter, go on board, go aboard, step aboard, climb on, mount, ascend, embark, catch; *informal* hop on, jump on; *formal* emplane, entrain, embus.
OPPOSITE get off.
2 *how are you getting on?* **fare**, manage, progress, advance, get along, do, cope, survive, muddle through/along; succeed, prosper, flourish; *informal* get by, make out.
3 *he just got on with his job* **continue**, proceed, go ahead, carry on, go on, keep on, press on, push on, press ahead, persist, persevere; keep at; *informal* stick with/at, soldier on with.
OPPOSITE give up.
4 *my father and I don't get on* **be friendly**, be on friendly terms, be in harmony, be compatible, get along, feel a rapport; agree, see eye to eye, concur, be in agreement, be in accord, be in sympathy, sympathize, be united, be as one man, accord; be of the same mind/opinion (as); *informal* hit it off, be on the same wavelength (as).

□ **get out 1** *several prisoners had got out* **escape**, break out, break free, get free, break loose, make a break for it, bolt, clear out, run away, run off, get away, flee, fly, take flight, make off, take off, decamp, abscond, take to one's heels, make a/one's escape, make good one's escape, make a/one's getaway, beat a hasty retreat, show a clean pair of heels, run for it, make a run for it; disappear, vanish, slip away, steal away, sneak away; get out of someone's clutches; *informal* bust, do a bunk, do a moonlight flit, cut and run, skedaddle, skip, head for the hills, do a disappearing/vanishing act, fly the coop, take French leave, scarper, vamoose, hightail it, leg it; *Brit. informal* do a runner, hook it; *N. Amer. informal* take a powder, go on the lam.
2 *the news has got out* **become known**, become common knowledge, become apparent, come to light, emerge, transpire, materialize, prove to be the case; come out, be discovered, be uncovered, be made public, be revealed, be divulged, be disclosed, be reported, be publicized, be released, leak out; *literary* be noised about/abroad.

□ **get out of** *he tried to get out of paying the survivors any compensation* **evade**, dodge, shirk, slide out of, avoid, escape, sidestep; *informal* duck, duck out of, wriggle out of, cop out of; *Brit. informal* skive off, funk; *N. Amer. informal* cut; *Austral./NZ informal* duck-shove; *archaic* decline.
OPPOSITE agree to.

□ **get over 1** *I have only just got over flu* **recover from**, recuperate from, get better after, pull through, shrug off, survive, come round from.
OPPOSITE sicken for.
2 *to get over this problem the architect angled the exit into the piazza slightly. See* GET ROUND *sense 2.*

□ **get something over** *that should get the point over to the manufacturers* **communicate**, get across, put over, impart, convey, transmit, make understood, make clear, express.

□ **get round 1** *he got round his mother and she bought it for him* **cajole**, persuade, wheedle, coax, manoeuvre, prevail on, win someone over, bring someone round, sway, beguile, blarney, flatter, seduce, lure, entice, charm, tempt, inveigle, induce, influence, woo; talk into; *informal* sweet-talk, soft-soap, butter up, twist someone's arm; *archaic* blandish.
2 *we can get round these difficulties* **overcome**, surmount, prevail over, triumph over, get the better of, master; get over, circumvent, find an/the answer to, find a/the solution to; sort out, take care of, resolve, solve, crack; deal with, cope with; *informal* lick.

□ **get together 1** *your job is to get together the best bunch of writers you can find* **collect**, gather, assemble, bring together, call together, rally, muster, marshal, line up, congregate, convene, amass, scrape together; *formal* convoke.
OPPOSITE disperse.
2 *we must get together soon* **meet**, meet up, have a meeting, rendezvous, see each other, socialize.

□ **get up** *Rose used to get up very early* **get out of bed**, rise, stir, rouse oneself, bestir oneself, get going; *informal* surface, show signs of life; *formal* arise.
OPPOSITE go to bed.

□ **get someone up** (*informal*) *he was got up in his finery* **dress**, clothe, attire, garb, fit out, turn out, deck, deck out, trick out/up, costume, array, robe, accoutre; *informal* doll up; *literary* bedizen; *archaic* apparel.

getaway ▶ **noun** *guards spotted the gunman as he tried to make his getaway* **escape**, breakout, break, bolt for freedom, running away, flight, bolting, absconding, decamping, fleeing, flit; disappearance, vanishing act; *rare* abscondment, decampment.

get-together ▶ **noun** *we're having a get-together after work* **party**, gathering, meeting, social occasion/event/gathering/meeting; *informal* do, bash; *Brit. informal* rave-up, thrash, knees-up, jolly, beanfeast, bunfight, beano.

get-up ▶ noun (*informal*) *I adore your get-up—such an amusing hat* **outfit**, clothes, costume, ensemble, suit, clothing, dress, attire, garments, garb, turnout, rig, uniform, livery, array, regalia, robes, finery; *informal* gear, togs, duds, glad rags; *Brit. informal* clobber, kit, strip, rig-out; *N. Amer. informal* threads; *formal* apparel; *literary* raiment, habiliments; *archaic* vestments, vesture, habit.

get-up-and-go ▶ noun (*informal*) *alas, I don't have the get-up-and-go to find the money to make a film* **drive**, initiative, enterprise, enthusiasm, eagerness, ambition, motivation, push, go, dynamism, energy, gusto, vigour, vitality, verve, fire, fervour; single-mindedness, will power, dedication, doggedness, tenacity, zeal, commitment, forcefulness, spirit; *informal* gumption, oomph, vim, pep, zing, zip, pizzazz, punch.
OPPOSITE lethargy.

ghastly ▶ adjective **1** *he is implicated in several ghastly stabbings* **terrible**, frightful, horrible, grim, awful, dire; frightening, terrifying, horrifying, alarming; distressing, shocking, appalling, harrowing; dreadful, fearful, hideous, horrendous, monstrous, unspeakable, gruesome, tragic, calamitous, grievous, grisly.
OPPOSITE pleasant.
2 *it's hard to escape the ghastly visitor centres* **unpleasant**, objectionable, offensive, disagreeable, distasteful, displeasing, unacceptable, off-putting, undesirable, obnoxious; **nasty**, disgusting, awful, terrible, dreadful, frightful, foul, repulsive, repellent, repugnant, revolting, abhorrent, loathsome, hateful, odious, detestable, reprehensible, deplorable, appalling, insufferable, intolerable, despicable, contemptible, beyond the pale, vile, obscene, unsavoury, unpalatable, sickening, nauseating, nauseous, noxious; *informal* horrible, horrid, sick-making; *Brit. informal* beastly; *archaic* disgustful, loathly; *rare* exceptionable, rebarbative.
OPPOSITE charming.
3 *the patient feels ghastly on getting out of bed* **ill**, unwell, washed out, peaky; sick, queasy, nauseous, nauseated, green about the gills; *Brit.* off, off colour, poorly; *informal* rough, lousy, rotten, terrible, awful, horrible, dreadful, crummy; *Brit. informal* grotty, ropy; *Scottish informal* wabbit, peely-wally; *Austral./NZ informal* crook; *dated* queer, seedy; *rare* peaked, peakish.
OPPOSITE fine.
4 *a ghastly mistake* **serious**, severe, grave, very bad, grievous, dreadful, terrible, awful, frightful, dire; unforgivable, inexcusable, indefensible, reprehensible, disgraceful, shameful; *archaic or humorous* parlous.
OPPOSITES trivial; excusable.
5 *her face had a ghastly pallor* **pale**, white, pallid, pasty, pasty-faced, wan, colourless, anaemic, bloodless, washed out, peaky, peakish, ashen, ashen-faced, ashy, chalky, chalk-white, grey, whitish, white-faced, whey-faced, waxen, waxy, blanched, drained, pinched, green, sickly, sallow, as white as a sheet, as white as a ghost, deathly pale, cadaverous, corpse-like, ghostlike, spectral; *informal* like death warmed up; *Scottish informal* peely-wally; *rare* livid, etiolated, lymphatic.
OPPOSITE healthy.

ghost ▶ noun **1** *it is said that his ghost still haunts the crypt* **spectre**, phantom, wraith, spirit, soul, shadow, presence; vision, apparition, hallucination; *Scottish & Irish* bodach; *German* Doppelgänger; *W. Indian* duppy; *informal* spook; *literary* phantasm, shade, revenant, visitant, wight; *rare* eidolon, manes, lemures.
2 *she gave the ghost of a smile* **trace**, hint, suggestion, impression, faint appearance, touch, suspicion, tinge, modicum, dash, soupçon; **glimmer**, semblance, shadow, breath, whiff, undertone, whisper.

WORD LINKS
fear of ghosts **phasmophobia**

ghostly ▶ adjective *a ghostly figure appeared at the end of the tunnel* **ghostlike**, **spectral**, phantom, wraithlike, phantasmal, phantasmic, unearthly, unnatural, supernatural, other-worldly, insubstantial, illusory, unreal, shadowy, eerie, weird, uncanny, mysterious, magical, mystic, strange, abnormal, freakish; frightening, spine-chilling, hair-raising, blood-curdling, scaring, terrifying, petrifying, chilling, sinister; *Scottish* eldritch; *informal* creepy, scary, spooky, freaky; *Brit. informal* rum.

ghoulish ▶ adjective *the torchlight gave his face a ghoulish appearance* **macabre**, grisly, gruesome, grotesque, ghastly, morbid, black; unhealthy, perverted, death-obsessed; horrible, unwholesome, revolting; *informal* sick.

giant *See centre pages for list of* **Giants**
▶ noun **colossus**, man mountain, behemoth, Brobdingnagian, mammoth, leviathan, monster, monstrosity, ogre; *informal* jumbo.
OPPOSITE dwarf.
▶ adjective *a dredger resembling a giant vacuum cleaner* **huge**, colossal, massive, enormous, gigantic, very big, very large, great, mammoth, vast, immense, tremendous, mighty, stupendous, monumental, epic, prodigious, mountainous, monstrous, titanic, towering, elephantine, king-sized, king-size, gargantuan, Herculean, Brobdingnagian; substantial, extensive, hefty, bulky, weighty, heavy, gross; *informal* mega, monster, whopping, whopping great, thumping, thumping great, humongous, jumbo, hulking, bumper, astronomical, astronomic; *Brit. informal* whacking, whacking great, ginormous.
OPPOSITE miniature.

gibber ▶ verb *what are you gibbering about?* **prattle**, rattle on, chatter, babble, ramble, drivel, jabber, patter, gabble, bumble, burble, twitter, flannel, go on, run on, mutter, mumble, maunder, prate, bleat, cackle; *Scottish & Irish* slabber; *informal* gab, yak, yap, yackety-yak, yabber, yatter, natter, yammer, blabber, jibber-jabber, blather, blether, blither, jaw, gas, shoot one's mouth off; *Brit. informal* witter, rabbit, chunter, waffle; *N. Amer. informal* run off at the mouth; *Austral./NZ informal* mag; *archaic* clack, twaddle, twattle.

gibberish ▶ noun *he just stared at her as if she was talking gibberish* **nonsense**, rubbish, balderdash, blather, blether; *informal* drivel, gobbledegook, mumbo-jumbo, rot, tripe, hogwash, baloney, bilge, bosh, bull, bunk, guff, eyewash, piffle, twaddle, poppycock, phooey, hooey, malarkey, dribble; *Brit. informal* cobblers, codswallop, cock, stuff and nonsense, double Dutch, tosh, cack; *Scottish & N. English informal* havers; *N. Amer. informal* garbage, flapdoodle, blathers, wack, bushwa, applesauce; *informal, dated* bunkum, tommyrot, cod, gammon, toffee; *vulgar slang* shit, bullshit, horseshit, crap, bollocks, balls; *Austral./NZ vulgar slang* bulldust.
OPPOSITE sense.

gibe ▶ noun & verb. *See* JIBE.

giddiness ▶ noun *I nearly fell down with giddiness* **dizziness**, light-headedness, loss of balance/equilibrium, spinning/swimming of the head; faintness, weakness at the knees, unsteadiness, shakiness, wobbliness; *Scottish* mirligoes, dwalm; *informal* wooziness, legs like jelly, rubbery legs; *technical* megrim, sturdy, scotoma; *archaic* turnsick; *rare* vertiginousness.
OPPOSITE steadiness.

giddy ▶ adjective **1** *she felt giddy with the sickly heat* **dizzy**, light-headed, faint, weak, weak at the knees, unsteady, shaky, wobbly, off balance; reeling, staggering, tottering, teetering; *informal* woozy, with legs like jelly, with rubbery legs; *rare* vertiginous.
OPPOSITE steady.
2 *she was so young and giddy that she had no understanding of the problem* **flighty**, silly, frivolous, skittish, irresponsible, flippant, whimsical, capricious, light-minded, feather-brained, scatterbrained, scatty; careless, thoughtless, heedless, carefree, insouciant; *informal* dippy, dopey, batty, dotty, nutty; *N. Amer. informal* ditzy.
OPPOSITE sensible.

gift ▶ noun **1** *he made the hospital a gift of £2 million* **present**, donation, offering, contribution, handout, presentation, bestowal, largesse, alms, charity, bonus, award, premium, bounty, boon, favour, bequest, legacy, inheritance, settlement, subsidy, grant, endowment, benefaction; tip, gratuity, baksheesh; giving; *French* pourboire; *informal* freebie, perk, prezzie, sweetener; *formal* perquisite; *archaic* conferment.
2 *he had a unique gift for melody* **talent**, flair, aptitude, facility, knack, technique, touch, bent, ability, expertise, capacity, capability, power, faculty; endowment, strength, strong point, forte, genius, brilliance; dexterity, adroitness, skill, cleverness, virtuosity, artistry.
▶ verb *he has gifted a new composition to the BBC Symphony Orchestra* **present**, give, bestow, confer, donate, contribute, endow, award, accord, grant; pledge, vouchsafe, furnish, bequeath, hand over, turn over, make over, leave, will.

gifted ▶ adjective *she was already a gifted artist* **talented**, skilful, skilled, accomplished, expert, consummate, master(ly), first-rate, polished, adroit, dexterous, able, competent, capable, apt, deft, adept, proficient; **intelligent**, clever, bright, brilliant, quick, sharp, perceptive; precocious, advanced for one's age, old beyond one's years, forward, ahead of one's peers, mature; *informal* crack, top-notch, top-drawer, top-hole, ace, wizard.
OPPOSITES inept, stupid.

gigantic ▶ adjective *the college is a gigantic Victorian building* **huge**, enormous, vast, extensive, expansive, broad, wide; very big/large, great, giant, massive, colossal, mammoth, immense, tremendous, mighty, stupendous, monumental; boundless, immeasurable, limitless, infinite; epic, prodigious, mountainous, monstrous, titanic, towering, elephantine, king-sized, king-size, gargantuan, Herculean, Brobdingnagian, substantial; *informal* mega, monster, whopping, whopping great, thumping, thumping great, humongous, jumbo, hulking, bumper, astronomical, astronomic; *Brit. informal* whacking, whacking great, ginormous.
OPPOSITE tiny.

giggle ▶ verb *Rory couldn't help but giggle at the ridiculous picture* **titter**, snigger, snicker, tee-hee, give a half-suppressed laugh, chuckle, chortle; smirk, sneer, simper.
▶ noun *she suppressed a giggle with difficulty* **titter**, snigger, snicker, tee-hee, half-suppressed laugh, chuckle, chortle; smirk, sneer, simper.

gigolo ▶ noun *their wives frivolously whittled away the family money on a succession of gigolos* **playboy**, beau, admirer; **(male) dancing partner**, (male) escort, (male) companion; *informal* fancy man; *Brit. informal* toy boy.

gild ▶ verb **1** (usually **gilded**) *the steeple was crowned by a gilded weathercock* **cover with gold**, paint gold, lacquer gold, inlay with gold.
2 *there was no need to gild the truth* **elaborate**, embellish, embroider, sugar-

coat, window-dress, camouflage, disguise, dress up, touch up, ginger up, colour, exaggerate, enlarge on, expand on; *informal* jazz up.

gimcrack ▶ adjective *they lived in gimcrack villas you'd be afraid to sneeze in* **shoddy**, jerry-built, badly built, flimsy, insubstantial, rickety, ramshackle, thrown together, makeshift, inferior, poor-quality, second-rate, third-rate, low-grade, cheap, cheapjack, tawdry, rubbishy, kitschy, trashy, crude, tinny; *informal* tacky, tatty, junky; *Brit. informal* ropy, duff, rubbish, grotty.
OPPOSITES sound, solid.

gimmick ▶ noun *a quality newspaper shouldn't have to resort to gimmicks like bingo* **publicity device**, stunt, contrivance, eye-catching novelty, scheme, trick, dodge, ploy, stratagem; loss-leader; *informal* shtick.

gingerly ▶ adverb *he stepped gingerly on to the ice* **cautiously**, carefully, with caution, with care, circumspectly, delicately, warily, charily, guardedly, prudently, judiciously, on one's guard, on the alert, on the lookout, on the qui vive, suspiciously, attentively, heedfully, watchfully, vigilantly, observantly, alertly, cannily; hesitantly, timidly, timorously.
OPPOSITES carelessly; recklessly.

G

gird ▶ verb (*literary*) **1** *Sir Hector girded on his sword* **fasten**, belt, bind, tie.
2 *the island was girded by treacherous rocks* **surround**, enclose, encircle, circle, ring, encompass, circumscribe, border, bound, edge, skirt, fringe, form a ring around, form a barrier round; close in, shut in, fence in, wall in, hem in, pen up/in, lock in, cut off, confine; *literary* girdle, engird, compass.
3 *the Persians girded themselves for an attack* **prepare**, get ready, make ready, gear up, nerve, steel, galvanize, brace, strengthen, fortify, bolster, buttress; *informal* psych oneself up.

girdle ▶ noun **1** *round his waist was a diamond-studded girdle* **belt**, sash, strap, cummerbund, waistband, band, girth, cord, fillet; *Japanese* obi; *rare* baldric, cincture, ceinture, cestus, cingulum, zone.
2 *her stockings were held up by her girdle* **corset**, corselet, foundation garment, panty girdle; *Medicine* truss.
▶ verb (*literary*) *a formal garden girdled the house* **surround**, enclose, encircle, circle, ring, encompass, circumscribe, border, bound, edge, skirt, fringe, form a ring around, form a barrier round; close in, shut in, fence in, wall in, hem in, pen up/in, lock in, cut off, confine; *literary* gird, engird, compass.

girl ▶ noun **1** *a five-year-old girl* **female child**; daughter; schoolgirl; *Scottish & N. English* lass, bairn; *informal* kid, kiddie, kiddiewink, nipper, tot, tiny tot; *derogatory* brat, chit.
2 *a tall dark girl got off the train* **young woman**, young lady, miss; *Scottish* lass, lassie; *Irish* colleen; *French* Mademoiselle; *Italian* signorina; *Spanish* señorita; *German* Fräulein; *informal* chick, girlie, filly; *Brit. informal* bird, bint, popsy; *N. Amer. informal* gal, broad, dame, jane, babe; *derogatory informal* tart, piece, bit, mare, baggage; *Austral./NZ informal* sheila; *black English* bitch, sister; *Brit. informal, dated* Judy; *N. Amer. dated* frail; *literary* maid, maiden, damsel, demoiselle; *archaic* wench, petticoat.
3 *his girl eloped with an accountant* **girlfriend**, sweetheart, woman, partner, lover, significant other, fiancée; *Italian* inamorata; *informal* steady; *Irish informal* mot; *Brit. informal* bird; *N. Amer. informal* squeeze, patootie; *Austral. informal* dona; *Indian informal* bibi; *dated* lady, lady friend, lady love, young lady, betrothed; *archaic* leman.

> **CHOOSE THE RIGHT WORD**
>
> **girl, woman, lady**
>
> *See* WOMAN.

girlfriend ▶ noun *Richard's split up with his girlfriend* **sweetheart**, woman, girl, partner, significant other, lover, fiancée; *Italian* inamorata; *informal* steady, date; *Brit. informal* bird; *Irish informal* mot; *N. Amer. informal* squeeze, patootie; *Austral. informal* dona; *Indian informal* bibi; *dated* lady, lady friend, lady love, young lady, betrothed; *archaic* leman.

girlish ▶ adjective *her girlish giggles* **youthful**, childlike, childish, immature; feminine; coquettish, flirtatious, kittenish; *informal* girly, flirty.

girth ▶ noun **1** *a tree that was 150 feet in height and 10 feet in girth* **circumference**, width, perimeter; size, bulk, measure.
2 *he tied the towel around his girth* **stomach**, midriff, middle, abdomen, belly, gut; *informal* tummy, tum.
3 *a horse's girth N. Amer.* cinch.

gist ▶ noun *the gist of his speech* **essence**, substance, quintessence, main idea/theme, central idea/theme, nub, core, heart, heart of the matter, nucleus, kernel, pith, marrow, meat, burden, crux, important point; thrust, direction, drift, sense, meaning, significance, import; *informal* nitty-gritty.

give ▶ verb **1** *he had given them nearly two thousand pounds* **present with**, provide with, supply with, furnish with, gift with; hand, let someone have; offer, proffer; award, grant, bestow, accord, confer; donate, contribute, put up; hand over, turn over, make over, leave, will, bequeath, pledge, vouchsafe; lend, slip; *informal* fork out, shell out, lay out, cough up; *Brit. informal* stump up; *N. Amer. informal* ante up, pony up.
OPPOSITES receive, accept, take; withhold.
2 *can I give him a message?* **convey**, pass on, impart, communicate, transmit, transfer; send, deliver, relay, purvey; tell.
3 *a baby given into their care* **entrust**, commit, put into someone's hands, consign, assign, render; *formal* commend.
4 *he gave his life for his country* **sacrifice**, give up, relinquish; devote, dedicate, set aside.
5 *he decided to give her time to think things over* **allow**, permit, let have, grant, accord; offer.
6 *this leaflet gives our opening times* **show**, display, set out, set forth, indicate, detail, give details of, list.
7 *the animals became docile and gave no further trouble* **cause**, be a source of, make, create, occasion.
8 *some salamis are wrapped in garlic which gives additional flavour* **produce**, yield, afford, result in; **impart**, lend.
9 *he gave a drinks party to celebrate* **organize**, arrange, lay on, provide, be responsible for; **throw**, host, hold, have.
10 *Dominic gave a small bow* **perform**, execute, carry out; make, do.
11 *she gave a warning shout* **utter**, let out, emit; produce, make.
12 *he gave Harry a beating* **administer**, deliver, deal; inflict, impose.
13 *the door gave after the fifth push* **give way**, cave in, collapse, break, fall apart, come apart; bend, buckle, sink.

□ **give someone/something away 1** *his face gave little away* **reveal**, disclose, divulge, let slip, leak, let out; give the game away.
2 *Luke would never forgive her if she gave him away* **betray**, inform on; *English Law* turn Queen's/King's evidence; *informal* split on, blow the whistle on, rat on, peach on, stitch up, do the dirty on, sell down the river, squeal on, squeak on; *Brit. informal* grass on, shop, sneak on; *N. Amer. informal* rat out, drop a/the dime on, finger, job; *Austral./NZ informal* dob on, pimp on, pool, shelf, put someone's pot on, point the bone at.

□ **give in** *in the end, he was forced to give in* **capitulate**, admit/concede defeat, give up, surrender, yield, submit, climb down, back down, give way, defer, acquiesce, relent, succumb, comply; *informal* throw in the towel/sponge.
OPPOSITE hold out.

□ **give something off/out** *a small fire burned, giving off more smoke than heat* **emit**, produce, send out, send forth, pour out, throw out; discharge, release, exude, exhale, vent; *rare* exsufflate.

□ **give out 1** *his strength was giving out* **run out**, be used up, be consumed, be exhausted, be depleted, come to an end, fail, flag; dry up.
2 *he gave out that he would hold a meeting* **announce**, declare, state, make known, notify, give notice, communicate, broadcast, report, publish; disclose, reveal, divulge, let it be known.

□ **give something out** *thousands of leaflets were given out* **distribute**, issue, hand out, pass round, dole out, dispense; mete out; allocate, allot, apportion, assign, share out, parcel out; disseminate; *informal* dish out.
OPPOSITE collect.

□ **give up** *he isn't the kind of man to give up easily* **admit defeat**, concede defeat, stop trying, call it a day, give in, surrender, capitulate, be beaten; despair, lose heart, abandon hope, give up hope; *informal* throw in the towel/sponge; *Austral. informal* drop one's bundle.

□ **give something up** *I'm determined to give up smoking | she gave up her job* **stop**, cease, discontinue, desist from, swear off, forbear from, abstain from, cut out, renounce, forswear, forgo, abandon, have done with; resign from, stand down from; *informal* quit, kick, leave off, knock off, pack in, lay off, jack in, chuck, ditch.
OPPOSITES take up; continue.

▶ noun (*informal*) *the jacket has a major drawback—there isn't enough give under the arms* **elasticity**, flexibility, stretch, stretchiness; slack, play.

give and take ▶ noun *there has to be some give and take on both sides* **compromise**, concession; cooperation, reciprocity, teamwork, interplay; adaptability, flexibility.
OPPOSITE intransigence.

given ▶ adjective **1** *a given number of years* **specified**, stated, designated, set, particular, specific, named, identified, delineated, prescribed; agreed, appointed, decided, prearranged, predetermined.
OPPOSITE unspecified.
2 *she was given to having temper tantrums* **prone**, liable, inclined, disposed, predisposed, apt, likely; in the habit of.
▶ preposition *given the complexity of the issues involved, a summary of the discussion is difficult* **considering**, taking into consideration, taking into account, in view of, bearing in mind, giving consideration to, keeping in mind, in the light of; making allowances for; assuming.
▶ noun *in this theory, aggression is taken as a given which must find some outlet* **established fact**, reality, certainty; *French* donnée.

giver ▶ noun **donor**, contributor, donator, benefactor, benefactress, provider; supporter, backer, subsidizer, patron, sponsor, subscriber; philanthropist, well-wisher, helper; *informal* angel, fairy godmother; *rare* benefactrice, benefactrix, philanthrope.
OPPOSITE recipient.

glacial ▶ adjective **1** *glacial conditions* **freezing**, bitterly cold, icy, ice-cold,

sub-zero, frozen, wintry; arctic, polar, Siberian; bitter, biting, piercing, raw, cutting; *literary* chill, frore; *rare* gelid, brumal, rimy, algid.
OPPOSITES tropical, hot.
2 *Polly's tone was glacial* **unfriendly**, frosty, icy, wintry, cold, chilly, frigid, hostile, unwelcoming; *rare* gelid.
OPPOSITES friendly, warm.

glad ▶ **adjective 1** *I'm really glad you're coming with me* **pleased**, **happy**, delighted, as pleased as Punch, well pleased, thrilled, overjoyed, cock-a-hoop, elated, like a dog with two tails, like a child with a new toy, gleeful; satisfied, contented, gratified, grateful, thankful; *French* enchanté; *informal* tickled pink, over the moon, as happy as Larry; *Brit. informal* chuffed; *N. English informal* made up; *N. Amer. informal* as happy as a clam; *Austral. informal* wrapped; *humorous* gruntled.
OPPOSITES dismayed; annoyed.
2 *I'd be glad to help* **more than willing**, eager, happy, pleased, delighted; ready, prepared, nothing loath; *informal* game.
OPPOSITES unwilling, reluctant.
3 *glad tidings* **pleasing**, welcome, happy, joyful, delightful, cheering, heart-warming, heartening, gratifying; *literary* gladsome.
OPPOSITES unwelcome, distressing.

gladden ▶ **verb** *it gladdened him to see her again* **delight**, please, make happy, make someone feel good, give someone pleasure, exhilarate, elate; **raise someone's spirits**, cheer, cheer up, hearten, do someone's heart good, warm the cockles of someone's heart, brighten up, buoy up, give someone a lift, uplift; gratify; *informal* give someone a buzz, give someone a kick, tickle someone pink, buck up; *archaic* glad.
OPPOSITES sadden, depress.

gladly ▶ **adverb** *I would gladly have given him the money* **with pleasure**, happily, cheerfully; **willingly**, readily, eagerly, freely, without hesitation, without reluctance, with good grace, ungrudgingly; *archaic* fain, lief.
OPPOSITES reluctantly, unwillingly.

glamorous ▶ **adjective 1** *a glamorous woman* **alluring**, beautiful, attractive, elegant, chic, smart, well dressed, stylish, fashionable; charming, charismatic, fascinating, intriguing, beguiling, appealing, lovely, bewitching, enchanting, entrancing, irresistible, seductive, tantalizing; *informal* classy, glitzy, ritzy, glam.
OPPOSITES plain, drab, dowdy.
2 *a glamorous lifestyle* **exciting**, stimulating, thrilling, fascinating, high profile, dazzling, glittering, glossy, tinselled; cosmopolitan, colourful, exotic; *informal* ritzy, glitzy, sexy, fast-lane, jet-setting.
OPPOSITES dull, boring.

glamour ▶ **noun 1** *she had undeniable glamour* **beauty**, **allure**, attractiveness, elegance, chic, style; charisma, charm, fascination, magnetism, seductiveness, desirability; *rare* witchery.
2 *the glamour of working in show business* **allure**, attraction, attractiveness, fascination, charm, enchantment, captivation, magic, romance, mystique, exoticism, spell; excitement, thrill, glitter, brilliance, the bright lights, the high life; *informal* glitz, pizzazz, glam.

glance ▶ **verb 1** *Rachel glanced at him nervously* **take a quick look**, look quickly, look briefly, peek, peep; glimpse, catch a glimpse of; *Scottish* keek; *informal* sneak a look, take a gander; *Brit. informal* take a dekko, have a shufti, take a butcher's; *Austral./NZ informal* squiz; *archaic* glance one's eye.
OPPOSITES gaze, scrutinize.
2 *I glanced through the report* **read quickly**, scan, have a quick look, run one's eye over; skim, leaf, flick, flip, thumb, browse; dip into; *informal* give something a/the once-over.
OPPOSITES study, pore over.
3 *a bullet glanced off the ice* **ricochet**, rebound, be deflected; fly, bounce; graze, clip, make contact with; *Billiards & Pool* cannon, carom; *rare* resile.
4 *the bright sunlight glanced off her copper hair* **reflect**, **flash**, gleam, glint, glitter, glisten, glimmer, shimmer, flicker, sparkle, twinkle; *rare* coruscate.
▶ **noun 1** *he took a quick glance at his watch* **peek**, peep, brief look, quick look; glimpse; *Scottish* keek; *French* coup d'œil; *informal* gander; *Brit. informal* dekko, shufti, butcher's; *Austral./NZ informal* squiz, geek.
2 (*literary*) *a glance of light* **flash**, gleam, glitter, glint, glimmer, shimmer, flicker, sparkle, twinkle.
□ **at first glance** *at first glance, nothing much seemed to have changed* **on the face of it**, on the surface, at first sight, to the casual eye, to all appearances, to go/judge by appearances; apparently, seemingly, outwardly, superficially, it seems (that), it would seem (that), it appears (that), it would appear (that), as far as one can see/tell, by all accounts, so it seems, to all intents and purposes.

gland ▶ **noun.** *See centre pages for list of human* **Glands**

WORD LINKS
relating to glands **glandular**
related prefix **adeno- (e.g. *adenoids, adenocarcinoma*)**

glare ▶ **verb 1** *she glared at him, her eyes flashing* **stare angrily**, scowl, glower, look daggers, frown, lour, give someone a black look, look threateningly/menacingly; *informal* give someone a dirty look; *archaic* glout; *Scottish archaic* glunch.
OPPOSITE smile.
2 *the sun glared out of a clear blue sky* **blaze**, be dazzling, be blinding, shine brightly, flare, flame, beam.
▶ **noun 1** *she gave Harley a cold glare* **angry stare**, scowl, glower, frown, black look, threatening/menacing look; *informal* dirty look.
OPPOSITE smile.
2 *the harsh glare of the arc lights* **strong light**, dazzling light, blaze, dazzle, shine, beam, flare; radiance, brilliance, luminescence, fluorescence.

glaring ▶ **adjective 1** *the glaring lights* **dazzling**, blinding, blazing, strong, extremely bright, harsh; fluorescent.
OPPOSITES dim, soft.
2 *a glaring omission* **obvious**, conspicuous, plain to see, unmistakable, obtrusive, striking, flagrant, blatant, staring someone in the face, as plain as a pikestaff, as plain as day, inescapable, unmissable, outrageous, gross; overt, patent, transparent, manifest, visible, apparent, unconcealed, undisguised; *informal* as plain as the nose on one's face, standing/sticking out like a sore thumb, standing/sticking out a mile, right under one's nose; *rare* egregious.
OPPOSITES inconspicuous, minor.

glass *See centre pages for lists of* **Drinking Vessels** **Glass** **Mirrors**
▶ **noun 1** *we sell china and glass* **glassware**, crystal, crystalware; *rare* vitrics.
2 (*Brit.*) *she put it on and looked at herself in the glass* **mirror**, looking glass.

WORD LINKS
relating to glass **vitreous**
fear of glass **nerophobia**
glass-fitter **glazier**

glasses *See centre pages for list of* **Glasses**
▶ **plural noun** *a pair of thick-lensed glasses* **spectacles**; *N. Amer.* eyeglasses; *informal* specs.

glasshouse ▶ **noun.** *See* GREENHOUSE.

glassy ▶ **adjective 1** *the glassy surface of the lake* **smooth**, mirror-like, glass-like, gleaming, shining, shiny, sheeny, glossy, polished; slippery, slick, icy, ice-covered; clear, crystal clear, transparent, translucent, limpid, pellucid; calm, still, flat, unruffled, even, waveless, like a millpond; *informal* slippy; *technical* vitreous, hyaloid.
OPPOSITES rough; murky.
2 *a glassy stare* **expressionless**, glazed, blank, empty, vacant, fixed, unmoving, motionless, emotionless, fishy, impassive, lifeless, wooden, dull, vacuous; deadpan.
OPPOSITE expressive.

glaze ▶ **verb 1** *the newly made pots are glazed when they are completely dry* **varnish**, enamel, lacquer, japan, shellac, paint, coat; gloss, make shiny.
2 *choux pastry glazed with caramel sauce* **cover**, coat; ice, frost.
3 *his eyes glazed over* **become glassy**, grow expressionless, go blank, be motionless; mist over, film over.
▶ **noun 1** *a pottery jar with a rich blue glaze* **varnish**, enamel, lacquer, finish, coating; lustre, shine, gloss.
2 *brush the cake with an apricot glaze* **coating**, topping; icing, frosting.

gleam ▶ **verb** *the new brass nameplate gleamed in the moonlight* **shine**, glimmer, glint, catch the light, glitter, shimmer, glow, sparkle, twinkle, flicker, blink, wink, glisten, flash, flare, beam, fluoresce; reflect light; *literary* glister; *rare* coruscate, scintillate, fulgurate, effulge, luminesce, incandesce, phosphoresce.
▶ **noun 1** *a gleam of light* **glimmer**, glint, shimmer, glow, twinkle, sparkle, flicker, blink, spark, flash, flare; beam, ray, shaft, finger, pencil.
2 *the gleam of polished brass* **shine**, lustre, gloss, sheen; glint, glitter, glimmer, sparkle, brightness, brilliance, radiance, glow, luminescence, luminosity, phosphorescence, incandescence; *literary* glister; *rare* lambency, scintillation, effulgence, refulgence, fulguration, coruscation.
3 *a gleam of hope appeared in Ray's eyes* **glimmer**, glimmering, flicker, ray, spark, trace, suggestion, hint, faint sign, scintilla.

glean ▶ **verb** *the information is gleaned from press cuttings* **obtain**, get, take, draw, derive, extract, cull, garner, gather, reap; select, choose, pick; learn, find out.

glee ▶ **noun** *Agnes clapped her hands together with glee* **delight**, pleasure, happiness, joy, joyfulness, gladness, elation, euphoria, exhilaration, cheerfulness, amusement, mirth, mirthfulness, merriment, joviality, jollity, jocularity; excitement, animation, gaiety, high spirits, exuberance, verve, liveliness, triumph, jubilation, relish, satisfaction, gratification; *German* Schadenfreude; *humorous* delectation; *rare* joyousness, jouissance.
OPPOSITES gloom, disappointment.

gleeful ▶ **adjective** *a gleeful chuckle* **delighted**, pleased, joyful, happy, glad, amused, mirthful, cheerful, overjoyed, elated, euphoric, exhilarated; merry, gay, high-spirited, in high spirits, jolly, jovial, exuberant; cock-a-hoop, jubilant; *informal* over the moon; *literary* joyous.
OPPOSITE gloomy.

glib ▶ **adjective** *the glib phrases rolled off his tongue | a glib PR official* **slick**, pat, neat, plausible, silky, smooth-talking, fast-talking; **smooth**, urbane, smooth-tongued, silver-tongued, smooth-spoken; **fluent**, voluble,

loquacious, having kissed the Blarney Stone; disingenuous, insincere, facile, shallow, superficial, simplistic, oversimplified, easy, ready, flippant; *informal* flip, sweet-talking, with the gift of the gab.
OPPOSITES sincere, thoughtful; inarticulate.

CHOOSE THE RIGHT WORD

glib, slick, smooth, urbane

These words, with varying degrees of disapproval, describe extreme ease and confidence in speech or manner.

- To be **glib** is always bad. The word most commonly describes utterances that are too easy, fluent, and inadequate to deal with the complexity of an issue, or are too readily produced to be sincere (*they should be on their guard against accepting glib answers*).
- **Slick** is used of a person or their actions or utterances; it indicates expertise and the assurance that that brings, but it usually implies that this is at the expense of content (*a slick public relations campaign*) or of honesty and altruism (*slick financiers and face-grinding industrialists*).
- Someone described as **smooth** is regarded as possibly insincere or too charming to be trusted (*he was too smooth, and his charm a little too insincere, to be a real gentleman*).
- **Urbane** is the most positive term. It is used of a person, action, or utterance and indicates a polished and relaxed ease and charm (*his urbane discourse is both enlivening and instructive*). *Urbane* is almost always used to describe men and not women.

G

glide ▶ verb **1** *two gondolas glided past* **slide**, move smoothly, slip, sail, float, drift, flow; coast, freewheel, roll; skim, skate, glissade.
OPPOSITE hurtle.
2 *seagulls gliding gracefully over the waves* **soar**, wheel, plane; fly.
3 *Toby glided out of the back door* **slip**, move lightly/quietly, steal, slink.
OPPOSITE stamp.

glimmer ▶ verb *moonlight glimmered on the lawn* **gleam**, shine, glint, flicker, shimmer, glisten, glow, twinkle, sparkle, glitter, catch the light, blink, wink, flash; *literary* glister; *rare* scintillate, coruscate, fulgurate, effulge, luminesce, incandesce, phosphoresce.
▶ noun **1** *a faint glimmer of light* **gleam**, glint, flicker, shimmer, glow, twinkle, sparkle, blink, flash, ray.
2 *a glimmer of hope* **gleam**, glimmering, flicker, ray, trace, faint sign, scintilla, suggestion, hint.

glimpse ▶ noun *a fleeting glimpse of her face* **brief look**, quick look; glance, peek, peep; sight, sighting; *French* coup d'œil.
▶ verb *he glimpsed a figure standing in the shade* **catch sight of**, catch/get a glimpse of, see briefly, get a sight of, notice, discern, spot, spy, sight, note, pick out, make out; *Brit. informal* clock; *literary* espy, descry.

glint ▶ verb *the diamond ring glinted in the sunlight* **shine**, gleam, catch the light, glitter, sparkle, twinkle, blink, wink, glimmer, shimmer, glow, flicker, glisten, flash; reflect light; *literary* glister; *rare* coruscate, scintillate, fulgurate, effulge, luminesce, incandesce, phosphoresce.
▶ noun *the glint of the silverware* **glitter**, gleam, sparkle, twinkle, blink, wink, glimmer, flash.

glisten ▶ verb *the sea glistened in the early morning light* **shine**, sparkle, twinkle, glint, glitter, catch the light, glimmer, shimmer, glow, flicker, blink, wink, flash; *literary* glister; *rare* coruscate, scintillate, fulgurate, effulge, luminesce, incandesce, phosphoresce.

glitter ▶ verb *silver and crystal glittered in the candlelight* **shine**, sparkle, twinkle, glint, gleam, shimmer, glimmer, flicker, blink, wink, catch the light, flash, spangle; *literary* glister; *rare* scintillate, coruscate, fulgurate, effulge, luminesce, incandesce, phosphoresce.
▶ noun **1** *the glitter of sunlight on the water* **sparkle**, twinkle, glint, gleam, shimmer, glimmer, flicker, blink, flash; brightness, brilliance, light, luminescence, phosphorescence, luminosity; *rare* lambency, scintillation, coruscation, fulguration, effulgence.
2 *the glitter of show business* **glamour**, excitement, thrills, attractions, appeal; showiness, dazzle, tinsel; *informal* razzle-dazzle, razzmatazz, glitz, glitziness, ritziness, pizzazz, flashiness.

gloat ▶ verb *she gloated over his recent humiliation | I hadn't time to gloat over my good fortune* **delight in**, relish, take great pleasure in, enjoy greatly, revel in, rejoice in, glory in, exult in, triumph over, crow over; boast about, brag about, feel self-satisfied about, be smug about, congratulate oneself on, preen oneself about, pat oneself on the back about; rub one's hands together; *informal* rub it in; *archaic* pique oneself on.

global ▶ adjective **1** *the global economy* **worldwide**, international, world, intercontinental; universal.
OPPOSITES national, local.
2 *a global view of the problem* **comprehensive**, overall, general, all-inclusive, all-encompassing, encyclopedic, universal, exhaustive, blanket; **broad**, wide-ranging, far-reaching, extensive, sweeping.
OPPOSITES partial, restricted.

globe ▶ noun **1** *a city full of tourists from every corner of the globe* **world**, earth, universe, planet; *literary* orb.
2 *the sun is a globe, not the flat disc it appears to be* **sphere**, orb, ball, spheroid, round; globule; *rare* spherule.

globular ▶ adjective *the plant's globular pinkish-green blooms* **spherical**, round, globe-shaped, ball-shaped, orb-shaped, rounded, bulbous, bulb-shaped; *rare* spheroid, spheroidal, spheric, globate, globose, globoid, orbicular, orbiculate.

globule ▶ noun *globules of sweat* **droplet**, drop, dewdrop, bead, tear, ball, bubble, pearl, particle; *informal* blob, glob; *technical* prill.

gloom ▶ noun **1** *Sharpe peered into the gloom* **darkness**, semi-darkness, dark, gloominess, dimness, blackness, murkiness, murk, shadows, shade, shadiness, obscurity; dusk, twilight, gloaming; *rare* tenebrosity.
OPPOSITE light.
2 *his gloom deepened* **despondency**, depression, dejection, downheartedness, dispiritedness, heavy-heartedness, melancholy, melancholia, unhappiness, sadness, glumness, gloominess, low spirits, dolefulness, misery, sorrow, sorrowfulness, forlornness, woefulness, woe, wretchedness, lugubriousness, moroseness, mirthlessness, cheerlessness; despair, pessimism, hopelessness, the slough of despond, negativity; *German* Weltschmerz; *informal* the blues, the dumps; *N. Amer. informal* the blahs; *rare* mopery.
OPPOSITE happiness.

gloomy ▶ adjective **1** *a gloomy room filled with mahogany furniture* **dark**, ill-lit, poorly lit, shadowy, sunless, dim, sombre, dingy, frowzy, drab, dismal, dreary, murky, depressing, unwelcoming, uninviting, cheerless, joyless, comfortless, funereal; grey, leaden, overcast, cloudy; *literary* crepuscular, tenebrous; *rare* Stygian, Tartarean, caliginous, subfusc.
OPPOSITES bright, sunny, well lit.
2 *Joanna looked gloomy | his gloomy expression* **despondent**, downcast, downhearted, dejected, disconsolate, dispirited, crestfallen, cast down, depressed, disappointed, disheartened, discouraged, demoralized, desolate, heavy-hearted, in low spirits, low-spirited, sad, unhappy, glum, full of gloom, doleful, melancholy, miserable, woebegone, mournful, sorrowful, forlorn, long-faced, fed up, in the doldrums, subdued, wretched, lugubrious, Eeyorish, morose, sepulchral, saturnine, dour, mirthless, woeful; *informal* blue, down, down in the mouth, down in the dumps; *Brit. informal* brassed off, cheesed off, looking as if one had lost a pound and found a penny; *literary* dolorous; *archaic* chap-fallen, adust.
OPPOSITES happy, cheerful.
3 *gloomy forecasts about the economy* **pessimistic**, depressing, downbeat, looking on the black side, disheartening, disappointing, dispiriting, unpromising, unfavourable, bleak, bad, dark, black, sombre, melancholy, saddening, distressing, grim, cheerless, comfortless, hopeless.
OPPOSITES optimistic, upbeat.

glorify ▶ verb **1** *their prime purpose is to glorify God* **give praise to**, praise, extol, exalt, laud, worship, revere, reverence, venerate, pay homage/tribute to, honour, adore, thank, give thanks to, bless; *archaic* magnify.
2 *a poem written to glorify the memory of those men killed in the war | a football video glorifying violence* **ennoble**, exalt, elevate, lift up, add dignity to, dignify, add lustre to, add distinction to, enhance, increase, augment, promote, boost; praise, sing/sound the praises of, celebrate, honour, extol, laud, eulogize, hymn, lionize, acclaim, applaud, hail; glamorize, aggrandize, idealize, romanticize, put on a pedestal, enshrine, apotheosize, canonize, immortalize; *black English* big up; *dated* cry up; *rare* emblazon, panegyrize, heroize.
OPPOSITES dishonour, vilify.

glorious ▶ adjective **1** *a glorious victory* **illustrious**, celebrated, famous, famed, renowned, acclaimed, distinguished, honoured, eminent, excellent, outstanding, great, magnificent, splendid, impressive, noble, supreme, sublime, triumphant; immortal, unforgettable.
OPPOSITE undistinguished.
2 *glorious views of the Cotswolds* **wonderful**, marvellous, magnificent, superb, sublime, spectacular, lovely, excellent, fine, delightful, enjoyable, pleasurable; *informal* super, great, smashing, amazing, stunning, fantastic, terrific, tremendous, incredible, sensational, heavenly, divine, gorgeous, dreamy, grand, fabulous, fab, fabby, fantabulous, awesome, magic, ace, out of this world; *Brit. informal* brilliant, brill; *N. Amer. informal* peachy, dandy, jim-dandy, neat; *Austral./NZ informal* beaut, bonzer; *Brit. informal, dated* capital, champion, wizard, corking, ripping, spiffing, top-hole, topping, beezer; *N. Amer. informal, dated* swell, keen; *literary* wondrous, beauteous; *archaic* goodly; *rare* frabjous, splendacious, splendiferous, splendorous.
OPPOSITES horrid, miserable.

glory ▶ noun **1** *a sport that has won him glory abroad* **renown**, fame, prestige, honour, distinction, kudos, eminence, pre-eminence, acclaim, acclamation, celebrity, praise, accolades, laurels, recognition, note, notability, credit, repute, reputation, name, illustriousness, lustre; *informal* bouquets; *rare* laudation.
OPPOSITES shame; obscurity.
2 *glory be to God in the highest* **praise**, worship, glorification, adoration, veneration, honour, reverence, exaltation, extolment, homage, tribute, thanksgiving, thanks, blessing; *rare* laudation, magnification.

3 *a late 17th century house restored to its former glory* **magnificence**, splendour, resplendence, grandeur, majesty, greatness, impressiveness, gloriousness, nobility, pomp, stateliness, sumptuousness, opulence, beauty, elegance, brilliance, gorgeousness, splendidness.
OPPOSITES lowliness, modesty.
4 *the glories of Vermont* **wonder**, beauty, delight, wonderful thing, glorious thing, marvel, phenomenon; sight, spectacle.
▶ verb *individuals who* **gloried in** *their independence* **take great pleasure in**, exult in, rejoice in, delight in, revel in; relish, savour, greatly enjoy; take great pride in, preen oneself on, congratulate oneself on, be proud of; boast about, crow about, gloat about; *informal* get a kick out of, get a thrill out of; *archaic* plume oneself on, pique oneself on.
OPPOSITE feel ashamed of.

gloss[1] ▶ noun **1** *the healthy gloss of her jet-black hair* **shine**, sheen, lustre, gleam, patina, shininess, glossiness, brightness, brilliance, shimmer, sparkle; polish, burnish, glaze, varnish.
OPPOSITE dullness.
2 *beneath the gloss of success was a tragic private life* **facade**, veneer, surface, front, show, camouflage, disguise, mask, semblance, smokescreen, outward appearance, false appearance; window dressing, attractive appearance.
▶ verb **1** *she licked her lips in order to gloss them* **make glossy**, shine, give a shine to; glaze, polish, burnish.
2 *the company has tried to* **gloss over** *the seriousness of the situation* **conceal**, cover up, hide, camouflage, disguise, mask, veil, draw a veil over, whitewash; explain away; evade, avoid, shrug off, brush aside, play down, downplay, minimize, understate, make light of, soft-pedal, de-emphasize; *informal* brush something under the carpet; *rare* gloze over.
OPPOSITES disclose; exaggerate.

gloss[2] ▶ noun *glosses are provided in the right-hand margin* **explanation**, interpretation, exegesis, explication, elucidation; annotation, note, marginal note, footnote, commentary, comment, critique; translation, paraphrase; *rare* scholium.
▶ verb *difficult words are glossed in a footnote* **explain**, give an explanation of, interpret, explicate, elucidate; annotate, add notes/footnotes to, add a commentary to, comment on; translate, paraphrase, construe; *rare* footnote, margin, marginalize.

glossy ▶ adjective **1** *the glossy wooden floor* **shiny**, shining, gleaming, lustrous, bright, brilliant, sparkling, shimmering, glistening, sleek, silky, silken, satiny, sheeny, smooth, glassy; polished, burnished, glazed, waxed, japanned, shellacked, lacquered; *rare* nitid, patinated.
OPPOSITES dull, lustreless; matt.
2 *a glossy fashion magazine* **expensive**, high-quality, well produced; stylish, fashionable, glamorous, sophisticated; attractive, artistic; *Brit.* upmarket; coffee-table; *informal* classy, ritzy, glitzy, arty.
OPPOSITES cheap, downmarket.

glove ▶ noun **mitten**, mitt, gauntlet; *Computing* dataglove.

glow ▶ verb **1** *lights glowed from the windows of the high-street shops* **shine**, radiate, shed a glow; gleam, glimmer, flicker, flare; *rare* incandesce, phosphoresce, luminesce.
2 *the remains of a fire glowed in the hearth* **radiate heat**, burn without flames, smoulder.
3 *her cheeks began to glow with embarrassment* **flush**, blush, redden, go red, colour, colour up, go pink, crimson, go scarlet, be suffused with colour; burn, radiate heat; *archaic* mantle.
OPPOSITE pale.
4 *she glowed with pride* **radiate**, tingle, thrill; beam.
▶ noun **1** *the golden glow of the fire* **radiance**, light, brightness, luminosity, shine, gleam, glimmer, incandescence, phosphorescence, luminescence; richness, vividness, brilliance; warmth, heat; *rare* lambency, lucency, irradiance.
2 *a delicate glow spread over her face* **flush**, blush, rosiness, pinkness, redness, crimson, scarlet, reddening, ruddiness, high colour; bloom, radiance; warmth.
OPPOSITE pallor.
3 *she felt a warm glow deep inside her* **happiness**, contentment, pleasure, satisfaction, gratification, gladness.

glower ▶ verb *she glowered at him suspiciously* **scowl**, glare, stare angrily, look daggers, frown, lour, give a someone black look, pull a face; *informal* give someone a dirty look; *archaic* glout; *Scottish archaic* glunch.
OPPOSITES smile, grin.
▶ noun *the icy glower on her father's face* **scowl**, glare, angry stare, frown, black look; *informal* dirty look.

glowing ▶ adjective **1** *glowing street lights | the glowing coals* **bright**, shining, radiant, glimmering, flickering, twinkling, incandescent, candescent, luminous, luminescent, phosphorescent; lit up, lighted, illuminated, ablaze; aglow, smouldering; *literary* lambent, lucent, rutilant, ardent, fervent, fervid.
2 *his glowing cheeks* **rosy**, pink, red, reddish, rose-red, flushed, blushing; healthy-looking, fresh, radiant, blooming, ruddy, high-coloured, florid; hot, burning; *archaic* sanguine; *rare* erubescent, rubescent, rubicund.
OPPOSITE pale.
3 *the glowing colours of the textiles* **vivid**, vibrant, bright, brilliant, colourful, rich, intense, strong, radiant, warm, flaming.
OPPOSITE dull.
4 *a glowing report* **highly complimentary**, highly favourable, enthusiastic, full of praise, commendatory, praising, admiring, lionizing, ecstatic, rapturous, rhapsodic, eulogistic, laudatory, acclamatory, adulatory; fulsome; *informal* rave; *rare* encomiastical, panegyrical, laudative.
OPPOSITES critical; unenthusiastic.

glue ▶ noun *a tube of glue* **adhesive**, fixative, gum, paste, cement; epoxy, epoxy resin, sealant, size, glair; *N. Amer.* mucilage; *N. Amer. informal* stickum.
▶ verb **1** *strips of plywood were glued together* **stick**, gum, paste; affix, fix, cement, epoxy; *rare* agglutinate, conglutinate.
2 (**be glued to**) (*informal*) *her eyes were glued to the television screen* **be riveted to/by**, be gripped by, be hypnotized by, be mesmerized by; be fixed on, be fastened on, be pinned to, be locked on.

glum ▶ adjective *Kenneth looked glum and resentful* **gloomy**, downcast, downhearted, dejected, disconsolate, dispirited, despondent, crestfallen, cast down, depressed, disappointed, disheartened, discouraged, demoralized, desolate, heavy-hearted, in low spirits, low-spirited, sad, unhappy, doleful, melancholy, miserable, woebegone, mournful, forlorn, long-faced, fed up, in the doldrums, wretched, lugubrious, morose, sepulchral, saturnine, dour, mirthless; *informal* blue, down, down in the mouth, down in the dumps; *Brit. informal* brassed off, cheesed off, looking as if one had lost a pound and found a penny; *literary* dolorous; *archaic* chap-fallen, adust.
OPPOSITES cheerful, merry.

glut ▶ noun *there is a glut of cars on the market* **surplus**, excess, surfeit, superfluity, overabundance, superabundance, oversupply, mountain; too many, too much, more than enough, plethora; *informal* more … than one can shake a stick at; *rare* nimiety.
OPPOSITES dearth, scarcity.
▶ verb *the factories for recycling paper are glutted* **cram full**, fill to excess, overfill, overload, oversupply, saturate, supersaturate, flood, inundate, deluge, swamp; choke, clog; *informal* stuff.

glutinous ▶ adjective *a glutinous liquid* **sticky**, viscous, tacky, glue-like, gluey, gummy, treacly; mucilaginous, mucous; cohesive, adhesive; *Brit.* claggy; *informal* gooey, gloopy, cloggy; *N. Amer. informal* gloppy; *rare* viscid, viscoid.
OPPOSITE dry.

glutton ▶ noun **gourmand**, gourmandizer, overeater, gorger, big eater; *informal* pig, greedy pig, hog, gannet, greedy guts, gutbucket, human dustbin, gobbler, guzzler; *N. Amer. informal* chowhound; *rare* trencherman.

gluttonous ▶ adjective **greedy**, gourmandizing, voracious, insatiable, wolfish; *informal* piggish, piggy, hoggish, gannet-like, with eyes bigger than one's stomach; *rare* edacious, esurient, gourmand, ventripotent.
OPPOSITES moderate, abstemious.

gluttony ▶ noun **greed**, greediness, overeating, gourmandism, gourmandizing, gluttonousness, voraciousness, voracity, wolfishness, insatiability; *informal* piggishness, hoggishness, gutsiness; *technical* polyphagia, hyperphagia; *rare* edaciousness, edacity, gulosity, esurience.
OPPOSITES moderation, abstinence.

gnarled ▶ adjective **1** *the gnarled trunk of an old crab-apple tree* **knobbly**, knotty, knotted, gnarly, lumpy, bumpy, nodular, rough; twisted, bent, crooked, distorted, contorted; *rare* knurled, nodulous, nodose.
2 *his gnarled hands* **twisted**, bent, arthritic, misshapen; knotty, rough, leathery, weather-beaten, weathered, wrinkled, wizened; *Scottish* thrawn; *archaic* wry.

gnash ▶ verb *she wailed and gnashed her teeth* **grind**, strike together, grate, rasp, grit; *archaic* gristbite.

gnaw ▶ verb **1** *the dog* **gnawed at** *a large piece of bone* **chew**, bite, nibble, munch, crunch, champ, chomp, masticate; worry, tear; *rare* manducate, chumble.
2 *pressures which are* **gnawing away** *the industry's independence* **erode**, wear away, wear down, eat away (at), chip away (at), bite into, corrode, consume, devour; *rare* fret.
3 *the doubts continued to* **gnaw at** *her* **prey on someone's mind**, nag, plague, torment, torture, trouble, distress, worry, haunt, oppress, weigh heavily on someone's mind, be a weight on someone's mind, burden, hang over, harry, bother, exercise, fret; niggle, rankle with; fester.

gnawing ▶ adjective *a gnawing pain in her abdomen | his gnawing doubts* **persistent**, nagging, niggling, lingering, constant, continual, unrelenting, unabating; worrying worrisome, troubling, disturbing.

go ▶ verb **1** *she went forwards, step by step | he's gone into town* **move**, proceed, make one's way, advance, progress, pass, walk, wend one's way; travel, journey; repair, remove, retire; *literary* betake oneself.
2 *the road goes to London* **extend**, continue, carry on, stretch, reach; lead.
3 *the money raised will go to charity* **be given**, be donated, be assigned, be allotted, be granted, be presented, be awarded; be applied, be devoted; be handed (over), be turned over, be made over, be ceded.
4 *it's time to go* **leave**, depart, take one's leave, take oneself off, go away, go off, withdraw, absent oneself, say one's goodbyes, quit, make an exit,

G

exit; set off, set out, start out, get going, get under way, be on one's way; decamp, retreat, beat a retreat, retire, make off, clear out, make oneself scarce, slope off, run off, run away, flee; *Brit.* make a move; *informal* make tracks, shove off, push off, clear off, beat it, take off, skedaddle, scram, split, scoot, up sticks, pack one's bags; *Brit. informal* sling one's hook; *N. Amer. informal* vamoose, hightail it, cut out; *rare* abstract oneself.
OPPOSITES arrive, come.
5 *three years went past* **pass**, pass by, elapse, slip by/past, roll by/past, tick away; wear on, march on; fly by/past.
6 *a golden age that has now gone for good* **come to an end**, cease to exist, disappear, vanish, be no more, be over, run its course, fade away, melt away, evaporate; blow over; finish, end, stop, cease, terminate; *rare* evanish.
OPPOSITE return.
7 *25 of their 80 staff have gone* **be dismissed**, be given (one's) notice, be made redundant, be laid off, be let go; *informal* get the sack, be sacked, be fired, be given the boot, be given the push, get one's marching orders, be booted out, be axed, get the axe/chop; *Brit. informal* be given one's cards.
8 *her purse had gone* **be stolen**, be taken; **go missing**, disappear, be lost, be mislaid.
9 *after a few weeks, all our money had gone* **be used up**, be spent, be finished, be at an end, be exhausted, be consumed, be drained, be depleted.
10 *I'd like to see my grandchildren before I go* **die**, pass away, pass on, expire, depart this life, be no more, breathe one's last, draw one's last breath, meet one's end, meet one's death, meet one's Maker, give up the ghost, go to the great beyond, cross the great divide, shuffle off this mortal coil, perish, go the way of the/all flesh, go to one's last resting place; *informal* kick the bucket, bite the dust, croak, conk out, buy it, turn up one's toes, cash in one's chips, go belly up; *Brit. informal* snuff it, peg out, pop one's clogs.
11 *there was no warning at all before the bridge went* **collapse**, give way, fall down, cave in, fall in, crumble, disintegrate, break, fall to pieces.
12 *his hair had gone grey* **become**, get, turn, grow, come to be; *literary* wax.
13 *he heard the bell go* **make a sound**, make a noise, sound, reverberate, sound out, resound; ring, chime, peal, toll, ding, clang.
14 *everything went well* **turn out**, work out, fare, progress, develop, come out; result, end, end up; *informal* pan out; *rare* eventuate.
15 *the carpet and curtains don't really go* **match**, go together, be harmonious, harmonize, blend, suit each other, be suited, complement each other, be complementary, coordinate with each other, be compatible.
16 *my car won't go* **function**, work, be in working order, run, operate, be operative, perform.
17 *where does the cutlery go?* **be kept**, belong, have a place, be found, be located; be situated, lie, stand.
18 *this all goes to prove my point* **contribute**, help, serve; incline, tend.

□ **go about** *Ruth went about her tasks enthusiastically* **set about**, begin, embark on, make a start on, start, address oneself to, get down to, get to work on, get going on, undertake; approach, tackle, attack; *informal* get cracking on/with; *formal* commence.

□ **go along with** *he seemed happy enough to go along with your plans* **agree to/with**, fall in with, comply with, concur with, cooperate with, acquiesce in, assent to, follow; submit to, bow to, yield to, defer to.

□ **go away** *just go away and leave me in peace* **leave**, go, depart, get going, get out, be off with you, shoo; *informal* scram, be on your way, run along, beat it, skedaddle, split, vamoose, scat, get lost, push off, buzz off, shove off, clear off, go (and) jump in the lake; *Brit. informal* hop it, bog off, naff off, on your bike, get along, sling your hook; *N. Amer. informal* bug off, light out, haul off, haul ass, take a powder, hit the trail, take a hike; *Austral. informal* nick off; *Austral./NZ informal* rack off; *S. African informal* voetsak, hamba; *vulgar slang* bugger off, piss off, fuck off; *Brit. vulgar slang* sod off; *literary* begone, avaunt.
OPPOSITE return.

□ **go back on** *she went back on her promise* **renege on**, break, fail to honour, default on, backtrack on, back out of, repudiate, retract; go back on one's word, break one's word, break one's promise, do an about-face; *informal* cop out (of), rat on.
OPPOSITES keep, honour.

□ **go by** *we have to go by the referee's decision* **obey**, abide by, comply with, observe, keep to, conform to, follow, be guided by, heed, take as a guide; defer to, respect.
OPPOSITE flout.

□ **go down 1** *the ship went down in a storm* **sink**, be submerged, founder, go under.
2 *interest rates are going down* **decrease**, get lower, fall, drop, be reduced, decline; plummet, plunge, slump.
OPPOSITE rise.
3 (*informal*) *they went down 2–1 in the first leg* **lose**, **be beaten**, be defeated, suffer defeat, be vanquished, collapse, come to grief.
OPPOSITE win.
4 *his name will go down in history* **be remembered**, be recorded, be commemorated, be immortalized.

□ **go down with** (*Brit.*) *she's gone down with flu* **fall ill with**, get, develop, contract, pick up, succumb to, fall victim to, be struck down with, become infected with; *informal* take ill with; *N. Amer. informal* take sick with.

□ **go far** *you're a smart girl—you'll go far* **be successful**, succeed, be a success, do well (for oneself), do all right for oneself, make progress, achieve a great deal, get on, get somewhere, get on in the world, get ahead, advance oneself, make good, set the world on fire; *informal* make a name for oneself, make it, make one's mark, find a place in the sun.

□ **go for 1** *I went for the grilled tuna* **choose**, pick, opt for, select, plump for, take, settle on, decide on.
OPPOSITE reject.
2 *he lost his temper and went for her* **attack**, assault, hit, strike, give someone a beating, beat up, assail, launch oneself at, set upon, spring at/on, rush at, let fly at, tear into, lash out at; *informal* lay into, rough up, let someone have it, beat the living daylights out of; *Brit. informal* have a go at, duff up; *N. Amer. informal* beat up on, light into.
3 *Philip's seeing Sarah—he goes for older women* **be attracted to**, find attractive, like, fancy; prefer, favour, choose, be drawn to, gravitate towards; *informal* have a thing about.
OPPOSITE dislike.

□ **go in for** *we don't normally go in for this sort of thing* **take part in**, participate in, be a participant in, engage in, get involved in, join in, enter into, occupy oneself with, play a part in, be a party to, undertake; practise, pursue; take up, espouse, adopt, embrace.

□ **go into** *you'll need to go into the subject in greater detail* **investigate**, examine, enquire into, look into, research, study, probe, explore, delve into, try to get to the bottom of; discuss, consider, review, analyse, weigh up.

□ **go off 1** *the bomb went off at 9.20* **explode**, detonate, blow up, burst, erupt; *informal* go bang.
2 (*Brit.*) *the milk's gone off* **go bad**, go stale, go sour, turn, spoil, go rancid; decompose, go mouldy, be rotten; be past its sell-by date.

□ **go on 1** *the lecture went on for three hours* **last**, continue, carry on, run on, proceed; endure, persist, stay, remain; take.
2 *she went on about how much she loved the sea* **talk at length**, ramble, rattle on, talk on and on, carry on talking, chatter, prattle, prate, gabble, maunder, blether, blather, twitter; *informal* gab, yak, yackety-yak, yabber, yatter, shoot one's mouth off; *Brit. informal* witter, rabbit, natter, waffle, chunter; *N. Amer. informal* run off at the mouth.
3 *I'm not sure what went on that night* **happen**, take place, occur, transpire; *N. Amer. informal* go down; *literary* come to pass, betide, chance; *rare* eventuate, hap.

□ **go out 1** *the lights went out | the fire had gone out* **be turned off**, be extinguished; stop burning, die out, be doused, be quenched.
2 *he's been going out with her for about two months* **see**, take out, be someone's boyfriend/girlfriend, be romantically involved with, go around with, keep company; *informal* **date**, go steady with, go with; *Austral. informal* track square with; *Brit. informal, dated* walk out with; *N. Amer. informal, dated* step out with; *dated* court, woo.

□ **go over 1** *I need to go over the figures* **examine**, study, scrutinize, inspect, read over, look at/over, scan, run over, check; analyse, consider, appraise, weigh up, review; *informal* give something the once-over.
2 *we spent the time going over our lines* **rehearse**, practise, read/run through.

□ **go round 1** *the wheels were still going round* **spin**, revolve, turn, rotate, whirl.
2 *there's a nasty rumour going round* **be spread**, be passed round, be circulated, be put about, be in circulation, circulate, pass round, be disseminated, be broadcast.

□ **go through 1** *no one can imagine what she and the children have gone through* **undergo**, experience, face, suffer, be subjected to, live through, endure, brave, bear, tolerate, stand, withstand, put up with, brook, cope with, weather, come in for, receive, sustain; *Scottish* thole.
2 *he went through hundreds of pounds of his mother's money* **spend**, use up, run through, get through, expend, consume, exhaust, deplete; waste, fritter away, squander.
3 *he went through Susie's bag* **search**, look through, hunt through, rummage in/through, rifle through, dig into, ferret (about/around) in, root about/around in, turn inside out; check; *informal* frisk, inspect; *Austral./NZ informal* fossick through.
4 *it took me three hours to go through the report* **examine**, study, scrutinize, inspect, read over, look at/over, scan, run over, check; analyse, consider, appraise, weigh up, review.
5 *the deal has finally gone through* **be completed**, be concluded, be brought to a conclusion, be carried through, be brought off, be pulled off; be approved, be signed, be rubber-stamped.

□ **go under** *over 1,000 businesses went under in the last three months* **go bankrupt**, cease trading, go into receivership, go into liquidation, become insolvent, be liquidated, be wound up, be closed (down), be shut (down); fail; *informal* go broke, go to the wall, go belly up, fold.

□ **go without 1** *I decided to go without breakfast* **abstain from**, forgo, refrain from, do without, deny oneself; give up, cut out, swear off.
2 *she tried to make sure the children did not go without* **lack for something**,

go short, go hungry, be in need, be deprived, be in want, suffer deprivation.

▶ **noun 1** *his second go* **attempt**, try, effort, bid, endeavour; *informal* shot, stab, crack, bash, whirl, whack; *formal* essay; *archaic* assay.
2 *he still has plenty of go in him* **energy**, vigour, vitality, life, liveliness, animation, vivacity, spirit, spiritedness, verve, enthusiasm, zest, vibrancy, spark, sparkle, effervescence, exuberance, brio, buoyancy, perkiness, sprightliness; stamina, dynamism, drive, push, determination; *informal* zip, zing, pep, pizzazz, punch, bounce, fizz, oomph, get-up-and-go, vim and vigour; *N. Amer. informal* feistiness.

goad ▶ **noun 1** *he applied his goad energetically to the cattle's hindquarters* **prod**, spiked stick, spike, staff, crook, pole, rod; *Indian* ankus; *archaic* prick.
2 *the offer of economic help acted as a goad to political change* **stimulus**, **incentive**, encouragement, stimulant, stimulation, inducement, fillip, impetus, impulse, spur, prod, prompt; incitement; motive, motivation; *informal* kick in the pants, kick up the backside, shot in the arm.
▶ **verb** *the government was finally goaded into action* **provoke**, spur, prick, sting, prod, egg on, hound, badger, incite, rouse, stir, move, stimulate, motivate, excite, inflame, work/fire up, impel, pressure, pressurize, dragoon, prompt, induce, encourage, urge, inspire.

go-ahead (*informal*) ▶ **noun** *officials have given the go-ahead for the scheme* **permission**, consent, leave, licence, dispensation, warrant, clearance; authorization, assent, acquiescence, agreement, approval, seal of approval, approbation, endorsement, sanction, blessing, imprimatur, acceptance, rubber stamp, accreditation; authority, right, power, mandate; *informal* the thumbs up, the OK, the green light, the nod, someone's say-so; *rare* permit, nihil obstat.
OPPOSITE refusal.
▶ **adjective** *this technology is now standard in go-ahead companies* **enterprising**, resourceful, imaginative, ingenious, inventive, original, creative, innovative; progressive, pioneering, modern, liberal, advanced, forward-looking, forward-thinking, enlightened; spirited, enthusiastic, ambitious, energetic, entrepreneurial, vigorous, vital, high-powered; bold, daring, audacious, courageous, intrepid, adventurous; rising, up-and-coming, new, dynamic, avant-garde; *informal* go-getting.
OPPOSITES conservative; unambitious.

goal ▶ **noun** *our long-term goal is a nuclear-free world* **aim**, objective, object, grail, holy grail, end, target, design, desire, desired result, intention, intent, plan, purpose, idea, point, object of the exercise; ambition, aspiration, wish, dream, hope; resolve; *French* raison d'être.

goat *See centre pages for list of* **Goats**
▶ **noun 1** *a herd of goats* billy goat, billy, nanny goat, nanny, kid.
2 (*Brit. informal*) *he was in the mood for playing the silly goat.* See FOOL.
3 (*informal*) *Sally, just you be careful of that old goat* **lecher**, lecherous man, lascivious man, libertine, womanizer, seducer, adulterer, pervert, debauchee, rake, roué, profligate, wanton, loose-liver, sensualist, sybarite, voluptuary, Don Juan, Casanova, Lothario, Romeo; *informal* lech, dirty old man, DOM, wolf, ladykiller; *dated* rip; *archaic* fornicator.

WORD LINKS

relating to goats	**caprine**
male	**billy goat**
female	**nanny goat**
young	**kid**
collective noun	**flock, herd, trip**

gobble ▶ **verb** *he paused only to gobble down his lunch* **eat greedily/hungrily**, guzzle, bolt, gulp, swallow hurriedly, devour, wolf, cram, gorge (oneself) on, gorge oneself; *informal* tuck into, put/pack away, demolish, polish off, scoff (down), down, stuff (down), murder, shovel down, stuff one's face (with), pig oneself (on), nosh; *Brit. informal* gollop, shift; *N. Amer. informal* scarf (down/up), snarf (down/up); *rare* gluttonize, gourmandize, ingurgitate.
OPPOSITE nibble.

gobbledegook ▶ **noun** (*informal*) *the authority wrote him a letter full of legal gobbledegook* **jargon**, unintelligible language, obscure language; **gibberish**, claptrap, nonsense, rubbish, balderdash, blather, blether, argle-bargle; *informal* mumbo-jumbo, drivel, rot, tripe, hogwash, baloney, bilge, bosh, bull, bunk, guff, eyewash, piffle, twaddle, poppycock, phooey, hooey, malarkey, dribble; *Brit. informal* cobblers, codswallop, cock, stuff and nonsense, double Dutch, tosh, cack; *Scottish & N. English informal* havers; *N. Amer. informal* garbage, flapdoodle, blathers, wack, bushwa, applesauce; *informal, dated* bunkum, tommyrot, cod, gammon, toffee; *vulgar slang* shit, bullshit, horseshit, crap, bollocks, balls; *Austral./NZ vulgar slang* bulldust.

go-between ▶ **noun** *an American firm acted as go-between in the transaction* **intermediary**, middleman, agent, representative, broker, dealer, factor, liaison, liaison officer, link, linkman, linkwoman, linkperson, messenger, contact, contact man/woman/person; negotiator, honest broker, interceder, intercessor, mediator; medium.

goblet ▶ **noun wine glass**, chalice; glass, beaker, tumbler, cup; *archaic* stoup; *Scottish archaic* tass; (**goblets**) *N. Amer.* stemware.

goblin ▶ **noun hobgoblin**, gnome, dwarf, troll, imp, elf, sprite, brownie, fairy, pixie; *Scottish* kelpie; *Irish* leprechaun, pooka; *archaic* bugbear, hob.

god ▶ **noun 1** *sacrifices were made to appease the gods* **deity**, goddess, divine being, celestial being, supreme being, divinity, immortal; creator, demiurge; godhead; daemon, numen; *Hinduism* avatar.
2 *wooden gods from the Congo* **idol**, graven image, icon, golden calf, totem, talisman, fetish, mascot, juju.

WORD LINKS

relating to gods	**divine**
study of God	**theology**
fear of God	**theophobia**

godforsaken ▶ **adjective** *I realize that you are bored in this godforsaken town* **wretched**, miserable, dreary, dismal, depressing, grim, cheerless, bleak, desolate, joyless, gloomy, uninviting, discouraging, disheartening, unpromising, hopeless, dire; **deserted**, abandoned, unfrequented, unvisited, neglected, solitary, lonely, isolated, forlorn, remote, in the back of beyond, backward; *Brit. informal* grotty; *literary* drear.
OPPOSITES charming; bustling.

godless ▶ **adjective 1** *the inhumanity and ruthlessness of a godless society* **atheistic**, unbelieving, non-believing, agnostic, sceptical, heretical, faithless, irreligious, ungodly, unholy, impious, profane; infidel, barbarian, barbarous, heathen, heathenish, idolatrous, pagan; satanic, devilish, fiendish, demonic, diabolical, infernal; *rare* nullifidian.
OPPOSITE religious.
2 *a mob reeling out from their godless pleasures* **immoral**, **wicked**, sinful, wrong, morally wrong, wrongful, evil, bad, iniquitous, corrupt, irreligious, unrighteous, sacrilegious, profane, blasphemous, impious, irreverent, criminal, nefarious, depraved, degenerate, reprobate, vice-ridden, debauched, dissolute, perverted, dissipated, intemperate, decadent, unprincipled, erring, fallen, impure, sullied, tainted; *rare* peccable.
OPPOSITE virtuous.

godlike ▶ **adjective** *the Titans were godlike giants who created order from chaos* **divine**, godly, angelic, seraphic, transcendent, superhuman; spiritual, heavenly, celestial, sacred, holy, saintly, beatific, blessed; *rare* empyrean, deiform, deific.
OPPOSITE mortal.

godly ▶ **adjective** *the Puritans' verbal assaults on their less godly neighbours* **religious**, devout, pious, reverent, faithful, devoted, committed, believing, God-fearing, dutiful, saintly, holy, prayerful, churchgoing, practising.
OPPOSITE irreligious.

godsend ▶ **noun** *hire purchase was a godsend to thousands of people* **boon**, blessing, bonus, good thing, benefit, help, aid, advantage, gain, asset, privilege, luxury; windfall, bonanza, stroke of luck, piece of good fortune; *informal* perk, plus, plus point, pro; *formal* perquisite; *literary* benison.
OPPOSITE scourge.

goggle ▶ **verb** *they goggled at the well-stocked liquor stores* **stare**, gape, stare open-mouthed, stare in wonder/amazement, gawk, gaze, ogle, look fixedly, look vacantly; *informal* rubberneck; *Brit. informal* gawp.
OPPOSITES glance; ignore.

going-over ▶ **noun** (*informal*) **1** *he is subjected to a comprehensive going-over in two biographies* **examination**, inspection, exploration, investigation, probe, check, check-up; assessment, review, discussion, study, analysis, appraisal, critique; treatment, consideration, coverage, handling; *informal* once-over.
2 *the flat needs a going-over before you have visitors* **clean**, wipe, sponge, mop, swab, flush, scrub, hose-down, swill, lather, soap; *informal* vacuum, once-over.
3 *the thugs gave him a good going-over* **beating**, thrashing, thumping, pounding, pummelling, drubbing, slapping, smacking, hammering, hitting, striking, punching, knocking, thwacking, cuffing, buffeting, battering, boxing, mauling, pelting, lambasting; assault, attack; flaying, whipping, horsewhipping, lashing, cudgelling, clubbing, birching; corporal punishment, chastisement; *N. Amer.* bullwhipping; *informal* beating-up, duffing-up, doing-over, belting, bashing, pasting, walloping, whacking, clobbering, slugging, tanning, biffing, bopping, hiding.

goings-on ▶ **plural noun** *all those disturbing goings-on in soap operas* **events**, happenings, affairs, business; behaviour, conduct; mischief, misbehaviour, misconduct, funny business, chicanery, dishonesty, deception, deceit, trickery, intrigue, skulduggery, subterfuge, machinations; *informal* monkey business, hanky-panky, shenanigans, carryings-on, carry-on, fooling around, playing around; *Brit. informal* jiggery-pokery, monkey tricks; *N. Amer. informal* monkeyshines; *archaic* knavery.

gold ▶ **noun** *Holland won the gold* **gold medal**, first prize.

WORD LINKS

relating to gold	**auric, aurous**
related prefixes	**aur-, chrys-**
containing gold	**auriferous**
fear of gold	**aurophobia, chrysophobia**

golden ▶ **adjective 1** *her beautiful golden hair* **gold-coloured**, blonde,

G

blonde, yellow, yellowish, fair, flaxen, tow-coloured; bright, gleaming, resplendent, brilliant, shining; *rare* aureate.
OPPOSITES brunette, dark.
2 *it was a golden time indeed* **successful**, prosperous, flourishing, thriving; favourable, propitious, auspicious, providential, encouraging, lucky, fortunate; happy, joyful, delightful, glorious, precious, treasured.
OPPOSITES unsuccessful; unhappy.
3 *it will be a golden opportunity for us* **excellent**, fine, superb, splendid, tremendous, special, unique, favourable, opportune, exciting, promising, bright, brilliant, rosy, full of promise, optimistic, hopeful, advantageous, profitable, valuable, fortunate, providential, auspicious, propitious.
4 *the golden girl of British tennis* **gifted**, talented, skilful, skilled, accomplished, brilliant, expert, consummate; **popular**, admired, attractive, favourite, favoured, cherished, beloved, pet, acclaimed, applauded, praised, lauded; *informal* blue-eyed, crack, top-notch, ace, wizard.

golf ▶ noun. *See centre pages for list of* **Golf Clubs**

gone ▶ adjective **1** *I wasn't gone long* **away**, absent, off, out, not present, non-attending, truant; missing, lacking, unavailable; *Latin* in absentia; *informal* AWOL.
OPPOSITE present.
2 *those days are gone* **past**, gone by, over, over and done with, no more, done, dead and buried, finished, completed, ended, forgotten, extinct.
OPPOSITES extant, here.
3 *the milk's all gone* **used up**, consumed, exhausted, finished, spent, depleted, drained, at an end.
4 *an aunt of mine, long since gone* **dead**, deceased, expired, departed, no more, passed on, passed away; late, lost, lamented; perished, fallen, slain, slaughtered, killed, murdered; lifeless, having breathed one's last, defunct, extinct; *informal* (as) dead as a doornail, six feet under, pushing up daisies, under the sod; *euphemistic* with God, asleep, at peace; *rare* demised, exanimate.
OPPOSITE alive.

goo ▶ noun (*informal*) *the treacly goo that stuck to my jacket* **sticky substance**, ooze, sludge, muck, slush, stickiness; *informal* gunk, yuck, crud, gook, gloop; *Brit. informal* gunge, grot; *N. Amer. informal* guck, glop.

good ▶ adjective **1** *there is always a market for a good product* **fine**, of high quality, of a high standard, quality, superior; **satisfactory**, acceptable, adequate, in order, up to scratch, up to the mark, up to standard, up to par, competent, not bad, all right; **excellent**, superb, outstanding, magnificent, of the highest quality, of the highest standard, exceptional, marvellous, wonderful, first-rate, first-class, superlative, splendid, admirable, worthy, sterling; *informal* great, OK, hunky-dory, A1, ace, terrific, tremendous, smashing, fantastic, fab, top-notch, tip-top, class, awesome, magic, wicked; *Brit. informal* brilliant, brill; *Austral. informal* beaut, bonzer; *Brit. informal, dated* spiffing, ripping, cracking, topping, top hole, wizard, capital, champion; *N. Amer. informal, dated* swell.
OPPOSITE bad.
2 *he is basically a good person* **virtuous**, righteous, moral, morally correct, ethical, upright, upstanding, high-minded, right-minded, right-thinking, principled, exemplary, clean, law-abiding, lawful, irreproachable, blameless, guiltless, unimpeachable, just, honest, honourable, unbribable, incorruptible; scrupulous, reputable, decent, respectable, noble, lofty, elevated, worthy, trustworthy, meritorious, praiseworthy, commendable, admirable, laudable; pure, pure as the driven snow, whiter than white, sinless, saintly, saintlike, godly, angelic; *informal* squeaky clean.
OPPOSITE wicked.
3 *the children are good with most of their teachers* **well behaved**, **obedient**, dutiful, well mannered, well brought up, polite, civil, courteous, respectful, deferential, manageable, compliant, acquiescent, tractable, malleable.
OPPOSITE naughty.
4 *it was a good thing to do* **right**, correct, proper, decorous, seemly; appropriate, fitting, apt, suitable; convenient, expedient, favourable, auspicious, propitious, opportune, felicitous, timely, well judged, well timed, seasonable; *archaic* meet.
5 *she's a good driver | that was good work* **capable**, able, proficient, adept, adroit, accomplished, seasoned, skilful, skilled, gifted, talented, masterly, virtuoso, expert, knowledgeable, qualified, trained; *informal* great, mean, wicked, deadly, nifty, crack, ace, wizard, magic; *N. Amer. informal* crackerjack; *vulgar slang* shit-hot.
6 *he's been a good friend to me* **reliable**, dependable, trustworthy, true, tried and true, faithful, devoted, steady, steadfast, staunch, unswerving, unwavering, constant, loyal, trusty, dutiful, dedicated, committed, unfailing.
7 *the dogs look in good condition* **healthy**, fine, sound, tip-top, hale, hale and hearty, hearty, lusty, fit, robust, sturdy, strong, vigorous.
OPPOSITES poor; ill; diseased.
8 *that was a good party* **enjoyable**, pleasant, agreeable, pleasing, pleasurable, delightful, great, nice, lovely, amusing, diverting, jolly, merry, lively, festive, cheerful, convivial, congenial, sociable; *informal* super, fantastic, fabulous, fab, terrific, glorious, grand, magic, out of this world, cool; *Brit. informal* brilliant, brill, smashing; *N. Amer. informal* peachy, neat, ducky; *Austral./NZ informal* beaut, bonzer; *Brit. informal, dated* capital, wizard, corking, spiffing, ripping, top-hole, topping, champion, beezer; *N. Amer. informal, dated* swell; *rare* frabjous.
OPPOSITE terrible.
9 *it was good of you to come* **kind**, kindly, kind-hearted, good-hearted, friendly, obliging, generous, charitable, magnanimous, gracious, sympathetic, benevolent, benign, altruistic, unselfish, selfless.
OPPOSITE unkind.
10 *tomorrow would be a good time to call* **convenient**, suitable, appropriate, fitting, fit, suited, agreeable; **opportune**, timely, well timed, favourable, advantageous, seasonable, expedient, felicitous, propitious, auspicious, happy, providential; *archaic* commodious.
OPPOSITE inconvenient.
11 *milk is good for you* **wholesome**, health-giving, healthful, healthy, nourishing, nutritious, nutritional, strengthening, beneficial, salubrious, salutary.
12 *are these eggs still good?* **edible**, safe to eat, fit to eat, fit to be eaten, fit for human consumption; fresh, wholesome, consumable, comestible.
13 *the restaurant provided good food* **delicious**, mouth-watering, appetizing, tasty, flavoursome, flavourful, delectable, toothsome, inviting, enjoyable, palatable; succulent, luscious, rich, sweet; savoury, piquant; *informal* scrumptious, delish, scrummy, yummy, yum-yum; *Brit. informal* moreish; *N. Amer. informal* finger-licking, nummy; *literary* ambrosial; *rare* ambrosian, nectareous, nectarean, flavorous, sapid.
14 *give me one good reason why I should go* **valid**, genuine, authentic, legitimate, sound, bona fide; **convincing**, persuasive, forceful, striking, telling, potent, powerful, strong, cogent, compelling; trenchant, weighty, important, meaningful, influential.
15 *we had to wait a good hour* **whole**, full, entire, complete, solid, not less than.
OPPOSITE part.
16 *a good number of them lost their lives* **considerable**, sizeable, substantial, appreciable, significant; goodly, tolerable, fair, reasonable, tidy, hefty; ample, plentiful, abundant, superabundant, great, large, lavish, profuse, generous; marked, noticeable; *informal* not to be sneezed at, OK; *literary* plenteous.
OPPOSITE small.
17 *this is something you would only tell a good friend* **close**, intimate, dear, bosom; close-knit, inseparable, attached, loving, devoted, faithful, constant; special, best, fast, firm, valued, treasured, cherished.
OPPOSITE distant.
18 *don't you go getting your good clothes grubby* **best**, finest, newest, nice, nicest, smart, smartest, special, party, Sunday, formal; *informal* dressy.
OPPOSITES casual; scruffy.
19 *good weather* **fine**, fair, dry; bright, clear, sunny, sunshiny, cloudless, unclouded, without a cloud in the sky; calm, windless, tranquil; warm, mild, balmy, summery, clement; agreeable, pleasant, nice, benign.

□ **in good part** *luckily the police took the joke in good part* **good-naturedly**, good-humouredly, without offence, amicably, favourably, with forbearance, patiently, tolerantly, indulgently, cheerfully, well; not be offended by, not take offence at, not be upset by, not be bothered by, not disapprove of, not resent, not mind, take kindly to.

□ **make good** *the working-class boy who made good* **succeed**, achieve success, be successful, be a success, do well, get ahead, reach the top, become famous, achieve recognition, distinguish oneself, set the world on fire; prosper, flourish, thrive, advance; *Brit.* set the Thames on fire; *informal* make it, make the grade, cut it, crack it, make a name for oneself, make one's mark, get somewhere, arrive, do all right for oneself, bring home the bacon, find a place in the sun.
OPPOSITE fail.

□ **make something good 1** *he promised to make good any damage* **repair**, mend, fix, patch up, put right, set right, put to rights, see to; restore, remedy, rectify, put back into its original condition, make as good as new; rebuild, reconstruct, remodel, refit, refurbish, recondition; *N. English* fettle.
2 *they made good their escape* **effect**, conduct, perform, implement, execute, carry out, perpetrate; **achieve**, accomplish, succeed in, realize, attain, manage, engineer, bring about, bring off, carry off, carry through; *rare* effectuate.
3 *they hope he will make good his promise of payment* **fulfil**, carry out, carry through, implement, execute, effect, discharge, perform, honour, redeem; keep, observe, abide by, comply with, obey, respect, conform to, stick to, act in accordance with, act according to, have regard to, heed, follow, pay attention to, defer to, take notice of, be bound by, keep faith with, live up to, stand by, adhere to.

▶ noun **1** *complex issues of good and evil* **virtue**, **righteousness**, virtuousness, goodness, morality, ethicalness, uprightness, upstandingness, integrity, principle, dignity, rectitude, rightness; honesty, truth, truthfulness, honour, incorruptibility, probity, propriety, worthiness, worth, merit; irreproachableness, blamelessness, purity, pureness, lack of corruption, justice, justness, fairness.

OPPOSITE wickedness.

2 *don't worry, it's all for your good* **benefit**, advantage, profit, gain, interest, welfare, well-being, enjoyment, satisfaction, comfort, ease, convenience; help, aid, assistance, use, usefulness, avail, service, behalf.
OPPOSITE disadvantage.

□ **for good** *those bad old days are gone for good* **forever**, permanently, for always, for good and all, perpetually, eternally, (for) evermore, for ever and ever, for all (future) time, until/to the end of time, world without end, endlessly, timelessly, for eternity, in perpetuity, everlastingly, enduringly, never to return; *Scottish* aye; *N. Amer.* forevermore; *informal* for keeps, until hell freezes over, until doomsday, until the cows come home; *archaic* for aye; *rare* immortally, deathlessly, imperishably, abidingly, sempiternally, perdurably.
OPPOSITE temporarily.

▶ **exclamation** *good, that's settled* **fine**, very well, all right, right, right then, right you are, yes, agreed; *informal* okay, OK, oke, okey-dokey, okey-doke, wilco, roger; *Brit. informal* righto, righty-ho; *Indian informal* acha.

goodbye ▶ **exclamation** *goodbye, safe journey!* **farewell**, adieu; *Austral./NZ* hooray; *S. African* check you; *French* au revoir; *Italian* ciao; *German* auf Wiedersehen; *Spanish* adios; *Japanese* sayonara; *Latin* vale; *informal* bye, bye-bye, so long, see you, see you later, catch you later; *Brit. informal* cheers, cheerio, ta-ta; *N. English informal* ta-ra; *N. Amer. informal* later, laters; *informal, dated* toodle-oo, toodle-pip, pip pip.
OPPOSITE hello.

good-for-nothing ▶ **adjective** *a good-for-nothing layabout* **useless**, worthless, incompetent, inefficient, inept, ne'er-do-well; lazy, idle, slothful, indolent, shiftless, spiritless, apathetic, aimless, unambitious, unenterprising; *informal* no-good, no-account, lousy.
OPPOSITE worthy.

▶ **noun** *he considered the workers lazy good-for-nothings* **ne'er-do-well**, layabout, do-nothing, idler, loafer, slob, lounger, sluggard, laggard, slugabed, malingerer, shirker; *informal* skiver, waster, slacker, lazybones, lead-swinger, couch potato; *Brit. informal* scrimshanker; *archaic* wastrel; *French archaic* fainéant.

good-humoured ▶ **adjective** *he was too good-humoured to be offended* **genial**, friendly, affable, cordial, congenial, amiable, warm, easy-going, approachable, sympathetic, well disposed, good-natured, cheerful, cheery, neighbourly, hospitable, companionable, comradely, bluff, easy to get along with; sociable, convivial, outgoing, extrovert, extroverted, gregarious, company-loving, hail-fellow-well-met; *informal* chummy, pally; *Brit. informal* matey; *N. Amer. informal* buddy-buddy, clubby, regular.
OPPOSITE grumpy.

good-looking ▶ **adjective** *she was still good-looking without her make-up* **attractive**, nice-looking, beautiful, pretty, as pretty as a picture, handsome, lovely, stunning, striking, arresting, gorgeous, prepossessing, winning, fetching, captivating, bewitching, beguiling, engaging, charming, charismatic, enchanting, appealing, delightful, irresistible; sexy, sexually attractive, sexual, seductive, alluring, tantalizing, ravishing, desirable, sultry, sensuous, sensual, erotic, arousing, luscious, lush, nubile; *Scottish & N. English* bonny; *informal* fanciable, beddable, tasty, hot, smashing, knockout, drop-dead gorgeous, out of this world, easy on the eye, come-hither, come-to-bed; *Brit. informal* fit; *N. Amer. informal* cute, foxy, bootylicious; *Austral./NZ informal* spunky; *literary* beauteous; *dated* taking, well favoured; *archaic* comely, fair; *rare* sightly, pulchritudinous.
OPPOSITE ugly.

goodly ▶ **adjective** *£1500 is a goodly sum* **fairly large**, sizeable, substantial, considerable, not inconsiderable, respectable, significant, largish, biggish, decent, decent-sized, generous, handsome; *Scottish & N. English* bonny; *informal* tidy, not to be sneezed at, serious.
OPPOSITE paltry.

good-natured ▶ **adjective** *the crowd was rowdy but good-natured* **warm-hearted**, friendly, amiable; neighbourly, benevolent, well disposed, favourably disposed, kind, kindly, kind-hearted, generous, magnanimous, unselfish, considerate, thoughtful, obliging, helpful, supportive, charitable; understanding, sympathetic, lenient, tolerant, easy-going, patient, accommodating; *Brit. informal* decent.
OPPOSITE malicious.

goodness ▶ **noun 1** *he was a dangerous criminal, but he had some goodness in him* **virtue**, virtuousness, good, righteousness, morality, ethicalness, uprightness, upstandingness, integrity, principle, dignity, rectitude, rightness; honesty, truth, truthfulness, honourableness, honourability, honour, incorruptibility, probity, propriety, decency, respectability, nobility, nobility of soul/spirit, nobleness, worthiness, worth, merit, trustworthiness, meritoriousness, irreproachableness, blamelessness, purity, pureness, lack of corruption; justice, justness, fairness, equity, equitableness, impartiality, lawfulness, legality.
OPPOSITE wickedness.

2 *God's goodness towards us* **kindness**, kindliness, kind-heartedness, warm-heartedness, tender-heartedness, humaneness, humanity, mildness, benevolence, benignity, tenderness, warmth, motherliness, fatherliness, affection, lovingness, love, goodwill; sympathy, compassion, care, concern, understanding, tolerance, patience, indulgence, generosity, charity, charitableness, leniency, clemency, forbearance, magnanimity; helpfulness, considerateness, thoughtfulness, consideration, niceness, courtesy, politeness, decency, graciousness, neighbourliness, pleasantness, public-spiritedness, friendliness, geniality, congeniality, amiability, cordiality.
OPPOSITE meanness.

3 *slow cooking can help to retain the goodness of the food* **nutritional value**, nutrition, nutrients, wholesomeness, nourishment; *rare* nutriment.

goods ▶ **plural noun 1** *the manufacturer then dispatches the goods to a wholesaler* **merchandise**, wares, stock, commodities, line, lot, produce, products, articles; imports, exports; *rare* vendibles.

2 *they had to dispose of the dead man's goods* **property**, possessions, personal possessions, personal effects, effects, worldly goods, chattels, goods and chattels, valuables, accoutrements, appurtenances, paraphernalia, trappings; *informal* things, stuff, junk, gear, kit, rubbish, bits and pieces, bits and bobs; *Brit. informal* clobber, gubbins; *vulgar slang* shit, crap.

3 (*Brit.*) *most goods went by train* **freight**, cargo; load, haul, consignment, delivery, shipment; *archaic* lading; *rare* freightage.

good-tempered ▶ **adjective** *he remained good-tempered in spite of being in such demand* **equable**, even-tempered, imperturbable, unexcitable; unruffled, unperturbed, unflustered, undisturbed, unagitated, untroubled, well balanced; easy-going, calm, relaxed, composed, collected, self-possessed, cool, {cool, calm, and collected}, at ease, as cool as a cucumber; nonchalant, insouciant, blithe, mellow, mild; serene, tranquil, placid, steady, stable, quiet, level-headed; *informal* unflappable, unfazed, together, laid-back; *rare* equanimous.
OPPOSITE excitable.

G

goodwill ▶ **noun** *the UN is dependent on the goodwill of its most powerful members* **benevolence**, compassion, kind-heartedness, big-heartedness, goodness, kindness, kindliness, consideration, charity; cooperation, collaboration, friendliness, thoughtfulness, decency, amity, sympathy, understanding, amenability, neighbourliness, mutual support.
OPPOSITE hostility.

goody-goody ▶ **adjective** (*informal*) *the goody-goody prefects will probably tell the headmistress* **self-righteous**, sanctimonious, pious, **prim and proper**, prim, proper, strait-laced, prudish, priggish, puritanical, moralistic, prissy, mimsy, niminy-piminy, shockable, Victorian, old-maidish, schoolmistressy, schoolmarmish, governessy; *informal* starchy, square, fuddy-duddy, stick-in-the-mud; *rare* Grundyish, Pecksniffian.

gooey ▶ **adjective** (*informal*) **1** *he wiped off the gooey mess with towels* **sticky**, viscous, viscid; **gluey**, tacky, gummy, treacly, syrupy; mucilaginous; *Brit.* claggy; *Scottish & N. English* clarty; *informal* gloopy, cloggy, gungy, icky; *N. Amer. informal* gloppy; *rare* viscoid.
OPPOSITES dry; hard.

2 *Mrs McSpadden got all gooey over young Kenneth* **sentimental**, mawkish, over-sentimental, overemotional, cloying, sickly, saccharine, sugary, syrupy; romantic, hearts-and-flowers; *Brit.* twee; *informal* slushy, sloppy, mushy, schmaltzy, cutesy, lovey-dovey, drippy, sloshy, soupy, treacly, cheesy, corny, icky, sick-making, toe-curling; *Brit. informal* soppy; *N. Amer. informal* cornball, sappy, hokey; *trademark* Mills-and-Boon.
OPPOSITES cold; undemonstrative.

goose ▶ **noun.** *See centre pages for list of* **Birds**

WORD LINKS

male	**gander**
female	**goose**
young	**gosling**
collective noun	**gaggle (on land), skein/team/wedge (in flight)**
relating to geese	**anserine**

gore[1] ▶ **noun** *the film's gratuitous gore* **blood**, bloodiness; bloodshed, slaughter, carnage, butchery; *rare* cruor, grume.

gore[2] ▶ **verb** *he was gored in the leg by the bull* **pierce**, stab, stick, impale, puncture, penetrate, spear, spit, horn.

gorge ▶ **noun** *here the river rushes through a gorge* **ravine**, canyon, gully, pass, defile, couloir, deep narrow valley; chasm, abyss, gulf; *S. English* chine, bunny; *N. English* clough, gill, thrutch; *Scottish* cleuch, heugh; *N. Amer.* gulch, coulee, flume; *American Spanish* arroyo, barranca, quebrada; *Indian* nullah, khud; *S. African* sloot, kloof, donga; *rare* khor.

▶ **verb 1** *they gorged themselves on Cornish cream teas* **stuff**, cram, fill; glut, satiate, sate, surfeit, overindulge, overfill, overeat; *informal* pig.

2 *huge carrion birds gorged on the flesh* **eat greedily/hungrily**, guzzle, gobble, bolt, gulp (down), swallow hurriedly, devour, wolf, cram; *informal* tuck into, put/pack away, demolish, polish off, scoff (down), down, stuff (down), murder, shovel down, stuff one's face (with), nosh; *Brit. informal* gollop, shift; *N. Amer. informal* scarf (down/up), snarf (down/up), inhale; *rare* raven, gluttonize, gourmandize, ingurgitate.
OPPOSITE nibble.

gorgeous ▶ **adjective 1** *a simply gorgeous man* **good-looking**, attractive, nice-looking, handsome, lovely, beautiful, pretty, as pretty as a picture, stunning, striking, arresting, prepossessing, winning, fetching, captivating, bewitching, beguiling, engaging, charming, charismatic, enchanting, appealing, delightful, irresistible; sexy, sexually attractive,

sexual, seductive, alluring, tantalizing, ravishing, desirable, sultry, sensuous, sensual, erotic, arousing, luscious, lush, nubile; *Scottish & N. English* bonny; *informal* fanciable, beddable, tasty, studly, hot, smashing, knockout, out of this world, easy on the eye, come-hither, come-to-bed; *Brit. informal* fit; *N. Amer. informal* cute, foxy, bootylicious; *Austral./NZ informal* spunky; *literary* beauteous; *dated* taking, well favoured; *archaic* comely, fair; *rare* sightly, pulchritudinous.
OPPOSITE ugly.
2 *a little restaurant with gorgeous views across the valley* **spectacular**, splendid, superb, wonderful, grand, impressive, awe-inspiring, awesome, astounding, astonishing, amazing, stunning, breathtaking, stupendous, incredible; *informal* sensational, out of this world, fabulous, fantastic; *literary* wondrous.
OPPOSITE uninteresting.
3 *gorgeous uniforms of scarlet and gold* **resplendent**, magnificent, stately, imposing, sumptuous, luxurious, elegant, opulent, dazzling, brilliant, glittering.
OPPOSITE drab.
4 (*informal*) *gorgeous weather* **excellent**, marvellous, superb, very good, first-rate, first-class, wonderful, delightful, outstanding, exceptional, magnificent, splendid, superlative, matchless, peerless; *informal* great, glorious, terrific, tremendous, smashing, fantastic, sensational, fabulous, ace, fab, A1, cool, awesome, magic, wicked, tip-top, top-notch, out of sight, out of this world, way-out, capital; *Brit. informal* brilliant, brill, wizard; *Austral./NZ informal* bonzer; *Brit. informal, dated* spiffing, topping, top-hole.
OPPOSITE terrible.

G

gorilla ▶ noun
WORD LINKS
mature male mountain gorilla **silverback**
collective noun **band**

gory ▶ adjective **1** *the ritual slaughter is a gory ceremony* **grisly**, gruesome, violent, bloodthirsty, bloody, brutal, savage; ghastly, frightful, horrid, horrifying, fearful, hideous, macabre, spine-chilling, horrible, horrendous, grim, awful, dire, dreadful, terrible, horrific; disgusting, repulsive, repugnant, revolting, repellent, sickening, distressing, shocking, appalling, abominable, loathsome, abhorrent, odious, monstrous, unspeakable; *informal* blood-and-thunder, blood-and-guts, sick, sick-making, gut-churning, gross; *archaic* sanguinary, disgustful, loathly.
OPPOSITES charming; uplifting.
2 *gory pieces of human skin and bone* **bloody**, bloodstained, bloodsoaked, blood-spattered.

gospel *See centre pages for list of Books of the* **Bible**
▶ noun **1** (**the gospel**) *the Gospel was spread informally by missionaries* **Christian teaching**, Christ's teaching, the life of Christ, the word of God, the good news, Christian doctrine, the New Testament, the writings of the evangelists.
2 *one should not treat any historical document as gospel* **the truth**, the whole truth, the naked truth, gospel truth, God's truth, the honest truth; fact, actual fact, what actually/really happened, reality, actuality, factuality, the case, so, verity, a certainty.
OPPOSITE a lie.
3 *the Dalai Lama's gospel of non-violence* **doctrine**, dogma, teaching, principle, ethic, creed, credo, theory, thesis, ideology, idea, ideal, position; belief, tenet, canon, conviction, persuasion, opinion.

gossamer ▶ noun *her dress swirled like gossamer* **cobweb**, spider's web; silk, silky substance, Japanese silk, gauze, tissue, chiffon; thistledown, down, feather.
▶ adjective *beautiful ladies in gossamer veils* **ultra-fine**, fine, diaphanous, gauzy, gauzelike, gossamer-thin, gossamer-like, gossamery, delicate, filmy, floaty, chiffony, cobwebby, feathery, silky, silken, wispy, thin, light, lightweight, insubstantial, papery, flimsy, frail; translucent, transparent, see-through, sheer; *rare* transpicuous, translucid.
OPPOSITES heavy; opaque.

gossip ▶ noun **1** *tell me all the gossip about the new tenants* **tittle-tattle**, tattle, rumour(s), whispers, stories, tales, canards, titbits; idle talk, scandal, hearsay; malicious gossip, whispering campaign, smear campaign; *French* bavardage, on dit; *German* Kaffeeklatsch; *W. Indian* labrish, shu-shu; *informal* dirt, buzz, mud-slinging; *Brit. informal* goss; *N. Amer. informal* scuttlebutt; *S. African informal* skinder; *rare* bruit.
OPPOSITES facts, the truth.
2 *they then adjourn to the pub for a glass and a gossip* **chat**, talk, conversation, chatter, heart-to-heart, tête-à-tête, powwow, blether, blather; conference, discussion, dialogue, exchange; *Indian* adda; *informal* chit-chat, jaw, gas, confab, goss; *Brit. informal* natter, chinwag, rabbit; *Scottish & N. English informal* crack; *N. Amer. informal* rap, bull session, gabfest; *Austral./NZ informal* mag, yarn; *rare* confabulation, colloquy.
3 *Myra is a dear, but she's also a gossip* **scandalmonger**, gossipmonger, tattler, tittle-tattler, busybody, muckraker; *informal* bad-mouth, bad-mouther; *rare* quidnunc, calumniator.
▶ verb **1** *she had gossiped about his wife's illness* **spread rumours**, spread gossip, circulate rumours, spread stories, tittle-tattle, tattle, talk, whisper, tell tales, muckrake; *informal* dish the dirt; *S. African informal* skinder; *literary* bruit something abroad/about.
2 *people sat around gossiping as they drank* **chat**, talk, converse, speak to each other, discuss things, have a talk, have a chat, have a tête-à-tête, have a conversation, engage in conversation; *informal* gas, have a confab, chew the fat/rag, jaw, rap, yak, yap; *Brit. informal* natter, have a chinwag, chinwag; *N. Amer. informal* shoot the breeze, shoot the bull, visit; *Austral./NZ informal* mag; *formal* confabulate.

gouge ▶ verb *a tunnel had been gouged out of the mountain* **scoop out**, burrow (out), hollow out, excavate; cut (out), hack (out), chisel (out), dig (out), scrape (out), claw (out), scratch (out); *literary* delve.

gourmand ▶ noun *gourmands who care more for quantity than quality* **glutton**, gourmandizer, overeater, big/good eater, (good) trencherman, (good) trencherwoman; *informal* pig, greedy pig, hog, gannet, greedy guts, gutbucket, human dustbin, gobbler, guzzler; *N. Amer. informal* chowhound.

gourmet ▶ noun *even the most demanding gourmets adore the restaurants on Lake Como* **gastronome**, epicure, epicurean; connoisseur; *French* bon vivant, bon viveur; *informal* foodie.

govern ▶ verb **1** *the Conservative Party governed the province for the next five years* **rule**, preside over, be in power over, reign over, control, exercise control over, have control of, be in control of, be in charge of, command, hold sway over, lead, be the leader of, dominate, run, head, direct, administer, order, manage, regulate, guide, conduct, oversee, supervise, superintend, be at the helm of, steer, pilot; *informal* be in the driving seat; *literary* sway.
2 *the rules governing social behaviour* **determine**, decide, control, regulate, direct, rule, dictate, condition, form, shape; affect, have an effect on, influence, exert influence on, be a factor in, sway, act on, work on, mould, modify, alter, touch, have an impact on, impact on.
3 *Maria made a fresh effort to govern her feelings* **control**, restrain, keep in check, check, curb, hold back, keep back, bridle, rein in, keep a tight rein on, subdue, constrain, contain.

governess ▶ noun **tutor**, instructress, duenna; *French* Mademoiselle; *archaic* tutoress, tutress, tutrice, tutrix.

government *See centre pages for lists of* **Governments** **Political Philosophies and Systems**
▶ noun **1** *the government has announced defence cuts of a billion pounds* **administration**, executive, regime, authority, powers that be, directorate, council, leadership, management; cabinet, ministry; rule, term of office, incumbency; *informal* top brass.
2 *the executive council was to assist him in the government of the country* **rule**, running, direction, administration, leadership, leading, control, regulation, guidance, guiding, management, conduct, supervision, superintendence, steering.

governor ▶ noun *the governor of the province | a prisoner governor* **administrator**, ruler, chief, leader, principal, head; premier, president, viceroy, chancellor; manager, director, chairman, chairwoman, chairperson, chair, superintendent, supervisor, commissioner, controller, master, warden, overseer, organizer; member of the board; *informal* boss.
WORD LINKS
relating to a governor **gubernatorial**

gown ▶ noun **dress**, frock, shift, robe; garment, costume.

grab ▶ verb **1** *Doreen grabbed his arm, swinging him round* **seize**, grasp, snatch, seize hold of, grab hold of, take hold of, catch hold of, lay hold of, lay (one's) hands on, get one's hands on, take a grip of, fasten round, grapple, grip, clasp, clutch; catch at, take, pluck; *informal* collar.
OPPOSITE release.
2 (*informal*) *Clint Eastwood grabbed a fistful of awards last night* **obtain**, acquire, come by, carry off, come to have, get, receive, gain, earn, win, come into, come in for, take possession of, take receipt of, be given; buy, purchase, procure, possess oneself of, secure, snap up; gather, collect, pick up, appropriate, amass, build up, hook, net, land; achieve, attain; *informal* get/lay one's hands on, get one's mitts on, get hold of, bag, score, swing, nab, collar, pull down, cop; *Brit. informal* blag.
▶ noun *she made a grab for his gun* **lunge for**, attempt to grab.
□ **up for grabs** (*informal*) *dozens of prizes are up for grabs* **available**, obtainable, to be had, there for the taking; up for sale, on the market, waiting to be bought; untaken, unengaged; *informal* yours for the asking, on tap, gettable.

grace ▶ noun **1** *she has the natural grace of a ballerina* **elegance**, stylishness, poise, finesse, charm; gracefulness, dexterity, adroitness; deftness, fluidity of movement, fluency, flow, suppleness, smoothness, ease, effortlessness, naturalness, neatness, precision, agility, nimbleness, light-footedness; *informal* poetry in motion; *rare* flowingness, lightsomeness.
OPPOSITES stiffness, inelegance.
2 *he at least had the grace to look sheepish* **courtesy**, courteousness, politeness, manners, good manners, mannerliness, civility, decorum, decency, propriety, breeding, respect, respectfulness; consideration, thought, thoughtfulness, tact, tactfulness, diplomacy, etiquette.
OPPOSITE effrontery.
3 *Americans found it hard to see another president fall from grace* **favour**,

approval, approbation, acceptance, commendation, esteem, regard, respect, preferment, liking, support, goodwill.
OPPOSITE disfavour.
4 *he was granted a house by grace of the king* **favour**, good will, generosity, kindness, benefaction, beneficence, indulgence.
5 *they have been given five days' grace to decide* **deferment**, deferral, postponement, suspension, putting off/back, adjournment, delay, shelving, rescheduling, interruption, arrest, pause; respite, stay, moratorium, reprieve; *N. Amer.* tabling; *N. Amer. Law* continuation; *rare* put-off.
6 *say grace* **prayer of thanks**, thanksgiving, blessing, benediction.
▶ **verb 1** *the occasion was graced by the presence of Lady Thomson* **dignify**, distinguish, add distinction to, add dignity to, honour, bestow honour on, favour, enhance, add lustre to, magnify, ennoble, glorify, elevate, make lofty, aggrandize, upgrade.
2 *the dolphin fresco may originally have graced the floor of an upper chamber* **adorn**, embellish, decorate, furnish, ornament, add ornament to, enhance; beautify, prettify, enrich, bedeck, deck (out), garnish, emblazon, gild, set off; *informal* get up, do up, do out; *literary* bejewel, bedizen, caparison, furbelow.

graceful ▶ **adjective 1** *her simple, graceful clothes have won legions of devotees* **elegant**, stylish, tasteful, refined, sophisticated, dignified, distinguished, discerning, with good taste, poised; fashionable, cultured, cultivated, beautiful, attractive, appealing, lovely, comely; charming, polished, suave, urbane, dashing; luxurious, sumptuous, opulent, grand, plush, exquisite; *informal* swanky.
OPPOSITE inelegant.
2 *graceful dancers* **fluid**, fluent, flowing, supple, smooth, easy, effortless, natural, elegant, stylish, neat, precise, agile, nimble, light-footed, deft, dexterous, adroit.
OPPOSITES stiff; ungainly.

graceless ▶ **adjective** *a loud, graceless teenager* **gauche**, maladroit, inept, socially awkward, socially inept, socially unsure, lacking in social graces, unpolished, unsophisticated, uncultured, uncultivated, unrefined; **clumsy**, awkward, ungainly, ungraceful, inelegant, uncoordinated, gawky, gangling, bumbling, blundering, lumbering; tactless, thoughtless, inconsiderate; inexperienced, raw, uneducated, unworldly; nervous, nervy, shy, bashful; *informal* cack-handed, ham-fisted, ham-handed, butterfingered.
OPPOSITES graceful; sophisticated.

gracious ▶ **adjective 1** *she was ever the gracious hostess* **courteous**, polite, civil, chivalrous, well mannered, decorous, gentlemanly, ladylike, civilized, tactful, diplomatic; **kind**, kindly, kind-hearted, warm-hearted, benevolent, considerate, thoughtful, obliging, accommodating, charitable, indulgent, magnanimous, beneficent, benign; **friendly**, pleasant, amiable, affable, cordial, hospitable; *informal* couth; *Brit. informal* decent; *dated* mannerly.
OPPOSITE ungracious.
2 *tree-lined avenues with gracious colonial buildings* **elegant**, stylish, tasteful, graceful, comfortable, luxurious, sumptuous, opulent, grand, plush, high-class, exquisite, smart, sophisticated, fashionable, modish, chic; *informal* swanky.
OPPOSITE homely.
3 *I am saved by God's gracious intervention* **merciful**, forgiving, compassionate, kind, kindly, lenient, clement, pitying, forbearing, humane, mild, soft-hearted, tender-hearted, sympathetic; patient, humanitarian, liberal, easy-going, permissive, tolerant, indulgent, generous, magnanimous, beneficent, benign, benignant, benevolent.
OPPOSITE cruel.

gradation ▶ **noun 1** *within the woodpecker family there is a gradation of drilling ability* **range**, scale, gamut, spectrum, sweep, compass, span; progression, sequence, succession, series; variety; hierarchy, ladder, ranking, pecking order.
2 *each of the bands has a number of gradations within it* **level**, rank, position, standing, status, station, degree, grade, stage, standard, echelon, rung, point, mark, step, notch; class, stratum, group, grouping, set, classification.

grade ▶ **noun 1** *hotels within the same grade* **category**, class, classification, grouping, group, set, section, bracket, division, type, brand.
2 *they appointed him to the lowest grade* **rank**, level, echelon, standing, station, position, placing, class, status, order; stage, step, rung, rung on the ladder, notch, stratum, tier; degree of proficiency, degree of quality, degree of merit.
3 (*N. Amer.*) *they got the best grades in the school* **mark**, score, grading, assessment, evaluation, appraisal.
4 (*N. Amer.*) *a kid in the fifth grade* **class**, form, study group, school group, set, stream, band; year.
5 (*N. Amer.*) *roads on steep grades* **slope**, gradient, incline, acclivity, declivity, tilt, angle; hill, rise, bank, ramp.
□ **make the grade** (*informal*) *he lacked the experience to make the grade* **come up to standard**, come up to scratch, qualify, pass, pass muster, measure up, measure up to expectation; succeed, be successful, come through, come through with flying colours, win through, get through; *informal* be up to snuff, cut it, cut the mustard, crack it.
OPPOSITE fail.
▶ **verb 1** *the weights were graded in the box by size* **classify**, class, categorize, bracket, sort, group, order, arrange, type, pigeonhole, brand, size; rank, evaluate, rate, value, range, graduate, calibrate.
2 (*N. Amer.*) *children should be told how they have been graded* **assess**, mark, score, judge, evaluate, appraise.
3 *all these categories grade into one another* **pass**, shade, change, merge, blend, transmute, turn.

gradient ▶ **noun 1** *the road was on a steep gradient* **slope**, incline, hill, rise, rising ground, bank, ramp, acclivity; drop, descent, declivity; *N. Amer.* grade.
2 *the gradient of the line* **steepness**, angle, slant, slope, inclination, leaning.

gradual ▶ **adjective 1** *the gradual transition from military to civilian rule* **slow**, moderate, measured, unhurried, restrained, cautious, circumspect, unspectacular; piecemeal, step by step, little by little, bit by bit; progressive, successive, continuous, systematic; regular, steady, even, consistent, uniform; *informal* softly-softly.
OPPOSITES sudden; abrupt.
2 *a gradual slope* **gentle**, not steep, moderate, slight, easy, subtle, imperceptible.
OPPOSITE steep.

gradually ▶ **adverb** *you can begin to introduce new ideas gradually* **slowly**, moderately, unhurriedly, cautiously, gently, gingerly, circumspectly, unspectacularly; piecemeal, step by step, little by little, bit by bit, inch by inch, piece by piece, drop by drop, by degrees; progressively, successively, continuously, systematically, slowly but surely; regularly, steadily, evenly, constantly, consistently, uniformly, at a regular pace; *rare* inchmeal, gradatim.
OPPOSITES suddenly, abruptly.

graduate ▶ **noun** *we need to recruit more graduates* **degree-holder**, person with a degree; Bachelor of Arts, BA, Bachelor of Science, BSc, Master of Arts, MA, Master of Science, MSc, doctor, PhD, DPhil.
▶ **verb 1** *he wants to be a teacher when he graduates* **qualify**, pass one's exams, pass, be certified, be licensed; take an academic degree, receive/get one's degree, become a graduate, complete one's studies.
2 *she wants to graduate to serious emotional drama* **progress**, advance, move up, go up, proceed, develop; gain promotion, be promoted.
OPPOSITES regress; be demoted.
3 *a proposal to graduate income tax* **arrange in a series**, arrange in order, order, group, classify, class, categorize, rank, grade, range.
4 *the thermometer was graduated in Fahrenheit* **calibrate**, mark off, measure off/out, divide into degrees, grade.

graft[1] ▶ **noun 1** *such grafts may die from lack of water* **scion**, cutting, shoot, offshoot, bud, slip, new growth, sprout, sprig.
2 *she had a skin graft* **transplant**, implant, implantation.
▶ **verb 1** *they graft on a bud higher up the stem* **affix**, slip, join, insert, splice; *rare* engraft.
2 *a technique in which living tissue is grafted on to the patient's cornea* **transplant**, implant, transfer.
3 *a Victorian mansion grafted on to a seventeenth-century farmhouse* **fasten**, attach, add, fix, join, insert.

graft[2] (*Brit. informal*) ▶ **noun** *he earned success through hard graft* **work**, effort, endeavour, toil, labour, exertion, the sweat of one's brow, drudgery, donkey work; perseverance, persistence; *informal* slog; *Austral./NZ informal* yakka.
▶ **verb** *the players are not frightened to graft for each other* **work hard**, exert oneself, toil, labour, hammer away, grind away, sweat; plod away, slave away, work like a Trojan, work like a dog, keep one's nose to the grindstone; persevere, persist, keep at it, stick with it; *informal* slog away, plug away, beaver away, put one's back into something, work one's socks off, work one's guts out, sweat blood, kill oneself; *Brit. informal* get one's head down; *Brit. vulgar slang* work one's balls/arse/nuts off; *N. Amer. vulgar slang* work one's ass/butt off; *archaic* drudge, travail, moil.

graft[3] ▶ **noun** *the new president has started a campaign against graft* **corruption**, bribery, bribing, dishonesty, deceit, fraud, fraudulence, subornation, unlawful practices, illegal means, underhand means; *N. Amer.* payola; *informal* palm-greasing, back-scratching, hush money, kickback, crookedness, shadiness, shady business, dirty tricks, dirty dealings, wheeling and dealing, sharp practices.
OPPOSITE honesty.

grain *See centre pages for list of* **Cereal Crops**
▶ **noun 1** *it's uneconomical for local farmers to grow grain* **cereal**, cereal crops.
2 *a grain of corn* **kernel**, seed, grist, fruit.
3 *grains of sand* **granule**, particle, speck, spot, mote, mite, dot; bit, piece; scrap, crumb, fragment, flake, morsel, iota, molecule, atom.
4 *there was a grain of truth in what he said* **trace**, hint, suggestion, suspicion, tinge, shadow; **small amount**, bit, little bit, soupçon; spark, scintilla, ounce, modicum, iota, jot, whit, scrap, shred, spot, drop, pinch; *Irish* stim; *informal* smidgen, smidge, tad; *archaic* scantling, scruple.

5 *the grain of the timber | a kind of leather with a fine grain* **texture**, intertexture, surface, finish, feel; **weave**, nap, fibre, fabric, pattern.
6 (archaic) *the grain of the man is also in his work* **disposition**, nature, character, make-up, mentality, essential quality, essence, spirit, ethos, complexion, kind, humour, temperament, manner, temper; inclination, turn, bent, cast; N. Amer. stripe; informal kidney.

grammar ▶ noun **syntax**, rules of language, morphology, semantics; linguistics, phonology; technical langue.

grammatical ▶ adjective **1** *the grammatical structure of a sentence* **syntactic**, morphological, semantic; linguistic, phonological.
2 *the report should be written in short grammatical sentences* **well formed**, correct, idiomatic, acceptable, allowable.
OPPOSITES ungrammatical, solecistic.

grand ▶ adjective **1** *a grand hotel* **magnificent**, imposing, impressive, awe-inspiring, splendid, resplendent, superb, striking, monumental, majestic, glorious; palatial, stately, large; luxurious, sumptuous, lavish, opulent, princely, fit for a king; Brit. upmarket; N. Amer. upscale; informal fancy, posh, plush, classy, swanky; Brit. informal swish.
OPPOSITES inferior, unimpressive.

2 *rousing speeches and grand schemes* **ostentatious**, grandiose, showy, extravagant, lordly, imperious; ambitious, bold, epic, big.
3 *a grand old lady* **august**, distinguished, illustrious, eminent, esteemed, great, elevated, exalted, honoured, venerable, dignified, refined, respectable; pre-eminent, prominent, leading, notable, renowned, highly regarded, celebrated, well thought of, of distinction, famous; aristocratic, noble, regal, upper-class, blue-blooded, high-born, well born, patrician, elite; informal posh, upper-crust, upmarket, top-drawer.
OPPOSITES humble, ordinary.
4 *we raised a grand total of £2,000* **complete**, comprehensive, total, all-inclusive, inclusive, exhaustive, final.
OPPOSITE partial.
5 *the grand staircase* **main**, principal, foremost, major, central, prime; biggest, largest.
OPPOSITES minor, secondary.
6 (informal) *you're doing a grand job* **excellent**, very good, marvellous, splendid, first-class, first-rate, wonderful, brilliant, outstanding, sterling, of the first water, fine, admirable, commendable, creditable; informal superb, terrific, great, super, top-notch, A1, fab, ace, tip-top, out of this world, wicked; Brit. informal smashing, brill, top-hole, champion, magic; N. Amer. informal bully; Austral./NZ informal beaut; rare applaudable.
OPPOSITE poor.
▶ noun (informal) *a cheque for ten grand* **thousand pounds/dollars**; informal thou, K; N. Amer. informal G, gee.

grandeur ▶ noun *the grandeur of formal royal occasions* **splendour**, magnificence, impressiveness, glory, gloriousness, resplendence, splendidness, superbness, majesty, greatness; stateliness, pomp, pomp and circumstance, ceremony, ceremonial, ceremoniousness.

grandfather ▶ noun **1** *his grandfather was a mathematician* patriarch; informal grandad, grandpa, grandpop; N. Amer. informal gramps, grand daddy.
2 *he was the grandfather of modern liberalism* **founder**, inventor, originator, creator, initiator, instigator, father, founding father, pioneer, framer, mastermind; literary begetter; rare establisher.
3 *our Victorian grandfathers* **forefather**, forebear, ancestor, progenitor, antecedent.
▶ verb (N. Amer. informal) *smokers who worked here before the ban have been grandfathered* **exempt**, excuse, make an exception of/for, give/grant immunity to, let off, release, exclude, exonerate; informal let off the hook.

grandiloquent ▶ adjective *their grandiloquent phrases failed to convince me* **pompous**, bombastic, magniloquent, pretentious, ostentatious, high-flown, high-sounding, rhetorical, orotund, fustian, florid, flowery; laboured, strained, overwrought, overblown, overdone; wordy, periphrastic; epic, Homeric, Miltonian; informal highfalutin, purple; rare tumid, pleonastic, euphuistic, aureate, hyperventilated.
OPPOSITES unpretentious; concise.

grandiose ▶ adjective **1** *the grandiose town hall* **magnificent**, impressive, grand, imposing, awe-inspiring, splendid, resplendent, superb, striking, monumental, majestic, glorious, elaborate; palatial, stately, large; luxurious, lavish, opulent; informal plush, classy, swanky, flashy, flash.
OPPOSITES unimpressive, humble.
2 *a grandiose plan of urban renewal* **ambitious**, bold, epic, big; overambitious, ostentatious, showy, extravagant, high-flown, high-sounding, flamboyant; informal over the top, OTT.
OPPOSITES modest, humble.

grandmother ▶ noun *my grandmother's ill* informal grandma, granny; (in Russia) babushka; N. Amer. Jewish bubbie; S. African ouma; Brit. informal gran, nana, nan; N. Amer. informal gramma.

grant ▶ verb **1** *he granted them leave of absence* **allow**, accord, permit, afford, concede, vouchsafe.
OPPOSITE refuse.
2 *the programme granted them £20 million* **bestow on**, confer on, give, impart to, present with; award to, present to, donate to, contribute to, provide with, endow with, hand out to; furnish with, supply with; allocate to, allot to, assign to.
3 *I grant that the difference is not absolute* **admit**, accept, concede, yield, cede, allow, appreciate, recognize, acknowledge, confess; agree, concur, go along with.
OPPOSITE deny.
▶ noun *he has received a grant for equipment from the council* **endowment**, subvention, award, donation, bursary, contribution, allowance, subsidy, handout, allocation, allotment, gift, present; scholarship, sponsorship; stipend; formal benefaction.

granular ▶ adjective *plant food in a new granular form* **powder**, powdered, powdery, grainy, granulated, gritty, sandy; technical comminuted.

granulate ▶ verb *all that's left to do is to granulate the tea leaves to make instant tea* **powder**, crush, crumble, pulverize, grind, pound, mince, shred, grate, mash, smash, fragment; technical triturate, comminute; archaic levigate, bray, powderize.

granule ▶ noun *minute granules of gold* **grain**, particle, fragment, bit, sliver; scrap, crumb, morsel, mite, mote, speck, spot, dot, molecule, atom, iota, jot, whit; informal smidgen, smidge.

grape *See centre pages for list of* **Wine and Grape Varieties**
▶ noun **1** *a bunch of grapes* berry.
2 (informal) *a glass of the grape* **wine**; informal vino, plonk.

WORD LINKS
farming of grapes **viticulture, viniculture**

graph ▶ noun *use graphs to analyse your data* **chart**, diagram, grid; histogram, bar chart, pie chart, scatter diagram, nomogram, nomograph.
▶ verb *we can calculate and graph new prices* **plot**, trace, draw up, delineate.

graphic ▶ adjective **1** *writing is a graphic representation of language* **visual**, **symbolic**, pictorial, depictive, illustrative, diagrammatic, drawn, written, in writing, delineative.
2 *a graphic account of the horrors of war* **vivid**, explicit, expressive, detailed, uninhibited, striking, forceful, powerful, punchy; lively, colourful, highly coloured, rich; lurid, shocking, startling; cogent, clear, lucid; realistic, descriptive, illustrative, pictorial, well defined, well delineated, well drawn, well expressed, photographic; telling, effective.
OPPOSITES vague; softened.
▶ noun (Computing) *this printer's good enough for churning out letters, and the odd graphic* **picture**, illustration, image; icon, logo; diagram, graph, chart.

graphic novel ▶ noun **comic**, comic book, cartoon; Japanese manga.

grapple ▶ verb **1** *he threw himself forward and grappled with him* **wrestle**, struggle, tussle; brawl, fight, scuffle, clash, combat, battle; close, engage.
2 *he launched into the crowd to grapple his unfortunate prey* **seize**, grab, lay hold of, take hold of, grip, hold, grasp, clasp, clench, catch hold of, catch, lay one's hands on, get one's hands on.
OPPOSITES let go of, release.
3 *a writer* ***grappling with*** *the problems of exile* **tackle**, confront, address oneself to, face, attend to, attack, get down to; deal with, cope with, get/come to grips with; concentrate on, focus on, apply oneself to, devote oneself to; informal get stuck into, get cracking on, get weaving on, have a crack at, have a go at, have a shot at, have a stab at.
OPPOSITE avoid.
4 (archaic) *the king wished to grapple this vessel and take it* **hook**, secure, fasten, make fast, pin.

grasp ▶ verb **1** *she grasped his hands* **grip**, clutch, clasp, hold, clench, lay hold of; catch, seize, grab, snatch, latch on to, catch at, grapple, get one's hands on.
OPPOSITE release.
2 *after the lectures she made sure everybody had grasped the important points* **understand**, comprehend, follow, take in, realize, perceive, see, apprehend, assimilate, absorb, make sense of, master, get to the bottom of, penetrate; informal get, catch on to, figure out, get one's head around, get a fix on, take on board, get the picture, get the drift, make head or tail of; Brit. informal twig, suss (out).
3 *Henry grasped the opportunity* **take advantage of**, act on; seize, grasp with both hands, grab (at), leap at, snatch, jump at, pounce on.
OPPOSITES miss, overlook.
▶ noun **1** *his grasp on her hand was fierce* **grip**, hold; clutch, clasp, clench.
2 *he broke free from his domineering mother's grasp* **control**, power, clutches, command, mastery, domination, dominion, rule, tyranny, evil embrace.
3 *a mighty prize lay within their grasp* **reach**, scope, capacity, power, limits, range, compass.
4 *your grasp of history impresses me* **understanding**, comprehension, perception, apprehension, awareness, grip, conception, realization, knowledge, cognizance, ken; mastery, command; insight, familiarity.

grasping ▶ adjective *a grasping corporate executive* **avaricious**, acquisitive, greedy, rapacious, grabbing, usurious, covetous, venal; mercenary, materialistic, money-orientated; mean, miserly, parsimonious, niggardly, scrimping, penny-pinching, cheese-paring, hoarding, selfish, possessive, close; N. Amer. forehanded; informal tight-fisted, tight, stingy, money-grubbing, money-grabbing, on the make; N. Amer. informal cheap, grabby; Austral./NZ informal hungry; vulgar slang tight-arsed.

OPPOSITES generous, altruistic.

grass *See centre pages for list of* **Grasses, Sedges, and Rushes**
▶ **noun 1** *he sat down on the grass* **turf**, greenery, green, sod; lawn, field, pasture, meadow, grassland, grasslands; blades of grass; *S. African* veld; *literary* sward, mead, lea.
2 (*informal*) *they spent their afternoons smoking grass.* See CANNABIS.
3 (*Brit. informal*) *few pubs were without a grass or an undercover policeman* **informer**, mole, stool pigeon; *informal* snitch, snout, stoolie, whistle-blower, snake in the grass, supergrass, rat, scab, nose; *Brit. informal* nark; *N. Amer. informal* fink.
▶ **verb 1** *the hill is completely grassed* **cover with grass**, grass over, turf, lay grass on.
2 (*Brit. informal*) *he was suspected of grassing on the airport robbers* **inform**, tell; give away, betray, denounce, sell out, be a Judas to; *informal* split, blow the whistle, rat, peach, squeal, squeak, do the dirty, grass up, tell tales about, spill the beans about, stitch up, sell down the river; *Brit. informal* sneak, shop; *N. Amer. informal* drop a/the dime, finger, rat out, job; *Austral./NZ informal* dob, pimp, pool, shelf, put someone's pot on, point the bone at; *N. Irish & Scottish informal* tout; *archaic* delate.
OPPOSITES keep quiet about; protect.

WORD LINKS
relating to grass **graminaceous**
study of grasses **agrostology**
grass-eating **graminivorous**

grate ▶ **verb 1** *she started to grate the cheese* **shred**, rub into pieces, pulverize, mince, grind, granulate, crush, crumble, mash, smash, fragment, macerate; *technical* triturate.
2 *he gripped her so hard that her bones grated together* **rasp**, scrape, jar, scratch, grind, rub, drag, grit; squeak, screech, creak.
3 *the jingly tune grates slightly* **irritate**, set someone's teeth on edge, jar; irk, exasperate, annoy, vex, nettle, peeve, rankle, anger, rub up the wrong way, chafe, fret, eat away at; *informal* get on someone's nerves, get under someone's skin, rile, aggravate, get someone's goat.

grateful ▶ **adjective 1** *I was most grateful for your hospitality* **thankful**, filled with gratitude, appreciative; indebted, obliged, obligated, under obligation, in your debt, beholden.
OPPOSITE ungrateful.
2 (*archaic*) *a grateful breeze came from the sea* **welcome**, **pleasant**, agreeable, pleasing, pleasurable, satisfying, gratifying, cheering, refreshing, acceptable, nice.
OPPOSITE unwelcome.

CHOOSE THE RIGHT WORD

grateful, thankful, appreciative

These words indicate various forms of awareness of having been fortunate or well treated.

- Someone who is **grateful** realizes that someone else has helped them or treated them kindly, and has warm feelings towards that person (*we're most grateful for your help | her whole family is grateful to the surgeons who saved her*). *Grateful*, in fact, suggests more of an impulse to thank someone than *thankful* does. It is also used in polite requests such as *I would be grateful if you could let me know.*
- **Thankful** is typically more concerned with a person's attitude to their good fortune than with their feelings towards anyone responsible for it. It suggests that someone is relieved or pleased about a situation or turn of events, often one for which no particular person can be identified as responsible (*she was thankful that she felt so much better | I have a lot to be thankful for*).
- The main use of **appreciative** is to say that someone recognizes the merits or appeal of something and expresses that recognition in actions or words (*they were the most appreciative audience we'd played to*). If what is appreciated is a kindness or service, *appreciative* is used with *of* and often also implies gratitude (*the team are very appreciative of your support*).

gratification ▶ **noun** *ours is the civilization of instant gratification* **satisfaction**, fulfilment, indulgence, relief, quenching, slaking, satiation, appeasement, assuagement; **pleasure**, enjoyment, thrill, relish; *informal* kicks.

gratify ▶ **verb 1** *it gratified him to be seen in her company* **please**, gladden, give pleasure to, make happy, make content, delight, make someone feel good, satisfy, warm the cockles of the heart, thrill; *informal* tickle someone pink, give someone a buzz/kick, buck someone up.
OPPOSITE displease.
2 *he was gratifying his strange desires* **satisfy**, fulfil, indulge, relieve, humour, comply with, pander to, cater to, give in to, quench, slake, satiate, pacify, appease, assuage, provide for, feed, accommodate.
OPPOSITE frustrate.

grating[1] ▶ **adjective 1** *pushing his chair from the table with a grating noise* **scraping**, scratching, grinding, rasping, creaking, jarring, abrasive.
2 *her high grating voice* **harsh**, raucous, strident, piercing, shrill, ear-piercing, screeching, squawking, squawky, squeaky, sharp; discordant, dissonant, cacophonous; brassy, blaring; hoarse, croaky, rough, gravelly.
OPPOSITES pleasing, harmonious.
3 *it's written in grating pseudo-teenspeak language* **irritating**, annoying, infuriating, rankling, vexatious, irksome, galling, exasperating, maddening, displeasing; **jarring**, discordant, inharmonious, out of place, unsuitable, inappropriate, ill suited; tiresome, troublesome, niggling, disagreeable, unpleasant, offensive; *informal* aggravating.
OPPOSITES pleasing; appropriate.

grating[2] ▶ **noun** *a strong iron grating* **framework**, grid, grate, network, grille, grillwork, lattice, trellis, criss-cross, matrix; mesh, gauze, netting, net, web, webbing, tracery, interlacing, reticulation, reticulum; *technical* plexus, graticule, decussation.

gratis ▶ **adverb** *a monthly programme was issued gratis to dancers* **free of charge**, free, without charge, for nothing, at no cost, without payment, without paying, freely, gratuitously; *informal* on the house, for free.
OPPOSITE for a fee.

gratitude ▶ **noun** *Maureen ought to show gratitude for the money* **gratefulness**, thankfulness, thanks, appreciation, recognition, acknowledgement, credit, regard, respect; sense of obligation, indebtedness.
OPPOSITE ingratitude.

gratuitous ▶ **adjective 1** *student demonstrations developed an edge of gratuitous violence* **unjustified**, without reason, uncalled for, unwarranted, unprovoked, undue; indefensible, unjustifiable; needless, unnecessary, superfluous, redundant, avoidable, inessential, non-essential, unmerited, groundless, ungrounded, causeless, without cause; senseless, careless, wanton, indiscriminate, unreasoning, brutish; excessive, immoderate, disproportionate, inordinate; unfounded, baseless, inappropriate; *French* de trop.
OPPOSITES justifiable, necessary.
2 *the worker is not there to offer gratuitous advice* **free**, gratis, complimentary, voluntary, volunteer, unpaid, unrewarded, unsalaried, free of charge, without charge, for nothing, at no cost, without payment; *Law* pro bono (publico); *informal* for free, on the house; *Brit. informal* buckshee.
OPPOSITES paid, professional.

gratuity ▶ **noun** (*formal*) *under no circumstances was any officer to receive a gratuity* **tip**, gift, present, donation, reward, handout, recompense, boon, baksheesh; fringe benefit, bonus, extra payment, little extra, bit extra; (**gratuities**) largesse, benefaction; *French* pourboire, douceur; *informal* perk; *formal* perquisite; *rare* guerdon, lagniappe.

grave[1] ▶ **noun** *a cross marks the grave* **burying place**, tomb, sepulchre, vault, burial chamber, burial pit, mausoleum, crypt, catacomb; last home, last resting place; *historical* tumulus, barrow; *rare* undercroft.

grave[2] ▶ **adjective 1** *a grave matter* **serious**, important, all-important, profound, significant, momentous, weighty, of great consequence; vital, crucial, critical, acute; urgent, pressing, exigent; pivotal, precarious, touch-and-go, life-and-death, in the balance; dire, terrible, awful, dreadful, alarming, drastic, sore; perilous, hazardous, dangerous, threatening, menacing, risky; *informal* dicey, hairy, iffy, chancy; *Brit. informal* dodgy; *rare* egregious.
OPPOSITE trivial.
2 *Jackie looked grave* **solemn**, earnest, serious, sombre, sober, severe; unsmiling, long-faced, stone-faced, grim-faced, grim, gloomy; preoccupied, thoughtful, dignified, staid, dour, aloof, forbidding.
OPPOSITES carefree, cheerful.

gravel ▶ **noun** *his boots crunched on the gravel* **shingle**, grit, pebbles, stones.

gravelly ▶ **adjective 1** *a gravelly beach* **shingly**, pebbly, gritty, containing gravel.
2 *his gravelly voice answered immediately* **husky**, gruff, throaty, deep, croaking, raspy, rasping, grating, harsh, low, rough, rough-sounding, thick, guttural.

gravestone ▶ **noun** **headstone**, tombstone, stone, monument, memorial, plaque, tablet.

graveyard ▶ **noun** **cemetery**, burial ground, churchyard, memorial park, necropolis, burial place, burying place, garden of remembrance; *Scottish* kirkyard; *informal* boneyard; *historical* potter's field, charnel house, urnfield; *archaic* God's acre.

gravitas ▶ **noun** *a man of gravitas* **dignity**, seriousness, solemnity, gravity, loftiness, grandeur, decorum, sobriety, sedateness.
OPPOSITE frivolity.

gravitate ▶ **verb** *he naturally gravitated towards Paris* **move**, head, be pulled, drift; tend, have a tendency, lean, incline, veer; be drawn to, be attracted to.

gravity ▶ **noun 1** *gravity attracts objects towards each other* **attraction**, attracting force, downward force, pull, weight, heaviness.
2 *I hope they realize the gravity of the situation* **seriousness**, importance, profundity, significance, momentousness, moment, weightiness, weight,

consequence, magnitude; criticalness, acuteness, cruciality; urgency, exigence; direness, terribleness, awfulness, dreadfulness; precariousness, perilousness, peril, hazard, danger, threat, menace, risk; *informal* hairiness, iffiness, chanciness; *Brit. informal* dodginess; *formal* egregiousness.
OPPOSITE triviality.
3 *she was baffled by the gravity of his demeanour* **solemnity**, seriousness, sombreness, sobriety, soberness, severity; unsmilingness, stone-facedness, long-facedness, grim-facedness, grimness, humourlessness, gloominess; preoccupation, thoughtfulness, dignity, staidness, dourness, aloofness.
OPPOSITES cheerfulness, levity.

graze[1] ▶ **verb** *a group of deer grazed* **feed**, eat, crop, browse, ruminate, pasture, nibble, take nourishment.

graze[2] ▶ **verb 1** *he grazed his knuckles on the corner of the fuse box* **scrape**, abrade, skin, scratch, chafe, bark, scuff, rasp, break the skin of, cut, nick, snick; *Medicine* excoriate.
2 *his shot grazed the far post* **touch**, touch lightly, brush, brush against, rub lightly, shave, skim, kiss, caress, sweep, scrape, glance off, clip.
▶ **noun** *cuts and grazes on the skin* **scratch**, scrape, abrasion, cut, injury, sore; *Medicine* trauma, traumatism.

G

grease ▶ **noun 1** *axle grease* **lubricant**, lubrication, unguent; *informal* lube.
2 *the kitchen was filmed with grease* **fat**, oil, cooking oil, animal fat; lard, suet, butter, margarine, dripping.
3 *his hair was smothered with grease* **oil**, ointment, lotion, cream; *trademark* Brylcreem.
▶ **verb** *grease a shallow baking dish* **lubricate**, oil, smear with grease/oil, make slippery, make smooth, make oily.

greasy ▶ **adjective 1** *a greasy fish supper* **fatty**, oily, fat, swimming in oil/fat, buttery, oleaginous; *technical* adipose, sebaceous, pinguid, unctuous.
OPPOSITES lean; crisp.
2 *a man with greasy grey hair* **oily**, shiny, glossy.
OPPOSITE dry.
3 *the game had made the pitch very greasy* **slippery**, slick, slimy, slithery, oily, glassy, smooth; *informal* slippy, skiddy.
OPPOSITE dry.
4 *that greasy little coward* **ingratiating**, fawning, grovelling, sycophantic, toadying, obsequious, cringing, flattering, effusive, gushing, gushy, abject, truckling, self-effacing, Uriah Heepish; unctuous, oily, smooth-tongued, smooth, glib, suave, slick, reptilian; *informal* slimy, smarmy, bootlicking, all over someone, soapy, sucky.

great ▶ **adjective 1** *academics waited with great interest for the book* **considerable**, substantial, pronounced, sizeable, significant, appreciable, serious, exceptional, inordinate, extraordinary, special.
OPPOSITE little.
2 *a great expanse of water* **large**, big, extensive, expansive, broad, wide, sizeable, ample, spacious; vast, immense, huge, enormous, gigantic, massive, colossal, mammoth, monstrous, prodigious, tremendous, stupendous, unlimited, boundless; *informal* humongous, whopping, whopping great, thumping, thumping great, dirty great; *Brit. informal* whacking, whacking great, ginormous.
OPPOSITE small.
3 *a great big house* **very**, extremely, exceedingly, exceptionally, especially, tremendously, immensely, extraordinarily, remarkably, really, truly; *informal* dirty.
4 *you great fool!* **absolute**, total, utter, out-and-out, downright, thorough, complete; perfect, pure, positive, prize, decided, arrant, sheer, rank, unmitigated, unqualified, unadulterated, unalloyed, consummate, veritable, egregious; *informal* thundering; *Brit. informal* right, proper.
5 *the great writers of the Romantic age* **prominent**, eminent, pre-eminent, important, distinguished, august, illustrious, noble; celebrated, noted, notable, noteworthy, famous, famed, honoured, esteemed, revered, renowned, acclaimed, admired, well known; **leading**, top, high, high-ranking, chief, major, main, principal, central; gifted, talented; outstanding, foremost, remarkable, exceptional, highly rated, first-rate, incomparable, superlative, unsurpassed, unexcelled, matchless, peerless, star, arch-; *N. Amer. informal* major league.
OPPOSITE minor.
6 *a great power with a formidable navy* **powerful**, dominant, influential, strong, potent, formidable, redoubtable; leading, important, illustrious, top rank, of the first rank, first rate; foremost, major, main, chief, principal, capital, paramount, primary.
OPPOSITE minor.
7 *the great castle of Montellana-Coronil* **magnificent**, imposing, impressive, awe-inspiring, grand, splendid, majestic, monumental, glorious, sumptuous, resplendent, lavish, beautiful.
OPPOSITE modest.
8 *he's a great sportsman* **expert**, skilful, skilled, adept, adroit, accomplished, talented, fine, able, masterly, master, brilliant, virtuoso, magnificent, marvellous, outstanding, first class, first rate, elite, superb, proficient, very good; *informal* crack, ace, wizard, A1, class, hot, top-notch, out of this world, mean, demon; *vulgar slang* shit hot.
OPPOSITE poor.
9 *I'm not really a great follower of fashion* **enthusiastic**, eager, keen, zealous, devoted, ardent, fervent, fanatical, passionate, dedicated, diligent, assiduous, intent, habitual, active, vehement, hearty, wholehearted, committed, warm.
OPPOSITE unenthusiastic.
10 *he's having a great time* **enjoyable**, amusing, delightful, lovely; pleasant, congenial, diverting; exciting, thrilling; **excellent**, marvellous, wonderful, superb, first-class, first-rate, admirable, fine, splendid, very good, good; *informal* terrific, tremendous, smashing, fantastic, fabulous, fab, super, glorious, grand, magic, out of this world, cool; *Brit. informal* brilliant, brill, champion; *Austral./NZ informal* bonzer, beaut; *Brit. informal, dated* capital, wizard, corking, spiffing, ripping, cracking, top-hole, topping, champion, beezer; *N. Amer. informal, dated* swell.
OPPOSITE bad.
11 *the great thing is to regret nothing* **important**, essential, crucial, critical, pivotal, vital, salient, significant, big; chief, main, principal, major, most important, uppermost, primary, prime, cardinal, central, key, supreme, paramount, overriding; momentous, weighty, dominant, consequential; *informal* number one.
OPPOSITE inessential.

greatly ▶ **adverb** *a frantic training programme greatly increases the risk of injury* **very much**, much, by a considerable amount, considerably, to a great extent, substantially, appreciably, significantly, markedly, sizeably, seriously, materially, signally, profoundly, to a great extent/degree; enormously, vastly, immensely, tremendously, hugely, mightily, abundantly, extremely, exceedingly, remarkably; *informal* plenty, majorly, well, to the nth degree.
OPPOSITES slightly; not at all.

greatness ▶ **noun 1** *a woman destined for greatness* **eminence**, distinction, pre-eminence, illustriousness, lustre, repute, reputation, status, standing, high standing; **importance**, significance, value, merit, worth; celebrity, noteworthiness, fame, prominence, renown.
OPPOSITES insignificance, obscurity.
2 *Wilde's greatness as a writer* **brilliance**, genius, prowess, talent, expertise, expertness, mastery, artistry, virtuosity, flair, skill, skilfulness, finesse, panache, power, adeptness, proficiency; calibre, distinction.
OPPOSITE mediocrity.
3 *a city fallen from greatness* **grandeur**, grandness, magnificence, impressiveness, splendour, gloriousness, glory, majesty, loftiness.

greed, **greediness** ▶ **noun 1** *wasting resources in order to satisfy human greed* **avarice**, acquisitiveness, covetousness, rapacity, graspingness, cupidity, avidity, possessiveness, materialism; mercenariness, predatoriness; *informal* money-grubbing, money-grabbing; *N. Amer. informal* grabbiness; *rare* Mammonism, pleonexia.
OPPOSITE generosity.
2 *her mouth began to water with unashamed greed* **gluttony**, hunger, ravenousness, voraciousness, voracity, insatiability; gourmandizing, gourmandism; intemperance, overeating, self-indulgence; *informal* swinishness, piggishness, hoggishness, gutsiness; *rare* edacity, esurience.
OPPOSITES temperance, asceticism.
3 *he appealed to their greed for power* **desire**, urge, need, appetite, hunger, craving, longing, yearning, hankering, hungering, thirst, pining; avidity, eagerness, enthusiasm, impatience; *informal* yen, itch.
OPPOSITE indifference.

greedy ▶ **adjective 1** *a greedy eater* **gluttonous**, ravenous, ravening, voracious, gourmandizing, gourmand, intemperate, self-indulgent, insatiable, insatiate, wolfish, gannet-like; *informal* piggish, piggy, swinish, hoggish, gutsy; *rare* esurient, edacious; (**be greedy**) have eyes bigger than one's stomach; *black English* have a/the big eye.
OPPOSITES temperate, ascetic.
2 *a greedy millionaire* **avaricious**, acquisitive, covetous, rapacious, grasping, venal, cupidinous, materialistic, mercenary, predatory, usurious, possessive; grabbing, hoarding, Scrooge-like; *informal* money-grubbing, money-grabbing; *N. Amer. informal* grabby; *rare* pleonectic, Mammonish, Mammonistic.
OPPOSITES generous, altruistic.
3 *she is greedy for a title* **eager**, avid, hungry, craving, longing, yearning, hankering, thirsty, pining, enthusiastic, impatient, anxious; desirous of; *informal* dying, itching, hot, gagging.
OPPOSITE indifferent.

green ▶ **adjective 1** *a green scarf* greenish, viridescent; olive green, pea green, emerald green, lime green, bottle green, Lincoln green, sea green, sage green, acid green, eau de Nil, aquamarine, aqua; *literary* virescent, glaucous.
2 *a pleasant green island* **verdant**, grassy, grass-covered, leafy, verdurous; rural, pastoral.
OPPOSITE barren.
3 (usually **Green**) *he has become preoccupied with Green issues* **environmentalist**, ecologist, conservationist, preservationist.
4 *a green alternative to powering cars with diesel* **environmentally friendly**, environmentally/ecologically sound, non-polluting, ozone-friendly.
OPPOSITE environmentally unfriendly.
5 *green bananas* **unripe**, not ripe, immature.

6 *green timber* **unseasoned**, not aged, unfinished; pliable, supple.
OPPOSITE dry.
7 *finely sliced green bacon* **raw**, fresh, unsmoked, uncured.
OPPOSITE cured.
8 *the new lieutenant was very green* **inexperienced**, unversed, callow, immature; new, raw, unseasoned, untried; inexpert, untrained, unqualified, ignorant; simple, unsophisticated, unpolished; **naive**, innocent, ingenuous, credulous, gullible, unworldly; *informal* wet behind the ears, born yesterday.
OPPOSITE experienced.
9 *his still green recollection of that memorable night* **vivid**, fresh, flourishing; remembered, unforgotten.
OPPOSITE dim.
10 *his aunt was still flourishing in a green old age* **vigorous**, strong, sturdy, sound, healthy, flourishing.
OPPOSITE weak.
11 *he went green, and I thought he was going to be sick* **pale**, wan, pallid, ashen, ashen-faced, pasty, pasty-faced, grey, whitish, washed out, whey-faced, waxen, waxy, blanched, drained, pinched, sallow; **sickly**, nauseous, ill, sick, unhealthy.
OPPOSITE ruddy.
▶ **noun 1** *that lovely canopy of green over Stratford Road* **foliage**, greenery, plants, leaves, leafage, vegetation; *rare* herbage, verdure, frondescence.
2 *a small village green* **lawn**, common, grassy area, sward, grass; *archaic* greensward, mead, lea.
3 (**greens**) *they had roast beef, potatoes, and greens for lunch* **vegetables**, leaf vegetables; *informal* veg, veggies.
4 (usually **Green**) *Greens are against multinationals* **environmentalist**, conservationist, preservationist, nature-lover, eco-activist; *informal, derogatory* econut, ecofreak, tree hugger.

WORD LINKS
related prefix **chloro-** (e.g. ***chlorophyll, chlorine***)

greenery ▶ **noun** *the hotel is surrounded by lush greenery* **foliage**, vegetation, plants, green, leaves, leafage, undergrowth, plant life, flora; *rare* herbage, verdure, frondescence.

greenhorn ▶ **noun** (*N. Amer. informal*) *as a greenhorn he was bound to make a few mistakes* **novice**, beginner, starter, tyro, neophyte, new recruit, raw recruit, fledgling, new boy/girl, novitiate; trainee, learner, student, pupil, probationer; *N. Amer.* tenderfoot; *informal* rookie, new kid (on the block), newie, newbie; *N. Amer. informal* punk.
OPPOSITE veteran.

greenhouse ▶ **noun** **hothouse**, glasshouse, conservatory.

green light ▶ **noun** *he was given* **the green light** *to implement his proposals* **authorization**, permission, approval, assent, consent, sanction; leave, clearance, warranty, agreement, imprimatur, one's blessing, the seal/stamp of approval, the rubber stamp; authority, licence, dispensation, empowerment, freedom, liberty; *informal* the OK, the go-ahead, the thumbs up, the say-so, the nod; *rare* permit, nihil obstat.
OPPOSITES the red light; refusal.

greet ▶ **verb 1** *she greeted Hank cheerily* **say hello to**, address, salute, hail, halloo; nod to, wave to, raise one's hat to, tip one's hat to, acknowledge the presence of.
OPPOSITE ignore.
2 *I greeted him at the door with a martini* **welcome**, meet, receive; show in, usher in, admit, accept, let in.
3 *the decision was greeted with a chorus of outrage* **receive**, acknowledge, respond to, react to, take; hear, listen to.

greeting ▶ **noun 1** *he shouted a greeting* **hello**, salute, salutation, address, welcome, hailing; nod, wave, acknowledgement.
OPPOSITE farewell.
2 (**greetings**) *they passed on birthday greetings* **best wishes**, good wishes, regards, kind/kindest regards, congratulations, compliments, respects, felicitations; *archaic* one's devoirs, remembrances.

gregarious ▶ **adjective 1** *he was fun-loving and gregarious* **sociable**, social, company-loving, companionable, convivial, clubbable; outgoing, friendly, affable, amiable, genial, congenial, cordial, hospitable, neighbourly, welcoming, warm, pleasant, comradely, hail-fellow-well-met; *Scottish* couthy; *informal* chummy, pally; *Brit. informal* matey, decent; *N. Amer. informal* clubby, buddy-buddy; *rare* conversable.
OPPOSITES unsociable; reserved.
2 *these fish are small and gregarious* **social**, organized, living in shoals/flocks/herds.

grey ▶ **adjective 1** *a grey suit* greyish, silvery; silver-grey, pearl-grey, pearly, gunmetal grey, slate-grey, smoke-grey, smoky, sooty.
2 *his thinning grey hair* **white**, silver, hoary.
3 *a grey old man* **grey-haired**, hoary, grizzled; **elderly**, old, aged, senior, ancient, venerable; in one's dotage, long in the tooth, as old as the hills; past one's prime, not as young as one was, not as young as one used to be; decrepit, doddering, doddery, not long for this world; *informal* past it, over the hill, no spring chicken; *formal* senescent.
OPPOSITE young.
4 *it was a dim, grey day* **cloudy**, overcast, dull, dim, dark, sunless; gloomy, dreary, dismal, sombre, drab, bleak, cheerless, depressing, glum; misty, foggy, murky.
OPPOSITES bright, sunny.
5 *her face looked grey* **ashen**, wan, pale, pasty, pallid, colourless, sallow, leaden, bloodless, anaemic, white, waxen, chalky; sickly, peaked, drained, sapped, washed-out, drawn, deathly, deathlike, ghostly; *informal* peaky.
OPPOSITE ruddy.
6 *if you drive the idiosyncrasies out of football, what is left can be grey indeed* **characterless**, colourless, nondescript, unremarkable, faceless; lifeless, soulless, passionless, spiritless, insipid, jejune, flat, bland, dry, stale; dull, uninteresting, unimaginative, boring, tedious, monotonous; neutral, anonymous, wishy-washy.
OPPOSITES colourful, lively.
7 *a grey area* **ambiguous**, doubtful, unclear, uncertain, indistinct, indefinite, indeterminate, open to question, debatable; mixed, neither one thing nor the other, neither fish nor fowl.
OPPOSITES black and white, certain.
8 *grey importing is not illegal* **unofficial**, informal, irregular, back-door.
▶ **verb** *health bills rose as the population greyed* **age**, get old, grow old, mature.

grid ▶ **noun 1** *the castings were placed on to a metal grid* **grating**, mesh, gauze, grille, grillwork, lattice, framework, network, criss-cross.
2 *the grid of streets* **matrix**, network, reticulation, reticulum; *technical* plexus, decussation, graticule.

grief ▶ **noun 1** *Amanda's grief for her father* **sorrow**, misery, sadness, anguish, pain, distress, agony, torment, affliction, suffering, heartache, heartbreak, broken-heartedness, heaviness of heart, woe, desolation, despondency, dejection, despair, angst, mortification; **mourning**, mournfulness, bereavement, lamentation, lament; remorse, regret, pining; *informal* blues; *literary* dolour, dole.
OPPOSITE joy.
2 (*informal*) *the police gave me loads of grief* **trouble**, annoyance, bother, irritation, vexation, harassment, nuisance; *informal* aggravation, aggro, hassle, headache.
□ **come to grief** *the scheme came to grief because of the opposition of the Cabinet Secretary* **fail**, meet with failure, meet with disaster, miscarry, go wrong, go awry, fall through, fall flat, be frustrated, break down, collapse, founder, fold, come to nothing, come to naught; *informal* come unstuck, come a cropper, flop, fizzle out, go phut, go down like a lead balloon, bomb, go to the wall, bite the dust; *Brit. informal* go pear-shaped; *N. Amer. informal* tank.
OPPOSITE succeed.

grief-stricken ▶ **adjective** *a grief-stricken widow* **sorrowful**, overcome with sorrow, heavy with grief, sorrowing, miserable, sad, anguished, pained, distressed, tormented, suffering, heartbroken, broken-hearted, heartsick, woeful, doleful, desolate, despondent, dejected, despairing, devastated, upset, inconsolable, dismal, angst-ridden, mortified, wretched, crushed; **mourning**, grieving, mournful, bereaved, lamenting; remorseful, regretful, pining; *informal* cut up; *Brit. informal* gutted; *literary* dolorous.
OPPOSITE joyful.

grievance ▶ **noun 1** *civil disorder could be the result of a real or imagined grievance* **injustice**, unjust act, wrong, injury, ill, offence, disservice, unfairness, evil, outrage, atrocity, damage; affront, insult, indignity.
2 *the phone line lets callers air grievances about public services* **complaint**, criticism, objection, protestation, charge, protest, grumble, moan, cavil, quibble, problem; grudge, ill feeling, hard feeling, bad feeling, resentment, bitterness, rancour, pique, umbrage; *informal* grouse, gripe, whinge, grouch, niggle, beef, bone to pick, chip on one's shoulder; *N. Amer. informal* crow to pluck; *literary* plaint.
OPPOSITE commendation.

grieve ▶ **verb 1** *she continued to grieve for Mary* **mourn**, lament, be mournful, be sorrowful, sorrow, be sad, be miserable; cry, sob, weep, shed tears, keen, weep and wail, beat one's breast; suffer, ache, be in anguish, be distressed, be in distress, eat one's heart out.
OPPOSITES be happy, rejoice.
2 *Alexander was grieved to lose such a good friend* **hurt**, wound, pain, harrow, sting, gall; **sadden**, upset, distress, devastate, cause suffering to, crush, break someone's heart, make someone's heart bleed, hit someone hard.
OPPOSITE please.

grievous ▶ **adjective 1** *no money can compensate her for her grievous injuries* **serious**, severe, grave, bad, critical, dreadful, terrible, awful; painful, agonizing, hurtful, afflicting, wounding, damaging, injurious; sharp, acute; *Medicine* peracute.
OPPOSITES slight, trivial.
2 *that is most grievous news* **disastrous**, calamitous; crushing, distressing, traumatic, harrowing; sorrowful, mournful, sad.
OPPOSITE good.
3 *a grievous sin* **heinous**, grave, deplorable, shocking, appalling, atrocious, gross, dire, outrageous, dreadful, egregious, iniquitous, nefarious, shameful, lamentable; flagrant, glaring; *rare* flagitious.

G

OPPOSITES trivial, venial.

grim ▶ adjective **1** *she took in his grim expression* **stern**, forbidding, uninviting, unapproachable, aloof, distant; formidable, strict, dour, harsh; steely, flinty, stony; fierce, ferocious, threatening, menacing; cross, churlish, crabbed, surly, sour, ill-tempered, unsmiling; cruel, ruthless, merciless.
OPPOSITES amiable, pleasant.
2 *she was caught between a rock and a hard place, she realized with grim humour* **black**, dark, mirthless, bleak, cynical, fatalistic.
OPPOSITE light-hearted.
3 *the asylum holds some grim secrets* **dreadful**, dire, ghastly, horrible, horrendous, horrid, terrible, awful, appalling, frightful, shocking, unspeakable, atrocious, harrowing; grisly, gruesome, hideous, disgusting, revolting, gory, macabre, morbid; depressing, distressing, upsetting, worrying, unpleasant, disagreeable.
4 *a grim little hovel* **bleak**, dreary, dismal, dingy, wretched, miserable, disheartening, depressing, cheerless, comfortless, joyless, gloomy, sombre, uninviting, drab; *informal* God-awful.
5 *two beasts locked in grim combat* **merciless**, cruel, ruthless, pitiless, savage, vicious, brutal, harsh, severe.
6 *there was grim determination in every line of her face* **resolute**, determined, firm, decided, steadfast, dead set; obstinate, stubborn, obdurate; unyielding, uncompromising, unbending, unwavering, unfaltering, unshakeable, intractable, adamant, inflexible; unrelenting, relentless, dogged, tenacious, inexorable, persistent, strong-willed.
OPPOSITE irresolute.

grimace ▶ noun *his mouth twisted into a grimace* **scowl**, frown, sneer, pout, moue, wince, distorted expression; face, wry face.
OPPOSITE smile.
▶ verb *Nina grimaced at Joe* **scowl**, frown, sneer, pout, wince, glower, lour; make a face, make faces, pull a face; *Brit.* gurn.
OPPOSITE smile.

grime ▶ noun *her skirt was smeared with grime* **dirt**, smut, soot, dust, mud, filth, mire, sludge, dross, pollution; *informal* muck, gunge, yuck, crud, goo; *Brit. informal* grot.
▶ verb *concrete grimed by diesel exhaust* **begrime**, blacken, dirty, make grimy, make dirty, make sooty, stain, soil, befoul, defile; *literary* besmirch.
OPPOSITE clean.

grimy ▶ adjective *reporters in grimy anoraks* **dirty**, grimed, begrimed, grubby, soiled, stained, smeared, filthy, uncleaned, messy; dirt-encrusted, smutty, sooty, dusty, muddy, muddied, mud-caked, polluted; *informal* mucky, yucky, cruddy; *Brit. informal* manky, grotty, gungy; *Austral./NZ* scungy; *literary* besmirched, besmeared.
OPPOSITE clean.

grin ▶ verb *Guy grinned merrily at her* **smile**, smile broadly, beam, grin from ear to ear, smile from ear to ear, grin like a Cheshire cat, smirk; *informal* be all smiles.
OPPOSITES frown; scowl.
▶ noun *a silly grin* **smile**, broad smile, smirk.
OPPOSITES frown; scowl.

grind ▶ verb **1** *grind the praline into a fine powder* **crush**, pound, pulverize, mill, powder, granulate, grate, mince, shred, crumble, pestle, mash, smash, press, fragment, kibble; *technical* triturate, comminute; *archaic* levigate, bray.
2 *a knife being ground on a wheel* **sharpen**, whet, make sharp/sharper, hone, file, strop; smooth, polish, sand, sandpaper.
3 *one tectonic plate grinds against another* **rub**, grate, scrape, rasp.
4 *Mitch ground his teeth in fury* **gnash**, grit.
5 *a car grinding up the other side of the hill* **move laboriously**, strain, struggle, drag oneself, fight one's way, labour; chug; *N. Amer. informal* putter.
□ **grind away** *he began to grind away in a job as a research assistant* **labour**, toil, slave (away), plod away, sweat, hammer away, work one's fingers to the bone, work like a Trojan, work like a dog, work like a slave, work day and night, keep one's nose to the grindstone; persevere, persist, keep at it, stick with it; *informal* slog, plug away, beaver away, peg away, put one's back into something, work one's socks off, sweat blood, kill oneself, work one's guts out; *Brit. informal* graft, get one's head down; *archaic* drudge, travail, moil.
□ **grind someone down** *I've never let male colleagues grind me down* **oppress**, persecute, tyrannize, suppress; afflict, maltreat, ill-treat, scourge; torture, torment, molest, harass, harry.
□ **grind on** *the meeting ground on* **drag on**, go on and on, plod on, pass slowly, move slowly, creep along, limp along, crawl, hang heavy, go at a snail's pace, wear on, go on too long; **continue**, carry on, go on, keep on, keep going, proceed.
OPPOSITES race by, fly.
□ **grind something out** *a hack grinding out newspaper copy* **produce**, generate, crank out, turn out; *informal* churn out, trot out, bang out.
▶ noun *teaching could be a grind* **chore**, slog, travail; **drudgery**, toil, hard work, donkey work, labour, slavery, exertion; *informal* fag, sweat.

grip ▶ verb **1** *she gripped the edge of the table* **grasp**, clutch, hold, clasp, grasp/take/lay hold of, latch on to, grab, seize, clench, cling to, catch, catch at, get one's hands on, pluck; squeeze, press; *archaic* gripe.
OPPOSITES release; hold lightly.
2 *Harry was gripped by a sneezing fit* **afflict**, affect, take over, beset, rack, torment, convulse.
3 *we were gripped by the drama* **engross**, enthral, entrance, absorb, rivet, spellbind, hold spellbound, bewitch, fascinate, hold, catch, compel, mesmerize, arrest, ensnare, enrapture; interest, intrigue, engage, distract, divert, entertain, amuse.
OPPOSITES repel; bore.
▶ noun **1** *she never released her grip on the handrail* **grasp**, hold, clutch, clasp, clench; *archaic* gripe.
2 *the car's back wheels lost all grip on the slick surface* **traction**, purchase, friction, adhesion, resistance.
3 *he was in the grip of an obsession he was powerless to resist* **control**, power, mastery, hold, stranglehold, clutches, domination, dominion, command, influence, possession; rule, tyranny, evil embrace.
4 *he took Moran's hand in a firm grip* **handshake**, hand grip, hand clasp.
5 *he was having difficulty getting a* **grip on** *what she was saying* **understanding of**, comprehension of, perception of, awareness of, grasp of, apprehension of, conception of, realization of, knowledge of, cognizance of, ken of, mastery of, command of; insight into, familiarity with.
6 *she watched him pack his grip* **travelling bag**, bag, holdall, overnight bag, overnighter, flight bag, kitbag, Gladstone bag, valise, portmanteau.
7 *he was offered a job as a grip at the studio* **stagehand**, theatrical assistant.
□ **come/get to grips with** *it's time the council got to grips with this problem* **deal with**, cope with, handle, grasp, grasp the nettle of; tackle, undertake, take on, grapple with, contend with, close with; face, face up to, meet head on, confront, encounter; take the bit between one's teeth.
OPPOSITE avoid.

gripe (*informal*) ▶ verb *he was griping about the boss* **complain**, grumble, moan, groan, protest, whine, bleat; *informal* grouse, bellyache, beef, bitch, grouch, whinge, kick up a fuss, knock; *Brit. informal* chunter, create, be on at someone; *N. Amer. informal* kvetch; *N. English informal* mither.
▶ noun *my only gripe is that the game is a little too easy* **complaint**, grumble, moan, groan, grievance, objection, protest, whine; cavil, quibble, niggle; *informal* grouse, beef, whinge, bellyaching, beefing, bitching, grouching, whingeing; *N. Amer. informal* kvetch.

gripping ▶ adjective *a gripping thriller* **engrossing**, enthralling, entrancing, absorbing, riveting, captivating, spellbinding, bewitching, fascinating, compulsive, addictive, compelling, mesmerizing, arresting; thrilling, exciting, action-packed, dramatic, stimulating; interesting, engaging, distracting, diverting, entertaining, amusing; *informal* unputdownable.
OPPOSITE boring.

grisly ▶ adjective *the grisly details of human sacrifices* **gruesome**, ghastly, frightful, horrid, horrifying, fearful, hideous, macabre, spine-chilling, horrible, horrendous, grim, awful, dire, dreadful, terrible, horrific; disgusting, repulsive, repugnant, revolting, repellent, sickening, distressing, shocking, appalling, abominable, loathsome, abhorrent, odious, monstrous, unspeakable; *informal* sick, sick-making, gut-churning, gross; *archaic* disgustful, loathly.
OPPOSITES pleasant; attractive.

gristly ▶ adjective *a gristly piece of meat* **stringy**, **sinewy**, fibrous, ropy; tough, leathery, leather-like, chewy; *technical* coriaceous.
OPPOSITE tender.

grit ▶ noun **1** *the grit from the paths got into her sandals* **gravel**, pebbles, stones, shingle, sand, dust, dirt.
2 (*informal*) *I'm very impressed by your grit* **courage**, courageousness, bravery, pluck, mettle, mettlesomeness, backbone, spirit, strength of character, strength of will, moral fibre, steel, nerve, gameness, valour, fortitude, toughness, hardiness, resolve, determination, resolution; stamina, doggedness, tenacity, perseverance, endurance; *informal* gumption, guts, spunk; *Brit. informal* bottle; *vulgar slang* balls.
▶ verb *Gina gritted her teeth to keep her temper under control* **clench**, clamp together, press together, shut tightly; grate, grind, gnash, scrape, rasp.

gritty ▶ adjective **1** *she filled the pots with gritty soil* **sandy**, grainy, granular, gravelly, pebbly, stony; powdery, dusty.
2 *his many gritty displays as an all-round cricketer* **courageous**, brave, plucky, mettlesome, stout-hearted, lionhearted, valiant, bold, spirited, intrepid, game, hardy, tough, steely, determined, resolute, purposeful; dogged, tenacious, enduring, unfaltering, unswerving, unyielding, unflinching; *informal* gutsy, spunky, ballsy, feisty; *rare* perseverant.

grizzle ▶ verb (*Brit. informal*) *the baby grizzled when she went away* **cry**, cry fretfully, weep, whimper, whine, whinge, mewl, moan, bleat, snivel, sob, wail, howl, bawl; *Scottish* greet; *informal* boohoo, blubber, blub, turn on the waterworks.

grizzled ▶ adjective *he tugged at his grizzled beard* **grey**, greying, greyish, silver, silvery, snowy, snowy-white, white, whitish, grizzly, hoary, hoar, salt-and-pepper; grey-haired, grey-headed; *rare* griseous, canescent.

groan ▶ verb **1** *Ashley groaned and put a hand to her stomach* **moan**,

murmur, whine, whimper, mewl, bleat, sigh; wail, howl, sob, cry, call out.
2 *she gets home and groans about the working day* **complain**, grumble, moan, mutter, lament, protest, object, make a fuss, find fault; *informal* grouse, gripe, niggle, beef, bellyache, bitch, whinge.
3 *the car juddered and groaned alarmingly* **creak**, grate, grind, jar; squeak, screech, squeal.
▶ **noun 1** *he uttered a groan of anguish* **moan**, murmur, whine, whimper, mewl, bleat, sigh; wail, howl, sob, cry, lamentation.
2 *she listens with sincerity to all their moans and groans* **complaint**, grumble, objection, protest, protestation, grievance, moan, mutter, muttering, carping; *informal* grouse, grouch, gripe, beef, beefing, bellyaching, bitching, whinge, whingeing.
3 *we could hear the groan of the elevator* **creaking**, creak, grating, grinding, jarring; squeak, screech, squeal, squealing.

groggy ▶ **adjective** *she is still feeling groggy from the anaesthetic* **dazed**, muzzy, stupefied, in a stupor, befuddled, fuddled, muddled, confused, bewildered, disoriented, disorientated, vague, benumbed, numb, stunned, dizzy, punch-drunk, shaky, staggering, reeling, unsteady, wobbly, weak, faint; *informal* dopey, woozy, woolly, woolly-headed, discombobulated, not with it.

groin ▶ **noun** *she kicked her attacker in the groin* **crotch**, crutch, genitals; lap.
WORD LINKS
relating to the groin **inguinal**

groom ▶ **verb 1** *her hair was groomed to a silken sheen* **brush**, comb, smooth, do, dress, arrange, adjust, put in order, tidy, make tidy, spruce up, smarten up, preen, primp, freshen up; *informal* fix.
2 *she groomed her dark bay pony* **curry**, brush, comb, rub, rub down.
3 *the youngsters were being groomed for stardom* **prepare**, prime, make ready, ready, condition, tailor; coach, train, instruct, tutor, drill, teach, educate, school.
▶ **noun 1** *he tossed his horse's reins to a groom* **stable hand**, stableman, stable lad, stable boy, stable girl; *historical* equerry.
2 *she walked out of the chapel with her groom* **bridegroom**, new husband, husband-to-be; newly-married man, newly-wed.

groove ▶ **noun 1** *water had worn a groove in the surface of the rock* **furrow**, channel, trench, trough, canal, gouge, hollow, indentation, rut, gutter, cutting, cut, score, fissure, seam; *technical* rabbet, rebate.
2 *the company had become stuck in a groove* **rut**, routine, boring routine, habit, dead end, humdrum existence, same old round, grind, daily grind, treadmill.

grooved ▶ **adjective** *the bark was wrinkled and grooved* **furrowed**, channelled, rutted, fluted, corrugated, ribbed, ridged; *technical* rabbeted.
OPPOSITE smooth.

grope ▶ **verb 1** *Ruth groped for her sunglasses* **fumble**, scrabble, fish, ferret (about/around), rummage (about/around/round), root about/around, feel, cast about/around/round, search, hunt, look; *Brit. informal* rootle around; *rare* grabble, roust around.
2 (*informal*) *he was accused of groping his secretaries* **fondle**, touch; **molest**, interfere with, assault, sexually assault, abuse, sexually abuse; *informal* paw, maul, feel up, touch up, goose.

gross ▶ **adjective 1** *I feel gross and even my legs feel flabby* **obese**, corpulent, overweight, fat, big, large, outsize, outsized, massive, immense, huge, colossal, fleshy, flabby, portly, bloated, bulky, hulking, lumpish; *informal* porky, pudgy, tubby, blubbery, roly-poly; *Brit. informal* podgy, fubsy; *N. Amer. vulgar slang* lard-assed; *rare* pursy, abdominous.
OPPOSITE slender.
2 *they used gross insults to intimidate her* **vulgar**, coarse, crude, obscene, rude, ribald, lewd, bawdy, dirty, filthy, earthy, smutty, risqué, indecent, indelicate, improper, impure, unseemly, offensive, pornographic; *informal* sleazy, porno, porn, raunchy, naughty, blue, steamy, spicy, locker-room; *Brit. informal* fruity, saucy, near the knuckle, close to the bone; *N. Amer. informal* gamy; *euphemistic* adult; *rare* concupiscent.
OPPOSITE pure.
3 *don't go throwing yourself at men of gross natures* **boorish**, loutish, oafish, thuggish, brutish, bearish, Neanderthal, philistine, coarse, uncouth, unsavoury, crass, vulgar, common, unrefined, unsophisticated, uncultured, uncultivated, undiscriminating, tasteless, insensitive, unfeeling, imperceptive, callous; *informal* cloddish, slobbish, plebby, clodhopping; *Brit. informal* yobbish; *Austral./NZ informal* ocker.
OPPOSITE refined.
4 (*informal*) *I threw up—it was gross* **disgusting**, repellent, repulsive, abhorrent, loathsome, detestable, sickening, nauseating, nauseous, stomach-churning, stomach-turning, off-putting, unpalatable, unappetizing, uninviting, unsavoury, distasteful, foul, nasty, obnoxious, odious; *N. Amer.* vomitous; *informal* yucky, icky, sick-making, gut-churning; *Brit. informal* grotty; *archaic* disgustful.
OPPOSITE lovely.
5 *the report is a gross distortion of the truth* **flagrant**, blatant, glaring, obvious, overt, evident, conspicuous; naked, barefaced, shameless, brazen, audacious, brass-necked; undisguised, unconcealed, patent, transparent, manifest, palpable; out and out, utter, complete; outrageous, scandalous, shocking, disgraceful, reprehensible, dreadful, terrible; enormous, heinous, atrocious, monstrous, wicked, iniquitous, villainous; *archaic* arrant.
OPPOSITE minor.
6 *tax is deducted from their gross income* **total**, whole, entire, complete, full, overall, comprehensive, combined, aggregate; before deductions, before tax.
OPPOSITE net.
▶ **verb** *he grosses over a million dollars a month* **earn**, make, bring in, take, get, receive, fetch, draw, collect; *informal* rake in, pull in, haul in, bag.

grotesque ▶ **adjective 1** *a grotesque creature with a flattened body and a squashed head* **malformed**, deformed, misshapen, misproportioned, distorted, twisted, gnarled, mangled, mutilated; ugly, unsightly, monstrous, hideous; **freakish**, unnatural, abnormal, bizarre, outlandish, strange, odd, peculiar; fantastic, fanciful, whimsical; *informal* weird, freaky; *Brit. informal* rum.
OPPOSITES ordinary, normal.
2 *stories of grotesque mismanagement and wasting of money* **outrageous**, monstrous, shocking, astonishing, preposterous, ridiculous, ludicrous, farcical, unbelievable, unthinkable, incredible; *informal* crazy.

grotto ▶ **noun** *a grotto had been hollowed out of the mountainside* **cave**, cavern, cavity, hollow, recess, alcove; tunnel, pothole, underground chamber.

grouch ▶ **noun** *he's an ill-mannered grouch* **grumbler**, complainer, moaner, discontent, malcontent, fault-finder, carper; grumpy person, miserable person, moper, pessimist, prophet of doom; *informal* grump, sourpuss, crosspatch, bear with a sore head, grouser, whinger, wet blanket, party-pooper, doom merchant; *Brit. informal* griper, misery; *N. Amer. informal* sorehead, kvetcher.
▶ **verb** *there's not a lot to grouch about* **grumble**, complain, grouse, moan, whine, bleat, carp, cavil, grieve, sigh; *informal* whinge, beef, bellyache, bitch, sound off, kick up a fuss, kick up a stink; *Brit. informal* gripe, grizzle, chunter, create; *N. Amer. informal* kvetch; *S. African informal* chirp.

grouchy ▶ **adjective** **grumpy**, cross, irritable, bad-tempered, crotchety, crabby, crabbed, cantankerous, curmudgeonly, moody, miserable, morose, sullen, surly, churlish; touchy, testy, tetchy, huffy, snappish, waspish, prickly; *informal* snappy, cranky; *Brit. informal* narky, ratty, eggy, like a bear with a sore head, whingy; *N. Amer. informal* soreheaded, sorehead, peckish; *Austral./NZ* snaky; *dated* miffy.
OPPOSITE easy-going.

ground ▶ **noun 1** *she stumbled and then collapsed on the ground* **floor**, earth, terra firma; flooring; *informal* deck.
2 *their feet sank into the soggy ground* **earth**, soil, topsoil, dirt, clay, loam, turf, clod, mould, sod, dust; land, terrain.
3 *the team won at their home ground* **stadium**, pitch, field, arena, park; track, course, racetrack, racecourse, ring, rink; *N. Amer.* bowl.
4 (**grounds**) *a balcony overlooking the embassy grounds* **estate**, gardens, lawns, park, parkland, land, acres, property, surroundings, domain, holding, territory; *archaic* demesne.
5 (**grounds**) *his actions constituted grounds for dismissal* **reason**, cause, basis, base, foundation, justification, rationale, argument, premise, occasion, factor, excuse, pretext, motive, motivation, inducement.
6 (**grounds**) *there were coffee grounds in the bottom of the cup* **sediment**, precipitate, settlings, dregs, lees, deposit, residue, sludge; *rare* grouts.
▶ **verb 1** *a bitter wind blew and the bombers were grounded* **prevent from flying**, keep on the ground.
2 *the boat grounded on a mud bank* **run aground**, become stranded, run ashore, beach, become beached, land, be high and dry.
OPPOSITES float; put to sea.
3 *this assertion was grounded on results of several studies* **base**, found, establish, set, settle, root, build, construct, form.
4 *her governess* **grounded** *her* **in** *Latin and Greek* **instruct**, coach, tutor, educate, school, train, drill, prime, prepare; teach, familiarize with, acquaint with, make conversant with, inform about; *informal* give the gen about, give the low-down on, gen up on, clue up on, clue in on, fill in on, put in the picture about.

groundless ▶ **adjective** *she dismissed their fears as groundless* **baseless**, without basis, without foundation, foundationless, ill-founded, unfounded, unsupported, uncorroborated, unproven, not backed up, empty, idle, vain, chimerical, imaginary, illusory, false, unsubstantiated, unwarranted, unjustified, unjustifiable, uncalled for, unprovoked, without cause, without reason, without justification, unreasonable, irrational, illogical, unsound, unreliable, questionable, misguided, spurious, specious, fallacious, erroneous.

groundwork ▶ **noun** *I had to do the groundwork for a revolutionary new project* **preliminary work**, preliminaries, preparations, preparatory measures, basic work, spadework, legwork, hard work, donkey work, hack work; planning, arrangements, organization, homework; basics, rudiments, essentials, fundamentals, underpinning, footing, foundation, cornerstone; *informal* nitty-gritty, nuts and bolts, brass tacks.

group *See centre pages for list of* **Collective Names for Animals**

G

▶ noun 1 *she sorted the coins into groups* **category**, class, classification, grouping, set, lot, batch, bracket, type, sort, kind, variety, family, species, genus, breed, style; grade, grading, rank, status.
2 *a group of passengers awaited their plane* **crowd**, band, company, party, body, gathering, congregation, assembly, collection, cluster, flock, pack, troop, gang, batch; *informal* bunch.
3 *a coup attempt was mounted by a group within the parliament* **faction**, division, section, clique, coterie, circle, set, ring, camp, bloc, caucus, cabal, junta, fringe movement, splinter group, minority group.
4 *the women's group meets in the early afternoon* **association**, club, society, league, guild, circle, union, consortium, cooperative, partnership, syndicate; *rare* consociation.
5 *a small group of islands off Brittany* **cluster**, knot, collection, mass, clump, bunch.
▶ verb 1 *patients were grouped according to their symptoms* **categorize**, classify, class, sort, bracket, pigeonhole, grade, rate, rank; designate, label, tag, brand; file, catalogue, list, tabulate, index, assign.
2 *she grouped the flowers beautifully in a small alcove* **assemble**, collect, gather together, mass, amass, cluster, clump, bunch; arrange, organize, marshal, range, line up, dispose.
3 *the two parties* ***grouped together*** *for negotiating purposes* **unite**, join up, join together, team up, join forces, pool resources, club together, get together, come together, gather; collaborate, work together, pull together, cooperate; link, ally, associate, fraternize, form an alliance, affiliate, federate; amalgamate, combine, merge, integrate, consolidate.
OPPOSITE split up.

grouse ▶ verb *she* ***groused about*** *having to sit next to Kim* **grumble**, complain, moan, groan, protest, whine, bleat, carp, cavil, lodge a complaint, make a complaint, make a fuss; object to, speak out against, rail at, oppose, lament, bewail, grieve over, sorrow about, sorrow for, sigh over; *informal* bellyache, beef, bitch, grouch, whinge, kick up a fuss, kick up a stink, sound off, go on; *Brit. informal* gripe, grizzle, chunter, create; *N. Amer. informal* kvetch; *S. African informal* chirp; *Brit. dated* crib, natter; *archaic* plain over.
▶ noun *our biggest grouse was about the noise* **grumble**, complaint, moan, groan, whine, grievance, objection, protest, protestation, cavil, quibble; *informal* beef, gripe, bellyache, whinge, grouch; *Law, Brit.* plaint.

WORD LINKS

male	**cock**
female	**hen**
young	**cheeper**
collective noun	**pack, covey**

grove ▶ noun *a villa sited in an olive grove* **copse**, wood, thicket, coppice, group of trees; orchard, plantation; *Brit.* spinney; *archaic* hurst, holt.

grovel ▶ verb 1 *George grovelled at his feet* **crawl**, creep, cringe, crouch, prostrate oneself, kneel, fall on one's knees; throw oneself at someone's feet.
2 *they dislike leaders who* ***grovel to*** *foreign patrons* **behave obsequiously**, be obsequious, be servile, be sycophantic, fawn, kowtow, bow and scrape, toady, truckle, abase oneself, humble oneself, prostrate oneself; curry favour with, flatter, court, woo, dance attendance on, make up to, play up to, ingratiate oneself with; *informal* crawl, creep, suck up, butter up, be all over, fall all over, lick someone's boots, rub up the right way; *archaic* blandish.

grow ▶ verb 1 *the baby is growing and looking healthy | the food mountains continue to grow* **get bigger**, get taller, get larger, increase in size, increase in weight, fill out, fatten; heighten, lengthen, enlarge, extend, expand, stretch, spread, widen; swell, increase, multiply, snowball, mushroom, balloon, augment, build up, mount up, pile up.
OPPOSITE shrink.
2 *grass and flowers grew among the rocks* **sprout**, shoot up, spring up, develop, bud, burst forth, germinate, bloom; emerge, arise, spread; flourish, thrive, run riot; *rare* pullulate, vegetate, burgeon.
OPPOSITE fail.
3 *he grew beautiful flowers in his garden* **cultivate**, produce, propagate, raise, rear, bring on, nurture, tend; farm, plant, sow.
4 *the family businesses grew over the years* **expand**, improve, advance, develop, progress, make progress, make headway; **flourish**, thrive, burgeon, prosper, succeed, be successful, get on well, boom; *informal* go great guns, rocket, skyrocket.
OPPOSITES decline; fail.
5 *the fable grew from an ancient Indian source* **originate**, stem, spring, arise, have its origin, emerge, issue, spread, extend; develop, evolve.
6 *after an hour of waiting Leonora grew bored* **become**, come to be, get to be, get, turn, start to feel.

growl ▶ verb 1 *the black dog growled at him* **snarl**, bark, yap, bay.
2 *'Get out of my pub,' growled Jim* **say roughly**, say brusquely, say nastily, say angrily, say abruptly, bark, snap, snarl, fling, hurl; round on someone; *informal* jump down someone's throat.

grown-up ▶ noun *she wanted to be treated like a grown-up* **adult**, grown person, grown-up person, mature person; woman, grown woman, mature woman, man, grown man, mature man, lady, gentleman.
OPPOSITE child.
▶ adjective *Christine has two grown-up daughters and seven grandchildren* **adult**, mature, of age, having reached one's majority; fully grown, full-grown, fully developed, fully fledged.
OPPOSITES infant, juvenile.

growth ▶ noun 1 *many countries have rapid population growth* **increase**, expansion, augmentation, proliferation, multiplication, enlargement, amplification, mushrooming, snowballing, rise, escalation, build-up; development, evolution.
OPPOSITE decrease.
2 *the hormone stimulates the growth of the pancreas* **growing**, extension, widening, thickening, broadening, heightening, swelling, magnification, ballooning.
OPPOSITE shrinking.
3 *harsh weather stunts the growth of plants* **development**, maturation, growing, germination, shooting up, springing up, sprouting; blooming, flourishing, thriving; *rare* vegetation, burgeoning, pullulation.
OPPOSITE withering.
4 *the marked growth of local enterprises* **expansion**, development, progress, advance, advancement, headway, improvement, furtherance, extension, spread, buildout, escalation; rise, success, thriving, flourishing, blooming; boom, upturn, upswing.
OPPOSITES decline; failure.
5 *he went to hospital to have a growth removed* **tumour**, cancerous growth, malignant growth, malignancy, cancer; lump, outgrowth, swelling, protuberance, protrusion, knob, nodule; cyst, polyp; *technical* process, bulla; *rare* excrescence, intumescence, tumescence, tumefaction.

WORD LINKS

prefix related to growth	**-plasia (e.g. *dysplasia, achondroplasia*)**
relating to growths	**onco- (e.g. *oncogenic*)**
suffix related to growths	**-oma (e.g. *carcinoma, melanoma*)**
branch of medicine concerned with growths	**oncology**

grub ▶ noun 1 *the grub becomes a fully grown beetle* **larva**, maggot; caterpillar.
2 (*informal*) *we had third helpings of delicious pub grub.* See FOOD.
▶ verb 1 *kids like* ***grubbing around in*** *the dirt* **dig**, excavate, burrow, tunnel; poke about/around, scratch about/around, rake through, sift through, explore, probe; *literary* delve.
2 *they* ***grub up*** *the old trees and replace them* **dig up**, unearth, disinter, uproot, root out, root up, pull up, pull out, tear out, take out of the ground; *literary* deracinate.
OPPOSITE plant.
3 *he began* ***grubbing about in*** *the waste-paper basket* **search**, hunt, delve, dig, rummage, scrabble, scour, probe, ferret (about/around), root, rifle, fish, poke; go through, turn upside down, turn inside out; *Brit. informal* rootle; *Austral./NZ informal* fossick through; *rare* roust.
4 *she achieved financial independence without having to grub for it* **slave**, toil, labour, grind, plod, sweat, struggle, strive, overwork oneself, work very hard, work one's fingers to the bone, work like a Trojan/dog, keep one's nose to the grindstone; *informal* slog away, plug away, peg away, kill oneself, put one's back into it, sweat blood, knock oneself out; *Brit. informal* graft, fag; *archaic* drudge, travail, moil.
OPPOSITE take it easy.

grubby ▶ adjective *grubby net curtains* **dirty**, grimy, filthy, unwashed, stained, soiled, smeared, spotted, muddy, dusty, sooty; messy, scruffy, shabby, untidy, unkempt, slovenly, slatternly, sordid, squalid; unhygienic, unsanitary, insanitary; *informal* mucky, cruddy, yucky, icky; *Brit. informal* manky, grotty, gungy; *literary* befouled, besmirched, besmeared, begrimed; *rare* feculent.
OPPOSITE clean.

grudge ▶ noun *the attack was carried out by someone with a grudge* **grievance**; resentment, bitterness, rancour, pique, umbrage, displeasure, dissatisfaction, disgruntlement, bad feelings, hard feelings, ill feelings, ill will, venom, hate, hatred, dislike, aversion, animosity, antipathy, antagonism, enmity, animus; *informal* a chip on one's shoulder.
▶ verb 1 *he grudged the time that the meetings involved* **begrudge**, resent, feel aggrieved/bitter about, be annoyed about, be angry about, be displeased about, be resentful of, mind, object to, take exception to, regret; give unwillingly, give reluctantly, give resentfully, give stintingly.
2 *I do not grudge you your success* **envy**, begrudge, resent, mind; be jealous of, be envious of, be resentful of.

grudging ▶ adjective *she offered a grudging apology* **reluctant**, unwilling, disinclined, forced, half-hearted, unenthusiastic, hesitant; begrudging, resentful, envious, jealous, sullen, sulky, sour, bitter.
OPPOSITE eager.

gruelling ▶ adjective *he undertook a gruelling three-mile run* **exhausting**, tiring, fatiguing, wearying, enervating, taxing, draining, sapping, debilitating; demanding, exacting, trying, difficult, hard, arduous, laborious, back-breaking, strenuous, harsh, severe, stiff, punishing, crushing, crippling, grinding, brutal, relentless, unsparing; *informal* killing, murderous, hellish; *Brit. informal* knackering; *rare* exigent.

gruesome ▶ adjective *the gruesome evidence of a recent massacre* **grisly**, ghastly, frightful, horrid, horrifying, fearful, hideous, macabre, spine-chilling, horrible, horrendous, grim, awful, dire, dreadful, terrible, horrific; disgusting, repulsive, repugnant, revolting, repellent, sickening, distressing, shocking, appalling, abominable, loathsome, abhorrent, odious, monstrous, unspeakable; *informal* sick, sick-making, gut-churning, gross; *archaic* disgustful, loathly.
OPPOSITE pleasant.

gruff ▶ adjective **1** *a gruff reply | his gruff exterior hid a sensitive nature* **abrupt**, brusque, curt, short, blunt, bluff, no-nonsense; laconic, taciturn; surly, churlish, grumpy, crotchety, crabby, crabbed, cross, bad-tempered, short-tempered, ill-natured, crusty, tetchy, bearish, sullen, sour, uncivil, rude, unmannerly, impolite, discourteous, ungracious, unceremonious, offhand; *informal* grouchy, off, offish.
OPPOSITES friendly; courteous.
2 *a gruff male voice bade them enter* **rough**, hoarse, harsh, guttural, throaty, husky, croaking, rasping, raspy, gravelly, growly, growling; low, thick.
OPPOSITES soft, mellow.

grumble ▶ verb **1** *the players* **grumble about** *the referee* **complain**, moan, groan, whine, mutter, grouse, bleat, carp, cavil, protest; object to, speak out against, find fault with; *informal* bellyache, beef, bitch, grouch, whinge, sound off, go on, pick holes in; *Brit. informal* gripe, grizzle, chunter, create; *N. English informal* mither; *N. Amer. informal* kvetch; *S. African informal* chirp; *Brit. dated* crib, natter; *archaic* plain over.
2 *my stomach was starting to grumble audibly* **rumble**, gurgle, murmur, growl, roar.
▶ noun **1** *he listens to his customers' grumbles* **complaint**, moan, groan, whine, muttering, grievance, objection, protest, protestation, cavil, quibble, criticism, charge, accusation; *informal* grouse, grouch, whinge, beef, beefing, bellyaching, bitching, grouching, whingeing; *Brit. informal* gripe; *Law, Brit.* plaint.
2 *the grumble of his stomach* **rumble**, gurgle, murmur, growl, roar.

grumpy ▶ adjective *she can be grumpy first thing in the morning* **bad-tempered**, ill-tempered, short-tempered, crotchety, crabby, crabbed, tetchy, testy, waspish, prickly, peppery, touchy, irritable, irascible, crusty, cantankerous, curmudgeonly, bearish, surly, churlish, ill-natured, ill-humoured, peevish, cross, as cross as two sticks, fractious, disagreeable, pettish; having got out of bed on the wrong side; *informal* grouchy, snappy, snappish, chippy, on a short fuse, short-fused; *Brit. informal* shirty, stroppy, narky, ratty, eggy, like a bear with a sore head; *N. Amer. informal* cranky, ornery, peckish, soreheaded; *Austral./NZ informal* snaky; *informal, dated* miffy, waxy.
OPPOSITE good-humoured.

guarantee ▶ noun **1** *all repairs have a one-year guarantee* **warranty**, warrant, contract, covenant, bond, assurance, promise.
2 *they gave their guarantee that the hospital would stay open* **promise**, assurance, word, word of honour, pledge, vow, oath, bond, commitment.
3 *banks usually demand a personal guarantee for loans* **collateral**, security, surety, guaranty, assurance, insurance, indemnity, indemnification; *archaic* gage, earnest.
4 *I will not venture to be your guarantee* **guarantor**, warrantor, underwriter, voucher, sponsor, supporter, backer; *Law* bondsman.
▶ verb **1** *they have to guarantee the loan with their own personal assets* **underwrite**, sponsor, support, back, insure, indemnify, vouch for, put up collateral for, give earnest money for, provide surety for, provide (financial) security for; *informal* be ready to pick up the tab for; *N. Amer. informal* bankroll.
2 *can you guarantee that he wasn't involved?* **promise**, swear, swear to the fact, pledge, vow, undertake, give one's word, give an assurance, give assurances, give an undertaking, give a pledge, swear an oath, take an oath, cross one's heart (and hope to die); *archaic* plight.

guarantor ▶ noun *a guarantor of the company's debts* **warrantor**, guarantee, underwriter, voucher, sponsor, supporter, backer; *Law* bondsman.

guard ▶ verb **1** *the infantry guarded the barricaded bridge* **protect**, stand guard over, watch over, look after, keep an eye on, take care of, cover, patrol, police, defend, shield, safeguard, preserve, save, keep safe, secure, screen, shelter; fortify, garrison, barricade; man, occupy.
2 *the prisoners were guarded by armed men* **keep under surveillance**, keep under guard, keep watch over, mind, supervise, restrain, control.
3 *the forest wardens have to* **guard against** *poachers* **beware of**, keep watch for, be alert to, take care for, keep an eye out for, be on the alert for, be on the qui vive for, be on the lookout for; *informal* keep one's eyes peeled/skinned for.
▶ noun **1** *the refugees were turned back by the border guards* **sentry**, sentinel, security guard, nightwatchman; protector, defender, guardian, custodian, keeper; scout, lookout, watch; garrison; *informal* bouncer; *archaic* watchman.
2 *she slipped easily past her prison guard* **jailer**, warder, wardress, warden, prison officer, keeper, incarcerator, captor, sentry; *informal* screw; *Law* detainer; *archaic* turnkey.
3 *he let his guard slip and they escaped* **vigilance**, vigil, watch, close watch, monitoring, policing, surveillance, sentry duty; watchfulness, caution, heed, attention, care, wariness.
4 *all machines must be fitted with a guard* **safety guard**, safety device, protective device, shield, bulwark, screen, fence, fender, bumper, buffer, cushion, pad.
□ **off (one's) guard** *he was caught off guard when the man charged towards him* **unprepared**, unready, inattentive, unwary, unwatchful, with one's defences down, by surprise, cold, unsuspecting; *informal* napping, asleep on the job, asleep at the wheel, on the hop.
OPPOSITE prepared.
□ **on one's guard** *police are urging horse owners to be on their guard* **vigilant**, alert, on the alert, wary, watchful, cautious, careful, heedful, chary, circumspect, on the lookout, on the qui vive, on one's toes, prepared, ready, wideawake, attentive, observant, keeping one's eyes peeled; *informal* all ears, beady-eyed, on the ball, not missing a trick, keeping a weather eye on things, cagey, leery; *rare* regardful, Argus-eyed.
OPPOSITE inattentive.

guarded ▶ adjective *his colleagues showed guarded enthusiasm for the proposal* **cautious**, careful, circumspect, wary, chary, reluctant, non-committal, reticent, restrained, reserved, controlled, moderate, discreet, unrevealing, vague, diplomatic, prudent, politic, tactful; with reservations; *informal* cagey, leery.
OPPOSITES revealing; obvious.

guardian ▶ noun *an indefatigable guardian of public morality* **protector**, defender, preserver, champion, custodian, warden, guard, keeper; conservator, curator, caretaker, steward, trustee, supervisor.

WORD LINKS
relating to a guardian **tutelary**

guerrilla ▶ noun *there was fierce fighting between guerrillas and government troops* **freedom fighter**, underground fighter, irregular soldier, irregular, resistance fighter, member of the resistance, partisan; rebel, radical, revolutionary, revolutionist; terrorist.

guess ▶ verb **1** *she was asked to guess the weight of the animal* **estimate**, calculate, approximate, make a guess at, make an estimate of; **hypothesize**, postulate, predict, speculate, conjecture, surmise, reckon, fathom; evaluate, judge, gauge, determine, rate, appraise, weigh up, form an opinion of; *informal* guesstimate, size up.
2 (*informal*) *I guess I owe you an apology* **suppose**, think, believe, imagine, expect, assume, presume, judge, consider, feel, suspect, dare say, fancy, divine, deem, conjecture, surmise, conclude, hazard a guess, be of the opinion, be given to understand; *N. Amer.* figure; *informal* reckon.
▶ noun *my guess is that he is a receiver of stolen cars* **hypothesis**, theory, prediction, postulation, conjecture; conclusion, belief, opinion, surmise, estimate, reckoning, judgement, supposition, assumption, speculation, notion, suspicion, impression, feeling; *informal* guesstimate.

guesswork ▶ noun *their estimates were based largely on guesswork* **guessing**, conjecture, surmise, supposition, assumption, presumption, suspicion, speculation, hypothesizing, theorizing, prediction, expectation; approximations, rough calculations; feelings, hunches; *informal* guesstimates; *N. Amer. informal* ballpark figures.

guest ▶ noun **1** *he took dinner with his guests* **visitor**, caller; company; *archaic* visitant.
OPPOSITE host.
2 *the hotel allowed two towels per guest* **patron**, client, person staying; **boarder**, lodger, resident, tenant, paying guest, PG; *N. Amer.* roomer.
OPPOSITES landlady, landlord.

guest house ▶ noun *she spent three nights in a Blackpool guest house* **boarding house**, bed and breakfast, B&B, hotel, motel; inn, hostelry.

guff ▶ noun (*informal*) *there's been a lot of nostalgic guff written about the sixties* **nonsense**, rubbish, garbage, claptrap, balderdash, blather, blether, moonshine; foolishness, silliness; *informal* rot, tripe, hogwash, baloney, drivel, bilge, bosh, bull, bunk, eyewash, piffle, poppycock, phooey, hooey, malarkey, twaddle, dribble; *Brit. informal* cobblers, codswallop, stuff and nonsense, tosh, cack; *Scottish & N. English informal* havers; *N. Amer. informal* flapdoodle, blathers, applesauce, wack, bushwa; *informal, dated* bunkum, tommyrot, cod, gammon, toffee; *vulgar slang* bullshit, crap, balls; *Brit. vulgar slang* bollocks; *Austral./NZ vulgar slang* bulldust.

guffaw ▶ verb *he guffawed at his own punchline* **laugh heartily**, laugh loudly, roar with laughter, hoot with laughter, laugh uncontrollably; roar, bellow, cackle, howl; *informal* laugh like a drain.
▶ noun *his joke brought a great guffaw from the youth* **hearty laugh**, loud laugh, roar of laughter, hoot of laughter, shriek of laughter, peal of laughter, belly laugh.

guidance ▶ noun **1** *she looked to her instructor for guidance* **advice**, counsel, direction, instruction, teaching, counselling, enlightenment, intelligence, information; recommendations, suggestions, tips, hints, pointers, guidelines, ideas, facts, data; *informal* info, gen, dope, the low-down, the inside story.
2 *we are working under the guidance of a strong chairman* **direction**, control, leadership, management, supervision, superintendence, government, regulation, orchestration, charge, rule, command; handling, conduct, running, overseeing.

guide ▸ noun **1** *this man will be your guide in the jungle* **escort**, attendant, conductor, courier, pilot, usher, chaperone; *rare* cicerone, convoy.
2 *the abbot is their inspiration and their guide* **adviser**, mentor, counsellor, guidance counsellor; confidant, tutor, teacher, guru, consultant; therapist; *informal* main man.
3 *their guide along the road was a faint, distant light* **pointer**, marker, indicator, signpost, key, clue, mark, landmark; **guiding light**, sign, signal, beacon, lodestar.
4 *the techniques outlined are meant as a guide* **model**, pattern, blueprint, template, archetype, prototype, sample, example, exemplar; standard, touchstone, measure, benchmark, yardstick, gauge, norm, paradigm, ideal, precedent, guiding principle.
5 *she studied a pocket guide of Washington* **guidebook**, tourist guide, travel guide, Baedeker, travelogue, directory, handbook, manual, ABC, A to Z; *Latin* vade mecum; *rare* enchiridion.
▸ verb **1** *could you guide me back to the house?* **lead**, lead the way, conduct, show, show someone the way, usher, shepherd, direct, steer, pilot, escort, accompany, attend; see, take, help, assist.
OPPOSITE follow.
2 *the chairman must guide the meeting* **direct**, steer, control, manage, command, lead, conduct, run, be in charge of, take charge of, take control of, have control of, govern, rule, preside over, superintend, supervise, oversee; handle, regulate, manipulate, manoeuvre.
3 *they guide adolescents through their critical years* **advise**, counsel, give advice to, give counsel to, give counselling to, direct, give direction to, make recommendations to, make suggestions to, give someone tips, give someone hints, give someone pointers, inform, give information to; illuminate, educate, instruct, teach, give instruction to, be responsible for the education of.

G

guidebook ▸ noun *they followed the tour in the museum guidebook* **guide**, travel guide, tourist guide, Baedeker, travelogue; visitor's guide, companion, handbook, directory, manual, ABC, A to Z; reference book; *Latin* vade mecum; *informal* bible; *rare* enchiridion, promptuary.

guideline ▸ noun *the planning authorities have fairly strict guidelines* **recommendation**, instruction, direction, suggestion, advice; regulation, rule, requirement, specification, prescription, precept, principle, guiding principle; standard, criterion, measure, gauge, yardstick, benchmark, touchstone; procedure, parameter, constraint, limit.

guild ▸ noun *a member of the Women's Cooperative Guild* **association**, society, union, league, alliance, coalition, federation, consortium, syndicate, combine, trust, organization, company, cooperative, partnership, fellowship, club, order, lodge, sisterhood, sorority, brotherhood, fraternity; *rare* consociation, sodality.

guile ▸ noun *they penetrated the city's defences by guile* **cunning**, craftiness, craft, artfulness, art, artifice, wiliness, slyness, deviousness, shrewdness, canniness, ingenuity; wiles, ploys, schemes, stratagems, manoeuvres, subterfuges, tricks, ruses; deception, deceit, duplicity, underhandedness, double-dealing, trickery, trickiness, sharp practice, treachery, chicanery, skulduggery, fraud; *informal* foxiness; *archaic* knavery, knavishness, management.
OPPOSITES honesty; candour.

guileless ▸ adjective *Paulette's questioning had the guileless innocence of a child* **artless**, ingenuous, open, honest, sincere, genuine, naive, natural, simple, childlike, innocent, unsophisticated, unworldly, unsuspicious, trustful, trusting; honourable, truthful, frank, candid, straightforward, forthright, unaffected, unpretentious; *N. Amer.* on the up and up.
OPPOSITE scheming.

guilt ▸ noun **1** *the new evidence made them doubt his guilt* **culpability**, guiltiness, blameworthiness, wrongdoing, wrong, wrongfulness, criminality, unlawfulness, misconduct, delinquency, sin, sinfulness, iniquity; responsibility, accountability, liability, answerability.
OPPOSITE innocence.
2 *eat your food and enjoy it without guilt* **self-reproach**, self-accusation, self-condemnation, feelings of guilt, guiltiness, a guilty conscience, a bad conscience, pangs of conscience; **remorse**, remorsefulness, regret, contrition, contriteness, repentance, penitence, compunction; shame, disgrace, dishonour; *archaic* rue.
OPPOSITE shamelessness.

guiltless ▸ adjective *I am entirely guiltless in this matter* **innocent**, blameless, free from guilt, free from blame, not to blame, without fault, above reproach, beyond criticism, above suspicion, in the clear, uncensurable, unimpeachable, irreproachable, faultless, sinless, spotless, stainless, immaculate, unsullied, uncorrupted, undefiled, untainted, unblemished, untarnished, impeccable; *informal* squeaky clean, whiter than white, as pure as the driven snow.
OPPOSITE guilty.

CHOOSE THE RIGHT WORD

guiltless, blameless, innocent

See INNOCENT.

guilty ▸ adjective **1** *he was found guilty of a criminal offence* **culpable**, to blame, blameworthy, blameable, at fault, in the wrong, responsible, answerable, accountable, liable; censurable, reproachable, condemnable, reprehensible, erring, errant, delinquent, offending, sinful, felonious, iniquitous, criminal, convicted; *archaic* peccant.
OPPOSITE innocent.
2 *he felt guilty at deceiving his family* **ashamed**, guilt-ridden, conscience-stricken, remorseful, sorry, regretful, contrite, repentant, penitent, rueful, abashed, shamefaced, sheepish, hangdog; mortified, discomfited, distressed, uncomfortable; in sackcloth and ashes; *informal* with one's tail between one's legs; *rare* compunctious.
OPPOSITE unrepentant.

guise ▸ noun **1** *the god appeared in the guise of a swan* **likeness**, external appearance, appearance, semblance, form, outward form, shape, image, aspect; disguise, false colours; costume, clothes, outfit, dress.
2 *the king sent forces into Flanders under the guise of a crusade* **pretence**, false show, false front, false display, show, front, facade, illusion, cover, blind, screen, smokescreen, masquerade, posture, pose, act, charade; *informal* put-on, put-up job.

gulf ▸ noun **1** *our ship sailed east into the gulf* **inlet**, creek, bight, fjord, estuary, sound, arm of the sea; bay, cove; *Scottish* firth, frith; (*in Orkney & Shetland*) voe; *technical* ria; *rare* fleet, armlet.
2 *the ice gave way and a gulf widened slowly* **opening**, gap, fissure, cleft, split, rift, crevasse, hole, pit, cavity, chasm, abyss, void; ravine, gorge, canyon, gully.
3 *there is a growing gulf between the rich and the poor* **divergence**, contrast, polarity, divide, division, separation, difference, wide area of difference; **schism**, breach, rift, split, severance, rupture, divorce; chasm, abyss, gap; *rare* scission.

gull ▸ verb *she knew she wouldn't be able to gull him* **hoodwink**, hoax, dupe, deceive, trick, fool, make a fool of, mislead, take in, delude, misguide; lead on, inveigle, seduce, ensnare, entrap, beguile; swindle, defraud, cheat, double-cross; *informal* pull the wool over someone's eyes, pull a fast one on, put one over on, sell a pup to, take to the cleaners, con, do, sting, gyp, rip off, diddle, swizzle, shaft, bilk, rook, bamboozle, finagle; *N. Amer. informal* sucker, snooker, stiff, euchre, bunco, hornswoggle; *Austral. informal* pull a swifty on; *archaic* cozen, sharp; *rare* mulct.
▸ noun *she is unaware of being the gull of John's plot* **dupe**, victim, pawn, puppet, instrument; fool, simpleton, innocent; *informal* sucker, stooge, sitting duck, sitting target, soft touch, pushover, chump, muggins, charlie, fall guy; *Brit. informal* mug; *N. Amer. informal* pigeon, patsy, sap, schlemiel, mark; *Austral./NZ informal* dill; *Brit. informal, dated* juggins.

gullet ▸ noun **oesophagus**, throat, pharynx; crop, craw, maw; *informal, dated* the red lane; *archaic* weasand, throttle, gorge, gula.

WORD LINKS

relating to the gullet **oesophageal**

gullible ▸ adjective *the swindler preyed upon gullible old women* **credulous**, over-trusting, over-trustful, trustful, easily deceived/led, easily taken in, exploitable, dupable, deceivable, impressionable, unsuspecting, unsuspicious, unwary, unguarded, unsceptical, ingenuous, naive, innocent, simple, inexperienced, unworldly, green, as green as grass, childlike, ignorant; foolish, silly; *informal* wet behind the ears, born yesterday.
OPPOSITES cynical; suspicious.

CHOOSE THE RIGHT WORD

gullible, credulous

- A **gullible** person is easy to deceive because they are too ready to believe or trust someone (*professional manipulators intent on pulling the wool over the eyes of a gullible public*). They are particularly likely to believe something that would be to their advantage or that they want to be true. *Gullible* carries a note of scornful pity at someone's foolish failure to examine the evidence critically.
- **Credulous** also describes people who are too ready to believe or accept what they are told (*the very incomprehensibility of the modern world has made us even more credulous*), but, unlike *gullible*, *credulous* does not necessarily imply that anyone is deliberately trying to take advantage of an easily-fooled person.

gully ▸ noun **1** *the climber plunged 300 feet down an icy gully* **ravine**, canyon, gorge, pass, defile, couloir, deep narrow valley; gulf, chasm, abyss; *S. English* chine, bunny; *N. English* clough, gill, thrutch; *Scottish* cleuch, heugh; *N. Amer.* gulch, coulee, flume; *S. African* sloot, kloof, donga.
2 *the water runs from the drainpipe into a gully* **channel**, conduit, trench, ditch, drain, culvert, cut, flume, gutter, furrow, groove, depression.

gulp ▸ verb **1** *Belinda gulped her juice* **swallow**, quaff, swill down, down; drain one's glass; *informal* swig, slug down, knock back, toss off.
OPPOSITE sip.
2 *the spaniels* **gulped down** *what was left on the plates* **gobble**, guzzle, bolt, wolf, cram, stuff; devour, gorge (oneself) on, eat greedily, eat hungrily;

informal tuck into, put away, pack away, demolish, polish off, stuff one's face with, pig oneself on, murder, shovel down; *Brit. informal* scoff, shift.
OPPOSITE pick at.
3 *Jenny gulped back her tears* **choke back**, fight back, hold back, hold in, keep back, restrain, suppress, stifle, smother, strangle, muffle, quench, curb, check, withhold, contain, bottle up.
OPPOSITE let out.
▶ **noun** *he took a gulp of the cold beer* **mouthful**, swallow, draught; *informal* swig.
OPPOSITE sip.

gum[1] ▶ **noun** *the photographs were stuck down with gum* **glue**, adhesive, fixative, paste, cement, resin, epoxy resin, superglue; *N. Amer.* mucilage; *N. Amer. informal* stickum.
▶ **verb** *the receipts were gummed into a special book* **stick**, glue, paste, cement; fix, affix, attach, fasten, post.
□ **gum something up 1** *check the valves to make sure that they don't get gummed up* **clog (up)**, choke (up), stop up, dam up, plug, congest, jam, obstruct, occlude, close; *informal* bung up, gunge up.
2 *perfectionism tends to gum up the works* **obstruct**, impede, hinder, interfere with, bring to a halt.

gum[2] ▶ **noun** (*Anatomy*)

WORD LINKS
relating to the gums **gingival**
inflammation of the gums **gingivitis**

gummy ▶ **adjective** *conifers exude a gummy substance* **sticky**, tacky, gluey, adhesive, resinous, viscous, viscid, glutinous, mucilaginous; *Brit.* claggy; *Scottish & N. English* clarty; *informal* gooey, gloopy, cloggy, gungy, icky; *N. Amer. informal* gloppy; *rare* viscoid.

gumption ▶ **noun** (*informal*) *she had the gumption to go and make a better life for herself* **initiative**, resourcefulness, enterprise, imagination, imaginativeness, ingenuity, inventiveness; cleverness, astuteness, shrewdness, acumen, discernment, understanding, reason, wisdom, sagacity, sense, common sense, wit, mother wit, native wit, native ability, practicality; spirit, forcefulness, backbone, pluck, mettle, nerve, courage; *informal* get-up-and-go, grit, spunk, oomph, nous, savvy, horse sense; *Brit. informal* loaf, common; *N. Amer. informal* smarts.
OPPOSITE stupidity.

gun *See centre pages for lists of* **Guns Projectiles and Projectile Weapons**
▶ **noun firearm**, weapon; *informal* shooter, cannon; *N. Amer. informal* piece, heater, gat, rod, roscoe, shooting iron.

WORD LINKS
seller of guns **gunsmith**

gunfire ▶ **noun** *they heard the distant sounds of gunfire* **gunshots**, shots, shooting, firing, sniping; artillery fire, strafing, shelling, bombardment.

gunman ▶ **noun** *the gunman broke into the bank through the roof* **armed robber**, hold-up man, bandit, gangster, terrorist, gunfighter; sniper, assassin, murderer, killer, liquidator; *informal* stick-up man, hit man, gun, hired gun, contract man, hatchet man, trigger man, gunslinger, mobster; *N. Amer. informal* shootist, hood, button man.

gurgle ▶ **verb 1** *the creek splashes and gurgles in a series of pools* **babble**, burble, tinkle, bubble, ripple, murmur, purl, lap, trickle, splash; *literary* plash.
2 *the baby gurgled and smiled at Ruth* **burble**, babble, chuckle, giggle, laugh, crow.
▶ **noun 1** *there was silence except for the gurgle of a small brook* **babble**, babbling, tinkle, bubbling, ripple, rippling, trickling, murmur, murmuring, purling, splashing; *literary* plashing.
2 *Catherine gave a gurgle of laughter* **chuckle**, chortle, burble, giggle; crow.

guru ▶ **noun 1** *his guru instructed him to set off on a pilgrimage* **spiritual teacher**, teacher, tutor, sage, counsellor, mentor, guiding light, spiritual leader, leader, master; *Indian* acharya, pandit; *Hinduism* swami, Maharishi; *Buddhism* Roshi; *Judaism* rabbi, rav, rebbe.
OPPOSITE disciple.
2 *a natural childbirth guru* **expert**, authority, leading light, professional, master, pundit; *informal* buff, whizz, boffin.
OPPOSITE amateur.

gush ▶ **verb 1** *the white waters gushed through the weir* **surge**, burst, spout, spurt, jet, stream, rush, pour, spill, well out, cascade, flood; flow, run, issue, emanate; *Brit. informal* sloosh; *rare* disembogue.
2 *they were gushing about her dress for the dance* **enthuse**, over-enthuse, be enthusiastic, be effusive, effuse; **rave**, rhapsodize, go into raptures, wax lyrical, effervesce, bubble over; get carried away, make too much of, overstate the case, praise to the skies; *informal* go mad, go crazy, go wild, get all worked up, go over the top; *N. Amer. informal* ballyhoo; *black English* big something up; *dated* cry something up.
▶ **noun** *the pipe sent forth a gush of water* **surge**, stream, spurt, jet, spout, outpouring, outflow, burst, rush, cascade, flood, torrent, sweep; *technical* flux, efflux.

gushing, gushy ▶ **adjective** *the gushing praise of the New York critics* **effusive**, over-effusive, enthusiastic, over-enthusiastic, unrestrained, unreserved, extravagant, fulsome, lavish, rhapsodic, lyrical, exuberant, ebullient, expansive; *informal* over the top, OTT, hyped up, laid on with a trowel.
OPPOSITE restrained.

gust ▶ **noun 1** *a sudden gust of wind* **flurry**, blast, puff, blow, rush, squall.
2 *a great gust of delighted laughter came from downstairs* **outburst**, burst, outbreak, gale, effusion, eruption, explosion, storm, surge, peal, howl, hoot, shriek, roar; fit, paroxysm.
▶ **verb** *the wind gusted around chimneys* **bluster**, flurry, blow, blast, roar.

gusto ▶ **noun** *he was attacking his breakfast with some gusto* **enthusiasm**, relish, appetite, enjoyment, delight, glee, pleasure, satisfaction, gratification, appreciation, liking, fondness; zest, zeal, fervour, verve, keenness, avidity; *humorous* delectation.
OPPOSITES apathy; distaste.

CHOOSE THE RIGHT WORD
gusto, zest, verve
See ZEST.

G

gusty ▶ **adjective** *a gusty autumnal night* **blustery**, breezy, windy, squally, gusting, blustering; stormy, tempestuous, wild, turbulent, violent; *informal* blowy.
OPPOSITE calm.

gut ▶ **noun 1** (also **guts**) *he had an ache in his gut* **stomach**, belly, abdomen; intestines, bowels, colon; *informal* tummy, tum, insides, innards, breadbasket; *Austral. informal* bingy; *Medicine* solar plexus.
2 (**guts**) *they threw away the fish heads and guts* **intestines**, entrails; **vital organs**, bodily organs, vital parts, viscera; offal; *informal* insides, innards; *Brit. archaic* numbles.
3 (**guts**) (*informal*) *Nicola had the guts to say exactly what she felt* **courage**, courageousness, bravery, valour, backbone, nerve, fortitude, pluck, pluckiness, mettle, mettlesomeness, spirit, boldness, audacity, daring, fearlessness, hardiness, toughness, forcefulness, determination, resolve, resolution; *informal* grit, gumption, spunk, gutsiness, gameness; *Brit. informal* bottle, ballsiness; *N. Amer. informal* moxie, cojones, sand; *vulgar slang* balls.
OPPOSITE cowardice.
▶ **adjective** (*informal*) *she had a gut feeling that something was not right* **instinctive**, instinctual, intuitive, impulsive, natural, basic, emotional, heartfelt, deep-seated; knee-jerk, automatic, involuntary, spontaneous, unthinking, unconditioned.
▶ **verb 1** *the pilchards had to be gutted and salted* **disembowel**, eviscerate, draw, dress, clean, remove the innards from, remove the guts from; *rare* embowel, disbowel, exenterate, gralloch, paunch.
2 *the entire church was gutted by fire* **devastate**, destroy, demolish, wipe out, lay waste to, ravage, consume, ruin, leave in ruins, wreck, raze, level, flatten; *literary* despoil.

WORD LINKS
relating to the gut **visceral, enteric**
related prefix **enter- (e.g. *enteritis, enterovirus*)**

gutless ▶ **adjective** (*informal*) *he's too gutless to stand up to them. See* COWARDLY.

gutsy ▶ **adjective** (*informal*) *he is a gutsy and popular player* **courageous**, brave, mettlesome, plucky, bold, valiant, valorous, intrepid, heroic, lionhearted, daring, fearless, daredevil, adventurous, audacious, undaunted, unflinching, unshrinking, unafraid, dauntless, indomitable, doughty, venturesome, stout-hearted, spirited; determined, resolute, forceful, death-or-glory; *N. Amer.* rock-ribbed; *informal* spunky, game, ballsy, have-a-go; *rare* venturous.
OPPOSITE gutless.

gutter ▶ **noun** *a tide of rainwater swept into the gutter* **drain**, sluice, sluiceway, culvert, spillway, flume, sewer; channel, conduit, pipe, duct, chute; trough, trench, ditch, furrow, cut.

guttersnipe ▶ **noun** *the child was a penniless guttersnipe* **urchin**, street urchin, ragamuffin, waif, stray, outcast, orphan; *informal* scarecrow; *dated* gamin; *archaic* mudlark, scapegrace, street Arab, wastrel, tatterdemalion.

guttural ▶ **adjective** *he heard guttural shouts in a foreign language* **throaty**, husky, gruff, gravelly, growly, growling, croaky, croaking, harsh, harsh-sounding, rough, rasping, raspy, grating, jarring; deep, low, thick.

guy ▶ **noun 1** (*informal*) *he's quite a handsome guy* **man**, fellow, gentleman; lad, youth, boy; individual, person, soul; *informal* fella, geezer, gent, character, customer, creature, sort, type; *Brit. informal* chap, bloke, bod; *N. Amer. informal* dude, hombre; *Austral./NZ informal* digger, bastard; *S. African informal* ou, oom, oke; *Indian informal* admi; *Brit. informal, dated* cove; *Brit. vulgar slang* sod, bugger; *archaic* wight; *Scottish archaic* carl.
2 (*Brit.*) *the kids asked passing workers for pennies for the guy* **effigy of Guy Fawkes**; effigy, figure, representation, likeness, image, model, dummy.
▶ **verb** *he didn't realize I was guying the whole idea* **ridicule**, make fun of, poke fun at, laugh at, make a joke of, mock, sneer at, jibe at, jeer at, deride, scorn, scoff at; satirize, lampoon; *informal* send up, rib, take off; *Brit. informal* take the mickey out of, rag; *N. Amer. informal* goof on, rag on; *Austral./NZ*

informal poke mullock at, sling off at; *Brit. vulgar slang* take the piss out of; *dated* make sport of.

guzzle ▶ verb **1** *he guzzled all that was on the table* **gobble (up)**, gulp, bolt, wolf, devour, eat greedily, eat hungrily, cram oneself with, stuff oneself with, gourmandize on; *informal* tuck into, put away, pack away, demolish, polish off, stuff one's face with, pig oneself on, murder, shovel down; *Brit. informal* scoff, shift.
2 *she guzzled down the orange juice* **gulp down**, swallow greedily, swallow, quaff, down, swill; drain one's glass; *informal* knock back, swig, slug down, toss off.

gymnastics ▶ noun. *See centre pages for list of* **Gymnastics Events**

gypsy, gipsy ▶ noun **Romany**, Rom, chal, chai, gitano, gitana, tzigane, Zingaro, Zigeuner, zingana, didicoi; traveller, New Age traveller, New Ager; nomad, migrant, rover, roamer, wanderer, wayfarer; Bedouin, Bohemian; *informal, derogatory* gyppo, gippy; *derogatory* transient, vagrant, vagabond, tinker.

gyrate ▶ verb *flashing lights gyrate above the dance floor* **rotate**, revolve, move in circles, go round in circles, circle, spiral, wheel round, turn round, whirl, pirouette, twirl, swirl, spin, swivel.

gyration ▶ noun *the gyration of the Earth on its own axis* **rotation**, revolution, turning, circling, convolution, spinning, swivelling; wheeling, whirling, pirouetting, twirling, swirling; *rare* circumrotation.

G

habit ▸ noun **1** *sensible eating habits* **practice**, custom, pattern, routine, style, convention, policy, wont, way, manner, mode, norm, tradition, matter of course, rule, usage; tendency, propensity, inclination, bent, proclivity, proneness, disposition, predisposition.
2 *his habit of pulling his ear as he made a point he thought important* **mannerism**, quirk, characteristic gesture, characteristic, foible, trick; trait, tendency, idiosyncrasy, peculiarity, singularity, oddity, eccentricity, way, feature, custom, practice.
3 *the scientific* ***habit of mind*** *helps us to deal intelligently with problems* **disposition**, temperament, character, nature, make-up, constitution, frame of mind, bent.
4 *they financed their drug habit through prostitution* **addiction**, dependence, dependency, craving, fixation, compulsion, obsession, weakness; *informal* monkey; *N. Amer. informal* jones.
5 *a monk's habit* **garment**, outfit, robe, costume, uniform, attire, dress, garb, clothes, clothing, garments; *informal* get-up, rig-out, gear, togs, clobber, rags; *formal* apparel.
□ **in the habit of** *they were in the habit of phoning each other regularly* **accustomed to**, used to, given to, habituated to, addicted to, no stranger to, not new to; wont to, inclined to.
OPPOSITE unaccustomed to.

habitable ▸ adjective *contractors worked around the clock to make the building habitable* **fit to live in**, inhabitable, fit to occupy, in good repair, usable, liveable in, suitable for residential use; *formal* tenantable.
OPPOSITE uninhabitable.

habitat ▸ noun *a record of new plants in their native habitat* **natural environment**, natural element, natural territory, natural surroundings, natural terrain, home, domain, haunt; *formal* habitation, abode.
OPPOSITE unnatural surroundings.

habitation ▸ noun **1** *the house is fit for human habitation* **occupancy**, occupation, residence, residency, living in, housing, billeting, quartering, tenure; *formal* dwelling; *rare* inhabitancy, habitancy, inhabitance, domiciliation.
2 (*formal*) *we walked for an hour without passing a single habitation* **house**, home, seat, lodging, lodging place, a roof over one's head, billet, quarters, living quarters, rooms, accommodation, housing; *informal* pad, digs, diggings; *formal* residence, place of residence, dwelling, dwelling place, abode, domicile.

habit-forming ▸ adjective *habit-forming drugs* **addictive**, causing addiction, causing dependency; compelling, compulsive; *Brit. informal* moreish.
OPPOSITE non-addictive.

habitual ▸ adjective **1** *father's habitual complaints and strictures* **constant**, persistent, continual, continuous, perpetual, non-stop, recurrent, repeated, frequent; interminable, incessant, ceaseless, endless, relentless, unrelenting, never-ending, unremitting, sustained, unabating; *informal* eternal.
OPPOSITE infrequent.
2 *habitual drinkers* **inveterate**, confirmed, addicted, compulsive, obsessive, incorrigible, hardened, ingrained, dyed-in-the-wool, chronic, by habit, regular; *informal* pathological, hooked.
OPPOSITE occasional.
3 *the commuters assembled in their habitual positions along the platform* **customary**, accustomed, regular, usual, normal, set, fixed, established, routine, common, ordinary, familiar, traditional, typical, general, characteristic, standard, time-honoured; *literary* wonted.
OPPOSITE unaccustomed.

habituate ▸ verb *school had* ***habituated*** *him* ***to*** *shabbiness and discomfort* **accustom**, make used, adapt, adjust, attune, acclimatize, acculturate, inure, harden; make familiar with, familiarize with; season; condition, teach, train, school, educate, discipline, break in; *N. Amer.* acclimate.

habitué ▸ noun *a habitué of the West End* **frequent visitor**, regular visitor, regular customer, regular patron, regular client, familiar face, regular, patron, frequenter, haunter.
OPPOSITES passing trade; tourist.

hack[1] ▸ verb **1** *Stuart hacked the padlock off | they had to hack their way through the jungle* **cut**, chop, hew, lop, saw; slash.
2 *he was wheezing and hacking* **cough**, bark, rasp, wheeze.
□ **hack it** (*informal*) *Adam moved out because he couldn't hack it* **cope**, manage, get on, get along, get by, carry on, muddle through, muddle along, come through, stand on one's own two feet, weather the storm; stand it, tolerate it, bear it, endure it, put up with it; *Scottish* thole it; *informal* make out, handle it, abide it, stick it; *Brit. informal* rub along, be doing with it.
□ **hack someone off** (*informal*) *it hacks him off when he misses a putt.* See ANNOY.
▸ noun *a smoker's hack* **cough**, bark, rasp, wheeze.

hack[2] ▸ noun **1** *he briefed the media's industry hacks before the party conference* **journalist**, reporter, correspondent, newspaperman, newspaperwoman, newsman, newswoman, writer, feature writer, contributor, columnist, Grub Street writer; *Brit.* pressman; *N. Amer.* legman, wireman; *Austral.* roundsman; *informal* news hound, journo, scribbler, scribe, hackette, stringer; *N. Amer. informal* newsy; *archaic* penny-a-liner.
2 *a hard-working, clerical hack* **drudge**, menial, menial worker, factotum, toiler, plodder, doormat, hewer of wood and drawer of water; servant, lackey, labourer, slave; *informal* dogsbody, skivvy, running dog, runner; *N. Amer.* peon, gofer; *archaic* scullion, servitor.
3 *the average riding-school hack* **nag**, inferior horse, tired-out horse, worn-out horse, Rosinante; *informal* bag of bones, crock; *N. Amer. informal* plug, crowbait; *Austral./NZ informal* moke; *Brit. informal, dated* screw; *archaic* jade, rip, keffel.
4 (*N. Amer.*) *they hailed an empty hack* **taxi**, cab, taxi cab, minicab, hackney cab; *Brit. formal* hackney carriage; *historical* fiacre.

hackle ▸ noun
□ **make someone's hackles rise** *his impatient reply made her hackles rise* **annoy**, irritate, exasperate, anger, irk, vex, put out, nettle, provoke, incense, gall, rile, infuriate, antagonize, get on someone's nerves, rub up the wrong way, make someone's blood boil, ruffle someone's feathers, ruffle, try someone's patience; offend, pique, peeve, rankle with; *informal* aggravate, needle, make someone see red, hack off, get someone's back up, get someone's goat, get under someone's skin, get up someone's nose, get in someone's hair, get someone's dander up, bug, get, miff; *Brit. informal* wind up, get at, nark, get across, get on someone's wick; *N. Amer. informal* tee off, tick off, burn up, rankle, ride, gravel; *informal, dated* give someone the pip; *vulgar slang* piss off; *rare* exacerbate, hump, rasp.
OPPOSITE appease.

hackneyed ▸ adjective *hackneyed old sayings* **overused**, overworked, overdone, worn out, time-worn, platitudinous, vapid, stale, tired, threadbare; **trite**, banal, hack, clichéd, hoary, commonplace, common, ordinary, stock, conventional, stereotyped, predictable; unimaginative, unoriginal, uninspired, prosaic, dull, boring, pedestrian, run-of-the-mill, routine, humdrum; *informal* old hat, corny, played out; *N. Amer. informal* cornball, dime-store; *rare* truistic, bromidic.
OPPOSITES original, fresh.

> **CHOOSE THE RIGHT WORD**
>
> **hackneyed, trite, stale**
>
> *See* TRITE.

Hades ▸ noun *the fires of Hades* **hell**, the underworld, the land/abode of the dead, the infernal regions, the netherworld, the nether regions, the abyss; eternal damnation, eternal punishment, perdition; *Biblical* Gehenna,

Tophet, Abaddon; *Judaism* Sheol; *Greek Mythology* Tartarus, Acheron; *Roman Mythology* Avernus; *Scandinavian Mythology* Niflheim; *Brit.* the other place; *literary* the pit, the shades; *archaic* the lower world.
OPPOSITE heaven.

haft ▶ noun *my fingers gripped the haft of the knife* **handle**, shaft, shank, hilt, butt, stock, grip, handgrip, helve.
OPPOSITES blade, head.

hag ▶ noun *the old hag lifted her skinny hand* **crone**, old woman, witch, gorgon; *informal* cow, old cow, old bag, old bat.

haggard ▶ adjective *he looked terrible, all grey and haggard* **careworn**, tired, drained, drawn, raddled; unwell, unhealthy, sickly, spent, sapped, washed out, rundown, exhausted; gaunt, grim, pinched, peaked, peaky, hollow-cheeked, hollow-eyed; pale, wan, grey, ashen, pallid, pasty-faced, sallow; thin, emaciated, wasted, cadaverous, ghastly, ghostlike, deathlike.
OPPOSITES fresh, healthy.

haggle ▶ verb *tourists haggled over exotic handicrafts* **barter**, bargain, negotiate, discuss terms, quibble, wrangle; beat someone down, drive a hard bargain; deal, wheel and deal, trade, traffic; *N. Amer.* dicker; *formal* treat; *archaic* chaffer, palter.

hag-ridden ▶ adjective *she was hag-ridden by her misgivings* **tormented**, troubled, anguished, agonized, distressed, tortured, harrowed, racked with suffering, angst-ridden, ground down, worn out, despairing.
OPPOSITE untroubled.

hail[1] ▶ verb **1** *a friend hailed him from the upper deck* **greet**, salute, address, halloo, speak to, call out to, shout to, say hello to, initiate a discussion with, talk to; nod to, wave to, smile at, signal to, lift one's hat to, acknowledge; accost, approach, waylay, stop, catch; *informal* collar, buttonhole; *Brit. informal* nobble.
OPPOSITE say goodbye to.
2 *he hailed a cab* **flag down**, wave down, signal to stop, gesture to stop, make a sign to; call to, shout to; summon, accost.
3 *the critics hailed the new film as a masterpiece* **acclaim**, praise, applaud, commend, rave about, extol, eulogize, vaunt, hymn, lionize, express approval of, express admiration for, pay tribute to, speak highly of, sing the praises of, make much of; **glorify**, cheer, salute, exalt, honour, hurrah, hurray, toast, welcome, pay homage to; *N. Amer. informal* ballyhoo; *black English* big up; *dated* cry up; *archaic* emblazon; *rare* laud, panegyrize.
OPPOSITES criticize, condemn.
4 *the band's twenty-six members all* **hail from** *Wales* **come from**, be from, be a native of, have been born in, originate in, have one's roots in; be … (by birth); live in, have one's home in, inhabit, be an inhabitant of, be settled in, reside in, be a resident of.
▶ noun *a hearty hail greeted me* **greeting**, hello, hallo, halloo, call, cry, shout, salutation; acknowledgement, welcome, salute.
OPPOSITE farewell.

hail[2] ▶ noun **1** *frequent heavy showers of rain and hail* **frozen rain**, hailstones, sleet, precipitation; hailstorm, hail shower.
2 *a hail of bullets* **barrage**, volley, shower, deluge, torrent, burst, stream, storm, flood, spate, rain, tide, avalanche, blaze, onslaught; bombardment, cannonade, battery, blast, broadside, salvo.
▶ verb *tons of dust* **hailed down on us** **beat**, shower, rain, fall, pour, drop; pelt, pepper, batter, bombard, volley, assail.

hail-fellow-well-met ▶ adjective *he was a hail-fellow-well-met type of guy* **convivial**, sociable, outgoing, gregarious, companionable, friendly, genial, affable, amiable, congenial, agreeable, good-humoured, extrovert, extroverted, uninhibited; *Scottish* couthy; *informal* backslapping, chummy, pally, clubbable, clubby, buddy-buddy; *Brit. informal* matey; *rare* conversable.
OPPOSITE unsociable.

hair *See centre pages for list of* **Hairstyles**
▶ noun **1** *thick black curly hair* **head of hair**, shock of hair, mop of hair, mane; locks, tresses, curls; wig, toupee, hairpiece, switch; *informal* rug, thatch; *Brit. informal* barnet; *rare* postiche.
2 *your hair looks lovely* **hairstyle**, haircut, cut, style, coiffure; *informal* hairdo, do, coif.
3 *muscular dogs with wide heads and short, blue-grey hair* **fur**, wool; coat, fleece, pelt, hide, skin; mane; *archaic* fell.
□ **a hair's breadth** *the American bison was saved from extinction by a hair's breadth* **the narrowest of margins**, a narrow margin, the skin of one's teeth, a split second, a fraction, a nose; *informal* a whisker.
OPPOSITE a wide margin.
□ **get in someone's hair** (*informal*) *she got in my hair until I couldn't bear it another day* **annoy**, irritate, gall, irk, pique, needle, nettle, bother, vex, provoke, displease, offend, affront, upset, anger, exasperate, disgruntle, ruffle, put someone's back up, get on someone's nerves, make someone's hackles rise, raise someone's hackles; *informal* peeve, aggravate, miff, get, get to, bug, nark, wind up, get under someone's skin, get up someone's nose, hack off, get someone's goat, ruffle someone's feathers, get on someone's wick, give someone the hump, rub up the wrong way, get across someone; *N. Amer. informal* tick off, rankle, ride, gravel; *vulgar slang* piss off; *Brit. vulgar slang* get on someone's tits; *rare* exacerbate, hump, rasp.
OPPOSITE appease.
□ **let one's hair down** (*informal*) *visitors young and old let their hair down and enjoyed the entertainment* **have a good time**, have a great time, enjoy oneself, have fun, make merry, have the time of one's life, let oneself go, have a fling; *informal* have a ball, whoop it up, make whoopee, paint the town red, live it up, have a whale of a time, let it all hang out; *Brit. informal* push the boat out, have a rave-up; *N. Amer. informal* hang loose, chill out; *S. African* jol.
□ **make someone's hair stand on end** *the dossier on him would make your hair stand on end* **horrify**, shock, appal, scandalize, dismay, stun; make someone's blood run cold, freeze someone's blood; *informal* make someone's hair curl; *Brit. informal* put the wind up someone.
OPPOSITE reassure.
□ **not turn a hair** *if I was told I'd been sacked, I wouldn't turn a hair* **remain calm**, keep calm, keep cool, remain composed, remain unruffled, appear unaffected, maintain one's equilibrium, keep control of oneself, not show emotion, not lose one's head, bite one's lip, keep a stiff upper lip; *informal* keep one's cool, not bat an eyelid; *Brit. informal* keep one's hair on.
OPPOSITE panic.
□ **split hairs** *a pompous professor who uses language to equivocate and split hairs* **quibble**, raise trivial objections, find fault, cavil, carp, niggle, argue over nothing; *informal* nit-pick; *archaic* pettifog.

WORD LINKS
relating to hair **capillaceous**
related prefix **tricho- (e.g. *trichology*)**
fear of hair **trichophobia**

hairdo ▶ noun (*informal*) **hairstyle**, haircut, cut, style, hair, coiffure; *informal* do, coif.

hairdresser ▶ noun **hairstylist**, stylist, barber; *French* coiffeur, coiffeuse, friseur; *informal* crimper; *rare* tonsor, tonsorialist.

hairless ▶ adjective **bald**, bald-headed; shaven, shaved, shorn, clean-shaven, smooth-shaven, beardless, smooth, smooth-faced, depilated; *Scottish & Irish* baldy; *technical* glabrous, glabrate; *archaic* tonsured, bald-pated.
OPPOSITE hairy.

hairpiece ▶ noun **wig**, toupee, false hair, extension, torsade, switch; *informal* rug; *rare* merkin, postiche.

hair-raising ▶ adjective *I thought ski jumping was hair-raising, but rafting beats it* **terrifying**, frightening, petrifying, alarming, chilling, horrifying, shocking, scaring, spine-chilling, blood-curdling, appalling, dreadful, fearsome, nightmarish; eerie, sinister, weird, ghostly, unearthly; *Scottish* eldritch; *informal* hairy, spooky, scary, creepy, spine-tingling.
OPPOSITES relaxing, pleasant.

hair-splitting ▶ adjective *legal experts have a particularly hair-splitting mentality* **quibbling**, fault-finding, niggling, cavilling, carping, captious, critical, criticizing, disapproving, censorious, judgemental, overcritical, hypercritical, pedantic, punctilious, pettifogging; *informal* **nit-picking**, pernickety, picky; *N. Amer. informal* persnickety; *archaic* nice, overnice.

hairstyle *See centre pages for list of* **Hairstyles**
▶ noun *she had a smart black dress and a sophisticated hairstyle* **haircut**, cut, style, hair, coiffure; *informal* hairdo, do, coif.

hairy ▶ adjective **1** *the shirt was unbuttoned, revealing a hairy chest | a rather hairy young man* **hirsute**, **shaggy**, bushy, hair-covered, long-haired; woolly, furry, fleecy, fuzzy; bearded, unshaven, unshorn, bewhiskered, stubbly, bristly; *technical* pilose, pileous, pappose; *rare* crinite, crinigerous.
OPPOSITES hairless; short-haired.
2 (*informal*) *it got very hairy when we ran into some troops guarding the border* **risky**, unsafe, dangerous, perilous, hazardous, high-risk, touch-and-go, fraught with danger; tricky, ticklish, difficult, awkward, uncertain, unpredictable, precarious; *Scottish* unchancy; *informal* chancy, dicey, sticky, iffy; *Brit. informal* dodgy; *N. Amer. informal* gnarly; *archaic or humorous* parlous.
OPPOSITE safe.

halcyon ▶ adjective **1** *hot, halcyon days of sunshine* **serene**, calm, pleasant, balmy, tranquil, peaceful, temperate, mild, quiet, gentle, placid, still, windless, stormless.
OPPOSITE stormy.
2 *the halcyon days of the 1960s* **happy**, carefree, blissful, golden, joyful, joyous, contented, idyllic, palmy; flourishing, thriving, prosperous, successful.
OPPOSITE troubled.

hale ▶ adjective *only just sixty, very hale and hearty* **healthy**, well, fit, fighting fit, in good health, bursting with health, in excellent shape, in fine fettle, fit as a fiddle, fit as a flea, in tip-top condition; flourishing, blooming, strong, robust, vigorous, hardy, sturdy, hearty, lusty, able-bodied; *informal* in the pink, right as rain, full of vim, up to snuff.
OPPOSITE unwell.

half ▶ noun *half a bar of chocolate* one of two equal parts of, fifty per cent of, bisection of.
OPPOSITE all.
□ **by halves** *he operated on a grand scale and never did anything by halves* **incompletely**, imperfectly, inadequately, insufficiently, partially, scrappily, skimpily, to a limited extent/degree.
OPPOSITE thoroughly.

□ **too ... by half** *Rosemary is too clever by half* **unduly**, overly, excessively, exceedingly, inordinately, disproportionately, far too, to too great an extent/degree, by an excessive amount; enormously, considerably, uncommonly, very, ultra-; *informal* too-too.

▶ **adjective** *he ate a half grapefruit for breakfast* **halved**, divided in two, part, partial; bisected, in two equal parts/portions.
OPPOSITE whole.

▶ **adverb 1** *the chicken is half cooked* **partially**, partly, incompletely, inadequately, insufficiently, slightly, barely, in part, part, to a limited extent/degree, in some measure; not totally, not wholly, not entirely, not fully.
OPPOSITE completely.
2 *I am half inclined to believe you* **to a certain extent/degree**, to a limited extent/degree, to some extent/degree, (up) to a point, in part, partly, in some measure; almost, nearly, very nearly, just about, all but.
OPPOSITE fully.

□ **not half** (*informal*) **1** *that doesn't half make you feel old!* **really**, certainly, definitely, decidedly, assuredly, surely, very much, to a great extent, to a considerable extent, for sure, indeed; undeniably, undoubtedly, indubitably, irrefutably, incontrovertibly, incontestably, unequivocally.
2 *the players are not half bad* **not at all**, not a bit, not in any way, by no means, absolutely not, most certainly not, not for a moment, not nearly, not the slightest bit, to no extent.

WORD LINKS
related prefixes **demi-** (e.g. ***demi-pension, demitasse***), **hemi-** (e.g. ***hemisphere, hemiola***), **semi-** (e.g. ***semicircle, semiconductor***)

half-baked ▶ **adjective 1** *half-baked moral theories* **not thought through**, not fully developed, undeveloped, unformed, hare-brained; poorly planned, unplanned, ill-conceived, ill-judged; impractical, unrealistic, unworkable, injudicious, ridiculous; *informal* crazy, crackpot, cock-eyed.
OPPOSITES sensible, well reasoned.
2 *her half-baked young nephew* **foolish**, stupid, silly, idiotic, doltish, asinine, simple-minded, feeble-minded, empty-headed, hare-brained, feather-brained, feather-headed, brainless, senseless, witless, unintelligent, ignorant; inexperienced, immature, callow, green, credulous; *informal* crazy, dim, dopey, dumb, thick, damfool, half-witted, dim-witted, birdbrained, lamebrained, dunderheaded, wet behind the ears, as thick as two short planks; *Brit. informal* gormless, daft, divvy, dozy; *Scottish & N. English informal* glaikit; *N. Amer. informal* dumb-ass, chowderheaded; *S. African informal* dof; *W. Indian informal* dotish.
OPPOSITE sensible.

half-hearted ▶ **adjective** *the plan received a half-hearted welcome* **unenthusiastic**, lukewarm, cool, apathetic, perfunctory, cursory, superficial, desultory, feeble, faint, weak, tepid; indifferent, unconcerned, listless, lacklustre, dispassionate, uninterested, unemotional, languid, passive; *rare* Laodicean.
OPPOSITE enthusiastic.

halfway ▶ **adjective** *the halfway point* **midway**, middle, mid, central, centre, intermediate, equidistant between two points; mean, median, average; *technical* medial, mesial; *rare* intermedial.

▶ **adverb 1** *he stopped halfway down the passage* **midway**, at the mid point, in the middle, in the centre; to the middle, to the mid point; part of the way, at some point, part-way.
2 *he seemed halfway friendly* **to some extent/degree**, to a certain extent/degree, in some measure, rather, relatively, comparatively, moderately, cautiously, somewhat, (up) to a point; in part, partly, part, just about, almost, nearly.

□ **meet someone halfway** *I was willing to meet him halfway* **reach a compromise**, find the middle ground, come to terms, come to an understanding, reach an agreement, make a deal, make concessions, find a happy medium, strike a balance; give and take; *informal* split the difference, go fifty-fifty.

halfwit ▶ **noun** (*informal*). *See* FOOL.

half-witted ▶ **adjective** (*informal*). *See* STUPID.

hall ▶ **noun 1** *hang your coat in the hall* **entrance hall**, hallway, entry, entrance, lobby, foyer, vestibule, reception area, atrium, concourse; passageway, passage, corridor; *N. Amer.* entryway.
2 *the building is used as a village hall* **assembly hall**, assembly room, meeting room, large public room, chamber; conference hall, lecture room, theatre, concert hall, auditorium, dance hall, church hall, village hall, town hall, guildhall.

hallmark ▶ **noun 1** *the hallmark on silver* **assay mark**, official mark, authentication mark, stamp of authenticity, stamp of authentication.
2 *the tiny bubbles are the hallmark of fine champagnes* **distinctive feature**, mark, sign, indicator, indication, sure sign, telltale sign; feature, characteristic, trait, attribute, property, quality; trademark, earmark, stamp, badge, symbol.

halloo ▶ **verb** *they hallooed and shouted as they passed* **call out**, shout, cry out, yell, bawl, bellow, scream, shriek, screech, roar, whoop; **call hello to**, hail, greet; *informal* holler, yoo-hoo, cooee.

hallowed ▶ **adjective** *water was sprayed over the hallowed ground* **holy**, sacred, consecrated, sanctified, blessed, blest; revered, reverenced, venerated, honoured, sacrosanct, worshipped, divine, inviolable.
OPPOSITE cursed.

CHOOSE THE RIGHT WORD
hallowed, blessed, sacred, holy
See SACRED.

hallucinate ▶ **verb** *the drug was making me hallucinate* **have hallucinations**, imagine things, see things, see visions, be delirious, have delirium tremens, fantasize, daydream, dream; *informal* have a trip, trip, see pink elephants, have daymares.

hallucination ▶ **noun** *a hallucination caused by trauma* **delusion**, illusion, figment of the imagination, vision, apparition, mirage, chimera, fantasy, dream, daydream; (**hallucinations**) delirium, phantasmagoria; *informal* trip, pink elephants; *literary* phantasm.

halo ▶ **noun ring of light**, nimbus, aureole, aureola, glory, crown of light, corona, disc, radiance, aura; *technical* halation; *rare* gloriole.

halt ▶ **verb 1** *Len halted and turned round* **stop**, come to a halt, come to a stop, come to a standstill, come to rest, pull up, draw up, stand still, draw to a stand.
OPPOSITES start; go.
2 *the restoration work has temporarily halted* **cease**, stop, finish, discontinue, terminate, conclude, come to an end, come to a halt, come to a stop, draw to a close, come to a standstill, be over, be abandoned; pause, be broken off, be suspended.
OPPOSITES start; continue.
3 *a further strike has halted production* **terminate**, end, stop, cease, finish, suspend, bring to a stop, bring to a close, bring to an end, put an end to, put a stop to, break off, wind up; arrest, impede, check, curb, stem, staunch, block, stall, hold back; *informal* pull the plug on, put the kibosh on.
OPPOSITES start; continue.

▶ **noun 1** *the car drew to a halt* **stop**, standstill.
2 *a halt in production* **cessation**, termination, stoppage, stopping, close, end, discontinuation, discontinuance; break, pause, interval, interruption, interlude, intermission, suspension, rest, respite, hiatus, breathing space, time out; *informal* breather.
OPPOSITES start; continuation.

halter ▶ **noun harness**, head collar, bridle; *N. Amer.* headstall; *technical* chase-halter.

halting ▶ **adjective 1** *a rather halting conversation | he spoke to us in halting English* **hesitant**, disjointed, faltering, hesitating, stumbling, stammering, stuttering; **broken**, non-fluent, imperfect, laboured.
OPPOSITE fluent.
2 *his halting gait* **unsteady**, awkward, uneven, faltering, stumbling, limping, hobbling.
OPPOSITES steady, adroit, nimble.

halve ▶ **verb 1** *halve the tomatoes and scoop out the pips* **cut in half**, divide into two equal parts, divide in two, split in two, sever in two, divide equally, share equally, bisect.
2 *interest rates have halved* **reduce by fifty per cent**, decrease by fifty per cent, lessen by fifty per cent.

halves ▶ **plural noun**

□ **by halves**. *See* HALF.

ham-fisted ▶ **adjective** *his ham-fisted handling of the situation* **clumsy**, bungling, incompetent, amateurish, inept, unskilful, inexpert, maladroit, gauche, awkward, inefficient, bumbling, useless, unhandy; *informal* cack-handed, butterfingered, ham-handed; *Brit. informal* all thumbs, all fingers and thumbs.
OPPOSITE expert.

hammer *See centre pages for list of* **Hammers**

▶ **noun** *they work the stone with hammer and chisel* mallet, beetle, gavel.

▶ **verb 1** *the alloy is hammered into a circular shape* **beat**, forge, shape, form, mould, fashion, make.
2 *Sally* ***hammered at*** *the door* **batter**, pummel, beat, bang, pound; strike, hit, knock on, thump on; cudgel, bludgeon, club, pelt, assail, thwack; *informal* bash, wallop, clobber, whack.
3 *they have been* ***hammering away at*** *their non-smoking campaign* **work hard**, labour, slog away, plod away, grind away, slave away, work like a Trojan, work like a dog, keep one's nose to the grindstone; persist with, persevere with, keep on with, press on with, not cease from; *informal* stick at, peg away at, beaver away at, plug away at, work one's socks off on, sweat blood for, soldier on with, kill oneself with; *Brit. informal* graft away at; *rare* drudge away at.
OPPOSITES give up on; abandon.
4 *anti-racism had been* ***hammered into*** *her* **drum**, instil, inculcate, knock, drive, din; drive home to, impress upon, teach repeatedly to, reiterate to; ingrain.

H

5 (*informal*) *he got hammered for an honest mistake* **criticize**, censure, attack, condemn, castigate, chastise, lambaste, pillory, reprimand, rebuke, admonish, remonstrate with, take to task, haul over the coals, berate, reproach, reprove; *informal* knock, slam, lay into, roast, cane, blast, bawl out, dress down; *Brit. informal* carpet, slate, slag off, rollick; *N. Amer. informal* chew out, ream out, pummel, cut up; *Austral./NZ informal* bag, monster; *rare* excoriate, objurgate, reprehend.
OPPOSITE praise.
6 (*informal*) *we have hammered them twice this season* **trounce**, defeat, beat, beat hollow, worst, best, overwhelm, rout, annihilate, bring someone to their knees; *informal* thrash, clobber, lick, demolish, slaughter, murder, paste, pound, drub, give someone a drubbing, wipe the floor with, take to the cleaners, run rings round, walk all over, make mincemeat of, turn something inside out; *Brit. informal* stuff, marmalize; *N. Amer. informal* shellac, cream, skunk, blow out.
OPPOSITE lose to.

□ **hammer something out** *the area chairmen hammered out a national plan* **thrash out**, work out, agree on, sort out, decide on, bring about, effect, produce, broker, negotiate, reach an agreement on, come to terms about, come to a decision on, come to a satisfactory conclusion on, form a resolution about.
OPPOSITE fail to agree about.

hamper[1] ▶ **noun** *a picnic hamper* **basket**, pannier, wickerwork basket; box, container, holder.

hamper[2] ▶ **verb** *an attempt to hamper the investigations* **hinder**, obstruct, impede, inhibit, retard, baulk, thwart, foil, curb, delay, set back, slow down, hold back, hold up, interfere with; restrict, restrain, constrain, block, check, curtail, frustrate, cramp, bridle, handicap, cripple, hamstring, shackle, fetter, encumber; *informal* stymie; *Brit. informal* throw a spanner in the works of; *N. Amer. informal* bork, throw a monkey wrench in the works of; *rare* cumber, trammel.
OPPOSITE help.

CHOOSE THE RIGHT WORD

hamper, hinder, impede, obstruct
See HINDER.

hamstring ▶ **verb 1** *the enemy was trying to hamstring his horse* **cripple**, lame, hock, disable, handicap, injure.
2 *we were hamstrung by a total lack of knowledge* **handicap**, constrain, restrict, cripple, shackle, fetter, encumber, block, frustrate, cramp, bridle; hamper, hinder, obstruct, impede, inhibit, retard, baulk, thwart, foil, curb, delay, set back, slow down, hold back, hold up; restrain, check, curtail; *informal* stymie; *N. Amer. informal* bork; *literary* trammel; *rare* cumber.
OPPOSITE help.

hand ▶ **noun 1** *big, strong hands* palm, fist; *informal* paw, mitt, duke, hook, meat hook; *Scottish & N. English* nieve; *technical* manus, metacarpus.
OPPOSITE foot.
2 *the clock's second hand* **pointer**, indicator, needle, arrow, marker, index.
3 (**hands**) *the concentration of wealth in the hands of the entrepreneurial class* **control**, power, charge, authority; command, responsibility, guardianship, management, care, supervision, jurisdiction; possession, keeping, custody, clutches, grasp; disposal; *informal* say-so; *literary* thrall.
4 *come and give me a hand with the tidying up* **help**, a helping hand, assistance, aid, support, succour, relief; a good turn, a favour, a kindness; *rare* abettance.
OPPOSITE hindrance.
5 (*informal*) *his fans gave him a big hand* **round of applause**, clap, handclap, ovation, standing ovation; applause, handclapping, praise, acclaim.
OPPOSITES booing; catcalls.
6 *the document was written in his own hand* **handwriting**, writing, script, longhand, letters, pen; penmanship, calligraphy, chirography.
7 *a factory hand* **worker**, factory worker, manual worker, unskilled worker, blue-collar worker, workman, workwoman, workperson, working man, labourer, operative, hired hand, hireling, roustabout, employee, artisan; farmhand, farm worker, field hand; crewman, sailor, deckhand; *Spanish-American* peon; *Austral./NZ* rouseabout; *Indian* mazdoor, khalasi; *archaic* mechanical.

□ **at hand 1** *you need to keep the manual close at hand* **readily available**, available, handy, to hand, near at hand, within reach, accessible, ready, close, close by, near, nearby, at the ready, at one's fingertips, at one's disposal, convenient; *informal* get-at-able, on tap.
OPPOSITE far away.
2 *the time for starting the campaign is at hand* **imminent**, close at hand, approaching, forthcoming, coming, coming soon, about to happen, nearly on us, just around the corner, on the horizon; impending.
OPPOSITE a long time away.

□ **by hand** *each chocolate is decorated by hand* **manually**, with one's hands, using one's hands, not by machine, not mechanically, freehand.
OPPOSITE by machine.

□ **from hand to mouth** *they live from hand to mouth—from one benefit day to the next* **precariously**, from day to day, not knowing where one's next meal is coming from, uncertainly, insecurely, in poverty, meagrely; improvidently; *Brit.* on the breadline.
OPPOSITES securely; without financial worries.

□ **hand in glove** *they were working hand in glove with our enemies* **in close collaboration**, in close association, in close cooperation, very closely, closely together, in partnership, in league, in collusion; *informal* in cahoots.

□ **hand in hand 1** *two small children were walking hand in hand* **holding hands**, clasping hands, with hands clasped, with hands joined; arm in arm.
2 *poverty goes hand in hand with war* **in close association**, closely together, together, in partnership, closely, conjointly, concurrently, side by side, in concert.

□ **hands down** *we won hands down* **easily**, effortlessly, with ease, with no trouble, with very little trouble, without effort, with very little effort; *informal* by a mile, no sweat.
OPPOSITE with difficulty.

□ **in hand 1** *the task in hand* **being dealt with**, receiving attention, being attended to, under way; under control.
2 *we have money in hand to cover next month's expenses* **available for use**, ready, available, put by; spare, in reserve.

□ **to hand** *the bullies pelted us with anything that was to hand* **readily available**, available, handy, near at hand, within reach, accessible, ready, close, close by, near, nearby, at the ready, at one's fingertips, at one's disposal, convenient; *informal* get-at-able.

□ **try one's hand** *I would like to try my hand at bonsai* **make an attempt at**, have a shot at; attempt, try, try out, give something a try; *informal* have a go at, have a crack at, have a stab at, have a bash at, give something a whirl; *formal* essay; *archaic* assay.

▶ **verb 1** *he handed each man a glass* **pass**, give, reach, let someone have, throw, toss; pass to, hand over to, deliver to, present to, transfer to, convey to; *informal* chuck, bung.
OPPOSITE take away from.
2 *he handed him into a carriage* **assist**, help, aid, give someone a hand, give someone a helping hand, give someone assistance; guide, convey, conduct, lead.

□ **hand something down** *the family jewellery is handed down from generation to generation* **pass on**, pass down; **bequeath**, will, leave, leave in one's will, make over, endow, gift, transfer, give, transmit; *Law* demise, devise.

□ **hand something on** *the drugs were handed on to a dealer* **give**, pass, hand, transfer, grant, cede, surrender, relinquish; part with, let go of; bequeath, will, leave.
OPPOSITE receive.

□ **hand something out** *the attendant handed out prayer books* **distribute**, hand round, give out, give round, pass out, pass round, share out, dole out, dish out, deal out, mete out, issue, circulate, dispense; allocate, allot, apportion, disburse, disseminate.
OPPOSITE collect in.

□ **hand something over** *it is suggested that he might hand over power to his son* **yield**, give, give up, pass, grant, entrust, surrender, relinquish, cede, turn over, deliver up, forfeit, sacrifice; confer on, bestow on.
OPPOSITE keep.

WORD LINKS

relating to the hands	**manual**
related prefix	**chiro-** (e.g. ***chirography, chiropody***)

handbag ▶ **noun** **bag**, shoulder bag, clutch bag, evening bag, pochette; flight bag, travelling bag, handgrip, overnighter; *French* minaudière, pompadour; *Brit.* holdall; *N. Amer.* purse, pocketbook; *rare* reticule, caba, keister, Dorothy bag, peggy bag, purse-bag, vanity bag.

handbill ▶ **noun** **notice**, advertisement, flyer, leaflet, circular, handout, bulletin, pamphlet, brochure; *N. Amer. & Austral.* dodger; *informal* ad, junk mail; *Brit. informal* advert.

handbook ▶ **noun** **manual**, instructions, instruction booklet, instruction manual, reference manual, ABC, A to Z, almanac, companion, directory, compendium; **guide**, guidebook, travel guide, tourist guide, Baedeker; *Latin* vade mecum; *rare* enchiridion, promptuary, desk-book.

handcuff ▶ **verb** *they handcuffed the prisoner to a warder* **manacle**, fetter, shackle; restrain, secure, put handcuffs on, put someone in irons, clap someone in irons, put someone in chains; *informal* cuff; *rare* enfetter, gyve.
OPPOSITE free.

handcuffs ▶ **plural noun** **manacles**, fetters, shackles, irons, bonds, restraints; *informal* cuffs, bracelets, darbies; *rare* gyves, wristlets, snips, stringers.

handful ▶ **noun 1** *we've received only a handful of letters* **a small number**, a small amount, a small quantity, a sprinkling, a smattering, a scattering, a trickle; a few, one or two, several, some, not many.
OPPOSITE a lot.
2 (*informal*) *the child is a real handful* **nuisance**, problem, bother, irritant, source of annoyance, thorn in someone's flesh, thorn in someone's side, bugbear; *informal* pest, headache, pain, pain in the neck, pain in the

backside, blister; *Scottish informal* nyaff, skelf; *N. Amer. informal* pain in the butt, nudnik, burr under/in someone's saddle; *Austral./NZ informal* nark; *Brit. vulgar slang* pain in the arse.
OPPOSITE blessing.

handgun ▶ noun **pistol**, revolver, gun, side arm, automatic pistol, six-shooter, thirty-eight, derringer, Browning automatic; *N. Amer. informal* piece, shooting iron, Saturday night special, rod, roscoe; *trademark* Colt, Webley, Luger.

handicap ▶ noun **1** *he was born with a significant visual handicap* **disability**, physical abnormality, mental abnormality, defect, impairment, affliction, disadvantage, deficiency.
2 *this legislation is a handicap to the competitiveness of the industry* **impediment**, hindrance, obstacle, barrier, bar, encumbrance; **disadvantage**, drawback, stumbling block, difficulty, shortcoming, obstruction, limitation, constraint, straitjacket, restriction, check, block, curb; ball and chain, albatross, millstone round someone's neck; *literary* trammel.
OPPOSITES benefit; advantage.
▶ verb *delivery of services has been handicapped by inadequate investment* **hamper**, impede, hinder, impair, disadvantage, put at a disadvantage, hamstring, curtail; **restrict**, check, obstruct, block, curb, bridle, hold back, constrain, limit, encumber; *informal* stymie; *N. Amer. informal* bork; *literary* trammel.
OPPOSITE help.

handicapped ▶ adjective *a special school for handicapped children* **disabled**, incapacitated, disadvantaged, infirm, invalid; *euphemistic* physically challenged, mentally challenged, differently abled.
OPPOSITE able-bodied.

handicraft ▶ noun *handicraft and sewing workshops* **craft**, handiwork, craftwork; craftsmanship, workmanship, artisanship, art, skill.

handiwork ▶ noun *this jewellery is the handiwork of Chinese smiths* **creation**, product, work, achievement, design, doing, action, result; **handicraft**, craft, craftwork.

handkerchief ▶ noun pocket handkerchief; tissue, paper handkerchief; *trademark* Kleenex; *Scottish & N. English* napkin; *French* mouchoir; *Indian* corah, Malabar, pullicate; *informal* **hanky**, nose rag, snot rag; *informal, dated* nose-wiper, sneezer, wipe, wiper; *literary* kerchief; *archaic* clout, muckender, monteith, fogle, foulard, stook, Barcelona.

handle ▶ verb **1** *bladed tools can cause serious injury if they are not handled and stored with care* **hold**, pick up, grasp, grip, lift; **feel**, touch, finger, thumb, toy with, play with; *informal* paw.
2 *she handled the car well on the wet roads* **control**, drive, steer, operate, manoeuvre, manipulate.
3 *she handled the job formidably* **deal with**, manage, cope with, tackle, take care of, take charge of, contend with, attend to, give one's attention to, see to, sort out, apply oneself to, take something in hand, control.
OPPOSITE neglect.
4 *the paper handled the race story with constraint* **treat**, examine, tackle, explore, go into, report, review, discuss, discourse on.
5 *the advertising company that is handling the account* **administer**, manage, control, conduct, direct, guide, supervise, oversee, be in charge of, take care of, look after.
6 *some dealers handle antiquities that lack honest pedigrees* **trade in**, deal in, do business in, buy, sell, supply, stock, carry, peddle, traffic in, purvey, hawk, tout, market; *informal* push; *Brit. informal* flog.
▶ noun *the handle of the knife* **haft**, shank, stock, shaft, grip, handgrip, hilt, helve, butt; knob.
OPPOSITES head; blade.

hand-me-down ▶ adjective *a faded hand-me-down dress* **second-hand**, used, nearly new, handed-down, passed-on, cast-off, worn, old, pre-owned; *Brit. informal* reach-me-down.
OPPOSITE new.

handout ▶ noun **1** (**handouts**) *she existed on handouts as her husband couldn't work* **charity**, aid, benefit, financial support, gifts of money, gifts of food, subsidies, payments, donations; *Brit. informal* dole; *historical* alms.
OPPOSITE earned income.
2 *a plastic carrier containing a selection of freebies and handouts* **free sample**, free gift, contribution, offering, present; *informal* freebie, perk, prezzie, sweetener; *archaic* perquisite.
OPPOSITE purchase.
3 *there are a number of handouts to read before the next session* **leaflet**, pamphlet, brochure, bulletin; advertising leaflet, handbill, flyer, notice, circular, mailshot; literature, printed matter.

hand-picked ▶ adjective *the lecture was attended by a hand-picked audience* **specially chosen**, specially selected, invited, screened, vetted; choice, elite, select.
OPPOSITE random.

handsome ▶ adjective **1** *a handsome, dark-haired young man* **good-looking**, nice-looking, attractive, personable, striking, stunning, fine, well-proportioned, well-formed; *informal* hunky, dishy, gorgeous, drop-dead gorgeous, tasty, fanciable, knockout; *Brit. informal* fit; *N. Amer. informal* cute; *Austral./NZ informal* spunky; *rare* sightly.
OPPOSITE ugly.
2 *a handsome woman of 30* **striking**, imposing, prepossessing, elegant, stately, dignified, statuesque, good-looking, nice-looking, attractive, personable.
OPPOSITE plain.
3 *the pub was running at a handsome profit | a handsome present* **substantial**, considerable, sizeable, large, big, ample, abundant, bumper, plentiful; generous, lavish, liberal, bountiful, princely; *Scottish & N. English* bonny; *informal* tidy, whopping, whopping great, thumping, thumping great, kingly, not to be sneezed at; *Brit. informal* whacking, whacking great, ginormous; *literary* plenteous, bounteous.
OPPOSITE meagre.

handwriting ▶ noun *clear and legible handwriting* **writing**, **script**, hand, longhand, letters, pen; penmanship, calligraphy, chirography; *informal* scrawl, scribble.

WORD LINKS
study of handwriting **graphology**

handy ▶ adjective **1** *a handy reference tool* **useful**, convenient, practical, easy-to-use, well-designed, user-friendly, user-oriented, helpful, functional, serviceable, utilitarian; *informal* neat, nifty.
OPPOSITE inconvenient.
2 *it has eight pockets to keep everything you need handy* **readily available**, available, at hand, to hand, near at hand, within reach, accessible, ready, close, close by, near, nearby, at the ready, at one's fingertips, at one's disposal, convenient; *informal* get-at-able, on tap.
3 *he's handy with a needle* **skilful**, skilled, dexterous, deft, nimble-fingered, adroit, practical, able, adept, proficient, capable; masterly, gifted, talented, expert; clever with one's hands, good with one's hands; *informal* nifty, wizard, ace; *N. Amer. informal* crackerjack; *vulgar slang* shit-hot; *rare* habile.
OPPOSITE inept.

handyman ▶ noun **odd-job man**, odd-jobber, factotum, jack of all trades, man of all work; DIY expert, DIYer; *Austral.* knockabout, rouseabout, loppy; *French* bricoleur; *informal* Mr Fixit.

hang ▶ verb **1** *lanterns hung from the ridgepole of the tent* **be suspended**, hang down, be pendent, dangle, swing, sway; *archaic* depend.
OPPOSITE rise.
2 *hang your pictures at eye level* **put up**, fix, attach, affix, fasten, post, display, suspend, stick up, pin up, tack up, nail up, put on a hook.
OPPOSITE take down.
3 *size the wall before you hang the wallpaper* **paste up**, glue on, stick up, fasten on, fix on, attach.
OPPOSITE peel off.
4 *the room was hung with banners and streamers* **decorate**, adorn, drape, festoon, deck out, trick out, bedeck, array, furnish, garland, swathe, cover, ornament; *informal* get up, do up, do out, tart up; *literary* bedizen, caparison, furbelow.
5 *they hanged the prisoners at a triple gallows* **execute by hanging**, hang by the neck, send to the gallows, send to the gibbet, send to the scaffold, gibbet, put to death; lynch; *informal* string up.
6 *pollutants hang in the air over the motorway* **hover**, float, drift, linger, remain static, be suspended, be poised.
OPPOSITE be dispersed.

□ **hang about/around/round** (*informal*) **1** *they spent most of their time hanging around restaurants or bars* **loiter in**, linger in, wait around in, spend time in, loaf (around/about) in, lounge (around/about) in; waste time, kill time, mark time, while away the/one's time, dally; kick one's heels, cool one's heels, twiddle one's thumbs; frequent, be a regular visitor to, be a regular client of, haunt; *informal* hang out in.
2 *hang about, see what it says here?* **wait**, hold on, wait a minute; *informal* hang on, hold your horses.
3 *he was hanging around with a fellow called Mick* **associate**, mix, go around, keep company, spend time, mingle, socialize, fraternize, consort, rub shoulders; *N. Amer.* rub elbows; *informal* hang out, run around, knock about/around, be thick, hobnob.
OPPOSITE have nothing to do with.

□ **hang back** *she hung back, scared to face the old woman* **stay back**, hold back, stay in the background, shrink back, shy away, be reluctant to come forward, hesitate, demur, recoil, turn away.

□ **hang fire** *we should hang fire for things to cool off* **delay**, hang back, hold back, hold on, stall, stop, pause, cease, halt, discontinue, procrastinate, vacillate, adopt Fabian tactics; *informal* hang about, hang around, sit tight, hold one's horses.

□ **hang on 1** *he hung on to the back of her coat* **hold on to**, hold fast to, grip, clutch, grasp, hold tightly, cling to, cling on to; *literary* cleave to.
OPPOSITE let go of.
2 *the whole credibility of electoral reform hangs on this decision* **depend on**, be dependent on, turn on, hinge on, rest on, be based on, be conditional on, be contingent upon, be determined by, be decided by, be conditioned by, revolve around.
3 *she hung on his every word* **listen closely to**, attend closely to, pay close

H

attention to, be very attentive to, concentrate hard on, pay heed to, lend an ear to, give ear to, be rapt by; *informal* be all ears for; *archaic* hearken to.
OPPOSITE pay no attention to.
4 *I will hang on until there are other people who can take the campaign forward* **persevere**, **hold out**, hold on, go on, carry on, keep on, keep going, keep at it, not give up; **continue**, persist, remain, stay the course, stay with it, struggle on, plod on, plough on; *informal* soldier on, plug away, peg away, stick at it, stick it out, hang in there, bash on.
OPPOSITE give up.
5 (*informal*) *hang on, let me think for a moment* **wait**, wait a minute, hold on, stop; hold the line; *informal* hold your horses, sit tight; *Brit. informal* hang about.
□ **hang out** (*informal*) *he spent a lot of time hanging out with musicians* **associate**, mix, go around, keep company, spend time, mingle, socialize, fraternize, consort, rub shoulders; *N. Amer.* rub elbows; *informal* hang around, run around, knock about/around, be thick, hobnob; *Brit. informal* hang about.
□ **hang something out** *you can hang out the washing in the laundry room* **peg out**, peg up, stick up, pin up, drape, fix, fasten.
□ **hang over 1** *two girls hung over the rail of the ferry* **lean over**, bend over, bend downwards, bend forwards, lean forwards, droop forwards, bow over.
2 *the threat of budget cuts is hanging over us* **be imminent**, threaten, approach, be close, be impending, impend, loom, draw near, be in prospect, be on the horizon, be just around the corner.

▸ **noun**
□ **get the hang of** (*informal*) *I never got the hang of roller skating* **get the knack of**, master, learn, acquire the technique of, acquire the skill of, learn the art of, become proficient in, become expert in, manage, catch on to, pick up; **understand**, grasp, comprehend.

hangdog ▸ **adjective** *the hangdog look of a condemned man* **shamefaced**, ashamed, guilty-looking, sheepish, abashed, abject, cowed, cringing, downcast, crestfallen, woebegone, disconsolate, embarrassed, uncomfortable; browbeaten, defeated, intimidated, wretched.
OPPOSITES confident, frank.

hanger-on ▸ **noun** **follower**, flunkey, toady, camp follower, sycophant, fawner, parasite, leech; henchman, minion, lackey, vassal, dependant, retainer, acolyte, underling; *N. Amer.* cohort; *informal* groupie, sponger, freeloader, passenger, sidekick; *Brit. informal* ligger; *archaic* liegeman, pursuivant.
OPPOSITE leader.

hanging ▸ **noun** *silk wall hangings* **drape**, curtain, drop, drop cloth, drop curtain, drop scene, tableau curtain, frontal, dossal; drapery; *informal* tab.
▸ **adjective** *hanging fronds of honeysuckle* **pendent**, suspended, supported from above, dangling, swinging, swaying, trailing, flowing, falling, tumbling; pendulous, drooping, droopy, sagging, flaccid; *rare* pensile.

hang-out ▸ **noun** *a student hang-out* **haunt**, stamping ground, favourite spot, meeting place, territory, domain, purlieu, resort; den, nook, nest, refuge, retreat, hideout; *informal* hidey-hole; *Brit. informal* local, patch, manor.

hangover ▸ **noun** headache; *informal* the morning after the night before, head; *literary* crapulence, crapulousness; *S. African* babalaas; *N. Amer. informal, dated* katzenjammer.

hang-up ▸ **noun** *people with hang-ups about their age* **neurosis**, preoccupation, fixation, obsession, phobia, mania; inhibition, mental block, psychological block, block, difficulty; *French* idée fixe; *informal* complex, thing, bee in one's bonnet.

hank ▸ **noun** *hanks of pale green yarn | a hank of hair* **coil**, skein, length, roll, bunch, clump, loop, twist, piece; shock, lock, ringlet, curl.

hanker ▸ **verb** *she still hankered to go back | they hankered for the bright lights of the capital* **yearn**, long, have a longing, have a hankering, crave, desire, wish, want, hunger, thirst, lust, ache, be aching, itch, be itching, burn, be burning, pant, want badly, be eager, be desperate, be hungry, be greedy, be thirsty, be consumed with a/the desire, be eating one's heart out; fancy, pine for, have one's heart set on; *informal* be dying, have a yen; *archaic* be desirous, be athirst; *rare* suspire.
OPPOSITE be averse.

> **CHOOSE THE RIGHT WORD**
> **hanker, yearn, long, pine**
> See YEARN.

hankering ▸ **noun** *a hankering for the sea* **longing**, yearning, craving, desire, wish, need, hunger, thirst, urge, ache, itch, lust, burning, pining, appetite, passion, fancy; *informal* yen; *rare* appetency, appetence.
OPPOSITE aversion.

hanky-panky ▸ **noun** (*informal*) *the public takes a dim view of hanky-panky among public officials* **goings-on**, funny business, mischief, misbehaviour, misconduct, chicanery, dishonesty, deception, deceit, trickery, intrigue, skulduggery, subterfuge, machinations; **extramarital sex**, infidelity, unfaithfulness, adultery, liaison, affair, fling; *informal* monkey business, shenanigans, carryings-on, carry-on, fooling around, playing around; *Brit. informal* jiggery-pokery, monkey tricks; *N. Amer. informal* monkeyshines; *archaic* fornication, knavery.
OPPOSITES good behaviour; fidelity.

haphazard ▸ **adjective** *things were strewn around in a haphazard fashion* **random**, unplanned, unsystematic, unmethodical, disorganized, disorderly, irregular, indiscriminate, chaotic, hit-and-miss, arbitrary, orderless, aimless, undirected, careless, casual, slapdash, slipshod; chance, accidental; *informal* higgledy-piggledy.
OPPOSITES methodical; systematic.

hapless ▸ **adjective** *the hapless victims of exploitation* **unfortunate**, unlucky, luckless, out of luck, ill-starred, ill-fated, jinxed, cursed, doomed; unhappy, forlorn, wretched, miserable, woebegone; *informal* down on one's luck; *literary* star-crossed.
OPPOSITE lucky.

> **CHOOSE THE RIGHT WORD**
> **hapless, unfortunate, unlucky, ill-starred**
> See UNFORTUNATE.

happen ▸ **verb 1** *she could not explain how the accident happened | this is what happens when the mechanism goes wrong* **occur**, take place, come about, come off, come into being; **ensue**, result, transpire, materialize, arise, be, crop up, come up, fall out, pan out, turn out, follow, develop, emerge, surface, present itself, supervene; *N. Amer. informal* go down; *literary* come to pass, betide, chance; *rare* eventuate, hap.
2 *I wonder what happened to Susie?* **become of**, be the fate of, be the lot of, overtake, be visited on; *literary* befall, betide.
3 *they happened to be in London when the news was received* **chance**, have the good/bad/ill fortune, have the good/bad/ill luck, be someone's fortune/misfortune.
4 *he happened on a linnet's nest* **discover unexpectedly**, find unexpectedly, find by chance, chance on, stumble on, hit on, light on, come on, come across, run across, blunder on, unearth, uncover, locate, bring to light; meet by chance, run into, encounter; *informal* bump into, dig up; *archaic* run against.

happening ▸ **noun** *he was a witness to these bizarre happenings* **occurrence**, event, incident, scene, affair, circumstance, phenomenon, episode, adventure, experience, occasion, action, activity, development, eventuality, accident, case, business, thing.
▸ **adjective** (*informal*) *nightclubs for the young are the happening thing* **fashionable**, modern, popular, new, latest, up to date, up to the minute, in fashion, in vogue; *French* de rigueur, le dernier cri; *informal* **trendy**, funky, hot, cool, with it, hip, in, big, now, groovy, sharp, swinging; *N. Amer. informal* kicky, tony, fly; *black English* down.
OPPOSITE old-fashioned.

happily ▸ **adverb 1** *the children played happily on the sand for hours* **contentedly**, merrily, delightedly, joyfully, gaily, cheerfully, cheerily, agreeably, blithely, light-heartedly, gleefully, blissfully, with pleasure, to one's heart's content; *literary* joyously.
OPPOSITE miserably.
2 *I will happily leave my car behind* **willingly**, gladly, readily, freely, cheerfully, ungrudgingly, unhesitatingly, with pleasure, with all one's heart and soul; *archaic* lief, fain.
OPPOSITE unwillingly.
3 *happily, we are living in enlightened times* **fortunately**, luckily, thankfully, mercifully, opportunely, providentially, felicitously, by chance, by good luck, by good fortune, as luck would have it; thank goodness, thank God, thank heavens, thank the stars.
OPPOSITE unfortunately.

happiness ▸ **noun** *her eyes shone with happiness* **contentment**, pleasure, contentedness, satisfaction, cheerfulness, cheeriness, merriment, merriness, gaiety, joy, joyfulness, joyousness, joviality, jollity, jolliness, glee, blitheness, carefreeness, gladness, delight, good spirits, high spirits, light-heartedness, good cheer, well-being, enjoyment, felicity; exuberance, exhilaration, elation, ecstasy, delirium, jubilation, rapture, bliss, blissfulness, euphoria, beatitude, transports of delight; heaven, paradise, seventh heaven, cloud nine; *humorous* delectation; *rare* jouissance.
OPPOSITE unhappiness.

happy ▸ **adjective 1** *Melissa came in looking happy and excited* **contented**, content, cheerful, cheery, merry, joyful, jovial, jolly, joking, jocular, gleeful, carefree, untroubled, delighted, smiling, beaming, grinning, glowing, satisfied, gratified, buoyant, radiant, sunny, blithe, joyous, beatific, blessed; cock-a-hoop, in good spirits, in high spirits, in a good mood, light-hearted, good-humoured; thrilled, exuberant, elated, exhilarated, ecstatic, blissful, euphoric, overjoyed, exultant, rapturous, rapt, enraptured, in seventh heaven, on cloud nine, over the moon, walking on air, beside oneself with joy, jumping for joy; *informal* chirpy, on top of the world, as happy as a sandboy, tickled pink, tickled to death, like a dog with two tails, as pleased as Punch, on a high, blissed out, sent; *Brit. informal* chuffed, as happy as Larry; *N. English informal* made up; *N. Amer. informal* as happy as a clam; *Austral. informal* wrapped; *dated* gay; *rare*

blithesome, jocose, jocund.
OPPOSITE sad.
2 *we will be happy to advise you* **willing**, **glad**, ready, pleased, delighted, contented; disposed, inclined; *informal* game.
OPPOSITE unwilling.
3 *by a happy coincidence the date was Richard's birthday | a happy choice of venue* **fortunate**, lucky, favourable, advantageous, opportune, timely, well-timed, convenient, propitious, felicitous, auspicious, beneficial, helpful; **appropriate**, apt, fitting, fit, good, right, apposite, proper, seemly, befitting.
OPPOSITE unfortunate.

happy-go-lucky ▶ **adjective** *their casual, happy-go-lucky manner* **easy-going**, carefree, casual, free and easy, devil-may-care, blithe, nonchalant, insouciant, blasé, unconcerned, untroubled, unworried, light-hearted; heedless, reckless, irresponsible, improvident; *informal* slap-happy, laid-back.
OPPOSITES anxious; serious.

harangue ▶ **noun** *father began a harangue about my monstrous behaviour* **tirade**, lecture, diatribe, homily, polemic, rant, fulmination, broadside, verbal attack, verbal onslaught, invective; criticism, berating, censure, admonition, reproval, admonishment; exhortation, declamation, oration, peroration, speech, talk, address; *informal* sermon, tongue-lashing, spiel, pep talk; *rare* philippic, obloquy.
OPPOSITE panegyric.
▶ **verb** *the union leaders harangued the workers over loudspeakers* **deliver a tirade to**, rant at, lecture, hold forth to, preach to, pontificate to, sermonize to, spout to, declaim to, give a lecture to; berate, castigate, criticize, attack, lambaste, censure, pillory, upbraid; *informal* earbash, speechify to, preachify to, sound off to, spiel to.

harass ▶ **verb** **1** *children always harass their mother* **pester**, badger, hound, harry, plague, torment, bedevil, persecute, bother, annoy, exasperate, worry, disturb, trouble, agitate, provoke, vex; stress, stress out, nag, keep on at, chivvy; tease, bait, molest; *informal* hassle, bug, give someone a hard time, drive someone up the wall, drive someone round the bend; *Brit. informal* drive someone round the twist; *N. English informal* mither; *N. Amer. informal* devil, ride.
OPPOSITE leave in peace.
2 *they were sent to harass the enemy flanks and rear* **harry**, attack repeatedly, raid, press hard, beleaguer, set upon, assail, maraud, ravage, oppress.

harassed ▶ **adjective** *the programme of activities is a godsend for harassed parents* **stressed**, strained, frayed, harried, stressed out, worn out, hard-pressed, careworn, worried, troubled, vexed, beleaguered, agitated, fretting, distraught; under stress, under pressure, at the end of one's tether, with one's back to the wall, with one's back up against the wall; *N. Amer.* at the end of one's rope; *informal* hassled.
OPPOSITE carefree.

harassment ▶ **noun** *he knows how to make a noise and claim police harassment* **persecution**, harrying, pestering, badgering, intimidation, bother, annoyance, aggravation, irritation, pressure, pressurization, force, coercion, molestation; *informal* hassle; *rare* bedevilment.
OPPOSITES cooperation; assistance.

harbinger ▶ **noun** *witch hazels are the harbingers of spring* **herald**, sign, indicator, indication, signal, prelude, portent, omen, augury, forewarning, presage, announcer; forerunner, precursor, messenger, usher; *French* avant-courier; *literary* foretoken.

harbour ▶ **noun** **1** *the boat was tied up in the harbour* **port**, dock, haven, marina, dockyard, boatyard, mooring, anchorage, roads, waterfront; jetty, quay, pier, slipway, wharf, landing stage; *rare* harbourage, moorage, roadstead, hithe.
2 *I am looking for a kind man who is a safe harbour for me* **refuge**, haven, safe haven, shelter, sanctuary, retreat, asylum, place of safety, place of security, port in a storm, oasis, sanctum.
▶ **verb** **1** *he was suspected of harbouring an escaped prisoner* **shelter**, conceal, hide, shield, protect, give asylum to, give sanctuary to, give shelter to, provide a refuge for; accommodate, lodge, put up, take in, billet, house.
OPPOSITE hand over.
2 *he had never harboured any hostile feelings against them* **bear**, nurse, nurture, cherish, entertain, foster, feel secretly, hold on to, cling to, possess, maintain, retain.

hard ▶ **adjective** **1** *the ground was as hard as a rock* **firm**, solid, dense, rigid, stiff, resistant, unbreakable, inflexible, unpliable, impenetrable, unyielding, solidified, hardened, compact, compacted, steely, tough, strong, stony, rock-like, flinty, close-packed, compressed, as hard as iron, as hard as stone; frozen; *rare* adamantine, unmalleable, renitent.
OPPOSITE soft.
2 *it was hard physical work* **arduous**, strenuous, tiring, fatiguing, exhausting, wearying, back-breaking, gruelling, heavy, laborious; difficult, taxing, exacting, testing, challenging, demanding, punishing, tough, formidable, onerous, rigorous, uphill, Herculean; *informal* murderous, killing, hellish; *Brit. informal* knackering; *rare* toilsome, exigent.
OPPOSITE easy.
3 *hard workers* **diligent**, hard-working, industrious, sedulous, assiduous, conscientious, energetic, keen, enthusiastic, zealous, earnest, persevering, persistent, unflagging, untiring, indefatigable; studious.
OPPOSITE lazy.
4 *we have a hard problem to solve* **difficult**, puzzling, perplexing, baffling, bewildering, mystifying, knotty, thorny, ticklish, problematic, enigmatic, complicated, complex, intricate, involved, tangled, insoluble, unfathomable, impenetrable, incomprehensible, unanswerable; *informal* spiny, mind-bending; *N. Amer. informal* gnarly; *rare* insolvable, wildering.
OPPOSITE simple.
5 *times are hard and jobs are scarce* **harsh**, **grim**, difficult, bad, bleak, dire, tough, austere, unpleasant, disagreeable, uncomfortable, intolerable, unendurable, unbearable, insupportable; straitened, spartan, dark, severe, distressing, painful, awful.
OPPOSITES comfortable; luxurious.
6 *he can be such a hard taskmaster* **strict**, harsh, firm, severe, stern, tough, rigorous, demanding, exacting, unkind, unfriendly, unsympathetic, cold, heartless, hard-hearted, cold-hearted, unfeeling, intransigent, unbending, uncompromising, inflexible, intolerant, implacable, stubborn, obdurate, unyielding, unrelenting, unsparing, lacking compassion, grim, ruthless, merciless, oppressive, tyrannical, pitiless, callous, cruel, vicious, unjust, unfair; standing no nonsense, ruling with a rod of iron; *informal* hard-boiled; *Austral./NZ informal* solid.
OPPOSITES easy-going; kind.
7 *a hard winter* **bitterly cold**, cold, bitter, harsh, severe, extreme, bleak, freezing, icy, icy-cold, arctic, polar, Siberian, glacial.
OPPOSITE mild.
8 *a hard blow to the head* **forceful**, heavy, strong, sharp, smart, violent, powerful, vigorous, mighty, hefty, tremendous.
OPPOSITE light.
9 *hard facts about the underclass are maddeningly elusive* **reliable**, definite, true, actual, confirmed, undeniable, indisputable, unquestionable, verifiable; plain, cold, bare, bold, harsh, unvarnished, unembellished.
OPPOSITE unverified.
10 *they do not touch hard liquor* **alcoholic**, strong, intoxicating, inebriating, stiff, potent, spirituous, vinous, intoxicant.
OPPOSITES non-alcoholic; low-alcohol.
11 *hard drugs* **addictive**, habit-forming, causing dependency; strong, harmful, narcotic.
OPPOSITE soft.
□ **hard and fast** *there are no hard-and-fast rules about this* **definite**, fixed, set, strict, rigid, binding, stringent, rigorous, clear-cut, cast-iron, established, inflexible, immutable, unalterable, invariable, unvarying, unchangeable, unchanging, incontestable, incontrovertible, uncompromising.
OPPOSITE flexible.
□ **hard feelings** *I had no hard feelings about being fired* **resentment**, animosity, ill feeling, ill feelings, ill will, bitterness, bad blood, resentfulness, rancour, malice, acrimony, antagonism, antipathy, animus, friction, anger, hostility, hate, hatred.
OPPOSITE goodwill.
▶ **adverb** **1** *George pushed her hard away from him* **forcefully**, forcibly, fiercely, roughly, powerfully, strongly, strenuously, heavily, sharply, vigorously, intensely, energetically, with all one's might, with might and main, with vigour, with force, with great effort.
OPPOSITE gently.
2 *they work hard at school* **diligently**, industriously, assiduously, conscientiously, sedulously, busily, intensely, enthusiastically, energetically, earnestly, persistently, doggedly, steadily, indefatigably, untiringly, all out, with application, with perseverance; *informal* like mad, like crazy, like billy-o.
OPPOSITE lackadaisically.
3 *this prosperity has been hard won* **with difficulty**, with effort, after a struggle, painfully, arduously, laboriously.
OPPOSITE easily.
4 *her death hit him hard* **severely**, badly, intensely, harshly, acutely, deeply, keenly, seriously, profoundly, violently, forcefully, grievously, gravely.
OPPOSITE slightly.
5 *it was raining hard* **heavily**, strongly, intensely, in torrents, in sheets, cats and dogs; steadily; *Brit. informal* buckets, bucketloads, stair rods; *N. Amer. informal* pitchforks.
OPPOSITE lightly.
6 *my mother looked hard at me* **closely**, attentively, intently, critically, carefully, keenly, searchingly, earnestly, sharply, scrutinizingly.
OPPOSITE casually.
□ **hard by** *a little shop, hard by the St Paul Hotel* **close to**, right by, close by, beside, near, near to, nearby, not far from, a short distance from, a step away from, a stone's throw from, on the doorstep of, in the vicinity of, in the neighbourhood of, round the corner from, within easy reach of, adjacent to; *informal* within spitting distance of, within sniffing distance of, {a hop, skip, and a jump away from}.
OPPOSITE far from.
□ **hard on/upon** *his banishment followed hard on the quarrel* **soon after**, hard on the heels of, quickly after, promptly after, shortly after, immediately

after, directly after, straight after, right after, a short time after, without delay after.
OPPOSITE long after.

□ **hard up** (informal) *I'm too hard up to buy fancy clothes* **poor**, short of money, short of cash, impoverished, impecunious, in financial difficulties, financially embarrassed, financially distressed, in reduced circumstances, in straitened circumstances, unable to make ends meet; penniless, moneyless, destitute, poverty-stricken, bankrupt, in the red, without a sou, without means of support; informal broke, stony broke, flat broke, bust, on one's beam-ends; Brit. informal skint, cleaned out, strapped for cash, on one's uppers, not having two pennies/farthings to rub together, in Queer Street, without a shot in one's locker, without a brass farthing; N. Amer. informal stone broke, without a red cent.
OPPOSITE rich.

WORD LINKS
related prefix **sclero-** (e.g. ***sclerosis, scleroderma***)

hardbitten ▸ adjective *a hardbitten war reporter* **hardened**, tough, cynical, hard-headed, callous, as hard as nails, unsentimental, lacking sentiment, world-weary, case-hardened, toughened by experience; informal hard-nosed, hard-boiled, as tough as old boots; rare indurate, indurated.
OPPOSITE sentimental.

hard-boiled ▸ adjective (informal) *a hard-boiled undercover agent* **cynical**, tough, hardened, hardbitten, hard-headed, callous, as hard as nails, unsentimental, lacking sentiment, world-weary, case-hardened, toughened by experience; informal hard-nosed, as tough as old boots; rare indurate, indurated.
OPPOSITE sentimental.

hard-core ▸ adjective *a hard-core following* **diehard**, staunch, dedicated, committed, steadfast, hard-line, dyed-in-the-wool, long-standing; extreme, entrenched, radical, intransigent, uncompromising, rigid; informal deep-dyed.
OPPOSITE moderate.

harden ▸ verb **1** *this glue will harden in four hours* **solidify**, set, become hard, become solid, congeal, clot, coagulate, stiffen, thicken, cake, freeze, bake, crystallize; strengthen, reinforce; technical anneal, vulcanize, ossify, petrify; rare indurate, inspissate, gelatinize.
OPPOSITE liquefy.
2 *their suffering had hardened them* **toughen**, desensitize, inure, make insensitive, make tough, make unfeeling, case-harden, harden someone's heart; deaden, numb, benumb, anaesthetize; brutalize, make callous; rare indurate.
OPPOSITE soften.

hardened ▸ adjective **1** *he was hardened to the violence he had seen and inflicted* **inured**, desensitized, deadened, accustomed, habituated, acclimatized, used; coarsened; rare indurate.
OPPOSITE unaccustomed.
2 *a hardened criminal* **inveterate**, seasoned, habitual, chronic, compulsive, confirmed, accustomed, dyed-in-the-wool; through and through; incorrigible, incurable, irredeemable, impenitent, unreformable, unregenerate, reprobate, obdurate, shameless.
OPPOSITE infrequent.
3 *the silos are hardened against air attack* **strengthened**, fortified, reinforced, toughened, thickened; literary girded; rare embastioned.
OPPOSITE unfortified.

hard-headed ▸ adjective *a hard-headed businessman* **unsentimental**, practical, pragmatic, businesslike, realistic, sensible, rational, tough, clear-thinking, cool-headed, hardbitten, down-to-earth, matter-of-fact, no-nonsense, with one's/both feet on the ground; shrewd, astute, sharp, sharp-witted; informal hard-nosed, hard-boiled.
OPPOSITE idealistic.

hard-hearted ▸ adjective *only the most hard-hearted man would not have offered comfort* **unfeeling**, heartless, cold, hard, unsympathetic, uncaring, unloving, unconcerned, indifferent, intolerant, unmoved, unkind, uncharitable, unemotional, stony, cold-hearted, cold-blooded, lacking compassion, mean-spirited, without sentiment, stony-hearted, with a heart of stone, hard as nails; cruel, brutal, callous, savage, inhuman, merciless, pitiless.
OPPOSITE compassionate.

hard-hitting ▸ adjective *the campaign against speeding included a hard-hitting television advertisement* **uncompromising**, blunt, forthright, frank, honest, direct, tough; critical, condemnatory, unsparing, strongly worded, straight-talking, all out, pulling no punches, no holds barred, not mincing one's words, not beating about the bush; informal upfront, straight from the shoulder.
OPPOSITE mild.

hardihood ▸ noun (dated) *the soldiers showed great hardihood and endurance* **bravery**, courage, boldness, daring, spirit, valour, mettle, heart, nerve, spine, pluck, dauntlessness, doughtiness, fortitude, courageousness, backbone, intrepidity, intrepidness, heroism, strength of character, moral fibre; informal guts, grit, spunk; Brit. informal bottle; N. Amer. informal moxie, cojones, sand; vulgar slang balls.
OPPOSITE timidity.

hardiness ▸ noun *this breed is renowned for its hardiness* **robustness**, healthiness, strength, toughness, vigour, ruggedness, sturdiness, resilience, stamina, good health.
OPPOSITE frailty.

hard-line ▸ adjective *a hard-line nationalist* **uncompromising**, strict, diehard, extreme, tough, inflexible, immoderate, intransigent, intractable, unyielding, undeviating, unwavering, single-minded, not giving an inch; rare indurate.
OPPOSITE moderate.

hardly ▸ adverb **1** *we hardly know each other | Dad had hardly got a word out before she cut him off* **scarcely**, barely, only just, not much, faintly, narrowly, slightly, rarely, little; by a very small margin, by the narrowest of margins, by the skin of one's teeth, by a hair's breadth, by a nose; almost not, not quite; informal by a whisker.
OPPOSITE fully.
2 *she could hardly sit up straight* **only with difficulty**, barely, scarcely, only with effort, only just, almost not; Brit. informal at a push.
OPPOSITE easily.

hardness ▸ noun **1** *the hardness of the ground* **firmness**, solidity, stiffness, rigidity, denseness, inflexibility, inelasticity, resistance.
OPPOSITE softness.
2 *there was a core of calculating hardness to this man* **hard-heartedness**, heartlessness, cold-heartedness, lack of compassion, lack of feeling, lack of sentiment, callousness, unkindness, flintiness, steeliness; harshness, severity, strictness, sternness, toughness.
OPPOSITES compassion, kindness.

hard-nosed ▸ adjective (informal) *hard-nosed businessmen* **tough-minded**, unsentimental, down-to-earth, no-nonsense, hard-headed, hardbitten, pragmatic, clear-thinking, realistic, practical, rational, shrewd, astute, businesslike; informal hard-boiled.
OPPOSITE sentimental.

hard-pressed ▸ adjective **1** *the hard-pressed French infantry* **under attack**, closely pursued, hotly pursued, harried, hounded.
2 *organizations that are hard-pressed financially* **in difficulties**, under pressure, under stress, troubled, beleaguered, harassed, with one's back to the wall, with one's back up against the wall, in a tight corner, in a tight spot, between a rock and a hard place; busy, overburdened, overworked, overloaded, overtaxed, rushed off one's feet; N. Amer. at the end of one's rope; informal pushed, up against it.
OPPOSITE untroubled.

hardship ▸ noun *the world depression caused severe hardship* **privation**, deprivation, destitution, poverty, austerity, penury, want, need, neediness, beggary, impecuniousness, impecuniosity, financial distress; misfortune, distress, suffering, affliction, trouble, pain, misery, wretchedness, tribulation, adversity, disaster, ruin, ruination, calamity; trials, trials and tribulations, dire straits; informal hassle; literary travails.
OPPOSITES prosperity; ease.

hardware ▸ noun *tanks and other military hardware* **equipment**, apparatus, gear, paraphernalia, tackle, kit, machinery; tools, articles, implements, instruments, appliances, gadgets; informal stuff, things; Brit. informal clobber, gubbins; rare equipage.

hard-wearing ▸ adjective *a hard-wearing fabric* **durable**, strong, tough, resilient, lasting, solid, stout, rugged, long-lasting, made to last, well made, wear-resistant, heavy-duty, strongly made; rare infrangible.
OPPOSITES delicate; flimsy.

hard-working ▸ adjective *loyal and hard-working employees* **diligent**, industrious, conscientious, assiduous, sedulous, painstaking, persevering, unflagging, untiring, tireless, indefatigable, studious; energetic, keen, enthusiastic, zealous, busy, with one's shoulder to the wheel, with one's nose to the grindstone; archaic laborious.
OPPOSITE lazy.

CHOOSE THE RIGHT WORD

hard-working, diligent, industrious

- **Hard-working** is the most general term but is typically applied to people in paid work (*you can search for an honest, hard-working mechanic in your area*).
- **Diligent** describes a careful, conscientious person (such as a *pupil, teacher, parent,* or *student*) or their actions (such as *research, enquiries, practice,* or a *search*). A *diligent* person typically works hard from a sense of duty or dedication (*she had been diligent about her piano lessons | skilled and diligent nursing staff*).
- **industrious** conveys an impression of worthiness (*she wanted energetic, industrious people around her*), being commonly used alongside *energetic, loyal, sober* or *obedient*.

hardy ▸ adjective *a couple of hardy outdoor types | hardy trees and shrubs*

robust, healthy, fit, strong, sturdy, tough, rugged, hearty, lusty, vigorous, hale and hearty, fit as a fiddle, fighting fit, in fine fettle, in good health, in good condition; *Brit.* in rude health; *dated* stalwart.
OPPOSITES delicate; tender.

hare *See centre pages for list of* **Rabbits and Hares**
▶ **noun**

WORD LINKS

male	**buck**
female	**doe**
young	**leveret**
home	**form**
collective noun	**down, mute, husk**
relating to hares	**leporine**

hare-brained ▶ **adjective 1** *a hare-brained scheme* **ill-judged**, rash, foolish, foolhardy, reckless, madcap, wild, silly, stupid, ridiculous, preposterous, absurd, idiotic, asinine, imprudent, impracticable, unworkable, unrealistic, unconsidered, half-baked, ill-thought-out, ill-advised, ill-conceived; *informal* daft, crackpot, crackbrained, cock-eyed, crazy, barmy.
OPPOSITE sensible.
2 *a hare-brained young girl* **foolish**, silly, idiotic, unintelligent, empty-headed, scatterbrained, feather-brained, birdbrained, pea-brained, brainless, giddy; *informal* dippy, dizzy, dopey, dotty, airheaded.
OPPOSITE intelligent.

harem ▶ **noun women's quarters;** (*in Muslim societies, formerly*) seraglio; (*in India & Persia*) zenana; (*in ancient Greece & Rome*) gynaeceum; *rare* haremlik, serai.

hark ▶ **verb** (*literary*) *hark, I hear a warning note* **listen**, lend an ear, pay attention, pay heed, attend, mark, note, notice; *archaic* hearken, give ear.
□ **hark back** *these newest styles* **hark back** *to the seventies* **recall**, call to mind, look back to, turn back to, cause one to remember, cause one to recollect, cause one to think back to.

harlequin ▶ **noun jester**, joker, merry andrew, droll; *rare* zany.
▶ **adjective** *a harlequin pattern* **varicoloured**, variegated, colourful, particoloured, multicoloured, multicolour, many-coloured, many-hued, rainbow, jazzy, kaleidoscopic, psychedelic, polychromatic, chequered; *informal* (looking) like an explosion in a paint factory; *rare* motley.
OPPOSITE plain.

harlot ▶ **noun** (*archaic*) **prostitute**, whore, call girl, sex worker, white slave; promiscuous woman, slut, hussy; *euphemistic* model, escort, masseuse; *French* fille de joie, demi-mondaine, grande horizontale; *Spanish* puta; *informal* tart, pro, tail, brass nail, tom, woman on the game, working girl, member of the oldest profession, floozie, moll; *Brit. informal* scrubber, slag, slapper; *N. Amer. informal* hooker, tramp, hustler, roundheel; *black English* ho; *dated* streetwalker, woman of the streets, woman of the night, scarlet woman, loose woman, fallen woman, woman of easy virtue, cocotte, wanton; *archaic* strumpet, courtesan, trollop, woman of ill repute, lady of pleasure, Cyprian, doxy, drab, quean, trull, wench.

harm ▶ **noun 1** *the voltage is not sufficient to cause harm* **injury**, hurt, pain, suffering, distress, anguish, trauma, torment, grief; **damage**, impairment, destruction, loss, ruin, defacement, defilement, mischief.
OPPOSITE benefit.
2 *I can't see any harm in it* **evil**, badness, wrong, mischief, wrongdoing, immorality, ill, wickedness, vice, iniquity, sin, sinfulness, nefariousness.
OPPOSITE good.
▶ **verb** *he's never harmed anybody in his life | this could harm his World Cup prospects* **injure**, hurt, wound, maltreat, mistreat, misuse, ill-treat, ill-use, abuse, molest, inflict pain on, inflict suffering on, handle/treat roughly, do violence to, lay a finger on; **damage**, spoil, mar, destroy, do mischief to, impair, deface, defile, blemish, tarnish, taint.
OPPOSITES benefit; improve.

harmful ▶ **adjective** *the harmful effects of cigarette smoking | a harmful influence* **damaging**, injurious, detrimental, dangerous, deleterious, unfavourable, negative, disadvantageous, unhealthy, unwholesome, hurtful, baleful, wounding, destructive; noxious, hazardous, poisonous, toxic, deadly, lethal; bad, evil, malign, malignant, malevolent, corrupting, subversive, pernicious; *rare* baneful, maleficent, malefic.
OPPOSITES beneficial; harmless.

harmless ▶ **adjective 1** *a harmless substance* **safe**, innocuous, benign, gentle, mild, wholesome, non-dangerous, non-toxic, non-poisonous, non-irritant, non-addictive; *rare* innoxious.
OPPOSITES dangerous; harmful.
2 *he seems harmless enough* **inoffensive**, innocuous, unobjectionable, unexceptionable, unoffending, tame, gentle.
OPPOSITE objectionable.

harmonious ▶ **adjective 1** *harmonious music* **tuneful**, melodious, melodic, sweet-sounding, pleasant-sounding, sweet-toned, mellifluous, dulcet, lyrical; **euphonious**, euphonic, harmonic, harmonizing, polyphonic, consonant; *informal* easy on the ear; *rare* symphonious, canorous, mellifluent.
OPPOSITE discordant.
2 *a harmonious relationship between business and customer* **friendly**, amicable, cordial, amiable, agreeable, congenial, easy, peaceful, peaceable, cooperative, good-natured; fraternal, compatible, sympathetic, united, attuned, in harmony, in rapport, in tune, in accord, of one mind, seeing eye to eye, free from disagreement.
OPPOSITE hostile.
3 *the decor is a harmonious blend of traditional and modern* **congruous**, coordinated, matching, balanced, proportional, in proportion, compatible, well matched, well proportioned, well balanced.
OPPOSITE incongruous.

harmonize ▶ **verb 1** *the colours harmonize well* **coordinate**, **go together**, match, fit together, blend, mix, balance, tone in; be compatible, be harmonious, be congruous, be consonant, be well coordinated, suit each other, set each other off.
OPPOSITE clash.
2 *the need to harmonize tax laws across Europe* **coordinate**, systematize, correlate, match, integrate, synchronize, homogenize, bring together, make consistent, bring in line (with), bring in tune (with), tie in; *rare* concert.
3 *he tried to harmonize relations between the quarrelling factions* **reconcile**, make harmonious, restore harmony to, make peaceful, patch up, repair, smooth out.

harmony ▶ **noun 1** *the quartet owes its air of tranquillity largely to the subtle harmony* **euphony**, polyphony, consonance; tunefulness, melodiousness, mellifluousness, mellifluence.
OPPOSITE dissonance.
2 *the simplicity of the individual parts focused attention on the harmony of the whole structure* **balance**, symmetry, congruity, consonance, coordination, blending, correspondence, compatibility.
OPPOSITE incongruity.
3 *the villagers live together in harmony | man and machine in perfect harmony* **concord**, accord, agreement, peace, peacefulness, amity, amicability, friendship, fellowship, comradeship, solidarity, cooperation, understanding, consensus, unity, sympathy, rapport, goodwill, like-mindedness; unison, union, concert, oneness, synthesis, concurrence.
OPPOSITE disagreement.

harness *See centre pages for list of parts of a horse's* **Harness**
▶ **noun** *a horse's harness* **tack**, tackle, equipment, trappings, straps, yoke; *informal* gear; *archaic* equipage.
□ **in harness** *it was good to be back in harness again* **at work**, working, employed, in an occupation, in action, active, busy.
OPPOSITE unemployed.
▶ **verb 1** *Dad harnessed a horse and put it between the shafts* **hitch up**, put something in harness, saddle, yoke, couple.
OPPOSITE unhitch.
2 *attempts to harness solar energy | organizations that try to harness the creativity of their workforce* **control**, exploit, utilize, use, make use of, put to use, render useful, make productive, turn to good account; channel, mobilize, employ, apply, capitalize on.
OPPOSITE underuse.

harp ▶ **noun.** *See centre pages for list of* **Stringed Instruments**
▶ **verb** *guys who are constantly* **harping on about** *the war* **keep on about**, go on about, persist in talking about, keep talking about, labour the point about, dwell on, expatiate on, elaborate on, expound on, make an issue of, discuss something at length; complain repeatedly about, nag someone about, badger someone about; *informal* witter on about, rabbit on about, hassle someone about.

WORD LINKS

harp player	**harpist, harper**

harpoon ▶ **noun spear**, trident, arrow, dart, barb; *rare* gaff, leister.

harridan ▶ **noun shrew**, **virago**, harpy, termagant, vixen, nag, hag, crone, dragon, ogress; fishwife, hellcat, she-devil, fury, gorgon, martinet, tartar, spitfire; *informal* old bag, old bat, old trout, old cow, bitch, battleaxe, witch; *rare* scold, Xanthippe.

harried ▶ **adjective** *it was full of harried women with crying children* **harassed**, hard-pressed, beleaguered, agitated, flustered, bothered, troubled, distressed, vexed, beset, hag-ridden, hounded, plagued, tormented; *informal* hassled, up against it.
OPPOSITE untroubled.

harrow ▶ **verb** *to read those words harrowed her very soul* **distress**, trouble, afflict, grieve, torment, torture, crucify, rack, sear, pain, wound, mortify, cause agony to, cause suffering to; *informal* cut up.
OPPOSITES calm; comfort.

harrowing ▶ **adjective** *harrowing pictures of starving children | a harrowing experience* **distressing**, traumatic, upsetting, heartbreaking, heart-rending, shocking, disturbing, painful, affecting, haunting, appalling, tragic, horrifying; *informal* gut-wrenching; *rare* distressful.
OPPOSITE heartening.

harry ▶ **verb 1** *after the battle, they harried the retreating enemy* **attack**, assail, assault, maraud, ravage, devastate, wreak havoc on; plunder, rob, sack,

ransack, raid, pillage, lay waste to; *literary* despoil; *rare* depredate, reave, spoliate.
2 *the government is being mercilessly harried by a new lobby* **harass**, hound, pressurize, bring pressure to bear on, put pressure on, lean on, keep on at, go on at, chivvy, bedevil, torment, pester, bother, disturb, worry, annoy, badger, nag, plague, persecute, molest; *informal* hassle, bug, give someone a hard time, drive someone round the bend, drive someone up the wall, be in someone's hair, get on someone's back, breathe down someone's neck; *Brit. informal* drive someone round the twist.
OPPOSITE leave in peace.

harsh ▶ adjective **1** *his shrill, harsh voice* **grating**, jarring, grinding, rasping, raspy, strident, raucous, brassy, jangling, metallic, ear-piercing, discordant, dissonant, disagreeable, unharmonious, cacophonous, unmelodious; screeching, shrill, tinny, squeaky, squawking; rough, coarse, guttural, hoarse, gruff, croaky, croaking, growly, growling; *rare* stridulant.
OPPOSITES soft; dulcet.
2 *drenched in a harsh white neon light | harsh colours* **glaring**, bright, dazzling, brilliant; loud, flashy, garish, gaudy, lurid, bold, showy, crude, vulgar.
OPPOSITE subdued.
3 *during his harsh rule, thousands were exiled* **cruel**, severe, savage, barbarous, despotic, dictatorial, tyrannical, tyrannous, ruthless, merciless, pitiless, relentless, unrelenting, hard, strict, intolerant, illiberal; hard-hearted, heartless, unkind, inhuman, inhumane, unfeeling, unsympathetic, unmerciful, unpitying; *rare* suppressive.
OPPOSITES enlightened; kind.
4 *politicians are taking harsh measures to clear the homeless from the streets* **severe**, stringent, firm, austere, punitive, draconian, stiff, cruel, brutal, hard, stern, rigid, rigorous, grim, uncompromising, inflexible.
OPPOSITE lenient.
5 *harsh words are exchanged when tempers get frayed* **rude**, discourteous, uncivil, impolite, unfriendly, sharp, acerbic, bitter, abusive, unkind, disparaging; abrupt, brusque, blunt, curt, gruff, short, surly, ungracious, disrespectful, ill-mannered, bad-mannered, offhand.
OPPOSITE friendly.
6 *the harsh conditions of the refugee camps* **austere**, grim, spartan, hard, rough, severe, comfortless, inhospitable, stark; bleak, desolate, barren, bitter, wild.
OPPOSITE comfortable.
7 *a harsh winter* **hard**, severe, cold, bitter, bitterly cold, bleak, freezing, icy, icy-cold, arctic, polar, Siberian, glacial, extreme, nasty.
OPPOSITE balmy.
8 *harsh cleaners scratch stains away* **abrasive**, strong, caustic; coarse, rough, bristly, hairy, scratchy.
OPPOSITES mild; smooth.

harum-scarum ▶ adjective (*informal*) *he was a harum-scarum young fellow* **reckless**, impetuous, impulsive, imprudent, rash, wild, daredevil, madcap, precipitous, precipitate, frivolous, hot-headed, hare-brained, giddy, foolhardy, thoughtless, incautious, careless, heedless, hasty, overhasty; *informal* devil-may-care, scatty, dotty, dippy; *Brit. informal* divvy; *rare* temerarious.
OPPOSITE cautious.

harvest ▶ noun **1** *the women and girls helped with the harvest* **gathering in of the crops**, harvesting, harvest time, harvest home; **reaping**, picking, collecting; *rare* garnering, ingathering, gleaning, culling.
2 *a poor harvest* **yield**, crop, vintage, year's growth; fruits, produce.
3 *in terms of science, Apollo yielded a meagre harvest* **return**, result, fruits; product, effect, consequence, output.
▶ verb **1** *once he's harvested the wheat crop, there are still the beans* **gather in**, gather, bring in, take in; reap, pick, collect; *rare* garner, ingather, glean, cull.
2 *he harvested a hat-trick of honours* **acquire**, obtain, gain, get, procure, secure, earn; accumulate, amass, gather, collect; *informal* land, net, bag, scoop, cop.

hash[1] ▶ noun *I used a whole hash of excuses* **mixture**, assortment, variety, array, mixed bag, mix, miscellany, random collection, motley collection, selection, medley, melange, mishmash, hotchpotch, hodgepodge, ragbag, pot-pourri, jumble, farrago, patchwork; *rare* gallimaufry, omnium gatherum, olio, olla podrida, salmagundi, macédoine, motley.
□ **make a hash of** (*informal*) *he made a hash of a simple penalty* **make a mess of**, bungle, botch, fluff, fumble, butcher, mess up; mismanage, mishandle, misdirect, misgovern, misconduct, mar, spoil, ruin, wreck; *informal* muff, muck up, foul up, screw up, louse up, bitch up, blow, foozle; *Brit. informal* make a muck of, make a pig's ear of, make a Horlicks of, cock up; *N. Amer. informal* flub, goof up, bobble; *vulgar slang* balls up, bugger up, fuck up.
OPPOSITE manage successfully.

hash[2] ▶ noun (*informal*) **cannabis**, marijuana, hashish, bhang, hemp, kef, kif, charas, ganja, sinsemilla; *informal* dope, grass, pot, blow, draw, stuff, Mary Jane, tea, the weed, gold, skunkweed, skunk, reefer, spliff, rope, smoke, gage, boo, charge, jive, mootah, pod; *Brit. informal* wacky backy; *N. Amer. informal* locoweed; *S. African* dagga, zol; *informal, dated* green, mezz.

hassle (*informal*) ▶ noun **1** *parking in the city centre is a hassle | the hassle of child care* **inconvenience**, bother, nuisance, problem, struggle, difficulty, annoyance, irritation, thorn in one's flesh/side, bane of one's life; trials and tribulations, fuss, trouble; *informal* aggravation, aggro, stress, headache, pain, pain in the neck/backside; *N. Amer. informal* pain in the butt; *Brit. vulgar slang* pain in the arse.
2 (*N. Amer.*) *you'd better not get into a hassle with that guy* **disagreement**, quarrel, argument, dispute, altercation, squabble, wrangle, shouting match, difference of opinion, contretemps, falling-out, war of words; fight, tussle, struggle, fracas, free-for-all, brawl; *Irish, N. Amer., & Austral.* donnybrook; *informal* tiff, set-to, run-in, spat, scrap, dust-up; *Brit. informal* row, barney, slanging match, ding-dong, bust-up, bit of argy-bargy, ruck; *Scottish informal* rammy; *N. Amer. informal* rhubarb; *archaic* broil, miff; *Scottish archaic* threap, collieshangie.
OPPOSITE agreement.
▶ verb *they were hassling him to pay up* **harass**, pester, nag, go on at, keep on at, keep after, badger, hound, harry, harp on at, chivvy, trouble, bother, worry, torment, annoy, plague, bedevil, persecute; *informal* bug, give someone a hard time, get in someone's hair, get on someone's case, get on someone's back, breathe down someone's neck; *N. English* mither; *N. Amer. informal* devil, ride; *Austral./NZ informal* heavy; *rare* discommode.
OPPOSITE leave in peace.

hassled ▶ adjective (*informal*) *he was hassled and rushed off his feet* **harassed**, stressed, stressed out, harried, frayed, hard-pressed, agitated, flustered, beleaguered, hounded, plagued, bothered, troubled, distressed, beset, hag-ridden, tormented; under stress, under pressure, at the end of one's tether, with one's back up against the wall; *N. Amer.* at the end of one's rope; *informal* up against it, in a state, hot and bothered.
OPPOSITES calm, relaxed.

haste ▶ noun *working with feverish haste* **speed**, hastiness, hurry, hurriedness, swiftness, rapidity, rapidness, quickness, promptness, briskness, immediateness; impetuosity, precipitateness, rush, rushing; *literary* celerity, fleetness; *rare* expedition, expeditiousness, promptitude.
OPPOSITES slowness, delay.
□ **in haste quickly**, rapidly, fast, speedily, with alacrity, with urgency, in a rush, in a hurry, with dispatch.

hasten ▶ verb **1** *we hastened back to Paris* **hurry**, go fast, go quickly, make haste, hurtle, dash, dart, race, rush, fly, flash, shoot, streak, bolt, bound, blast, charge, chase, career, hurry up, speed up, scurry, scramble, scamper, scuttle, sprint, run, gallop, go like lightning, go hell for leather; *Brit.* scutter; *informal* whizz, whoosh, vroom, tear, scoot, hare, pelt, zip, whip, zoom, belt, beetle, buzz, get a move on, step on it, hotfoot it, leg it, burn rubber, go like a bat out of hell; *Brit. informal* bomb, bucket, shift, put one's foot down, go like the clappers; *Scottish informal* wheech; *N. Amer. informal* hightail, barrel, boogie, clip, lay rubber, get the lead out; *N. Amer. vulgar slang* drag/tear/haul ass; *informal, dated* cut along; *archaic* post, hie, fleet.
OPPOSITES dawdle; crawl.
2 *stress chemicals can hasten ageing* **speed up**, make faster, accelerate, quicken, precipitate, expedite, advance, hurry on, step up, push forward, urge on, spur on; facilitate, aid, assist, help, boost; *informal* crank up, gee up.
OPPOSITES delay; slow down.

hastily ▶ adverb **1** *Meg retreated hastily as the blades began to rotate* **quickly**, hurriedly, fast, swiftly, rapidly, speedily, briskly, expeditiously, without delay, post-haste, at high speed, at full speed, with all speed, at full tilt, at the speed of light, as fast as possible, with all possible haste, like a whirlwind, like an arrow from a bow, at breakneck speed, as fast as one's legs can carry one, at a run, at a gallop, hotfoot, on the double; cursorily, perfunctorily, briefly, fleetingly, sketchily, superficially; *informal* double quick, in double quick time, p.d.q. (pretty damn quick), nippily, like (greased) lightning, hell for leather, like mad, like crazy, like blazes, like the wind, like a bomb, like nobody's business, like a scalded cat, like the deuce, a mile a minute, like a bat out of hell; *Brit. informal* at a rate of knots, like the clappers, like billy-o; *N. Amer. informal* lickety-split; *literary* apace.
OPPOSITE slowly.
2 *an agreement was hastily drawn up* **hurriedly**, speedily, quickly; impetuously, impulsively, recklessly, precipitately, precipitously, rashly, incautiously, imprudently, on the spur of the moment, prematurely.
OPPOSITES carefully, deliberately.

hasty ▶ adjective **1** *Fran took several hasty steps backwards* **quick**, hurried, fast, swift, rapid, speedy, brisk, hurrying, expeditious; cursory, perfunctory, brief, short, fleeting, passing, flying, transitory; *literary* fleet, rathe.
OPPOSITE slow.
2 *hasty decisions* **rash**, impetuous, impulsive, reckless, precipitate, precipitous, incautious, imprudent, spur-of-the-moment, premature, ill-considered, unconsidered, unthinking, ill-advised, ill-judged, injudicious; *rare* temerarious.
OPPOSITE considered.

hat *See centre pages for list of* **Hats**
▶ **noun** *Brit. informal* titfer.

WORD LINKS
seller of hats **hatter**
seller of women's hats **milliner**

hatch ▶ **verb 1** *the duck hatched a clutch of eggs* **incubate**, brood, sit on, cover; bring forth.
2 *the little plot that you and Sylvia* **hatched up** *last night* **devise**, conceive, contrive, concoct, brew, invent, plan, design, formulate; think up, make up, dream up, trump up, put together; *informal* cook up.

hatchet ▶ **noun axe**, cleaver, mattock, tomahawk; *Brit.* chopper.

hate ▶ **verb 1** *the boys hate each other* **loathe**, detest, dislike greatly, abhor, abominate, despise, execrate, feel aversion towards, feel revulsion towards, feel hostile towards, be repelled by, be revolted by, regard with disgust, not be able to bear/stand, be unable to stomach, find intolerable, shudder at, recoil from, shrink from; *informal* hate someone's guts; *rare* disrelish.
OPPOSITES love; like.
2 *I hate to bother you* **be sorry**, be reluctant, be loath, be unwilling, be disinclined; regret, dislike, not like, hesitate.
▶ **noun 1** *feelings of hate and revenge* **loathing**, hatred, detestation, dislike, distaste, abhorrence, abomination, execration, resentment, aversion, hostility, ill will, ill feeling, bad feeling; enmity, animosity, antagonism, antipathy, bitterness, animus, revulsion, disgust, contempt, repugnance, odium, rancour; *rare* disrelish.
OPPOSITES love; liking.
2 *Richard's* **pet hate** *is filling in his tax returns* **bugbear**, bane, bogey, bugaboo, pet aversion, thorn in one's flesh/side, bane of one's life; *French* bête noire.
OPPOSITE favourite thing.

hateful ▶ **adjective** *that hateful arrogant old woman* **detestable**, horrible, horrid, unpleasant, awful, nasty, disagreeable, despicable, objectionable, insufferable, revolting, rotten, loathsome, abhorrent, abominable, damnable, execrable, odious, repugnant, repellent, repulsive, disgusting, distasteful, obnoxious, offensive, foul, vile, heinous; *informal* ghastly; *Brit. informal* beastly, God-awful, yucky; *vulgar slang* shitty; *archaic* loathly, disgustful.
OPPOSITES delightful; lovable.

hatred ▶ **noun** *full of hatred and bitterness* **loathing**, hate, detestation, dislike, distaste, abhorrence, abomination, execration, resentment, aversion, hostility, ill will, ill feeling, bad feeling; enmity, animosity, antagonism, antipathy, bitterness, animus, revulsion, disgust, contempt, repugnance, odium, rancour; *rare* disrelish.
OPPOSITES love; liking.

WORD LINKS
related prefix **mis-** (e.g. ***misogyny, misanthrope***)

haughtiness ▶ **noun arrogance**, pride, conceit, hubris, self-importance, egotism, sense of superiority, pomposity, high-handedness, swagger, boasting, bumptiousness, bluster, condescension, disdain, contempt, imperiousness; vanity, immodesty; loftiness, lordliness, snobbishness, snobbery, superciliousness, smugness; pretension, pretentiousness, affectation; scorn, mocking, sneering, scoffing; *informal* snootiness, uppitiness, big-headedness.
OPPOSITE modesty.

haughty ▶ **adjective** *his bearing was both haughty and disdainful* **proud**, vain, arrogant, conceited, snobbish, stuck-up, pompous, self-important, superior, egotistical, supercilious, condescending, lofty, patronizing, smug, scornful, contemptuous, disdainful, overweening, overbearing, imperious, lordly, cavalier, high-handed, full of oneself, above oneself; *informal* snooty, sniffy, hoity-toity, uppity, uppish, cocky, big-headed, swollen-headed, puffed up, high and mighty, la-di-da, on one's high horse, too big for one's boots; *Brit. informal* toffee-nosed; *N. Amer. informal* chesty; *informal, dated* too big for one's breeches; *literary* vainglorious.
OPPOSITES modest; humble.

haul ▶ **verb 1** *she hauled the laden basket up the slope* **drag**, pull, tug, heave, hump, trail, draw, tow, manhandle; *informal* lug; *N. Amer. informal* schlep; *archaic* hale.
OPPOSITE push.
2 *a contract to haul coal over a five-year period* **transport**, convey, cart, carry, ship, ferry, move, shift, take.
▶ **noun** *the thieves were forced to abandon their haul* **booty**, loot, plunder; spoils, stolen goods, gains, ill-gotten gains; *informal* swag, the goods, hot goods, boodle.

haunches ▶ **plural noun rump**, rear, rear end, backside, seat; buttocks, thighs, hips, hindquarters; *Brit.* bottom; *French* derrière; *German* Sitzfleisch; *informal* behind, sit-upon, stern, BTM, tochus; *Brit. informal* bum, botty, prat, jacksie; *N. Amer. informal* butt, fanny, tush, tushie, tail, duff, buns, booty, caboose, heinie, patootie, keister, tuchis; *W. Indian informal* batty; *humorous* fundament, posterior; *black English* rass, rusty dusty; *Brit. vulgar slang* arse; *N. Amer. vulgar slang* ass; *technical* nates; *archaic* breech.

haunt ▶ **verb 1** *a ghost haunts this eighteenth-century house* **appear in**, materialize in; visit; *informal* spook.
2 *he haunts street markets* **frequent**, spend time in, patronize, visit regularly, be a regular visitor to, be a regular client of, loiter in, linger in; *informal* hang around/round/out in; *Brit. informal* hang about in.
3 *the sight haunted me for years* **torment**, obsess, oppress, disturb, trouble, worry, plague, burden, beset, beleaguer, bedevil, besiege, torture; prey on, weigh on, gnaw at, nag at, weigh heavily on, lie heavy on; prey on one's mind, weigh heavily on one's mind, be a weight on one's mind; *informal* bug.
▶ **noun** *a favourite haunt of artists of the time* **hang-out**, stamping ground, meeting place, territory, domain, purlieu, resort, den, retreat, favourite spot; *informal* hidey-hole; *Brit. informal* local, patch, manor.

haunted ▶ **adjective 1** *a haunted house* **possessed**, cursed, jinxed; ghostly, eerie, unearthly, other-worldly; *informal* spooky.
2 *haunted eyes stared at her* **tormented**, anguished, troubled, plagued, bedevilled, beleaguered, oppressed, obsessed, tortured, preoccupied, worried, disturbed.
OPPOSITE untroubled.

haunting ▶ **adjective** *the sweet haunting sound of pan pipes* **evocative**, affecting, moving, touching, emotive, expressive, powerful, stirring, atmospheric, soul-stirring; **poignant**, nostalgic, wistful, plaintive; memorable, unforgettable, indelible, not/never to be forgotten.
OPPOSITES unaffecting; unmemorable.

hauteur ▶ **noun** *his natural coolness and aristocratic hauteur* **haughtiness**, superciliousness, loftiness, arrogance, pride, conceit, snobbery, snobbishness, superiority, self-importance, disdain, disdainfulness, condescension, contempt, scorn; airs, airs and graces; *informal* snootiness, uppitiness, uppishness, la-di-da; *Brit. informal* side.

have ▶ **verb 1** *he had a new car and a boat* **possess**, own, be in possession of, be the owner of, be the (proud) possessor of, have in one's possession, have to one's name, count among one's possessions, be blessed with, boast, enjoy; keep, maintain, retain, hold, use, utilize, occupy.
OPPOSITE be bereft of.
2 *the flat has five rooms* **comprise**, consist of, contain, include, incorporate, be composed of, be made up of, be formed of; embrace, embody, encompass, take in; *formal* comprehend.
3 *they had beans on toast | we had three cups of tea* **eat**, consume, devour, partake of; **drink**, empty, drain, quaff; *informal* demolish, dispose of, put away, get outside of, scoff (down), pack away, tuck away; imbibe, sink, knock back; *Brit. informal* shift, bevvy; *N. Amer. informal* scarf (down/up), snarf (down/up), inhale; *rare* ingurgitate, bib.
4 *she had a letter from Mark* **receive**, get, be given, be sent, obtain, acquire, procure, come by, take receipt of.
OPPOSITES send; give.
5 *we've decided to have a party* **organize**, arrange, hold, give, host, throw, provide, put on, lay on, set up, fix up, make arrangements for, make preparations for, pencil in, prepare for, plan for.
OPPOSITE cancel.
6 *she's going to have a baby* **give birth to**, bear, produce, be delivered of, bring into the world; *informal* drop; *archaic* be brought to bed of, bring forth, beget.
7 *we are having guests for dinner* **entertain**, be host to, cater for, receive; invite round, invite over, ask round, ask over, show hospitality to, invite to a meal, invite to a party, wine and dine; **accommodate**, put up, take in, give a bed to.
OPPOSITE visit.
8 *the driver had trouble finding the restaurant* **experience**, encounter, undergo, face, meet, find, go through, run into, come across, be subjected to, have experience of, be faced with.
9 *I have a headache* **be suffering from**, be afflicted by, be affected by, be troubled with, be a sufferer from; *informal* be a martyr to.
10 *I went to a few parties and had a good time* **experience**, enjoy, taste.
11 *many pilots have doubts about the safety of the new computer system* **harbour**, feel, entertain, foster, nurse, cherish, nurture, bear, sustain, maintain, keep in one's mind.
12 *he had little patience with technological gadgetry* **manifest**, show, display, exhibit, demonstrate, express, evince.
13 *he had his bodyguards throw Chris out* **cause to**, **make**, ask to, request to, get to, tell to, require to, persuade to, induce to, prevail upon someone to; order to, command to, direct to, enjoin to, oblige to, force to, compel to, coerce to.
14 *I can't have you insulting Tom like that* **tolerate**, endure, bear, support, accept, put up with, go along with, take, countenance, brook; permit to, allow to; *informal* stand, abide, stick, stomach, hold with; *Brit. informal* be doing with.
15 *I* **have to** *get up at 6.30 tomorrow morning* **must**, have got to, be obliged to, be required to, be compelled to, be forced to, be bound to, be duty-bound to, be under an obligation to.
16 (*informal*) *I realized I'd been had* **trick**, fool, deceive, cheat, dupe, take in, outwit, double-cross, hoodwink, swindle; *informal* do, con, diddle, bilk, rip off, shaft, pull a fast one on, put one over on, take to the cleaners; *N. Amer. informal* sucker, snooker, stiff.

□ **have done with** *the drug scene is behind me—I have done with it* **be finished with**, have finished with, be done with, be through with, want no more to do with, be no longer involved with/in, have given up, have no further dealings with, have turned one's back on, have washed one's hands of, have no more truck with.
OPPOSITE get into.

□ **have had it** (*informal*) **1** *in private they admit that they've had it* **have no chance**, have no hope, have failed, be finished, be out, be defeated, have lost, have no chance of success, have come to nothing; *informal* have flopped, have bitten the dust, have come a cropper.
OPPOSITE succeed.
2 *if you ever let this information get out to the public, you've had it* **be in trouble**, be going to be punished, be going to suffer the consequences, be going to pay the price, be in for a scolding, be going to answer for something; *informal* be for it, be for the high jump, be in hot water, be in deep water, be in (deep) shtook, be going to take the rap, be going to catch it.

□ **have (got) nothing on** (*informal*) *I am not worried—they've got nothing on me* **have no evidence against**, know nothing bad about, know nothing damning about, have no incriminating information about.

□ **have someone on** (*Brit. informal*) *that's just too neat—you're having me on* **play a trick on**, play a joke on, joke with, trick, tease, rag, pull someone's leg, fool about/around; *informal* kid, rib, take the mickey out of, make a monkey out of, take for a ride, lead up the garden path; *Brit. informal* wind up; *N. Amer. informal* put on, pull someone's chain; *Brit. vulgar slang* take the piss out of; *dated* make sport of.

□ **have (got) something on 1** *she had a blue dress on* **be wearing**, be dressed in, be clothed in, be garbed in, be attired in, be turned out in, be decked out in, be tricked out in, be robed in; *archaic* be apparelled in.
2 (*Brit.*) *I have got a lot on at the moment* **be committed to**, have arranged, have planned, have organized, have fixed up, have on the agenda, have made arrangements for.

haven ▸ **noun 1** *they stopped off in small harbours and havens* **anchorage**, harbour, port, mooring, roads; cove, inlet, bay, fjord; *rare* harbourage, moorage, roadstead, hithe.
2 *a safe haven in times of trouble* **refuge**, retreat, shelter, sanctuary, asylum, place of safety, place of security, port in a storm, harbour, oasis, sanctum.

haversack ▸ **noun knapsack**, rucksack, backpack, pack, kitbag.

havoc ▸ **noun 1** *the hurricane ripped through Florida causing havoc* **devastation**, destruction, damage, desolation, depredation, despoliation, ruination, ruin, disaster, ravagement, waste, catastrophe.
2 *hyperactive children create havoc wherever they go* **disorder**, chaos, disruption, mayhem, bedlam, pandemonium, turmoil, tumult, confusion, uproar; commotion, upheaval, furore, shambles; *informal* hullabaloo, a madhouse; *N. Amer. informal* a three-ring circus.
OPPOSITE peace.

hawk ▸ **verb** *street traders were hawking costume jewellery* **peddle**, sell, tout, vend, trade in, deal in, traffic in, push, offer for sale, sell from door to door; *Brit. informal* flog.

WORD LINKS

young	**chick, eyas**
collective noun	**cast**

hawker ▸ **noun** (*dated*) **trader**, seller, dealer, purveyor, vendor, tout, barrow boy, door-to-door salesman, travelling salesman; *W. Indian* higgler; *informal* pusher; *dated* pedlar; *archaic* chapman, packman; *rare* huckster, crier, colporteur.

hawk-eyed ▸ **adjective** *a hawk-eyed policeman saved the lives of dozens of shoppers* **vigilant**, observant, alert, sharp-eyed, keen-eyed, gimlet-eyed, eagle-eyed, lynx-eyed, with one's eyes open, on the alert, on the lookout, with one's eyes opened/skinned/peeled; *informal* beady-eyed, not missing a trick, on the ball, leery; *rare* regardful, Argus-eyed.
OPPOSITE inattentive.

hay ▸ **noun forage**, dried grass, pasturage, herbage, silage, fodder, straw.

□ **make hay while the sun shines** make the most of an opportunity, exploit an opportunity, take advantage of an opportunity, capitalize on an advantage, strike while the iron is hot, seize the day; *Latin* carpe diem.

haywire ▸ **adjective** (*informal*) *a bug that makes computers go haywire* **out of control**, out of order, erratic, faulty, not functioning properly; **chaotic**, confused, crazy, wild, disorganized, disordered, topsy-turvy; *informal* on the blink, shambolic; *Brit. informal* up the spout, wonky.
OPPOSITES in order; under control.

hazard ▸ **noun 1** *the hazards of high-energy radiation* **danger**, risk, peril, threat, menace; difficulty, problem, pitfall; jeopardy, perilousness, endangerment, imperilment.
2 *we can form no calculation concerning the laws of hazard* **chance**, probability, fortuity, luck, fate, destiny, fortune, providence, serendipity, accident; *N. Amer.* happenstance.
▸ **verb 1** *he hazarded a guess* **venture**, put forward, proffer, advance, volunteer; conjecture, speculate, surmise; *formal* opine.
2 *the cargo business is too risky to hazard money on* **risk**, put at risk, jeopardize, chance, gamble, stake, bet, take a chance with; **endanger**, imperil, expose to danger, put in jeopardy.
OPPOSITE keep safe.

> CHOOSE THE RIGHT WORD
>
> **hazard, danger, peril, risk**
>
> *See* DANGER.

hazardous ▸ **adjective 1** *we work in hazardous conditions* **dangerous**, risky, unsafe, perilous, precarious, insecure, tricky, unpredictable, uncertain, high-risk, touch-and-go, fraught with danger; *informal* dicey, hairy, sticky, iffy; *Brit. informal* dodgy; *N. Amer. informal* gnarly; *archaic or humorous* parlous.
OPPOSITES safe; secure.
2 *a hazardous venture* **chancy**, uncertain, undependable, unpredictable, precarious, speculative.
OPPOSITE certain.

haze ▸ **noun 1** *there was a thick haze on this October morning* **mist**, fog, cloud, smog; cloudiness, mistiness, fogginess, smokiness, vapour, steam.
2 *the evening passed in a haze of euphoria* **blur**, daze, confusion, vagueness, muddle, befuddlement; obscurity, dimness, indistinctness.

hazy ▸ **adjective 1** *it was a beautiful day but quite hazy* **misty**, foggy, cloudy, clouded, smoggy, murky, overcast.
OPPOSITES bright, sunny.
2 *hazy memories* **vague**, indistinct, unclear, faint, dim, indefinite, ill-defined, nebulous, shadowy, blurred, fuzzy, muzzy, woolly, confused, muddled.
OPPOSITE clear.

> CHOOSE THE RIGHT WORD
>
> **hazy, indistinct, vague**
>
> *See* VAGUE.

head ▸ **noun 1** *she was hurt when her head hit the ground* skull, cranium, crown; *informal* **nut**, noodle, noddle, nob, noggin, dome; *Brit. informal* bonce, napper; *Scottish & N. English informal* poll; *informal, dated* bean, conk; *archaic* pate, Costard, crumpet.
2 *this new job meant he had to use his head* **brain**, brains, brainpower, intellect, intelligence, intellectual capacity, mental capacity, powers of reasoning; wit, wits, wisdom, mind, sense, reasoning, rationality, mentality, understanding, common sense; *informal* nous, grey matter, savvy, brainbox, brain cells, upper storey; *Brit. informal* loaf; *N. Amer. informal* smarts; *S. African informal* kop.
3 *she had a good head for business* **aptitude**, faculty, flair, talent, gift, capacity, ability, knack, bent; mind, brain.
4 *the head of the Dutch Catholic Church* **leader**, chief, boss, controller, master, supervisor, governor, superintendent, foreman, forewoman, headman; commander, commanding officer, captain; director, managing director, chief executive, manager; principal, head teacher, headmaster, headmistress; president, premier, prime minister, ruler; chair, chairman, chairwoman, chairperson; *N. Amer.* chief executive officer, CEO; *informal* boss man, kingpin, top dog, big cheese, bigwig, Mr Big, skipper; *Brit. informal* gaffer, guv'nor; *N. Amer. informal* numero uno, head honcho, padrone, sachem, big white chief, big kahuna, big wheel, high muckamuck.
OPPOSITE subordinate.
5 *at the head of the queue* **front**, beginning, start, fore, forefront, top, leading position, foremost position.
OPPOSITES back, bottom.
6 *the head of the River Thames* **source**, origin, well head, headspring, headwater, headwaters; *S. African* eye; *literary* wellspring, fount, fountain.
OPPOSITE mouth.
7 *beer with a creamy head* **froth**, foam, bubbles, spume, fizz, effervescence, lather, suds.
8 (*Nautical*) *they were cleaning out the heads. See* TOILET.

□ **at the head of** *his years at the head of the company* **in charge of**, in control of, in command of, at the top of, at the helm of, at the controls of, as leader of, in the driving seat of, at the wheel of, responsible for, accountable for, liable for; **managing**, running, administering, directing, supervising, overseeing, controlling, commanding, leading, heading up, looking after, taking care of.

□ **come to a head** *the violence came to a head with the deaths of six youths* **reach a crisis**, come to a climax, reach a critical point, reach a turning point, reach a crossroads; *informal* come to the crunch.

□ **go to someone's head 1** *the wine has gone to my head* **intoxicate**, inebriate, befuddle, make someone intoxicated, make someone drunk, make someone dizzy, make someone's head spin; *informal* make someone woozy.
2 *her victory went to her head* **make someone conceited**, make someone arrogant, turn someone's head, make someone full of themselves, puff someone up.

□ **keep one's head** *he takes chances but keeps his head* **keep/stay calm**, keep/stay cool, remain unruffled, keep control of oneself, keep one's self-control, maintain one's equilibrium, maintain one's composure; *informal* keep one's cool, keep one's shirt on.
OPPOSITE lose control of oneself.

□ **lose one's head** *I lost my head and started a big fuss* **lose control of oneself**, lose one's composure, lose one's self-control, lose one's equilibrium, lose control of the situation, go to pieces, fall to pieces; panic, go mad, get flustered, get confused, get angry, get excited, get hysterical; *informal* lose one's cool, freak out, crack up; *Brit. informal* go into a (flat) spin, throw a wobbly.
OPPOSITE keep control of oneself.

▶ **adjective** *the head waiter* **chief**, principal, leading, main, first, front, prime, premier, foremost, top, topmost, highest, supreme, pre-eminent, high-ranking, top-ranking, most important; *N. Amer.* ranking; *informal* top-notch.
OPPOSITE subordinate.

▶ **verb 1** *the St George's Day procession was headed by the mayor* **be at the front of**, lead, be the leader of, be at the head of; be first, go first, lead the way.
OPPOSITES be at the back of, bring up the rear of.
2 *an organizational unit headed by a line manager* **be in charge of**, be at the head of, be in command of, command, be in control of, control, lead, be the leader of, run, manage, direct, administer, supervise, superintend, oversee, preside over, rule, govern, captain, be the boss of, be at the helm of.
OPPOSITE be subordinate.
3 *he was heading for the exit* **move towards**, go towards, make for, aim for, make one's way towards, go in the direction of, direct one's steps towards, be bound for, steer for, make a beeline for; set out in the direction of, set out for, start out for.
OPPOSITE move away from.

□ **head someone/something off 1** *he ran up the road to head off approaching cars* **intercept**, divert, deflect, redirect, re-route, turn aside, draw away, turn away, cut off.
2 *they headed off a row by ordering further study of both plans* **forestall**, avert, ward off, fend off, stave off, hold off, nip in the bud, keep at bay; prevent, avoid, stop, check, thwart.
OPPOSITE precipitate.

WORD LINKS

related prefix	**cephalo-** (e.g. ***cephalopod***)
measurement of the head	**cephalometry**

headache ▶ **noun 1** *I've got a splitting headache* **sore head**, migraine; neuralgia; *informal* head; *rare* cephalalgy, hemicrania.
2 (*informal*) *their disruptive behaviour was a headache for Mr Jones* **nuisance**, trouble, problem, bother, bugbear, hassle, pain, pest, worry, inconvenience, vexation, irritant, source of irritation, source of annoyance, bane of one's life, thorn in one's flesh; *informal* aggravation, bind, pain in the neck/backside; *N. Amer. informal* pain in the butt; *Austral./NZ informal* nark; *Brit. vulgar slang* pain in the arse.
OPPOSITE blessing.

head case ▶ **noun** (*informal*) **madman/madwoman**, maniac, lunatic; *informal* loony, nut, nutcase, nutter, fruitcake, basket case, headbanger, schizo, crank, crackpot, oddball, weirdo, weirdie, sicko; *Brit. informal* odd bod; *N. Amer. informal* screwball, crazy, kook, geek, nutso, meshuggener, wacko, wack; *N. Amer. & Austral./NZ informal* dingbat; *informal, dated* case.

head first ▶ **adjective & adverb 1** *she dived head first into the water* **head foremost**, headlong, on one's head; diving.
OPPOSITE feet first.
2 *don't plunge head first into a new relationship* **without thinking**, without forethought, precipitately, precipitously, impetuously, rashly, recklessly, carelessly, heedlessly, hastily, in haste, head over heels, headlong.
OPPOSITE cautiously.

heading ▶ **noun 1** *chapter headings* **title**, caption, legend, subtitle, subheading, wording, rubric, inscription, name, headline, banner headline.
2 *this topic falls under four main headings* **category**, division, classification, class, categorization, head, section, group, grouping, subject, topic, branch, department.

headland ▶ **noun cape**, promontory, point, head, foreland, peninsula, ness, spit, tongue, horn, bill, bluff; *Scottish* mull.

headlong ▶ **adverb 1** *he fell headlong into the tent* **head foremost**, head first, on one's head; diving.
OPPOSITE feet first.
2 *those who rush headlong to join in the latest craze* **without thinking**, without forethought, precipitately, precipitously, impetuously, rashly, recklessly, carelessly, heedlessly, hastily, in haste, head first, head over heels.
OPPOSITE cautiously.

▶ **adjective** *a headlong dash through the house* **breakneck**, whirlwind; reckless, precipitate, precipitous, rash, impetuous, hasty, careless, heedless.
OPPOSITE cautious.

headman ▶ **noun chief**, chieftain, leader, ruler, head, overlord, master, commander, suzerain, seigneur, lord, liege, liege lord, potentate; (*among American Indians*) sachem.
OPPOSITE underling.

head-on ▶ **adjective 1** *a head-on collision* **direct**, involving the front of a vehicle, front-to-front.
2 *the advantage of this proposal is that it avoids a head-on confrontation* **direct**, face to face, personal; *informal* eyeball to eyeball.

headquarters ▶ **plural noun head office**, main office, HQ, base, nerve centre, mission control; general headquarters, GHQ, command post, depot, centre of operations.

headstone ▶ **noun gravestone**, tombstone, stone, monument, memorial, plaque, tablet.

headstrong ▶ **adjective** *she has been rather headstrong and argumentative* **wilful**, self-willed, strong-willed, contrary, perverse, wayward, unruly, refractory, ungovernable, unyielding, stubborn, obstinate, obdurate; reckless, heedless, rash, capricious, impulsive, wild.
OPPOSITE tractable.

CHOOSE THE RIGHT WORD

headstrong, wilful, obstinate, stubborn
See **OBSTINATE**.

head teacher ▶ **noun headmaster**, **headmistress**, head, principal, director, master, mistress; dean, rector, warden, chancellor, vice-chancellor, president, provost, governor; *N. Amer. informal* prexy, prex.

headway ▶ **noun**
□ **make headway** *they appear to be making headway in bringing the rebels under control* **make progress**, make strides, gain ground, progress, advance, proceed, move, get on, get ahead, come on, come along, shape up, take shape, move forward in leaps and bounds; *informal* be getting there.
OPPOSITES retrogress; stagnate.

heady ▶ **adjective 1** *several bottles of heady local wine* **potent**, intoxicating, inebriating, strong, alcoholic, spirituous, vinous, intoxicant.
OPPOSITE non-alcoholic.
2 *she felt heady with excitement* **exhilarated**, thrilled, elated, excited, euphoric, ecstatic, enraptured, overwhelmed, overjoyed, overpowered, in seventh heaven, on cloud nine; *informal* over the moon, on top of the world, on a high.
OPPOSITE bored.
3 *the heady days of my youth* **exhilarating**, exciting, thrilling, stimulating, invigorating, galvanizing, electrifying, rousing, arousing; *informal* mind-blowing.
OPPOSITE boring.

heal ▶ **verb 1** *his concern is to heal sick people* **make better**, make well, cure, treat successfully, restore to health, get someone back on their feet, put someone on the road to recovery; make good, mend, remedy, restore.
OPPOSITE make worse.
2 *he would have to wait until his knee had healed* **get better**, get well, be cured, become healthy, recover, mend, be on the mend, improve, show improvement, be restored.
OPPOSITE get worse.
3 *time will eventually heal the pain of grief* **alleviate**, assuage, palliate, relieve, ameliorate, ease, help, soften, lessen, mitigate, attenuate, allay, salve.
OPPOSITE aggravate.
4 *we've been trying to heal the rift between them* **put right**, set right, put to rights, repair, remedy, resolve, correct, settle, make good, patch up, soothe, conciliate, reconcile, harmonize.
OPPOSITE worsen.

healing ▶ **adjective** *this flower is said to have healing properties* **curative**, therapeutic, medicinal, remedial, curing, corrective, reparative; restorative, tonic, health-giving, healthful, beneficial, salubrious; *rare* sanative, analeptic, iatric.
OPPOSITE harmful.

WORD LINKS

related prefix	**iatro-** (e.g. ***iatrogenic, iatrochemistry***)

health ▶ **noun 1** *he was restored to health* **good physical condition**, healthiness, fitness, physical fitness, well-being, haleness, good trim, good shape, fine fettle, good kilter; robustness, strength, vigour, soundness, salubrity.
OPPOSITE illness.
2 *bad health forced him to retire* **state of health**, physical state, physical health, physical shape, condition, constitution, form.

WORD LINKS

health-giving	**salubrious**
relating to health	**sanitary**

healthful ▶ **adjective** *garlic was considered very healthful in winter* **good for one**, good for one's health, healthy, health-giving, beneficial, salubrious, salutary; wholesome, nourishing, nutritious.

OPPOSITE unhealthy.

healthy ▶ adjective **1** *feeling fit and healthy* **in good physical condition**, in good health, well, all right, fine, fit, physically fit, in good trim, in good shape, in fine fettle, in good kilter, in top form, in tip-top condition; flourishing, blooming, thriving, hardy, hale, hearty, robust, strong, vigorous, hale and hearty, fighting fit, fit as a fiddle, fit as a flea, bursting with health, the picture of health; Brit. in rude health; informal OK, in the pink, right as rain, up to snuff.
OPPOSITE ill.
2 *a healthy balanced diet* **good for one**, good for one's health, health-giving, healthful, wholesome, nutritious, nourishing, beneficial, salubrious, salutary.
OPPOSITE unwholesome.
3 *the island has a healthy climate* **beneficial**, health-giving, healthful, salubrious, salutary; invigorating, bracing, refreshing, tonic, stimulating; hygienic, clean, sanitary.
OPPOSITE unhealthy.

heap ▶ noun **1** *a disordered heap of boxes* **pile**, stack, mass, mound, mountain, quantity, load, lot, bundle, jumble; collection, accumulation, gathering; assemblage, store, stock, supply, stockpile, hoard, aggregation, agglomeration, accrual, conglomeration; Scottish, Irish, & N. English rickle; Scottish bing; rare amassment.
2 *we have heaps of room | a heap of troubles* **a lot**, **lots**, a large amount, a fair amount, much, a good/great deal, a deal, a great quantity, quantities, an abundance, a wealth, a profusion, plenty, masses; **many**, a great many, a large number, a considerable number, a huge number, numerous, scores, hundreds, thousands, millions, billions; informal a load, loads, loadsa, a pile, piles, oodles, stacks, scads, reams, wads, pots, oceans, a mountain, mountains, miles, tons, zillions, gazillions, bazillions, more ... than one can shake a stick at; Brit. informal a shedload, lashings; N. Amer. informal gobs; Austral./NZ informal a swag; vulgar slang a shitload.
OPPOSITES a little, not much; a few, not many.
▶ verb *she heaped logs on the fire* **pile up**, pile, stack up, stack, make a pile of, make a stack of, make a mound of; assemble, accumulate, collect, amass; store, store up, stock up, stockpile, hoard.
□ **heap something on/upon** *they heaped praise on her* **shower on**, lavish on, load on; **bestow on**, confer on, give, grant, vouchsafe, assign to, award to, favour with, furnish with.

hear ▶ verb **1** *behind her she could hear men's voices* **perceive**, catch, get, make out, take in, apprehend, discern; overhear; listen to, attend to, give ear to.
2 *they heard that I had moved* **be informed**, be told, find out, discover, learn, gather, glean, ascertain, get word, be made aware, be given to understand, hear tell, get wind, pick up.
OPPOSITE be unaware.
3 *an all-woman jury heard the case* **try**, judge, sit in judgement on; adjudicate (on), adjudge, pass judgement on, give a ruling on.

hearing ▶ noun **1** *people who have very acute hearing* **ability to hear**, faculty of hearing, sense of hearing, aural faculty, auditory perception.
2 *she had moved out of hearing* **earshot**, hearing distance, hearing range, carrying range, range of one's voice, auditory range, sound, range.
3 *I think I had a fair hearing* **chance to speak**, opportunity to be heard, opportunity to express one's point of view, opportunity to put one's case, chance to put one's side of the story; interview, audience.
4 *he gave evidence at the hearing* **trial**, court case, inquiry, inquest, tribunal, legal proceedings; investigation, review, examination, inquisition.

WORD LINKS

relating to hearing	**auditory, audial, aural, acoustic**
related prefix	**audio-**
branch of medicine to do with hearing	**audiology**
measurement of hearing	**audiometry**

hearsay ▶ noun *a story based only on hearsay* **rumour**, gossip, tittle-tattle, tattle, idle chatter, idle talk, mere talk, report; stories, tales, titbits; French bavardage, on dit; German Kaffeeklatsch; W. Indian labrish, shu-shu; informal buzz, the grapevine; Brit. informal goss; N. Amer. informal scuttlebutt; Austral./NZ informal furphy; S. African informal skinder; rare bruit.
OPPOSITE confirmed facts.

heart *See centre pages for list of parts of the* **Heart**
▶ noun **1** *his heart had stopped beating* seat of the emotions; informal ticker.
2 *he poured out his heart to me | she captured my heart* **emotions**, feelings, sentiments, soul, mind, bosom, breast; **love**, affection, passion; sympathy, pity, concern, compassion.
3 *he has no heart* **compassion**, sympathy, humanity, feeling(s), fellow feeling, concern for others, brotherly love, tender feelings, tenderness, empathy, understanding; kindness, kindliness, goodwill, benevolence, humanitarianism.
4 *they may lose heart as the work mounts up* **enthusiasm**, keenness, eagerness, spirit, determination, resolution, resolve, purpose, courage, backbone, spine, nerve, stomach, will, will power, fortitude, bravery, stout-heartedness; informal guts, spunk, grit; Brit. informal bottle; vulgar slang balls.
5 *right in the heart of the city* **centre**, central part, middle, hub, core, nucleus, kernel, eye, bosom, navel.
OPPOSITE edge.
6 *the heart of the matter* **essence**, quintessence, crux, core, nub, root, gist, meat, marrow, pith, substance, sum and substance, essential part, intrinsic nature, kernel, nucleus; informal nitty-gritty.
OPPOSITE peripherals.
□ **after one's own heart** *he looked like a man after my own heart* **like-minded**, of the same mind, similar to oneself, kindred, compatible, congenial, sharing one's tastes; **to one's liking**, of the kind that one likes, attractive to one, desirable, attractive, appealing, pleasing; informal on the same wavelength.
OPPOSITES dissimilar; unappealing.
□ **at heart** *he's a good lad at heart* **basically**, fundamentally, essentially, at bottom, deep down, in essence, intrinsically, innately; **really**, actually, truly, in fact, in truth; French au fond; informal when you get right down to it.
OPPOSITE superficially.
□ **by heart** *I know the poem by heart* **from memory**, off pat, by rote, off by heart, word for word, verbatim, parrot-fashion, word-perfect.
□ **do one's heart good** *it did the rector's heart good to see so many at church* **give one pleasure**, make one happy, cheer, cheer one up, delight, please, gladden, hearten, gratify, satisfy, make one feel good, raise one's spirits, give one a lift, bring joy to; informal give one a buzz, tickle one pink, buck one up.
OPPOSITE sadden.
□ **eat one's heart out** *I stayed in London, eating my heart out for you* **pine**, long, ache, brood, mope, fret, sigh, sorrow, suffer, bleed, yearn, agonize, weep and wail, regret someone's loss/absence; grieve, mourn, lament, shed tears; be filled with envy; informal die; literary repine.
□ **from the (bottom of one's) heart** *I have told the truth from the bottom of my heart | she spoke from the heart* **sincerely**, with all one's heart, earnestly, fervently, passionately, truly, truthfully, genuinely, devoutly, heartily, heart and soul, with all sincerity.
□ **give/lose one's heart to** *he lost his heart to a French girl* **fall in love with**, fall for, become infatuated with, be smitten by; informal fall head over heels for, be swept off one's feet by, develop a crush on.
□ **have a change of heart** *you can have your money back if you have a change of heart* **change one's mind**, change one's tune, have second thoughts, have a rethink, think again, think differently, think twice; informal get cold feet.
□ **have a heart** *have a heart—this is my last chance* **be compassionate**, be kind, be merciful, be lenient, be sympathetic, be considerate, take pity, have mercy.
□ **heart and soul** *they had committed themselves heart and soul to the project* **wholeheartedly**, enthusiastically, eagerly, zealously, unreservedly, absolutely, thoroughly, completely, entirely, fully, totally, utterly, body and soul, to the hilt, with open arms, one hundred per cent, all the way.
□ **set one's heart on** *she had set her heart on going to college. See* SET.
□ **take heart** *Mary took heart from the encouragement handed out* **be encouraged**, be heartened, be comforted, derive comfort, derive satisfaction; cheer up, brighten up, perk up, liven up, become livelier, revive; informal buck up.
OPPOSITE lose heart.
□ **with one's heart in one's mouth** *she watched with her heart in her mouth as the plane lost height* **in alarm**, in fear, fearfully, with apprehension, apprehensively, on edge, in a state of agitation, in a state of nerves, in fear and trembling, with trepidation, in suspense, in a cold sweat, with bated breath, on tenterhooks, with one's stomach in knots; informal with butterflies in one's stomach, in a state, in a stew, all of a dither, in a sweat; Brit. informal having kittens; N. Amer. informal in a twit; Brit. vulgar slang shitting bricks, bricking oneself; dated overstrung.

WORD LINKS

relating to the heart	**cardiac**
related prefix	**cardio-**
branch of medicine to do with the heart	**cardiology**
inflammation of the heart	**carditis**
relating to the arteries of the heart	**coronary**
fear of heart disease	**cardiophobia**

heartache ▶ noun **anguish**, grief, suffering, distress, unhappiness, misery, sorrow, sadness, heartbreak, pain, hurt, agony, angst, wretchedness, despondency, despair, woe, desolation, torment, torture; anxiety, worry; literary dolour.
OPPOSITE happiness.

heartbreak ▶ noun *an unforgettable tale of joy and heartbreak* **distress**, grief, suffering, unhappiness, misery, sorrow, sadness, anguish, trauma, heartache, pain, hurt, agony, angst, wretchedness, bitterness, despondency, despair, woe, dejection, devastation, desolation, torment, torture; literary dolour.
OPPOSITE happiness.

heartbreaking ▶ adjective *it would be heartbreaking to see it all collapse* **distressing**, upsetting, disturbing, heart-rending, sad, tragic, painful,

saddening, traumatic, agonizing, desolating, harrowing, excruciating; pitiful, piteous, poignant, plaintive, affecting, moving, tear-jerking; *rare* distressful.
OPPOSITE comforting.

heartbroken ▶ adjective *I was heartbroken at his death* **anguished**, devastated, broken-hearted, heavy-hearted, suffering, grieving, grief-stricken, grieved, inconsolable, crushed, shattered, desolate, despairing; upset, distressed, miserable, sorrowful, sad, dejected, dispirited, disheartened, downcast, disconsolate, crestfallen, disappointed, despondent, in low spirits; *informal* choked, down in the mouth, down in the dumps, cut up; *Brit. informal* gutted; *literary* dolorous, heartsick; *archaic* chap-fallen.
OPPOSITE delighted.

heartburn ▶ noun **indigestion**, dyspepsia, acidity, hyperacidity; *technical* pyrosis.

hearten ▶ verb *their success greatly heartened him* **cheer up**, cheer, raise someone's spirits, encourage, comfort, reassure, console, boost, buoy up, perk up, ginger up; invigorate, revitalize, energize, animate, rouse, revivify, exhilarate, uplift, elate; *informal* buck up, pep up, give a shot in the arm to; *rare* inspirit.
OPPOSITE dishearten.

heartfelt ▶ adjective *our heartfelt thanks* **sincere**, genuine, unfeigned, deeply felt, from the heart; earnest, profound, deep, wholehearted, ardent, fervent, passionate, enthusiastic, eager, kindly, warm, cordial; honest, bona fide; *rare* full-hearted.
OPPOSITE insincere.

heartily ▶ adverb **1** *this development is something that we should heartily welcome* **wholeheartedly**, sincerely, genuinely, unfeignedly, warmly, cordially, deeply, profoundly, from the bottom of one's heart, from the heart, with all one's heart, heart and soul; **eagerly**, enthusiastically, with eagerness, with enthusiasm, zealously, energetically, earnestly, vigorously, ardently, resolutely.
OPPOSITES with reservations; half-heartedly.
2 *they were heartily sick of the whole subject* **very**, very much, completely, entirely, totally, absolutely, extremely, thoroughly, fully, decidedly, really, exceedingly, immensely, uncommonly, extraordinarily, most, downright, one hundred per cent; *Scottish* unco; *N. Amer.* quite; *French* très; *informal* right, too ... for words, seriously, majorly; *Brit. informal* jolly, ever so, dead, well, fair; *N. Amer. informal* real, mighty, plumb, powerful, way; *S. African informal* lekker; *informal, dated* devilish; *archaic* exceeding.

heartless ▶ adjective *heartless thieves stole the pushchair of a two-year-old boy* **unfeeling**, unsympathetic, unkind, uncaring, unloving, unmoved, unconcerned, insensitive, inconsiderate, hard-hearted, stony-hearted, cold-hearted, cold-blooded, with a heart of stone, lacking compassion, mean-spirited, without sentiment, hard as nails; cold, hard, harsh, stern, callous, cruel, brutal, merciless, pitiless, ruthless, inhuman.
OPPOSITE compassionate.

heart-rending ▶ adjective *a heart-rending cry of torment* **distressing**, upsetting, disturbing, heartbreaking, sad, tragic, painful, saddening, traumatic, agonizing, desolate, harrowing, excruciating; pitiful, piteous, poignant, plaintive, affecting, moving, tear-jerking; *rare* distressful.
OPPOSITE comforting.

heartsick ▶ adjective (*literary*) *weary and heartsick, she forced herself to search through the remains of the village* **despondent**, dejected, dispirited, disheartened, discouraged, depressed, desolate, downcast, down, disappointed, grieving, forlorn, unhappy, sad, upset, miserable, crestfallen, wretched, woebegone, inconsolable, sick at heart, heavy-hearted, broken-hearted, grief-stricken, in low spirits, low-spirited; *literary* heartsore, dolorous; *archaic* chap-fallen.
OPPOSITES happy, cheerful.

heart-throb ▶ noun (*informal*) **idol**, pin-up, popular figure, darling, star, superstar, hero, heroine; *informal* dreamboat.

heart-to-heart ▶ adjective *a heart-to-heart chat* **intimate**, candid, frank, open, unreserved, personal, honest, truthful, sincere, man-to-man, woman-to-woman.
OPPOSITE guarded.
▶ noun *they had a long heart-to-heart in the garden* **private conversation**, private word, cosy chat, tête-à-tête, one-on-one, one-to-one, head-to-head, conversation, chat, talk, word; *informal* confab, chit-chat, chinwag; *Brit. informal* natter.

heart-warming ▶ adjective *the sympathy in his voice was heart-warming* **touching**, moving, affecting, heartening, stirring, rewarding, uplifting, pleasing, cheering, gladdening, encouraging, gratifying, satisfying, warming, soul-stirring; *literary* gladsome.
OPPOSITE distressing.

hearty ▶ adjective **1** *a hearty and boisterous character* **exuberant**, cheerful, jovial, ebullient, backslapping, unreserved, uninhibited, effusive, lively, loud, animated, vivacious, energetic, spirited, dynamic, enthusiastic, eager; warm, cordial, friendly, affable, amiable, warm-hearted, good natured.
OPPOSITE introverted.
2 *he expressed his hearty agreement* | *hearty congratulations* **wholehearted**, heartfelt, sincere, genuine, real, true, unfeigned, from the heart, complete, total, absolute, thorough; **earnest**, fervent, ardent, enthusiastic, warm, cordial.
OPPOSITE half-hearted.
3 *a formidably hearty spinster of fifty-five* **robust**, healthy, hardy, hale, hale and hearty, fit, flourishing, blooming, spirited, fighting fit, fit as a fiddle, fit as a flea, bursting with health; **active**, energetic, vigorous, sturdy, strong, sound; *Brit.* in rude health; *informal* full of vim; *dated* stalwart.
OPPOSITE frail.
4 *they end each day with a hearty meal* **substantial**, ample, sizeable, filling, large, abundant, generous, square, solid; **wholesome**, nutritious, nourishing, healthy, health-giving, good for one's health.
OPPOSITES light; unhealthy.

heat ▶ noun **1** *it is sensitive to both heat and cold* **hotness**, warmth, warmness, high temperature; fever, feverishness; *rare* calefaction.
OPPOSITE cold.
2 *the oppressive heat was making both men sweat* **hot weather**, hotness, warm weather, warmth, warmness, sultriness, closeness, mugginess, humidity, swelter; heatwave, hot spell; *literary* dog days; *rare* torridness, torridity.
OPPOSITE cold weather.
3 *conciliation services are designed to take the heat out of disputes* **passion**, intensity of feeling, ardour, fervour, vehemence, warmth, intensity, animation, earnestness, eagerness, enthusiasm, excitement, agitation; anger, fury, violence; *rare* fervency, ardency, passionateness.
OPPOSITE apathy.
▶ verb **1** *the room faces north and is difficult to heat* | *the food was heated on a portable stove* **warm**, warm up, heat up, make hot, make warm, raise something's temperature; reheat, cook, boil, bake, roast, toast, stew, fry, grill; *informal* hot, hot up.
OPPOSITE cool.
2 *the pipes expand as they* **heat up** **become hot**, become warm, grow hot, grow warm, become hotter, become warmer, get hotter, get warmer, increase in temperature, rise in temperature; *informal* hot up.
OPPOSITE cool down.
3 *he seemed to calm down as quickly as he had* **heated up** **become impassioned**, become excited, become animated, grow passionate, grow vehement; get angry, become enraged, get annoyed.
OPPOSITE calm down.
4 (*archaic*) *this discourse had heated them* **excite**, inflame, arouse, rouse, stir up, work up, whip up, agitate, animate, stimulate, impassion, fire; anger, make angry, enrage, annoy, provoke.
OPPOSITE calm.

WORD LINKS
relating to heat **thermal, caloric**
related prefixes **therm- (e.g.** ***thermionic*****), calor- (e.g.** ***calorimeter, calorific*****)**
fear of heat **thermophobia**

heated ▶ adjective **1** *a heated swimming pool* | *heated milk* **made warm**, made hot, warmed up; reheated; hot, piping hot.
OPPOSITE cooled.
2 *she had a heated argument with an official* **vehement**, passionate, impassioned, animated, spirited, 'lively', intense, fiery; **angry**, bitter, furious, fierce, violent, frenzied, raging, stormy, tempestuous; *rare* fervid, perfervid, passional, full-hearted.
OPPOSITE half-hearted.
3 *Robert grew heated as he spoke of the risks* **excited**, roused, animated, inflamed, worked up, wound up, keyed up; angry, furious, enraged; *informal* het up, in a state, uptight.
OPPOSITE calm.

heater ▶ noun **warmer**, radiator, convector, fire, brazier; electric heater, gas heater, convector heater, fan heater, storage heater, water heater, geyser, immersion heater, block heater; *Austral./NZ* chip heater.
OPPOSITE cooler.

heath ▶ noun **moor**, heathland, moorland, scrub, scrubs, common land, open country, upland.

heathen ▶ noun **1** *bringing Christianity to the heathens* **pagan**, infidel, idolater, idolatress; **unbeliever**, non-believer, disbeliever, atheist, agnostic, sceptic, heretic; *rare* paynim, nullifidian.
OPPOSITES Christian; believer.
2 *heathens who spoil the flavour of good whisky with ice* **philistine**, boor, oaf, ignoramus, lout, yahoo, vulgarian, plebeian; **barbarian**, savage, beast, brute; *informal, derogatory* pleb, peasant; *Brit. informal* oik.
OPPOSITE civilized person.
▶ adjective *it is a heathen practice to worship idols* **pagan**, infidel, idolatrous, heathenish; **unbelieving**, non-believing, atheistic, agnostic, heretical, faithless, godless, irreligious, ungodly, unholy; **barbarian**, barbarous, savage, uncivilized, uncultured, unenlightened, primitive, ignorant, philistine, brutish, barbaric; *rare* nullifidian.
OPPOSITES Christian; civilized.

heave ▶ verb **1** *she heaved the sofa back into place* **haul**, pull, lug,

manhandle, drag, draw, tug; lift, raise, hoist, heft; *informal* hump, yank; *rare* upheave.
OPPOSITE push.
2 (*informal*) *she heaved half a brick at him* **throw**, fling, cast, toss, hurl, lob, pitch, send, dash, let fly; *informal* bung, chuck, sling; *N. Amer. informal* peg; *Austral. informal* hoy; *NZ informal* bish.
3 *he heaved a euphoric sigh of relief* **let out**, breathe, give, sigh, gasp, emit, utter.
4 *the sea heaved up and down beneath her* **rise and fall**, roll, swell, surge, churn, boil, seethe, swirl, billow.
5 *she crawled to the rail and heaved into the sea* **vomit**, retch, gag, bring up, cough up; *Brit.* be sick; *N. Amer.* get sick; *informal* throw up, puke, chunder, chuck up, hurl, spew, do the technicolor yawn, keck; *Brit. informal* honk, sick up; *Scottish informal* boke; *N. Amer. informal* spit up, barf, upchuck, toss one's cookies.

heaven ▶ **noun 1** *those who practised good deeds would receive the reward of a place in heaven* **paradise**, nirvana, the kingdom of heaven, the promised land, the heavenly kingdom, the City of God, the celestial city, the abode of God, the abode of the saints, the abode of the angels, Zion, Abraham's bosom, the empyrean; the beyond the hereafter, the next world, the next life, the afterworld, the afterlife; (*among American Indians*) happy hunting ground; *Christianity* the New Jerusalem; *Hinduism* Swarga; *Classical Mythology* Elysium, the Elysian Fields, the Islands of the Blessed; *Scandinavian Mythology* Valhalla; *Arthurian Legend* Avalon.
OPPOSITES hell, purgatory.
2 *lying by the pool with a good book is my idea of heaven* **ecstasy**, bliss, rapture, contentment, happiness, delight, joy, felicity, supreme happiness, supreme joy, perfect contentment, seventh heaven, cloud nine; paradise, Eden, Utopia, nirvana, Shangri-La, idyll; *literary* Arcadia, Arcady.
OPPOSITES misery; hell on earth.
3 (usually **the heavens**) *Galileo used a telescope to observe the heavens* **the sky**, the skies, the upper atmosphere, the stratosphere; *literary* the firmament, the vault of heaven, the blue, the (wide) blue yonder, the welkin, the ether, the empyrean, the azure, the upper regions, the sphere, the celestial sphere.
□ **in seventh heaven ecstatic**, euphoric, thrilled, elated, delighted, overjoyed, on cloud nine/seven, walking/treading on air, jubilant, rapturous, beside oneself with joy, jumping for joy, exultant, transported, delirious, enraptured, blissful, in raptures, like a child with a new toy; *informal* over the moon, on top of the world, on a high, tickled pink, as pleased as Punch, cock-a-hoop, as happy as a sandboy; *Brit. informal* as happy as Larry; *N. English informal* made up; *N. Amer. informal* as happy as a clam; *Austral. informal* wrapped.
□ **move heaven and earth** (*informal*) *if he had truly loved her he would have moved heaven and earth to get her back* **try one's hardest**, try as hard as one can, do one's best, do one's utmost, do all one can, give one's all, make every effort, spare no effort, put oneself out; strive, struggle, exert oneself, work hard, endeavour, try; *informal* bend over backwards, do one's damnedest, go all out, pull out all the stops, bust a gut, break one's neck, kill oneself; *N. Amer. informal* do one's darnedest/durnedest; *Austral./NZ informal* go for the doctor.

WORD LINKS
relating to heaven **celestial, empyrean**
fear of heaven **uranophobia**

heavenly ▶ **adjective 1** *they saw visions of angels and heavenly choirs* **divine**, holy, celestial, godlike, godly, angelic, seraphic, cherubic, blessed, blest, beatific, immortal; *literary* empyrean, empyreal; *rare* paradisical, paradisaical, deiform, deific.
OPPOSITES mortal; infernal.
2 *heavenly constellations* **celestial**, cosmic, stellar; planetary; extraterrestrial, extramundane, unearthly, other-worldly; *literary* empyrean, empyreal; *rare* superterrestrial.
OPPOSITES terrestrial, earthly.
3 (*informal*) *it was a heavenly morning for a ride | a combination of heavenly blues and yellows* **delightful**, wonderful, marvellous, glorious, perfect, excellent, ideal, superb, sublime, idyllic, first-class, first-rate; blissful, pleasurable, enjoyable, gratifying, rapturous; **exquisite**, beautiful, lovely, gorgeous, sensational, enchanting, entrancing, ravishing, alluring; *informal* divine, super, great, fantastic, fabulous, smashing, terrific, wicked, out of this world; *Brit. informal* brilliant, brill.
OPPOSITES dreadful; ugly.

heaven-sent ▶ **adjective** *she was so afraid of losing this heaven-sent opportunity* **auspicious**, providential, propitious, felicitous, opportune, golden, favourable, advantageous, serendipitous, lucky, happy, good, right, fortunate, timely, well timed.
OPPOSITE inopportune.

heavily ▶ **adverb 1** *Dad walked heavily towards the door* **laboriously**, slowly, ponderously, steadily, deliberately, woodenly, stiffly, with heavy steps, with leaden steps; with difficulty, painfully, awkwardly, clumsily; gloomily, dejectedly, sluggishly, dully.
OPPOSITES easily, quickly.
2 *our troops were heavily defeated* **decisively**, utterly, completely, thoroughly, totally, conclusively, roundly, soundly, absolutely.
OPPOSITE narrowly.
3 *he started drinking heavily* **excessively**, to excess, immoderately, copiously, inordinately, intemperately, a great deal, too much, very much, overmuch, to a great extent, to too great an extent, without restraint, without control.
OPPOSITE moderately.
4 *the area is heavily planted with pine trees* **densely**, closely, thickly, compactly.
OPPOSITE lightly.
5 *I became heavily involved in politics* **deeply**, extremely, very, greatly, exceedingly, enormously, terribly, tremendously, awfully, profoundly; *informal* seriously; majorly; *Brit. informal* jolly, ever so.
OPPOSITE to a limited extent.

heavy ▶ **adjective 1** *the pan was too heavy for me to carry* **weighty**, hefty, big, large, substantial, massive, ponderous; solid, dense, leaden; burdensome; *informal* hulking, weighing a ton.
OPPOSITE light.
2 *he was a heavy man of about sixty* **overweight**, large, bulky, stout, stocky, portly, plump, paunchy, fleshy, fat, obese, corpulent, of ample build, ample, well upholstered, well padded, broad in the beam, Falstaffian; *informal* hulking, tubby, beefy, porky, pudgy, blubbery, poddy; *Brit. informal* podgy; *archaic* pursy.
OPPOSITE thin.
3 *a heavy blow to the head* **forceful**, hard, strong, violent, powerful, vigorous, mighty, hefty, tremendous, sharp, smart, severe, grievous.
OPPOSITE gentle.
4 *a gardener comes in to do the heavy work for me* **arduous**, hard, physical, laborious, demanding, difficult, exacting, strenuous, tough, onerous, back-breaking, tiring, fatiguing, exhausting, wearying, gruelling; *informal* murderous, killing, hellish; *Brit. informal* knackering; *rare* toilsome, exigent.
OPPOSITE easy.
5 *a heavy burden of responsibility* **onerous**, burdensome, demanding, challenging, difficult, formidable, weighty, worrisome, wearisome, stressful, trying, crushing, exacting, oppressive; *rare* toilsome, exigent.
OPPOSITE undemanding.
6 *the helicopter ran into heavy fog* **dense**, thick, opaque, soupy, murky, smoggy, impenetrable.
OPPOSITES light, wispy.
7 *a heavy thundery sky* **overcast**, cloudy, clouded, clouded over, overclouded, sunless, grey, dull, gloomy, murky, dark, darkened, black, stormy, leaden, louring, promising rain; *literary* tenebrous.
OPPOSITES sunny, bright.
8 *we had heavy overnight rain* **torrential**, relentless, copious, intense, teeming, excessive, strong, severe.
OPPOSITE light.
9 *the summer weather is very heavy here* **humid**, sultry, muggy, close, sticky, clammy, steamy, oppressive, airless, like a Turkish bath, like a sauna.
OPPOSITES fresh; arid.
10 *this tool is ideal for breaking up heavy soil* **clayey**, clay, viscous, viscid, muddy, sticky, glutinous, gluey, difficult, wet; *Brit.* claggy; *Scottish & N. English* clarty; *informal* gooey, gloopy, cloggy; *N. Amer. informal* gloppy.
OPPOSITES friable; dry.
11 *heavy losses | a heavy fine* **sizeable**, substantial, hefty, colossal, big, considerable; stiff; *informal* tidy, whopping (great), steep, astronomical; *Brit. informal* whacking (great).
OPPOSITE small.
12 *the boat encountered very heavy seas* **tempestuous**, turbulent, wild, violent, rough, stormy, storm-tossed, choppy, squally.
OPPOSITE calm.
13 *the battalion was involved in heavy fighting* **intense**, intensive, fierce, vigorous, concentrated, relentless, all-out, severe, serious, excessive, considerable, immoderate.
OPPOSITE half-hearted.
14 *he is a heavy drinker* **immoderate**, intemperate, overindulgent, unrestrained, uncontrolled, excessive.
OPPOSITE moderate.
15 *you shouldn't eat a heavy meal after 6 pm* **substantial**, filling, hearty, large, big, ample, sizeable, generous, square, solid.
OPPOSITE light.
16 *the Japanese diet is* **heavy on** *soybeans and vegetables* **abounding in**, abundant in, lavish with, generous with, liberal with, profuse with, extravagant with, free with, unstinting with, using a lot of; overabundant in, using too much of, overusing.
OPPOSITE light on.
17 *he felt heavy and very tired* **lethargic**, listless, sluggish, torpid, languid, apathetic, lacking in energy.
OPPOSITES energetic; animated.
18 *I left him with a heavy heart* **sad**, sorrowful, melancholy, gloomy, downcast, downhearted, heartbroken, disheartened, dejected, disconsolate, demoralized, discouraged, despondent, depressed, crestfallen, crushed, disappointed, desolate, grief-stricken, grieving;

informal blue, down, down in the mouth, down in the dumps; *literary* dolorous; *archaic* heartsick, heartsore.
OPPOSITE cheerful.
19 *these poems are dull and heavy | the editors of the heavy dailies* **tedious**, difficult, dull, dry, serious, over-serious, heavy-going, dreary, boring, turgid, uninteresting, wearisome, dry as dust; *informal* deadly.
OPPOSITE readable.
20 *branches heavy with blossoms* **laden**, loaded, covered, filled, groaning, bursting, teeming, abounding, weighed down, weighted down.
21 *we had a heavy crop of good quality fruit* **bountiful**, plentiful, abundant, large, bumper, handsome, lavish, rich, copious, considerable, sizeable, profuse; *informal* whopping, thumping; *Brit. informal* whacking; *literary* plenteous, bounteous.
OPPOSITE meagre.
22 *he had a big moustache and heavy features* **coarse**, rough, rough-hewn, ungraceful, unrefined, inelegant; rugged, craggy.
OPPOSITE delicate.

heavy-handed ▸ adjective **1** *they tend to be heavy-handed with the equipment* **clumsy**, awkward, maladroit, unhandy, inept, unskilful, inexpert, graceless, ungraceful; *informal* ham-handed, ham-fisted, cack-handed; *Brit. informal* all thumbs, all fingers and thumbs.
OPPOSITE dexterous.
2 *heavy-handed policing* **insensitive**, oppressive, overbearing, high-handed, harsh, hard, stern, severe, tyrannical, despotic, autocratic, ruthless, merciless; tactless, undiplomatic, thoughtless, inconsiderate, inept.
OPPOSITE sensitive.

heavy-hearted ▸ adjective **melancholy**, sad, sorrowful, melancholic, mournful, lugubrious, gloomy, pensive; depressed, desolate, despondent, dejected, down, downhearted, downcast, crestfallen, disconsolate, glum, sunk in gloom, miserable, wretched, dismal, dispirited, discouraged, low, in low spirits, in the doldrums, blue, morose, funereal, woeful, woebegone, doleful, wistful, unhappy, joyless, low-spirited, sombre; *informal* down in the dumps, down in the mouth, blue; *literary* dolorous; *archaic* heartsick, heartsore, chap-fallen.
OPPOSITE cheerful.

heckle ▸ verb *he was booed and heckled when he tried to address the demonstrators* **jeer**, taunt, jibe at, shout down, shout at, boo, hiss, disrupt, interrupt, harass; shout catcalls at; *Brit. & Austral./NZ* barrack; *informal* give someone a hard time.
OPPOSITE cheer.

hectic ▸ adjective *a hectic business schedule | a hectic street market* **frantic**, frenetic, frenzied, feverish, manic, restless, very busy, very active, fast and furious; lively, brisk, bustling, buzzing, vibrant, crowded.
OPPOSITES leisurely; quiet.

hector ▸ verb *he hectored the witness into incoherence* **bully**, intimidate, browbeat, cow, badger, chivvy, harass, torment, plague; coerce, pressurize, strong-arm, threaten, menace, ride roughshod over, use strong-arm tactics on, dragoon; *informal* bulldoze, railroad, steamroller; *N. Amer. informal* bullyrag.

hedge ▸ noun **1** *houses concealed behind high hedges* **hedgerow**, row of bushes, fence; windbreak, barrier, barricade, boundary; *Brit.* quickset.
2 *he sees the new fund as an excellent hedge against a fall in sterling* **safeguard**, protection, shield, screen, guard, buffer, cushion; cover, insurance, security, provision, insurance cover.
3 *his analysis is full of hedges like 'probably' and 'perhaps'* **equivocation**, evasion, fudge, quibble, qualification, qualifying expression; temporizing, uncertainty, prevarication, vagueness.
OPPOSITES absolute, certainty.
▸ verb **1** *the fields were hedged with hawthorn* **surround**, enclose, encircle, circle, ring, border, edge, bound; *literary* gird, girdle, engird.
2 *she was* **hedged in** *by her imperfect education* **confine**, restrict, limit, hinder, obstruct, impede, constrain, trap; hem in, shut in, close, keep within bounds.
3 *he hedged at every new question* **prevaricate**, equivocate, vacillate, quibble, hesitate, stall, evade the issue, dodge the issue, fudge the issue, sidestep the issue, be non-committal, be evasive, be indecisive, be vague, hedge one's bets, beat about the bush, parry questions, pussyfoot around, mince one's words, shilly-shally; *Brit.* hum and haw; *informal* sit on the fence, duck the question; *Brit. informal* waffle, flannel; *rare* tergiversate.
OPPOSITE come to the point.
4 *the company hedged its investment position on the futures market* **safeguard**, protect, shield, guard, cushion, cover, insure, take out insurance, take out insurance cover.
OPPOSITE expose to risk.

hedgehog ▸ noun
WORD LINKS
relating to hedgehogs **erinaceous**

hedonism ▸ noun **self-indulgence**, indulgence, pursuit of pleasure, pleasure-seeking, lotus-eating, epicureanism, epicurism, self-gratification; lack of self-restraint, intemperance, intemperateness, immoderation, overindulgence, excess, extravagance; luxury, the high life, high living; sensualism, voluptuousness; *Italian* la dolce vita; *rare* sybaritism.
OPPOSITE self-restraint.

hedonist ▸ noun **sybarite**, sensualist, voluptuary, pleasure seeker, pleasure lover; libertine, playboy, debauchee, loose-liver; epicure, gastronome, gourmand; *French* bon viveur, bon vivant.
OPPOSITE ascetic.

hedonistic ▸ adjective **self-indulgent**, indulgent, pleasure-seeking, pleasure-loving, sybaritic, lotus-eating, epicurean; luxurious, unrestrained, intemperate, immoderate, overindulgent, excessive, extravagant; sensual, voluptuous, decadent.
OPPOSITE ascetic.

heed ▸ verb *he should have heeded the warnings* **pay attention to**, take notice of, take note of, pay heed to, be heedful of, attend to, listen to, notice, note, pay regard to, bear in mind, be mindful of, mind, mark, consider, take into account, take into consideration, be guided by, follow, obey, keep, keep to, adhere to, abide by, observe, take to heart, give ear to, be alert to; be cautious of, watch out for.
OPPOSITE disregard.
▸ noun *if he heard, he paid no heed* **attention**, notice, note, regard, heedfulness, attentiveness, consideration, thought, care.

heedful ▸ adjective *on every side they cast a heedful eye* **attentive**, careful, mindful, cautious, prudent, circumspect, alert, aware, wary, chary, observant, watchful, vigilant, taking notice, paying attention, on guard, on the alert, on one's toes, on the qui vive; *rare* regardful.
OPPOSITES heedless; inattentive.

heedless ▸ adjective *someone had stayed behind, heedless of the warnings* **unmindful of**, taking no notice of, paying no heed to, careless of, disregardful of, regardless of, unheeding of, neglectful of, unconscious of, oblivious to, inattentive to, blind to, deaf to; incautious, imprudent, rash, reckless, foolhardy, blithe, precipitate, unthinking, thoughtless, improvident, unwary, unobservant, unwatchful.
OPPOSITES heedful; attentive.

CHOOSE THE RIGHT WORD
heedless, careless, thoughtless
See CARELESS.

heel¹ ▸ noun **1** *shoes with low heels* heel piece, lower back part of shoe; wedge, wedge heel, stiletto, stiletto heel, platform heel, spike heel, Cuban heel, kitten heel, Louis heel, stacked heel.
2 *there was the heel of a loaf in the cupboard* **tail end**, crust, end, remnant, remainder, remains, stump, butt, vestige.
3 (*informal, dated*) *what kind of a heel do you think I am?* **scoundrel**, rogue, rascal, good-for-nothing, reprobate; *informal* villain, bastard, beast, son of a bitch, s.o.b., rat, louse, swine, skunk, snake, snake in the grass, wretch, scumbag, bad egg, stinker; *N. English informal* scally; *Scottish informal* scrote; *Irish informal* sleeveen, spalpeen; *N. Amer. informal* rat fink; *informal, dated* rotter, bounder, blighter; *vulgar slang* shit, bugger; *N. Amer. vulgar slang* motherfucker, mother, mofo; *dated* cad, ne'er-do-well; *archaic* blackguard, miscreant, knave, dastard, vagabond, varlet, wastrel, rapscallion, whoreson.
□ **take to one's heels** *he shouted a warning and took to his heels* **run away**, run off, make a run for it, run for it, take flight, make off, take off, make a break for it, bolt, flee, beat a (hasty) retreat, make a quick exit, make one's getaway, escape, head for the hills; *informal* beat it, clear off, clear out, vamoose, skedaddle, split, cut and run, leg it, hightail it, hotfoot it, show a clean pair of heels, turn tail, scram, hook it, fly the coop, skip off, do a fade; *Brit. informal* do a runner, scarper, do a bunk; *N. Amer. informal* light out, bug out, cut out, peel out, take a powder, skidoo; *Austral. informal* go through, shoot through; *archaic* fly, levant.
OPPOSITE stay put.

heel² ▸ verb *the ship was beginning to heel to starboard* **lean over**, list, cant, careen, tilt, tip, incline, slant, slope, keel over, be at an angle.

heft ▸ verb *Donald hefted a stone jar of whisky into position* **lift**, lift up, raise, raise up, heave, hoist, haul, manhandle; carry, cart, lug, tote; *informal* hump, yank; *rare* upheave.
OPPOSITE put down.

hefty ▸ adjective **1** *a hefty young man* **burly**, heavy, sturdy, strapping, bulky, brawny, husky, strong, muscular, large, big, massive, weighty, solid, well built, solidly built, powerfully built; portly, stout; *informal* hulking, hunky, beefy; *literary* stalwart, thewy.
OPPOSITES slight, gaunt.
2 *he aimed a hefty kick at the door* **powerful**, violent, hard, forceful, heavy, vigorous, mighty, thunderous.
OPPOSITE feeble.
3 *the horses hauled hefty loads of timber and metal* **heavy**, weighty, bulky, leaden, big, large, substantial, massive, ponderous; unwieldy, cumbersome, burdensome, awkward; *informal* hulking, weighing a ton.
OPPOSITE light.
4 *they face a hefty fine* **substantial**, sizeable, considerable, stiff, high-cost, extortionate, inflated, large, huge, excessive, colossal; *Brit.* over the odds;

informal steep, astronomical, whopping, thumping; *Brit. informal* whacking, whacking great.
OPPOSITES small, paltry.

hegemony ▶ noun *Germany was united under Prussian hegemony after 1871* **leadership**, dominance, dominion, supremacy, ascendancy, predominance, primacy, authority, mastery, control, power, sway, rule, sovereignty; *rare* predomination, paramountcy, prepotence, prepotency, prepollency.
OPPOSITE self-government.

height ▶ noun **1** *we measured the height of the wall | three metres in height* **highness**, tallness, loftiness, distance upwards, extent upwards, vertical measurement, elevation, stature, altitude, distance above the ground; vertical distance above sea level.
2 *his eyes swept around the mountain heights* **summit**, top, peak, crest, crown, tip, cap, pinnacle, apex, vertex, brow, ridge, highest point, hilltop, mountain top; *French* aiguille, serac.
OPPOSITE base.
3 *they were at the height of their fame* **high point**, highest point, crowning moment, culminating point, peak, acme, apotheosis, zenith, apogee, pinnacle, climax, culmination, consummation, high water mark.
OPPOSITES nadir, low point.
4 *it would be the height of bad manners not to attend the wedding* **epitome**, acme, zenith, quintessence, limit, very limit, culmination, ultimate, utmost; *Latin* ne plus ultra.
5 (**heights**) *he is terrified of heights* **high places**, sheer drops, steep inclines, high ground, steep ground; precipices, cliffs.

WORD LINKS
related prefixes **acro- (e.g. *acropolis*), hypso-, alti-**
measurement of height **altimetry, hypsometry**
fear of heights **acrophobia**

heighten ▶ verb **1** *raising the floor level meant the roof had to be heightened* **make higher**, raise, lift, lift up, elevate, upraise.
OPPOSITE lower.
2 *the pleasure was heightened by the sense of guilt that accompanied it* **intensify**, increase, enhance, make greater, add to, raise, augment, boost, strengthen, sharpen, deepen, magnify, amplify, reinforce; aggravate, make worse, worsen, exacerbate, inflame, compound.
OPPOSITE reduce.

heinous ▶ adjective *child abuse is considered a most heinous offence* **odious**, wicked, evil, atrocious, monstrous, disgraceful, abominable, detestable, contemptible, reprehensible, despicable, horrible, horrific, horrifying, terrible, awful, abhorrent, loathsome, outrageous, shocking, shameful, hateful, hideous, unspeakable, unpardonable, unforgivable, inexcusable, execrable, ghastly, iniquitous, villainous, nefarious, beneath contempt, beyond the pale; *rare* egregious, flagitious.
OPPOSITE admirable.

heir, **heiress** ▶ noun *his eldest son and heir* **successor**, next in line, inheritor, heir apparent, heir presumptive, heir-at-law, descendant, beneficiary, legatee, scion; *Law* devisee, grantee, parcener, coparcener; *Scottish Law* heritor.
OPPOSITE predecessor.

WORD LINKS
relating to an heir **hereditary**

helix ▶ noun **spiral**, coil, curl, corkscrew, twist, twirl, loop, gyre, whorl, scroll, curlicue, convolution; *technical* volute, volution.

hell ▶ noun **1** *they feared they would be consumed by flames in hell* **the netherworld**, the land/abode of the dead, the infernal regions, the Inferno, the nether regions, the abyss; the abode of the damned, eternal damnation, eternal punishment, perdition; hellfire, fire and brimstone; *Biblical* Gehenna, Tophet, Abaddon; *Judaism* Sheol; *Greek Mythology* Hades, Tartarus, Acheron; *Roman Mythology* Avernus; *Scandinavian Mythology* Niflheim; *literary* the pit, the shades; *archaic* the lower world.
OPPOSITE heaven.
2 *he made her life hell* **a misery**, purgatory, hell on earth, torture, agony, a torment, a nightmare, an ordeal, a trauma; suffering, affliction, anguish, wretchedness, woe, tribulation, trials and tribulations.
OPPOSITE paradise.

□ **get hell** (*informal*) *later he got hell from his father* **be severely reprimanded**, be upbraided, be scolded, get a scolding, be admonished, be castigated, be rebuked, be chastised, be censured, be criticized severely, be taken to task, get into trouble, be hauled over the coals; *informal* catch it, get what for, be told off, get into hot/deep water, get into shtook, get a dressing-down, get an earful, get a roasting, get a rocket, get a rollicking, get a rap over the knuckles, get a slap on the wrist.
OPPOSITES be praised, be commended.

□ **give someone hell** (*informal*) **1** *when the truth came out I gave him hell* **reprimand severely**, rebuke, admonish, chastise, chide, upbraid, reprove, reproach, scold, remonstrate with, berate, take to task, pull up, castigate, lambaste, read someone the Riot Act, give someone a piece of one's mind, haul over the coals, lecture, criticize, censure; *informal* tell off, give someone a talking-to, give someone a telling-off, dress down, give someone a dressing-down, give someone an earful, give someone a roasting, give someone a rocket, give someone a rollicking, rap, rap over the knuckles, slap someone's wrist, send someone away with a flea in their ear, let someone have it, bawl out, come down hard on, blow up, pitch into, lay into, lace into, give someone a caning, blast, rag, keelhaul; *Brit. informal* tick off, have a go at, carpet, give someone a mouthful, tear someone off a strip, give someone what for, give someone some stick, wig, give someone a wigging; *N. Amer. informal* chew out, ream out; *Austral. informal* monster; *Brit. vulgar slang* bollock, give someone a bollocking; *N. Amer. vulgar slang* chew someone's ass, ream someone's ass; *dated* call down, rate, give someone a rating, trim; *rare* reprehend, objurgate.
OPPOSITES praise, commend.
2 *she gave me hell when I was her junior* **harass**, hound, plague, badger, harry, pester, bother, worry, annoy, trouble, bully, intimidate, pick on, bait, molest, bedevil, victimize, terrorize; *N. Amer.* devil; *informal* hassle, give someone a hard time, get on someone's back, make it/things hot for someone; *Austral. informal* heavy.
OPPOSITE leave in peace.

□ **hell for leather** *the cars went hurtling down the lane, hell for leather* **as fast as possible**, as quickly as possible, very fast, very quickly, very rapidly, very speedily, very swiftly, hurriedly, at full speed, at the double, at full tilt, at full pelt, headlong, hotfoot, post-haste, pell-mell, helter-skelter, at the speed of light, at breakneck speed, like an arrow from a bow; *informal* like a bat out of hell, at a lick, like the wind, like greased lightning, like a bomb, like mad, like crazy, like blazes; *Brit. informal* like the clappers, at a rate of knots, like billy-o; *N. Amer. informal* lickety-split; *literary* apace, hurry-scurry.
OPPOSITE at moderate speed.

□ **raise hell** (*informal*) **1** *they were hollering and raising hell* **cause a disturbance**, cause a commotion, be loud and noisy, run riot, run wild, behave wildly, go on the rampage, get out of control; have a (wild) party, party, carouse, revel; *informal* raise the roof, raise Cain.
OPPOSITE keep the peace.
2 *he raised hell with real estate developers and polluters* **remonstrate**, expostulate, be very angry, be furious, be enraged, argue, protest loudly to, object noisily to, complain vociferously to; *informal* kick up a fuss, kick up a stink.

WORD LINKS
relating to hell **infernal**
fear of hell **hadephobia, stygiophobia**

hell-bent ▶ adjective *why are you hell-bent on leaving?* **intent**, bent, determined, set, dead set, insistent, fixed, resolved, settled; firm about, single-minded about, inflexible about, obsessive about, fanatical about, fixated on.
OPPOSITE half-hearted.

hellish ▶ adjective **1** *the hellish face of Death* **infernal**, Hadean; **devilish**, diabolical, diabolic, fiendish, satanic, demonic, demoniac, demoniacal, Mephistophelian, ungodly, evil, wicked; *Greek Mythology* Stygian; *rare* cacodemonic.
OPPOSITES godly, angelic.
2 (*informal*) *it had been a hellish week* **horrible**, rotten, awful, terrible, dreadful, ghastly, horrid, vile, foul, abominable, appalling, atrocious, horrendous, frightful; difficult, unpleasant, nasty, disagreeable; stressful, taxing, demanding, trying, tough, hard, heavy, pressured, testing, frustrating, fraught, traumatic, arduous, tiring, gruelling; *informal* murderous, a bitch of a, a stinker of a, a bummer of a, from hell; *Brit. informal* grotty, beastly; *N. Amer. informal* hellacious, lousy.
OPPOSITES wonderful; easy.
▶ adverb (*informal, dated*) *it's hellish hard work* **very**, extremely, exceedingly, exceptionally, extraordinarily, tremendously, immensely, hugely, intensely, acutely, uncommonly, unusually, decidedly, particularly, remarkably, really, truly, mightily, thoroughly; all that, to a great extent, to a fault, in the extreme, most, so; *Scottish* unco; *French* très; *N. English* right; *informal* terrifically, awfully, fearfully, terribly, devilishly, majorly, seriously, mega, ultra, oh-so, stinking, mucho, damn, damned; *informal, dated* devilish, frightfully; *Brit. informal* ever so, well, bloody, dead; *N. Amer. informal* real, mighty, powerful, awful, plumb, darned, way, bitching; *S. African informal* lekker; *archaic* exceeding.
OPPOSITE moderately.

helm ▶ noun *the second mate took the helm* **tiller**, wheel; steering gear, rudder.

□ **at the helm** *they are family-run empires whose founders remain at the helm* **in charge**, in command, in control, responsible, at the top, in authority, in the seat of authority, at the wheel, in the driving seat, in the saddle; **managing**, running, administering, directing, supervising, overseeing, controlling, commanding, leading, heading up; *informal* holding the reins, running the show, pulling the strings, calling the shots.

help ▶ verb **1** *they helped her with domestic chores | can you help me please?* **assist**, aid, help out, lend a hand to, lend a helping hand to, give assistance to, come to the aid of, succour, aid and abet; be of service to, be of use to, be useful to; **do someone a favour**, do someone a service, do someone a good turn, bail/bale someone out, come to someone's

rescue, give someone a leg up; cooperate with, do one's bit for, rally round, pitch in, chip in; *informal* get someone out of a tight spot, save someone's bacon, save someone's skin; *Brit. informal* muck in with, get stuck in with.
OPPOSITE hinder.
2 *using this affinity card helps cancer research* **support, contribute to,** give money to, give a donation to; promote, boost, give a boost to, back, give backing to, forward, encourage, further the interests of; *N. Amer. informal* bankroll.
OPPOSITE impede.
3 *sore throats can be helped by gargles* **relieve**, soothe, ameliorate, alleviate, make better, ease, improve, assuage, palliate, lessen, mitigate; **remedy**, cure, heal, restore.
OPPOSITES worsen, aggravate.
4 *can I help you?* **serve**, be of assistance to, be of help to, be of service to, give help to.
□ **cannot help** *he could not help laughing* **be unable to stop**, be unable to prevent oneself from, be unable to refrain from, be unable to keep from, be unable to forbear from, be unable to break the habit of.
□ **help oneself to** *he helped himself to the wages she had brought home* **steal**, take, appropriate, take possession of, 'borrow', 'liberate', pocket, purloin, commandeer, make free with, use without asking; *informal* swipe, nab, filch, snaffle, blag, walk off with, run off with; *Brit. informal* nick, pinch, whip, knock off; *N. Amer. informal* heist, glom; *W. Indian informal* tief.
▶ **noun 1** *I asked for help from my neighbours | this could be of help to you* **assistance**, aid, a helping hand, support, succour, advice, guidance; **benefit**, use, advantage, service, comfort, avail; cooperation, collaboration, backing, encouragement; *informal* a shot in the arm.
OPPOSITE hindrance.
2 *he sought help for his eczema* **relief**, amelioration, alleviation, easing, improvement, assuagement, mitigation, healing; **a remedy**, a cure, a balm, a salve, a restorative, a corrective.
OPPOSITE irritant.
3 *they treated the help like dirt* **domestic worker**, domestic help, domestic servant, cleaner, cleaning woman, cleaning lady, home help, maid, housemaid, housekeeper, servant, hired help, helper, assistant, employee, worker; *Brit. informal* daily, daily woman, skivvy, Mrs Mop; *Brit. dated* charwoman, charlady, char; *archaic* scullion, abigail.

CHOOSE THE RIGHT WORD

help, aid, assist, support

- **Help** is the most general term for acting in such a way as to make it easier for someone else to do something or, more generally, to make their life more comfortable (*she helped him to find a job | helping the poor*). When followed by an infinitive, as in the first example above, *to* can be omitted (*we can help give these youngsters a better start in life*).
- **Aid** is used in more formal contexts, and typically in the case of help in the achievement of something (*these posters aid employees in the identification of pests*). It is often used with impersonal or abstract subjects and objects (*some additions have been made to the text to aid understanding*), and as *aided* in constructions such as *computer-aided design*.
- **Assist** is also a more formal term for *help* (*a charge of murder was brought against him for assisting a woman to commit suicide | two approaches might assist in tackling the problem*), and it can be used specifically to indicate that someone plays a subordinate part in a joint action (*a subcommittee should be appointed to assist the chairman*).
- To **support** someone or something is to show one's approval or agreement and, where necessary, to give practical, especially financial, assistance (*we want to support all efforts for peace | we should show our gratitude for God's gifts by supporting a charity*). Often the suggestion is that the help provided is important or essential for something's survival or success (*he could not have earned enough to support his family*). *Support* is also used of giving emotional help and comfort (*his wife has supported him through many difficult periods*).

helper ▶ **noun** *there was no shortage of helpers to relieve us during breaks* **assistant**, co-worker, fellow worker, workmate, teammate, helpmate, helpmeet, associate, aider, aide, colleague, supporter, partner, collaborator, abetter; **subordinate**, deputy, auxiliary, second, second in command, number two, right-hand man, right-hand woman, attendant, junior, acolyte; accessory, accomplice, henchman; *informal* sidekick.

helpful ▶ **adjective 1** *the staff are friendly and helpful* **obliging**, eager to help, eager to please, friendly, pleasant, kind, accommodating, considerate, thoughtful, supportive, cooperative, sympathetic, caring, hospitable, neighbourly, charitable, benevolent, beneficent.
OPPOSITES unobliging, unsympathetic.
2 *we find it very helpful to receive comments* **useful**, of use, of service, of benefit, beneficial, valuable, profitable, fruitful, advantageous, worthwhile, productive, constructive, practical; informative, instructive.
OPPOSITE useless.
3 *we recommend this helpful new power tool* **handy**, useful, convenient, practical, easy-to-use, well-designed, user-friendly, user-oriented, functional, serviceable, utilitarian; *informal* neat, nifty.
OPPOSITE inconvenient.

helping ▶ **noun** *there will be enough for six to eight helpings* **portion**, serving, piece, slice, share, spoonful, plate, plateful, bowlful, ration, allocation; *informal* dollop.

helpless ▶ **adjective** *the cubs are born blind and helpless* **dependent**, **incapable**, powerless, impotent, weak, weakly, feeble; **defenceless**, unprotected, vulnerable, exposed, easily hurt, easily destroyed, open to attack; paralysed, disabled.
OPPOSITES independent, capable of looking after oneself.

helpmate ▶ **noun 1** *a crowing rooster was the helpmate of the goddess of the sun* **companion**, partner, associate, assistant, helper, helpmeet, attendant, escort; supporter, friend.
2 *she couldn't survive on her own and happily submitted to the role of helpmate once again* **spouse**, partner, consort, mate, husband, wife; *informal* other half, better half.

helter-skelter ▶ **adverb** *the children ran helter-skelter down the valley* **headlong**, pell-mell, hotfoot, post-haste, hastily, hurriedly, as fast as possible, as quickly as possible, at full speed, at full pelt, at full tilt, hell for leather, recklessly, precipitately, impetuously, impulsively, carelessly, heedlessly, wildly; *informal* like a bat out of hell, at a lick, like the wind, like greased lightning, like a bomb, like mad, like crazy, like blazes; *Brit. informal* like the clappers, at a rate of knots, like billy-o; *N. Amer. informal* lickety-split; *literary* apace, hurry-scurry.
OPPOSITE at moderate speed.
▶ **adjective** *the village was a helter-skelter collection of dwellings* **disordered**, disorderly, chaotic, muddled, jumbled, untidy, haphazard, disorganized, unorganized, disarranged, topsy-turvy; in a mess, in a muddle, in a shambles, at sixes and sevens, out of order; *informal* higgledy-piggledy, all over the place; *Brit. informal* shambolic, all over the shop; *N. Amer. informal* all over the map, all over the lot; *rare* orderless.
OPPOSITE orderly.

hem ▶ **noun** *she let down the hem of her dress* **edge**, edging, border, trim, trimming; fringe, frill, flounce, valance.
▶ **verb** *Nanna taught me to hem skirts* **edge**, put a hem on, border, trim, bind, fringe.
□ **hem someone/something in 1** *the bay was hemmed in by pine trees* **surround**, border, edge, encircle, circle, ring, enclose, skirt, flank, fringe, encompass; *literary* gird, girdle, engird.
2 *he was hemmed in by the furniture | we were hemmed in by the rules* **restrict**, confine, trap, close in, shut in, hedge in, fence in, pen in, box in, keep within bounds, immure; constrain, restrain, limit, circumscribe, curb, check; *N. Amer.* corral; *rare* compass.

he-man ▶ **noun** (*informal*) **muscleman**, strongman, macho, macho man, iron man, Hercules, Atlas, Samson, Tarzan; *informal* **hunk**, tough guy, beefcake, stud, bruiser; *N. Amer. informal* studmuffin.
OPPOSITE wimp.

hence ▶ **adverb** *many vehicle journeys (and hence a lot of pollution) would be saved* **in consequence**, consequently, as a consequence, for this reason, therefore, thus, so, accordingly, as a result, because of that, that being so, that being the case, on that account; *Latin* ergo.

henceforth ▶ **adverb** *henceforth the director will be solely responsible for the whole establishment* **from now on**, as of now, after this, in future, in the future, hence, henceforward, subsequently, from this day on, from this time on, from this day forth, from this day forward; *formal* hereafter, hereinafter.

henchman ▶ **noun** *the local dictator arrived with a group of henchmen* **follower**, supporter, assistant, aide, helper, adjutant, right-hand man; subordinate, underling, minion, lackey, flunkey, toady, stooge, acolyte, satellite, shadow; bodyguard, minder, protector; *informal* sidekick, crony, heavy, man/girl Friday.
OPPOSITE leader.

henpecked ▶ **adjective** *he was a henpecked husband at the end of his tether* **browbeaten**, downtrodden, bullied, dominated, nagged, subjugated, oppressed, repressed, intimidated, ground down, without a mind of one's own, tied to someone's apron strings, under someone's heel; meek, timid, docile, cringing, cowering, abject; *informal* under someone's thumb, led by the nose, treated like dirt.
OPPOSITE domineering.

herald ▶ **noun 1** *a herald announced the armistice* **messenger**, courier, bearer of tidings; proclaimer, announcer, crier, town crier.
2 *they considered the first primroses as the herald of spring* **harbinger**, sign, indicator, indication, signal, prelude, portent, omen, augury, forewarning, presage, announcer; forerunner, precursor, messenger, usher; *French* avant-courier; *literary* foretoken.
▶ **verb 1** *screams and shouts heralded their approach* **proclaim**, announce, broadcast, publicize, declare, trumpet, make public, make known, blazon; advertise, promote, beat the drum about.

2 *the speech heralded a change in policy* **signal**, indicate, announce, point to, spell, presage, augur, portend, promise, prefigure, foreshadow, foretell, usher in, show in, pave the way for, open the way for, be a harbinger of, be a forerunner, be a precursor of; precede, come before; *rare* forebode, foretoken, betoken, harbinger.

herb ▶ noun. *See centre pages for lists of* **Herbs** **Spices**

Herculean ▶ adjective **1** *a Herculean task* **arduous**, gruelling, laborious, back-breaking, onerous, strenuous, difficult, formidable, burdensome, hard, tough, huge, heavy, massive, uphill, Sisyphean; demanding, exhausting, taxing, exacting, wearying, wearisome, fatiguing; *informal* killing; *Brit. informal* knackering; *archaic* toilsome.
OPPOSITE easy.
2 *he was a man of Herculean build* **strong**, muscular, muscly, powerful, sturdy, robust, solid, well built, powerfully built, solidly built, strapping, brawny, burly, broad-shouldered, as strong as an ox, as strong as a horse, as strong as a lion; *informal* hunky, beefy, hulking; *literary* stalwart, thewy, stark.
OPPOSITE puny.

herd ▶ noun **1** *large farms with big dairy herds* drove, flock, pack, group, collection, fold.
2 (*archaic*) *they were obliged to employ herds for their cattle* **stockman**, herdsman, herdswoman, herder, drover, cattleman, cowherd, cowhand, cowman, cowboy, rancher; shepherd; *N. Amer.* sheepman; (*in Spanish-speaking America*) gaucho, llanero, ranchero, vaquero; *N. Amer. informal* cowpuncher, cowpoke, broncobuster; *N. Amer. dated* buckaroo.
3 *we ran into a herd of movie actors* **crowd**, group, bunch, horde, mass, mob, host, pack, multitude, throng, swarm, army, company, press.
4 (**the herd**) *they consider themselves above the herd* **the common people**, the masses, the public, the people, the rank and file, the populace, the multitude, the crowd, the commonality, the commonalty, the third estate, the plebeians; *derogatory* the hoi polloi, the mob, the proletariat, the common herd, the rabble, the riff-raff, the canaille, the ragtag (and bobtail), the great unwashed, the proles, the plebs, the peasants.
OPPOSITE the elite.
▶ verb **1** *he and the boys herded the sheep into the pen* **drive**, round up, shepherd, gather, collect, assemble, guide.
2 *we all herded into a storage room* **crowd**, pack, flock; cluster, huddle, group, gather.
3 *they live by herding reindeer* **look after**, take care of, keep, tend, watch, watch over, mind, guard.
OPPOSITE neglect.

herdsman, herdswoman ▶ noun **stockman**, herder, drover, shepherd, cattleman, cowherd, cowhand, cowman, cowboy, rancher; *N. Amer.* sheepman; (*in Spanish-speaking America*) gaucho, llanero, ranchero, vaquero; *N. Amer. informal* cowpuncher, cowpoke, broncobuster; *N. Amer. dated* buckaroo; *archaic* herd.

here ▶ adverb **1** *they have lived here most of their lives* **at/in this place**, at/in this spot, at/in this location.
2 *I am here now* **present**, in attendance, attending, at hand, available.
OPPOSITE absent.
3 *come here tomorrow morning* **to this place**, to this spot, to this location, to here, over here, near, nearer, close, closer; *literary* hither.
4 *here is your opportunity* **now**, at this moment, at this point, at this point in time, at this time, at this juncture, at this stage.
□ **here and there 1** *a landscape of ferns with clumps of heather here and there* **in various places**, in different places, hither and thither, at random.
2 *they darted here and there, adjusting and correcting* **from place to place**, around, about, to and fro, hither and thither, back and forth, in all directions, from pillar to post.

hereafter ▶ adverb (*formal*) *nothing I say hereafter is intended to relate to the second decision* **from now on**, after this, as of now, from this day on, from this time on, from this moment forth, from this day forth, from this day forward, subsequently, in future, in the future, hence, henceforth, henceforward; *formal* hereinafter.
▶ noun (**the hereafter**) *suffering is part of our preparation for the hereafter* **life after death**, the afterlife, the life to come, the afterworld, the next world, the beyond; immortality, eternity, heaven, paradise.

hereditary ▶ adjective **1** *in the past, the aristocracy had a hereditary right to elect the king* **inherited**, obtained by inheritance; bequeathed, willed, handed-down, passed-down, passed-on, transferred, transmitted; ancestral, family, familial; *rare* lineal.
2 *cystic fibrosis is our most common fatal hereditary disease* **genetic**, genetical, congenital, inborn, inherent, inherited, inbred, innate, in the family, in the blood, in the genes.

heredity ▶ noun *the relative influence of heredity and environment* **congenital characteristics**, congenital traits, genetics, genetic make-up, genes; ancestry, descent, extraction, parentage.

heresy ▶ noun *Huss was burned for heresy* **dissension**, dissent, dissidence, blasphemy, nonconformity, unorthodoxy, heterodoxy, apostasy, freethinking, schism, faction; scepticism, agnosticism, atheism, non-belief, unbelief, idolatry, paganism, separatism, sectarianism, revisionism; *rare* tergiversation, recreancy, recusancy.
OPPOSITE orthodoxy.

heretic ▶ noun *he was condemned as a heretic and executed at the stake* **dissident**, dissenter, nonconformist, unorthodox thinker, heterodox thinker, apostate, freethinker, iconoclast, schismatic, renegade; sceptic, agnostic, atheist, non-believer, unbeliever, idolater, idolatress, pagan, heathen; separatist, sectarian, revisionist; *rare* tergiversator, recreant, recusant, nullifidian; *archaic* paynim.
OPPOSITES conformist; believer.

heretical ▶ adjective *he was punished for his heretical views* **dissident**, dissenting, nonconformist, unorthodox, heterodox, apostate, freethinking, iconoclastic, schismatic, renegade; sceptical, agnostic, atheistical, non-believing, unbelieving, idolatrous, pagan, heathen, impious; separatist, sectarian, revisionist; *rare* recreant, recusant, nullifidian; *archaic* paynim.
OPPOSITE orthodox.

heritage ▶ noun **1** *they had stolen his heritage* **inheritance**, birthright, patrimony; legacy, bequest, endowment, estate, bequeathal; *Law* devise, hereditament.
2 *Europe's varied cultural heritage* **tradition**, history, background, culture, customs, past.
3 *he felt the pull of his Greek heritage* **ancestry**, lineage, descent, extraction, parentage, roots, background, heredity, pedigree.

hermaphrodite ▶ noun epicene; *technical* bisexual, gynandromorph; *rare* androgyne.
▶ adjective *hermaphrodite creatures in classical sculpture* **androgynous**, hermaphroditic, epicene; *technical* bisexual, monoclinous, gynandrous, gynandromorphic.

hermetic ▶ adjective *a hermetic seal that ensures perfect waterproofing* **airtight**, tight, sealed, shut; watertight, waterproof.

hermit ▶ noun **recluse**, solitary, loner, ascetic; *rare* anchorite, anchoress, eremite, stylite, pillarist, pillar hermit, pillar saint, solitudinarian.

WORD LINKS
relating to a hermit **eremitic**

hermitage ▶ noun **retreat**, refuge, haven, sanctuary, sanctum, asylum, hideaway, hideout, hiding place, shelter; *Latin* sanctum sanctorum; *informal* hidey-hole.

hero ▶ noun **1** *his father was a war hero* **brave man**, champion, man of courage, great man, man of the hour, conquering hero, victor, winner, conqueror, lionheart, warrior, paladin, knight; *French* chevalier.
OPPOSITES coward; loser.
2 *a football hero* **star**, idol, superstar, megastar, celebrity, luminary, lion; ideal, ideal man, paragon, exemplar, shining example, perfect example; favourite, darling; knight in shining armour, knight on a white charger; *French* beau idéal; *informal* celeb.
3 *the hero of the film is a young pianist* **male protagonist**, principal male character; principal male role, lead actor, lead, leading man, leading role, male lead, star role, starring role, star part, male star.
OPPOSITE villain.

heroic ▶ adjective **1** *a national flag can motivate citizens to heroic deeds | heroic rescuers* **brave**, courageous, valiant, valorous, intrepid, bold, daring, audacious, superhuman, Herculean, fearless, doughty, undaunted, dauntless, unafraid, plucky, indomitable, stout-hearted, lionhearted, mettlesome, venturesome, gallant, stalwart, chivalrous, noble; *N. Amer.* rock-ribbed; *informal* gutsy, spunky, ballsy, feisty; *rare* venturous.
OPPOSITES cowardly; fearful.
2 *a heroic achievement* **prodigious**, grand, enormous, huge, massive, titanic, colossal, monumental, stupendous; epic, Homeric; *informal* mega.
OPPOSITE modest.
3 (*literary*) *the fabulous narrations of the ancient heroic times* **classical**, Homeric, mythological, mythical, mythic, legendary, fabulous, fabled.
OPPOSITE modern.

heroine ▶ noun **1** *Nicky was a heroine—she saved my baby from being snatched* **brave woman**, hero, woman of courage, great woman, woman of the hour; victor, winner, conqueror.
OPPOSITES coward; loser.
2 *the literary heroine of Moscow* **star**, idol, superstar, megastar, celebrity, luminary, lion; ideal, ideal woman, paragon, exemplar, shining example, perfect example, favourite, darling; *informal* celeb.
3 *the film's heroine takes a feminist stand* **female protagonist**, principal female character; principal female role, lead actress, lead, leading lady, leading role, female lead, star role, starring role, star part, female star, prima donna, diva.
OPPOSITE villain.

heroism ▶ noun *many of the women distinguished themselves by great acts of heroism* **bravery**, braveness, courage, courageousness, valour, valiance, intrepidity, intrepidness, boldness, daring, audacity, audaciousness, fearlessness, doughtiness, dauntlessness, pluck, indomitability, stout-heartedness, lionheartedness; backbone, spine, spirit, fortitude, mettle, gallantry, chivalry; *informal* guts, grit, spunk, gutsiness; *Brit. informal* bottle, ballsiness; *N. Amer. informal* moxie, cojones, sand; *vulgar slang* balls.

OPPOSITES cowardliness; fearfulness.

hero-worship ▶ noun *the hero-worship of the fans gathered at the airport* **idolization**, adulation, admiration, idealization, awe, high esteem, high regard, putting on a pedestal; worship, adoration, glorification, exaltation, veneration, reverence; *rare* magnification.
OPPOSITES disparagement, lack of respect.

herself ▶ pronoun
□ **by herself**. *See* BY ONESELF *at* BY.

hesitancy ▶ noun **1** *they gave the impression of hesitancy and doubt* **uncertainty**, hesitation, hesitance, unsureness, doubt, doubtfulness, dubiousness, irresolution, irresoluteness, indecision, indecisiveness, equivocation, vacillation, wavering, scepticism, nervousness, second thoughts; **dithering**, stalling, shilly-shallying, temporizing, temporization, pausing, delay, hanging back, waiting; *Brit.* havering, humming and hawing; *Scottish* swithering; *informal* dilly-dallying, blowing hot and cold; *rare* dubiety, incertitude, cunctation.
OPPOSITES certainty, resolution.
2 *there was a little hesitancy in her voice* **reluctance**, unwillingness, disinclination, unease, uneasiness, ambivalence, demurral, compunction; misgivings, qualms, scruples, reservations.
OPPOSITE willingness.

hesitant ▶ adjective **1** *clients are hesitant about buying* **uncertain**, undecided, unsure, doubtful, in doubt, dubious, tentative, half-hearted, ambivalent, sceptical, reluctant, nervous, having misgivings, having qualms, hanging back, stalling, delaying; **irresolute**, hesitating, indecisive, dithering, vacillating, wavering, oscillating, shilly-shallying, in two minds, in a quandary, in a dilemma, on the horns of a dilemma; *Brit.* havering, humming and hawing; *informal* iffy, dilly-dallying, blowing hot and cold; *rare* cunctatory.
OPPOSITES certain; decisive.
2 *she was timid and hesitant* **lacking confidence**, diffident, timid, shy, bashful, insecure, self-effacing; stammering, stuttering, stumbling, faltering.
OPPOSITE confident.

hesitate ▶ verb **1** *she hesitated, unsure of what to say* **pause**, delay, hang back, wait, shilly-shally, dither, stall, temporize, be in two minds, be in a quandary, be in a dilemma, be on the horns of a dilemma; **be uncertain**, be hesitant, be unsure, be doubtful, be indecisive, equivocate, vacillate, oscillate, waver, have second thoughts; *Brit.* haver, hum and haw; *Scottish* swither; *informal* dilly-dally, blow hot and cold.
OPPOSITES be resolute, be certain.
2 *please do not hesitate to contact me* **be reluctant**, be unwilling, be disinclined, scruple; have misgivings about, have qualms about, be ambivalent about, feel uneasy about, shrink from, demur from, hang back from, think twice about, be diffident about, baulk at, boggle at.
OPPOSITE be willing.

hesitation ▶ noun **1** *she answered without hesitation* **pausing**, delay, hanging back, waiting, shilly-shallying, dithering, stalling, temporizing, temporization; **uncertainty**, hesitancy, hesitance, unsureness, doubt, doubtfulness, dubiousness, irresolution, irresoluteness, indecision, indecisiveness, equivocation, vacillation, oscillation, wavering, scepticism, nervousness, second thoughts; *Brit.* havering, humming and hawing; *Scottish* swithering; *informal* dilly-dallying, blowing hot and cold; *rare* dubiety, incertitude, cunctation.
OPPOSITES resolution, certainty.
2 *I have no hesitation in recommending him* **reluctance**, misgivings, qualms, scruples, reservations, compunction, unwillingness, disinclination, ambivalence, unease, uneasiness, demurral.
OPPOSITE willingness.

heterodox ▶ adjective *public expression of such heterodox views is impossible* **unorthodox**, heretical, dissenting, dissident, blasphemous, nonconformist, apostate, freethinking, iconoclastic, schismatic, rebellious, renegade, separatist, sectarian, revisionist; sceptical, agnostic, atheistical, non-believing, unbelieving, idolatrous, pagan, heathen, impious; *archaic* paynim; *rare* recreant, recusant, nullifidian.
OPPOSITE orthodox.

heterogeneous ▶ adjective *a large and heterogeneous collection* **diverse**, diversified, varied, varying, miscellaneous, assorted, mixed, sundry, contrasting, disparate, different, differing, divergent, unrelated, variegated, wide-ranging; motley; *literary* divers, myriad, legion; *rare* contrastive.
OPPOSITE homogeneous.

heterosexual ▶ adjective *informal* **straight**, hetero, het.
OPPOSITES homosexual, gay.

hew ▶ verb **1** *master carpenters would hew the logs with an axe* **chop**, hack, chop down, hack down, cut down, saw down, fell, lop, axe, cleave.
2 *steps had been hewn into the rock wall* **cut**, carve, shape, fashion, form, chip, hammer, chisel, sculpt, sculpture, model, whittle, rough-hew.

heyday ▶ noun *the paper has lost millions of readers since its heyday in 1964* **prime**, peak, height, high point, high spot, peak of perfection, pinnacle, acme, zenith, day, time, bloom, flowering, culmination, crowning point; prime of life, best days, best years, salad days.
OPPOSITE low point.

hiatus ▶ noun **1** *there has been a hiatus in space exploration following the Viking missions* **pause**, break, interval, interruption, suspension, intermission, interlude, gap, lacuna, lull, rest, respite, breathing space, time out; *N. Amer.* recess; *informal* breather, let-up; *archaic* surcease.
2 (*Medicine*) *the diaphragmatic hiatus was larger than necessary* **opening**, aperture, cavity, hole, gap, cleft, breach, fissure; *Medicine* foramen.

hibernate ▶ verb *some species hibernate in tree roosts* **lie dormant**, lie torpid, sleep, winter, overwinter, hole up.

hidden ▶ adjective **1** *they watched the action through a hidden camera* **concealed**, secret, not visible, invisible, unseen, not on view, out of sight, covered, camouflaged, disguised, masked, shrouded, veiled, unrevealed.
OPPOSITE visible.
2 *what is the hidden meaning behind his words?* **unknown**, not obvious, unclear, concealed, obscure, indistinct, indefinite, vague, unfathomable, inexplicable; **cryptic**, mysterious, secret, covert, abstruse, arcane, recondite, ulterior, deep, subliminal, coded, under wraps.
OPPOSITES obvious, clear.

WORD LINKS
related prefix **crypto-** (e.g. ***cryptogram, cryptozoology***)

hide¹ ▶ verb **1** *he hid the money in the house* **conceal**, secrete, put in a hiding place, put out of sight, camouflage; lock up, bury, store away, stow away, cache; *informal* stash.
OPPOSITES flaunt, expose.
2 *they eluded the police by hiding in an air vent* **conceal oneself**, secrete oneself, hide out, take cover, keep hidden, find a hiding place, keep out of sight; go into hiding, lie low, go to ground, go to earth, go underground, lurk; *informal* hole up; *Brit. informal* lie doggo.
OPPOSITE remain visible.
3 *clouds rolled up and hid the moon* **obscure**, block out, blot out, obstruct, cloud, shroud, veil, blanket, envelop, darken, eclipse; *literary* enshroud.
OPPOSITE reveal.
4 *Herbert could hardly hide his dislike* **keep secret**, keep unknown, conceal, cover up, keep dark, keep quiet about, hush up, bottle up, suppress, repress, withhold; **disguise**, mask, camouflage, veil, dissemble; *informal* keep mum about, keep under one's hat, keep a/the lid on.
OPPOSITE disclose.

hide² ▶ noun *the hide should be tanned as soon as possible* **skin**, pelt, coat, fur, fleece; **leather**; *archaic* fell.

hideaway ▶ noun *a mass of shrubs creates a secluded hideaway* **retreat**, refuge, hiding place, hideout, den, shelter, sanctuary, sanctum, hermitage, cache, bolt-hole, lair, nest, nook; *Latin* sanctum sanctorum; *informal* hidey-hole.

hidebound ▶ adjective *the hidebound traditionalists refused to accept the changes* **conservative**, reactionary, conventional, orthodox, fundamentalist, diehard, hard-line, dyed-in-the-wool, ultra-conservative, fixed in one's views, set in one's opinions, set in one's ways; narrow-minded, narrow, petty-minded, small-minded, intolerant, intractable, uncompromising, rigid, prejudiced, bigoted, strait-laced; *Brit.* blimpish.
OPPOSITES liberal, broad-minded.

hideous ▶ adjective **1** *his smile made him look more hideous than ever* **ugly**, unsightly, repulsive, repellent, revolting, gruesome, disgusting, grotesque, monstrous, grim, ghastly, macabre, misshapen, misproportioned, reptilian; *informal* weird, freaky, as ugly as sin; *Brit. informal* like the back end of a bus.
OPPOSITE beautiful.
2 *hideous cases of torture continue to be reported* **horrific**, terrible, appalling, awful, dreadful, frightful, fearful, horrible, horrendous, horrifying, shocking, sickening, gruesome, ghastly, very bad, terribly bad, unspeakable, outrageous, abhorrent, monstrous, heinous, abominable, foul, vile, odious, loathsome, contemptible, execrable, indescribable; *informal* God-awful; *Brit. informal* beastly; *rare* egregious.
OPPOSITE pleasant.

hideout ▶ noun *the kidnappers did not want their hideout discovered* **hiding place**, hideaway, retreat, refuge, shelter, bolt-hole, foxhole, lair, safe house, sanctuary, sanctum, hermitage; *Latin* sanctum sanctorum; *informal* hidey-hole.

hiding¹ ▶ noun (*informal*) *they took off after him, caught him, and gave him a hiding* **beating**, battering, thrashing, thumping, pounding, pummelling, drubbing, slapping, smacking, spanking, hammering, cuffing, thwacking, mauling, pelting; flogging, flaying, whipping, caning, lashing, cudgelling, clubbing, birching; *informal* licking, belting, bashing, pasting, lathering, larruping, walloping, whacking, clobbering, tanning, biffing, bopping, horsewhipping; *N. Amer. informal* whaling.

hiding² ▶ noun
□ **in hiding** *the fugitive priest was in hiding* **hidden**, concealed, lying low, gone to ground, gone to earth, gone underground, in a safe house; in seclusion, in retreat; *Brit. informal* lying doggo.

hiding place ▶ noun *they passed within inches of my hiding place* **hideaway**, hideout, retreat, refuge, den, shelter, sanctuary, bolt-hole, foxhole, lair, safe house, asylum, sanctum, hermitage, oasis, haven, harbour, place of safety; *informal* hidey-hole.

hie ▶ **verb** (*archaic*) *they heard voices and hied away* **hurry**, hasten, go quickly, run, race, rush, dash, speed, hare, hurtle, fly, wing, pelt, scurry, scramble; *informal* hotfoot it, leg it; *literary* fleet, post.
OPPOSITES go slowly, amble.

hierarchy ▶ **noun** *the initiative was with those lower down in the hierarchy* **pecking order**, ranking, grading, ladder, social order, social stratum, social scale, class system.

hieroglyphic ▶ **noun** (**hieroglyphics**) **1** *his exploits were recorded in hieroglyphics on a stone monument* **symbols**, signs, ciphers, code; **cryptograms**, cryptographs, runes.
2 *tattered notebooks filled with illegible hieroglyphics* **scribble**, scrawl, illegible writing, squiggles, jottings, writing, shorthand.
▶ **adjective** **1** *the piece is inlaid with hieroglyphic brass ornamentation* **symbolic**, stylized, figurative, emblematic.
2 *he wrote the prescription in hieroglyphic handwriting* **illegible**, indecipherable, unreadable, scribbled, scrawled, squiggly.

higgledy-piggledy (*informal*) ▶ **adjective** *a higgledy-piggledy mountain of newspapers* **disordered**, disorderly, untidy, disorganized, messy, chaotic, jumbled, muddled, confused, unsystematic, irregular, cluttered, littered; out of order, out of place, in disarray, in a mess, in a jumble, in a muddle, upside-down, at sixes and sevens, haywire, haphazard; *informal* all over the place, like a bomb's hit it; *Brit. informal* shambolic, all over the shop; *N. Amer. informal* all over the map, all over the lot; *rare* orderless.
OPPOSITES tidy, ordered.
▶ **adverb** *the cars were parked higgledy-piggledy* **in disorder**, in a muddle, in a jumble, in disarray, in a disorganized manner, untidily, haphazardly, indiscriminately, in a mess, in confusion, in a heap, anyhow, any old how, pell-mell, topsy-turvy; *informal* all over the place, every which way; *Brit. informal* all over the shop; *N. Amer. informal* all over the map, all over the lot.
OPPOSITES tidily, in an orderly fashion.

high ▶ **adjective** **1** *the top of a high mountain* **tall**, lofty, towering, soaring, elevated, giant, big; multi-storey, high-rise, sky-scraping.
OPPOSITE short.
2 *he is in a high position in the government* **high-ranking**, high-level, leading, top, top-level, prominent, eminent, pre-eminent, foremost, senior, influential, distinguished, powerful, important, elevated, notable, principal, prime, premier, chief, main, upper, ruling, exalted, illustrious; *N. Amer.* ranking; *informal* top-notch.
OPPOSITES low-ranking, lowly.
3 *you should hold on to your high principles* **high-minded**, noble-minded, lofty, moral, ethical, honourable, admirable, upright, principled, honest, virtuous, righteous.
OPPOSITE amoral.
4 *shop around to avoid high prices* **inflated**, excessive, unreasonable, overpriced, sky-high, unduly expensive, dear, costly, top, exorbitant, extortionate, outrageous, prohibitive; *Brit.* over the odds; *informal* steep, stiff, pricey, over the top, OTT, criminal.
OPPOSITE reasonable.
5 *I have always insisted upon high standards* **excellent**, outstanding, exemplary, exceptional, admirable, fine, great, good, very good, first-class, first-rate, superior, superlative, superb, commendable, laudable, praiseworthy, meritorious, blameless, faultless, flawless, impeccable, irreproachable, unimpeachable, perfect, unequalled, unparalleled; *informal* tip-top, A1, top-notch; *rare* applaudable.
OPPOSITES poor, deplorable.
6 *it was freezing cold with high winds* **strong**, powerful, violent, intense, extreme, forceful, sharp, stiff; blustery, gusty, stormy, squally, tempestuous, turbulent; *rare* boisterous.
OPPOSITES light; calm.
7 *he lived the high life among the London glitterati* **luxurious**, lavish, extravagant, rich, grand, sybaritic, hedonistic, opulent; prodigal, overindulgent, intemperate, immoderate; *Brit.* upmarket; *N. Amer.* upscale; *informal* fancy, classy, swanky.
OPPOSITE abstemious.
8 *I have a high opinion of your talents* **favourable**, good, positive, approving, admiring, complimentary, commendatory, appreciative, flattering, glowing, adulatory, approbatory, rapturous, full of praise; *rare* panegyrical, acclamatory, laudative, encomiastical.
OPPOSITE unfavourable.
9 *the voices rose to hit a high note* **high-pitched**, high-frequency, soprano, treble, falsetto, shrill, acute, sharp, piping, piercing, penetrating.
OPPOSITES low-pitched, deep.
10 (*informal*) *some of them were already high on alcohol and Ecstasy* **intoxicated**, inebriated, on drugs, drugged, stupefied, befuddled, delirious, hallucinating; *informal* on a high, stoned, turned on, on a trip, tripping, hyped up, freaked out, spaced out, zonked, wasted, wrecked, high as a kite, off one's head, out of one's mind, flying, charged up.
OPPOSITE sober.
11 *the partridges were pretty high* **gamy**, smelly, strong-smelling; stinking, reeking, rank, malodorous, going bad, going off, off, rotting, spoiled, tainted; *Brit. informal* pongy, niffy, whiffy; *N. Amer. informal* funky; *literary* noisome, miasmic.
OPPOSITES fresh; aromatic.
□ **high and dry** *your family would be left high and dry by the death of the breadwinner* **destitute**, bereft, helpless, without help, without assistance, without resources, in the lurch, in difficulties, forsaken, abandoned, stranded, marooned.
OPPOSITE well provided for.
□ **high and mighty** (*informal*) *her family were high and mighty and gave themselves airs* **self-important**, condescending, patronizing, disdainful, supercilious, superior, snobbish, snobby, haughty, arrogant, proud, conceited, above oneself, egotistic, egotistical, imperious, overweening, overbearing; *informal* stuck-up, snooty, snotty, hoity-toity, la-di-da, uppity, uppish, too big for one's boots; *Brit. informal* posh, toffee-nosed.
OPPOSITES unassuming, modest.
□ **in high dudgeon**. *See* DUDGEON.
▶ **noun** *commodity prices were actually at a rare high* **high level**, high point, record level, peak, record, high water mark; top, pinnacle, zenith, apex, acme, apogee, apotheosis, culmination, climax, height, summit.
OPPOSITE low.
□ **on a high** (*informal*) *he was on a high following his team's triumph* **ecstatic**, euphoric, delirious, elated, thrilled, overjoyed, beside oneself, walking on air, on cloud nine/seven, in seventh heaven, jumping for joy, in transports of delight, carried away, transported, rapturous, in raptures, exultant, jubilant, in a frenzy of delight; excited, overexcited, hysterical, wild with excitement, frenzied; *informal* blissed out, over the moon, on top of the world; *N. Amer. informal* wigged out; *Austral./NZ informal* wrapped; *rare* corybantic.
OPPOSITE depressed.
▶ **adverb** *a jet was flying high overhead* **at great height**, high up, far up, way up, at altitude; in the air, in the sky, on high, aloft, overhead, above one's head, over one's head.
OPPOSITE low.
□ **high and low** *we searched for her high and low* **everywhere**, all over, all around, in all places, in every place, far and wide, far and near, {here, there, and everywhere}, extensively, exhaustively, thoroughly, widely, broadly, in every nook and cranny; *informal* all over the place, every which way; *Brit. informal* all over the shop; *N. Amer. informal* all over the map.
OPPOSITE in a cursory way.

WORD LINKS
fear of high places **acrophobia, hypsophobia**
fear of high buildings **batophobia**

high-born ▶ **adjective** *a high-born Portuguese family* **noble**, aristocratic, of noble birth, noble-born, well born, titled, patrician, blue-blooded, upper-class; *Brit.* county; *informal* posh, upper-crust, top-drawer; *archaic* gentle, of gentle birth.
OPPOSITES plebeian, working-class.

highbrow ▶ **adjective** *innovatory art had a small, mostly highbrow following* **intellectual**, scholarly, bookish, cultured, cultivated, academic, educated, studious, serious, donnish, bluestocking, well read, widely read, well informed, sophisticated, erudite, learned; *informal* brainy, egghead; *archaic* lettered, clerkly.
OPPOSITES lowbrow, unsophisticated.
▶ **noun** *highbrows who squirm when they hear popular music* **intellectual**, scholar, academic, bluestocking, bookish person, man/woman of letters, don, thinker, pedant; *informal* egghead, brain, bookworm; *Brit. informal* brainbox, boffin; *N. Amer. informal* brainiac, rocket scientist, Brahmin.
OPPOSITES lowbrow, philistine.

high-class ▶ **adjective** *a high-class boarding school* **superior**, upper-class, first-rate, high-quality, top-quality, high-grade, excellent, select, elite, exclusive, choice, premier, top, top-flight, grade A; luxurious, de luxe, elegant, fancy; *Brit.* upmarket; *N. Amer.* high-toned; *informal* tip-top, top-notch, top-drawer, A1, super, super-duper, classy, posh; *Brit. informal* top-hole; *Austral./NZ informal* bonzer; *Brit. informal, dated* spiffing, topping.
OPPOSITES low-class, ordinary.

higher-up ▶ **noun** (*informal*) *he gave staff a vacation without getting approval from higher-ups* **superior**, senior, supervisor, controller, overseer, administrator, manager, boss, chief, superintendent; *informal* bossman, skipper; *Brit. informal* gaffer, guv'nor; *N. Amer. informal* honcho.
OPPOSITE subordinate.

highfalutin ▶ **adjective** (*informal*) *the report was cloaked in highfalutin language* **pretentious**, affected, high-sounding, high-flown, lofty, grandiose, magniloquent grandiloquent, ornate, florid, flowery, overblown, overdone, overwrought, verbose, inflated, rhetorical, oratorical, turgid; **pompous**, bombastic, declamatory, sonorous, portentous, pedantic, boastful, boasting, bragging; *informal* windy, purple, la-di-da, hoity-toity; *Brit. informal* poncey, posh; *rare* fustian, euphuistic, orotund, tumid.
OPPOSITE unpretentious.

high-flown ▶ **adjective** *his novels seem high-flown and absurd* **grand-sounding**, high-sounding, extravagant, exaggerated, elaborate, flowery,

florid, ornate, overblown, overdone, overwrought, grandiloquent, magniloquent, grandiose, lofty, rhetorical, oratorical, verbose, inflated, affected, pretentious, turgid, bombastic, declamatory; *informal* windy, purple, highfalutin, la-di-da; *rare* fustian, euphuistic, orotund, tumid.
OPPOSITE plain.

high-handed ▶ adjective *people are becoming disenchanted with his high-handed approach* **imperious**, arbitrary, peremptory, arrogant, haughty, domineering, bossy, overbearing, overweening, heavy-handed, high and mighty, lordly, inflexible, rigid; **autocratic**, authoritarian, dictatorial, oppressive, repressive, despotic, tyrannical; *informal* pushy, cocky; *rare* pushful.
OPPOSITE liberal.

high jinks ▶ plural noun *they get up to all kinds of high jinks on their trips away* **antics**, **pranks**, larks, escapades, stunts, practical jokes, tricks, romps, frolics; **fun**, fun and games, skylarking, mischief, horseplay, silliness, foolish behaviour, tomfoolery, foolery, clowning, buffoonery; *informal* shenanigans, capers; *Brit. informal* monkey tricks, monkey business; *N. Amer. informal* didoes; *archaic* harlequinades.

highland ▶ noun *Peru's Andean highland* **uplands**, highlands, mountains, hills, heights, moors, hilly country, mountainous region; plateau, upland, tableland, mesa, elevated plain, ridge; *Brit.* wolds.
OPPOSITE lowland.

highlight ▶ noun **1** *he views that season as the highlight of his career* **high point**, high spot, best part, climax, culmination, peak, pinnacle, height, top, acme, zenith, apex, summit, apogee, apotheosis, crowning moment, high water mark, most memorable part, most outstanding feature; *Latin* ne plus ultra.
OPPOSITES lowest point, nadir.
2 *the highlight of the lunch will be a speech by the minister* **main feature**, focal point, focus, focus of attention, centre of interest, most interesting part, cynosure.
▶ verb *this has highlighted a number of shortcomings in the technical arrangements* **call attention to**, focus attention on, focus on, spotlight, foreground, underline, underscore, feature, point up, play up, show up, bring out, accentuate, accent, give prominence to, bring to the fore, zero in on, bring home to one, stress, emphasize, place emphasis on, give emphasis to.
OPPOSITE play down.

highly ▶ adverb **1** *a highly dangerous substance* **very**, most, really, thoroughly, extremely, exceedingly, particularly, tremendously, hugely, greatly, decidedly, distinctly, exceptionally, immensely, eminently, supremely, inordinately, singularly, extraordinarily, vastly, overly; very much, to a great extent; *Scottish* unco; *French* très; *N. English* right; *informal* terrifically, awfully, terribly, devilishly, madly, majorly, seriously, desperately, mega, ultra, oh-so, too-too, stinking, mucho, damn, damned, too ... for words; *informal, dated* devilish, hellish, frightfully; *Brit. informal* ever so, well, bloody, dead, dirty, jolly, fair; *N. Amer. informal* real, mighty, powerful, awful, plumb, darned, way, bitching; *S. African informal* lekker; *archaic* exceeding, sore.
OPPOSITE slightly.
2 *he was highly regarded by his colleagues* **favourably**, well, warmly, appreciatively, admiringly, approvingly, positively, glowingly, enthusiastically, with praise, with admiration, with approbation.
OPPOSITES unfavourably, disparagingly.

highly strung ▶ adjective *a young artist with a highly strung temperament* **nervous**, nervy, excitable, temperamental, sensitive, unstable, brittle, easily upset, easily agitated, on edge, edgy, jumpy, keyed up, irritable, fidgety, restive, restless, anxious, overanxious, tense, taut, stressed, overwrought, neurotic; *informal* uptight, twitchy, wired, wound up, het up; *Brit. informal* strung up; *Austral./NZ informal* toey; *dated* overstrung.
OPPOSITE easy-going.

high-minded ▶ adjective *high-minded civil libertarians* **high-principled**, principled, honourable, moral, upright, upstanding, right-minded, right-thinking, noble-minded, good, honest, decent, ethical, righteous, virtuous, worthy, idealistic.
OPPOSITE unprincipled.

high-mindedness ▶ noun *he had a reputation for honour and high-mindedness* **integrity**, **principle**, honour, honourableness, morals, morality, uprightness, right-mindedness, noble-mindedness, decency, goodness, honesty, righteousness, rectitude, probity, virtue, nobility, scrupulousness, incorruptibility.
OPPOSITE dishonourableness.

high-pitched ▶ adjective *his voice was high-pitched* **high**, high-frequency, soprano, treble, falsetto, shrill, acute, sharp, piping, piercing, penetrating.
OPPOSITES low-pitched, deep.

high-powered ▶ adjective *the women described themselves as high-powered careerists* **dynamic**, energetic, ambitious, go-ahead, assertive, fast-track, effective, enterprising, vigorous, forceful, aggressive, pushy, pushing, driving; *informal* go-getting, full of get-up-and-go, high-octane; *N. Amer. informal* go-go.
OPPOSITE unambitious.

high-pressure ▶ adjective *unscrupulous salesmen using high-pressure tactics* **forceful**, insistent, persistent, persuasive, pressurizing, pushy, pushing, intensive, high-powered, importunate, aggressive, bludgeoning, coercive, compelling, thrusting, not taking no for an answer; *rare* pushful.
OPPOSITE laid-back.

high-priced ▶ adjective *there is a growing market for high-priced wines* **expensive**, costly, high-cost, dear, overpriced, exorbitant, extortionate, immoderate, extravagant; *Brit.* upmarket, over the odds; *informal* pricey, steep, stiff, costing an arm and a leg, costing the earth, costing a bomb.
OPPOSITE inexpensive.

high-sounding ▶ adjective *they clouded the issues with high-sounding words* **grand-sounding**, grandiloquent, magniloquent, high-flown, extravagant, exaggerated, elaborate, flowery, florid, ornate, overblown, overdone, overwrought, grandiose, lofty, rhetorical, oratorical; verbose, inflated, affected, pretentious, turgid, bombastic, declamatory; *informal* windy, purple, highfalutin, la-di-da; *rare* fustian, euphuistic, orotund, tumid.
OPPOSITE plain.

high-speed ▶ adjective *a modern high-speed train operates between the major cities* **fast**, fast-moving, quick, rapid, speedy, swift, breakneck, lightning, whistle-stop, brisk, prompt, expeditious; turbo, sporty; express, non-stop, direct, uninterrupted; *informal* nippy, zippy, souped-up, supersonic; *rare* fleet, tantivy, alacritous, volant.
OPPOSITES slow; indirect.

high-spirited ▶ adjective *he is just an ordinary, high-spirited little boy* **lively**, spirited, full of life, full of fun, fun-loving, animated, vibrant, vital, zestful, dynamic, active, energetic, vigorous, boisterous, bouncy, bubbly, sparkling, vivacious, effervescent, buoyant, cheerful, joyful, exuberant, ebullient, jaunty, irrepressible; *informal* chirpy, peppy, sparky, bright-eyed and bushy-tailed, bright and breezy, full of beans, full of vim and vigour; *N. Amer. informal* peart; *archaic* frolicsome.
OPPOSITES lifeless, apathetic.

high spirits ▶ plural noun *they were young, strong, and bursting with high spirits* **liveliness**, vitality, spirit, spiritedness, animation, zest, dynamism, energy, vigour, boisterousness, bounciness, sparkle, vivacity, buoyancy, cheerfulness, good cheer, good humour, joy, joyfulness, exuberance, ebullience, verve; *French* joie de vivre; *informal* go, pep, oomph, pizzazz, zing, zip, fizz.
OPPOSITES lifelessness, apathy.

highwayman ▶ noun (*historical*) **bandit**, brigand, robber, outlaw, ruffian, desperado, plunderer, marauder, raider, ravager, pillager, freebooter, criminal, thug, gangster; *Spanish* bandolero, ladrone; *Indian* dacoit; *informal, dated* knight of the road, footpad, land-pirate, tobyman; *archaic* reaver, snaphance, thief errant; *Scottish archaic* mosstrooper.

hijack ▶ verb *three armed men hijacked a white van* **commandeer**, seize, take over, take possession of, skyjack; appropriate, expropriate, confiscate; *informal* snatch.

hike ▶ noun *a 21-mile hike on the North Yorkshire Moors* **walk**, trek, tramp, trudge, traipse, slog, footslog, plod, march, journey on foot; ramble, wander, stroll; *Brit. informal* yomp; *archaic* peregrination, perambulation.
OPPOSITE drive.
▶ verb *they hiked across the moors for miles* **walk**, go on foot, trek, tramp, trudge, traipse, slog, footslog, plod, march; ramble, wander, stroll; *informal* hoof it, leg it, take Shanks's pony; *Brit. informal* yomp, trog; *rare* peregrinate, perambulate.
OPPOSITE drive.
□ **hike something up 1** *Roy hiked up his trousers to reveal his socks* **hitch up**, pull up, jerk up, lift, raise, hoist; *informal* yank up.
OPPOSITE pull down.
2 *the government hiked up the price of milk by 40 per cent* **increase**, raise, up, put up, mark up, push up, make higher, inflate; *informal* jack up, bump up; *dated* advance.
OPPOSITE lower.

hilarious ▶ adjective **1** *she told hilarious stories about her friends* **very funny**, extremely amusing, hysterically funny, hysterical, uproarious, riotous, farcical, side-splitting, rib-tickling, too funny for words; humorous, entertaining, comic; *informal* priceless, a scream, a hoot; *dated* killing, killingly funny.
OPPOSITE sad.
2 *we had a really hilarious evening* **amusing**, entertaining, animated, high-spirited, lively, funny, witty, droll, merry, jolly, jovial, jocular, mirthful, cheerful, vivacious, sparkling, uproarious, boisterous, noisy, rowdy; *informal* wacky.
OPPOSITE serious.

hilarity ▶ noun *his incredulous expression was the cause of much hilarity* **amusement**, mirth, laughter, merriment, light-heartedness, levity, fun, humour, jocularity, jollity, joviality, gaiety, delight, glee, comedy, frivolity, exuberance, boisterousness, high spirits; *dated* sport.
OPPOSITE seriousness.

hill ▶ noun **1** *he lived in a big house at the top of the hill* **high ground**, rising ground, prominence, eminence, elevation, rise, hillock, mound, mount,

knoll, hummock, tor, tump, fell, pike, mesa; bank, ridge, hogback, saddleback, whaleback; (**hills**) **heights**, downs, downland, foothills; *Geology* drumlin, inselberg, monadnock; *Brit.* wold; *Scottish & Irish* drum; *Scottish* brae; *N. Amer. or technical* butte; *S. African* koppie, berg; (*in N. Africa & the Middle East*) jebel; *archaic* holt.
OPPOSITE plain.
2 *they were climbing a steep hill in low gear* **slope**, rise, drop, incline, gradient, elevation, acclivity, declivity, ascent, descent, eminence, hillside, hillock, sloping ground, rising ground.
OPPOSITE flat ground.
3 *a hill of rubbish* **heap**, pile, stack, mass, mound, mountain, quantity, load; *Scottish, Irish, & N. English* rickle; *Scottish* bing; *rare* amassment.

hillock ▶ noun **mound**, small hill, prominence, eminence, elevation, rise, knoll, hummock, hump, tump, dune, barrow, tumulus; bank, ridge; *N. English* howe; *N. Amer.* knob; *S. African* koppie; *archaic* knap, monticle.

hilt ▶ noun **handle**, haft, handgrip, grip, shaft, shank, stock, helve.
OPPOSITES head, blade.
□ **to the hilt** *we will support our leaders to the hilt* **completely**, fully, wholly, totally, entirely, utterly, unreservedly, unconditionally, in every respect, in all respects, one hundred per cent, every inch, to the full, to the maximum extent, all the way, body and soul, heart and soul.
OPPOSITES partially, to a limited extent.

himself ▶ pronoun
□ **by himself**. *See* BY ONESELF *at* BY.

hind ▶ adjective *the horse shied and stood up on its hind legs* **back**, rear, hinder, hindmost, posterior; *technical* dorsal, caudal, posticous.
OPPOSITES fore, front.

hinder ▶ verb *technical difficulties have hindered our progress* **hamper**, be a hindrance to, obstruct, impede, inhibit, retard, baulk, thwart, foil, baffle, curb, delay, arrest, interfere with, set back, slow down, hold back, hold up, forestall, stop, halt; restrict, restrain, constrain, block, check, curtail, frustrate, cramp, handicap, cripple, hamstring, shackle, fetter, encumber; *informal* stymie; *Brit. informal* throw a spanner in the works of, throw a spoke in the wheel of; *N. Amer. informal* bork, throw a monkey wrench in the works of; *rare* cumber, trammel.
OPPOSITES help; facilitate.

CHOOSE THE RIGHT WORD

hinder, hamper, impede, obstruct

All these words apply to making progress slower or more difficult.

- **Hinder** refers generally to the creation of difficulties or delays that hold people back from doing something or prevent processes from proceeding smoothly (*ministers were suspected of deliberately hindering the progress of the bill*).
- **Hamper** is typically used of physical burdens that weigh someone down or make their movement awkward (*he was laden with parcels and further hampered by an enormous umbrella*), and, by extension, it is applied to problems and handicaps that interfere with effective action (*they were hampered by shortage of funds*). It rarely refers to a deliberate action or has a person as its subject.
- **Impede** refers to slowing something down or getting in the way (*rivers impeded north–south communications | in what ways did economic factors impede progress?*).
- **Obstruct** is used primarily of a physical object that literally blocks the way (*the horse charged between the trees which obstructed its path*). Its use is extended to the typically deliberate creation of non-physical obstacles, making something difficult though usually not impossible (*he was charged with obstructing the police investigation*), and is often used in legal or criminal contexts.

hindmost ▶ adjective *you should all follow the stroke of the hindmost oar in the boat* **furthest back**, last, rear, rearmost, end, endmost, final, tail, aftermost, nearest the rear, at the end, furthest behind.
OPPOSITES first, leading.

hindrance ▶ noun *the bad weather was a major hindrance to the relief effort* **impediment**, obstacle, barrier, bar, obstruction, handicap, block, check, curb, brake, hurdle, restraint, restriction, limitation, encumbrance, deterrent, complication, delay, interruption, stoppage; drawback, setback, difficulty, inconvenience, snag, catch, hitch, stumbling block; *informal* fly in the ointment, hiccup, facer; *Brit. informal* spanner in the works; *N. Amer. informal* monkey wrench in the works; *literary* trammel, cumber.
OPPOSITES help; advantage.

hinge ▶ verb *the future of the industry could* **hinge on** *the outcome of next month's election* **depend**, hang, rest, turn, pivot, centre, be based, be contingent, be dependent, be conditional; be subject to, be determined by, be decided by, revolve around.

hint ▶ noun **1** *he had given no hint that he was going to leave* **clue**, inkling, suggestion, indication, indicator, sign, signal, pointer, intimation, insinuation, innuendo, mention, allusion, whisper, a word to the wise.
2 *handy hints about what to buy* **tip**, suggestion, piece of advice, word of advice, pointer, clue, cue, guideline, recommendation; advice, help; *informal* how-to, wrinkle.
3 *the wine had a fresh flavour, with a hint of mint* **trace**, touch, suspicion, suggestion, dash, soupçon, tinge, modicum, breath, whiff, taste, scent, whisper, undertone; *informal* smidgen, sniff, tad.
OPPOSITE lashings.
▶ verb *he has hinted that his ambitions lie in Hollywood | what are you hinting at?* **imply**, insinuate, intimate, suggest, indicate, signal, whisper, give a clue, give an inkling, let it be known, allude to the fact, make a reference to the fact, refer to the fact, give someone to understand, give someone to believe; **allude to**, refer to, drive at, mean; *informal* get at.

CHOOSE THE RIGHT WORD

hint, suggestion, innuendo, insinuation

- A **hint** is a message that one person conveys to another without stating it explicitly, often because it is a request or involves something that they are embarrassed to say directly. It may be conveyed verbally or through someone's behaviour (*the girl dropped increasingly blatant hints about her affair | she picked up her book, but Sandra did not take the hint*). *Hint* can also refer to an explicit piece of practical advice or information given (*handy hints for home buyers*) or a trace of something (*smoked gammon with a hint of chilli*).
- A **suggestion** is an idea put forward for consideration without any implication of indirectness or concealment (*he shrugged off suggestions that he was planning to quit politics*). This sense tends to merge with that of a 'piece of advice' (*Louise made her suggestion that Nora leave the girl behind*).
- **Innuendo** is an indirect way of conveying an idea through the undertones and implications of what is said. The message conveyed typically has a sexual content or is to someone's discredit (*walk away, unless you are in the mood to parry age-old male posturings and sexual innuendo | innuendos about his sources of finance*).
- **Insinuation** is the most consistently negative of these words. Whereas *innuendo* may sometimes refer to an exploitation of implicit meanings that is intended simply to amuse, an *insinuation* is always meant to hurt or distress someone by implying (but not directly stating) something to their discredit (*she faced insinuations about the immorality of her private life*).

hinterland ▶ noun *early settlers were driven from the coastal areas into the hinterland* **the back of beyond**, the middle of nowhere, the backwoods, the wilds, the bush, remote areas, a backwater; *Austral./NZ* the outback, the back country, the backblocks, the booay; *S. African* the backveld, the platteland; *informal* the sticks; *N. Amer. informal* the boondocks, the boonies, the tall timbers; *Austral./NZ informal* Woop Woop, beyond the black stump.
OPPOSITE civilization.

hip ▶ adjective (*informal*) *it's becoming hip to be environmentally conscious* **fashionable**, popular, all the rage, in fashion, in vogue, up to the minute; *informal*, trendy, cool, with it, in, hot, big, happening, now, groovy, funky, sharp, the in thing; *N. Amer. informal* kicky, tony, fly; *black English* down; *Brit. informal, dated* swagger.
OPPOSITES unfashionable, unpopular.

hippy ▶ noun **flower child**, bohemian, dropout, free spirit, nonconformist, unconventional person; (**hippies**) flower people.

hips ▶ plural noun **pelvis**, hindquarters, haunches, thighs, loins, buttocks, posterior, rear.

WORD LINKS
relating to the hips **sciatic**

hire ▶ verb **1** *we hired a car and drove to Wales* **rent**, lease, charter, pay for the use of; *dated* engage.
OPPOSITE buy.
2 *management hired and fired labour in line with demand* **employ**, engage, recruit, appoint, take on, sign on, sign up, enrol, commission, enlist, take into employment, secure the services of, put on the payroll.
OPPOSITE dismiss.
▶ noun *the agreed rate for the hire of the machine* **rent**, rental, hiring, lease, leasing, charter; *dated* engagement, engaging.
OPPOSITE purchase.

hire purchase ▶ noun *these schemes are a flexible form of hire purchase* **instalment plan**, instalment-payment plan, HP, credit, finance, instalments, deferred payment, easy terms; *N. Amer.* instalment buying; *Brit. informal* the never-never.

hirsute ▶ adjective *the rest of his body was similarly hirsute* **hairy**, shaggy, bushy, hair-covered, long-haired, woolly, furry, fleecy, fuzzy; bearded, unshaven, unshorn, bewhiskered, stubbly, bristly; *technical* pilose, pileous, pappose, hispid; *rare* crinite, crinigerous.
OPPOSITES hairless; short-haired.

hiss ▶ verb **1** *the escaping gas was now hissing* **fizz**, fizzle, whistle, wheeze, buzz, shrill; *rare* sibilate.
2 *the audience hissed loudly at the mention of his name* **jeer**, catcall, utter catcalls, whistle, shout disapproval; scoff, taunt, hoot, jibe, deride; *informal* blow raspberries.
OPPOSITE cheer.
▶ noun **1** *the hiss of the escaping steam* **fizz**, fizzing, whistle, hissing, sibilance, wheeze, wheezing, buzz, buzzing; *rare* sibilation.
2 *the speaker received hisses and boos* **jeer**, catcall, whistle, shout of derision, raspberry; (**hisses**) abuse, scoffing, taunting, derision; *Brit. informal* the bird.
OPPOSITE cheer.

historian ▶ noun **chronicler**, annalist, archivist, recorder, biographer, historiographer, palaeographer, antiquarian, chronologist.

historic ▶ adjective *we are standing on a historic site | historic events* **famous**, famed, important, significant, notable, celebrated, renowned, momentous, consequential, outstanding, extraordinary, memorable, unforgettable, remarkable, landmark, groundbreaking, epoch-making, red-letter, of importance, of significance, of consequence, earth-shaking, earth-shattering.
OPPOSITE insignificant.

historical ▶ adjective **1** *the historical background to such studies* **documented**, recorded, chronicled, attested, factual, verified, confirmed, archival, authentic, actual, true.
OPPOSITE legendary.
2 *famous historical figures* **past**, bygone, ancient, old, former, prior, from the past; *literary* of yore.
OPPOSITE contemporary.

history ▶ noun **1** *this is a wonderful opportunity to use my interest in history* **the past**, former times, historical events, days of old, the old days, the good old days, time gone by, bygone days, yesterday, antiquity; *literary* days of yore, the olden days, yesteryear; *archaic* the eld.
OPPOSITE the future.
2 *I was reading a history of the Civil War* **chronicle**, archive, record, report, narrative, story, account, study, tale, saga; memoir, biography, autobiography; public records, annals.
3 *Kirsty calmly related the details of her history* **background**, past, family background, life story, antecedents; experiences, adventures, fortunes.

WORD LINKS
Muse **Clio**

histrionic ▶ adjective *a histrionic outburst* **melodramatic**, theatrical, affected, dramatic, exaggerated, actressy, stagy, showy, artificial, overacted, overdone, unnatural, mannered, stilted, unreal; *informal* hammy, ham, camp.
OPPOSITE unaffected.

histrionics ▶ plural noun **dramatics**, drama, theatrics, theatricality, tantrums; **affectation**, staginess, artificiality, unnaturalness.

hit ▶ verb **1** *the woman hit her child for stealing sweets* **strike**, slap, smack, cuff, punch, beat, thrash, thump, batter, belabour, drub, hook, pound, smash, slam, welt, pummel, hammer, bang, knock, swat, whip, flog, cane, sucker-punch, rain blows on, give someone a (good) beating/drubbing, box someone's ears; *informal* whack, wallop, bash, biff, bop, clout, clip, clobber, sock, swipe, crown, lick, beat the living daylights out of, give someone a (good) hiding, belt, tan, lay one on, lay into, pitch into, lace into, let someone have it, knock into the middle of next week, lam, whomp, deck, floor; *Brit. informal* stick one on, dot, slosh, twat; *N. Amer. informal* slug, boff, bust, whale; *Austral./NZ informal* dong, quilt, king-hit; *literary* smite, swinge; *dated* baste, buffet, birch.
2 *a car hit the barrier* **crash into**, run into, bang into, smash into, smack into, knock into, bump into, cannon into, plough into, collide with, meet head-on; *N. Amer.* impact; *N. Amer. informal* barrel into.
3 *the banking sector has been hit by the recession | the tragedy has hit her hard* **affect badly**, devastate, damage, harm, hurt, ruin, leave a mark on, have a negative effect on, have a negative impact on, do harm to, impinge on; **upset**, shatter, crush, shock, overwhelm, traumatize, touch, make suffer; *informal* knock back, knock for six, knock sideways, knock the stuffing out of.
OPPOSITE have no effect on.
4 (*informal*) *capital spending this year is likely to hit £1,800 million* **reach**, attain, touch, arrive at, get to, rise to, climb to; achieve, accomplish, gain, secure.
OPPOSITE fall to.
5 *I was a mile away when it hit me that I had forgotten to get the information I needed* **occur to**, strike, dawn on, come to; enter one's head, enter one's mind, cross one's mind, come to mind, spring to mind, flash across one's mind, come into one's consciousness.
□ **hit back** *prison officers hit back at the critical report* **retaliate against**, respond to, reply to, react to, strike back at, counter, defend oneself against; *rare* controvert.
OPPOSITE turn the other cheek.
□ **hit home** *she could see that her remark had hit home* **have the intended effect**, make the intended impression, strike home, hit the mark, be registered, be understood, be comprehended, get through, sink in.
OPPOSITE have no effect.
□ **hit it off** (*informal*) *they make an unlikely pair, but they've always hit it off* **get on well**, get on, get along, be on good terms, be friends, be friendly, be compatible, relate well to each other, feel a rapport, see eye to eye, take to each other, warm to each other, find things in common; *informal* click, get on like a house on fire, be on the same wavelength.
OPPOSITE rub someone up the wrong way.
□ **hit on/upon** *she hit on a novel idea for fund-raising* **discover**, come up with, think of, conceive of, dream up, work out, invent, create, originate, develop, devise, design, pioneer, uncover, contrive, realize; stumble on, chance on, light on, come upon, blunder on, arrive at; *informal* put one's finger on.
□ **hit out at** *he hit out at the government's lack of action* **criticize**, attack, denounce, lash out at, rant at, inveigh against, rail against, fulminate against, run down, find fault with; condemn, censure, harangue, berate, upbraid, castigate, vilify, malign, assail, lambaste; *informal* knock, slam, hammer, blast, lay into, pitch into, lace into, bawl out, bad-mouth, tear someone off a strip, give someone hell, give someone a roasting; *Brit. informal* slate, slag off, have a go at, rubbish; *N. Amer. informal* pummel, cut up; *Austral./NZ informal* bag, monster; *dated* rate, reprobate; *rare* vituperate, excoriate, arraign, objurgate, asperse, anathematize, animadvert on, denunciate.
OPPOSITE praise.
▶ noun **1** *he took a few minutes to recover after a hit from behind | few structures can withstand a hit from a speeding car* **blow**, thump, punch, knock, bang, thwack, box, cuff, slap, smack, spank, tap, crack, stroke, welt; impact, collision, bump, crash; *informal* whack, wallop, bash, belt, biff, clout, sock, swipe, clip, clobber; *Brit. informal* slosh; *N. Amer. informal* boff, bust, slug, whale; *Austral./NZ* dong; *dated* buffet.
2 *he could not resist a hit at his friend's religiosity* **jibe**, taunt, jeer, sneer, barb, cutting remark, barbed remark, attack, insult; *informal* dig, put-down, crack, wisecrack.
OPPOSITE compliment.
3 *he was the director of many big hits* **success**, box-office success, sell-out, winner, triumph, sensation; best-seller; *French* tour de force; *informal* knockout, crowd-puller, smash, smash hit, smasher, cracker, wow, biggie.
OPPOSITES failure, flop.

hitch ▶ verb **1** *she hitched the blanket around her* **pull**, jerk, hike, lift, raise; *informal* yank.
2 *Thomas hitched the pony to his cart* **harness**, yoke, couple, fasten, connect, attach, tie, tether, bind.
OPPOSITE unhitch.
3 (*informal*) *they hitched there and back* **hitch-hike**; *informal* thumb a lift, hitch a lift.
▶ noun *everything went without a hitch* **problem**, difficulty, snag, setback, catch, hindrance, obstacle, obstruction, complication, impediment, barrier, stumbling block, block, trouble; **hold-up**, interruption, delay, check, stoppage; *informal* headache, glitch, hiccup; *Brit. informal* spanner in the works; *N. Amer. informal* monkey wrench in the works.

hither ▶ adverb (*literary*) *a change of fortune summoned me hither* **here**, to this place, to this spot, to this location, to here, over here, near, nearer, close, closer.

hitherto ▶ adverb *hitherto a part of French West Africa, Benin achieved independence in 1960* **previously**, formerly, earlier, so far, thus far, before, beforehand, to date, as yet; until now, until then, up until now, up until then, till now, till then, up to now, up to then; *rare* heretofore.

hit-or-miss ▶ adjective *her work can be rather hit-or-miss* **haphazard**, disorganized, undisciplined, erratic, unmethodical, uneven, careless, slapdash, slipshod, casual, offhand, remiss, cursory, lackadaisical, perfunctory, random, aimless, undirected, indiscriminate, trial-and-error; *informal* sloppy, all over the place, slap-happy; *Brit. informal* all over the shop.
OPPOSITES meticulous, systematic.

hoard ▶ noun *they found a secret hoard of paintings and porcelain* **cache**, stockpile, stock, store, collection, supply, reserve, reservoir, fund, accumulation, heap, pile, mass, aggregation, conglomeration, treasure house, treasure trove; *informal* stash; *rare* amassment.
▶ verb *many of the boat people had hoarded rations* **store**, store up, stock up on, stockpile, put aside, put by, put away, lay by, lay in, lay up, set aside, stow away, buy up, cache, amass, heap up, pile up, stack up; **collect**, save, gather, garner, accumulate, husband, squirrel away, put to one side, put away for a rainy day; *informal* stash away, salt away.
OPPOSITE squander.

hoard or horde?
These words are quite distinct in meaning despite their identical pronunciation. A **hoard** is a secret stock or store of something, as in *a hoard of treasure*. **Horde**, on the other hand, is a disparaging word for a large group of people, as in *hordes of fans descended on the stage*.

hoarder ▶ noun **collector**, saver, gatherer, accumulator, magpie, squirrel.

hoar frost ▶ **noun** **frost**, ground frost, rime, rime frost, verglas; *informal* Jack Frost; *archaic* hoar.

hoarse ▶ **adjective** *their voices were hoarse from shouting* **rough**, harsh, croaky, croaking, throaty, gruff, husky, guttural, gravelly, growly, cracked, grating, rasping, raucous; *rare* stridulant.
OPPOSITES mellow; soft.

hoary ▶ **adjective 1** *majestic old oaks and hoary willows* **greyish-white**, grey, white, silver, silvery; frost-covered, frosty, rimy.
2 *he began to think of himself as a hoary ancient* **elderly**, aged, old, getting on, ancient, venerable, long in the tooth, of an advanced age, advanced in years; grey-haired, white-haired, silvery-haired, grizzled, grizzly; *informal* past it, over the hill; *rare* longevous, senescent.
OPPOSITE young.
3 *the hoary old adage often used by Fleet Street editors* **trite**, hackneyed, clichéd, banal, platitudinous, vapid, ordinary, commonplace, common, stock, conventional, stereotyped, predictable, overused, overdone, overworked, stale, worn out, time-worn, tired, threadbare, hack, unimaginative, unoriginal, derivative, uninspired, prosaic, routine, pedestrian, run-of-the-mill; *informal* old hat, corny, played out; *N. Amer. informal* cornball, dime-store; *rare* truistic, bromidic.
OPPOSITE original.

hoax ▶ **noun** *they recognized the plan as a hoax* **practical joke**, joke, jest, prank, trick, jape; **ruse**, deception, fraud, imposture, cheat, swindle, bluff, humbug, confidence trick; *informal* con, spoof, scam, fast one, put-on.
▶ **verb** *on April 1st the radio station hoaxed its listeners* **play a practical joke on**, play a joke on, play a jest on, play a prank on, trick, fool; **deceive**, hoodwink, delude, dupe, take in, lead on, cheat, bluff, gull, humbug; *informal* con, kid, have on, pull a fast one on, put one over on, take for a ride, lead someone up the garden path, pull the wool over someone's eyes; *informal, dated* gammon; *N. Amer. informal* sucker, snooker, hornswoggle; *Austral. informal* pull a swifty on; *vulgar slang* bullshit; *archaic* cozen.

hoaxer ▶ **noun** **practical joker**, joker, prankster, trickster; fraudster, impostor, hoodwinker, swindler, cheat, confidence trickster; *informal* spoofer, con man; *N. Amer. informal* bunco artist; *Austral. informal* illywhacker.

hobble ▶ **verb** *he was hobbling around on crutches* **limp**, walk with a limp, walk with difficulty, move unsteadily, walk unevenly, walk lamely, walk haltingly; shuffle, shamble, falter, totter, dodder, stagger, stumble, reel, lurch; *Scottish* hirple.
OPPOSITE stride.

hobby ▶ **noun** *her hobbies are reading and gardening* **pastime**, leisure activity, leisure pursuit, leisure interest, amateur interest, sideline, diversion, avocation, divertissement, enthusiasm; recreation, relaxation, entertainment, amusement; *informal* thing.
OPPOSITES work, job.

hobgoblin ▶ **noun** **imp**, sprite, goblin, elf, brownie, pixie, leprechaun, gnome, dwarf; bogey, bogeyman, troll, evil spirit; *Scottish* kelpie; *rare* hob, nix, nixie, elfin.

hobnob ▶ **verb** (*informal*) *he was hobnobbing with the great and good* **associate**, mix, fraternize, socialize, go around, keep company, spend time, mingle, consort, rub shoulders; *N. Amer.* rub elbows; *informal* hang around/round/out, run around, knock about/around, pal up, pal around, chum around, be thick with.

hocus-pocus ▶ **noun 1** *he is a master of legal hocus-pocus* **jargon**, unintelligible language, obscure language, mumbo-jumbo, argle-bargle, gibberish, balderdash, claptrap, nonsense, rubbish, twaddle; *informal* gobbledegook, double Dutch, hokum, bull, rot, garbage, tripe; *N. Amer. informal* flapdoodle; *informal, dated* bunkum.
2 *the hocus-pocus was just for the show* **magic words**, magic formula, mumbo-jumbo, abracadabra, incantation, chant, invocation, charm.

hodgepodge ▶ **noun**. See HOTCHPOTCH.

hog ▶ **noun** **pig**, sow, swine, porker, piglet, boar; *children's word* piggy; *rare* grunter, baconer.
▶ **verb** (*informal*) *he never hogged the limelight* **monopolize**, keep to oneself, dominate, take over, corner, control; *N. Amer. informal* bogart.
OPPOSITE share.

hogwash ▶ **noun** (*informal*) *some of the statements in the article are undiluted hogwash*. See NONSENSE.

hoi polloi ▶ **noun** (**the hoi polloi**) *royalty are reluctant to let the hoi polloi into their homes* **the masses**, the common people, the populace, the public, the people, the multitude, the rank and file, the lower orders, the crowd, the commonality, the commonalty, the commons, the third estate, the plebeians; *derogatory* the mob, the proletariat, the common herd, the herd, the rabble, the riff-raff, the canaille, the great unwashed, the many, the ragtag (and bobtail), the plebs, the proles, the peasants.
OPPOSITES the elite, the aristocracy.

hoist ▶ **verb** *as we travelled north we hoisted a large mainsail* **raise**, raise up, lift, lift up, haul up, heave up, jack up, hike up, winch up, pull up, upraise, uplift, elevate, erect; *rare* upheave.
OPPOSITE lower.
▶ **noun** *mechanical lifts or hoists for firefighting purposes* **lifting gear**, crane, winch, tackle, block and tackle, pulley, windlass, davit, derrick.

hoity-toity ▶ **adjective** (*informal*) *he's too hoity-toity to make friends with his fellow cadets* **snobbish**, haughty, condescending, disdainful, patronizing, snobby, conceited, proud, arrogant, supercilious, superior, imperious, above oneself, self-important, overweening, lordly, lofty; *informal* high and mighty, snooty, uppity, uppish, la-di-da; *Brit. informal* toffee-nosed, posh.
OPPOSITES modest, unassuming.

hold ▶ **verb 1** *she was holding a brown leather suitcase* **clasp**, hold on to, clutch, grasp, grip, clench, cling to, have in one's hand; **carry**, bear; *literary* cleave to.
OPPOSITES release, let go of.
2 *I wanted to hold her in my arms* **embrace**, hug, clasp, cradle, fold, enfold, envelop, squeeze, hold tight, hold in one's arms; *literary* embosom.
3 *candidates must hold a clean driving licence* **possess**, have, own, bear, carry, be the owner of, have in one's possession, be in possession of, have to one's name.
4 *I reached up to the nearest branch which seemed likely to hold my weight* **support**, bear, carry, take, hold up, keep up, sustain, prop up, bolster up, shore up, buttress, brace.
5 *the police were holding him on a murder charge* **detain**, hold in custody, imprison, lock up, shut up, put behind bars, put in prison, put in jail, incarcerate, keep under lock and key, confine, impound, immure, intern, constrain, keep under constraint; *informal* put away, put inside.
OPPOSITE let go.
6 *their minimal costumes are a way of holding an audience's attention* **maintain**, keep, keep up, keep alive, occupy, engross, absorb, interest, captivate, fascinate, enthral, rivet, monopolize; engage, catch, capture, grip, arrest.
OPPOSITE lose.
7 *he held a senior post in the Foreign Office* **occupy**, have, be in, fill; *informal* hold down.
8 *the tank held twenty-four gallons | the church is big enough to hold 400 people* **have a capacity of**, take, have room for, have space for, contain, comprise; **accommodate**, fit, seat, have seats for.
9 *they hold that all literature is empty of meaning | the Court of Appeal held that there was no evidence to support the judge's assessment* **believe**, think, consider, take the view, feel, maintain, swear, deem, be of the opinion, subscribe to the opinion; **adjudge**, judge, rule, decide; *N. Amer.* figure; *informal* reckon; *formal* esteem, opine.
10 *let's hope the good weather holds for the rest of the week* **continue**, carry on, go on, hold on, hold out, keep up, keep going, last, persist, endure, stay, remain, remain unchanged.
OPPOSITE end.
11 *I'll have that coffee now, if the offer still holds* **remain available**, remain valid, remain in force, hold good, stand, apply, remain, exist, operate, obtain, be the case, be in force, be in operation, be in effect.
OPPOSITE be no longer valid.
12 *the president held a meeting with party leaders* **convene**, call, assemble, summon; **conduct**, have, organize, run, preside over, officiate at; *formal* convoke.
OPPOSITE disband.
□ **hold back** *he held back, remembering the mistake he had made before* **hesitate**, pause, stop oneself, restrain oneself, desist, forbear, discontinue, withhold from doing something, refrain from doing something.
OPPOSITE carry on.
□ **hold someone back** *my lack of experience held me back a bit* **hinder**, hamper, inhibit, impede, obstruct, check, curb, block, thwart, baulk, hamstring, restrain, frustrate, retard, delay, prevent from making progress, stand in someone's way; *informal* stymie; *N. Amer. informal* bork; *literary* trammel.
OPPOSITES help, facilitate.
□ **hold something back 1** *Jane struggled to hold back the tears* **suppress**, keep back, hold in, bite back, fight back, choke back, stifle, smother, subdue, rein in, repress, restrain, check, curb, control, keep in check, keep under control, keep a tight rein on; *informal* keep the lid on, button up, cork up.
OPPOSITE release.
2 *you're not holding anything back from me, are you?* **withhold**, hide, conceal, keep back, keep secret, keep hidden, keep silent about, keep quiet about, hush up, refuse to disclose, suppress; *informal* sit on, keep under one's hat.
OPPOSITE disclose.
□ **hold someone/something dear** *fidelity is something most of us hold dear* **cherish**, treasure, prize, appreciate, value highly, rate highly, care very much for/about, place a high value on, attach great importance to, set great store by; *informal* put on a pedestal.
OPPOSITE think little of.
□ **hold someone down** *the people are held down by a repressive military regime* **oppress**, repress, suppress, subdue, tyrannize, dominate, subjugate, keep down, keep under, keep in subjection, keep in submission.
□ **hold something down 1** *he is determined to hold down inflation* **keep**

down, keep low, keep at a low level, peg down, freeze, fix.
2 (*informal*) *holding down two jobs was proving tiring for him* **occupy**, hold, have, be in, fill.

□ **hold forth** *he was holding forth about the qualities of good wine* **speak at length**, talk at length, speak, talk, go on, sound off; **declaim**, discourse, spout, expatiate, pontificate, orate, preach, sermonize; lecture, harangue, fulminate; *informal* spiel, speechify, preachify, drone on; *rare* perorate.

□ **hold off 1** *fortunately, the rain held off until the evening* **be delayed**, keep off, stay away, not begin, not occur, not happen, not arrive.
OPPOSITE start.
2 *if I was in their shoes, I'd hold off for a couple of days* **wait**, hold back, pause, delay, hang back, hang fire, take no action, bide one's time, play a waiting game; postpone, defer, refrain from, put something off, keep from doing something, avoid doing something; *informal* hold one's horses, sit tight.
OPPOSITE proceed.

□ **hold something off** *he held off a late challenge by Vose to win by thirteen seconds* **resist**, repel, repulse, rebuff, parry, deflect, keep off, fend off, stave off, ward off, keep at bay.
OPPOSITES submit to, be overpowered by.

□ **hold on 1** *hold on a minute, I'll be right back!* **wait**, wait a minute, just a moment, just a second, stay here, stay put, remain here; hold the line; *informal* hang on, hang around, stick around, sit tight, hold your horses; *Brit. informal* hang about; *dated* tarry.
2 *if only they could hold on a little longer* **keep going**, keep on, survive, last, continue, persevere, struggle on, carry on, go on, hang on, hold out, not give up, see it through, stay the course; *informal* soldier on, stick at it, stick it out, hang in there.
OPPOSITE give up.

□ **hold on to 1** *he held on to the back of a chair* **clutch**, hold, hang on to, clasp, grasp, grip, cling to; *literary* cleave to.
OPPOSITES release, let go of.
2 *the industry is trying to hold on to experienced staff* **retain**, keep, hang on to, keep possession of, retain possession of, retain use of, retain ownership of, not sell, not give away, keep for oneself.
OPPOSITE lose.

□ **hold one's own**. *See* OWN.

□ **hold out 1** *British troops* **held out against** *constant attacks* **resist**, withstand, hold off, fight off, fend off, keep off, keep at bay, stand up to, square up to, fight against, bear up against, stand fast against, stand firm against, hold the line against.
OPPOSITE yield to.
2 *we can stay here as long as our supplies hold out* **last**, remain, be extant, continue.
OPPOSITE run out.

□ **hold something out** *Celia held out her hand* **extend**, proffer, offer, present, outstretch, reach out, stretch out, put out, hold forth; *literary* outreach.
OPPOSITE withdraw.

□ **hold something over** *the usual family gathering was held over until late January* **postpone**, put off, put back, delay, defer, adjourn, suspend, shelve, hold in abeyance; *N. Amer.* put over, table, take a rain check on; *informal* put on ice, put on the back burner, put in cold storage, mothball; *rare* remit, respite.
OPPOSITE bring forward.

□ **hold up** *their views still seem to hold up extremely well* **be convincing**, be logical, hold, hold water, bear examination, survive investigation, be verifiable, be provable.
OPPOSITE be unconvincing.

□ **hold something up 1** *they held up the trophy for all to see* **display**, hold aloft, exhibit, show, show off, put on show, present, flourish, flaunt, brandish; *informal* flash.
OPPOSITE keep out of sight.
2 *concrete pillars hold up the elevated section of the motorway* **support**, hold, bear, carry, take, sustain, keep up, prop up, bolster up, shore up, buttress.
3 *our return flight was held up for seven hours* **delay**, detain, make late, set back, keep back, retard, slow down, slow up.
OPPOSITE speed up.
4 *a lack of cash has held up progress* **obstruct**, **impede**, hinder, hamper, inhibit, baulk, thwart, curb, hamstring, frustrate, foil, baffle, be a hindrance to, interfere with, put a brake on, stop; *informal* stymie; *Brit. informal* throw a spanner in the works of, put a spoke in the wheel of; *N. Amer. informal* bork, throw a monkey wrench in the works of.
OPPOSITE facilitate.
5 *a masked raider held up the post office* **rob**, commit armed robbery on, make an armed raid on; waylay, mug; *informal* stick up.

□ **hold water**. *See* WATER.

□ **hold with** *I don't hold with fighting or violence* **approve of**, agree with, be in favour of, go along with, endorse, accept, countenance, support, give support to, subscribe to, give one's blessing to, take kindly to; *informal* stand for, give the thumbs up to, give the okay to; *Brit. informal* be doing with; *N. Amer. rare* approbate.
OPPOSITE disapprove of.

▶ **noun 1** *the little girl kept a firm hold on my hand | he lost his hold and fell* **grip**, grasp, clasp, clutch; **purchase**, foothold, footing, toehold.
2 *he discovered that Tom had some kind of hold over his father* **influence**, power, control, dominance, pull, sway, mastery, authority, leverage; *informal* clout.
3 *military forces tightened their hold on the capital* **control**, grip, power, stranglehold, dominion, authority, ascendancy.

□ **get hold of** (*informal*) **1** *if you can't get hold of ripe tomatoes, add some tomato purée* **obtain**, acquire, get, find, come by, pick up, procure, get possession of; buy, purchase; *informal* get one's hands on, lay one's hands on, get one's mitts on.
2 *I'll try and get hold of Mark* **contact**, get in touch with, communicate with, make contact with, approach, reach, notify, be in communication with; phone, call, speak to, talk to, write to; *Brit.* ring (up), get on to; *informal* drop a line to.

□ **put something on hold** *the proposed rematch has been put on hold* **postpone**, put off, put back, hold off, defer, delay, adjourn, shelve, suspend, hold in abeyance; *N. Amer.* put over, take a rain check on; *informal* put on ice, put on the back burner, put in cold storage, mothball; *rare* remit, respite.
OPPOSITE bring forward.

holder ▶ **noun 1** *a large knife in a leather holder* **container**, receptacle, case, casing, cover, covering, housing, sheath; stand, rest, support, base, rack.
2 *a British passport holder | the holder of the office of commander-in-chief* **bearer**, owner, possessor, keeper, proprietor; **incumbent**, occupant, custodian.

holdings ▶ **plural noun** *they have UK gilts and holdings in offshore funds* **possessions**, belongings, valuables; **stock**, property, capital, estate; **assets**, funds, resources, savings, investments, securities, equities, bonds, stocks and shares, reserves.

hold-up ▶ **noun 1** *I ran into a hold-up and nearly didn't get here* **delay**, setback, hitch, snag, difficulty, problem, trouble, wait, waiting period, stoppage; **traffic jam**, jam, bottleneck, tailback, gridlock, congestion; *informal* snarl-up, glitch, hiccup.
2 *there has been another bank hold-up* **robbery**, raid, armed robbery, armed raid, theft, burglary, mugging; *informal* stick-up, snatch; *N. Amer. informal* heist.

hole ▶ **noun 1** *there was a hole in the roof where the tiles had fallen away* **opening**, aperture, gap, space, orifice, slot, vent, outlet, chink, breach; **break**, crack, leak, rift, rupture; puncture, perforation, cut, incision, split, gash, rent, slit, cleft, crevice, fissure; spyhole, peephole, keyhole; *Medicine* foramen; *archaic* loophole.
2 *they were digging a hole in the ground* **pit**, ditch, trench, cavity, crater, depression, hollow; well, borehole, excavation, shaft, mineshaft, dugout; cave, cavern, pothole, chamber, gorge, chasm, canyon, ravine.
3 *they dug the badger out of his hole* **burrow**, lair, den, covert, earth, sett, drey, retreat, shelter, cave.
4 *the captives were thrown into a black hole* **dungeon**, cell, underground cell, oubliette, prison.
5 *a recent article highlighted some holes in their argument* **flaw**, fault, defect, weakness, weak point, shortcoming, inconsistency, discrepancy, loophole, error, mistake, fallacy.
6 (*informal*) *I was living in a real hole* **hovel**, slum, shack, mess; *informal* dump, dive, pigsty, tip, joint.
OPPOSITE palace.
7 (*informal*) *they have been known to embezzle their clients' money when they are in a hole* **predicament**, difficult situation, awkward situation, mess, corner, tight corner, quandary, dilemma, muddle, emergency, crisis, imbroglio; difficulty, trouble, plight, dire straits; *informal* fix, jam, bind, spot, tight spot, scrape, pickle, sticky situation, hot water, deep water; *Brit. informal* spot of bother.

□ **pick holes in** (*informal*) *it's really not too difficult to pick holes in the plan* **find fault with**, criticize, attack, condemn; disparage, denigrate, deride, belittle, run down, complain about, quibble about, carp about, cavil at, scoff at, moan about, grouse about, grouch about, grumble about, whine about; *informal* knock, bad-mouth, do down, gripe about, beef about, bellyache about, bitch about, whinge about, nit-pick over, sound off about, pull to pieces; *Brit. informal* slag off, have a go at, rubbish.
OPPOSITE praise.

▶ **verb** *a fuel tank was holed by the attack and a fire started* **puncture**, make a hole in, perforate, pierce, penetrate, rupture, spike, stab, split, slit, rent, lacerate, gash, gore.

□ **hole up 1** *it was getting time for the bears to hole up* **hibernate**, lie dormant, winter, overwinter, lie torpid, go to sleep.
2 (*informal*) *the snipers holed up in a nearby farmhouse* **hide**, hide out, hide oneself, conceal oneself, secrete oneself, shelter, take cover, lie low, go to ground, go to earth, go underground; *Brit. informal* lie doggo.
OPPOSITE come out into the open.

hole-and-corner ▶ **adjective** *they expressed regret at the hole-and-corner tactics being used* **secret**, secretive, in secret, private, clandestine; **underhand**, surreptitious, covert, furtive, devious, stealthy, sneaky,

backstairs, closet, undercover, hugger-mugger, cloak-and-dagger, behind-the-scenes, under-the-table, under-the-counter; *informal* hush-hush.
OPPOSITES open, above board.

holiday *See centre pages for list of* **Festivals**
▶ **noun 1** *she took a 10-day holiday* **vacation**, break, rest, period of leave, day off, week off, month off, recess, school holiday, half-term; **time off**, time out, leave, leave of absence, furlough, sabbatical; trip, tour, journey, expedition, voyage; *informal* hols, vac; *formal* sojourn.
OPPOSITES working time; term time.
2 *in Antigua the twenty-fourth of May is a holiday* **public holiday**, bank holiday, festival, festival day, feast day, gala day, carnival day, fête, fiesta, festivity, celebration, anniversary, jubilee; saint's day, holy day, religious festival, day of observance.
OPPOSITE working day.

CHOOSE THE RIGHT WORD

holiday, vacation, leave, break

- **Holiday** denotes a period when someone does not have to work. It can refer to: a day when most businesses are closed by law or custom (*10 June is a public holiday*), a period of time allowed off work (*staff are entitled to 24 working days' holiday per year*), time in between school terms (*the school summer holidays*), or a leisure trip away from home (*a driving holiday in France*).
- **Vacation** is used for the period between two law or university terms (*many students found jobs in the long vacation*), and is in addition the American term for a trip away from home (*your dream vacation in Mexico*).
- **Leave** is time off duty in the armed forces (*Joe was home on leave*) or a formal term for time off work for a variety of reasons (*sick leave | annual leave*).
- A **break** means any sort of pause, a short period of rest from work (*he wanted to talk to her during the coffee break*), or a shorter-than-average leisure trip away from home (*a weekend countryside break*).

holier-than-thou ▶ **adjective** *they had quite a critical, holier-than-thou approach* **sanctimonious**, self-righteous, complacent, smug, self-satisfied, priggish, pious, pietistic, Pharisaic; *Scottish* unco guid; *informal* goody-goody, preachy; *rare* religiose.
OPPOSITES humble, meek.

holiness ▶ **noun** *a life of holiness and total devotion to God* **sanctity**, divinity, godliness, saintliness, sanctitude, sacredness, faith, devotion, devoutness, divineness, blessedness, spirituality, religiousness, piety, piousness, righteousness, goodness, perfection, virtue, virtuousness, purity, sinlessness.
OPPOSITE wickedness.

holler (*informal*) ▶ **verb** *he hollers when he wants feeding* **shout**, yell, cry, cry out, call, call out, roar, howl, bellow, bawl, bark, shriek, scream, screech, bay, wail, whoop, boom, thunder, raise one's voice, call at the top of one's voice; *rare* vociferate.
OPPOSITE whisper.
▶ **noun** *the audience responded with whoops and hollers* **shout**, cry, yell, roar, howl, bellow, bawl, shriek, scream, screech, bay, wail, whoop; *rare* vociferation.
OPPOSITE whisper.

hollow ▶ **adjective 1** *each fibre has a hollow core* **empty**, not solid, void, unfilled, vacant, hollowed out.
OPPOSITE solid.
2 *her cheeks were hollow and her face bony* **sunken**, deep-set, concave, depressed, dented, indented, caved in; *rare* incurvate.
3 *'Goodbye,' he said in a hollow voice* **dull**, low, flat, toneless, expressionless; muffled, muted; deep, rumbling, echoing, sepulchral.
4 *the result was a hollow victory* **meaningless**, empty, valueless, worthless, useless, pyrrhic, futile, of no use, of no value, of no avail, fruitless, profitless, pointless, unavailing; *archaic* bootless.
OPPOSITE worthwhile.
5 *the women believed it was nothing but a hollow promise* **insincere**, hypocritical, feigned, pretended, artificial, false, dissembling, dissimulating, deceitful, sham, cynical, counterfeit, spurious, untrue, unsound, flimsy, two-faced, double-dealing; *informal* phoney, pretend.
OPPOSITE sincere.
□ **beat someone hollow** *he was a mere boy, but he beat them hollow* **trounce**, defeat utterly, beat, annihilate, drub, give a drubbing to, crush, rout, worst, overwhelm, outclass; *informal* hammer, clobber, thrash, lick, best, paste, pound, pulverize, crucify, slaughter, massacre, murder, flatten, demolish, destroy, walk over, wipe the floor with, take to the cleaners, make mincemeat of, turn inside out; *Brit. informal* stuff, marmalize; *N. Amer. informal* shellac, cream, skunk, blow out.
OPPOSITE lose to.
▶ **noun 1** *a hollow at the base of a large tree* **hole**, pit, cavity, crater, trough, cave, cavern; **depression**, indentation, concavity, dent, dint, dip, dimple, dish, basin, niche, nook, cranny, recess.
2 *a village nestled in a hollow in the Cotswolds* **valley**, vale, dale; *Brit.* dene, combe, slade; *N. English* clough; *Scottish* glen, strath; *literary* dell, dingle.
▶ **verb** *a tunnel hollowed out in a mountain range* **gouge out**, scoop out, dig out, cut out, excavate, channel.

holocaust ▶ **noun** *apocalyptic thoughts have surfaced due to the spectre of a nuclear holocaust* **cataclysm**, disaster, catastrophe, destruction, devastation, demolition, annihilation, ravaging; inferno, fire, conflagration; massacre, slaughter, mass murder, carnage, butchery, extermination, liquidation, genocide, ethnic cleansing.

holy ▶ **adjective 1** *people from all over the Muslim world visit the tombs of the holy men* **saintly**, godly, saintlike, pious, pietistic, religious, devout, God-fearing, spiritual, canonized, beatified, ordained, deified; righteous, good, virtuous, moral, sinless, pure, perfect.
OPPOSITES sinful, irreligious.
2 *the Wailing Wall is the most important Jewish holy place* **sacred**, consecrated, hallowed, sanctified, venerated, revered, reverenced, divine, religious, blessed, blest, dedicated.
OPPOSITES unsanctified, cursed.

CHOOSE THE RIGHT WORD

holy, sacred, hallowed, blessed

See SACRED.

homage ▶ **noun** *he intended his book as an act of homage* **respect**, recognition, admiration, esteem, adulation, acclaim, acclamation, commendation, honour, reverence, worship; **tribute**, acknowledgement, eulogy, accolade, panegyric, paean, encomium, salute; *rare* laudation.
OPPOSITE criticism.
□ **pay homage to** *they paid homage to the local boy who became president* **honour**, acclaim, applaud, praise, commend, extol, salute, celebrate, commemorate, glorify, laud, magnify, pay tribute to, sing the praises of, give recognition to, speak highly of, take one's hat off to.
OPPOSITE criticize.

home *See centre pages for lists of* **Homes** **Homes for Animals**
▶ **noun 1** *the floods forced people to flee their homes* **place of residence**, accommodation, property, a roof over one's head; quarters, lodgings, rooms; address, location, place; *informal* pad; *Brit. informal* digs; *formal* residence, domicile, abode, dwelling, dwelling place, habitation.
2 *there is a growing demand for new homes* **house**, flat, apartment, bungalow, cottage, terraced house, semi-detached house, detached house; *informal* semi.
3 *I spent long stretches of time far from my home* **native land**, homeland, home town, birthplace, roots, fatherland, motherland, mother country, country of origin, land of one's fathers, the old country.
4 *a private home for the elderly* **institution**, residential home, nursing home, old people's home, retirement home, convalescent home, rest home, children's home; hospice, shelter, refuge, retreat, asylum, hostel.
5 *Piedmont is the home of Italy's finest red wines* **domain**, realm, place of origin, source, cradle, fount, fountainhead.
6 *Montana is home to a surprising number of rare animals* **natural habitat**, natural environment, natural territory, habitat, home ground, stamping ground, haunt.
□ **at home 1** *I told him I'd be at home most of the day* **in**, in one's house, present, available, indoors, inside, here.
OPPOSITE out.
2 *Milan was one of the big cities where she felt very much at home* **at ease**, comfortable, relaxed, content, confident, at peace, in one's element.
OPPOSITE ill at ease.
3 *he was not particularly at home with mathematics* **confident with**, conversant with, proficient in, competent at, used to, familiar with, au fait with, au courant with, skilled in, experienced in, well versed in; *informal* well up on.
OPPOSITE unused to.
4 *she took to her room and was not at home to friends* **entertaining**, receiving, playing host to, showing hospitality to.
□ **bring something home to someone** *Art's illness brought home to them the gravity of the situation* **make someone realize**, make someone understand, make someone aware of, make someone conscious of, make something clear to someone, drive home, press home, impress upon someone, draw attention to, focus attention on, point up, underline, highlight, spotlight, foreground, emphasize, stress.
□ **hit home**. *See* HIT.
□ **nothing to write home about** (*informal*) *his looks were nothing to write home about* **unexceptional**, mediocre, ordinary, common, commonplace, indifferent, average, middle-of-the-road, run-of-the-mill, middling, medium, moderate, everyday, workaday, tolerable, passable, adequate, fair, nothing out of the ordinary; *informal* OK, so-so, bog-standard, fair-to-middling, (plain) vanilla, no great shakes, not so hot, not up to much; *Brit. informal* common or garden; *N. Amer. informal* ornery; *NZ informal* half-pie.
OPPOSITE exceptional.

▸ adjective **1** *we need to stimulate demand within the UK home market* **domestic**, internal, local, national, interior, native.
OPPOSITES foreign, international.
2 *a sale of home produce* **home-made**, home-grown, locally produced, family, local.
▸ verb
□ **home in on** *a teaching style which homes in on what is of central importance for each pupil* **focus on**, focus attention on, concentrate on, zero in on, centre on, fix on, aim at, highlight, spotlight, underline, pinpoint; *informal* zoom in on.

WORD LINKS
fear of home **oikophobia**

homeland ▸ noun *he left his homeland to settle in London* **native land**, native country, country of origin, home, fatherland, motherland, mother country, land of one's fathers, the old country.

homeless ▸ adjective *the plight of young homeless people* **without a roof over one's head**, on the streets, vagrant, sleeping rough, living rough; destitute, down and out, derelict, itinerant; *Brit. informal* dossing; *formal* of no fixed abode.
▸ noun (**the homeless**) *charities for the homeless* **homeless people**, vagrants, down-and-outs, tramps, beggars, vagabonds, itinerants, transients, migrants, derelicts, drifters, beachcombers; *N. Amer.* hobos; *Austral.* bagmen, knockabouts, overlanders, sundowners, whalers; *informal* bag ladies; *Brit. informal* dossers; *N. Amer. informal* bums, bindlestiffs; *Austral./NZ informal* derros; *S. African informal* outies; *formal* people of no fixed abode.

homely ▸ adjective **1** *a modern hotel with a homely atmosphere* **cosy**, homelike, homey, comfortable, snug, welcoming, friendly, congenial, hospitable, informal, relaxed, intimate, warm, pleasant, cheerful; *N. Amer.* down-home, homestyle; *informal* comfy.
OPPOSITES uncomfortable, formal.
2 *he interested himself in the homely pursuits of keeping chickens* **unsophisticated**, everyday, ordinary, domestic, plain, simple, modest, natural, down-to-earth, homespun, folksy, unrefined, unpretentious, unaffected, unassuming.
OPPOSITE sophisticated.
3 (*N. Amer.*) *the girl is clumsy, homely, and desperate for a date* **unattractive**, plain, plain-featured, plain-looking, plain as a pikestaff, ordinary-looking, unprepossessing, unlovely, ill-favoured, ugly; *informal* not much to look at, short on looks; *Brit. informal* no oil painting; *Austral./NZ informal* drack.
OPPOSITE attractive.

Homeric ▸ adjective *some of us exert a Homeric effort* **epic**, large-scale, grand, monumental, vast, heroic, impressive, imposing.

homespun ▸ adjective *he was a source of homespun rural philosophy* **unsophisticated**, unpolished, unrefined, plain, simple, rustic, folksy, artless, modest, natural; coarse, rough, rude, crude, rudimentary.
OPPOSITE sophisticated.

homey ▸ adjective **1** *the house is homey yet elegant* **cosy**, homelike, homely, comfortable, snug, welcoming, friendly, congenial, hospitable, informal, relaxed, intimate, warm, pleasant, cheerful; *N. Amer.* down-home, homestyle; *informal* comfy.
OPPOSITES uncomfortable, formal.
2 *an idealized vision of traditional peasant life as simple and homey* **unsophisticated**, homely, unrefined, unpretentious, ordinary, plain, simple, modest, down-to-earth, homespun.
OPPOSITE sophisticated.

homicidal ▸ adjective *he had homicidal tendencies* **murderous**, violent, brutal, savage, ferocious, fierce, vicious, bloody, bloodthirsty, barbarous, barbaric, cruel; mortal, deadly, lethal, death-dealing; *dated* cut-throat; *archaic* sanguinary, fell.
OPPOSITE peaceable.

homicide ▸ noun **1** *he was charged with homicide. See* MURDER.
2 (*dated*) *a convicted homicide. See* MURDERER.

homily ▸ noun *she delivered her homily about the need for patience* **sermon**, lecture, discourse, address, lesson, talk, speech, oration, declamation; preaching, teaching; *informal* spiel; *rare* peroration, allocution, postil.

homogeneity ▸ noun *the cultural homogeneity of Europe* **uniformity**, homogeneousness, similarity, similar nature, similitude, likeness, alikeness, sameness, identicalness, consistency, resemblance, comparability, correspondence; *rare* analogousness.
OPPOSITES variety, difference.

homogeneous ▸ adjective **1** *the elderly are far from a homogeneous group* **uniform**, identical, unvaried, unvarying, consistent, similar, undistinguishable; alike, all alike, of the same kind, much the same, all the same, the same, all one, all of a piece; *informal* much of a muchness.
OPPOSITE heterogeneous.
2 *you must consider cost efficiency to compete with homogeneous products* **similar**, comparable, equivalent, like, analogous, corresponding, correspondent, parallel, matching, kindred, related, correlative, congruent, cognate.
OPPOSITES different; dissimilar.

homogenize ▸ verb *they wanted to wipe out the differences between towns and villages—to homogenize society* **make uniform**, make similar, unite, integrate, fuse, merge, blend, meld, coalesce, amalgamate, synthesize, combine, join together; *literary* commingle; *archaic* commix.
OPPOSITE diversify.

homogenous ▸ adjective. *See* HOMOGENEOUS.

homologous ▸ adjective *the cell has two sets of homologous chromosomes* **similar**, comparable, equivalent, like, analogous, corresponding, correspondent, parallel, matching, kindred, related, correlative, congruent, cognate.
OPPOSITES different, dissimilar.

homosexual ▸ adjective **gay**, lesbian; *informal* queer, camp, pink, lavender, limp-wristed, swinging the other way, homo, lezzy, les, lesbo, butch, dykey; *Brit. informal* bent, poofy; *N. Amer. informal* fruity; *rare* homophile, Uranian, sapphic.
OPPOSITE heterosexual.
▸ noun **gay**, lesbian; *W. Indian* zami; *informal* queer, homo, queen, friend of Dorothy, pansy, nancy, nelly, dyke, les, lesbo, lezzie, butch, femme; *Brit. informal* poof, poofter, ponce, jessie, woofter, shirtlifter; *N. Amer. informal* cupcake, swish, twinkie; *Austral. informal* wonk; *S. African informal* moffie; *W. Indian informal* batty boy, batty man; *rare* tribade, homophile.
OPPOSITE heterosexual.

WORD LINKS
fear of homosexuals **homophobia**

hone ▸ verb *he was carefully honing the curved blade* **sharpen**, make sharper, make sharp, whet, strop, grind, file, put an edge on; *rare* edge, acuminate.
OPPOSITE blunt.

honest ▸ adjective **1** *I did the only right and honest thing | he is an honest man* **morally correct**, upright, honourable, moral, ethical, principled, righteous, right-minded, respectable; **virtuous**, good, worthy, decent, law-abiding, high-minded, upstanding, just, fair, incorruptible, truthful, true, veracious, trustworthy, trusty, reliable, conscientious, scrupulous, reputable, dependable, loyal, faithful; *informal* on the level, honest-to-goodness.
OPPOSITE dishonest.
2 *I haven't been totally honest with you* **truthful**, sincere, candid, frank, direct, open, forthright, straight, straightforward, genuine, blunt, plain-spoken, plain-speaking, matter-of-fact, outspoken, as straight as a die, straight from the shoulder; *informal* upfront; *archaic* free-spoken.
OPPOSITE insincere.
3 *he'd made an honest mistake* **genuine**, real, authentic, actual, true; legitimate, above board, fair and square; *Latin* bona fide; *informal* legit, kosher, on the level, honest-to-goodness.
OPPOSITE intentional.
4 *they had given their honest opinion* **objective**, impartial, unbiased, balanced, unprejudiced, disinterested, even-handed, fair, just, equitable.
OPPOSITE biased.

honestly ▸ adverb **1** *he'd come by the money honestly* **fairly**, lawfully, legally, legitimately, honourably, decently, ethically, morally, by fair means, by just means, without corruption, in good faith, by the book, in accordance with the rules; *informal* on the level.
OPPOSITE dishonestly.
2 *we honestly believe this is the best investment you will ever make* **frankly**, candidly, sincerely, genuinely, truthfully, truly, wholeheartedly, freely, openly, plainly, straight out, straight from the shoulder; *informal* straight up.
3 *quite honestly, I'm not very interested in men* **truthfully**, really, truly, actually, to be honest, to tell you the truth, to be frank, speaking truthfully, speaking frankly, in all honesty, in all sincerity, in plain language, in plain English; without pretence, without dissembling; *informal* Scout's honour; *dated* honest Injun.

honesty ▸ noun **1** *a character reference should provide evidence of honesty* **moral correctness**, uprightness, honourableness, honour, integrity, morals, morality, ethics, principle, (high) principles, nobility, righteousness, rectitude, right-mindedness, upstandingness; **virtue**, goodness, probity, worthiness, high-mindedness, justness, fairness, incorruptibility, truthfulness, truth, veracity, trustworthiness, reliability, conscientiousness, scrupulousness, reputability, dependability, loyalty, faithfulness, fidelity.
OPPOSITE dishonesty.
2 *they spoke with convincing honesty about their fears* **truthfulness**, truth, sincerity, candour, frankness, directness, forthrightness, openness, straightforwardness, plainness, genuineness, bluntness, outspokenness.
OPPOSITE insincerity.

honey ▸ noun

WORD LINKS
honey production **apiculture**
yielding or producing honey **melliferous**
honey-eating **mellivorous**

honeyed ▸ adjective *he wooed her with honeyed words* **sweet**, sweet-sounding, saccharine, sugary, pleasant, agreeable, flattering, adulatory,

unctuous; dulcet, soothing, soft, mellow, lyrical, mellifluous.
OPPOSITE harsh.

honorarium ▶ noun **fee**, payment, consideration, allowance; remuneration, pay, expenses, compensation, recompense, reward; *formal* emolument.

honorary ▶ adjective **1** *he received an honorary doctorate from Harvard University* **titular**, nominal, in name only, in title only, unofficial, token, so-called; *Latin* honoris causa, ex officio.
2 *she took office as honorary treasurer* **unpaid**, unsalaried, without pay, without payment, for nothing; voluntary, volunteer, unrewarded; *Law* pro bono (publico).
OPPOSITE paid.

honour ▶ noun **1** *the general's record shows that he was a man of honour* **integrity**, honourableness, honesty, uprightness, ethics, morals, morality, principle, (high) principles, righteousness, rectitude, nobility, high-mindedness, right-mindedness, noble-mindedness; **virtue**, goodness, decency, probity, scrupulousness, worthiness, worth, fairness, justness, justice, truthfulness, trustworthiness, reliability, dependability, faithfulness, fidelity.
OPPOSITE dishonour.
2 *he earned the honour of having the archive named after him | a mark of honour* **distinction**, privilege, glory, tribute, kudos, cachet, prestige, fame, renown, merit, credit, importance, illustriousness, notability; **respect**, esteem, approbation.

OPPOSITE disgrace.
3 *our national honour is at stake* **reputation**, good name, name, character, repute, prestige, image, kudos, cachet, standing, stature, status; *Indian* izzat.
4 *he was welcomed with honour by the king* **acclaim**, acclamation, commendation, applause, accolades, tributes, compliments, congratulations, salutes, plaudits, bouquets, paeans, homage, praise, glory, eulogy, adoration, reverence, veneration, adulation, exaltation, glorification; *rare* extolment, laudation, eulogium.
OPPOSITE contempt.
5 *Mrs Young had the honour of being received by the Queen* **privilege**, pleasure, pride, satisfaction, joy, compliment, favour, source of pleasure, source of pride.
OPPOSITE shame.
6 *the highest military honours* **accolade**, award, reward, prize, decoration, distinction, order, title, medal, ribbon, star, laurel, laurel wreath, bay, palm; *Military, informal* fruit salad; *Brit. informal* gong.
7 *she died defending her honour* **chastity**, virginity, virtue, maidenhood, maidenhead, purity, innocence, modesty; *informal* cherry; *Theology* immaculateness.
▶ verb **1** *we should love and honour our parents* **hold in great respect**, hold in high esteem, have a high regard for, esteem, respect, admire, defer to, look up to, think highly of; appreciate, value, prize, cherish; reverence, revere, venerate, worship; *informal* put on a pedestal.
OPPOSITE dishonour.
2 *talented writers were honoured at a special ceremony* **applaud**, acclaim, praise, salute, recognize, celebrate, commemorate, commend, glorify, hail, lionize, exalt, eulogize, give credit to, pay homage to, pay tribute to, show appreciation of, give accolades to, sing the praises of, sing paeans to; *archaic* magnify; *rare* laud, panegyrize, emblazon.
OPPOSITES disgrace, criticize.
3 *make sure the franchisees honour the terms of the contract* **fulfil**, observe, keep, discharge, implement, perform, execute, effect, obey, heed, follow, carry out, carry through, keep to, abide by, adhere to, comply with, conform to, act in accordance with, be true to, be faithful to, live up to; *rare* effectuate.
OPPOSITE disobey.
4 *the bank informed him that the cheque would not be honoured* **cash**, **accept**, take, clear, pass, encash, convert into cash, convert into money.
OPPOSITE bounce.

honourable ▶ adjective **1** *he took the honourable course and resigned | a decent and honourable man* **morally correct**, honest, moral, ethical, principled, righteous, right-minded, full of integrity; decent, respected, respectable, venerable, virtuous, good, upstanding, upright, worthy, noble, high-principled, fair, just, truthful, trustworthy, trusty, law-abiding, incorruptible, reliable, reputable, dependable, faithful.
OPPOSITES dishonourable, crooked.
2 *a long and honourable career* **illustrious**, distinguished, eminent, great, admirable, glorious, prestigious, noble, notable, creditable, renowned, esteemed.
OPPOSITE deplorable.

hood ▶ noun **head covering**, cowl, snood, scarf, head scarf.

hoodlum ▶ noun **1** *a bunch of hoodlums just looking for trouble* **hooligan**, thug, lout, delinquent, tearaway, vandal, ruffian, rowdy; *Austral./NZ* larrikin; *informal* tough, rough, bruiser, roughneck; *Brit. informal* yob, yobbo, bovver boy, lager lout; *Scottish & N. English informal* keelie, ned; *Austral./NZ informal* roughie.
2 *Pesci plays a hoodlum for whom killing is a pleasure* **gangster**, gang member, mobster, criminal, gunman, thug, racketeer, ruffian, member of a criminal gang, member of the Mafia, Mafioso, Yardie; (*in Japan*) yakuza; *informal* hit man, hatchet man, heavy, gorilla; *N. Amer. informal* hood, goon.

hoodoo ▶ noun *she's working some hoodoo on us* **witchcraft**, magic, black magic, sorcery, wizardry, devilry, voodoo, necromancy; *N. Amer.* mojo; *NZ* makutu; *S. African* muti; *rare* witchery, demonry, thaumaturgy, theurgy.

hoodwink ▶ verb *he kept on the lookout for the young man who had hoodwinked him* **deceive**, trick, dupe, outwit, fool, delude, cheat, take in, bluff, hoax, mislead, misguide, lead on, defraud, double-cross, swindle, gull, finagle, get the better of; *informal* con, bamboozle, do, have, sting, gyp, diddle, fiddle, swizzle, shaft, bilk, rook, rip off, lead up the garden path, pull a fast one on, put one over on, take for a ride, pull the wool over someone's eyes, throw dust in someone's eyes, sell a pup to, take to the cleaners; *N. Amer. informal* sucker, snooker, stiff, euchre, bunco, hornswoggle, make a sucker of; *Austral. informal* pull a swifty on; *archaic* cozen, sharp, befool; *rare* mulct.

hoof ▶ noun *there was a clatter of hoofs as a rider came up to us* trotter, foot, cloven hoof; *technical* ungula, cloot.

WORD LINKS
relating to hooves **ungual**

hook ▶ noun **1** *she hung her jacket on the hook* **peg**, holder.
2 *the back of the dress fastens with a hook and eye* **fastener**, fastening, catch, clasp, hasp, clip, pin, buckle, hook and eye; *Archaeology* fibula.
3 *I had a fish on the end of my hook* **fish hook**, barb, snare, trap.
4 *he used a hook to clear the undergrowth* **billhook**, scythe, sickle.
5 (*archaic*) *it lies up in a little hook in the river* **bend**, curve, bow, crook, elbow, angle, arc, loop, dog-leg, oxbow, horseshoe bend.
6 *a perfectly timed right hook to the chin* **punch**, blow, hit, box, cuff, thump, smack, crack, knock, thwack; *Scottish & N. English* skelp; *informal* belt, bop, biff, sock, clout, whack, wallop, plug, slug, whop; *Brit. informal* slosh, dot; *N. Amer. informal* boff; *Austral./NZ informal* dong.
□ **by hook or by crook** *the government intends, by hook or by crook, to hold on to the land* **by any means**, by any means whatsoever, somehow, somehow or other, no matter how, in one way or another, by fair means or foul.
□ **hook, line, and sinker** *he fell hook, line, and sinker for this year's April Fool joke* **completely**, totally, utterly, entirely, absolutely, thoroughly, wholly, through and through, one hundred per cent, {lock, stock, and barrel}.
OPPOSITE to a limited extent.
□ **off the hook** (*informal*) *I lied to get him off the hook* **out of trouble**, free, in the clear, under no obligation; **acquitted**, cleared, reprieved, exonerated, absolved, vindicated, found not guilty; *informal* let off.
▶ verb **1** *they hooked baskets onto the ladder rungs* **attach**, fix, hitch, fasten, secure, clasp; *archaic* hasp, grapple.
OPPOSITE unhitch.
2 *he hooked his thumbs in his belt* **curl**, bend, crook, loop, angle, curve.
3 *he hooked a 24 lb pike* **catch**, take, land, net, bag, snare, ensnare, trap, entrap.
OPPOSITE release.

hookah ▶ noun **pipe**, water pipe, hubble-bubble, chillum, narghile, kalian.

hooked ▶ adjective **1** *he had a hooked nose* **curved**, hook-shaped, hook-like, aquiline, bent, bowed, angular; *technical* falcate, falciform, uncinate.
OPPOSITE straight.
2 (*informal*) *they are **hooked on** cocaine* **addicted to**, dependent on, with a ... habit; *informal* using; *US black slang* have a jones for.
OPPOSITE clean.
3 (*informal*) *he has been **hooked on** crosswords since his teens* **very keen on**, very enthusiastic about, devoted to, addicted to, obsessed with, fixated on, fanatical about; *informal* mad about, crazy about, gone on, wild about, nuts about, potty about, dotty about, a sucker for; *N. Amer. informal* nutso over; *Austral./NZ informal* shook on.
OPPOSITE indifferent.

hooligan ▶ noun *the violence was caused by football hooligans* **hoodlum**, thug, lout, delinquent, tearaway, vandal, ruffian, rowdy, troublemaker; *Austral./NZ* larrikin; *informal* tough, rough, bruiser, roughneck; *Brit. informal* yob, yobbo, bovver boy, lager lout; *Scottish & N. English informal* keelie, ned; *Austral./NZ informal* roughie.

hoop ▶ noun **ring**, band, circle, circlet, loop, wheel, round, girdle; *technical* annulus.

hoot ▶ noun **1** *she heard the hoot of an owl* **cry**, call, screech, tu-whit tu-whoo.
2 *the hoot of a horn was followed by the roar of an engine* **blast**, blare, sound, beep, honk, toot.
3 *there were hoots of derision* **shout**, yell, cry, howl, scream, shriek, whoop, whistle; **boo**, hiss, jeer, mock, taunt, catcall; *informal* raspberry.
OPPOSITE cheer.
4 (*informal*) *your mum's a real hoot—I always have a giggle with her* **amusing person**, character, clown, somebody very funny; **amusing situation**, piece of fun, something very funny; *informal* scream, laugh, card, case, one, riot, giggle, lark, barrel of laughs; *informal, dated* caution.
□ **give a hoot** (*informal*) *I don't give a hoot about what anyone else thinks* **care**, be

concerned, mind, be bothered, be interested; *informal* give a damn, give a rap, give a hang, give a tinker's curse/damn, give a monkey's, lose sleep, get worked up.
OPPOSITE be unconcerned.
▸ verb **1** *in the stillness of the night an owl hooted* **cry**, call, utter a hoot, screech, tu-whit tu-whoo.
2 *a car horn hooted, frightening her* **sound**, blare, blast, beep, honk, toot, make a loud sound.
3 *the delegates hooted in disgust* **shout**, yell, cry, howl, scream, shriek, whoop, whistle; **boo**, hiss, jeer, mock, taunt, catcall; *informal* blow raspberries.
OPPOSITE cheer.

hop ▸ verb **1** *he hopped along beside her* **jump**, bound, spring, bounce, skip, jig, trip, flit, leap, prance, caper, dance, frolic, gambol.
2 (*informal*) *she hopped over the Atlantic for a bit for shopping* **go**, dash, rush; *informal* **pop**, whip; *Brit. informal* nip.
▸ noun **1** *put the rabbit on the floor to have a hop around* **jump**, bound, bounce, prance, leap, spring, skip, gambol.
2 (*informal*) *it's just a short hop here by taxi* **journey**, distance, ride, drive, run, trip, jaunt; flight, plane trip; *informal* spin.
3 (*informal*) *what about coming to the hop on Saturday* **dance**, social, party, jamboree, gathering, function, disco; *informal* bash, bop, shindig, shindy, do; *Brit. informal* rave-up, knees-up, beanfeast, beano, bunfight.
□ **on the hop** (*Brit. informal*) **1** *he was caught on the hop* **unprepared**, unready, off guard, unawares, by surprise, with one's defences down; *informal* napping, asleep at the wheel; *Brit. informal* with one's trousers down; *N. Amer. informal* with one's pants down.
OPPOSITE prepared.
2 *we were always kept on the hop* **busy**, occupied, employed, working, at work, rushed off one's feet, hard-pressed, on the job; *informal* busy as a bee, on the go.
OPPOSITE idle.

hope ▸ noun **1** *I had high hopes of making the Olympic team* **aspiration**, desire, wish, expectation, ambition, aim, plan, dream, daydream, pipe dream; longing, yearning, craving, hankering.
2 *most of us begin married life filled with hope* **hopefulness**, optimism, expectation, expectancy; confidence, faith, trust, belief, conviction, assurance.
3 *he does see some hope for the future* **optimism**, grounds for hope, promise, light at the end of the tunnel.
OPPOSITE pessimism.
▸ verb **1** *he's hoping for an offer of compensation* **expect**, anticipate, look for, wait for, be hopeful of, pin one's hopes on, want; wish for, dream of, hope against hope for.
OPPOSITE despair of.
2 *we're hoping to address all these issues* **aim**, intend, be looking, have the/every intention, have in mind, plan, aspire.

hopeful ▸ adjective **1** *he remained hopeful that something could be worked out* **optimistic**, full of hope, confident, positive, buoyant, sanguine, bullish, cheerful, assured, expectant, anticipative, disposed to look on the bright side; *informal* upbeat.
OPPOSITE pessimistic.
2 *there are some hopeful signs of recovery in the US market* **promising**, encouraging, heartening, reassuring, auspicious, favourable, optimistic, propitious, gladdening, cheering, bright, rosy, full of promise, full of hope.
OPPOSITE discouraging.

CHOOSE THE RIGHT WORD

hopeful, confident, sanguine, optimistic
See CONFIDENT.

hopefully ▸ adverb **1** *he rode on hopefully* **optimistically**, with hope, full of hope, confidently, expectantly, with anticipation, with assurance, buoyantly, sanguinely, bullishly.
OPPOSITE pessimistically.
2 *hopefully it should be finished by next year* **all being well**, it is to be hoped that, if all goes well, if everything turns out all right, God willing, most likely, with luck, probably, conceivably, feasibly; *informal* touch wood, fingers crossed.

hopeless ▸ adjective **1** *Jess looked at him in mute hopeless appeal* **despairing**, without hope, in despair, desperate, dejected, downhearted, despondent, demoralized, disconsolate, downcast, wretched, woebegone, forlorn, negative, pessimistic, defeatist, resigned.
OPPOSITE optimistic.
2 *she gave up on him as a hopeless case* **irremediable**, beyond hope, lost, beyond remedy, beyond repair, beyond recovery, irreparable, irreversible, incorrigible, despaired of; **past cure**, incurable, grave, fatal, deadly.
OPPOSITES remediable; curable.
3 *although the situation was hopeless, they sent in more troops* **impossible**, beyond hope, with no chance of success, useless, no-win, futile, unworkable, impracticable, forlorn, pointless, vain; *archaic* bootless, parlous.
OPPOSITE hopeful.
4 *Joseph was hopeless at school* **very bad**, very poor, awful, terrible, dreadful, appalling, frightful, atrocious, inferior, incompetent, inadequate, ineffective; *informal* pathetic, useless, lousy, rotten, a dead loss, abysmal, dire; *Brit. informal* duff, rubbish, a load of pants, unable to do something for toffee, unable to do something to save one's life.
OPPOSITE accomplished.

hopelessly ▸ adverb **1** *she began to cry hopelessly* **despairingly**, without hope, in despair, in anguish, in distress, desperately, dejectedly, downheartedly, despondently, disconsolately, wretchedly, miserably, forlornly, resignedly, pessimistically.
OPPOSITE optimistically.
2 *she was hopelessly confused and lost* **utterly**, completely, irretrievably, impossibly; extremely, very, desperately, totally, awfully, terribly, tremendously, frightfully, dreadfully; *informal* chronically.
OPPOSITE slightly.

horde ▸ noun *a horde of paparazzi burst into the office* **crowd**, large group, mob, pack, gang, troop, army, swarm, mass; throng, multitude, host, drove, band, flock, gathering, assemblage, press; *informal* crew, tribe, load; *archaic* rout.

horde or hoard?
See HOARD.

H

horizon ▸ noun **1** *the sun rose above the horizon* **skyline**, range of vision, field of view, vista, view.
2 *she wanted to leave home and broaden her horizons* **range of experience**, **outlook**, perspective, scope, perception, compass, sphere, ambit, orbit, purview.
□ **on the horizon** *trouble could be on the horizon* **imminent**, impending, close, near, approaching, coming, forthcoming, in prospect, at hand, on the way, about to happen, upon us, in the offing, in the pipeline, in the air, in the wind, in the wings, just around the corner; brewing, looming, threatening, menacing; *informal* on the cards.

horizontal ▸ adjective **1** *draw a horizontal line near the top of the wall* **parallel**, level, even, straight, plane, flush.
OPPOSITE vertical.
2 *she was stretched horizontal on a sun lounger* **flat**, supine, prone, prostrate, lying down.
OPPOSITE upright.

hormone ▸ noun. *See centre pages for list of* **Hormones**

horn ▸ noun
WORD LINKS
like horn **corneous**

horny ▸ adjective (*informal*) *she was making him very horny* **aroused**, **sexy**, sexually aroused, excited, stimulated, titillated, amorous, inflamed, impassioned, lustful; *informal* turned on, on fire, raunchy, hot, sexed up; *Brit. informal* randy; *N. Amer. informal* squirrelly, foxy; *rare* concupiscent.
OPPOSITE turned off.

horrendous ▸ adjective *she suffered horrendous injuries | a horrendous sight.* *See* HORRIBLE.

horrible ▸ adjective **1** *there was a horrible murder here earlier this year* **dreadful**, **horrifying**, horrific, horrendous, frightful, fearful, awful, terrible, shocking, appalling, hideous, grim, grisly, ghastly, harrowing, gruesome, heinous, vile, nightmarish, macabre, unspeakable, hair-raising, spine-chilling; loathsome, monstrous, abhorrent, detestable, hateful, execrable, abominable, atrocious, sickening, nauseating.
2 *the tea tasted horrible | a horrible little man* **nasty**, disagreeable, unpleasant, horrid, awful, dreadful, terrible, appalling, horrendous, disgusting, foul, revolting, repulsive, repellent, ghastly; obnoxious, hateful, odious, objectionable, offensive, insufferable, vile, loathsome, abhorrent; *informal* frightful, lousy, God-awful, hellish; *Brit. informal* beastly, grotty, bitchy, catty; *N. Amer. informal* hellacious; *archaic* disgustful, loathly; *rare* rebarbative.
OPPOSITES pleasant; agreeable.

horrid ▸ adjective **1** *horrid apparitions. See* HORRIBLE *sense* 1.
2 *the teachers at school were horrid. See* HORRIBLE *sense* 2.

horrific ▸ adjective *he lay in a coma following a horrific car crash* **dreadful**, horrendous, horrifying, horrible, frightful, awful, terrible, fearful, shocking, appalling, atrocious, hideous, grim, grisly, ghastly, harrowing, gruesome, unspeakable, monstrous, nightmarish, sickening, nauseating.

horrify ▸ verb **1** *she loved to horrify us with tales of ghastly happenings* **frighten**, scare, terrify, petrify, alarm, panic, terrorize, scare stiff, scare/frighten to death, fill with fear, scare someone out of their wits, scare/frighten the living daylights out of, throw into a panic, make someone's hair stand on end, make someone's blood run cold; *informal* scare the pants off, make someone's hair curl; *Brit. informal* throw into a blue funk,

put the wind up; *Irish informal* scare the bejesus out of; *N. Amer. informal* spook; *vulgar slang* scare shitless, scare the shit out of; *archaic* affright.
2 *Lucien was horrified by her remarks, but said nothing* **shock**, appal, outrage, scandalize, offend, dismay, throw off balance; disgust, revolt, repel, nauseate, sicken; *informal* rattle, faze, knock sideways, knock for six; *archaic* pother.
OPPOSITE please.

> **CHOOSE THE RIGHT WORD**
>
> **horrify, appal, dismay**
> *See* DISMAY.

horror ▸ noun **1** *children screamed in horror* **terror**, fear, fear and trembling, fearfulness, fright, alarm, panic, dread, trepidation.
OPPOSITE delight.
2 *to her horror she found that a thief had stolen the machine* **dismay**, consternation, perturbation, alarm, distress; disgust, outrage, shock.
OPPOSITE satisfaction.
3 *photographs showed the horror of the tragedy* **awfulness**, frightfulness, cruelty, savagery, gruesomeness, ghastliness, hideousness; atrocity, outrage, crime, barbarity.
4 (*informal*) *that little horror Zach was around* **rascal**, devil, imp, monkey, scamp; *informal* terror, holy terror, scallywag; *Brit. informal* perisher; *N. English informal* tyke, scallion; *N. Amer. informal* varmint, hellion; *archaic* scapegrace, rapscallion.

□ **have a horror of** *Laura had a horror of pubs* **hate**, detest, loathe, greatly dislike, have a strong aversion to, abhor, abominate, be unable to bear/stand.
OPPOSITE love.

horror-struck, **horror-stricken** ▸ adjective *horror-struck, she stared at him with frightened eyes* **horrified**, terrified, petrified, frightened, afraid, fearful, scared, panic-stricken, terror-struck, scared/frightened to death, scared stiff, scared witless, scared out of one's wits; shocked, stunned, stupefied, awestruck, aghast, appalled; *vulgar slang* scared shitless, shit-scared.
OPPOSITES delighted; relaxed.

horse *See centre pages for lists relating to* **Horses** *and lists of* **Equestrian Sports** *and* **Harness**
▸ noun **mount**, charger, yearling; cob, draught horse, carthorse, packhorse, racehorse; pony, foal, colt, stallion, gelding, mare, filly; nag, hack; *N. Amer.* bronco; *Austral./NZ* moke, yarraman; *archaic* steed, jade; *children's word* gee-gee.
▸ verb
□ **horse around/about** (*informal*) *they were talking silly and horsing around* **fool around/about**, play the fool, act foolishly, act the clown, act the fool, play about/around, clown about/around, monkey about/around, play tricks, indulge in horseplay, engage in high jinks; *informal* mess about/around, lark (about/around); *Brit. informal* muck about/around; *N. Amer. informal* cut up; *Brit. vulgar slang* piss about/around, arse about/around, bugger about/around; *dated* play the giddy goat.
OPPOSITE be serious.

WORD LINKS	
relating to horses	**equine, hippic**
related prefix	**hippo-** (e.g. ***hippodrome, hippopotamus***)
male	**stallion**
castrated male	**gelding**
female	**mare**
young	**foal**
young male	**colt**
young female	**filly**
collective noun	**drove, string, stud, team**
relating to riding horses	**equestrian**
fear of horses	**hippophobia**
seller of horses	*Brit. archaic* **horse-coper**

horseman, **horsewoman** ▸ noun **rider**, equestrian, horse rider, jockey; cavalryman, horse soldier, trooper, dragoon, knight; *archaic* hussar, cavalier.

horseplay ▸ noun *this ridiculous horseplay has gone far enough* **fooling around**, foolish behaviour, clowning, fooling, tomfoolery, buffoonery; pranks, practical jokes, antics, larks, capers, high jinks; rough and tumble, romping, skylarking; *informal* shenanigans, monkey business; *Brit. informal* monkey tricks; *N. Amer. informal* didoes.

horse riding ▸ noun. *See centre pages for list of* **Equestrian Sports**

horse sense ▸ noun (*informal*) *she has the horse sense to keep Dan from those wild schemes* **common sense**, good sense, sense, sensibleness, native wit, native intelligence, mother wit, wit, judgement, sound judgement, level-headedness, prudence, discernment, acumen, sharpness, sharp-wittedness, canniness, astuteness, shrewdness, judiciousness, wisdom, insight, intuition, intuitiveness, perceptiveness, perspicacity, vision, understanding, intelligence; *informal* nous, gumption, savvy, know-how, the sense one was born with; *Brit. informal* common; *N. Amer. informal* smarts; *rare* sapience, arguteness.
OPPOSITE stupidity.

hortatory ▸ adjective *the hortatory moralism of many contemporary churchmen* **exhortatory**, exhortative, exhorting, moralistic, homilectic, didactic, pedagogic; *informal* preachy.

horticulture ▸ noun **gardening**, floriculture, arboriculture, agriculture, cultivation, cultivation of plants, garden management.

hosanna ▸ noun *their hosannas rose up to the heavens* **shout of praise**, alleluia, hurrah, hurray, cheer, paean, glorification; *archaic* huzza; *rare* laudation.

hose ▸ noun **1** *a thirty-foot garden hose* **pipe**, piping, tube, tubing, conduit, channel, line, duct, outlet, pipeline, siphon.
2 *her hose had been laddered. See* HOSIERY.

hosiery ▸ noun **stockings**, tights, stay-ups, nylons; hose; **socks**, knee socks, ankle socks; *N. Amer.* pantyhose.

hospitable ▸ adjective *two friendly, hospitable brothers run the hotel* **welcoming**, friendly, congenial, genial, sociable, convivial, cordial, gracious, amicable, well disposed, amenable, helpful, obliging, accommodating, neighbourly, warm, warm-hearted, kind, kindly, kind-hearted, generous, liberal, bountiful, open-handed.
OPPOSITES inhospitable; unfriendly.

hospital ▸ noun **medical institution**, medical centre, health centre, clinic, infirmary, sanatorium, nursing home, convalescent home, hospice; *Brit.* cottage hospital; *Austral./NZ* base hospital; *Military* field hospital; *archaic* lazaretto.

hospitality ▸ noun **1** *Scotland is renowned for its hospitality* **friendliness**, hospitableness, welcome, warm reception, helpfulness, neighbourliness, warmth, warm-heartedness, kindness, kind-heartedness, congeniality, geniality, sociability, conviviality, cordiality, amicability, amenability, generosity, liberality, bountifulness, open-handedness.
OPPOSITE unfriendliness.
2 *the inn's hospitality includes a selection of real ales, bar menu, and live music on Thursday nights* entertainment, catering, food, accommodation.

host[1] ▸ noun **1** *the host greeted the new guests* **party-giver**, entertainer, hostess.
OPPOSITE guest.
2 *he was the host of a half-hour TV series* **presenter**, compère, master of ceremonies, MC, anchor, anchorman, anchorwoman, announcer, link person; *informal* emcee.
▸ verb **1** *the Queen hosted a dinner for 600 hundred guests* **give**, throw, have, hold, provide, put on, lay on, arrange, organize.
OPPOSITE be a guest at.
2 *the show is hosted by Angus Deayton* **present**, introduce, compère, front, anchor, announce, be the presenter of; *informal* emcee.

host[2] ▸ noun **1** *a host of memories rushed into her mind* **multitude**, myriad, lot, large number, great quantity, score, abundance, wealth, flood, profusion, array; *informal* load, heap, mass, pile, ton; *Brit. informal* shedload; *Austral./NZ informal* swag.
OPPOSITE small number.
2 *she joined a host of other stars at the London fashion show* **crowd**, throng, pack, band, flock, herd, drove, swarm, troop, horde, mob, army, legion, crush, press; collection, assembly, assemblage, gathering; *archaic* rout.
OPPOSITE small group.

hostage ▸ noun *the hijackers released all the hostages* **captive**, prisoner, detainee, internee; pawn, security, surety, pledge.

hostel ▸ noun **cheap hotel**, youth hostel, YMCA, YWCA, bed and breakfast, B&B, boarding house, guest house, pension; hall of residence, dormitory.

hostile ▸ adjective **1** *he wrote a ferociously hostile attack* **antagonistic**, aggressive, confrontational, belligerent, bellicose, pugnacious, militant, truculent, combative, warlike; **unfriendly**, unkind, bitter, unsympathetic, malevolent, malicious, vicious, spiteful, rancorous, venomous, biting, wrathful, angry; *literary* malefic, maleficent.
OPPOSITES friendly; mild.
2 *he painted a grim picture of hardship in hostile climatic conditions* **unfavourable**, adverse, bad, harsh, grim, hard, tough, inhospitable, forbidding, uncomfortable, unwelcoming.
OPPOSITE favourable.
3 *people are very hostile to the idea* **opposed**, averse, antagonistic, ill-disposed, unsympathetic, antipathetic, inimical; opposing, against, dead set against, at odds with; *informal* anti, down on.
OPPOSITE in favour of.

hostility ▸ noun **1** *the boy glared at her with hostility* **antagonism**, **unfriendliness**, bitterness, malevolence, malice, unkindness, spite, spitefulness, rancour, rancorousness, venom, wrath, anger, hatred; aggression, aggressiveness, belligerence, bellicosity, pugnaciousness, militancy, truculence, warlikeness.

OPPOSITE friendliness.
2 *there is a great amount of hostility to the present regime* **opposition**, antagonism, animosity, antipathy, animus, ill will, ill feeling, bad feeling, resentment, aversion, enmity, inimicalness.
OPPOSITE approval.
3 (**hostilities**) *he called for an immediate cessation of hostilities* **fighting**, conflict, armed conflict, combat, warfare, war, bloodshed, violence, action, military action, battles, strife.
OPPOSITE peace.

hot ▶ adjective **1** *they provided plenty of good hot food* **heated**, piping, piping hot, sizzling, steaming, roasting, boiling, boiling hot, searing, scorching, scalding, red-hot.
OPPOSITE cold.
2 *it was a beautiful hot day* **very warm**, balmy, summery, tropical, boiling, boiling hot, blazing hot, baking, scorching, roasting, searing, flaming, parching, blistering, oven-like; sweltering, torrid, sultry, humid, muggy, close, airless, oppressive, stifling.
OPPOSITE chilly.
3 *she felt hot and her throat was parched* **feverish**, fevered, febrile, burning, flushed; *informal* with a temperature; *rare* pyretic.
4 *a very hot dish cooked with green chilli* **spicy**, spiced, peppery, piquant, highly seasoned, sharp, fiery, strong, pungent, aromatic.
OPPOSITE mild.
5 *hot rage surged through him again* **angry**, indignant, furious, fiery, seething, raging, boiling, fuming; wrathful, enraged, infuriated, inflamed.
OPPOSITE calm.
6 *it remains the subject of hot debate* **animated**, heated, fierce, 'lively', intense, passionate, impassioned, spirited, ardent, fervent, feverish; **furious**, violent, ferocious, acrimonious, stormy, tempestuous, savage; *rare* fervid, passional.
OPPOSITE dispassionate.
7 *he found the competition too hot* **fierce**, intense, keen, competitive, cut-throat, dog-eat-dog, ruthless, aggressive, strong, powerful.
OPPOSITE weak.
8 (*informal*) *the romance was the hottest story in Fleet Street* **new**, fresh, recent, late, up to date, up to the minute; brand new, just out, just released, just issued, hot off the press; *informal* bang up to date.
OPPOSITE old.
9 (*informal*) *this band is seriously hot* **popular**, in demand, sought-after, in favour, well liked, well loved; **fashionable**, in fashion, in vogue, all the rage; *informal* big, in, now, hip, trendy, cool; *Brit. informal, dated* all the go.
OPPOSITES unpopular, out of fashion.
10 (*informal*) *Tony is* **hot on** *local history* **knowledgeable about**, well informed about, au fait with, up on, well versed in, au courant with; skilled at, expert at, enthusiastic about, keen on; *informal* clued up about, genned up about.
OPPOSITES ill-informed; apathetic.
11 (*informal*) *computer hardware is the most saleable category of hot goods* **stolen**, illegally obtained, under the counter, illegal, illicit, unlawful, smuggled, bootleg, contraband; *Brit. informal* dodgy.
OPPOSITE lawful.
□ **blow hot and cold** (*informal*) *he had been stringing her along, blowing hot and cold* **vacillate**, keep changing one's mind, dither, shilly-shally, oscillate, waver, be indecisive, be irresolute, be undecided, be uncertain, be unsure, hesitate; *Brit.* haver, hum and haw; *Scottish* swither; *informal* dilly-dally.
OPPOSITE be decisive.
□ **hot on the heels of** *critique followed hot on the heels of this pioneering work* **close behind**, soon after, shortly after, directly after, right after, straight after, immediately after, hard on the heels of, following closely.
OPPOSITE far behind.
□ **hot under the collar** (*informal*) *Nick got really hot under the collar about the issue* **angry**, **annoyed**, furious, irate, infuriated, incensed, enraged, cross, in a temper, irritated, put out, fed up, aggrieved; *informal* aggravated, peeved, miffed, mad, riled, hacked off, peed off; *Brit. informal* cheesed off, brassed off, narked, ratty, shirty; *N. Amer. informal* teed off, ticked off, sore, bent out of shape; *Austral./NZ informal* snaky, crook; *vulgar slang* pissed off; *literary* ireful.
OPPOSITE pleased.
□ **make it/things hot for someone** (*informal*) *make it hot for her and she'll soon go away* **harass**, hound, plague, badger, harry, pester, bother, bully, intimidate, pick on, persecute, victimize, terrorize; *N. Amer.* devil; *informal* hassle, give someone hell, give someone a hard time, get on someone's back; *Austral. informal* heavy.
OPPOSITE leave in peace.

hot air ▶ noun (*informal*) *they dismissed the theory as a load of hot air* **nonsense**, rubbish, empty talk, wind, froth, blarney, blather, blether, claptrap, moonshine, drivel, balderdash, gibberish; **pomposity**, **bombast**, verbiage, verbosity; *informal* guff, bosh, hogwash, gobbledegook, poppycock, bilge, twaddle; *Brit. informal* cobblers, codswallop, stuff and nonsense, tosh, double Dutch, flannel, waffle; *Scottish & N. English informal* havers; *N. Amer. informal* garbage, flapdoodle; *informal, dated* bunkum, tommyrot; *vulgar slang* bullshit; *Austral./NZ vulgar slang* bulldust.
OPPOSITE sense.

hotbed ▶ noun *the country was a hotbed of revolt and dissension* **breeding ground**, nursery, cradle, nest, den, seedbed, forcing house.

hot-blooded ▶ adjective *hot-blooded young lovers* **passionate**, impassioned, amorous, amatory, sensual, sexy, ardent; **lustful**, libidinous, lecherous, sex-hungry; *informal* horny, randy, raunchy; *rare* concupiscent, lickerish.
OPPOSITES cold, frigid.

hotchpotch, **hodgepodge** ▶ noun *it was a rambling hotchpotch of roof lines and gables* **mixture**, mix, mixed bag, assortment, assemblage, collection, selection, jumble, ragbag, miscellany, medley, patchwork, pot-pourri; melange, mess, mishmash, confusion, clutter, farrago; *rare* gallimaufry, olio, olla podrida, salmagundi.

hotel ▶ noun **inn**; motel, boarding house, guest house, lodge, bed and breakfast, B&B, hostel; aparthotel, boatel; *French* pension, auberge; *Spanish* parador, posada; *Portuguese* pousada; *Italian* pensione; *German* Gasthaus.

hotfoot ▶ adverb *he rushed hotfoot to the planning office to object* **hastily**, hurriedly, speedily, quickly, fast, rapidly, swiftly, without delay, in haste, at top speed, at full tilt, as fast as possible; headlong, post-haste, pell-mell, helter-skelter; *informal* at a lick, like the wind, like greased lightning, like a bomb, like mad, like crazy, like blazes; *Brit. informal* like the clappers, at a rate of knots, like billy-o; *N. Amer. informal* lickety-split; *literary* apace, hurry-scurry.
OPPOSITE at moderate speed.
▶ verb
□ **hotfoot it** (*informal*) *we hotfooted it after him* **hurry**, dash, run, race, sprint, bolt, dart, gallop, career, charge, shoot, hurtle, hare, bound, fly, speed, zoom, streak, make haste, hasten; *informal* tear, belt, pelt, scoot, zap, zip, whip, leg it, steam, go like a bat out of hell, burn rubber; *Brit. informal* bomb, bucket; *Scottish informal* wheech; *N. Amer. informal* boogie, hightail it, clip, barrel; *N. Amer. vulgar slang* drag/tear/haul ass; *archaic* post, hie, haste.
OPPOSITE dawdle.

hothead ▶ noun *a few hotheads urged their comrades to break the police roadblocks* **madcap**, daredevil; *Brit.* tearaway; *informal* loony, nut, nutter; *N. Amer. informal* screwball; *dated* desperado, hotspur.

hot-headed ▶ adjective *a number of hot-headed youths caused the bother* **impetuous**, impulsive, headstrong, reckless, rash, irresponsible, foolhardy, madcap, wild, excitable, volatile, precipitate, overhasty, unruly, fiery, hot-tempered, quick-tempered; *informal* harum-scarum, crazy, crackpot; *archaic* hasty.
OPPOSITE cool-headed.

hothouse ▶ noun **greenhouse**, glasshouse, conservatory, orangery, vinery, alpine house, winter garden; summer house, gazebo, pavilion, belvedere.
▶ adjective *the school's isolated location has encouraged a hothouse atmosphere* **intense**, oppressive, stifling; oversheltered, overprotected, pampered, coddled, shielded.

hotly ▶ adverb **1** *the rumours were hotly denied* **vehemently**, vigorously, strenuously, fiercely, passionately, heatedly, with a vengeance; angrily, indignantly, furiously, in anger, with indignation.
OPPOSITE calmly.
2 *he rushed out, hotly pursued by Boris* **closely**, swiftly, quickly, hotfoot, without delay; eagerly, enthusiastically, energetically.

hot-tempered ▶ adjective *he is arrogant, hot-tempered, and capable of violence* **irascible**, quick-tempered, short-tempered, irritable, fiery, impatient, huffy, brusque, ill-tempered, bad-tempered, ill-natured, ill-humoured, touchy, volatile, testy, tetchy, fractious, snarling, waspish, prickly, crusty, peppery, bilious, liverish, dyspeptic, splenetic, choleric; *informal* snappish, snappy, chippy, on a short fuse; *Brit. informal* narky, ratty, eggy, like a bear with a sore head; *N. Amer. informal* peckish, soreheaded; *Austral./NZ informal* snaky; *informal, dated* miffy.
OPPOSITE easy-going.

hound *See centre pages for list of* **Dogs**
▶ noun **1** **dog**, hunting dog, canine, mongrel, cur; *informal* doggy, pooch, mutt; *Austral. informal* mong, bitzer.
2 (*informal, dated*) *go, you monstrous hound!* **scoundrel**, rogue, villain, wretch, reprobate, good-for-nothing; *informal* beast, pig, swine, rat, creep, louse, snake, snake in the grass, skunk, dog, weasel, lowlife, scumbag, heel, stinker, stinkpot, bad lot, son of a bitch, s.o.b., nasty piece of work; *Scottish informal* scrote; *Irish informal* spalpeen, sleeveen; *N. Amer. informal* rat fink, fink; *Austral. informal* dingo; *informal, dated* rotter, cad, bounder, blighter; *vulgar slang* shit, bastard; *archaic* blackguard, dastard, vagabond, knave, varlet.
▶ verb **1** *she was hounded by the Italian press* **harass**, persecute, harry, pester, bother, trouble, annoy, badger, torment, bedevil, keep after; nag, bully, browbeat, chivvy, keep on at, go on at; *informal* hassle, bug, give someone a hard time; *N. Amer. informal* devil, ride; *Austral. informal* heavy.
OPPOSITE leave in peace.
2 *his opponents used the allegations to hound him out of office* **force**, drive, pressure, pressurize, propel, push, urge, coerce, impel, dragoon, strong-

arm; *informal* bulldoze, railroad; *Brit. informal* bounce; *N. Amer. informal* hustle.
3 *he led the race from start to finish but was hounded all the way by Phillips* **pursue**, chase, follow, shadow, give chase to, follow on the heels of, be hot on someone's heels; hunt, hunt down, stalk, track, trail; *informal* tail.

WORD LINKS
collective noun **pack, cry**

hour ▶ noun. *See centre pages for list of* **Canonical Hours**

house *See centre pages for list of* **Homes**
▶ noun **1** *the new estate comprises 200 houses* **home**, place of residence, homestead, lodging place, a roof over one's head; *formal* habitation, residence, dwelling, dwelling place, abode, domicile.
2 *make yourself scarce before you wake the whole house* **household**, family, family circle, ménage, clan, tribe; *informal* brood.
3 *the power and prestige of the house of Stewart* **clan**, kindred, family, tribe, race, strain; dynasty, line, lineage, ancestry, ancestors, bloodline, descent, family tree.
4 *the publishing and printing house grew to become self-financing* **firm**, business, company, corporation, enterprise, establishment, institution, concern, organization, operation; *informal* outfit, set-up.
5 *the sixty-member National Council, the country's upper house* **legislative assembly**, legislative body, chamber, council, parliament, diet, congress, senate.
6 *the house burst into applause* **audience**, crowd, those present, listeners, spectators, viewers, gathering, assembly, assemblage, congregation; gallery, stalls; *informal* punters.
7 *the house offers a wide variety of real ales* **inn**, bar, tavern, hostelry, taproom; restaurant, hotel, eating house; *Brit.* pub, public house; *informal* eatery, boozer; *historical* alehouse, taphouse, beerhouse; *N. Amer. historical* saloon.
□ **on the house** (*informal*) *our first rounds always came on the house* **free**, free of charge, without payment, without charge, at no cost, for nothing, gratis; courtesy, complimentary; *informal* for free; *N. Amer. informal* comp.
OPPOSITE paid for.
▶ verb **1** *they converted a disused cinema to house twelve employees* **accommodate**, provide accommodation for, provide with accommodation, give accommodation to, make space for, make room for, give someone a roof over their head, provide a roof over someone's head, provide with a place to work, harbour; lodge, quarter, board, billet, take in, provide shelter for, shelter; sleep, put up, give a bed to, provide with a place to sleep.
OPPOSITE evict.
2 *the rear panel houses the selector switch* **contain**, hold, store, cover; protect, enclose, encase, sheathe, keep safe.
OPPOSITE expose.

household ▶ noun *the whole household was asleep* **family**, house, family circle, ménage, clan, tribe; *informal* brood.
▶ adjective *they had all kinds of household goods on offer* **domestic**, family, workaday, ordinary, everyday, usual, common, run-of-the-mill; *Brit.* common or garden.
OPPOSITE exotic.

householder ▶ noun **homeowner**, owner, occupant, resident, head of the household; tenant, leaseholder; proprietor, landlady, landlord, freeholder; *Brit.* occupier, owner-occupier; *formal* dweller.

housekeeping ▶ noun *she did as much of the cooking and housekeeping as she could* **household management**, domestic work, domestic duties, homemaking, the running of the home; home economics, domestic science; *rare* housecraft, housewifery.

houseman ▶ noun (*Brit.*) **junior doctor**, house doctor, newly qualified doctor, medical officer, MO; *Brit.* house officer; *N. Amer.* intern, resident.

house-trained ▶ adjective (*Brit.*) *the cat is not completely house-trained yet* **domesticated**, trained; *N. Amer.* housebroken.

housing ▶ noun **1** *they invest in housing and other ventures* **homes**, houses, places of residence, buildings; accommodation, living quarters; *formal* dwellings, dwelling places, habitations, abodes, domiciles.
2 *the large spheres provide protective housing for the radio antennae* **casing**, covering, case, cover, encasement, container, enclosure, holder, sheath, jacket, shell, capsule; *technical* integument.

hovel ▶ noun *people were living in rat-infested hovels* **shack**, slum, shanty, hut, shed, cabin; *informal* dump, hole; *Scottish* bothy.

hover ▶ verb **1** *army helicopters hovered overhead* **be suspended**, be poised, hang, float, levitate, drift, fly, flutter.
2 *she hovered anxiously in the background* **linger**, loiter, wait about, stay nearby; *informal* hang around, stick around; *Brit. informal* hang about.

however ▶ adverb **1** *people tend to put on weight in middle age—however, gaining weight is not inevitable* **but**, **nevertheless**, nonetheless, still, yet, though, although, even so, (but) for all that, (but) despite that, (but) in spite of that; anyway, anyhow, be that as it may, having said that, notwithstanding; *informal* still and all; *archaic* howbeit, withal, natheless.
2 *however you look at it, you can't criticize that* **in whatever way**, regardless of how, no matter how.

howl ▶ noun **1** *at midnight she heard the howl of a wolf* **baying**, bay, howling, crying, cry, yowl, yowling, bark, barking, yelp, yelping.
2 *he let out a howl of anguish* **wail**, cry, yell, yelp, yowl, bawl, bellow, roar, shout, shriek, scream, screech, caterwaul; *informal* holler; *rare* ululation.
▶ verb **1** *they heard dogs howling in the distance* **bay**, cry, yowl, bark, yelp.
2 *a baby started to howl* **wail**, cry, yell, yelp, yowl, bawl, bellow, roar, shout, shriek, scream, screech, caterwaul; *informal* holler; *rare* ululate.
3 *the audience howled and whooped with laughter* **laugh**, guffaw, roar, laugh loudly, roar with laughter, dissolve into laughter, be creased up, be doubled up, split one's sides; *informal* fall about, crack up, be in stitches, be rolling in the aisles, laugh fit to bust.

howler ▶ noun (*informal*) *the occasional schoolboy howler would amuse the examiners* **mistake**, error, blunder, fault, gaffe, slip, slip of the pen; *Latin* lapsus calami; *informal* slip-up, boo-boo, boner, botch, fluff; *Brit. informal* boob, bloomer, clanger; *N. Amer. informal* blooper, bloop, goof; *vulgar slang* fuck-up; *technical* malapropism, solecism.

hub ▶ noun **1** *the spokes radiate from the hub of the wheel* **pivot**, axis, fulcrum, centre, centre point.
2 *the kitchen was the hub of family life* **centre**, centre of activity, core, heart, focus, focal point, middle, nucleus, kernel, nerve centre.
OPPOSITE periphery.

hubbub ▶ noun **1** *his wife's voice could be heard above the hubbub* **noise**, loud noise, din, racket, commotion, clamour, ruckus, cacophony, babel; *informal* rumpus; *Brit. informal* row; *rare* vociferation.
2 *she fought through the hubbub* **confusion**, chaos, pandemonium, bedlam, mayhem, uproar, disorder, turmoil, tumult, fracas, hurly-burly, havoc, brouhaha; *Scottish & N. English* stramash; *W. Indian* bangarang; *informal* hullabaloo.
OPPOSITE calm.

hubris ▶ noun *the self-assuring hubris among economists was shaken in the late 1960s* **arrogance**, conceit, conceitedness, haughtiness, pride, vanity, self-importance, self-conceit, pomposity, superciliousness, feeling of superiority; *French* hauteur; *informal* uppitiness, big-headedness.
OPPOSITE modesty.

huckster ▶ noun (*rare*) **trader**, dealer, seller, purveyor, vendor, barrow boy, salesman, door-to-door salesman; *W. Indian* higgler; *informal* pusher; *dated* pedlar, hawker; *archaic* chapman, packman; *rare* crier, colporteur.

huddle ▶ verb **1** *they huddled together for warmth* **crowd**, gather, throng, flock, herd, pile, bunch, cluster, collect, group, congregate; press, pack, squeeze, cram, jam; *rare* foregather.
OPPOSITE disperse.
2 *he huddled beneath the sheets* **curl up**, snuggle, cuddle, nestle, hunch up; *N. Amer.* snug down.
OPPOSITE stretch out.
▶ noun **1** *a huddle of passengers gathered round the information desk* **crowd**, gathering, throng, flock, herd, swarm, press, pack; cluster, bunch, knot, band, collection, circle, small group, assemblage; *informal* gaggle.
2 *a huddle of barns and outbuildings* **collection**, group, cluster, number, mass, selection, array; jumble, confusion, muddle, heap, tangle, mess.
3 (*informal*) *each team went into a huddle and then wrote down its answer* **consultation**, discussion, debate, talk, parley, meeting, conference; *informal* confab, powwow; *rare* confabulation.

hue ▶ noun **1** *seaweeds are found in a variety of hues* **colour**, tone, shade, tint, tinge, cast, tincture.
2 *men of all political hues submerged their feuds* **complexion**, type, kind, sort, cast, light, stamp, nuance, aspect, character, nature.

hue and cry ▶ noun *her relatives raised a hue and cry after the accident* **commotion**, outcry, uproar, fuss, clamour, racket, storm, ado, stir, furore, ruckus, ballyhoo, brouhaha, palaver, pother; *informal* hoo-ha, hullabaloo, to-do, flap, song and dance, rumpus, splash; *Brit. informal* kerfuffle, carry-on, row, stink; *NZ informal* bobsy-die.

huff ▶ noun *she walked off in a huff* **bad mood**, sulk, fit of bad humour, fit of pique, pet, temper, tantrum, rage, fury, passion; *informal* grump, snit; *Brit. informal* strop, paddy; *N. Amer. informal* blowout, hissy fit; *Brit. informal, dated* bate, wax; *archaic* paddywhack, miff.
OPPOSITE good mood.

huffy ▶ adjective *he was huffy with me for ages* **irritable**, irritated, annoyed, cross, grumpy, huffish, bad-tempered, crotchety, crabby, crabbed, cantankerous, curmudgeonly, moody, petulant, miserable, morose, sullen, surly, churlish; touchy, testy, tetchy, crusty, snappish, waspish, prickly; *informal* snappy, cranky; *Brit. informal* narky, narked, miffed, ratty, eggy, shirty, like a bear with a sore head, whingy; *N. Amer. informal* soreheaded, peckish; *Austral./NZ* snaky; *vulgar slang* pissed off; *dated* miffy.
OPPOSITES cheerful, friendly.

hug ▶ verb **1** *people kissed and hugged each other* **embrace**, cuddle, squeeze, clasp, clutch, cling to, hold someone close, hold someone tight, take someone in one's arms, enfold someone in one's arms, clasp/press someone to one's bosom; *literary* embosom.
2 *I headed north, hugging the coastline all the way* **keep close to**, stay near to, follow closely, follow the course of.
OPPOSITE keep away from.
3 *we hugged the comforting thought that we were safe from foreign foes* **cling**

to, hold on to, cherish, harbour, nurture, nurse, foster, retain, maintain, keep in one's mind.
OPPOSITE abandon.
▶ noun *there were hugs and tears as they were reunited* **embrace**, cuddle, squeeze, bear hug, hold, clasp, clutch, clinch, caress.

huge ▶ adjective *a huge amount of raw materials come from abroad | a huge slab of rock* **enormous**, vast, immense, very large, very big, great, massive, colossal, prodigious, gigantic, gargantuan, mammoth, monumental, tremendous, stupendous; **giant**, towering, hefty, bulky, weighty, heavy, gross, monstrous, elephantine, mountainous, titanic; epic, Herculean, Brobdingnagian; princely, generous, handsome; *informal* jumbo, mega, monster, whopping, whopping great, thumping, thumping great, humongous, hulking, bumper, almighty, astronomical, astronomic; *Brit. informal* whacking, whacking great, ginormous.
OPPOSITES insignificant; tiny.

hugely ▶ adverb *they are fighting a hugely expensive legal battle* **very**, most, really, thoroughly, extremely, exceedingly, particularly, tremendously, highly, greatly, decidedly, distinctly, exceptionally, immensely, eminently, supremely, inordinately, singularly, extraordinarily, vastly, overly; very much, to a great extent; *Scottish* unco; *French* très; *N. English* right; *informal* terrifically, awfully, terribly, devilishly, madly, majorly, seriously, desperately, mega, ultra, oh-so, too-too, stinking, mucho, damn, damned, too ... for words; *informal, dated* devilish, hellish, frightfully; *Brit. informal* ever so, well, bloody, dead, dirty, jolly, fair; *N. Amer. informal* real, mighty, powerful, awful, plumb, darned, way, bitching; *S. African informal* lekker; *archaic* exceeding, sore.
OPPOSITE slightly.

hugger-mugger ▶ adjective **1** *a spirit of careless frivolity where all was hugger-mugger* **disorderly**, confused, disorganized, chaotic, muddled, haphazard, in a mess, in a shambles, in disarray, topsy-turvy, at sixes and sevens; *informal* higgledy-piggledy; *Brit. informal* shambolic.
OPPOSITE orderly.
2 *no more hugger-mugger dealings for me!* **clandestine**, secret, covert, furtive, cloak-and-dagger, hole-in-the-corner, behind-the-scenes, under-the-table, sneaky, sly, underhand; undercover, underground; *informal* hush-hush.
OPPOSITE above board.

hulk ▶ noun **1** *the rusting hulks of ships* **wreck**, shipwreck, ruin, shell, skeleton, hull, frame, framework, derelict.
2 *a great clumsy hulk of a man* **oaf**; *informal* clodhopper, ape, gorilla; *N. Amer. informal* lummox, klutz; *N. Amer. & Scottish informal* galoot; *archaic* lubber, clodpole.

hulking ▶ adjective (*informal*) *a hulking man stood aside as I entered* **large**, big, heavy, heavily built, well built, solidly built, powerfully built, sturdy, burly, brawny, hefty, strapping, bulky, weighty, massive, ponderous, overgrown; clumsy, awkward, ungainly, lumbering, lumpish, loutish, oafish; *informal* hunky, beefy, clodhopping; *literary* thewy, stark; *archaic* lubberly.
OPPOSITES light, small.

hull[1] ▶ noun *the wooden hull of the ship* **framework**, body, frame, skeleton, shell, structure, basic structure; exterior.

hull[2] ▶ noun **shell**, husk, pod, case, casing, covering, seed case; rind, skin, peel; *N. Amer.* shuck; *technical* pericarp, capsule, legume; *rare* integument.
▶ verb *a beak which the bird uses effectively in hulling seeds* **shell**, husk, peel, pare, skin; *N. Amer.* shuck; *technical* decorticate.

hullabaloo ▶ noun (*informal*) *there was a terrific hullabaloo over the by-election* **fuss**, commotion, uproar, hubbub, outcry, furore, ruckus, ado, palaver, brouhaha, hue and cry; pandemonium, mayhem, tumult, turmoil, hurly-burly; roar, racket, din, noise, clamour, bedlam, babel; *informal* rumpus, ruction, hoo-ha, to-do, song and dance; *Brit. informal* kerfuffle, carry-on, row.

hum ▶ verb **1** *the engine was humming and ready to go* **purr**, whirr, throb, vibrate, murmur, buzz, thrum, drone; *literary* susurrate, bombinate.
2 *humming a tune* sing, croon, murmur, drone.
3 *the repair shops are humming as the tradesmen set about their various tasks* **be busy**, be active, be lively, buzz, bustle, be bustling, be a hive of activity, throb, vibrate, pulsate, pulse.
OPPOSITE be quiet.
4 (*Brit. informal*) *when the wind drops this stuff really hums* **smell**, stink, stink to high heaven, reek, have a bad smell, be malodorous; *Brit. informal* pong.
□ **hum and haw** (*Brit.*) *they waste a lot of time humming and hawing before going into action* **be indecisive**, hesitate, dither, vacillate, procrastinate, equivocate, prevaricate, waver, falter, fluctuate; *Brit.* haver; *Scottish* swither; *informal* shilly-shally, dilly-dally, blow hot and cold, pussyfoot around; *dated* tarry.
OPPOSITE be decisive.
▶ noun *a low hum of conversation* **murmur**, murmuring, drone, droning, vibration, purr, purring, buzz, buzzing, whirr, whirring, throb, throbbing, thrum, thrumming; *literary* susurration, susurrus, bombination.

human *See centre pages for list of early* **Humans**
▶ adjective **1** *the survival of the human race* anthropoid.
OPPOSITE animal.
2 *they're only human and therefore mistakes do occur | accidents due to human frailty* **mortal**, flesh and blood; **fallible**, weak, frail, imperfect, vulnerable, susceptible, erring, error-prone; physical, bodily, fleshly, carnal, corporal.
OPPOSITE infallible.
3 *the human side of politics is getting stronger* **compassionate**, humane, kind, kindly, kind-hearted, considerate, understanding, sympathetic, tolerant; approachable, accessible.
OPPOSITE inhuman.
▶ noun *the complex link between humans and animals* **person**, human being, personage, mortal, member of the human race; man, woman, child; individual, living soul, soul, being; earthling; *Latin* Homo sapiens; *informal, dated* body; *archaic* wight.
OPPOSITES animal; alien.

WORD LINKS

related prefix	**anthropo-**
study of humankind	**anthropology**
measurement of the human body	**anthropometry**
eating of other humans	**anthropophagous, cannibalistic**

humane ▶ adjective *regulations ensuring the humane treatment of animals* **compassionate**, kind, kindly, kind-hearted, considerate, understanding, sympathetic, tolerant, civilized, good, good-natured, gentle; lenient, forbearing, forgiving, merciful, mild, tender, clement, benign, humanitarian, benevolent, charitable, generous, magnanimous; approachable, accessible; *rare* benignant.
OPPOSITES cruel; inhumane.

humanitarian ▶ adjective **1** *they sought his release on humanitarian grounds | a humanitarian act* **compassionate**, humane; unselfish, altruistic, generous, magnanimous, benevolent, civilized, merciful, kind, good, sympathetic; *rare* benignant.
OPPOSITE selfish.
2 *a humanitarian organization* **charitable**, philanthropic, public-spirited, socially concerned, doing good works, welfare.
OPPOSITE for profit.
▶ noun **philanthropist**, altruist, benefactor, social reformer, do-gooder, good Samaritan; *historical* almsgiver; *rare* philanthrope, Maecenas.
OPPOSITE self-seeker.

humanities ▶ plural noun **liberal arts**, arts, literature; classics, classical studies, classical languages, classical literature; *Latin* literae humaniores.

humanity ▶ noun **1** *humanity evolved from the higher apes* **humankind**, the human race, the human species, mankind, man, people, mortals; *Latin* Homo sapiens.
OPPOSITE the animal kingdom.
2 *the humanity of Christ* **human nature**, humanness, mortality, flesh and blood.
3 *he praised them for their standards of humanity, care, and dignity* **compassion**, brotherly love, fellow feeling, humaneness, kindness, kind-heartedness, consideration, understanding, sympathy, tolerance, goodness, good-heartedness, gentleness, leniency, mercy, mercifulness, pity, tenderness, benevolence, charity, generosity, magnanimity.
OPPOSITES cruelty; inhumanity.

humanize ▶ verb *schools should try to humanize their pupils* **civilize**, improve, better; educate, enlighten, edify, instruct, sophisticate, socialize, refine, polish; *informal* rub the rough edges off.

humankind ▶ noun **the human race**, the human species, humanity, mankind, man, people, mortals; *Latin* Homo sapiens.
OPPOSITE the animal kingdom.

humble ▶ adjective **1** *her bearing was very humble and apologetic* **meek**, deferential, respectful, submissive, self-effacing, unassertive, unpresuming; **modest**, unassuming, self-deprecating, free from vanity, hiding one's light under a bushel; obsequious, sycophantic, servile; *Scottish* mim; *archaic* resistless.
OPPOSITES proud, overbearing.
2 *she came from a humble, unprivileged background* **low-ranking**, low, lowly, lower-class, plebeian, proletarian, working-class, undistinguished, poor, mean, ignoble, of low birth, low-born, of low rank; common, commonplace, ordinary, simple, inferior, unimportant, unremarkable, insignificant, inconsequential; *informal* plebby; *archaic* baseborn.
OPPOSITE noble.
3 *welcome to my humble abode* **unpretentious**, modest, unostentatious, plain, simple, ordinary.
OPPOSITE grand.
▶ verb **1** *I knew he had humbled himself to ask for my help* **humiliate**, abase, demean, belittle, lower, degrade, debase, bring down, bring low; mortify, shame, put to shame, abash, subdue, chasten, make someone eat humble pie, take down a peg or two; *informal* put down, cut down to size, settle someone's hash; *N. Amer. informal* make someone eat crow.
2 *Wales were humbled at Cardiff Arms Park by Romania* **defeat**, beat, beat hollow, crush, trounce, conquer, vanquish, rout, smash, overwhelm, get the better of, give a drubbing to, bring to one's knees; *informal* lick, clobber, hammer, slaughter, murder, massacre, crucify, wipe the floor with, walk all over; *N. Amer. informal* shellac, blow out, cream, skunk.

H

OPPOSITE be victorious over.

humbug ▶ noun **1** *to dress it all up as a 'green' tax is sheer humbug* **hypocrisy**, hypocritical talk/behaviour, sanctimoniousness, posturing, cant, empty talk; insincerity, dishonesty, falseness, falsity, sham, deceit, deception, deceptiveness, imposture, pretence; fraud, trickery, cheating; *informal* phoneyness, con, kidology; *Irish informal* codology; *rare* Tartufferie.
2 *you are a coward as well as a humbug* **hypocrite**, hypocritical person, plaster saint, whited sepulchre; charlatan, impostor, fraud, cheat, deceiver, dissembler, fake, sham; *informal* con man, con artist, phoney; *rare* Tartuffe.
▶ verb *poor Dave is easily humbugged* **deceive**, trick, delude, mislead, fool, hoodwink, dupe, hoax, take in, beguile, bamboozle, gull, cheat; *informal* con, kid, put one over on, have on, pull the wool over someone's eyes; *vulgar slang* bullshit; *archaic* cozen.

humdrum ▶ adjective *humdrum routine work* **mundane**, dull, dreary, boring, tedious, monotonous, banal, ho-hum, tiresome, wearisome, prosaic, unexciting, uninteresting, uneventful, unvarying, unvaried, unremarkable, repetitive, repetitious, routine, ordinary, everyday, day-to-day, quotidian, run-of-the-mill, commonplace, common, workaday, usual, pedestrian, customary, regular, normal; *N. Amer.* garden variety; *informal* typical, vanilla, plain vanilla; *Brit. informal* common or garden; *rare* banausic.
OPPOSITES remarkable; exciting.

H

humid ▶ adjective *a hot and humid day* **muggy**, close, sultry, sticky, steamy, oppressive, airless, stifling, suffocating, stuffy, clammy, soupy, heavy, fuggy, like a Turkish bath, like a sauna; damp, dank, moist, wet, misty.
OPPOSITES fresh; arid.

humidity ▶ noun *a climate of warm temperatures and high humidity* **mugginess**, humidness, closeness, sultriness, stickiness, steaminess, airlessness, stuffiness, clamminess; dampness, damp, dankness, moisture, moistness, wetness, mistiness.
OPPOSITES freshness; aridity.

WORD LINKS
measurement of humidity **hygrometry, psychrometry**

humiliate ▶ verb *you'll humiliate me in front of the whole school* **embarrass**, mortify, humble, show up, shame, make ashamed, put to shame; disgrace, discomfit, chasten, subdue, abash, abase, debase, demean, degrade, deflate, crush, quash, squash, bring down, bring low, cause to feel small, cause to lose face, make someone eat humble pie, take down a peg or two; *informal* put down, cut down to size, settle someone's hash; *N. Amer. informal* make someone eat crow.
OPPOSITE aggrandize.

humiliating ▶ adjective *a humiliating election defeat* **embarrassing**, mortifying, humbling, ignominious, inglorious, shaming, shameful; discreditable, undignified, discomfiting, chastening, debasing, demeaning, degrading, deflating, crushing, quashing, squashing, bringing down, bringing low; *informal* blush-making; *rare* humiliatory.
OPPOSITE glorious.

humiliation ▶ noun *only a few go through the humiliation of having the bailiffs at the door* **embarrassment**, mortification, shame, indignity, ignominy, disgrace, dishonour, discomfiture, degradation, discredit, obloquy, opprobrium, loss of pride, loss of face; affront, insult, rebuff, snub, put-down, blow to one's pride, slap in the face, smack in the face, kick in the teeth; *informal* brush-off; *rare* disesteem, reprobation, vitiation.
OPPOSITE honour.

humility ▶ noun *he needs the humility to accept that their way may be better* **modesty**, humbleness, modestness, meekness, lack of pride, lack of vanity, diffidence, unassertiveness.
OPPOSITE pride.

hummock ▶ noun **hillock**, hump, mound, knoll, tump, prominence, eminence, elevation, rise, dune, barrow, tumulus; *N. Amer.* knob; *S. African* koppie; *archaic* knap, monticle.

humorist ▶ noun **comic writer**, writer of comedy, wit, wag; funny man, funny woman, comic, comedian, comedienne, joker, jokester, clown, jester; cartoonist, caricaturist; *informal* card, laugh, scream, hoot, riot, barrel of laughs; *informal, dated* caution.

humorous ▶ adjective *the novel is a humorous account of a developing relationship* **amusing**, funny, entertaining, comic, comical, diverting, witty, jocular, light-hearted, tongue-in-cheek, wry, waggish, whimsical, playful; hilarious, uproarious, riotous, zany, facetious, farcical, absurd, droll; *informal* priceless, wacky, side-splitting, rib-tickling, a scream, a hoot, a laugh, a barrel of laughs; *informal, dated* killing; *rare* jocose.
OPPOSITES serious; boring.

humour ▶ noun **1** *the humour of the situation is central to the film* **comical aspect**, comic side, funny side, comedy, funniness, hilarity, jocularity; absurdity, absurdness, ludicrousness, drollness, facetiousness; satire, irony.
OPPOSITE seriousness.

CHOOSE THE RIGHT WORD

humorous, funny, witty, comical

All these words refer to the quality of being amusing, but the nature and source of the amusement vary.

- Something that is **humorous** has typically been created intentionally to amuse (*a collection of humorous sketches*).
- **Funny** is the most general and informal word for someone or something found amusing (*a funny story* | *a naturally funny man*). It concentrates on the effect of making people laugh rather than the intention behind it, and covers a range of causes from highly intellectual jokes to slapstick and amusing accidents. In a negative construction, *funny* can mean that something is unpleasant or wrong (*stealing other people's work isn't funny*). The word has a very close sense of 'strange, curious', which is often difficult to distinguish from 'amusing' (*I do get some funny looks* | *funny ha-ha or funny peculiar?*).
- **Witty** is reserved for the clever and inventive exploitation of the potential of language to amuse (*a stylish and witty black comedy*).
- **Comical** suggests that the amusement is caused by a perception of oddness or incongruity (*his astonishment was almost comical* | *they remembered the comical dog on the beach*).

2 *the familiar stories are spiced up with humour* **jokes**, joking, jests, jesting, quips, witticisms, witty remarks, funny remarks, puns; **wit**, wittiness, comedy, jocularity, waggishness, drollery, repartee, badinage, banter, raillery; *French* doubles entendres, bons mots; *informal* gags, wisecracks, cracks, one-liners.
3 *his good humour was infectious* **mood**, temper, disposition, temperament, frame of mind, state of mind; spirits.
4 (*archaic*) *variations caused by the different humours of particular men* **inclination**, whim, caprice, fancy, whimsy, foible, vagary, quirk, peculiarity, oddity, idiosyncrasy, eccentricity, propensity, kink, crotchet, bent; *informal* hang-up, thing; *rare* megrim, singularity.
▶ verb *she was always humouring him to prevent trouble* **indulge**, pander to, yield to, bow to, cater to, give way to, give in to, go along with, comply with, adapt to, accommodate; **pamper**, spoil, overindulge, cosset, coddle, mollycoddle, mollify, soothe, placate, gratify, satisfy.
OPPOSITE stand up to.

humourless ▶ adjective *she was thought of as a hard-working, humourless academic* **serious**, serious-minded, solemn, earnest, sober, sombre, grave, stern, grim, dour, morose, unsmiling, stony-faced; **gloomy**, glum, depressed, sad, melancholy, dismal, doleful, mournful, dejected, despondent, joyless, cheerless, lugubrious, in low spirits, with a long face; boring, tedious, dull, dry, heavy-going.
OPPOSITES light-hearted; jovial.

hump ▶ noun *his back rose into a kind of hump at the base of the spine* **protuberance**, lump, bump, knob, protrusion, prominence, projection, bulge, swelling, hunch, nodule, node, mass, growth, outgrowth, excrescence; *rare* tumescence, tumefaction, intumescence.
□ **give someone the hump** (*informal*). See ANNOY.
□ **over the hump** *now we have reached this point we are over the hump* **over the worst part**, over the worst of it, out of the woods, on the road to recovery, on the up and up, on the way up, getting better, making progress, in the clear.
OPPOSITE in difficulties.
▶ verb **1** *he turned and humped his body to avoid a rope* **arch**, curve, hunch, bend, bow, curl, crook.
OPPOSITE straighten.
2 (*informal*) *he continued to hump cases up and down the hotel corridor* **carry**, lug, heave, lift, shoulder, hoist, heft, tote; *informal* schlep; *Scottish informal* humph; *rare* upheave.

humped ▶ adjective *he had a grotesquely humped back* **arched**, bent, bowed, curved, rounded, hunched; humpbacked, hunchbacked; *technical* kyphotic; *literary* embowed, crookbacked; *rare* curviform.
OPPOSITE straight.

hunch ▶ verb **1** *he thrust his hands in his pockets, hunching his shoulders* **arch**, curve, hump, bend, bow, curl, crook.
OPPOSITE straighten.
2 *I* **hunched up** *as small as I could* **crouch**, huddle up, curl up, hunker down, bend, stoop, squat.
OPPOSITE stretch out.
▶ noun **1** *he had a hunch on his back* **protuberance**, hump, lump, bump, knob, protrusion, prominence, projection, bulge, swelling, nodule, node, mass, growth, outgrowth, excrescence; *rare* tumescence, tumefaction, intumescence.
2 *my hunch is that these may not be the end of the changes* **feeling**, guess, suspicion, sneaking suspicion, impression, inkling, idea, notion, fancy, presentiment, premonition, intuition; *informal* gut feeling, feeling in one's bones, funny feeling, sixth sense.

hundred ▶ cardinal number century; *informal* ton.

WORD LINKS

related prefixes **centi-** (e.g. ***centimetre, centipede***), **hecto-** (e.g. ***hectogram***)

relating to a hundred **centenary, centennial**

hunger ▶ noun **1** *she was faint with hunger* **lack of food**, need for food, hungriness, ravenousness, emptiness; starvation, famine, malnutrition, malnourishment, undernourishment; *rare* famishment, inanition.
2 *there is a global hunger for news* **desire**, craving, longing, yearning, pining, hankering, thirst, appetite, lust, ache, want, need; *informal* itch, yen; *rare* appetence, appetency.
OPPOSITE aversion.
▶ verb (*archaic*) *when he had fasted forty days and forty nights, he afterwards hungered* **feel hunger**, be hungry, be famished, be starving, be ravenous.
□ **hunger after/for** *all actors hunger for such a role* **desire**, crave, have a craving for; long for, yearn for, have a yearning for, pine for, ache for, thirst for, have an appetite for, hanker after, lust after, want, need; *informal* have a yen for, itch for, be dying for, be gagging for; *archaic* be athirst for, be desirous of.
OPPOSITE have an aversion to.

hungry ▶ adjective **1** *I was feeling ravenously hungry* **ravenous**, empty, hollow, faint from hunger; starving, starved, famished, dying from hunger, deprived of food, half-starved, malnourished, undernourished, underfed; *informal* peckish, able to eat a horse, with one's stomach thinking one's throat's cut; *rare* sharp-set, esurient.
OPPOSITES full; well fed.
2 *the new team are* ***hungry for*** *success* **eager**, keen, avid, longing, yearning, pining, aching, greedy, thirsting, with an appetite; craving, desiring, desirous of, covetous of, hankering after, lusting after, in need of, in want of; *informal* itching, dying, gagging, hot, with a yen; *archaic* athirst.
OPPOSITES averse to; indifferent to.

hunk ▶ noun **1** *the soup was served with a hunk of bread* **chunk**, large piece, slab, wedge, block, lump, mass, square, gobbet, dollop, portion; *Scottish* dod; *Brit. informal* wodge; *N. Amer. informal* gob; *rare* nub.
2 (*informal*) *the calendar gives you a different hunk each month* **muscleman**, strongman, macho, macho man, iron man, Hercules, Atlas, Samson, Tarzan; *informal* tough guy, he-man, beefcake, stud, bruiser; *N. Amer. informal* studmuffin.
OPPOSITE wimp.

hunt ▶ verb **1** *in the autumn they hunted deer* **chase**, give chase to, pursue, stalk, course, hunt down, run down; track, trail, follow, shadow, hound, dog; *informal* tail.
2 *police are* ***hunting for*** *her attacker* **search**, look, look high and low, scour around; seek, try to find; cast about/around/round, rummage (about/around/round), root about/around, fish about/around, forage about/around, ferret (about/around); *Brit. informal* rootle about/around.
▶ noun **1** *they enjoyed the thrill of the hunt* **chase**, pursuit, stalking, course, coursing; tracking, trailing, shadowing; *informal* tailing.
2 *police have stepped up the hunt for the killer* **search**, look, quest; seeking, rummaging, foraging, ferreting (about/around).

hunted ▶ adjective *his eyes had a hunted look* **harassed**, persecuted, harried, hounded, besieged, beleaguered, troubled, stressed, tormented; careworn, haggard, downtrodden, browbeaten, distraught, desperate; *informal* hassled, up against it.
OPPOSITE carefree.

hunter ▶ noun **huntsman**, **huntswoman**, stalker, trapper, woodsman; nimrod, Orion; predator; *French* chasseur; *Indian* shikari; *rare* venator, venerer.

hunting ▶ noun **blood sports**, field sports, stalking, trapping, coursing, fox-hunting, the chase; poaching; *Indian* shikar; *archaic* venery.

hurdle ▶ noun **1** *he hit a hurdle and cut his leg badly* **fence**, jump, barrier, barricade, bar, railing, rail, wall, hedge, hedgerow.
2 *this was the final hurdle to overcome in the college's bid for university status* **obstacle**, difficulty, problem, barrier, bar, snag, stumbling block, impediment, obstruction, complication, handicap, hindrance; *informal* hiccup, headache, fly in the ointment; *Brit. informal* spanner in the works; *N. Amer. informal* monkey wrench in the works.

hurl ▶ verb *rioters hurled a brick through the windscreen of a car* **throw**, toss, fling, pitch, cast, lob, launch, flip, catapult, shy, dash, send, bowl, aim, direct, project, propel, fire, let fly; *informal* chuck, heave, sling, buzz, whang, bung; *N. Amer. informal* peg; *Austral. informal* hoy; *NZ informal* bish.
OPPOSITES catch, hold.

hurly-burly ▶ noun *they wanted to escape from the hurly-burly of city life* **bustle**, hustle, commotion, hubbub, confusion, chaos, disorder, fuss, turmoil, uproar, tumult, turbulence, pandemonium, mayhem, bedlam, furore, brouhaha; upheaval, unrest, disruption, trouble, agitation; *informal* hoo-ha, hullabaloo, ballyhoo, rumpus; *Brit. informal* kerfuffle.
OPPOSITES calm, order.

hurricane ▶ noun **cyclone**, typhoon, tornado, storm, tropical storm, tempest, windstorm, gale, squall, whirlwind; *N. Amer. informal* twister; *Austral./NZ informal* willy-willy.

hurried ▶ adjective **1** *he left in long, hurried strides | hurried glances* **quick**, fast, swift, rapid, speedy, brisk, hasty, hurrying, expeditious, breakneck; cursory, perfunctory, brief, short, fleeting, passing, flying, superficial; *literary* fleet, rathe.
OPPOSITES slow, leisurely.
2 *a hurried decision* **hasty**, rushed, speedy, quick; **rash**, impetuous, impulsive, reckless, precipitate, precipitous, incautious, imprudent, spur-of-the-moment, premature; *rare* temerarious.
OPPOSITE considered.

hurriedly ▶ adverb *she got up and dressed hurriedly* **hastily**, speedily, quickly, fast, rapidly, swiftly, briskly, expeditiously, without delay, in haste, at a run, at a gallop, at top speed, at full tilt, at the double, as fast as possible; headlong, hotfoot, post-haste, pell-mell, helter-skelter; *informal* at a lick, like the wind, like greased lightning, like a bomb, like mad, like crazy, like blazes, double quick, in double quick time; *Brit. informal* like the clappers, at a rate of knots, like billy-o; *N. Amer. informal* lickety-split; *literary* apace, hurry-scurry.
OPPOSITES slowly; at moderate speed.

hurry ▶ verb **1** *you'd better hurry or you'll be late* **be quick**, hurry up, move quickly, go fast, hasten, make haste, speed, speed up, lose no time, press on, push on, run, dash, rush, hurtle, dart, race, fly, flash, shoot, streak, bolt, bound, blast, charge, chase, career, scurry, scramble, scamper, scuttle, sprint, gallop, go hell for leather, go like lightning; *Brit.* scutter; *informal* whizz, whoosh, vroom, tear, scoot, hare, pelt, zip, whip, zoom, belt, beetle, buzz, get a move on, step on it, get cracking, get moving, shake a leg, go like a bat out of hell, hotfoot it, leg it, burn rubber; *Brit. informal* bomb, bucket, shift, put one's foot down, get one's skates on, go like the clappers, stir one's stumps; *Scottish informal* wheech; *N. Amer. informal* hightail, barrel, boogie, clip, lay rubber, get the lead out, get a wiggle on; *S. African informal* put foot; *N. Amer. vulgar slang* drag/tear/haul ass; *informal, dated* cut along; *archaic* post, hie, fleet.
OPPOSITES move slowly; dawdle.
2 *she hurried him across the landing* **hustle**, hasten, push (on), urge (on), drive on, spur on, goad, prod; *informal* gee up.
OPPOSITES slow down; delay.
▶ noun *in all the hurry, we forgot the picnic* **haste**, flurry, bustle, confusion, commotion, hubbub, hustle, urgency, agitation, turmoil; **rush**, race, scramble, scurry; speed, swiftness, rapidity, quickness; *literary* fleetness, celerity; *archaic* hurry scurry, pother.
OPPOSITE calmness.

hurt ▶ verb **1** *my back hurts* **be painful**, be sore, be tender, cause pain, cause discomfort, ache, smart, sting, burn, tingle, throb; *informal* be killing, be playing up.
OPPOSITE be healed.
2 *Dad had hurt his leg* **injure**, wound, damage, disable, incapacitate, impair, maim, mutilate, cause injury to, cause pain to; bruise, cut, gash, graze, scrape, scratch, lacerate; abuse, torture, maltreat, ill-treat, molest.
OPPOSITE heal.
3 *his cruel words hurt her deeply* **distress**, pain, wound, offend, sting, upset, sadden, devastate, mortify, grieve, aggrieve, be hurtful to, hurt someone's feelings, cause sorrow, cause suffering, cause anguish, make unhappy, give offence to, cut to the quick.
OPPOSITES please; comfort.
4 *high interest rates are hurting the local economy* **harm**, damage, do harm to, be detrimental to, weaken, spoil, mar, blemish, blight, impair, impede, jeopardize, undermine, ruin, wreck, sabotage, cripple; *informal* foul up.
OPPOSITES benefit, improve.
▶ noun **1** *rolling properly into a fall minimizes hurt | he rubbed the hurt on his chin* **harm**, injury, wounding, pain, suffering, discomfort, soreness, aching, smarting, stinging, throbbing, pangs; bruise, graze, scrape, cut, gash, scratch, laceration.
2 *she loved him, in spite of all the hurt he had caused her* **distress**, pain, suffering, grief, misery, anguish, torment, trauma, woe, upset, sadness, sorrow, wretchedness; harm, damage, injury, trouble, misfortune, affliction, wrong, detriment, disadvantage; *informal* mischief.
OPPOSITE joy.
▶ adjective **1** *the doctor looked at my hurt hand* **injured**, wounded, bruised, grazed, scratched, cut, gashed, lacerated, sore, painful, aching, burning, smarting, throbbing.
OPPOSITE healed.
2 *Anne's hurt expression spoke volumes* **pained**, distressed, aggrieved, displeased, disgruntled, anguished, resentful, offended, piqued, upset, sad, saddened, sorrowful, grief-stricken; *informal* miffed, peeved, narked, browned off, hacked off; *Brit. informal* cheesed off; *N. Amer. informal* sore; *vulgar slang* pissed off.
OPPOSITE pleased.

hurtful ▶ adjective **1** *hurtful words* **upsetting**, distressing, wounding, painful; **unkind**, cruel, nasty, mean, malicious, spiteful, snide, acerbic, cutting, biting, barbed, vicious, offensive; *informal* catty, bitchy; *Brit. informal* sarky; *N. Amer. informal* snarky; *rare* acidulous, mordacious.
OPPOSITES pleasant; comforting.

2 *such a move would be hurtful to the interests of women* **detrimental**, harmful, damaging, injurious, disadvantageous, unfavourable, prejudicial, baleful, deleterious, destructive, disastrous, pernicious, ruinous, inimical; *literary* malefic, maleficent; *rare* baneful, prejudicious.
OPPOSITE beneficial.

hurtle ▶ verb *a runaway car hurtled towards them* **speed**, rush, race, chase, bolt, bowl, dash, career, careen, cannon, sweep, whizz, buzz, zoom, flash, blast, charge, shoot, streak, run, gallop, stampede, hare, fly, wing, scurry, scud, go like the wind; *informal* belt, pelt, tear, scoot, tool, zap, zip, whip, burn rubber, go like a bat out of hell; *Brit. informal* bomb, bucket, shift, go like the clappers; *N. Amer. informal* clip, boogie, hightail, barrel; *archaic* post, hie.
OPPOSITE go slowly.

husband ▶ noun **spouse**, partner, mate, consort, man; groom, bridegroom; *informal* hubby, old man, one's better half; *Brit. informal* other half; *humorous* lord and master; *archaic* helpmate, helpmeet.
▶ verb *reserves of oil and gas should be husbanded* **use economically**, use sparingly, economize on, be frugal with, manage thriftily; **conserve**, preserve, save, safeguard, save for a rainy day, put aside, put by, lay in, reserve, store, stockpile, hoard.
OPPOSITES squander, waste.

husbandry ▶ noun **1** *farmers have no money to invest in new methods of husbandry* **farm management**, farming, agriculture, land management, agronomy, agronomics, agribusiness, cultivation, tillage; animal husbandry.
2 *they have gained some reward from the careful husbandry of their slender resources* **conservation**, careful management, good housekeeping, economy, thrift, thriftiness, frugality; saving, budgeting; *rare* sparingness.
OPPOSITE wastefulness.

hush ▶ verb **1** *he placed a finger before pursed lips to hush her* **silence**, quieten, quieten down, shush; gag, muzzle; *informal* shut up.
2 *the lights dimmed and everyone hushed* **fall silent**, become silent, stop talking, quieten, quieten down; *informal* pipe down, shut up.
OPPOSITE become noisy.
3 *she tried to hush their fears* **calm**, allay, assuage, still, quieten, soften, ease, soothe, lessen, reduce, moderate.
OPPOSITE aggravate.
4 *management took steps to* **hush up** *the dangers* **keep secret**, conceal, hide, suppress, cover up, keep dark, keep quiet about, not divulge, stifle, squash, whitewash, smother, obscure, veil, sweep under the carpet; *informal* sit on, keep under one's hat.
OPPOSITE disclose.
▶ exclamation *Hush! Someone will hear you* **be quiet**, keep quiet, quieten down, be silent, stop talking, hold your tongue; *informal* shut up, shut your face, shut your mouth, shut your trap, button your lip, pipe down, cut the cackle, put a sock in it, give it a rest, not another word; *Brit. informal* shut your gob, wrap it up, wrap up; *N. Amer. informal* save it.
OPPOSITE speak up.
▶ noun *a hush descended over the crowd* **silence**, quiet, quietness, quietude, soundlessness, noiselessness; stillness, still, peacefulness, peace, calmness, calm, tranquillity.
OPPOSITE noise.

hush-hush ▶ adjective (*informal*) *this is meant to be hush-hush* **secret**, top secret, confidential, strictly confidential, classified, restricted, under wraps, off the record, not for publication/circulation, not to be made public, not to be disclosed; unrevealed, undisclosed, unpublished, untold, unknown; *Latin* sub rosa.
OPPOSITES public, on the record.

husk ▶ noun **shell**, hull, pod, case, casing, covering, seed case; rind, skin, peel; (**husks**) chaff, bran; *N. Amer.* shuck; *technical* pericarp, capsule, legume; *rare* integument.

husky ▶ adjective **1** *his voice deepened to a husky growl* **throaty**, gruff, deep, gravelly, hoarse, coarse, croaking, croaky, rough, rough-sounding, thick, guttural, harsh, rasping, raspy.
OPPOSITES shrill; soft.
2 *Paddy looked a husky guy* **strong**, muscular, muscly, muscle-bound, brawny, hefty, burly, hulking, chunky, strapping, thickset, solid, powerful, heavy, robust, rugged, sturdy, Herculean, big and strong, broad-shouldered, well built, powerfully built, solidly built; *informal* beefy, hunky; *dated* stalwart; *literary* thewy, stark.
OPPOSITE puny.

hussy ▶ noun **minx**, madam, coquette, tease, seductress, Lolita, Jezebel; trollop, slut, loose woman; *informal* floozie, tart, puss; *Brit. informal* scrubber, slapper, slag; *N. Amer. informal* tramp, vamp; *archaic* baggage, hoyden, fizgig, jade, quean, wanton, strumpet.

hustle ▶ verb **1** *they were hissed and hustled as they went* **jostle**, push, push roughly, bump, knock, shove, nudge, elbow, shoulder; crowd, mob.
2 *I was hustled away to a cold cell* **manhandle**, push, shove, thrust, frogmarch, bulldoze; rush, hurry, hasten, whisk, sweep; *informal* bundle.
3 (*informal*) *don't be hustled into anything unless you really want to do it* **coerce**, force, compel, pressure, pressurize, badger, pester, hound, harass, nag, harry, urge, goad, prod, spur; browbeat, bludgeon, bulldoze, steamroller, dragoon, prevail on, strong-arm; *informal* railroad; *Brit. informal* bounce; *N. Amer. informal* fast-talk.
▶ noun *we were tired of the hustle and bustle of city life* **activity**, bustle, hustle and bustle, hurly-burly, commotion, tumult, hubbub, brouhaha, busyness, action, liveliness, animation, movement, life, excitement, agitation, fuss, flurry, stir, whirl; *informal* toing and froing, comings and goings, rumpus, ballyhoo, hoo-ha, hullabaloo, to-do; *archaic* hurry scurry, pother.
OPPOSITE peace.

hut ▶ noun **shack**, shanty, cabin, log cabin, shelter, shed, lean-to, den, hovel; *Scottish* bothy, shieling, shiel; *N. Amer.* cabana; *Canadian* tilt; *S. African* hok; *Austral.* gunyah, mia-mia, humpy; *NZ* whare; *American Indian* hogan, wickiup; (*in Brazil*) favela; *N. Amer. archaic* shebang.

hybrid ▶ noun *this is a hybrid between a brown and albino mouse* **cross**, cross-breed, mixed-breed, half-breed, half-blood; mixture, blend, meld, amalgam, amalgamation, combination, composite, compound, conglomerate, fusion, synthesis.
▶ adjective *hybrid varieties of rose* **composite**, cross-bred, interbred; mixed, compound, combined, blended, mongrel, impure; half-caste, half-breed, of mixed breed.
OPPOSITE pure-bred.

hybridize ▶ verb *a few gardeners hybridize their roses* **cross-breed**, cross, interbreed, mix, intermix, blend, combine, amalgamate; cross-fertilize, cross-pollinate.

hygiene ▶ noun *poor standards of food hygiene* **cleanliness**, personal hygiene, personal cleanliness, purity, sterility, disinfection, sanitation, sanitariness; public health, environmental health, sanitary measures.
OPPOSITE uncleanliness.

hygienic ▶ adjective *this will leave the whole kitchen clean and hygienic* **sanitary**, clean, germ-free, dirt-free, disinfected, sterilized, sterile, antiseptic, aseptic, uninfected, unpolluted, uncontaminated, salubrious, healthy, pure, wholesome; *informal* squeaky clean, as clean as a whistle.
OPPOSITES dirty; insanitary.

hymn ▶ noun **religious song**, **anthem**, song of praise, canticle, chorale, psalm, carol, chant; antiphon, introit, doxology, spiritual, paean, plainsong; *rare* lay, miserere.

WORD LINKS
Muse **Erato**

hype (*informal*) ▶ noun *she relied on hype and headlines to stoke up interest in her music* **publicity**, advertising, promotion, marketing, puff, puffery, propaganda, exposure; boost, push, fanfare, build-up; *informal* plug, plugging, razzmatazz, ballyhoo.
▶ verb *this was another stunt to hype a new product* **publicize**, advertise, promote, push, boost, merchandise, give publicity to, give a puff to, puff, puff up, build up, talk up, beat/bang the drum for; *informal* plug.
OPPOSITE play down.

hyperbole ▶ noun *the media hyperbole which accompanied their European Championship match* **exaggeration**, overstatement, magnification, amplification, embroidery, embellishment, overplaying, excess, overkill; *informal* purple prose, puffery.
OPPOSITE understatement.

hypercritical ▶ adjective *he was a sarcastic, hypercritical man* **carping**, captious, overcritical, fault-finding, hair-splitting, cavilling, niggling, quibbling, pedantic, pettifogging, fussy, finicky, over-censorious, over-exacting, over-rigorous, over-particular, over-strict; *informal* **picky**, nit-picking, pernickety; *N. Amer. informal* persnickety; *archaic* nice, overnice.
OPPOSITES easy-going; uncritical.

hypnosis ▶ noun **mesmerism**, hypnotism, hypnotic suggestion, auto-suggestion.

hypnotic ▶ adjective *her voice had a hypnotic quality* **mesmerizing**, mesmeric, spellbinding, entrancing, bewitching, fascinating, irresistible, compelling; **soporific**, sleep-inducing, sleep-producing, somnolent, somniferous, sedative, numbing; *Medicine* stupefacient, stupefactive; *rare* somnific.
OPPOSITE invigorating.

hypnotism ▶ noun **mesmerism**, hypnosis, hypnotic suggestion, auto-suggestion.

hypnotize ▶ verb **1** *a witness had been hypnotized to enhance his memory* **mesmerize**, send into a trance, put under, put out, put to sleep.
2 *they were hypnotized by the dancers* **fascinate**, entrance, beguile, spellbind, hold spellbound, enthral, transfix, be unable to take one's eyes off, captivate, bewitch, enrapture, grip, rivet, absorb, magnetize; *informal* bowl over, knock out.
OPPOSITE bore.

hypochondria ▶ noun **imagined ill health**, **valetudinarianism**, anxiety about one's health, preoccupation with one's health, health obsession; neurosis; *rare* hypochondriasis, hypochondriacism.

hypochondriac ▶ noun *she was a hypochondriac who could not manage without her pills* **valetudinarian**, valetudinary, neurotic; *French* malade

imaginaire; *archaic* melancholico; *rare* hypochondriast.
▶ **adjective** *her tiresome hypochondriac husband* **valetudinarian**, valetudinary, malingering, neurotic, health-obsessed, obsessed with one's health, preoccupied with ill health, anxious about one's health; *rare* hypochondriacal, hypochondric.

hypocrisy ▶ **noun** *plain speaking was important to him—he hated hypocrisy* **sanctimoniousness**, sanctimony, pietism, piousness, affected piety, affected superiority, false virtue, cant, humbug, pretence, posturing, speciousness, empty talk; insincerity, falseness, falsity, deceptiveness, deceit, deceitfulness, deception, dishonesty, dissembling, dissimulation, duplicity, imposture, two-facedness, double-dealing; *informal* phoneyness; *rare* Pharisaism, Tartufferie.
OPPOSITES honesty; sincerity.

hypocrite ▶ **noun** *he condemned her as superficial and a hypocrite* **sanctimonious person**, pietist, whited sepulchre, plaster saint, humbug, pretender, deceiver, dissembler, impostor; *informal* phoney, Holy Willie; *Brit. informal* creeping Jesus; *N. Amer. informal* bluenose; *rare* Pharisee, Tartuffe, Pecksniff, canter.

hypocritical ▶ **adjective** *a hypocritical morality regarding sexual behaviour* **sanctimonious**, pious, pietistic, self-righteous, holier-than-thou, superior, insincere, specious, feigned, pretended, hollow, false; deceitful, deceptive, dishonest, untruthful, lying, dissembling, duplicitous, two-faced, double-dealing, untrustworthy; *informal* phoney, pretend; *rare* Pharisaic, Pharisaical, Tartuffian, Janus-faced, canting.
OPPOSITE sincere.

hypodermic ▶ **noun** **needle**, syringe; *informal* hype, spike.

hypothesis ▶ **noun** *his 'steady state' hypothesis of the origin of the universe* **theory**, theorem, thesis, conjecture, supposition, speculation, postulation, postulate, proposition, premise, surmise, assumption, presumption, presupposition; notion, concept, idea, contention, opinion, view, belief.

hypothetical ▶ **adjective** *a hypothetical case | the hypothetical tenth planet* **theoretical**, **speculative**, conjectured, imagined, notional, suppositional; supposed, assumed, presumed, putative; made up, unreal; academic.
OPPOSITES real, actual.

hysteria ▶ **noun** *his voice had an edge of hysteria* **frenzy**, wildness, feverishness, irrationality; **hysterics**, loss of control; panic, panic attack, alarm, outburst/fit of agitation, loss of reason, fit of madness, neurosis, delirium, derangement, mania, distress, mental distress; *Brit. informal* the screaming abdabs/habdabs.
OPPOSITES calmness, self-possession.

hysterical ▶ **adjective** **1** *Janet became hysterical and began screaming | hysterical laughter* **overwrought**, emotional, uncontrolled, uncontrollable, out of control, unrestrained, unrestrainable, frenzied, in a frenzy, frantic, wild, feverish; beside oneself, driven to distraction, in a panic, agitated, neurotic; mad, crazed, berserk, maniac, maniacal, manic, delirious, unhinged, deranged, out of one's mind, out of one's wits, raving; *informal* in a state.
OPPOSITES calm, self-possessed.
2 (*informal*) *her attempts to teach them to dance were hysterical* **hilarious**, uproarious, very funny, very amusing, comical, comic, farcical; *informal* hysterically funny, side-splitting, rib-tickling, killing, killingly funny, screamingly funny, a scream, a hoot, a laugh, a barrel of laughs, a laugh a minute.
OPPOSITE serious.

hysterics ▶ **plural noun** (*informal*) **1** *she was throwing a fit of screaming hysterics* **hysteria**, wildness, feverishness, irrationality, frenzy, loss of control, loss of reason; neurosis, delirium, derangement, mania, distress, mental distress; *Brit. informal* the screaming abdabs/habdabs.
OPPOSITES calmness, self-possession.
2 *this started them both giggling and they fled upstairs in hysterics* **fits of laughter**, gales of laughter, peals of laughter, uncontrollable laughter, convulsions, fits, guffawing, howling; *informal* stitches, hooting; *rare* cachinnation.

ice ▶ noun **1** *the lake was covered with ice* **frozen water**; icicle, iceberg, glacier; black ice, glaze, verglas, frost, rime.
2 *assorted ices* **ice cream**; sorbet, water ice; N. Amer. sherbet.
3 *the ice in her voice had no effect on him* **coldness**, coolness, frost, frostiness, iciness, chilliness, glaciality, frigidity, lack of warmth; hostility, unfriendliness, stiffness, distance, stand-offishness, aloofness.
□ **on ice** (informal) *Govan's transfer to the City team was still on ice last night* **in abeyance**, pending, ongoing, (up) in the air, (still) open, hanging fire, in the balance; in suspension, in a state of suspension, suspended, put to one side, in a state of uncertainty, in limbo, betwixt and between; deferred, postponed, put off; awaiting attention, awaiting decision, awaiting action, unattended to, outstanding, unfinished, incomplete; unresolved, undetermined, undecided, unsettled, unconcluded, uncertain; informal on the back burner, in cold storage.
OPPOSITE in hand.
□ **with ice** *would you like your Scotch with ice?* informal **on the rocks**.
▶ verb **1** *the lake has iced over* **freeze**, freeze over, turn into ice, harden, solidify; archaic glaciate.
OPPOSITE thaw.
2 (usually **iced**) *a refreshingly iced lemonade* **cool**, chill, make cold, refrigerate, add ice to.
OPPOSITE hot.
3 *she had iced the cake and written 'Good Luck' on it* **cover with icing**, glaze; N. Amer. frost, spread frosting over.

WORD LINKS
relating to ice **gelid, glacial**
fear of ice **cryophobia**

ice-cold ▶ adjective *the ice-cold waters of the fjord* **icy**, freezing, bitterly cold, glacial, sub-zero, frozen, wintry; arctic, polar, Siberian; bitter, biting, piercing, raw, cutting, chilly; refreshing, bracing, invigorating; literary chill, frore; rare gelid, brumal, rimy, algid.
OPPOSITES hot, warm.

icing ▶ noun *a big cake with white icing* **glaze**, sugar paste; royal icing, butter icing, glacé icing, fondant icing; N. Amer. frosting.

icon ▶ noun *an icon of the Madonna hangs on the wall* **image**, idol, portrait, likeness, representation, symbol, figure, statue, model.

iconoclast ▶ noun *she is an iconoclast, called to shatter the myth of restaurants she feels are too popular* **critic**, sceptic, questioner; heretic, nonconformist, dissident, dissenter, dissentient; malcontent, rebel, subversive, renegade, mutineer; maverick; original, innovator.

iconoclastic ▶ adjective *a fresh, even an iconoclastic, influence could work wonders* **critical**, sceptical, questioning; heretical, irreverent, nonconformist, dissident, dissenting, dissentient; malcontent, rebellious, subversive, renegade, mutinous; maverick, original, innovative, groundbreaking.
OPPOSITE conformist.

icy ▶ adjective **1** *icy roads* **frozen**, frozen over, iced over, ice-bound, ice-covered, iced up, frosty, frosted, glassy, like a sheet of glass, slippery; informal slippy; literary rimy.
2 *an icy wind* **freezing**, frigid, chill, chilly, chilling, frosty, biting, bitter, raw, arctic, glacial, Siberian, polar, gelid.
OPPOSITES hot, warm.
3 *'What did you say?' said an icy voice* **unfriendly**, unwelcoming, inhospitable, hostile, forbidding; cold, cool, chilly, frigid, frosty, glacial, wintry; stiff, aloof, distant, unsympathetic, disdainful, haughty, stony, stern, hard, fierce; rare gelid.
OPPOSITE friendly.

idea ▶ noun **1** *the idea of death scares her* **concept**, notion, conception, conceptualization, thought, image, mental picture, visualization, abstraction, perception; hypothesis, postulation.
2 *our idea is to open a new shop* **plan**, design, scheme, project, proposal, proposition, suggestion, recommendation, aim, intention, objective, object, purpose, end, goal, target.
3 *Elizabeth had other ideas on the subject* **thought**, theory, view, viewpoint, opinion, feeling, outlook, belief, judgement, conclusion.
4 *you had an idea that it might happen?* **sense**, feeling, suspicion, fancy, inkling, hunch, understanding, theory, hypothesis, thesis, interpretation, assumption, presumption, supposition, surmise, postulation, conclusion, deduction, inference, notion, impression.
5 *the idea of the letter was to get patients to protest* **purpose**, point, aim, object, objective, goal, intention, end, end in view, design, reason, use, utility, sense, motive; value, advantage.
6 *could you give me some idea of the cost?* **estimate**, estimation, guess, approximation, conjecture, rough calculation, rough idea, surmise; guesswork; informal guesstimate; N. Amer. informal a ballpark figure.

CHOOSE THE RIGHT WORD

idea, concept, notion

- **Idea** has the widest range of these words, with uses dividing roughly into ways of understanding something and plans or intentions. An *idea* may be a belief or opinion, in particular someone's impression of what something is like (*most people form their idea of reality from experience*). This often merges into feelings about what something ideally should be (*a cookery course wasn't her idea of fun*). An idea can also be a thought or suggestion about something that should be done, typically one arrived at as a possible solution to a problem, and this sense extends to that of a plan, hope, or intention (*it might be a good idea to get more rest | the idea is to reduce costs*).
- A **concept** is an understanding of what something is, usually quite a broad subject; it is more fully and consciously worked out than an *idea* (*his theories rest on his concept of consciousness | modern concepts of democracy*).
- **Notion** may refer either to beliefs about matters of fact or to ideas and wishes about things to do (*the notion that public bodies should be representative*). A *notion* is generally vaguer or more tentatively held than an *idea*, and there may be a suggestion, not present in the other two words, that the beliefs in question are mistaken or absurd (*the misguided notion that the policy would remove the problem of homelessness | he rejects any notion of de-skilling*).

ideal ▶ adjective **1** *it was ideal flying weather* **perfect**, best possible, consummate, supreme, absolute, complete, copybook, flawless, faultless, without fault, exemplary, classic, archetypal, model, ultimate, quintessential.
OPPOSITE bad.
2 *a unified European culture remained as an ideal concept that inspired future kings and emperors* **abstract**, **theoretical**, conceptual, notional, intellectual, metaphysical, philosophical, academic; hypothetical, speculative, conjectural, conjectured, suppositional, putative; rare suppositious, suppositive, ideational.
OPPOSITE concrete.
3 *the film-makers portray an ideal world* **unattainable**, unachievable, impracticable, unworkable, unfeasible; **unreal**, fictitious, hypothetical, theoretical, ivory-towered, imaginary, idealized, Utopian, romantic, quixotic, visionary, fanciful, fairy-tale.
OPPOSITES attainable; real.
▶ noun **1** *she endeavoured to be what she imagined was his ideal* **perfection**, paragon, epitome, ne plus ultra, beau idéal, nonpareil, crème de la crème, the last word, the ultimate, a dream; informal one in a million, the tops, the best/greatest thing since sliced bread, the bee's knees; archaic a nonsuch.

2 *an ideal to aim at* **model**, pattern, exemplar, example, paradigm, archetype, prototype, criterion, yardstick.
3 *the service of others is the highest ideal* **principle**, standard, rule of living, moral value, belief, conviction, persuasion; (**ideals**) morals, morality, ethics, code of behaviour, code of honour, ideology, creed; integrity, uprightness, high-mindedness, righteousness, virtue, probity, rectitude, sense of honour, honour, decency, conscience, sense of duty, scruples.

idealism ▶ **noun** *the Liberal Party had about it the idealism of youth* **Utopianism**, wishful thinking, romanticism, fantasizing, quixotism, daydreaming, impracticability.
OPPOSITES realism; cynicism; defeatism.

idealist ▶ **noun** *he came to power with the reputation of a left-wing idealist* **Utopian**, visionary, wishful thinker, pipe-dreamer, fantasist, fantasizer, romantic, romanticist, romancer, castle-builder, Walter Mitty, Don Quixote, dreamer, daydreamer, impractical person, unrealistic person; *rare* fantast, reverist.
OPPOSITES realist; cynic; defeatist.

idealistic ▶ **adjective** *idealistic young doctors who went to work for the Afghan rebels* **Utopian**, visionary, romantic, quixotic, dreamy, unrealistic, impractical, castle-building.
OPPOSITES realistic; cynical; defeatist.

idealize ▶ **verb** *they tend to idealize the post-war years* **romanticize**, romance, be unrealistic about, look at something through rose-tinted/rose-coloured spectacles, paint a rosy picture of, glamorize; idolize, apotheosize, deify.

ideally ▶ **adverb** *ideally, everyone should have enough to live on* **in a perfect world**, in a Utopia; preferably, if possible, for preference, by preference, from choice, by choice, as a matter of choice, much rather, rather; all things being equal, theoretically, hypothetically, in theory, in principle, on paper; *French* en principe.
OPPOSITES in practice, in reality.

idée fixe ▶ **noun** (*French*) *his other idée fixe was his belief in the existence of a ninth planet* **obsession**, fixation, ruling/consuming passion, passion, mania, compulsion, preoccupation, enthusiasm, infatuation, addiction, fetish, craze, hobby horse; phobia, complex, neurosis; *informal* bee in one's bonnet, hang-up, thing, bug.

identical ▶ **adjective 1** *a contingent of businessmen wearing identical lapel badges* **similar**, alike, (exactly) the same, indistinguishable, uniform, twin, interchangeable, undifferentiated, homogeneous, of a piece, cut from the same cloth; corresponding, correspondent, commensurate, equivalent, matching, like, parallel, analogous, comparable, cognate, equal; *informal* like (two) peas in a pod, much of a muchness, (like) Tweedledum and Tweedledee.
OPPOSITES different, unlike.
2 *try again, using the identical technique* **the same**, the very same, one and the same, the selfsame, the very; **aforementioned**, previously mentioned, aforesaid, aforenamed, previously described, above, above-stated; foregoing, preceding, precedent, earlier, previous.
OPPOSITE different.

identifiable ▶ **adjective** *there are no easily identifiable features on the shoreline* **distinguishable**, recognizable, known, noticeable, perceptible, discernible, appreciable, detectable, observable, perceivable, visible, notable, measurable; **distinct**, marked, conspicuous, unmistakable, clear, apparent, evident; *archaic* sensible.
OPPOSITES unrecognizable; inconspicuous.

identification ▶ **noun 1** *the identification of the suspect by the victim carries great weight* **recognition**, singling out, picking out, spotting, pointing out, pinpointing, naming, placing; discerning, distinguishing, discovery, finding, location; *N. Amer. informal* fingering.
2 *early identification of problems was important* **determining**, establishment, ascertainment, finding out, discovery, fixing, settling, diagnosis, divination, discerning, distinguishing; verification, confirmation.
3 *may I see your identification?* **ID**, papers, identity papers, identification papers, bona fides, documents, credentials; ID card, identity card, pass, badge, warrant, licence, permit, passport, proof of identity; proof of qualifications, certificate, diploma, references, testimonial, letter of introduction, letter of recommendation.
4 *the identification of Nonconformity with Victorian values* **association**, link, linkage, connection, tie, bracketing, relatedness, interrelation, interconnection, interdependence.
5 *his identification with the music is evident from the opening bars* **empathy**, rapport, fellow feeling, togetherness, unity, bond of sympathy, sympathetic cord, sympathy, understanding; *informal* good vibes.

identify ▶ **verb 1** *she identified her attacker in a police line-up* **recognize**, single out, pick out, spot, point out, pinpoint, pin down, put one's finger on, put a name to, name, place, know, know again, know by sight, discern, distinguish, discover, find, locate; remember, recall, recollect, call to mind; *informal* put the finger on; *N. Amer. informal* finger.
2 *I was able to identify four problem areas* **determine**, establish, ascertain, find out, discover, learn, fix, settle, decide, make out, ferret out, diagnose, deduce, divine, intuit, discern, distinguish; verify, confirm, make certain of, certify; *informal* figure out, get a fix on.
3 *tobacco sponsorship is aimed at a market that **identifies** sport **with** glamour* **associate**, link, connect, couple, relate, bracket, think of together; think of in connection with, draw a parallel with, mention in the same breath as, set side by side with.
OPPOSITE distinguish.
4 *children usually **identify with** the hero* **empathize**, be in tune, have a rapport, feel togetherness, feel at one, commune, sympathize, be in sympathy; be on the same wavelength as, speak/talk the same language as; understand, relate to, feel for, have insight into; *informal* put oneself in the shoes of.
5 *it is tempting to **identify** him **with** an Athenian painter of the same name* **equate with**, identify someone as, consider someone/something to be, regard as being the same as, regard as being identical to.

identity ▶ **noun 1** *they eventually discovered the identity of the owner* **name**; specification.
2 *she was afraid of losing her identity if she became his wife* **individuality**, self, selfhood, ego, personality, character, originality, distinctiveness, distinction, singularity, peculiarity, uniqueness, differentness.
3 *a case of mistaken identity* **identification**, recognition, naming, singling out, picking out, pinpointing, placing; discerning, distinguishing; *N. Amer. informal* fingering.
4 *management need to secure an identity of interests with shareholders* **identicalness**, sameness, selfsameness, oneness, congruity, congruence, indistinguishability, interchangeability; likeness, alikeness, uniformity, similarity, closeness, accordance, alignment, parallelism, symmetry.
OPPOSITE mismatch.

ideology ▶ **noun** *the horrors spawned by Nazi ideology* **beliefs**, ideas, ideals, principles, doctrine, creed, credo, teaching, dogma, theory, thesis, tenets, canon(s); conviction(s), persuasion, opinions, position, ethics, morals.

idiocy ▶ **noun 1** *to reduce funding by a further 20% would seem to be the height of idiocy | the idiocies of mankind* **stupidity**, folly, foolishness, foolhardiness, madness, insanity, lunacy, silliness, brainlessness, thoughtlessness, senselessness, lack of sense, indiscretion, irresponsibility, injudiciousness, imprudence, rashness, recklessness, ineptitude, inaneness, inanity, irrationality, illogicality, absurdity, nonsense, ludicrousness, ridiculousness, fatuousness, fatuity, asininity, pointlessness, meaninglessness, futility, fruitlessness; *informal* craziness; *Brit. informal* daftness.
OPPOSITE sense.
2 (*dated*) *idiocy was once considered possession by devils* **feeble-mindedness**, weak-mindedness, imbecility, very low intelligence, stupidity.
OPPOSITE intelligence.

idiom ▶ **noun 1** *'Far out,' she replied, using a rather dated idiom* **expression**, idiomatic expression, turn of phrase, set phrase, fixed expression, phrase; *formal* locution.
2 *the poet's idiom is elegantly terse* **language**, mode of expression, style of speech, speech, talk, -speak, way/manner of speaking, usage, phraseology, phrasing, choice of words, vocabulary, parlance, tongue, vernacular, jargon, patter, argot, patois, cant; *French* façon de parler; *informal* lingo; *formal* locution.

idiomatic ▶ **adjective** *the texts have been translated from Italian into idiomatic English* **natural**, native-speaker, grammatical, correct; vernacular, colloquial, everyday, conversational.
OPPOSITE unidiomatic.

idiosyncrasy ▶ **noun** *his idiosyncrasies included the recycling of cigar butts | sleep patterns show a high degree of idiosyncrasy* **peculiarity**, individual/personal trait, oddity, eccentricity, mannerism, quirk, whim, whimsy, fancy, fad, vagary, notion, conceit, caprice, kink, twist, freak, fetish, passion, bent, foible, crotchet, habit, characteristic, speciality, quality, feature; individuality; unconventionality, unorthodoxy; *archaic* megrim; *rare* singularity.

idiosyncratic ▶ **adjective** *each researcher had his or her own idiosyncratic interest | some might think this a rather idiosyncratic approach* **distinctive**, **individual**, characteristic, distinct, distinguishing, peculiar, individualistic, different, typical, special, specific, representative, unique, personal, private, essential; **eccentric**, unconventional, uncommon, abnormal, irregular, aberrant, anomalous, odd, quirky, queer, strange, weird, bizarre, outlandish, freakish, extraordinary; *rare* singular.

idiot ▶ **noun 1** (*informal*) *that idiot was driving far too fast* **fool**, ass, halfwit, nincompoop, blockhead, dunce, dolt, ignoramus, cretin, imbecile, dullard, moron, simpleton, clod; *informal* dope, ninny, chump, dimwit, goon, dumbo, dummy, dum-dum, dumb-bell, loon, dork, jackass, bonehead, fathead, numbskull, dunderhead, chucklehead, knucklehead, muttonhead, pudding-head, thickhead, wooden-head, airhead, pinhead, lamebrain, pea-brain, birdbrain, zombie, jerk, nerd, dipstick, donkey, noodle; *Brit. informal* nit, nitwit, twit, clot, plonker, berk, prat, pillock, wally, git, wazzock, divvy, nerk, twerp, charlie, mug, muppet; *Scottish informal* nyaff, balloon, sumph, gowk; *Irish informal* gobdaw; *N. Amer. informal* schmuck, bozo, boob, turkey, schlepper, chowderhead, dumbhead, goofball, goof, goofus, galoot, lummox, klutz, putz, schlemiel, sap, gink, cluck, clunk, ding-dong, dingbat, wiener, weeny, dip, simp, spud, coot,

palooka, poop, squarehead, yo-yo, dingleberry; *Austral./NZ informal* drongo, dill, hoon, alec, galah, nong, bogan, poon, boofhead; *S. African informal* mompara; *archaic* tomfool, noddy, clodpole, loggerhead, spoony, mooncalf.
OPPOSITE genius.
2 (*dated*) *the village idiot* **mentally handicapped person**; *dated* halfwit, simpleton, imbecile, cretin; *N. Amer. dated* retardate.
OPPOSITE intellectual.

idiotic ▶ **adjective** *I'm trying to stop Suzanne making an idiotic mistake* **stupid**, silly, foolish, half-witted, witless, brainless, mindless, thoughtless, imprudent, incautious, irresponsible, injudicious, indiscreet, unwise, unintelligent, unreasonable; ill-advised, ill-considered, impolitic, rash, reckless, foolhardy; absurd, senseless, pointless, nonsensical, inane, fatuous, ridiculous, laughable, risible, derisible; *informal* dumb, dim, dim-witted, dopey, gormless, damfool, half-baked, hare-brained, crackbrained, pea-brained, wooden-headed, thickheaded, nutty, mad, crazy, dotty, batty, dippy, cuckoo, screwy, wacky; *Brit. informal* barmy, daft; *Scottish & N. English informal* glaikit; *N. Amer. informal* dumb-ass, chowderheaded; *W. Indian informal* dotish.
OPPOSITE sensible.

idle ▶ **adjective 1** *an idle fellow* **lazy**, indolent, slothful, work-shy, shiftless, loafing, inactive, inert, sluggish, lethargic, languorous, listless, torpid; remiss, negligent, slack, lax, lackadaisical, impassive, good-for-nothing, do-nothing; leisurely; *informal* bone idle; *French archaic* fainéant; *rare* otiose.
OPPOSITE industrious.
2 *'I was getting bored with being idle,' she told her new employer* **unemployed**, jobless, out of work, out of a job, redundant, between jobs, workless, unwaged, unoccupied; *Brit. informal* on the dole, signing on, 'resting'; *Austral./NZ informal* on the wallaby track.
OPPOSITE employed.
3 *instead of leaving the machine idle, I sold it* **not in use**, out of use, not operating, not working, inactive, out of action, inoperative, non-functioning, out of service, unused, unoccupied, unemployed; disused, no longer in use, fallen into disuse, mothballed.
OPPOSITE working.
4 *they filled their idle hours with endless gossiping sessions* **unoccupied**, spare, empty, vacant, unfilled, available.
OPPOSITES busy; full.
5 *he didn't indulge in idle remarks or mere social chit-chat* **frivolous**, trivial, trifling, minor, petty, foolish, lightweight, shallow, superficial, insignificant, unimportant, worthless, valueless, pointless, paltry, niggling, peripheral, without depth, inane, fatuous, senseless, meaningless, purposeless, unnecessary, time-wasting.
OPPOSITES serious; meaningful.
6 *she was not a woman to make idle threats* **empty**, meaningless, aimless, pointless, worthless, useless, vain, in vain, insubstantial, futile, ineffective, ineffectual; groundless, without grounds, baseless, without/lacking foundation.
OPPOSITE serious.
▶ **verb 1** *Lily idled on the window seat: she hated Sundays* **do nothing**, be inactive, vegetate, sit back, take it easy, rest on one's oars, mark time, kick one's heels, twiddle one's thumbs, kill time, languish, laze (around/about), lounge (around/about), loll (around/about), loaf (around/about), slouch (around/about); go to seed, degenerate, moulder, stagnate; *informal* hang around, veg out; *Brit. informal* hang about, mooch about/around, slummock; *N. Amer. informal* bum around, bat around/about, lollygag, lay on one's oars.
2 *the men idled their time away on street corners* **fritter**, while, laze, loiter; **pass**, spend, use, employ, use up, occupy, take up, fill up, fill in, fill, beguile, expend, devote, waste, dissipate, kill.
3 *Robert idled along the pavement* **saunter**, stroll, dawdle, drift, potter, amble, go/walk slowly, loiter, maunder, wander, straggle; *informal* mosey, tootle; *Brit. informal* pootle, mooch, swan; *N. Amer. informal* putter.
4 *he slowed the car at a junction, letting the engine idle* **tick over**, run slowly in neutral.

WORD LINKS
fear of being idle **thassophobia**

CHOOSE THE RIGHT WORD
idle, lazy, indolent
See LAZY.

idleness ▶ **noun 1** *he was birched for his idleness at school* **laziness**, indolence, slothfulness, sloth, shiftlessness, inertia, sluggishness, lethargy, languor, torpidity, torpor; remissness, negligence, slackness, laxity; *French archaic* fainéance; *rare* otiosity, hebetude.
OPPOSITE industry.
2 *we suffered a period of enforced idleness* **inactivity**, inaction, unemployment, rest, repose.
OPPOSITE activity.

idler ▶ **noun** *you were not brought into this world to be an idler—you'll have to set your mind to something* **loafer**, layabout, good-for-nothing, ne'er-do-well, do-nothing, lounger, shirker, sluggard, laggard, slugabed, malingerer; *informal* skiver, waster, slacker, cyberslacker, slowcoach, slob, lazybones; *N. Amer. informal* slowpoke; *archaic* wastrel; *French archaic* fainéant.
OPPOSITES workaholic; swot.

idol ▶ **noun 1** *an idol in a shrine* **icon**, god, image, likeness, fetish, totem, statue, figure, figurine, doll, carving; graven image, false god, effigy, golden calf.
2 *the pop world's latest idol* **hero**, **heroine**, star, superstar, icon, celebrity; favourite, darling, beloved, pet, apple of one's eye; *informal* pin-up, heart throb, blue-eyed boy/girl, golden boy/girl; *N. Amer. informal* fair-haired boy/girl.

idolatrous ▶ **adjective 1** *idolatrous religions* **idol-worshipping**, icon-worshipping, fetishistic; pagan, heathen, heretical, infidel, sacrilegious.
2 *America's idolatrous worship of the auto* **idolizing**, fetishistic; adulatory, adoring, reverential, glorifying, uncritical, lionizing; worshipping, worshipful, hero-worshipping.
OPPOSITE vilifying.

idolatry ▶ **noun 1** *Jeremiah preached against idolatry* **idol worship**, idolatrism, fetishism, iconolatry, icon worship; paganism, heathenism, heresy, sacrilege, ungodliness.
2 *our idolatry of art* **idolization**, idolizing, fetishization, worship, worshipping, adulation, adoration, adoring, reverence, glorification, lionizing, lionization, love, admiration, loving, admiring, hero-worshipping.
OPPOSITE vilification.

idolize ▶ **verb** *he idolized professional wrestlers* **hero-worship**, worship, revere, venerate, deify, lionize, adulate, adore, stand in awe of, reverence, look up to, admire, exalt, love, dote upon; *informal* put on a pedestal.
OPPOSITE vilify.

idyll ▶ **noun 1** *he looked back on this time as an idyll | they lived in an idyll unspoilt by machines* **perfect time**, ideal time, wonderful time, moment of bliss, honeymoon; **paradise**, heaven, heaven on earth, Garden of Eden, Shangri-La, fairyland, Utopia; *literary* Arcadia, Arcady, Erewhon.
OPPOSITE hell on earth.
2 *the poem began as a two-part idyll* **pastoral**, eclogue, georgic, rural poem.

idyllic ▶ **adjective** *their idyllic times together | the idyllic English countryside* **perfect**, ideal, idealized, wonderful, blissful, halcyon, happy; heavenly, paradisal, Utopian, Elysian; peaceful, picturesque, pastoral, rural, rustic, bucolic, unspoilt; *literary* Arcadian, sylvan.
OPPOSITE hellish.

if ▶ **conjunction 1** *if the weather is fine, we can walk to the village* **on condition that**, provided (that), providing (that), presuming (that), supposing (that), assuming (that), on the assumption that, allowing (that), as long as, given that, with the provision/proviso that, with/on the understanding that, if and only if, contingent on, in the event that, allowing that.
OPPOSITE unless.
2 *if I go out she gets nasty* **whenever**, every time.
3 *I wonder if he noticed* **whether**, whether or not.
4 *a useful, if unintended innovation* **although**, albeit, but, even though, even if, despite being, in spite of being, yet, whilst.
▶ **noun** *there is of course one if in all this* **uncertainty**, doubt, lack of certainty, hesitation, vagueness; **condition**, stipulation, provision, proviso, constraint, prerequisite, precondition, requirement, specification, restriction, supposition, modification.

iffy ▶ **adjective** (*informal*) **1** *the windscreen's a bit iffy, but it's a good car* **substandard**, second-rate, low-grade, low-quality, of low quality, of poor quality; **doubtful**, dubious, questionable; *informal* not up to much; *Brit. informal* dodgy, ropy, not much cop.
OPPOSITE perfect.
2 *that date is a bit iffy* **tentative**, undecided, unsettled, unsure, unreliable, unresolved, in doubt, in the balance; *informal* up in the air.
OPPOSITE settled.

ignite ▶ **verb 1** *he got to safety moments before the petrol ignited* **catch fire**, catch, burst into flames, be set off, erupt, explode; burn up, burn, flame up; *rare* kindle.
OPPOSITE go out.
2 *he lit a cigarette which ignited the petrol fumes* **light**, set fire to, set on fire, set alight, set burning, fire, kindle, inflame, touch off; *informal* set/put a match to.
OPPOSITE extinguish.
3 *the campaign failed to ignite voter interest* **arouse**, kindle, trigger, spark, instigate, excite, provoke, foment; agitate, stimulate, stir up, work up, whip up, incite, fuel, animate.
OPPOSITE dampen.

ignoble ▶ **adjective** *the war is being fought over an ignoble cause* **dishonourable**, unworthy, base, shameful, contemptible, despicable, shabby, abject, low, sordid, degraded, corrupt, mean, wrong; improper, unprincipled, unchivalrous, uncharitable, discreditable, blameworthy, reprehensible.
OPPOSITE noble.

ignominious ▸ adjective **1** *the leader's ignominious defeat* **humiliating**, undignified, embarrassing, mortifying, shameful, disgraceful, dishonourable, discreditable, ignoble, inglorious, abject, sorry, wretched, miserable, pitiful; *rare* humiliatory.
OPPOSITE glorious.
2 *the regime's most ignominious crimes* **heinous**, infamous, scandalous, disgraceful, shameful, contemptible, despicable, shabby, wicked, vile, villainous, base, low, ignoble, wretched.
OPPOSITE admirable.

ignominy ▸ noun *the ignominy of a public trial* **shame**, humiliation, embarrassment, mortification; disgrace, dishonour, stigma, disrepute, discredit, degradation, abasement, opprobrium, obloquy, scandal, infamy, indignity, ignobility, loss of face.
OPPOSITE honour.

CHOOSE THE RIGHT WORD

ignominy, shame, disgrace, dishonour
See DISGRACE.

ignoramus ▸ noun *he was a foul-mouthed ignoramus. See* FOOL.

ignorance ▸ noun **1** *his ignorance of economics* **incomprehension**, unawareness, unconsciousness, inexperience, innocence; unfamiliarity with, lack of enlightenment about, lack of knowledge about, lack of information about; *informal* cluelessness; *literary* nescience.
OPPOSITES knowledge, education.
2 *their attitudes are based on ignorance and fear* **lack of knowledge**, lack of education; unenlightenment, benightedness; lack of intelligence, unintelligence, stupidity, foolishness, idiocy, denseness, brainlessness, mindlessness, slow-wittedness; *informal* thickness, dimness, dumbness, dopiness, doziness.
OPPOSITES knowledge, education.

ignorant ▸ adjective **1** *an ignorant country girl* **uneducated**, unknowledgeable, untaught, unschooled, untutored, untrained, illiterate, unlettered, unlearned, unread, uninformed, unenlightened, unscholarly, unqualified, benighted, backward; inexperienced, unworldly, unsophisticated; unintelligent, stupid, simple, empty-headed, mindless; *informal* pig-ignorant, thick, airheaded, (as) thick as two short planks, dense, dumb, dim, dopey, wet behind the ears, slow on the uptake, dead from the neck up, a brick short of a load, two sandwiches short of a picnic; *Brit. informal* dozy, divvy, daft, not the full shilling; *Scottish & N. English informal* glaikit; *N. Amer. informal* chowderheaded, dumb-ass; *W. Indian informal* dotish; *S. African informal* dof; *rare* hebete.
OPPOSITES educated, knowledgeable.
2 *middle-class women were ignorant of working-class life* **without knowledge**, unaware, unconscious, insensible; unfamiliar with, unacquainted with, unconversant with, inexperienced in, uninitiated in, blind to, oblivious to, naive about, innocent about, green about, a stranger to; uninformed about, unenlightened about, unschooled in; *informal* in the dark about, clueless about, not knowing the first thing about, not having the faintest about; *literary* nescient, strange to.
OPPOSITE knowledgeable about.
3 (*informal*) *she could be very ignorant, and he had no intention of getting in an argument* **rude**, impolite, ill-mannered, bad-mannered, unmannerly, ungracious, discourteous, insensitive, uncivil, ill-humoured, surly, sullen; boorish, oafish, loutish, crude, coarse, vulgar, gross.
OPPOSITE polite.

ignore ▸ verb **1** *he ignored the customers and began counting money* **disregard**, take no notice of, pay no attention to, pay no heed to, pass over, shut one's eyes to, be oblivious to, turn a blind eye to, turn a deaf ear to, brush aside, shrug off, push aside, never mind; look the other way.
OPPOSITE pay attention to.
2 *he was ignored by the countess* **snub**, slight, spurn, shun, disdain, look right through, look past, turn one's back on, give someone the cold shoulder, cold-shoulder, freeze out, steer clear of; *Brit.* send to Coventry; *informal* give someone the brush-off, cut, cut dead, knock back, give someone the go-by; *Brit. informal* blank.
OPPOSITE acknowledge.
3 *doctors ignored her husband's instructions* **set aside**, pay no attention to, take no account of, veto; break, contravene, fail to comply with, fail to observe, disobey, breach, defy, flout, fly in the face of; omit, leave out, bypass, overlook, neglect, disregard, exclude; *informal* skip.
OPPOSITE obey.

ilk ▸ noun *Mrs Taylor and her ilk talk utter tripe* **type**, sort, class, category, group, set, bracket, genre, kidney, grain, species, race, strain, vintage, make, model, brand, stamp, variety, family.

ill ▸ adjective **1** *Mama was seriously ill | she had begun to feel rather ill* **unwell**, sick, not (very) well, ailing, poorly, sickly, peaky, afflicted, indisposed, infirm, liverish; out of sorts, not oneself, not in good shape, not up to par, under/below par, bad, in a bad way; bedridden, invalided, on the sick list, valetudinarian; queasy, nauseous, nauseated; weak, feeble, frail; diseased, infected; *Brit.* off colour; *informal* under the weather, not up to snuff, laid up, dicky, funny, peculiar, iffy, crummy, lousy, rough, groggy, green about the gills, at death's door, like death warmed up; *Brit. informal* ropy, grotty; *Scottish informal* wabbit; *Austral./NZ informal* crook; *dated* queer, seedy.
OPPOSITES well, healthy.
2 *the ill effects of tobacco smoke* **harmful**, damaging, detrimental, deleterious, adverse, injurious, hurtful, destructive, pernicious, inimical, dangerous, ruinous, calamitous, disastrous, malign, malignant; unhealthy, unwholesome, poisonous, noxious, cancerous; *literary* malefic, maleficent, nocuous, baneful.
OPPOSITES good, beneficial.
3 *the ill feeling between him and the Woodvilles* **hostile**, antagonistic, acrimonious, inimical, antipathetic, poisonous; belligerent, bellicose, aggressive, pugnacious, truculent, contentious; unfriendly, unkind, unsympathetic, harsh, cruel; rancorous, resentful, spiteful, malicious, vindictive, vitriolic, malevolent, bitter, mean, nasty; *informal* bitchy, catty.
OPPOSITES friendly, warm.
4 *a bird of ill omen* **unlucky**, adverse, unfavourable, unfortunate, unpropitious, inauspicious, unpromising, infelicitous, bad, gloomy; threatening, menacing, ominous, sinister, disturbing, dire, evil, baleful, forbidding, portentous; *archaic* direful; *rare* minatory, minacious.
OPPOSITE auspicious.
5 *the ill manners of her spouse* **rude**, discourteous, unmannerly, impolite; bad, objectionable, unpleasant, disagreeable; impertinent, insolent, impudent, audacious, uncivil, disrespectful, churlish, crass, ungracious, graceless, boorish; *informal* ignorant.
OPPOSITES good, polite.
6 *the ill management of their finances* **bad**, poor, unsatisfactory, incompetent, unacceptable, inadequate, deficient, defective, faulty, unskilful, inexpert, amateurish.
OPPOSITES good, competent.
□ **ill at ease** *he looked ill at ease in morning dress* **awkward**, uneasy, uncomfortable, self-conscious, out of place, unnatural, inhibited, gauche, strained; embarrassed, shy, bashful, blushing, retiring, shrinking; unsure, uncertain, unsettled, hesitant, faltering; restless, restive, fidgety, unrelaxed, disquieted, disturbed, discomfited, troubled, worried, anxious, on edge, edgy, nervous, tense, on tenterhooks; apprehensive, distrustful; *informal* fazed, discombobulated, twitchy, on pins and needles, jittery, nervy; *N. Amer. informal* antsy; *rare* unquiet.
OPPOSITES at ease, comfortable.
▸ adverb **1** *it ill became the king to behave as a vassal* **poorly**, badly, imperfectly; wrongly, unsuccessfully.
OPPOSITE well.
2 *the look on her face boded ill for anyone who crossed her path* **unfavourably**, adversely, badly, unhappily, inauspiciously.
OPPOSITES well, auspiciously.
3 *he can ill afford the loss of income* **barely**, scarcely, hardly, just, only just, just possibly, narrowly; with difficulty, only with effort; *Brit. informal* at a push.
OPPOSITE easily.
4 *if things go ill, it's all over* **badly**, adversely, unsuccessfully, unfavourably; unfortunately, unluckily, hard, inauspiciously.
OPPOSITE well, according to plan.
5 *we are ill prepared for floods* **inadequately**, unsatisfactorily, insufficiently, imperfectly, deficiently, defectively, poorly, badly, negligently.
OPPOSITES well, satisfactorily.
□ **speak ill of** *nobody wants to speak ill of the dead* **denigrate**, disparage, cast aspersions on, criticize, be critical of, speak badly of, speak of with disfavour, be unkind about, be malicious about, be spiteful towards, blacken the name of, blacken the character of, besmirch, run down, insult, abuse, attack, slight, revile, malign, vilify; *N. Amer.* slur; *informal* bad-mouth, slate, bitch about, do a hatchet job on, pull to pieces, sling mud at, throw mud at, drag (someone's name) through the mud; *Brit. informal* rubbish, slag off, have a go at, have a pop at; *rare* asperse, derogate, vilipend, vituperate.
OPPOSITES compliment, extol.
▸ noun **1** (**ills**) *the government had failed to cure many of society's ills* **problems**, troubles, difficulties, misfortunes, strains, trials, tribulations, trials and tribulations, worries, anxieties, concerns; pain, suffering, hardship, misery, woe, affliction, distress, disquiet, malaise; *informal* headaches, probs, hassles; *archaic* travails.
2 *he wished them no ill* **harm**, hurt, injury, damage, mischief, pain, trouble, unpleasantness, misfortune, grievance, suffering, distress, anguish, trauma, grief.
3 (**ills**) *the body's ills* **illnesses**, ill/poor health; ailments, disorders, complaints, afflictions, sicknesses, diseases, maladies, infirmities, indispositions; infections, contagions.

ill-advised ▸ adjective *an ill-advised business venture* **unwise**, injudicious, misguided, imprudent, impolitic, incautious, ill-considered, ill-judged, ill-conceived, ill-thought-out, badly planned, inexpedient; foolhardy, hare-

brained, rash, hasty, overhasty, short-sighted, thoughtless, unthinking, careless, reckless; foolish, silly, asinine, wrong-headed; *informal* crazy, crackpot, crackbrained, cock-eyed; *Brit. informal* daft.
OPPOSITES wise, judicious.

> CHOOSE THE RIGHT WORD
>
> **ill-advised, unwise, imprudent, injudicious**
> *See* UNWISE.

ill-assorted ▶ adjective *an ill-assorted travelling party* **mismatched**, ill-matched, incongruous, unsuited, incompatible, inharmonious, discordant, clashing, discrepant; dissimilar, unlike, unalike, varying, varied, at variance, disparate, divergent, diverse, contrasting, distinct.
OPPOSITES well matched, similar.

ill-bred ▶ adjective *she was unlikely to be amused by ill-bred behaviour* **ill-mannered**, bad-mannered, rude, unmannerly, impolite, discourteous, uncivil; boorish, churlish, loutish, vulgar, common, coarse, crass, gross, uncouth, crude, unpolished, uncivilized, ungentlemanly, unladylike, unsophisticated, unrefined, ungallant, indelicate, indecorous, unseemly; *informal* yobbish, ignorant, plebby, cloddish; *Brit. informal* common as muck.
OPPOSITES well bred, genteel.

ill-considered ▶ adjective *the government can force through this ill-considered legislation* **rash**, unconsidered, ill-advised, ill-judged, injudicious, imprudent, unwise, hasty, overhasty; misjudged, ill-conceived, badly thought out, not thought through, unthought-out, unguarded, wild, hare-brained; *literary* temerarious.
OPPOSITE judicious.

ill-defined ▶ adjective *the boundary between the two manors was rather ill-defined* **vague**, indistinct, unclear, imprecise, inexplicit; blurry, blurred, fuzzy, hazy, woolly, nebulous, shadowy, dim.
OPPOSITES well defined, sharp.

ill-disposed ▶ adjective *the court may be ill-disposed to foreign companies* **hostile**, antagonistic, unfriendly, unsympathetic, antipathetic, inimical, unfavourable; opposing, opposed, averse, contrary, at odds; *informal* anti, down on.
OPPOSITES well disposed, friendly.

illegal ▶ adjective **1** *gangs operating illegal gambling* **unlawful**, illicit, illegitimate, criminal, lawbreaking, actionable, felonious; unlicensed, unauthorized, unsanctioned, unwarranted, unofficial; outlawed, banned, forbidden, barred, prohibited, interdicted, proscribed, not allowed, not permitted; contraband, black-market, under the counter, bootleg; *Law* malfeasant; *German* verboten; *informal* crooked, shady; *Brit. informal* bent, dodgy; *rare* non licet.
OPPOSITES legal; lawful.
2 *illegal play will be penalized by surrendering possession of the ball* **foul**, against the rules; unfair, unsporting, unsportsmanlike, below the belt, dirty, dishonourable, dishonest, underhand, cheating.
OPPOSITES legal; legitimate.

> CHOOSE THE RIGHT WORD
>
> **illegal, unlawful, illicit**
>
> - An **illegal** action, activity, or object is one that is specifically forbidden by law, especially criminal law (*illegal drug use | he was accused of possessing illegal weapons*).
> - Anything that is *illegal* is necessarily also **unlawful**. However, *unlawful* has a wider application than *illegal*, referring also to actions that are not sanctioned by the law (*sue the commissioner for unlawful arrest | the use of unlawful violence*).
> - **Illicit** can be used synonymously with *illegal* (*use of heroin or other illicit drugs*). It may also, however, refer to the breach of a moral code or to things that are disapproved of by custom or society (*the temptations of an illicit romance | the gang indulged in games of Dare and illicit cigarettes*). In these contexts, *illicit* suggests the allure of something clandestine or forbidden.

illegible ▶ adjective *an illegible signature* **unreadable**, indecipherable, unintelligible, hard to read; scrawled, scribbled, squiggly, crabbed, hieroglyphic, obscure; *informal* clear as mud.
OPPOSITES legible; clear.

illegitimate ▶ adjective **1** *illegitimate share trading* **illegal**, unlawful, illicit, criminal, lawbreaking, actionable, felonious; unlicensed, unauthorized, unsanctioned, unwarranted, unofficial; banned, forbidden, barred, prohibited, outlawed, interdicted, proscribed, not allowed, not permitted, against the rules; contraband, black-market, under the counter, bootleg; fraudulent, corrupt, dishonest, dishonourable; *German* verboten; *Law* malfeasant; *informal* crooked, shady; *Brit. informal* bent, dodgy.
OPPOSITES legitimate, lawful.
2 *an illegitimate child* **born out of wedlock**, born of unmarried parents; love; *dated* born on the wrong side of the blanket, unfathered; *archaic* bastard, natural, misbegotten, baseborn, spurious, nameless; *rare* adulterine.
OPPOSITE legitimate.
3 *it is quite illegitimate to treat such a person as a swindler* **incorrect**, illogical, invalid, unsound, spurious, wrongly inferred, wrongly deduced.
OPPOSITES legitimate, correct.

ill-fated ▶ adjective *an ill-fated rebellion* **doomed**, blighted, condemned, damned, cursed, ill-starred, ill-omened, jinxed; unlucky, luckless, unfortunate, hapless, unhappy; *literary* star-crossed.

ill-favoured ▶ adjective *an ill-favoured old woman* **unattractive**, plain, unappealing, ugly, ugly looking, hideous, unsightly, unlovely, plain as a pikestaff; *N. Amer.* homely; *informal* not much to look at, short on looks; *Brit. informal* no oil painting; *Austral./NZ informal* drack.
OPPOSITE attractive.

ill-founded ▶ adjective *your faith in his expertise was ill-founded* **baseless**, groundless, without foundation, foundationless, without basis, unjustified, unsupported; unsubstantiated, unproven, unverified, uncorroborated, unconfirmed, unauthenticated, not backed up by evidence, speculative, conjectural; unsound, unreliable, questionable, misinformed, misguided, spurious, trumped-up.
OPPOSITE well-founded.

ill humour ▶ noun *the downward tilt to her mouth betrayed her ill humour* **bad mood**, bad temper, ill temper, irritability, irascibility, cantankerousness, peevishness, petulance, pettishness, pique, fit of pique, querulousness, crabbiness, testiness, tetchiness, fractiousness, snappishness, waspishness, touchiness, moodiness, sullenness, sulkiness, surliness, resentment, rancour, spleen, dyspepsia, biliousness, sourness, annoyance, anger, crossness.
OPPOSITE good humour.

ill-humoured ▶ adjective *an ill-humoured little man* **bad-tempered**, ill-tempered, short-tempered, hot-tempered, quick-tempered, in a (bad) mood, cross, as cross as two sticks; irritable, irascible, tetchy, testy, crotchety, touchy, thin-skinned, scratchy, cantankerous, curmudgeonly, peevish, fractious, waspish, prickly, peppery, pettish, shrewish; grumpy, grouchy, crabbed, crabby, disagreeable, volatile, splenetic, dyspeptic, choleric, bilious, liverish, cross-grained; *informal* snappish, snappy, chippy, on a short fuse, short-fused; *Brit. informal* shirty, stroppy, narky, ratty, eggy, like a bear with a sore head; *N. Amer. informal* cranky, ornery, peckish, soreheaded; *Austral./NZ informal* snaky; *informal, dated* waxy, miffy.
OPPOSITES good-humoured, amiable.

illiberal ▶ adjective *the government moved towards more illiberal policies* **intolerant**, narrow-minded, unenlightened, puritanical, fundamentalist; reactionary, conservative, hidebound; undemocratic, authoritarian, strict, repressive, totalitarian, despotic, tyrannical, draconian, oppressive, fascist.
OPPOSITE liberal.

illicit ▶ adjective **1** *illicit drugs* **illegal**, unlawful, illegitimate; outlawed, banned, forbidden, prohibited, interdicted, proscribed, not allowed, not permitted; criminal, lawbreaking, actionable, felonious; unlicensed, unauthorized, unsanctioned, unwarranted, unofficial; contraband, black-market, under the counter, bootleg; *Law* malfeasant; *German* verboten; *rare* non licet.
OPPOSITES licit, legal.
2 *an illicit love affair* **taboo**, forbidden, ruled out, impermissible, not acceptable, unacceptable, against the rules; secret, clandestine, furtive, sly; *German* verboten; *Islam* haram; *NZ* tapu.
OPPOSITE above board.

> CHOOSE THE RIGHT WORD
>
> **illicit, illegal, unlawful**
> *See* ILLEGAL.

illimitable ▶ adjective *the great illimitable space we were in* **limitless**, unlimited, without limits, unbounded; endless, unending, never-ending, without end, infinite, immeasurable, inestimable.
OPPOSITE limited.

illiteracy ▶ noun **1** *the ineffective educational system meant that illiteracy was widespread* **illiterateness**, inability to read or write.
OPPOSITE literacy.
2 *his economic illiteracy* **ignorance**, unawareness, inexperience, unenlightenment, benightedness, lack of knowledge, lack of education; *informal* cluelessness; *literary* nescience.

illiterate ▶ adjective **1** *he was no illiterate peasant* **unable to read or write**, unlettered, analphabetic, functionally illiterate.
OPPOSITE literate.
2 *a politically illiterate youth* **ignorant**, unknowledgeable, uneducated, untaught, unschooled, untutored, untrained, uninstructed, uninformed, unlearned, unread, unenlightened, benighted, backward; *literary* nescient.
OPPOSITES literate; knowledgeable.

ill-judged ▶ adjective *she flinched at his ill-judged choice of words* **ill-**

considered, ill-thought-out, ill-conceived; unwise, imprudent, incautious, injudicious, misguided, ill-advised, impolitic, inexpedient; foolhardy, foolish, rash, hasty, overhasty, short-sighted, thoughtless, unthinking, careless, reckless, spur of the moment.
OPPOSITES judicious, well thought out.

ill-mannered ▶ adjective *ill-mannered children* **bad-mannered**, rude, unmannerly, mannerless, impolite, discourteous, uncivil, abusive, disagreeable; insolent, impertinent, impudent, cheeky, audacious, presumptuous, disrespectful; badly behaved, ill-behaved, boorish, loutish, oafish, uncouth, uncivilized, ill-bred, coarse, gross; *informal* ignorant.
OPPOSITES well mannered, polite.

ill-natured ▶ adjective *a disagreeable, ill-natured girl* **mean**, nasty, spiteful, malicious, disagreeable, bitter, poisonous, venomous; ill-tempered, bad-tempered, ill-humoured, moody, irritable, irascible, surly, sullen, peevish, petulant, cross, fractious, crabbed, crabby, tetchy, testy, grouchy, waspish; perverse, disobliging.
OPPOSITE good-natured.

illness *See centre pages for lists of* **Illnesses** **Phobias**
▶ noun *he was making a steady recovery from his recent illness* **sickness**, disease, ailment, disorder, complaint, malady, affliction, attack, infection, contagion, disability, indisposition; ill health, poor health, infirmity, valetudinarianism; *informal* bug, virus; *Brit. informal* lurgy; *Austral. informal* wog.
OPPOSITE good health.

WORD LINKS
related suffix **-pathy (e.g. *neuropathy*), noso- (e.g. *nosography*)**
fear of illness **nosophobia**

illogical ▶ adjective *he drew a strange and illogical conclusion* **irrational**, unreasonable, unsound, unreasoned, unfounded, groundless, unjustifiable, unjustified; incorrect, erroneous, wrong, invalid, spurious, faulty, flawed, fallacious, unscientific, inconsistent, unproved; specious, sophistic, casuistic; absurd, preposterous, untenable, implausible, impossible, beyond belief, beyond the bounds of possibility; senseless, meaningless, nonsensical, insane, ridiculous, idiotic, stupid, foolish, silly, inane, imbecilic; *informal* crazy, off beam, way out, full of holes; *Brit. informal* daft, barmy.
OPPOSITE logical.

ill-starred ▶ adjective *some people have lost everything because they invested in that ill-starred venture* **ill-fated**, doomed, blighted, ill-omened, foredoomed, infelicitous; unlucky, unfortunate, hapless, luckless, bedevilled, damned; inauspicious, unpropitious, unpromising, ominous; *informal* jinxed; *literary* star-crossed.
OPPOSITES destined for success; blessed.

CHOOSE THE RIGHT WORD
ill-starred, unfortunate, unlucky, hapless
See UNFORTUNATE.

ill temper ▶ noun *her ill temper was caused by an argument with her boyfriend* **bad mood**, annoyance, irritation, vexation, exasperation, indignation, huff, moodiness, pet, pique, fit of pique, displeasure; anger, crossness, fury, rage, outrage, bad temper, tantrum; irritability, irascibility, peevishness, tetchiness, testiness, dyspepsia, spleen; *informal* grump; *Brit. informal* paddy, strop; *N. Amer. informal* blowout, hissy fit; *Brit. informal, dated* bate, wax.
OPPOSITES good mood; calmness.

ill-tempered ▶ adjective *an ill-tempered woman* **bad-tempered**, short-tempered, hot-tempered, quick-tempered, ill-humoured, moody; in a (bad) mood, cross, as cross as two sticks, annoyed; irritable, irascible, tetchy, testy, crotchety, touchy, crusty, thin-skinned, scratchy, cantankerous, curmudgeonly, peevish, fractious, waspish, shrewish, prickly, peppery, sharp, pettish; grumpy, grouchy, crabbed, crabby, disagreeable, volatile, splenetic, dyspeptic, choleric, bilious, liverish, cross-grained; *informal* snappish, snappy, chippy, on a short fuse, short-fused; *Brit. informal* shirty, stroppy, narky, ratty, eggy, like a bear with a sore head; *N. Amer. informal* cranky, ornery, peckish, soreheaded; *Austral./NZ informal* snaky; *informal, dated* waxy, miffy.
OPPOSITES good-tempered, amiable.

ill-timed ▶ adjective *their ill-timed foray into overseas property markets* **untimely**, mistimed, badly timed; premature, early, hasty; inopportune, inconvenient, awkward, unwelcome; inappropriate, unsuitable, inapt; disadvantageous, unfavourable, unfortunate, inept.
OPPOSITES opportune; timely.

ill-treat ▶ verb *her mother had ill-treated her when she was young* **abuse**, mistreat, maltreat, treat badly, ill-use, misuse, victimize; manhandle, handle roughly, mishandle, maul, molest; harm, injure, damage; *informal* knock about/around.
OPPOSITE pamper.

ill-treatment ▶ noun *he died from medical neglect and ill-treatment* **abuse**, mistreatment, maltreatment, bad treatment, ill use, ill usage, misuse, victimization; manhandling, rough treatment, mishandling.
OPPOSITE pampering.

illuminate ▶ verb **1** *the bundle of clothes was illuminated by the officer's torch* **light**, light up, throw light on, cast light upon, brighten, make brighter, shine on, flood with light, floodlight, irradiate; *literary* illumine.
OPPOSITE darken.
2 *the manuscripts are illuminated in brilliant inks* **decorate**, illustrate, embellish, adorn, ornament, enhance, emblazon, highlight.
3 *documents often illuminate people's thought processes* **clarify**, elucidate, explain, reveal, make clear, shed light on, cast light on, give insight into, clear up; make explicit, spell out, explicate, expound, rationalize.
OPPOSITES conceal; confuse.

illuminating ▶ adjective *an illuminating account of the writer's style* **informative**, enlightening, revealing, explanatory, instructive, instructional, helpful, educational, educative, edifying, rewarding, enriching.

illumination ▶ noun **1** *the flickering illumination of the match | a floodlamp provided additional illumination* **light**, lighting, radiance, gleam, glitter, brilliance, glow, glare, dazzle, flash, shimmer; shining, gleaming, glowing; irradiation, luminescence, incandescence, fluorescence, phosphorescence; *rare* illumining, irradiance, lucency, lambency, effulgence, refulgence, coruscation, fulguration.
OPPOSITE darkness.
2 *the illumination of a medieval manuscript* **decoration**, illustration, embellishment, adornment, ornamentation.
3 *these books form the most sustained analysis and illumination of the subject* **clarification**, elucidation, explanation, revelation, explication, exposition, exegesis, rationalization.
4 *there were moments of real illumination* **enlightenment**, insight, revelation, discovery; understanding, awareness; explanation, instruction; learning, education, information, knowledge, edification.
OPPOSITE ignorance.

illusion ▶ noun **1** *I was under no illusion about the difficulty of my job | he had destroyed her illusions* **delusion**, misapprehension, misconception, deception, false impression, mistaken impression; fantasy, dream, chimera, fool's paradise, self-deception, castles in the air, castles in Spain; fallacy, error, misjudgement, fancy.
2 *the lighting helps to increase the illusion of depth* **appearance**, impression, imitation, semblance, pretence, sham; false appearance, deceptive appearance, deception, misperception; *rare* simulacrum.
OPPOSITE reality.
3 *the magical illusion is created using mirrors, lights, and paint* **mirage**, hallucination, apparition, phantasm, phantom, vision, spectre, fantasy, figment of the imagination, will-o'-the-wisp, trick of the light; *Latin* ignis fatuus.
4 *he is keen to dispel any impression that his illusions are achieved using TV trickery* **magic trick**, conjuring trick, trick, deception, (**illusions**) magic, conjuring, sleight of hand, legerdemain, trickery.

illusory ▶ adjective *the comfort these theories give is illusory* **delusory**, delusional, delusive; illusionary, imagined, imaginary, fancied, non-existent, unreal, hallucinatory; sham, hollow, deceptive, deceiving, false, fallacious, fake, bogus, mistaken, erroneous, misleading, misguided, untrue, specious, fanciful, notional, chimerical; *rare* illusive, Barmecide.
OPPOSITES real, genuine.

illustrate ▶ verb **1** *the etchings and photographs that illustrate the book are gruesome* **decorate**, adorn, ornament, embellish, accompany; add pictures/drawings/sketches to, provide artwork for.
2 *the complex interplay of such pressures can be illustrated through a brief example* **explain**, elucidate, clarify, make clear, make plain, demonstrate, point up, show, bring home, emphasize, interpret; describe, sum up, summarize, gloss; *informal* get across, get over.
3 *he possessed a quicksilver wit, as illustrated by his remark to Lucy* **exemplify**, show, demonstrate, display, instance, encapsulate, represent; *rare* instantiate.

illustrated ▶ adjective *an illustrated weekly magazine* **with illustrations**, with pictures, with drawings, with sketches, pictorial; decorated, adorned, ornamented, embellished.

illustration ▶ noun **1** *the illustrations in children's books* **picture**, drawing, sketch, figure, graphic; plate, print, engraving, etching, cut, woodcut, linocut, photogravure, duotone, half-tone.
OPPOSITE text.
2 *the way in which tax relief is obtained can best be described by way of illustration* **exemplification**, demonstration, showing, instancing; example, typical case, representative case, case in point, instance, specimen, sample, exemplar, analogy.
3 *students interested in a career in illustration* **artwork**, design, graphic design; ornamentation, decoration, embellishment, adornment.

illustrative ▶ adjective *historians provide illustrative details and examples* **exemplifying**, explanatory, explaining, elucidatory, elucidative, explicative, expository, interpretative, illuminative, exegetic; *rare* evincive.

illustrious ▶ adjective *an illustrious general* **eminent**, distinguished,

acclaimed, noted, notable, noteworthy, prominent, pre-eminent, foremost, leading, paramount, prestigious, important, significant, influential, lionized; renowned, famous, famed, well known, celebrated; esteemed, honoured, respected, exalted, venerable, august, highly regarded, well thought of, of distinction, of repute, of high standing; splendid, brilliant, remarkable, outstanding, great, noble, glorious, grand, lofty.
OPPOSITES unknown, obscure.

ill will ▶ noun *he didn't bear his wife any ill will* **animosity**, hostility, enmity, acrimony, animus, hatred, hate, loathing, detestation, antipathy; ill feeling, bad blood, antagonism, unfriendliness, unkindness, aversion, dislike; spite, spitefulness, rancour, resentment, hard feelings, bitterness, venom, poison, bile, vitriol, malice, malevolence, odium; *archaic* disrelish.
OPPOSITE goodwill.

image ▶ noun **1** *an image of the Madonna* **likeness**, resemblance; **depiction**, portrayal, representation; statue, statuette, sculpture, bust, effigy, figure, figurine, doll, carving; painting, picture, portrait, drawing, sketch.
2 *Voyager 2 sent back images of the planet Neptune* **picture**, facsimile, photograph, snapshot, photo; optical representation, reproduction.
3 *he contemplated his image in the mirrors* **reflection**, mirror image, likeness; echo.
4 *the world has an image of this country as democratic* **conception**, impression, idea, concept, perception, notion; mental picture, mental representation, conceptualization, vision, fancy, thought.
5 *his poetry is constructed around biblical images* **simile**, **metaphor**, metonymy; figure of speech, trope, figurative expression, turn of phrase, rhetorical device, conceit; word painting, word picture.
6 *everyone expects him to live up to his heart-throb image* **public perception**, public conception, public impression, persona, profile, face, identity, front, facade, mask, guise, role, part; portrayal, depiction.
7 *Ma says I'm the image of my grandfather* **double**, living image, replica, lookalike, clone, copy, reproduction, twin, duplicate, exact likeness, facsimile, counterpart, mirror image; *German* Doppelgänger; *informal* very spit, dead spit, spitting image, chip off the old block, ringer, dead ringer; *archaic* similitude.
8 *a graven image* **idol**, icon, fetish, false god, golden calf, totem, talisman.
▶ verb *she imaged imposing castles and cathedrals* **envisage**, envision, imagine, conceive of, picture, dream up, see in one's mind's eye.

WORD LINKS
related prefix **icono-**
study of images **iconography, iconology**

imaginable ▶ adjective *the most severe weather conditions imaginable* **thinkable**, conceivable, supposable, believable, credible, creditable, comprehensible; possible, plausible, feasible, tenable, within the bounds/realms of possibility, under the sun; *rare* cogitable.
OPPOSITES unimaginable, inconceivable.

imaginary ▶ adjective *the imaginary world of the novel* **unreal**, non-existent, fictional, fictitious, pretend, make-believe, mythical, mythological, legendary, storybook, fanciful, fantastic; made-up, dreamed-up, invented, concocted, fabricated, fancied, the product of someone's imagination; illusory, illusive, figmental, hallucinatory, phantasmal, phantasmic, a figment of someone's imagination; dreamy, dreamlike, shadowy, unsubstantial, chimerical, ethereal; virtual, notional, hypothetical, theoretical; assumed, supposed, suppositious; *archaic* visionary.
OPPOSITES real, actual.

imagination ▶ noun **1** *he had a very vivid imagination* **imaginative faculty**, creative power, fancy; *informal* mind's eye.
2 *the government needs imagination in dealing with these problems* **creativity**, imaginativeness, creativeness; vision, inspiration, insight, inventiveness, invention, resourcefulness, initiative, ingenuity, enterprise; originality, innovation, innovativeness; individuality, unorthodoxy, nonconformity; cleverness, wit, quick-wittedness, genius, flair, panache; artistry, artistic power.
3 *every once in a while an album captures the public's imagination* **interest**, fascination, attention, passion, curiosity, preoccupation.

imaginative ▶ adjective *a strong, imaginative storyline | an imaginative solution* **creative**, visionary, inspired, insightful, inventive, resourceful, ingenious, enterprising; original, innovative, innovatory, individual, unorthodox, unconventional, nonconformist, unusual, out of the ordinary; fanciful, whimsical; *informal* blue-sky.
OPPOSITES unimaginative; pedestrian.

imagine ▶ verb **1** *one can imagine the cloud-capped towers of the castle* **visualize**, envisage, envision, picture, form a picture of, see in the mind's eye, conjure up, conceptualize; dream about, fantasize about; dream up, think up, conceive, think of; plan, project, scheme.
2 *I imagine he was at home with his wife* **assume**, presume, expect, take it, take it for granted, take it as read, take it as given, presuppose; suppose, think it likely, dare say, think, surmise, conjecture, believe, be of the opinion that, fancy, feel, be of the view, be under the impression; *N. Amer.* figure; *informal* guess, reckon; *formal* opine; *archaic* ween.
OPPOSITE doubt.

imbalance ▶ noun *the political imbalance between North and South* **disparity**, variance, unevenness, polarity, contrast, variation, disproportion, lopsidedness, lack of proportion, lack of harmony, lack of relation; gulf, breach, split, gap.
OPPOSITES balance, parity.

imbecile (*informal*) ▶ noun *I'd have to be an imbecile to do such a thing* **fool**, idiot, cretin, moron, dolt, halfwit, ass, dunce, dullard, simpleton, nincompoop, blockhead, ignoramus, clod; *informal* dope, thickhead, ninny, chump, dimwit, dummy, dum-dum, dumb-bell, jackass, bonehead, fathead, numbskull, dunderhead, airhead, pinhead, lamebrain, pea-brain, birdbrain, dipstick, donkey, noodle; *Brit. informal* nit, nitwit, twit, clot, muppet, plonker, berk, prat, pillock, wally, wazzock, divvy; *N. Amer. informal* bozo, turkey, goofus.
OPPOSITE genius.
▶ adjective *try not to make imbecile remarks* **stupid**, foolish, idiotic, silly, doltish, half-witted, witless, dull, brainless, mindless, unintelligent, unwise; senseless, absurd, crazy, mad, fatuous, inane, asinine, ridiculous; *informal* dense, dumb, thickheaded, dim, dim-witted, dopey, gormless, half-baked, hare-brained, crackbrained, pea-brained, nutty, dotty, batty, dippy, cuckoo, screwy, wacky; *Brit. informal* barmy, daft.
OPPOSITE intelligent.

imbed ▶ verb. *See* EMBED.

imbibe ▶ verb **1** *he was flushed from the Scotch he'd imbibed* **drink**, consume, sup, sip, quaff, swallow, down, guzzle, gulp (down), swill, lap, slurp; *informal* swig, knock back, sink; *Brit. informal* neck.
2 *he had imbibed too liberally* **drink alcohol**, drink, take strong drink, indulge, tipple, swill; *informal* booze, hit the bottle, take to the bottle, knock a few back, wet one's whistle; *Brit. informal* bevvy; *N. Amer. informal* bend one's elbow; *archaic* wassail, tope.
3 *he has spent a lifetime imbibing his local club's history* **assimilate**, absorb, soak up, take in, digest, ingest, drink in, learn, acquire, grasp, gain, pick up, familiarize oneself with.

imbroglio ▶ noun **1** *a man caught up in a political imbroglio* **complicated situation**, complication, complexity, problem, difficulty, predicament, plight, trouble, entanglement, confusion, muddle, mess, quandary, dilemma; *informal* bind, jam, pickle, fix, scrape, corner, tight corner, hole, sticky situation, mare's nest, hot water, deep water.
2 (*archaic*) *an imbroglio of papers* **confused heap**, jumble, muddle, mess, bundle, clutter, hodgepodge, hotchpotch, mishmash, farrago; *rare* gallimaufry.

imbue ▶ verb *a society imbued with a sense of fairness* **permeate**, saturate, diffuse, suffuse, pervade; impregnate, inject, inculcate, instil, ingrain, inspire, inform; fill, charge, load.

imitate ▶ verb **1** *it was quite acceptable for artists to imitate other artists* **emulate**, copy, take as a model, model oneself on, take as a pattern, pattern oneself on/after, follow the example of, take as an example, take as a role model, take after, follow, follow in someone's steps/footsteps; echo, parrot; follow suit, take a leaf out of someone's book; *informal* rip off.
2 *he was a splendid mimic, and loved to imitate Winston Churchill* **mimic**, do an impression of, impersonate, ape; parody, caricature, burlesque, travesty, mock; masquerade as, pose as, pass oneself off as; *informal* take off, send up, spoof, do; *N. Amer. informal* make like; *archaic* monkey; *rare* personate.
3 *the tombs imitated houses* **resemble**, look like, be like, simulate; match, echo, mirror; bring to mind, remind one of.

imitation ▶ noun **1** *she wore an imitation of a sailor's hat* **copy**, simulation, reproduction, replica; counterfeit, forgery, fake.
2 *learning by imitation* **emulation**, copying, following, echoing, parroting.
3 *he did a perfect imitation of Francis* **impersonation**, impression, parody, mockery, caricature, burlesque, travesty, lampoon, pastiche; mimicry, mimicking, imitating, aping, mocking; *informal* send-up, take-off, spoof.
▶ adjective *imitation ivory | imitation Louis Quinze furniture* **artificial**, synthetic, simulated, man-made, manufactured, ersatz, substitute; reproduction, replica, repro, facsimile, model; mock, sham, fake, counterfeit, bogus, spurious; *informal* pseudo, phoney, dummy; *Brit. informal* cod.
OPPOSITES real, genuine.

imitative ▶ adjective **1** *the fear that young people would be provoked into imitative crime by television* **similar**, like; **mimicking**, mimetic, mimic, parrot-like; *informal* **copycat**.
2 *I found the film empty and imitative* **derivative**, unoriginal, uninventive, non-innovative, unimaginative, uninspired, plagiarized, plagiaristic, copied, second-hand, rehashed, warmed-up; clichéd, hackneyed, stale, trite, tired, worn out, flat, banal, stock; *informal* cribbed, old hat.
OPPOSITE original.
3 *words which are imitative, like 'peewit'* **onomatopoeic**, echoic.

imitator ▶ noun **1** *the show's success has sparked off many imitators* **copier**, copyist, emulator, follower, mimic, plagiarist, ape, parrot, echo; *informal* copycat; *rare* epigone.
2 *an Elvis imitator* **impersonator**, impressionist, mimicker; parodist, caricaturist, lampooner, lampoonist.

immaculate ▶ adjective **1** *an immaculate white shirt* **clean**, spotless, pristine, unsoiled, unstained, unsullied, speckless, ultra-clean; whiter than white, snowy-white, lily-white; shining, shiny, gleaming; neat, tidy, neat and tidy, spick and span, neat as a new pin; *informal* squeaky clean, as clean as a whistle.
OPPOSITES dirty, grubby.
2 *a guitar in immaculate condition* **perfect**, pristine, mint, as good as new; flawless, faultless, without blemish, unblemished, unimpaired, unspoilt, undamaged, unmarred; excellent, impeccable, prime, peak; *informal* tip-top, A1.
OPPOSITES bad; damaged.
3 *that wouldn't look good on his otherwise immaculate record* **unblemished**, spotless, pure, impeccable, unsullied, undefiled, untarnished, stainless; innocent, virtuous, incorrupt, guiltless, sinless; *informal* squeaky clean, as pure as the driven snow.
OPPOSITE blameworthy.

immanent ▶ adjective **1** *the material insecurity immanent in the forced commodification of labour* **inherent**, intrinsic, innate, built-in, latent, essential, fundamental, basic, ingrained, natural.
2 *God is immanent in His creation* **pervasive**, pervading, permeating; omnipresent, ubiquitous, present everywhere; *rare* permeative, suffusive, permeant.
OPPOSITE transcendent.

immaterial ▶ adjective **1** *the difference in our ages was immaterial* **irrelevant**, unimportant, inconsequential, insignificant, of no matter/moment, of little account, beside the point, not to the point, neither here nor there, inapposite, not pertinent, not germane; trivial, trifling, petty, superficial; peripheral, tangential, extraneous.
OPPOSITES important, significant.
2 *he believed in the immortality of an immaterial soul* **intangible**, incorporeal, not material, bodiless, unembodied, disembodied, impalpable, ethereal, unsubstantial, insubstantial, airy, aerial; spiritual, ghostly, spectral, wraithlike, transcendental, unearthly, supernatural; *rare* discarnate, disincarnate, unbodied, phantasmal, phantasmic.
OPPOSITES physical, tangible.

immature ▶ adjective **1** *white Stilton is a very young, immature Stilton* **unripe**, not ripe, not mature, not matured, unmellowed; undeveloped, unformed, imperfect, unfinished, incomplete; crude, raw, green.
OPPOSITES ripe, mature.
2 *she is an extremely shy and immature girl* **childish**, babyish, infantile, juvenile, puerile, jejune, callow, green, inexperienced, unsophisticated, unworldly, naive, ingenuous; *informal* wet behind the ears, born yesterday.
OPPOSITE mature.

immaturity ▶ noun **1** *the immaturity of the fruit | the immaturity of the technology* **unripeness**, greenness, sourness; newness, rawness, crudeness, crudity, imperfection, incompleteness, lack of completion, lack of development.
2 *they were shocked by such immaturity in a grown man* **childishness**, babyishness, infantilism, juvenility, puerility, lack of experience, inexperience, unworldliness, naivety, ingenuousness.

immeasurable ▶ adjective *he dreamed of possessing immeasurable riches* **incalculable**, inestimable, innumerable, unfathomable, fathomless, indeterminable, measureless, untold; limitless, boundless, unbounded, unlimited, illimitable, infinite, endless, never-ending, interminable, inexhaustible, bottomless; vast, immense, great, abundant; *informal* no end of; *literary* myriad; *rare* innumerous, unnumberable.
OPPOSITE few.

immediate ▶ adjective **1** *the UN resolution called for immediate action* **instant**, instantaneous, on-the-spot, prompt, swift, speedy, rapid, quick, expeditious; sudden, hurried, hasty, precipitate, abrupt; lightning, whirlwind, overnight; *informal* snappy, p.d.q. (pretty damn quick); *literary* fleet, rathe; *rare* alacritous.
OPPOSITES delayed; gradual.
2 *there are no immediate plans to launch the product* **current**, present, existing, existent, actual, extant; urgent, pressing; *archaic* instant.
OPPOSITES past; future.
3 *the immediate past is of more importance than a remoter period* **recent**, not long past, just gone; occurring recently.
OPPOSITE remote.
4 *they have strong ties with their immediate neighbours* **nearest**, near, close, closest, next-door; adjacent, adjoining, abutting, contiguous, proximate.
OPPOSITE distant.
5 *the coroner identified the immediate cause of death* **direct**, primary.
OPPOSITE indirect.

immediately ▶ adverb **1** *it was necessary to make a decision immediately* **straight away**, at once, right away, right now, instantly, now, directly, promptly, forthwith, this/that (very) minute, this/that instant, there and then, here and now, in a flash, without delay, without hesitation, without further ado, post-haste; quickly, as fast as possible, fast, speedily, with all speed, as soon as possible, a.s.a.p.; *French* tout de suite; *informal* before you can say Jack Robinson, pronto, double quick, in double quick time, p.d.q (pretty damn quick), toot sweet; *Indian informal* ekdam; *archaic* straightway, instanter, forthright.
2 *I sat immediately behind him* **directly**, right, exactly, precisely, squarely, just, dead; close, closely, at close quarters; *informal* slap bang; *N. Amer. informal* smack dab.

immemorial ▶ adjective *an immemorial custom* **ancient**, old, very old, age-old, antediluvian, timeless, dateless, archaic, long-standing, long-lived, time-worn, time-honoured; ancestral, traditional, atavistic; of yore, rooted in the past.
OPPOSITE recent.

immense ▶ adjective *an immense brick church dominates the town* **huge**, vast, massive, enormous, gigantic, colossal, great, very large, very big, extensive, expansive, monumental, towering, mountainous, tremendous, prodigious, substantial; giant, elephantine, monstrous, mammoth, titanic, Brobdingnagian, king-size, king-sized; *informal* mega, monster, whopping, whopping great, thumping, thumping great, humongous, jumbo, hulking; *Brit. informal* whacking, whacking great, ginormous.
OPPOSITE tiny.

immensely ▶ adverb *it was an immensely difficult decision* **extremely**, very, exceedingly, exceptionally, especially, extraordinarily, tremendously, vastly, hugely, abundantly, intensely, acutely, singularly, significantly, distinctly, outstandingly, uncommonly, unusually, decidedly, particularly, eminently, supremely, highly, remarkably, really, truly, mightily, thoroughly, to a fault, in the extreme, extra; all that, to a great extent, most, so; *Scottish* unco; *French* très; *N. English* right; *informal* terrifically, awfully, fearfully, terribly, devilishly, majorly, seriously, mega, ultra, oh-so, stinking, mucho, damn, damned; *informal, dated* devilish, hellish, frightfully; *Brit. informal* ever so, well, bloody, dead, dirty, jolly, fair; *N. Amer. informal* real, mighty, powerful, awful, plumb, darned, way, bitching; *S. African informal* lekker; *archaic* exceeding.
OPPOSITES slightly; by no means.

immerse ▶ verb **1** *litmus paper turns red on being immersed in acid* **submerge**, plunge, dip, dunk, duck, sink; douse, souse, soak, drench, imbue, saturate, cover, rinse, wet.
2 *the new Christian would be immersed in the river* **baptize**, christen; purify; *informal, dated* dip; *rare* lustrate.
3 *Elliot was immersed in his work* **absorb**, engross, occupy, engage, involve, engulf, bury; busy, employ, distract, divert, preoccupy; *informal* lose oneself in, get lost in.

immigrant ▶ noun *the country traditionally welcomes immigrants* **newcomer**, settler, incomer, new arrival, migrant, emigrant; non-native, foreigner, alien, outsider, stranger; naturalized citizen, expatriate; *informal* expat.
OPPOSITE native.

imminent ▶ adjective *there was speculation that a ceasefire was imminent* **impending**, at hand, close, near, approaching, fast approaching, coming, forthcoming, on the way, about to happen, upon us, in store, in the offing, in the pipeline, on the horizon, in the air, in the wind, brewing, looming, looming large; threatening, menacing; expected, anticipated; *informal* on the cards.
OPPOSITE remote.

immobile ▶ adjective **1** *she sat immobile for a long time* **motionless**, unmoving, without moving, still, stock-still, static, stationary, at rest, at a standstill, dormant; rooted to the spot, fixed to the spot, rigid, frozen, stiff, riveted, transfixed, like a statue, as if turned to stone, not moving a muscle, immobilized.
OPPOSITE moving.
2 *she dreaded being immobile and physically dependent* **unable to move**, immobilized, immovable; paralysed, crippled, handicapped; *technical* immotile, immotive.
OPPOSITE mobile.

immobilize ▶ verb *the officer wanted to immobilize their vehicle* **put out of action**, disable, prevent from moving/working, make inoperative, render inactive, inactivate, deactivate, paralyse, cripple; bring to a standstill, bring to a halt, halt, stop; clamp, wheel-clamp; *rare* disenable.

immoderate ▶ adjective *they were concerned about his immoderate drinking* **excessive**, heavy, intemperate, unrestrained, unrestricted, uncontrolled, unlimited, unbridled, uncurbed, self-indulgent, overindulgent, imprudent, reckless, wild; undue, inordinate, unreasonable, unjustified, unwarranted, uncalled for, outrageous, egregious; extravagant, lavish, prodigal, profligate, wanton, dissipative.
OPPOSITE moderate.

immoderation ▶ noun *he paid a high price for his immoderation* **excess**, excessiveness, intemperance, intemperateness, lack of restraint, lack of self-control, self-gratification, self-indulgence, overindulgence, lavishness, extravagance, decadence, profligacy, wantonness, dissipation, dissoluteness, dissolution.
OPPOSITE moderation.

immodest ▶ adjective *her clothes and manner were most immodest* **indecorous**, improper, indecent, indelicate, indiscreet, immoral; forward, bold, brazen, impudent, unblushing, unchaste, unvirtuous, shameless, loose, wanton; *informal* fresh, cheeky, naughty, saucy.

immolate ▶ verb *ancient Chinese kings would immolate vast numbers of* *animals* **sacrifice**, offer up, offer as a sacrifice, kill as a sacrifice; kill, slaughter, burn.

immoral ▶ adjective *they deplored immoral behaviour among the upper classes* **unethical**, bad, morally wrong, wrongful, wicked, evil, unprincipled, unscrupulous, dishonourable, dishonest, unconscionable, iniquitous, disreputable, fraudulent, corrupt, depraved, vile, villainous, nefarious, base, unfair, underhand, devious; sinful, impure, unchaste, unvirtuous, shameless, degenerate, debauched, abandoned, dissolute, reprobate, perverted, indecent, lewd, licentious, wanton, bawdy, lustful, promiscuous, whorish; *informal* shady, low-down; *Brit. informal* dodgy, crooked, not cricket; *archaic* miscreant.
OPPOSITES moral, ethical; chaste.

immoral or amoral?
See AMORAL.

immorality ▶ noun *he believed his father had been punished by God for his immorality* **wickedness**, immoral behaviour, badness, evil, vileness, iniquity, corruption, dishonesty, dishonourableness; sinfulness, sin, impurity, unchastity, depravity, vice, turpitude, degeneracy, debauchery, dissolution, perversion, indecency, lewdness, licentiousness, lustfulness, wantonness, promiscuity, shamelessness; *informal* shadiness; *Brit. informal* crookedness.
OPPOSITES morality; chastity.

I

immortal ▶ adjective **1** *they believe that their souls are immortal* **undying**, never dying, deathless, eternal, ever living, everlasting, never-ending, endless, perpetual, lasting, enduring, constant, abiding; imperishable, indestructible, inextinguishable, unfading, immutable, indissoluble; *rare* sempiternal, perdurable.
OPPOSITE mortal.
2 *the immortal children's classic 'The Wind in the Willows'* **timeless**, perennial, evergreen, classic, traditional, ageless, time-honoured, abiding, enduring, unforgettable, memorable, remembered; **famous**, famed, renowned, legendary, great, eminent, outstanding, acclaimed, celebrated, commemorated, honoured.
OPPOSITES forgettable; obscure.
▶ noun **1** *the many Greek temples of the immortals* **god**, **goddess**, deity, divine being, immortal being, celestial being, supreme being, divinity; Olympian.
OPPOSITE mortal.
2 *he will always be one of the immortals of soccer* **great**, hero, Olympian; genius, celebrity.

immortality ▶ noun **1** *eating the fruit gave the gods immortality* **eternal life**, everlasting life, deathlessness, everlastingness, endlessness, perpetuity; indestructibility, imperishability.
2 *occasionally a guide book has achieved immortality* **timelessness**, legendary status; lasting fame/renown/repute/glory; durability, permanence.

immortalize ▶ verb *the battle was immortalized in prose by Pushkin* **commemorate**, memorialize, keep alive the memory of, eternalize, perpetuate, preserve, enshrine; celebrate, pay tribute to, pay homage to, honour, salute, exalt, laud, glorify; *literary* eternize.

immovable ▶ adjective **1** *it's best to lock your bike to something immovable* **fixed**, secure, stable, rooted, riveted, moored, anchored, braced, set firm, set fast, fast, firm; stuck, jammed, stiff, unbudgeable.
OPPOSITE mobile.
2 *she shook him but he sat immovable* **motionless**, unmoving, stationary, still, stock-still, at a standstill, not moving a muscle, rooted to the spot, dead still, statue-like; transfixed, paralysed, frozen.
OPPOSITE moving.
3 *she was so immovable in her loyalties* **steadfast**, unwavering, unswerving, resolute, determined, adamant, firm, unshakeable, unfailing, dogged, tenacious, stubborn, obdurate, inflexible, unyielding, unbending, uncompromising, unrelenting, inexorable, iron-willed, strong-willed, steely, dead set; *N. Amer.* rock-ribbed; *informal* stiff-necked; *rare* indurate.
OPPOSITES fickle; unsure.

immune ▶ adjective *they are* **immune to** *hepatitis B | our business is* **immune to** *the economic conditions* **resistant**, not subject, not liable, unsusceptible, not vulnerable, not open, not exposed; protected from, safe from, secure against, not in danger of, exempt from, clear of, free from, unaffected by, proof against; freed from, absolved from, released from, excused from, relieved of, spared from, excepted from, exempted from; *informal* let off.
OPPOSITE susceptible.

immunity ▶ noun **1** *the children have an* **immunity to** *malaria* **resistance to**, resilience to, non-susceptibility to, lack of susceptibility to, protection from, ability to fight off, ability to withstand, ability to counteract, defences against; immunization against, inoculation against.
OPPOSITE susceptibility to.
2 *the rebels were given* **immunity from** *prosecution* **exemption**, exception, freedom, release, impunity, dispensation, exoneration; non-liability for; *informal* a let-off; *rare* derogation.
3 *he could not be sued since he possessed diplomatic immunity* **indemnity**, privilege, prerogative, special treatment, right, liberty, licence, permission; asylum; legal exemption, impunity, protection, freedom; *French* carte blanche; *Law, historical* droit.

WORD LINKS
branch of medicine to do with immunity **immunology**

immunize ▶ verb *he* **immunized** *the children* **against** *measles* **vaccinate**, inoculate, inject; protect from, shield from, safeguard from; *informal* give someone a jab, give someone a shot.

immure ▶ verb *the monks were immured in Newgate jail* **confine**, intern, shut up, lock up, incarcerate, imprison, jail, put away, put behind bars, put under lock and key, hold captive, hold prisoner; coop up, mew up, fence in, wall in, close in; detain, keep, hold, trap.

immutable ▶ adjective *a precise and immutable set of rules* **unchangeable**, fixed, set, rigid, inflexible, unyielding, unbending, permanent, entrenched, established, well-established, unshakeable, irremovable, indelible, ineradicable; **unchanging**, unchanged, changeless, unvarying, unvaried, undeviating, static, constant, lasting, abiding, enduring, persistent, perpetual.
OPPOSITE variable.

imp ▶ noun **1** *imps are thought to sprout from Satan* **demon**, little devil, devil, fiend; hobgoblin, goblin, elf, sprite, puck; *archaic* bugbear; *rare* cacodemon.
2 *the child's a cheeky young imp* **rascal**, scamp, monkey, fiend, demon, devil, mischief-maker, troublemaker, prankster, rogue, wretch, brat, urchin, whippersnapper, tearaway; minx, chit; *informal* monster, horror, mischief, holy terror; *Brit. informal* perisher; *Irish informal* spalpeen; *N. English informal* tyke, scally; *N. Amer. informal* hellion, varmint; *archaic* scapegrace, jackanapes, rapscallion, rip.

impact ▶ noun (stress on the first syllable) **1** *car parts were spread by the impact over a wide region* **collision**, crash, smash, clash, bump, bang, knock, jolt, thump, whack, thwack, slam, smack; contact.
2 *no car can withstand the impact of a train* **force**, full force, shock, brunt, impetus, pressure, weight.
3 *the job losses will have a major impact | the impact of agriculture on wildlife* **effect**, influence, impression; results, consequences, repercussions, ramifications, reverberations; *informal* pay-off.
▶ verb (stress on the second syllable) **1** (*N. Amer.*) *a comet impacted the earth sixty million years ago* **crash into**, smash into, collide with, be in collision with, hit, strike, ram, smack into, slam into, bang into, cannon into, plough into, meet head-on, dash against.
2 *high interest rates have* **impacted on** *retail spending* **affect**, influence, have an effect, have an influence, exert influence, make an impression, act, work; strike, hit, touch, change, alter, modify, transform, shape, control, govern, determine, decide, sway, bias.

impair ▶ verb *even one drink can impair driving performance* **damage**, harm, diminish, reduce, weaken, lessen, decrease, blunt, impede, hinder, mar, spoil, disable; undermine, compromise, threaten; *informal* foul up, put the kibosh on; *rare* vitiate.
OPPOSITES improve, enhance.

impaired ▶ adjective *they care for themselves despite being physically impaired* **disabled**, handicapped, incapacitated; debilitated, infirm, weak, weakened, enfeebled; paralysed, immobilized; *euphemistic* challenged, differently abled.

impairment ▶ noun *the baby has a visual impairment* **disability**, handicap, abnormality, defect, deficiency, flaw; affliction, disadvantage, problem; *formal* dysfunction; *rare* vitiation.

impale ▶ verb *his head was impaled on a pike for all to see* **stick**, skewer, spear, spike, pin, transfix; pierce, stab, run through, bayonet, harpoon, lance; gore, disembowel; puncture, perforate; *rare* transpierce.

impalpable ▶ adjective *a glimpse of an idea that remained as impalpable as a dream* **intangible**, insubstantial, incorporeal, unable to be touched, imperceptible to the touch; **indefinable**, elusive, hard to define/describe, undescribable; *rare* immaterial, unbodied, discarnate.
OPPOSITE palpable.

impart ▶ verb **1** *she had news that she couldn't wait to impart* **communicate**, pass on, convey, transmit, relay, relate, recount, set forth, present, tell, make known, make public, go public with, report, announce, proclaim, spread, disseminate, circulate, promulgate, broadcast; disclose, reveal, divulge, bring into the open; *informal* let on about, tell all about, blab, spill; *archaic* discover, unbosom.
OPPOSITE keep to oneself.
2 *the brush imparts a good sheen to the dog's coat* **give**, bestow, confer, grant, lend, accord, afford, provide, supply, offer, yield, contribute.
OPPOSITE remove.

impartial ▶ adjective *the referee is obliged to be impartial* **unbiased**, unprejudiced, neutral, non-partisan, non-discriminatory, disinterested, uninvolved, uncommitted, detached, dispassionate, objective, open-minded, equitable, even-handed, fair, fair-minded, just; without favouritism, free from discrimination, with no axe to grind, without fear or favour; *informal* on the fence.

OPPOSITES biased, partisan.

impassable ▸ adjective *many roads were impassable after the flood* **blocked**, closed, obstructed, impenetrable; pathless, trackless; unnavigable, untraversable, unpassable.

impasse ▸ noun *the negotiations seemed to have reached an impasse* **deadlock**, dead end, stalemate, checkmate, stand-off; standstill, halt, stop, stoppage, full stop.

impassioned ▸ adjective *she made an impassioned plea for the return of her abducted child* **emotional**, heartfelt, wholehearted, from the heart, earnest, sincere, fervent, ardent, vehement, intense, burning, urgent, passionate, feverish, frantic, emotive, zealous; *rare* fervid, perfervid, passional, full-hearted.
OPPOSITE half-hearted.

impassive ▸ adjective *she smiled at him, but his features remained impassive* **expressionless**, unexpressive, inexpressive, inscrutable, blank, deadpan, poker-faced, straight-faced, dispassionate; stony, wooden, unresponsive; empty, vacant, glazed, fixed, lifeless.
OPPOSITE expressive.

impatience ▸ noun **1** *he was shifting in his seat with impatience* **restlessness**, restiveness, frustration, agitation, nervousness, edginess, jitteriness, excitability; **eagerness**, keenness, avidity, hunger, greed, longing, yearning.
2 *she crumpled up the pages in a burst of impatience* **irritability**, testiness, tetchiness, snappiness, irascibility, querulousness, peevishness, intolerance, disgruntlement, frustration, exasperation, annoyance, pique, discontent, dissatisfaction, displeasure; abruptness, brusqueness, shortness, curtness; *informal* aggravation.

impatient ▸ adjective **1** *the hours ticked by and Melissa grew impatient* **restless**, restive, agitated, nervous, anxious, ill at ease, fretful, edgy, jumpy, jittery, worked up, keyed up; *Brit.* nervy; *informal* twitchy, uptight.
OPPOSITES calm; indifferent.
2 *they are impatient to get back home* **anxious**, **eager**, keen, avid, desirous, yearning, longing, aching; *informal* itching, dying, raring, gagging, straining at the leash.
OPPOSITE reluctant.
3 *he dismissed them with an impatient gesture* **irritated**, annoyed, angry, testy, tetchy, snappy, cross, crabby, moody, grumpy, querulous, fretful, peevish, peeved, piqued, discontented, displeased, disgruntled; intolerant, short-tempered, quick-tempered; abrupt, curt, brusque, terse, short; *informal* aggravated, grouchy; *Brit. informal* narked, narky, ratty, eggy, shirty.
OPPOSITE pleased.

impeach ▸ verb **1** (*N. Amer.*) *congressional moves to impeach the president* **indict**, charge, accuse, bring a charge against, bring a case against, lay charges against, prefer charges against, arraign, take to court, put on trial, bring to trial, prosecute; *informal* have the law on.
OPPOSITE acquit.
2 *the headlines did much to impeach their clean image* **challenge**, question, call into question, cast doubt on, raise doubts about.
OPPOSITE confirm.

impeccable ▸ adjective *a youth of impeccable character* **flawless**, faultless, unblemished, spotless, stainless, untarnished, perfect, exemplary, ideal, model; **virtuous**, pure, moral, sinless, upright, irreproachable, unimpeachable, blameless, guiltless, above suspicion, beyond reproach, beyond criticism, incorrupt, uncorrupted; *informal* squeaky clean, whiter than white, lily-white, as pure as the driven snow.
OPPOSITES imperfect; sinful.

impecunious ▸ adjective *she came from a respectable but impecunious family* **penniless**, penurious, in penury, poor, impoverished, indigent, insolvent, moneyless, hard up, poverty-stricken, needy, in need, in want, destitute; poor as a church mouse, without a sou, in straitened circumstances, on one's beam ends, unable to make ends meet; *Brit.* on the breadline, without a penny (to one's name); *informal* broke, flat broke, strapped for cash, cleaned out, strapped, on one's uppers, without two pennies/brass farthings to rub together; *Brit. informal* skint, boracic, stony broke, in Queer Street; *N. Amer. informal* stone broke; *rare* pauperized, beggared.
OPPOSITE wealthy.

impede ▸ verb *the programme has been impeded by several problems* **hinder**, obstruct, hamper, handicap, hold back, hold up, delay, interfere with, disrupt, retard, slow, slow down, brake, put a brake on, restrain, fetter, shackle, hamstring, cramp, cripple; block, check, bar, curb, stop, thwart, frustrate, baulk, foil, derail, stand in the way of; *informal* stymie, foul up, screw up; *Brit. informal* scupper, throw a spanner in the works of; *N. Amer. informal* bork, throw a monkey wrench in the works of; *rare* cumber.
OPPOSITE facilitate.

> **CHOOSE THE RIGHT WORD**
>
> **impede, obstruct, hinder, hamper**
>
> See HINDER.

impediment ▸ noun **1** *the country's debt was a serious impediment to economic improvement* **hindrance**, obstruction, obstacle, barrier, bar, handicap, block, check, curb, brake, restraint, restriction, limitation, encumbrance, deterrent; drawback, setback, difficulty, snag, catch, hitch, stumbling block; *informal* fly in the ointment, hiccup, facer; *Brit. informal* spanner in the works; *N. Amer. informal* monkey wrench in the works; *rare* cumber.
OPPOSITE benefit.
2 *she spoke with an impediment* **speech defect**, speech impediment, stammer, stutter, lisp; hesitancy, faltering.

impedimenta ▸ plural noun *all the tedious impedimenta of a teacher's working life* **paraphernalia**, trappings, equipment, accoutrements, appurtenances, accessories, bits and pieces, bits and bobs, odds and ends, things, tackle, effects, possessions, belongings, goods, movables; baggage, luggage; *informal* stuff, gear, traps, junk, rubbish; *Brit. informal* clobber, gubbins, odds and sods; *archaic* equipage.

impel ▸ verb **1** *her sense of duty impelled her to keep up appearances* **force**, compel, constrain, oblige, necessitate, require, demand, make, urge, exhort, press, apply pressure, pressure, pressurize, drive, push, spur, prod, goad, incite, prompt, persuade, inspire.
2 *vital energies impel him in unforeseen directions* **propel**, drive, drive forwards, move forwards, move, actuate, set in motion, get going, get moving.

impending ▸ adjective *she had a strange feeling of impending danger* **imminent**, at hand, close, close at hand, near, nearing, approaching, coming, forthcoming, upcoming, to come, on the way, about to happen, upon us, in store, in the offing, in the pipeline, on the horizon, in the air, in the wind, brewing, looming, looming large, threatening, menacing; *informal* on the cards.

impenetrable ▸ adjective **1** *the ships had impenetrable armoured plating* **impervious**, impermeable, solid, dense, thick, hard, unyielding, unbreakable, indestructible, puncture-proof, unpierceable, resistant; invulnerable, impregnable, inviolable, unattackable, unassailable; waterproof, closed, sealed, hermetically sealed, tight; secure, safe.
OPPOSITES permeable; vulnerable.
2 *a dark, impenetrable forest* **impassable**, unpassable, inaccessible, unnavigable, untraversable, pathless, trackless, untrodden; dense, thick, overgrown, jungly, jungle-like; *archaic* thickset.
OPPOSITES accessible; sparse.
3 *an impenetrable clique* **exclusive**, closed, secretive, secret, private; restrictive, restricted, limited; *rare* discriminative.
OPPOSITE open.
4 *these statistics can seem impenetrable and tedious* **incomprehensible**, impossible to understand, unfathomable, fathomless, inexplicable, unintelligible, unclear, baffling, bewildering, puzzling, perplexing, confusing, abstruse, obscure, opaque, recondite, inscrutable, mysterious, cryptic, Delphic; complex, complicated, difficult, hard; *archaic* wildering; *rare* insolvable.
OPPOSITE clear.

impenitent ▸ adjective *I am quite impenitent at having encouraged her rebellion* **unrepentant**, unrepenting, without regret/remorse, uncontrite, remorseless, unremorseful, shameless, unashamed, unblushing, unapologetic, unabashed, brazen, conscienceless.
OPPOSITE penitent.

imperative ▸ adjective **1** *it is imperative that you find him* **vitally important**, of vital importance, all-important, vital, crucial, critical, essential, of the essence, a matter of life and death, of great consequence, necessary, indispensable, exigent, pressing, urgent; required, compulsory, mandatory, obligatory.
OPPOSITES unimportant; optional.
2 *the imperative note in her voice was unmistakable* **peremptory**, commanding, imperious, authoritative, masterful, lordly, magisterial, autocratic, dictatorial, domineering, overbearing, assertive, firm, insistent, bossy, high-handed, overweening.
OPPOSITE submissive.

imperceptible ▸ adjective *the change was slow and imperceptible* **unnoticeable**, undetectable, indistinguishable, indiscernible, unapparent, inappreciable, invisible, inaudible, impalpable, unobtrusive, impossible to detect; slight, small, subtle, faint, fine, inconsequential, negligible, tiny, minute, minuscule, microscopic, infinitesimal; indistinct, unclear, obscure, vague, indefinite, shadowy, hard to make out.
OPPOSITES obvious, noticeable.

imperfect ▸ adjective **1** *the goods were returned as imperfect* **faulty**, flawed, defective, shoddy, unsound, unsaleable, unfit, inferior, second-rate, below par, below standard, substandard; damaged, impaired, blemished, broken, cracked, torn, scratched, deformed, warped, shabby; inoperative, malfunctioning, not functioning, not working, out of order, in a state of disrepair; *informal* not up to snuff, not up to scratch, tenth-rate, crummy, lousy; *Brit. informal* duff, ropy, rubbish, not much cop.
OPPOSITE perfect.
2 *the manuscript was published in imperfect form in 1888 and fully in 1947* **incomplete**, abridged, not whole, not entire, partial, unfinished, half-

done; deficient, lacking, wanting, unpolished, unrefined, patchy, rough, crude.
OPPOSITE complete.
3 *she spoke imperfect Arabic* **broken**, disjointed, faltering, halting, hesitant, rudimentary, limited, non-fluent, deficient.
OPPOSITES perfect, fluent.

imperfection ▶ **noun 1** *the glass is free from bubbles and other imperfections* **defect**, fault, flaw, deformity, discoloration, disfigurement; crack, break, scratch, chip, dent, pit, notch, nick; blemish, stain, spot, mark, streak.
2 *he was aware of his own imperfections* **flaw**, fault, failing, deficiency, weakness, weak point, weak spot, shortcoming, fallibility, frailty, infirmity, foible, inadequacy, limitation; Achilles heel, chink in one's armour; *informal* hang-up.
OPPOSITE strength.
3 *nature is full of imperfection* **flaws**, faults, faultiness, irregularity, abnormality, distortion, deformity, malformation, misshapenness; ugliness, disfigurement.
OPPOSITE perfection.
4 *the imperfection of the fossil record* **incompleteness**, patchiness, partialness, deficiency; roughness, crudeness.
OPPOSITE completeness.

WORD LINKS
fear of imperfection **atelophobia**

CHOOSE THE RIGHT WORD
imperfection, blemish, flaw
See BLEMISH.

imperial ▶ **adjective 1** *the symbol figured on the imperial banners* **royal**, regal, monarchal, monarchial, monarchical, sovereign, kingly, queenly, princely, majestic; *rare* imperatorial.
2 *her imperial bearing* **majestic**, grand, dignified, proud, stately, noble, aristocratic, regal; magnificent, great, distinguished, imposing, impressive, august, lofty.
3 *our customers thought we were imperial and uninterested in them* **imperious**, high-handed, commanding, peremptory, dictatorial, domineering, bossy, arrogant, overweening, overbearing, authoritarian, tyrannical, authoritative, lordly, officious.

imperil ▶ **verb** *a radiation leak would imperil life and health over a wide area* **endanger**, jeopardize, risk, put at risk, put in danger, expose to danger, put in jeopardy, expose, leave vulnerable, put someone's life on the line; threaten, pose a threat to, be a danger to, be detrimental to, damage, injure, harm, do harm to; *archaic* peril.

CHOOSE THE RIGHT WORD
imperil, endanger, jeopardize, risk
See ENDANGER.

imperious ▶ **adjective** *he spoke to her in a very imperious manner* **peremptory**, high-handed, commanding, imperial, overbearing, overweening, domineering, authoritarian, dictatorial, authoritative, lordly, officious, assertive, dominating, bullish, forceful, bossy, arrogant; *informal* pushy, high and mighty, throwing one's weight around; *rare* pushful.
OPPOSITE meek.

imperishable ▶ **adjective** *the fruits of his inspired labours are imperishable* **enduring**, everlasting, undying, deathless, immortal, timeless, ageless, perennial, lasting, long-lasting; indestructible, inextinguishable, ineradicable, unfading, undiminished, permanent, never-ending, never dying, without end; *rare* sempiternal, perdurable.

impermanent ▶ **adjective** *life has value precisely because it is impermanent* **temporary**, non-permanent, not permanent, transient, transitory, passing, fleeting, momentary, ephemeral, fugitive, fading; short-lived, short-term, short, brief, here today and gone tomorrow; *literary* evanescent, fugacious.
OPPOSITE permanent.

impermeable ▶ **adjective** *the product is packaged in impermeable containers* **watertight**, waterproof, damp-proof, water-resistant, water-repellent, airtight, tight, sealed, hermetically sealed, closed; impenetrable, impregnable, inviolable, resistant; *rare* imperviable.
OPPOSITE permeable.

impersonal ▶ **adjective 1** *the hand of fate is brutal but impersonal* **neutral**, unbiased, non-partisan, non-discriminatory, unprejudiced, unswayed, objective, detached, disinterested, dispassionate, free from discrimination, without favouritism, with no axe to grind, without fear or favour; fair, just, equitable, balanced, even-handed.
OPPOSITE biased.
2 *even his children found him strangely impersonal* **aloof**, distant, remote, reserved, withdrawn, unemotional, unfeeling, unsentimental, dispassionate, passionless, cold, cool, frigid, unresponsive, indifferent, unconcerned; **formal**, stiff, rigid, wooden, starchy, stilted, restrained, self-controlled, matter-of-fact, businesslike, clinical; *informal* stand-offish; *rare* gelid.
OPPOSITES warm; emotional.

impersonate ▶ **verb** *she tried to impersonate her boss* **imitate**, mimic, do an impression of, ape; parody, caricature, burlesque, travesty, mock, satirize, lampoon; masquerade as, pose as, pass oneself off as, profess to be, purport to be, represent oneself as; *informal* take off, do, spoof, send up; *N. Amer. informal* make like; *archaic* monkey; *rare* personate.

impersonation ▶ **noun** *he did an impersonation of Fred Astaire* **impression**, imitation; parody, caricature, mockery, burlesque, travesty, lampoon, pastiche; *informal* take-off, send-up, spoof; *rare* personation.

impertinence ▶ **noun** *they gasped at the impertinence of the suggestion* **rudeness**, insolence, impoliteness, unmannerliness, bad manners, lack of civility, discourtesy, discourteousness, disrespectfulness, incivility; **impudence**, cheek, cheekiness, audacity, temerity, effrontery, nerve, gall, boldness, brazenness, brashness, shamelessness, presumptuousness, presumption, forwardness; *informal* brass, brass neck, neck, face, front, cockiness; *Brit. informal* sauce; *Scottish informal* snash; *N. Amer. informal* sass, sassiness, nerviness, chutzpah; *informal, dated* hide, crust; *archaic* malapertness; *rare* procacity, assumption.
OPPOSITE politeness.

impertinent ▶ **adjective 1** *she asked a lot of impertinent questions* **rude**, insolent, impolite, unmannerly, ill-mannered, bad-mannered, uncivil, discourteous, disrespectful; **impudent**, cheeky, audacious, bold, brazen, brash, shameless, presumptuous, forward, pert; tactless, undiplomatic, unsubtle, personal; *informal* brass-necked, fresh, flip; *Brit. informal* saucy; *N. Amer. informal* sassy, nervy; *archaic* malapert, contumelious; *rare* mannerless.
OPPOSITE polite.
2 (*formal*) *talk of 'rhetoric' is impertinent to this process* **irrelevant**, inapplicable, inapposite, inappropriate, immaterial, unrelated, unconnected, not germane; beside the point, out of place, nothing to do with it, neither here nor there.
OPPOSITES relevant, pertinent.

imperturbable ▶ **adjective** *my father was a solid, imperturbable man* **self-possessed**, composed, collected, calm, {cool, calm, and collected}, as cool as a cucumber, cool-headed, self-controlled, poised, tranquil, serene, relaxed, easy-going, unexcitable, even-tempered, placid, sedate, phlegmatic; unperturbed, unflustered, untroubled, unbothered, unruffled, undismayed, unagitated, undisturbed, unmoved, nonchalant, at ease; *informal* unflappable, unfazed, together, laid-back; *rare* equanimous.
OPPOSITES edgy; excitable.

impervious ▶ **adjective 1** *he seemed impervious to the chill wind | she is impervious to his suggestions* **unaffected by**, untouched by, immune to, invulnerable to, insusceptible to, not susceptible to, proof against, unreceptive to, closed to, resistant to, indifferent to, heedless of, unresponsive to, oblivious to, unmoved by, deaf to.
OPPOSITES receptive to, susceptible to.
2 *an impervious damp-proof course* **impermeable**, impenetrable, impregnable, waterproof, watertight, water-resistant, water-repellent; sealed, hermetically sealed; *rare* imperviable.
OPPOSITE permeable.

CHOOSE THE RIGHT WORD
impetuous, impulsive, precipitate, headlong
These words all refer to haste and lack of forethought.

- **Impetuous** and **impulsive** are very similar in meaning, applying to people, their characters, or their actions, but *impetuous* emphasizes the irresponsibility involved (*I was a bit impetuous offering him the job just like that | she might live to regret this impetuous decision*), while to be *impulsive* can be endearing (*an act of impulsive generosity | they married as young, impulsive teenagers*).
- **Precipitate** is used of actions, not people; a *precipitate* act is typically undesirable and lacks proper planning or consideration of its possible effect (*the danger of inappropriate and precipitate intervention which fails to protect the child*).
- When used as an adjective, **headlong** applies only to actions, not to people. It describes actions which, after their initial impetus, are not guided by any plan and quickly get out of control (*our headlong rush to develop and industrialize the world*). As an adverb, *headlong* can also apply to people in this sense (*I'm going to enjoy each day while it lasts, instead of dashing headlong into the future*).

impetuous ▶ **adjective 1** *she might live to regret this impetuous decision* **impulsive**, rash, hasty, overhasty, reckless, heedless, foolhardy, incautious, imprudent, injudicious, ill-conceived, ill-considered, unplanned, unreasoned, unthought-out, unthinking; spontaneous, impromptu, spur-of-the-moment, precipitate, precipitous, headlong, hurried, rushed.

OPPOSITES cautious, considered.
2 *an impetuous flow of water* **torrential**, powerful, forceful, vigorous, violent, raging, rampant, relentless, unrestrained, uncontrolled, unbridled; rapid, fast, fast-flowing, rushing.
OPPOSITES sluggish, weak.

impetus ▶ noun **1** *the flywheel lost all its impetus* **momentum**, propulsion, impulsion, impelling force, motive force, driving force, drive, thrust, continuing motion; energy, force, power, push, steam, strength.
2 *new products were introduced to give the sales force fresh impetus* **motivation**, stimulus, incitement, incentive, inducement, inspiration, encouragement, boost; urging, pressing, goading, spurring, prodding; *informal* a shot in the arm.

impiety ▶ noun **1** *a world of impiety and immorality* **godlessness**, ungodliness, unholiness, irreligion, sinfulness, sin, vice, immorality, unrighteousness, sacrilege, profaneness, irreverence, disrespect; apostasy, atheism, agnosticism, paganism, heathenism, non-belief, disbelief, unbelief, scepticism, doubt.
OPPOSITES piety; faith.
2 *one impiety will cost me my eternity in paradise* **sin**, transgression, wrongdoing, evil-doing, wrong, misdeed, misdemeanour, bad deed, act of wickedness, immoral act, fall from grace; profanity, blasphemy.
OPPOSITE good deed.

impinge ▶ verb **1** *these issues impinge on all of us* **affect**, have an effect on, have a bearing on, touch, influence, exert influence on, make an impression on, make an impact on, leave a mark on.
2 *the proposed fencing would impinge on a public bridleway* **encroach on**, intrude on, infringe, invade, trespass on, obtrude into, make inroads into, cut through, interfere with; violate; *informal* muscle in on; *archaic* entrench on.
3 (*technical*) *electrically charged particles impinge on the lunar surface* **strike**, hit, dash against, collide with.

impious ▶ adjective *the church was shamefully plundered by impious villains* **godless**, ungodly, unholy, irreligious, sinful, immoral, unrighteous, sacrilegious, profane, blasphemous, irreverent, disrespectful; apostate, atheistic, agnostic, pagan, heathen, faithless, non-believing, unbelieving, disbelieving, doubting; *rare* nullifidian.
OPPOSITE pious.

impish ▶ adjective **1** *he takes an impish delight in shocking the press* **mischievous**, naughty, wicked, devilish, rascally, roguish, prankish, playful, waggish; mischief-making, full of mischief, troublemaking; *archaic* sportive.
2 *she has an engaging impish grin* **elfin**, elflike, elfish, elvish, pixieish, pixie-like, puckish; mischievous, roguish, arch.

implacable ▶ adjective *he was their most implacable critic* **unappeasable**, unpacifiable, unplacatable, unmollifiable, unforgiving, unsparing, grudge-holding; **inexorable**, intransigent, adamant, determined, unshakeable, unswerving, unwavering, inflexible, unyielding, unbending, uncompromising, unrelenting, relentless, ruthless, remorseless, merciless, pitiless, heartless, cruel, hard, harsh, stern, steely, tough.

implant ▶ verb (stress on the second syllable) **1** *the collagen is implanted under the skin* **insert**, embed, bury, lodge, place, put in place, install, introduce; graft, engraft.
OPPOSITE extract.
2 *he implanted the idea in my mind* **instil**, inculcate, insinuate, introduce, inject, plant, sow, sow the seeds of, infuse, impress, imprint, root, lodge.
▶ noun (stress on the first syllable) *the hormone encourages the bone and the implant to bond* **transplant**, graft, implantation, insert.

implausible ▶ adjective *they despaired of his adherence to implausible theories* **unlikely**, not likely, improbable, questionable, doubtful, debatable; hard to believe, unconvincing, far-fetched, unrealistic, incredible, unbelievable, unimaginable, inconceivable, fantastic, fanciful, ridiculous, absurd, preposterous; *informal* hard to swallow, cock and bull, tall.
OPPOSITES plausible, convincing.

implement ▶ noun *garden implements* **tool**, utensil, instrument, device, apparatus, contrivance, gadget, contraption, appliance, machine, labour-saving device; *informal* gizmo.
▶ verb *the cost of implementing the new law* **execute**, apply, put into effect/action, put into practice, carry out, carry through, perform, enact, administer; fulfil, discharge, accomplish, bring about, achieve, realize, contrive, effect; enforce, impose; *rare* effectuate.

implementation ▶ noun *I became responsible for the implementation of the plan* **execution**, application, carrying out, carrying through, performance, enactment, administration; fulfilment, fulfilling, discharge, accomplishment, achievement, realization, contrivance, prosecution, effecting; enforcement, imposition; *rare* effectuation.

implicate ▶ verb **1** *he had been implicated in a financial scandal* **incriminate**, compromise; involve, connect, embroil, enmesh, ensnare; expose; *archaic* inculpate.
OPPOSITE absolve.
2 *viruses are known to be* **implicated in** *the development of certain cancers* **involve in**, concern with, associate with, connect with, tie up with.
3 *when one asks a question one implicates that one desires an answer.* See IMPLY.

implication ▶ noun **1** *he was smarting at their implication that he didn't believe in what he was doing* **suggestion**, inference, insinuation, innuendo, hint, intimation, imputation, indication; connotation, overtone, undertone, hidden meaning, secondary meaning.
OPPOSITE explicit statement.
2 *there was a meeting to discuss the implications of the ban* **consequence**, result, ramification, repercussion, reverberation, effect.
3 *at the first whiff of implication in a murder case he'd probably burn everything* **incrimination**, involvement, connection, entanglement, association; *archaic* inculpation.

implicit ▶ adjective **1** *the implicit assumptions of much sociological writing on women* **implied**, indirect, inferred, understood, hinted, suggested, deducible; unspoken, unexpressed, undeclared, unstated, unsaid, tacit, unacknowledged, silent, taken for granted, taken as read, assumed.
OPPOSITES explicit, direct.
2 *there are a number of assumptions implicit in the way the questions are asked* **inherent**, latent, underlying, inbuilt, incorporated; fundamental.
OPPOSITES explicit, direct.
3 *an implicit trust in human nature* **absolute**, complete, entire, total, wholehearted, perfect, sheer, utter; unqualified, unconditional, unreserved, unadulterated, unalloyed, undiluted, positive; unshaken, unshakeable, unhesitating, unquestioning, firm, steadfast, constant.
OPPOSITE limited.

CHOOSE THE RIGHT WORD

implicit, tacit, unspoken

These words all describe ideas that can be understood despite not being directly expressed.

- A meaning or message that is **implicit** is not stated openly but can be worked out by reasoning from what has been said (*the speech contained an implicit condemnation of nuclear weapons*). Similarly, an *implicit* attitude or belief can be inferred from the behaviour that it prompts (*we must examine assumptions implicit in the way the questions are asked*).
- **Tacit**, from the Latin for 'silent', is typically used to describe situations involving agreement or cooperation in which the underlying attitude, though not expressed directly, is nevertheless understood and accepted by the parties involved (*the government depended on a tacit agreement with other parties | tacit support for the rebels*).
- **Unspoken** basically means that something is not said aloud (*'It was Father's,' she said to his unspoken question*), and depending on context it can have opposite implications. Something may be unspoken because it is to be kept secret (*unspoken resentment*), or it may describe a message that is made very clear and is possibly all the more effective for not being explicit (*there was always an element of unspoken threat*).

implicitly ▶ adverb *he trusted Sarah implicitly* **completely**, absolutely, totally, wholeheartedly, utterly, unconditionally, unreservedly, without reservation, without reserve, without qualification, one hundred per cent; *informal* all the way.

implied ▶ adjective *there was implied criticism of the king's choice of commanders* **implicit**, indirect, hinted, suggested, insinuated, deducible, inferred, understood; oblique, unspoken, unexpressed, undeclared, unstated, unsaid, tacit, unacknowledged, not spelt out, silent, taken for granted, taken as read, assumed.
OPPOSITES explicit, direct.

implore ▶ verb **1** *his mother implored him to continue studying* **plead with**, beg, entreat, beseech, appeal to, pray, ask, request, solicit, supplicate, importune, call on; exhort, urge, enjoin, press, push, petition, encourage, bid; *rare* obtest, obsecrate, impetrate.
2 (*archaic*) *she implored pity* **beg for**, plead for, appeal for, call for, crave; ask for, request, sue for, press for.

imply ▶ verb **1** *she seemed to be implying that he was mad* **insinuate**, suggest, hint, intimate, implicate, say indirectly, indicate, give someone to understand, give someone to believe, convey the impression, signal; *informal* make out.
2 *the forecast traffic increase implied more roads and more air pollution* **involve**, entail; mean, point to, signify, indicate, signal; necessitate, require.

imply or infer?
See INFER.

impolite ▶ adjective *it would have been impolite to leave in the middle of the band's set* **rude**, bad-mannered, ill-mannered, unmannerly, discourteous, uncivil, disrespectful, inconsiderate, boorish, churlish, ill-bred,

I

ungentlemanly, unladylike, ungracious, ungallant; insolent, impudent, impertinent, cheeky, pert, audacious, brassy, offensive, insulting, derogatory; loutish, rough, crude, unrefined, indelicate, indecorous, brash, vulgar; *informal* ignorant, fresh, lippy; *archaic* malapert, contumelious; *rare* underbred, mannerless.
OPPOSITE polite.

impolitic ▶ **adjective** *it would be impolitic not to make amends with this man* **imprudent**, unwise, injudicious, incautious, irresponsible; ill-judged, ill-advised, misguided, ill-considered, careless, rash, reckless, foolhardy, foolish, short-sighted; undiplomatic, indiscreet, indelicate, tactless.
OPPOSITES prudent, wise.

import ▶ **verb** (stress on the second syllable) *the UK imports 95 per cent of its charcoal* **buy from abroad**, bring from abroad, bring in, buy in, ship in, source from abroad.
OPPOSITE export.
▶ **noun** (stress on the first syllable) **1** *a tax levied on imports* **imported commodity**, foreign commodity, non-domestic commodity.
OPPOSITE export.
2 *a ban on the import of foreign books* **importation**, importing, introduction, bringing in, bringing from abroad, buying from abroad, sourcing from abroad, shipping in.
OPPOSITE export.
3 *a matter of great import* **importance**, significance, consequence, moment, momentousness, magnitude, substance, weight, weightiness, note, noteworthiness, gravity, seriousness.
OPPOSITE insignificance.
4 *Seb suddenly realized the full import of her words* **meaning**, sense, essence, gist, drift, purport, message, thrust, substance, sum and substance, implication, signification, point, burden, tenor, spirit; pith, core, nub; *informal* nitty-gritty.

importance ▶ **noun 1** *the signing of the treaty was an event of immense importance* **significance**, momentousness, import, consequence, note, noteworthiness, substance, value; seriousness, graveness, gravity, weightiness, urgency.
OPPOSITES unimportance, insignificance.
2 *she had a fine sense of her own importance* **power**, influence, authority, sway, weight, dominance; prominence, eminence, pre-eminence, notability, worth, account; prestige, high rank, status, standing, stature, superiority, mark, fame, renown, greatness, grandness; *informal* clout, pull.
OPPOSITES unimportance, insignificance.

important ▶ **adjective 1** *an important meeting* **significant**, consequential, momentous, of great moment, of import, of great import, of great consequence, far-reaching, major; critical, crucial, vital, pivotal, decisive, urgent, epoch-making, historic, seminal; serious, grave, substantial, weighty, signal, material.
OPPOSITES unimportant, trivial.
2 *the important thing is that you do well in your A levels* **main**, chief, principal, key, major, salient, prime, dominant, foremost, supreme, predominant, paramount, overriding, cardinal, crucial, vital, indispensable, critical, essential, significant, urgent; central, fundamental, basic; *informal* number-one.
OPPOSITES unimportant, inessential.
3 *the school was important to the community* **of value**, valuable, valued, useful, of use, beneficial, necessary, essential, indispensable, vital, of the essence; **of concern**, of interest, relevant, pertinent, material, germane.
OPPOSITES unimportant, irrelevant.
4 *he was an important man* **powerful**, influential, of influence, well-connected, high-ranking, high-level, top-level, controlling, dominant, formidable; prominent, eminent, pre-eminent, notable, noteworthy, of note; distinguished, esteemed, respected, prestigious, celebrated, famous, great, grand; leading, foremost, outstanding; *informal* big, big time, major league, big league.
OPPOSITES unimportant, insignificant.

importunate ▶ **adjective** *an importunate beggar* **persistent**, insistent, tenacious, persevering, dogged, unremitting, unrelenting, tireless, indefatigable; stubborn, intransigent, obstinate, obdurate; pressing, urgent, demanding, entreating, nagging, exacting, clamorous, clamant; aggressive, high-pressure; *informal* pushy; *formal* exigent, pertinacious, suppliant.

importune ▶ **verb 1** *he importuned her for some spare change* **beg**, beseech, entreat, implore, plead with, appeal to, apply to, call on, supplicate, solicit, petition, enjoin; **harass**, pester, beset, press, dun, badger, bother, torment, plague, hound, nag, harry, go on at, harp on at; *N. English* mither; *informal* hassle, bug; *rare* obsecrate.
2 *they arrested me for importuning* **solicit**, make sexual advances, offer one's services as a prostitute; accost, approach; *informal* proposition; *N. Amer. informal* hustle.

impose ▶ **verb 1** *he imposed his ideas on the art director* **foist**, force, thrust, inflict, obtrude, press, urge; *informal* saddle someone with, land someone with, lumber someone with.
2 *new taxes will be imposed on all non-renewable forms of energy* **levy**, charge, exact, apply, enforce; set, establish, fix, put, lay, institute, introduce; decree, ordain, enact, promulgate, bring into effect, bring to bear; *informal* clap, slap.
3 *how dare you impose on me like this!* **take advantage of**, abuse, exploit, take liberties with, misuse, ill-treat, treat unfairly, manipulate; bother, trouble, disturb, inconvenience, put out, put to trouble, take for granted; be a burden on, prey on; *informal* walk all over.
□ **impose oneself** *he struggled to impose himself on a fractious party* **force oneself**, foist oneself, thrust oneself; intrude, break in, obtrude, interlope, trespass, impinge, butt in, barge in; control, gain control of, take charge of; *informal* gatecrash, crash, horn in, muscle in, call the shots, call the tune, be in the driving seat, be in the saddle, run the show, pull the strings, rule the roost.

imposing ▶ **adjective** *an imposing mansion | his imposing physical presence* **impressive**, striking, arresting, eye-catching, dramatic, spectacular, staggering, stunning, awesome, awe-inspiring, remarkable, formidable; splendid, grand, majestic, august, lofty, stately, dignified, resplendent.
OPPOSITES unimposing, modest.

imposition ▶ **noun 1** *the imposition of an alien culture on the indigenous inhabitants* **imposing**, foisting, forcing, inflicting, obtruding, pressing.
2 *the imposition of VAT on domestic fuel* **levying**, charging, exacting, application, applying, enforcement, enforcing; setting, establishment, fixing, laying, introduction, institution; decreeing, ordainment, enactment, promulgation; *informal* slapping, clapping.
3 *it would be no imposition, I assure you* **burden**, load, onus, encumbrance, strain, demand, pressure, charge, bother, worry; *informal* hassle.
4 *the government began levying special impositions* **tax**, levy, duty, charge, tariff, toll, excise, tithe, fee, impost, exaction, payment; *rare* mulct.

impossible ▶ **adjective 1** *gale force winds made fishing impossible* **not possible**, beyond the bounds of possibility, out of the question, not worth considering; unfeasible, impractical, impracticable, non-viable, unworkable, beyond one; unthinkable, unimaginable, inconceivable; paradoxical, illogical, irrational; *informal* undoable.
OPPOSITES possible; easy.
2 *six months ago his ambition had seemed an impossible dream* **unattainable**, unachievable, unobtainable, hopeless, impractical, implausible, far-fetched, impracticable, unworkable; forlorn, vain; incredible, unbelievable, absurd, ludicrous, ridiculous, laughable, risible, preposterous, outlandish, outrageous; wild, hare-brained.
OPPOSITES possible, attainable.
3 *a ban on buses would have made life impossible for many residents* **unbearable**, intolerable, unendurable, unsustainable; *informal* no-win.
OPPOSITES bearable, tolerable.
4 (*informal*) *your mother is the most impossible woman in the world* **unmanageable**, intractable, recalcitrant, wayward, objectionable, difficult, demanding, awkward, perverse, ungovernable; intolerable, unbearable, unendurable; exasperating, maddening, infuriating.
OPPOSITES manageable, easy to please.

impostor, **imposter** ▶ **noun** **impersonator**, masquerader, pretender, deceiver, hoaxer; fake, fraud, sham, humbug; charlatan, quack, mountebank; trickster, fraudster, swindler, hoodwinker, bluffer, deluder, duper, cheat, cheater, defrauder, exploiter, rogue, wolf in sheep's clothing; *informal* phoney, con man, con artist, flimflammer, flimflam man; *dated* confidence man/woman.

imposture ▶ **noun** *by the time the imposture had been discovered the real prince had fled* **misrepresentation**, pretence, deceit, deception, duping, cheating, trickery, artifice, subterfuge; hoax, trick, ruse, dodge, blind, wile; fraudulence, fraud, swindling; charlatanry, quackery; *informal* con, con trick, scam, sting, flimflam, kidology; *Brit. informal* wheeze; *Irish informal* codology.

impotent ▶ **adjective 1** *the legal sanctions are regarded as impotent* **powerless**, ineffective, ineffectual, inadequate, weak, useless, worthless, vain, futile, unavailing, unsuccessful, profitless, fruitless; *literary* impuissant.
OPPOSITES powerful, effective.
2 *there are powerful natural forces which man is impotent to control* **unable**, incapable, helpless, powerless, incompetent, unfit, unfitted.
OPPOSITE able.
3 *an impotent opposition party* **weak**, powerless, ineffective, lame, feeble, effete; *informal* past it.
OPPOSITES strong, effective.

impound ▶ **verb 1** *officials began impounding documents yesterday* **confiscate**, appropriate, take possession of, seize, commandeer, expropriate, requisition, sequester, sequestrate, take; *Law* distrain, disseize, attach; *Scottish Law* poind.
2 *the cattle were rounded up and impounded* **pen in**, shut up/in, fence in, coop up, hem in, box in, hedge in, rail in; cage, enclose, confine; *N. Amer.* corral.
3 *the poor unfortunates impounded in the prison* **lock up**, incarcerate, imprison, confine, intern, immure, hold captive, hold prisoner, put under lock and key; *informal* put behind bars.

impoverish ▶ **verb 1** *a widow who had been impoverished by inflation* **make poor**, make penniless, reduce to penury, reduce to destitution, bring to

ruin, bring someone to their knees, bankrupt, ruin, make insolvent; wipe out, clean out, break, cripple; *rare* pauperize, beggar.
OPPOSITE make wealthy.
2 *the trees were considered to be impoverishing the soil* **weaken**, sap, exhaust, drain, empty, diminish, deplete, enervate, suck dry; *informal* bleed.
OPPOSITES strengthen, enrich.

impoverished ▶ adjective **1** *an impoverished peasant farmer* **poor**, poverty-stricken, penniless, penurious, destitute, indigent, impecunious, needy, pauperized, in distressed/reduced/straitened circumstances, in want, in need, down and out, on the breadline; bankrupt, ruined, insolvent, wiped out, cleaned out, broken, crippled, without a penny to one's name; *informal* broke, flat broke, stony broke, on one's uppers, strapped (for cash), on one's beam ends, bust, hard up, without two pennies/farthings to rub together, without a bean, without a sou, as poor as a church mouse, on skid row; *Brit. informal* skint, without a shot in one's locker; *Brit. rhyming slang* boracic (lint); *N. Amer. informal* stone broke, without a red cent; *rare* beggared.
OPPOSITES rich, wealthy.
2 *the soil is impoverished* **weakened**, exhausted, drained, sapped, diminished, depleted, enervated, sucked dry, used up, spent, played out; barren, unproductive, unfertile, arid, uncultivatable.
OPPOSITES rich, fertile.

impracticable ▶ adjective *my colleagues thought it an impracticable plan* **unworkable**, non-viable, impossible to carry out, unfeasible, inoperable, out of the question, not worth considering, unachievable, unattainable, unrealizable; impractical; *informal* undoable.
OPPOSITES workable, feasible.

impracticable or impractical?
See IMPRACTICAL.

impractical ▶ adjective **1** *an impractical suggestion* **unrealistic**, unworkable, unfeasible, non-viable, impracticable; ill-considered, ill-thought-out, illogical, unreasonable, far-fetched, impossible, silly, foolish, absurd, wild; *informal* cock-eyed, crackpot, crazy, half-baked.
OPPOSITES practical, sensible.
2 *she wore impractical white ankle boots* **unsuitable**, not sensible, inappropriate, unserviceable.
OPPOSITES practical, sensible.
3 *an unworldly and impractical scholar* **unrealistic**, idealistic, head-in-the-clouds, out of touch with reality, romantic, dreamy, fanciful, starry-eyed, visionary, quixotic; *informal* airy-fairy.
OPPOSITES practical, down to earth.

impractical or impracticable?
Although similar in spelling, these words have distinct meanings. **Impractical** means 'not sensible or realistic', and applies either to things that are not designed to be useful in everyday situations or to an outlook that does not take the realities of life into account (*Paul was impractical and dreamy | you're wearing rather impractical clothes*). **Impracticable**, on the other hand, describes an idea or plan that is impossible to put into action (*the small population made it impracticable to provide separate schools for boys and girls*). An *impractical dreamer* might well be preoccupied with *impracticable projects*.

imprecation ▶ noun (*formal*) **1** *he cursed himself with the most dreadful imprecations* **curse**, malediction, anathema; *N. Amer.* hex; *Irish* cess; *archaic* execration, malison, ban.
OPPOSITE bless.
2 *he abused her with a stream of imprecations* **swear word**, curse, expletive, oath, profanity, four-letter word, obscenity, epithet, dirty word; (**imprecations**) swearing, cursing, blaspheming, blasphemy, sacrilege, bad language, foul language, strong language, colourful language; *N. Amer.* cuss word; *archaic* execration.

imprecise ▶ adjective **1** *this is a rather imprecise definition* **vague**, loose, indefinite, inexplicit, indistinct, non-specific, unspecific, broad, general, sweeping; hazy, fuzzy, blurred, unfocused, woolly, nebulous; confused, ambiguous, equivocal, uncertain, non-committal.
OPPOSITES precise, narrow.
2 *an imprecise estimate* **inexact**, approximate, estimated, rough; inaccurate, incorrect, wrong, erroneous, wide of the mark, off target, out; *N. Amer. informal* ballpark.
OPPOSITES precise, exact.

impregnable ▶ adjective **1** *such a castle must have been impregnable* **invulnerable**, impenetrable, unattackable, unassailable, inviolable, secure, strong, stout, safe, well fortified, well defended; invincible, unconquerable, unbeatable, indestructible.
OPPOSITE vulnerable.
2 *an impregnable parliamentary majority* **unassailable**, unbeatable, undefeatable, unshakeable, invincible, indomitable, unconquerable, unstoppable, invulnerable.
OPPOSITE vulnerable.
3 *as a working theory, this is impregnable* **irrefutable**, incontrovertible, undeniable, indisputable, incontestable, unquestionable, unassailable, beyond question, beyond doubt, indubitable; flawless, faultless, watertight, airtight, foolproof, without loopholes.
OPPOSITE flawed.

impregnate ▶ verb **1** *a pad impregnated with natural oils* **infuse**, soak, steep, saturate, drench; permeate, suffuse, imbue, pervade, fill, load, charge.
2 *he was obliged to marry the woman he had impregnated* **make pregnant**, get pregnant, inseminate, fertilize; *informal* put in the family way; *Brit. informal* get up the duff, put in the club, get up the spout, get up the stick; *N. Amer. informal* knock up; *informal, dated* get into trouble; *archaic* fecundate, get with child.

impresario ▶ noun *a theatrical impresario* **organizer**, manager, producer, stage manager; promotor, publicist, showman; controller, arranger, fixer; financier, moneyman; director, conductor, maestro.

impress ▶ verb **1** *Hazel had impressed him mightily* **make an impression on**, have an impact on, influence, affect, leave a mark on, move, stir, rouse, excite, inspire, galvanize; dazzle, overcome, overwhelm, overpower, awe, overawe, take someone's breath away, take someone aback, amaze, astonish; (**be impressed**) feel admiration, feel respect; *informal* grab, stick in someone's mind.
OPPOSITE disappoint.
2 *goldsmiths impressed his likeness on medallions* **imprint**, print, stamp, mark, engrave, emboss, punch, etch, carve, inscribe, cut, chisel.
3 *you must impress upon her that she has to come to school* **emphasize to**, stress to, bring home to, establish in someone's mind, fix deeply in someone's mind, instil in, inculcate in, drum into, knock into, drive into, din into, ingrain in, leave in no doubt.

impression ▶ noun **1** *he got the impression that she was hiding something* **feeling**, sense, fancy, suspicion, sneaking suspicion, inkling, intuition, hunch, apprehension; notion, idea, thought, belief, opinion, conviction; *informal* funny feeling, gut feeling, feeling in one's bones, sixth sense.
2 *she had formed a favourable impression of him* **opinion**, view, conception, image, picture, perception, judgement, verdict, estimation.
3 *school made a profound impression on me* **impact**, effect, influence.
4 *the cap had left a circular impression on his hair* **indentation**, dent, hollow, concavity, depression, dip, mark, outline, stamp, stamping, imprint.
5 *he did a good impression of their science teacher* **impersonation**, imitation, mimicry; parody, caricature, burlesque, travesty, mockery, lampoon, pastiche; *informal* take-off, send-up, spoof; *rare* personation.
6 *an artist's impression of the finished gardens* **representation**, portrayal, depiction, rendition, rendering, interpretation, picture, drawing.
7 *a revised impression of the 1981 edition* **print run**, printing, imprinting, imprint, reprint, issue, edition, version, publication.

impressionable ▶ adjective *an impressionable adolescent girl* **easily influenced**, easily led, suggestible, susceptible, receptive, persuadable, pliable, malleable, pliant, mouldable; vulnerable, exploitable, ingenuous, trusting, naive, credulous, gullible.
OPPOSITE unimpressionable.

impressive ▶ adjective **1** *the hall is an impressive building* **magnificent**, majestic, imposing, splendid, spectacular, grand, august, awe-inspiring, stirring, stunning, breathtaking; stately, monumental, palatial, noble, dignified.
OPPOSITES unimpressive, ordinary.
2 *they played some impressive football* **admirable**, accomplished, expert, skilled, skilful, masterly, consummate; excellent, formidable, outstanding, first-class, first-rate, fine; *informal* great, mean, nifty, cracking, crack, ace, wizard; *N. Amer. informal* crackerjack.
OPPOSITES unimpressive, mediocre.

imprint ▶ verb (stress on the second syllable) **1** *patterns can be imprinted in the clay* **stamp**, print, impress, mark, engrave, emboss.
2 *he knew he'd always have this ghastly image imprinted on his mind* **fix**, establish, stick, lodge, implant, embed; stamp, impress, etch, engrave, print.
▶ noun (stress on the first syllable) **1** *her feet left imprints on the floor* **impression**, print, mark, indentation.
2 *colonialism has left its imprint* **impact**, lasting effect, influence, impression.

imprison ▶ verb *she was imprisoned for sedition* **incarcerate**, put in prison, send to prison, jail, lock up, take into custody, put under lock and key, put away, intern, confine, detain, hold prisoner, hold captive, hold, put into detention, put in chains, put in irons, clap in irons; *Brit.* detain at Her Majesty's pleasure; *informal* send down, put behind bars, put inside; *Brit. informal* bang someone up; *rare* immure.
OPPOSITES free, release.

imprisoned ▶ adjective *an imprisoned dissident* **incarcerated**, in prison, in jail, jailed, locked up, in custody, under lock and key, interned, confined, detained, held prisoner, captive, held captive, in chains, in irons, clapped

in irons; *Brit.* detained at Her Majesty's pleasure; *informal* sent down, behind bars, doing time, inside, away; *Brit. informal* doing porridge, doing bird, banged up; *rare* immured.
OPPOSITE free.

imprisonment ▶ **noun** *he was sentenced to two months' imprisonment* **incarceration**, internment, confinement, detention, custody, captivity; penal servitude, hard labour; *informal* time; *Brit. informal* porridge, bird, chokey; *archaic* durance, duress.
OPPOSITE freedom.

improbability ▶ **noun** *his belief in the improbability of war in Europe* **unlikelihood**, implausibility; doubtfulness, uncertainty, dubiousness; unthinkability, inconceivability, incredibility.
OPPOSITES probability, certainty.

improbable ▶ **adjective 1** *it seemed improbable that the hot weather should continue much longer* **unlikely**, not likely, doubtful, dubious, debatable, questionable, uncertain; difficult to believe, implausible, far-fetched, fanciful; unthinkable, inconceivable, unimaginable, incredible.
OPPOSITES probable, certain.
2 *the impression created by some advertisers is an improbable exaggeration* **inauthentic**, unconvincing, unbelievable, incredible, ridiculous, absurd, preposterous; contrived, laboured, strained, forced; *informal* hard to swallow.
OPPOSITES believable, realistic.

impromptu ▶ **adjective** *he gave an impromptu lecture* **unrehearsed**, unprepared, unscripted, extempore, extemporized, improvised, improvisational, improvisatory, improvisatorial, spontaneous, unstudied, unpremeditated, unarranged, unplanned, on the spot, snap, ad lib; ad hoc, thrown together, cobbled together, rough and ready; *Latin* ad libitum; *informal* off-the-cuff, spur-of-the-moment; *rare* extemporaneous.
OPPOSITES prepared, rehearsed.
▶ **adverb** *they played the song impromptu* **extempore**, spontaneously, without preparation, without rehearsal, on the spur of the moment, offhand, ad lib; *Latin* ad libitum; *informal* off the cuff, off the top of one's head; *rare* extemporaneously.

improper ▶ **adjective 1** *it was improper for policemen to accept gifts* **inappropriate**, unacceptable, unsuitable, unprofessional, irregular, illegitimate, against the rules; unethical, corrupt, immoral, dishonest, dishonourable, unscrupulous; *informal* crooked, not cricket.
OPPOSITES acceptable, proper.
2 *it would have been thought improper for two young ladies to drive a young man home* **unseemly**, indecorous, unbecoming, unfitting, out of keeping, unladylike, ungentlemanly, indiscreet, indelicate, impolite, undignified; indecent, unwholesome, immodest, immoral; outrageous, scandalous, shocking, offensive, distasteful; forward, bold, brazen, shameless; *informal* fresh, cheeky.
OPPOSITE proper.
3 *he recited an extremely improper poem* **indecent**, risqué, off colour, indelicate, suggestive, naughty, ribald, earthy, Rabelaisian, smutty, dirty, filthy, vulgar, crude, rude, obscene, lewd, pornographic; *informal* blue, raunchy, steamy, near the knuckle/bone, nudge-nudge; *Brit. informal* fruity, saucy.
OPPOSITE decent.

impropriety ▶ **noun 1** *he was outraged at any suggestion of impropriety* **wrongdoing**, misconduct, dishonesty, corruption, unscrupulousness, illegitimacy, unprofessionalism, irregularity; inappropriateness; unseemliness, indecorousness, indiscretion, indelicacy, injudiciousness, indecency, immorality, unwholesomeness, immodesty, indecorum, bad taste, impoliteness.
OPPOSITE propriety.
2 *the director was jailed for a list of fiscal improprieties* **transgression**, misdemeanour, offence, misdeed, improper act, sin, crime, felony; indiscretion, mistake, slip, error, blunder, lapse, peccadillo; *archaic* trespass.

improve ▶ **verb 1** *staff looked for ways to improve the service* **make better**, better, ameliorate, upgrade, refine, enhance, boost, build on, help, raise, revamp, brush up, polish up, perk up, tweak; *informal* give a facelift to; *rare* meliorate.
OPPOSITES worsen, impair.
2 *communications improved during the 18th century* **get better**, become better, advance, progress, develop; make headway, come along, make progress, take steps forward, pick up, rally, perk up, make strides; *informal* look up.
OPPOSITES worsen, deteriorate.
3 *the dose is not repeated for as long as the patient continues to improve* **recover**, get better, get well, recuperate, convalesce, gain strength, rally, revive, strengthen, regain one's strength/health, get back on one's feet, get over something; be on the road to recovery, be on the mend; *informal* turn the corner, take a turn for the better, take on a new lease of life; *Brit. informal* be on the up and up.
OPPOSITES deteriorate, become ill.
4 *resources are needed to improve the offer* **increase**, make larger, make bigger, raise, put up, add to, augment, supplement, top up, enlarge; *informal* up, jack up, hike up, bump up, crank up, step up.
OPPOSITE decrease.
□ **improve on** *I cannot improve on his comments* **surpass**, better, do better than, outdo, exceed, beat, top, trump, cap, outstrip, overshadow, go one better than.

improvement ▶ **noun** *an improvement in the quality of Britain's rivers | many areas in the design could do with improvement* **advance**, development, upgrade, change for the better, refinement, enhancement, furtherance, advancement, forwarding; boost, augmentation, raising; correction, rectification, rectifying, upgrading, amelioration; rally, recovery, upswing, breakthrough.
OPPOSITE deterioration.

improvident ▶ **adjective** *a feckless and improvident lifestyle* **spendthrift**, thriftless, unthrifty, wasteful, prodigal, profligate, extravagant, squandering, uneconomical, free-spending, lavish, immoderate, excessive; shiftless, feckless; imprudent, irresponsible, incautious, careless, reckless, rash, impetuous, hasty, thoughtless.
OPPOSITES thrifty; cautious.

improvisation ▶ **noun** *some of the best things in the film came out of improvisation* **extemporization**, ad-libbing, spontaneity, lack of premeditation; *rare* autoschediasm.

improvise ▶ **verb 1** *she was improvising in front of the cameras* **extemporize**, ad lib, speak impromptu, make it up as one goes along, think on one's feet, take it as it comes; *informal* speak off the cuff, speak off the top of one's head, play it by ear, busk it, wing it.
2 *she improvised a sandpit for the children to play in* **contrive**, devise, throw together, cobble together, concoct, rig, jury-rig, put together; *Brit. informal* knock up; *informal* whip up, fix up, rustle up.

improvised ▶ **adjective 1** *an improvised short speech* **impromptu**, improvisational, improvisatory, unrehearsed, unprepared, unscripted, extempore, extemporized, spontaneous, unstudied, unpremeditated, unarranged, unplanned, on the spot, ad lib; *Latin* ad libitum; *informal* off-the-cuff, spur of the moment; *rare* improvisatorial.
OPPOSITES prepared, rehearsed.
2 *an improvised shelter* **makeshift**, thrown together, cobbled together, devised, rigged, jury-rigged, rough and ready, make-do, emergency, stopgap, temporary, short-term, pro tem; *Latin* ad hoc, pro tempore, ad interim.

imprudent ▶ **adjective** *the banks were imprudent in making the loans* **unwise**, injudicious, incautious, unwary; ill-considered, ill-judged, ill-conceived, impolitic, misguided, ill-advised; thoughtless, unthinking, improvident, irresponsible, short-sighted, foolish, careless, hasty, overhasty, rash, reckless, heedless, foolhardy.
OPPOSITES prudent, sensible.

> **CHOOSE THE RIGHT WORD**
>
> **imprudent, unwise, injudicious, ill-advised**
>
> *See* UNWISE.

impudence ▶ **noun** **impertinence**, insolence, effrontery, cheek, audacity, temerity, brazenness, shamelessness, immodesty, pertness; presumption, presumptuousness, disrespect, insubordination, irreverence, flippancy, bumptiousness, brashness, boldness; rudeness, impoliteness, ill manners, bad manners, unmannerliness, discourteousness, gall, ill breeding; *informal* freshness, cockiness, brass neck, sauce, sauciness, lip, mouth, face, nerve; *N. Amer. informal* sassiness, chutzpah, nerviness.

impudent ▶ **adjective** *these impudent youngsters* **impertinent**, insolent, cheeky, audacious, brazen, shameless, immodest, pert; presumptuous, forward, disrespectful, insubordinate, irreverent, flippant, bumptious, brash, bold, bold as brass; rude, impolite, ill-mannered, bad-mannered, unmannerly, discourteous, insulting, ill-bred; *informal* fresh, cocky, brass-necked, saucy, lippy, mouthy, flip; *N. Amer. informal* sassy, nervy; *archaic* malapert, contumelious.
OPPOSITES polite, respectful.

impugn ▶ **verb** *he had impugned the Prime Minister's honour* **call into question**, challenge, question, dispute, query, take issue with, impeach.
OPPOSITE support.

impulse ▶ **noun 1** *she had an impulse to run and hide somewhere* **urge**, instinct, drive, compulsion, need, itch; whim, caprice, desire, fancy, notion.
2 *he was a man of impulse* **spontaneity**, impetuosity, wildness, recklessness, irresponsibility, rashness.
OPPOSITES premeditation, carefulness.
3 *passions provide the main impulse of poetry and music* **inspiration**, stimulation, stimulus, incitement, motivation, encouragement, fillip, spur, prod, catalyst.
4 *neurons conduct impulses from the spinal cord to the muscles* **pulse**, current, wave; **signal**, message, brainwave, communication.
□ **on (an) impulse** *Valerie and I married on impulse* **impulsively**,

spontaneously, on the spur of the moment, without forethought, without planning, without thinking twice, without premeditation, unpremeditatedly.
OPPOSITE with forethought.

impulsive ▸ adjective **1** *he had an impulsive nature* **impetuous**, spontaneous, hasty, passionate, emotional, uninhibited, unrepressed, abandoned; rash, reckless, foolhardy, madcap, devil-may-care, daredevil, hot-headed, wild, daring, adventurous.
OPPOSITE cautious.
2 *his impulsive decision to leave his job and join the army* **impromptu**, snap, spontaneous, unpremeditated, spur-of-the-moment, extemporaneous; impetuous, precipitate, hasty, headlong, rash, reckless, incautious, imprudent, injudicious; sudden, quick, ill-considered, ill-thought-out, unplanned, thoughtless, unthinking.
OPPOSITE premeditated.

CHOOSE THE RIGHT WORD

impulsive, impetuous, precipitate, headlong
See IMPETUOUS.

impunity ▸ noun *the impunity enjoyed by military officers implicated in civilian killings* **immunity**, indemnity, exemption from punishment, freedom from punishment, exemption, non-liability, licence; amnesty, dispensation, pardon, reprieve, stay of execution, exoneration; privilege, special treatment, favouritism; *French* carte blanche.
OPPOSITES liability, responsibility.
□ **with impunity** *criminals who appear to flout the law with impunity* with no ill consequences, with no ill effects, without being punished, without punishment; scot-free, unpunished.

impure ▸ adjective **1** *a small amount of impure gold* **adulterated**, mixed, combined, blended, alloyed; debased, degraded, defiled; *technical* admixed.
OPPOSITE pure.
2 *the water was impure* **contaminated**, polluted, tainted, infected, sullied, defiled, unwholesome, poisoned; dirty, filthy, unclean, foul; unhygienic, unsanitary, insanitary; *literary* befouled; *rare* feculent.
OPPOSITES pure, clean.
3 *they cleared their minds of any impure notions* **immoral**, corrupt, sinful, wrongful, wicked, dishonourable; depraved, degenerate, debauched, dissolute; **unchaste**, lustful, lecherous, lewd, lascivious, prurient, obscene, dirty, indecent, unclean, wanton, ribald, risqué, smutty, improper, crude, vulgar, coarse, gross, pornographic; *rare* concupiscent.
OPPOSITES pure, chaste.

impurity ▸ noun **1** *the brittleness of cast iron resulted from its impurity* **adulteration**, debasement, degradation.
OPPOSITE purity.
2 *the impurity of the air breathed by pitmen* **contamination**, pollution; dirtiness, filthiness, uncleanliness, foulness, unwholesomeness; *rare* feculence.
OPPOSITES purity, cleanliness.
3 *all the impurities are left in the beer* **contaminant**, adulterant, pollutant, foreign body; dross, dirt, filth, grime, scum; (**impurities**) bits, foreign matter.
4 *a struggle to rid the soul of sin and impurity* **immorality**, corruption, sin, sinfulness, vice, wickedness, dishonour; depravity, degeneracy, debauchery, dissolution; **unchastity**, lustfulness, lechery, lecherousness, lewdness, lasciviousness, prurience, obscenity, dirtiness, indecency, wantonness, ribaldry, smut, smuttiness, impropriety, crudity, crudeness, vulgarity, coarseness, grossness; *rare* concupiscence.
OPPOSITES purity, chastity.

impute ▸ verb *he imputes selfish views to me* **attribute**, ascribe, assign, credit, accredit, chalk up; connect with, associate with, lay on, lay at the door of; *informal* pin on, stick on.

in ▸ preposition **1** *she was hiding in a wardrobe* **inside**, within, in the middle of, within the bounds/confines of; surrounded by, enclosed by.
OPPOSITE outside.
2 *he was covered in mud* **with**, by.
3 *he put a fruit gum in his mouth* **into**, inside, into the interior of.
4 *they met in 1921* **during**, in the course of, in the time of, over.
5 *I'll see you in half an hour* **after**, at the end of, following, subsequent to; within, in less than, in under, in no more than, before a … is up.
6 *the tax is charged at ten pence in the pound* **to**, per, every, each.
□ **in for** *she is in for a huge pay rise* **due for**, in line for, likely to receive; expecting, about to receive, about to experience; up for, ready for.
□ **in for it** *we're in for it now!* **in trouble**, about to be punished, about to suffer the consequences, about to pay the price, in for a scolding; *informal* for it, for the high jump, in hot water, in deep water, in (deep) shtook, about to take the rap, about to catch it.
□ **in on** *now you're in on my secret* **privy to**, aware of, acquainted with, informed about/of, advised of, apprised of, mindful of, sensible of; *informal* wise to, clued in on, up on, in the know about, hip to, in the loop; *archaic* ware of.
▸ adverb **1** *his mum walked in* **inside**, indoors, into the interior, into the room/house/building, within.
OPPOSITE out.
2 *the tide's in* **high**, at its highest level, rising.
OPPOSITES out, low.
▸ adjective **1** *we knocked at the door but there was no one in* **present**, home, at home; **inside**, indoors, in the house/room.
OPPOSITE out.
2 (*informal*) *back when beards were in* **fashionable**, in fashion, in vogue, voguish, stylish, in style, popular, (bang) up to date, up to the minute, modern, modish, trendsetting, chic; *French* à la mode, de rigueur; *informal* trendy, all the rage, with it, cool, the in thing, hot, hip, happening, now, swinging; *Brit. informal, dated* all the go.
OPPOSITES unfashionable, out.
3 *I was in with all the right people* **in favour**, popular, friendly, friends; favoured by, liked by, approved of by, admired by, accepted by; *informal* in someone's good books.
OPPOSITE unpopular.
▸ noun
□ **ins and outs** *our instructors will teach novices the ins and outs of the sport* **details**, particulars, facts, features, points, characteristics, traits, nuts and bolts, particularities; intricacies, peculiarities, idiosyncrasies; *informal* nitty gritty, ABC, A to Z.

inability ▸ noun **lack of ability**, incapability, incapacity, powerlessness, impotence, helplessness; incompetence, ineptitude, inaptitude, unfitness, ineffectiveness, uselessness, inefficacy; *Medicine* insufficiency.
OPPOSITE ability.

inaccessible ▸ adjective **1** *an inaccessible woodland site* **unreachable**, out of reach, beyond reach; cut-off, isolated, remote, in the middle of nowhere, in the back of beyond, out of the way, off the map, lonely, godforsaken; secluded, sequestered; *informal* unget-at-able; *archaic* unapproachable.
OPPOSITE accessible.
2 *the radio station was accused of being elitist and inaccessible* **esoteric**, obscure, abstruse, recondite, recherché, arcane, rarefied; cerebral, intellectual; elitist, exclusive, pretentious, snobby, snobbish.

inaccuracy ▸ noun **1** *the inaccuracy of recent opinion polls* **incorrectness**, inexactness, inexactitude, imprecision, erroneousness, mistakenness, fallaciousness, faultiness.
OPPOSITES accuracy, correctness.
2 *the article contained a number of inaccuracies* **error**, mistake, miscalculation, fallacy, slip, oversight, fault, blunder, gaffe, defect, flaw; erratum, typographical error, slip of the pen, printer's error, literal, corrigendum; slip of the tongue; *Latin* lapsus calami, lapsus linguae; *informal* slip-up, foul-up, clanger, howler, boob, boo-boo, typo; *N. Amer. informal* blooper, goof; *Brit. informal, dated* bloomer.

inaccurate ▸ adjective *the maps were notoriously inaccurate* **inexact**, imprecise, incorrect, wrong, erroneous, faulty, imperfect, flawed, defective, unsound, unreliable; out, adrift, wide of the mark, off target; fallacious, false, mistaken, untrue, not true, not right; falsified, distorted, garbled; *informal* off beam, full of holes.
OPPOSITE accurate.

inaction ▸ noun *wildlife is threatened by government inaction* **inactivity**, passivity, non-intervention; neglect, negligence, disregard, apathy; inertia, indolence, laziness, idleness, sloth, slothfulness, sluggishness, lethargy, torpor.
OPPOSITE action.

inactivate ▸ verb *coffee tends to inactivate homeopathic remedies* **disable**, deactivate, render inactive, make inoperative, prevent from working, halt, stop, immobilize; *informal* scupper.
OPPOSITE activate.

inactive ▸ adjective **1** *over the next few days I was horribly inactive* **idle**, indolent, lazy, lifeless, slothful, lethargic, inert, slow, sluggish, stagnant, dozy, unenergetic, listless, languishing, vegetating, torpid; immobile.
OPPOSITE active.
2 *the device remains inactive while the computer is started up* **inoperative**, non-functioning, idle, turned off, dormant; not working, out of service, unused, out of use, not in use, unoccupied, unemployed, inert, dead.
OPPOSITES active, in use.

inactivity ▸ noun **1** *don't suddenly take up violent exercise after years of inactivity* **idleness**, indolence, laziness, lifelessness, slothfulness, shiftlessness, lethargy, inertia, slowness, sluggishness, stagnancy, doziness, listlessness; immobility; *Italian* dolce far niente.
OPPOSITE activity.
2 *people are frustrated with government inactivity* **inaction**, passivity, non-intervention, laissez-faire; neglect, negligence, disregard, apathy.
OPPOSITES activity, action.

inadequacy ▸ noun **1** *the inadequacy of available resources* **insufficiency**, deficiency, scantness, scarcity, scarceness, sparseness, dearth, paucity, poverty, shortage, want, lack, undersupply; paltriness, meagreness, niggardliness; sketchiness, incompleteness, limitedness, restrictedness;

I

rare exiguity, exiguousness.
OPPOSITES abundance, surplus.
2 *her feelings of personal inadequacy* **incompetence**, incapability, unfitness, ineffectiveness, ineffectuality, inefficiency, inefficacy, inexpertness, lack of skill, lack of proficiency, ineptness, uselessness, hopelessness, impotence, powerlessness; amateurishness, inferiority, unsatisfactoriness, substandardness.
OPPOSITE competence.
3 *the inadequacies of the present system* **shortcoming**, defect, fault, failing, weakness, weak point, limitation, flaw, imperfection, Achilles heel; loophole.
OPPOSITE strong point.

inadequate ▶ adjective **1** *inadequate water supplies | inadequate wages* **insufficient**, not enough, deficient, poor, scant, scanty, scarce, sparse, too little, too few, short, in short supply; paltry, meagre, niggardly; skimpy, sketchy, incomplete, restricted, limited; *informal* measly, pathetic, piddling; *rare* exiguous.
OPPOSITES adequate, sufficient.
2 *inadequate staff* **incompetent**, incapable, unsatisfactory, not good enough, no good, found wanting, not up to scratch, lacking, leaving much to be desired, unfit, ineffective, ineffectual, inefficient, unskilful, inexpert, inept, unproficient, amateurish, substandard, poor, bad, hopeless, useless, inferior; impotent, powerless; *informal* not up to snuff, lousy; *Brit. informal* duff, not much cop, no great shakes; *vulgar slang* half-arsed.
OPPOSITE competent.

I

inadmissible ▶ adjective *inadmissible evidence* **not allowable**, invalid, not acceptable, unacceptable, unallowable, impermissible, disallowed, forbidden, prohibited, precluded; inappropriate, inapplicable, inapposite, irrelevant, immaterial, impertinent, not germane, beside the point.
OPPOSITE admissible.

inadvertent ▶ adjective *an inadvertent omission* **unintentional**, unintended, accidental, unpremeditated, unplanned, unmeant, innocent, uncalculated, unconscious, unthinking, unwitting, involuntary; chance, coincidental; careless, thoughtless.
OPPOSITES deliberate, intentional.

inadvertently ▶ adverb *his name had been inadvertently omitted from the list* **accidentally**, by accident, unintentionally, unwittingly; unawares, without noticing, in all innocence; by mistake, mistakenly.
OPPOSITE deliberately.

inadvisable ▶ adjective *an economically inadvisable move* **unwise**, ill-advised, imprudent, ill-judged, ill-considered, injudicious, impolitic, inexpedient, foolish, incautious, misguided, misconceived, wrong-headed, silly, thoughtless, foolhardy.
OPPOSITES shrewd, wise.

inalienable ▶ adjective *the inalienable rights of every citizen* **inviolable**, absolute, sacrosanct, unchallengeable, unassailable; **untransferable**, non-transferable, non-negotiable; inherent; *Law* imprescriptible, indefeasible.

inane ▶ adjective *an inane remark* **silly**, foolish, stupid, fatuous, idiotic, absurd, ridiculous, ludicrous, laughable, risible, imbecilic, moronic, cretinous, unintelligent, witless, asinine, pointless, senseless, frivolous, nonsensical, brainless, mindless, thoughtless, vacuous, vapid, empty-headed; childish, puerile, infantile, jejune; *informal* daft, dumb, dim, half-baked, gormless, damfool; *Brit. informal* divvy; *Scottish & N. English informal* glaikit; *N. Amer. informal* dumb-ass; *S. African informal* dof.
OPPOSITES intelligent, sensible.

inanimate ▶ adjective *inanimate objects* **lifeless**, insentient, insensate, without life, inert, motionless; inorganic, non-organic, mineral; dead, defunct, extinct; *rare* exanimate, abiotic.
OPPOSITE living.

inapplicable ▶ adjective *inapplicable moral criteria* **irrelevant**, immaterial, not germane, not pertinent, unrelated, unconnected, extraneous, beside the point, nothing to do with it; inadmissible; inappropriate, inapposite, inapt; *rare* impertinent.
OPPOSITES relevant, applicable.

inapposite ▶ adjective *a singularly inapposite remark* **inappropriate**, unsuitable, inapt, out of place, infelicitous, misplaced, misguided, ill-considered, ill-judged, ill-advised; irrelevant, immaterial, not germane, not pertinent, inapplicable; *rare* impertinent.
OPPOSITE appropriate.

inappreciable ▶ adjective *an inappreciable difference* **imperceptible**, barely perceptible, minute, tiny, minuscule, slight, small, infinitesimal, microscopic; **insignificant**, inconsequential, unimportant, immaterial, negligible, petty, trivial, trifling, minor, paltry, of no account, not worth mentioning, not worth bothering about; *informal* piddling, piffling; *rare* exiguous.
OPPOSITES considerable; significant.

inappropriate ▶ adjective *inappropriate behaviour | inappropriate clothes for the office* **unsuitable**, unfitting, ill-suited, unseemly, unbecoming, unprofessional, unfit, unbefitting, indecorous, improper, lacking in propriety, ungentlemanly, unladylike; **incongruous**, out of place, out of keeping, wrong, amiss, inapposite, inapt; inexpedient, inadvisable, injudicious, ill-advised, ill-judged, ill-considered, infelicitous, unfortunate, regrettable, misguided, misplaced, ill-timed, untimely, inopportune, undue, untoward, tactless, tasteless, in poor/bad taste, undesirable; *informal* out of order; *rare* malapropos.
OPPOSITES appropriate, suitable.

inapt ▶ adjective *an inapt remark. See* INAPPROPRIATE.

inarticulate ▶ adjective **1** *an inarticulate young man* **tongue-tied**, lost for words, at a loss for words, unable to express oneself, unable to get a word out, poorly spoken; mute, dumb, speechless; *rare* mumchance.
OPPOSITES articulate, silver-tongued.
2 *an inarticulate reply* **unintelligible**, incomprehensible, incoherent, unclear, indistinct, mumbled, muttered, muffled; hesitant, faltering, hesitating, halting, stumbling, stuttering, stammering; confused, garbled, muddled, rambling, disjointed, jumbled.
OPPOSITES articulate, fluent.
3 *I was filled with inarticulate rage* **unspoken**, silent, unexpressed, wordless, unvoiced, unsaid, unuttered, unvocalized; voiceless, soundless.
OPPOSITE vocal.

inattention ▶ noun **1** *a moment of inattention which could have cost lives* **lack of concentration**, distraction, inattentiveness, preoccupation, absent-mindedness, daydreaming, dreaminess, reverie, wool-gathering, abstraction, staring into space, obliviousness; brown study.
OPPOSITES attention, concentration.
2 *his inattention to duty* **negligence**, neglect, neglectfulness, disregard, slackness, remissness, laxness; forgetfulness, carelessness, thoughtlessness, heedlessness; indifference, unconcern, inconsideration; *rare* oscitation.
OPPOSITE care.

inattentive ▶ adjective **1** *an inattentive pupil* **not concentrating**, distracted, lacking concentration, preoccupied, absent-minded, daydreaming, dreamy, dreaming, wool-gathering, lost in thought, off in a world of one's own, in a brown study, with one's head in the clouds, abstracted, distrait, oblivious, not with us, unheeding; *informal* miles away.
OPPOSITES attentive, alert.
2 *I was disappointed by the food and the inattentive service* **negligent**, neglectful, remiss, slack, sloppy, slapdash, lackadaisical, lax; forgetful, careless, thoughtless, heedless, unthinking; indifferent, unconcerned, inconsiderate.
OPPOSITE attentive.

inaudible ▶ adjective *Michelle's response was inaudible* **unheard**, not heard, out of earshot; hard to hear, hard to make out, indistinct, imperceptible, faint, muted, soft, low, muffled, stifled, whispered, muttered, murmured, mumbled.
OPPOSITE audible.

inaugural ▶ adjective *the inaugural meeting of the Geographical Society* **first**, initial, introductory, initiatory, launching; **opening**, maiden; dedicatory.
OPPOSITES final; closing.

inaugurate ▶ verb **1** *he inaugurated a new policy of trade and exploration* **initiate**, begin, start, institute, launch, start off, set in motion, get going, get under way, get off the ground, establish, originate, lay the foundations of, lay the first stone of, lay the cornerstone of, bring up the curtain on; bring in, usher in; *informal* kick off; *formal* commence.
OPPOSITES end, wind up.
2 *the new President will be inaugurated in January* **admit to office**, install, instate, induct, swear in; invest, ordain; crown, enthrone.
3 *the museum was inaugurated on September 12* **open**, open officially, declare open; dedicate, consecrate; unveil, take the wraps off; *rare* hansel.
OPPOSITE close.

inauguration ▶ noun **1** *the inauguration of an independent prosecution service* **initiation**, institution, setting up, launch, establishment, foundation, founding, origination, formation; beginning, start, inception; *formal* commencement.
OPPOSITES demise, winding up.
2 *the President's inauguration* **installation**, instatement, induction, swearing in; investiture; coronation, enthronement, crowning.
3 *the inauguration of the Modern Art Museum* **opening**; dedication, consecration; unveiling.
OPPOSITE closure.

inauspicious ▶ adjective *an inauspicious start to the season* **unpromising**, unpropitious, unfavourable, adverse, unfortunate, infelicitous, unhappy, ill-omened, ominous, ill-fated, ill-starred, untoward, untimely, inopportune, disadvantageous; discouraging, disheartening, gloomy, bleak, black, bad; *Scottish* unchancy.
OPPOSITES promising, auspicious.

inborn ▶ adjective *a child's inborn linguistic ability* **innate**, congenital, existing from birth; inherent, inherited, hereditary, in the family, in one's genes, bred in the bone, inbred; natural, native, constitutional, deep-seated, deep-rooted, ingrained, in one's blood, inbuilt, instinctive, instinctual, unlearned; *rare* connate, connatural.

OPPOSITES acquired, learned.

inbred ▸ adjective *his inbred courtesy.* See INBORN.

inbuilt ▸ adjective **1** *a personal computer with an inbuilt CD-ROM drive* **built-in**, integral, incorporated.
OPPOSITE add-on.
2 *our inbuilt survival instinct* **inherent**, intrinsic, innate, ingrained, congenital, natural, native; basic, fundamental, essential, deep-rooted; *rare* connatural, connate.

incalculable ▸ adjective *archaeological treasures of incalculable value* **inestimable**, indeterminable, untold, immeasurable, uncountable, incomputable, not to be reckoned; infinite, endless, without end, limitless, measureless, boundless, fathomless, bottomless; enormous, immense, huge, vast, innumerable, countless, without number, numberless, multitudinous; *rare* innumerous, unnumberable, unnumbered, unsummed.
OPPOSITE limited.

incandescent ▸ adjective **1** *incandescent fragments of lava* **white-hot**, intensely hot, red-hot, burning, fiery, on fire, blazing, ablaze, aflame; glowing, aglow, radiant, bright, brilliant, dazzling, shining, luminous, gleaming; *literary* fervid, fervent, ardent, rutilant, lucent, candescent.
2 *the minister was said to be incandescent* **furious**, enraged, raging, very angry, incensed, seething, infuriated, fuming, boiling, inflamed, irate, wrathful, in a temper, beside oneself; in high dudgeon, indignant, outraged; *informal* livid, hot under the collar, up in arms, foaming at the mouth, mad, hopping mad, wild, as cross as two sticks, apoplectic, riled, aerated, on the warpath, steamed up, in a lather, in a paddy, fit to be tied, up the wall; *N. Amer. informal* bent out of shape, soreheaded; *Austral./NZ informal* ropeable, snaky, crook; *W. Indian informal* vex; *Brit. informal, dated* in a bate; *literary* ireful, wroth.
OPPOSITE calm.

incantation ▸ noun **1** *he muttered some weird incantations* **chant**, invocation, conjuration, magic spell, magic formula, rune; abracadabra, open sesame; *N. Amer.* hex, mojo; *NZ* makutu.
2 *the ritual incantation of such words* **chanting**, intonation, recitation.

incapable ▸ adjective **1** *a manager must train staff without making them feel stupid or incapable* **incompetent**, inept, lacking ability, no good, inadequate, not good enough, leaving much to be desired, inexpert, unproficient, unskilful, ineffective, ineffectual, inefficacious, feeble, unfit, unfitted, unqualified, inferior; unequal to the task; *informal* not up to scratch, out of one's depth, not up to it, not up to snuff, useless, hopeless, pathetic, a dead loss, cack-handed, ham-fisted; *Brit. informal* not much cop; *Brit. vulgar slang* not knowing one's arse from one's elbow, half-arsed, not capable of organizing a piss-up in a brewery.
OPPOSITES capable, competent.
2 *he was judged to be mentally incapable* **incapacitated**, helpless, powerless, impotent.
3 *she was* **incapable of** *fending for herself* **unable to**, not capable of, lacking the ability to, not equipped to, lacking the experience to.
OPPOSITES capable of, able to.
4 *a problem which is* **incapable of** *solution* **not open to**, not admitting of, not susceptible to, resistant to, impervious to.
OPPOSITES capable of, open to.

incapacitated ▸ adjective *Richard was temporarily incapacitated* **disabled**, debilitated, indisposed, unfit; **immobilized**, crippled, paralysed, out of action, out of commission; *French* hors de combat; *informal* laid up.
OPPOSITE fit.

incapacity ▸ noun **1** *evidence of his mental incapacity* **disability**, incapability, inability, debility, impairment, indisposition, unfitness; powerlessness, impotence, helplessness, weakness; incompetence, inadequacy, ineffectiveness, ineffectuality, inefficiency.
OPPOSITES ability, capability.
2 *legal incapacity* **disqualification**, lack of entitlement, lack of legal right.
OPPOSITE qualification.

incarcerate ▸ verb **1** *he was incarcerated for expressing counter-revolutionary opinions* **imprison**, put in prison, send to prison, jail, lock up, take into custody, put under lock and key, put away, intern, confine, detain, hold, put into detention, immure, put in chains, clap in irons, hold prisoner, hold captive; *Brit.* detain at Her Majesty's pleasure; *informal* send down, put behind bars, put inside; *Brit. informal* bang someone up.
OPPOSITES free, release.
2 *the long evening incarcerated below decks had given her a headache* **confine**, shut away, shut up, coop up; immure, cage.

incarceration ▸ noun *eight years of incarceration in a Soviet jail* **imprisonment**, internment, confinement, detention, custody, captivity, restraint; penal servitude, hard labour; *informal* time; *Brit. informal* porridge, chokey; *archaic* durance, duress.
OPPOSITE freedom.

incarnate ▸ adjective *she looked at me as though I were the devil incarnate* **in human form**, in the flesh, in physical form, in bodily form, made flesh, made manifest; corporeal, physical, fleshly, embodied.

incarnation ▸ noun **1** *Beethoven was seen as the incarnation of artistic genius* **embodiment**, personification, exemplification, type, epitome; manifestation, bodily form, representation in the flesh; *rare* avatar.
2 *they believed they had been together in a previous incarnation* **lifetime**, life, existence.

incautious ▸ adjective *his anger made him incautious* **rash**, unwise, careless, heedless, thoughtless, reckless, unthinking, imprudent, misguided, ill-advised, ill-judged, injudicious, impolitic, unguarded, foolhardy, foolish; unwary, unwatchful, off-guard, inattentive, unobservant; *informal* asleep on the job, asleep at the wheel, leading with one's chin.
OPPOSITES cautious, circumspect.

incendiary ▸ adjective **1** *an incendiary bomb* **combustible**, flammable, inflammable, fire-producing, fire-raising.
2 *her incendiary speech provoked more rioting* **inflammatory**, rabble-rousing, provocative, seditious, subversive, revolutionary, insurrectionary, insurrectionist; arousing, stirring; contentious, controversial.
OPPOSITE conciliatory.
▸ noun **1** *an aircraft loaded with incendiaries* **explosive**, bomb, incendiary device.
2 *incendiaries set the village on fire* **arsonist**, fire-bomber, fire-setter; pyromaniac; *Brit.* fire-raiser; *informal* firebug, pyro; *N. Amer. informal* torch.
3 *a political incendiary* **agitator**, demagogue, rabble-rouser, firebrand, troublemaker, revolutionary, revolutionist, insurgent, subversive, instigator, inciter, soapbox orator; *French* agent provocateur; *informal* tub-thumper, stirrer.

incense[1] ▸ verb (stress on the second syllable) *the glint of amusement in his eyes incensed her* **enrage**, infuriate, anger, madden, send into a rage, outrage, inflame, exasperate, antagonize, provoke, irritate greatly, rile, gall; *informal* make someone see red, make someone's blood boil, make someone's hackles rise, get someone's back up, hack off, drive mad/crazy, drive up the wall, get someone's dander up, get someone's goat, get up someone's nose, rattle someone's cage; *Brit. informal* wind up, get on someone's wick, nark; *N. Amer. informal* burn up, tick off, gravel; *vulgar slang* piss off; *Brit. vulgar slang* get on someone's tits; *rare* empurple.
OPPOSITES placate; please.

incense[2] ▸ noun (stress on the first syllable) *Corbett caught a whiff of incense* **perfume**, fragrance, scent; aroma, bouquet, redolence, balm.

incensed ▸ adjective *Leonora glared back at him, incensed* **enraged**, very angry, irate, furious, infuriated, angered, in a temper, raging, incandescent, fuming, seething, beside oneself, outraged, in high dudgeon; *informal* mad, hopping mad, wild, livid, as cross as two sticks, boiling, apoplectic, aerated, hot under the collar, on the warpath, up in arms, with all guns blazing, foaming at the mouth, steamed up, in a lather, in a paddy, in a filthy temper, fit to be tied; *Brit. informal* shirty, stroppy; *N. Amer. informal* sore, bent out of shape, soreheaded, ticked off; *Austral./NZ informal* ropeable, snaky, crook; *W. Indian informal* vex; *Brit. informal, dated* in a bate, waxy; *vulgar slang* pissed off; *N. Amer. vulgar slang* pissed; *literary* wrathful, ireful, wroth.
OPPOSITE calm.

incentive ▸ noun *tax laws which give factories a financial incentive to reduce pollution* **inducement**, motivation, motive, reason, stimulus, stimulant, spur, impetus, encouragement, impulse; incitement, goad, provocation; attraction, lure, bait; *informal* carrot, sweetener, come-on; *rare* premium, douceur.
OPPOSITES deterrent, disincentive.

inception ▸ noun *the inception of the EEC in 1958* **establishment**, institution, foundation, founding, formation, initiation, setting up, origination, constitution, inauguration, opening; **beginning**, start, starting point, outset; birth, dawn, genesis, origin, rise; debut, day one; *informal* kick-off; *formal* commencement.
OPPOSITE end.

incessant ▸ adjective *incessant rain fell for several days* **ceaseless**, unceasing, constant, continual, unabating, interminable, endless, unending, never-ending, everlasting, eternal, perpetual, continuous, non-stop, uninterrupted, unbroken, ongoing, unremitting, persistent, relentless, unrelenting, unrelieved, sustained, unflagging, unwearying, untiring; recurrent.
OPPOSITES intermittent, occasional.

incessantly ▸ adverb *she talked about him incessantly* **constantly**, continually, all the time, non-stop, without stopping, without a break, interminably, unremittingly, round the clock, ceaselessly, endlessly, without cessation, unceasingly, perpetually; *informal* 24-7.
OPPOSITE occasionally.

incidence ▸ noun *an increased incidence of heart disease in women in their thirties* **occurrence**, prevalence, commonness; **rate**, frequency; amount, degree, quantity, extent.

incident ▸ noun **1** *his memories of incidents from his youth* **event**, occurrence, occasion, episode, experience, happening, proceeding, eventuality, affair, business; adventure, exploit, escapade, deed, feat; matter, circumstance, fact, development.
2 *police are now investigating the incident* **disturbance**, fracas, melee,

commotion, rumpus, scene; fight, skirmish, clash, brawl, free-for-all, encounter, conflict, confrontation, altercation, contretemps; *Irish, N. Amer., & Austral.* donnybrook; *W. Indian* bangarang; *informal* ruction, ruckus, argy-bargy; *Law, dated* affray.
3 *the journey was not without incident* **excitement**, adventure, exciting experiences, drama; danger, peril, dangerous/perilous experiences.

incidental ▶ adjective **1** *incidental details* **less important**, of less importance, secondary, subsidiary, subordinate, ancillary, auxiliary; **minor**, peripheral, background, by-the-way, by-the-by, non-essential, inessential, unimportant, insignificant, inconsequential, unnecessary, trivial, trifling, negligible, petty, tangential, extrinsic, extraneous, dispensable, expendable.
OPPOSITES crucial; essential.
2 *the implications of this incidental discovery* **chance**, by chance, accidental, by accident, random, casual, fortuitous, serendipitous, adventitious, coincidental, unlooked-for; *rare* fluky; *rare* aleatory.
OPPOSITE deliberate.
3 *the risks necessarily* **incidental to** *a fireman's job* **connected with**, related to, associated with, accompanying, attending, attendant on, concomitant to.
▶ noun (**incidentals**) *an allowance to cover meals, taxis, and other incidentals* **extras**, contingencies, odds and ends; expenses.

incidentally ▶ adverb **1** *incidentally, I haven't had a reply from Hartley yet* **by the way**, by the by(e), in passing, en passant, speaking of which, while on the subject; parenthetically; *informal* BTW, as it happens.
2 *the infection was discovered incidentally at post-mortem examination* **by chance**, by accident, accidentally, fortuitously, by a fluke, as luck would have it, by a twist of fate; coincidentally, by coincidence; *N. Amer.* by happenstance.

incinerate ▶ verb *household waste should be incinerated to generate electricity* **burn**, burn up, reduce to ashes, consume by fire, carbonize; cremate.

incipient ▶ adjective *a system to detect incipient problems early* **developing**, impending, growing, emerging, emergent, dawning; just beginning, starting, inceptive, initial; nascent, embryonic, fledgling, in its infancy, germinal; rudimentary, inchoate; *rare* embryonal.
OPPOSITE full-blown.

incise ▶ verb **1** *the abdomen of each rat was incised* **cut**, cut into, make an incision in, slit, slit open, lance; gash, slash.
2 *an inscription incised in Roman letters* **engrave**, etch, carve, cut, chisel, inscribe, score, chase, notch; *archaic* scotch.

incision ▶ noun **1** *a surgical incision* **cut**, opening, slit.
2 *the incisions were made on the underside of the jar* **notch**, nick, snick, scratch, scarification; gash, slash; *archaic* scotch.

incisive ▶ adjective *an incisive political commentator* **penetrating**, acute, sharp, sharp-witted, razor-sharp, keen, rapier-like, astute, shrewd, trenchant, piercing, perceptive, insightful, percipient, perspicacious, discerning, analytical, intelligent, canny, clever, smart, quick; concise, succinct, pithy, to the point, crisp, clear; *informal* punchy, on the ball; *N. Amer. informal* heads-up; *rare* argute, sapient.
OPPOSITES rambling, vague.

incite ▶ verb **1** *Rico was arrested for inciting racial hatred* **stir up**, whip up, work up, encourage, fan the flames of, stoke up, fuel, kindle, ignite, inflame, stimulate, instigate, provoke, excite, arouse, awaken, waken, inspire, trigger, spark off, ferment, foment, agitate for/against; cause, generate, bring about; *literary* enkindle.
OPPOSITE suppress.
2 *she had incited him to commit murder* **egg on**, encourage, urge, goad, provoke, spur on, drive on, stimulate, push, prod, prompt, induce, impel, motivate, make, influence; arouse, rouse, excite, inflame, stir up, sting, prick; *informal* put up to; *N. Amer. informal* root on; *Law* procure.
OPPOSITES dissuade, deter.

incitement ▶ noun *this amounted to an incitement to commit murder* **egging on**, urging, goading, spurring on, motivation, persuasion, inducement; **instigation**, encouragement, stirring up, whipping up, stoking up, kindling, fuelling, stimulation, provocation, arousing, rousing, fomentation; *literary* enkindling.
OPPOSITES suppression, discouragement.

incivility ▶ noun *lateness, absenteeism, and incivility on the part of staff will not be tolerated* **rudeness**, discourtesy, discourteousness, impoliteness, lack of politeness; **bad manners**, ill-manneredness, lack of manners, unmannerliness, disrespect, disrespectfulness, boorishness, uncouthness, lack of refinement, ungraciousness, lack of social grace, ungentlemanly behaviour, unladylike behaviour; insolence, impertinence, impudence.
OPPOSITES politeness, good manners.

inclement ▶ adjective *the work was delayed by the inclement weather* **cold**, chilly, bitter, bleak, raw, wintry, freezing, snowy, icy; **wet**, rainy, drizzly, damp; stormy, blustery, wild, rough, squally, tempestuous, windy; unpleasant, bad, foul, nasty, filthy, severe, extreme, harsh, adverse.
OPPOSITES fine, mild, sunny.

inclination ▶ noun **1** *his political inclinations often got him into trouble | she showed no inclination to leave* **tendency**, propensity, proclivity, leaning; predisposition, disposition, predilection, weakness, proneness; desire, wish, readiness, impulse; bent; *archaic* list, humour; *rare* velleity.
OPPOSITES aversion, disinclination.
2 *she had no inclination for housework* **liking**, penchant, partiality, preference, appetite, fancy, fondness, affection, love; interest, affinity; stomach, taste; *informal* yen; *rare* appetency.
OPPOSITE dislike.
3 *an inclination of his head* **bowing**, bow, bending, nod, nodding, lowering, dip.
4 *an inclination in excess of 90 degrees* **gradient**, incline, slope, pitch, ramp, bank, ascent, rise, acclivity, descent, declivity; slant, lift, tilt; cant, camber, bevel; angle.

incline ▶ verb (stress on the second syllable) **1** *his prejudice inclines him to overlook obvious facts* **predispose**, lead, make, make of a mind to, dispose, bias, prejudice; prompt, induce, influence, sway; persuade, convince.
2 *I* **incline to** *the opposite view* **prefer**, have a preference for, favour, be favourably disposed to, go for, have a penchant for, have a liking for; tend, lean, swing, veer, gravitate, be drawn, be attracted; *N. Amer.* trend.
3 *he inclined his head* **bend**, bow, nod, bob, lower, dip.
OPPOSITES raise, lift.
4 *the columns incline several degrees away from the vertical* **lean**, tilt, angle, tip, slope, slant, bend, curve, bank, cant, bevel; list, heel; deviate.
▶ noun (stress on the first syllable) *a steep incline* **slope**, gradient, pitch, ramp, bank, ascent, rise, acclivity, upslope, dip, descent, declivity, downslope; hill; *N. Amer.* grade, downgrade, upgrade.

inclined ▶ adjective **1** *I'm inclined to believe her* **disposed**, minded, of a mind, willing, ready, prepared; predisposed.
OPPOSITE disinclined.
2 *she's inclined to gossip with complete strangers* **liable**, likely, prone, disposed, given, apt, wont, with a tendency; in the habit of.
OPPOSITE unlikely.

include ▶ verb **1** *extra-curricular activities include sports, drama, music, and chess* **incorporate**, comprise, encompass, cover, embrace, involve, take in, number, contain; consist of, be made up of, be composed of; *formal* comprehend.
OPPOSITES exclude, omit.
2 *don't forget to include the cost of tyres and bodywork repairs* **allow for**, count, take into account, take into consideration.
OPPOSITES exclude, leave out.
3 *include your name, address, and telephone number* **add**, insert, put in, append, enter, build in.
OPPOSITE leave out.

including ▶ preposition *a wide range of sports facilities, including squash, tennis, and badminton* **which include(s)**, inclusive of, counting; as well as, plus, together with.
OPPOSITE excluding.

inclusion ▶ noun *material suitable for inclusion in the programme* **incorporation**, addition, insertion, introduction; involvement, taking in, encompassing.
OPPOSITES exclusion, omission.

inclusive ▶ adjective **1** *the company quoted an inclusive price | an inclusive definition* **all-in**, all-inclusive, with everything included, comprehensive, in toto; overall, full, all-round, across the board, umbrella, blanket, catch-all, all-encompassing, all-embracing, without exception.
OPPOSITE exclusive.
2 *prices are* **inclusive of** *VAT* **including**, incorporating, taking in, counting, taking account of; comprising, covering, embracing.
OPPOSITE excluding.

incognito ▶ adjective & adverb *he travelled incognito* **under an assumed name**, under a false name, with one's identity concealed, in disguise, disguised, under cover, in plain clothes, camouflaged; unrecognized, unidentified; secretly, covertly, anonymously; *informal* incog.

incognizant ▶ adjective (*rare*) *she was incognizant of his presence* **unaware**, unconscious, oblivious, ignorant, unmindful; unknowing, unsuspecting, unenlightened; *rare* nescient.
OPPOSITE aware.

incoherent ▶ adjective **1** *a long and incoherent speech* **unclear**, confused, muddled, unintelligible, incomprehensible, hard to follow, disjointed, disconnected, unconnected, disordered, mixed up, garbled, jumbled, scrambled; rambling, wandering, discursive, disorganized, uncoordinated, illogical; inarticulate, mumbled, muttered, stuttered, stammered, slurred; *rare* inchoate.
OPPOSITES coherent, lucid, intelligible.
2 *Melanie was incoherent and shivering violently* **delirious**, raving, babbling, hysterical, irrational.
OPPOSITE lucid.

incombustible ▶ adjective **non-flammable**, non-combustible, not inflammable, unburnable; fireproof, fire resistant, fire retardant; flameproof, flame resistant, flame retardant; heatproof, ovenproof; *informal* non-flam; *rare* asbestine.
OPPOSITES flammable, inflammable.

income ▶ noun *each spouse is responsible for paying tax on their own income* **earnings**, salary, pay, remuneration, wages, stipend, emolument; **revenue**, receipts, takings, profits, gains, proceeds, turnover, yield, dividend, incomings, money received; means; N. Amer. take.
OPPOSITES expenditure, outgoings.

incoming ▶ adjective **1** *the incoming train* **arriving**, entering; **approaching**, coming, coming in.
OPPOSITE outgoing.
2 *the incoming president* **succeeding**, new, next, future, soon to take office; elect, to-be, designate, elected.
OPPOSITE outgoing.
▶ noun (**incomings**) *keep an account of your incomings and outgoings.* See INCOME.

incommensurate ▶ adjective *the penalty is* ***incommensurate with*** *his crime* **out of proportion to**, not in proportion to, disproportionate to, relatively too large/small for, not appropriate for; out of keeping with, at odds with; insufficient, inadequate; excessive, inordinate, unreasonable, uncalled for, undue, unfair.
OPPOSITE proportional.

incommunicable ▶ adjective *his incommunicable grief* **indescribable**, inexpressible, unutterable, unspeakable, undefinable, ineffable, beyond words, beyond description; overwhelming, intense, profound.

incomparable ▶ adjective *the incomparable beauty of Venice* **without equal**, beyond compare, unparalleled, matchless, peerless, without peer, unmatched, without match, without parallel, beyond comparison, second to none, in a class of its own, unequalled, unrivalled, inimitable, nonpareil; transcendent, superlative, surpassing, unsurpassed, unsurpassable, supreme, top, outstanding, consummate, unique, singular, rare, perfect; French par excellence, hors concours; informal one-in-a-million; rare unexampled.
OPPOSITES ordinary, commonplace.

incomparably ▶ adverb *this beach is incomparably superior to the others on the island* **far and away**, by far, infinitely, immeasurably, beyond compare, beyond comparison, easily; inimitably, unbeatably, supremely, superlatively, transcendently, uniquely.
OPPOSITE slightly.

incompatible ▶ adjective **1** *she and McBride are totally incompatible* **unsuited**, mismatched, ill-matched, poles apart, worlds apart, like day and night; ill-assorted; Brit. like chalk and cheese.
OPPOSITES well matched, suited.
2 *incompatible economic objectives* **irreconcilable**, conflicting, opposed, opposite, contradictory, antagonistic, antipathetic; clashing, inharmonious, discordant; mutually exclusive.
OPPOSITES compatible; complementary.
3 *his theory was* ***incompatible with*** *that of his predecessor* **inconsistent with**, at odds with, out of keeping with, different to, differing from, divergent from, at variance with, incongruous with, inconsonant with, contrary to, in conflict with, in opposition to, diametrically opposed to, counter to, not in accord with, irreconcilable with, not able to be reconciled with, alien to; rare repugnant to, oppugnant to.
OPPOSITE consistent.

incompetence ▶ noun *allegations of professional incompetence* **ineptitude**, ineptness, inability, lack of ability, incapability, incapacity, lack of skill, lack of proficiency, amateurishness, inexpertness, clumsiness, ineffectiveness, inadequacy, deficiency, inefficiency, ineffectuality, ineffectualness, insufficiency; informal cack-handedness, ham-fistedness, uselessness, hopelessness.
OPPOSITES competence, prowess.

incompetent ▶ adjective *he lost his job due to his incompetent performance* **inept**, unskilful, unskilled, inexpert, amateurish, unprofessional, lacking ability, bungling, blundering, clumsy, unproficient, inadequate, substandard, inferior, ineffective, deficient, inefficient, ineffectual, no good, not good enough, wanting, lacking, leaving much to be desired; incapable, unfitted, unfit, unsuitable, unqualified; informal useless, pathetic, cack-handed, ham-fisted, not up to it, a dead loss, not up to scratch, not up to snuff; Brit. informal unable to do something for toffee, unable to do something to save one's life, not much cop; vulgar slang half-arsed, not knowing one's arse from one's elbow, not capable of organizing a piss-up in a brewery.
OPPOSITES competent, skilful.

incomplete ▶ adjective **1** *the monument was still incomplete ten years after his death* **unfinished**, uncompleted, not finished, not completed, half-finished, half-done, half-completed, partially finished, partially complete, partial, not concluded; unaccomplished, undone, unexecuted, unperformed.
OPPOSITES complete, finished.
2 *inaccurate or incomplete information* **deficient**, insufficient, imperfect, defective, partial, patchy, sketchy, fragmentary, fragmented, scrappy, bitty; lacking, wanting, not entire, not whole, not total, abridged, shortened; qualified, restricted.
OPPOSITE full.

incomprehensible ▶ adjective **1** *April muttered something incomprehensible* **unintelligible**, indecipherable; incoherent, inarticulate.
OPPOSITES intelligible, comprehensible.
2 *legalistic and largely incomprehensible documents* **unintelligible**, impossible to understand, impenetrable, unclear, too difficult/hard to understand, beyond comprehension, beyond one, beyond one's grasp, unfathomable, unaccountable, inexplicable, inscrutable, baffling, bewildering, mystifying, puzzling, confusing, perplexing, abstruse, obscure, opaque, esoteric, recondite, arcane, mysterious, Delphic; complicated, complex, involved, intricate; informal over one's head, all Greek to someone; Brit. informal double Dutch; archaic wildering.
OPPOSITES intelligible, understandable, clear.

inconceivable ▶ adjective *it seemed inconceivable that the president had been unaware of what was going on* **beyond belief**, unbelievable, extremely difficult to believe, scarcely credible, incredible, unthinkable, unimaginable, extremely unlikely, not in the least likely, extremely implausible, extremely doubtful; impossible, beyond the bounds of possibility, out of the question, preposterous, ridiculous, ludicrous, absurd, incomprehensible; informal hard to swallow, mind-boggling.
OPPOSITE likely.

inconclusive ▶ adjective *their findings were inconclusive* **indecisive**, proving nothing, resolving nothing, leaving matters open; indefinite, indeterminate, undetermined, unresolved, unproved, unsettled, still open to question, still open to doubt, debatable, unconfirmed, not yet established; moot; vague, ambiguous; informal up in the air, left hanging.
OPPOSITES conclusive, open-and-shut.

incongruity ▶ noun *the incongruity of his fleshy face and skinny body disturbed her* **inappropriateness**, incongruousness, unsuitability, lack of harmony, discordance, inharmoniousness, dissonance, incompatibility, inconsistency, difference, disparity, discrepancy, irreconcilability; strangeness, oddity, absurdity, bizarreness, extraneousness; rare disconsonance.
OPPOSITE appropriateness.

incongruous ▶ adjective **1** *the women looked incongruous in their smart hats and fur coats* **out of place**, out of keeping, inappropriate, unsuitable, unsuited, not in harmony; discordant, dissonant, conflicting, clashing, jarring, wrong, at odds, in opposition, contrary, contradictory, irreconcilable; strange, odd, absurd, bizarre, off-key, extraneous; informal like a fish out of water, sticking/standing out a mile; rare disconsonant.
OPPOSITE appropriate.
2 *an incongruous collection of objects* **ill-matched**, ill-assorted, mismatched, unharmonious, inconsistent, incompatible, different, dissimilar, contrasting, disparate, discrepant.
OPPOSITE harmonious.

inconsequential ▶ adjective *inconsequential scraps of information* **insignificant**, unimportant, of little/no importance, of little/no consequence, of little/no account, of no moment, neither here nor there, incidental, inessential, non-essential, immaterial, irrelevant; negligible, inappreciable, inconsiderable, slight, minor, trivial, trifling, petty, paltry, nugatory, not worth mentioning, not worth bothering about, not worth speaking of, insubstantial, silly, lightweight; informal piddling, fiddling, piffling; N. Amer. informal small-bore, picayune.
OPPOSITES significant, important.

inconsiderable ▶ adjective *a not inconsiderable amount of money* **insignificant**, negligible, trifling, small, tiny, little, minuscule, nominal, token, petty, slight, niggling, minor, inappreciable, insubstantial, not worth mentioning, not worth bothering about, inconsequential; paltry, derisory, pitiful, niggardly, beggarly; informal piffling, piddling, fiddling, pathetic, measly, mingy; Brit. informal poxy; N. Amer. informal nickel-and-dime, small-bore; rare exiguous.
OPPOSITES considerable, large.

inconsiderate ▶ adjective *his inconsiderate behaviour hurt her dreadfully* **thoughtless**, unthinking, insensitive, selfish, self-centred, self-seeking, unsympathetic, uncaring, unthoughtful, unconcerned, heedless, unmindful, unkind, uncharitable, ungracious, impolite, discourteous, rude, disrespectful; tactless, undiplomatic, indiscreet, indelicate; callous, heartless, unfair; informal ignorant.
OPPOSITES considerate, thoughtful.

inconsistency ▶ noun **1** *he earned a reputation for political inconsistency* **unpredictability**, inconstancy, lack of consistency, changeableness, variability, instability, irregularity, unevenness, unsteadiness; self-contradiction, self-contradictoriness, contradiction, contrariety; capriciousness, fickleness, unreliability, undependability, flightiness, volatility; rare erraticism.
OPPOSITE consistency.
2 *the inconsistency between his expressed attitudes and his actual behaviour* **incompatibility**, conflict, difference, dissimilarity, lack of similarity, disagreement, lack of accord, opposition, clash, irreconcilability, lack of congruence, incongruity, lack of harmony, mismatch, discordance, disparity, discrepancy; rare disconsonance, inconsonance, repugnancy, oppugnancy.
OPPOSITES consistency, harmony.

I

inconsistent ▶ adjective **1** *his behaviour was inconsistent and irrational* **erratic**, changeable, unpredictable, variable, varying, changing, inconstant, unstable, irregular, fluctuating, unsteady, unsettled, uneven; self-contradictory, contradictory, paradoxical; capricious, fickle, flighty, whimsical, unreliable, undependable, mercurial, volatile, ever-changing, protean, chameleon-like, chameleonic; *informal* blowing hot and cold, up and down; *technical* labile; *rare* changeful, fluctuant.
OPPOSITES consistent, predictable.
2 *this finding is* **inconsistent with** *the conclusions of previous surveys* **incompatible with**, conflicting with, in conflict with, at odds with, at variance with, differing from, different to, in disagreement with, disagreeing with, not in accord with, contrary to, in opposition to, opposed to, irreconcilable with, not in keeping with, out of keeping with, out of place with, out of step with, not in harmony with, incongruous with, discordant with, discrepant with; antithetical to, diametrically opposed to; *rare* disconsonant with, inconsonant with, repugnant to, oppugnant to.
OPPOSITE consistent.

inconsolable ▶ adjective *normally stoic in the face of adversity, Tom was inconsolable* **heartbroken**, broken-hearted, unable to be comforted, unable to be consoled, grief-stricken, prostrate with grief, beside oneself with grief, devastated, wretched, sick at heart, desolate, despairing, distraught, comfortless; miserable, unhappy, sad; *literary* heartsick, dolorous.

inconspicuous ▶ adjective *Isabel tried to remain as inconspicuous as possible | an inconspicuous building* **unobtrusive**, unnoticeable, unremarkable, unspectacular, unostentatious, unimposing, undistinguished, unexceptional, modest, unassuming, discreet, hidden, concealed; ordinary, plain, run-of-the-mill, insignificant, characterless, forgettable, unmemorable; in the background, unnoticed, unseen, behind the scenes, out of the public eye, out of the spotlight, backstage, out of the limelight, low-profile, low-key; quiet, retiring.
OPPOSITES conspicuous, noticeable; high-profile.

inconstant ▶ adjective **1** *the exact dimensions are not easily measured since they are inconstant* **variable**, varying, changeable, changing, irregular, shifting, fluctuating, inconsistent, not constant, unsettled, unfixed, mutable, unstable, unsteady; *technical* labile; *rare* changeful, fluctuant, variational.
OPPOSITES constant, consistent.
2 *an inconstant lover* **fickle**, faithless, unfaithful, false, false-hearted, wayward, undependable, unreliable, untrustworthy, changeable, capricious, volatile, mercurial, flighty, chameleon-like, unpredictable, erratic, unstable; *informal* blowing hot and cold, cheating, two-timing.
OPPOSITES faithful, dependable.

CHOOSE THE RIGHT WORD

inconstant, changeable, capricious, fickle

These words all indicate that someone or something is liable to change and cannot be relied upon.

- **Inconstant** is a rather literary word suggesting that changes are not only sudden and frequent but also inexplicable. It is applied particularly to someone who is not faithful in love (*a widely held belief that women were by nature inconstant*).
- **Changeable** is a more common word for people and things liable to frequent variation (*she experienced changeable moods and panic attacks | conflicting and changeable political objectives*) and is often used of the weather (*outlook for tomorrow: changeable with rain at times*).
- **Capricious** emphasizes the fact that someone's changes of mind and behaviour spring from irrational and unpredictable whims, making them totally unreliable (*it was hopeless to try and argue with her capricious husband*). A *capricious* person is irresponsible and inconsiderate, possibly to the point of cruelty (*a capricious and often brutal administration*).
- **Fickle**, deriving from an Old English word meaning 'deceitful', is a disapproving description of someone who changes their views or allegiances very rapidly or readily (*the fickle Viennese public had once flocked to hear Mozart*). A *fickle lover* is shallow and transfers their affections repeatedly from one person to another (*men are so fickle, always on the lookout for someone new*).

incontestable ▶ adjective *finally, we had incontestable proof of their guilt* **incontrovertible**, indisputable, undeniable, irrefutable, unassailable, beyond dispute, unquestionable, beyond question, indubitable, not in doubt, beyond doubt, beyond a shadow of a doubt; compelling, convincing, clinching, airtight, watertight, unarguable, undebatable, unanswerable, emphatic, categorical; unequivocal, unambiguous, unmistakable, clear, clear-cut, certain, sure, definite, definitive, proven, demonstrable, self-evident, positive, decisive, conclusive, final, ultimate; *rare* inarguable, irrefragable, apodictic.
OPPOSITE questionable.

incontinent ▶ adjective **1** *incontinent patients* lacking bladder/bowel control.
OPPOSITE continent.
2 *their incontinent hysteria* **unrestrained**, uncontrolled, lacking self-restraint, unbridled, unchecked, ungoverned, uncurbed, unsuppressed, unfettered, untrammelled; uncontrollable, ungovernable.
OPPOSITE restrained.

incontrovertible ▶ adjective *their judgement is based on the evidence of incontrovertible facts* **indisputable**, incontestable, undeniable, irrefutable, unassailable, beyond dispute, unquestionable, beyond question, indubitable, not in doubt, beyond doubt, beyond a shadow of a doubt, unarguable, inarguable, undebatable, unanswerable; unequivocal, unambiguous, unmistakable, certain, sure, definite, definitive, proven, positive, decisive, conclusive, final, ultimate; clear, clear-cut, straightforward, plain, as plain as a pikestaff, transparent, obvious, manifest, evident, self-evident, staring one in the face, patent, demonstrative, demonstrable, observable, palpable; uncontroversial, accepted, acknowledged; marked, pronounced, express, emphatic, categorical, compelling, convincing, clinching, airtight, watertight; *rare* irrefragable, apodictic.
OPPOSITE questionable.

inconvenience ▶ noun **1** *we apologize for any inconvenience caused* **trouble**, bother, problems, disruption, nuisance value, disadvantage, difficulty, embarrassment, disturbance, vexation, harassment, worry, anxiety, distress, concern, disquiet, unease, irritation, annoyance, stress, agitation, unpleasantness; *informal* aggravation, hassle.
OPPOSITE help.
2 *his early arrival was clearly an inconvenience to his hosts* **nuisance**, trouble, bother, source of disruption/vexation/irritation/annoyance, vexation, worry, trial, tribulation, bind, pest, bore, plague, irritant, thorn in someone's flesh, cross to bear, the bane of someone's life, burden, hindrance, problem; *informal* headache, pain, pain in the neck, pain in the backside, drag, aggravation, hassle; *N. Amer. informal* pain in the butt, burr under/in someone's saddle; *Austral./NZ informal* nark; *Brit. informal, dated* blister; *vulgar slang* pain in the arse.
OPPOSITE convenience.
▶ verb *the general public was not greatly inconvenienced by the demonstration* **trouble**, bother, put out, put someone to trouble, be a problem to, disrupt, be a nuisance to, disadvantage, cause someone difficulty, impose on, burden, harass, plague, beset, embarrass, disturb; vex, worry, annoy, upset, irritate; *informal* hassle; *Austral./NZ informal* heavy; *rare* discommode.
OPPOSITE help.

inconvenient ▶ adjective *visitors often park their cars in inconvenient places* **awkward**, difficult, unsuitable, inappropriate, troublesome, bothersome, problematic, disruptive; inopportune, untimely, ill-timed, unfavourable, unseasonable, inexpedient, unfortunate, disadvantageous; tiresome, irritating, vexing, annoying, worrisome, distressing, embarrassing; *informal* aggravating.
OPPOSITE convenient.

incorporate ▶ verb **1** *part of Ukraine was incorporated into Moldavian territory* **absorb**, include, subsume, assimilate, integrate, take in, swallow up, engulf, consolidate.
OPPOSITE separate.
2 *the most expensive model incorporates some advanced features* **embody**, include, comprise, contain, embrace, build in, encompass.
3 *a small amount of salt is uniformly incorporated with the butter* **blend**, mix, mingle, combine, put together, merge, fuse, unite, unify, join, bring together, amalgamate, integrate; fold in, stir, whisk; meld, marry, mesh, compound, alloy, coalesce, homogenize, emulsify, intermingle, intermix; *informal* blunge; *rare* commingle, commix.

incorporeal ▶ adjective *millions believe in a supreme but incorporeal being* **intangible**, impalpable, non-material, non-physical; bodiless, unembodied, disembodied; ethereal, unsubstantial, insubstantial, airy, aerial; spiritual, ghostly, spectral, phantom, wraithlike, transcendental, unearthly, supernatural; unreal, imaginary, illusory, chimerical, hallucinatory; *rare* immaterial, discarnate, disincarnate, unbodied, phantasmal, phantasmic.
OPPOSITE tangible.

incorrect ▶ adjective **1** *an incorrect answer* **wrong**, **mistaken**, in error, erroneous, inaccurate, not accurate, inexact, not exact, imprecise, invalid, untrue, false, fallacious, wide of the mark, off target; misleading, illogical, unsound, unfounded, without foundation, faulty, flawed; *informal* off beam, out, way out, full of holes, iffy; *archaic* abroad.
OPPOSITE correct.
2 *most food contamination is caused by incorrect storage at home | incorrect behaviour* **inappropriate**, wrong, unsuitable, inapt, inapposite, undesirable; **ill-advised**, ill-considered, ill-judged, impolitic, injudicious, infelicitous, unacceptable, beyond the pale, unwarranted, unfitting, out of keeping, improper, unseemly, unbecoming, indecorous, lacking in propriety; *informal* out of order.

incorrigible ▶ adjective *she's an incorrigible flirt* **inveterate**, habitual, confirmed, hardened; incurable, unreformable, irreformable,

irredeemable, intractable, hopeless, beyond hope/redemption; chronic, diehard, deep-dyed, dyed-in-the-wool, long-standing, addicted, hard-core; impenitent, uncontrite, unrepentant, unapologetic, unashamed; *informal* impossible.
OPPOSITES occasional; repentant.

incorruptibility ▶ noun *he claimed that his Ministers enjoyed an untarnished reputation for incorruptibility* **honesty**, honour, trustworthiness, scrupulousness, conscientiousness, correctness, rectitude, probity, integrity, uprightness, high-mindedness, righteousness, right-mindedness, virtue, nobility, respectability, decency.
OPPOSITE venality.

incorruptible ▶ adjective **1** *a conscientious and incorruptible detective* **unbribable**, honest, trustworthy, scrupulous, conscientious, principled, high-principled, proper, correct, honourable, upright, straight, upstanding, high-minded, righteous, right-minded, moral, ethical, good, virtuous, just, noble, respectable, decent.
OPPOSITE venal.
2 *as it was incorruptible, gold was considered special* **imperishable**, indestructible, non-biodegradable, not decaying, non-corroding, indissoluble, durable, made to last, enduring, everlasting, eternal; *rare* perdurable.
OPPOSITE perishable.

increase ▶ verb (stress on the second syllable) **1** *gas demand is likely to increase* **grow**, get bigger, get larger, become greater, enlarge, expand, swell; rise, climb, escalate, soar, surge, rocket, shoot up, spiral; improve, intensify, strengthen; heighten, lengthen, extend, stretch, spread, widen; multiply, snowball, mushroom, proliferate, balloon, build up, mount up, pile up, accrue, accumulate; *literary* wax.
OPPOSITE decrease.
2 *higher expectations will increase user demand* **add to**, make larger, make bigger, make greater, augment, supplement, top up, build up, enlarge, expand, extend, raise, multiply, elevate, swell, inflate; magnify, intensify, strengthen, amplify, heighten, escalate; improve, make better, boost, ameliorate, enhance, enrich, upgrade; worsen, make worse, exacerbate, aggravate, inflame, compound, reinforce; *informal* up, jack up, hike up, hike, bump up, crank up, step up.
OPPOSITE reduce.
▶ noun (stress on the first syllable) *the increase in size | an increase in demand* **growth**, rise, enlargement, expansion, extension, multiplication, elevation, swelling, inflation; increment, addition, augmentation; magnification, intensification, strengthening, amplification, stepping up, step up, heightening; climb, escalation, surge, upsurge, upswing, spiral; improvement, boost, amelioration, enhancement, upgrade, upturn; worsening, exacerbation, aggravation; development, advance, boom, spurt, snowballing, mushrooming; *informal* hike.
OPPOSITES decrease, reduction.

increasingly ▶ adverb *the regime became increasingly draconian* **more and more**, progressively, to an increasing extent, steadily more, continuously more, gradually more; *rare* growingly.
OPPOSITE less and less.

incredible ▶ adjective **1** *to be honest, I find his story incredible* **unbelievable**, beyond belief, hard to believe, scarcely credible, unconvincing, far-fetched, strained, laboured, implausible, improbable, highly unlikely, not in the least likely, questionable, dubious, doubtful, inconceivable, unthinkable, unimaginable, impossible, astonishing, astounding, breathtaking, staggering, absurd, preposterous, phenomenal, extraordinary; unheard of, fictitious, mythical, fanciful, fantastic, unrealistic; feeble, weak, unsound, thin, transparent, poor, tame, paltry, lame, trifling, shallow, inadequate, unsatisfactory, ineffectual, half-baked, pathetic; *informal* hard to swallow/take, tall, cock and bull.
OPPOSITES believable; likely.
2 *an incredible feat of engineering* **magnificent**, wonderful, marvellous, spectacular, remarkable, phenomenal, prodigious, miraculous, sublime; **breathtaking**, dazzling, amazing, stunning, astounding, astonishing, awe-inspiring, staggering, extraordinary, unbelievable; formidable, imposing, impressive, supreme, great, awesome, superhuman; *Scottish* unco; *informal* fantastic, terrific, tremendous, stupendous, mind-boggling, mind-blowing, out of this world, unreal; *literary* wondrous; *archaic* awful.
OPPOSITE unspectacular.

incredulity ▶ noun *reports of UFO sightings were met with incredulity* **disbelief**, incredulousness, lack of belief, unbelief, lack of credence, doubt, doubtfulness, dubiety, dubiousness, lack of conviction; distrust, mistrust, suspicion, questioning, lack of trust, cynicism, scepticism, wariness, chariness.
OPPOSITES credulity; belief.

incredulous ▶ adjective *he was frankly incredulous when told the cost* **disbelieving**, unbelieving, doubtful, dubious, unconvinced; distrustful, distrusting, mistrustful, mistrusting, suspicious, questioning, lacking trust, cynical, sceptical, wary, chary.
OPPOSITE credulous.

increment ▶ noun *an annual salary increment* **increase**, addition, gain, augmentation, step up, supplement, addendum, adjunct, accretion, accrual; enlargement, enhancement, boost, advance; *informal* hike.
OPPOSITE reduction.

incriminate ▶ verb *Drury persuaded one witness to incriminate Cooper* **implicate**, involve; blame, accuse, denounce, inform against, blacken the name of; entrap; *informal* frame, set up, point the finger at, stick/pin the blame on, grass on, rat on; *Brit. informal* fit up; *archaic* inculpate.
OPPOSITES absolve, clear.

inculcate ▶ verb **1** *parents try to* **inculcate** *a sense of responsibility* **in** *their children* **instil**, implant, fix, ingrain, infuse, impress, imprint, introduce; engender, produce, generate, induce, inspire, promote, foster; hammer into, drum into, drive into, drill into, din into.
2 *he tries to inculcate students with a sense of the beauty and joy of the subject* **imbue**, infuse, inspire, instil; brainwash, indoctrinate; teach.

inculpate ▶ verb (*archaic*). See INCRIMINATE.

incumbent ▶ adjective **1** *it is incumbent on the government to give a clear lead* **binding**, obligatory, mandatory, necessary, compulsory, required, requisite, essential, imperative.
OPPOSITE optional.
2 *the incumbent President had been defeated* **current**, existing, present, in office, in power; reigning.
OPPOSITES past; future.
▶ noun *the first incumbent of the post was appointed in 1961* **holder**, bearer, occupant; office-holder, office-bearer, officer, functionary, official.

incur ▶ verb *the company incurred a loss of two million pounds | kicking one's opponent incurs a 25-point penalty* **suffer**, sustain, experience, bring upon oneself, expose oneself to, lay oneself open to; run up, collect; attract, invite, provoke, earn, arouse, induce, cause, give rise to, bring on, be liable/subject to, meet with, draw.
OPPOSITE avoid.

incurable ▶ adjective **1** *an incurable illness* **untreatable**, inoperable, irremediable, beyond cure; terminal, fatal, deadly, mortal; chronic, persistent, long-standing, constantly recurring, long-term; *rare* immedicable.
OPPOSITE curable.
2 *an incurable romantic* **inveterate**, dyed-in-the-wool, confirmed, entrenched, established, long-established, long-standing, deep-rooted, diehard, complete, absolute, utter, thorough, thoroughgoing, out-and-out, true blue, through and through; firm, unshakeable, staunch, steadfast, committed, devoted, dedicated, loyal, faithful, unswerving, unwavering, unfaltering; unashamed, unapologetic, unrepentant, incorrigible, hopeless, beyond hope; *N. Amer.* full-bore; *informal* deep-dyed, card-carrying, mad keen, keen as mustard; *archaic* arrant; *rare* right-down.

incursion ▶ noun *the first Ottoman* **incursion into** *Europe* **attack on**, assault on, raid on, invasion of, storming of, overrunning of, foray into, blitz on, sortie into, sally against/into, advance on/into, push into, thrust into, descent on; intrusion into, trespass on, infiltration of, obtrusion into, appropriation of.
OPPOSITE retreat.

indebted ▶ adjective *I shall always be indebted to them for their help* **beholden**, under an obligation, obliged, obligated, bound, duty-bound, honour-bound, grateful, thankful, filled with gratitude, appreciative; in someone's debt, owing someone a debt of gratitude.

indecency ▶ noun *a man was up in court this week on a charge of indecency* **indecent behaviour**, gross indecency, pornography; **obscenity**, rudeness, coarseness, dirtiness, smuttiness, vulgarity, grossness, crudity, crudeness, bawdiness, lewdness, raciness, salaciousness, wickedness, impropriety, indelicacy, unseemliness, impurity, ribaldry, lasciviousness, licentiousness; prurience, profanity, foulness, vileness.

indecent ▶ adjective **1** *he was fined for importing indecent material* **obscene**, dirty, filthy, rude, coarse, vulgar, gross, crude, bawdy, lewd, racy, risqué, salacious, wicked, improper, indelicate, unseemly, impure, smutty, spicy, raw, off colour, ribald, Rabelaisian, lascivious, licentious; pornographic, offensive, prurient, sordid, scatological, low, profane, foul, vile; *informal* blue, naughty, near the knuckle/bone, nudge-nudge, porn, porno, X-rated, raunchy, skin; *Brit. informal* fruity, saucy; *euphemistic* adult.
OPPOSITES decent, proper.
2 *most of her clothes are rather indecent* **revealing**, short, brief, skimpy, scanty, insubstantial, low-cut, flimsy, thin, see-through; erotic, arousing, sexy, suggestive, titillating.
OPPOSITE modest.
3 *the company took her pass and desk away from her with indecent haste* **unseemly**, improper, indecorous, unceremonious, indiscreet, indelicate, demeaning, unbecoming, ungentlemanly, unladylike, unworthy, unfitting, unbefitting, degrading, debasing, cheapening, belittling, lowering, shaming, shameful, humiliating, mortifying, dishonourable, ignominious, undignified, discreditable, ignoble, inglorious, scandalous, disgraceful, outrageous; untoward, unsuitable, inappropriate; in bad taste, tasteless, unacceptable, offensive, crass.

indecipherable ▶ adjective *the taxi driver scribbled something indecipherable upon the back of a cigarette packet* **illegible**, unreadable, hard to read, indistinguishable, indiscernible, unclear, indistinct; scribbled, scrawled,

I

hieroglyphic, squiggly, shaky, small, cramped, crabbed, pinched, bad; unintelligible, unfathomable, impenetrable, enigmatic, puzzling, mystifying, inexplicable, baffling, bewildering.
OPPOSITE legible.

indecision ▶ **noun** *she was rooted to the spot, torn by indecision* **indecisiveness**, irresolution, irresoluteness, lack of resolution, hesitancy, hesitation, tentativeness; ambivalence, doubt, doubtfulness, unsureness, uncertainty; vacillation, equivocation, oscillation, wavering, teetering, fluctuation, faltering, second thoughts; delay, hanging back, waiting, shilly-shallying, dithering, stalling, temporizing, temporization; *Brit.* havering, humming and hawing; *Scottish* swithering; *informal* dilly-dallying, blowing hot and cold, sitting on the fence; *rare* dubiety, incertitude, cunctation.
OPPOSITES decision, decisiveness.

indecisive ▶ **adjective 1** *these experimental results are indecisive* **inconclusive**, proving nothing, settling nothing, open, indeterminate, undecided, unsettled, borderline, indefinite, unclear, ambiguous, contradictory, ambivalent, conflicting, confusing, two-edged, double-edged, paradoxical; *informal* up in the air.
OPPOSITE decisive.
2 *he came across as a weak, indecisive leader* **irresolute**, hesitant, tentative, weak; vacillating, equivocating, dithering, wavering, teetering, fluctuating, faltering, shilly-shallying; ambivalent, divided, in two minds, in a dilemma, in a quandary, torn; doubtful, unsure, uncertain; undecided, uncommitted, unresolved, undetermined; *informal* iffy, blowing hot and cold, sitting on the fence.
OPPOSITE decisive.

I

indecorous ▶ **adjective** *kissing in public is considered indecorous in many countries* **improper**, unseemly, unbecoming, undignified, immodest, indecent, indelicate, indiscreet, immoral, shameless, loose, wanton, unvirtuous; inappropriate, incorrect, wrong, unsuitable, inapt, inapposite, undesirable, unfitting, out of keeping, unacceptable, impolite, discourteous, in bad taste, ill-bred, ill-mannered, beyond the pale.
OPPOSITE decorous.

indecorum ▶ **noun** *it would have been the height of indecorum to send one's daughter unchaperoned to a ball* **impropriety**, unseemliness, unbecomingness, indignity, immodesty, indecency, indelicacy, indiscretion, immorality, shamelessness; inappropriateness, incorrectness, unsuitability, inaptness, inappositeness, undesirability, unacceptability, impoliteness, discourtesy, bad taste, ill breeding, bad manners; *rare* improperness.
OPPOSITE decorum.

indeed ▶ **adverb 1** *there was, indeed, quite a furore* **as expected**, to be sure, in fact, in point of fact, as a matter of fact, in truth, truly, actually, really, in reality, as it happens/happened, certainly, surely, for sure, undeniably, veritably, nay, if truth be told, you could say; *archaic* in sooth, verily.
2 *'Are you well?' 'Indeed!' | indeed I did* **yes**, **certainly**, assuredly, emphatically, absolutely, exactly, precisely, of course, definitely, quite, positively, naturally, without (a) doubt, without question, unquestionably, undoubtedly, doubtlessly, indubitably; by all means; *informal* you bet, you got it, I'll say.
3 *Ian's future with us looked rosy indeed* **very**, extremely, exceedingly, exceptionally, especially, extraordinarily, to a fault, in the extreme, extra, tremendously, immensely, singularly, significantly, distinctly, outstandingly, uncommonly, unusually, decidedly, particularly, eminently, supremely, highly, remarkably, really, truly, mightily, thoroughly; all that, to a great extent, most, so; *Scottish* unco; *French* très; *N. English* right; *informal* terrifically, awfully, fearfully, terribly, devilishly, majorly, seriously, mega, ultra, oh-so, mucho, damn, damned; *informal, dated* devilish, hellish, frightfully; *Brit. informal* ever so, well, bloody, dead, jolly, fair; *N. Amer. informal* real, mighty, powerful, awful, plumb, darned, way, bitching; *S. African informal* lekker; *archaic* exceeding.
OPPOSITES moderately, slightly; by no means.

indefatigable ▶ **adjective** *he is one of those indefatigable researchers who won't take no for an answer* **tireless**, untiring, never-tiring, unwearied, unwearying, unflagging; energetic, dynamic, enthusiastic; unrelenting, relentless, unremitting, unswerving, unfaltering, unshakeable, indomitable; persistent, tenacious, determined, dogged, single-minded, assiduous, industrious.
OPPOSITES idle; feeble.

indefensible ▶ **adjective 1** *indefensible cruelty* **inexcusable**, unjustifiable, unjustified, unpardonable, unforgivable, inexpiable; uncalled for, unprovoked, gratuitous, without justification, without cause, without reason, unreasonable, unnecessary; regrettable, unacceptable, unworthy, remiss, blameworthy, culpable, reprehensible, censurable, unwarrantable; excessive, immoderate, unconscionable, outrageous.
OPPOSITES justifiable, excusable.
2 *an indefensible system of dual justice* **untenable**, insupportable, unsustainable, unwarrantable, unwarranted, unjustifiable, unjustified, unadmissible, unsound, ill-founded, unfounded, groundless, baseless, flimsy, weak, shaky, flawed, faulty, defective, invalid, specious, arbitrary, implausible, absurd, illogical, irrational, preposterous, senseless, unacceptable.
OPPOSITE tenable.
3 *an indefensible island* **undefendable**, defenceless, undefended, unfortified, unguarded, unprotected, unshielded, unarmed, without arms, without weapons, without defences; vulnerable, exposed, assailable, open to attack, wide open, open, endangered, in danger, in peril, in jeopardy, at risk, insecure; *rare* pregnable.
OPPOSITES defensible; well protected.

indefinable ▶ **adjective** *the curious, indefinable quality which sets his sculptures apart* **hard to define**, hard to describe, indescribable, inexpressible, nameless; vague, obscure; indefinite, unanalysable, intangible, impalpable, incorporeal, elusive, fugitive.
OPPOSITE definable.

indefinite ▶ **adjective 1** *an indefinite period* **unknown**, **indeterminate**, unspecified, unlimited, unrestricted, undecided, undetermined, undefined, unfixed, unsettled, unresolved, uncertain; limitless, infinite, endless, immeasurable.
OPPOSITES fixed, limited.
2 *a word with an indefinite meaning* **vague**, ill-defined, unclear, loose, general, imprecise, inexact, nebulous, blurred, fuzzy, hazy, confused, obscure, ambiguous, equivocal, doubtful, dubious.
OPPOSITE clear.

indefinitely ▶ **adverb 1** *the trial has been postponed indefinitely* **for an unspecified time/period**, for an unlimited time/period, without a fixed limit; *Law* sine die.
2 *the state of affairs could continue indefinitely* **forever**, for always, for good, for good and all, evermore, for ever and ever, for all time, until the end of time, eternally, undyingly, permanently, perpetually, in perpetuity; *Brit.* for evermore; *N. Amer.* forevermore; *informal* for keeps, until the cows come home, until hell freezes over, until the twelfth of never, until doomsday, until kingdom come; *archaic* for aye.
OPPOSITE temporarily.

indelible ▶ **adjective** *indelible ink | the story made an indelible impression on me* **ineradicable**, inerasable, ineffaceable, unexpungeable, indestructible, permanent, lasting, persisting, enduring, stubborn, ingrained, unfading, imperishable; unforgettable, haunting, memorable, not/never to be forgotten.
OPPOSITE erasable.

indelicacy ▶ **noun** *the magazine printed the photographs with manifest indelicacy for commercial ends* **impropriety**, unseemliness, unbecomingness, indignity, immodesty, indecency, obscenity, indecorum, indiscretion, immorality, shamelessness; insensitivity, tactlessness; undesirability, unacceptability, impoliteness, discourtesy, bad taste, ill breeding, bad manners.
OPPOSITES delicacy; propriety.

indelicate ▶ **adjective 1** *forgive me if I am indelicate in asking* **insensitive**, tactless, undiplomatic, impolitic, indiscreet.
OPPOSITE tactful.
2 *an indelicate sense of humour* **vulgar**, coarse, rude, gross, crude, bawdy, racy, risqué, ribald, Rabelaisian, earthy, indecent, improper, indecorous, unseemly, unrefined, off colour, obscene, dirty, filthy, impure, smutty, lewd, salacious, raw, lascivious, licentious; *informal* blue, naughty, near the knuckle/bone, nudge-nudge, raunchy; *Brit. informal* fruity, saucy.
OPPOSITES clean; polite.

indemnify ▶ **verb 1** *he should be indemnified for his losses in the war* **reimburse**, compensate, recompense, repay, pay back, remunerate, recoup, requite, make restitution/amends to; settle up with, settle accounts with.
2 *the author is required to indemnify the publishers against any such loss* **insure**, assure, guarantee, protect, secure, make secure, give security to, warrant; agree to pay.

indemnity ▶ **noun 1** *an outgoing partner should insist on indemnity against future liabilities of the firm* **insurance**, assurance, protection, security, indemnification, surety, endorsement, guarantee, warranty, safeguard.
2 *those charged with political offences were granted indemnity from prosecution* **immunity**, exemption, exception, dispensation, exclusion, freedom, release, relief, absolution, exoneration; special treatment, privilege, favouritism; impunity; *informal* a let-off; *rare* derogation.
3 *the public purse would be saved the burden of paying indemnity* **reimbursement**, compensation, recompense, repayment, restitution, payment, remuneration, requital, redress, reparation(s), damages; *N. Amer. informal* comp; *archaic* guerdon, meed; *rare* solatium.

indent ▶ **verb** (stress on the second syllable) **1** *the first line of a paragraph is indented by using the tab key* **move to the right**, move further from the margin, start in from the margin.
2 *the many lochs that indent the isle of Mull* **notch**, nick, make an indentation in, make notches/nicks in, scallop, serrate, pink, cut, mark, score, incise, carve, engrave, scratch, gash, slit, snick, gouge, groove, furrow, dent.

3 *you'll have to **indent** for a new uniform* **order**, put in an order for, requisition, apply for, put in for, request, put in a request for, ask for, claim, put in a claim for, call for, demand.

▶ **noun** (stress on the first syllable) (*Brit.*) *he cancelled the indent for silk scarves* **order**, requisition, purchase order, request, call, application; claim, demand, summons.

indentation ▶ **noun** *there was a slight indentation in his chin | indentations in the coastline* **hollow**, depression, dent, dint, cavity, concavity, dip, pit, trough, crater; dimple; cleft, slot, snick, notch; nick, mark, cut, gouge, gash; recess, alcove, niche, bay; inlet, cove, creek, fjord, firth, ria; *Anatomy* fossa, lacuna.

indenture ▶ **noun** *the indenture allowed for moneys to be returned in certain circumstances* **contract**, agreement, covenant, compact, bond, pledge, promise, warrant, undertaking, commitment, settlement, arrangement, understanding; lease, guarantee, warranty; certificate, deed, document, instrument; *rare* engagement.

independence ▶ **noun 1** *the struggle for American independence* **self-government**, self-rule, home rule, self-legislation, self-determination, sovereignty, autonomy, non-alignment, freedom, liberty; *rare* autarky.
OPPOSITES dependence; subservience.
2 *one disadvantage of marriage is the individual's lack of independence* **self-sufficiency**, self-reliance, self-support, self-sustenance, self-standing.
OPPOSITE dependence.
3 *you must be able to rely on an adviser's independence* **impartiality**, neutrality, disinterest, disinterestedness, uninvolvement, detachment, dispassionateness, lack of bias, lack of prejudice, objectivity, open-mindedness, even-handedness, fairness, fair-mindedness, justice; *rare* equitableness.
OPPOSITE partiality.
4 *there is a tendency for select committees to show some greater independence of spirit* **individualism**, unconventionality, unorthodoxy; freedom, liberation, boldness, unconstraint, lack of constraint/restraint; indiscipline, unruliness, wilfulness, contrariness.
OPPOSITES constraint; orthodoxy.

> **CHOOSE THE RIGHT WORD**
>
> **independence, liberty, freedom**
>
> *See* LIBERTY.

independent ▶ **adjective 1** *an independent country* **self-governing**, self-legislating, self-determining, sovereign, autonomous, autonomic, autarkic, free, non-aligned.
OPPOSITES dependent; subservient.
2 *the auditing of a company's accounts is done by independent accountants* **unconnected**, unrelated, unassociated, dissociated, unattached, separate.
OPPOSITE connected.
3 *the Institute will quickly become a fully independent unit* **separate**, discrete, different, distinct, free-standing, self-contained, complete.
OPPOSITE subordinate.
4 *an independent school* **private**, public, non-state-controlled, non-state-run, non-public, private-sector, private-enterprise, fee-paying, commercial; privatized, denationalized.
OPPOSITES private; state-run.
5 *one has to be very careful about offering money to proud and independent old folk* **self-sufficient**, self-supporting, self-sustaining, self-reliant, self-standing, able to stand on one's own two feet; self-contained, self-made; *informal* living on one's hump.
OPPOSITE dependent.
6 *an independent financial adviser* **impartial**, unbiased, unprejudiced, neutral, disinterested, uninvolved, uncommitted, detached, dispassionate, objective, open-minded, equitable, non-partisan, even-handed, fair, fair-minded, just; without favouritism, free from discrimination, non-discriminatory, with no axe to grind, without fear or favour; *informal* on the fence.
OPPOSITES biased; tied.
7 *entrepreneurs are independent spirits* **freethinking**, individualistic, unconventional, maverick; free, liberated, bold, unconstrained, unrestrained, unfettered, untrammelled, unhampered; undisciplined, wild, wilful, headstrong, contrary.
OPPOSITES constrained; orthodox.

independently ▶ **adverb** *he prefers to work independently | we'll get there independently and then meet up* **alone**, all alone, on one's own, in a solitary state, separately, singly, solitarily, unaccompanied, solo; unaided, unassisted, without help, without assistance, by one's own efforts, under one's own steam, single-handed(ly), off one's own bat, on one's own initiative, autonomously, as one's own boss; *informal* by one's lonesome; *Brit. informal* on one's tod, on one's lonesome, on one's jack, on one's Jack Jones; *formal* severally.
OPPOSITES accompanied; jointly; assisted.

indescribable ▶ **adjective** *the indescribable thrill of the chase* **inexpressible**, undefinable, beyond words/description, beggaring description, nameless, incommunicable, ineffable, unutterable, unspeakable; intense, extreme, acute, strong, powerful, profound; incredible, extraordinary, remarkable, prodigious; indefinite, unanalysable, intangible, impalpable, elusive, fugitive.

indestructible ▶ **adjective** *indestructible plastic containers | the indestructible spirit of man* **unbreakable**, shatterproof, non-breakable; toughened, sturdy, stout, hard-wearing, heavy-duty, resistant, durable, lasting, made to last; enduring, everlasting, perennial, deathless, undying, immortal, endless, inextinguishable, imperishable, ineradicable, long-lasting; *literary* adamantine; *rare* infrangible.
OPPOSITES fragile; ephemeral.

indeterminate ▶ **adjective 1** *a woman of indeterminate age* **undetermined**, undefined, unspecified, unfixed, unsettled, indefinite, unknown, uncounted, uncertain, unpredictable.
OPPOSITE known.
2 *indeterminate background noise* **vague**, indefinite, unspecific, unclear, obscure, nebulous, indistinct, some kind of; ambiguous, ambivalent, equivocal; amorphous, shapeless, formless, unformed, unshaped, structureless, unstructured; inexact, imprecise, inexplicit, ill-defined; hazy, faint, shadowy, dim; *rare* nebulose.
OPPOSITES definite, clear.

index ▶ **noun 1** *the book has a very complete index* **register**, list, listing, inventory, directory, guide, key, catalogue, table of contents.
2 *literature is an index to the condition of civilization* **guide**, clue, hint, indication, indicator, lead, sign, signal, mark, token, evidence, symptom, implication, intimation, suggestion.
3 *the index jumped up the dial* **pointer**, indicator, needle, hand, finger, marker.

indicate ▶ **verb 1** *sales indicate a growing market for such art | the scowl on his face indicated his displeasure* **demonstrate**, show, point to, be a sign of, be evidence of, evidence, testify to, bear witness to, be a symptom of, be symptomatic of, denote, connote, mark, signal, signify, suggest, imply; manifest, reveal, betray, evince, display, reflect, represent; *literary* bespeak, betoken.
2 *the Prime Minister indicated that the government would take no further action* **state**, declare, make (it) known, announce, communicate, mention, say, reveal, divulge, disclose, register, record, put it on record; admit; *informal* come out with.
3 *please indicate your choice of prize* **designate**, specify, stipulate; show.
4 *he indicated the room to me* **point to**, point out, gesture towards.

indicated ▶ **adjective** *these remedies can be of great value, even when surgery is indicated* **advisable**, desirable, recommended, suggested, desired, preferable, best, sensible, wise, commonsensical, prudent; appropriate, suitable; helpful, useful, effective, advantageous, beneficial, valuable, profitable, gainful, in someone's (best) interests; **necessary**, needed, required, called for, essential.

indication ▶ **noun 1** *pain may be an indication of injury* **sign**, indicator, symptom, mark, manifestation, signal, demonstration, evidence, attestation, proof; omen, augury, portent, warning, forewarning, pointer, guide, hint, clue.
2 *her face was turned away as an indication of her contempt* **expression**, demonstration, show, exhibition, display, manifestation, revelation, disclosure, register, record; declaration, communication, intimation.

indicative ▶ **adjective** *the President's visit was indicative of improving diplomatic relations* **symptomatic**, expressive, suggestive, evocative, typical, characteristic, representative, symbolic, emblematic; *archaic* indicatory.

indicator ▶ **noun 1** *these tests are a reliable indicator of performance* **measure**, gauge, barometer, index, mark, sign, signal; guide to; standard, touchstone, yardstick, benchmark, criterion, point of reference, guideline, test, litmus test.
2 *the depth indicator is calibrated in metres* **meter**, measuring instrument, measuring device, measure, gauge, dial, display, scale, index.
3 *a red position indicator points at flap settings* **pointer**, needle, hand, arrow, marker, index.

indict ▶ **verb** *he was indicted for murder* **charge with**, accuse of, arraign for, take to court for, put on trial for, bring to trial for, prosecute for; summons, cite, make accusations about, lay charges against, file charges against, prefer charges against; *N. Amer.* impeach for.
OPPOSITE acquit.

indictment ▶ **noun** *the indictment named only one defendant* **charge**, accusation, arraignment, citation, summons; allegation, imputation; *Brit.* plaint; *N. Amer.* impeachment; *N. Amer. informal* beef; *archaic* inculpation.
OPPOSITE acquittal.

indifference ▶ **noun 1** *he has a total indifference to public opinion* **lack of concern about**, unconcern about, apathy about/towards, nonchalance about, lack of interest in, disregard for, obliviousness to, uninvolvement in/with; heedlessness of, mindlessness of, carelessness of, dismissiveness of; boredom with, weariness of, unresponsiveness to, lack of enthusiasm about; impassiveness, impassivity, dispassionateness, aloofness, insouciance, detachment, distance, coldness, coolness, unresponsiveness,

I

passionlessness, emotionlessness, lack of feeling, lack of sympathy, callousness; *rare* poco-curantism.
OPPOSITES heed; care.
2 *the indifference of the team's midfield players* **mediocrity**, ordinariness, commonplaceness, lack of inspiration, passableness, adequacy; **inferiority**, lack of distinction, amateurism.
OPPOSITE brilliance.

indifferent ▸ adjective **1** *Government cannot be* ***indifferent to*** *the long-term success of business* **unconcerned about**, apathetic about/towards, uncaring about, casual about, nonchalant about, offhand about, uninterested in, uninvolved in/with; heedless of, mindless of, careless of, regardless of, oblivious to; reckless about, cavalier about, frivolous about, dismissive of; unimpressed by, bored by, weary of, unmoved by, unresponsive to, lukewarm about, unenthusiastic about, phlegmatic about; impassive, dispassionate, aloof, insouciant, detached, distant, cold, cool, unresponsive, passionless, unemotional, emotionless, unmoved, unfeeling, unsympathetic, callous; *rare* poco-curante.
OPPOSITES heedful; caring.
2 *both players played indifferent shots* **mediocre**, ordinary, commonplace, average, middle-of-the-road, middling, medium, moderate, everyday, workaday, tolerable, passable, adequate, fair; **inferior**, second-rate, uninspired, undistinguished, unexceptional, unexciting, unremarkable, run-of-the-mill, not very good, pedestrian, prosaic, lacklustre, forgettable, amateur, amateurish; *informal* OK, so-so, bog-standard, fair-to-middling, (plain) vanilla, nothing to write home about, no great shakes, not so hot, not up to much; *NZ informal* half-pie.
OPPOSITE brilliant.

I

indigence ▸ noun *he did valuable work towards the relief of indigence* **poverty**, penury, impoverishment, impecuniousness, impecuniosity, destitution, pennilessness, privation, hand-to-mouth existence, pauperism; insolvency, bankruptcy, ruin, ruination; need, neediness, want, reduced/straitened/narrow circumstances, dire straits, deprivation, disadvantage, hardship, distress, financial distress, difficulties; beggary, mendicancy, vagrancy; *rare* pauperdom.
OPPOSITE wealth.

indigenous ▸ adjective *indigenous peoples are being slowly wiped out as prospectors invade their lands* **native**, aboriginal, local; original, earliest, first, initial; ancient, primitive, primeval, primordial; *rare* autochthonous, autochthonic.
OPPOSITES expatriate; migrant; adventitious.

> **CHOOSE THE RIGHT WORD**
>
> **indigenous, native, aboriginal**
> *See* NATIVE.

indigent ▸ adjective *the first state pensions were given to indigent people over seventy* **poor**, impecunious, destitute, penniless, impoverished, poverty-stricken, down and out, pauperized, without a penny to one's name, without two farthings/pennies to rub together; insolvent, ruined; needy, in need, in want, hard up, on the breadline, hard-pressed, in reduced/straitened circumstances, deprived, disadvantaged, distressed, badly off; beggarly, beggared; *informal* on one's uppers, up against it, broke, flat broke, strapped (for cash), without a brass farthing, without a bean, without a sou, as poor as a church mouse, on one's beam-ends; *Brit. informal* stony broke, skint, boracic (lint); *N. Amer. informal* stone broke, without a red cent, on skid row; *formal* penurious.
OPPOSITE rich.

indigestion ▸ noun *crisps give me indigestion* **dyspepsia**, hyperacidity, acidity, heartburn, (a) stomach ache, (an) upset stomach, (a) stomach upset, a gastric upset; *informal* (a) bellyache, (a) tummy ache, collywobbles; *technical* pyrosis.

indignant ▸ adjective *he was indignant at the way he was being treated* **aggrieved**, resentful, affronted, disgruntled, discontented, dissatisfied, angry, distressed, unhappy, disturbed, hurt, pained, upset, offended, piqued, in high dudgeon, riled, nettled, vexed, irked, irritated, annoyed, put out, chagrined; *informal* peeved, miffed, aggravated, in a huff; *Brit. informal* cheesed off, browned off; *N. Amer. informal* sore, steamed; *vulgar slang* pissed off; *N. Amer. vulgar slang* pissed.
OPPOSITE content.

indignation ▸ noun *she was filled with indignation at having been blamed so unjustly* **resentment**, umbrage, affront, disgruntlement, anger, distress, unhappiness, discontent, dissatisfaction, displeasure, hurt, pain, upset, offence, pique, spleen, crossness, exasperation, vexation, irritation, annoyance, chagrin; *informal* aggravation; *literary* ire.
OPPOSITE contentment.

indignity ▸ noun *Annie has suffered the indignity of being dumped by her husband* **shame**, humiliation, loss of self-respect, loss of pride, embarrassment, mortification, abasement, degradation; disgrace, dishonour, stigma, disrepute, discredit, opprobrium, scandal, infamy, ignobility, loss of face; affront, insult, abuse, mistreatment, injury, offence, injustice, outrage, slight, snub, contempt, disrespect, discourtesy; *informal* slap in the face, kick in the teeth; *rare* obloquy.
OPPOSITES honour; glory.

indirect ▸ adjective **1** *motherhood has an indirect effect on pay* **incidental**, accidental, unintended, secondary, subordinate, ancillary, collateral, concomitant, accompanying, contingent, resulting, resultant, consequential, derived, derivative.
OPPOSITE direct.
2 *the indirect route is usually less congested* **roundabout**, circuitous, deviant, divergent, wandering, meandering, serpentine, winding, curving, tortuous, zigzag; *rare* anfractuous.
OPPOSITE direct.
3 *an indirect attack on the Archbishop* **oblique**, inexplicit, roundabout, circuitous; implicit, implied, allusive.

indirectly ▸ adverb **1** *the losses suffered by Lloyd's members indirectly affect us all* **incidentally**, accidentally, secondarily, concomitantly, contingently, consequentially.
OPPOSITE directly.
2 *I heard of the damage indirectly* **second-hand**, at second hand, in a roundabout way, from others; *informal* on the grapevine, on the bush/jungle telegraph.
3 *both writers refer, if only indirectly, to a wealth of other art* **obliquely**, by implication, by hinting, allusively.

indiscernible ▸ adjective **1** *the transition from brush to pen is indiscernible* **unnoticeable**, imperceptible, invisible, undetectable, indistinguishable, unapparent, inappreciable, barely perceptible, impalpable, unobtrusive, impossible to detect, hidden; tiny, minute, minuscule, microscopic, infinitesimal, negligible, inconsequential, slight, subtle, faint, fine.
OPPOSITE discernible.
2 *an indiscernible shape among the shadows | his words were indiscernible in the din* **indistinct**, unclear, fuzzy, obscure, vague, indefinite, nebulous, amorphous, shadowy, dim, hard to make out; unintelligible, incomprehensible, hard to understand, inaudible; *archaic* blear.
OPPOSITE distinct.

indiscreet ▸ adjective **1** *I wouldn't be so indiscreet as to reveal my source | an indiscreet remark* **imprudent**, impolitic, unwise, injudicious, incautious, irresponsible; ill-judged, ill-advised, misguided; ill-considered, careless, rash, unwary, hasty, reckless, precipitate, impulsive, foolhardy, foolish, short-sighted; undiplomatic, indelicate, tactless, insensitive; inexpedient, untimely, infelicitous.
OPPOSITE discreet.
2 *he looked long into her eyes—remarkably indiscreet behaviour with his wife present* **immodest**, indecorous, improper, indecent, indelicate, unseemly; forward, bold, brazen, impudent, unblushing, shameless; *informal* fresh, cheeky, naughty, saucy.
OPPOSITE decorous.

indiscretion ▸ noun **1** *they were obsessed with the need for secrecy and the dangers of indiscretion* **imprudence**, injudiciousness, lack of caution, incaution, irresponsibility; carelessness, rashness, unwariness, haste, recklessness, precipitateness, impulsiveness, foolhardiness, foolishness, folly, poor judgement, short-sightedness; indelicacy, tactlessness, lack of diplomacy, insensitivity.
OPPOSITE discretion.
2 *he admitted his past indiscretions to investigators* **blunder**, lapse, gaffe, mistake, error, breach of etiquette, slip, miscalculation, impropriety; misdemeanour, transgression, peccadillo, offence, misdeed, crime, felony, sin; (**indiscretions**) wrongdoing, misconduct, mischief, mischievousness, wickedness, misbehaviour, bad behaviour; *French* faux pas; *informal* slip-up; *archaic* trespass.

indiscriminate ▸ adjective *the indiscriminate bombing of cities | the furnishings were an indiscriminate mess* **non-selective**, unselective, undiscriminating, uncritical, aimless, hit-or-miss, haphazard, random, unsystematic, unmethodical; wholesale, general, sweeping, blanket; broad-based, wide, catholic, eclectic, varied, miscellaneous, heterogeneous, motley, confused, chaotic; thoughtless, unthinking, unconsidered, casual, careless; *rare* promiscuous.
OPPOSITES selective, discriminating; systematic.

indiscriminately ▸ adverb *his armies slaughtered men, women, and children indiscriminately* **randomly**, at random, unsystematically, aimlessly, unmethodically, without method, haphazardly, blindly, uncritically, undiscriminatingly, non-selectively, injudiciously; chaotically, erratically, casually, desultorily, arbitrarily; carelessly, unthinkingly, thoughtlessly, mindlessly; wholesale, without exception, across the board; *rare* undiscerningly, unselectively, promiscuously.
OPPOSITES selectively; systematically.

indispensable ▸ adjective *education is indispensable for the preservation of democracy* **essential**, crucial, necessary, key, vital, needed, required, called for, requisite, important, all-important, vitally important, of the utmost importance, of great consequence, of the essence, critical, life-and-death,

imperative, mandatory, compulsory, obligatory, compelling, urgent, pressing, burning, acute, paramount, pre-eminent, high-priority, significant, consequential.
OPPOSITES dispensable, superfluous, non-essential.

CHOOSE THE RIGHT WORD
indispensable, necessary, requisite, essential
See NECESSARY.

indisposed ▶ adjective **1** *the billed soloist was indisposed* **ill**, unwell, sick, on the sick list, infirm, poorly, ailing, not (very) well, not oneself, not in good shape, out of sorts, not up to par, under/below par; in bed, bedridden, confined to bed, laid up, out of commission, out of action; *Brit.* off, off colour; *French* hors de combat; *informal* under the weather.
OPPOSITE well.
2 *she was indisposed to criticize the same fault in others* **reluctant**, unwilling, disinclined, loath, unprepared, not ready, not disposed, not keen, not minded, not in the mood; slow, hesitant, afraid; averse, antipathetic, resistant, opposed; nervous about, not in favour of, unenthusiastic about.
OPPOSITE willing.

indisposition ▶ noun **1** *due to an indisposition, Herr Gesner will not be able to continue his performance* **illness**, ailment, disorder, sickness, affliction, malady, infirmity, malaise, disease, infection, upset; condition, complaint, problem, trouble; ill health; *informal* bug, virus; *Brit. informal* lurgy; *Austral. informal* wog.
2 *an utter **indisposition to do** anything whatever* **reluctance**, unwillingness, disinclination, unpreparedness; slowness, hesitation, hesitancy; aversion, resistance, opposition; nervousness about, antipathy towards, dislike of, distaste for, lack of enthusiasm for.
OPPOSITE willingness.

indisputable ▶ adjective *there is indisputable evidence that terrorists are to blame* **incontrovertible**, incontestable, undeniable, irrefutable, unassailable, beyond dispute, unquestionable, beyond question, indubitable, not in doubt, beyond doubt, beyond a shadow of a doubt, unarguable, inarguable, undebatable, unanswerable; unequivocal, unambiguous, unmistakable, certain, sure, definite, definitive, proven, positive, decisive, conclusive, final, ultimate; clear, clear-cut, straightforward, plain, as plain as a pikestaff, transparent, obvious, manifest, evident, self-evident, staring one in the face, patent, demonstrative, demonstrable, observable, palpable; uncontroversial, accepted, acknowledged; marked, pronounced, express, emphatic, categorical, compelling, convincing, clinching, airtight, watertight; *rare* irrefragable, apodictic.
OPPOSITE questionable.

indistinct ▶ adjective **1** *the distant shoreline behind them was indistinct* **blurred**, out of focus, fuzzy, hazy, misty, foggy, cloudy, shadowy, smoky, dim, nebulous; unclear, obscure, vague, faint, indefinite, indistinguishable, barely perceptible, undefined, lacking definition, hard to see, hard to make out; *archaic* blear; *rare* obfuscated, nebulose.
OPPOSITES distinct; clear.
2 *the last two digits of the number are indistinct* **indecipherable**, illegible, barely legible, unreadable, unintelligible, unfathomable, hard to read, hard to make out; undefined, ill-defined, lacking definition, formless, indeterminate; pale, faded, smudged; *informal* as clear as mud.
OPPOSITE legible.
3 *indistinct sounds emerged from the building* **muffled**, muted, dull, low, quiet, soft, faint, weak, feeble, inaudible, scarcely audible, scarcely perceptible, hard to hear, hard to make out; muttered, mumbled, stifled, strangled, smothered, suppressed.
OPPOSITES loud; clear.

CHOOSE THE RIGHT WORD
indistinct, vague, hazy
See VAGUE.

indistinguishable ▶ adjective **1** *the two girls were indistinguishable* **identical**, almost identical, the same, alike, very similar; cut from the same cloth, two of a kind, difficult to tell apart; *informal* as like as two peas in a pod, like Tweedledum and Tweedledee.
OPPOSITES dissimilar; easy to tell apart.
2 *in choral music the words are frequently indistinguishable* **unintelligible**, incomprehensible, hard to understand, hard to make out, indistinct, unclear, indefinite; inappreciable, indiscernible, imperceptible, inaudible.
OPPOSITES clear, distinguishable.

individual ▶ adjective **1** *exhibitions devoted to individual artists* **single**, separate, discrete, independent; sole, lone, solitary, isolated.
2 *he had his own individual style of music* **characteristic**, distinctive, distinct, typical, particular, peculiar, personal, personalized, special; *rare* especial.
OPPOSITE collective.
3 *he has a chic and highly individual apartment* **original**, unique, exclusive, singular, idiosyncratic, different, unusual, novel, unorthodox, atypical, out of the ordinary.
OPPOSITE ordinary.
▶ noun **1** *Peter was a rather stuffy individual* **person**, human being, human, being, mortal, soul, creature, thing; man, gentleman, boy, woman, lady, girl; figure, personage; *informal* character, type, sort, beggar, cookie, customer, guy, devil, bunny, bastard; *Brit. informal* bod, geezer, gent, punter; *informal, dated* body, dog, cove; *Brit. vulgar slang* sod, bugger; *archaic* wight.
2 *she enjoyed the freedom of being an individual* **individualist**, free spirit, nonconformist, original, eccentric, character, bohemian, maverick, rare bird, rarity; loner, lone wolf, outsider; *Latin* rara avis; *Brit. informal* one-off, oner.

individualism ▶ noun *collectivism is a more powerful force for productivity than individualism* **independence**, self-direction, self-reliance, freethinking, free thought, originality; unconventionality, eccentricity; libertarianism.

individualist ▶ noun *he was regarded as not merely an individualist but something of a crank* **free spirit**, individual, nonconformist, unorthodox person, unconventional person, original, eccentric, bohemian, maverick, rare bird, rarity; lone wolf, outsider; *Latin* rara avis; *Brit. informal* one-off, loner.
OPPOSITE conformist.

individualistic ▶ adjective *he took an individualistic approach to his subject* **unconventional**, unorthodox, uncommon, atypical, singular, unique, original, nonconformist, independent, freethinking, liberated, unconstrained, unfettered, untrammelled, pioneering, groundbreaking; eccentric, bohemian, maverick, strange, odd, peculiar, idiosyncratic.

individuality ▶ noun *we are motivated by the need to assert our individuality* **uniqueness**, originality, singularity, particularity, peculiarity, distinctiveness, distinction, differentness, separateness; personality, character, identity, self.

individually ▶ adverb *a panel will look at all of the applications individually* **one at a time**, one by one, singly, separately, independently, discretely, apart; *Latin* seriatim; *formal* severally.
OPPOSITE together.

indoctrinate ▶ verb *they use alien dogmas to indoctrinate the masses* **brainwash**, propagandize, proselytize, inculcate, re-educate, persuade, convince, condition, discipline, mould; instruct, teach, school, drill, ground.

indolence ▶ noun *my failure is probably due to my own indolence* **laziness**, idleness, slothfulness, sloth, shiftlessness, inactivity, inaction, inertia, lifelessness, sluggishness, lethargy, languor, languidness, torpor, torpidity, slowness, dullness; remissness, negligence, slackness, laxity; *rare* otiosity, hebetude.
OPPOSITES industriousness; energy.

indolent ▶ adjective *the pub is full of indolent young men* **lazy**, idle, slothful, loafing, work-shy, shiftless, apathetic, lackadaisical, inactive, inert, lifeless, sluggish, lethargic, listless, languid, torpid, slow, slow-moving, dull, plodding; slack, lax, remiss, negligent, good-for-nothing; *informal* bone idle; *French archaic* fainéant; *rare* otiose.
OPPOSITES industrious; energetic.

CHOOSE THE RIGHT WORD
indolent, lazy, idle
See LAZY.

indomitable ▶ adjective *these indomitable warriors have never been subjugated by an invading force* **invincible**, unconquerable, unbeatable, unassailable, impregnable, invulnerable, unsurpassable, unshakeable; indefatigable, unyielding, unbending, stalwart, stout-hearted, lionhearted, strong-willed, strong-minded, staunch, resolute, firm, steadfast, determined, intransigent, inflexible, adamant; unflinching, courageous, brave, valiant, heroic, intrepid, fearless, plucky, mettlesome, gritty, steely.
OPPOSITES submissive; weak.

indubitable ▶ adjective *he furnished indubitable evidence of his identity* **unquestionable**, undoubtable, indisputable, unarguable, inarguable, undebatable, incontestable, undeniable, irrefutable, incontrovertible, unmistakable, unequivocal, certain, sure, positive, definite, absolute, conclusive, emphatic, categorical, compelling, watertight, clear, clear-cut; beyond doubt, beyond the shadow of a doubt, beyond dispute, beyond question, not in question, not in doubt; *rare* irrefragable, apodictic.
OPPOSITE doubtful.

induce ▶ verb **1** *the pickets induced many workers to stay away* **persuade**, convince, prevail upon, get, make, prompt, move, inspire, instigate, influence, exert influence on, press, urge, incite, encourage, impel, actuate, motivate; coax into, wheedle into, cajole into, talk into, prod into; *Law* procure; *informal* twist someone's arm.
OPPOSITE dissuade.
2 *these activities induce a feeling of social togetherness* **bring about**, bring on,

cause, be the cause of, produce, effect, create, give rise to, generate, originate, instigate, engender, occasion, set in motion, develop, lead to, result in, have as a consequence, have as a result, trigger off, spark off, whip up, stir up, kindle, arouse, rouse, foster, promote, encourage; *literary* beget, enkindle; *rare* effectuate.
OPPOSITE prevent.

> **CHOOSE THE RIGHT WORD**
> **induce, convince, persuade**
> *See* CONVINCE.

inducement ▶ **noun** *shopkeepers began offering free gifts as an inducement to trade* **incentive**, attraction, encouragement, temptation, incitement, stimulation, stimulus, bait, lure, pull, draw, spur, goad, impetus, motive, motivation, provocation; bribe, reward; *informal* carrot, come-on, sweetener, perk; *rare* douceur.
OPPOSITE deterrent.

induct ▶ **verb 1** *eighteen new junior ministers were* **inducted into** *the government* **admit to**, allow into, introduce to, initiate into, install in, instate in, swear into; appoint to; be engaged by, be taken on by.
OPPOSITE bar from.
2 *my master* **inducted** *me* **into** *the skills of magic* **introduce to**, acquaint with, familiarize with, make familiar with, make conversant with, make aware of, inform of, give information about; ground in, instruct in, teach in, educate in, school in; *informal* fill in on, gen up on, clue up on, clue in on, put in the picture about.

indulge ▶ **verb 1** *Sally indulged her passion for long walks* **satisfy**, gratify, fulfil, satiate, quench, appease, feed, accommodate; go along with, yield to, give in to, give way to, pander to, cater to, comply with.
OPPOSITE frustrate.
2 *she* **indulged in** *a fit of sulks* **wallow in**, give oneself up to, give way to, yield to, abandon oneself to, give rein to, give free rein to; luxuriate in, revel in, lose oneself in.
OPPOSITE stifle.
3 *she did not like her children to be indulged* **pamper**, spoil, overindulge, coddle, mollycoddle, cosset, nanny, nursemaid, mother, baby, pet, spoon-feed, feather-bed, wrap in cotton wool; pander to, humour, wait on someone hand and foot, cater to someone's every whim, kill someone with kindness; *archaic* cocker.
□ **indulge oneself** *a man should indulge himself now and then* **treat oneself**, give oneself a treat, luxuriate in something, give oneself up to pleasure; splash out; *informal* have a spree, go to town, splurge.
OPPOSITE deny oneself.

indulgence ▶ **noun 1** *he squandered his money on the indulgence of all his desires* **satisfaction**, satisfying, gratification, gratifying, fulfilment, fulfilling, satiation, appeasement, assuagement, quenching, slaking; accommodation.
OPPOSITE denial.
2 *he took exercise as an antidote to excess indulgence* **self-gratification**, self-indulgence, overindulgence, intemperance, immoderation, immoderateness, dissipation, dissolution, dissoluteness, debauchery, excess, excessiveness, lack of restraint, prodigality, extravagance, decadence, pleasure-seeking, wantonness, lack of self-control; *rare* sybaritism.
OPPOSITE moderation.
3 *they viewed holidays abroad as an indulgence* **extravagance**, luxury, treat, comfort, non-essential, extra, frill.
OPPOSITE necessity.
4 *her indulgence left him spoilt* **pampering**, coddling, mollycoddling, cosseting, babying, mothering, nannying; spoiling, humouring, catering to someone's every whim; partiality.
5 *his parents view his lapses with indulgence* **tolerance**, forbearance, humanity, compassion, kindness, understanding, sympathy, liberalness, liberality, forgiveness, leniency, lenience, clemency, mercy, mercifulness.
OPPOSITE severity.

indulgent ▶ **adjective** *she had a very indulgent father* **permissive**, easy-going, broad-minded, liberal, tolerant, forgiving, forbearing, lenient, merciful, clement, mild, humane, kind, kindly, soft-hearted, caring, compassionate, understanding, sympathetic; fond, doting, pampering, mollycoddling, cosseting, soft; compliant, obliging, accommodating.
OPPOSITES strict; intolerant.

industrial ▶ **adjective 1** *the industrial areas of the city* **manufacturing**, factory; **commercial**, business, trade.
2 (*Brit.*) *their colleagues voted for industrial action* **strike**, protest.

industrialist ▶ **noun** **manufacturer**, producer, factory owner, factory boss; captain of industry, big businessman, top executive, magnate, tycoon, capitalist, financier, investor; *informal, derogatory* fat cat.

industrious ▶ **adjective** *he was honest, sober, and industrious* **hard-working**, diligent, assiduous, sedulous, conscientious, steady, painstaking, persistent, persevering, pertinacious, unflagging, untiring, tireless, indefatigable, studious; busy, busy as a bee, active, bustling, energetic, on the go, vigorous, determined, dynamic, zealous, productive; with one's shoulder to the wheel, with one's nose to the grindstone; *archaic* laborious.
OPPOSITE indolent.

> **CHOOSE THE RIGHT WORD**
> **industrious, diligent, hard-working**
> *See* HARD-WORKING.

industry ▶ **noun 1** *the decline of British industry* **manufacturing**, production, fabrication, construction.
2 *the publishing industry* **business**, trade, field, line, line of work, line of business, commercial enterprise, service; profession, occupation, craft; *informal* racket.
3 *the kitchen was a hive of industry* **hard work**, industriousness, diligence, assiduity, application, sedulousness, sedulity, conscientiousness, steadiness, tirelessness, persistence, pertinacity, perseverance, dedication, determination, rigour, rigorousness; **activity**, busyness, energy, vigour, effort, labour, dynamism, zeal, productiveness; *archaic* laboriousness, continuance; *rare* perseveration.
OPPOSITE indolence.

inebriated ▶ **adjective** *they helped to put the inebriated man to bed* **drunk**, intoxicated, inebriate, drunken, tipsy, the worse for drink, under the influence; blind drunk, dead drunk, rolling drunk, roaring drunk, as drunk as a lord, as drunk as a skunk; sottish, gin-soaked; *informal* tight, merry, the worse for wear, pie-eyed, three sheets to the wind, plastered, smashed, hammered, sloshed, soused, sozzled, well oiled, paralytic, wrecked, wasted, blotto, stewed, pickled, tanked up, soaked, blasted, ratted, off one's face, out of one's head, out of one's skull; *Brit. informal* legless, bevvied, Brahms and Liszt, half cut, out of it, bladdered, trolleyed, well away, squiffy, tiddly, out of one's box; *Scottish informal* fou; *N. Amer. informal* loaded, trashed, out of one's gourd; *Brit. vulgar slang* pissed, rat-arsed; *informal, dated* in one's cups, lit up; *euphemistic* tired and emotional; *archaic* sotted, foxed, screwed; *rare* crapulent, crapulous, bibulous, ebriate.
OPPOSITE sober.

inebriation ▶ **noun** *he's in a state of extreme inebriation* **intoxication**, drunkenness, insobriety, tipsiness; *informal* tightness; *rare* crapulence.
OPPOSITE sobriety.

inedible ▶ **adjective** *they were served with inedible fruit* **uneatable**, indigestible, unconsumable, unpalatable, unwholesome, unsavoury; stale, not fit to eat, rotten, off, bad, putrid, rancid.
OPPOSITE edible.

ineffable ▶ **adjective 1** *the ineffable natural beauty of the Everglades* **inexpressible**, indescribable, beyond words, beyond description, beggaring description; undefinable, unutterable, untold, unheard of, unthought of, unimaginable; overwhelming, marvellous, wonderful, breathtaking, staggering, astounding, amazing, astonishing, fantastic, fabulous.
2 *the ineffable name of God* **unutterable**, not to be uttered, not to be spoken, not to be said, unmentionable; taboo, forbidden, off limits, out of bounds; *informal* no go.

ineffective ▶ **adjective 1** *they made an ineffective attempt to resolve the issue* **unsuccessful**, non-successful, unproductive, fruitless, profitless, unprofitable, abortive, failed, futile, purposeless, worthless, useless, ineffectual, inefficient, inefficacious, inadequate, vain, unavailing, to no effect; idle, feeble, weak, inept, lame; *archaic* bootless; *rare* unfructuous, inutile.
OPPOSITE effective.
2 *he was a weak and ineffective president* **ineffectual**, inefficient, inefficacious, unsuccessful, powerless, impotent, inadequate, incompetent, incapable, unfit, inept, lame, feeble, weak, poor; *informal* useless, hopeless.
OPPOSITE effective.

ineffectual ▶ **adjective 1** *the state was under the control of ineffectual rulers* **inefficient**, ineffective, inefficacious, unsuccessful, powerless, impotent, inadequate, inept, incompetent, incapable, unfit, lame, feeble, weak, poor; *informal* useless, hopeless, rotten, lousy, no good.
2 *she made an ineffectual effort to escape* **ineffective**, unproductive, unsuccessful, non-successful, profitless, fruitless, futile, failed, abortive, vain, unavailing, useless, worthless, inadequate, inefficient, inefficacious, lame, inept, bungled, bungling; *archaic* bootless; *rare* unfructuous, inutile.

inefficacious ▶ **adjective** *the old way of doing things was suddenly inefficacious. See* INEFFECTIVE.

inefficient ▶ **adjective 1** *my boss thinks I'm inefficient* **ineffective**, ineffectual, inefficacious, incompetent, inept, incapable, unfit, unsuitable, unskilled, unskilful, inexpert, amateurish; disorganized, badly organized, unprepared, undisciplined, negligent, lax, slipshod, sloppy, slack, remiss, careless; *informal* lousy, useless; *Brit. vulgar slang* not capable of organizing a piss-up in a brewery.

OPPOSITE efficient.
2 *a series of elaborate and inefficient processes* **uneconomical**, wasteful, purposeless, unproductive, time-wasting, slow, slow-moving, awkward, unwieldy, cumbersome, badly arranged, deficient, disorganized, unsystematic.
OPPOSITE efficient.

inelegant ▶ adjective **1** *Amanda gave an inelegant bellow of laughter* **unrefined**, uncouth, unsophisticated, unpolished, uncultured, uncultivated, gauche; crude, ill-bred, coarse, vulgar, rude, impolite, unmannerly.
OPPOSITES refined; polite.
2 *she danced in a stiff and inelegant way* **ungraceful**, graceless, ungainly, uncoordinated, gawky, gangling, awkward, clumsy, lumbering, blundering; inept, unskilful, inexpert; *informal* with two left feet, like a bull in a china shop.
OPPOSITE elegant.

ineligible ▶ adjective **1** *students are ineligible for housing benefit* **unqualified**, ruled out, disqualified, legally disqualified, disentitled; *Law* incompetent.
OPPOSITE eligible.
2 (*dated*) *she was in love with someone who was ineligible* **unmarriageable**, unavailable, not available for marriage, married; **unsuitable**, unacceptable, undesirable, inappropriate, unworthy, not good enough; *informal* not up to scratch, not up to snuff.
OPPOSITES eligible; suitable.

inept ▶ adjective *my attempts at baking were inept but I fumbled on* **incompetent**, unskilful, unskilled, inexpert, amateurish, crude, rough; clumsy, awkward, maladroit, unhandy, heavy-handed, bungling, blundering, bumbling, botched; unproductive, unsuccessful, ineffectual, inadequate, inferior, substandard, wanting, lacking, not up to scratch; *informal* cack-handed, ham-fisted, ham-handed, butterfingered; *Brit. informal* all thumbs, all fingers and thumbs; *N. Amer. informal* klutzy.
OPPOSITE competent.

inequality ▶ noun **1** *a society without social inequality* **imbalance**, inequity, unevenness, disproportion, inconsistency, variation, variability; divergence, polarity, disparity, discrepancy, dissimilarity, difference, contrast, distinction, differential; bias, prejudice, discrimination, unfairness, unfair treatment.
OPPOSITES equality; uniformity.
2 (*archaic*) *the inequality of the ground hindered their footing* **unevenness**, irregularity, roughness.
OPPOSITE evenness.

inequitable ▶ adjective *a crude and inequitable process for setting salary rates* **unfair**, unjust, discriminatory, preferential, one-sided, unequal, uneven, unbalanced, loaded, weighted, slanted, non-objective, biased, partisan, partial, prejudiced.
OPPOSITES fair; impartial.

inequity ▶ noun *we wish to emphasize the inequity of the present law* **unfairness**, injustice, unjustness, one-sidedness, partisanship, partiality, favouritism, bias, prejudice, discrimination.

inert ▶ adjective **1** *she lay inert in her bed* **unmoving**, motionless, immobile, still, stock-still, stationary, static, dormant, sleeping; unconscious, out cold, comatose, lifeless, inanimate, insensible, senseless, insensate, insentient; inactive, idle, indolent, slack, lazy, loafing, slothful, dull, sluggish, lethargic, stagnant, languid, listless, torpid; unconcerned, apathetic, indifferent; *informal* dead to the world; *French archaic* fainéant; *rare* soporose, soporous, otiose.
OPPOSITES moving; active.
2 *the inert gases in meteorites* **chemically inactive**.

inertia ▶ noun *he showed signs of lapsing into inertia* **inactivity**, inaction, inactiveness, inertness, passivity, apathy, accidie, malaise, stagnation, dullness, enervation, sluggishness, lethargy, languor, languidness, listlessness, torpor, torpidity, idleness, indolence, laziness, sloth, slothfulness; motionlessness, immobility, lifelessness; *French archaic* fainéance; *rare* stasis, otiosity, hebetude.
OPPOSITES activity; energy.

inescapable ▶ adjective *they concluded that political reform was inescapable* **unavoidable**, inevitable, ineluctable, inexorable, assured, sure, certain, bound to happen, sure to happen, preordained, predestined, predetermined; necessary, required, compulsory, mandatory; *rare* ineludible.
OPPOSITE avoidable.

inessential ▶ adjective *he cut out the inessential details* **unnecessary**, not necessary, not essential, non-essential, not needed, not required, unwanted, uncalled-for, needless, redundant, superfluous, excessive, excess, surplus, dispensable, expendable, optional, ornamental, cosmetic; unimportant, minor, secondary, peripheral; *rare* supererogatory.
OPPOSITE essential.

inestimable ▶ adjective *he believes the diet brings inestimable benefits* **immeasurable**, incalculable, innumerable, unfathomable, fathomless, indeterminable, measureless, untold; limitless, boundless, unbounded, unlimited, illimitable, infinite, endless, never-ending, interminable, inexhaustible, bottomless; vast, immense, great, abundant; *informal* no end of; *literary* myriad; *rare* innumerous, unnumberable.
OPPOSITE few.

inevitable ▶ adjective *his resignation was inevitable* **unavoidable**, inescapable, bound to happen, sure to happen, inexorable, assured, certain, for sure, sure, fated, predestined, predetermined, preordained, ineluctable; necessary, compulsory, required, obligatory, mandatory, prescribed; *rare* ineludible.
OPPOSITES avoidable; uncertain.

inevitably ▶ adverb *the poor crop will inevitably affect the price of the wine* **naturally**, automatically, as a matter of course, necessarily, of necessity, by force of circumstance, inescapably, unavoidably, ineluctably, certainly, surely, definitely, incontrovertibly, undoubtedly; as a result, as a consequence, consequently, accordingly; *Latin* nolens volens; *informal* like it or not; *formal* perforce.

inexact ▶ adjective *his description of the procedure is inexact* **imprecise**, not accurate, not exact, approximate, rough, crude, general, vague, hazy, woolly; incorrect, erroneous, wrong, false, fallacious, wide of the mark, off target, off, out, wanting, lacking; *N. Amer. informal* ballpark.
OPPOSITE exact.

inexcusable ▶ adjective *Geoffrey's behaviour was inexcusable* **indefensible**, unjustifiable, unjustified, unwarrantable, unwarranted, unpardonable, unforgivable, inexpiable; blameworthy, censurable, reprehensible, deplorable, unconscionable, outrageous, disgraceful, regrettable, unacceptable, unreasonable, unworthy; uncalled-for, unprovoked, gratuitous, without cause, without reason, without justification.
OPPOSITE excusable.

inexhaustible ▶ adjective **1** *her patience seemed inexhaustible* **unlimited**, limitless, illimitable, without limit, infinite, unbounded, boundless, endless, never-ending, unending, without end, unfailing, everlasting, bottomless, measureless, immeasurable, incalculable, inestimable, untold; copious, abundant.
OPPOSITE limited.
2 *the dancers were inexhaustible* **tireless**, indefatigable, untiring, unwearying, weariless, unfaltering, unfailing, unflagging, unwavering, unremitting, persevering, persistent, dogged.
OPPOSITES weary; lacking stamina.

inexorable ▶ adjective **1** *the inexorable advance of science* **relentless**, unstoppable, unavoidable, inescapable, inevitable, irrevocable; persistent, continuous, non-stop, steady, unabating, interminable, incessant, unceasing, unending, unremitting, unrelenting.
2 *fifty debtors were detained by inexorable creditors* **intransigent**, unbending, unyielding, inflexible, unswerving, unwavering, adamant, obdurate, determined, immovable, unshakeable, implacable, unappeasable, unpacifiable, unplacatable, unmollifiable, unforgiving, unsparing, uncompromising; strict, severe, iron-handed, stringent, harsh, hard, tough, exacting, rigorous, draconian, cruel, ruthless, relentless, unrelenting, pitiless, merciless, remorseless; *rare* indurate.

inexpedient ▶ adjective *it was inexpedient to antagonize these people* **unadvisable**, injudicious, unwise, impolitic, imprudent, incautious, irresponsible, thoughtless, careless, foolhardy, foolish, silly, wrong-headed, short-sighted; ill-advised, ill-judged, ill-considered; undiplomatic, tactless, indiscreet, inappropriate; disadvantageous, detrimental, prejudicial, harmful, damaging.
OPPOSITES advisable; wise.

inexpensive ▶ adjective *a retail chain specializing in inexpensive furniture* **cheap**, low-priced, low-price, low-cost, economical, economic, competitive, affordable, reasonable, reasonably priced, moderately priced, keenly priced, budget, economy, cheap and cheerful, bargain, cut-rate, cut-price, half-price, sale-price, sale, reduced, on special offer, marked down, discounted, discount, rock-bottom, giveaway; *informal* bargain-basement, slashed, going for a song, dirt cheap.
OPPOSITE expensive.

inexperience ▶ noun *his mistakes will be put down to youthful inexperience* **ignorance**, unawareness, unenlightenment, lack of knowledge, lack of education; unworldliness, naivety, naiveness, innocence, rawness, freshness, greenness, immaturity; *informal* cluelessness; *literary* nescience.

inexperienced ▶ adjective *the new secretary was enthusiastic but inexperienced* **inexpert**, unpractised, lacking experience, untrained, untutored, unschooled, unqualified, unskilled, amateur, uninitiated; uninformed, ignorant, unacquainted, unversed, unfledged, untried, unseasoned; naive, unsophisticated, callow, immature, fresh, green, raw; *informal* wet behind the ears, wide-eyed, out of one's depth, born yesterday.
OPPOSITE experienced.

inexpert ▶ adjective *the crane was manoeuvred by inexpert operators* **unskilled**, unskilful, amateur, amateurish, unprofessional, untrained, unpractised, unqualified, inexperienced; inept, incompetent, maladroit, clumsy, awkward, bungling, bumbling, blundering, heavy-handed, unhandy; *informal* cack-handed, ham-fisted, ham-handed, butterfingered; *Brit. informal* all fingers and thumbs, all thumbs.

OPPOSITE expert.

inexplicable ▶ adjective *she had had an inexplicable change of heart* **unaccountable**, unexplainable, incomprehensible, unfathomable, impenetrable, insoluble, unsolvable, baffling, puzzling, perplexing, mystifying, bewildering, mysterious, strange, weird, abstruse, enigmatic; beyond comprehension, beyond understanding; *archaic* wildering; *rare* insolvable.
OPPOSITE understandable.

inexpressible ▶ adjective *he felt inexpressible gratitude towards her* **indescribable**, undefinable, unutterable, unspeakable, incommunicable, ineffable; beyond words, beyond description, beggaring description; unimaginable, inconceivable, unthinkable, untold, overwhelming, intense, profound.

inexpressive ▶ adjective *their faces were utterly inexpressive* **expressionless**, unexpressive, impassive, inscrutable, unreadable, emotionless, blank, bland, vacant, empty, glazed, fixed, lifeless, inanimate, deadpan, wooden, stony; poker-faced, straight-faced.
OPPOSITE expressive.

inextinguishable ▶ adjective *he's known for his inextinguishable good humour* **irrepressible**, unquenchable, imperishable, indestructible, undying, unfading, unfailing, unceasing, ceaseless, enduring, lasting, everlasting, eternal, persistent, incessant.

inextricable ▶ adjective **1** *the past and the present are inextricable* **inseparable**, impossible to separate, indivisible, entangled, tangled, ravelled, mixed up, confused.
2 *an inextricable situation* **inescapable**, impossible to escape from, unavoidable.

I

infallible ▶ adjective **1** *she had an infallible sense of timing* **unerring**, error-free, unfailing, faultless, flawless, impeccable, perfect, true, uncanny, precise, accurate, meticulous, scrupulous; *Brit. informal* spot on; *N. Amer. informal* on the money.
2 *infallible cures for a variety of ailments* **unfailing**, never failing, always effective, guaranteed, dependable, trustworthy, reliable, sure, certain, safe, sound, tried and tested, foolproof, effective, efficacious; *informal* sure-fire.

infamous ▶ adjective **1** *a portrait of an infamous mass murderer* **notorious**, disreputable, ill-famed, of ill-repute; legendary, fabled, well-known.
OPPOSITE reputable.
2 *they disqualified the doctor for infamous misconduct* **abominable**, outrageous, shocking, shameful, disgraceful, dishonourable, discreditable, unworthy, unprincipled, unscrupulous; monstrous, atrocious, appalling, dreadful, terrible, heinous, detestable, disgusting, loathsome, hateful, wicked, vile, base, unspeakable, unforgivable, iniquitous, criminal, odious, nefarious, scandalous; *informal* dirty, filthy, low-down; *Brit. informal* beastly; *formal* egregious, flagitious, exceptionable.
OPPOSITE honourable.

infamy ▶ noun **1** *these acts brought him fame and infamy* **notoriety**, disrepute, disreputableness, ill repute, ill fame, loss of reputation, disgrace, discredit, shame, dishonour, ignominy, scandal, censure, blame, disapprobation, condemnation, contempt; humiliation, loss of face; *rare* disesteem.
OPPOSITES honour; anonymity.
2 *she was to be suitably punished for her infamy* **wickedness**, evil, baseness, sordidness, vileness, iniquity, iniquitousness, depravity, degeneracy, turpitude, immorality, unscrupulousness, corruption, dissolution; sin, wrong, offence, violation, abuse, indignity.
OPPOSITE virtue.

infancy ▶ noun **1** *her two daughters died in infancy* **babyhood**, early childhood; one's early years, one's early days.
OPPOSITE old age.
2 *the infancy of radio broadcasting* **beginnings**, very beginnings, early days, early stages, seeds, roots; start, launch, debut, rise, emergence, outset, onset, dawn, dawning, birth, cradle, inception, conception, genesis; *formal* commencement.
OPPOSITE end.

infant ▶ noun *she picked up the fretful infant* **baby**, newborn, young child, little child, little one; *Scottish & N. English* bairn, wean; *informal* tot, tiny tot, tiny, sprog; *literary* babe, babe in arms; *technical* neonate.
▶ adjective *the protection of infant industries* **developing**, emergent, emerging, dawning, embryonic, nascent, new, fledgling, budding, burgeoning, growing, up-and-coming.

infantile ▶ adjective *he refused to play their infantile games* **childish**, babyish, immature, puerile, juvenile, adolescent; silly, foolish, inane, fatuous, jejune.
OPPOSITE mature.

infantry ▶ noun *casualties were high among the infantry* **infantrymen**, foot soldiers, foot guards; the ranks, the rank and file, cannon fodder; (*in the US*) GIs; *Brit. informal* Tommies; *military slang* infanteers, grunts; *US informal, dated* dogfaces, doughboys; *historical* footmen.

infatuated ▶ adjective *Sarah seemed to be* **infatuated with** *John* **besotted**, in love, head over heels in love, hopelessly in love, obsessed, taken; passionate about, consumed with desire for, (greatly) enamoured of, very attracted to, devoted to, charmed by, captivated by, enchanted by, beguiled by, bewitched by, fascinated by, enraptured by, under the spell of, hypnotized by; *informal* smitten with, sweet on, keen on, gone on, mad about, wild about, crazy about, nuts about, potty about, stuck on, hung up on, turned on by, swept off one's feet by, bowled over by, carrying a torch for.

infatuation ▶ noun *he was aware of his brother's* **infatuation with** *Joan | an* **infatuation with** *motorcycles* **passion for**, love for, adoration of, desire for, fondness for, feeling for, regard for, devotion to, penchant for, preoccupation with, obsession with, fixation with, craze for, mania for, addiction to; fancy, passing fancy; *informal* crush on, thing about, hang-up about; pash, puppy love, calf love; *rare* mash.
OPPOSITE indifference to.

infect ▶ verb **1** *people with HIV can infect their partners* **pass infection to**, transmit infection to, spread disease to, contaminate; cause infection in, cause disease in.
2 *the nitrates were infecting more and more river systems* **contaminate**, pollute, make impure, taint, foul, dirty, blight, spoil, mar, impair, damage, ruin; poison, radioactivate; *rare* vitiate.
OPPOSITES purify; disinfect.
3 *his high spirits often infect all those present* **affect**, have an effect on, influence, have an impact on, impact on, touch, take hold of; excite, inspire, stimulate, animate.

infection ▶ noun **1** *she was treated for a kidney infection* **disease**, virus, contagion; disorder, condition, affliction, problem, complaint, illness, ailment, sickness, infirmity, indisposition; *informal* bug; *Brit. informal* lurgy.
2 *an attempt to reduce the infection in his head wounds* **contamination**, poison; **septicity**, septicaemia, ulceration, suppuration, inflammation; germs, bacteria, microbes; *technical* sepsis.

infectious ▶ adjective **1** *the control of infectious disease by vaccination* **contagious**, communicable, transmittable, transmissible, transferable, conveyable, spreadable, spreading; *informal* catching; *technical* epidemic, pandemic, epizootic; *dated* infective.
2 *infectious body fluids* **contaminating**, germ-laden, polluting, pestilential, virulent; poisonous, toxic, noxious.
3 *her laughter is infectious* **irresistible**, compelling; **contagious**, catching, spreading, communicable.

infelicitous ▶ adjective *his infelicitous use of certain phrases* **unfortunate**, regrettable, unsuitable, inappropriate, inapposite, inapt, inadvisable, injudicious, untimely, inopportune; imprudent, incautious, indiscreet, indelicate, tactless, insensitive.
OPPOSITES felicitous; appropriate.

infelicity ▶ noun *I bear full responsibility for any infelicities in the text* **mistake**, error, blunder, slip, lapse, solecism, misusage, impropriety.

infer ▶ verb *the judge inferred that the deceased was murdered* **deduce**, reason, work out, conclude, come to the conclusion, draw the inference, conjecture, surmise, theorize, hypothesize; gather, understand, presume, assume, take it, come to understand, glean, extrapolate, reckon; read between the lines; *N. Amer.* figure; *Brit. informal* suss, suss out; *archaic* collect.

> **infer or imply?**
>
> **Infer** is often used as though it meant the same as **imply**, but the two are in fact quite distinct. To *infer* something is to work it out from a statement or other evidence that suggests or entails it but does not make it explicit (*if he gives no explanation of his action the court may infer that he had no good reason*). To *imply* something, on the other hand, is to allow it to be understood from what one says without making it explicit (*you implied that I was free to go*). *Infer* and *imply* can describe the same event of someone's deducing an unspoken message from a statement, but *infer* looks at it from the viewpoint of the person who does the interpreting, while *imply* looks at it from the viewpoint of the one conveying the message.

inference ▶ noun *the doctor's inference appears legitimate* **deduction**, conclusion, reasoning, conjecture, speculation, surmise, thesis, theorizing, hypothesizing, presumption, assumption, supposition, reckoning, extrapolation, reading between the lines; guesswork, guessing; *informal* guesstimate; *rare* ratiocination.

inferior ▶ adjective **1** *they are regarded as inferior by other staff* **lower in status**, lesser, second-class, second-fiddle, minor, subservient, lowly, humble, menial, not very important, not so important, below someone, beneath someone, under someone's heel; lower-ranking, lower in rank, subordinate, junior, secondary, subsidiary, ancillary.
OPPOSITES superior; senior.
2 *I had to put up with inferior accommodation* **second-rate**, substandard, low-quality, low-grade, downmarket, indifferent, mediocre, unsatisfactory, shoddy, shabby, deficient, flawed, imperfect, unsound; poor, bad, awful, dreadful, disagreeable, deplorable, wretched, leaving much to be desired; *informal* grotty, crummy, dire, rotten, lousy, poxy,

third-rate, God-awful, not up to much, not up to snuff, the pits; *Brit. informal* duff, rubbish, ropy, pants, a load of pants.
OPPOSITES first-rate, high quality.
▶ **noun** *how dare she treat him as an inferior?* **subordinate**, junior, underling, minion, menial.
OPPOSITE superior.

inferiority ▶ **noun 1** *he was overcoming his feelings of inferiority* **lowliness**, inferior status, inferior position, secondary status, secondary position, subordination, subservience, subjection, servitude.
OPPOSITE superiority.
2 *the inferiority of the goods they sold* **shoddiness**, second-rateness, substandardness, unfitness, unsatisfactoriness, poorness, cheapness, mediocrity, indifference; imperfection, faultiness, deficiency; *Brit. informal* grottiness.

infernal ▶ **adjective 1** *the infernal regions* **of hell**, **hellish**, lower, nether, subterranean, underworld; Hadean, Plutonic, Plutonian, Stygian, Styxian, Tartarean, Acherontic, Avernal; *rare* chthonic, helly.
2 (*informal*) *you're an infernal nuisance* **damned**, damn, damnable, wretched, accursed, rotten, horrible; annoying, irritating, infuriating, exasperating; *informal* flaming, blasted, blessed, dratted, cussed, pesky, pestiferous, pestilential, aggravating; *Brit. informal* blinking, bloody, bleeding, blooming, flipping, effing, chuffing; *Austral./NZ informal* plurry; *Brit. informal, dated* bally, ruddy, deuced, dashed, cursed; *vulgar slang* frigging, fucking.

infertile ▶ **adjective 1** *their land has infertile, stony soil* **barren**, non-fertile, unfruitful, unproductive, non-productive, uncultivatable, lifeless, sterile, impoverished, arid; *rare* unfructuous.
OPPOSITE fertile.
2 *she was infertile as a result of the illness* **sterile**, barren; childless; *Medicine* infecund.
OPPOSITE fertile.

infest ▶ **verb** *a plague of field mice infested the housing estate* **overrun**, spread through, take over, overspread, swarm over, crawl over, run riot over; invade, penetrate, infiltrate, pervade, permeate, inundate, overwhelm; beset, pester, plague.

infested ▶ **adjective** *her house is infested with cockroaches* **overrun**, swarming, teeming, crawling, bristling, alive, ridden, infiltrated, permeated; plagued, beset; *rare* vermined.

infidel ▶ **noun** *a holy war against the infidels* **unbeliever**, disbeliever, non-believer, heathen, pagan, idolater, idolatress, heretic, agnostic, atheist, nihilist, apostate, freethinker, libertine, dissenter, nonconformist; *archaic* paynim; *rare* nullifidian.

infidelity ▶ **noun** *her husband never knew of her infidelity* **unfaithfulness**, adultery, unchastity, cuckoldry, extramarital relations, extramarital sex; faithlessness, disloyalty, falseness, breach of trust, treachery, double-dealing, duplicity, deceit, perfidy, perfidiousness; affair, liaison, intrigue, amour; *informal* fooling around, playing around, playing the field, cheating, two-timing, hanky-panky, a bit on the side; *archaic* fornication.
OPPOSITES fidelity, faithfulness.

infiltrate ▶ **verb 1** *he sought to infiltrate the smuggling operation* **insinuate oneself into**, worm one's way into, sneak into, slip into, creep into, invade, intrude on, impinge on, trespass on, butt into; *informal* gatecrash, muscle in on.
2 *mineral solutions infiltrate the rocks* **permeate**, penetrate, pervade, filter through, percolate through, spread through, seep into, seep through, soak into, flow into, pass into, get into, enter.

infiltrator ▶ **noun** *the constant vigilance needed to outwit enemy infiltrators* **spy**, agent, secret agent, undercover agent, operative, plant, intruder, interloper, subversive, informant, informer, mole, entrist, entryist; *informal* gatecrasher; *N. Amer. informal* spook; *archaic* intelligencer.

infinite ▶ **adjective 1** *the universe is spatially infinite* **boundless**, unbounded, unlimited, limitless, without limit, without end, never-ending, interminable; measureless, immeasurable, fathomless, unfathomed, bottomless; extensive, vast.
OPPOSITE limited.
2 *an infinite number of small birds* **countless**, uncountable, inestimable, indeterminable, innumerable, numberless, immeasurable, incalculable, untold, very many; great, vast, enormous, immense, prodigious, multitudinous; *rare* innumerous, unnumberable.
OPPOSITES limited; small.
3 *she bathed the wound with infinite care* **very great**, immense, supreme, absolute, total, real; endless, unending, unlimited; *informal* no end of.
OPPOSITE very little.

infinitesimal ▶ **adjective** *a tiny fish with infinitesimal white scales* **minute**, tiny, minuscule, extremely small, very small; microscopic, barely perceptible, imperceptible, inappreciable, indiscernible, invisible to the naked eye; *Scottish* wee; *informal* teeny, teeny-weeny, teensy-weensy, eensy-weensy, itsy-bitsy, itty-bitty, tiddly; *Brit. informal* titchy; *N. Amer. informal* little-bitty.
OPPOSITE huge.

infinity ▶ **noun 1** *she stared out into the infinity of space* **endlessness**, infinitude, infiniteness, boundlessness, limitlessness, unlimitedness, extensiveness, vastness, immensity; infinite distance.
2 *an infinity of different molecules* **infinite number**, unlimited number, very great number, abundance, profusion, host, multitude, mass, wealth; *informal* heap, stack, ton; *Brit. informal* shedload.
OPPOSITE limited number.

WORD LINKS
fear of infinity **apeirophobia**

infirm ▶ **adjective 1** *she looks after elderly and infirm people* **frail**, weak, feeble, enfeebled, weakly, debilitated, decrepit, disabled, bedridden; ill, unwell, sick, sickly, poorly, indisposed, in poor/declining health, failing, ailing; crippled, lame, doddering, doddery, tottering, wobbly, unsteady, unstable.
OPPOSITES strong, healthy.
2 (*archaic*) *he was infirm of purpose* **weak**, hesitant, uncertain, unsettled; indefinite, indecisive, irresolute, unresolved, undetermined, wavering, vacillating, fluctuating, faltering, undecided.
OPPOSITES strong, certain.

infirmity ▶ **noun 1** *they excused themselves on grounds of age and infirmity* **frailty**, weakness, feebleness, enfeeblement, delicacy, fragility, debility, debilitation, decrepitude, disability, impairment; illness, sickness, indisposition, poor health, declining health; lameness, dodderiness, shakiness, unsteadiness, instability.
OPPOSITES strength, good health.
2 *the infirmities of old age* **ailment**, malady, illness, disease, disorder, sickness, affliction, complaint, upset, condition, indisposition.
3 *he struggled throughout his life with his own infirmity of will* **weakness**, hesitation, uncertainty, inconstancy; indecision, irresolution, irresoluteness, vacillation, fluctuation.
OPPOSITES strength, certainty.

inflame ▶ **verb 1** *the play's impact inflames anti-Semitism* **incite**, arouse, rouse, provoke, animate, stir up, work up, whip up, kindle, fire, ignite, touch off, foment, actuate, inspire; stimulate, agitate, spur on.
OPPOSITES dampen, calm.
2 *he made comments that inflamed what was already a sensitive situation* **aggravate**, exacerbate, intensify, worsen, make worse, compound; add fuel to the flames, fan the flames, rub salt in the wound.
OPPOSITE soothe.
3 *his opinions so inflamed his rival that they came to blows* **enrage**, incense, anger, infuriate, exasperate, madden, send into a rage, provoke, antagonize, rile, gall; *informal* make someone see red, make someone's blood boil, drive mad/crazy; *rare* empurple.
OPPOSITE placate.

inflamed ▶ **adjective 1** *they treated her inflamed skin* **swollen**, puffed up; **red**, reddened, raw, hot, burning, itchy, itching, chafing, smarting, stinging, angry, angry-looking; sore, painful, tender, sensitive; infected, festered, septic.
2 *her face was inflamed with rage* **red**, flushed, high coloured, burning, flaming, florid.

inflammable ▶ **adjective** *inflammable gases* **flammable**, combustible, incendiary, explosive; unstable, volatile; *rare* burnable, ignitable, deflagrable.
OPPOSITES incombustible, fireproof, non-flammable.

inflammation ▶ **noun** *inflammation of the gums* **swelling**, puffiness; redness, rawness, hotness, heat, burning, smarting, stinging; soreness, pain, painfulness, tenderness, sensitivity; infection, festering, eruption, suppuration, septicity.

inflammatory ▶ **adjective 1** *an inflammatory lung condition* **causing inflammation**, causing swelling; irritant; *technical* erythrogenic.
2 *a play containing inflammatory material* **provocative**, provoking, inflaming, incendiary, inciting, agitating, stirring, rousing, instigative, fomenting; like a red rag to a bull; rabble-rousing, demagogic, hate-mongering, seditious, mutinous, revolutionary, rebellious, insurgent, anarchic; fiery, passionate, emotional, emotive; controversial, contentious.
OPPOSITE uncontroversial.

inflate ▶ **verb 1** *we started to inflate the balloons | the mattress inflated* **blow up**, **fill with air**, aerate, fill up, puff up, puff out, pump up; dilate, distend, swell.
OPPOSITE deflate.
2 *one effect of the demand for second homes was to inflate prices* **increase**, raise, put up, boost, escalate, step up; *informal* hike up, jack up, bump up.
OPPOSITES decrease, depress.
3 *numbers have been greatly inflated by the local press* **exaggerate**, magnify, pump up, overplay, overstate, dramatize, elaborate, enhance, embellish, touch up, blow up, blow up out of all proportion; increase, extend, amplify, augment, expand, intensify, swell; stretch the truth; *informal* make a big thing out of.
OPPOSITES play down, understate.

I

inflated ▶ adjective **1** *an inflated balloon* **blown up**, aerated, filled, puffed up, puffed out, pumped up; dilated, distended, stretched, expanded, engorged, enlarged, swollen.
OPPOSITE deflated.
2 *consumers pay inflated food prices* **increased**, raised, boosted; **high**, excessive, sky-high, unreasonable, unwarranted, disproportionate, prohibitive, outrageous, overinflated, exorbitant, extortionate; *Brit.* over the odds; *informal* over the top, OTT, steep.
OPPOSITES reduced, low.
3 *he had an inflated opinion of his worth* **exaggerated**, magnified, aggrandized, unwarranted, immoderate, pumped up, overblown, overstated, overplayed.
OPPOSITES low, humble.
4 *inflated language* **high-flown**, extravagant, exaggerated, elaborate, flowery, florid, ornate, overblown, overdone, overwrought, grandiloquent, magniloquent, grandiose, lofty, rhetorical, oratorical, verbose, affected, pretentious, turgid, bombastic, declamatory; *informal* windy, purple, highfalutin, la-di-da; *rare* fustian, euphuistic, orotund, tumid.
OPPOSITES plain, simple.

inflection ▶ noun **1** *these distinctions are often encoded in verbal inflections* **conjugation**, declension; form, ending, case.
2 *his voice was completely without inflection* **stress**, cadence, rhythm, accentuation, intonation, emphasis, modulation, metre, measure, rise and fall, swing, lilt, beat, change of pitch, change of tone, change of timbre.
3 (*technical*) *a point of inflection* **curving**, curvature, bending, turning; curve, bend, turn, bow, crook, angle, arc, arch.

I

inflexible ▶ adjective **1** *the committee's inflexible attitude* **stubborn**, obstinate, obdurate, intractable, intransigent, unbending, immovable, inexorable, unadaptable, unaccommodating; hidebound, set in one's ways, blinkered, single-minded, pig-headed, mulish; uncompromising, dogged, adamant, firm, resolute, diehard, steely, iron-willed, dyed-in-the-wool; *formal* refractory.
OPPOSITES flexible, accommodating.
2 *a landlady with inflexible house rules* **unalterable**, unchangeable, unvarying, unwavering, unshakeable, entrenched; firm, fixed, set, established, hard and fast, uncompromising; stringent, rigorous, strict, severe, inexorable, immutable.
OPPOSITE flexible.
3 *an inflexible metal plate* **rigid**, stiff, non-flexible, unyielding, unbending, unbendable, taut, hard, firm, inelastic; *rare* impliable, unmalleable.
OPPOSITES flexible, pliable.

inflict ▶ verb **1** *I came close to inflicting a serious injury on Frank* **administer to**, deal out to, mete out to, serve out to, deliver to, apply to; lay, impose, exact, wreak; cause to, give to.
2 *I had no desire to inflict an alcoholic parent on my children* **impose**, force, press, thrust, foist; saddle someone with, land someone with, lumber someone with, burden someone with.

infliction ▶ noun **1** *there is no need for the infliction of pain on a horse* **inflicting**, administering, administration, dealing out, meting out, serving out, delivering, application, applying; exaction, imposition, wreaking, perpetration.
2 (*informal, dated*) *they bore the infliction with heroism* **affliction**, trial, problem, inconvenience, nuisance, trouble, annoyance, bother, irritant; suffering, hurt, torture, torment, tribulation, punishment, penalty.

influence ▶ noun **1** *the influence of parents on their children* **effect**, impact; control, sway, hold, power, authority, ascendancy, mastery, domination, supremacy, leadership; guidance, direction, pressure.
2 *she has been denounced as a bad* **influence on** *young girls* **example to/for**, exemplar for, role model for, model for, guide for, inspiration to.
3 *he had used his political influence in the firm's interests* **power**, authority, sway, leverage, weight, standing, prestige, stature, rank, ranking, position, social position, station, connections, contacts; *informal* clout, pull, muscle, teeth; *N. Amer. informal* drag.
▶ verb **1** *bosses can influence the careers of subordinates* **affect**, have an effect on, exert influence on; determine, guide, control, form, shape, govern, decide, regulate; change, alter, modify, transform, impact on.
2 *an attempt to influence the jury* **sway**, bias, affect, prejudice, colour, predispose, suborn; bring pressure to bear on, pressurize, coerce, lean on; *informal* pull strings with, twist someone's arm; *Brit. informal* nobble.
3 *some voters were influenced to change their allegiances* **persuade**, convince, talk round, talk into, win over, bring round, sway, coax, induce, inveigle, impel, incite, entice, tempt, lure, cajole, manipulate, prompt; coerce, dragoon, intimidate, browbeat, brainwash.

influential ▶ adjective **1** *China's most influential political leader* **powerful**, authoritative, dominant, controlling, strong; **important**, prominent, predominant, leading, prestigious, distinguished, noteworthy.
OPPOSITES unimportant, insignificant.
2 *her school had been very influential in shaping her enthusiasm for physics* **significant**, important, crucial, pivotal; instrumental, guiding, persuasive, inspiring.
OPPOSITE insignificant.

influx ▶ noun **1** *we have a large influx of tourists in the summer* **inundation**, inrush, rush, stream, flood, incursion, ingress; invasion, intrusion.
2 *the lakes are fed by influxes of meltwater* **inflow**, inrush, flood, inundation.

inform ▶ verb **1** *she informed him that she was ready to leave | we'll keep you informed of any new developments* **tell**, let someone know, notify, apprise, advise, announce to, impart to, communicate to; brief, prime, enlighten, send word to, keep posted; *informal* put in the picture, fill in, clue in/up, give the low-down to.
2 *he* **informed on** *two well-known villains* **denounce**, give away, betray, incriminate, inculpate, report, tell the authorities/police about; double-cross, sell out, stab in the back, be a Judas to, give someone a Judas kiss; *English Law* turn Queen's/King's evidence; *informal* rat, squeal, squeak, blab, split, tell, tell tales about, blow the whistle, spill the beans, put the finger on, sell down the river, nark, snitch, peach, stitch up, do the dirty on; *Brit. informal* grass, shop, sneak; *Scottish informal* clype; *N. Amer. informal* rat out, drop a/the dime on, finger, job; *Austral./NZ informal* dob, pimp, pool, shelf, put someone's pot on, point the bone at; *rare* delate.
3 *half of the articles were informed by feminism* **suffuse**, pervade, permeate, infuse, imbue, saturate; illuminate, animate; characterize, typify.

informal ▶ adjective **1** *an informal discussion* **casual**, relaxed, easy-going, natural, unceremonious, unofficial, non-formal, unstudied, unaffected; open, friendly, intimate; simple, unpretentious, easy; *informal* unstuffy, unbuttoned, chummy, pally, matey.
OPPOSITES formal, official.
2 *an informal speech style* **colloquial**, vernacular, idiomatic, demotic, non-standard, popular, dialectal, non-literary; simple, natural, familiar, everyday, unofficial, unpretentious; *informal* slangy, chatty, folksy.
OPPOSITES formal, literary.
3 *the guys wore very informal clothes* **casual**, relaxed, comfortable, everyday, sloppy, leisure; *French* sportif; *informal* comfy, laid-back, sporty.
OPPOSITES formal, smart.
4 *an informal job sector has developed* **unofficial**, irregular, grey, black, back-door, illegal, illicit.

informality ▶ noun *the informality of the occasion | his genial informality* **lack of ceremony**, casualness, unceremoniousness, non-formality, unpretentiousness; homeliness, cosiness; **ease**, ease of manner, naturalness, relaxedness, approachability, accessibility.
OPPOSITE formality.

information ▶ noun *for further information write to the address below* **details**, particulars, facts, figures, statistics, data; knowledge, intelligence; instruction, advice, guidance, direction, counsel, enlightenment; news, notice, word; material, documentation, documents; *informal* info, gen, the low-down, the dope, the inside story, the latest, bumf.

informative ▶ adjective *an informative booklet* **instructive**, instructional, illuminating, enlightening, revealing, explanatory, telling, communicative, factual; educational, educative, edifying, didactic, improving; chatty, gossipy; *informal* newsy.

informed ▶ adjective *an informed society* **knowledgeable**, enlightened, illuminated, literate, well informed, well educated, educated, schooled, instructed; sophisticated, cultured; well briefed, well versed, abreast of the facts, primed, up to date, up to speed, in the picture, in the know; *French* au courant, au fait; *informal* clued up, genned up, filled in; *Brit. informal* switched-on, sussed; *US black English* down.
OPPOSITES ill-informed, ignorant.

informer ▶ noun *the police had a good network of informers* **informant**; betrayer, traitor, Judas, collaborator, double-crosser, fifth columnist, double agent, spy, infiltrator, plant, turncoat; *N. Amer.* tattletale; *informal* rat, squealer, stool pigeon, stoolie, telltale, taleteller, whistle-blower, snake in the grass, canary, snitch, peacher; *Brit. informal* grass, supergrass, nark, snout, nose; *Scottish informal* clype; *Scottish & N. Irish informal* tout; *N. Amer. informal* fink; *Austral./NZ informal* fizgig, pimp, shelf; *archaic* intelligencer, beagle.

infraction ▶ noun *an infraction of the rules* **infringement**, contravention, breach, violation, transgression, breaking; neglect, dereliction, non-observance, failure to observe, non-compliance; *Law* delict, contumacy.

infrequent ▶ adjective *his infrequent trips abroad* **rare**, uncommon, unusual, exceptional, few and far between, few, like gold dust, as scarce as hens' teeth; unaccustomed, unwonted; isolated, scarce, thin on the ground, scattered; sporadic, irregular, intermittent, fitful; *Brit.* out of the common; *N. Amer.* sometime; *informal* once in a blue moon; *dated* seldom.
OPPOSITES frequent, common.

infringe ▶ verb **1** *the takeover bid infringed EU competition rules* **contravene**, violate, transgress, break, breach, commit a breach of, disobey, defy, flout, fly in the face of, ride roughshod over, kick against; fail to comply with, fail to observe, disregard, take no notice of, ignore, neglect; go beyond, overstep, exceed; *Law* infract; *informal* cock a snook at.

OPPOSITES obey, comply with.
2 *such widespread surveillance could infringe personal liberties* **undermine**, erode, diminish, weaken, impair, damage, compromise; limit, curb, check, place a limit on, encroach on, interfere with, disturb, disrupt.
OPPOSITES preserve, strengthen.
3 *he shall be restrained from ever infringing your territory* **trespass on**, encroach on, impinge on, intrude on, enter, invade; barge in on, burst in on; *archaic* entrench on.

infringement ▶ noun **1** *an infringement of the law* **contravention**, violation, transgression, breach, breaking, non-observance, non-compliance, neglect, dereliction, failure to observe; *Law* infraction, delict.
OPPOSITE compliance.
2 *an infringement of his liberty* **undermining**, erosion, weakening, compromise; limitation, curb, check, encroachment, disruption, disturbance.
OPPOSITES preservation, strengthening.

infuriate ▶ verb *his arrogance was beginning to infuriate her* **enrage**, incense, anger, madden, inflame, send into a rage, make someone's blood boil, stir up, fire up; **exasperate**, antagonize, provoke, rile, make one's hackles rise, annoy, irritate, nettle, gall, get on someone's nerves, rub up the wrong way, ruffle someone's feathers, try someone's patience, irk, vex, pique; *N. Amer.* rankle, ride; *informal* aggravate, make one see red, get someone's back up, get someone's dander up, get someone's goat, peeve, needle, get under someone's skin, get up someone's nose, hack off; *Brit. informal* wind up, get at, nark, get across, get on someone's wick, brown off, cheese off; *N. Amer. informal* bug, tick off, gravel; *vulgar slang* piss off.
OPPOSITES please; soothe.

infuriating ▶ adjective *his infuriating know-it-all attitude* **exasperating**, maddening, provoking, annoying, irritating, irksome, vexing, vexatious, trying, tiresome, bothersome; *informal* aggravating, pesky, cussed, confounded, infernal, pestiferous, plaguy, pestilent.

infuse ▶ verb **1** *she was infused with a sense of exhilaration* **fill**, pervade, permeate, suffuse, charge, saturate, imbue, inspire, inundate.
2 *his arrival infused new life and energy into the group* **instil**, breathe, inject, impart, inculcate, introduce, implant, add.
3 *infuse the dried leaves in boiling water* **steep**, brew, stew, soak, immerse, marinate, souse; *Brit. informal* mash.

ingenious ▶ adjective *an ingenious engineer | an ingenious solution* **inventive**, creative, imaginative, original, innovative, resourceful, enterprising, insightful, inspired, perceptive, intuitive; clever, intelligent, bright, smart, brilliant, masterly, talented, gifted, skilful, capable; sharp, astute, sharp-witted, razor-sharp, quick, quick-witted, shrewd; elaborate, sophisticated, trailblazing, pioneering; *informal* on the ball, thinking outside the box.
OPPOSITE unimaginative.

ingenuity ▶ noun *considerable ingenuity must be employed in writing software* **inventiveness**, creativity, imagination, originality, innovation, resourcefulness, enterprise, insight, inspiration, perceptiveness, perception, intuition, flair, finesse, artistry, genius; cleverness, intelligence, brilliance, mastery, talent, skill; sharpness, astuteness, acumen, acuity, sharp-wittedness, quick-wittedness, quickness, shrewdness; sophistication; *informal* thinking outside the box.

ingenuous ▶ adjective *he looked at her with wide, ingenuous eyes* **naive**, innocent, simple, childlike, trusting, trustful, over-trusting, unwary, unsuspicious, unguarded, unsceptical, uncritical, unworldly, wide-eyed, inexperienced, green; open, sincere, honest, frank, candid, undeceitful; direct, forthright, artless, guileless, genuine, unaffected, unstudied, unsophisticated.
OPPOSITES disingenuous; artful.

ingenuous or disingenuous?

Although **ingenuous** is sometimes used as though it meant **disingenuous**, the words are almost opposite in meaning. *Ingenuous* means 'innocent, unsuspecting, and straightforward' (*his love for her was plain on his ingenuous face*). *Disingenuous*, on the other hand, means 'dishonest and devious', often suggesting that someone is concealing something (*the Minister's argument is disingenuous*). The confusion may be due partly to the similarity between *ingenuous* and *ingenious*, the idea being that concealment and insincerity call for clever planning.

CHOOSE THE RIGHT WORD

ingenuous, naive, artless

See NAIVE.

inglorious ▶ adjective *an inglorious retreat* **shameful**, dishonourable, ignominious, discreditable, disgraceful, humiliating, mortifying, demeaning, shaming, ignoble, abject, unheroic, undignified, wretched, shabby; scandalous, shocking.
OPPOSITE glorious.

ingrain, **engrain** ▶ verb *societal norms were ingrained in his mind* **entrench**, establish, fix, inculcate, instil, implant, root; drive home, hammer home, drill into, drive into, din into.

ingrained, **engrained** ▶ adjective **1** *his ingrained attitudes towards women* **entrenched**, established, fixed, implanted, deep-rooted, rooted, deep-seated, settled, firm, unshakeable, ineradicable, driven in; inveterate, dyed-in-the-wool, abiding, enduring, stubborn, unfading; inbred, instinctive, intrinsic, gut.
OPPOSITE transient.
2 *the ingrained dirt on the flaking paintwork* **ground-in**, fixed, infixed, planted, implanted, embedded; permanent, indelible, ineradicable, ineffaceable, inexpungible.
OPPOSITE superficial.

ingratiate ▶ verb
□ **ingratiate oneself** *he was determined to* **ingratiate himself with** *Stephen* **curry favour with**, find the favour of, cultivate, win over, get on the good side of, get in someone's good books; toady to, crawl to, grovel to, fawn over, be obsequious towards, kowtow to, bow and scrape to, play up to, truckle to, pander to, be a yes man/woman to, be a sycophant to, flatter, court, dance attendance on; *informal* keep someone sweet, suck up to, rub up the right way, lick someone's boots.

ingratiating ▶ adjective *he sidled up to her with an ingratiating smile* **sycophantic**, toadying, fawning, crawling, creeping, unctuous, obsequious, servile, submissive, Uriah Heepish; flattering, insincere, smooth, smooth-talking, smooth-tongued, honey-tongued, silver-tongued, slick, slippery; cloying, nauseating, sickening, greasy, oily, saccharine; wheedling, cajoling; *informal* smarmy, slimy, creepy, sucky, bootlicking; *N. Amer. informal* brown-nosing.

ingratitude ▶ noun *Harry was fuming at her ingratitude* **ungratefulness**, thanklessness, unthankfulness, lack of gratitude, lack of appreciation, non-recognition.
OPPOSITE gratitude.

ingredient ▶ noun *investment is an essential ingredient of corporate success* **constituent**, component, component part, element; part, piece, integral part, bit, section, strand, portion, unit, item, feature, aspect, attribute; (**ingredients**) contents, makings; *rare* integrant.

ingress ▶ noun **1** *two large doors offered ingress to the station* **entry**, entrance, access, means of entry, admittance, admission; way in, approach, means of approach; right of entry.
OPPOSITES egress, exit.
2 *the joints are sealed against the ingress of water* **seepage**, leakage, inundation, inrush, intrusion, incursion, entry, entrance.

inhabit ▶ verb *the greater part of this area is inhabited by Kurds* **live in**, occupy; settle in, settle, people, populate, colonize, make one's home in, set up home in; dwell in, reside in, tenant, lodge in, have one's home in, be an inhabitant of, be established in, be ensconced in; *formal* be domiciled in, abide in.

inhabitable ▶ adjective *an inhabitable apartment* **habitable**, fit to live in, fit to occupy, usable, liveable-in, suitable for residential use; *formal* tenantable.
OPPOSITE uninhabitable.

inhabitant ▶ noun *the inhabitants of the village* **resident**, occupant, occupier, dweller, settler; local, native; (**inhabitants**) population, populace, people, public, community, citizenry, folk, townsfolk, townspeople; *humorous* denizen, burgher; *rare* residentiary, habitant, oppidan, indweller.

inhale ▶ verb *he inhaled smoke deeply* **breathe in**, draw in, suck in, sniff in, gasp, gulp, inspire, drink in; *rare* inbreathe.
OPPOSITES exhale, expire.

inharmonious ▶ adjective **1** *inharmonious sounds* **unmelodious**, unharmonious, unmusical, tuneless, discordant, dissonant, off-key; harsh, grating, jarring, jangling, cacophonous, screeching, raucous, strident; *rare* horrisonant, absonant.
OPPOSITES harmonious, musical.
2 *the inharmonious modern building on the south of the square* **out of place**, unsuitable, inappropriate, ill suited, clashing, conflicting, incompatible, mismatched, ill-matched, contradictory, irreconcilable, jarring, discordant.
OPPOSITES harmonious, fitting.
3 *a family whose relationships are inharmonious* **antagonistic**, quarrelsome, argumentative, disputatious, captious, cantankerous, confrontational, belligerent, bellicose, combative.
OPPOSITES harmonious, congenial.

inherent ▶ adjective *his belief in the inherent goodness of man* **intrinsic**, innate, immanent, built-in, inborn, ingrained, deep-rooted; essential, fundamental, basic, implicit, structural, characteristic, organic;

inseparable, permanent, indelible, ineradicable, ineffaceable, inexpungible; natural, instinctive, instinctual, congenital, native; *rare* connate, connatural.
OPPOSITES acquired; alien.

CHOOSE THE RIGHT WORD

inherent, intrinsic, essential, innate

These words are all applied to qualities or features that are a central element in something's or someone's nature.

- **Inherent** is typically used to qualify words having negative connotations (*any form of mountaineering has its inherent dangers | the anti-male sexism inherent in some areas of child care*). It tends to be used as a warning, indicating the undesirable features or consequences of something.
- **Intrinsic** is a more general term for an element regarded as central to something's nature. A feature or quality described as *intrinsic* is typically either neutral or good (*access to the arts is intrinsic to a high quality of life*). *Intrinsic* is often used to emphasize that something possesses a quality in its own right, not through external or incidental factors (*the analysis is worthwhile because of its intrinsic interest*).
- An **essential** feature of someone or something is one that is so important to their nature that without it they would not be the same person or thing (*ensuring that others have their turn is an essential feature of citizenship | human expertise is essential to any organization*). Something may therefore be defined or summarized by reference to an *essential* element (*his essential point is that those who hold information hold power*). *Essential* may be used to suggest that a characteristic is in fact fundamental to someone, even if more superficial characteristics conceal or contradict it (*a belief in the essential goodness of human nature*).
- An **innate** characteristic is literally one with which someone is born, contrasted with one that is acquired at some later stage in life (*everything speaks of innate good taste | students with innate ability*). *Innate* is also used in a weakened sense of 'great' or 'deep-seated' (*he had an innate respect for a fellow professional sportsman*).

inherit ▶ verb **1** *she inherited her uncle's farm* **become heir to**, fall heir to, come into/by, be bequeathed, be left, be willed; *Law* be devised.
2 *his older brother inherited the title* **succeed to**, accede to, assume, take over, come into; be elevated to, have conferred on one.

inheritance ▶ noun **1** *he came into a comfortable inheritance* **legacy**, bequest, endowment, birthright, estate, heritage, bestowal, bequeathal, benefaction, provision, patrimony; *Law* devise, hereditament.
2 *his inheritance of the title* **succession to**, accession to, assumption of, taking over of, elevation to.

WORD LINKS
relating to inheritance **hereditary**

inheritor ▶ noun **heir**, **heiress**, legatee, recipient, receiver; successor, next in line; *Law* devisee, grantee, parcener, coparcener, cestui que trust; *Scottish Law* heritor.

inhibit ▶ verb **1** *the obstacles which inhibit change* **impede**, hinder, hamper, hold back, discourage, interfere with, obstruct, put a brake on, slow, slow down, retard; curb, check, suppress, repress, restrict, restrain, constrain, bridle, rein in, shackle, fetter, cramp, baulk, frustrate, arrest, stifle, smother, prevent, block, thwart, foil, quash, stop, halt, put an end/stop to, nip in the bud.
OPPOSITES assist, encourage.
2 *no one need feel inhibited from taking part* **prevent**, disallow, exclude, forbid, prohibit, preclude, ban, bar, debar, interdict, proscribe.
OPPOSITE allow.

inhibited ▶ adjective *older people are sometimes inhibited about discussing the past* **shy**, reticent, self-conscious, reserved, diffident, bashful, coy, embarrassed, uneasy, wary, reluctant, uncomfortable, hesitant, apprehensive, nervous, insecure; unconfident, unassertive, timid, timorous, subdued, withdrawn, tongue-tied; repressed, constrained, restrained, undemonstrative; *informal* uptight, hung up.
OPPOSITES uninhibited; extrovert.

inhibition ▶ noun **1** (usually **inhibitions**) *not everyone managed to overcome their inhibitions* **shyness**, reticence, self-consciousness, reserve, diffidence, bashfulness, coyness, embarrassment, unease, wariness, reluctance, discomfort, hesitance, hesitancy, apprehension, nerves, nervousness, insecurity; lack of confidence, unassertiveness, timidity, timorousness; repression, restraint, constraint, reservation, mental block, psychological block; *informal* hang-up.
2 *the inhibition of news publishing by libel laws* **hindrance**, hampering, holding back, discouragement, obstruction, impediment, retardation; curbing, checking, suppression, repression, restriction, restraint, constraint, bridling, shackling, fettering, cramping, baulking, frustration, arrest, stifling, smothering, prevention, blocking, thwarting, foiling, quashing, stopping, halting, putting an end/stop to, nipping in the bud; curb, check, bar, barrier, straitjacket.
OPPOSITES encouragement, promotion.

inhospitable ▶ adjective **1** *the inhospitable landscape* **uninviting**, unwelcoming; bleak, lonely, empty, forbidding, cheerless, hostile, harsh, inimical; uninhabitable, barren, bare, sterile, desolate, austere, severe, stark, spartan.
2 *forgive me if I seem inhospitable, but I'm very busy* **unwelcoming**, unfriendly, unsociable, unsocial, antisocial, unneighbourly, uncongenial, cool, cold, chilly, frosty, glacial, aloof, stand-offish, haughty, disdainful, distant, remote, indifferent, offhand; uncivil, discourteous, ungracious; ungenerous, unkind, unsympathetic, ill-disposed; hostile, inimical, xenophobic.
OPPOSITES hospitable, welcoming.

inhuman ▶ adjective **1** *the inhuman treatment meted out to political prisoners* **cruel**, harsh, inhumane, brutal, callous, sadistic, severe, savage, vicious, barbaric, barbarous; bestial, monstrous, fiendish, diabolical, evil, wicked, heinous; merciless, ruthless, pitiless, unpitying, remorseless, cold-blooded, heartless, hard-hearted, stone-hearted, with a heart of stone, unforgiving; unkind, unkindly, inconsiderate, unsympathetic, unfeeling, uncaring; *informal* hard-boiled, hard-nosed; *Brit. informal, dated* beastly; *archaic* dastardly, sanguinary; *rare* egregious, flagitious.
OPPOSITES humane, compassionate.
2 *the macabre, inhuman vampires of old films* **non-human**, non-mortal, monstrous, devilish, demonic, demoniac, ghostly; subhuman, animal; strange, odd, bizarre, unearthly.
OPPOSITE human.

inhumane ▶ adjective *torture and inhumane treatment are banned in this country* **cruel**, harsh, brutal, callous, sadistic, severe, savage, vicious, barbaric, barbarous; bestial, monstrous, inhuman, fiendish, diabolical, evil, wicked, heinous; merciless, ruthless, pitiless, unpitying, remorseless, cold-blooded, heartless, hard-hearted, stone-hearted, with a heart of stone, unforgiving; unkind, unkindly, inconsiderate, unsympathetic, unfeeling, uncaring; *informal* hard-boiled, hard-nosed; *Brit. informal, dated* beastly; *archaic* dastardly, sanguinary; *rare* egregious, flagitious.
OPPOSITES humane, compassionate.

inhumanity ▶ noun *the vicious inhumanity of the apartheid system* **cruelty**, harshness, brutality, callousness, sadism, severity, savagery, viciousness, barbarity, barbarism; bestiality, monstrousness, fiendishness, evil, evilness, wickedness, heinousness; mercilessness, ruthlessness, pitilessness, remorselessness, cold-bloodedness, heartlessness, hard-heartedness, stone-heartedness, unforgivingness; unkindness, unkindliness, inconsiderateness, uncaringness, lack of compassion, lack of feeling, lack of sympathy; *Brit. informal, dated* beastliness; *archaic* dastardliness; *rare* egregiousness, flagitiousness.
OPPOSITES humanity, compassion.

inhumation ▶ noun **1** *cremation took over from inhumation as the dominant burial rite* **burial**, burying, interment, committal, entombment, laying to rest, consignment to the grave; *rare* sepulture, exequies.
OPPOSITE exhumation.
2 *the burial chamber contained two inhumations* **corpse**, body, dead body, cadaver, carcass, skeleton; remains, relics; *archaic* corse.

inhume ▶ verb (*literary*) *no hand his bones shall gather or inhume* **bury**, inter, lay to rest, consign to the grave, entomb, earth up; *rare* sepulchre, ensepulchre, inearth.

inimical ▶ adjective **1** *party politics are inimical to genuine democracy* **harmful**, injurious, detrimental, deleterious, pernicious, damaging, hurtful, dangerous, destructive, ruinous, calamitous; antagonistic, contrary, antipathetic, unfavourable, adverse, opposed, hostile, at odds, not conducive, prejudicial; *literary* malefic, maleficent.
OPPOSITES helpful, advantageous.
2 *he fixed her with an inimical gaze* **hostile**, unfriendly, antagonistic, ill-disposed, unkind, unsympathetic, malevolent, malign; inhospitable, unwelcoming, cold, icy, frosty, glacial.
OPPOSITES friendly, warm.

inimitable ▶ adjective *in his own inimitable style he provides sound advice* **unique**, distinctive, individual, special, idiosyncratic, quirky, exclusive, rare; incomparable, unparalleled, unrivalled, matchless, unmatched, peerless, unequalled, unsurpassed, unsurpassable, superlative, supreme, without equal, without match, beyond compare, beyond comparison, second to none, in a class of one's own; model, faultless, perfect, consummate, ideal, unexampled, nonpareil.

iniquitous ▶ adjective **1** *we protest against this iniquitous decision* **wicked**, sinful, evil, immoral, improper; villainous, criminal, heinous, nefarious; vile, foul, base, odious, abominable, execrable, atrocious, dreadful, egregious, malicious; outrageous, monstrous, obscene, intolerable, shocking, scandalous, reprehensible; unjust, unfair; *Law* malfeasant; *humorous* dastardly; *archaic* facinorous.
OPPOSITE good.
2 *his iniquitous uncle* **dishonourable**, unprincipled; wicked, evil, criminal, lawless; degenerate, corrupt, reprobate, immoral, dissolute; devilish,

diabolical, fiendish; *informal* crooked; *archaic* blackguardly.
OPPOSITE virtuous.

iniquity ▸ **noun 1** *the iniquity of his conduct* **wickedness**, sinfulness, immorality, impropriety, vice, evil, sin; villainy, criminality, crime, heinousness, nefariousness, knavery; vileness, foulness, baseness, odiousness, atrociousness, dreadfulness, egregiousness; outrageousness, outrage, monstrousness, obscenity, reprehensibility; ungodliness, godlessness, impiety, devilry.
OPPOSITES goodness, virtue.
2 *I will forgive their iniquity* **sin**, crime, transgression, wrongdoing, wrong, offence, injury, vice, violation, atrocity, outrage.
OPPOSITE virtue.

initial ▸ **adjective** *we are at the initial stages* **beginning**, opening, commencing, starting, inceptive, embryonic, fledgling; first, early, earliest, prime, primary; preliminary, elementary, foundational, preparatory, rudimentary; introductory, inaugural, incipient, inchoate; pilot, test, trial.
OPPOSITE final.
▸ **noun** *the initials stand for the State Earnings Related Pension* **initial letter**, beginning letter; (**initials**) **abbreviation**, acronym, initialism.
▸ **verb 1** *he initialled the three warrants* **put one's initials on**, sign, countersign, autograph, endorse, put one's mark on, inscribe, superscribe, witness; *archaic* underwrite.
2 *Greece and the United States initialled a new agreement* **ratify**, accept, approve, agree to, consent to, authorize, validate, recognize.
OPPOSITES reject, repeal.

initially ▸ **adverb** *initially, Steve cleared tables and washed up* **at first**, at the start, at the outset, in/at the beginning, to begin with, to start with, originally, in the early stages, in the first instance.
OPPOSITES finally, in the end.

initiate ▸ **verb 1** *the government has initiated an extensive programme* **begin**, start off, commence, take action on, usher in; **institute**, inaugurate, launch, open, instigate, bring about, get under way, set in motion, trigger off, actuate; establish, set up, lay the foundations of, lay the first stone of, lay the cornerstone of, sow the seeds of, start the ball rolling; originate, pioneer; *informal* get cracking on, get going on, kick off.
OPPOSITES complete, finish.
2 *he had been newly initiated into a cult* **introduce**, admit, let, induct, install, instate, incorporate, ordain, invest, enlist, enrol, recruit, sign up, swear in; convert.
OPPOSITE expel.
3 *they were **initiated into** the mysteries of mathematics* **teach about**, instruct in, coach in, tutor in, school in, train in, drill in, prime in, ground in, familiarize with, acquaint with, make conversant with, make aware of; indoctrinate, inculcate; *informal* break someone in, show someone the ropes.
▸ **noun** *an initiate in the cult of an Egyptian god* **novice**, starter, beginner, newcomer; learner, student, pupil, trainee, apprentice, probationer; new boy, new girl, new recruit, raw recruit, recruit, tyro, neophyte; member; *Christianity* postulant, novitiate; *informal* rookie, new kid (on the block), newie, newbie; *N. Amer. informal* greenhorn.

initiation ▸ **noun 1** *the initiation of a programme to privatize state monopolies* **beginning**, starting, commencement; institution, inauguration, launch, opening, instigation, actuation, origination, devising, inception; establishment, setting up; *informal* kick-off.
OPPOSITES completion, finish.
2 *a rite of initiation into the tribe* **induction**, introduction, admission, admittance, installation, incorporation, ordination, investiture, investment, enlistment, enrolment, recruitment; baptism.
OPPOSITE expulsion.

initiative ▸ **noun 1** *interviewers are looking for enthusiasm and initiative* **enterprise**, inventiveness, resourcefulness, capability; imagination, imaginativeness, ingenuity, originality, creativity; drive, dynamism, ambition, ambitiousness, motivation, spirit, verve, dash, energy, vitality, vigour, leadership, vision; *informal* get-up-and-go, zing, push, pep, zip, punch, pizzazz.
OPPOSITE unimaginativeness.
2 *he had lost the initiative* **advantage**, upper hand, edge, lead, whip hand, trump card; first step, first move, first blow, opening move, opening gambit, gambit; beginning, start, commencement.
3 *a recent initiative on recycling* **plan**, scheme, strategy, stratagem, measure, technique, proposal, step, action, act, manoeuvre, gambit; approach, tack, tactic; *French* démarche.

inject ▸ **verb 1** *the doctor was about to inject a dose of codeine* **administer**, introduce; administer a drug to; inoculate, vaccinate; *drug-users' slang* shoot, shoot up, mainline, fix (up), pop.
2 *a pump which injects air into the compartment* **insert**, introduce, place, push, force, drive, shoot, feed.
3 *he injected new life and enthusiasm into the department* **introduce**, instil, bring in, infuse, imbue, inculcate, breathe.

injection ▸ **noun 1** *an anti-tetanus injection* **inoculation**, vaccination, vaccine, immunization, booster, dose; *informal* jab, shot, hype; *drug-users' slang* fix, hit, pop.
2 *the injection of adrenalin into the circulation* **administration**, introduction.
3 *the injection of a note of enthusiasm can alter the whole tenor of a meeting* **introduction**, instilling, infusion, imbuing, inculcation.

injudicious ▸ **adjective** *he will probably pay dearly for his injudicious comments* **imprudent**, unwise, inadvisable, ill-advised, misguided; ill-considered, ill-judged, incautious, hasty, rash, spur-of-the-moment, unguarded, foolish, foolhardy, hare-brained, hot-headed; indiscreet, tactless, inappropriate, unsuitable, wrong, wrong-headed; impolitic, inexpedient, undesirable; *informal* dumb.
OPPOSITES judicious, prudent.

CHOOSE THE RIGHT WORD

injudicious, unwise, imprudent, ill-advised
See UNWISE.

injunction ▸ **noun** *a High Court injunction to prevent Sunday trading* **order**, ruling, direction, directive, command, instruction, demand; decree, edict, prescription, dictum, dictate, fiat, mandate, ordainment, enjoinment, exhortation, admonition, precept, ultimatum; (*in Tsarist Russia*) ukase; *rare* monition, firman, decretal, irade.

injure ▸ **verb 1** *she was injured in a road accident | he injured his foot* **hurt**, wound, harm, damage; cripple, lame, disable; maim, mutilate, deform, mangle, crush, shatter, smash, break, do mischief to; *Brit. informal* knacker; *archaic* scathe.
OPPOSITE heal.
2 *she worried that her son would injure his health by overstudy* **harm**, damage, impair, undermine, diminish, impede, weaken, enfeeble; have a bad effect on, have a negative effect on, do harm to; *rare* vitiate.
3 *a libel calculated to injure the company's reputation* **damage**, mar, spoil, ruin, blight, blemish, besmirch, tarnish, blacken.
4 *I have injured no one save myself by my folly* **wrong**, do an injury to, do an injustice to, offend against, be detrimental to; abuse, maltreat, mistreat, ill-treat, treat badly, ill-use; *informal* do the dirty on.

injured ▸ **adjective 1** *an injured player | his injured arm* **hurt**, wounded, harmed, sore, damaged, bruised, on the sick list; crippled, lame, disabled; maimed, mutilated, deformed, mangled, crushed, shattered, smashed, broken, fractured; *Brit. informal* knackered, gammy; *Austral./NZ informal* crook; *dated* game.
OPPOSITES healthy, fit.
2 *they were required to render compensation to the injured party* **wronged**, offended, abused, maltreated, mistreated, ill-treated, ill-used, harmed; defamed, vilified, maligned, insulted, dishonoured, impugned, denigrated.
OPPOSITE offending.
3 *'No doubt you would' she replied in an injured tone* **upset**, hurt, wounded, reproachful, offended, piqued, pained, aggrieved; unhappy, cut to the quick, put out, disgruntled, displeased.

injurious ▸ **adjective** *food which is injurious to health* **harmful**, damaging, deleterious, detrimental, hurtful, dangerous; disadvantageous, unfavourable, undesirable, adverse, inimical, unhealthy, unwholesome, destructive, pernicious, malignant; *literary* malefic, maleficent.
OPPOSITE favourable.

injury ▸ **noun 1** *he was taken to hospital with minor injuries* **wound**, bruise, cut, gash, tear, rent, slash, gouge, scratch, graze, laceration, abrasion, contusion, lesion, sore; *technical* trauma.
2 *they are reasonably safe from personal injury* **harm**, hurt, wounding, damage, pain, suffering, impairment, affliction, disablement, incapacity, disability; disfigurement.
3 *compensation for injury to feelings* **offence**, abuse; wrong, wrongdoing, injustice, disservice, grievance; affront, insult, slight, snub, indignity, slap in the face, outrage.

WORD LINKS
fear of injury **traumatophobia**

injustice ▸ **noun 1** *he was protesting at the injustice of the world* **unfairness**, unjustness, inequity, corruption; cruelty, brutality, tyranny, despotism, repression, suppression, exploitation; bias, prejudice, bigotry, favouritism, partiality, one-sidedness, discrimination, partisanship, intolerance.
OPPOSITE justice.
2 *his sacking was an injustice* **wrong**, injury, offence, unjust act, evil, villainy, crime, sin, iniquity, misdeed, outrage, atrocity, scandal, disgrace, monstrosity, affront, grievance.

inkling ▸ **noun** *I had an inkling of what was going on | they had no inkling of his intentions* **idea**, vague idea, notion, glimmering; sense, impression, suggestion, indication, whisper, suspicion, sneaking suspicion, fancy, hunch; knowledge, slight knowledge; hint, clue, intimation, sign, pointer, insinuation, innuendo; *Brit. informal* the foggiest idea, the foggiest, the faintest idea, the faintest.

I

inky ▸ adjective **1** *the inky darkness of the tunnel* **black**, jet-black, jet, pitch-black, pitch-dark, pitch, black as pitch, coal-black, black as night, sable, ebony, dark; *literary* Stygian, Cimmerian; *rare* nigrescent.
2 *a man with inky fingers* **ink-stained**, stained.

inlaid ▸ adjective *a plaque inlaid with mother of pearl | an inlaid mahogany sideboard* **inset**, set, enchased, ornamented, decorated, studded, lined, panelled, tiled; tessellated, mosaic, intarsia, marquetry, parquetry; *rare* damascened, empaestic.

inland ▸ adjective **1** *we enjoyed exploring the inland areas* **interior**, non-coastal, central, inshore, internal, upcountry.
OPPOSITE coastal.
2 *inland trade* **domestic**, internal, home, local.
OPPOSITES international, foreign.
▸ adverb *the goods were carried inland by barges* **towards the interior**, away from the coast.

inlet ▸ noun **1** **arm of the sea**, cove, bay, bight, creek, estuary, fjord, sound; (*in Orkney & Shetland*) voe; *Scottish* firth, sea loch; *technical* ria; *rare* fleet, armlet.
2 *a fresh air inlet* **vent**, flue, shaft, conduit, duct, channel, pipe, pipeline, passage, tube.
OPPOSITE outlet.

inmate ▸ noun **1** *the inmates of the hospital* **patient**, inpatient, hospital case; convalescent; resident, inhabitant, occupant.
2 *the prison's 1,300 inmates* **prisoner**, convict, captive, detainee, internee; *informal* jailbird, con; *Brit. informal* lag; *N. Amer. informal* yardbird.

inmost ▸ adjective. *See* INNERMOST.

inn ▸ noun **tavern**, bar, hostelry, taproom; hotel, guest house; *Brit.* pub, public house; *Scottish* howff; *Canadian* beer parlour; *informal* watering hole; *historical* alehouse, pot-house, taphouse, beerhouse.

innards ▸ plural noun (*informal*) *he scales the fish and removes the innards* **entrails**, internal organs, vital organs, viscera, intestines, bowels, guts; *informal* insides; *Brit. archaic* numbles.

innate ▸ adjective *people differ in terms of their innate abilities* **inborn**, natural, inbred, congenital, inherent, intrinsic, instinctive, intuitive, spontaneous, unlearned, untaught; hereditary, inherited, in the blood, in the family; quintessential, organic, essential, basic, fundamental, constitutional, built-in, inbuilt, ingrown, deep-rooted, deep-seated; *rare* connate, connatural.
OPPOSITE acquired.

> **CHOOSE THE RIGHT WORD**
>
> **innate, inherent, intrinsic, essential**
>
> *See* INHERENT.

inner ▸ adjective **1** *she lives in inner London* **central**, innermost, mid, middle, interior, nuclear; the centre of, the middle of, the heart of.
OPPOSITE outer.
2 *the major went to close the inner gates* **internal**, interior, inside, inmost, innermost, intramural.
OPPOSITES external, outer.
3 *the inner circle of the Imperial court* **privileged**, restricted, exclusive, secret, private, confidential, intimate.
OPPOSITE outer.
4 *a reinterpretation of the inner meaning of the Christian faith* **unapparent**, veiled, obscure, esoteric, hidden, secret, unrevealed; deep, profound, underlying.
OPPOSITE apparent.
5 *the uniqueness of an individual's inner life* **mental**, intellectual, psychological, psychic, spiritual, emotional; of the mind, of the heart; *rare* psychical, mindly.

innermost, **inmost** ▸ adjective **1** *the innermost shrine of the Temple* **central**, middle, internal, interior; furthest in, deepest within.
2 *she was ashamed to reveal her innermost feelings* **deepest**, deep, deep-seated, profound, inward, underlying, intimate, private, personal, secret, hidden, veiled, masked, concealed, unexpressed, unrevealed, unapparent; true, real, honest; *informal* bottled up.

innkeeper ▸ noun (*archaic*) **landlord**, **landlady**, hotelier, hotel owner, hotel keeper, proprietor, manager, manageress, host; publican, pub owner, licensee, barman, barmaid, barperson, barkeeper, restaurateur; *archaic* alewife.

innocence ▸ noun **1** *the accused protested his innocence* **guiltlessness**, blamelessness, freedom from guilt, freedom from blame, irreproachability, clean hands.
OPPOSITE guilt.
2 *they questioned the innocence of our motives* **harmlessness**, innocuousness, lack of malice, inoffensiveness.
3 *the youthfulness and innocence of his bride* **virginity**, chastity, chasteness, purity, lack of sin, sinlessness, impeccability, spotlessness; virtue, virtuousness, integrity, honour, righteousness, morality, decency, wholesomeness; *Christianity* immaculateness.
4 *he had taken advantage of Isabel's innocence* **naivety**, naiveness, ingenuousness, credulity, credulousness, trustfulness, inexperience, gullibility, simpleness, simplicity, unworldliness, lack of experience, lack of sophistication, guilelessness, greenness, childlikeness.
OPPOSITE experience.

innocent ▸ adjective **1** *the police realized he was entirely innocent* **guiltless**, guilt-free, not guilty, blameless, not to blame, in the clear, unimpeachable, irreproachable, above suspicion, beyond criticism, without fault, faultless; honourable, honest, upright, upstanding, law-abiding, incorrupt; *informal* squeaky clean.
OPPOSITE guilty.
2 *the game was nothing but innocent fun* **harmless**, innocuous, safe, non-injurious, unobjectionable, inoffensive, playful.
3 *those perverts pick on the nice innocent girls* **virtuous**, pure, sinless, free of sin, moral, decent, righteous, upright, wholesome, demure, modest, chaste, virginal, virgin, impeccable, pristine, spotless, stainless, unblemished, unsullied, incorrupt, uncorrupted, uncontaminated, undefiled; *informal* squeaky clean, whiter than white, as pure as the driven snow; *Christianity* immaculate.
OPPOSITE sinful.
4 *she is genuinely innocent of guile* **free from**, without, lacking (in), empty of, clear of, unacquainted with, ignorant of, unaware of, unfamiliar with, untouched by; *rare* nescient of.
5 *he took advantage of innocent foreigners* **naive**, ingenuous, trusting, trustful, over-trusting, credulous, unsuspicious, unsuspecting, unwary, unguarded, unsceptical, impressionable, gullible, easily deceived, easily taken in, easily led; inexperienced, unworldly, unsophisticated, green, wide-eyed; simple, artless, guileless, childlike, frank, open; *informal* wet behind the ears, born yesterday, as green as grass.
OPPOSITE worldly.
6 *innocent tumours made up of blood vessels* **benign**, non-cancerous, non-malignant, non-dangerous, harmless, not life-threatening; curable, remediable, treatable; *technical* benignant.
OPPOSITE malignant.
▸ noun *I was an innocent let loose in a strange land* **unworldly person**, naive person; child; novice, greenhorn; *French* ingénue; *literary* babe in arms, babe.

> **CHOOSE THE RIGHT WORD**
>
> **innocent, blameless, guiltless**
>
> - **Innocent** is the most general word for someone who has not done wrong. It can be used, both generally and as a legal term, to declare someone not responsible for a particular wrongful act (*fabricating evidence against men whom they know to be innocent*). More generally, it indicates that someone has no malicious intentions or is not corrupt. It is often used to suggest the unfairness of harm done to people who have not harmed anyone themselves (*the innocent victims of terrorist anarchy*).
> - **Blameless** is a more unusual word, which typically refers to a general way of life that does not lay someone open to reproach of any kind (*they have all three led blameless lives*).
> - **Guiltless** is also not a very common word, It can indicate an absence of actual guilt (*Isabelle was guiltless: I was to blame for everything*) or an absence of any guilty feeling (*lavish menus for those who enjoy guiltless eating*).

innocuous ▸ adjective **1** *an innocuous fungus that grows on trees* **harmless**, safe, non-dangerous, non-poisonous, non-toxic, non-irritant, non-injurious, innocent; edible, eatable, wholesome; *rare* innoxious.
OPPOSITE harmful.
2 *an innocuous young man | an innocuous comment* **inoffensive**, unobjectionable, unexceptionable, unoffending, harmless, mild, peaceful, gentle, tame, insipid; anodyne, bland, unremarkable, commonplace, run-of-the-mill.
OPPOSITE obnoxious.

innovation ▸ noun *they favoured the traditional approach and resisted innovation* **change**, alteration, revolution, upheaval, transformation, metamorphosis, reorganization, restructuring, rearrangement, recasting, remodelling, renovation, restyling, variation; **new measures**, new methods, new devices, novelty, newness, unconventionality, modernization, modernism; a break with tradition, a shift of emphasis, a departure, a change of direction; *informal* a shake up; *N. Amer. informal* a shakedown; *humorous* transmogrification.

innovative ▸ adjective *the store's products are innovative and effective* **original**, innovatory, innovational, new, novel, fresh, unconventional, unorthodox, unusual, unfamiliar, unprecedented, avant-garde, experimental, inventive, ingenious; advanced, modern, modernistic, ultra-modern, state-of-the-art, futuristic, pioneering, groundbreaking, trailblazing, revolutionary, radical, newfangled; *rare* new-fashioned, neoteric.

innovator ▸ noun *the 19th century's prolific scientific innovators* **pioneer**, developer, groundbreaker, trailblazer, pathfinder, front runner, spearhead, prime mover; modernizer, reformer, reformist, progressive, progressivist; experimenter, inventor, creator.

innuendo ▸ noun *he became the butt for their smutty innuendoes* **insinuation**, implication, hint, suggestion, intimation, overtone, undertone, whisper, allusion, nuance, reference, imputation, aspersion, slur.

> CHOOSE THE RIGHT WORD
>
> **innuendo, hint, suggestion, insinuation**
>
> *See* HINT.

innumerable ▸ adjective *she served on innumerable committees* **countless**, numerous, very many, manifold, multitudinous, multifarious, untold, incalculable, numberless, unnumbered, beyond number; a great number of, incalculable numbers of, endless numbers of, a multitude of, a multiplicity of, a raft of, more than one can count, too many to be counted; *informal* umpteen, masses of, oodles of, no end of, loads of, stacks of, heaps of, bags of, zillions of; *N. Amer. informal* a slew of, a whole bunch of, gazillions of, bazillions of; *S. African informal* lank; *literary* myriad, legion, divers; *rare* innumerous, unnumberable.
OPPOSITE few.

inoculate ▸ verb *he **inoculated** his patients **against** smallpox* **immunize**, vaccinate, inject; protect from, shield from, safeguard from; *informal* give someone a jab, give someone a shot.

inoculation ▸ noun **immunization**, vaccination, vaccine, injection, booster; *informal* jab, shot.

WORD LINKS
fear of inoculation **trypanophobia, vaccinophobia**

inoffensive ▸ adjective *the victim was an inoffensive law-abiding citizen* **harmless**, innocuous, unobjectionable, unexceptionable, unoffending, non-aggressive, non-violent, non-combative; mild, peaceful, peaceable, gentle, tame, innocent; unremarkable.

inoperable ▸ adjective **1** *an inoperable brain tumour* **untreatable**, incurable, beyond cure, beyond surgery, irremediable; malignant; terminal, fatal, deadly, lethal, mortal; *rare* immedicable.
OPPOSITES operable, curable.
2 *the airfield was bombed and left inoperable* **unusable**, out of action, out of order, out of service, not in service, not operative, not in operation, not working, non-active, unable to be used.
3 *the unions say the agreement is now inoperable* **impractical**, unworkable, unfeasible, unrealistic, non-viable, impracticable, unserviceable, unsuitable, inappropriate, inconvenient.
OPPOSITE workable.

inoperative ▸ adjective **1** *the ventilating fan is inoperative* **not working**, not in working order, not functioning, broken, broken-down, out of order, out of service, out of commission, acting up, unserviceable, faulty, defective, non-functional, in disrepair; down; *informal* conked out, bust, (gone) kaput, gone phut, on the blink, gone haywire, shot; *Brit. informal* knackered, jiggered, wonky; *N. Amer. informal* on the fritz, out of whack; *Brit. vulgar slang* buggered.
OPPOSITES operative, working.
2 *their actions rendered the contract inoperative* **void**, null and void, nullified, ineffective, invalid, cancelled, revoked, rescinded, terminated, discontinued, not binding, not in force, non-viable; worthless, useless, valueless, vain, pointless, nugatory, futile, unproductive, abortive.
OPPOSITE valid.

inopportune ▸ adjective *she turned up at the most inopportune moment* **inconvenient**, untimely, ill-timed, badly timed, mistimed, unseasonable, inappropriate, unsuitable, inapt, ill-chosen, infelicitous, unfavourable, unfortunate, unpropitious, inauspicious, inexpedient, disadvantageous; awkward, difficult, troublesome, bothersome, problematic, disruptive, disturbing.
OPPOSITES opportune, convenient.

inordinate ▸ adjective *the job had taken an inordinate amount of time* **excessive**, undue, unreasonable, unjustifiable, unwarrantable, disproportionate, out of all proportion, unconscionable, unwarranted, unnecessary, needless, uncalled for, exorbitant, extreme, outrageous, preposterous; immoderate, overabundant, superfluous, extravagant, unrestrained, unrestricted, unlimited; *informal* over the top, OTT.
OPPOSITES moderate; limited.

inorganic ▸ adjective *the spontaneous generation of life from inorganic matter* **inanimate**, not living, lifeless, dead, defunct, extinct, inert; not natural, not organic, mineral, man-made.
OPPOSITE organic.

input ▸ noun *the program has an error resulting from invalid input* **data**, details, material, resources; facts, figures, information, statistics, particulars, specifics; *informal* info.
▸ verb *you must input data into a named database file* **feed in**, put in, load, insert; key in, type in; code, capture, process, store.

inquest ▸ noun *they held an inquest into the death of her daughter* **inquiry**, investigation, inquisition, probe, review, study, survey, analysis, examination, exploration, scrutinization; hearing, case.

inquire ▸ verb. *See* ENQUIRE.

inquiring ▸ adjective. *See* ENQUIRING.

inquiry ▸ noun. *See* ENQUIRY.

inquisition ▸ noun *she sat down opposite him and started on her inquisition* **interrogation**, questioning, quizzing, cross-examination, cross-questioning, catechism; investigation, inquiry, inquest, fact-finding; *informal* grilling, pumping, giving someone the third degree; *Law* examination.

inquisitive ▸ adjective *their inquisitive neighbours had gathered at the gate* **curious**, intrigued, interested, burning with curiosity, agog; over-curious, over-interested, prying, spying, scrutinizing, eavesdropping, intrusive, interfering, busybody, meddling, meddlesome; inquiring, questioning, probing; *informal* nosy, nosy-parker, snooping, snoopy; *rare* busy.
OPPOSITE uninterested.

insalubrious ▸ adjective *he moved from one insalubrious dwelling to another* **seedy**, unsavoury, sordid, seamy, sleazy, unpleasant, dingy, mean, wretched, dismal; **slummy**, slum-like, squalid, shabby, ramshackle, tumbledown, run down, down at heel, dilapidated, neglected, uncared-for, unmaintained, crumbling, decaying, gone to rack and ruin; *informal* scruffy, scuzzy, crummy, grungy, shambly; *Brit. informal* grotty; *N. Amer. informal* shacky, skanky.
OPPOSITES salubrious; smart.

insane ▸ adjective **1** *she was examined by three doctors and declared insane* **mentally ill**, severely mentally disordered, of unsound mind, certifiable, psychotic, schizophrenic; mad, mad as a hatter, mad as a March hare, deranged, demented, out of one's mind, out of one's head, not in one's right mind, sick in the head, unhinged, unbalanced, unstable, disturbed, crazed, crazy, hysterical; *Latin* non compos mentis; *informal* raving mad, stark staring/raving mad, away with the fairies, not all there, bonkers, cracked, batty, bats, cuckoo, loony, loopy, nuts, nutty, nutty as a fruitcake, screwy, bananas, off one's rocker, off one's head, off one's chump, off one's nut, off the wall, round the bend; *Brit. informal* crackers, barmy, barking, barking mad, off one's trolley, round the twist, as daft as a brush, not the full shilling; *N. Amer. informal* buggy, nutsy, nutso, out of one's tree, wacko, squirrelly; *Canadian & Austral./NZ informal* bushed; *NZ informal* porangi.
OPPOSITE sane.
2 *he made an insane suggestion* **extremely foolish**, idiotic, stupid, silly, senseless, nonsensical, pointless, absurd, ridiculous, ludicrous, farcical, laughable, preposterous, weird, bizarre, fatuous, inane, imbecilic, moronic, asinine, mindless, hare-brained, half-baked, ill-conceived; impracticable, untenable, implausible, unreasonable, irrational, illogical, unrealistic, unthinkable; *informal* potty, crazy, mad, off beam, way out, full of holes, cock-eyed; *Brit. informal* daft, barmy.
OPPOSITE sensible.
3 *the fly's buzzing had been driving me insane* **mad**, crazy; angry, annoyed, irritated, cross, vexed, exasperated, incensed, enraged; *informal* aggravated, hot under the collar, foaming at the mouth; *Brit. informal* spare, crackers.
OPPOSITE calm.

insanitary ▸ adjective *disease spreads quickly in crowded and insanitary conditions* **unhygienic**, unsanitary, dirty, filthy, unclean, impure, contaminated, polluted, foul, feculent, infected, infested, germ-ridden, disease-ridden, unhealthy, insalubrious, unwholesome, deleterious, detrimental, harmful; *informal* germy.
OPPOSITES sanitary, hygienic.

insanity ▸ noun **1** *insanity runs in her family* **mental illness**, mental disorder, mental derangement, madness, insaneness, dementia, dementedness, lunacy, instability, unsoundness of mind, loss of reason; delirium, hysteria, mania, psychosis; *informal* craziness; *archaic* crazedness; *rare* deliration.
OPPOSITE sanity.
2 *it would be pure insanity to take this loan* **folly**, foolishness, foolhardiness, idiocy, stupidity, imbecility, asininity, lunacy, madness, silliness, senselessness, brainlessness, thoughtlessness, irrationality, illogicality, absurdity, ludicrousness, ridiculousness; *informal* craziness; *Brit. informal* daftness.
OPPOSITE sense.

WORD LINKS
fear of insanity **lyssophobia, maniphobia**

insatiable ▸ adjective *Steve had an insatiable appetite for apple pudding* **unquenchable**, unappeasable, uncontrollable, voracious, prodigious, gluttonous, greedy, hungry, ravenous, ravening, wolfish, avid, eager, keen; never satisfied, unable to be satisfied; *informal* piggish, piggy, hoggish, swinish, gutsy; *Brit. informal* gannet-like; *rare* insatiate, edacious, esurient.

inscribe ▸ verb **1** *his name was now inscribed above the door* **carve**, **write**, engrave, etch, cut, chisel, chase, score, incise; imprint, stamp, impress, mark, brand; *archaic* scotch.

I

2 (archaic) *he demanded to be inscribed on the list of conscripts* **enrol**, enlist; enter, register, record, write, list, note down, mark down.
3 *the book was personally inscribed to him by the author* **dedicate**, address, name, sign.

inscription ▶ noun **1** *she read the inscription on the marble sarcophagus* **engraving**, **wording**, writing, lettering, legend, epitaph, epigraph, etching, carving; words.
2 *the book had an inscription in green ink* **dedication**, address, message; signature, autograph.

inscrutable ▶ adjective **1** *her inscrutable face gave nothing away* **enigmatic**, unreadable, impenetrable, mysterious, impossible to interpret, cryptic; unexpressive, inexpressive, emotionless, unemotional, expressionless, impassive, blank, vacant, deadpan, dispassionate; *informal* poker-faced.
OPPOSITE expressive.
2 *the ways of the gods are inscrutable* **mysterious**, inexplicable, unexplainable, incomprehensible, beyond comprehension, beyond understanding, impossible to understand, unintelligible, impenetrable, unfathomable, fathomless, opaque, puzzling, perplexing, baffling, bewildering, confusing, abstruse, arcane, obscure; *literary* sibylline; *archaic* wildering.
OPPOSITE transparent.

insect *See centre pages for lists of* **Butterflies** **Butterfly Types** **Insects** **Moths**

WORD LINKS

related prefix	**entomo-**
study of insects	**entomology**
collective noun	**flight, swarm**
insect-eating	**insectivorous, entomophagous**
fear of insects	**entomophobia**
substance that kills insects	**insecticide**

insecure ▶ adjective **1** *a gauche, rather insecure young man* **unconfident**, lacking confidence, lacking self-confidence, not self-assured, diffident, self-effacing, self-conscious, unforthcoming, uncertain, unsure, doubtful, self-doubting, hesitant, unassertive, retiring, shrinking, shy, timid, timorous, meek, passive, inhibited, introverted; anxious, fearful, apprehensive, worried, ill at ease; *informal* mousy.
OPPOSITE confident.
2 *burglars can gain access through insecure doors and windows* **unguarded**, unprotected, ill-protected, vulnerable, defenceless, undefended, unshielded, exposed, assailable, open to attack, in danger; unlocked, unbolted, unfastened, unsecured; *rare* pregnable.
OPPOSITE secure.
3 *an insecure footbridge* **unstable**, unsecured, loose, rickety, rocky, wobbly, shaky, unsteady, precarious; unsubstantial, weak, flimsy, frail, fragile, spindly, decrepit, unsound, unsafe; *informal* jerry-built, teetery; *Brit. informal* wonky, dicky, dodgy.
OPPOSITES secure, stable.

insecurity ▶ noun **1** *he tried to conceal his insecurity* **lack of confidence**, lack of self-confidence, self-doubt, diffidence, unassertiveness, humility, humbleness, meekness, timidity, timidness, timorousness, uncertainty, nervousness, hesitancy, inhibition, self-consciousness; anxiety, apprehension, worry, unease, uneasiness.
2 *we were conscious of the insecurity of our situation* **vulnerability**, defencelessness, unguardedness, lack of protection, perilousness, peril, danger, riskiness; instability, fragility, frailty, shakiness, rockiness, unsteadiness, unreliability, tenuousness; *informal* chanciness, iffiness; *Brit. informal* dodginess.

insensate ▶ adjective *the patient was permanently insensate. See* INSENSIBLE.

insensible ▶ adjective **1** *I found her insensible on the floor* **unconscious**, insensate, senseless, insentient, comatose, knocked out, passed out, blacked out, inert, stupefied, stunned; numb, benumbed, numbed, lacking feeling, lacking sensation; *informal* out, out cold, out for the count, out of it, zonked (out), dead to the world; *Brit. informal* spark out; *rare* soporose, soporous.
OPPOSITES conscious; responsive.
2 *they were not* ***insensible of*** *the problem | he was* ***insensible to*** *the risks* **unaware of**, ignorant of, without knowledge of, unconscious of, unmindful of, mindless of, oblivious to; indifferent to, impervious to, deaf to, blind to, careless of, unmoved by, untouched by, unaffected by, unresponsive to; *informal* in the dark about; *rare* insensitive of, negligent of.
OPPOSITES aware; heedful.
3 *he filled even the most insensible person with terror* **insensitive**, dispassionate, cool, passionless, emotionless, unfeeling, unconcerned, detached, indifferent, aloof, hard, hardened, hard-hearted, stony-hearted, as hard as nails, with a heart of stone, tough, cruel, callous; *informal* hard-boiled; *rare* marble-hearted.
OPPOSITES caring, sensitive.
4 *the almost insensible result of the various improvements* **imperceptible**, unnoticeable, undetectable, indistinguishable, indiscernible, unapparent, inappreciable, invisible, inaudible, impalpable, unobtrusive, impossible to detect; slight, small, subtle, faint, fine, inconsequential, negligible, tiny, minute, minuscule, microscopic, infinitesimal.

insensitive ▶ adjective **1** *their leader is an insensitive bully* **heartless**, unfeeling, inconsiderate, thoughtless, thick-skinned, hard-hearted, stony-hearted, cold-hearted, cold-blooded, with a heart of stone, as hard as nails, lacking compassion, compassionless, uncaring, unconcerned, unsympathetic, unkind, callous, hard, harsh, cruel, merciless, pitiless, unpitying, uncharitable, inhuman.
OPPOSITES sensitive; compassionate.
2 *he was* ***insensitive to*** *his son's feelings* **impervious to**, oblivious to, unaware of, unappreciative of, unresponsive to, indifferent to, unaffected by, unmoved by, untouched by, immune to; *informal* in the dark about; *rare* incognizant of, nescient of.

insentient ▶ adjective *insentient beings* **inanimate**, lifeless, inorganic, inert; insensate, lacking physical sensation; unconscious, comatose, anaesthetized, desensitized, numb; stupefied, knocked out, passed out, blacked out; *informal* dead to the world, out, out cold, out for the count, out of it; *Brit. informal* spark out.

inseparable ▶ adjective **1** *the three girls were inseparable friends* **devoted**, bosom, close, fast, firm, good, best, intimate, confidential, boon, constant, loyal, faithful; *informal* as thick as thieves.
2 *their moral and religious laws are inseparable* **indivisible**, indissoluble, inextricable, entangled, ravelled, mixed up, impossible to separate; the same, one and the same.

insert ▶ verb (stress on the second syllable) **1** *he inserted a tape in the recorder* **put**, place, press, push, thrust, slide, slip, load, fit, position, slot, lodge, install; drive, wedge, work, tuck; *informal* pop, stick, shove, bung, jam.
OPPOSITES take out, extract.
2 *John has inserted a clause to that effect into the contract* **enter**, put, introduce, incorporate, interpolate, interpose, interject, inset, infix, build.
OPPOSITE remove.
▶ noun (stress on the first syllable) *the local newspaper carried an insert* **enclosure**, insertion, inset, inlay, addition, supplement; circular, advertisement, notice, slip, pamphlet, leaflet; *informal* ad.

insertion ▶ noun **1** *the insertion of a catheter into the portal vein* **introduction**, introducing, putting, placing, installing, fitting, positioning, lodging, sliding.
2 *the fair was advertised on special newspaper insertions. See* INSERT.

inside ▶ noun (stress on the second syllable) **1** *my breath misted up the inside of my visor | the inside of a volcano* **interior**, inner part, inner side, inner surface; centre, core, middle, heart, nucleus.
OPPOSITES outside, exterior.
2 (**insides**) (*informal*) *my insides are out of order* **stomach**, gut, bowels, intestines; internal organs, viscera, entrails; *informal* belly, tummy, guts, bread basket.
▶ adjective (stress on the first syllable) **1** *he took an envelope from his inside pocket* **inner**, interior, internal, inmost, innermost; on the inside.
OPPOSITE outer.
2 *the directors used inside information to their own advantage* **confidential**, classified, restricted, reserved, privileged, private, internal, secret, top secret, exclusive, off the record, not for publication; *informal* hush-hush; *archaic* privy.
OPPOSITE public.
▶ adverb (stress on the second syllable) **1** *the old woman ushered me inside* **indoors**, within, in; into the interior, into the house, into the building, into the room.
OPPOSITE outside.
2 *don't let them know how you feel inside* **inwardly**, within, secretly, privately, deep down, at heart, in one's heart, in one's mind, emotionally, intuitively, instinctively.
OPPOSITE outwardly.
3 (*informal*) *if I commit another offence I'll be back inside* **in prison**, in jail, in custody, under lock and key; locked up, imprisoned, incarcerated; *informal* behind bars, doing time; *Brit. informal* doing porridge, doing bird, banged up.

WORD LINKS
related prefix **intra-** (e.g. ***intravenous, intraday***)

insider ▶ noun *a Home Office insider leaked the information* **member**, staff member, member of staff, worker, employee, representative; participant; person in the know; *informal* one of the in-crowd.
OPPOSITE outsider.

insidious ▶ adjective *the insidious erosion of rights and liberties* **stealthy**, subtle, surreptitious, sneaking, cunning, crafty, Machiavellian, artful, guileful, sly, wily, tricky, slick, deceitful, deceptive, dishonest, underhand, backhanded, indirect; *informal* sneaky.
OPPOSITE straightforward.

insight ▶ noun **1** *your knowledge and insight have been invaluable to us* **intuition**, perception, awareness, discernment, understanding, comprehension, apprehension, appreciation, cognizance, penetration, acumen, astuteness, perspicacity, perspicaciousness, sagacity, sageness, discrimination, judgement, shrewdness, sharpness, sharp-wittedness,

acuity, acuteness, flair, breadth of view, vision, far-sightedness, prescience, imagination; *informal* nous, horse sense, savvy; *rare* sapience, arguteness.
2 *the book provides a rare* **insight into** *the complexities of government* **understanding of**, appreciation of, revelation about, illumination of; introduction to, experience of, description of; *informal* eye-opener.

insightful ▶ adjective *he gives an insightful analysis of the text* **intuitive**, perceptive, discerning, penetrating, penetrative, astute, percipient, perspicacious, sagacious, wise, judicious, shrewd, sharp, sharp-witted, razor-sharp, keen, incisive, acute, imaginative, appreciative, intelligent, thoughtful, sensitive, deep, profound; visionary, far-sighted, prescient; *informal* savvy; *rare* sapient, argute.

insignia ▶ noun *his tunic bore the insignia of the Légion d'Honneur* **badge**, crest, emblem, symbol, sign, device, mark, seal, colours; decoration, medal, medallion, pin, ribbon, star, award; *military slang* fruit salad; *Brit. informal* gong.

insignificant ▶ adjective *too many articles are devoted to insignificant details* **unimportant**, of minor importance, of no importance, of little importance, of little import, trivial, trifling, footling, negligible, inconsequential, of little consequence, of no consequence, of no account, of no moment, inconsiderable, not worth mentioning, not worth speaking of, nugatory, meagre, paltry, scanty, petty, insubstantial, unsubstantial, flimsy, frivolous, pointless, worthless, irrelevant, immaterial, peripheral, extraneous, non-essential; *informal* piddling; *N. Amer. informal* dinky.
OPPOSITE significant.

insincere ▶ adjective *an insincere smile | insincere political rhetoric* **false**, fake, hollow, artificial, feigned, pretended, put-on, exaggerated, overdone, lacking sincerity, not candid, not frank; **disingenuous**, dissembling, dissimulating, devious, hypocritical, cynical, deceitful, deceptive, duplicitous, dishonest, underhand, double-dealing, faithless, disloyal, treacherous, two-faced, lying, untruthful, mendacious, evasive, shifty, slippery; *informal* phoney, pretend, pseud.
OPPOSITE sincere.

insinuate ▶ verb **1** *he insinuated that she lied* **imply**, suggest, hint, intimate, whisper, indicate, convey the impression, give a clue, give an inkling, allude to the fact, make reference to the fact, let it be known, give someone to understand, give someone to believe; *informal* make out, tip someone the wink.
2 *he insinuated his right hand under her arm* **slide**, slip, manoeuvre, insert, edge, work, move into position.
□ **insinuate oneself into** *he was insinuating himself into their family* **worm one's way into**, work one's way into, ingratiate oneself with, curry favour with; foist oneself on, introduce oneself into, squeeze oneself into, edge one's way into; infiltrate, invade, sneak into, intrude on, impinge on; *informal* get in with, muscle in on.

insinuation ▶ noun *he winced at the insinuation that he was past it* **implication**, inference, suggestion, hint, intimation, imputation, innuendo, reference, allusion, indication, undertone, overtone; aspersion, slur, allegation.

CHOOSE THE RIGHT WORD

insinuation, hint, suggestion, innuendo

See HINT.

insipid ▶ adjective **1** *they drank endless mugs of insipid coffee* **tasteless**, flavourless, unflavoured, savourless, bland, weak, thin, watery, watered-down, unappetizing, unpalatable; *informal* wishy-washy; *Scottish, dated* wersh.
OPPOSITE tasty.
2 *a rather insipid little boy* **uninteresting**, boring, vapid, dull, spiritless, zestless, bloodless, lifeless, characterless, lacking personality, lacking charisma, anaemic, wishy-washy, pathetic; ordinary, commonplace, middle-of-the-road, run-of-the mill, not amounting to much.
OPPOSITE interesting.
3 *many artists continued to churn out insipid works* **unimaginative**, uninspired, uninspiring, characterless, flat, bland, vapid, uninteresting, unexciting, lacklustre, lustreless, dull, prosaic, boring, monotonous, tedious, wearisome, dry, dry as dust, jejune, humdrum, run-of-the-mill, commonplace, pedestrian, trite, banal, tired, hackneyed, stale, lame, tame, poor, inadequate, half-hearted, bloodless, sterile, anaemic, barren; *Brit. informal* common or garden.
OPPOSITES imaginative; interesting.

insist ▶ verb **1** *if they won't see you, be prepared to insist* **stand firm**, be firm, stand one's ground, make a stand, stand up for oneself, be resolute, be determined, show determination, hold on, hold out, be emphatic, not take no for an answer, brook no refusal; persevere, persist, not give up, keep on at someone; *informal* stick to one's guns, stick it out, hang in there.
OPPOSITE give up.
2 *Tom insisted that the fees be paid within thirty days* **demand**, command, require, dictate; importune, entreat, urge, exhort.
3 *he insisted that he knew nothing about the plot* **maintain**, assert, hold, contend, argue, protest, claim, aver, avow, vow, swear, state, declare, announce, pronounce, proclaim, propound, be emphatic, emphasize, stress, repeat, reiterate; *archaic* avouch; *rare* asseverate, represent.

insistence ▶ noun **1** *she sat beside Julia at Anne's insistence* **demand**, bidding, command, dictate, instruction, requirement, request, entreaty, urging, exhortation, importuning; *informal* say-so, arm-twisting; *literary* behest, hest.
2 *there was too much vehemence in his insistence that he loved her* **assertion**, declaration, contention, statement, claim, proclamation, announcement, pronouncement, assurance, attestation, affirmation, avowal, averment, profession, swearing, emphasis, stress; *rare* maintenance, asseveration.

insistent ▶ adjective **1** *Tony's insistent questioning | she was very insistent that I call her* **persistent**, determined, adamant, importunate, tenacious, unyielding, obstinate, dogged, unrelenting, unfaltering, unwavering, inexorable; demanding, urgent, pressing; emphatic, determined, firm, assertive, decided, resolute, resolved; *informal* pushy; *rare* pushful, exigent.
2 *the insistent buzzing of the bees* **incessant**, constant, unremitting, iterative, repeated, repetitive; clamorous, vociferous, loud, noisy, obtrusive, intrusive.

insobriety ▶ noun *he had a tendency to insobriety* **drunkenness**, intoxication, inebriation, tipsiness; intemperance, overindulgence, debauchery; hard drinking, serious drinking, heavy drinking, alcoholism, alcohol abuse, dipsomania; *rare* inebriety, sottishness, bibulousness, crapulence.
OPPOSITE sobriety.

insolence ▶ noun *I will not stand for your insolence!* **impertinence**, impudence, cheek, cheekiness, bad manners, ill-manneredness, unmannerliness, rudeness, impoliteness, incivility, lack of civility, discourtesy, discourteousness, disrespect, insubordination, contempt; audacity, boldness, brazenness, brashness, pertness, forwardness, effrontery, gall, presumptuousness, presumption; insults, abuse, offensiveness; *informal* brass, brass neck, neck, face, front, cockiness, freshness, backchat, bad-mouthing; *Brit. informal* sauce; *Scottish informal* snash; *N. Amer. informal* chutzpah, sass, sassiness, nerviness; *informal, dated* hide, crust; *archaic* contumely, malapertness.
OPPOSITE politeness.

insolent ▶ adjective *the girl had been continually insolent* **impertinent**, impudent, cheeky, ill-mannered, bad mannered, unmannerly, rude, impolite, uncivil, lacking civility, discourteous, disrespectful, insubordinate, contemptuous, presumptuous; audacious, bold, brazen, brash, pert, forward; insulting, abusive, offensive; *informal* fresh, flip, cocky, lippy; *Brit. informal* saucy; *N. Amer. informal* sassy, nervy; *archaic* contumelious, malapert; *rare* mannerless.
OPPOSITE polite.

insoluble ▶ adjective **1** *we must face the fact that some problems are insoluble* **unsolvable**, insolvable, unable to be solved, without a solution, unanswerable, unresolvable; unfathomable, impenetrable, unexplainable, inscrutable; baffling, puzzling, perplexing, enigmatic, obscure, mystifying, mysterious, inexplicable.
2 *these minerals are relatively insoluble* **not soluble**, indissoluble, incapable of dissolving.

insolvency ▶ noun *the firm is on the brink of insolvency* **bankruptcy**, liquidation, failure, collapse, ruin, financial ruin, ruination; pennilessness, penury, impecuniousness, beggary; *Brit.* administration, receivership; *informal* folding; *rare* pauperdom.
OPPOSITE solvency.

insolvent ▶ adjective *the bank was declared insolvent* **bankrupt**, unable to pay one's debts, ruined, collapsed, defaulting, liquidated, wiped out; penniless, impoverished, penurious, impecunious, without a sou; *Brit.* in the hands of the receivers, in receivership, in administration, without a penny (to one's name); *informal* bust, broke, flat broke, belly-up, gone under, gone to the wall, on the rocks, in the red, hard up, strapped for cash; *Brit. informal* skint, in Queer Street, stony broke, cleaned out, without two pennies to rub together; *Brit. informal, dated* in Carey Street; *rare* pauperized, beggared.
OPPOSITE solvent.

insomnia ▶ noun *Anna was suffering from anxiety and insomnia* **sleeplessness**, wakefulness, restlessness; inability to sleep; *archaic* watchfulness.

insouciance ▶ noun *his anxieties increased, despite Jen's insouciance* **nonchalance**, unconcern, lack of concern, indifference, heedlessness, relaxedness, calm, calmness, equanimity, coolness, composure, casualness, ease, easy-going attitude, airiness, carefreeness, frivolousness, carelessness; *informal* cool.
OPPOSITES anxiety, concern.

insouciant ▶ adjective *he had an insouciant attitude to their money problems* **nonchalant**, untroubled, unworried, unruffled, unconcerned, lacking concern, indifferent, blasé, heedless, relaxed, calm, equable, equanimous, serene, composed, casual, easy, easy-going, airy, breezy, carefree, free and

easy, free from care, free from worry, happy-go-lucky, light-hearted, frivolous, unserious; *informal* cool, laid back, upbeat.
OPPOSITES anxious, concerned.

inspect ▸ verb *the safety equipment is inspected by officials each year* **examine**, check (over), scrutinize, vet, investigate, test, monitor, survey, study, go over, look over, look at, take a look at, pore over, view, scan, observe, explore, probe, subject to an examination, subject to an inspection, go over with a fine-tooth comb; assess, appraise, review; *informal* check out, give something the once-over, give something a going-over, give something a look-see.

inspection ▸ noun *he ordered an inspection of all aircraft | all reactors require regular inspection* **examination**, check, check-up, survey, scrutiny, look-over, probe, exploration, perusal, view, scan, observation, investigation, assessment, appraisal, review, evaluation; examining, checking, surveying, vetting, investigating, assessing, appraising, consideration; *informal* once-over, going-over, look-see, overhaul.

inspector ▸ noun *the machinery was not acceptable to the factory inspector* **examiner**, checker, scrutinizer, scrutineer, investigator, surveyor, assessor, appraiser, reviewer, analyst; observer, overseer, supervisor, monitor, watchdog, ombudsman; auditor; *rare* examinant, scrutinator.

inspiration ▸ noun **1** *her idea proved a real inspiration to others* **stimulus**, stimulation, motivation, motivating force, fillip, encouragement, influence, muse, goad, spur, lift, boost, incentive, incitement, impulse, catalyst; example, model, guiding light; *informal* shot in the arm; *rare* afflatus.
2 *these writings lack inspiration* **creativity**, inventiveness, innovation, innovativeness, ingenuity, imagination, imaginativeness, originality, individuality; artistry, expressiveness, creative power, creative talent, creative skill, genius, insight, vision, wit, finesse, flair, brilliance, sophistication.
3 *Emily racked her brain and had a sudden inspiration* **bright idea**, brilliant idea, timely thought, revelation; *informal* brainwave; *N. Amer. informal* brainstorm.
4 *she experiences pain on deep inspiration* **inhalation**, breathing in, drawing in of breath; respiration, breathing.

inspire ▸ verb **1** *the landscape inspired Hardy to write this fine poem* **stimulate**, motivate, cause, incline, persuade, encourage, influence, rouse, move, stir, spur (on), goad, energize, galvanize, incite, impel; animate, fire the imagination of, fire with enthusiasm; *rare* inspirit, incentivize, fillip.
2 *the film inspired a musical on the London stage* **give rise to**, lead to, result in, bring about, cause, be the cause of, prompt, produce, spawn, engender; be the inspiration for; *literary* beget.
3 *Charles inspired awe in those who worked with him* **arouse**, awaken, prompt, cause, induce, ignite, trigger, kindle, produce, generate, bring out, bring about, give rise to, sow the seeds of; *literary* enkindle.
OPPOSITE extinguish.

inspired ▸ adjective *an inspired performance | she is an inspired gardener* **outstanding**, wonderful, marvellous, excellent, magnificent, fine, exceptional, formidable, first-class, first-rate, virtuoso, supreme, superlative, dazzling, exciting, thrilling, enthralling, memorable; gifted, talented, creative, imaginative, inventive, innovative, innovatory, innovational, ingenious, original, resourceful, enterprising; *informal* tremendous, superb, super, smashing, ace, A1, mean, wicked, awesome, magic, out of this world; *Brit. informal* brilliant, brill.
OPPOSITES mediocre, poor.

inspiring ▸ adjective *he was an inspiring example to his pupils* **inspirational**, encouraging, heartening, uplifting, stirring, rousing, stimulating, electrifying, exhilarating, exciting; moving, affecting, memorable, striking, impressive, influential; *rare* stimulative.
OPPOSITES uninspiring; dull.

instability ▸ noun **1** *the instability of political life* **unreliability**, uncertainty, unpredictability, unpredictableness, precariousness, unsteadiness, insecurity, vulnerability, perilousness, riskiness; impermanence, temporariness, transience, inconstancy, changeability, variability; fluidity, fluctuation, rise and fall, rising and falling; *informal* chanciness, iffiness; *Brit. informal* dodginess; *literary* mutability.
OPPOSITE stability.
2 *her emotional instability* **changeableness**, variability, capriciousness, volatility, flightiness, fitfulness, vacillation, oscillation, unpredictability, unpredictableness; moodiness, a tendency to blow hot and cold; unsoundness, frailty, infirmity, weakness, irregularity, abnormality; *rare* erraticism.
OPPOSITE stability.
3 *the instability of the building's foundations* **unsteadiness**, unsoundness, shakiness, ricketiness, wobbliness, frailty, fragility, flimsiness, insubstantiality.
OPPOSITES stability; soundness.

install ▸ verb **1** *a colour photocopier was installed in the office* **put**, position, place, put in place, set in place, fix, fit, locate, situate, station, site, lodge, establish; insert; *informal* plonk, park.
OPPOSITE remove.
2 *the National Congress installed a new president* **swear in**, induct, instate, inaugurate, invest, institute, introduce, appoint, admit to office, take on; ordain, consecrate, anoint; enthrone, crown.
OPPOSITE remove.
3 *Katie installed herself behind the table* **ensconce**, establish, position, settle, seat, lodge, plant, plump; sit, sit down, take a seat, take a chair, perch; *informal* plonk, park; *Brit. informal* take a pew.

installation ▸ noun **1** *the installation of a central heating system* **installing**, fitting, putting in, putting in place; insertion; attachment.
2 *the installation of the new chancellor* **swearing in**, induction, instatement, inauguration, investiture, appointment; ordination, consecration; enthronement, crowning, coronation.
3 *the computer installation was new to the company* **equipment**, machinery; unit, appliance, fixture, piece of equipment.
4 *a local army installation* **base**, camp, station, post, depot, centre, facility, establishment, premises; *informal* outfit, set-up.

instalment ▸ noun **1** *they agreed to pay by monthly instalments* **part payment**, partial payment; instalment plan, instalment-payment plan, deferred payment; *Brit.* hire purchase, HP; *N. Amer.* instalment buying; *Brit. informal* the never-never.
2 *the paper published his letters in weekly instalments* **part**, portion, section, segment, division, bit; chapter, episode, volume, issue.

instance ▸ noun **1** *there was not a single instance of religious persecution* **example**, occasion, occurrence, case, representative case, typical case, case in point, illustration, specimen, sample, exemplar, exemplification.
2 *criminal investigations are conducted by the police* **in the first instance place**; stage, step; **initially**, at first, at the start, at the outset, in/at the beginning, to begin with, to start with, originally, in the early stages.
3 (*formal*) *proceedings were launched at the instance of the Director of Public Prosecutions* **instigation**, prompting, suggestion; request, entreaty, solicitation; wish, desire; urging, importuning, pressure; demand, insistence.
▸ verb *as an example of this type of play, I would instance 'Measure for Measure'* **cite**, quote, refer to, make reference to, mention, allude to, adduce, give, give as an example, point to, point out; specify, name, identify; bring up, invoke, draw attention to, call attention to, put forward, present, offer, advance, propose.

instant ▸ adjective **1** *instant access to your money* **immediate**, instantaneous, on-the-spot, prompt, direct, swift, speedy, rapid, quick, expeditious, express, lightning, sudden, precipitate, abrupt; *informal* snappy, p.d.q. (pretty damn quick); *literary* fleet, rathe; *rare* alacritous.
OPPOSITES delayed; long-term.
2 *the additives in instant meals* **pre-prepared**, ready prepared, ready mixed, pre-cooked, fast, easy/quick to prepare, easy/quick to make, microwaveable, convenience, TV.
▸ noun **1** *there'll never be an instant quite like this again* **moment**, time, point in time, moment in time, minute, second, hour; stage, phase, juncture, point.
2 *it all happened in an instant* **short time**, little while, bit, moment, minute, second, split second, trice, twinkling, twinkling of an eye, flash, (less than) no time, no time at all; *informal* sec, jiffy, jiff, two shakes of a lamb's tail, the blink of an eye; *Brit. informal* mo, two ticks; *N. Amer. informal* snap.
OPPOSITE eternity.
□ **on the instant**. *See* INSTANTLY.

instantaneous ▸ adjective *it may be difficult for you to make an instantaneous response to what is said* **immediate**, instant, on-the-spot, prompt, direct, swift, speedy, rapid, quick, expeditious, express, lightning; sudden, hurried, hasty, precipitate, abrupt; *informal* snappy, p.d.q. (pretty damn quick); *literary* fleet, rathe; *rare* alacritous.
OPPOSITES delayed; long-term.

instantly ▸ adverb *she fell asleep almost instantly* **immediately**, at once, straight away, right away, instantaneously, suddenly, abruptly, all of a sudden, on the instant, at a stroke, forthwith, then and there, there and then, here and now, this/that (very) minute, this/that instant; quickly, rapidly, swiftly, speedily, directly, without delay, promptly; in an instant, in a moment, in a (split) second, in a minute, in a trice, in a fraction of a second, in/like a flash, quick as lightning, like a shot, in a wink, in the blink of an eye, in the twinkling of an eye, in two shakes (of a lamb's tail), in (less than) no time, before you know it, on the double, at the speed of light, like an arrow from a bow; *French* tout de suite; *informal* in a jiffy, pronto, before you can say Jack Robinson, double quick, in double quick time, p.d.q. (pretty damn quick), like (greased) lightning, toot sweet; *Indian informal* ekdam; *archaic* straightway, instanter, forthright.
OPPOSITES eventually; slowly.

instead ▸ adverb *people should leave their cars at home and travel by train instead* **as an alternative**, as a substitute, as a replacement, in lieu, alternatively; **rather**, by contrast, for preference, by choice, from choice; on second thoughts; all things being equal, ideally; *N. Amer.* alternately.
OPPOSITE as well.
□ **instead of** *their menus are written in English instead of French* **as an**

alternative to, as a substitute for, as a replacement for, in place of, in lieu of, in preference to; **rather than**, as opposed to, in contrast with, as against, as contrasted with, before.
OPPOSITE as well as.

instigate ▶ verb **1** *the Commission instigated formal proceedings | he accused union leaders of instigating the disturbances* **set in motion**, put in motion, get under way, get going, get off the ground, get in operation, start, begin, initiate, launch, institute, lay the foundations of, lay the first stone of, sow the seeds of, set up, inaugurate, found, establish, organize, get working, get functioning, activate; trigger off, set off, spark off, inspire, foment, kindle, stir up, whip up, actuate, generate, cause, bring about; start/get/set the ball rolling; *informal* kick off; *formal* commence.
OPPOSITE halt.
2 *the clergy were criticized for instigating men to refuse allegiance* **incite**, encourage, urge, goad, provoke, spur on, drive on, egg on, entice, stimulate, push, press, prod, prompt, induce, impel, prevail upon, constrain, motivate, make, influence, persuade, sway; arouse, rouse, excite, inflame, stir up, sting, prick; *informal* put up to; *N. Amer. informal* root on; *Law* procure.
OPPOSITE dissuade.

instigation ▶ noun **1** *the whole team became involved at David's instigation* **prompting**, suggestion; request, entreaty, solicitation; wish, desire; urging, importuning, pressure, persuasion; demand, insistence; *formal* instance.
2 *the Interior Ministry spoke of foreign instigation of the disorder* **initiation**, incitement, provocation, stirring up, whipping up, kindling, fuelling, fomentation, encouragement, inducement; actuation, devising, inception.

instigator ▶ noun *Ricardou has been credited as the instigator of this development | the instigators of the revolt* **initiator**, prime mover, motivator, architect, designer, deviser, planner, shaper, inventor, maker, producer, contriver, mastermind, originator, author, creator, founder, pioneer, father, mother, founding father, agent; inciter, agitator, fomenter, troublemaker, agent provocateur, ringleader, leader; *literary* begetter.

instil ▶ verb **1** *all parents must instil in their children the need to be vigilant* **inculcate**, implant, fix, ingrain, infuse, impress, imprint, introduce; engender, produce, generate, induce, inspire, promote, foster; hammer into, drum into, drive into, drill into, din into.
2 *Boudin instilled Monet with the love of nature* **imbue**, inspire, infuse, inculcate; brainwash, indoctrinate; teach.
3 *she was told how to instil eye drops* **administer**, introduce, add gradually, infuse, inject.

instinct ▶ noun **1** *Michael showed no instinct to conform | some instinct told me that I must be careful* **natural tendency**, inborn tendency, inherent tendency, inclination, inner prompting, urge, drive, compulsion, need; **intuition**, natural feeling, sixth sense, second sight, insight, nose.
2 *he already has a good instinct for acting* **talent**, gift, ability, capacity, facility, faculty, aptitude, skill, flair, feel, genius, knack, bent.

instinctive ▶ adjective *an instinctive understanding of machines | his instinctive reaction is to blame someone else* **intuitive**, natural, innate, inborn, inherent, inbred, instinctual, unconscious, subconscious, subliminal, emotional, intuitional, untaught, unlearned; **automatic**, reflex, knee-jerk, mechanical, spontaneous, involuntary, impulsive, unconditioned, unthinking, unpremeditated; *informal* gut.
OPPOSITES learned; conscious; voluntary.

institute ▶ noun *a research institute* **organization**, establishment, institution, foundation, centre; academy, school, college, university, conservatory, seminary, centre of learning, seat of learning; society, association, federation, group, circle, fellowship, body, league, union, alliance, guild, consortium, concern, corporation.
▶ verb **1** *Lowell instituted a search for this unknown planet* **set in motion**, put in motion, get under way, get going, get off the ground, get in operation, start, begin, initiate, launch, lay the foundations of, lay the first stone of, sow the seeds of, set up, inaugurate, found, establish, organize, get working, get functioning, activate, actuate, generate, cause, bring about; start/get/set the ball rolling; *informal* kick off; *formal* commence.
OPPOSITES halt; cancel; end.
2 *he will be instituted as vicar of Saltburn* **install**, instate, induct, invest, inaugurate, introduce, admit into office, swear in, initiate; ordain, consecrate, anoint; enthrone, crown; appoint, put in, create.
OPPOSITES dismiss; defrock.

institution ▶ noun **1** *an academic institution | a savings institution* **organization**, establishment, institute, foundation, centre; academy, school, college, university, conservatory, seminary, centre of learning, seat of learning; society, association, federation, group, circle, fellowship, body, league, union, alliance, guild, consortium, concern, corporation.
2 *young people who have spent most of their lives in institutions* **home**, residential care organization. *See also* HOME, HOSPITAL, ASYLUM, PRISON.
3 *the institution of the new rector* **installation**, instatement, induction, investiture, inauguration, introduction, swearing in, initiation; ordination, consecration, anointing; enthronement, coronation, crowning; appointment, putting in, creation.
OPPOSITES dismissal; defrocking.
4 *until 1926 English law did not recognize the institution of adoption* **practice**, custom, phenomenon, fact, procedure, convention, usage, tradition, rite, ritual, fashion, use, habit, wont; method, system, routine, way, policy, idea, notion, concept; rule, law; *Latin* modus operandi; *formal* praxis.
5 *the institution of legal proceedings* **initiation**, launch, launching, start, starting, beginning, setting in motion, putting in motion, getting under way, getting going, getting off the ground, instigation, setting up, inauguration, founding, foundation, establishment, organization, activation, actuation, generation, origination; *formal* commencement.
OPPOSITES halting; cancellation; ending.

institutional ▶ adjective **1** *the new organization would provide an institutional framework for discussions* **organized**, established, bureaucratic, accepted, orthodox, conventional, procedural, prescribed, set, routine, customary, formal, systematic, systematized, methodical, businesslike, ready, orderly, coherent, structured, regulated; *informal* establishment.
2 *the school food is OK, if rather institutional* **unappetizing**, unpalatable, inedible, uneatable, distasteful, unsavoury, insipid, bland, tasteless, flavourless, savourless; unappealing, uninviting, off-putting, unattractive, uninteresting, dull, unpleasant, disagreeable; uniform, unvarying, unvaried, unchanging, monotonous, regimented; *informal* wishy-washy.
OPPOSITES appetizing; attractive.
3 *the house might have remained forever coated in institutional chocolate-coloured paint* **dreary**, dingy, dismal, gloomy, drab, colourless, grey, grim, cheerless, joyless, sombre, cold, depressing, impersonal, formal, off-putting, unwelcoming, uninviting, forbidding; desolate, austere, severe, stark, spartan, bare, clinical, sterile.
OPPOSITES bright; cheerful.

instruct ▶ verb **1** *a union may instruct its members to work to rule* **order**, command, direct, tell, enjoin, give the order to, give orders to, give the command to, require, call on, mandate, charge; dictate; *literary* bid.
2 *nobody instructed him in how to operate and maintain the baler* **teach**, school, give lessons to, coach, train, ground, enlighten, illuminate, inform, verse, edify, educate, tutor, guide, prepare, prime, din something into; drill, discipline, put someone through their paces.
3 *when she reached the age of 16, she exercised her right to instruct solicitors and counsel of her own choice* **employ**, authorize to act for one, brief, give information to.
4 *I should not have to instruct typists that all my documents are confidential* **inform**, tell, let someone know, notify, apprise, advise, announce to, impart to, relate to, communicate to; acquaint, familiarize, brief, prime, ground, enlighten, make conversant, make knowledgeable, send word to; *informal* put in the picture, fill in, clue in/up, put wise.

instruction ▶ noun **1** *if a prisoner disobeys an instruction, he will be punished* **order**, command, directive, direction, decree, edict, injunction, mandate, dictate, commandment, diktat, demand, bidding, requirement, stipulation, charge, ruling, mandate, pronouncement; summons, writ, subpoena, warrant; *informal* say-so; *literary* behest; *rare* rescript.
2 (**instructions**) *read the instructions to find out* **directions**, key, guide, recipe, specification; handbook, manual, guide, booklet, reference manual, ABC, A to Z, companion; *Latin* vade mecum; *informal* bible; *rare* enchiridion.
3 *an officer in the Royal Engineers provided instruction in demolition work* **teaching**, tuition, coaching, tutoring, education, schooling, tutelage; lessons, classes, tutorials, lectures; training, drill, drilling, discipline; preparation, grounding, priming; direction, guidance, information, enlightenment, edification.

instructive ▶ adjective *a recent study of cooperatives makes instructive reading* **informative**, instructional, informational, illuminating, enlightening, revealing, explanatory, telling; educational, educative, edifying, didactic, pedagogic, doctrinal, preceptive, improving, heuristic; moralistic, homiletic; useful, helpful; *rare* propaedeutic.
OPPOSITE unenlightening.

instructor ▶ noun *a flying instructor* **trainer**, teacher, tutor, coach, demonstrator, adviser, counsellor, guide; schoolteacher, schoolmaster, schoolmistress, educator, lecturer, professor; *archaic* pedagogue, preceptor.
OPPOSITE pupil.

instrument *See centre pages for lists of* **Brass Instruments** **Keyboard Instruments** **Orchestral Instruments** **Organs** **Percussion Instruments** **Stringed Instruments** **Wind Instruments**
▶ noun **1** *the wound appeared to have been made with a sharp instrument* **implement**, tool, utensil, device, apparatus, contrivance, gadget, contraption, appliance, mechanism; *informal* gizmo.
2 *when you have climbed to 800 feet you must check all the cockpit instruments again* **measuring device**, gauge, meter, measure; indicator, dial, display.
3 *drama is both a creative art form and an instrument of learning* **agent**, agency, catalyst, cause, factor, channel, force, medium, means, mechanism, vehicle, organ.
4 *he was a mere instrument acting under coercion* **pawn**, puppet, creature, dupe, hostage, counter, cog; tool, cat's paw; *informal* **stooge**.

instrumental ▶ adjective *he was instrumental in developing new diagnostic procedures | the company's record was instrumental in its ultimate failure*

involved, active, influential, contributory; helpful, of help/assistance, useful, of use/service; significant, important; (**be instrumental in**) **play a part in**, contribute to, be a factor in, be (partly) responsible for, have a hand in; add to, help, promote, advance, further, forward, oil the wheels of, open the door for, be conducive to, make for; lead to, cause, give rise to; *formal* conduce to.
OPPOSITES uninvolved; obstructive.

insubordinate ▶ adjective *he soon found a means of dealing with his insubordinate son* **disobedient**, unruly, wayward, errant, badly behaved, disorderly, undisciplined, delinquent, troublesome, rebellious, defiant, mutinous, recalcitrant, refractory, uncooperative, non-compliant, wilful, unbiddable, intractable, ungovernable, unmanageable, uncontrollable, obstreperous, awkward, difficult, perverse, contrary; naughty, mischievous, impish, roguish, rascally; *Brit. informal* bolshie; *archaic or Law* contumacious.
OPPOSITE obedient.

insubordination ▶ noun *a soldier could be shot for insubordination* **disobedience**, unruliness, waywardness, indiscipline, bad behaviour, misbehaviour, misconduct, delinquency, troublemaking; rebellion, rebelliousness, defiance, mutiny, revolt; recalcitrance, lack of cooperation, non-compliance, wilfulness, intractability, ungovernability, uncontrollability, obstreperousness, awkwardness, perversity, perverseness, contrariness; naughtiness, mischievousness, mischief, impishness, roguery; *informal* carryings-on, acting-up; *archaic or Law* contumacy, infraction.
OPPOSITE obedience.

I

insubstantial ▶ adjective **1** *these insubstantial structures cannot be converted into satisfactory dwellings* **flimsy**, slight, light, fragile, breakable, weak, frail, shaky, unstable, wobbly, tottery, rickety, ramshackle, makeshift; **jerry-built**, badly built, thrown together, cheap, shoddy, gimcrack.
OPPOSITE sturdy.
2 *insubstantial evidence* **weak**, flimsy, feeble, poor, inadequate, insufficient, thin, slight, tenuous, insignificant, inconsequential, unsubstantial, unconvincing, implausible, unsatisfactory, paltry, trifling, trivial, shallow.
OPPOSITE sound.
3 *she felt worried, in an insubstantial yet unsettling way | the flickering light made her face seem insubstantial* **intangible**, impalpable, indefinable, indescribable, vague, obscure, unclear, indistinct; untouchable, imperceptible to the touch, unsubstantial, incorporeal; imaginary, imagined, fancied, fanciful, figmental, unreal, non-existent, illusory, illusive, delusive, hallucinatory, phantom, spectral, ghostlike, visionary, chimerical, airy, vaporous; *rare* immaterial, unbodied, discarnate, phantasmal, phantasmic, inexistent, illusionary.
OPPOSITES tangible; real.

insufferable ▶ adjective **1** *an insufferable glare of publicity* **intolerable**, unbearable, unendurable, insupportable, unacceptable, oppressive, overwhelming, overpowering, impossible, not to be borne, past bearing, too much to bear, more than one can stand, more than flesh and blood can stand, enough to try/test/tax the patience of a saint; unspeakable, dreadful, excruciating, grim, outrageous; *informal* too much.
OPPOSITES bearable; congenial.
2 *his triumph had made him insufferable* **conceited**, arrogant, boastful, cocky, cocksure, full of oneself, above oneself, self-important, immodest, swaggering, strutting; vain, self-satisfied, self-congratulatory, pleased with oneself, self-loving, in love with oneself, self-admiring, self-regarding, smug, complacent; *informal* swollen-headed, big-headed, too big for one's boots; *literary* vainglorious; *rare* peacockish.
OPPOSITE modest.

insufficiency ▶ noun *there was an insufficiency of evidence* **lack**, inadequacy, shortage, want, dearth, deficit, shortfall; scarcity, scarceness, scantiness, paucity, absence, undersupply, sparseness, deprivation, meagreness, shortness; *rare* exiguity, exiguousness.
OPPOSITE sufficiency.

insufficient ▶ adjective *there was insufficient time available | insufficient resources* **inadequate**, not enough, too little; too few, too small, deficient, poor, scant, scanty; scarce, sparse, short, in short supply, at a premium; lacking, wanting; paltry, meagre, niggardly; skimpy, sketchy, incomplete, restricted, limited; *informal* measly, pathetic, piddling; *rare* exiguous.
OPPOSITE sufficient.

insular ▶ adjective **1** *a stubbornly insular group of people* **narrow-minded**, limited, blinkered, restricted, inward-looking, conventional, parochial, provincial, small-town, localist, small-minded, petty-minded, petty, close-minded, short-sighted, myopic, hidebound, dyed-in-the-wool, diehard, set, set in one's ways, inflexible, dogmatic, rigid, entrenched, illiberal, intolerant, prejudiced, bigoted, biased, partisan, sectarian, xenophobic, discriminatory; *Brit.* parish-pump, blimpish; *French* borné; *N. Amer. informal* jerkwater; *rare* claustral.
OPPOSITES broad-minded; tolerant.
2 *an insular community which has few links with the rest of the world* **isolated**, inaccessible, cut off, closed, separate, segregated, detached, solitary, lonely, insulated, self-contained, self-sufficient.
OPPOSITES accessible; cosmopolitan.

insularity ▶ noun **1** *he was untrammelled by the insularity which bedevilled the art world* **narrow-mindedness**, blinkered approach/attitude, parochialism, provincialism, localism, narrowness, small-mindedness, pettiness, short-sightedness, myopia, inflexibility, dogmatism, illiberality, intolerance, prejudice, bigotry, bias, partisanship, sectarianism, xenophobia, discrimination.
OPPOSITES broad-mindedness; tolerance.
2 *the valley's insularity has proved a blessing* **isolation**, inaccessibility, separation, segregation, detachment, solitariness, loneliness, insulation, self-sufficiency.
OPPOSITE accessibility.

insulate ▶ verb **1** *pipes in the attic must be insulated* **wrap**, cover, encase, enclose, envelop, swathe, sheathe, bundle up; lag, heatproof, soundproof, muffle, make shockproof, pad, cushion; *literary* lap.
2 *the Netherlands was largely insulated from the full impact of the Great War* **protect**, keep safe, keep from harm, save, safeguard, shield, defend, shelter, screen, cushion, cocoon; isolate, segregate, separate, sequester, detach, exclude, cut off, cloister.

insulation ▶ noun **1** *his life in Attleborough afforded him insulation from the rigours of inner-city life* **protection**, defence, shelter, screen, cushion, shield, shielding, safe keeping, safeguarding; isolation, segregation, separation, setting apart, sequestration, closeting, detachment, exclusion, quarantine.
OPPOSITE exposure.
2 *lofts should have at least 100mm of insulation* **lagging**, blanket, jacket, wrap.

insult ▶ verb (stress on the second syllable) *you are insulting the woman I love* **offend**, give/cause offence to, affront, abuse, be rude to, call someone names, slight, disparage, discredit, libel, slander, malign, defame, denigrate, cast aspersions on, impugn, slur, revile, calumniate; hurt, hurt someone's feelings, mortify, humiliate, wound; snub, rebuff, spurn, shun, treat disrespectfully, ignore, cut dead, give someone the cold-shoulder, turn one's back on; *informal* bad-mouth; *Brit. informal* slag off; *N. Amer. informal* trash-talk; *rare* asperse, derogate, miscall.
OPPOSITES compliment; flatter.
▶ noun (stress on the first syllable) *he hurled insults at us* **abusive remark**, jibe, affront, slight, snub, barb, slur, backhanded compliment, injury, libel, slander, defamation, abuse, disparagement, depreciation, impugnment, revilement, humiliation, indignity, insolence, rudeness; aspersions; *informal* dig, put-down, slap in the face, kick in the teeth; *archaic* contumely.
OPPOSITE compliment.

insulting ▶ adjective *they directed foul and insulting comments at the referee* **abusive**, rude, vulgar, offensive, wounding, mortifying, humiliating, disparaging, belittling, derogatory, depreciating, deprecatory, disrespectful, denigratory, uncomplimentary, pejorative, vituperative; disdainful, derisive, scornful, contemptuous; defamatory, slanderous, libellous, scurrilous, blasphemous, discrediting; *informal* bitchy, catty; *archaic* contumelious.
OPPOSITES complimentary; polite.

CHOOSE THE RIGHT WORD

insulting, offensive, derogatory

See OFFENSIVE.

insuperable ▶ adjective *there should be no insuperable obstacle to the purchase* **insurmountable**, unconquerable, invincible, unassailable; overwhelming, hopeless, impossible.
OPPOSITE surmountable.

insupportable ▶ adjective **1** *this view appears insupportable* **unjustifiable**, without justification, indefensible, inexcusable, unforgivable, unpardonable, unwarrantable, unreasonable; **groundless**, unfounded, without foundation, foundationless, baseless, without basis, unsupported, unsubstantiated, unconfirmed, uncorroborated, invalid, untenable, implausible, weak, shaky, flawed, specious, defective.
OPPOSITE justified.
2 *the heat in Cairo was insupportable* **intolerable**, insufferable, unbearable, unendurable, unacceptable, oppressive, overwhelming, overpowering, impossible, not to be borne, past bearing, too much to bear, more than one can stand, more than flesh and blood can stand; unspeakable, dreadful, excruciating; *informal* too much.
OPPOSITES bearable; congenial.

insurance ▶ noun **1** *insurance on his new car was going to cost him £750* **assurance**, indemnity, indemnification, (financial) protection, security, surety, cover.
2 *the high defence expenditure was considered a reasonable insurance against a third World War* **protection**, defence, safeguard, safety measure, shelter, security, precaution, provision, preventive measure, immunity; guarantee, warranty; *informal* backstop.

insure ▸ verb *they had failed to insure the building against fire* **protect**, indemnify, cover, underwrite, assure, guarantee, warrant.

insure or ensure?
See ENSURE.

insurgent ▸ adjective *insurgent forces have captured the north of the country* **rebellious**, rebel, revolutionary, mutinous, mutinying; traitorous, renegade, rioting, seditious, subversive; *rare* insurrectionary, insurrectionist.
OPPOSITES loyal; government.
▸ noun *government troops were fighting insurgents* **rebel**, revolutionary, revolutionist, mutineer, agitator, subversive, guerrilla, anarchist, terrorist, rioter; freedom fighter, resistance fighter; traitor, renegade; (*in Mexico, historical*) Zapatista; (*in S. America, historical*) Montonero; *rare* insurrectionist, insurrectionary.
OPPOSITE loyalist.

insurmountable ▸ adjective *there are insurmountable difficulties in ensuring equal opportunities for all pupils* **insuperable**, unconquerable, invincible, unassailable; overwhelming, hopeless, impossible.
OPPOSITE surmountable.

insurrection ▸ noun *the leaders of the insurrection surrendered* **rebellion**, revolt, uprising, mutiny, revolution, insurgence, insurgency, rising, rioting, riot, sedition; civil disobedience, civil disorder, unrest, anarchy, fighting in the streets; coup; *French* coup d'état, jacquerie; *German* putsch.

intact ▸ adjective *something struck the window but the glass stayed intact* | *his reputation was intact* **whole**, entire, complete, unbroken, undamaged, unharmed, uninjured, unimpaired, unflawed, faultless, flawless, unscathed, untouched, unspoilt, unmutilated, unsevered, unblemished, unmarred, unmarked, perfect, pristine, inviolate, unviolated, undefiled, unsullied, in one piece; sound, solid; *rare* scatheless.
OPPOSITES broken; damaged.

intangible ▸ adjective **1** *the moonlight made things seem intangible* **impalpable**, untouchable, imperceptible to the touch, non-physical, bodiless, incorporeal, unembodied, disembodied, abstract, invisible; ethereal, insubstantial, airy, aerial; spiritual, ghostly, spectral, phantom, wraithlike, transcendental, unearthly, supernatural; *rare* immaterial, unbodied, discarnate, disincarnate, phantasmal, phantasmic.
OPPOSITE tangible.
2 *an intangible atmosphere of dread and doom* **indefinable**, indescribable, inexpressible, nameless; vague, obscure, unclear, hazy, dim, mysterious; indefinite, unanalysable, subtle, elusive, fugitive.
OPPOSITE clear.

integral ▸ adjective **1** *communicating is an integral part of all human behaviour* **essential**, fundamental, basic, intrinsic, inherent, constitutive, innate, structural; vital, indispensable, necessary, requisite.
OPPOSITES incidental; peripheral.
2 *the travelling hairdryer has integral cord storage* **built-in**, inbuilt, integrated, incorporated, fitted, component, constituent; *rare* integrant.
OPPOSITE add-on.
3 *an integral approach to users and their needs* **unified**, integrated, comprehensive, organic, composite, combined, aggregate, undivided, overall, gross, entire, complete, whole, total, full, intact.
OPPOSITES fragmented; partial.

integrate ▸ verb *he proposes to integrate our reserve forces more closely with the regular forces* **combine**, amalgamate, merge, unite, join, fuse, blend, mingle, coalesce, consolidate, meld, intermingle, mix, intermix, incorporate, affiliate, unify, assimilate, homogenize, harmonize, mesh, desegregate; *literary* commingle.
OPPOSITE separate.

integrated ▸ adjective **1** *an integrated package of support services* **unified**, united, consolidated, amalgamated, joined, combined, merged, fused, blended, meshed, coherent, homogeneous, homogenized, mutually dependent, assimilated, cohesive, concatenated; federal, federated, confederate, confederated.
OPPOSITES unconnected; separate.
2 *an integrated school* **desegregated**, non-segregated, unsegregated, racially mixed, racially balanced; non-discriminatory.
OPPOSITE segregated.

integration ▸ noun **1** *the integration of images and text as camera-ready copy* **combination**, amalgamation, incorporation, unification, consolidation, merger, fusing, blending, meshing, homogenization, homogenizing, coalescing, assimilation, concatenation.
OPPOSITE separation.
2 *the report focused attention on the integration of children with special educational needs* **desegregation**, inclusion.
OPPOSITE segregation.

integrity ▸ noun **1** *I never doubted his integrity* **honesty**, uprightness, probity, rectitude, honour, honourableness, upstandingness, good character, principle(s), ethics, morals, righteousness, morality, nobility, high-mindedness, right-mindedness, noble-mindedness, virtue, decency, fairness, scrupulousness, sincerity, truthfulness, trustworthiness.
OPPOSITE dishonesty.
2 *internal racial unrest threatened the integrity of the federation* **unity**, unification, wholeness, coherence, cohesion, undividedness, togetherness, solidarity, coalition.
OPPOSITE division.
3 *the structural integrity of the aircraft* **soundness**, robustness, strength, sturdiness, solidity, solidness, durability, stability, stoutness, toughness.
OPPOSITE fragility.

intellect ▸ noun **1** *it's a film that appeals more to the intellect than to the gut* **mind**, brain, brains, head, intelligence, reason, understanding, comprehension, thought, brainpower, sense, judgement, wisdom, wits; *informal* nous, grey matter, brainbox, brain cells, upper storey; *Brit. informal* loaf; *N. Amer. informal* smarts; *S. African informal* kop.
OPPOSITE emotion.
2 *one of the most sophisticated intellects of the century* **thinker**, intellectual, bluestocking, academic, scholar, sage; mind, brain.

intellectual ▸ adjective **1** *he is a man of formidable intellectual capacity* **mental**, cerebral, cognitive; rational, psychological, abstract, conceptual, theoretical, analytical, logical; academic; *rare* mindly, phrenic, ratiocinative.
OPPOSITE physical.
2 *a remarkably intellectual man* **intelligent**, clever, academic, well educated, well read, widely read, erudite, cerebral, learned, knowledgeable, literary, bookish, donnish, highbrow, scholarly, studious, cultured, cultivated, civilized, enlightened, sophisticated; *informal* brainy; *archaic* lettered, clerkly.
OPPOSITES stupid; illiterate.
▸ noun *intellectuals are appalled by the mentality of the popular soap operas* **intelligent person**, learned person, highbrow, academic, bookworm, bookish person, man of letters, woman of letters, bluestocking, thinker, brain, scholar, sage; **genius**, Einstein, polymath, expert, prodigy, gifted child; mastermind; *Hindu* pandit; *informal* egghead, brains, bright spark, whizz, wizard, walking encyclopedia; *Brit. informal* brainbox, clever clogs, boffin; *N. Amer. informal* brainiac, rocket scientist, maven, Brahmin, pointy-head; *archaic* bookman.
OPPOSITE dunce.

intelligence ▸ noun **1** *a man of great intelligence* **intellectual/mental capacity**, intellect, mind, brain, brains, brainpower, powers of reasoning, judgement, reason, reasoning, understanding, comprehension, acumen, wit, sense, insight, perceptiveness, perception, perspicaciousness, perspicacity, penetration, discernment, sharpness, quickness of mind, quick-wittedness, smartness, canniness, astuteness, intuition, acuity, alertness, cleverness, brilliance, aptness, ability, giftedness, talent; *informal* braininess.
OPPOSITE stupidity.
2 *the lack of intelligence received from the Eighth Army* **information**, facts, details, particulars, data, figures, statistics, knowledge, report(s); *informal* info, gen, dope.
3 *a former agent for British military intelligence* **information gathering**, surveillance, observation, reconnaissance, spying, espionage, undercover work, infiltration, ELINT, Humint; *informal* recon.

intelligent ▸ adjective **1** *Breuer is an intelligent writer* **clever**, bright, brilliant, sharp, quick, quick-witted, quick on the uptake, smart, canny, astute, intuitive, thinking, acute, alert, keen, insightful, perceptive, perspicacious, penetrating, discerning; ingenious, inventive; knowledgeable; apt, able, gifted, talented; *informal* brainy; (**be intelligent**) *informal* have a good head on one's shoulders, there are no flies on …; *Brit. informal* know how many beans make five.
OPPOSITE stupid.
2 *an extraterrestrial intelligent being* **rational**, capable of thought, higher-order.
OPPOSITE non-rational.
3 *intelligent machines* **robotic**, automatic, self-regulating, capable of learning; *informal* smart.

intelligentsia ▸ plural noun *there is a distrust of the intelligentsia and of theoretical learning* **intellectuals**, intelligent people, academics, scholars, learned people, literati, culturati, men and women of letters, cognoscenti, illuminati, highbrows, bluestockings, thinkers, brains; the intelligent; *informal* eggheads; *Brit. informal* boffins.
OPPOSITE masses.

intelligibility ▸ noun *documents of varying degrees of complexity and intelligibility* **comprehensibility**, ease of understanding, accessibility, digestibility, user-friendliness; lucidity, lucidness, clarity, clearness, coherence, transparency, plainness, simplicity, perspicuity, explicitness, precision, lack of ambiguity, unambiguity.
OPPOSITE unintelligibility.

intelligible ▸ adjective *statutes were drafted so as to be intelligible only to lawyers* **comprehensible**, understandable; easy to understand, accessible, digestible, user-friendly; lucid, clear, crystal clear, coherent, transparent, plain, simple, perspicuous, explicit, precise, unambiguous, self-

I

explanatory, penetrable, fathomable, graspable.
OPPOSITE unintelligible.

intemperance ▶ noun **1** *the friars were frequently criticized for personal intemperance* **overindulgence**, intemperateness, immoderation, lack of restraint, abandon, lack of self-control; excess, excessiveness, extravagance, prodigality, profligacy, lavishness; self-indulgence, self-gratification; debauchery, decadence, wantonness, dissipation, dissolution, dissoluteness.
OPPOSITE moderation.
2 *the Temperance Movement argued that intemperance was a disease* **drinking**, hard/heavy drinking, alcoholism, alcohol abuse, dipsomania; drunkenness, intoxication, inebriation, insobriety, tipsiness; *rare* inebriety, sottishness, bibulousness, crapulence.
OPPOSITE temperance.

intemperate ▶ adjective *I drank, I confess, an intemperate amount of beer | his intemperate language* **immoderate**, excessive, undue, inordinate, unreasonable, unjustified, unwarranted, uncalled for; extreme, unrestrained, unrestricted, uncontrolled, unbridled, uncurbed; self-indulgent, overindulgent, extravagant, lavish, prodigal, profligate, imprudent, reckless, wild, outrageous, egregious; dissolute, debauched, wanton, dissipated, dissipative.
OPPOSITE moderate.

intend ▶ verb *Charlie intends to buy a bungalow | the goods are intended for export* **plan**, mean, have the/every intention, have in mind, have in view, have plans, aim, propose, aspire, hope, expect, be looking, be going, be resolved, have resolved, be determined, have set out, purpose, be plotting; desire, want, wish; contemplate, think of, envisage; design, earmark, set apart.

intended ▶ adjective *the foul was not intended* **deliberate**, intentional, calculated, conscious, done on purpose, planned, considered, studied, knowing, wilful, wanton, purposeful, purposive, premeditated, pre-planned, thought out in advance, prearranged, preconceived, predetermined; aforethought; voluntary, volitional; *Law, dated* prepense.
OPPOSITE accidental.
▶ noun (*informal, dated*) *can you share your inner thoughts with your intended?* **fiancée**, **fiancé**, wife-to-be, husband-to-be, bride-to-be, future wife/husband, prospective wife/husband, prospective spouse; *formal* betrothed.

intense ▶ adjective **1** *the subject of intense interest | intense heat* **great**, acute, enormous, fierce, severe, extreme, high, exceptional, extraordinary, harsh, strong, powerful, potent, vigorous; major, profound, deep, concentrated, consuming; *informal* serious.
OPPOSITE mild.
2 *a very intense young man* **passionate**, impassioned, ardent, earnest, fervent, fervid, hot-blooded, zealous, vehement, fiery, heated, feverish, emotional, heartfelt, eager, keen, enthusiastic, excited, animated, spirited, vigorous, strong, energetic, messianic, fanatical, committed; *rare* perfervid, passional.
OPPOSITE apathetic.

intensification ▶ noun *he warned of the intensification of terrorist activity* **escalation**, stepping up, boosting, increase, pickup, build-up, sharpening, strengthening, augmentation, concentration, reinforcement; heightening, deepening, broadening, widening, extension, expansion, amplification, magnification, enlargement; aggravation, exacerbation, worsening, deterioration, compounding.
OPPOSITES lessening, abatement.

intensify ▶ verb *Henry intensified his attack on the church | the violence intensified* **escalate**, step up, boost, increase, raise, sharpen, strengthen, augment, add to, concentrate, reinforce; gain strength, pick up, build up, heighten, deepen, broaden, widen, extend, expand, amplify, magnify; aggravate, exacerbate, make worse, worsen, inflame, compound.
OPPOSITES lessen, abate.

intensity ▶ noun **1** *the intensity of the sun* **strength**, power, powerfulness, potency, vigour, force, forcefulness; severity, ferocity, vehemence, fierceness, violence, harshness; magnitude, greatness, high degree, concentration, extremity, acuteness; seriousness, gravity, graveness, severeness, grievousness.
2 *his eyes seared hers with a glowing intensity* **passion**, ardour, fervour, fervency, zeal, vehemence, fire, heat, fever, emotion, eagerness, keenness, enthusiasm, excitement, animation, spirit, vigour, earnestness, strength, energy; fanaticism.
OPPOSITES apathy; indifference.

intensive ▶ adjective *an intensive course in Russian | an intensive search of the area* **thorough**, in-depth, concentrated, rigorous, exhaustive, all-out, concerted, thoroughgoing; all-embracing, all-encompassing, all-inclusive, comprehensive, complete, full, total, all-absorbing; serious, vigorous, strenuous, detailed, minute, close, meticulous, scrupulous, assiduous, conscientious, painstaking, methodical, careful, sedulous, elaborate, extensive, widespread, sweeping, searching, high-pressure, determined, resolute, persistent, insistent.
OPPOSITES superficial; cursory; partial.

intent ▶ noun *he tried to divine his father's intent in asking the question* **aim**, purpose, intention, objective, object, goal, target, end; design, plan, scheme; resolve, resolution, determination; wish, desire, ambition, idea, dream, aspiration, hope.
□ **to all intents and purposes** *to all intents and purposes a newborn human baby is helpless* **in effect**, effectively, in essence, essentially, virtually, practically, in practical terms, for all practical purposes, in all important respects; more or less, just about, all but, as good as, in all but name, as near as dammit; almost, nearly, verging on, bordering on, well nigh, nigh on; *S. African* plus-minus; *informal* pretty much, pretty nearly, pretty well.
OPPOSITES fully; by no means.
▶ adjective **1** *he was intent on proving his point* **bent**, set, determined, insistent, fixed, resolved, hell-bent, keen; firm about, committed to; single-minded about, inflexible about, obsessive about, obsessed with, fanatical about, fixated on; determined to, resolved to, anxious to, impatient to.
OPPOSITES half-hearted; reluctant.
2 *she had an intent look on her face* **attentive**, absorbed, engrossed, fascinated, enthralled, enrapt, rapt, focused, earnest, concentrated, concentrating, intense, studious, fixed, steady, steadfast, occupied, preoccupied, wrapped up, alert, watchful, observant.
OPPOSITE vacant.

intention ▶ noun **1** *it is his intention to be leader* **aim**, purpose, intent, objective, object, goal, target, end; design, plan, scheme; resolve, resolution, determination; wish, desire, ambition, idea, dream, aspiration, hope.
2 *Milton manages, with or without intention, to build up a wonderfully vivid and intriguing portrait of Satan* **deliberateness**, intentionality, intent, design, calculation; premeditation, preconception, forethought, plan, planning, pre-planning, advance planning, prearrangement, malice aforethought.
OPPOSITES inadvertency; accident.

intentional ▶ adjective *there shall be no intentional physical contact between teams* **deliberate**, calculated, conscious, done on purpose, intended, planned, meant, considered, studied, knowing, wilful, wanton, purposeful, purposive, purposed, premeditated, pre-planned, thought out in advance, prearranged, preconceived, predetermined; aforethought; voluntary, volitional; *Law, dated* prepense.
OPPOSITES unintentional, accidental.

intentionally ▶ adverb *she would never intentionally hurt anyone* **deliberately**, on purpose, purposely, purposefully, by design, knowingly, wittingly, consciously; premeditatedly, calculatedly, in cold blood, wilfully, wantonly; with malice aforethought.
OPPOSITE accidentally.

intently ▶ adverb *she listened intently to Harry's story* **attentively**, closely, keenly, with fascination, raptly, earnestly, concentratedly, hard, studiously, fixedly, steadily, steadfastly, alertly, watchfully, observantly, carefully.
OPPOSITES absently; casually.

inter ▶ verb *his remains were interred in the new cemetery* **bury**, lay to rest, consign to the grave, entomb, inurn; earth up; *informal* put six feet under, plant; *N. Amer. informal* deep-six; *literary* sepulchre, ensepulchre, inhume, inearth.
OPPOSITE exhume.

intercede ▶ verb *several nations offered to intercede on the captives' behalf* **mediate**, act as an intermediary, intermediate, negotiate, arbitrate, moderate, conciliate, act as honest broker, intervene, interpose, step in, become/get involved, act, take action, take measures, take a hand; plead, petition, entreat, supplicate.

intercept ▶ verb *an Italian naval vessel intercepted the gunrunners' boat* **stop**, head off, cut off; catch, seize, grab, snatch, expropriate, commandeer; obstruct, impede, interrupt, block, check, detain; attack, ambush, take on, challenge, pounce on, swoop down on, waylay, accost, tackle, confront; *informal* buttonhole.

intercession ▶ noun *he made contact with the Austrians through the intercession of the Serbs* **mediation**, intermediation, negotiation, arbitration, conciliation, intervention, interposition, involvement, action; pleading, petition, entreaty, supplication, good offices, agency, shuttle diplomacy; *rare* mediatorship.

intercessor ▶ noun *they act as priests, intercessors between the people and the gods* **mediator**, moderator, go-between, negotiator, middleman, intermediary, intervenor, interceder, arbitrator, arbiter; conciliator, reconciler, broker, honest broker, petitioner, supplicant, liaison officer, peacemaker.

interchange ▶ verb (stress on the third syllable) **1** *superiors and subordinates freely interchange ideas and information* **exchange**, trade, swap, change, barter, bandy, reciprocate; *archaic* truck.
2 *the terms 'tone' and 'colour' are often wrongly interchanged* **substitute**, transpose, exchange, change, switch, swap (round), reverse, invert, turn about/around, change (round), move (around), rearrange, reorder, replace, supplant.
▶ noun (stress on the first syllable) **1** *the interchange of ideas between the*

producers and the end users **exchange**, trading, trade, swap, swapping, barter, bandying, give and take, traffic, trafficking, reciprocation, reciprocity; *archaic* truck.
2 *the interchange of the ninth and tenth columns* **substitution**, transposition, exchange, switch, switching, swap, swapping, reversal, inversion, change, rearrangement, reordering, replacement, replacing; *N. Amer.* trade.
3 *a motorway interchange* **junction**, intersection, crossing; turn-off, exit; *N. Amer.* cloverleaf.

interchangeable ▶ adjective **1** *the very latest paint gun has three interchangeable barrels* **exchangeable**, transposable, replaceable.
OPPOSITE incompatible.
2 *you can follow one of two more or less interchangeable roads back into the valley* **identical**, similar, alike, (exactly) the same, indistinguishable, uniform, twin, undifferentiated, homogeneous, of a piece, cut from the same cloth; corresponding, correspondent, commensurate, equivalent, matching, like, parallel, analogous, comparable, cognate, equal; *informal* like (two) peas in a pod, much of a muchness, (like) Tweedledum and Tweedledee.
OPPOSITE different.

intercourse ▶ noun **1** *the market was an important focus of social intercourse* **dealings**, relations, relationships, association, connections, contact, interchange, communication, intercommunication, communion, correspondence, negotiations, bargaining, transactions, proceedings; **trade**, trading, business, commerce, traffic, trafficking; *informal* truck, doings.
2 *she did not consent to intercourse with him* **sexual intercourse**, sex, lovemaking, making love, sex act, act of love, sexual relations, intimate relations, intimacy, coupling, mating, going to bed with someone, sleeping with someone; *informal* nooky; *Brit. informal* bonking, rumpy pumpy, a bit of the other, how's your father; *S. African informal* pata-pata; *vulgar slang* screwing, fucking; *Brit. vulgar slang* shagging; *formal* coitus, coition, copulation; *archaic* fornication, carnal knowledge, (sexual) congress, commerce.

interdict ▶ noun *they breached an interdict banning them from organizing mass pickets* **prohibition**, ban, bar, veto, proscription, interdiction, embargo, moratorium, injunction, restraining order; *Brit.* exclusion order.
OPPOSITE permission.
▶ verb **1** *the Portuguese interdicted all foreign commerce* **prohibit**, forbid, ban, bar, veto, proscribe, make illegal, place an embargo on, embargo, disallow, debar, outlaw, stop, put a stop to, put an end to, block, suppress; *Law* enjoin, estop, restrain.
OPPOSITE permit.
2 (*N. Amer.*) *efforts to interdict asylum seekers before they ever reach the US* **intercept**, stop, head off, cut off; obstruct, impede, interrupt, block, check, detain.

interest ▶ noun **1** *the children listened to the story with great interest* **attentiveness**, undivided attention, absorption, engrossment, heed, regard, notice, scrutiny; curiosity, inquisitiveness; enjoyment, delight.
OPPOSITE boredom.
2 *the region has many places of interest to the tourist* **attraction**, appeal, fascination, charm, beauty, allure, allurement, temptation, tantalization.
3 *this account may only be of interest to those involved* **concern**, **importance**, import, consequence, moment, momentousness, significance, substance, note, relevance, value, weight, gravity, priority, urgency.
4 *her interests include reading and music* **hobby**, pastime, leisure activity, leisure pursuit, recreation, entertainment, diversion, amusement, relaxation; passion, enthusiasm; *informal* thing, bag, scene, cup of tea.
5 *he has a financial interest in the firm* **stake**, share, portion, claim, investment, stock, equity; involvement, participation, concern.
6 *you must declare your interest in the case* **involvement**, partiality, partisanship, preference, loyalty; one-sidedness, favouritism, bias, prejudice.
7 *his attorney zealously guarded his interests* **concern**, business, business matter, matter, care; **(interests)** affairs.
8 *put your cash in a savings account where it will earn interest* **dividends**, profits, returns; a percentage, a gain.
□ **in someone's interests** *the merger is in the interests of both regiments* **of benefit to**, to the advantage of, for the sake of, for the benefit of.
▶ verb **1** *write about a topic that interests you* **be of interest to**, appeal to, attract, be attractive to, intrigue, fascinate; absorb, engross, rivet, grip, hold, captivate; amuse, divert, entertain; arouse one's curiosity, whet one's appetite, hold one's attention, engage one's attention; *informal* float someone's boat, tickle someone's fancy, light someone's fire.
OPPOSITE bore.
2 *can I* **interest** *you* **in** *an aerial photograph of your house?* **arouse someone's interest in**, persuade to buy, sell.

interested ▶ adjective **1** *an interested crowd had gathered round the buskers* **attentive**, intent, absorbed, engrossed, fascinated, riveted, gripped, captivated, rapt, agog, intrigued, inquiring, inquisitive, curious, burning with curiosity; earnest, keen, eager; *informal* all ears, beady-eyed, nosy, snoopy.
OPPOSITES bored, uninterested.
2 *the government must consult with interested bodies before formulating a legislative measure* **concerned**, involved, implicated, affected, connected, related.
3 *no interested party can judge the contest* **partisan**, partial, biased, prejudiced, one-sided, preferential, discriminatory.
OPPOSITE disinterested.

interesting ▶ adjective *it is one of the most interesting novels of its time* **absorbing**, engrossing, fascinating, riveting, gripping, compelling, compulsive, spellbinding, captivating, engaging, enthralling, entrancing, beguiling; appealing, attractive, amusing, entertaining, stimulating, thought-provoking, diverting, exciting, intriguing, action-packed; *informal* unputdownable.
OPPOSITES boring, uninteresting.

interfere ▶ verb **1** *we can't let personal feelings* **interfere with** *our duty* **impede**, obstruct, get in the way of, stand in the way of, hinder, be a hindrance to, inhibit, restrict, restrain, constrain, hamper, handicap, cramp, check, block, frustrate, thwart, baulk, hold back, hold up; disturb, disrupt, influence, affect, confuse; *Brit. informal* throw a spanner in the works of; *N. Amer. informal* throw a monkey wrench in the works of; *rare* trammel, cumber.
2 *she tried not to* **interfere in** *her children's lives* **butt into**, barge into, pry into, nose into, be nosy about, intrude into, intervene in, get involved in, intercede in, encroach on, impinge on, impose oneself on; meddle in, tamper with; tread on someone's toes, step on someone's toes; *informal* poke one's nose into, mess with, horn in on, muscle in on, stick one's oar in, gatecrash; *N. Amer. informal* kibitz on; *archaic* entrench on.
3 (*Brit. euphemistic*) *he was accused of* **interfering with** *local children* **sexually abuse**, abuse, sexually assault, indecently assault, assault, molest, grope; harm, damage; *informal* feel up, touch up, paw, maul.

I

interference ▶ noun **1** *they resent state interference in religious affairs* **intrusion**, intervention, intercession, involvement, impinging, encroaching, trespass, trespassing, obtrusion; butting in, barging in; meddling, meddlesomeness, tampering, prying, poking around, nosing around; *informal* horning in, muscling in, gatecrashing.
2 *the cable helps to suppress radio interference* **disruption**, disturbance, static, fading.

interfering ▶ adjective *they wanted to be free from their interfering relatives* **meddlesome**, meddling, intrusive, intruding, prying, probing, nosy, inquisitive, over-curious, over-interested, busybody; *informal* nosy-parker, snoopy, snooping; *archaic* intermeddling; *rare* obtrusive, busy.

interim ▶ noun *in the interim they agreed to carry out further research* **meantime**, meanwhile, intervening time, interval, interlude; interregnum.
▶ adjective *he appointed an interim advisory committee* **provisional**, temporary, pro tem, stopgap, short-term, fill-in, caretaker, acting, intervening, transitional, changeover, make-do, makeshift, improvised, impromptu, emergency; *Latin* pro tempore, ad interim; *rare* provisory, provisionary.
OPPOSITE permanent.

interior ▶ adjective **1** *the house has a lovely oak staircase and interior panelling* **inside**, inner, internal, intramural; on the inside.
OPPOSITE exterior.
2 *the interior basin deserts of the western United States* **inland**, inshore, upcountry, non-coastal, inner, innermost, central; remote, wild.
OPPOSITE outer.
3 *he controlled the country's interior affairs* **internal**, home, domestic, national, state, civil, local.
OPPOSITE foreign.
4 *individuals are driven by interior forces* **inner**, spiritual, mental, psychological, emotional, private, personal, intimate, secret, hidden; instinctive, intuitive, impulsive, involuntary, spontaneous; *informal* gut.
▶ noun **1** *a hatch led to the interior of the yacht* **inside**, inner part, inner area, depths, recesses, bowels, belly; centre, middle, nucleus, core, heart; *informal* innards.
OPPOSITES exterior, outside.
2 *he went on treks to the country's interior* **centre**, heartland, hinterland; wilderness, wilds; (*in Australia and Africa*) bush.
OPPOSITE borderland.

interject ▶ verb **1** *at one point in his story she interjected a comment* **interpose**, introduce, throw in, insert, interpolate, add.
2 *Christina felt bound to interject before there was open warfare* **interrupt**, intervene, cut in, break in, butt in, chime in; have one's say, put one's oar in; remark, comment; *Brit. informal* chip in, put one's pennyworth in; *N. Amer. informal* put one's two cents in.

interjection ▶ noun **1** *there were astonished interjections from the crowd* **exclamation**, ejaculation, sudden utterance, cry, shout, roar, call; *rare* vociferation.
2 *the interjection of a question here and there* **interposition**, interposing, interpolation, interpolating, insertion, inserting, addition, adding, introduction, introducing.

interlock ▶ verb *the fixed panel should interlock with the sliding section* **engage**, interconnect, interlink, mesh, intermesh, fit together, join

together, join, unite, connect, yoke, mate, couple.
OPPOSITE disengage.

interloper ▶ noun *they were a close community and could not abide interlopers* **intruder**, encroacher, trespasser, invader, infiltrator, unwanted person, unwanted visitor, uninvited guest; outsider, stranger, immigrant, foreigner, alien, newcomer; *informal* gatecrasher.

interlude ▶ noun *a peaceful interlude in her busy day* **interval**, intermission, break, recess, pause, respite, rest, breathing space, halt, gap, stop, stoppage, hiatus, lull; *informal* breather, let-up, time out, down time; *Austral./NZ informal* smoko; *archaic* surcease.

intermediary ▶ noun *they concluded the deal through an intermediary* **mediator**, go-between, negotiator, intervenor, interceder, intercessor, arbitrator, arbiter, conciliator, peacemaker; middleman, broker, agent, liaison, linkman, linkwoman, linkperson; *rare* negotiant.

intermediate ▶ adjective *an intermediate stage in the cell's development* **halfway**, in-between, middle, mid, midway, median, intermediary, intervening, interposed, transitional; in the middle, at the halfway point, equidistant between two points/stages; *technical* medial; *rare* intermedial.

interment ▶ noun *his body was taken for interment* **burial**, burying, committal, entombment, inhumation; a funeral; funeral rites, obsequies; *rare* sepulture, exequies.
OPPOSITE exhumation.

interminable ▶ adjective **1** *Wednesday was a day of interminable meetings* **seemingly endless**, endless, never-ending, unending, without end, non-stop, everlasting, ceaseless, unceasing, incessant, constant, continual, uninterrupted, unbroken, sustained; monotonous, tedious, wearisome, boring, long-winded, long-drawn-out, overlong, rambling, meandering, laborious, ponderous.
2 *he was back from one of his interminable job interviews* **countless**, numerous, many, untold, manifold, multitudinous, multifarious, innumerable, numberless, unmeasured, unnumbered, incalculable, indeterminable; *literary* myriad, legion; *rare* innumerous, unnumberable.

intermingle ▶ verb *the two species of finch rarely intermingle | continue cooking to intermingle the flavours* **mix**, intermix, mingle, unite, affiliate, associate, fraternize, get together, link up; blend, fuse, merge, combine, amalgamate, compound, marry; *rare* commingle, commix, admix, interflow.

intermission ▶ noun *after the first film there was an intermission | the work goes on without intermission* **interval**, interlude, entr'acte, break, recess, pause, rest, respite, breathing space, lull, gap, stop, stoppage, halt; cessation, suspension, stopping, pausing, breaking off, discontinuation; *informal* let-up, breather, time out, down time; *Austral./NZ informal* smoko; *archaic* surcease.

intermittent ▶ adjective *they heard intermittent bursts of gunfire* **sporadic**, irregular, fitful, spasmodic, broken, fragmentary, discontinuous, disconnected, isolated, odd, random, patchy, scattered; on again and off again, on and off, in fits and starts; occasional, periodic, cyclic, recurrent, recurring.
OPPOSITES continuous, steady.

intern ▶ verb *they have been interned without trial* **imprison**, incarcerate, impound, jail, put in jail, put behind bars, detain, take into custody, hold in custody, hold captive, hold, lock up, keep under lock and key, confine; *Brit.* detain at Her Majesty's pleasure; *informal* put away, put inside, send down; *Brit. informal* bang up; *rare* immure.
OPPOSITE release.
▶ noun (*N. Amer.*) *he worked as an intern for a local magazine* **trainee**, apprentice, probationer, student, novice, learner, beginner; person doing work experience.

internal ▶ adjective **1** *the offices faced each other across a large internal courtyard* **inner**, interior, inside, intramural; central, middle.
OPPOSITE external.
2 *she died of internal injuries* **inside**, inner; within the body, inside the body.
OPPOSITE external.
3 *the provinces retain autonomy in their internal affairs* **domestic**, home, interior, civil, local; national, state; in-house, in-company.
OPPOSITE foreign.
4 *she was waging an internal battle with herself* **mental**, psychological, emotional; personal, private, secret, hidden, intimate.

WORD LINKS
related prefix **endo-** (e.g. ***endoskeleton, endocrine***)

international ▶ adjective *the international business community | the international flavour of the exhibition* **global**, worldwide, intercontinental; cosmopolitan, multiracial, multinational, universal, catholic, wide-ranging, far-reaching, all-embracing.
OPPOSITES national; local.

internecine ▶ adjective *internecine feuds between aspirants to the throne* **deadly**, bloody, violent, fierce, destructive, ruinous; civil, internal, family.

interplay ▶ noun *the interplay between military and civilian populations* **interaction**, interchange, teamwork, cooperation, reciprocation, reciprocity, give and take, compromises, concessions; flexibility, adaptability.

interpolate ▶ verb *the illustrations were interpolated in the text* **insert**, interpose, introduce, enter, add, incorporate, inset, implant, build, put.

interpose ▶ verb **1** *he interposed himself between her and the stairs* **insinuate**, place, put.
2 *at this point it is necessary to interpose a note of caution* **introduce**, insert, interject, inject, add, throw in, put in, work in.
3 *the legislature interposed to suppress the custom* **intervene**, intercede, step in, mediate, involve oneself; interfere, intrude, obtrude, butt in, cut in; *informal* barge in, horn in, muscle in.

interpret ▶ verb **1** *the rabbis interpreted the Jewish laws* **explain**, elucidate, expound, explicate, clarify, make clear, make plain, illuminate, shed light on, throw light on; gloss, simplify, spell out.
2 *the remark was interpreted as a reference to the government* **understand**, construe, take to mean, take, read, see, regard, explain.
3 *the symbols are difficult to interpret* **decipher**, decode, solve, resolve, untangle, unravel, make intelligible; understand, comprehend, make sense of; *informal* crack.
4 *the book was interpreted for English-speaking readers* **translate**, transcribe, transliterate, rewrite, convert; paraphrase.
5 *few ballets have so fully interpreted the thoughts of a poet* **portray**, depict, present, perform, execute, enact, render.

interpretation ▶ noun **1** *the interpretation and application of the Bible's teaching* **explanation**, elucidation, expounding, exposition, explication, exegesis, clarification, definition; simplification.
2 *she did not care what interpretation he put on her haste* **meaning**, understanding, construal, connotation, reading, explanation, inference, conclusion, supposition.
3 *the interpretation of experimental findings* **analysis**, reading, evaluation, review, study, examination, diagnosis; decoding, deciphering; *rare* anatomization.
4 *the interpretation of foreign texts* **translation**, transcription, transliteration; paraphrasing.
5 *Davis was admirable in his interpretation of the sonata* **rendition**, rendering, execution, presentation, performance, reading, playing, singing; enactment, portrayal, depiction.

interpreter ▶ noun **1** *a fluent Japanese speaker acted as their interpreter* **translator**, transcriber, transliterator, decipherer; *rare* dragoman.
2 *she was the most important vocal interpreter of his music* **performer**, presenter, portrayer, exponent; singer, player.
3 *interpreters of Soviet history* **analyst**, evaluator, reviewer, commentator, annotator; *rare* exegete, scholiast, glossator.

interrogate ▶ verb *the police wished to interrogate her* **question**, put questions to, cross-question, cross-examine, quiz, probe, catechize, sound out; interview, examine, debrief; *informal* pump, grill, give someone the third degree, put someone through the third degree, put the screws on, put someone through the wringer, worm something out of someone.

interrogation ▶ noun *he was driven to the police station for interrogation* **questioning**, cross-questioning, cross-examination, quizzing, probing, inquisition, catechism; investigation, interviewing, interview, debriefing; *informal* pumping, grilling, the third degree; *Law* examination.

interrogative ▶ adjective *he gazed at me with a hard interrogative stare* **questioning**, inquiring, inquisitive, inquisitorial, probing, searching, quizzing, quizzical, curious, intrigued, investigative; *rare* catechistic, catechistical.

interrupt ▶ verb **1** *she opened her mouth to interrupt | I'm sorry to interrupt your chat* **cut in (on)**, break in (on), barge in (on), intrude (on), interfere (with), intervene (in); heckle, put one's oar in, have one's say; *Brit.* put one's pennyworth in; *N. Amer.* put one's two cents in; *informal* butt in (on), chime in (on), horn in (on), muscle in (on); *Brit. informal* chip in (on).
2 *the band had to interrupt their US tour* **suspend**, adjourn, discontinue, break off, hold up, delay, lay aside, leave off, postpone, put off, put back, defer, shelve; stop, put a stop to, halt, bring to a halt, bring to a standstill, cease, end, bring to an end, bring to a close, cancel, sever, dissolve, terminate; *informal* take a breather from, put on ice, put on a back burner, put in cold storage.
3 *the coastal plain is interrupted by large lagoons* **break up**, break, punctuate, intersperse; pepper, strew, dot, scatter.
4 *their view is to be interrupted by a new housing estate* **obstruct**, impede, block, interfere with, cut off, get in the way of, limit, restrict.

interruption ▶ noun **1** *he was not best pleased at her interruption* **cutting in**, interference, intervention, intrusion, obtrusion, disturbance; *informal* butting in, barging in, muscling in, horning in, sticking one's oar in.
2 *the system is protected against interruption of the power supply* **discontinuance**, discontinuation, breaking off, suspension, stopping, halting, ceasing, cessation, termination.
3 *she is returning to education after an interruption in her career* **interval**, interlude, break, pause, recess, gap, hiatus.

intersect ▶ verb **1** *the lines intersect at right angles* **cross**, criss-cross; converge, meet, connect, join, link up, come together; *technical* decussate.

2 *the cornfield is intersected by a farm track* **bisect**, divide, halve, cut in two, cut in half, cut across, cut through; cross, traverse, span.

intersection ▶ noun **1** *the intersection of the supply and demand curves* **crossing**, criss-crossing; convergence, meeting, joining.
2 *the driver stopped at an intersection* **road junction**, junction, T-junction, interchange, crossroads, crossing; level crossing, railway crossing; *Brit.* roundabout.

intersperse ▶ verb **1** *giant lobelia were interspersed among crags of rock* **scatter**, distribute, disperse, spread, strew, dot, sprinkle, pepper, litter; *literary* bestrew.
2 *the beech trees are interspersed with conifers* **intermix**, mix, mingle; **vary**, diversify, variegate, punctuate.

interstice ▶ noun *the interstices between the soil particles* **space**, gap, interval, aperture, opening, hole, cranny, crevice, chink, slit, slot, crack, breach, vent.

intertwine ▶ verb *a wreath of laurel, intertwined with daffodils* **entwine**, interweave, interlace, interthread, interwind, intertwist, twist, coil, twirl, ravel, lace, braid, plait, knit; *rare* convolute.

interval ▶ noun **1** *I returned to my balcony seat after the interval* **intermission**, interlude, entr'acte, break, recess, pause, gap; lull, respite; half-time.
2 *polling day was a week away and Baldwin made two speeches in the interval* **interim**, interlude, intervening time, intervening period, meantime, meanwhile; interregnum.
3 *the rapids have some short intervals of still water* **stretch**, distance, span, area; space, gap, interspace.

intervene ▶ verb **1** *had the war not intervened, they might have married* **occur**, happen, take place, arise, crop up, materialize, come about; result, ensue, follow, supervene; *literary* come to pass, befall, betide; *archaic* hap.
2 *she intervened in the row and drew up new guidelines* **intercede**, involve oneself, get involved, interpose oneself, insinuate oneself, step in, cut in; mediate, arbitrate, conciliate, negotiate, act as peacemaker, act as an intermediary; interfere, intrude.

intervention ▶ noun *they would suffer no state intervention in their private business* **involvement**, intercession, interceding, interposing, interposition; mediation, mediatorship, arbitration, conciliation, peacemaking; interference, intrusion, meddling; *rare* arbitrament.

interview ▶ noun *all applicants will be called for an interview | the journalists were granted an interview with the bishop* **meeting**, discussion, conference, question and answer session, examination, evaluation, interrogation; **audience**, talk, dialogue, exchange; talks; *informal* rap session, confab; *formal* confabulation, interlocution.
▶ verb *the reporter interviewed him about his book | we interviewed seventy subjects for the survey* **talk to**, have a discussion with, have a dialogue with, hold a meeting with, confer with; **question**, put questions to, probe, interrogate, cross-examine; poll, canvass, survey, sound out, ascertain the opinions of; *informal* grill, pump, give the third degree to; *Law* examine.

interviewer ▶ noun *the interviewer had a long list of questions* **questioner**, interrogator, examiner, evaluator, assessor, appraiser; journalist, reporter, correspondent; *rare* examinant.

interweave ▶ verb **1** *the threads attached to the kite are interwoven* **intertwine**, entwine, interlace, interthread, splice, braid, plait; twist together, weave together, twine together, wind together; *Nautical* marry.
2 *their fates were interwoven* **interlink**, link, connect, associate; intermix, mix, merge, blend, fuse, interlock, knit, bind together.

intestinal ▶ adjective *he died from an intestinal complaint* **enteric**, gastro-enteric, duodenal, coeliac, gastric, ventral, stomach, abdominal, visceral; *rare* stomachic, stomachical.

intestines ▶ plural noun *colic is a sharp pain in a baby's stomach or intestines* **gut**, guts, entrails, viscera; small intestine, large intestine, bowel, colon; *informal* insides, innards; *Brit. archaic* numbles.

WORD LINKS

relating to the intestines	**enteric, visceral**
related prefix	**entero-**
incision into the intestine	**enterotomy**
inflammation of the intestines	**enteritis**

intimacy ▶ noun **1** *the sisters instantly re-established their old intimacy* **closeness**, togetherness, affinity, rapport, attachment, familiarity, confidentiality, close association, close relationship, close attachment, close friendship, friendliness, comradeship, companionship, amity, affection, mutual affection, warmth, warm feelings, understanding, fellow feeling; *informal* chumminess, palliness; *Brit. informal* mateyness.
2 *she flushed at the memory of their earlier intimacy* **sexual relations**, sexual intercourse, sex, intercourse, lovemaking, act of love, carnal knowledge, sexual congress, congress; *formal* coition, coitus, copulation.

intimate[1] (rhymes with 'ultimate') ▶ adjective **1** *an intimate friend of Picasso's* **close**, bosom, boon, dear, cherished, familiar, confidential, faithful, constant, devoted, fast, firm, favourite, special; *informal* chummy, pally, as thick as thieves.
OPPOSITE distant.
2 *the hotel has an intimate atmosphere* **friendly**, warm, welcoming, hospitable, harmonious, relaxed, informal, easy; cosy, comfortable, snug; tête-à-tête; *informal* comfy.
OPPOSITES formal; cold.
3 *they divulged their intimate thoughts* **personal**, private, confidential, secret; innermost, inmost, inner, inward, deep, deepest, darkest, deep-seated; unspoken, undeclared, undisclosed, unvoiced.
4 *he has an intimate knowledge of the coal industry* **detailed**, thorough, exhaustive, deep, in-depth, profound; experienced, personal, first-hand, direct, immediate.
OPPOSITE scant.
5 *he had intimate relations with his friend's wife* **sexual**, carnal, amorous, amatory, romantic; *rare* fornicatory.
▶ noun *his background was common knowledge among his intimates* **close friend**, best friend, bosom friend, constant companion, alter ego, confidant, confidante, close associate; *informal* chum, pal, buddy, crony, sidekick, cully, spar, main man; *Brit. informal* mate, mucker, china, oppo, butty; *N. English informal* marrow, marrer, marra; *N. Amer. & S. African informal* homeboy, homegirl; *S. African informal* gabba; *Austral./NZ informal* offsider; *rare* fidus Achates.

intimate[2] (rhymes with 'imitate') ▶ verb **1** *he intimated to the committee his decision to retire* **announce**, state, proclaim, set forth, make known, make public, make plain, impart, disclose, reveal, divulge; tell, inform.
2 *her feelings were subtly intimated in various ways* **imply**, suggest, hint at, insinuate, indicate, signal, allude to, refer to, communicate, convey; give someone an inkling of; *informal* tip someone the wink about, get at, drive at.

intimation ▶ noun **1** *the early intimation of training session dates* **announcement**, statement, communication, notification, notice, report, reporting, publishing, broadcasting, proclamation; disclosure, revelation, divulging; *archaic* annunciation.
2 *the first intimation of discord in the family* **suggestion**, hint, indication, sign, signal, inkling, suspicion, impression; reference to, allusion to, pointer to, clue to, overtone of, undertone of, whisper of.

intimidate ▶ verb *he paid them to intimidate his political rivals* **frighten**, menace, terrify, scare, alarm, terrorize, overawe, awe, cow, subdue, discourage, daunt, unnerve; **threaten**, domineer, browbeat, bully, pressure, pressurize, harass, harry, hound, hector, torment, plague; tyrannize, persecute, oppress; *informal* push around/about, lean on, bulldoze, steamroller, railroad, twist someone's arm, use strong-arm tactics on; *N. Amer. informal* bullyrag.

CHOOSE THE RIGHT WORD

intimidate, threaten, menace
See THREATEN.

intimidation ▶ noun *there had been blatant intimidation of witnesses* **frightening**, menacing, terrifying, scaring, alarming, terrorization, terrorizing, cowing, subduing, daunting, unnerving; **threatening**, domineering, browbeating, bullying, pressuring, pressurizing, pressurization, coercion, harassment, harrying, hounding, tormenting, plaguing; tyrannization, persecution, oppression; *informal* strong-arm tactics, arm-twisting, bulldozing, steamrollering, railroading.

intolerable ▶ adjective *the drilling noise had become intolerable* **unbearable**, insufferable, unsupportable, insupportable, unendurable, beyond endurance, unacceptable, impossible, more than flesh and blood can stand, too much to bear, past bearing, not to be borne, overpowering; *informal* too much, enough to try the patience of a saint, enough to try the patience of Job.
OPPOSITES bearable, tolerable.

intolerance ▶ noun **1** *they are protesting at political and religious intolerance* **bigotry**, narrow-mindedness, small-mindedness, parochialism, provincialism, insularity, fanaticism, dogmatism, illiberality; prejudice, bias, partiality, partisanship, sectarianism, one-sidedness, inequality, unfairness, injustice, discrimination.
2 *she was tested for lactose intolerance* **sensitivity**, hypersensitivity, oversensitivity; allergy, allergic reaction.

intolerant ▶ adjective **1** *Sophia was intolerant in religious matters* **bigoted**, narrow-minded, small-minded, parochial, provincial, insular, blinkered, illiberal, inflexible, dogmatic, rigid, uncompromising, unforgiving, unsympathetic; prejudiced, biased, partial, partisan, one-sided, sectarian, discriminatory, unfair, unjust.
2 *limit those foods to which you are intolerant* **allergic**, sensitive, hypersensitive, oversensitive.

intonation ▶ noun **1** *she read the sentence with the wrong intonation | his*

voice was low with a faint regional intonation **inflection**, pitch, tone, timbre, cadence, cadency, lilt, rise and fall, modulation, speech pattern; accentuation, emphasis, stress; accent, brogue.
2 *the intonation of hymns of praise* **chanting**, incantation, recitation, singing; *rare* cantillation.

intone ▶ **verb** *grace before the meal was intoned in Gaelic* **chant**, intonate, sing, recite; *rare* cantillate.

intoxicate ▶ **verb 1** *one glass of wine was enough to intoxicate him* **inebriate**, make drunk, make intoxicated, make inebriated; befuddle, fuddle, stupefy, go to someone's head, make someone's head spin; *informal* make legless, make woozy.
OPPOSITE sober someone up.
2 *he was intoxicated by cinema from the start* **exhilarate**, thrill, elate, delight, captivate, enthral, entrance, enrapture, invigorate, animate, enliven, excite, stir, rouse, move, inspire, inflame, electrify; fire with enthusiasm, fire someone's imagination; *informal* give someone a buzz, give someone a kick, bowl over, tickle someone pink; *N. Amer. informal* give someone a charge.
OPPOSITE bore.

intoxicated ▶ **adjective** *he was cautioned for being intoxicated while on duty* **drunk**, inebriated, inebriate, drunken, tipsy, the worse for drink, under the influence; blind drunk, dead drunk, rolling drunk, roaring drunk, as drunk as a lord, as drunk as a skunk; sottish, gin-soaked; *informal* tight, merry, the worse for wear, pie-eyed, three sheets to the wind, plastered, smashed, hammered, sloshed, soused, sozzled, well oiled, paralytic, wrecked, wasted, blotto, stewed, pickled, tanked up, soaked, blasted, ratted, off one's face, out of one's head, out of one's skull; *Brit. informal* legless, bevvied, Brahms and Liszt, half cut, out of it, bladdered, trolleyed, well away, squiffy, tiddly, out of one's box; *Scottish informal* fou; *N. Amer. informal* loaded, trashed, out of one's gourd; *Brit. vulgar slang* pissed, rat-arsed; *informal, dated* in one's cups, lit up; *euphemistic* tired and emotional; *archaic* sotted, foxed, screwed; *rare* crapulent, crapulous, bibulous, ebriate.
OPPOSITE sober.

intoxicating ▶ **adjective 1** *they abstain from intoxicating drink* **alcoholic**, containing alcohol; strong, hard, potent, stiff; *rare* inebriating, intoxicant, spirituous, spiritous, vinous.
OPPOSITE non-alcoholic.
2 *an intoxicating sense of freedom prevailed* **heady**, exhilarating, thrilling, exciting, rousing, stirring, stimulating, invigorating, electrifying, inspiring, galvanizing; strong, powerful, potent; *informal* mind-blowing.
OPPOSITE dull.

intoxication ▶ **noun** *he left the pub in a state of intoxication* **drunkenness**, inebriation, insobriety, tipsiness, stupefaction; *informal* tightness; *rare* inebriety, crapulence.
OPPOSITE sobriety.

intractable ▶ **adjective 1** *their problems have become more acute and intractable* **unmanageable**, uncontrollable, ungovernable, out of control, out of hand, impossible to cope with; difficult, awkward, complex, troublesome, demanding, burdensome.
OPPOSITE manageable.
2 *there was no budging this intractable man* **stubborn**, obstinate, obdurate, inflexible, unadaptable, unmalleable, unbending, unyielding, uncompromising, unaccommodating, uncooperative, difficult, awkward, perverse, contrary, disobedient, indomitable, refractory, recalcitrant, pig-headed, bull-headed, wilful; *N. Amer.* rock-ribbed; *informal* stiff-necked; *Brit. informal* bloody-minded; *N. Amer. informal* balky.
OPPOSITES compliant; obedient.

intransigent ▶ **adjective** *his intransigent attitude led to the quarrels with his friends* **uncompromising**, inflexible, unbending, unyielding, unshakeable, unwavering, resolute, unpersuadable, unmalleable, unaccommodating, uncooperative, stubborn, obstinate, obdurate, pig-headed, bull-headed, single-minded, iron-willed, hard-line, hard and fast, diehard, immovable, unrelenting, inexorable, inveterate, rigid, tough, firm, determined, adamant, tenacious; *informal* stiff-necked; *Brit. informal* bloody-minded; *N. Amer. informal* balky; *rare* indurate.
OPPOSITES compliant; flexible.

intrench ▶ **verb.** See ENTRENCH.

intrenched ▶ **adjective.** See ENTRENCHED.

intrepid ▶ **adjective** *the intrepid band braved a precipitous mountain track* **fearless**, unafraid, undaunted, dauntless, undismayed, unalarmed, unflinching, unshrinking, unblenching, unabashed, bold, daring, audacious, adventurous, dashing, heroic, dynamic, spirited, mettlesome, confident, indomitable; **brave**, courageous, valiant, valorous, stout-hearted, lionhearted, stalwart, plucky; *informal* gutsy, spunky, game, ballsy, go-ahead, have-a-go; *archaic* doughty; *rare* venturous.
OPPOSITES fearful; cowardly.

intricate ▶ **adjective** *intricate Arabic patterns | the intricate relationships between plants and animals* **complex**, complicated, convoluted, tangled, entangled, ravelled, twisted, knotty, maze-like, labyrinthine, winding, serpentine, circuitous, sinuous; elaborate, ornate, detailed; Byzantine, Daedalian, Gordian, involved, mixed up, difficult, hard; *informal* fiddly; *rare* involute, involuted.
OPPOSITES simple, straightforward.

> **CHOOSE THE RIGHT WORD**
>
> **intricate, complicated, complex, involved**
>
> See COMPLICATED.

intrigue ▶ **verb** (stress on the second syllable) **1** *other people's houses always intrigued her* **interest**, be of interest to, fascinate, be a source of fascination to, arouse someone's curiosity, engage someone's attention, attract, draw, lure, tempt, tantalize; rivet, absorb, engross, charm, captivate; divert, titillate.
OPPOSITE bore.
2 *the ministers were intriguing for their own gains* **plot**, hatch a plot, conspire, take part in a conspiracy, make secret plans, lay plans, scheme, manoeuvre, connive, collude, work hand in glove; *rare* complot, cabal, machinate.
▶ **noun** (stress on the first syllable) **1** *the intrigue that accompanied the selection of a new leader | they implicated him in a nasty intrigue* **plotting**, planning, conspiracy, collusion, conniving, scheming, machination, trickery, sharp practice, double-dealing, unscrupulousness, underhandedness, deviousness, subterfuge; plot, scheme, stratagem, ruse, wile, artifice, manoeuvre; *informal* dirty tricks; *rare* complot, cabal, covin.
2 *the king's intrigues with his nobles' wives* **secret love affair**, affair, affair of the heart, liaison, amour, amorous entanglement, romantic entanglement, fling, flirtation, dalliance; adultery, infidelity, unfaithfulness; *informal* fooling around, playing around, playing away, hanky-panky; *Brit. informal* carryings-on, carry-on, bit on the side.

intriguer ▶ **noun** *he was revealed to be a political intriguer* **conspirator**, co-conspirator, conspirer, plotter, schemer, colluder, collaborator, conniver; manipulator, exploiter; *rare* machinator, Machiavelli, Machiavellian, cabalist, intrigant(e).

intriguing ▶ **adjective** *a wealth of intriguing stories appear in this book* **interesting**, fascinating, absorbing, compelling, gripping, riveting, captivating, engaging, enthralling, diverting, titillating, tantalizing; stimulating, thought-provoking.

intrinsic ▶ **adjective** *pride was an intrinsic component of his personal make-up* **inherent**, innate, inborn, inbred, congenital, natural, native, constitutional, built-in, ingrained, deep-rooted, inseparable, permanent, indelible, ineradicable, ineffaceable; **integral**, basic, fundamental, underlying, constitutive, elemental, essential, vital, necessary; *rare* connate, connatural.
OPPOSITES extrinsic; acquired.

> **CHOOSE THE RIGHT WORD**
>
> **intrinsic, inherent, essential, innate**
>
> See INHERENT.

introduce ▶ **verb 1** *he has tried to introduce a new system of joint consultation* **institute**, initiate, launch, inaugurate, establish, found, instigate; bring in, bring into being, usher in, set in motion, start, begin, commence, get going, get under way, phase in; organize, develop, originate, pioneer, take the lead in; *informal* kick off.
OPPOSITE abolish.
2 *you can introduce new ideas* **propose**, put forward, suggest, submit, advance, table, move; raise, broach, bring up, set forth, moot, mention, open, air, ventilate, float.
3 *she* **introduced** *Lindsey* **to** *the young man* **present**, present formally, make known; acquaint with, make acquainted with, bring into contact with.
4 *a device used to introduce nitrogen into canned beer* **insert**, inject, put, place, push, force, drive, shoot, feed.
OPPOSITE remove.
5 *she tried to introduce a note of severity into her voice* **instil**, infuse, inject, add, insert, bring; interpose.
6 *the same presenter introduces the programme each week* **announce**, present, give an introduction to; preface, precede, lead into, commence, start off, begin, open, launch.

introduction ▶ **noun 1** *the introduction of democratic reforms* **institution**, establishment, initiation, launch, inauguration, foundation, instigation; start, commencement, inception; development, origination, pioneering.
OPPOSITE abolition.
2 *he wished for an introduction to the king* **presentation**, formal presentation; meeting, audience, interview, encounter.
3 *he wrote an introduction to the catalogue* **foreword**, preface, preamble, prologue, prelude, front matter, lead-in; opening, beginning, start, opening statement; *informal* intro, prelims, curtain-raiser; *formal* prolegomenon, proem, exordium, prolusion.
OPPOSITES afterword, appendix.

4 *the handbook will include an* ***introduction to*** *the history of the period* **basic explanation of**, brief account of, description of; the basics, the rudiments, the fundamentals, the groundwork.
5 *he had hoped for a gentle introduction to the life of the school* **initiation**, induction, baptism, inauguration, debut.

introductory ▶ adjective **1** *the introductory chapter* **opening**, initial, starting, commencing, initiatory, first, earliest; prefatory, preliminary, precursory, lead-in; *rare* prefatorial, precursive, prodromal, prodromic, preambular, preambulatory, preludial, prelusive, prelusory, exordial, proemial, prolegomenal.
OPPOSITE final.
2 *a one-day introductory course* **elementary**, basic, rudimentary, fundamental; initiatory, preparatory, primary; *rare* rudimental.
OPPOSITE advanced.

introspection ▶ noun *he wasn't given to introspection* **brooding**, self-analysis, soul-searching, heart-searching, introversion, self-observation, self-absorption; contemplation, thoughtfulness, pensiveness, thought, thinking, musing, rumination, meditation, pondering, reflection, cogitation; *informal* navel-gazing.

introspective ▶ adjective *a shy and introspective man* **inward-looking**, self-analysing, self-examining, self-observing, brooding; introverted, introvert, self-contained; contemplative, thoughtful, pensive, musing, ruminative, meditative, reflective; *informal* navel-gazing; *rare* indrawn.
OPPOSITES outward-looking, extrovert.

introverted ▶ adjective *an introverted and thoughtful person* **shy**, reserved, withdrawn, reticent, diffident, retiring, quiet, timid, timorous, meek, bashful, unsociable; introspective, introvert, inward-looking, self-contained, self-absorbed, self-interested; contemplative, thoughtful, pensive, ruminative, meditative, reflective; *rare* indrawn.
OPPOSITE extroverted.

intrude ▶ verb **1** *the press believe they have the right to* ***intrude on*** *people's privacy* **encroach**, impinge, trespass, infringe, obtrude, thrust oneself in; invade, violate; interfere with, disturb, disrupt; *informal* horn in, muscle in; *archaic* entrench.
OPPOSITE withdraw.
2 *he intruded his own personality into his work* **force**, push, introduce, obtrude, impose, thrust.
OPPOSITE remove.

intruder ▶ noun *the intruder had rifled through drawers* **trespasser**, interloper, invader, prowler, infiltrator, encroacher, violator; burglar, housebreaker, thief, raider, robber, cat burglar.

intrusion ▶ noun *she didn't want his constant* ***intrusion into*** *her life* **encroachment on**, trespass on, obtrusion into; invasion of, incursion into, violation of, interruption of, intervention in, interference with, disturbance of, disruption of, infringement of, impingement on.
OPPOSITE withdrawal.

intrusive ▶ adjective **1** *an intrusive journalist* **intruding**, invasive, obtrusive, interrupting, trespassing, unwanted, unwelcome; meddlesome, meddling, interfering, busybody; inquisitive, prying, curious; *informal* pushy, nosy.
2 *in those days opinion polls played a much less intrusive role in elections* **invasive**, impossible to ignore, high-profile, prominent, unavoidable, inescapable, interrupting, disturbing; annoying, irritating, irksome; *informal* in one's face.
OPPOSITE low-key.
3 *some parents reacted badly to the intrusive questions* **personal**, prying, forward, impudent, impertinent, offensive; *informal* nosy, nosy-parker, snooping, snoopy.

intuition ▶ noun **1** *he works according to intuition* **instinct**, intuitiveness; sixth sense, divination, clairvoyance, second sight, ESP (extrasensory perception).
OPPOSITE intellect.
2 *this confirms an intuition I had* **hunch**, feeling, feeling in one's bones, gut feeling, funny feeling, inkling, sneaking suspicion, suspicion, impression; premonition, presentiment, foreboding; *Buddhism* satori; *informal* feeling in one's water.

intuitive ▶ adjective *he had an intuitive grasp of people's moods* **instinctive**, intuitional, instinctual; innate, inborn, inherent, untaught, unlearned, natural, congenital, inbuilt, built-in, ingrown; automatic, unconscious, subconscious, involuntary, spontaneous, impulsive, unthinking; *informal* gut.

intumescence ▶ noun (*rare*) *the intumescence of the abdomen on the right side* **swelling**, bulging, bloating, distension, dilatation, turgidity; *rare* turgescence, tumefaction.

inundate ▶ verb **1** *many buildings were inundated* **flood**, deluge, overflow, overrun, swamp, submerge, engulf, drown, immerse, cover; saturate, soak, drench.
2 *we have been inundated by complaints* **overwhelm**, overpower, overburden, overrun, overload, swamp, bog down, besiege, snow under, bury, bombard, glut.

inundation ▶ noun **1** *the annual inundation of the Nile* **flood**, overflow, deluge, torrent, influx; tidal wave, flash flood, freshet; *Brit.* spate.
2 *this inundation of classical pedantry soon infected poetry* **onslaught**, outpouring, flood, deluge, hail, avalanche, flow, barrage, battery, effusion; overabundance, superabundance, plethora, excess, superfluity, surplus, glut; *informal* tons, heaps.

inure ▶ verb *they became inured to poverty* **harden**, toughen, season, temper, condition; accustom, habituate, familiarize, acclimatize, adjust, adapt, attune; desensitize, dehumanize, brutalize, case-harden; *rare* indurate.
OPPOSITE sensitize.

invade ▶ verb **1** *the island was invaded by the Axis powers* **occupy**, **conquer**, capture, seize, take (over), annex, win, gain, secure; march into, overrun, overwhelm, storm, descend on, swoop on, swarm over, surge over, make inroads on; attack, assail, assault, raid, plunder, maraud.
OPPOSITE withdraw from.
2 *I was angry that someone had invaded our privacy* **intrude on**, violate, encroach on, infringe on, trespass on, obtrude on, burst in on, interrupt, disturb, disrupt; *informal* horn in on, muscle in on; *archaic* entrench on.
OPPOSITE respect.
3 *the feeling of betrayal that had invaded my being* **permeate**, pervade, fill, spread through/over, diffuse through, imbue, perfuse, be disseminated through, flow through; assail, attack, take over.

invader ▶ noun **1** *the northern frontier was overrun by invaders* **attacker**, raider, plunderer, pillager, marauder, looter; occupier, conqueror; assailant, assaulter; intruder.
2 *she held herself stiffly, repelling any invader of her personal space* **intruder**, trespasser, violator, encroacher, infringer.

invalid[1] (stress on the first syllable) ▶ noun *my mother is an invalid* **ill person**, infirm person, sick person, valetudinarian, sufferer, patient, convalescent.
▶ adjective *her invalid husband* **ill**, sick, ailing, unwell, infirm, valetudinarian, valetudinary, in poor health; incapacitated, disabled, handicapped, bedridden; frail, feeble, weak, debilitated, sickly; *informal* poorly.
OPPOSITE healthy.
▶ verb *an officer invalided by a chest wound* **disable**, incapacitate, indispose, hospitalize, put out of action, lay up, cripple, paralyse, lame, put on the sick list; injure, wound, hurt, weaken, enfeeble.

invalid[2] (stress on the second syllable) ▶ adjective **1** *the by-law was invalid because it infringed rights of common* **void**, legally void, null, null and void, unenforceable, not binding, inoperative, worthless; illegitimate, incorrect, improper, unacceptable, inapplicable; annulled, nullified, cancelled, revoked, rescinded, abolished, repealed.
OPPOSITES valid, binding.
2 *the whole theory is invalid* **false**, untrue, inaccurate, faulty, fallacious, spurious, inadequate, unconvincing, unsound, weak, wrong, wrongly inferred, wide of the mark, off target; unjustified, unsubstantiated, unwarranted, untenable, baseless, ill-founded, unfounded, groundless; illogical, irrational, unscientific, absurd, preposterous, inconsistent; *informal* off beam, out, way out, full of holes, bogus.
OPPOSITES true, accurate.

invalidate ▶ verb **1** *a low turnout invalidated the ballot* **render invalid**, void, nullify, annul, negate, cancel, quash, veto, overturn, overrule, override, undo, reverse; revoke, rescind, abolish, repeal, repudiate, terminate.
OPPOSITE validate.
2 *this case is exceptional, and does not invalidate the general argument* **disprove**, show/prove to be false, refute, explode, contradict, rebut, negate, gainsay, belie, give the lie to, discredit, expose, debunk, knock the bottom out of, drive a coach and horses through; weaken, undermine, compromise; *informal* shoot full of holes, shoot down (in flames); *formal* confute, negative.
OPPOSITES validate, support.

invaluable ▶ adjective *an invaluable member of the organization* **indispensable**, crucial, critical, key, vital, irreplaceable, extremely useful, extremely helpful, all-important, vitally important, of the utmost importance.
OPPOSITES dispensable, superfluous.

invariable ▶ adjective *his routine was invariable* **unvarying**, unchanging, changeless, unvaried, invariant; constant, stable, set, steady, fast, static, uniform, predictable, regular, consistent, undeviating, unfluctuating, unwavering; unchangeable, unalterable, immutable, fixed.
OPPOSITES varied, variable.

invariably ▶ adverb *he is invariably described as 'down to earth'* **always**, every time, each time, on every occasion, at all times, without fail, without exception, whatever happens, universally; everywhere, in all places, in all cases, in every case, in all instances, in every instance; regularly, consistently, repeatedly, habitually, unfailingly, {day in, day out}, infallibly, inevitably, dependably.
OPPOSITES sometimes; never.

invasion ▶ noun **1** *the invasion of the islands took place in April* **occupation**, conquering, capture, seizure, annexation, annexing, takeover, appropriation, expropriation, arrogation; overrunning, overwhelming,

I

storming; attack, incursion, offensive, assailing, assault, onslaught; foray, sortie, raid.
OPPOSITE withdrawal.
2 *every year the valley suffers an invasion of cars* **influx**, inundation, inrush, rush, flood, torrent, deluge, stream, avalanche.
3 *it was a terrible invasion of your privacy* **violation**, infringement, interruption, disturbance, disruption, breach, infraction; intrusion into, encroachment on, trespass on, obtrusion into, interference with.

invective ▶ noun *she poured forth a string of invective* **abuse**, insults, vituperation, expletives, swear words, swearing, curses, bad language, foul language; denunciation, censure, revilement, vilification, castigation, recrimination, reproach, reproval, admonition; *informal* tongue-lashing; *archaic* contumely, billingsgate, obloquy.
OPPOSITE praise.

inveigh ▶ verb *he went on to* **inveigh against** *pornography and violence in the cinema* **fulminate**, declaim, protest, rail, rage, remonstrate, storm; denounce, censure, condemn, decry, criticize, complain vehemently about; disparage, denigrate, run down, revile, abuse, vilify, impugn; *informal* lash, tongue-lash, kick up a fuss about, kick up a stink about, bellyache about, beef about, grouch about, sound off about.
OPPOSITE support.

inveigle ▶ verb *he was attempting to inveigle them into doing his will* **cajole**, wheedle, coax, persuade, convince, talk; tempt, lure, allure, entice, ensnare, seduce, flatter, beguile, dupe, fool; *informal* sweet-talk, soft-soap, butter up, twist someone's arm, con, bamboozle; *N. Amer. informal* sucker; *archaic* blandish.

I

invent ▶ verb **1** *Louis Braille invented an alphabet to help blind people* **originate**, create, innovate, design, devise, contrive, formulate, develop; conceive, think up, come up with, hit on, mastermind, pioneer; discover, find; coin, mint; *informal* dream up.
2 *he admitted that they invented the story for a laugh* **make up**, fabricate, concoct, hatch, dream up, trump up, manufacture; *informal* cook up.

invention ▶ noun **1** *the invention of the telescope* **origination**, creation, innovation, devising, contriving, contrivance, formulation, development, design; conception, masterminding, pioneering, introduction; discovery, finding.
2 *medieval inventions included the spinning wheel* **innovation**, origination, creation, design, contraption, contrivance, construction, device, gadget, apparatus, machine; discovery; coinage; *informal* brainchild, gizmo, widget.
3 *his invention was flagging* **inventiveness**, originality, creativity, creativeness, imagination, imaginativeness, inspiration; ingenuity, ingeniousness, resourcefulness, initiative, enterprise; genius, brilliance, vision.
4 *the movement was never more than a journalistic invention* **fabrication**, concoction, fiction, piece of fiction, yarn, story, tale, figment of one's imagination; lie, untruth, falsehood, fib, trumped-up story; myth, fantasy; *informal* tall story, fairy story, fairy tale, cock and bull story, red herring; kidology.

inventive ▶ adjective **1** *the most inventive composer of his time* **creative**, original, innovational, innovative, imaginative, fertile, ingenious, resourceful; artistic, inspired, gifted, talented, virtuoso, accomplished, masterly, skilful, clever.
OPPOSITES unimaginative, uninventive.
2 *a fresh, inventive comedy* **original**, innovative, unusual, fresh, novel, new; experimental, offbeat, quirky, avant garde, forward-looking, groundbreaking; unfamiliar, unorthodox, unconventional, alternative, fringe; *N. Amer.* left-field.
OPPOSITE hackneyed.

inventiveness ▶ noun **1** *they valued his vigour and inventiveness* **creativity**, originality, innovation, invention, imagination, imaginativeness, creative power, creative talent, creative gift, fertility, ingeniousness, resourcefulness, enterprise; artistry, inspiration, giftedness, talent, virtuosity, accomplishment, mastery, skill, cleverness.
OPPOSITE unimaginativeness.
2 *the outstanding inventiveness of Irish literature* **originality**, innovation, unusualness, freshness, novelty, newness, break with tradition; quirkiness, unfamiliarity, unconventionality, unorthodoxy.
OPPOSITE unoriginality.

inventor ▶ noun *the inventor of the seed drill* **originator**, creator, innovator; designer, deviser, developer, maker, planner, framer, producer; author, architect; pioneer, mastermind, father, prime mover; scientist, discoverer; *informal* boffin; *literary* begetter.

inventory ▶ noun *a complete inventory of all their belongings* **list**, listing, catalogue, directory, record, register, checklist, tally, roster, file, log, account, archive, description, statement.
▶ verb *I inventoried his collection of drawings* **list**, catalogue, record, register, make a list of, file, log, tally.

inverse ▶ adjective *inverse snobbery | an inverse correlation between the size and frequency of words* **reverse**, reversed, inverted, opposite, converse, contrary, counter, antithetical, transposed, retroverted.
▶ noun *alkalinity is the inverse of acidity* **opposite**, converse, obverse, antithesis, other side; *informal* flip side, other side of the coin.

inversion ▶ noun *a hypocrite's inversion of the truth* **reversal**, transposition, turning about, turning upside down; reverse, contrary, antithesis, converse, transposal; *rare* contrareity, antipode.

invert ▶ verb *the crew inverted the yacht's mast* **turn upside down**, upturn, upend, turn around, turn about, turn inside out, turn back to front, reverse, flip (over), transpose.

invest ▶ verb **1** *he* **invested in** *a cotton mill* **put money into**, sink money into, lay out money on, plough money into; provide capital for, spend money on, fund, back, finance, underwrite, subsidize, support, pay for; buy into, buy shares in, buy/take a stake in; *informal* get a piece of, splash out on.
2 *they invested £18 million to redesign their retail outlets* **spend**, expend, lay out, put in, plough in, use up, devote; venture, speculate, risk, gamble; contribute, donate, give.
3 *the words were invested with as much sarcasm as she could muster* **imbue**, infuse, perfuse, charge, steep, saturate, suffuse, pervade, fill, endow.
4 *by virtue of the powers* **invested in** *me, I grant your request* **vest in**, endow in, confer on, bestow on, grant to, entrust to, give to, consign to, put in someone's hands.
5 *bishops whom the king had invested* **admit to office**, instate, install, induct, swear in; ordain, anoint; crown, enthrone.
6 (*archaic*) *he stands before you invested in the full canonicals of his calling* **clothe**, attire, dress, garb, robe, gown, drape, swathe, adorn, deck, deck out, accoutre, outfit, fit out, costume; *archaic* apparel, bedizen, caparison, habit, trap out.
7 (*archaic*) *he proceeded to invest the fort of Arcot* **besiege**, lay siege to, beleaguer, beset, surround, enclose.

investigate ▶ verb *police were investigating the death of a woman* **enquire into**, look into, go into, look over, probe, explore, scrutinize, conduct an investigation into, conduct an inquiry into, make inquiries about, try to get to the bottom of; inspect, analyse, study, examine, consider, research, search/sift the evidence concerning, pore over, delve into; audit, evaluate; follow up; *informal* check out, suss out, give something the once-over; *N. Amer. informal* scope out.

investigation ▶ noun *this claim requires further investigation | an investigation into the accident* **examination**, inquiry, study, inspection, exploration, consideration, analysis, appraisal; research, scrutiny, scrutinization, scanning, perusal, sifting, fact-finding; probe, review, survey, search; inquest, hearing, questioning, interrogation, inquisition; audit, evaluation; *informal* snoop, snooping, post-mortem, recce.

investigator ▶ noun *social security fraud investigators* **inspector**, examiner, inquirer, explorer, analyser; researcher, scrutineer, scrutinizer, factfinder, prober, surveyor, searcher, checker, monitor; detective, questioner, inquisitor.

investiture ▶ noun *the investiture of archbishops* **inauguration**, appointment, installation, instatement, induction, initiation, swearing in; ordination, consecration; crowning, enthroning, enthronement, accession.

investment ▶ noun **1** *you can lose money pretty fast by bad investment* **investing**, speculation; expenditure, outlay, funding, backing, financing, underwriting; buying shares.
2 *I'm satisfied that it's a good investment* **venture**, speculation, risk, gamble; asset, buy, acquisition, holding, possession; bargain; *Brit. informal* flutter, punt.
3 *an investment of £305,000* **stake**, share, portion, interest, money/capital invested; *informal* ante.
4 *a substantial investment of time and energy* **sacrifice**, surrender, foregoing, loss, relinquishment, forfeiture.

inveterate ▶ adjective **1** *an inveterate gambler* **confirmed**, hardened, chronic, hard-core, incorrigible; habitual, addicted, compulsive, obsessive, obsessional; *informal* pathological, hooked.
2 *an inveterate Democrat* **staunch**, steadfast, committed, devoted, dedicated; deep-dyed, dyed-in-the-wool, thorough, thoroughgoing, out and out, diehard, long-standing.
3 *mankind's inveterate pride and stupidity* **ingrained**, deep-seated, deep-rooted, deep-set, entrenched, established, long-established, congenital; ineradicable, incurable, irredeemable.

invidious ▶ adjective **1** *I didn't want to put her in an invidious position* **unpleasant**, awkward, difficult; undesirable, unenviable.
OPPOSITES pleasant, desirable.
2 *an invidious comparison* **unfair**, unjust, prejudicial, discriminatory, iniquitous, weighted, one-sided; offensive, objectionable; deleterious, detrimental, unwarranted.
OPPOSITE fair.

invigorate ▶ verb *we were invigorated by the fresh air* **revitalize**, energize, refresh, revive, vivify, brace, rejuvenate, enliven, liven up, perk up, wake up, animate, galvanize, electrify, stimulate, motivate, rouse, exhilarate, excite; rally, hearten, uplift, encourage, fortify, strengthen, put new strength/life/heart in; *informal* buck up, pep up, give a new lease of life to.
OPPOSITE tire.

invigorating ▶ adjective *we drank in the invigorating cold air* **revitalizing**, energizing, refreshing, reviving, vivifying, bracing, rejuvenating, enlivening, restorative; galvanizing, electrifying, stimulating, rousing, exhilarating, exciting; rallying, heartening, uplifting, encouraging, fortifying, strengthening, health-giving, healthy, tonic.
OPPOSITE tiring.

invincible ▶ adjective *an invincible warrior* **invulnerable**, indestructible, unconquerable, unbeatable, indomitable, unassailable; unyielding, unflinching, unbending, unshakeable, indefatigable, dauntless; impregnable, inviolable, secure, safe.
OPPOSITES vulnerable, defenceless.

inviolable ▶ adjective *the inviolable right to life* **inalienable**, absolute, untouchable, unalterable, unchallengeable, unbreakable, impregnable; sacrosanct, sacred, holy, hallowed; *rare* intemerate.
OPPOSITE partial.

inviolate ▶ adjective *his home remained inviolate* **untouched**, undamaged, unhurt, unharmed, unscathed; unmarred, unspoilt, unimpaired, unflawed, unsullied, unstained, undefiled, unpolluted, unprofaned, perfect, pristine, pure, virgin; intact, unbroken, whole, entire, complete, sound, solid; *rare* scatheless.

invisible ▶ adjective *an invisible gas | he lounged in the doorway, invisible in the dark* **not visible**, unseeable; undetectable, indiscernible, indistinguishable, inconspicuous, unnoticeable, imperceptible; unseen, unnoticed, unobserved, hidden, concealed, obscured, out of sight, secret.
OPPOSITE visible.

invitation ▶ noun **1** *she'd received an invitation to dinner* request to attend; call, bidding, summons; *informal* invite.
2 *he left the door open—an invitation to an opportunistic thief* **encouragement**, provocation, temptation, lure, magnet, bait, enticement, attraction, draw, pull, allure; *informal* come-on.
OPPOSITE discouragement.

invite ▶ verb (stress on the second syllable) **1** *they invited us to Sunday brunch* **ask**, bid, summon; request someone's company at, request someone's presence at, request someone's appearance at, request the pleasure of someone's company, have someone over/round.
2 *applications are invited for the post of director* **ask for**, request, call for, look for, appeal for, solicit, seek, petition, summon.
OPPOSITE refuse.
3 *airing such views in public would invite trouble* **cause**, induce, provoke, create, generate, engender, foster, encourage, lead to, call forth, make happen; draw, attract, incite, elicit, bring on, bring on oneself, arouse; tempt, court, allure, entice.
▶ noun (stress on the first syllable) (*informal*) *no one turns down an invite to one of Mickey's parties.* See INVITATION sense 1.

inviting ▶ adjective *an inviting smell of coffee wafted into the room* **tempting**, enticing, alluring, beguiling, winning; attractive, appealing, pleasant, agreeable, delightful; appetizing, mouth-watering; fascinating, engaging, enchanting, entrancing, bewitching, captivating, intriguing, irresistible, ravishing, seductive, tantalizing.
OPPOSITES repellent, offensive.

invocation ▶ noun **1** *her invocation of themes favoured by the grass-roots supporters* **citation**, mention, acknowledgement, calling on; appeal to, reference to, allusion to.
2 *the invocation of rain by tribal people* **summoning**, bringing, calling, conjuring (up).
3 *an invocation to the Holy Ghost* **prayer**, request, intercession, supplication, call, entreaty, solicitation, petition, appeal, suit; incantation, chant; *archaic* orison; *rare* imploration, adjuration, obsecration, epiclesis.

invoice ▶ noun *an invoice for the goods supplied* **bill**, account, statement, statement of charges, itemization, reckoning, tally; *N. Amer.* check; *informal* tab; *archaic* score.
▶ verb *we'll invoice you for the damage* **bill**, charge, debit, send an invoice/bill to.

invoke ▶ verb **1** *he invoked his statutory right to complain to the district auditor* **cite**, refer to, adduce, instance; resort to, have recourse to, turn to, call into use, use, put into effect/use.
OPPOSITE waive.
2 *I closed my eyes and invoked the Madonna* **pray to**, call on, appeal to, plead with, supplicate, entreat, solicit, beseech, beg, implore, importune, petition; call for, request; *rare* obtest, obsecrate, impetrate.
3 *she was walking in a circle as though invoking the spirits of the place* **summon**, call (up), bring, conjure (up).
4 *middle-class moralities invoke peculiar anxieties* **bring forth**, bring on, elicit, induce, cause, kindle, bring out.

involuntary ▶ adjective **1** *she gave an involuntary shudder* **reflex**, reflexive, automatic, knee-jerk, mechanical, unconditioned; spontaneous, instinctive, instinctual, impulsive, unconscious, unthinking; unintentional, unintended, unplanned, inadvertent, uncontrolled, uncontrollable.
OPPOSITES voluntary, deliberate.
2 *a policy of involuntary repatriation* **compulsory**, obligatory, mandatory, forced, coerced, coercive, compelled, exacted, imposed, demanded, required, constrained, ordained, prescribed; unwilling, unconsenting, against one's will, against one's wishes, reluctant, grudging.
OPPOSITES voluntary; optional; willing.

involve ▶ verb **1** *the research involved the assembly of information on unemployment* **require**, necessitate, demand, call for; **entail**, mean, imply, presuppose, presume, assume; appertain to, pertain to, relate to, concern.
OPPOSITE preclude.
2 *I try to involve everyone in key decisions* **include**, count in, take in, bring in, draw in, take into account, take account of, take note of, allow for; cover, incorporate, encompass, deal with, touch on; embrace, comprise, contain, comprehend.
OPPOSITE exclude.
3 *many drug addicts involve themselves in crime* **implicate**, incriminate, inculpate; associate, connect, concern; embroil, entangle, enmesh, ensnare; *informal* mix up.

involved ▶ adjective **1** *social workers* **involved in** *the case* **associated with**, connected with, concerned with, participating in, taking part in.
OPPOSITE unconnected.
2 *he had been involved in burglaries* **implicated**, incriminated, inculpated, embroiled, entangled, caught up, enmeshed, ensnared; *informal* mixed up.
3 *a long and involved story* **complicated**, intricate, complex, elaborate; confused, confusing, bewildering; jumbled, tangled, entangled, convoluted, knotty, mixed up, impenetrable, unfathomable, tortuous, labyrinthine, Byzantine; difficult, hard.
OPPOSITES straightforward, simple.
4 *they were both totally* **involved in** *their work* **engrossed**, absorbed, immersed, caught up, rapt, interested; preoccupied by, busy with, engaged in/with, riveted by, gripped by, intent on; *informal* up to one's ears in.
OPPOSITE uninterested.

CHOOSE THE RIGHT WORD

involved, complicated, complex, intricate

See COMPLICATED.

involvement ▶ noun **1** *he is in prison for his involvement in a plot to overthrow the government* **participation**, action, hand; collaboration, collusion, complicity, connivance, implication, incrimination, inculpation; association, connection, attachment, embroilment, entanglement, inclusion.
2 *a nurse has to avoid emotional involvement with the patient* **attachment**, connection, friendship, intimacy, entanglement; relationship, relations, bond.

invulnerable ▶ adjective *no state in the region is invulnerable to attack by another* **impervious**, insusceptible, immune, insensitive; indestructible, impenetrable, impregnable, unassailable, unattackable, inviolable, invincible, unshakeable, secure, safe, safe and sound, strong; proof against.
OPPOSITES vulnerable, defenceless.

inward ▶ adjective **1** *a small inward indentation* **towards the inside**, going in, ingoing; concave.
OPPOSITE outward.
2 *he allowed himself an inward smile* **internal**, inner, interior, inside, innermost; private, personal, hidden, secret, veiled, masked, concealed, unexpressed, unrevealed; intimate, confidential; *informal* bottled up; *archaic* privy.
OPPOSITE external.
▶ adverb *the door opened inward.* See INWARDS.

WORD LINKS
related prefix **intro-** (e.g. ***introduce, introvert***)

inwardly ▶ adverb *inwardly, George blamed himself* **inside**, internally, within, deep down (inside), deep within, at heart, in one's heart (of hearts), in one's mind, to oneself; privately, secretly, confidentially.
OPPOSITES outwardly; out loud.

inwards ▶ adverb *light spilled inwards from the porch* **inside**, towards the inside, into the interior, inward, within.

iota ▶ noun *nothing she said seemed to make an iota of difference* **bit**, mite, speck, scrap, shred, ounce, scintilla, atom, jot, tittle, jot or tittle, whit, little bit, tiniest bit, particle, fraction, morsel, grain; *French* soupçon; *informal* smidgen, smidge, tad; *archaic* scruple, scantling.

irascible ▶ adjective *an irascible young man* **irritable**, quick-tempered, short-tempered, bad-tempered, ill-tempered, hot-tempered, thin-skinned, snappy, snappish, tetchy, testy, touchy, edgy, crabby, waspish, dyspeptic; surly, cross, crusty, crabbed, grouchy, crotchety, cantankerous, curmudgeonly, ill-natured, ill-humoured, peevish, querulous, captious, fractious, bilious; *informal* narky, prickly, ratty, hot under the collar; *rare* iracund, iracundulous.

irate ▶ adjective *an irate customer* **angry**, very angry, furious, infuriated,

incensed, enraged, incandescent, fuming, seething, ireful, cross, mad; raging, ranting, raving, frenzied, in a frenzy, beside oneself, outraged, up in arms; indignant, annoyed, irritated, aggrieved, vexed, exasperated, frustrated, irked, piqued; *informal* foaming at the mouth, hot under the collar, hacked off; *literary* wrathful, wroth.
OPPOSITES calm, composed.

ire ▶ noun (*literary*) *the plans provoked the ire of conservationists* **anger**, rage, fury, wrath, hot temper, outrage, temper, crossness, spleen; annoyance, exasperation, irritation, vexation, displeasure, chagrin, pique; indignation, resentment; *literary* choler.

Ireland ▶ noun Eire, the Republic of Ireland, the Irish Republic, southern Ireland; Northern Ireland; *informal* the Emerald Isle; *Latin* Hibernia; *literary* Erin.

WORD LINKS
related prefix **Hiberno- (e.g. *Hiberno-English*)**

iridescent ▶ adjective *the iridescent films of oil on top of puddles* **shimmering**, shimmery, glittering, sparkling, dazzling, shining, gleaming, glowing, lustrous, scintillating, dancing, opalescent, opaline; multicoloured, kaleidoscopic, rainbow-like, rainbow-coloured, many-hued, prismatic, colourful, psychedelic; variegated, shot; *literary* glistering; *rare* coruscating, coruscant, fulgurating, effulgent, scintillant.

irk ▶ verb *her reticence about certain things irked him* **irritate**, annoy, vex, gall, rattle, pique, rub up the wrong way, exasperate, try someone's patience, put out, displease; anger, infuriate, madden, incense, make someone's blood boil, get on someone's nerves, make angry, make cross; ruffle, ruffle someone's feathers, make someone's hackles rise, raise someone's hackles, discountenance; antagonize, provoke, goad; *informal* get someone's goat, get/put someone's back up, peeve, miff, rile, aggravate, nettle, needle, get, get to, bug, hack off, get under someone's skin, get up someone's nose, put someone's nose out of joint, give someone the hump, rattle someone's cage, get someone's dander up, drive mad/crazy, drive round the twist, drive up the wall, make someone see red; *Brit. informal* wind up, brown off, cheese off, nark, get across, get on someone's wick; *N. Amer. informal* tee off, tick off, burn up, rankle, ride, gravel; *vulgar slang* piss off; *Brit. vulgar slang* get on someone's tits; *informal, dated* give someone the pip.
OPPOSITE please.

irksome ▶ adjective *an irksome task* **irritating**, annoying, vexing, vexatious, galling, exasperating, displeasing, grating, disagreeable; tiresome, wearisome, tedious, trying, troublesome, burdensome, bothersome, awkward, inconvenient, difficult, boring, uninteresting; infuriating, maddening; *informal* pesky, cussed, confounded, infernal, pestiferous, plaguy, pestilent.
OPPOSITES pleasant, agreeable.

iron ▶ noun **1** *an ocean liner built of iron* metal; pig iron, bog iron, cast iron, wrought iron, soft iron, hoop iron.
2 *she needed some iron in her soul* **strength**, toughness, resilience, fortitude, firmness, robustness, hardiness, steel; *informal* guts, grit, grittiness, spunk.
OPPOSITE weakness.
3 *a soldering iron* **tool**, implement, utensil, device, apparatus, appliance, contrivance, contraption, mechanism.
4 *an iron that is too hot will melt nylon* **flat iron**, electric iron, steam iron, smoothing iron.
5 (**irons**) *you will be clapped in irons* **manacles**, shackles, fetters, chains, restraints, handcuffs; *informal* cuffs, bracelets; *rare* trammels.
▶ adjective **1** *an iron key* **made of iron**; ferric, ferrous.
2 *an iron law of politics* **inflexible**, unbreakable, absolute, unconditional, categorical, unquestionable, incontrovertible, infallible.
OPPOSITE flexible.
3 *he ruled over his employees with an iron will* **uncompromising**, unrelenting, unyielding, unbending, resolute, resolved, determined, firm, rigid, steadfast, unwavering, unvacillating; stern, strict.
OPPOSITES weak, flexible.
▶ verb *she even used to iron his shirts* **press**.
□ **iron something out 1** *John had ironed out all the minor snags* **resolve**, straighten out, sort out, clear up, settle, put right, set right, set to rights, find a solution to, solve, remedy, heal, cure, rectify; *informal* patch up, fix, mend, clean up, crack, figure out; *archaic* compose.
2 *the new directive will iron out differences in national systems* **eliminate**, eradicate, erase, get rid of, smooth over; harmonize, reconcile.

WORD LINKS
related prefixes **ferro- (e.g. *ferroconcrete*), ferri- (e.g. *ferrimagnetic*), sidero- (e.g. *siderophore*)**

ironic ▶ adjective **1** *Edward's tone was ironic* **sarcastic**, sardonic, dry, caustic, sharp, stinging, scathing, acerbic, acid, bitter, trenchant, mordant, cynical; mocking, satirical, scoffing, ridiculing, derisory, derisive, scornful, sneering; wry, double-edged, backhanded, tongue-in-cheek; *Brit. informal* sarky.
OPPOSITE sincere.
2 *I just wanted to go out and experience life, so it's ironic that I've ended up writing* **paradoxical**, incongruous, odd, strange, weird, peculiar, unexpected.
OPPOSITES logical, to be expected.

CHOOSE THE RIGHT WORD
ironic, sarcastic, sardonic, caustic
See SARCASTIC.

irony ▶ noun **1** *that note of irony in her voice* **sarcasm**, sardonicism, dryness, causticity, sharpness, acerbity, acid, bitterness, trenchancy, mordancy, cynicism; mockery, satire, ridicule, derision, scorn, sneering; wryness, backhandedness; *Brit. informal* sarkiness.
OPPOSITE sincerity.
2 *the irony of the situation hit her* **paradox**, paradoxical nature, incongruity, incongruousness, peculiarity.
OPPOSITE logic.

irradiate ▶ verb **1** *the patients were irradiated* **treat with radiation**, expose to radiation, X-ray.
2 *he was irradiated by a steady glow* **illuminate**, light up, light, brighten, cast light upon, throw light on, shine on, flood with light; *literary* illumine.

irrational ▶ adjective *she told herself that it was an irrational fear* **unreasonable**, illogical, groundless, baseless, unfounded, unjustifiable, unsound; absurd, ridiculous, ludicrous, silly, foolish, senseless, nonsensical, laughable, idiotic, stupid, wild; untenable, implausible, unscientific, arbitrary; *informal* crazy, mad; *Brit. informal* barmy, daft.
OPPOSITES rational, logical.

irreconcilable ▶ adjective **1** *the affair revealed irreconcilable views about the duties of government* **incompatible**, at odds, at variance, incongruous, conflicting, clashing, discordant, antagonistic, mutually exclusive; opposite, contrary, opposing, antithetical, diametrically opposed; different, disparate, variant, dissimilar, poles apart, polar; *rare* oppugnant.
OPPOSITES compatible, similar.
2 *irreconcilable enemies* **implacable**, unappeasable, uncompromising, inexorable, intransigent, inflexible, remorseless, relentless, unrelenting, hard-line; mortal, bitter, deadly, sworn, out-and-out; *informal* at each other's throats.

irrecoverable ▶ adjective *an irrecoverable bad debt* **unrecoverable**, unreclaimable, irretrievable, irredeemable, irrevocable, unrestorable, unsalvageable, irremediable, lost, lost and gone, gone for ever, beyond cure, beyond hope, hopeless; written off.
OPPOSITE recoverable.

irrefutable ▶ adjective *there is irrefutable evidence that there will be a shortfall* **indisputable**, undeniable, unquestionable, incontrovertible, incontestable, unassailable, impregnable, beyond question, indubitable, beyond doubt, beyond dispute, indisputable; conclusive, definite, definitive, decisive, certain, sure, positive, sound, flawless, watertight, unmistakable, palpable, patent, manifest, obvious, evident, plain, clear, forceful, telling; *rare* irrefragable, apodictic.
OPPOSITE unreliable.

irregular ▶ adjective **1** *he had strong, irregular features | an irregular coastline* **asymmetrical**, non-uniform, uneven, crooked, misshapen, lopsided, contorted, twisted; twisting, serpentine, curving; broken, jagged, ragged, craggy, serrated, sawtooth, saw-edged, notched, nicked, indented.
OPPOSITES regular; straight.
2 *three coats of varnish are used on very irregular surfaces* **rough**, bumpy, uneven, coarse; pitted, rutted, rutty, holed, holey; lumpy, knobby, knobbly, gnarled.
OPPOSITES regular; smooth.
3 *an irregular heartbeat | an irregular ferry service* **inconsistent**, unsteady, uneven, shaky, fitful, patchy, variable, varying, changeable, changing, ever-changing, on-and-off, off-and-on, inconstant, erratic, haphazard, unstable, unsettled, spasmodic, sporadic, episodic, intermittent, occasional, unpunctual, wavering, fluctuating, aperiodic, unsystematic, unmethodical, capricious; desultory, casual.
OPPOSITES regular; steady.
4 *his appointment was most irregular* **against the rules**, contrary to the rules, out of order, improper, incorrect, illegitimate, unscrupulous, unethical, unprofessional; unofficial, back-door, grey; not done, unacceptable, wrong, beyond the pale, unorthodox, unconventional, abnormal; *informal* not on, a bit much, shady; *Brit. informal* a bit thick, off, not cricket; *Austral./NZ informal* over the fence.
OPPOSITE above board.
5 *an irregular army* **guerrilla**, underground; unofficial, paramilitary; resistance, partisan, mercenary.
OPPOSITE regular.
▶ noun *scruffy, gun-toting irregulars refused to allow traffic through the town* **guerrilla**, underground fighter; paramilitary; resistance fighter, partisan, mercenary.
OPPOSITE regular.

irregularity ▸ noun **1** *the irregularity of the coastline* **asymmetry**, lack of symmetry, non-uniformity, unevenness, crookedness, lopsidedness, contortion, deformity, jaggedness, raggedness, cragginess, indentation.
OPPOSITES regularity; straightness.
2 *the irregularity of the road surface* **roughness**, bumpiness, unevenness, coarseness; lumpiness, knobbliness; *rare* knobbiness.
OPPOSITES regularity; smoothness.
3 *any irregularities in the concrete will be masked by the soft board on top* **bump**, lump, bulge, hump, knob, knot, projection, prominence, eminence, ridge, protuberance, kink; **hole**, hollow, pit, crater, depression, dip, indentation, trough, dent, dint; gap, space, break, crack, chink, fissure, cranny; *informal* sticky-out bit; *rare* concavity.
4 *villagers complained about the irregularity of the bus service* **inconsistency**, unsteadiness, unevenness, fitfulness, patchiness, haphazardness, inconstancy, instability, variability, changeableness, fluctuation, unpunctuality, unpredictability, unreliability, volatility, fickleness, caprice; casualness, desultoriness; *technical* aperiodicity; *rare* erraticism, intermittence, intermittency.
OPPOSITES regularity; steadiness.
5 *the monitor showed every little irregularity of her baby's heartbeat* **fluctuation**, flutter, waver, flicker, falter, quiver, tremor, tremble, hiccup.
6 *there has been irregularity in the conduct of the election | a probe into alleged financial irregularities at the club* **impropriety**, incorrectness, wrongdoing, misconduct, illegitimacy, dishonesty, corruption, immorality, unscrupulousness, unprofessionalism; inappropriateness, unacceptability, unseemliness, indecorousness, indiscretion, indelicacy; unorthodoxy, unconventionality; *informal* shadiness, crookedness.
OPPOSITE correctness.
7 *staff kept a vigilant watch and noted any irregularity in operation* **abnormality**, unusualness, uncommonness, strangeness, waywardness, oddness, unexpectedness, singularity, atypicality, anomaly, anomalousness, deviation, divergence, aberrancy, aberration, freakishness, peculiarity, curiousness, eccentricity, idiosyncrasy, quirkiness, unorthodoxy.

irregularly ▸ adverb **1** *the first plate is irregularly hexagonal* **asymmetrically**, unevenly, lopsidedly.
2 *his heart was playing up, beating irregularly* **erratically**, at irregular intervals, intermittently, in/by fits and starts, on and off, off and on, fitfully, patchily, haphazardly, unsystematically, unmethodically, inconsistently, unsteadily, unevenly, variably, sporadically, spasmodically, episodically, discontinuously, interruptedly, occasionally, piecemeal; *rare* inconstantly, aperiodically.

irrelevance ▸ noun *people are bored at school because of the irrelevance of the curriculum to their own life* **inapplicability**, unconnectedness, unrelatedness, peripherality, extraneousness; inappropriateness, inappositeness, inaptness; unimportance, inconsequentiality, insignificance; *rare* impertinence.
OPPOSITE relevance.

irrelevant ▸ adjective *students must avoid wasting time on irrelevant detail* **beside the point**, not to the point, immaterial, not pertinent, not germane, off the subject, neither here nor there, unconnected, unrelated, peripheral, tangential, extraneous, inapposite, inapt, inapplicable; unimportant, inconsequential, insignificant, of no matter/moment, of little account, trivial, negligible, minor, trifling, petty, superficial; *rare* impertinent.
OPPOSITE relevant.

irreligious ▸ adjective *an irreligious world* **atheistic**, unbelieving, non-believing, agnostic, sceptical, heretical, faithless, godless, ungodly, unholy, impious, profane, infidel, barbarian, barbarous, heathen, heathenish, idolatrous, pagan; **immoral**, wicked, sinful, morally wrong, evil, bad, iniquitous, corrupt, unrighteous, sacrilegious, blasphemous, irreverent, depraved, degenerate, reprobate, vice-ridden, debauched, dissolute, perverted, dissipated, intemperate, decadent, unprincipled, erring, fallen, impure, sullied, tainted; *rare* peccable, nullifidian.
OPPOSITES pious, religious.

irreparable ▸ adjective *if the pump runs dry, irreparable damage can be done* **irreversible**, irremediable, unrectifiable, irrevocable, irretrievable, irredeemable, unrestorable, irrecoverable, unrecoverable, unrepairable, beyond repair, past mending; hopeless, past hope, beyond hope; written off.
OPPOSITE repairable.

irreplaceable ▸ adjective *if you make a mistake, you may ruin an irreplaceable recording* **unique**, unrepeatable, incomparable, unparalleled, priceless, invaluable, beyond price, without price, inestimably precious, of incalculable value/worth, of inestimable value/worth, of immeasurable value/worth, worth its weight in gold; treasured, prized, cherished.
OPPOSITE replaceable.

irrepressible ▸ adjective **1** *the desire for freedom is irrepressible* **inextinguishable**, unquenchable, uncontainable, uncontrollable, unstoppable, indestructible, imperishable, undying, unfading, unfailing, enduring, lasting, everlasting, eternal, persistent.
OPPOSITES ephemeral; fragile.
2 *his irrepressible personality* **ebullient**, exuberant, buoyant, sunny, breezy, jaunty, light-hearted, in high spirits, high-spirited, bubbling over, sparkling, effervescent, vivacious, animated, full of life, lively, vigorous, zestful, joyful, cheerful, cheery, merry; *informal* bubbly, bouncy, peppy, zingy, upbeat, chipper, chirpy, sparky, full of beans; *N. Amer. informal* peart; *dated* gay; *literary* gladsome, blithe, blithesome; *archaic* as merry as a grig, of good cheer.
OPPOSITE gloomy.

irreproachable ▸ adjective *he was awarded the medal in recognition of thirty years' irreproachable service* **impeccable**, exemplary, model, copybook, immaculate, outstanding, exceptional, admirable, meritorious, honourable, consummate, perfect, ideal; above reproach, beyond reproach, blameless, faultless, flawless, guiltless, unimpeachable, unblemished, untarnished, stainless, spotless, pure, sinless, innocent; *informal* squeaky clean, whiter than white, snow white.
OPPOSITE reprehensible.

irresistible ▸ adjective **1** *her irresistible smile* **tempting**, enticing, alluring, inviting, seductive; attractive, desirable, fetching, glamorous, appealing; captivating, ravishing, beguiling, enchanting, fascinating, tantalizing; *informal, dated* come-hither.
2 *it was an irresistible impulse—I couldn't stop myself* **uncontrollable**, overwhelming, overpowering, compelling, compulsive, besetting, irrepressible, ungovernable; unavoidable, inescapable, unpreventable, inexorable, driving, forceful, potent, oppressive, imperative, urgent; obsessive.

irresolute ▸ adjective *she stood irresolute outside his door* **indecisive**, hesitant, tentative, nervous, weak; vacillating, equivocating, dithering, wavering, teetering, fluctuating, faltering, shilly-shallying; ambivalent, divided, in two minds, in a dilemma, in a quandary, torn; doubtful, in doubt, full of doubt, unsure, uncertain; undecided, uncommitted, unresolved, undetermined; *informal* iffy, blowing hot and cold, sitting on the fence.
OPPOSITE decisive.

irresolution ▸ noun *'I'll go,' she said after several minutes of irresolution* **indecisiveness**, indecision, irresoluteness, lack of resolution, hesitancy, hesitation, tentativeness; ambivalence, doubt, doubtfulness, unsureness, uncertainty; vacillation, equivocation, oscillation, wavering, teetering, fluctuation, faltering, second thoughts; delay, hanging back, waiting, shilly-shallying, dithering, stalling, temporizing, temporization; *Brit.* havering, humming and hawing; *Scottish* swithering; *informal* dilly-dallying, blowing hot and cold, sitting on the fence; *rare* dubiety, incertitude, cunctation.
OPPOSITE decisiveness.

irrespective ▸ adjective *each member has one vote, irrespective of the number of shares held* **regardless of**, without regard to/for, disregarding, ignoring, notwithstanding, whatever, no matter what, without reference to, without consideration of, setting aside, discounting; *informal* irregardless of.
OPPOSITE according to.

irresponsible ▸ adjective **1** *such irresponsible behaviour will not be tolerated* **reckless**, rash, careless, thoughtless, incautious, unwise, imprudent, ill-advised, ill-considered, injudicious, misguided, heedless, unheeding, inattentive, hasty, overhasty, precipitate, precipitous, wild, foolhardy, impetuous, impulsive, daredevil, devil-may-care, hot-headed, negligent, delinquent, neglectful, remiss, careless of one's duty, lax, slack, uncaring, casual, insouciant; *N. Amer.* derelict; *rare* disregardful, inadvertent, oscitant.
OPPOSITES responsible; sensible.
2 *if Rose wants to behave like an irresponsible teenager, that's her affair* **immature**, naive, foolish, hare-brained, feather-brained; carefree, blasé; unreliable, undependable, untrustworthy, flighty, giddy, scatterbrained, erratic; *Brit.* tearaway; *informal* harum-scarum, slap-happy.
OPPOSITES responsible; serious.

irretrievable ▸ adjective *the situation was now irretrievable* **irreversible**, unrectifiable, irremediable, irrevocable, irredeemable, irrecoverable, unrecoverable, irreparable, unrepairable, beyond repair; irreclaimable, lost, lost and gone, gone forever, hopeless, past hope, beyond hope.
OPPOSITES reversible, reparable.

irreverence ▸ noun *wacky irreverence is the hallmark of any comedy show worth its salt* **disrespect**, lack of respect, disdain, scorn, contempt, derision, mockery, ridicule, disparagement; insolence, impudence, impertinence, cheek, flippancy, insubordination, presumptuousness, presumption, forwardness; rudeness, impoliteness, discourtesy, incivility, abuse; *informal* lip, nerve.
OPPOSITES reverence, respect.

irreverent ▸ adjective *an irreverent attitude to tradition* **disrespectful**, disdainful, scornful, contemptuous, derisive, disparaging; insolent, impudent, impertinent, cheeky, flippant, flip, insubordinate, presumptuous, forward; rude, impolite, discourteous, uncivil, insulting, abusive; *informal* fresh, lippy.

OPPOSITES reverent, respectful.

irreversible ▸ adjective *a priority is to stop irreversible damage to the natural environment | an irreversible decision* **irreparable**, unrepairable, beyond repair, unrectifiable, irremediable, irrevocable; permanent, lasting, enduring, abiding; **unalterable**, unchangeable, invariable, immutable, final, binding, absolute, categorical; *Law* peremptory, unappealable.
OPPOSITES reversible; temporary.

irrevocable ▸ adjective *an irrevocable step | an irrevocable commitment* **irreversible**, unrectifiable, irremediable, irreparable, unrepairable, beyond repair; **unalterable**, unchangeable, immutable, final, binding, absolute, permanent, lasting; *Law* peremptory, unappealable.
OPPOSITES reversible; temporary.

irrigate ▸ verb *the scheme aims to divert water from the river to irrigate agricultural land* **water**, bring water to; spray, soak, deluge, flood, inundate; make fertile.

irritability ▸ noun *apart from occasional irritability, there were no major disagreements among them* **irascibility**, tetchiness, testiness, touchiness, scratchiness, grumpiness, moodiness, grouchiness, crotchetiness, a (bad) mood, cantankerousness, curmudgeonliness, churlishness, bad temper, ill temper, ill nature, ill humour, peevishness, crossness, pique, impatience, fractiousness, pettishness, crabbiness, waspishness, prickliness, pepperiness, crustiness, spleen, shrewishness, short temper, hot temper, quick temper; *informal* snappishness, snappiness, chippiness, a short fuse; *Brit. informal* shirtiness, stroppiness, rattiness; *N. Amer. informal* crankiness, orneriness, soreheadedness; *Austral./NZ informal* snakiness; *informal, dated* miffiness; *literary* choler.
OPPOSITES good humour; placidity.

I

irritable ▸ adjective *being out of work made him irritable* **bad-tempered**, irascible, tetchy, testy, touchy, scratchy, grumpy, grouchy, moody, crotchety, in a (bad) mood, cantankerous, curmudgeonly, ill-tempered, ill-natured, ill-humoured, peevish, having got out of bed the wrong side, cross, as cross as two sticks, fractious, disagreeable, pettish, crabbed, crabby, waspish, prickly, peppery, crusty, splenetic, shrewish, short-tempered, hot-tempered, quick-tempered, dyspeptic, choleric, bilious, liverish, cross-grained; *informal* snappish, snappy, chippy, on a short fuse, short-fused; *Brit. informal* shirty, stroppy, narky, ratty, eggy, like a bear with a sore head; *N. Amer. informal* cranky, ornery, peckish, soreheaded; *Austral./NZ informal* snaky; *informal, dated* waxy, miffy.
OPPOSITES good-humoured; easy-going.

irritant ▸ noun *in 1966 Vietnam was becoming an irritant to the Labour government* **annoyance**, irritation, source of irritation, source of vexation, source of annoyance, thorn in someone's side/flesh, pinprick, pest, bother, trial, torment, plague, inconvenience, nuisance, menace; *informal* aggravation, peeve, pain, pain in the neck, bind, bore, headache, hassle; *Scottish informal* nyaff, skelf; *N. Amer. informal* pain in the butt, nudnik, burr in/under someone's saddle; *Austral./NZ informal* nark; *Brit. vulgar slang* pain in the arse.
OPPOSITES help; pleasure.

irritate ▸ verb **1** *if you are feeling slightly down, the smallest things are likely to irritate you* **annoy**, vex, make angry, make cross, anger, exasperate, bother, irk, gall, pique, put out, displease, get/put someone's back up, antagonize, get on someone's nerves, rub up the wrong way, try someone's patience, ruffle, ruffle someone's feathers, make someone's hackles rise, raise someone's hackles; enrage, infuriate, madden, incense, make someone's blood boil, drive to distraction, goad, provoke; *informal* aggravate, peeve, hassle, miff, rile, nettle, needle, get, get to, bug, hack off, get under someone's skin, get in someone's hair, get up someone's nose, put someone's nose out of joint, get someone's goat, give someone the hump, rattle someone's cage, get someone's dander up, drive mad/crazy, drive round the bend/twist, drive up the wall, drive bananas, make someone see red; *Brit. informal* wind up, nark, get across, get on someone's wick; *N. Amer. informal* tee off, tick off, burn up, rankle, ride, gravel; *Brit. informal* get on someone's tits; *informal, dated* give someone the pip; *vulgar slang* piss off; *rare* exacerbate, hump, rasp.
OPPOSITE pacify.
2 *some sand got into the car and irritated my eyes* **inflame**, aggravate; hurt, pain; chafe, abrade, fret, gall, rub painfully, rub against, scratch, rasp, scrape, graze, grate; *rare* excoriate.
OPPOSITE soothe.

> **CHOOSE THE RIGHT WORD**
>
> **irritate, annoy, aggravate, vex, peeve**
>
> *See* ANNOY.

irritated ▸ adjective *she was irritated with herself for having behaved so pettily* **annoyed**, cross, angry, vexed, exasperated, irked, piqued, displeased, put out, fed up, disgruntled, in a bad mood, in a temper, testy, in high dudgeon, huffy, in a huff, resentful, aggrieved; furious, irate, infuriated, incensed, enraged, wrathful, choleric; *informal* aggravated, peeved, nettled, miffed, miffy, mad, riled, hacked off, peed off, hot under the collar, foaming at the mouth; *Brit. informal* browned off, cheesed off, brassed off, narked, ratty, shirty, eggy; *N. Amer. informal* teed off, ticked off, sore, bent out of shape; *Austral./NZ informal* snaky, crook; *W. Indian informal* vex; *vulgar slang* pissed off; *N. Amer. vulgar slang* pissed; *literary* ireful; *archaic* snuffy, wrath.
OPPOSITES contented; good-humoured.

irritating ▸ adjective *the railway companies have the irritating habit of addressing passengers as customers* **annoying**, infuriating, exasperating, maddening, trying, tiresome, vexing, vexatious, irksome, galling, troublesome, bothersome, provoking, displeasing; awkward, difficult, inconvenient; *informal* aggravating, pesky, cussed, accursed, confounded, infernal, pestiferous, plaguy, pestilent.
OPPOSITES helpful; pleasing.

irritation ▸ noun **1** *'I found it for myself,' she said, trying not to show her irritation* **annoyance**, infuriation, exasperation, vexation, indignation, impatience, crossness, displeasure, resentment, gall, chagrin, pique; anger, rage, fury, wrath, outrage, temper; *informal* aggravation; *literary* ire.
OPPOSITE delight.
2 *I realize my presence here is an irritation for you* **irritant**, source of irritation, source of vexation, annoyance, source of annoyance, thorn in someone's side/flesh, pinprick, pest, bother, trial, torment, plague, inconvenience, nuisance, bugbear, menace; *informal* aggravation, peeve, pain, pain in the neck, bind, bore, headache, hassle; *Scottish informal* nyaff, skelf; *N. Amer. informal* pain in the butt, nudnik, burr in/under someone's saddle; *Austral./NZ informal* nark; *Brit. vulgar slang* pain in the arse.
OPPOSITE pleasure.

island ▸ noun **isle**, islet; atoll; (*in the Caribbean*) key; (*in Spanish America*) cay; *Brit.* ait, holm; *Scottish* skerry; (**islands**) archipelago, chain, group.
OPPOSITES mainland, continent.

> **WORD LINKS**
>
> *relating to an island* **insular**

isolate ▸ verb **1** *she tried to isolate herself from her family | the area was evacuated and isolated until the danger had passed* **separate**, set apart, segregate, detach, cut off, keep apart, cocoon, insulate, quarantine, keep in solitude, sequester, cloister, seclude, divorce, shut away, alienate, distance, exclude, keep out; cordon off, form a ring around, put a cordon sanitaire around, seal off, close off, fence off, rope off, screen off, tape off, curtain off, shut off, partition off.
OPPOSITE integrate.
2 *even in a stream of traffic the laser beam can isolate the offending vehicles* **identify**, single out, pick out, spot, point out, recognize, pinpoint, pin down, put one's finger on, discern, distinguish, discover, find, locate; sort out, filter out, separate out, weed out.
OPPOSITE confuse.

isolated ▸ adjective **1** *railways are not flexible enough to be able to serve isolated communities* **remote**, out of the way, outlying, off the beaten track, secluded, in the depths of ..., hard to find, lonely, in the back of beyond, in the hinterlands, off the map, in the middle of nowhere, godforsaken, obscure, inaccessible, cut-off, unreachable; faraway, far-flung; *N. Amer.* in the backwoods, lonesome; *S. African* in the backveld, in the platteland; *Austral./NZ* in the backblocks, in the booay; *informal* ungetatable, in the sticks; *N. Amer. informal* jerkwater, in the tall timbers; *Austral./NZ informal* Barcoo, beyond the black stump; *archaic* unapproachable.
OPPOSITE accessible.
2 *he lived a very isolated existence and was something of a recluse* **solitary**, lonely, companionless, unaccompanied, by oneself, on one's own, (all) alone, friendless; secluded, cloistered, sequestered, segregated; protected, cocooned, sheltered, insulated, immune; antisocial, unsociable, withdrawn, reclusive, introverted, hermitic; *N. Amer.* lonesome.
OPPOSITE sociable.
3 *police believe the attack is an isolated incident* **unique**, single, lone, sole, only, one, solitary, individual; unusual, uncommon, exceptional, anomalous, abnormal, odd, atypical, untypical; random, unrelated, stray, freak; *informal* one-off.
OPPOSITES common; multiple.

isolation ▸ noun **1** *there were two single rooms reserved for patients who needed isolation* **separation**, segregation, setting apart, keeping apart; quarantine; insulation, seclusion, closeting, protection, shielding, partitioning.
2 *the isolation experienced by those bringing up children alone* **solitariness**, loneliness, friendlessness, lack of contact, (sense of) exile, aloneness.
OPPOSITE contact.
3 *some mental hospitals are considered to be non-viable on the grounds of their isolation* **remoteness**, seclusion, loneliness, inaccessibility.
OPPOSITE accessibility.

issue ▸ noun **1** *the committee has yet to meet to discuss the issue* **matter**, matter in question, affair, business, subject, topic, question, point, point at issue, item, thing, case, concern, theme; proceeding, situation, occasion, circumstance; problem, bone of contention, controversy, argument.
2 *the victory was celebrated with the issue of a special stamp* **issuing**, issuance, publication, publishing; circulation, distribution, supplying, supply,

sending out, delivery; appearance.
3 *the latest issue of our magazine* **edition**, number, instalment, copy; printing, imprint, impression, version, publication.
4 (*Law*) *she died without issue in 1635* **offspring**, descendants, heirs, successors, children, sons or daughters, progeny, scions, family, youngsters, babies; *informal* kids; *derogatory* spawn; *archaic* seed, fruit, fruit of one's loins.
5 *an issue of blood* **discharge**, emission, release, outflow, outflowing, outpouring, outrush, rush, flood, deluge, spurt, jet, cascade, stream, torrent, gush; flow, flux, outflux, welling; leakage, escape, drain, drainage; excretion, secretion, ejection, disgorgement, debouchment, emanation, exudation, exuding, venting, effluence, effluent, effusion; *technical* efflux.
6 (*dated*) *his perseverance certainly merited a favourable issue* **result**, outcome, consequence, end result, net result, upshot, effect, after-effect, aftermath, conclusion, end, denouement; *informal* pay-off.

□ **at issue** *at issue here is the definition of a work of art* **in question**, in dispute; being discussed, under discussion, under consideration; on the agenda, for debate, to be discussed, to be decided, unsettled.

□ **take issue** *I* ***take issue with*** *your assertion* **disagree**, fail to agree, be in dispute, be in contention, be at variance, be at odds, be at loggerheads, not see eye to eye, argue, quarrel; challenge, dispute, question, call into question, oppose, object to, take exception to, protest against, contradict, gainsay, differ from, dissent from, diverge from; *archaic* disaccord.
OPPOSITE agree.

▶ **verb 1** *writs were issued against the contractors | the minister issued a statement* **send out**, put out; release, deliver; publish, announce, proclaim, broadcast, promulgate, communicate, impart, purvey, circulate, distribute, spread, disseminate; *literary* bruit about/abroad, utter.
OPPOSITE withdraw.
2 *the captain* ***issued*** *the crew* ***with*** *side arms* **supply**, provide, furnish, arm, equip, fit out, rig out, kit out, accoutre, outfit, fit up; provision, stock, purvey, accommodate; present, invest, endow, favour; *informal* fix up.
OPPOSITE withdraw.
3 *savoury smells began to issue from the kitchen | soft music issued from overhead speakers* **emanate**, emerge, proceed, exude, discharge, flow (out/forth), pour (out/forth), gush (out/forth), come (out/forth), seep (out/forth), ooze (out/forth), spread out; be uttered, be emitted, be transmitted.
4 *surprising profits might* ***issue from*** *the unwinding of a few giant companies* **result**, follow, ensue, develop, stem, spring, arise, start, derive, evolve, proceed, emerge, emanate, flow; be got, be had, be taken; be caused by, be the result of, be brought on/about by, be produced by, originate in, have its origin in, attend, accompany, be consequent on; *Philosophy* supervene on.
OPPOSITE bring about.

Italy ▶ **noun**

WORD LINKS

related prefix	**Italo-**
hatred or fear of Italian people and things	**Italophobia**
lover of Italian people and things	**Italophile**

itch ▶ **noun 1** *scratch my back—I have an itch* tingling, irritation, itchiness, stinging, prickling, tickling; *Medicine* paraesthesia; *rare* formication.
2 (*informal*) *he had the itch to write fiction* **longing**, yearning, pining, craving, ache, burning, hunger, thirst, urge, lust, hankering, need, eagerness, zeal, covetousness; wish, fancy, desire; hope, aspiration, dream; *informal* yen.

▶ **verb 1** *the heat made their chilblains itch* tingle, be irritated, be itchy, sting, prickle, tickle.
2 (*informal*) *he itched to do something to help | they were* ***itching for*** *a good game* **long**, yearn, pine, ache, burn, hanker for/after, hunger, thirst, lust, pant, hope, be eager, be desperate, be consumed with desire, be unable to wait, would give one's eye teeth, wish, have a fancy; crave, need, lust after, dream of, set one's heart on, be bent on, eat one's heart out over, covet; want, desire, fancy, set one's sights on; *informal* have a yen, be dying, be gagging.

WORD LINKS

fear of itching **acarophobia**

item ▶ **noun 1** *an item of farm equipment | earthworms are the main item in a badger's diet* **thing**, article, object, unit, module, artefact, piece, commodity, product, bit; element, constituent, component, ingredient.
2 *the meeting was ill-prepared to discuss the item* **issue**, matter, affair, business, subject, topic, question, point, detail, particular, thing, case, concern, consideration, theme, feature; proceeding, situation, occasion, circumstance.
3 *a news item* **report**, story, account, description, article, piece, write-up, paragraph, column, flash, brief, release, newscast, headline, communication, communiqué, bulletin, feature; message, dispatch, statement; *informal* scoop.
4 *the exceptional items in the profit and loss account* **entry**, record, statement, note, listing, thing.

itemize ▶ **verb 1** *Steinburg itemized thirty-two design faults in the reactor type* **list**, catalogue, inventory, record, set out, set forth, spell out, document, register, tabulate, detail, particularize, specify, identify, cite, name, mention, give; enumerate, number.
2 *they sent back the bill with a request to itemize it* **analyse**, break down, split up, dissect, take apart, deconstruct.

iterate ▶ **verb** *the process is iterated until a convincing agreement is reached* **repeat**, recapitulate, go through again, go over again, run through again, rehearse; say again, restate, reiterate; *informal* recap; *rare* reprise, ingeminate.

itinerant ▶ **adjective** *a market for both local and itinerant traders* **travelling**, peripatetic, wandering, wayfaring, roving, roaming, rambling, touring, nomadic, gypsy, migrant, migratory, ambulatory; vagrant, vagabond, homeless, of no fixed address/abode, displaced; footloose, rootless, drifting, floating, unsettled, restless; globetrotting, jet-setting; *archaic* errant.
OPPOSITES sedentary; settled.

▶ **noun** *an itinerants' lodging house* **traveller**, wanderer, wayfarer, roamer, rover, nomad, gypsy, Bedouin; migrant, transient, drifter, vagabond, vagrant, tramp; refugee, displaced person, DP, homeless person; *dated* bird of passage.

itinerary ▶ **noun** *the ancient university town of Cambridge should be on every visitor's itinerary* **planned route**, route, journey, way, road, path, course; travel plan, schedule, timetable, programme, travel arrangements, flight plan; tour, circuit, round.

itself ▶ **pronoun**

□ **by itself**. *See* BY ONESELF *at* BY.

I

jab ▶ **verb** *he jabbed the Englishman twice in the ribs | he jabbed his forefinger at Melanie* **poke**, prod, dig, nudge, tap, butt, ram, elbow, shove, punch, jolt; prick; thrust, stab, push, plunge, stick, insert, drive, lunge.
▶ **noun** *he gave me a jab in my ribs with his rifle butt* **poke**, prod, dig, nudge, tap, butt, elbow, shove, punch, jolt; prick; thrust, stab, push, plunge, drive, lunge.

jabber ▶ **verb** *they jabbered non-stop to each other over the radio* **prattle**, babble, chatter, twitter, prate, gabble, go on, run on, rattle on/away, yap, jibber-jabber, patter, blather, maunder, ramble, drivel, blab; talk rapidly, talk incoherently, talk unintelligibly; *informal* yak, yackety-yak, yabber, yatter, blabber; *Brit. informal* witter, rabbit, chunter, natter, waffle; *Scottish & Irish informal* slabber; *Austral./NZ informal* mag; *archaic* twaddle, clack, twattle.
▶ **noun** *stop your jabber and get on with your breakfast* **prattle**, babble, chatter, chattering, twitter, twittering, prating, gabble, jibber-jabber, patter, blather, rambling, twaddle, drivel; rapid talk, unintelligible talk; *informal* yak, yackety-yak, yabbering, yatter, blabber; *Brit. informal* wittering, rabbiting, nattering, waffle, waffling; *Austral./NZ informal* mag; *archaic* clack, twattle.

jack ▶ **verb**
□ **jack something up 1** *thieves jacked up the car and stole the wheels* **raise**, hoist, lift, lift up, raise aloft, haul up, winch up, lever up, heave up, hike up, hitch up, pull up, take up, upraise, uplift, elevate; *rare* upheave, uprear, upthrust.
2 (*informal*) *he may need to jack up interest rates further* **increase**, raise, put up, push up, up, mark up, make higher, boost, step up, lift, augment, inflate, escalate; *informal* hike (up), bump up.
OPPOSITE lower.

jacket *See centre pages for list of* **Coats, Cloaks, and Jackets**
▶ **noun** *a jacket for your hot-water tank will save at least £15 a year* **wrapping**, wrapper, wrap, sleeve, sheath, sheathing, envelope, cover, covering; casing, case, shell, housing, encasement, capsule; *technical* integument.

jackpot ▶ **noun** *this week's lottery jackpot is over £14 million* **top prize**, main prize, first prize; kitty, pool, pot, bank, bonanza, windfall.
□ **hit the jackpot** (*informal*) **win a large prize**, win a lot of money, strike it lucky, make a large profit, make a/one's fortune, make money, be successful, be lucky; *informal* clean up, strike it rich, rake it in, make a/one's pile, make a killing, make a packet, make a bundle, make a pretty penny, hit the big time; *Brit. informal* make a bomb; *N. Amer. informal* make big bucks.

jaded ▶ **adjective 1** *there are soups exotic enough for the most jaded palate* **satiated**, sated, surfeited, glutted, cloyed, gorged; **dulled**, blunted, deadened, benumbed.
2 *she has an eye for the detail that a more jaded journalist might overlook* **tired**, weary, tired out, wearied, worn out, exhausted, fatigued, overtired, sleepy, drowsy, sapped, dog-tired, spent, drained, jet-lagged, debilitated, prostrate, enervated, low; *informal* all in, done (in/up), dead, dead beat, dead tired, dead on one's feet, asleep on one's feet, ready to drop, played out, fagged out, bushed, pooped, worn to a frazzle, shattered, burnt out; *Brit. informal* knackered, whacked; *N. Amer. informal* tuckered out.
OPPOSITE fresh.

jag ▶ **noun** *a head of rye, all jags and bristles* **sharp projection**, point, snag, jagged bit; barb, thorn, tooth, spur; *informal* sticky-out bit.

jagged ▶ **adjective** *the jagged end of a broken bone* **spiky**, spiked, barbed, snaggy, nicked, pointed, ragged, craggy, rough, uneven, irregular, broken; serrated, sawtooth, saw-edged, toothed, notched, indented, denticulate.
OPPOSITE smooth.

jail, gaol ▶ **noun** *he was arrested and thrown into jail* **prison**, penal institution, place of detention, lock-up, place of confinement, guardhouse, correctional facility, detention centre; young offender institution, youth custody centre; *N. Amer.* penitentiary, jailhouse, boot camp, stockade, house of correction; *informal* the clink, the slammer, inside, stir, the jug, the big house, the brig, the glasshouse; *Brit. informal* the nick; *N. Amer. informal* the can, the pen, the cooler, the joint, the pokey, the slam, the skookum house, the calaboose, the hoosegow; *Brit. informal, dated* chokey, bird, quod; *historical* pound, roundhouse; *Brit. historical* approved school, borstal, bridewell; *Scottish historical* tollbooth; *French, historical* bastille; *N. Amer. historical* reformatory.
▶ **verb** *she was jailed for killing her husband* **imprison**, put in prison, send to prison, incarcerate, lock up, take into custody, put under lock and key, put away, intern, confine, detain, hold prisoner, hold captive, hold, put into detention, constrain, immure, put in chains, put in irons, clap in irons; *Brit.* detain at Her Majesty's pleasure; *informal* send down, put behind bars, put inside; *Brit. informal* bang up.
OPPOSITES acquit; release.

jailer, gaoler ▶ **noun** *the jailer had discovered the loss of his prisoners* **prison officer**, (prison) warder, (prison) wardress, (prison) warden, (prison) guard, keeper, incarcerator, captor, sentry; *informal* screw; *Law* detainer; *archaic* turnkey.

jam[1] ▶ **verb 1** *he jammed a finger in each ear* **stuff**, shove, force, ram, thrust, wedge, press, push, stick, squeeze, compress, confine, cram, pack, sandwich, insert.
2 *several hundred friends and celebrities* **jammed into** *the shop | students soon jammed the streets* **crowd**, pack, pile, press, squeeze, cram; throng, occupy, fill, overfill, overcrowd; obstruct, block, clog, congest; *N. Amer.* mob.
3 *the rudder had jammed* **stick**, become stuck, catch, seize (up), become immobilized, become unable to move, become fixed, become wedged, become lodged, become trapped.
4 *even dust could jam the mechanism* **immobilize**, paralyse, disable, cripple; deactivate, put out of action, make inoperative; stop, halt, bring to a halt, bring to a standstill.
OPPOSITE free.
▶ **noun 1** *a traffic jam* **tailback**, line, stream, hold-up, obstruction, congestion, bottleneck, stoppage; *N. Amer.* gridlock; *informal* snarl-up.
2 (*informal*) *I'd tell you if we ever got into a real jam* **predicament**, plight, tricky situation, ticklish situation, awkward situation, spot of trouble, bit of bother, difficulty, problem, puzzle, quandary, dilemma, muddle, mess, quagmire, mire, imbroglio, mare's nest, dire straits; with nowhere to turn; *W. Indian* comess; *informal* pickle, stew, sticky situation, fix, hole, scrape, bind, (tight) spot, (tight) corner, fine kettle of fish, how-do-you-do, hot water, deep water; *Brit. informal* spot of bother.

jam[2] ▶ **noun** *raspberry jam* **preserve**, conserve, jelly, marmalade; *N. Amer.* dulce; *rare* confiture, confection.

jamb ▶ **noun** *he leaned against the door jamb* **post**, doorpost, upright, frame, pillar.

jamboree ▶ **noun** *the world Scout jamboree* **rally**, gathering, get-together, convention, conference; festival, fête, fiesta, gala, party, carnival, celebration; *informal* bash, shindig, shindy, jolly, junket.

jammy ▶ **adjective** (*Brit. informal*) *that jammy pig's won a million quid! See* LUCKY.

jangle ▶ **verb 1** *keys jangled at his waist* **clank**, clink, jingle, tinkle, ding, ping, clang, clash, clatter, rattle, vibrate, ring, chime; *rare* tintinnabulate.
2 *the sound of merriment jangled her nerves* **grate on**, jar on, irritate, disturb, assault, fray, rasp, put/set on edge, shred, rub raw, test, rattle, stretch tight, wreak havoc on; *informal* get on.
▶ **noun** *the jangle of his chains and bells* **clank**, clanking, clink, clinking, chink, chinking, jangling, jingle, jingling, clash, clashing, clang, clanging, rattle, rattling, clangour; **cacophony**, din, racket, noise, discord, dissonance, discordance, caterwauling, raucousness, stridency, stridor; *rare* tintinnabulation.

janitor ▶ **noun** **caretaker**, custodian, porter, concierge, doorkeeper, doorman, steward, warden, watchman; cleaner, maintenance man; *N. Amer.* superintendent.

January ▶ noun

WORD LINKS
birthstone **garnet**

jar¹ ▶ noun *a jar of honey* **glass/earthenware container**, pot, crock, urn, pitcher, jug, flask, decanter, carafe, flagon, ewer, drum, canister; vessel, container, receptacle, repository; *N. Amer.* creamer; *historical* jorum; *archaic* reservatory.

jar² ▶ verb **1** *each step jarred my whole body* **jolt**, jerk, shake, vibrate; bang.
2 *his daughter's shrill, childish voice* **jarred on** *him* **grate on**, set someone's teeth on edge; irritate, annoy, upset, irk, exasperate, nettle, vex, disturb, rattle, discompose; jangle; *informal* rile, aggravate, get on someone's nerves, get someone's goat.
OPPOSITE please.
3 *the play's symbolism* **jarred with** *the realism of its setting* **clash**, conflict, be incompatible, be at variance, be at odds, be inconsistent, be incongruous, be in opposition, be in conflict, disagree, contrast, collide; differ from, diverge from; not match, not go, be discordant; *informal* scream at.
OPPOSITES blend; match.

jargon ▶ noun *the instructions are written in electrician's jargon* **specialized language**, technical language, slang, cant, idiom, argot, patter, patois, vernacular; computerese, legalese, bureaucratese, journalese, psychobabble; unintelligible language, obscure language, gobbledegook, gibberish, double Dutch; *informal* lingo, -speak, -ese, mumbo-jumbo.

jarring ▶ adjective *the jarring juxtaposition of opposites* **clashing**, conflicting, contrasting, incompatible, incongruous; discordant, dissonant, inharmonious; harsh, grating, jangling, strident, shrill, cacophonous; out of place, unsuitable, inappropriate; disagreeable, unpleasant, offensive.
OPPOSITES harmonious; pleasing.

jaundiced ▶ adjective *a jaundiced view of the world* **bitter**, resentful, cynical, soured, distorted, disenchanted, disillusioned, disappointed, pessimistic, sceptical, distrustful, suspicious, misanthropic; jealous, envious; narrow-minded, bigoted, prejudiced, intolerant, discriminatory.
OPPOSITES optimistic; charitable.

jaunt ▶ noun *his wife went off for a jaunt round Oxford* **trip**, pleasure trip, outing, excursion, expedition, day trip, day out, mini holiday, short break; tour, mystery tour, drive, ride, run, turn, cruise, sally; *informal* junket, spin, tootle, joyride, tool; *Scottish informal* hurl.

jaunty ▶ adjective *he wore a cap pushed to one side to give him a jaunty air* **cheerful**, cheery, happy, merry, jolly, joyful, gleeful, glad; **lively**, vivacious, perky, full of life, bright, sunny, buoyant, bubbly, bouncy, breezy, frisky, full of the joys of spring, in good spirits, exuberant, ebullient, effervescent, sparkling, sparkly, sprightly, spry; **carefree**, unworried, untroubled, without a care in the world, blithe, airy, light-hearted, nonchalant, insouciant, happy-go-lucky, free and easy, easy-going, blasé, devil-may-care, casual, relaxed; *informal* bright-eyed and bushy-tailed, full of beans, sparky, upbeat, go-go, chirpy, chipper, peppy, zippy, zappy, full of vim and vigour; *N. Amer. informal* peart; *dated* gay; *archaic* blithesome, perk, as merry/lively as a grig, wick.
OPPOSITES depressed; serious; sedate.

javelin ▶ noun. *See centre pages for lists of* **Projectiles** **Weapons**

jaw ▶ noun **1** *he sustained a broken jaw* **jawbone**, lower jaw, mandible; maxilla, upper jaw.
2 (**jaws**) *the whale seized a struggling seal pup in its jaws* **mouth**, maw, muzzle, lips; *informal* chops.
3 (*informal*) *we ought to have a jaw. See* CHAT.
▶ verb (*informal*) *Tommaso was the type to jaw about whatever new scheme had taken his fancy. See* CHAT.

WORD LINKS
relating to the jaw **mandibular, maxillary**

jazz *See centre pages for list of* **Jazz Genres**
▶ verb
□ **jazz something up** (*informal*) *why not jazz up your documents with a few unusual typefaces?* **enliven**, liven up, brighten up, make more interesting, make more exciting, put some spirit into, make more attractive, add (some) colour to, wake up, give a lift/boost to, lift, ginger up; improve, enhance, embellish, dress up, beautify, gild, season, leaven, add spice to, spice up, revitalize, vitalize; *informal* perk up, pep up.

jazzy ▶ adjective *their range of ceramic jars uses a jazzy combination of spots and stripes* **bright**, colourful, brightly coloured, bright-coloured, brilliant, striking, strong, eye-catching, stimulating, exciting, interesting, effective, imaginative, graphic, vivid, lively, vibrant, bold, flamboyant, flashy, glaring, showy, gaudy, lurid, garish; *informal* (looking) like an explosion in a paint factory.
OPPOSITE dull.

jealous ▶ adjective **1** *he was jealous of his brother's popularity* **envious**, covetous, desirous; resentful, grudging, begrudging; jaundiced, bitter, malicious, spiteful; green with envy, green, green-eyed; greedy, selfish, acquisitive; *formal* emulous.
OPPOSITES admiring; proud.
2 *a jealous lover* **suspicious**, distrustful, mistrustful, doubting, insecure, anxious; apprehensive of rivals, possessive, proprietorial, overprotective, clinging, controlling, dominating.
OPPOSITES trusting, understanding.
3 *they are very jealous of their rights* **protective**, defensive, vigilant, watchful, heedful, mindful, careful, solicitous, attentive.
OPPOSITES careless, unconcerned.

jealousy ▶ noun **1** *he was consumed with jealousy at the younger man's superior talents* **envy**, enviousness, covetousness, desire; resentment, resentfulness, bitterness, discontent, spite, grudge; *informal* the green-eyed monster.
OPPOSITES admiration; pride.
2 *their relationship survived the understandable jealousy of his long-suffering wife* **suspicion**, suspiciousness, distrust, mistrust, doubt, insecurity, anxiety; apprehension about rivals, possessiveness, overprotectiveness.
OPPOSITES trust, understanding.
3 *such hierarchies produce an intense jealousy of status* **protectiveness**, defensiveness, vigilance, watchfulness, heedfulness, mindfulness, care, solicitousness, attentiveness.
OPPOSITES unconcern, carelessness.

WORD LINKS
fear of jealousy **zelotypophobia**

jeans ▶ plural noun **denims**, blue jeans; cut-offs; *trademark* Levi's, Wranglers.

jeer ▶ verb *the crowd* **jeered at** *the referee* | *the demonstrators jeered the police* **taunt**, mock, scoff at, ridicule, laugh at, sneer at, deride, tease, insult, abuse, jibe (at), scorn, shout disapproval (at); heckle, interrupt, shout at/down, hector, catcall (at), boo (at), hoot at, whistle at, hiss (at), blow raspberries (at); *informal* knock, give someone a hard time; *archaic* flout at.
OPPOSITES cheer; applaud.
▶ noun *the jeers of the crowd* **taunt**, sneer, insult, shout, jibe, boo, hiss, catcall; mockery, ridicule, derision, teasing, scoffing, hectoring, shouting, abuse, scorn, disapproval, interruption, heckling, catcalling, booing, hissing; *Brit. & Austral./NZ* barracking; *informal* knocking.
OPPOSITES cheer; applause; approval.

jejune ▶ adjective **1** *their entirely predictable and usually jejune opinions* **naive**, simple, innocent, artless, guileless, unworldly, childlike, ingenuous, unsophisticated; inexperienced, ignorant, green, immature, callow, trusting, trustful, unsuspicious, unwary, unguarded; credulous, gullible, easily taken in; unaffected, without airs, open, frank, uninhibited, natural, unpretentious, spontaneous, down-to-earth; childish, immature, juvenile, puerile, silly, infantile; *informal* wet behind the ears.
OPPOSITES sophisticated, mature.
2 *the following poem now seems to me rather jejune* **boring**, dull, dull as ditchwater, tedious, dreary; uninteresting, unexciting, uneventful, uninspiring, unstimulating, unimaginative; humdrum, run-of-the-mill, mundane, commonplace, workaday, quotidian, routine; stodgy, lacklustre, dry, dry as dust, arid, sterile, lifeless, vapid, insipid, flat, drab, bland, banal, trite, prosaic, colourless, monochrome, monotonous, unrelieved, lacking variety, lacking variation; tiresome, tiring, wearisome; *informal* deadly, nothing to write home about; *Brit. informal* samey; *Scottish informal* dreich; *N. Amer. informal* dullsville, ornery.
OPPOSITES fascinating, inspired.

jell ▶ verb. *See* GEL.

jeopardize ▶ verb *relocating outside London will jeopardize their competitiveness* **threaten**, endanger, imperil, menace, risk, put at risk, expose to risk, put in danger, expose to danger, put in jeopardy, put on the line; leave vulnerable, leave unprotected; compromise, prejudice, be prejudicial to; be a danger to, pose a threat to; **damage**, injure, harm, do harm to, be detrimental to; *archaic* peril.
OPPOSITE safeguard.

CHOOSE THE RIGHT WORD
jeopardize, endanger, imperil, risk
See ENDANGER.

jeopardy ▶ noun *the peace talks are* **in jeopardy** **danger**, peril; at risk; endangerment, imperilment, insecurity; perilousness, riskiness, precariousness, uncertainty, instability, vulnerability, threat, menace.
OPPOSITES safety, security.

jerk ▶ noun **1** *she gave the reins a jerk* **yank**, tug, pull, wrench, snatch, heave, drag, tweak, twitch.
2 *he let the clutch in with a jerk* **jolt**, lurch, bump, start, jar, jog, bang, bounce, shake, shock; *rare* jounce.
3 (*informal*) *I was left behind, feeling a complete jerk. See* FOOL.
▶ verb **1** *she jerked her arm free* **yank**, tug, pull, wrench, wrest, heave, haul, drag, tweak, twitch, pluck, snatch, seize, rip, tear, whisk; *informal* whip.
OPPOSITE ease.
2 *the car jerked along in the traffic* **jolt**, lurch, bump, jog, bang, rattle, bounce, shake; *rare* jounce.
OPPOSITE glide.

jerky ▶ adjective **1** *the jerky movements of a frightened horse* **convulsive**,

J

spasmodic, fitful, twitchy, paroxysmal, shaking, shaky, tremulous, uncontrolled, uncontrollable.
OPPOSITES fluid, smooth.
2 *the coach drew to a jerky halt* **jolting**, lurching, bumpy, bouncy, jarring, rough; *rare* jouncing.
OPPOSITE smooth.

jerry-built ▶ adjective *they lived in tents and jerry-built shacks* **shoddy**, badly built, gimcrack, flimsy, insubstantial, rickety, unstable, ramshackle, crude, carelessly built, thrown together, makeshift, defective, faulty, flawed; inferior, poor-quality, second-rate, third-rate, low-grade, cheap, cheapjack; *informal* tacky, junky; *Brit. informal* ropy, rubbish, grotty.
OPPOSITES well made, sturdy, substantial.

jersey ▶ noun. *See centre pages for list of* **Pullovers**

jest ▶ noun **1** *the men talk cheerfully and jests are bandied about freely* **joke**, witticism, funny remark, gag, quip, sally, pun, play on words; *French* bon mot; *informal* crack, wisecrack, one-liner, funny, comeback; repartee, banter.
2 *he wished that Lady Lavinia had not practised this jest upon him* **prank**, joke, practical joke, piece of mischief, hoax, trick, jape; *informal* leg-pull, put-on, lark; *N. Amer. informal* dido.
□ **in jest** *he could tell from the others' smirks that it was meant in jest* **in fun**, as a joke, tongue in cheek, playfully, jokingly, light-heartedly, facetiously, flippantly, frivolously, for a laugh; to tease, teasingly, banteringly, whimsically.
OPPOSITE seriously.
▶ verb **1** *'It's good weather when it doesn't snow before half-time,' he jests* **joke**, crack, quip, gag, sally, pun; tell jokes, crack jokes, banter; *informal* wisecrack.
2 *she began to fear that they had not been jesting* **fool**, fool about/around, play a prank, play a practical joke, tease, hoax; *informal* kid, wind up, have on, pull someone's leg, make a monkey out of; *N. Amer. informal* pull someone's chain, fun, shuck.

J

jester ▶ noun **1** (*historical*) *a court jester* **fool**, court fool, court jester; clown, harlequin, pantaloon; *archaic* buffoon, merry andrew, merryman, motley.
2 *teachers don't usually like the class jester* **joker**, comedian, comic, humorist, wag, wit, funny man/woman, prankster, jokester, clown, buffoon, character; *informal* card, case, caution, hoot, scream, laugh, kidder, wisecracker, riot, barrel of laughs; *Austral./NZ informal* hard case.

jet[1] ▶ noun **1** *a jet of water went down his neck* **stream**, spurt, squirt, spray, fountain, spout; gush, outpouring, rush, surge, burst, spill, flow, flood, cascade, torrent, current.
2 *the carburettor jets can get clogged* **nozzle**, head, spray, rose, atomizer, sprinkler, sprinkler head, spout, nose; *technical* sparkler, spile.
3 *they found an executive jet to fly me back* **jet plane**, jetliner; aircraft, plane; *Brit.* aeroplane.
▶ verb **1** *they jetted out of Heathrow last night* **fly**, travel/go by jet, travel/go by plane, travel/go by air.
2 *little puffs of gas jetted out* **squirt**, spurt, shoot, spray, fountain, erupt; gush, pour, stream, rush, pump, surge, spew, spill, flow, course, well, spring, burst, issue, emanate; *Brit. informal* sloosh.

jet[2] ▶ adjective *her glossy jet hair* **black**, jet-black, pitch-black, as black as pitch, pitchy, pitch-dark, inky, ink-black, sloe-black, coal-black, ebony, raven, sable, sooty.

jettison ▶ verb **1** *six aircraft jettisoned their loads into the sea* **dump**, drop, ditch, discharge, eject, throw out, empty out, pour out, tip out, unload, throw overboard, throw over the side.
OPPOSITE load.
2 *he sorted out his desk, jettisoning unwanted papers | the scheme was jettisoned* **discard**, dispose of, throw away, throw out, get rid of, toss out; reject, scrap, dispense with, cast aside/off, abandon, relinquish, drop, have done with, shed, slough off, shrug off, throw on the scrap heap; *informal* chuck (away/out), fling, dump, ditch, axe, bin, junk, get shut of; *Brit. informal* get shot of; *N. Amer. informal* trash.
OPPOSITES keep, retain.

jetty ▶ noun **pier**, landing stage, landing place, landing, quay, wharf, dock, berth, staithe, stair(s), finger, pontoon, marina, harbour; breakwater, mole, groyne, dyke; *N. Amer.* dockominium, levee; (*in Venice*) traghetto.

Jew ▶ noun
OPPOSITE Gentile.

WORD LINKS
relating to Jews **Judaic, Semitic**
related prefix **Judaeo- (e.g. *Judaeo-Christian*)**

jewel *See centre pages for lists of* **Gems** **Jewellery**
▶ noun **1** *a crown encrusted with priceless jewels* **gem**, gemstone, precious stone, semi-precious stone, stone, brilliant; baguette, cabochon; *informal* sparkler, rock; *archaic* bijou.
2 *the Crown jewels* **piece of jewellery**, ornament; trinket.
3 *the jewel of his collection | a jewel of a poem* **finest example/specimen**, choicest example/specimen, best example/specimen, showpiece, pearl, flower, pride, pride and joy, cream, crème de la crème, jewel in the crown, nonpareil, glory, wonder, prize, boast, pick; masterpiece, chef d'oeuvre, pièce de résistance; outstanding example, shining example; *Latin* ne plus ultra; *informal* the pick of the bunch.
4 *the girl is a jewel* **treasure**, saint, angel, paragon, marvel, find, godsend, someone/something worth their weight in gold; darling, dear; *informal* one in a million, one of a kind, a star, the bee's knees, the tops; *archaic* nonsuch.

jeweller ▶ noun *rare* lapidary, gemmologist.

jewellery *See centre pages for lists of* **Gems** **Jewellery**
▶ noun **jewels**, gems, gemstones, precious stones, semi-precious stones, bijouterie; treasure, regalia; **ornaments**, trinkets, costume jewellery, diamanté; *archaic* bijoux.

Jezebel ▶ noun **immoral woman**, hussy; seductress, temptress, femme fatale, Delilah; *informal* vamp, maneater; *N. Amer. informal* roundheel, tramp; *informal, derogatory* tart; *Brit. informal, derogatory* scrubber, slapper, slag; *dated* scarlet woman, loose woman, woman of easy virtue, woman of ill repute, fallen woman, wanton, strumpet, trollop; *archaic* harlot, jade.

jib ▶ verb **1** *the horse **jibbed at** the final fence* **stop at**, stop short at, baulk at, shy at, retreat from; refuse.
OPPOSITE clear.
2 *some struggling farmers **jib at** paying large veterinary bills* **baulk at**, fight shy of, shy away from, recoil from, shrink from, draw back from, stop short of; be unwilling to, be reluctant to, demur at, be loath to, not want to; *informal* boggle at.
OPPOSITE be willing to.

jibe ▶ noun *the cruel jibes of his former colleagues* **snide remark**, cutting remark, taunt, sneer, jeer, insult, barb; *informal* dig, wisecrack, crack, put-down.
▶ verb *'What accomplishments?' Simon jibed in his sarcastic way* **jeer**, taunt, mock, scoff, sneer.

jiffy ▶ noun (*informal*)
□ **in a jiffy** *I'll be back in a jiffy* **very soon**, soon, in a second, in a minute, in a moment, in a trice, in a flash, shortly, directly, any second, any minute, any minute now, in a short time, in an instant, in the twinkling of an eye, in no time, in no time at all, in less than no time, before you know it, before long; *N. Amer.* momentarily; *informal* in a sec, in a jif, in two shakes, in two shakes of a lamb's tail, before you can say Jack Robinson, in the blink of an eye, in a blink, in the wink of an eye, in a wink, before you can say knife; *Brit. informal* in a tick, in two ticks, in a mo; *N. Amer. informal* in a snap, in jig time; *archaic* anon.

jig ▶ verb *Joan **jigged about** with excitement* **bob up and down**, leap up and down, jump up and down, spring up and down, skip, hop; prance, caper, bounce; *rare* curvet, rollick, capriole, jounce.

jiggle ▶ verb **1** *Barrett jiggled his foot, looking anywhere but at Bill* **shake**, jig, joggle, jog, waggle, wiggle; jerk.
2 *Thomas jiggled excitedly* **fidget**, wriggle, squirm, move restlessly; *informal* have ants in one's pants.

jilt ▶ verb *the man I thought loved me jilted me and stole my money* **leave**, walk out on, throw over, finish with, break up with, reject, cast aside; desert, abandon, leave in the lurch, leave high and dry; betray; *informal* chuck, ditch, dump, drop, run out on, do the dirty on, give someone the push, give someone the old heave-ho, give someone the elbow, give someone the big E; *archaic* forsake.

jingle ▶ noun **1** *the jingle of money in the till* **clink**, chink, tinkle, jangle, rattle.
2 *the jingle of the bell above the shop door made her jump* **tinkle**, ring, ding, ping, ting-a-ling, chime; *rare* tintinnabulation.
3 *advertising jingles* **slogan**, catchline, catchphrase; **ditty**, song, rhyme, tune, verse; chorus, refrain; limerick, piece of doggerel; *N. Amer.* tag line.
▶ verb **1** *her bracelets jingled noisily | he jingled the coins in his pocket* **clink**, chink, tinkle, jangle, rattle, clank.
2 *the bell jingled* **tinkle**, ring, ding, ping, go ting-a-ling, chime; *rare* tintinnabulate.

jingoism ▶ noun *the jingoism of Hollywood war films* **extreme patriotism**, blind patriotism, chauvinism, extreme nationalism, flag-waving, excessive loyalty to one's country, xenophobia; isolationism, sectarianism; hawkishness, militarism, warmongering, belligerence, bellicosity.

jinx ▶ noun *the jinx struck six days later, when fire gutted the building* **curse**, spell, hoodoo, malediction, plague, affliction; the evil eye, black magic, voodoo, bad luck, evil fortune; *Irish* cess; *N. Amer.* hex; *informal* the kiss of death; *archaic* malison.
▶ verb *some people believe the family is jinxed* **curse**, cast a spell on, put the evil eye on, hoodoo, bewitch; *Austral.* point the bone at; *N. Amer.* hex; *Austral. informal* mozz, put the mozz on; *rare* accurse.

jitters ▶ plural noun (*informal*) *a fit of opening-night jitters* **nervousness**, nerves, fit of nerves, edginess, uneasiness, anxiety, anxiousness, tension, agitation, fretfulness, restlessness, fidgeting, trembling, shaking, jumpiness; stage fright; *N. Amer.* buck fever; *informal* butterflies (in one's stomach), the willies, collywobbles, the heebie-jeebies, the shakes, the DTs, the jumps, the yips, jitteriness, the jim-jams, twitchiness; *Brit. informal*

the (screaming) abdabs; *Austral. rhyming slang* Joe Blakes; *N. Amer. archaic* worriment.
OPPOSITES calmness, serenity.

jittery ▶ **adjective** (*informal*). See NERVOUS.

job ▶ **noun 1** *my job involves a lot of travelling* **position of employment**, position, post, situation, place, appointment, posting, placement; **occupation**, profession, trade, career, work, field of work, line of work, line of business, means of livelihood, means of earning a living, walk of life, métier, pursuit, craft; vocation, calling; vacancy, opening; *Scottish* way; *informal* berth; *Austral. informal* grip; *archaic* employ.
2 *a job that will take him three months to complete* **task**, piece of work, assignment, project; chore, errand; undertaking, venture, operation, enterprise, activity, business, affair; *Military* detail.
3 *it's your job to protect her* **responsibility**, **duty**, charge, concern, task; role, function, contribution, capacity, mission, commission; *informal* department; *Brit. informal* pigeon; *dated* office.
4 (*informal*) *it was a job to get here on time* **difficult task**, problem, trouble, struggle, strain, hard time, trial, bother; *informal* headache, hassle, performance, pain, hard mountain to climb, hard row to hoe.
5 (*informal*) *a series of daring bank jobs* **crime**, felony; raid, robbery, hold-up, burglary, break-in, theft; *informal* stick-up, smash-and-grab (raid); *N. Amer. informal* heist.
□ **just the job** (*Brit. informal*) **the very thing**, just the thing, just right, exactly what's needed; *informal* just what the doctor ordered, just the ticket; *Austral. informal* just the glassy.

WORD LINKS
relating to a job **vocational**

CHOOSE THE RIGHT WORD
job, task, chore, duty
See TASK.

jobless ▶ **adjective** *sixteen per cent of the town's workforce is jobless* **unemployed**, out of work, without work, out of a job, without paid employment, unwaged, workless, between jobs, redundant, laid off; *N. Amer.* on welfare, collecting unemployment; *Brit. informal* signing on, on the dole, 'resting'; *Austral./NZ informal* on the wallaby track; *N. Amer. informal* collecting; *rare* disemployed.
OPPOSITES in work, employed.

jockey ▶ **noun** **rider**, horseman, horsewoman, equestrian; *Austral. informal* hoop.
▶ **verb 1** *I jockeyed the stone into position | he jockeyed himself into a position on the team* **manoeuvre**, ease, edge, manipulate, work, steer; engineer, inveigle, insinuate, ingratiate, wheedle, coax, cajole; *informal* finagle.
2 *members of the Cabinet began jockeying for position* **compete**, contend, vie; **struggle**, fight, tussle, scramble, push, jostle.

jocular ▶ **adjective** *jocular comments | a jocular mood* **humorous**, funny, witty, comic, comical, amusing, droll, entertaining, diverting, joking, jesting, hilarious, facetious, tongue-in-cheek; playful, light-hearted, jolly, jovial, cheerful, cheery, merry, mirthful, roguish, waggish, whimsical, teasing; *informal* jokey; *dated* sportive; *rare* jocose, ludic.
OPPOSITES solemn, serious, earnest.

jocund ▶ **adjective** (*literary*). See CHEERFUL.

jog ▶ **verb 1** *he began to jog along the road* **run slowly**, jogtrot, dogtrot, trot, lope; go jogging.
2 *things seem to be jogging along quite nicely here* **continue**, proceed, go, go on, carry on.
3 *a hand jogged his elbow* **nudge**, prod, poke, push, elbow, tap; bump, jar.
4 *I think it was seeing you that jogged her memory* **stimulate**, prompt, stir, activate, arouse; refresh.
5 *she jogged her foot up and down* **joggle**, jiggle, bob, bounce, jolt, jerk, shake; *rare* jounce.
▶ **noun** *he set off along the bank at a jog* **run**, jogtrot, dogtrot, trot, lope.

joie de vivre ▶ **noun** (*French*) *Mediterranean joie de vivre is not a quality found in the typical Briton* **gaiety**, cheerfulness, cheeriness, merriment, light-heartedness, happiness, joy, joyfulness, joyousness, delight, pleasure, high spirits, spiritedness, jollity, jolliness, joviality, exuberance, ebullience, liveliness, vivacity, enthusiasm, enjoyment, verve, gusto, relish, animation, effervescence, sparkle, buoyancy, sprightliness, jauntiness, zest, zestfulness; *informal* pep, zing, get-up-and-go, being full of the joys of spring, perkiness; *literary* gladsomeness, blitheness, blithesomeness.
OPPOSITES depression; sobriety.

join ▶ **verb 1** *the two parts of the mould are joined with clay* **connect**, unite, fix, affix, attach, add, annex, fasten, stick, glue, fuse, knit, weld, amalgamate, consolidate, combine, bond, append, link, bridge, secure, lock, make fast, tie, bind, string, lash, couple, marry, pair, yoke, team, chain, merge, dovetail, splice, blend; *formal* conjoin.
OPPOSITE separate.
2 *here the path joins a major road* **meet**, touch, reach, extend to, abut, adjoin, border (on), converge (with); rejoin.
OPPOSITE leave.
3 *I'm off to join the search party* **become a member of**, help in, participate in, join in, get involved in, contribute to, have a hand in; enlist (in), join up (with), sign up (with), affiliate to, team up (with), join forces (with), play a part (in); band together, get together, ally.
OPPOSITE leave.
▶ **noun**. *See* JOINT.

joint *See centre pages for list of joints of* **Meat**
▶ **noun 1** *a leaky joint in the metal guttering* **join**, junction, juncture, intersection, link, linkage, connection, nexus; weld, knot, seam; coupling, coupler; bracket, brace, hinge; *Anatomy* commissure, suture.
2 *the hip joint* ball-and-socket joint, hinge joint; *technical* articulation.
3 (*informal*) *L'Alouette looked like a pretty classy joint* **establishment**, restaurant, bar, club, nightclub; *informal* clip joint, dive; *N. Amer. informal* honky-tonk; (*in the US, historical*) speakeasy.
4 (*informal*) *he rolled a joint* **cannabis cigarette**, marijuana cigarette; *informal* spliff, reefer, bomb, bomber, stick; *S. African* zol; *black English* blunt.
▶ **adjective** *matters of joint interest | a joint effort* **common**, shared, communal, collective, corporate; mutual, reciprocal; cooperative, collaborative, concerted, joined, combined, allied, united.
OPPOSITES separate, individual.
▶ **verb** *use a sharp knife to joint the carcass* **cut up**, chop up, butcher, carve.

WORD LINKS
related prefixes **arthro-** **(e.g.** ***arthropod, arthroscope*****)** **zygo-** **(e.g.** ***zygomatic*****)**

jointly ▶ **adverb** *a survey organized jointly by the WWF and the Forestry Commission* **together**, in partnership, in cooperation, cooperatively, in collaboration, in conjunction, in concert, in combination, as one, mutually; in alliance, in league, in collusion; *informal* in cahoots.

joke ▶ **noun 1** *they sat round the table telling jokes* **funny story**, jest, witticism, quip, pleasantry; pun, play on words; shaggy-dog story, old chestnut, double entendre; in-joke; *informal* **gag**, wisecrack, crack, funny, one-liner, rib-tickler, killer, knee-slapper, thigh-slapper; *N. Amer. informal* boffola; *rare* blague.
2 *he was given to playing stupid jokes on people* **trick**, practical joke, prank, stunt, hoax, jape; *informal* leg-pull, lark, spoof; *Austral. informal* goak; *N. Amer. informal, dated* cutup; *archaic* quiz; *Scottish archaic* cantrip.
3 (*informal*) *he soon became a joke to most of us because he was so pedantic* **laughing stock**, figure of fun, source of amusement, object of ridicule; *Brit.* Aunt Sally.
4 (*informal*) *the present system is nothing short of a joke* **farce**, travesty, waste of time; standing joke; *informal* laugh; *N. Amer. informal* shuck.
▶ **verb 1** *she laughed and joked with the guests* **tell jokes**, crack jokes; jest, banter, quip; *informal* wisecrack, josh.
2 *don't panic—I'm only joking* **fool**, fool about/around, play a prank, play a trick, play a joke, play a practical joke, tease, hoax, pull someone's leg, mess someone about/around; *informal* kid, make a monkey out of someone; *Brit. informal* mess, have someone on, wind someone up; *N. Amer. informal* fun, shuck someone, pull someone's chain, put someone on; *Brit. informal, dated* rot someone.

joker ▶ **noun** *he had a reputation as the family joker* **humorist**, comedian, comedienne, comic, funny man/woman, wag, wit, jester; prankster, practical joker, hoaxer, trickster, clown; *informal* card, jokester, wisecracker; *archaic* quiz, droll, merry andrew; *rare* quipster, gagster, jokesmith, punster, kidder, farceur.

jolly ▶ **adjective** *a big, jolly woman | he returned home in a jolly mood* **cheerful**, happy, cheery, good-humoured, jovial, merry, sunny, bright, joyful, light-hearted, in high spirits, in good spirits, sparkling, bubbly, exuberant, effervescent, ebullient, breezy, airy, lively, vivacious, full of life, sprightly, jaunty; glad, cock-a-hoop, gleeful; smiling, grinning, laughing, mirthful, radiant; happy-go-lucky, genial, carefree, unworried, untroubled, without a care in the world, full of the joys of spring, fun-loving, buoyant, optimistic, hopeful, positive; *informal* chipper, chirpy, perky, smiley, upbeat, peppy, sparky, zippy, zingy, bright-eyed and bushy-tailed, full of beans, full of vim and vigour; *N. Amer. informal* peart; *dated* gay; *literary* gladsome, jocund, joyous, jocose, blithe, blithesome; *archaic* of good cheer, perk, as merry/lively as a grig; *rare* Pickwickian.
OPPOSITES miserable, gloomy.
▶ **verb** (*informal*) *he tried to jolly her along* **encourage**, urge, coax, cajole, persuade, wheedle.
▶ **adverb** (*Brit. informal*) *that's a jolly good idea*. *See* VERY.

jolt ▶ **verb 1** *the train stopped suddenly, jolting the passengers to one side | he jolted his injured ankle* **push**, thrust; **jar**, bump, knock, bang, jostle; shake, joggle, jog, nudge.
2 *the car jolted along the rough wet roads* **bump**, bounce, jerk, rattle, lurch, shudder, vibrate; *Brit.* judder; *rare* jounce.
3 *she was jolted out of her reverie | the anger in his tone jolted her* **startle**, surprise, shock, stun, shake, take aback; astonish, astound, amaze, stagger, stop someone in their tracks; upset, disturb, perturb, disconcert, discompose, unnerve, throw off balance, set someone back on their heels; galvanize, electrify; *informal* rock, floor, knock for six, knock sideways.

J

▶ noun 1 *a series of sickening jolts that jarred every bone in her body* **bump**, bounce, shake, jerk, lurch, vibration; impact; *Brit.* judder; *rare* jounce.
2 *he woke up with a jolt* **start**, jerk, jump, abrupt movement, convulsive movement.
3 *the sight of the dagger gave him a jolt* **fright**, the fright of one's life, shock, scare; *informal* turn.
4 *it had been an unpleasant jolt, but Susan recovered quickly* **shock**, surprise, bombshell, bolt from the blue, thunderbolt, rude awakening, eye-opener; blow, upset, setback; *informal* whammy.

jostle ▶ verb 1 *she stepped aside to avoid being jostled by a crowd of noisy students* **bump into/against**, knock into/against, bang into, collide with, cannon into, plough into, jolt; **push**, shove, elbow, hustle; mob; *N. Amer. informal* barrel into.
2 *I jostled my way to the exit* **push**, thrust, barge, shove, force, squeeze, elbow, shoulder, bulldoze.
3 *people jostled for the best position* **struggle**, vie, jockey, scramble, crowd one another; *informal* scrum.

jot ▶ verb *I've jotted down a few details* **write down**, note down, make a note of, take down, set down, put down, put on paper, mark down; log, record, list, register, enter; scribble, scrawl.
▶ noun *they have not produced a jot of evidence | she didn't care a jot about him* **iota**, scrap, shred, whit, grain, crumb, ounce, little bit, bit, tiniest bit, jot or tittle, fraction, speck, atom, particle, scintilla, trace, hint, mite; any; rap, hoot, fig; *Irish* stim; *French* soupçon; *informal* smidgen, smidge, tad, damn, tinker's cuss, monkey's; *Austral./NZ informal* skerrick; *archaic* scantling, scruple, smitch.

journal ▶ noun 1 *a medical journal* **periodical**, publication, magazine, gazette, digest, professional organ, review, newsletter, news-sheet, bulletin; **newspaper**, paper; daily, weekly, monthly, quarterly.
2 *while abroad, he kept a journal* **diary**, day-by-day account, daily record, log, logbook, weblog, blog, yearbook; chronicle, register; notebook, commonplace book; annals, history; *N. Amer.* daybook.

J

journalism ▶ noun 1 *a career in journalism* **the newspaper business**, the newspaper world, the press, the print media, the fourth estate; radio journalism, television journalism; *Brit.* Fleet Street.
2 *his incisive style of journalism* **reporting**, writing, reportage, feature writing, news coverage; investigative journalism; articles, reports, features, pieces, stories.

journalist ▶ noun **reporter**, correspondent, newsman, newswoman, newspaperman, newspaperwoman, columnist, writer, commentator, reviewer, blogger; investigative journalist, photojournalist, war correspondent, lobby correspondent; editor, subeditor, copy editor; paparazzo; *Brit.* pressman; *N. Amer.* legman, wireman; *Austral.* roundsman; *informal* news hound, hack, hackette, stringer, journo, talking head; *N. Amer. informal* newsy, thumbsucker; *dated* publicist; (**journalists**) the commentariat.

journey ▶ noun *his three-year journey round the world* **trip**, expedition, period of travelling, tour, trek, voyage, cruise, safari, ride, drive; crossing, passage, flight; travels, wandering, roaming, roving, globetrotting; odyssey, pilgrimage; excursion, outing, jaunt; *rare* peregrination.
▶ verb *they journeyed south* **travel**, go, voyage, sail, cruise, fly, hike, trek, ride, drive, make one's way, wend one's way; go on a trip, take a trip, go on an expedition, go on an excursion, go on a tour, tour, go on safari; globetrot, backpack; roam, rove, ramble, wander, meander; *rare* peregrinate.

joust (*historical*) ▶ verb *knights jousted with lances and shields* **enter the lists**, tourney, tilt, break a lance; fight, spar, contend, clash.
▶ noun *a medieval joust* **tournament**, tourney, tilt, the lists; combat, contest, fight, encounter, duel, passage of arms.

jovial ▶ adjective *a stout, jovial man | his jovial manner* **cheerful**, jolly, happy, cheery, good-humoured, convivial, genial, good-natured, friendly, amiable, affable, sociable, outgoing, clubbable; smiling, grinning, laughing, mirthful, merry, sunny, bright, joyful, high-spirited, exuberant, ebullient, lively, vivacious, full of life, sprightly, jaunty, breezy; happy-go-lucky, carefree, unworried, untroubled, without a care in the world, full of the joys of spring, fun-loving, buoyant, optimistic, positive; *informal* chipper, chirpy, perky, smiley, upbeat, peppy, sparky, bright-eyed and bushy-tailed, full of beans, full of vim and vigour; *N. Amer. informal* peart; *dated* gay; *literary* gladsome, jocund, joyous, jocose, blithe, blithesome; *archaic* of good cheer, perk, as merry/lively as a grig; *rare* Pickwickian.
OPPOSITES miserable, gloomy.

joy ▶ noun 1 *whoops of joy | the look of joy on her face* **delight**, great pleasure, joyfulness, jubilation, triumph, exultation, rejoicing, happiness, gladness, glee, exhilaration, ebullience, exuberance, elation, euphoria, bliss, ecstasy, transports of delight, rapture, radiance; enjoyment, gratification, felicity; cloud nine, seventh heaven; *French* joie de vivre; *humorous* delectation; *literary* joyousness; *rare* jouissance, ravishment, jocundity.
OPPOSITES misery, despair.
2 *it was a joy to be with her* **pleasure**, source of pleasure, delight, treat, thrill; *informal* buzz, kick.
OPPOSITES trial, tribulation.
3 (*informal*) *if you still have no joy, you may have to resort to the courts* **success**, satisfaction, luck, successful result, positive result; accomplishment, achievement.

joyful ▶ adjective 1 *his joyful mood* **cheerful**, happy, jolly, merry, bright, sunny, joyous, light-hearted, in good spirits, in high spirits, sparkling, bubbly, effervescent, exuberant, ebullient, cock-a-hoop, breezy, airy, cheery, sprightly, jaunty, smiling, grinning, beaming, laughing, mirthful, radiant; jubilant, overjoyed, beside oneself with joy, thrilled, ecstatic, euphoric, blissful, on cloud nine/seven, elated, delighted, glad, gleeful, gratified; jovial, genial, good-humoured, happy-go-lucky, carefree, unworried, untroubled, without a care in the world, full of the joys of spring; buoyant, optimistic, hopeful, full of hope, positive; content, contented; *informal* upbeat, chipper, chirpy, peppy, smiley, sparky, over the moon, on top of the world; *N. Amer. informal* peart; *dated* gay; *Austral./NZ informal* wrapped; *literary* jocund, gladsome, blithe, blithesome; *archaic* of good cheer.
OPPOSITES sad, miserable.
2 *the joyful news about his forthcoming marriage* **pleasing**, glad, happy, good, cheering, gladdening, gratifying, welcome, heart-warming, delightful; *literary* gladsome.
OPPOSITE distressing.
3 *a joyful occasion* **happy**, cheerful, merry, jolly, festive, celebratory, joyous; *dated* gay.
OPPOSITES sad, depressing.

joyless ▶ adjective 1 *a narrow-minded, joyless man* **gloomy**, melancholy, morose, lugubrious, glum, sombre, saturnine, sullen, dour, mirthless, humourless; unhappy, sad, miserable, depressed, despondent, sunk in gloom, heavy-hearted, doleful, downcast, dejected, dispirited.
OPPOSITES cheerful, fun-loving.
2 *a joyless room filled with yellowing oil paintings* **depressing**, cheerless, gloomy, dreary, bleak, dispiriting, drab, dismal, desolate, wretched, comfortless, austere, stark, sombre, grim; unwelcoming, uninviting, inhospitable; *literary* drear.
OPPOSITES pleasant, welcoming.

joyous ▶ adjective *her joyous expression.* See JOYFUL.

jubilant ▶ adjective *crowds of jubilant fans ran on to the pitch* **overjoyed**, exultant, triumphant, joyful, jumping for joy, rejoicing, cock-a-hoop, exuberant, elated, thrilled, gleeful, euphoric, ecstatic, beside oneself with happiness, enraptured, in raptures, rhapsodic, transported, walking on air, in seventh heaven, on cloud nine; crowing, gloating, triumphal, triumphalist; *informal* over the moon, on top of the world, blissed out, on a high, tickled pink; *N. Amer. informal* wigged out; *Austral. informal* wrapped.
OPPOSITES downcast, despondent.

jubilation ▶ noun *Arlene was unable to conceal her jubilation* **exultation**, triumph, joy, joyousness, rejoicing, elation, euphoria, ecstasy, rapture, transports of delight, glee, gleefulness, exuberance.
OPPOSITE despondency.

jubilee ▶ noun **anniversary**, commemoration; **celebration**, festival, gala, carnival, jamboree, feast day, holiday; festivities, revelry.

Judas ▶ noun **traitor**, betrayer, back-stabber, double-crosser, false friend; turncoat, quisling, renegade; *archaic* traditor; *rare* tergiversator, renegado.

judge ▶ noun 1 *the judge sentenced him to five years* justice, magistrate, His/Her/Your Honour; Law Lord, Lord Justice; (**judges**) the judiciary; (*in England & Wales*) recorder; (*in Scotland*) sheriff; (*in the Isle of Man*) deemster; (*in the Channel Islands*) jurat; *N. Amer.* jurist, surrogate; *Spanish* alcalde; *informal* beak, m'lud; *historical* reeve; *Scottish historical* sheriff-depute, bailie.
2 *a distinguished panel of judges will select the winning design* **adjudicator**, arbiter, assessor, evaluator, appraiser, examiner, moderator; umpire, referee, mediator; expert, connoisseur, authority, specialist, pundit; *Latin* arbiter elegantiarum.
▶ verb 1 *I judged that she was simply exhausted | voters were asked what factors they judged to be most important* **form the opinion**, come to the conclusion, conclude, decide, determine; consider, believe, think, deem, view; deduce, gather, infer, gauge, tell, see, say, estimate, assess, guess, surmise, conjecture; regard as, hold, see as, look on as, take to be, rate as, rank as, class as, count; *informal* reckon, figure, guesstimate.
2 *other cases were judged by tribunal* **try**, hear, sit in judgement on; adjudicate, decide, give a ruling/verdict on, pass judgement on.
3 *she was judged innocent of murder* **adjudge**, pronounce, decree, rule, find.
4 *the competition will be judged by Alan Amey* **adjudicate**, arbitrate, umpire, referee, mediate, moderate; officiate.
5 *entries will by judged by a panel of experts* **assess**, appraise, evaluate, weigh up; examine, review, criticize; *informal* size up.

judgement ▶ noun 1 *the incident showed the extent to which his temper could affect his judgement* **discernment**, acumen, shrewdness, astuteness, common sense, good sense, sense, perception, perspicacity, percipience, penetration, acuity, discrimination, wisdom, wit, native wit, judiciousness, prudence, sagacity, understanding, intelligence, awareness, canniness, sharpness, sharp-wittedness, cleverness, powers of reasoning, reason, logic; *informal* nous, savvy, know-how, horse sense, gumption, grey

matter; *Brit. informal* common; *N. Amer. informal* smarts; *rare* sapience, arguteness.
2 *a county-court judgement* **verdict**, decision, adjudication, ruling, pronouncement, decree, finding, conclusion, determination; sentence.
3 *the critical judgement of work by artists and designers* **assessment**, evaluation, appraisal; review, analysis, criticism, critique.
4 *the crash had been a judgement on them for their wickedness* **punishment**, retribution, penalty; just deserts.
□ **against one's better judgement reluctantly**, unwillingly, grudgingly, under protest; despite oneself.
□ **in my judgement** *in my judgement, such things should be forbidden* **in my opinion**, to my mind, in my view, to my way of thinking, I believe, I think, as I see it, if you ask me, personally, in my book, for my money, in my estimation.

judgemental ▶ **adjective** *I don't like to sound judgemental but it really was a big mistake* **critical**, fault-finding, censorious, condemnatory, disapproving, disparaging, deprecating, negative, overcritical, hypercritical, scathing.

judicial ▶ **adjective** *a judicial inquiry* **legal**, judiciary, juridical, judicatory, forensic, jurisdictive; official.

judicious ▶ **adjective** *a judicious course of action* **wise**, sensible, prudent, politic, shrewd, astute, canny, sagacious, common-sense, commonsensical, sound, well advised, well judged, well thought out, considered, thoughtful, perceptive, discerning, clear-sighted, insightful, far-sighted, percipient, discriminating, informed, intelligent, clever, enlightened, logical, rational; discreet, careful, cautious, circumspect, diplomatic; strategic, expedient, practical, advisable, in one's (best) interests; *informal* smart, savvy; *Scottish & N. English informal* pawky; *N. Amer. informal* heads-up; *dated, informal* long-headed; *rare*; argute, sapient.
OPPOSITES injudicious, foolish, ill-advised.

jug ▶ **noun pitcher**, ewer, crock, jar, urn; carafe, flask, flagon, decanter; vessel, receptacle, container; toby jug; *N. Amer.* creamer; *historical* amphora, jorum, greybeard.

juggle ▶ **verb** *defence chiefs juggled the figures on bomb tests* **misrepresent**, tamper with, falsify, misstate, distort, change round, alter, manipulate, rig, massage, fudge; *informal* fix, doctor, cook the books; *Brit. informal* fiddle.

juice ▶ **noun 1** *squeeze the juice from two lemons* **liquid**, fluid, sap; extract; *Winemaking* taille.
2 (**juices**) *digestive juices* **secretions**; serum.
3 (**juices**) *strain the cooking juices into a pan* **liquid**, liquor.
4 (*informal*) *he ran out of juice*. See PETROL.

juicy ▶ **adjective 1** *a juicy steak | a juicy peach* **succulent**, tender, moist; ripe, luscious, lush, sappy; *archaic* mellow.
OPPOSITE dry.
2 (*informal*) *juicy gossip* **very interesting**, fascinating, intriguing, sensational, lurid, thrilling, exciting, colourful, entertaining; **scandalous**, racy, risqué, spicy, piquant, provocative, suggestive; *informal* hot, shock-horror.
OPPOSITE dull.
3 (*informal*) *a juicy severance package* **large**, substantial, sizeable, generous; lucrative, profitable, remunerative; *informal* fat, tidy, whopping (great), thumping (great); *Brit. informal* whacking (great).
OPPOSITE small.

July ▶ **noun**
WORD LINKS
birthstone **ruby**

jumble ▶ **noun 1** *the books were in a chaotic jumble | a jumble of ideas and impressions* **untidy heap**, confused heap, clutter, muddle, mess, confusion, welter, disarray, disarrangement, tangle, litter; hodgepodge, hotchpotch, mishmash, miscellany, motley collection, mixture, mixed bag, medley, farrago; *Brit. informal* dog's dinner, dog's breakfast; *rare* gallimaufry, mingle-mangle, congeries, macédoine.
2 (*Brit.*) *bags of jumble* **junk**, bric-a-brac, bits and pieces; *Brit.* lumber; *rare* rummage.
▶ **verb** *the photographs are all jumbled up in an envelope* **mix up**, muddle up, disarrange, disorganize, disorder, confuse, put in disarray, throw into chaos, make a shambles of; shuffle.

jumbo ▶ **adjective** (*informal*) *a jumbo packet of crisps* See HUGE.

jump ▶ **verb 1** *the cat jumped off his lap | Flora began to jump about all over the kitchen* **leap**, spring, bound, hop, bounce; skip, bob, caper, dance, prance, gambol, frolic, frisk, cavort.
2 *the youth jumped the fence and ran across the yard* **vault (over)**, leap over, clear, sail over, hop over, go over, leapfrog; pole-vault, hurdle.
3 *pre-tax profits jumped from £51,000 to £1.03 million* **rise**, go up, leap up, shoot up, soar, surge; climb, increase, mount, escalate, spiral; *informal* skyrocket.
OPPOSITES fall, plummet.
4 *an owl hooted nearby, making her jump* **start**, jerk, jolt, flinch, recoil, twitch, wince; shudder, shake, quiver; *informal* jump out of one's skin.
5 *Polly jumped at the chance to go* **accept eagerly**, leap at, welcome with open arms, seize on, snap up, grab, snatch, pounce on, go for enthusiastically, show enthusiasm for.
6 (*informal*) *he jumped at least seven red lights* **ignore**, disregard, fail to stop at, drive through, overshoot; *informal* run.
□ **jump the gun** (*informal*) **act prematurely**, act too soon, be overhasty, be precipitate; *informal* be previous, be ahead of oneself.
□ **jump to it** (*informal*) **hurry up**, get a move on, be quick; *informal* get cracking, get moving, get on with it, shake a leg, look lively, look sharp, get/pull one's finger out, get weaving, rattle one's dags; *Brit. informal* get your skates on, stir one's stumps; *N. Amer. informal* get a wiggle on; *Austral./NZ informal* get a wriggle on; *S. African informal* put foot; *dated* make haste.
▶ **noun 1** *in making the short jump across the gully, he lost his balance* **leap**, spring, vault, bound, hop; bounce, skip.
2 *the horse cleared the last jump with ease* **obstacle**, barrier; fence, hurdle, rail, hedge, gate.
3 *a fifty-one per cent jump in annual profits* **rise**, leap, increase, upturn, upsurge, upswing, spiralling, lift, escalation, elevation, boost, advance, augmentation; *informal* hike.
OPPOSITES fall, drop.
4 *I woke up with a jump* **start**, jerk, sudden movement, involuntary movement, convulsive movement, spasm, twitch, wince; shudder, quiver, shake.

jumper ▶ **noun**. *See centre pages for list of* **Pullovers**

jumpy ▶ **adjective 1** (*informal*) *he was tired and jumpy* **nervous**, on edge, edgy, tense, anxious, ill at ease, unrelaxed, in a state of nerves, in a state of agitation, fretful, uneasy, restless, fidgety, worked up, keyed up, overwrought, wrought up, strung out, on tenterhooks, on pins and needles, with one's stomach in knots, worried, apprehensive, strained; shaky, shaking, trembling, quivering; *Brit.* nervy; *informal* with butterflies in one's stomach, a bundle of nerves, jittery, like a cat on a hot tin roof, twitchy, in a state, in a stew, uptight, wired, het up, all of a dither, all of a doodah, all of a lather, in a tizz/tizzy, stressed out, white-knuckled; *Brit. informal* strung up, windy, like a cat on hot bricks; *N. Amer. informal* spooky, squirrelly, antsy; *Austral./NZ informal* toey; *dated* overstrung.
OPPOSITES calm, relaxed.
2 *jumpy black-and-white footage* **jerky**, jolting; lurching, bumpy, jarring; fitful, convulsive; *rare* jouncing.

junction ▶ **noun 1** *the junction between the roof and the adjoining walls* **join**, joint, intersection, link, bond, weld, seam, coupling, connection, union, juncture; brace, bracket, hinge; *Anatomy* commissure, suture, synapse.
2 *the junction of the two rivers* **confluence**, convergence, meeting, meeting point, conflux, juncture, watersmeet; *Indian* sangam.
3 *turn right at the next junction* **crossroads**, crossing, intersection, interchange, T-junction, box junction, gyratory; level crossing; turn, turn-off, exit; *Brit.* roundabout; *N. Amer.* turnout, cloverleaf.

juncture ▶ **noun 1** *at this juncture, I am unable to give any further information | a critical juncture in her career* **point**, point in time, time, moment, moment in time, stage; period, phase.
2 *the juncture of the pipes*. See JUNCTION sense 1.
3 *the juncture of the rivers*. See JUNCTION sense 2.

June ▶ **noun**
WORD LINKS
birthstone **pearl**

jungle ▶ **noun 1** *the Amazon jungle* **tropical forest**, (tropical) rainforest; wilderness, wilds, the bush.
2 *the jungle of third world bureaucracy* **complexity**, confusion, complication, mess, chaos; **labyrinth**, maze, tangle, snarl, web.
□ **the law of the jungle the survival of the fittest**, each/every man for himself, dog-eat-dog.

junior ▶ **adjective 1** *the junior members of the family* **younger**, youngest.
OPPOSITES senior, older.
2 *a junior minister | part of my function is to supervise those junior to me* **low-ranking**, lower-ranking, subordinate, sub-, lesser, lower, minor, secondary, inferior; beneath, under.
OPPOSITES higher-ranking, senior.
3 *John White Junior* **the Younger**; *Brit.* minor; *N. Amer.* II.
OPPOSITE Senior.

junk (*informal*) ▶ **noun** *an attic full of all kinds of junk* **useless things**, **discarded things**, rubbish, clutter, stuff, odds and ends, bits and pieces, bric-a-brac, oddments, flotsam and jetsam, white elephants; garbage, refuse, litter, scrap, waste, debris, detritus, dross; leavings, leftovers, remnants, cast-offs, rejects; *Brit.* lumber; *N. Amer.* trash; *Austral./NZ* mullock; *informal* dreck; *Brit. informal* gubbins, odds and sods; *vulgar slang* crap, shit; *archaic* rummage.
▶ **verb** *sort out what can be sold off and junk the rest* **throw away/out**, discard, get rid of, dispose of, scrap, toss out, jettison, dispense with; *informal* chuck (away/out), dump, ditch, bin, get shut of; *Brit. informal* bung away/out, get shot of.

junket ▶ **noun** (*informal*) *a media junket organized to stir up interest in the film* **celebration**, party, jamboree, feast, festivity, revelry; spree, excursion, outing, trip, jaunt; *informal* do, bash, shindy, shindig, shebang; *Brit. informal* beanfeast, jolly, thrash, bunfight, beano; *Austral. informal* jollo, shivoo;

J

informal, dated ding-dong.

junta ▶ noun *the military junta took power in a coup last February* **faction**, group, cabal, clique, party, set, ring, gang, league, confederacy; *historical* junto; *rare* camarilla.

jurisdiction ▶ noun **1** *an area under French jurisdiction* **authority**, control, power, dominion, rule, administration, command, sway, leadership, sovereignty, ascendancy, hegemony, mastery; say, influence.
2 *the extradition of criminals from foreign jurisdictions* **territory**, region, province, district, area, zone; domain, realm, orbit, sphere; *historical* soke, leet.

just ▶ adjective **1** *a just and democratic society | Max was a just man* **fair**, fair-minded, equitable, even-handed, impartial, unbiased, objective, neutral, disinterested, unprejudiced, open-minded, non-partisan, non-discriminatory; honourable, upright, upstanding, decent, honest, righteous, ethical, moral, virtuous, principled, full of integrity, good, right-minded, straight, reasonable, scrupulous, trustworthy, incorruptible, truthful, sincere; *informal* square.
OPPOSITES unjust, unfair.
2 *a just reward | his just deserts* **deserved**, well deserved, well earned, merited, earned; rightful, due, proper, fitting, appropriate, apt, suitable, befitting; *formal* condign; *archaic* meet.
OPPOSITE undeserved.
3 *just criticism* **valid**, sound, well founded, well grounded, justified, justifiable, warranted, warrantable, defensible, defendable, legitimate, reasonable, logical; *rare* vindicable.
OPPOSITES unfair, wrongful.
▶ adverb **1** *I just saw him* **a moment ago**, a second ago, a short time ago, very recently, not long ago, lately, only now.
2 *that's just what I need | she's just right for him* **exactly**, precisely, absolutely, completely, totally, entirely, perfectly, utterly, wholly, thoroughly, altogether, in every way, in every respect, in all respects, quite; *informal* down to the ground, to a T, bang on, dead; *N. Amer. informal* on the money.
3 *we just made it* **by a narrow margin**, narrowly, only just, by inches, by a hair's breadth, by the narrowest of margins; barely, scarcely, hardly; *informal* by the skin of one's teeth, by a whisker.
4 *she's just a child | it's just you and me now* **only**, merely, simply, but, nothing but, no more than; at best, at most; alone, to the exclusion of everyone/everything else, and no one else, and nothing else; *N. English* nobbut; *S. African informal* sommer.
5 *the colour's just fantastic* **really**, absolutely, completely, entirely, totally, altogether, positively, quite, one hundred per cent; indeed, truly.
□ **just about** (*informal*) *that's just about all the money I've got left* **nearly**, almost, practically, all but, virtually, as good as, more or less, close to, nigh on, to all intents and purposes, not far off; not quite; *informal* pretty much; *literary* well-nigh.

> **CHOOSE THE RIGHT WORD**
>
> **just, fair, equitable**
> *See* FAIR.

justice ▶ noun **1** *ideas of social justice | I appealed to his sense of justice* **fairness**, justness, fair play, fair-mindedness, equity, equitableness, even-handedness, egalitarianism, impartiality, impartialness, lack of bias, objectivity, neutrality, disinterestedness, lack of prejudice, open-mindedness, non-partisanship; honour, uprightness, decency, integrity, probity, honesty, righteousness, ethics, morals, morality, virtue, principle, right-mindedness, propriety, scrupulousness, trustworthiness, incorruptibility.
OPPOSITE injustice.
2 *the justice of his case* **validity**, justification, soundness, well-foundedness, legitimacy, legitimateness, reasonableness.
3 *an attempt to pervert the course of justice* **judicial proceedings**, administration of the law.
4 *an order made by the justices* **judge**, magistrate, His/Her/Your Honour; Law Lord, Lord Justice; (*in England & Wales*) recorder; (*in Scotland*) sheriff; (*in the Isle of Man*) deemster; (*in the Channel Islands*) jurat; *N. Amer.* jurist, surrogate; *Spanish* alcalde; *informal* beak, m'lud; *historical* reeve; *Scottish historical* sheriff-depute, bailie.

WORD LINKS

relating to a system of justice	**judicial**
fear of justice	**dikephobia**

justifiable ▶ adjective *justifiable criticism* **valid**, legitimate, warranted, well founded, justified, just, sound, reasonable, sensible; **defensible**, arguable, tenable, able to hold water, defendable, supportable, sustainable, warrantable, vindicable, acceptable, plausible; lawful, legal; explainable, understandable, forgivable, venial.
OPPOSITES unjustifiable, indefensible.

justification ▶ noun *the justification for government action* **grounds**, reason, just cause, basis, rationale, premise, rationalization, vindication, warrant, foundation, explanation, excuse; defence, argument, apologia, apology, case.

justify ▶ verb **1** *marketing directors were pressed to justify the expenditure* **give grounds for**, give reasons for, give a justification for, show just cause for, explain, give an explanation for, account for, show/prove to be reasonable, provide a rationale for, rationalize; defend, answer for, vindicate, substantiate, uphold, sustain; establish, legitimize, legitimatize.
2 *the situation was grave enough to justify further investigation* **warrant**, be good reason for, be a justification for; bear out, confirm, validate.

justly ▶ adverb **1** *a man who is justly proud of his achievement* **justifiably**, with reason, with good reason, legitimately, rightly, rightfully, properly, deservedly, by rights.
OPPOSITE unjustifiably.
2 *they deserve to be treated justly* **fairly**, with fairness, equitably, even-handedly, impartially, without bias, objectively, without prejudice, without fear or favour; by the book, in accordance with the rules; *informal* fairly and squarely.
OPPOSITE unjustly.

jut ▶ verb *a rock jutted out from the side of the bank* **stick out**, project, protrude, poke out, bulge out, overhang, beetle (over), obtrude; extend; *rare* be imminent, protuberate, impend.

juvenile ▶ adjective **1** *juvenile offenders* **young**, teenage, teenaged, adolescent, junior, under age, pubescent, prepubescent.
OPPOSITE adult.
2 *his juvenile behaviour* **childish**, immature, puerile, infantile, babyish; jejune, inexperienced, callow, green, unsophisticated, naive, foolish, silly, stupid, asinine; *N. Amer.* sophomoric; *informal* wet behind the ears.
OPPOSITE mature.
▶ noun *cases of assault in which the victims are juveniles* **young person**, youngster, child, teenager, adolescent, minor, junior; boy, girl, schoolboy, schoolgirl; *informal* kid.
OPPOSITE adult.

juxtapose ▶ verb *her work juxtaposes images from serious and popular art* **place/set side by side**, place/set close to one another, mix; compare, contrast, place/set against one another; *Linguistics* collocate, colligate.

juxtaposition ▶ noun *the juxtaposition of considerable wealth and severe deprivation* **comparison**, contrast; **proximity**, nearness, closeness; *Linguistics* collocation, colligation; *rare* contiguity.

Accents

name	example in use	accent	example in use
acute	é	grave	è
breve	ŭ	háček	ř
cedilla	ç	macron	ā
circumflex	î	tilde	ñ
diaeresis/umlaut	ö		

Acids
Types of Acid

See also **Amino Acids**

amino acid
carboxylic acid
dibasic acid
fatty acid
Lewis acid
mineral acid
monobasic acid
nucleic acid
organic acid
tribasic acid

Actors
Types of Actor

See also **Roles in the Theatre**

actor-director
actor-manager
actress
body double
character actor
comedian
comedienne
comic actor
double
extra
farceur
film actor
film star
guisor
ham actor
hambone
ingénue
juvenile
leading lady
leading man
leading woman
matinee idol
mummer
mute
principal
showgirl
stage actor
stage performer
stage player
stager
star
starlet
stunt double
stuntman
stuntwoman
super
supernumerary
synthespian
tragedian
tragedienne
trouper
understudy
walk-on

Administrative Districts

See **Districts**

Ages

See **Geological Ages**

Agricultural Workers

bondager
boundary rider
bracero
broncobuster
broomie
buckaroo
bullocky
bullwhacker
cattleman
charro
contadino
cottar
cottier
cotton-picker
cowboy
cowgirl
cowherd
cowman
cowpoke
cowpuncher
dairymaid
dairyman
farmhand
field hand
gaucho
goatherd
grape-picker
grieve
harvester
haymaker
herdboy
hind
Hodge
hopper
hop-picker
jackaroo
jillaroo
kanaka
kisan
knockabout
land girl
llanero
milker
milkmaid
musterer
outrider
oxherd
peasant
peon
pigman
ploughman
potato-picker
ranchero
reaper
ringer
rouseabout
serf
shedhand
sheepman
shepherd
shepherdess
station hand
stockman
swineherd
thresher
trail boss
vaquero
vendangeur
vine dresser
vintager
wrangler

Agriculture

See **Farming**

Aircraft

aerodyne
aerostat
airliner
airship
amphibian
autogiro
balloon
biplane
blimp
bomber
chopper
convertiplane
delta-wing
dirigible
dive bomber
drone
fighter
fighter-bomber
floatplane
flying boat
flying wing
freighter
glider
ground-attack aircraft
gunship
gyrocopter
gyroplane
hang-glider
helicopter
hot-air balloon
hydroplane
interceptor
interdictor
jet
jetliner
jet plane
jumbo jet
jump jet
landplane
microlight
minelayer
monocoque
monoplane
multiplane
night fighter
ornithopter
paraglider
paramotor
prop jet
sailplane
seaplane
ski-plane
spaceplane
spotter
stealth bomber
strike fighter
swept-wing
swing-wing
taildragger
tanker
tank killer
taxiplane
towplane
trainer
trijet
triplane
troop carrier
tug
turbofan
turbojet
turboprop
warbird
warplane
water bomber
whirlybird
widebody
Zeppelin

Aircraft Parts

See also **Engines**

aerofoil
aileron
air brake
airfoil
airframe
air intake
airscrew
airspeed indicator
altimeter
artificial horizon
astrodome
astrohatch
balance tab
belly
black box
bomb bay
bombsight
bubble canopy
bulkhead
cabin
canard
canopy
cockpit
cockpit voice recorder
collective pitch control
control column
cowl
cowling
cyclic pitch control
delta wing
droop-snoot
drop tank
ejector seat
elevator
elevon
emergency chute
empennage
engine
escape hatch
fairing
fin
firing button
flap
flexwing
flight control
flight deck
flight recorder
float
former
fuel tank
fuselage
glareshield
gondola
hatch
head-up display (HUD)
heat shield
hold
joystick
landing gear
landing lights
leading edge
longeron
mainplane
nacelle
navaid
nose
nose cone
pod
pontoon
porthole
prop
propeller
pylon
radome
rate-of-climb indicator
rib
rotary wing
rotor
rotor blade
rudder
rudder bar
skid
skin
spar
spinner
spoiler
sponson
stabilator
stabilizer
strake
stringer
swept wing
swing-wing
tab
tail
tail boom
tail fin
tailplane
tail rotor
tail skid
throttle
trailing edge
tricycle undercarriage
trim tab
undercarriage
undercart
ventral fin
vertical stabilizer
viewport
wing
winglet
wing tip
yoke

Alcohol

See **Drinks** **Beers** **Cocktails** **Sherries** **Whiskies** **Wines**

Algae

arame
badderlocks
bladderwrack
blanket weed
blue-green algae
brown algae
bull kelp
carrageen/carragheen (moss)
Ceylon moss
chlamydomonas
chlorella
coenocyte
coralline alga/seaweed
desmid
diatom
dulse
fucoid
fucus
green algae
gulfweed
kelp
knotted wrack
kombu
laver
nori

- nullipore
- oarweed
- pepper dulse
- pond scum
- red algae
- sargassum
- sea lettuce
- seaweed
- spirogyra
- sugar kelp
- tangle
- varec
- wrack

Alloys

- aluminium brass
- aluminium bronze
- babbitt metal
- bell metal
- bidri
- billon
- brass
- Britannia metal
- bronze
- constantan
- cupro-nickel
- Dutch metal
- electrum
- eureka
- German silver
- gunmetal
- kamacite
- magnox
- manganese bronze
- misch metal
- mosaic gold
- nickel brass
- nitinol
- ormolu
- permalloy
- pewter
- phosphor bronze
- pinchbeck
- platinoid
- red gold
- shakudo
- silver solder
- similor
- solder
- speculum metal
- spiegeleisen
- stainless steel
- steel
- terne
- tin
- tombac
- type metal
- white gold
- white metal
- zircaloy

Alphabets

See **Letters (Greek and Hebrew)**

Amino Acids

- alanine
- arginine
- asparagine
- aspartic acid
- cysteine
- dopa
- gamma-aminobutyric acid
- glutamic acid
- glutamine
- glycine
- histidine
- homocysteine
- isoleucine
- leucine
- lysine
- methionine
- ornithine
- phenylalanine
- proline
- sarcosine
- serine
- taurine
- threonine
- tryptophan
- tyrosine
- valine

Ammunition

See **Bombs and Mines** **Bullets and Shot** **Explosives** **Projectiles**

Amphibians

- alpine salamander
- amphiuma
- bullfrog
- caecilian/coecilian
- cane toad
- cave salamander
- clawed frog
- crested newt
- eft
- fire-bellied toad
- fire salamander
- flying frog
- frog
- giant salamander
- goliath frog
- hairy frog
- hellbender
- horned toad
- hyla
- leopard frog
- lungless salamander
- marsh frog
- midwife toad
- mole salamander
- mud puppy
- natterjack toad
- newt
- olm
- palmate newt
- peeper
- platanna
- poison-arrow frog
- salamander
- siren
- smooth newt
- spadefoot toad
- Suriname toad
- tiger salamander
- toad
- toadlet
- tree frog
- triton
- waterdog
- Xenopus

Anchors

- bower
- Bruce anchor (*trademark*)
- Danforth anchor
- double-fluked anchor
- drag anchor
- drift anchor
- floating anchor
- grapnel
- grapple
- kedge
- killick
- mushroom anchor
- projectile anchor
- sea anchor
- sheet anchor
- stocked anchor
- stockless anchor
- stream anchor

Angels

The Ninefold Hierarchy of Angels

- seraphim
- cherubim
- thrones
- dominations
- principalities
- powers
- virtues
- archangels
- angels

Animals

Male and Female Terms

See also **Amphibians** **Bats** **Bears** **Birds** **Cats** **Cattle** **Deer and Antelopes** **Dogs** **Fish** **Fowl** **Foxes** **Goats** **Horses and Ponies** **Insects** **Marsupials** **Molluscs** **Monkeys and Apes** **Pigs** **Lemurs and Other Prosimians** **Rabbits and Hares** **Reptiles** **Rodents** **Seals, Sea Lions, and Sea Cows** **Sharks** **Sheep** **Snakes** **Spiders and Other Arachnids** **Squirrels** **Weasels and Similar Animals** **Whales and Dolphins** **Worms** **Young Animals** *and* **Chinese Calendar**

animal	male	female
antelope	buck	doe
badger	boar	sow
bear	boar	sow
bobcat	tom	lioness
buffalo	bull	cow
camel	bull	cow
caribou	stag	doe
cat	tom	queen
cattle	bull	cow
chicken	cock	hen
cougar	tom	lioness
coyote	dog	bitch
deer	stag	doe
dog	dog	bitch
donkey	jackass	jennyass
duck	drake	duck
elephant	bull	cow
ferret	jack	jill
fish	cock	hen
fox	fox	vixen
giraffe	bull	cow
goat	billygoat	nannygoat
goose	gander	goose
hare	buck	doe
hartebeest	bull	cow
horse	stallion	mare
impala	ram	ewe
jackrabbit	buck	doe
kangaroo	buck	doe
leopard	leopard	leopardess
lion	lion	lioness
lobster	cock	hen
moose	bull	cow
peafowl	peacock	peahen
pheasant	cock	hen
pig	boar	sow
rhinoceros	bull	cow
seal	bull	cow
sheep	ram	ewe
swan	cob	pen
tiger	tiger	tigress
weasel	boar	cow
whale	bull	cow
wolf	dog	bitch
zebra	stallion	mare

Antelopes

See **Deer**

Apes

See **Monkeys and Apes**

Arachnids

See **Spiders and Other Arachnids**

Architectural Styles

- Art Deco
- Art Nouveau
- baroque
- Bauhaus
- Beaux Arts
- brutalist
- Byzantine
- Cape Dutch
- Carolingian
- Churrigueresque
- cinquecento
- classical
- collegiate Gothic
- colonial
- composite
- Corinthian
- Decorated
- Doric
- Early English
- Edwardian
- Elizabethan
- Empire
- Federation
- flamboyant

functional
Georgian
Gothic
Gothic Revival
Graeco-Roman
Grecian
Greek Revival
international
Ionic
Islamic
Jacobean
mannerist
Manueline
medieval
modernist
Moorish
Moresque
Mozarabic
Mudejar
neoclassical
neo-Gothic
Norman
Palladian
Perpendicular
postmodernist
quattrocento
Queen Anne
rayonnant
Regency
Renaissance
rococo
Roman
Romanesque
Saxon
Spanish-Colonial
Spanish Mission
transitional
Tudor
Tudorbethan
Tuscan
Usonian
vernacular
Victorian Gothic

Architectural Terms

See also **Church Parts Towers Vaulting Windows**

abacus
amphiprostyle
ancon
annulet
architrave
archivolt
astragal
astylar
atlas
baguette
bas-relief
beading
boss
buttress
campanile
capital
capstone
cartouche
caryatid
cavetto
clerestory
colonnade
column
conch
coping
corbel
cornice
cove
coving
cresting
crocket
crow steps
cruck
cupola
cusp
cusping
dado
decastyle
dentil
dipteral
dog-tooth
dome
dosseret
dripstone
echinus
embrasure
encrustation
entablature
entablement
entasis
entresol
epistyle
extrados
facade
fascia
fenestration
fillet
finial
flaunching
flute
flying buttress
frieze
frontispiece
gable
gambrel
gargoyle
half-timbered
hammer beam
haunch
hexastyle
hipped roof
hood mould
hypaethral
hypostyle
hypotrachelium
inglenook
intercolumniation
intrados
jerkin head
keystone
king post
lacunar
lancet arch
lantern
linenfold
lintel
loggia
long-and-short work
lunette
machicolation
mansard
manteltree
mezzanine
moulding
mullion
obelisk
octastyle
octofoil
ogee
ogive
onion dome
pediment
pent roof
peripteral
peristyle
perron
pilaster
pillar
plinth
polychromy
porch
portico
prostyle
queen post
quoin
respond
reticulated
rope-moulding
rustication
saddleback
scotia
scroll
scuncheon
sedilia
severy
socle
soffit
spandrel
springer
squinch
stringboard
string course
stucco
stylobate
talon
tambour
telamon
tetrastyle
tie beam
tracery
transom
trefoil
truss
tympanum
vault
vaulting
vignette
volute
voussoir

Areas, Administrative

See **Districts**

Armour
Parts of a Suit of Armour

basinet
beaver
bracer
brassard
breastplate
brigandine
burgonet
camail
casque
chain mail
chausses
coif
corselet
coutere
cuirass
cuisse
gauntlet
gorget
greave
habergeon
hauberk
helmet
jambeau
lance rest
mail
morion
nasal
neck guard
nosepiece
pectoral
plastron
poleyn
pouldron
rerebrace
sabaton
sallet
solleret
tasses
vambrace
ventail
visor

Arms

See **Bombs and Mines Guns Projectiles Weapons**

Army

See **Ranks Soldiers**

Art Schools and Movements

abstract expressionism
Aesthetic Movement
Art Deco
art nouveau
Arte Povera
Arts and Crafts Movement
Ashcan School
avant-garde
Barbizon School
baroque
Blaue Reiter
Bloomsbury Group
Camden School
chinoiserie
classicism
constructivism
cubism
Dada
Danube School
De Stijl
Euston Road
expressionism
fauvism
Florentine school
futurism
Graecism
Grand Manner
Group of Seven
High Renaissance
Impressionism
International Gothic
intimisme
Jugendstil
magic realism
Mannerism
metaphysical painting
minimalism
modernism
Nabi Group
naive art
naturalism
Nazarenes
neoclassicism
neoexpressionism
neo-Impressionism
neoplasticism
neo-realism
neoromanticism
Neue Sachlichkeit
Norwich School
op art
Orphism
performance art
photorealism
plein-air painting
pop art
post-Impressionism
postmodernism
Precisionism
Pre-Raphaelitism
primitive art
Purism
Rayonism
realism
Renaissance art
rococo
romanticism
seicento
Sezession
Sienese school
socialist realism
social realism
Sturm und Drang
suprematism
surrealism
symbolism
Synchromism
tenebrism
transavant-garde
ukiyo-e
Umbrian school
Venetian school
verism
Vorticism

Art Techniques and Media

See also **Painting Techniques and Methods**

acrylic painting
action painting
airbrushing
aquatint
batik
brass rubbing
calligraphy
cartooning
ceramics
cloisonné
collage
collotype
colour print
colour wash
Conté
divisionism
drawing
dry-point
enamelling
encaustic
engineering drawing
engraving
etching
finger-painting
fresco
frottage
illumination
intaglio
lino cut
lithography
lost wax
marbling
marquetry
metalwork
mezzotint
montage
mosaic
painting
pastel
photography
photogravure
photomontage
photoprint
screen printing
sculpture
scumbling
sgraffito
silk-screen printing
sketching
soft-ground etching
stained glass
tachism
tapestry
technical drawing
trompe l'œil
wood carving
woodcut
wood engraving
zincography

Arteries

See **Veins and Arteries**

Artistes

See **Entertainers**

Athletics Events

biathlon
caber, tossing the
cross-country running
decathlon
discus
fell-running
field event
half-marathon
hammer
heptathlon
high jump
hurdles
javelin
long jump
marathon
middle-distance race
pentathlon
pole vault
relay race
shot-put
sprint
steeplechase
tetrathlon
track event
triathlon
triple jump
tug of war
walking

Atmosphere

Layers of the Earth's Atmosphere

See also **Cloud Formations** **Weather Phenomena**

D-layer
E-layer
exosphere
F-layer
ionosphere
mesosphere
ozone layer
ozonosphere
stratosphere
thermosphere
troposphere

Backbone

See **Vertebrae**

Ball Games

American football
Association Football
Australian Rules football
bagatelle
baseball
basketball
beach volleyball
billiards
bocce
boule/boules
bowling
bowls
broomball
camogie
Canadian football
carom billiards
clock golf
cricket
croquet
crown-green bowls
Eton fives
five-a-side football
fivepin bowling
fives
flat-green bowls
football
French cricket
Gaelic football
goalball
golf
handball
hockey
hurling
jai alai
korfball
lacrosse
lawn tennis
mini rugby
netball
ninepins
paddleball
paddle tennis
pall-mall
pelota
pétanque
polo
pool
rackets
raquetball
real tennis
roller hockey
rounders
Rugby fives
rugby league
rugby union
shinty
short tennis
skittles
snooker
soccer
softball
speedball
squash
stoolball
table tennis
tennis
tenpin bowling
touch football
touch rugby
volleyball
water polo

Ballet Steps and Positions

arabesque
assemblé
attitude
balancé
ballon
balloné
ballotté
battement
battement frappé
battement tendu
batterie
bourrée
brisé
brisé volé
cabriole
chaîné
changement (de pieds)
chassé
dégagé
développé
écarté
échappé
elevation
enchaînement
entrechat
fifth position
first position
fondu
fouetté
fourth position
frappé
glissade
glissé
grand battement
grand batterie
grand jeté
jeté
pas de basque
pas de bourrée
pas de chat
pas de cheval
pas de deux
petit battement
petit batterie
petit jeté
piqué
pirouette
plié
pointe work
port de bras
relevé
retiré
rond de jambe à terre
rond de jambe en l'air
sauté
second position
sissonne
soubresaut
temps
temps levé
third position
tour en l'air

Bats

barbastelle
blossom bat
bulldog bat
butterfly bat
Daubenton's bat
disk-wing bat
epauletted fruit bat
false vampire
fisherman bat
flower bat
flying fox
free-tailed bat
fruit bat
funnel-eared bat
ghost bat
golden bat
hairless bat
hammer-headed bat
hog-nosed bat
hollow-faced bat
horseshoe bat
leaf-nosed bat
Leisler's bat
long-eared bat
mastiff bat
mouse-eared bat
mouse-tailed bat
moustached bat
myotis
naked bat
Natterer's bat
noctule
painted bat
particoloured bat
pipistrelle
roussette
sac-winged bat
serotine bat
sheath-tailed bat
short-tailed bat
slit-faced bat
smoky bat
spotted bat
sucker-footed bat
tomb-bat
Trident bat
tube-nosed bat
vampire bat
whiskered bat
white bat

Beans, Pulses, and Peas

adzuki/aduki bean
asparagus pea
black bean
black-eyed bean
borlotti bean
broad bean
butter bean
cannellini bean
chickpea
cowpea
fava bean
field bean
field pea
flageolet
French bean
garbanzo bean
garden pea
haricot bean
horsebean
jack bean
kidney bean
lentil
lima bean
mangetout
marrowfat pea
mesquite bean
mung bean
navy bean
partridge pea
pea bean
petit pois
pinto bean
puy lentil
red bean
runner bean
scarlet runner
snap bean
snow pea
soybean
string bean
sugar bean
sugar pea
sugar snap pea
tick bean
waxpod

Beards and Moustaches

burnsides
five o'clock shadow
goatee beard
handlebar moustache
Hitler moustache
imperial
Kaiser (Bill/Wilhelm) moustache
kesh
mustachios
Old Bill moustache
pencil moustache
soup-strainer
spade beard
toothbrush moustache
Vandyke beard
walrus moustache
Zapata moustache

Bears

black bear
brown bear
cinnamon bear
giant panda
grizzly bear
honey bear
Kodiak bear
musquaw
polar bear
red panda
sloth bear
spectacled bear
sun bear

Beds

bassinet
bedstead
berth
bunk bed
camp bed
carrycot
chaise longue
charpoy
cot
couchette
cradle
crib
daybed
divan
feather bed
four-poster
futon
half-tester
hammock
king-size bed
pallet
palliasse
pipe berth/cot
rollaway
shakedown
sleeper
sleigh bed
sofa bed
takht
truckle bed
trundle bed
waterbed
Z-bed

Beers

ale
barley wine
bitter
bock
brown ale
cask beer
chicha
craft beer
draught beer
gueuze
heavy
ice beer
India pale ale (IPA)
keg beer
lager
lambic
light ale
lite
microbrew
mild
milk stout
pale ale
Pils
Pilsner/Pilsener
porter
Rauchbier
real ale
shandy
small beer
spruce beer
stout
wheat beer

Berries

See **Fruit**

Beverages

See **Drinks**

Bible

Books of the Bible

Old Testament

Genesis
Exodus
Leviticus
Numbers
Deuteronomy
Joshua
Judges
Ruth
Samuel I
Samuel II
Kings I
Kings II
Chronicles I
Chronicles II
Ezra
Nehemiah
Esther
Job
Psalms
Proverbs
Ecclesiastes
Song of Solomon
Isaiah
Jeremiah
Lamentations
Ezekiel
Daniel
Hosea
Joel
Amos
Obadiah
Jonah
Micah
Nahum
Habakkuk
Zephaniah
Haggai
Zechariah
Malachi

Apocrypha

Esdras I
Esdras II
Tobit
Judith
Additions to the Book of Esther
Wisdom of Solomon
Ecclesiasticus
Baruch
Letter of Jeremiah
Song of the Three Holy Children
Susanna
Bel and the Dragon
Prayer of Manasses
Maccabees I
Maccabees II

New Testament

Matthew
Mark
Luke
John
Acts
Romans
Corinthians I
Corinthians II
Galatians
Ephesians
Philippians
Colossians
Thessalonians I
Thessalonians II
Timothy I
Timothy II
Titus
Philemon
Hebrews
James
Peter I
Peter II
John I
John II
John III
Jude
Revelation

Bicycle Components

bottom bracket
brake
brake block
brake caliper
carrier
cassette
chain
chain gear
chainring
crank
derailleur
drop handlebars
dynamo
fork
frame
frameset
freehub
freewheel
gear
gearwheel
groupset
handlebars
headset
hub
inner tube
mudguard
pannier
pedal
reflector
saddle
spokes
sprocket
stabilizers
toe clip
twist-grip
tyre
wheel

Birds

See also **Fowl**

accentor
accipiter
adjutant bird
albatross
amazon
American eagle
ani
Anna's hummingbird
antbird
ant-thrush
apostlebird
aracari
Arctic tern
argus pheasant
asity
auk
auklet
avadavat
avocet
babbler
bald eagle
Baltimore oriole
bananaquit
barbet
barnacle goose
barn owl
barwing
bateleur
baya weaver
baza
bean goose
bearded tit
becard
bee-eater
bellbird
Bewick's swan
bird of paradise
bishop bird
bittern
blackbird
blackcap
black grouse
black guillemot
black kite
blackpoll
black swan
black vulture
bleeding heart dove
bluebill
bluebird
blue bonnet
blue crane
blue jay
bluethroat
blue tit
boatbill
bobolink
bobwhite (quail)
bokmakierie
boobook
booby
boubou (shrike)
bowerbird
brainfever bird
brambling
brent goose
bristlebird
broadbill
brolga
bronzewing
brown owl
brubru
brush turkey
budgerigar
buffalo weaver
bufflehead
bulbul
bullfinch
bunting
burrowing owl
bushchat
bush-hen
bushtit
bustard
butcher-bird
buteo
button-quail
buzzard
cacique
cahow
calandra
Canada goose
canary
canvasback
Cape Barren goose
Cape hen
capercaillie
Cape sparrow
caracara
cardinal
Carolina parakeet
carrion crow
cassowary
catbird
cattle egret
Cetti's warbler
chachalaca
chaffinch
chanting goshawk
chat
chickadee
chicken
chiffchaff
chimney swift
chipping sparrow
chough
chuck-will's-widow
chukar
cicadabird
cirl bunting
cisticola
citril
clapper rail
coal tit
cochoa
cockatiel
cockatoo
cock-of-the-rock
collared dove
condor
conure
coot
corella
cormorant
corn bunting
corncrake
coscoroba swan
cotinga
coucal
courser
cowbird
crab plover
crake
crane
crested tit
crocodile bird
crombec
crossbill
crow
crowned crane
crowned pigeon
crow-pheasant
cuckoo
cuckoo-roller
cuckoo shrike
curassow
curlew
currawong
cut-throat weaver
dabbling duck
dabchick
darter
Dartford warbler
demoiselle crane
diamond bird
dickcissel
dipper
diver
diving duck
diving petrel
dollarbird
dotterel
dove
dowitcher
drongo
duck
dunlin
dunnock
eagle
eagle owl
egret
Egyptian goose
Egyptian plover
Egyptian vulture
eider duck
Eleonora's falcon
elf owl
emperor penguin
emu
emu wren
erne
Eskimo curlew
fairy bluebird
fairy penguin
fairy tern
fairy wren
falcon
fantail
fernbird
ferruginous duck
fieldfare
figbird
fig parrot
finch
finfoot
fireback
firecrest
firefinch
fish eagle
flamingo
flammulated owl
flatbill
flicker
florican
flowerpecker
flufftail
flycatcher
fody
forktail
francolin
friarbird
frigate bird
frogmouth
fruitcrow
fruit dove
fruit pigeon
fulmar
gadwall
galah
gallinule
gannet
gardener bowerbird
garden warbler
garganey
gentoo penguin
giant petrel
gibberbird
glaucous gull
glossy starling
gnatcatcher
godwit
goldcrest
goldenback
golden eagle
goldeneye
golden oriole
golden pheasant
golden plover
goldfinch
gonolek
goosander
goose
goshawk
grackle
grassbird
grasshopper warbler
grass parrot
grassquit
great crested grebe
great tit
grebe
greenbul
greenfinch
greenlet
greenshank
green woodpecker
grey jay
greylag goose
grey parrot
griffon vulture
grosbeak
ground dove
grouse
guan
guillemot
guineafowl
gull
gyrfalcon
hadada
hamerkop/ hammerkop
hardhead
harlequin duck
harpy eagle
harrier
Harris' hawk
Hawaiian goose
hawfinch
hawk
hawk eagle
hawk owl
hazel grouse
hedge sparrow
helmet bird
hen
hen harrier
hermit thrush
heron
herring gull
hillstar
hoatzin
hobby
honeybird
honey buzzard
honeycreeper
honeyeater
honeyguide
honeysucker
hooded crow
hoopoe
hoot owl
hornbill
horned owl
hornero
houbara
house finch
house martin
house sparrow
huia
hummingbird
ibis
ibisbill
iiwi
imperial pigeon
inca
indigobird
iora
jabiru
jacamar

jacana
jackdaw
jack snipe
Jacky Winter
jacobin
jaeger
Java sparrow
jay
junco
junglefowl
kagu
kaka
kakapo
kea
Kentish plover
kereru
kestrel
killdeer
kingbird
king eider
kingfisher
kinglet
king penguin
kiskadee
kite
kittiwake
kiwi
knot
koel
kokako
kookaburra
korhaan
kori
lammergeier
landrail
lanner
lapwing
lark
laughing jackass
laughing thrush
leafbird
leaflove
leaf warbler
leiothrix
lily-trotter
limpkin
linnet
little auk
little grebe
little owl
loggerhead shrike
logrunner
longbill
longclaw
longspur
long-tailed duck
long-tailed tit
loon
lorikeet
lotusbird
lovebird
lyrebird
macaroni penguin
macaw
magpie
malcoha
malimbe
mallard
malleefowl
manakin
mandarin duck
manucode
marabou stork
marsh harrier
martial eagle
martin
meadowlark
meadow pipit
megapode
merganser
merlin
mesia
minivet
mistle thrush
mistletoebird
mockingbird
monal
monarch flycatcher
Montagu's harrier
moorcock
moorfowl
moorhen
Mother Carey's chicken
motmot
mountain gem
mourning dove
mousebird
mud-nester
munia
murre
murrelet
Muscovy duck
musk duck
mute swan
mutton bird
mynah bird
needletail
nene
nighthawk
night heron
nightingale
nightjar
noddy
notornis
nunbird
nutcracker
nuthatch
oilbird
openbill
orangequit
oriole
oropendola
ortolan
osprey
ostrich
ou
ouzel
ovenbird
owl
owlet
oxpecker
oystercatcher
parakeet
pardalote
parrot
parrotbill
partridge
pauraque
peacock
peafowl
peewee
peewit
pelican
penguin
pepper-shrike
peregrine falcon
petrel
phalarope
pheasant
phoebe
piapiac
piculet
pied wagtail
piet-my-vrou
pigeon
pilot bird
pintail
pipit
plains-wanderer
plover
pochard
poorwill
potoo
prairie chicken
pratincole
prion
prothonotary warbler
ptarmigan
puffback
puffbird
puffin
quail
quelea
quetzal
racket-tail
rail
raven
razorbill
red-backed shrike
redhead
red kite
redpoll
redshank
redstart
redwing
reed-bird
reed bunting
reed warbler
rhea
rhinoceros bird
rifle bird
rifleman
ringdove
ringed plover
ringneck
ring ouzel
roadrunner
robin
robin-chat
rock dove
rockfowl
rockhopper
rock thrush
roller
rook
roseate spoonbill
roseate tern
rosefinch
rosella
rosy finch
rubythroat
ruddy duck
ruddy shelduck
ruff
Sabine's gull
sabrewing
sacred ibis
saddleback
sage grouse
sakabula
saker
sanderling
sandgrouse
sand martin
sandpiper
sand plover
sandwich tern
sapsucker
saw-whet owl
scaup
scimitarbill
scissortail
scops owl
scoter
screamer
screech owl
scrub turkey
sea eagle
seagull
secretary bird
sedge warbler
seriema
serin
shag
shama
shearwater
sheathbill
shelduck
shikra
shoebill
shorelark
shortwing
shoveler
shrike
sibia
sicklebill
silverbill
silvereye
siskin
sittella
skimmer
skua
skylark
smew
snakebird
snipe
snowbird
snow bunting
snowcap
snow goose
snowy owl
song thrush
sooty tern
sora
sparrow
sparrowhawk
spinetail
spinifexbird
spoonbill
spotted flycatcher
sprew
spurfowl
starling
steamer duck
stifftail
stilt
stint
stitchbird
stock dove
stonechat
stone curlew
stork
storm petrel
sugarbird
sunbird
sunbittern
sungrebe
surfbird
swallow
swamphen
swan
swift
swiftlet
swordbill
tailorbird
takahe
tanager
tawny owl
tchagra
teal
tern
thickhead
thornbill
thorntail
thrasher
thrush
tinamou
tinkerbird
tit
titihoya
titlark
titmouse
toco
tody
toucan
toucanet
towhee
tragopan
treecreeper
tree pie
tree pipit
tree sparrow
triller
trogon
tropicbird
troupial
trumpeter
tufted duck
tui
turaco
turkey
turkey vulture
turnstone
turtle dove
twinspot
twite
tyrannulet
tyrant flycatcher
umbrellabird
vanga
veery
verdin
vireo
vulture
wagtail
waldrapp
wallcreeper
warbler
water rail
waterthrush
wattlebird
wattle-eye
waxbill
waxwing
weaver bird
wedgebill
weebill
weka
wheatear
whimbrel
whinchat
whipbird
whippoorwill
whistler
whistling swan
white eye
whitefront
whitehead
whitethroat
whooper
whooping crane
whydah
widowbird
wigeon
willet
willow warbler
woodchat
woodcock
wood duck
woodgrouse
wood ibis
woodlark
woodpecker
wood pigeon
woodstar
woodswallow
wood warbler
wren
wrentit
wrybill
wryneck
yellowbill
yellowhammer
yellowhead
yellowlegs
yellowthroat
zebra finch

extinct birds

dodo
elephant bird
great auk
huia
ichthyornis
moa
passenger pigeon
solitaire

Birds
Game Birds

black grouse
bobwhite (quail)
capercaillie
duck
francolin
golden pheasant
goose
grouse
guineafowl
hazel grouse
moorfowl
partridge
peafowl
pheasant
ptarmigan
quail
red grouse
ringneck pheasant
ruffed grouse
sage grouse
spurfowl
turkey
waterfowl
willow grouse
woodcock
woodgrouse

Birthstones

month	birthstone	month	birthstone
January	garnet	July	ruby
February	amethyst	August	sardonyx
March	bloodstone	September	sapphire
April	diamond	October	opal
May	emerald	November	topaz
June	pearl	December	turquoise

Biscuits

Bath Oliver (*trademark*)
bourbon
brandy snap
cracknel
cream cracker
crispbread
custard cream
digestive
Florentine
fortune cookie
garibaldi
ginger nut
ginger snap
graham cracker
langue de chat
macaroon
marie biscuit
matzo
Nice biscuit
oatcake
petit beurre
pretzel
ratafia
rusk
saltine
ship's biscuit
shortbread/shortcake
Shrewsbury biscuit
soda cracker
sweetmeal biscuit
tollhouse cookie
tuile
water biscuit
wholemeal biscuit

Blood Cells

acidophil
basophil
eosinophil
erythrocyte *or* red blood cell
granulocyte
killer cell
leucocyte *or* white blood cell
lymphocyte
macrophage
megaloblast
microcyte
microphage
monocyte
neutrophil
plasma cell
platelet
reticulocyte

Board Games

backgammon
checkers
chess
Chinese chequers
Chinese chess
Cluedo (*trademark*)
draughts
fox and geese
go
halma
kriegspiel
ludo
mah-jong
mancala
Monopoly (*trademark*)
nine men's morris
pachisi
peggotty
Pictionary (*trademark*)
Risk (*trademark*)
Scrabble (*trademark*)
shogi
snakes and ladders
solitaire
tric-trac
Trivial Pursuit (*trademark*)
wari
wei ch'i

Boats

See **Ships and Boats** **Sailing Ships and Boats**

Body

Parts of the Body

See **Blood Cells** **Bones** **Brain** **Digestive System** **Ear** **Eye** **Glands** **Heart** **Nervous System** **Tooth** **Veins and Arteries** **Vertebrae**

Bombs and Mines

See also **Explosives** **Projectiles**

A-bomb
acoustic mine
atom/atomic bomb
Bangalore torpedo
blockbuster
car bomb
claymore
cluster bomb
daisy-cutter
depth charge
dirty bomb
doodlebug
firebomb
flying bomb
fragmentation bomb/grenade
fuel-air bomb
fusion bomb
gas shell
gelignite
grenade
hand grenade
H-bomb
hydrogen bomb
incendiary bomb
JDAM (joint direct attack munition)
landmine
laser-guided bomb
letter bomb
limpet mine
magnetic mine
mail bomb
Mills bomb
Molotov cocktail
napalm bomb
neutron bomb
nuclear bomb/device
parcel bomb
payload
petard
petrol bomb
pipe bomb
plastic bomb
RPG (rocket-propelled grenade)
satchel charge
shaped charge
shell
smart bomb
smoke bomb
sonic mine
stick grenade
thermobaric bomb
thermonuclear bomb/device
time bomb
torpedo
vacuum bomb
warhead

Bones

Human Bones

See also **Vertebrae**

astragalus
calcaneum (*or* heel bone)
capitate
carpal
carpus
cheekbone
clavicle (*or* collarbone)
concha
costa
cranium
cuboid
cuneiform bones
ethmoid
femur (*or* thigh bone)
fibula
floating rib
frontal bone
hallux
hamate
humerus
hyoid
ilium
incus (*or* anvil)
innominate bone
ischium
jawbone
lacrimal
lunate bone
malleus (*or* hammer)
mandible
maxilla
metacarpal
metatarsal
navicular bone
occipital bone
palatine bone
parietal bone
patella (*or* kneecap)
pelvis
phalanx
pisiform bone
pubis
rachis
radius
rib
sacrum
scaphoid
scapula (*or* shoulder blade)
sesamoid bone
skull
sphenoid
spinal column
spine (*or* backbone)
stapes (*or* stirrup)
sternum (*or* breastbone)
talus (*or* ankle bone)
tarsal
tarsus
temporal bone
tibia (*or* shin bone)
trapezium
trapezoid
triquetral
ulna
vertebra
vertebral column
vomer
zygomatic bone

Books

See **Stories and Novels**

Boots

See **Footwear**

Bottles

See **Wine Bottles**

Bracelets

See **Jewellery**

Brain

Parts and Regions of the Human Brain

amygdala
appestat
association area
basal ganglia
brainstem
Broca's area
caudate nucleus
central sulcus
cerebellum
cerebral aqueduct
cerebral cortex
cerebral hemisphere
cerebrum
choroid plexus
cingulum
claustrum
commissure
cornu
corpus callosum
corpus striatum
crus cerebri
culmen
Deiters' nucleus
diencephalon
ependyma
flocculus
forebrain
fornix
frontal lobe
globus pallidus
grey matter
gyrus
hindbrain
hippocampus
hypercolumn
hypothalamus
infundibulum
insula
lateral ventricle
limbic system
lobe
medulla oblongata
meninges
mesencephalon
midbrain
motor cortex
neencephalon
occipital lobe
optic chiasma
optic cup
palaeencephalon
parietal lobe
pineal body
pituitary gland
pons Varolii
prosencephalon
putamen
rhombencephalon
satiety centre
speech centre
splenium
sulcus
Sylvian fissure
telencephalon
temporal lobe
thalamus
third ventricle
vasomotor centre
ventricle
vermis
white matter

Brass Instruments

althorn
baritone
bombardon
bugle
clarion
cornet
cornopean
euphonium
flugelhorn
French horn
handhorn
helicon
horn
lur
mellophone
ophicleide
post horn
sackbut
sarrusophone
saxhorn
saxotromba
slide trombone
sousaphone
trombone
trumpet
tuba
Wagner tuba
zinke

Bread and Bread Rolls

azyme
bagel
baguette
bannock
bap
bara brith
barmbrack
barm cake
barracouta
bialy
billy-bread
bloomer
boxty
bridge roll
brioche
bun
challah
chapatti
ciabatta
cob
cornbread
cottage loaf
crumpet
damper
farl
farmhouse loaf
flatbread
focaccia
French stick
fruit loaf
granary bread (*trademark*)
hoagie
injera
johnnycake
kaiser
kulcha
malt loaf
manchet
matzo
milk loaf
muffin
nan
pan dulce
panettone
panino
pan loaf
paratha
petit pain
pikelet
piki
pitta
platzel
pone
poppadom
pumpernickel
puri
quartern loaf
roti
rye bread
soda bread
sourdough
split tin
spoon bread
stollen
stotty
wholemeal

Bridges

air bridge
aqueduct
Bailey bridge
bascule bridge
bridge of boats
cantilever bridge
catenary bridge
catwalk
chain bridge
clapper bridge
drawbridge
floating bridge
flyover
footbridge
gangway
girder bridge
humpback bridge
linkspan
overbridge
overpass
pontoon
skew bridge
skyway
suspension bridge
swing bridge
toll bridge
transporter bridge
underbridge
viaduct

Building

See **Architectural Styles** **Architectural Terms** **Bridges** **Towers**

Bullets and Shot

ball
baton round
birdshot
buckshot
canister
cannonball
case-shot
chain shot
dumdum bullet
dust shot
grapeshot
lead shot
pellet
plastic bullet
round-nose
round shot
rubber bullet
shell
slug
soft-nosed bullet
tracer
wadcutter

Bushes

See **Flowering Plants and Shrubs** **Trees and Shrubs**

Butterflies

See also **Moths**

Adonis blue
alpine
angle wings
apollo
arctic
argus
azure
birdwing
blue
brimstone
brown
buckeye
cabbage white
Camberwell beauty
chalkhill blue
checkerspot
cleopatra
clouded yellow
comma
copper
diana
dog face
dryad
Duke of Burgundy
dusky wing
elfin
emperor
festoon
fritillary
gatekeeper
grayling
hairstreak
heath
julia
large blue
map butterfly
marbled white
mazarine blue
meadow brown
metalmark
milkweed
monarch
morpho
mourning cloak
nettle-tree butterfly
nymph
orange tip
owl butterfly
painted lady
peacock butterfly
pearly eye
plain tiger
purple emperor
red admiral
ringlet
satyr
Scotch argus
silver-studded blue
skipper
snout butterfly
speckled wood
sulphur
swallowtail
tortoiseshell
two-tailed pasha
wall brown
white admiral
wood nymph
zebra

Butterfly Types

danaid
lycaenid
nymphalid
papilionid
pierid
satyrid
vanessid

Cabinets

See **Cupboards and Cabinets**

Cactuses

cholla
Christmas cactus
epiphyllum
hedgehog cactus
night-blooming cereus
nopal
opuntia
organ pipe cactus
peyote
pitahaya
prickly pear
saguaro
strawberry pear
tuna
Turk's cap

Cakes, Puddings, and Desserts

almond cake
angel cake
angel food cake
apfelstrudel
apple charlotte
apple pie
baba
baked Alaska
Bakewell tart
baklava
banana split
Banbury cake
banoffi pie
Battenberg
bavarois
beignet
Berliner
black bun
Black Forest gateau
blancmange
bombe
bouchée
brack
brandy snap
bread-and-butter pudding
bread pudding
Brown Betty
brownie
bun
butterfly cake
cabinet pudding
cannoli
cassata
charlotte
charlotte russe
cheesecake
clafoutis
cobbler
college pudding
compote
cream puff
crème brûlée
crème caramel
crêpe
crêpe Suzette
croquembouche
cruller
crumble
crumpet
cupcake
custard pie
Danish pastry
death by chocolate
devil's food cake
Dobos Torte
doughnut/donut
drop scone
dumpling
Dundee cake
Eccles cake
eclair
egg custard
Eskimo pie (*US trademark*)
Eve's pudding
fairy cake
fancy
firni
flapjack
floating island
flummery
fool
frangipane
frozen yogurt
fruit cocktail
fruit salad
frumenty
funnel cake
gateau
gelato
Genoa cake
gingerbread
granita
halwa
hasty pudding
hoecake
hokey-pokey
hot cross bun
ice cream
ice milk
jello
jelly
johnny cake
junket
khir
kissel
Knickerbocker Glory
koeksister
kulfi
lady's finger
lamington
lardy cake
layer cake
macédoine
Madeira cake
madeleine
maid of honour
marble cake
marquise
meringue
milk pudding
millefeuille
mince pie
Mississippi mud pie
moon cake
mousse
mousseline
napoleon
palacsinta
pancake
pandowdy
panettone
panforte
parfait
parkin
pashka
pavlova
peach Melba
petit fours
plum cake
plum duff
plum pudding
popover
pound cake
profiteroles
puftaloon
queen cake
queen of puddings
ras malai
rice pudding
rock cake
roly-poly
Sachertorte
sago pudding
Sally Lunn
sandwich (cake)
savarin
scone
seed cake
semolina
shoo-fly pie
shortcake
simnel cake
singing hinny
snowball
sorbet
soufflé
sponge (cake)
sponge pudding
spotted dick
spumoni

steamed pudding
stollen
streusel
strudel
suet pudding
suji
summer pudding
sundae
Swiss roll
syllabub
tapioca pudding
tart
tarte Tatin
tartlet
tartufo
tipsy cake
tiramisu
torte
treacle tart
trifle
turnover
tutti-frutti
upside-down cake
Victoria sponge
waffle
water ice
whip
yogurt
yule log
zabaglione
zuppa inglese

Cameras

APS camera
box camera
camcorder
cine camera
compact camera
digicam (*trademark*)
digital camera
disc camera
Gatso
instant camera
miniature camera
minicam
movie camera
pinhole camera
Polaroid (*trademark*) camera
reflex camera
rostrum camera
single-lens reflex (SLR)
single-use camera
speed camera
Steadicam (*trademark*)
stereo camera
television camera
twin-lens reflex
video camera
webcam

Canonical Hours

matins
lauds
terce
sext
none
vespers
compline

Caps

See **Hats**

Car Components

accelerator pedal
air conditioning
alternator
anti-lock braking system (ABS)
anti-roll bar
automatic choke
automatic transmission
axle
battery
bench seat
big end
blinker
bodywork
bonnet (*Brit.*)
boot (*Brit.*)
brake
brake disc
brake drum
brake light
brake pad
brake pedal
brake shoe
brush bar
bucket seat
bull bar
bumper
cam belt
camshaft
carburettor
catalytic converter
central locking system
chassis
clutch
clutch pedal
connecting rod
con rod (*Brit.*)
courtesy light
cowling
crank
crankcase
cruise control
crumple zone
cubbyhole (*S. African*)
cylinder
cylinder block
cylinder head
damper
dashboard/dash
differential gear
differential lock
dimmer (*N. Amer.*)
dip switch (*Brit.*)
disc brake
distributor
doorbin
door mirror
drivetrain
driving wheel
drum brake
engine
exhaust pipe
fan
fan belt
fascia (*Brit.*)
fender (*N. Amer.*)
filler cap
final drive
floorpan
flywheel
fog lamp/fog light
footbrake
four-wheel drive
front-wheel drive
fuel gauge
fuel injection pump
fuel tank
gasket
gas tank (*N. Amer.*)
gate
gear
gearbox
gear change
gear lever/gearstick (*Brit.*)
gear shift (*N. Amer.*)
generator
glovebox
grille
handbrake
hatch
hazard warning lights
headlight/headlamp
heater
hood (*N. Amer.*)
hooter (*Brit.*)
horn
hubcap
hypoid gear
ignition
ignition key
immobilizer
indicator
instrument panel
kick-down (*Brit.*)
licence plate
lite (*N. Amer.*)
loadspace
manifold
milometer
monocoque
muffler (*N. Amer.*)
number plate
odometer
oil gauge
overdrive
overrider (*Brit.*)
parcel shelf
pedal
petrol tank
piston
pneumatic tyre
points
power brakes
power steering
propshaft/propeller shaft
pushrod
quarter-light (*Brit.*)
rack-and-pinion
radial tyre
radiator
radiator grille
radius rod
rear-view mirror
rear-wheel drive
reflector
registration plate (*Brit.*)
rocker
rocker panel
roll bar
roof light
rotor arm
running board
running lights
safety cage
seat
seat belt
shaft
shift/shifter (*N. Amer.*)
shock absorber
sidelight (*Brit.*)
sidescreen
silencer
sill
solenoid
spare tyre
spare wheel
spark plug
speedometer
spoiler
starter
starter motor
steering column
steering gear
steering rack
steering wheel
stick
stick shift (*N. Amer.*)
stop light
subframe
sump
sunroof
suspension
switchgear
tachometer
tag (*N. Amer.*)
tailgate
tail light/tail lamp
tailpipe
tappet
thermostat
tie rod
tow bar
track rod
trafficator (*Brit.*)
transaxle
transmission
trim
trunk (*N. Amer.*)
turbocharger
tyre
underframe
valance
valve
vanity mirror
viscous coupling
wheel
wheel nut
windscreen (*Brit.*)
windscreen washer (*Brit.*)
windscreen wiper (*Brit.*)
windshield (*N. Amer.*)
windshield washer (*N. Amer.*)
windshield wiper (*N. Amer.*)
wing
wing mirror
winker (*Brit.*)
wishbone

Cars

automatic
bubble car
cabriolet
compact
concept car
convertible
coupé
cruiser
dragster
drophead
estate
fastback
four-wheel drive
GTi
hardtop
hatchback
hot rod
kit car
limousine
low-rider
microcar
minicab
multi-purpose vehicle (MPV)
notchback
off-roader
people carrier
phaeton
racing car
ragtop
rally car
roadster
runabout
saloon
sedan
shooting brake
soft top
sports car
sportster
sport utility vehicle (SUV)
station wagon
stock car
stretch limo
supercar
supermini
targa
taxi
tourer
touring car

Card Games

See also **Poker Hands** **Suits of Cards**

all fours
auction bridge
baccarat
beggar-my-neighbour
bezique
blackjack
Black Maria
Boston
brag
bridge
canasta
Canfield
cheat
chemin de fer
cooncan
cribbage
donkey
duplicate bridge
écarté
euchre
fan-tan
faro
five hundred
gin rummy
happy families
hearts
high-low
hoy
klobbiyos
Klondike
lansquenet
loo
Michigan
monte
nap
napoleon
Newmarket
old maid
ombre
panguingue
patience
Pedro Sancho
Pelmanism
penny ante
pinochle
piquet
pitch
poker
pontoon
Pope Joan
primero
quinze
racing demon
red dog
rouge et noir
rubber bridge
rummy
Russian Bank
short whist
skat
skin
snap
solitaire
solo whist
strip Jack naked
strip poker
stud poker
thirty-one
three-card monte
trente et quarante
twenty-five
twenty-one
vingt-et-un
whist

Carpets and Rugs

Aubusson
Axminster
broadloom
Brussels
dhurrie
drugget
flokati
hearthrug
ingrain
kaross
Kidderminster
kilim
Kirman
numdah
Persian
prayer mat *or* rug
rag rug
runner
Savonnerie

scatter rug
shagpile
sheepskin
Soumak
tiger-skin
Turkish
Turkoman
twist
vase
velvet
Wilton
Yarkand

Carriages and Carts

See also **Trains and Rolling Stock**

barouche
brake
breaking cart
britzka
brougham
buckboard
buggy
cab
cabriolet
caleche
caravan
carriole
chaise
chariot
clarence
coach
coach-and-four
Conestoga wagon
coupé
covered wagon
curricle
dog cart
dray
droshky
fiacre
fly
four-in-hand
gharry
gig
hackney
handcart
hansom
haywain
jaunting car
jinker
landau
ox cart
phaeton
post-chaise
prairie schooner
rickshaw
stagecoach
stanhope
sulky
surrey
tarantass
tilbury
trailer
trap
trishaw
tumbril
unicorn
Victoria
vis-à-vis
wagon
wagonette

Cash

See **Coins Currency Units**

Casseroles

See **Stews**

Cats

breeds

Abyssinian
angora
Balinese
Birman
Burmese
Burmilla
chinchilla
colourpoint
Cornish Rex
Devon Rex
ginger cat
Japanese Bobtail
Maine Coon
Maltese
Manx
marmalade cat
Persian
Ragdoll
Rex
Russian Blue
sealpoint
Siamese
smoke Persian
Somali
Sphynx
tabbypoint
Tiffanie
Tonkinese
Turkish Van

wild cats

bobcat
caracal
catamount
cheetah
clouded leopard
cougar
eyra
fishing cat
Geoffroy's cat
golden cat
jaguar
jaguarundi
jungle cat
leopard
liger
lion
lynx
manul
margay
mountain lion
ocelot
ounce
Pallas's cat
panther
puma
ringtail
sabre-toothed tiger (*extinct*)
sand cat
serval
snow leopard
Temminck's golden cat
tiger
tigon
wildcat

Catapults

See **Projectile Weapons**

Cattle

breeds

Aberdeen Angus
Afrikander
Andalusian
Ayrshire
Bangus
Barrosã
beefalo
Beef Shorthorn
Belgian Blue
Belted Galloway
Belted Welsh
Blonde d'Aquitaine
Brahmin
British White
Brown Swiss
Charolais
Chianina
Danish Red
Devon
Dexter
Droughtmaster
Durham
Friesian
Galician Blond
Galloway
German Yellow
Guernsey
Hereford
Highland
Holstein
Illawarra shorthorn
Irish Moiled
Jamaica Hope
Jersey
Kerry
Kyloe
Limousin
Lincoln Red
longhorn
Luing
Maine Anjou
Meuse-Rhine-Ijssel
Miranda
Mongolian
Murray Grey
N'Dama
Pinzgauer
Red-and-White Friesian
Red Poll
Romagnola
Sahiwal
Santa Gertrudis
Shetland
shorthorn
Simmental
South Devon
Sussex
Swedish Red-and-White
Texas longhorn
Welsh Black
West Highland
White Galloway
White Park

wild cattle

anoa
aurochs
banteng
bison
Brahmin
buffalo
dzo/dzho/zho
gaur
gayal
kouprey
musk ox
ox
park cattle
sapi-utan
seladang
takin
tamarau
tsine
water buffalo
wisent
yak
zebu

Cells

See **Blood Cells**

Ceramics

See **Pottery and Porcelain**

Cereal Crops

barley
blue corn
cockspur grass
corn
durra/dhurra
durum (wheat)
einkorn
emmer
flint corn
mabela
maize
millet
milo
oats
pearl millet
rice
rye
sorghum
spelt
sudan grass
sweet corn
teff
triticale
wheat

Cetaceans

See **Whales and Dolphins**

Chairs and Stools

armchair
BarcaLounger (*US trademark*)
barrel chair
bar stool
bath chair
bench
bentwood chair
box seat
bucket seat
buffet
button-back chair
canapé
carver
chaise longue
chesterfield
club chair
comb-back
couch
davenport
deckchair
dining chair
divan
donkey stool
duchesse
easy chair
faldstool
footstool
high chair
ladder-back
lawn chair
Lloyd Loom chair
lounger
love seat
milking stool
Morris chair
music stool
nursing chair
panel-back chair
pew
pouffe
recliner
rocking chair *or* rocker
settee
settle
side chair
slingback chair
sofa
sofa bed
spindle-back chair
stall
stool
studio couch
sugan
swivel chair
tabouret
tailor's chair
throne
tripod
tub chair
tuffet
wheelback chair
wheelchair
Windsor chair
wing chair

Cheeses

Ami du Chambertin
Beaufort
Bel Paese (*trademark*)
blue Brie
blue cheese
blue vinny
Boursin (*trademark*)
Brie
Caerphilly
Cambozola (*trademark*)
Camembert
Cantal
Chaumes
Cheddar
Cheshire
chèvre
Colby
Cotswold
cottage cheese
cream cheese
crowdie *or* crowdy
curd cheese
Danish blue
Derby
Dolcelatte (*trademark*)
Double Gloucester
Dunlop
Edam
Emmental
feta *or* fetta
fontina
fromage blanc
fromage frais
Gervais
Gjetost
Gloucester
Gorgonzola
Gouda
grana
green cheese
Gruyère
halloumi
Ilchester
Jarlsberg (*trademark*)
Lancashire
Leerdammer
Leicester
Liederkranz
Limburger
Liptauer
Livarot
mascarpone
Monterey Jack
mozzarella
Neufchâtel
Oka
paneer *or* panir
Parmesan
Parmigiano Reggiano
pecorino
Pont l'Évêque
Port Salut
pot cheese
provolone
quark
reblochon
Red Leicester
ricotta
Romano
Roquefort (*trademark*)
sage Derby
Saint Agur
Sainte Honoré
Saint Nectaire
Samsoe
Stilton
stracchino
taleggio
Tillamook
Tilsit
tomme (de Savoie)
tvorog
Vacherin
vignotte
Wensleydale
Windsor Red

Chemicals

See also **Acids Compounds Elements Poisonous Substances and Gases Sugars Vitamins**

common name	chemical name
acetic acid	ethanoic acid
acetone	propanone
acetylene	ethyne
alcohol	ethanol
alum	potash alum
alumina	aluminium oxide
aqua fortis (*archaic*)	nitric acid
baking soda	sodium bicarbonate
baryta	barium hydroxide
bicarbonate of soda	sodium bicarbonate
blue vitriol (*archaic*)	copper sulphate
boracic acid	boric acid
borax	sodium borate
Borazon (*trademark*)	boron nitride
calomel	mercurous chloride
carbolic acid	phenol
carbonic acid gas (*archaic*)	carbon dioxide
carbon tetrachloride	tetrachloromethane
carborundum	silicon carbide
caustic potash	potassium hydroxide
caustic soda	sodium hydroxide
Chile saltpetre	sodium nitrate
chloroform	trichloroethane
chrome yellow	lead chromate
cinnabar	mercuric sulphide
common salt	sodium chloride
copperas	ferrous sulphate *or* iron(II) sulphate
copper vitriol (*archaic*)	copper sulphate
corrosive sublimate (*dated*)	mercuric chloride
corundum	aluminium oxide
cream of tartar	potassium hydrogen tartrate
cyanide	sodium (*or* potassium) cyanide
dry ice	(solid) carbon dioxide
Epsom salts	magnesium sulphate
ether	diethyl ether
ethyl alcohol	ethanol
firedamp	methane
flowers of zinc	zinc oxide
folic acid	pteroylglutamic acid
formaldehyde	methanal
formic acid	methanoic acid
Glauber's salt	sodium sulphate
glycerine	glycerol
green vitriol (*archaic*)	ferrous sulphate *or* iron(II) sulphate
gypsum	calcium sulphate
jeweller's rouge	ferric oxide
laughing gas	dinitrogen monoxide
litharge	lead monoxide
lithia	lithium oxide
lunar caustic (*archaic*)	silver nitrate
magnesia	magnesium oxide
marsh gas	methane
massicot	lead monoxide
muriatic acid (*archaic*)	hydrochloric acid
nitric oxide	nitrogen monoxide
oil of vitriol (*archaic*)	sulphuric acid
peroxide	hydrogen peroxide
phosphorous acid	phosphoric acid
plaster of Paris	calcium sulphate
potash	potassium carbonate *or* potassium hydroxide
prussic acid (*dated*)	hydrocyanic acid
quicklime	calcium oxide
red lead	lead oxide
sal ammoniac (*dated*)	ammonium chloride
salt	sodium chloride
saltpetre	potassium nitrate
silica	silicon dioxide
slaked lime	calcium hydroxide
soda	sodium carbonate
spirits of salt (*archaic*)	hydrochloric acid *or* hydrogen chloride
strontia	strontium oxide
sugar	sucrose
sugar of lead (*dated*)	lead acetate
sulphuretted hydrogen (*archaic*)	hydrogen sulphide
tartar emetic	potassium antimony tartrate
thoria	thorium dioxide
titanium white	titanium dioxide
verdigris	copper carbonate
vitriol (*archaic*)	sulphuric acid
washing soda	sodium carbonate
white arsenic	arsenic trioxide
white vitriol (*archaic*)	zinc sulphate
xylene	dimethylbenzene
zaffre	cobalt oxide
zirconia	zirconium dioxide

Chickens

See **Fowl**

China

See **Pottery and Porcelain**

Chinese Calendar
Animals of the Chinese Calendar

rat
buffalo
tiger
rabbit/hare
dragon
snake
horse
goat/sheep
monkey
rooster
dog
pig

Christian Denominations, Past and Present

Abode of Love
Adventists
African & Afro-Caribbean Churches
African Orthodox Church

Agapemone
Albigenses
American Baptist Churches
American Orthodox Church
Amish
Amish Mennonites
Anabaptists
Anglican Communion
Anglo-Catholics
Apostolic Brethren
Armenian Church
Assemblies of God
Assumptionists
Assyrian Church
Baptists
Bogomils
Bohemian Brethren
Brethren (Dunkers)
Brethren in Christ
Buchanites
Calvinistic Methodists
Cameronians
Camisards
Catholic Apostolic Church
Catholics
Celtic Church
Chaldaean Christians
Cherubim & Seraphim Churches
Christadelphians
Christian Brethren
Christian Science
Church Army
Churches of Christ
Churches of God
Church in Wales
Church of Christ Scientist
Church of England
Church of Ireland
Church of Jesus Christ of Latter-day Saints
Church of North India
Church of Scotland
Church of South India
Church of the Nazarene
Church of the New Jerusalem
Congregationalists
Conservative Baptists
Coptic Orthodox Church
Countess of Huntingdon's Connexion
Covenanters
Cumberland Presbyterian Church
Disciples of Christ
Doppers
Doukhobors
Dunkers
Dutch Reformed Church
Eastern Orthodox Church
Episcopal Church of Scotland
Episcopal Church of USA
Ethiopian Orthodox Church
Evangelical Churches
Family of Love
Fifth Monarchy Men
Free Church
Free Church of Scotland
Free Presbyterian Church of Scotland
Free Will Baptists
Gideons
Glassites
Greek Orthodox Church
Huguenots
Hussites
Hutterites
Independent Methodists
Jehovah's Witnesses
Jesus People
Jumpers
Lollards
Lutherans
Malabar Christians
Maronites
Mennonites
Methodists
Millennial Church
Moravian Church
Muggletonians
Nazarenes
Nestorians
New Testament Assembly
Old Believers
Old Catholics
Oriental Orthodox Churches
Orthodox Church
Particular Baptists
Paulicians
Pentecostal Churches
Plain People, the
Plymouth Brethren
Presbyterians
Primitive Methodists
Protestants
Puritans
Quakers
Ranters
Reformed Churches
Religious Society of Friends
River Brethren
Roman Catholics
Rosicrucians
Russian Orthodox Church
Salvation Army
Sandemanians
Seventh-Day Adventists
Shakers
Society of Friends
Southern Baptist Church
Swedenborgians
Syrian Orthodox Church
Uniates
Unitarians
Unitarian Universalists
Unitas Fratrum
United Church of Christ
United Free Church
United Reformed Church
Waldenses
Wesleyans

Christian Doctrinal Movements and Heresies

Abelianism
Adoptionism
Ambrosianism
Antinomianism
Antipaedobaptism
Apollinarianism
Arianism
Arminianism
Augustinianism
Barclayism
Basilidianism
Biblicism
Brownism
Calvinism
Catharism
Charismatic Movement
Chiliasm
Cursillo
Docetism
Ebionitism
Ecumenical Movement
Evangelicalism
Fundamentalism
Gallicanism
Gnosticism
Hussitism
Iconoclasm
Jansenism
Latitudinarianism
Liberation Theology
Liturgical Movement
Lullism
Mandeism
Manichaeism
Millenarianism
Monarchianism
Monophysitism
Monothelitism
Montanism
Moral Majority
Moral Rearmament
Mormonism
Nestorianism
Nonconformism
Oxford Group
Oxford Movement
Paulicianism
Pelagianism
Pentecostalism
Pietism
Protestantism
Puritanism
Sabellianism
Tractarianism
Trinitarianism
Ultramontanism

Christian Religious Orders

Antonians
Augustinian Hermits
Austin Friars
Barnabites
Benedictines
Bernardines
Black Friars
Black Monks
Blue Nuns
Bonhommes
Brethren of the Common Life
Brigittines
Brothers Hospitallers
Camaldolites
Canons Regular
Capuchins
Carmelites
Carthusians
Christian Brothers
Cistercians
Cluniacs
Conceptionists
Conventuals
Culdees
Doctrinarians
Dominicans
Franciscans
Friars Minor
Friars Preachers
Gilbertines
Grey Friars
Grey Nuns
Hieronymites
Hospitallers
Ignorantines
Jacobins
Jesuits
Knights Templar
Little Brothers of Jesus
Marianists
Marists
Minims
Minorites
Norbertines
Oratorians
Passionists
Paulines
Piarists
Poor Clares
Poor Soldiers of the Temple
Premonstratensians
Salesians
Servites
Sisters of Charity
Sisters of the Love of God
Sisters of the Sacred Cross
Somascans
Studites
Sulpicians
Sylvestrines
Theatines
Trappists
Trinitarians
Ursulines
Visitandines
White Friars

Church
Parts of a Church

See also **Architectural Terms** **Places of Worship**

aisle
ambo
ambulatory
antechapel
apse
atrium
aumbry
baptistery/baptistry
belfry
buttress
chancel
chantry
chapel
chevet
choir
choir stall
ciborium
clerestory
confessional
crossing
crypt
dome
fenestella
flèche
flying buttress
font
galilee
gallery
Gospel side
high altar
iconostasis
Jesse window
Lady chapel
Lady altar
loft
naos
narthex
nave
organ loft
parclose
parvis/parvise
pew
piscina
predella
presbytery
prothesis
pulpit
retrochoir
rood loft
rood screen
sacrarium
sacristy
sanctuary
sedilia
spire
squint
stall
steeple
tabernacle
tambour
tower
transept
traverse
tribune
triforium
undercroft
vault
vestibule
vestry

Cinema

See **Film Types, Versions, and Genres**

Clergy

See **Priests**

Climatic Zones

arid
boreal
continental humid
desert
equatorial rainforest
highland
ice cap
Marine West Coast
Mediterranean
monsoon
polar
semi-arid
steppe
subarctic
subtropical humid
temperate rainy
trade-wind littoral
tropical savannah
tropical wet
tropical wet-dry
tundra

Cloaks

See **Coats, Cloaks, and Jackets**

Clocks and Watches

alarm clock
analogue watch/clock
astronomical clock
atomic clock
bracket clock
caesium clock
calendar clock
carriage clock
chronograph
chronometer
clepsydra
clock radio
cuckoo clock
digital watch/clock
egg-timer
fob watch
grandfather clock
grandmother clock
half-hunter watch
hourglass
hunter watch
impulse clock
journeyman clock
lever watch
long-case clock
pendulum clock
pocket watch
quartz-crystal clock
quartz watch/clock
repeater
sandglass
sidereal clock
stem-winder
stopwatch
sundial
tabernacle clock
time clock
travelling clock
turnip
water clock
wristwatch

Cloth

See **Fabrics and Fibres**

Cloud Formations

altocumulus
altostratus
anvil cloud
cirrocumulus
cirrostratus
cirrus
cloud street
cumulonimbus
cumulostratus
cumulus
funnel cloud
lenticular cloud
mackerel sky
mare's tails
nimbostratus
nimbus
noctilucent cloud
rain cloud
storm cloud
stratocirrus
stratocumulus
stratus
thundercloud
thunderhead
wrack

Clubs

See **Golf Clubs** **Weapons**

Coaches

See **Carriages and Carts** **Vehicles** **Trains and Rolling Stock**

Coats, Cloaks, and Jackets

achkan
Afghan coat
anorak
baju
balmacaan
Barbour (*trademark*)
bedjacket
biker jacket
blanket coat
blazer
blouson
body warmer
bolero
bomber jacket
British warm
Burberry (*trademark*)
burka
burnous/burnoose
bush jacket
cagoule/kagoul
cape
capote
Capuchin
car coat
chlamys
coatee
coat of mail
combat jacket
cope
covert coat
cowl
Crombie coat
cutaway
dinner jacket (DJ)
djellaba/jellaba
dolman
domino
donkey jacket
doublet
dreadnought
dress coat
duffel coat
dustcoat
duster (coat)
Eisenhower jacket
Eton jacket
flak jacket
fleece
flying jacket
frock coat
fur coat
gaberdine/gabardine
gi
gilet
greatcoat
hacking jacket
haik/haick
haori
happi (coat)
Harrington
hoody
hunting jacket
jean jacket
jerkin
jibba/djibba
jumper
kebaya
kirtle
leather jacket
letter jacket
loafer
loden
lumberjacket
mac
macfarlane
mackinaw
mackintosh/macintosh
mandarin jacket
manteau
mantle
mantlet
Mao jacket
matinee coat
maud
mess jacket
mink
monkey jacket
morning coat
Mother Hubbard
mozzetta
Nehru jacket
Norfolk jacket
nor'wester
oilskin
opera cloak
overcoat
pakamac
pallium
parka
pea jacket
pelerine
pelisse
peplum
pilot jacket
poncho
Puffa (jacket) (*Brit. trademark*)
raglan
raincoat
rainproof
redingote
reefer (jacket)
riding jacket
sack coat
safari jacket
sarape/serape
scapular
shawl
sheepskin
shell jacket
sherwani
shooting coat
shooting jacket
shrug
slicker
smoking jacket
spencer
sportcoat
sports coat/jacket
suba
surcoat
surtout
swagger coat
swing coat
tabard
tailcoat
tent coat
tippet
topcoat
trench coat
tunic
tux
tuxedo
ulster
undercoat
waistcoat
waterproof
waxed jacket
windbreaker (*US trademark*)
windcheater
workcoat
wrap

Cocktails and Mixed Drinks

alcoholic

Alaska
Astoria
bee's kiss
Bellini
black velvet
Bloody Friday
Bloody Mary
brandy Alexander
Bronx
Broughton punch
Buck's Fizz
bullshot
caipirinha
Caruso
Castro
champagne cocktail
cobbler
Collins fizz
Collins sour
Copenhagen
cosmopolitan
Cuba libre
Cuban Island
daiquiri
Dom Pedro
egg-flip
egg-nog
El Diablo
Gibson
gimlet
gin and it
gin sling
glögg
gloom raiser
Harvey Wallbanger
highball
horse's neck
James Bond
John Collins
Kir
Kir Royale
Long Island iced tea
mai tai
manhattan
margarita
Martini (*trademark*)
Mary Pickford
Metropolitan
mimosa
mint julep
mojito
monkey gland
moose milk
Moscow mule
negroni
New England iced tea
old-fashioned
orange blossom
pina colada
pink gin
pink lady
planter's punch
Presidente
Prince of Wales
punch
rattlesnake
red-eye
rickey
Rob Roy
rum and black
rusty nail
salty dog
sangria
Sazarac
screwdriver
sea breeze
September morn
Shirley Temple
sidecar
Singapore sling
snakebite
snowball
spritzer
stinger
swizzle
tequila slammer
tequila sunrise
Tom and Jerry
Tom Collins
whisky mac
whisky sour
White Lady
White Russian
yellow bird
yellow fever
zombie

non-alcoholic

mud
prairie oyster
St Clements
Virgin Mary

Coffee Drinks

café au lait
café noir
caffè latte
caffè macchiato
cappuccino
decaffeinated coffee
drip coffee
espresso
filter coffee
Gaelic coffee
Greek coffee
instant coffee
Irish coffee
latte
latte macchiato
mocha
mochaccino
percolated (*or* perked) coffee
Turkish coffee

Coins

See also **Currency Units**

angel
as
aureus
bawbee
bezant
chervonets
copper
crown
denarius
denier
dime
double eagle

double napoleon
doubloon
ducat
dupondius
eagle
farthing
florin
follis
groat
groschen
guinea
half-crown
halfpenny
half-sovereign
joey
krugerrand
liard
loonie
louis d'or
maravedi
Maundy money
minim
moidore
napoleon
nickel
noble
obol
picayune
pistole
quarter
scudo
sequin
sestertius
shilling
siliqua
sixpence
soldo
solidus
sou
sovereign
spade guinea
spur royal
stater
stiver
tanner
threepenny bit
tickey

Collective Names for Animals

Many of these are fanciful or humorous terms which probably never had any real currency but have been popularized in books such as Sports and Pastimes of England *(1801) by Joseph Strutt.*

shrewdness of **apes**
herd/pace of **asses**
troop of **baboons**
cete of **badgers**
sloth of **bears**
swarm/drift/hive/erst of **bees**
flock/flight/pod of **birds**
herd/gang/obstinacy of **buffalo**
bellowing of **bullfinches**
drove of **bullocks**
army of **caterpillars**
clowder/glaring of **cats**
herd/drove of **cattle**
brood/clutch/peep of **chickens**
chattering of **choughs**
rag/rake of **colts**
covert of **coots**
herd of **cranes**
bask of **crocodiles**
murder of **crows**
litter of **cubs**
herd of **curlew**
herd/mob of **deer**
pack/kennel of **dogs**
school of **dolphins**
trip of **dotterel**
flight/dole/piteousness of **doves**
paddling of **ducks** (on water)
safe of **ducks** (on land)
fling of **dunlins**
herd/parade of **elephants**
herd/gang of **elk**
busyness of **ferrets**
charm of **finches**
shoal/run of **fish**
swarm/cloud of **flies**
skulk of **foxes**
gaggle of **geese** (on land)
skein/team/wedge of **geese** (in flight)
herd of **giraffes**
cloud of **gnats**
flock/herd/trip of **goats**
band of **gorillas**
pack/covey of **grouse**
down/mute/husk of **hares**
cast of **hawks**
siege of **herons**
bloat of **hippopotami**
drove/string/stud/team of **horses**
pack/cry/kennel of **hounds**
flight/swarm of **insects**
fluther/smack of **jellyfish**
mob/troop of **kangaroos**
kindle/litter of **kittens**
desert of **lapwings**
bevy/exaltation of **larks**
leap/lepe of **leopards**
pride/sawt of **lions**
tiding of **magpies**
sord/suit of **mallard**
stud of **mares**
richesse of **martens**
labour of **moles**
troop of **monkeys**
span/barren of **mules**
watch of **nightingales**
parliament/stare of **owls**
yoke of **oxen**
pandemonium of **parrots**
covey of **partridges**
muster of **peacocks**
muster/parcel/rookery of **penguins**
bevy/head of **pheasants**
kit of **pigeons** (in flight)
litter/herd of **pigs**
congregation/stand/wing of **plovers**
rush/flight of **pochards**
pod/school/herd/turmoil of **porpoises**
covey of **ptarmigan**
litter of **pups**
bevy/drift of **quail**
bury of **rabbits**
string of **racehorses**
unkindness of **ravens**
crash of **rhinoceros**
bevy of **roe deer**
parliament/building/rookery of **rooks**
hill of **ruffs**
pod/herd/rookery of **seals**
flock/herd/trip/mob of **sheep**
dopping of **sheldrake**
wisp/walk of **snipe**
host of **sparrows**
murmuration of **starlings**
flight of **swallows**
game/herd of **swans** (on land)
wedge of **swans** (in flight)
drift/herd/sounder of **swine**
spring of **teal**
knot of **toads**
hover of **trout**
rafter of **turkeys**
bale/turn of **turtles**
bunch/knob of **waterfowl**
school/herd/pod/gam of **whales**
company/trip of **wigeon**
sounder of **wild boar**
dout/destruction of **wild cats**
team of **wild ducks** (in flight)
bunch/trip/plump/knob of **wildfowl**
pack/rout of **wolves**
fall of **woodcock**
descent of **woodpeckers**
herd of **wrens**
zeal of **zebras**

Colours

See also **Dyes Horse Colours Rainbow**

almond
almond green
amaranth
amber
amethyst
anthracite
apple green
apricot
aqua
aquamarine
ash blonde
aubergine
auburn
avocado
azure
baby blue
baby pink
bay
beige
biscuit
bisque
bistre
black
blaze
blonde
blood-red
blue
blush
bottle green
brindle/brindled
bronze
brown
bubblegum pink
buff
burgundy
burnt ochre
burnt sienna
burnt umber
buttermilk
butternut
cadmium yellow
café au lait
Cambridge blue
camel
canary yellow
candy-apple red
caramel
cardinal red
carmine
carnation
carnelian
carrot
celadon
cerise
cerulean
champagne
charcoal
chartreuse
cherry
chestnut
chocolate
cinnabar
cinnamon
citron
clair-de-lune
claret
cobalt blue
cocoa
coffee
Copenhagen blue
copper
coral
cornflower blue
cream
crimson
cyan
cyclamen
daffodil
damask
damson
dove
drab
duck-egg blue
dun
eau de Nil
ebony
ecru
eggshell
electric blue
emerald
fallow
fawn
flame
flesh
fuchsia
gamboge
gentian
ginger
gold
green
grenadine
grey
gunmetal
hazel
heather
heliotrope
henna
honey
ice blue
incarnadine
indigo
iris
iron grey
ivory
jade
jasmine
jet
khaki
kingfisher blue
lapis lazuli
lavender
leaf green
lemon
lilac
lily white
lime green
Lincoln green
liver
lovat green
magenta
magnolia
mahogany
maroon
mauve
mazarine blue
midnight blue
mocha
mouse
mulberry
mushroom
mustard
nankeen
navy blue
Nile blue
Nile green
nut-brown
nutmeg
oatmeal
ochre
off-white
old gold
old rose
olive
opal
orange
oxblood
Oxford blue
oyster pink
oyster white
palomino
pansy
paprika
parchment
peach
peach-bloom
peacock blue
pea green
pearl
periwinkle
perse
petrol blue
pewter
pine green
pink
pistachio
platinum
plum
poppy
powder blue
primrose
puce
purple
putty
raspberry
raven
red
robin's-egg blue
rose
royal blue
royal purple
ruby
russet
rust
sable
saffron
salmon
sand
sanguine
sapphire
saxe blue
scarlet
sea green
seal brown
sepia
shell pink
sienna
silver
sky blue
slate
snow-white
sorrel
spice
steel blue
steel grey
stone
straw
strawberry
strawberry blonde
tan
tangerine
tawny
teak
teal
tea rose
terracotta
Titian
topaz
tortoiseshell
Turkey red
turquoise
Tyrian purple
ultramarine
umber
Venetian red
verditer
vermilion
violet
viridian
walnut
Wedgwood blue
white
wine
yellow

Compost

See **Fertilizers**

Compounds
Types of Chemical Compound

See also **Acids** **Amino Acids** **Sugars**

acetate
acid
alcohol
aldehyde
alkaloid
alkane
alkene
alkyne
amine
base
bromide
carbide
carbohydrate
carbonate
chloride
chlorofluorocarbon (CFC)
cyanide
epoxide
ester
fluoride
hydrocarbon
hydroxide
iodide
ketone
nitrate
nitride
nitro compound
oxide
paraffin
phosphate
salt
silicate
silicone
sulphate
sulphide

Computer Parts and Peripherals

See also **Programs**

accelerator board/card
acoustic coupler
analogue to digital converter
arithmetic and logic unit (ALU)
bar-code reader
bubblejet printer
bubble memory
buffer
bus
cache memory
card
CD-ROM
CD-RW (read-write) disk/drive
central processing unit (CPU)
chip
console
control unit
coprocessor
digital to analogue converter
digitizer
DIMM (dual in-line memory module)
disk
disk drive
diskette
dot-matrix printer
drum scanner
DVD (digital videodisc)
dynamic memory
dynamic RAM (DRAM)
erasable programmable ROM (EPROM)
expansion card/board
fax modem
firmware
fixed disk
flash memory
floating-point unit (FPU)
floppy disk
graphics card
graphics pad
hard disk
hard drive
imagesetter
inkjet printer
input-output device
input-output port
joystick
keyboard
laser printer
light pen
line printer
maths coprocessor
memory
microprocessor
minidisc
minitower
mobo
modem
monitor
motherboard
mouse
mouse mat
non-volatile memory
optical disk
option card
plotter
port
printed circuit
printed circuit board (PCB)
printer
processor
random-access memory (RAM)
raster image processor (RIP)
read-only memory (ROM)
register
removable disk
scanner
sequencer
serial port
silicon chip
SIMM (single in-line memory module)
software
solid-state memory
sound card
static RAM (SRAM)
synchronous dynamic RAM (SDRAM)
tape streamer
terminal
TFT (thin film transistor) screen
touch pad
touch screen
trackball
transistor
video card
visual display unit (VDU)
voice synthesizer
wand
Winchester disk
Winchester disk drive
Zip disk (*trademark*)
Zip drive (*trademark*)

Confectionery

See **Sweets and Confectionery**

Contraceptives

barrier method
birth control pill
birth pill
cap
coil
coitus interruptus
combined pill
condom
contraceptive jelly
diaphragm
douche
douche bag
Durex (*trademark*)
Dutch cap
female condom
Femidom (*trademark*)
French letter
intrauterine device (IUD)
karezza
Lippes loop
mini-pill
morning-after pill
Norplant (*trademark*)
oral contraceptive
pessary
the pill
prophylactic
protective
rhythm method
sheath
spermicidal cream/jelly
spermicide
sponge
sympto-thermal method
withdrawal method

Cooking Methods

baking
barbecuing
blanching
boiling
braising
broasting
broiling
browning
caramelizing
casseroling
charbroiling
coddling
currying
deep-frying
dry-frying
fricasséeing
frying
griddling
grilling
marinating
microwaving
oven-roasting
pan-frying
parboiling
poaching
pot-roasting
pre-cooking
pressure-cooking
reheating
roasting
sautéing
scrambling
searing
simmering
slow-cooking
smoking
spit-roasting
steaming
stewing
stir-frying
sweating
tandoori
toasting

Cooking Vessels

bain-marie
billy
billycan
casserole
cauldron
chafing dish
coal pot
cocotte
Crockpot (*trademark*)
dixie
double boiler
dutchie
Dutch oven
fish kettle
frying pan
frypan
karahi
marmite
mess tin
pattypan
pipkin
poacher
potjie
pressure cooker
pudding basin
ramekin (dish)
saucepan
scallop
skillet
slow cooker
steamer
stewpot
stockpot
tagine
tian
wok

Corn

See **Cereal Crops**

Cows

See **Cattle**

Cricket Roles and Positions

all-rounder
bat
batsman/batswoman
bowler
cover
cover point
deep midwicket
deep square leg
extra cover
fielder
fieldsman
fine leg
gully
keeper
last man
leg-side fielder
leg slip
leg spinner
long field
long leg
long off
long on
longstop
medium pacer
mid-off
mid-on
midwicket
nightwatchman
non-striker
offside fielder
off spinner
opener
opening batsman
pace bowler
paceman
point
runner
seam bowler
seamer
short leg
short midwicket
silly mid-off
silly mid-on
silly point
slip
spin bowler
spinner
square leg
striker
tail-ender
third man
twelfth man
wicketkeeper

Crockery

See **Pottery and Porcelain**

Crustaceans

acorn barnacle
barnacle
blue crab
Chinese mitten crab
crab
crawdad
crawfish
cray
crayfish
crevette
Cyclops

daphnia
Dungeness crab
edible crab
euphausiid
fairy shrimp
fiddler crab
fish louse
freshwater crayfish
ghost crab
goose barnacle
gribble
hermit crab
horseshoe crab
king crab
king prawn
kreef
krill
land crab
langouste
lobster
mantis shrimp
marron
mitten crab
mudbug
mysid
nipper
Norway lobster
opossum shrimp
pea crab
phyllopod
pill woodlouse
porcelain crab
prawn
robber crab
Sally Lightfoot
sand crab
sandhopper
sea slater
shore crab
shrimp
slater
snow crab
softshell crab
spider crab
spiny lobster
stone crab
swimming crab
tiger prawn
velvet swimming crab
woodlouse
yabby

Crust of the Earth

See **Earth's Crust**

Cultivation

See **Farming and Cultivation**

Cupboards and Cabinets

almirah
armoire
aumbry
buffet
canterbury
cassone
cellaret/cellarette
chest
chest of drawers
chiffonier
closet
commode
console
credenza
dresser
highboy
hope chest
larder
locker
lowboy
pantry
press
safe
sea chest
sideboard
tabernacle
tallboy
tansu
wardrobe
Welsh dresser
whatnot

Cups

See **Drinking Vessels**

Currency Units

See also **Coins**

afghani
agora
anna
at
avo
baht
baiza
balboa
ban
birr
bolivar
boliviano
butut
cedi
cent
centas
centavo
centesimo
centésimo
centime
centimo
CFA franc
chetrum
colón
cordoba
crore
cruzado
cruzeiro
dalasi
denar
Deutschmark
dinar
diram
DM
D-mark
dobra
dollar
dong
drachma
dram
ecu/ECU
escudo
euro
Eurodollar
European currency unit
eyrir
fen
filler
fils
florin
forint
franc
gopik
gourde
groschen
grosz
guarani
guilder
guinea
gulden
halala
haler
halier
heller
hryvna/hryvnia
inti
jeon
jiao
jun
khoum
kina
kip
kobo
kopek/kopeck/copecks
kopiyka
koruna
krona
krone
kroon
kuna
kurus
kwacha
kwanza
kyat
lari
lat
lek
lempira
leone
lepton
leu
lev/leva
likuta
lilangeni
lipa
lira
litas
loti
luma
lwei
manat
mark
markka
metical
mill
millieme
milreis
mongo
naira
nakfa
ngultrum
ngwee
øre
öre
Ostmark
ouguiya
pa'anga
paisa
para
pataca
pengö
penni
penny
peseta
pesewa
peso
petrodollar
pfennig
piastre
pice
pie
poisha
pound
pul
pula
punt
pya
qintar
quetzal
qursh
rand
rappen
real
Reichsmark
renminbi
rial/riyal
riel
ringgit
rouble
rufiyaa
rupee
rupiah
santim
satang
schilling
sen
sene
seniti
sent
sente
shekel
shilling
simoleon
sol
soldo
som
somoni
sov
stotin
stotinka
sucre
tael
taka
tala
talent
tambala
tein
tenesi
tenge
tetri
thebe
tiyin
toea
tolar
tugrik
vatu
won
xu
yen
yuan
zaire
zloty

Curves

arc
Archimedean spiral
bell curve
bow
brachistochrone
cardioid
catenary
characteristic curve
circle
cissoid
conchoid
crescent
Cupid's bow
cycloid
demilune
ellipse
entasis
epicycloid
equiangular spiral
evolute
folium of Descartes
Gaussian curve
half-moon
helix
horseshoe
hyperbola
hypocycloid
involute
lemniscate
logarithmic spiral
logistic curve
normal curve
ogive
oval
parabola
polar curve
roulette
sigmoid curve
sine curve/sine wave
sinusoid
solidus
spiral
spline
transition curve
trochoid
whaleback
witch of Agnesi

Daggers

See **Knives and Daggers**

Dances and Types of Dancing

See also **Ballet Steps and Positions**

allemande
Apache
ballet
ballroom
barn dance
basse danse
beguine
belly dance
black bottom
body popping
bolero
boogaloo
boogie
bop
bossa nova
Boston
bourrée
branle
break-dancing
buck-and-wing
bunny hug
cachucha
cakewalk
cancan
capoeira
carioca
ceroc
cha-cha
cha-cha-cha
chaconne
character dance
charleston
circle dance
clog dance
conga
contradance
contredanse
corroboree
Cossack dance
cotillion
country dance
courante
csardas
cueca
cumbia
Dashing White Sergeant
devil dance
disco
do-si-do
double shuffle
ecossaise
eightsome reel
excuse-me
fan dance
fandango
farandole
farruca
flamenco
fling
folk dance
formation dancing
foxtrot
frug
galliard
gallopade
galop
gavotte
Gay Gordons
gigue
goombay
gopak
habanera
haka
hay
(Helston) floral dance
(Helston) furry
Highland fling
hoedown
hokey-cokey
hora
hornpipe
hula-hula
hully gully
hustle
Irish jig
Irish reel
jaleo
jazz dance
jig
jitterbug
jive
jota
juba
Kathak
Kathakali
kazachoc
kolo
kwela
lambada
Lambeth Walk
lancers

ländler
lap dance
limbo
Lindy Hop
lion dance
Madison
malagueña
mambo
mashed potato
maxixe
maypole dance
mazurka
merengue
Mexican hat
military two-step
minuet
moonstomp
moonwalk
morris dance
mosh
musette
nautch
old-time
one-step
palais glide
pantsula
pas de deux
pas de quatre
pas de trois
paso doble
passepied
pas seul
pata-pata
Paul Jones
pavane
polka
polonaise
quadrille
quickstep
rain dance
reel
rigadoon
ring-shout
robotic dancing
rock and roll
ronde
round dance
roundelay
rumba
sakkie-sakkie
salsa
saltarello
samba
saraband
seguidilla
sequence dance
shag
shake
Shango
shimmy
shuffle
siciliano/siciliana
Sir Roger de Coverley
skank
slam dance
snake dance
soft-shoe shuffle
square dance
stomp
strathspey
strip the willow
strut
sun dance
sword dance
sytarki
tambourin
tango
tap dance
tarantella
tickey-draai
torch
turkey trot
twist
twosome reel
two-step
veleta
vogueing
volta
waltz
war dance
Watusi
zambra
zapateado

Deer and Antelopes

addax
ariel
axis deer
barasingha
beira
beisa
blackbuck
blesbok
bongo
bontebok
brocket
bubal
bushbuck
caribou
chamois
chevrotain
Chinese water deer
chinkara
chiru
chital
Clark's gazelle
dama gazelle
dibatag
dik-dik
dorcas gazelle
duiker
eland
elk
fallow deer
gazelle
gemsbok
gerenuk
gnu
goa
goat-antelope
goral
grysbok
guemal
hartebeest
hirola
hog deer
impala
klipspringer
kob
kongoni
kudu
lechwe
marsh deer
moose
mountain goat
mouse deer
mule deer
muntjac
musk deer
musk ox
nilgai
nyala
okapi
oribi
oryx
Père David's deer
pronghorn (antelope)
pudu
puku
red deer
reedbuck
reindeer
rhebok
roan antelope
roe deer
royal antelope
royal stag
rusa
sable (antelope)
saiga
sambar
sasin
scimitar oryx
serow
sika
sitatunga
sorel
springbok
steenbok
steinbock
suni
swamp deer
takin
thamin
Thomson's gazelle
topi
tsessebi
tufted deer
wapiti
waterbuck
water deer
white-tailed deer
wildebeest

Denominations

See **Christian Denominations**

Dentists

See **Doctors and Dentists**

Desks

See **Tables and Desks**

Desserts

See **Cakes, Puddings, and Desserts**

Diacritics

See **Accents**

Dietary Habits

term	thing eaten
anthropophagous	fellow humans
cannibalistic	members of the same species
carnivorous	meat
coprophagous	faeces
detritivorous	plant detritus
entomophagous	insects
folivorous	leaves
frugivorous	fruit
fungivorous	fungi
graminivorous	grass
herbivorous	plants
insectivorous	insects, worms, and other invertebrates
mellivorous	honey
nectarivorous	nectar
omnivorous	all kinds of plants and meat
omophagous	raw food, especially raw meat
piscivorous	fish
planktivorous	plankton
vermivorous	worms

Digestive System

Parts of the Human Digestive System

alimentary canal
anus
buccal cavity
colon
duodenum
gall bladder
ileum
intestine
jejunum
liver
mouth
oesophagus
pancreas
rectum
salivary glands
stomach
teeth
tongue

Dinosaurs

alamosaurus
albertosaurus
allosaurus
anchiceratops
anchisaurus
ankylosaur
apatosaurus
barosaurus
brachiosaurus
brontosaurus
camarasaurus
camptosaurus
carnosaur
ceratops
ceratosaurus
cetiosaurus
chasmosaurus
coelophysis
coelosaur
compsognathus
conodont
corythosaurus
deinonychus
dilophosaurus
diplodocus
dromaeosaur
dryosaurus
duck-billed dinosaur
edmontosaurus
fabrosaurus
gallimimus
hadrosaur
heterodontosaurus
hypsilophodont
iguanodon
kentrosaurus
leptoceratops
megalosaurus
melanorosaurus
microvenator
monoclonius
ornithischian
ornitholestes
ornithomimus
ornithopod
ostrich dinosaur
oviraptor
pachycephalosaur
parasaurolophus
pentaceratops
plateosaurus
pliosaur
procompsognathus
prosauropod
protoceratops
psittacosaurus
pteranodon
pterodactyl
quetzalcoatlus
raptor
rhamphorhyncoid
riojasaurus
saurischian
saurolophus
sauropod
scelidosaurus
seismosaurus
staurikosaurus
stegoceras
stegosaur
styracosaurus
syntarsus
tarbosaurus
theropod
thescelosaurus
titanosaurus
torosaurus
triceratops
troodon
tyrannosaur
ultrasaurus
utahraptor
velociraptor

Diseases

See **Illnesses**

Districts of a City

arrondissement
barrio
block
borough
business park
Cabbagetown
cardboard city
Chinatown
civic centre
clubland
council estate
dockland
downtown
edge city
estate
exurb
exurbia
faubourg
garden suburb
ghetto
group area
hood
housing estate
industrial estate
inner city
jhuggi jhopri
kasbah
liberty
locality
medina
mohalla
nabe
neighbourhood
outskirts
pedestrian precinct
precinct
quarter
quartier
red-light district
rookery
school district
science park
seafront
sector
skid row
slum
smokeless zone
suburb
suburbia
technology park
theatreland
township
trading estate
twilight zone
uptown
village
waterfront

Districts, Administrative

archbishopric
archdeaconry
archdiocese
arrondissement
autonomy
bailiwick
Bantustan
barony
bishopric
borough
canton
century
chapelry
circuit
civil parish
classis
colony
commonwealth
commune
constituency
county
county borough
County Palatine
cure
deme
department
diocese
district
division
dominion
duchy
dukedom
earldom
electorate
emirate
eparchy
exarchate
group area
homeland
hundred
island area
jagir
jurisdiction
krai/kray
Land
manor
marquisate/marquessate
metropolitan county
metropolitan district
minor county
nomarchy
nome
oblast
okrug
palatinate
pargana/pergunnah/pergana
parish
pocket borough
prefecture
presbytery
province
rape
rectory
regality
region
riding
rotten borough
rural district
sanjak
satrapy
seat
see
sheading
shire
shire county
situs
soke
state
stewartry/stewardry
taluk/taluka
tehsil/tahsil
territory
theme
tithing
township
tribe
union
unitary authority
unitary council
urban district
vicus
vilayet
viscounty
wapentake
ward
zamindari/zemindari/zamindary
zilla/zillah

Doctors and Dentists

allergist
anaesthesiologist
anaesthetist
audiologist
aurist
brain surgeon
cardiologist
chiropodist
chiropractor
clinician
consultant
dental surgeon
dentist
dermatologist
diagnostician
embryologist
endocrinologist
endodontist
ENT (ear, nose, & throat) doctor
epidemiologist
exodontist
extern
flying doctor
forensic pathologist
gastroenterologist
general practitioner (GP)
geriatrician
gerontologist
gynaecologist
haematologist
heart surgeon
hospital doctor
houseman
house officer
immunologist
intern
junior doctor
laryngologist
medical examiner
medical officer (MO)
nephrologist
neurologist
neuropathologist
neurosurgeon
nosologist
obstetrician
oculist
oncologist
ophthalmologist
orthodontist
orthopaedist
orthotist
osteologist
otolaryngologist
otologist
otorhinolaryngologist
paediatrician
paedodontist
parasitologist
pathologist
perinatologist
periodontist
physician
plastic surgeon
podiatrist
proctologist
prosthodontist
radiologist
radiotherapist
registrar
rheumatologist
senior registrar
serologist
specialist
surgeon
teratologist
trichologist
urologist
venereologist

Dogs

breeds

Aberdeen terrier
affenpinscher
Afghan hound
Airedale terrier
Akita
Alsatian
Australian terrier
basenji
basset hound
beagle
bearded collie
Bedlington terrier
Belgian sheepdog
Bernese mountain dog
bichon frise
black and tan
Blenheim spaniel
bloodhound
Border collie
Border terrier
borzoi
Boston terrier
bouvier
boxer
Briard
Brussels griffon
bulldog
bull mastiff
bull terrier
cairn terrier
Cape hunting dog
carriage dog
Cavalier King Charles spaniel
chihuahua
chow
Clumber spaniel
Clydesdale
coach dog
cocker spaniel
collie
coonhound
corgi
dachshund
Dalmatian
Dandie Dinmont
deerhound
Dobermann pinscher
dray hound
elk hound
English setter
English springer
field spaniel
Finnish spitz
foxhound
fox terrier
French bulldog
German Shepherd
golden retriever
Gordon setter
Great Dane
greyhound
griffon
Groenendael
harrier
husky
Ibizan hound
Irish setter
Irish terrier
Irish wolfhound
Istrian pointer
Ivicene
Jack Russell terrier
keeshond
kelpie
Kerry blue
King Charles spaniel
Komondor
Kuvasz
Labrador retriever
laika
Lakeland terrier
Leonberg
Lhasa apso
malamute/malemute
Maltese dog/terrier
Manchester terrier
mastiff
Mexican hairless
Munsterlander
Newfoundland
Norfolk terrier
Norwich terrier
Old English sheepdog
otter dog/hound
papillon
peke
Pekinese/Pekingese
Pharaoh hound
pit bull terrier
pointer
Pomeranian
poodle
pug dog
puli
Pyrenean mountain dog
Pyrenean sheepdog
Pyrenean wolfhound
Queensland blue heeler
redbone
red setter
retriever
Rhodesian ridgeback
Rottweiler
rough collie
St Bernard dog
saluki
Samoyed
schipperke
schnauzer
Scottie dog
Scottish terrier
Sealyham terrier
setter
Shar Pei
sheepdog
sheltie
Shetland sheepdog
shih-tzu
Skye terrier
sleuth hound
spaniel
Spinone
spitz
springer spaniel
Staffordshire bull terrier
staghound
terrier
Tibetan mastiff
Tibetan spaniel
Tibetan terrier
tosa
vizsla
Weimaraner
Welsh corgi
Welsh hound
Welsh springer
Welsh terrier
West Highland terrier
wheaten terrier
whippet
wolfhound
Yorkshire terrier

wild dogs

African wild dog
bush dog
Cape hunting dog
coyote
dhole
dingo
dire wolf (extinct)
golden jackal
grey wolf
jackal
lobo
maned wolf
raccoon dog
red dog
red wolf
Simien jackal/fox
timber wolf

Dolphins

See **Whales and Dolphins**

Drama

See **Plays**

Dresses

baby-doll dress
backless dress
ballgown
button-through dress
chemise
cheongsam
coat dress
cocktail dress
dinner gown
dirndl
Empire line dress
evening gown
gymslip
kaftan
kimono
maternity dress
maxidress
minidress
Mother Hubbard
muumuu
overdress
pinafore dress
polonaise
pouf dress
sack dress
sari
sarong
shamma
sheath dress
shift dress
shirt dress
shirtwaister
short waist
skimmer
slip dress
smock
strapless dress
sundress
tea gown
tent dress
tube dress
wedding dress
yukata

Dressings
Salad Dressings

balsamic vinaigrette
blue cheese dressing
Caesar dressing
French dressing
mayonnaise
oil and vinegar
ranch dressing
remoulade
salad cream
Thousand Island dressing
vinaigrette

Drinking Vessels

balloon (glass)
beaker
cannikin
chalice
coffee cup
copita
cup
demitasse
dock glass
drinking horn
flagon
flute
glass
globe
goblet
gourd
kylix
lady's waist
loving cup
middy
moustache cup
mug
pannikin
pint pot
pony
quaich
rummer
schooner
seidel
shot glass
sippy cup
snifter
stein
stirrup cup
stoup
tankard
tass
tassie
taster
tastevin
tazza
teacup
toby jug
tumbler
tyg
yard of ale

Drinks (Alcoholic)

See also **Beers** **Cocktails and Mixed Drinks** **Sherries** **Whiskies** **Wines**

absinthe
advocaat
aguardiente
alcopop
amaretto
anisette
applejack
aquavit
Armagnac
arrack/arak
bourbon
brandy
cachaca
Calvados
cassis
champagne
chartreuse
cherry brandy
cider
cognac
crème de cacao
crème de menthe
curaçao
fine champagne
fraise
framboise
genever
gin
ginger wine
goldwasser
grappa
Hollands
hydromel
kirsch
koumiss
kümmel
kvass
liqueur
makkoli
maraschino
marc
mead
mescal
metheglin
noyau
ouzo
pacharán
palm wine
pastis
perry
pisco
pombe
port
poteen
pulque
raki
ratafia
reposado
rum
sake
sambuca
schnapps
scrumpy
sercial
shochu
slivovitz
sloe gin
tafia
tej
tequila
triple sec
vermouth
vodka
witblits

Drinks (Soft)

See also **Coffee Drinks** **Teas**

water or water-based

barley water
bitter lemon
carbonated water
cherryade
citron pressé
club soda (*trademark*)
coffee
cola
cordial
cream soda
crush
dandelion and burdock
fruit juice
fruit tea
ginger ale
ginger beer
herbal tea/infusion
horchata
iced tea
isotonic drink
lemonade
lemon tea
limeade
maté
mineral water
orangeade
orgeat
prairie oyster
pressé
root beer
St Clements
sarsaparilla
seltzer water
sherbet
soda water
sports drink
spring water
squash
tea
tisane
tonic water
Vichy water

milk or milk-based

buttermilk
cocoa
drinking chocolate
hot chocolate
ice milk
lassi
malted milk
milkshake
smoothie (*informal*)
soya milk

Drugs
Narcotic Drugs

acid
amphetamine (sulphate)
angel dust
basuco
betel
bhang/bang
blow
burley (tobacco)
cannabis (resin)
cavendish
charas
charlie
chaw
coca
cocaine
crack (cocaine)
crystal meth
dagga
designer drug
dope
downer
draw
dynamite
E *or* Es
Ecstasy
eight ball
euphoriant, euphoriants
filler
freebase (cocaine)
ganja
gateway drug
gear
GHB
grass
green
H
hashish
hemp
henbane
heroin
hop
horse
ibogaine
junk
kava
khat
kif/kef
kinnikinnick
locoweed
LSD
lysergic acid diethylamide (LSD)
marijuana/marihuana
Mary Jane
mescaline/mescalin
meth
methamphetamine
methylenedioxymethamphetamine (MDMA)
muscimol
narceine
nicotine
nose candy
opiate, opiates
opium
paan/pan
perique
peyote
peyote buttons
pot
psilocybin
psychedelic drug
rappee
reefer
rock
shag (tobacco)
sinsemilla
skag/scag
skunkweed
smack
snow
snuff
speed
speedball
spliff
sugar
tendu leaf
Thai stick
tobacco
toot
upper
wacky baccy
weed
whizz
wild dagga
X
zarda

Drums

See **Percussion Instruments**

Ducks

See **Fowl**

Dwellings

See **Homes**

Dyes

See also **Colours**

alizarin
alkanet
aniline dye
annatto
azo dye
basic dye
cochineal
copper sulphate
diazo compound
eosin
flavin
fluorescein
fuchsin
fustic
garancin
gentian violet
henna
indigo
induline
kermes
litmus
madder
magenta
orchil
orpiment
Perkin's mauve
phthalocyanine dye
picric acid
Prussian blue
purpurin
reddle
rhodamine
rosanaline
saffron
sappanwood
Saxon blue
tartrazine
Turkey red
turmeric
Tyrian purple
weld
woad
xanthene dye
zedoary

Ear

Parts of the Human Ear

auditory canal
auditory nerve
auricle *or* pinna
basilar membrane
cochlea
eardrum *or* tympanic membrane
endolymph
Eustachian tube
hair cell
incus *or* anvil
inner ear
malleus *or* hammer
middle ear
organ of Corti
outer ear
perilymph
saccule
semicircular canal
stapes *or* stirrup
tectorial membrane
utricle
vestibule

Earth's Crust

Layers of the Earth's Crust

asthenosphere
continental crust
lithosphere
lower mantle
Mohorovičić discontinuity
oceanic crust
sial
transition zone
upper mantle

Earthenware

See **Pottery and Porcelain**

Elements

Chemical Elements and Their Symbols

Element	Symbol
actinium*	Ac
aluminium	Al
americium*	Am
antimony	Sb
argon	Ar
arsenic	As
astatine*	At
barium	Ba
berkelium*	Bk
beryllium	Be
bismuth	Bi
bohrium*	Bh
boron	B
bromine	Br
cadmium	Cd
caesium	Cs
calcium	Ca
californium*	Cf
carbon	C
cerium	Ce
chlorine	Cl
chromium	Cr
cobalt	Co
copper	Cu
curium*	Cm
dubnium*	Db
dysprosium	Dy
einsteinium*	Es
erbium	Er
europium	Eu
fermium*	Fm
fluorine	F
francium*	Fr
gadolinium	Gd
gallium	Ga
germanium	Ge
gold	Au
hafnium	Hf
hassium*	Hs
helium	He
holmium	Ho
hydrogen	H
indium	In
iodine	I
iridium	Ir
iron	Fe
krypton	Kr
lanthanum	La
lawrencium*	Lr
lead	Pb
lithium	Li
lutetium	Lu
magnesium	Mg
manganese	Mn
meitnerium*	Mt
mendelevium*	Md
mercury	Hg
molybdenum	Mo
neodymium	Nd
neon	Ne
neptunium*	Np
nickel	Ni
niobium	Nb
nitrogen	N
nobelium*	Nb
osmium	Os
oxygen	O
palladium	Pd
phosphorus	P
platinum	Pt
plutonium*	Pu
polonium*	Po
potassium	K
praseodymium	Pr
promethium*	Pm
protactinium*	Pa
radium*	Ra
radon*	Rn
rhenium	Re
rhodium	Rh
rubidium	Rb
ruthenium	Ru
rutherfordium*	Rf
samarium	Sm
scandium	Sc
seaborgium*	Sg
selenium	Se
silicon	Si
silver	Ag
sodium	Na
strontium	Sr
sulphur	S
tantalum	Ta
technetium*	Tc
tellurium	Te
terbium	Tb
thallium	Tl
thorium*	Th
thulium	Tm
tin	Sn
titanium	Ti
tungsten	W
uranium*	U
vanadium	V
xenon	Xe
ytterbium	Yb
yttrium	Y
zinc	Zn
zirconium	Zr

* *radioactive*

Embroidery

See **Sewing Techniques and Stitches**

Energy and Fuels

acetylene
anthracite
atomic power
avgas
benzol
bio-diesel
biofuel
biogas
biomass energy
briquette
butane
Calor gas (*trademark*)
chemical energy
coal
coal gas
Coalite (*trademark*)
coke
derv
diesel
electrical power
electromagnetic energy
firewood
fission energy
fossil fuel
four-star petrol
fuel oil
fuel rod
fusion energy
gas
gasohol
gas oil
gasoline
geothermal energy
heat
hydroelectric power
hydrogen
kerosene
kinetic energy
leaded petrol
lead replacement petrol (LRP)
light
lignite
liquefied petroleum gas (LPG)
methane
MOX
natural gas
nitromethane
nuclear power
oil
Orimulsion (*trademark*)
paraffin
peat
petrol
petroleum
photosynthesis
potential energy
producer gas
propane
renewable energy
solar energy
steam power
Sterno (*US trademark*)
synfuel
tidal power
town gas
turf
unleaded petrol
water gas
water power
wave power
whale oil
wind power

Engineering

Branches of Engineering

aerodynamics
aeronautical engineering
aerospace engineering
agricultural engineering
astronautics
automotive engineering
chemical engineering
civil engineering
cosmonautics
electrical engineering
electronics engineering
environmental engineering
ergonomics
fluid dynamics
geotechnics
hydraulics
mechanical engineering
mining engineering
naval engineering
nuclear engineering
process engineering
production engineering
structural engineering

Engines

See also **Trains and Rolling Stock**

aero engine
auxiliary power unit (APU)
beam engine
diesel engine
donkey engine
double-acting engine
dynamo
electric motor

external-combustion engine
flat-four engine
flathead engine
four-stroke (engine)
gas turbine
generator
heat engine
hyperdrive
inboard
internal-combustion engine (ICE)
ion engine
jato
jet engine
linear motor
magneto
oil engine
outboard
Otto engine
petrol engine
piston engine
prop jet
pulse jet
radial engine
ramjet
rebore
reciprocating engine
rocket engine
rotary engine
scramjet
stationary engine
steam engine
steam turbine
sterndrive
Stirling engine
straight-eight
straight-six
thruster
triple expansion engine
turbine
turbo diesel
turbofan
turbogenerator
turbojet
turboprop
turboshaft
twin-cam engine
two-stroke (engine)
ullage rocket
V engine
Wankel engine

Entertainers

See also **Actors** **Musicians** **Singers**

acrobat
actor
aerialist
bullfighter
busker
chorine
chorus girl
circus artist
clown
comedian
comedienne
comic
commère
compère
conjuror
contortionist
dancer
deejay
disc jockey (DJ)
diseuse
drag artist
drum major
drum majorette
emcee
equilibrist
escape artist
escapologist
exotic dancer
female impersonator
fire-eater
funambulist
gladiator
gleeman
go-go dancer
griot
harlequin
hypnotist
illusionist
impersonator
impressionist
instrumentalist
jester
jongleur
juggler
Kathak
lap dancer
lion tamer
magician
masker/masquer
MC
Meistersinger
merry andrew
mime artist
mimic
mind reader
minstrel
mixmaster
musician
one-man band
organ grinder
player
puppeteer
raconteur
raconteuse
rapper
redcoat
retiarius
rhapsode
ringmaster
rope-walker
samplist
selector/selecta
showman
singer
singsong girl
snake charmer
song-and-dance act
stand-up comedian
storyteller
stripper
striptease artist
strongman
stuntman
stuntwoman
sword-swallower
taleteller
tightrope walker
toaster
trapeze artist
tumbler
tummler
turntablist
unicyclist
vaudevillian
ventriloquist
wire-walker

Epochs

See **Geological Ages**

Eponyms

eponym	person
America	Amerigo Vespucci (Italian explorer)
Baedeker	Karl Baedeker (German publisher)
Bailey bridge	Donald Bailey (English engineer)
biro (*trademark*)	László Bíró (Hungarian inventor)
bloomers	Amelia Bloomer (American reformer)
bobby	Robert Peel (British statesman)
bowdlerization	Dr Thomas Bowdler (English editor of Shakespeare)
boycott	Capt. Charles Boycott (Irish land agent)
boysenberry	Robert Boysen (American horticulturist)
Braille	Louis Braille (French educationalist)
Bunsen burner	Robert Bunsen (German chemist)
Caesarean section	Julius Caesar (Roman general and statesman)
cardigan	James Brudenell, 7th Earl of Cardigan (English soldier)
chauvinism	Nicolas Chauvin (French soldier)
clerihew	Edmund Clerihew Bentley (English writer)
Colt (*trademark*)	Samuel Colt (American inventor)
Cyrillic script	St Cyril (Greek missionary)
daguerreotype	Louis Daguerre (French physicist and painter)
Derby (horse race)	Edward Stanley, 12th Earl of Derby (its founder)
derringer	Henry Derringer (American gunsmith)
diesel	Rudolf Diesel (French-born German engineer)
dolomite	Dieudonné Dolomieu (French geologist)
Dow Jones index	Charles Dow and Edward Jones (American economists)
dunce	John Duns Scotus (Scottish theologian)
epicure	Epicurus (Greek philosopher)
Everest, Mount	George Everest (British surveyor general of India)
filbert	St Philibert (French saint)
Fosbury flop	Richard Fosbury (American high jumper)
galvanization	Luigi Galvani (Italian anatomist)
garibaldi biscuit	Giuseppe Garibaldi (Italian leader)
Gatling gun	Richard Gatling (American inventor)
Geiger counter	Hans Geiger (German nuclear physicist)
gerrymandering	Elbridge Gerry (Governor of Massachusetts)
Granny Smith (apple)	Maria Smith (Australian grower)
greengage	William Gage (English botanist)
guillotine	Joseph-Ignace Guillotin (French physician)
guppy	R. J. Lechmere Guppy (Trinidadian clergyman)
guy	Guy Fawkes (English conspirator)
guyot	Arnold H. Guyot (Swiss geographer)
hansom cab	Joseph A. Hansom (English architect)
Hobson's choice	Thomas Hobson (English carrier)
Hoover (*trademark*)	William Hoover (American industrialist)
jacuzzi (*trademark*)	Candido Jacuzzi (Italian-born American inventor)
Kalashnikov	Mikhail Kalashnikov (Russian weapon designer)
leotard	Jules Léotard (French trapeze artist)
loganberry	John H. Logan (American horticulturist)
lynch	William Lynch (American planter)
macadam	John L. McAdam (British surveyor)
macadamia	John Macadam (Australian chemist)
Mach number	Ernst Mach (Austrian physicist)
mackintosh	Charles Macintosh (Scottish inventor)
magnolia	Pierre Magnol (French botanist)
martinet	Jean Martinet (French drill master)
masochism	Leopold von Sacher-Masoch (Austrian novelist)
Mason–Dixon Line	Charles Mason and Jeremiah Dixon (English astronomers)
Mauser (*trademark*)	Paul von Mauser (German inventor)
mausoleum	Mausolus (King of Caria)
maverick	Samuel Maverick (Texan rancher)
Melba sauce and Melba toast	Nellie Melba (Australian opera singer)
mesmerism	Franz Mesmer (Austrian physician)
Molotov cocktail	Vyacheslav Molotov (Soviet statesman)
Morse code	Samuel Morse (American inventor)
nicotine	Jean Nicot (French diplomat)
Nissen hut	Peter N. Nissen (British engineer)
orrery	Charles Boyle, 4th Earl of Orrery (patron of its inventor)
pasteurization	Louis Pasteur (French bacteriologist)
pavlova	Anna Pavlova (Russian ballerina)
peach Melba	Nellie Melba (Australian opera singer)
pinchbeck	Christopher Pinchbeck (English watchmaker)
platonic	Plato (Greek philosopher)
Plimsoll line	Samuel Plimsoll (English politician)
pompadour	Madame de Pompadour (French noblewoman)
praline	Marshal de Plessis-Praslin (French soldier)
Pullman	George Pullman (its American designer)
pyrrhic victory	Pyrrhus (King of Epirus)
Queensberry Rules	John Douglas, 9th Marquess of Queensberry (their sponsor)
quisling	Vidkun Quisling (Norwegian puppet ruler)
Rachmanism	Peter Rachman (London landlord)
Rastafarianism	Emperor Haile Selassie (born Tafari Makonnen)
Rubik's cube (*trademark*)	Erno Rubik (Hungarian inventor)
sadism	Marquis de Sade (French writer and soldier)
sandwich	John Montague, 4th Earl of Sandwich (its supposed inventor)
saxhorn and saxophone	Charles and Antoine-Joseph Sax (Belgian instrument-makers)
shrapnel	Henry Shrapnel (British general)
sideburns	Ambrose Burnside (American general)

eponym	person
silhouette	Étienne de Silhouette (French author and politician)
sousaphone	John Philip Sousa (American composer)
spoonerism	Revd W. A. Spooner (English scholar)
Stakhanovite	Alexei Stakhanov (Russian coal miner)
Stetson (*trademark in US*)	John B. Stetson (American hat manufacturer)
stroganoff	Count Pavel Stroganov (Russian diplomat)
tarmac (tarmacadam)	John L. McAdam (British surveyor)
teddy bear	Theodore (Teddy) Roosevelt (American president and bear-hunter)
thespian	Thespis (Greek dramatic poet)
tommy gun	John Thompson (American general)
wellington boot	Arthur Wellesley, 1st Duke of Wellington (British soldier)
Winchester rifle	Oliver Winchester (American weapons manufacturer)
Yale lock (*trademark*)	Linus Yale, Jr (American locksmith)
Zeppelin	Count Ferdinand von Zeppelin (German army officer)

Equestrian Sports

Arab racing
competitive trail riding
cross-country
dressage
endurance riding
eventing
flat racing *or* the flat
gymkhana
harness racing
haute école
horse racing
hunting
marathon driving
one-day eventing
plating
point-to-point
polo
puissance
rodeo
showing
showjumping
skijoring
steeplechasing
three-day eventing
trotting

Eras

See **Geological Ages**

Explosives

amatol
blasting gelatin
cordite
dynamite
fuel-air explosive
gelignite
guncotton
gunpowder
high explosive (HE)
lyddite
nitroglycerine
plastic explosive
plastique
RDX
Semtex
thermobaric explosive
trinitrotoluene (TNT)

Eye

Parts of the Human Eye

aqueous humour
blind spot
central retinal artery
central retinal vein
choroid
ciliary body
cone
conjunctiva
cornea
dilator muscle
extrinsic muscle
eyeball
eyelash
eyelid
fovea
iris
lens
limbus
optic foramen
optic nerve
orbit
pupil
retina
rod
sclera
sinus venosus sclerae
stroma
suspensory ligament
tarsal plate
tear (*or* lacrimal) glands
vitreous humour
zonular ligament

Fabrics and Fibres

acetate
Acrilan (*trademark*)
acrylic
aida
alpaca
angora
Antron (*trademark*)
Arnel (*trademark*)
asbestos
astrakhan
bafta
baize
balbriggan
barathea
barège
barkcloth
batiste
beaver (cloth)
Bedford cord
bengaline
blanketing
bobbinet
bobbin lace
bombazine
Botany wool
bouclé
brilliantine
broadcloth
broadtail
brocade
brocatelle
brown holland
buckram
bunting
burlap
butter muslin
byssus
calamanco
calico
Cambrelle (*trademark*)
cambric
camel hair
candlewick
canvas
cashmere
cavalry twill
challis
chambray
Chantilly lace
charmeuse
cheesecloth
chenille
cheviot
chiffon
chinchilla
chino
chintz
ciré
cloqué
coconut matting
coir
CoolMax (*trademark*)
cord
Cordura (*trademark*)
corduroy
cotton
crêpe
crêpe de Chine
crépon
cretonne
crewel
Crimplene (*trademark*)
crinoline
crushed velvet
cupro
Dacron (*trademark*)
damask
denim
devoré
dimity
doeskin
Donegal tweed
drab
Dralon (*trademark*)
drill
drugget
duchesse lace
duchesse satin
duffel
dungaree
dupion
elastane
faille
felt
filoselle
fishnet
flannel
flannelette
flax
fleece
flock
floss silk
foulard
frieze
fustian
gaberdine
gauze
georgette
gimp
gingham
Gore-tex (*trademark*)
gossamer
grasscloth
grenadine
grogram
grosgrain
gros point
guipure
gunny
haircloth
Harris tweed (*trademark*)
hemp
herringbone
hessian
hodden
holland
Honiton lace
hopsack
horsehair
huckaback
ikat
ixtle
jaconet
jacquard
jean
jersey
jute
kalamkari
kapok
karakul
Kasha (*trademark*)
kemp
kenaf
Kendal Green
kente
kersey
kerseymere
khadi
khaki
khanga
kikoi
kincob
kitenge
lace
lambswool
lamé
lampas
lawn
leathercloth
leatherette (*trademark*)
leno
Lincoln green
linen
linsey-woolsey
lint
lisle
loden
Lurex (*trademark*)
lustring
Lycra (*trademark*)
madras
marocain
marquisette
Marseilles
matting
Mechlin
melton
merino
microfibre
micromesh
Milanese silk
modacrylic
mohair
moiré
moleskin
moquette
moreen
mousseline
Moygashel (*trademark*)
mungo
muslin
nainsook
nankeen
Naugahyde (*US trademark*)
needlecord
net
ninon
Nottingham lace
nylon
oakum
oilcloth
oiled silk
oilskin
organdie
organza
organzine
Orlon (*trademark*)
osnaburg
ottoman
Oxford cloth
packthread
paduasoy
paisley
pandanus
panne velvet
paper taffeta
parramatta
pashmina
peau-de-soie
percale
Persian silk
Pertex (*trademark*)
petersham
phulkari
pillow lace
pilot cloth
piqué
plaid
plush
plush velvet
point lace
polycotton
polyester
pongee
poplin
poult
prunella
raffia
ramie
rayon
rep
ripstop
rose-point
sackcloth
sacking
sailcloth
samite
sarsenet
sateen
satin
satinette
saxony
schappe
sea-island cotton
seersucker
sendal
sennit
serge
shahtoosh
shantung
sharkskin
sheer
Shetland wool
shoddy
silk
sisal
slipper satin
slub
Spandex (*trademark*)
spun silk
stammel
stockinet
stroud
suede
sunn
Supplex (*trademark*)
surah
swansdown
tabaret
tabby
taffeta
tailor's twist
tapestry
tarlatan
tarpaulin
tattersall
tatting
Tencel (*trademark*)
terry
Terylene (*Brit. trademark*)
ticking
tiffany
toile
toile de Jouy
toquilla
torchon
towelling
Trevira (*trademark*)
Tricel (*trademark*)
tricot
Tricotine (*US trademark*)
tulle
tussore
tweed
twill
Utrecht velvet
Valenciennes
Velcro (*trademark*)
velour
velvet
velveteen
vicuña
viscose
Viyella (*trademark*)
voile
waxcloth
webbing
whipcord
wild silk
wincey
winceyette
wool
worsted
zari

Factories and Workshops

armoury
assembly line
assembly shop
atelier
backlot
bakehouse
bakery
bindery
bloomery
boatyard
body shop
brewery
brewhouse
brickfield
brickworks
brickyard
cannery
chop shop
creamery
distillery
fab
fitting shop
forge
foundry
gasworks
gristmill
hydro
ironworks
malthouse
maquiladora
microbrewery
mill
mint
oil mill
paint shop
paper mill
pattern room/shop
pottery
power station
printery
printing works
printworks
private press
refinery
rolling mill
rope-walk
rope-yard
sail loft
saltern
salt works
sawmill
sewage farm
shipyard
shop floor
smithery
smithy
stamp mill
steelworks
strip mill
studio
sweatshop
tannery
tide mill
windmill
winery
workstation

Family

See **Relatives**

Farming

Types of Farming and Cultivation

agribusiness
agroforestry
agro-industry
animal husbandry
apiculture
aquaculture
arable farming
arboriculture
battery farming
biodynamics
citriculture
crofting
dairy farming
dairying
dry-land farming
extensive farming
factory farming
fish farming
floriculture
forestry
horticulture
hydroponics
intensive farming
livestock farming
mariculture
market gardening
monoculture
orcharding
organic farming
pisciculture
polyculture
pomiculture
sericulture
sharecropping
share farming
shifting cultivation/agriculture
silviculture
smallholding
strip cropping
subsistence farming
tank-farming
viniculture
viticulture

Fears

See **Phobias**

Female Animals

See **Animals—Male and Female Terms**

Fertilizers

agrochemical
ammonium nitrate
base dressing
basic slag
blood, fish, and bone
blood meal
bone ash
bonemeal
calcium phosphate
compost
dung
fishmeal
green manure
growmore
guano
lime
manure
marl
muck
mulch
nitrochalk
oilcake
superphosphate
tankage
top dressing

Festivals

Religious Festivals and Holy Days

Buddhism

Bodhi Day
Dhammacakka
Vesak

Christianity

All Saints' Day *or* All Hallows
Annunciation
Ash Wednesday
Candlemas
Christmas
Easter
Epiphany
Good Friday
Holy Innocents' Day
Pentecost *or* Whit Sunday
Shrove Tuesday

Hinduism

Diwali
Dusshera
Holi
Janmashtami
Mahashivaratri
Navaratri
New Year
Raksha Bandhan
Rama Naumi

Islam

Eid ul-Adha
Eid ul-Fitr
Lailat ul-Bara'h
Lailat ul-Isra wal Mi'raj
Lailat ul-Qadr
Milad
Muharram

Judaism

Hanukkah
Lag b'Omer
Passover *or* Pesach
Purim
Rosh Hashana
Shavuoth
Succoth
Yom Kippur *or* Day of Atonement

pagan

Beltane
Lammas
Samhain

Sikhism

Baisakhi
Birthday of Guru Gobind Singh
Birthday of Guru Nanak
Holi Mohalla
Martyrdom of Guru Arjan
Martyrdom of Guru Tegh Bahadur

Fibres

See **Fabrics and Fibres**

Figures of Speech

See **Rhetorical Devices and Figures of Speech**

Film Types, Versions, and Genres

actioner
animatic
anime
biopic
bioscope
blockbuster
B-movie
buddy movie
caper
cartoon
chick flick
cinéma-vérité
costume drama
director's cut
docudrama
docutainment
epic
feature (film)
featurette
film noir
filmstrip
flick
fly-through
home movie
horse opera
kidult
kinescope
master
mockumentary
musical
nasty
neo-realism
newsreel
oater
peep show
policier
preview
promo
remake
re-release
road movie
romance
romcom
romp
rough cut
rushes
semi-documentary
sequel
shockumentary
shoot-'em-up
short
short subject
showreel
skin flick
slasher
snuff movie
spaghetti western
spoof
supporting film
swashbuckler
talkie
talking picture
telefilm
tie-in
toon
trail
trailer
weepy
western

Firearms

See **Guns**

Fireworks

banger
Bengal light
Catherine wheel
cracker
firecracker
fizgig
fountain
girandole
golden rain
jumping jack
maroon
petard
Pharaoh's serpent
pinwheel
rocket
Roman candle
skyrocket
sparkler
squib
thunderflash
torpedo
volcano
whizz bang

Fish

See also **Sharks**

acara
aholehole
albacore
alewife
alligator fish
allis shad
amberjack
anchoveta
anchovy
anemone fish
angelfish
angel shark
anglerfish
arapaima
archerfish
argentine
argus fish
asp
ballan wrasse
balloonfish
bandfish
barbel
barracouta
barracuda
barramundi
barrelfish
bass
basslet
batfish
beaconfish
beardfish
beluga
bib
bichir
bigeye
billfish
bitterling
black bass
black durgon
blackfish
bleak
blenny
bloodfin
blowfish
bluefin
bluefish
bluegill
bluehead
boarfish
bonefish
bonito
bonnetmouth
bowfin
boxfish
bream
brill
brisling
brown trout
buffalo fish
bullhead
bull trout
bumblebee fish
bummalo
burbot
burrfish
butterfish
butterfly fish
butterfly ray
cabezon
callop
candiru
candlefish
capelin
cardinal fish
carp
catfish
cat shark
cavefish
cero
channel cat
characin
charr
chimera
chinook salmon
chromide
chub
chum salmon
cisco
climbing perch
clingfish
clownfish
coalfish
cobia
cockabully
cod
coelacanth
coho
coley
comber
combfish
coney
conger eel
cornetfish
corvina
cowfish
crappie
crestfish
crucian carp
cunner
cusk
cutlassfish
dab
dace
daggertooth
damselfish
danio
darter
dealfish
devil ray
discus
Dolly Varden
dolphinfish
dorado
dory
Dover sole
dragonet
dragonfish
driftfish
drumfish
eagle ray
eel
eelpout
electric eel
electric ray
elephant fish
elephant-snout fish
escolar
espada
fallfish
featherback
ferox
fighting fish
filefish
fingerfish
firefish
flagfish
flatfish
flathead
flounder
fluke
flying fish
flying gurnard
four-eyed fish
frogfish
fugu
galjoen
gambusia
gaper
garden eel
garfish
garibaldi
garpike
glassfish
globefish
goatfish
goby
goggle-eye
goldfish
goosefish
gourami
grass carp
grayling
greeneye
Greenland halibut
greenling
grenadier
grey mullet
grouper
grunion
grunt
gudgeon
guitarfish
gulper eel
gunnel
guppy
gurnard
gwyniad
haddock
hagfish
hake
halfbeak
halibut
harlequin fish
hatchetfish
hawkfish
headstander
herring
high hat
hogfish
hoki
horse mackerel
houndfish
houting
huchen
humpback salmon
icefish
ide
inanga
inconnu
jackfish
jackknife fish
jack mackerel
jawfish
jewelfish
jewfish
John Dory
kaapenaar
kabeljou
killifish
kingclip
kingfish
klipfish
knifefish
kob
koi carp
kokanee
labyrinth fish
ladyfish
lake trout
lampern
lamprey
lancetfish
lanternfish
leaf fish
leatherjacket
leervis
lemon sole
ling
lingcod
lionhead
lizardfish
loach
louvar
luderick
lumpsucker
lungfish
lyrefish
mackerel
mado
madtom
mahimahi
mahseer
man-of-war fish
manta
marari
margate
marlin
medaka
medusa fish
megrim
menhaden
midshipman
milkfish
miller's thumb
minnow
mirror carp
mojarra
molly
monkfish
moon-eye
moonfish
Moorish idol
moray eel
morwong
mosquito fish
mudfish
mudminnow
mudskipper
mullet
mulloway
mummichog
Murray cod
muskellunge
musselcracker
nannygai
needlefish
neon tetra
Nile perch
numbfish
oarfish
oilfish
old wife
opah
orfe
oscar
ouananiche
pacu
paddlefish
paradise fish
parrotfish
pearleye
pearlfish
perch
permit
pickerel
pigfish
pike
pikeperch
pilchard
pilotfish
pipefish
piranha
plaice
platy
poacher
poenskop
pollack
pollan
pollock
pomfret
pompano
pope
porcupine fish
porgy
pout
powan
prickleback
prowfish
puffer fish
pumpkinseed
pupfish
queenfish
rabbitfish
ragfish
rainbow trout
rascasse
ratfish
ray
razorfish
redfin
redfish
red mullet
red snapper
remora
ribbonfish
rivulus
roach
rock bass
rockfish
rockling
rock snapper
roman fish
ronquil
rosefish
rouget
roughy
rudd
ruffe
sablefish
sailfin molly
sailfish
saithe
salmon
salmon trout
sand dab
sand eel
sandfish
sardine
sargassum fish
sauger
saury
sawfish
scabbardfish
scad
scaldfish
scat
schelly
scissortail
scorpionfish
sculpin
scup
sea bass
sea bream
sea horse
sea moth
sea perch
sea robin
sea trout
sergeant fish
sergeant major
sevruga
sewin
shad
shanny
shark
shark-sucker
sheepshead
shiner
shovelhead
shubunkin
sild
silverside
skate
skilfish
skipjack tuna
skipper
smelt
snaggle-tooth
snailfish
snake mackerel
snakehead
snapper
snipe eel
snipefish
snook
soapfish
sockeye salmon
soldierfish
sole
spadefish
Spanish mackerel
sparling
spearfish
splake
sprat
square-tail
squawfish
squirrelfish
stargazer
steelhead
steenbras
sterlet
stickleback
stingaree
stingray
stockfish
stonefish
striped bass
stumpnose
sturgeon
sucker
sunfish
surfperch
surgeonfish
surmullet
swallower
sweeper
sweetlips
swordfish
swordtail
tai
tailorfish
taimen
tang
tarakihi
tarpon
tarwhine
tautog
tench
tenpounder
tetra
thornback
threadfin
tiger fish
tilapia
tilefish
toadfish
tomcod
tonguefish
toothcarp
topminnow
torpedo ray
torsk
trevally
triggerfish
trout
trumpeter
trumpetfish
trunkfish
tubesnout
tullibee
tuna
tunny
turbot
twaite shad
unicorn fish
vendace
viperfish
wahoo
walleye
warbonnet
warehou
weakfish
weatherfish
weever
wels
whitebait
white bass
whitefish
whiting
windowpane
winter flounder
witch
wolf fish
wormfish
wrasse
wreckfish
wrymouth
X-ray fish
yellowfin
yellowtail
zander
zebra fish

extinct fish

acanthodian
ostracoderm
placoderm

Fish Types

bony fish
carangid
cartilaginous fish
Chondrichthyes
cichlid
clupeoid
crossopterygian
cyprinid
cyprinoid
elasmobranch
gadid
gadoid
ganoid
haplochromine
livebearer
lobe-finned fish
mouthbrooder
Osteichthyes
percid
percoid
ray-finned fish
salmonid
salmonoid
sciaenid
scombroid
selachian
serranid
siluroid
sparid
teleost

Flies

See **Insects**

Flowering Plants and Shrubs

Aaron's rod
abelia
abutilon
acacia
acanthus
achimenes
aconite
African daisy
African violet
agapanthus
agave
agrimony
ajowan
akebia
albizzia
alkanet
allamanda
aloe
alstroemeria
alyssum
amaranth
amaryllis
anchusa
anemone
angelica
angel's trumpet
anthurium
aquilegia
arabis
arbutus
arnica
arrowgrass
arum lily
asphodel
aspidistra
aster
astilbe
astrantia
aubretia
autumn crocus
avens
azalea
baby's breath
bachelor's buttons
balsam
baneberry
banksia
barberry
Barberton daisy
barrenwort
bauera
bearberry
bear's breech
bedstraw
begonia
belladonna
bellflower
bergamot
bergenia
betony
bignonia
bilberry
bindi-eye
bindweed
bird of paradise flower
bird's-eye primrose
bird's-eye speedwell
bird's-foot trefoil
bird's-nest
birthwort
bistort
bittersweet
black-eyed Susan
blackthorn
blazing star
bleeding heart
bloodroot
bluebell
blue-eyed grass
blue-eyed Mary
bluet
bog asphodel
bog rosemary
boneset
borage
boronia
bottlebrush
bougainvillea
bramble
brooklime
brookweed
broom
broomrape
bryony
buckeye
buddleia
bugbane
bugle
bugloss
bulrush
bunchberry
bunchflower
burdock
bur-marigold
burnet
busy Lizzie
butterbur
buttercup
butterfly bush
butterwort
buttonbush
cabbage rose
cactus
calamint
calamondin
calceolaria
calendula
California poppy
camas
camellia
camomile
campanula
campion
canary creeper
candytuft
canna lily
Canterbury bell
Cape primrose
cardinal flower
carnation
carrion flower
catchfly
catmint
cattleya
ceanothus
celandine
centaury
chaffweed
champak
charlock
checkerberry
Cherokee rose
chervil
chickweed
chicory
chinaberry
chincherinchee
Chinese lantern
chionodoxa
chives
choisya
chokeberry
cholla
Christmas cactus
Christmas rose
chrysanthemum
cicely
cinchona
cineraria
cinquefoil
cistus
clarkia
clematis
clianthus
clivia
cloudberry
clove pink
clover
cockscomb
coltsfoot
columbine
comfrey
coneflower
convolvulus
coralberry
coral tree
coreopsis
corncockle
cornflower
corydalis
cotoneaster
cottonweed
cow parsley
cowslip
cranesbill
creeping Jenny
crocus
crosswort
crowfoot
crown imperial
crown of thorns
cuckooflower
cuckoo pint
cupid's dart
cyclamen
cymbidium
cyphel
daffodil
dahlia
daisy
damask rose
dandelion
daphne
datura
day lily
deadly nightshade
delphinium
desert rose
deutzia
devil's bit scabious
dianthus
dill
dittany
dock
dogbane
dog rose
dog's mercury
dog violet
dropwort
duckweed
Dutchman's breeches
echinacea
edelweiss
eglantine
elder
epiphyllum
escallonia
eschscholzia
eucryphia
evening primrose
eyebright
felwort
feverfew
figwort
firethorn
flax
fleabane
flixweed
fluellen
forget-me-not
forsythia
foxglove
frangipani
fraxinella
freesia
fritillary
fuchsia
fumitory
furze
gaillardia
gardenia
gazania
geebung
genista
gentian
geranium
gerbera
gillyflower
gladdon
gladiolus
globeflower
globe thistle
glory-of-the-snow
gloxinia
goat's beard
godetia
golden rod
goldilocks
gorse
grape hyacinth
grass of Parnassus
gromwell
groundsel
guelder rose
gypsophila
gypsywort
harebell
hare's-foot
hawkbit
hawksbeard
hawkweed
hawthorn
heartsease
heather
hebe
helenium
helianthemum
helianthus
heliconia
heliotrope
hellebore
helleborine
hemlock
hemp agrimony
hepatica
herb Christopher
herb Paris
herb Robert
heuchera
hibiscus
hobblebush
hogweed
holly
hollyhock
honesty
honeysuckle
honeywort
hop
hosta
Hottentot fig
hound's tongue
houseleek
hoya
hyacinth
hydrangea
ice plant
Indian pipe
iris
ixia
jacaranda
Jack-by-the-hedge
Jacob's ladder
japonica
jasmine
jonquil
juneberry
Kaffir lily
kalanchoe
kalmia
kangaroo paw
karo
kayakeet
kerria
kidney vetch
kingcup
knapweed
knotgrass
kudzu
laburnum
lady's bedstraw
lady's finger
lady's mantle
lady's slipper
lady's smock
lady's tresses
larkspur
laurustinus
lavatera
lavender
lemon balm
leopard lily
lilac
lily
lily of the valley
lobelia
London pride
loosestrife
loranthus
lords and ladies
lotus
lovage
love-in-a-mist
love-in-idleness
love-lies-bleeding
lungwort
lupin
madonna lily
magnolia
mahonia
mallow
malope
mandrake
marguerite
marigold
mariposa tulip
marsh marigold
marshwort
marvel of Peru
may
mayapple
mayflower
mayweed
meadow rue
meadow saffron
meadowsweet
Michaelmas daisy
mignonette
milfoil
milkwort
mimosa
mint
mistletoe
mock orange
moly
monkey flower
monkshood
montbretia
moonflower
morning glory
moschatel
motherwort
mullein
musk rose
myrtle
narcissus
nasturtium
nemesia
nettle
nicotiana
nigella
night-scented stock
nightshade
nopal
num-num
ocotillo
old man's beard
oleander
orchid
organ pipe cactus
orpine
ox-eye daisy
oxlip
ox tongue
oyster plant
paloverde
pansy
Parma violet
parsley
pasque flower
passion flower
paulownia
pelargonium
pennyroyal
penstemon
peony
peppermint
periwinkle
petunia
peyote
phacelia
pheasant's eye
phlox
pieris
pimpernel
pincushion
pinesap
pink
pitcher plant
plantain
plumbago
poinsettia
pokeweed
polyanthus
poppy
potentilla
prickly pear
prickly poppy
primrose
primula
privet
protea
pulsatilla
purslane
pyracantha
pyrethrum
Queen Anne's lace
rabbitbrush
rafflesia
ragged robin
ragweed
ragwort
rampion
ramsons
rape
red-hot poker
red rattle
restharrow
rhododendron
rhodora
rock rose
rose
rosebay willowherb
rose of Sharon
rudbeckia
rugosa
safflower
saffron crocus
saguaro
sainfoin
St John's wort
St Patrick's cabbage
salal
salpiglossis
salvia
samphire
sandwort
sarcococca
sasanqua
saw-wort
saxifrage
scabious
scarlet pimpernel
schizanthus
scilla
sea holly
sedum
shamrock
sheep's-bit
shepherd's needle
shooting star
shrimp plant
silverberry
silversword
skimmia
skullcap
skyflower
slipperwort
snakeroot
snapdragon
sneezeweed
snowdrop
snowflake
snow-in-summer
soapwort
soldanella
Solomon's seal
sorrel
sowbread
sowthistle
Spanish bayonet
sparaxis
spatterdock
speedwell
spider flower
spider plant
spiderwort
spignel
spikenard
spiraea
spurge
spurrey
squill

stapelia
star of Bethlehem
starwort
stephanotis
stitchwort
stock
stonecrop
storax
storksbill
strawflower
streptocarpus
sundrops
sunflower
sweetbriar
sweet cicely
sweet pea
sweet rocket
sweet sultan
sweet william
tansy
tea rose
teasel
thistle
thorn apple
thrift
tiger lily
toadflax
tormentil
touch-me-not
tradescantia
Transvaal daisy
traveller's joy
trefoil
trillium
tuberose
tulip
turnsole
turtle-grass
turtlehead
twayblade
valerian
velvetleaf
Venus flytrap
verbena
veronica
vervain
vetch
viburnum
violet
viper's bugloss
wallflower
waratah
water lily
water violet
weigela
willowherb
wintergreen
winter jasmine
wintersweet
wisteria/wistaria
witch hazel
wolfsbane
wood anemone
wood avens
woodruff
wood sage
wood sorrel
woody nightshade
wormwood
yarrow
yellow archangel
yellow rattle
yellow-wort
yerba buena
yucca
yulan
zinnia

Flower Parts

androecium
anther
calyx
capitulum
carpel
carpophore
catkin
corolla
corymb
cyathium
cyme
dichasium
filament
floret
glume
gynoecium
hypanthium
involucel
involucre
lemma
lip
monochasium
nectary
nucellus
ovary
ovule
palea
panicle
pedicel
peduncle
perianth
petal
pistil
placenta
pollen
pollen grain
pollinium
raceme
rachis
receptacle
sepal
spadix
spathe
spike
spikelet
spur
stamen
stigma
style
tassel
tepal
torus
umbel
whorl

Food

See **Beans, Pulses, and Peas Biscuits Bread and Bread Rolls Cakes, Puddings, and Desserts Cereal Crops Cheeses Dietary Habits Fish Fruit Fungi, Mushrooms, and Toadstools Herbs Meals Meat Nuts Pasta Pies Sauces and Dips Sausages Soups Spices Stews Sugars Sweets and Confectionery Vegetables Vitamins**

Footwear
Shoes and Boots

alpargatas
ankle boots
Arctics
babouches
ballet shoes
balmorals
beetle-crushers
Birkenstocks (*trademark*)
bluchers
bootees
bovver boots
brogans
brogues
brothel creepers
buckskins
buskins
carpet slippers
chappals
Chelsea boots
cleats
clogs
combat boots
court shoes
cowboy boots
crepe-soled shoes
Cuban heels
daps
deck shoes
Derbies
desert boots
Dr Martens (DMs) (*trademark*)
elevator shoes
espadrilles
field boots
flip-flops
galoshes
ghillies
gumboots
half-boots
Hessian boots
high-lows
high-tops
hobnail boots
huaraches
jackboots
jandals (*NZ trademark*)
jelly shoes
kitten heels
kletterschuhe
lace-ups
loafers
Mary Janes
moccasins
moon boots
mukluks
mules
napoleons
opankas
overboots
overshoes
Oxfords
pattens
peep-toes
penny loafers
platforms
plimsolls
pumps
rubbers
sabots
saddle shoes
sandals
shoepacks
slingbacks
slip-ons
slippers
sneakers
snow boots
snowshoes
spikes
step-ins
stilettos
stogies
tap shoes
tennis shoe
thongs
top boots
track shoes
trainers
Turkish slippers
waders
walking boots/shoes
wedges
wedgies
wellington boots
winkle-pickers
zoris

Forests
Types of Forest and Wood

ancient forest
boreal forest
broadleaf forest
chaparral
cloud forest
coniferous forest
copse
deciduous forest
dry tropical forest
evergreen forest
gallery forest
garigue
high forest
jungle
maquis
Mediterranean scrub
mixed forest
monsoon forest
montane rainforest
rainforest
scrub
selva
subtropical forest
taiga
temperate rainforest
terai
thorn forest
tropical deciduous forest
tropical rainforest

Fossils

See also **Dinosaurs Humans**

acanthodian
aepyornis
amber
ammonite
ammonoid
anoplothere
anthracothere
archaeopteryx
archelon
arsinoitherium
arthrodire
baluchitherium
barylambda
belemnite
bioclast
brontops
brontothere
caenolestid
calamite
cave bear
cave lion
cephalaspid
ceratite
chalicothere
condylarth
conodont
coprolite
corallite
creodont
cryptoclidus
cygnognathus
cynodont
deinotherium
diatryma
dicynodont
dimetrodon
dimorphodon
dinocephalian
dinornis
diprotodon
dire wolf
Dryopithecus
elasmosaur
elephant bird
eohippus
eryops
eurypterid
giant elk
glyptodont
gomphotherium
goniatite
graptolite
ground sloth
gryphaea
hesperornis
hyracotherium
ichthyornis
ichthyosaur
ichthyostega
labyrinthodont
lepidodendron
lepidosaur
lepospondyl
litoptern
lycaenops
mammoth
mastodon
megaloceros
megatherium
merychippus
mesohippus
mesosaur
miacid
microfossil
microsaur
moeritherium
morganucodon
moropus
mosasaur
moschops
multituberculate
mylodon
nannofossil
nothosaur
notoungulate
nummulite
Nutcracker man
orthocone
osteostracan
ostracoderm
pantodont
pareiasaur
pelycosaur
phororhacos
phytosaur
placoderm
placodont
plesiadapid
plesiosaur
pliopithecus
pliosaur
propliopithecus
psilophyton
pteranodon
pteridosperm
pterodactyl
pterosaur
quetzalcoatlus
rudist
rugose coral
sabretooth
seymouriamorph
sivatherium
smilodon
stereospondyl
stigmaria
stone-lily
stromatolite
symmetrodont
synapsid
taeniodont
temnospondyl
thecodont
therapsid
thylacosmilus
tinoceratid
titanothere
toxodont
trilobite
uintatherium
woolly mammoth
woolly rhinoceros
zeuglodont

Fowl
Breeds of Fowl

chickens

Ancona
Andalusian
Australorp
Bantam
Booted
Brahmaputra
Bresse
Campine
Cochin
Crèvecour
Croad Langshan
Dorking
Faverolle
Frizzles
Hamburg
Houdan
Indian Game
Ixworth
Jersey Giant
Jubilee Indian Game
La Fleche
Lakenfelder
Leghorn

Malay
Malines
Marans
Marsh Daisy
Minorca
Modern Game
Modern Langshan
Nankin
New Hampshire Red
Norfolk Grey
North Holland Blue
Old English Game
Old English Pheasant Fowl
Orloff
Orpington
Phoenix
Plymouth Rock
Poland
Redcap
Rhode Island Red
Rosecomb
Rumpless
Scots Dumpy
Scots Grey
Sebright
Sicilian Buttercup
Silkie
Spanish
Sultan
Sumatra Game
Sussex
Transylvanian Naked Necks
Welsummer
Wyandotte
Yokohama

ducks

Aylesbury
Black East Indian
Cayuga
Crested
Indian Runner
Khaki Campbell
Magpie
Muscovy
Orpington
Rouen
Welsh Harlequin
Whalesbury

geese

Brecon Buff
Chinese
Embden
Pilgrim
Roman
Sebastopol
Toulouse

guineafowl

Lavender
Pearl Grey
White

turkeys

Black Norfolk
Bourbon Red
Broad-Breasted Bronze
Broad-Breasted White
Cambridge Bronze
Mammoth Bronze
Narragansett
Nicholas
White Austrian
White Holland

Foxes

Arctic fox
Azara's fox
bat-eared fox
Blanford's fox
blue fox
Colpeo fox
corsac fox
crab-eating fox
cross fox
fennec
grey fox
hoary fox
kit fox
pale fox
red fox
Samson fox
sand fox
silver fox
swift fox
zorro

Fractures of Human Bones

Colles' fracture
comminuted fracture
compound fracture
greenstick fracture
impacted fracture
march fracture
multiple fracture
open fracture
Pott's fracture
simple fracture
spiral fracture
stress fracture

Friars

See **Christian Religious Orders**

Frogs

See **Amphibians**

Fruit

Edible Fruits

ackee
alligator pear
ananas
apple
apricot
Asian pear
avocado
azarole
babaco
bael
bakeapple
banana
beach plum
bilberry
blackberry
blackcurrant
blood orange
blueberry
boysenberry
breadfruit
bullace
cantaloupe
Cape gooseberry
carambola
cashew apple
chayote
checkerberry
cherimoya
cherry
cherry plum
Chinese gooseberry
citron
clementine
cloudberry
coconut
Costard
cowberry
crab apple
cranberry
crowberry
currant
custard apple
damson
date
dewberry
durian
elderberry
feijoa
fig
galia melon
geebung
genip
genipap
gooseberry
gourd
granadilla
grape
grapefruit
greengage
guava
hackberry
honeydew melon
huckleberry
jaboticaba
jackfruit
jamun
jujube
juneberry
kaki
kiwi fruit
kumquat
lemon
lime
lingonberry
loganberry
longan
loquat
lychee
mammee
mandarin
mango
mangosteen
manzanilla
maypop
medlar
melon
minneola
mombin
mulberry
muscat
musk melon
myrobalan
naseberry
nashi
navel orange
nectarine
Ogen melon
olive
orange
ortanique
papaya
partridgeberry
passion fruit
pawpaw
peach
pear
persimmon
physalis
pineapple
pippin
pitahaya
plantain
plum
pomegranate
pomelo
prickly pear
pumpkin
quandong
quince
rambutan
raspberry
redcurrant
roseapple
salmonberry
sapodilla
satsuma
sea grape
serviceberry
sharon fruit
sloe
sorb
soursop
star apple
starfruit
strawberry
sugar apple
sweetsop
tamarillo
tamarind
tangelo
tangerine
tayberry
thimbleberry
tomatillo
tomato
Ugli fruit (*trademark*)
veitchberry
Victoria plum
watermelon
white currant
whortleberry
wineberry
youngberry

Fuels

See **Energy and Fuels**

Fungi, Mushrooms, and Toadstools

See also **Poisonous Plants and Fungi**

agaric
amethyst deceiver
anise cap
armillaria
artist's fungus
beefsteak fungus
bird's-nest fungus
black bulgar
blewit
blusher
bolete
boletus
bonnet
bootlace fungus
bracket fungus
brain fungus
brown hay cap
brown roll rim
butter cap
button mushroom
Caesar's mushroom
cage fungus
candle snuff fungus
cauliflower fungus
cep
champignon
chanterelle
charcoal burner
chicken of the woods
club foot
coral fungus
coral spot
cramp balls
cup fungus
dead man's fingers
death cap
destroying angel
dryad's saddle
ear pick fungus
earth ball
earth fan
earthstar
elf cup
ergot
fairies' bonnets
fairy ring fungus
false chanterelle
false morel
field mushroom
fly agaric
funnel cap
ghost fungus
giant puffball
grisette
hedgehog fungus
herald of the winter
honey fungus
horn of plenty
horsehair toadstool
horse mushroom
ink cap
jelly babies
jelly fungus
jelly tongue
Jew's ear
King Alfred's cakes
lawyer's wig mushroom
liberty cap
lorchel
meadow mushroom
milk cap
miller
morel
mousseron
old man of the woods
oyster mushroom
panther cap
parasol mushroom
parrot toadstool
penny bun
peppery bolete
plums and custard
poached egg fungus
poison pie
polypore
porcelain fungus
porcini
portobello
prince
puffball
reishi
russet shank
russula
saffron milk cap
St Anthony's fire
St George's mushroom
scarlet elf cup
scarlet hood
shaggy ink cap
shaggy parasol
shiitake
sickener
slimy beech cap
slippery jack
spike cap
stag's-horn fungus
stinkhorn
stinking parasol
straw mushroom
sulphur tuft
tartufo
tawny grisette
tinder fungus
tough shank
truffle
tuckahoe
velvet shank
verdigris agaric
wax cap
weeping widow
white truffle
witches' butter
wood blewit
wood mushroom
wood woolly foot
yellow stainer

Furniture

See **Beds Chairs and Stools Cupboards and Cabinets Tables and Desks**

Furniture Types and Styles

Bauhaus
Biedermeier
Cape Dutch
Chippendale
Empire
Gothic Revival
Hepplewhite
Jacobean
Louis Quatorze
Louis Quinze
Louis Seize
Louis Treize
Queen Anne
Regency
reproduction
Scandinavian
Shaker
Sheraton

Games

See also **Ball Games Board Games Card Games Sports**

Aunt Sally
bagatelle
bingo
Botticelli
British bulldog
bumble-puppy
charades
chicken
chuck-a-luck
computer game
consequences
crambo
craps
crown and anchor
darts
deck quoits
deck tennis
diabolo
dice
dodgeball
dominoes
dreidel
ducks and drakes
dumb crambo
dungeons and dragons
fan-tan
fantasy football
fivestones
forfeits
frisbee (*trademark*)
hazard
housey-housey
jacks
jackstraws
jukskei
kabaddi
keno
liar dice
mah-jong
matador
MUD
mumblety-peg
nim
pachinko
Pac-Man (*trademark*)
paintball
panel game
parlour game
pinball
pitch-and-toss
poker dice
pool
quoits
roulette
round game
shove-halfpenny
shovelboard
sic bo
spillikins
spin the bottle
Subbuteo (*trademark*)
swy
table football
thimblerig
tiddlywinks
tipcat
trapball
treasure hunt
Trivial Pursuit (*trademark*)
tug of war
twenty questions
two-up

Games (Children's)

battleships
blind man's buff
catch
cat's cradle
Chinese whispers
conkers
cops and robbers
follow-my-leader
grandmother's footsteps
hangman
hide-and-seek
hoopla
hopscotch
hunt the slipper
I spy
it
King of the Castle
leapfrog
lotto
marbles
murder in the dark
musical bumps
musical chairs
noughts and crosses
pass the parcel
pat-a-cake
peekaboo
peever
piggy in the middle
Poohsticks
postman's knock
prisoner's base
ring-a-ring o' roses
sardines
Simon Says
statues
tag
taw
tic-tac-toe/tick-tack-toe
tig
tok-tokkie

Gardens
Types of Garden

allotment
alpine garden
arboretum
beer garden
bog garden
botanic/botanical garden
bottle garden
cottage garden
flower garden
herb garden
Italian garden
Japanese garden
kaleyard
kitchen garden
knot garden
market garden
physic garden
potager
rockery
rock garden
roof garden
rosarium
rose garden
shrubbery
sunken garden
tea garden
vegetable garden
walled garden
water garden
wild garden
winter garden
xeriscape

Gases

See also **Poisonous Substances and Gases**

acetylene
afterdamp
ammonia
argon
arsine
biogas
blister gas
butadiene
butane
butene
Calor gas (*trademark*)
carbon dioxide
carbon monoxide
chlorine
chlorofluorocarbon (CFC)
coal gas
compressed natural gas (CNG)
CS gas
cyanogen
cyclopropane
diazomethane
diborane
ethane
ethylene
fluorine
formaldehyde
greenhouse gas
halon
helium
hydrogen
isobutane
ketene
krypton
laughing gas
lewisite
liquefied natural gas (LNG)
liquefied petroleum gas (LPG)
marsh gas
methane
mustard gas
natural gas
neon
nerve gas
nitrogen
nitrogen dioxide
nitrous oxide
oil gas
oxygen
ozone
phosgene
phosphine
producer gas
propane
propylene
radon
sarin
silane
soman
steam
sulphur dioxide
tabun
tail gas
tear gas
tetrafluoroethylene
town gas
vinyl chloride
water gas
xenon

Geese

See **Fowl**

Gems

See also **Minerals Rocks**

agate
alexandrite
almandine
amber
amethyst
aquamarine
balas ruby
beryl
bloodstone
cairngorm
carbuncle
carnelian
cat's-eye
chalcedony
chrysolite
chrysoprase
corundum
diamond
emerald
fire opal
garnet
girasol
greenstone
jacinth
jade
jasper
lapis lazuli
marcasite
moonstone
morganite
moss agate
onyx
opal
pyrope
rhodolite
ruby
sapphire
sardonyx
smoky quartz
spessartine
spiderweb
sunstone
tanzanite
topaz
tourmaline
turquoise
uvarovite
zircon

Geography
Branches of Geography

biogeography
cartography
climatology
cultural geography
demography
economic geography
geology
geomorphology
geopolitics
glaciology
historical geography
human geography
hydrology
hypsography
meteorology
oceanography
oceanology
orography
physical geography
political geography
seismology
social geography
topography
volcanology

Geological Ages

Archaean/Azoic period
Cambrian period
Carboniferous period
Cenozoic era
Cretaceous period
Devonian period
Eocene epoch
Holocene epoch
Jurassic period
Mesozoic era
Miocene epoch
Oligocene epoch
Ordovician period
Palaeocene epoch
Palaeozoic era
Permian period
Phanerozoic aeon
Pleistocene epoch
Pliocene epoch
Precambrian era
Proterozoic aeon
Quaternary period
Silurian period
Tertiary period
Triassic period

Giants

Antaeus
Atlas
Blunderbore
Briareus
Cyclops
Enceladus
Fafner
Fasolt
Gargantua
Gog
Goliath
Jotun
King Kong
Magog
Mimas
Orion
Pantagruel
Polyphemus
Ymir

Glands
Human Glands

adrenal gland
apocrine gland
Bartholin's gland
Brunner's gland
buccal gland
corpus luteum
Cowper's gland
ductless gland
eccrine gland
endocrine gland
exocrine gland
gastric gland
islets of Langerhans
lacrimal gland
Lieberkühn's gland
liver
mammary gland
meibomian gland
ovary
pancreas
parathyroid gland
parotid gland
pineal gland
pituitary gland
preputial gland
prostate gland
salivary gland
sebaceous gland
sublingual gland
submandibular/ submaxillary gland
sweat gland
testis
thyroid gland

Glass
Types of Glass

aventurine
blown glass
borosilicate
bottle glass
bulletproof glass
cameo glass
crown glass
crystal
cullet
cut glass
favrile glass
fibreglass
flint glass
float glass
frosted glass
ground glass
hobnail
lace glass
laminated glass
latticinio
lead crystal
lead glass
milk glass
millefiori
mirror glass
opal glass
opaline
optical glass
peach-blow
plate glass
Pyrex (*trademark*)
quartz glass
ruby glass
safety glass
sheet glass
smalt
stained glass
toughened glass
triplex (*trademark*)
Waterford glass

Glasses

bifocals
cheaters
contact lenses
dark glasses
goggles
granny glasses
horn-rimmed glasses
lorgnette(s)
monocle
pince-nez
Polaroids (*trademark*)
Raybans (*trademark*)
reading glasses
safety glasses
shades
shooting glasses
single-vision glasses
sunglasses
sunnies
trifocals
varifocals

Goats

breeds

Anglo-Nubian
Angora
Apulian
Bagot
Chamois Coloured
Dutch White
French Alpine
Golden Guernsey
Grisons Striped
Kashmiri
Murcian
Nubian
Saanen
Somali
Soviet Mohair
Syrian Mountain
Telemark
Toggenburg
Valais Blackneck

wild goats

bezoar
ibex
markhor
Spanish ibex
tahr
tur

goat-antelopes

chamois
goral
mountain goat
musk ox
serow
takin

Golf Clubs

brassie
cleek
driver
driving iron
iron
jigger
lofter
mashie
midiron
niblick
putter
sand iron
sand wedge
spoon
wedge
wood

Goose

See **Fowl**

Governments
Types and Systems of Government

See also **Political Philosophies and Systems**

autocracy	by an absolute ruler
bureaucracy	by state officials
constitutionalism	according to a constitution
democracy	by elected representatives
despotism	by a despot
diarchy	by two independent authorities
dictatorship	by a dictator
fascism	by a right-wing, nationalistic regime
federalism	according to federal principles
gynarchy	by women
heptarchy	by seven rulers
hierocracy	by priests
imperialism	by an emperor or empire
meritocracy	by people of proven ability
monarchy	by a monarch
monocracy	by one person
ochlocracy	by the populace or mob
octarchy	by eight people
oligarchy	by a small group of people
plutocracy	by the rich
stratocracy	by the army
synarchy	by two or more people or groups
theocracy	by priests representing a deity
timocracy	by property owners
totalitarianism	by an absolute ruler or regime
tyranny	by a tyrant

Grain

See **Cereal Crops**

Grapes

See **Wine and Grape Varieties**

Grasses, Sedges, and Rushes

bamboo
barley
beach grass
beard grass
bent
Bermuda grass
bluegrass
bristle grass
brome
broomcorn
buffalo grass
bulrush
bunch grass
button grass
canary grass
carex
cat's-tail grass
cheat grass
China grass
chufa
clubrush
cocksfoot
cogon
cordgrass
corn
cotton grass
couch grass
crabgrass
cutgrass
cutting grass
danthonia
darnel
deergrass
dogstail
dropseed
durra
elephant grass
esparto
feather grass
fescue
finger grass
fiorin
flowering rush
fog
foxtail
gama grass
hair grass
hare's-tail grass
Indian corn
Job's tears
kangaroo grass
kikuyu grass
lemon grass
lyme grass
maize
marram grass
meadow fescue
meadow grass
melick
millet
milo
moor grass
oat
oat grass
orchard grass
palmarosa
pampas grass
panic grass
papyrus
paspalum
pearl millet
quack grass
quaking grass
quitch grass
razor glass
redtop
reed
reed grass
reed mace
rice
rooigras
rush
rye
ryegrass
sawgrass
sedge
sheep's fescue
small-reed
sorghum
sour grass
spartina
spear grass
spelt
spinifex
squirrel-tail grass

star grass
sugar cane
switchgrass
sword grass
teff
teosinte
timothy grass
tussock grass
twitch grass
umbrella plant
vernal grass
wheat
wild oat
wild rice
wire grass
witch grass
woodrush
Yorkshire fog
zoysia

Groups

See **Collective Names for Animals**

Guns

air gun/pistol/rifle
AK-47
anti-aircraft gun
anti-tank gun
Armalite (*trademark*)
artillery
assault gun
assault rifle
automatic
bazooka
Big Bertha
blunderbuss
Bofors gun
breech-loader
Bren (gun)
Brown Bess
Browning
burp gun
cannon
carbine
carronade
chain gun
chassepot
Colt (*trademark*)
derringer
double-barrelled gun
duelling pistol
elephant gun
Enfield rifle
express rifle
falconet
field gun
firelock
flintlock
forty-five
fowling piece
fusil
Garand (rifle)
Gatling (gun)
hackbut
handgun
harpoon gun
harquebus/arquebus
horse pistol
Hotchkiss (gun)
howitzer
Kalashnikov
Lee–Enfield (rifle)
Lewis gun
Luger (*US trademark*)
M-1 (rifle/carbine)
M-16 (rifle)
M-60 (machine gun)
machine gun
magazine rifle
matchlock
Mauser (*trademark*)
Maxim gun
mine-thrower
mortar
musket
muzzle-loader
Oerlikon (*trademark*)
Owen (gun)
Parabellum (*trademark*)
pepperbox
pistol
pistolet
pom-pom
pump-action shotgun
pump gun
rail gun
repeating rifle
revolver
rifle
Saturday night special
sawn-off shotgun
Schmeisser
self-loader
self-loading rifle (SLR)
semi-automatic shotgun
sidearm
siege gun
six-shooter
small arms
Smith & Wesson (*trademark*)
smooth-bore
Springfield (rifle)
starting pistol
Sten gun
Steyr
sub-machine gun
swivel-gun
thirty-eight
Thompson sub-machine gun
tommy gun
trench mortar
Uzi
Very pistol
Vickers (gun)
Walther
Webley (*trademark*)
Winchester (*trademark*)
zip gun

Gymnastics Events and Disciplines

artistic gymnastics
asymmetric bars
beam
floor exercises
high bar
horse vault
parallel bars
pommel horse
rhythmic gymnastics
rings
side horse vault
sports acrobatics
sports aerobics
trampolining
tumbling

Hairstyles

Afro
bangs
beehive
big hair
bob
body wave
bouffant
braids
bun
bunches
buzz cut
chignon
combover
cornrows
crew cut
crop
dreadlocks *or* dreads
elf-locks
Eton crop
feathercut
flat-top
French plait
French pleat/roll
fringe
marcel wave
Mohican/Mohawk
mullet
number one, two, etc.
pageboy
perm/permanent
pigtail
plait
pompadour
ponytail
quiff
rat's tails
razor cut
ringlets
shag
shingle
short back and sides
tonsure
topknot
whiffle cut
widow's peak

Hammers

ball peen/pein hammer
beetle
claw hammer
cross peen/pein
gavel
jackhammer
Kango (*trademark*)
mallet
plexor
pneumatic hammer
priest
sledge(hammer)
steam hammer
tenderizer
tilt hammer
trip hammer

Hares

See **Rabbits and Hares**

Harness

Parts of a Horse's Harness or Tack

backband
bearing rein
bellyband
bit
blinders
blinkers
breastband
breast collar
breastplate
breeching
bridle
bridoon
cavesson
cheekpiece
cinch
collar
crupper
curb bit
double bit
double bridle
eggbutt snaffle
frontlet
girth
hackamore
halter
hames
head collar
headstall
martingale
noseband
pelham
reins
saddle
saddlepad
snaffle (bit)
surcingle
throatlatch
traces
Weymouth bit

Harps

See **Stringed Instruments**

Hats and Other Headgear

agal
aigrette
Akubra (*trademark*)
Alice band
amice
babushka
balaclava
balmoral
bandeau
baseball cap
beanie
bearskin
beaver hat
beret
billycock
biretta
boater
bobble hat
bonnet
Borsalino
bowler hat
bucket hat
busby
calash
cap
caubeen
caul
chapeau
chapeau-bras
chaplet
cheese-cutter cap
circlet
cloche
cloth cap
cocked hat
cockscomb
coif
coolie hat
coonskin hat
coronal
coronet
cowl
crash helmet
crown
deerstalker
derby
diadem
doek
Dolly Varden hat
do-rag
dunce's cap
Dutch cap
earmuffs
fedora
fez
fillet
flat cap
forage cap
frontlet
garland
garrison cap
gibus hat
gimme cap
glengarry
hairband
hairnet
hard hat
headband
headscarf
headtie
helmet
high hat
hijab
homburg
hood
jester's cap
jockey cap
Juliet cap
Kangol (*trademark*)
keffiyeh
kepi
kippa
leghorn hat
lum hat
mantilla
mitre
mob cap
mortar board
mutch
nightcap
opera hat
pagri
panama
peaked cap
petasus
Phrygian bonnet
picture hat
pillbox
pixie hat
poke bonnet
pork-pie hat
puggaree
rebozo
sailor hat
shako
shapka
shemagh
shovel hat
skimmer
skullcap
slouch hat
snap-brim hat
snood
sola topi
sombrero
sou'wester
square
Stetson (*US trademark*)
stocking cap
stovepipe hat
sun bonnet
sun hat
sun helmet
taenia
taj
tam
tammy
tam-o'-shanter
tarboosh
ten-gallon hat
terai
tiara
tignon
top hat
topi
topper
toque
tricorne
trilby
triple crown
tuque
turban
veil
velour
watch cap
wideawake
wimple
wreath
yarmulke
zucchetto

Heart
Parts of the Heart

aortic valve
atrium
epicardium
mitral valve
myocardium
pericardium
pulmonary artery
pulmonary vein
semilunar valve
sino-atrial node
tricuspid valve
upper chamber
vena cava
ventricle
ventricular septum

Herbs
Culinary Herbs

See also **Spices**

angelica
anise
basil
bay leaf
bergamot
borage
camomile
chervil
chicory
chives
cilantro
clary
comfrey
coriander
dandelion greens
dill
dittany
dong quai
fennel
flat-leaf/flat-leaved parsley
hyssop
lavender
lemon balm
lemon grass
lemon mint
lovage
marjoram
mint
oregano
parsley
peppermint
rosemary
rue
saffron
sage
savory
sorrel
spearmint
sweet balm
sweet cicely
tarragon
thyme
vervain
yerba buena

Holidays

See **Festivals**

Holy Books

See **Bible** **Sacred Texts and Holy Books**

Homes

adobe
A-frame
apartment
back-to-back
barracks
bastide
bedsit
bedsitter
bed-sitting room
bi-level
black house
blockhouse
bungalow
cabin
caravan
casita
castle
chalet
chateau
condo
condominium
cottage
country house
crannog
dacha
deanery
detached house
donga
duplex
farmhouse
fibro
flat
flatlet
floatel
frame house
gîte
grange
hacienda
hermitage
hogan
homestead
hostel
hotel
house
houseboat
hovel
hut
igloo
jhuggi
lake dwelling
lodge
log cabin
longhouse
maisonette
manoir
manor
manse
mansion
messuage
mobile home
motel
mud hut
palace
parsonage
penthouse
pied-à-terre
pile dwelling
prefab
presbytery
priory
ranch (house)
rancher
rath
rectory
rest home
rondavel
semi-detached house
shack
shanty
side split
single end
skerm
split
stately home
stilted house
studio flat
tenement
tent
tepee
terrace
terraced house
terramare
town house
trailer
tree house
tupik
two-up two-down
vicarage
villa
whare
wigwam
yurt

Homes for Animals

animal	home
ant	anthill
badger	sett/earth
bear	den
beaver	lodge
bee	beehive/apiary
bird	nest/aviary
cow	byre
dog	kennel
dove	dovecote
eagle	eyrie
fish	aquarium
fox	earth/hole/burrow
hare	form
hen	coop
horse	stable
lion	den
otter	holt
pig	sty
rabbit	burrow/warren
sheep	fold/pen
squirrel	drey
wasp	nest/vespiary

Hormones

abscisic acid
adrenalin
adrenocorticotrophic hormone (ACTH)
aldosterone
anabolic steroid
androgen
androstenedione
androsterone
antidiuretic hormone (ADH)
auxin
bovine growth hormone (BGH)
bovine somatotrophin (BST)
calcitonin
cholecystokinin (CCK)
chorionic gonadotrophin
corticosteroid
corticosterone
cortisone
deoxycorticosterone
dihydrotestosterone (DHT)
ecdysone
endorphin
erythropoietin
follicle-stimulating hormone (FSH)
gastrin
gibberellin
glucagon
gonadotrophin
growth hormone
human chorionic gonadotrophin (HCG)
human growth hormone (HGH)
hydrocortisone
inhibin
insulin
lipotropin
luteinizing hormone (LH)
melanocyte-stimulating hormone
melatonin
mifepristone
neurohormone
noradrenaline
oestradiol
oestriol
oestrogen
oestrone
oxytocin
pancreozymin
parathormone
prednisolone
progesterone
progestogen
prolactin
relaxin
secretin
somatomedin
somatostatin
somatotrophin
stilboestrol
sympathin
testosterone
thromboxane
thyroid-stimulating hormone (TSH)
thyrotropin
thyrotropin-releasing hormone (TRH)
thyroxine
triiodothyronine
vasopressin

Horse
Points of a Horse

cannon bone
cheek
chest
chestnut
chin groove
coffin bone
coronet
crest
croup
dock
elbow
ergot
feathers
fetlock
fetlock joint
flank
forearm
forelock
frog
gaskin
gullet
heel
hindquarters
hock
hoof
knee
loin
mane
navicular bone
pastern
pedal bone
point of hip
point of shoulder
poll
ribs
shank
sheath
shoulder
splint bone
stifle
tail
tendon
windpipe
withers

Horse Colours

albino
bay
blue roan
chestnut
dapple grey
dun
grey
iron grey
liver chestnut
piebald
pinto
roan
skewbald
sorrel
strawberry roan

Horse Family

ass
burro
cuddy
donkey
hinny
horse
hyracotherium
jackass
kiang
kulan
mule
onager
quagga
zebra

Horse Riding

See **Equestrian Sports**

Horses and Ponies

American Saddle Horse
Andalusian
Anglo-Arab
Appaloosa
Arab
Barb
Basuto pony
Breton
brumby
Camargue
Caspian
Cleveland Bay
Clydesdale
Comtois
Conestoga
Connemara pony
criollo
Dales pony
Dartmoor pony
Dutch draught
Dutch warmblood
Exmoor pony
Falabella
Fell pony
Fjord
Friesian
Galiceño
Galloway
Gelderlander
Gotland
Hackney
Haflinger
Hanoverian
Highland pony
Holstein
Huçul
hunter
Iceland pony
Irish draught
Irish hunter
Jutland
Kabardin
Karabakh
Kathiawari
Kazakh
Lipizzaner/ Lippizaner
Lokai
Lundy Island
Mangalarga
Manipur pony
Mérens pony
miniature Shetland
Missouri fox-trotting horse
Morgan
mustang
New Forest pony
Nonius
Noriker
Norwegian racing trotter
Oldenburger
Orlov trotter
palomino
Paso Fino
Percheron
Pinto
Pinzgauer
Plateau Persian
polo pony
pony of the Americas
Przewalski's horse
Quarter Horse
Russ
Russian heavy draught
Russian warmblood
Sable Island
Saddlebred
Salerno
Sandalwood pony
Schleswig
Shetland pony
shire horse
Standardbred
Suffolk Punch
Swedish warmblood
Tartar pony
Tennessee Walking Horse
Tersky
thoroughbred
Timor pony
Trakehner
trotter
Viatka
Waler
warmblood
Welsh cob
Welsh mountain pony
Yorkshire coach horse

extinct horses

hyracotherium *or* eohippus
miohippus
pliohippus
tarpan

Hounds

See **Dogs**

Hours

See **Canonical Hours**

Houses

See **Homes**

Humans

Early Humans

Aegyptopithecus
Australopithecus
Boxgrove man
Cro-Magnon man
Gigantopithecus
Heidelberg man
Homo erectus
Homo habilis
Homo sapiens
Java man
Kabwe man
Lucy
Neanderthal man
Nutcracker man
Paranthropus
Peking man
Pithecanthropus
Proconsul
protohuman
Ramapithecus
Sinanthropus
Zinjanthropus

Illnesses (Physical)

(Illnesses and Conditions)

achondroplasia
acidosis
acne
acromegaly
Addison's disease
agammaglobulinaemia
agranulocytosis
ague
Aids (acquired immune deficiency syndrome)
Aids-related complex (ARC)
ainhum
albuminuria
alopecia
altitude sickness
alveolitis
Alzheimer's disease
amaurosis
amoebiasis
anaemia
ancylostomiasis
anergy
Angelman's syndrome
angina (pectoris)
ankylosing spondylitis
ankylosis
anthrax
anuria
aplastic anaemia
appendicitis
arc eye
arteriosclerosis
arteritis
arthritis
asbestosis
ascariasis
ascites
aspergillosis
asthenia
asthma
ataxia
atheroma
atherosclerosis
athetosis
athlete's foot
avitaminosis
bacteraemia
bacteriuria
balanitis
barber's itch/rash
Barcoo rot
Barcoo sickness
bartholinitis
Bell's palsy
the bends
benign prostatic hyperplasia (BPH)
beriberi
berylliosis
bilharzia
bird fancier's lung
black lung
blackwater fever
blastomycosis
blepharitis
blood poisoning
Bornholm disease
botulism
brain fever
Bright's disease
Broca's aphasia
bronchiolitis
bronchitis
bronchopneumonia
brucellosis
bubonic plague
Buerger's disease
Burkitt's lymphoma
bursitis
byssinosis
cachexia
caecitis
calenture
cancer
candidiasis
canker
carcinogenesis
carcinomatosis
cardiac tamponade
cardiomegaly
cardiomyopathy
carditis
carpal tunnel syndrome (CTS)
cataract
cat scratch fever/ disease
cerebral palsy (CP)
Chagas' disease
chancroid
chickenpox
chikungunya (fever)
chill
Chinese restaurant syndrome
chloracne
chlorosis
cholera
chorea
Christmas disease
chronic fatigue syndrome (CFS)
chronic obstructive pulmonary disease (COPD)
ciguatera
cirrhosis
claw foot
coccidioidomycosis
coeliac disease
cold
colic
colitis
coloboma
common cold
conjunctivitis
consumption
coronary heart disease (CHD)
cor pulmonale
coryza
cough
cowpox
Creutzfeldt–Jakob disease (CJD)
Crohn's disease
croup
cryptococcosis
cryptosporidiosis
Cushing's disease
Cushing's syndrome
cyanosis
cystic fibrosis (CF)
cystitis
decompression sickness
deep-vein thrombosis (DVT)
deficiency disease
dengue (fever)
dermatitis
dermatomycosis
dermatosis
dhobi itch
diabetes
diabetes insipidus
diabetes mellitus
diarrhoea
diphtheria
diverticular disease
diverticulitis
double pneumonia
Down's syndrome
dry eye
Duchenne muscular dystrophy (DMD)
duodenitis
Dupuytren's contracture
dysentery
Ebola (fever/virus)
eclampsia
eczema
elephantiasis
emphysema
empyema
encephalitis
encephalopathy
endocarditis
endometriosis
endometritis
enteritis
enteropathy
epidermolysis
epilepsy
ergotism
erysipelas
erythroblastosis
erythroleukaemia
Ewing's tumour/ sarcoma
falciparum (malaria)
farmer's lung
fascioliasis
fetal alcohol syndrome (FAS)
fever
fibromyalgia
fibrositis
filariasis
flu
fluorosis
flux
food poisoning
fragile X syndrome
frozen shoulder
full-blown Aids
gangrene
gastric flu
gastritis
gastro-enteritis
Gaucher's disease
general paralysis of the insane (GPI)
German measles
giardiasis
gigantism
gingivitis
glandular fever
glaucoma
glomerulonephritis
glue ear
glycaemia
glycosuria
goitre
gonorrhoea
gout
Graves' disease

Guillain–Barré syndrome
Gulf War syndrome
haematemesis
haematuria
haemochromatosis
haemolytic disease of the newborn
haemophilia
Hansen's disease
Hashimoto's disease
hay fever
heat stroke
helminthiasis
hepatitis (A/B/C)
hepatoma
hernia
herpes
herpes simplex
Hirschsprung's disease
histoplasmosis
hives
Hodgkin's disease
hookworm
Horner's syndrome
hospital fever
Huntington's disease
Hurler's syndrome
hyaline membrane disease
hydramnios
hydrocephalus
hydrophobia
hyperglycaemia
hypertension
hyperthyroidism
hypocalcaemia
hypoglycaemia
hypokalaemia
hypomagnesaemia
hypopituitarism
hypothermia
hypothryroidism
hypoxia
ichthyosis
ileitis
impetigo
infantile paralysis
infectious mononucleosis
influenza
insulitis
intertrigo
iodism
iritis
irritable bowel syndrome (IBS)
ischaemia
jaundice
jungle fever
kala-azar
Kaposi's sarcoma (KS)
Kawasaki disease
keratitis
ketonaemia
ketosis
Klinefelter's syndrome
kuru
kwashiorkor
kyphosis
labyrinthitis
lactosuria
Laennec's cirrhosis
laryngitis
Lassa fever
lathyrism
lead poisoning
legionella
legionnaires' disease
leishmaniasis
leprosy
leptospirosis
Lesch–Nyhan syndrome
leukaemia
lichen
lipaemia
lipidosis
listeria
listeriosis
locomotor ataxia
loiasis
lordosis
Lou Gehrig's disease
lues (venerea)
lupus
lupus vulgaris
Lyme disease
lymphadenopathy
lymphangitis
lymphoma
malaria
mal de mer
malignant pustule
marasmus
Marburg disease/virus
Marfan's syndrome
marsh fever
mastitis
mastoiditis
measles
melaena
Ménière's disease
meningitis
meningoencephalitis
methaemoglobinaemia
milk fever
Minamata disease
molluscum contagiosum
mononucleosis
morning sickness
motor neuron disease
mountain sickness
multiple sclerosis (MS)
mumps
muscular dystrophy
myalgic encephalomyelitis (ME)
myasthenia (gravis)
mycetoma
mycosis
myelitis
myelopathy
myocarditis
myopathy
myositis
myotonic dystrophy
myxoedema
nappy rash
narcolepsy
necrotizing fasciitis
neoplasia
nephritis
nephrosis
neurofibromatosis
neuropathy
neurosyphilis
neutropenia
new variant Creutzfeldt–Jakob disease (nvCJD)
non-Hodgkin's lymphoma
non-specific urethritis (NSU)
obstructive jaundice
oedema
oesophagitis
oophoritis
ophthalmia
ophthalmitis
optic neuritis
orchitis
oriental sore
osteoarthritis
osteogenesis imperfecta
osteomyelitis
osteoporosis
otosclerosis
Paget's disease
pancreatitis
pancytopenia
parainfluenza
paratyphoid (fever)
paresis
Parkinson's disease
parotitis
Patau's syndrome
pellagra
pelvic inflammatory disease (PID)
pemphigoid
pemphigus
pericarditis
periostitis
peritonitis
pernicious anaemia
Perthes disease
pertussis
Peyronie's disease
pharyngitis
phenylketonuria (PKU)
phlebitis
phthisis
phycomycosis
Pick's disease
pink disease
pink-eye
pityriasis
plague
pleocytosis
pleurisy
pleuropneumonia
pneumoconiosis
pneumocystitis carinii pneumonia (PCP)
pneumonia
pneumonic plague
pneumonitis
pneumothorax
podagra
poliomyelitis
polycythaemia
polymyositis
polyneuritis
polyposis
Pontiac fever
porphyria
postviral (fatigue) syndrome (PVS)
Prader–Willi syndrome
prickly heat
proctitis
progeria
prostatitis
proteinuria
prurigo
pruritus
psittacosis
psoriasis
puerperal fever
pulmonary emphysema
purpura
pyaemia
pyelitis
pyelonephritis
pyoderma
pyrexia
pyuria
Q fever
quinsy
rabies
radiation sickness
rat-bite fever
Raynaud's disease/ syndrome/ phenomenon
Reiter's syndrome
relapsing fever
repetitive strain injury (RSI)
respiratory distress syndrome (RDS)
retinitis
retinitis pigmentosa
retinopathy
Reye's syndrome
rhabdomyolysis
rheumatic fever
rheumatism
rheumatoid arthritis
rhinitis
rickets
ringworm
river blindness
roseola
roseola infantum
rubella
St Vitus's dance
salmonella
salpingitis
Sanfilippo's syndrome
sarcoid
sarcoidosis
scabies
scarlet fever
schizophrenia
sciatica
scleritis
scleroderma
sclerosing cholangitis
sclerosis
scoliosis
scrofula
scrub typhus
scurvy
seasonal affective disorder (SAD)
sepsis
septicaemia
serositis
serum hepatitis
serum sickness
severe acute respiratory syndrome (SARS)
severe combined immune deficiency (SCID)
sexually transmitted disease (STD)
shingles
sick building syndrome (SBS)
sickle-cell anaemia/ disease
silicosis
sinusitis
Sjögren's syndrome
sleeping sickness
sleepy sickness
smallpox
soft sore
Spanish flu/influenza
spasmophilia
spina bifida
splenitis
spondylosis
sporotrichosis
spotted fever
sprue
status asthmaticus
status epilepticus
steatosis
stenosis
stomatitis
strabismus
strangury
strongyloidiasis
sudden infant death syndrome (SIDS)
sunburn
sunstroke
swamp fever
sweating sickness
sycosis
Sydenham's chorea
synovitis
syphilis
syringomyelia
systemic lupus erythematosus (SLE)
tamponade | cardiac tamponade
tardive dyskinesia
Tay–Sachs disease
tendinitis
tenosynovitis
tetanus
tetany
tetter
thalassaemia
thrombophlebitis
thrombosis
thrush
tick fever
tonsillitis
torticollis
Tourette's syndrome
toxaemia
toxic shock syndrome (TSS)
toxocariasis
toxoplasmosis
tracheitis
trachoma
trench fever
trench foot
trench mouth
trichinosis
trichomoniasis
trigeminal neuralgia
trisomy-21
trypanosomiasis
tuberculosis (TB)
tuberous sclerosis
Turner's syndrome
typhlitis
typhoid (fever)
typhus
undulant fever
uraemia
urethritis
urolithiasis
urticaria
uveitis
vaccinia
vaginismus
vaginitis
vaginosis
valvulitis
variant Creutzfeldt–Jakob disease (vCJD)
varioloid
vasculitis
venereal disease (VD)
vibration white finger
viraemia
vitiligo
von Recklinghausen's disease
von Willebrand's disease/factor
vulvitis
Waldenström's macroglobulinaemia/ disease
Wegener's granulomatosis
Weil's disease
Werdnig–Hoffmann disease
Werner's syndrome
Wernicke's encephalopathy/ syndrome
whooping cough
wool-sorters' disease
wryneck
xeroderma
yaws
yellow fever
Zollinger–Ellison syndrome
zoonosis

Illnesses (Psychological)
(Illnesses and Conditions)

See also **Phobias**

anorexia nervosa
Asperger's syndrome
attention deficit hyperactivity disorder (ADHD)
autism
body dysmorphic disorder
bulimia nervosa
catatonia
clinical depression
combat fatigue
de Clerambault's syndrome
dementia
dysphoria
dysthymia
eating disorder
erotomania
false memory syndrome
gender dysphoria
hebephrenia
hyperactivity
hyperkinesis
hypomania
Korsakoff's syndrome
manic depression
megalomania
multiple-personality disorder
Munchausen's syndrome
Munchausen's syndrome by proxy
obsessive–compulsive disorder
panic disorder
paramnesia
paranoia
paraphilia
pica
post-natal depression
post-traumatic stress disorder (PTSD)
psychosis
schizo-affective disorder
schizophrenia
seasonal affective disorder (SAD)
shell shock

Insects

See also **Butterflies** **Moths**

agrion
alderfly
amazon ant
ambrosia beetle
animated stick
anopheles
ant
ant lion
aphid
Argentine ant
army ant
army worm
asparagus beetle
assassin bug
backswimmer
bark beetle
bat fly
bedbug
bee
bee beetle
bee fly
bee louse
beetle
biscuit beetle
biting midge
black ant
black beetle
blackfly
blister beetle
bloodworm
bloody-nosed beetle
blowfly
bluebottle
body louse
boll weevil
bombardier beetle
booklouse
bookworm
borer
botfly
braconid
bristletail
buffalo gnat
bulb fly
bulldog ant
bumblebee
burying beetle
bush cricket
butterfly
cabbage root fly
cabbageworm
caddis fly
cadelle
camel cricket
cankerworm
carabid
cardinal beetle
carpenter ant
carpenter bee
carpet beetle
carrion beetle
carrot fly
chafer
chalcid wasp
cheese fly
chigger
chinch bug
Christmas beetle
churchyard beetle
cicada
cigarette beetle
click beetle
cluster fly
cockchafer
cockroach
Colorado beetle
conehead
corn borer
corn earworm
cotton-leaf worm
cotton stainer
crab louse
crane fly
cricket
cuckoo bee
cuckoo wasp
curculio
cutworm
daddy-long-legs
damsel bug
damselfly
darkling beetle
darner
darter
death-watch beetle
deer fly
demoiselle
devil's coach-horse
digger wasp
diving beetle
dobsonfly
dor beetle
dragonfly
driver ant
drone fly
drosophila
dung beetle
dung fly
earwig
elm bark beetle
emperor dragonfly
fairy fly
field cricket
fig wasp
fire ant
firebrat
firefly
flea
flea beetle
flesh fly
flour beetle
flower beetle
fly
forest fly
frit fly
froghopper
fruit fly
fungus beetle
furniture beetle
gadfly
gall midge
gall wasp
garden chafer
glow-worm
gnat
gold beetle
goliath beetle
grain borer
grain weevil
grasshopper
greenbottle
greenfly
greenhead
ground beetle
groundhopper
harvester ant
hawker
head louse
Hercules beetle
Hessian fly
hide beetle
honey ant
honeybee
honeypot ant
hornet
horntail
hornworm
horsefly
housefly
hoverfly
ichneumon
Japanese beetle
jewel beetle
June bug
katydid
ked
khapra beetle
kissing bug
lace bug
lacewing
lac insect
ladybird
lantern fly
larder beetle
leaf beetle
leafcutter ant
leafcutter bee
leafhopper
leaf insect
leaf miner
leatherjacket
lightning bug
locust
longhorn beetle
louse
louse fly
mantis
Maori bug
mason bee
mason wasp
May bug
mayfly
meal beetle
mealworm
mealy bug
meat ant
midge
mining bee
minotaur beetle
mole cricket
mopane worm
mosquito
moth
mud dauber
museum beetle
musk beetle
nostril fly
oil beetle
onion fly
paper wasp
pharaoh ant
phylloxera
pill beetle
pinhole borer
pismire
plant hopper
plant louse
pond skater
potato beetle
potter wasp
powder-post beetle
praying mantis
rainfly
raspberry beetle
rat-tailed maggot
rhinoceros beetle
robber fly
root fly
rose chafer
rove beetle
St Mark's fly
sandfly
sand wasp
saucer bug
sawfly
sawyer
scale insect
scarab
scorpion fly
screech beetle
screw worm
sexton beetle
shield bug
silverfish
skin beetle
slave-making ant
snake fly
snipe fly
snow flea
soldier beetle
soldier fly
Spanish fly
spider beetle
spider-hunting wasp
spittlebug
springtail
spruce budworm
squash bug
stable fly
stag beetle
stick insect
stilt bug
stink bug
stonefly
stylops
tarantula hawk
tent caterpillar
termite
thrips
thunderbug
thunderfly
tiger beetle
timberman
tobacco beetle
tortoise beetle
treehopper
tsetse fly
tumblebug
turtle bug
vedelia beetle
velvet ant
warble fly
wart-biter
wasp
wasp beetle
water beetle
water boatman
water cricket
water measurer
water scorpion
water strider
weaver ant
web-spinner
webworm
weevil
weta
whirligig
white ant
whitefly
wireworm
witchetty grub
wood ant
woodwasp
woodworm
woolly bear
yellow jacket

Instruments

See **Brass Instruments** **Keyboard Instruments** **Orchestral Instruments** **Organs** **Percussion Instruments** **Stringed Instruments** **Wind Instruments**

Jackets

See **Coats, Cloaks, and Jackets**

Jazz Genres

acid jazz
Afro-Cuban
avant-garde
barrelhouse
bebop
bop
cool
Dixieland
free jazz
fusion
Harlem
harmolodics
honky-tonk
hot jazz
jazz funk
mainstream
modern jazz
progressive jazz
razzmatazz
rooty-toot
skiffle
swing
third stream
trad jazz
west coast

Jerseys

See **Pullovers**

Jewellery

See also **Gems**

amulet
anklet
armlet
band
bangle
beads
bijou
bracelet
breastpin
brooch
cameo
chain
charm bracelet
choker
circlet
Claddagh ring
clip
cuff link
diadem
dress watch
ear stud
earring
engagement ring
eternity ring
fibula
friendship bracelet
friendship ring
hair slide
hatpin
hei-tiki
kara
keeper
labret
locket
lunula

manilla
marquise
medallion
mourning ring
necklace
necklet
nose ring
nose stud
pavé
pendant
phalera
pin
posy ring
rakhi
ring
rivière
sautoir
scarf ring
seal ring
signet ring
slave bangle
sleeper
stickpin
strand
stud
tiara
tiepin
toe ring
torc
wedding ring
wristlet

Joints of Meat

See **Meat Cuts and Joints**

Jumpers

See **Pullovers**

Keyboard Instruments

accordion
American organ
calliope
carillon
celesta
chamber organ
cinema organ
clavichord
clavicytherium
clavier
computer organ
dulcitone
electric organ
electronic organ
fortepiano
grand piano
Hammond organ (*trademark*)
harmonium
harpsichord
mellotron
melodeon
melodica
Moog synthesizer (*trademark*)
Novachord
ondes martenot
organ
pianino
piano
piano accordion
pianoforte
pianola
pipe organ
player-piano
portative organ
positive organ
reed organ
spinet
stylophone
synthesizer
upright piano
virginals
Wurlitzer (*trademark*)

Killers

See **Murderers**

Knitting Stitches

cable stitch
garter stitch
loop stitch
moss stitch
plain stitch
purl stitch
ribbing
shell stitch
slip stitch
stocking stitch
trellis stitch

Knives and Daggers

athame
bayonet
bistoury
bolo
bowie knife
bread knife
butter knife
butterfly knife
carver
carving knife
case knife
clasp knife
cleaver
commando knife
craft knife
dagger
dirk
drawknife
fish knife
flensing knife
flesher
flick knife
Frenchman
hunting knife
jackknife
kirpan
kris
kukri
lancet
machete
misericord
panga
paperknife
parang
penknife
pocket knife
poniard
pruning knife
sai
scalpel
scramasax
sheath knife
skean-dhu
Stanley knife (*trademark*)
steak knife
stiletto
Swiss army knife (*trademark*)
switchblade
table knife
tanto
ulu
utility knife
X-acto knife (*trademark*)

Knots

bend
Blackwall hitch
blood knot
bow
bowknot
bowline
bowline on the bight
carrick bend
cat's paw
clinch knot
clove hitch
diamond knot
Englishman's tie
figure-of-eight knot
fisherman's bend
fisherman's knot
granny knot
half hitch
hangman's knot
harness hitch
hawser bend
Hercules knot
hitch
loop knot
love knot
Matthew Walker
mesh knot
overhand knot
prusik
reef knot
rolling hitch
round turn and two half hitches
running bowline
running knot
sailor's knot
sheepshank
sheet bend
shoulder knot
shroud-knot
slip knot
slippery hitch
square knot
surgeon's knot
swab hitch
thumb knot
timber hitch
true-love knot
Turk's head
wale knot
wall knot
water knot
weaver's knot
Windsor knot

Ladders

accommodation ladder
cat ladder
companion ladder
etrier
fish ladder
folding ladder
Jacob's ladder
kitchen steps
monkey bars
pair of steps
quarter ladder
ratline
rope ladder
salmon ladder
scaling ladder
stepladder
steps
turntable ladder

Lamps and Lights

Aldis lamp (*trademark*)
anchor light
anglepoise (*trademark*)
arc lamp
Argand lamp
brake light
chandelier
Chinese lantern
Coleman lantern
courtesy light
cross light
crusie/cruisie
Davy lamp
desk lamp
discharge lamp
diya
downlighter
electrolier
fairy lights
fill light
flambeau
flare
flashgun
flash lamp
flashlight
floodlight
floor lamp
fluorescent light
fog lamp/light
follow spot
footlight
gaslight
halogen light
hazard (warning) lights
headlight/headlamp
hurricane lamp
idiot light
indicator
jack light
jack-o'-lantern
klieg
landing lights
lantern
lava lamp
luminaire
mercury vapour lamp
navigation lights
neon light
night light
occulting light
oil lamp
parachute flare
parking light
pendant
penlight
pilot light
pressure lamp
quartz lamp
reversing light
riding light
ring flash
running lights
safelight
safety lamp
sanctuary lamp
searchlight
sidelight
slit lamp
sodium-vapour lamp
spirit lamp
spotlight
standard lamp
stop light/lamp
storm lantern
street light/lamp
strip light
strobe/stroboscope
sunlamp
table lamp
tail light/lamp
tilley lamp (*trademark*)
torch
track lighting
traffic lights
uplighter
Very light

Lawyers

Types of Lawyer

advocate
advocate-depute
advocate-general
ambulance-chaser
amicus (curiae)
articled clerk
attorney
Attorney General (AG)
barrister
barrister-at-law
bencher
cadi
canonist
Chief Justice (CJ)
civil lawyer
commissioner for oaths
Common Serjeant
conveyancer
counsel
counselor-at-law
county commissioner
criminal lawyer
Crown prosecutor
custos rotulorum
defence lawyer
defending counsel
Director of Public Prosecutions (DPP)
district attorney (DA)
hakim
high sheriff
judge
judge advocate
Judge Advocate General (JAG)
junior barrister
jurisconsult
jurist
Justice of the Peace (JP)
justiciar
law agent
law lord
Law Officer (of the Crown)
leading counsel
Lord Chancellor
Lord Justice (LJ)
Lord Justice of Appeal
Lord of Session
master
Master of the Rolls (MR)
moulvi

mufti
munsif
notary
notary public (NP)
official (principal)
ordinary
paralegal
proctor
procurator
procurator fiscal
prosecuting counsel
prosecution lawyer
prosecutor
prosecutrix
public defender
public prosecutor
pupil-master
QC
Queen's Counsel
recorder
registrar
resident magistrate (RM)
senator
serjeant-at-law
sheriff
sheriff-depute
silk
solicitor
solicitor General (SG)
Solicitor in the Supreme Court (SSC)
state's attorney
surrogate
trial lawyer
undersheriff
vakil
writer to the Signet

Laxatives

(bitter) aloes
cascara
castor oil
colocynth
croton oil
Epsom salts
gamboge
Glauber's salt(s)
glycerol
Gregory powder
ipecacuanha
jalap
lactulose
liquid paraffin
magnesia
manna
Milk of Magnesia (*trademark*)
mineral oil
phenolphthalein
psyllium
scammony
Seidlitz powder
senna
syrup of figs

Leathers

buckskin
buff
calfskin
capeskin
chamois
chrome leather
cordovan
cowhide
crocodile
deerskin
doeskin
dogskin
goatskin
grain leather
kid
kidskin
Levant morocco
mocha
morocco
nappa
Nubuck
oxhide
patent leather
pigskin
ponyskin
rawhide
roan
Russia leather
shagreen
sheepskin
suede
tree calf
wash leather
whitleather

Lemurs and Other Prosimians

angwantibo
aye-aye
bushbaby
colugo
dwarf lemur
flying lemur
galago
indri
lemur
loris
mouse lemur
potto
ring-tailed lemur
ruffed lemur
sifaka
slender loris
slow loris
spectral tarsier
tarsier
tree shrew

Lens Shapes

biconcave
biconvex
concave
concavo-convex
convex
convexo-concave
planoconcave
planoconvex

Letters
Types of Correspondence

acknowledgement
air letter
begging letter
billet-doux
bread-and-butter letter
business letter
chain letter
circular
cover letter
covering letter/note
dead letter
Dear John letter
email
encyclical
fan mail
form letter
junk mail
letter-card
letter of introduction
letter of recommendation
love letter
mailshot
mash note
memo
memorandum
newsletter
notelet
open letter
pastoral
poison pen letter
postcard
reference
rejection slip
reminder
reply
sick note
thank-you letter

Letters of the Alphabet
Names of Greek and Hebrew Letters

Greek			Hebrew	
Α	α	alpha	א	aleph
Β	β	beta	ב	beth
Γ	γ	gamma	ג	gimel
Δ	δ	delta	ד	daleth
Ε	ε	epsilon	ה	he
Ζ	ζ	zeta	ו	waw
Η	η	eta	ז	zayin
Θ	θ	theta	ח	heth
Ι	ι	iota	ט	teth
Κ	κ	kappa	י	yodh
Λ	λ	lambda	כ	kaph
Μ	μ	mu	ל	lamedh
Ν	ν	nu	מ	mem
Ξ	ξ	xi	נ	nun
Ο	ο	omicron	ס	samekh
Π	π	pi	ע	àyin
Ρ	ρ	rho	פ	pe
Σ	σ, ς	sigma	צ	sadhe
Τ	τ	tau	ק	qoph
Υ	υ	upsilon	ר	resh
Φ	φ	phi	שׂ	śin
Χ	χ	chi	שׁ	shin
Ψ	ψ	psi	ת	taw
Ω	ω	omega		

Lights

See **Lamps and Lights**

Liquor

See **Drinks**

Lists

active list
agenda
A-list
Army List
back catalogue
backlist
balance sheet
baronage
baronetage
bibliography
bill
bill of costs
bill of fare
bill of lading
blacklist
B-list
calendar
call-over
card index
catalogue
catalogue raisonné
charts
chronology
class list
code book
codex
concordance
contents
contingency table
credits
criminal record
critical list
danger list
dean's list
disabled list
draw sheet
dump
electoral register
electoral roll
ephemeris
errata
ethogram
filmography
formulary
glossary
handlist
hit list
hit parade
honours list
hotlist
key
knightage
laundry list
league table
leet
legend
life list
life table
longlist
mailing list
manifest
market basket
martyrology
masthead
mathematical tables
menu
multiplication table
muster roll
necrology
notitia
pace notes
panel
paradigm
payroll
periodic table
playbill
playlist
price list
programme
racecard
rate card
ready reckoner
receipt
recipe
reckoner
rent roll
retail price index
roll
roll-call
roster
rota
sampling frame
schedule
scheme
score
scorebook
scorecard
scoresheet
shopping list
shortlist
sick list
signal book
slate
standings
station bill
statistical tables
stop list
subject catalogue
syllabus
tab
tales
tariff
terrier
thematic catalogue
tide table
timetable
transfer book
transfer list

undercard
union catalogue
vocabulary
waiting list
wait list
want list
watch list
waybill
white list
who's who
wine list
wish list

Literary Schools, Movements, and Groups

Acmeism
Aesthetic Movement
Angry Young Men
Augustans
beat generation
Bloomsbury group
Cavalier poets
classicism
Dadaism
existentialism
expressionism
futurism
Georgian poets
Harlem Renaissance
imagism
Kailyard School
Lake poets
Liverpool poets
magic/magical realism
mannerism
medievalism
metaphysical poets
minimalism
modernism
Movement, the
naturalism
neoclassicism
neo-realism
Neue Sachlichkeit
occultism
Parnassians
Pléiade, la
postmodernism
post-structuralism
Pre-Raphaelitism
pre-Romanticism
primitivism
realism
Renaissance humanism
Romanticism
Russian formalism
Scottish Chaucerians
social realism
socialist realism
structuralism
Sturm und Drang
surrealism
symbolism
transcendentalism
verismo
Vorticism

Loaves

See **Bread and Bread Rolls**

Locks

barrel lock
Chubb lock (*trademark*)
combination lock
cylinder lock
D-lock
double lock
drawback lock
lever-tumbler lock
mortise lock
night latch
padlock
radial pin-tumbler lock
rim lock
shackle lock
snap-lock
spring lock
stock-lock
time lock
tumbler lock
twist-lock
U-lock
warded lock
Yale lock (*trademark*)

Lords

See **Nobles**

Lorries

See **Vehicles**

Machine Guns

See **Guns**

Male Animals

See **Animals—Male and Female terms**

Manure

See **Fertilizers**

Maps

Map Types and Projections

atlas
A to Z
azimuthal projection
cadastral map
cartogram
chart
choropleth map
conical/conic projection
contour map
equal-area map
equidistant projection
globe
ichnography
ispoleth map
key map
mappemonde
Mercator projection
Mollweide projection
orthomorphic projection
Peters projection
photomap
photomosaic
plane chart
planisphere
plat
relief map
road map
sketch map
street map
topographical map
town plan
weather map/chart
zenithal projection

Marsupials

antechinus
bandicoot
bettong
bilby
boodie
brushtail
brush-tailed bettong
brush-tailed possum
cuscus
dasyure
dibbler
dunnart
flying phalanger
glider
honey possum
kangaroo
koala
kowari
kultarr
marsupial cat
marsupial mole
marsupial mouse
marsupial rat
mouse opossum
mulgara
numbat
opossum
pademelon
phalanger
phascogale
planigale
possum
potoroo
pygmy possum
quokka
quoll
rat kangaroo
ringtail
rock wallaby
sminthopsis
Tasmanian devil
thylacine (*or* Tasmanian tiger/wolf)
Virginia opossum
wallaby
wallaroo
wombat
woylie
yapok

Martial Arts and Combat Sports

aikido
ba gua
boxing
capoeira
fencing
jousting
judo
ju-jitsu
karate
kendo
kick-boxing
kung fu
pa-kua
Silat
sumo wrestling
tae kwon do
t'ai chi chu'an
tang soo do
Thai boxing
wrestling

Material

See **Fabrics and Fibres**

Mathematics

Branches of Mathematics

algebra
applied mathematics
arithmetic
calculus
catastrophe theory
chaos theory
combinatorics
conics
differential calculus
game theory
geodesy
geometry
integral calculus
mechanics
nomography
number theory
numerical analysis
probability theory
pure mathematics
set theory
statistics
topology
trigonometry

Meals

afternoon tea
banquet
barbecue
barbie
braaivleis
breakfast
brunch
buffet
burgoo
clambake
continental breakfast
cookout
cream tea
cut lunch
dinner
dinner party
elevenses
evening meal
feast
finger buffet
fork supper
harvest supper
high tea
lunch
luncheon
midday meal
packed lunch
picnic
safari supper
smorgasbord
supper
takeaway
tapas
tea
TV dinner
wedding breakfast

Measurement

Types of Measurement

process	phenomenon measured
acidimetry	strength of acid
actinometry	power of radiant energy
aerometry	properties of air
alcoholometry	concentration of alcohol
alkalimetry	strength of alkali
altimetry	height or altitude
anemometry	speed of wind
anthropometry	the human body
astrometry	positions and magnitudes of stars
audiometry	range and sensitivity of hearing
barometry	atmospheric pressure
bathymetry	depth of water in seas and lakes
bolometry	power of radiant energy
calorimetry	heat involved in a chemical reaction
campimetry	field of vision
cephalometry	the head and face
chronometry	time
colorimetry	intensity of colour
coulometry	number of coulombs used in electrolysis
craniometry	the skull
cytophotometry	light passing through cells
densitometry	optical density of a material
diffractometry	diffraction
dosimetry	absorption of ionizing radiation
ergometry	electrical potential of a circuit
eudiometry	changes in volumes of gas
fluorometry	intensity of fluorescence
galvanometry	galvanic currents
goniometry	angles
gravimetry	weight
hydrometry	density of liquids
hygrometry	humidity of air or a gas
hypsometry	height or altitude
interferometry	displacement of light or sound waves
keratometry	the cornea
lichenometry	lichens
longimetry (*archaic*)	distances
magnetometry	magnetic forces
manometry	pressure in a gas or liquid
microcalorimetry	small amounts of heat
microdensitometry	density of small areas of a photographic image
micrometry	minute objects
microphotometry	intensity of light in very small areas
morphometry	external shape and dimensions of landforms, living organisms, etc.
nepheleometry	turbidity of a liquid or gas
odorimetry	intensity of odours
olfactometry	intensity of odours or sensitivity to odours
olfactronics	vapours
ophthalmometry	the eye
optometry	eyesight
orometry	topographical features
oscillometry	blood pressure
osmometry	osmotic pressure
osteometry	bones
oximetry	oxygenated haemoglobin in the blood
pelvimetry	the pelvis
perimetry	field of vision
photoclinometry	brightness distribution in aerial photographs
photometry	intensity of light
planimetry	area of a plane figure
plastometry	plasticity of a substance
pneumotachography	rate of airflow during breathing
polarimetry	polarization of light
porosimetry	porosity of materials
potentiometry	electrical potential
profilometry	roughness of a surface
psychrometry	humidity
pupillometry	the pupil of the eye
pyrometry	high temperatures
quantitative analysis	quantities of constituents present in a substance
radiometry	intensity or force of radiation
reflectometry	reflected pulses of energy
refractometry	refractivity
respirometry	respiration
sensitometry	sensitivity of photographic equipment to light
spectrometry	spectra
spectrophotometry	intensity of light in a part of the spectrum
sphygmomanometry	blood pressure
spirometry	air capacity of the lungs
stereometry	solid bodies
stoichiometry	relative quantities of substances in a reaction or compound
tachometry	speed of an engine
tensiometry	surface tension of a liquid
thermometry	temperature
turbidimetry	turbidity of a liquid suspension
velocimetry	velocity
viscometry	viscosity of liquids

Meat Cuts and Joints

back rib
baron of beef
belly
best end
brisket
chateaubriand
chine
chop
chuck
collar
cutlet
entrecôte
escalope
fillet
flank
fore rib
fricandeau
gigot
hand
hock
hough
knuckle
leg
loin
neck
noisette
porterhouse steak
rack
rib
riblets
round
round steak
rump
saddle
shank
shin
shoulder
side
silverside
sirloin
skirt
spare rib
T-bone
tenderloin
topside
tournedos
undercut

Meat Types and Products

See also **Sausages**

bacon
beef
beefburger
brawn
bresaola
burger
bushmeat
chicken
chitterlings
corned beef
duck
faggot
fries
game
gammon
goose
ham
hamburger
haslet
kidney
lamb
lamb's fry
lights
liver
luncheon meat
mince
mutton
offal
oxtail
tongue
Parma ham
pâté
pig's trotters
pork
poultry
prosciutto
rabbit
rissole
salt pork
sidemeat
spam (*trademark*)
steak
sweetbread
tripe
turkey
veal
venison

Medication, Forms of

balsam
cachet
caplet
capsule
collyrium
cream
draught
drench
drip
drops
ear drops
enema
eye drops
gargle
hypodermic
inhalant
injectable
linctus
lotion
lozenge
microcapsule
nasal spray
nebulizer
ointment
pastille
pessary
pill
poultice
powder
rub
salve
spray
suppository
syrette
tablet

Medication Types

See also **Laxatives**

abortifacient
addictive
alpha blocker
anaesthetic
analeptic
analgesic
anaphrodisiac
anodyne
anovulant

antacid
anthelmintic
antibacterial
antibiotic
anticholinergic
anticoagulant
anticonvulsant
antidepressant
antidiarrhoeal
antidote
anti-emetic
anti-epileptic
antifungal
antihistamine
anti-infective
anti-inflammatory
antipruritic
antipsychotic
antipyretic
antiretroviral
antiscorbutic
antiseptic
antispasmodic
antitussive
antiviral
anxiolytic
aperient
aphrodisiac
appetite suppressant
arsenical
beta blocker
booster
bronchodilator
calefacient
calmative
carminative
cathartic
contraceptive
convulsant
counterirritant
curative
cure-all
decongestant
depressant
diaphoretic
digestive
dilator
diuretic
ecbolic
emetic
emollient
euphoriant
evacuant
expectorant
febrifuge
fungicide
germicide
immunosuppressive
laxative
lenitive
mercurial
muscle relaxant
narcotic
nervine
neuroleptic
nootropic
painkiller
palliative
placebo
preventive
prophylactic
psychotomimetic
psychotropic
relaxant
resolvent
restorative
roborant
sedative
sleeping draught
sleeping pill
soporific
sorbefacient
spasmolytic
steroid
stimulant
stupefacient
sudatory
sudorific
suppressant
sympatholytic
tonic
tranquillizer
vasoconstrictor
vasodilator
vermifuge

Medicine
Branches of Medicine

See also **Therapies**

allopathy
anaesthesiology
audiology
cardiology
chiropody
community medicine
dermatology
embryology
endocrinology
epidemiology
gastroenterology
geriatrics
gynaecology
haematology
immunology
laryngology
nephrology
neurology
neuropathology
neurosurgery
nuclear medicine
obstetrics
oncology
ophthalmology
orthopaedics
orthotics
paediatrics
parasitology
pathology
pharmacology
physiotherapy
plastic surgery
proctology
prosthetics
psychiatry
psychosurgery
radiology
surgery
therapeutics
trichopathy
urology
venereology
veterinary medicine

alternative and complementary

acupressure
acupuncture
Alexander technique
aromatherapy
Ayurveda
Bach flower remedies
balneotherapy
Bates method
bioenergetics
bodywork
bush medicine
chiropractic
colour therapy
craniosacral therapy
crystal healing/therapy
electro-acupuncture
eurhythmics
faith healing
Feldenkrais method
Gerson therapy
Hay diet
herbalism
homeopathy
hydropathy
iridology
McTimoney chiropractic
nature cure
naturopathy
neurolinguistic programming
organotherapy
osteopathy
psionic medicine
radionics
rebirthing
reflexology
reiki
Rolfing
shiatsu
thalassotherapy
zone therapy

Merchants

See **Sellers of Goods**

Metals and Their Chemical Symbols

aluminium	Al	lead	Pb	strontium	Sr
antimony	Sb	lithium	Li	tantalum	Ta
barium	Ba	magnesium	Mg	thallium	Tl
beryllium	Be	manganese	Mn	thorium	Th
bismuth	Bi	mercury	Hg	tin	Sn
cadmium	Cd	molybdenum	Mo	titanium	Ti
calcium	Ca	nickel	Ni	tungsten/wolfram	W
chromium	Cr	niobium	Nb	uranium	U
cobalt	Co	platinum	Pt	vanadium	V
copper	Cu	potassium	K	zinc	Zn
gold	Au	silver	Ag	zirconium	Zr
iron	Fe	sodium	Na		

Metals
Types of Metal

actinide
alkali metal
alkaline earth (metal)
alloy
amalgam
base metal
heavy metal
lanthanide
noble metal
platinum metal
precious metal
rare earth (metal)
transition metal

Military

See **Ranks** **Soldiers**

Milk Drinks

See **Drinks**

Minerals

See also **Gems** **Rocks**

actinolite
agate
alabaster
albite
allanite
andalusite
andradite
anhydrite
anorthite
antigorite
apatite
apophylite
aragonite
arsenopyrite
asbestos
augite
autunite
aventurine
azurite
baddeleyite
baryte
bastnaesite
bentonite
beryl
biotite
bloodstone
Blue John
borax
bornite
brucite
bytownite
cairngorm
calcite
carnallite
carnotite
cassiterite
chabazite
chalcedony
chalcopyrite
chiastolite
chlorite
chloritoid
chromite
chrysoberyl
chrysocolla
chrysoprase
chrysotile
cinnabar
clinopyroxene
colemanite
columbite
cordierite
corundum
covellite
crocidolite
crocoite
cryolite
cummingtonite
cuprite
diamond
diopside
dioptase
dolomite
dumortierite
emery
enargite
enstatite
epidote
fayalite
feldspar
ferberite
fluorite
fluorspar
fool's gold
forsterite
gadolinite
galena
garnet
garnierite
geyserite
gibbsite
glauconite
glaucophane
goethite
graphite
greenockite
grossular
gypsum
haematite
halite
hemimorphite
hiddenite
hornblende
hydroxyapatite
hypersthene
iddingsite
idocrase
illite
ilmenite
ilvaite
jacinth
jadeite
jargoon
jasper
kainite
kaolinite
kernite
kieserite
kunzite
kyanite
labradorite
lazurite
lepidocrocite
lepidolite
leucite
limonite
magnesite
magnetite
malachite
manganite
marcasite
mica
microcline
millerite
mimetite
molybdenite
monazite
montmorillonite
muscovite
natron
nepheline
nephrite
oligoclase
olivine
onyx
opal
orpiment
orthoclase
orthopyroxene
pentland

periclase
peridot
perovskite
phlogopite
piemontite
pigeonite
pitchblende
plagioclase
pyrargyrite
pyrites
pyrolusite
pyromorphite
pyroxene
pyrrhotite
quartz
realgar
rhodochrosite
rhodonite
riebeckite
rock salt
rutile
sanidine
sard
scheelite
serpentine
siderite
sillimanite
skutterudite
smaltite
smectite
smithsonite
smoky quartz
sodalite
spectrolite
sphalerite
sphene
spinel
spodumene
staurolite
steatite
stibnite
stishovite
strontianite
sylvite
talc
tantalite
tennantite
tetrahedrite
thenardite
topaz
tourmaline
tremolite
trona
tungstite
tyuyamunite
ulexite
uraninite
vanadinite
verminculite
vesuvianite
vivianite
willemite
witherite
wolframite
wollastonite
wulfenite
wurzite
xenotime
zeolite
zincite
zircon
zoisite

Mines

See **Bombs and Mines**

Ministers of Religion

See **Priests, Religious Officials, and Members of Religious Orders**

Mirrors

cheval glass/ mirror
door mirror
full-length mirror
handglass
heliograph
heliostat
mirrorball
one-way mirror
periscope
pier glass
rear-view mirror
speculum
two-way mirror
vanity mirror
wing mirror

Missiles

See **Bombs and Mines** **Bullets and Shot** **Projectiles**

Molluscs

abalone
angel wings
argonaut
ark (shell)
auger (shell)
basket shell
bittersweet shell
bivalve
bubble (shell)
canoe shell
carpet shell
carrier shell
cephalopod
chink shell
chiton
clam
cockle
cone shell
coquina (clam)
cowrie
cuttlefish
date mussel
dog cockle
dog whelk
dove shell
drill
drupe
duck mussel
edible snail
file shell
gaper
gastropod
geoduck
giant clam
hard clam
harp (shell)
helmet (shell)
horn shell
jewel box
jingle (shell)
lamp shell
limpet
lion's paw
mitre (shell)
moon shell
murex
mussel
nautilus
necklace shell
nerite
Noah's ark
nudibranch
octopus
olive (shell)
ormer
otter shell
oyster
pandora
paper nautilus
paua
pearl mussel
pearl oyster
pearly nautilus
pelican's foot shell
pen shell
periwinkle
pheasant shell
piddock
pipi
pteropod
quahog
ramshorn snail
razor shell
round clam
scallop
scaphopod
scungille
sea butterfly
sea hare
sea lemon
sea slug
shipworm
slipper limpet
slit limpet
slug
snail
softshell clam
spindle shell
spire shell
squid
sundial (shell)
swan mussel
tellin
teredo
thorny oyster
top shell
tridacna
triton
trough shell
trumpet shell
tulip shell
tun (shell)
turban (shell)
turret (shell)
tusk shell
vase shell
venus
Venus (clam/ shell)
wedge shell
wentletrap
whelk
wing oyster
winkle
worm shell
zebra mussel

Money

See **Coins** **Currency Units**

Monkeys and Apes

agile gibbon
baboon
Barbary ape
bonobo
capuchin monkey
chacma baboon
chimpanzee
colobus
Diana monkey
douroucouli
drill
gelada
gibbon
gorilla
green monkey
grivet
guenon
hamadryas
hanuman langur
hoolock
howler monkey
langur
lar gibbon
leaf monkey
macaque
mandrill
mangabey
marmoset
mona monkey
New World monkey
night monkey
Old World monkey
orang-utan
owl-faced monkey
patas monkey
proboscis monkey
rhesus monkey
saki
samango
siamang
spider monkey
squirrel monkey
talapoin
tamarin
titi
uakari
vervet
wanderoo
woolly monkey
woolly spider monkey

Monks

See **Christian Religious Orders**

Monsters

See **Giants** **Mythological and Fictional Creatures**

Moths

See also **Butterflies**

angle shades
atlas moth
bagworm
bogong
brimstone (moth)
brown-tail (moth)
buff-tip
burnet
burnished brass
cabbage moth
cecropia (moth)
cinnabar (moth)
clearwing (moth)
Clifden nonpareil
clothes moth
codling/codlin moth
common heath
corn borer
crescent
dagger
death's head hawkmoth
diamondback moth
drinker (moth)
dun-bar
eggar
emerald (moth)
emperor
ermine (moth)
festoon
flour moth
footman
forester
fox moth
garden carpet
garden tiger
geometer (moth)
geometrid
ghost moth
goat moth
gypsy moth
hawkmoth
heath
hooktip
hornet moth
io moth
Kentish moth
kitten
lackey (moth)
lappet (moth)
leaf miner
leaf roller
leopard moth
lobster moth
luna moth
magpie moth
meal moth
merveille du jour
minor
moon moth
Mother Shipton
noctuid
oak eggar
old lady
owlet
peach blossom
peppered moth
pine beauty
pink bollworm
plume moth
processionary (moth)
prominent (moth)
pug
puss moth
pyralid
rivulet
rustic
sallow
saturniid
shark (moth)
silk moth
silver-line
silver Y
snout (moth)
sphingid
swallow-tailed moth
swift (moth)
tabby
tapestry moth
thorn
tiger moth
tortrix (moth)
triangle
turnip moth
tussock moth
tussore moth
umber
underwing (moth)
vapourer (moth)
wainscot
wax moth
white spot
winter moth
yellow-tail (moth)
yellow underwing
yucca moth

Motors

See **Engines**

Motor Sports

autocross
cross-country
demolition derby
dirt-track racing
drag racing
enduro
Formula One (F1)
go-karting
Grand Prix (GP)
hill-climbing
Indy/Indycar
karting
motocross
motorcycle racing
off-roading
rallycross
rallying
scrambling
sidecar racing
speedway
stock-car racing
Tourist Trophy (TT)
trials

Motor Vehicles

See **Cars Vehicles**

Mouse

See **Rodents**

Moustaches

See **Beards and Moustaches**

Murderers

Types of Murderer

assassin
axeman
Bluebeard
butcher
button man
contract killer
cut-throat
deicide
filicide
fratricide
highbinder
hired gun
hit man
infanticide
killer
matricide
parricide
patricide
regicide
ripper
serial killer
spree killer
tyrannicide
uxoricide

Muscles

Human Muscles

muscle	location	muscle	location
biceps	arm	pectoral	chest
buccinator	cheek	peroneal muscle	leg
deltoid	shoulder	psoas	spine/groin
detrusor	bladder	quadriceps	leg
digastric	jaw	rectus (abdominis)	abdomen
gastrocnemius	leg	rhomboideus	shoulder
gluteus	buttock	sartorius	leg
gracilis	leg	scalenus	neck/ribs
iliacus	pelvis/groin	soleus	leg
intercostal	ribs	splenius	neck/back
latissimus	back	temporalis	jaw
masseter	cheek/jaw	teres	shoulder/arm
obturator	pelvis	trapezius	neck/shoulders
opponent muscle	hand	triceps	arm

Muscle Types

abductor
adductor
agonist
antagonist
constrictor
depressor
dilator
elevator
erector
extensor
flexor
levator
pronator
rotator
skeletal
sphincter
supinator

Mushrooms

See **Fungi, Mushrooms, and Toadstools**
Poisonous Plants and Fungi

Musical Directions

term	translation
a battuta	return to strict time
a cappella	unaccompanied
accel(erando)	accelerating
adagietto	fairly slowly
adagio	slowly
ad lib(itum)	at will
affettuoso	tenderly
agitato	agitated
al fine	to the end
allargando	broadening
allegretto	fairly lively
allegro	lively
al segno	as far as the sign
amoroso	tenderly
andante	moderately slow
andantino	slightly faster than andante
animato	spirited
arco	with the bow
arioso	in a sustained singing style
assai	very
a tempo	in the original tempo
attacca	continue without a pause
bis	repeat
calando	becoming quieter and slower
cantabile	in a smooth singing style
capriccioso	freely
coda	final part of a movement
col legno	with the stick of the bow
con amore	tenderly
con brio	with vigour
con fuoco	fiery
con moto	with movement
con sordino	with a mute
cresc(endo)	becoming louder
da capo *or* DC	from the beginning
dal segno *or* DS	from the sign
decresc(endo)	becoming quieter
dim(inuendo)	becoming quieter
dolce	sweetly and softly
dolente	sorrowfully
doppio	double
espressivo	with expression of feeling
fine	end (not at the end of the score)
f(orte)	loudly
forte piano	loudly and then immediately softly
fortissimo *or* ff	very loudly
furioso	furiously and wildly
giocoso	playfully
glissando	sliding
in modo di	in the manner of
larghetto	fairly slowly
largo	very slowly
legato	tied/smoothly
leggiero	lightly
lento	slowly
maestoso	majestically
marcato	accented
marcia	march
meno	less
meno mosso	less quickly
mezza voce	at half vocal strength
mezzo	half
mezzo forte *or* mf	fairly loudly
mezzo piano *or* mp	fairly softly
moderato	at a moderate pace
molto	very
morendo	dying away
mosso	fast and with animation
moto	motion
niente	gradually fading to nothing
nobilmente	nobly

term	translation
non troppo	not too much
obbligato	not to be omitted
parlando	in the manner of speech
ped.	pedal
pesante	heavily
pianissimo *or* pp	very soft
p(iano)	soft
più	more
pizz(icato)	plucked
poco	a little
portamento	carrying one note into the next
prestissimo	as fast as possible
presto	very fast
rall(entando)	slowing down
ravvivando	quickening
rinforzando *or* rfz	accentuated
rit(ardando)	slowing down
ritenuto	suddenly more slowly
scherzando	playfully
segno	sign
semplice	simply
sempre	always/throughout
senza	without
sf(orzando) *or* sfz	strongly accented
smorzando	dying away
sordino	with a mute
sost(enuto)	sustained
sotto voce	in an undertone
spiccato	bouncing the bow on the strings
stacc(ato)	detached
stretto	in quicker time
stringendo	faster and more intensely
subito	immediately
tacet	voice/instrument remains silent
tanto	too much
tempo	speed/beat
ten(uto)	held
tranquillo	tranquilly
tremolando	trembling
troppo	too much
tutti	all players/singers
una corda	using the soft pedal (on a piano)
vivace	lively
zoppa	syncopated

Musical Forms

See also **Dances Musical Directions**

air
anthem
aria
arietta
aubade
bagatelle
ballad
ballet
barcarole
berceuse
brindisi
cabaletta
calypso
canon
canticle
canzone
canzonetta
capriccio
carol
catch
cavatina
chaconne
chanson
chant
chorale
chorus
concertino
concerto
concerto grosso
coronach
courante
dead march
descant
dirge
ditty
dringing song
duet
dumka
duo
entr'acte
entrée
étude
fado
fancy
fanfare
fantasia
fantasy
finale
five-finger exercise
flourish
frottola
fugato
fugue
glee
gradual
humoresque
hymn
impromptu
interlude
intermezzo
introit
jingle
karanga
lament
Lied
lullaby
madrigal
march
mass
medley
monody
motet
moto perpetuo
movement
musette
nocturne
nonet
octet
opera
operetta
oratorio
overture
partita
part-song
passacaglia
passion
pastoral
pibroch
postlude
prelude
psalm
quartet
quintet
quodlibet
rag
raga
rap
recitative
refrain
requiem
reverie
rhapsody
ricercar/ ricercare
ritornello
romance
rondo
round
roundelay
scena
scherzo
septet
serenade
serenata
setting
sextet
shanty
signature tune
sinfonia
sinfonia concertante
sinfonietta
Singspiel
solo
sonata
sonatina
song
song cycle
spiritual
study
suite
symphonic poem
symphony
terzetto
threnody
thumri
tiento
toccata
tone poem
trio
trio sonata
variation
verset
villanella/ villanelle
voluntary
waiata

Musical Genres

See also **Jazz Genres**

absolute music
acid house
acid rock
alt.country
ambient
AOR
arioso
bachata
baggy
ballet music
barbershop
baroque
bel canto
benga
bhangra
bluegrass
blues
boogie-woogie
breakbeat
Britpop
calypso
Cantopop
chamber music
chant
choral music
church music
classical music
comic opera
contrapuntal music
country
country and western
country rock
cowpunk
crossover
cumbia
dance floor
dancehall
death metal
dhrupad
disco
dodecaphonic music
doo-wop
drum and bass
dub
easy listening
electro
emo/emocore
flamenco
folk
free jazz
funk
funkadelic
fusion
gagaku
galant
gangsta (rap)
garage
glam rock
go-go
gospel
Goth
grand opera
grunge
gumbo
hardcore
harmolodics
heavy metal
highlife
hip hop
honky-tonk
house
indie
industrial
jazz
jit
jive
juju
jump blues
jungle
klezmer
Krautrock
kwaito
kwela
light opera
liturgical music
marabi
mariachi
mbaqanga
mento
merengue
minimalism
motet
Motown
multiculti
musique concrète
New Age
New Romantic
new wave
norteño
northern soul
oi
old-time
opera
opera buffa
opera seria
orbital
orchestral music
Palm Court
parang
pibroch
pogo
pop
popular music
programme music
progressive
psychedelic
psychobilly
punk
qawwali
queercore
ragamuffin/ ragga
ragtime
rai
ranchera
rap
rave
reggae
rhythm and blues (R & B)
rock
rockabilly
rock and roll
rocksteady
sacred music
sakkie-sakkie
salsa
serialism
sijo
ska
skiffle
soca
soukous
soul
surf
swing
symphonic music
taarab
talking blues
tasso
techno
technofunk
Tejano
Tex-Mex
thrash (metal)
trance
trip hop
twelve-note/ twelve-tone music
vocalese
western swing
world music
zouk
zydeco

Musical Instruments

See **Brass Instruments Keyboard Instruments Orchestral Instruments Organs Percussion Instruments Stringed Instruments Wind Instruments**

Musicians
Instrumentalists

See also **Singers** **Voices**

player	instrument
accordionist	accordion
banjoist	banjo
bassist	bass guitar *or* double bass
bassoonist	bassoon
cellist	cello
clarinettist	clarinet
cornetist	cornet
cymbalist	cymbal
drummer	drum
fiddler	violin
flautist	flute
guitarist	guitar
harper	harp
harpist	harp
harpsichordist	harpsichord
keyboardist	keyboard
lutenist, lutist	lute
lyrist	lyre
mandolinist	mandolin
oboist	oboe
organist	organ
percussionist	percussion
pianist	piano
piper	bagpipes
saxist	saxophone
saxophonist	saxophone
tambourinist	tambourine
timpanist	timpani
trombonist	trombone
trumpeter	trumpet
vibist, vibraphonist	vibraphone
violinist	violin
violist	viola *or* viol
xylophonist	xylophone

Mythological and Fictional Creatures

See also **Giants** **Nymphs**

Abominable Snowman
amazon
amphisbaena
banshee
basilisk
Bigfoot *or* Sasquatch
bugbear
bunyip
centaur
Cerberus
Charybdis
chimera
cockatrice
dragon
dwarf
dybbuk
elf
erl-king
fairy
firedrake
Frankenstein's monster
the Furies
genie
giant/giantess
gnome
goblin
golem
gorgon
Grendel
griffin
harpy
hippogriff
hobbit
hobgoblin
Hydra
jinn
kelpie
kobold
kraken
kylin
lamia
leprechaun
leviathan
Lilith
Loch Ness monster
lycanthrope
manticore
Medusa
mermaid
merman
Midgard's serpent
Minotaur
naga
ogre/ogress
orc
Pegasus
peri
phoenix
pixie
pooka
roc
Scylla
sea serpent
selkie
simurg
siren
sphinx
taniwha
Tiamat
tokoloshe
troll
unicorn
Valkyrie
vampire
werewolf
windigo
wyvern
yeti
zombie

Names
Types of Name

See also **Eponyms**

agnomen
alias
anonym
assumed name
baptismal name
brand name
byname
Christian name
code name
cognomen
cryptonym
eponym
family name
first name
forename
given name
hypocorism
last name
maiden name
matronymic/metronymic
microtoponym
middle name
nickname
nom de guerre
nom de plume
nom de théâtre
patronymic
pen name
personal name
pet name
place name
professional name
proper name
proprietary name
pseudonym
second name
sobriquet/soubriquet
stage name
surname
toponym
trade name
username

Narcotics

See **Drugs**

Needlework

See **Sewing Techniques and Stitches**

Nervous System
Parts of the Human Nervous System

abducens nerve
accessory nerve
autonomic nervous system
brain
central nervous system
cranial nerves
femoral nerve
glossopharyngeal nerve
hypoglossal nerve
motor nerves
nerve cell *or* neuron(e)
oculomotor nerve
olfactory nerve
optic nerve
parasympathetic nervous system
peripheral nervous system
peroneal nerve
radial nerve
sciatic nerve
sensory nerves
solar plexus
spinal cord
spinal nerves
sympathetic nervous system
tibial nerve
trigeminal/trifacial nerve
trochlear nerve
ulnar nerve
vestibulocochlear nerve

Nets

butterfly net
cast net
dip net
dragnet
drift net
fyke (net)
gill net
keepnet
kiddle
landing net
mosquito net
otter trawl
pod
purse net
purse seine
safety net
scoop net
seine (net)
set-net
stake net
torpedo net
tow net
trammel net
trawl (net)
trek net
tuck-net/tuck-seine
tunnel-net

Newspapers
Types of Newspaper

broadsheet
daily
eveninger
evening paper
extra
final
free sheet
gazette
gutter press
heavy
journal
local paper
national
news-sheet
organ, organs
print
provincial
quality
red top
regional
scandal sheet
special edition
Sunday
tab
tabloid
weekly

Nobles

See also **Rulers' Titles**

baron
baroness
baronet
begum
bey
boyar
burgrave
castellan
commander
contessa
count
countess
don
duchess
duke
earl
esquire
grand duke
grandee
hidalgo
Junker
knight
knight commander
life peer
life peeress
maid of honour
marchesa
marchese
marchioness
margrave
margravine
marquesa
marquess
marquis
marquise
Mistress of the Robes
nawab
paladin

palsgrave
prince
rangatira
royal duke
seigneur/seignior
squire
thakur
thane
vicomte
vicomtesse
viscount
viscountess

Nuclear Reactors

advanced gas-cooled reactor (AGR)
boiling-water reactor (BWR)
breeder reactor
CANDU
converter reactor
fast breeder (reactor)
fast reactor
Magnox reactor
pressurized-water reactor (PWR)
slow reactor
stellarator
thermal reactor
tokamak

Nuns

See **Christian Religious Orders**

Nurses

accoucheur
auxiliary nurse
candy-striper
charge nurse
dental nurse
district nurse
geriatric nurse
health visitor
hospital nurse
licensed practical nurse (LPN)
matron
midwife
night nurse
nurse practitioner
nurse midwife
nursing officer
practical nurse (PN)
registered general nurse (RGN)
registered nurse (RN)
scrub nurse
senior nursing officer
sick nurse
sister
staff nurse
state enrolled nurse (SEN)
state registered nurse (SRN)
theatre nurse
veterinary nurse

Nuts

acorn
almond
areca nut
beechnut
betel nut
bitternut
Brazil (nut)
breadnut
burrawang nut
butternut
candlenut
cashew (nut)
chestnut
chincapin
cobnut
coco de mer
coconut
coffee nut
cohune nut
cola nut
conker
coquilla nut
double coconut
dwarf chestnut
earthnut
filbert
groundnut
grugru nut
gum nut
hazelnut
hickory nut
hognut
horse chestnut
ivory nut
lychee nut
macadamia (nut)
mockernut
monkey nut
palm nut
peanut
pecan
pine nut
piñon
pistachio (nut)
quandong
Queensland nut
sal nut
saouari nut
sweet chestnut
walnut
water chestnut
white walnut

Nymphs

dryad
hamadryad
naiad
nereid
Oceanid
oread
sprite
sylph
undine

Oils

ajowan
almond oil
arachis oil
attar
baby oil
bergamot oil
brilliantine
cajuput/cajeput
castor oil
chaulmoogra
citronella
coconut oil
cod liver oil
copaiba
corn oil
creosote
croton oil
crude (oil)
Danish oil
diesel oil
drying oil
essential oil
eucalyptus oil
fatty oil
fixed oil
fuel oil
fusel oil
gas oil
geranial
grapeseed oil
grease
heavy oil
jojoba
lavender oil
linseed oil
Macassar
mineral oil
multigrade
naphtha
neat's-foot oil
neroli oil
nut oil
oil of cloves
oil of juniper
oil of turpentine
oil of wintergreen
olive oil
otto
palmarosa oil
palm oil
patchouli
peanut oil
petitgrain
petroleum
rape oil
rapeseed oil
safflower oil
sandalwood oil
sesame oil
shale oil
shea
sperm oil
stand oil
sunflower oil
suntan oil
tanning oil
tar oil
tea oil
train oil
tung oil
turpentine
turps
vanaspati
vegetable oil
vetiver/vetivert
volatile oil
walnut oil
whale oil
white oil
wintergreen
ylang-ylang/ilang-ilang

Operations

Surgical Operations

technical name	procedure
adenoidectomy	removal of adenoids
angioplasty	repair of blood vessel
appendectomy/appendicectomy	removal of appendix
arteriotomy	incision of artery
blepharoplasty	repair or reconstruction of eyelid
Caesarean (section)	incision of wall of mother's abdomen to deliver child
cheiloplasty	repair of lips
cholecystectomy	removal of gall bladder
cholecystotomy	incision of gall bladder
colectomy	removal of colon
colostomy	opening of colon
craniotomy	incision of skull
cystectomy	removal of bladder/removal of cyst
cystoplasty	repair of bladder
cystostomy	opening of bladder
cystotomy	incision of bladder
dermatoplasty	repair of skin
embolectomy	removal of blood clot
enterostomy	opening of small intestine
enterotomy	incision of intestine
episiotomy	incision of vaginal opening
gastrectomy	removal of stomach
gastroplasty	repair of stomach
gastrostomy	opening of stomach
gastrotomy	incision of stomach
glossectomy	removal of tongue
haemorrhoidectomy	removal of haemorrhoids
hepatectomy	removal of liver
hepaticostomy	opening of bile duct
hysterectomy	removal of womb
hysterotomy	incision of womb
keratotomy	incision of cornea
laminectomy	removal of back of vertebra/vertebrae
laparotomy	incision of abdomen
laryngectomy	removal of larynx
laryngotomy	incision of larynx
lithotomy	removal of kidney stone
lobectomy	removal of lobe of an organ
lobotomy	incision of prefrontal lobe of brain
lumpectomy	removal of breast tumour
mammaplasty	reshaping of breast
mastectomy	removal of breast
myotomy	incision of muscle
nephrectomy	removal of kidney
nephrostomy	opening of kidney
nephrotomy	incision of kidney
neurectomy	removal of nerve
neurotomy	incision of nerve
oesophagectomy	opening of oesophagus
oophorectomy	removal of ovary
orchidectomy	removal of testis
orchidotomy	incision of testis
ostectomy	removal of bone
osteotomy	incision of bone
otoplasty	repair or reshaping of ear
ovariectomy	removal of ovary
ovariotomy	incision of ovary
palatoplasty	repair of cleft palate
pancreatectomy	removal of pancreas

technical name	procedure
pericardiectomy/ pericardectomy	removal of membrane around heart
pericardiotomy	incision of membrane around heart
perineoplasty	repair of vaginal opening
phalloplasty	repair of penis
pharyngectomy	removal of pharynx
phlebotomy	incision of vein
pleurotomy	incision of pleural membrane
pneumonectomy	removal of lung
polypectomy	removal of polyp
prostatectomy	removal of prostate gland
rhinoplasty	repair of nose
salpingectomy	removal of fallopian tube
salpingostomy	opening of fallopian tube
splenectomy	removal of spleen
tenotomy	incision of tendon
thoracoplasty	repair of thorax
thoracotomy	incision of chest cavity
thrombectomy	removal of blood clot
thymectomy	removal of thymus gland
thyroidectomy	removal of all or part of thyroid gland
tonsillectomy	removal of tonsils
tonsillotomy	incision of tonsil
tracheostomy	opening of windpipe
tracheotomy	incision of windpipe
ureterectomy	removal of ureter
ureterostomy	opening of ureter
ureterotomy	incision of ureter
urethroplasty	repair of urethra
urethrotomy	incision of urethra
vagotomy	incision of vagus nerve
valvotomy	incision of heart valve
varicotomy	removal of varicose vein
vasectomy	removal of vas deferens
vitrectomy	removal of vitreous humour from eyeball

Orchestral Instruments

bass clarinet
bass drum
basset horn
bassoon
bass tuba
celesta
cello
clarinet
contrabassoon
cor anglais
cymbals
double bass
flute
French horn
glockenspiel
harp
kettledrums
oboe
oboe d'amore
piccolo
side drum
snare drum
tam-tam
timpani *or* kettledrums
triangle
trombone
trumpet
tuba
tubular bells
viola
viola d'amore
violin
Wagner tuba

Organs
Musical Organs

American organ
barrel organ
chamber organ
cinema organ
electric organ
electronic organ
Hammond organ (*trademark*)
hand organ
harmonica
harmonium
melodeon
mouth organ
piano organ
pipe organ
portative organ
positive organ
reed organ
steam organ
Wurlitzer (*trademark*)

Organ Stops

bombarde
bourdon
carillon
clarabella
clarinet
clarion
cor anglais
cornet
diapason
dulcian
dulciana
echo
fagott
fifteenth
flute
gedeckt
gemshorn
hautboy
horn
mixture
oboe
open diapason
principal
quint
reed
salicet
salicional
solo stop
stopped diapason
tierce
tromba
trombone
trumpet
tuba
viola
vox angelica
vox humana

Oxen

See **Cattle**

Paints

acrylic
antifouling
cellulose
colour wash
Day-Glo (*trademark*)
distemper
eggshell
emulsion
enamel (paint)
face paint
finger-paint
gloss (paint)
gouache
masonry paint
matt paint
metallic paint
oil paint
poster paint
powder paint
primer
tempera
undercoat
vinyl emulsion
watercolour
whitewash

Paintings
Types and Forms of Painting

altarpiece
annunciation
capriccio
cave painting
cityscape
cloudscape
conversation piece
crucifixion
diorama
diptych
Ecce Homo
écorché
fête galante
fresco
half-length
icon
kakemono
landscape
miniature
mural
nativity
nocturne
noli me tangere
nude
old master
panorama
paysage
pietà
polyptych
portrait
predella
retable
riverscape
seascape
skyscape
still life
tondo
townscape
triptych
trompe l'œil
vanitas
wall painting

Painting Techniques and Methods

acrylic painting
action painting
aquarelle
chiaroscuro
colour-field painting
colour wash
divisionism
encaustic
genre painting
gouache
grisaille
grotesque
impasto
miniature painting
mural painting
oil painting
pointillism
polychromy
sand painting
scumbling
secco
silk painting
spray-can painting
sumi-e
tempera
tenebrism
watercolour
Yamato-e

Papers
Types of Paper

See also **Newspapers**

art paper
blotting paper
bond (paper)
bromide (paper)
brown paper
carbon (paper)
cartridge (paper)
construction paper
crêpe paper
drawing paper
filter paper
flimsy
flypaper
gelatin paper
gift wrap
glassine
glasspaper
graph paper
greaseproof (paper)
India paper
Japanese paper
kitchen paper
kraft (paper)
laid (paper)
litmus paper
Manila (paper)
manuscript paper
mourning paper
notepaper
oaktag
oil paper
onion-skin paper
parchment (paper)
rag paper
ricepaper
sandpaper
satin paper
squared paper
stamp paper
thermal paper
tissue (paper)
toilet paper
tracing paper
transfer paper
vellum
wallpaper
waxed paper
woodchip (paper)
wove (paper)
wrapping paper
writing paper

Particles
Subatomic Particles

See also **Quarks**

antielectron
antineutron
antiparticle
antiproton
antiquark
axion
baryon
boson
electron
fermion
gluon
hadron
Higgs (boson/ particle)
hyperon
kaon
lambda particle
lepton
meson
muon

neutrino
neutron
nucleon
photon
pion
positron
proton
psi particle
quark
strange particle
tau particle
WIMP

Pasta Types

agnolotti
angel hair
annellini
bigoli
bucatini
cannelloni
capelli
capellini
cappelletti
casareccie
conchiglie
cravattine
ditali
ditalini
ditaloni
farfalle
farfalline
fedelini
fettucce
fettuccine
fidelini
fusilli
gramigna
lasagne
linguine
lumache
macaroni
mafalde
manicotti
maruzze
mezzani
mostaccioli
noodles
orecchiette
orzo
paglia e fieno
pappardelle
penne
pipe
ravioli
rigatoni
risoni
rotelle
rotini
spaghetti
spaghettini
spaghettone
stelline
tagliatelle
tagliolini
taglioni
tortellini
tortelloni
tortiglioni
trenette
tuffoloni
vermicelli
ziti

Pastries

See **Cakes**

Patterns

See also **Shapes**

anthemion
argyle
banding
basket weave
bird's-eye
bow tie
chalk-stripe
check
chequers
clock
counterchange
crackle
diaper
dog-tooth
fret
Greek key
herringbone
honeycomb
houndstooth
log cabin
meander
microcheck
millefleurs
mottle
overcheck
paisley
pinstripe
plaid
polka dot
Prince of Wales check
shepherd's plaid
spiral
spreite
starburst
sunburst
swirl
tartan
veining
waffle
woodgrain

Peas

See **Beans, Pulses, and Peas**

Peers

See **Nobles**

Pens

See **Writing Implements**

Percussion Instruments

agogo
angel chimes
anvil
balafon
banana drum
barrel drum
bass drum
bells
bhaya
bodhrán
bongos
castanets
celesta
changko
chengcheng
chime bar
Chinese block
clappers
claves
conga drum
cowbell
crotales
cylindrical drums
cymbals
dhol
djembe
drum
dulcimer
frame drum
gamelan
glockenspiel
gong
gong chimes
goombay
handbell
hi-hat (cymbals)
idiophone
Jew's harp
kettledrum
kick drum
lithophone
maracas
mbira
mridangam
piano
rattle
rommelpot
rototom
santoor
saron
scraper
sekere
shaker
side drum
sistrum
sleigh bells
slit drum
snare drum
stamping tube
steel drum
tabla
tabor
taiko
tambour
tambourine
tam-tam
tassa drum
tenor drum
temple block
thumb piano
timbales
timpani
tom-tom
triangle
tubular bells
Turkish crescent
vibraphone
vibraslap
washboard
whip
wobbleboard
wood block
xylophone
xylorimba

Performers

See **Actors** **Entertainers** **Musicians** **Singers**

Periods

See **Geological Ages**

Philosophy

Branches of Philosophy

aesthetics
analytical philosophy
axiology
bioethics
cosmology
deontology
epistemology
ethics
formal logic
gnosiology
legal ethics
linguistic philosophy
logic
medical ethics
metaethics
metaphysics
metempirics
modal logic
moral philosophy
ontology
pataphysics
phenomenology
philosophy of language
philosophy of law
philosophy of mathematics
philosophy of mind
philosophy of psychology
philosophy of religion
philosophy of science
political philosophy
teleology

Phobias

object of fear or dislike	phobia
air travel	aerophobia
American people and things	Americophobia
animals	zoophobia
bacteria	bacteriophobia
beards	pogonophobia
beating	mastigophobia
bed	clinophobia
bees	apiphobia
being buried alive	taphephobia
birds	ornithophobia
blood	haemophobia
blushing	erythrophobia
body odour	bromidrosiphobia
bridges	gephyrophobia
bullets	ballistophobia
cancer	carcinophobia
cats	ailurophobia
childbirth	tocophobia
children	paedophobia
Chinese people and things	Sinophobia
church	ecclesiophobia
clouds	nephophobia
coitus	coitophobia
cold	cheimaphobia
colour	chromophobia
comets	cometophobia
computers	cyberphobia
constipation	coprostasophobia
corpses	necrophobia
correspondence	epistolophobia

object of fear or dislike	phobia
crowds	demophobia/ochlophobia
dampness	hygrophobia
darkness	scotophobia
dawn	eosophobia
death	thanatophobia
depth	bathophobia
dirt	mysophobia
disease	pathophobia/nosophobia
dogs	cynophobia
dreams	oneirophobia
drink	potophobia
drugs	pharmacophobia
dust	koniophobia
electricity	electrophobia
enclosed places	claustrophobia
English people and things	Anglophobia
everything	panophobia/pantophobia
eyes	ommetaphobia
faeces	coprophobia
failure	kakorrhaphiaphobia
fatigue	kopophobia
fear	phobophobia
feathers	pteronophobia
fever	febriphobia
fire	pyrophobia
fish	ichthyophobia
flesh	selaphobia
floods	antlophobia
flowers	anthophobia
fog	homichlophobia
food	cibophobia/sitophobia
foreigners	xenophobia
freedom	eleutherophobia
French people and things	Francophobia/Gallophobia
fur	doraphobia
German people and things	Germanophobia/Teutophobia
germs	bacteriophobia
ghosts	phasmophobia
giving birth to monsters	teratophobia
glass	nelophobia
God	theophobia
gold	chrysophobia/aurophobia
hair	trichophobia
heart disease	cardiophobia
heat	thermophobia
heaven	uranophobia
hell	hadephobia/stygiophobia
heredity	patroiophobia
high buildings	batophobia
high places	acrophobia/hypsophobia
home	oikophobia
homosexuals	homophobia
horses	hippophobia
ice	cryophobia
ideas	ideophobia
idleness	thassophobia
illness	nosophobia
imperfection	atelophobia
infinity	apeirophobia
injury	traumatophobia
inoculation	trypanophobia/vaccinophobia
insanity	lyssophobia/maniphobia
insects	entomophobia
insect stings	cnidophobia
Italian people and things	Italophobia
itching	acarophobia
jealousy	zelotypophobia
justice	dikephobia
lakes	limnophobia
leprosy	leprophobia
lice	pediculophobia
light	photophobia
lightning	astrapophobia

object of fear or dislike	phobia
lists	pinaciphobia/katastichophobia
loneliness	autophobia/ermitophobia
machinery	mechanophobia
magic	rhabdophobia
marriage	gamophobia
men	androphobia
metal	metallophobia
mice	musophobia
microbes	bacillophobia/microbiophobia
mirrors	eisoptrophobia
mites	acarophobia
mobs	ochlophobia
money	chrematophobia
motion	kinetophobia
music	musicophobia
names	onomatophobia
narrowness	anginophobia
needles	belonephobia
new things	neophobia
night	nyctophobia
nudity	gymnophobia
open places	agoraphobia
pain	algophobia
parasites	parasitophobia
people	anthropophobia
philosophy	philosophobia
pins	enetophobia
places	topophobia
pleasure	hedonophobia
poison	toxiphobia
politics	politicophobia
Pope	papaphobia
poverty	peniaphobia
precipices	cremnophobia
priests	hierophobia
punishment	poinephobia
rabies	hydrophobophobia
rail travel	siderodromophobia
religious works of art	iconophobia
reptiles	batrachophobia
responsibility	hypegiaphobia
ridicule	katagelophobia
rivers	potamophobia
robbers	harpaxophobia
ruin	atephobia
Russian people and things	Russophobia
saints	hagiophobia
Satan	Satanophobia
scabies	scabiophobia
Scottish people and things	Scotophobia
sea	thalassophobia
sex	erotophobia
shadows	sciophobia
sharpness	acrophobia
shock	hormephobia
sin	hamartophobia
skin disease	dermatosiophobia/dermatopathophobia
sleep	hypnophobia
slime	blennophobia
small things	microphobia
smell	olfactophobia/osmophobia
smothering	pnigerophobia
snakes	ophidiophobia
snow	chionophobia
solitude	eremophobia
sound	acousticophobia
sourness	acerophobia
speech	lalophobia/glossophobia/phonophobia
speed	tachophobia
spiders	arachnophobia
standing	stasophobia
stars	siderophobia
stealing	kleptophobia

object of fear or dislike	phobia
string	linonophobia
stuttering	laliophobia
sun	heliophobia
swallowing	phagophobia
symmetry	symmetrophobia
taste	geumatophobia
technology	technophobia
teeth	odontophobia
telephone	telephonophobia
thinking	phronemophobia
thirteen	triskaidekaphobia
thunder	brontophobia/tonitrophobia/keraunophobia
time	chronophobia
touch	haptophobia
travel	hodophobia
tuberculosis	phthisiophobia
tyrants	tyrannophobia
vehicles	ochophobia
venereal disease	syphilophobia
voids	kenophobia
vomiting	emetophobia
water	hydrophobia
waves	cymophobia
weakness	asthenophobia
wind	anemophobia
women	gynophobia
words	logophobia
work	ergophobia
worms	helminthophobia
writing	graphophobia

Pies

Savoury Pies

cottage pie
coulibiac
fidget pie
game pie
pirog
pork pie
pot pie
Scotch pie
shepherd's pie
squab pie
stargazy pie
steak and kidney pie
tourtière

Pigs

breeds

Berkshire
British Lop
British Saddleback
Chester White
Duroc
Gloucester Old Spot
Hampshire
Landrace
Middle White
Oxford Sandy and Black
Pietrain
Poland China
Saddleback
Tamworth
Vietnamese Pot-Bellied
Welsh

wild pigs

babirusa
bush pig
hog
peccary
razorback
warthog
wild boar

Places of Worship

abbey
balmyard
baptistery/baptistry
basilica
cathedral
chantry
chapel
chapel of ease
chapel royal
chorten
church
collegiate church
dargah
duomo
fane
feretory
gurdwara
heiau
holy of holies
house of God
joss house
kirk
kiva
mandir
marabout
marae
martyry
masjid
meeting house
minster
Mithraeum
monopteros
mosque
nymphaeum
oracle
oratory
pagoda
pantheon
peculiar
sacrarium
sanctuary
sanctum sanctorum
shrine
shul
stupa
synagogue
tabernacle
temple
teocalli
tirtha/tirth
valhalla
vihara
wat

Planes

See **Aircraft**

Plant Parts

bark
bract
flower
fruit
guard cell
lateral root
leaf
phloem
root
root cap
root hair
stem
stoma
tap root
vascular bundle
xylem

Plant Types

See also **Flowering Plants and Shrubs** **Fruit** **Fungi, Mushrooms, and Toadstools** **Grasses** **Nuts** **Poisonous Plants and Fungi** **Trees and Shrubs** **Vegetables**

algae
angiosperms
bryophytes
clubmosses
conifers
cycads
ferns
fungi
gymnosperms
hornworts
horsetails
lichens
liverworts
mosses
pteridophytes
vascular plants

Plays

Types of Play and Drama

antimasque
burlesque
closet play
comedy
comedy of manners
commedia dell'arte
docudrama
dumbshow
duologue
fabula
farce
Grand Guignol
Greek drama
harlequinade
improvisation
kabuki
kitchen-sink drama
kyogen
masque
melodrama
mime
miracle play
monodrama
morality play
mummers' play
music drama
mystery play
nativity play
Noh
pantomime
passion play
psychodrama
school drama
sociodrama
teleplay
tragedy
tragicomedy
two-hander
verse drama

Poems

Types of Poem

See also **Verse Forms** **Verse Metres**

aubade
ballad
ballade
bucolic
chanson
clerihew
dirge
dithyramb
dramatic monologue
eclogue
elegy
encomium
epic
epigram
epithalamium
epode
epyllion
georgic
ghazal
haiku
idyll
lay
limerick
lyric
madrigal
monody
nursery rhyme
ode
palinode
pastoral
prothalamium
quatorzain
renga
rondeau
roundel
roundelay
saga
sapphics
satire
sestina
sonnet
tanka
threnody
triolet
vilanelle
virelay

Poets

See **Writers**

Poisonous Plants and Fungi

aconite
baneberry
belladonna
black bryony
buttercup
cowbane
deadly nightshade
death cap
desert rose
destroying angel
dog's mercury
fly agaric
fool's parsley
foxglove
greater celandine
hellebore
hemlock
henbane
Indian poke
laburnum
lucky bean
manchineel
meadow saffron
mezereon
monkshood
naked boys
naked ladies
oleander
panther cap
poison ivy
privet
the sickener
spurge laurel
stavesacre
thorn apple
upas (tree)
water dropwort
water hemlock
white snakeroot
wolfsbane

Poisonous Substances and Gases

aconitine
afterdamp
Agent Orange
aldrin
allyl alcohol
ammonia
antifreeze
arsenic
arsine
atropine
bleach
blister gas
bromine
cacodyl
cacodylic acid
carbon disulphide
carbon monoxide
caustic soda
chlordane
chlorine
coniine
curare
cyanic acid
cyanide
cyanogen
diazomethane
diborane
digitalin
digoxin
dioxane
endrin
ethylene oxide
fluorine
formaldehyde
hydrocyanic acid
hydrogen cyanide
hydrogen sulphide
hyoscyamine
iodine
lewisite
lindane
mercuric chloride
methanol
muscarine
nerve gas
nitric acid
nitrogen dioxide
osmium tetroxide
ouabain
oxalic acid
paraquat
parathion
Paris green
perchloric acid
perchloroethylene
phenol
phosgene
quinine
rat poison
ricin
rotenone
santonin
sarin
solanine
strophanthin
strychnine
sulphur dioxide
tartar emetic
tetrodotoxin
turpentine
veratrine
warfarin
white spirit
zinc chromate

Poker Hands

royal flush
straight flush
4 of a kind
full house
flush
straight
3 of a kind
2 pairs
1 pair

Police Officers and Forces

askari
assistant chief constable
bomb squad
Bow Street Runner/Officer
cadet
captain
carabiniere/carabinieri
chief (of police)
chief constable
chief inspector
chief superintendent
CID (Criminal Investigation Department)
commander
commissaire
commissioner
community police officer
constable
constabulary
crime squad
deputy chief constable
desk sergeant
detective chief inspector
detective chief superintendent
detective constable
detective inspector
detective sergeant
detective superintendent
drug/drugs squad
faujdar/faujidar
flying squad
fraud squad
Garda/Gardai
gendarme
gendarmerie
Gestapo
GPU
havildar
Homicide
inspector
investigating officer
Keystone Kops
KGB
LAPD (Los Angeles Police Department)
lieutenant
marshal
master-at-arms
Met
military police (MP)
military policeman/policewoman (MP)
Mountie
murder squad
NKVD
NYPD (New York Police Department)
pointsman
police constable
police department
port police
provost
provost guard
provost marshal
redcap
Royal Canadian Mounted Police
roundsman
Scotland Yard
secret police
Securitate
security police
sepoy
sergeant
snatch squad
SOCO (scene-of-crime officer)
special
special constable
SS
Stasi
station sergeant
strike force
super
superintendent
Sûreté
SWAT team
Sweeney
Texas Ranger
transport police
trooper
vice squad
Vopo
woman police constable

Political Philosophies and Systems

See also **Government**

absolutism
anarchism
anarcho-syndicalism
authoritarianism
Bolshevism
collectivism
communism
conservatism
democracy
egalitarianism
Eurocommunism
fascism
federalism
imperialism
individualism
laissez-faire
leftism
Leninism
liberalism
libertarianism
Maoism
Marxism
meritocracy
monarchism
nationalism
neo-Marxism
pluralism
plutocracy
populism
republicanism
rightism
situationism
social democracy
socialism
Sovietism
Stalinism
state capitalism
state socialism
statism
syndicalism
technocracy
Thatcherism
theocracy
the third way
timocracy
Titoism
totalitarianism
Trotskyism
utilitarianism
Utopianism

Porcelain

See **Pottery and Porcelain**

Pottery

Types of Pottery and Porcelain

Arita
barbotine
basalt
biscuit (ware)
bisque ware
black-figure ware
bone china
Capo di Monte
Castleford ware
celadon
champlevé
Chelsea ware
Chün
cloisonné
Coalport
creamware
Crown Derby
delft
(Royal) Doulton (*trademark*)
Dresden china
earthenware
faience
famille jaune/noire/rose/verte
graniteware
greenware
grooved ware
Halaf ware
Imari
ironstone
Iznik ware
jasper/jasperware
Kakiemon ware
Kutani ware
lustreware
maiolica
majolica
Martinware
Meissen
Ming
Minton (*trademark*)
Nabeshima ware
Parian ware
pearlware
Peterborough ware
queensware
raku
red-figure ware
Rockingham ware
Samian ware
Satsuma ware
Seto ware
Sèvres
slipware
spatterware
Spode (*trademark*)
Staffordshire ware
stone china
stoneware
terracotta
terra sigillata
Toft ware
transferware
Wedgwood (*trademark*)
willowware
(Royal) Worcester (*trademark*)

Poultry

See **Fowl**

Prayers

act of contrition
Agnus Dei
Amidah
Ave Maria
benedicite
benediction
Benedictus
bidding prayer
blessing
collect
Confiteor
Creed
decade
doxology
Gloria
grace
Habdalah/Havdalah
Hail Mary
Kaddish
Kiddush
Kol Nidre
Kyrie (eleison)
Litany
miserere
namaz
Our Father
paternoster
requiescat
rogation
salat
Salve Regina
secret
shahada/shahadah
suffrages

Priests, Religious Officials, and Members of Religious Orders

See also **Christian Religious Orders**

ancient Roman

augur
flamen
haruspex
oracle
pontifex
Pythia

ancient Celtic

Druid
ovate

Buddhist

Dalai Lama
lama
Panchen Lama
pongyi
talapoin

Christian

abbess
abbott
acolyte
almoner
anchoress
anchorite
archbishop
archdeacon
archimandrite
area dean
beadle
bishop
brother
canon
canoness
cantor
cardinal
chaplain
churchwarden
confessor
curate
deacon
deaconess
dean
elder
friar
lay brother
lay sister
mendicant
minister
monk
Monsignor
mother superior
nun
nuncio
padre
patriarch
pope
precentor
prelate
presbyter
primate
prior
prioress
rector
rural dean
sacristan
seminarist/seminarian
sexton
sister
succentor
thurifer
verger
vicar

Hindu

rishi
Brahman
guru
mahant
panda
pandit
pujari
rishi

Jewish

cantor
chief rabbi
dayan
hazzan
kohen/cohen
Levite
Maggid
rabbi
rebbe
rebbetzin

Muslim

ayatollah
bilal
caliph
fakir
imam
muezzin
mullah
sheikh

Sikh

guru

voodoo

houngan
mamaloi
mambo
papaloi

Zoroastrian/Parsee

dastur
magus

general/other

archpriest
cleric
hierarch
hierophant
high priest
preacher
priest
priestess
santero
witch
witch doctor

Printing Processes

autography
autotype
blind stamping/tooling
bubblejet printing
collotype
diazo/diazotype
die-stamping
dry mounting
dyeline
flexography
four-colour process
hot metal
inket printing
intaglio
laser printing
letterpress
letterset
linocutting
lithography
nature printing
offset
offset lithography
photogravure
photolithography
photo-offset
planography
process printing
relief printing
rotogravure
screen-printing
serigraphy
sheet printing
silk-screen
thermal printing
thermography
three-colour process
web offset
web printing
xerography
Xerox (*trademark*)
xylography

Programs
Types of Computer Program

agent
applet
application
application programming interface
assembler
BIOS
bloatware
bot
browser
cancelbot
chatterbot
client
converter
courseware
crawler
cross-assembler
cross-compiler
daemon
database management system
debugger
diagnostic
dialler
disassembler
driver
droid
editor
executable
expert system
filter
firewall
firmware
freeware
garbage collector
generator
gopher
graphic equalizer
groupware
hack
interface
interpreter
knowbot
linker
loop
macro
mailer
malware
manager
microbrowser
microprogram
middleware
nagware
navigator
newsreader
object program
outliner
packet sniffer
parametric equalizer
parser
personal information manager
plug-in
preprocessor
rotoscope
routine
run-time
scheduler
script
search engine
servlet
shareware
shell program
shovelware
simulator
sniffer
source program
spellchecker
spreadsheet
suite
telnet
text editor
tool
translator
Trojan Horse
user interface
utility
vaccine
vapourware
virus
walk-through
warez
word processor
workalike
worm

Projectiles and Projectile Weapons

See also **Bombs and Mines** **Bullets and Shot** **Guns**

projectiles

arrow
assegai
bolas
bolt
boomerang
brickbat
brinny
bullet
cruise missile
dart
flare
flechette
flying bomb
gig
Greek fire
guided missile
harpoon
heat-seeking missile
javelin
jerid
kierie
kylie
missile
mortar bomb/shell
pellet
rocket
shrapnel
shuriken
smoke ball
spear
star shell
torpedo
woomera
whiz-bang

projectile weapons

arbalest
ballista
bazooka
blowpipe
bow
catapult
crossbow
gun
harpoon gun
longbow
mangonel
missile launcher
mortar
rail gun
rocket launcher
sling
trebuchet

Prosimians

See **Lemurs and Other Prosimians**

Psychology
Branches of Psychology

abnormal psychology
Adlerian psychology
analytical psychology
apperceptionism
applied psychology
associationism
behaviourism
biopsychology
child psychology
clinical psychology
cognitive psychology
comparative psychology
configurationism
developmental psychology
educational psychology
ethology
experimental psychology
Freudianism
gestalt therapy
group psychology
Horneyan psychology
humanistic psychology
industrial and organizational psychology
introspection psychology
Jungian psychology
Lacanian psychology
metapsychology
neuropsychology
object-relations theory
occupational psychology
orgone theory
parapsychology
Pavlovian psychology
physiological psychology
psychoacoustics
psychoanalysis
psychobiochemistry
psychobiography
psychobiology
psychodynamics

psychogenetics
psychography
psycholinguistics
psychometry
psychopathology
psychopharmacology
psychophysiology
Reichian psychology
Skinnerian psychology
social psychology
structuralism
Watsonian psychology

Puddings

See **Cakes, Puddings, and Desserts**

Pullovers

cardigan
Cowichan sweater
crew neck
gansey
golfer
guernsey
jersey
jumper
maillot
polo neck
roll-neck
shrug
Siwash sweater
skinny-rib
slipover
sloppy joe
sweater
sweatshirt
turtleneck
V-neck
woolly

Punctuation Marks

accent
apostrophe
asterisk
asterism
backslash
brace
bracket
caret
colon
comma
dagger
dash
diacritical mark
ellipsis
em dash/rule
en dash/rule
exclamation mark
full stop/point
hyphen
inverted comma
obelus
omission mark
parenthesis
period
point
printer's mark
question mark
quotation mark
semicolon
solidus
square bracket
stop
stroke
swung dash
virgule

Punishments

See also **Torture Instruments**

attainder
auto-da-fé
banishment
bastinado
belt
birch
blackballing
blacklisting
boxing someone's ears
boycott
branks
cane
capital punishment
confiscation
corporal punishment
Coventry, sending to
crucifixion
cucking stool
damnation
death penalty
debagging
decimation
demotion
detention
ducking
ducking stool
endorsement
excommunication
execution
fatigues
fine
firing squad
flogging
gallows
gating
gauntlet, running the
gibbet
grounding
hanging
hanging, drawing, and quartering
hard labour
hiding
internal exile
jankers
kadaitcha/kurdaitcha
keelhauling
kneecapping
knout
kurbash
lash
lethal injection
life sentence
lines
lynching
mastheading
necktie party
noose
noyade
order mark
ostracism
pack drill
paddle
peine forte et dure
penal servitude
penalty point
penance
perdition
rod
rope
rustication
sanction
scaffold
scourging
self-flagellation
sequestration
six of the best
solitary confinement
spanking
spud-bashing
stocks
strap
strappado
suspended sentence
tarring and feathering
tawse
torture
transportation
wheel
whipping

Quarks

Flavours and Colours of Quarks and Antiquarks

beauty
blue
bottom
charm
down
green
minus-blue
minus-green
minus-red
red
strangeness
top
truth
up

Rabbits and Hares

angora
Arctic hare
Belgian hare
brown hare
chinchilla
cottontail
European rabbit
jackrabbit
mountain hare
pika
snowshoe hare

Radiation Types

alpha radiation
background radiation
backscatter
beta radiation
bremsstrahlung
Cerenkov radiation
coherent radiation
cosmic rays
electromagnetic radiation
gamma radiation
gravitational radiation
Hawking radiation
infrared (IR) radiation
insolation
ionizing radiation
light
microwaves
radar waves
radio waves
submillimetre radiation
synchrotron radiation
ultraviolet (UV) radiation
visible radiation
X-rays

Rainbow

Colours of the Rainbow

red orange yellow green blue indigo violet

Ranks

Military Ranks

British Army

Field Marshal
General
Lieutenant General
Major General
Brigadier
Colonel
Lieutenant Colonel
Major
Captain
Lieutenant
Second Lieutenant
Warrant Officer
Staff Sergeant
Sergeant
Corporal/Bombardier
Lance Corporal/Lance Bombardier
Private/Gunner

Royal Navy

Admiral of the Fleet
Admiral
Vice Admiral
Rear Admiral
Commodore
Captain
Commander
Lieutenant Commander
Lieutenant
Sub Lieutenant
Midshipman
Warrant Officer
Chief Petty Officer
Petty Officer
Leading Rating
Able Rating
Ordinary Rating

Royal Air Force

Marshal of the Royal Air Force
Air Chief Marshal
Air Marshal
Air Vice-Marshal
Air Commodore
Group Captain
Wing Commander
Squadron Leader
Flight Lieutenant
Flying Officer
Pilot Officer
Acting Pilot Officer
Warrant Officer
Flight Sergeant
Sergeant
Senior Aircraftman/Aircraftwoman
Leading Aircraftman/Aircraftwoman
Aircraftman/Aircraftwoman

US Army and Air Force

Chief of Staff
General
Lieutenant General
Major General
Brigadier General
Colonel
Lieutenant Colonel
Major
Captain
First Lieutenant
Second Lieutenant

Warrant Officer
Sergeant
Corporal
Private First Class
Private

US Navy

Chief of Naval Operations
Fleet Admiral
Admiral
Vice Admiral
Rear Admiral
Captain
Commander
Lieutenant Commander
Lieutenant
Lieutenant junior grade
Ensign
Warrant Officer
Master Chief Petty Officer
Senior Chief Petty Officer
Petty Officer
Seaman

Rats

See **Rodents**

Regions, Administrative

See **Districts**

Relatives

aunt
babyfather
babymother
brother
brother-german
brother-in-law
brother uterine
co-parent
cousin
daughter
daughter-in-law
father
father-in-law
first cousin
full brother
full sister
genitor
grandchild
granddaughter
grandfather
grandmother
grandparent
grandson
great-aunt
great-grandchild
great-granddaughter
great-grandfather
great-grandmother
great-grandparent
great-grandson
great-nephew
great-niece
great-uncle
half-brother
half-sister
husband
in-law
mother
mother-in-law
nephew
niece
parallel cousin
parent
sibling
sister
sister-german
sister-in-law
sister uterine
son
son-in-law
spouse
stepbrother
stepchild
stepdaughter
stepfather
stepmother
step-parent
stepsister
stepson
uncle
widow
widower
wife

Religions and Sects

See also **Christian Denominations Christian Doctrinal Movements Christian Religious Orders**

Baha'i

Babism

Buddhism

Falun Gong
Hinayana
Lamaism
Mahayana
Nichiren
Rinzai Zen
Soka Gakkai
Soto Zen
Tantrism
Theravada
Tibetan Buddhism
Zen

Christianity

Confucianism

neo-Confucianism

Hinduism

Brahmanism
Krishna Consciousness
Saivism
Shaktism/Saktism
Shivaism/Sivaism
Tantrism
Vaishnavism
Vedantism
Vishnuism

Islam

Druzes
Ismailis
Mahdism
Salafi
Senussi
Shia
Sufism
Sunni
Wahhabism

Jainism

Digambara
Svetambara

Judaism

Conservative Judaism
Essenes
Falashas
Hasidism
Kabbalah
Karaism
Messianic Judaism
Orthodox Judaism
Pharisaism
Rabbinism
Reconstructionism
Reform Judaism
Samaritanism
Zionism

Shinto

Sikhism

Taoism

Zoroastrianism

Mazdaism
Parseeism

other

ancestor worship
animism
candomblé
cargo cult
Druidism
Eleusinian mysteries
Ghost Dance cult
Hau-Hauism
Macumba
Mithraism
Myalism
Neopaganism
Orphism
Paganism
Pocomania
Rastafarianism
Ratana Church
Sabaism
Scientology (*trademark*)
Shamanism
Shango
Shango
Spiritualism
Subud
Theosophy
Totemism
Umbanda
Unification Church ('Moonies')
Voodoo
Wicca
Yezidism

Reptiles

See also **Snakes**

agama
alligator
alligator lizard
anole
axolotl
barking gecko
basilisk
bearded dragon
bearded lizard
blindworm
bloodsucker
box turtle
caiman
chameleon
chuckwalla
collared lizard
cooter
crocodile
diamondback terrapin
earless lizard
false gharial
fence lizard
flapshell
flying lizard
freshie
frilled lizard
Galapagos giant tortoise
galliwasp
gecko
gharial
giant tortoise
giant zonure
Gila monster
girdled lizard
glass lizard
goanna
green lizard
green turtle
hawksbill
horned toad
iguana
Jacky lizard
Komodo dragon
land mullet
leatherback
legless lizard
legless skink
leguan
lizard
loggerhead turtle
map turtle
marine iguana
matamata
moloch
monitor lizard
morocoy
mud turtle
mugger
musk turtle
night lizard
Nile crocodile
Nile monitor
padloper
painted turtle
perentie
pond turtle
racerunner
ridley turtle
rock lizard
saltwater lizard
sand lizard
scalyfoot
seps
shingleback
side-necked turtle
skink
slider
slow-worm
snake lizard
snapping turtle
softshell turtle
stinkpot turtle
sungazer
tegu
terrapin
tokay
tortoise
tuatara
turtle
twenty-four hours
viviparous lizard
wall lizard
whiptail
worm lizard
zonure

Restaurants

automat
bistro
brasserie
buffet
cafe
cafe bar
cafeteria
canteen
carry-out
carvery
chophouse
churrascaria
coffee shop
crêperie
cyber cafe
diner
drive-in
estaminet
gastropub
grillroom
internet cafe
luncheonette
mess
noodle bar
oyster bar
pizzeria
pull-in
rotisserie
snack bar
steakhouse
supper club
sushi bar
takeaway
tandoori
taqueria
taverna
tea room
tea shop
transport cafe
trattoria
truck stop

Rhetorical Devices and Figures of Speech

allegory
alliteration
anacoluthon
anadiplosis
anaphora
anastrophe
antiphrasis
antistrophe
antithesis
antonomasia
aporia
apostrophe
assonance
bathos
cacophemism
catachresis
chiasmus
circumlocution
diacope
dysphemism
echoism
ellipsis
enallage
epanalepsis
epanorthosis
epiphora
epistrophe
epizeuxis
euphemism
euphony
euphuism
hendiadys
homeoteleuton
hypallage
hyperbaton
hyperbole
hysteron proteron
innuendo
irony
isocolon
litotes
meiosis
metaphor
metonymy
onomatopoeia
oxymoron
paradox

paralipsis
paronomasia
periphrasis
personification
pleonasm
prolepsis
prosopopoeia
pun
rhetorical question
sarcasm
simile
syllepsis
symploce
synecdoche
tautology
transferred epithet
trope
zeugma

Rigging

See also **Sails**

backstay
baggywrinkle
bibb
bitt
bobstay
boom
bottlescrew
bowline
brace
brails
bullseye
buntline
burton
chainplate
cheek
claw ring
cleat
cordage
cringle
crossjack
crosstree
crowfoot
deadeye
downhaul
eye
fairlead
foot rope
foresheet
forestay
furling line
gaff
gantline
garland
gasket
gooseneck
halyard
hank
horse
hound
inhaul
jackstay
jibsheet
kicking strap
lanyard
lazy jack
lutchet
mainstay
martingale
mouse
outhaul
parrel
passaree
pendant/pennant
pole
preventer
ratlines
reefing line
reefpoint
sail tie
sheer pole
sheet
shroud
spar
spider
spider hoop
spreader
sprit
stay
step
stirrup
stopper knot
tabernacle
thimble
top
topping lift
track
traveller
trestletree
truck
truss
turnbuckle
uphaul
vangs
wishbone
yard
yardarm
yard sling

Roads

A-road
access road
accommodation road
approach road
arterial road/route
artery
Autobahn
autopista
autoroute
autostrada
avenue
B-road
backstreet
beef road
beltway
blind alley
boreen
bottleneck
boulevard
broadway
bypass
byroad
byway
cart track
causeway
clearway
close
concession road
corduroy road
corniche
corso
crescent
cul-de-sac
dead end
divided highway
drag
drive
driveway
drove road
dual carriageway
escape road
expressway
feeder
flyover
freeway
frontage road
hard
haul road
high road
high street
highway
interstate (highway)
lane
loop (road)
main drag
main road
main street
marg
motorway
national road
off-ramp
one-way street
orbital
overpass
parade
parkway
perimeter road
pike
private road
prospekt
Queen's highway
radial (road)
ramp
rat run
red route
relief road
ridgeway
ring road
Roman road
row
service road
side road
side street
single carriageway
skid road
skyway
slip road
speedway
spur
street
strip
superhighway
terrace
thoroughfare
throughway/thruway
toll road
tollway
trackway
tram road
tramway
trunk road
turnpike (road)
unadopted road
underpass
viaduct
woonerf

Rocks

See also **Gems** **Minerals**

sedimentary

arenite
argillite
breccia
chalk
chert
claystone
coal
conglomerate
diatomite
dolomite
flint
ironstone
limestone
marl
mudstone
oil shale
oolite
phosphorite
pisolite
radiolarite
rag
rudite
sandstone
shale
siltstone
tillite

metamorphic

amphibolite
blueschist
eclogite
epidiorite
epidosite
gneiss
granulite
hornfels
lapis lazuli
marble
mica schist
mylonite
phyllite
psammite
pyroxenite
quartzite
schist
serpentinite
slate
verdite

igneous

andesite
anorthosite
aplite
basalt
breccia
diorite
dolerite
dunite
elvan
felsite
gabbro
granite
greenstone
kimberlite
lamprophyre
lava
monzonite
obsidian
ophiolite
pegmatite
peridotite
phonolite
picrite
porphyry
pumice
rhyolite
syenite
tephrite
tonalite
trachyte
trap
tuff
variolite
vitrophyre

Rodents

See also **Squirrels**

acouchi
agouti
bamboo rat
bandicoot rat
bank vole
beaver
black rat
brown rat
cane rat
capybara
cavy
chinchilla
climbing mouse
common rat
cotton rat
coypu
deer mouse
degu
desert rat
dormouse
field mouse
field vole
gerbil
gopher
grasshopper mouse
guinea pig
gundi
hamster
harvest mouse
hopping mouse
house mouse
hutia
jerboa
jird
jumping mouse
kangaroo mouse
kangaroo rat
lemming
mara
marmot
meadow vole
mole rat
mountain beaver
mouse
muskrat
naked mole rat
Norway rat
paca
pacarana
pine vole
pocket mouse
porcupine
pouched rat
rat
red-backed vole
rice rat
snow vole
spiny mouse
springhaas
springhare
steppe lemming
stick-nest rat
swamp rat
tuco-tuco
vesper rat
viscacha
vole
water rat
water vole
white-footed mouse
white mouse
wood mouse
woodrat

Roles in the Theatre

anti-hero
anti-heroine
bit part
cameo
character part
chorus
comic relief
co-star
dame
deuteragonist
extra
feed
figurant
harlequin
hero
heroine
ingénue
lead
love interest
nayaka
Pantaloon
pantomime horse
Pierrot
principal boy
principal girl
prologue
protagonist
Punch
Punchinello
soubrette
spear carrier
star
stock character
super
supernumerary
title role
tritagonist
underpart
understudy
villain
walking gentleman
walking lady
walk-on

Rolls

See **Bread and Bread Rolls**

Rooms

anteroom
assembly room
atrium
attic
ballroom
basement
bathroom
bedchamber
bedroom
bedsit
bed-sitting room
boardroom
boiler room
boudoir
box room
breakfast room
buttery
card room
carrel
casemate
cell
cellar
changing room
chill-out room

classroom
cloakroom
common room
conference room
conservatory
consulting room
cutting room
darkroom
day room
decompression chamber
den
dinette
dining hall
dining room
dormitory
drawing room
dressing room
echo chamber
edit suite
engine room
family room
fitting room
Florida room
foyer
front room
gallery
garret
gas chamber
gatehouse
green room
guardroom
guest room
gunroom
hall
kitchen
kitchenette
landing
larder
lavatory
lecture room
library
living room
lobby
locker room
loft
loggia
loo
lounge
lumber room
meeting room
morning room
nursery
office
orderly room
oubliette
pantry
parlour
playroom
presence chamber
pump room
reception room
recreation room
restroom
robing room
rumpus room
sacristy
salon
saloon
sanatorium
schoolroom
scriptorium
scullery
sickbay
sickroom
sitting room
smoking room
snug
solarium
spare room
stateroom
still room
stockroom
storeroom
studio
study
study-bedroom
sun lounge
tack room
tambour
taproom
toilet
torture chamber
utility room
vestiary
vestibule
waiting room
ward
winter garden
withdrawing room
workroom

Ropes

backstay
bobstay
bolt rope
bowline
brace
brail
breeching
buntline
cable
catenary
cord
cordage
downhaul
foot rope
foresheet
forestay
gantline
guest rope
guide rope
guy
halyard
hawser
hobble
inhaul
jackstay
jib sheet
lanyard
lariat
lasso
lazy jack
leg-rope
manrope
marline
noose
outhaul
painter
ratline
rawhide
rode
runner
running rope
seizing
sheet
shroud
slip rope
span
stay
sugan
tack
tackle fall
tether
topping lift
top rope
tow rope
vang
warp

Rugby Players

attacker
back row
back-row forward
ball carrier
blocker
breakaway
centre
defender
eighthman
five-eighth
flanker
fly half
forward
front row
front-row forward
fullback
halfback
hooker
jumper
left centre three-quarter
left wing three-quarter
lock (forward)
loose forward
loose head (prop)
number eight
prop (forward)
punter
right centre three-quarter
right wing three-quarter
scrum half
second row
second-row forward
stand-off half
three-quarter
tight end
tight head (prop)
winger
wing forward
wing (three-quarter)

Rugs

See **Carpets and Rugs**

Rulers' Titles

See also **Nobles**

aga
archduke
caesar
caliph
chief
elector
electress
emir
emperor
empress
Führer
grand duke
kaiser
khan
khedive
king
maharaja
mikado
mogul
nawab
negus
nizam
pharaoh
prince
princess
queen
raja
rani
regent
satrap
shah
sheikh
shogun
sultan
tenno
tsar/czar
vicereine
viceroy

Sacred Texts and Holy Books

See also **Bible**

text	religion
Analects of Confucius	Confucianism
Atharva Veda	Hinduism
Bhagavadgita	Hinduism
Bible	Christianity
Guru Granth Sahib	Sikhism
I Ching	Confucianism
Koran	Islam
Li Chi	Confucianism
Mahabharata	Hinduism
Ramayana	Hinduism
Rig Veda	Hinduism
Sama Veda	Hinduism
Shih Ching	Confucianism
Shu Ching	Confucianism
Talmud	Judaism
Tao Te Ching	Taoism
Torah	Judaism
Tripitaka	Buddhism
Yajur Veda	Hinduism

Sailing Ships and Boats

See also **Ships and Boats**

barque
barquentine
bawley
brig
brigantine
caique
caravel
carrack
catamaran
catboat
clipper
cutter
daysailor
dhoni
dhow
dinghy
dromond
East Indiaman
felucca
frigate
full-rigger
galleon
galley
galliot
hermaphrodite brig
hooker
Indiaman
jolly (boat)
junk
keelboat
ketch
lateen
longboat
longship
lugger
man-of-war
monohull
motorsailer
multihull
nuggar
pink
pinnace
polacre
pram
proa
razee
rigger
sabot
schooner
scow
shallop
sharpie
skiff
skipjack
sloop
sloop of war
smack
snekkja
square-rigger
tall ship
tartan
training ship
trimaran
windjammer
xebec
yacht
yawl

Sails

course
fore-and-aft sail
fore-course
fore-royal
foresail
forestaysail
fore-topgallant-sail
foretopsail
gaff foresail
gaff topsail
genny
genoa (jib)
gunter
headsail
jib
jigger
kite
lateen sail
lugsail
main course
mainsail
maintopsail
mizzen
moonraker
royal sail
skysail
spanker
spinnaker
spritsail
square sail
staysail
storm sail
studdingsail
topgallant
topsail
trysail

Sauces and Dips

aioli
apple sauce
baba ghanoush
barbecue sauce
Béarnaise sauce
béchamel sauce
bolognese sauce
bordelaise sauce
bread sauce

brown sauce
carbonara sauce
catsup
chasseur sauce
chaud-froid
chawan mushi
cheese sauce
chilli sauce
cranberry sauce
demi-glace
gravy
guacamole
harissa
hoisin sauce
hollandaise sauce
horseradish sauce
hummus
ketchup
mayonnaise
milanese sauce
mint sauce
mornay sauce
mousseline sauce
mustard sauce
onion sauce
parsley sauce
pebre
pepper sauce
pesto
pizzaiola sauce
ragù
salsa verde
satay sauce
sauce ravigote
sauce remoulade
skordalia
soubise
soy sauce
sweet and sour sauce
Tabasco sauce
taramasalata
tartare sauce
Teriyaki sauce
tomato ketchup
tzatziki
velouté
white sauce
Worcester sauce

Sausages

andouille
baloney/boloney
black pudding
blood pudding
blood sausage
boerewors
bologna
bratwurst
cervelat
chipolata
chorizo
crépinette
Cumberland sausage
frank
frankfurter
keilbasa
knackwurst
merguez
mortadella
pepperoni
salami
saucisson
saveloy
slim jim
summer sausage
weenie
Weisswurst
white pudding
wiener
wurst

Saws

bandsaw
bench saw
bowsaw
chainsaw
circular saw
compass saw
coping saw
cross-cut saw
dovetail saw
frame saw
fretsaw
grooving saw
hacksaw
handsaw
hole saw
jigsaw
keyhole saw
padsaw
panel saw
pitsaw
pruning saw
rabbet saw
ripsaw
sawbench
scroll saw
Swede saw
tenon saw
whipsaw

Scale

See **Tonic Sol-Fa Notes**

Schools

boarding school
board school
charity school
charter school
cheder
choir school
church school
City Technology College (CTC)
co-educational school
college
comprehensive (school)
conservatory
convent
county school
day school
direct-grant school
elementary school
farm school
finishing school
first school
free school
grade school
grammar school
grant-maintained school (GM school)
high school
infant school
junior high school
junior school
kindergarten
lower school
magnet school
middle school
night school
nursery school
parochial school
preparatory/prep school
pre-school
primary school
private school
public school
residential school
secondary modern (school)
secondary school
seminary
senior high school
separate school
sixth-form centre/college
special school
state school
Talmud Torah
upper school
voluntary school
yeshiva

Science
Branches of Science

See also **Engineering Geography Mathematics Medicine Psychology**

acoustics
aerodynamics
agriscience
anatomy
anthropology
astronomy
astrophysics
atomic physics
bacteriology
behavioural science
biochemistry
biology
botany
chemistry
climatology
computer science
conchology
cosmology
cryogenics
crystallography
cybernetics
cytology
dendrology
dynamics
earth science
ecology
economics
electrical engineering
electrodynamics
electronics
endocrinology
engineering
entomology
epidemiology
ethnology
ethology
evolutionary psychology
exobiology
fluid mechanics
forensics
genetic engineering
genetics
geochemistry
geochronology
geography
geology
geomorphology
geophysics
glaciology
haematology
herpetology
histology
holography
hydrodynamics
hydrology
hydrostatics
ichthyology
immunology
information technology
limnology
linguistics
marine biology
mathematics
mechanics
medical physics
medicine
metallurgy
meteorology
microbiology
mineralogy
molecular biology
mycology
natural history
nephology
neurochemistry
neurology
neuroscience
nuclear chemistry
nuclear physics
oceanography
oncology
ophthalmology
optics
ornithology
palaeobotany
palaeoclimatology
palaeontology
palynology
parasitology
particle physics
pathology
pedology
petrology
pharmacology
photochemistry
physics
physiography
physiology
phytology
phytopathology
psychiatry
psychology
quantum mechanics
radiochemistry
radiology
robotics
seismology
sociobiology
sociology
soil science
spectroscopy
statistics
stratigraphy
taxonomy
tectonics
thermodynamics
toxicology
veterinary medicine
virology
volcanology/vulcanology
zoogeography
zoology
zymurgy

Scotch

See **Whiskies**

Scripture

See **Bible Sacred Texts and Holy Books**

Seals, Sea Lions, and Sea Cows

Baikal seal
bearded seal
common seal
crabeater seal
dugong
elephant seal
fur seal
grey seal
harbour seal
harp seal
hooded seal
leopard seal
manatee
monk seal
ringed seal
Ross seal
sea cow
sea elephant
seal
sea lion
Steller's sea cow
walrus
Weddell seal

Seashells

See **Shells**

Sects

See **Religions and Sects**

Sellers of Goods

seller	goods
apothecary	medicines
baker	bread
bibliopole	books
bowyer	archers' bows
butcher	meat
chandler	candles
cheesemonger	dairy products
chocolatier	chocolate
clothier	clothes
colporteur	books etc.
confectioner	confectionery
cosmetician	cosmetics
costermonger	fruit and vegetables
couturier	clothes
cutler	cutlery
dairyman	dairy products
draper	textile fabrics
druggist	medicinal drugs
fishmonger	fish
fishwife	fish
fletcher	arrows
florist	cut flowers
flower girl	flowers
fruiterer	fruit
furnisher	furniture
furrier	furs
glazier	glass
greengrocer	fruit and vegetables
grocer	food and small household goods
gunsmith	firearms
haberdasher	sewing items (*Brit.*)
haberdasher	men's clothes (*N. Amer.*)
hatter	hats
herbalist	medicinal herbs
horse-coper	horses
hosier	hosiery
iceman	ice
ironmonger	hardware
jeweller	jewels and jewellery
licensed victualler	alcohol
mercer	fabrics
milkman	milk
milliner	women's hats
newsagent	newspapers
perfumer	perfume
pieman	pies
plumassier	ornamental feathers
poulterer	poultry
salter	salt
seedsman	seeds
ship (*or* ship's) chandler	nautical supplies and equipment
skinner	animal skins
slaver	slaves
stationer	stationery
tobacconist	tobacco
victualler	food
woolman	wool

Sewing Techniques and Stitches

appliqué
backstitch
bar tack
basting
binding
blackwork
blanket stitch
blind stitch
bullion knot
buttonhole stitch
chain stitch
chikan
couching
crewel work
crocheting
cross stitch
crow's foot
cutwork
darning
dart
drawn work
embroidery
facing
faggoting
feather stitch
fine-drawing
Florentine stitch
French knot
fulling
gathering
gros point
hemstitch
herringbone stitch
ladder stitch
laid work
lazy daisy stitch
lock stitch
loop stitch
mitring
needlepoint
overcasting
overlocking
oversewing
overstitch
patchwork
petit point
pleating
purl
quilting
ruching
ruffling
running stitch
saddle stitch
satin stitch
scalloping
shadow stitch
shirring
slip stitch
smocking
stay stitch
stem stitch
straight stitch
Swiss darning
tacking
tapestry
tent stitch
topstitch
treble
tucking
tufting
whipstitch
whitework
wool work

Shapes

Geometric Shapes

See also **Curves Lens Shapes Patterns Triangles**

annulus
circle
decagon
diamond
dodecagon
ellipse
hendecagon
heptagon
hexagon
kite
lozenge
nonagon
oblong
octagon
ovoid
parallelogram
pentagon
pentagram
pentangle
polygon
quadrangle
quadrant
quadrilateral
rectangle
rhomboid
rhombus
roundel
semicircle
square
tetragon
trapezium
trapezoid
triangle
trigon
undecagon

Sharks

basking shark
blue shark
bonnethead
bramble shark
carpet shark
cat shark
cow shark
dogfish
frilled shark
great white shark
gummy
hammerhead
huss
mako
megamouth
nurse hound
nurse shark
porbeagle
requiem shark
sand shark
sea-angel
selachian
smooth hound
spur-dog
thresher
tiger shark
tope
whaler
whale shark
wobbegong/ wobbegon

Sheep

breeds

Abyssinian
Afrikander
Altai
Askanian
Australian Merino
Awassi
Berber
Bergamo
Beulah Speckled Face
Biella
Blackface
Blackhead Persian
Black Welsh Mountain
Blue-faced Leicester
Border Leicester
Boreray
Bosnian Mountain
Brazilian Woolless
Brecknock Hill Cheviot
British Blue du Maine
British Charollais
British Friesland
British Milksheep
British Oldenburg
British Texel
British Vendéen
Broadtail
Cambridge
Campanian Barbary
Cannock Chase
Castlemilk Moorit
Caucasian
Cheviot
Chios
Clun Forest
Colbred
Columbia
Corriedale
Cotswold
Dalesbred
Dartmoor
Derbyshire Gritstone
Devon Closewool
Devon Longwool
Dorper
Dorset Down
Dorset Horn
Dubrovnik
East Friesland
English Halfbred
English Longwool
Exmoor Horn
Finnish Landrace
French Blackheaded
Galway
Greek Zackel
Hampshire Down
Hebridean
Herdwick
Hexham Leicester
Hill Radnor
Icelandic
Île-de-France
Island Pramenka
Jacob
Karakachan
Karakul
Kent
Kerry Hill
Kivircik
Lacaune
Lacho
Lamon
Leicester
Lincoln Longwool
Llanwenog
Lleyn
Longwool
Lonk
Lourdes
Manech
Manx Loghtan
Masai
Masham
Merino
Mongolian
Mug
Mule
Norfolk Horn
North Country Cheviot
North Ronaldsay
Old Norwegian
Orkney
Oxford Down
Panama
Persian
Poll Dorset
Polwarth
Portland
Précoce
Radnor

Rambouillet
Red Karaman
Rhiw Hill
Romanov
Romeldale
Romney Marsh
Rouge de l'Ouest
Rough Fell
Ryeland
St. Kilda
Sardinian
Scottish Blackface
Scottish Halfbred
Shetland
Shropshire
Sicilian
Soay
South Devon
Southdown
South Wales Mountain
Spanish Merino
Suffolk
Swaledale
Swedish Landrace
Swiss White Alpine
Swiss White Mountain
Talavera
Targhee
Teeswater
Texel
Tibetan
Tsigai
Tyrol Mountain
Welsh Halfbred
Welsh Hill Speckled
Welsh Mountain
Welsh Mountain Badger-faced
Welsh Mule
Wensleydale
Whiteface Dartmoor
Whiteface Woodlands
Wicklow Mountain
Wiltshire Horn

wild sheep

aoudad
argali
Barbary sheep
bharal
bighorn
blue sheep
Dall/Dall's sheep
mouflon
mountain sheep
urial
white sheep

Shells
Seashells

abalone
angel wing
ark shell
auger
basket shell
bonnet
bubble shell
canoe shell
carpet shell
carrier shell
cask shell
chambered nautilus
chank
clam
coat-of-mail
cockle
cock's-comb oyster
conch
cone
cowrie
cup-and-saucer
date mussel
dog whelk
dove shell
drill
drupe
ear shell
fighting conch
fig shell
file shell
flamingo tongue
frog shell
furrow shell
gaper
giant clam
hard clam
harp
heart cockle
helmet
hoof shell
horn shell
horse mussel
jewel box
jingle shell
junonia
keyhole limpet
lima
limpet
lion's paw
lucine
marginella
mitre
money cowrie
moon shell
murex
mussel
nautilus
necklace shell
nerite
Noah's ark
nutmeg shell
nut shell
olive
ormer
otter shell
oyster
oyster drill
partridge shell
pearly nautilus
pelican's foot
pen shell
periwinkle
pheasant shell
piddock
puka (shell)
pyramid shell
quahog
queen scallop
razor shell
rock shell
saddle oyster
scallop
sea snail
slipper limpet
slit limpet
slit shell
spider conch
spindle shell
spire shell
staircase shell
sundial
sunset shell
tellin
thorny oyster
tiger cowrie
tooth shell
top shell
tower shell
triton
triton's trumpet
trough shell
trumpet shell
tulip shell
tun
turban
turkey wing
turret shell
tusk shell
umbrella shell
vase shell
venus
Venus shell/clam
violet sea snail
volute
wedge shell
wentletrap
whelk
wing oyster
winkle
worm shell
zebra mussel

Sherries

amontillado
amoroso
cream sherry
fino
manzanilla
oloroso
palo cortado
vino de pasto

Ship Parts

See also **Anchors**

after deck
anchor
berth
bilge
bilge keel
bitt
board
boat deck
boiler room
bollard
bow
bridge
brig
bulkhead
bullseye
bulwarks
cabin
caboose
capstan
carline
cathead
cat hole
centreboard
chain locker
chart room
cleat
companion ladder
companionway
counter
crow's nest
daggerboard
davit
dodger
engine room
false keel
figurehead
fin keel
flight deck
forecastle/fo'c'sle
freeboard
funnel
futtock
galley
gangplank
gangway
glory hole
guard rail
gudgeon
gun deck
gunwale/gunnel
half-deck
hatch
hatchway
hawsehole
hawsepipe
hawser
head
hold
keel
keelson
larboard
lazaretto
limber
limber hole
mainmast
maintop
mast
mizzenmast
mizzentop
monkey rail
oar
orlop deck
outboard
outrigger
paddle wheel
painter
pilot house
pintle
planking
Plimsoll line
poop
poop deck
porthole
portside
promenade deck
propeller
propeller shaft
prow
quarter rail
quarters
radio room
rail
riding lamp
rigger
round house
rowlock
rudder
rudderpost
scupper
skeg
spanker
stabilizer
stack
stanchion
starboard
stateroom
stern
sternpost
strake
stretcher
stringer
thole
tiller
transom
trunnion
turtleback
wardroom
washboard
washstrake
waterline
weatherboard
weather deck
wheel
winch
windlass

Ships and Boats

See also **Sailing Ships and Boats**

airboat
aircraft carrier
amphibious assault ship
amphibious landing craft
auxiliary
banker
barge
bateau mouche
bathyscaphe
bathysphere
battlecruiser
battleship
bidarka
bireme
boatel
bulk carrier
bumboat
butty
cabin cruiser
cable ship
canal boat
canoe
capital ship
cargo ship
catamaran
chain ferry
chalupa
coaler
coal ship
coaster
coble
cockboat
cockle
cockleshell
cog
collier
container ship
coracle
corvette
crabber
cruiser
cruise ship
cutter
dahabeeyah
destroyer
dinghy
diving bell
dory
double-ender
dragon boat
dreadnought
dredger
drifter
dromond
dugout
DUKW/duck
E-boat
factory ship
ferry
flag boat
flagship
flat boat
freighter
frigate
galliot
gig
gondola
gunboat
helicopter carrier
hooker
hospital ship
houseboat
hovercraft
hydrofoil
hydroplane
iceboat
ice-breaker
inboard
Indiaman
inflatable dinghy
ironclad
jetboat
jetfoil
jet ski (*trademark*)
johnboat
jolly (boat)
kayak
keelboat
keeler
laker
landing craft
lapstrake
lateen
launch
liberty boat
lifeboat
life raft
lighter
lightship
liner
longboat
longliner
longship
mailboat
man-of-war
merchantman
merchant ship
minehunter
minelayer
minesweeper
monitor
monkey-boat
monohull
mosquito boat
motor boat
motorsailer
motor torpedo boat (MTB)
motor yacht
multihull
narrowboat
oiler
oil tanker
outboard
outrigger
packet boat
paddle boat
paddle steamer
passenger ship
pedal boat
pedalo
pilot boat
pinnace
pirogue
pitpan
pocket battleship
pontoon
powerboat
pram
prawner
privateer
proa
PT boat
punt
quinquereme
Q-ship
raft
randan
revenue cutter
RIB
riverboat
roll-on roll-off
rowing boat
rubber dinghy
safety boat
sailing boat
sailing ship
sampan
school ship
schooner
scow
scull
sculler
sealer
shallop
sharpie
shell
shikara
ship of the line
ship's boat
showboat
shrimper
side-wheeler
single-hander
ski boat
skiff
skipjack
slaver

sloop
smack
sneakbox
speedboat
squirt boat
stake boat
steamboat
steamer
steamship
sternwheeler
submarine
submersible
supertanker
supply ship
surfboat
tall ship
tanker
tartan
tender
three-decker
torpedo boat
trader
traghetto
train ferry
tramp steamer
trawler
trimaran
trireme
troop carrier
troopship
tub
tugboat
umiak
vaporetto
warship
water bus
water taxi
weekender
whaleboat
whaler
wherry
windjammer
workboat
yacht

Shirts

aloha shirt
blouse
banyan
boiled shirt
button-down
choli
dashiki
dress shirt
evening shirt
grandad shirt
guayabera
hair shirt
kaftan
kurta
long-sleeved shirt
middy blouse
nightshirt
olive-drab shirt
overblouse
overshirt
plastron
polo shirt
sark
short-sleeved shirt
skivvy
smock
sports shirt
sweatshirt
tee
T-shirt

Shoes

See **Footwear**

Shops
Specialist Shops

See also **Sellers of Goods**

shop	goods sold
bakery	bread and cakes
bodega	wine and food
boutique (*Brit.*)	clothes
boutique (*N. Amer.*)	specialist goods
butcher's	meat
cantina	wine
chandlery	candles
charcuterie	cold cooked meats
charity shop	second-hand goods
chemist (*Brit.*)	medicinal drugs
confectioner's	sweets
convenience store	household goods and groceries
corner shop (*Brit.*)	household goods and groceries
creamery	dairy products
dairy	dairy products
delicatessen	speciality foods
dime store (*N. Amer.*)	cheap merchandise
drugstore (*N. Amer.*)	medicinal drugs and toiletries
factory shop/outlet	surplus factory stock
fishmonger	fish
five-and-dime (*N. Amer.*)	household goods
florist's	cut flowers
greengrocer's	fruit and vegetables
grocery	food and household goods
haberdashery (*Brit.*)	dressmaking and sewing goods
haberdashery (*N. Amer.*)	men's clothing
heel bar	shoe repairs
ironmonger (*Brit.*)	tools and household implements
jeweller's	jewels and jewellery
junk shop	second-hand goods
newsagent	newspapers
off-licence	alcoholic drink
parfumerie	perfume
patisserie	pastries and cakes
perfumery	perfume
pharmacy	medicinal drugs
saddlery	saddles etc.
smoke shop (*N. Amer.*)	tobacco and smoking equipment
snackette	snacks and groceries
soda fountain (*N. Amer.*)	soft drinks
stationer	stationery
supermarket	food
tabac	tobacco
thrift shop	second-hand goods
tobacconist	tobacco and smoking equipment
tuck shop (*Brit.*)	sweets

Shot

See **Bullets and Shot**

Shrubs

See **Flowering Plants and Shrubs** **Trees and Shrubs**

Singers

See also **Voices**

balladeer
choirboy
choirgirl
chorister
chorus boy
chorus girl
coloratura
crooner
diva
folk singer
gleeman
Heldentenor
jongleur
Meistersinger
minstrel
opera singer
pop singer
pop star
precentor
prima donna
primo uomo
singer-songwriter
soloist
spinto
troubadour

Sins
The Seven Deadly Sins

See also **Virtues**

anger
covetousness
envy
gluttony
lust
pride
sloth

Skeleton

See **Bones** **Vertebrae**

Skirts

A-line skirt
ballet skirt
crinoline
dirndl
divided skirt
filibeg
flared skirt
full skirt
fustanella
gathered skirt
gored skirt
grass skirt
hobble skirt
hoop skirt
hula skirt
kilt
lungi
maxi
midi
mini
miniskirt
overskirt
pencil skirt
piupiu
pleated skirt
puffball skirt
rah-rah skirt
sarong
skort
slit skirt
sports skirt
straight skirt
tennis skirt
tutu
underskirt
wrap-around skirt

Snakes

adder
Aesculapian snake
anaconda
asp
bandy-bandy
black mamba
blind snake
boa
boa constrictor
boomslang
brown snake
bull snake
bushmaster
carpet python
carpet snake
cerastes
coachwhip
cobra
colubrid
constrictor
copperhead
coral snake
corn snake
cottonmouth
death adder
diamondback (rattlesnake)
diamond python
dugite
egg-eating snake
Egyptian cobra
false coral snake
fer de lance
file snake
flowerpot snake
flying snake
Gaboon viper
garter snake

gopher snake
grass snake
green snake
hamadryad
highland moccasin
hognose snake
horned snake
indigo snake
keelback
king cobra
krait
mamba
massasauga
milk snake
night adder
pine snake
pipe snake
pit viper
puff adder
python
racer
rat snake
rattlesnake
reticulated python
rinkhals
rock python
rubber boa
Russell's viper
sea krait
sea snake
shieldtail snake
sidewinder
skaapsteker
smooth snake
spitting cobra
swamp snake
taipan
tiger snake
tree snake
viper
wart snake
water moccasin
water snake
whip snake
wolf snake
woma
worm snake

Snow Types and Conditions

breakable crust
champagne powder
corn snow
crust
firn
graupel
névé
piste
powder (snow)
slush
snow-ice
spring snow
wind pack
windslab

Soldiers
Types of Soldier

See also **Ranks**

archer
artilleryman
banneret
beefeater
blue helmet
bowman
brave
cadet
cannoneer
carabineer
cataphract
cavalier
cavalryman
centurion
chasseur
commando
conscript
cuirassier
doughboy
draftee
dragoon
drum major
enlisted man
ensign
evzone
fencible
foot soldier
freelance
fugleman
fusilier
galloglass
grenadier
guardsman
guerrilla
gunner
halberdier
havildar
hoplite
hussar
infantryman
irregular
janissary
jawan
kern
klepht
knight
lancer
landsknecht
legionary
legionnaire
marine
mercenary
military policeman/policewoman
militiaman
miner
musketeer
NCO
officer
orderly
other ranks
paratrooper
partisan
pistoleer
point man
ranger
ranker
recruit
redcap
redcoat
regular
reservist
rifleman
sabreur
samurai
sapper
scout
SEAL
sentinel
sentry
sepoy
spahi
spearman
swordsman
Territorial
tirailleur
trooper
uhlan
vedette
yeoman

Songs

See **Musical Forms**

Soups

bisque
borscht
bouillabaisse
bouillon
broth
burgoo
callaloo
chowder
cock-a-leekie
congee
consommé
Cullen skink
gazpacho
goulash
gumbo
madrilene
menudo
minestrone
mock turtle soup
mulligatawny
oxtail
petite marmite
pistou
potage
pot-au-feu
rasam
sancoche
Scotch broth
shchi
skilly
stracciatella
vichyssoise

Spears

See **Projectiles** **Weapons**

Spectacles

See **Glasses**

Spices

See also **Herbs**

ajowan
allspice
black pepper
capers
caraway seeds
cardamom
cassia
cayenne pepper
chilli
cinnamon
cloves
coriander
cumin
curcuma
fennel seeds
fenugreek
five-spice
galangal
garam masala
garlic
ginger
ginseng
grains of Paradise
green pepper
jalapeño (pepper)
juniper berries
mace
mustard
nutmeg
paprika
pepper
pimento
star anise
sumac
turmeric
vanilla
white pepper

Spiders and Other Arachnids

baboon spider
beetle mite
bird-eating spider
black widow
button spider
camel spider
cardinal spider
chigger
cobweb spider
crab spider
diadem spider
false scorpion
funnel-web spider
harvestman
harvest mite
hunting spider
huntsman spider
itch mite
jockey spider
jumping spider
katipo
mite
money spider
mygalomorph
orb weaver
orb-web spider
raft spider
redback
red spider mite
retiary spider
scorpion
scorpion spider
solifuge
spider
spider mite
sun spider
tarantula
tick
trapdoor spider
varroa
violin spider
water scorpion
water spider
whip scorpion
white-tailed spider
wind scorpion
wolf spider
wood tick
zebra spider

Spirits

See **Drinks** **Whiskies**

Sports

See also **Athletics Events** **Ball Games** **Equestrian Sports** **Gymnastics Events** **Martial Arts** **Motor Sports**

aerobatics
aerobics
Alpine skiing
American football
angling
aquaplaning
archery
Association Football
athletics
Australian Rules football
badminton
ballooning
baseball
base-jumping
basketball
beach volleyball
beagling
billiards
BMX
bobsleighing
bocce
boule/boules
bowling
bowls
boxing
broomball
bullfighting
bungee jumping
caber tossing
Canadian football
canoe racing
canyoning
carom billiards
caving
clay-pigeon shooting
climbing
clock golf
coarse fishing
coursing
cricket
croquet
crossbow archery
cross-country running
crown-green bowls
curling
cycle racing
cycling
cyclo-cross
darts
dinghy racing
diving
downhill racing
Eton fives
falconry
fencing
field hockey
figure-skating
fishing
five-a-side football
fivepin bowling
fives
flat-green bowls
fly-fishing
football
fowling
freediving
free skating
freestyle skiing
French cricket
Gaelic football
game fishing
gliding
goalball
golf
greyhound racing
gymnastics
handball
hang-gliding
hiking
hockey
hurling
hydrospeed
ice climbing
ice dancing
ice hockey
ice skating
jai alai
jet-skiing
kabaddi
kayaking
kiteboarding
kitesurfing
korfball
lacrosse
langlauf
lawn tennis
luge
match fishing
mountain biking
mountaineering

netball
ninepins
Nordic skiing
orienteering
paddleball
paddle tennis
pall-mall
parachuting
paragliding
parapente/parapenting
parasailing
parascending
paraskiing
pelota
pétanque
pigeon racing
pistol shooting
pool
potholing
powerboat racing
quoits
rackets
racquetball
rafting
real tennis
ringette
rock climbing
rollerblading
roller hockey
roller skating
roller skiing
rounders
rowing
Rugby fives
rugby league
rugby union
sailing
sailplaning
scuba-diving
sculling
sea fishing
shinny
shinty
shooting
short tennis
skateboarding
skeet
ski-bob racing
skiing
skijoring
ski jumping
skin diving
skittles
skydiving
sky surfing
slalom
sled-dog racing
snooker
snorkelling
snowboarding
soccer
softball
speedball
speed skating
spelunking
sprinting
squash
stoolball
surfing
swimming
synchronized swimming
table tennis
tennis
tenpin bowling
tobogganing
touch football
trap shooting
volleyball
wakeboarding
walking
water polo
waterskiing
weightlifting
white-water rafting
wildfowling
wild-water racing
windsurfing
wrestling
yacht racing

Squirrels and Related Rodents

anomalure
chickaree
chipmunk
flying squirrel
giant squirrel
gopher
grey squirrel
groundhog
ground squirrel
marmot
mountain beaver
palm squirrel
petaurist
pocket gopher
prairie dog
red squirrel
scaly-tailed squirrel
souslik
sun squirrel
tree squirrel
woodchuck

Star Types

astrometric binary
binary star
brown dwarf
cepheid
collapsar
dark star
double star
dwarf star
eclipsing binary
flare star
giant
lodestar
magnetar
neutron star
nova
polar
polar star
pulsar
quasar
red dwarf
red giant
supergiant
supernova
variable star
visual binary
white dwarf

Stews

boeuf bourguignon
bouillabaisse
bredie
Brunswick stew
burgoo
callaloo
carbonnade
casserole
cassoulet
chilli con carne
coq au vin
daube
étouffée
feijoada
fricassée
goulash
grillade
hopping john
hotpot
Irish stew
jollof rice
Lancashire hotpot
lobscouse
mannish water
mulligan
navarin
olio
olla podrida
osso bucco
pepper pot
potjie
pot pie
ragout
salmi
slumgullion
smoor
stifado
stovies
tsimmes

Stitches

See **Sewing Techniques and Stitches**

Stones

See **Birthstones** **Gems** **Rocks**

Stools

See **Chairs and Stools**

Stories
Types of Story and Novel

adventure story
Aga saga
allegory
antinovel
autobiography
bedtime story
Bildungsroman
black comedy
blockbuster
bodice-ripper
bonkbuster
cliffhanger
comedy
conte
crime story
detective story/novel
dime novel
epic
epistolary novel
exemplum
fable
fabliau
fairy story
fairy tale
fantasy
folk story
folk tale
ghost story
gothic novel
graphic novel
heartbreaker
historical novel
horror story
just-so story
legend
Märchen
mystery
myth
nancy story
nouveau roman
novelette
novelization
novella
parable
photonovel
picaresque novel
police procedural
policier
roman-à-clef
roman-à-thèse
romance
roman expérimental
roman-fleuve
roman noir
romantic novel
saga
short story
spine-chiller
stream of consciousness
sword and sorcery
tearjerker
techno-thriller
thriller
true story
urban myth
western
whodunnit

Stringed Instruments

See also **Keyboard Instruments**

acoustic guitar
aeolian harp
archlute
arpeggione
autoharp
balalaika
bandora/bandura
banjo
banjolele/banjulele
banjolin
baryton
bass guitar
bass lute
bass viol
biwa
bouzouki
cello
Celtic harp
charango
chitarrone
cimbalom
citole
cittern
clarsach
classical guitar
contrabass
cuatro
dobro (*trademark*)
double bass
dulcimer
electric guitar
erhu
fiddle
gamba
gittern
guitar
gusli
harp
Hawaiian guitar
hurdy-gurdy
kanoon
kantele
kithara
kora
koto
lute
lyre
mandola
mandolin
orpharion
oud
pedal steel guitar
pipa
psaltery
rebab
rebec
requinto
samisen
santoor
sarangi
sarod
saz
sitar
steel/steel-string guitar
string bass
tamboura
tamburitza
theorbo
trigon
triple harp
twelve-string guitar
ukulele
veena
vihuela de arco
vihuela de mano
viol
viola
viola bastarda
viola da gamba
viola d'amore
violetta
violin
violoncello
violone
Welsh harp
wind harp
zither

Sugar
Types of Edible Sugar

beet sugar
brown sugar
candy (*Brit.*)
cane sugar
caster/castor sugar
crystallized sugar
cube sugar
demerara (sugar)
fruit sugar
golden syrup
granulated sugar
gur
icing sugar
jaggery
lump sugar
maple sugar
molasses
muscovado (sugar)
palm sugar
penuche/panocha
powdered sugar
preserving sugar
refined sugar
syrup
treacle
white sugar

Sugars
Biochemical Sugars

arabinose
deoxyribose
dextrose
disaccharide
fructose
galactosamine
galactose
glucose
grape sugar
hexose
inulin
invert sugar
lactose
lactulose
laevulose
maltose
mannose
monosaccharide
pectose
pentose
photosynthate
raffinose
rhamnose
ribose

ribulose
saccharose
sorbose
sucrose
tetrose
trehalose
triose
trisaccharide
xylose

Suits of Cards

standard pack

clubs
diamonds
hearts
spades

tarot pack

cups
pentacles/coins/discs
swords
trumps
wands/batons

Surgical Instruments

bistoury
bougie
burr
cannula
colposcope
curette
depressor
dilator
forceps
gouge
guillotine
haemostat
lancet
laparoscope
osteotome
probe
raspatory
retractor
scalpel
scarificator
scoop
sigmoidoscope
snare
tenaculum
trepan
trephine
trocar

Surgical Operations

See **Operations**

Sweaters

See **Pullovers**

Sweets and Confectionery

See also **Cakes, Puddings, and Desserts**

acid drop
aniseed ball
barley sugar
boiled sweet
brittle
bullseye
burfi
butterscotch
candy cane
candyfloss
caramel
chew
chewing gum
chocolate
chocolate drop
coconut ice
comfit
cracknel
crystallized fruit
dolly mixtures
dragée
Easter egg
fondant
fruit drop
fruit gum
fruit pastille
fudge
gobstopper
gulab jamun
gumdrop
halva
hazlenut whirl
humbug
jalebi
jelly
jelly baby
jelly bean
jujube
Kendal mint cake
laddu
lemon sherbert
liquorice
liquorice allsort
lollipop
lolly
marshmallow
marzipan
mint
nougat
pastille
patty
pear drop
peppermint
peppermint cream
Pontefract cake
praline
rasgulla
rock
sherbert
sherbert dip
sugared almond
toffee
toffee apple
truffle
Turkish delight
wine gum

Swimming Strokes, Kicks, and Dives

Australian crawl
backcrawl
backstroke
breaststroke
butterfly
crawl
doggy-paddle
dolphin kick
duck-dive
fishtail kick
frog kick
front crawl
jackknife
overarm stroke
recovery stroke
scissors kick
sidestroke
swallow dive
swan dive
trudgen

Swords

See **Weapons**

Symbols

See **Elements and Their Symbols**

Tables and Desks

altar
bedside table
billiard table
bonheur du jour
bureau
card table
coffee table
console table
credence table
davenport
dresser
dressing table
drop-leaf table
duchesse
dumb waiter
escritoire
gaming table
gateleg table
kneehole desk
lap desk
lectern
loo table
nightstand
night table
operating table
partners' desk
pedestal table
Pembroke table
piecrust table
pier table
pinball table
prothesis
refectory table
rent table
roll-top desk
secretaire
steam table
tabouret
teapoy
tea table
trestle table
trivet table
vanity table
writing desk

Taxes

advance corporation tax (ACT)
airport tax
alternative minimum tax (AMT)
capital gains tax (CGT)
capital levy
capital transfer tax(CTT)
capitation
carbon tax
community charge
corporation tax
council tax
countervailing duty
customs (duty)
death duty
estate duty
estate tax
excise
goods and services tax (GST)
groundage
income tax
inheritance tax
inland duty
insurance tax
landfill tax
land tax
metage
murage
nagative income tax
octroi
pavage
PAYE (pay as you earn)
Peter's pence
poll tax
poor rate
post-war credit
property tax
purchase tax
rates
road tax
sales tax
ship money
stallage
stamp duty
supertax
surtax
taille
tallage
tarrif
tithe
toll
transit duty
uniform business rate (UBR)
VAT (value added tax)
vehicle excise duty (VED)
wealth tax
windfall tax
window tax
withholding tax
zakat

Teas

Assam
black tea
bohea
bush tea
camomile tea
Ceylon
China
congou
Darjeeling
Earl Grey
fruit tea
green tea
gunpowder tea
herbal tea
hyson
iced tea
Indian
jasmine tea
Keemun
Labrador tea
Lapsang Souchong
lemon tea
maté
mint tea
oolong
orange pekoe
pekoe
peppermint tea
post-and-rail tea
pouchong
rooibos tea
rosehip tea
Russian tea
sage tea
souchong
tilleul
tisane
yerba buena
yerba maté

Telescopes

almucantar
altazimuth telescope
astronomical telescope
Cassegrain telescope
cathetometer
collimator
coudé telescope
Dobsonian telescope
equatorial telescope
finder
Galilean telescope
Gregorian telescope
heliometer
Maksutov telescope
meridian circle
monocular
Newtonian telescope
radio telescope
reflecting telescope
refracting telescope
Schmidt telescope
Schmidt–Cassegrain telescope
space telescope
telescopic sight
terrestrial telescope

Television Components

aerial
amplifier
cabinet
cathode-ray tube
chrominance signal extractor
colour decoder
control
deflector coil
downconverter
electron gun
loudspeaker
luminance signal amplifier
phosphor dots
scanning current generator
screen
set-top box
shadow mask
sound demodulator
synchronizing pulse separator
tuner
V-chip

Temples

See **Places of Worship**

Tennis Strokes

ace
backhand
cross-court
dink
drive
drop shot
forehand
groundstroke
half-volley
lob
overhead
passing shot
serve
slice
smash
stop volley
volley

Tents

barrel-vaulted tent
bell tent
big top
bivvy
box tent
conical tent
dome tent
frame tent
kibitka
lodge
marquee
mat tent
oxygen tent
pandal
pavilion
pup tent
ridge tent
shamiana
tabernacle
tepee/teepee/tipi
touring tent
trailer tent
tunnel tent
tupik
wall tent
wigwam
yurt

Textiles

See **Fabrics and Fibres**

Theatre

Parts of a Theatre

See also **Plays**

acting area
aisle
apron (stage)
auditorium
backstage
balcony
the boards
box
box office
bridge
catwalk
circle
coulisse
curtain
cut drop
cyclorama
dais
dress circle
dressing room
drop curtain
fire curtain
the flies
floats
fly gallery
fly tower
footlights
forestage
foyer
front of house
gallery
the gods
green room
gridiron
house lights
iron
lighting gallery
loge
mezzanine
orchestra pit
orchestra stalls
parquet
parterre
pass door
picture-frame stage
pit
prompt box
proscenium
proscenium arch
proscenium stage
revolve
revolving stage
safety curtain
scene dock
set
skene
stage
stage door
stalls
tableau curtains
tabs
thrust stage
trap
upper circle
upstage
velarium
vomitorium
vomitory
wings

Therapies

See also **Medicine**

acupressure
acupuncture
Alexander technique
allopathy
aromatherapy
art therapy
auriculotherapy
autogenic training
aversion therapy
Ayurveda
balneotherapy
Bates method
behavioural therapy
behaviour therapy
bibliotherapy
bioenergetics
biofeedback
bodywork
brachytherapy
bush medicine
chemotherapy
chiropractic
chronotherapy
co-counselling
cognitive behavioural therapy (CBT)
cognitive therapy
colour therapy
combination therapy
confrontation therapy
counter-conditioning
craniosacral therapy
cryotherapy
crystal healing/therapy
cupping
detoxification
drama therapy
electro-acupuncture
electroconvulsive therapy (ECT)
electroplexy
electroshock therapy
electrotherapy
eurhythmics
faith healing
family therapy
gene therapy
Gerson therapy
gestalt therapy
group therapy
heat treatment
heliotherapy
herbalism
homeopathy
hormone replacement therapy (HRT)
humanistic therapy
hydropathy
hydrotherapy
hypnotherapy
immunotherapy
insulin shock therapy
irradiation
McTimoney chiropractic
mechanotherapy
megavitamin therapy
metrazol shock therapy
moxibustion
music therapy
narcotherapy
nature cure
naturopathy
neurolinguistic programming
occupational therapy (OT)
organotherapy
osteopathy
pharmacotherapy
phototherapy
physical therapy
physiotherapy
play therapy
polarity therapy
primal therapy
psychoanalysis
psychotherapy
radiation therapy
radionics
radiotherapy
rational-emotive therapy
rebirthing
recreational therapy
reflexology
regression therapy
reiki
relaxation therapy
release therapy
Rogerian therapy
Rolfing
sex therapy
shiatsu
shock therapy
shock treatment
sleep therapy
sound therapy
speech therapy
spiritual healing
supportive therapy
thalassotherapy
zone therapy

Ties

(Neckties)

ascot (tie)
bandanna
black tie
bolo tie
bootlace tie
bow tie
cravat
dicky bow
foulard
four-in-hand
kipper tie
neckerchief
old school tie
stock
string tie
white tie
Windsor tie

Timepieces

See **Clocks and Watches**

Titles

See **Rulers' Titles**

Toads

See **Amphibians**

Tonic Sol-Fa Notes

doh
ray
mi
fah
soh
lah
te

Tools

See also **Hammers Knives Saws**

adze
Allen key (*trademark*)
auger
awl
axe
bastard file
bevel (square)
billhook
biscuit jointer
blowlamp
blowtorch
bodkin
borer
brace (and bit)
bradawl
burin
burnisher
burr
capstan lathe
centre bit
centre punch
chisel
chopper
clamp
cleaver
copper bit
cramp
crowbar
croze
cultivator
cutter
dibber
dibble
diestock
dovetailer
drill
drill press
edge tool
edging shears
edging tool
file
flail
float
fly cutter
fork
former
froe
fuller
G-clamp
G-cramp
gimlet
glass cutter
graver
grinder
grouter
grozing iron
hack
hammer
hammer drill

hand-axe
handspike
hatchet
hedge clipper/ trimmer
hex key
hob
hoe
(hot-)air gun
jack
jemmy
jointer
knife
lap
lathe
lawnmower
lever
loppers
marlinspike
mattock
mitre
nailer
nail punch
needle
nibbler
nippers
paint gun
panga
perforator
pestle
pick
pickaxe
pincers
pitchfork
plane
pliers
pruning hook
punch
rake
ram
rasp
reamer
riddle
riffler
ripper
roller
roulette
router
rule
sander
sandpaper
sash cramp
saw
scarifier
scraper
screwdriver
screw tap
scribe (awl)
scythe
secateurs
shave
shavehook
shears
shovel
sickle
slasher
sley
snarling iron
socket wrench
soldering iron
spade
spanner
spokeshave
square
staple gun
strickle
swage
swingle
tinsnips
torque wrench
trowel
tweezers
vice
wedge
wheel brace
wire cutter
wire stripper
woodcarver
wrecking bar
wrench

Tooth
Types of Human Tooth

bicuspid
canine
cuspid
eye tooth
incisor
milk tooth
molar
permanent tooth
premolar
primary tooth
tricuspid
wisdom tooth

Tooth Parts
Parts of a Human Tooth

apex
cingulum
crown
cusp
dentine
enamel
neck
nerve
pulp
pulp artery
pulp cavity
pulp horn
pulp vein
root
root canal

Torture Instruments

See also **Punishments**

bastinado
boot
branks
cucking-stool
iron maiden
necklace
pilliwinks
rack
scold's bridle
screws
stocks
strappado
thumbscrew
wheel

Towers

barbican
bastion
belfry
bell tower
belvedere
broch
campanile
church tower
clock tower
column
control tower
cooling tower
demi-bastion
donjon
gate tower
gopura
high-rise building
keep
lighthouse
lookout tower
Martello tower
mast
minar
minaret
mirador
nuragh
pagoda
peel/pele (tower)
pylon
shikhara
shot tower
silo
skyscraper
spire
stair tower
steeple
tower block
turret
watchtower
water tower
ziggurat

Toys

action figure
Advent calendar
agate
ally
balloon
beanbag
bear
board game
bobskate
box kite
brick
building block
catapult
cuddly toy
diabolo
doll
doll's house
dreidel
Dutch doll
flannelboard
frisbee (*trademark*)
glove puppet
golliwog
hobby horse
hoop
hula hoop
humming top
jack-in-the-box
jigsaw
jumping bean
jumping jack
kaleidoscope
kite
marble
marionette
ocarina
party popper
pea-shooter
pedal car
peery
pegtop
playhouse
plaything
Pog
pogo (stick)
popgun
puppet
puzzle
rag doll
rattle
rattlebox
ride-on
rocking horse
Russian doll
scooter
see-saw
skipping rope
slot car
snowstorm
squirt gun
Swanee whistle
tangram
teddy (bear)
teeter-totter
teetotum
thaumatrope
tin soldier
top
tumbler
water gun
water pistol
Wendy house
whipping top
whirligig
windmill
yo-yo
zoetrope

Trains and Rolling Stock

aerotrain
armoured train
baggage car
banker
bi-level carriage
boat train
bogie
boxcar
brake van
buffet car
bullet train
cable car
caboose
car
carriage
chair car
club car
coach
couchette
day coach/car
diesel-electric
diesel-hydraulic
diesel locomotive
diesel multiple unit (DMU)
dining car
double-header
drive-on train
electric train
express
flatcar
freight car
freight train
goods train
goods wagon
guard's van
handcar
high-speed train (HST)
hopper
hospital train
hovertrain
jerkwater train
jigger
light engine
luggage van
maglev
mail coach
mail train
metro
Metroliner
milk train
monorail
motor coach
non-smoker
non-stop
observation car
palace car
pannier tank
parlor car
passenger train
Pullman
railbus
railcar
restaurant car
saddle tank
saloon car
shunter
sleeper
sleeping car/ carriage
slip carriage
slow train
smoker
steam locomotive
steam train
stopping train
subway train
switcher
tank engine
tender
traction unit
the tube
turbotrain
underground train
unit train
wagon-lit

Transport

See **Aircraft** **Cars** **Carriages and Carts** **Sailing Ships and Boats** **Ships and Boats** **Trains and Rolling Stock** **Vehicles**

Traps

booby trap
crab pot
deadfall
gin
leghold trap
light trap
lobster pot
mantrap
mousetrap
net
noose
radar trap
snare
speed trap
springe
trapline
tripwire

Treatments

See **Therapies** **Medicine**

Trees and Shrubs

See also **Flowering Plants and Shrubs**

abele
abura
acacia
acer
ackee
afara
afrormosia
ailanthus
albizzia
alder
alerce
allspice
almond
ambatch
angelica
anise
annatto
antiar
apple
apricot
araucaria
arbutus
argan
arolla (pine)
ash
aspen
assegai (wood)
avocado
azalea
axe-breaker
azarole
babul

balata
balsa
balsam fir
balsam poplar
bamboo
banksia
banyan
baobab
basswood
bay tree
bebeeru
beech
beefwood
belah
bergamot (orange)
birch
blackbutt
blackthorn
bloodwood
bluegum
bog oak
boldo
bo/bodh tree
bottlebrush
bottle tree
box
box elder
breadfruit
brigalow
bristlecone pine
broom
buckeye
buckthorn
bullace
bunya (pine) *or* bunya bunya
bur oak
butternut
buttonwood (tree)
cacao
cajuput
calabash
camellia
camphor tree
camwood
candelabra tree
candleberry
candlenut
caragana
carambola
carob (tree)
cascara (sagrada)
cashew
cassava
cassia
casuarina
catalpa
cecropia
cedar
ceiba
celery(-top) pine
champak/ chempaka
chaulmoogra
cheesewood
cherimoya
cherry
cherry laurel
cherry plum
chestnut
chinaberry
chinar/chenar
chinquapin/ chinkapin
chinar
choke cherry
cinchona
cinnamon
citron
clove
coachwood
cockspuar thorn
cocobolo
coco de mer
coconut palm
coffee tree
cola/kola
coolibah/ coolabah
copper beech
coral tree
cork oak
corkwood
cornel
coromandel
cottonwood
courida
cow tree
crab apple
crack willow
criollo (tree)
croton
cryptomeria
curry leaf
custard apple
cypress
damiana
damson
danewort
dawn redwood
deodar
desert oak
devil's walking stick
dhak
diamond willow
divi-divi
dogwood
Douglas fir/pine/ spruce
dove tree
dragon tree
eaglewood
ebony
elder
elm
Engelmann spruce
eucalyptus
eucryphia
eugenia
euonymus
false acacia
fatsia
feijoa
fever tree
ficus
fig
filbert
fir
firethorn
flamboyant
flame of the forest
flame tree
forastero (tree)
frangipani
fringe tree
fuchsia
fustic
gaboon
gean
geebung
genip/genipap
genipapo/ genipap
gidgee
ginkgo
goat willow
gomuti
gopherwood
gorse
grapefruit
greengage
greenheart
grevillea
guaiacum
guava
guayule
gum tree
gurjun
hackberry
hackmatack
handkerchief tree
hawthorn
hazel
hemlock fir/ spruce
hevea
hiba
hickory
hinoki
hog plum
holly
holly oak
holm oak
honey locust
honeysuckle
hop tree
hornbeam
horse chestnut
Huon pine
hydrangea
idigbo
ilex
immortelle
incense tree
Indian bean tree
iroko
ironbark
ironwood
ivorywood
jacaranda
jackfruit
jack pine
jamun (tree)
japonica
jarrah
jarul
jasmine
jelutong
Jerusalem thorn
jojoba
Joshua tree
Judas tree
jujube
juniper
kaffirboom
kahikatea
kaki
kalmia
kamahi
kanuka
kapok
kapur
karaka
karree/karee
karri
katsura
kauri (pine)
kawa-kawa
keaki
kermes oak
keruing
keurboom
kiaat
koa
kowhai
kumquat
kurrajong
laburnum
lacebark
lacquer tree
lancewood
lantana
larch
laurel
Lawson's cypress
leatherwood
lemon
lemonwood
lentisc
Leyland cypress
leylandii
lilac
lilly-pilly
limber pine
lime
linden
liquidambar
liriodendron
live oak
loblolly (pine)
locust (tree)
lodgepole pine
logwood
Lombardy poplar
London plane
longleaf pine
loquat
lychee
logwood
macadamia
macrocarpa
madroño
magnolia
mahoe
mahogany
mahua
maidenhair tree
mako
mallee
mammee (apple)
mammee sapote
manchineel
mandarin/ mandarine
mango
mangosteen
mangrove
manna ash
manuka
maple
maritime pine
marri
mastic (tree)
matai
maté
may
medlar
melaleuca
merbau
mesquite
mimosa
minnerichi/ minnaritchi
mirabelle
miro
monkey orange
monkey puzzle (tree)
moosewood
mopane/mopani
Moreton Bay chestnut
mountain ash
mpingo
msasa
mulberry
mulga
musk tree
myall
myrobalan (plum)
myrtle
nectarine
neem
nettle tree
ngaio
Nigerian pearwood
nipa (palm)
nonda
Nootka cypress
Norfolk (Island) pine
Norway maple
Norway spruce
nutmeg
nux vomica
oak
obeche
ocotillo
oleaster
olive
opepe
opopanax
Osage orange
osier
padauk
pagoda tree
palm
palmyra
paloverde
pandanus
papaya
paperbark
paper mulberry
paulownia
pawpaw
pear (tree)
pea tree
pedunculate oak
peepul
pepperidge
pepper tree
persimmon
pin oak
piñon
pistachio
pitch pine
pine
plane
plum
podocarp
pohutukawa
poinciana
pomegranate
pomelo
ponderosa (pine)
poplar
Port Jackson willow
poui
prickly ash
pride of India
primavera
privet
protea
puriri
pussy willow
pyinkado
quandong
quassia
quebracho
quince
quiver tree
rain tree
rambutan
ramin
rata
rauli
redbud
red cedar
redwood
rewarewa
rhododendron
ribbonwood
rimu
robinia
roseapple
rosewood
rowan
royal palm
rubber plant
rubber tree
sabicu
sal
sally/sallee
sallow
sandalwood
sandbox (tree)
sapele
sapodilla
sappanwood
saskatoon
sassafras
satinwood
sausage tree
savin
schefflera
Scots pine
sea grape
senna
sequoia
service tree
shagbark hickory
shea
shisham (tree)
silk-cotton tree
silk tassel bush
silky oak
silver birch
silver fir
silver tree
Sitka cypress
Sitka (spruce)
slash pine
slippery elm
simaruba
smoke tree
snakebark maple
snakewood
sneezewood
snowbell
soapbark
soapberry
sorbus
sorrel tree
soursop
sourwood
spindle
spruce
star anise
stinking cedar
stinkwood
stone pine
storax
strawberry tree
stringybark
styrax/storax
sugar maple
sugar pine
sumac/sumach
sweet chestnut
sweet gum
sycamore
tacamahac
tallow tree
tallow-wood
tamarack
tamarind
tamarisk
tambotie
tangerine
tawa
teak
tea tree
terebinth
thorn tree
thuja
tilleul
toothache tree
toquilla
totara
towai
tragacanth
tree of heaven
trembling poplar
trumpet tree
tulip tree
tulipwood
tung
tupelo
turkey oak
turpentine tree
ulmo
umbrella tree
upas
utile
valonia (oak)
varnish tree
viburnum
waboom
wahoo (elm)
walnut
wattle
wax tree
wayfaring tree
weeping willow
wellingtonia
whitebeam
wig tree
wilga
willow
wine palm
wing nut
winter sweet
witch hazel
woollybutt
wych elm
yarran
yaupon (holly)
yellow-wood
yew
ylang-ylang
yohimbe
yucca
zebrawood

Triangles

acute-angled
circular
congruent triangles
equilateral
isosceles
obtuse-angled
right
right-angled
scalene
similar triangles
spherical

Trousers

baggies
bags
bell-bottoms
Bermuda shorts
bloomers
board shorts
breeches
breeks
buckskins
capri pants
cargo pants
carpenter trousers
chaparajos/chaps
chinos
churidars
cigarette pants
clamdiggers
combat trousers
cords/corduroys
culottes
cut-offs
cycling shorts
denims
dhoti
drabs
drainpipes
drawstring trousers
ducks
dungarees
flannels
flares
galligaskins
gharara
gym pants
hakama
harem pants
hip-huggers
hipsters
hot pants
jeans
jodhpurs
joggers
jogging pants
khakis
knee breeches
knickerbockers
kuccha
lederhosen
leggings
loons
moleskins
nankeens
overtrousers
Oxford bags
palazzo pants
pantaloons
pedal pushers
pegtops
plus fours
pyjama
riding breeches
salopettes
salwar/shalwar
sharara
shorts
short trousers
ski pants
skort
slacks
slim jims
slops
stirrup pants
sweatpants
toreador pants
Turkish trousers
velveteens
zoaves

Typefaces

Albertina
Albertus
Aldine
American Typewriter
Antique Olive
Arial
Ashley Script
Avant Garde
Balmoral
Baskerville
Bauhaus
Bell
Bembo
Bodoni
Bookman
Boston
Broadway
Calisto
Caslon
Centaur
Century Gothic
Century Schoolbook
Chicago
Clarendon
Clearface
Cloister
Colonna
Cooper Black
Courier
Dante
Delphian
Ehrhardt
Engravers
Festival
Flash
Folio
Fournier
Fraktur
Franklin Gothic
Futura
Galliard
Garamond
Gill Sans
Gothic
Goudy
Grotesque
Helvetica
Hobo
Imprint
Joanna
Klang
Korinna
Lubalin Graph
Lucida Bright
Melior
Novarese
Old English
Optima
Othello
Palace Script
Palatino
Peignot
Perpetua
Photina
Pilgrim
Plantin
Prestige
Rockwell
Sabon
Serifa
Showbill
Souvenir
Spartan
Stone
Swift
Swing
Times New Roman
Trump
Typewriter
Univers
University Roman
Van Dijck
Vivaldi
Vogue
Walbaum
Windsor
Zapf Chancery

Underwear

bikini briefs
bloomers
bodice
body
body stocking
boxer shorts
bra
brassiere
briefs
BVDs (*trademark*)
camiknickers
camisole
chemise
chemisette
choli
chuddies
combination
combs
corselette
corset
crinoline
Directoire drawers
drawers
farthingale
fleshings
foundation garment
French knickers
frillies
girdle
G-string
hold-ups
jockey shorts
jocks
jockstrap
kecks
knickers
liberty bodice
long johns
maillot
Mother Hubbard
nylons
pantalettes
panties
pants
panty girdle
pantyhose
petticoat
posing pouch
roll-on
scanties
semmit
shift
shorts
skivvy
spencer
stays
string vest
suspender belt
suspenders
tanga (briefs)
T-back
teddy
thermals
thong
tights
underpants
undershirt
undershorts
undervest
underwire
union suit
vest
waspie
Y-fronts (*trademark*)

Units

acre
acre-foot
air mile
ampere
angstrom
are
astronomical unit
atmosphere
atomic mass unit
bale
bar
barleycorn
barn
barrel
bath
baud
becquerel
bel
bigha
bit
board foot
Board of Trade Unit
bovate
brake horsepower
British thermal unit
bushel
butt
byte
cable
calorie
candela
candle
carat
cental
centiare
centigram
centilitre
centimetre
centner
century
chain
cord
coulomb
cran
cubit
cup
cupful
curie
cusec
cycle
dalton
daraf
darcy
day
debye
decade
decalitre
decametre
decibel
decigram
decilitre
decimetre
degree
degree-day
denarius
denier
dessertspoon
dioptre
drachm
dunam
dyne
electronvolt
ell
em
en
ephah
epoch
erg
farad
faraday
fathom
fermi
firkin
fluid drachm
fluid ounce
fluidram
foot
foot-pound
fresnel
furlong
gal
gallon
gamma
gauss
geographical mile
gigabyte
gigaelectronvolt
gigaflop
gigawatt
gilbert
gill
grade
grain
gram
gram-molecular weight
gray
hand
hank
hectare
hectogram
hectolitre
hectometre
henry
hertz
hide
hin
hogshead
Hoppus foot
horsepower
hour
hundredweight
inch
jansky
joule
kelvin
kilderkin
kilobit
kilobyte
kilocalorie
kilocycle
kilo-electronvolt
kilogram
kilohertz
kilojoule
kilolitre
kilometre
kiloton/kilotonne
kilovolt
kilowatt-hour
kip
knot
lambert
last
lea
league
libra
light year
line
link
litre
lumen
lux
Mach number
magneton
maxwell
megabyte
mega-electronvolt
megaflop
megahertz
megaton
megavolt
megawatt
megohm
metre
metric ton
mho
microfarad
microgram
microlitre
micrometre
micron
microsecond
mil
mile
millennium
milliampere
millibar
milligram
millilitre
millimetre
millimicron
millisecond
millivolt
milliwatt
minim
minute
MIPS
mole
month
morgan
morgen
mutchkin
nail
nanometre
nanosecond
nautical mile
neper
newton
nit
noggin
oersted
ohm
oka/oke
okta
ounce
parsec
pascal
peck
pennyweight
perch
petabyte
phon
phot
pica
pint
pipe
ploughland
point
poise
pole
pound
poundal
probit
puncheon
quantum bit
quart
quarter
quartern
quintal
rad
radian
rem
rod
roentgen
rood
rutherford
sabin
scruple
sea mile
second
section
seer
siemens
sievert
sone
span
spindle
square
stack
stadium
standard
steradian
stere
stilb
stokes
stone
Svedberg
tablespoon
teaspoon
teraflop
terawatt
tesla
therm
tierce
tog
ton
tonne
torr
troy ounce
tsubo
tun
verst
virgate
volt
watt
weber
week
wey
x-unit
yard
year
yoke

Vaulting Types

barrel
cross
domical
fan
Gothic
groin/groined
intersecting
lierne
neo-Gothic
ogival
palm
parabolic
pendentive
quadripartite
rib/ribbed
Romanesque
segmental
sexpartite
tunnel
underpitch
wagon

Vegetables

ackee
acorn squash
adzuki/aduki bean
alfalfa
artichoke
asparagus
aubergine
avocado pear
bamboo shoots
batata
bean
beet
beetroot
black bean
black-eyed bean
borlotti bean
breadfruit
broad bean
broccoli
Brussels sprout
butter bean
buttercup squash
butterhead lettuce
butternut squash
cabbage
cabbage lettuce
calabrese
cannellini bean
capsicum
cardoon
carrot
cassava
cauliflower
celeriac
celery
chard
chayote
chervil
chickpea
chicory
Chinese artichoke
Chinese cabbage
Chinese leaves
choko
collard
corn on the cob
cos lettuce
courgette
cress
cucumber
curly kale
cush-cush
custard marrow
dishcloth gourd
drumhead
earthnut
eggplant
endive
escarole
fennel
flageolet
French bean
garbanzo
garden pea
garlic
gherkin
globe artichoke
gobo
gourd
green onion
gumbo
haricot bean
Jerusalem artichoke
jicama
kale
kidney bean
kohlrabi
leek
lentil
lettuce
lima bean
lollo rosso
mangetout
manioc
marrow
marrowfat pea
marrow squash
mizuna
mooli
mung bean
mustard
oak leaf (lettuce)
okra
onion
orache
oyster plant
pak choi
parsnip
pattypan (squash)
pea
pea bean
pearl onion
pepper
petits pois
pimiento
pinto bean
plantain
potato
puha
pumpkin
puy lentil
radicchio
radish
romaine
runner bean
rutabaga
salsify
samphire
savoy cabbage
scallion
scorzonera
Scotch kale
sea kale
shallot
snap bean
snow pea
soybean
spinach
spinach beet
spring greens
spring onion
sprue
squash
string bean
succory
sugar bean
sugar snap peas
swede
sweetcorn
sweet pepper
sweet potato
tannia
taro
tiger nut
tomato
turnip
turnip tops/ greens
vegetable spaghetti
wasabi
water chestnut
watercress
waxpod
yam
yam bean
zucchini

Vehicles

Motor Vehicles

See also **Cars** **Carriages and Carts** **Trains and Rolling Stock**

all-terrain vehicle (ATV)
ambulance
armoured car
articulated lorry
automobile
autorickshaw
battlebus
beach buggy
Black Maria
bloodmobile
bookmobile
bowser (*trademark*)
bulldozer
bus
cab
camper (van)
car
caravanette
carryall
car transporter
charabanc
coach
combination
crash wagon
delivery truck
digger
dirt bike
dolmus
double-decker bus
DUKW/duck
dumper truck
dump truck
dune buggy
dustcart
earth mover
fire engine
flatbed (truck)
float
forklift truck
four-by-four
four-wheel drive (4WD)
garbage truck
go-kart
golf cart/buggy
gritter
hackney cab
half-track
hearse
heavy goods vehicle (HGV)
horsebox
hot rod
JCB (*trademark*)
Jeep (*trademark*)
juggernaut
kart
large goods vehicle (LGV)
lorry
low-loader
low-rider
lunar roving vehicle (LRV)
milk float
minelayer
moped
motorbike/ motorcycle
motor caravan
multi-purpose vehicle (MPV)
off-road vehicle (ORV)
omnibus
pantechnicon
passenger-carrying vehicle (PCV)
people carrier
personnel carrier
pickup (truck)
public service vehicle (PSV)
quad bike
recreational vehicle (RV)
refrigerated van
removal van
roadroller
road train
rover
scooter
scout car
scrambler
semitrailer
shooting brake
skidsteer loader
skimobile
snowcat
snowmobile
snowplough
sport utility vehicle (SUV)
steamroller
streetcar
superbike
tank
tanker
taxi/taxicab
tow truck
tracklayer
tractor
trail bike
trailer
tram
transporter
trolleybus
troop carrier
truck
tuk-tuk
utility
van
wagon/waggon
wrecker

Veins and Arteries

Main Human Veins and Arteries

aorta
axillary artery
axillary vein
azygos vein
basilic vein
brachial artery
brachial vein
carotid artery
cephalic artery
cephalic vein
coeliac artery
coronary artery
crural artery
crural vein
cubital vein
digital artery
digital vein
dorsal metatarsal artery
dorsal venous arch
femoral artery
femoral vein
gastric artery
gastroepiploic vein
hepatic artery
hepatic portal vein
iliac artery
iliac vein
inferior vena cava
innominate artery
innominate vein
jugular vein
long thoracic artery
median cubital vein
(inferior/ superior) mesenteric artery
(inferior/ superior) mesenteric vein
ovarian artery
ovarian vein
palmar arch
palmar network
peroneal artery
plantar artery
popliteal artery
popliteal vein
portal vein
pulmonary artery
pulmonary vein
radial artery
renal artery
renal vein
(great/short) saphenous vein
splenic artery
subclavian artery
subclavian vein
superior vena cava
suprarenal vein
testicular artery
testicular vein
tibial artery
ulnar artery
ulnar vein
vena cava
vertebral artery

Verse Forms

See also **Poems**

alcaics (*or* alcaic verse)
alexandrine verse
alliterative verse
Anacreontics
ballad
ballade
blank verse
Clerihew
dactylics (*or* dactylic verse)
doggerel
dramatic monologue
echo verse
elegy
epic
epigram
epode
epopee
fixed form
free verse
haiku
heroic verse
Horatian ode
iambics (*or* iambic verse)
Leonines
limerick
lyric
macaronics (*or* macaronic verse)
madrigal
monody
ode
ottava rima
pantoum/pantun
Petrarchan sonnet
Pindaric
quatorzain
rhyme royal
ritornello
rondeau
roundel
sapphics
secondary epic
sequidilla
sestina
sonnet
Spenserian stanza
tail rhyme
tanka
terza rima
triolet
triplet
trochaics (*or* trochaic verse)
villanelle
virelay

Verse Metres and Metrical Feet

alexandrine
amphibrach
amphimacer
anapaest/ anapest
choree
choriamb/ choriambus
cretic
dactyl
decasyllable
dimeter
dipody
distich
disyllable
duple metre
elegiac couplet
elegiac distich
heptameter
heroic couplet

hexameter
iamb/iambus
iambic pentameter
ionic
monometer
octameter
paeon
pentameter
pyrrhic
spondee
tetrameter
tribrach
trimeter
trisyllable
trochee

Vertebrae

vertebra	number	
cervical	7	
thoracic	12	
lumbar	5	
sacral	5	(fused, forming the sacrum)
coccygeal	4	(fused, forming the coccyx)

Vessels

See **Drinking Vessels** **Sailing Ships and Boats** **Ships and Boats** **Veins and Arteries**

Vestments

Clerical Vestments

Christianity

alb
amice
biretta
cassock
chasuble
chimere
clerical collar
cope
cotta
cowl
dalmatic
dog collar
frock
Geneva bands
Geneva gown
habit
hood
infula
maniple
mantle
mitre
mozzetta
pallium
rochet
scapular
shovel hat
skullcap
soutane
stole
superhumeral
surplice
tippet
tunicle
wimple
zucchetto

Judaism

ephod
kippa *or* kipa
pectoral
skullcap
tallith
yarmulke

Virtues

See also **Sins**

cardinal virtues

fortitude
justice
prudence
temperance

theological virtues

charity
faith
hope

Viruses

actinophage
adenovirus
alphavirus
arbovirus
arenavirus
bacteriophage
baculovirus
Borna disease virus
coronavirus
Coxsackie virus
cytomegalovirus
Ebola virus
echovirus
enterovirus
Epstein–Barr virus (EBV)
filovirus
hantavirus
herpes simplex virus
herpesvirus
herpes zoster virus
human immunodeficiency virus (HIV)
human papilloma virus (HPV)
influenza virus
Lassa virus
lentivirus
leukovirus
maedi virus
Marburg virus
mengovirus
morbillivirus
myxovirus
Norwalk virus
oncornavirus
orbivirus
papillomavirus
papovavirus
parainfluenza virus
paramyxovirus
parvovirus
picornavirus
poliovirus
polyoma virus
poxvirus
reovirus
retrovirus
rhabdovirus
rhinovirus
Ross River virus
rotavirus
Sendai virus
Shope virus
slow virus
tobacco mosaic virus (TMV)
togavirus
tumour virus
ultravirus
varicella virus
West Nile virus

Vitamins

A	retinol
B1	thiamine
B2	riboflavin
B3	niacin
B6	pyridoxine
B12	cyanocobalamin
B complex	folic acid, pantothenic acid, biotin, inositol, choline, pteroylglutamic acid
C	ascorbic acid
D2	calciferol
D3	cholecalciferol
E	tocopherol
H	biotin
K1	phylloquinone
K2	menaquinone/menadione
M	folic acid
P	citrin, bioflavonoid

Voices

Types of Singing Voice

See also **Singers**

alto
baritone
bass
basso profundo
boy soprano
castrato
contralto
countertenor
falsetto
mezzo
mezzo-soprano
soprano
tenor
treble

Watches

See **Clocks and Watches**

Weapons

Personal Weapons

See also **Bombs and Mines** **Bullets and Shot** **Guns** **Knives and Daggers** **Projectiles and Projectile Weapons**

axe
backsword
baseball bat
baton
battleaxe
bayonet
bilbo
bill
blackjack
blade
bludgeon
bowie knife
brass knuckles
broadsword
chopper
claymore
club
commando knife
cosh
cudgel
cutlass
dagger
danda
dirk
épée
falchion
flick knife
foil
gisarme
gun
halberd
harpoon
hatchet
javelin
kierie
kleywang
knife
knobkerrie
knuckleduster
kris
kukri
lance
lathi
life preserver
mace
machete
nulla-nulla
panga
parang
partisan
pike
poleaxe
poniard
quarterstaff
rapier
sabre
scimitar
shillelagh
sjambok
skean
skean-dhu
slung shot
small sword
snickersnee
spear
staff
stave
stick
stiletto
sword
swordstick
tomahawk
truncheon
yataghan

Weasels and Similar Animals

badger
beech marten
civet
cusimanse
ermine
ferret
ferret-badger
fisher
fossa
genet
glutton
grison
hog badger
honey badger
kolinsky
linsang
marbled polecat
marten
meerkat
mink
mongoose
muishond
otter
palm civet
pine marten
polecat
ratel
sable
sea otter
skunk
stink badger
stoat
suricate
tayra
teledu
toddy cat
weasel
wolverine
zorilla

Weather Phenomena

See also **Climatic Zones** **Cloud Formations** **Winds**

anticyclone
blocking high
cold front
cyclone
deep depression
depression
filling depression
frontal system
high pressure
jet stream
low pressure
occlusion
pressure system
ridge
shallow depression
stationary depression
stationary high
temperature inversion
thermal
trough
turbulence
warm front
warm sector

Whales and Dolphins

Amazon dolphin
baleen whale
beaked whale
beluga
blue whale
boto/boutu
bottlenose dolphin
bottlenose whale
bowhead whale
cachalot
dusky dolphin
finback whale
fin whale
grampus
Greenland right whale
grey whale
humpback whale
killer whale
minke whale
narwhal
orca
pilot whale
porpoise
right whale
Risso's dolphin
river dolphin
rorqual
sei whale
sperm whale
spinner dolphin
toothed whale
tucuxi
whalebone whale
white-sided dolphin
white whale

Whiskies

blended whisky
bourbon
corn whisky
grain whisky
Irish whiskey
malt (whisky)
rye (whisky)
Scotch (whisky)
single malt (whisky)
sour mash (whiskey)
vatted malt (whisky)

Wind Instruments

See also **Brass Instruments**

alpenhorn
altohorn
bagpipes
barrel organ
basset horn
bassoon
bombarde
clarinet
contrabassoon
cor anglais
cornetto
didgeridoo
fife
fipple flute
flageolet
flute
harmonica
heckelphone
kazoo
krummhorn
lysarden
melodica
mouth organ
oboe
oboe d'amore
ocarina
piccolo
piffero
pipe
racket
recorder
reed pipe
sarrusophone
saxophone
serpent
shawm
stock-and-horn
tin whistle
whistle

Windows

arrow slit
bay window
bow window
bullseye
casement
Catherine wheel
clerestory window
compass window
deadlight
dormer window
double-hung window
embrasure
eyelet
fanlight
fenestella
French window
gable window
garret window
grisaille
guichet
Jesse window
lancet window
lattice window
leaded light
lucarne
lunette
mullion/mullioned window
oculus
oeil-de-boeuf
opera window
oriel window
oval window
Palladian window
picture window
porthole
quarter-light
roof light
rose window
roundel
sash window
sidelight
skylight
squint
stained-glass window
storm window
top light
transom window
viewport
wheel window

Winds

berg wind
bise
bora
brickfielder
buran
Cape doctor
chinook
Etesian
föhn/foehn
ghibli
haboob
harmattan
khamsin
levanter
libeccio
maestrale
meltemi
mistral
monsoon
nor'wester
pampero
Perth doctor
shamal
simoom/simoon/samiel
sirocco
solano
southerly buster
tramontana
wet chinook
williwaw
willy-willy
zonda

Wine and Grape Varieties

See also **Sherries** *and Dessert* **Wines**

white wines and grapes

Aligoté
Asti
Auslese
Barsac
Beerenauslese
Blanc de blancs
Blanc Fumé
Bourgogne Blanc
Bucelas
Burgundy
Catawba
Cava
Chablis
Champagne
Chardonnay
Chasselas
Chenin Blanc
Clairette
Colombard
Condrieu
Crémant
Eiswein
Entre-deux-Mers
Frascati
Furmint
Gavi
Gewürztraminer
Graves
Grüner Veltliner
Hárslevelü
Heuriger
Hock
Johannisberg
Jurançon
Kabinett
Kerner
Liebfraumilch
Lutomer Riesling
Mâcon
Mâcon Villages
Malvasia Bianca
Malvoisie
Manseng
Marsanne
Mauzac
Meursault
Minervois
Montrachet
Morio-Muskat
Moselle
Müller-Thurgau *or* Rivaner
Muscadelle
Muscadet
Muscat Blanc
Muscat d'Alexandrie
Muscatel
Niersteiner
Orvieto
Palomino
Pedro Ximenez
Piesporter
Pinot Blanc
Pinot Grigio
Pouilly-Fuissé
Pouilly-Fumé
Retsina
Riesling
Rioja
Roussette
Rueda
sack
Sancerre
Saumur
Sauvignon
Scheurebe
Scuppernong
Sekt
Sémillon
Sercial
Seyval Blanc
Soave
Spätlese
Spumante
Steen
Sylvaner
Symphony
Tocai-Friulano
Tokay
Traminer
Trebbiano
Trockenbeerenauslese
Verdejo
Verdelho
Verdello
Verdicchio
Verduzzo
Vermentino
Vernaccia
Vernaccia di San Gimignano
Villard
Vinho Verde
Viognier
Viura
Vouvray
Welschriesling *or* Olasz Rizling *or* Laski Rizling

red wines and grapes

Aleatico
Amarone
Aramon
Bandol
Banyuls
Barbaresco
Barbera
Bardolino
Barolo
Beaujolais
Beaune
Blauer Portugieser
Blaufränkisch/Kékfrankos
Bourgogne Rouge
Bourgueil
Brouilly
Brunello de Montalcino
Bull's Blood
Burgundy
Cabernet Franc
Cabernet Sauvignon
Cahors
Carema
Carignan
Chianti
Cinsault
claret
Concord
Corvina
Côtes du Rhône
Crozes-Hermitage
Dão
Dolcetto
Faugères
Fitou
Fleurie
Gaillac
Gamay
Gattinara
Gevrey-Chambertin
Gigondas
Graves
Grenache
Grignolino
Lambrusco
Malbec
Malvasia
Malvoisie Rouge
Mammolo
Mandelaria
Manseng
Margaux
Médoc
Merlot
Meunier
Montepulciano
Mourvèdre
Nebbiolo
Negroamoro
Nuits St George
Pauillac
Pinot Noir
Pinotage
Pomerol
Pommard
Rioja
Rofosco
Saint-Émilion
Saint-Estèphe
Sangiovese
Shiraz/Syrah
Tempranillo
Valdepeñas
Valpolicella
Vino Nobile di Montepulciano
Zinfandel
Zweigelt *or* Blauer Zweigelt

rosé wines

Rosé d'Anjou
Rosé de Syrah
Tavel

Wine Bottles

bottle	capacity (normal bottles)
magnum	2
jeroboam	4
rehoboam	6
methuselah	8
salmanazar	12
balthazar	16
nebuchadnezzar	20

Wines, Dessert

Bual
canary wine
Grenache
hanepoot
jerepigo
Madeira
malmsey
Marsala
Monbazillac
moscato
muscat
Muscat de Beaumes-de-Venise
muscatel
Sauternes
Sercial
Verdelho
vin de paille
vin santo

Wolves

See **Dogs**

Woods

See **Forests**

Woodwind

See **Wind Instruments**

Wool

See **Fabrics and Fibres**

Workers

See **Agricultural Workers**

Workshops

See **Factories and Workshops**

Worms

acanthocephalan
acorn worm
annelid
arrow worm
ascarid
bamboo worm
beard worm
bladder worm
blood fluke
bloodworm
bootlace worm
brandling
bristle worm
catworm
chaetognath
dungworm
earthworm
eelworm
eye worm
fan worm
feather duster (worm)
filaria
fireworm
flatworm
fluke
gapeworm
gordian worm
Guinea worm
hairworm
heartworm
helminth
hookworm
horsehair worm
horseshoe worm
kidney worm
leech
liver fluke
lobworm
lugworm
lungworm
mesozoan
mopane worm
nematode (worm)
nemertean
nereid
oligochaete
paddle worm
palolo worm
parchment worm
peacock worm
peanut worm
phoronid
pinworm
platyhelminth
pognophoran
polychaete
pot worm
proboscis worm
pterobranch
ragworm
rainworm
redworm
rhombozoan
ribbon worm
roundworm
scale worm
sea mouse
serpulid
sipunculid
spiny-headed worm
spoonworm
straw worm
strongyle
tapeworm
thorny-headed worm
threadworm
tongue worm
toxocara
trematode
trichina
tube worm
tubifex
vinegar eel
whipworm
white worm

Writers

Types of Writer

adaptor
agony aunt
amorist
annalist
author
authoress
bard
best-seller
biographer
chronicler
city editor
co-author
columnist
comedist
commentator
continuator
contributor
copywriter
correspondent
crime writer
critic
cub reporter
diarist
draftsman
dramatist
dramaturge
editor
editress
encyclopedist
epilogist
essayist
evangelist
fabulist
farceur
gagster
ghostwriter
glossator
glossographer
hack
hackette
hagiographer
herbalist
humorist
hymnographer
journalist
lexicographer
littérateur
lobby correspondent
lyricist
lyrist
memorialist
Minnesinger
mythographer
necrologist
newsman
newspaperman
novelist
pamphleteer
pastoralist
playwright
poet
poetess
Poet Laureate
pressman
programmer
prosaist
psalmist
publicist
recorder
remembrancer
reporter
reviewer
rhymester
scenarist
screenwriter
scribe
scriptwriter
skald
sob sister
songster
songwriter
sonneteer
speech-writer
story editor
sub
synoptic
synoptist
tragedian
troubadour
trouvère
war correspondent
war poet
wireman
wordsmith
writer-in-residence
Yahwist

Writing Implements

ballpoint
biro
chinagraph pencil
crayon
crow quill
dip pen
felt-tip pen
fibre tip
fountain pen
highlighter
lead pencil
mapping pen
marker (pen)
pen
pencil
propelling pencil
quill
rollerball
slate pencil
stylograph
stylus

Young Animals

young	animal
calf	antelope/buffalo/camel/cattle/elephant/elk/giraffe/hartebeest/rhinoceros/seal/whale
cheeper	grouse/quail/partridge
chick	chicken/hawk/pheasant
colt	horse
cub	badger/bear/fox/leopard/lion/tiger/walrus/wolf
cygnet	swan
duckling	duck
eaglet	eagle
elver	eel
eyas	hawk
fawn	caribou/deer
filly	horse
foal	horse/zebra
fry	fish
gilt	pig
gosling	goose
joey	kangaroo/wallaby/possum
kid	goat/roedeer
kit	beaver/fox/weasel/ferret/mink
kitten	bobcat/cat/cougar/rabbit/skunk
lamb	sheep
leveret	hare
owlet	owl
parr	salmon
peachick	peafowl
pickerel	pike
piglet	pig
porkling	pig
pup	dog/wolf/seal/rat
puppy	dog/coyote
scrod	cod/haddock
smolt	salmon
squab	pigeon
squeaker	pigeon
tadpole	frog/toad
whelp	dog/wolf

Kk

kaleidoscopic ▶ adjective **1** *the branches refracted the light from the street lamps into kaleidoscopic shapes on the pavement* **multicoloured**, many-coloured, multicolour, many-hued, variegated, particoloured, varicoloured, prismatic, psychedelic, rainbow, rainbow-like, polychromatic, harlequin, motley, many-splendoured; *informal* (looking) like an explosion in a paint factory.
OPPOSITE monochrome.
2 *the country's kaleidoscopic political landscape* **ever-changing**, changeable, shifting, fluid, protean, mutable, variable, varying, inconstant, unstable, fluctuating, mobile, unsteady, unpredictable, ever-moving, chameleon-like, chameleonic, impermanent, indefinite; *technical* labile; *rare* changeful.
OPPOSITES fixed, constant, immutable.
3 *children's questions about the kaleidoscopic world they are living in* **multifaceted**, many-faceted, varied, manifold, multifarious; **complex**, intricate, complicated, convoluted; confused, chaotic, muddled, disordered, disorganized, disarranged, jumbled, confusing.

kaput (*informal*) ▶ adjective *the TV's kaput* **broken**, malfunctioning, broken-down, inoperative; ruined, destroyed, smashed, wrecked, useless; finished, at an end, defunct, extinct, dead; *informal* done for.
□ **go kaput break down**, go wrong, stop working, go haywire, give out; be ruined, be spoiled, be wrecked; *informal* have had it, conk out.

keel ▶ verb
□ **keel over 1** *it's going to take more wind to make this boat keel over* **capsize**, turn turtle, turn upside down, turn topsy-turvy, founder, list, heel over, lean over; overbalance, topple over, overturn, turn over, tip over, fall over.
2 *the slightest activity made him keel over* **collapse**, faint, fall down in a faint, pass out, black out, lose consciousness; *literary* swoon.
▶ noun *she sat on the upturned keel of the boat* **base**, bottom, bottom side, underside.

keen[1] ▶ adjective **1** *his publishers were keen to capitalize on his success* **eager**, anxious, impatient, determined, desirous, longing, wishing, itching, dying, yearning, ambitious, ready; intent on; *informal* raring.
OPPOSITE reluctant.
2 *I had been a keen birdwatcher since I was a boy* **enthusiastic**, avid, eager, ardent, passionate, fervent, fervid, impassioned, wholehearted, zestful, zealous; willing, conscientious, committed, dedicated; diligent, earnest, industrious, assiduous, intent.
OPPOSITES apathetic, half-hearted.
3 *her sisters are* **keen on** *horses | he had a girl in Kentucky he was* **keen on** **enthusiastic about**, interested in, passionate about, fascinated by; **attracted to**, fond of, taken with, smitten with, enamoured of, attached to, devoted to, infatuated with; eager for, hungry for; *informal* struck on, sweet on, gone on, mad about, crazy about, nuts about, into.
OPPOSITES unenthusiastic, indifferent.
4 *a keen cutting edge* **sharp**, sharp-edged, sharpened, honed, razor-like, razor-sharp, whetted, fine-edged.
OPPOSITE blunt.
5 *nimble fingers and keen eyesight are required for the work* **acute**, sharp, penetrating, discerning, sensitive, perceptive, piercing, clear, observant; powerful.
OPPOSITES weak, defective.
6 *an able administrator with a keen mind* **acute**, penetrating, astute, incisive, sharp, perceptive, piercing, rapier-like, razor-like, razor-sharp, perspicacious, shrewd, subtle, finely honed, quick-witted, sharp-witted, discerning, clever, intelligent, brilliant, bright, smart, wise, canny, percipient, insightful, sagacious, sapient; *informal* brainy.
OPPOSITES dull, stupid.
7 *the magazines are spoken of with keen derision* **cutting**, scathing, mordant, caustic, withering, acerbic, stinging, searing, acid, biting, tart, astringent, pointed, trenchant, pungent, incisive, virulent, devastating; sardonic, sarcastic, satirical; *rare* mordacious.
OPPOSITES gentle, mild.
8 *a keen wind cut through their coats* **cold**, icy, freezing, harsh, raw, bitter; penetrating, piercing, biting, sharp, stinging.
9 *there is keen competition for places on these committees | a keen sense of duty* **intense**, acute, extreme, fierce, violent, passionate, consuming, burning, fervent, fervid, ardent; strong, powerful, profound, deep-seated.

CHOOSE THE RIGHT WORD

keen, eager, enthusiastic, avid
See EAGER.

keen, acute, penetrating

- **Keen** is used of sensitive and powerful perception, both physical and mental (*his keen hearing caught the whirring of the tape | he enjoyed exercising his keen intellect in analysing the controversies of the day*); when applied to someone's eyes, it often suggests an appearance of alertness and perceptiveness as well as actual power (*his keen eyes went from Thomas to Ralf*). The impressions or attitudes resulting from *keen* mental perception are intense (*young people show a keen awareness of animal welfare | lawyers with a keen sense of the value of good political connections*).
- Someone whose physical or mental perception is **acute** can detect small details that are not readily apparent to others (*young children have a particularly acute sense of smell | Simon's vague manner concealed an agile and acute mind*). An *acute observer* can produce *acute criticism*, identifying central issues and making perceptive points about them. Intense and insistent emotion may be described as *acute* (*acute grief at the loss of her parents*).
- **Penetrating** eyes may or may not have good sight, but they look as though they can see through you (*she was unable to meet his penetrating eyes*). A *penetrating mind* enables one to see deeply into a problem and think up *penetrating questions*, calculated to reveal important truths.

keen[2] ▶ verb *the bereaved gathered around the graves to keen* **lament**, mourn, weep, cry, sob, sorrow, grieve; wail, moan, whine, whimper, groan, howl; *Scottish* greet; *archaic* plain; *rare* ululate.

keenness ▶ noun **1** *the company has signalled its keenness to sign a deal* **eagerness**, willingness, readiness, desire, wish, anxiety, impatience; enthusiasm, fervour, wholeheartedness, zest, zeal, ardour, passion, devotion, avidity; earnestness, diligence, assiduity, conscientiousness, intentness.
OPPOSITE reluctance.
2 *the keenness of the blade* **sharpness**, razor-sharpness.
OPPOSITE bluntness.
3 *keenness of hearing* **acuteness**, sharpness, sensitivity, perceptiveness, discrimination, clarity.
4 *the keenness of his mind* **acuity**, sharpness, subtlety, incisiveness, astuteness, perspicacity, perceptiveness, quick-wittedness, sharp-wittedness, shrewdness, penetration, insight, cleverness, discernment, intelligence, brightness, brilliance, canniness, sagacity.
OPPOSITES dullness, obtuseness.
5 *the keenness of her wit* **incisiveness**, causticity, tartness, sharpness, mordancy, acidity, acerbity, trenchancy, pungency, virulence, sarcasm, sardonicism, satire.
OPPOSITES gentleness, insipidity.
6 *the keenness of his sense of loss* **intensity**, acuteness, extremity, strength, power, violence, profundity, depth, ferocity.

keep[1] ▶ verb **1** *he kept the ball as a memento of the match | you should keep all the old forms* **retain**, hold on to, keep for oneself, retain possession of,

keep possession of, retain in one's possession, keep hold of, not part with, hold fast to, hold back; **save**, store, store up, save up, hoard, put by, put aside, lay aside, set aside, reserve, keep in reserve, lay down; collect, accumulate, amass, pile up, stockpile, garner; *N. Amer.* set something by; *informal* hang on to, stash away.
OPPOSITES lose, throw away.
2 *I was trying desperately to keep calm* **remain**, continue to be, stay, carry on being, go on being, persist in being, not cease to be.
3 *he keeps going on about the murder* **persist in**, go on, keep on, carry on, continue, do something constantly, do something incessantly, do something continually, not stop doing something, persevere.
OPPOSITES give up, stop.
4 *I shan't keep you long* **detain**, cause to stay, cause to wait, keep waiting, keep back, hold back, restrain; **delay**, hold up, retard, make late, set back, slow down, slow up, hinder, obstruct, check, impede, block, hamper, constrain.
5 *he had to keep his promise | some people kept the rules and some never tried* **comply with**, obey, respect, observe, conform to, abide by, stick to, act in accordance with, act according to, have regard to, heed, follow, pay attention to, defer to, take notice of; **fulfil**, carry out, act on, make good, be bound by, honour, keep to, redeem, keep faith with, stand by, adhere to; execute, discharge, perform; *rare* effectuate.
OPPOSITES break, disobey.
6 *I like to keep the old traditions* **preserve**, keep alive, keep going, continue, keep up, carry on, hold on to, perpetuate, maintain, uphold, sustain, conserve, cherish, nurture.
OPPOSITES abandon, discard.
7 *the stand where her umbrella was kept* **store**, house, stow, keep a place for, put away, place, put, deposit, stack, pile.
8 *the shop keeps a good stock of parchment* **stock**, have in stock, carry, have, have for sale, hold, sell, deal in, trade in, handle, market, supply, provide, offer for sale.
9 *he has to steal to keep his family* **provide for**, support, provide food for, provide sustenance for, provide board for, feed, keep alive, maintain, sustain, subsidize, finance; take care of, look after, nurture, nourish.
10 *she kept rabbits in the back garden* **breed**, rear, raise, farm; own, have as a pet, keep as a pet, look after, tend.
11 *his parents kept a shop* **manage**, run, own, be the proprietor of, be in charge of, administer, organize, direct, keep up, maintain, operate, look after, superintend.
12 *the boy keeps the sheep | 'God keep you,' he muttered* **tend**, look after, care for, take care of, mind, watch over, have charge of, be responsible for; **protect**, keep safe, keep from harm, preserve, defend, guard, shield, shelter, safeguard, save.
13 *today's consumers do not keep the Sabbath* **observe**, respect, honour, hold sacred, recognize, acknowledge; celebrate, mark, solemnize, ritualize, ceremonialize, commemorate.
OPPOSITES ignore, neglect.

□ **keep at** *start work early and keep at it* **persevere with**, persist with, be persistent in, keep going with, keep on at, be pertinacious in, show determination in, be resolute in, be steadfast in, not give up, not cease from, not falter in, carry on with, press on with, work away at, continue with, see through, struggle on with; *informal* stick at, soldier on with, slave away at, peg away at, plug away at, hammer away at, bash on with, plough through.
OPPOSITE give up.

□ **keep something back 1** *every week she kept back a portion of the money he gave her* **reserve**, keep in reserve, put by, save, save up, store up, put aside, lay aside, set aside, hoard, treasure; **retain**, hold back, keep, keep for oneself, hold on to, not part with, keep in one's possession; *N. Amer.* set by; *informal* keep for a rainy day, stash away.
2 *she kept back the details from Ann* **conceal**, keep secret, keep hidden, hide, withhold, suppress, keep quiet about, not tell, not reveal, not divulge, hush up.
OPPOSITES disclose, divulge.
3 *she could hardly keep back her tears* **suppress**, stifle, withhold, choke back, fight back, hold back/in, restrain, repress, check, keep in check, keep under control, contain, curb, smother, swallow, bottle up, bite back.
OPPOSITE let out.

□ **keep from** *Dinah bit her lip to keep from screaming* **refrain from**, stop oneself, restrain oneself from, prevent oneself from, manage not to, forbear from, resist the temptation to, forgo, avoid.

□ **keep someone from something 1** *worry kept her from sleeping | he could hardly keep himself from laughing* **prevent**, stop, hinder, impede, hamper; **restrain**, check, curb, hold back, halt.
OPPOSITES enable, allow.
2 *keep him from harm* **preserve**, protect, keep safe, afford protection to, guard, shield, shelter, save, safeguard, secure, defend.
OPPOSITE endanger.

□ **keep something from someone** *now you know what your mother tried to keep from you* **keep secret**, keep hidden, hide, conceal, withhold, hush up, not tell, suppress, censor; *informal* keep dark, not breathe a word of.
OPPOSITES tell, divulge.

□ **keep off 1** *he'd tell the boy to keep off private land* **stay off**, not enter, keep away from, stay away from, not trespass on, remain at a distance from, not go near.
OPPOSITE enter.
2 *Maud tried to keep off political subjects* **avoid**, steer clear of, stay away from, shun, evade, skirt round, sidestep, dodge, pass over, bypass; *informal* duck.
OPPOSITES raise, mention.
3 *the first thing she told me was to keep off alcohol* **abstain from**, go without, do without, renounce, refrain from, give up, forgo, forswear, resist, turn aside from, swear off, not touch; *informal* quit.
OPPOSITE take up.
4 *it'll be great if the rain keeps off* **stay away**, hold off, not start, not begin, not come, not happen.
OPPOSITE start.

□ **keep on 1** *they preferred to keep on working* **continue**, go on, carry on, persist in, persevere in, keep going with; soldier on, struggle on, see something through.
OPPOSITE stop.
2 *the commander kept on about vigilance* **talk constantly**, talk endlessly, talk repeatedly, keep talking, go on, go on talking, go on and on, dwell on the subject, refer to repeatedly, repeat oneself, ramble on, rant on; *informal* harp on, witter on, rabbit on.

□ **keep someone on** *the boss decided to keep the man on* **continue to employ**, keep employing, carry on employing, retain in one's service, not dismiss, not sack, keep in one's employ, retain the services of.
OPPOSITE dismiss.

□ **keep on at** *they kept on at him to hurry up* **nag**, go on at, keep at, harp on at, badger, chivvy, harass, hound, bully, pester, scold; *informal* hassle; *N. Amer. informal* ride.

□ **keep to 1** *I've got to keep to the rules* **obey**, abide by, observe, follow, comply with, adhere to, act in accordance with, conform to, be governed by, respect, defer to; **honour**, keep, fulfil, act on, stand by, stick to, be bound by, be true to, keep faith with, make good, carry out.
2 *keep to the path by the hedge* **follow**, follow closely, stick to, stay on.
OPPOSITE stray from.
3 *speakers should keep to the point* **stick to**, restrict oneself to, confine oneself to.
OPPOSITE deviate from.

□ **keep someone under** *the local people are kept under by the army* **keep in subjection**, keep in submission, hold down, keep down, keep under one's thumb, subdue, subject, suppress, repress, oppress, tyrannize over, tyrannize; *informal* squash, squelch, trample on.

□ **keep up** *he had to run to keep up* **keep pace**, keep abreast.
OPPOSITE lag behind.

□ **keep something up** *keep up the good work | she kept up a continuous conversation* **continue**, keep on with, continue with, go on with, carry on with, persist with, persevere with; maintain, carry on, keep going, sustain.
OPPOSITE cease from.

□ **keep up with 1** *she walked fast to keep up with him* **keep pace with**, keep abreast of; rival, challenge, compete with, vie with, match, touch, equal.
OPPOSITE lag behind.
2 *even while travelling he kept up with events at home* **keep informed about**, keep up to date with, keep in touch with, not lose track of, keep abreast of, keep an eye on, learn about, retain an interest in; *informal* keep tabs on, keep a tab on.
OPPOSITE lose touch with.
3 *they kept up with him by means of Christmas cards* **remain in contact with**, stay in touch with, maintain contact with, remain in correspondence with, remain in communication with, keep up one's friendship with, remain acquainted with.
OPPOSITE lose touch with.

▶ **noun** *he had no money to pay for his keep* **maintenance**, upkeep, support, sustenance, subsistence, board, board and lodging, food, nourishment, nurture; living, livelihood, means.

□ **for keeps** (*informal*) *his performance earned him the trophy for keeps* **forever**, for ever, for all time, for ever and ever, for always, once and for all, for good, for good and all, permanently, in perpetuity; *N. Amer.* forevermore; *informal* until kingdom come, until hell freezes over, until doomsday; *archaic* for aye.
OPPOSITES temporarily, for the time being.

keep[2] ▶ **noun** *enemies storming the keep* **fortress**, fort, stronghold, tower, donjon, castle, citadel, bastion, fortification, fastness; *archaic* hold, dungeon.

keeper ▶ **noun 1** *he was made keeper of the archives at court* **curator**, conservator, custodian, guardian, administrator, overseer; steward, caretaker, superintendent; governor, warden, attendant.
2 *he was keeper of an inn* **proprietor**, owner, holder, possessor, master/mistress, landlord/landlady.
3 *she's not a child and you're not her keeper* **guardian**, protector, defender,

K

guard, bodyguard, escort, minder, attendant, chaperone, carer, nursemaid, nurse.
4 *the prisoners' keepers would sometimes confiscate books* **jailer**, prison officer, guard, warder, warden, custodian, sentry; *informal* screw.

keeping ▶ **noun** *the document is in the keeping of the county archivist* **safe keeping**, care, custody, charge, keep, possession, trust, protection, safeguard; guardianship, trusteeship, tutelage, supervision, protectorship.
□ **in keeping with** *a trend to the left which was in keeping with the political atmosphere of the time* **consistent with**, in harmony with, in accord with, in accordance with, in agreement with, in line with, in character with, true to, compatible with, congruent with, commensurate with; appropriate to, befitting, as befits, suitable for, suited to.
OPPOSITE at odds with.

keepsake ▶ **noun** *she gave him a lock of her hair as a keepsake* **memento**, token of remembrance, souvenir, reminder, something to remember someone by, remembrance, relic, memorial, token; *archaic* remembrancer, favour.

keg ▶ **noun** **barrel**, cask, vat, butt, tun, drum, hogshead, firkin, tub, tank, container, vessel.

ken ▶ **noun** *their talk hinted at mysteries beyond my ken* **knowledge**, awareness, perception, understanding, grasp, comprehension, realization, apprehension, appreciation, consciousness, recognition, notice.

kernel ▶ **noun 1** *the squirrel cracks the nut's shell and extracts the rich kernel* seed, grain, heart, core, stone; nut.
2 *the foreword contained the kernel of the policy* **essence**, core, heart, essential part, essentials, quintessence, fundamentals, basics, nub, gist, substance, burden, heart of the matter, marrow, meat, pith, crux; *informal* nitty-gritty, nuts and bolts, brass tacks.
3 *there may be a kernel of truth in what he says* **nucleus**, centre, germ, grain, nugget.

K

key ▶ **noun 1** *I put my key in the lock* door key, latchkey, pass key, master key, skeleton key.
2 *the* **key** *to the mystery lay elsewhere | customer satisfaction is the* **key to** *success* **answer**, clue, solution, explanation, pointer, cue, lead; **basis of**, foundation for, requisite for; condition, precondition, essential, means, way, route, path, passport, secret, formula; **guide**, gloss, glossary, interpretation, explication, translation, clarification, exposition, annotation, index, legend, code.
3 (*Music*) *a song in a minor key* **tone**, pitch, timbre, tonality, tone colour, modulation.
4 *it was like the sixties all over again, in a more austerely intellectual key* **style**, character, mood, vein, spirit, feel, feeling, flavour, quality, humour, atmosphere.
▶ **adjective** *he was a key figure in formulating policy* **crucial**, central, essential, indispensable, basic, fundamental, pivotal, critical, decisive, dominant, vital, principal, salient, prime, chief, major, leading, main, important, significant.
OPPOSITES secondary, peripheral.

keyboard ▶ **noun.** *See centre pages for list of* **Keyboard Instruments**

keynote ▶ **noun** *the keynote of the paper was 'positive planning'* **theme**, salient point, point, gist, substance, burden, tenor, heart of the matter, pith, marrow, topic, policy line; essence, heart, core, basis, essential feature/element, defining characteristic, centre, kernel, nucleus.

keystone ▶ **noun 1** *a carved head formed the keystone of the door* **cornerstone**, central stone, quoin.
2 *cooperation remains the keystone of the government's security policy* **foundation**, basis, linchpin, cornerstone, base, principle, guiding principle, core, heart, centre, crux, fundament, mainspring, priority.

kibosh ▶ **noun** (*informal*)
□ **put the kibosh on** *his boss put the kibosh on the deal* **put a stop to**, check, curb, stop, halt, bring to an end, put an end to, nip in the bud, quash, block, cancel, scotch, thwart, frustrate, prevent, quell, suppress; *informal* squelch, put paid to, scupper, spike, stymie.

kick ▶ **verb 1** *her attacker punched and kicked her | she kicked a box in his direction* **boot**, punt, strike with the foot; propel, drive, knock, send; *Scottish* blooter; *informal* put the boot into.
2 (*informal*) *he was struggling to kick his drug habit* **give up**, break, get out of, abandon, end, escape from; stop, cease, leave off, desist from, renounce, forgo, do without, eschew; *informal* shake, pack in, lay off, quit.
OPPOSITES take up, start.
3 *the gun kicked so hard that he flinched* **recoil**, spring back, fly back.
□ **kick against** *young people are expected to kick against the establishment* **resist**, rebel against, oppose, struggle/fight against, refuse to accept; protest against, complain about, rage against, grumble about, object to; defy, disobey, reject, spurn; *informal* gripe about, grouse about, beef about, bitch about.
OPPOSITE accept.
□ **kick someone/something around** (*informal*) **1** *we feel we are undervalued and get kicked around* **abuse**, mistreat, maltreat, treat disrespectfully, treat inconsiderately, push around/about, boss about/around, trample on, take for granted; *informal* mess about/around, walk all over.
2 *they began to kick around the idea of sending a man into space* **discuss**, talk over, debate, thrash out, consider, moot, toy with, play with, argue the pros and cons of.
□ **kick back** (*N. Amer. informal*) *take a moment to kick back and enjoy an ice cream* **relax**, unwind, take it easy, rest, take one's ease, slow down, let up, ease up/off, be at leisure, sit back, laze, enjoy oneself; *N. Amer. informal* chill out, hang loose.
□ **kick off** (*informal*) *the festival kicks off on Monday | the installation kicks off a three-year project* **start**, begin, get going, get off the ground, get under way; open, start off, set going, set in motion, launch, initiate, introduce, inaugurate, usher in, start the ball rolling; *informal* get the show on the road; *formal* commence.
□ **kick someone out** (*informal*) *he was kicked out of his regiment for insubordination* **expel**, send away, eject, turn out, throw out, force out, oust, evict, put out, get rid of; dismiss, discharge; *informal* chuck out, send packing, boot out, show the door to, give someone their marching orders, throw someone out on their ear, sack, fire, give someone the boot, axe; *Brit. informal* turf out; *N. Amer. informal* give someone the bum's rush.
▶ **noun 1** *he gave the ball a kick* boot, punt.
2 (*informal*) *I get a kick out of driving a racing car | the murderer was a lunatic who killed for kicks* **thrill**, excitement, stimulation, tingle; fun, enjoyment, amusement, pleasure, gratification; *informal* buzz, high; *N. Amer. informal* charge.
3 (*informal*) *caffeine-free cola for those who want the taste without the kick | mustard is mixed into the dough to give the roll a delicious kick* **potency**, stimulant effect, alcoholic effect, strength, power, punch; tang, zest, bite, piquancy, edge, pungency, spice, savour; *informal* zip, zing, zap, pep, oomph.
4 (*informal*) *their parents had gone on a health kick and refused to buy junk food* **craze**, enthusiasm, obsession, mania, passion, preoccupation, fixation; fashion, vogue, trend; *informal* fad, jag.

kickback ▶ **noun 1** *the kickback from the gun punches at your shoulder* **recoil**, kick, rebound.
2 (*informal*) *the businessmen were accused of paying kickbacks to politicians to obtain public contracts* **bribe**, payment, reward, recompense, inducement; *N. Amer.* payola; *informal* pay-off, sweetener, backhander, cut, graft.

kick-off ▶ **noun** (*informal*) *this weekend is the kick-off for Japan's holiday season* **beginning**, start, outset, opening, starting point, initiation, inception; *formal* commencement.
OPPOSITE end.

kid[1] ▶ **noun** (*informal*) *she is married with three kids* **child**, youngster, little one, young one, baby, toddler, infant, boy/girl, young person, minor, juvenile, adolescent, teenager, youth, stripling; offspring, son/daughter; *Scottish* bairn, wean; *informal* kiddie, nipper, tot, tiny, kiddiewink, shaver, young 'un; *Brit. informal* sprog; *N. Amer. informal* rug rat; *Austral./NZ* ankle-biter; *derogatory* brat, urchin; *literary* babe.

kid[2] ▶ **verb** (*informal*) **1** *the village is called Hell—I'm not kidding* **joke**, tease, jest, chaff, be facetious; pretend, play, fool about/around; *informal* pull someone's leg, wind up, have on, rib, josh; *N. Amer. informal* pull someone's chain, fun, shuck.
2 *why did I kid myself that I'd succeed?* **delude**, deceive, fool, trick, take in, hoodwink, hoax, beguile, dupe, gull, bamboozle; *informal* con, pull the wool over someone's eyes; *literary* cozen.

kidnap ▶ **verb** *militants kidnapped the daughter of a minister* **abduct**, carry off, capture, seize, snatch, hold to ransom, take as hostage, hijack; run off/away with; *informal* nobble, shanghai.

kidney ▶ **noun**

WORD LINKS

relating to kidneys	**renal, nephritic**
related prefix	**nephro-**
branch of medicine concerning the kidneys	**nephrology**
inflammation of the kidneys	**nephritis**
removal of kidney	**nephrectomy**
removal of kidney stone	**lithotomy**

kill ▶ **verb 1** *gangs killed twenty-seven people* **murder**, cause the death of, take/end the life of, do away with, make away with, assassinate, do to death, eliminate, terminate, dispatch, finish off, put to death, execute; slaughter, butcher, massacre, wipe out, destroy, annihilate, erase, eradicate, exterminate, extirpate, decimate, mow down, shoot down, cut down, cut to pieces; put down, put to sleep; *informal* bump off, polish off, do in, do for, knock off, top, take out, croak, stiff, blow away, liquidate, dispose of; *N. Amer. informal* ice, off, rub out, waste, whack, scrag, smoke; *literary* slay.
2 *media hostility would kill all hopes of progress* **destroy**, put an end to, bring to an end, be the end of, end, extinguish, dash, quell, quash, ruin, wreck, shatter, smash, crush, scotch; stop, block, frustrate, thwart, put a

stop to, prevent, defeat, derail; *informal* put paid to, do for, put the lid on, put the kibosh on, stymie, queer; *Brit. informal* scupper, dish.
OPPOSITE facilitate.
3 *we had to kill several hours at the airport* **while away**, use up, fill up, fill in, fill, occupy, beguile, pass, spend, expend; fritter away, waste.
4 *you must rest or you'll kill yourself* **exhaust**, wear out, tire out, overtax, overtire, fatigue, weary, sap, drain, tax, strain, debilitate, enervate, prostrate; *informal* knock out, fag out, shatter; *Brit. informal* knacker.
OPPOSITES refresh, revitalize.
5 (*informal*) *my feet were killing me* **hurt**, give pain to, cause pain to, cause agony to, pain, torture, torment, cause discomfort to; be agonizing, be excruciating, be painful, be sore, be uncomfortable.
6 (*informal*) *the music kills me every time I hear it* **overwhelm**, take someone's breath away, leave speechless, shake, move, stir, stun, amaze, astonish, stagger, dumbfound; *informal* bowl over, blow away, knock sideways, blow someone's mind, knock for six, flabbergast.
7 *the captain kept the engines at a low rev to kill the noise* **muffle**, deaden, stifle, dampen, damp down, smother, reduce, diminish, decrease, suppress, abate, tone down, moderate, silence, mute, still, quieten, soften, quell.
OPPOSITE amplify.
8 *she gave me a shot to kill the pain* **alleviate**, assuage, soothe, allay, take the edge off, mitigate, dull, blunt, mask, deaden, stifle, suppress, subdue, weaken, abate, quell, get rid of, put an end to.
OPPOSITE intensify.
9 (*informal*) *if a message has been killed, the file contains only the header* **delete**, wipe out, erase, remove, destroy, rub out, cut out, cut, cancel, get rid of, expunge, obliterate, eliminate; *informal* zap.
10 (*informal*) *Congress killed an anti-tobacco bill* **veto**, defeat, vote down, rule against, reject, throw out, overrule, stop, block, put a stop to, put an end to, quash, overturn, disallow; *informal* give the thumbs down to, squash.
OPPOSITES pass, accept.
11 (*informal*) *Noel parked and killed the engine* **turn off**, switch off, stop, stop working, shut off, shut down, cut, cut out, deactivate; put out, turn out, extinguish.
OPPOSITE start.
▶ **noun 1** *the hunter proudly flung down his kill* **prey**, quarry, victim, bag.
2 *the wolf was moving in for the kill* **death blow**, killing, act of killing, dispatch; conclusion, ending, finish, end, climax; *French* coup de grâce.

WORD LINKS
person or substance that kills **-cide (e.g. *insecticide*)**
killing of someone **-cide (e.g. *regicide, suicide*)**

killer *See centre pages for list of* **Murderers**
▶ **noun 1** *police are searching for clues to help find the killer* **murderer**, slaughterer, destroyer, liquidator, exterminator, terminator, executioner; *literary* slayer; *dated* homicide.
2 *the major killers are coronary disease, stroke, and cancer* **cause of death**, fatal/deadly illness, destroyer, threat to life, menace, plague, scourge, peril.

killing ▶ **noun** *the community was shocked by the brutal killing* **murder**, taking of life, assassination, homicide, manslaughter, liquidation, elimination, putting/doing to death, execution, dispatch, martyrdom; **slaughter**, massacre, butchery, carnage, bloodshed, destruction, decimation, extermination, eradication, annihilation, wiping out, extinction; patricide, matricide, parricide, infanticide, filicide; *literary* slaying.
□ **make a killing** (*informal*) *investors are set to make a killing in the sell-off* **make a large profit**, make a/one's fortune, gain, profit, make money, be successful, be lucky; *informal* clean up, strike it rich, rake it in, make a/one's pile, make a packet, make a bundle, make a pretty penny; *Brit. informal* make a bomb; *N. Amer. informal* make big bucks.
▶ **adjective 1** *a killing blow* **deadly**, lethal, fatal, mortal, death-dealing, causing death, life-threatening, final, destructive, dangerous; murderous, homicidal; *literary* deathly.
2 (*informal*) *the Minister has a killing schedule* **exhausting**, gruelling, punishing, taxing, draining, wearing, prostrating, sapping, crushing, tiring, fatiguing, debilitating, enervating, arduous, tough, demanding, onerous, strenuous, rigorous, relentless, unsparing, grinding, formidable; *informal* murderous, back-breaking; *Brit. informal* knackering.
3 (*informal*) *the suspense will be killing* **unbearable**, intolerable, unendurable, not to be borne, more than one can bear, more than flesh and blood can stand, insupportable, impossible; cruel, heartbreaking, painful, excruciating, agonizing, grievous.
4 (*informal, dated*) *'I think he's absolutely killing,' said Muriel* **hilarious**, hysterically funny, outrageously funny, too funny for words, uproarious, riotous, comic, comical, amusing, laughable, absurd, ludicrous, outrageous; *informal* priceless, side-splitting, a scream, a hoot, rib-tickling, killingly funny, screamingly funny.

killjoy ▶ **noun** *sun worshippers feel the anti-sun lobby are just killjoys* **spoilsport**, moaner, complainer, mope, prophet of doom, Cassandra, Jeremiah, death's head at a feast; puritan, prig, prude; *Austral./NZ* wowser; *informal* wet blanket, party-pooper, misery, dog in the manger.

kilter ▶ **noun**
□ **out of kilter** *daylight saving throws everyone's body clock out of kilter* **awry**, off balance, unbalanced, out of order, not in working order, disordered, confused, disorderly, disorganized, muddled, in poor shape; disharmonious, discordant, out of tune, out of step.

kin ▶ **noun** *mothers left their children with grandmothers or other kin* **relatives**, relations, family, family members, kindred, connections, clan, tribe, kith and kin, one's own flesh and blood, nearest and dearest; kinsfolk, kinsmen/kinswomen; *informal* folks; *dated* people.
▶ **adjective** *my uncle was kin to the brothers* **related**, akin, allied, close, connected with, cognate with; *rare* consanguineous, consanguine.

kind[1] ▶ **noun 1** *she brought all kinds of gifts | he named the kinds of bird that could be seen* **sort**, type, variety, style, form, class, category, genre; genus, species, race, breed, family, strain, order, natural kind; brand, make, model, design, version, line, mark.
2 *the trials were different in kind from any that preceded them | the book was the first of its kind* **character**, nature, essence, quality, disposition, make-up, calibre; type, style, stamp, manner, description, mould, cast, temperament, ilk, kidney, persuasion; *N. Amer.* stripe; *archaic* grain.
□ **kind of** (*informal*) *it got kind of cosy* **rather**, quite, fairly, moderately, somewhat, a little, slightly, a shade; in a way, in a manner of speaking, after a fashion, as one might say; *informal* sort of, a bit, kinda, pretty, a touch, a thought, a tad.

kind[2] ▶ **adjective** *she's a kind girl and often rings me | it was so kind of him to help out* **kindly**, good-natured, kind-hearted, tender-hearted, warm-hearted, soft-hearted, good-hearted, tender, caring, feeling, affectionate, loving, warm, gentle, mellow, mild; **considerate**, helpful, thoughtful, obliging, unselfish, selfless, altruistic, good, cooperative, accommodating, attentive; compassionate, sympathetic, understanding, big-hearted, benevolent, benign, friendly, neighbourly, courteous, agreeable, pleasant, nice, amiable, hospitable, well meaning, well intentioned, public-spirited, well meant; generous, magnanimous, indulgent, tolerant, charitable, gracious, lenient, humane, merciful, clement, pitying, forbearing, long-suffering, patient; liberal, open-handed, lavish, bountiful, unsparing, unstinting, beneficent, munificent, giving; philanthropic; handsome, princely; *Brit. informal* decent; *literary* bounteous; *rare* benignant.
OPPOSITES unkind, inconsiderate, mean, cruel.

CHOOSE THE RIGHT WORD

kind, kindly, benevolent

These words all describe people who care about and try to promote the well-being and happiness of others.

- A **kind** person shows consideration for others, either by behaving helpfully, thoughtfully, and generously (*it was very kind of you to make her a cake*) or by being gentle and caring, especially to someone in trouble or distress (*Mrs Melburn was kind to them after their father died*). *Kind* is also used rather formulaically in polite requests, where the speaker is not in fact concerned with the generous or considerate feelings of the person addressed (*please be so kind as to excuse me*). It is the only one of these words that can be used to someone's face to express appreciation; one can say *you are very kind*, but not *you are kindly*.
- **Kindly** (as an adjective) is a much less common word and is often used of older people. It tends to refer to their general manner rather than actual generous acts, and suggests a gentle, warm, and tolerant kindness (*she was kindly, almost motherly | Adams was a kindly man who took a keen interest in his staff*).
- A person described as **benevolent** is often one in a position of authority. A *benevolent ruler* has the good of their subjects at heart and acts to promote it. *Benevolent* can also be used of an older person who is detached from but pleased by the happiness of younger or less experienced people (*he was like a benevolent uncle*).

kind-hearted ▶ **adjective** *she was friendly and kind-hearted* **kind**, caring, warm-hearted, tender-hearted, soft-hearted, kindly, benevolent, good-natured, good-hearted, mild, tender, warm, feeling, gentle, compassionate, sympathetic, understanding; indulgent, humane, altruistic, patient, tolerant, lenient, merciful, benign, mellow, beneficent, amiable; *rare* benignant.
OPPOSITE hard-hearted.

kindle ▶ **verb 1** *he kindled a fire of dry grass* **light**, **ignite**, set alight, set light to, set on fire, set fire to, put a match to, set burning, get going, start, touch off, spark; *informal* torch.
OPPOSITES douse, extinguish, put out.
2 *it was Elvis who kindled my interest in music* **rouse**, arouse, wake, waken, awaken, quicken; **stimulate**, inspire, stir up, call forth, call/bring into being, draw forth, bring out, excite, evoke, pique, whet, stir, provoke, spur, fire, inflame, trigger, prompt, induce, encourage, actuate, activate, touch off, spark off, set off, set going, incite, promote, engender, generate; *literary* enkindle.

kindliness ▸ noun *she was grateful for his kindliness and care* **kindness**, benevolence, warmth, benignity, gentleness, mildness, tenderness, care, humanity, humaneness, sensitivity, sympathy, compassion, understanding; generosity, charity, kind-heartedness, warm-heartedness, soft-heartedness, tender-heartedness, thoughtfulness, concern, solicitousness.
OPPOSITE unkindness.

kindly ▸ adjective *the children were adopted by a kindly old lady | he smiled in a kindly manner* **benevolent**, kind, kind-hearted, warm-hearted, generous, good-natured, humane; **gentle**, warm, mild, compassionate, caring, tender-hearted, soft-hearted, tender, loving, loving and giving, motherly, fatherly, benign, mellow, well meaning, genial; indulgent, understanding, sympathetic, lenient, tolerant, charitable, magnanimous, easy-going, patient; helpful, thoughtful, considerate, good, good-hearted, nice, friendly, neighbourly, pleasant, amiable, agreeable, affable, amicable; *Brit. informal* decent; *rare* benignant.
OPPOSITES unkind, cruel.
▸ adverb 1 *'Welcome,' she said kindly | someone kindly lent us a car* **benevolently**, good-naturedly, warmly, affectionately, tenderly, lovingly, compassionately; considerately, thoughtfully, helpfully, obligingly, generously, selflessly, unselfishly, graciously, indulgently, sympathetically, leniently, charitably.
OPPOSITES unkindly, harshly.
2 *kindly explain what you mean by that* **please**, if you please, if you would be so good, if you wouldn't mind, have the goodness to, pray; *French* s'il vous plaît; *archaic* prithee.
□ **not take kindly to** *she does not take kindly to criticism* **resent**, dislike, object to, take umbrage at, take exception to, be offended by, take offence at, be annoyed/irritated by, be displeased by, be affronted by, feel aggrieved about, take something amiss, be upset by, be put out by; *informal* be miffed at.

CHOOSE THE RIGHT WORD

kindly, kind, benevolent
See KIND.

kindness ▸ noun 1 *he thanked her for her kindness and support* **kindliness**, kind-heartedness, warm-heartedness, tender-heartedness, goodwill, affectionateness, affection, warmth, gentleness, tenderness, concern, care; consideration, considerateness, helpfulness, thoughtfulness, unselfishness, selflessness, altruism, compassion, sympathy, understanding, big-heartedness, benevolence, benignity, friendliness, neighbourliness, hospitality, amiability, courteousness, public-spiritedness; generosity, magnanimity, indulgence, patience, tolerance, charitableness, graciousness, lenience, humaneness, mercifulness; *Brit. informal* decency; *literary* bounteousness.
OPPOSITES unkindness, meanness.
2 *she has done us many a kindness* **kind act**, good deed, act of kindness, good turn, favour, act of assistance, service, help, aid.
OPPOSITE disservice.

kindred ▸ noun 1 *he owed his popularity to his mother's kindred* **family**, relatives, relations, kin, family members, connections, kith and kin, one's own flesh and blood, clan, tribe, house, lineage; *informal* folks; *dated* people; *formal* kinsfolk, kinsmen/kinswomen.
2 *ties of kindred* **kinship**, family ties, being related, relationship, relatedness, blood relationship, ties of blood, consanguinity, common ancestry, common lineage.
▸ adjective 1 *the centre collects works on industrial relations and kindred subjects* **related**, allied, connected, closely connected/related, comparable, similar, like, alike, parallel, associated, corresponding, cognate, analogous, interconnected, affiliated.
OPPOSITE unrelated.
2 *she was glad to find a kindred spirit to confide in* **like-minded**, sympathetic, in sympathy, in harmony, in agreement, in tune, of one mind, akin, similar, like, congenial, compatible, understanding, agreeable; *informal* on the same wavelength.
OPPOSITES uncongenial, unsympathetic, alien.
3 (*archaic*) *the tenants were members of an allied and kindred clan* **related**, akin, kin, connected, of the same blood, of the same family, with a common ancestor, of the same lineage, cognate; *rare* agnate, consanguineous, consanguine.
OPPOSITE unrelated.

king ▸ noun 1 *Edward made a bid to be crowned king of France* **ruler**, sovereign, monarch, supreme ruler, crowned head, majesty, Crown, head of state, royal personage, emperor, prince, potentate, overlord, liege lord, lord, leader, chief.
2 (*informal*) *he has become king of world football* **star**, leading light, luminary, superstar, mogul, giant, master, kingpin, celebrity, lion; *informal* supremo, megastar, top dog, VIP, celeb, big name, bigwig, big cheese; *N. Amer. informal* big wheel.
□ **a king's ransom** *the perfume cost a king's ransom* **a fortune**, a small fortune, a huge amount, a vast sum, millions, billions; *informal* a mint, a bundle, a packet, a pretty penny, a tidy sum; *Brit. informal* a bomb, loadsamoney, shedloads; *N. Amer. informal* big bucks, big money, gazillions; *Austral. informal* big bickies.

WORD LINKS
relating to a king **regal**

kingdom ▸ noun 1 *his kingdom covered many countries* **realm**, domain, dominion, country, land, nation, state, sovereign state, province, territory; empire, principality, palatinate, duchy.
2 *the third floor was Henry's little kingdom* **domain**, province, realm, sphere, sphere/field of influence, dominion, area of power, department, territory, field, arena, zone, orbit.
3 *homeopathic remedies are drawn from the plant and mineral kingdoms* **division**, category, classification, grouping, group; class, family, genus, kind, order, branch.

kingly ▸ adjective 1 *kingly power* **royal**, regal, of a king, monarchical, sovereign, imperial, princely, crowned, supreme, absolute.
2 *kingly robes* **regal**, **majestic**, stately, august, noble, lordly, proud, dignified, distinguished, courtly; splendid, magnificent, fit for a king, grand, glorious, rich, gorgeous, resplendent, princely, superb, sumptuous, opulent, costly, fine, grandiose, imposing, impressive; *informal* splendiferous, posh.
3 (*informal*) *the kingly sum of 2,500 guineas* **vast**, princely, huge, enormous, generous, lavish, handsome, prodigious, substantial, tremendous, massive; *informal* astronomical, whopping, whopping great, thumping, thumping great; *Brit. informal* whacking, whacking great, ginormous.
OPPOSITE measly.

kink ▸ noun 1 *your fishing line should have no kinks or frays* **curl**, crimp, twist, twirl, ringlet, wave, frizz; knot, tangle, entanglement, coil, loop, crinkle, wrinkle, warp, distortion, irregularity.
2 *go round the kink in the road* **bend**, corner, angle, dog-leg, crook, twist, turn, curve, loop, zigzag; *Brit.* hairpin bend.
3 *though the system is making headway, there are still some kinks to iron out* **flaw**, defect, imperfection, problem, difficulty, complication, hitch, snag, shortcoming, weak point/spot, weakness, catch; *informal* hiccup, glitch.
4 *I haven't come here to talk about my sartorial kinks* **peculiarity**, quirk, idiosyncrasy, eccentricity, oddity, foible, whim, whimsy, caprice, vagary, twist, crotchet, mannerism, fad; aberration, irregularity, deviation, perversion, fetish; *informal* hang-up, thing; *rare* singularity.

kinky ▸ adjective 1 (*informal*) *a kinky lover | she was involved in a kinky relationship with a couple of older women* **abnormal**, unusual, weird, bizarre, peculiar, strange, odd, funny; **perverted**, deviant, unnatural, warped, twisted, depraved, degenerate, perverse, unhealthy, aberrant, sadistic, masochistic, corrupt, immoral; *informal* sick, pervy, sicko; *rare* deviative.
2 (*informal*) *kinky underwear* **provocative**, sexy, sexually arousing, sexually exciting, erotic, seductive, suggestive, inviting, tempting, tantalizing, alluring, titillating, indecent, immodest; *informal* tarty, saucy, naughty.
3 *Catriona's long kinky hair* **curly**, crimped, curled, curling, frizzy, frizzed, wavy, ringletted, ringletty; twisted, bent, coiled, crinkled.
OPPOSITE straight.

kinsfolk ▸ noun *his kinsfolk in England* **relatives**, relations, kin, kindred, family members, family, kith and kin, kinsmen/kinswomen, one's own flesh and blood, blood relatives, connections; *informal* folks; *dated* people.

kinship ▸ noun 1 *ties of descent and kinship* **relationship**, relatedness, being related, family ties, family connections, blood relationship, blood ties, common ancestry, common lineage, kindred, connection; *formal* consanguinity, propinquity.
2 *she could not feel kinship with people who were not decisive* **affinity**, sympathy, kindred, rapport, harmony, understanding, alliance, association, empathy, closeness, fellow feeling, bond, community, communion, compatibility, link, accord, friendship, togetherness; similarity, likeness, parallel, parallelism, connection, correspondence, concordance, equivalence, agreement, symmetry, analogy, uniformity.

kinsman, kinswoman ▸ noun *his namesake and distant kinsman* **relative**, relation, blood relation/relative, family member, one's own flesh and blood, next of kin; cousin, uncle, nephew, aunt, niece.

kiosk ▸ noun *he's buying an ice cream from the kiosk* **booth**, stand, stall, counter, refreshments kiosk, news-stand, bookstall, telephone kiosk; box, compartment, cubicle, cabin, hut, enclosure.

kismet ▸ noun *what chance did I stand against kismet?* **fate**, destiny, fortune, providence, the stars, God's will, what is written in the stars, one's doom, one's portion, one's lot, one's lot in life, karma, predestination, preordination, predetermination, what is to come, the writing on the wall; luck, chance; *archaic* one's dole; *rare* predestiny.

kiss ▸ verb 1 *he kissed her on the lips | close by a couple were kissing* give a kiss to, plant a kiss on, brush one's lips against, blow a kiss to, air-kiss; *informal* peck, give a peck to, give a smacker to, smooch, canoodle, neck, pet, kiss and cuddle, bill and coo; *Brit. informal* snog; *N. Amer. informal* buss; *informal, dated* spoon; *rare* osculate.
2 *allow your foot just to kiss the floor* **brush against**, brush, caress, touch

gently, touch lightly, touch, stroke, graze, scrape, shave, skim over, glance off.

▶ **noun 1** *she gave him a kiss on the cheek* air kiss; French kiss, soul kiss; X; *informal* peck, smack, smacker, smackeroo, smooch; *Brit. informal* snog; *N. Amer. informal* buss; *rare* osculation.
2 *the kiss of the flowers against her cheeks* **gentle touch**, light touch, caress, brush, stroke; **graze**, glance, scrape, shave.

kit ▶ **noun 1** *his tool kit* **equipment**, tools, implements, instruments, gadgets, utensils, appliances, tools of the trade, materials, aids, gear, tackle, hardware, paraphernalia, appurtenances; outfit, rig, set of tools, apparatus, set; *informal* things, stuff, the necessary; *Military* accoutrements.
2 *boys in football kit* **clothes**, clothing, rig, outfit, dress, costume, garments, attire, garb; uniform, colours, regimentals, livery, trappings; *Brit.* strip; *informal* togs, things, gear, get-up, stuff, duds; *Brit. informal* rig-out; *formal* apparel; *literary* raiment, array, habiliments.
3 *the children were building a model chalet from a kit* **set of parts**, set of components, set, outfit, DIY kit, do-it-yourself kit, self-assembly set, flat-pack.
4 (*informal*) *we packed up all our kit and set off* **belongings**, luggage, baggage, paraphernalia, effects, supplies, provisions, trappings, appurtenances, impedimenta; *informal* things, stuff, clobber, gear.

▶ **verb**

□ **kit someone/something out** *the studio is kitted out with six cameras | we were all kitted out in life jackets* **equip**, fit, fit out, fit up, fix up, furnish, stock, supply, provide, provision, issue; outfit, get up, rig out, turn out, dress, clothe, array, costume, attire, accoutre, deck out; arm.

kitchen ▶ **noun** *they sat drinking cocoa in the kitchen* kitchenette, kitchen-diner, cooking area, galley, cookhouse, bakehouse, scullery; *N. Amer.* cookery.

kittenish ▶ **adjective** *girls on radio had to be kittenish and girly* **playful**, fun-loving, light-hearted, skittish, mischievous, roguish, impish, frisky, lively; coquettish, flirtatious, cute, coy, arch, teasing, cheeky, naughty; frivolous, flippant, superficial, trivial, shallow, giddy, empty-headed, scatterbrained, feather-brained, silly; *informal* flirty, dizzy; *archaic* frolicsome, sportive, gamesome, frolic; *rare* ludic.
OPPOSITES serious, solemn, staid.

knack ▶ **noun 1** *some people have a knack for making money | it takes practice to acquire the knack* **gift**, talent, flair, genius, instinct, faculty, ability, capability, capacity, aptitude, aptness, bent, forte, facility, dexterity, adroitness, readiness, quickness, ingenuity, proficiency, expertness, competence; **technique**, method, trick, skill, art, secret, approach, way, skilfulness, mastery, expertise, handiness, deftness; *informal* know-how, the hang of something.
OPPOSITE inability.
2 *he has a knack of getting injured at the wrong time* **tendency to**, propensity for, habit of, way of, proneness to, aptness to, bent for, liability to, leaning towards, predisposition to, disposition to, inclination to, penchant for, readiness to.

knackered ▶ **adjective** (*Brit. informal*) **1** *you look absolutely knackered.* See EXHAUSTED.
2 *the computer was knackered.* See BROKEN sense 3.

knapsack ▶ **noun** **rucksack**, backpack, haversack, pack, kitbag, duffel bag, satchel, shoulder bag, holdall.

knave ▶ **noun** (*archaic*) *don't let yourself by hoodwinked by that knave* **scoundrel**, rogue, villain, rascal, good-for-nothing, wretch, ne'er-do-well, unprincipled person, reprobate, scapegrace, wrongdoer, evil-doer, charlatan, cheat, swindler, fraudster; *informal* swine, louse, hound, cur, rat, scumbag, wrong'un, bastard, beast, son of a bitch, s.o.b., skunk, nasty piece of work, ratbag; *Scottish informal* scrote; *Irish informal* spalpeen, sleeveen; *N. Amer. informal* fink, rat fink; *W. Indian informal* scamp; *N. English informal* scally; *informal, dated* cad, heel, rotter, bounder, bad egg, dastard, stinker, blighter; *archaic* blackguard, miscreant, varlet, vagabond, rapscallion, whoreson.

knavery ▶ **noun** (*archaic*) *no system can protect a fool from the knavery of others* **villainy**, unscrupulousness, baseness, roguishness, badness, wickedness, viciousness, iniquity, depravity, evil, vileness, devilishness, rascality, delinquency, corruption, corruptness; wrongdoing, evil-doing, misconduct, mischief, roguery, devilry, turpitude; dishonesty, deceit, deception, fraud, trickery, chicanery, cheating, swindling, duplicity, double-dealing, imposture; *informal* crookedness; *archaic* knavishness.
OPPOSITES honesty, virtue, honour.

knavish ▶ **adjective** (*archaic*) *his knavish behaviour* **dishonourable**, unprincipled, unscrupulous, ignoble, untrustworthy, roguish, rascally, scoundrelly, mischievous, reprobate, unregenerate, villainous, wicked, depraved, bad, immoral, fiendish, devilish; dishonest, deceitful, fraudulent, corrupt, lying, deceptive; base, contemptible, despicable, discreditable, shabby; *informal* shady, crooked; *archaic* scurvy, dastardly.
OPPOSITES honourable, noble, virtuous.

knead ▶ **verb 1** *turn the dough on to a floured board and knead* **pummel**, work, pound, squeeze, wring, twist, crush, form, shape, mould, mix, blend; *rare* malaxate, malax.
2 *she put her hands on his shoulders and kneaded the base of his neck* **massage**, press, manipulate, palpate, rub, handle, stroke, feel.

kneel ▶ **verb** *they knelt down and prayed* **fall to one's knees**, get down on one's knees, genuflect, bow, bow down, make obeisance, kowtow, curtsy, show reverence, show deference; crouch, squat, hunch down, hunker down.

knell ▶ **noun 1** *the knell of the ship's bell* **toll**, tolling, ringing, chime, clang, dong, peal, stroke, resounding, reverberation, clangour, boom; death knell; *archaic* knoll, tocsin.
2 *no politician wants to be remembered as the one who sounded the knell for the NHS* **end**, beginning of the end, presage of the end, death knell; **death sentence**, death warrant; omen, evil omen, ill omen, portent, warning.

knickers *See centre pages for list of* **Underwear**
▶ **plural noun** (*Brit.*) **underpants**, briefs, bikini briefs, drawers, French knickers, tanga briefs, camiknickers; *Brit.* **pants**; *informal* panties, knicks; *historical* bloomers, Directoire drawers, pantalettes.

knick-knack ▶ **noun** *knick-knacks for the tourist trade* **ornament**, novelty, gewgaw, piece of bric-a-brac, bibelot, trinket, trifle, bauble, gimcrack, bagatelle, curio, curiosity, plaything, toy; memento, souvenir; *N. Amer.* kickshaw; *French* objet, objet d'art; *informal* oojah, whatnot, thingamajig, thingamabob, dingle-dangle; *N. Amer. informal* tchotchke, tsatske; *Brit. informal* doobry, doodah; *archaic* gaud, folderol, whim-wham, bijou.

knife *See centre pages for list of* **Knives and Daggers**
▶ **noun** *peel the oranges using a sharp knife* **cutting tool**, blade, cutter, carver.
▶ **verb** *the victims had been knifed more than seventy times* **stab**, hack, gash, run through, slash, lacerate, cut, tear, gouge, pierce, spike, impale, transfix, bayonet, spear, skewer, wound.

knight ▶ **noun** *knights in armour* **chevalier**, cavalier, cavalryman, horseman, equestrian; gallant, champion, paladin, banneret, knight errant; lord, noble, nobleman.

□ **knight in shining armour** *she's still waiting for her knight in shining armour* **Sir Galahad**, knight on a white charger, protector, rescuer, saviour, preserver, champion, defender, guardian, guardian angel, deliverer, liberator; hero.

knightly ▶ **adjective 1** *tales of chivalry and knightly deeds* **gallant**, noble, valiant, heroic, courageous, brave, bold, intrepid, dauntless, fearless, stout-hearted; **chivalrous**, courtly, courteous, gracious, honourable, noble-minded; *literary* valorous.
OPPOSITES ignoble, cowardly, ungallant.
2 *conflict between knightly and non-knightly classes* **upper-class**, **well born**, high-born, noble, of noble birth, aristocratic, lordly, patrician, blue-blooded, titled; *archaic* gentle, of gentle birth.
OPPOSITES low-born, common.

knit *See centre pages for list of* **Knitting Stitches**
▶ **verb 1** *disparate regions had begun to knit together | their experience knitted the men together* **unite**, become united, unify, become unified, become one, come together, become closer, band together, bond, combine, coalesce, merge, meld, blend, amalgamate, league; bind, weld together, bring together, draw together, ally, link, join, fuse, connect, consolidate.
2 *we expect broken bones to knit* **heal**, mend, join, fuse, draw together, unite, become whole.
3 *Marcus knitted his brows* **furrow**, tighten, contract, gather, draw in, wrinkle, pucker, knot, screw up, crease, scrunch up.
▶ **noun** *silky knits in pretty shades* **knitted garment**, woollen; *informal* woolly.

knob ▶ **noun 1** *the drakes have a black bill with a knob at the base* **lump**, bump, protuberance, projection, protrusion, bulge, swelling, knot, node, nodule, gnarl, growth, outgrowth, excrescence, carbuncle, tumour; boss, stud, ball, knop, nub; *technical* umbo; *rare* tumescence.
2 *he fiddled with the knobs on the radio* **dial**, button, switch, on/off switch, key.
3 *she turned the knob and pushed open the door* **doorknob**, handle, door handle, grip, pull.
4 *spread a few knobs of butter over the surface* **nugget**, nub, nubble, lump, pat, cake, ball, cube, chunk, gobbet, dollop, piece, bit, portion, wedge, hunk, bar, slab; *Brit. informal* wodge, gob.

knock ▶ **verb 1** *he knocked on the door marked 'Enquiries'* **bang**, tap, rap, thump, pound, hammer; strike, hit, beat, batter, buffet, pummel.
2 *she knocked her knee painfully on the table* **bump**, bang, hit, strike, crack; **injure**, hurt, damage, bruise; *informal* bash, thwack.
3 *he knocked into an elderly man with a walking stick* **collide with**, bump into, bang into, knock against, hit, strike, be in collision with, run into, crash into, smash into, plough into, slam into, dash against, ram, jolt; *N. Amer.* impact; *informal* bash into.
4 (*informal*) *I'm not knocking the company—it's first-class* **criticize**, find fault with, run down, disparage, belittle, depreciate, deprecate, detract from, give a bad press to, cast aspersions on, scoff at, deride, jeer at, carp at, cavil at; lambaste, censure, condemn, denounce, revile, attack; *informal* slam, pan, bash, pull to pieces, pull apart, pick holes in, maul, savage, flay, throw brickbats at, shoot down, give something a battering, talk something down, have a go at, bad-mouth; *Brit. informal* slate, rubbish, slag off; *N. Amer. informal* trash, pummel; *Austral./NZ informal* bag.

K

OPPOSITE praise.

□ **knock about/around** (*informal*) **1** *for a couple of years we knocked around the Mediterranean* **wander**, roam, rove, range, travel, travel idly, journey, voyage, globetrot, drift, coast, meander, gad about, gallivant, jaunt, take a trip, go on a trip; ramble, stroll, saunter, maunder, amble, traipse, dawdle, potter; traverse, travel round, roam around, range over; *rare* peregrinate, perambulate, vagabond.
2 *she knocked around with artists* **associate**, consort, keep company, go around, mix, socialize, have dealings, have to do with, accompany, escort; be friends, be friendly; *informal* hobnob, hang out, run around, be thick with, chum around, pal around, pal up.

□ **knock someone/something about/around** *her husband was a brute who used to knock her about* **beat up**, beat, batter, strike, hit, punch, thump, thrash, smack, slap, cuff, buffet, pummel, belabour; **maltreat**, mistreat, abuse, ill-treat, ill-use, treat roughly, assault, attack, maul, manhandle; injure, damage, cause injury to, hurt, harm, wound, bruise; *N. Amer.* beat up on; *informal* rough up, do over, lay into, lace into, give someone a hiding, clobber, clout, bash, belt, whack, wallop, sock, plug, deck; *archaic* smite.

□ **knock something back** (*informal*) *she knocked back her gin* **swallow**, gulp down, drink up, swill down, swill, quaff, guzzle, toss off, consume, finish; *informal* down, swig; get one's laughing gear round; *N. Amer. informal* scarf (down/up), snarf (down/up); *rare* ingurgitate, bib.

□ **knock someone down** *two men knocked him down | their son was knocked down by a car* **fell**, floor, flatten, bring down, prostrate, topple, knock to the ground, throw to the ground; mug, attack, assault, set upon, beat up; knock over, run over, run down.

□ **knock something down 1** *the shop was closed and knocked down* **demolish**, pull down, bring down, take down, tear down, destroy; raze, raze to the ground, level, flatten, knock to the ground, topple, fell, bulldoze.
2 (*informal*) *the firm has knocked down the prices of its machines* **reduce**, lower, cut, decrease, bring down, drop, put down, diminish, mark down; *informal* slash, down.

□ **knock off** (*Brit. informal*) *they knock off at 5 o'clock* **stop work**, finish work, finish working, clock off, close shop, shut down, leave work, finish the working day; take a break, break, break off, rest, pause, stop, halt, finish; *informal* call it a day, have a breather, take five.
OPPOSITE clock on.

□ **knock someone off** (*informal*) *the person who slugged me was the one who knocked off Maloney* **kill**, murder, assassinate, do to death, do away with, make away with, get rid of, dispose of, eliminate, liquidate, terminate, finish off; *informal* do in, bump off, top, polish off, croak, stiff; *N. Amer. informal* waste, blow away, ice, off, rub out; *literary* slay.

□ **knock something off** (*informal*) **1** *someone knocked off the video recorder* **steal**, purloin, take, make off with, abscond with, pilfer, misappropriate; thieve, rob; *informal* nab, snitch, snaffle, swipe, filch, lift, souvenir; *Brit. informal* pinch, nick, half-inch, whip, nobble; *N. Amer. informal* heist, glom; *Austral. informal* snavel; *W. Indian informal* tief.
2 *we expect you to knock off three stories a day* **produce**, make, turn out, create, construct, assemble, fashion, put together, fabricate; complete, finish; mass-produce.
3 *I've always been able to knock off several years from my age* **deduct**, take off, subtract, take away, dock, debit, remove.
OPPOSITE add on.

□ **knock it off!** (*informal*) *'Oh, knock it off,' she snapped* **stop it**; *informal* cut it out, give it a rest, leave off, pack it in, lay off, quit; *Brit. informal* give over.

□ **knock someone out 1** *I hit him with the axe and knocked him out* **stun**, strike unconscious, knock unconscious, render unconscious, knock senseless, stupefy, daze, lay out, floor, prostrate, level; *informal* KO, kayo, knock cold, put out cold.
2 *England had been knocked out of the World Cup* **eliminate**; **beat**, defeat, vanquish, overwhelm, overthrow, overcome, get the better of, trounce.
3 (*informal*) *walking that far knocked her out* **exhaust**, wear out, tire out, overtire, overtax, tire, fatigue, weary, enervate, drain, sap, debilitate, enfeeble, prostrate; *informal* do in, take it out of, fag out, frazzle; *Brit. informal* knacker; *N. Amer. informal* poop.
4 (*informal*) *the view from my window knocked me out* **overwhelm**, overpower, stun, stupefy, amaze, astound, astonish, stagger, take someone's breath away, leave someone open-mouthed, dumbfound, confound, take aback; impress, dazzle, enchant, entrance; *informal* bowl over, flabbergast, knock sideways, knock for six, hit like a ton of bricks, floor, blow away.

□ **knock up** *they were knocking up before the tennis match* **warm up**, practise, have a practice game, hit a ball around.

□ **knock someone up 1** (*Brit. informal*) *we were knocked up at five in the morning* **wake**, wake up, waken, awaken, call, rouse, arouse, get out of bed, get up; *informal* give someone a shout.
2 (*informal*) *he's going to marry her—he's knocked her up* **make pregnant**, impregnate, inseminate; *informal* put in the family way; *Brit. informal* get in the club; *archaic* get with child.

□ **knock something up 1** (*Brit. informal*) *I could knock up some frames* **make quickly**, put together quickly, prepare hastily, build rapidly, whip up, rig up, jerry-build, throw together, cobble together, improvise, devise, contrive; make, prepare, produce, get, get ready, assemble, put together; *informal* fix, rustle up.
2 (*informal*) *Gloucester knocked up their biggest win of the season* **achieve**, attain, accomplish, gain, win, succeed in making, reach, make, get, obtain; score, chalk up, tally, record; *informal* clock up, notch up, rack up, bag.

▶ **noun 1** *there was a sharp knock at the door* **tap**, rap, rat-tat, rat-tat-tat, knocking, bang, banging, beating, pounding, hammering, drumming, thump, thud.
2 *the casing is tough enough to withstand knocks* **bump**, blow, bang, striking, beating, jolt, jar, jarring, shock; collision, crash, smash, impact.
3 *a knock on the ear* **blow**, bang, stroke, hit, slap, smack, crack, buffet, punch, cuff, thump, box; *informal* clip, clout, wallop, thwack, belt, bash.
4 (*informal*) *this isn't a knock on Dave, he's the best player we've got* **criticism**, disparagement, stricture, fault-finding, denigration, censure, reproach, reproval, condemnation, lambasting; *informal* slamming, panning, slagging off, rubbishing, slating, flak, brickbats.
OPPOSITE praise.
5 *life's hard knocks* **setback**, reversal, reverse of fortune, rebuff, rejection, defeat, failure, difficulty, misfortune, bad luck, stroke of bad luck, mishap, bad experience, blow, body blow, disaster, calamity, disappointment, grief, sorrow, trouble, hardship; *informal* kick in the teeth, one in the eye, whammy.

knockout ▶ **noun 1** *forty-three of Rocky's matches were won by a knockout* **stunning blow**, finishing blow; *French* coup de grâce; *informal* KO, kayo.
2 *before the third round knockout punters were growing bored* **elimination match**, tie, elimination competition.
3 (*informal*) *she's nice-looking but not a knockout* **beauty**, vision, picture, sensation, joy to behold, dream; *informal* stunner, dish, looker, good-looker, lovely, peach, eyeful, smasher, cracker.
4 (*informal*) *the binoculars are a technical knockout* **masterpiece**, sensation, marvel, wonder, triumph, winner, success, feat, coup, master stroke; smash hit, hit, attraction; *French* tour de force, coup de maître; *informal* smasher, cracker.
OPPOSITES failure, flop.

knoll ▶ **noun** *she walked up the grassy knoll* **hillock**, mound, rise, hummock, hill, hump, knob, tor, tump, barrow, outcrop, bank, ridge, dune, elevation, acclivity, eminence; *Geology* drumlin; *Scottish* brae; *S. African* koppie.

knot *See centre pages for list of* **Knots**
▶ **noun 1** *tie a small knot in the yarn* **tie**, twist, loop, bow, splice, splicing, join, link, fastening, bond, intertwinement, interlacement, ligature, joint, connection; tangle, entanglement.
2 *a knot in the wood* **nodule**, gnarl, knurl, node, lump, knob, swelling, growth, gall, protuberance, bump; *archaic* knar.
3 *there was a knot of people around Catherine* **cluster**, group, band, huddle, bunch, circle, ring, set, collection; party, gathering, company, crowd, throng, swarm, host, flock, gang, assemblage, mob, pack.
4 *a pretty garden with knots of lavender* **clump**, tuft, cluster, bunch, tuffet, tussock, bush.
▶ **verb** *their scarves were knotted round their throats* **tie**, make/tie a knot in, make a bow in, loop, lace; fasten, secure, bind, make fast, tie up, do up, lash, tether.
OPPOSITE untie.

knotted ▶ **adjective** *her wild knotted hair* **tangled**, tangly, knotty, entangled, matted, snarled, ravelled, twisted, entwined, coiled, unkempt, uncombed, tousled; *informal* mussed up.

knotty ▶ **adjective 1** *a knotty legal problem* **complex**, complicated, involved, intricate, convoluted, Byzantine, tangled, tortuous; **difficult**, hard, thorny, taxing, awkward, tricky, problematic, troublesome, perplexing, baffling, mystifying, obscure, unfathomable, unanswerable, insoluble, impenetrable; *formal* involute, involuted.
OPPOSITES straightforward, simple.
2 *knotty roots of gorse bushes* **gnarled**, knotted, knurled, nodular, knobbly, lumpy, bumpy, rugged, rough, coarse; *rare* nodulous, nodose.
3 *a knotty piece of thread* **knotted**, tangled, tangly, twisted, entangled, ravelled, snarled, matted.

know ▶ **verb 1** *she doesn't know I'm here* **be aware**, realize, be conscious, have knowledge, be informed, have information; notice, perceive, see, sense, recognize, understand, appreciate; *informal* savvy, latch on to something.
2 *I would write to him if I knew his address* **have knowledge of**, be aware of, be cognizant of, be informed of, be apprised of.
3 *he asked whether I knew French | they know the game* **be familiar with**, be conversant with, be acquainted with, have knowledge of, be versed in, be knowledgeable about, have mastered, have a grasp of, grasp, understand, comprehend, apprehend; have learned, have memorized,

have learned by heart; *informal* be clued up on, have something taped.
4 *I don't know many people here | we know him well* **be acquainted with**, have met, be familiar with; be friends with, be friendly with, be on good terms with, be close to, be intimate with, socialize with, associate with, have dealings with; understand, have insight into, be in sympathy with, empathize with; *Scottish* ken; *informal* be thick with.
5 *a man who had known better times* **experience**, have experience of, go through, undergo, live through, meet, meet with, encounter, taste.
6 *my brothers don't know a saucepan from a frying pan* **distinguish**, tell apart, differentiate, tell, tell which is which, discriminate; recognize, pick out, identify, make out, discern, see.

know-all ▶ noun (*informal*) *you're such a know-all—you tell me!* *informal* **smart alec**, wise guy, smarty, smarty-pants; *Brit. informal* clever clogs, clever Dick, smart-arse, smarty-boots; *N. Amer. informal* know-it-all, smart-ass; *archaic* wiseacre.

know-how ▶ noun (*informal*) *know-how in high-tech fields will help build better vehicles* **knowledge**, expertise, skill, skilfulness, expertness, proficiency, understanding, mastery, art, accomplishment, technique; finesse; ability, capability, competence, capacity, adeptness, dexterity, deftness, aptitude, adroitness, ingenuity, faculty, knack, talent, gift, flair, bent; *French* savoir faire; *N. Amer. informal* savvy.
OPPOSITES ignorance, incompetence.

knowing ▶ adjective **1** *she gave a knowing smile* **significant**, meaningful, eloquent, expressive, suggestive, speaking; **arch**, sly, cunning, mischievous, impish, teasing, playful; enigmatic.
2 *she's a very knowing child* **sophisticated**, worldly, worldly-wise, urbane, unprovincial, experienced, seasoned; knowledgeable, well informed, enlightened; shrewd, astute, acute, canny, sharp, wily, aware, perceptive, perspicacious; *informal* having been around.
OPPOSITES ingenuous, innocent.
3 *a knowing infringement of the rules* **deliberate**, intentional, conscious, intended, calculated, wilful, volitional, purposeful, done on purpose, premeditated, preconceived, pre-planned, planned, aforethought.
OPPOSITE accidental.

knowingly ▶ adverb *the chairman denied that the company knowingly misled the public* **deliberately**, intentionally, consciously, wittingly, with full knowledge, in full awareness, with one's eyes open, on purpose, by design, calculatedly, premeditatedly, studiedly, wilfully, purposefully, willingly.
OPPOSITES accidentally, unawares.

knowledge ▶ noun **1** *his knowledge of history was small | technical knowledge* **understanding**, comprehension, grasp, grip, command, mastery, apprehension; **expertise**, skill, proficiency, expertness, accomplishment, adeptness, capacity, capability, *French* savoir faire, *informal* know-how.
OPPOSITE ignorance.
2 *people anxious to display their knowledge* **learning**, erudition, education, scholarship, letters, schooling, science; wisdom, enlightenment, philosophy.
OPPOSITES ignorance, illiteracy.
3 *he slipped away without my knowledge* **awareness**, consciousness, realization, recognition, cognition, apprehension, perception, appreciation; *formal* cognizance.
OPPOSITE unawareness.
4 *National Trust staff develop an intimate* **knowledge of** *the countryside* **familiarity with**, acquaintance with, conversance with, intimacy with.
5 *it is your duty to inform the police of your knowledge* **information**, facts, data, intelligence, news, reports; lore; *informal* info, gen, low-down.

WORD LINKS
relating to knowledge **gnostic**
science of knowledge **epistemology**

knowledgeable ▶ adjective **1** *a knowledgeable old man* **well informed**, informed, learned, with great knowledge, well read, well educated, educated, widely read, erudite, scholarly, cultured, cultivated, enlightened, aware.
OPPOSITE ignorant.
2 *we need to appoint someone who is* **knowledgeable about** *modern art* **acquainted with**, familiar with, with a knowledge of, with an understanding of, conversant with, au courant with, au fait with; skilled, expert, competent, proficient; up on, up to date with, abreast of, at home with, no stranger to; experienced in, practised in, well versed in, seasoned; *informal* clued up about, genned up about; *Brit. informal* switched on to.
OPPOSITE ill-informed.

known ▶ adjective **1** *a known fact | a known criminal* **recognized**, **well known**, widely known, generally known, publicly known, noted, celebrated, notable, notorious; admitted, acknowledged, confessed, self-confessed, avowed, declared, overt, proclaimed, published, revealed, publicized.
OPPOSITE secret.
2 *the known world* **familiar**, known about, well known; studied, investigated.
OPPOSITE unknown.

knuckle ▶ verb
□ **knuckle under** *bombing does not always make the victims knuckle under* **surrender**, submit, capitulate, give in, give up, yield, give way, succumb, climb down, back down, quit, admit defeat, lay down one's arms, be defeated, be overcome, acquiesce, accede, accept, defer; *informal* throw in the towel, raise the white flag, throw in the sponge.
OPPOSITE resist.

kowtow ▶ verb **1** *a Russian envoy refused to* **kowtow to** *the Chinese Emperor* **prostrate oneself**, bow, bow down before, genuflect, do/make obeisance, fall on one's knees before, get down on one's knees before, kneel before; salaam, throw oneself at someone's feet, fall down before someone, curtsy, bow and scrape; pay homage, show reverence, show deference, humble oneself before someone, worship.
2 *she didn't have to* **kowtow to** *a boss* **grovel**, behave obsequiously, be obsequious, be servile, be sycophantic, fawn on, bow and scrape, toady, truckle, abase oneself, humble oneself, prostrate oneself; curry favour with, flatter, court, woo, dance attendance on, make up to, play up to, ingratiate oneself with; *informal* crawl, creep, suck up to, butter up, be all over, fall all over, lick someone's boots; *N. Amer. informal* brown-nose; *Austral./NZ informal* smoodge to; *archaic* blandish.

kudos ▶ noun *much kudos is attached to the position* **prestige**, cachet, glory, honour, status, standing, distinction, prestigiousness, fame, celebrity, reputation, repute, renown, notability; admiration, respect, esteem, acclaim, acclamation, applause, praise, credit, approbation, tribute.
OPPOSITES obscurity, infamy.

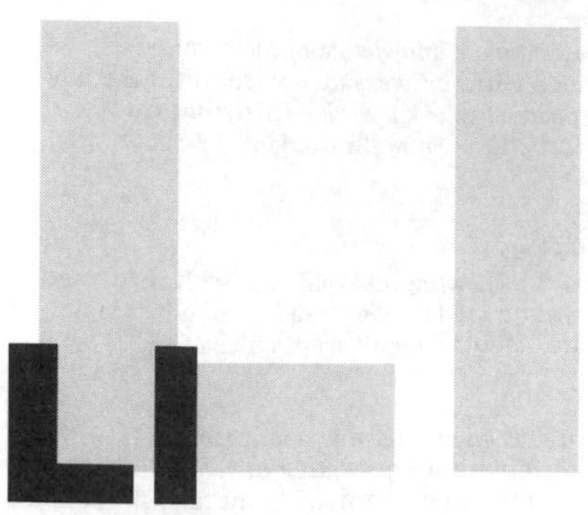

label ▶ noun **1** *the price is clearly stated on the label* **tag**, ticket, tab, sticker, marker, docket, chit, chitty, flag, stamp; document, documentation.
2 *they offer both function and fashion under their label* **brand**, brand name, trade name, trademark, proprietary name, line, make, logo.
3 *I always resented the label of 'shock jock' that the media came up with for me* **designation**, denomination, description, characterization, identification, tag; name, epithet, nickname, title, sobriquet, pet name, byname; *formal* appellation, cognomen.
▶ verb **1** *label each jar with the date* **tag**, attach labels to, put labels on, tab, ticket, stamp, mark, put stickers on, docket, flag.
2 *tests that will* **label** *him* **as** *an underachiever | he'll always be labelled 'bluesman'* **categorize**, classify, class, characterize, describe, designate, identify; mark, stamp, pronounce, brand, condemn, pigeonhole, stereotype, typecast, compartmentalize, typify; call, name, term, dub, nickname.

WORD LINKS
matchbox label collector **phillumenist**

laborious ▶ adjective **1** *tunnelling was a laborious and dangerous job* **arduous**, hard, heavy, difficult, strenuous, gruelling, murderous, punishing, exacting, tough, formidable, onerous, burdensome, back-breaking, trying, uphill, relentless, stiff, challenging, Herculean; tiring, fatiguing, exhausting, wearying, wearing, taxing, enervating, demanding, wearisome; tedious, boring, irksome; *Brit. informal* knackering; *archaic* toilsome; *rare* exigent.
OPPOSITES easy, simple.
2 *Doug's slow laborious style* **laboured**, strained, forced, contrived, affected, studied, stiff, stilted, unnatural, artificial, overdone, overwrought, heavy, ponderous, convoluted, not fluent, elaborate, over-elaborate, intricate, ornate, prolix.
OPPOSITES effortless, natural.

labour ▶ noun **1** *the aristocratic disdain for manual labour* **work**, toil, employment, exertion, industry, industriousness, toiling, hard work, hard labour, drudgery, effort, the sweat of one's brow, donkey work, menial work; *informal* slog, grind, sweat, elbow grease; *Brit. informal* graft; *archaic* travail, moil.
OPPOSITES rest, leisure, ease, idleness.
2 *the conflict of interest between capital and labour* **workers**, employees, workmen, workforce, staff, working people, blue-collar workers, hands, labourers, labour force, hired hands, proletariat, wage-earners, manpower, human resources, personnel; *humorous* liveware.
OPPOSITE management.
3 *the labours of Hercules* **task**, job, chore, undertaking, mission, commission, assignment.
4 *Gina had a long and difficult labour* **childbirth**, birth, birthing, delivery, nativity; contractions, labour pains, labour pangs, labour throes; *technical* parturition; *archaic* confinement, accouchement, lying-in, childbed, travail.
▶ verb **1** *a project on which he had laboured for many years* **work (hard)**, toil, slave (away), grub away, plod away, grind away, sweat away, struggle, strive, exert oneself, overwork, work one's fingers to the bone, work like a Trojan/dog/slave, keep one's nose to the grindstone; *informal* slog away, kill oneself, plug away, put one's back into something, peg away; *Brit. informal* graft; *archaic* drudge, travail, moil.
OPPOSITES rest, relax, laze.
2 *Newcastle laboured to break down the home team's defence* **strive**, struggle, endeavour, work, try hard, make every effort, do one's best, do one's utmost, do all one can, give (it/something) one's all, go all out, fight, push, be at pains, put oneself out, apply oneself, exert oneself; *informal* bend/fall/lean over backwards, give it one's best shot, pull out all the stops.
3 *enough has been said, and there is no need to labour the point* **overemphasize**, belabour, overstress, place/lay too much emphasis on, overdo, strain, over-elaborate, overplay, attach too much importance/weight to, make too much of, exaggerate, dwell on, harp on (about), expound on, expand.
4 *Rex was* **labouring under** *a misapprehension* **suffer from**, be a victim of, be burdened by, be overburdened by, be disadvantaged by, be under.

CHOOSE THE RIGHT WORD
labour, work, toil
See WORK.

laboured ▶ adjective **1** *his harsh, laboured breathing* **strained**, difficult, forced, laborious, heavy, awkward.
OPPOSITE easy.
2 *a rather laboured joke* **contrived**, stiff, strained, stilted, forced, unnatural, artificial, mannered, studied, affected, overdone, overworked, heavy, ponderous, over-elaborate, over-embellished, long-winded, awkward, clumsy, inelegant, turgid, laborious, overwrought, not spontaneous, unconvincing, convoluted, complex, intricate, ornate, elaborate, prolix.
OPPOSITE natural.

labourer ▶ noun **workman**, worker, working man, hand, manual worker, unskilled worker, blue-collar worker, hired hand, hired man, roustabout, labouring man, drudge, menial; *Spanish-American* peon; *Austral./NZ* rouseabout; *Indian* mazdoor, khalasi; (*in Asian countries*) coolie; *dated* navvy; (*in Scotland & Ireland, historical*) cottar; (*in Australia, historical*) kanaka; *archaic* mechanic, cottier.

labyrinth ▶ noun **1** *a labyrinth of little streets* **maze**, warren, network, complex, web, coil, entanglement.
2 *the labyrinth of conflicting laws and regulations* **tangle**, web, morass, jungle, snarl, twist, turn, complexity, confusion, complication, entanglement, convolution, intricacy; jumble, mishmash, hotchpotch, hodgepodge; *archaic* perplexity.

labyrinthine ▶ adjective **1** *the stadium's labyrinthine corridors* **maze-like**, winding, twisting, serpentine, meandering, wandering, rambling, mazy, sinuous, zigzag.
2 *a labyrinthine criminal justice system* **complicated**, intricate, complex, involved, tortuous, convoluted, tangled, elaborate, knotty; confusing, puzzling, perplexing, mystifying, bewildering, baffling; inextricable, entangled, impenetrable, thorny, Byzantine, Daedalian, Gordian; *rare* involute, involuted.
OPPOSITES straightforward, simple.

lace ▶ noun **1** *a dress trimmed with white lace* openwork, lacework, tatting, netting, net, tulle, meshwork, mesh, webbing; Chantilly lace, Brussels lace, fishnet, filigree, passementerie, bobbinet, needlepoint (lace), point lace, filet, bobbin lace, pillow lace, duchesse lace, Honiton lace, Nottingham lace, Shetland lace, guipure, rosaline.
2 *brown shoes with laces* **shoelace**, bootlace, shoestring, lacing, string, cord, thong, twine, tie; *archaic* latchet.
▶ verb **1** *he* **laced up** *his running shoes* **fasten**, do up, tie up, secure; bind, knot, truss.
OPPOSITE undo.
2 *he laced his fingers into mine* **entwine**, intertwine, twine, entangle, interweave, interlink, link; criss-cross, braid, plait.
3 *tea laced with rum* **flavour**, mix (in), blend, fortify, strengthen, stiffen, season, spice (up), imbue, infuse, enrich, enliven, liven up; doctor, adulterate, contaminate, drug; *informal* spike, boost.
4 *her brown hair was laced with grey* **streak**, stripe, striate, band, line; mark, smear, daub.
□ **lace into** (*informal*) **1** *Danny laced into him and punched him in the stomach* **set upon**, fall on, attack, assault, assail, beat, thrash, tear into, turn on, set about, lash out at, round on, drub, thump, batter, hammer, pummel, hit

out at, strike out at, (let) fly at, weigh into, belabour; *informal* lay into, light into, sail into, pitch into, paste, let someone have it; *Brit. informal* have a go at.
2 *the newspaper laced into the prime minister* **castigate**, censure, condemn, lambaste, criticize, harangue, rant/rave/rail at, attack; scold, berate, upbraid, reprimand, rebuke, chide, reprove, admonish; *informal* lay into, pitch into; *Brit. informal* have a go at; *N. Amer. informal* light into.

lacerate ▶ **verb 1** *jagged edges that lacerated their arms* **cut (open)**, gash, slash, tear, rip, rend, mangle, mutilate, maim, maul, shred, score, scratch, scrape, graze, incise; knife, gouge, split, cleave, hack, stab, tear apart, butcher, savage, wound, injure, hurt, damage.
2 *the author's feelings have been lacerated by criticism* **hurt**, wound, distress, pain, harrow, torture, torment, crucify, tear to pieces/shreds.

laceration ▶ **noun 1** *the laceration of her hand* **cutting (open)**, gashing, slashing, tearing, ripping, mangling, mutilation, maiming, mauling, scratching, scraping, grazing, incision, splitting, cleaving, hacking, stabbing, tearing apart, butchery, savaging, wounding, injury, damaging.
2 *a bleeding laceration on the animal's back* **gash**, cut, wound, injury, tear, slash, mutilation, scratch, scrape, abrasion, graze, score, incision, slit, puncture; *Medicine* lesion, trauma, traumatism.

lachrymose ▶ **adjective 1** *she gets quite lachrymose at the mention of his name* **tearful**, weeping, crying, teary, with tears in one's eyes, close to tears, on the verge of tears, sobbing, snivelling, whimpering; emotional, sad, mournful, woeful, unhappy, depressed, gloomy, melancholy, low-spirited, despondent, downcast, low, glum, morose, sorrowful, joyless, disconsolate, doleful, maudlin, miserable, forlorn, grief-stricken, lugubrious; *informal* weepy, blubbering, down, down in the mouth, blue; *literary* dolorous; *rare* larmoyant.
OPPOSITES cheerful, laughing, happy.
2 *a lachrymose novel* **tragic**, sad, poignant, heart-rending, tear-jerking, moving, melancholy, depressing, plaintive; mawkish, sentimental; *Brit. informal* soppy.
OPPOSITE comic.

lack ▶ **noun** *a lack of cash* **absence**, want, need, deficiency, dearth, insufficiency, shortage, shortfall, scarcity, paucity, unavailability, scarceness, undersupply, deficit, scantiness, sparseness, meagreness, inadequacy, shortness, deprivation, destitution, privation, famine, drought, poverty, non-existence, rareness, infrequency, uncommonness; *rare* exiguity, exiguousness.
OPPOSITES abundance; sufficiency.
▶ **verb** *she's immature and lacks judgement* **be without**, have need of, be in need of, need, be lacking, require, want, feel the want of, be short of, be deficient in, stand in need of, go without, be bereft of, be deprived of, be low on, be pressed for, not have enough of, be devoid of, have insufficient, cry out for; miss; *informal* be clean/fresh out of, be strapped for.
OPPOSITES have, own, possess, enjoy.

lackadaisical ▶ **adjective** *I was lackadaisical about my training* **careless**, **lazy**, lax, unenthusiastic, half-hearted, uninterested, lukewarm, indifferent, uncaring, unconcerned, casual, offhand, blasé, insouciant, leisurely, relaxed; apathetic, languid, languorous, lethargic, limp, listless, sluggish, enervated, spiritless, aimless, bloodless, torpid, passionless, idle, indolent, shiftless, inert, impassive, feeble; *informal* laid back, couldn't-care-less, easy going, slap-happy; *Brit. vulgar slang* half-arsed; *rare* Laodicean, poco-curante.
OPPOSITES enthusiastic, excited.

lackey ▶ **noun 1** *lackeys were waiting to help them from their carriage* **servant**, flunkey, footman, manservant, valet, liveried servant, steward, butler, equerry, retainer, vassal, page, attendant, houseboy, domestic, drudge, factotum; *informal* skivvy; *archaic* scullion.
2 *a rich man's lackey* **toady**, flunkey, sycophant, flatterer, minion, doormat, dogsbody, spaniel, stooge, hanger-on, lickspittle, parasite; tool, puppet, instrument, pawn, subordinate, underling, creature, cat's paw; *informal* yes-man, bootlicker.

lacking ▶ **adjective 1** *proof was lacking* **absent**, missing, non-existent, not present, unavailable, not to be found.
OPPOSITES present, plentiful.
2 *the advocate general found the government lacking on two counts* **deficient**, defective, inadequate, wanting, limited, flawed, faulty, insufficient, unacceptable, impaired, imperfect, second-rate, restricted, inferior.
OPPOSITE perfect.
3 *the game was* **lacking in** *atmosphere* **without**, devoid of, bereft of, bankrupt of, destitute of, empty of, deprived of, free from/of; **deficient in**, low on, short on, in need of; *informal* minus.
OPPOSITE full of.

lacklustre ▶ **adjective** *a limp and lacklustre speech* **uninspired**, uninspiring, unimaginative, dull, humdrum, colourless, characterless, bland, insipid, vapid, flat, dry, lifeless, listless, tame, tired, prosaic, mundane, run-of-the-mill, commonplace, spiritless, lustreless, apathetic, torpid, unanimated; uninteresting, boring, monotonous, dreary, tedious, wearisome.
OPPOSITES inspired, brilliant.

laconic ▶ **adjective 1** *his laconic comment* **brief**, concise, terse, succinct, short, economical, elliptical, crisp, pithy, to the point, incisive, short and sweet, compendious; abrupt, blunt, curt, clipped, monosyllabic, brusque, pointed, gruff, sharp, tart; epigrammatic, aphoristic, gnomic.
OPPOSITES verbose, long-winded.
2 *their laconic press officer* **taciturn**, of few words, uncommunicative, reticent, quiet, untalkative, reserved, silent, speechless, tight-lipped, unforthcoming, brusque.
OPPOSITE loquacious.

lad ▶ **noun** (*informal*) **1** *a young lad of eight* **boy**, schoolboy, youth, youngster, juvenile, stripling, young fellow, junior, whippersnapper; *informal* kid, nipper, little shaver; *Scottish informal* laddie; *derogatory* brat, urchin.
2 *a hard-working lad trying to make ends meet* **man**, young man; *informal* guy, fellow, geezer, customer, gent; *Brit. informal* chap, bloke; *N. Amer. informal* dude, hombre; *Austral./NZ informal* digger; *S. African informal* oke, ou; *Indian informal* admi; *Brit. informal, dated* cove; *Scottish archaic* carl.

ladder *See centre pages for list of* **Ladders**
▶ **noun** *I began to edge my way up the academic ladder* **hierarchy**, scale, set of stages, stratification, pecking order, grading, ranking, spectrum.

laden ▶ **adjective** *a tray laden with plates* **loaded**, burdened, weighed down, overloaded, weighted, piled high, fully charged, encumbered, hampered, oppressed, taxed; full, filled, packed, stuffed, crammed; *informal* chock-full, chock-a-block.
OPPOSITE empty.

la-di-da ▶ **adjective** (*informal*) *a la-di-da Cambridge graduate* **snobbish**, refined, over-refined, pretentious, affected, mannered, pompous, conceited, superior, haughty, precious; *informal* snooty, stuck-up, high and mighty, hoity-toity, uppity, snotty, snot-nosed, highfalutin; *Brit. informal* posh, toffee-nosed.
OPPOSITES common, gorblimey.

ladle ▶ **noun** *a soup ladle* **spoon**, scoop, dipper, bailer.
▶ **verb** *he was* **ladling out** *the contents of the pot* **spoon out**, scoop out, dish up/out, serve; bail out.

lady ▶ **noun 1** *he gave the ladies presents of flowers from his garden* **woman**, member of the fair/gentle sex, female; *Scottish & N. English* lass, lassie; *informal* biddy, filly; *Brit. informal* bird, bint; *Scottish & N. English informal* besom, wifie; *N. Amer. informal* dame, broad, jane; *Austral./NZ informal* sheila; *archaic* maid, damsel; *archaic or humorous* wench; *archaic* gentlewoman, petticoat.
2 *lords and ladies and royalty were once entertained at the house* **noblewoman**, gentlewoman, duchess, countess, peeress, viscountess, baroness, dame, grand dame.

CHOOSE THE RIGHT WORD

lady, woman, girl

See WOMAN.

ladylike ▶ **adjective** *her antics were considered very undignified by her ladylike peers* **genteel**, **polite**, refined, well bred, cultivated, polished, decorous, proper, correct, respectable, seemly, well mannered, cultured, sophisticated, courteous, civil, elegant, urbane, civilized, courtly, dignified, gracious; *Brit. informal* posh.
OPPOSITES coarse, unmannerly.

lag ▶ **verb** *Elizabeth had not walked over to the villa with the other guests, but lagged behind* **fall behind**, straggle, fall back, trail (behind), linger, dally, dawdle, hang back, delay, move slowly, loiter, drag one's feet, take one's time, not keep pace, idle, dither, saunter, bring up the rear; *informal* dilly-dally, shilly-shally; *dated* tarry.
OPPOSITES lead; keep up; hurry.

laggard ▶ **noun** **straggler**, loiterer, lingerer, dawdler, sluggard, snail, delayer, idler, loafer, lounger, shirker, layabout, lagger; *informal* lazybones, skiver, do-nothing, waster, slacker, slowcoach; *N. Amer. informal* slowpoke; *archaic* wastrel; *French archaic* fainéant.

lagoon ▶ **noun** *the yachts on the lagoon* inlet of the sea, inland sea, bay, lake, bight, pool, pond, swim; *Scottish* loch; *Anglo-Irish* lough; *N. Amer.* bayou; *literary* mere.

laid-back ▶ **adjective** (*informal*) **relaxed**, at ease, easy-going, equable, free and easy, easy, casual, informal, friendly, nonchalant, insouciant, unexcitable, imperturbable, unemotional, unruffled, blasé, blithe, cool, collected, {cool, calm, and collected}, calm, composed, self-possessed, level-headed, self-controlled, unperturbed, unflustered, unworried, unconcerned, placid, peaceful, tranquil, serene, low-key, understated, downbeat; leisurely, unhurried; stoical, phlegmatic, mellow, forbearing, live-and-let-live, tolerant; *informal* unflappable, together.
OPPOSITES tense, edgy, uptight.

laid up ▶ **adjective** *he was laid up for six weeks in the Middlesex Hospital* **bedridden**, ill in bed, confined to bed, on the sick list, out of action/commission, housebound, immobilized, incapacitated, injured, disabled; ill, sick, unwell, sickly, poorly, infirm, ailing, off colour, afflicted, indisposed.

lair ▶ **noun 1** *the lair of a large python* **den**, burrow, hole, lie, covert, tunnel,

dugout, hollow, cave, haunt.
2 *the lair of a villain* **hideaway**, hiding place, hideout, refuge, sanctuary, haven, cache, shelter, retreat; *informal* hidey-hole.

laissez-faire ▶ **noun** *laissez-faire is an economic system based on individualism and self-interest* **free enterprise**, private enterprise, free trade, individualism, non-intervention, free-market capitalism, private ownership, market forces, deregulation; non-interference, non-involvement, indifference.
▶ **adjective** *a belief in laissez-faire economics* **non-interventionist**, non-interventional, non-interfering, non-restrictive, liberal, libertarian, uninvolved, indifferent, lax, loose, permissive, live-and-let-live; *informal* hands-off.
OPPOSITE interventionist.

lake ▶ **noun** **pond**, pool, tarn, reservoir, lagoon, waterhole, inland sea, swim; *Scottish* loch, lochan; *Anglo-Irish* lough; *N. Amer.* bayou, pothole (lake); *NZ* moana; *Indian* sagar; *literary* mere.

WORD LINKS
relating to lakes **lacustrine**
study of lakes **limnology**

lam ▶ **verb** (*informal*) *the usher lammed me on the head with his flashlight. See* HIT.

lambaste ▶ **verb** *the manager fiercely lambasted his team* **criticize**, castigate, chastise, censure, condemn, take to task, harangue, attack, rail at, rant at, revile, fulminate against, haul/call over the coals; upbraid, scold, reprimand, rebuke, chide, reprove, admonish, berate; *informal* rap someone's knuckles, slap someone's wrist, lay into, pitch into, tear into, lace into, dress down, give someone a dressing-down, carpet, tell off, bawl out; *Brit. informal* tick off, have a go at, slag off; *N. Amer. informal* chew out; *rare* reprehend, excoriate, objurgate.

lame ▶ **adjective 1** *a lame and sickly child | the mare went lame* **limping**, hobbling; crippled, game, disabled, incapacitated, handicapped, debilitated, infirm, deformed, mutilated, maimed, defective; *informal* gammy; *euphemistic* physically challenged; *archaic* halt.
OPPOSITE able-bodied.
2 *a lame excuse* **feeble**, weak, thin, flimsy, transparent, poor, puny; **unconvincing**, implausible, unlikely, hollow, hard to believe; *informal* pathetic, half-baked, hard to swallow.
OPPOSITES convincing, persuasive.

L

lament ▶ **noun 1** *the widow's laments* **wail**, wailing, lamentation, moan, moaning, groan, weeping, crying, sob, sobbing, keening, howl, complaint; *rare* jeremiad, ululation.
2 *he sang a lament for the dead* **dirge**, requiem, elegy, funeral song/chant, burial hymn, dead march, keen, plaint, knell; *Scottish* coronach; *rare* threnody, monody, epicedium.
▶ **verb 1** *the mourners lamented a life taken so suddenly* **mourn**, grieve (for/over), weep for, shed tears for; sorrow, wail, moan, groan, weep, cry, sob, keen, plain, howl, pine for, beat one's breast; *rare* ululate.
OPPOSITES celebrate, rejoice.
2 *he lamented the modernizing of the old buildings* **bemoan**, bewail, complain about, deplore, regret, rue; protest against, speak out against, object to, oppose, disagree with, fulminate against, inveigh against, rail at, make a fuss about, denounce.

lamentable ▶ **adjective** *a lamentable lack of funds* **deplorable**, regrettable, tragic, terrible, awful, wretched, woeful, sorrowful, unfortunate, distressing, grievous, dire, disastrous, calamitous, desperate, grave, appalling, dreadful; intolerable, ignominious, pitiful, shameful; *rare* egregious.

lamentation ▶ **noun** **weeping**, **wailing**, crying, sobbing, moaning, moan, sob, wail, lament, sorrow, complaint, keening, grief, grieving, mourning, howling, howl, plaint; *rare* ululation.

laminate ▶ **verb** *we will laminate your photos in clear plastic* **cover**, overlay, coat, surface, face; veneer, glaze.

lamp ▶ **noun.** *See centre pages for list of* **Lamps and Lights**

lampoon ▶ **verb** *he was mercilessly lampooned for his absurd get-ups* **satirize**, mock, ridicule, make fun of, poke fun at, caricature, burlesque, parody, take off, guy, make a fool of, rag, tease; *informal* send up; *rare* pasquinade.
▶ **noun** *a lampoon of student life in the early twenties* **satire**, burlesque, parody, skit, caricature, imitation, impersonation, impression, travesty, take-off, mockery, squib; *informal* send-up, spoof; *rare* pasquinade.

lance ▶ **noun** *a knight with a lance* **spear**, pike, javelin, bayonet, shaft; harpoon.
▶ **verb** *the boil may be lanced to drain the pus* **cut**, cut open, slit, incise, puncture, prick, nick, notch, pierce, stab, skewer, spike.

land ▶ **noun 1** *Lyme Park has 1323 acres of land | a campaign to ban fox-hunting on publicly owned land* **grounds**, ground, fields, open space, open area; property, acres, acreage, estate, estate, lands, realty, real property, real estate, landholding, holding; countryside; unbuilt land, rural area, green area, green belt; *archaic* demesne.
2 *a small patch of fertile land* **soil**, earth, loam, sod, dirt, clay, turf, topsoil, humus, marl.
3 (**the land**) *so many people are leaving the land and going to work in the city* **the countryside**, the country, rural areas, farmland, agricultural land.
4 *Tunisia is a land of variety* **country**, nation, state, nation state, fatherland, motherland, homeland, realm, kingdom, empire, republic, commonwealth, province, territory, district, region, area, domain.
5 *the lookout sighted land at last* **terra firma**, dry land, solid ground; coast, coastline, shore.
OPPOSITE sea.
▶ **verb 1** *Allied troops had landed in France* **disembark**, reach the shore, go ashore, debark, alight, get off; arrive.
OPPOSITE embark.
2 *the ship landed at Le Havre* **berth**, dock, moor, anchor, drop anchor, tie up, beach, put in, reach the shore, come in to land; arrive.
OPPOSITES put to sea, sail, depart.
3 *their plane landed at Chicago airport* **touch down**, alight, make a landing, come in to land, come down, come to rest, arrive.
OPPOSITE take off.
4 *a bird landed on the window sill* **perch**, settle, come down, come to rest, alight.
OPPOSITE fly off.
5 *landing a plane was no problem for me* **bring down**, make a landing, put down, take down.
6 (*informal*) *Nick had landed the job of editor* **obtain**, get, acquire, procure, secure, be appointed to, gain, net, win, earn, achieve, attain, bag, come by, draw, pick up; carry off, catch, capture, grab, hook; *informal* get/lay one's hands on, get hold of, get one's mitts on, score, swing, nab, collar, pull down; *Brit. informal* blag.
7 (*informal*) *that habit landed her in juvenile custody* **bring**, lead, drive, cause to be in, cause to arrive in.
8 (*informal*) *she hoped he wouldn't land her with the bill* **burden**, saddle, encumber, trouble, tax, load; *informal* dump something on someone; *Brit. informal* lumber.
9 (*informal*) *John tried to land a punch on Brian's chin* **inflict**, deal, deliver, administer, deposit, dispense, give, catch, mete out; *informal* fetch.
□ **land up** *many of them land up in prison* **finish up**, arrive, find oneself, end up, turn up, come, go, appear; *informal* wind up, fetch up, show up, roll up, blow in.

WORD LINKS
relating to land **terrestrial**

landing ▶ **noun 1** *during the forced landing the aircraft was substantially damaged | the Apollo 11 moon landing* **alighting**, arrival, coming in, deplaning; disembarkation, docking; re-entry, touchdown, splashdown; *informal* greaser.
OPPOSITES take-off, departure.
2 *I steered the boat into the south landing* **harbour**, berth, dock, jetty, landing stage, landing place, pier, quay, wharf, slipway, marina, anchorage, haven, platform.

landlady, **landlord** ▶ **noun 1** *the landlord of the pub* **publican**, licensee, innkeeper, manager, manageress, pub-owner, proprietor; hotel-keeper, hotelier, host, mine host, restaurateur, bar-keeper; barman, barmaid, barperson.
2 *he had just been booted out of his digs because the landlady had objected to the noise* **property owner**, proprietor, proprietress, lessor, letter, householder, freeholder, landowner, landholder, master, mistress, lady of the house; *rare* proprietrix.
OPPOSITES tenant, lodger.

landmark ▶ **noun 1** *the spire was once a landmark for ships sailing up the river* **marker**, mark, indicator, guiding light, leading light, signal, beacon, lodestar, sign.
2 *the Tower of London, one of London's most famous landmarks* **monument**, distinctive/prominent feature, sight, spectacle.
3 *the landmarks which separated the two states had been removed* **boundary marker**, demarcator, boundary line, boundary fence, pale, picket; *Architecture* terminus.
4 *the ruling was hailed as a landmark by human rights activists* **turning point**, milestone, watershed, critical point, historic event, major achievement; crisis, divide.

landscape ▶ **noun** *the landscape of east Norfolk* **scenery**, countryside, topography, country, land, terrain, environment; outlook, view, prospect, aspect, vista, panorama, perspective, sweep.

landslide ▶ **noun 1** *floods and landslides killed several hundred people* landslip, rockfall, mudslide, earthslip, earthfall; avalanche.
2 *the 1906 election produced a Liberal landslide* **decisive victory**, runaway victory, overwhelming majority, grand slam, triumph, walkover.
OPPOSITES narrow victory; hung parliament.

lane ▶ **noun 1** *she walked along the country lanes* **byroad**, byway, bridleway, bridle path, path, pathway, footpath, way, towpath, trail, track, road, street, alley, alleyway, roadway, passage, thoroughfare; *Scottish* vennel; *N. English* ginnel, snicket, twitten; *Scottish & N. English* wynd; *W. Indian & N. Amer.* trace.
2 *cycle lanes | a three-lane highway* **track**, strip, way, course, channel, road division.

language ▶ **noun 1** *the grammatical structure of language* **speech**, **writing**,

communication, verbal expression, verbalization, vocalization, conversation, speaking, talking, words, utterance, vocabulary, articulation, enunciation, pronunciation, talk, discourse, interchange, intercourse, interaction; *archaic* converse.
2 *the English language* **tongue**, speech, mother tongue, native tongue; *Indian* bhasha; *informal* lingo.
3 *the language of tabloid journalism | different varieties of language* **wording**, diction, phrasing, phraseology, style, vocabulary, terminology, expressions, turns of phrase, parlance, manner of writing/speaking, way of talking, form/mode of expression, usages, locutions, idiolect, choice of words, rhetoric, oratory; speech, dialect, vernacular, regionalisms, provincialisms, localisms, patois, lingua franca, slang, idioms, colloquialisms, jargon, argot, barbarisms, vulgarisms, cant, newspeak; pidgin English, Creole; *informal* lingo, legalese, journalese, technospeak, gobbledegook.

WORD LINKS

related suffix	**-glot** (e.g. ***polyglot***)
relating to language	**linguistic**
scientific study of language	**linguistics**

languid ▶ adjective **1** *his languid demeanour irritated her | a languid wave of the hand* **relaxed**, unhurried, languorous, unenergetic, lacking in energy, slow, slow-moving; listless, lethargic, phlegmatic, torpid, sluggish, lazy, idle, slothful, inactive, indolent, lackadaisical, apathetic, indifferent, uninterested, impassive; *informal* laid back; *rare* otiose, poco-curante, Laodicean.
OPPOSITES energetic, active.
2 *languid days in the Italian sun* **leisurely**, peaceful, languorous, relaxed, restful, lazy.
OPPOSITES energetic, action-packed.
3 *pale, languid individuals* **sickly**, weak, faint, feeble, frail, delicate, debilitated, flagging, drooping; tired, weary, fatigued, enervated.
OPPOSITES energetic, vigorous.

CHOOSE THE RIGHT WORD

languid, lethargic, listless

These words are all used of people who are (or appear to be) lacking in enthusiasm or energy.

- **Languid** is typically used to describe someone other than oneself, or their movements or a part of their body (*the languid and willowy pre-Raphaelite heroine | she lifted a languid hand to push back her flowing hair*). It represents how they appear to an observer rather than how they actually feel. It is typically an attractive quality.
- **Lethargic** is more commonly used to describe a person's own feeling of lacking energy (*he felt lethargic, unable for the moment to move*). It is more common to say that one feels *lethargic* than that one feels *languid* or *listless*, the implication being that *lethargy* tends to be something that one can observe in oneself, while *languor* and *listlessness* are more often observed in others.
- A person described as **listless** usually lacks both energy and interest in their surroundings, the suggestion being that their malaise is psychological as well as physical (*a desperate young woman clutching a pale, listless child | she saw youngsters sitting listless and dejected outside their homes*).

languish ▶ verb **1** *the plants languished and died* **weaken**, grow weak, deteriorate, decline, go into a decline; wither, droop, flag, wilt, fade, fail, waste away; *informal* go downhill.
OPPOSITES thrive, flourish.
2 *the general is now languishing in prison* **waste away**, rot, decay, wither away, moulder, be abandoned, be neglected, be forgotten, suffer; be disregarded, experience hardship.
3 (*archaic*) *she still* ***languished after*** *Richard* **pine for**, yearn for, ache for, long for, sigh for, desire, want, hanker after, carry a torch for; grieve for, mourn, miss; *literary* repine.

languor ▶ noun **1** *she clenched her jaw to kill the sultry languor that was stealing over her* **lassitude**, lethargy, listlessness, tiredness, torpor, fatigue, weariness; laziness, idleness, indolence, inactivity, inertia, sluggishness; sleepiness, drowsiness, somnolence, enervation, lifelessness, apathy.
OPPOSITE vigour.
2 *the languor of a hot, breezeless day* **stillness**, tranquillity, calm, calmness, lull, silence, windlessness, oppressiveness, heaviness.

lank ▶ adjective **1** *the man had lank, brown, greasy hair* **limp**, lifeless, lustreless; straggling, straggly, dull, unkempt, untidy; straight, long; *informal* ratty.
OPPOSITES glossy, lustrous.
2 *his long, lank figure.* See LANKY.

lanky ▶ adjective *a pale-skinned, lanky youth* **tall**, **thin**, slender, slim, lean, lank, skinny, spindly, spare, gangling, gangly, scrawny, skeletal, scraggy, emaciated, bony, gaunt, raw-boned, gawky, rangy, skin-and-bones, angular, pinched, attenuated; *informal* weedy.
OPPOSITES short, fat, stocky.

lap[1] ▶ noun *Henry was sitting on his gran's lap* **knee**, knees, thighs.
□ **in the lap of the gods** *the result is in the lap of the gods now* **out of one's hands**, beyond one's control, in the hands of fate, open to chance, not one's responsibility.
□ **live in the lap of luxury** *Katie was living in the lap of luxury in Paris* **lead a very comfortable life**, be very rich, want for nothing, live off the fat of the land; *informal* live the life of Riley; *Irish informal* be on the pig's back; *N. Amer. informal* live high on the hog.

lap[2] ▶ noun *Nicky led the race for eight laps* **circuit**, leg, stretch, tour, circle, revolution, round, part, portion, segment, section, stage, phase, step, loop.
▶ verb **1** *she raced around the track, lapping some of the other runners* **overtake**, overhaul, outstrip, outdistance, leave behind, pass, go past, get/pull ahead of; catch up with.
2 *he was lapped in blankets* **wrap**, swathe, cover, envelop, enfold, encase, wind, swaddle, twist, surround.

lap[3] ▶ verb **1** *the sound of waves lapping against the sea wall* **splash**, wash, swish, slap, slosh, break, purl; beat, strike, dash, surge, rush, ripple, roll, flow; *literary* plash.
2 *the dog lapped water out of a puddle* **drink**, lick up, sip, sup, swallow, slurp, gulp, swill, suck.
□ **lap something up** *he was lapping up the accolades* **relish**, revel in, savour, delight in, luxuriate in, bask in, wallow in, glory in, enjoy, indulge in.

lapse ▶ noun **1** *a momentary lapse of concentration* **failure**, failing, slip, error, mistake, blunder, fault, omission, oversight, negligence, dereliction; *informal* slip-up.
2 *his lapse into petty crime* **decline**, downturn, fall, falling, falling away, slipping, drop, deterioration, worsening, degeneration, dereliction, backsliding, regression, retrogression, decay, descent, sinking, slide, ebb, waning, corruption, debasement, tainting, corrosion, impairment.
3 *after this lapse of time I can look at it more calmly* **interval**, gap, pause, intermission, interlude, lull, hiatus, break; passage, course, passing, period, term, span, spell.
▶ verb **1** *the applicants let the planning permission lapse* **expire**, become void, become invalid, run out, terminate, become obsolete.
2 *do not let friendships lapse* **end**, cease, come to an end, stop, terminate, vanish, disappear, pass, fade, fall away, dwindle, wilt, wither, die.
3 *morality has lapsed* **deteriorate**, decline, fall, fall off, drop, worsen, degenerate, decay, rot, backslide, regress, retrogress, get worse, sink, wane, slump, fail; *informal* go downhill, go to pot, go to the dogs, go down the toilet, hit the skids.
OPPOSITES improve, strengthen.
4 *she lapsed into silence* **revert**, relapse, fall back; **drift**, slide, slip, sink, subside.

lapsed ▶ adjective **1** *a lapsed Catholic* **non-practising**, lacking faith, backsliding, recidivist, apostate; *formal* quondam.
OPPOSITES practising, devout.
2 *a lapsed season ticket* **expired**, void, invalid, run out, out of date, terminated, discontinued, unrenewed.
OPPOSITES current, valid.

larceny ▶ noun **theft**, stealing, robbery, pilfering, thieving, thievery, purloining; burglary, housebreaking, breaking and entering; appropriation, expropriation, misappropriation; *informal* lifting, filching, swiping; *Brit. informal* nicking, pinching, half-inching, blagging; *rare* peculation.

larder ▶ noun **pantry**, storage room, storeroom, store, food store, cupboard; cooler, scullery; *Brit.* buttery, still room, butlery; *archaic* spence.

large ▶ adjective **1** *a large house | large numbers of people* **big**, great, huge, of considerable size, sizeable, substantial, immense, enormous, colossal, massive, mammoth, vast, goodly, prodigious, tremendous, gigantic, giant, monumental, stupendous, gargantuan, elephantine, titanic, mountainous, monstrous; towering, tall, high, lofty; mighty, epic, inordinate, voluminous, unlimited, king-size, king-sized, giant-size, giant-sized, man-size, man-sized, outsize, oversized, overgrown, considerable, major, Brobdingnagian; cumbersome, unwieldy; *informal* jumbo, whopping, whopping great, thumping, thumping great, mega, humongous, monster, astronomical, dirty great; *Brit. informal* whacking, whacking great, ginormous.
OPPOSITE small.
2 *a large red-faced man* **big**, burly, heavy, tall, bulky, thickset, heavyset, chunky, strapping, powerfully built, hulking, hefty, muscular, muscle-bound, brawny, muscly, husky, solid, powerful, sturdy, solidly built, broad-shouldered, strong, big and strong, rugged, Herculean; fat, plump, overweight, chubby, stout, weighty, meaty, fleshy, portly, rotund, flabby, well fed, paunchy, Falstaffian, obese, gross, corpulent; buxom; *informal* hunky, beefy, roly-poly, tubby, pudgy, porky, well upholstered, broad in the beam; *Brit. informal* podgy, fubsy; *N. Amer. informal* zaftig, corn-fed, lard-assed.
OPPOSITES small; thin.
3 *a large supply of wool* **abundant**, copious, plentiful, ample, liberal, generous, lavish, profuse, bountiful, bumper, boundless, teeming,

L

overflowing, good, considerable, superabundant, opulent, handsome, galore, sufficient; *informal* tidy; *literary* plenteous.
OPPOSITES meagre, scanty.
4 *the measure has large economic implications* **wide-reaching**, far-reaching, wide-ranging, wide, sweeping, large-scale, broad, extensive, comprehensive, exhaustive, wholesale, global.
OPPOSITES trivial, petty.
□ **at large 1** *fourteen criminals are still at large* **at liberty**, free, on the loose, on the run, fugitive; unconfined, unrestrained, roaming, loose, unbound, unrestricted, untied, unchained, unshackled, unfettered, set loose, wild; *N. Amer. informal* on the lam.
OPPOSITES confined, in prison.
2 *society at large* **as a whole**, as a body, generally, in general, in the main.
OPPOSITES in particular, specifically.
3 *he speaks at large of the choroid plexus* **in detail**, with full details, exhaustively, at length, extensively.
□ **by and large** *the children, by and large, treated him well* **on the whole**, generally, in general, altogether, all things considered, all in all, taking everything into consideration, for the most part, in the main, as a rule, overall, usually, normally, ordinarily, almost always, customarily, habitually, typically, mainly, mostly, basically, chiefly, predominantly, principally, substantially; on average, in most cases, on balance, to all intents and purposes.

WORD LINKS
related prefixes **macro-** (e.g. ***macroeconomics, macrocephaly***), **mega-** (e.g. ***megalith, megabucks***), **megalo-** (e.g. ***megalosaurus, megalomaniac***)

largely ▸ **adverb** *the engineer William Jessop was largely responsible for this pioneering work* **mostly**, mainly, to a large extent, to a great extent, to a great degree, on the whole, chiefly, generally, in general, predominantly, substantially, primarily, overall, for the most part, in the main, principally, in great measure, preponderantly, first and foremost, for all intents and purposes, basically; usually, typically, commonly.

large-scale ▸ **adjective 1** *a large-scale privatization programme* **extensive**, wide-reaching, wide-ranging, sweeping, broad, far-reaching, wholesale, comprehensive, exhaustive, expansive, mass, nationwide, global, universal.
OPPOSITES small-scale, minor.
2 *a large-scale map* **enlarged**, blown-up, magnified.

largesse ▸ **noun 1** *Tupper took advantage of his friend's largesse* **generosity**, liberality, munificence, bounty, bountifulness, beneficence, benefaction, altruism, charity, philanthropy, magnanimity, benevolence, charitableness, open-handedness, kindness, big-heartedness, great-heartedness, lavishness, free-handedness, unselfishness, selflessness, self-sacrifice, self-denial; *historical* almsgiving.
OPPOSITES meanness, miserliness.
2 *he had distributed largesse to the locals* **gifts**, presents, donations, handouts, endowments, grants, aid, alms, offerings, favours, contributions; patronage, sponsorship, backing, help.

lark (*informal*) ▸ **noun 1** *I only went along for a lark | we were just having a bit of a lark* **fun**, amusement, amusing time, laugh, giggle, joke; escapade, prank, trick, game, jape, skylark, practical joke, stunt; *informal* leg-pull, put-on, gag, crack; (**larks**) **antics**, high jinks, horseplay, fooling about/around, mischief, devilry, roguery, clowning, tomfoolery; *informal* shenanigans; *Brit. informal* monkey tricks, monkey business; *N. Amer. informal* didoes; *dated* sport.
2 *I've got this snowboarding lark sussed* **activity**, undertaking, thing to do; hobby, pastime, task; *informal* business, caper.
▸ **verb** *he's always joking and larking about* **fool about/around**, play tricks, indulge in horseplay, make mischief, monkey about/around, footle about/around, clown about/around, have fun, cavort, caper, romp, frolic, skylark; *informal* mess about/around, play up, act the (giddy) goat; *Brit. informal* muck about/around, fanny about/around; *Brit. vulgar slang* bugger about/around, piss about/around, arse about/around; *archaic or humorous* disport oneself.

larynx ▸ **noun**

WORD LINKS
relating to the larynx **laryngeal**
branch of medicine concerning the larynx **laryngology**
inflammation of the larynx **laryngitis**

lascivious ▸ **adjective** *there was a lascivious glint in his eyes* **lecherous**, lewd, lustful, licentious, libidinous, goatish, salacious, wanton, lubricious, prurient, dirty, smutty, filthy, naughty, suggestive, indecent, ribald; debauched, depraved, degenerate, dissolute, dissipated, unchaste, loose; *informal* horny, blue; *Brit. informal* randy; *rare* concupiscent, lickerish.
OPPOSITES puritanical, ascetic.

lash ▸ **verb 1** *removing his leather belt, he lashed her repeatedly across buttocks and thighs* **whip**, flog, beat, thrash, horsewhip, scourge, birch, switch, flay, belt, strap, cane, leather; strike, hit, clout, batter, welt, hammer, pummel, belabour; *informal* wallop, whack, lam, tan someone's hide, give someone a (good) hiding, larrup; *N. Amer. informal* whale; *archaic* smite, stripe, flagellate.
2 *rain lashed the window panes* **beat against**, dash against, crash against, pound, batter, buffet, smack against, strike, hit, knock.
3 *the tiger began to growl and lash his tail* **swish**, flick, twitch, switch, whip, wave, wag.
4 *fear lashed them into a frenzy* **provoke**, incite, arouse, excite, agitate, stir up, whip up, work up, egg on, goad.
5 *two punts were lashed to rings embedded in the stonework* **fasten**, bind, tie, tie up, tether, hitch, attach, knot, rope, strap, leash, truss, fetter, make fast, secure; chain, pinion, join, connect, couple.
□ **lash out 1** *the president **lashed out at** her for publicly opposing his economic policy* **criticize**, castigate, chastise, censure, attack, condemn, denounce, lambaste, harangue, rant at, rail at, haul over the coals, fulminate against, pillory, let fly; berate, upbraid, scold, rebuke, chide, reprove, reproach, take to task; *informal* lay into, round on, pitch into, lace into, carpet, bawl out; *Brit. informal* slate; *N. Amer. informal* chew out, ream out.
2 *Norman **lashed out at** Terry with a chisel* **hit out**, strike, let fly, take a swing; set upon, set about, turn on, round on, attack, weigh into; *informal* lay into, tear into, pitch into, lace into, sail into.
3 *he considered lashing out on a taxi* **spend lavishly**, be extravagant, pay out, spend a lot of money; *informal* **splash out**, push the boat out, splurge, shell out, squander money, waste money, fritter money away, go on a spending spree, go on a shopping binge.
▸ **noun 1** *he brought the lash down upon the prisoner's back* **whip**, horsewhip, bullwhip, switch, scourge, flagellum, cat-o'-nine-tails, cat, thong, flail, strap, birch, cane; *historical* knout.
2 *he was sentenced to 50 lashes with a bamboo cane* **stroke**, blow, hit, strike, welt, bang, thwack, thump; *informal* swipe, wallop, whack; *archaic* stripe.

lass ▸ **noun** (*Scottish & N. English*) **girl**, young woman, young lady; schoolgirl, miss; *Scottish* lassie; *Irish* colleen; *informal* chick, girlie, filly; *Brit. informal* bird, bint, popsy; *N. Amer. informal* dame, babe, doll, gal, broad, patootie, tomato; *Austral./NZ informal* sheila; *derogatory* baggage, piece, bit, tart; *literary* maid, maiden, damsel; *archaic or humorous* wench.

lassitude ▸ **noun** *prolonged periods of lassitude which she ascribed to the heat* **lethargy**, listlessness, weariness, languor, sluggishness, enervation, tiredness, exhaustion, fatigue, sleepiness, drowsiness, torpor, torpidity, ennui, lifelessness, sloth, apathy.
OPPOSITES vigour, energy.

last[1] ▸ **adjective 1** *the last woman in the queue* **rearmost**, rear, hindmost, bringing up the rear, nearest the rear, at the end, furthest back, at the back (of the queue), aftermost, endmost, furthest behind, final, ultimate, most remote, remotest, furthest, utmost, extreme.
OPPOSITES first, leading.
2 *Rembrandt spent his last years in Amsterdam* **closing**, concluding, final, ending, end, finishing, ultimate, terminal, terminating; valedictory; later, latter.
OPPOSITES early, initial.
3 *I'd be the last person to say anything against him* **least likely**, most unlikely, most improbable, most reluctant; least suitable, most unsuitable, most inappropriate, least appropriate, least wanted, least favourite.
OPPOSITES first, most likely.
4 *he scored a hat-trick last year* **previous**, preceding; latest, most recent; prior, former.
OPPOSITE next.
5 *this was his last chance to prove it* **final**, only remaining, only one left.
□ **the last word 1** *you'll marry my daughter over my dead body, and that's my last word* **final decision**, summation, final statement, definitive statement, conclusive comment; ultimatum.
2 *she turned, determined to leave having had the last word* **concluding remark**, final remark, final say, closing statement, parting shot, Parthian shot.
3 *the spa is the last word in luxury and efficiency* **the best**, the peak, the acme, the epitome, the quintessence, the most fashionable, the most up to date, the latest, the newest; the pinnacle, the apex, the apogee, the cream, the ultimate, the height, the zenith, the utmost, the nonpareil, the crème de la crème, the ne plus ultra, the dernier cri, the beau idéal; *archaic* the nonsuch.
▸ **adverb** *the candidate coming last is eliminated* **at the end**, at the rear, in the rear, behind, after.
▸ **noun** *the most important business was left to the last* **end**, ending, finish, close, conclusion, completion, finale, termination; bitter end.
OPPOSITES beginning, opening.
□ **at last** *at last the storm died away* **finally**, in the end, eventually, ultimately, at long last, after a long time, after a considerable time, in time, at the end of the day, in the fullness of time; lastly, in conclusion.

last[2] ▸ **verb 1** *the hearing is expected to last for a number of days* **continue**, go on, carry on, keep on, keep going, run on, proceed, be prolonged; take; stay, remain, persist, endure.
OPPOSITES finish, end, stop.
2 *she managed to **last out** until the end of the programme | how long does he*

reckon he'll last as manager? **survive**, endure, hold on, hold out, keep going, persevere, exist; *informal* stick it out, hang on, stay around, hack it.
3 *the car is built to last* **endure**, wear well, stand up, keep going, bear up; withstand, resist; *informal* go the distance.
OPPOSITE wear out.

last³ ▸ **noun** *the iron lasts on which he mended our shoes* **mould**, model, pattern, form, matrix; anvil; *N. English* hobbing foot/boot.

last-ditch ▸ **adjective** *a last-ditch attempt to save the plan from collapse* **last-minute**, last-chance, eleventh-hour, last-resort, desperate, frantic, frenzied, wild, struggling, straining, final, extreme, all-out, do-or-die; *informal* last-gasp.

lasting ▸ **adjective** *a lasting peace* **enduring**, long-lasting, long-lived, lifelong, abiding, continuing, remaining, long-term, surviving, persisting, permanent, deep-rooted, indelible, ingrained; durable, constant, stable, established, secure, fast, firm, fixed, long-standing; unchanging, never-changing, irreversible, immutable, eternal, undying, everlasting, perennial, perpetual, unending, never-ending, endless, immortal, imperishable, unfading, changeless, indestructible, ceaseless, unceasing, unwavering, unfaltering, non-stop, steady, steadfast, uninterrupted, unbroken, interminable; dependable, reliable; *rare* sempiternal, perdurable.
OPPOSITES short-lived, ephemeral.

lastly ▸ **adverb** *lastly, I would like to thank my parents for making me what I am* **finally**, in conclusion, to conclude, in closing, to sum up, to end, in drawing things to a close, in winding up, last, ultimately, in fine, last but not least.
OPPOSITE firstly.

latch ▸ **noun** *lifting the latch, she pushed the gate open* **fastening**, catch, fastener; clasp, hasp, hook, bar, bolt, clip; lock, padlock, deadlock; *Scottish* sneck, snib.
▸ **verb** *Jess latched the back door* **fasten**, secure, make fast, bar, bolt; lock, padlock, deadlock; *Scottish & Irish* sneck, snib.

late ▸ **adjective 1** *the train was one and a half hours late | he was late for work* **behind time**, behind schedule, behind, behindhand; not on time, unpunctual, tardy, running late, overdue, belated, delayed; slow, dilatory.
OPPOSITES punctual, early, fast.
2 *her late husband* **dead**, deceased, departed, lamented, passed on/away, lost, expired, gone, extinct, perished.
OPPOSITES alive, existing.
3 *he was Minister for Education in the late government* **previous**, preceding, former, past, prior, earlier, sometime, one-time, ex-, erstwhile, old, defunct, precedent, foregoing, no longer extant; *French* ci-devant; *formal* quondam; *archaic* whilom.
OPPOSITE current.
▸ **adverb 1** *she had arrived late* **behind schedule**, behind time, behindhand, unpunctually, belatedly, tardily, at the last minute, at the tail end; dilatorily, slowly, recently.
OPPOSITES early, betimes.
2 *I was working late* **after hours**, after office hours, overtime, past the usual finishing/stopping/closing time.
3 *I won't have you staying out late* **late at night**, till the early hours of the morning; *informal* till the wee small hours, till all hours.
□ **of late** *she'd been drinking too much of late* **recently**, lately, latterly, in the past few days, in the last couple of weeks, in recent times; newly, freshly, not long ago.

lately ▸ **adverb** *divorced people have had a bad press lately* **recently**, of late, latterly, in the past few days, in the last couple of weeks, in recent times; newly, freshly, not long ago.
OPPOSITE long ago.

lateness ▸ **noun** **unpunctuality**, tardiness, belatedness, delay, retardation, dilatoriness.
OPPOSITES punctuality, timeliness, earliness.

latent ▸ **adjective** *they have a huge reserve of latent talent* **dormant**, quiescent, inactive, untapped, unused; **undiscovered**, hidden, unrevealed, unexpressed, concealed, unapparent, indiscernible, imperceptible, invisible, inert, covert, unseen, veiled, masked, lurking, undeveloped, unrealized, unfulfilled, potential, not activated, inoperative, in abeyance, suppressed, repressed; possible, likely, underlying, inherent, innermost, immanent, inchoate, unacknowledged, subconscious, unconscious, sleeping.
OPPOSITES manifest, obvious; active.

later ▸ **adjective** *this question will be dealt with in a later chapter* **subsequent**, following, succeeding, future, upcoming, to come, ensuing, next; *archaic* after; *rare* posterior.
OPPOSITES earlier, prior.
▸ **adverb 1** *later, the film rights were sold* **subsequently**, eventually, then, next, later on, after this/that, afterwards, following this/that, at a later time, at a later date, at a future time/date, at some point in the future, in the future, in time to come, in due course.
2 *two days later a letter arrived* **afterwards**, later on, after, after that, subsequently, following; by and by, in a while, in time, after a bit; *formal* thereafter, thereupon.

lateral ▸ **adjective 1** *lateral movements* **sideways**, sidewise, sidelong, sideward, edgewise, edgeways, side, flank, wing, indirect, oblique, slanting.
2 *lateral thinking* **unorthodox**, inventive, creative, imaginative, original, innovative, ingenious.

latest ▸ **adjective** *the latest fashion* **most recent**, newest, brand new, just out, just released, fresh, present-day, up to date, up to the minute, state-of-the-art, current, modern, contemporary, modernistic, fashionable, in fashion, in vogue, voguish, bang up to date, in; *French* à la mode; *informal* with it, trendy, hip, hot, happening, cool, now.
OPPOSITES old, unfashionable.

lather ▸ **noun 1** *a rich lather of rose-scented suds* **foam**, froth, suds, soapsuds, bubbles; cream, head; *literary* spume.
2 *the mare was covered with lather* **sweat**, perspiration, moisture; *technical* diaphoresis, hidrosis.
3 (*informal*) *Dad was in a right lather* **panic**, nervous state, state of agitation, state of anxiety, fluster, flutter, fret, fuss, frenzy, fever, pother; *informal* flap, sweat, tizzy, dither, twitter, state, stew; *N. Amer. informal* twit.

latitude ▸ **noun 1** *Toronto shares the same latitude as Nice* parallel, grid line.
OPPOSITES longitude, meridian.
2 *he gave them much latitude in day-to-day operations* **freedom**, **scope**, leeway, elbow room, breathing space, space, room, flexibility, liberty, independence, play, slack, free rein, free play, licence, self-determination, room to manoeuvre, scope for initiative, freedom of action, freedom from restriction, a free hand, margin, leisure, unrestrictedness, indulgence, laxity; *French* carte blanche.
OPPOSITES constraint, restriction.

latter ▸ **adjective 1** *the latter half of the season* **later**, hindmost, closing, end, concluding, final.
2 *the latter years of the last century* **latest**, most recent, modern.
3 *Russia chose the latter option* **last-mentioned**, second-mentioned, second of the two, second, last, later.
OPPOSITES former, prior.

latter-day ▸ **adjective** *a latter-day puritan* **modern**, present-day, present-time, current, contemporary; *French* de nos jours.
OPPOSITE old-time.

latterly ▸ **adverb 1** *latterly, she had been in more pain* **recently**, lately, of late, in the past few days, in the last couple of weeks, in recent times.
OPPOSITE formerly.
2 *he worked on the paper for fifty years, latterly as its political editor* **ultimately**, finally, towards the end, at the end.

lattice ▸ **noun** *honeysuckle was growing up a lattice round the door* **grid**, latticework, fretwork, open framework, openwork, trellis, trelliswork, network, mesh, web, webbing, netting, net, tracery, interlacing, reticulation, reticulum, grate, grating, grille, grillwork, criss-cross, matrix; espalier, filigree; *technical* plexus, graticule, reticule, reticle, decussation.

laud ▸ **verb** *the single was lauded by the music press* **praise**, extol, hail, applaud, acclaim, commend, admire, approve of, make much of, sing the praises of, lionize, speak highly of, pay tribute/homage to, eulogize, sing paeans to; cheer, celebrate, welcome, salute, glorify, exalt, rhapsodize over/about, honour, adore, revere, venerate, idolize; *informal* put on a pedestal, rave about; *black English* big someone/something up; *dated* cry someone/something up; *archaic* magnify; *rare* panegyrize.
OPPOSITES condemn, criticize.

laudable ▸ **adjective** *a laudable attempt to get more women into Parliament* **praiseworthy**, commendable, admirable, meritorious, worthy, deserving, creditable, worthy of admiration, estimable, of note, noteworthy, exemplary, reputable, honourable, excellent, sterling; *rare* applaudable.
OPPOSITES blameworthy, shameful.

laudation ▸ **noun** (*rare*) *he was singled out for laudation* **praise**, honour, extolment, applause, acclaim, acclamation, adulation, commendation, admiration, homage, distinction, prestige, approval, credit, kudos, glory, esteem, approbation, tribute, congratulations, plaudits, salutes, veneration, eulogy, panegyric, paean, encomium.

laudatory ▸ **adjective** *a laudatory front-page endorsement* **full of praise**, complimentary, congratulatory, praising, extolling, acclamatory, adulatory, commendatory, admiring, approving, approbatory, flattering, celebratory, glorifying, eulogizing, eulogistic, panegyric, panegyrical; fulsome; *informal* glowing, rave; *rare* encomiastic, encomiastical.
OPPOSITES disparaging, damning.

laugh ▸ **verb 1** *he started to laugh excitedly* **chuckle**, chortle, guffaw, giggle, titter, snigger, snicker, cackle, howl, roar, ha-ha, tee-hee, burst out laughing, roar/hoot with laughter, shake with laughter, be convulsed with laughter, dissolve into laughter, split one's sides, hold one's sides, be doubled up; *informal* be in stitches, die laughing, be rolling in the aisles, laugh like a drain, bust a gut, break up, be creased up, crease up, fall about, crack up.
OPPOSITE cry.
2 *people laughed at Henry and his theories* **ridicule**, mock, deride, scoff at,

L

jeer at, sneer at, jibe at, make fun of, poke fun at, make jokes about, heap scorn on, scorn, pooh-pooh; lampoon, satirize, caricature, parody; taunt, tease, torment; *informal* send up, take the mickey out of; *Austral./NZ informal* poke mullock at; *Brit. vulgar slang* take the piss out of; *dated* make sport of.

□ **laugh something off** *she laughed off criticism with good humour* **dismiss**, make a joke of, make light of, refuse to acknowledge, overlook, turn a blind eye to, discount, ignore, disregard, shrug off, brush aside, scoff at, pooh-pooh, take no notice of, pay no attention to, play down, never mind; *informal* cock a snook at.
OPPOSITE take something to heart.

▶ **noun 1** *he gave a short laugh* **chuckle**, chortle, guffaw, giggle, titter, ha-ha, tee-hee, snigger, roar of laughter, hoot of laughter, shriek of laughter, peal of laughter, belly laugh.
2 (*informal*) *he was a right laugh* **joker**, comedian, comic, comedienne, humorist, wag, wit, entertainer, clown, funny man, funny woman, jester, prankster, character; *informal* card, case, caution, hoot, scream, riot, barrel of laughs; *Austral./NZ informal* hard case.
OPPOSITES bore, misery.
3 (*informal*) *I entered the contest for a laugh* **joke**, **prank**, piece of fun, jest, escapade, adventure, caper, romp, practical joke, trick, bit of mischief; shenanigans, horseplay; *informal* lark, giggle, hoot.

laughable ▶ **adjective 1** *the idea that nuclear weapons deter anyone is laughable* **ridiculous**, ludicrous, absurd, risible, preposterous, irrational, worthy of scorn, derisory; foolish, silly, idiotic, daft, stupid, nonsensical, senseless, asinine, fatuous, crazy, insane, hare-brained, scatterbrained, outrageous; *informal* cock-eyed.
2 *if it wasn't so tragic, it'd be laughable* **amusing**, funny, humorous, hilarious, uproarious, comical, comic, entertaining, diverting, farcical, droll, side-splitting; *informal* rib-tickling, jokey, killing, priceless; *rare* jocose.
OPPOSITE serious.

laughing stock ▶ **noun** *they have become the laughing stock of world sport* **figure of fun**, object of ridicule, dupe, butt, fool, joke, standing joke, everybody's fool, stooge; fair game, everybody's target, victim, Aunt Sally; exhibition, spectacle; *informal* fall guy; *Brit. informal* goat.

L

laughter ▶ **noun 1** *the sound of conversation and laughter* **laughing**, chuckling, chortling, guffawing, giggling, tittering, sniggering, howling, convulsions, fits; *informal* hysterics, hooting; *rare* cachinnation.
2 *a source of laughter* **amusement**, entertainment, humour, mirth, merriment, gaiety, hilarity, glee, jollity, jocularity, fun, enjoyment, pleasure, delight, joy, festivity, light-heartedness, blitheness.
OPPOSITES despair, gloom, misery.

launch ▶ **verb 1** *he ordered his crewmen to launch a boat* **set afloat**, float; put to sea, put into the water, send down the slipway.
2 *they've launched the shuttle* **send into orbit**, put into orbit; blast off, take off, lift off.
3 *a chair was launched at him* **throw**, hurl, fling, pitch, lob, toss, cast, let fly, propel, project; fire, shoot; *informal* chuck, heave, sling.
4 *Amnesty International has launched an emergency appeal* **set in motion**, get going, get under way, start, begin, embark on, usher in, initiate, instigate, institute, inaugurate, set up, bring out, organize, introduce, open; establish, found, originate, create, pioneer, lay the foundations of, lay the first stone of, bring into being, activate, mastermind, float, debut, roll out; start the ball rolling; *informal* kick off; *formal* commence.
5 *he* ***launched into*** *a tirade against the government* **start**, burst into, break into, begin, embark on, get going on; *formal* commence.

launder ▶ **verb** *the used sheets are taken away to be laundered* **wash**, clean, wash and iron, wash and press, dry-clean.

laundry ▶ **noun 1** *a big pile of laundry* **dirty washing**, washing, wash, dirty clothes, clothes to be cleaned; *Brit. dated* bagwash.
2 *communal accommodation includes a kitchen, a laundry, and two bathrooms* **washroom**, laundry room, launderette, dry cleaner's, public wash house, Chinese laundry; *N. Amer. trademark* laundromat.

laurels ▶ **plural noun** *she has rightly won laurels for this perceptive first novel* **honours**, awards, trophies, prizes, rewards, tributes, praise, plaudits, accolades, decorations, titles; kudos, acclaim, acclamation, commendation, credit, glory, honour, distinction, fame, renown, prestige, recognition; *informal* brownie points; *rare* laudation.

lavatory ▶ **noun** **toilet**, WC, water closet, (public) convenience, cloakroom, facilities, powder room, urinal, privy, latrine, outhouse, earth closet, jakes; *N. Amer.* washroom, bathroom, rest room, men's room, ladies' room, commode, comfort station; *French* pissoir; *Nautical* head; *informal* little girls' room, little boys' room, smallest room; *Brit. informal* loo, bog, the Ladies, the Gents, khazi, lav, throne, thunderbox; *N. English informal* netty; *N. Amer. informal* can, john, honey bucket; *Austral./NZ informal* dunny, little house; *vulgar slang* pisser, shithouse; *archaic* closet, garderobe.

lavish ▶ **adjective 1** *he held lavish dinner parties at his home* **sumptuous**, luxurious, luxuriant, lush, gorgeous, costly, opulent, grand, elaborate, splendid, rich, regal, ornate, expensive; pretentious, showy, fancy; *informal* posh.
OPPOSITE meagre.
2 *he was lavish with his hospitality* **generous**, liberal, bountiful, open-handed, unstinting, unsparing, ungrudging, free, munificent, handsome; extravagant, prodigal, fulsome; *informal* over the top.
OPPOSITES frugal, mean.
3 *lavish amounts of the best quality olive oil* **abundant**, copious, ample, superabundant, plentiful, profuse, liberal, prolific, generous; *literary* plenteous.
OPPOSITE scant.

▶ **verb** *she has always lavished money on her children* **give freely**, spend, expend, heap, shower, pour, deluge, give generously, give unstintingly, bestow freely; *informal* blow.
OPPOSITES economize, begrudge.

law ▶ **noun 1** *the law of the land* **rules and regulations**, system of laws, body of laws, constitution, legislation, code, legal code, charter; jurisprudence.
OPPOSITE anarchy.
2 *a new law was passed to make divorce easier and simpler* **regulation**, **statute**, enactment, act, bill, decree, edict, rule, ruling, resolution, promulgation, measure, motion, dictum, command, order, stipulation, commandment, directive, pronouncement, ratification, proclamation, dictate, diktat, fiat, covenant, demand, by-law; *N. Amer.* ordinance; (*in Tsarist Russia*) ukase; (*in Spain & Spanish-speaking countries*) pronunciamento.
3 (**the law**) *a career in the law* **the legal profession**, the bar, barristers and solicitors collectively.
4 *he's got to pay for it, or I'll take him to law* **litigation**, legal action, legal proceedings, lawsuit, justice.
5 (**the law**) (*informal*) *on the run from the law* **the police**, the officers of the law, the forces of law and order, law-enforcement officers, police officers, policemen, policewomen, the police force, the constabulary; *black English derogatory* Babylon; *informal* the cops, the fuzz, the boys in blue, the long arm of the law; *Brit. informal* the (Old) Bill, the bobbies, the busies, the bizzies, the coppers, the rozzers, the force, plod, PC Plod; *N. Amer. informal* the heat; *informal, derogatory* the pigs, the filth.
6 *the laws of the game* **rule**, regulation, principle, convention, direction, instruction, guideline, practice.
7 *a moral law* **principle**, rule, precept, directive, direction, injunction, instruction, commandment, prescription, standard, criterion, belief, creed, credo, ethic, maxim, formula, tenet, doctrine, canon; *Judaism* mitzvah.

WORD LINKS
relating to laws **legal, judicial, juridical, jural**

law-abiding ▶ **adjective** *decent law-abiding citizens* **well behaved**, lawful, righteous, honest, honourable, correct, upright, upstanding, good, decent, proper, solid, virtuous, moral, ethical; high-minded, right-minded, principled, worthy, orderly, above board, clean-living, peaceable, peaceful, civilized; dutiful, duteous, obedient, compliant, manageable, deferential, respectful, disciplined.
OPPOSITES lawless, criminal.

lawbreaker ▶ **noun** **criminal**, felon, wrongdoer, evil-doer, offender, delinquent, malefactor, reprobate, culprit; villain, rogue, ruffian, hoodlum, desperado, outlaw; rascal, transgressor, sinner, trespasser, violator, convict; *informal* crook, con, jailbird, crim, wrong 'un, baddy; *Law* malfeasant, infractor; *archaic* miscreant.

law court ▶ **noun** **court**, court of law, court of justice, tribunal, judicature.

WORD LINKS
relating to law courts **judicial, juridical**

lawful ▶ **adjective 1** *the jury delivered a verdict of lawful killing* **legitimate**, legal, licit, just, permissible, permitted, allowable, allowed, rightful, proper, constitutional, legalized, sanctioned, authorized, warranted, justified, justifiable, approved, recognized, admissible, above board, within the law, going by the rules; *informal* legit, kosher, by the book.
OPPOSITES illegal, prohibited.
2 *a lawful political organization* **law-abiding**, righteous, honourable, good, decent, proper, solid, virtuous, moral, ethical, orderly, well behaved, peacekeeping, peaceful, civilized, dutiful, duteous, obedient, compliant, complying, disciplined.
OPPOSITES lawless, criminal.

lawless ▶ **adjective 1** *an unruly and lawless rabble* **anarchic**, anarchical, disorderly, ungovernable, unruly, without law and order, disruptive, insurrectionary, insurgent, revolutionary, rebellious, insubordinate, riotous, mutinous, mutinying, seditious, revolting, terrorist.
OPPOSITE orderly.
2 *any member associated with any subversive or lawless activities shall be expelled* **illegal**, unlawful, lawbreaking, illicit, illegitimate, criminal, felonious, indictable, delinquent, culpable, villainous, transgressing, violating; *informal* crooked, shady, bent; *archaic* miscreant.
OPPOSITE law-abiding.

lawlessness ▶ **noun** **anarchy**, disorder, chaos, unruliness, lack of control, lack of restraint, wildness, riot, criminality, crime, rebellion,

revolution, mutiny, insurgency, insurrection, misrule.
OPPOSITE order.

lawsuit ▶ noun **legal action**, suit, suit at law, case, action, cause, legal proceeding, proceedings, judicial proceedings, litigation, trial, legal process, legal dispute, legal contest, bringing to book, bringing of charges, indictment.

lawyer *See centre pages for list of* **Lawyers**
▶ noun legal practitioner, attorney, legal officer, legal adviser, legal representative, agent, member of the bar; *informal* brief.

lax ▶ adjective *lax discipline in schools* **slack**, slipshod, negligent, neglectful, remiss, careless, heedless, unmindful, inattentive, slapdash, offhand, casual; easy-going, lenient, permissive, soft, liberal, non-restrictive, indulgent, overindulgent, complaisant, over-tolerant, irresponsible; *informal* sloppy.
OPPOSITES stern, careful.

laxative *See centre pages for list of* **Laxatives**
▶ noun **purgative**, lenitive, aperient, cathartic, evacuant; *rare* eccoprotic.

lay[1] ▶ verb **1** *Curtis laid the empty can on the passenger seat* **put**, place, set, put down, set down, deposit, rest, situate, sit, settle, stow, balance, station, drop, leave, let fall, throw down, fling down, deploy, locate, position; *informal* plant, stick, dump, bung, park, plonk, pop, shove.
OPPOSITE pick up.
2 *the Act which laid the foundation for the modern education system* **set in place/position**, put in place/position, set out, position; establish, set up.
3 *I'll* ***lay money*** *that Michelle will be there* **bet**, wager, gamble, stake, hazard, risk, chance, venture; give odds, speculate, game; *informal* punt, have a flutter.
4 *he had been the first to lay formal charges* **bring**, bring forward, put forward, submit, advance, present, press, prefer, offer, lodge, register, place, file, table; accuse, charge, indict; *N. Amer.* impeach.
5 *he* ***laid the blame for*** *the crisis firmly at the Prime Minister's door* **assign**, attribute, ascribe, allocate, allot, impute, attach, impose, fix; hold someone responsible, hold someone accountable, hold someone answerable, condemn, find guilty of, pin the blame on.
OPPOSITES exonerate, hold blameless.
6 *we laid plans for the next voyage* **devise**, arrange, contrive, make, prepare, work out, hatch, concoct, design, plan, scheme, plot, organize, frame, think up, dream up, cook up, brew, conceive, make ready, get ready, put together, draw up, produce, develop, compose, formulate.
7 *the new section laid a responsibility on the court to consider whether financial obligations should be terminated* **impose**, apply, entrust, vest, place, put; inflict, encumber, saddle, tax, charge, burden.
OPPOSITE excuse.
8 *the eagles laid two eggs* **produce**; *technical* oviposit.
□ **lay something aside 1** *payments for farmers who lay aside areas for conservation* **put aside**, put to one side, keep, save, store, hold in abeyance.
2 *producers must lay aside the conservatism that hindered development in the past* **abandon**, cast aside, reject, renounce, repudiate, dismiss, disregard, ignore, forget, discard; *archaic* forsake.
OPPOSITE take up.
3 *Protestants opposed it strongly enough to lead the government to lay the idea aside* **defer**, shelve, hold over, suspend, put on ice, mothball, set aside, put off, put aside, put out of one's mind, wave aside, put back, adjourn; *informal* put on the back burner, put in cold storage; *rare* remit.
OPPOSITES pursue; promote; progress.
□ **lay something bare** *the secrets of his heart will be laid bare* **reveal**, disclose, divulge, show, expose, exhibit, bring to light, uncover, unveil, unmask, manifest, express, highlight, pinpoint, put the spotlight on, betray, give away, smoke out, let slip, blurt out, publish, acknowledge, make a clean breast of, make known, make public.
OPPOSITE conceal.
□ **lay something down 1** *he laid down his glass* **put down**, set down, place down, deposit, drop, station, leave, rest; *informal* dump, bung down, plonk down.
2 *they were forced to* ***lay down their weapons*** **relinquish**, surrender, give up, yield, cede, turn over; **disarm**, give in, submit, capitulate, raise/show the white flag, throw in the towel/sponge, demilitarize.
3 *the ground rules laid down by the Civil Aviation Authority* **formulate**, stipulate, set down, draw up, frame; prescribe, order, command, ordain, dictate, decree, enjoin, assert; pronounce, announce, proclaim, promulgate; enact, pass, direct, decide, determine, impose, establish, institute, specify, fix, codify.
4 *I like to buy young wines and lay them down for a few years* **store**, put into store, keep for future use, keep, save.
□ **lay down the law** *when his father tried to lay down the law, he rebelled* **order someone about/around**, tell someone what to do, boss someone about/around, ride roughshod over someone, be dogmatic, be domineering; call the shots, call the tune; *informal* throw one's weight about/around, push someone about/around.
□ **lay eyes on** *(informal) I've never laid eyes on him before!* **see**, spot, observe, regard, notice, catch sight of, view, perceive, discern, spy; *informal* clap/set eyes on, clock; *literary* behold, espy, descry.
□ **lay hands on 1** *wait till I lay my hands on you!* **catch**, lay hold of, get one's hands on, get hold of, seize, grab, snatch, clutch, grip, grasp, capture.
OPPOSITES let go; leave alone.
2 *it's not easy to lay your hands on decent champagne around here* **obtain**, acquire, get, come by, find, locate, discover, unearth, uncover, bring to light, run to earth, turn up, pick up, come up with, secure, procure, hit on, ferret out, get one's hands on, encounter, get possession of, buy, purchase; *informal* get one's mitts on.
3 *the pastor will lay hands on those who come before him* **bless**, consecrate; confirm; ordain.
□ **lay something in** *Bill proposed that we should lay in a lot of good meat, and keep it for the winter* **stock up with/on**, stockpile, store (up), amass, heap up, hoard, save, stow, put aside, garner, accumulate, pile up, mass, assemble, stack up, put away, stow away, husband, reserve, preserve, conserve, collect, muster, put by, put by for a rainy day, squirrel away; *informal* salt away, stash (away).
□ **lay into** *(informal)* **1** *a policeman laying into a protestor* **attack**, assail, hit, strike, let fly at, tear into, lash out at, set about, set upon, fall on, turn on, assault, beat, thrash, pound, pummel, wallop, hammer, pounce on, round on, pelt, drub; *informal* lace into, sail into, pitch into, let someone have it, get stuck into, paste, do over, knock about/around, rough up; *Brit. informal* have a go at.
OPPOSITE leave in peace.
2 *there was no reason for him to lay into her with a string of insults* **criticize harshly**, castigate, censure, lambaste, harangue, condemn, pillory, rant at, rave at; berate, upbraid, rebuke, chide, reproach, reprove, scold; *informal* pitch into, crucify, rubbish, slag off; *Brit. informal* have a go at; *N. Amer. informal* light into, bad-mouth, bawl out; *rare* objurgate.
OPPOSITES praise, extol.
□ **lay it on** *(informal)* ***lay it on thick*** *about what you'll do for them* **exaggerate**, stretch the truth, overdo it, overstate one's case, embellish the truth; flatter, pay extravagant compliments, give fulsome praise, over-praise, soft-soap; *informal* pile it on, lay it on with a trowel/shovel, ham it up, sweet-talk.
OPPOSITE understate.
□ **lay off** *(informal) you should lay off smoking* **give up**, stop, refrain from, abstain from, not continue, desist from, leave alone, cut out; *N. Amer.* quit; *informal* pack in, leave off, kick, give over, knock off.
OPPOSITES start, take up.
□ **lay someone off** *cutbacks forced the museum to lay off 244 employees* **make redundant**, dismiss, let go, discharge, give notice to, pay off, release; *informal* sack, give someone the sack, fire, give someone their cards, give someone their marching orders, send packing, give someone the boot, give someone the bullet, give someone the push, give someone the (old) heave-ho, boot out.
OPPOSITES take on, hire.
□ **lay something on** *they arrived at the club to find no refreshments laid on* **provide**, supply, furnish, give, fix up, line up, organize, prepare, produce, come up with, dispense, purvey, bestow, impart, make available; cater.
□ **lay someone out** *(informal) he belted him, laid him out flat* **knock out**, knock unconscious, knock down, fell, floor, flatten, prostrate; *informal* KO, kayo, knock for six.
□ **lay something out 1** *Robyn laid the plans out on the desk* **spread out**, set out, arrange, display, exhibit, distribute, line up, order.
OPPOSITES fold up, put away.
2 *a pamphlet which tells you how to lay out election leaflets* **design**, plan, set out, arrange; map out, outline, sketch out, rough out, block out, detail, draw up, formulate, work out, frame, draft, plot out, trace out.
3 *(informal) he had to lay out $70 on antibiotics* **spend**, expend, pay, disburse, contribute, part with, invest, put in, devote, use up, donate, give; lavish, squander, waste, dissipate; *informal* shell out, fork out, dish out, splurge; *Brit. informal* stump up; *N. Amer. informal* ante up, pony up.
□ **lay waste** *the army* ***laid waste to*** *hundreds of villages* **devastate**, wipe out, destroy, demolish, annihilate, raze, ruin, leave in ruins, wreck, level, flatten, gut, consume, ravage, pillage, sack, wreak havoc on; *literary* despoil; *rare* depredate.

lay[2] ▶ adjective **1** *a lay preacher* **non-clerical**, non-ordained, non-ecclesiastical, secular, temporal; civil, civilian; *rare* laic, laical.
OPPOSITE ordained.
2 *I cannot explain to a lay audience the techniques I used to study these genes* **non-professional**, amateur, non-specialist, non-technical, untrained, unqualified, inexpert; dilettante.
OPPOSITES qualified, professional.

layabout ▶ noun **idler**, good-for-nothing, ne'er-do-well, do-nothing, loafer, lounger, shirker, sluggard, laggard, slugabed, malingerer, parasite, leech; *informal* skiver, waster, slacker, lazybones, lead-swinger, slob, couch potato; *Austral./NZ informal* bludger; *Brit. informal, chiefly Military* scrimshanker; *archaic* wastrel; *French archaic* fainéant.
OPPOSITE workaholic.

layer ▶ noun *the walls were topped by a layer of concrete* **coating**, sheet, coat, surface, film, covering, blanket, skin, veneer, thickness.

layman ▶ noun. See LAYPERSON.

lay-off ▶ noun *a strike in protest over lay-offs* **redundancy**, dismissal, discharge; notice; unemployment; *informal* sacking, firing; marching orders; the sack, the boot, the bullet, the axe, the (old) heave-ho, the elbow, the bounce.
OPPOSITES recruitment, hiring.

layout ▶ noun **1** *she seems familiar with the layout of the house* **arrangement**, geography, design, organization, make-up, shape; plan, map.
2 *the magazine's layout and typography give it a stylish look* **design**, arrangement, presentation, style, format; structure, organization, composition, formation, configuration, set-up; pattern, outline, plan, sketch.

layperson ▶ noun **1** *a book for laypeople that explains the church's policies* **unordained person**, member of the congregation, parishioner; layman, laywoman.
OPPOSITE clergyman.
2 *engineering sounds highly specialized to the layperson* **non-expert**, layman, non-professional, amateur, non-specialist, man in/on the street; dilettante, enthusiast, dabbler.
OPPOSITES professional, expert.

laze ▶ verb *I was just* ***lazing around*** *on beaches* **relax**, unwind, idle, do nothing, loaf (around/about), lounge (around/about), loll (around/about), lie (around/about), take it easy; waste time, kill time, mark time, while away the hours, fritter away time, twiddle one's thumbs; *informal* hang around/round, skive, veg (out); *Brit. informal* hang about; *N. Amer. informal* bum (around).
OPPOSITE work.

laziness ▶ noun **idleness**, indolence, slothfulness, sloth, shiftlessness, inactivity, inertia, sluggishness, lethargy, languor, torpidity, slowness, heaviness, dullness; remissness, negligence, slackness, laxity.
OPPOSITES industriousness, energy.

lazy ▶ adjective **idle**, indolent, slothful, work-shy, shiftless, loafing, inactive, inert, sluggish, lethargic, languorous, listless, torpid, enervated, slow-moving, slow, heavy, dull, plodding; remiss, negligent, slack, lax, lackadaisical, impassive, good-for-nothing, do-nothing; leisurely; *informal* bone idle; *French archaic* fainéant; *rare* otiose.
OPPOSITES active, industrious, energetic.

L

CHOOSE THE RIGHT WORD

lazy, idle, indolent

People described as any of these words are reluctant to expend any energy or go to any trouble over work they have to do.

- **Lazy** is the most general word (*he's too lazy to mow the lawn*). Of the three words, only *lazy* can also be used to describe something done without much effort (*lazy speaking leads to lazy writing*). Uncritically, it can be used of a time when little effort is expended (*what better way to liven up these lazy summer days*) or, figuratively, of inanimate objects (*the Neapolitan Riviera extends in a lazy curve around the coast*).
- **Idle** can be more strongly critical than *lazy* (*you're an idle scrounger*) but is normally used in more formal contexts. Care is sometimes needed to avoid confusion with the sense 'out of work', as in *10.3 per cent of the workforce is now idle*.
- **Indolent** is rarer, and more formal still (*their leaders and functionaries have been indolent, self-serving, or downright corrupt*). It can sometimes indicate slow, even graceful movements (*she moved across the room with an indolent, hip-swaying saunter*).

lazybones ▶ noun (*informal*) **idler**, loafer, layabout, lounger, good-for-nothing, do-nothing, shirker, sluggard, laggard, slugabed; *informal* skiver, waster, slacker, slowcoach, slob, couch potato; *Austral./NZ informal* bludger; *archaic* wastrel; *French archaic* fainéant.

leach ▶ verb *nitrate is leached from the soil by rainfall* **drain**, filter, percolate, filtrate, discharge, strain, leak, separate; trickle, dribble, drip, ooze, seep; *rare* osmose, lixiviate.

lead[1] (rhymes with 'feed') ▶ verb **1** *Michelle let them lead her into the porch* **guide**, conduct, show, show someone the way, lead the way, usher, escort, steer, pilot, marshal, shepherd; accompany, see, take, help, assist.
OPPOSITE follow.
2 *we are led to believe that lack of finance is to blame* **cause**, induce, prompt, move, persuade, sway, influence, prevail on, bring round, make willing, motivate, drive, condition, determine, make, impel, give, force; incline, dispose, predispose, bias.
3 *they feared that the Marshall Plan would* ***lead to*** *Germany's industrial revival* **result in**, cause, bring on, bring about, call forth, give rise to, be the cause of, make happen, create, produce, occasion, effect, engender, generate, contribute to, be conducive to, add to, be instrumental in, have a hand in, have a part in, help, promote, advance; precipitate, hasten, accelerate, quicken, push forward, prompt, expedite, further, speed up; provoke, stir up, spark off, trigger (off), set off, touch off, arouse, rouse, excite, foment, instigate; cost, involve, necessitate, invite, risk, elicit, entail; *rare* effectuate, conduce to.
4 *he intended to lead a march to the city centre* **be at the head of**, be at the front of, head, spearhead.
OPPOSITE follow.
5 *the Prime Minister led a coalition of republican radicals* **be the leader of**, be the head of, preside over, hold sway over, head; command, direct, govern, rule, be in charge of, be in command of, be in control of, have control of, have charge of, regulate, supervise, superintend, oversee, chair, run, mastermind, orchestrate, control, conduct, guide, be at the helm of, take the chair of; administer, organize, manage; dominate, master, reign over, domineer, be in power over; *informal* head up, run the show, call the shots.
OPPOSITE serve in.
6 *he fired in breaks of 52 and 65 to lead 8–54* **be ahead**, be winning, be in front, be out in front, be in the lead, be first, come first.
OPPOSITES be losing, lose.
7 *the champion steeplechaser was leading the field as usual* **be at the front of**, be first in, be ahead of, head; outdistance, outrun, outstrip, outpace, leave behind, get (further) ahead of, draw away from, shake off; outdo, excel, exceed, surpass, outclass, transcend, top, trump, cap, beat, better; widen the gap; *informal* leave standing, walk away from, run rings around; *archaic* outrival, outvie.
OPPOSITES follow, trail.
8 *right now, all I want is to lead a normal life* **experience**, have, live, pass, spend, undergo.
9 *a path through the park* ***leads to*** *the beach* **open on to**, give on to, connect with/to, provide a route to, communicate with.

□ **lead something off** *they watched his dramatic announcement lead off the Nine O'Clock News* **begin**, start, start off, open, get going; *informal* kick off; *formal* commence.
OPPOSITES end, conclude.

□ **lead someone on** *he knew she was leading him on* **deceive**, mislead, delude, hoodwink, dupe, trick, take in, fool, pull the wool over someone's eyes, gull; ensnare, entrap, entice, allure, lure, beguile, inveigle, tempt, tantalize, tease, flirt with, seduce; *informal* **string along**, lead up the garden path, take for a ride, put one over on.

□ **lead the way 1** *he led the way to the kitchen* **guide**, conduct, show the way.
2 *Britain has often led the way in aerospace technology* **take the first step**, initiate things, break (new) ground, blaze a trail, lay the foundation, lay the first stone, set in motion, prepare the way, set the ball rolling, take the initiative, make the first move, make a start; develop, introduce, start, begin, launch, instigate, institute, originate.
OPPOSITE follow.

□ **lead up to** *she wondered if he was leading up to suggesting that they go together* **prepare the way for**, pave the way for, open the way for, lay the groundwork for, set the scene for; work round/up to, make overtures about, make advances about, hint at, approach the subject of, introduce the subject of; suggest, hint, imply.

▶ noun **1** *I found myself* ***in the lead*** *early in the back straight* **leading position**, leading place, first place, advance position, van, vanguard; ahead, in front, winning, leading the field, to the fore; *informal* up front.
OPPOSITES last, losing.
2 *they took the lead in the personal computer market* **first position**, head place, forefront, primacy, dominance, superiority, precedence, ascendancy; pre-eminence, supremacy, advantage, edge, upper hand, whip hand; head start.
OPPOSITE last position.
3 *Newcastle built up a 3-0 half-time lead* **winning margin**, margin, gap, interval.
4 *sixth-formers are supposed to give a lead to younger pupils* **example**, model, pattern, exemplar, paradigm, standard of excellence; role model.
5 *she is going to be playing the lead in Glen's movie* **leading role**, star/starring role, star part, title role, principal part; star, principal character, male lead, female lead, leading man, leading lady, hero, heroine, protagonist.
OPPOSITES bit part, extra.
6 *a Labrador on a lead* **leash**, tether, rein, cord, rope, chain, line.
7 *detectives were following up a new lead in their hunt for the killers* **clue**, pointer, guide, hint, tip, tip-off, suggestion, indication, indicator, sign, signal, intimation, inkling; (**leads**) evidence, information.

▶ adjective *we lost the lead position due to a combination of circumstances* **leading**, first, top, foremost, front, head; chief, principal, main, most important, premier, paramount, prime, primary.
OPPOSITE last.

lead[2] (rhymes with 'bed') ▶ noun *he was removing the lead from the man's chest* **bullet**, pellet, ball, slug; shot, buckshot, ammunition.

WORD LINKS

relating to lead **plumbic, plumbous**
related prefix **plumb- (e.g. *plumbate*)**

leaden ▶ adjective **1** *he levered himself up from the armchair, his eyes leaden with sleep* **dull**, heavy, weighty; listless, lifeless, inactive, inert.
2 *on leaden feet, he moved back to the staircase* **sluggish**, heavy, lumbering, plodding, cumbersome, slow, torpid; laboured.
OPPOSITES light, springy.
3 *he avoids the leaden prose which so many academics affect* **boring**, dull, unimaginative, uninspired, uninteresting, tedious, monotonous, insipid, heavy, laboured, stilted, wooden, prosaic, stodgy.
OPPOSITES interesting, lively.
4 *a dour and leaden sky* **grey**, greyish, grey-coloured, black, dark, ashen; **cloudy**, gloomy, overcast, sombre, dim, sunless, starless, louring, oppressive, threatening, dreary, dismal, dingy, bleak, dull, murky, sullen, cheerless, depressing; *literary* tenebrous; *rare* Cimmerian, caliginous.
OPPOSITES bright, cheerful.

leader ▶ noun **1** *the leader of the Democratic Party* **chief**, head, principal, boss; commander, captain; figurehead, controller, superior, kingpin, headman, mover and shaker; chairman, chairwoman, chairperson, chair, convener, moderator; director, managing director, MD, manager, superintendent, supervisor, overseer, administrator, employer, master, mistress, foreman; president, premier, governor; ruler, monarch, king, queen, sovereign, emperor, tsar, prince, princess, lord, lord and master; elder, patriarch; guru, mentor, authority; *informal* boss man, skipper, gaffer, guv'nor, top dog, number one, big cheese, big noise, bigwig, big shot; *N. Amer. informal* honcho, Mister Big, numero uno, sachem, padrone.
OPPOSITES follower, supporter.
2 *a world leader in the use of video conferencing* **pioneer**, front runner, innovator, trailblazer, pathfinder, groundbreaker, trendsetter, leading light, guiding light, torch-bearer, pacemaker, originator, initiator, developer, discoverer, founder, architect.

leadership ▶ noun **1** *she won the leadership of the Conservative Party* **headship**, directorship, direction, governorship, governance, administration, jurisdiction, captaincy, superintendency, control, ascendancy, rule, command, power, mastery, domination, dominion, premiership, sovereignty.
2 *we need firm and committed leadership* **guidance**, direction, authority, control, management, superintendence, supervision; organization, government, orchestration, initiative, influence.

leading ▶ adjective **1** *he played the leading role in his team's narrow victory* **main**, chief, major, prime, most significant, principal, foremost, key, supreme, paramount, dominant, superior, ruling, directing, guiding, controlling, essential, cardinal, central, focal; momentous, noteworthy, notable; *informal* number-one.
OPPOSITES secondary, subordinate.
2 *the leading industrially developed countries* **most powerful**, most important, foremost, greatest, chief, outstanding, pre-eminent, richest, principal, dominant, most influential, most illustrious, paramount, top-rank, of the first rank, first-rate.
OPPOSITES minor, secondary; second-rate.
3 *last season's leading scorer* **top**, highest, best, first; superlative, unsurpassed, unexcelled, front, in first place, lead, unparalleled, matchless, peerless, incomparable, star, arch-.
OPPOSITES last; worst.

leaf ▶ noun **1** *sycamore leaves* **frond**; flag, needle, pad, blade, bract, leaflet; *technical* cotyledon, foliole.
2 *as he handled the book, a sheaf of loose leaves fell from the back* **page**, sheet, folio, flyleaf.
□ **turn over a new leaf** *I see fatherhood as a chance to turn over a new leaf* **reform**, improve, amend; mend one's ways, become a better person, change completely, make a fresh start, change for the better, reconstruct oneself; *informal* go straight, get back on the straight and narrow.
OPPOSITE be set in one's ways.
▶ verb **1** *he leafed through a pile of documents* **flick**, flip, thumb, skim, browse, glance, look, riffle; read, scan, dip into, run one's eye over, have a look at, peruse.
2 *many plants need a period of dormancy before they leaf and flower* **put out leaves**, bud, burst into leaves; *rare* foliate.

WORD LINKS

related prefix	**phyllo- (e.g. *phylloxera*)**
related suffix	**-phyll (e.g. *chlorophyll*)**
relating to leaves	**foliar**
resembling leaves	**foliaceous**
decorated like leaves	**foliate**
leaf-eating	**folivorous, phyllophagous**

leaflet ▶ noun **pamphlet**, booklet, brochure, handbill, circular, flyer, handout, advertisement, bulletin, mailshot, bill, notice; *N. Amer.* folder; *informal* advert, ad, bumf; *N. Amer. & Austral. informal* dodger.

league ▶ noun **1** *he tried to form a league of chieftains* **alliance**, confederation, confederacy, federation, union, association, coalition, combine, consortium, affiliation, guild, corporation, conglomerate, cooperative, partnership, fellowship, syndicate, compact, band, group, circle, ring; bloc, faction, axis, congress, entente; brotherhood, society, fraternity, coterie, lodge; *rare* consociation, sodality.
2 *we won the league last year | the football league* **championship**, competition, contest; group, band, association.
3 *the store is not in the same league as the major supermarkets* **class**, group, category, ability group, level of ability, level.
□ **in league with** *they confessed to being in league with foreign powers* **collaborating with**, cooperating with, in cooperation with, in alliance with, allied with, conspiring with, leagued with, linked with, hand in glove with, in collusion with; *informal* in cahoots with.
▶ verb *Oscar had* ***leagued together*** *with other construction companies* **ally**, join forces, join together, unite, form an association, band together, affiliate, combine, amalgamate, form a federation, confederate, collaborate, team up, join up.

leak ▶ verb **1** *oil leaking from the tanker* **seep (out)**, escape, ooze (out), exude, discharge, emanate, issue, drip, dribble, drain, bleed; spill, stream, gush (out), spurt, spout, squirt, spew, jet.
2 *ageing underground tanks are leaking gasoline into the area* **discharge**, exude, emit, eject, release, drip, dribble, pour out, send forth, ooze, excrete, secrete.
3 (*informal*) *civil servants who leak information are criticized by politicians for a breach of trust* **disclose**, divulge, reveal, make known, make public, tell, impart, pass on, relate, communicate, expose, broadcast, publish, release, unveil, give away, betray, admit, confess, let slip, blurt out, bring into the open, bring to light; let on; *informal* take the lid off, blow wide open, blab, let the cat out of the bag, spill the beans, blow the gaff.
▶ noun **1** *check that there are no leaks in the bag* **hole**, opening, puncture, perforation, prick, cut, gash, slit, nick, rent, break, rift, crack, crevice, chink, fissure, rupture, aperture.
2 *a gas leak was discovered* **discharge**, leakage, leaking, oozing, seeping, seepage, drip, percolation; escape, gush, issue, flow, outflow, emanation; *technical* efflux.
3 (*informal*) *a series of leaks to the media* **disclosure**, revelation, divulgence, uncovering, admission, confession, exposé.

leaky ▶ adjective **leaking**, dripping; cracked, split, holed, holey, punctured, perforated; porous, permeable.
OPPOSITE watertight.

lean[1] ▶ verb **1** *Polly leaned against the door* **rest**, be propped up, recline, be supported.
2 *a line of palm trees leaning in the wind* **slant**, incline, bend, tilt, be at an angle, slope, tip, bank, list, heel, careen, cant, bias, veer, sway, angle.
3 *he* ***leans towards*** *existentialist philosophy* **tend**, incline, gravitate, have a tendency; have a propensity for, have a proclivity for, have a preference for, have a penchant for, be partial to, be attracted to, have a liking for, have an affinity with, be prone to.
4 *Jack had always been there, a strong shoulder to* ***lean on*** **depend**, be dependent, rely, count, bank, pin one's faith; have faith in, trust, have every confidence in, swear by, cling to; not manage without.
5 (*informal*) *I got* ***leaned on*** *by villains many times* **intimidate**, coerce, domineer, browbeat, bully, tyrannize, pressurize, threaten, compel, pressure, put pressure on, force, drive, impel, constrain; *informal* twist someone's arm, put the frighteners on, put the screws on, strong-arm, push around, squeeze, bulldoze.

lean[2] ▶ adjective **1** *a tall, lean, aristocratic man* **slim**, thin, slender, rangy, spare, wiry, slight; lissom, svelte, willowy, sylphlike; skinny, scrawny, scraggy, lanky, lank, bony, gaunt, emaciated, skin and bones, raw-boned, rangy, gangling, spindly, skeletal, angular, pinched.
OPPOSITE fat.
2 *lean meat* **non-fatty**, unfatty.
OPPOSITE fatty.
3 *a lean harvest* **meagre**, scanty, sparse, poor, scant, mean, inadequate, insufficient, paltry, limited, restricted, modest, deficient, insubstantial, slight.
OPPOSITES abundant, plentiful.
4 *too often in lean times the poorest are asked to make the largest sacrifices* **unproductive**, unfruitful, unprofitable, unremunerative, arid, barren; hard, bad, difficult, tough, impoverished, poverty-stricken, moneyless.
OPPOSITES productive, prosperous.

leaning ▶ noun *his early leanings towards socialism were evident in the articles he wrote* **inclination**, tendency, bent, proclivity, propensity, penchant, predisposition, predilection, proneness, partiality, preference, disposition, orientation, bias, attraction, liking, fancy, fondness, taste; weakness, hankering, appetite, thirst.

leap ▶ verb **1** *he leapt over the gate* **jump over**, jump, vault over, vault, spring over, bound over, hurdle, skip (over), cross over, sail over, hop (over), leapfrog, high jump, clear, negotiate.
2 *Claudia leapt to her feet* **spring**, jump, jump up, bound, dart; lunge.
3 *we leapt to the rescue* **rush**, hurry, hasten, hurtle.
4 *she had* ***leapt at*** *the chance* **accept eagerly**, grasp, grasp with both hands, grab, take advantage of, seize (on), snatch, jump at, pounce on.
OPPOSITE reject.
5 *she had* ***leapt to*** *conclusions which could be hopelessly wide of the mark* **arrive at hastily**, reach hurriedly, come to overhastily, form hastily, hurry, hasten, jump, rush, reach.

L

6 *profits leapt by 55%* **increase rapidly**, soar, rocket, skyrocket, shoot up, escalate, mount, surge, spiral, grow rapidly, rise rapidly.
OPPOSITES fall, plummet.
▶ **noun 1** *he had cleared the brook in an easy leap* **jump**, vault, spring, bound, hop, skip; *Ballet* entrechat; *rare* curvet.
2 *the figures unveiled last week showed a leap of 33%* **sudden rise**, rapid increase, escalation, soaring, surge, upsurge, upswing, upturn; increment, elevation; revival.
OPPOSITE drop.
□ **in/by leaps and bounds** *productivity can be improved in leaps and bounds* **rapidly**, swiftly, quickly, speedily, at an amazing rate, exponentially; *informal* in no time (at all).
OPPOSITE slowly.

learn ▶ **verb 1** *a scheme to encourage people to learn a foreign language* **acquire a knowledge of**, gain an understanding of, acquire skill in, become competent in, become proficient in, grasp, master, take in, absorb, assimilate, pick up, digest, familiarize oneself with; become expert in, know inside out, know backwards, comprehend; study, read up on, work at, apply oneself to, be taught, have lessons in, pursue; *informal* get the hang of, get clued up about, get the point of.
2 *if I want to learn a poem I stick it on the fridge* **memorize**, learn by heart, learn by rote, commit to memory, become word-perfect in, learn word for word, learn parrot-fashion, get off/down pat, have off/down pat, know, retain; *informal* get off by heart; *archaic* con.
OPPOSITE forget.
3 *he learned that the school would shortly be closing* **discover**, find out, become aware, be made aware, be informed, have it brought to one's attention, hear, be given to understand, get to know, come to know, hear tell; gather, understand, ascertain, establish, realize, determine; *informal* get wind of the fact, get wise to the fact; *Brit. informal* suss out; *N. Amer. informal* dope out.

learned ▶ **adjective** *a learned and formidable intellectual | learned academic books* **scholarly**, erudite, well educated, knowledgeable, well read, widely read, well versed, well informed, lettered, cultured, cultivated, civilized, intellectual, intelligent, clever, academic, literary, bookish, highbrow, studious, sage, wise, sagacious, discerning, donnish, cerebral, enlightened, illuminated, sophisticated, pedantic; esoteric, obscure, recondite; *informal* brainy; *rare* sapient.
OPPOSITES ignorant, ill-educated.

learner ▶ **noun beginner**, trainee, apprentice, pupil, student, novice, newcomer, starter, probationer, tyro, fledgling, fresher, freshman, freshwoman, neophyte, initiate, new recruit, raw recruit, new boy/girl; *N. Amer.* tenderfoot, novitiate; *informal* newbie; *N. Amer. informal* greenhorn, rookie.
OPPOSITES veteran, expert.

learning ▶ **noun 1** *the importance of the library as a centre of learning* **study**, studying, education, schooling, tuition, teaching, academic work, instruction, training; research, investigation; *Brit. informal* swotting.
2 *his second book displayed the astonishing range of his learning* **scholarship**, knowledge, education, erudition, culture, intellect, academic attainment, acquirements, enlightenment, illumination, edification, book learning, insight, information, understanding, sageness, wisdom, sophistication; pedantry; letters.
OPPOSITE ignorance.

lease ▶ **noun** *they were able to acquire a 15-year lease on a factory* **leasehold**, rental agreement, hire agreement, charter, contract; **rental**, tenancy, tenure, booking; period of occupancy, period of occupation.
OPPOSITE freehold.
▶ **verb 1** *the film crew leased a large hangar and used it as their headquarters* **rent**, hire, charter, engage, take, borrow, pay for the use of.
OPPOSITE buy.
2 *they leased the mill to a reputable family* **rent out**, rent, let, let out, hire, hire out, sublet, sublease, farm out, charge for the use of.
OPPOSITE sell.

leash ▶ **noun 1** *you should always keep your dog on a leash* **lead**, rein, tether, rope, cord, chain, line, strap; restraint; *archaic* lyam.
2 *the adolescent Wolfgang found himself off the parental leash* **control**, restraint, check, curb, rein, hold, discipline.
□ **straining at the leash** *each year some 300 youngsters are straining at the leash to get into professional golf* **eager**, impatient, anxious, enthusiastic; *informal* itching, dying, gagging.
▶ **verb 1** *she called the dog to heel so that she could leash him* **put a leash on**, put a lead on, fasten, hitch up, tether, tie up, secure, bind, fetter; confine, restrain.
OPPOSITES unleash, release.
2 *the ire in her face was barely leashed* **curb**, control, keep under control, check, restrain, hold back, suppress.
OPPOSITES unleash, release.

least ▶ **determiner** *I have not the least idea what this phrase could mean* **slightest**, smallest, minimum, minimal, minutest, tiniest, littlest.
OPPOSITES greatest, most.
□ **at least** *check in at least one hour before take-off* **at the minimum**, no less than, not less than; as a conservative estimate, at rock-bottom; more than.

leather *See centre pages for list of* **Leathers**
▶ **noun** *his leather jacket | a volume bound in leather* **skin**, hide.
▶ **verb** *he caught me and leathered me black and blue* **beat**, strap, belt, thrash, flog, whip, lash, scourge, horsewhip, birch, cane, strike, hit, clout, batter, spank; *informal* wallop, whack, tan someone's hide, give someone a (good) hiding, lather.

leathery ▶ **adjective 1** *he was about fifty, with soulful eyes and leathery skin* **rough**, rugged, wrinkled, wrinkly, furrowed, lined, wizened, weather-beaten, callous, hard, hardened, thickened, gnarled, leather-like; *technical* coriaceous.
2 *leathery sides of beef* **tough**, hard, hardened, fibrous, gristly, chewy, sinewy, stringy, leather-like; *technical* coriaceous.

leave[1] ▶ **verb 1** *I left the hotel* **depart from**, go away from, go from, withdraw from, retire from, take oneself off from, exit from, take one's leave of, pull out of, quit, be gone from, decamp from, disappear from, abandon, vacate, absent oneself from, evacuate; say one's farewells/goodbyes, make off, clear out, make oneself scarce, check out; abscond from, run away from, flee (from), fly from, bolt from, go AWOL, take French leave, escape (from); *informal* push off, shove off, cut, cut and run, do a bunk, do a disappearing act, split, vamoose, scoot, clear off, take off, make tracks, up sticks, pack one's bags, flit; *Brit. informal* sling one's hook.
OPPOSITES arrive, come, stay.
2 *the next morning we left for Leicester* **set off**, head, make, begin one's journey, set sail.
3 *he's left his wife* **abandon**, desert, discard, turn one's back on, cast aside, cast off, jilt, leave in the lurch, leave high and dry, throw over, leave stranded, brush off; *informal* dump, ditch, chuck, drop, walk out on, run out on, rat on, leave flat; *archaic* forsake.
OPPOSITE stay with.
4 *he left his job in November* **quit**, give up, abandon, move from, resign from, retire from, bow out of, step down from, withdraw from, get out of, pull out of, back out of.
OPPOSITE stay in.
5 *she left her handbag on a bus* **leave behind**, omit to take, forget, lose, mislay.
6 *I thought I'd leave it to the experts* **entrust**, hand over, pass on, refer; delegate; assign, consign, allot, give, commit.
7 *when he died he left her £100,000* **bequeath**, will, endow, hand down, transfer, convey, make over; *Law* demise, devise.
8 *the speech left some feelings of disappointment* **cause**, produce, generate, give rise to, result in.
□ **leave someone in the lurch** *I wouldn't have left the club if it meant leaving them in the lurch* **leave in trouble**, let down, leave helpless, leave stranded, leave high and dry, abandon, desert, betray; *N. Amer. informal* bail on; *archaic* forsake.
OPPOSITES help, support, come to the aid of.
□ **leave off** (*informal*) *I wish he would leave off hanging around with them* **stop**, cease, finish, desist from, keep from, break off, lay off, give up, discontinue, refrain from, restrain oneself from, hold back from, swear off, resist the temptation to, stop oneself from, withhold from, eschew; conclude, terminate, suspend, bring to an end, renounce, forswear, forbear, relinquish; *N. Amer.* quit; *informal* give over, knock off, jack something in.
OPPOSITES continue, go on.
□ **leave someone/something out 1** *Adam left out the address on the letter* **miss out**, omit, omit by accident, fail to include, overlook, pass over, neglect to notice, leave unnoticed, forget; skip, miss, jump.
OPPOSITE include.
2 *he was left out of the England squad* **exclude**, omit, except, eliminate, drop, count out, disregard, ignore, reject, pass over, neglect, cut out, do away with, bar, debar, keep out.
OPPOSITE include.

CHOOSE THE RIGHT WORD

leave, permission, consent, authorization
See PERMISSION.

leave, holiday, vacation, break
See HOLIDAY.

leave[2] ▶ **noun 1** *the judge granted leave to appeal* **permission**, consent, authorization, sanction, warrant, dispensation, concession, indulgence, approval, clearance, blessing, agreement, backing, assent, acceptance, confirmation, ratification, mandate, licence, acquiescence, concurrence, liberty, freedom; *informal* the go-ahead, the green light, the OK, the rubber stamp.
2 *he was on leave from the Royal Engineers* **holiday**, vacation, break, time off, furlough, sabbatical, leave of absence, a day/week/month off, leisure

L

time, respite, breathing space; half-term, bank holiday, recess; *informal* hols, vac.
3 *if you will excuse me, I will now take my leave of you* **departure**, leaving, leave-taking, parting, withdrawal, exit, farewell, goodbye, adieu, valediction.

leaven ▶ noun *leaven is added to the dough and the dough is left to rise* **leavening**, ferment, fermentation agent, raising agent, yeast, barm, baking powder.
▶ verb **1** *the biscuits are light because they use both yeast and baking powder to leaven the flour* **raise**, make rise, ferment, work, lighten, puff up, expand, swell, inflate.
2 *his humour was sharp, but often leavened with a touch of self-mockery* **permeate**, infuse, pervade, penetrate, imbue, suffuse, transform, modify; **enliven**, lighten, quicken, inspire, stimulate, liven up, invigorate, vivify, ginger up, energize, electrify, galvanize, perk up, brighten up, cheer up, season, spice; *informal* buck up, pep up, add zest to, add zing to.

leavings ▶ plural noun *the leavings of their hasty meal* **residue**, remainder, remains, remnants, leftovers, scrapings, scraps, oddments, odds and ends, fragments, cast-offs, excess, surplus, rejects, junk, waste, dregs, refuse, rubbish, litter, debris, sweepings, detritus, lees; *rare* orts.

lecher ▶ noun **lecherous man**, libertine, womanizer, seducer, adulterer, debauchee, rake, roué, profligate, wanton, loose-liver, sensualist, sybarite, voluptuary, Don Juan, Casanova, Lothario, Romeo; pervert; *informal* lech, dirty old man, DOM, goat, wolf, ladykiller; *dated* rip; *archaic* fornicator.
OPPOSITE puritan.

lecherous ▶ adjective *a lecherous old man* **lustful**, licentious, lascivious, libidinous, prurient, lewd, salacious, lubricious, debauched, dissolute, wanton, loose, fast, impure, unchaste, intemperate, dissipated, degenerate, sinful, depraved, crude, goatish; sensual, libertine, promiscuous, carnal; dirty, filthy, perverted, coarse, corrupt, indecent; *informal* randy, horny, raunchy, pervy, naughty; *rare* concupiscent, lickerish.
OPPOSITES chaste, pure.

lechery ▶ noun **lust**, lustfulness, licentiousness, lasciviousness, lewdness, salaciousness, libertinism, libidinousness, debauchery, dissoluteness, wantonness, intemperance, dissipation, degeneracy, depravity, impurity, unchastity, immorality, looseness, immodesty; promiscuity, carnality, womanizing, rakishness; sensuality, sensualness, sexual desire, desire, sexual appetite, libido; *informal* randiness, horniness, raunchiness, the hots, leching; *rare* concupiscence, lubricity, salacity.
OPPOSITE chastity.

lecture ▶ noun **1** *a lecture on children's literature* **speech**, talk, address, discourse, disquisition, presentation, oration, lesson, recitation, monologue, sermon, homily.
2 *Dad got a severe lecture for wasting his money* **scolding**, chiding, reprimand, rebuke, reproof, reproach, remonstration, upbraiding, berating, castigation, tirade, diatribe, harangue, admonition, admonishment, lambasting, obloquy; *informal* dressing-down, telling-off, talking-to, tongue-lashing; *Brit. informal* rocket, wigging.
OPPOSITES commendation, pat on the back.
▶ verb **1** *he visited schools to lecture on the dangers of drugs* **give a lecture**, give a talk, talk, give a speech, make a speech, speak, give an address, discourse, expound, hold forth, declaim, expatiate, give a sermon, sermonize, pontificate; *informal* speechify, preachify, spout, jaw, sound off, spiel, drone on.
2 *she lectures in Communications at Dublin University* **teach**, tutor in, instruct in, give instruction in, give lessons in.
3 *he was lectured by the headmaster in front of the whole school* **scold**, chide, reprimand, rebuke, reprove, reproach, remonstrate with, upbraid, berate, castigate, chastise, admonish, lambaste, nag, haul over the coals, take to task, read someone the Riot Act; *informal* give someone a dressing-down, give someone a talking-to, tell off; *Brit. informal* tick off, carpet; *N. Amer. informal* bawl out.

lecturer ▶ noun **1** *this year's Reith lecturer is a journalist* **public speaker**, speaker, speech-maker, orator, declaimer, preacher; rhetorician.
2 *a lecturer in economics* **university teacher**, college teacher, tutor, reader, instructor, scholar, don, professor, fellow, doctor, researcher; academic, academician, pedagogue, educator, educationalist; *informal* boffin, egghead; *rare* preceptor.

ledge ▶ noun *she arranged the plants in a row on the ledge | a cliff ledge* **shelf**, sill, mantel, mantelpiece, mantelshelf, shelving; **projection**, protrusion, overhang, extension, ridge, step, prominence, spur, jut, bulge, flange.

ledger ▶ noun *a sales ledger* **book**, account book, record book, register, registry, log; records, archives, books; balance sheet, financial statement.

lee ▶ noun *they sat in the lee of the wall* **shelter**, protection, cover, refuge, safety, security, sanctuary, haven, shield.

leech ▶ noun *the smug faces of leeches feeding off the hard-working majority* **parasite**, clinger, barnacle, bloodsucker, cadger, passenger, layabout; extortioner; sycophant, toady, hanger-on, fawner, yes man; *informal* **scrounger**, sponger, freeloader, ligger; *N. Amer. informal* mooch, moocher.

leer ▶ verb *Henry leered at her* **ogle**, look lasciviously, look suggestively, give sly looks to, eye, watch, stare, goggle; *informal* give someone the glad eye, give someone a/the once-over, lech after/over, drool over, undress someone with one's eyes; *Brit. informal* gawp, gawk; *Austral./NZ informal* perv on.
▶ noun *he gave me a sly leer* **lecherous look**, lascivious look, suggestive look, ogle, sly glance, stare; *informal* the glad eye, the once-over.

leery ▶ adjective (*informal*) *he was a bit leery of her from the buffeting she'd given him earlier* **wary**, cautious, careful, guarded, chary, suspicious, distrustful, mistrusting, dubious, sceptical; worried, anxious, apprehensive.
OPPOSITES heedless, trustful.

lees ▶ plural noun *the lees in the bottom of the cask* **sediment**, dregs, deposit, grounds, settlings, residue, remains, accumulation, silt, sludge; *technical* precipitate, sublimate, residuum; *rare* draff, grouts.

leeway ▶ noun *this has left the police with some leeway to interpret the law for themselves* **freedom**, **scope**, room to manoeuvre, latitude, elbow room, slack, space, room, liberty, room to spare, room to operate, scope for initiative, freedom of action, freedom from restriction, a free hand, flexibility, independence, licence, self-determination, free rein, free play, unrestrictedness, indulgence, margin, play, give, laxity, leisure; *French* carte blanche.
OPPOSITES constraint, restriction.

left ▶ adjective *my left arm* **left-hand**, sinistral; *Nautical* port; *Nautical, archaic* larboard; *Heraldry* sinister, sinistrous.
OPPOSITES right; starboard; dexter.

WORD LINKS
relating to the left **sinistral**
related prefixes **laevo- (e.g. *laevorotatory*), sinistro- (e.g. *sinistrorse*)**

left-handed ▶ adjective **1** *a left-handed golfer* sinistral; *informal* southpaw.
OPPOSITE right-handed.
2 *a left-handed compliment* **backhanded**, ambiguous, equivocal, uncertain, double-meaning, double-edged; dubious, indirect, enigmatic, cryptic, paradoxical, ironic, sardonic, insincere, hypocritical.
OPPOSITE forthright.

leftover ▶ noun **1** *she looks like a leftover from Woodstock in her flowery dress* **residue**, **survivor**, legacy, vestige, trace.
2 (**leftovers**) *she saves leftovers in a plastic container* **leavings**, **uneaten food**, remainder, unused supplies, scraps, remnants, remains, scourings, slops, crumbs, dregs; excess, surplus, overage; rejects, offcuts, tail ends, odds and ends, bits and bobs, oddments.
▶ adjective *leftover food* **remaining**, left; uneaten, unconsumed; excess, surplus, superfluous, extra, additional, unused, unwanted, spare, in reserve, excessive; residual, surviving.

left-wing ▶ adjective *a left-wing political group* **socialist**, **communist**, communistic, Bolshevik, leftist; radical, revolutionary, militant, red; progressive, liberal, reforming, social-democrat, politically correct; Labour, Labourite; Marxist, Leninist, Marxist–Leninist, Trotskyite, Maoist; *informal, derogatory* Commie, Lefty, pink, bolshie.
OPPOSITES right-wing, conservative, reactionary.

leg ▶ noun **1** *he broke his leg in a football match* **lower limb**, shank; limb, member; *technical* crus; *informal* stump, peg, pin.
2 *a gilded table leg* **upright**, support, prop, brace, underpinning, column.
3 *the first leg of a European tour* **part**, **stage**, portion, segment, section, bit, phase, stretch, lap, step, instalment; passage, subdivision, subsection, juncture.
□ **give someone a leg up** *parents want to give their kids a leg up in the world* **help/assist someone**, act as someone's support, give someone assistance, lend someone a helping hand, come to someone's aid; give someone a boost, boost, advance, raise, kick-start, give someone a flying start.
□ **on its last legs 1** *your car looked as though it was on its last legs* **dilapidated**, worn out, rickety, about to break, about to fall apart, about to collapse.
OPPOSITE in good condition.
2 *a foundry business that was on its last legs* **about to fail**, failing, about to go bankrupt, near to ruin, going to the wall; *informal* **going bust**, going down the toilet.
OPPOSITE thriving.
□ **pull someone's leg** *it's all right, Robbie, I was only pulling your leg* **tease**, rag, make fun of, chaff, trick, joke with, play a joke on, play a trick on, play a practical joke on, taunt, jest; hoax, fool, deceive, misguide, lead on, hoodwink, dupe, beguile, gull; *informal* kid, have on, rib, wind up, take for a ride, lead up the garden path, take the mickey out of, make a monkey out of; *N. Amer. informal* put on.
□ **stretch one's legs** *after two days on the bus we were glad of the chance to stretch our legs* **go for a walk**, take a walk, go for a stroll, walk, stroll, move about, promenade, get some exercise, get some air, take the air.
▶ verb
□ **leg it** (*informal*) **1** *if the dog starts growling, leg it!* **run away**, run, flee, make off, make a break for it, escape, hurry, decamp; *informal* hightail it, hotfoot it, make a run for it, make tracks, cut and run, skedaddle, vamoose, show a clean pair of heels, split, scoot, scram, hook it; *Brit. informal* scarper, do a runner, have it away (on one's toes), get cracking, get a move on.

L

OPPOSITE stay.
2 *I am part of a sales team legging it around London* **walk**, march, tramp, trek, trudge, plod, wander, ramble, go on foot; *informal* go on Shanks's pony.

WORD LINKS
relating to a leg **crural**

legacy ▸ noun **1** *a legacy from a great aunt had paid for their house* **bequest**, inheritance, heritage, bequeathal, bestowal, benefaction, endowment, gift, patrimony, heirloom, settlement, birthright, provision; *Law* devise, hereditament.
2 *the rancorous legacy of the Vietnam war | a legacy of the British Empire* **consequence**, effect, outcome, upshot, spin-off, repercussion, aftermath, by-product, product, result; residue, fruits.

legal ▸ adjective **1** *the Government possessed no legal power to close down this newspaper* **lawful**, legitimate, licit, within the law, legalized, valid; permissible, permitted, allowable, allowed, above board, admissible, acceptable; authorized, sanctioned, warranted, licensed, official, enforceable, constitutional, statutory, statutable, ex cathedra, binding, bona fide, genuine; right, proper, sound, just, fair, rightful, de jure, honest, upright; *informal* legit, kosher.
OPPOSITES illegal, criminal.
2 *the legal profession* **judicial**, juridical, jurisdictive, judicatory, forensic.

legality ▸ noun *provisions governing the legality of strikes and unions* **lawfulness**, legitimacy, legitimateness, licitness, validity, rightness, rightfulness, soundness, admissibility, admissibleness, permissibility, constitutionality; justice, fairness, justness, equity, properness.

legalize ▸ verb *a campaign to legalize marijuana* **make legal**, decriminalize, legitimize, legitimatize, legitimate, validate, ratify, permit, allow, admit, accept, authorize, sanction, warrant, license, approve, countenance, pronounce lawful, give the stamp of approval to; regularize, regulate, normalize; *informal* OK, give the go-ahead to, give the thumbs up to, give the OK to, give the green light to, say the word, give one's blessing to.
OPPOSITE prohibit.

legate ▸ noun *a papal legate* **envoy**, emissary, agent, ambassador, representative, nuncio, commissioner, commissary, delegate, proxy, surrogate, deputy, spokesperson, plenipotentiary, messenger; *Scottish* depute; *informal* go-between.

legatee ▸ noun *his will made her his sole legatee* **beneficiary**, inheritor, heir, heiress, recipient, receiver, payee, assignee; *Law* devisee, grantee; *Scottish Law* heritor.

legation ▸ noun **1** *the train carrying the British legation to Istanbul* **diplomatic mission**, mission, embassy, consulate, ministry, delegation, deputation, representation, contingent, commission; envoys, delegates, deputies, diplomats, aides.
2 *the legations in the capital were besieged* **embassy**, consulate, diplomatic establishment.

legend ▸ noun **1** *the Arthurian legends* **myth**, saga, epic, folk tale, folk story, traditional story, tale, story, fairy tale, narrative, fable, romance; folklore, lore, mythology, fantasy, oral history, tradition, folk tradition, old wives' tales; *technical* mythos, mythus; *informal* yarn.
2 *pop legends like the Beatles* **celebrity**, star, superstar, icon, famous person, great, genius, phenomenon, luminary, giant, big name; *informal* celeb, megastar.
3 *'the most distinguished address in Ireland' boasted the legend on the desk notepad* **caption**, **inscription**, dedication, motto, slogan, device, heading, head, title, wording, subtitle, subheading, rubric, colophon.
4 *the experimental conditions were as described in the legend to Figure 5* **explanation**, key, code, cipher, table of symbols, guide, glossary.

legendary ▸ adjective **1** *the legendary high kings of Ireland* **fabled**, heroic, ancient, traditional, fairy-tale, storybook, romantic, mythical, mythological.
OPPOSITES factual, historical.
2 *a legendary figure in the trade-union movement* **famous**, **celebrated**, famed, renowned, acclaimed, illustrious, esteemed, honoured, exalted, lauded, lionized, vaunted, venerable, notable, noted, well known, popular, prominent, distinguished, great, eminent, pre-eminent, outstanding, revered, glorious, remembered, immortal, unforgettable.
OPPOSITES unknown, obscure, unsung.

legerdemain ▸ noun **1** *stage magicians practising legerdemain* **sleight of hand**, juggling, conjuring, magic, prestidigitation, wizardry, illusion, dexterity; *rare* thaumaturgy.
2 *a classic piece of management legerdemain* **trickery**, cunning, artfulness, craftiness, craft, wiles, chicanery, skulduggery, deceit, deception, artifice, cheating, dissimulation, double-dealing, artful argument, specious reasoning, sophistry, humbug, flimflam; *Brit. informal* jiggery-pokery; *archaic* stratagem.

legibility ▸ noun *type design and layout clearly affect the legibility of the text* **readability**, clarity, readableness, ease of reading, decipherability, clearness, legibleness, plainness, neatness.

legible ▸ adjective *she had large, legible handwriting* **readable**, easily read, easy to read, decipherable, easily deciphered, clear, distinct, plain, carefully written, neat, sharp, vivid, intelligible, understandable, comprehensible; printed.
OPPOSITE illegible.

legion ▸ noun **1** *a Roman legion* **brigade**, regiment, battalion, company, troop, division, squadron, squad, platoon, contingent, unit, force, corps, garrison, section, group, detachment, commando, battery, band, outfit, cohort.
2 *there were legions of photographers and TV cameras* **horde**, host, throng, multitude, crowd, drove, mass, mob, rabble, gang, swarm, flock, herd, body, pack, score, mountain, army, sea, abundance, profusion.
▸ adjective *her fans, who are legion, will love it* **numerous**, countless, innumerable, incalculable, immeasurable, untold, endless, limitless, boundless, myriad, many, abundant, plentiful, thick on the ground; *informal* umpteen.

legislate ▸ verb *the parliament will have powers to legislate for Scotland's domestic affairs* **make laws**, pass laws, enact laws, formulate laws, establish laws, codify laws, ratify laws, constitutionalize, put laws in force; decree, order, ordain, prescribe, authorize, make provision, rule, lay down laws.

legislation ▸ noun **1** *it will require legislation to change this situation* **law-making**, law enactment, law formulation, codification, prescription, ratification.
2 *he demanded the repeal of anti-union legislation* **law**, body of laws, constitution, rules, rulings, regulations, acts, bills, statutes, enactments, charters, ordinances, measures, canon, code; jurisprudence.

legislative ▸ adjective *a legislative assembly* **law-making**, law-giving, judicial, juridical, jurisdictive, parliamentary, congressional, senatorial, deliberative, governmental, policy-making, administrative; *rare* legislatorial.

legislator ▸ noun **lawmaker**, lawgiver, parliamentarian, politician, representative, minister, statesman, stateswoman; (*in the UK*) Member of Parliament, MP; (*in the US*) congressman, congresswoman, senator.

legitimate ▸ adjective **1** *they have been given permission to run gambling halls, the only legitimate gambling in the area* **legal**, lawful, licit, legalized, authorized, permitted, permissible, allowable, allowed, admissible, recognized, sanctioned, approved, licensed, statutory, constitutional, within the law, going by the rules, above board, valid, honest, upright; *informal* legit, by the book.
OPPOSITES illegal, illegitimate.
2 *the legitimate heir* **rightful**, lawful, genuine, authentic, real, true, proper, correct, authorized, sanctioned, warranted, acknowledged, recognized, approved, just; *informal* legit, kosher, pukka.
OPPOSITES false, fraudulent.
3 *these are legitimate grounds for unease* **valid**, sound, admissible, acceptable, well founded, justifiable, reasonable, sensible, tenable, defensible, supportable, just, warrantable, fair, bona fide, proper, genuine, plausible, credible, believable, reliable, understandable, logical, rational.
OPPOSITES invalid, unjustifiable.

legitimize ▸ verb *the formal recognition of a union legitimizes workers' resistance to intimidation* **validate**, legitimate, permit, warrant, authorize, sanction, license, give the stamp of approval to, condone, justify, vindicate, endorse, approve, support, sustain; legalize, pronounce lawful, declare legal, decriminalize, normalize.
OPPOSITE outlaw.

leisure ▸ noun *whenever Paul had leisure he worked on the manuscript | the trade-off between leisure and work* **free time**, spare time, spare moments, time to spare, idle hours, time off, freedom, holiday, vacation, breathing space, breathing spell, respite, relief, ease, peace, quiet; **recreation**, relaxation, inactivity, amusement, entertainment, pleasure, diversion, distraction, fun, games, fun and games; *informal* time to kill, R and R.
OPPOSITE work.
□ **at your leisure** *wander at your leisure through the wide selection of shops* **at your convenience**, when it suits you, in your own (good) time, when you can fit it in, without need for haste, without haste, unhurriedly, without hurry, when you get round to it, when you want to; in due course.

leisurely ▸ adjective *the journey was taken at a leisurely pace | a leisurely stroll* **unhurried**, relaxed, unrushed, easy, easy-going, gentle, sedate, comfortable, restful, effortless, undemanding, slow, lazy, lackadaisical, languid, languorous, lingering; measured, steady; *informal* laid-back.
OPPOSITES brisk, hurried.

lemur ▸ noun. *See centre pages for list of* **Lemurs and Other Prosimians**

lend ▸ verb **1** *I'll lend you my towel* **loan**, give someone the loan of, let someone use, let someone have the use of; **advance**; *Brit. informal* sub.
OPPOSITES borrow; withhold.
2 *these examples lend weight to his assertions* **add**, impart, give, bestow, confer, provide, grant, supply, furnish, accord, offer, contribute, afford, bring, donate.
OPPOSITE detract.

L

□ **lend an ear listen**, keep one's ears open, prick up one's ears; **pay attention**, take notice, be attentive, attend, concentrate, heed, pay heed, give ear, give one's undivided attention; *informal* be all ears, pin back one's ears; *archaic* hearken.
□ **lend a hand** *an agricultural student who had come to lend a hand with the harvest* **help**, help out, give a helping hand, assist, give assistance, aid, make a contribution, do someone a favour, take part, do one's bit; cooperate; *informal* pitch in, muck in, get stuck in, get involved.
□ **lend itself to** *the landscape does not lend itself to long-distance walking or riding* **be suitable for**, be suited to, be appropriate for, be adaptable to, have the right characteristics for, be applicable for, be easily used for, be readily used for, be serviceable for.

length ▶ noun **1** *some of these amphibians grew to a length of three or four metres | from the plane she was able to see the whole length of the valley* **extent**, extent lengthwise, distance, distance lengthwise, linear measure, span, reach; area, expanse, stretch, range, scope.
2 *there has been a tremendous increase in the length of time spent on remand* **period**, **duration**, stretch, term, span.
3 *a length of pale blue silk* **piece**, swatch, portion, section, measure, segment, roll.
4 *MPs criticized the length of the speech* **protractedness**, lengthiness, extent, extensiveness, elongation; prolixity, prolixness, wordiness, verbosity, verboseness, long-windedness.
OPPOSITES conciseness, brevity.
□ **at length 1** *he spoke at length of his suitability for the job* **for a long time**, for ages, for hours, on and on, interminably, endlessly, incessantly, ceaselessly, constantly, continually, unendingly, eternally, forever.
OPPOSITE briefly.
2 *when questioned at length he insisted he had no links with terrorists* **thoroughly**, fully, in detail, in depth, comprehensively, exhaustively, completely, extensively, to the fullest extent.
3 *his search had led him, at length, to the headquarters in Seattle* **after a long time**, after a considerable time, eventually, in time, in the long run, in the fullness of time; finally, at last, at long last, lastly, in the end, ultimately, in conclusion.
OPPOSITES immediately, straight away.
□ **go to any length(s)** *they'll go to any lengths to obtain money to buy drugs* **do absolutely anything**, go to any extreme, go to any limits, observe no limits.

lengthen ▶ verb **1** *he followed her, lengthening his stride to keep up* **elongate**, make longer, stretch out, extend; expand, widen, broaden, enlarge.
OPPOSITE shorten.
2 *they flower in the spring when the days are lengthening* **grow longer**, get longer, draw out, stretch.
OPPOSITES contract, decrease.
3 *you'll need to lengthen the cooking time* **prolong**, make longer, increase, extend, expand, protract, stretch out, draw out, drag out, spin out.
OPPOSITES curtail, truncate.

lengthy ▶ adjective **1** *a lengthy civil war* **long**, very long, of considerable length, long-lasting, prolonged, extended, extensive.
OPPOSITE short.
2 *the board held lengthy discussions on the report* **protracted**, very long, overlong, long-drawn-out; diffuse, discursive, verbose, wordy, garrulous, prolix, long-winded, ponderous, digressive, rambling, dragged out; **tedious**, boring, interminable, wearisome.
OPPOSITES brief, concise.

leniency, lenience ▶ noun *the judge rejected pleas for greater leniency* **mercifulness**, mercy, clemency, lenity, forgiveness; tolerance, forbearance, moderateness, lack of severity, moderation, humanity, charity, indulgence, gentleness, mildness, sufferance, acceptance; pity, sympathy, compassion, understanding, concern, consideration, kindness, kind-heartedness, benevolence; soft-heartedness, permissiveness, liberality, liberalness.
OPPOSITES mercilessness, strictness, severity.

lenient ▶ adjective *the courts may be more lenient with female offenders* **merciful**, clement, sparing, forgiving, forbearing, tolerant, moderate, charitable, humane, indulgent, easy-going, magnanimous, sympathetic, compassionate, pitying, kind, kindly, kind-hearted, benevolent, gentle; liberal, permissive, soft, soft-hearted.
OPPOSITES merciless, severe, strict.

lens ▶ noun. *See centre pages for list of* **Lens Shapes**

leper ▶ noun *a social leper* **outcast**, social outcast, pariah, untouchable, undesirable, exile, reject, non-person, unperson, persona non grata.

leprechaun ▶ noun **pixie**, **goblin**, elf, sprite, fairy, gnome, imp, brownie, puck, devil; (**leprechauns**) the little people.

lesbian ▶ noun **homosexual woman**, gay woman; *W. Indian* zami; *informal* les, lesbo, butch, femme; *derogatory, informal* lezzy, dyke, bulldyke; *rare* tribade.
OPPOSITE heterosexual.
▶ adjective **homosexual**, gay; *informal* les, lesbo, butch; *derogatory, informal* lezzy, dykey, queer, bent; *rare* tribadic.
OPPOSITES heterosexual, straight.

lesion ▶ noun *he lost a lot of weight and the purple-black lesions on his skin began to spread* **wound**, injury, bruise, abrasion, contusion, scratch, scrape, cut, gash, laceration, tear, puncture; ulcer, ulceration, sore, running sore, abscess, carbuncle, canker; mark; *technical* trauma.

less ▶ pronoun *the fare is less than £1* **a smaller amount**; not so much as, not as much as, under, below.
OPPOSITE more.
▶ determiner *there was less noise now in the town* **not so much**, not so great, smaller, slighter, shorter, reduced; fewer.
OPPOSITE more.
▶ adverb *we must consider the alternatives available so we can use the car less* **to a lesser degree**, to a smaller extent, not so much, not as much; rarely, barely, little, not much.
OPPOSITE more.
▶ preposition *normally the buyer purchases at list price less 10 per cent* **minus**, subtracting, excepting, without, lacking.
OPPOSITE plus.

> **less or fewer?**
> In standard English, **less** should be used only with mass nouns, as in *I have less money than I thought*, or with numbers or expressions of time, as in *less than three weeks*. With countable nouns, **fewer** should be used, as in *customers with fewer than five items*.

lessen ▶ verb **1** *exercise lessens the risk of coronary heart disease* **reduce**, **make less**, minimize, make smaller, decrease; allay, assuage, alleviate, attenuate, palliate, ease, dull, deaden, blunt, take the edge off, moderate, mitigate, check, dampen, depress, soften, tone down, dilute, relax, mollify, temper, weaken, tame, erode; narrow, lower, discount; curtail, prune, pare down, truncate; *informal* slash.
OPPOSITES increase, magnify.
2 *the pain in his chest began to lessen* **grow less**, get less, grow smaller, decrease, diminish, decline, subside, abate, moderate; fade, die down/off, let up, ease off, tail off, drop, drop off/away, fall, dwindle, taper off, peter out, go/come down, shrink, contract; ebb, wane, erode, waste away, flag, attenuate, slacken, lighten, quieten, recede, relent, remit, desist; sink, slump, plummet; *informal* nosedive.
OPPOSITES increase, grow.
3 *his behaviour lessened him in their eyes* **diminish**, lower, reduce, minimize, degrade, discredit, devalue, belittle, humble.
OPPOSITES aggrandize, make more important.

lesser ▶ adjective **1** *a lesser offence* **less important**, minor, secondary, subsidiary, marginal, ancillary, auxiliary, supplementary, supplemental, peripheral; inferior, slighter, insignificant, unimportant, petty; lower, lower-level, lower-grade, second-rate.
OPPOSITES greater, primary.
2 *you look down your nose at us lesser mortals* **subordinate**, minor, inferior, second-class, subservient, lowly, humble, servile, menial, mean; junior.
OPPOSITE superior.

lesson ▶ noun **1** *a maths lesson* **class**, session, seminar, tutorial, lecture, period; period of instruction, period of teaching, period of coaching, period of tutoring, period of schooling.
2 *they should be industrious at their lessons* **exercise**, assignment, school task, drill; (**lessons**) school work, homework.
3 *she would always volunteer to read the lesson in assembly* **Bible reading**, Bible passage, scripture, text, reading.
4 *Stuart's accident should be a lesson to all parents* **warning**, deterrent, caution; example, exemplar; message, moral, precept.
5 (**lessons**) *it was a tough time, and it taught her some hard lessons* **knowledge**, wisdom, enlightenment, experience, truths.

lest ▶ conjunction *he cut the remark out of the final programme lest it should offend listeners* **in case**, just in case, for fear that, in order to avoid, to avoid the risk of.

let ▶ verb **1** *let him sleep for now* **allow**, permit, give permission to, give leave to, authorize, sanction, grant, grant the right to, warrant, license, empower, enable, entitle; assent to, consent to, agree to, acquiesce in, accede to, approve of, tolerate, countenance, suffer, brook, admit of, give one's blessing to, give assent to; cause, make; *informal* give the green light to, give the go-ahead to, give the thumbs up to, give someone/something the nod, say the magic word, OK.
OPPOSITES prevent, prohibit.
2 *Wilcox pushed open the door to let her through* **allow to go**, permit to pass; make way for.
3 *they hired an agent to let their flat* **rent out**, let out, rent, lease, hire, hire out, loan, give on loan, sublet, sublease, farm out, contract, charge for the use of.
□ **let someone down** *it's his players who have let the team down* **fail**, fail to support, fall short of expectation; **disappoint**, disillusion, disenchant; abandon, desert, leave stranded, leave in the lurch, leave high and dry,

L

betray, neglect, jilt; stab in the back; *N. Amer. informal* bail on; *archaic* forsake.
OPPOSITES support, satisfy; do one's bit.

□ **let something down** *I put on a skirt which Sylvie had let down for me* **lengthen**, make longer.
OPPOSITE take up.

□ **let fly 1** *he let fly with a brick* **hurl**, fling, throw, propel, pitch, lob, toss, launch, cast, shy, project, catapult, bowl; shoot, fire, blast, discharge; *informal* chuck, sling, heave.
2 *she let fly at Geoffrey* **lose one's temper with**, lash out at, scold, criticize, condemn, chastise, chide, rant at, inveigh against, rail against, abuse, revile; explode, burst out, erupt with anger, let someone have it, give free rein to one's emotions, keep nothing back, give vent to one's emotions; *informal* carpet, give someone a rocket, tear someone off a strip, tear into; *rare* excoriate.

□ **let go** *apply the brakes before you let go of the pushchair* **release**, release one's hold on, loose/loosen one's hold on, relinquish, unhand, surrender, give up.
OPPOSITE hold tight.

□ **let someone go** *I was upset about letting him go, but he assured me he'd find another job* **make redundant**, dismiss, discharge, lay off, give notice to, pay off, remove, release; *informal* sack, give someone the sack, fire, give someone their cards, give someone their marching orders, send packing, give someone the boot, give someone the bullet, give someone the push, give someone the (old) heave-ho, boot out, axe.
OPPOSITE retain.

□ **let someone in** *a young lady came to open the gate and let me in* **allow to enter**, allow in, admit, take in, open the door to, grant entrance to, give access to, allow entry to, permit entry to, give right of entry to; receive, welcome, greet, accept.
OPPOSITE refuse admission to.

□ **let someone in on something** *he asked to be let in on the joke* **include**, count in, admit; **allow to share in**, let participate in, take in, inform about, tell about, bring up to date about.

□ **let something off** *some members of the family let off fireworks in the background* **detonate**, discharge, explode, set off, fire off.

□ **let someone off 1** *I'll let you off this time, but don't try a trick like that again* **pardon**, forgive, grant an amnesty to; release, discharge; deal leniently with, be lenient on/to, be merciful to, show mercy to, have mercy on; acquit, absolve, exonerate, clear, exculpate, vindicate; let bygones be bygones, bear no malice, harbour no grudge, bury the hatchet; *informal* let someone off the hook, go easy on.
2 *he let me off work for the day* **excuse from**, relieve from, exempt from, spare from.

□ **let on** (*informal*) **1** *I never let on that Uncle Joe made me feel anxious* **reveal**, make known, tell, disclose, mention, divulge, let out, let slip, give away, leak, proclaim, blurt out, expose, bring to light, uncover, make public; blab; *informal* let the cat out of the bag, give the game away, sing, squeal.
OPPOSITES conceal, keep quiet about.
2 *they all let on they didn't hear me* **pretend**, feign, affect, make out, make believe, simulate, fake.

□ **let something out 1** *I let out a cry of triumph* **utter**, emit, give vent to, produce, give, issue, express, air, voice, verbalize, release, pour out, come out with.
OPPOSITE suppress.
2 *she let out that he'd given her a lift home* **reveal**, make known, tell, disclose, mention, divulge, let slip, give away, let it be known, leak, blurt out, expose, bring to light, uncover, make public, blab.
OPPOSITE keep quiet about.

□ **let someone out** *they should never have let Carolyn out of hospital like that* **release**, liberate, free, set free, let go, discharge; set/turn/let loose, allow to leave, open the door for, grant exit to; uncage, unfetter, unshackle.
OPPOSITE imprison.

□ **let up** (*informal*) **1** *the rain had let up, so we walked* **abate**, lessen, decrease, diminish, subside, moderate, decline, relent, slacken, die down/off, ease (off), tail off, taper off, drop off/away, peter out; ebb, wane, dwindle, fade, quieten (down), calm (down), weaken; stop, cease, finish, come to a stop, come to an end, terminate.
OPPOSITE continue.
2 *you never let up, do you?* **relax one's efforts**, relax, ease up/off, do less, slow down; **pause**, break (off), take a break, take a breath; adjourn, desist, rest, hold back, stop; *informal* take a breather.
3 *I promised you I'd let up on him* **treat less severely**, be more lenient with, be kinder to; *informal* go easy on.
OPPOSITE treat harshly.

let-down ▶ **noun** *it's a big let-down when bonfire parties fizzle out* **disappointment**, disillusionment, anticlimax, comedown, non-success, non-event, fiasco, setback, frustration, blow; *informal* washout, damp squib.
OPPOSITES triumph, climax.

lethal ▶ **adjective** *a lethal weapon | those pills were lethal* **fatal**, deadly, mortal, causing death, death-dealing, life-threatening, murderous, homicidal, killing, terminal, final, incurable; poisonous, toxic, virulent, noxious, venomous; dangerous, destructive, harmful, pernicious, malignant, disastrous, calamitous, ruinous; *literary* deathly, nocuous, mephitic; *archaic* baneful.
OPPOSITES harmless, safe.

lethargic ▶ **adjective** *she became depressed and lethargic* **sluggish**, inert, inactive, slow, torpid, lifeless, dull; **languid**, listless, lazy, idle, indolent, shiftless, slothful, phlegmatic, apathetic, passive, weary, tired, fatigued, sleepy, drowsy, enervated, somnolent, narcotic.
OPPOSITES vigorous, energetic, animated.

> **CHOOSE THE RIGHT WORD**
>
> **lethargic, languid, listless**
>
> *See* LANGUID.

lethargy ▶ **noun** *with an effort, Miles shook off the lethargy that had been creeping over him since his wife's death* **sluggishness**, inertia, inactivity, inaction, slowness, torpor, torpidity, lifelessness, dullness, listlessness, languor, languidness, stagnation, laziness, idleness, indolence, shiftlessness, sloth, phlegm, apathy, passivity, ennui, weariness, tiredness, lassitude, fatigue, sleepiness, drowsiness, enervation, somnolence, narcosis; *rare* hebetude.
OPPOSITES vigour, energy, animation.

letter *See centre pages for lists of* **Letters (Correspondence)** **Letters of the Alphabet (Greek and Hebrew)**
▶ **noun 1** *a gold chain which spelled out Zara in half-inch letters* **alphabetical character**, character, sign, symbol, mark, type, figure, device, rune; *technical* grapheme.
2 *she received a letter from the king* **written message**, message, written communication, communication, note, line, missive, epistle, dispatch, report, bulletin; correspondence, news, information, intelligence, word; post, mail.
3 (**letters**) *a man of letters* **learning**, scholarship, erudition, education, knowledge, book learning, academic training; intellect, intelligence, enlightenment, illumination, wisdom, sagacity, culture, cultivation; literature, books, humanities, belles-lettres.

□ **to the letter** *he followed her instructions to the letter* **strictly**, precisely, exactly, accurately, closely, faithfully, religiously, punctiliously, literally, with a literal interpretation, with strict attention to detail, word for word, letter for letter, verbatim, in every detail, by the book.
OPPOSITES in general terms, approximately.

WORD LINKS

relating to alphabetical letters	**literal**
relating to letters (correspondence)	**epistolary**

lettered ▶ **adjective** *my mother was not a lettered woman, but she knew the importance of a good education* **learned**, erudite, academic, well educated, educated, literate, well read, widely read, knowledgeable, intellectual, schooled, well schooled, enlightened, illuminated, sophisticated, accomplished, versed, cultured, cultivated, civilized, scholarly, scholastic, literary, bookish, highbrow, studious; *informal* brainy.
OPPOSITES ignorant, ill-educated.

let-up ▶ **noun** (*informal*) *there can be no let-up in the war against drugs* **abatement**, lessening, decrease, diminishing, diminution, subsidence, moderation, decline, relenting, remission, slackening, weakening, relaxation, dying down, easing off, tailing off, tapering off, dropping away/off, ebbing, waning, dwindling; respite, break, interval, hiatus, suspension, cessation, stop, pause, breathing space, lull, interlude, intermission.
OPPOSITES continuation, escalation.

level ▶ **adjective 1** *these wallcoverings need to be hung on a smooth and level surface* **flat**, smooth, even, uniform, plane, flush, plumb, regular, true; (as) flat as a pancake; perfectly horizontal; perfectly vertical.
OPPOSITES uneven, bumpy.
2 *he did his best to keep his voice level* **unchanging**, steady, unvarying, stable, even, uniform, regular, consistent, constant; invariable, unalterable, unaltering, unfluctuating; calm, unemotional, composed, equable, unruffled, serene, tranquil.
OPPOSITES unsteady, shaky.
3 *he missed a penalty when the scores were level | just four minutes later Spurs were level* **equal**, even, drawn, tied, balanced, all square, on a level, in a position of equality; close together, neck and neck, level pegging, nip and tuck, side by side, on a par, evenly matched, with nothing to choose between them; *informal* even-steven(s).
OPPOSITES unequal, uneven.
4 *his eyes were level with hers* **aligned**, on the same level as, on a level, at the same height as, in line, balanced; abreast, side by side.
OPPOSITES above, below, uneven.
▶ **noun 1** *the post, which is at research-officer level, will be for two years* **rank**, standing, status, position; echelon, station, degree, grade, gradation, stage, standard, rung, point, mark, step; class, stratum, group, grouping, set, classification; level of achievement, degree of competence.
2 *they allowed a high level of employment* **quantity**, **amount**, extent,

measure, degree, volume, size; magnitude, intensity, pitch, strength; proportion.
3 *the lock is being opened so that the level of water is raised allowing a boat to pass through* **height**, highness, altitude, elevation, distance upward.
4 *the museum tour begins on the sixth level and continues on the floors above* **floor**, storey, tier, deck.
□ **on the level** (*informal*) **genuine**, straight, honest, above board, fair, true, legitimate, sincere, straightforward, proper, honest-to-goodness; *informal* upfront, kosher; *N. Amer. informal* on the up and up.
OPPOSITE dishonest.
▶ **verb 1** *tilt the tin to level the mixture* **make level**, level out, level off, make even, even off, even out, make flat, flatten, smooth, smooth out, plane, make uniform, make regular, regularize; polish, face.
2 *terrorists could have levelled the base* **raze**, raze to the ground, demolish, flatten, gut, topple, lay waste, destroy, wipe out, blow up, blow to bits, bomb; tear down, knock down, pull down, bring down, bulldoze, fell, dismantle, break up, wreck, pulverize, obliterate.
OPPOSITES raise, build.
3 *he levelled his opponent with a single blow* **knock down**, knock to the ground, throw to the ground, lay out, prostrate, flatten, floor, fell, knock out; *informal* KO, kayo.
4 *Carl levelled the score with an ice-cool goal* **equalize**, make equal, equal, even, even up, make level.
5 *he levelled his pistol at me* **aim**, point, direct, train, sight, focus, turn, beam, zero in on, draw a bead on; take aim.
6 *I knew you'd level with me sooner or later* **be frank**, be open, be honest, be above board, tell the truth, tell all, hide nothing, keep nothing back, be straightforward, put all one's cards on the table; *informal* be upfront.
WORD LINKS
related prefix **plano-** (e.g. ***planographic, planoconcave***)

level-headed ▶ **adjective sensible**, practical, realistic, prudent, circumspect, pragmatic, wise, reasonable, rational, mature, commonsensical, full of common sense, judicious, sound, sober, businesslike, no-nonsense, sane, composed, calm, cool, collected, {cool, calm, and collected}, serene, relaxed, at ease, confident, well balanced, equable, moderate, unworried, unmoved, unemotional, cool-headed, hard-headed, balanced, self-possessed, unruffled, even-tempered, imperturbable, reliable, dependable, with one's feet on the ground; *informal* unflappable, together.
OPPOSITE excitable.

lever ▶ **noun 1** *you can insert a lever and prise the rail off* **crowbar**, bar, handspike, jemmy; crank, arm, shaft, spindle, crankshaft.
2 *he pulled the lever which unlocked the bonnet* **handle**, grip, pull, switch, joystick, key, knob.
▶ **verb** *he found a crowbar and levered the cottage door open | they levered the inert body up* **prise**, force, wrench, pull, wrest, twist, rip, strain, tug, jerk, heave, move, shift, dislodge, jemmy; **raise**, lift, hoist, haul; *N. Amer.* pry, jimmy.

leverage ▶ **noun 1** *the long handles provide increased leverage* **grip**, purchase, hold, grasp; contact, attachment, support, anchorage, force, strength; resistance, friction.
2 *the high levels of unionization gave workers significant leverage in workplace negotiations* **influence**, power, authority, weight, sway, control, say, ascendancy, dominance, advantage, pressure, edge, standing, prestige, rank; *informal* pull, clout, muscle, teeth, beef.

levitate ▶ **noun** *the casket suddenly levitated a metre above the ground* **float**, rise into the air, rise, hover, be suspended, glide, waft, drift, hang, defy gravity, fly, soar up.

levity ▶ **noun 1** *he did much to inject a note of levity into a very hard-working production cycle* **light-heartedness**, carefreeness, light-mindedness, high spirits, vivacity, liveliness, conviviality, cheerfulness, cheeriness, humour, gaiety, fun, jocularity, hilarity, frivolity, frivolousness, amusement, mirth, laughter, merriment, glee, comedy, funniness, wit, wittiness, jollity, joviality, joking, drollery, good cheer, sportiveness, nonsense, irreverence, facetiousness, flippancy, blitheness, triviality, silliness, foolishness, childishness, giddiness, skittishness.
OPPOSITES seriousness, gravity.
2 *he was distressed by the levity of her nature* **fickleness**, inconstancy, instability, unsteadiness, variability, changeability, unreliability, undependability, inconsistency, flightiness.
OPPOSITE constancy.

levy ▶ **verb 1** *a proposal to levy VAT on fuel* **impose**, charge, exact, demand, raise, collect, gather; tax; *rare* mulct.
2 (*archaic*) *they levied troops for less grand operations* **conscript**, call up, enlist, mobilize, rally, muster, marshal, press, recruit, raise, assemble, round up; *N. Amer.* draft.
OPPOSITES demobilize, disband.
▶ **noun 1** *the troubles had been caused by the levy of taxation for the defence of the realm* **imposition**, charging, exaction, raising, collection, gathering.
2 *the record industry's call for a levy on blank audio tapes* **tax**, tariff, toll, excise, duty, fee, imposition, impost, exaction, assessment, tithe, payment; *rare* mulct; (**levies**) taxation, customs, dues.
3 (usually **levies**) (*archaic*) *these were not shire levies, but professional soldiers* **conscripts**, troops, forces, armed forces, army, militia, guard.

lewd ▶ **adjective 1** *a lewd old man* **lecherous**, lustful, licentious, lascivious, dirty, prurient, salacious, lubricious, libidinous; immoral, impure, debauched, depraved, degenerate, unchaste, wanton, of easy virtue, decadent, disgusting, dissipated, dissolute, corrupt, perverted, sinful, wicked; bestial, goatish, wolfish; *informal* horny; *Brit. informal* randy; *rare* concupiscent, lickerish.
OPPOSITE chaste.
2 *a lewd limerick* **vulgar**, crude, smutty, dirty, filthy, obscene, pornographic, coarse, tasteless, indecorous, indelicate, off colour, unseemly, indecent, salacious, gross, disgusting, sordid, low, foul, vile; rude, racy, risqué, naughty, wicked, arousing, earthy, erotic, sexy, suggestive, titillating, spicy, bawdy, ribald, raw, taboo, explicit, near the bone, near the knuckle; *informal* blue, raunchy, X-rated, nudge-nudge, porno; *euphemistic* adult.
OPPOSITES decent, clean.

lexicon ▶ **noun dictionary**, wordbook, vocabulary list, glossary, word-finder; reference book, phrase book, concordance, thesaurus, encyclopedia.

liability ▶ **noun 1** *journalists cannot avoid liability for defamation merely by avoiding the naming of names* **accountability**, **responsibility**, legal responsibility, answerability; incrimination, blame, blameworthiness, culpability, guilt, onus, fault; *informal* the rap.
OPPOSITE immunity.
2 *they have some huge assets and some equally big liabilities* **financial obligation**, debt, indebtedness, debit; (**liabilities**) **debts**, arrears, dues.
OPPOSITE asset.
3 *she had come to be seen as an electoral liability* **hindrance**, encumbrance, burden, handicap, nuisance, inconvenience; obstacle, impediment, drawback, drag, disadvantage, weakness, shortcoming, problem, weak spot/point; millstone round one's neck, stumbling block, cross to bear, cross, albatross; Achilles heel; *informal* minus, fly in the ointment; *archaic* cumber.
OPPOSITES asset, advantage.
4 *their liability to the disease* **susceptibility**, vulnerability, proneness, tendency, predisposition, propensity; risk, chance, likelihood, threat.
OPPOSITE immunity.

liable ▶ **adjective 1** *he held the defendants liable for negligence* **responsible**, legally responsible, accountable, answerable, chargeable, blameworthy, at fault, culpable, subject, guilty, faulty, censurable.
OPPOSITES exempt, unaccountable.
2 *my income is liable to fluctuate wildly* **likely**, inclined, tending, disposed, apt, predisposed, prone, given; *informal* on the cards.
OPPOSITE unlikely.
3 *you are more **liable to** injury when you exercise infrequently* **exposed**, open, prone, subject, susceptible, vulnerable, in danger of, at risk of, at the mercy of.
OPPOSITES immune; above.

liaise ▶ **verb** *social services liaised with the police* **cooperate**, work together, collaborate; **communicate**, intercommunicate, exchange information, network, interface, link up, hook up.

liaison ▶ **noun 1** *the Bank of England works in very close liaison with the Treasury* **cooperation**, contact, association, connection, collaboration; communication, interchange, affiliation, alliance, partnership, link, linkage, tie-up, hook-up.
2 *Dave was my White House liaison and all-round troubleshooter* **intermediary**, mediator, middleman, contact, contact man/woman/person, link, linkman, linkwoman, linkperson, go-between, representative, agent, interceder, factor.
3 *she abandoned her loyalty to her absent husband in favour of a liaison with William* **love affair**, affair, relationship, romance, attachment, fling, intrigue, amour, affair of the heart, involvement, amorous entanglement, romantic entanglement, entanglement; flirtation, dalliance; *informal* hanky-panky; *Brit. informal* bit on the side, carry-on.

liar ▶ **noun deceiver**, fibber, falsifier, teller of lies, teller of untruths, perjurer, false witness, fabricator, equivocator, prevaricator, spinner of yarns; romancer, fabulist; *informal* storyteller; *rare* fibster.
WORD LINKS
compulsive liar **mythomaniac**

libation ▶ **noun 1** *dressed in their priestly robes, they pour libations into the holy well* **liquid offering**, offering, tribute, dedication, oblation; sacrifice.
2 (*humorous*) *would Madame honour me with her company for a small libation?* **drink**, beverage, alcoholic drink, liquid refreshment, bracer; dram, draught, nip, tot, swallow, sip, gulp; *informal* swig, tincture, tipple; *archaic* potation.

libel ▶ **noun** *she sued two national newspapers for libel | a company's reputation could be injured by a libel* **defamation**, defamation of character, character assassination, calumny, misrepresentation, scandalmongering; aspersions, denigration, vilification, disparagement, derogation, insult, slander, malicious gossip, tittle-tattle, traducement; lie, slur, smear,

L

untruth, false insinuation, false report, smear campaign, slight, innuendo, rumour; *informal* mud-slinging; *N. Amer. informal* bad-mouthing; *archaic* contumely.

▶ **verb** *she alleged the magazine had libelled her* **defame**, malign, slander, give someone a bad name, blacken someone's name, sully someone's reputation, speak ill/evil of, write false reports about, traduce, smear, cast aspersions on, fling mud at, drag someone's name through the mud/mire, besmirch, tarnish, taint, do a hatchet job on, tell lies about, spread tales about, spread scandal about, stain, vilify, calumniate, denigrate, disparage, run down, derogate, stigmatize, discredit, slight; *N. Amer.* slur; *rare* asperse.

> **CHOOSE THE RIGHT WORD**
>
> **libel, slander, malign, defame, traduce**
>
> *See* MALIGN.

libellous ▶ **adjective** *we reserve the right to edit correspondence and to remove potentially libellous statements* **defamatory**, denigratory, vilifying, disparaging, derogatory, aspersive, calumnious, calumniatory, slanderous, false, untrue, misrepresentative, traducing, maligning, insulting, scurrilous, slurring, smearing; *informal* mud-slinging, muckraking.

liberal ▶ **adjective 1** *the values of a liberal society* **tolerant**, unprejudiced, unbigoted, broad-minded, open-minded, enlightened, forbearing; **permissive**, free, free and easy, easy-going, laissez-faire, libertarian, latitudinarian, unbiased, impartial, non-partisan, indulgent, lenient, lax, soft.
OPPOSITES narrow-minded, bigoted.
2 *he launched a liberal social agenda* **progressive**, advanced, modern, forward-looking, forward-thinking, progressivist, go-ahead, enlightened, reformist, radical; left-wing, leftist, freethinking, politically correct, PC; *informal* right-on.
OPPOSITES conservative, reactionary.
3 *the provision of liberal adult education* **wide-ranging**, broad-based, general, humanistic.
4 *a liberal interpretation of divorce laws* **flexible**, broad, loose, rough, non-restrictive, free, general, non-literal, non-specific, not literal, not strict, not close; inexact, imprecise, vague, indefinite, ill-defined, unrigorous, unmeticulous.
OPPOSITES strict, to the letter.
5 *liberal coatings of paint* **abundant**, copious, ample, plentiful, generous, lavish, luxuriant, profuse, considerable, prolific, rich; galore; excessive, immoderate, superabundant, overabundant; *informal* over the top; *literary* plenteous.
OPPOSITE scant.
6 *they had been liberal with their cash* **generous**, magnanimous, open-handed, unsparing, unstinting, ungrudging, lavish, free, munificent, bountiful, beneficent, benevolent, big-hearted, kind-hearted, kind, philanthropic, charitable, altruistic, unselfish; extravagant, overgenerous, generous to a fault, immoderate, wasteful, overabundant, profligate, prodigal, thriftless, improvident, intemperate, unrestrained, wild; *informal* over the top; *literary* bounteous.
OPPOSITES miserly, careful.

L

liberate ▶ **verb** *Lincoln's proclamation liberating the slaves* **set free**, free, release, let out, let go, discharge, set/let loose, deliver, save, rescue, extricate; unshackle, unfetter, unchain, untie, unmanacle, unbind, unyoke; emancipate, enfranchise, give rights to; ransom; *historical* manumit; *rare* disenthral.
OPPOSITES confine; enslave, subjugate.

liberation ▶ **noun 1** *the liberation of prisoners* **freeing**, release, discharge, deliverance, salvation, rescue, relief, extrication, setting free; loosing, unloosing, unshackling, unfettering, unchaining, untying, unbinding; freedom, liberty; emancipation; ransom; *French* laissez-aller; *historical* manumission; *rare* disenthralment.
OPPOSITES confinement; slavery, subjugation.
2 *the battle for women's liberation* **freedom**, **equality**, equal rights, non-discrimination, emancipation, enfranchisement, independence.
OPPOSITE oppression.

liberator ▶ **noun rescuer**, saviour, deliverer, freer, emancipator, messiah, champion, knight in shining armour, Good Samaritan; *historical* manumitter.
OPPOSITES enslaver, oppressor.

libertine ▶ **noun** *'Don Giovanni' ends with the unrepentant libertine being dragged down to hell by demons* **philanderer**, ladies' man, playboy, rake, roué, loose-liver, Don Juan, Lothario, Casanova, Romeo; **lecher**, seducer, womanizer, adulterer, debauchee, sensualist, voluptuary, hedonist; profligate, wanton, reprobate, degenerate; *informal* stud, skirt-chaser, ladykiller, lech, wolf; *dated* rip, blood, gay dog; *archaic* fornicator.
OPPOSITE puritan.

▶ **adjective** *they were careful to insist that free love was not to be confused with libertine sexual intercourse* **licentious**, lustful, libidinous, lecherous, lascivious, lubricious, dissolute, dissipated, debauched, immoral, wanton, shameless, degenerate, depraved, debased, profligate, promiscuous, unchaste, lewd, prurient, salacious, indecent, immodest, impure, carnal, intemperate, abandoned, unrestrained, unprincipled, reprobate; rakish, decadent, sensual, voluptuary, hedonistic; *informal* loose, fast, goatish, randy, horny, raunchy; *rare* concupiscent, lickerish.
OPPOSITES chaste, puritanical.

liberty ▶ **noun 1** *individuals should enjoy the liberty to pursue their own interests and preferences* **freedom**, independence, free rein, freeness, licence, self-determination; free will, latitude, option, choice; volition, non-compulsion, non-coercion, non-confinement; leeway, margin, scope, elbow room.
OPPOSITES constraint.
2 *parliamentary government is the essence of British liberty* **independence**, freedom, autonomy, sovereignty, self government, self rule, self determination, home rule; civil liberties, civil rights, human rights; *rare* autarky.
OPPOSITE dependence, subjugation.
3 *no man who was born free would be contented to be penned up and denied the liberty to go where he pleases* **right**, birthright, opportunity, facility, prerogative, entitlement, privilege, permission, sanction, leave, consent, authorization, authority, licence, clearance, blessing, dispensation, exemption, faculty; *French* carte blanche.
OPPOSITE constraint.

□ **at liberty 1** *he was at liberty for three months before he was recaptured* **free**, **on the loose**, loose, set loose, at large, unconfined, roaming; unbound, untied, unchained, unshackled, unfettered, unrestrained, unrestricted, wild, untrammelled; escaped, out; *informal* sprung.
OPPOSITES in captivity; imprisoned.
2 *your great aunt was at liberty to divide her estate how she chose* **free**, **permitted**, allowed, authorized, able, entitled, eligible, fit; unconstrained, unrestricted, unhindered, without constraint.
OPPOSITE forbidden.

□ **take liberties** *you've already taken too many liberties with me* **act with overfamiliarity**, act with familiarity, show disrespect, act with impropriety, act indecorously, be impudent, commit a breach of etiquette, act with boldness, act with impertinence, show insolence, show impudence, show presumptuousness, show presumption, show forwardness, show audacity, be unrestrained; take advantage of, exploit.
OPPOSITES be polite; show consideration.

> **CHOOSE THE RIGHT WORD**
>
> **liberty, freedom, independence**
>
> All these words denote absence of constraint or coercion.
>
> - **Liberty** denotes the desirable state of being free, within society, from oppressive restrictions imposed by authority on one's behaviour or political views (*we believe in civil and religious liberty for everyone*). It may also mean the power or scope to act as one pleases (*individuals should enjoy the liberty to pursue their own preferences*). To be *at liberty* to do something is to be allowed or entitled to do it (*I'm not at liberty to say*).
> - **Freedom** is a more general word for the absence of constraint (*decentralization would give local managers more freedom | freedom of expression | freedom to organize their affairs*). *Freedom* can also indicate the absence of a particular evil or constraint (*freedom from fear | freedom from interference*) or the state of being unrestricted in movement (*the shorts have a side split for freedom of movement*). Both *freedom* and *liberty* can also mean the state of not being imprisoned or enslaved (*the teenager committed fifty-six crimes before he lost his freedom | the mayor remained at liberty pending a decision as to his place of confinement*).
> - The principal meaning of **independence** is the absence of control of a nation or corporate body by an outside power (*recognition of Azerbaijan's independence | the independence of the judiciary*). When used in relation to individuals, *independence* may denote a freedom from commitments (*could she pursue her independence if Chester needed her?*) or the personal quality of not relying on others (*parents should foster their child's independence*).

libidinous ▶ **adjective** *he couldn't come to terms with his own libidinous impulses* **lustful**, lecherous, lascivious, lewd, carnal; **erotic**, sexual, sensual, venereal, hot, fleshly, voluptuous; salacious, prurient, licentious, libertine, lubricious, dissolute, debauched, depraved, degenerate, decadent, dissipated, wanton, promiscuous, immoral, unchaste, unvirtuous, loose, impure, intemperate, abandoned, incontinent, gross, ruttish, goatish, wolfish; *informal* horny; *Brit. informal* randy; *rare* concupiscent, lickerish.
OPPOSITE chaste.

libido ▶ **noun** *in men, heavy drinking can result in loss of libido* **sex drive**, sexual appetite, sexual passion, sexual urge, sexual longing; sexual desire, desire, passion, sexiness, sensuality, sexuality, lust, lustfulness, carnality, eroticism, ardour; *informal* horniness, the hots; *Brit. informal* randiness; *rare* concupiscence.

licence ▶ **noun 1** *a driving licence* **permit**, certificate, document, documentation, authorization, warrant, voucher, diploma, imprimatur; certification, credentials; pass, papers.
2 *I went in dread of the beatings that teachers had licence to administer* **permission**, authority, discretion, right, a free hand, leave, consent, authorization, sanction, approval, assent, entitlement, privilege, prerogative, blessing, exemption, mandate; liberty, freedom; power, empowerment, dispensation; *French* carte blanche; *informal* a blank cheque; *rare* warranty.
3 *they manufacture high-fashion footwear under licence* **franchise**, permission, consent, sanction, warrant, warranty, charter; seal of approval.
4 *the government was criticized for giving the army too much licence* **freedom**, liberty, free rein, latitude, choice, option, independence, self-determination, scope, impunity, margin, leisure; *French* carte blanche.
OPPOSITE restriction.
5 *he may have used a little poetic licence to embroider a good yarn* **disregard for the facts**, deviation from the truth, departure from the truth; inventiveness, invention, creativity, imagination, fancy; fancifulness, resourcefulness, ingenuity, inspiration; freedom, looseness.
6 *churchmen and dissenters cooperated against the licence of the age* **licentiousness**, dissoluteness, dissipation, debauchery, immorality, impropriety, decadence, profligacy, immoderation, intemperateness, indulgence, self-indulgence, excess, excessiveness, lack of restraint, lack of control, irresponsibility, abandon, laxness, laxity, disorder, disorderliness, unruliness, lawlessness, anarchy.
OPPOSITES restraint, decorum.

license ▶ **verb** *he was licensed to sell liquor* **permit**, allow, authorize, grant/give a licence to, grant/give a permit to, grant/give authorization to, grant/give authority to, grant/give the right to, grant/give leave to, grant/give permission to; warrant, certify, accredit, empower, give power to, entitle, enable, validate, charter, franchise, give the stamp of approval to, give approval to, let; recognize, qualify, sanction; *informal* OK, rubber-stamp.
OPPOSITES ban, forbid.

licentious ▶ **adjective** *he was a puritan in a licentious age* **dissolute**, dissipated, debauched, degenerate, salacious, immoral, wanton, decadent, depraved, profligate, impure, sinful, wicked, corrupt, indecent, libertine; **lustful**, lecherous, lascivious, libidinous, prurient, lubricious, lewd, promiscuous, unchaste, carnal, fleshly, intemperate, abandoned; ribald, risqué, smutty, dirty, filthy, coarse, perverted; *informal* horny, raunchy, naughty, pervy; *Brit. informal* randy; *rare* concupiscent, lickerish.
OPPOSITES moral, virtuous.

licit ▶ **adjective** *licit marital sexual intercourse* | *a warehouse filled with all manner of licit and illicit goods* **legitimate**, permissible, admissible, allowable, acceptable; **permitted**, valid, allowed, approved, sanctioned, authorized, warranted, recognized, bona fide, genuine, rightful, right, proper, above board, going by the rules; **lawful**, legal, constitutional, statutory, statutable, legalized, within the law, licensed, official; *informal* legit, kosher, by the book.
OPPOSITES illicit, forbidden.

lick ▶ **verb 1** *the spaniel leapt to lick his face* | *Pete licked the gravy from his hand* pass one's tongue over, touch with one's tongue, clean with one's tongue, tongue, wet, moisten, wash, clean; taste, lap, slurp.
2 *she sat looking into the flames licking round the coal* **flicker**, play, flick, flit, dart, ripple, dance.
3 (*informal*) *they licked the home side 3-0* **defeat**, beat, best, conquer, trounce, thrash, rout, vanquish, overcome, overwhelm, overpower, destroy, drub, get the better of, triumph over, prevail over, gain a victory over, win over/against, worst, subdue, quash, crush; *informal* slaughter, murder, kill, clobber, hammer, whip, paste, crucify, demolish, wipe the floor with, make mincemeat of, take to the cleaners, walk (all) over, run rings around; *Brit. informal* stuff, marmalize; *N. Amer. informal* shellac, skunk.
4 (*informal*) *the Prime Minister claimed that the government had inflation licked* **overcome**, get the better of, solve, find an answer to, find a solution to, conquer, beat, quell, control, govern, master, curb, check, bridle, tame.
▶ **noun 1** *the building itself had changed little, apart from a lick of paint here and there* **dab**, bit, drop, dash, spot, touch, hint, dribble, splash, sprinkle, trickle; little; *informal* smidgen, tad.
OPPOSITE lashings.
2 (*informal*) *you came up that last bit at a fair lick* **speed**, rate, pace, tempo, velocity, momentum; *informal* clip.

licking ▶ **noun** (*informal*) **1** *Arsenal can take a licking as much as any other club* **defeat**, loss, beating, trouncing, thrashing, drubbing; rout; *informal* hiding, pasting, caning, hammering, demolition, slaughter, massacre, annihilation; *N. Amer. informal* shellacking.
OPPOSITE victory.
2 *when his father heard what he had done, Ray got the worst licking of his life* **thrashing**, beating, flogging, whipping, slapping, spanking, thumping; *informal* walloping, hiding, tanning, pasting, hammering, clobbering, lathering, larruping, working-over; *N. Amer. informal* whaling.

lid ▶ **noun** *the lid of a saucepan* **cover**, top, cap, covering; cork, stopper, bung, plug.
□ **put a/the lid on** (*informal*) *they're wondering what they've got to do to put a lid on the rumours* **stop**, control, finish, end, put an end to, be the end of, put a stop to, put paid to, destroy.
□ **lift the lid off/on** (*informal*) *lifting the lid on what happened between Jett and Moira all those years ago* **expose**, reveal, bring to light, make known, make public, bring into the open, leak, disclose, divulge, broadcast, publish, release; *informal* take the lid off, blow wide open, let the cat out of the bag, spill the beans, blow the gaff, blab.
OPPOSITE keep secret.

lie¹ ▶ **noun** *Len's loyalty to his mates had made him tell lies* **untruth**, falsehood, fib, fabrication, deception, made-up story, trumped-up story, invention, piece of fiction, fiction, falsification, falsity, fairy story/tale, cock and bull story, barefaced lie; (little) white lie, half-truth, exaggeration, prevarication, departure from the truth; yarn, story, red herring, fable, myth, flight of fancy, figment of the imagination; pretence, pretext, sham; (**lies**) misinformation, disinformation, perjury, dissimulation, mendacity, gossip, propaganda; *informal* tall story, tall tale, whopper; *Brit. informal* porky, pork pie, porky pie; *humorous* terminological inexactitude; *vulgar slang* bullshit; *Austral./NZ vulgar slang* bulldust.
OPPOSITES truth, fact.
□ **give the lie to** *the success of our manufactured exports gives the lie to the Opposition's portrayal of manufacturing* **disprove**, contradict, negate, deny, refute, rebut, gainsay, belie, invalidate, show/prove to be false, explode, discredit, debunk, quash, knock the bottom out of, drive a coach and horses through; challenge, call into question; *informal* shoot full of holes, shoot down (in flames); *rare* controvert, confute, negative.
OPPOSITES show to be true, verify, confirm.
▶ **verb** *he had lied to the police as to his whereabouts* **say something untrue**, tell an untruth, tell a lie, tell a falsehood, fib, fabricate, invent a story, make up a story, falsify, dissemble, dissimulate, bear false witness; tell a white lie, prevaricate, exaggerate, stretch the truth; perjure oneself, commit perjury, forswear oneself, be forsworn; bluff, pretend, depart from the truth; deceive, delude, mislead, trick, hoodwink, hoax, take in, lead astray, throw off the scent, send on a wild goose chase, put on the wrong track, pull the wool over someone's eyes; *informal* lie through one's teeth, con; *humorous* be economical with the truth, tell a terminological inexactitude; *vulgar slang* bullshit.
OPPOSITE tell the truth.

lie² ▶ **verb 1** *he was lying on a bed* **recline**, lie down, lie back, be recumbent, be prostrate, be supine, be prone, be stretched out, stretch oneself out, lean back, sprawl, rest, repose, relax, lounge, loll, bask.
OPPOSITE stand.
2 *her handbag lay on a chair at the other end of the room* **be placed**, be set, be situated, be positioned, rest, repose, be.
3 *the tiny principality which lies on the border of Switzerland and Austria* **be situated**, be located, be placed, be positioned, be found, be sited, be established, be.
4 *his body lies in a crypt below our headquarters* **be buried**, be interred, be laid to rest, rest, be entombed; *rare* be inhumed, be sepulchred.
5 *the difficulty lies in building real quality into the products* **consist**, be inherent, inhere, be present, be contained, exist, reside, have its existence/being.
□ **lie heavy on** *it was the loss of human life that lay heavy on him* **trouble**, worry, bother, torment, oppress, nag, prey on one's mind, plague, niggle at, gnaw at, haunt; be a burden to, burden, press down on, weigh down, be a great weight on, weigh heavily on someone's mind, cause anxiety to; *informal* bug, aggravate.
□ **lie low** *we'll have to lie low and wait for dark* **hide**, go into hiding, hide out, find a hiding place, conceal oneself, keep out of sight, keep a low profile, take cover, go to earth, go to ground, go underground, cover one's tracks, lurk, skulk; *informal* hole up; *Brit. informal* lie doggo.

liege ▶ **noun** **liege lord**, lord, feudal lord, seigneur, suzerain, overlord, master, chief, chieftain, superior, monarch, sovereign, baron, ruler.

lieutenant ▶ **noun** *he began his criminal career as the lieutenant of a notorious mob boss* **deputy**, second in command, right-hand man/woman, number two, assistant, aide, henchman, henchwoman, subordinate; *informal* sidekick.

life ▶ **noun 1** *only a mother can appreciate the joy of giving life to a child* **existence**, being, living, animation, aliveness, animateness; entity, sentience, creation, survival, viability; *rare* esse.
OPPOSITES death, non-existence.
2 *armaments that threaten to eliminate life on the planet* **living things**, living beings, living creatures, the living; human/animal/plant life, fauna, flora, ecosystems, creatures, wildlife; human beings, humanity, humankind, mankind, man, human activity; *literary* flesh.
3 *inshore fishing isn't an easy life* **way of life**, way of living, manner of living, lifestyle, situation, position, state, station, condition, set of circumstances, fate, lot; sphere, field, line, career, business.
4 *I hadn't talked to my father for the last nine months of his life* **lifetime**, life span, days, duration of life, allotted span, course of life, time on earth,

existence, one's time, one's career, threescore years and ten, this mortal coil; *informal* one's born days.
5 *the Parliament Bill introduced a limit of five years for the life of any Parliament* **duration**, active life, lifetime, existence, functioning period, period of effectiveness, period of usefulness, validity, efficacy.
6 *he is happy and full of life in his new job* **vivacity**, animation, liveliness, vitality, verve, high spirits, sparkle, exuberance, zest, buoyancy, effervescence, enthusiasm, energy, vigour, dynamism, go, elan, gusto, brio, bounce, spirit, spiritedness, activity, fire, panache, colour, dash, drive, push; business, bustle, hustle and bustle, movement, stir; *informal* oomph, pizzazz, pep, zing, zip, vim, get-up-and-go.
7 *his mother would be the life of the party* **moving spirit**, moving force, animating spirit, vital spirit, spirit, vital spark, life force, lifeblood, essence, core, heart, soul, strength, quintessence, substance; *French* élan vital.
8 *more than 1,500 lives were lost in the accident* **person**, human being, individual, mortal, soul, creature.
9 *I was reading a life of Chopin* **biography**, autobiography, life story, life history, memoir, history, profile; diary, journal, confessions; record, chronicle, account, report, portrayal, depiction, portrait; *informal* biog, bio.
10 *I'll miss you, but there it is, that's life* **the way of the world**, the world, the way things go, the way of it, the human condition, the times we live in, the usual state of affairs, the school of hard knocks; fate, destiny, providence, kismet, karma, fortune, luck, chance; *N. Amer. informal* the way the cookie crumbles.

□ **come to life 1** *he could hear the familiar sounds of a barracks coming to life* **become active**, become lively, come alive, wake up, awaken, waken, show signs of life, arouse, rouse, stir, emerge.
OPPOSITES be dormant, be quiescent.
2 *it was as though the carved angel by the lectern had suddenly come to life* **become animate**, come alive, become a living creature; revive, resurrect.

□ **for dear life** *she was holding on for dear life* **desperately**, with all one's might, with might and main, urgently, with urgency, vigorously, with as much vigour as possible, for all one is worth, as fast/hard as possible, like the devil.

L

□ **give one's life 1** *he's devoted to his queen and would give his life for her* **die**, lay down one's life, sacrifice oneself; die to save, offer one's life, surrender one's life.
2 *he gave his life to the company and could have expected some support from them* **dedicate oneself**, devote oneself, give oneself, commit oneself, pledge oneself, surrender oneself.

WORD LINKS

related prefix	**bio-** (e.g. ***biosphere***)
having life	**animate**
essential for life	**vital**

life-and-death ▶ **adjective** *a life-and-death decision* **vital**, of vital importance, crucial, critical, urgent, pivotal, momentous, of great moment, important, all-important, key, serious, grave, significant, decisive, far-reaching, historic, weighty, consequential, of great consequence, epoch-making, apocalyptic, fateful, portentous; *informal* earth-shattering, world-shattering, earth-shaking, world-shaking.
OPPOSITES trivial, unimportant.

lifeblood ▶ **noun** *fast, accurate information is the lifeblood of the economy* **life force**, life, essential part/component/constituent, animating spirit, moving force, driving force, dynamic force, vital spark, vital fluid, inspiration, stimulus, centre, animus, essence, crux, heart, soul, core, kernel, marrow, pith; *French* élan vital; *informal* guts; *Philosophy* quiddity.

life-giving ▶ **adjective** *their view of karma as a life-giving force that flows from life to life* **vitalizing**, animating, vivifying, energizing, invigorating, enlivening, stimulating; life-preserving, life-sustaining.
OPPOSITE destructive.

lifeless ▶ **adjective 1** *they dropped the lifeless body into the shallow grave* **dead**, deceased, defunct, departed, late, extinct, perished, gone, no more, passed on/away, stiff, cold, (as) dead as a doornail; *rare* demised, exanimate.
OPPOSITE alive.
2 *a lifeless rag doll* **inanimate**, inorganic, without life, inert, insentient, insensate, wooden, mechanical, abiotic; nerveless.
OPPOSITE animate.
3 *a lifeless planet | the lifeless, emotionless city of the future* **barren**, sterile, bare, desolate, stark, arid, infertile, uncultivated, empty, uninhabited, unoccupied; cold, bleak, joyless, colourless, characterless, soulless.
4 *he spoke in a dull, lifeless voice | a lifeless performance* **lacklustre**, spiritless, lacking vitality, apathetic, torpid, lethargic; dull, monotonous, boring, tedious, dreary, insipid, unexciting, wearisome, bland, drab, dry, flat, static, stiff, wooden, mechanical, uninspired, inexpressive, expressionless, emotionless, colourless, characterless, two-dimensional, uninspiring.
OPPOSITES lively, vibrant.
5 *lifeless hair* **lank**, lustreless.

lifelike ▶ **adjective** *a lifelike sketch* **realistic**, true to life, representational, faithful, authentic, exact, precise, detailed, vivid, graphic, natural, naturalistic, convincing, undistorted; photographic, cinematic, filmic; speaking; factual.
OPPOSITE unrealistic.

lifelong ▶ **adjective** *a lifelong friendship* **lasting**, for all one's life, lifetime's, long-lasting, long-standing, long-term, long-running, persisting, prevailing, durable, constant, stable, established, steady, steadfast, secure, fast, firm, fixed, deep-rooted, enduring, continuing, abiding, remaining; permanent, eternal, immutable.
OPPOSITES ephemeral, short-lived, temporary.

lifestyle ▶ **noun** *the privileged lifestyle of rich New York youngsters* **way of life**, way of living, manner of living, life, situation, position, state, station, condition, set of circumstances, fate, lot; conduct, behaviour; customs, habits, ways, mores.

lifetime ▶ **noun 1** *he made an exceptional contribution to the conservation of nature during his lifetime* **lifespan**, life, days, duration of life, allotted span, course of life, time on earth, existence, one's time, one's career, one's threescore years and ten, this mortal coil; *informal* one's born days.
2 *the lifetime of workstations will generally be between three and five years* **duration**, life, active life, existence, life expectancy, functioning period, period of effectiveness/usefulness/validity/efficacy.
3 *it takes a lifetime to do it properly* **all one's life**, a very long time, an eternity; hours, days, months, years, aeons, hours/days/months on end; *informal* ages (and ages), an age.

lift ▶ **verb 1** *holding the sling in your left hand, lift the pack on to your back* **raise**, hoist, heave, haul up, uplift, heft, boost, raise up/aloft, upraise, elevate, thrust, hold high, bear aloft; pick up, grab, take up, scoop up, gather up, snatch up; winch up, jack up, lever up; carry, manhandle; *informal* hump; *rare* upheave.
OPPOSITES drop, put down.
2 *a few cocktails had lifted his flagging spirits* **boost**, raise, buoy up, elevate, give a lift to, cheer up, perk up, enliven, uplift, brighten up, lighten, ginger up, gladden, encourage, stimulate, arouse, revive, restore; *informal* buck up, jazz up.
OPPOSITE subdue.
3 *they seem able to lift their game for the big occasions* **improve**, boost, enhance, make better, invigorate, revitalize, upgrade, ameliorate.
OPPOSITES worsen, impair.
4 *by now the fog had lifted* **clear**, rise, disperse, dissipate, disappear, vanish, dissolve, be dispelled, thin out, scatter.
OPPOSITE appear.
5 *a draft law lifting the ban on political parties* **cancel**, raise, remove, withdraw, revoke, rescind, annul, void, discontinue, countermand, relax, end, stop, terminate.
OPPOSITES establish, impose.
6 *the end of September is the time to lift and store carrots* **dig up**, pick, pull up, dig out of the ground, root out, unearth, take up.
OPPOSITES plant, sow.
7 *they needed far more supplies than the RAF could lift in the required time scale* **airlift**, transport by air, transport, move, transfer, fly, convey, shift.
8 *he lifted his voice slightly* **amplify**, raise, make louder, louden, increase.
OPPOSITES soften, quieten.
9 (*informal*) *he lifted portions of his book nearly verbatim from a 1986 article* **plagiarize**, pirate, copy, reproduce, poach, steal, borrow; *informal* crib, rip off, nick, pinch.
10 (*informal*) *he could lift a wallet better than anyone I've ever known* **steal**, thieve, rob, pilfer, purloin, pocket, snatch, take, appropriate, abstract, help oneself to; *informal* swipe, nab, filch, snaffle, blag, walk off with, 'borrow', 'liberate', rip something off; *Brit. informal* pinch, nick, half-inch, whip, knock off, trouser; *N. Amer. informal* glom; *W. Indian informal* tief.

□ **lift off** *the helicopters lifted off at 1030 hours* **take off**, be launched, blast off, leave the ground, become airborne, take to the air, take wing.
OPPOSITES land, touch down.

▶ **noun 1** *Alice went up to the second floor in the lift* **elevator**, hoist; paternoster (lift); dumb waiter.
2 *give me a lift up, Martha* **push**, hoist, heave, thrust, shove, uplift, a helping hand.
3 *he gave me a lift to the airport* **car ride**, ride, run, drive, transportation, journey; *informal* hitch.
4 *he scored an excellent goal, which will give his confidence a real lift* **boost**, fillip, pick-me-up, stimulus, impetus, encouragement, spur, reassurance, aid, help, push; improvement, enhancement, upgrading, amelioration; *informal* shot in the arm.
OPPOSITE discouragement.

light[1] *See centre pages for list of* **Lamps and Lights**

▶ **noun 1** *the houses had only the shadowy light of candles and oil lamps* **illumination**, brightness, luminescence, luminosity, shining, gleaming, gleam, brilliance, radiance, lustre, glowing, glow, blaze, glare, dazzle; incandescence, phosphorescence; sunlight, moonlight, starlight, lamplight, firelight, electric light, gaslight; ray of light, shaft of light, beam of light; *rare* effulgence, refulgence, lambency, fulguration.
OPPOSITE darkness.

2 *there was a light on in the hall | he shone his light into Oliver's face* **lamp, torch**, flashlight; headlight, headlamp, sidelight; standard lamp, wall light; street light, floodlight; lantern, candle, taper, beacon.
3 *have you got a light?* **match, (cigarette) lighter**, flame, spark, source of fire.
4 *don't worry, we'll be driving in the light and we won't have to go fast* **daylight**, light of day, natural light, sunlight; **daylight hours**, daytime, day, hours of sunlight.
OPPOSITES darkness, night-time.
5 *he saw the problem in a different light | the work sheds new light on the early history of the library* **aspect**, angle, slant, approach, interpretation, viewpoint, standpoint, context, point of view, vantage point; appearance, guise, hue, complexion.
6 *light dawned on Loretta, and she launched herself into her part* **understanding**, enlightenment, illumination, comprehension, insight, awareness, knowledge, elucidation, explanation, clarification, edification.
OPPOSITE ignorance.
7 *an eminent legal light* **expert**, authority, master, leader, guru; leading light, guiding light, luminary, celebrity, dignitary, public figure, worthy, VIP, big name, star; *informal* bigwig, big gun, big shot, big noise, celeb.
8 *he served his party loyally according to his lights* **talent**, skill, ability; intelligence, mental powers, intellect, knowledge, understanding.
□ **bring something to light** *a serious case of corruption within government was first brought to light by an internal audit* **reveal**, disclose, expose, uncover, show up, lay bare, unveil, manifest, unearth, dig up, dig out, turn up, bring to notice, detect, identify, dredge up, smoke out, root out, ferret out, hunt out, nose out.
OPPOSITES hush up, keep secret.
□ **come to light** *the thefts came to light early last year* **be discovered**, be uncovered, be unearthed, appear, come out, transpire, become known, become apparent, materialize, emerge, crop up, turn up, show up, pop up.
OPPOSITES remain secret, remain hidden.
□ **in the light of** *I see no reason, in the light of these reports, to abandon our current policy* **taking into consideration**, considering, taking into account, bearing in mind, keeping in mind, mindful of, taking note of, in view of.
□ **throw/cast/shed light on** *no one could shed any light on the mysterious car accident* **explain**, elucidate, clarify, clear up, offer/give an explanation for/of, make clear, make plain, interpret, comment on.
▶ **verb** *Alan gathered sticks and lit a fire | Rickie lit a cigarette* **set alight**, set light to, set burning, set on fire, set fire to, put/set a match to, ignite, kindle, burn, spark (off), fire, touch off, start, torch; *archaic* enkindle.
OPPOSITES extinguish, put out.
□ **light up** *the dashboard lit up* **become bright**, brighten, become brighter, lighten, flash, shine, gleam, flare, blaze, glint, sparkle, flicker, shimmer, glisten, scintillate, glare, beam; *rare* coruscate, fulgurate.
□ **light something up 1** *a flare lit up the night sky* **make bright**, brighten, illuminate, make brighter, lighten, throw/cast/shed light on, shine on, irradiate, flood with light, floodlight; *literary* illumine.
2 *her enthusiasm lit up her face* **animate**, irradiate, brighten, make cheerful, cheer up, enliven.
▶ **adjective 1** *a cool and light breakfast room adjoins the bar* **bright**, full of light, well lit, well lighted, well illuminated, sunny, sunshiny, undimmed, brilliant.
OPPOSITES dark, gloomy.
2 *a subtle colour scheme of light pastel shades* **light-coloured**, light-toned, pale, pale-coloured, pastel, pastel-coloured, whitish, faded, faint, weak, bleached.
OPPOSITE dark.
3 *a young woman with light hair* **fair**, light-coloured, blonde, golden, flaxen, yellow.
OPPOSITES dark, brunette.

WORD LINKS

related prefixes	**photo-, lumin-** (e.g. *luminescent*), **luc-** (e.g. *Lucifer*)
study of behaviour of light	**optics**
measurement of the intensity of light	**photometry**
fear of light	**photophobia**

light[2] ▶ **adjective 1** *it's light, portable, and you can use it anywhere | you're as light as a feather!* **easy to lift**, not heavy, weighing very little, lightweight; easy to carry, portable, transportable, weightless, insubstantial, airy.
OPPOSITE heavy.
2 *a light cotton robe* **flimsy**, lightweight, insubstantial, thin; delicate, floaty, gauzy, sheer, gossamer, diaphanous, transparent, translucent, see-through.
OPPOSITES heavy, thick.
3 *she seemed as light on her feet as a dancer* **nimble**, deft, agile, lithe, limber, lissom, flexible, supple, adroit, graceful, acrobatic, lively, active, quick, quick-moving, spry, sprightly; light-footed, fleet-footed; *informal* twinkle-toed, nippy; *literary* fleet, lightsome.
OPPOSITE clumsy.
4 *cotton lavender needs a dry sunny situation in light soil* **friable**, sandy, easily dug, workable; crumbly, not dense, loose, porous.
OPPOSITE dense.
5 *a light dinner* **small**, modest, scanty, simple, skimpy, frugal, not heavy, not rich, not large; easily digested, digestible.
OPPOSITES heavy, rich.
6 *I was put on light duties* **easy**, simple, undemanding, untaxing, unexacting, not burdensome, moderate, endurable, bearable, tolerable; *informal* cushy.
OPPOSITES hard, burdensome.
7 *his eyes gleamed with light mockery* **gentle**, mild, moderate, slight; **playful**, light-hearted, easy-going; witty, dry.
OPPOSITE serious.
8 *light entertainment | light reading* **entertaining, lightweight**, diverting, recreative, undemanding, easily understood, middle-of-the-road; amusing, humorous, funny, witty, light-hearted; frivolous, unserious, superficial, trivial, trifling.
OPPOSITES serious, deep.
9 *I pitched into the chores with a light heart* **carefree**, light-hearted, cheerful, cheery, happy, merry, jolly, blithe, bright, sunny, untroubled; buoyant, vivacious, bubbly, jaunty, bouncy, breezy, optimistic, positive, upbeat, ebullient, easy-going, free and easy, happy-go-lucky; *dated* gay.
10 *this is no light matter* **unimportant**, insignificant, trivial, trifling, petty, worthless, inconsequential, inconsiderable, superficial.
OPPOSITES serious, important.
11 *he heard light footsteps | she leaned up and planted a light kiss on Dave's mouth* **gentle, delicate**, soft, dainty, graceful; faint, indistinct.
OPPOSITE heavy.
12 *her heart was pounding and her head felt light* **dizzy**, giddy, light-headed, faint, unsteady; *informal* woozy, funny; *dated* queer; *rare* vertiginous.
13 (*archaic*) *he found the room full of soldiers and light women* **promiscuous**, loose, wanton, unchaste, licentious.
OPPOSITE chaste.

light[3] ▶ **verb**
□ **light into 1** (*informal*) *we started lighting into our attackers* **assault**, set upon, fall on, attack, assail, turn on, lash out at, round on, strike, beat; thrash, drub, thump, batter, hammer, pummel, hit out at, strike out at, (let) fly at, weigh into, belabour; *informal* lay into, tear into, sail into, lace into, pitch into, paste, let someone have it; *Brit. informal* have a go at.
2 *my father really lit into me for being late* **scold**, berate, upbraid, castigate, censure, condemn, lambaste, criticize, reprimand, rebuke, chide, reprove, admonish, harangue, take to task, lay into, rant at, rave at, rail at, revile, fulminate against, haul/call over the coals; *informal* pitch into, rap someone's knuckles, slap someone's wrist, dress down, give someone a dressing-down, carpet, tell off, bawl out; *Brit. informal* tick off, have a go at, slag off; *N. Amer. informal* chew out; *rare* reprehend, excoriate, objurgate.
□ **light on/upon** *we will suppose that the author has lighted upon important new material* **come across**, chance on, hit on, happen on, stumble on/across, blunder on, find, discover, uncover, arrive at, encounter, think of, come up with.

lighten[1] ▶ **verb 1** *the sky was beginning to lighten* **become lighter**, grow brighter, brighten.
OPPOSITE darken.
2 *the first touch of dawn lightened the sky* **make lighter**, make brighter, brighten, light up, illuminate, throw/cast/shed light on, shine on, irradiate, flood with light, floodlight; *literary* illumine.
OPPOSITE darken.
3 *he sometimes used lemon juice to lighten his hair* **whiten**, make white(r), bleach, peroxide, blanch, make pale(r), remove colour from, fade, wash out, decolour, decolorize.
OPPOSITE blacken.
4 (*rare*) *it thundered and lightened* **emit lightning**, flash lightning; *rare* fulgurate.

lighten[2] ▶ **verb 1** *we intend to lighten the burden of taxation* **make lighter**, lessen, reduce, decrease, diminish, moderate, soften, ease, temper; alleviate, mitigate, allay, relieve, palliate, assuage, soothe, calm, subdue.
OPPOSITES increase, intensify.
2 *an attempt to lighten her spirits* **cheer (up)**, brighten, gladden, hearten, perk up, lift, ginger up, enliven, boost, buoy (up), elate, inspire, uplift, sweeten, revive, restore, revitalize, stimulate; enhance, improve, leaven; *informal* jazz up; *rare* inspirit.
OPPOSITE depress.

light-fingered ▶ **adjective** *a security system which prevents light-fingered customers from making off with the goods* **thieving**, thievish, stealing, pilfering, shoplifting, pocket-picking; dishonest; *informal* crooked, filching, sticky-fingered.
OPPOSITE honest.

light-footed ▶ **adjective** *these dogs are light-footed and agile* **nimble**, light on one's feet, agile, deft, graceful, lithe, spry, sprightly, light of foot, limber, lissom, acrobatic; swift, fast, quick, quick-moving; *informal* twinkle-toed, nippy; *literary* fleet of foot, fleet-footed.
OPPOSITES clumsy, slow.

light-headed ▶ adjective *the pain had left him feeling light-headed* **dizzy**, giddy, faint, unsteady, light in the head, weak-headed, muzzy; shaky, reeling, staggering; *informal* woozy; *rare* vertiginous.

light-hearted ▶ adjective *light-hearted banter | a light-hearted comedy* **carefree**, cheerful, cheery, happy, merry, glad, playful, jolly, jovial, joyful, jocund, gleeful, ebullient, high-spirited, lively, perky, blithe, bright, sunny, buoyant, vivacious, bubbly, effervescent, jaunty, bouncy, breezy; optimistic, positive; easy-going, free and easy, happy-go-lucky, in good spirits, untroubled, genial; entertaining, amusing, funny, comic, humorous, witty, mirthful, diverting; *informal* chirpy, upbeat; *dated* gay; *archaic* frolicsome.
OPPOSITES miserable, gloomy, serious, solemn.

lighthouse ▶ noun light-tower, warning light, guiding light, beacon, pharos, phare; lightship, floating light, light vessel; light, signal, danger/warning signal; *archaic* watchtower, fanal.

lightly ▶ adverb **1** *Maisie kissed him lightly on the cheek* **softly**, gently, faintly, delicately; gingerly, timidly.
OPPOSITES hard, heavily.
2 *season very lightly with salt and pepper | lightly cooked salmon* **sparingly**, slightly, sparsely, moderately, softly, thinly, delicately.
OPPOSITES intensely, abundantly.
3 *he has got off lightly* **without severe punishment**, easily, leniently, mildly.
OPPOSITE severely.
4 *her views are not to be dismissed lightly* **carelessly**, airily, readily, heedlessly, without consideration, uncaringly, indifferently, unthinkingly, thoughtlessly, flippantly, facilely, breezily, frivolously; light-heartedly, gaily, blithely, nonchalantly, cheerfully.
OPPOSITE seriously.

lightweight ▶ adjective **1** *a comfortable lightweight jacket* **thin**, light, flimsy, insubstantial; summery; feathery, airy, delicate, fine, floaty, gauzy, sheer, gossamer, diaphanous, transparent, translucent, see-through.
OPPOSITES heavy, thick.
2 *snobs will dismiss the show as lightweight, contrived pap* **trivial**, insubstantial, trifling, frothy, superficial, shallow, unintellectual, undemanding, frivolous, insignificant; of no account, unimportant, of no consequence, inconsequential, minor, paltry, petty, slight, negligible, immaterial, of no merit, of no value, valueless, worthless.
OPPOSITES profound, heavyweight.

L

likable ▶ adjective. *See* LIKEABLE.

like[1] ▶ verb **1** *I rather like Colonel Maitland* **be fond of**, be attached to, have a soft spot for, have a fondness for, have a liking for, have regard for, think well of, look on with favour, hold in esteem, admire, respect, esteem; be attracted to, fancy, find attractive, be keen on, be taken with; *informal* take a shine to, be into, rate.
OPPOSITES dislike, hate.
2 *Maisie likes veal | she likes gardening* **enjoy**, have a taste for, have a preference for, have a liking for, have a weakness for, be partial to, delight in, find/take pleasure in, be keen on, find agreeable, derive pleasure from, be pleased by, have a penchant for, have a passion for, derive satisfaction from, find enjoyable, take to, appreciate; love, adore, relish, savour, lap up, revel in; *informal* get a kick from/out of, have a thing about, be into, get off on, go for, be mad about/for, dig, groove on, get a charge from/out of, get a buzz from/out of, get a bang out of, be hooked on, go a bundle on.
OPPOSITES dislike, hate.
3 *feel free to say what you like* **choose**, please, prefer, wish, want, desire, see fit, think fit, care to, fancy, be/feel inclined, will.
OPPOSITE reject.
4 *how would she like it if someone did that to her picture?* **feel about**, regard, think about, consider.

like[2] ▶ preposition **1** *you're just like a teacher* **similar to**, the same as, identical to.
OPPOSITE unlike.
2 *the figure landed like a cat* **in the same way as**, in the manner of, in the same manner as, in the same way that, in a similar way to, after the fashion of, along/on the lines of, as, tantamount to.
OPPOSITE unlike.
3 *physical decay extends across whole areas of cities like Birmingham, Glasgow, and Leeds* **such as**, for example, for instance, in particular, as, namely, viz.
OPPOSITE except for.
4 *Richard sounded mean and spiteful, which isn't like him* **characteristic of**, typical of, in character with.
OPPOSITE unlike.
▶ noun *well, we shan't see his like again* **equal**, match, equivalent, counterpart, opposite number, fellow, twin, mate, parallel, peer; *rare* compeer.
OPPOSITES inferior; superior.
▶ adjective *a like situation* **similar**, much the same, more or less the same, not unlike, comparable, corresponding, correspondent, resembling, alike, approximating, analogous, parallel, equivalent, cognate, related, of a kind, akin, kindred; interchangeable, indistinguishable, identical, same, matching.
OPPOSITES different, dissimilar.

WORD LINKS
related suffixes **-esque (e.g. *carnivalesque, Pythonesque*)**, **-ish (e.g. *amateurish, girlish*)**, **-oid (e.g. *asteroid, rhomboid*)**

likeable, likable ▶ adjective *a lively and very likeable young woman* **pleasant**, nice, friendly, agreeable, affable, amiable, genial, civil, personable, charming, popular, clubbable, good-natured, engaging, warm, pleasing, appealing, endearing, convivial, congenial, winning, delightful, enchanting, attractive, winsome, fetching, captivating, lovable, adorable, sweet; *Scottish* couthy; *Italian & Spanish* simpatico; *informal* chummy, pally, darling, lovely.
OPPOSITES hateful, unpleasant.

likelihood ▶ noun *solicitors also fear that the changes could increase the likelihood of a miscarriage of justice* **probability**, chance, prospect, possibility, likeliness, odds, feasibility, plausibility, conceivability; risk, threat, hazard, danger, fear, peril, liability; hope, opportunity, promise.
OPPOSITE unlikeliness.

likely ▶ adjective **1** *it seemed likely that a scandal of some sort would eventually break | the likely outcome of the vote* **probable**, distinctly possible, to be expected, odds-on, on, possible, credible, plausible, believable, within the bounds of possibility, imaginable; expected, anticipated, natural, prospective, predictable, predicted, foreseeable, ten to one, liable; sure, destined, fated; in the wind, in the air; *informal* on the cards, a pound to a penny.
OPPOSITES unlikely, impossible; improbable.
2 *a more likely explanation for the slump can be found in the shaky financial structure of the club* **plausible**, reasonable, feasible, acceptable, believable, credible, tenable, conceivable.
OPPOSITES incredible, unbelievable.
3 *(ironic) Gone running has he? A likely story!* **unlikely**, implausible, unbelievable, incredible, untenable, unacceptable, inconceivable.
OPPOSITE believable.
4 *it was a likely place for a romantic-minded young girl to frequent* **suitable**, appropriate, apposite, fit, fitting, acceptable, proper, right; reasonable, promising, hopeful.
5 *what would I be needing money for with a likely lad like Tom here to support me?* **likely to succeed**, **promising**, talented, gifted; *informal* up-and-coming.
▶ adverb *he was most likely dead* **probably**, in all probability, presumably, no doubt, doubtlessly; *informal* like enough, (as) like as not.

liken ▶ verb *these sculptures have been likened to seashells* **compare**, equate, show the resemblance/similarity between, analogize, draw an analogy between, make an analogy of/between, draw a parallel between, parallel, correlate, match; link, associate, make connections between, bracket together, think of together, regard as similar, set beside, mention in the same breath; set side by side.
OPPOSITE contrast.

likeness ▶ noun **1** *her likeness to Anne is quite uncanny* **resemblance**, similarity, alikeness, sameness, similitude, congruity, affinity, correspondence, analogy, parallelism, agreement, relationship, identity, identicalness, uniformity, conformity, equivalence.
OPPOSITE dissimilarity.
2 *the arm of the chair had been carved in the likeness of a naked woman* **semblance**, guise, appearance, outward form, form, shape, image, aspect, character, mien.
3 *a few coins which bear the likeness of the last president* **representation**, image, depiction, portrayal, delineation, profile; picture, drawing, sketch, painting, portrait, photograph, study, bust, statue, statuette, sculpture, icon.

likewise ▶ adverb **1** *an ambush was out of the question, likewise poison* **also**, in addition, too, as well, by the same token, to boot; besides, moreover, furthermore, further, into the bargain.
2 *we hope you will continue to support the Society, and encourage your family and friends to do likewise* **the same**, similarly, correspondingly, in the same way, in like manner, in similar fashion.
OPPOSITE the opposite.

liking ▶ noun *he had a ruddy complexion due to his liking for port* **fondness**, love, affection, penchant, attachment; enjoyment, appreciation, taste; preference, partiality, predilection, proclivity, propensity, proneness, predisposition, tendency, bias; desire, fancy, inclination, bent, leaning, hankering, affinity, attraction; passion, longing, urge, itch; *informal* thing.
OPPOSITES dislike, aversion, hatred.

lilt ▶ noun *the lilt of his Scottish accent* **cadence**, rise and fall, inflection, intonation, upswing, emphasis, stress, rhythm, swing, sway, beat, pulse, measure, metre, tempo.

limb ▶ noun **1** *he was stretching his sore limbs* **arm**, **leg**; wing; extremity, appendage, protuberance, projection; *archaic* member.

2 *the bare limbs of a high tree* **branch**, bough.
3 *local job centres act as limbs of the Ministry of Employment* **section**, branch, offshoot, arm, wing, part, subdivision; department, division, office, member.

□ **out on a limb 1** *the portrayal of Scotland as being out on a limb from the rest of Britain* **isolated**, stranded, segregated, set apart, separate, marooned, cut off; solitary, sequestered, high and dry.
OPPOSITE a central part of.
2 *I don't think the government would be prepared to go out on a limb on his behalf* **in a precarious position**, in a weak position, in a risky situation, vulnerable; *informal* sticking one's neck out.
OPPOSITE in a safe position/situation.

WORD LINKS
relating to a limb **appendicular**

limber ▶ **adjective** *I have to practise to keep myself limber* **lithe, supple**, nimble, lissom, flexible, fit, spry, sprightly, agile, acrobatic, quick-moving, deft, willowy, graceful, loose-jointed, loose-limbed; active, lively, in good condition; *informal* in good nick.
OPPOSITES stiff, unfit.
▶ **verb**
□ **limber up** *they had been limbering up for their evening's training schedule* **warm up**, loosen up, get into condition, get into shape, get ready, prepare, practise, train, drill; stretch, exercise, work out.

limbo ▶ **noun** *unbaptized infants are thought to live in limbo* abode of the souls of unbaptized infants; non-existence, void, oblivion; neither heaven nor hell.
□ **in limbo** *the measure has been in limbo since Congress took a 10-day break* **in abeyance**, unattended to, unfinished, incomplete; suspended, deferred, postponed, put off, pending, in a state of suspension, awaiting action, on ice, in cold storage; unresolved, undetermined, in a state of uncertainty, up in the air, betwixt and between; ongoing, outstanding, hanging fire; abandoned, forgotten, left out, neglected; *informal* on the back burner, on hold.
OPPOSITES in hand, under way, continuing.

limelight ▶ **noun** (**the limelight**) *she couldn't conceal her excitement at being back in the limelight* **the focus of attention**, public attention, public notice, public interest, the public eye, media attention, media interest; public recognition, publicity, the glare of publicity, prominence, exposure, hype, glare, the spotlight; fame, renown, celebrity, stardom, notability, eminence.
OPPOSITE obscurity.

limit ▶ **noun 1** *a campus outside the city limits* **boundary**, border, boundary line, bound, bounding line, partition line, frontier, edge, demarcation line, end point, cut-off point, termination; perimeter, outside, outline, confine, periphery, margin, rim, extremity, fringe, threshold, compass.
OPPOSITE centre.
2 *for Saturday's match the police have set a limit of 4,500 supporters* **maximum**, ceiling, limitation, upper limit; restriction, curb, check, control, curtailment, restraint; damper, brake, rein.
OPPOSITE minimum.
3 *resources are stretched to the limit* **utmost**, breaking point, extremity, greatest extent, ultimate, end point, the bitter end.
4 (**the limit**) *that really is the limit!* **the last straw**, the straw that broke the camel's back, enough, more than enough; *informal* the end, it.
▶ **verb** *the pressure to limit costs | Congress's power to legislate may be limited by the Constitution* **restrict**, curb, check, place a limit on, cap, keep within bounds, hold in check, restrain, put a brake on, hold, freeze, peg; regulate, control, govern, delimit, demarcate, circumscribe, ration; arrest, bridle, inhibit, damp (down), fetter, tie down; *rare* trammel.
OPPOSITES increase, allow to grow unchecked.

limitation ▶ **noun 1** *there have been calls for a limitation on the number of newcomers* **restriction**, curb, restraint, constraint, control, check, clampdown; hindrance, impediment, obstacle, obstruction, bar, barrier, block, deterrent, inhibition, damper, brake, rein.
OPPOSITES extension, increase.
2 *the critic must be aware of his own limitations* **imperfection**, flaw, defect, failing, shortcoming, weak point, inability, incapability, deficiency, failure, incapacity, frailty, weakness; disability, foible, vice, disadvantage, drawback.
OPPOSITES strength, strong point.

limited ▶ **adjective 1** *the competition for limited resources | space is limited* **restricted, finite**, bounded, little, narrow, tight, lean, slight, slender, in short supply, short; meagre, scanty, sparse, insubstantial, deficient, inadequate, insufficient, paltry, poor, miserly; basic, rudimentary, patchy, sketchy, minimal; cramped, small.
OPPOSITES ample, boundless, unlimited.
2 *the limited powers of the council* **restricted**, curbed, checked, controlled, restrained, constrained, confined; delimited, defined, qualified.
OPPOSITES unlimited, absolute.

limitless ▶ **adjective** *he's got limitless ability* **boundless**, unbounded, unlimited, without limit, illimitable; infinite, endless, never-ending, unending, everlasting, untold, immeasurable, measureless, incalculable, inestimable, bottomless, fathomless; immense, vast, huge, great, extensive; unceasing, unflagging, interminable, without end, inexhaustible, constant, perpetual; *literary* myriad.
OPPOSITES limited, little.

limp¹ ▶ **verb** *she limped out of the house* **hobble**, walk with a limp, walk with difficulty, walk lamely, walk haltingly, walk unevenly, falter; shuffle, shamble, totter, dodder, stagger, stumble; *Scottish* hirple.
▶ **noun** *he walked with a limp* **lameness**, hobble, uneven gait, shuffle; *rare* claudication.

limp² ▶ **adjective 1** *a limp handshake | a posy of limp flowers* **soft, flaccid**, loose, slack, lacking firmness, lax, unfirm, pliable, not taut, relaxed; **floppy**, drooping, droopy, sagging, hanging, pendulous.
OPPOSITES firm, stiff.
2 *we were all limp with exhaustion* **tired**, fatigued, weary, exhausted, worn out; lethargic, listless, spiritless, without energy, spent, weak, enervated, flagging.
OPPOSITE energetic.
3 *a limp and lacklustre speech* **uninspired**, uninspiring, insipid, flat, lifeless, vapid, half-hearted.
OPPOSITES inspired, stirring.

limpid ▶ **adjective 1** *a limpid pool | her limpid eyes* **clear**, transparent, glassy, glass-like, crystal clear, crystalline, see-through, translucent, pellucid, unclouded, uncloudy.
OPPOSITES opaque; muddy.
2 *the limpid clarity of his later novels* **lucid**, clear, plain, understandable, intelligible, comprehensible, perceptible, coherent, explicit, unambiguous, simple, vivid, sharp, direct, clear-cut, crystal clear, luminous, straightforward, distinct, perspicuous; *rare* luculent.
OPPOSITE unintelligible.
3 *it was a limpid, beautiful day* **calm**, still, serene, tranquil, placid, peaceful, untroubled, fair, fine.
OPPOSITES stormy; murky.

line¹ ▶ **noun 1** *he drew a line through the name | a pattern of wavy lines* dash, rule, bar, score; underline, underscore, stroke, slash, virgule, solidus; stripe, strip, band, streak, belt, striation; *technical* stria; *Brit.* oblique.
2 *there were new lines round her eyes and mouth* **wrinkle**, furrow, crease, crinkle, crow's foot, groove, corrugation; scar.
3 (usually **lines**) *the classic lines of its exterior* **contour**, **outline**, configuration, shape, figure, delineation, silhouette, profile, features.
4 *he headed the ball over the line | the county line* **boundary**, boundary line, limit, border, borderline, bound, bounding line, frontier, partition, demarcation line, dividing line, end point, cut-off point, termination, edge, pale, margin, perimeter, periphery, rim, extremity, fringe, threshold.
5 (usually **lines**) *they were behind enemy lines* **position**, formation, disposition, front, front line, firing line; trenches.
6 *he put the washing on the line | a fishing line* **cord**, rope, string, cable, wire, thread, twine, strand, filament, ligature.
7 *a line of soldiers* **file**, rank, column, string, chain; train, convoy, procession; row, queue; *Brit. informal* crocodile.
8 *a line of figures* **column**, row.
9 *it seemed to be the latest in a long line of crass decisions* **series**, sequence, succession, chain, string, train; progression, course, set, cycle.
10 *it stopped right in the line of flight of some bees* **course**, route, track, channel, path, way, run; trajectory, bearing, orientation.
11 *they took a very tough line with the industry right from the word go | ministers are obliged to follow the party line* **course of action**, course, procedure, MO, technique, way, tactic, tack, system, method, process, manner; **policy**, practice, scheme, approach, plan, programme, position, stance, philosophy, argument, avenue; *Latin* modus operandi.
12 *she had not been listening, but pursuing her own line of thought* **course**, direction, drift, tack, tendency, trend, bias, tenor.
13 *oh, come on, don't give me that line* **patter**, story, pitch, piece of fiction, fabrication; *informal* spiel.
14 (**lines**) *he couldn't seem to remember his lines* **words**, role, part, script, speech, dialogue.
15 *there are no jobs nowadays in my line* **line of work**, line of business, business, field, trade, occupation, employment, profession, work, job, calling, vocation, career, pursuit, activity, walk of life; **specialty**, forte, province, department, sphere, area, area of expertise, domain, realm; *French* métier; *informal* line of country, game, thing, bag, pigeon, racket.
16 *he's introduced his own line of cologne* **brand**, kind, sort, type, variety, make, label, trade name, trademark, registered trademark.
17 *a man from a noble line claiming royal descent* **ancestry**, family, parentage, birth, descent, lineage, extraction, derivation, heritage, genealogy, roots, house, dynasty, origin, background; stock, strain, race, bloodline, blood, breeding, pedigree, succession.
18 *the opening line of Wilfred Owen's 'Anthem for Doomed Youth'* **sentence**, phrase, group of words, prosodic unit, construction, clause, utterance; passage, extract, quotation, quote, citation, section, piece, part, snippet, sound bite, fragment, portion.

19 *perhaps I should drop Ralph a line* **note**, letter, card, postcard, message, bulletin, communication, epistle, missive, memorandum, dispatch, report; correspondence, word; *informal* memo.

□ **draw the line at** *I draw the line at the fish-hook method on humanitarian grounds* **stop short of**, refuse to accept, draw a line in the sand, baulk at; object to, take issue with, take exception to; *informal* put one's foot down about.
OPPOSITE approve of.

□ **in line 1** *the poor still had to stand in line for food stamps* **in a queue**, in a row, in a column, in a file.
2 *the adverts are in line with the editorial style of the magazines* **in agreement**, in accord, in accordance, in harmony, in step, in conformity; in compliance, in obedience.
OPPOSITES different, out of step.
3 *hold the front sight directly in line with the bullseye* **in alignment**, aligned, level, balanced, at the same height, straight; plumb, true; abreast, side by side.
4 *the referee seemed determined to keep him in line* **under control**, in order, in check, obedient, conforming with the rules.

□ **in line for** *he was now in line for promotion* **a candidate for**, in the running for, on the shortlist for, shortlisted for, being considered for, under consideration for, next in succession for, likely to receive, up for, ready for.

□ **lay it on the line** *soon, I'm going to have to lay it on the line, tell them what really has been happening* **speak frankly**, be direct, speak honestly, pull no punches, be blunt, not mince one's words, call a spade a spade; *informal* give it to someone straight, tell it like it is.
OPPOSITES equivocate, shilly-shally.

□ **on the line** *we should protect police officers whose lives are on the line* **at risk**, in danger, endangered, imperilled.

□ **toe the line** *sooner or later a boy has to learn to toe the line* **conform**, obey the rules, comply with the rules, observe the rules, abide by the rules, adhere to the rules, act in accordance with the rules, follow the rules, keep to the rules, stick to the rules; submit, yield; *informal* play it by the book, play by the rules, keep in step.
OPPOSITE misbehave.

▶ **verb 1** *her face was lined with age* **furrow**, wrinkle, crease, mark with lines, cover with lines, crinkle, pucker, corrugate.
2 *the driveway was lined by poplars* **border**, edge, fringe, bound, skirt, hem, rim.

□ **line up** *we entered the building and lined up* **form a queue**, form a line, form lines, get into rows/columns, file, queue up, group together, fall in, straighten up; *Military* dress; *Brit. informal* form a crocodile.

□ **line someone/something up 1** *they lined them up and shot them* **arrange in a line**, arrange in lines, put in rows, arrange in columns; group, marshal, align, range, straighten up, arrange, array, dispose; *Military* dress.
2 *we've lined up an all-star cast* **assemble**, get together, organize, prepare, arrange, lay on; get, obtain, procure, secure, produce, come up with, fix up, prearrange; book, schedule, timetable.

line[2] ▶ **verb** *a cardboard box lined with a blanket* **cover**, put a lining in, back, put a backing on, interline, face, panel, inlay, reinforce, encase; paper, decorate; stuff, fill, pack, pad; *archaic* ceil.

□ **line one's pockets** (*informal*) *he had lined his pockets with campaign funds* **make money**; accept bribes; embezzle money, siphon off money; *informal* feather one's nest, graft, be on the make, be on the take.

lineage ▶ **noun** *a Dutch nobleman of ancient lineage* **ancestry**, family, parentage, birth; **descent**, line, extraction, derivation, heritage, genealogy, roots, house, dynasty, origin, background; stock, strain, race, bloodline, blood, breeding, pedigree, succession.

lineaments ▶ **plural noun** *the lineaments of his face* **distinctive features**, features, distinguishing characteristics, hallmarks, properties, traits; **form**, outline, lines, contours; configuration, physiognomy, profile, face, countenance, visage.

lined[1] ▶ **adjective 1** *a pad of lined paper* **ruled**, feint; scored, striped, stripy, banded, streaked, striated.
OPPOSITES plain, blank.
2 *his lined, weather-worn face* **wrinkled**, wrinkly, furrowed, creased, marked with lines, covered with lines, crinkled, wizened, leathery, worn, puckered, grooved, corrugated; scarred.
OPPOSITE smooth.

lined[2] ▶ **adjective** *lined curtains* **covered**, backed, interlined; faced, panelled, inlaid; reinforced, encased, papered, decorated; stuffed, filled, packed, padded; *archaic* ceiled.

liner ▶ **noun 1** *the luxury liner QE II* **ship**, ocean liner, passenger vessel, boat.
2 *her eyes were ringed with liner* **eyeliner**, eye pencil, kohl pencil, kohl, eyeshadow, eyebrow pencil, lipliner.

line-up ▶ **noun 1** *they saw the star-studded line-up as an opportunity to boost viewing figures* **list of performers**, list, listing, cast, bill, programme.
2 *United's starting line-up* **list of players**, team, squad, side, selection.
3 *you've got a long line-up of customers at the ticket window* **queue**, line, row, column; *Brit. informal* crocodile.

linger ▶ **verb 1** *the crowd lingered for a long time, until it was almost dark* **wait around**, stay, remain, stay put, wait; loiter, dawdle, dally, take one's time, lag behind, straggle, dither, potter about/around/round, pause; procrastinate, stall, delay; *informal* dilly-dally, stick around, hang around/round, hang on, hang back; *dated* tarry.
OPPOSITE leave.
2 *the infection can linger for many years | ten years later, the memory lingers on* **persist**, continue, remain, stay; be protracted, endure, carry on, last, keep on/up, hold; survive, abide; *informal* hang around/round.
OPPOSITES vanish, disappear.

> **CHOOSE THE RIGHT WORD**
>
> **linger, loiter, dawdle**
>
> The idea common to these words is that of prolonging an activity or staying longer than necessary.
>
> - A person may **linger** somewhere because they are enjoying being there, not merely because they are wasting time (*just linger over your coffee and liqueurs*). If something such as a person's *fingers, eyes,* or *look* linger, they stay in one place for a long time (*her fingers linger on his | Merrill's gaze lingered on his mouth*). *Linger* is also used of something, typically an abstract noun, that lasts longer than normal or expected (*the memory lingered on*); the adjectival form *lingering* is often used in this sense (*a lingering death*).
> - **Loiter** is always used in a spatial sense: it is to stay somewhere too long and typically be up to no good (*teenagers loitering in front of a newsagent's, drinking shandy and smoking*).
> - **Dawdling** is normally used of slow, idle movement (*a handful of people crossed the square, dawdling on their way home*) and often implies that someone is wasting time (*don't dawdle over your breakfast*).

lingerie ▶ **noun** *fine silk lingerie* **women's underwear**, underclothes, underclothing, undergarments, nightwear, nightclothes; *informal* undies, frillies, underthings, unmentionables; *Brit. informal* smalls; *rare* underlinen.

lingering ▶ **adjective 1** *there were still some lingering doubts in my mind* **remaining**, surviving, persisting, abiding, nagging, niggling, gnawing, lasting, residual.
2 *a lingering recession* **protracted**, persistent, prolonged, long-drawn-out, long-lasting, lasting, dragging, chronic, unabating, long-standing.
OPPOSITE short-lived.

lingo (*informal*) ▶ **noun 1** *it doesn't matter if you can't speak the lingo* **language**, tongue, speech, parlance, vocabulary, mother tongue, native tongue; dialect, idiom, vernacular, slang, patois; *informal* patter.
2 *the hacker lingo makes this magazine indecipherable* **jargon**, terminology, idiom, slang, argot, cant; *informal* -ese, -speak, mumbo-jumbo, gobbledegook.

linguistic ▶ **adjective** *the meanings of linguistic expressions | a child's linguistic ability* **language-producing**, semantic, lingual, semasiological; rhetorical, verbal, poetic, expressive.

lining ▶ **noun** *a cape with a fur lining* **backing**, interlining, facing, inlay, reinforcement, liner; panelling; quilting, cushioning, padding, wadding, stuffing, filling.

link ▶ **noun 1** *a chain made of steel links* **loop**, ring, connection, connective, connector, coupling, joint, knot.
2 *the links between transport and the environment* **connection**, relationship, relatedness, association, linkage, tie-up.
3 *they cultivated their links with the labour movement* **bond**, tie, attachment, connection, relationship, association, affiliation; mutual interest, liaison; nexus.
4 *one of the links in the organization* **component**, constituent, element, part, piece, member, division.

▶ **verb 1** *four boxes were linked together* **join**, connect, fasten, attach, bind, unite, combine, amalgamate; clamp, secure, fix, affix, tie, stick, hitch, bond, knit, glue, cement, fuse, weld, solder, couple, yoke.
OPPOSITES detach, separate.
2 *there wasn't a scrap of evidence linking him with the body* **associate**, connect, relate, join, bracket, draw a connection between, marry, wed.

lion ▶ **noun 1** *a lion stands ready to attack* big cat; king of the beasts; lioness.
2 *my lord was a lion amongst men* **hero**, man of courage, brave man, lionheart, lionhearted man; conqueror, champion, conquering hero, warrior, knight, paladin.
3 *he hobnobbed with all the lions of the symphony hall* **celebrity**, person of note, dignitary, notable, VIP, personality, public figure, pillar of society, luminary; star, superstar, big name, leading light, idol, magnate; *informal* big shot, bigwig, big noise, big wheel, big cheese, big gun, somebody, celeb, hotshot, megastar.

□ **beard the lion in his den defy danger**, face up to danger, brave danger, confront danger, stand up to danger; court destruction, tempt providence; *informal* face the music, bell the cat, bite the bullet.

□ **the lion's share** *the lion's share of the profits* **most**, the majority, the larger part/number, the greater part/number, the best/better part, the main part, more than half, the bulk, the preponderance.

WORD LINKS
relating to lions **leonine**
collective noun **pride, sawt**
home **den**

lionhearted ▶ **adjective** *the lionhearted champion of freedom* **brave**, courageous, valiant, gallant, intrepid, valorous, fearless, bold, daring; stout-hearted, stalwart, staunch, heroic, audacious, resolute, undaunted, dauntless, doughty, plucky, game, mettlesome, assertive; *informal* gutsy, spunky.
OPPOSITES cowardly, timid, mousy.

lionize ▶ **verb** *the band's leader has been lionized by the media* **celebrate**, fête, glorify, honour, bestow honour on, exalt, acclaim, admire, commend, sing/sound the praises of, praise, extol, applaud, hail, make a fuss of/over, make much of, cry up, venerate, eulogize, sing paeans to, reverence, pay homage to, pay tribute to, put on a pedestal, hero-worship, worship, idolize, adulate; aggrandize; *rare* laud, panegyrize.
OPPOSITE vilify.

lip ▶ **noun 1** *the lip of the coffee pot | the lip of the crater* **edge**, rim, brim, margin, border, verge, brink; boundary, perimeter; mouth.
OPPOSITE centre.
2 (*informal*) *I'll tan your hide if I have any more of your lip* **insolence**, impertinence, impudence, cheek, rudeness, audacity, effrontery, disrespect, presumptuousness, temerity, brazenness; *informal* sauce, backchat, mouth, brass neck, gall.
OPPOSITE politeness.

□ **keep a stiff upper lip keep control of oneself**, not show emotion, appear unaffected, bite one's lip; *informal* keep one's cool.

WORD LINKS
relating to the lips **labial**
related prefix **labio-** (e.g. *labiodental*)

liquefy ▶ **verb** *above a certain temperature it is impossible to liquefy a gas | the wine was warm and the cheese had liquefied* **make/become liquid**, condense, dissolve, precipitate; liquidize, melt; deliquesce, run.
OPPOSITES solidify, coagulate; gasify.

CHOOSE THE RIGHT WORD

liquid, fluid

Just as these two words are close in their scientific senses, they have similar figurative meanings.

- Scientifically, **liquid** is the narrower term, denoting a fluid, such as water or oil, that flows but has constant volume (at constant temperature and pressure). A liquid has no fixed shape and yields easily to external pressure; thus we can talk metaphorically about *liquid assets* (such as shares or commodities) that can easily be converted into cash, while *a liquid market* features much trading and continual price movements. *Liquid* is also used of things that are clear to the eye or ear (*liquid blue eyes | the liquid song of a bird*).
- In its scientific sense, **fluid** denotes anything that flows, including gases, which can change shape more dramatically than liquids. In figurative uses, a *fluid situation* is also very volatile, while *fluid pricing*, to which airline flights and package holidays in particular are now subject, means that their prices are varied continually, according to the demand from customers or the cash-flow requirements of the business. *Fluid* is also used to indicate effortless and graceful movement (*in one fluid movement, he picked up the bag and its contents*).

liquid ▶ **adjective 1** *liquid fuels* **fluid**, flowing, running; runny, watery, thin, sloppy, aqueous, liquefied; melted, molten, thawed, dissolved, uncongealed; *technical* hydrous.
OPPOSITES solid; gaseous.
2 *her liquid eyes* **clear**, transparent, limpid, crystal clear, crystalline, see-through; translucent, pellucid, unclouded, uncloudy; bright, shining, brilliant, glowing, gleaming.
OPPOSITES cloudy; opaque.
3 *her liquid voice* **pure**, clear, smooth, fluent, distinct, clarion; **mellifluous**, dulcet, mellow, sweet, sweet-sounding, sweet-toned, soft, melodious, honeyed, soothing, tuneful, musical, lilting, lyrical, harmonious, euphonious; *rare* mellifluent.
OPPOSITES cacophonous, disharmonious.
4 *liquid assets* **convertible**, negotiable, disposable, usable, realizable, obtainable, spendable.
OPPOSITES unavailable, tied up.

▶ **noun** *a vat of liquid* **fluid**; moisture, wet, wetness, damp, dampness; liquor; solution; juice, sap, secretion.
OPPOSITES solid; gas.

WORD LINKS
science of moving liquids **hydraulics**

liquidate ▶ **verb 1** *if the company was liquidated, there would be enough funds released to honour the debts* **close down**, wind up, put into liquidation, dissolve, break up, disband, terminate.
2 *he would normally have liquidated his share portfolio* **convert to cash**, convert, cash, cash in, sell off, sell up, realize.
3 *the fund was raided for purposes other than liquidating the public debt* **pay off**, pay, pay in full, settle, clear, discharge, square, make good, honour, defray, satisfy, account for; remit.
4 (*informal*) *nationalist rivals were liquidated in bloody purges*. See KILL.

liquidize ▶ **verb** *liquidize a large raw carrot to a smooth paste* **purée**, cream, liquefy, pulp, crush, press; blend, process.
OPPOSITE condense.

liquor *See centre pages for list of* **Drinks**
▶ **noun 1** *it is not permitted to sell liquor to a person under 18* **alcohol**, spirits, alcoholic drink, strong drink, drink, intoxicating liquor, intoxicant; *informal* booze, hard stuff, shorts, the demon drink, firewater, juice, grog; *N. Amer. informal* the sauce, hooch.
2 *carefully strain the cooking liquor into the sauce* **stock**, broth, bouillon, juice, gravy, liquid, infusion, extract, concentrate, decoction.

lissom ▶ **adjective** *she had the lissom body of a dancer* **supple**, lithe, limber, graceful, elegant, spry, flexible, loose-limbed, agile, nimble, deft, dexterous, fit; **slim**, slender, thin, willowy, sylphlike, sleek, trim.
OPPOSITE portly.

list[1] *See centre pages for list of* **Lists**
▶ **noun** *a list of the world's wealthiest people* **catalogue**, inventory, record, register, roll, file, index, directory, listing, checklist, tally, docket, ticket, enumeration, table, tabulation; series, litany, recital.
▶ **verb** *the accounts are listed alphabetically* **record**, register, make a list of, note down, write down, set down, enter; itemize, enumerate, recite, catalogue, file, log, minute, tabulate, categorize, inventory, schedule, chronicle; classify, group, arrange, sort, rank, alphabetize, index.

list[2] ▶ **verb** *the boat listed to one side* **lean**, lean over, tilt, tip, heel, heel over, careen, cant, pitch, toss, roll, incline, slant, slope, be at an angle, bank, keel over.
OPPOSITE be on an even keel.

listen ▶ **verb 1** *I've just been listening to the news* **hear**, pay attention, be attentive, attend, concentrate on, concentrate on hearing, give ear to, lend an ear to; hang on someone's words; keep one's ears open, prick up one's ears; *informal* be all ears, pin back one's ears, get a load of, tune in; *literary* hark, hearken.
2 *policy-makers should listen to popular opinion* **pay attention**, take heed, heed, give heed, take notice, take note, mind, observe, watch, follow, notice, mark, bear in mind, give a thought to, take into consideration, take into account, take to heart, hang on, accept, believe; obey, do as one is told by.
OPPOSITES ignore, be deaf to.

□ **listen in** *anyone with the right radio receiver can listen in on calls* **eavesdrop**, spy; overhear, tap, wiretap, bug, monitor; *informal* snoop.

listless ▶ **adjective** *she was pale and listless | a listless performance* **lethargic**, enervated, lackadaisical, spiritless, unenergetic, lifeless, vigourless, lacking energy, limp, effete; **languid**, languorous, languishing, inactive, inert, sluggish, torpid, supine, half-hearted, lukewarm, indifferent, uninterested, impassive; indolent, idle, apathetic, shiftless, slothful; passive, dull, heavy.
OPPOSITES energetic, lively.

CHOOSE THE RIGHT WORD

listless, languid, lethargic

See LANGUID.

litany ▶ **noun 1** *the lips of others had moved also, repeating the litany* **prayer**, invocation, petition, supplication, devotion, entreaty; *archaic* orison.
2 *a litany of complaints* **recital**, recitation, repetition, enumeration, account, refrain; **list**, listing, catalogue, inventory, roll.

literacy ▶ **noun** *tests of literacy and numeracy* **ability to read and write**, reading/writing ability, reading/writing proficiency; learning, book learning, education, scholarship, schooling; letters.
OPPOSITE illiteracy.

literal ▶ **adjective 1** *those who believe in the literal truth of the biblical Genesis | it is unique, in the literal sense of that word* **strict**, **factual**, plain, simple, bare, exact, straightforward, stark; unvarnished, unexaggerated, unembellished, undistorted, unadulterated; objective, narrow, correct, true, truthful, faithful, accurate, genuine, authentic, veritable, veracious, gospel.
OPPOSITES metaphorical, figurative; loose, approximate.

L

2 *a literal translation* **word-for-word**, verbatim, line-for-line, letter-for-letter; exact, precise, faithful, close, strict, to the letter, undeviating, true, accurate; *rare* literatim.
OPPOSITES loose, liberal, vague.
3 *his literal, unrhetorical manner* **literal-minded**, down-to-earth, factual, matter-of-fact, no-nonsense, unsentimental, level-headed, hard-headed; prosaic, unimaginative, colourless, pedestrian, tedious, boring, dull, humdrum, uninspired, uninspiring, prosy.
OPPOSITE whimsical.
▶ **noun** *William read through the article, correcting two literals* **misprint**, error, mistake, slip, slip of the pen, printing/typographical/typesetting/keyboarding/keying/typing error/mistake, corrigendum, erratum; *informal* typo, howler.

literally ▶ **adverb** *their name, translated literally, means 'the river'* **verbatim**, word for word, line for line, letter for letter, to the letter; exactly, precisely, faithfully, closely, strictly, strictly speaking, accurately, rigorously; *rare* literatim.
OPPOSITES loosely, imprecisely; metaphorically.

literary ▶ **adjective 1** *an established canon of literary works* **written**; poetic, artistic, dramatic; published, printed, in print.
2 *her literary friends | a literary magazine* **scholarly**, learned, intellectual, cultured, erudite, bookish, highbrow, studious, cerebral, lettered, academic, cultivated, civilized; well read, widely read, knowledgeable, educated, well educated; *informal* brainy.
OPPOSITES ill-educated; popular.
3 *literary language* **formal**, written; **poetic**, dramatic, dignified, solemn; elaborate, ornate, flowery, purple.
OPPOSITES informal, colloquial, vernacular.

literate ▶ **adjective 1** *their parents were barely literate* **able to read and write**.
OPPOSITE illiterate.
2 *a literate, informed public* **educated**, well educated, well read, widely read, scholarly, learned, schooled, knowledgeable, intellectual, intelligent, erudite, lettered, cultured, cultivated, sophisticated, well informed.
OPPOSITE ignorant.
3 *a literate and readable study* **well written**, articulate, lucid, eloquent, stylish, polished.
OPPOSITE badly written.

L

literature *See centre pages for lists of*
Literary Schools, Movements, and Groups **Plays** **Poems** **Stories**
▶ **noun 1** *a lecturer in English literature* **written works**, writings, (creative) writing, literary texts, compositions, letters, belles-lettres; printed works, published works; humanities, arts, liberal arts.
2 *the literature on prototype theory* **publications**, published writings, texts, reports, studies, relevant works.
3 *noticeboards have been covered with election literature* **printed matter**, brochures, leaflets, pamphlets, circulars, flyers, handouts, handbills, mailshots, bulletins, documentation, publicity, blurb, notices, information, data, facts; *informal* bumf, junk mail.

lithe ▶ **adjective** *his tall lithe figure* **agile**, graceful, supple, limber, loose-limbed, nimble, deft, spry, flexible, pliant, pliable, lissom, willowy, acrobatic, fit; *rare* lithesome.
OPPOSITES clumsy, stiff.

litigant ▶ **noun** *a litigant in civil proceedings* **litigator**, opponent in law, opponent, contestant, contender, disputant, plaintiff, claimant, complainant, petitioner, apellant, respondent, party, interest, defendant, accused.

litigation ▶ **noun** *he objected to some passages in the book, but did not resort to litigation* **legal proceeding(s)**, legal action, lawsuit, legal dispute, legal case, case, legal contest, action, cause, judicial proceeding(s), suit, suit at law, legal process, prosecution, bringing of charges, indictment, trial.

litter ▶ **noun 1** *always clear up after a picnic and never drop litter* **rubbish**, refuse, junk, waste, debris, odds and ends, scraps, leavings, fragments, detritus, flotsam, discarded matter, dross, muck; *N. Amer.* trash, garbage.
2 *she looked at the litter of glasses around her* **clutter**, jumble, muddle, mess, tangle, heap, disorder, untidiness, confusion, hotchpotch, disarray, disorganization, disarrangement, turmoil; *informal* shambles; *rare* olla podrida.
3 *a litter of kittens* **brood**, family; young, offspring, progeny, issue; *rare* progeniture.
4 *threshed straw had to be taken from the barns to the horses for use as litter* **animal bedding**, bedding, straw, floor covering.
5 *he was conveyed the rest of the way in a horse-drawn litter* **sedan chair**, palanquin; stretcher, portable bed/couch.
▶ **verb** *clothes and newspapers littered the floor* **make untidy**, mess up, make a mess of, clutter up, throw into disorder, be strewn about, be scattered about, be jumbled, be disarranged; *informal* make a shambles of, trash; *literary* bestrew, besmirch.

little ▶ **adjective 1** *a little writing desk* **small**, small-scale, compact; mini, miniature, tiny, minute, minuscule; toy, baby, pocket, undersized, dwarf, midget; bijou, dainty, cute, sweet, dear; *Scottish* wee; *informal* teeny, teeny-weeny, teensy, teensy-weensy, itsy-bitsy, tiddly, half-pint, dinky; *Brit. informal* titchy, ickle; *N. Amer. informal* little-bitty, vest-pocket.
OPPOSITES big, large.
2 *the smile vanished from the little man's face* **short**, small, slight, thin, petite, diminutive, tiny; squat, stubby; elfin, dwarf, dwarfish, midget, pygmy, bantam, homuncular, Lilliputian; *Scottish* wee; *informal* teeny, teeny-weeny, pint-sized, knee high to a grasshopper.
OPPOSITES big, large.
3 *my little sister* **young**, younger, junior, small, baby, infant, minor.
OPPOSITES big, old, elder.
4 *I was a bodyguard for a little while* **brief**, short, short-lived; fleeting, momentary, transitory, transient, ephemeral, evanescent, infinitesimal; fast, quick, hasty, cursory; *Scottish* wee.
OPPOSITE long.
5 *this car does have a few little problems* **minor**, **unimportant**, insignificant, trivial, trifling, petty, paltry, inconsequential, negligible, inconsiderable, nugatory, of minor importance, of little/no account.
OPPOSITES significant, important.
▶ **determiner** *they have low status and little political influence* **hardly any**, not much, slight, small, scant, limited, restricted, modest, little or no, minimal, negligible; insufficient, inadequate.
OPPOSITES considerable, a great deal of.
□ **a little 1** *if it's too thick, add a little water* **some**, **a small amount of**, a bit of, a touch of, a soupçon of, a dash of, a taste of, a dab of, a spot of, a modicum of, a morsel of, a fragment of, a snippet of, a tinge of, a particle of, a jot of, a shade of, a suggestion of, a trace of, a hint of, a suspicion of; a dribble of, a splash of, a driblet of; a pinch of, a sprinkling of, a sprinkle of, a grain of, a speck of; *informal* a smidgen of, a tad of.
OPPOSITES a lot of, a great deal of.
2 *after a little, Oliver came in* **a short time**, a little while, a bit, an interval, a short spell, a short period; a minute, a moment, a second, a split second, an instant, a flash; *informal* a sec, a mo, a jiffy, a jiff.
OPPOSITE a long time.
3 *the whole scene does remind me a little of the Adriatic* **slightly**, faintly, remotely, vaguely; moderately, somewhat, a little bit, quite, to some degree, fairly; *informal* sort of, kind of, kinda.
OPPOSITE a great deal.
□ **little by little** *little by little, the town was turning into ruins* **gradually**, slowly, by degrees, by stages, step by step, piecemeal, progressively, bit by bit, inch by inch, inchmeal; subtly, imperceptibly, unnoticeably.
OPPOSITES immediately, all at once.
▶ **adverb 1** *he is little known as a teacher* **hardly**, barely, scarcely, not much, only slightly, slightly, only just.
OPPOSITE well.
2 *this disease is little seen nowadays* **rarely**, seldom, infrequently, hardly ever, hardly, scarcely ever, scarcely, not much.
OPPOSITE often.

liturgical ▶ **adjective** *liturgical music* **ceremonial**, ritual, solemn, sacramental, hieratic, church, for use in church.
OPPOSITE secular.

liturgy ▶ **noun** *the Anglican liturgy* **ritual**, worship, service, ceremony, rite, observance, celebration, ordinance, office, sacrament, solemnity, ceremonial; formulation, form, custom, practice, tradition, rubric.

live[1] (rhymes with 'give') ▶ **verb 1** *he was one of the greatest mathematicians who ever lived* **exist**, **be alive**, be, have being, have life; breathe, draw breath, walk the earth; be extant; *informal* be in the land of the living.
OPPOSITES die, be dead.
2 *I live in central London | about 38,000 people live in the area* **reside**, have one's home, have one's residence, be settled; be housed, lodge, board; inhabit, occupy, populate; *Scottish* stay; *informal* hang out, hang one's hat, put up; *formal* dwell, sojourn, be domiciled; *archaic* bide.
3 *he lived quietly during his remaining years* **pass one's life**, spend one's life, lead one's life, have a life, have a lifestyle; behave, conduct oneself, comport oneself.
4 *she had lived a difficult life* **experience**, spend, pass, lead, have, go through, undergo.
5 *old people living on small fixed pensions | Freddy lived by his wits* **survive**, make a living, earn one's living, eke out a living; subsist, support oneself, sustain oneself; keep alive, stay alive, maintain oneself, make ends meet, keep body and soul together.
6 *couldn't we just forget about work for one afternoon and live a little?* **enjoy oneself**, enjoy life, have fun, be happy, live life to the full; flourish, prosper, thrive, make the most of life.
□ **live it up** (*informal*) *those two are living it up in Hawaii* **live extravagantly**, live in the lap of luxury, live in clover; **carouse**, revel, overindulge, party, enjoy oneself, celebrate, have a good time, roister; *informal* go on a spree, push the boat out, paint the town red, have a ball, make whoopee, go overboard, make a pig of oneself; *N. Amer. informal* live high on/off the hog; *archaic* wassail.
□ **live off/on** *scavenging seabirds live off discarded fish* **subsist on**, feed on/off,

rely for nourishment on, thrive on, depend on; **eat**, consume, use.

live[2] (rhymes with 'five') ▶ adjective **1** *the use of live bait* **living**, alive, having life, breathing; animate, organic, biological, sentient; existing, existent, extant; *informal* in the land of the living, among the living; *archaic* quick.
OPPOSITES dead, inanimate.
2 *this is her first live appearance in Britain | a live radio phone-in* **in the flesh**, personal, in person, actual; **not pre-recorded**, not recorded, unedited; not delayed, real-time; with an audience.
OPPOSITE recorded.
3 *he touched a live rail while working on the track* **electrified**, charged, powered, connected, active, switched on; *informal* hot.
OPPOSITE inactive.
4 *the fire grate was full of live coals* **hot**, **glowing**, red hot, aglow, smouldering; burning, alight, flaming, aflame, blazing, fiery, ignited, on fire, afire.
5 *a live grenade* **unexploded**, explosive, explodable, active; loaded, charged, primed; unstable, volatile.
OPPOSITE inactive.
6 *gay rights has become a live issue across America* **topical**, current, of current interest, contemporary; **burning**, pressing, important, vital; relevant, pertinent; controversial, debatable, unsettled.
□ **live wire** *she's a real live wire* **energetic person**; *informal* **ball of fire**, fireball, human dynamo, busy bee, eager beaver, go-getter, whizz-kid, mover and shaker, powerhouse, life and soul of the party, tiger, demon.

livelihood ▶ noun *many people in the area relied on the coconut plantations for their livelihood* **income**, source of income, means of support, means, living, subsistence, keep, maintenance, sustenance, nourishment, daily bread, upkeep; job, work, employment, occupation, trade, profession, career; *informal* bread and butter.

livelong ▶ adjective (*literary*) *we decided to hunt and play together the livelong day* **entire**, whole, total, complete, full, long; unbroken, undivided, continuous.

lively ▶ adjective **1** *the bride was an attractive and lively young woman* **energetic**, active, animated, vigorous, dynamic, full of life, outgoing, spirited, high-spirited, vivacious, enthusiastic, vibrant, buoyant, exuberant, effervescent, cheerful; bouncy, bubbly, perky, sparkling, sprightly, spry, youthful, zesty, zestful, frisky, skittish; fun, fun-loving; *informal* bright-eyed and bushy-tailed, full of beans, chirpy, go-go, chipper, peppy, zippy, zappy, full of vim and vigour; *N. Amer. informal* peart.
OPPOSITES listless, lifeless, apathetic.
2 *a lively West End bar* **busy**, crowded, bustling, hectic, swarming, teeming, astir, buzzing, thronging; **vibrant**, boisterous, jolly, festive; *informal* hopping, jumping, buzzy.
OPPOSITES quiet, dead.
3 *a lively debate* **heated**, vigorous, stimulating, animated, spirited, enthusiastic, forceful; exciting, stirring, interesting, eventful, memorable.
OPPOSITES lifeless, dull.
4 *a lively portrait of the local community* **vivid**, colourful, striking, stirring, graphic, bold, strong, interesting, effective, imaginative.
OPPOSITES lifeless, dull.
5 *he bowled at a lively pace* **brisk**, quick, fast, rapid, swift, speedy, smart, vigorous, fast and furious; *informal* nippy, snappy.
OPPOSITE slow.
6 *the press is making things lively for the Government* **awkward**, tricky, difficult, challenging; **eventful**, exciting, busy; *informal* hairy.
OPPOSITES easy, peaceful.

liven ▶ verb
□ **liven up** *at this, he seemed to liven up* **brighten up**, cheer up, perk up, wake up, revive, rally, pick up, become lively, bounce back; *informal* buck up.
□ **liven someone/something up** *he could do with a drink to liven him up* **brighten up**, cheer up, enliven, put some life into, animate, put some spark into, raise someone's spirits, perk up, spice up, ginger up, make lively, waken/wake up, hearten, gladden, invigorate, give a boost to, rejuvenate, vitalize, restore, revive, refresh, vivify, put some zest into, galvanize, stimulate, stir up, get going; *informal* buck up, pep up, jazz up, hot up.
OPPOSITE calm someone down.

liver ▶ noun

WORD LINKS

relating to the liver	**hepatic**
related prefix	**hepato-** (e.g. ***hepatotoxic***)
inflammation of the liver	**hepatitis**
removal of the liver	**hepatectomy**

livery ▶ noun *pageboys in scarlet and green livery* **uniform**, regalia, costume, dress, attire, habit, garb, clothes, clothing, outfit, suit, garments, ensemble, robes, finery; *informal* get-up, gear, togs, clobber, duds, kit; *formal* apparel; *literary* raiment, array; *archaic* vestments.

livid ▶ adjective **1** (*informal*) *he was livid at finding himself back on the bench* **furious**, angry, infuriated, irate, fuming, raging, seething, incensed, enraged, angered, beside oneself, wrathful, ireful, maddened, cross, annoyed, irritated, exasperated, indignant; *informal* mad, boiling, wild, seeing red, hot under the collar, up in arms, foaming at the mouth, on the warpath, steamed up, fit to be tied.
2 *Quinn had a livid bruise on the side of his jaw* **purplish**, bluish, dark, discoloured, black and blue, purple, greyish-blue; bruised; angry.

living ▶ noun **1** *she was cleaning floors for a living* **livelihood**, income, source of income, means of support, means, subsistence, keep, maintenance, sustenance, nourishment, daily bread, upkeep; job, work, employment, occupation, trade, profession, career; *informal* bread and butter.
2 *making informed choices about healthy living | urban living* **way of life**, lifestyle, manner of living, way of living, mode of living, life; conduct, behaviour, activities; customs, habits, ways.
▶ adjective **1** *living organisms* **alive**, live, having life; animate, organic, biological, sentient; breathing, moving; existing, existent; *informal* in the land of the living, among the living, alive and kicking; *archaic* quick.
OPPOSITES dead, inanimate, extinct.
2 *English, unlike Latin, is a living language* **current**, contemporary, present; **in use**, operative, active, operating, ongoing, continuing, surviving, extant, persisting, remaining, abiding; existing, existent, in existence.
OPPOSITES dead, obsolete, extinct.
3 *he committed to paper a living image of the man* **exact**, faithful, true to life, speaking, authentic, genuine; close, near, similar, like, alike.
OPPOSITE inaccurate.

living room ▶ noun *the television was on in the living room* **sitting room**, lounge, parlour, front room, drawing room, morning room, reception room, salon, family room; TV room; common room.

lizard ▶ noun

WORD LINKS

relating to lizards **saurian**

load ▶ noun **1** *MacDowell's got a load to deliver | the rear seats can be folded forward to carry larger loads* **cargo**, freight, freightage, charge, burden; pack, bundle, parcel, bale; consignment, haul, delivery, shipment, batch; goods, merchandise, payload; contents; lorryload, truckload, shipload, boatload, containerload, busload, vanload; *archaic* lading.
2 (*informal*) *I bought* ***a load of*** *clothes | a hot dog with* ***loads of*** *fried onions* **a lot**, **a great deal**, a great/large amount, a large quantity, a number, an abundance, a wealth, a profusion, a mountain; many, plenty, reams; ample; *informal* a heap, a mass, a pile, an ocean, a stack, a ton, lots, heaps, masses, piles, oceans, stacks, tons, oodles, scads; *Brit. informal* a shedload, lashings; *Austral./NZ informal* a swag; *vulgar slang* a shitload.
OPPOSITE few.
3 *a heavy teaching load* **commitment**, responsibility, duty, obligation, onus, charge, weight; burden, encumbrance, cross, millstone, albatross; trouble, worry, strain, pressure.
▶ verb **1** *she began to load the washing machine | we quickly loaded the van with our diving gear* **fill**, fill up, pack, stuff, cram, pile, heap, stack; lade, freight, charge; stock.
OPPOSITE unload.
2 *Larry loaded boxes into the jeep* **pack**, stow, store, stack, bundle, stuff, cram, squeeze, jam, wedge; place, deposit, put away.
OPPOSITE unload.
3 *loading the committee with responsibilities means some subjects receive less attention than others* **burden**, weigh down, weight, saddle, charge; overburden, overwhelm, encumber, hamper, handicap, tax, strain, oppress, trouble, worry; *rare* trammel.
4 *within a few weeks, Richard was loading Marshal with honours* **reward**, ply, regale, shower; supply, provide.
5 *he began to load a gun* **prime**, charge, arm, fill, prepare to fire/use.
OPPOSITE unload.
6 *load the cassette into the camcorder* **insert**, put, place, fit, slide, slot.
OPPOSITE remove.
7 *the dice are loaded against him* **bias**, rig, fix, set up; weight.

loaded ▶ adjective **1** *a loaded freight train | a loaded tray* **full**, filled, laden, packed, burdened, stuffed, crammed, brimming, freighted, stacked; supplied, stocked; *informal* chock-full, chock-a-block.
OPPOSITE empty.
2 *a loaded gun* **primed**, charged, armed, filled, containing ammunition, ready to fire, ready for use.
OPPOSITE unloaded.
3 (*informal*) *they could have afforded to buy the stuff—their parents were all loaded* **rich**, wealthy, well off, well-to-do, affluent, prosperous, moneyed, with deep pockets, of means; *informal* well heeled, rolling in it, made of money, flush, in clover, on easy street.
OPPOSITE poor.
4 (*N. Amer. informal*) *it was an excuse for everyone to get loaded.* See DRUNK.
OPPOSITE sober.
5 *loaded dice* **biased**, rigged, fixed; weighted; *informal* crooked.
OPPOSITE honest.
6 *a loaded question | 'green' is a politically loaded word* **charged**, meaningful, pregnant; tendentious, emotive, sensitive, difficult, delicate.
OPPOSITES ingenuous, straightforward.

loaf[1] ▶ noun. *See centre pages for list of* **Bread and Bread Rolls**

loaf[2] ▶ verb *he was loafing around his father's yards* **laze**, lounge, loll; do nothing, take things easy, idle, be idle, shirk one's duties; waste time, fritter away time, kill time, while away the time, twiddle one's thumbs, sit on one's hands, dawdle, dally; *informal* hang around/round, skive; *Brit. informal* hang about, mooch about/around; *N. Amer. informal* bum around.
OPPOSITES work, toil.

loafer ▶ noun **idler**, layabout, good-for-nothing, ne'er-do-well, do-nothing, lounger, shirker, sluggard, laggard, slugabed, malingerer; *informal* skiver, waster, slacker, cyberslacker, slob, lazybones.

loan ▶ noun *a loan to purchase industrial goods* **credit**, advance; mortgage, overdraft; debenture; **lending**, moneylending, advancing; *Brit. informal* sub.
▶ verb **1** *a friend loaned me £1,500 | works of art will be loaned to the new museum for a period of twenty years* **lend**, advance, give credit, credit, allow; give on loan, give someone the loan of, let someone have the use of, let out, lease, charter, hire; *Brit. informal* sub.
OPPOSITE borrow.
2 *the majority of exhibits have been loaned from the Kelvingrove Art Gallery* **borrow**, ask for the loan of, receive/take on loan, use temporarily.

loath ▶ adjective *the batsmen were loath to take risks* **reluctant**, unwilling, disinclined, ill-disposed, not in the mood; hesitant; against, averse, opposed, resistant, hostile, antagonistic; resisting.
OPPOSITES willing, eager.

loathe ▶ verb *the staff at school loathed him | cats loathe vinegar* **hate**, detest, abhor, despise, abominate, dislike greatly, execrate; have a strong aversion to, feel repugnance towards, not be able to bear, not be able to stand, shrink from, recoil from, be repelled by, be unable to stomach, find intolerable.
OPPOSITES love, like.

loathing ▶ noun *his face was filled with loathing for the man in front of him* **hatred**, hate, detestation, abhorrence, abomination, execration, odium; antipathy, dislike, hostility, animosity, ill will, ill feeling, bad feeling, malice, animus, enmity, aversion; repugnance, disgust, revulsion.
OPPOSITE love.

loathsome ▶ adjective *a foul and loathsome beast | a loathsome crime against innocent people* **hateful**, detestable, abhorrent, repulsive, odious, repugnant, repellent, disgusting, revolting, sickening, nauseating, abominable, despicable, contemptible, reprehensible, execrable, damnable; hideous, ghastly, vile, horrible, nasty, frightful, obnoxious, gross, foul, offensive, disagreeable; *informal* horrid, yucky; *literary* noisome.
OPPOSITES lovable, delightful, pleasant.

lob ▶ verb *they lobbed grenades on to the gun platform* **throw**, toss, fling, pitch, shy, hurl, pelt, sling, loft, cast, let fly with, flip; launch, propel, impel; bowl; *informal* chuck, bung, heave.

lobby ▶ noun **1** *they went into the hotel lobby* **entrance hall**, hallway, hall, entrance, vestibule, foyer, reception area, outer room, waiting room, anteroom, antechamber, porch; corridor, passage, passageway.
2 *the anti-hunt lobby* **pressure group**, interest group, interest, movement, campaign, crusade, lobbyists, supporters; faction, camp, bloc, clique; *Brit.* ginger group.
▶ verb **1** *readers are urged to lobby their MPs on the issue* **seek to influence**, try to persuade, bring pressure to bear on, importune, persuade, influence, sway; petition, solicit, appeal to, call on, urge, press, pressure, pressurize, push.
2 *a group lobbying for better rail services* **campaign**, crusade, press, push, drum up support, speak, clamour, ask, call, drive; promote, advocate, recommend, speak/plead/argue in favour of, champion, urge, insist on, demand.

local ▶ adjective **1** *the local council* **community**, district, neighbourhood, regional, city, town, municipal, provincial, village, parish, parish-pump, parochial; domestic, internal, home.
OPPOSITES national, global.
2 *a local restaurant* **neighbourhood**, nearby, near, at hand, close by, in the area; accessible, handy, convenient.
3 *a local infection* **confined**, restricted, contained, limited, localized; circumscribed, delimited, specific, particular.
OPPOSITE general.
▶ noun **1** *the police had complaints from the locals* **local person**, native, inhabitant, resident, parishioner, citizen; *humorous* denizen, burgher; *derogatory, informal* local yokel.
OPPOSITE outsider.
2 (*informal*) *he arranged to meet her at his local* **pub**, public house, bar, inn, tavern, hostelry, saloon, wine bar; *informal* boozer, watering hole, drinker.

locale ▶ noun *the photography conveys the atmosphere of the locale effectively* **place**, site, spot, area; position, location, setting, scene, venue, milieu, background, backdrop; neighbourhood, district, region, environs, locality, environment, territory; *technical* locus.

locality ▶ noun **1** *other schools in the locality* **vicinity**, surrounding area, area, neighbourhood, district, region, environs, zone, locale, territory; community; *informal* neck of the woods; *technical* locus.
2 *the locality of the property* **position**, place, situation, location, spot, point, site, scene, setting; whereabouts, bearings; *technical* locus.

localize ▶ verb *the policy of non-intervention had succeeded in localizing the conflict* **limit**, restrict, confine, contain, restrain, constrain, circumscribe, concentrate, delimit, delimitate; isolate.
OPPOSITES generalize, globalize.

locate ▶ verb **1** *he had no difficulty in locating the missing men* **find**, discover, pinpoint, detect, track down, run to earth, unearth, hit on, come across, reveal, bring to light, sniff out, smoke out, search out, ferret out, turn up, uncover, come up with, lay one's hands on, pin down; light on, stumble across/on, chance on; *informal* put one's finger on.
2 *a company located near Pittsburgh* **situate**, site, position, place, base; put, build, establish, found, fix, station, install, lodge, set, settle, seat.

location ▶ noun *the property is set in a convenient location* **position**, **place**, situation, site, locality, locale, spot, whereabouts, point, placement; scene, setting, area, environment; bearings, orientation; venue, address; *technical* locus.

lock[1] *See centre pages for list of* **Locks**
▶ noun *she turned the key in the lock* **bolt**, catch, fastener, clasp, bar, hasp, latch.
▶ verb **1** *he locked the door behind him* **bolt**, fasten, bar, secure, make secure, make fast, seal; padlock, latch, chain.
OPPOSITES unlock, open.
2 *wedge-shaped pins are driven in to* **lock** *the parts* **together** **join**, interlock, mesh, engage, link, unite, connect, combine, yoke, mate; couple.
OPPOSITES separate, divide.
3 *the wheels locked and the car careered across the road* **become stuck**, stick, jam, become/make immovable, become/make rigid.
4 *he locked her in an ecstatic embrace* **clasp**, clench, grasp, embrace, hug, squeeze.
□ **lock something in** *the beach is locked in by headlands at each end* **enclose**, encircle, surround, encompass, bound, ring, circle, envelop; shut in, hem in, hedge in.
□ **lock someone out** *she was locked out of her office | people locked out of the job market* **keep out**, shut out, refuse entrance to, deny admittance to; **exclude**, bar, debar, ban, ostracize, banish, exile.
□ **lock someone up** *he was locked up for burglary* **imprison**, jail, incarcerate, send to prison, put behind bars, put under lock and key, put in chains, put/throw into irons, clap in irons, hold captive; detain, remand, intern, impound, immure, shut up, shut in, confine, cage, pen, coop up, fence in, pen in, wall in, mew (up); *informal* send down, put away, put inside.

lock[2] ▶ noun *a lock of hair* **tress**, tuft, curl; ringlet, kiss-curl, lovelock, forelock, plait; hank; strand, wisp; snippet.

locker ▶ noun *she stowed her shirt in a locker* **cupboard**, cabinet, chest, safe, box, case, coffer; compartment, storeroom, storage room.

lock-up ▶ noun **1** *the old red-brick police station was the site of the village lock-up* **jail**, prison, cell, police cell, place of detention, place of confinement, detention centre; *N. Amer.* jailhouse; *informal* cooler, slammer, jug, can, nick, stir, clink, quod, chokey, pen.
2 *they had some spare space in a lock-up in a basement car park* **storeroom**, store, warehouse, depository, storage space, garage.

locomotion ▶ noun *spider monkeys have prehensile tails used in posture, locomotion, and grasping | steam locomotion* **movement**, motion, moving, shifting, stirring, action; travel, travelling; mobility, motility; walking, ambulation, perambulation, running; progress, progression, passage, transit, transport, headway.

lodestar ▶ noun *she dominated his existence, as chief muse and intellectual lodestar | maximizing profits is management's lodestar* **guide**, guiding star, guiding light, role model, model, luminary, exemplar, ideal, inspiration; criterion, aim, guiding principle, standard, pattern.

lodge ▶ noun **1** *the porter's lodge* **gatehouse**, cottage, toll house.
2 *a hunting lodge* **house**, cottage, cabin, chalet; *Brit.* shooting box.
3 *a beaver's lodge* **den**, lair, hole, sett; retreat, haunt, shelter.
4 *a Masonic lodge* **section**, branch, chapter, wing; association, society, group, club, union, guild, fraternity, brotherhood, sorority, alliance, coterie, league; *rare* sodality.
▶ verb **1** *William lodged at our house* **reside**, **board**, stay, have lodgings, have rooms, take a room, put up, live, be quartered, stop; occupy; *N. Amer.* room; *informal* have digs; *formal* dwell, be domiciled, sojourn; *archaic* abide.
2 *Mrs Gould, her maid, and the baby were lodged at an inn in Newcastle* **accommodate**, provide accommodation for, put up, take in, house, board, billet, quarter, shelter, harbour, provide shelter for; cater for, entertain.
3 *I intend to lodge an official complaint* **submit**, register, enter, put forward, place, advance, lay, present, press, bring, prefer, tender, proffer, put on record, record, table, file.

4 *the trophy was lodged in the vault of a local bank* **deposit**, put, bank, entrust, consign; stash, store, stow, put away, lay in, squirrel away; *rare* reposit.
5 *shrapnel slashed his neck and lodged in his spine* **become fixed**, embed itself, become embedded, become implanted, get/become stuck, stick, catch, wedge, become caught, become settled, anchor itself, become anchored, come to rest, remain.
6 *the power of the Crown is always lodged in a single person* **vest**, entrust, place, put, lay, transfer, consign.

lodger ▶ noun *she took in a lodger* **boarder**, paying guest, PG, guest, tenant, resident, inmate; *N. Amer.* roomer.

lodging ▶ noun *she lives in sumptuous lodging in London | he lived alone in a tiny lodging* **accommodation**, rooms, chambers, living quarters, quarters, apartments; place, place to stay, place of residence, establishment, flat, suite; shelter, board, housing; a roof over one's head; *informal* digs, pad; *formal* abode, residence, dwelling, dwelling place, habitation.

lofty ▶ adjective **1** *the buildings have lofty towers and spires* **tall**, high, giant, towering, soaring, sky-high, sky-scraping; imposing, magnificent, majestic.
OPPOSITES low, short.
2 *lofty ideals* **noble**, exalted, high, high-minded, grand, fine, sublime, elevated, worthy.
OPPOSITES base, lowly.
3 *he has obtained a lofty position in Hollywood* **eminent**, prominent, leading, distinguished, illustrious, renowned, celebrated, elevated, esteemed, honoured, respected.
OPPOSITE base.
4 *they looked on with lofty disdain* **haughty**, proud, aloof, arrogant, disdainful, supercilious, condescending, patronizing, scornful, contemptuous, self-important, conceited, snobbish; lordly, grandiose, imperious, pompous, magisterial, overweening, overbearing; *informal* high and mighty, stuck-up, snooty, snotty, toffee-nosed, uppity, uppish, hoity-toity; *literary* vainglorious; *archaic* contumelious.
OPPOSITE modest.

log ▶ noun **1** *she tripped over a fallen log* **chunk of wood**, branch, tree trunk, bole, stump; block of wood, billet; timber.
2 *the ship's log | we require a log of calls to be maintained* **record**, register, logbook, journal, diary, chronicle, daybook, record book, ledger; chart, account, tally; minutes; *informal* write-up.
▶ verb **1** *details of the problem will be logged by the help-desk staff* **register**, record, make a note of, note down, write down, jot down, book down, set down, put down, put in writing; enter, file, minute, chart, tabulate, catalogue.
2 *the pilot had logged 95 hours* **attain**, achieve, chalk up, make, do, go, cover.

loggerheads ▶ plural noun
□ **at loggerheads** *local councillors have found themselves at loggerheads with the Government* **in disagreement**, at odds, at variance, in opposition, at cross purposes, out of step, quarrelling, clashing, at outs; in conflict, at war, at daggers drawn, fighting, wrangling, feuding, conflicting, locking horns, estranged; *informal* at each other's throats, like cat and dog.

logic ▶ noun **1** *this case appears to defy all logic | he accepted the logic of the shipowners' argument* **reason**, judgement, logical thought, rationality, cognition, wisdom, sagacity, sound judgement, sense, good sense, common sense, rationale, sanity, deduction, inference, syllogistic reasoning; coherence, relevance; *informal* horse sense.
2 *the logic of the Marxist argument is as follows* **reasoning**, line of reasoning, chain of reasoning, process of reasoning, argument, argumentation.
3 *the study of logic* **science of reasoning**, science of deduction, science of thought, dialectics, argumentation, ratiocination.

logical ▶ adjective **1** *conclusions based on evidence and logical argument | information displayed in a simple and logical fashion* **reasoned**, well reasoned, rational, sound, cogent, well thought out, valid; lucid, coherent, clear, well organized, systematic, orderly, methodical, articulate, consistent, relevant; syllogistic, deductive, inductive, inferential; *informal* joined-up.
OPPOSITES irrational, illogical.
2 *the move into production seems the logical outcome* **natural**, unsurprising, only to be expected, understandable, reasonable, sensible; predictable, most likely, likeliest, obvious; right, correct, practical.
OPPOSITES unlikely, surprising.
3 *his logical mind* **reasoning**, thinking, straight-thinking, rational, objective, analytical, cerebral, insightful; intelligent, judicious, wise, sensible, hard-headed.

logistics ▶ plural noun *the logistics of deploying forces in foreign territory are daunting* **organization**, planning, plans, management, arrangement, administration, masterminding, direction, orchestration, regimentation, engineering, coordination, execution, handling, running; strategy, tactics.

logo ▶ noun *the company logo* **emblem**, trademark; device, symbol, design, sign, mark, figure, stamp, monogram; insignia, crest, seal, coat of arms, shield, badge, motif, hallmark, logotype, colophon.

loiter ▶ verb **1** *he loitered in the parking lot* **linger**, potter, wait, skulk; loaf, lounge, idle, laze, waste time, kill time, while away time; *informal* hang around/round; *Brit. informal* hang about, mooch about/around; *dated* tarry.
2 *the weather had tempted them out to loiter along the river bank* **dawdle**, dally, stroll, saunter, loll, go slowly, take one's time, go/move at a snail's pace, drag one's feet, delay; *informal* dilly-dally, mosey; *Brit. informal* mooch.

> **CHOOSE THE RIGHT WORD**
>
> **loiter, linger, dawdle**
> See LINGER.

loll ▶ verb **1** *Louis lolled at ease in one of the deckchairs* **lounge**, sprawl, drape oneself, stretch oneself, lie, sit, flop; slouch, slump; laze, luxuriate, put one's feet up, lean back, recline, relax, take it easy, repose, rest; loaf, idle, vegetate; *informal* hang around/round; *Brit. informal* hang about.
2 *a dog lay down by the side of the building, its tongue* **lolling out** *with thirst* **hang down**, hang, hang loosely, dangle, droop, sag, flap, flop, drop.

lone ▶ adjective **1** *a lone police officer | a lone tree* **solitary**, single, solo, unaccompanied, unescorted, alone, all alone, by oneself/itself, sole, without companions, companionless; individual, distinct, detached, isolated, unique; lonely.
2 *a lone parent* **single**, unmarried, unattached, without a partner/husband/wife, partnerless, husbandless, wifeless; separated, divorced, widowed.
3 (*literary*) *a cowboy on the lone prairie* **deserted**, uninhabited, unfrequented, lonely, unpopulated, desolate, barren, isolated, remote, marooned, out of the way, secluded, sequestered, off the beaten track, in the back of beyond, in the middle of nowhere, godforsaken.
OPPOSITES populous, crowded.

loneliness ▶ noun **1** *he sought refuge in drink because of his loneliness* **isolation**, friendlessness, lack of friends/companions, forsakenness, abandonment, rejection; unpopularity; sadness, unhappiness, forlornness, despondency; *N. Amer.* lonesomeness.
2 *the enforced loneliness of a prison cell* **solitariness**, solitude, lack of company, aloneness, separation.
3 *the loneliness of the village* **isolation**, remoteness, inaccessibility, seclusion, secludedness; desertedness.

> **WORD LINKS**
> *fear of loneliness* **autophobia, ermitophobia**

lonely ▶ adjective **1** *a sad and lonely man | I felt very lonely* **isolated**, alone, all alone, friendless, companionless, without friends/companions, with no one to turn to, outcast, forsaken, abandoned, rejected, unloved, unwanted; unpopular; sad, unhappy, forlorn, despondent; *N. Amer.* lonesome.
OPPOSITE popular.
2 *the lonely life of a writer* **solitary**, unaccompanied, alone, lone, by oneself/itself, without companions, companionless.
OPPOSITE sociable.
3 *a lonely road* **deserted**, uninhabited, unfrequented, unpopulated, desolate, barren, isolated, remote, out of the way, secluded, sequestered, off the beaten track, in the back of beyond, in the middle of nowhere, godforsaken; *literary* lone.
OPPOSITES populous, crowded.

loner ▶ noun *I don't want my child to turn into an antisocial loner* **recluse**, introvert, lone wolf, hermit, solitary, misanthrope, outsider; maverick, nonconformist, individual; *rare* eremite, coenobite, anchorite, stylite, solitudinarian.

long[1] ▶ adjective **1** *a tall girl with long brown hair | this was followed by a long tense silence* **lengthy**, of considerable length, extended, prolonged, extensive, stretched out, spread out; long-lasting, lasting.
OPPOSITE short.
2 *the white rhinoceros can reach 17 feet long* **in length**, lengthways, lengthwise.
3 *the couple fought a long battle to get welfare benefits | a long speech* **prolonged**, protracted, lengthy, overlong, extended, long-drawn-out, drawn-out, spun-out, dragged-out, seemingly endless, lingering, interminable; tedious, boring, wearisome.
OPPOSITES short, brief.
□ **before long** *before long, others will follow* **soon**, shortly, presently, in the near future, in a short time, in a little while, in a minute, in a moment; in an instant, in the twinkling of an eye, in (less than) no time, in no time (at all), before you know it, any minute (now); by and by; *informal* in a jiffy, in two shakes, in two shakes of a lamb's tail, before you can say Jack Robinson; *archaic or informal* anon; *archaic* ere long.

long[2] ▶ verb *all through the exams I* **longed for** *the holidays | she had longed to be invited to the party* **yearn**, pine, ache, wish, burn, hanker for/after, hunger, thirst, itch, pant, hope, be eager, be desperate, be consumed with desire, be unable to wait, would give one's eye teeth; crave, need, lust after, dream of, set one's heart on, be bent on, eat one's heart out over, covet; want, desire, set one's sights on; *informal* have a yen, be dying, yen.

> **CHOOSE THE RIGHT WORD**
> **long, yearn, pine, hanker**
> *See* YEARN.

long-drawn-out ▶ **adjective** *his trial was a long-drawn-out affair* **prolonged**, protracted, lengthy, lasting, long-lasting, marathon, overlong, extended, drawn-out, spun-out, dragged-out, dragging, time-consuming, seemingly endless, lingering, interminable; tedious, boring, wearisome.

longing ▶ **noun** *urban dwellers clearly have a longing for the countryside* **yearning**, pining, craving, ache, burning, hunger, thirst, itch, urge, lust, hankering, need, eagerness, zeal, covetousness; wish, fancy, desire, want; hope, aspiration, dream; *informal* yen.
▶ **adjective** *a longing look* **yearning**, desirous, pining, craving, hungry, thirsty, hankering, avid, covetous; wishful, hopeful, wistful.

long-lasting ▶ **adjective** *our long-lasting friendship* **enduring**, lasting, long-lived, long-running, long-established, long-standing, lifelong; permanent, abiding, surviving, deep-rooted, established; strong, durable, stable, fast, firm, reliable; time-honoured, traditional.
OPPOSITES short-lived, ephemeral.

long-lived ▶ **adjective** *the long-lived success of the organization* lasting, enduring, abiding; durable, hardy.
OPPOSITE short-lived.

long-standing ▶ **adjective** *a long-standing friendship* **well established**, long-established, established, fixed; time-honoured, time-hallowed; abiding, enduring, long-lived, surviving, persistent, prevailing, durable, perennial; firm, constant, deep-rooted, steady, stable, staunch, long-term.
OPPOSITES new, recent.

long-suffering ▶ **adjective** *his long-suffering wife* **patient**, forbearing, tolerant, uncomplaining, with the patience of Job, stoical, resigned; easy-going, indulgent, charitable, accommodating, forgiving; submissive, deferential, acquiescent, meek, docile, compliant, mild.
OPPOSITES impatient, complaining.

long-winded ▶ **adjective** *a long-winded speech* **lengthy**, long, overlong, prolonged, protracted, long-drawn-out, interminable, tedious, wearisome, boring; discursive, diffuse, rambling, meandering, repetitious, tautological, periphrastic, circumlocutory, tortuous, verbose, wordy, prolix; *informal* windy; *rare* pleonastic, ambagious, sesquipedalian.
OPPOSITES concise, succinct, laconic.

look ▶ **verb 1** *Mrs. Wright* **looked at** *him | she looked out of the window* **glance**, gaze, stare, gape, peer, fix one's gaze, focus; peep, peek, take a look; **watch**, examine, study, inspect, scan, scrutinize, survey, check, contemplate, consider; see, observe, view, regard, pay attention to, take note of, mark; glimpse, spot, spy, lay one's eyes on, catch sight of, eye, take in, ogle; *informal* take a gander, give someone/something a/the once-over, have a squint, get a load of, rubberneck, recce; *Brit. informal* take a dekko, take a butcher's, take a shufti, clock, gawp; *N. Amer. informal* eyeball; *archaic* behold, espy, descry.
OPPOSITE ignore.
2 *a pair of windows looked north over Madison Avenue | the breakfast room looks out on to a small patio* **command a view**, face, overlook, front.
3 *both visitors looked shocked* **seem**, seem to be, appear, appear to be, have the appearance/air of being, give the impression of being, give every appearance/indication of being, look to be, present as being, strike someone as being.

□ **look after** *I had to look after my brother after his accident* **take care of**, care for, attend to, tend, mind, minister to, take charge of, supervise, protect, guard; keep an eye on, keep safe, be responsible for; watch, sit with, nurse, babysit, childmind.

□ **look back on** *I look back on my early teenage years with some amazement* **reflect on**, think about, remember, recall, bring to mind, muse on, brood on, ponder on, reminisce about, be nostalgic about, hark back to.

□ **look down on** *my mother had social pretensions and looked down on most of our neighbours* **disdain**, scorn, hold in disdain, regard with contempt, treat with contempt, sneer at, spurn, shun, disparage, pooh-pooh, despise; *informal* look down one's nose at, turn up one's nose at.
OPPOSITE look up to.

□ **look for 1** *she looked for her comb, but couldn't find it | police are looking for two suspects* **search for**, hunt for, seek, look about/around/round for, cast about/around/round for, try to find, try to track down, forage for, scout out, quest for/after.
2 *Jeremiah and Ezekiel looked for the day when God would forge a new covenant with men* **anticipate**, expect, await, count on, reckon on, watch for, hope for, look forward to, contemplate, prepare for, envisage.

□ **look forward to** *I was looking forward to seeing Ted* **await with pleasure**, anticipate, wait for, be unable to wait for, count the days until, long for, hope for; *informal* lick one's lips over.
OPPOSITE dread.

□ **look into** *the authorities promised to look into the complaints* **investigate**, explore, research, enquire about, make enquiries about, find out about, ask questions about, ask about; probe, search into, go into, delve into, dig into, examine, study, scrutinize, check, analyse, follow up, check up on, pore over, take stock of; vet, audit; *N. Amer.* check out.

□ **look like** *in his overcoat he looks like an undertaker* **resemble**, bear a resemblance to, look similar to, have a look of, have the appearance of, remind one of, put one in mind of, make one think of, be the image of, echo, have (all) the hallmarks of, simulate; take after; *informal* be the spitting image of, be the spit of, be a dead ringer for, favour.

□ **look on/upon** *people he looked on as friends took advantage of him* **regard**, consider, think of, deem, judge, count, see, view, take, reckon, believe to be.

□ **look out** *you'll be trampled on if you don't look out* **beware**, watch out, be on (one's) guard, be alert, be wary, be vigilant, be careful, be cautious, pay attention, take heed, heed, keep one's eyes open, keep one's eyes peeled/skinned, keep an eye out, be on the qui vive.

□ **look something over** *he looked over the reports from the engineer* **inspect**, examine, check, monitor, read through, look through, scan, run through, cast an eye over, leaf through, flick through, flip through, browse, give something/someone a/the once-over, take stock of, view, peruse; *informal* take a dekko at; *N. Amer.* check out; *N. Amer. informal* eyeball.

□ **look to 1** *we must look to the future* **consider**, give thought to, think about, turn one's thoughts to, take heed of, pay attention to, attend to, mind, heed.
2 *they got themselves into trouble and now look to the government for help* **turn to**, resort to, have recourse to, fall back on, avail oneself of, make use of.

□ **look up** *things are looking up for opera these days* **improve**, show improvement, get better, pick up, advance, develop, come along/on, progress, make progress, make headway, shape up, perk up, rally, take a turn for the better.

□ **look someone up** (*informal*) *Moira said you were going up to Leeds to look up some old friends* **visit**, pay a visit to, call on, go to see, look in on; *N. Amer.* visit with, go see; *informal* drop in on.

□ **look up to** *Jerry looked up to me* **admire**, have a high opinion of, think highly of, hold in high regard, regard highly, rate highly, respect, hold in esteem, esteem, value; honour, revere, venerate, idolize, worship, hero-worship, adulate, put on a pedestal, lionize.
OPPOSITE look down on.

▶ **noun 1** *have a look at this report* **glance**, observation, view, examination, study, inspection, scan, survey, sight, peep, peek, glimpse, gaze, stare, gape, ogle; *informal* eyeful, gander, look-see, once-over, squint, recce; *Brit. informal* shufti, dekko, butcher's; *Austral./NZ informal* geek, squiz.
2 *the puzzled look on her face turned to one of irritation* **expression**, mien.
3 *he had a shifty look about him | the kitchen has that rustic look Mary's so fond of* **appearance**, air, aspect, bearing, cast, manner, mien, demeanour, features, semblance, guise, facade, impression, effect; atmosphere, mood, quality, ambience, feeling, flavour.
4 *the latest look for this season is lean and elegant* **fashion**, style, vogue, mode, trend, fad, craze, rage, mania.

WORD LINKS
fear of being looked at **scopophobia**

lookalike ▶ **noun** *a Charlie Chaplin lookalike* **double**, twin, exact likeness, image, living image, mirror image, exact match, replica, clone, imitation, duplicate, copy, facsimile; *German* Doppelgänger; *informal* spitting image, spit, spit and image, ringer, dead ringer.

lookout ▶ **noun 1** *a signal station used as a lookout during the Napoleonic Wars* **observation post**, lookout point, lookout station, lookout tower, watchtower, tower, post; coastguard station.
2 *the lookout sighted sails on the western horizon* **watchman**, guard, watch, sentry, sentinel, night watchman, scout, picket; *historical* vedette.
3 (*informal*) *it would be a poor lookout for the men of the fleet if they didn't return to shore before the rain struck* **outlook**, prospect, view of the future, future; chances, expectations.
4 (*informal*) *I doubt if she'll fit in, but that's her own lookout* **problem**, concern, business, affair, responsibility, worry, difficulty; *informal* pigeon, funeral, headache.

□ **be on the lookout/keep a lookout** *he kept a sharp lookout for enemy fighters* **keep watch**, keep/be on one's guard, beware, keep an eye out, keep a vigil, be alert, be observant, be attentive, be on the qui vive; *informal* keep one's eyes peeled/skinned.

loom ▶ **verb 1** *ghostly shapes loomed out of the fog* **emerge**, appear, become visible, come into view, take shape, materialize, reveal itself, appear indistinctly, come to light, take on a threatening shape.
2 *the church* **loomed above** *him* **soar**, tower, rise, rise up, mount, rear up; overhang, overshadow, hang over, dominate.
3 *without reforms, disaster looms* **be imminent**, be on the horizon, impend, be impending, be close, be ominously close, threaten, be threatening, menace, brew, be just around the corner.

loop ▶ noun **1** *make a loop in the twine | a loop of rope* **coil**, hoop, ring, circle, noose, oval, spiral, curl, twirl, whorl, twist, hook, zigzag, helix, convolution, incurvation.
2 *the flex has a loop in it* **bend**, curve, kink, arc.
▶ verb **1** *loop a heavy rope around its hind legs* **coil**, wind, twist, snake, wreathe, spiral, form a hoop with, form hoops with, make a circle with, make circles with, bend into spirals/whorls.
2 *the driveway looped around the house* **wind**, curve, bend, twist, turn, snake, meander, coil, spiral, corkscrew; **encircle**, form a ring round, surround, encompass; *rare* incurvate.
3 *he took two cables and looped them together* **fasten**, tie, join, connect, knot, bind, secure, tether, lash, leash.

loophole ▶ noun **1** *they've taken advantage of a loophole in the regulations* **means of evasion/avoidance**, means of escape, escape clause, escape route; **ambiguity**, omission, inadequacy, flaw, fault, defect, crack, inconsistency, discrepancy, shortcoming, slip; *informal* let-out, let-out clause, dodge.
2 (*archaic*) *loopholes in the walls* **hole**, gap, opening, aperture, chink, slit, slot.

loose ▶ adjective **1** *a loose floorboard* **not fixed in place**, not secure, insecure, unsecured, unattached; detached, unfastened; wobbly, rickety, unsteady, movable.
OPPOSITES secure, tight.
2 *she wore her hair loose* **untied**, unpinned, unbound, hanging free, down, flowing, floppy.
3 *there's a wolf loose in the woods* **free**, at large, at liberty, on the loose, escaped; unconfined, untied, unchained, untethered, unsecured, unshackled, unfastened, unrestricted, unbound; freed, let go, liberated, released, set loose.
OPPOSITE secure.
4 *the loose interpretation of a particular ruling* **vague**, indefinite, inexact, imprecise, ill-defined, unrigorous, unmeticulous; broad, general, rough, non-specific, inexplicit; liberal.
OPPOSITES literal, narrow.
5 *a loose jacket* **baggy**, loose-fitting, easy-fitting, generously cut, slack, roomy; oversized, shapeless, bagging, lax, hanging, sagging, sloppy.
OPPOSITE tight.
6 (*dated*) *a loose woman* **promiscuous**, sexually indiscriminate, of easy virtue, fast, wanton, no better than one should be, unchaste, immoral, impure; libidinous, licentious, dissolute; *informal* easy; *N. Amer. informal* roundheeled; *dated* fallen; *derogatory* whorish, sluttish; *archaic* light.
OPPOSITE chaste.
□ **at a loose end** *why don't you stay to eat, if you're at a loose end?* **with nothing to do**, unoccupied, unemployed, at leisure, idle, purposeless, aimless, adrift, with time to kill; bored, twiddling one's thumbs, kicking one's heels.
OPPOSITE busy.
□ **break loose** *the tethered horses broke loose* **escape**, make one's escape, get away, get free, break free, free oneself; run off, run away, make a break for it, make a run for it, bolt, take to one's heels.
□ **let loose 1** *she let the python loose* **free**, set free, unloose, turn loose, set loose, let go, release, liberate; untie, unchain, unfetter, untether, unfasten, unpen, unleash.
2 *she let loose a graceless snort* **emit**, give, burst out with, give forth, send forth; shout, yell, bellow.
□ **on the loose** *a serial killer was on the loose* **free**, at liberty, at large, escaped, set loose, unconfined, unrestrained, roaming, unbound, unrestricted, untied, unchained, unshackled, unfettered; on the run, fugitive; *informal* on the lam.
▶ verb **1** *the cattle were loosed on the common* **free**, set free, unloose, turn loose, set loose, let loose, let go, release, liberate; untie, unchain, unfetter, untether, unfasten, unpen, unleash.
OPPOSITE confine.
2 *he loosed the reins a little | the steel fingers loosed their hold* **relax**, slacken, loosen; weaken, lessen, reduce, diminish, moderate, soften.
OPPOSITE tighten.
3 *Brian* **loosed off** *a shot though the back of the car* **fire**, discharge, shoot, eject, catapult, let go, let fly with.

loose-limbed ▶ adjective *he was loose-limbed and lean* **supple**, limber, lithe, lissom, willowy, flexible, pliant, pliable, loose-jointed; agile, nimble, deft.

loosen ▶ verb **1** *to open it up, you simply loosen two screws* **make slack**, slacken, slack, unstick; **unfasten**, detach, release, disconnect, undo, unclasp, unlatch, unbolt.
OPPOSITE tighten.
2 *her fingers loosened* **become slack**, slacken, become loose, let go, unbind, ease; work loose, work free.
OPPOSITE tighten.
3 *he had loosened his tie and undone his top button* **unfasten**, undo, release, unhook, slacken, let out.
OPPOSITE tighten.
4 *Philip loosened his grip | the extension of the franchise helped loosen the grip of the aristocracy* **weaken**, relax, slacken, loose, lessen, reduce, moderate, diminish, soften, alleviate, dilute.
OPPOSITE tighten.
5 *you need to* **loosen up**, *get rid of some inhibitions* **relax**, become relaxed, unwind, ease up/off, become less rigid; *informal* let up, hang loose, lighten up, go easy.

loot ▶ noun *a treasure chest brimming over with loot* **booty**, spoils, plunder, stolen goods, contraband, pillage; haul, prize; *informal* swag, the goods, hot goods, ill-gotten gains, boodle.
▶ verb *troops rushed in and looted the cathedral* **plunder**, pillage, ransack, sack, raid, rifle, rob, burgle, steal from; maraud, ravage, devastate, lay waste to, wreak havoc on, vandalize; gut, strip, fleece, clear out; *literary* despoil; *rare* depredate, spoliate.

lop ▶ verb **1** *workmen have* **lopped off** *more branches in an effort to save the tree* **cut**, chop, hack, saw, hew, slice, pare; prune, sever, clip, trim, snip, dock, crop, remove, detach, excise.
2 *it will* **lop** *an hour* **off** *journey times to the continent* **remove**, cut, slash, axe, take, trim, prune, dock, truncate, eliminate.

lope ▶ verb *he loped off down the corridor* **stride**, run, bound; lollop.

lopsided ▶ adjective *he gave a rather lopsided grin* **asymmetrical**, unsymmetrical, uneven, unevenly balanced, unbalanced, off-balance, off-centre, unequal, askew, skew, skewed, squint, tilted, tilting, crooked, sloping, slanted, aslant, one-sided, out of true, out of line, to one side, awry; *informal* skew-whiff, cock-eyed.
OPPOSITES even, level, balanced.

loquacious ▶ adjective *he was a loquacious and precocious boy* **talkative**, garrulous, voluble, over-talkative, long-winded, wordy, verbose, profuse, prolix, effusive, gushing, rambling; communicative; chatty, gossipy, gossiping, chattering, chattery, babbling, blathering, gibbering; *informal* with the gift of the gab, having kissed the blarney stone, yakking, big-mouthed, gabby, gassy; *rare* multiloquent, multiloquous.
OPPOSITES reticent, taciturn.

> **CHOOSE THE RIGHT WORD**
>
> **loquacious, talkative, chatty, garrulous**
>
> *See* TALKATIVE.

loquacity ▶ noun *he had a dim recollection of talking with drunken loquacity of his adventures* **talkativeness**, over-talkativeness, garrulousness, garrulity, volubility, long-windedness, wordiness, prolixity, verbosity, verbiage, effusiveness, profuseness; chattiness, chattering, babble, blathering, gibbering; *informal* the gift of the gab, yackety-yak, yakking, big mouth, blah-blah, gabbiness, gassiness; *rare* logorrhoea, multiloquence.
OPPOSITES taciturnity, succinctness.

lord *See centre pages for list of* **Nobles**
▶ noun **1** *lords and ladies were entertained here* **noble**, nobleman, peer, aristocrat, patrician, grandee; feudal lord, landowner, lord of the manor, seigneur; duke, earl, viscount.
OPPOSITE commoner.
2 *leave it to us, my lord | the lord of the manor* **master**, lord and master, ruler, leader, chief, superior, monarch, sovereign, king, emperor, prince, governor, commander, captain, overlord, suzerain, baron, potentate, liege, liege lord.
OPPOSITES servant, inferior.
3 *our Lord's parable of the lost sheep* **God**, the Father, Jehovah, the Almighty, the Supreme Being, the Deity; **Jesus**, Jesus Christ, Christ, Christ the Lord, the Messiah, the Saviour, the Son of God, the Redeemer, the Lamb of God, the Prince of Peace, the King of Kings.
4 *a press lord* **magnate**, tycoon, mogul, captain, baron, king, nabob, grandee, mandarin; industrialist, proprietor, entrepreneur, executive, chief, leader; *informal* big shot, bigwig, honcho; *derogatory* fat cat; *N. Amer. informal* big wheel.
▶ verb
□ **lord it over someone** *when we were at school, you used to lord it over us* **order about/around**, boss about/around, give orders to, domineer, dominate, dictate to, pull rank on, tyrannize, bully, browbeat, oppress, repress, ride roughshod over, have under one's thumb; be overbearing, put on airs, swagger; *informal* throw one's weight about/around, act big.
OPPOSITE be submissive.

lordly ▶ adjective **1** *the symbols of lordly status | lordly titles* **noble**, aristocratic, princely, kingly, regal, royal, imperial, courtly, stately; magnificent, majestic, grand, august, lofty, exalted, dignified, imposing, impressive.
OPPOSITE lowly.
2 *I called a taxi and in lordly tones asked to be taken to Lansdowne Road* **imperious**, arrogant, haughty, proud, self-important, swaggering; snobbish, supercilious, disdainful, scornful, contemptuous, condescending, patronizing, cavalier, aloof, superior, high-handed, overbearing, overweening, overconfident, pompous; dictatorial, authoritarian, bossy, peremptory, autocratic, tyrannical; refined; *informal*

L

high and mighty, stuck-up, snooty, uppity, hoity-toity, toffee-nosed, pushy.
OPPOSITE humble.

lore ▶ noun **1** *he had a passion for Arthurian legend and lore* **mythology**, myths, legends, stories, traditions, folklore, culture, beliefs, sayings, superstitions, fantasy, oral tradition; *technical* mythos, mythus.
2 *cricket lore was passed down from Yorkshire father to son* **knowledge**, learning, wisdom; *informal* know-how, how-to.

lorry *See centre pages for list of* **Vehicles**
▶ noun *the lorry was rumbling over Tower Bridge* **truck**; *Brit.* juggernaut.

lose ▶ verb **1** *I've lost my watch* **mislay**, misplace, be unable to find; drop, forget, overlook, lose track of, leave (behind), fail to keep/retain, fail to keep sight of.
OPPOSITE find.
2 *he's lost a lot of blood but his life is not in danger | she was suffering from flu and had lost her voice* **be deprived of**, suffer the loss of, no longer have, stop having.
OPPOSITE regain.
3 *by this time the fans had managed to lose the police* **escape from**, evade, elude, dodge, avoid, give someone the slip, shake off, throw off, throw off the scent, duck, get rid of; leave behind, outdistance, outstrip, outrun, outpace, get ahead of; *informal* ditch; *archaic* bilk.
4 *she still sometimes* **loses her way** *in the maze* **stray from**, wander from, depart from, go astray from, fail to keep to, fail to keep in sight; **get lost**, lose one's bearings.
5 *he never lost an opportunity to poke fun at her* **neglect**, waste, squander, fail to grasp, fail to take, fail to take advantage of, let pass, miss, forfeit, give up, ignore, disregard; *informal* pass up, lose out on.
6 *Leeds lost twice to Rangers in the European Cup | he lost the party leadership contest* **be defeated**, be beaten, suffer defeat, be the loser, be conquered, be vanquished, be trounced, be worsted, be bested by, get/have the worst, come off second-best, lose out, fail, come to grief, meet one's Waterloo; *informal* come a cropper, go down, take a licking.
□ **lose out** *the town has* **lost out on** *a major tourist opportunity* **be unable to take advantage of**, fail to benefit from; be unsuccessful, be defeated, be the loser, be disadvantaged; *informal* miss out on.
□ **lose out to** *Celtic have lost out to rivals Rangers* **be defeated by**, be beaten by, be conquered by, be vanquished by, be trounced by, be worsted by, be bested by, be beaten into second place by.

L

loser ▶ noun **1** *candidates compete against each other, so there are winners and losers* **defeated person**, also-ran, the defeated, the vanquished; runner-up.
OPPOSITE winner.
2 (*informal*) *he's a complete loser* **failure**, nonachiever, underachiever, ne'er-do-well, born loser, dead loss, nonentity, nobody; write-off, has-been; *informal* flop, dud, non-starter, no-hoper, washout, lemon, two-time loser.
OPPOSITE success.

loss ▶ noun **1** *the loss of the documents appears to be a serious breach of security* **mislaying**, misplacement, dropping, forgetting, overlooking.
OPPOSITES recovery, finding.
2 *insurance covering loss of earnings | loss of dignity* **deprivation**, disappearance, losing, privation, forfeiture, waste, squandering, dissipation; **diminution**, erosion, reduction, impoverishment, depletion.
3 *she mourned the loss of her husband* **death**, **demise**, passing (away/on), decease, end, expiry, expiration; bereavement; *rare* quietus.
4 (usually **losses**) *they were able to inflict severe losses on enemy troops | British losses in the war were 400,000* **casualty**, fatality, mortality, victim; dead; missing; **death toll**, number killed/dead/wounded.
5 *the club were facing a loss of £15,000 a year* **deficit**, debit, debt, indebtedness, lack of profit, deficiency, losing, depletion, minus sum of money; cost, expense, sacrifice.
OPPOSITES profit, gain.
□ **at a loss** *I am at a loss to explain this contradiction* **baffled**, nonplussed, mystified, stumped, stuck, puzzled, perplexed, bewildered, bemused, uncomprehending, (all) at sea, at sixes and sevens, at one's wits' end, without ideas, confused, dumbfounded, blank; *informal* clueless, flummoxed, bamboozled, discombobulated, fazed, floored, beaten.

lost ▶ adjective **1** *they were all searching for her lost keys | a lost cat* **missing**, strayed, gone missing/astray, mislaid, misplaced, vanished, disappeared, forgotten, nowhere to be found; absent, not present, gone.
2 *his spirit still walks among the hills, searching for lost travellers | I went for a walk in the woods and I got lost* **stray**, astray, off-course, off-track, off the right track, disorientated, disoriented, having lost one's bearings, adrift, going round in circles, at sea.
3 *a lost opportunity* **missed**, forfeited, neglected, wasted, squandered, dissipated, gone by the board; *informal* down the drain.
4 *lost traditional values* **bygone**, past, former, one-time, previous, old, olden, departed, vanished, forgotten, unremembered, unrecalled, consigned to oblivion, extinct, dead, lost and gone, lost in time; out of date, outmoded; *French* passé.
5 *a lament over lost species and habitats* **extinct**, died out, defunct, vanished, gone, perished; **destroyed**, wiped out, ruined, wrecked, crushed, finished, demolished, obliterated, effaced, exterminated, eradicated, annihilated, extirpated.
6 *a lost cause* **hopeless**, beyond hope, failed, despaired of, beyond remedy, beyond recovery.
7 *lost souls* **damned**, fallen, cursed, accursed, irredeemable, irreclaimable, irretrievable, past hope, past praying for, condemned, doomed, excommunicated.
8 *he was a person entirely* **lost to** *all sense of decency* **impervious**, immune, closed, unreceptive, unaffected by, unmoved by, untouched by.
9 *Father Reynard was* **lost in** *his own thoughts* **engrossed**, absorbed, rapt, immersed, deep, intent, engaged, wrapped up; preoccupied by, taken up by, spellbound by, distracted by, entranced by, fascinated by, enthralled by, captivated by, riveted by; abstracted, dreamy, distrait, absent-minded, daydreaming, wool-gathering, somewhere else, not there, not with us, in a world of one's own, with one's head in the clouds, in a brown study; *informal* miles away.

lot ▶ pronoun (**a lot/lots**) *he had obviously spent a lot of money | she had lots of friends* **a large amount**, a fair amount, a good/great deal, a deal, a great quantity, quantities, an abundance, a wealth, a profusion, plenty, masses; **many**, a great many, a large number, a considerable number, numerous, scores, hundreds, thousands, millions, billions; *informal* loads, loadsa, heaps, a pile, piles, oodles, stacks, scads, reams, wads, pots, oceans, a mountain, mountains, miles, tons, zillions, gazillions, more ... than one can shake a stick at; *Brit. informal* a shedload, lashings; *N. Amer. informal* gobs, a bunch, gazillions, bazillions; *Austral./NZ informal* a swag; *vulgar slang* a shitload.
OPPOSITES a little, not much; a few, not many.
▶ adverb (**a lot/lots**) *I work in pastels a lot* **a great deal**, a good deal, to a great extent, much; often, frequently, regularly, many times.
OPPOSITES a little, not much.
▶ noun **1** (*informal*) *I will not be dictated to by that lot up at the mansion* **group**, set, crowd, circle, clique, bunch, band, gang, crew, mob, pack, company; *Brit. informal* shower.
2 *it was auctioned off as a single lot* **batch**, set, collection, load, group, bundle, bunch, consignment, quantity, assortment, parcel, aggregate.
3 *he was discontented with his lot in life* **fate**, destiny, fortune, doom; situation, circumstances, state, condition, position, plight, predicament.
4 *they were to have one lot, and one lot only* **share**, portion, quota, ration, allowance, allocation, percentage, part, piece; *informal* cut.
5 (*N. Amer.*) *some youngsters playing ball in a vacant lot* **patch of ground**, tract of land, allotment, piece of ground, plot, area, tract, acreage, parcel, building lot; *N. Amer.* plat.
□ **draw/cast lots** *the players draw lots to decide who goes first* **decide randomly**, spin/toss a coin, throw dice, draw straws, cut straws, decide on the toss of a coin, decide on the throw of a die, dice, decide on the drawing of straws.
□ **throw in one's lot with** *he threw in his lot with the conspirators* **join forces with**, join up with, form an alliance with, ally with, align oneself with, link up with, go into league with, combine with, join fortunes with, make common cause with.

lotion ▶ noun *she rubbed some lotion into the skin* **ointment**, cream, salve, balm, rub, emollient, moisturizer, lubricant, unguent, liniment, embrocation, poultice; pomade; hand lotion, body lotion, eye lotion.

lottery ▶ noun *Dad had won £7,000 in a lottery* **raffle**, (prize) draw, sweepstake, sweep, bingo, lotto, tombola, drawing of lots, pools; gamble, speculation, game of chance, competition.

loud ▶ adjective **1** *there was loud music in the lounge* **noisy**, blaring, booming, deafening, roaring, thunderous, thundering, tumultuous, clamorous, blasting, head-splitting, ear-splitting, ear-piercing, piercing; cacophonous, harsh, raucous; strident, resounding, reverberating, reverberant, carrying, clearly audible; sonorous, deep, ringing, lusty, powerful, forceful, stentorian; rowdy; *Music* forte, fortissimo.
OPPOSITES quiet, soft.
2 *the resulting congestion of business led to loud complaints of the law's delays* **vociferous**, clamorous, insistent, vehement, emphatic, urgent, importunate, demanding.
OPPOSITE gentle.
3 *a loud T-shirt* **garish**, gaudy, flashy, bold, flamboyant, lurid, glaring, showy, ostentatious, obtrusive; vulgar, tasteless; *informal* flash, naff, kitsch, tacky.
OPPOSITES sober, tasteful.

loudly ▶ adverb *the audience cheered loudly | music played loudly* **at the top of one's voice**, **at full volume**, at top volume; **noisily**, blaringly, boomingly, deafeningly, thunderously, thunderingly, tumultuously, clamorously, piercingly; cacophonously, harshly, raucously; stridently, resoundingly; sonorously, deeply, ringingly, lustily, powerfully, forcefully; *Music* forte, fortissimo; *informal* as if to wake the dead.
OPPOSITES quietly, softly.

loudmouth ▶ noun (*informal*) **1** *if he wins, the press, who have dismissed him as an untested loudmouth, will have to sit up and take note* **braggart**, boaster, blusterer, swaggerer; *informal* windbag, big mouth, blowhard, gasbag, bag of wind, show-off, big-head; *N. Amer. informal* showboat; *vulgar slang*

bullshitter; *literary* braggadocio, gasconader.
2 *I approached him in the strictest confidence, but all too quickly I learned that he is just a gin-sodden loudmouth* **gossip**, gossipmonger, scandalmonger, blabbermouth, blabber, busybody, chatterer, prattler, babbler; *N. Amer.* blatherskite; *informal* gasbag.

loudspeaker ▶ **noun** *a muffled announcement was made over the loudspeaker* **public address system**, PA system, speaker, speaker unit, speaker system, microphone; loud hailer, megaphone; *informal* mike, mic.

lounge ▶ **verb** *the room was empty except for one man lounging in a comfortable chair | I spent the day lounging around the pool* **laze**, lie, loll, lie back, lean back, recline, stretch oneself, drape oneself, relax, rest, repose, take it easy, put one's feet up, unwind, luxuriate; sprawl, slump, slouch, flop; loaf, idle, do nothing.
▶ **noun 1** *she returned to the lounge to say goodnight* **living room**, sitting room, parlour, front room, drawing room, morning room, reception room, salon, family room.
2 *the hotel has a lounge, TV room, and cocktail bar* **public room**, sitting room, common room; cocktail lounge.

lour, **lower** ▶ **verb** *the lofty statue lours at patients in the infirmary* **scowl**, frown, look sullen, glower, glare, grimace, give someone black looks, look daggers, look angry; *informal* give someone dirty looks.
OPPOSITE smile.

louring ▶ **adjective** *the louring sky* **overcast**, dark, leaden, grey, cloudy, clouded, sunless, gloomy, threatening, menacing, promising rain.
OPPOSITES sunny, bright.

louse ▶ **noun**

WORD LINKS

relating to or infested with lice	**pedicular**
infestation with lice	**pediculosis**
fear of lice	**pediculophobia**
chemical used to kill lice	**pediculicide**

lousy ▶ **adjective 1** (*informal*) *he had been a lousy husband* **awful**, terrible, appalling, abysmal, very bad, atrocious, desperate, unspeakable, frightful, miserable; poor, incompetent, inadequate, unsatisfactory, inferior, not up to scratch, careless, second-rate, shoddy, slovenly; *informal* rotten, pathetic, useless, hopeless; *Brit. informal* duff, poxy, rubbish, pants, a load of pants.
OPPOSITES good, competent.
2 (*informal*) *the lousy, double-crossing snake!* **despicable**, contemptible, dirty, low, mean, base, low-down, hateful, detestable, loathsome, vile, wicked, vicious; *informal* rotten, no-good.
OPPOSITES good, decent.
3 *lousy bedclothes* **lice-infested**, lice-ridden, lice-infected; *rare* pedicular, pediculous.
OPPOSITES clean, fumigated.
4 (*informal*) *Doc Reid dishes me out a few vitamin pills when I'm feeling lousy* **ill**, unwell, poorly, sick, nauseous, nauseated, queasy, bad; *Brit.* off, off colour; *informal* rough, rotten, awful, out of sorts, under the weather; *Brit. informal* grotty, ropy.
OPPOSITES well, healthy.
□ **lousy with** (*informal*) *the town is lousy with tourists* **full of**, crowded with, overrun by, overflowing with, swarming with, teeming with, alive with, crawling with, hopping with, bristling with, thronged with, packed with, rife with, well supplied with, awash with, abounding in, abundant in, knee-deep in, rolling in.
OPPOSITE devoid of.

lout ▶ **noun** *a crowd of drunken louts* **ruffian**, hooligan, thug, boor, oaf, hoodlum, rowdy, bully boy; *informal* yob, yobbo, tough, roughneck, bruiser, gorilla, yahoo; *N. Amer. informal* lug; *Austral. informal* ocker.
OPPOSITES smoothie, gentleman.

loutish ▶ **adjective** *a loutish youth | his loutish behaviour* **uncouth**, rude, impolite, unmannerly, ill-mannered, ill-bred, coarse; **thuggish**, boorish, oafish, rowdy, bullying, uncivilized, wild, rough, vulgar, philistine, common, crass; *informal* yobbish, slobbish.
OPPOSITES polite, well behaved.

lovable ▶ **adjective** *a lovable teddy bear | she was so lovable and funny* **adorable**, dear, sweet, cute, charming, darling, lovely, likeable, attractive, delightful, captivating, enchanting, engaging, bewitching, pleasing, appealing, winsome, winning, fetching, taking, endearing, cherished; affectionate, warm-hearted, cuddly; *Italian & Spanish* simpatico; *French* sympathique; *German* sympatisch; *N. Amer. dated* cunning.
OPPOSITES hateful, loathsome.

love ▶ **noun 1** *his friendship with Helen grew into love | she has a great love for her children* **deep affection**, fondness, tenderness, warmth, intimacy, attachment, endearment; devotion, adoration, doting, idolization, worship; passion, ardour, desire, lust, yearning, infatuation, adulation, besottedness.
OPPOSITE hatred.
2 *her love of fashion* **liking**, weakness, partiality, bent, leaning, proclivity, inclination, disposition; enjoyment, appreciation, soft spot, taste, delight, relish, passion, zeal, appetite, zest, enthusiasm, keenness, predilection, penchant, fondness.
3 *their love for their fellow human beings* **compassion**, care, caring, regard, solicitude, concern, warmth, friendliness, friendship, kindness, charity, goodwill, sympathy, kindliness, altruism, philanthropy, unselfishness, benevolence, brotherliness, sisterliness, fellow feeling, humanity.
4 *don't fret, my love | he was her one and only true love* **beloved**, loved one, love of one's life, dear, dearest, dear one, darling, sweetheart, sweet, sweet one, angel, honey; lover, boyfriend, girlfriend, significant other, betrothed, paramour, inamorata, inamorato.
5 *he is confident that their love can survive* **relationship**, **love affair**, affair, romance, liaison, affair of the heart, intrigue, amour.
6 *my mother sends her love to you* **best wishes**, regards, good wishes, greetings, kind/kindest regards, felicitations, salutations, compliments, best, respects.
□ **fall in love with** *the moment they met he fell in love with her* **become infatuated with**, give/lose one's heart to, become smitten with; *informal* fall for, fall head over heels in love with, be swept off one's feet by, develop a crush on.
□ **in love with** *I'm in love with Gillian* **besotted with**, infatuated with, enamoured of, smitten with, passionate about, with a passion for, consumed with desire for; captivated by, bewitched by, enthralled by, entranced by; devoted to, doting on; *informal* mad/crazy/nuts/wild/potty about, bowled over by, carrying a torch for.
▶ **verb 1** *I love you, Rory | she loves her family* **be in love with**, be infatuated with, be smitten with, be besotted with, be passionate about; **care very much for**, feel deep affection for, hold very dear, adore, think the world of, be devoted to, dote on, cherish, worship, idolize, treasure, prize; *informal* be mad/crazy/nuts/wild/potty about, have a pash on, carry a torch for.
OPPOSITES hate, loathe, detest.
2 *Laura had always loved painting* **like very much**, delight in, enjoy greatly, have a passion for, take great pleasure in, derive great pleasure from, have a great liking for, be addicted to, relish, savour; have a weakness for, be partial to, have a soft spot for, have a taste for, be taken with, have a predilection for, have a proclivity for, have a penchant for; *informal* get a kick from/out of, have a thing about/for, be mad for/about, be crazy/nuts/wild/potty about, be hooked on, go a bundle on, get off on, get a buzz from/out of.

WORD LINKS

relating to love	**amatory**
related prefix	**phil(o)- (e.g. *philanthrope, philogynist*)**
related suffixes	**-phile (e.g. *bibliophile, Francophile*),**
	-philia (e.g. *paedophilia*),
	-phily (e.g. *scripophily*)

love affair ▶ **noun 1** *he had a love affair with a teacher* **relationship**, affair, romance, liaison, affair of the heart, intrigue, fling, amour, involvement, amorous entanglement, romantic entanglement, entanglement; flirtation, dalliance; *French* affaire de/du cœur; *Brit. informal* carry-on.
2 *I have had a love affair with the motor car all of my life* **enthusiasm**, mania, devotion, passion, liking, appreciation.

loveless ▶ **adjective** *she feels trapped in a loveless marriage* **passionless**, unloving, unfeeling, heartless, undemonstrative, unresponsive, cold, cold-hearted, icy, frigid.
OPPOSITES loving, passionate.

lovelorn ▶ **adjective** *a lovelorn teenager* **lovesick**, unrequited in love, crossed in love; spurned, jilted, rejected, neglected, forsaken, yearning; pining, moping, languishing, mooning, frustrated, miserable, unhappy.

lovely ▶ **adjective 1** *a lovely young woman | you look lovely* **beautiful**, pretty, as pretty as a picture, attractive, good-looking, appealing, handsome, adorable, exquisite, sweet, personable, charming; enchanting, engaging, bewitching, winsome, seductive, gorgeous, alluring, ravishing, glamorous; *Scottish & N. English* bonny; *informal* tasty, knockout, stunning, smashing, drop-dead gorgeous; *Brit. informal* fit; *N. Amer. informal* cute, foxy; *formal* beauteous; *archaic* comely, fair; *rare* sightly, pulchritudinous.
OPPOSITES ugly, hideous.
2 *there's a lovely view across the town* **scenic**, picturesque, pleasing, easy on the eye; magnificent, stunning, splendid.
3 (*informal*) *it was a lovely warm summer's day* **delightful**, very pleasant, very nice, very agreeable, marvellous, wonderful, sublime, superb, fine, magical, enchanting, captivating; *informal* terrific, fabulous, fab, heavenly, divine, amazing, glorious.
OPPOSITES horrible, disagreeable.

lovemaking ▶ **noun sexual intercourse**, sex, intercourse, making love, sexual relations, sex act, act of love, intimate relations, intimacy, sexual union, coupling, sexual congress, congress, mating, going to bed with someone, sleeping with someone; *informal* it, the other, nooky, rumpy pumpy; *Brit. informal* bonking, how's your father; *vulgar slang* fucking, screwing; *Brit. vulgar slang* shagging; *formal* coitus, coition, copulation; *archaic* fornication, carnal knowledge.

lover ▶ **noun 1** *sometimes I think she had a secret lover* **boyfriend**, **girlfriend**, man friend, woman friend, lady friend, lady-love, beau, loved one, beloved, love, darling, sweetheart; mistress, paramour, other man, other woman; partner, significant other; *Italian* inamorata, inamorato; *informal* bit

L

on the side, bit of fluff, toy boy, fancy man, fancy woman, sugar daddy, bird, fella; *archaic* swain, concubine, doxy, leman, courtesan; *rare* cicisbeo.
2 *he was a great lover of country sports | a dog lover* **devotee**, admirer, fan, enthusiast, aficionado, follower, supporter, fanatic, addict, hound; *informal* buff, freak, nut.

WORD LINKS
lover of ... **-phile (e.g. *bibliophile*)**

lovesick ▶ **adjective** *he was mooning around like a lovesick teenager* **lovelorn**, pining, languishing, longing, yearning, infatuated; frustrated.

loving ▶ **adjective 1** *her loving husband* **affectionate**, fond, devoted, adoring, doting, solicitous, demonstrative; caring, tender, warm, warm-hearted; amorous, ardent, passionate, lustful, amatory.
OPPOSITES cold, cold-hearted.
2 *a loving family life* **caring**, warm, tender, close-knit, close, supportive, nurturing; *informal* touchy-feely.
OPPOSITES cold, cruel.

low[1] ▶ **adjective 1** *a low fence* **short**, small, little; squat, stubby, stunted, truncated, dwarfish, knee-high; shallow.
OPPOSITE high.
2 *a narrow tract of low land* **low-lying**, ground-level, sea-level, flat; sunken, depressed, subsided, nether.
OPPOSITE high.
3 *the low neckline of her blouse* **low-cut**, skimpy, revealing; plunging.
4 *grain prices are still low* **cheap**, inexpensive, low-priced, low-cost, economical, moderate, reasonable, modest, bargain, cut-price, bargain-basement, rock-bottom.
OPPOSITES expensive, high.
5 *her money supplies were low* **scarce**, scanty, scant, skimpy, meagre, sparse, few, little, paltry, measly, trifling; reduced, depleted, diminished; deficient, inadequate, insufficient.
OPPOSITES plentiful, abundant.
6 *much of the work was of a very low standard* **inferior**, substandard, poor, bad, low-grade, low-quality, below par, second-rate, inadequate, unacceptable, unsatisfactory, deficient, defective; wanting, lacking, leaving much to be desired.
OPPOSITES superior, high.
7 *a woman of low birth | a man low in the social scale* **humble**, lowly, low-born, low-bred, low-ranking, plebeian, proletarian, peasant, poor; common, ordinary, simple, plain, unpretentious; inferior, subordinate.
OPPOSITES noble, superior.
8 *adults have low expectations of children's ability to explain things* **unambitious**, unaspiring, modest.
OPPOSITES high, ambitious.
9 *most Americans have a low opinion of New York City* **unfavourable**, poor, bad, adverse, negative, hostile.
OPPOSITES good, favourable, high.
10 *she considered it a rather low thing to have done* **despicable**, contemptible, reprehensible, lamentable, disgusting, shameful, mean, abject, unworthy, shabby, uncharitable, base, dishonourable, unprincipled, ignoble, sordid, wretched; nasty, cruel, foul, bad, wrong, immoral, vile; *informal* rotten, beastly, low-down; *archaic* dastardly, scurvy.
OPPOSITES admirable, decent.
11 *down-at-heel theatres that put on low comedy* **crude**, coarse, vulgar, indecent, ribald, smutty, bawdy, suggestive, off colour, rude, rough, unrefined, indelicate, improper; gross, obscene, pornographic, offensive, profane, filthy, dirty; *informal* blue.
OPPOSITES high, exalted.
12 *he was speaking in a low voice* **quiet**, soft, faint, muted, subdued, muffled, hushed, quietened, whispered, stifled, murmured, gentle, dulcet, indistinct, inaudible.
OPPOSITE loud.
13 *going from a low note to a high note without using valves is difficult* **bass**, low-pitched, deep, deep-toned, low-toned, full-toned, resonant, rich, rumbling, booming, resounding, sonorous.
14 *Fran felt low and unhappy* **depressed**, dejected, despondent, downhearted, downcast, low-spirited, down, sorrowful, gloomy, glum, unhappy, sad, melancholy, blue, fed up, morose, moody, miserable, dismal, heavy-hearted, mournful, forlorn, woebegone; disheartened, discouraged, crestfallen, dispirited, without energy, enervated, flat, sapped, weary; ill, unwell, poorly, out of sorts; *informal* down in the mouth, down in the dumps; *Brit. informal* brassed off, cheesed off.
OPPOSITE cheerful.
▶ **noun** *the news caused the dollar to fall to an all-time low* **nadir**, low point, lowest point, all-time low, lowest level, low-water mark, bottom, rock bottom.
OPPOSITES zenith, acme.

low[2] ▶ **verb** *the sound of cattle lowing* **moo**, bellow.

lowbrow ▶ **adjective** *a lowbrow action movie* **mass-market**, tabloid, pop, popular, intellectually undemanding, lightweight, easy to understand, accessible, unpretentious, simple, simplistic; downmarket, uncultured, unsophisticated, rubbishy, trashy, philistine, plebeian, cheap; *informal* dumbed-down.
OPPOSITES highbrow, intellectual.

low-down (*informal*) ▶ **adjective** *a dirty low-down trick* **unfair, mean**, despicable, reprehensible, contemptible, lamentable, disgusting, shameful, low, abject, unworthy, shabby, uncharitable, base, dishonourable, unprincipled, ignoble, sordid, wretched, loathsome, odious, treacherous, underhand; nasty, cruel, bad, immoral, wicked, wrong, evil, sinful, vile, foul, vicious, nefarious, heinous; *informal* rotten, dirty, stinking, beastly; *archaic* dastardly, scurvy.
OPPOSITES kind, altruistic, unselfish.
▶ **noun** (**the low-down**) *he gave us the low-down on his life as Britain's top comedian* **inside information**, the whole story, the facts; **data**, information, facts and figures, intelligence, the news; **a briefing**, a brief, guidance; *informal* info, the score, the gen, the latest, the word, the rundown; *N. Amer. informal* the poop, the dope.

lower[1] (rhymes with 'mower') ▶ **adjective 1** *the lower house of the German parliament* **subordinate**, inferior, lesser, junior, minor, secondary, lower-level, lower-grade, subsidiary, ancillary, second-fiddle, subservient; second-class, second-rate.
OPPOSITES upper, senior.
2 *the curtain covers the lower half of the window | Flora stuck out her lower lip* **bottom**, bottommost, under, underneath, further down, beneath, nether.
OPPOSITES top, upper, higher.
3 *you may have to accept a lower price* **cheaper**, reduced, decreased, lessened, curtailed, pruned, cut, slashed.
OPPOSITES higher, increased.

lower[2] (rhymes with 'mower') ▶ **verb 1** *she lowered the mask* **move down**, let down, take down, haul down, drop, let fall, let sink.
OPPOSITES raise, lift up.
2 *the crowd had lowered their voices* **soften**, modulate, quieten, hush, tone down, muffle, turn down, mute.
OPPOSITES raise, intensify.
3 *demand could be stimulated by lowering taxes* **reduce**, decrease, lessen, bring down, diminish, curtail, prune, pare (down), ease up on, cause to fall, slim down, mark down, cut, slash, axe.
OPPOSITE increase.
4 *the water level lowered* **subside**, fall (off), recede, ebb, wane; abate, die down, let up, moderate, diminish, lessen.
5 *he must really love her to lower himself in this way* **degrade**, debase, demean, abase, humble, humiliate, downgrade, discredit, shame, dishonour, disgrace; belittle, cheapen, devalue; (**lower oneself**) **condescend**, deign, stoop, sink, descend, vouchsafe.
OPPOSITE boost.

lower[3] (rhymes with 'power') ▶ **verb.** *See* LOUR.

low-grade ▶ **adjective** *low-grade coal | low-grade jobs* **poor-quality**, inferior, substandard, below standard, second-rate; shoddy, cheap, shabby, reject, rubbishy, trashy, junky, bargain-basement, gimcrack; poor, bad, unsatisfactory, not up to par, not up to scratch; mediocre; *informal* tinpot; *Brit. informal* duff, ropy, twopenny-halfpenny; *N. Amer. informal* two-bit, bum, cheapjack, a dime a dozen, low-rent, tinhorn.
OPPOSITES top-quality, first-class.

low-key ▶ **adjective** *the councils' low-key approach had saved them from widespread media hostility* **restrained**, modest, understated, muted, subtle, quiet, low-profile, inconspicuous, unostentatious, unobtrusive, discreet, circumspect, played-down, toned-down, self-effacing, relaxed, downbeat, easy-going, modulated, softened; *informal* laid-back.
OPPOSITES ostentatious, showy.

lowly ▶ **adjective 1** *it was unheard of for a tradesman of such lowly status to threaten his customers in such a fashion* **humble**, low, low-born, low-bred, low-ranking, plebeian, proletarian, peasant, poor; common, ordinary, simple, plain; inferior, ignoble, subordinate, obscure.
OPPOSITES noble, aristocratic.
2 *I'm just a lowly civil servant* **average**, modest, simple, plain, ordinary, commonplace, run-of-the-mill; unambitious, unpretentious, unaspiring.

low-spirited ▶ **adjective** *she sounded a little low-spirited* **depressed**, dejected, despondent, downhearted, downcast, low, down, sorrowful, gloomy, glum, unhappy, sad, melancholy, blue, fed up, morose, moody, miserable, dismal, heavy-hearted, mournful, forlorn, woebegone; disheartened, discouraged, crestfallen, dispirited, without energy, enervated, flat; *informal* down in the mouth, down in the dumps; *Brit. informal* brassed off, cheesed off.
OPPOSITE cheerful.

CHOOSE THE RIGHT WORD

loyal, faithful, constant, true
See FAITHFUL.

loyal ▶ **adjective** *she was loyal to her country* **faithful**, true, true-hearted, tried and true, true-blue, devoted; **constant**, steadfast, fast, staunch, dependable, reliable, trusted, trustworthy, trusty, dutiful, unchanging, unwavering, unswerving, dedicated, committed, firm, stable, steady,

unfailing; patriotic.
OPPOSITES disloyal, treacherous.

loyalty ▶ noun *he owes his primary loyalty to the party* **allegiance**, faithfulness, fidelity, obedience, fealty, adherence, homage, devotion, bond; trueness, true-heartedness; steadfastness, fastness, staunchness, dependability, reliability, trustiness, trustworthiness, duty, constancy, dedication, commitment; firmness, stability, steadiness; patriotism; *archaic* troth.
OPPOSITES disloyalty, treachery.

lozenge ▶ noun **1** *the patterns comprise mosaics, lozenges, and crosses* **rhombus**, diamond shape, diamond.
2 *she was always taking throat lozenges and cough mixtures* **pastille**, tablet, pill, capsule, pilule, drop; **cough sweet**, cough drop, gum, gumdrop, jujube; *Medicine* troche, bolus; *rare* trochisk, trochiscus.

lubberly (*archaic*) ▶ adjective *a great lubberly fellow* **clumsy**, awkward, blundering, bumbling, lumbering, ungainly, gawky, graceless, ungraceful, inelegant, maladroit, inept, bungling, uncoordinated, hulking, oafish, clownish, doltish, boorish, lumpish, lumpen, gauche, like a bull in a china shop, all fingers and thumbs, heavy-handed; *informal* yobbish, slobbish, clodhopping, butterfingered.
OPPOSITES graceful, dexterous.

lubricant ▶ noun *the pipe ends had been smeared with lubricant* **grease**, oil, lubricator, lubrication, emollient, lotion, unguent; lard, fat; moisturizer.

lubricate ▶ verb **1** *lubricate the washer with silicone grease* **oil**, **grease**, make slippery, make smooth, smear with oil, cover with oil, rub with oil, moisturize, wax, polish.
2 *firms would invite clients in the hope that the goodwill created would lubricate some future deal* **facilitate**, ease, ready, make smooth, smooth the way for, oil the wheels for, pave the way for.
OPPOSITES impede, obstruct.

lucid ▶ adjective **1** *a lucid introduction to the philosophy of mind* **intelligible**, comprehensible, understandable, cogent, coherent, communicative, articulate, eloquent; clear, clear-cut, crystal clear, transparent; plain, simple, direct, vivid, sharp, straightforward, perspicuous, unambiguous, graphic, explicit; *informal* joined-up.
OPPOSITES confusing, unclear, ambiguous.
2 *occasionally she has these lucid moments where she's herself again* **rational**, sane, in one's right mind, in possession of one's faculties, of sound mind, able to think clearly; normal, balanced, well balanced, sensible, clear-headed, right-minded, sober; *Latin* compos mentis; *informal* all there, with all one's marbles.
OPPOSITE muddled.
3 (*literary*) *the lucid stars* **bright**, shining, gleaming, luminous, radiant, brilliant, glowing, dazzling, lustrous, luminescent, phosphorescent; *literary* lucent, lambent; *rare* effulgent, refulgent.
OPPOSITES dark, dull.

luck ▶ noun **1** *with luck you'll be in Marseilles tomorrow night | best of luck, John!* **good fortune**, good luck, success, successfulness, prosperity, advantage, advantageousness, felicity; a stroke of luck; *informal* fluke, a lucky break.
OPPOSITES bad luck, misfortune.
2 *she sent up a silent prayer that her luck had changed* **fortune**, fate, destiny, lot, stars, what is written in the stars, karma, kismet; fortuity, serendipity; chance, accident, a twist of fate, contingency, circumstances; *Austral./NZ informal* mozzle.

□ **in luck** *I was in luck—the lift was working* **fortunate**, lucky, blessed, favoured, born under a lucky star; successful, prosperous, happy, opportune, timely, blessed with good luck; *Brit. informal* jammy.
OPPOSITES unlucky, out of luck.

□ **out of luck** *you're out of luck—you've missed the evening edition* **unfortunate**, unlucky, luckless, hapless, cursed with ill-luck, unsuccessful, disadvantaged, miserable; *informal* down on one's luck.
OPPOSITES lucky, in luck.

luckily ▶ adverb *luckily, our ship was not badly damaged* **fortunately**, happily, providentially, opportunely, by good luck, by good fortune, as luck would have it, propitiously; mercifully, thankfully; thank goodness, thank God, thank heavens, thank the stars.
OPPOSITE unfortunately.

luckless ▶ adjective *the novel's luckless hero ends tragically without wife, mistress, or home* **unlucky**, unfortunate, unsuccessful, out of luck, down on one's luck, jinxed, cursed, doomed, hapless, ill-fated, ill-starred, star-crossed; disadvantaged; unhappy, miserable, wretched, forlorn.
OPPOSITES lucky, fortunate.

lucky ▶ adjective **1** *I'm lucky to have such a caring family | fifty lucky winners have received T-shirts* **fortunate**, in luck, blessed, blessed with good luck, favoured, born under a lucky star, charmed; successful, prosperous, happy; advantaged, born with a silver spoon in one's mouth; *Brit. informal* jammy.
OPPOSITES unlucky, unfortunate.
2 *I had a lucky escape | it was just a lucky guess* **providential**, fortunate, advantageous, timely, opportune, serendipitous, expedient, heaven-sent, auspicious, propitious, felicitous, convenient, apt; chance, fortuitous, accidental, unexpected, unanticipated, unforeseen, unlooked-for, coincidental; *informal* fluky.
OPPOSITE unfavourable.

lucrative ▶ adjective *a lucrative business* **profitable**, profit-making, gainful, remunerative, moneymaking, paying, high-income, well paid, high-paying, bankable, cost-effective; productive, fruitful, rewarding, worthwhile, advantageous; thriving, flourishing, successful, booming, going.
OPPOSITE unprofitable.

lucre ▶ noun *he had seen the inheritance simply as a source of lucre* **money**, cash, hard cash, ready money, funds, capital, finances, riches, wealth, spoils, ill-gotten gains, Mammon; profit, profits, gain, proceeds, winnings; *informal* dough, bread, loot, the ready, readies, moolah; *Brit. informal* dosh, brass, lolly, spondulicks, wonga, ackers; *archaic* pelf.

ludicrous ▶ adjective *a ludicrous idea* **absurd**, ridiculous, farcical, laughable, risible, preposterous, foolish, idiotic, stupid, inane, silly, asinine, nonsensical; *informal* crazy, mad, insane; *rare* derisible.
OPPOSITE sensible.

lug ▶ verb *they lugged the baskets of laundry upstairs* **carry**, lift, bear, tote, heave, hoist, shoulder, manhandle; haul, drag, pull, tug, tow, transport, move, take, bring, convey, shift, fetch; *informal* hump, schlep; *Scottish informal* humph.

luggage ▶ noun *David hauled their luggage off the back seat* **baggage**, bag and baggage, things, gear, belongings, kit, effects, goods and chattels, impedimenta, paraphernalia, accoutrements, rig, tackle; bags, suitcases, cases, trunks; *informal* stuff, clobber. *See also* BAG *sense* 3.

lugubrious ▶ adjective *his lugubrious expression | a lugubrious hymn* **mournful**, gloomy, sad, unhappy, doleful, Eeyorish, glum, melancholy, melancholic, woeful, miserable, woebegone, forlorn, despondent, dejected, depressed, long-faced, sombre, solemn, serious, sorrowful, morose, dour, mirthless, cheerless, joyless, wretched, dismal, grim, saturnine, pessimistic; funereal, sepulchral, dirge-like, elegiac; *informal* down in the mouth, down in the dumps, blue; *Brit. informal* looking as if one had lost a pound and found a penny; *literary* dolorous.
OPPOSITES cheerful, joyful.

lukewarm ▶ adjective **1** *they drank bitter lukewarm coffee* **tepid**, slightly warm, warmish, blood-hot, blood-warm, at room temperature, at skin temperature; *French* chambré.
OPPOSITES hot; cold.
2 *elsewhere in the country, however, the idea met with a lukewarm response* **indifferent**, cool, half-hearted, apathetic, unenthusiastic, tepid, uninterested, unconcerned, offhand, lackadaisical, perfunctory, phlegmatic, impassive, dispassionate, emotionless, passionless, limp, non-committal, unresponsive, unmoved; *informal* laid-back, unenthused, couldn't-care-less; *Brit. vulgar slang* half-arsed; *rare* Laodicean.
OPPOSITE enthusiastic.

lull ▶ verb **1** *the sound of the bells lulled us to sleep* **soothe**, quiet, hush, lullaby; rock to sleep.
OPPOSITES waken, agitate.
2 *he had been unable to lull his wife's anxiety about her fading beauty* **assuage**, allay, ease, alleviate, pacify, palliate, mitigate, placate, mollify; soothe, quiet, quieten, silence, calm, settle, hush, still, quell, quash, stifle, deaden, repress; temper, reduce, check, diminish.
OPPOSITE aggravate.
3 *the noise from the fair had lulled* **abate**, die down, subside, let up, moderate, slacken, lessen, dwindle, decrease, diminish, ebb, fade away, wane, taper off, lower.
OPPOSITE increase.
▶ noun **1** *for two days there had been a lull in the fighting* **pause**, respite, interval, break, hiatus, suspension, cessation, interlude, intermission, breathing space, moratorium, lacuna; *Prosody* caesura; *informal* let-up, breather.
2 *the lull before the storm* **calm**, calmness, stillness, quiet, quietness, tranquillity, peace, peacefulness, silence, hush.
OPPOSITE activity.

lullaby ▶ noun *I remembered a lullaby my mother sang to me* **cradle song**, soothing song, gentle song, quiet song; *French* berceuse.

lumber[1] ▶ verb *she watched him lumber blindly down the steep narrow staircase* **lurch**, stumble, shamble, shuffle, reel, waddle; **trudge**, clump, stump, plod, tramp, walk heavily/clumsily, stamp, stomp, thump, thud, bang; *informal* galumph.

lumber[2] ▶ noun **1** *a spare room packed with lumber* **jumble**, clutter, odds and ends, bits and pieces, bits and bobs, rummage, bric-a-brac, oddments, miscellanea, sundries, knick-knacks, flotsam and jetsam, cast-offs, white elephants, stuff, things; rejects, trash, refuse, rubbish, litter; *informal* junk, odds and sods, gubbins, clobber.
2 *they have diversified into lumber and cattle ranching in the Amazon* **timber**, wood, planks, planking.
▶ verb (*Brit. informal*) *a career would be less easy once she was lumbered with a husband and child* **burden**, saddle, encumber, hamper, impose on, load, oppress, trouble, tax; *informal* land, dump something on someone.

L

lumbering ▶ adjective *he was a lumbering bear of a man* **clumsy**, awkward, heavy-footed, blundering, bumbling, inept, maladroit, uncoordinated, ungainly, oafish, like a bull in a china shop, ungraceful, gauche, lumpish, hulking, cumbersome, ponderous, laborious, stolid; *informal* clodhopping; *archaic* lubberly.
OPPOSITES nimble, agile.

luminary ▶ noun *the luminaries of the art world* **leading light**, guiding light, inspiration, leader, expert, master, panjandrum, dignitary, VIP; star, superstar, megastar, celebrity, big name, household name, somebody, name; notable, public figure, important personage, lion, legend, great, giant; *informal* bigwig, big shot, big cheese, biggie, celeb.
OPPOSITES nobody, pleb.

luminous ▶ adjective **1** *a cluster of luminous stars | he checked the luminous dial on his alarm clock* **shining**, bright, brilliant, radiant, dazzling, glowing, gleaming, scintillating, lustrous, luminescent, phosphorescent, incandescent; vivid, intense, resplendent; lighted, lit, illuminated; *literary* lambent, lucent; *rare* coruscating, refulgent, effulgent, candescent, luminiferous.
OPPOSITE dark.
2 *a luminous account of such phenomena* **lucid**, illuminating, intelligible, comprehensible, understandable, cogent, coherent, communicative, articulate, eloquent; clear, clear-cut, crystal clear, transparent; plain, simple, direct, vivid, graphic, sharp, straightforward, perspicuous, unambiguous.
OPPOSITES obscure, confusing.

lump[1] ▶ noun **1** *a lump of coal* **chunk**, wedge, hunk, piece, mass, block, slab, cake, nugget, ball, brick, cube, dab, pat, knob, clod, gobbet, dollop, wad, clump, cluster, mound, concentration; bit, segment, portion; *informal* gob, glob.
2 *he had a huge lump on his head* **swelling**, bump, bulge, protuberance, protrusion, growth, outgrowth, carbuncle, hump, tumour, wen, boil, blister, wart, corn, eruption, node, contusion; *rare* tumescence.
▶ verb *the media tend to* **lump together** *women singer-songwriters* **combine**, put, group, bunch, aggregate, unite, pool, mix, blend, merge, mass, join, fuse, conglomerate, coalesce, consolidate, collect, throw, consider together.

lump[2] (*informal*) ▶ verb
□ **lump it** *we're going to the swimming pool tomorrow, like it or lump it* **put up with it**, bear it, endure it, take it, tolerate it, suffer it, accept it, make allowances for it, abide it, brook it, weather it, countenance it; *Scottish* thole it; *informal* stick it, stomach it, stand it, swallow it, hack it, wear it.

lumpish ▶ adjective **1** *lumpish furniture* **cumbersome**, unwieldy, heavy, hulking, clumsily formed, awkwardly shaped.
OPPOSITE elegant.
2 *a lumpish Belgian girl* **stupid**, obtuse, dense, dim-witted, dull-witted, slow-witted, slow, obtuse, moronic, half-baked, doltish; lethargic, bovine, stolid; *informal* thick, dumb, dopey, slow on the uptake; *Brit. informal* dozy.
OPPOSITES quick-witted, sharp.

lumpy ▶ adjective **1** *a lumpy mattress* **bumpy**, knobbly, bulging, uneven, covered with lumps, full of lumps.
2 *lumpy custard* **clotted**, curdled, full of lumps, congealed, coagulated; granular, grainy; *rare* nodose.

lunacy ▶ noun **1** *the survivors descended into despair and lunacy* **insanity**, madness, mental illness, derangement, dementia, dementedness, insaneness, loss of reason, unsoundness of mind, mental instability, mania, frenzy, psychosis; *informal* craziness.
OPPOSITE sanity.
2 *such an economic policy would be sheer lunacy* **folly**, foolishness, foolhardiness, stupidity, idiocy, imbecility, irrationality, illogicality, senselessness, nonsense, absurdity, absurdness, madness, insanity; silliness, inanity, ridiculousness, ludicrousness; *informal* craziness; *Brit. informal* daftness.
OPPOSITES sense, prudence.

lunatic ▶ noun **1** *a dangerous lunatic* **maniac**, madman, madwoman, psychopath, psychotic; *informal* loony, loon, nut, nutter, nutcase, head case, headbanger, screwball, psycho.
2 *when I'm in a bad mood I drive like a lunatic* **fool**, idiot, imbecile, moron.
▶ adjective **1** *a lunatic prisoner. See* MAD.
2 *a lunatic idea. See* FOOLISH.

lunch ▶ noun *I had lunch with John* **midday meal**, luncheon, brunch, snack; *Brit.* dinner.

WORD LINKS
relating to a meal **prandial**

lung ▶ noun

WORD LINKS

relating to the lungs	**pulmonary**
related prefixes	**pneumo- (e.g. *pneumoconiosis*), pneumon- (e.g. *pneumonitis*)**
removal of a lung	**pneumonectomy**
measurement of lung capacity	**spirometry**

lunge ▶ noun *Harry made a lunge for the dagger* **thrust**, pounce, dive, jump, spring, leap, rush, sudden movement, grab.
▶ verb *McCulloch raised his cudgel and lunged at him* **thrust**, pounce, dive, launch oneself, jump, spring, leap, rush, charge, move suddenly, make a grab.

lurch ▶ verb **1** *he lurched into the kitchen* **stagger**, stumble, sway, reel, roll, weave, totter, flounder, falter, wobble, slip, move clumsily.
OPPOSITE tiptoe.
2 *Scott was hurled across a bulkhead as the ship lurched* **sway**, reel, list, roll, pitch, toss, keel, veer, labour, flounder, heel, swerve, make heavy weather; *Nautical* pitchpole.

lure ▶ verb *consumers are frequently lured into debt by clever advertising* **tempt**, entice, attract, induce, coax, persuade, inveigle, allure, seduce, win over, cajole, beguile, bewitch, ensnare, captivate, enrapture; decoy, draw, lead (on); whet someone's appetite.
OPPOSITES deter, put off.
▶ noun *Les could never resist the lure of the stage* **temptation**, enticement, attraction, pull, draw, appeal; inducement, allurement, fascination, interest; decoy, incentive, bait, magnet, siren song, drawing card, carrot, snare, trap; *informal* come-on.

CHOOSE THE RIGHT WORD
lure, tempt, entice
See TEMPT.

lurid ▶ adjective **1** *a lurid birthday card* **brightly coloured**, bright, over-bright, brilliant, glaring, fluorescent, flaming, dazzling, vivid, intense; showy, gaudy, loud.
OPPOSITES muted, subtle.
2 *a lurid account of the prostitution trade | lurid details* **sensational**, sensationalist, melodramatic, exaggerated, overdramatized, extravagant, colourful, trashy, rubbishy, cheap, pulp, tasteless, kitschy; **salacious**, graphic, explicit, unrestrained, prurient, ribald, suggestive, shocking, startling, dirty, filthy; **gruesome**, gory, grisly, macabre, repugnant, revolting, disgusting, ghastly, morbid, unearthly, grotesque, hideous, horrifying, appalling; *informal* tacky, shock-horror, juicy, full-frontal.
OPPOSITES restrained, discreet.

lurk ▶ verb *a ruthless killer still lurked in the darkness* **skulk**, loiter, lie in wait, lie low, hide, conceal oneself, take cover, keep out of sight; sneak, sidle, slink, prowl, steal, move furtively, move with stealth.

luscious ▶ adjective **1** *luscious fruits and vegetables* **delicious**, succulent, lush, juicy, mouth-watering, sweet, tasty, flavourful, flavoursome, appetizing, delectable, palatable, toothsome, choice; *informal* scrumptious, scrummy, yummy, moreish; *N. Amer. informal* nummy; *literary* ambrosial; *rare* ambrosian, nectareous, nectarean.
OPPOSITE unappetizing.
2 *a luscious Swedish beauty* **sexy**, sexually attractive, nubile, ravishing, gorgeous, desirable, alluring, sultry, sensuous, beautiful, stunning, attractive; voluptuous, curvaceous, shapely, buxom; *informal* beddable, fanciable, curvy; *N. Amer. informal* foxy, cute, bootylicious; *Austral./NZ informal* spunky.
OPPOSITES plain; scrawny.

lush[1] ▶ adjective **1** *the hills are covered in lush vegetation* **luxuriant**, rich, abundant, superabundant, profuse, exuberant, riotous, prolific, teeming, flourishing, thriving, vigorous; dense, thick, rank, rampant, overgrown, jungle-like; verdant, green; *informal* jungly.
OPPOSITES barren, meagre.
2 *a lush ripe peach* **succulent**, luscious, juicy, fleshy, pulpy, soft, tender, ripe, fresh.
OPPOSITE shrivelled.
3 *a lush apartment in the best residential section* **luxurious**, luxury, de luxe, sumptuous, grand, palatial, opulent, lavish, elaborate, extravagant, fancy; *informal* plush, ritzy, classy, posh, swanky; *Brit. informal* swish; *N. Amer. informal* swank.
OPPOSITE austere.

lush[2] ▶ noun *a cheerful but notorious lush* **alcoholic**, heavy drinker, hard drinker, problem drinker, drinker, drunk, drunkard, sot, tippler, inebriate, dipsomaniac, imbiber; *informal* alky, boozer, barfly, sponge, souse, dipso, tosspot, wino, soak; *Austral./NZ informal* hophead; *vulgar slang* piss artist; *archaic* toper.
OPPOSITE teetotaller.

lust ▶ noun **1** *he was watching her with undisguised lust* **sexual desire**, sexual appetite, sexual longing, sexual passion, lustfulness, ardour, desire, passion; libido, sex drive, sexuality, biological urge; **lechery**, lecherousness, lasciviousness, lewdness, carnality, licentiousness, salaciousness, prurience; *informal* horniness, raunchiness, the hots; *Brit. informal* randiness; *rare* salacity, concupiscence, nympholepsy.
2 *a lust for power* **greed**, greediness, desire, craving, covetousness, eagerness, keenness, avidness, avidity, cupidity, longing, yearning, hunger, thirst, appetite, hankering.
OPPOSITE aversion.
▶ verb **1** *he* **lusted after** *his employer's wife* **desire**, be consumed with desire

for, find sexually attractive, find sexy, crave, covet, want, wish for, long for, yearn for, hunger for, thirst for, ache for, burn for, pant for; *informal* have the hots for, lech after/over, fancy, have a thing about/for, drool over, have the horn for.
2 *she* ***lusted after*** *some unbridled adventure* **crave**, **desire**, be consumed with desire for, covet, have one's heart set on, want, wish for, long for, yearn for, dream of, hanker for, hanker after, hunger for, thirst for, ache for.
OPPOSITE be averse to.

lustful ▶ adjective *a lustful look* **lecherous**, lascivious, lewd, libidinous, licentious, lubricious, salacious, goatish; wanton, unchaste, impure, immodest, indecent, dirty, prurient; passionate, ardent, amorous, amatory, hot-blooded, sensual, sexy, erotic; *informal* horny, randy, raunchy, naughty; *rare* concupiscent, lickerish.
OPPOSITES chaste, pure.

lustily ▶ adverb *the crew cheered lustily* **heartily**, vigorously, loudly, at the top of one's voice, with all one's might, with might and main, powerfully, forcefully, strongly; *informal* like mad, like crazy.
OPPOSITES faintly, quietly.

lustre ▶ noun **1** *her hair lost its lustre* **sheen**, gloss, glossiness, shine, brightness, radiance, burnish, polish, patina, glow, gleam, glimmer, shimmer.
OPPOSITE dullness.
2 *the lustre of the Milky Way* **brilliance**, brightness, sparkle, dazzle, flash, glitter, glint, gleam, radiance, luminousness, luminosity, luminescence, light; *rare* effulgence, refulgence, lambency, coruscation.
OPPOSITE darkness.
3 *the lustre of their achievements* **honour**, glory, illustriousness, credit, merit, prestige, éclat, distinction, eminence, pre-eminence, notability, consequence, renown, fame.
OPPOSITE dishonour.
4 *a ginger jar in pink lustre with embossed flowers* **glaze**, lacquer, shellac, varnish, enamel, patina, coat, coating, covering, finish.

lustreless ▶ adjective *a pallid face and lustreless eyes | lustreless black boots* **dull**, lacklustre, matt, unburnished, unpolished, tarnished, dingy, dim, dark, drab.
OPPOSITES lustrous, bright.

lustrous ▶ adjective *lustrous black hair* **shiny**, shining, satiny, glossy, gleaming, burnished, polished, radiant, bright, brilliant, luminous; dazzling, sparkling, glistening, twinkling, shimmering, scintillating; *literary* lucent, irradiant; *rare* effulgent, refulgent.
OPPOSITE dull.

lusty ▶ adjective **1** *lusty young men* **healthy**, **strong**, **fit**, vigorous, robust, hale and hearty, hearty, energetic, vital, lively, bursting with good health, blooming, in good condition, in fine fettle; rugged, sturdy, tough, stalwart, brawny, muscular, muscly, strapping, hefty, husky, burly, solidly built, well built, well made, solid, substantial, powerful; virile, red-blooded; *informal* beefy.
OPPOSITE weak.
2 *he sang a few bars in a lusty baritone* **loud**, vigorous, hearty, strong, powerful, forceful, stentorian; strident.
OPPOSITES quiet, weak.

luxuriant ▶ adjective *luxuriant green vegetation* **lush**, rich, abundant, superabundant, profuse, exuberant, prolific, teeming, flourishing, fecund, thriving, vigorous, riotous; dense, thick, rank, rampant, overgrown; verdant, green; *informal* jungly.
OPPOSITES barren, meagre, sparse.

luxuriant or luxurious?
See LUXURIOUS.

luxuriate ▶ verb *run a hot bath and* ***luxuriate in*** *it* **revel**, bask, delight, take pleasure, wallow, indulge oneself, enjoy, relish, savour, appreciate, lap up; *informal* get a kick out of, get a thrill out of, get a charge out of.
OPPOSITES dislike, find intolerable.

luxurious ▶ adjective **1** *a luxurious New York hotel* **opulent**, sumptuous, affluent, expensive, rich, costly, de luxe, lush, grand, palatial, splendid, magnificent, lavish, lavishly appointed, well appointed, extravagant, ornate, fancy, stylish, elegant; *informal* plush, posh, upmarket, classy, ritzy, swanky; *Brit. informal* swish; *N. Amer. informal* swank; *rare* palatian.
OPPOSITES poor; austere, spartan.
2 *a luxurious lifestyle* **self-indulgent**, sensual, pleasure-loving, comfort-seeking, epicurean, hedonistic, sybaritic, lotus-eating, decadent, extravagant, immoderate.
OPPOSITE abstemious.

luxurious or luxuriant?
You may find *luxuriant foliage* in the conservatory of a *luxurious home*, but the two words have quite different meanings.
- **Luxurious** denotes things that are extremely comfortable, elegant, and pleasurable (usually with a hint that they may be self-indulgent and unnecessarily expensive), as in *the luxurious villas of the rich and famous*.
- **Luxuriant**, on the other hand, is used mainly with reference to the growth of plants (*luxuriant creepers climbed up the wall*), though it may also refer to a person's hair (*she tossed her luxuriant hair back contemptuously*).

luxury ▶ noun **1** *we'll live in luxury for the rest of our lives* **opulence**, luxuriousness, sumptuousness, richness, costliness, grandeur, grandness, splendour, magnificence, lavishness, lap of luxury, bed of roses, milk and honey; comfort, security; affluence, wealth, prosperity, prosperousness, plenty; *informal* the life of Riley.
OPPOSITES austerity; poverty.
2 *the luxury of a long night's rest* **joy**, delight, bliss, blessing, benefit, advantage, boon; satisfaction, comfort, ease.
3 *a TV is his only luxury* **indulgence**, extravagance, self-indulgence, treat, extra, non-essential, frill; refinement.
OPPOSITE necessity.

lying ▶ noun *she was no good at lying* **untruthfulness**, fabrication, fibbing, perjury, white lies, little white lies; falseness, falsity, dishonesty, mendacity, mendaciousness, perfidy, perfidiousness, lack of veracity, telling stories, invention, misrepresentation, deceit, duplicity, dissimulation, dissembling, pretence, artifice, guile, double-dealing, underhandedness; *informal* kidology.
OPPOSITES telling the truth, honesty.
▶ adjective *he's a lying, cheating snake in the grass* **untruthful**, false, dishonest, mendacious, perfidious, deceitful, deceiving, deceptive, duplicitous, dissimulating, dissembling, double-dealing, two-faced, guileful, underhand, disingenuous; *informal* crooked, bent, sneaky, tricky; *archaic* hollow-hearted.
OPPOSITES truthful, honest.

WORD LINKS
compulsion to lie **mythomania**

lynch ▶ verb *six policemen were lynched by angry crowds* **hang**, hang by the neck; execute, put to death, kill, murder; *informal* **string up**, do in, bump off, knock off; *literary* slay; *rare* gibbet.

lyric ▶ adjective **1** *lyric poems of extraordinary beauty* **melodic**, songlike, musical, melodious, lyrical, rhapsodic, poetic; **expressive**, emotional, deeply felt, personal, subjective, passionate.
2 *lyric voices* **light**, silvery, clear, lilting, flowing, dulcet, euphonious, sweet, sweet-toned, sweet-sounding, honeyed, mellifluous, mellow, lyrical; *rare* mellifluent.
OPPOSITES harsh, cacophonous.

lyrical ▶ adjective **1** *lyrical love poetry* **songlike**, lyric, melodic, musical, melodious, rhapsodic, poetic; **expressive**, emotional, deeply felt, personal, subjective, passionate.
2 *she was lyrical about her success* **enthusiastic**, rhapsodic, effusive, rapturous, ecstatic, euphoric, carried away, emotional, passionate, impassioned.
OPPOSITE unenthusiastic.

lyrics ▶ plural noun *the lyrics of the song* **words**, libretto, book, text, lines.

L

Mm

macabre ▶ adjective **1** *a macabre ritual* **gruesome**, grisly, grim, gory, morbid, ghastly, unearthly, lurid, grotesque, hideous, horrific, horrible, horrifying, horrid, horrendous, terrifying, frightening, frightful, fearsome, shocking, dreadful, appalling, loathsome, repugnant, repulsive, sickening.
2 *a macabre joke* **black**, **weird**, unhealthy, sick.

mace ▶ noun **staff**, club, cudgel, stick, shillelagh, bludgeon, blackjack, truncheon, cosh, life preserver.

macerate ▶ verb *macerate the seeds in a vinegar solution* **pulp**, mash, squash, soften, liquefy, soak, steep, infuse.

Machiavellian ▶ adjective *there were press accusations of Machiavellian deception* **devious**, cunning, crafty, artful, wily, sly, scheming, designing, conniving, opportunistic, insidious, treacherous, perfidious, two-faced, tricky, double-dealing, unscrupulous, deceitful, dishonest; *informal* foxy.
OPPOSITES straightforward, ingenuous.

machinations ▶ plural noun *they attributed the unrest to the machinations of the communists* **schemes**, plotting, plots, intrigues, conspiracies, designs, plans, devices, ploys, ruses, tricks, wiles, stratagems, tactics, manoeuvres, manoeuvring, contrivances, expedients; *rare* complots.

machine ▶ noun **1** *a special pincer machine for this work* **apparatus**, appliance, instrument, tool, utensil, device, unit, contraption, contrivance, gadget, mechanism, engine, motor, lever, pulley; *informal* gizmo.
2 *a machine can perform these tasks better than a human being* **robot**, automaton, computer.
3 *an efficient publicity machine* **organization**, system, structure, arrangement, agency, machinery; *informal* set-up.

WORD LINKS
relating to machines **mechanical**
fear of machines **mechanophobia**

machine gun ▶ noun. *See centre pages for list of* **Guns**

machinery ▶ noun **1** *a paper mill equipped with modern machinery* **equipment**, apparatus, hardware, plant, mechanism, gear, tackle, instruments, tools, gadgetry, technology; *rare* enginery.
2 *the machinery of local government* **workings**, organization, system, structure, administration, institution, agency, channel, vehicle; *informal* set-up, nuts and bolts, brass tacks, nitty-gritty.

WORD LINKS
fear of machinery **mechanophobia**

machinist ▶ noun *a machinist in a local paper mill* **operator**, operative, machine operator, machine-minder, worker.

machismo ▶ noun *a woman following her career can challenge a husband's machismo* **(aggressive) masculinity**, toughness, chauvinism, male chauvinism, sexism, laddishness; virility, manliness.

macho ▶ adjective *a macho, non-caring image* **(aggressively) male**, (unpleasantly) masculine; manly, virile, red-blooded, swashbuckling; *informal* butch, laddish.
OPPOSITE wimpish.
▶ noun **1** *he was a macho at heart* **red-blooded male**, macho man, muscleman; *informal* he-man, tough guy, stud; *N. Amer. vulgar slang* cocksman.
OPPOSITES wimp, milksop.
2 *macho is out. See* MACHISMO.

mackintosh ▶ noun **raincoat**, overcoat, gaberdine, trench coat; anorak, cagoule, cape, oilskin, waterproof; *Brit.* pakamac; *Brit. informal* mac; *N. Amer. informal* slicker; *trademark* Burberry, Drizabone.

macrocosm ▶ noun **1** *the law of the macrocosm* **universe**, cosmos, world, wide world, globe, creation, solar system, galaxy, outer space.
OPPOSITE microcosm.
2 *the individual is a microcosm of the social macrocosm* **system**, structure, totality, entirety, complex.

macula ▶ noun **spot**, dot, fleck, mark, speck, speckle, smudge, splash, stain, macule.

mad ▶ adjective **1** *he felt he was going mad* **insane**, mentally ill, certifiable, deranged, demented, of unsound mind, out of one's mind, not in one's right mind, sick in the head, not together, crazy, crazed, lunatic, non compos mentis, unbalanced, unhinged, unstable, disturbed, distracted, stark mad, manic, frenzied, raving, distraught, frantic, hysterical, delirious, psychotic, psychopathic, mad as a hatter, mad as a March hare, away with the fairies, foaming at the mouth; *informal* mental, off one's head, out of one's head, off one's nut, nuts, nutty, nutty as a fruitcake, off one's rocker, not (quite) right in the head, round the bend, stark staring/raving mad, raving mad, bats, batty, bonkers, dotty, cuckoo, cracked, loopy, loony, bananas, loco, dippy, screwy, schizoid, touched, gaga, up the pole, off the wall, not all there, not right upstairs; *Brit. informal* barmy, crackers, barking, barking mad, round the twist, off one's trolley, as daft as a brush, not the full shilling; *N. Amer. informal* buggy, nutsy, nutso; out of one's tree, meshuga, squirrelly, wacko; *Canadian & Austral./NZ informal* bushed; *NZ informal* porangi; (**be mad**) *informal* have a screw loose, have bats in the/one's belfry; *Austral. informal* have kangaroos in the/one's top paddock.
OPPOSITE sane.
2 (*informal*) *I'm still mad at him for what he did* **angry**, furious, infuriated, irate, raging, enraged, fuming, blazing, flaming mad, blazing mad, in a towering rage, incensed, wrathful, seeing red, cross, indignant, exasperated, irritated, berserk, out of control, beside oneself; *informal* livid, spare, wild, aerated; *informal, dated* waxy, in a wax; *N. Amer. informal* sore.
OPPOSITES calm, unruffled.
3 *what sort of mad scheme are you working on?* **foolish**, insane, stupid, lunatic, foolhardy, idiotic, irrational, unreasonable, illogical, zany, senseless, nonsensical, absurd, impractical, silly, inane, asinine, ludicrous, wild, unwise, imprudent, preposterous; *informal* crazy, daft, crackpot, crackbrained.
OPPOSITE sensible.
4 (*informal*) *he's* **mad about** *jazz* **enthusiastic**, passionate, impassioned, keen on; ardent, zealous, fervent, avid, eager, fervid, fanatical, addicted to, devoted to, infatuated with, in love with, hot for; *informal* crazy, potty, dotty, nuts, wild, hooked on, gone on; *N. Amer. informal* nutso.
OPPOSITE indifferent.
5 *we made mad, passionate love* **unrestrained**, uncontrolled, uninhibited, wild, abandoned, overpowering, overwhelming, excited, frenzied, frantic, frenetic, ebullient, energetic, boisterous.

□ **go mad 1** *he subsequently went mad and threw himself in front of a train* **become insane**, lose one's reason, lose one's mind, take leave of one's senses, go off one's head, go crazy; *informal* go doolally (tap), lose one's marbles; *Brit. informal* go barmy, go off one's trolley, go round the twist, go crackers.
2 (*informal*) *when I told her I was going to be an actor, my mother went mad* **become very angry**, lose one's temper, get in a rage, rant, rant and rave, fulminate; go crazy; *informal* explode, burst, go off the deep end, go ape, flip, flip one's lid; *Brit. informal* do one's nut; *N. Amer. informal* flip one's wig; *vulgar slang* go apeshit.
3 *the crowd went mad with excitement* **become frenzied**, become uncontrollable, lose control, erupt, boil over.

□ **like mad** (*informal*) **1** *the two men turned towards me, and I ran like mad* **fast**, furiously, as fast as possible, as fast as one's legs can carry one, hurriedly, quickly, rapidly, speedily, hastily.
2 *he had to fight like mad to get away* **energetically**, enthusiastically, madly, with a will, for all one is worth, passionately, intensely, ardently, fervently; *informal* like crazy, hammer and tongs; *Brit. informal, dated* like billy-o.

madcap ▶ adjective **1** *a madcap scheme* **reckless**, rash, hot-headed, daredevil, impulsive, wild, daring, adventurous, heedless, thoughtless,

incautious, imprudent, indiscreet, ill-advised, hasty, foolhardy, foolish, senseless, impractical, hare-brained; *informal* crazy, crackpot, crackbrained.
2 *a madcap comedy* **zany**, eccentric, ridiculous, unconventional, weird.
▶ **noun** *she was a boisterous madcap* **eccentric**, crank, madman/madwoman, maniac, lunatic, psychotic; oddity, odd fellow, character, individual; hothead, daredevil; *informal* crackpot, oddball, weirdo, loony, nut, nutter; *N. Amer. informal* screwball; *Austral./NZ informal* dingbat.

madden ▶ **verb 1** *what maddens people most is his vagueness* **infuriate**, exasperate, irritate; incense, anger, enrage, send into a rage, inflame, annoy, provoke, upset, agitate, vex, irk, pique, gall, make someone's hackles rise, raise someone's hackles, make someone's blood boil, make someone see red, get someone's back up; *informal* aggravate, bug, get up someone's nose, make livid; *Brit. informal* nark.
2 *they were maddened with pain* **drive mad**, drive insane, derange, unhinge, unbalance; *informal* drive someone off their head, drive round the bend.

maddening ▶ **adjective** *she put the remaining coins back into her purse with maddening slowness* **infuriating**, exasperating, irritating, annoying, provoking, upsetting, vexing, irksome, unsettling, disturbing, troublesome, bothersome, vexatious, galling; *informal* aggravating, pestilential.

made-up ▶ **adjective 1** *a made-up story* **invented**, fabricated, trumped-up, concocted, devised, manufactured, fictitious, fictional, false, untrue, unreal, sham, specious, spurious, bogus, apocryphal, imaginary, mythical.
2 *a heavily made-up woman* **painted**, done up, powdered, rouged.

madhouse ▶ **noun 1** *his father is shut up in a madhouse* **mental hospital**, mental institution, psychiatric hospital, asylum; *informal* nuthouse, funny farm, loony bin; *dated* lunatic asylum.
2 *the place was a total madhouse* **bedlam**, mayhem, babel, chaos, pandemonium, uproar, turmoil, wild disarray, scene of confusion, disorder, hurly-burly, tumult, jumble, pell-mell, hullabaloo, hubbub, whirlwind, maelstrom, madness, all hell broken loose; *N. Amer.* three-ring circus.

madly ▶ **adverb 1** *she was smiling madly* **insanely**, frantically, hysterically, deliriously, wildly, like a lunatic; *informal* crazily, barmily.
2 *it was fun, hurtling madly downhill* **fast**, furiously, hurriedly, quickly, speedily, hastily, energetically; *informal* like mad, like crazy.
3 (*informal*) *Tara is madly in love with you* **intensely**, fervently, wildly, unrestrainedly, enthusiastically, completely; with all one's heart, to distraction, fantastically.
OPPOSITE slightly.
4 (*informal*) *his job isn't madly glamorous* **very**, extremely, exceedingly, excessively, absurdly, ridiculously, fantastically, wildly, outrageously; all that, terribly, terrifically, awfully, tremendously, hugely.

madman, **madwoman** ▶ **noun lunatic**, maniac, imbecile, psychotic, psychopath, schizophrenic; *informal* loony, nut, nutter, nutcase, head case, basket case, headbanger, psycho, schizo, crank, crackpot; *N. Amer. informal* screwball; *N. Amer. & Austral./NZ informal* dingbat.

madness ▶ **noun 1** *today madness is called mental illness* **insanity**, insaneness, dementia, mental illness, derangement, dementedness, instability, unsoundness of mind, lunacy, distraction, depression, mania, hysteria, frenzy, psychosis, psychopathy, schizophrenia, hydrophobia; *informal* craziness; *N. Amer. informal* meshugaas; *Austral./NZ informal* dingbats; *rare* moon-madness, cynanthropy, deliration, lycanthropy, zoanthropy.
OPPOSITE sanity.
2 *it would be madness to do otherwise* **folly**, foolishness, stupidity, insanity, lunacy, midsummer madness, foolhardiness, idiocy, imprudence, irrationality, unreasonableness, illogicality, senselessness, nonsense, nonsensicalness, absurdness, absurdity, silliness, inanity, ludicrousness, wildness, preposterousness; *informal* craziness; *Brit. informal* daftness.
OPPOSITES common sense, good sense.
3 *it's absolute madness in here* **bedlam**, mayhem, chaos, pandemonium, babel, uproar, turmoil, wild disarray, disorder, hurly-burly; scene of confusion, madhouse, tumult, jumble, pell-mell, hullabaloo, hubbub, whirlwind, maelstrom, all hell broken loose; *N. Amer. informal* three-ring circus.

madrigal ▶ **noun** *a group of five-part madrigals* **song**, anthem, carol, ballad, canzone, chanson, motet, chant; hymn, psalm.

maelstrom ▶ **noun 1** *we headed south, with one eye on the maelstrom to starboard* **whirlpool**, vortex, eddy, swirl; *literary* Charybdis.
2 *they were caught up in the maelstrom of war* **turbulence**, tumult, turmoil, uproar, commotion, disorder, jumble, disarray, chaos, confusion, upheaval, seething mass, welter, pandemonium, bedlam, whirlwind, swirl.

maestro ▶ **noun** *the orchestra took to the great maestro | blues maestro Eric Clapton* **conductor**, director; **virtuoso**, master, expert, genius, wizard, prodigy; *informal* ace, whizz; *Brit. informal* dab hand.
OPPOSITES tyro, beginner.

magazine ▶ **noun** *she leafed through the magazines* **journal**, publication, periodical, paper, proceedings; organ, supplement, colour supplement, number, copy, issue, title, weekly, fortnightly, monthly, quarterly, comic; *informal* glossy, book, rag, mag, 'zine, fanzine; *rare* magalogue.

magenta ▶ **adjective reddish-purple**, purplish-red, crimson, mauvish-crimson, carmine red, fuchsia, fuchsin.

maggot ▶ **noun grub**, larva; caterpillar.

magic ▶ **noun 1** *do you believe in magic?* **sorcery**, witchcraft, wizardry, necromancy, enchantment, spell-working, incantation, the supernatural, occultism, the occult, black magic, the black arts, devilry, divination, malediction, voodoo, hoodoo, sympathetic magic, white magic, witching, witchery; charm, hex, spell, jinx; *N. Amer.* mojo, orenda; *NZ* makutu; *S. African informal* muti; *rare* sortilege, thaumaturgy, theurgy.
2 *he does magic at children's parties* **conjuring tricks**, sleight of hand, legerdemain, illusion, prestidigitation, deception, trickery, juggling; *informal* jiggery-pokery.
3 *the magic of the stage* **allure**, allurement, attraction, excitement, enchantment, entrancement, fascination, charm, glamour, magnetism, enticement.
OPPOSITE dullness.
4 *a taste of soccer magic* **skill**, skilfulness, brilliance, ability, accomplishment, adeptness, competence, adroitness, deftness, dexterity, aptitude, expertise, expertness, art, finesse, experience, professionalism, talent, cleverness, smartness.
OPPOSITES clumsiness, incompetence.
▶ **adjective 1** *a magic spell* **supernatural**, enchanted, occult, Druidical; *rare* necromantic, thaumaturgic, thaumaturgical, sorcerous.
2 *a magic place* **fascinating**, captivating, charming, glamorous, magical, enchanting, entrancing, spellbinding, magnetic, irresistible, hypnotic.
3 (*informal*) *we had a magic time* **marvellous**, wonderful, excellent, admirable; *informal* terrific, fabulous, fab, brilliant, brill.

WORD LINKS
fear of magic **rhabdophobia**

magical ▶ **adjective 1** *he began uttering magical incantations* **supernatural**, magic, occult, mystical, mystic, paranormal, preternatural, other-worldly, spectral, ghostly, secret, dark, cryptic, uncanny, cabbalistic, shamanistic; *rare* necromantic, thaumaturgic, thaumaturgical, sorcerous, extramundane.
2 *the news had an instant and magical effect* **extraordinary**, remarkable, exceptional, outstanding, incredible, phenomenal, unbelievable, inconceivable, unimaginable, amazing, astonishing, astounding, stunning, staggering, marvellous, magnificent, wonderful, sensational, breathtaking, miraculous, singular, uncommon, unheard of, unique, unparalleled, unprecedented, unusual, unusually good, too good to be true, superlative, prodigious, surpassing, rare; *informal* fantastic, fabulous, stupendous, out of this world, terrific, tremendous, brilliant, mind-boggling, mind-blowing, awesome, stellar; *literary* wondrous.
3 *this magical small land in the heart of Europe* **enchanting**, entrancing, spellbinding, bewitching, beguiling, fascinating, captivating, alluring, enthralling, charming, attractive, appealing, magnetic, irresistible, intriguing, engaging, hypnotic, mesmerizing, mesmeric, intoxicating, heady, seductive, inviting, idyllic, wonderful, magnificent, superb, glorious, sublime, lovely, delightful, beautiful, too good to be true; *informal* dreamy, heavenly, divine, gorgeous, mind-blowing.
OPPOSITES dull, boring.

magician ▶ **noun 1** *the person the magician wishes to influence* **sorcerer**, sorceress, witch, wizard, warlock, enchanter, enchantress, necromancer, spell-caster, Druid, shaman, witch doctor, magus, alchemist; (*in southern Africa*) sangoma, inyanga; *rare* thaumaturge, theurgist.
2 *the magician fools his audience with sleight of hand* **conjuror**, illusionist, juggler, prestidigitator.
3 (*informal*) *he is the greatest bowler in modern cricket—a magician* **genius**, master, virtuoso, expert, marvel, wizard, maestro; *informal* ace, whizz.

magisterial ▶ **adjective 1** *a magisterial pronouncement* **authoritative**, masterful, lordly, judgelike.
2 *his magisterial style of questioning* **domineering**, dictatorial, autocratic, imperious, bossy, overbearing, peremptory, pompous, lofty, overweening, high-handed, arrogant, haughty; confident, self-confident, overconfident, supercilious, patronizing.
OPPOSITES hesitant, tentative.

magnanimity ▶ **noun** *Herbert's magnanimity in making do with the smaller bedroom* **generosity**, charitableness, charity, benevolence, beneficence, open-handedness, big-heartedness, great-heartedness, liberality, humanity, nobility, chivalry, kindness, munificence, bountifulness, bounty, largesse, altruism, philanthropy; **unselfishness**, selflessness, self-sacrifice, self-denial; **clemency**, mercy, leniency, forgiveness, indulgence.
OPPOSITES meanness, selfishness.

magnanimous ▶ **adjective** *she was magnanimous in victory* **generous**, charitable, benevolent, beneficent, open-handed, big-hearted, great-hearted, munificent, bountiful, liberal, handsome, princely, altruistic, kind, kindly, philanthropic, chivalrous, noble; **unselfish**, selfless, self-sacrificing, ungrudging, unstinting; **forgiving**, merciful, lenient, indulgent, clement; *literary* bounteous.

M

OPPOSITES mean-spirited, selfish.

magnate ▶ noun *the real power lay in the hands of a few rich magnates and landowners* **industrialist**, tycoon, mogul, captain of industry, baron, lord, king, proprietor, entrepreneur, merchant prince, financier, top executive; chief, leader, VIP, notable, magnifico, nabob, grandee, noble, prelate; *informal* big shot, bigwig, honcho; *N. Amer. informal* big wheel; *derogatory* fat cat.

magnet ▶ noun **1** *the principle of magnets repelling each other* **lodestone**, magnetite; field magnet, bar magnet, horseshoe magnet, transverse magnet, electromagnet, electret, solenoid, diamagnet, antiferromagnet, magnetoid, wiggler.
2 *the waterfront has become a magnet for tourists* **attraction**, focus, focal point, enticement, pull, crowd-pleaser, draw, lure, allurement, temptation, invitation, fascination; *informal* crowd-puller.

magnetic ▶ adjective **1** *a magnetic compass* electromagnetic, biomagnetic, paramagnetic, ferrimagnetic, ferromagnetic, archaeomagnetic, geomagnetic, gyromagnetic, hydromagnetic, palaeomagnetic, antiferromagnetic.
2 *his magnetic personality* **alluring**, attractive, fascinating, captivating, enchanting, enthralling, appealing, charming, prepossessing, engaging, entrancing, tempting, tantalizing, seductive, inviting, irresistible, magic, magical, bewitching, charismatic, hypnotic, mesmeric.

WORD LINKS
measurement of magnetic forces **magnetometry**

magnetism ▶ noun *the sheer magnetism of his physical presence* **allure**, attraction, fascination, enchantment, appeal, draw, drawing power, pull, charm, seductiveness, sexual magnetism, animal magnetism, magic, spell, charisma; hypnotism, mesmerism.

WORD LINKS
measurement of magnetic force **magnetometry**

magnification ▶ noun **1** *the fine lines were visible only under high magnification* **enlargement**; increase, augmentation, extension, expansion, amplification, intensification, heightening, deepening, broadening, widening, dilation, boost, enhancement; macrophotography, photomacrography.
OPPOSITE reduction.
2 *the magnification of the marginal details in the play* **exaggeration**, overstatement, amplification, overemphasis, overplaying, dramatization, overdramatization, colouring, embroidery, embellishment, enhancement, extravagance, inflation, hyperbole, aggrandizement; gilding the lily; *informal* blowing up, blowing up out of all proportion, making a big thing out of something.
OPPOSITE understatement.

magnificence ▶ noun *the magnificence of eighteenth-century Bath* **splendour**, resplendence, grandeur, greatness, impressiveness, imposingness, glory, gloriousness, majesty, nobility, pomp, pomp and circumstance, stateliness, sumptuousness, opulence, luxuriousness, luxury, lavishness, richness, brilliance, radiance, dazzle, beauty, elegance, distinction, spectacle, pageantry, splendidness, gorgeousness, éclat, elevation, transcendence, transcendency; *informal* splendiferousness, ritziness, poshness.
OPPOSITES tawdriness, cheapness.

magnificent or munificent?
Magnificent and **munificent** are different in meaning but sometimes confused. *Magnificent* denotes something exceptionally good or beautiful, especially in an impressive or striking style (*a magnificent mansion | a magnificent performance*). *Munificent* means 'extremely generous' (*munificent financial support*). However, there is some overlap between the things to which they apply: a *munificent gift* might well consist of some *magnificent jewellery*.

magnificent ▶ adjective **1** *a magnificent view of the mountains* **splendid**, **spectacular**, impressive, striking, glorious, superb, majestic, awesome, awe-inspiring, breathtaking.
OPPOSITE uninspiring.
2 *a magnificent apartment overlooking the lake* **sumptuous**, resplendent, grand, impressive, imposing, monumental, palatial, noble, proud, stately, exalted, royal, regal, kingly, imperial, princely, opulent, fine, luxurious, lavish, rich, brilliant, radiant, dazzling, beautiful, elegant, gorgeous, elevated, transcendent; *informal* splendiferous, ritzy, posh; *rare* splendacious, magnolious.
OPPOSITES modest, tawdry, cheap.
3 *a magnificent act of heroism* **admirable**, fine, great, wonderful, notable.
OPPOSITES feeble, weak.
4 *a magnificent performance* **masterly**, skilful, virtuoso, splendid, excellent, impressive, fine, marvellous, wonderful, tremendous; *informal* terrific, glorious, superb, brilliant, great, out of this world, (like) a million dollars.
OPPOSITES poor, weak.

magnify ▶ verb **1** *the image is magnified by an eyepiece* **enlarge**, boost, enhance, maximize, increase, augment, extend, expand, amplify, intensify, heighten, deepen, broaden, widen, dilate; *informal* blow up.
OPPOSITE reduce.
2 *she tended to magnify the defects of those she disliked* **exaggerate**, overstate, overemphasize, overplay, dramatize, colour, embroider, embellish, enhance, inflate, amplify, make a mountain out of (a molehill); *informal* make a big thing out of, blow up, blow up out of all proportion; *archaic* draw the long bow.
OPPOSITES minimize, understate.
3 *my soul doth magnify the lord* **praise**, bless, worship, venerate, adore, extol.

magniloquence ▶ noun **grandiloquence**, loftiness, grandiosity, pompousness, pomposity, pretentiousness, bombast, rhetoric, turgidity, boastfulness, pretension, ornateness; *rare* orotundity, fustian, braggadocio.

magniloquent ▶ adjective *a magniloquent lawyer | his magniloquent phraseology* **grandiloquent**, high-sounding, high-flown, lofty, heroic, grandiose, ornate, pompous, pretentious, bombastic, overblown, rhetorical, oratorical, orotund, declamatory, sonorous, rotund, stilted, turgid, boastful, bragging, braggart, Falstaffian; *informal* highfalutin; *rare* fustian.
OPPOSITES terse, crisp.

magnitude ▶ noun **1** *they felt daunted by the magnitude of the task* **immensity**, vastness, hugeness, enormity, enormousness, expanse; size, extent, greatness, largeness, bigness.
OPPOSITE smallness.
2 *events of tragic magnitude* **importance**, import, significance, weight, moment, consequence, mark, notability, note, greatness, distinction, eminence, fame, renown, intensity, power.
OPPOSITE triviality.
3 *electorates of less than average magnitude* **size**, extent, measure, proportions, dimensions, breadth, volume, weight, quantity, mass, bulk; amplitude, capacity, strength, degree, gauge, measurement, extension.
4 *its brightest star is only of magnitude 4.2* **brightness**, brilliance, radiance, luminosity; absolute magnitude, apparent magnitude.
5 *the magnitude of each economic variable could be determined* **value**, index, indicator, measure, norm, order, quantity, number, vector, figure.
□ **of the first magnitude** **of the utmost importance**, of the greatest significance, very important, of importance, of significance, of note, of great moment, of great consequence.

WORD LINKS
measurement of magnitude of stars **astrometry**

maid ▶ noun **1** *the maid cleared the table* **female servant**, maidservant, housemaid, parlourmaid, serving maid, lady's maid, chambermaid, maid-of-all-work, domestic, drudge, menial; help, cleaner, cleaning woman/lady, housekeeper, au pair; *Indian* amah, bai; *Brit. informal* daily, skivvy, Mrs Mop; *Brit. dated* charwoman, charlady, char, cook-general, cook-maid, tweeny; *archaic* abigail.
2 (*archaic*) *a village maid and her swain* **girl**, young woman, young lady, lass, miss, nymphet, slip of a girl, shepherdess; *Scottish* (wee) lassie; *literary* damsel, nymph; *archaic* maiden, wench.
3 (*archaic*) *she was no longer a maid* **virgin**, vestal virgin, chaste woman, unmarried girl, celibate; *Latin* virgo intacta; *archaic* maiden.

maiden ▶ noun (*archaic*). *See* MAID *senses 2 & 3.*
▶ adjective **1** *a maiden aunt* **unmarried**, spinster, unwed, unwedded, single, husbandless, spouseless, celibate.
2 *the maiden voyage of the Titanic* **first**, initial, inaugural, introductory, initiatory, proving.

maidenhood ▶ noun (*archaic*) *the loss of her maidenhood* **virginity**, purity, chastity, virtue, honour, celibacy; *informal* cherry; *archaic* maidenhead.

maidenly ▶ adjective *her delicate mannerisms and maidenly demeanour* **virginal**, immaculate, intact, chaste, pure, undefiled, virtuous, unsullied, vestal; **demure**, reserved, retiring, decorous, seemly.
OPPOSITES blowsy, tarty.

mail[1] ▶ noun *this letter came in the mail* **post**, letters, packages, parcels, correspondence, communications, airmail; postal system, postal service, post office; registered mail, special delivery, recorded delivery; delivery, collection, mail drop, mailshot, mailing, first class, second class, third class, electronic mail, email, voicemail, Pony Express; *informal* snail mail; *N. Amer. & W. Indian* the mails; *Indian* dak, tappal.
▶ verb *we mailed the six packages* **send**, post, send by mail/post, dispatch, direct, forward, remit, transmit, email, airmail.

mail[2] ▶ noun (*historical*) *warriors in mail shirts* **armour**, coat of mail, chain mail, chain armour; *rare* brigandine, hauberk, byrnie, habergeon, camail.

maim ▶ verb *they are prepared to kill and maim innocent people in pursuit of their cause* **injure**, wound, hurt, cripple, disable, put out of action, lame, incapacitate, impair, mar, mutilate, lacerate, disfigure, deform, mangle.

main ▶ adjective **1** *the main office | the main issue* **principal**, chief, head, leading, foremost, most important, major, ruling, dominant, central, focal, key, prime, master, premier, primary, first, high, grand, fundamental, supreme, predominant, (most) prominent, pre-eminent, paramount, overriding, cardinal, crucial, vital, critical, capital, pivotal,

salient, elemental, essential, staple, intrinsic, urgent.
OPPOSITES subsidiary, minor.
2 *they dragged him away by main force* **sheer**, pure, utter, downright, mere, plain, brute, stark, absolute, out-and-out, direct.
▶ **noun** (*literary*) *the Spanish Main* **sea**, ocean, deep, brine; *informal, dated* the drink; *Brit. informal, dated* the briny.
□ **in the main**. *See* MAINLY.

mainly ▶ **adverb** *the people are mainly visitors* **mostly**, for the most part, in the main, on the whole, largely, by and large, to a large extent, to a great degree, predominantly, chiefly, principally; generally, usually, typically, commonly, as a rule, on average.

mainspring ▶ **noun** *the mainspring of anti-communism* **motive**, motivation, impetus, driving force, incentive, impulse, cause, prime mover, reason, origin, fountain, fount, beginning, root, generator, basis.

mainstay ▶ **noun 1** *agriculture was the mainstay of the economy* **central component**, centrepiece, prop, linchpin, cornerstone, pillar, bulwark, buttress, chief support, backbone, anchor, foundation, base, bastion.
2 *he is the mainstay of the Arsenal defence* **tower of strength**, key player, sinew, right-hand man/woman, right arm, Atlas.

mainstream ▶ **adjective** *the author never strays far from mainstream physics* **normal**, conventional, ordinary, orthodox, conformist, accepted, established, recognized, common, usual, prevailing, popular.

maintain ▶ **verb 1** *the need to maintain close links between industry and schools* **continue**, keep, keep going, keep up, keep alive, keep in existence, carry on, preserve, conserve, prolong, perpetuate, sustain, bolster (up), prop up, retain, support, bear.
OPPOSITE break off.
2 *the roads are maintained at public expense* **keep in good condition**, keep in repair, keep up, service, rebuild, conserve, preserve, keep intact, care for, take good care of, look after.
OPPOSITE neglect.
3 *the costs of maintaining a family* **support**, provide for, keep, finance; **nurture**, feed, nourish, sustain.
OPPOSITE neglect.
4 *he always maintained his innocence* | *he maintains that he is innocent* **insist (on)**, declare, assert, protest, state, aver, say, announce, affirm, avow, profess, claim, allege, contend, argue, swear (to), hold to; *rare* asseverate.
OPPOSITE deny.
5 *the King swears he will maintain the laws of God* **uphold**, defend, fight for, champion, support, back, advocate.
OPPOSITE abandon.

maintenance ▶ **noun 1** *the maintenance of law and order* **preservation**, conservation, continuation, continuance, continuity, keeping up, carrying on, prolongation, perpetuation.
OPPOSITE breakdown.
2 *a water softener requires regular servicing and maintenance* **upkeep**, service, servicing, repair(s); improvement, care, aftercare.
OPPOSITE neglect.
3 *the maintenance and education of his children* **nurture**, feeding, life support; **financing**, supporting, support, keeping, upkeep; *rare* sustentation, alimentation, appanage, corrody.
OPPOSITE neglect.
4 *absent fathers are forced to pay maintenance* **financial support**, child support, alimony, provision, allowance, keep, upkeep, subsistence, living expenses.

majestic ▶ **adjective** *majestic mountain scenery* | *his father's majestic presence* **exalted**, august, great, awesome, elevated, sublime, lofty; **stately**, dignified, distinguished, striking, magisterial, solemn, maestoso, magnificent, grand, splendid, resplendent, glorious, sumptuous, impressive, awe-inspiring, monumental, palatial; statuesque, Olympian, imposing, marvellous, sonorous, resounding, heroic, portentous, superb, proud; regal, royal, kingly, queenly, princely, imperial, noble, lordly, sovereign.
OPPOSITES pitiful, pathetic.

majesty ▶ **noun 1** *the majesty of the procession* **stateliness**, dignity, magnificence, pomp, solemnity, grandeur, grandness, splendour, resplendence, glory, impressiveness, superbness, awesomeness, awe, loftiness, sublimity, regalness, regality, royalty, royalness, kingliness, queenliness, nobility, nobleness, augustness, exaltedness, exaltation, pride.
2 *the majesty invested in the monarch* **sovereignty**, authority, power, dominion, supremacy.
3 *Your Majesty* **Royal Highness**, Highness, Serene Highness, Serenity, Magnificence.

major ▶ **adjective 1** *the major English poets* **greatest**, **best**, finest, most important, chief, main, prime, principal, capital, cardinal, leading, star, foremost, outstanding, first-rate, notable, eminent, pre-eminent, arch-, supreme, uppermost.
OPPOSITE minor.
2 *an issue of major importance* **crucial**, vital, great, considerable, paramount, utmost, prime, extensive.
OPPOSITES little; unimportant.
3 *the use of drugs is a major problem* **important**, big, significant, weighty, crucial, key, sweeping, substantial.
OPPOSITE trivial.
4 *major surgery* **serious**, radical, complicated, difficult.
OPPOSITE minor.
□ **major part**. *See* MAJORITY *sense* 1.

majority ▶ **noun 1** *in the majority of cases* **larger part/number**, greater part/number, best/better part, main part, most, more than half; bulk, mass, weight, (main) body, preponderance, predominance, generality, lion's share; (**the majority**) (the) people, the masses, the silent majority.
OPPOSITE minority.
2 *Labour retained the seat by a large majority* **(winning) margin**, superiority of numbers/votes; landslide.
3 *a girl who has not yet reached her majority* **coming of age**, legal age, seniority, adulthood, manhood/womanhood, maturity; age of consent.

make ▶ **verb 1** *he makes model steam engines* **construct**, build, assemble, put together, manufacture, produce, fabricate, create, form, fashion, model, mould, shape, forge, bring into existence.
OPPOSITE destroy.
2 *she made me drink it* **force**, compel, coerce, press, drive, pressure, pressurize, oblige, require; have someone do something, prevail on, dragoon, bludgeon, strong-arm, impel, constrain, urge, will, steamroller, browbeat, intimidate, use strong-arm tactics on, bully, hector, blackmail; *informal* railroad, bulldoze, put the heat on, put the screws on, turn/tighten the screw/screws on.
3 *don't make such a noise* **cause**, create, give rise to, produce, bring about, generate, engender, occasion, effect, set up, establish, institute, found, develop, originate, frame; *literary* beget.
4 *she pirouetted and made a little bow* **perform**, execute, give, do, accomplish, achieve, bring off, carry out, effect, practise, engage in, commit, act, prosecute.
5 *they made him chairman* **appoint**, designate, name, nominate, select, elect, vote in, install, place, post; induct, institute, invest, ordain, assign, cast as; detail, draft, engage, hire, employ, recruit, retain, enrol, enlist, sign up.
6 *I've made a will and left you everything* **formulate**, frame, draw up, devise, make out, prepare, compile, compose, put together; draft, write, pen, produce.
7 *I'm sorry, I've* **made a mistake** **perpetrate**, commit, be responsible for, be guilty of, be to blame for; blunder, err, trip up, put a foot wrong, nod, miscalculate; *informal* slip up, bloop, make a boo-boo, blow it, foul up, goof (up); *Brit. informal* boob, drop a clanger; *N. Amer. informal* screw up, drop the ball.
8 *he had a great talent for making money* **acquire**, obtain, gain, get, realize, secure, win, earn; gross, fetch, bring in, take (in); take home, pocket, net, clear.
OPPOSITE lose.
9 *he made lunch for us all* **prepare**, get ready, put together, concoct, cook, dish up, throw together, whip up, brew; *Brit. informal* mash; *N. Amer. informal* fix.
10 *parliament makes laws* **formulate**, draw up, write, frame, draft, form, enact, pass, lay down, establish, institute, found, originate.
OPPOSITE repeal.
11 *that makes £100* **add up to**, amount to, come to, total, count as; *Brit.* tot up to.
12 *what do you make the total?* **compute**, calculate, work out; estimate, count up, determine, gauge, reckon, put a figure on, give a figure to, forecast, predict.
13 *what do you* **make of** *him?* **think of/about**; appraise, evaluate, assess, size up, adjudge, look on, view, regard, consider, judge, deem; figure (out), value, rate, think, sum up, weigh up.
14 *we've got to make a decision* **reach**, come to, settle on, determine on, conclude, establish, seal.
15 *I've been asked to make a speech* **utter**, give, deliver, give voice to, enunciate, recite, pronounce.
16 *he'll make a great leader* | *the sofa makes a good bed* **be**, act as, serve as, function as, constitute, perform the function of, do duty for, play the part of, represent, embody, form.
17 *he'll make the first eleven* **gain a place in**, get into, gain access to, enter; achieve, attain.
18 *he believed he could still make the night train* **catch**, get, arrive/be in time for, arrive at, reach; get to.
OPPOSITE miss.
□ **make as if/though** *he made as if to run away* **feign**, pretend, give the impression, make a show/pretence of, affect, feint, make out; *informal* put it on.
□ **make away with 1** *he could have made away with her and dumped the body* **kill**, murder, put to death, slaughter, dispatch, execute, eliminate; *informal* bump off, do away with, do in, do for, knock off, take out, finish off, top, croak, stiff, liquidate, blow away; *N. Amer. informal* ice, off, rub out, smoke, waste; *literary* slay.
2 *they made away with the evidence* **dispose of**, get rid of, destroy, throw

M

away, jettison, ditch, dump, eliminate; *informal* do away with.

□ **make believe pretend**, fantasize, indulge in fantasy, daydream, build castles in the air, build castles in Spain, dream, imagine, romance, fancy, play-act, play.

□ **make do 1** *we have very little but we make do* **scrape by/along**, get by/along, manage, cope, survive, muddle through/along, fare all right, make the best of a bad job, improvise, make ends meet, keep the wolf from the door, keep one's head above water, shift for oneself; *informal* make out.
2 *you'll have to make do with an old car* **make the best of**, get by with/on, put to the best use, make the most of.

□ **make for 1** *she made for the door* **go towards**, head for/towards, aim for, make one's way towards, move towards, direct one's steps towards, steer a course towards, be bound for, set out for, make a beeline for, take to.
2 *constant arguing doesn't make for a happy marriage* **contribute to**, be conducive to, produce, promote, facilitate, further, advance, forward, foster, favour; *formal* conduce to.

□ **make fun of** *it is easy to make fun of politicians* **taunt**, poke fun at, chaff, tease, make jokes about, ridicule, mock, laugh at, guy, mimic, parody, caricature, lampoon, satirize, rag, quiz, be sarcastic about, deride, scoff at, jeer at, jibe at; *informal* take the mickey out of, send up, rib, josh, wind up, pull someone's leg, make a monkey of; *N. Amer. informal* goof on, rag on, pull someone's chain, razz; *Austral./NZ informal* poke mullock at, sling off at; *Brit. informal, dated* rot, twit; *dated* make sport of; *archaic* smoke, rally.

□ **make it 1** *he never really made it as a doctor* **succeed**, be successful, prosper, distinguish oneself, be a success, get ahead, make good; *informal* make the grade, arrive, crack it, cut it, find a place in the sun.
2 *she's very ill—is she going to make it?* **survive**, come through, pull through, get better, recover, rally, recuperate.

□ **make love have sex**, have sexual intercourse, go to bed (together), sleep together; *Brit. informal* bonk, do it, make whoopee, get one's oats; *N. Amer. informal* get it on; *vulgar slang* fuck, screw, shag, hump, do the business, have it away/off; *Brit. vulgar slang* knob, roger; *formal* copulate; *dated* couple; *archaic* fornicate.

□ **make off** *on seeing the police they made off* **run away/off**, take to one's heels, beat a hasty retreat, flee, make one's getaway, make a quick exit, make a run for it, run for it, take off, take flight, bolt, fly, make oneself scarce, leave, abscond, decamp, do a disappearing act; *informal* clear off/out, beat it, do a runner, leg it, make tracks, cut and run, skedaddle, vamoose, hightail it, hotfoot it, show a clean pair of heels, fly the coop, split, scoot, scram; *Brit. informal* scarper, have it away (on one's toes); *N. Amer. informal* light out, bug out, cut out, peel out, take a powder; *Brit. informal, dated* hook it.
OPPOSITE turn up.

□ **make off with** *burglars made off with all the wedding presents* **take**, **steal**, purloin, pilfer, abscond with, appropriate, run away/off with, carry off, snatch; kidnap, abduct; *informal* walk away/off with, swipe, filch, snaffle, nab, lift, 'liberate', 'borrow', snitch; *Brit. informal* pinch, half-inch, nick, whip, knock off, nobble, bone; *N. Amer. informal* heist, glom; *Austral. informal* snavel; *W. Indian informal* tief; *archaic* crib, hook.

□ **make out 1** *how did you make out?* **get on**, get along, fare, do, proceed, go, progress, manage, survive, cope, get by.
2 (*N. Amer. informal*) *they were making out on the sofa* **make love**, have sex, have sexual intercourse; kiss and cuddle, caress, French kiss, pet, engage in heavy petting; *informal* canoodle, neck, smooch; *Brit. informal* snog, bonk, do it, make whoopee, get one's oats; *N. Amer. informal* get it on; *vulgar slang* fuck, screw, hump, do the business, have it away/off; *Brit. vulgar slang* roger; *informal, dated* spoon, couple; *formal* copulate; *archaic* fornicate.

□ **make something out 1** *I could just make out a figure in the distance* **see**, discern, distinguish, perceive, pick out, detect, notice, observe, recognize, catch sight of, glimpse, discover; *literary* descry, espy, behold.
2 *he couldn't make out what she was saying* **understand**, comprehend, follow, grasp, fathom, work out, figure out, make sense of, interpret, decipher, make head or tail of, get, get the drift of, catch; *Brit. informal* suss out.
3 *she made out that he was violent* **allege**, claim, assert, declare, maintain, affirm, aver, suggest, imply, hint, insinuate, indicate, intimate, impute, make as if/though, pretend.
4 *how do you make that out?* **demonstrate**, show to be true, establish, substantiate, prove, verify, validate, authenticate, corroborate.
5 *he made out a receipt for $20* **write out**, fill out, fill in, complete, draw up, draft, inscribe.

□ **make something over to someone** *he made over the whole property to his son* **transfer**, sign over, turn over, hand over, hand on, give, hand down, leave, bequeath, bestow, pass on, devolve, transmit, cede, deliver, assign, consign, convey, entrust.

□ **make up** *come now, pet, let's kiss and make up* **be friends again**, bury the hatchet, declare a truce, make peace, forgive and forget, shake hands, become reconciled, settle one's differences, mend fences, call it quits.
OPPOSITE quarrel.

□ **make something up 1** *women make up 56 per cent of the student body* **comprise**, form, compose, constitute, account for.
2 *he brought another girl with him to make up a foursome* **complete**, round off, finish.
3 *the pharmacist made up the prescription* **prepare**, mix, concoct, put together.
4 *I'll have to make up an excuse* **invent**, fabricate, concoct, dream up, think up, hatch, trump up; devise, manufacture, formulate, frame, construct, coin; *informal* cook up.
5 *she made up her face carefully* **apply make-up/cosmetics to**, powder, rouge; (**make oneself up**) *informal* put on one's face, do one's face, paint one's face, tart oneself up, do oneself up, apply one's warpaint, doll oneself up.

□ **make up for 1** *she tried to make up for what she'd said earlier* **atone for**, make amends for, compensate for, make recompense for, make reparation for, make redress for, make restitution for, expiate; *formal* requite.
2 *hard work can more than make up for a lack of intellectual brilliance* **offset**, counterbalance, counterweigh, counteract, compensate for; balance, neutralize, cancel out, even up, redeem.

□ **make up one's mind** *stop dithering and make up your mind* **decide**, be decisive, come to a decision, make a decision, reach a decision; determine, resolve, settle on a plan of action, come to a conclusion, reach a conclusion.

□ **make up to** (*informal*) *she spent the whole evening making up to Adam* **flirt with**, chase after, run after, pursue, make romantic advances to, court, woo, vamp; *informal* chat up, make eyes at, make sheep's eyes at, give the come-on to, come on to, be all over; *dated* set one's cap at.

□ **make way** *please make way for the king* **move aside**, clear the way, make a space, make room, stand back; allow to pass, allow through.

▶ **noun 1** *a different make of car* **brand**, marque, model, mark, sort, type, kind, variety, style, label.
2 *a man of a different make from his brother* **character**, nature, temperament, temper, disposition, cast/turn of mind, humour, make-up, kidney, mould, stamp.

WORD LINKS

making or causing ... **-facient**, (e.g. ***abortifacient***), **-fic** (e.g. ***soporific***), **-genic** (e.g. ***hallucinogenic***), **-faction** (e.g. ***liquefaction***)

make-believe ▶ **noun** *if that was make-believe I can't wait to sample the real thing* **fantasy**, **pretence**, pretending, daydreaming, dreaming, imagination, invention, fancy, dream, unreality, romancing, fabrication, play-acting, charade, masquerade, self-deception, illusion, delusion.
OPPOSITE reality.
▶ **adjective** *Heather loved reading stories and was always having make-believe adventures* **imaginary**, imagined, pretended, made-up, fantasy, fantasized, fancied, dream, dreamed-up, unreal, fanciful, fictitious, fictive, mythical, feigned, fake, mock, sham, simulated, pseudo, false, spurious; *informal* pretend, phoney; *S. African* play-play.
OPPOSITES real, actual.

Maker ▶ **noun** *he had gone to meet his Maker* **God**, Creator, Prime Mover, master of the universe.

maker ▶ **noun** *the maker's name is stamped on the back* **creator**, manufacturer, builder, constructor, producer, fabricator, author, architect, designer, framer, originator, inventor, founder, father.

makeshift ▶ **adjective** *a huge makeshift scaffold had been erected in front of the palace* **temporary**, make-do, provisional, stopgap, standby, rough and ready, substitute, emergency, improvised, ad hoc, impromptu, extemporary, extempore, thrown together, cobbled together; *Nautical* jury-rigged, jury; *informal* quick and dirty.
OPPOSITE permanent.

make-up ▶ **noun 1** *she was pale in spite of her excessive make-up* **cosmetics**, greasepaint; foundation, pancake, panstick, powder, loose powder, pressed powder, blusher, rouge, concealer; mascara, eye make-up, eyeliner, eyeshadow, eyebrow pencil, kohl; lipstick, lip gloss, lip pencil, nail varnish/polish; blackface, whiteface; *informal* paint, warpaint, face paint, slap; *rare* maquillage.
2 *the cellular make-up of plants and trees* **composition**, constitution, configuration, form, arrangement, format, structure, construction, formation, assembly, organization, fabric, framework.
3 *jealousy doesn't seem to be part of his make-up* **character**, nature, temperament, temper, personality, disposition, constitution, mentality, persona, psyche, psychology, make, stamp, mould, cast/turn of mind; *informal* kidney, what makes someone tick; *archaic* humour, grain.

making ▶ **noun 1** *the making of the cars* **manufacture**, manufacturing, mass production, building, construction, assembly, production, producing, creation, creating, putting together, modelling, fabrication, invention, forming, formation, moulding, forging, composition.
OPPOSITE destruction.
2 (**makings**) *does she have the makings of a champion?* **qualities**, characteristics, ingredients, potential, promise, capacity, capability; **essentials**, essence, beginnings, rudiments, basics, materials, stuff.

□ **in the making** *he was a major heroic actor in the making* **budding**, burgeoning, coming, emergent, growing, developing, nascent, potential, promising, up and coming, incipient.

maladjusted ▶ adjective *a school for maladjusted pupils* **disturbed**, unstable, ill-adjusted, neurotic, alienated, muddled, confused, unbalanced; *informal* mixed up, screwed up, untogether, hung up, messed up; *vulgar slang* fucked up.
OPPOSITES well adjusted, together.

maladministration ▶ noun *a long battle against maladministration and incompetence* **mismanagement**, mishandling, misgovernment, misrule, incompetence, inefficiency, bungling, blundering; malpractice, misconduct, corruption, dishonesty; *Law* malfeasance, misfeasance; *rare* malversation.
OPPOSITES probity, efficiency.

maladroit ▶ adjective *both men are unhappy about the maladroit way the matter has been handled* **bungling**, awkward, inept, clumsy, bumbling, incompetent, unskilful, heavy-handed, ungainly, inelegant, inexpert, graceless, ungraceful, gauche, unhandy, uncoordinated, gawky, cloddish, clodhopping, all fingers and thumbs, flat-footed, lumbering; like a bull in a china shop, tactless, insensitive, thoughtless, inconsiderate, undiplomatic, impolitic, injudicious; *informal* butterfingered, ham-fisted, ham-handed, cack-handed; *archaic* lubberly.
OPPOSITES adroit, skilful.

malady ▶ noun *sea sickness, a malady with no respect for rank or courage* **illness**, sickness, ailment, disorder, complaint, disease, infection, indisposition, affliction, infirmity; *informal* lurgy, bug, virus; *Austral. informal* wog.

malaise ▶ noun *a society afflicted by a deep cultural malaise* **unhappiness**, restlessness, uneasiness, unease, melancholy, depression, despondency, dejection, disquiet, trouble, anxiety, anguish, angst; ailment(s), ills; lassitude, listlessness, languor, weariness, enervation, doldrums; weakness, feebleness, debility, indisposition, infirmity, illness, sickness, disease, discomfort; *German* Weltschmerz; *French* ennui.
OPPOSITES comfort, well-being.

malapropism ▶ noun **wrong word**, **solecism**, error, misuse, misusage, misapplication, infelicity, slip of the tongue.

malapropos ▶ adjective **inappropriate**, unsuitable, inapposite, infelicitous, inapt, unseemly, inopportune, ill-timed, untimely, uncalled for, tactless.

malcontent ▶ noun *the trouble was caused by a group of malcontents* **troublemaker**, mischief-maker, agitator, dissentient, dissident, rebel; discontent, complainer, grumbler, moaner, fault-finder, carper; *informal* stirrer, whinger, grouch, grouser, griper, nit-picker, bellyacher, beefer; *N. Amer. informal* kvetch.
▶ adjective *a malcontent employee* **disaffected**, discontented, dissatisfied, disgruntled; **fed up**, restive, unhappy, annoyed, irritated, displeased, vexed, peeved, piqued, put out, malcontented, resentful; rebellious, dissentious, factious, troublemaking, grumbling, complaining, fault-finding, carping; *informal* nit-picking, bellyaching; *Brit. informal* browned off, cheesed off, brassed off; *N. Amer. informal* hacked off, teed off, ticked off; *vulgar slang* pissed off, peed off.
OPPOSITE happy.

male *See centre pages for list of male and female* **Animals**
▶ adjective *male sexual jealousy* **masculine**, to do with men, he-; **virile**, manly, macho, red-blooded.
OPPOSITE female.
▶ noun. *See* MAN.

male chauvinist ▶ noun **sexist**, chauvinist, anti-feminist, misogynist, woman-hater; *informal* male chauvinist pig, MCP.

malediction ▶ noun *the simple villagers were terrified by his maledictions* **curse**, oath, imprecation, execration; anathema, voodoo, spell; cursing, damning, damnation; *N. Amer.* hex; *archaic* malison.
OPPOSITE blessing.

malefactor ▶ noun *most malefactors are the victims of their environment* **criminal**, culprit, wrongdoer, offender, villain, lawbreaker, felon, evil-doer, convict, delinquent, sinner, transgressor, outlaw; scoundrel, wretch, reprobate, rogue, rascal; *informal* crook, baddy; *Austral. informal* crim; *Law* malfeasant, misfeasor; *archaic* miscreant, trespasser.

malevolence ▶ noun *there was a sinister atmosphere, a feeling of oppressive malevolence* **malice**, **spite**, spitefulness, hostility, hatred, hate, ill will, bitterness, enmity, ill feeling, balefulness, venom, rancour, maliciousness, malignance, malignity, ill nature, vindictiveness, viciousness, revengefulness, vengefulness, cruelty, nastiness, unfriendliness; *literary* maleficence.
OPPOSITE benevolence.

malevolent ▶ adjective *she shot a malevolent glare at her companion* **malicious**, **spiteful**, hostile, evil-minded, baleful, bitter, evil-intentioned, poisonous, venomous, evil, malign, malignant, rancorous, vicious, vindictive, revengeful, vengeful, pernicious; cruel, fierce, nasty, unfriendly, unkind, ill-natured; *literary* malefic, maleficent.
OPPOSITE benevolent.

malformation ▶ noun *a congenital malformation of the larynx* **deformity**, distortion, crookedness, misshapenness, disfigurement, misproportion, abnormality, irregularity, oddity, warp, freak (of nature).

malformed ▶ adjective *usually it is the weak, undersized, and malformed beasts that are weeded out* **deformed**, distorted, crooked, contorted, wry, misshapen, twisted, warped, out of shape, bent, bandy, skewed, asymmetrical, irregular, misproportioned, ill-proportioned, ill-shaped, disfigured, hunchbacked, abnormal, grotesque, monstrous; *Scottish* thrawn.

malfunction ▶ verb *the computer has malfunctioned* **crash**, develop a fault, go wrong, break down, break, act up, be defective, be faulty, fail, cease to function/work, stop working; *informal* conk out, go kaput, fall over; *Brit. informal* play up, pack up.
▶ noun *a major computer malfunction* **crash**, breakdown, fault, failure, defect, flaw, collapse, impairment; *informal* glitch.

malice ▶ noun *the malice of evil men who hated his good qualities* **spitefulness**, spite, malevolence, maliciousness, animosity, hostility, ill will, ill feeling, hatred, hate, bitterness, venom, vindictiveness, vengefulness, revenge, malignity, malignance, evil intentions, animus, enmity, devilment, devilry, bad blood, backbiting, gall, rancour, spleen, grudge; *informal* bitchiness, cattiness; *literary* maleficence.
OPPOSITE benevolence.

malicious ▶ adjective *he bore their malicious insults with dignity* **spiteful**, malevolent, hostile, bitter, venomous, poisonous, evil-intentioned, ill-natured, evil, baleful, vindictive, vengeful, vitriolic, rancorous, malign, malignant, pernicious, mean, nasty, harmful, hurtful, mischievous, destructive, wounding, cruel, unkind, defamatory; *informal* bitchy, catty; *literary* malefic, maleficent.
OPPOSITE benevolent.

malign ▶ verb *he accused them of maligning an innocent man* **defame**, slander, libel, blacken someone's name/character, smear, run a smear campaign against, vilify, speak ill of, spread lies about, accuse falsely, cast aspersions on, run down, misrepresent, calumniate, traduce, denigrate, disparage, slur, derogate, abuse, revile; *informal* bad-mouth, knock, drag through the mud/mire, throw/sling/fling mud at, do a hatchet job on; *Brit. informal* rubbish, slag off; *rare* asperse, vilipend.
OPPOSITE praise.
▶ adjective *a malign influence* **harmful**, evil, bad, baleful, hostile, inimical, destructive, malevolent, evil-intentioned, malignant, injurious, spiteful, malicious, vicious; *literary* malefic, maleficent.
OPPOSITE beneficial.

CHOOSE THE RIGHT WORD

malign, defame, slander, libel, traduce

All these verbs involve making unfair or damaging critical remarks about someone.

- **Malign** is a non-legal term for making false or unjustifiable criticisms (*teenagers are much maligned, but the support these youngsters gave was tremendous*). One can malign someone unintentionally (*I could be maligning the lad—I haven't seen much of him*).
- To **defame** someone is to make an unfair critical or accusatory remark about them which will damage their reputation, even if this is not the intention (*he convinced the jurors that he had been defamed by the article*).
- In legal usage, **slander** and **libel** are particular forms of defamation: to *slander* someone is to defame them in speech (*they were accused of insulting and slandering the head of state*), whereas to *libel* someone is to defame them in written form, which is now taken to encompass any 'permanent' form, including broadcasting and the Internet (*Samuelson claims he was libelled in the same article*).
- **Traduce** is a more literary term for the deliberate telling of damaging untruths (*he is traducing his colleagues with his unsubstantiated accusations*).

malignant ▶ noun **1** *a malignant growth in her left kidney* **cancerous**, non-benign, metastatic.
OPPOSITE benign.
2 *a malignant disease* **virulent**, infectious, invasive, uncontrollable, dangerous, harmful, pernicious; deadly, fatal, life-threatening, lethal, terminal, incurable.
3 *one of the most malignant glares she had ever seen* **spiteful**, hostile, malevolent, malicious, malign, evil-intentioned, baleful, full of hate, vicious, nasty, poisonous, venomous, acrimonious, rancorous, splenetic, cruel.
OPPOSITE benevolent.

malinger ▶ verb *the doctor alleged that the plaintiff was malingering* **pretend to be ill**, feign/fake illness, pretend to be an invalid, sham, shirk, skulk; *informal* put it on; *Brit. informal* skive, swing the lead; *N. Amer. informal* goldbrick.

malingerer ▶ noun *patients for whom no specific diagnosis can be made tend to be regarded as malingerers* **shirker**, slacker, idler, layabout; *Brit. informal* skiver, lead-swinger; *N. Amer. informal* gold brick.

mall ▶ noun **shopping precinct**, shopping centre, shopping complex, arcade, galleria; *N. Amer.* plaza, strip mall.

malleable ▶ adjective **1** *a malleable substance* **pliable**, ductile, plastic, pliant, soft, workable, shapable, mouldable, tractile, tensile.
OPPOSITE hard.
2 *a malleable young woman* **easily influenced**, suggestible, susceptible, impressionable, amenable, cooperative, adaptable, compliant, pliable, tractable, accommodating; biddable, docile, obedient, complaisant, manageable, manipulable, persuadable, governable, influenceable, like putty in someone's hands.
OPPOSITE intractable.

malnutrition ▶ noun *there is a real danger of hunger and even malnutrition* **undernourishment**, malnourishment, poor diet, inadequate diet, unhealthy diet, lack of food, inanition; starvation, hunger, famine; anorexia.

malodorous ▶ adjective *the rubbish was already malodorous despite being in sealed bags* **foul-smelling**, evil-smelling, fetid, smelly, stinking, stinking to high heaven, reeking, reeky, pungent, acrid, rank, high, putrid, noxious; *W. Indian* fresh; *informal* stinky; *Brit. informal* niffing, niffy, pongy, whiffy, humming; *N. Amer. informal* funky; *literary* noisome, mephitic; *rare* miasmic, miasmal, olid.
OPPOSITE fragrant.

malpractice ▶ noun *victims of medical malpractice* **wrongdoing**, dereliction of duty, professional misconduct, breach of ethics, unprofessional behaviour, unprofessionalism, unethical behaviour; negligence, carelessness, incompetence.

maltreat ▶ verb *Keith was a bully and occasionally maltreated his wife* **ill-treat**, mistreat, abuse, ill-use, misuse, treat badly; handle/treat roughly, knock about/around, hit, beat, strike, mishandle, manhandle, maul; bully, torture, injure, harm, hurt, persecute, molest; *informal* beat up, rough up, do over.

maltreatment ▶ noun *the maltreatment and execution of prisoners* **ill-treatment**, mistreatment, abuse, ill use, ill usage, misuse, bad treatment; rough handling, beating, mishandling, manhandling, mauling; bullying, torture, injury, harm, persecution, molestation.

M

mammoth ▶ adjective *a mammoth task | a crisis of mammoth proportions* **huge**, enormous, gigantic, giant, colossal, massive, vast, immense, mighty, stupendous, monumental, Herculean, epic, prodigious, mountainous, monstrous, titanic, towering, elephantine, king-sized, king-size, gargantuan, Brobdingnagian; *informal* mega, monster, whopping great, thumping, thumping great, humongous, jumbo, bumper, astronomical, astronomic; *Brit. informal* whacking, whacking great, ginormous.
OPPOSITE tiny.

man ▶ noun **1 male**, adult male, gentleman, youth; *informal* guy, fellow, geezer, gent, mother's son; *Brit. informal* bloke, chap, lad, cove; *N. Amer. informal* dude, bozo, hombre; *Austral./NZ informal* digger; *S. African informal* oke, ou, oom; *Indian informal* admi; *Scottish & Irish informal* bodach; *Scottish archaic* carl.
2 *all men are mortal* **human being**, human, person, mortal, individual, personage, soul.
3 *the evolution of man* **the human race**, the human species, Homo sapiens, humankind, humanity, human beings, humans, people, mankind.
4 *the men voted to go on strike* **worker**, workman, labourer, helper, hand, blue-collar worker. *See also* STAFF.
5 *have you met her new man?* **boyfriend**, partner, husband, spouse, lover, admirer, fiancé, amour, inamorato; common-law husband, escort, live-in lover, significant other, cohabitee; *informal* fancy man, toy boy, sugar daddy; *N. Amer. informal* squeeze; *S. African informal* jong; *dated* beau, steady, young man; *informal, dated* intended; *archaic* leman.
6 *his man brought him a cocktail* **manservant**, valet, gentleman's gentleman, attendant, retainer; page, footman, flunkey, Jeeves; *Military, dated* batman; *N. Amer.* houseman.
□ **man to man frankly**, openly, honestly, directly, candidly, plainly, forthrightly, without beating about the bush; woman to woman.
□ **to a man with no exceptions**, without exception, bar none, one and all, everyone, each and every one, unanimously, as one.
▶ verb **1** *the office is manned from 9 a.m. to 5 p.m.* **staff**, crew, occupy, people.
2 *firemen manned the pumps* **operate**, work, use, utilize.

WORD LINKS

relating to men	**male, masculine, virile**
related prefix	**andro-**
centred on men	**androcentric**
fear of men	**androphobia**
hatred of men	**misandry**
rule by men	**androcracy**

manacle ▶ verb *Bosley and Hughes knelt on him and manacled his hands behind his back* **shackle**, fetter, chain, chain up, put in chains, put/clap in irons, handcuff, restrain; tie, secure; *informal* cuff.

manacles ▶ plural noun *the soldiers were already putting manacles around Rachel's wrists* **handcuffs**, shackles, chains, irons, fetters, restraints, bonds; *informal* cuffs, bracelets; *archaic* darbies, gyves.

manage ▶ verb **1** *she manages a staff of 80 people* **be in charge of**, run, be head of, head, direct, control, preside over, lead, govern, rule, command, superintend, supervise, oversee, administer, organize, conduct, handle, guide, be at the helm of; *informal* head up.
2 *he's good at managing his money* **organize**, take care of, administer, regulate, deal with efficiently.
OPPOSITE squander.
3 *how much work can you manage this week?* **accomplish**, achieve, do, carry out, perform, undertake, bring about/off, effect, finish, succeed in, contrive, engineer.
4 *will you be able to manage without him?* **cope**, get along/on, make do, be/fare/do all right, carry on, survive, deal with the situation, scrape by/along, muddle through/along, fend for oneself, shift for oneself, make ends meet, weather the storm; *informal* make out, get by, hack it.
5 *she can't manage that horse* **control**, handle, master, influence, manipulate; cope with, deal with.

manageable ▶ adjective **1** *a manageable amount of work* **achievable**, **doable**, practicable, possible, feasible, reasonable, attainable, viable.
OPPOSITES impracticable, impossible.
2 *a manageable child* **controllable**, compliant, tractable, pliant, pliable, malleable, biddable, docile, amenable, manipulable, governable, tameable, accommodating, acquiescent, complaisant, yielding, submissive.
OPPOSITE unmanageable.
3 *a manageable tool* **user-friendly**, easy to use, handy; *rare* wieldy.
OPPOSITE unwieldy.

management ▶ noun **1** *he's responsible for the management of the firm* **administration**, running, managing, organization; charge, care, direction, leadership, control, governing, governance, ruling, command, superintendence, supervision, overseeing, conduct, handling, guidance, operation.
2 *the workers are in dispute with the management* **managers**, employers, directors, board of directors, board, directorate, executives, administrators, administration; owners, proprietors; *informal* bosses, top brass.
OPPOSITE workers.

manager ▶ noun **1** *the works manager* **executive**, head of department, line manager, supervisor, principal, administrator, head, boss, director, managing director, employer, superintendent, foreman, forewoman, overseer; proprietor; *informal* chief, head honcho, governor; *Brit. informal* gaffer, guv'nor; *N. Amer. informal* high muckamuck, straw boss.
2 *the band's manager* **organizer**, controller, comptroller; impresario.

mandate ▶ noun **1** *he called an election to seek a mandate for his policies* **authority**, approval, acceptance, ratification, endorsement; sanction, authorization.
2 *a mandate from the UN was necessary* **instruction**, directive, direction, decree, command, order, injunction, edict, charge, commission, bidding, warrant, ruling, ordinance, law, statute, fiat; (*in Tsarist Russia*) ukase; (*in Spanish-speaking countries*) pronunciamento.

mandatory ▶ adjective *the concept of mandatory retirement* **obligatory**, compulsory, binding, required; inescapable, unavoidable; requisite, necessary, essential, imperative.
OPPOSITE optional.

manful ▶ adjective *his manful attempt to smile* **brave**, courageous, bold, plucky, gallant, heroic, intrepid, fearless, valiant, valorous, dauntless, doughty; **resolute**, with gritted teeth, grim, determined, manly, stout, stout-hearted, lionhearted, stalwart; *informal* gutsy, ballsy, spunky.
OPPOSITES cowardly, timorous.

manfully ▶ adverb *he began to struggle manfully upwards* **bravely**, courageously, boldly, gallantly, pluckily, heroically, intrepidly, fearlessly, valiantly, dauntlessly; **resolutely**, determinedly, stoutly, stout-heartedly, stalwartly, hard, strongly, vigorously, with might and main, like a Trojan; with all one's strength, to the best of one's abilities, as best one can, desperately, with desperation, with all the stops out.
OPPOSITE timorously.

mange ▶ noun **scabies**, scab, itch, rash, eruption, skin infection.

manger ▶ noun **trough**, feeding trough, fodder rack, feeder, crib.

mangle ▶ verb **1** *the bodies were mangled beyond recognition* **mutilate**, maim, disfigure, damage, injure, crush, crumple; hack, cut about, lacerate, tear apart, rend, chop (up), butcher, deform, maul, wreck.
2 *he's mangling the English language* **spoil**, ruin, mar, mutilate, bungle, mess up, make a mess of, wreck; *informal* murder, make a hash of, muck up, screw up, butcher.

mangy ▶ adjective **1** *a mangy cat* **scabby**, scaly, scabious, diseased.
2 *a mangy old armchair* **scruffy**, moth-eaten, shabby, worn, unkempt, shoddy, sorry, dirty, squalid, filthy, sleazy, seedy; *informal* tatty, the worse for wear, scuzzy, grungy, yucky; *Brit. informal* grotty; *N. Amer. informal* raggedy.

manhandle ▸ verb **1** *he was manhandled by a gang of youths* **jostle**, shove, hustle, handle roughly, push, pull; **maltreat**, ill-treat, mistreat, abuse, maul, molest, injure, damage, beat, knock about/around, batter; *informal* paw, beat up, rough up; *N. Amer. informal* roust.
2 *we manhandled the piano down the stairs* **heave**, haul, push, shove; pull, tug, drag, move, carry, lift, manoeuvre; *informal* hump, lug.

manhood ▸ noun **1** *the transition from boyhood to manhood* **maturity**, sexual maturity, adulthood.
2 *an insult to his manhood* **virility**, manliness, machismo, masculinity, maleness; mettle, spirit, fortitude, resolution, determination, manfulness, bravery, courage, strength, intrepidity, valour, heroism, boldness.

mania ▸ noun **1** *she suffered from fits of mania* **madness**, derangement, dementia, insanity, lunacy, dementedness, psychosis, schizophrenia, mental illness, delirium, frenzy, hysteria, raving, violence, wildness.
2 *he has a mania for gadgets* **obsession**, compulsion, fixation, fetish, fascination, preoccupation, passion, enthusiasm, desire, urge, craving, craze, fad, rage; *informal* thing, yen; *rare* cacoethes.

maniac ▸ noun **1** *a homicidal maniac* **lunatic**, madman, madwoman, mad person, deranged person, psychopath, psychotic; *informal* loony, fruitcake, nutcase, nut, nutter, psycho, screwball, head case, headbanger, sicko; *N. Amer. informal* crazy, kook, meshuggener, nutso.
2 (*informal*) *a football maniac* **enthusiast**, fan, addict, devotee, aficionado; *informal* freak, fiend, nut, buff.

manic ▸ adjective **1** *a manic grin* **mad**, insane, deranged, demented, maniacal, lunatic, crazed, wild, demonic, demoniacal, hysterical, raving, neurotic, unhinged, unbalanced; *informal* crazy.
OPPOSITE sane.
2 *scenes of manic activity* **frenzied**, feverish, frenetic, hectic, intense; *informal* hyper, mad.
OPPOSITE calm.

manifest ▸ verb **1** *she manifested signs of depression* **display**, **show**, exhibit, demonstrate, betray, present, evince, reveal, indicate, make plain, express, declare.
OPPOSITE hide.
2 *disputes and strikes manifest bad industrial relations* **be evidence of**, be a sign of, indicate, show, attest, reflect, bespeak, prove, establish, evidence, substantiate, corroborate, verify, confirm; *literary* betoken.
OPPOSITES mask; deny.
▸ adjective *his manifest lack of interest in the proceedings* **obvious**, clear, plain, apparent, evident, patent, palpable, distinct, definite, blatant, overt, glaring, barefaced, explicit, transparent, conspicuous, undisguised, unmistakable, unquestionable, undeniable, noticeable, perceptible, visible, recognizable, observable.
OPPOSITES hidden, secret.

manifestation ▸ noun **1** *the manifestation of anxiety* **display**, demonstration, showing, show, exhibition, presentation, indication, illustration, exemplification, exposition, disclosure, declaration, expression, profession.
2 *manifestations of global warming* **sign**, indication, evidence, proof, token, symptom, testimony, substantiation, mark, symbol, reflection, example, instance.
3 *a supernatural manifestation* **apparition**, appearance, materialization, visitation.

manifesto ▸ noun **policy statement**, platform, programme, declaration, proclamation, pronouncement, announcement, publication, notification; (*in Spanish-speaking countries*) pronunciamento.

manifold ▸ adjective **many**, numerous, multiple, multifarious, multitudinous, multiplex, legion, diverse, various, several, varied, different, miscellaneous, assorted, sundry, copious, abundant; *literary* myriad, divers.

manikin ▸ noun **dwarf**, midget, little man, homunculus, pygmy, Tom Thumb.

manipulate ▸ verb **1** *the workman manipulated some knobs and levers* **operate**, handle, work, control, use, employ, utilize.
2 *she used her hands to manipulate the muscles of his back* **massage**, rub, knead, feel, palpate.
3 *the government tried to manipulate the situation* **exploit**, **control**, influence, use/turn to one's advantage, manoeuvre, engineer, steer, direct, guide, twist round one's little finger, work, orchestrate, choreograph.
4 *they accused him of manipulating the data* **falsify**, rig, distort, alter, change, doctor, massage, juggle, tamper with, fiddle with, tinker with, interfere with, misrepresent, fudge, corrupt; *informal* cook, fiddle.

manipulative ▸ adjective **1** *a ruthlessly manipulative woman* **scheming**, calculating, cunning, crafty, wily, shrewd, devious, designing, conniving, Machiavellian, artful, guileful, slippery, slick, sly, unscrupulous, disingenuous; *informal* foxy.
OPPOSITE ingenuous.
2 *a manipulative skill such as typing* **manual**, done with one's hands, dexterous.

manipulator ▸ noun *a ruthless political manipulator* **exploiter**, puller of strings, user, manoeuvrer, conniver, intriguer, puppet master, puppeteer, wheeler-dealer; *informal* operator, thimblerigger.

mankind ▸ noun **the human race**, man, humanity, human beings, humans, Homo sapiens, humankind, the human species, people, men and women.

manliness ▸ noun **1** *he felt that his manliness was threatened* **virility**, masculinity, vigour, strength, muscularity, ruggedness, toughness, robustness, powerfulness, brawniness, hardihood; *informal* hunkiness.
OPPOSITE femininity.
2 *he used military discipline and drill to instil Christian manliness into unruly boys* **resoluteness**, steadfastness, mettle, spirit, dauntlessness, doughtiness, determination, fortitude, stalwartness; bravery, courage, boldness, valour, fearlessness, pluck, machismo, manhood, manfulness, daring, intrepidity, heroism, gallantry, chivalrousness, stout-heartedness; *informal* guts, grit, spunk; *N. Amer. informal* cojones.
OPPOSITES cowardice, funk.

manly ▸ adjective **1** *his manly physique* **virile**, masculine, strong, all-male, muscular, muscly, strapping, well built, sturdy, robust, rugged, tough, hardy, powerful, brawny, red-blooded, vigorous; *informal* hunky.
OPPOSITE feminine.
2 *their manly deeds* **brave**, courageous, bold, valiant, valorous, fearless, plucky, macho, manful, intrepid, daring, lionhearted, heroic, gallant, chivalrous, swashbuckling, adventurous, stout-hearted, stout, dauntless, doughty, mettlesome, resolute, determined, stalwart; *informal* Ramboesque, gutsy, ballsy, spunky.
OPPOSITES effeminate, cowardly, weak.

man-made ▸ adjective *a blend of 80% wool and 20% man-made fibres* **artificial**, synthetic, manufactured, fabricated; imitation, ersatz, faux, simulated, mock, fake, plastic.
OPPOSITES natural; real.

CHOOSE THE RIGHT WORD

man-made, artificial, synthetic
See ARTIFICIAL.

mannequin ▸ noun **1** *mannequins in a shop window* **dummy**, model, figure.
2 *mannequins on the catwalk* **model**, fashion model, supermodel; *informal* clothes horse.

manner ▸ noun **1** *the matter was dealt with in a very efficient manner* **way**, fashion, mode, means, method, system, style, approach, technique, procedure, process, methodology, modus operandi, form, routine, practice.
2 (*archaic*) *what manner of person is he?* **kind**, sort, type, variety, form, nature, breed, brand, stamp, class, category, genre, order.
3 *she had a rather unfriendly manner* **demeanour**, air, aspect, attitude, appearance, look, bearing, cast, deportment, behaviour, conduct; comportment, mien.
4 (**manners**) *the life and manners of Victorian society* **customs**, habits, ways, practices, conventions, usages.
5 (**manners**) *it's bad manners to stare* **social behaviour**, behaviour, conduct, way of behaving, form, social habit.
6 (**manners**) *you ought to teach him some manners* **correct behaviour**, etiquette, social graces, good form, protocol, politeness, decorum, propriety, gentility, civility, formalities, niceties, Ps and Qs, breeding; *French* politesse; *informal* the done thing; *archaic* convenances.
OPPOSITES rudeness, bad behaviour.

mannered ▸ adjective *Dornford Yates's highly artificial, mannered prose style* **affected**, pretentious, unnatural, artificial, contrived, stilted, stiff, forced, put-on, insincere, theatrical, elaborate, precious, posed, stagy, camp; *informal* pseudo.
OPPOSITES natural, unpretentious.

mannerism ▸ noun *he has the mannerisms of a bishop without actually having become one* **idiosyncrasy**, quirk, oddity, foible, trait, peculiarity, habit, characteristic, characteristic gesture, trick.

mannerly ▸ adjective (*dated*) *he woke them up in as mannerly a way as he knew how* **polite**, courteous, well mannered, well behaved, civil, gentlemanly, ladylike, genteel, decorous, respectful, well bred, refined, polished, civilized, cultivated, gracious, chivalrous, urbane, well brought up.
OPPOSITE rude.

mannish ▸ adjective *her gruff, mannish exterior* **manlike**, masculine, unfeminine, unwomanly, unladylike, Amazonian; *informal* **butch**, dykey; *rare* viraginous, viragoish.
OPPOSITES feminine, girlish.

manoeuvre ▸ verb **1** *I manoeuvred the car into a parking space* **steer**, guide, drive, negotiate, navigate, pilot, direct, manipulate, move, work, jockey.
2 *he had manoeuvred things to suit himself* **manipulate**, contrive, manage, engineer, devise, plan, plot, fix, organize, arrange, set up, orchestrate, choreograph, stage-manage; *informal* wangle.

M

3 *he began manoeuvring for the party leadership* **intrigue**, plot, scheme, plan, lay plans, conspire, pull strings; *N. Amer.* pull wires; *rare* machinate.
▶ **noun 1** *a tricky parking manoeuvre* **operation**, exercise, activity, move, movement, action.
2 *a series of diplomatic manoeuvres* **stratagem**, **tactic**, gambit, ploy, trick, dodge, ruse, plan, scheme, operation, device, plot, machination, artifice, subterfuge, intrigue, manipulation; *French* démarche; *informal* wangle.
3 (**manoeuvres**) *large-scale military manoeuvres* **training exercises**, exercises, war games, operations.

manse ▶ **noun** (*Scottish*) **minister's house**; vicarage, parsonage, rectory, deanery; *archaic* glebe-house.

manservant ▶ **noun valet**, attendant, retainer, equerry, gentleman's gentleman, man, Jeeves; steward, butler, footman, flunkey, page, houseboy, lackey; *Military, dated* batman; *N. Amer.* houseman.

mansion ▶ **noun** *a lavish Beverly Hills mansion* **residence**, hall, abode, stately home, seat, manor, manor house, country house, villa, castle; *French* château, manoir; *Italian* palazzo; *German* schloss; *informal* palace, pile.
OPPOSITE hovel.

manslaughter ▶ **noun killing**, murder; *literary* slaying.

mantle ▶ **noun 1** *a dark green velvet mantle* **cloak**, cape, shawl, wrap, stole; *rare* pelisse, pelerine; *S. American* poncho, serape; *archaic* mantlet.
2 *houses covered in a thick mantle of snow* **covering**, **layer**, blanket, sheet, veil, curtain, canopy, cover, cloak, pall, shroud, screen, mask, cloud, overlay, envelope.
3 *the mantle of leadership* **role**, burden, onus, duty, responsibility, function, position, capacity, task, job.
▶ **verb** *heavy mists mantled the forest* **cover**, envelop, veil, cloak, curtain, shroud, swathe, wrap, blanket, screen, cloud, conceal, hide, disguise, mask, obscure, surround, overlay, clothe; *literary* enshroud.

manual ▶ **adjective 1** *manual work* **done with one's hands**, labouring, physical, blue-collar.
2 *a manual typewriter* **hand-operated**, hand, non-automatic.
OPPOSITES automatic, mechanical.
▶ **noun** *a training manual* **handbook**, set of instructions, instructions, instruction book, guide, companion, reference book, ABC, guidebook; *Latin* vade mecum; *informal* bible; *rare* enchiridion.

manufacture ▶ **verb 1** *the company manufactures laser printers* **make**, **produce**, mass produce, build, construct, assemble, put together, create, fabricate, prefabricate, turn out, process, form, fashion, model, mould, shape, forge, engineer.
2 *the story was manufactured by the press* **make up**, **invent**, fabricate, concoct, hatch, dream up, think up, trump up, devise, formulate, frame, contrive, construct, coin; *informal* cook up.
▶ **noun** *the manufacture of aircraft engines* **production**, **making**, manufacturing, mass-production, construction, building, assembly, creation, fabrication, prefabrication, processing, putting together, turning out, engineering, forging.

manufacturer ▶ **noun maker**, **producer**, builder, constructor, processor, creator, fabricator; factory owner, industrialist, captain/baron of industry.

manure *See centre pages for list of* **Fertilizers**
▶ **noun dung**, muck, droppings, ordure, guano, cowpats; *N. Amer. informal* cow chips, horse apples; *vulgar slang* shit, crap.

manuscript ▶ **noun document**, text, script, paper, typescript; codex, parchment, palimpsest, vellum, scroll; autograph, holograph.
OPPOSITES publication, published work.
WORD LINKS
study of manuscripts **codicology**

many ▶ **determiner & adjective 1** *he has many faults* **numerous**, a great/good deal of, a lot of, a large/great number of, great quantities of, plenty of, countless, innumerable, scores of, crowds of, droves of, an army of, a horde of, a multitude of, a multiplicity of, multitudinous, numberless, multiple, untold; several, various, sundry, diverse, assorted, multifarious; copious, abundant, profuse, an abundance of, a profusion of; frequent; *informal* lots of, umpteen, loads of, masses of, stacks of, scads of, heaps of, piles of, bags of, tons of, oodles of, dozens of, hundreds of, thousands of, millions of, billions of, zillions of, more ... than one can shake a stick at; *Brit. informal* shedload; *N. Amer. informal* a slew of, gazillions of, bazillions of, gobs of; *Austral./NZ informal* a swag of; *vulgar slang* a shitload of; *literary* myriad, divers.
OPPOSITE few.
2 (**the many**) *sacrificing the individual for the sake of the many* **the people**, the common people, the masses, the multitude, the majority, the populace, the public, the rank and file, the crowd, the commonalty, the commonality; *derogatory* the hoi polloi, the common herd, the mob, the proletariat, the rabble, the riff-raff, the great unwashed, the canaille, the proles, the plebs.
OPPOSITE aristocracy.
WORD LINKS
related prefixes **multi- (e.g. *multicoloured, multibuy*), poly- (e.g. *polytechnic, polyunsaturated*)**

map *See centre pages for list of* **Map Types and Projections**
▶ **noun plan**, chart.
▶ **verb** *the region was mapped from the air* **chart**, plot, delineate, draw, depict, portray, survey.
□ **map something out** *he mapped out a plan of campaign* **outline**, set out, lay out, sketch out, trace out, rough out, block out, delineate, detail, draw up; formulate, work out, frame, draft, plan, plot out; arrange, design, programme, think out, think through, organize.
WORD LINKS
relating to maps **cartographic**
making of maps **cartography**

mar ▶ **verb 1** *an ugly scar marred his features* **spoil**, ruin, impair; **disfigure**, detract from, flaw, blemish, scar, mutilate, deface, deform.
OPPOSITES improve, enhance.
2 *the celebrations were marred by violence* **spoil**, ruin, impair, upset, damage, wreck; **harm**, hurt, blight, taint, tarnish, sully, stain, pollute, vitiate; *informal* foul up.

maraud ▶ **verb** *bands of robbers crossed the river to maraud* **plunder**, go looting, go pillaging, foray, raid, ravage, harry, go on forays/raids, freeboot; *archaic* reave.

marauder ▶ **noun** *they placed chains across the river mouth to keep out marauders* **raider**, plunderer, pillager, looter, robber, pirate, freebooter, buccaneer, corsair, rover, bandit, brigand, rustler, highwayman, ravager; *Scottish historical* cateran, mosstrooper; *archaic* reaver, snaphance.

marauding ▶ **adjective** *reservists are being called up to protect civilians from marauding gunmen* **predatory**, rapacious, thieving, vulturine, plundering, pillaging, looting, freebooting, piratical; *rare* plunderous.

marble ▶ **noun**
WORD LINKS
relating to marble **marmoreal**

March ▶ **noun**
WORD LINKS
birthstone **bloodstone**

march ▶ **verb 1** *a squadron of soldiers marched past* **stride**, walk, troop, step, pace, tread; footslog, slog, tramp, hike, trudge; parade, file, process, promenade; *Brit. informal* yomp.
2 *she marched in without even knocking* **stalk**, strut, stride, flounce, storm, stomp, sweep, swagger.
3 *time marches on* **move forward**, advance, progress, forge ahead, make headway, go on, continue on, roll on, develop, evolve.
▶ **noun 1** *a 20-mile march across open country* **hike**, trek, tramp, slog, footslog, walk; route march, forced march; *Brit. informal* yomp.
2 *a march by veterans and sailors through the centre of the city | a protest march against racism* **parade**, procession, march past, promenade, cortège; **demonstration**, protest; *informal* demo; *Indian* morcha.
3 *the march of technology* **progress**, advance, progression, passage, continuance, development, evolution, headway.

marches ▶ **plural noun** *the Welsh marches* **borders**, boundaries, borderlands, frontiers, limits, confines; *historical* marchlands.

margin ▶ **noun 1** *the margin of the lake* **edge**, side, bank, verge, border, perimeter, brink, brim, rim, fringe, boundary, limits, periphery, bound, extremity; *literary* marge, bourn, skirt.
2 *there was no margin for error* **leeway**, latitude, scope, room, room for manoeuvre, room to spare, space, allowance, extra, surplus.
3 *they won by a narrow margin* **gap**, majority, amount, difference, measure/degree of difference.

marginal ▶ **adjective 1** *the difference is marginal* **slight**, small, tiny, minute, low, minor, insignificant, minimal, negligible.
OPPOSITES vast, gross.
2 *a very marginal case* **borderline**, disputable, questionable, doubtful.

marijuana ▶ **noun cannabis**, hashish, bhang, hemp, kef, kif, charas, ganja, sinsemilla; *informal* dope, hash, grass, pot, blow, draw, stuff, Mary Jane, tea, the weed, gold, skunkweed, skunk, reefer, rope, smoke, gage, boo, charge, jive, mootah, pod; *Brit. informal* wacky backy; *N. Amer. informal* locoweed; *S. African* dagga, zol; *informal, dated* green, mezz.

marinate ▶ **verb** *marinate the fruit in the rum for 30 minutes* **souse**, soak, steep, immerse, marinade.

marine ▶ **adjective 1** *marine plants* **saltwater**, seawater, sea, oceanic, aquatic; *rare* pelagic, thalassic.
OPPOSITE freshwater.
2 *a marine insurance company* **maritime**, nautical, naval, seafaring, seagoing, ocean-going.

mariner ▶ **noun sailor**, seaman, seafarer, seafaring man; *informal* Jack tar, tar, sea dog, salt, bluejacket, matelot, matlow, matlo; *N. Amer. informal* shellback.

marital ▶ **adjective** *as children leave home marital satisfaction tends to pick up again* **matrimonial**, married, wedded, conjugal, connubial, nuptial, marriage, wedding; *Law* spousal; *literary* hymeneal, epithalamic.

maritime ▶ **adjective 1** *maritime law* **naval**, marine, nautical, seafaring,

seagoing, sea, ocean-going.
2 *maritime regions* **coastal**, seaside, littoral.

mark ▸ noun **1** *a dirty mark on the tablecloth | a chestnut mare with a white mark on her forehead* **blemish**, streak, spot, fleck, dot, blot, stain, smear, trace, speck, speckle, blotch, smudge, smut, smirch, fingermark, fingerprint, impression, imprint; bruise, discoloration, scar, pit, pockmark, pock, scratch, dent, chip, notch, nick, line, score, cut, incision, gash; marking, blaze, stripe; birthmark; *informal* splotch, splodge; *technical* stigma.
2 *a punctuation mark* **symbol**, sign, character; exclamation mark, question mark, quotation mark; diacritic, diacritical mark.
3 *he signed his mark in the visitors' book* **signature**, autograph, cross, X, scribble, squiggle, initials, imprint.
4 *books bearing the mark of a well-known bookseller* **logo**, seal, stamp, imprint, symbol, emblem, device, insignia, badge, brand, trademark, token, monogram, hallmark, logotype, watermark, label, tag, flag, motto.
5 *unemployment had passed the three million mark* **point**, level, stage, degree.
6 *the flag was lowered as a mark of respect* **sign**, token, symbol, indication, badge, emblem, symptom, feature, evidence, proof, clue, hint.
7 *the war left its mark on him* **impression**, imprint, traces, vestiges, effect, impact, influence.
8 *it is the mark of a civilized society to treat its elderly members well* **characteristic**, feature, trait, attribute, quality, hallmark, badge, stamp, property, peculiarity, indicator.
9 *he got very good marks for maths and physics* **grade**, grading, rating, score, percentage; assessment, evaluation.
10 *the bullet missed its mark | his comment hit the mark* **target**, goal, aim, bullseye, objective, object, end, purpose, intent, intention.
11 *his work hasn't been up to the mark* **required standard**, standard, norm, par, level, criterion, gauge, yardstick, rule, measure, scale.
□ **of mark** (*dated*) *a man of mark* **important**, distinguished, eminent, pre-eminent, prominent, notable, famous, great, prestigious; of importance, of consequence, of note, of high repute, of high standing, of distinction, of renown.
□ **make one's mark** *he has made his mark in the financial world* **be successful**, **distinguish oneself**, succeed, gain success, be a success, prosper, get ahead, get on, make good, achieve recognition, attain distinction; *informal* make it, make the grade, find a place in the sun.
□ **quick off the mark alert**, quick, quick-witted, bright, clever, perceptive, sharp, sharp-witted, observant, wide awake; *informal* on the ball, on one's toes, quick on the uptake.
OPPOSITES slow-witted, dozy.
□ **wide of the mark 1** *his answer was wide of the mark* **inaccurate**, incorrect, wrong, erroneous, inexact, off-target, off-beam, out, fallacious, mistaken, misguided, misinformed; *archaic* abroad.
OPPOSITE spot on.
2 *the observations were wide of the mark* **irrelevant**, inapplicable, inapposite, inappropriate, inapt, immaterial, not to the point, beside the point, off the subject, extraneous, neither here nor there.
OPPOSITE to the point.
▸ verb **1** *be careful not to mark the paintwork* **discolour**, stain, smear, smudge, streak, blotch, blot, blemish; dirty, smirch, damage, deface, disfigure, pockmark, pit, bruise, scrape, scratch, scar, dent, chip, nick, notch, score, cut, gash; *informal* splotch, splodge.
2 *all her possessions were clearly marked* **put one's name on**, name, initial, put one's seal on, label, tag, hallmark, watermark, brand, stamp, earmark.
3 *I've marked the relevant passages | a bronze cross marks the grave* **indicate**, label, flag, tab, tick, show the position of, show, identify, designate, delineate, denote.
4 *the city held a festival to mark its 200th anniversary* **celebrate**, observe, recognize, acknowledge, keep, honour, solemnize, pay tribute to, salute, commemorate, remember, memorialize.
5 *the incidents marked a new phase in the terrorists' campaign* **represent**, signify, be an indication of, be a sign of, indicate, herald.
6 *his style is marked by simplicity and concision* **characterize**, distinguish, identify, typify, brand, signalize, stamp.
7 *an examiner may have hundreds of papers to mark* **assess**, evaluate, appraise, correct; *N. Amer.* grade.
8 *it'll cause trouble, you mark my words!* **take heed of**, pay heed to, heed, listen to, take note/notice of, pay attention to, attend to, note, mind, bear in mind, give (a) thought to, take into consideration, take to heart; *archaic* regard.
□ **mark something down 1** *prices have been marked down for quick sale* **reduce**, decrease, lower, cut, put down, take down, discount; *informal* slash.
OPPOSITE increase.
2 *some shops have marked the trainers down* **lower the price of**, make cheaper, sell at a giveaway price, put in a sale; *informal* knock down.
OPPOSITE mark something up.
□ **mark someone out 1** *his honesty marked him out from the rest of them* **set apart**, separate, single out, differentiate, distinguish.
2 *she is marked out for fame* **destine**, ordain, predestine, preordain.
□ **mark something out** *the pitch had already been marked out* **delineate**, outline, delimit, demarcate, measure out, mark the boundaries/limits of, mark off, define, describe, stake out.
□ **mark something up 1** *they marked up the price by 66 per cent* **increase**, raise, up, put up, hike (up), escalate; *informal* jack up.
OPPOSITE mark something down.
2 *editors marked up the text in pencil* **annotate**, correct, label.

marked ▸ adjective *a marked deterioration in her health* **noticeable**, pronounced, decided, distinct, striking, clear, glaring, blatant, unmistakable, obvious, plain, manifest, patent, palpable, considerable, remarkable, prominent, signal, significant, great, substantial, strong, conspicuous, notable, noted, pointed, salient, recognizable, identifiable, distinguishable, discernible, apparent, evident, open, written all over one.
OPPOSITES imperceptible, inconspicuous.

markedly ▸ adverb *the birth rate declined markedly* **noticeably**, decidedly, strikingly, distinctly, remarkably, clearly, plainly; blatantly, glaringly, unmistakably, conspicuously, pointedly, obviously, manifestly, patently, palpably, signally, significantly, greatly, considerably, substantially, recognizably, discernibly, notably, apparently, evidently, to a marked extent, to a great extent; *informal* seriously.
OPPOSITE imperceptibly.

market ▸ noun **1 shopping centre**, marketplace, mart, retail outlet, flea market, fair, bazaar, piazza, plaza; *Arabic* souk; *historical* agora; *archaic* emporium.
2 *there's no market for such expensive goods* **demand**, call, want, desire, need, requirement.
3 *the market is sluggish* **trade**, trading, business, commerce, buying and selling, dealing.
▸ verb *the product was marketed worldwide* **sell**, retail, offer for sale, put up for sale, vend, merchandise, trade, peddle, hawk; advertise, promote.
□ **in the market for wishing to buy**, in need of, seeking, wanting, lacking, wishing for, desiring.
□ **on the market on sale**, up for sale, for sale, on offer, purchasable, available, obtainable; *N. Amer.* on the block.

marketable ▸ adjective **1** *marketable fruit* **saleable**, sellable, merchantable; *rare* vendible.
2 *marketable skills* **in demand**, sought-after, wanted.

marksman, markswoman ▸ noun **sniper**, sharpshooter, good shot; *Italian* bersagliere; *informal* crack shot, dead shot; *N. Amer. informal* deadeye, shootist.

maroon ▸ verb *a novel about English schoolboys marooned on a desert island* **strand**, leave stranded, cast away, cast ashore, abandon, leave behind, leave, leave in the lurch, desert, turn one's back on, leave isolated; *informal* leave high and dry; *archaic* forsake.

marriage ▸ noun **1** *a proposal of marriage* **matrimony**, holy matrimony, wedlock, married state, conjugal bond.
2 *the marriage took place at St Margaret's Church* **wedding**, wedding ceremony, marriage ceremony, nuptials, union; *archaic* espousal.
OPPOSITES divorce, splitting up.
3 *the piece is a marriage of jazz, pop, and gospel* **union**, alliance, fusion, amalgamation, combination, affiliation, association, connection, coupling, merger, unification; *informal* hook up.
OPPOSITES sundering, separation.

WORD LINKS

relating to marriage	**marital, matrimonial, nuptial, conjugal, connubial, spousal**
fear of marriage	**gamophobia**
obsession with marriage	**gamomania**

married ▸ adjective **1** *a married couple* **wedded**, wed, joined in marriage, united in wedlock; *informal* spliced, hitched.
OPPOSITES unmarried, single.
2 *married bliss* **marital**, matrimonial, connubial, conjugal, nuptial, spousal.

marrow ▸ noun **1** *bone marrow.*
2 *the marrow of his statement* **essence**, core, nucleus, pith, kernel, heart, centre, soul, spirit, quintessence, gist, substance, sum and substance, meat, nub, stuff; *informal* nitty-gritty, nuts and bolts.

marry ▸ verb **1** *the couple married last year* **get/be married**, wed, be wed, become man and wife, plight/pledge one's troth; *informal* tie the knot, walk down the aisle, take the plunge, get spliced, get hitched, get yoked, say 'I do'; *archaic* become espoused.
2 *John wanted to marry her* **wed**, take to wife/husband, lead to the altar; *informal* make an honest woman of; *archaic* espouse, wive.
OPPOSITE divorce.
3 *the show marries poetry with art* **join**, join together, unite, ally, merge, unify, amalgamate, combine, affiliate, associate, link, connect, fuse, weld,

M

couple, knit, yoke.
OPPOSITES split, separate.

marsh ▶ noun **swamp**, marshland, bog, peat bog, swampland, morass, mire, quagmire, quag, slough, fen, fenland, wetland, sump; salt marsh, saltings, salina; *N. Amer.* bayou, pocosin, moor; *Scottish & N. English* moss; *Irish* corcass; *archaic* marish.

WORD LINKS
relating to marshes **paludal**

marshal ▶ verb **1** *the Mercian king marshalled a formidable army* **gather**, gather together, assemble, collect, muster, mass, amass, call together, draw up, line up, align, array, organize, group, set/put in order, set/put into position, arrange, deploy, position, order; dispose, rank, mobilize, rally, round up.
OPPOSITES disperse, scatter.
2 *guests were marshalled to their seats* **usher**, guide, escort, conduct, lead, shepherd, steer, take.

marshy ▶ adjective **boggy**, swampy, muddy, squelchy, soggy, waterlogged, oozy, squashy, miry, fenny; *Scottish & N. English* mossy; *technical* paludal, paludine; *rare* marish, quaggy, uliginous.
OPPOSITES dry; firm.

marsupial ▶ noun. *See centre pages for list of* **Marsupials**

martial ▶ adjective **1** *their martial exploits* **military**, soldierly, soldier-like, army, naval, fighting, service; courageous, brave, valiant, valorous, heroic.
OPPOSITES civil, civilian.
2 *one of the most powerful and martial tribes* **warlike**, combative, belligerent, bellicose, aggressive, pugnacious, gung-ho, militant, militaristic.
OPPOSITE peaceable.

martial arts ▶ plural noun. *See centre pages for list of* **Martial Arts and Combat Sports**

martinet ▶ noun **disciplinarian**, slave-driver, stickler for discipline, taskmaster, taskmistress, authoritarian, tyrant; drill sergeant.

martyr ▶ verb *she was martyred for her faith* **put to death**, kill, make a martyr of, martyrize; burn, burn at the stake, stone, immolate, throw to the lions, crucify, put on the rack.
▶ noun
□ **be a martyr to** (*informal*) *he's a martyr to migraine* **suffer from**, be a constant sufferer from, have chronic ...; be seriously affected by, be afflicted with, be troubled by, get.

martyrdom ▶ noun **death**, **suffering**, torture, torment, agony, persecution, ordeal, anguish; killing, putting to death, martyrization, sacrifice, crucifixion, immolation, burning, burning at the stake; *Portuguese* auto-da-fé; *archaic* passion.
OPPOSITE apostasy.

marvel ▶ verb *she marvelled at their courage* **be amazed**, be filled with amazement, be astonished, be surprised, be awed, stand in awe, wonder, be full of wonder, stare, gape, goggle, not believe one's eyes/ears, not know what to say, be dumbfounded; **admire**, applaud, think highly of, respect, venerate, appreciate; *informal* be flabbergasted.
OPPOSITES be indifferent; disregard.
▶ noun *the marvels of technology | I don't know how she did it—she's a marvel* **wonder**, **miracle**, wonderful thing, amazing thing, sensation, spectacle, phenomenon; genius, miracle worker, prodigy, paragon, virtuoso, wizard; *informal* something else, something to shout about, something to write home about, eye-opener; whizz, whizz-kid.

marvellous ▶ adjective **1** *his solo climb was marvellous* **amazing**, astounding, astonishing, awesome, breathtaking, sensational, remarkable, spectacular, stupendous, staggering, stunning; phenomenal, prodigious, miraculous, extraordinary, incredible, unbelievable; *literary* wondrous.
OPPOSITE ordinary.
2 *we had marvellous weather* **excellent**, splendid, wonderful, magnificent, superb, glorious, sublime, lovely, delightful, beautiful, too good to be true; *informal* super, great, smashing, amazing, fantastic, terrific, tremendous, phenomenal, sensational, heavenly, gorgeous, dreamy, grand, fabulous, fab, fabby, fantabulous, awesome, to die for, magic, ace, cool, mean, bad, wicked, mega, crucial, mind-blowing, far out, A1, sound, out of this world, marvy; *black English* dope, def, phat; *Brit. informal* brilliant, brill; *N. Amer. informal* neat, badass, bodacious, boss, radical, rad, peachy, boffo, bully, bitching, dandy, jim-dandy; *Austral./NZ informal* beaut, bonzer; *informal, dated* groovy, spanking, divine; *Brit. informal, dated* capital, champion, wizard, corking, ripping, cracking, spiffing, top-hole, topping, beezer; *N. Amer. informal, dated* swell, keen; *S. African informal* kif, lank; *archaic* goodly.
OPPOSITE awful.

masculine ▶ adjective **1** *a masculine trait* **male**, manly, manlike, of men, man's, men's, male-oriented.
OPPOSITE feminine.
2 *a powerfully masculine man* **virile**, macho, manly, all-male, muscular, muscly, strong, strapping, well built, rugged, robust, brawny, powerful, red-blooded, vigorous; *informal* hunky.
OPPOSITES weak; timid.
3 *a rather masculine woman* **mannish**, manlike, unfeminine, unwomanly, unladylike, Amazonian; *informal* butch, dykey; *archaic* viraginous, viragoish.
OPPOSITES feminine; effeminate.

masculinity ▶ noun **virility**, manliness, maleness, vigour, strength, muscularity, ruggedness, toughness, robustness.
OPPOSITE femininity.

mash ▶ verb *mash the potatoes* **pulp**, crush, purée, cream, smash, squash, pound, beat, macerate, liquidize, liquefy, whip, grind, mince, soften, mangle, chew.
▶ noun *first pound the garlic to a mash* **pulp**, purée, mush, paste, pâté, crush, slush, liquid; *derogatory* pap.

mask ▶ noun **1** *she wore a mask to conceal her face* **disguise**, **veil**, false face, domino, stocking mask, fancy dress; *historical* visor; *archaic* vizard.
2 *wear a mask to avoid inhaling dust* **face mask**, protective mask, gas mask, oxygen mask, fencing mask, iron mask, ski mask, dust mask; safety goggles, welding goggles, welding mask, surgical mask, eye mask, visor.
3 *de Craon had dropped his mask of good humour* **pretence**, semblance, veil, screen, front, false front, facade, veneer, blind, false colours, disguise, guise, concealment, cover, cover-up, cloak, camouflage.
4 *a mask that blocks out part of the image* **matte**, photomask, shadow mask, masking, masking tape.
▶ verb *people carried herbs to mask the stench* **hide**, conceal, disguise, cover up, obscure, screen, cloak, camouflage, veil, mantle, blanket, enshroud.
OPPOSITE enhance, reinforce.

masquerade ▶ noun **1** *a grand masquerade organized by Lord Tylney at Wanstead House* **masked ball**, masque, fancy-dress party.
2 *I doubt if he could have kept up the masquerade for much longer* **pretence**, deception, pose, act, front, facade, disguise, dissimulation, cover-up, bluff, subterfuge, play-acting, make-believe; *informal* put-on.
▶ verb *a journalist **masquerading as** a man in distress* **pretend to be**, pose as, pass oneself off as, impersonate, disguise oneself as, simulate, profess to be; *rare* personate.

Mass ▶ noun **Eucharist**, Holy Communion, Communion, the Lord's Supper.

mass ▶ noun **1** *a thick soggy mass of fallen leaves* **pile**, heap, stack, clump, cloud, bunch, bundle, lump; concentration, conglomeration, accumulation, aggregation, concretion, accretion, assemblage, collection, stockpile, build-up; *rare* amassment.
2 *a mass of cyclists* **large number**, abundance, profusion, multitude, group, crowd, mob, rabble, horde, barrage, throng, huddle, host, troop, army, herd, flock, drove, swarm, pack, press, crush, mountain, flood.
3 *the mass of people voted against* **majority**, larger part/number, greater part/number, best/better part, major part, most, bulk, main body, preponderance, almost all, lion's share.
4 (**the masses**) **the common people**, the populace, the public, the people, the multitude, the rank and file, the crowd, the commonalty, the commonality, the third estate, the plebeians; *derogatory* the hoi polloi, the mob, the proletariat, the common herd, the rabble, the riff-raff, the canaille, the great unwashed, the ragtag (and bobtail), the proles, the plebs.
OPPOSITES elite, oligarchy.
5 *one tenth of the mass of the star* **weight**, size, magnitude, bulk, dimensions, capacity, density, extent, scope, greatness, bigness, hugeness, amount, matter.
▶ adjective *mass hysteria* **wholesale**, universal, widespread, general, large-scale, extensive, pandemic.
▶ verb *both countries began massing troops in the region* **accumulate**, assemble, amass, collect, gather, gather together, draw together, join together; marshal, muster, round up, mobilize, rally.
OPPOSITES disperse, disband.

massacre ▶ noun **1** *a cold-blooded massacre of innocent civilians* **slaughter**, wholesale slaughter, mass slaughter, wholesale killing, indiscriminate killing; murder, murdering, mass murder, mass homicide, execution, mass execution, destruction, mass destruction, annihilation, extermination, liquidation, decimation, carnage, butchery, bloodbath, bloodletting, pogrom, genocide, ethnic cleansing, holocaust, Shoah, night of the long knives; *literary* slaying; *rare* battue, hecatomb.
2 (*informal*) *the match was an 8–0 massacre. See* ROUT *sense 2.*
▶ verb **1** *thousands were brutally massacred by the soldiers* **slaughter**, butcher, murder, kill, annihilate, exterminate, execute, liquidate, eliminate, destroy, decimate, kill off, wipe out, mow down, cut down, cut to pieces, put to the sword, put to death, send to the gas chambers; *literary* slay.
2 (*informal*) *they were absolutely massacred in the final. See* TROUNCE.

massage ▶ noun **rub-down**, rubbing, rub, kneading, palpation, manipulation, pummelling; *technical* shiatsu, reflexology, acupressure, hydromassage, Swedish massage, osteopathy, chiropractic treatment,

effleurage, tapotement, Rolfing.
▶ **verb 1** *he massaged her tired muscles* **rub**, rub down, knead, palpate, manipulate, pummel, work; *rare* embrocate.
2 *the statistics have been massaged* **alter**, tamper with, manipulate, doctor, falsify, juggle, fiddle with, tinker with, distort, change, rig, interfere with, misrepresent; *informal* fix, cook, fiddle.

massive ▶ **adjective** *these burial chambers were massive structures* **huge**, enormous, gigantic, very big, very large, great, giant, colossal, mammoth, vast, immense, tremendous, mighty, stupendous, monumental, epic, prodigious, mountainous, monstrous, titanic, towering, elephantine, king-sized, king-size, gargantuan, Herculean, Brobdingnagian, substantial, extensive, hefty, bulky, weighty, heavy, gross; *informal* mega, monster, whopping, whopping great, thumping, thumping great, humongous, jumbo, hulking, bumper, astronomical, astronomic; *Brit. informal* whacking, whacking great, ginormous.
OPPOSITE tiny.

mast ▶ **noun 1** *a ship's mast* spar, boom, yard, gaff, foremast, mainmast, topmast, mizzenmast, mizzen, royal mast; *archaic* stick.
2 *the mast on top of the building* **flagpole**, flagstaff, pole, post, rod, support, upright; aerial, transmitter, pylon.

master ▶ **noun 1** *he acceded to his master's wishes* **lord**, overlord, lord and master, ruler, sovereign, monarch, liege, liege lord, suzerain; overseer, superintendent, director, manager, controller, leader, governor, commander, padrone, captain, head, headman, boss, principal, employer, foreman; *informal* chief, top dog, honcho, head honcho, Big Chief, Big Daddy; *Brit. informal* gaffer, guv'nor; *N. Amer. informal* kahuna, sachem.
OPPOSITES servant; underling.
2 *he's a master of disguise | a chess master* **expert**, adept, genius, past master, maestro, virtuoso, professional, doyen, authority, pundit, master hand, prodigy, grandmaster, champion, star; *informal* ace, pro, wizard, whizz, wiz, hotshot; *Brit. informal* dab hand; *N. Amer. informal* maven, crackerjack.
OPPOSITES amateur, novice.
3 *the dog's pining for his master* **owner**, keeper.
4 *the master of the ship* **captain**, skipper, commander.
5 *the geography master* **teacher**, schoolteacher, schoolmaster, tutor, instructor, pedagogue; *rare* preceptor.
OPPOSITE pupil.
6 *they regarded him as their spiritual master* **guru**, teacher, spiritual leader, guide, mentor, torch-bearer, swami, Roshi, Maharishi.
OPPOSITES acolyte, disciple.
7 *you can make a copy from the master* **original**, archetype, prototype.
OPPOSITE copy.
▶ **verb 1** *I managed to master my fears* **overcome**, conquer, beat, quell, quash, suppress, control, repress, restrain, overpower, triumph over, subdue, vanquish, subjugate, prevail over, govern, curb, check, bridle, tame, defeat, get the better of, get a grip on, get over, gain mastery over; *informal* lick.
OPPOSITE give way to.
2 *it took him ages to master the technique* **learn**, learn thoroughly, become proficient in, know inside out, know backwards, become expert in, acquire, pick up, grasp, understand; *informal* get the hang of, get clued up about, get off by heart.
▶ **adjective 1** *a master craftsman* **expert**, adept, proficient, skilled, skilful, deft, dexterous, adroit, practised, experienced, masterly, accomplished, demon, brilliant; *informal* crack, ace, mean, wizard; *N. Amer. informal* crackerjack; *vulgar slang* shit-hot; *archaic or humorous* compleat.
2 *the master bedroom* **principal**, main, chief, leading, prime, predominant, foremost, great, grand, most important, biggest.
3 *his master plan* **controlling**, ruling, directing, commanding, dominating, overall.

masterful ▶ **adjective 1** *he looked self-assured and masterful* **commanding**, powerful, controlling, imposing, magisterial, lordly, authoritative, dominating, domineering, overbearing, overweening, imperious, bossy, peremptory, high-handed, arrogant, autocratic, dictatorial, tyrannical, despotic; *informal* pushy.
OPPOSITES weak, meek, wimpish.
2 *their masterful handling of the situation* **expert**, adept, clever, masterly; **skilful**, skilled, adroit, proficient, deft, dexterous, accomplished, polished, excellent, superb, superlative, consummate, first-rate, peerless, fine; *informal* crack, ace.
OPPOSITES incompetent, inept.

masterful or masterly?
Some writers use **masterful** only in the sense 'powerful and able to control others' (*a masterful tone of voice*) in order to maintain the distinction from **masterly**. In practice, however, the two words are used almost equally in this sense.

masterly ▶ **adjective** *a masterly analysis of the problem* **expert**, adept, clever, masterful; **skilful**, deft, adroit, skilled, dexterous, accomplished, polished, excellent, superb, superlative, consummate, first-rate, brilliant, intelligent, fine, talented, gifted; *informal* crack, ace.
OPPOSITES incompetent, inept.

masterly or masterful?
See MASTERFUL.

mastermind ▶ **verb** *he masterminded the whole campaign* **control**, **plan**, direct, be in charge of, run, conduct, organize, arrange, administer, regulate, supervise, superintend, preside over, orchestrate, stage-manage, engineer, manage, coordinate, conceive, devise, put together, forge, originate, initiate, think up, create, work out, dream up, frame, hatch, generate, come up with, have the bright idea of; *informal* be the brains behind.
▶ **noun** *the mastermind behind the project* **genius**, mind, intellect, author, architect, engineer, director, planner, organizer, deviser, originator, manager, prime mover, initiator, inventor; *informal* brain, brains, bright spark; *Brit. informal* brainbox.

masterpiece ▶ **noun** *'La Gioconda' is Leonardo's masterpiece* **finest work**, best work, masterwork, greatest creation; work of art, object of vertu; *Latin* magnum opus; *French* chef-d'œuvre, pièce de résistance, tour de force.
OPPOSITE hack work.

master stroke ▶ **noun** **act of genius**, coup, successful manoeuvre, triumph, victory, complete success; *French* coup de maître.

mastery ▶ **noun 1** *her mastery of the French language* **proficiency**, ability, capability; **knowledge**, understanding, comprehension, familiarity, command, grasp, grip.
2 *they played with tactical mastery* **skill**, skilfulness, expertise, dexterity, finesse, adroitness, virtuosity, prowess, deftness, proficiency; *informal* know-how.
3 *man's mastery over nature* **control**, superiority, domination, command, ascendancy, supremacy, pre-eminence, triumph, victory, the upper hand, the whip hand, rule, government, power, sway, authority, jurisdiction, dominion, sovereignty.

masticate ▶ **verb** *this lizard eats a wide variety of plants but does not masticate the food* **chew**, munch, champ, chomp, crunch, eat; ruminate, chew the cud; *technical* manducate, triturate; *rare* chumble.

masturbate ▶ **verb** practise self-abuse, indulge in self-stimulation; *formal* practise onanism; *informal* play with oneself, touch oneself; *vulgar slang* **wank**, jerk off, jack off, toss off, bring oneself off, beat one's/the meat, beat off, frig, whack off.

masturbation ▶ **noun** auto-eroticism, self-abuse, self-gratification, self-stimulation; *informal* playing with oneself; *formal* onanism; *vulgar slang* **wanking**, wank, handjob, frig, frigging, beating one's/the meat, hand relief.

mat ▶ **noun 1** *the wooden floor was covered by two mats* **rug**, runner, carpet, drugget; **doormat**, welcome mat, hearthrug, bath mat, rag rug, scatter rug; bearskin, sheepskin; *Indian* dhurrie, numdah; *Turkish & Persian* kilim; *Greek* flokati; *Azerbaijani* Soumak; *N. Amer.* floorcloth; *S. African* kaross.
2 *he put the casserole on a mat to protect the table* **table mat**, place mat; **coaster**, beer mat, drip mat, doily.
3 *a thick mat of hair* **mass**, tangle, knot, mop, thatch, shock, mane, cluster, mesh.
▶ **verb** *his hair was matted with blood* **tangle**, entangle, knot, ravel, snarl up.

match ▶ **noun 1** *a football match | a boxing match* **contest**, **competition**, game, tournament, tie, cup tie, event, fixture, trial, test, test match, meet, bout, fight, duel; quarter-final, semi-final, final, Cup Final; friendly, derby, local derby; play-off, replay, rematch; *Canadian & Scottish* playdown; *N. Amer.* split; *informal, dated* mill; *archaic* tourney.
2 *he was no match for the champion* **equal**, rival, equivalent, peer, counterpart; *rare* compeer.
3 *the vase was an exact match of the one she already owned* **replica**, copy, lookalike, double, twin, duplicate, equivalent, facsimile, like; mate, fellow, companion, counterpart, pair, complement; *informal* spitting image, spit and image, spit, dead spit, ringer, dead ringer.
4 *theirs is definitely a love match* **marriage**, betrothal, relationship, partnership, union, pairing, alliance, compact, contract, affiliation, combination.
5 *he would be a very suitable match for any of their daughters* **prospective husband/wife**, prospect, candidate; *informal* catch.
▶ **verb 1** *the curtains matched the duvet cover* **go with**, coordinate with, complement, harmonize with, blend with, tone with, team with, be the same as, be similar to, suit.
2 *these socks don't match* **be a pair**, be a set, be the same, go together.
3 *did their statements match?* **correspond**, be in agreement, tally, agree, match up, coincide, accord, conform, square, harmonize, be consonant, be compatible.
4 *they matched suitable applicants with firms having vacancies* **combine**,

M

match up, link, bring/put together, unite, marry, pair up, yoke, team, couple, pair, ally; *formal* conjoin.
5 *no one can match him at chess* **equal**, be equal to, be the equal of, be a match for, measure up to, compare with, parallel, be in the same league as, be in the same category as, be on a par with, touch, keep pace with, keep up with, emulate, rival, vie with, compete with, contend with; *informal* hold a candle to.

□ **match against/with** *Spain was matched against France* pit/set against, draw against, play off against.

□ **match up to** *the film didn't match up to my expectations* **come up to**, measure up to, meet with, be equal to, be as good as, satisfy, fulfil, answer to.

matching ▶ adjective *he picked up a cup and then identified the matching saucer | she was wearing a navy-blue blazer and matching skirt* **corresponding**, equivalent, parallel, analogous, coordinating, complementing, complementary, harmonizing, blending, toning, harmonious, the same, paired, twin, coupled, double, duplicate, identical, (all) of a piece, like, like (two) peas in a pod, alike, comparable, similar, correlative, congruent, tallying, agreeing, concordant, consonant.
OPPOSITES different, clashing.

matchless ▶ adjective *her sister's matchless beauty* **incomparable**, unrivalled, inimitable, beyond compare, unparalleled, unequalled, without equal, peerless, unmatched, beyond comparison, second to none, unsurpassed, unsurpassable, nonpareil, unique, consummate, perfect, rare, exquisite, transcendent, surpassing, superlative, supreme; *rare* unexampled.
OPPOSITES ordinary, run-of-the-mill.

matchmaker ▶ noun **marriage broker**, marriage bureau, dating agency; **go-between**, pandar, Pandarus; *Jewish* shadchan.

mate ▶ noun **1** (*Brit. informal*) *he's gone off to the pub with his mates* **friend**, companion, boon companion, comrade, intimate, familiar, confidant, alter ego, second self; playmate, classmate, schoolmate, workmate, team-mate, flatmate, room-mate; *informal* pal, chum, buddy, bosom pal, sidekick, cully, spar, crony, main man; *Brit. informal* china, mucker, butty, oppo; *N. Amer. informal* amigo, compadre, paisan, cohort; *S. African informal* gabba, homeboy; *N. English & Scottish informal* marrow, marrer; *archaic* compeer; *rare* fidus Achates.
2 (*Brit. informal*) *see you later, mate* **man**, my friend; *informal* pal, chum; *Brit. informal* cock, squire, matey; *Brit. informal, dated* old fellow, old bean, old boy, old chap, old fruit; *Welsh & Irish informal* boyo; *N. Amer. informal* bud, buster, amigo, Mac, bro, bubba, bo, jack, partner; *Austral./NZ informal* cobber, digger; *Indian informal* bhai, yaar; *S. African informal* jong, okie.
3 *she's finally found her ideal mate* **partner**, husband, wife, spouse, lover, live-in lover, amour, significant other, inamorato, inamorata, companion, helpmate, helpmeet, consort; *informal* POSSLQ (person of the opposite sex sharing living quarters), other half, better half, hubby, missus, missis, old man, old lady, old woman; *Brit. informal* dutch, trouble and strife.
4 *I can't find the mate to this sock* **match**, fellow, twin, companion, pair, one of a pair, other half, equivalent, counterpart.
5 *a plumber's mate* **assistant**, helper, apprentice, subordinate; collaborator, accomplice, aider and abetter; *informal* sidekick.
▶ verb **1** *pandas rarely mate in captivity* **breed**, couple; *formal* copulate.
2 *the cow was mated with a Charolais bull* **couple**, pair, join, bring together.
3 *people tend to* **mate with** *people from their own social class* **marry**, get married to; wed, pair up, form a relationship; *informal* shack up.

material *See centre pages for list of* **Fabrics**
▶ noun **1** *the decomposition of organic material* **matter**, substance, stuff, medium.
2 *the materials for a new building* **constituent**, raw material, element, component.
3 (**materials**) *cleaning materials* **things**, items, articles, stuff, necessaries; *Brit. informal* gubbins.
4 *samples of curtain material* **fabric**, cloth, stuff, textiles.
5 *she's collecting material for a magazine article* **information**, data, facts, facts and figures, statistics, evidence, subject matter, ideas, details, particulars; background, notes, documentation, documents, papers; *informal* info, gen, dope, low-down, dirt.
▶ adjective **1** *the material rather than the spiritual world* **physical**, corporeal, tangible, non-spiritual, mundane, worldly, earthly, temporal, concrete, real, solid, substantial, secular, lay; *rare* sublunary.
OPPOSITES spiritual, abstract.
2 *she was too fond of material pleasures* **sensual**, carnal, materialistic, corporal, fleshly, physical, bodily.
OPPOSITES aesthetic, intellectual.
3 *the storms caused material damage to the crops* **significant**, major, important, of consequence, consequential, momentous, weighty, vital, essential, key, meaningful.
OPPOSITES unimportant, insignificant, inconsequential.
4 *information that could be material to a murder inquiry* **relevant**, applicable, pertinent, apposite, germane; apropos, to the point, to the purpose; *Latin* ad rem; *rare* appurtenant.
OPPOSITES immaterial, irrelevant.

materialistic ▶ adjective *a materialistic society that worships consumer goods* **worldly**, consumerist, money-oriented, money-grubbing; capitalistic, bourgeois; acquisitive, greedy, grasping, avaricious, rapacious; *informal, derogatory* yuppie.
OPPOSITES spiritual, religious, intellectual; aesthetic.

materialize ▶ verb **1** *the forecast investment boom did not materialize* **happen**, occur, come about, take place, come into being, transpire, arise, be realized, take shape; *informal* come off, shape up; *archaic* come to pass; *rare* eventuate.
2 *Harry suddenly materialized at the kitchen door* **appear**, turn up, arrive, make/put in an appearance, present oneself/itself, come into view/sight, emerge, surface, loom, become visible, show oneself/itself, reveal oneself/itself, show one's face, come to light, pop up; *informal* show up, fetch up, pitch up, blow in.
OPPOSITE disappear.

materially ▶ adverb *this will materially affect our plans* **significantly**, greatly, much, very much, to a great extent, considerably, substantially, a great deal, appreciably, markedly, seriously, gravely, essentially, fundamentally.
OPPOSITE negligibly.

maternal ▶ adjective **1** *the baby aroused her maternal instincts* **motherly**, maternalistic; protective, caring, nurturing, loving, devoted, affectionate, fond, warm, tender, gentle, kind, kindly, comforting, compassionate.
2 *his maternal grandparents* **on one's mother's side**, on the distaff side.
OPPOSITE paternal.

maternity ▶ noun **motherhood**, parenthood; motherliness.

mathematical ▶ adjective **1** arithmetical, arithmetic, numerical, statistical, algebraic, geometric, geometrical, trigonometric, trigonometrical, topological.
2 *he arranged everything with mathematical precision* **rigorous**, meticulous, scrupulous, punctilious, scientific, strict, precise, exact, accurate, pinpoint, correct, careful, unerring.
OPPOSITES vague, imprecise.

mathematics ▶ plural noun. *See centre pages for list of branches of* **Mathematics**

mating ▶ noun *after mating, the female butterfly lays between 50 and 1000 eggs* **copulation**, copulating, coupling, sexual intercourse, intercourse, sex, procreation; pairing, breeding, union; *formal* coitus, coition.
▶ adjective *a mating pair of mute swans* **sexually active**, breeding.

matrimonial ▶ adjective *the matrimonial home* **marital**, conjugal, connubial, married, wedded; shared, jointly owned; *Law* spousal.

matrimony ▶ noun (*formal*) *the sacrament of holy matrimony* **marriage**, wedlock, union; bridal vows, nuptials.
OPPOSITE divorce.

matted ▶ adjective *his greasy, matted hair* **tangled**, tangly, entangled, knotted, knotty, tousled, dishevelled, uncombed, unkempt, felted, ratty, greasy, dirty; *black English* natty.
OPPOSITES straight; neat.

matter ▶ noun **1** *decaying vegetable matter* **material**, substance, stuff, medium.
2 *let's get to the heart of the matter* **affair**, business, proceeding, situation, circumstance, event, happening, occurrence, incident, episode, occasion, experience, thing; **subject**, topic, issue, question, point, point at issue, item, case, concern, theme.
3 *it is of little matter now* **importance**, consequence, significance, note, import, moment, weight, interest.
4 (**the matter**) *is anything the matter? | what's the matter?* **problem**, trouble, difficulty, upset, distress, worry, bother, complication.
5 *the matter of the sermon* **content**, subject matter, text, argument, substance, thesis, sense, purport, gist, pith, essentials, burden.
6 *an infected wound full of matter* **pus**, suppuration, purulence, discharge, secretion; *rare* sanies.

□ **as a matter of fact actually**, in actual fact, in fact, in point of fact, as it happens, really, believe it or not, in reality, in truth, to tell the truth, truly.

□ **no matter it doesn't matter**, it makes no difference/odds, it's unimportant, never mind, don't apologize, don't worry about it, don't mention it.

▶ verb **1** *it doesn't matter what you wear* **make any difference**, make a difference, be important, be of importance, be of consequence, signify, be of significance, be relevant, be of account, carry weight, count; *informal* cut any ice.
2 *she was trying to make an impression on the people who mattered* **be influential**, have influence, be important.

WORD LINKS
science of matter **physics**

matter-of-fact ▶ adjective **unemotional**, practical, down-to-earth, sensible, realistic, rational, sober, unsentimental, pragmatic, businesslike, commonsensical, level-headed, hard-headed, no-nonsense, factual, literal, straightforward, plain, unembellished, unvarnished, unadorned, prosaic, mundane, unimaginative, uncreative, deadpan, flat,

dull, dry, pedestrian, lifeless, humdrum.
OPPOSITE airy-fairy.

mature ▶ adjective **1** *she is now a mature woman* **adult**, grown-up, grown, fully grown, full-grown, of age, fully developed, fully fledged, in one's prime, in full bloom, nubile.
OPPOSITES immature, growing, adolescent.
2 *he's very mature for his age* **sensible**, responsible, adult, level-headed, reliable, dependable; discriminating, shrewd, practical, wise, sagacious, experienced, sophisticated.
OPPOSITES immature, childish.
3 *mature Cheddar cheese* **ripe**, ripened, mellow, ready, seasoned, full-flavoured.
OPPOSITES fresh, unripe.
4 *on mature reflection, he decided not to go* **careful**, thorough, deep, considered, methodical.
OPPOSITES impulsive, unthinking.
▶ verb **1** *kittens mature when they are about a year old* **be fully grown**, be full-grown, be fully developed, develop fully, come of age, become adult, reach adulthood, reach maturity.
2 *he has matured since he left home* **become more sensible/responsible/adult**, grow up; bloom, blossom.
3 *leave the cheese to mature* **ripen**, grow ripe, become ripe, mellow, become mellow, age.
4 *their friendship did not have time to mature* **develop**, grow, evolve, bloom, blossom, flourish, thrive, come to fruition.

maturity ▶ noun **1** *her progress from childhood to maturity* **adulthood**, full growth, majority, coming-of-age, matureness, manhood/womanhood, puberty, pubescence.
OPPOSITES childhood, youth.
2 *he displayed a maturity beyond his years* **sense of responsibility**, sense, level-headedness, responsibleness, matureness, wisdom, adultness; discrimination, shrewdness, practicality, sagacity, sensibleness, sophistication, experience.
OPPOSITE childishness.
3 *many fruits change colour when they reach maturity* **ripeness**, matureness, mellowness.

maudlin ▶ adjective **1** *a bout of maudlin self-pity* **sentimental**, over-sentimental, emotional, overemotional, tearful, lachrymose; *informal* weepy.
OPPOSITES austere, undemonstrative.
2 *a maudlin Irish ballad* **mawkish**, sentimental, over-sentimental, cloying, sickly, saccharine, sugary, syrupy, sickening, nauseating, banal, trite; *Brit.* twee; *informal* mushy, slushy, sloppy, schmaltzy, weepy, cutesy, lovey-dovey, gooey, drippy, sloshy, soupy, treacly, cheesy, corny, icky, sick-making, toe-curling; *Brit. informal* soppy; *N. Amer. informal* cornball, sappy, hokey, three-hankie.
OPPOSITES understated, dry, prosaic.

maul ▶ verb **1** *he had been mauled by a lion* **savage**, attack, tear to pieces, lacerate, claw, mutilate, mangle, scratch.
2 *she hated being mauled by men* **molest**, feel, fondle; handle roughly, handle clumsily, manhandle; *informal* **grope**, paw, touch up, goose.
3 *his book was mauled by the critics* **criticize**, denigrate, attack, censure, condemn, find fault with, give a bad press to, pillory, lambaste, flay, savage; *informal* knock, slam, pan, bash, take/pull to pieces, take apart, crucify, hammer, lay into, roast, skewer; *Brit. informal* slate, rubbish, slag off; *N. Amer. informal* pummel, cut up; *Austral./NZ informal* bag, monster; *rare* excoriate.

maunder ▶ verb **1** *he maundered on about his problems* **ramble**, prattle, prate, blather, blether, blither, drivel, rattle, chatter, jabber, gabble, babble; *Scottish & Irish* slabber; *informal* gab, yak, yackety-yak, yabber, yatter; *Brit. informal* rabbit, witter, waffle, natter, chunter; *archaic* twaddle, clack.
2 *she maundered across the road* **wander**, drift, meander, amble, dawdle, potter, straggle; *Brit. informal* mooch.
OPPOSITE march.

mausoleum ▶ noun **tomb**, sepulchre, crypt, vault, charnel house, burial chamber, catacomb, undercroft.

maverick ▶ noun *he was too much of a maverick to fit into any formal organization* **individualist**, nonconformist, free spirit, unorthodox person, unconventional person, original, trendsetter, bohemian, eccentric, outsider; rebel, dissenter, dissident.
OPPOSITE conformist.

maw ▶ noun *a gigantic wolfhound with a fearful, gaping maw* **mouth**, jaws, muzzle, throat, gullet; *informal* trap, chops, kisser; *Brit. informal* gob.

mawkish ▶ adjective *a long and mawkish poem* **sentimental**, over-sentimental, overemotional, cloying, sickly, saccharine, sugary, syrupy, sickening, nauseating, maudlin, lachrymose, banal, trite; *Brit.* twee; *informal* mushy, slushy, sloppy, schmaltzy, weepy, cutesy, lovey-dovey, gooey, drippy, sloshy, soupy, treacly, cheesy, corny, icky, sick-making, toe-curling; *Brit. informal* soppy; *N. Amer. informal* cornball, sappy, hokey, three-hankie.
OPPOSITES cool, dry.

maxim ▶ noun *'You are what you eat' is a favourite maxim* **saying**, adage, aphorism, proverb, motto, saw, axiom, dictum, precept, epigram; catchphrase, slogan, byword, watchword; truism, platitude, cliché; *French* bon mot; *rare* apophthegm.

maximum ▶ adjective *the vehicle's maximum speed* **greatest**, highest, biggest, largest, top, topmost, most, utmost, supreme, maximal, paramount, extreme.
OPPOSITE minimum.
▶ noun *production levels are near their maximum* **upper limit**, limit, utmost, uttermost, greatest, most, extreme, extremity, peak, height, ceiling, top, summit, pinnacle, crest, apex, vertex, apogee, acme, zenith.

May ▶ noun
WORD LINKS
birthstone **emerald**

maybe ▶ adverb **perhaps**, possibly, conceivably, it could be (that), it is possible (that), for all one knows; *N. English* happen; *literary* peradventure, perchance, mayhap, haply; *rare* percase.

mayhem ▶ noun *furious TV bosses watched stunned as the band created mayhem onstage* **chaos**, disorder, confusion, havoc, bedlam, pandemonium, tumult, uproar, turmoil, madness, madhouse, hullabaloo, all hell broken loose, wild disarray, disorganization, maelstrom, trouble, disturbance, commotion, riot, anarchy, destruction, violence.

maze ▶ noun **1** *a maze in the castle grounds* **labyrinth**, network of paths.
2 *a maze of corridors | a maze of petty regulations* **complex network**, labyrinth, web, tangle, warren, mesh, jungle, snarl, imbroglio.

meadow ▶ noun **field**, pasture, paddock, water meadow, pastureland, grassland; *literary* lea, mead; *Irish & Canadian* bawn.

meagre ▶ adjective **1** *they were forced to supplement their meagre earnings* **inadequate**, scanty, scant, paltry, limited, restricted, modest, insufficient, sparse, spare, deficient, negligible, insubstantial, skimpy, short, little, lean, small, slight, slender, poor, miserable, pitiful, puny, miserly, niggardly, beggarly; *informal* measly, stingy, pathetic, piddling; *rare* exiguous.
OPPOSITE abundant.
2 *a tall, meagre man* **thin**, thin as a rake, lean, skinny, spare, scrawny, scraggy, gangling, gangly, spindly, stringy, lanky, reedy, bony, raw-boned, gaunt, underweight, emaciated, skeletal, starved, underfed, undernourished, attenuated, wraithlike, cadaverous, wasted, anorexic.
OPPOSITE fat.

CHOOSE THE RIGHT WORD

meagre, sparse, scanty

All these words are used when there is less of something than there could or should be.

- **Meagre** is generally used of necessities such as food, money, or something else which is provided or available for people. It suggests that there is not enough (*these men were unable to save out of their meagre earnings*) or that what there is is of poor quality (*prisoners queue for their meagre rations of thin soup*).
- **Sparse** means 'thinly dispersed'—that is, small or few in relation to the area covered or the space to be filled (*a sparse and scattered population*) and therefore, by extension, 'in short supply' (*it was a sparse audience | for the first half of the nineteenth century the evidence is sparse*).
- **Scanty** refers particularly to the smallness of the thing that is inadequate (*there are only scanty remains of any of the great palaces*) and is often used of skimpy or revealing clothing (*the ridiculously scanty nightdress threatened to fall off her shoulders altogether*).

meagreness ▶ noun **inadequacy**, scantiness, paucity, paltriness, dearth, limitedness, restrictedness, insufficiency, sparseness, spareness, scarcity, deficiency, slightness, skimpiness, leanness, poorness, poverty, pitifulness, miserliness, puniness, beggarliness; *informal* measliness, stinginess; *rare* exiguity.
OPPOSITE abundance.

meal *See centre pages for list of* **Meals**
▶ noun **repast**, snack; something to eat; *informal* spread, blowout, bite, bite to eat, nosh, feed; *Brit. informal* nosh-up, tuck-in; *N. Amer. informal* square; *Indian* khana; *formal* collation, refection.
WORD LINKS
relating to meals **prandial**

mean[1] ▶ verb **1** *the flashing lights mean that the road is blocked* **signify**, convey, denote, designate, indicate, connote, show, express, spell out, stand for, represent, symbolize, imply, purport, suggest, allude to, intimate, hint at, insinuate, drive at, refer to; *informal* get at; *literary* betoken.
2 *she didn't mean to break it* **intend**, aim, plan, design, have in mind, have

in view, contemplate, think of, purpose, propose, have plans, set out, aspire, desire, want, wish, expect.
3 *he was hit by a bullet meant for a soldier* **destine**, predestine, fate, preordain, ordain; intend, design.
4 *the closures will mean a rise in unemployment* **entail**, involve, necessitate, lead to, result in, give rise to, bring about, cause, engender, produce, effect.
5 *this means a lot to me* **matter**, have importance, have significance, be important, be significant; have an input on.
6 *a red sky in the morning usually means rain* **presage**, portend, foretell, augur, promise, foreshadow, herald, signal, bode; *rare* betoken, foretoken, forebode, adumbrate.

mean[2] ▶ adjective **1** *he's too mean to leave a tip* **miserly**, niggardly, close-fisted, parsimonious, penny-pinching, cheese-paring, ungenerous, penurious, illiberal, close, grasping, greedy, avaricious, acquisitive, Scrooge-like; *Austral./NZ & Scottish* miserable; *informal* tight-fisted, stingy, tight, mingy, money-grubbing, skinflinty; *N. Amer. informal* cheap, grabby; *Austral. informal* hungry; *Brit. vulgar slang* tight-arse, tight-arsed, tight as a duck's arse; *archaic* near, niggard.
OPPOSITES generous, extravagant, munificent.
2 *why are you being so mean to me? | that was a mean trick* **unkind**, **nasty**, spiteful, foul, malicious, malevolent, despicable, contemptible, obnoxious, vile, odious, loathsome, disagreeable, unpleasant, unfriendly, uncharitable, shabby, unfair, callous, cruel, vicious, base, low; *informal* horrible, horrid, hateful, rotten, low-down; *Brit. informal* beastly, bitchy, catty; *vulgar slang* shitty.
OPPOSITE kind.
3 *the truth was obvious to even the meanest intelligence* **inferior**, poor, limited, restricted, meagre.
4 *her flat was mean and cold* **squalid**, shabby, dilapidated, sordid, seedy, slummy, sleazy, insalubrious, poor, sorry, wretched, dismal, dingy, miserable, mangy, broken-down, run down, down at heel; *informal* scruffy, scuzzy, crummy, grungy, ratty, tacky; *Brit. informal* grotty.
OPPOSITES luxurious, palatial.
5 *a man of mean birth* **lowly**, humble, ordinary, low, low-born, lower-class, modest, common, base, proletarian, plebeian, obscure, undistinguished, ignoble; *archaic* baseborn.
OPPOSITE noble.
6 (*informal*) *he's a mean cook* **excellent**, marvellous, magnificent, superb, fine, wonderful, outstanding, exceptional, formidable, first-class, first-rate, virtuoso, skilful, masterful, masterly; *informal* great, terrific, tremendous, super, smashing, amazing, fantastic, sensational, fabulous, fab, ace, crack, A1, awesome, magic, bad, wicked, out of this world; *Brit. informal* brilliant, brill; *N. Amer. informal* neat, badass, boss; *Austral. informal* bonzer; *Brit. informal, dated* wizard, spiffing, ripping, topping, champion, capital, top-hole; *N. Amer. informal, dated* swell, keen; *vulgar slang* shit-hot.
OPPOSITES bad, awful, terrible, dreadful.

mean[3] ▶ noun *trying to find a mean between frankness and rudeness* **middle course**, middle way, mid point, central point, middle, happy medium, golden mean, compromise, balance, median, norm, average.
▶ adjective *the mean temperature* **average**, median, middle, halfway, centre, central, intermediate, medial, medium, normal, standard, middling.

meander ▶ verb **1** *the river meandered gently through the meadow* **zigzag**, wind, twist, turn, curve, curl, bend, snake.
2 *we meandered along the path* **stroll**, saunter, amble, wander, roam, ramble, rove, drift, maunder, stray, straggle; *Scottish & Irish* stravaig; *Irish* streel; *informal* mosey, tootle; *rare* vagabond.
3 *she meandered on about the difficulties* **ramble**, **prattle**, maunder, prate, blather, blether, blither, drivel, chatter, rattle, drift; *Brit. informal* witter, waffle, rabbit, natter.
▶ noun **1** *the river flows in sweeping meanders* **bend**, loop, curve, twist, turn, turning, coil, zigzag, oxbow, convolution; *rare* anfractuosity, flexuosity.
2 *a leisurely meander* **wander**, ramble, stroll, saunter, amble; *informal* mosey, tootle.

meandering ▶ adjective **1** *a meandering stream* **winding**, windy, zigzag, zigzagging, twisting, turning, curving, serpentine, sinuous, snaking, snaky, twisty, tortuous; *rare* anfractuous, flexuous, meandrous.
OPPOSITE straight.
2 *meandering reminiscences* **rambling**, circuitous, roundabout, digressive, discursive, indirect, diffuse, tortuous, convoluted; *rare* anfractuous.
OPPOSITE succinct.

meaning ▶ noun **1** *the poem has a hidden meaning | I didn't understand the meaning of his remark* **significance**, sense, signification, import, thrust, drift, gist, implication, tenor, message, essence, substance, purport, intention.
2 *the word has several different meanings* **definition**, sense, explanation, denotation, connotation, interpretation, elucidation, explication.
3 *my life has no meaning* **value**, validity, worth, consequence, account, use, usefulness, significance, point.
4 *his smile was full of meaning* **expressiveness**, significance, eloquence, implications, intimations, insinuations.
▶ adjective *she gave him a meaning look* **meaningful**, significant, pointed, eloquent, expressive, pregnant, speaking, telltale, revealing, suggestive.
OPPOSITE vacant.

WORD LINKS
relating to meaning **semantic**
study of meaning **semantics**

meaningful ▶ adjective **1** *a meaningful remark* **significant**, relevant, important, consequential, material, telling, pithy, weighty, valid, worthwhile, purposeful.
OPPOSITE inconsequential.
2 *a meaningful relationship* **sincere**, deep, serious, in earnest, significant, important.
3 *a meaningful glance* **expressive**, eloquent, pointed, significant, meaning; deep, pregnant, speaking, telltale, revealing, suggestive.
OPPOSITE meaningless.

meaningless ▶ adjective **1** *a meaningless statement* **unintelligible**, incomprehensible, incoherent, illogical, senseless, unmeaning, foolish, silly, absurd, fatuous, ridiculous, nonsensical, idle.
OPPOSITE meaningful.
2 *she felt her life was meaningless* **futile**, pointless, aimless, empty, hollow, vain, purposeless, motiveless, valueless, useless, of no use, worthless, trivial, trifling, vacuous, unimportant, insignificant, inconsequential, insubstantial, nugatory, fruitless, profitless, barren, unproductive, unprofitable.
OPPOSITE worthwhile.

meanness ▶ noun **1** *his careful attitude towards money bordered on meanness* **miserliness**, niggardliness, close-fistedness, parsimony, parsimoniousness, penny-pinching, cheese-paring, penury, illiberality, greed, avarice, acquisitiveness; *informal* stinginess, tight-fistedness, tightness, minginess; *N. Amer.* cheapness; *archaic* nearness.
OPPOSITE generosity.
2 *the filth and meanness of the place* **squalor**, squalidness, shabbiness, dilapidation, sordidness, seediness, sleaziness, insalubriousness, wretchedness, dismalness, dinginess, poverty; *informal* scruffiness, scuzziness, crumminess, grunginess, tackiness; *Brit. informal* grottiness.
3 *his meanness of temper* **nastiness**, mean-spiritedness, spitefulness, disagreeableness, unpleasantness, unkindness.

means ▶ plural noun **1** *the drugs were obtained by illegal means | modern means of communication such as television* **method**, way, manner, mode, measure, fashion, process, procedure, technique, expedient, agency, medium, instrument, mechanism, channel, vehicle, avenue, course.
2 *she doesn't have the means to support herself* **money**, resources, capital, income, finance, funds, cash, the wherewithal, assets; *informal* dough, bread, dibs, moolah, shekels, gelt, loot, oof, scratch, splosh; *Brit. informal* dosh, brass, lolly, spondulicks, wonga, ackers; *N. Amer. informal* dineros, jack, mazuma; *Austral./NZ informal* Oscar.
3 *a man of means* **wealth**, riches, affluence, substance, fortune, property, money, capital.
□ **by all means** *of course*, certainly, definitely, surely, absolutely, naturally, with pleasure, assuredly; *N. Amer. informal* sure thing.
□ **by means of** *the load was raised by means of a crane* **using**, utilizing, employing, through, with the help of, with the aid of, as a result of, by dint of, by way of, by virtue of, via.
□ **by no means** *the result is by no means certain* **not at all**, in no way, not in the least, not in the slightest, not the least bit, not by a long shot, certainly not, absolutely not, definitely not, on no account, under no circumstances; *Brit.* not by a long chalk; *informal* no way.

meantime ▶ adverb. *See* MEANWHILE.

meanwhile ▶ adverb **1** *something will turn up—meanwhile we shall keep an eye on him* **for now**, for the moment, for the present, for the time being, meantime, in the meantime, in the intervening period, in the interim, in the interval, in the meanwhile, the while, temporarily; *Latin* pro tem, ad interim; *French* en attendant.
2 *Moore's old club, meanwhile, are trying to persuade him to rejoin them* **at the same time**, simultaneously, concurrently, the while.

measurable ▶ adjective **1** *physically measurable aspects of human behaviour* **quantifiable**, assessable, gaugeable, appraisable, computable, fathomable, resolvable.
2 *a measurable improvement* **appreciable**, noticeable, significant, visible, tangible, perceptible, obvious, striking, material, moderate, reasonable.
OPPOSITE negligible.

measure ▶ verb **1** *they measured the length and width of the room* **take the measurements of**, calculate, compute, estimate, count, meter, quantify, weigh, size, evaluate, rate, assess, appraise, gauge, plumb, measure out, determine, judge, survey.
OPPOSITES guess, estimate.
2 *I had better measure my words* **choose carefully**, select with care, consider, think carefully about, plan, calculate.
3 *she did not need to measure herself against some ideal* **compare with**,

contrast with, put into competition with; pit, set, match, test, judge.
4 (archaic) *we must measure twenty miles today* **travel**, cover, put behind one, get under one's belt.

□ **measure something off** *the assistant measured off the required length* **mark off**, mark the boundaries/limits of, measure out, demarcate, delimit, delineate, outline, describe, define, stake out.

□ **measure something out** *measure out and mix the ingredients* **pour out**, dole out, deal out; **dispense**, administer, issue.

□ **measure up** *he was sacked because he didn't measure up* **come up to standard**, achieve the required standard, fulfil expectations, fit/fill the bill, pass muster, do well; be capable, be acceptable, be satisfactory, be adequate, be suitable; *informal* come up to scratch, make the grade, cut the mustard, be up to snuff.
OPPOSITE fall short.

□ **measure something up 1** *I must measure up the windows for some new curtains* **survey**, quantify, take the measurements of, weigh, appraise, determine; estimate, count, meter.
2 *the two men shook hands and silently measured each other up* **evaluate**, rate, assess, appraise, judge, adjudge, weigh up, size up, survey.

□ **measure up to** *we didn't measure up to the standards they set* **achieve**, meet, come up to, equal, be equal to, match, rival, vie with, bear comparison with, be on a level with, serve, satisfy, fulfil, comply with.
OPPOSITE fall short of.

▶ **noun 1** *cost-cutting measures* **action**, act, course, course of action, deed, proceeding, procedure, step, means, expedient; manoeuvre, initiative, programme, operation, control, legal action.
2 *the Senate passed the measure* **statute**, act, bill, law, legislation.
3 *the original dimensions were in imperial measure, 15 inches on each side* **system**, **standard**, units, scale.
4 *use a measure to check the size* **ruler**, **tape measure**, rule, gauge, meter, scale, level, yardstick.
5 *a measure of egg white* **portion**, **quantity**, amount, quota, ration, allowance, allocation.
6 *the states retain a measure of independence* **certain amount**, amount, degree, quantity.
7 *sales are the measure of the company's success* **yardstick**, test, standard, norm, barometer, touchstone, litmus test, criterion, benchmark.
8 *poetic measure* **metre**, cadence, rhythm, foot.
9 (archaic) *now tread we a measure* **dance**, step, caper, hop.

□ **beyond measure** *it irritates him beyond measure that she is nearly always right* **immensely**, extremely, vastly, greatly, excessively, immeasurably, incalculably, infinitely, limitlessly, boundlessly, inexhaustibly.

□ **for good measure** *she added a couple of chilli peppers for good measure* **as a bonus**, as an extra, into the bargain, to boot, in addition, besides, as well.

□ **get/have the measure of** *she wants to get the measure of Kate before they meet at the Olympics* **evaluate**, assess, gauge, judge, weigh up; understand, fathom, read, be wise to, not be deceived by, see through; *informal* have someone's number, not fall for, know someone's (little) game.

measured ▶ **adjective 1** *the measured tread of the warder in the corridor* **regular**, steady, even, uniform, rhythmic, rhythmical, unfaltering, constant, sustained, slow, dignified, resolute, stately, sedate, leisurely, unhurried, firm, deliberate, ponderous.
OPPOSITE erratic.
2 *he began to speak in carefully measured tones* **guarded**, studied, thoughtful, careful, carefully chosen, selected with care, well thought out, calculated, planned, considered, judicious, restrained, deliberate, reasoned.
OPPOSITES thoughtless, careless.

measureless ▶ **adjective** *Otto turned out to have measureless charm* **boundless**, limitless, without limit, unlimited, unbounded, untold, immense, vast, great, endless, unending, never-ending, without end, inexhaustible, infinite, interminable, unceasing, everlasting, illimitable, immeasurable, incalculable.
OPPOSITES limited, restricted.

measurement *See centre pages for lists of* **Measurement Units**
▶ **noun 1** *measurement of the effect is difficult* **quantification**, quantifying, computation, calculation, mensuration; estimation, evaluation, assessment, appraisal, gauging; weighing, sizing.
2 *all measurements are given in metric form | he wrote down my measurements* **size**, dimension, proportions, magnitude, amplitude; mass, bulk, volume, capacity, extent, expanse; **value**, amount, quantity, area, length, height, depth, weight, width, range, acreage, footage, mileage, tonnage.

WORD LINKS
related suffixes **-metry** (e.g. ***telemetry, calorimetry***), **-metric** (e.g. ***volumetric, geometric***)
study of measurement **metrology**

meat *See centre pages for lists of* **Meat** **Sausages**
▶ **noun 1 flesh**, muscle.
2 *meat and drink* **food**, nourishment, sustenance, provisions, rations, fare, foodstuff(s), nutriment, daily bread, feed; *informal* grub, eats, chow, nosh, scoff; *formal* comestibles, provender; *archaic* victuals, viands, commons; *rare* aliment.
3 *the meat of the matter* **substance**, pith, marrow, heart, kernel, core, nucleus, nub; **essence**, essentials, point, gist, fundamentals, basics; *informal* nitty-gritty, nuts and bolts.

WORD LINKS
meat-eating **carnivorous**

meaty ▶ **adjective 1** *a tall, meaty young man* **beefy**, fleshy, brawny, burly, muscular, muscly, powerful, sturdy, rugged, husky, strapping, well built, solidly built, stout, thickset.
OPPOSITES weedy, feeble.
2 *the meaty character roles she'd love to play* **full of interest**, interesting, three-dimensional, stimulating, giving food for thought; **substantial**, pithy, satisfying, meaningful, profound, deep, involved, significant.
OPPOSITES insubstantial, one-dimensional.

mechanic ▶ **noun technician**, **engineer**, artificer, repairman, serviceman, greaser; *informal* mech, grease monkey.

mechanical ▶ **adjective 1** *the invention of the mechanical clock in the fourteenth century* **mechanized**, machine-driven, automated, automatic, motor-driven, power-driven, self-propelled.
OPPOSITE manual.
2 *she stopped the mechanical brushing of her hair* **automatic**, machine-like, unthinking, unemotional, unconscious, involuntary, instinctive, routine, matter-of-fact, habitual, inattentive; unfeeling, impersonal, inhuman, lifeless, soulless, uninspired, unanimated, casual; perfunctory, cursory, careless, unimaginative, negligent.
OPPOSITES conscious, emotional, careful.

mechanism ▶ **noun 1** *an electrical mechanism for long-distance signalling* **apparatus**, machine, appliance, tool, device, implement, utensil, instrument, contraption, contrivance, gadget, tackle, structure, system; *informal* gizmo.
2 *the train's safety mechanism had jammed* **machinery**, workings, works, movement, motion, action, gear, gears, wheels, components, motor, engine, power source; *informal* innards, guts.
3 *a formal mechanism for citizens to lodge complaints* **procedure**, process, system, operation, method, technique, workings, means, medium, agency, channel, channels, vehicle, structure.

mechanize ▶ **verb** *agriculture started to become mechanized* **automate**, industrialize, motorize, computerize, equip with machines, tool.

medal ▶ **noun** *he won his first gold medal in 1998* **honour**, **decoration**, ribbon, star, order, badge, pin, laurel, wreath, palm, colours, insignia, plaque, award, trophy; *military slang* fruit salad; *Brit. informal* gong.

meddle ▶ **verb 1** *I don't want him meddling in our affairs* **interfere**, butt in, intrude, intervene, interlope, pry, poke, nose, busybody, interpose, obtrude, thrust; *informal* stick one's nose in, horn in, muscle in, snoop, put/stick one's oar in, mess with; *N. Amer. informal* kibitz; *archaic* intermeddle.
OPPOSITE mind one's own business.
2 *you have no right to come in here meddling with my things* **fiddle**, interfere, tamper, tinker, monkey; touch/handle without permission, finger; *informal* dick around; *Brit. informal* muck about/around.
OPPOSITE leave alone.

meddlesome ▶ **adjective** *a growing demand for more efficient and less meddlesome government* **interfering**, meddling, intrusive, prying, inquisitive, officious, importunate; *informal* snooping, nosy; *archaic* pragmatic, intermeddling; *rare* obtrusive, busy.

mediate ▶ **verb 1** *Austria tried to mediate between the belligerents* **arbitrate**, conciliate, moderate, umpire, referee, act as peacemaker, reconcile differences, restore harmony, make peace, bring to terms, liaise; intervene, step in, intercede, act as an intermediary, interpose; *archaic* temporize.
2 *a tribunal was set up to mediate disputes* **resolve**, settle, arbitrate in, umpire, reconcile, mend, clear up, patch up.
3 *he had attempted to mediate a solution to the conflict* **negotiate**, bring about, effect, make happen; *rare* effectuate.
4 *the important ministry of mediating the power of the word* **convey**, transmit, communicate, put across/over, impart, pass on, hand on, relate, reveal.

mediation ▶ **noun** *mediation between victims and offenders* **conciliation**, arbitration, reconciliation, intervention, intercession, interposition, good offices; negotiation, shuttle diplomacy; *archaic* temporization.

mediator ▶ **noun** *a mediator in a dispute over teachers' pay* **arbitrator**, arbiter, negotiator, conciliator, go-between, middleman, intermediary, moderator, intervenor, interceder, intercessor, reconciler, broker, honest broker, liaison officer, peacemaker, umpire, referee, adjudicator, judge.

medicinal ▶ **adjective** *medicinal herbs* **curative**, healing, curing, remedial, therapeutic, restorative, corrective, health-giving; medical, healthy; *rare* sanative, analeptic, iatric.

medicine *See centre pages for lists of* **Laxatives** *, types and forms of* **Medication** *, branches of* **Medicine** *, and* **Therapies**
▶ **noun 1** *she poured out a dose of medicine for her mother* **medication**, medicament, remedy, cure, nostrum, patent medicine, quack remedy,

M

panacea, cure-all, placebo, drug, prescription, dose, treatment; *archaic* physic; *rare* medicinal.
2 *the remarkable achievements of modern medicine* **medical science**, practice of medicine, healing, therapeutics, therapy, treatment, healing art.
□ **give someone a dose/taste of their own medicine get even (with)**, get back at, get, let someone see how it feels, have/get/take one's revenge (on), be revenged (on), revenge oneself (on), hit back (at); even the score (with), settle a/the score, settle accounts (with), get one's own back (on), give as good as one gets, play tit for tat (with), pay someone back, repay, reciprocate, retaliate (against), take reprisals (against), exact retribution (on); *informal* give someone their comeuppance.
□ **take one's medicine accept one's punishment**, take the consequences of one's actions; *informal* take the rap, take it on the chin.

WORD LINKS

relating to medicines	**pharmaceutical**
related prefix	**iatro- (e.g.** ***iatrogenic, iatrochemistry*****)**
seller of medicines	**pharmacist;** *Brit.* **chemist;** *N. Amer.* **druggist**
shop selling medicines	**pharmacy;** *Brit.* **chemist's;** *N. Amer.* **drugstore**

medieval ▸ adjective **1 of the Middle Ages**, Middle Age, of the Dark Ages, Dark-Age, 11th to 14th century, 6th to 14th century, Gothic, early.
OPPOSITE modern.
2 (*informal*) *the plumbing's a bit medieval, I'm afraid* **primitive**, antiquated, prehistoric, archaic, antique, antediluvian, old-fashioned, out of date, outdated, outmoded, anachronistic, passé, obsolescent, obsolete; *informal* out of the ark; *N. Amer. informal* horse-and-buggy, mossy, clunky.
OPPOSITE modern.

mediocre ▸ adjective *the difference between a world record and a mediocre performance* **ordinary**, common, commonplace, indifferent, average, middle-of-the-road, middling, medium, moderate, everyday, workaday, tolerable, passable, adequate, fair; **inferior**, second-rate, uninspired, undistinguished, unexceptional, unexciting, unremarkable, run-of-the-mill, not very good, pedestrian, prosaic, lacklustre, forgettable, amateur, amateurish; *informal* OK, so-so, bog-standard, fair-to-middling, (plain) vanilla, nothing to write home about, no great shakes, not so hot, not up to much; *NZ informal* half-pie.
OPPOSITES exceptional, excellent.

mediocrity ▸ noun **1** *the mediocrity of her work* **ordinariness**, commonplaceness, lack of inspiration, passableness, adequacy, indifference; **inferiority**, amateurism, amateurishness.
OPPOSITE excellence.
2 *a brilliant woman surrounded by mediocrities* **nonentity**, nobody, nothing, lightweight, cipher, second-rater, amateur; *informal* no-hoper, non-starter.
OPPOSITE star.

meditate ▸ verb *he went off to meditate on the idea* **contemplate**, think about, consider, ponder, cogitate, muse; revolve, weigh up; reflect, deliberate, chew over, ruminate, chew the cud, digest, turn over, pore over, brood, mull over; engage in contemplation, be in a thoughtful state, be in a brown study, be lost in thought, debate with oneself, puzzle, speculate; have in mind, intend, purpose, propose, plan, project, design, devise, scheme, plot; *informal* put on one's thinking cap; *rare* cerebrate.

meditation ▸ noun *cultivating the presence of God in meditation and prayer* **contemplation**, thought, thinking, musing, pondering, consideration, reflection, prayer, deliberation, study, rumination, cogitation, brooding, mulling over, reverie, brown study, concentration, speculation; *rare* cerebration.

meditative ▸ adjective *yogic meditative techniques* **contemplative**, prayerful, reflective, musing, pensive, cogitative, thinking, thoughtful, studious, rapt, introspective, brooding, philosophical, ruminative, deliberative, ruminant, speculative, wistful; *rare* lucubratory.

medium ▸ noun **1** *television is the most powerful medium available* **means of communication**, means/mode of expression, means, method, way, form, agency, channel, forum; avenue, approach, vehicle; voice, organ, instrument, implement, mechanism, apparatus, instrumentality.
2 *these organisms were growing in their natural medium* **habitat**, element, environment, surroundings, milieu, setting, conditions, circumstances, ambience, atmosphere.
3 *two mediums told me they could see bags of money over my head* **spiritualist**, clairvoyant, mind-reader, fortune teller, seer, necromancer; *rare* spiritist.
4 *a happy medium between what is too easy and what is too difficult* **middle way**, middle course, middle ground, middle, mean, median, mid point, central point, centre, average, norm, standard; **compromise**, balance, happy medium, golden mean.
OPPOSITE extreme.
▸ adjective *he is of medium height* **average**, middling, medium-sized, middle-sized, moderate, fair, normal, standard, usual.
OPPOSITE extreme.

medley ▸ noun *a medley of Beatles songs* **assortment**, miscellany, mixture, melange, blend, variety, mixed bag, mix, diversity, collection, selection, assemblage, combination, motley collection, pot-pourri, conglomeration, jumble, mess, confusion, mishmash, hotchpotch, hodgepodge, ragbag, pastiche, patchwork, farrago, hash; *informal* scissors-and-paste job; *rare* gallimaufry, omnium gatherum, olio, salmagundi, macédoine.

meek ▸ adjective **1** *they used to call her Miss Mouse because she was so meek and mild* **patient**, long-suffering, forbearing, resigned; **gentle**, quiet, shy, retiring, reverent, peaceful, peaceable, docile, lamblike, mild, demure, modest, humble, lowly, diffident, unassuming, self-effacing, unpretentious, unambitious, unobtrusive.
OPPOSITES impatient, assertive.
2 *the meek compliance of our politicians* **submissive**, yielding, unresisting, obedient, compliant, tame, biddable, tractable, acquiescent, deferential, weak, timid, frightened, spineless, spiritless, unprotesting, like a lamb to the slaughter; *informal* weak-kneed, wimpish.
OPPOSITES assertive, overbearing.

meekness ▸ noun *the meekness and gentleness of Christian religious practice* **patience**, long-suffering, forbearance, resignation; **gentleness**, mildness, softness, peacefulness, docility, diffidence, modesty, humility, humbleness, unpretentiousness, lowliness; **submissiveness**, submission, self-effacement, self-abasement, lack of resistance, compliance, obedience, acquiescence, tameness, deference; *archaic* mansuetude.

meet ▸ verb **1** *I met an old friend on the train* **encounter**, meet up with, come face to face with, make contact with, run into/across, come across/upon, chance on, happen on, light on, stumble across/on; *informal* bump into.
OPPOSITE avoid.
2 *she first met Paul at a party* **get to know**, be introduced to, make the acquaintance of.
3 *the committee will meet on Saturday* **gather**, assemble, come together, get together, congregate, convene, muster, rally; *rare* foregather.
OPPOSITE disperse.
4 *the curtains don't quite meet* **come together**, converge, connect, touch, link up, reach, abut, butt, adjoin, join, unite, intersect, cross.
OPPOSITE separate.
5 *he met death bravely* **face**, encounter, undergo, experience, go through, bear, suffer, endure.
6 *the announcement was met with widespread hostility* **greet**, receive, answer, deal with, handle, treat, face, cope with, approach.
7 *he just does not meet the requirements of the job* **fulfil**, satisfy, fill, measure up to, match (up to), conform to, come up to, perform, comply with, answer.
8 *shipowners would meet the cost of oil spills* **pay**, settle, clear, honour, liquidate, satisfy, discharge, pay off, square, account for.
□ **meet someone halfway**. *See* HALFWAY.
▸ noun *an international meet in Wales* **event**, tournament, game, match, contest, competition; bout, fight, encounter, engagement; hunt; gathering, convention, conclave, rally, congress, convocation, muster, quiz.

meeting ▸ noun **1** *he stood up to address the meeting* **gathering**, assembly, conference, congregation, convention, summit, forum, convocation, conclave, council of war; *N. Amer.* caucus; *informal* get-together; *N. Amer. informal* confab.
2 *she demanded a meeting with the housing minister* **consultation**, audience, interview.
3 *he intrigued her on their first meeting* **encounter**, contact, introduction, appointment, assignation, rendezvous, tryst.
4 *the meeting of land and sea* **convergence**, coming together, confluence, conjunction, union, junction, abutment, concourse, intersection, T-junction, crossing.
5 *an athletics meeting* **event**, meet, rally, competition, match, game, contest.

megalomania ▸ noun *demanding changes in the script was an example of the stars' megalomania* **delusions of grandeur**, obsessionalism, grandiosity, grandioseness; self-importance, egotism, conceit, conceitedness; *French* folie de grandeur.
OPPOSITES modesty, humility.

melancholy ▸ adjective *Mozart's exquisitely melancholy clarinet concerto | a tall, bony old man with a long melancholy face* **sad**, sorrowful, desolate, melancholic, mournful, lugubrious, gloomy, pensive; despondent, dejected, depressed, depressing, down, downhearted, downcast, disconsolate, glum, sunk in gloom, miserable, wretched, dismal, dispirited, discouraged, low, in low spirits, in the doldrums, blue, morose, funereal, woeful, woebegone, doleful, wistful, unhappy, joyless, heavy-hearted, low-spirited, sombre, defeatist, pessimistic; *informal* down in the dumps, down in the mouth, morbid.
OPPOSITES cheerful, happy.
▸ noun *a feeling of melancholy descended on him* **desolation**, sadness, pensiveness, woe, sorrow, melancholia; unhappiness, dejection, depression, gloom, gloominess, misery, low spirits, moroseness, doldrums, defeatism, pessimism, dejectedness, dispiritedness, despondency; *informal* the dumps, the blues.
OPPOSITES cheerfulness, happiness.

melange ▸ noun *the population is a melange of different cultures* **mixture**, medley, blend, variety, mixed bag, mix, miscellany, diversity, collection, selection, assortment, assemblage, combination, motley collection, pot-pourri, conglomeration, jumble, mess, confusion, mishmash, hotchpotch, hodgepodge, ragbag, pastiche, patchwork, farrago, hash; *informal* scissors-and-paste job; *rare* gallimaufry, omnium gatherum, olio, salmagundi, macédoine.

melee, mêlée ▶ **noun** *a number of people were trampled to death during the subsequent melee* **tumult**, disturbance, rumpus, commotion, disorder; **brawl**, fracas, fight, affray, fray, scuffle, breach of the peace, struggle, skirmish, free-for-all, tussle, quarrel; *Irish, N. Amer., & Austral.* donnybrook; *W. Indian* bangarang; *informal* scrap, set-to, ruction, shindy, shindig, punch-up, dust-up; *Scottish informal* rammy; *N. Amer. informal* rough house; *archaic* broil, bagarre.

mellifluous ▶ **adjective** *his low, mellifluous voice was instantly recognizable* **sweet-sounding**, sweet-toned, dulcet, honeyed, mellow, soft, liquid, soothing, rich, smooth, euphonious, lyric, harmonious, tuneful, musical; *rare* mellifluent.
OPPOSITE cacophonous.

mellow ▶ **adjective 1** *the splendid mellow brickwork of the Tudor gatehouse* **seasoned**, conditioned, mature, aged, old; rich in texture, warm.
OPPOSITE fresh.
2 *the mellow tone of his voice* **dulcet**, sweet-sounding, tuneful, euphonious, lyric, melodious, mellifluous; fruity, smooth, warm, full, rich, well rounded; *rare* mellifluent.
OPPOSITE harsh.
3 *mellow apples* **ripe**, mature, soft, lush, juicy, tender, luscious, sweet, full-flavoured, flavoursome.
OPPOSITES green, unripe.
4 *I believe you are growing mellow with age* **easy-going**, tolerant, amicable, amiable, warm-hearted, warm, sympathetic, good-natured, affable, gracious, gentle, pleasant, kindly, kind-hearted.
5 *he was in a mellow mood* **genial**, jovial, jolly, cheerful, happy, merry.
OPPOSITE nasty, irritable.
6 *he was feeling mellow after two glasses of wine* **tipsy**, slightly drunk, full of well-being; *informal* happy, merry; *Brit. informal* tiddly, squiffy.
▶ **verb 1** *eight years had done nothing to mellow him* **relax**, calm, settle, mature, improve; soften, sweeten.
2 *age has mellowed the buildings* **condition**, season, age, improve.

melodious ▶ **adjective** *a quiet melodious voice* **harmonious**, tuneful, melodic, musical, dulcet, round, sweet-sounding, sweet-toned, silvery, silvery-toned, euphonious, mellifluous, lyrical, soothing; *informal* easy on the ear; *rare* mellifluent.
OPPOSITES discordant, grating.

melodramatic ▶ **adjective** *he flung the door open with a melodramatic flourish* **exaggerated**, histrionic, extravagant, overdramatic, overdone, over-sensational, sensationalized, overemotional, sentimental; theatrical, stagy, actressy; *informal* hammy.
OPPOSITES calm, stoical.

melody ▶ **noun 1** *he's playing the melody from that new film* **tune**, music, air, strain, theme, subject, line, part, song, refrain, jingle, piece.
2 *his unique gift for melody* **musicality**, musicalness, melodiousness, tunefulness, lyricism, sweetness, euphony.

melt ▶ **verb 1** *the snow was beginning to melt | how long does the cheese take to melt?* **liquefy**, thaw, unfreeze, defrost, soften, run, flux, fuse, render, clarify, dissolve, deliquesce.
2 *her charm melted the old lady's heart* **soften**, touch, disarm, mollify, relax, affect, move.
3 *the crowd melted away | the figure melted into thin air* **vanish**, vanish into thin air, disappear, fade away; dissipate, disperse, go away, peter out, pass, dissolve, evaporate, evanesce.

member ▶ **noun 1** *a member of the club* **subscriber**, associate, representative, attender, insider, fellow, comrade, adherent, life member, founder member, card-carrying member; supporter, follower, upholder, advocate, disciple, sectary.
2 *a member of a mathematical set* **constituent**, element, component, part, portion, piece, unit, factor, feature, attribute.
3 (*archaic*) *many victims had injured members* **limb**, part of the body, organ; arm, leg; appendage, extremity, projection, protuberance, process; penis.

membership ▶ **noun 1** *he recently resigned his membership of the Academy* **belonging**, associateship; community, integration, clanship; shirt, cap, cloth, seat, whip.
2 *less than half the membership bothered to vote* **members**, subscribers, associates, representatives, attenders, fellows, comrades, followers; fold, congregation, electorate, party, body.

membrane ▶ **noun layer**, laminate, sheet, skin, film, veil, diaphragm, partition, drum, tissue, pellicle, integument, overlay, covering, coat; peritoneum, amnion, caul, hymen.

memento ▶ **noun souvenir**, keepsake, reminder, remembrance, token, memorial; testimonial, trophy, relic, vestige; *archaic* memorandum.

memoir ▶ **noun 1** *her touching memoir of a London childhood in the 1870s* **account**, historical account, history, record, chronicle, annal(s), commentary, narrative, story, report, portrayal, depiction, sketch, portrait, life, life story, profile, biography.
2 (**memoirs**) *he published his memoirs in 1955* **autobiography**, life story, life, memories, recollections, personal recollections, reminiscences, experiences, journal, diary, log, weblog, blog.

memorable ▶ **adjective unforgettable**, catchy, haunting, indelible, not/never to be forgotten, signal, special; momentous, significant, historic, notable, noteworthy, important, consequential, remarkable, outstanding, extraordinary, striking, vivid, arresting, impressive, distinctive, distinguished, famous, celebrated, renowned, notorious, illustrious, glorious; immortal, undying, everlasting, eternal, unfading, perpetual, imperishable, timeless; brilliant, supreme, superlative, dazzling, exciting, thrilling, enthralling, wonderful, marvellous; *informal* out of this world.
OPPOSITES forgettable, run-of-the-mill, commonplace.

memorandum ▶ **noun 1** *the two countries signed a memorandum of understanding* **record**, minute, note, contract, agreement; aide-memoire, reminder, memory jogger, jotting, chit; *N. Amer. informal* tickler.
2 *a memorandum from the managing director to all staff* **message**, communication, note, email, letter, epistle, missive; *informal* memo.

memorial ▶ **noun 1** *meet me at the war memorial* **monument**, shrine, mausoleum, cenotaph; statue, plaque, brass, cairn; tombstone, gravestone, headstone, trophy.
2 *a National Land Fund was established as a memorial to those who lost their lives* **tribute**, testimonial, remembrance, memento, souvenir.
3 (*archaic*) *the council sent a strongly worded memorial to the Chancellor of the Exchequer* **petition**, representation, call, appeal, application, address, statement.
▶ **adjective** *a memorial service* **commemorative**, remembrance, celebratory, commemorating, monumental.

memorize ▶ **verb** *Paula listened, memorizing every detail* **commit to memory**, remember, retain, learn by heart, get by heart, learn off, learn, learn by rote, impress on the memory, study, become word-perfect in, get off pat; *archaic* con.

memory ▶ **noun 1** *she is losing her memory* **ability to remember**, powers of recall, recall, powers of retention, retention, mind.
OPPOSITE forgetfulness.
2 *my memory of the events is faint* **recollection**, remembrance, reminiscence, evocation, reminder, souvenir, echo, impression.
3 *the town built a statue in memory of him* **commemoration**, remembrance, honour, tribute, recognition, observance, respect.
4 *a computer's memory* **memory bank**, store, cache, disk, RAM, ROM.

WORD LINKS
relating to memory **mnemonic**

menace ▶ **noun 1** *an atmosphere full of menace* **threat**, ominousness, intimidation, warning, ill-omen; *rare* commination.
2 *it's a menace to British society* **danger**, peril, risk, hazard, threat; jeopardy, source of apprehension/dread/fright/fear/terror.
3 *the child next door is a menace* **nuisance**, pest, source of annoyance, annoyance, plague, torment, troublemaker, mischief-maker, a thorn in someone's side/flesh.
▶ **verb 1** *serious bush fires menaced the suburbs of Sydney* **threaten**, be a danger to, put at risk, jeopardize, imperil, loom over.
2 *she menaced me with a fire extinguisher* **bully**, intimidate, issue threats to, threaten, frighten, scare, alarm, terrify; browbeat, cow, terrorize.

CHOOSE THE RIGHT WORD

menace, threaten, intimidate

See THREATEN.

menacing ▶ **adjective 1** *she shot him a menacing look* **threatening**, ominous, black, thunderous, glowering, brooding, sinister, intimidating, frightening, terrifying, fearsome, alarming, forbidding, baleful, warning; *rare* minatory, minacious.
2 *a menacing storm* **looming**, louring, in the wind, impending, brewing, black, dark, heavy, portentous, ugly, imminent; *rare* bodeful.
OPPOSITES friendly, auspicious.

mend ▶ **verb 1** *workmen were mending faulty cabling* **repair**, fix, put back together, piece together, patch up, restore, sew (up), stitch, darn, patch, cobble, botch, vamp (up); rehabilitate, renew, renovate, redevelop, overhaul, recondition, rebuild, refurbish; make whole, make well, cure, heal; *N. English* fettle, spetch; *Scottish & N. English* ranter; *archaic* clout, tinker, beet.
OPPOSITES break, tear.
2 *'How's Walter?' 'He'll mend.' | foot injuries can take months to mend* **get better**, get well, recover, be on the road to recovery, pull through, recuperate, convalesce, improve, be well, be cured, be all right, heal, knit, draw together.
OPPOSITE worsen.
3 *quarrels could be mended by talking* **put/set right**, set straight, make up, straighten out, sort out, put in order, rectify, remedy, right, redress, resolve, square, settle, put to rights, correct, amend, emend, retrieve,

M

improve, make better, better, make good, ameliorate, reform.
OPPOSITE make worse.
4 *he mended the fire* **stoke (up)**, make up, charge, fuel.

mendacious ▶ adjective *mendacious propaganda* **lying**, untruthful, dishonest, deceitful, false, dissembling, insincere, disingenuous, hypocritical, fraudulent, double-dealing, two-faced, two-timing, duplicitous, perjured, perfidious; untrue, fictitious, falsified, fabricated, fallacious, invented, made up, hollow; *humorous* economical with the truth, terminologically inexact; *rare* unveracious.
OPPOSITE truthful.

mendacity ▶ noun **lying**, untruthfulness, dishonesty, deceit, deceitfulness, deception, dissembling, insincerity, disingenuousness, hypocrisy, fraud, fraudulence, double-dealing, two-timing, duplicity, perjury, perfidy; untruth, fictitiousness, falsity, falsehood, falseness, fallaciousness, hollowness; *informal* kidology; *Irish informal* codology; *humorous* economy with the truth, terminological inexactitude; *rare* unveracity.

mendicant ▶ noun **beggar**, beggarman, beggarwoman, tramp, vagrant, vagabond, cadger; *informal* scrounger, sponger; *N. Amer.* hobo; *N. Amer. informal* schnorrer, mooch, moocher, bum; *rare* clochard.
▶ adjective **begging**, cadging; *informal* scrounging, sponging; *N. Amer. informal* mooching.

menial ▶ adjective *he took a menial job in a factory* **unskilled**, lowly, humble, low-grade, low-status, routine, humdrum, boring, dull; degrading, mean, inferior, unworthy; *N. Amer.* blue-collar.
OPPOSITES noble, elevated, skilled.
▶ noun *they were treated like menials* **servant**, domestic servant, domestic, drudge, maid of all work; wage slave, labourer, minion, junior, slave, underling, subordinate, inferior, hireling, vassal, serf, lackey, flunkey, factotum, stooge; hewers of wood and drawers of water; *informal* dogsbody, skivvy; *N. Amer. informal* peon, gofer; *archaic* scullion, servitor.
OPPOSITE master.

menstruation ▶ noun **period**, menstrual cycle; *informal* the curse, monthlies, one's/the time of the month, being on the rag; *technical* **menses**, menarche, show, menorrhoea; *archaic* time; *rare* catamenia, flowers.

mensuration ▶ noun *for many artisans mensuration was a more necessary skill than writing* **measurement**, measuring, calculation, computation, estimating, quantification, quantifying, weighing, sizing; evaluation, assessment, appraisal, gauging.

M

mental ▶ adjective **1** *the limits of his mental ability are clear* **intellectual**, cerebral, brain, rational, psychological, cognitive, abstract, conceptual, theoretical; *rare* mindly, phrenic.
OPPOSITE physical.
2 *a mental hospital | mental illness* **psychiatric**, psychogenic, lunatic, for the insane.
3 (*informal*) *he's completely mental. See* MAD.

WORD LINKS
measurement of mental capacity **psychometrics**

mentality ▶ noun **1** *I simply can't understand the mentality of these people* **way of thinking**, cast of mind, frame of mind, turn of mind, way someone's mind works, mind, mind set, psychology, mental attitude; **outlook**, personality, persona, psyche, disposition, make-up, temperament, temper.
2 *machines can possess mentality* **intellect**, intellectual capabilities, intelligence, intelligence quotient, IQ, brainpower, brain, brains, mind, comprehension, understanding, wit, wits, reasoning, rationality, powers of reasoning, wisdom, sense, perception, imagination; *informal* grey matter; *Brit. informal* loaf; *rare* ratiocination.

mentally ▶ adverb *mentally, I was prepared to deal with the situation* **in the/one's mind**, in the/one's brain, in the/one's head, inwardly, intellectually, cerebrally, cognitively, psychologically, psychically.
OPPOSITES emotionally, spiritually.

mention ▶ verb **1** *don't mention the war* **allude to**, refer to, touch on/upon, speak briefly of, hint at; bring up, raise, broach, introduce, moot.
2 *Nigel mentioned that his father had been a teacher* **state**, say, let someone/anyone know, declare, disclose, divulge, let out, reveal, intimate, indicate; put forward, advance, present, propound; **tell**, speak about/of, utter, communicate, breathe a word of; *informal* let on about.
3 *I'll gladly mention your work to my friends* **recommend**, commend, endorse, advertise, put in a good word for, speak well of; *informal* puff, hype (up), plug.
□ **don't mention it** **don't apologize**, it doesn't matter, it makes no difference/odds, it is unimportant, that's all right, never mind, don't worry.
□ **not to mention** *lives may be lost, not to mention the ship* **in addition to**, as well as; not counting, not including, to say nothing of, aside from, besides.
▶ noun **1** *he made no mention of your request* **reference to**, allusion to, comment on, remark about; statement, announcement, indication.
2 *a mention in dispatches* **tribute**, citation, acknowledgement, recognition, honourable mention.
3 *my book got a mention on the show* **recommendation**, commendation, endorsement, a good word.

mentor ▶ noun **1** *one of the prime minister's early political mentors* **adviser**, guide, confidant, confidante, counsellor, consultant, therapist; master, spiritual leader, rav, rebbe, guru, swami, maharishi, acharya.
2 *regular meetings between mentor and trainee* **trainer**, teacher, tutor, coach, instructor.

menu ▶ noun **bill of fare**, tariff, card; carte du jour, set menu, table d'hôte, specials board; wine list.

mephitic ▶ adjective (*literary*) *the mephitic, sulphurous stench of the crater* **foul-smelling**, evil-smelling, fetid, smelly, stinking, reeking, reeky, rank, high, off, rancid, putrid, fusty, musty, stale, noxious, malodorous, ill-smelling; *Brit. informal* niffy, pongy, whiffy, humming; *literary* noisome; *rare* miasmic, miasmal, olid.
OPPOSITE fragrant.

mercantile ▶ adjective **1** *the mercantile community of Bordeaux* **commercial**, trade, trading, business, merchant, sales.
2 *the metaphysical poets expressed discontentment with the mercantile age they lived in* **profit-oriented**, money-oriented, profit-making, for-profit, mercenary, capitalistic; worldly, greedy, materialistic.
OPPOSITES idealistic, unworldly.

mercenary ▶ adjective **1** *research suggests that buyers are unashamedly mercenary* **money-oriented**, grasping, greedy, acquisitive, avaricious, covetous, rapacious, bribable, venal, materialistic; *informal* money-grubbing.
OPPOSITES altruistic, philanthropic.
2 *mercenary soldiers* **hired**, paid, bought, professional, venal, hireling; *historical* freelance.
▶ noun *a force of two thousand mercenaries* **soldier of fortune**, professional soldier, hired soldier, hireling; private army; *informal* merc, hired gun; *historical* freelance, condottiere; *archaic* adventurer, lance-knight.
OPPOSITES volunteer; conscript.

merchandise ▶ noun *retailers were looking for new merchandise to attract people into their stores* **goods**, wares, stock, commodities, lines, produce, product; *rare* vendibles.
▶ verb *such items should be merchandised to form a distinct section of your shop* **promote**, market, sell, retail, distribute; advertise, publicize, push; *informal* hype (up), plug, puff, give a puff to.

merchant *See centre pages for list of* **Sellers of Goods**
▶ noun *a wine merchant* **trader**, dealer, trafficker, wholesaler, broker, agent, seller, buyer, buyer and seller, salesman/saleswoman/salesperson, vendor, retailer, shopkeeper, tradesman, distributor, representative, commercial traveller, marketer, marketeer; magnate, mogul, baron; *dated* pedlar, hawker.

WORD LINKS
relating to merchants **mercantile, commercial**

merchantable ▶ adjective *the goods must be of merchantable quality* **saleable**, sellable, marketable, merchandisable; *rare* vendible.

merciful ▶ adjective **1** *God is merciful* **forgiving**, compassionate, gracious, lenient, clement, pitying, forbearing, humane, mild, soft-hearted, tender-hearted, kind, kindly, sympathetic; patient, humanitarian, liberal, easy-going, permissive, tolerant, indulgent, generous, magnanimous, beneficent, benign, benignant, benevolent.
OPPOSITES merciless, cruel.
2 *her death came as a merciful release* **welcome**, blessed, acceptable.
□ **be merciful to** **show mercy to**, have mercy on, have pity on, spare, pardon, forgive, let off, be lenient on/to, deal leniently with; *informal* go/be easy on.

mercifully ▶ adverb *mercifully, the event passed off without incident* **luckily**, fortunately, happily, thank goodness/God/heavens.

merciless ▶ adjective *Mithra was merciless to his enemies* **ruthless**, remorseless, pitiless, unmerciful, unforgiving, uncharitable, unsparing, unpitying, implacable, inexorable, relentless, inflexible, barbarous, inhumane, inhuman, cold-blooded, hard-hearted, stony-hearted, heartless, harsh, callous, cruel, brutal, cut-throat, unsympathetic, unfeeling, illiberal, intolerant, rigid, severe, stern.
OPPOSITES merciful, compassionate.

mercurial ▶ adjective *a mercurial temperament* **volatile**, capricious, temperamental, excitable, fickle, changeable, unpredictable, variable, protean, mutable, erratic, quicksilver, inconstant, inconsistent, unstable, unsteady, fluctuating, ever-changing, kaleidoscopic, fluid, wavering, vacillating, moody, flighty, wayward, whimsical, giddy, impulsive; *technical* labile.
OPPOSITES stable, steady, constant.

mercy ▶ noun **1** *the boy was begging for mercy* **leniency**, lenience, clemency, compassion, grace, pity, charity, forgiveness, forbearance, quarter, humanity, humaneness, humanitarianism; mildness, soft-heartedness, tender-heartedness, kindness, sympathy, liberality, indulgence, tolerance, generosity, magnanimity, beneficence.

OPPOSITES ruthlessness, cruelty, inhumanity.
2 *we must be thankful for small mercies* **blessing**, godsend, boon, favour, piece/stroke of luck.

□ **at the mercy of 1** *they found themselves at the mercy of the tyrant* **in the power of**, under/in the control of, in the clutches of, in the palm of someone's hand, under the heel of, subject to.
2 *men who lived and died at the mercy of the violent and unpredictable Australian climate* **defenceless against**, unprotected against, vulnerable to, threatened by, exposed to, susceptible to, prey to, (wide) open to, an easy target for.

mere ▶ adjective **1** *it costs a mere £29.95* **trifling**, meagre, bare, trivial, paltry, basic, scant, scanty, skimpy, minimal, slender; no more than, just, only.
2 *I was a mere boy at the time* **no more than**, nothing more than, no better than, no more important than, just, only, merely; unimportant, insignificant, inconsequential.

merely ▶ adverb *they were merely exercising their rights* **only**, purely, solely, simply, entirely, just, but.

meretricious ▶ adjective *the meretricious glitter of the whole charade* **flashy**, pretentious, gaudy, tawdry, trashy, garish, chintzy, Brummagem, loud, tinselly, cheap, tasteless, kitschy; false, artificial, fake, faked, fraudulent, imitation, bogus, spurious, sham, specious, plastic; *informal* tacky.

meretricious or meritorious?

Similar in form, these words are opposite in meaning. **Meretricious** is used of something with a superficial attractiveness that conceals its essential worthlessness (*the artist had been content to churn out meretricious souvenirs for tourists*). **Meritorious**, on the other hand, means 'deserving reward, worthy' (*he received a medal for meritorious conduct*).

merge ▶ verb **1** *the Communist League decided to merge with the Independent Labour Party* **join (together)**, join forces, amalgamate, consolidate, integrate, unite, unify, combine, incorporate, affiliate, coalesce, meld, agglutinate, team up, link (up), band (together), ally, league, federate.
OPPOSITES separate, split.
2 *a decision was taken to merge the two organizations* **amalgamate**, bring together, join, consolidate, conflate, unite, combine, incorporate, coalesce, meld, pool, link (up), knit, yoke.
3 *the two colours merged* **mingle**, blend, fuse, run/melt/fade into one another, mix, intermix, intermingle, commingle, converge, integrate, coalesce, compound, homogenize, emulsify, lump (together), mass, conglomerate.

merger ▶ noun *a merger between an aerospace company and a car company* **amalgamation**, combination, merging, union, fusion, coalition, affiliation, coupling, unification, incorporation, coalescence, consolidation, confederation, hook-up, link-up; alliance, association, connection.
OPPOSITES split, break-up.

merit ▶ noun **1** *composers of outstanding merit* **excellence**, goodness, standard, quality, level, grade, high quality, calibre, worth, good, credit, eminence, worthiness, value, virtue, distinction, account, deservingness, meritoriousness.
OPPOSITE inferiority.
2 *the merits of the scheme* **good point**, strong point, advantage, benefit, value, profit, asset, plus, advisability; advantageousness.
OPPOSITES fault, disadvantage.
▶ verb *the accusation did not merit a response* **deserve**, earn, be deserving of, warrant, rate, justify, be worthy of, be worth, be entitled to, have a right to, have a claim to/on, be qualified for.

CHOOSE THE RIGHT WORD

merit, deserve, earn

See EARN.

meritorious ▶ adjective *the captain was awarded a medal for meritorious conduct* **praiseworthy**, laudable, commendable, admirable, estimable, creditable, worthy, worthwhile, deserving, excellent, exemplary, good.
OPPOSITES worthless, discreditable.

meritorious or meretricious?

See MERETRICIOUS.

merriment ▶ noun *her eyes were dancing with merriment* **high spirits**, high-spiritedness, exuberance; **cheerfulness**, gaiety, fun, effervescence, euphoria, exhilaration, elation, verve, buoyancy, carefreeness, blitheness, levity, zest, sportiveness, liveliness, cheer, joy, joyfulness, joyousness, jolliness, jollity, happiness, gladness, exultation, rejoicing, jocundity, jocularity, conviviality, festivity, merrymaking, revelry, mirth, mirthfulness, glee, gleefulness, laughter, hilarity, light-heartedness, amusement, pleasure; *informal* larking about.
OPPOSITES doom and gloom, misery.

merry ▶ adjective **1** *the narrow streets were dense with merry throngs of students* **cheerful**, cheery, in good spirits, high-spirited, blithe, bright, sunny, light-hearted, buoyant, bubbly, lively, carefree, without a care in the world, joyful, joyous, rejoicing, jolly, jocund, convivial, festive, mirthful, gleeful, happy, glad, laughing; *informal* chirpy; *dated* gay; *archaic* frolicsome, sportive, blithesome.
OPPOSITES miserable, sad, gloomy.
2 *after three beers he began to feel quite merry* **tipsy**, mellow, slightly drunk; *Brit. informal* tiddly, squiffy.

□ **make merry have fun**, have a good time, enjoy oneself, have a party, party, celebrate, carouse, feast, {eat, drink, and be merry}, revel, roister, rejoice, go on a spree; *informal* have a ball, make whoopee; *dated* spree.

merry-go-round ▶ noun **carousel**; *Brit.* roundabout; *archaic* whirligig.

mesh ▶ noun **1** *the wire mesh of a chicken run* **netting**, net, network, tracery, reticulation; web, webbing, lattice, latticework, lacework, openwork, tatting, filigree, trellis, screen, plexus, tangle, mat.
2 *he was caught in the mesh of political intrigue* **entanglement**, net, tangle, web, snare, trap.
▶ verb **1** *one gear meshes with the input gear* **engage**, be engaged, mate, connect, lock, interlock.
2 *I don't want to get meshed in the weeds* **entangle**, enmesh, ensnare, snare, net, trap, entrap, catch.
3 *our ideas just do not mesh* **harmonize**, fit together, go together, coordinate, match, be on the same wavelength, dovetail.

mesmerize ▶ verb *they were mesmerized by his performance* **enthral**, spellbind, entrance, hold spellbound, dazzle, bewitch, charm, captivate, enrapture, enchant, fascinate, transfix, transport, grip, magnetize, hypnotize; *informal* get under someone's skin.

mess ▶ noun **1** *please clear up the mess in the kitchen* **untidiness**, disorder, disarray, clutter, heap, shambles, litter, tangle, jumble, muddle, mishmash, chaos, confusion, disorganization, turmoil; *informal* muck, fright, sight; *Brit. informal* dog's dinner/breakfast, tip.
2 *there was cat mess all over the room* **excrement**, dung, muck, faeces, excreta, dirt.
3 *I've got to get out of this mess* **plight**, predicament, emergency, tight spot, tight corner, difficulty, straits, trouble, quandary, dilemma, problem, muddle, mix-up, confusion, complication, imbroglio, entanglement, mire; *informal* jam, fix, pickle, stew, hot water, hole, pretty/fine kettle of fish, scrape.
4 *what a mess he made of the project* **muddle**, botch, bungle, wreck; *informal* hash, muck, foul-up, screw-up; *Brit. informal* cock-up; *N. Amer. informal* snafu; *vulgar slang* fuck-up, balls-up.

□ **make a mess of** *she felt she had made a complete mess of her life* **mismanage**, mishandle, misdirect, misgovern, misconduct, bungle, botch, fluff, fumble, mess up, mar, spoil, ruin, wreck; *informal* make a hash of, muff, muck up, foul up, screw up, bitch up; *Brit. informal* make a muck of, make a pig's ear of, make a Horlicks of, cock up; *vulgar slang* balls up, bugger up, fuck up.
▶ verb

□ **mess about/around potter about**, amuse oneself, pass the time, do nothing very much, fiddle about/around, footle about/around, play about/around, fool about/around; fidget, toy, trifle, tamper, tinker, interfere, meddle, monkey (about/around); *informal* piddle about/around; *Brit. informal* muck about/around, lark (about/around), fanny about/around; *vulgar slang* frig about/around, fuck about/around; *Brit. vulgar slang* piss about/around, arse about/around, bugger about/around.

□ **mess something up 1** *he had completely messed up my kitchen* **dirty**, befoul, litter, besmirch, pollute; clutter up, disarrange, jumble, throw into disorder/confusion, muss, dishevel, rumple, tumble.
2 *Eddie has messed things up* **bungle**, botch, fluff, fumble, make a mess of, mismanage, mishandle, misdirect, misgovern, misconduct, mar, spoil, ruin, mangle, wreck; *informal* make a hash of, muff, muck up, foul up, screw up, bitch up; *Brit. informal* make a muck of, make a pig's ear of, make a Horlicks of, cock up; *vulgar slang* balls up, bugger up, fuck up.

message ▶ noun **1** *are there any messages for me?* **communication**, piece of information, news, word, note, memorandum, memo, email, letter, line, missive, report, bulletin, communiqué, dispatch, intelligence, notification, announcement.
2 *a campaign to get the message about home security across* **meaning**, sense, import, idea; **point**, thrust, gist, essence, spirit, content, subject (matter), substance, implication, tenor, drift, purport, intimation, theme, moral, lesson, precept.
3 (*Scottish*) *he would run messages to the pub or the bookie* **errand**, task, job, commission, chore, mission; shopping.

□ **get the message** *I realized that he'd never get the message—he was too thick* **understand**, get the point, get the drift, comprehend; take the hint; *informal* understand what's what, catch on, latch on, get it, get the picture.

messenger ▶ noun **message-bearer**, message-carrier, postman, courier, errand boy/girl, runner, dispatch rider, envoy, emissary, agent, go-between, legate, nuncio, herald, harbinger.

messy ▶ adjective **1** *messy oil spills and grease marks | messy hair* **dirty**, filthy, grubby, soiled, grimy, begrimed; mucky, muddy, slimy, sticky, sullied, spotted, stained, smeared, smudged, tarnished; **dishevelled**, blowsy, scruffy, rumpled, matted, unkempt, tousled, bedraggled, tangled, slapdash, slovenly; *informal* yucky; *Brit. informal* gungy.
OPPOSITE clean.
2 *a messy kitchen* **disorderly**, disordered, muddled, in a muddle, chaotic, confused, disorganized, in disarray, in turmoil, disarranged; **untidy**, cluttered, littered, in a jumble, jumbled; *informal* like a bomb's hit it; *Brit. informal* shambolic.
OPPOSITES tidy, orderly.
3 *a messy legal battle* **chaotic**, convoluted, complex, intricate, tangled, tortuous, confused, confusing, difficult; **unpleasant**, nasty, bitter, acrimonious, spiteful.
OPPOSITES straightforward, amicable.

metal ▶ noun. *See centre pages for lists of* **Alloys** **Metals**

metallic ▶ adjective **1** *a metallic sound* **tinny**, jangling, jangly, jingling, jingly, plinky; grating, harsh, jarring, dissonant, raucous.
2 *metallic paint* **metallized**, burnished; shiny, gleaming, glossy, lustrous, pearlescent, polished.

metamorphose ▶ verb *in the painting Queen Maria Luisa is metamorphosed into a barn owl* **transform**, change, mutate, transmute, transfigure, convert, alter, vary, modify, remodel, recast, restyle, reconstruct, reorder, reorganize, undergo a sea change, translate; *humorous* transmogrify; *formal* transubstantiate.

metamorphosis ▶ noun **transformation**, mutation, transmutation, transfiguration, change, alteration, conversion, variation, modification, remodelling, restyling, reconstruction, reordering, reorganization, sea change; *humorous* transmogrification; *formal* transubstantiation.

metaphor *See centre pages for list of* **Rhetorical Devices and Figures of Speech**
▶ noun **figure of speech**, figurative expression, image, trope, allegory, parable, analogy, comparison, symbol, emblem, word painting, word picture; *literary* conceit.

metaphorical ▶ adjective *there is no clear line between literal and metaphorical senses* **figurative**, allegorical, analogous, symbolic, emblematic; imaginative, fanciful, extended; *rare* parabolic, tropical.
OPPOSITE literal.

metaphysical ▶ adjective **1** *the metaphysical question of the nature of the mind* **abstract**, theoretical, conceptual, notional, philosophical, speculative, intellectual, academic; unpractical, abstruse, recondite.
OPPOSITE empirical.
2 *Good and Evil are inextricably linked in a metaphysical battle* **transcendental**, spiritual, supernatural, paranormal; extramundane, unearthly, ethereal, incorporeal.
OPPOSITE physical.

mete ▶ verb
□ **mete something out** *the judges were unwilling to mete out harsh punishment* **dispense**, hand out, apportion, distribute, issue, deal out, dole out, measure out, divide out, divide up, parcel out, share out, split up, give out, portion out, dish out, allocate, allot, bestow, assign, administer.

meteor ▶ noun **falling star**, shooting star, fireball, meteorite, bolide, meteoroid, comet.

meteoric ▶ adjective *her meteoric rise to fame* **rapid**, lightning, swift, fast, quick, speedy, breakneck, fast-track, accelerated, overnight, instant, whirlwind, mushrooming, sudden, spectacular; momentary, fleeting, transient, ephemeral, evanescent, brief, short-lived.
OPPOSITES slow, gradual, long-drawn-out.

meteorologist ▶ noun **weather forecaster**, met officer, weatherman, weatherwoman, nowcaster, weather prophet; *informal* weathergirl, met man.

method ▶ noun **1** *they use very old-fashioned methods* **procedure**, technique, system, practice, routine, modus operandi, method of working, formula, process, means, medium, mechanism; tack, approach, way, line, course of action, route, road; strategy, tactic, plan, recipe, rule.
2 *there's method in his madness* **order**, orderliness, organization, arrangement, structure, form, system, logic, planning, plan, design, purpose, pattern, routine, discipline.
OPPOSITES chaos, disorder.

methodical ▶ adjective *a methodical approach to the evaluation of computer systems* **orderly**, well ordered, well organized, well thought out, planned, well planned, efficient, businesslike, coherent, systematic, scientific, structured, logical, analytic, formal, regular, well regulated, disciplined; meticulous, punctilious, tidy, neat.
OPPOSITES disorganized, chaotic, inefficient.

meticulous ▶ adjective *meticulous attention to detail* **careful**, conscientious, diligent, ultra-careful, scrupulous, punctilious, painstaking, demanding, exacting, accurate, correct; **thorough**, studious, rigorous, detailed, perfectionist, fastidious, methodical, particular, strict; pedantic, fussy; *archaic* nice, laborious.
OPPOSITES careless, sloppy, slapdash.

métier ▶ noun **1** *he had another métier besides the priesthood* **occupation**, job, work, profession, specialism, business, employment, employ, career, calling, vocation, mission, trade, craft, walk of life, line (of work), field, province, area; *N. Amer.* specialty.
2 *television is more my métier* **forte**, strong point, strength, long suit, strong suit, speciality, talent, skill, gift, bent; *informal* bag, thing, cup of tea.

metropolis ▶ noun **1** *their trip to London gave them nine days in the metropolis* **capital (city)**, chief town, state/regional/provincial capital, county town, county borough, administrative centre.
2 *compared to Farafra, Bahriyah was a metropolis* **big city**, conurbation, megalopolis, urban sprawl, concrete jungle; *informal* big smoke; *archaic* wen.

mettle ▶ noun **1** *Sir Charles, a man of mettle, did not surrender without a struggle* **spirit**, fortitude, tenacity, strength of character, moral fibre, steel, determination, resolve, resolution, steadfastness, indomitability, backbone, hardihood, pluck, nerve, gameness, courage, courageousness, bravery, gallantry, valour, intrepidity, fearlessness, boldness, daring, audacity; *informal* guts, grit, spunk; *Brit. informal* bottle.
2 *Frazer's disciple was of a very different mettle* **calibre**, character, disposition, nature, temperament, temper, personality, make-up, stamp, kind, sort, variety, mould, kidney, grain.

mettlesome ▶ adjective *a rider who likes a mettlesome horse* **spirited**, game, gritty, intrepid, fearless, courageous, hardy, brave, plucky, gallant, valiant, valorous, bold, daring, audacious, heroic; tenacious, steely, determined, resolved, resolute, steadfast, indomitable.

mew ▶ verb **1** *the cat mewed plaintively* **miaow**, meow, mewl, yowl, cry.
2 *above them, seagulls mewed* **cry**, screech, squawk.

mewing ▶ noun **1** *the mewing of the cat* **miaowing**, meowing, mewling, yowling; caterwauling, noise.
2 *the mewing of gulls* **cry**, crying, screech, screeching, squawking.

mewl ▶ verb *the baby fretted and mewled* **whimper**, cry, whine, squall; *informal* grizzle; *literary* pule.

miasma ▶ noun **stink**, reek, stench, smell, odour, malodour; *Brit. informal* pong, niff, whiff; *Scottish informal* guff.

miasmic, miasmal ▶ adjective (*rare*) *the miasmic smog* **foul-smelling**, evil-smelling, fetid, smelly, stinking, stinking to high heaven, reeking, rank, high, putrid, noxious, malodorous; *literary* noisome, mephitic; *Brit. informal* niffing, niffy, pongy, whiffy; *rare* olid.

microbe ▶ noun *microbes which cause dangerous diseases* **micro-organism**, bacillus, bacterium, virus, germ; *informal* bug.
WORD LINKS
fear of microbes **microphobia, bacillophobia**

microscopic ▶ adjective *protozoa are microscopic amoeba-like organisms* **tiny**, very small, minute, infinitesimal, minuscule, invisible to the naked eye; little, micro, diminutive; *Scottish* wee; *informal* teeny, teeny-weeny, teensy, teensy-weensy, weeny, itsy-bitsy, itty-bitty, eensy, eensy-weensy, tiddly, pint-sized, bite-sized, knee-high to a grasshopper; *Brit. informal* titchy; *N. Amer. informal* little-bitty.
OPPOSITES huge, enormous, gigantic.

midday ▶ noun **noon**, twelve noon, twelve midday, twelve o'clock, high noon, noontide, noontime, noonday, twelve hundred, twelve hundred hours, one-two-double-O.
OPPOSITE midnight.
WORD LINKS
relating to midday **meridional**

middle ▶ noun **1** *a shallow dish with a spike in the middle* **centre**, mean, median, mid point, halfway point, dead centre, focal point, focus, hub, nucleus, midst; eye, heart, core, kernel, bosom, interior, depths, thick, bullseye.
OPPOSITES outside, circumference.
2 *he had a towel round his middle* **midriff**, waist, waistline, belly, gut, stomach, paunch, pot belly, beer belly; *informal* tummy, tum, pot, bread basket.
▶ adjective **1** *the middle point between two extremes* **central**, mid, mean, medium, medial, median, midway, halfway, equidistant, mesial.
2 *there is a dearth of talent at middle level* **intermediate**, intermedial, intermediary, inner, inside.
WORD LINKS
related prefix **meso- (e.g. *mesoblast, Meso-America*)**

middleman ▶ noun *we give value for money by cutting out the middleman and selling direct* **intermediary**, go-between; **dealer**, broker, representative, agent, factor, wholesaler, distributor; mediator, liaison officer.

middling ▶ adjective *a spa town of the middling kind, neither rich nor poor* **average**, standard, normal, middle-of-the-road, in-between, medium; moderate, ordinary, common, commonplace, everyday, workaday, tolerable, passable, adequate; run-of-the-mill, fair, indifferent, mediocre, pedestrian, prosaic, uninspired, undistinguished, unexceptional, unexciting, unremarkable, lacklustre, forgettable, inferior, second-rate, amateur, amateurish; *informal* OK, so-so, bog-standard, fair-to-middling, (plain) vanilla, nothing to write home about, no great shakes, not so hot, not up to much; *NZ informal* half-pie.

midget ▶ noun *these earth houses were so small that their inhabitants must have been midgets* **small person**, dwarf, homunculus, Lilliputian, manikin, gnome, pygmy, Tom Thumb; *informal* shrimp.
▶ adjective **1** *a midget lettuce* **dwarf**, miniature, baby.
2 *a story about midget matadors in Spain* **diminutive**, dwarfish, petite, elfin, very small, pocket, toy, pygmy; *informal* pint-sized, sawn-off.
3 *a midget camera* **miniature**, pocket.
OPPOSITE giant.

midnight ▶ noun **twelve midnight**, twelve at night, twelve o'clock, dead of night, the middle of the night, zero hours, the witching hour.
OPPOSITE midday.

midst ▶ noun (*literary*) **1** *the anecdote occurs* **in the midst of** *a digression* **middle**, centre, midpoint, halfway point, kernel, nub, focal point; interior, depth(s), thick; **in the course of**, halfway through, at the heart of, at the core of.
2 *a stranger* **in our midst** **among us**, between us, amid us, in our group, with us, surrounded by us, in the centre; heart, bosom, core.

midway ▶ adverb *he froze in an awkward position midway across the room* **halfway**, in the middle, at the mid point, in the centre, equidistant; betwixt and between, part-way, at some point.

mien ▶ noun *a low-browed, frowning mien* **appearance**, look, expression, countenance, face, front, aspect, aura, demeanour, comportment, attitude, air, presence, manner, bearing, carriage, deportment, stance.

miffed ▶ adjective (*informal*) *she was slightly miffed at not being invited* **annoyed**, displeased, offended, aggrieved, piqued, riled, nettled, vexed, irked, irritated, upset, hurt, pained, put out, in a huff, fed up, chagrined, disgruntled, discontented, resentful; *informal* peeved, narked, browned off, hacked off; *Brit. informal* cheesed off; *N. Amer. informal* sore; *vulgar slang* pissed off.
OPPOSITE pleased.

might ▶ noun *she hit him with all her might* **strength**, force, power; vigour, energy, brawn, sinew, muscularity; stamina, stoutness, mightiness, powerfulness, forcefulness, potency, toughness, robustness, sturdiness.
OPPOSITE feebleness.
□ **with might and main with all one's strength**, with everything one has got, to the best of one's ability, as hard as one can, as hard as possible, all out, with maximum force, (with) full force, full blast, with all the stops out, forcefully, powerfully, strongly, vigorously, enthusiastically; *informal* hammer and tongs, like crazy, like mad.

mightily ▶ adverb **1** *he is a mightily impressive election campaigner* **extremely**, exceedingly, enormously, vastly, immensely, tremendously, hugely, markedly, remarkably, abundantly; awfully, dreadfully; very, very much, most, to a great extent; *informal* majorly, mega, oh-so; *informal, dated* devilish; *N. Amer. informal* mighty, plumb.
2 *Ann and I laboured mightily to no avail* **strenuously**, energetically, powerfully, heavily, hard, with all one's might, with might and main, all out, heartily, vigorously, with vigour, forcefully, with force, forcibly, with great effort, fiercely, intensely, eagerly, industriously, diligently, assiduously, conscientiously, enthusiastically, sedulously, with application, earnestly, with perseverance, persistently, indefatigably; *informal* like billy-o, like mad, like crazy.

mighty ▶ adjective **1** *a mighty blow to the back of the head* **powerful**, forceful, violent, ferocious, fierce, brutal, vicious, vigorous, hefty, thunderous, savage, destructive, damaging, painful; lethal, deadly.
OPPOSITE feeble.
2 *a mighty warrior* **fearsome**, ferocious; big, tough, robust, manful, potent, sturdy, muscular, strapping, Herculean; vigorous, energetic, stout.
OPPOSITES puny, tiny.
3 *three mighty industrial countries* **dominant**, influential, strong, powerful, important, leading, authoritative, controlling, predominant, prestigious.
OPPOSITE insignificant.
4 *mighty oak trees* **huge**, enormous, massive, gigantic, big, large, great, giant, colossal, mammoth, vast, immense, tremendous, stupendous, monumental, prodigious, mountainous, monstrous, titanic, towering, elephantine, king-sized, king-size, gargantuan, Brobdingnagian, substantial; *informal* mega, monster, whopping, whopping great, thumping, thumping great, humongous, jumbo(-sized), hulking, bumper, astronomical, astronomic; *Brit. informal* whacking, whacking great, ginormous.
OPPOSITE tiny.
▶ adverb (*N. Amer.*) *I'm mighty pleased to see you* **extremely**, exceedingly, enormously, vastly, immensely, tremendously, hugely, markedly, remarkably, abundantly, deadly, awfully, dreadfully, mightily, very, very much, most, so, to a great extent; *informal* majorly, mega, oh-so, way, stinking, bitching; *Brit. informal* well, jolly; *N. Amer. informal* plumb; *S. African informal* lekker; *informal, dated* frightfully, devilish.

migrant ▶ noun *economic migrants were sent back home* **immigrant**, **emigrant**, incomer, newcomer, asylum seeker, settler, expatriate, expat, exile; nomad, itinerant, gypsy, traveller, vagrant, transient, rover, wayfarer, wanderer, drifter, displaced person, DP, homeless person.
▶ adjective *the arrival of migrant birds from further south | migrant workers* **travelling**, wandering, moving, migrating, migratory, expatriate; drifting, nomadic, roving, roaming, itinerant, gypsy, peripatetic, vagrant, transient, floating, unsettled, on the move, displaced, homeless.
OPPOSITE indigenous.

migrate ▶ verb **1** *rural populations have migrated to urban areas* **relocate**, resettle, move, move house; emigrate, go abroad, go overseas, be posted, defect, trek; *N. Amer.* pull up stakes; *Brit. informal* up sticks, flit; *formal* remove.
2 *wildebeest migrate around the Serengeti Plains* **roam**, wander, drift, rove, travel (around), voyage, journey, trek, hike, itinerate, globetrot.

migration ▶ noun **1** *new workers were found through migration from the Commonwealth* **relocation**, resettling, population movement, transhumance, moving, moving abroad, emigration, expatriation, posting, exodus, departure, hegira, defection, trek, diaspora; *German* Völkerwanderung.
2 *the swallows start flocking before they begin their winter migration* **departure**, passage; flight, run.

migratory ▶ adjective *migratory birds* **migrant**, migrating, translocating, relocating, moving, travelling.

mild ▶ adjective **1** *he continued in the same mild tone of voice* **gentle**, tender, soft, soft-hearted, tender-hearted, sensitive, sympathetic, warm, warm-hearted, unassuming, conciliatory, placid, meek, modest, docile, calm, tranquil, serene, peaceful, peaceable, pacific, good-natured, amiable, affable, genial, easy, easy-going, mellow.
OPPOSITE harsh.
2 *a mild punishment* **lenient**, clement, light; **compassionate**, pitying, forgiving, merciful, forbearing, humane.
OPPOSITES cruel, harsh.
3 *he was eyeing her with mild interest* **slight**, faint, vague, minimal, half-hearted, paltry, meagre, superficial, nominal, token, feeble, indifferent, imperceptible.
OPPOSITE strong.
4 *mild weather* **warm**, balmy, equable, temperate, gentle, soft, moderate, favourable, clement.
OPPOSITES severe, cold.
5 *a mild curry* **bland**, insipid, flavourless, tasteless, savourless, spiceless; thin, watery, watered down.
OPPOSITE spicy.

mildewy ▶ adjective *two ounces of mildewy cheese* **mouldy**, mildewed, blighted, smutty, smutted, musty, fetid, fusty, rotting, rotten, decaying, putrid, putrescent, stale, damp.

mildness ▶ noun **1** *there are moments when mildness of manner is not enough* **gentleness**, tenderness, softness, soft-heartedness, sensitivity, warmth, warmness, compassion, meekness, modesty, docility, calmness, tranquillity, placidity, serenity, peaceableness, amiability, affability, geniality, mellowness.
OPPOSITES cruelty, harshness.
2 *the exceptional mildness of the past winter* **warmth**, balminess, equability, temperateness, gentleness, softness, moderation.
OPPOSITE severity.

milieu ▶ noun *the social, political, and artistic milieu in Britain* **environment**, background, backdrop, setting, context, atmosphere, scene; location, locale, conditions, surroundings, habitat, environs; sphere, world, territory, home, domain, preserve, province, circle, element.

militant ▶ adjective *the exuberance of his more militant supporters* **aggressive**, violent, belligerent, bellicose, assertive, pushy, vigorous, forceful, active, ultra-active, fierce, combative, pugnacious; radical, extremist, extreme; enthusiastic, zealous, fanatical.
OPPOSITES restrained; apathetic.
▶ noun *they threatened to kill the hostages if three imprisoned militants were not released* **activist**, extremist, radical, enthusiast, supporter, follower, devotee, Young Turk, zealot, fanatic, sectarian, partisan.
OPPOSITES centrist, conformist, conservative.

militaristic ▶ adjective *the militaristic image of the current leadership* **warmongering**, war-loving, warlike, martial, hawkish, pugnacious, combative, aggressive, belligerent, bellicose; jingoistic, flag-waving, chauvinistic; *informal* gung-ho.
OPPOSITE peaceable.

military *See centre pages for lists of* **Ranks** **Soldiers**
▶ adjective *all forces were put under US military command* **fighting**, service, army, armed, defence, warrior, soldierly, soldier-like, martial.
OPPOSITE civilian.
▶ noun (**the military**) *the zone was set up in 1967 at the insistence of the military*

armed forces, army, forces, services, militia, soldiery; navy, air force, marines, special forces.

militate ▶ verb *anger may **militate against** sexual satisfaction* **tend to prevent**, work against, resist, hinder, discourage, oppose, counter, cancel out, foil, prejudice, operate/work/go/tell against, be detrimental to, be disadvantageous to.
OPPOSITE reinforce.

militate or mitigate?
See MITIGATE.

milk *See centre pages for list of* **Drinks (Soft)**
▶ noun *informal* cow juice.
▶ verb **1** *milk a little of the liquid from the cylinder* **draw off**, siphon, bleed, pump off, tap, drain, extract, withdraw.
2 *phoney psychics can milk their rich clients for years* **exploit**, take advantage of, cash in on, impose on, bleed, suck dry, fleece, squeeze, wring, blackmail.

WORD LINKS
relating to milk **dairy, lactic**
related prefix **lacto-** (e.g. ***lactoprotein, lacto-vegetarian***)

milksop ▶ noun *would a boy brought up by his mother grow up a milksop?* **namby-pamby**, coward, weakling, Milquetoast; *informal* drip, mummy's boy, sissy, pansy, jellyfish, wimp, crybaby; *Brit. informal* **wet**, big girl's blouse, chinless wonder; *N. Amer. informal* candy-ass, pantywaist, pussy; *archaic* poltroon.

milky ▶ adjective *not a blemish marred her milky skin* **pale**, white, milk-white, snow-white, whitish, off-white, cream, creamy, chalky, pearly, nacreous, ivory, alabaster, opaque, clouded, cloudy, misty, blanched, bloodless, anaemic, ashen, pallid, drained, pasty, wan, waxen, faded.
OPPOSITE swarthy.

mill ▶ noun **1** *a paper mill | a steel mill* **factory**, plant, processing plant, works, workshop, shop, foundry, industrial centre, industrial unit.
2 *a pepper mill* **grinder**, quern, crusher.
▶ verb *the wheat is milled into flour* **grind**, pulverize, powder, granulate, kibble; grate, pound, crush, crunch, press; *rare* comminute, triturate, bray, levigate.

□ **mill around/about** *people were milling about in the streets* **throng**, swarm, seethe, crowd, stream, surge.

millstone ▶ noun *she had become a millstone round his neck* **burden**, unwanted responsibility, encumbrance, dead weight, load, onus; duty, obligation, liability, trouble, problem, misfortune, affliction; cross to bear, albatross; *archaic* cumber.

mime ▶ noun *he performed a brief mime of someone fencing* **dumb show**, pantomime, mummery.
▶ verb *she mimed picking up a phone* **act out**, pantomime, use gestures to indicate, gesture, simulate, represent, indicate by dumb show, indicate by sign language.

WORD LINKS
Muse of mime **Polyhymnia**

mimic ▶ verb **1** *she mimicked his broad northern accent* **imitate**, copy, impersonate, do an impression of, take off, do an impersonation of, do, ape, caricature, mock, make fun of, parody, satirize, lampoon, burlesque, travesty; *informal* send up, spoof; *archaic* monkey.
2 *most hoverflies are patterned so as to mimic bees and wasps* **resemble**, look like, have/take on the appearance of, simulate, mirror, echo; *N. Amer. informal* make like.
▶ noun *he had a dry wit and was a superb mimic* **impersonator**, impressionist, imitator, mimicker; parodist, caricaturist, lampooner, lampoonist; copier, copyist; *informal* copycat; *archaic* ape, zany; *rare* epigone.
▶ adjective *they were waging mimic war* **simulated**, mock, imitation, make-believe, sham, imitative, mimetic; *informal* pretend, copycat.

mimicry ▶ noun *some birds specialize in vocal mimicry* **imitation**, imitating, impersonation, take-off, impression, copying, aping, caricature, mockery, parody, satire, lampoon, burlesque; *informal* send-up, spoof; *rare* apery, pasquinade.

minatory ▶ adjective (*rare*) *his minatory look* **menacing**, threatening, baleful, intimidating, ominous, admonitory, warning, cautionary; *rare* minacious, comminatory, minatorial.

mince ▶ verb **1** *mince the meat and mix in the remaining ingredients* **chop up**, cut up, chop/cut into small pieces; **grind**, dice, crumble, cube; *N. Amer.* hash.
2 *she stood up and minced out of the room* **walk affectedly**, walk in an affected/dainty way, teeter, waddle, skip; *N. Amer. informal* sashay.
□ **not mince (one's) words talk straight**, not beat about the bush, call a spade a spade, speak straight from the shoulder, pull no punches, make no bones about something, get to the point; *informal* tell it like it is; *N. Amer. informal* talk turkey.

mincing ▶ adjective *he had a strange, mincing walk, his hips slightly swaying* **affected**, fastidious, dainty, effeminate, niminy-piminy, chichi, foppish, dandyish; pretentious, precious; *informal* camp, sissy, la-di-da, campy; *Brit. informal* poncey.

mind ▶ noun **1** *my mind was full of dark thoughts | a good teacher must stretch pupils' minds* **brain**, **intelligence**, intellect, intellectual capabilities, mental capacity, brains, brainpower, wits, wit, powers of reasoning, powers of comprehension, powers of thought, understanding, reasoning, judgement, sense, mentality, perception; head, imagination, subconscious, psyche, ego; *informal* grey matter, brainbox, brain cells; *Brit. informal* loaf; *N. Amer. informal* smarts; *S. African informal* kop; *rare* ratiocination.
OPPOSITE body.
2 *he found it hard to keep his mind on the job* **attention**, thoughts, concentration, thinking, attentiveness.
3 *the tragedy has affected her mind* **sanity**, mental balance, mental faculties, senses, wits, reason, reasoning, judgement, rationality; *informal* marbles.
4 *his words stuck in her mind* **memory**, recollection, powers of recall.
5 *one of the greatest minds of his time* **intellect**, thinker, brain, scholar, academic, intellectual, sage.
6 *I've a mind to write in and complain* **inclination**, desire, wish, urge, notion, fancy, disposition, intention, intent, will, aim, purpose, design.
7 *everyone was of the same mind* **opinion**, way of thinking, outlook, attitude, view, viewpoint, point of view, belief, judgement, thoughts, feeling, sentiment, persuasion.
□ **be in two minds** *I was in two minds whether to hit him* **be undecided**, be uncertain, be unsure, be hesitant, be ambivalent, hesitate, waver, vacillate, dither, be on the horns of a dilemma; *Brit.* haver, hum and haw; *Scottish* swither; *informal* dilly-dally, shilly-shally, blow hot and cold.
□ **bear/keep in mind remember**, note, make a mental note of, be mindful of, do not forget, take into account/consideration, consider, take cognizance of, take note of, be cognizant of.
□ **cross one's mind** *it never crossed his mind that this would upset her* **occur to one**, come to one, come to mind, spring to mind, enter one's mind/head, strike one, hit one, dawn on one, come into one's consciousness, suggest itself.
□ **give someone a piece of one's mind reprimand**, rebuke, scold, reprove, reproach, chastise, castigate, upbraid, berate, read someone the Riot Act, haul over the coals; *informal* tell off, bawl out, blow up, give someone hell, give someone a talking-to, dress down, give someone a telling-off, give someone a dressing-down, give someone an earful, give someone a roasting, give someone a rocket, give someone a rollicking, give someone a row; *Brit. informal* tick off, carpet, give someone a mouthful; *N. Amer. informal* chew out; *Austral. informal* monster; *Brit. vulgar slang* bollock; *N. Amer. vulgar slang* chew someone's ass.
□ **have something in mind** *did you have anything specific in mind?* **think of**, contemplate; intend, aim, plan, design, propose, purpose, aspire, desire, want, wish, set out.
□ **out of one's mind 1** *if you think I'll agree to this you must be out of your mind!* **mad**, insane, deranged, demented, not in one's right mind, non compos mentis, unbalanced, mad as a hatter, mad as a March hare, away with the fairies; *informal* crazy, mental, off one's head, out of one's head, off one's nut, nuts, nutty, off one's rocker, not (quite) right in the head, round the bend, raving mad, bats, batty, bonkers, cuckoo, loopy, loony, bananas, loco, with a screw loose, touched, gaga, off the wall, not all there, out to lunch, not right upstairs; *Brit. informal* barmy, crackers, barking, barking mad, round the twist, off one's trolley, not the full shilling; *N. Amer. informal* buggy, nutsy, nutso, out of one's tree, meshuga, squirrelly, wacko; *Canadian & NZ informal* bushed; *NZ informal* porangi.
2 *I've been out of my mind with worry* **frantic**, beside oneself, berserk, distraught, in a frenzy; *informal* crazy.
□ **put someone in mind of remind of**, cause to remember, recall, conjure up, suggest, evoke, summon up, call up; **resemble**, look like.
□ **to my mind in my opinion**, in my view, as I see it, (according) to my way of thinking, from my standpoint, personally, in my estimation, in my judgement, in my book, for my money, if you ask me.
▶ verb **1** *do you mind if I smoke? | I don't mind if you're late* **care**, **object**, be bothered/troubled/annoyed, be upset, be offended, take offence, be affronted, be resentful, disapprove, resent it, dislike it, look askance; *informal* give/care a damn, give/care a toss, give/care a hoot, give a monkey's, give/care a rap, give a tinker's curse/damn; *vulgar slang* give a shit.
2 *mind the step!* **be careful of**, **watch out for**, look out for, beware of, take care with, be on one's guard for, be cautious of, be wary of, be watchful of, keep one's eyes open for.
OPPOSITES ignore, miss.
3 ***mind you*** *wipe your feet before you come in* **be/make sure (that)**, see (that), take care that; **remember to**, be/make sure to, don't forget to, take care to.
OPPOSITE forget.
4 *she left her husband to mind the baby* **look after**, take care of, keep an eye on, attend to, care for, tend, watch, have/take charge of, guard, protect.
OPPOSITE neglect.

5 *mind what your mother says* **pay attention to**, take heed of, heed, pay heed to, attend to, take note/notice of, be heedful of, note, mark, concentrate on, listen to, observe, have regard for, respect, be mindful of; obey, follow, comply with, adhere to; *archaic* regard.
OPPOSITES disregard, take no notice of.

□ **mind out** *mind out—there's a car coming* **take care**, be careful, watch out, look out, beware, be on one's guard, be wary, be watchful, keep one's eyes open, be cautious.

□ **never mind 1** *never mind the cost* **don't bother about**, pay no attention to, don't worry about, don't concern yourself with, disregard, forget, don't take into consideration, don't give a second thought to, don't think twice about.
2 *never mind, it's all right now* **don't apologize**, forget it, don't worry about it, it doesn't matter, don't mention it, it's unimportant.

WORD LINKS

relating to the mind	**mental, cognitive**
study of the mind	**psychology**
branch of medicine to do with the mind	**psychiatry**

mindful ▶ adjective *he was mindful of the difficulties involved* **aware of**, conscious of, alive to, sensible of, alert to, awake to, acquainted with, heedful of, watchful of, careful of, wary of, chary of, cognizant of; *informal* wise to, hip to; *rare* regardful of, recognizant of.
OPPOSITES heedless, oblivious.

mindless ▶ adjective **1** *some mindless idiot nearly drove into me* **stupid**, idiotic, brainless, imbecilic, imbecile, asinine, witless, foolish, empty-headed, vacuous, unintelligent, half-witted, dull, slow-witted, obtuse, weak-minded, feather-brained, doltish, blockish; *informal* dumb, moronic, pig-ignorant, dead from the neck up, brain-dead, cretinous, thick, thickheaded, birdbrained, pea-brained, pinheaded, dopey, dim, dim-witted, dippy, pie-faced, fat-headed, blockheaded, boneheaded, lamebrained, chuckleheaded, dunderheaded, wooden-headed, damfool, muttonheaded; *Brit. informal* divvy; *Scottish & N. English informal* glaikit; *N. Amer. informal* dumb-ass, chowderheaded; *S. African informal* dof; *W. Indian informal* dotish.
OPPOSITE intelligent.
2 *mindless acts of vandalism* **unthinking**, thoughtless, senseless, gratuitous, careless, wanton, indiscriminate, unreasoning, uncalled for, brutish, barbarous, barbaric.
OPPOSITES thoughtful, considered, premeditated.
3 *a mindless, repetitive task* **mechanical**, automatic, routine, robotic; tedious, boring, monotonous, brainless, mind-numbing.
OPPOSITE interesting.

□ **mindless of** *she was mindless of the consequences of her actions* **indifferent to**, heedless of, unaware of, unmindful of, careless of, insensible to, blind to.

mine *See centre pages for list of* **Bombs and Mines**
▶ noun **1** **pit**, colliery, excavation, quarry, workings, diggings, lode, vein, seam, deposit, shaft, mineshaft; coalfield, goldfield, opencast mine; *N. Amer.* open-pit mine, strip mine.
2 *the book is a mine of information* **rich source**, repository, store, storehouse, reservoir, gold mine, mint, treasure house, treasury, reserve, fund, wealth, vein, stock, supply, hoard, accumulation; wellspring.
3 *a mine was built under the fortifications* **tunnel**; *historical* sap.
▶ verb **1** *the iron ore was mined from shallow pits* **quarry**, excavate, dig (up), extract, unearth, remove, draw, scoop out; strip-mine.
2 *medical data was mined for relevant statistics* **search**, ransack, delve into, rake through, scour, scan, read, look through, survey.
3 *the entrance to the harbour had been mined* **defend with mines**, protect with mines, lay with mines, sow with mines.

miner ▶ noun **pitman**, digger, collier, haulier; faceworker, headsman, surfaceman, topman; tinner; *Austral.* dry-blower; *dated* hewer; *rare* groover.

mineral ▶ noun. *See centre pages for lists of* **Gems** **Minerals** **Rocks**

mingle ▶ verb **1** *fact and fiction are skilfully mingled in his novels | the sound of voices mingled with a scraping of chairs* **mix**, blend, intermingle, commingle, intermix, interweave, interlace, combine, merge, fuse, unite, join, amalgamate, meld, marry, mesh, compound, coalesce, interblend; *rare* admix, commix, interflow.
OPPOSITES separate, be separated.
2 *wedding guests mingled in the marquee* **socialize**, circulate, fraternize, associate with others, rub shoulders, get together, consort with others; *informal* hobnob, hang out.
OPPOSITES separate, part.

miniature ▶ adjective *a miniature railway* **small-scale**, scaled-down, mini; tiny, little, small, minute, baby, toy, pocket, midget, dwarf, pygmy, minuscule, microscopic, micro, diminutive, reduced, Lilliputian; *Scottish* wee; *N. Amer.* vest-pocket; *informal* teeny, teeny-weeny, teensy, teensy-weensy, weeny, itsy-bitsy, itty-bitty, eensy, eensy-weensy, tiddly, pint-sized, bite-sized; *Brit. informal* titchy; *N. Amer. informal* little-bitty.
OPPOSITE giant.

minimal ▶ adjective *the committee approved the report with minimal alteration* **very little**, minimum, the smallest amount of; slightest, least, least possible, minutest, tiniest, littlest; nominal, token, negligible, next to no.
OPPOSITE maximal.

minimize ▶ verb **1** *the aim is to minimize costs* **keep down**, keep at/to a minimum, reduce, decrease, cut back on, cut down, lessen, curtail, diminish, prune, pare down, shrink; *informal* slash.
OPPOSITES maximize, increase.
2 *we should not minimize the value of his contribution* **belittle**, make light of, play down, underestimate, underrate, make little of, downplay, underplay, undervalue, detract from, sell short, de-emphasize, understate, discount, soft-pedal, reduce, lessen, brush aside, gloss over, trivialize, decry, disparage, deprecate, depreciate, denigrate; *informal* pooh-pooh; *archaic* hold cheap; *rare* derogate, misprize, minify.
OPPOSITE exaggerate.

minimum ▶ noun *operating costs will be kept to the minimum* **lowest level**, lower limit, bottom level, bottom, base, least, lowest, rock bottom, slightest, depth, nadir.
OPPOSITE maximum.
▶ adjective *the minimum amount of effort* **minimal**, least, smallest, least possible, slightest, lowest, rock-bottom, minutest, littlest.
OPPOSITES maximum, most.

minion ▶ noun *Inspector Cotton and his minion Sergeant Mack* **underling**, **henchman**, flunkey, lackey, hanger-on, follower, camp follower, servant, hireling, vassal, stooge, creature, toady, sycophant, flatterer, fawner, lickspittle, myrmidon; *informal* yes-man, bootlicker; *Brit. informal* poodle, dogsbody; *N. Amer. informal* gofer, suck-up, brown-nose; *Indian informal* chamcha; *Brit. vulgar slang* arse-licker, bum-sucker; *N. Amer. vulgar slang* ass-kisser.
OPPOSITE peer.

minister *See centre pages for list of* **Priests**
▶ noun **1** *a government minister* **member of the government**, political leader, cabinet minister, secretary of state, secretary, undersecretary, department head, privy counsellor, politician; *Indian* diwan.
2 *a minister of religion* **clergyman**, clergywoman, cleric, ecclesiastic, pastor, vicar, rector, priest, parson, father, man/woman of the cloth, man/woman of God, churchman, churchwoman; curate, chaplain, curé, divine, evangelist, preacher; *Scottish* kirkman; *informal* reverend, padre, Holy Joe, sky pilot; *Austral. informal* josser.
3 *the British minister in Egypt* **ambassador**, chargé d'affaires, plenipotentiary, envoy, emissary, legate, diplomat; consul, delegate, representative, aide, dignitary, official.
▶ verb *doctors were busy* ***ministering to*** *the injured | he selflessly* ***ministered to*** *her needs* **tend**, care for, take care of, look after, nurse, treat, attend to, see to, administer to, help, assist, succour; cater to, serve, wait on, accommodate, be solicitous of, pander to; *informal* doctor.

ministrations ▶ plural noun *her mother's anxious ministrations* **attention**, treatment, help, assistance, aid, care, services, succour, relief, support.

ministry ▶ noun **1** *the ministry for foreign affairs* **government department**, department, bureau, agency, office.
2 *he's training for the ministry* **holy orders**, the priesthood, the cloth, the church.
3 *the life and ministry of Jesus* **teaching**, preaching, evangelism.
4 *Gladstone's first ministry* **period of office**, term (of office), administration, incumbency.

minor ▶ adjective **1** *minor structural alterations | a relatively minor problem* **slight**, small; **unimportant**, insignificant, inconsequential, inconsiderable, of little account, peripheral, subsidiary, negligible, trivial, trifling, paltry, petty, footling; *N. Amer.* nickel-and-dime; *informal* piffling, piddling.
OPPOSITE major.
2 *a minor poet* **little known**, unknown, lesser; **unimportant**, insignificant, obscure, lightweight, subordinate; *N. Amer.* minor-league; *informal* small-time, penny-ante; *N. Amer. informal* two-bit, picayune, bush-league.
OPPOSITES important, considerable.
3 (*Brit.*) *Smith minor* **junior**, younger.
▶ noun *the heir to the throne being a minor, there would have to be a regency* **child**, infant, youth; adolescent, teenager, boy, girl, lad, lass, schoolboy, schoolgirl; *informal* kid, kiddie.
OPPOSITE adult.

minstrel ▶ noun (*historical*) **musician**, **singer**, balladeer; *historical* bard, troubadour, jongleur; *rare* joculator.

mint ▶ noun **1** **coinage factory**, money factory, coining works; *rare* coinery.
2 (**a mint**) (*informal*) *the bank made a mint out of the deal* **a fortune**, a vast sum of money; millions, billions, a king's ransom; *informal* a small fortune, pots of money, stacks of money, heaps of money, a tidy sum, a bundle, a wad, a pile; *Brit. informal* a bomb, a packet, loadsamoney, shedloads; *N. Amer. informal* big bucks, big money, gazillions; *Austral. informal* big bickies, motser, motza.
▶ adjective *in mint condition* **brand new**, as new, pristine, perfect, immaculate, unblemished, undamaged, untarnished, unmarked,

unmarred, unused, fresh, first-class, excellent; *informal* spanking.
▶ **verb 1** *the shilling was minted in 1742* **coin**, stamp, stamp out, strike, cast, punch, die, forge, make, manufacture, produce.
2 *the slogan had been freshly minted for the occasion* **create**, invent, make up, think up, dream up, hatch, devise, frame, originate, come up with, fabricate, fashion, produce.

minuscule ▶ **adjective** *the newsroom was minuscule, not much more than a cubbyhole* **tiny**, minute, microscopic, very small, little, micro, diminutive, miniature, baby, toy, midget, dwarf, pygmy, Lilliputian, infinitesimal; *Scottish* wee; *informal* teeny, teeny-weeny, teensy, teensy-weensy, weeny, itsy-bitsy, itty-bitty, eensy, eensy-weensy, tiddly; *Brit. informal* titchy; *N. Amer. informal* little-bitty.
OPPOSITES vast, huge.

minute[1] (stress on the first syllable) ▶ **noun 1** *it'll only take a minute* **moment**, short time, little while, second, bit, instant; *informal* sec, jiffy, jiff; *Brit. informal* tick, mo, two ticks.
2 *at that minute, Tony walked in* **point in time**, point, moment, instant, time, juncture, stage.
3 (**minutes**) *their objection was noted in the minutes* **record(s)**, proceedings, log, notes, transactions, account; transcript, summary, résumé.
□ **at the minute at present**, at the moment, at the present moment/time, now, currently, this minute, presently.
□ **in a minute very soon**, in a moment, in a second, in a trice, in a flash, shortly, any minute, any minute now, in a short time, in an instant, in the twinkling of an eye, in (less than) no time, in no time at all, before you know it, before long; *N. Amer.* momentarily; *informal* in a jiffy, in two shakes, in two shakes of a lamb's tail, in the blink of an eye, in a blink, in the wink of an eye, in a wink, before you can say Jack Robinson, before you can say knife; *Brit. informal* in a tick, in a mo, in two ticks; *N. Amer. informal* in a snap; *archaic or informal* anon; *archaic* ere long.
□ **this minute at once**, immediately, directly, this moment, this second, instantly, straight away, right away, right now, without further/more ado, forthwith; *French* tout de suite; *Latin* instanter; *informal* pronto, straight off, right off, toot sweet; *archaic* straight.
□ **up to the minute latest**, newest, up to date, modern, fashionable, smart, chic, stylish, all the rage, in vogue, trendsetting, ultra-modern, modish, voguish; *French* à la mode; *informal* trendy, with it, in, bang up to date, now, hip.
□ **wait a minute be patient**, wait a moment/second, just a moment/minute/second, hold on; *informal* **hang on**, hold your horses; *Brit. informal* hang about.

M

minute[2] (stress on the second syllable) ▶ **adjective 1** *minute particles of gold dust | her handwriting is minute* **tiny**, minuscule, microscopic, very small, little, micro, diminutive, miniature, baby, toy, midget, dwarf, pygmy, Lilliputian; *Scottish* wee; *informal* teeny, teeny-weeny, teensy, teensy-weensy, weeny, itsy-bitsy, itty-bitty, eensy, eensy-weensy, tiddly, pint-sized, bite-sized, knee-high to a grasshopper; *Brit. informal* titchy; *N. Amer. informal* little-bitty.
OPPOSITE huge.
2 *a minute chance of success* **negligible**, slight, infinitesimal, minimal, trifling, trivial, paltry, petty, insignificant, inappreciable; *informal* piffling, piddling; *N. Amer. informal* picayune.
OPPOSITE significant.
3 *considering the proposal in minute detail* **exhaustive**, painstaking, systematic, meticulous, rigorous, scrupulous, punctilious, detailed; close, fine, strict, exact, precise, accurate, critical.
OPPOSITES superficial, cursory.

WORD LINKS
measurement of minute objects **micrometry**

minutely ▶ **adverb** *every document was examined minutely* **exhaustively**, painstakingly, systematically, meticulously, rigorously, scrupulously, punctiliously, in detail; closely, finely, precisely, accurately, critically; *informal* with a fine-tooth comb.

minutiae ▶ **plural noun** *the captain cannot be concerned with the minutiae of shipboard life* **details**, **niceties**, subtleties, finer points, particulars, specifics; trivia, trivialities, trifles, technicalities, non-essentials.

minx ▶ **noun tease**, seductress, coquette, trollop, slut, Lolita, loose woman, hussy; *informal* tramp, floozie, tart, puss; *Brit. informal* scrubber, madam; *N. Amer. informal* princess, vamp; *vulgar slang* cock-teaser, prick-teaser; *archaic* baggage, hoyden, fizgig, jade, quean, wanton, strumpet.

miracle ▶ **noun 1** *a painting of Christ's first miracle* **supernatural phenomenon**, mystery, prodigy, sign.
2 *Germany's economic miracle* **wonder**, marvel, sensation, phenomenon, astonishing feat, amazing achievement.

miraculous ▶ **adjective 1** *an attack was repulsed, according to legend, with the miraculous help of St Blaise* **supernatural**, preternatural, superhuman, inexplicable, unaccountable, fantastic, magical, phenomenal, prodigious; *rare* thaumaturgic.
2 *it is miraculous that you have finished | a miraculous escape* **amazing**, astounding, remarkable, extraordinary, incredible, unbelievable, sensational; unparalleled, unprecedented, unheard of, providential, marvellous, wonderful; *informal* fantastic, fabulous, mind-boggling, mind-blowing.

mirage ▶ **noun optical illusion**, hallucination, phantasmagoria, apparition, fantasy, chimera, trick, vision; delusion, figment of the imagination, misconception, pipe dream, day dream; *literary* phantasm.

mire ▶ **noun 1** *when it's wet it's a mire out there* **swamp**, bog, morass, peat bog, quagmire, quag, slough, sump, quicksand, fen, fenland, swampland, marshland, wetland, salt marsh, saltings, salina; *N. Amer.* bayou, moor.
2 *her horse was spattered with mire* **mud**, slime, sludge, dirt, filth, ooze, muck.
3 *struggling to pull Russia out of the mire caused by decades of hard-line Communist rule* **mess**, difficulty, plight, predicament, emergency, tight spot, tight corner, mass of problems, straits, trouble, quandary, dilemma, problem, muddle, mix-up, confusion, complication, imbroglio, entanglement; *informal* jam, fix, pickle, spot, stew, hot water, hole, pretty/fine kettle of fish, scrape.
▶ **verb 1** *Frank's horse* **got mired** *in a bog hole* **get bogged down**, sink, sink down, stick in the mud.
2 *the children were mired from playing outside* **dirty**, soil, muddy, begrime, spatter, smear, make muddy/dirty, cake with dirt/soil.
3 *since his fall from grace he had been mired in lawsuits* **entangle**, tangle up, embroil, enmesh, catch up, mix up, involve, bog down.

mirror *See centre pages for list of* **Mirrors**
▶ **noun 1** *a quick look in the mirror* **looking glass**, reflector, reflecting surface; *Brit.* glass.
2 *he felt that the Frenchman's life was a mirror of his own* **reflection**, twin, double, exact likeness, image, replica, copy, clone, match, parallel; *informal* spitting image, spit, dead spit, dead ringer for.
▶ **verb** *pop music mirrored the mood of Britain's desperation | these circumstances are mirrored all over the country* **reflect**, repeat, match, reproduce, imitate, simulate; reiterate, follow; copy, mimic, echo, parallel, correspond to; impersonate.

WORD LINKS
relating to mirrors **catoptric, specular**
fear of mirrors **eisoptrophobia**

mirth ▶ **noun** *she giggled, making an effort to control her mirth* **merriment**, high spirits, mirthfulness, cheerfulness, cheeriness, cheer, hilarity, glee, laughter, jocularity, levity, gaiety, buoyancy, blitheness, euphoria, exhilaration, elation, light-heartedness, joviality, joy, joyfulness, joyousness, fun, enjoyment, amusement, pleasure, merrymaking, jollity, festivity, revelry, frolics, frolicsomeness; *dated* sport.
OPPOSITES gloom, misery.

mirthful ▶ **adjective merry**, high-spirited, in high spirits, cheerful, cheery, hilarious, gleeful, laughter-filled, jocular, buoyant, carefree, blithe, euphoric, exhilarated, elated, light-hearted, jovial, joyous, fun-filled; enjoyable, amusing, pleasurable, jolly, festive, playful; *archaic* frolicsome, sportive.
OPPOSITES miserable, dejected.

mirthless ▶ **adjective** *his lips twisted into a mirthless grin* **humourless**, unamused, grim, glum, moody, sour, surly, dour, sullen, sulky, gloomy, scowling, glowering, sombre, lugubrious, mournful, melancholy, melancholic, doleful, miserable, dismal, grumpy, churlish, grouchy.
OPPOSITES cheerful, smiling.

miry ▶ **adjective** *the roads were miry and troublesome in winter* **muddy**, oozy, slushy, slimy, swampy, marshy, boggy, fenny, watery, sodden, sopping, saturated, squelchy, waterlogged, soggy, soft, heavy; mucky, dirty, filthy; *rare* quaggy.

misadventure ▶ **noun** *a verdict of death by misadventure | a series of misadventures* **accident**, **problem**, difficulty, misfortune, mishap, mischance; unfortunate incident, setback, reverse, reverse of fortune, stroke of bad luck, blow; trouble, failure, disaster, tragedy, calamity, woe, trial, tribulation, catastrophe, contretemps, reversal, upset, debacle.
OPPOSITE piece of good luck.

misanthrope, **misanthropist** ▶ **noun hater of mankind**, cynic, sceptic, churl, grouch, grump, recluse, hermit, anchorite.

misanthropic ▶ **adjective** *his misanthropic gloom* **antisocial**, unsociable, unfriendly, reclusive, uncongenial, unneighbourly, inhospitable, cynical, suspicious, distrustful, sceptical, jaundiced, narrow-minded.
OPPOSITE sociable.

misanthropy ▶ **noun hatred of mankind**, antisocial behaviour, cynicism, scepticism, reclusiveness.

misapply ▶ **verb** *the idea of permissiveness has been overstated, exaggerated, or misapplied* **misuse**, make bad use of, mishandle, misemploy, misappropriate, abuse, exploit, pervert, prostitute; distort, garble, warp, misinterpret, misconstrue, misrepresent; squander, waste, dissipate.

misapprehend ▶ **verb** *I do not think that I misapprehend your meaning* **misunderstand**, misinterpret, put a wrong interpretation on, misconstrue, misconceive, mistake, misread, miss, confuse, confound, take amiss; miscalculate, err, be mistaken, get the wrong idea, get it/someone wrong, take something the wrong way, receive a false impression, be under a delusion, get (hold of) the wrong end of the stick, be at cross purposes; *informal* be barking up the wrong tree.

misapprehension ▶ noun *you seem to be under the misapprehension that I approve* **misunderstanding**, mistake, error, misinterpretation, misconstruction, misreading, misjudgement, misconception, misbelief, miscalculation, confusion, mix-up, the wrong idea, false impression, fallacy, illusion, delusion.

misappropriate ▶ verb *he confessed to having misappropriated $2.2bn from his clients' portfolios* **embezzle**, expropriate, steal, thieve, pilfer, swindle, pocket, help oneself to, abscond with, make off with, have one's hand/fingers in the till; *informal* skim, swipe, lift, filch, rip off, snitch; *Brit. informal* pinch, half-inch, nick, whip, knock off, bone; *rare* peculate, defalcate.

misappropriation ▶ noun *the alleged misappropriation of funds* **embezzlement**, expropriation, swindle, stealing, theft, thieving, pilfering, unauthorized removal; *rare* peculation, defalcation.

misbegotten ▶ adjective **1** *it is a disgrace that the hospital is included in this misbegotten scheme* **ill-conceived**, ill-advised, ill-made, badly planned, badly thought-out, hare-brained, abortive.
2 *you little misbegotten bundle of dog food!* **contemptible**, despicable, wretched, miserable, confounded, blithering, footling, infernal, damned, cursed, accursed, flaming; *vulgar slang* fucking, frigging, pissing, shitty; *N. Amer. vulgar slang* chickenshit, pissant.
3 (*archaic*) *the king's misbegotten children* **illegitimate**, bastard, born out of wedlock; *dated* natural, born on the wrong side of the blanket, unfathered; *archaic* baseborn, spurious, nameless.

misbehave ▶ verb *the manager appears powerless to prevent his players misbehaving on the field* **behave badly**, be misbehaved, be bad, be naughty, be disobedient, get up to mischief, get up to no good, misconduct oneself, forget oneself, be guilty of misconduct; be bad-mannered, show bad/poor manners, be rude, fool around; *informal* carry on, act up.
OPPOSITE behave oneself.

misbehaviour ▶ noun *as soon as the misbehaviour begins, turn away from your child* **bad behaviour**, misconduct, disorderly conduct, badness, naughtiness, disobedience, mischief, mischievousness, delinquency; misdeed, misdemeanour; bad/poor manners, rudeness, fooling around; *informal* carryings-on, acting-up, shenanigans.

misbelief ▶ noun *it is a misbelief that alcohol problems are confined to drinkers* **false belief**, unorthodoxy, heresy, wrong belief, delusion, illusion, fallacy, error, mistake, misconception, misapprehension.
OPPOSITE orthodoxy.

miscalculate ▶ verb *he had grossly miscalculated the time it would take* **misjudge**, make a mistake (about), calculate wrongly, estimate wrongly, overestimate, underestimate, overvalue, undervalue; go wrong, err, make an error, blunder, be wide of the mark; *informal* slip up, make a boo-boo, make a howler; *Brit. informal* boob.
OPPOSITE get it right.

miscalculation ▶ noun *it is Government miscalculations that are to blame* **error of judgement**, misjudgement, misreading of the situation, mistake, blunder, faux pas, overestimate, underestimate; *informal* slip-up, boo-boo; *rare* misreckoning.

miscarriage ▶ noun **1** *she's had a miscarriage* **spontaneous abortion**, stillbirth.
2 *Gould's impatience stemmed from the miscarriage of a good project | a miscarriage of justice* **failure**, foundering, ruin, ruination, collapse, breakdown, thwarting, frustration, undoing, reversal, setback, unsuccessfulness, aborting, non-fulfilment, misfiring, mismanagement, perversion.

miscarry ▶ verb **1** *the shock caused her to miscarry* **lose one's baby**, have a miscarriage, abort, have a spontaneous abortion.
2 *our plan miscarried* **go wrong**, go awry, go amiss, be unsuccessful, fail, misfire, abort, be abortive, founder, come to nothing, come to grief, meet with disaster, fall through, be ruined, fall flat, boomerang, rebound, backfire, recoil; *informal* flop, bite the dust, go up in smoke, go phut.
OPPOSITE succeed.

miscellaneous ▶ adjective *a variety of miscellaneous tasks* **various**, varied, different, assorted, mixed, diverse, disparate, sundry, many and different, variegated, diversified, motley, multifarious, jumbled, confused, indiscriminate, heterogeneous; *literary* divers; *rare* farraginous.

miscellany ▶ noun *a miscellany of poems by several hands* **assortment**, mixture, melange, blend, variety, mixed bag, mix, medley, diversity, collection, selection, assemblage, combination, motley collection, pot-pourri, conglomeration, jumble, mess, confusion, mishmash, hotchpotch, hodgepodge, ragbag, pastiche, patchwork, farrago, hash; *informal* scissors-and-paste job; *rare* gallimaufry, omnium gatherum, olio, salmagundi, macédoine.

mischance ▶ noun *we lost it by mischance | a life full of mischances* **accident**, misfortune, mishap, misadventure, unfortunate incident, setback, failure, disaster, tragedy, calamity, catastrophe, contretemps, reversal, upset, blow, debacle; bad luck, ill fortune.
OPPOSITE good fortune.

mischief ▶ noun **1** *the boys are always getting up to mischief* **naughtiness**, badness, bad behaviour, misbehaviour, mischievousness, misconduct, misdemeanour, perversity, disobedience, pranks, tricks, larks, capers, nonsense, roguery, devilry, funny business; *French* diablerie; *informal* monkey tricks, monkey business, shenanigans, goings-on, hanky-panky; *Brit. informal* carry-on, carryings-on, jiggery-pokery; *archaic* deviltry.
OPPOSITE good behaviour.
2 *he could see mischief in her eyes* **impishness**, roguishness, devilment; *rare* rascality.
OPPOSITE solemnity.
3 (*informal*) *be careful, or you'll do yourself a mischief* **harm**, hurt, an injury; impairment, damage, detriment, ill, trouble.

mischievous ▶ adjective **1** *a mischievous child* **naughty**, bad, badly behaved, misbehaving, disobedient, troublesome, vexatious, full of mischief; rascally, roguish, prankish, delinquent.
OPPOSITES well behaved, good.
2 *a mischievous smile* **playful**, teasing, wicked, impish, puckish, roguish, waggish, arch.
3 *mischievous gossip* **malicious**, malevolent, hostile, spiteful, bitter, venomous, poisonous, evil-intentioned, ill-natured, evil, baleful, vindictive, vengeful, vitriolic, rancorous, malign, malignant, pernicious, mean, nasty, harmful, hurtful, destructive, wounding, cruel, unkind, defamatory; *informal* bitchy, catty; *literary* malefic, maleficent.
OPPOSITES harmless, well intentioned.

misconceive ▶ verb *many lawyers misconceive their own role* **misunderstand**, misinterpret, put a wrong interpretation on, misconstrue, misapprehend, mistake, misread, miss, confuse, confound, take amiss; miscalculate, err, be mistaken, get the wrong idea, get it/someone wrong, receive a false impression, be under a delusion, be misguided about, get (hold of) the wrong end of the stick, be at cross purposes; *informal* be barking up the wrong tree.

misconception ▶ noun *a popular misconception about science* **misapprehension**, misunderstanding, mistake, error, mix-up, misinterpretation, misconstruction, misreading, misjudgement, misbelief, miscalculation, false impression, illusion, fallacy, delusion; the wrong idea.

misconduct ▶ noun **1** *allegations of misconduct by the security forces* **wrongdoing**, delinquency, unlawfulness, lawlessness, crime, felony, criminality, sin, sinfulness, evil, evil-doing; unprofessional behaviour, unprofessionalism, unethical behaviour, malpractice, maladministration, dereliction of duty, negligence, breach of ethics, impropriety, immorality, abuse; *rare* malversation.
2 *misconduct in the classroom was punished by detention* **misbehaviour**, bad behaviour, misdeeds, misdemeanours, disorderly conduct, badness, mischief, naughtiness, rudeness.

misconstruction ▶ noun *his misconstruction of the legislation* **misunderstanding**, misinterpretation, misapprehension, misconception, misreading, misjudgement, misbelief, miscalculation; mistake, error, mix-up, false impression, illusion, fallacy, delusion; the wrong idea.

misconstrue ▶ verb *his indifference can easily be misconstrued as arrogance* **misunderstand**, misinterpret, put a wrong interpretation on, misconceive, misapprehend, mistake, misread, miss, confuse, confound, take amiss; miscalculate, err, be mistaken, get the wrong idea, get it/someone wrong, receive a false impression, be under a delusion, get (hold of) the wrong end of the stick, be at cross purposes; *informal* be barking up the wrong tree.

miscreant ▶ noun (*archaic*) *the village stocks, where miscreants of olden days were pelted with rotten garbage* **criminal**, culprit, wrongdoer, malefactor, offender, villain, lawbreaker, evil-doer, convict, delinquent, sinner, transgressor, outlaw, trespasser, scoundrel, wretch, reprobate, rogue, rascal; *Law* malfeasant, misfeasor.

misdeed ▶ noun *he repented of his misdeeds and vowed to change his ways* **wrongdoing**, wrong, evil deed, crime, felony, criminal act, misdemeanour, misconduct, offence, violation, error, peccadillo, transgression, sin; *archaic* trespass.

misdemeanour ▶ noun *he preferred to turn a blind eye to his son's misdemeanours* **wrongdoing**, evil deed, crime, felony, criminal act; misdeed, misconduct, offence, violation, error, peccadillo, transgression, sin; *archaic* trespass.

miser ▶ noun *a typical miser, he hid his money in the house in various places* **penny-pincher**, pinchpenny, niggard, cheese-parer, Scrooge; **hoarder**, saver, collector, gatherer, accumulator, magpie, squirrel; ascetic, puritan; *informal* **skinflint**, meanie, money-grubber, cheapskate; *N. Amer. informal* tightwad; *vulgar slang* tight-arse.
OPPOSITES spendthrift; philanthropist.

miserable ▶ adjective **1** *I'm too miserable to eat* **unhappy**, sad, sorrowful, dejected, depressed, downcast, downhearted, down, despondent, despairing, disconsolate, out of sorts, desolate, bowed down, wretched, glum, gloomy, dismal, blue, melancholy, melancholic, low-spirited, mournful, woeful, woebegone, doleful, forlorn, crestfallen, broken-

hearted, heartbroken, inconsolable, luckless, grief-stricken; *informal* down in the mouth, down in the dumps.
OPPOSITES happy, contented.
2 *their miserable surroundings* **dreary**, dismal, dark, gloomy, drab, sombre, wretched, depressing, grim, cheerless, godforsaken, bleak, desolate, joyless, uninviting, discouraging, disheartening, unpromising, hopeless, dire, pathetic, tragic, distressing, grievous; mean, poor, shabby, squalid, filthy, foul, sordid, seedy, dilapidated.
OPPOSITE luxurious.
3 *those planning day trips face four miserable wet or windy days* **unpleasant**, disagreeable, displeasing, depressing, uncomfortable; wet, rainy, stormy; *informal* rotten.
OPPOSITES glorious, lovely.
4 *he was a good leader, but a miserable old prune on a bad day* **grumpy**, sullen, sulky, gloomy, bad-tempered, ill-tempered, in a bad mood, dour, surly, sour, glum, moody, unsmiling, humourless, uncommunicative, taciturn, unresponsive, unsociable, scowling, glowering, ill-humoured, sombre, sober, saturnine, pessimistic, lugubrious, dismal, irritable, churlish, cantankerous, crotchety, cross, crabbed, crabby, grouchy, testy, snappish, peevish, crusty, waspish; *N. English informal* mardy; *informal, dated* mumpish.
OPPOSITES cheerful, good-natured.
5 *the agricultural working class were forced to work for miserable wages* **inadequate**, meagre, scanty, scant, paltry, limited, restricted, insufficient, deficient, negligible, insubstantial, skimpy, short, little, lean, small, slight, slender, poor, lamentable, pitiful, puny, niggardly, beggarly; *informal* measly, stingy, lousy, pathetic, piddling; *rare* exiguous.
OPPOSITES generous, adequate.
6 *all that fuss about a few miserable mushrooms* **wretched**, **contemptible**, despicable, confounded; *informal* blithering, flaming, footling, infernal, damned, cursed, accursed.

miserliness ▶ noun *miserliness and greed are quickly followed by fear of losing the money* **avarice**, acquisitiveness, parsimony, parsimoniousness, penny-pinching, cheese-paring, thrift; **meanness**, niggardliness, close-fistedness, closeness, penuriousness, illiberality, greed; asceticism, puritanism, masochism; *informal* stinginess, minginess, tightness, tight-fistedness; *N. Amer.* cheapness; *archaic* nearness.
OPPOSITE generosity.

miserly ▶ adjective **1** *his miserly great-uncle proved to be worth nearly a million* **mean**, niggardly, parsimonious, close-fisted; **penny-pinching**, cheese-paring, grasping, greedy, avaricious, Scrooge-like, ungenerous, illiberal, close; ascetic, puritanical, masochistic; *informal* stingy, mingy, tight, tight-fisted, money-grubbing, money-grabbing; *N. Amer. informal* cheap; *vulgar slang* tight-arsed; *archaic* near.
OPPOSITES spendthrift, generous.
2 *the prize for the winner of the women's championship will be a miserly £3,500* **meagre**, inadequate, paltry, limited, insufficient, deficient, negligible, insubstantial, skimpy, miserable, lamentable, pitiful, puny, niggardly, beggarly; *informal* measly, stingy, lousy, pathetic, piddling; *rare* exiguous.
OPPOSITES lavish, huge.

misery ▶ noun **1** *I went through periods of intense misery* **unhappiness**, distress, wretchedness, hardship, suffering, affliction, anguish, anxiety, angst, torment, torture, hell, agony, pain, discomfort, deprivation, poverty, grief, heartache, heartbreak, heartbrokenness, despair, despondency, dejection, depression, desolation, gloom, gloominess, low spirits, moroseness, doldrums, melancholy, melancholia, woe, sadness, sorrow; *informal* the dumps, the blues; *literary* dolour.
OPPOSITES contentment, pleasure.
2 *the miseries of war* **affliction**, misfortune, difficulty, problem, adversity, ordeal, trouble, hardship, deprivation; pain, sorrow, burden, load, blow, trial, tribulation, woe, torment, catastrophe, calamity, disaster, misadventure, mischance, accident, reverse, reverse of fortune, mishap.
3 (*Brit. informal*) *he's a real old misery* **killjoy**, dog in the manger, damper, dampener, spoilsport, pessimist, prophet of doom, complainer, moaner, mope; *informal* sourpuss, grouch, grump, wet blanket, party-pooper, doom merchant; *rare* melancholiac.

misfire ▶ verb *his plan had misfired* **go wrong**, go awry, go amiss, be unsuccessful, fail, abort, be abortive, founder, come to nothing, come to grief, meet with disaster, fall through, be ruined, fall flat; boomerang, rebound, backfire, recoil; *informal* flop, bite the dust, go up in smoke, go phut.

misfit ▶ noun *a refuge for failures, freeloaders, and misfits* **fish out of water**, square peg in a round hole, round peg in a square hole; **nonconformist**, eccentric, maverick, individualist, deviant, exception, outsider; *informal* **oddball**, odd fish, weirdo, weirdie, freak; *N. Amer. informal* screwball, kook.

misfortune ▶ noun *they endured many misfortunes* **problem**, difficulty, trouble, setback, reverse, adversity, reverse of fortune, misadventure, mishap, stroke of bad luck, blow, failure, accident, disaster, tragedy, affliction, sorrow, misery, woe, trial, tribulation, catastrophe, calamity.
OPPOSITE piece of luck.

misgiving ▶ noun *despite occasional misgivings, he was optimistic* **qualm**, doubt, reservation, scruple; suspicion, distrust, mistrust, lack of faith, lack of confidence, diffidence, second thoughts; trepidation, scepticism, worry, unease, uneasiness, anxiety, apprehension, uncertainty, niggle, disquiet, disquietude, hesitation, hesitance, hesitancy.
OPPOSITE confidence.

misguided ▶ adjective **1** *the whole selection policy had been misguided* **erroneous**, fallacious, unwarranted, unfounded, unsound, misplaced, misconceived, ill-advised, inadvisable, ill-considered, ill-judged, inappropriate, impolitic, unwise, injudicious, imprudent, rash, foolish.
OPPOSITE well judged.
2 *the misguided teacher might well believe that self-expression was all that was needed* **misinformed**, misled, misdirected, labouring under a delusion/misapprehension, wrong, mistaken, deluded, ill-advised, foolish.
OPPOSITE well informed.

mishandle ▶ verb **1** *he was accused of mishandling the allocation of land for development* **botch**, bungle, fluff, fumble, make a mess of; **mismanage**, misdirect, misgovern, misconduct, mar, spoil, ruin, mangle, wreck; *informal* make a hash of, muff, mess up, muck up, foul up, screw up, bitch up; *Brit. informal* make a muck of, make a pig's ear of, make a Horlicks of, cock up; *vulgar slang* balls up, fuck up.
2 *he mishandled people and pushed them about* **bully**, persecute, treat badly, ill-treat, mistreat, maltreat, abuse, ill-use, misuse, knock about/around, hit, beat, strike, manhandle, maul, molest, injure, harm, hurt; *informal* beat up, rough up, do over.
3 *the equipment could be dangerous if mishandled* **misuse**, abuse, use inexpertly, misapply, handle/treat roughly.

mishap ▶ noun *a fair proportion of major accidents are generated by minor mishaps* **accident**, trouble, problem, difficulty, setback, reverse, adversity, reverse of fortune, misadventure, misfortune, mischance, stroke of bad luck, blow; failure, disaster, tragedy, affliction, woe, trial, tribulation, catastrophe, contretemps, upset, calamity.

mishmash ▶ noun *a bizarre mishmash of colours and patterns* **jumble**, mess, confusion, hotchpotch, hodgepodge, ragbag, pastiche, patchwork, farrago, hash, assortment, medley, miscellany, mixture, melange, blend, variety, mixed bag, mix, diversity, collection, selection, assemblage, combination, motley collection, pot-pourri, conglomeration; *informal* scissors-and-paste job; *rare* gallimaufry, omnium gatherum, olio, salmagundi, macédoine.

misinform ▶ verb *I'm afraid you have been misinformed* **mislead**, misguide, misdirect, give wrong information to, delude, take in, deceive, lie to, fool, hoodwink, lead astray, throw off the scent, send on a wild goose chase, put on the wrong track, pull the wool over someone's eyes, pull someone's leg; *informal* bamboozle, lead up the garden path, take for a ride; *N. Amer. informal* give someone a bum steer.

misinformation ▶ noun *a lot of misinformation was received in Moscow* **disinformation**, false information, misleading information, deception; lie, fib, false rumour, gossip, red herring, false trail; *informal* kidology; *N. Amer. informal* bum steer.

misinterpret ▶ verb *he explained that his proposal had been misinterpreted* **misunderstand**, misconceive, misconstrue, misapprehend, mistake, misread, put a wrong interpretation on; miss, confuse, confound, take amiss; miscalculate, err, be mistaken, get the wrong idea, get it/someone wrong, receive a false impression, be under a delusion, get (hold of) the wrong end of the stick, be at cross purposes; *informal* be barking up the wrong tree.

misjudge ▶ verb *she had misjudged her nearness to the wall and crashed into it* **get the wrong idea about**, get wrong, get the wrong end of the stick about, judge incorrectly, jump to the wrong conclusion about, estimate wrongly; overestimate, underestimate, overvalue, undervalue, underrate, be wrong about, miscalculate, misconstrue, misread, misapprehend; wrong, do someone an injustice, belittle.

mislay ▶ verb *I seem to have mislaid my driving licence* **lose**, misplace, put in the wrong place, lose track of, miss; drop, forget, be unable to find, be unable to lay one's hands on, forget the whereabouts of, forget where one has put something.
OPPOSITES find; keep.

mislead ▶ verb *it seemed that Caroline had deliberately misled her* **deceive**, delude, take in, lie to, fool, hoodwink, lead astray, throw off the scent, send on a wild goose chase, put on the wrong track, pull the wool over someone's eyes, pull someone's leg, misguide, misdirect, misinform, give wrong information to; *informal* bamboozle, lead up the garden path, take for a ride; *N. Amer. informal* give someone a bum steer.

misleading ▶ adjective *the leaflet was full of misleading statements* **deceptive**, confusing, deceiving, equivocal, ambiguous, fallacious, specious, spurious, false, mock, pseudo, illusory, delusive, evasive; casuistic, sophistical.

mismanage ▶ verb *the campaign had been badly mismanaged* **botch**, bungle, fluff, fumble, make a mess of, mishandle, misdirect, misgovern, misconduct, mar, spoil, ruin, mangle, wreck; *informal* make a hash of, muff, mess up, muck up, foul up, screw up, bitch up; *Brit. informal* make a muck of, cock up, make a pig's ear of, make a Horlicks of; *vulgar slang* fuck up, balls up.

M

mismatch ▶ noun *there is still a mismatch between policy and practice* **discrepancy**, lack of congruence, inconsistency, contradiction, incongruity, incongruousness, conflict, discord, irreconcilability, misalliance, mismarriage, mésalliance, bad match.

mismatched ▶ adjective *mismatched kitchen units* **ill-assorted**, ill-matched, incongruous, unsuited, incompatible, inharmonious, conflicting, inconsistent, opposed, at odds; out of keeping, clashing, discrepant; uneven, dissimilar, unlike, unalike, different, varying, variant, at variance, disparate, unrelated, divergent, deviating, diverse, various, contrasting, distinct.
OPPOSITES matching, compatible.

misogynist ▶ noun *a bachelor and renowned misogynist* **woman-hater**, anti-feminist, male chauvinist, male supremacist, chauvinist, sexist; *informal* male chauvinist pig, MCP.

misplace ▶ verb *he had misplaced the tickets* **lose**, mislay, put in the wrong place, lose track of, miss, drop, forget, be unable to find, be unable to lay one's hands on, forget the whereabouts of, forget where one has put something.
OPPOSITES find; keep.

misplaced ▶ adjective **1** *his comments turned out to be misplaced* **misguided**, unwise, misconceived, ill-advised, ill-considered, ill-judged; **inappropriate**, unsuitable, untoward, inapt.
2 *her misplaced keys* **lost**, mislaid, missing, nowhere to be found.

misprint ▶ noun *the book is full of misprints* **mistake**, error, printing mistake/error, typographical mistake/error, typesetting mistake/error, keyboarding mistake/error, keying mistake/error, typing mistake/error, corrigendum, erratum; *Brit.* literal; *informal* typo, howler; *Brit. informal* boob.

misquote ▶ verb *my original statement has been misquoted* **misreport**, misrepresent, misstate, quote incorrectly, take/quote out of context, distort, twist, slant, bias, put a spin on, pervert, falsify, garble, muddle, mistranslate; *rare* misrender.

misrepresent ▶ verb *you are misrepresenting the views of the government* **give a false account of**, give a false idea of, misstate, misreport, misquote, quote/take out of context, garble, misinterpret, put a spin on, falsify, fudge, pervert, belie, distort, warp, strain, colour, manipulate, parody, travesty, conceal, disguise.

misrule ▶ noun **1** *the 1484 Act is scathing about the misrule of Edward IV* **bad government**, misgovernment, mismanagement, misdirection, mishandling, maladministration, negligence, incompetence, malpractice.
2 *the weekly carnival of misrule at contemporary football games* **lawlessness**, anarchy, disorder, chaos, confusion, mayhem, turmoil, tumult.
OPPOSITE order.

miss[1] ▶ verb **1** *the shot he fired missed her by inches* **fail to hit**, be wide of, go wide of, fall short of.
OPPOSITE hit.
2 *Mandy missed the catch and flung the ball back rather crossly* **fail to catch**, drop, fumble, fluff, bungle, mishandle, misfield, mishit.
OPPOSITE catch.
3 *I'll miss my bus now* **be too late for**, fail to catch/get.
OPPOSITE catch.
4 *I'm sorry, I missed what you said* **fail to hear**, fail to take in, mishear, misunderstand.
5 *you can't miss the station because it's so big* **fail to see/notice**, overlook, pass over, forget.
OPPOSITES see, notice.
6 *she never missed a meeting that I remember* **fail to attend**, be too late for, absent oneself from, be absent from, play truant from, take French leave from, cut, skip, omit; *Brit. informal* skive off.
OPPOSITE attend.
7 *don't miss this exciting opportunity!* **fail to take advantage of**, fail to seize/grasp/take, let slip, let go/pass, forfeit, pass up, lose out on, overlook, disregard.
8 *I left my flat early to try to miss the rush-hour traffic* **avoid**, beat, evade, escape, dodge, sidestep, elude, get round, circumvent, steer clear of, give a wide berth to, find a way round, bypass, skirt, cheat, duck.
OPPOSITE get caught up in.
9 *she loved her father and missed him when he was away* **pine for**, yearn for, ache for, long for, long to see, regret the absence/loss of, feel the loss of, feel nostalgic for, need.
10 *we did not miss the children until darkness fell* **notice the absence of**, find missing.
□ **miss someone/something out leave out**, exclude, fail to include, except, miss, miss off, fail to mention, pass over, skip; *Brit. informal* give something a miss.
▶ noun *one hit and three misses* **failure**, omission, slip, blunder, error, mistake, fiasco; *informal* flop.
OPPOSITE hit.

miss[2] ▶ noun *that little miss knows more than she lets on* **young woman**, young lady, girl, schoolgirl, slip of a girl; girlie, missy, lass, maiden, maid; nymphet, belle, baby doll; *Scottish* lassie; *Irish* colleen; *informal* babe, chick, bit, doll, teeny-bopper; *Brit. informal* popsy, bird, bint, poppet; *N. Amer. informal* broad, dame, patootie; *Irish informal* mot; *Austral./NZ informal* sheila; *dated, informal* filly, baggage; *N. Amer. dated, informal* bobby-soxer; *literary* damsel, nymph; *archaic or humorous* wench.

misshapen ▶ adjective *his bowed legs and misshapen feet* **deformed**, malformed, distorted, crooked, contorted, wry, twisted, warped, out of shape, bent, bandy, asymmetrical, irregular, misproportioned, ill-proportioned, ill-shaped, disfigured, hunchbacked, abnormal, grotesque, monstrous; *Scottish* thrawn.
OPPOSITES well proportioned, well built.

missile *See centre pages for lists of* **Bombs and Mines** **Bullets and Shot** **Projectiles**
▶ noun *a player was hit by a missile thrown by a spectator* **projectile**; *rare* trajectile.

missing ▶ adjective **1** *his clothes and wallet are also missing* **lost**, mislaid, misplaced, nowhere to be found, absent, not present, gone, gone astray, unaccounted for.
OPPOSITE to hand.
2 *passion was an element that had been* **missing from** *her life for too long* **absent from**, not present in, not to be found in, lacking in, wanting from; in short supply.
OPPOSITES present, plentiful.

mission ▶ noun **1** *two Alton drivers are among a team on a mercy mission to Romania* **assignment**, commission, expedition, journey, trip, errand, undertaking, operation; task, job, labour, work, chore; business, duty, charge, trust; *Scottish & Irish* message.
2 *her mission in life is to heal the sick* **vocation**, calling, pursuit, goal, aim, quest, undertaking, purpose, function.
3 *a trade mission* **delegation**, deputation, commission, task force, legation, representation, delegacy.
4 *he returned to southern Africa as a mission teacher* missionary post, missionary station, missionary organization.
5 *a bombing mission* **sortie**, operation, raid.

missionary ▶ noun *methods employed by Christian missionaries to convert Hindus* **evangelist**, apostle, proselytizer, preacher, televangelist, minister, priest; **campaigner**, crusader, champion, converter, promoter, advocate, proponent.

missive ▶ noun *a missive from the Foreign Office* **message**, communication, letter, word, note, memorandum, line, report, bulletin, communiqué, dispatch, intelligence, piece of information, news, notification, announcement, greeting, epistle; *informal* memo; *literary* tidings.

misspent ▶ adjective *his misspent youth* **wasted**, dissipated, squandered, thrown away, frittered away, prodigal, misused, misapplied, irregular; idle, profitless, unprofitable.
OPPOSITES well regulated, fruitful, profitable.

misstate ▶ verb *they were accused of misstating the underlying purpose of the transaction* **misreport**, misrepresent, take/quote out of context; distort, twist, slant, bias, put a spin on, pervert, falsify; garble, muddle, mistranslate; *rare* misrender.

mist ▶ noun *the mist was clearing and the sun began to peep through* **haze**, **fog**, smog, murk, cloud, cloudiness, mistiness, Scotch mist, haar, vapour, drizzle, spray; steam, condensation, film; *N. English* (sea) fret; *literary* brume, fume.
▶ verb
□ **mist over/up** *her glasses were misting up* **steam up**, become misty, fog over/up, become covered with condensation, haze over, film over, cloud over, become cloudy, become blurred.

mistake ▶ noun **1** *I assumed it had been a mistake on the part of the overworked staff* **error**, fault, inaccuracy, omission, slip, blunder, miscalculation, misunderstanding, flaw, oversight, misinterpretation, fallacy, gaffe, faux pas, solecism, misapprehension, misconception, misreading; *informal* slip-up, boo-boo, howler, boner; *Brit. informal* boob, clanger; *N. Amer. informal* goof; *Brit. informal, dated* bloomer; *rare* misreckoning.
2 *a couple of spelling mistakes* **misprint**, printing error/mistake, typographical error/mistake, typesetting error/mistake, keyboarding error/mistake, keying error/mistake, typing error/mistake, corrigendum, erratum; *Brit.* literal; *informal* typo.
□ **make a mistake go wrong**, err, make an error, blunder, be wide of the mark, go astray, miscalculate; *informal* slip up, make a boo-boo, make a howler; *Brit. informal* boob.
▶ verb **1** *men were so apt to mistake their own feelings* **misunderstand**, misinterpret, get wrong, put a wrong interpretation on, misconstrue, misapprehend, misread, miss, take amiss.
2 *children often* **mistake** *vitamin pills* **for** *sweets* **confuse with**, mix up with, take for, misinterpret as, confound with.
□ **be mistaken** *I'm afraid you are mistaken—I've never been here before* **be wrong**, be in error, be at fault, be under a misapprehension, be misinformed, be misguided, be wide of the mark, be barking up the wrong tree, get the wrong end of the stick.
OPPOSITE be right.

mistaken ▶ adjective *there is a mistaken but widespread belief that manufacturing is still shrinking* **wrong**, erroneous, inaccurate, incorrect,

M

inexact, off-target, off-beam, out, false, fallacious, unsound, unfounded, misguided, misinformed, wide of the mark.
OPPOSITES correct, accurate.

mistakenly ▶ adverb **1** *we often mistakenly imagine that when a problem is diagnosed it is solved* **wrongly**, in error, erroneously, incorrectly, falsely, fallaciously, inaccurately, imprecisely, inappropriately.
OPPOSITES correctly, accurately.
2 *Mr Perkins had mistakenly opened a package addressed to the actor* **by accident**, accidentally, inadvertently, unintentionally, unwittingly, unknowingly, unconsciously, by mistake, by chance, misguidedly.
OPPOSITE intentionally.

mistimed ▶ adjective *his mistimed floral tribute upset her greatly* **ill-timed**, badly timed, inopportune, inappropriate, untimely, unseasonable, inconvenient; awkward, unwelcome, unfavourable, unfortunate, inapt.
OPPOSITES opportune, timely.

mistreat ▶ verb *foreign nationals held hostage in the country had been mistreated* **ill-treat**, maltreat, abuse, ill-use, misuse, treat badly, handle/treat roughly, knock about/around, hit, beat, strike, mishandle; manhandle, maul, molest, injure, harm, hurt, bully, persecute; *informal* beat up, rough up, do over.

mistreatment ▶ noun *reforms designed to protect detainees from mistreatment or torture* **ill-treatment**, maltreatment, abuse, ill use, ill usage, beating, rough handling, mishandling, manhandling; molestation, injury, harm, bullying, persecution.

mistress ▶ noun *his wife never found out about his mistress* **lover**, girlfriend, paramour, kept woman, live-in lover; courtesan, concubine, inamorata, hetaera, sultana; *informal* **fancy woman**, bit on the side, gun moll, (little) bit of fluff; *dated* lady-love; *archaic* doxy, leman.

mistrust ▶ verb **1** *I mistrust his motives* **be suspicious of**, be mistrustful of, be distrustful of, be sceptical of, be wary of, be chary of, harbour suspicions about, be uneasy about, distrust, have doubts about, have misgivings about, have reservations about, have qualms about, suspect, wonder about; *informal* be leery of.
OPPOSITE trust.
2 *we are taught to mistrust our impulses* **question**, challenge, doubt, disbelieve, have no confidence/faith in, query.
▶ noun **1** *mistrust of Russia was widespread* **suspicion**, **distrust**, doubt, misgivings, wariness, circumspection.
OPPOSITE trust.
2 *does this reflect mistrust of David's competence?* **questioning**; lack of confidence/faith in, doubt about, disbelief in.

mistrustful ▶ adjective *such youngsters may often be mistrustful of those who try to help them* **suspicious**, chary, wary, uncertain, unsure, distrustful, untrusting, doubtful, dubious, uneasy, cautious, hesitant, sceptical, unbelieving; *informal* leery.
OPPOSITE trusting.

misty ▶ adjective **1** *misty weather* **hazy**, **foggy**, cloudy, smoggy, steamy, murky, smoky.
OPPOSITE clear.
2 *hovering in the darkness was a misty figure* **blurry**, fuzzy, blurred, dim, indistinct, unclear, vague, obscure, lacking definition, out of focus, nebulous.
OPPOSITE sharp.
3 *a few misty memories* **vague**, unclear, indefinite, obscure, hazy, nebulous; tenuous, slight, rough, approximate, imprecise.
OPPOSITE clear.

misunderstand ▶ verb *she misunderstood his motives | I must have misunderstood—I thought you were anxious to leave* **misapprehend**, misinterpret, put a wrong interpretation on, misconstrue, misconceive, mistake, misread, miss, confuse, confound, take amiss; miscalculate, err, be mistaken, get the wrong idea, get it/someone wrong, take something the wrong way, receive a false impression, be under a delusion, get (hold of) the wrong end of the stick, be at cross purposes; *informal* be barking up the wrong tree.
OPPOSITES grasp, understand correctly, get the right idea.

misunderstanding ▶ noun **1** *the proposals are based on a fundamental misunderstanding of juvenile crime* **misinterpretation**, misconstruction, misreading, misapprehension, misconception; mistake, error, misjudgement, misbelief, miscalculation, confusion, mix-up, the wrong idea, false impression, fallacy, illusion, delusion.
2 *there have been misunderstandings but they have been sorted out* **disagreement**, difference, difference of opinion, variance, clash of views, dispute, disputation, falling-out, quarrel, argument, altercation, squabble, wrangle, row, clash, conflict; *informal* ruction, spat, scrap, tiff.
OPPOSITE harmony.

misuse ▶ verb **1** *the mayor was found guilty of misusing public funds* **put to wrong use**, misapply, misemploy, embezzle, use fraudulently; abuse, exploit, squander, waste, dissipate.
2 *she had been misused by her husband* **ill-treat**, maltreat, mistreat, abuse, ill-use, treat badly, handle/treat roughly, knock about/around, hit, beat, strike, mishandle, manhandle, maul, molest, injure, harm, hurt, bully, persecute; *informal* beat up, rough up, do over.
OPPOSITES look after, treat well.
▶ noun **1** *the misuse of public funds* **wrong use**, misemployment, embezzlement, fraud; exploitation, squandering, waste, dissipation.
2 *the misuse of drugs* **illegal use**, wrong use, abuse, misapplication.
3 *only drastic curbs on foreigners would prevent the misuse and injury of the indigenous people* **ill-treatment**, maltreatment, abuse, ill-use, ill-usage, beating, rough handling, mishandling, manhandling, molestation, injury, harm, bullying, persecution.

mite ▶ noun

WORD LINKS
fear of mites and ticks **acarophobia**
study of mites and ticks **acarology**

mitigate ▶ verb *drugs which mitigated the worst symptoms of the disease* **alleviate**, reduce, diminish, lessen, weaken, lighten, attenuate, take the edge off, allay, ease, assuage, palliate, cushion, damp, deaden, dull, appease, soothe, relieve, help, soften, temper, still, quell, quieten, quiet, tone down, blunt, dilute, moderate, modify, abate, lull, pacify, placate, mollify, sweeten, tranquillize, remit, extenuate, excuse, commute.
OPPOSITES aggravate, increase, intensify.

mitigate or militate?

Mitigate and **militate** are frequently confused on account of their similarity in form, but their meanings are quite different. *Mitigate* means 'make (something bad) less severe', as in *drainage schemes have helped to mitigate this problem*, while *militate* is nearly always used in constructions with *against* to mean 'be a powerful factor in preventing', as in *these disagreements will militate against the two communities coming together.*

mitigating ▶ adjective *he would have faced a prison sentence but for mitigating circumstances* **extenuating**, exonerative, justificatory, justifying, vindicatory, vindicating, exculpatory, palliative, qualifying, moderating, modifying, tempering, lessening.
OPPOSITE aggravating.

mitigation ▶ noun **1** *the mitigation of the problems of rural unemployment* **alleviation**, reduction, diminution, lessening, easing, weakening, lightening, assuagement, palliation, cushioning, dulling, deadening; soothing, softening, relief.
OPPOSITE intensification.
2 *in mitigation, she said her client had been deeply depressed* **extenuation**, explanation, excuse; appeasement.

mix ▶ verb **1** *mix all the ingredients together | oil and water don't mix* **blend**, mingle, combine, put together, stir, jumble, merge; fuse, unite, unify, join, amalgamate, incorporate, fold in, meld, marry, mesh, compound, alloy, coalesce, homogenize, intermingle, intermix, interweave, interpenetrate, interlace; cross, cross-breed, hybridize, integrate, emulsify, premix; shuffle, shift around; *informal* blunge; *rare* admix, commingle, interflow, commix.
OPPOSITES separate, divide.
2 *she mixes with all sorts* **associate**, **socialize**, mingle, meet, get together, have dealings, fraternize, circulate, keep company, rub shoulders, consort, move, go out; *N. Amer.* rub elbows; *informal* hang out/around, knock about/around, hobnob; *Brit. informal* hang about.
OPPOSITE keep oneself to oneself.
3 *we're like oil and water—we just don't mix* **be compatible**, get along/on, go (together), fit together, be in harmony, be like-minded, be of the same mind, be of like mind, see eye to eye, agree; *informal* hit it off, click, be on the same wavelength.
□ **mix something up 1** *mix up the filler paste with its catalyst* **blend**, mingle, combine, put together, stir, jumble, merge; fuse, unite, unify, join, amalgamate, incorporate, fold in, meld, marry, mesh, compound, alloy, coalesce, homogenize, intermingle, intermix, interweave, interpenetrate, interlace; cross, cross-breed, hybridize, integrate, emulsify, premix; shuffle, shift around; *informal* blunge; *rare* admix, commingle, interflow, commix.
2 *I'm sorry, I mixed up the dates* **confuse**, get confused, muddle, muddle up, get muddled up, get jumbled up, scramble, mistake.
□ **mixed up in** *I'm sure he was mixed up in this business* **involved in**, embroiled in, entangled in, drawn into, caught up in, a party to.
▶ noun *the decor is a fascinating mix of antique and modern* **mixture**, blend, mingling, combination, compound, fusion, composition, concoction, brew, alloy, merger, union, amalgamation, amalgam, coalition, cross, hybrid; medley, melange, diversity, collection, selection, assortment, variety, mixed bag, miscellany, assemblage, motley collection, pot-pourri, conglomeration, jumble, mess, confusion, mishmash, hotchpotch, hodgepodge, ragbag, pastiche, patchwork, farrago, hash; *informal* scissors-and-paste job; *rare* gallimaufry, omnium gatherum, olio, salmagundi, macédoine.

mixed ▶ adjective **1** *a mixed collection of artefacts* **assorted**, varied, variegated, miscellaneous, different, differing, disparate, diverse,

diversified, motley, sundry, jumbled, haphazard, heterogeneous.
OPPOSITE homogeneous.
2 *the original chickens were of mixed breed* **hybrid**, half-caste, half-breed, cross-breed, cross-bred, interbred, mongrel, impure; *dated* underbred.
OPPOSITE pure.
3 *he had mixed reactions* **ambivalent**, equivocal, unsure, uncertain, doubtful, contradictory, conflicting, confused, muddled.
OPPOSITE unequivocal.

mixed up ▶ **adjective** *she's a crazy mixed-up kid* **confused**, at sea, befuddled, bemused, bewildered, confounded, muddled, perplexed; maladjusted, ill-adjusted, disturbed, neurotic, unbalanced; *informal* screwed up, untogether, hung up, messed up; *vulgar slang* fucked up; *archaic* mazed. See also MIX.

mixer ▶ **noun 1** *a kitchen mixer* **blender**, food processor, liquidizer, stirrer, beater, churn, whisk.
2 *she was a very private person, never really a mixer* **sociable person**, socializer, mingler, extrovert, social butterfly, socialite, life and soul of the party.
OPPOSITE loner.

mixture ▶ **noun 1** *every member of the family would stir the pudding mixture* **blend**, mix, brew, combination, concoction; jumble, fusion, composition, compound, alloy, amalgam.
2 *it's hard to imagine a stranger mixture of people* **assortment**, miscellany, medley, melange, blend, variety, mixed bag, mix, diversity, collection, selection, assemblage, combination, motley collection, pot-pourri, conglomeration, jumble, mess, confusion, mishmash, hotchpotch, hodgepodge, ragbag, pastiche, patchwork, farrago, hash; *rare* gallimaufry, omnium gatherum, olio, salmagundi, macédoine.
3 *other animals were a mixture of genetic strands* **cross**, cross-breed, mongrel, hybrid, half-breed, half-caste.

mix-up ▶ **noun** *there's been a mix-up over rules governing foreign players* **confusion**, muddle, misunderstanding, mistake, error, mess, jumble.

moan ▶ **noun 1** *Katherine's soft moans of pain* **groan**, wail, whimper, sob, cry, whine, howl, lament, lamentation, keen.
2 *the moan of the wind* **sough**, sigh, murmur, whisper, groan.
3 *there were moans about the car's feeble ventilation* **complaint**, complaining, grouse, grousing, moans and groans, grouch, grouching, grumble, grumbling, whine, whining, carping, muttering, murmur, murmuring, whispering; *informal* gripe, griping, bellyache, bitch, whinge, whingeing, beef, beefing.
▶ **verb 1** *the injured man moaned in agony* **groan**, wail, whimper, sob, cry, whine, howl, keen.
2 *the wind moaned in the trees* **sough**, sigh, murmur, whisper, groan.
3 *you're always moaning about the weather* **complain**, grouse, grouch, grumble, whine, carp, mutter, murmur, whisper; *informal* gripe, bellyache, bitch, beef, whinge, *N. English informal* mither.

mob ▶ **noun 1** *troops were called in to disperse the mob* **crowd**, horde, multitude, rabble, mass, body, throng; group, host, pack, press, crush, jam, gang, gathering, swarm, assemblage; *archaic* rout.
2 *the mob, the dregs, were to be firmly excluded from political life* **the common people**, the masses, the populace, the public, the multitude, the rank and file, the commonality, the commonalty, the third estate, the plebeians, the proletariat, the peasantry, the crowd; the hoi polloi, the lower classes, the common herd, the rabble, the riff-raff, the canaille, the great unwashed, the dregs of society, the ragtag (and bobtail), the proles, the plebs.
3 (*Brit. informal*) *don't you get any firearms training in your mob?* **group**, set, crowd, lot, circle, coterie, in-crowd, clan, faction, pack, band, ring, fraternity, brotherhood, society, troop, company, team; *informal* gang, bunch, lads; *Brit. informal* shower.
▶ **verb 1** *Chancellor Kohl was mobbed when he visited East Berlin* **surround**, swarm around, besiege, jostle; harass, set upon, fall on, worry.
2 *the reporters mobbed the gift shop like a crowd of souvenir-starved tourists* **crowd (into)**, cram full, fill to overflowing, fill, pack, throng, press into, squeeze into.

WORD LINKS
fear of mobs **demophobia, ochlophobia**

mobile ▶ **adjective 1** *both patients had been mobile up to the day of surgery* **able to move**, able to move around, moving, walking, ambulant, ambulatory; lively, sprightly, spry, energetic, vigorous; *Zoology* motile.
OPPOSITES immobile, motionless, inert.
2 *her mobile face registered sorrow and concern* **expressive**, eloquent, suggestive, meaning, speaking, revealing, telltale, animated, changing, ever-changing.
OPPOSITE expressionless.
3 *a mobile library* **travelling**, transportable, transferable, portable, movable, locomotive, manoeuvrable; itinerant, peripatetic, nomadic, peregrine, wandering, roving, rangy; airborne, mechanized, motorized, waterborne, seaborne.
OPPOSITE stationary.
4 *these groups consist of highly mobile young people and families* **adaptable**, flexible, versatile, changing, fluid, moving, on the move, adjustable, transplantable.
OPPOSITE static.

mobility ▶ **noun 1** *elderly people may become socially isolated as a result of restricted mobility* **ability to move**, movability, moveableness, motility, vigour, strength, potency.
2 *the gleeful mobility of Billy's face* **expressiveness**, eloquence, animation.
3 *the mobility of the product* **transportability**, portability, manoeuvrability.
4 *an increasing mobility in the workforce* **adaptability**, flexibility, versatility, adjustability.

mobilize ▶ **verb 1** *the government mobilized regular troops and reservists* **marshal**, deploy, muster, rally, call to arms, call up, summon, assemble, mass, organize, make ready, prepare, ready.
2 *he used the press to mobilize support for his party* **bring into play**, bring into service, arouse, generate, induce, cause, resort to, awaken, deploy, waken, excite, incite, provoke, foment, prompt, stimulate, stir up, impel, galvanize, urge, encourage, inspire, whip up.

mock ▶ **verb 1** *the local children taunted and mocked the old people in the home* **ridicule**, jeer at, sneer at, deride, treat with contempt, treat contemptuously, scorn, make fun of, poke fun at, laugh at, make jokes about, laugh to scorn, scoff at, pillory, be sarcastic about, tease, taunt, make a monkey of, rag, chaff, jibe at; *Austral./NZ* chiack; *informal* kid, rib, josh, twit; *Brit. informal* wind up, take the mickey out of; *Brit. vulgar slang* take the piss out of; *N. Amer. informal* goof on, rag on, razz, pull someone's chain; *Austral./NZ informal* poke mullock at, sling off at; *dated* make sport of.
2 *they still mock the slow way he speaks* **parody**, ape, guy, take off, caricature, satirize, lampoon, imitate, mimic; *informal* send up, spoof.
▶ **adjective** *a mock leather armchair* **imitation**, artificial, man-made, manufactured, simulated, synthetic, ersatz, plastic, so-called, fake, false, faux, reproduction, replica, facsimile, dummy, model, toy, make-believe, sham, spurious, bogus, counterfeit, fraudulent, forged, pseudo, pretended; *informal* pretend, phoney.
OPPOSITE genuine.

mockery ▶ **noun 1** *a note of mockery in his voice* **ridicule**, derision, jeering, sneering, contempt, scorn, scoffing, joking, teasing, taunting, sarcasm, ragging, chaffing, jibing; *Austral./NZ* chiacking; *informal* kidding, kidology, ribbing, joshing; *Brit. informal* winding up; taking the mickey; *Brit. vulgar slang* taking the piss; *N. Amer. informal* goofing, razzing.
2 *the trial was a mockery* **travesty**, charade, farce, parody, laughing stock, caricature, lampoon, burlesque, apology, excuse, poor substitute.

CHOOSE THE RIGHT WORD

mockery, ridicule, derision

These three words reflect increasing degrees of scorn.

- **Mockery** is the least severe. While it is usually intended to humiliate (*stung by her mockery, Frankie hung his head*), it can also express affectionate amusement (*'Liar,' he said with soft mockery*). It can also mean 'a worthy object of mockery' in the phrase *a mockery of* (*after a mockery of a trial, he was executed*), but the sense is usually considerably weakened, especially (however serious the subject) in the cliché *make a mockery of* (*modern technology has made a mockery of the 1959 Obscene Publications Act*).
- **Ridicule** is more intense, the aim being not so much to provoke or tease the victim as to cause others to laugh at them (*Puritans were frequently subjected to ridicule and abuse at the hands of their contemporaries*).
- **Derision** is still crueller and more contemptuous (*Eline would forget the hurtful words spoken in derision*). The phrase *of derision* is commonly used to qualify a description of a scornful noise (*the answer was a snort of derision*).

mocking ▶ **adjective** *a mocking smile* **sneering**, derisive, contemptuous, scornful, sardonic, insulting, satirical, sarcastic, ironic, ironical, quizzical, teasing, taunting.
OPPOSITES friendly, open, good-humoured.

mode ▶ **noun 1** *an extremely informal mode of policing* **manner**, way, fashion, means, method, system, style, approach, technique, procedure, process, methodology, modus operandi, form, routine, practice.
2 *with the camera in manual mode you can zoom in fast* **function**, position, operation, role, capacity.
3 *the mode for active wear took hold in the seventies* **fashion**, **vogue**, current/latest style, style, look, trend, latest thing, latest taste; craze, rage, fad, general tendency, convention, custom, practice; *French* dernier cri.

model ▶ **noun 1** *a working model of a train* **replica**, copy, representation, mock-up, dummy, imitation, double, duplicate, lookalike, reproduction; **toy**, miniature, facsimile.
2 *the American model of airline deregulation* **prototype**, stereotype, archetype, type, version, style; mould, template, framework, pattern, design, guide, blueprint, paradigm; sample, example, exemplar.
3 *she was an absolute model as a teacher* **ideal**, paragon, perfect example,

specimen, perfect specimen; personification, embodiment, perfection, acme, the epitome; *French* beau idéal, nonpareil, crème de la crème; *informal* pick of the bunch.
4 *she was too small to be a top model* **fashion model**, supermodel, mannequin; *informal* clothes horse.
5 *he used his wife as a model for his pictures* **sitter**, poser, subject, artist's model, photographic model.
6 *he changes his car every year for the latest model* **version**, type, design, mark, configuration, variety, kind, sort.
7 *this dress is a model, so not for sale, I'm afraid* **original**, original design, exclusive; *informal* one-off.
▶ **adjective 1** *a competition for model hot-air balloons* **replica**, **toy**, miniature, mock-up, dummy, imitation, duplicate, lookalike, reproduction, facsimile; artificial, fake, make-believe, sham, false, spurious, bogus, counterfeit; *informal* pretend, phoney.
2 *ten model farms have been set up as a showcase for alternative production methods* **prototypical**, prototypal, archetypal, illustrative.
3 *a model teacher* **ideal**, perfect, exemplary, classic, flawless, faultless, consummate, impeccable.
OPPOSITES deficient, imperfect.

moderate ▶ **adjective 1** *the club enjoyed moderate success* **average**, modest, medium, middling, ordinary, common, commonplace, everyday, workaday; tolerable, passable, adequate, fair, decent; **mediocre**, indifferent, uninspired, undistinguished, unexceptional, unexciting, unremarkable, run-of-the-mill, lacklustre, forgettable, inferior, second-rate; *informal* OK, so-so, bog-standard, fair-to-middling, (plain) vanilla, nothing to write home about, no great shakes, not so hot, not up to much; *NZ informal* half-pie.
OPPOSITES great, massive.
2 *moderate demands | moderate prices* **reasonable**, within reason, acceptable, non-excessive, within due limits; **inexpensive**, low, cheap, bargain-basement, fair, modest; abstemious, temperate, restrained.
OPPOSITES outrageous, unreasonable.
3 *a man of moderate views* **dispassionate**, non-extreme, middle-of-the-road, non-radical, non-reactionary, open to reason, equitable, impartial.
OPPOSITE extreme.
4 *moderate behaviour* **restrained**, controlled, temperate, sober, steady, regular, not given to excesses; easy, even, mild, tolerant, lenient.
OPPOSITES unreasonable, immoderate.
▶ **verb 1** *the wind has moderated* **die down**, abate, let up, calm down, lessen, grow less, decrease, diminish, slacken; ebb, recede, dwindle, weaken, subside.
OPPOSITES get up, increase.
2 *you can do something to moderate the anger* **curb**, control, check, keep in check, keep under control, hold in, temper, regulate, restrain, restrict, subdue; still, damp, repress, tame, break, lessen, deaden, decrease, lower, reduce, diminish, remit, mitigate, alleviate, allay, appease, assuage, ease, palliate, soothe, soften, calm, modulate, pacify, mellow, mince, tone down.
OPPOSITES exacerbate, aggravate.
3 *the Speaker moderates the assembly* **chair**, take the chair of, preside over; **arbitrate**, mediate, referee, judge.

moderately ▶ **adverb** *a moderately successful small farmer* **somewhat**, quite, rather, fairly, reasonably, comparatively, relatively, to a limited extent/degree, to a certain degree, to some extent, within reason, within limits, tolerably, passably, adequately, satisfactorily; *informal* pretty, kind of, sort of.
OPPOSITES massively, hugely.

moderation ▶ **noun 1** *he was anxious to contrast his moderation with the sabre-rattling of his opponent* **self-restraint**, restraint, self-control, self-discipline; moderateness, temperateness, temperance, abstemiousness, non-indulgence, leniency, fairness.
OPPOSITE extremism.
2 *he called for a moderation of the Government's confrontational style* **relaxation**, easing (off), reduction, abatement, weakening, slackening, diminution, diminishing, lessening, decrease, lightening, subsidence, contraction; tailing off, waning, decline, modulation, ebb, alleviation, attenuation, modification, mitigation, allaying, appeasement, assuagement, palliation, cushioning, damping, deadening, dulling; soothing, relief, softening, tempering, stilling, quelling, calming, pacification, placation, mollification, remission, extenuation; *informal* let-up.
OPPOSITE stepping up.
□ **in moderation** *wine, if drunk in moderation, can be beneficial to health* **in moderate quantities**, in moderate amounts, within reasonable limits, within sensible limits, within limits, within bounds, within due limits; moderately, up to a point.

modern ▶ **adjective 1** *in modern times* **present-day**, contemporary, present-time, present, current, twenty-first-century, latter-day, recent, latest.
OPPOSITE past.
2 *her clothes are very modern* **fashionable**, in fashion, in, in style, in vogue, up to date, up to the minute, all the rage, trendsetting, stylish, voguish, modish, chic, smart, the latest, new, newest, newfangled, new-fashioned, fresh, modernistic, advanced, progressive, forward-looking; *French* à la mode; *informal* trendy, cool, flash, with it, swinging, now, hip, happening, snazzy, natty, nifty, go-ahead; *N. Amer. informal* tony.
OPPOSITES out of date, old-fashioned.

modernity ▶ **noun** **contemporaneity**, contemporaneousness, modernness, modernism, currency, freshness, novelty, fashionableness, vogue; *informal* trendiness, coolness, snazziness.

modernize ▶ **verb 1** *the company is investing $9m to modernize its manufacturing facilities* **update**, bring up to date, bring/drag/lead/march into the twenty-first century, streamline, rationalize, overhaul, develop; **renovate**, rebuild, reindustrialize, remodel, refashion, retouch, remake, redo, refresh, revamp, make over, rejuvenate, redecorate, refurbish; *informal* do over, tart up.
2 *if we don't modernize, we will lose our competitive edge* **get up to date**, move with the times, innovate, make changes/alterations; *informal* get in the swim, drag oneself into the twenty-first century, get on the ball, get with it.

modest ▶ **adjective 1** *she was always modest about her poetry* **self-effacing**, self-deprecating, humble, unpretentious, unassuming, unpresuming, unostentatious, low-key, free from vanity, keeping one's light under a bushel; **shy**, bashful, self-conscious, diffident, timid, reserved, retiring, reticent, quiet, coy, embarrassed, shamefaced, blushing, fearful, meek, docile, mild, apologetic; *Scottish* mim.
OPPOSITES boastful, conceited.
2 *a period of modest success* **moderate**, fair, tolerable, passable, adequate, satisfactory, acceptable, unexceptional, small; light, limited, scanty, skimpy, frugal, meagre, sparse.
OPPOSITES great, runaway.
3 *a modest house* **small**, ordinary, simple, plain, humble, homely; inexpensive, low-cost, cheap, poor; unostentatious, unpretentious, unimposing.
OPPOSITES grand, grandiose.
4 *the full-length skirt of her modest navy blue suit* **decorous**, decent, seemly, demure, sober, severe; coy, proper, discreet, delicate, chaste, virtuous.
OPPOSITES immodest, flamboyant.

modesty ▶ **noun 1** *Hannah's innate modesty cloaks many talents* **self-effacement**, humility, lack of vanity, lack of pretension, unpretentiousness; **shyness**, bashfulness, self-consciousness, reserve, reticence, timidity, meekness.
OPPOSITE boastfulness.
2 *Gandhi's political tactics obscured the modesty of his political aspirations* **limited scope**, moderation, fairness, acceptability, smallness.
OPPOSITE grandeur.
3 *it is appropriate to contrast the modesty of his home with those of more affluent politicians* **unpretentiousness**, simplicity, plainness, lack of pretension, inexpensiveness, lack of extravagance.
OPPOSITE grandeur.
4 *they jeered at her maidenly modesty* **decorum**, decorousness, decency, seemliness, demureness, sobriety, severity; coyness, propriety, discreetness, delicacy, chasteness, virtue.
OPPOSITES immodesty, flamboyance.

modicum ▶ **noun** *people with only a modicum of scientific knowledge* **little bit**, small amount, particle, degree, speck, fragment, scrap, crumb, grain, morsel, taste, soupçon, shred, mite, dash, drop, pinch, ounce, touch, tinge, dab, jot, iota, whit, tittle, jot or tittle, atom, inch, snippet, sliver, smattering, scintilla, hint, suggestion, whisper, trifle; *informal* smidgen, smidge, tad; *archaic* scantling, scruple.

modification ▶ **noun 1** *the design of the engine is undergoing extensive modification* **alteration**, adjustment, change, adaptation, improvement, refinement, revision, recasting, reshaping, refashioning, restyling, revamping, reworking, remodelling, remoulding, reconstruction, reorganization; variation, conversion, transformation; tailoring, customization.
2 *the proposal was passed after some minor modifications had been made* **revision**, refinement, variation, improvement, amendment, adaptation, adjustment, change, alteration.
3 *there was some modification of his views on communism* **softening**, moderation, tempering, qualification, restriction, lessening, reduction, decrease, diminishing, lowering, abatement, mitigation.

modify ▶ **verb 1** *their economic policy has been substantially modified* **alter**, make alterations to, change, adjust, make adjustments to, adapt, amend, improve, revise, recast, reform, reshape, refashion, redesign, restyle, revamp, rework, remake, remodel, remould, redo, reconstruct, reorganize, refine, reorient, reorientate, vary, transform, convert; customize, tailor; *informal* tweak; *technical* permute; *rare* permutate.
2 *he was forced to modify his more extreme views* **moderate**, revise, temper, soften, tone down, blunt, dull, qualify, restrict, limit, lessen, reduce, decrease, diminish, lower, abate, mitigate.

modish ▶ **adjective** **fashionable**, stylish, smart, chic, modern, contemporary, designer, all the rage, in vogue, trendsetting, voguish, up to the minute; *French* à la mode; *informal* trendy, cool, with it, in, now, hip, happening, snazzy, natty, nifty; *N. Amer. informal* kicky, tony; *Brit. informal, dated* all the go, swagger.

modulate ▶ verb **1** *the cells modulate the body's immune response* **regulate**, adjust, set, attune, balance, harmonize, temper, modify, moderate.
2 *she modulated her voice so as to speak more gently* **adjust**, change the tone of, vary, inflect.

modus operandi ▶ noun (*Latin*) **method of working**, method, way, MO, manner, technique, style, procedure, approach, course of action, plan of action, methodology, mode, fashion, process, means, strategy, plan, formula, recipe, practice; *rare* praxis.

mogul ▶ noun *Hollywood movie moguls* **magnate**, tycoon, VIP, notable, notability, personage, baron, captain, king, lord, grandee, mandarin, nabob; *informal* bigwig, big shot, big noise, big cheese, big gun, big wheel, big fish, top dog, Big Chief, Big Daddy, biggie, heavy, fat cat; *N. Amer. informal* kahuna, top banana, big enchilada, macher.

moist ▶ adjective **1** *the air was moist and heavy | moist, well-drained soil* **damp**, dampish, steamy, humid, muggy, clammy, dank, moisture-laden, wet, wettish, rainy, drizzly, drizzling, dewy, dripping, soggy, sweaty, sticky.
OPPOSITE dry.
2 *a rich, moist fruit cake* **succulent**, juicy, soft, spongy.
3 *her dark eyes grew moist* **tearful**, teary, dewy-eyed, watery, misty.

moisten ▶ verb *the compost should be moistened before use* **dampen**, wet, damp, dew, water, soak, irrigate, humidify; *literary* bedew; *rare* sparge, humify, humect, moistify.
OPPOSITE dry.

moisture ▶ noun *dehumidifiers will remove moisture from the air* **wetness**, wet, water, liquid, condensation, steam, vapour, dampness, damp, humidity, clamminess, mugginess, dankness, wateriness; rain, dew, drizzle, precipitation, spray; perspiration, sweat.

WORD LINKS
related prefix **hygro-**
instrument for measuring moisture in the air **hygrometer, hygroscope**

moisturizer ▶ noun *a moisturizer which hydrates the skin for up to 12 hours* **lotion**, cream, balm, emollient, salve, unguent, lubricant; hand lotion, body lotion, baby oil, cold cream, aftershave, aftersun; pomade, pomatum; *technical* humectant.

mole[1] ▶ noun *he had a small mole on his left cheek* **mark**, freckle, blotch, discoloration, spot, blemish.

mole[2] ▶ noun **1** *moles have burrowed under the lawn* *dialect* mouldwarp, mouldywarp.
2 *they planted a mole in the other side's operation* **spy**, agent, secret agent, double agent, undercover agent, operative, plant, infiltrator; *N. Amer. informal* spook; *archaic* intelligencer.

WORD LINKS
collective noun (for the animals) **labour**

mole[3] ▶ noun *a mole was built to protect the harbour from storms* **breakwater**, groyne, dyke, pier, jetty, sea wall, embankment, causeway.

molest ▶ verb **1** *the crowd were shouting abuse and molesting the police officers* **harass**, harry, pester, beset, persecute, torment, plague; *N. Amer. informal* roust.
2 *he was charged with molesting a ten-year-old boy* **abuse**, sexually abuse, assault, sexually assault, interfere with, rape, violate, attack, hurt, harm, injure; *informal* maul, grope, paw; *dated* ravish.

mollify ▶ verb **1** *nature reserves were set up to mollify local conservationists* **appease**, placate, pacify, conciliate, humour, soothe, calm, calm down, still, quieten, propitiate; *Austral.* square someone off.
OPPOSITE enrage.
2 *the government's undertaking mollified the fears of the public* **allay**, assuage, alleviate, mitigate, ease, lessen, reduce, moderate, lull, temper, tone down, cushion, quell, soften, blunt.
OPPOSITES inflame, aggravate.

mollusc ▶ noun. *See centre pages for list of* **Molluscs**

mollycoddle ▶ verb *his parents have mollycoddled him since he was a baby* **pamper**, cosset, coddle, spoil, indulge, overindulge, pet, baby, wait on hand and foot, wrap in cotton wool, spoon-feed, kill with/by kindness, nanny, nursemaid, feather-bed; *archaic* cocker.
▶ noun *the boy's a mollycoddle!* **milksop**, namby-pamby, crybaby, baby, coward, weakling, Milquetoast; *informal* sissy, weed, softie, nancy, nancy boy, pansy, ponce; *Brit. informal* wet, mummy's boy, chinless wonder, jessie; *N. Amer. informal* pantywaist, cupcake, pussy; *Austral./NZ informal* sook; *S. African informal* moffie; *archaic* poltroon.

molten ▶ adjective *a stream of molten metal* **liquefied**, liquid, fluid, melted, flowing, soft.

moment ▶ noun **1** *he thought for a moment before answering* **little while**, short time, bit, minute, second, instant, split second; *informal* sec, jiffy, jiff; *Brit. informal* tick, mo, two ticks.
2 *she would always remember the moment they met* **point in time**, point, time, hour, juncture, stage.
3 *the issues were of little moment to the voters* **importance**, import, significance, consequence, substance, note, mark, prominence, value, weight, concern, interest, gravity, seriousness.
□ **in a moment very soon**, in a minute, in a second, in a trice, in a flash, shortly, any minute, any minute now, in a short time, in an instant, in the twinkling of an eye, in (less than) no time, in no time at all, before you know it, before long; *N. Amer.* momentarily; *informal* in a jiffy, in two shakes, in two shakes of a lamb's tail, before you can say Jack Robinson, in the blink of an eye, in a blink, in the wink of an eye, in a wink, before you can say knife; *Brit. informal* in a tick, in two ticks, in a mo; *N. Amer. informal* in a snap; *archaic or informal* anon; *archaic* ere long.

momentarily ▶ adverb **1** *as he passed her door, he paused momentarily* **briefly**, temporarily, fleetingly, for a moment, for a second, for an instant, for a minute, for a little while.
2 (*N. Amer.*) *my husband will pick me up momentarily* **(very) soon**, in a minute, in a second, in a trice, in a flash, shortly, any minute, any minute now, in a short time, in an instant, in the twinkling of an eye, in (less than) no time, in no time at all, before you know it, before long; *informal* in a jiffy, in two shakes, in two shakes of a lamb's tail, before you can say Jack Robinson, in the blink of an eye, in a blink, in the wink of an eye, in a wink, before you can say knife; *Brit. informal* in a tick, in two ticks, in a mo; *N. Amer. informal* in a snap; *archaic or informal* anon; *archaic* ere long.

momentary ▶ adjective *Jamieson didn't see the momentary flash of panic in her eyes* **brief**, short, short-lived, quick, fleeting, passing, transient, transitory, ephemeral, evanescent, fugitive, temporary, impermanent; *rare* fugacious.
OPPOSITES lengthy, lasting, permanent.

momentary or momentous?
Momentary and **momentous** are both derived from *moment*, but in different senses. *Momentary* is related to *moment* in the sense 'a very brief time', and means 'lasting only for a very short time' (*after a momentary hesitation she nodded*). *Momentous*, derived from *moment* in the sense of 'importance', means 'of great importance or significance', and applies particularly to events with profound implications for future developments (*a decade of momentous political change*).

momentous ▶ adjective *a momentous decision* **important**, significant, epoch-making, historic, apocalyptic, fateful, portentous, critical, crucial, vital, life-and-death, decisive, pivotal, serious, grave, weighty, consequential, big, great, far-reaching, of importance, of moment, of significance, of consequence; earth-shaking, earth-shattering, world-shaking, world-shattering.
OPPOSITES unimportant, trivial, insignificant.

momentous or momentary?
See MOMENTARY.

momentum ▶ noun *the vehicle gained momentum as the road dipped* **impetus**, energy, force, power, strength, drive, thrust, push, driving power, steam, impulse, speed, velocity.

monarch ▶ noun **sovereign**, ruler, Crown, crowned head, potentate; king, queen, emperor, empress, prince, princess, tsar.

monarchy ▶ noun **1** *the country is a constitutional monarchy* **kingdom**, sovereign state, principality, empire; realm.
2 *few questioned the moral justification of hereditary monarchy* **kingship**, sovereignty, autocracy, monocracy, absolutism, absolute power, despotism; royalism, monarchism.

monastery ▶ noun **religious house**, religious community; friary, abbey, priory, cloister, convent, nunnery; *Buddhism* vihara, lamasery; *Islam* tekke; *Indian* ashram; *historical* charterhouse, cell; *rare* coenobium, coenoby.

monastic ▶ adjective **1** *a monastic community* **cloistered**, conventual, cloistral, claustral, canonical, monastical; *rare* coenobitic, monachal.
2 *he was a shy man and led a rather monastic existence* **austere**, ascetic, simple, solitary, monkish, celibate, quiet, cloistered, sequestered, secluded, reclusive, withdrawn, hermit-like, eremitic, anchoritic, hermitic, contemplative, meditative.
OPPOSITE sybaritic.

monetary ▶ adjective **financial**, fiscal, pecuniary, money, cash, economic, budgetary, capital.

money *See centre pages for lists of* **Coins** **Currency Units**
▶ noun **1** *I haven't got enough money to buy it* **cash**, hard cash, ready money; **the means**, the wherewithal, funds, capital, finances, (filthy) lucre; banknotes, notes, paper money, coins, change, coin, coinage, silver, copper, currency, legal tender; *Brit.* sterling; *N. Amer.* bills; *N. Amer. & Austral.* roll; *informal* dough, bread, loot, the ready, readies, shekels, moolah, the

M

necessary, wad, boodle, dibs, gelt, ducats, rhino, gravy, scratch, stuff, oof, folding money; *Brit. informal* dosh, brass, lolly, spondulicks, wonga, ackers; *N. Amer. informal* dinero, greenbacks, simoleons, bucks, jack, mazuma; *Austral./NZ informal* Oscar; *informal, dated* splosh, green, tin; *Brit. dated* l.s.d.; *N. Amer. informal, dated* kale, rocks, shinplasters; *formal* specie; *archaic* pelf.
2 *she married him for his money* **wealth**, riches, fortune, affluence, assets, liquid assets, resources, substance, means, prosperity.
3 *I took the job here because the money was better* **pay**, salary, wages, remuneration, fee, stipend; *rare* emolument.

□ **for my money** *for my money, they are the better team* **in my opinion**, to my mind, in my view, as I see it, (according) to my way of thinking, from my standpoint, personally, in my estimation, in my judgement, in my book, if you ask me.

□ **in the money** **rich**, wealthy, affluent, well-to-do, well off, prosperous, moneyed, in clover, opulent; *informal* rolling in it, rolling in money, loaded, stinking rich, well heeled, flush, made of money, in/on easy street; *informal, dated* oofy; *Brit. informal* quids in.

WORD LINKS
relating to money **pecuniary, monetary**
collector of notes and coins **numismatist**
fear of money **chrematophobia**

moneyed ▶ adjective *the industrial revolution created a new moneyed class* **rich**, wealthy, affluent, well-to-do, well off, with deep pockets, prosperous, in clover, opulent, of means, of substance; *informal* in the money, rolling in it, rolling in money, loaded, stinking/filthy rich, well heeled, flush, made of money, in/on easy street; *Brit. informal* quids in; *informal, dated* in the chips, on velvet, oofy.
OPPOSITES penniless, poor, impoverished.

money-grubbing ▶ adjective *(informal) his money-grubbing relatives* **acquisitive**, avaricious, grasping, money-grabbing, greedy, rapacious, mercenary, materialistic; *N. Amer. informal* grabby; *rare* quaestuary, Mammonish, Mammonistic.

moneymaking ▶ adjective *a moneymaking scheme* **profitable**, profit-making, remunerative, lucrative, gainful, paying, successful, financially rewarding, productive, thriving, going; commercial, for-profit.
OPPOSITE loss-making.

mongrel ▶ noun *a rough-haired mongrel with a dash of Airedale* **cross-breed**, cross, mixed breed, half-breed, hybrid; tyke, cur, mutt; *N. Amer.* yellow dog; *NZ* kuri; *Asian* pye-dog, pariah dog; *informal* Heinz 57; *Austral. informal* mong, bitzer; *technical* bigener.
▶ adjective *a mongrel bitch* **cross-bred**, of mixed breed, half-breed, hybrid.
OPPOSITE pedigree.

monitor ▶ noun **1** *a heart monitor | a bank of monitors covered various areas of the building* **detector**, scanner, recorder; security system, security camera, CCTV.
2 *UN monitors declared that the election had been fair* **observer**, watchdog, overseer, invigilator, supervisor.
3 *a computer monitor* **screen**, VDU, visual display unit.
4 *(Brit.) a school monitor* **prefect**, praepostor; senior boy, senior girl, senior pupil.
▶ verb *equipment was installed to monitor air quality | his movements were closely monitored* **observe**, watch, keep an eye on, keep track of, track, keep under observation, keep watch on, keep under surveillance, surveil, check, keep a check on, scan, examine, study, record, note, oversee, supervise, superintend; *informal* keep tabs on, keep a tab on, keep a beady eye on.

monk *See centre pages for list of* **Christian Religious Orders**
▶ noun brother, male member of a religious order, religious, contemplative; friar; abbot, prior; novice, oblate, postulant; Benedictine, Black Monk, Cluniac, Carthusian, Cistercian, White Monk, Culdee; *Buddhism* lama, talapoin; *Islam* marabout; *historical* mendicant; *rare* coenobite, cloisterer, religioner, religieux.

WORD LINKS
relating to a monk **monastic**

monkey *See centre pages for list of* **Monkeys and Apes**
▶ noun **1** **simian**, primate, ape.
2 *where have you been, you little monkey!* **rascal**, imp, wretch, mischief-maker, devil, rogue; *informal* scamp, scallywag, horror, tyke, monster; *Brit. informal* perisher; *N. Amer. informal* varmint, hellion; *informal, dated* rip; *Brit. informal, dated* pickle; *archaic* scapegrace, rapscallion.

□ **make a monkey (out) of** **make someone look a fool**, make someone look foolish, make a fool of, make a laughing stock of, ridicule, deride, make fun of, poke fun at; set someone up, play a trick on.

▶ verb *(informal)*

□ **monkey about/around** *we were just monkeying around upstairs* **fool about/around**, play about/around, clown about/around, fiddle-faddle, footle about/around; *informal* mess about/around, horse about/around, lark (about/around), screw around, puddle about/around; *Brit. informal* muck about/around, fanny about/around; *Brit. vulgar slang* piss about/around, arse about/around, bugger about/around.

□ **monkey with** *don't monkey with that lock* **tamper with**, fiddle with, interfere with, meddle with, tinker with, touch/handle without permission, play with, fool with, trifle with; *informal* mess with, dick around with; *Brit. informal* muck about/around with.

WORD LINKS
relating to monkeys **simian**
collective noun **troop**

monkey business ▶ noun *(informal) if they try any monkey business with me they'll soon find out who's in charge* **mischief**, misbehaviour, mischievousness, devilry, devilment, rascality, tomfoolery; dishonesty, trickery, misconduct, misdemeanour, chicanery, skulduggery; *informal* shenanigans, funny business, hanky-panky, goings-on; *Brit. informal* monkey tricks, carry-on, carryings-on, jiggery-pokery; *N. Amer. informal* monkeyshines.

monocle ▶ noun **eyeglass**, glass; *historical* lorgnette, quizzing glass.

monolith ▶ noun **standing stone**, menhir, sarsen (stone), megalith.

monolithic ▶ adjective **1** *a monolithic building* **massive**, huge, vast, colossal, gigantic, immense, giant, enormous, mammoth, monumental; **featureless**, characterless, faceless.
2 *the old monolithic Communist party had become an anachronism* **inflexible**, rigid, unbending, unchanging, intractable, immovable, impenetrable, fossilized, hidebound; undifferentiated, uniform, unitary.

monologue ▶ noun *the skilfully varied tone and pace of her 40-minute monologue* **soliloquy**, speech, address, lecture, oration, sermon, homily; dramatic monologue, interior monologue; *informal* spiel.

monomania ▶ noun *his profound interest in the subject verges on monomania* **obsession**, fixation, idée fixe, ruling passion, consuming passion, mania, compulsion, fetish, preoccupation, hobby horse; *informal* bee in one's bonnet, thing.

monopolize ▶ verb **1** *the company has monopolized the market* **corner**, control, take over, gain control/dominance over, have sole/exclusive rights in, exercise a monopoly over; *archaic* engross.
2 *he has a tendency to monopolize the conversation* **dominate**, take over, not let anyone else take part in; not let anyone else get a word in edgeways; *informal* hog.
3 *she monopolized the guest of honour for most of the evening* **take up all the attention of**, keep to oneself, have all to oneself, not allow to associate with others; *informal* tie up.
OPPOSITE share.

monotonous ▶ adjective **1** *a monotonous job* **tedious**, boring, dull, uninteresting, unexciting, wearisome, tiresome, repetitive, repetitious, unvarying, unchanging, unvaried, lacking variety, without variety, humdrum, ho-hum, routine, mechanical, mind-numbing, soul-destroying, prosaic, run-of-the-mill, uneventful, unrelieved, dreary, plodding, colourless, featureless, dry as dust, uniform, monochrome; *informal* deadly; *Brit. informal* samey; *N. Amer. informal* dullsville.
OPPOSITES varied, interesting, exciting.
2 *a monotonous voice* **toneless**, flat, unvarying, uninflected, droning, soporific.

CHOOSE THE RIGHT WORD
monotonous, boring, tedious, dull
See BORING.

monotony ▶ noun **1** *the monotony of everyday life* **tedium**, tediousness, lack of variety, dullness, boredom, lack of variation, repetitiveness, repetitiousness, repetition, sameness, unchangingness, uniformity, routine, routineness, wearisomeness, tiresomeness, humdrumness, lack of interest, lack of excitement, prosaicness, uneventfulness, dreariness, colourlessness, featurelessness; *informal* deadliness; *Brit. informal* sameyness.
OPPOSITES variety, excitement.
2 *the monotony of her voice* **tonelessness**, flatness, lack of inflection, drone.

monster *See centre pages for lists of* **Giants** **Mythological and Fictional Creatures**
▶ noun **1** *legendary sea monsters* **frightening imaginary creature**, fabulous creature, mythical creature.
2 *her husband is an absolute monster* **brute**, fiend, beast, ogre, devil, demon, barbarian, savage, villain, sadist, animal, bogeyman; *informal* bastard, swine, pig; *vulgar slang* shit.
3 *Christian's only a year old, but he's already a little monster* **rascal**, imp, wretch, mischief-maker, rogue, devil; *informal* horror, scamp, scallywag, tyke, monkey; *archaic* rip, scapegrace, rapscallion; *Brit. informal* perisher; *Brit. informal, dated* pickle; *N. Amer. informal* varmint, hellion.
4 *he was huge, a monster of a man* **giant**, mammoth, colossus, leviathan, behemoth, titan, Brobdingnagian, monstrosity; *informal* jumbo.
▶ adjective *the film is sure to be a monster hit | a monster 16 kg carp* **huge**, enormous, massive, gigantic, big, large, great, giant, colossal, mammoth, vast, immense, tremendous, mighty, stupendous, monumental, epic, prodigious, mountainous, monstrous, titanic, towering, elephantine,

M

king-sized, king-size, gargantuan, Herculean, Brobdingnagian; *informal* mega, whopping, whopping great, thumping, thumping great, humongous, jumbo, hulking, bumper, astronomical, astronomic; *Brit. informal* whacking, whacking great, ginormous.

WORD LINKS
related prefix **terato-** (e.g. ***teratogenic, teratology***)

monstrosity ▶ noun **1** *the shopping centre was a multi-storey concrete monstrosity* **eyesore**, horror, blot on the landscape, carbuncle, excrescence.
2 *a biological monstrosity* **mutant**, mutation, freak, freak of nature, monster, abortion, malformation; *Latin* lusus naturae; *rare* abnormity, miscreation.

monstrous ▶ adjective **1** *a monstrous creature with great leathery wings and a horny head* **grotesque**, hideous, ugly, ghastly, gruesome, horrible, horrid, horrific, horrendous, horrifying, grisly, disgusting, repulsive, repellent, revolting, nightmarish, dreadful, frightening, terrifying, fearsome, freakish, malformed, misshapen, unnatural, abnormal, mutant, miscreated; *rare* teratoid.
OPPOSITES lovely, beautiful, normal.
2 *a monstrous tidal wave engulfed the countryside* **huge**, enormous, massive, great, gigantic, giant, colossal, mammoth, vast, immense, tremendous, mighty, stupendous, monumental, epic, prodigious, mountainous, titanic, towering, elephantine, king-sized, king-size, gargantuan, Herculean, Brobdingnagian, substantial; *informal* mega, monster, whopping, whopping great, thumping, thumping great, humongous, jumbo, hulking; *Brit. informal* whacking, whacking great, ginormous.
OPPOSITES tiny, minute.
3 *could he be guilty of such monstrous acts?* **appalling**, abhorrent, heinous, evil, wicked, abominable, terrible, horrible, dreadful, hideous, foul, vile; outrageous, shocking, disgraceful, scandalous, atrocious; villainous, nasty, ghastly, odious, loathsome, shameful, infamous, nefarious, iniquitous, unspeakable, intolerable, contemptible, despicable, vicious, cruel, savage, brutish, bestial, barbaric, barbarous, base, inhuman, depraved, fiendish, devilish, diabolical, satanic, ruthless, merciless; *Brit. informal* beastly; *rare* egregious, flagitious.
OPPOSITES admirable, good, kind.

monument ▶ noun **1** *a stone monument was built to mark the site* **memorial**; statue, pillar, column, obelisk, cross; cairn, dolmen, cromlech, monolith, megalith, henge, stone circle; cenotaph, tomb, mausoleum, shrine, sepulchre, reliquary; *Buddhism* chorten.
2 *a monument of granite was placed over the grave* **gravestone**, headstone, tombstone.
3 *the restored airfield is a monument to a past era of aviation | a musical work which is an astonishing monument of skill and industry* **testament**, record, reminder, remembrance, memorial, commemoration, witness, token; example, exemplar, model, archetype, pattern, nonpareil, paragon.

monumental ▶ adjective **1** *a monumental task* **huge**, great, enormous, gigantic, massive, colossal, mammoth, immense, tremendous, mighty, stupendous, vast, prodigious, Herculean, titanic, gargantuan, staggering, exceptional, extraordinary; *Brit. informal* ginormous.
2 *a monumental error of judgement* **terrible**, dreadful, awful, colossal, staggering, huge, enormous; catastrophic, unforgivable, indefensible; *informal* whopping; *rare* egregious.
3 *the ballet is one of his most monumental works* **impressive**, striking, outstanding, remarkable, magnificent, marvellous, majestic, stupendous, prodigious, ambitious, large-scale, grand, awe-inspiring, awesome, important, significant, distinguished, classic, memorable, transcendent, exalted, unforgettable, enduring, lasting, abiding, permanent, immortal, historic, epoch-making.
4 *a monumental inscription* **commemorative**, memorial, celebratory, commemorating, funerary.

mood ▶ noun **1** *she was in a very good mood that morning* **frame of mind**, state of mind, emotional state, humour, temper; disposition, spirit, tenor, vein.
2 *he's obviously in a mood* **bad mood**, temper, bad temper, fit of bad/ill temper, sulk, pet, the sulks, fit of pique, low spirits, depression, bout of moping, the doldrums, the blues; *informal* the dumps, grump; *Brit. informal* paddy; *Brit. informal, dated* bate, wax.
3 *the soundtrack captures the mood of the film* **atmosphere**, feeling, spirit, ambience, aura, character, tenor, flavour, quality, climate, feel, tone, key.
□ **in the mood** *I'm not **in the mood** for sightseeing | Jane was **in the mood** to talk* **in the right frame of mind for/to**, feeling like, ready for/to, wanting to, inclined to, disposed to, minded to, interested in, keen on/to, eager to, enthusiastic about, willing to, game for.

moody ▶ adjective *teenagers tend to get a bad name for being moody and irresponsible* **unpredictable**, temperamental, emotional, volatile, capricious, changeable, mercurial, unstable, fickle, flighty, inconstant, undependable, unsteady, erratic, fitful, impulsive; **sullen**, sulky, morose, gloomy, glum, moping, mopey, mopish, depressed, dejected, despondent, blue, melancholic, doleful, dour, dismal, sour, saturnine, lugubrious, introspective; *informal* down in the dumps, down in the mouth; *N. English informal* mardy; *informal, dated* mumpish; *archaic* kittle.
OPPOSITES cheerful, happy, equable.

moon ▶ noun **satellite**.
▶ verb **1** *stop mooning about and get on with some work* **waste time**, fiddle, loaf, idle, mope, drift, stooge around; *Brit. informal* mooch; *N. Amer. informal* lollygag, bat.
2 *he's mooning over her photograph as if he was a schoolboy* **mope**, pine, languish, brood, daydream, fantasize, be in a reverie, be in a brown study.
□ **many moons ago** (*informal*) **a long time ago**, ages ago, years ago; *Brit. informal* donkey's years ago, yonks ago; *S. African* before the rinderpest.
□ **once in a blue moon** (*informal*) **hardly ever**, almost never, scarcely ever, rarely, very seldom.
□ **over the moon** (*informal*) *Eve was over the moon when I broke the news* **ecstatic**, euphoric, thrilled, overjoyed, elated, delighted, on cloud nine/seven, walking/treading on air, in seventh heaven, jubilant, rapturous, beside oneself with joy, jumping for joy, exultant, transported, delirious, enraptured, blissful, in raptures, as pleased as Punch, cock-a-hoop, as happy as a sandboy, as happy as Larry, like a child with a new toy; *informal* on top of the world, on a high, tickled pink; *N. English informal* made up; *N. Amer. informal* as happy as a clam; *Austral. informal* wrapped.

WORD LINKS
relating to the moon **lunar**
scientific study of the moon **selenology**

moonshine ▶ noun *David Bates, prosecuting, dismissed the story as moonshine* **nonsense**, rubbish, balderdash, claptrap, blarney, blather, blether; *informal* hogwash, rot, baloney, tripe, drivel, bilge, bosh, bull, bunk, guff, hot air, eyewash, piffle, poppycock, phooey, malarkey, twaddle, dribble; *Brit. informal* cobblers, codswallop, cock, stuff and nonsense, tosh, taradiddle; *Scottish & N. English informal* havers; *N. Amer. informal* garbage, flapdoodle, blathers, bushwa, wack, applesauce; *informal, dated* bunkum, tommyrot, cod, gammon; *vulgar slang* shit, bullshit, crap, bollocks, balls; *Austral./NZ vulgar slang* bulldust.

moor[1] ▶ verb *a boat was moored to the end of the dock* **tie up**, secure, make fast, fix firmly, fasten, anchor, berth, dock; lash, hitch.

moor[2] ▶ noun **1 upland**, moorland, heath, plateau; *Brit.* fell, wold; grouse moor.
2 (*archaic*) **bog**, fen, marsh, marshland, mire, swamp; *Scottish & N. English* moss, carr.

moot ▶ adjective *whether the temperature rise is due to the greenhouse effect is a moot point* **debatable**, open to debate, open to discussion, arguable, questionable, at issue, open to question, open, doubtful, open to doubt, disputable, contestable, controvertible, problematic, problematical, controversial, contentious, vexed, disputed, unresolved, unsettled, up in the air, undecided, yet to be decided, undetermined, unconcluded.
▶ verb *the idea was first mooted in the 1930s* **raise**, bring up, broach, mention, put forward, introduce, advance, present, propose, suggest, submit, propound, air, ventilate.

mop ▶ noun **1** *a mop and bucket* **sponge**, swab, squeegee.
2 *her tousled mop of hair* **shock**, mane, thatch, tangle, mass, mat.
▶ verb *a man was mopping the floor* **wash**, clean, wipe, swab, sponge, squeegee.
□ **mop something up 1** *I mopped up the spilt coffee* **wipe up**, clean up, soak up, absorb, sop up, sponge up.
2 *troops mopped up the last pockets of resistance* **finish off**, deal with, make an end of, dispose of, account for, take care of, clear up, eliminate, dispatch.

mope ▶ verb **1** *it's no use moping—things could be worse* **brood**, sulk, be miserable, be gloomy, be sad, be despondent, pine, eat one's heart out, fret, grieve, despair; *informal* be down in the dumps, be down in the mouth; *literary* repine.
2 *she spends too much time moping about the house* **languish**, moon, droop, idle, loaf, fiddle, drift, stooge; *Brit. informal* mooch; *N. Amer. informal* lollygag, bat.
▶ noun *many people regarded her as a mope* **melancholic**, depressive, pessimist, prophet of doom, killjoy, moaner; *informal* sourpuss, wet blanket, party-pooper, spoilsport, grouch, grump; *Brit. informal* misery; *rare* melancholiac.

moral ▶ adjective **1** *moral issues* **ethical**; social, behavioural; to do with right and wrong.
2 *a very moral man* **virtuous**, good, righteous, upright, upstanding, high-minded, right-minded, principled, proper, honourable, honest, just, noble, incorruptible, scrupulous, respectable, decent, irreproachable, truthful, law-abiding, clean-living, chaste, pure, blameless, sinless.
OPPOSITES immoral, bad, dishonourable.
3 *moral support* **psychological**, emotional, mental.
▶ noun **1** *the moral of the story* **lesson**, message, meaning, significance, signification, import, point, precept, teaching.
2 (**morals**) *he has no morals and cannot be trusted* **moral code**, code of ethics, moral standards, moral values, principles, principles of right and wrong, rules of conduct, standards/principles of behaviour, standards, morality, sense of morality, scruples, ideals.

M

morale ▶ noun *morale in the team was higher than it had been for a long time* **confidence**, self-confidence, self-esteem; spirit, spirits, esprit de corps, team spirit, state of mind; heart, optimism, hope, hopefulness, determination.

moral fibre ▶ noun *an ineffectual man with no moral fibre* **strength of character**, resolution, fortitude, resolve, backbone, spine, mettle, firmness of purpose, toughness of spirit, steel.
OPPOSITES weakness, cowardice.

morality ▶ noun **1** *the morality of the possession of nuclear weapons* **ethics**, rights and wrongs, correctness, ethicality.
2 *the past few years have seen a sharp decline in morality* **virtue**, goodness, good behaviour, righteousness, rectitude, uprightness; morals, principles, honesty, integrity, propriety, honour, justice, fair play, justness, decency, probity, chasteness, chastity, purity, blamelessness.
OPPOSITE immorality.
3 *orthodox Christian morality* **moral standards**, morals, moral code, ethics, principles of right and wrong, rules of conduct, standards/principles of behaviour, ethos, mores, standards, ideals.

moralize ▶ verb *doctors should not moralize but simply deal with the patient's medical condition* **pontificate**, sermonize, philosophize, lecture, preach; *informal* preachify; *rare* ethicize.

morass ▶ noun **1** *he managed to free himself from the muddy morass* **quagmire**, swamp, bog, marsh, mire, quag, marshland, peat bog, fen, slough, quicksand; *Scottish & N. English* moss, carr; *Irish* corcass; *N. Amer.* bayou, pocosin, moor; *archaic* marish.
2 *we were stuck in a morass of procedure and paperwork* **confusion**, chaos, muddle, tangle, entanglement, imbroglio, mix-up, jumble, clutter; mire, quagmire; *W. Indian* comess.

moratorium ▶ noun *a temporary moratorium on all nuclear testing* **embargo**, ban, prohibition, suspension, postponement, stay, stoppage, halt, freeze, standstill, respite, hiatus, delay, deferment, deferral, adjournment.

morbid ▶ adjective **1** *a morbid fascination with the horrors of contemporary warfare* **ghoulish**, macabre, unhealthy, gruesome, grisly, grotesque, ghastly, horrible, unwholesome, death-obsessed; *informal* sick.
OPPOSITE wholesome.
2 *during the months leading up to my 40th birthday, I felt decidedly morbid* **gloomy**, glum, sunk in gloom, melancholy, lugubrious, pessimistic, morose, given to looking on the black side, dismal, funereal, defeatist, sombre, doleful, melancholic, despondent, dejected, sad, blue, depressed, downcast, down, disconsolate, desolate, miserable, unhappy, heavy-hearted, downhearted, dispirited, in low spirits, low-spirited, low, in the doldrums; *informal* down in the dumps, down in the mouth.
OPPOSITE cheerful.
3 *a morbid condition* **diseased**, pathological.
OPPOSITE healthy.

mordant ▶ adjective *a mordant sense of humour* **caustic**, trenchant, biting, cutting, acerbic, sardonic, sarcastic, scathing, acid, sharp, keen, tart, pungent, stinging, astringent, incisive, devastating, piercing, rapier-like, razor-edged; critical, bitter, polemic, virulent, vitriolic, venomous, waspish, corrosive; *rare* acidulous, mordacious.
OPPOSITES vague; uncritical.

more ▶ determiner *more water came pouring through the gap | I could do with some more clothes* **additional**, further, added, extra, increased, fresh, new, other, supplementary, supplemental, spare, alternative.
OPPOSITES less, fewer.
▶ adverb **1** *he was able to concentrate more on his writing* **to a greater extent**, further, longer, some more, better.
2 *he was rich, and more, he was handsome* **moreover**, furthermore, besides, what's more, in addition, also, as well, too, to boot, additionally, on top of that, over and above that, into the bargain; *archaic* withal, forbye.
▶ pronoun *that's not enough—we're going to need more* **extra**, an additional amount/number, a greater quantity/number; an addition, a supplement, an increase.
OPPOSITES less, fewer.
□ **more or less approximately**, roughly, nearly, almost, close to, about, of the order of, in the region of, give or take a few; *S. African* plus-minus.

moreover ▶ adverb **besides**, furthermore, what's more, in addition, also, as well, too, to boot, additionally, on top of that, over and above that, into the bargain, at that, more; *archaic* withal, forbye.

mores ▶ plural noun (*Latin*) *factors that shaped the social mores of the community* **customs**, conventions, ways, way of life, way of doing things, traditions, practices, custom and practice, procedures, habits, usages; *formal* praxis.

morgue ▶ noun *the body, still unidentified, was taken to the morgue* **mortuary**, funeral parlour, funeral chapel, funeral home; *Brit.* chapel of rest; *archaic* charnel house, dead house, lich-house.

moribund ▶ adjective **1** *the patient was moribund* **dying**, expiring, on one's deathbed, near death, near the end, at death's door, breathing one's last, fading/sinking fast, not long for this world, failing rapidly, on one's last legs, in extremis; *informal* with one foot in the grave.
OPPOSITES thriving; recovering.
2 *the country's moribund shipbuilding industry* **declining**, in decline, on the decline, waning, dying, stagnating, stagnant, decaying, crumbling, atrophying, obsolescent, on its last legs; *informal* on the way out.
OPPOSITE flourishing.

morning ▶ noun **1** *I've got a meeting this morning* **before noon**, before lunch(time), a.m.; *literary* morn; *Nautical & N. Amer.* forenoon.
2 *a hint of light showed that morning was on its way* **dawn**, daybreak, sunrise, break of day, first light; *N. Amer.* sunup; *literary* cockcrow, dayspring, dawning, aurora.
□ **morning, noon, and night all the time**, without a break, constantly, continually, always, forever, incessantly, ceaselessly, perpetually, unceasingly; *informal* 24-7; *archaic* without surcease.

WORD LINKS
relating to the morning **matutinal, antemeridian**

moron ▶ noun (*informal*) *why don't you look where you're going, you moron!* **fool**, oaf, nincompoop, clown, dunce, dolt, dullard, ignoramus, simpleton; *informal* idiot, cretin, imbecile, nitwit, halfwit, ninny, dope, dimwit, dumbo, dummy, ass, jerk, nerd, dum-dum, loon, chump, goon, jackass, fathead, blockhead, numbskull, dunderhead, meathead, dipstick, bonehead, chucklehead, clod, goop, knucklehead, lamebrain, pea-brain, pudding-head, thickhead, wooden-head, pinhead, airhead, birdbrain, dumb-bell, donkey, stupe, noodle; *informal, dated* muttonhead, noddy; *Brit. informal* nit, clot, twit, muppet, plonker, berk, prat, pillock, wally, git, wazzock, divvy, nerk, dork, twerp, charlie, mug; *Scottish informal* nyaff, balloon, sumph, gowk, galoot; *Irish informal* gobdaw; *N. Amer. informal* schmuck, bozo, boob, schlepper, chowderhead, dumbhead, goofball, goof, lummox, klutz, putz, schlemiel, sap, gink, cluck, ding-dong, wiener, weeny, dip, simp, spud, coot, palooka, poop, retardate, squarehead, yo-yo, goofus, clunk, dingleberry, turkey; *Austral. informal* alec, galah, nong, bogan, poon, boofhead; *Austral./NZ informal* dingbat, drongo, dill, hoon; *S. African informal* mompara; *vulgar slang* dickhead, fuckwit, fuckhead, shit for brains, dildo; *Brit. vulgar slang* arsehole, arse, dick, tit, tosser; *N. Amer. vulgar slang* asshole; *Irish vulgar slang* gobshite; *archaic* tomfool, retard, clodpole, loggerhead, spoony, mooncalf.

moronic ▶ adjective (*informal*) *an endless succession of moronic game shows* **stupid**, **foolish**, senseless, brainless, mindless, idiotic, imbecilic, imbecile, insane, lunatic, asinine, ridiculous, ludicrous, absurd, preposterous, silly, inane, witless, half-baked, empty-headed, unintelligent, half-witted, slow-witted, weak-minded; *informal* crazy, daft, dumb, dead from the neck up, brain-dead, cretinous, doltish, thick, thickheaded, birdbrained, pea-brained, pinheaded, dopey, dim, dim-witted, dippy, pie-faced, fat-headed, blockheaded, boneheaded, lamebrained, chuckleheaded, dunderheaded, wooden-headed, muttonheaded, damfool; *Brit. informal* divvy; *Scottish & N. English informal* glaikit; *N. Amer. informal* dumb-ass, chowderheaded; *S. African informal* dof; *W. Indian informal* dotish.
OPPOSITE intelligent.

morose ▶ adjective *Louis sat alone at a table, looking morose* **sullen**, sulky, gloomy, bad-tempered, ill-tempered, in a bad mood, dour, surly, sour, glum, moody, unsmiling, humourless, uncommunicative, taciturn, unresponsive, unsociable, scowling, glowering, ill-humoured, sombre, sober, saturnine, pessimistic, lugubrious, Eeyorish, mournful, melancholy, melancholic, doleful, miserable, dismal, depressed, dejected, despondent, downcast, unhappy, low-spirited, in low spirits, low, with a long face, blue, down, fed up, grumpy, irritable, churlish, cantankerous, crotchety, cross, crabbed, crabby, grouchy, testy, snappish, peevish, crusty, waspish; *informal* down in the mouth, down in the dumps; *Brit. informal* narky; *N. English informal* mardy; *informal, dated* mumpish.
OPPOSITES cheerful, happy, communicative.

morsel ▶ noun **mouthful**, bite, nibble, bit, small piece, soupçon, taste, sample, spoonful, forkful, crumb, grain, particle, fragment, fraction, scrap, sliver, shred, pinch, drop, dollop, whit, atom, granule, segment, spot, modicum, gobbet; titbit, bonne bouche; *informal* smidgen, smidge; *Austral./NZ informal* skerrick.

mortal ▶ adjective **1** *the coffin held the mortal remains of her uncle | all men are mortal* **perishable**, physical, bodily, corporeal, fleshly, corporal, earthly; human, earth-born; impermanent, temporal, worldly, transient, ephemeral, passing; *rare* sublunary.
OPPOSITE immortal.
2 *a mortal blow* **deadly**, fatal, lethal, death-dealing, killing, murderous, destructive, terminal, incurable.
3 *mortal enemies* **irreconcilable**, deadly, to the death, sworn, bitter, out-and-out, implacable, relentless, unrelenting, unappeasable, remorseless, merciless.
4 *a mortal sin* **unpardonable**, unforgivable, irremissible.
OPPOSITE venial.
5 *in the developing countries, parents live in mortal fear of such diseases* **extreme**, very great, great, enormous, terrible, awful, dreadful, intense, severe, grave, dire, inordinate, unbearable, agonizing.
6 *the punishment is out of all mortal proportion to the offence* **conceivable**, imaginable, perceivable, possible, earthly.
▶ noun *mere mortals may entreat God to perform miracles on their behalf* **human**

being, human, person, man/woman, being, creature, individual; earthling; *informal, dated* body.
OPPOSITES immortal, god.

mortality ▸ noun **1** *her death filled him with a sense of his own mortality* **impermanence**, temporality, transience, ephemerality, impermanency, perishability; humanity; corporeality, earthliness; *rare* corporality.
OPPOSITE immortality.
2 *the causes of mortality among infants and young children* **death**, loss of life, dying.

mortification ▸ noun **1** *scarlet with mortification, Leonora looked away* **embarrassment**, humiliation, chagrin, discomfiture, discomposure, awkwardness, shame, loss of face.
2 *the mortification of the flesh* **subduing**, suppression, subjugation, control, controlling, restraint; **disciplining**, chastening, punishment, denying.

mortify ▸ verb **1** *I'd be mortified if my friends found out I was learning ballroom dancing* **embarrass**, humiliate, chagrin, shame, discomfit, abash, horrify, appal, crush.
OPPOSITES be pleased, be proud.
2 *he was mortified at the prospect of being excluded from the meeting* **hurt**, wound, affront, offend, put out, pique, irk, pain, annoy, displease, vex, gall; *informal* rile; *Brit. informal* nark.
OPPOSITE gratify.
3 *an ascetic who consistently chooses to mortify the flesh* **subdue**, suppress, subjugate, control, restrain, get under control; **discipline**, chasten, punish, deny.
OPPOSITE indulge.
4 *the cut in his arm had mortified* **become gangrenous**, fester, putrefy, gangrene, rot, decay, decompose; *rare* necrose, sphacelate.
OPPOSITE heal.

mortuary ▸ noun *three of the bodies have been taken to the mortuary* **morgue**, funeral parlour, funeral chapel, funeral home; *Brit.* chapel of rest; *archaic* charnel house, dead house, lich-house.

moss ▸ noun
WORD LINKS
study of mosses **bryology, muscology**

most ▸ pronoun *she spends most of her time in London | most of the guests brought flowers* **nearly all**, almost all, the greatest quantity/part/number, the majority, the bulk, the lion's share, the mass, the preponderance.
OPPOSITES little, few.
□ **for the most part** *the path for the most part sticks to the coast* **mostly**, mainly, in the main, on the whole, largely, by and large, to a large extent, to a great degree, predominantly, chiefly, principally, basically, substantially, overall, in general, effectively, to all intents and purposes, especially, primarily, generally, usually, typically, commonly, as a rule, altogether, all in all, on balance, on average.

mostly ▸ adverb **1** *the other passengers were mostly businessmen* **mainly**, for the most part, on the whole, in the main, almost entirely, largely, chiefly, predominantly, principally, primarily, substantially.
2 *I mostly wear jeans and trousers, not skirts* **usually**, generally, in general, as a general rule, as a rule, ordinarily, normally, commonly, customarily, typically, most of the time, almost always, more often than not, most often.
OPPOSITE rarely.

mote ▸ noun **speck**, particle, grain, spot, fleck, atom, scintilla, mite.
OPPOSITE beam

moth ▸ noun. *See centre pages for lists of* **Moths** **Butterflies**

moth-eaten ▸ adjective *a moth-eaten tweed jacket* **threadbare**, worn out, well worn, worn, old, shabby, scruffy, decrepit, tattered, ragged, holey, frayed, mangy, unkempt; *informal* tatty, the worse for wear, ratty, scuzzy, grungy; *N. Amer. informal* raggedy.

mother ▸ noun **1 female parent**, materfamilias, matriarch; biological mother, birth mother, foster mother, adoptive mother, stepmother, surrogate mother; *informal* ma, mam, mammy, old dear, old lady, old woman; *Brit. informal* mum, mummy, mumsy; *N. Amer. informal* mom, mommy; *Brit. informal, dated* mater; *dated* mama, mamma; *Indian* Mata; *Indian informal* amma; *rare* progenitress, progenitrix.
2 *it was time for the foal to be separated from its mother* **dam**.
3 *the wish was mother of the deed* **source**, origin, genesis, fount, fountainhead, inspiration, stimulus; *literary* wellspring.
▸ verb **1** *she mothered her husband, insisting he take cod liver oil* **look after**, care for, take care of, nurture, nurse, protect, cherish, tend, raise, rear; **pamper**, coddle, cosset, baby, overprotect, fuss over, indulge, spoil.
OPPOSITE neglect.
2 *she mothered an illegitimate daughter* **give birth to**, have, deliver, bear, produce, bring forth; *N. Amer.* birth; *informal* drop; *archaic* be brought to bed of.
WORD LINKS
relating to a mother **maternal**
related prefix **matri-** (e.g. ***matrilineal***)
killing of one's mother **matricide**

motherly ▸ adjective **maternal**, maternalistic, protective, caring, nurturing, loving, devoted, affectionate, fond, warm, tender, gentle, kind, kindly, comforting, understanding, compassionate.

motif ▸ noun **1** *a black chenille sweater with a colourful tulip motif* **design**, pattern, decoration, figure, shape, logo, monogram, device, emblem, ornament.
2 *the room is one of the recurring motifs in Pinter's work* **theme**, idea, concept, subject, topic, leitmotif, element, motive.

motion ▸ noun **1** *the rocking motion of the boat | a planet's motion around the sun* **movement**, moving, locomotion, rise and fall, shifting, stirring, to and fro, toing and froing, coming and going; **progress**, passage, passing, transit, course, flow, going, travel, travelling; motility, mobility.
2 *she made a little fluttering motion with her hands* **gesture**, gesticulation, movement, signal, sign, indication; wave, nod; body language, kinesics.
3 *the motion failed to obtain an absolute majority in the Assembly* **proposal**, proposition, submission, recommendation, suggestion.
▸ verb *he motioned her to sit down* **gesture**, gesticulate, signal, sign, direct, indicate; wave, beckon, nod.
□ **in motion** *do not distract the driver while the vehicle is in motion* **moving**, on the move, going, travelling, not at rest, running, functioning, operational; under way.
OPPOSITE stationary.
□ **set/put in motion** *the Home Secretary set in motion a review of the law* **start**, begin, activate, institute, initiate, launch, get under way, get going, get in operation, get working/functioning, get off the ground, start/get/set the ball rolling; trigger off, set off, spark off, generate, cause, bring about; *formal* commence.
WORD LINKS
relating to motion **kinetic**
fear of motion **kinetophobia**

motionless ▸ adjective *Rob and Graham remained motionless, not daring to look at each other* **unmoving**, still, stationary, stock-still, at a standstill, immobile, immovable, static, at rest, halted, stopped, not moving a muscle, rooted to the spot, transfixed, paralysed, frozen, inert, inanimate, quiescent, lifeless.
OPPOSITES moving, mobile, active.

motivate ▸ verb **1** *she was primarily motivated by the desire for profit | I asked him what had motivated the theme of his current exhibition* **prompt**, drive, move, inspire, stimulate, influence, lead, persuade, actuate, activate, impel, push, propel, spur (on); provoke, trigger, cause, bring about, occasion, induce, incite.
2 *it's the teacher's job to motivate the child at school* **inspire**, stimulate, encourage, spur (on), galvanize, arouse, rouse, excite, stir (up), fire with enthusiasm, fire the imagination of; *rare* inspirit, incentivize.
OPPOSITE demotivate.

motivation ▸ noun **1** *the motivation for taking part in the training was often financial* **motive**, motivating force, incentive, stimulus, stimulation, inspiration, impulse, inducement, incitement, spur, goad, provocation; reason, rationale, ground(s).
2 *keep staff up to date to maintain their interest and motivation* **enthusiasm**, drive, ambition, initiative, determination, enterprise, sense of purpose; *informal* get-up-and-go.

motive ▸ noun **1** *the motive for the attack is still unknown* **reason**, motivation, motivating force, rationale, grounds, cause, basis, occasion, thinking, the whys and wherefores, object, purpose, intention, design; incentive, inducement, impulse, incitement, influence, lure, inspiration, stimulus, stimulation, spur, goad, provocation, pressure, persuasion, consideration.
2 *religious motives in art* **motif**, theme, idea, concept, subject, topic, leitmotif, element.
▸ adjective *the machinery supplying the motive power for the hydraulic cranes* **kinetic**, driving, impelling, propelling, propulsive, operative, moving, motor.

motley ▸ adjective **1** *a motley collection of old clothes* **miscellaneous**, disparate, diverse, assorted, sundry, varied, mixed, diversified, heterogeneous.
OPPOSITES homogeneous, uniform.
2 *a motley coat* **multicoloured**, many-coloured, multicolour, colourful, particoloured, many-hued, variegated, harlequin, kaleidoscopic, rainbow, psychedelic, prismatic, polychromatic; *informal* (looking) like an explosion in a paint factory.
OPPOSITE monochrome.

motor ▸ noun. *See centre pages for list of* **Engines**

motor sport ▸ noun. *See centre pages for list of* **Motor Sports**

motor vehicle ▸ noun. *See centre pages for lists of* **Cars** **Vehicles**

mottled ▸ adjective *her mottled skin | the bird's mottled reddish-brown plumage* **blotchy**, blotched, spotted, spotty; **speckled**, streaked, streaky, marbled, flecked, freckled, dappled, stippled, piebald, skewbald, pied, brindled, brindle, tabby, marled; patchy, variegated, multicoloured, particoloured; *N. Amer.* pinto; *informal* splotchy, splodgy; *rare* jaspé.

motto ▸ noun **1** *he adopted the motto 'work hard and play hard' | their school*

M

motto **maxim**, saying, proverb, aphorism, adage, saw, axiom, formula, expression, phrase, rule, dictum, precept, epigram, gnome; slogan, catchphrase, watchword, byword, cry, battle cry; truism, cliché, platitude; *rare* apophthegm.
2 *cracker mottoes* **joke**, witticism, one-liner.

mould[1] ▶ **noun 1** *the molten metal is poured into a mould* **cast**, die, form, matrix, shape, container; **framework**, template, pattern, frame.
2 *an actress in the traditional Hollywood mould* **pattern**, form, shape, format, structure, configuration, construction, frame, build, model, design, arrangement, organization, formation, figure, cast, kind, brand, make, line, type, cut, style; archetype, paradigm, prototype.
3 *he is a figure of heroic mould* **character**, nature, temperament, temper, disposition, cast/turn of mind, mettle; calibre, kind, sort, variety, stamp, type, kidney, grain, ilk.
▶ **verb 1** *a figure moulded from clay* **shape**, form, fashion, model, work, construct, frame, make, create, configure, manufacture, design, sculpt, sculpture, throw; forge, cast, stamp, die-cast.
2 *the professionals who were helping to mould US policy* **determine**, direct, control, guide, lead, influence, shape, form, fashion, affect, make.

mould[2] ▶ **noun** *whitewashed walls stained with mould* **mildew**, fungus, must, mouldiness, mustiness; blight, smut; dry rot, wet rot.

mould[3] ▶ **noun** *the ground was damp, with old leaves thick in the mould* **earth**, soil, dirt, loam, humus.

moulder ▶ **verb** *his body still lay mouldering in some forgotten field in France* | *the buildings had mouldered away* **decay**, decompose, rot, rot away, go mouldy, perish, go off, go bad, spoil, putrefy; crumble, disintegrate, fall apart, fall to pieces, deteriorate, fall into decay, go to rack and ruin.

mouldy ▶ **adjective** *a lump of mouldy cheese* **mildewed**, mildewy, musty, mouldering, fusty; blighted, smutty; decaying, decayed, rotting, rotten, bad, spoiled, spoilt, decomposing, decomposed, rancid, rank, putrid, putrescent, putrefying; *rare* mucid.

mound ▶ **noun 1** *a mound of leaves and garden rubbish* **heap**, pile, stack; mass, collection, accumulation, aggregation, assemblage; mountain, pyramid; *Scottish, Irish, & N. English* rickle; *Scottish* bing.
2 *he built his castle high on the mound* **hillock**, hill, knoll, rise, hummock, hump, embankment, bank, ridge, dune, tor, elevation, acclivity; *Geology* drumlin; *Scottish* brae; *N. Amer. or technical* butte; *rare* tump.
3 *a burial mound* | *a low mound marks the site of the meeting place* **barrow**, **tumulus**; motte; *Middle East* tell; *Russian* kurgan.
▶ **verb** *mound up the rice on a serving plate* **pile**, pile up, heap, heap up.

M

mount ▶ **verb 1** *he mounted the stairs* **go up**, ascend, climb, climb up, scale, clamber up, make one's way up, move up.
OPPOSITE descend.
2 *the master of ceremonies mounted the platform* **climb on to**, jump on to, clamber on to, get on to; board, step aboard.
3 *they mounted their horses and made their way back* **get astride**, straddle, get on the back of, bestride, get on to, hop on to.
4 *the museum is mounting an exhibition of 16th-century drawings* **put on display**, display, exhibit, present, put in place, install; organize, put on, stage, prepare.
5 *the company successfully mounted a takeover bid* **organize**, stage, prepare, arrange, set up, produce, get up; launch, set in motion, initiate.
6 *their losses mounted rapidly* **increase**, grow, rise, escalate, soar, spiral, leap up, shoot up, rocket, climb, accumulate, accrue, pile up, build up, multiply, intensify, swell; *literary* wax.
OPPOSITES decrease, diminish.
7 *cameras were mounted above the door* **install**, place, fix, set, erect, put up, attach, put in position, secure.
▶ **noun 1** *he hung on to his mount's bridle* **horse**; *archaic* steed.
2 *a decorated photograph mount* **setting**, backing, support, mounting, fixture, frame, stand, base.

mountain ▶ **noun 1** **peak**, height, elevation, eminence, prominence, summit, pinnacle, alp, horn; **(mountains)** range, massif, sierra, cordillera, ridge; *N. English* fell; *Scottish* ben, Munro; *S. African* berg; (*in N. Africa*) jebel; *Geology* inselberg; *archaic* mount.
2 *a mountain of paperwork* | *mountains of dirty dishes* **a great deal**, a lot, heap, pile, mound, stack; **profusion**, abundance, quantity; backlog, logjam; *informal* lots, loads, heaps, piles, tons, masses, oodles, scads; *Brit. informal* shedload; *N. Amer. informal* slew, gobs; *Austral./NZ informal* swag; *vulgar slang* shitload.
3 *a butter mountain* **surplus**, surfeit, glut, excess, overabundance, oversupply.
OPPOSITE molehill.
□ **move mountains 1** *faith can move mountains* **perform miracles**, work/do wonders, achieve the impossible.
2 *his fans move mountains to catch as many of his performances as possible* **make every effort**, pull out all the stops, do one's utmost/best; *informal* bend/lean over backwards.

WORD LINKS
related prefix **oro- (e.g. *orogeny*)**
relating to mountains **orographic**

mountainous ▶ **adjective 1** *a mountainous region* | *mountainous terrain* **hilly**, craggy, rocky, alpine, high, steep, precipitous; upland, highland.
OPPOSITE flat.
2 *mountainous waves* **huge**, enormous, gigantic, massive, very big, very large, great, giant, colossal, mammoth, vast, immense, tremendous, mighty, formidable, staggering, monumental, Herculean, epic, prodigious, monstrous, titanic, towering, king-sized, king-size, gargantuan, substantial; *informal* mega, monster, whopping, whopping great, thumping, thumping great, humongous, jumbo, hulking, astronomical, astronomic; *Brit. informal* whacking, whacking great, ginormous.
OPPOSITES tiny, minute.

mountebank ▶ **noun** **swindler**, charlatan, confidence trickster, confidence man, fraud, fraudster, impostor, trickster, racketeer, hoaxer, sharper, quack, rogue, villain, scoundrel; *informal* con man, shark, flimflammer, sharp; *Brit. informal* twister; *N. Amer. informal* grifter, bunco artist, chiseller; *Austral. informal* shicer, magsman, illywhacker; *rare* defalcator.

mourn ▶ **verb 1** *Isobel mourned her husband* **grieve for**, sorrow over, lament for, weep for, shed tears for/over, wail/keen over; *archaic* plain for.
2 *he mourned the loss of the beautiful medieval buildings* **deplore**, bewail, bemoan, rue, regret, sigh over.
OPPOSITE rejoice.

mournful ▶ **adjective** *a mournful expression* | *mournful music* **sad**, sorrowful, sorrowing, doleful, melancholy, melancholic, woeful, grief-stricken, miserable, unhappy, heartbroken, broken-hearted, heavy-hearted, gloomy, dismal, tragic, desolate, dejected, despondent, depressed, downcast, disconsolate, woebegone, forlorn, rueful, lugubrious, sombre, joyless, cheerless, mirthless; funereal, elegiac, plaintive, plangent, dirge-like; *rare* threnodic; *literary* heartsick, dolorous.
OPPOSITES happy, joyful, cheerful.

mourning ▶ **noun 1** *a period of national mourning* **grief**, grieving, sorrowing, lamentation, lament, keening, wailing, weeping; sorrow, sadness, misery, melancholy, heartache, anguish, despair, despondency, desolation, woefulness; *Judaism* shiva; *archaic* dole.
2 *she was dressed in mourning* **black clothes**, black; *archaic* widow's weeds, weeds, sackcloth and ashes, sables.

mouse ▶ **noun.** *See centre pages for list of* **Rodents**

WORD LINKS
relating to mice **murine**
fear of mice **musophobia**

moustache *See centre pages for list of* **Beards and Moustaches**
▶ **noun** *informal* tash; *N. Amer. informal* stash; *Scottish & N. Amer.* mouser.

mousy ▶ **adjective 1** *mousy hair* **lightish brown**, brownish, brownish-grey, dun-coloured; colourless, neutral, drab, dull, lacklustre.
2 *he had a small, mousy wife* **timid**, quiet, meek, fearful, timorous, shy, self-effacing, diffident, ineffectual, unassertive, unconfident, unforthcoming, reticent, shrinking, hesitant, withdrawn, introverted, introvert, unobtrusive.
OPPOSITES bold, brazen, ferocious.

mouth ▶ **noun 1** lips, jaws; maw, muzzle; *informal* trap, chops, kisser, yap; *Brit. informal* gob, cakehole, mush; *N. Amer. informal* puss, bazoo.
2 *the mouth of the cave* **entrance**, opening, entry, way in, entryway, inlet, access, ingress; door, doorway, gateway, gate, portal, aperture, orifice, vent; way out, exit.
3 *the mouth of the bottle* **opening**, rim, lip.
4 *the mouth of the river* **outfall**, outlet, debouchment, embouchure, debouchure; **estuary**, firth.
5 *he's not all mouth—he gets results* **boasting**, bragging, empty talk, idle talk, bombast, fustian; *informal* hot air, gas; *literary* braggadocio, rodomontade.
6 *you've got more mouth than any woman I've ever known* **impudence**, cheek, cheekiness, insolence, impertinence, effrontery, audacity, audaciousness, boldness, presumption, presumptuousness, sauciness, incivility, rudeness, disrespect; *informal* lip, nerve, neck, brass neck; *Brit. informal* sauce, backchat; *N. Amer. informal* sass, sassiness, back talk, smart mouth; *archaic* malapertness.
□ **down in the mouth unhappy**, dejected, sad, miserable, down, downhearted, downcast, depressed, blue, melancholy, gloomy, glum, dispirited, discouraged, disheartened, despondent, disconsolate, with a long face, forlorn, crestfallen, woebegone, subdued, fed up, out of sorts, low, in low spirits, in the doldrums, heavy-hearted; *informal* down in the dumps; *Brit. informal* brassed off, cheesed off, browned off, peed off; *N. Amer. informal* teed off, ticked off; *vulgar slang* pissed off.
□ **keep one's mouth shut say nothing**, keep quiet, not breathe a word, not tell a soul, not give the game away, keep it under one's hat; *informal* keep mum, play/keep one's cards close to one's chest, not let the cat out of the bag.
▶ **verb** *he mouthed platitudes in soothing tones* **utter**, speak, say; pronounce, enunciate, articulate, voice, express, vocalize, verbalize; say insincerely,

say for form's sake.
□ **mouth off** (*informal*) *he was mouthing off about school, teachers, and society in general* **rant**, spout, declaim, rave, jabber, sound off.

WORD LINKS
relating to the mouth **oral, buccal**
scientific study of the mouth **stomatology**

mouthful ▶ **noun 1** *a mouthful of pizza* **bite**, nibble, taste, bit, piece; spoonful, forkful, morsel, sample.
2 *a mouthful of beer* **draught**, sip, swallow, sup, drop, pull, gulp; *informal* swig, slug, swill.
3 *'sesquipedalian' is a bit of a mouthful* **tongue-twister**, long word, difficult word.
OPPOSITE monosyllable.

mouthpiece ▶ **noun 1** *the flute's mouthpiece* **embouchure**.
2 *he's just a mouthpiece for the government* **spokesperson**, spokesman, spokeswoman, agent, representative, propagandist, organ, voice; negotiator, intermediary, mediator, intermediator.

movable ▶ **adjective 1** *movable objects* **portable**, transportable, transferable; mobile; adjustable, flexible, detachable; *rare* portative.
OPPOSITE immovable.
2 *a calendar for all religious feasts, both fixed and movable* **variable**, changeable, alterable, unfixed, floating.
OPPOSITES fixed, immovable.

movables ▶ **plural noun possessions**, belongings, effects, property, goods, chattels, things, stuff, paraphernalia, impedimenta; *informal* gear; *rare* plenishings.
OPPOSITES fixtures, fittings.

move ▶ **verb 1** *she stood up and moved to the door | stay there—don't move!* **go**, walk, proceed, progress, advance, pass; budge, stir, shift, change position, make a move; *rare* locomote.
OPPOSITE stay put.
2 *he moved the chair closer to the fire* **carry**, transport, transfer, transpose, shift, switch.
3 *for some people, things were moving too fast* **progress**, make progress, make headway, advance, develop.
OPPOSITE stagnate.
4 *he urged the council to move quickly* **take action**, act, take steps, make a move, do something, take measures, take the initiative; *informal* get moving.
OPPOSITE do nothing.
5 *she's moved—she lives in Cambridge now* **relocate**, move house, move away/out, change address/house, leave, go away, decamp; change jobs; migrate, emigrate; *Scottish & N. English* flit; *informal* split; *Brit. informal* up sticks; *N. Amer. informal* pull up stakes.
6 *I was deeply moved by the story* **affect**, touch, strike, impress, shake, upset, disturb, hit, disquiet, agitate, stir, make an impression on, have an impact on, tug at someone's heartstrings.
OPPOSITES be unaffected (by), be indifferent (to).
7 *she attended a lecture on meditation and was moved to find out more about it* **inspire**, prompt, stimulate, motivate, provoke, influence, rouse, actuate, incline, persuade, urge, lead, cause, impel, induce, incite, excite.
8 *they are not prepared to move on this issue* **change**, budge, shift one's ground, change one's tune, sing a different song, change one's mind, change one's opinion, have second thoughts; do a U-turn, do an about-face, reconsider, climb down, back-pedal; *Brit.* do an about-turn.
9 *she moves in the pop and art worlds* **circulate**, mix, go round, socialize, fraternize, keep company, associate; *informal* hang out, hang around; *Brit. informal* hang about.
10 *I move that we all adjourn to my sitting room* **propose**, submit, suggest, put forward, advocate, recommend, request, urge.
▶ **noun 1** *his eyes followed her every move* **movement**, motion, action, activity; gesture, gesticulation.
2 *his recent move from Geneva to London* **relocation**, change of house/address/job, removal, transfer, posting; *Scottish & N. English* flit, flitting.
3 *the latest move in the war against illegal drugs* **initiative**, step, action, act, measure, tack, manoeuvre, tactic, stratagem, deed, gambit, ploy, ruse, trick, dodge.
4 *it's your move* **turn**, go, play; opportunity, chance; *informal* shot.
□ **get a move on** (*informal*) **hurry up**, speed up, move faster; *informal* get cracking, get moving, make it snappy, step on it, step on the gas, shake a leg, rattle one's dags; *Brit. informal* get one's skates on, stir one's stumps; *N. Amer. informal* get a wiggle on; *S. African informal* put foot; *dated* make haste.
□ **make a move 1** *each army was waiting for the other side to make a move* **do something, take action**, act, take measures, take the initiative; *informal* get moving.
2 *it's getting late—I think I'd better be making a move* **leave**, take one's leave, take oneself off, be on one's way, get going, depart, be off, set off, take one's farewells; *informal* push off, skedaddle, scram, shove off, split.
□ **on the move 1** *she's always on the move* **travelling**, in transit, moving, in motion, journeying, on the road, on the wing; *informal* on the go.
OPPOSITE in one place.
2 *the economy appears to be on the move at last* **progressing**, making progress, proceeding, advancing, developing, moving/going forward.
OPPOSITE stagnating.

movement ▶ **noun 1** *Rachel made a sudden movement | the scene was almost devoid of movement* **motion**, move, manoeuvre; gesture, gesticulation, sign, signal; action, activity.
2 *the movement of supplies by foreign military units* **transportation**, shift, shifting, conveyance, moving, transfer, transferral, relocation, repositioning.
3 *the labour movement* **political group**, party, faction, organization, grouping, wing, front, lobby, camp; coalition.
4 *a movement to declare war on poverty* **campaign**, crusade, drive, push.
5 *there have been movements in the financial markets* **development**, change, fluctuation, rise, fall, variation.
6 *the movement towards greater sexual equality* **trend**, tendency, drift, swing, current, course.
7 *he believes that some movement in the case will be made by the end of the month* **progress**, progression, advance, step forward, breakthrough.
8 *a symphony in three movements* **part**, section, division, passage.
9 *the clock's movement* **mechanism**, machinery, works, workings, action, wheels, motion; *informal* innards, guts.

WORD LINKS
relating to movement **kinetic**
fear of movement **kinetophobia**

movie ▶ **noun 1** *a horror movie* **film**, picture, motion picture, feature, feature film; *informal* flick, talkie; *dated* moving picture.
2 (**the movies**) *the growth of the movies as mass entertainment* **the cinema**, the pictures, the silver screen, the big screen; *informal* the flicks.

moving ▶ **adjective 1** *the moving parts of the machine | a moving train* **in motion**, operating, operational, working, going, on the move, active; kinetic; movable, mobile, motile, unfixed.
OPPOSITES immobile, fixed, stationary, motionless.
2 *an unforgettable and moving book* **affecting**, touching, emotive, poignant, heart-warming, heart-rending, emotional, upsetting, disturbing; effective, telling, striking, impressive, inspiring, inspirational, stimulating, arousing, stirring, soul-stirring, exciting, thrilling, dramatic; *informal* tear-jerking.
OPPOSITE unemotional.
3 *he has been the party's moving force since its foundation* **driving**, motivating, dynamic, impelling, stimulating, inspirational, stimulative.

CHOOSE THE RIGHT WORD

moving, touching, affecting

All three words relate to the arousing of emotions, generally ones in which pleasure and pain are mixed.

- The emotions aroused by something **moving** are typically of sadness or sympathy with someone else's suffering (*a moving display of drawings by children in a concentration camp*). They are generally both painful and uplifting (*a moving tribute to the power of the human spirit*), and can be of a religious or artistic nature (*the torchlight procession round the church after Mass was a very moving experience | Philip Bond gives a wonderful and moving portrayal of jaded professor Frank*).
- Something **touching** inspires feelings of tenderness, sometimes verging on the sentimental (*there was a touching air of innocence about the boy*). *Touching* is less intense than *moving*. It can also convey gratitude for an unexpected service or tribute (*your concern is most touching*).
- **Affecting** is similiar in meaning to *moving* but rarer and more literary (*an infectious and affecting tale of romantic doom*).

mow ▶ **verb** *someone had mown the grass* **cut**, cut down, scythe, shear, trim; crop, clip.
□ **mow someone/something down** *they were mown down by government troops* **kill**, gun down, shoot down, cut down, cut to pieces, butcher, slaughter, massacre, decimate, annihilate, exterminate, liquidate, wipe out, destroy; *informal* blow away; *N. Amer. informal* smoke; *literary* slay.

much ▶ **determiner** *did you get much help?* **a lot of**, a great/good deal of, a great/large amount of, plenty of, ample, copious, abundant, plentiful, considerable, substantial; *informal* lots of, loads of, heaps of, masses of, a pile of, piles of, oodles of, tons of, more … than one can shake a stick at; *Brit. informal* lashings of, a shedload of; *N. Amer. informal* gobs of; *vulgar slang* a shitload of.
OPPOSITE little.
▶ **adverb 1** *it didn't hurt much* **greatly**, to a great extent/degree, a great deal, a lot, exceedingly, considerably, appreciably, decidedly, indeed.
2 *does he come here much?* **often**, frequently, many times, on many/numerous occasions, repeatedly, recurrently, regularly, habitually, customarily, routinely, usually, normally, commonly; for long, for a long time; *informal* a lot.
▶ **pronoun** *she doesn't eat much | he did so much for our team* **a lot**, a great/good

M

deal, plenty; *informal* lots, loads, heaps, masses, oodles, tons.
□ **much of a muchness very similar**, much the same, more or less the same, very alike, practically identical, practically indistinguishable.

muck ▶ **noun 1** *I'll just clean the muck off the windscreen* **dirt**, grime, filth, mud, slime, sludge, scum, mire, mess, rubbish; *informal* crud, gunk, grunge, gloop, gook, goo, yuck; *Brit. informal* gunge, grot; *N. Amer. informal* guck, glop.
2 *the spreading of muck on the fields* **dung**, manure, ordure, excrement, excreta, droppings, faeces, cowpats, guano, sewage; *N. Amer. informal* cow chips, horse apples; *vulgar slang* shit, crap; *rare* feculence.
▶ **verb**
□ **muck something up** (*informal*) *I was convinced she would muck the whole thing up* **make a mess of**, mess up, botch, bungle, spoil, ruin, wreck, mishandle, mismanage; *informal* make a hash of, muff, fluff, foul up, screw up, louse up, bitch up, blow, foozle; *Brit. informal* make a muck of, make a pig's ear of, cock up, make a Horlicks of; *N. Amer. informal* flub, goof up; *vulgar slang* fuck up, bugger up, balls up.
□ **muck about/around** (*Brit. informal*) **1** *he was mucking about with his mates* **fool about/around**, play about/around, fiddle about/around, amuse oneself, clown about/around, footle about/around; *informal* mess about/around, horse about/around, lark (about/around), screw around, puddle about/around; *Brit. informal* fanny about/around; *vulgar slang* frig about/around, fuck about/around; *Brit. vulgar slang* piss about/around, arse about/around, bugger about/around.
2 *someone's been mucking about with the video* **interfere**, fiddle (about/around), play about/around, tamper, meddle, tinker, monkey (about/around); *informal* mess (about/around), dick around.

mucky ▶ **adjective** *a pair of mucky boots* **dirty**, filthy, grimy, muddy, mud-caked, grubby, messy, soiled, stained, smeared, smeary, scummy, slimy, sticky, sooty, dusty, unclean, foul, begrimed, bespattered, befouled, polluted, squalid, insanitary; *informal* cruddy, grungy, yucky, icky, gloopy, crummy; *Brit. informal* manky, gungy, grotty; *Austral./NZ informal* scungy; *literary* besmirched; *rare* feculent.
OPPOSITE clean.

mud ▶ **noun mire**, sludge, slush, ooze, silt, clay, gumbo, dirt, soil; *Scottish & N. English* clart; *Irish* slob.

muddle ▶ **verb 1** *the papers seem to have got muddled up* **confuse**, mix up, jumble, jumble up, disarrange, disorganize, disorder, disturb, throw into disorder, get into a tangle, scramble, mess up.
OPPOSITE be in (good) order.
2 *I won't explain—it'll only muddle you* **bewilder**, confuse, bemuse, perplex, puzzle, baffle, nonplus, mystify, confound, disorientate, disorient, befuddle, daze, addle.
OPPOSITE enlighten.
□ **muddle along/through** *we're muddling along as best we can* **cope**, manage, get by/along, scrape by/along, make do, make the best of a bad job.
▶ **noun 1** *the files are in a bit of a muddle* **mess**, confusion, jumble, tangle, clutter, hotchpotch, mishmash, mare's nest, chaos, disorder, disarray, welter, disorganization.
2 *a bureaucratic muddle* **bungle**, mix-up, misunderstanding, mistake; *informal* hash, foul-up, screw-up; *N. Amer. informal* snafu; *vulgar slang* fuck-up; *Brit. vulgar slang* balls-up.

muddled ▶ **adjective 1** *a muddled pile of photographs* **jumbled**, in a jumble, in a muddle, in a mess, chaotic, in disorder, in disarray, topsy-turvy, disorganized, disordered, disorderly, out of place, out of order, mixed up, upside-down, at sixes and sevens, untidy, messy, scrambled, tangled; *informal* higgledy-piggledy.
OPPOSITE orderly.
2 *she felt muddled and couldn't keep track of her thoughts* **confused**, in a state of confusion, bewildered, bemused, perplexed, disorientated, disoriented, at sea, in a muddle, befuddled, dazed; *informal* discombobulated; *Canadian & Austral./NZ informal* bushed.
3 *muddled thinking* **incoherent**, confused, muddle-headed, woolly, jumbled, disjointed.
OPPOSITES clear, lucid.

muddy ▶ **adjective 1** *we picked our way through the muddy ground* **waterlogged**, boggy, marshy, swampy, squelchy, squishy, mucky, miry, oozy, slushy, slimy, sodden, spongy, wet, soft, heavy, sloughy; *Scottish & N. English* mossy, clarty; *rare* quaggy.
2 *they changed their muddy boots* **mud-caked**, mud-spattered, muddied, dirty, filthy, mucky, grubby, grimy, soiled, begrimed.
OPPOSITE clean.
3 *muddy water* **murky**, cloudy, muddied, turbid, opaque, impure; *N. Amer.* riled, roily, roiled.
OPPOSITE clear.
4 *the original colours had faded to a muddy pink* **dingy**, dirty, drab, dull, sludgy, washed out, flat.
5 *some sentences are so muddy that their meaning can only be guessed* **incoherent**, confused, muddled, jumbled, woolly, vague, fuzzy.
▶ **verb 1** *you can step ashore without muddying your boots* **make muddy**, cake with mud/dirt, dirty, soil, begrime, grime, mire, spatter, bespatter; *literary* smirch, besmirch, bemire.
2 *the results muddy rather than clarify the situation* **make unclear**, **obscure**, confuse, obfuscate, blur, cloud, befog, mix up.
OPPOSITE clarify.

muff ▶ **verb** *the administration muffed several of its biggest projects* **mishandle**, mismanage, mess up, make a mess of, bungle, botch; miss, mishit, fumble; *informal* make a hash of, fluff, foul up, screw up, louse up, bitch up, blow, foozle; *Brit. informal* make a muck of, make a pig's ear of, cock up, make a Horlicks of; *N. Amer. informal* flub, goof up, bobble; *vulgar slang* fuck up, bugger up, balls up, bollix up.

muffle ▶ **verb 1** *it was cold and everyone was muffled up in coats and scarves* **wrap**, wrap up, swathe, swaddle, enfold, envelop, cloak, cover up.
2 *the sound of their footsteps was muffled by the fog | unions fear their voice within the party is being muffled* **deaden**, dull, dampen, damp down, mute, soften, quieten, hush, silence, still, tone down, mask, stifle, smother, subdue, suppress, gag, muzzle.

muffled ▶ **adjective** *muffled shouts* **indistinct**, faint, muted, dull, dim, soft, strangled, stifled, smothered, suppressed.
OPPOSITES loud, clear.

mug[1] ▶ **noun 1** *a china mug* **beaker**, cup; tankard, glass, stein, flagon, pot, pint pot, toby jug; *dated* seidel; *archaic* stoup.
2 (*informal*) *I never want to see your ugly mug again* **face**, features, countenance, physiognomy; *informal* clock; *Brit. informal* mush, phiz, phizog, dial; *Brit. rhyming slang* boat race; *Scottish & Irish informal* coupon; *N. Amer. informal* puss, pan; *literary* visage; *archaic* front.
3 (*informal*) *he's no mug—he's got it all worked out* **fool**, simpleton, innocent, dupe, gull; *informal* sucker, soft/easy touch, pushover, chump, noddle, dummy, dope, dimwit, dumbo, nerd, knucklehead, lamebrain, pea-brain, pudding-head, thickhead, wooden-head, pinhead, airhead, birdbrain; *Brit. informal* muggins, juggins, charlie; *N. Amer. informal* patsy, sap, schlemiel, pigeon, mark; *Austral./NZ informal* dill.
▶ **verb** *he was mugged by three youths who stole his bike* **assault**, attack, set upon, beat up, knock down, rob; *informal* jump, rough up, lay into, work over, steam; *Brit. informal* duff up, do over; *N. Amer. informal* stick up.

mug[2] ▶ **verb**
□ **mug something up** *she's mugging up the Highway Code* **study**, get up, read up, cram; *informal* bone up (on); *Brit. informal* swot; *archaic* con.

muggy ▶ **adjective** *an unpleasantly muggy evening* **humid**, close, sultry, sticky, steamy, oppressive, airless, stifling, suffocating, stuffy, clammy, damp, moist, soupy, heavy, fuggy, like a Turkish bath, like a sauna.
OPPOSITES fresh, airy.

mulish ▶ **adjective** *George could sometimes be rather mulish* **obstinate**, stubborn, stubborn as a mule, pig-headed, recalcitrant, refractory, intransigent, intractable, unyielding, inflexible, unbending, bull-headed, stiff-necked, headstrong, difficult, wilful, self-willed, cross-grained; *Brit. informal* bloody-minded, bolshie; *archaic* contumacious.
OPPOSITES docile, tractable; obliging.

mull ▶ **verb**
□ **mull something over** *Barney sat there for a while, mulling things over* **ponder**, consider, think over/about, reflect on, contemplate, deliberate, turn over in one's mind, chew over, weigh up, consider the pros and cons of, cogitate on, meditate on, muse on, ruminate over/on, brood on, have one's mind on, give some thought to, evaluate, examine, study, review, revolve; *archaic* pore on; *rare* cerebrate.

multicoloured ▶ **adjective kaleidoscopic**, psychedelic, colourful, multicolour, many-coloured, many-hued, rainbow, jazzy, particoloured, varicoloured, variegated, harlequin, motley, prismatic, polychromatic; pied, piebald, skewbald, dappled, brindled, brindle, tabby; *N. Amer.* pinto; *informal* (looking) like an explosion in a paint factory.
OPPOSITE monochrome.

multifarious ▶ **adjective** *the multifarious local and ethnic traditions that are found in the USA* **diverse**, many, numerous, various, varied, diversified, multiple, multitudinous, multiplex, manifold, multifaceted, legion, different, heterogeneous, eclectic, sundry, miscellaneous, assorted, variegated; *literary* myriad, divers.
OPPOSITE homogeneous.

multiple ▶ **adjective** *words with multiple meanings* **numerous**, many, various, different, diverse, several, sundry, miscellaneous, manifold, multifarious, multitudinous, compound, collective; *literary* myriad, divers.

WORD LINKS
related prefixes **multi-** (e.g. ***multidirectional, multibuy***), **poly-** (e.g. ***polygon, polyethnic***)
related suffix **-fold** (e.g. ***fourfold***)

multiplicity ▶ **noun** *the multiplicity of species found in the rainforests* **abundance**, scores, mass, host, array, variety, myriad, a lot; range, diverseness, numerousness, heterogeneity, plurality; profusion, quantities; *informal* lots, loads, stacks, heaps, piles, masses, tons, oodles, hundreds, thousands, millions, billions; *Brit. informal* shedload; *N. Amer. informal* slew, gazillions, gobs; *Austral./NZ informal* swag; *vulgar slang* shitload.

multiply ▶ **verb 1** *the difficulties seem to be multiplying by the minute* **increase**, increase exponentially, grow, become more numerous,

M

accumulate, proliferate, mount up, mushroom, snowball, burgeon, spread, expand; *literary* wax.
OPPOSITES decrease, diminish.
2 *rabbits were introduced here and multiplied* **breed**, reproduce, procreate, propagate.

multitude ▶ **noun 1** *a multitude of problems | multitudes of birds* **a lot**, a great/large number, a great/large quantity, host, horde, mass, mountain, droves, swarm, army, legion, sea, abundance, profusion; scores, quantities; *informal* lots, loads, masses, stacks, heaps, tons, dozens, hundreds, thousands, millions, billions, zillions; *Brit. informal* shedload; *N. Amer. informal* slew, gazillions, bazillions, gobs; *Austral./NZ informal* swag; *vulgar slang* shitload.
2 *Father Peter addressed the multitude* **crowd**, gathering, assembly, group, assemblage, congregation, flock, throng, horde, mob; *rare* concourse.
3 (**the multitude**) *placing political power in the hands of the multitude* **the common people**, the populace, the public, the people, the masses, the rank and file, the crowd, the commonality, the commonalty, the third estate, the plebeians; the hoi polloi, the mob, the proletariat, the common herd, the rabble, the riff-raff, the canaille, the great unwashed, the ragtag (and bobtail), proles, plebs.
OPPOSITE the elite.

multitudinous ▶ **adjective** *the multitudinous stars* **numerous**, many, abundant, profuse, prolific, copious, legion, teeming, multifarious, a thousand and one, innumerable, countless, uncounted, infinite, numberless, unnumbered, untold, incalculable; *informal* umpteen; *S. African informal* lank; *literary* divers, myriad; manifold; *rare* innumerous, unnumberable.

mum¹ ▶ **noun** (*Brit. informal*). *See* MOTHER.

mum² ▶ **adjective** (*informal*) *he was keeping mum about his future plans* **silent**, quiet, mute, dumb, tight-lipped, close-mouthed, uncommunicative, unforthcoming, reticent, secretive; *archaic* mumchance.
▶ **noun**
□ **mum's the word say nothing**, keep quiet, don't breathe a word, don't tell a soul, don't give the game away, keep it secret, keep it to yourself, keep it under your hat, play dumb; *Scottish* play the daft baddie/lassie; *informal* don't let on, keep shtum, don't let the cat out of the bag.

mumble ▶ **verb** *the old man shuffled away, mumbling to himself* **mutter**, murmur, speak indistinctly, talk under one's breath, speak sotto voce, talk to oneself; *rare* maffle.

mumbo-jumbo ▶ **noun** *the instructions are complete mumbo-jumbo* **nonsense**, gibberish, claptrap, rubbish, balderdash, blather, blether; rigmarole; **jargon**, unintelligible language, obscure language, hocus-pocus; *informal* gobbledegook, double Dutch, argle-bargle, bull.

munch ▶ **verb** *he munched his sandwich in a dream* **chew**, champ, chomp, masticate, crunch, scrunch, eat; *rare* chumble, manducate, triturate.

mundane ▶ **adjective 1** *the mundane aspects of daily life* **humdrum**, dull, boring, tedious, monotonous, tiresome, wearisome, prosaic, unexciting, uninteresting, uneventful, unvarying, unvaried, unremarkable, repetitive, repetitious, routine, ordinary, everyday, day-to-day, quotidian, run-of-the-mill, commonplace, common, workaday, usual, pedestrian, customary, regular, normal; unimaginative, banal, hackneyed, trite, stale, platitudinous; *informal* typical, vanilla, plain vanilla; *rare* banausic.
OPPOSITES extraordinary, imaginative.
2 *the mundane world* **earthly**, worldly, terrestrial, material, temporal, secular, non-spiritual, fleshly, carnal, sensual; *rare* sublunary.
OPPOSITE spiritual.

municipal ▶ **adjective** *land use is controlled by the municipal authorities* **civic**, civil, metropolitan, urban, city, town, borough, community, district, local, council, public; *rare* oppidan.
OPPOSITE rural.

municipality ▶ **noun** *each municipality has its own quota of subsidy* **borough**, town, city, district, administrative division; *N. Amer.* precinct, township; *Scottish* burgh; *French* arrondissement.

munificence ▶ **noun** *the munificence of our host* **generosity**, bountifulness, open-handedness, magnanimity, magnanimousness, princeliness, lavishness, free-handedness, liberality, philanthropy, charity, charitableness, largesse, big-heartedness, beneficence, benevolence; *literary* bounty, bounteousness.
OPPOSITES meanness, niggardliness.

munificent ▶ **adjective** *a munificent bequest* **generous**, bountiful, open-handed, magnanimous, philanthropic, princely, handsome, lavish, unstinting, free-handed, unstinted, liberal, free, charitable, big-hearted, beneficent, ungrudging; *literary* bounteous.
OPPOSITES mean, niggardly, miserly.

munificent or magnificent?
See MAGNIFICENT.

murder ▶ **noun 1** *the brutal murder of a German holidaymaker* **killing**, homicide, assassination, liquidation, extermination, execution, slaughter, butchery, massacre; manslaughter; patricide, matricide, parricide, fratricide, sororicide, filicide, infanticide, uxoricide, regicide; *literary* slaying.
2 (*informal*) *driving there was murder* **hell**, hell on earth, a nightmare, an ordeal, a trial, a frustrating/unpleasant/difficult experience, misery, torture, agony.
▶ **verb 1** *someone tried to murder him* **kill**, put/do to death, assassinate, execute, liquidate, eliminate, neutralize, dispatch, butcher, cut to pieces, slaughter, massacre, wipe out, mow down; *informal* bump off, do in, do away with, do for, knock off, blow away, blow someone's brains out, stiff, take out, top, croak, give someone the works, dispose of, hit, zap; *N. Amer. informal* ice, rub out, smoke, waste, off, whack, scrag; *N. Amer. euphemistic* terminate with extreme prejudice; *literary* slay.
2 (*informal*) *Anna was murdering a Mozart sonata. See* BUNGLE.
3 (*informal*) *he murdered his lacklustre opponent. See* TROUNCE.

murderer, **murderess** *See centre pages for list of types of* **Murderer**
▶ **noun killer**, liquidator, terminator, slaughterer; *dated* homicide; *literary* slayer.

murderous ▶ **adjective 1** *a murderous attack* **homicidal**, brutal, violent, savage, ferocious, fierce, vicious, bloodthirsty, barbarous, barbaric, cruel, inhuman; fatal, lethal, deadly, mortal, killing, death-dealing, bloody; *literary* fell; *archaic* sanguinary.
2 (*informal*) *the team had a murderous schedule of four games in ten days* **arduous**, gruelling, strenuous, punishing, onerous, back-breaking, crushing, exhausting, taxing, difficult, hard, laborious, rigorous, stressful, formidable, intolerable, unbearable, harrowing; *informal* killing, hellish; *Brit. informal* knackering.
OPPOSITES easy, light.

murky ▶ **adjective 1** *a murky winter afternoon* **dark**, **gloomy**, grey, leaden, dull, dim, overcast, cloudy, clouded, sunless, foggy, misty, dismal, dreary, bleak, louring, threatening, cheerless, depressing, shadowy, sombre; *literary* tenebrous, crepuscular; *rare* caliginous, Cimmerian.
OPPOSITES bright, sunny.
2 *murky water* **dirty**, **muddy**, cloudy, turbid, opaque; *N. Amer.* riled, roily, roiled.
OPPOSITE clear.
3 *a government minister with a murky past* **questionable**, **suspicious**, suspect, dubious, dark, mysterious, secret; *informal* shady.
OPPOSITE innocent.

murmur ▶ **noun 1** *his voice was little more than a murmur* **whisper**, undertone, mutter, mumble.
2 *there were murmurs in Tory ranks* **complaint**, grumble, moan, grouse; mutter, muttering; *informal* gripe, beef, bitch.
3 *the murmur of the river* **burble**, babble, purl, gurgle; *literary* plash.
4 *the murmur of bees* **hum**, humming, buzz, buzzing, whirr, thrum, thrumming, drone, sigh; *rare* susurration, murmuration, susurrus.
▶ **verb 1** *he heard them murmuring in the hall* **mutter**, mumble, whisper, talk under one's breath, speak in an undertone, speak softly, speak sotto voce, speak in hushed tones; breathe, purr.
OPPOSITES shout, yell.
2 *no one murmured at the delay* **complain**, moan, mutter, grumble, grouse, carp, whine, bleat; *informal* gripe, beef, bitch, whinge; *Brit. informal* chunter, grizzle; *N. English informal* mither.
3 *the wind was murmuring through the trees* **rustle**, whirr, burble, purl, rumble, sigh; *literary* whisper, breathe.

muscle *See centre pages for lists of* **Muscles** **Muscle Types**
▶ **noun 1** *I've pulled a muscle in my leg literary* thew.
2 *he had muscle but no brains* **strength**, power, muscularity, brawn, brawniness, burliness, huskiness; *informal* beef, beefiness; *literary* thew.
3 *they used financial muscle to secure senior UN posts* **influence**, power, strength, might, force, forcefulness, weight, potency; *informal* clout, beef, pull.
▶ **verb**
□ **muscle in** *he was determined to* **muscle in** *on the union's affairs* **interfere with**, force one's way into, elbow one's way in on, butt in on, impose oneself on, encroach on; *informal* horn in on.

WORD LINKS

related prefix	**myo-** (e.g. ***myocardial***)
branch of medicine to do with muscles	**orthopaedics**
incision into muscle	**myotomy**

muscular ▶ **adjective 1** *muscular tissue* **fibrous**, sinewy.
2 *he's tall, blonde, and very muscular* **strong**, brawny, muscly, sinewy, well built, powerfully built, well muscled, burly, strapping, sturdy, rugged, powerful, broad-shouldered, athletic, well knit, muscle-bound, Herculean, manly; *informal* hunky, beefy, husky; *dated* stalwart; *literary* thewy; *Physiology* mesomorphic.
3 *a muscular economy* **vigorous**, robust, strong, powerful, dynamic, potent, energetic, active, aggressive.
OPPOSITES weak, puny, feeble.

muse¹ ▶ **noun** *the poet's muse* **inspiration**, creative influence, stimulus, stimulation; *rare* afflatus.

M

muse[2] ▶ verb *I mused on Toby's story as I walked home* **ponder**, consider, think over/about, mull over, reflect on, contemplate, deliberate, turn over in one's mind, chew over, weigh up, meditate on, ruminate over/on, brood on, give some thought to, cogitate on, evaluate, examine, study, review; think, debate with oneself, be lost in contemplation/thought, be in a brown study, daydream, be in a reverie; *archaic* pore on; *rare* cerebrate.

mush ▶ noun **1** *she was eating some sort of greyish mush* **pap**, pulp, slop, paste, purée, slush, swill, mash, pomace; *informal* gloop, goo, gook; *N. Amer. informal* glop.
2 *the film's just romantic mush* **sentimentality**, mawkishness; *informal* schmaltz, corn, slush, hokum, sob stuff, cheese; *N. Amer. informal* slop.

mushroom *See centre pages for lists of* **Fungi, Mushrooms, and Toadstools** **Poisonous Plants and Fungi**
▶ verb *the ecotourism industry mushroomed in the 1980s* **proliferate**, grow/develop rapidly, burgeon, spread, increase, expand, spring up, shoot up, sprout, burst forth, boom, explode, snowball, rocket, skyrocket; thrive, flourish, prosper.
OPPOSITES contract; fail.

mushy ▶ adjective **1** *cook until the fruit is mushy* **soft**, **semi-liquid**, pulpy, pappy, slushy, sloppy, spongy, squashy, squelchy, squishy; *informal* gooey, gloopy; *Brit. informal* squidgy; *rare* pulpous.
OPPOSITES hard, firm.
2 *a mushy film* **sentimental**, mawkish, over-sentimental, emotional, cloying, sickly, saccharine, sugary, syrupy; *Brit.* twee; *informal* slushy, sloppy, schmaltzy, weepy, cutesy, lovey-dovey, gooey, drippy, sloshy, soupy, treacly, cheesy, corny, icky, sick-making, toe-curling; *Brit. informal* soppy; *N. Amer. informal* cornball, sappy, hokey, three-hankie.
OPPOSITES unsentimental, gritty.

music ▶ noun. *See centre pages for lists of* **Dances** **Jazz Genres** **Musical Genres** **Musical Forms** **Musical Directions** **Tonic Sol-Fa Notes**

WORD LINKS
Muse of flutes **Euterpe**
Muse of hymns **Erato**
fear of music **musicophobia**

musical ▶ adjective **tuneful**, melodic, melodious, harmonious, sweet-sounding, sweet, mellifluous, dulcet, lyrical, lilting, liquid, euphonious, euphonic; *rare* mellifluent.
OPPOSITES discordant, harsh, grating.
▶ noun **musical comedy**.

musical instrument ▶ noun. *See centre pages for lists of* **Brass Instruments** **Keyboard Instruments** **Orchestral Instruments** **Organs** **Percussion Instruments** **Stringed Instruments** **Wind Instruments**

musician *See centre pages for lists of* **Musicians (Instrumentalists)** **Singers** **Voices**
▶ noun **player**, performer, instrumentalist, accompanist, soloist, virtuoso, maestro, conductor; composer; *archaic* minstrel.

musing ▶ noun **meditation**, thinking, contemplation, deliberation, pondering, reflection, rumination, cogitation, introspection, daydreaming, dreaming, reverie, brown study, abstraction, preoccupation, brooding, wool-gathering; *rare* cerebration.

muss ▶ verb *the wind was mussing up his hair* **ruffle**, tousle, dishevel, rumple, mess up, make a mess of, disarrange, make untidy, tumble, put out of place, disorder.
OPPOSITE tidy.

must[1] ▶ verb *I must go* **ought to**, should, have to, have got to, need to, be obliged to, be required to, be compelled to, be under an obligation to.
▶ noun (*informal*) *this video is a must* **not to be missed**, very good; necessity, essential, necessary thing, sine qua non, requirement, requisite.
OPPOSITE option.

must[2] ▶ noun *a smell of must* **mould**, mustiness, mouldiness, mildew, fustiness, decay.

muster ▶ verb **1** *they had mustered 50,000 troops* **assemble**, bring together, call together, marshal, mobilize, rally, round up, raise, summon, gather, gather together, mass, collect, convene, call up, call to arms, recruit, conscript, draft; *formal* convoke; *archaic* levy.
OPPOSITE disperse.
2 *reporters mustered outside her house* **congregate**, assemble, gather together, come together, meet, collect together, convene, mass, cluster together, flock together, rally; *rare* foregather.
3 *mustering her courage, she marched into the office* **summon up**, summon, screw up, gather together, call up, rally.
▶ noun *the colonel called a muster* **roll-call**, **assembly**, rally, meeting, round-up, convocation, mobilization, gathering, assemblage, congregation, convention; parade, review.
□ **pass muster be good enough**, come up to standard, come up to scratch, measure up, be acceptable/adequate, be sufficient, fill/fit the bill, do, qualify; *informal* make the grade, come/be up to snuff, cut the mustard.

musty ▶ adjective **1** *the room smelled musty* **mouldy**, stale, fusty, damp, dank, mildewed, mildewy, decayed, smelly, stuffy, airless, unventilated; *Brit.* frowsty; *N. Amer. informal* funky; *rare* mucid.
OPPOSITES fresh, fragrant.
2 *when I read it again, the play seemed musty* **unoriginal**, uninspired, unimaginative, hackneyed, stale, flat, tired, banal, trite, clichéd, dry as dust, old-fashioned, antiquated, antediluvian, out of date, outdated, hoary, moth-eaten, worn out, threadbare, out of fashion, behind the times, obsolete; *French* passé, vieux jeu; *informal* old hat.
OPPOSITES fresh, modern.

mutable ▶ adjective *the mutable nature of fashion* **changeable**, variable, varying, fluctuating, shifting, inconsistent, unpredictable, inconstant, uncertain, fluid, erratic, irregular, uneven, unsettled, unstable, unsteady, protean, chameleon-like, chameleonic; capricious, fickle, faithless, flighty, unreliable, undependable, mercurial, volatile; *technical* labile; *rare* changeful, fluctuant.
OPPOSITES constant, invariable.

mutant ▶ noun **freak**, freak of nature, deviant, oddity, monstrosity, monster, mutation, variant, variation; *Latin* lusus naturae; *rare* miscreation.

mutate ▶ verb *rhythm and blues mutated into rock and roll* **change**, metamorphose, evolve, undergo a sea change; transmute, transform, transfigure, recast, reconstruct, convert; *humorous* transmogrify.

mutation ▶ noun **1** *cells that have undergone mutation* **alteration**, change, variation, modification, transformation, metamorphosis, transmutation, transfiguration, sea change, evolution; *humorous* transmogrification.
2 *a genetic mutation* **mutant**, variant, variation, freak, freak of nature, deviant, monstrosity, monster, deformity; anomaly, departure; *Latin* lusus naturae; *rare* miscreation.

mute ▶ adjective **1** *although I longed for details, Yasmin remained mute* **silent**, speechless, dumb, unspeaking, wordless, voiceless, tongue-tied, at a loss for words, tight-lipped, close-mouthed, taciturn, uncommunicative; *informal* mum; *archaic* mumchance.
OPPOSITES voluble, talkative.
2 *she gazed at him in mute appeal* **wordless**, silent, dumb, tacit, unspoken, inarticulate, unvoiced, unsaid, unexpressed, unuttered.
OPPOSITE spoken.
3 *the church was mute and dark* **quiet**, silent, noiseless, soundless, hushed.
OPPOSITE noisy.
4 *he had been bullied into silence—people wondered if he was actually mute* **dumb**, unable to speak; *technical* aphasic, aphonic.
▶ verb **1** *the noise of the traffic was muted by the heavy curtains* **deaden**, **muffle**, mask, dull, dampen, damp down, soften, quieten, silence; stifle, smother, suppress, lower, reduce, diminish, decrease.
OPPOSITE amplify.
2 *Bruce had muted his criticisms* **restrain**, soften, subdue, tone down, make less intense, moderate, temper, soft-pedal.
OPPOSITE intensify.

muted ▶ adjective **1** *the muted hum of distant traffic* **muffled**, faint, indistinct, quiet, soft, softened, low, dull; hushed, whispered, lowered, stifled, suppressed.
OPPOSITE amplified.
2 *muted tones of grey and powder blue* **subdued**, **pastel**, delicate, faded, dusty, subtle, toned down, understated, discreet, unobtrusive, restrained, low-key.
OPPOSITE garish.

mutilate ▶ verb **1** *many of the bodies had been mutilated* **mangle**, maim, disfigure, cut to pieces, cut up, hack up, butcher, dismember, tear limb from limb, tear apart, lacerate, cripple, lame, disable.
2 *the 14th-century carved screen had been mutilated* **vandalize**, damage, deface, spoil, mar, ruin, destroy, wreck, violate, desecrate; *N. Amer. informal* trash; *rare* disfeature.

mutilation ▶ noun **maiming**, disfigurement, dismembering; damage, vandalization, desecration.

mutinous ▶ adjective *mutinous troops seized three military bases* **rebellious**, insubordinate, subversive, seditious, insurgent, insurrectionary, insurrectionist, rebel, revolutionary; anarchistic, lawless, riotous, rioting, traitorous, factious; disobedient, defiant, wilful, recalcitrant, refractory, restive, disaffected, up in arms, unruly, disorderly, out of control, uncontrollable, ungovernable, unmanageable, unbiddable; *Brit. informal* bolshie; *archaic* contumacious.
OPPOSITES obedient, compliant.

mutiny ▶ noun *the mutiny over pay arrears had spread to the armed forces* **insurrection**, **rebellion**, revolt, riot, revolution, uprising, rising, coup, coup d'état, putsch, protest, strike; insurgence, insurgency, subversion, sedition, anarchy, disorder, insubordination, disobedience, resistance, defiance.
▶ verb *thousands of soldiers mutinied* **rise up**, **rebel**, revolt, riot, take part in an insurrection/uprising, resist/oppose authority, disobey/defy authority, refuse to obey orders; be insubordinate, protest, strike, go on strike.

mutt ▶ noun (*informal*) **1** *a long-haired mutt of doubtful pedigree* **mongrel**, hound, dog, cur, tyke; *informal* pooch; *Austral. informal* mong, bitzer.

2 *he pitied the poor mutt who fell for her charms.* See FOOL.

mutter ▶ verb **1** *a group of men stood muttering in one corner of the room* **talk under one's breath**, murmur, mumble, whisper, speak in an undertone, speak sotto voce, speak in hushed tones; talk to oneself.
OPPOSITE speak out.
2 *backbenchers muttered about the reshuffle* **grumble**, moan, complain, grouse, carp, whine, bleat; *informal* gripe, beef, bitch, whinge, sound off; *Brit. informal* chunter, grizzle; *N. English informal* mither; *N. Amer. informal* kvetch.

mutual ▶ adjective *a partnership based on mutual respect and understanding* **reciprocal**, reciprocated, requited, returned, give-and-take, interchangeable, interactive, complementary, correlative; common, joint, shared.

muzzle ▶ noun **1** *she patted the dog's velvety muzzle* **snout**, nose, mouth, jaws, maw.
2 *the law says that pit bull terriers have to wear a muzzle* **gag**, restraint.
▶ verb *clumsy attempts to muzzle the media* **gag**, silence, censor, suppress, stifle, inhibit, restrain, check, curb, fetter.

muzzy ▶ adjective **1** *she was shivering and felt muzzy* **groggy**, light-headed, faint, dizzy, shaky, confused, muddled, fuddled, befuddled, addled, befogged; *informal* dopey, woozy, not with it.
OPPOSITE clear-headed.
2 *a slightly muzzy picture* **blurred**, blurry, fuzzy, unfocused, unclear, indistinct, ill-defined, woolly, foggy, hazy, faint.
OPPOSITE clear.

myopic ▶ adjective **1** *thick lenses may restrict a myopic patient's field of view* **short-sighted**; *N. Amer.* nearsighted; *informal* as blind as a bat; *archaic* purblind.
OPPOSITE long-sighted.
2 *the government still has a myopic attitude to public spending* **unimaginative**, uncreative, unadventurous, narrow-minded, lacking foresight, small-minded, short-term, narrow; insular, parochial, provincial.
OPPOSITE far-sighted.

myriad ▶ noun *myriads of insects danced around the light* **multitude**, a large/great number/quantity, a lot, scores, quantities, mass, crowd, throng, host, droves, horde, army, legion, sea, swarm; *informal* lots, loads, masses, stacks, tons, oodles, hundreds, thousands, millions, billions, zillions, more ... than one can shake a stick at; *N. Amer. informal* gazillions, bazillions.
▶ adjective *the myriad lights of the city* **innumerable**, countless, infinite, numberless, unlimited, untold, limitless, unnumbered, immeasurable, multitudinous, numerous, manifold, multiple, legion, several, many, various, sundry, diverse, multifarious; *literary* divers; *rare* innumerous, unnumberable.

myself ▶ pronoun
□ **by myself**. *See* BY ONESELF *at* BY.

mysterious ▶ adjective **1** *his colleague had vanished in mysterious circumstances* **puzzling**, **strange**, peculiar, curious, funny, queer, odd, weird, bizarre, mystifying, inexplicable, baffling, perplexing, bewildering, confusing, uncanny, dark, impenetrable, incomprehensible, unexplainable, unfathomable, Delphic, sibylline, unaccountable, insoluble, obscure; arcane, recondite, secret, esoteric, occult, cryptic, hidden, concealed, supernatural, mystical.
OPPOSITE straightforward.
2 *he was being very mysterious about his whereabouts* **enigmatic**, inscrutable, secretive, sphinx-like, cloak-and-dagger, reticent, non-committal, discreet, evasive, furtive, surreptitious, covert.
OPPOSITE open.

mystery ▶ noun **1** *his death remains a mystery* **puzzle**, **enigma**, conundrum, riddle, secret, unsolved problem, problem, question, question mark, closed book; *informal* poser.
2 *much of her past is shrouded in mystery* **secrecy**, darkness, obscurity, ambiguity, ambiguousness, uncertainty, impenetrability, vagueness, nebulousness; inscrutability, inscrutableness, unfathomableness, mystique, romance.
3 *a 1920s murder mystery entitled 'The Ghost Train'* **thriller**, detective story/novel, murder story; *informal* whodunnit.

mystic, **mystical** ▶ adjective **1** *a mystic experience* **spiritual**, religious, transcendental, transcendent, paranormal, other-worldly, supernatural, preternatural, non-rational, occult, metaphysical, ineffable.
2 *mystic rites* **symbolic**, symbolical, allegorical, representational, metaphorical, emblematic, emblematical, non-literal.
3 *a geometric figure of mystical significance* **cryptic**, concealed, hidden, abstruse, arcane, esoteric, recondite, inscrutable, inexplicable, unfathomable, mysterious, secret, enigmatic, occult, cabbalistic, obscure, unrevealed.

mystify ▶ verb *I was completely mystified by his disappearance* **bewilder**, puzzle, perplex, baffle, confuse, confound, bemuse, obfuscate, nonplus, throw, get; *informal* flummox, be all Greek to, stump, bamboozle, beat, faze, fox; *archaic* wilder, gravel, maze.

CHOOSE THE RIGHT WORD

mystify, puzzle, perplex, baffle
See PUZZLE.

mystique ▶ noun *a certain mystique still surrounds the family* **charisma**, glamour, romance, mystery, fascination, magic, spell, charm, appeal, allure, awe.

myth ▶ noun **1** *ancient Greek myths* **folk tale**, story, folk story, legend, tale, fable, saga, allegory, parable, tradition, lore, folklore; *technical* mythos, mythus.
2 *there are still plenty of myths surrounding pregnancy and childbirth* **misconception**, fallacy, mistaken belief, false notion, misbelief, old wives' tale, fairy story, fairy tale, fiction, fantasy, delusion, figment of the imagination; invention, fabrication, falsehood, untruth, lie; *informal* story, tall story, tall tale, fib, cock and bull story, kidology.

WORD LINKS
study of myths mythology

mythical ▶ adjective **1** *dragons and other mythical beasts* **legendary**, mythological, fabled, fabulous, folkloric, fairy-tale, storybook, chimerical; fantastical, imaginary, imagined, fictitious; allegorical, symbolic, symbolical, parabolic.
2 *the girl claimed that Tyler was the father of her mythical child* **imaginary**, fictitious, make-believe, fantasy, fanciful, invented, fabricated, made-up, unreal, untrue, non-existent; *informal* pretend.
OPPOSITES real, actual.

mythological ▶ adjective **fabled**, fabulous, folkloric, fairy-tale, legendary, mythical, mythic, heroic, traditional; fictitious, imaginary, imagined; allegorical, symbolic, symbolical, parabolic.

mythology *See centre pages for lists of* **Giants** **Mythological and Fictional Creatures** **Nymphs**
▶ noun **myth(s)**, legend(s), folklore, folk tales, folk stories, lore, tradition, stories, tales; *technical* mythos.

M

nab ▶ **verb** (*informal*) *police nabbed him when he got back home* **catch**, capture, apprehend, arrest, take into custody, place under arrest, seize, take in, bring in; *informal* nail, pinch, cop, run in, pull in, pick up, collar, bust; *Brit. informal* nick, nobble.

nabob ▶ **noun** *a Wall Street nabob* **very rich person**, tycoon, magnate, millionaire, billionaire, multimillionaire, plutocrat; *informal* zillionaire, fat cat, moneybags; *rare* Croesus, Dives.

nadir ▶ **noun** *it was the nadir of his career* **the lowest point**, the all-time low, the lowest level, low-water mark, the bottom, as low as one can get, rock-bottom, the depths; zero; *informal* the pits.
OPPOSITES zenith, acme, climax.

nag[1] ▶ **verb 1** *I don't want to nag you but you really should eat something* **harass**, keep on at, go on at, harp on at, badger, keep after, give someone a hard time, get on someone's back, persecute, chivvy, hound, harry, bully, pick on, criticize, find fault with, keep complaining to, moan (on) at, grumble at, henpeck, carp at, scold, upbraid, berate; *informal* hassle; *N. Amer. informal* ride; *Austral. informal* heavy.
2 *one question has been nagging me for weeks* **trouble**, worry, bother, plague, torment, niggle, prey on one's mind, gnaw at, hang over, haunt, weigh down, weigh heavily on, lie heavy on, burden, cause anxiety to; annoy, irritate, vex, irk, rankle with; *N. English* mither; *informal* bug, aggravate.
▶ **noun** *she's such a nag* **shrew**, nagger, harpy, termagant, harridan; moaner, complainer, grumbler, fault-finder, carper, caviller; *N. Amer. informal* kvetch; *archaic* scold.

nag[2] ▶ **noun** *she can ride any old nag and get the best out of it* **worn-out horse**, old horse, hack, Rosinante; *informal* bag of bones; *N. Amer. informal* plug, crowbait; *Austral./NZ informal* moke; *Brit. informal, dated* screw; *archaic* jade, rip, keffel.

nagging ▶ **adjective 1** *his nagging wife* **shrewish**, complaining, grumbling, fault-finding, scolding, carping, cavilling, criticizing.
2 *there was a nagging pain in his chest* **persistent**, continuous, lingering, niggling, troublesome, unrelenting, unremitting, unabating; aching, painful, distressing, worrying.

nail ▶ **noun 1** tack, spike, pin, rivet; hobnail; screw; *Brit.* panel pin, tin tack; *technical* brad, sprig, clout nail, sparable.
2 fingernail, thumbnail, toenail; claw, talon, nipper, pincer; *technical* unguis, chela.
□ **hard as nails callous**, hard-hearted, heartless, with a heart of stone, stony, stony-hearted, unfeeling, unsympathetic, uncaring, insensitive, unsentimental, cold-hearted, cold, hardbitten, tough, unforgiving, lacking compassion, uncharitable, inflexible, unbending, implacable.
□ **on the nail immediately**, at once, without delay, straight away, right away, promptly, on the spot, directly, now, this minute; *N. Amer.* on the barrelhead.
▶ **verb 1** *a large blackboard was nailed to the wall* **fasten**, attach, fix, affix, secure, tack, hammer, pin, post.
2 (*informal*) *a device which could help police to nail their suspects* **catch**, capture, apprehend, arrest, take into custody, seize, take in, bring in; *informal* collar, nab, pinch, cop, run in, pull in, pick up, bust; *Brit. informal* nick, nobble.
3 *the paper's exclusive pictures had nailed the lie* **expose**, reveal, uncover, unmask, bring to light, lay bare, smoke something out, unearth, detect, identify; *archaic* discover.

WORD LINKS
relating to the nails **ungual**

naive ▶ **adjective** *I was very naive to begin with, but I learnt fast* **innocent**, unsophisticated, artless, ingenuous, inexperienced, guileless, unworldly, childlike, trusting, trustful, dewy-eyed, starry-eyed, wide-eyed, fond, simple, natural, unaffected, unpretentious; **gullible**, credulous, easily taken in, easily deceived, unsuspecting, over-trusting, over-trustful, born yesterday, unsuspicious, deceivable, dupable, immature, callow, raw, green, as green as grass, ignorant; *informal* wet behind the ears.
OPPOSITES sophisticated, disingenuous, experienced, worldly.

CHOOSE THE RIGHT WORD

naive, artless, ingenuous

- **Naive** is by far the most common of these adjectives. It is generally used critically or pityingly of people lacking experience, wisdom, or judgement, or of their actions (*the rather naive young man had been totally misled | it may be naive to think that much of the population really believes specific election pledges*). It can, however, also be used more approvingly of a person seen as natural and unaffected (*Andy had a sweet, naive look when he smiled*).
- **Ingenuous** is a more literary term, expressing approval or acceptance of people or actions that are innocent and unsuspecting (*an ingenuous young art student, fresh from college*).
- **Artless** is quite rare and means 'without guile or deception', the opposite of the much more common *artful* (*what she knew of him was picked up from his wife's artless prattle*). Again approvingly, it can mean 'without effort or pretentiousness' (*the children had been directed to give very real, artless performances*). However, an older sense denoting things or actions that are considered to lack aesthetic imagination or practical skill is enjoying a revival (*this awful, artless building*).

naivety ▶ **noun innocence**, lack of sophistication, lack of experience, ingenuousness, guilelessness, lack of guile, unworldliness, childlikeness, trustfulness, simplicity, naturalness; **gullibility**, credulousness, credulity, over-trustfulness, lack of suspicion, blind faith, immaturity, callowness, greenness, ignorance.
OPPOSITE sophistication.

CHOOSE THE RIGHT WORD

naked, nude, bare

These words are all used to refer to a person's unclothed state.

- **Naked** is the standard word for someone who isn't wearing any clothes. It also has several well-established metaphorical uses, always placed before the noun: *the naked eye* is unaided by a telescope or similar instrument, while a *naked light bulb* is not shielded or dimmed by a shade. *Naked* feelings or behaviour are openly expressed or at least undisguised (*he saw in her eyes naked fear | naked self-interest*).
- **Nude** is slightly more formal or euphemistic than *naked*. It is used especially with reference to paintings and photographs of naked people (*she posed as a nude model in magazines*) or to swimming and sunbathing (*nude bathing is illegal*).
- **Bare** is used typically to refer to just a part of the body (*running about in bare feet*). However, doing something *with your bare hands* implies that you are not using any tools, rather than not wearing gloves. In its metaphorical uses, *bare* suggests the removal of everything that is not absolutely indispensable (*the bare bones of a news story | emissions are kept to a bare minimum*).

naked ▶ **adjective 1** *a naked woman* **nude**, bare, in the nude, stark naked, with nothing on, stripped, unclothed, undressed, uncovered, in a state of nature, disrobed, unclad, undraped, exposed; *French* au naturel; *informal* without a stitch on, in one's birthday suit, in the raw, in the altogether, in the buff, as naked as the day one was born, in the nuddy, mother

naked; *Brit. informal* starkers; *Scottish informal* in the scud, scuddy; *N. Amer. informal* bare-assed, buck naked; *Austral. informal* bollocky; *Brit. vulgar slang* bollock-naked.
OPPOSITES clothed, dressed.
2 *each man was carrying a naked sword | a naked flame* **unprotected**, uncovered, exposed, open, unguarded; **unsheathed**, drawn.
OPPOSITES covered, sheathed.
3 *the naked branches of the trees* **bare**, barren, stark, denuded, stripped, uncovered; treeless, grassless; *rare* defoliated.
4 *I felt naked and exposed as I crossed the deserted square* **vulnerable**, helpless, weak, powerless, defenceless, exposed, unprotected, undefended, open to attack.
5 *the naked truth | naked hostility blazed in his eyes* **undisguised**, plain, unadorned, unvarnished, unveiled, unqualified, stark, bald, unexaggerated, simple; overt, obvious, open, patent, evident, apparent, manifest, unmistakable, palpable, blatant, glaring, flagrant, barefaced, out-and-out, unmitigated.

WORD LINKS
related prefix **gymno-** (e.g. *gymnosophist*)
fear of being naked **gymnophobia**

nakedness ▸ noun **1** *she tried to cover her nakedness* **nudity**, state of undress, bareness; *French* déshabillé; *informal* one's birthday suit.
2 *the nakedness of the landscape* **bareness**, barrenness, starkness.

namby-pamby ▸ adjective *we don't want a club full of namby-pamby bleeding hearts* **weak**, feeble, spineless, effeminate, effete, limp-wristed, womanish, prim, prissy, mincing, simpering, niminy-piminy, vapid, insipid, colourless, anaemic, ineffectual; sentimental, over-sentimental, mawkish, maudlin; *informal* wet, wishy-washy, weedy, wimpish, wimpy, sissy, sissified; *N. Amer. informal* candy-assed.

name *See centre pages for lists of* **Names** **Eponyms**
▸ noun **1** *her name's Gemma* denomination, designation, honorific, title, tag, epithet, label; *Indian* naam; *informal* moniker, handle; *formal* appellation; *rare* agnomen, allonym, anonym, appellative.
2 *the top names in the British fashion industry* **celebrity**, star, superstar, VIP, famous person, important person, leading light, big name, luminary, mogul, person of note, dignitary, personage, worthy; expert, authority, lion; *informal* celeb, somebody, megastar, big noise, big shot, bigwig, big cheese, big gun, big wheel, big fish.
3 *he made his name as one of the greatest steeplechase jockeys of our time | this may damage the good name of the firm* **reputation**, character, repute, standing, stature, honour, esteem, prestige, cachet, kudos; fame, celebrity, renown, popularity, notability, note, distinction, eminence, prominence; *Indian* izzat.
▸ verb **1** *they named the child Phoebe* **call**, give a name to, dub; label, style, term, title, entitle; baptize, christen; *archaic* clepe; *rare* denominate.
2 *the driver of the car was later named as Jason Penter* **identify**, specify, cite, give, mention.
3 *on March 19th, he named his successor* **choose**, select, pick, decide on, nominate, designate, appoint, delegate, assign.

WORD LINKS
relating to names **nominal, onomastic**
related suffix **-onym (e.g. *pseudonym, synonym*)**
fear of names **onomatophobia**

named ▸ adjective **1** *a girl named Anne | a condition named 'myasthenic syndrome'* **called**, by the name of, baptized, christened, known as, under the name of; dubbed, entitled, styled, termed, described as, labelled.
2 *documentary sources able to supply information about named individuals* **specified**, designated, identified, cited, given, mentioned, selected, nominated, chosen, singled out; *rare* individuated.

nameless ▸ adjective **1** *the pictures were taken by a nameless photographer | a nameless grave* **unnamed**, unidentified, anonymous, incognito, unspecified, unacknowledged, uncredited; unknown, unheard of, unsung, uncelebrated, inglorious, obscure; untitled, undesignated, unlabelled, untagged; *rare* innominate.
OPPOSITES well known, famous.
2 *he had become a prey to nameless fears* **unspeakable**, unutterable, inexpressible, unmentionable, indescribable, abominable, horrible, dreadful, appalling, shocking, awful, terrible, frightful; **indefinable**, vague, obscure, unspecified, unspecifiable.
OPPOSITE specific.

namely ▸ adverb *he has something rare to offer, namely charisma* **that is**, that is to say, to be specific, specifically, in other words, viz., to wit, sc.; *Latin* id est, videlicet, scilicet.

nanny ▸ noun **nursemaid**, nurse, nurserymaid, au pair, childminder, childcarer; governess; *Indian* ayah, amah; *Jewish* metapelot; *informal* nursey; *French dated* bonne.
▸ verb *stop nannying me* **mollycoddle**, be overprotective towards, cosset, coddle, wait on hand and foot, wrap in cotton wool, baby, feather-bed, nursemaid; spoil, pamper, indulge, overindulge; *archaic* cocker.

nap[1] ▸ verb *they arrived to find her napping on the sofa* **doze**, sleep (lightly), take a nap, catnap, rest, take a siesta, drowse; *informal* snooze, snatch forty winks, drop off, nod off, get some shut-eye; *Brit. informal* kip, have a kip, zizz, get some zizz; *N. Amer. informal* catch some/a few Zs; *literary* slumber.
▸ noun *she'd been awake all night and was looking forward to taking a nap* **(light) sleep**, catnap, siesta, doze, lie-down, rest; *informal* snooze, forty winks, shut-eye; *Brit. informal* kip, zizz; *literary* slumber.
□ **catch someone napping catch off guard**, catch unawares, take by surprise, surprise, catch in an unguarded moment, catch out, find unprepared; *informal* catch someone with their trousers/pants down; *Brit. informal* catch on the hop.

nap[2] ▸ noun *use a wire brush to raise the nap of the suede* **pile**, fibres, threads, weave, shag, texture, feel, surface, grain.

nappy ▸ noun *N. Amer.* diaper; *Brit. dated* napkin.

narcissism ▸ noun **vanity**, self-love, self-admiration, self-adulation, self-absorption, self-obsession, conceit, self-conceit, self-centredness, self-regard, egotism, egoism, egocentricity, egomania.
OPPOSITES modesty, diffidence.

narcissistic ▸ adjective **vain**, in love with oneself, self-loving, self-admiring, wrapped up in oneself, self-absorbed, self-obsessed, conceited, self-centred, self-regarding, egotistic, egotistical, egoistic, egocentric, egomaniac.
OPPOSITES modest, self-effacing.

narcotic *See centre pages for list of* **Drugs**
▸ noun **soporific drug**, opiate, sleeping pill, soporific; painkiller, pain reliever, analgesic, anodyne, palliative, anaesthetic; tranquillizer, sedative; *informal* downer; *dated* sleeping draught; *literary* nepenthes; *rare* stupefacient, stupefactive.
▸ adjective **soporific**, sleep-inducing, opiate, hypnotic; painkilling, pain-relieving, analgesic, anodyne, anaesthetic, stupefying, numbing, dulling, tranquillizing, sedative, calming; *rare* stupefacient, stuporific, stupefactive.

narked ▸ adjective (*Brit. informal*) *he was just narked that I hadn't told him about it. See* ANNOYED.

narrate ▸ verb *the story is narrated by an ageing English butler* **tell**, relate, recount, give an account of, unfold, set forth/out, describe, detail, sketch out, portray, chronicle, give a report of, report, relay, retail, delineate, rehearse, recite; voice-over.

narration ▸ noun **1** *the first chapter is taken up with a narration of past events in his life* **account**, narrative, story, tale, chronicle, description, portrayal, report, sketch, recital, recitation, rehearsal; telling, relation, story telling, chronicling, detailing; *rare* recountal.
2 *he introduces the story with a narration that sets the tone for the entire film* **voice-over**, reading, commentary.

narrative ▸ noun *a chronological narrative of Stark's life* **account**, story, tale, chronicle, history, description, record, portrayal, sketch, portrait, statement, report, rehearsal, recital, rendering.

narrator ▸ noun **1** *the narrator of 'the Arabian Nights'* **storyteller**, teller of tales, recounter, relater, describer, chronicler, romancer, reporter, annalist; raconteur; *Austral. informal* magsman; *rare* anecdotist, anecdotalist.
OPPOSITES listener, audience.
2 *the film's narrator* **voice-over**, commentator.

narrow ▸ adjective **1** *the path became narrower and more overgrown* small, tapered, tapering, narrowing, narrow-gauged; *archaic* strait.
OPPOSITES wide, broad.
2 *he slid his arm around her narrow waist* **slender**, slim, lean, slight, spare, attenuated, thin; *rare* attenuate.
OPPOSITE broad.
3 *he eased himself out of the narrow space* **confined**, cramped, tight, close, restricted, limited, constricted, confining, pinched, squeezed, meagre, scant, scanty, spare; *rare* incommodious, exiguous, incapacious.
OPPOSITE spacious.
4 *a narrow range of products | her experience of life was very narrow* **limited**, restricted, circumscribed, straitened, small, inadequate, insufficient, deficient, lacking, wanting; select, exclusive.
OPPOSITES wide, broad.
5 *a narrow view of the world. See* NARROW-MINDED.
6 *this is nationalism in the narrowest sense of the word* **strict**, literal, exact, precise, close, faithful, true.
7 *a narrow victory | a narrow escape* marginal; lucky.
▸ verb *the path narrowed and we had to proceed in single file | it narrowed the gap between rich and poor* **get/become/make narrower**, get/become/make smaller, taper, diminish, decrease, reduce, contract, shrink, constrict; *archaic* straiten.

narrowly ▸ adverb **1** *one bullet struck the car, narrowly missing him* **only just**, just, barely, scarcely, hardly, by a hair's breadth, by a very small margin, by the narrowest of margins, by the skin of one's teeth, by a nose; *informal* by a whisker.
2 *she looked at me narrowly* **closely**, carefully, searchingly, scrutinizingly, attentively; meticulously, scrupulously, painstakingly.

narrow-minded ▸ adjective **intolerant**, illiberal, reactionary, conservative, ultra-conservative, conventional, parochial, provincial,

insular, small-town, localist, small-minded, petty-minded, petty, close-minded, short-sighted, myopic, blinkered, inward-looking, narrow, hidebound, dyed-in-the-wool, diehard, limited, restricted, inflexible, dogmatic, rigid, entrenched, prejudiced, bigoted, biased, partisan, sectarian, discriminatory; prudish, priggish, strait-laced, stuffy, puritanical, moralistic, prim, starchy, prissy, shockable; racist, racialist, chauvinistic, chauvinist, sexist, nationalistic; *Brit.* parish-pump, blimpish; *French* borné; *N. Amer. informal* jerkwater; *rare* claustral.
OPPOSITES broad-minded, tolerant.

narrows ▶ plural noun **strait(s)**, sound, neck, channel, waterway, passage, sea passage.

nascent ▶ adjective *the nascent economic recovery* **just beginning**, budding, developing, growing, embryonic, incipient, young, in its infancy, fledgling, evolving, emergent, emerging, rising, dawning, advancing, burgeoning; *rare* naissant.

nastiness ▶ noun **1** *my mother tried to shut herself off from reality and from nastiness* **unpleasantness**, disagreeableness, offensiveness, vileness, foulness, unsavouriness, ugliness, squalor, filthiness, filth, pollution.
OPPOSITES niceness, pleasantness.
2 *he was bewildered by her uncharacteristic nastiness* **unkindness**, unpleasantness, unfriendliness, disagreeableness, hostility, rudeness, churlishness, spite, spitefulness, malice, maliciousness, meanness, mean-spiritedness, ill temper, ill nature, bad temper, bad-temperedness, viciousness, ill humour, malevolence, venom, venomousness, malignancy, cantankerousness, cruelty, abusiveness; *informal* bitchiness, cattiness.
OPPOSITES niceness, kindness.
3 *for some real nastiness this week, you had to watch 'The Sex Hunters'* **obscenity**, indecency, offensiveness, impropriety, indelicacy, crudity, vulgarity, grossness, pornography, smuttiness, smut, salaciousness, lewdness, licentiousness.

nasty ▶ adjective **1** *there was a nasty smell in the kitchen* **unpleasant**, disagreeable, disgusting, distasteful, awful, dreadful, horrible, terrible, vile, foul, abominable, frightful, loathsome, revolting, repulsive, odious, sickening, nauseating, nauseous, repellent, repugnant, horrendous, hideous, appalling, atrocious, offensive, objectionable, obnoxious, unpalatable, unsavoury, unappetizing, off-putting, uninviting, dirty, filthy, squalid; noxious, evil-smelling, foul-smelling, smelly, stinking, rank, rancid, fetid, malodorous, acrid; *informal* ghastly, horrid, gruesome, putrid, diabolical, yucky, sick-making, God-awful, gross, icky, stinky; *Brit. informal* beastly, grotty, whiffy, pongy, niffy; *N. Amer. informal* lousy, skanky, funky; *Austral. informal* on the nose; *literary* noisome, mephitic; *archaic* disgustful, loathly; *rare* miasmal, olid.
OPPOSITES nice, delightful, lovely, pleasant.
2 *the weather turned nasty* **unpleasant**, disagreeable, foul, filthy, inclement; wet, rainy, stormy, cold, foggy, blustery, squally.
OPPOSITES fine, sunny.
3 *sometimes, she can be really nasty* **unkind**, unpleasant, unfriendly, disagreeable, inconsiderate, uncharitable, rude, churlish, spiteful, malicious, mean, mean-spirited, ill-tempered, ill-natured, ill-humoured, bad-tempered, hostile, vicious, malevolent, evil-minded, surly, obnoxious, poisonous, venomous, vindictive, malign, malignant, cantankerous, hateful, hurtful, cruel, wounding, abusive; *informal* bitchy, catty; *vulgar slang* shitty.
OPPOSITES charming, agreeable, nice, likeable.
4 *her father's had a nasty accident | she's got a nasty cut on her head* **serious**, dangerous, bad, awful, dreadful, terrible, frightful, critical, severe, grave, alarming, worrying; painful, ugly.
OPPOSITES slight, minor.
5 *she had a nasty habit of suddenly appearing and staring at him* **annoying**, irritating, infuriating, unwelcome, disagreeable, unpleasant, unfortunate, maddening, exasperating, irksome, vexing, vexatious; *informal* aggravating, pesky.
6 *they got hold of spray cans and wrote nasty things on the back of the headstones* **obscene**, indecent, offensive, improper, indelicate, crude, rude, off colour, dirty, filthy, vulgar, foul, vile, gross, disgusting, pornographic, smutty, salacious, risqué, lewd, lascivious, licentious, X-rated; scatological, profane; *informal* blue, sick.

nation ▶ noun **country**, **state**, land, sovereign state, nation state, kingdom, empire, republic, confederation, federation, commonwealth, power, superpower, polity, domain; fatherland, motherland; people, race, civilization, tribe, society, community, population, body politic, populace, public; *Law* realm; *Latin* res publica.

WORD LINKS
related prefix **ethno- (e.g. *ethnocentric, ethnolinguistics*) ethnic**

national ▶ adjective **1** *national politics | national and international news* **state**, public, federal, governmental; civic, civil, domestic, internal, home; popular; ethnic, racial, cultural, tribal, indigenous, native, ethnological.
OPPOSITES local; international.
2 *a one-day national strike* **nationwide**, countrywide, state, coast-to-coast, general, widespread, overall, comprehensive.
OPPOSITE local.
▶ noun *a French national* **citizen**, subject, native, resident, inhabitant; voter.

nationalism ▶ noun *the resurgence of nationalism in Europe and in other parts of the world* **patriotism**, patriotic sentiment, allegiance/loyalty to one's country, loyalism, nationality; **xenophobia**, chauvinism, jingoism, flag-waving, isolationism; ethnocentrism, ethnocentricity.

nationalistic ▶ adjective *Russian foreign policy was becoming increasingly nationalistic* **patriotic**, nationalist, loyal to one's country, pro one's country; **xenophobic**, chauvinistic, jingoistic, flag-waving, isolationist; ethnocentric.

nationality ▶ noun **1** *individuals seeking British nationality* **citizenship**; the right to hold a passport.
2 *all the main nationalities of Ethiopia* **ethnic group**, ethnic minority, tribe, clan, race, nation; *rare* ethnos.

nationwide ▶ adjective *a nationwide conservation scheme* **national**, countrywide, state, coast-to-coast, general, widespread, overall, comprehensive, all-embracing, extensive, across the board.

native ▶ noun *a native of Sweden | New York in the summer was too hot even for the natives* **inhabitant**, resident, local; aborigine; **citizen**, national; *formal* dweller; *rare* autochthon, indigene.
OPPOSITES foreigner, outsider, alien.
▶ adjective **1** *the island's native population* **indigenous**, aboriginal, original, first, earliest; *rare* autochthonous, autochthonic.
OPPOSITE immigrant.
2 *honey, eggs and other native produce | native plants* **domestic**, **home-grown**, home-made, home, local; indigenous, endemic.
OPPOSITE imported.
3 *his vagueness masked a shrewd native instinct for politics* **innate**, inherent, inborn, intrinsic, instinctive, instinctual, intuitive, natural, natural-born, deep-seated, deep-rooted; hereditary, inherited, in the blood, in the family, natal, congenital, bred in the bone, inbred, ingrained, built-in; *rare* connate, connatural.
OPPOSITES acquired, learned.
4 *her native tongue* **mother**, vernacular.

CHOOSE THE RIGHT WORD

native, indigenous, aboriginal

These words all describe someone or something associated with a particular place by birth or origin.

- **Native**, related to *nativity* (meaning 'birth'), refers to the place where an individual was born (*he left his native Germany in his teens*). It often refers to a quality or ability that someone has possessed or learned since birth (*she possessed a certain amount of native wit | she spoke English and French fluently, as well as Farsi, her native language*) or to a person in relation to the language they grew up speaking (*only 45 per cent of the Web's users are native speakers of English*). *Native* also denotes people or other living things which originated in the region or country being discussed (*native fauna*). *Native peoples*, with their *native cultures*, were looked down on in the days of the British Empire, so that *native* became a derogatory word for a person, but it is usually acceptable, as an adjective or a noun, when the place is specified (*a native Australian | a 23-year-old native of Montreal*).
- **Indigenous** is a more technical word, used to refer to populations of people, plants, or animals that naturally occur in a particular place, and to things associated with them (*indigenous Arctic folk | the indigenous languages of Nigeria*).
- **Aboriginal** refers to the earliest known inhabitants of a place, such as those present when colonists arrived. It is almost always used before its noun (*the inherent right of aboriginal peoples to self-government*), and is not used of plants or animals. It is usually capitalized when used of *Australian Aboriginals*.

nativity ▶ noun **birth**, childbirth, delivery; *technical* parturition; *rare* nascence, nascency.

natter (*Brit. informal*) ▶ verb *they nattered away as if they had all the time in the world* **chatter**, chat, talk idly, prattle, prate, go on, run on, rattle on/away, gossip, tittle-tattle, tattle, ramble, gabble, jabber, babble, blather, blether, blither, twitter, maunder, drivel, patter, yap, jibber-jabber, cackle; *Brit.* talk nineteen to the dozen; *Scottish & Irish* slabber; *informal* chit-chat, jaw, gas, gab, yak, yackety-yak, yabber, yatter, yammer, chew the fat, chew the rag, shoot one's mouth off, blabber; *Brit. informal* witter, rabbit, chunter, waffle, talk the hind leg off a donkey; *N. Amer. informal* run off at the mouth, shoot the breeze, shoot the bull, visit; *Austral./NZ informal* mag; *archaic* twaddle, clack, twattle, claver.
▶ noun *she was always ringing me up for a natter. See* CHAT.

natty ▶ adjective *Stephen looked very natty in a lightweight grey suit and shiny black shoes* **smart**, stylish, fashionable, dapper, debonair, dashing, jaunty, rakish, spruce, well turned out, well dressed, chic, modish, elegant, trim; *informal* snazzy, trendy, cool, sharp, snappy, with it, nifty, groovy; *N. Amer.*

informal sassy, spiffy, fly, kicky; *dated* as if one had just stepped out of a bandbox; *archaic* trig.
OPPOSITE scruffy.

natural ▶ adjective **1** *a natural occurrence* **normal**, ordinary, everyday, usual, regular, common, commonplace, typical, routine, standard, established, customary, accustomed, habitual, run-of-the-mill, stock, unexceptional.
OPPOSITES abnormal, unnatural, exceptional.
2 *her policy of using fresh, natural produce* **unprocessed**, organic, pure, wholesome, unrefined, pesticide-free, chemical-free, additive-free, unbleached, unmixed, real, plain, virgin, crude, raw.
OPPOSITES artificial, refined.
3 *Alex is a natural leader* **born**, naturally gifted, untaught.
4 *his natural instincts* **innate**, inborn, inherent, native, native-born, intrinsic, instinctive, instinctual, intuitive, natural-born, ingrained, built-in; gut; hereditary, inherited, inbred, congenital; *rare* connate, connatural.
OPPOSITE acquired.
5 *she's very natural | the conversation was natural and easy* **unaffected, spontaneous**, uninhibited, straightforward, relaxed, unselfconscious, genuine, open, artless, guileless, ingenuous, unsophisticated, unpretentious, without airs, easy; unstudied, unforced, uncontrived, unmannered, unstilted, unconstrained.
OPPOSITES affected, false; stilted, strained; awkward, self-conscious.
6 *it was quite natural for him to think she admired him* **reasonable**, logical, understandable, unsurprising, expected, (only) to be expected, predictable; inevitable.
OPPOSITE unreasonable.
7 *his natural son* **illegitimate**, born out of wedlock; *informal, dated* born on the wrong side of the blanket; *archaic* bastard, misbegotten, baseborn, spurious; *rare* adulterine.
OPPOSITE legitimate.

naturalist ▶ noun **natural historian, life scientist**, wildlife expert; biologist, botanist, zoologist, ornithologist, entomologist, ecologist, conservationist, environmentalist, preservationist; birdwatcher; *N. Amer.* birder; *informal* twitcher.

naturalist or naturist?
Unwary **naturalists** might be embarrassed to come across **naturists** when they were looking for specimens. Despite their similar spelling, the two words have quite different meanings: a *naturalist* is someone interested in or knowledgeable about natural history, while *naturist* is a less common term for *nudist*.

naturalistic ▶ adjective *naturalistic painting | a naturalistic drama* **realistic**, real-life, true-to-life, lifelike, vivid, graphic, representational, photographic; factual; *French* vérité; *informal* kitchen-sink, warts and all; *rare* verisimilar, veristic.
OPPOSITE abstract.

naturalize ▶ verb **1** *he emigrated to London before the Second World War and was naturalized in 1950* **grant citizenship to**, make a citizen, endow with the rights of citizenship, confer citizenship on, give a passport to, enfranchise; *rare* endenizen, denizen, citizenize.
2 *coriander has been naturalized in southern Britain* **establish**, introduce, acclimatize, domesticate; *N. Amer.* acclimate.
3 *he saw myth as the process by which ideology is naturalized* **assimilate**, absorb, incorporate, adopt, accept, take in, homogenize; *rare* acculturate.

naturally ▶ adverb **1** *he's naturally shy* **by nature**, by character, inherently, innately, congenitally, instinctively.
2 *try and act naturally* **normally**, in a natural manner/way, unaffectedly, spontaneously, genuinely, artlessly, unpretentiously; *informal* natural.
OPPOSITES awkwardly, self-consciously, pretentiously.
3 *naturally, they wanted everything kept quiet* **of course**, as might be expected, as you/one would expect, needless to say, not unexpectedly, as was anticipated, as a matter of course; obviously, clearly, it goes without saying; *informal* natch.
OPPOSITE surprisingly.

naturalness ▶ noun *she was different—she'd lost a certain naturalness* **unselfconsciousness**, lack of affectation, spontaneity, spontaneousness, lack of inhibition, straightforwardness, genuineness, openness, ingenuousness, simplicity, lack of sophistication, unpretentiousness, lack of pretension.
OPPOSITES affectation, awkwardness, self-consciousness, pretentiousness.

nature ▶ noun **1** *the beauty of nature* **the natural world**, the living world, Mother Nature, creation, the world, the environment, the earth, Mother Earth, the universe, the cosmos, natural forces; wildlife, flora and fauna, countryside, landscape, scenery.
2 *such crimes are, by their very nature, difficult to hide* **essence**, inherent/basic/essential characteristics, inherent/basic/essential qualities, inherent/basic/essential attributes, inherent/basic/essential features, sum and substance, character, identity, complexion.
3 *it was not in Daisy's nature to be bitchy* **character**, personality, disposition, temperament, temper, humour, make-up, cast/turn of mind, persona, psyche, constitution, fibre.
4 *experiments of a similar nature* **kind**, sort, type, variety, description, category, ilk, class, classification, species, genre, style, cast, order, kidney, mould, stamp, grain; *N. Amer.* stripe.

naturist ▶ noun **nudist**, sun worshipper; *informal* nudie.
OPPOSITE textile.

naturist or naturalist?
See NATURALIST.

naught ▶ noun (*archaic*) *all his efforts will have been for naught* **nothing**, nothing at all, nought, nil, zero; *N. English* nowt; *informal* zilch, sweet Fanny Adams, sweet FA, not a dicky bird, nix; *Brit. informal* damn all, not a sausage; *N. Amer. informal* zip, zippo, nada, diddly-squat, a goose egg; *Brit. vulgar slang* bugger all, fuck all, sod all.

naughty ▶ adjective **1** *a naughty boy* **badly behaved, disobedient**, bad, misbehaved, misbehaving, wayward, defiant, unruly, insubordinate, wilful, self-willed, delinquent, undisciplined, unmanageable, uncontrollable, ungovernable, unbiddable, disorderly, disruptive, mutinous, fractious, refractory, recalcitrant, errant, wild, wicked, obstreperous, difficult, troublesome, awkward, contrary, perverse, exasperating, incorrigible; bad-mannered, rude, impolite; **mischievous**, full of mischief, playful, impish, roguish, puckish, rascally, prankish, tricksy; *informal* brattish, scampish; *Scottish informal* gallus; *archaic* contumacious.
OPPOSITES good, well behaved, obedient.
2 *naughty jokes* **indecent, risqué**, rude, racy, ribald, bawdy, broad, spicy, suggestive, titillating, improper, indelicate, indecorous, off colour; vulgar, dirty, filthy, smutty, crude, offensive, salacious, coarse, obscene, lewd, pornographic, X-rated; *informal* blue, raunchy; *Brit. informal* fruity, near the knuckle, saucy; *N. Amer. informal* gamy; *euphemistic* adult.
OPPOSITE decent.

nausea ▶ noun **1** *symptoms include a loss of appetite, nausea, and a severe headache* **sickness**, biliousness, queasiness; vomiting, retching, gagging; travel-sickness, seasickness, carsickness, airsickness, motion sickness, morning sickness, altitude sickness; *informal* throwing up, puking; *rare* qualms.
2 *intended to induce a feeling of nostalgia, it only induces in me a feeling of nausea* **disgust**, revulsion, repugnance, repulsion, distaste, aversion, loathing, abhorrence, detestation, odium; *archaic* disrelish.

N

nauseate ▶ verb *the smell of the meat nauseated her* **sicken**, make sick, turn someone's stomach, make someone's gorge rise, make someone's stomach rise, revolt, disgust, repel, repulse, be repugnant to, offend; *informal* make someone want to throw up; *N. Amer. informal* gross out.

nauseating ▶ adjective *the smell in the compartment was nauseating | his nauseating self-pity* **sickening**, stomach-turning, stomach-churning, nauseous, emetic, sickly; **disgusting**, revolting, repulsive, repellent, repugnant, offensive, loathsome, abhorrent, odious, obnoxious, nasty, foul, vile, appalling, abominable; *N. Amer.* vomitous; *informal* sick-making, ghastly, putrid, horrid, God-awful, gross, gut-churning, yucky; *Brit. informal* beastly; *literary* noisome; *archaic* disgustful, loathly.

nauseous ▶ adjective **1** *the thought of food made her feel nauseous* **sick**, nauseated, queasy, bilious, sick to one's stomach, green, green about/at the gills, ill, unwell, bad; seasick, carsick, airsick, travel-sick; *informal* about to throw up; *N. Amer. informal* barfy; *rare* qualmish.
2 *a nauseous stench | that doesn't mean I have to be involved in this nauseous business* **sickening**, nauseating, stomach-turning, stomach-churning, emetic, sickly; **disgusting**, revolting, repulsive, repellent, repugnant, offensive, loathsome, abhorrent, odious, obnoxious, nasty, foul, vile, appalling, abominable; *N. Amer.* vomitous; *informal* sick-making, ghastly, putrid, horrid, God-awful, gross, gut-churning, yucky; *Brit. informal* beastly; *literary* noisome; *archaic* disgustful, loathly.
OPPOSITES charming, pleasing.

nautical ▶ adjective **maritime**, marine, naval, seafaring, seagoing, ocean-going; yachting, boating, sailing.

navel ▶ noun **1** *informal* belly button, tummy button; *technical* umbilicus.
2 *Cyprus was the navel of Byzantine culture* **centre**, central point, middle, midpoint, hub, nub, focal point, focus, pivot, nucleus, heart, core, eye; *rare* omphalos.

WORD LINKS
relating to the navel **umbilical**
related prefix **omphalo- (e.g. *omphalocele*)**

navigable ▶ adjective *all of the main tributaries of the Vistula were navigable* **passable**, negotiable, traversable, able to be sailed/travelled on, crossable; clear, open, free from obstruction, unobstructed, unblocked.

navigate ▶ verb **1** *they navigated by the stars* **steer**; plot a route/course; *Nautical* helm.
2 *he navigated the yacht across the Atlantic with nothing more than an astrolabe* **steer**, pilot; guide, manoeuvre, direct, handle, drive; skipper, captain; *Nautical* con, helm.
3 *the upper reaches of the river are dangerous to navigate* **sail across/over**, sail, cruise, travel/journey/voyage across/over; cross, traverse, negotiate.
4 *I'll drive—you can navigate* **map-read**, give directions, plan the route.

navigation ▶ noun **1** *the navigation of the ship* **steering**, piloting, pilotage, sailing, guiding, directing, guidance, manoeuvring.
2 *Cooper learned the skills of navigation* **helmsmanship**, steersmanship, seamanship, map-reading, chart-reading.

navigator ▶ noun **helmsman**, steersman, pilot, guide, seaman, mariner; *N. Amer.* wheelman.

navvy ▶ noun **labourer**, day labourer, manual worker, workman, worker, digger, hand, roustabout; *Brit.* hodman, ganger; *Spanish-American* peon; *Austral./NZ* rouseabout; *Indian* mazdoor, khalasi; (*in Asian countries*) coolie; *archaic* mechanic.

navy ▶ noun **1** *a 600-ship navy* **fleet**, flotilla, armada, naval (task) force, squadron.
2 *sober shades of grey, black, and navy* **navy blue**, dark blue, indigo, midnight blue, ink blue.

nay ▶ adverb *it is difficult, nay, impossible, to understand* **or rather**, and more than that, (and) indeed, and even, in fact, in point of fact, actually, in truth.

near ▶ adverb **1** *her children all live near* **close by**, close, nearby, close/near at hand, not far off/away, in the neighbourhood, in the vicinity, at hand, within reach, within close range, on the doorstep, within earshot, within sight, a stone's throw away, at close quarters, alongside; *informal* within spitting distance, {a hop, skip, and a jump away}, within sniffing distance; *archaic* nigh.
OPPOSITE far away.
2 *near perfect conditions* **almost**, just about, nearly, practically, virtually, all but; *literary* well-nigh.
▶ preposition *a family-run hotel near the seafront* **close to**, close by, not far (away) from, a short distance from, in the vicinity of, in the neighbourhood of, within reach of, a stone's throw away from, next to, adjacent to, alongside, bordering on, adjoining, abutting, contiguous with; *informal* within spitting distance of, {a hop, skip, and a jump away from}, within sniffing distance of.
▶ adjective **1** *they carried her to the nearest house* **close**, nearby, not far off/away, close/near at hand, at hand, a stone's throw away, within reach, within range, accessible, handy, convenient, local, neighbouring, adjacent, next-door, adjoining, bordering, abutting, contiguous, proximate; *informal* within spitting distance.
OPPOSITE far.
2 *the final judgement is near* **imminent**, forthcoming, in the offing, close/near at hand, at hand, (just) round the corner, approaching, impending, upcoming, coming, looming.
OPPOSITES distant, remote.
3 *a near relation of hers | our nearest and dearest* **closely related**, close, related, connected.
OPPOSITE distant.
4 *apparently it had been a near escape* **narrow**, close, by a hair's breadth; *informal* by a whisker.
5 *she's too near to spend that much money* **mean**, **miserly**, niggardly, close-fisted, penny-pinching, cheese-paring, ungenerous, penurious, illiberal, close, grasping, Scrooge-like, stinting, sparing, frugal; *informal* tight-fisted, stingy, tight, mingy, money-grubbing, skinflinty; *N. Amer. informal* cheap; *Brit. vulgar slang* tight-arsed, tight as a duck's arse.
▶ verb **1** *by dawn the next day we were nearing Moscow* **approach**, draw near/nearer to, get near/nearer to, get close/closer to, come towards, move towards, advance towards, close in on.
2 *the death toll is nearing 3,000* **verge on**, border on, approach, get close to, approximate to.

nearby ▶ adjective *a boy from one of the nearby villages* **not far away/off**, close/near at hand, close by, close, near, within reach, at hand, neighbouring, adjacent; accessible, handy, convenient.
OPPOSITE faraway.
▶ adverb *her mother lives nearby* **close by**, not far off/away, close, close/near at hand, near, a short distance away, in the neighbourhood, in the vicinity, at hand, within reach, on the doorstep, (just) round the corner.

nearly ▶ adverb *dinner's nearly ready* **almost**, just about, about, more or less, practically, virtually, all but, as good as, next to, close to, near, nigh on, not far from, not far off, to all intents and purposes, approaching, bordering on, verging on, nearing; not quite; *informal* pretty nearly, pretty much, pretty well; *literary* well-nigh.

near miss ▶ noun *two airliners were involved in a near miss yesterday* **close thing**, near thing, narrow escape, close call, nasty moment; *informal* close shave; *Brit. informal* narrow squeak.

nearness ▶ noun **1** *the town's geographical nearness to Rome* **closeness**, proximity, propinquity, adjacency; accessibility, handiness; *rare* contiguity, contiguousness, vicinity, vicinage.
2 *the nearness of death focuses the mind* **imminence**, closeness, immediacy, immediateness.
3 *a marriage is also void on the ground of nearness of relationship* **consanguinity**, closeness.

nearsighted ▶ adjective (*N. Amer.*) **short-sighted**, myopic; *informal* as blind as a bat; *archaic* purblind, mope-eyed.

neat ▶ adjective **1** *the bedroom was neat and scrupulously clean* **tidy**, neat and tidy, as neat as a new pin, orderly, well ordered, in (good) order, well kept, shipshape (and Bristol fashion), in apple-pie order, immaculate, spick and span, uncluttered, straight, trim, spruce; *archaic* tricksy.
OPPOSITES disorderly, untidy.
2 *he's very neat* **smart**, spruce, dapper, trim, well groomed, well turned out, besuited; organized, well organized, tidy, methodical; fastidious; *informal* natty; *dated* as if one had just stepped out of a bandbox; *archaic* trig.
OPPOSITE shabby.
3 *her neat, italic script | the neat white contours of the building* **well formed**, regular, precise, crisp, clean-cut, elegant, well proportioned, simple, unadorned, unornamented.
4 *this neat little gadget* **compact**, well designed, well made, handy, easy to use; *Brit. informal* dinky.
5 *his neat footwork* **skilful**, deft, dexterous, adroit, adept, expert, practised, accurate, precise, nimble, agile, graceful, stylish; *informal* nifty.
OPPOSITE clumsy.
6 *a neat solution to the problem* **clever**, ingenious, inventive, resourceful, good, apt, efficient; slick.
7 *a small glass of neat gin* **undiluted**, straight, unmixed, unadulterated, unblended, pure, uncut; *N. Amer. informal* straight up.
8 (*N. Amer. informal*) *we had a really neat time.* See WONDERFUL, MARVELLOUS.

neaten ▶ verb *we neatened ourselves up for dinner* **tidy (up)**, make neat/neater, straighten (up), smarten (up), spruce up, groom, arrange, put in order, put to rights, trim; *N. Amer. informal* fix up; *archaic* trig (up).

neatly ▶ adverb **1** *she was neatly dressed in a tweed suit and a cashmere jersey | neatly arranged papers* **tidily**, smartly, sprucely; methodically, systematically.
2 *the point was neatly put* **cleverly**, aptly, nicely, elegantly, well.
3 *a neatly executed back header* **skilfully**, deftly, adroitly, adeptly, expertly, precisely, nimbly, agilely, gracefully, effortlessly; *informal* niftily.

neatness ▶ noun **1** *I was struck with the neatness of the cottage* **tidiness**, orderliness, trimness, spruceness, immaculateness, unclutteredness, absence of clutter, straightness.
2 *neatness, grooming, and deportment were important* **smartness**, spruceness, trimness, tidiness, fastidiousness, simplicity.
3 *the neatness of her movements* **grace**, gracefulness, nimbleness, precision, deftness, dexterity, adroitness, agility, light-footedness, skill, accuracy, stylishness; *literary* lightsomeness.

nebulous ▶ adjective **1** *the figure was still nebulous—she couldn't quite see it* **indistinct**, indefinite, unclear, vague, hazy, cloudy, fuzzy, misty, lacking definition, blurred, blurry, out of focus, foggy, faint, shadowy, dim, obscure, shapeless, formless, unformed, amorphous; *rare* nebulose.
OPPOSITE clear.
2 *his nebulous ideas about salvation* **vague**, ill-defined, unclear, hazy, uncertain, indefinite, indeterminate, imprecise, unformed, muddled, confused, ambiguous, inchoate, opaque, muddy.
OPPOSITE well defined.

necessarily ▶ adverb **1** *an increase in the money supply will not necessarily have much effect on spending* **automatically**, as a direct consequence/result, as an automatic consequence/result, as a matter of course, by definition, certainly, surely, definitely, incontrovertibly, undoubtedly, axiomatically.
2 *the timetable may, necessarily, be subject to amendment* **unavoidably**, of necessity, by force of circumstance, by force majeure, inevitably, inescapably, ineluctably; willy-nilly; *Latin* nolens volens; *informal* like it or not; *formal* perforce.
OPPOSITE possibly.

necessary ▶ adjective **1** *planning permission is necessary | I don't want to go unless it's absolutely necessary* **obligatory**, requisite, required, compulsory, mandatory, imperative, demanded, needed, called for, needful; **essential**, indispensable, vital, of the essence, incumbent; *French* de rigueur.
OPPOSITES unnecessary, non-essential, dispensable.
2 *their fate was a necessary consequence of progress* **inevitable**, unavoidable, certain, sure, inescapable, inexorable, ineluctable, fated, destined, predetermined, predestined, preordained.
OPPOSITE possible.

N

▶ **noun** (**the necessary**) (*informal*) *could you lend me the necessary?* **money**, cash, the wherewithal, funds, finances, capital, means, resources; *informal* dough, bread, loot, the ready, the readies; *Brit. informal* dosh. *See also* MONEY.

CHOOSE THE RIGHT WORD

necessary, requisite, essential, indispensable

- Something that is **necessary** must be accepted or done, whether we like it or not. The word denotes something without which a condition cannot be fulfilled, often something that is needed for a particular purpose, rather than generally (*carrying out the necessary repairs | a general election was necessary*). *Necessary* is the only one of these words that can be used in the phrase *if necessary* (*do a dummy run if necessary*).
- **Requisite** has a very similar meaning to *necessary*, but it is more formal and often refers to something required by regulations rather than an inherent need (*each event must be staffed by the requisite number of officials*). Unlike the other three words here, *requisite* is almost always used before its noun.
- **Essential** is the strongest way to say that something is necessary (*it is essential to keep up-to-date records*). Some uses merge with the older meaning of 'fundamental to the nature of something' (*fibre is an essential ingredient of our diet*): see INHERENT. Of these four words, it is normal to use only *essential* or *necessary* with the anticipatory subject *it* in a construction such as *it is essential to read a daily newspaper*.
- **Indispensable** is typically used of someone or something that is already present, and implies contemplation of having to do without them (*you've been absolutely indispensable to me | electricity is an indispensable source of energy which we take for granted in our everyday lives*).

necessitate ▶ **verb** *such a level of public expenditure would necessitate tax increases* **make necessary**, entail, involve, mean, require, demand, call for, be grounds for, warrant, leave no choice but to, oblige, compel, constrain, exact, force.

necessitous ▶ **adjective** *2.5 tons of dried milk was supplied to necessitous mothers* **needy**, in need, poor, badly off, hard up, short of money, disadvantaged, underprivileged, unable to make ends meet, needful, in reduced/straitened circumstances, impoverished, poverty-stricken, penurious, penniless, impecunious, destitute, indigent, on one's beam-ends, as poor as a church mouse; *Brit.* on the breadline, without a penny to one's name; *informal* on one's uppers; *Brit. informal* without two pennies/(brass) farthings to rub together, in Queer Street; *rare* pauperized, beggared.
OPPOSITES wealthy, rich, well off.

necessity ▶ **noun 1** *considered a luxury in the 70s, the VCR is now regarded as a necessity* **essential requirement**, prerequisite, indispensable thing/item, essential, requisite, necessary, fundamental, basic; *Latin* sine qua non, desideratum.
2 *the necessity of taking expert advice | the necessity for young people to grow up with respect for the law* **indispensability**, need, needfulness.
3 *political necessity forced him to consider it* **force/pressure of circumstance**, need, obligation, call, exigency; crisis, emergency, urgency; *French* force majeure.
4 *the necessity of growing old* **inevitability**, unavoidability, certainty, inescapability, inexorability, ineluctability.
5 *necessity made them steal* **poverty**, need, neediness, want, deprivation, privation, penury, destitution, indigence.
□ **of necessity** *such institutional changes will, of necessity, lead to a review of the Arts Council's role* **necessarily**, inevitably, unavoidably, by force of circumstance, inescapably, ineluctably; by definition, as a matter of course, naturally, automatically, certainly, surely, definitely, incontrovertibly, undoubtedly, axiomatically; willy-nilly; *Latin* nolens volens; *informal* like it or not; *formal* perforce.

neck ▶ **noun** nape, scruff; *technical* cervix; *archaic* scrag, halse.
□ **neck and neck** *the six contestants are neck and neck* **level**, **equal**, tied, nip and tuck, side by side, with nothing to choose between them, close together; *Brit.* level pegging; *informal* even-steven(s).
▶ **verb** (*informal*) **kiss**, caress, pet; *informal* smooch, canoodle; *Brit. informal* snog; *N. Amer. informal* play kissy-face, make out; *dated* spoon.

WORD LINKS
relating to the neck **cervical, jugular**

necklace ▶ **noun chain**, choker, necklet, beads, pearls, pendant, locket; *French* rivière, sautoir, lavallière; *Maori* hei-tiki; *historical* torc, torque, carcanet, negligée.

necromancer ▶ **noun sorcerer**, sorceress, (black) magician, wizard, warlock, witch, diviner, occultist, enchanter, enchantress; spiritualist, spiritist, medium; *rare* thaumaturge, thaumaturgist, theurgist.

necromancy ▶ **noun sorcery**, (black) magic, the black arts, witchcraft, wizardry, the occult, occultism, enchantment, divination, demonology, voodooism, voodoo, hoodoo, witchery, witching; spiritualism, spiritism; *rare* thaumaturgy, theurgy.

necropolis ▶ **noun cemetery**, graveyard, churchyard, burial place, burial ground, burying ground, garden of remembrance; *Scottish* kirkyard; *N. Amer.* memorial park; *informal* boneyard; *historical* urnfield, charnel house; *archaic* God's acre, potter's field.

née ▶ **adjective** *Rachel Watts, née Goldstraw* **born**, formerly, previously; *formal* heretofore.

need ▶ **verb 1** *the house still needs a lot of work | do you need money?* **require**, be in need of, stand in need of, have need of, want, be in want of, be crying out for, be desperate for; demand, call for, necessitate, entail, involve; have occasion for/to; lack, be without, be short of, miss.
2 *you needn't come if you don't want to* **have to**, be under an obligation to, be obliged to, be compelled to, be under a compulsion to; *archaic* have need to.
3 *she needed him so much that it seemed as if her entire heart and soul were crying out to him* **yearn for**, pine for, long for, crave for, desire, miss.
▶ **noun 1** *there's no need to apologize | the need to safeguard the environment* **necessity**, obligation, requirement, call, demand; *rare* exigency.
2 *the basic human needs of food and shelter* **requirement**, essential, necessity, want, requisite, prerequisite, wish, demand; *Latin* desideratum.
3 *a family whose need was particularly pressing* **neediness**, want, poverty, deprivation, privation, hardship, penury, destitution, indigence, impecuniousness.
4 *please don't abandon me in my hour of need* **difficulty**, trouble, distress; **crisis**, emergency, urgency, extremity, dire/desperate straits; *rare* exigency.
□ **in need** *the organization provides food and clothing to people in need* **needy**, requiring help, deprived, disadvantaged, underprivileged, in want, poor, badly off, unable to make ends meet, in reduced/straitened circumstances, unable to keep the wolf from the door, impoverished, poverty-stricken, destitute, penurious, impecunious, indigent; *Brit.* on the breadline; *rare* necessitous.

needed ▶ **adjective** *funds are desperately needed | planning permission is needed* **necessary**, required, wanted, desired, lacking, called for; essential, requisite, compulsory, obligatory, mandatory.
OPPOSITE optional.

needful ▶ **adjective** *I'm willing to do what's needful* **necessary**, needed, required, requisite; essential, imperative, vital, indispensable; stipulated.

needle ▶ **noun 1** *a needle and thread* sewing needle, darning needle, darner, bodkin; knitting needle.
2 *the virus is easily transmitted via needles* hypodermic needle; *informal* hype, spike.
3 *the needle on the meter barely moved* **indicator**, pointer, marker, arrow, hand.
4 *she lowered the needle on to the record* stylus.
▶ **verb** (*informal*) *why had she allowed Leo to needle her into telling him?* **goad**, provoke, bait, taunt, pester, harass, prick, prod, sting; **irritate**, annoy, anger, vex, irk, nettle, pique, exasperate, infuriate, get on someone's nerves, rub up the wrong way, get/put someone's back up, ruffle someone's feathers, try someone's patience; *informal* aggravate, rile, niggle, get in someone's hair, hassle, get to, bug, miff, peeve, get under someone's skin, get up someone's nose, hack off; *Brit. informal* wind up, get at, nark, get across; *N. Amer. informal* ride; *vulgar slang* piss off; *rare* exacerbate, hump, rasp.

WORD LINKS
fear of needles **belonephobia**

needless ▶ **adjective** *there's no point going into needless detail* **unnecessary**, inessential, non-essential, unneeded, undesired, unwanted, too much, uncalled for, gratuitous, pointless, useless, purposeless, to no purpose; dispensable, expendable, superfluous, redundant, excessive; avoidable; *French* de trop; *rare* supererogatory.
OPPOSITES necessary, essential, indispensable, useful.
□ **needless to say of course**, as might be expected, as you/one would expect, not unexpectedly, it goes without saying, obviously, naturally, clearly; *informal* natch.

needlework *See centre pages for list of* **Sewing Techniques and Stitches**
▶ **noun sewing**, embroidery, needlepoint, needlecraft, tapestry, crocheting, fancy-work, patchwork, wool work, stitching, tatting, crewel work.

needy ▶ **adjective** *the food went to needy families in the area* **poor**, deprived, disadvantaged, underprivileged, in want, needful, badly off, hard up, in reduced/straitened circumstances, unable to make ends meet, unable to keep the wolf from the door, poverty-stricken, indigent, impoverished, on one's beam-ends, as poor as a church mouse, dirt poor, destitute, penurious, impecunious, penniless, moneyless; *Brit.* on the breadline, without a penny to one's name; *informal* on one's uppers, broke, flat broke, strapped for cash, strapped, cleaned out; *Brit. informal* skint, stony broke, without two pennies/(brass) farthings to rub together, in Queer Street; *N. Amer. informal* stone broke; *rare* necessitous, pauperized.

OPPOSITES wealthy, affluent, rich, well off.

ne'er-do-well ▶ noun **good-for-nothing**, layabout, loafer, idler, shirker, sluggard, slugabed, drone; black sheep; rascal, rogue, scoundrel; informal waster, lazybones; Brit. informal skiver; N. English informal scally; N. Amer. informal bum, gold brick, goof-off; archaic wastrel; French archaic fainéant.

nefarious ▶ adjective *the nefarious activities of the bodysnatchers* **wicked**, evil, sinful, iniquitous, villainous, criminal, heinous, atrocious, appalling, abhorrent, vile, foul, base, abominable, odious, depraved, corrupt, shameful, scandalous, monstrous, fiendish, diabolical, devilish, unholy, ungodly, infernal, satanic, dark, unspeakable, despicable, outrageous, shocking, disgraceful; archaic knavish, dastardly; rare egregious, flagitious.
OPPOSITES good, admirable.

negate ▶ verb **1** *legislators immediately took steps to negate the effects of the Court's ruling* **invalidate**, nullify, render null and void, render invalid, make ineffective, neutralize, cancel (out); **undo**, reverse, annul, void, revoke, rescind, abrogate, repeal, retract, countermand, overrule, overturn; Law avoid.
OPPOSITES confirm, support, validate.
2 *negating the political nature of education* **deny**, dispute, call into question, contradict, refute, rebut, discredit, disclaim, reject, repudiate; formal gainsay; rare controvert.
OPPOSITES confirm, ratify.

negation ▶ noun **1** *there should be confirmation—or negation—of the findings* **denial**, contradiction, repudiation, disproving, refutation, refuting, rebuttal, countering, disclaiming; nullification, cancellation, voiding, revocation, rescinding, abrogation, repeal, retraction; Law disaffirmation; rare disproval.
OPPOSITES confirmation, affirmation, substantiation.
2 *evil is not merely the negation of goodness* **opposite**, reverse, antithesis, contrary, inverse, converse; absence, lack, want, deficiency.
3 *a life full of negation* **nothingness**, nothing, nullity, blankness, void, non-existence, vacuity.

negative ▶ adjective **1** *the petition produced a negative reply from the Home Office* **saying 'no'**, in the negative, rejecting, refusing; dissenting, dissentient, contrary, anti-, opposing, opposed; denying; formal gainsaying; rare dissentious.
OPPOSITES positive, affirmative.
2 *he was criticized for being negative* **pessimistic**, **defeatist**, gloomy, gloom-ridden, cynical, bleak, fatalistic, dismissive, anti, antipathetic, uncooperative, obstructive; **unenthusiastic**, cool, cold, uninterested, unresponsive, apathetic.
OPPOSITES positive, optimistic, constructive, enthusiastic.
3 *the crisis had an immediate and negative effect on the economy* **harmful**, bad, adverse, damaging, detrimental, unfortunate, unfavourable, disadvantageous.
OPPOSITES favourable, good.
▶ noun *he murmured something sufficiently incomprehensible for her to take it as a negative* **'no'**, refusal, rejection, veto; dissension, contradiction; denial.
▶ verb **1** *the bill was negatived on the second reading by 130 votes to 129* **reject**, turn down, say 'no' to, refuse, veto, squash; informal give the thumbs down to, give the red light to.
OPPOSITES accept, ratify, pass.
2 *the insurer's main arguments were negatived by Lawrence* **disprove**, show/prove to be false, give the lie to, belie, invalidate, call into question, refute, rebut, discredit, explode; **contradict**, deny, negate; formal gainsay.
OPPOSITES prove, substantiate.
3 (rare) *would-be vendors inevitably raise selling prices to negative the effect of the tax* **cancel out**, neutralize, counteract, nullify, negate, render ineffective; offset, balance, counterbalance, balance out, equalize.

negativity ▶ noun *one person's negativity and intolerance can have a knock-on effect* **pessimism**, **defeatism**, gloom, gloominess, cynicism, negative thinking, hopelessness, despair, despondency, bleakness, blackness, world-weariness; lack of enthusiasm, apathy, indifference; German Weltschmerz; rare negativeness.
OPPOSITES optimism, positiveness.

neglect ▶ verb **1** *she smoked and drank, and neglected the children* **fail to look after**, fail to care for, fail to provide for, leave alone, abandon; archaic forsake.
OPPOSITES cherish, look after, care for.
2 *he's been neglecting his work for the past couple of days* **pay little/no attention to**, let slide, not attend to, be remiss about, be lax about, leave undone, lose sight of, skimp on, shirk, skip.
OPPOSITE concentrate on.
3 *neglect our advice at your peril!* **disregard**, ignore, pay no attention to, take no notice of, pay no heed to, discount, set aside, overlook, turn a deaf ear to, throw to the winds; disdain, pass over, pass by, scorn, slight, spurn, rebuff, turn one's back on.
OPPOSITES attend (to), heed.
4 *she's just irritable because I neglected to inform her that you were coming* **fail**, omit, forget, not remember; archaic pretermit.
OPPOSITE remember.
▶ noun **1** *the whole place had a hopeless air of neglect* **disrepair**, dilapidation, deterioration, shabbiness, disuse, abandonment; rare desuetude.
2 *her doctor had been guilty of serious neglect* **negligence**, failure to take proper care, lack of proper care and attention, dereliction of duty, non-performance/non-fulfilment of duty, failure to take proper action, remissness, neglectfulness, carelessness, heedlessness, lack of concern, unconcern, laxity, laxness, slackness, irresponsibility; Scottish Law culpa; formal delinquency.
OPPOSITE care.
3 *the relative* **neglect** *of women in studies of redundancy* **disregard**, ignoring, overlooking, failure to pay attention to, inattention to, indifference to, oversight, heedlessness; disdaining, scorning, slighting, spurning, rebuff.
OPPOSITE attention.

neglected ▶ adjective **1** *RSPCA officers found more than eighty neglected, underweight, and suffering animals* **uncared for**, mistreated, abandoned, forsaken.
OPPOSITE well cared for.
2 *a neglected 16th-century cottage | the neglected garden behind Merrill's flat* **run down**, derelict, dilapidated, tumbledown, ramshackle, untended, unmaintained; overgrown, uncultivated, unweeded, wild; rare weedgrown.
OPPOSITES neat, well tended.
3 *a neglected masterpiece of seventeenth-century devotional prose* **disregarded**, **forgotten**, overlooked, ignored, unrecognized, unnoticed, unsung, underestimated, undervalued, unappreciated, passed over, spurned; out in the cold.

neglectful ▶ adjective *children whose parents were abusive or neglectful* **negligent**, remiss, failing to show proper care and attention, lax, careless, irresponsible, indifferent, uncaring, heedless, thoughtless, inattentive, unmindful, forgetful; N. Amer. derelict; formal delinquent; rare disregardful, inadvertent, oscitant.
OPPOSITES dutiful, conscientious, attentive, careful.

negligence ▶ noun *the company was accused of negligence* **carelessness**, lack of care, lack of proper care and attention, dereliction of duty, non-performance of duty, non-fulfilment of duty, remissness, neglectfulness, neglect, laxity, laxness, irresponsibility, inattention, inattentiveness, heedlessness, thoughtlessness, unmindfulness, forgetfulness; slackness, sloppiness; Law contributory negligence; Scottish Law culpa; Maritime Law barratry; formal delinquency; rare disregardfulness, inadvertence, inadvertency, oscitation.
OPPOSITES conscientiousness, attention to duty.

negligent ▶ adjective *she claimed that her solicitor had been negligent* **careless**, failing to take proper care, remiss, neglectful, lax, irresponsible, inattentive, heedless, thoughtless, unmindful, forgetful; slack, sloppy, slapdash, slipshod; N. Amer. derelict; Maritime Law barratrous; formal delinquent; rare disregardful, inadvertent, oscitant.
OPPOSITES careful, attentive, conscientious.

negligible ▶ adjective *the damage to the BMW turned out to be negligible* **trivial**, trifling, insignificant, unimportant, minor, of no account, of no consequence, of no importance, not worth bothering about, not worth mentioning, inconsequential, minimal, small, slight, tiny, minute, inappreciable, imperceptible, infinitesimal, nugatory, petty; token, nominal; paltry, inadequate, insufficient, meagre, derisory, pitiful, pathetic, miserable; informal minuscule, piddling, piffling, measly, mingy, poxy; N. Amer. informal nickel-and-dime; rare exiguous.
OPPOSITES significant, considerable.

negotiable ▶ adjective **1** *part-time barman required, hours and salary negotiable* **open to discussion**, subject to discussion, flexible, open to modification, discussable; unsettled, undecided, debatable.
2 *the gulley was negotiable, though it was a tough scramble up the far side* **passable**, navigable, crossable, traversable; free from obstruction, open, clear, unblocked, unobstructed.
3 *negotiable cheques* transferable, usable as legal tender; valid.

negotiate ▶ verb **1** *the government refused to negotiate* **discuss terms**, hold talks, discuss a settlement, talk, consult together, try to reach a compromise, parley, confer, debate; mediate, intercede, arbitrate, moderate, conciliate, act as honest broker; bargain, haggle, wheel and deal, dicker; informal powwow; formal treat with someone; archaic chaffer, palter.
2 *Peter decided to remain with the company after negotiating a new contract* **arrange**, **work out**, thrash out, hammer out, reach an agreement on, agree on, come to terms about, reach terms on, broker; settle, clinch, conclude, contract, pull off, bring off, bring about, transact; informal sort out, swing.
3 *he came down, managing with difficulty to negotiate the obstacles on the stairs* **get round/past/over**, make one's way round/past/over, make it round/past/over, clear, cross, pass over; surmount, overcome, deal with, cope with.

negotiation ▶ noun **1** *the negotiations are due to resume in Geneva next week* **discussion(s)**, talks, consultation(s), parleying, deliberation(s), conference, debate, dialogue; mediation, arbitration, intercession,

conciliation; bargaining, haggling, wheeling and dealing, dickering.
2 *the negotiation of the deal* **working out**, discussing the terms of, arrangement, arranging, thrashing out, hammering out, brokering; settlement, conclusion, completion, clinching, pulling off, bringing off, transaction.

negotiator ▶ noun *a team of negotiators from the UN Security Council sought to resolve the situation* **mediator**, arbitrator, arbiter, moderator, go-between, middleman, intermediary, intercessor, interceder, intervener, conciliator; representative, spokesperson, agent, broker, honest broker, ambassador, diplomat, peacemaker; bargainer, haggler, wheeler-dealer; *rare* negotiant.

neigh ▶ verb **whinny**, bray, nicker, snicker, whicker; *Scottish archaic* nicher; *rare* hinny.

neighbourhood ▶ noun **1** *a quiet neighbourhood* **district**, area, locality, locale, quarter, community, part, region, zone; *informal* neck of the woods, parts; *Brit. informal* manor; *N. Amer. informal* hood, nabe.
2 *in the neighbourhood of Canterbury* **vicinity**, surrounding district/area, environs, purlieus, precincts, proximity; *N. Amer.* vicinage.

□ **in the neighbourhood of** *the cost was believed to be in the neighbourhood of $4.5m* **approximately**, about, around, roughly, in the region of, of the order of, not far off, nearly, almost, close to, just about, practically, more or less, or so, there or thereabouts, as near as dammit to; *Brit.* getting on for; *Latin* circa; *N. Amer. informal* in the ballpark of.

neighbouring ▶ adjective *the owner of the neighbouring property | neighbouring villages* **adjacent**, nearest, closest, next-door, next, adjoining, bordering, connecting, abutting, contiguous, proximate; **nearby**, near, very near, close/near at hand, not far away, in the vicinity, in close proximity, surrounding; *rare* conjoining, approximate, vicinal.
OPPOSITES distant, remote, faraway.

neighbourly ▶ adjective **obliging**, helpful, friendly, kind, kindly, amiable, amicable, affable, genial, easy to get on/along with, agreeable, hospitable, sociable, companionable, well disposed, civil, warm, warm-hearted, cordial, convivial, good-natured, nice, pleasant, generous; considerate, thoughtful, accommodating, unselfish, supportive; *Brit. informal* decent.
OPPOSITES unfriendly, unhelpful, curmudgeonly.

nemesis ▶ noun **1** *this could prove to be the bank's nemesis* **downfall**, undoing, ruin, ruination, destruction, Waterloo.
2 *the nemesis that his crime deserved* **retribution**, vengeance, retributive justice, punishment, just deserts; fate, destiny.

neologism ▶ noun **new word**, new expression, new term, new phrase, coinage, newly coined word, made-up word, invented word, invention, nonce-word; portmanteau word.

neophyte ▶ noun **1** *a neophyte of the monastery of St James* **novice**, novitiate; postulant, proselyte, catechumen.
2 *four-day cooking classes are offered to neophytes and experts alike* **beginner**, learner, novice, newcomer, new member, new entrant, new recruit, raw recruit, new boy/girl, initiate, tyro, fledgling; trainee, apprentice, probationer; *informal* rookie, new kid, newbie, newie; *N. Amer. informal* tenderfoot, greenhorn, punk.

ne plus ultra ▶ noun (*Latin*) *jeans were the ne plus ultra of the modish and modern* **the last word**, the ultimate example, the best example, the perfect example, the ultimate, the height, the acme, the zenith, the culmination, the epitome, the quintessence, perfection, the nonsuch; *French* le dernier cri.

nepotism ▶ noun **favouritism**, preferential treatment, keeping it in the family, the old boy network, looking after one's own, bias, partiality, partisanship, patronage; unfairness; *Brit.* jobs for the boys, the old school tie.
OPPOSITE impartiality.

nerd ▶ noun (*informal*) *it needs care to wear a tie like this without looking like a nerd* **bore**, dull person; *informal* dork, dweeb, geek; *Brit. informal* anorak, spod; *N. Amer. informal* Poindexter.

nerve *See centre pages for list of parts of the human* **Nervous System**
▶ noun **1** *the nerves that transmit pain and physical feeling* nerve fibre; *technical* axon.
2 *the match will be a test of nerve, strength, and skill* **self-confidence**, confidence, assurance, self-assurance, coolness, cool-headedness, self-possession; courage, bravery, pluck, pluckiness, boldness, courageousness, braveness, intrepidity, intrepidness, fearlessness, valour, daring, dauntlessness, doughtiness, gameness; determination, strength of character, firmness of purpose, will power, spirit, backbone, fortitude, mettle, heart, endurance, tenacity, resolution, resoluteness, stout-heartedness, steadfastness, staunchness, hardihood; *informal* grit, guts, spunk, gumption, gutsiness; *Brit. informal* bottle, ballsiness; *N. Amer. informal* moxie, cojones, sand; *vulgar slang* balls.
OPPOSITES timidity, faint-heartedness.
3 *he had the nerve to try and pick up the casting director at his first audition* **audacity**, **cheek**, barefaced cheek, effrontery, gall, temerity, presumption, presumptuousness, boldness, brazenness, impudence, impertinence, insolence, pertness, forwardness, front, arrogance, cockiness; *informal* face, neck, brass neck, brass, sauce; *N. Amer. informal* chutzpah; *informal, dated* hide; *Brit. informal, dated* crust; *rare* procacity, assumption.
OPPOSITES shyness, bashfulness; politeness.
4 (**nerves**) *an attack of pre-wedding nerves* **anxiety**, **tension**, nervousness, nervous tension, strain, tenseness, stress, worry, cold feet; **apprehensiveness**, apprehension, jumpiness, fright; *informal* butterflies (in one's stomach), collywobbles, the jitters, the willies, the heebie-jeebies, the shakes, the jumps, jim-jams, the yips; *Brit. informal* the (screaming) abdabs/habdabs; *Austral. rhyming slang* Joe Blakes.
OPPOSITES calmness, nonchalance.

□ **get on someone's nerves** **irritate**, annoy, irk, anger, bother, vex, provoke, displease, upset, exasperate, infuriate, gall, get/put someone's back up, put out, pique, rankle with, nettle, needle, ruffle someone's feathers, stroke someone's hair the wrong way, make someone's hackles rise, try someone's patience; jar on, grate on; *Brit.* rub up the wrong way; *informal* aggravate, get, get to, bug, miff, peeve, rile, get under someone's skin, get in someone's hair, get up someone's nose, hack off, get someone's goat; *Brit. informal* nark, get on someone's wick, give someone the hump, wind up, get across; *N. Amer. informal* rankle, ride, gravel; *vulgar slang* piss off; *Brit. vulgar slang* get on someone's tits; *rare* exacerbate, hump, rasp.

▶ verb
□ **nerve oneself** *Morag nerved herself to go on* **brace oneself**, steel oneself, summon/gather/screw up/muster one's courage, screw one's courage to the sticking place, gear oneself up, prepare oneself, get in the right frame of mind; fortify oneself, bolster oneself; *informal* psych oneself up; *literary* gird (up) one's loins.
OPPOSITE lose one's nerve.

WORD LINKS

relating to nerves in the body	**neural**
related prefix	**neur(o)-**
inflammation of a nerve	**neuritis**
branches of medicine to do with the nerves	**neurology, neuropathology, neurosurgery**
surgical removal of a nerve	**neurectomy**
surgical cutting of a nerve	**neurotomy**

nerveless ▶ adjective **1** *he took the gun from her suddenly nerveless fingers* **inert**, lifeless, lacking feeling; weak, powerless, feeble.
2 *a nerveless lack of restraint* **confident**, self-confident, self-assured, self-possessed, cool, cool-headed, calm, collected, {cool, calm, and collected}, composed, controlled, relaxed.
OPPOSITES nervous, worried, anxious.

nerve-racking ▶ adjective *meeting him for the first time was nerve-racking to say the least* **stressful**, anxious, worrying, fraught, nail-biting, tense, difficult, trying, worrisome, disquieting, daunting, alarming, frightening; *informal* scary, hairy, anxious-making.

nervous ▶ adjective **1** *a thin, nervous woman who always wore black* **highly strung**, easily frightened, easily agitated, anxious, edgy, tense, excitable, jumpy, skittish, brittle, neurotic, hysterical; timid, timorous, mousy, shy, fearful, frightened, frightened of one's own shadow, apprehensive, scared; *Brit.* nervy; *informal* trepidatious.
OPPOSITES calm, relaxed, easy-going.
2 *the day Richard started teaching, he was so nervous he couldn't eat breakfast* **anxious**, **worried**, **apprehensive**, on edge, edgy, tense, strained, stressed, agitated, in a state of nerves, in a state of agitation, uneasy, restless, worked up, keyed up, overwrought, wrought up, strung out, jumpy, on tenterhooks, with one's stomach in knots, fidgety, fearful, frightened, scared, with one's heart in one's mouth, like a cat on a hot tin roof, quaking, trembling, shaking, shaking in one's shoes, shaky, on pins and needles, in a cold sweat, fevered, febrile; *informal* with butterflies in one's stomach, jittery, twitchy, in a state, uptight, wired, in a stew, all of a dither, all of a doodah, in a sweat, in a flap, in a tizz/tizzy, all of a lather, het up, in a twitter; *Brit. informal* strung up, windy, having kittens, like a cat on hot bricks; *N. Amer. informal* spooky, squirrelly, in a twit; *Austral./NZ informal* toey; *Brit. vulgar slang* shitting bricks, bricking oneself; *dated* overstrung.
OPPOSITES cool, calm, relaxed, laid-back.
3 *a nervous disorder* **neurological**, neural, neuro-.

nervous breakdown ▶ noun **mental collapse**, breakdown, collapse, nervous collapse, nervous exhaustion, nervous tension, period of mental illness, crisis, personal crisis, psychological trauma; *informal* crack-up.

nervousness ▶ noun *as he ate, she found herself chattering away to him out of nervousness* **anxiety**, edginess, tension, nervous tension, agitation, strain, stress, tenseness, worry, restlessness, jumpiness, apprehensiveness, apprehension, uneasiness, disquiet, fear, fearfulness, trepidation, perturbation, alarm; *Brit.* nerviness; *informal* jitteriness, twitchiness, butterflies (in one's stomach), collywobbles, the jitters, the willies, the heebie-jeebies, the jumps, the shakes, jim-jams, the yips; *Brit. informal* the (screaming) abdabs/habdabs; *Austral. rhyming slang* Joe Blakes.

OPPOSITE calmness.

nervy ▶ adjective *Harriet isn't the nervy type | when I interviewed Ed, he was very nervy* **nervous, anxious, tense**, on edge, edgy, strained, stressed, agitated, apprehensive, in a state of nerves, in a state of agitation, uneasy, restless, worked up, keyed up, overwrought, wrought up, strung out, jumpy, on tenterhooks, with one's stomach in knots, fidgety, fearful, frightened, scared, with one's heart in one's mouth, like a cat on a hot tin roof, quaking, trembling, shaking, shaking in one's shoes, shaky, on pins and needles, in a cold sweat, fevered, febrile; excitable, neurotic, highly strung; *informal* in a state, uptight, wired, in a stew, all of a dither, in a sweat, in a flap, in a tizz/tizzy, all of a lather, het up, in a twitter; *Brit. informal* strung up, windy, having kittens, all of a doodah, like a cat on hot bricks; *N. Amer. informal* spooky, squirrelly, in a twit; *Austral./NZ informal* toey; *Brit. vulgar slang* shitting bricks, bricking oneself; *dated* overstrung.
OPPOSITES calm, relaxed, laid-back, easy-going.

nest ▶ noun **1** *in May and June, the females build a nest and incubate their eggs* roost, eyrie; nest box, nesting box; *N. Amer.* bird house.
2 *usually the animals will awake and disperse rapidly from the nest if disturbed* **lair**, den, drey, lodge, burrow, set, form.
3 *a cosy little love nest* **hideaway**, hiding place, hideout, retreat, shelter, refuge, snuggery, nook, den, haunt; *informal* hidey-hole.
4 *the place was a perpetual nest of intrigue* **hotbed**, den, breeding ground, cradle, seedbed, forcing house.
5 *a nest of tables* **cluster**, set, group, assemblage.

nest egg ▶ noun **savings**, life savings, money put by/saved for a rainy day, cache, funds, reserve.

nestle ▶ verb *he nestled up against her* **snuggle**, cuddle (up), curl up, huddle, nuzzle, settle, lie close, burrow; *N. Amer.* snug down.

nestling ▶ noun fledgling, chick, baby bird; *Falconry* eyas; *Scottish archaic* gorlin; *rare* pullus, birdling, broodling.

net[1] *See centre pages for list of* **Nets**
▶ noun **1** *a dress of dark green voile and net* **netting**, meshwork, mesh, webbing, tulle, fishnet, openwork, lace, lacework, latticework, lattice.
2 *one civil servant, at least, managed to escape the net* **trap**, booby trap, snare; *literary* toils.
▶ verb *drug busts that netted big criminals both in Panama and America* **catch**, capture, take captive, trap, entrap, snare, ensnare, bag, hook, land; *informal* nab, collar.

net[2] ▶ adjective **1** *their net earnings* **after taxes, after deductions**, take-home, clear, final; *Brit.* nett; *informal* bottom line.
OPPOSITE gross.
2 *the net result is difficult to predict* **final**, end, ultimate, concluding, closing; **overall**, actual, effective.
▶ verb *the once-struggling actress has netted £50,000 from interviews since the news broke* **earn**, make, get, gain, obtain, acquire, accumulate, take home, bring in, pull in, clear, pocket, realize, make a profit of, be paid; fetch, yield, raise; *informal* rake in.

nether ▶ adjective *the nether reaches of a vast, vaulted interior* **lower**, low, lower-level, bottom, bottommost, under; underground, basement; *technical* basal.
OPPOSITE upper.

netherworld ▶ noun *their souls were forever doomed to wander in the netherworld* **hell**, the underworld, the infernal regions, the nether regions, the abyss, the land of the dead; the abode of the damned, eternal damnation, perdition; *Biblical* Gehenna, Tophet, Abaddon; *Judaism* Sheol; *Greek Mythology* Hades, Tartarus, Acheron; *Brit.* the other place; *literary* the pit; *archaic* the lower world.
OPPOSITES heaven, paradise.

nettle ▶ verb **irritate**, annoy, irk, gall, vex, anger, exasperate, infuriate, bother, provoke; **upset**, displease, offend, affront, get/put someone's back up, disgruntle, rankle with, pique, needle, ruffle, get on someone's nerves, try someone's patience, ruffle someone's feathers, make someone's hackles rise, raise someone's hackles, chafe; *Brit.* rub up the wrong way; *N. Amer.* rankle, ride, gravel; *informal* peeve, aggravate, miff, rile, get, get to, bug, get under someone's skin, get in someone's hair, get up someone's nose, hack off, get someone's goat, drive up the wall; *Brit. informal* nark, get on someone's wick, give someone the hump, wind up, get across someone; *N. Amer. informal* tick off; *vulgar slang* piss off; *Brit. vulgar slang* get on someone's tits; *rare* exacerbate, hump, rasp.

nettled ▶ adjective **irritated**, annoyed, cross, put out, irked, galled, vexed, exasperated, infuriated; **upset**, displeased, offended, affronted, disgruntled, piqued, aggrieved, stung, huffy, in a huff; *informal* peeved, aggravated, miffed, miffy, riled, hacked off, peed off; *Brit. informal* cheesed off, browned off, brassed off, narked, eggy; *N. Amer. informal* teed off, ticked off, sore; *W. Indian informal* vex; *vulgar slang* pissed off; *archaic* snuffy.

network ▶ noun **1** *the network of arteries at the base of the brain* **web**, criss-cross, grid, lattice, net, matrix, mesh, webbing, tracery, trellis; webwork, meshwork, latticework, openwork, filigree, fretwork; *French* réseau; *technical* reticulum, plexus, rete, reticulation, reticule, graticule.
2 *a network of narrow, winding lanes* **maze**, labyrinth, warren, jungle, tangle.
3 *a network of friends and relations* **system**, complex, interconnected system/structure, complex system/arrangement, nexus, web; neural net; *informal* grapevine, bush telegraph, old boy network, the old school tie.

neurosis ▶ noun *Max was said to be in the grip of some sort of neurosis* **mental illness**, mental disorder, psychological disorder, mental disturbance, mental derangement, mental instability, psychological maladjustment, psychoneurosis, psychopathy; obsession, phobia, fixation; *rare* neuroticism.

neurotic ▶ adjective **1** *the treatment of anxiety in neurotic patients* **mentally ill**, mentally disturbed, mentally deranged, unstable, unbalanced, maladjusted, psychoneurotic; psychopathic, phobic.
OPPOSITES stable, well balanced.
2 *she seemed a neurotic, self-obsessed woman* **overanxious**, anxious, nervous, tense, highly strung, jumpy, oversensitive, paranoid; **obsessive**, compulsive, phobic, fixated, hysterical, overwrought, manic, irrational; *Brit.* nervy; *informal* twitchy.
OPPOSITES calm, laid-back, level-headed.

neuter ▶ adjective *I did not feel male, but rather, neuter* **asexual**, sexless, unsexed; **androgynous**; *rare* androgyne, epicene.
▶ verb *vets encourage owners to have their pets neutered* **castrate**, geld, cut, emasculate; **spay**, sterilize; fix, desex; *N. Amer. & Austral.* alter; *informal* doctor; *rare* caponize, eunuchize, ovariectomize, oophorectomize.

neutral ▶ adjective **1** *Dorothy has no axe to grind. She's completely neutral* **impartial**, unbiased, unprejudiced, objective, without favouritism, open-minded, non-partisan, non-discriminatory, disinterested, even-handed, equitable, fair, fair-minded, dispassionate, detached, impersonal, unemotional, clinical, indifferent, removed; uninvolved, uncommitted.
OPPOSITES biased, partisan.
2 *during the Second World War, Portugal remained neutral* **unaligned**, non-aligned, unaffiliated, unallied, non-allied, non-participating, uninvolved, non-interventionist; **non-combatant**, non-belligerent, non-combative, non-fighting.
OPPOSITES combatant, belligerent.
3 *she racked her brain desperately for a neutral topic of conversation* **inoffensive**, bland, unobjectionable, unexceptionable, anodyne, unremarkable, ordinary, commonplace, run-of-the-mill, everyday; safe, harmless, innocuous.
OPPOSITES provocative, offensive.
4 *a neutral background will make any small splash of colour stand out* **pale**, pastel, light-toned; beige, cream, taupe, oatmeal, ecru, buff, fawn, grey, greige, sand, stone-coloured, stone, mushroom, putty; colourless, uncoloured, washed out, indefinite, indistinct, indeterminate, neither one thing nor the other, insipid, nondescript, toneless, dull, drab; *rare* achromatic, achromic.
OPPOSITES bright, colourful.

neutrality ▶ noun **1** *the tradition of civil service neutrality* **impartiality**, lack of bias, lack of prejudice, objectivity, open-mindedness, disinterestedness, even-handedness, fairness, fair-mindedness, detachment.
OPPOSITES partiality, bias.
2 *our long-term interests will be served best by maintaining our neutrality in the war* **non-alignment**, non-participation, non-involvement, non-intervention, non-interventionism, non-combativeness.
OPPOSITES participation, taking sides.

neutralize ▶ verb *the strategy of the first half of the campaign was to neutralize the appalling economic news* **counteract**, offset, counterbalance, balance (out), counterpoise, countervail, compensate for, make up for; **cancel out**, make/render ineffective, nullify, negate, annul, undo, invalidate, be an antidote to, wipe out; equalize, even up, square up; *rare* negative, counterweigh.

never ▶ adverb **1** *his room is never tidy* **at no time**, not at any time, not ever, not once, on no occasion; *literary* ne'er.
OPPOSITES always, forever.
2 *your mother would never agree to it* **not at all**, certainly not, not for a moment, not under/in any circumstances, under/in no circumstances, on no account; *informal* no way, not on your life, not in a million years, not for love or money; *Brit. informal* not on your nelly.
OPPOSITES certainly, definitely.

never-ending ▶ adjective **1** *the never-ending noise of the city* **incessant**, continuous, unceasing, ceaseless, constant, continual, perpetual, unfaltering, permanent, uninterrupted, without interruption, unbroken, steady, unremitting, relentless, persistent, interminable, non-stop, without ceasing, endless, unending, without end, everlasting, eternal.
2 *you need to avoid getting carried away by the never-ending tasks that could fill your day* **endless**, countless, innumerable, myriad, without number, numberless, infinite, unlimited, untold, limitless, boundless, measureless.

never-never ▶ noun
□ **the never-never** (*Brit. informal*) **instalments**, instalment plan/system,

instalment-payment plan, credit, finance, deferred payment, easy terms; *Brit.* hire purchase, HP; *N. Amer.* instalment buying.

nevertheless ▶ **adverb** *nevertheless, it makes sense to take a few precautions* **in spite of that/everything**, nonetheless, even so, however, but, still, yet, though, be that as it may, for all that, despite that/everything, after everything, having said that, that said, just the same, all the same, at the same time, in any event, come what may, at any rate, notwithstanding, regardless, anyway, anyhow; *informal* still and all; *archaic* howbeit, withal, natheless.

new ▶ **adjective 1** *Roger used new techniques of measuring and recording growth* **recently developed**, newly discovered, brand new, up to the minute, up to date, latest, current, state-of-the-art, contemporary, present-day, advanced, recent, modern; newly arrived, newborn.
OPPOSITES old, existing.
2 *the committee is generally tolerant of new ideas* **novel**, fresh, original, unhackneyed, imaginative, creative, experimental, new-fashioned, contemporary, modernist, up to date; newfangled, modish, ultra-modern, avant-garde, futuristic; *informal* way out, far out.
OPPOSITES old-fashioned, stale, hackneyed.
3 *you have to decide whether to buy your boat new or second-hand* **unused**, brand new, as new, pristine, fresh, mint, in mint condition.
OPPOSITES second-hand, used.
4 *new neighbours had recently moved in | she started her new job on Monday* **different**, another, alternative, changed, unfamiliar, unknown, strange, unaccustomed, untried.
OPPOSITE present.
5 *the school has just had a new classroom built* **additional**, added, extra, increased, more, supplementary, supplemental, further, another, fresh.
OPPOSITE existing.
6 *I went into hospital feeling very poorly and came out a new woman* **reinvigorated**, restored, revived, improved, refreshed, regenerated, reborn, renewed, remodelled.

WORD LINKS
related prefix **neo-** (e.g. ***neonatal, neo-Gothic***)
fear of new things **neophobia**

CHOOSE THE RIGHT WORD

new, novel, fresh, original, newfangled

The more specific synonyms emphasize different aspects of being **new**.

- What is **novel** is interestingly new or unusual; the word may hint at surprise and approval (*an interesting and novel solution*).
- **Fresh** can mean 'new and different', and usually all the more welcome for being so (*the trial was reopened to consider fresh evidence | a variety of dramatic outfits that reflect fresh design ideas*) or simply 'another' (*she lit a fresh cigarette*). It can also mean 'good or active because new' (*the memory was still fresh in their minds*).
- **Original** is used for something that is ingenious and not derived from anything else (*an interesting and original line of argument*).
- What is **newfangled** is new, but disapproved of or unwanted (*expecting them to sing newfangled and jolly hymns*). Someone who describes something as *newfangled* risks being thought of as a fuddy-duddy or technophobe.

newborn ▶ **adjective** *all newborn babies are screened for the condition* **just born**, newly/recently born.
▶ **noun** *the bacteria can be fatal to newborns and the elderly* **newly born child**, new/young/tiny baby, infant, young; *technical* neonate; *literary* babe.

newcomer ▶ **noun 1** *she was a newcomer to the village* **(new) arrival**, immigrant, settler, stranger, outsider, foreigner, alien, intruder, parvenu, interloper; *Brit.* incomer; *N. English* offcomer; *informal* johnny-come-lately, the new kid on the block; *Austral. informal* blow-in.
2 *we have some tips for the newcomer to fish photography* **beginner**, novice, learner, trainee, apprentice, probationer, new recruit, raw recruit, new member, tyro, initiate, neophyte; novitiate, new boy/girl, proselyte; *informal* rookie, newbie, the new kid on the block, johnny-come-lately; *N. Amer. informal* tenderfoot, greenhorn.

newfangled ▶ **adjective** *not all hi-fi enthusiasts want newfangled digital technology* **new**, the latest, modern, novel, the newest, ultra-modern, up to the minute, state-of-the-art, advanced, contemporary, fashionable, new-fashioned, gimmicky; *informal* trendy, flash, snazzy, nifty.
OPPOSITES dated, old-fashioned.

CHOOSE THE RIGHT WORD

newfangled, new, novel, fresh, original

See NEW.

newly ▶ **adverb** *steam and ash began to erupt from a newly formed crater* **recently**, just, just recently, only just, lately, freshly, not long ago, (just) a short time ago, (just) a moment ago, only now, of late, new-.

news ▶ **noun** *colleagues were stunned by the news of his death* **report**, **announcement**, story, account; (news) item, article, news flash, newscast, headlines, press release, communication, communiqué, bulletin; message, dispatch, statement, intelligence; disclosure, revelation, word, talk, notice, intimation, the latest, gossip, tittle-tattle, rumour, scandal, exposé; *informal* scoop; *literary* tidings; *archaic* advices.

newspaper *See centre pages for list of types of* **Newspaper**
▶ **noun paper**; *informal* print, rag.

newsworthy ▶ **adjective** *press releases can help to ensure that newsworthy events receive publicity* **interesting**, topical, notable, noteworthy, important, significant, momentous, historic, remarkable, sensational.
OPPOSITE unremarkable.

next ▶ **adjective 1** *we shall turn to this issue in the next chapter | the first residents move in next week* **following**, succeeding, to come, upcoming.
OPPOSITES previous, preceding.
2 *a brick wall separated the garden of the next house from ours* **neighbouring**, **adjacent**, adjoining, next-door, bordering, abutting; contiguous, connected, connecting, attached; closest, nearest, proximate.
▶ **adverb** *people argued about where to go next* **then**, after this/that, following that/this, after, afterwards, after that time, later, at a later time, subsequently, at a subsequent time; *formal* thereafter, thereupon.
OPPOSITE before.
□ **next to** *she sat down next to a window* **beside**, next door to, alongside, by/at the side of, abreast of, by, adjacent to, cheek by jowl with, side by side with; close to, near, nearest to, neighbouring, adjoining, abutting; connected to, connecting with, contiguous with, attached to.
OPPOSITE away from.

nibble ▶ **verb 1** *she sat at her desk, nibbling her sandwich | the monkeys nibbled at mango fruits* **take small bites (from)**, pick (at), gnaw (at), peck at, pick over, eat listlessly, toy with, eat like a bird; taste, sample; eat between meals, graze (on); *informal* snack on.
OPPOSITES gobble, guzzle.
2 *the bird chirped and nibbled his finger* **peck**, nip, bite.
▶ **noun 1** *the fish enjoyed a nibble on the lettuce* **bite**, gnaw, peck, taste.
2 *I took a nibble from one of the sandwiches | sherry is perfect with nuts and nibbles* **morsel**, mouthful, bite, crumb, grain; snack, titbit, a little something, canapé, hors d'oeuvre, bonne bouche; refreshments.

nice ▶ **adjective 1** *have a nice time | it's a nice part of the country* **enjoyable**, **pleasant**, pleasurable, agreeable, delightful, satisfying, gratifying, acceptable, to one's liking, entertaining, amusing, diverting, marvellous, good; *Scottish* bonny, couthy; *informal* lovely, great; *N. Amer. informal* neat; *S. African informal* lekker, mooi; *black English, informal* irie.
OPPOSITE unpleasant.
2 *they were such nice people* **pleasant**, **likeable**, agreeable, personable, charming, delightful, amiable, affable, friendly, kindly, genial, congenial, good-natured, engaging, gracious, sympathetic, understanding, compassionate, good.
OPPOSITE nasty.
3 *he's got very nice manners* **polite**, courteous, civil, refined, cultivated, polished, genteel, elegant.
OPPOSITES unrefined, rough.
4 *that's a rather nice distinction to make* **subtle**, fine, delicate, minute, precise, exact, accurate, strict, close, careful, meticulous, rigorous, scrupulous, ultra-fine.
OPPOSITES rough, approximate.
5 *it's a nice day* **fine**, dry, sunny, cloudless, warm, mild, pleasant, agreeable.
OPPOSITES stormy, nasty, rough.

nicely ▶ **adverb 1** *the brooch goes nicely with my scarf* **attractively**, pleasantly, pleasingly, agreeably, delightfully, beautifully, well, enjoyably, amusingly.
OPPOSITES badly, so as to clash.
2 *talking to him nicely doesn't work* **politely**, courteously, civilly.
OPPOSITE rudely.
3 *we should manage nicely* **satisfactorily**, satisfyingly, fittingly, acceptably.

niceness ▶ **noun 1** *niceness gets you nowhere in the do-or-die modern world* **pleasantness**, **friendliness**, agreeableness, charm, amiability, affability, kindness, decency, geniality, cordiality, warmth, sympathy, understanding, compassion.
OPPOSITE nastiness.
2 *nice chap, right sort of background, but is niceness enough?* **politeness**, courtesy, civility, gentility, refinement, respectability.
OPPOSITE rudeness.

nicety ▶ **noun 1** *legal niceties are wasted on him* **fine point**, subtlety, nuance, fine distinction, shade, refinement, detail.
2 *great nicety of control was called for* **precision**, accuracy, exactness, meticulousness, rigour, rigorousness.

niche ▶ **noun 1** *in a niche in the wall is a statue of St John* **recess**, alcove, nook, cranny, slot, slit, hollow, bay, cavity, cubbyhole, pigeonhole,

opening, aperture; *Islam* mihrab.
2 *he feels he has found his niche in life* **ideal position**, calling, vocation, métier, place, function, job, slot, opportunity.

nick ▶ noun **1** *there was a slight nick half way up the blade* **cut**, scratch, abrasion, incision, snick, scrape; notch, chip, score, gouge, gash; dent, indentation; flaw, mark, blemish, defect.
2 (*Brit. informal*) *you'll end up in the nick*. See PRISON.
3 (*Brit. informal*) *she was down at Lewisham nick, helping police with their enquiries* **police station**, station; *N. Amer.* precinct, station house, substation; *Indian* kotwali, thana; *informal* cop shop.
4 (*Brit. informal*) *the car's in fairly good nick* **condition**, repair, shape, state, state of health, order, working order, form, fettle, trim.
▶ verb **1** *I didn't nick my skin even though I shaved quickly* **cut**, scratch, abrade, incise, snick, scrape; notch, chip, gouge, gash, score.
2 (*Brit. informal*) *he says you nicked his wallet*. See STEAL.
3 (*Brit. informal*) *Steve's been nicked*. See ARREST.
□ **in the nick of time** *they arrived in the nick of time* **just in time**, not a moment too soon, almost too late, at the critical moment; *N. Amer. informal* under the wire; *archaic* in the Godspeed, in the very nick.

nickname ▶ noun **sobriquet**, byname, tag, label, familiar name, epithet; pet name, diminutive, term of endearment, endearment, affectionate name; *informal* moniker; *formal* appellation, cognomen; *archaic* byword, agnomen, eke-name, to-name.

nifty ▶ adjective (*informal*) **1** *the film has some nifty lenswork* **skilful**, capable, agile.
OPPOSITE clumsy.
2 *the wallpaper trimming wheel is a nifty little gadget* **useful**, effective, practical.
3 *a nifty Kevlar tracksuit* **fashionable**, stylish, smart.

niggardliness ▶ noun **1** *he condemned the Government's niggardliness about funding* **meanness**, miserliness, parsimony, parsimoniousness, close-fistedness, penny-pinching, cheese-paring, penury, illiberality; *informal* stinginess, tight-fistedness, tightness, minginess; *N. Amer.* cheapness; *archaic* nearness.
OPPOSITE generosity.
2 *he was disappointed at the niggardliness of his reward* **meagreness**, inadequacy, scantiness, paltriness, limitedness, restrictedness, insufficiency, sparseness, spareness, deficiency, shortness, slightness, skimpiness, leanness, poorness, poverty, pitifulness, puniness, beggarliness; *informal* measliness; *rare* exiguity.
OPPOSITES lavishness, abundance.

N

niggardly ▶ adjective **1** *the critic must not be niggardly with his advice* **mean**, miserly, parsimonious, close-fisted, penny-pinching, cheese-paring, penurious, grasping, greedy, avaricious, Scrooge-like, ungenerous, illiberal, close; *informal* stingy, mingy, tight, tight-fisted, money-grubbing, money-grabbing; *N. Amer. informal* cheap; *vulgar slang* tight-arsed; *archaic* near.
OPPOSITE generous.
2 *his men complained of niggardly rations* **meagre**, inadequate, scanty, scant, paltry, limited, restricted, modest, insufficient, sparse, spare, deficient, negligible, insubstantial, skimpy, short, little, lean, small, slight, slender, poor, miserable, pitiful, puny; *informal* measly, stingy, pathetic, piddling; *rare* exiguous.
OPPOSITES lavish, abundant.

niggle ▶ verb **1** *it does niggle me that we cannot play whenever and wherever we like* **irritate**, annoy, worry, trouble, bother, provoke, exasperate, upset, gall, irk, rankle with; *informal* rile, get up someone's nose, hack off, get, get to, bug.
2 *he niggles on about the unemployed* **complain**, object, moan, fuss, nag, carp, cavil, find fault, grumble, grouse; *informal* nit-pick.
▶ noun *there were niggles about the lack of trim and equipment on some diesel cars* **minor criticism**, **quibble**, trivial objection, trivial complaint, adverse comment, moan, grumble, grouse, cavil; *informal* gripe, beef, grouch, nit-picking; *archaic* pettifogging, amphibology.

night ▶ noun night-time, darkness, dark, hours of darkness, dead of night.
OPPOSITES day, light.
□ **night and day all the time**, the entire time, around the clock, day and night, {morning, noon, and night}, {day in, day out}, without a break, ceaselessly, endlessly, incessantly, interminably, constantly, unceasingly, perpetually, permanently, continuously, continually, eternally, unremittingly, remorselessly, relentlessly; *informal* 24-7; *archaic* without surcease.

WORD LINKS

relating to night	**nocturnal**
related prefix	**nyct(o)- (e.g. *nyctalopia*)**
fear of the night	**nyctophobia**

nightclub ▶ noun **night spot**, **disco**, discotheque, cabaret, club, supper club, bar; *N. Amer.* cafe; *informal* hot spot, niterie.

nightfall ▶ noun *we can be back in the city before nightfall* **dusk**, twilight, sunset, evening, close of day, dark; *N. Amer.* sundown; *literary* eventide, gloaming, crepuscule, evenfall.
OPPOSITE dawn.

nightly ▶ adjective **1** *we were subjected to almost nightly raids* **every night**, each night, night after night, {night in, night out}.
OPPOSITE occasional.
2 *the badgers' nightly wanderings* **nocturnal**, night-time, at night.
OPPOSITE daytime.
▶ adverb *a Tyrolean band plays there nightly* **every night**, each night, night after night, {night in, night out}.

nightmare ▶ noun **1** *she had woken from a nightmare* **bad dream**, night terrors; *archaic* incubus; *rare* ephialtes.
2 *the long journey home was a nightmare* | *paperwork is most farmers' nightmare* **ordeal**, horror, torment, trial; burden, curse, bane, bogey, pet hate, dread, phobia; hell, purgatory, misery, agony, torture, murder; *French* bête noire.

nightmarish ▶ adjective *Grant fired at the nightmarish, clawing figure before him* **unearthly**, monstrous, ghostly, spine-chilling, horrific, macabre, hideous, unspeakable, gruesome, grisly, ghastly, harrowing, hair-raising, disturbing, Kafkaesque; *informal* scary, creepy; *rare* phantasmagorical.

nihilism ▶ noun **1** *he could not accept Bacon's nihilism, his insistence that man is a futile being* **negativity**, cynicism, pessimism; rejection, repudiation, renunciation, denial, abnegation; disbelief, non-belief, unbelief, scepticism, lack of conviction, absence of moral values, agnosticism, atheism.
2 *the roots of this decline lay deep in the moral nihilism of the 1960s* **anarchy**, disorder, chaos, absence of government, lawlessness, mobocracy.

nihilist ▶ noun *it is this approach which leads to the denunciation of Derrida as a nihilist* **disbeliever**, unbeliever, non-believer, sceptic, agnostic, atheist; negativist, cynic, pessimist; anarchist.

nil ▶ noun **nothing**, none; **nought**, zero, 0; *Tennis* love; *Cricket* a duck; *N. English* nowt; *informal* zilch, nix, not a dicky bird; *Brit. informal* damn all, (sweet) Fanny Adams, sweet F.A., not a sausage; *N. Amer. informal* zip, nada, a goose egg; *Brit. vulgar slang* bugger all, sod all, fuck all; *Computing* null character; *literary* null; *dated* cipher; *archaic* naught.

nimble ▶ adjective **1** *he was surprisingly nimble on his feet* | *she tore off the ring with nimble fingers* **agile**, lithe, sprightly, acrobatic, light-footed, nimble-footed, light, light on one's feet, fleet-footed, spry, lively, active, quick, quick-moving, graceful, supple, limber, lissom, flexible, skilful, deft, dexterous, adroit; *informal* nippy, zippy, twinkle-toed; *literary* fleet, lightsome.
OPPOSITES stiff, clumsy.
2 *the boy had a nimble mind* **quick-thinking**, quick-witted, quick, nimble-witted; alert, alive, lively, wide awake, ready, quick off the mark, observant, astute, perceptive, perspicacious, penetrating, discerning, shrewd, sharp, sharp-witted; intelligent, bright, clever, gifted, able, brainy, brilliant; *informal* smart, on the ball, on one's toes, quick on the uptake.
OPPOSITE dull.

nimbleness ▶ noun *he used his nimbleness to make sure he got on to the sofa first* **agility**, litheness, sprightliness, light-footedness, nimble-footedness, lightness, spryness, liveliness, activeness, quickness, smartness; grace, gracefulness, suppleness, limberness, lissomness, flexibility, skill, deftness, dexterity, adroitness; *informal* nippiness, zippiness; *literary* fleetness, lightsomeness.
OPPOSITE clumsiness.

nimbly ▶ adverb *she watched him climb nimbly over the wall* **agilely**, lithely, acrobatically, lightly, easily, spryly, actively, quickly, smartly, briskly; gracefully, supply, lissomly, flexibly, skilfully, deftly, dexterously, adroitly; *informal* nippily, zippily; *literary* fleetly, lightsomely.
OPPOSITE clumsily.

nincompoop ▶ noun *don't be such a nincompoop*. See FOOL, IDIOT.

nine ▶ cardinal number **nonet**; *rare* ennead, ninesome.

WORD LINKS

related prefix	**nona- (e.g. *nonagenarian*)**
relating to nine	**nonary**
nine-sided figure	**nonagon**

nip ▶ verb **1** *the dog nipped her ankle* **bite**, nibble, peck, pinch, tweak, squeeze, grip.
2 (*Brit. informal*) *I'll just nip out and see what's going on* **go**, **rush**, dash, dart, hurry, scurry, scamper; drop by/in/into/round, stop by, visit; *informal* tootle, pop, whip.
□ **nip something in the bud** *let's nip this unpleasantness in the bud before it goes any further* **curtail**, cut short, strangle at birth, check, cut off, thwart, beat, frustrate, curb, stop, halt, arrest, stifle, obstruct, impede, block, squash, quash, subdue, quell, crack down on, stamp out; *informal* squelch, put the kibosh on, clobber.
□ **nip something off** *carefully nip off older flowers on cyclamens and African violets* **cut off**, snip (off), trim, clip, prune, hack off, chop off, saw off, lop (off), dock, crop, sever, separate, detach, remove, take off.
▶ noun *rockhopper penguins have a strong beak that can deliver a serious nip* **bite**, nibble, peck, pinch, tweak, squeeze, grip.

nipple ▶ noun **teat**, dug; *informal* tit; *technical* mamilla; *archaic* pap, papilla, udder.

WORD LINKS
relating to a nipple **mamillary**

nippy ▶ adjective (*informal*) **1** *so big a man is never going to be exactly nippy* **agile**, lithe, sprightly, acrobatic, light-footed, nimble-footed, light, light on one's feet, fleet-footed, spry, lively, active, graceful, supple, limber, lissom, flexible, skilful, deft, dexterous, adroit; *informal* twinkle-toed; *literary* fleet, lightsome.
OPPOSITES lumbering, clumsy.
2 *a nippy three-door hatchback* **with good acceleration**, **fast**, quick, brisk, lively; *informal* zippy.
OPPOSITE slow.
3 *it's a bit nippy this morning* **cold**, chilly, icy, bitter, raw.
OPPOSITE warm.

nirvana ▶ noun *there are no short cuts to nirvana* **paradise**, heaven, Eden, the promised land; bliss, blessedness, ecstasy, joy, peace, serenity, tranquillity; enlightenment, oblivion.
OPPOSITES hell, purgatory.

nit-picking ▶ adjective (*informal*) *nurses can be driven spare by the nit-picking hierarchies in hospitals.* See PEDANTIC sense 1.

nitty-gritty ▶ noun (*informal*) *she is no longer involved in the nitty-gritty of running the company* **basics**, essentials, essence, essential part, main point, fundamental point, fundamentals, substance, heart of the matter, nub, core, heart, centre, quintessence, point, crux, gist, salient point, focal point, nucleus, meat, pith, kernel, marrow, burden; hard work, slog, toil, labour, donkey work, drudgery; *informal* brass tacks, nuts and bolts.

nitwit ▶ noun (*informal*) *I want nothing to do with that bunch of nitwits!* See FOOL, IDIOT.

no ▶ adverb no indeed, absolutely not, most certainly not, of course not, under no circumstances, by no means, not at all, negative, never, not really, no thanks; *Scottish* nae; *informal* nope, nah, not on your life, no way; *Brit. informal* no fear, not on your nelly; *N. Amer. informal* no siree; *Scottish, N. English, & N. Amer. informal* naw; *archaic* nay.
OPPOSITE yes.

nobble ▶ verb (*Brit. informal*) **1** *he was convicted for nobbling the jury* **bribe**, corrupt, suborn, buy, buy off, pay off, get at, induce, lure, entice, grease someone's palm, oil someone's palm/hand; **influence**, persuade, win over, secure someone's support, sway, swing, affect, control, manipulate.
2 *a stable lad was persuaded to nobble the horse* **drug**, dope; tamper with, interfere with, disable, incapacitate, weaken.
3 *what's to stop him nobbling Rose's money?* **steal**, thieve, rob, embezzle.
4 *they would nobble him and throw him on the train* **abduct**, seize, capture, kidnap, catch, apprehend, arrest, take into custody, take in, bring in; *informal* **snatch**, nab, nail, pinch, cop, run in, pull in, pick up, collar; *Brit. informal* nick.

nobility ▶ noun **1** *many of the nobility owned property in the area* **aristocracy**, aristocrats, lords, ladies, peerage, peers, peers of the realm, peeresses, nobles, noblemen, noblewomen, titled men/women/people, members of the aristocracy/nobility/peerage, patricians; *informal* aristos; *Brit. informal* nobs.
2 *the nobility of his deed* **virtue**, goodness, honour, honesty, decency, integrity, magnanimity, generosity, selflessness, bravery.
3 *he lacked any nobility of vision* **loftiness**, grandness.
4 *this type of trumpet lacks nobility of tone* **magnificence**, splendour, impressiveness, imposingness, majesty, grandeur, stateliness, dignity, distinction, glory, gloriousness, splendidness.

noble *See centre pages for lists of* **Nobles** **Rulers' Titles**
▶ adjective **1** *she came from a noble family* **aristocratic**, noble-born, of noble birth, titled, patrician, blue-blooded, high-born, well born; *archaic* gentle, of gentle birth.
OPPOSITE humble.
2 *they were fighting for a noble cause* **righteous**, virtuous, good, honourable, honest, upright, upstanding, decent, worthy, noble-minded, uncorrupted, moral, ethical, reputable, magnanimous, unselfish, generous, self-sacrificing, brave.
OPPOSITE dishonourable.
3 *noble thoughts* **lofty**, exalted, elevated, grand, sublime, imposing.
OPPOSITES ignoble, base.
4 *there is nothing more noble than a mature pine forest* **magnificent**, splendid, grand, stately, imposing, dignified, distinguished, proud, striking, impressive, majestic, glorious, marvellous, awe-inspiring, awesome, monumental, palatial, statuesque, heroic; regal, royal, kingly, queenly, princely, imperial.
OPPOSITE unimpressive.
5 *this noble grape variety lends weight and body to the wine* **excellent**, splendid, marvellous, magnificent, superb, fine, wonderful, exceptional, formidable, sublime, prime, first-class, first-rate, high-grade, grade A, superior, supreme, flawless, choice, select, finest, superlative, model; *informal* tip-top, A1, top-notch.
OPPOSITE poor.
▶ noun *seven Scottish nobles were killed in that battle* **aristocrat**, nobleman, noblewoman, lord, lady, peer, peeress, peer of the realm, patrician, titled man/woman/person; *informal* aristo; *Brit. informal* nob.

nod ▶ verb **1** *all she could do was nod her head* **incline**, bob, bow, dip, wag, duck.
2 *he nodded to me to start* **signal**, gesture, gesticulate, motion, sign, indicate.
3 *even Homer nods* **make a mistake**, be mistaken, be in error, be wrong, be incorrect, get something wrong, make an error, make a slip, err, trip up, stumble; be careless, be inattentive, be negligent; *informal* slip up.
□ **nod off** *the audience began to nod off* **fall asleep**, go to sleep, get to sleep, doze off, drop off; *informal* go off, drift off, crash out, flake out, go out like a light, conk out; *N. Amer. informal* sack out, zone out.
OPPOSITE stay awake.
▶ noun **1** *at a nod from the manager, she dimmed the lights* **signal**, indication, sign, cue; gesture.
2 *he greeted Ivan with a quick nod of his head* **inclination**, bob, bow, dip, duck; greeting, acknowledgement.
□ **get the nod** *Clarke got the nod, and really proved himself during the series* **be selected**, be chosen, be picked, make the grade; *Brit.* be capped; *Austral. informal* get a guernsey.
□ **give someone the nod 1** *Ronny Johnsen was given the nod in preference to David May* **select**, choose, pick, go for; *Brit.* cap.
2 *the chances are that the Lords will give the treaty the nod* **approve**, agree to, sanction, ratify, endorse, say yes to, give one's approval to, rubber-stamp; *informal* give something the go-ahead, give something the green light, OK, give something the OK, give something the thumbs up.
OPPOSITE reject.

node ▶ noun *the intersection of two or more such arteries would become major traffic nodes* **junction**, fork, branching, intersection, interchange, confluence, convergence, meeting point, crossing, criss-crossing, vertex, apex.

noise ▶ noun **sound**, loud sound, din, hubbub, clamour, racket, uproar, tumult, commotion, pandemonium, clangour; crash, clatter, clash, babble, shouting, yelling, babel; *W. Indian* bangarang; *informal* hullabaloo; *Brit. informal* row.
OPPOSITE silence.

noisome ▶ adjective (*literary*) *he had spent six long weeks in this noisome dungeon* **unpleasant**, disagreeable, nasty, distasteful, displeasing, objectionable, off-putting, uninviting, obnoxious, abominable, disgusting, offensive, repulsive, repellent, repugnant, revolting, abhorrent, loathsome, hateful, detestable, execrable, odious, vile, foul, unsavoury, unpalatable, sickening, nauseating, nauseous, ugly; noxious, fetid, rank, rancid, malodorous; *informal* ghastly, horrible, horrid, gross, putrid, sick-making, yucky, God-awful; *Brit. informal* beastly; *Austral. informal* on the nose; *N. Amer. informal* skanky; *literary* mephitic; *archaic* disgustful, loathly.
OPPOSITES pleasant, sweet-smelling.

noisy ▶ adjective **1** *cats loathe noisy homes | a noisy crowd* **rowdy**, rackety, clamorous, boisterous, roisterous, obstreperous, turbulent, brash, clattering, chattering, talkative, vociferous, shouting, screaming, shrieking, bawling.
OPPOSITE quiet.
2 *play some sweet music, not noisy pop* **loud**, fortissimo, blaring, booming, blasting, brassy, deafening, thunderous, tumultuous, clamorous, resounding, reverberating, ear-splitting, piercing, strident, harsh, cacophonous, raucous.
OPPOSITE soft.

nomad ▶ noun **itinerant**, traveller, migrant, wanderer, wayfarer, roamer, rover, gypsy, Bedouin; transient, drifter, vagabond, vagrant, tramp; refugee, displaced person, DP, homeless person; *dated* bird of passage.

nominal ▶ adjective **1** *he remained as the nominal head of the Bush campaign* **in name/title only**, titular, formal, official, ceremonial; theoretical, purported, supposed, ostensible; self-styled, so-called, would-be.
OPPOSITE real.
2 *agricultural workers have a cottage either free or for a nominal rent* **token**, symbolic, emblematic, peppercorn; **tiny**, minute, minimal, small, infinitesimal, insignificant, trifling, not worth mentioning, not worth bothering about; *informal* minuscule, piddling, piffling; *N. Amer. informal* nickel-and-dime; *rare* exiguous.
OPPOSITES considerable, substantial.

nominate ▶ verb **1** *any member of a branch may nominate a candidate* **propose**, put forward, put up, submit, present, recommend, suggest, name.
2 *he wished to nominate his own assistant* **appoint**, designate, make, assign, name, dub, delegate, select, choose, decide on, elect, commission, promote.

non-aligned ▶ adjective *the non-aligned countries of the Third World* **neutral**, impartial, non-partisan, uninvolved, unallied, unattached, unaffiliated, uncommitted, floating, independent; *informal* sitting on the fence.

non-believer ▶ noun *I was an absolute non-believer in spiritualism* **sceptic**, doubter, doubting Thomas, unbeliever, disbeliever, cynic, nihilist; atheist,

N

agnostic, freethinker, libertine; infidel, pagan, heathen; *archaic* paynim.

nonce ▶ noun

□ **for the nonce** *work on the bridge had been suspended for the nonce because of other commitments* **for the time being**, for the interim, for a while, for now, for the moment, for the present, at present, just now, in the meanwhile, the while, meantime, in the meantime, in the intervening period, provisionally, temporarily, pro tem; *Latin* ad interim; *French* en attendant.

nonchalance ▶ noun *she shrugged, feigning nonchalance* **calmness**, coolness, insouciance, unconcern, casualness, airiness, sangfroid, calm, indifference, dispassionateness, lack of emotion, composure, detachment, imperturbability; *informal* one's cool.
OPPOSITES anxiety, concern.

nonchalant ▶ adjective *he had tried to appear nonchalant about the risks he was taking* **calm**, cool, unconcerned, collected, {cool, calm, and collected}, cool as a cucumber, composed, airy; **indifferent**, unemotional, blasé, dispassionate, detached, apathetic, casual, offhand, insouciant; *informal* laid-back.
OPPOSITES anxious, concerned.

non-combatant ▶ adjective *the President sent US armed forces as non-combatant military advisers* **non-fighting**, non-participating, civilian, non-belligerent, pacifist, neutral, non-aligned.
OPPOSITES combatant, fighting.

non-committal ▶ adjective *she remained silent, apart from a few non-committal remarks* **evasive**, equivocal, temporizing, guarded, circumspect, reserved; cautious, wary, careful, prudent; discreet, unrevealing, uncommunicative, politic, tactful, diplomatic, vague; *informal* cagey.
OPPOSITES revealing, careless, indiscreet.

□ **be non-committal** *Alf was non-committal about their chances of success* **prevaricate**, give nothing away, play one's cards close to one's chest, straddle an issue, dodge the question/issue, sidestep the issue, hedge, fence, pussyfoot, beat about the bush, equivocate, temporize, shilly-shally, vacillate, waver; *Brit.* hum and haw; *informal* duck the question, sit on the fence.

non compos mentis ▶ adjective (*Latin*) *Roger had become non compos mentis through drink and age. See* MAD *sense 1.*

nonconformist ▶ noun *if the employees feel industrial action is warranted, they will not tolerate nonconformists* **dissenter**, dissentient, protester, rebel, renegade, freethinker, apostate, heretic, schismatic, recusant, seceder, individualist, free spirit, maverick, unorthodox person, eccentric, original, deviant, misfit, hippy, dropout, fish out of water, outsider; *informal* freak, oddball, odd fish, weirdo, weirdie; *N. Amer. informal* screwball, kook.
OPPOSITE conformist.

nondescript ▶ adjective *a little room in a nondescript Victorian terraced house* **undistinguished**, featureless, characterless, unremarkable, unexceptional, unmemorable, blending into the background; **ordinary**, commonplace, average, mediocre, run-of-the-mill, mundane; uninteresting, boring, uninspiring, dull, colourless, grey, anaemic, insipid, bland; *informal* bog-standard; *Brit. informal* common or garden.
OPPOSITES distinctive, extraordinary.

none ▶ pronoun **1** *none of the fish are unusual* **not one**, not a one.
OPPOSITES all, many, some.
2 *none of this concerns me* **no part**, not a part, not a bit, not any.
OPPOSITES all, some.
3 *none of these five-year-olds could read at that stage | none can know better than you* **not one**, not a one, never a one, not a soul, not a single person, no one, nobody, no man.
OPPOSITES all, many, some.

▶ adverb

□ **none the ...** *the family wrote to the Home Secretary for information but were left none the wiser* **not at all**, not a bit, not the slightest bit, in no way, to no extent, by no means any, not for a moment.
OPPOSITE much.

nonentity ▶ noun *without bargaining skills, a president will be a nonentity in the White House* **unimportant person**, person of no importance, person of no account, nobody, cipher, non-person, man of straw, nothing, small fry, lightweight; mediocrity, second-rater; *informal* no-hoper, non-starter; *Brit. informal* small beer.
OPPOSITES somebody, celebrity, heavyweight.

non-essential ▶ adjective *killing seals for non-essential products cannot be justified* **unnecessary**, inessential, unessential, needless, unneeded, not required, superfluous, uncalled for, redundant, dispensable, expendable, peripheral, unimportant, incidental, optional, extraneous, cosmetic; *French* de trop; *rare* supererogatory.
OPPOSITES essential, indispensable.

nonetheless ▶ adverb *the story behind the rumour is so curious, however, that it is worth telling nonetheless* **in spite of that/everything**, nevertheless, even so, however, but, still, yet, though, be that as it may, for all that, despite that/everything, after everything, having said that, just the same, all the same, at the same time, in any event, come what may, at any rate, notwithstanding, regardless, anyway, anyhow; *informal* still and all; *archaic* howbeit, withal, natheless.

non-existent ▶ adjective *she carefully brushed a non-existent piece of lint from her skirt* **imaginary**, imagined, unreal, fictional, fictitious, made up, invented, hypothetical, suppositional, fancied, fanciful; fantastic, fantasy, mythical, mythological, legendary; illusory, illusive, hallucinatory, chimerical, figmental, notional, shadowy, spectral, ghostly, insubstantial; missing, absent; *rare* phantasmal, phantasmic; inexistent, illusionary, unsubstantial.
OPPOSITES real, actual.

non-intervention ▶ noun **laissez-faire**, neutrality, non-alignment, non-participation, non-interference, non-interventionism, non-involvement, a hands-off approach, inaction, passivity; free enterprise, private enterprise, free trade, market forces; live and let live.
OPPOSITE interventionism.

non-observance ▶ noun *society deems these rules so important as to lay down sanctions for non-observance* **infringement**, **breach**, breaking, violation, contravention, transgression, non-compliance, non-performance, dereliction, neglect, ignoring, disobedience; *Law* infraction.

nonpareil ▶ adjective *Gould is a nonpareil storyteller* **incomparable**, matchless, unrivalled, unparalleled, unequalled, without equal, peerless, unmatched, beyond comparison, beyond compare, second to none, unsurpassed, unsurpassable, unbeatable, inimitable; unique, consummate, perfect, rare, exquisite, transcendent, surpassing, superlative, supreme; *rare* unexampled.
OPPOSITE mediocre.

▶ noun *he was a great player, Britain's nonpareil of the 1980s* **best**, finest, paragon, crème de la crème, peak of perfection, elite, jewel, jewel in the crown, gem; *Latin* ne plus ultra; *informal* the best/finest this side of ...; *archaic* nonsuch.
OPPOSITE mediocrity.

nonplus ▶ verb *young Lewis seemed remarkably nonplussed by the whole affair* **surprise**, stun, dumbfound, confound, astound, astonish, amaze, take aback, disconcert, stop someone in their tracks, throw, throw/catch off balance; **puzzle**, perplex, baffle, mystify, confuse, bemuse, bewilder; *informal* faze, flummox, floor, flabbergast, discombobulate, stump, bamboozle, fox.

nonsense ▶ noun **1** *don't talk complete nonsense, please!* **rubbish**, balderdash, gibberish, claptrap, blarney, guff, blather, blether; *informal* hogwash, rot, baloney, tripe, drivel, gobbledegook, bilge, bosh, bull, bunk, hot air, eyewash, piffle, poppycock, phooey, hooey, malarkey, twaddle, dribble; *Brit. informal* cobblers, codswallop, cock, stuff and nonsense, tosh, double Dutch, flannel, waffle; *Scottish & N. English informal* havers; *N. Amer. informal* garbage, flapdoodle, blathers, wack, bushwa, applesauce; *informal, dated* bunkum, tommyrot, cod, gammon, toffee; *vulgar slang* shit, bullshit, crap, bollocks, balls; *Austral./NZ vulgar slang* bulldust.
OPPOSITE sense.
2 *modern, mechanized methods would make economic nonsense on a smallholding* **ridiculousness**, stupidity, absurdity, ludicrousness, inanity, fatuity, pointlessness, foolishness, folly, foolhardiness, silliness, idiocy, senselessness, insanity, madness.
OPPOSITES sense, wisdom.
3 *Elaine could not see the villagers putting up with any nonsense from her* **mischief**, mischievousness, naughtiness, badness; **bad behaviour**, misbehaviour, misconduct, misdemeanour, perversity, pranks, tricks, larks, capers, joking, jesting, clowning, buffoonery, roguery, devilry, funny business; *French* diablerie; *informal* tomfoolery, monkey tricks, monkey business, shenanigans, goings-on, hanky-panky; *Brit. informal* carry-on, carryings-on, jiggery-pokery; *archaic* deviltry.

nonsensical ▶ adjective **1** *he would laugh at her soft, nonsensical way of talking* **meaningless**, senseless, illogical, unmeaning.
OPPOSITES logical, rational.
2 *this last comment is really a nonsensical generalization* **foolish**, insane, stupid, lunatic, idiotic, illogical, irrational, zany, senseless, absurd, silly, inane, asinine, hare-brained, ridiculous, ludicrous, wild, preposterous, fatuous; *informal* crazy, crackpot, crackbrained, nutty, wacky; *Brit. informal* daft.
OPPOSITES sane, sensible.

non-stop ▶ adjective *you can look forward to non-stop fun and entertainment* **continuous**, incessant, unceasing, ceaseless, constant, continual, perpetual, unfaltering, permanent, uninterrupted, without interruption, round-the-clock, unbroken, steady, unremitting, relentless, persistent.
OPPOSITES occasional, intermittent.

▶ adverb *we worked non-stop on the books* **continuously**, all the time, incessantly, unceasingly, ceaselessly, constantly, continually, perpetually, unfalteringly, permanently, uninterruptedly, without interruption, round the clock, steadily, unremittingly, relentlessly, persistently, without ceasing; *informal* 24-7.
OPPOSITE intermittently.

nook ▶ noun **1** *he hoped to lose his followers in the bookshop's maze of nooks and*

N

crannies **recess**, **corner**, alcove, cranny, crevice, niche, hollow, bay, inglenook, cavity, cubbyhole, pigeonhole, opening, gap, aperture.
2 *there are quiet riverside nooks for meditation* **hideaway**, hiding place, hideout, retreat, refuge, shelter, nest, snuggery, snug, den, haunt; *informal* hidey-hole.

noon ▶ **noun** *the railway operates between noon and 5 p.m. daily* **midday**, twelve noon, twelve midday, twelve o'clock, high noon, noontime, noontide, noonday, twelve hundred, twelve hundred hours, one-two-double-O.
OPPOSITE midnight.

WORD LINKS
relating to noon **meridional**

no one ▶ **pronoun** *there was no one about* **nobody**, not a soul, not anyone, not a person, not a single person, never a one, no man, none.
OPPOSITE everyone.

norm ▶ **noun 1** *talks intended to establish norms of diplomatic behaviour* **convention**, **standard**, criterion, measure, gauge, yardstick, benchmark, point of reference, touchstone, barometer, litmus test, basis, scale, rule, formula, pattern, guide, guideline, model, exemplar, type.
2 (**the norm**) *child protection teams are now the norm in local authorities* **standard**, **usual**, normal, typical, average, the rule, predictable, unexceptional, par for the course, what one would expect, expected, (only) to be expected.
OPPOSITE the exception.

normal ▶ **adjective 1** *the new library system will issue books in the normal way* **usual**, standard, typical, stock, common, ordinary, customary, conventional, habitual, accustomed, expected, wonted, everyday, regular, routine, day-to-day, daily, established, settled, set, fixed, traditional, quotidian, prevailing.
OPPOSITE unusual.
2 *to anyone looking at them, they must seem like a perfectly normal couple* **ordinary**, average, run-of-the-mill, standard, typical, middle-of-the-road, common, conventional, mainstream, unremarkable, unexceptional, plain, simple, homely, homespun, workaday; *N. Amer.* garden-variety; *informal* bog-standard, vanilla, plain vanilla, a dime a dozen; *Brit. informal* common or garden; *N. Amer. informal* ornery.
OPPOSITE abnormal.
3 *Mr Lowe was convinced that the man was not normal* **sane**, in one's right mind, right in the head, of sound mind, in possession of all one's faculties, able to think/reason clearly, lucid, rational, coherent, balanced, well balanced; *Latin* compos mentis; *informal* **all there**.
OPPOSITES insane, irrational.

normality ▶ **noun 1** *after yesterday's bomb scare, normality returned to the town centre this morning* **a normal state of affairs**, business as usual, the daily round, routine, a normal pattern, order, regularity; *N. Amer.* normalcy.
2 *people begin to wonder about the normality of the sufferer* **sanity**, soundness of mind, mental health, balance, lucidity, reason, rationality.
OPPOSITE insanity.

normally ▶ **adverb 1** *she wanted to walk normally again* **as usual**, as normal, ordinarily, naturally, conventionally, regularly.
OPPOSITE abnormally.
2 *normally, airlines keep quiet about terrorist threats* **usually**, ordinarily, commonly, as a rule, as a general rule, generally, in general, in the general run of things, mostly, for the most part, by and large, mainly, most of the time, almost always, more often than not, on the whole; **typically**, habitually, customarily, historically, traditionally, routinely.
OPPOSITE exceptionally.

north ▶ **adjective** *the north coast of the island | the north wind* **northern**, northerly, northwardly, Arctic, polar; *technical* boreal; *literary* hyperborean; *rare* borean, hyperboreal.
OPPOSITE south.
▶ **adverb** *I have to go up north tomorrow* **to the north**, northward, northwards, northwardly.
OPPOSITE south.

nose ▶ **noun 1** snout, muzzle, proboscis, trunk; *informal* beak, conk, snoot, schnozzle, hooter, sniffer, snitch; *Scottish & N. English informal* neb; *informal, dated* bracket; *N. Amer. informal, dated* bugle.
2 *he has a very good nose* **sense of smell**, olfactory sense.
3 *he had a nose for scandal* **instinct**, feeling, gift for discovering/detecting, sixth sense, intuition, insight, perception.
4 *a thin wine with an agreeably fruity nose* **smell**, bouquet, aroma, fragrance, perfume, scent, odour.
5 *the plane's nose dipped as it started descending* nose cone; bow, prow, front end; *Brit.* bonnet; *N. Amer.* hood; *informal* droop-snoot.
□ **by a nose** *all the appliances tested do the job well, but our best buy wins by a nose* **just**, only just, barely, narrowly, by a narrow margin, by the narrowest of margins, by a very small margin, by a hair's breadth, by the skin of one's teeth; *informal* by a whisker.
OPPOSITE by miles.
□ **on the nose** (*N. Amer.*) *the van pulled up at ten on the nose* **exactly**, precisely, sharp, on the dot; **promptly**, prompt, dead (on), on the stroke of ..., on the dot of ...; *informal* bang (on), spot on ...; *N. Amer. informal* on the button.
▶ **verb 1** *the dog nosed the carcass briefly* **nuzzle**, nudge, push, prod.
2 *she's always* **nosing into** *your business* **pry**, inquire impertinently, be inquisitive, inquire; be curious, poke about/around, mind someone else's business, be a busybody, stick/poke one's nose in; interfere (in), meddle (in), intrude (on); *informal* be nosy (about), nosy, snoop; *Austral./NZ informal* stickybeak.
3 *the submarine nosed around the island's waters | he nosed the car out into the traffic* **move slowly**, ease, inch, edge, move, manoeuvre, steer, slip, squeeze, slide; guide, push, tuck.
□ **nose around/about/round** *the others were no doubt nosing around the wreck* **investigate**, explore, ferret (about/around) in, rummage in, search, delve into, peer into, prowl around, have a good look at; *informal* snoop about/around/round.
□ **nose something out** *he has a rare gift of nosing out little-recorded composers* **detect**, find, search out, discover, disclose, bring to light, track down, dig up, hunt out, ferret out, root out, uncover, unearth, disinter, smell out, sniff out, follow the scent of, scent out, run to earth/ground.

WORD LINKS

relating to the nose	**nasal, rhinal**
related prefixes	**naso- (e.g. *nasogastric*), rhin(o)- (e.g. *rhinoceros*)**
inflammation in the nose	**rhinitis**
surgical repair of the nose	**rhinoplasty**
branch of medicine concerning the ear, nose, and throat	**otorhinolaryngology**

nosedive ▶ **noun 1** *the pilot put the plane into a nosedive and ejected* **dive**, drop, plunge, descent, plummet.
OPPOSITES climb, zoom.
2 (*informal*) *sterling took a nosedive* **sharp fall**, drop, plunge, plummet, tumble, decline, slump; *informal* crash.
OPPOSITE rise.
▶ **verb 1** *the engine stopped and the device nosedived to earth* **dive**, plunge, pitch (down), drop rapidly, swoop, plummet, crash-dive.
OPPOSITES soar, climb, zoom.
2 (*informal*) *building costs have nosedived* **fall sharply**, take a nosedive, take a header, drop, sink, plunge, plummet, tumble, slump, go down, decline, subside; *informal* crash.
OPPOSITES rise, soar.

nosegay ▶ **noun** *she carried a nosegay of white roses* **posy**, bouquet, spray, bunch, sprig, buttonhole, corsage; *French* boutonnière; *rare* tussie-mussie.

nosh (*informal*) ▶ **noun 1** *all kinds of lovely nosh* **food**, sustenance, nourishment, nutriment, fare, daily bread, groceries, rations, iron rations; snacks, titbits, eatables; *informal* nibbles, eats, grub, bread, chow; *Brit. informal* scoff; *N. Amer. informal* chuck; *archaic* victuals, vittles, meat, viands, commons.
2 *I could have had a nosh in any pub in town* **meal**, snack; something to eat; *informal* spread, blowout, bite, bite to eat, nosh-up, feed; *Brit. informal, dated* tuck-in; *N. Amer. informal* square.
▶ **verb** *the privileged can nosh smoked salmon while watching the proceedings* **eat**, munch (on), ingest, consume, take, partake of, taste, swallow, devour, feast on, gulp (down), gobble (down), wolf (down), scoff (down), tuck in/into, breakfast (on), lunch (on), dine (on); have breakfast, have lunch, have dinner, have tea, have supper; *informal* get stuck into, get one's laughing gear round; *Brit. informal* shift, gollop, bevvy; *N. Amer. informal* scarf (down/up), snarf (down/up), inhale; *rare* ingurgitate, bib.

nostalgia ▶ **noun** *there is a nostalgia for traditional values* **wistfulness**, longing/yearning/pining for the past, regret, regretfulness, reminiscence, remembrance, recollection, homesickness, sentimentality.

nostalgic ▶ **adjective** *the smell of the sea evoked nostalgic memories of childhood holidays* **wistful**, evocative, longing/yearning/pining for the past, romantic, sentimental, emotional about the past, regretful, dewy-eyed, maudlin, homesick.

nostrum ▶ **noun 1** *the pill pedlars will have to show that their nostrums work* **patent medicine**, quack remedy, potion, elixir, panacea, cure-all, cure for all ills, universal remedy, sovereign remedy, wonder drug, magic bullet; *rare* catholicon, diacatholicon, panpharmacon.
2 *his successes resulted from such right-wing nostrums as a wage freeze and cutting public spending* **remedy**, cure, prescription, answer, magic formula, recipe, recipe for success.

nosy ▶ **adjective** *he had to whisper in order to avoid being overheard by their nosy neighbours* **prying**, inquisitive, curious, busybody, probing, spying, eavesdropping, intrusive; *informal* snooping, snoopy.

notability ▶ **noun 1** *the village has always enjoyed a notability out of all relation to its size* **noteworthiness**, momentousness, memorability, impressiveness, extraordinariness; **prominence**, importance, significance, eminence; **fame**, publicity, renown, notoriety, stature, media attention/interest.
2 *the enterprise enjoyed the patronage of notabilities and aristocrats* **celebrity**, public figure, important person, VIP, personality, personage, notable,

N

dignitary, leading light, star, superstar, name, big name, famous name, household name; lion, worthy, grandee, luminary, panjandrum; *informal* celeb, somebody, bigwig, big shot, big noise, big cheese, big gun, big fish, biggie, heavy, megastar; *Brit. informal* nob; *N. Amer. informal* kahuna, macher, high muckamuck, high muckety-muck.
OPPOSITE nonentity.

notable ▶ adjective **1** *there were no notable examples of townships with high unemployment* **noteworthy**, remarkable, outstanding, important, significant, momentous, memorable, unforgettable, pronounced, marked, striking, glaring, obvious, impressive, uncommon, unusual, particular, special, extraordinary, exceptional, conspicuous, rare, signal.
OPPOSITES insignificant, unremarkable.
2 *Dr Butler was a notable headmaster* **prominent**, important, well known, famous, famed, noted, distinguished, great, eminent, pre-eminent, illustrious, consequential, respected, well thought of, esteemed, honoured, renowned, celebrated, acclaimed, influential, prestigious; in the public eye, of high standing, of distinction, of note, of repute, of mark, of importance, of consequence.
OPPOSITE obscure.
▶ noun *the hotel was a favoured haunt for kings, queens, movie stars, authors, and other notables* **celebrity**, public figure, important person, VIP, personality, personage, notability, dignitary, leading light, star, superstar, name, big name, famous name, household name, lion, worthy, grandee, luminary, panjandrum; *informal* celeb, somebody, bigwig, big shot, big noise, big cheese, big gun, big fish, biggie, heavy, megastar; *Brit. informal* nob; *N. Amer. informal* kahuna, macher, high muckamuck, high muckety-muck.
OPPOSITE nonentity.

notably ▶ adverb **1** *other industrialized countries, notably the USA, agreed to the measures* **in particular**, particularly, especially, specially, primarily, principally, above all.
2 *the flightless emu and ostrich are notably short-lived among birds* **remarkably**, strikingly, impressively, especially, specially, very, extremely, exceptionally, singularly, particularly, peculiarly, distinctly, significantly, unusually, extraordinarily, uncommonly, uniquely, outstandingly, amazingly, incredibly, awfully, terribly, really, markedly, decidedly, surprisingly, conspicuously, spectacularly, signally; *informal* seriously, majorly, mucho; *Brit. informal* jolly, dead, well; *informal, dated* devilish, frightfully.

notation ▶ noun **1** *notation is essential for communication* **system of symbols**, alphabet, syllabary, script; symbols, signs, code, cipher, hieroglyphics.
2 *flicking through, he noticed the notations in the margin* **annotation**, jotting, inscription, comment, footnote, entry, minute, record, item, memo, gloss, explanation, explication, elucidation; marginalia, exegesis; *rare* scholium.

N

notch ▶ noun **1** *there was a notch in the end of the arrow for the bowstring* **nick**, cut, mark, incision, score, scratch, gash, slit, snick, slot, gouge, groove, furrow, cleft, indentation, dent.
2 *her opinion of Nicole dropped a further few notches* **degree**, step, level, rung, point, mark, measure, grade, gradation, stage.
▶ verb *notch the wood* **nick**, cut, mark, score, incise, carve, engrave, scratch, gash, slit, slot, snick, gouge, groove, furrow, indent, make an indentation in, dent.
□ **notch something up** *the world champion notched up four wins and five draws* **score**, achieve, attain, secure, rack up, chalk up, gain, earn, make, register, record.

note *See centre pages for list of* **Tonic Sol-Fa Notes**
▶ noun **1** *she took out her diary and made a note of the time of the meeting* **record**, account, entry, item, notation, minute, jotting, inscription; memorandum, reminder, aide-memoire; *informal* memo.
2 (**notes**) *he may be asked to take notes of the meeting* **minutes**, records, jottings, report, account, commentary, transcript, proceedings, transactions; observations, impressions, details, data; synopsis, precis, summary, sketch, outline.
3 *there were some notes scribbled in the margins* **annotation**, footnote, commentary, comment, gloss, explanation, explication, exposition, elucidation; marginalia, exegesis; *rare* scholium.
4 *he dropped me a note the day he left* **message**, communication, letter, missive, epistle, line; email.
5 (*Brit.*) *a £20 note* **banknote**; *N. Amer.* bill, greenback; *N. Amer. or historical* Treasury note; *archaic* flimsy; (**notes**) paper money.
6 *only two developments are worthy of note* **attention**, consideration, notice, heed, observation, thought, regard, care, attentiveness, mindfulness.
7 *he was a composer of considerable note* **distinction**, importance, eminence, pre-eminence, influence, illustriousness, greatness, prestige, fame, acclaim, celebrity, renown, repute, reputation, stature, standing, position, rank, consequence, account.
8 *there was a note of hopelessness in her voice* **tone**, intonation, inflection, sound, hint, indication, sign, element, streak, strain, vein, suggestion, suspicion.
▶ verb **1** *we shall be delighted to note your suggestion* **bear in mind**, be mindful of, consider, observe, take into account/consideration, take note of, listen to; heed, take notice of, pay attention to, take in, pay regard to, be guided by.
OPPOSITES ignore, disregard.
2 *a final communiqué noted the ministers' concern* **mention**, make mention of, refer to, allude to, touch on, hint at, indicate, point out, make known, state.
3 *you had better note the date in your diary* **write down**, put down, jot down, take down, set down, mark down, inscribe, enter, mark, record, register, scribble, scrawl, pencil; put in writing, put down on paper, commit to paper, put in black and white.

notebook ▶ noun **notepad**, exercise book, register, logbook, log, diary, daybook, journal, commonplace book, memorandum book, record book, personal organizer; *Brit.* jotter, pocketbook; *N. Amer.* scratch pad; *French* cahier; *informal* memo pad; *trademark* Filofax.

noted ▶ adjective **1** *a noted French economist* **eminent**, **famous**, well known, famed, prominent; distinguished, illustrious, great, celebrated, acclaimed, esteemed, august, recognized, pre-eminent, important, of high standing, of distinction, of repute, considerable.
OPPOSITES unknown, unheard of, obscure.
2 *the district is noted for its antique shops, boutiques, and restaurants* **renowned**, **well known**, famous, noteworthy, notable, of note, important, recognized; well thought of, celebrated; notorious.

noteworthy ▶ adjective *other noteworthy features include the carved capitals of the chancel arch* **notable**, worthy of note, interesting, of particular interest, significant, worthy of mention, worth taking a look at, noticeable; **remarkable**, impressive, important, striking, outstanding, memorable, unique, special, prominent, conspicuous; unusual, extraordinary, out of the ordinary, singular, different, rare, uncommon.
OPPOSITES unexceptional, boring, insignificant, ordinary.

nothing ▶ noun **1** *there's nothing I can do about it* **not a thing**, not a single thing, not anything, nothing at all, nil, zero; *N. English* nowt; *informal* zilch, sweet Fanny Adams, sweet FA, nix, not a dicky bird; *Brit. informal* damn all, not a sausage; *N. Amer. informal* zip, nada, a goose egg, bupkis; *Brit. vulgar slang* bugger all, sod all, fuck all; *archaic* nought, naught.
OPPOSITE something.
2 *really, please forget it, it's nothing* **a matter of no importance/consequence**, a trifling matter, a trifle, a piece of trivia, a (mere) bagatelle; neither here nor there; *informal* no big deal.
3 *he seemed to treat her as nothing* **a person of no importance**, an unimportant person, a person of no account, a nobody, a nonentity, a cipher, a non-person; a lightweight; *Brit.* small beer.
OPPOSITE celebrity.
4 *the value of the shares is unlikely to fall to nothing* **zero**, nought, 0; *Tennis* love; *Cricket* a duck.
□ **be/have nothing to do with 1** *it has nothing to do with your enquiries* **be unconnected with**, be unrelated to; be irrelevant to, be extraneous to, be inapplicable to, be inapposite to, be extrinsic to; *rare* be malapropos of.
2 *he's a hard, ruthless man and I'll have nothing to do with him* **avoid**, have no dealings with, have no truck with, avoid dealing with, have no contact with, steer clear of, give a wide berth to.
□ **for nothing 1** *the former TV presenter agreed to host the show for nothing, but then demanded £1,000* **free**, gratis, without charge, without payment, free of charge, at no cost; *informal* for free, on the house.
2 *I've taken all this trouble for nothing* **in vain**, to no avail, to no purpose, with no result, needlessly, pointlessly, futilely; *archaic* bootlessly.
□ **nothing but** *he was nothing but a nuisance to her* **merely**, only, just, solely, simply, purely, no more than.

nothingness ▶ noun **1** *the total nothingness of death* **oblivion**, non-existence, non-being, non-life; **nullity**, blankness; void, vacuum; *rare* nihility.
OPPOSITES existence, being.
2 *the nothingness of it all overwhelmed him* **unimportance**, insignificance, triviality, pointlessness, uselessness, worthlessness, valuelessness.
OPPOSITES importance, value, significance.

notice ▶ noun **1** *no aspect connected with the running of his companies escaped his notice | two points are worthy of notice* **attention**, observation, awareness, consciousness, perception, cognizance, heed, note; regard, consideration, scrutiny, interest, thought, mindfulness, watchfulness, vigilance, attentiveness.
2 *a notice was pinned up outside the church* **information sheet**, bill, handbill, poster, advertisement, announcement, bulletin, broadsheet, circular, flyer, leaflet, pamphlet, sign, placard; card, sticker; handout; *French* affiche; *N. Amer. & Austral.* dodger; *informal* ad; *Brit. informal* advert.
3 *itineraries are subject to change without notice* **notification**, (advance) warning, announcement, apprisal, intimation; information, news, communication, intelligence, word.
4 *I handed in my notice yesterday* **resignation**, letter of resignation.
5 *governors can require the education authority to give notice to a teacher* **dismissal**, discharge, termination/ending of employment, one's

marching orders; *informal* **the sack**, the boot, the bullet, the axe, the (old) heave-ho, the elbow, the push, the bounce; *Brit. informal* one's cards, the chop.
6 *the film did not get universally good notices* **review**, write-up, critique, criticism; *French* compte rendu; *Brit. informal* crit.

□ **take no notice (of)** *he took no notice of anything I said* **pay no attention (to)**, **ignore**, disregard, pay no heed (to), take no account (of), turn a deaf ear (to), brush aside, shrug off, set aside, turn a blind eye (to), shut one's eyes (to), pass over, let pass, let go, overlook, look the other way, pretend not to notice; *informal* not want to know.
OPPOSITES heed, pay attention (to).

▶ **verb** *I noticed that the front door was open | she slipped back inside, hoping no one would notice her* **observe**, perceive, note, see, become aware of, discern, detect, spot, distinguish, catch sight of, make out, take notice of, mark, remark; pay attention to, take note of, heed, take heed of, pay heed to; *Brit. informal* clock; *literary* behold, descry, espy.
OPPOSITES overlook, ignore, disregard.

noticeable ▶ **adjective** *there has been a noticeable shift in public opinion lately* **perceptible**, discernible, detectable, distinguishable, observable, perceivable, visible, easily seen, appreciable, recognizable, notable, measurable; **distinct**, evident, obvious, apparent, manifest, patent, plain, clear, clear-cut, marked, significant, conspicuous, unmistakable, undeniable, palpable, pronounced, decided, prominent, salient, striking, arresting; *archaic* sensible.
OPPOSITES imperceptible, unobtrusive, inconspicuous.

> CHOOSE THE RIGHT WORD
> **noticeable, perceptible, palpable, appreciable**
> *See* PERCEPTIBLE.

noticeboard ▶ **noun** pinboard, cork board; hoarding, display site, advertisement board; *N. Amer.* bulletin board.

notification ▶ **noun 1** *the notification of the victim's next of kin* **informing**, telling, apprising, apprisal, alerting, warning.
2 *she received notification that her letter had been passed to the chairman of the advisory committee* **information**, word, notice, advice, news, intelligence; communication, message, report, account, story; *literary* tidings.
3 *matters relating to the notification of births and deaths* **announcement**, reporting, declaration, communication, disclosure, divulgence, publication, publishing.

notify ▶ **verb 1** *we will notify you as soon as possible | parents must be notified of the education authority's decision* **inform**, tell, advise, apprise, let someone know, put in the picture; alert, warn, caution; acquaint with, send word of.
2 *in the UK, export agreements are meant to be notified to the Office of Fair Trading* **make known**, report, announce, declare, communicate, give notice of, disclose, reveal, divulge, broadcast, publish.

notion ▶ **noun 1** *these figures give the lie to the notion that the country is strike-ridden | he had a notion that something very odd was going on* **idea**, belief, concept, conception, conviction, opinion, view, thought, impression, image, perception, mental picture; assumption, presumption, hypothesis, theory, supposition; feeling, funny feeling, suspicion, sneaking suspicion, hunch.
2 *Claire had no notion of what he meant* **understanding**, idea, awareness, knowledge, clue, inkling; *Brit. informal* the foggiest idea.
3 *you can't expect us to fire any of our staff just because you get a notion to come back* **impulse**, inclination, whim, desire, wish, fancy, caprice, whimsy.

> CHOOSE THE RIGHT WORD
> **notion, idea, concept**
> *See* IDEA.

notional ▶ **adjective** *the notional dividing line between the eastern and western zones* **hypothetical**, theoretical, speculative, conjectural, suppositional, putative, conceptual, abstract; supposed, conjectured, assumed; ideal; imaginary, fanciful, fancied, unreal, illusory, unsubstantiated; *rare* suppositious, ideational.
OPPOSITES actual, genuine, real.

notoriety ▶ **noun** *the book earned him undeserved notoriety* **infamy**, bad reputation/name, disrepute, ill repute, ill fame, dishonour, discredit, obloquy, opprobrium; fame, renown.
OPPOSITES anonymity, a low profile.

notorious ▶ **adjective** *the country's most notorious drug trafficker | she was notorious for having lots of love affairs* **infamous**, of ill repute, with a bad reputation/name, ill-famed, scandalous; **well known**, famous, famed, celebrated, renowned, fabled, legendary, noted, talked about, prominent.
OPPOSITES unknown, anonymous, faceless.

notwithstanding ▶ **preposition** *notwithstanding his many activities, Alan finds time to be a dedicated husband and father* **in spite of**, despite, regardless of, for all.
▶ **adverb** *she tells us she is an intellectual—notwithstanding, she faces the future as unprovided for as a beauty queen* **nevertheless**, nonetheless, even so, all the same, in spite of this/that, despite this/that, after everything, however, still, yet, be that as it may, having said that, that said, for all that, just the same, anyway, in any event, at any rate, at all events, when all is said and done; *archaic* withal, howbeit.
▶ **conjunction** *notwithstanding that Sir Henry had sold much land, his debts were still on the increase* **although**, in spite of the fact that, despite the fact that, even though, though, for all that.

nought ▶ **noun 1** *the past forty years have all been for nought* **nothing**, nothing at all, naught; no point, no purpose, no effect, no end result; *N. English* nowt; *informal* zilch, sweet Fanny Adams, sweet FA, not a dicky bird, nix; *Brit. informal* damn all, not a sausage; *N. Amer. informal* zip, nada, a goose egg; *Brit. vulgar slang* bugger all, fuck all, sod all.
2 *Richard Scott went for nought, caught behind by Bishop* **nil**, zero, 0; *Tennis* love; *Cricket* a duck; *dated* cipher.

noun ▶ **noun**
WORD LINKS
relating to nouns **nominal**

nourish ▶ **verb 1** *it is important that all patients are well nourished prior to surgery* **feed**, provide for, sustain, maintain; *rare* nutrify.
OPPOSITE starve.
2 *by investing in education we nourish the talents of children* **promote**, foster, encourage, stimulate, nurture, boost, further, advance, forward, contribute to, be conducive to, assist, help, aid, cultivate, strengthen, enrich.
3 *the hopes Ursula had nourished in his absence had been dashed* **cherish**, nurture, foster, harbour, nurse, keep in one's mind, entertain, maintain, sustain, hold, have.
OPPOSITES repress, discourage.

nourishing ▶ **adjective** *eating regular, nourishing meals is important to keep yourself fit and well* **nutritious**, good for one, full of nourishment, full of nutrients, nutritive, wholesome, healthy, health-giving, healthful, beneficial, sustaining, strengthening; *rare* nutrimental, nutrient, alimentary, alible.
OPPOSITES unwholesome, unhealthy.

nourishment ▶ **noun** *she denied wilful neglect by failing to provide the boy with sufficient nourishment* **food**, sustenance, nutriment, nutrition, subsistence, provisions, fare, daily bread; means of keeping body and soul together; *Scottish* vivers; *informal* grub, nosh, chow, eats; *Brit. informal* scoff; *N. Amer. informal* chuck; *formal* provender, comestibles; *archaic* victuals, viands, meat, vittles, commons; *rare* aliment, pabulum.

nouveau riche ▶ **plural noun** *the nouveau riche of today buy leather-covered volumes by the metre* the new rich; parvenus, arrivistes, upstarts, social climbers, vulgarians.

novel[1] *See centre pages for list of* **Stories** *(Types of Story and Novel)*
▶ **noun book**, paperback, hardback; **story**, tale, narrative, romance, work of fiction; best-seller; *informal* blockbuster; *historical* yellowback, three-decker.

novel[2] ▶ **adjective** *the practice would not be considered unusual today, but in 1945 it was novel* **new**, **original**, unusual, unfamiliar, unconventional, unorthodox, different, fresh, imaginative, creative, innovative, innovatory, innovational, inventive, modern, ultra-modern, state-of-the-art, advanced, avant-garde, futuristic, pioneering, groundbreaking, trailblazing, revolutionary; rare, unique, singular, unprecedented, uncommon; experimental, untested, untried, unknown, surprising, strange, exotic, out of the ordinary, newfangled; *N. Amer.* left-field; *rare* new-fashioned, neoteric.
OPPOSITES old; traditional.

> CHOOSE THE RIGHT WORD
> **novel, new, fresh, original, newfangled**
> *See* NEW.

novelist *See centre pages for list of types of* **Writer**
▶ **noun author**, writer of fiction, creative writer, man/woman of letters; *French* littérateur; *informal* penman, scribbler; *rare* fictionist, fictioneer.

novelty ▶ **noun 1** *they liked the novelty of our approach* **originality**, newness, freshness, unconventionality, unfamiliarity, unusualness, difference, imaginativeness, creativity, creativeness, innovativeness, innovation, modernity, modernness, break with tradition.
OPPOSITE conservatism.
2 *their products include handmade chocolates, figurines, and seasonal novelties* **knick-knack**, trinket, bauble, toy, trifle, gewgaw, gimcrack, ornament, curiosity; memento, souvenir; *N. Amer.* kickshaw; *archaic* gaud, folderol.

November ▶ noun
WORD LINKS
birthstone **topaz**

novice ▶ noun **1** *a 5-day course during which novices learn enough to skipper a yacht safely* **beginner**, learner, inexperienced person, neophyte, newcomer, new member, new recruit, raw recruit, new boy/girl, initiate, tyro, fledgling; apprentice, trainee, probationer, student, pupil; *N. Amer.* tenderfoot; *informal* rookie, new kid, newie, newbie; *N. Amer. informal* greenhorn, punk.
OPPOSITES expert, veteran.
2 *a novice who had never achieved ordination* neophyte, novitiate; postulant, proselyte, catechumen.

novitiate ▶ noun **1** *in 1868 he began a three-year novitiate* **probationary period**, probation, trial period, test period, apprenticeship, training period, traineeship, training, initiation.
2 *two young novitiates* **novice**, neophyte; postulant, proselyte, catechumen.

now ▶ adverb **1** *I'm afraid I'm extremely busy now, but I could see you in the morning* **at the moment**, at present, just now, right now, at the present time, at the present moment, at this time, at this moment in time, currently, here and now; *N. Amer.* presently; *Brit. informal* at the minute.
2 *television is now the main source of political information for most people* **nowadays**, today, these days, in this day and age; in the present climate, things being what they are, in the present circumstances; *rare* contemporarily.
3 *it would be best if you leave now* **at once**, straight away, right away, right now, this minute, this instant, immediately, instantly, directly, without further/more ado, promptly, without delay, as soon as possible; *French* tout de suite; *informal* pronto, straight off, a.s.a.p., toot sweet; *archaic* straightway, instanter.
□ **as of now** *as of now, cigarettes are banned in this house* **from this time on**, from now on/onwards, henceforth, henceforward, from this day forward, in future; *formal* hereafter.
□ **for now** *that will be all for now, thank you* **for the time being**, for the moment, for the present, for the meantime, for a little while; *archaic* for the nonce.
□ **not now** *I promise I will, but not now* **later**, later on, sometime, one day, some day, one of these days, at some time in the future, at a future time/date, one of these fine days, sooner or later, in due course, by and by, eventually, ultimately.
OPPOSITE immediately.
□ **now and again** *I go and stay with my sister now and again* **occasionally**, now and then, from time to time, sometimes, every so often, (every) now and again, at times, on occasion(s), on the odd occasion, (every) once in a while; at intervals, periodically, on and off; once in a blue moon; *archaic* ever and anon.

nowadays ▶ adverb *nowadays all graduates are computer literate* **these days**, today, in these times, at this time, in this day and age, now, just now, right now, currently, at the moment, at present, at this moment in time; in the present climate, things being what they are; *N. Amer.* presently.

noxious ▶ adjective *the discharge of noxious effluents into streams and rivers | noxious fumes* **poisonous**, toxic, deadly, virulent; **harmful**, dangerous, pernicious, damaging, destructive; **very unpleasant**, nasty, disgusting, awful, dreadful, horrible, terrible, vile, revolting, foul, sickening, nauseating, nauseous, appalling, offensive, foul-smelling, evil-smelling, malodorous, fetid, putrid, rancid, unwholesome, unhealthy, insalubrious; *informal* ghastly, horrid; *literary* noisome, mephitic; *archaic* disgustful; *rare* miasmal, miasmic, nocuous, olid.
OPPOSITES innocuous, safe; pleasant.

nuance ▶ noun *the expression of subtle nuances of thought* **fine distinction**, subtle distinction/difference, shade, shading, gradation, variation, modulation, degree; subtlety, nicety, refinement, overtone.

nub ▶ noun *the nub of his argument* **crux**, **central point**, main point, most important point, core, heart, heart of the matter, centre, nucleus, essence, essential part, quintessence, kernel, marrow, meat, pith; gist, substance, sum and substance; *informal* nitty-gritty.

nubile ▶ adjective *a nubile young girl* **sexually mature**, marriageable; **sexually attractive**, desirable, sexy, luscious, lush, voluptuous, ripe; *informal* beddable.

nuclear reactor *See centre pages for list of* **Nuclear Reactors**
▶ noun *dated* atomic pile.

nucleus ▶ noun **1** *the nucleus of the international banking world* **core**, centre, central part, most important part, heart, nub, hub, middle, midpoint, eye, kernel, focus, focal point, pivot, crux; *literary* navel; *rare* omphalos.
2 *a nucleus of non-party men were prepared to support him* **small group**, caucus, cell, coterie, clique, faction, cabal.

nude ▶ adjective **naked**, in the nude, stark naked, bare, with nothing on, stripped, unclothed, undressed, uncovered, in a state of nature, disrobed, unclad, undraped, exposed; *French* au naturel; *informal* without a stitch on, in one's birthday suit, in the raw, in the altogether, in the buff, as naked as the day one was born, in the nuddy, mother naked; *Brit. informal* starkers; *Scottish informal* in the scud, scuddy; *N. Amer. informal* bare-assed, buck naked; *Austral. informal* bollocky; *Brit. vulgar slang* bollock-naked.
OPPOSITES dressed, fully clothed.
WORD LINKS
fear of nudity **gymnophobia**

CHOOSE THE RIGHT WORD
nude, naked, bare
See NAKED.

nudge ▶ verb **1** *he nudged Ben in the ribs* **poke**, elbow, dig, prod, jog, jab, butt.
2 *the canoe nudged a bank of reeds* **touch**, bump (against), push (against), run into.
3 *enthusiastic reviewers have been known to nudge recalcitrant publishers into action* **prompt**, encourage, coax, stimulate, prod, jog.
4 *unemployment was nudging 3 million* **approach**, come/get close to, be verging on, border on, near.
▶ noun **1** *Maggie gave him a nudge* **poke**, dig in the ribs, dig, prod, jog, jab, butt, push.
2 *after a little nudge from me, she remembered Lilian* **reminder**, prompt, prompting, push, prod, encouragement.

nudity ▶ noun **nakedness**, bareness, state of undress, undress; *French* déshabillé; *informal* one's birthday suit.

nugatory ▶ adjective **1** *a nugatory and pointless observation* **worthless**, of no value, of no importance, unimportant, inconsequential, of no consequence, valueless, trifling, trivial, insignificant, meaningless.
2 *the teacher shortages will render nugatory the hopes of implementing the new curriculum* **futile**, useless, vain, unavailing, null and void, null, invalid; *archaic* bootless.

nugget ▶ noun *gold nuggets | savoury scones filled with nuggets of potato and cheese* **lump**, chunk, small piece, hunk, mass, clump, wad, gobbet, globule; *Scottish* dod; *Brit. informal* wodge; *N. Amer. informal* gob; *rare* nub.

nuisance ▶ noun *don't you find these long journeys a nuisance? | I'm terribly sorry to be such a nuisance* **source of annoyance/irritation**, annoyance, inconvenience, bore, bother, irritant, problem, difficulty, trouble, trial, burden; pest, plague, thorn in one's side/flesh; *informal* pain, pain in the neck, pain in the backside, headache, hassle, bind, drag, aggravation, menace; *Scottish informal* nyaff, skelf; *N. Amer. informal* pain in the butt, nudnik, burr under/in someone's saddle; *Austral./NZ informal* nark; *Brit. vulgar slang* pain in the arse; *Brit. informal, dated* blister; *rare* infliction.
OPPOSITES help, blessing.

null ▶ adjective **1** *his previous marriage was declared null* **invalid**, null and void, void; annulled, nullified, cancelled, abolished, revoked, rescinded, repealed.
OPPOSITE valid.
2 *his curiously null life* **lacking in character**, empty, characterless, blank, colourless, expressionless, vacuous, insipid, vapid, inane.
OPPOSITES full, colourful, interesting.

nullify ▶ verb **1** *the ANC warned that it would nullify the legislation* **annul**, declare null and void, render null and void, void, invalidate, render invalid; **repeal**, reverse, rescind, revoke, set aside, cancel, abolish, undo, abrogate; countermand, veto, dissolve, cast aside, do away with, bring to an end, terminate, quash, obliterate; *Law* vacate; *archaic* recall; *rare* disannul.
OPPOSITES ratify, validate, confirm.
2 *the costs of preparing the case would more than nullify any tax relief gained* **cancel out**, neutralize, negate, render ineffective, make of no use or value; *rare* negative.

nullity ▶ noun **1** *nullity of marriage must be carefully distinguished from divorce* **invalidity**, non-validity; illegality; *rare* voidness.
OPPOSITE validity.
2 *her bright yellow hair contrasted strongly with her pallor and the nullity of her features* **characterlessness**, emptiness, blankness, expressionlessness, vacuity, insipidity, vapidity, inanity.

numb ▶ adjective *his fingers were numb with cold | she felt numb with fear* **deprived of sensation**, without feeling, numbed, benumbed, dead, deadened, desensitized, insensible, insensate, senseless, unfeeling; anaesthetized, drugged; dazed, stunned, stupefied, in shock, paralysed, petrified, immobilized, frozen, chilled; *rare* torpefied.
OPPOSITES sensitive, responsive.
▶ verb *the cold had numbed her senses | I sat there, numbed by what had happened* **deaden**, deprive of sensation, benumb, desensitize, render insensitive, dull; anaesthetize, drug; daze, stun, stupefy, paralyse, petrify, immobilize, freeze, chill; *rare* torpefy, obtund.
OPPOSITE sensitize.

number ▶ noun **1** **numeral**, integer, figure, digit; character, symbol; whole number, decimal number, decimal, unit; cardinal number, ordinal

number; Roman number, Arabic number; *rare* cipher.
2 *they received a large number of complaints | the number of accidents involving cyclists has increased* **amount**, quantity; **total**, sum total, aggregate, tally; quota.
3 *the men were celebrating the wedding of one of their number* **group**, company, crowd, circle, party, body, band, crew, set; *informal* gang, tribe.
4 *a copy of the current number of the Society's quarterly magazine* **edition**, issue, copy; printing, imprint, impression, publication.
5 *in the background she could hear the band performing another number* **song**, piece of music, musical item, piece, tune, track; turn, item, routine, sketch, dance, act.
▶ **verb 1** *visitors to the cathedral numbered more than 2.25 million last year* **add up to**, amount to, total, come to.
2 *he numbers the editor of Vogue among his close friends* **include**, count; reckon, deem, look on.
3 *each paragraph is numbered consecutively* **assign a number to**, categorize by number, specify by number, mark with a number; itemize, enumerate.
4 *the number of published texts on the subject may be numbered on the fingers of both hands | he numbers the fleet at a thousand* **count**, add up, total, calculate, compute, enumerate, reckon, tell, tally; assess; *Brit.* tot up.
5 *his days are numbered* **limit**, limit in number, restrict, fix.
□ **a number of** *there are a number of reasons why many crimes are not reported to the police* **several**, various, quite a few, sundry, diverse; *literary* divers.
□ **without number** *I have crossed that road times without number* **countless**, innumerable, unlimited, endless, limitless, untold, an infinite number of, an incalculable number of, more than one can count, too many to be counted, numberless, uncountable, uncounted; numerous, many, multiple, manifold, legion; *rare* unnumbered, unnumberable, innumerous, unsummed.

WORD LINKS
relating to numbers **numerical**

numberless ▶ **adjective** *there are numberless questions to be answered* **innumerable**, countless, unlimited, endless, limitless, untold, an infinite number of, an incalculable number of, more than one can count, too many to be counted, without number, uncountable, uncounted; numerous, many, multiple, manifold, legion; *informal* more ... than one can shake a stick at; *literary* multitudinous, myriad; *rare* unnumbered, unnumberable, innumerous, unsummed.

numbing ▶ **adjective 1** *the menthol in the oil has a slight numbing action on the nerve | a deep, numbing fear* **deadening**, **desensitizing**, benumbing, anaesthetizing, anaesthetic; paralysing; *rare* torpefying.
2 *the numbing cold of the bitter wind* **freezing**, glacial, raw, piercing, cutting, bitter, arctic, polar.
3 *six days of numbing boredom and inactivity* **stupefying**, mind-numbing, stultifying, paralysing; sleep-inducing, soporific.

numbness ▶ **noun lack of sensation**, lack of feeling, deadness, insensibility; paralysis, stupefaction, immobility.
OPPOSITES feeling, sensation.

numbskull ▶ **noun** (*informal*) *the system seems to be organized and operated exclusively by numbskulls. See* FOOL, IDIOT.

numeral ▶ **noun number**, integer, figure, digit; character, symbol, unit; Roman numeral, Arabic numeral; *rare* cipher.

numerous ▶ **adjective** *numerous studies have been published on the subject* **many**, a lot of, a great many, very many, countless, scores of, innumerable; several, quite a few, various, diverse; a great number of, a great deal of, plenty of, copious, a quantity of, quantities of, an abundance of, a profusion of, a multitude of; frequent; *informal* lots of, umpteen, loads of, masses of, stacks of, heaps of, piles of, bags of, tons of, oodles of, scads of, dozens of, hundreds of, thousands of, millions of, billions of, zillions of, more ... than one can shake a stick at; *Brit. informal* a shedload of; *N. Amer. informal* a slew of, a bunch of, gazillions of, bazillions of; *Austral./NZ informal* a swag of; *vulgar slang* a shitload of; *literary* myriad, multitudinous; *rare* numberless, innumerous.
OPPOSITES few, occasional, rare.

numinous ▶ **adjective** *the strange, numinous beauty of this ancient landmark* **spiritual**, religious, divine, holy, sacred; mysterious, other-worldly, unearthly, awe-inspiring, transcendent.

nun *See centre pages for list of* **Christian Religious Orders**
▶ **noun** sister, novice, abbess, prioress, Mother Superior, Reverend Mother; bride of Christ, religious, conventual, contemplative; *Roman Catholic Church* canoness; *literary* vestal; *historical* anchoress, ancress; *rare* vowess.

nuncio ▶ **noun (papal) ambassador**, envoy, legate, messenger.

nunnery ▶ **noun convent**; priory, abbey, religious house, religious community, cloister; *rare* coenobium, coenoby, beguinage.

nuptial ▶ **adjective** *the nuptial festivities | moments of nuptial bliss* **matrimonial**, marital, marriage, wedding, conjugal, connubial, bridal; married, wedded; *literary* hymeneal, epithalamic; *Law* spousal.

nuptials ▶ **plural noun** *Queen Sofia arrived in Seville yesterday for her daughter's nuptials* **wedding**, wedding ceremony, marriage, marriage ceremony, union; *archaic* espousal, spousals, bridal(s).

nurse *See centre pages for list of* **Nurses**
▶ **noun 1** *a team of skilled doctors and nurses* **carer**, caregiver, attendant; *informal* Florence Nightingale, nursey; *N. Amer. informal* candy-striper.
2 *she had been his nurse when he was a little boy* **nanny**, childminder, governess, au pair, nursemaid, crèche worker, childcarer, babysitter, nursery nurse; *Indian* ayah, amah; *Jewish* metapelot; *informal* nursey; *French dated* bonne.
▶ **verb 1** *they had nursed smallpox patients* **care for**, take care of, look after, tend, attend to, minister to.
2 *I nursed my damaged finger* **treat**, medicate, tend, attend to, cure, heal; dress, bandage, soothe; *informal* doctor.
3 *Rosa was nursing a baby in her arms* **breastfeed**, suckle, wet-nurse, feed.
4 *the settlers still nursed old grievances* **harbour**, foster, entertain, brood over, bear, have, hold (on to), cherish, cling to, maintain, retain.
5 *our political unity needs to be protected and nursed* **encourage**, nurture, promote, boost, further, advance, contribute to, assist, help, cultivate, stimulate; protect, safeguard, keep alive.
OPPOSITE neglect; hinder.

nursemaid ▶ **noun nanny**, governess, nursery nurse, nurserymaid, childminder, au pair, childcarer; *Indian* ayah, amah; *Jewish* metapelot; *informal* nursey; *French dated* bonne.

nurture ▶ **verb 1** *giving birth to children and nurturing them into adulthood* **bring up**, care for, provide for, take care of, attend to, look after, rear, support, raise, foster, parent, mother, tend; feed, nourish; *rare* provender.
OPPOSITE neglect.
2 *we've nurtured different varieties of plant* **cultivate**, grow, keep, tend.
3 *my father nurtured my love of art* **encourage**, promote, stimulate, develop, foster, cultivate, further, advance, boost, forward, contribute to, be conducive to, assist, help, aid, abet, strengthen, advantage, fuel.
OPPOSITE hinder.
4 *the classical Hindu tradition in which Gandhi was nurtured* **educate**, school, train, tutor, coach.
▶ **noun 1** *we are all what nature and nurture have made us* **upbringing**, bringing up, care, fostering, tending, rearing, raising, training, education; *rare* alimentation.
OPPOSITES nature, innate disposition, inherited characteristics.
2 *the nurture of ideas* **encouragement**, promotion, fostering, development, cultivation, boosting, furtherance, advancement.
3 *a good base camp where one may receive nurture and rest* **food**, nourishment, nutrition, nutriment, diet, sustenance, feeding, subsistence; *rare* alimentation.

nut *See centre pages for list of* **Nuts**
▶ **noun 1** *nuts in their shells* kernel.
2 (*informal*) *he cracked him on the nut with a poker* **head**, skull, cranium; *informal* noodle, noddle, nob, noggin, dome; *Brit. informal* bonce, napper; *Scottish & N. English informal* poll; *informal, dated* bean, conk; *archaic* pate, Costard, crumpet.
3 (*informal*) *some nut arrived at the office screaming about communist propaganda* **madman/madwoman**, maniac, lunatic; eccentric; *informal* loony, nutcase, nutter, fruitcake, head case, basket case, headbanger, schizo, crank, crackpot, oddball, weirdo, weirdie; *Brit. informal* odd bod; *N. Amer. informal* screwball, crazy, kook, nutso, meshuggener, wacko, wack; *N. Amer. & Austral./NZ informal* dingbat.
4 (*informal*) *he's a movie nut* **enthusiast**, fan, fanatic, addict, devotee, aficionado; *informal* freak, fiend, maniac, buff, -head, a great one for; *N. Amer. informal* geek, jock; *S. African informal* fundi.
□ **do one's nut** (*informal*) *for God's sake don't tell Bea—she'd do her nut* **be very angry**, be furious, lose one's temper, go into a rage, breathe fire; *informal* go mad, go crazy, be hopping mad, be livid, go wild, go bananas, have a fit, blow one's top, blow a fuse, blow a gasket, hit the roof, go through the roof, go up the wall, go off the deep end, go ape, flip, flip one's lid, lose one's rag, be fit to be tied, go non-linear; *Brit. informal* go spare, go crackers, get one's knickers in a twist; *N. Amer. informal* flip one's wig; *vulgar slang* go apeshit.
OPPOSITE keep calm.
□ **off one's nut** (*informal*) *she's off her blooming nut. See* MAD *sense* 1, CRAZY *sense* 1.

nutriment ▶ **noun** *the egg contains sufficient nutriment for the chick up to the time of hatching* **nourishment**, nutrients, sustenance, goodness, nutrition, food; *archaic* aliment.

nutrition ▶ **noun** *the child was not receiving sufficient nutrition* **nourishment**, nutriment, nutrients, sustenance, food, daily bread; *informal* grub, chow, nosh; *Brit. informal* scoff; *archaic* victuals, vittles, viands; *rare* aliment.

WORD LINKS
relating to nutrition **trophic**

nutritious ▶ **adjective** *porridge is both cheap and nutritious* **nourishing**, good for one, full of nourishment, full of nutrients, nutritive, wholesome, healthy, health-giving, healthful, beneficial, sustaining, strengthening; *rare* nutrimental, nutrient, alimentary, alible.
OPPOSITE unwholesome.

N

nuts ▶ adjective (*informal*) **1** *they must have thought we were nuts. See* MAD *sense* 1, CRAZY *sense* 1.
2 *he's still* **nuts about** *her* **very keen on**, devoted to, infatuated with, in love with, smitten with, enamoured of, hot for; enthusiastic, passionate, impassioned, ardent; *informal* mad, crazy, potty, wild, nutty, hooked on, gone on; *Brit. informal* dotty, daft; *N. Amer. informal* nutso.
OPPOSITE indifferent.

nuts and bolts ▶ plural noun *the nuts and bolts of running an airline* **practical details**, basic details, fundamentals, basics, practicalities, essentials, mechanics; *informal* the nitty-gritty, the ins and outs, the brass tacks.

nutty ▶ adjective (*informal*) **1** *they're all as nutty as each other. See* MAD *sense* 1, CRAZY *sense* 1.
2 *she confessed that she wasn't as* **nutty about** *Elvis as her husband* **very keen on**, devoted to, infatuated with, in love with, smitten with, enamoured of, hot for; enthusiastic, passionate, impassioned, ardent; *informal* mad, crazy, potty, nuts, wild, hooked on, gone on; *Brit. informal* dotty, daft; *N. Amer. informal* nutso.
OPPOSITE indifferent.

nuzzle ▶ verb **1** *the horse nuzzled at her coat pocket* **nudge**, nose, prod, push.
2 *a girl was* **nuzzling up to** *her boyfriend* **snuggle**, cuddle (up), nestle, curl up, settle down, snug down, burrow, embrace, hug, lie close to.

nymph *See centre pages for list of* **Nymphs**
▶ noun **1** *Iris was depicted as a nymph with golden winged sandals* **sprite**, sylph, wood nymph, water nymph.
2 *a skinny nymph with deep-brown eyes* **girl**, belle, maiden, maid, nymphet, sylph; young woman, young lady; *Scottish & N. English* lass, lassie; *Irish* colleen; *Brit. dated* rosebud; *literary* maid, maiden, damsel; *archaic* demoiselle.

N

oaf ▸ noun *the thoughtless actions of a few loud-mouthed oafs* **lout**, boor, barbarian, Neanderthal, churl, clown, gawk, hulk, bumpkin, yokel; **fool**, dolt, dullard; *Irish* bosthoon; *informal* idiot, imbecile, halfwit, cretin, ass, jackass, goon, jerk, oik, yahoo, ape, gorilla, baboon, bear, lump, clodhopper, clod, blockhead, meathead, bonehead, chucklehead, knucklehead, lamebrain; *informal, dated* muttonhead, noddy, hobbledehoy; *Brit. informal* clot, twit, muppet, plonker, berk, prat, pillock, wally, git, wazzock, nerk, dork, yob, yobbo; *Scottish informal* nyaff, sumph, gowk, galoot; *Irish informal* gobdaw; *N. Amer. informal* bozo, schmuck, boob, chowderhead, dumbhead, lummox, klutz, putz, schlemiel, gink, cluck, ding-dong, wiener, weeny, dip, spud, coot, palooka, poop, squarehead, hick, goofus, clunk, dingleberry, turkey, stumblebum; *Austral. informal* dingbat, alec, galah, nong, bogan, poon, boofhead, drongo, dill, hoon; *S. African informal* skate, mompara; *vulgar slang* dickhead, fuckwit, fuckhead, shit for brains, dildo; *Brit. vulgar slang* arsehole, arse, dick, tit, tosser; *Irish vulgar slang* gobshite; *archaic* clodpole, lubber.

oafish ▸ adjective *her oafish idiot of a son* **stupid**, foolish, idiotic, cretinous; **ungainly**, loutish, clumsy, awkward, gawkish, lumbering, ape-like, bearish, cloddish, clownish, doltish, Neanderthal, uncouth, uncultured, boorish, lumpen, rough, coarse, crass, brutish, blockish, rough-hewn, ill-mannered, badly behaved, unrefined, unsophisticated; *informal* clodhopping, blockheaded, moronic, boneheaded, half-witted, dumb, lamebrained, chuckleheaded, thickheaded; *Brit. informal* yobbish; *N. Amer. informal* chowderheaded; *archaic* lubberly.
OPPOSITES smart, clever, neat.

oasis ▸ noun **1** *the oasis of Bahriyah is over 200 miles from Cairo* **watering hole**, watering place, water hole, spring; *Austral.* gnamma, claypan.
2 *a miniature woodland that offers a cool oasis in a hot summer* **refuge**, haven, safe haven, retreat, sanctuary, sanctum, shelter, resting place, hiding place, harbour, asylum, hideaway, hideout.

oath ▸ noun **1** *an oath of allegiance to the king* **vow**, sworn statement, promise, pledge, avowal, affirmation, attestation, word of honour, word, bond, guarantee, guaranty; *archaic* troth.
2 *he uttered a stream of unrepeatable oaths* **swear word**, profanity, expletive, four-letter word, dirty word, obscenity, imprecation, curse, malediction, blasphemy; vulgarism, vulgarity; swearing, bad/foul language, strong language; *informal* cuss, cuss word.

obdurate ▸ adjective *I argued with him but he was obdurate* **stubborn**, obstinate, unyielding, unbending, inflexible, intransigent, implacable, pig-headed, bull-headed, mulish, stiff-necked, headstrong, wilful, unshakeable, unmalleable, intractable, unpersuadable, unrelenting, relentless, immovable, inexorable, uncompromising, hard, stony, iron, iron-willed, adamant, firm, fixed, determined; *Brit. informal* bloody-minded; *rare* indurate.
OPPOSITES amenable, compliant, malleable, tractable.

obedience ▸ noun *Louise was so accustomed to obedience that she could not prevent herself from hurrying to carry out his orders* **compliance**, acquiescence, tractability, tractableness, amenability; **dutifulness**, deference, duty, respect, respectfulness, observance of the law/rules, discipline, biddableness, duteousness; malleability, pliability, conformity, conformance, conformability, submissiveness, submission, docility, tameness, meekness, passivity, passiveness, subservience, obsequiousness, servility.
OPPOSITES disobedience, rebellion, recalcitrance.

obedient ▸ adjective *Lucinda had always been very obedient* **compliant**, acquiescent, tractable, amenable; **dutiful**, good, law-abiding, deferential, respectful, duteous, under control, well trained, well disciplined, disciplined, observant, manageable, governable, conformable; **docile**, biddable, submissive, tame, meek, passive, unresisting, malleable, pliable, pliant, yielding, subservient, obsequious, servile.
OPPOSITES disobedient, rebellious, unruly.

CHOOSE THE RIGHT WORD

obedient, biddable, docile, compliant, dutiful

- Children and animals may be expected to be **obedient**, but nowadays the word is seldom used to describe adults without an implication of subservience (*'I was waiting for you to tell me. The obedient wife,' she said*) except when it is used of obedience to rules, the law, or a faith (*she seeks to be obedient to the Lord*).
- The critical note is still stronger in **biddable**: a biddable person (typically a woman or girl) is excessively meek and ready to obey any instruction, without questioning either its wisdom or the authority of the person giving it (*she'd been so meek, so biddable to this man*). It is also used of animals (*the golden retriever is both biddable and intelligent*).
- **Docile**, being used more commonly of animals, has similar implications, but in addition to unquestioning obedience it suggests a general reluctance to complain or rebel, even where such behaviour would be justified (*employers depended on the regime for a cheap and docile workforce*).
- **Compliant** means 'disposed to agree with others or obey rules' and typically has a disparaging tone, criticising the compliant person for not having the willpower to stand up for themselves and show some independence by expressing their own views (*compliant MPs loyally following party policy*).
- Even **dutiful**, though applied to a large extent to family members (*daughter, son, wife, parent, mother, father*), may suggest a dull but worthy individual or the perfunctory fulfilment of an obligation (*a dutiful postcard to his mother*).

obeisance ▸ noun **1** *they paid obeisance to the Prince | a gesture of obeisance* **respect**, homage, worship, adoration, reverence, veneration, respectfulness, honour, submission, deference.
2 *she made a deep obeisance* **bow**, curtsy, bob, genuflection, salaam, salutation; *Indian* namaskar; *Chinese, historical* kowtow; *archaic* reverence.

obelisk ▸ noun **column**, pillar, needle, shaft, monolith, monument, memorial.

obese ▸ adjective *he ate excessively and became obese* **fat**, overweight, corpulent, gross, stout, fleshy, outsize, massive, heavy, plump, portly, chubby, rotund, roly-poly, paunchy, pot-bellied, beer-bellied, big, large, ample, well upholstered, well padded, broad in the beam, bulky, bloated, flabby, Falstaffian; *informal* porky, pudgy, tubby, blubbery, poddy; *Brit. informal* podgy, fubsy; *N. Amer. informal* lard-assed; *archaic* pursy; *rare* abdominous.
OPPOSITES thin, skinny, emaciated, anorexic.

obesity ▸ noun *somehow, his famous charm made one ignore his years and his obesity* **fatness**, corpulence, stoutness, fleshiness, heaviness, plumpness, portliness, chubbiness, rotundity, bulkiness, flabbiness, grossness; size, bulk, weight, avoirdupois, weight problem; *informal* tubbiness, pudginess; *Brit. informal* podginess; *archaic* embonpoint.
OPPOSITES emaciation, anorexia.

obey ▸ verb **1** *I was so frightened that I obeyed him without question* **do what someone says**, take/accept orders from, carry out/follow the orders of, be dutiful to, heed; **submit to**, defer to, be ruled by, bow to, give way/in to, yield to, surrender to, truckle to.
2 *the officer was convicted for refusing to obey an order* **carry out**, perform, act on, execute, discharge, put into effect, implement, fulfil, meet.
3 *health and safety regulations have to be obeyed* **comply with**, adhere to, observe, abide by, act in accordance with, conform to, respect, acquiesce in, consent to, agree to, follow, accept, keep to, stick to; play it by the book, toe the line.

OPPOSITES disobey, defy, contravene.

obfuscate ▸ verb **1** *the debate all too often obfuscates the issue* **obscure**, confuse, make obscure/unclear, blur, muddle, jumble, complicate, garble, muddy, cloud, befog; muddy the waters.
OPPOSITE clarify.
2 *it is more likely to obfuscate people than enlighten them* **bewilder**, mystify, puzzle, perplex, baffle, confound, bemuse, befuddle, nonplus; *informal* flummox; *archaic* wilder, maze, gravel.

obituary ▸ noun **death notice**, eulogy; *informal* obit; *rare* necrology, necrologue.

object ▸ noun (stress on the first syllable) **1** *wooden objects* **thing**, article, item, piece, device, gadget, entity, body; *informal* thingamajig, thingamabob, thingummy, whatsit, whatchamacallit, what-d'you-call-it, thingy; *Brit. informal* doodah, doobry, gubbins; *N. Amer. informal* doodad, doohickey, doojigger; *N. Amer. & S. African informal* dingus.
OPPOSITES abstract idea, notion.
2 *he became the object of fierce criticism* **target**, butt, focus, recipient, victim.
3 *the Institute was opened with the object of promoting scientific study* **purpose**, objective, aim, goal, target, end, end in view, plan, object of the exercise; ambition, design, intent, intention, idea, point.
▸ verb (stress on the second syllable) *some teachers* **objected to** *the scheme | no reasonable person could have objected* **protest (against)**, lodge a protest (against), raise/express objections (to), express disapproval (of), express disagreement (with), oppose, be in opposition (to), take exception (to), take issue (with), take a stand against, argue (against), remonstrate (against), make a fuss (about), quarrel with, disapprove (of), condemn, draw the line (at), demur, mind, complain (about), moan (about), grumble (about), grouse (about), cavil (at), quibble (about); beg to differ; *informal* kick up a fuss/stink (about), beef (about), gripe (about); *N. Amer. informal* kvetch (about).
OPPOSITES approve, accept, acquiesce.

objection ▸ noun *the search was carried out regardless of her objections* **protest**, protestation, demur, demurrer, remonstrance, remonstration, exception, complaint, grievance, moan, grumble, grouse, cavil, quibble, expostulation; **opposition**, argument, counter-argument, demurral, disapproval, dissent, disagreement; *informal* niggle, gripe, beef, grouch.
OPPOSITES approval, acceptance, acquiescence.

objectionable ▸ adjective *I thought Randolph was one of the most objectionable people I had ever met* **offensive**, **unpleasant**, disagreeable, distasteful, displeasing, unacceptable, off-putting, undesirable, obnoxious; **nasty**, disgusting, awful, terrible, dreadful, frightful, repulsive, repellent, repugnant, revolting, abhorrent, loathsome, hateful, detestable, reprehensible, deplorable, appalling, insufferable, intolerable, despicable, contemptible, beyond the pale, odious, vile, obscene, foul, unsavoury, unpalatable, sickening, nauseating, nauseous, noxious; *informal* ghastly, horrible, horrid, sick-making; *Brit. informal* beastly; *archaic* disgustful, loathly; *rare* exceptionable, rebarbative.
OPPOSITES pleasant, agreeable, acceptable.

objective ▸ adjective **1** *an interviewer must try to be objective* **impartial**, unbiased, unprejudiced, non-partisan, disinterested, non-discriminatory, neutral, uninvolved, even-handed, equitable, fair, fair-minded, just, open-minded, dispassionate, detached, impersonal, unemotional, clinical.
OPPOSITES biased, partial, prejudiced.
2 *the world of objective knowledge* **factual**, actual, real, empirical, verifiable, existing, manifest.
OPPOSITE subjective.
▸ noun *our objective is to build a profitable business* **aim**, intention, purpose, target, goal, intent, object, end, end in view, grail, holy grail; idea, design, plan, scheme, ambition, aspiration, desire, hope; the point, the object of the exercise.

objectively ▸ adverb *the bank will do all it can to investigate your complaint objectively* **impartially**, with objectivity, without bias, without prejudice, with impartiality, disinterestedly, even-handedly, with detachment, dispassionately, detachedly, equitably, fairly, justly, open-mindedly, with an open mind, without fear or favour, neutrally.

objectivity ▸ noun *the ideals of journalistic accuracy and objectivity* **impartiality**, absence of bias/prejudice, fairness, fair-mindedness, equitableness, equitability, even-handedness, justness, justice, open-mindedness, disinterest, disinterestedness, detachment, dispassion, dispassionateness, neutrality.
OPPOSITES subjectivity, bias, prejudice.

oblation ▸ noun *the priest spread his hands over the oblation* **religious offering**, offering, sacrifice, peace offering, burnt offering, thank offering, first fruits, libation; *Hinduism* prasad, puja; *Judaism* Omer, sin-offering.

obligate ▸ verb *the medical establishment is obligated to take action in the best interests of the public* **oblige**, compel, commit, bind, require, constrain, force, impel, make.

obligation ▸ noun **1** *I have an obligation to look after her | he seemed able to fulfil his professional obligations* **duty**, commitment, responsibility, moral imperative; **function**, task, job, chore, assignment, commission, business, burden, charge, onus, liability, accountability, requirement, debt, engagement; *dated* office; *archaic* devoir; *literary* trust.
2 *she took him in solely out of a sense of obligation* **duty**, compulsion, indebtedness, duress, necessity, pressure, constraint.
3 *the company's export obligations* **contract**, agreement, deed, covenant, bond, treaty, deal, pact, compact, understanding, transaction.
□ **under an obligation** *she didn't want to be* **under an obligation** *to him* **owing someone a favour**, obliged, beholden, in someone's debt, indebted, obligated, owing someone a debt of gratitude, duty-bound, honour-bound, grateful, owing someone thanks.

obligatory ▸ adjective **1** *use of seat belts in cars is now obligatory* **compulsory**, mandatory, prescribed, required, demanded, statutory, enforced, binding, incumbent; requisite, necessary, imperative, unavoidable, inescapable, essential.
OPPOSITES voluntary, optional.
2 *after the obligatory preamble on the weather he got down to business* **customary**, traditional, usual, accustomed, routine, familiar, regular, habitual; *French* de rigueur; *literary* wonted.

oblige ▸ verb **1** *courts are obliged to act in accordance with the strict rules of the law | he was obliged to resign* **require**, compel, bind, make, constrain, obligate, force, put under an obligation, leave someone no option, impel, coerce, pressure, pressurize.
2 *will you oblige me by filling in this form?* **do someone a favour**, do someone a kindness, do someone a service, accommodate, indulge, gratify, gratify the wishes of, help, assist, serve, humour, meet the wants/needs of, put oneself out for; be kind enough to.

> **CHOOSE THE RIGHT WORD**
> **oblige, compel, force, coerce**
> *See* COMPEL.

obliged ▸ adjective *if you should hear from her I'd be obliged if you'd let me know* **thankful**, grateful, appreciative; **beholden**, indebted, in someone's debt, under an obligation, obligated.
□ **much obliged thank you**, thanks, many thanks, thanks a lot, thanks very much, thank you kindly; *informal* cheers, thanks a million; *Brit. informal* ta.

obliging ▸ adjective *Roger was a cheerful, obliging sort of chap* **helpful**, eager to help/please, accommodating, willing, cooperative, considerate, complaisant, agreeable, amenable, generous, friendly, kind, neighbourly, hospitable, pleasant, good-natured, amiable, gracious, unselfish, civil, courteous, polite, indulgent, benevolent; *Brit. informal* decent.
OPPOSITES disobliging, obstructive, unhelpful, uncooperative.

oblique ▸ adjective **1** *an oblique line* **slanting**, slanted, sloping, at an angle, angled, diagonal, aslant, slant, slantwise, sloped, inclined, inclining, tilted, tilting, atilt, skew, on the skew, askew; *Scottish* squint; *N. Amer.* cater-cornered, catty-cornered, kitty-corner.
OPPOSITE straight.
2 *an oblique reference to the president* **indirect**, inexplicit, roundabout, circuitous, circumlocutory, implicit, implied, elliptical, evasive, backhanded; *rare* circumlocutionary, ambagious.
OPPOSITES direct, explicit.
3 *he cast her an oblique glance* **sidelong**, sideways, furtive, covert, sly, surreptitious.
▸ noun slash, solidus, oblique line/stroke, backslash, diagonal, virgule, slant.

obliquely ▸ adverb **1** *the morning sun shone obliquely across the tower* **diagonally**, at an angle, slantwise, sideways, sidelong, aslant, athwart; *literary* aslope.
2 *he referred obliquely to the war as 'an unfortunate period'* **indirectly**, in a roundabout way, circuitously, evasively, not in so many words, not outright.
OPPOSITE directly.

obliterate ▸ verb **1** *the memory was so painful that he obliterated it from his mind* **erase**, eradicate, expunge, efface, blot out, rub out, wipe out, remove all traces of, blank out, block out, delete, strike out, cancel, cross out, ink out, score out.
2 *a nuclear explosion that would obliterate a city* **destroy**, wipe out, annihilate, exterminate, extirpate, demolish, eliminate, eradicate, kill, decimate, liquidate, wipe off the face of the earth, wipe off the map; *informal* zap.
OPPOSITES create, establish.

obliteration ▸ noun **1** *the complete and intentional obliteration of a will or any part of it* **eradication**, erasing, erasure, effacing, rubbing out, blotting out, wiping out, removal, expunging, effacement, blanking out, blocking out, deletion, striking out, cancellation, crossing out, inking out, scoring out; *rare* expunction, expungement.
2 *pressure from environmentalists has saved one of the country's national parks from obliteration* **destruction**, wiping out, annihilation, extermination, extirpation, elimination, eradication, killing, decimation, liquidation,

O

demolition; *informal* zapping.

oblivion ▶ noun **1** *he closed his eyes again and sank back into oblivion* **unconsciousness, insensibility**, stupor, stupefaction, senselessness, blankness, darkness; coma, blackout; obliviousness, unawareness, ignorance, amnesia; *literary* the waters of Lethe.
OPPOSITES consciousness, awareness.
2 *their words have been consigned to oblivion | they rescued him from artistic oblivion* **obscurity**, non-existence, limbo, void, vacuum, nothingness, nihility, nullity, extinction, anonymity, neglect, disregard.
OPPOSITE fame.

oblivious ▶ adjective *they were clearly oblivious to the danger | she was totally oblivious of her surroundings* **unaware**, unconscious, heedless, unmindful, insensible, unheeding, ignorant, blind, deaf, unsuspecting, unobservant, disregardful, unconcerned, impervious, unaffected, insensitive, indifferent, detached, removed; *rare* incognizant.
OPPOSITES aware, conscious.

obloquy ▶ noun **1** *he endured years of contempt and obloquy* **vilification**, opprobrium, vituperation, condemnation, castigation, denunciation, abuse, criticism, censure, flak, defamation, denigration, disparagement, derogation, slander, revilement, reviling, calumny, calumniation, execration, excoriation, lambasting, upbraiding, bad press, character assassination, attack, invective, libel, insults, aspersions; *informal* mud-slinging, bad-mouthing, tongue-lashing; *Brit. informal* stick, verbal, slagging off; *archaic* contumely; *rare* animadversion, objurgation.
OPPOSITE praise.
2 *conduct to which no moral obloquy could reasonably attach* **disgrace**, dishonour, shame, discredit, stigma, humiliation, loss of face, ignominy, odium, opprobrium, disfavour, disrepute, ill repute, infamy, notoriety, scandal, stain; *rare* disesteem.
OPPOSITE honour.

obnoxious ▶ adjective *a thoroughly obnoxious man | the smell was particularly obnoxious* **unpleasant**, disagreeable, nasty, distasteful, offensive, objectionable, unsavoury, unpalatable, dislikeable, off-putting, awful, terrible, dreadful, frightful, revolting, repulsive, repellent, repugnant, disgusting, odious, vile, foul, abhorrent, loathsome, nauseating, nauseous, sickening, hateful, detestable, execrable, abominable, insufferable, intolerable, unacceptable, despicable, contemptible, beyond the pale, poisonous, noxious, obscene, base, hideous, scabrous; *informal* ghastly, horrible, horrid, gruesome, gross, putrid, sick-making, yucky, God-awful; *Brit. informal* beastly; *N. Amer. informal* skanky; *literary* noisome; *archaic* disgustful, loathly.
OPPOSITES delightful, pleasant, charming.

obscene ▶ adjective **1** *obscene literature | obscene jokes* **pornographic, indecent**, salacious, smutty, X-rated, lewd, rude, dirty, filthy, vulgar, foul, coarse, crude, gross, vile, nasty, disgusting, offensive, shameless, immoral, improper, immodest, impure, indecorous, indelicate, unwholesome, scabrous, off colour, lubricious, risqué, ribald, bawdy, suggestive, titillating, racy, erotic, carnal, sensual, sexy, lascivious, lecherous, licentious, libidinous, goatish, degenerate, depraved, amoral, debauched, dissolute, prurient; scatological, profane; *informal* blue, porn, porno, raunchy, sick; *Brit. informal* near the knuckle, fruity, saucy; *euphemistic* adult; *rare* ithyphallic, Fescennine, Cyprian.
OPPOSITES pure, decent.
2 *it was the most obscene crime he had ever encountered* **shocking**, scandalous, vile, foul, atrocious, outrageous, heinous, wicked, evil, odious, abhorrent, abominable, disgusting, hideous, repugnant, repulsive, revolting, repellent, obnoxious, offensive, objectionable, loathsome, hateful, nauseating, sickening, awful, dreadful, terrible, frightful, ghastly; *archaic* disgustful, loathly.

obscenity ▶ noun **1** *the book was banned on the grounds of obscenity* **indecency**, immorality, impropriety, salaciousness, smuttiness, smut, lewdness, rudeness, vulgarity, dirtiness, dirt, filthiness, filth, foulness, coarseness, crudeness, grossness, vileness, nastiness, impurity, immodesty, indelicacy, indecorousness, unwholesomeness, scabrousness, ribaldry, bawdiness, suggestiveness, eroticism, carnality, lasciviousness, lechery, licentiousness, libidinousness, degeneracy, depravity, amorality, debauchery, dissoluteness, prurience; scatology, profanity, profaneness; *rare* bawdry, salacity, lubricity.
2 *he spoke of the 'murderous obscenities' of the terrorists* **atrocity**, act of brutality, act of savagery, evil, crime, outrage, offence, abomination, enormity.
3 *the men scowled and muttered obscenities* **curse**, oath, swear word, expletive, profanity, four-letter word, dirty word, blasphemy, imprecation, malediction, vulgarism, vulgarity; swearing, bad/foul language, strong language; *informal* cuss, cuss word.

obscure ▶ adjective **1** *he was born about 1650 though his origins and parentage remain obscure* **unclear**, uncertain, unknown, in doubt, doubtful, dubious, mysterious, hazy, vague, indeterminate, concealed, hidden.
2 *obscure references to Proust* **abstruse**, recondite, arcane, esoteric, recherché, occult; enigmatic, mystifying, puzzling, perplexing, baffling, ambiguous, cryptic, equivocal, Delphic, oracular, riddling, oblique, opaque, elliptical, unintelligible, uninterpretable, incomprehensible, impenetrable, unfathomable, inexplicable; unexplained; *informal* as clear as mud.
OPPOSITES clear, plain.
3 *an obscure Peruvian painter* **little known**, unknown, unheard of, undistinguished, insignificant, unimportant, inconsequential, inconspicuous, unnoticed, nameless, anonymous, minor, humble, lowly, unrenowned, unsung, unrecognized, unhonoured, inglorious, forgotten.
OPPOSITES famous, renowned.
4 *grey and obscure on the horizon rose a low island | the far end of the room was obscure* **indistinct**, faint, vague, ill-defined, unclear, blurred, blurry, misty, hazy, foggy, veiled, cloudy, clouded, nebulous, fuzzy; dark, dim, unlit, black, murky, sombre, gloomy, shady, shadowy; *literary* dusky, tenebrous, darkling, crepuscular; *rare* caliginous, Cimmerian.
OPPOSITE distinct.
▶ verb **1** *grey clouds obscured the sun* **hide**, conceal, cover, veil, shroud, screen, mask, cloak, cast a shadow over, shadow, envelop, mantle, block, block out, blank out, obliterate, eclipse, overshadow; *literary* enshroud, bedim, benight; *rare* obnubilate, adumbrate.
OPPOSITE reveal.
2 *recent events have obscured rather than illuminated the issue* **confuse**, complicate, obfuscate, cloud, blur, muddy; muddy the waters; *literary* becloud, befog.
OPPOSITES clarify, illuminate.

CHOOSE THE RIGHT WORD

obscure, abstruse, recondite, esoteric, arcane

- **Obscure** is a general term for something that is difficult to understand (*causation of much mental handicap is obscure | some obscure, niggling, unexplained bitterness*), or, more critically, it can refer to something that is not sufficiently clearly expressed (*the legislation is ambiguous or obscure*).
- **Abstruse** means much the same but is a more literary word (*maths is a mix of abstruse theory and detailed calculation | the extreme snobbery of this abstruse observation*).
- **Recondite**, an even more literary word, denotes topics that are not known, let alone understood, by more than a few experts and are therefore so obscure that they are beyond criticism (*recondite though her theme may be, she demonstrates that it is not without relevance*).
- **Esoteric** is used for subjects and activities that are intended for, or likely to be understood by, only a few people, who, it is sometimes implied, are therefore to be looked up to (*the esoteric world of technical and scientific supercomputing | Acanthus spinosus is so classy-looking as to be favoured by plantsmen with the most esoteric tastes*).
- **Arcane** also means 'understood by few people' but often has an added air of mystery (*the arcane language of philosophical hermeneutics | he had drawn several arcane symbols round the boundary of the circle*).

obscurity ▶ noun **1** *he brought the club back to the big time after years of obscurity* **insignificance**, inconspicuousness, unimportance, anonymity, lack of fame/renown/honour/recognition, non-recognition, ingloriousness, limbo, twilight, oblivion.
OPPOSITE fame.
2 *poems of impenetrable obscurity* **incomprehensibility**, impenetrability, unintelligibility, obscureness, complexity, intricacy, opacity, opaqueness, unclearness; abstruseness, reconditeness, arcaneness, deepness, esotericism.
OPPOSITE clarity.
3 *the obscurities in his poems and plays* **enigma**, puzzle, mystery, difficulty, problem, complication, intricacy, ambiguity; crux.
4 *the brightness of the light on stage left the recesses of the wings in obscurity* **darkness**, blackness, dimness, gloom, gloominess, murk, murkiness, shadow, shadowiness; *rare* tenebrosity.

obsequies ▶ plural noun **funeral rites**, funeral service, funeral, burial ceremony/service, burial; interment, entombment, inhumation, last offices; *formal* exequies; *archaic* sepulture.

obsequious ▶ adjective *an obsequious manservant welcomed them* **servile**, ingratiating, unctuous, sycophantic, fawning, toadying, oily, oleaginous, greasy, grovelling, cringing, toadyish, sycophantish, subservient, submissive, slavish, abject, Uriah Heepish; *informal* slimy, bootlicking, smarmy, sucky, soapy; *N. Amer. informal* brown-nosing; *Brit. vulgar slang* arse-licking, bum-sucking; *N. Amer. vulgar slang* kiss-ass, ass-kissing.
OPPOSITE domineering.

observable ▶ adjective *this kind of behaviour is readily observable in all wild and domestic creatures* **noticeable**, visible, perceptible, perceivable, detectable, discernible, recognizable, obvious, evident, manifest, patent, clear, distinct, plain, overt, conspicuous, palpable, distinguishable, unmistakable, unconcealed, apparent; *archaic* sensible.
OPPOSITE hidden.

observance ▶ noun **1** *strict observance of the rules* **compliance with**,

O

adherence to, conformity to, obedience to, acquiescence in, accordance with, respect for; keeping, obeying, observation, fulfilment of, following, performance, honouring, heeding; *archaic* abidance by.
OPPOSITE disregard.
2 *religious observances* **rite**, ritual, ceremony, ceremonial, celebration, practice, service, office, festival, tradition, custom, convention, usage, habit, formality, form; *formal* praxis.
3 *her baby's motionless observance of me* **scrutiny**, observation, examination, inspection, watching, viewing, eyeing, looking.

observant ▸ **adjective 1** *lifeguards should be observant and stop risky situations before they start* **alert**, sharp-eyed, sharp, eagle-eyed, hawk-eyed, with eyes like a hawk, keen-eyed, watchful, on the lookout, on the qui vive, on guard, attentive, vigilant, with one's eyes open/peeled/skinned, awake, heedful, mindful, aware; *informal* beady-eyed, not missing a trick, on the ball; *rare* regardful.
OPPOSITES inattentive, dreamy.
2 *an observant Jew* **practising**, obedient, dutiful, conformist, conforming; committed, devout, orthodox, law-abiding.

observation ▸ **noun 1** *she was brought into hospital for observation | detailed observation of the animal's behaviour* **watching**, **monitoring**, scrutiny, examination, inspection, scrutinization, viewing, survey, surveillance, surveying, attention, consideration, study, review.
2 *his observations were concise and to the point | record all your observations carefully* **remark**, comment, statement, utterance, pronouncement, declaration; **opinion**, impression, thought, feeling, reflection; finding, result; note, annotation; *Law* obiter dictum.
3 *the* **observation of** *the law* **observance**, adherence to, compliance with, keeping, conformity to, obeying, heeding, obedience to, fulfilment of, following, honouring, accordance with, respect for, acquiescence in; *archaic* abidance by.

observe ▸ **verb 1** *she observed that almost all the chairs were occupied* **notice**, see, note, perceive, discern, remark, spot, detect, discover, distinguish, make out; *literary* espy, descry, behold.
OPPOSITES overlook, fail to see.
2 *Rob stood in the hall, from where he could observe the happenings on the street* **watch**, see, look at, eye, contemplate, view, survey, regard, witness, keep an eye on, scrutinize, keep under observation, keep watch on, keep under surveillance, monitor, keep under scrutiny, watch like a hawk, keep a weather eye on, spy on, check out, reconnoitre; *informal* get a load of, keep tabs on, keep a tab on, case, keep a beady eye on; *Brit. informal* clock, take a dekko/butcher's/gander/shufti at, recce; *N. Amer. informal* eyeball; *archaic* twig; *rare* surveil.
3 *'You look tired,' she observed* **comment**, remark, say, mention, note, declare, announce, state, utter, pronounce, interpose, interject; *formal* opine.
4 *the European Council called on the parties involved to observe the ceasefire* **comply with**, abide by, keep, obey, adhere to, conform to, heed, honour, respect, be heedful of, pay attention to, follow, acquiesce in, consent to, accept, defer to, fulfil, stand by.
OPPOSITES disregard, ignore, break.
5 *relations gathered to observe the funeral rites* **participate in**, partake in, be present at, celebrate, keep; commemorate, solemnize, mark, memorialize, remember, recognize.

observer ▸ **noun spectator**, onlooker, watcher, looker-on, fly on the wall, viewer, witness, eyewitness, bystander, sightseer; commentator, reporter, blogger, monitor; *informal* rubberneck; *literary* beholder.
OPPOSITE participant.

obsess ▸ **verb** *thoughts of his own mortality obsessed him* **preoccupy**, be uppermost in someone's mind, prey on someone's mind, prey on, possess, haunt, consume, plague, torment, hound, bedevil, take control of, take over, become an obsession with, have a hold on, engross, eat up, have a grip on, grip, dominate, rule, control, beset, monopolize.
□ **be obsessed** *she's* **obsessed with** *him | he became* **obsessed by** *the urge to avenge his friend* **be fixated**, be preoccupied, be infatuated, be possessed, be haunted, be consumed, be plagued, be tormented, be bedevilled, be eaten up, be gripped, be in the grip of, be dominated, be beset; *informal* be hung up about/on, have a thing about, have something/someone on the brain, have a bee in one's bonnet; *N. Amer. informal* be hipped.

obsession ▸ **noun** *the idea grew in his mind until it became an obsession* **fixation**, ruling/consuming passion, passion, mania, idée fixe, compulsion, preoccupation, enthusiasm, infatuation, addiction, fetish, craze, hobby horse; phobia, complex, neurosis; *informal* bee in one's bonnet, hang-up, thing, bug.

obsessive ▸ **adjective** *reckless and obsessive love | an obsessive gambler* **all-consuming**, consuming, compulsive, dominating, controlling, obsessional, addictive, fanatical, fanatic, neurotic, excessive, besetting, gripping, haunting, tormenting, inescapable; *informal* pathological.

obsolescent ▸ **adjective** *industries regarded by policy makers as obsolescent* **dying out**, becoming obsolete, going out of use, going out of fashion, on the decline, declining, waning, on the wane, disappearing, past its prime, ageing, moribund, on its last legs, out of date, outdated, old-fashioned, outmoded; *informal* on the way out, past it.

obsolete ▸ **adjective** *this remarkable aircraft will render all other fighters obsolete* **out of date**, outdated, outmoded, old-fashioned; **no longer in use**, disused, fallen into disuse, superannuated, outworn, antiquated, antediluvian, anachronistic, discarded, discontinued, old, dated, antique, archaic, ancient, fossilized, extinct, defunct, dead, bygone, out of fashion, out, behind the times; *French* démodé, passé, vieux jeu; *informal* old hat, out of the ark, geriatric, prehistoric; *Brit. informal* past its sell-by date.
OPPOSITES contemporary, current, modern, new, up to date.

obstacle ▸ **noun** *lack of childcare provision was cited as a major obstacle for women who wish to participate in training initiatives* **barrier**, hurdle, stumbling block, bar, block, impediment, hindrance, snag, catch, drawback, hitch, handicap, deterrent, complication, difficulty, problem, disadvantage, baulk, curb, check, stop, interference; obstruction, barricade, blockade; *informal* fly in the ointment, hiccup, facer; *Brit. informal* spanner in the works; *N. Amer. informal* monkey wrench in the works; *dated* cumber; *literary* trammel.
OPPOSITES advantage, asset, aid.

obstinacy ▸ **noun** *Urquhart was irritated by her obstinacy* **stubbornness**, inflexibility, intransigence, intractability, intractableness, obduracy, mulishness, pig-headedness, bull-headedness, wilfulness, self-will, strong-mindedness, contrariness, perversity, perverseness, uncooperativeness, recalcitrance, refractoriness, unmanageableness, stiffness, rigidity, steeliness, implacability, relentlessness, immovability, persistence, persistency, tenacity, tenaciousness, doggedness, pertinacity, pertinaciousness, single-mindedness, firmness, steadfastness, determination; *Brit. informal* bloody-mindedness, bolshiness, stroppiness; *archaic* frowardness, contumaciousness, contumacy; *rare* induracy.

obstinate ▸ **adjective** *I don't think you'll succeed in changing his mind—he's very obstinate* **stubborn**, headstrong, wilful, unyielding, inflexible, unbending, intransigent, intractable, obdurate, mulish, stubborn as a mule, pig-headed, bull-headed, self-willed, strong-minded, strong-willed, contrary, perverse, recalcitrant, refractory, uncooperative, unmanageable, cross-grained, stiff-necked, stiff, rigid, steely, iron-willed, uncompromising, implacable, relentless, unrelenting, unpersuadable, immovable, unmalleable, unshakeable, inexorable, with one's toes/feet dug in, persistent, persevering, tenacious, pertinacious, dogged, single-minded, adamant, firm, steadfast, determined; *Brit. informal* bloody-minded, bolshie, stroppy; *N. Amer. informal* balky; *archaic* froward, contumacious; *rare* contrarious, indurate.
OPPOSITES compliant, amenable, tractable.

CHOOSE THE RIGHT WORD

obstinate, stubborn, headstrong, wilful

These words express a more or less exasperated reaction to someone's determination to have their own way in the face of persuasion or pressure to the contrary.

- Someone who is **obstinate** resolutely refuses to heed others (*he sensed obstinate refusal rather than a willingness to bargain*) or, occasionally, their own self-interest (*she went to the stake for an obstinate adherence to her views*).
- Someone who is **stubborn** is even more obstinate than someone who is *obstinate*. *Stubborn* can imply deliberate or irrational obstructiveness, rather than a mere refusal to comply with persuasion (*you're not in a fit state to drive, but I assumed you'd be stubborn about it*), or it can refer to an obstinacy that has nothing to do with volition (*he tried to make a stubborn mule climb the gangway*). *Stubbornness* can be seen as a good quality, however, or at least as doing no harm to anyone else (*I am quite ill nowadays, but just too stubborn to give up the thrill of the rallies!*).
- Whereas *obstinate* and *stubborn* imply refusal to act in accordance with the wishes of others, **headstrong** says little about others but concentrates, sometimes with grudging admiration, on the determination of the person being described, who may not be actually flouting anyone's wishes but is simply ignoring or even completely unaware of them. It is typically used of girls or young women (*how did one stop a person like Harriet, headstrong, independent, beholden to no one?*).
- Someone described as **wilful** is being condemned, often as immature, for their determination to do what they want regardless of its effects, especially on others (*she was wilful, determined, exciting, and manipulative*).

obstreperous ▸ **adjective** *obstreperous customers who have had a drop too much to drink* **unruly**, unmanageable, disorderly, undisciplined, uncontrollable, unrestrained, rowdy, uncontrolled, disruptive, truculent, difficult, refractory, rebellious, mutinous, out of hand, riotous, out of control, wild, turbulent, uproarious, tumultuous, tempestuous, unbridled, irrepressible, boisterous, roisterous, rackety; noisy, loud, clamorous, raucous, vociferous; *Brit. informal* stroppy, bolshie, rumbustious;

N. Amer. informal rambunctious; *archaic* rampageous.
OPPOSITES calm, quiet, restrained.

obstruct ▶ verb **1** *wheelchairs obstructed the aisles | ensure that air bricks and vents are not obstructed* **block**, block up, clog, clog up, get/stand in the way of, cut off, shut off, jam, bung up, gum up, choke, barricade, bar, dam up; *Brit. informal* gunge up; *dated* cumber; *technical* occlude, obturate.
OPPOSITE clear.
2 *police took him into custody on a charge of obstructing the traffic* **hold up**, bring to a standstill, stop, halt, block.
3 *environmentalists accused the government of obstructing the passage of the EC pollution laws* **impede**, hinder, interfere with, hamper, block, interrupt, hold up, hold back, stand in the way of, frustrate, thwart, baulk, inhibit, hamstring, sabotage, encumber, slow, slow down, retard, delay, stonewall, forestall, stall, arrest, check, stop, halt, stay, derail, restrict, limit, curb, put a brake on, bridle, fetter, shackle; *informal* stymie; *N. Amer. informal* bork; *rare* trammel.
OPPOSITES facilitate, help, further.

CHOOSE THE RIGHT WORD

obstruct, hinder, hamper, impede
See HINDER.

obstruction ▶ noun *the issue was the major obstruction to progress on the peace process* **obstacle**, barrier, stumbling block, hurdle, bar, block, impediment, hindrance, snag, difficulty, catch, drawback, hitch, handicap, deterrent, curb, check, stop, baulk, restriction; blockage, stoppage, congestion, bottleneck, hold-up; *Medicine* occlusion; *informal* fly in the ointment; *Brit. informal* spanner in the works; *N. Amer. informal* monkey wrench in the works; *dated* cumber.

obstructive ▶ adjective *you're being deliberately obstructive!* **making difficulties, unhelpful**, uncooperative, awkward, difficult, unaccommodating, disobliging, unconstructive, perverse, contrary; *Scottish* thrawn; *Brit. informal* bloody-minded, bolshie; *N. Amer. informal* balky; *archaic* froward, contrarious.
OPPOSITES helpful, supportive, cooperative.

obtain ▶ verb **1** *the newspaper obtained a copy of the letter* **get**, acquire, come by, secure, procure, come into the possession of, pick up, be given; gain, derive, earn, achieve, attain, win, draw, reap; buy, purchase; *informal* get/lay hold of, get/lay one's hands on, get one's mitts on, grab, bag, land, net; *Brit. informal* blag; *S. African informal* schlenter.
OPPOSITES lose, relinquish.
2 *the rules obtaining in other jurisdictions* **prevail**, be in force, apply, exist, be in use, be established, be customary, be effective, be prevalent, stand, hold, be the case.

obtainable ▶ adjective *frozen food is acceptable if fresh vegetables or meat are not obtainable* **available**, to be had, in circulation, on the market, on offer, in season, at one's disposal, at hand, gettable, procurable, securable, acquirable, realizable, accessible, achievable, attainable, ready; *informal* up for grabs, on a plate, on tap, get-at-able.

obtrusive ▶ adjective *the proposed quarry would be very obtrusive* **conspicuous**, prominent, noticeable, obvious, pronounced, unmistakable, inescapable; out of place, intrusive; thrusting, protruding, protuberant, sticking out; bold, loud, showy, garish, gaudy, lurid, flashy; *informal* standing/sticking out a mile, standing/sticking out like a sore thumb.
OPPOSITES unobtrusive, inconspicuous.

obtuse ▶ adjective *I wondered if he was too obtuse to pick up what I was driving at* **stupid**, dull, slow-witted, slow, dull-witted, unintelligent, witless, half-baked, half-witted, doltish, lumpish, blockish, imperceptive; uncomprehending, bovine, stolid, crass, insensitive, thick-skinned; *informal* dim, dense, thick, thickheaded, dim-witted, slow on the uptake, dumb, dopey, dead from the neck up, boneheaded, blockheaded, lamebrained, chuckleheaded, dunderheaded, wooden-headed, pig-ignorant, log-headed, muttonheaded; *Brit. informal* divvy, dozy; *Scottish & N. English informal* glaikit; *N. Amer. informal* dumb-ass, chowderheaded; *S. African informal* dof; *W. Indian informal* dotish; *rare* hebete.
OPPOSITES clever, astute, shrewd, bright.

obviate ▶ verb *the settlement obviated the need for the separate cases to be heard in court* **preclude**, prevent, remove, get rid of, do away with, get round, rule out, eliminate, make unnecessary, take away, foreclose, avoid, avert, counter.

obvious ▶ adjective *the reason was blindingly obvious | it's obvious that Bob's keen on her* **clear**, plain, plain to see, crystal clear, evident, apparent, manifest, patent, conspicuous, pronounced, transparent, clear-cut, palpable, prominent, marked, decided, salient, striking, distinct, bold, noticeable, perceptible, perceivable, visible, discernible, detectable, observable, tangible, recognizable; unmistakable, indisputable, self-evident, incontrovertible, incontestable, axiomatic, demonstrable, undeniable, as plain as a pikestaff, staring someone in the face, writ large, beyond doubt, beyond question, written all over one, as clear as day, blinding, inescapable; overt, open, undisguised, unconcealed, frank, glaring, blatant, flagrant; *informal* as plain as the nose on one's face, standing/sticking out like a sore thumb, standing/sticking out a mile, right under one's nose.
OPPOSITES imperceptible, inconspicuous, obscure.

obviously ▶ adverb *obviously, she didn't want to see you | he was obviously in great pain* **clearly**, evidently, plainly, patently, visibly, discernibly, manifestly, noticeably; unmistakably, undeniably, indubitably, incontrovertibly, demonstrably, unquestionably, undoubtedly, without doubt; of course, naturally, needless to say, it goes without saying, doubtless.
OPPOSITE perhaps.

occasion ▶ noun **1** *she consulted him on a number of occasions* **instance**, time, moment, juncture, point; event, happening, occurrence, affair, incident, episode, experience, situation, case, circumstance.
2 *the perfect venue for a special occasion | family occasions such as weddings* **social event**, event, affair, function, celebration, party, ceremony, get-together, gathering; *informal* do, bash; *Brit. informal* rave-up, thrash, knees-up, jolly, beanfeast, bunfight, beano, lig.
3 *I doubt if the occasion will arise* **opportunity**, suitable/opportune time, right moment, chance, opening, window.
4 *it's the first time I've had occasion to complain* **reason**, cause, call, grounds, justification, need, necessity, requirement, excuse, pretext, stimulus, inducement, provocation, motive.
▶ verb *her situation occasioned a good deal of sympathy* **cause**, give rise to, bring about, result in, lead to, prompt, provoke, evoke, elicit, call forth, produce, create, arouse, make (for), generate, engender, originate, effect, bring on, induce, precipitate, stir up, inspire, spark off, trigger, breed; *literary* beget; *rare* effectuate.
□ **on occasion**. *See* OCCASIONALLY.

occasional ▶ adjective *there was very little chance of her returning to the village, except for occasional visits* **infrequent**, intermittent, irregular, periodic, sporadic, odd, random, casual, desultory, incidental, uncommon, episodic, few and far between, fitful, spasmodic, isolated, rare; *N. Amer.* sometime; *dated* seldom.
OPPOSITES regular, frequent.

occasionally ▶ adverb *he's got a flat in London now, though he still comes home occasionally* **sometimes**, from time to time, (every) now and then, (every) now and again, at times, every so often, (every) once in a while, on occasion, on occasions, on the odd occasion, periodically, at intervals, irregularly, sporadically, spasmodically, infrequently, intermittently, on and off, off and on; *archaic* ever and anon.
OPPOSITES often, frequently.

occlude ▶ verb *thick make-up can occlude the pores* **block**, block up, stop, stop up, obstruct, clog, clog up, close, shut, fill, bung up, choke, seal, plug.

occlusion ▶ noun *the occlusion of a major coronary artery* **blockage**, obstruction, obstructing, blocking (up), closing (up), closure.

occult ▶ noun (**the occult**) *his sister was a spiritualist with a strong interest in the occult* **the supernatural**, the paranormal, supernaturalism, magic, black magic, witchcraft, sorcery, necromancy, wizardry, the black arts, Kabbalah, cabbalism, occultism, diabolism, devil worship, devilry, voodoo, hoodoo, white magic, witchery, witching, orenda, mysticism; *NZ* makutu; *rare* theurgy.
▶ adjective *occult powers | an occult ceremony* **supernatural**, magic, magical, mystical, mystic, paranormal, psychic, necromantic, preternatural, transcendental; secret, hidden, dark, concealed, veiled, invisible, obscure, recondite, cryptic, arcane, abstruse, esoteric, cabbalistic; inexplicable, unexplainable, unfathomable, incomprehensible, impenetrable, unrevealed, puzzling, perplexing, mystifying, mysterious, enigmatic, hermetic.

occupancy ▶ noun *rents paid by individuals are directly related to their occupancy of council houses* **occupation**, tenancy, tenure, residence, residency, inhabitation, habitation, lease, possession, holding, owner-occupancy, multi-occupancy, use, term; *formal* dwelling; *rare* inhabitancy, habitancy, inhabitance, domiciliation.

occupant ▶ noun **resident**, inhabitant, owner, householder, tenant, renter, leaseholder, lessee, lodger, boarder, inmate, user; addressee; incumbent, holder; *Brit.* occupier, owner-occupier; *N. Amer.* roomer; *formal* dweller; *humorous* denizen; *rare* indweller.

occupation ▶ noun **1** *his father's name and occupation are unknown* **job**, profession, work, line of work, line of business, trade, employment, position, post, situation, business, career, métier, vocation, calling, craft, skill, field, province, walk of life; *Scottish* way; *informal* racket, game; *Austral. informal* grip; *archaic* employ.
2 *among her leisure occupations is birdwatching* **pastime**, activity, leisure activity, hobby, pursuit, interest, entertainment, recreation, diversion, amusement, divertissement; *archaic* resource.

3 *a property suitable for occupation by older people* **residence**, residency, habitation, inhabitation, occupancy, tenancy, tenure, lease, living in; possession, use; incumbency, holding; *formal* dwelling; *rare* inhabitancy, habitancy, inhabitance, domiciliation.
4 *the Roman occupation of Britain* **conquest**, capture, invasion, seizure, takeover, annexation, overrunning, subjugation, subjection, appropriation; **colonization**, possession, rule, control, suzerainty.

occupational ▶ adjective *the project aims to expand girls' occupational horizons | occupational pensions* **job-related**, work, professional, vocational, employment, business, career.

occupied ▶ adjective **1** *a steady stream of clients kept her occupied until the middle of the afternoon* **busy**, engaged, working, employed, at work, on the job, hard-pressed, active; absorbed, engrossed, interested, involved, immersed, preoccupied; *informal* tied up, hard at it, wrapped up, on the go, on the trot; *Brit. informal* on the hop.
2 *all the tables were occupied* **in use**, full, engaged, taken, unavailable.
3 *only two of the flats are occupied* **inhabited**, lived-in, tenanted, settled.
OPPOSITES free, idle, vacant, empty.

> CHOOSE THE RIGHT WORD
> **occupied, busy, engaged, active**
> *See* BUSY.

occupy ▶ verb **1** *Carol occupied the basement flat* **live in**, inhabit, be the tenant of, tenant, lodge in, be established/ensconced in, establish/ensconce oneself in, take up residence in, make one's home in, settle in, move into; people, populate, settle; *Scottish & S. African* stay in; *formal* reside in, dwell in.
2 *two long windows occupied almost the whole of the end wall* **take up**, fill, fill up, cover, extend over, use up, utilize.
3 *he occupies a senior post at the Treasury* **hold**, be in, fill, have; *informal* hold down.
4 *I need something to occupy my mind* **engage**, busy, employ, distract, absorb, engross, preoccupy, hold, hold the attention of, immerse, interest, involve, entertain, divert, amuse, beguile.
5 *the region was occupied by Soviet troops* **capture**, seize, take possession of, conquer, invade, overrun, take over, colonize, garrison, annex, dominate, subjugate, hold, commandeer, requisition.
OPPOSITES leave, abandon, quit.

occur ▶ verb **1** *the accident occurred at about 3.30 p.m* **happen**, take place, come about, transpire, materialize, chance, arise, crop up, turn out, fall, come, fall out, pass off; *N. Amer. informal* go down; *literary* come to pass, befall, betide; *archaic* hap; *rare* eventuate.
2 *the disease occurs chiefly in tropical climates* **be found**, be present, exist, be met with, appear, prevail, present itself, show itself, manifest itself, turn up; *formal* obtain.
3 *an idea occurred to her | didn't it occur to you that I might have made other arrangements?* **enter one's head/mind**, cross one's mind, come to mind, spring to mind, come to one, strike one, hit one, dawn on one, suggest itself, present itself, come into one's consciousness.

O

occurrence ▶ noun **1** *vandalism used to be a rare occurrence* **event**, incident, happening, phenomenon, affair, matter, experience, circumstance, development, contingency, eventuality.
2 *the occurrence of cancer increases with age* **existence**, instance, appearance, manifestation, materialization, development, springing up; frequency, incidence, rate, prevalence; *Statistics* distribution.

ocean ▶ noun **1 (the) sea**; *informal* the drink; *Brit. informal* the briny; *N. Amer. informal* salt chuck; *literary* the deep, the waves, the main, the foam, the profound; *NZ* moana.
2 *she had oceans of energy* **a lot**, a great/large amount, a great/good deal, plenty, quantities, an abundance, a profusion; *informal* lots, loads, heaps, bags, masses, stacks, oodles, tons, scads; *Brit. informal* lashings, a shedload; *N. Amer. informal* gobs; *Austral./NZ informal* a swag; *vulgar slang* a shitload.
WORD LINKS
relating to the ocean **oceanic, marine, maritime, pelagic, thalassic**

October ▶ noun
WORD LINKS
birthstone **opal**

odd ▶ adjective **1** *the neighbours thought him very odd* **strange**, peculiar, weird, queer, funny, bizarre, eccentric, unusual, abnormal, idiosyncratic, unconventional, outlandish, offbeat, freakish, quirky, quaint, zany, off-centre; *informal* wacky, freaky, kooky, screwy, kinky, oddball, cranky; *N. Amer. informal* off the wall, wacko, bizarro; *Austral./NZ informal, dated* dilly.
OPPOSITES normal, conventional.
2 *quite a few odd things had happened in the last two days* **strange**, unusual, peculiar, funny, curious, bizarre, weird, uncanny, queer, unexpected, unfamiliar, abnormal, atypical, anomalous, untypical, different, out of the ordinary, out of the way, foreign, exceptional, rare, extraordinary, remarkable, puzzling, mystifying, mysterious, perplexing, baffling, unaccountable, incongruous, uncommon, irregular, singular, deviant, aberrant, freak, freakish; suspicious, dubious, questionable; eerie, unnatural; *Scottish* unco; *French* outré; *informal* fishy, creepy, spooky; *Brit. informal* rum.
OPPOSITES ordinary, usual.
3 *odd numbers* **uneven**, not divisible by two.
4 *we have the odd drink together | he does odd jobs for friends* **occasional**, casual, irregular, isolated, incidental, random, sporadic, seasonal, periodic, part-time; miscellaneous, various, varied, sundry.
OPPOSITE regular.
5 *when you've got an odd five minutes, could I have a word* **spare**, unoccupied, free, not committed, available; between engagements, between appointments.
6 *he's wearing odd shoes* **mismatched**, unmatched, unpaired; single, lone, solitary, extra, surplus, leftover, remaining, unused; *Scottish* orra.
□ **odd man out outsider**, exception, oddity, nonconformist, maverick, individualist, misfit, eccentric, fish out of water, square peg in a round hole, round peg in a square hole; *informal* freak.

> CHOOSE THE RIGHT WORD
> **odd, strange, curious, peculiar**
> *See* STRANGE.

oddity ▶ noun **1** *she was regarded as a bit of an oddity* **eccentric**, crank, misfit, fish out of water, square peg in a round hole, round peg in a square hole, maverick, nonconformist, original, rare bird; *Latin* rara avis; *informal* character, odd/queer fish, oddball, weirdo, weirdie, crackpot, nut, nutter, freak; *Brit. informal* odd bod, oner; *N. Amer. informal* screwball, kook, nutso, wacko, wack; *informal, dated* case.
OPPOSITE conformist.
2 *his most influential work remains an oddity in some respects* **anomaly**, aberration, curiosity, rarity.
3 *he was struck by the oddity of the collection* **strangeness**, peculiarity, oddness, curiousness, weirdness, bizarreness, abnormality, unusualness, eccentricity, queerness, freakishness, unnaturalness, incongruity, incongruousness, outlandishness, extraordinariness, unconventionality, singularity, individuality, anomalousness; *informal* wackiness, kookiness.
4 *the oddities of human nature* **peculiarity**, idiosyncrasy, eccentricity, quirk, irregularity, twist, kink, crotchet, mannerism.

oddments ▶ plural noun **1** *oddments of material* **scraps**, remnants, odds and ends, bits, pieces, bits and pieces, bits and bobs, leftovers, fragments, snippets, offcuts, ends, shreds, slivers, stubs, tail ends; *Brit. informal* fag ends.
2 *the cellar was full of oddments he couldn't bring himself to part with* **odds and ends**, bits and pieces, bits and bobs, stuff, paraphernalia, things, miscellanea, bric-a-brac, sundries, knick-knacks, souvenirs, keepsakes, mementoes, lumber, flotsam and jetsam; *informal* junk; *Brit. informal* odds and sods, gubbins, clobber; *vulgar slang* crap, shit; *archaic* rummage, truck; *rare* knick-knackery.

odds ▶ plural noun **1** *the odds are that he is no longer alive* **likelihood**, probability, chances, chance, balance.
2 *the odds are in our favour* **advantage**, lead, edge, superiority, supremacy, ascendancy.
□ **at odds 1** *he found himself at odds with his colleagues* **in conflict**, in disagreement, on bad terms, at cross purposes, at loggerheads, quarrelling, arguing, clashing, at daggers drawn, at each other's throats, at outs, estranged; *N. Amer.* on the outs.
2 *his behaviour is at odds with the interests of the company* **at variance**, not in keeping, out of keeping, out of line, out of step, in opposition, conflicting, clashing, disagreeing, differing, contrary, incompatible, contradictory, inconsistent, irreconcilable, incongruous, discrepant.
□ **odds and ends bits and pieces**, bits and bobs, bits, pieces, stuff, paraphernalia, things; **sundries**, miscellanea, bric-a-brac, knick-knacks, oddments, fragments, remnants, scraps, offcuts, cuttings, snippets, leftovers, leavings, remains, flotsam and jetsam, debris, detritus, rubbish, litter; *informal* junk; *Brit. informal* odds and sods, clobber, gubbins; *vulgar slang* shit, crap; *archaic* rummage, truck; *rare* knick-knackery.

odious ▶ adjective *the odious methods they had used to suppress dissent* **revolting**, repulsive, repellent, repugnant, disgusting, offensive, objectionable, vile, foul, abhorrent, loathsome, nauseating, nauseous, sickening, hateful, detestable, execrable, abominable, monstrous, appalling, reprehensible, deplorable, insufferable, intolerable, unacceptable, despicable, contemptible, beyond the pale, unspeakable, poisonous, noxious, obscene, base, hideous, grisly, gruesome, horrendous, heinous, atrocious, awful, terrible, dreadful, frightful, obnoxious, unsavoury, unpalatable, unpleasant, disagreeable, nasty, distasteful, dislikeable, off-putting, displeasing; *informal* ghastly, horrible, horrid, gross, putrid, sick-making, yucky, God-awful; *Brit. informal* beastly; *N. Amer. informal* skanky; *literary* noisome; *archaic* disgustful, scurvy, loathly.
OPPOSITES delightful, pleasant, agreeable, charming.

odium ▶ noun *his job had made him the target of public hostility and odium*

disgust, abhorrence, repugnance, revulsion, repulsion, loathing, detestation, hatred, hate, execration, obloquy, dislike, disapproval, disapprobation, distaste, disfavour, aversion, antipathy, animosity, animus, enmity, hostility, contempt, censure, condemnation; disgrace, shame, opprobrium, discredit, dishonour, disrepute, ill repute, infamy, notoriety, ignominy, stigma, loss of face, humiliation, unpopularity; *rare* disesteem, reprobation.
OPPOSITES approval, delight.

odorous ▸ adjective **1** *odorous fumes* **foul-smelling**, evil-smelling, smelly, stinking, reeking, reeky, malodorous, pungent, acrid, fetid, rank; *informal* stinky; *Brit. informal* pongy, whiffy, niffy, niffing; *N. Amer. informal* funky; *literary* noisome, mephitic; *rare* olid, odoriferous, miasmal, miasmic.
2 *an odorous cloud of damp talcum powder* **fragrant**, scented, perfumed, aromatic, balmy, tangy, redolent.

odour ▸ noun **1** *a delicious odour of coffee | the odour of sweat* **smell**, scent, aroma, perfume, fragrance, bouquet, savour, nose, tang, essence, redolence; stench, stink, reek, fetor, malodour, miasma; *Brit. informal* pong, whiff, niff, hum; *Scottish informal* guff; *N. Amer. informal* funk; *rare* mephitis.
2 *an odour of suspicion* **atmosphere**, air, aura, quality, spirit, flavour, savour, emanation, hint, suggestion, impression, whiff, ambience, tone.

WORD LINKS
relating to odour **osmic, olfactory**
measurement of intensity of odour **odorimetry**

odourless ▸ adjective *a clear, odourless gel* **unscented**, unperfumed, inodorous, deodorized, fragrance-free.

odyssey ▸ noun **journey**, voyage, trek, travels, quest, crusade, pilgrimage, wandering, journeying; *rare* peregrination.

off ▸ adverb **1** *the youths scrambled out of the car and ran off* **away**, to a distance, from here, from there.
2 *David took a day off* **away**, absent, out, unavailable, not working, not at work, off duty, on holiday, on leave, free, at leisure, idle; *N. Amer.* on vacation.
▸ adjective **1** *strawberries are off* **unavailable**, unobtainable, finished, sold out.
OPPOSITE available.
2 *due to a waterlogged pitch, the game was off* **cancelled**, postponed, called off, abandoned, shelved.
OPPOSITE on.
3 *the fish/milk is off* **rotten**, bad, stale, mouldy, high, sour, rancid, turned, spoiled, putrid, putrescent.
OPPOSITE fresh.
4 (*Brit.*) *I felt decidedly off.* See OFF COLOUR.
5 (*informal*) *his boss deducted the money from his pay, which was a bit off* **unfair**, unjust, uncalled for, below the belt, unacceptable, unjustified, unjustifiable, unreasonable, unsatisfactory, unwarranted, unnecessary, inequitable; *informal* a bit much; *Brit. informal* out of order, a bit thick; *Austral./NZ informal* over the fence.
OPPOSITES fair, reasonable.
6 (*informal*) *he was being really off with me* **unfriendly**, aloof, cool, cold, distant, chilly, frosty, hostile, frigid, unresponsive, unapproachable, uncommunicative; *informal* stand-offish, offish.
OPPOSITE friendly.
□ **off and on** *the book he has been working at, off and on, for over 20 years* **periodically**, at intervals, on and off, (every) once in a while, every so often, (every) now and then/again, from time to time, occasionally, on occasion, on occasions, on the odd occasion, at times, sometimes, sporadically, spasmodically, erratically, irregularly, intermittently, in/by fits and starts, fitfully, discontinuously, piecemeal; interruptedly.
OPPOSITE regularly.

offbeat ▸ adjective *the suggestion was a little offbeat but he agreed to put it to his bosses for consideration* **unconventional**, unorthodox, unusual, eccentric, outré, idiosyncratic, strange, bizarre, weird, peculiar, odd, freakish, outlandish, out of the ordinary, Bohemian, alternative, left-field, hippy, zany, quirky; avant-garde, novel, innovative; *informal* wacky, freaky, kinky, way-out, far out, kooky, oddball; *N. Amer. informal* off the wall, bizarro.
OPPOSITES ordinary, conventional, run-of-the-mill.

off colour ▸ adjective **1** (*Brit.*) *I'm feeling a bit off colour* **unwell**, ill, poorly, bad, out of sorts, indisposed, not oneself, sick, queasy, nauseous, nauseated, peaky, liverish, green about the gills, run down, washed out; *Brit.* off; *informal* under the weather, below par, not up to par, funny, peculiar, rough, lousy, rotten, awful, terrible, dreadful, crummy; *Brit. informal* grotty, ropy; *Scottish informal* wabbit, peely-wally; *Austral./NZ informal* crook; *dated* seedy.
OPPOSITES well, fit.
2 *off-colour jokes* **smutty**, dirty, rude, filthy, crude, suggestive, indecent, indelicate, indecorous, risqué, racy, bawdy, naughty, spicy, blue, vulgar, ribald, broad, salacious, coarse, obscene, pornographic; *informal* raunchy; *Brit. informal* fruity, near the knuckle, saucy; *euphemistic* adult.

offence ▸ noun **1** *he denied having committed any offence* **crime**, illegal/unlawful act, misdemeanour, breach/violation/infraction of the law, felony, wrongdoing, wrong, act of misconduct, misdeed, delinquency, peccadillo, sin, transgression, infringement, act of dereliction, shortcoming, fault, lapse; *Law* malfeasance; *archaic* trespass; *rare* malefaction.
2 *the outcome is an offence to basic justice* **affront**, slap in the face, insult, outrage, injury, hurt, injustice, indignity, slight, snub.
3 *I do not want to cause offence* **annoyance**, anger, resentment, indignation, irritation, exasperation, wrath, displeasure, disapproval, dislike, hard/bad/ill feelings, disgruntlement, animosity, pique, vexation, umbrage, antipathy, aversion, opposition, enmity; *literary* ire.
4 *strategic offence arsenals* **attack**, offensive, assault, act of aggression, aggression, onslaught, thrust, charge, sortie, sally, invasion, incursion, foray.
□ **take offence** *he went out, making it clear he'd taken offence* **be/feel offended**, take exception, take something personally, be/feel aggrieved, be/feel affronted, take something amiss, take umbrage, get/be/feel upset, get/be/feel annoyed, get/be/feel angry, be/feel indignant, be/feel put out, be/feel insulted, be/feel hurt, be/feel wounded, feel piqued, be/feel resentful, be/feel disgruntled, get/go into a huff, get huffy; *informal* be/feel miffed, have one's nose put out of joint, be/feel riled; *Brit. informal* get the hump.

offend ▸ verb **1** *I'm sorry if anything I said offended him* **hurt someone's feelings**, give offence to, affront, upset, displease, distress, hurt, wound, pain, injure, be an affront to, get/put someone's back up, disgruntle, put out, annoy, anger, exasperate, irritate, vex, pique, gall, irk, provoke, rankle with, nettle, needle, peeve, tread on someone's toes, ruffle, ruffle someone's feathers, rub up the wrong way, make someone's hackles rise, insult, humiliate, embarrass, mortify, scandalize, shock, outrage, spite; *informal* rile, miff, rattle, aggravate, put someone's nose out of joint, get up someone's nose, get under someone's skin, hack off, get someone's goat, get to, bug; *Brit. informal* nark, get on someone's wick; *N. Amer. informal* tick off; *vulgar slang* piss off.
2 *he didn't smoke and the smell of ash offended him* **displease**, be displeasing to, be distasteful to, be disagreeable to, be offensive to, cause offence to, upset, put off, disgust, repel, revolt, be repugnant to, repulse, turn someone's stomach, sicken, nauseate, make sick, make someone's gorge rise; *informal* turn off; *N. Amer. informal* gross out.
OPPOSITES please, delight.
3 *a small hard core of criminals who offend again and again* **break the law**, commit a crime, do wrong, sin, go astray, fall from grace, err, transgress; *archaic* trespass.

offended ▸ adjective *she was so offended she asked him to leave at once* **upset**, hurt, wounded, injured, insulted, aggrieved, affronted, pained, displeased, distressed, disgruntled, put out, annoyed, angered, angry, cross, exasperated, indignant, irritated, vexed, piqued, irked, stung, galled, nettled, needled, peeved, ruffled, resentful, in a huff, huffy, in high dudgeon, fed up; *W. Indian* vex; *informal* riled, miffed, miffy, rattled, aggravated, peed off, hacked off; *Brit. informal* narked, eggy, cheesed off, browned off, brassed off; *N. Amer. informal* sore, teed off, ticked off; *vulgar slang* pissed off; *archaic* snuffy.
OPPOSITE pleased.

offender ▸ noun *one of his main concerns was the problem of persistent offenders* **wrongdoer**, **criminal**, lawbreaker, malefactor, felon, delinquent, culprit, guilty party, sinner, transgressor, evil-doer, reprobate, outlaw; juvenile delinquent, young offender; *informal* crook; *Austral. informal* crim; *Law* malfeasant, misfeasor; *archaic* miscreant, trespasser.

offensive ▸ adjective **1** *he described the remarks as deeply offensive* **insulting**, rude, derogatory, disrespectful, hurtful, wounding, abusive, objectionable, displeasing, annoying, exasperating, irritating, vexing, galling, provocative, provoking, humiliating, impertinent, impudent, insolent, personal, discourteous, uncivil, impolite, unmannerly, unacceptable, shocking, scandalous, outrageous; crude, vulgar, coarse, indecent, improper; *rare* exceptionable.
OPPOSITES complimentary, polite.
2 *an offensive smell* **unpleasant**, disagreeable, nasty, distasteful, displeasing, objectionable, off-putting, uninviting, awful, terrible, dreadful, frightful, obnoxious, abominable, disgusting, repulsive, repellent, repugnant, revolting, abhorrent, loathsome, hateful, detestable, execrable, odious, vile, foul, unsavoury, unpalatable, sickening, nauseating, nauseous, ugly, unsightly; noxious, fetid, rank, rancid, malodorous, mephitic; *informal* ghastly, horrible, horrid, gross, putrid, sick-making, yucky, God-awful; *Brit. informal* beastly; *Austral. informal* on the nose; *N. Amer. informal* skanky; *literary* noisome; *archaic* disgustful, loathly.
OPPOSITES pleasant, delightful.
3 *an offensive air action against another country* **hostile**, **attacking**, aggressive, invading, incursive, combative, threatening, martial, warlike, belligerent, bellicose, antagonistic, on the attack.
OPPOSITE defensive.
▸ noun *a military offensive against the guerrillas* **attack**, assault, onslaught, drive, invasion, push, thrust, charge, sortie, sally, foray, raid, offence, act of war, act of aggression, incursion, blitz, campaign.

O

□ **take the offensive** *security forces took the offensive ten days ago* **begin to attack**, attack first, be aggressive, strike the first blow, start a war/battle/quarrel; *informal* be on the warpath.

CHOOSE THE RIGHT WORD

offensive, derogatory, insulting

These words all describe remarks or behaviour that cause offence or distress, unconsciously or intentionally.

- **Offensive** remarks or behaviour make someone hurt, upset, or angry, whether or not the speaker realizes or intends this (*the wording was unnecessarily offensive | the work is trite and offensive to women*). An *offensive* term for a person, such as someone of a particular ethnic type, may offend others, not just those of that ethnicity.
- A **derogatory** comment is deliberately intended to express a low opinion of someone or something (*derogatory racial remarks | I found myself repelled by the use of derogatory nicknames*).
- **Insulting** language or behaviour shows a lack of respect (*the Minister's reply is arrogant and insulting | the cartoon is insulting to men*). It is generally, but not necessarily, intended to upset or annoy.

offer ▶ verb **1** *the manager is always at hand to offer advice and information* **provide**, put forward, give, proffer, present, extend, suggest, recommend, propose, propound, advance, submit, tender, render, come up with.
OPPOSITES withdraw, refuse, withhold.
2 *a local man offered to help* **volunteer**, volunteer one's services, be at someone's disposal, be at someone's service, make oneself available, present oneself, step/come forward, show willing.
3 *the product is offered at a very competitive price* **put up for sale**, put on the market, sell, market, make available, put under the hammer, ask for bids for; *Law* vend.
4 *he offered $200* **bid**, tender, put in a bid of, put in an offer of.
5 *a job offering good career prospects* **provide**, **afford**, supply, give, furnish, present, give an opportunity for, purvey, make available, hold out.
6 *she offered no resistance when he kissed her firmly on the lips* **attempt**, try, give, show, express; *formal* essay.
7 *the birds were occasionally offered to the gods* **sacrifice**, offer up, immolate, give.
8 *he distinguished himself whenever an occasion offered* **occur**, present itself, arrive, appear, happen, show itself.
▶ noun **1** *sympathetic offers of help | a job offer* **proposal**, proposition, suggestion, submission, approach, overture; *literary* proffer.
2 *the government rejected the highest offer* **bid**, tender, bidding price.
□ **on offer on sale**, up for sale, on the market, purchasable, available, obtainable, to be had; *N. Amer.* on the block.

O

offering ▶ noun **1** *you may also place offerings in the charity box* **contribution**, donation, benefaction, gift, present, handout, widow's mite, subscription; charity; *historical* alms; *rare* donative.
2 *during this time, many offerings were made to the goddess of the dead* **sacrifice**, oblation, burnt offering, peace offering, thank-offering, immolation, libation, first fruits, tribute, dedication; *Hinduism* prasad, puja; *Judaism* Omer, sin-offering.

offhand ▶ adjective *an offhand comment that she regretted almost immediately* **indifferent**, **casual**, careless, uninterested, unconcerned, cool, distant, aloof, nonchalant, blasé, insouciant, offhanded, cavalier, glib, perfunctory, cursory, unceremonious, ungracious, curt, abrupt, terse, brusque, dismissive, discourteous, uncivil, impolite, rude; impromptu, off-the-cuff, spontaneous, extempore, unpremeditated, extemporaneous, unthinking, unstudied; *informal* off, offish, couldn't-care-less, take-it-or-leave-it; *rare* poco-curante.
▶ adverb *I can't think of a better answer offhand* **without preparation**, on the spur of the moment, without consideration, without checking, extempore, impromptu, ad lib; extemporaneously, without rehearsal, spontaneously; *Latin* ad libitum; *informal* off the cuff, off the top of one's head, just like that, at the drop of a hat.

office ▶ noun **1** *it was only a few minutes' walk to her office in Aldersgate Street* **place of business**, place of work, workplace, workroom, studio; headquarters, base, centre.
2 *the Paris office of the New York Herald Tribune* **branch**, division, section, bureau, department; agency.
3 *he assumed the office of President on May 20* **post**, position, appointment, job, occupation, role, place, situation, station, function, capacity.
4 *the offices of a nurse* **chore**, duty, job, task, obligation, assignment, service, responsibility, charge, commission; work, employment.
5 (**offices**) *his family escaped to Canada through the good offices of a Jewish agency* **assistance**, help, aid, services, intervention, intercession, mediation, intermediation, agency, support, backing, patronage, aegis, auspices, advocacy.

officer ▶ noun **1** *an officer in the army* military officer, army officer, naval officer, air force officer, commissioned officer, non-commissioned officer, NCO, commanding officer, CO.
2 *all officers carry warrant cards* **police officer**, policeman, policewoman, PC, WPC, officer of the law, detective, DC; *Brit.* constable; *N. Amer.* roundsman, trooper, peace officer, lawman; *French* gendarme, flic; *informal* cop, pig, woodentop; *Brit. informal* copper, busy, bizzy, plod, rozzer, bobby; *N. Amer. informal* narc, gumshoe, bear, uniform; *Austral./NZ informal* demon, walloper, John Hop; *informal, dated* tec, dick, flatfoot, flattie; *archaic* peeler, bluebottle, finger, bogey, runner.
3 *the officers of the society are under considerable pressure* **committee member**, **official**, office-holder, office-bearer, board member, public servant, administrator, commissioner, executive, functionary, bureaucrat, dignitary; *derogatory* apparatchik.
4 *an officer of the county court* **representative**, agent, deputy, messenger, envoy.

official ▶ adjective **1** *an official inquiry into the state of the hospital | until probate is granted the will is not official* **authorized**, accredited, approved, validated, authenticated, authentic, certified, endorsed, documented, sanctioned, licensed, formal, recognized, authoritative, accepted, verified, legitimate, legal, lawful, valid, bona fide, proper, true, ex cathedra, {signed, sealed, and delivered}, signed and sealed; *informal* kosher.
OPPOSITES unofficial, unauthorized.
2 *they were arrayed in all their finery for some official function* **ceremonial**, formal, solemn, ritualistic, ceremonious; pompous, stiff, bureaucratic, proper; *informal* stuffed-shirt.
OPPOSITE informal.
▶ noun *a union official* **officer**, office-holder, office-bearer, administrator, executive, appointee, functionary; bureaucrat, dignitary, mandarin; representative, agent; *derogatory* apparatchik; *Brit.* jack-in-office.

official or officious?
See OFFICIOUS.

officiate ▶ verb **1** *Kathy Dyson* ***officiated at*** *the opening ceremony | he officiated in both World Cups* **preside (over)**, take charge, be in charge (of), be responsible (for), direct, head (up), manage, oversee, superintend, supervise, conduct, run, lead, chair, take the chair; umpire, referee, judge, adjudicate, moderate, mediate; *N. Amer. informal* emcee.
2 *the Pope* ***officiated at*** *a public mass on October 11* **conduct**, perform, celebrate, solemnize, concelebrate.

officious ▶ adjective *an officious maître d' told him to wait at the bar* **self-important**, bumptious, self-assertive, overbearing, overzealous, dictatorial, bossy, domineering, interfering, intrusive, meddlesome, meddling, importunate, forward, opinionated; *informal* pushy; *archaic* pragmatic, intermeddling; *rare* obtrusive, busy.
OPPOSITE self-effacing.

officious or official?

One may well be unfortunate enough to encounter an **officious** person acting in an **official** capacity; but this is a matter of human nature and does not mean that the words have the same meaning. An *officious* person is excessively fond of asserting his or her authority, especially in relation to trivial matters (*the local bureaucrats are an officious lot*). *Official*, on the other hand, means 'relating to the responsibilities and authority of public office' (*his official duties | the Prime Minister's official engagements*) or 'approved or issued by an authority' (*the official unemployment figures*).

offing ▶ noun
□ **in the offing** *important changes were in the offing* **likely to happen**, on the way, coming soon, coming up, (close) at hand, just near, imminent, in prospect, on the horizon, in the wings, just around the corner, in the air, in the wind, brewing, upcoming, forthcoming; *informal* on the cards.

off-key ▶ adjective **1** *a slightly off-key rendition of an old family favourite* **out of tune**, flat, tuneless, unmusical, unmelodic, discordant, dissonant, unharmonious.
OPPOSITE in tune.
2 *some of the cinematic effects are distractingly off-key* **incongruous**, inappropriate, unsuitable, discordant, out of place, out of keeping, jarring, dissonant, inharmonious.
OPPOSITE harmonious.

offload ▶ verb **1** *the ship offloaded 500 tonnes of coal ash into the North Sea* **unload**, **dump**, jettison, discharge, unship, deposit, empty (out), tip (out), drop, get rid of; *archaic* unlade; *rare* disburden.
2 *it's expected that the government will offload most of its BT shares* **dispose of**, dump, jettison, get rid of, transfer, shift; palm off, foist, fob off.

off-putting ▶ adjective *a rather off-putting aroma | while not exactly threatening, her manner was off-putting* **unpleasant**, unappealing, uninviting, unattractive, disagreeable, offensive, distasteful, unsavoury, unpalatable, unappetizing, objectionable, nasty, disgusting, obnoxious, repellent; **discouraging**, disheartening, demoralizing, dispiriting, daunting, dismaying, forbidding, intimidating, frightening, formidable; *informal* horrid, horrible; *rare* rebarbative.

offset ▶ **verb** *profits and losses on each investment tend to offset each other* **counterbalance**, balance, balance out, cancel, cancel out, even out/up, counteract, counterpoise, countervail, equalize, neutralize, nullify, compensate for, make up for, make good, redeem, indemnify; atone for, redress, make amends for, make restitution for; *rare* equilibrize.

offshoot ▶ **noun 1** *the cactus grew some offshoots* **side shoot**, shoot, sucker, tendril, runner, scion, slip, offset, sprout, sprig, stem, twig, branch, bough, limb, spur; *technical* stolon.
OPPOSITE trunk.
2 *an offshoot of Thomas Cromwell's line* **descendant**, scion, relation, relative.
3 *offshoots of big firms or finance houses* **subsidiary**, branch, derivative, adjunct, appendage.
4 *one practical offshoot of the growth of interest in heritage is the growth of tourism* **outcome**, result, effect, consequence, upshot, product, by-product, spin-off, ramification, development, outgrowth.

offspring ▶ **noun 1** *anxious parents watching over their offspring* **children**, sons and daughters, progeny, family, youngsters, babies, brood; descendants, heirs, successors, scions; young, litter, fry; *Law* issue; *informal* kids, quiverful; *derogatory* spawn; *archaic* seed, fruit, fruit of one's loins.
2 *he obviously had great expectations for his latest offspring* **child**, baby, infant, son, daughter, youngster, little one, tot, tiny tot; descendant, heir, successor; *Scottish & N. English* bairn, wean; *black English* pickney; *informal* kid, kiddie, kiddiewink, nipper, brat, lad, shaver, munchkin, tiny, chick; *Brit. informal* sprog; *S. African informal* outjie, lighty; *literary* babe.

often ▶ **adverb** *he often asked after you* **frequently**, many times, many a time, on many/numerous occasions, a lot, in many cases/instances, repeatedly, again and again, time and again, time and time again, time after time, over and over, over and over again, {day in, day out}, {week in, week out}, all the time, regularly, recurrently, continually, usually, habitually, commonly, generally, ordinarily, as often as not; *N. Amer.* oftentimes; *informal* lots; *literary* oft, oft-times.
OPPOSITES seldom, rarely, never.

ogle ▶ **verb** *he'd been ogling her ever since she'd entered the room* **leer at**, stare at, gaze at, eye, make eyes at, make sheep's eyes at; *informal* eye up, give someone the glad eye, give someone a/the once-over, lech after/over, undress with one's eyes, give someone the come-on; *Brit. informal* gawp at, gawk at; *Austral./NZ informal* perv on.

ogre ▶ **noun 1** *an ogre with two heads* **monster**, giant, troll, bogeyman, bogey, demon, devil; *archaic* bugbear.
2 *her friends represented Maclean as an ogre* **brute**, **fiend**, monster, beast, devil, demon, barbarian, savage, sadist, animal, tyrant, villain, scoundrel; *informal* bastard, swine, pig; *vulgar slang* shit; *archaic* blackguard.

ogress ▶ **noun 1 monster**, giantess.
2 *the French teacher was a real ogress* **harridan**, tartar, termagant, shrew, harpy, gorgon, virago; *informal* battleaxe.

oil *See centre pages for list of* **Oils**
▶ **noun** *make sure the car has enough oil* **lubricant**, lubrication, grease; fuel, petroleum; *N. Amer. informal* black gold; *N. Amer. & Austral. informal* lube.
▶ **verb** *I'll oil that gate for you tomorrow* **lubricate**, grease; *N. Amer. & Austral. informal* lube.

WORD LINKS
related prefix **oleo- (e.g. *oleochemical, oleograph*)**

oily ▶ **adjective 1** *his dark oily skin | oily substances* **greasy**, oleaginous; slippery, slimy; *technical* sebaceous, pinguid, unctuous.
2 *a plateful of oily moussaka* **greasy**, fatty, buttery, swimming in oil/fat, oleaginous.
3 *an oily man with plump little hands* **unctuous**, fawning, ingratiating, smooth, smooth-talking, fulsome, flattering, glib, obsequious, sycophantic, soapy, oleaginous, servile, subservient; *informal* smarmy, slimy, sucky; *rare* saponaceous.

ointment ▶ **noun lotion**, cream, salve, liniment, embrocation, rub, gel, petroleum jelly, balm, emollient, unguent, balsam; pomade, pomatum; calamine lotion, zinc ointment; *Medicine* demulcent, humectant; *trademark* Vaseline, Tiger balm; *historical* spikenard; *archaic* unction.

OK, **okay** (*informal*) ▶ **exclamation** *OK, I'll go with him* **all right**, right, right then, right you are, very well, yes, very good, fine, agreed; *informal* oke, okey-dokey, okey-doke, roger; *Brit. informal* righto, righty-ho; *Indian informal* acha.
▶ **adjective 1** *the film was OK | is everything OK?* **satisfactory**, all right, fine, in order, acceptable, up to scratch, up to the mark, up to standard, up to par, competent; adequate, tolerable, passable, reasonable, quite good, fair, decent, not bad, average, middling, moderate, unremarkable, unexceptional; *informal* hunky-dory, so-so, fair-to-middling, (plain) vanilla; *Brit. informal, dated* tickety-boo; *N. Amer. & Austral./NZ informal* jake.
OPPOSITES unsatisfactory, unacceptable, inadequate.
2 *Jo's feeling OK now* **fine**, all right, well, in good shape, in good health, fit, healthy, as fit as a fiddle, as fit as a flea, in fine fettle, up to snuff; *informal* in the pink; *Brit. informal* as right as a trivet.
OPPOSITES ill, unwell.
3 *it is OK for me to come* **permissible**, allowable, acceptable, all right, in order, permitted, fine, fitting, suitable, appropriate.
▶ **adverb** *'How's the job going?' 'Okay.'* **all right**, fine, well, well enough, satisfactorily, passably, tolerably, acceptably.
▶ **noun** *he's just given me the OK* **authorization**, approval, seal of approval, agreement, consent, assent, permission, endorsement, ratification, sanction, approbation, acquiescence, confirmation, blessing, leave, imprimatur; *informal* the go-ahead, the green light, the thumbs up, say-so.
OPPOSITES refusal, denial.
▶ **verb** *the move must be okayed by the president* **authorize**, approve, agree to, consent to, sanction, pass, ratify, endorse, allow, give something one's consent, say yes to, accede to, give something one's approval, give something the nod, rubber-stamp; *informal* give something the go-ahead, give something the green light, give something the thumbs up, give something one's say-so.
OPPOSITES refuse, forbid, veto.

old ▶ **adjective 1** *old people* **elderly**, mature, aged, older, senior, advanced in years, up in years, getting on; in one's dotage, long in the tooth, grey, grey-haired, grey-bearded, grizzled, hoary; past one's prime, not as young as one was, ancient, decrepit, doddering, doddery, not long for this world, ripe, senescent, senile, superannuated, venerable, septuagenarian, octogenarian, nonagenarian, centenarian; *informal* past it, over the hill, no spring chicken; *rare* longevous.
OPPOSITE young.
2 *old farm buildings* **historic**, antiquated; dilapidated, broken-down, run down, tumbledown, ramshackle, decaying, crumbling, disintegrating.
OPPOSITES new, modern.
3 *old clothes* **worn**, worn out, shabby, threadbare, holey, torn, frayed, patched, tattered, moth-eaten, ragged, yellowed; old-fashioned, out of date, outmoded; cast-off, hand-me-down; *French* démodé; *informal* tatty.
OPPOSITES new, fashionable.
4 *old cars* **antique**, veteran, vintage.
OPPOSITES new, modern.
5 *she is old for her years | he's an old hand* **mature**, wise, sensible, experienced, worldly-wise, knowledgeable, well versed, familiar, practised, skilled, skilful, adept, expert, veteran.
OPPOSITES young, ingenuous, inexperienced.
6 *in the old days* **bygone**, past, former, olden, of old, remote, previous, early, earlier, earliest; medieval, ancient, classical, primeval, primordial, prehistoric, antediluvian, forgotten, immemorial.
OPPOSITES modern, recent.
7 *political worthies spew out the same old phrases* **hackneyed**, hack, banal, trite, overused, overworked, cut and dried, tired, worn out, time-worn, stale, stereotyped, clichéd, platitudinous, unoriginal, unimaginative, commonplace, common, pedestrian, prosaic, run-of-the-mill, stock, conventional; out of date, outdated, old-fashioned, outmoded, archaic, obsolete, defunct, extinct, antiquated, antediluvian, superannuated, hoary; *French* passé; *informal* old hat, out of the ark, corny, fuddy-duddy, played out.
OPPOSITES fresh, innovative, new.
8 *I love the good old tunes* **time-honoured**, old-time, long-established, age-old, long-standing, long-lived, enduring, lasting; **familiar**, customary, conventional, established, ritual, ritualistic, habitual, set, fixed, routine, usual, wonted, historic, folk, old-world, ancestral.
9 *an old girlfriend* **former**, previous, ex-, one-time, sometime, erstwhile, once, then, lapsed; *formal* quondam.
OPPOSITE new.
□ **old age declining years**, advanced years, elderliness, age, agedness, oldness, winter/autumn of one's life, senescence, senility, dotage.
OPPOSITES youth, childhood.
□ **old man 1 senior citizen**, pensioner, OAP, elder, elderly man, grandfather; patriarch; *Scottish & Irish* bodach; *informal* greybeard, gaffer, old codger, old boy, old chap, old geezer, old bloke, wrinkly; *Brit. informal* buffer, josser; *N. Amer. informal* old coot; *archaic* grandsire, ancient; *literary* senex.
OPPOSITES youth, boy, young man.
2 (*informal*) *her old man was away fighting* **husband**, man; *informal* hubby, better half; *Brit. informal* other half; *humorous* lord and master; *archaic* lord.
3 (*informal*) *the old man's still on the bridge* **captain**, **owner**, boss, employer, foreman, manager, overseer, superintendent, director, controller, head, headman, principal; *informal* head honcho; *Brit. informal* gaffer, guv'nor; *N. Amer. informal* sachem.
□ **old person senior citizen**, senior, pensioner, old-age pensioner, OAP, elder, geriatric, old fogey, dotard, Methuselah; *N. Amer.* golden ager; *informal* old stager, old-timer, oldie, wrinkly, crock, crumbly; *N. Amer. informal* oldster, woopie.
OPPOSITE youngster.
□ **old woman 1 senior citizen**, pensioner, OAP, elderly woman, crone; *Russian* babushka; *informal* old dear; *archaic* beldam, grandam, gammer, mother.

O

OPPOSITES girl, young woman.
2 (*informal*) *his old woman threw him out* **wife**, spouse, bride, squaw; *informal* old lady, wifey, better half, missus, the little woman; *Brit. informal* other half, her indoors, (old) dutch, trouble and strife; *N. Amer. informal* mama, mamma; *dated* lady, memsahib.
3 (*informal*) *my old woman took me to all sorts of doctors when I was a kid* **mother**; *Indian* amma; *informal* mum, mummy, ma, mam, mammy, mumsy, old dear, old lady; *N. Amer. informal* mom, mommy; *dated* mama, mamma, mater.
4 *he's such an old woman* **worrier**, **perfectionist**, stickler, grumbler; *informal* **fusspot**; *N. Amer. informal* fussbudget.

WORD LINKS

relating to old age	**gerontic**
relating to old people	**geriatric**
branch of medicine concerning old people	**geriatrics**
study of old age	**gerontology**
government by old people	**gerontocracy**
deteriorate with old age	**senesce**
related prefixes	**archaeo- (e.g. *archaeology, archaeopteryx*), palaeo- (*palaeography, Palaeocene*)**

old-fashioned ▶ adjective *a black-and-white photograph of a woman in old-fashioned clothes* **out of date**, outdated, dated, out, out of fashion, outmoded, unfashionable, last year's, frumpish, frumpy, out of style, outworn, old, old-time, old-world, behind the times, archaic, obsolescent, obsolete, ancient, antiquated, superannuated, defunct; medieval, prehistoric, antediluvian, old-fogeyish, old-fangled, conservative, backward-looking, quaint, anachronistic, crusted, feudal, fusty, moth-eaten, olde worlde; *French* passé, démodé, vieux jeu; *informal* old hat, square, not with it, out of the ark, creaky, mouldy; *N. Amer. informal* horse-and-buggy, clunky, rinky-dink, mossy; *archaic* square-toed.
OPPOSITES modern, up to date, fashionable.

old-time ▶ adjective *old-time dancing* **old style**, former, past, bygone, historic, heritage, antique, antiquarian, early, classical, traditional, folk, old-world, ancestral, time-honoured, ancient, veteran, vintage, quaint.
OPPOSITE modern.

old-world ▶ adjective *old-world charm | old-world cottages* **old-fashioned**, old, archaic, traditional, past, bygone, classical; **picturesque**, quaint.

Olympian ▶ adjective *Kerr himself preserved a attitude of Olympian detachment* **aloof**, distant, remote, stand-offish, unfriendly, unamiable, unaffable, uncongenial, unneighbourly, inhospitable, reclusive, solitary, misanthropic, uncommunicative, unforthcoming, reticent, withdrawn, cold, cool, chilly.
OPPOSITES affable, friendly, chummy.

omen ▶ noun *the ferocious storm began on our wedding day: perhaps it was an omen of things to come* **portent**, sign, signal, token, forewarning, warning, foreshadowing, prediction, forecast, prophecy, harbinger, augury; straw in the wind, writing on the wall, indication, hint, auspice, presage, threat, ill omen, menace; *literary* foretoken.

ominous ▶ adjective *ominous black clouds gathered on the horizon* **threatening**, menacing, baleful, forbidding, sinister, doomy, inauspicious, unpropitious, portentous, unfavourable, dire, unpromising; black, dark, wintry, gloomy, ugly; *archaic* direful; *rare* minatory, minacious.
OPPOSITES promising, auspicious, propitious.

omission ▶ noun **1** *there also appear to be some significant omissions from the Commission's report* **deletion**, cut, exclusion, gap, blank, lacuna, hiatus; oversight.
OPPOSITES addition, inclusion.
2 *the omission of the verb gives the sentence immediacy* **leaving out**, **exclusion**, exception, non-inclusion, deletion, erasure, cut, excision, elimination, absence; *Linguistics* aphesis, apheresis, apocope, apostrophe, asyndeton, elision, ellipsis, gapping, haplography, haplology, lipography, syncope; *rare* expunction.
OPPOSITES addition, inclusion.
3 *the damage to the goods was not caused by any act or omission by the carrier* **negligence**, neglect, neglectfulness, dereliction, forgetfulness, oversight, disregard, non-fulfilment, default, lapse, failure; *Law* nonjoinder; *rare* delinquency, misprision.
OPPOSITE conscientiousness.

omit ▶ verb **1** *they omitted his name from the list* **leave out**, **exclude**, fail to include, except, shut out, leave off, take out, miss out, miss, fail to mention, pass over, drop, delete, cut, erase, eliminate, elide, expunge, rub out, cross out, strike out, dispense with; *informal* give something a miss; *archaic* overleap, pretermit.
OPPOSITES add, include.
2 *I am sorry I omitted to mention our guest lecturer* **forget**, neglect, fail; leave undone, overlook, ignore, skip.
OPPOSITE remember.

omnipotence ▶ noun *traditional doctrines of divine omnipotence* **all-powerfulness**, almightiness, supremacy, pre-eminence, supreme power, absolute/unlimited power, undisputed sway, divine right; dictatorship, despotism, totalitarianism, autocracy, autarchy; invincibility.
OPPOSITE powerlessness.

omnipotent ▶ adjective *an omnipotent deity* **all-powerful**, almighty, supreme, most high, pre-eminent; dictatorial, despotic, totalitarian, autocratic, autarchic; invincible, unconquerable.

omnipresent ▶ adjective *in fairy tales, evil is as omnipresent as virtue* **present everywhere**, **ubiquitous**, general, universal, worldwide, global, all-pervasive, all-present, infinite, boundless; rife, prevalent, predominant, common, extensive, wide-ranging, far-reaching.

omniscient ▶ adjective *the story is told by an omniscient fictional narrator* **all-knowing**, all-wise, all-seeing.

omnivorous ▶ adjective **1** *most duck species are omnivorous* with a mixed/varied diet, able to eat anything, all-devouring; *rare* pantophagous, pamphagous, pantophagic, omnivorant.
2 *David was an omnivorous reader* **undiscriminating**, indiscriminate, unselective, uncritical.

on ▶ preposition **1** *there was a book on the table* **supported by**, resting on, in contact with.
OPPOSITES underneath, on the underside of.
2 *she put the book on the table* **on to**.
OPPOSITE off.
▶ adjective *the light was still on* **functioning**, in operation, working, in use, operating.
OPPOSITE off.
▶ adverb *she droned on* **interminably**, at length, for a long time, continuously, endlessly, ceaselessly, without a pause/break.
□ **on and off** *she had been working on that painting, on and off, for a long time.* See **OFF AND ON**.
□ **on and on** *she blabbered on and on* **for a long time**, for ages, for hours, at (great) length, incessantly, ceaselessly, constantly, continuously, continually, endlessly, unendingly, eternally, forever; **interminably**, unremittingly, relentlessly, indefatigably, without let-up, without a pause/break, without cease.

once ▶ adverb **1** *I saw him only once* **on one occasion**, one time, one single time.
OPPOSITES twice, many times.
2 *he did not once help* **ever**, at any time, on any occasion, at all, under any circumstances, on any account, in a million years.
3 *they were friends once* **formerly**, previously, in the past, at one time, at one point, once upon a time, on a former occasion, on one occasion, one time, in one case, time was when, in days/times gone by, back in the day, in times past, in the (good) old days, long ago; *archaic* sometime, erst, erstwhile, whilom; *literary* in days/times of yore, of yore.
OPPOSITE now.
□ **at once 1** *you must leave at once* **immediately**, right away, right now, this moment/instant/second/minute, now, straight away, instantly, instantaneously, directly, suddenly, abruptly, summarily, forthwith, promptly, without delay/hesitation, without further ado; quickly, as fast as possible, as soon as possible, fast, speedily, with all speed; *informal* like a shot, in/like a flash, before you can say Jack Robinson, in two shakes (of a lamb's tail).
OPPOSITES later, in due course.
2 *all the guests arrived at once* **at the same time**, at one and the same time, at the same instant/moment, (all) together, simultaneously; as a group, in unison, in concert, in chorus.
OPPOSITES singly, in dribs and drabs.
▶ conjunction *he'll be all right once she's gone* **as soon as**, when, after, immediately after, the instant/moment/second/minute; *Brit. informal* immediately.
□ **once and for all 1** *you must decide once and for all* **conclusively**, decisively, finally, positively, absolutely, determinedly, definitely, definitively, irrevocably.
2 *he has gone once and for all* **for good**, for always, forever, permanently, finally, in perpetuity; *informal* for keeps.
□ **once in a while** *once in a while a car went past* **occasionally**, from time to time, (every) now and then/again, every so often, every once in a while, on occasion, on occasions, on the odd occasion, at times, sometimes, off and on, at intervals, periodically, sporadically, spasmodically, erratically, irregularly, intermittently, in/by fits and starts, fitfully, discontinuously, piecemeal; *rare* interruptedly.

oncoming ▶ adjective *he lost control on a bend and collided with an oncoming car | the piercing March wind and the oncoming rain* **approaching**, advancing, coming, nearing, arriving, onrushing; forthcoming, upcoming, on the way, prospective, imminent, impending, looming, gathering, immediate, proximate; close, (close) at hand, about to happen/be, in the offing, in the wind, to come.

one ▶ cardinal number **1** **unit**, item; *technical* monad.
2 *only one person came* **a single**, a solitary, a sole, a lone.
3 *her one concern was her daughter* **only**, single, solitary, sole.

4 *one day they'll come* **some**, any, a certain.
5 *they are now one* **united**, a unit, amalgamated, consolidated, integrated, combined, incorporated, affiliated, allied, federated, linked, joined, unified, in league, in partnership; bound, wedded, married.

WORD LINKS
related prefixes **mono-** (e.g. ***monologue, monovalent***), **uni-** (e.g. ***unicellular, unicycle***)
relating to one **unitary**
obsession with one thing **monomania**

one and a half

WORD LINKS
related prefix **sesqui-** (e.g. ***sesquicentenary***)

onerous ▸ adjective *the task proved to be more onerous than she had expected* **burdensome**, heavy, inconvenient, troublesome, awkward, crushing, back-breaking, oppressive; weighty, arduous, strenuous, uphill, difficult, hard, severe, formidable, laborious, Herculean, exhausting, tiring, taxing, demanding, punishing, gruelling, exacting, wearing, stiff, stressful, wearisome, fatiguing; *archaic* toilsome; *rare* exigent.
OPPOSITES easy, effortless.

oneself ▸ pronoun
□ **by oneself**. *See* BY.

one-sided ▸ adjective 1 *foreign publications have been criticized for alleged one-sided reporting* **biased**, prejudiced, partisan, partial, preferential, discriminatory, coloured, inequitable, unfair, influenced, slanted, unjust, narrow-minded, bigoted.
OPPOSITE fair-minded.
2 *a one-sided game* **unequal**, uneven, unbalanced, lopsided.

one-time ▸ adjective *a one-time county cricketer* **former**, ex-, old, previous, sometime, erstwhile, once, then, lapsed; *formal* quondam.

ongoing ▸ adjective 1 *two laboratories have been refurbished as part of an ongoing programme of modernization* **in progress**, under way, going on, continuing, happening, occurring, taking place, proceeding, being done, being worked on, being performed, current, extant, existing, existent, progressing, advancing, evolving, growing, developing; pending, outstanding, to be done, unfinished, remaining.
OPPOSITES finished, abandoned.
2 *residents face the ongoing problem of shoppers parking outside their homes* **continuous**, continuing, uninterrupted, unbroken, non-stop, round-the-clock, incessant, unending, constant, ceaseless, unceasing, endless, never-ending, everlasting, eternal, perpetual, unremitting, relentless, unfaltering.
OPPOSITE intermittent.

onlooker ▸ noun *an onlooker described the scene as one of utter devastation* **eyewitness**, witness, observer, looker-on, fly on the wall, spectator, watcher, viewer, sightseer, bystander, non-participant; *informal* rubberneck; *literary* beholder.
OPPOSITE participant.

only ▸ adverb 1 *there was only enough for two* **at most**, at best, (only) just, no/not more than, as little as; no longer ago than, not until; barely, scarcely, hardly, narrowly, by a hair's breadth, by the skin of one's teeth.
2 *he only works on one picture at a time* **exclusively**, solely, entirely, uniquely, wholly, to the exclusion of everything else.
3 *you're only saying that* **merely**, simply, just, purely.
▸ adjective *he is their only son* **sole**, single, one (and only), solitary, lone, unique, only possible, individual, exclusive.

onomatopoeic ▸ adjective *'slap' is an onomatopoeic word* **imitative**, echoic.

onset ▸ noun *treatment was administered soon after the onset of symptoms* **start**, beginning, arrival, (first) appearance, opening, outset, inception; outbreak, dawn, birth, infancy, genesis, creation, day one, emergence, rise; *formal* commencement.
OPPOSITES end, termination.

onslaught ▸ noun *the relentless onslaught on the city was taking a heavy toll* **assault**, attack, offensive, aggression, advance, charge, onrush, rush, storming, sortie, sally, raid, descent, incursion, invasion, foray, push, thrust, drive, blitz, bombardment, barrage, salvo, storm, volley, shower, torrent, broadside; *archaic* onset.

onus ▸ noun *the onus is on the plaintiff to obtain the police report* **burden**, responsibility, liability, obligation, duty, weight, load, charge, mantle, encumbrance; cross to bear, millstone round one's neck, albatross.

ooze ▸ verb 1 *blood oozed from a long scratch on his forehead* **seep**, discharge, flow, exude, trickle, drip, dribble, issue, filter, percolate, escape, leak, drain, empty, bleed, sweat, well, leach; *Medicine* extravasate; *rare* filtrate, transude, exudate.
2 *she was positively oozing charm* **exude**, **gush**, drip, pour forth, give out, send out, emit, breathe, let loose, display, exhibit, demonstrate, manifest.
▸ noun 1 *the ooze of pus* **seepage**, seeping, discharge, flow, exudation, trickle, trickling, drip, dribble, filtration, percolation, excretion, escape, leak, leakage, drainage, emptying, bleeding, sweating, welling, leaching, secretion; *Medicine* extravasation.
2 *the skeletons of zooplankton accumulate in ooze on the ocean floor* **mud**, slime, alluvium, silt, mire, bog, sludge, slush, muck, dirt, deposit; *Scottish & N. English* clart; *Irish* slob.

opacity ▸ noun 1 *the opacity of water may arise from a variety of materials in suspension* **opaqueness**, non-transparency, lack of transparency; cloudiness, filminess, haziness, mistiness, blur, blurredness, dirtiness, dinginess, muddiness, griminess, smeariness.
OPPOSITES transparency, translucence, clarity.
2 *the opacity of much philosophical writing* **lack of clarity**, obscurity, abstruseness, unclearness, density, impenetrability, enigma, unintelligibility, incomprehensibility, reconditeness.
OPPOSITES clarity, limpidity.

opalescent ▸ adjective *the dress is embroidered with opalescent sequins* **multicoloured**, many-hued, prismatic, rainbow-like, kaleidoscopic, iridescent, lustrous, shimmering, glittering, sparkling, scintillating, variegated, shot, moiré, opaline, milky, pearly, nacreous, pearlescent.

opaque ▸ adjective 1 *the bottle was made of opaque glass so that the contents could not be seen* **non-transparent**, cloudy, filmy, blurred, smeared, hazy, misty, dirty, dingy, muddy, muddied, grimy, smeary.
OPPOSITES transparent, translucent, clear.
2 *federalism renders the decision-making process opaque and bureaucratic* **obscure**, **unclear**, dense, uncertain, indeterminate, mysterious, puzzling, perplexing, baffling, mystifying, confusing, enigmatic, inexplicable, unexplained, concealed, hidden, unfathomable, incomprehensible, impenetrable, vague, ambiguous, Delphic, indefinite, indistinct, hazy, foggy, nebulous, equivocal, doubtful, dubious, oblique, elliptical, oracular, cryptic, deep, abstruse, recondite, arcane, esoteric, recherché; *informal* as clear as mud.
OPPOSITES limpid, clear.

open ▸ adjective 1 *the door's open* **not shut**, not closed, unlocked, unbolted, unlatched, off the latch, unfastened, unbarred, unsecured; ajar, wide open, agape, gaping, yawning.
OPPOSITES shut, closed.
2 *a blue silk shirt, open at the neck* **unfastened**, not done up, undone, unbuttoned, unzipped, loose; unbuckled, untied, unlaced.
3 *the council used several tonnes of grit in a bid to keep the main roads open* **clear**, **passable**, navigable, unblocked, free from obstructions, unobstructed; snow-free, ice-free.
OPPOSITE blocked.
4 *an eighteenth-century farmhouse with lovely views over open countryside | her love of open spaces* **unenclosed**, rolling, sweeping, extensive, wide, wide open, broad, unfenced, exposed, unsheltered; spacious, airy, uncrowded, uncluttered; undeveloped, unbuilt-up.
OPPOSITES enclosed, built-up, developed.
5 *a map of the area was open beside him* **spread out**, unfolded, unfurled, unrolled, straightened out; extended, stretched out.
OPPOSITES closed, put away.
6 *the shop is open daily* **open for business**, open to the public.
OPPOSITES shut, closed.
7 *I could keep the position open for a week or two, to give you time to think* **available**, vacant, free, unfilled, unoccupied; *informal* on hold, up for grabs.
8 *he criticized the system for being open to abuse* **at risk of**, vulnerable, subject, susceptible, allowing of, permitting, liable, an easy target for, exposed, at the mercy of.
OPPOSITE immune.
9 *she was quite open about her feelings* **frank**, **candid**, honest, forthright, direct, unreserved, blunt, plain-spoken, outspoken, free-spoken, downright, not afraid to call a spade a spade; straightforward, genuine, natural, ingenuous, innocent, artless, transparent, guileless, simple; communicative, forthcoming, uninhibited; *informal* upfront; *archaic* round.
OPPOSITES secretive, deep, devious.
10 *they eyed one another with open hostility* **overt**, obvious, patent, manifest, palpable, conspicuous, plain, undisguised, unconcealed, unhidden, clear, noticeable, visible, apparent, evident; blatant, flagrant, barefaced, brazen.
OPPOSITE concealed.
11 *the case is still open* **unresolved**, not yet settled, yet to be settled, undecided, unsettled, up in the air; open to debate, open for discussion, arguable, debatable, moot.
OPPOSITES decided, concluded.
12 *I'm keeping an open mind on the subject* **impartial**, unbiased, unprejudiced, objective, disinterested, uncommitted, non-partisan, non-discriminatory, neutral, dispassionate, detached.
OPPOSITE biased.
13 *I'm always open to suggestions* **receptive**, amenable, willing/ready/disposed to listen, responsive.
14 *what other options are open to us?* **available**, accessible, on hand, obtainable, on offer.
15 *they are required by law to hold an open meeting* **public**, general, unrestricted, non-exclusive, accessible to everyone, non-restrictive.
OPPOSITE private.

▶ **verb 1** *she opened the front door* **unfasten**, unlatch, unlock, unbolt, unbar; throw wide.
OPPOSITES close, shut.
2 *when Katherine opened the parcel, she found a copy of 'Daisy Miller'* **unwrap**, undo, untie, unseal.
3 *shall I open another bottle?* **uncork**, broach, crack (open).
4 *Adam opened the Ordnance Survey map* **spread out**, unfold, unfurl, unroll, straighten out; extend, stretch out.
OPPOSITES close, fold up.
5 *a statement in which he opened his heart as never before* **reveal**, uncover, expose, lay bare, bare, pour out, exhibit, show, disclose, divulge.
6 *we're hoping to open next month* **start trading**, open for business, be ready for customers/visitors, admit customers, begin business, set up shop, put up one's plate; *N. Amer. informal* hang out one's shingle.
7 *Sir Bryan opened the meeting by welcoming the Commissioner | the film opens with a long sex scene* **begin**, start, initiate, set in motion, launch, get going, get under way, start/get/set the ball rolling, get off the ground; inaugurate; *informal* kick off, get the show on the road; *formal* commence.
OPPOSITES end, finish.
8 *the lounge opens on to a terrace* **give access**, give on to, lead, be connected, communicate with; command a view of, face, overlook.

WORD LINKS
fear of open places **agoraphobia**

open-air ▶ **adjective** *an open-air swimming pool* **outdoor**, out-of-doors, outside, alfresco, in the open air; *French* en plein air; *Italian* al fresco; *rare* hypaethral.
OPPOSITES inside, indoor.

open-handed ▶ **adjective** *a combination of hard-headed business sense and open-handed philanthropy* **generous**, magnanimous, charitable, benevolent, beneficent, big-hearted, great-hearted, munificent, bountiful, liberal, handsome, princely; altruistic, kind, kindly, philanthropic, chivalrous, noble, unselfish, selfless, self-sacrificing, generous to a fault, ungrudging, unstinting; *literary* bounteous.
OPPOSITE tight-fisted.

opening ▶ **noun 1** *the large hall is lit by an opening in the centre of the roof* **hole**, gap, aperture, space, orifice, vent, slot, window, crack, slit, gash, split, fissure, perforation, cleft, crevice, cut, incision, rent, cavity, cranny, groove, chink, eye, mouth; loophole, spyhole, peephole, judas; interstice; *Medicine* hiatus, foramen.
2 *she was still heading towards the dark opening in the wall* **doorway**, gateway, portal, way, entrance, entry, entryway, means of entry, way in, entrée, access, means of access, exit, egress, way out.
3 *United created openings but were unable to score* **opportunity**, chance, favourable time/occasion/moment, right set of circumstances, moment, occasion, window (of opportunity), possibility, turn, time; *informal* break, lucky break, shot.
4 *I'm looking for an opening with a stockbroker* **vacancy**, position, job, opportunity.
5 *the opening of the session had been repeatedly postponed* **beginning**, start, outset, inception, launch, birth, dawn; introduction, preliminary, preface, prelude, foreword, preamble, prefatory remarks, opening statement, opening remarks, prologue; *informal* kick-off; *formal* commencement; *rare* proem, prolegomenon.
OPPOSITES closure, close, end, termination.
6 *he crashes gallery openings for a bite of smoked salmon* **opening ceremony**, official opening, launch, initiation, inauguration, institution, foundation, establishment, setting up, formation, constitution, opening night, premiere, first night, first showing; private view, vernissage.

openly ▶ **adverb 1** *dangerous drugs were openly on sale* **publicly**, in public, in full view of people, for all to see, undisguisedly, blatantly, flagrantly, brazenly, with no attempt at concealment, overtly, boldly, audaciously; unashamedly, shamelessly, unabashedly, wantonly, immodestly.
OPPOSITE secretly.
2 *he could no longer speak openly of his problems* **frankly**, candidly, explicitly, honestly, truly, sincerely, forthrightly, directly, straightforwardly, bluntly, plainly, in plain language, unreservedly, without constraint, truthfully, without dissembling, to someone's face, straight from the shoulder, without beating about the bush, with no holds barred, man to man, woman to woman; *informal* on the level; *Brit. informal* straight up.
OPPOSITES indirectly, allusively.

open-minded ▶ **adjective 1** *they have sympathetic, open-minded attitudes to young people* **unbiased**, unprejudiced, prejudice-free, accepting, non-partisan, neutral, non-aligned, non-judgemental, non-discriminatory, objective, disinterested, dispassionate, detached; **tolerant**, liberal, permissive, broad-minded, undogmatic, unprescriptive.
OPPOSITES prejudiced, judgemental.
2 *the musicians have got to be open-minded enough to take some suggestions from the producers* **receptive**, open, open to suggestions, open to new ideas, amenable, flexible, responsive, willing to change, undogmatic.
OPPOSITES narrow-minded, opinionated.

open-mouthed ▶ **adjective** *they stare at us open-mouthed, as if we are completely insane* **astounded**, amazed, in amazement, surprised, stunned, bowled over, staggered, thunderstruck, aghast, stupefied, dazed, taken aback, shocked, in shock, nonplussed, speechless, dumbfounded, dumbstruck, tongue-tied, at a loss for words, agape, goggle-eyed, wide-eyed, staring; *informal* flabbergasted; *Brit. informal* gobsmacked.

operate ▶ **verb 1** *he can operate the machine* **work**, make go, run, set off, use, utilize, employ, handle, control, wield, ply, manage, be in charge of; drive, steer, guide, pilot, manipulate, manoeuvre, exercise.
2 *the machine ceased to operate* **function**, work, go, run, perform, act, be in action, behave, be in working/running order, be operative.
OPPOSITES break down, fail.
3 *the research will examine how the law operates in practice* **take effect**, act, be in effect, be in force, be in operation, stand, apply, be applied, run, be/remain valid, be current, function, be efficacious, hold good, be the case.
4 *Hechstetter continued to operate the mines until about 1634* **direct**, control, manage, run, conduct, carry on, govern, administer, superintend, head (up), lead, look after, supervise, oversee, preside over, be in control/charge of.
5 *when the results of the X-rays are known, doctors will decide whether to operate on Adis* carry out an operation, perform surgery; *informal* put under the knife.

operation *See centre pages for list of surgical* **Operations**
▶ **noun 1** *the slide bars are machined to ensure smooth operation* **functioning**, working, running, performance, action, behaviour.
2 *those responsible for the operation of the factory* **management**, running, direction, control, governing, administration, supervision.
3 *legislation to curtail the operation of the closed shop* **effect**, force, potency, power, effectiveness.
4 *a heart bypass operation* **surgery**, surgical operation, surgical intervention, major surgery, minor surgery.
5 *a carefully planned military operation* **action**, activity, exercise, affair, business, undertaking, step, enterprise, task, job, process, procedure, manoeuvre, campaign.
6 *the company's South American mining operation* **business**, enterprise, company, firm, organization, concern; *informal* outfit, set-up.
□ **in operation** *only the starboard engine was in operation* **functioning**, working, running, up and running, operative, in use, in action, going; operational, workable, serviceable, functional, usable, in working order/condition, viable; in force, effective, in effect, valid.

operational ▶ **adjective** *the two reactors became operational in 1983* **up and running**, running, working, functioning, operative, in operation, in use, in action, going; **in working order**, workable, serviceable, functional, usable, viable, ready for action, prepared.
OPPOSITES broken, out of order.

operative ▶ **adjective 1** *although the act has been passed by parliament, it is not operative at the moment* **in force**, in operation, effective, in effect, valid.
OPPOSITE invalid.
2 *the steam railway is still operative* **functioning**, working, running, up and running, in operation, in use, in action, going; operational, workable, serviceable, functional, usable, in working order/condition, viable.
OPPOSITE out of order.
3 *'might' is the operative word* **key**, significant, relevant, applicable, pertinent, apposite, germane, apropos, crucial, critical, main, chief, major, central, pivotal, fundamental, vital, important, essential.
OPPOSITE irrelevant.
▶ **noun 1** *the operatives clean the machines at the end of every shift* **machinist**, (machine) operator, mechanic, engineer, driver, worker, workman, (factory) hand, artisan, craftsman, craftswoman, blue-collar worker; *Brit.* machine-minder.
2 (*N. Amer.*) *a special operative of the CIA* **agent**, secret agent, undercover agent, spy, mole, plant, double agent, counterspy; *N. Amer. informal* spook; *archaic* intelligencer; *archaic, informal* beagle.
3 (*N. Amer.*) *employ a private operative* **detective**, private detective, investigator, private investigator, sleuth, shadow; *Brit.* enquiry agent; *informal* private eye, tail; *N. Amer. informal, dated* gumshoe, bogey, dick.

operator ▶ **noun 1** *a machine operator* **machinist**, mechanic, operative, engineer, driver, worker; *Brit.* machine-minder.
2 *a tour operator* **contractor**, entrepreneur, promoter, impresario, arranger, fixer, trader, dealer, director, manager, partner, businessman, businesswoman, financier, venture capitalist, speculator.
3 *nationalism has always been the ally of the ruthless operator* **manipulator**, manoeuvrer, mover, worker, string-puller, mover and shaker, wheeler-dealer; *N. Amer.* wirepuller.

opiate ▶ **noun** *six of the patients used an opiate during the radiotherapy* **drug**, narcotic, mind-altering drug, sedative, tranquillizer, depressant, sleeping pill, soporific, anaesthetic, painkiller, analgesic, anodyne; barbiturate, bromide, morphine, opium, laudanum; *Medicine* calmative, palliative, stupefacient; *informal* dope, downer; *literary* nepenthes; *dated* sleeping draught.

opine ▶ **verb** *the headmistress opined that the outing would make a nice change* **suggest**, submit, advance, propose, venture, volunteer, put forward,

O

moot, propound, posit, air, hazard, say, declare, observe, comment, remark; **think**, believe, consider, maintain, imagine, be of the view, be of the opinion, reckon, guess, estimate, conjecture, fancy, suspect, feel, have a/the feeling, assume, presume, take it, suppose, expect, gather; contend, be convinced, be of the conviction, reason, deduce, conclude, theorize, hypothesize, take as a hypothesis; N. Amer. informal allow; archaic ween.

opinion ▶ noun *she did not share her husband's opinion* **belief**, judgement, thought(s), school of thought, thinking, way of thinking, mind, point of view, view, viewpoint, outlook, angle, slant, side, attitude, stance, perspective, position, standpoint; theory, tenet, conclusion, verdict, estimation, thesis, hypothesis, feeling, sentiment, impression, reflections, idea, notion, assumption, speculation, conception, conviction, contention, persuasion, creed, dogma.

□ **a matter of opinion** *whether this is desirable or not is a matter of opinion* **open to question**, a debatable point, debatable, open to debate, a moot point, open to/for discussion, up to the individual.

□ **be of the opinion** *I'm of the opinion that this is not necessary* **believe**, think, consider, maintain, imagine, be of the view, reckon, guess, estimate, conjecture, fancy, suspect, feel, have a/the feeling, assume, presume, take it, suppose, expect, gather; contend, put forward, be convinced, be of the conviction, reason, deduce, conclude, theorize, hypothesize, take as a hypothesis; N. Amer. informal allow; formal opine; archaic ween.

□ **in my opinion** *we have very little choice, in my opinion* **as I see it**, in my view, to my mind, (according) to my way of thinking, from my standpoint, personally, in my estimation, in my judgement, in my book, for my money, if you ask me.

opinionated ▶ adjective *the boy was dutiful and punctilious, however opinionated* **dogmatic**, of fixed views, of preconceived ideas, pontifical, doctrinaire, dictatorial, domineering, assertive, cocksure, pompous, self-important, adamant, arrogant; inflexible, uncompromising, prejudiced, biased, bigoted.
OPPOSITE open-minded.

opponent ▶ noun **1** *he beat his Republican opponent by a landslide* **rival**, **adversary**, opposer, the opposition, fellow contestant, (fellow) competitor, other competitor/contestant/player/candidate, enemy, foe, antagonist, combatant, contender, challenger, critic, dissenter, disputant, objector.
OPPOSITES ally, partner, colleague.
2 *an opponent of the economic reforms* **opposer**, objector, dissident, dissenter.
OPPOSITE supporter.

opportune ▶ adjective *it would seem an opportune moment to impose stricter regulation* **auspicious**, propitious, favourable, advantageous, heaven-sent, golden, good, right, lucky, happy, fortunate, benign, providential, felicitous; **timely**, well timed, ripe, seasonable, convenient, expedient, suitable, appropriate, apt, fitting, relevant, applicable, pertinent.
OPPOSITES disadvantageous, ill-timed.

CHOOSE THE RIGHT WORD

opportune, timely, auspicious

- **Opportune** is used mainly to denote a favourable *time* or *moment* for doing something (*I waited for an opportune moment to discuss the idea*). When applied to actions or events occurring at favourable moments, it can suggest the role of chance in producing a happy outcome (*an opportune visit from the manager allowed him to air his views*).
- A **timely** action or event occurs at a moment when it can make the greatest difference to a situation (*the assassins were stopped only by the timely intervention of a patrol*). A *timely reminder* is given when it is much needed, if not overdue.
- **Auspicious** is used where all the circumstances are conducive to the success of a new undertaking, and it is used typically to describe a point in time (*he is waiting for the most auspicious moment to call an election*). It is often used precisely when circumstances are *not* conducive to success, especially when referring to the start of something (*he did not make the most auspicious of starts to the season*).

opportunism ▶ noun *many are saying that the early election was prompted by political opportunism* **expediency**, exploitation, taking advantage, Machiavellianism, manoeuvring, pragmatism, realism, unscrupulousness; striking while the iron is hot, making hay while the sun shines, making the best of a bad job; informal ad-hockery.

opportunity ▶ noun *staff will have the opportunity to discuss the matter | it's an opportunity you shouldn't miss* **chance**, lucky chance, good time, golden opportunity, time, occasion, moment, favourable time/occasion/moment, right set of circumstances, appropriate time/occasion/moment, suitable time/occasion/moment, opportune time/occasion/moment, opening, option, window (of opportunity), slot, turn, go, (clear) run, field day; possibility, scope, freedom, latitude, room to manoeuvre, elbow room; N. Amer. & Austral./NZ show; Canadian a kick at the can/cat; informal shot, break, look-in.

oppose ▶ verb *the council received letters of protest from residents who opposed the scheme* **be against**, object to, be hostile to, be anti, be in opposition to, disagree with, dislike, disapprove of; resist, take a stand against, put up a fight against, stand up to, take on, fight, withstand, defy, set one's face against, stand up and be counted against, go against, counter, cross, confront, challenge, contend with, attack, counterattack, combat, fly in the face of; take issue with, contradict, dispute, rebut, argue with/against, quarrel with; formal gainsay; rare controvert.
OPPOSITES support, defend, promote.

opposed ▶ adjective **1** *a large proportion of the population is opposed to the construction of nuclear power plants* **against**, (dead) set against; in opposition, averse, hostile, antagonistic, inimical, antipathetic, unsympathetic, resistant; informal anti.
OPPOSITES in favour of, favourably disposed to.
2 *their interests were opposed* **conflicting**, contrasting, incompatible, irreconcilable, antithetical, contradictory, clashing, contrary, different, differing, at variance, at odds, divergent, dissimilar, disagreeing, opposing, opposite, poles apart, polar; rare oppugnant.

□ **as opposed to** *the concrete as opposed to the abstract* **in contrast with**, as against, as contrasted with, as an alternative to, rather than, instead of.

opposing ▶ adjective **1** *the two opposing points of view* **conflicting**, contrasting, opposite, incompatible, irreconcilable, contradictory, antithetical, clashing, contrary, different, differing, at variance, at odds, divergent, dissimilar, disagreeing, opposed, poles apart, polar; rare oppugnant.
2 *children whose parents had fought on opposing sides in the war* **rival**, opposite, combatant, enemy, antagonistic.
OPPOSITE allied.
3 *on the opposing page there were two addresses* **opposite**, facing.

opposite ▶ adjective **1** *she and Alice sat opposite each other* **facing**, face to face with, across from; informal eyeball to eyeball with; archaic fronting.
2 *the drawing on the opposite page* **facing**, opposing.
3 *other authors have expressed opposite views* **conflicting**, contrasting, incompatible, irreconcilable, inconsistent, antithetical, converse, contradictory, clashing, contrary, at variance, at odds, different, differing, divergent, dissimilar, unlike, unalike, disagreeing, opposed, opposing, poles apart, polar, obverse; rare oppugnant.
OPPOSITES same, identical, like.
4 *opposite sides in a war* **rival**, opposing, combatant, enemy, antagonistic.
OPPOSITE allied.
▶ noun *forecasters expected it to be a year of recovery—in fact the opposite was true | his nature is the opposite of his father's* **reverse**, converse, antithesis, contrary, inverse, obverse, contradiction; the other extreme, the other side of the coin; Italian per contra; informal flip side; rare antipode, antipodes.

WORD LINKS
related prefixes **contra-** (e.g. ***contraception, contraflow***), **counter-** (e.g. ***counter-attack, counterclockwise***)

opposition ▶ noun **1** *the proposal met with considerable opposition* **resistance**, hostility, antagonism, antipathy, enmity, objection, dissent, criticism, defiance, non-compliance, obstruction, obstructiveness, counteraction; dislike, disapproval, demurral.
2 *the home team made short work of the opposition* **opponents**, opposing side, other side, other team, competition, competitors, opposers, rivals, adversaries, antagonists, enemies; literary foes.
3 *the opposition between the public and the private domains* **conflict**, clash, difference, contrast, disparity, antithesis, polarity.

oppress ▶ verb **1** *the Russians had participated in the dismemberment of Poland and oppressed its people* **persecute**, abuse, maltreat, ill-treat, treat harshly, be brutal to, be cruel to, tyrannize, crush, repress, suppress, subjugate, subdue, subject, enslave; scourge, exploit, hold down, keep down, grind down, rule with a rod of iron, rule with an iron hand, trample on, trample underfoot, bring people to their knees, ride roughshod over; informal walk all over.
2 *the gloom in the chapel oppressed her* **depress**, make gloomy/despondent, weigh down, lie heavy on, weigh heavily on, cast down, dampen someone's spirits, hang over, prey on, burden, crush, dispirit, dishearten, discourage, sadden, make desolate, get down, bring down, trouble, afflict; archaic deject.

oppressed ▶ adjective *oppressed racial minorities* **persecuted**, downtrodden, abused, maltreated, ill-treated, tyrannized, subjugated, repressed, subdued, crushed, enslaved, exploited, victimized, misused; disadvantaged, underprivileged, ground down, browbeaten.

oppression ▶ noun *years of violence and oppression* **persecution**, abuse, maltreatment, ill-treatment, tyranny, despotism, repression, suppression, subjection, subjugation, enslavement, exploitation; cruelty, ruthlessness, harshness, brutality, injustice, hardship, misery, suffering, pain, anguish, wretchedness.
OPPOSITES freedom, democracy.

oppressive ▶ adjective **1** *an oppressive dictatorship | oppressive laws* **harsh**, cruel, brutal, repressive, crushing, tyrannical, tyrannous, iron-fisted, domineering, autocratic, dictatorial, despotic, draconian, punitive; ruthless, relentless, merciless, pitiless, severe, inexorable; unjust, unfair, undemocratic.
OPPOSITES lenient, humane.
2 *an oppressive sense of despair* **overwhelming**, overpowering, hard to bear, unbearable, burdensome, unendurable, intolerable, heavy; uncomfortable, grinding.
3 *the day was grey and oppressive* **muggy**, close, heavy, hot, humid, sticky, steamy, soupy, fuggy, airless, stuffy, stifling, suffocating, sultry, torrid.
OPPOSITES fresh, airy.

oppressor ▶ noun **persecutor**, tyrant, despot, autocrat, bully, slave-driver, hard taskmaster, iron hand, scourge, dictator, tormentor, torturer, intimidator, subjugator.

opprobrious ▶ adjective *a couple of students shouted opprobrious remarks at him* **abusive**, vituperative, derogatory, disparaging, denigratory, pejorative, deprecatory, insulting, offensive, defamatory, slanderous, libellous, scurrilous, scandalous, vitriolic, venomous; **scornful**, contemptuous, derisive; *informal* bitchy; *archaic* contumelious; *rare* calumnious, calumniatory, aspersive.

opprobrium ▶ noun **1** *the government endured months of opprobrium* **vilification**, abuse, vituperation, condemnation, criticism, censure, castigation, denunciation, defamation, denigration, disparagement, obloquy, derogation, slander, revilement, reviling, calumny, calumniation, execration, excoriation, lambasting, upbraiding, bad press, character assassination, attack, invective, libel, insults, aspersions; *informal* flak, mud-slinging, bad-mouthing, tongue-lashing; *Brit. informal* stick, verbal, slagging off; *archaic* contumely; *rare* animadversion, objurgation.
OPPOSITE praise.
2 *the opprobrium of being associated with gangsters and thugs* **disgrace**, shame, dishonour, discredit, stigma, humiliation, loss of face, ignominy, odium, obloquy, disfavour, disrepute, ill repute, infamy, notoriety, scandal, stain; *rare* disesteem.
OPPOSITE honour.

opt ▶ verb *she opted for a cream silk shirt* **choose**, select, pick, pick out, decide on, go for, settle on, plump for/on, single out, take, fix on; *Brit.* pitch on.

optimism ▶ noun *such statements reflect the growing optimism among members of the profession* **hopefulness**, hope, confidence, buoyancy, cheer, good cheer, cheerfulness, sanguineness, positiveness, positive attitude.
OPPOSITE pessimism.

optimistic ▶ adjective **1** *always optimistic, Anne felt sure that she would see him* **cheerful**, cheery, positive, confident, hopeful, sanguine, bullish, buoyant, bright; disposed to look on the bright side, inclined to look through rose-coloured spectacles, always expecting the best, full of hope, Pollyannaish, Panglossian; *informal* upbeat; *archaic* of good cheer.
OPPOSITES pessimistic, negative.
2 *the forecast is certainly more optimistic* **encouraging**, promising, hopeful, bright, rosy, reassuring, favourable, auspicious, propitious.
OPPOSITES pessimistic, gloomy, ominous.

> **CHOOSE THE RIGHT WORD**
>
> **optimistic, hopeful, confident, sanguine**
> *See* CONFIDENT.

optimum ▶ adjective *the optimum pupil-teacher ratio* **best**, most favourable, most advantageous, most appropriate, ideal, perfect, prime, optimal, model; finest, superlative, peak, top, supreme, excellent, flawless, first-class; *informal* tip-top, A1, top-notch.

option ▶ noun *the way I see it, we have two options | she was given the option of resigning or being dismissed* **choice**, alternative, recourse, possibility, course of action; freedom of choice, power to choose, right to choose; *informal* bet.

optional ▶ adjective *registration was obligatory but voting was optional* **voluntary**, non-compulsory, at one's discretion, discretionary, not required, up to the individual, elective, non-mandatory, free, open, unforced; *Law* permissive; *rare* discretional.
OPPOSITES compulsory, obligatory, mandatory, required.

opulence ▶ noun **1** *he was taken aback by the sheer opulence of the room* **luxuriousness**, sumptuousness, lavishness, richness, lushness, luxury, luxuriance, splendour, magnificence, grandeur, splendidness, grandiosity, costliness, fanciness; *informal* plushness, plushiness, ritziness, swankiness, poshness, classiness.
OPPOSITES restraint, simplicity.
2 *a display of opulence* **wealth**, affluence, wealthiness, richness, riches, prosperity, prosperousness, money, fortune.
OPPOSITE poverty.

opulent ▶ adjective **1** *his parents' opulent home in Beverly Hills* **luxurious**, sumptuous, palatial, lavishly appointed, lavish, de luxe, rich, lush, luxuriant, splendid, magnificent, grand, grandiose, costly, expensive, fancy; *informal* plush, plushy, ritzy, swanky, posh, classy; *Brit. informal* swish; *N. Amer. informal* swank.
OPPOSITES stark, spartan, restrained, ascetic.
2 *an opulent family* **wealthy**, rich, affluent, well off, well-to-do, moneyed, with deep pockets, prosperous, of means, of substance; *informal* well heeled, rolling in it, rolling in money, loaded, in clover, stinking/filthy rich, flush, made of money, in/on easy street; *Brit. informal* quids in; *informal, dated* in the chips, oofy, on velvet.
OPPOSITES penniless, poor, impoverished, penurious.
3 *he stroked her opulent red hair* **copious**, abundant, profuse, prolific, plentiful, luxuriant; *literary* plenteous.
OPPOSITE sparse.
4 *the opulent curves of her body* **voluptuous**, shapely, full, rounded, ample, Rubensesque, lush, luscious, buxom; *informal* curvaceous, curvy.
OPPOSITES thin, emaciated.

opus ▶ noun *his acclaimed opus 'In Search of Excellence'* **composition**, work, work of art, oeuvre, piece, creation, production; *rare* opuscule.

oracle ▶ noun **1** *Hercules consulted the oracle of Apollo* **prophet**, **prophetess**, sibyl, seer, augur, prognosticator, diviner, soothsayer, wise man, wise woman, sage, fortune teller; *rare* oracler.
2 *the Colonial Office's oracle on Africa* **authority**, expert, specialist, pundit, guru, mentor, adviser, mastermind, connoisseur; *informal* wizard, high priest.

oracular ▶ adjective **1** *his every utterance was given oracular significance by his fans* **prophetic**, prophetical, sibylline, predictive, prescient, prognostic, divinatory, augural; *rare* vatic, mantic, fatidical, fatidic, haruspical, pythonic.
2 *his hesitation and oracular responses are not good advertisements for privatization* **enigmatic**, cryptic, abstruse, unclear, obscure, confusing, mystifying, puzzling, perplexing, baffling, mysterious, arcane; ambiguous, equivocal, two-edged, Delphic.

oral ▶ adjective *an oral agreement* **spoken**, verbal, unwritten, by mouth, vocal, viva voce, uttered, said.
OPPOSITE written.
▶ noun *a French oral* **oral examination**; *Brit.* viva, viva voce.

orate ▶ verb *he strode up and down the aisle as he orated* **declaim**, make a speech, hold forth, speak, discourse, pontificate, preach, sermonize, sound off, spout off; *informal* spiel, speechify, mouth off; *rare* perorate.

oration ▶ noun *his eloquent funeral oration* **speech**, address, lecture, talk, homily, sermon, discourse, declamation, recitation, disquisition, peroration, monologue, valedictory, harangue, tirade, diatribe, rant; *N. Amer.* salutatory; *informal* spiel; *rare* allocution, predication.

orator ▶ noun *an eloquent and persuasive orator* **speaker**, public speaker, speech-maker, lecturer, declaimer, rhetorician; *informal* spieler; *historical* demagogue, rhetor.

oratorical ▶ adjective *he adopted a rather oratorical style* **rhetorical**, grandiloquent, magniloquent, high-flown, high-sounding, sonorous, lofty, orotund, bombastic, grandiose, pompous, pretentious, overblown, turgid, extravagant, flowery, florid, declamatory, Ciceronian; *informal* highfalutin; *rare* epideictic, fustian, euphuistic, aureate, Demosthenic, Demosthenean.
OPPOSITES plain-spoken, simple, unadorned.

oratory ▶ noun *he whipped the meeting up into a frenzy with his oratory* **rhetoric**, eloquence, grandiloquence, magniloquence, public speaking, speech-making, declamation, way with words, the gift of the gab, fluency.

orb ▶ noun *the red orb of the sun sank beneath the horizon* **sphere**, globe, ball, circle, ring, spheroid, spherule, round.

orbit ▶ noun **1** *the earth's orbit around the sun* **course**, path, circuit, track, trajectory, rotation, revolution, circle, cycle, round; *rare* circumgyration.
2 *the problem comes within the Ombudsman's orbit* **sphere**, sphere of influence, area of activity, range, reach, scope, ambit, compass, sweep, jurisdiction, authority, remit, span of control, domain, realm, province, territory, preserve, department, turf; *informal* bailiwick.
▶ verb *Mercury orbits the sun* **revolve round**, circle round, go round, travel round; *rare* encircle.

orchestra *See centre pages for list of* **Orchestral Instruments**
▶ noun **ensemble**; *informal* band.

orchestrate ▶ verb **1** *the piece may have been subsequently orchestrated by Mozart* **arrange**, adapt, score; *rare* instrument.
2 *he threatened to orchestrate a campaign of civil disobedience* **organize**, arrange, put together, plan, set up, bring about, manage, mobilize, mount, stage, stage-manage, mastermind, choreograph, coordinate, direct, engineer; *rare* concert.

ordain ▶ verb **1** *the Church of England voted to ordain women* **confer holy orders on**, appoint, induct, install, invest, anoint, consecrate; *archaic* frock.
2 *the path ordained by God* **predetermine**, predestine, preordain, foreordain, destine, prescribe, fate, will, determine, designate.
3 *it was ordained that anyone hunting in the forest without permission was to*

pay a fine **decree**, rule, order, command, enjoin, lay down, set down, establish, fix, enact, legislate, dictate, prescribe, pronounce.

ordeal ▶ noun *both women were understandably shaken by their ordeal* **painful/unpleasant experience**, trial, tribulation, test, nightmare, trauma, baptism of fire, hell, hell on earth, misery, trouble, difficulty, torture, torment, agony.

order ▶ noun **1** *the list is in alphabetical order* **sequence**, arrangement, organization, disposition, structure, system, series, succession; grouping, classification, categorization, codification, systematization, disposal, form; layout, array, set-up, line-up.
2 *I tried to restore the room to some semblance of order* **tidiness**, neatness, orderliness, trimness, harmony, apple-pie order.
OPPOSITES chaos, disarray, untidiness.
3 *6,000 police were needed to keep order* **peace**, **control**, lawful behaviour, law and order, law, lawfulness, discipline, calm, quiet, peace and quiet, quietness, peacefulness, peaceableness, tranquillity, serenity.
OPPOSITE disorder.
4 *the idea appealed to his sense of order* **orderliness**, organization, method, system; symmetry, pattern, uniformity, regularity, routine.
5 *all the equipment was in good order* **condition**, state, repair, shape, situation.
6 *I had no choice but to obey his orders* **command**, instruction, directive, direction, decree, edict, injunction, mandate, dictate, commandment; law, rule, regulation, ordinance, statute, fiat, diktat; demand, bidding, requirement, stipulation; summons, writ, warrant; (in Spanish-speaking countries) pronunciamento; (in Tsarist Russia) ukase; informal say-so; literary behest; rare rescript.
7 *winning the order would mean about £60 million worth of work for the company* **commission**, purchase order, request, requisition, demand, call; booking, reservation, application.
8 *the upper and lower orders of society* **class**, level, rank, caste, grade, degree, position, station, category.
9 *the established social order* **system**, class system, hierarchy, pecking order, grouping, grading, ranking, scale.
10 *the higher orders of insects* **taxonomic group**, class, subclass, family, species, breed; technical taxon.
11 *the head of a religious order* **community**, brotherhood, sisterhood.
12 *the Independent Orange Order* **organization**, association, society, fellowship, body, fraternity, confraternity, sorority, brotherhood, sisterhood, lodge, guild, league, union, club; denomination, sect; rare sodality.
13 *diplomatic skills of a very high order* **type**, kind, sort, nature, variety, ilk, genre, cast, style, brand, vintage; quality, calibre, standard.

□ **in order 1** *list the points you intend to cover and put them in order* **in sequence**, in alphabetical order, in numerical order, in order of priority, in order of merit, in order of seniority.
2 *when he switched on the light and went in, he found everything in order* **tidy**, neat, neat and tidy, orderly, straight, trim, shipshape (and Bristol fashion), in apple-pie order, spick and span; in position, in place.
3 *I think it's in order for me to take the credit, don't you?* **appropriate**, fitting, suitable, right, correct, proper; **acceptable**, all right, permissible, permitted, allowable; French comme il faut; informal okay.

□ **out of order 1** *the lift's out of order* **not working**, not in working order, not functioning, broken, broken-down, out of service, out of commission, acting up, unserviceable, faulty, defective, non-functional, inoperative, in disrepair; down; informal conked out, bust, (gone) kaput, gone phut, on the blink, gone haywire, shot; Brit. informal knackered, jiggered, wonky; N. Amer. informal on the fritz, out of whack; Brit. vulgar slang buggered.
2 *he wanted to sack her on the spot—that's really out of order* **unacceptable**, unfair, unjust, unjustified, uncalled for, below the belt, out of turn, not done, unreasonable, unwarranted, unnecessary, wrong, beyond the pale, improper, irregular; informal not on, a bit much; Brit. informal a bit thick, off, not cricket; Austral./NZ informal over the fence.

▶ verb **1** *he ordered me to return at once* **instruct**, command, direct, enjoin, give the order to, give the command to, tell, require, charge, adjure; literary bid.
2 *Judge Butler ordered that assets worth £23,000 be confiscated under the Drugs Trafficking Act* **decree**, ordain, rule, legislate, lay down, dictate, prescribe, pronounce, determine; rare enact.
3 *you can order your tickets by phone* **request**, apply for, send away/off for, write off for, put in an order for, place an order for, requisition; book, reserve; commission, contract for; rare bespeak.
4 *Derek struggled to order his thoughts | the messages are ordered alphabetically* **organize**, put in order, set in order, arrange, sort out, straighten out, marshal, dispose, lay out, regulate; group, classify, categorize, catalogue, codify, systematize, systemize, tabulate; rare methodize.

□ **order someone about/around tell someone what to do**, give orders to, boss about/around, bully, lord it over, dictate to, ride roughshod over, dominate, domineer, browbeat; throw one's weight about/around, lay down the law; informal push about/around.

orderly ▶ adjective **1** *an orderly room* **neat**, **tidy**, well ordered, in order, trim, in apple-pie order, as neat as a new pin, spick and span, well kept, straight; Brit. informal, dated shipshape (and Bristol fashion).
OPPOSITES disorderly, untidy, chaotic, messy.
2 *Robert had been an orderly man | the orderly presentation of information* **well organized**, organized, efficient, businesslike, methodical, systematic, careful, meticulous, punctilious; coherent, structured, logical, well planned, well regulated, systematized; French rangé.
OPPOSITE disorganized.
3 *the crowd was quiet and orderly* **well behaved**, law-abiding, disciplined, peaceful, peaceable, non-violent, controlled, restrained, civilized, well mannered, polite, courteous, decorous; archaic ruly.
OPPOSITES disorderly, unruly.

ordinance ▶ noun **1** *the president issued a series of ordinances in 1944* **edict**, decree, law, injunction, fiat, command, order, rule, ruling, dictum, dictate, directive, mandate, enactment, statute, act, canon, regulation; (in Tsarist Russia) ukase; (in Spanish-speaking countries) pronunciamento.
2 *religious ordinances* **rite**, ritual, ceremony, sacrament, observance, service, usage, institution, practice.

ordinarily ▶ adverb *he ordinarily worked outside Great Britain* **usually**, normally, as a rule, generally, as a general rule, in general, in the general run of things, for the most part, by and large, mainly, mostly, most of the time, customarily, typically, habitually, commonly, routinely.
OPPOSITES exceptionally, unusually.

ordinary ▶ adjective **1** *the ordinary course of events* **usual**, normal, standard, typical, stock, common, customary, habitual, accustomed, expected, wonted, everyday, regular, routine, day-to-day, daily, established, settled, set, fixed, traditional, quotidian, prevailing.
OPPOSITE abnormal.
2 *he's just an ordinary middle-aged man | my life seemed very ordinary* **average**, normal, run-of-the-mill, standard, typical, middle-of-the-road, common, conventional, mainstream, unremarkable, unexceptional, unpretentious, modest, plain, simple, homely, homespun, workaday, undistinguished, nondescript, characterless, colourless, commonplace, humdrum, mundane, unmemorable, pedestrian, prosaic, quotidian, uninteresting, uneventful, dull, boring, uninspiring, bland, suburban, hackneyed, stale, mediocre, middling, indifferent; N. Amer. garden-variety; informal OK, so-so, bog-standard, vanilla, plain vanilla, nothing to write home about, a dime a dozen, no great shakes, not up to much; Brit. informal common or garden; N. Amer. informal ornery.
OPPOSITES unusual, extraordinary, unique, exceptional.

□ **out of the ordinary** *nothing out of the ordinary happened* **unusual**, exceptional, remarkable, extraordinary, unexpected, surprising, unaccustomed, uncommon, unfamiliar, abnormal, atypical, unwonted, out of the way, anomalous, different, special, exciting, memorable, striking, noteworthy, unique, singular, unheard of, impressive, outstanding, unconventional, unorthodox, exotic, strange, peculiar, odd, queer, curious, bizarre, offbeat, weird, outlandish.

ordnance ▶ noun **guns**, cannon, artillery, weapons, arms, munitions, military supplies, materiel.

ordure ▶ noun **excrement**, excreta, dung, manure, muck, droppings, faeces, stools, cowpats, guano, night soil, sewage, dirt, filth, jakes, doings, scat; informal pooh, doo-doo, jobbie; Brit. informal cack, whoopsie, big jobs; N. Amer. informal poop; vulgar slang shit, crap, turds; rare feculence, egesta.

organ *See centre pages for lists of* **Organs** **Organ Stops**
▶ noun **1** *the internal organs* **part of the body**, body part, biological structure.
2 *the official organ of the Chinese Communist Party* **newspaper**, paper, journal, periodical, magazine, newsletter, gazette, bulletin, publication, means of communication, mouthpiece, voice, forum, vehicle, medium, channel, instrument, agency; informal rag.

organic ▶ adjective **1** *organic matter* **living**, live, animate, biological, natural; technical biotic.
OPPOSITE inorganic.
2 *organic vegetables | organic farming* **pesticide-free**, additive-free, chemical-free, non-chemical, natural.
3 *the love scenes were an organic part of the drama and important in the story telling* **essential**, fundamental, basic, integral, intrinsic, vital, indispensable, inherent, constitutive, innate, structural.
OPPOSITE incidental.
4 *a society is an organic whole* **structured**, organized, coherent, integrated, coordinated, ordered, systematic, systematized, methodical, orderly, consistent, harmonious, methodized.
OPPOSITE disparate.

organism ▶ noun **1** *fish and other organisms* **living thing**, being, creature, animal, plant, structure, life form, entity, body.
2 *parliament is a complex political organism* **structure**, **system**, organization, entity, whole, set-up.

organization ▶ noun **1** *the organization of conferences and seminars* **planning**, arrangement, coordination, structuring, administration, organizing, running, management, logistics; establishment, formation, development, assembling, assembly, regulation.

2 *the overall organization of the book* **structure**, arrangement, scheme, plan, pattern, order, form, format, framework, system, composition, constitution, shape, make-up, configuration; systematization, methodization, categorization, classification, codification.
3 *his lack of organization* **efficiency**, order, orderliness, sense of order, method, system, tidiness, planning.
4 *a large international organization* **company**, firm, concern, operation, corporation, institution, group, establishment, consortium, conglomerate, combine, syndicate, body, agency, federation, confederation, alliance, coalition, association, movement, society, league, club, network, confederacy; informal outfit, set-up.

organize ▶ verb 1 *try to organize your thoughts | our primary objective is to collect, organize, and disseminate information* **put in order**, order, arrange, sort, sort out, assemble, marshal, put straight, group, dispose, classify, collocate, categorize, catalogue, codify, tabulate, compile, systematize, systemize, regulate, regiment, standardize, structure, shape, mould, lick/knock into shape, pigeonhole; rare methodize.
OPPOSITES jumble, disorganize.
2 *a local man organized a search party | I'll organize the transport* **make arrangements for**, arrange, coordinate, sort out, put together, fix up, get together, orchestrate, choreograph, be responsible for, be in charge of, take care of, look after, see to, see about, deal with, direct, run, manage, conduct, administrate, set up, mobilize, mastermind, engineer; institute, develop, form, create, establish, found, originate, begin, start; schedule, timetable, programme; rare concert.

organized ▶ adjective *a highly organized campaign | she used to be so organized* **well ordered**, in order, ordered, well run, well regulated, orderly, efficient, neat, tidy, methodical, businesslike, planned, systematic, structured, arranged; informal together.
OPPOSITES disorganized, inefficient.

orgiastic ▶ adjective *a place remarkable for its wild parties and orgiastic festivals* **debauched**, wild, riotous, wanton, abandoned, dissolute, depraved, bacchanalian, Bacchic, saturnalian, Dionysiac, Dionysian.
OPPOSITES puritanical, ascetic.

orgy ▶ noun 1 *a drunken orgy* **wild party**, debauch, carousal, carouse, revel, revelry, bacchanalia, bacchanal, saturnalia, Dionysiacs; Scottish skite; informal binge, jag, booze-up, bender, spree, drunk, love-in, gang bang; Brit. informal rave-up; N. Amer. informal toot; archaic wassail.
2 *a shopping orgy | an orgy of violence* **bout**, excess, surfeit, overindulgence; informal spree, splurge, binge.

orient, orientate ▶ verb 1 *there were no street names to enable her to orient herself* **get/find one's bearings**, get the lie of the land, establish one's location, feel one's way.
2 *you will need time to orientate yourself to your new way of life* **adapt**, adjust, accommodate, familiarize, acclimatize, accustom, attune, habituate, condition, find one's feet; Brit. play oneself in; N. Amer. acclimate.
3 *magazines oriented to the business community* **aim**, direct, slant, angle, pitch, steer, design, intend.
4 *the fires are oriented in direct line with the midsummer sunset* **align**, place, position, put, dispose, situate, set.

oriental ▶ adjective **eastern**, Far Eastern, Asian, Asiatic; subcontinental; literary orient.

orientation ▶ noun 1 *the orientation of the radar station | a north-easterly orientation* **positioning**, location, position, situation, lie, bearings, angle, placement, direction, alignment, emplacement, locating, situating.
2 *his orientation to his new way of life* **adaptation**, adjustment, accommodation, familiarization, acclimatization, settling in.
3 *a movement that was broadly Marxist in orientation* **attitude**, inclination, direction, aim, intention.
4 *only a small fraction of the workforce received any orientation* **induction**, training, guidance, introduction, initiation, briefing.

orifice ▶ noun **opening**, hole, aperture, crack, slot, slit, cleft, cranny, chink, gap, space, vent, breach, break, rent, fissure, mouth, crevice, rift, perforation, pore.

origin ▶ noun 1 *the origins of life and the physical universe | social problems that had their origin in the decline in the economy* **beginning**, start, origination, genesis, birth, dawning, dawn, emergence, inception, launch, creation, birthplace, cradle, early stages, conception, inauguration, foundation, outset; **source**, basis, base, cause, root, roots, spring, mainspring, well head, fountainhead, fountain, fount, head, seat, seed, germ; Latin fons et origo; formal commencement; literary wellspring; rare radix.
OPPOSITES end, conclusion, termination.
2 *the Latin origin of the word* **source**, derivation, root, roots, provenance, etymology; N. Amer. provenience.
3 *his Scottish origins* **descent**, **ancestry**, parentage, pedigree, lineage, line, line of descent, heritage, birth, extraction, background, family, stock, blood, bloodline, genealogy, beginnings; rare filiation, stirps.

original ▶ adjective 1 *the original inhabitants of Canada* **indigenous**, native, aboriginal; **first**, earliest, early, initial, primary, primordial, primal, primeval, primitive; rare autochthonic, autochthonous.
OPPOSITES latest, last.
2 *original Rembrandts* **authentic**, genuine, actual, real, true, pukka, bona fide, veritable, not copied, archetypal, prototypical, master; informal kosher.
3 *the film is challenging and highly original* **innovative**, creative, imaginative, innovatory, innovational, inventive, ingenious; **new**, novel, fresh, refreshing; unusual, unconventional, unorthodox, unfamiliar, unprecedented, groundbreaking, pioneering, avant-garde, seminal, fertile, unique, individual, individualistic, distinctive.
OPPOSITES commonplace, conventional, unimaginative.
▶ noun 1 *the portrait may be a copy of the original* **archetype**, prototype, source, master, paradigm, model, pattern, standard.
2 *he really is an original* **individualist**, individual, eccentric, nonconformist, free spirit, bohemian, rare bird, maverick, oddity; Latin rara avis; informal character, oddball, odd/queer fish, nut, weirdo, weirdie; Brit. informal one-off, odd bod, oner; N. Amer. informal wacko, wack, screwball, kook; informal, dated card, case.

WORD LINKS
related prefixes **proto-** (e.g. ***prototype, prototherian***), **ur-** (e.g. ***urtext***)

CHOOSE THE RIGHT WORD

original, new, novel, fresh, newfangled
See NEW.

originality ▶ noun *the originality of his ideas* **inventiveness**, ingenuity, creativeness, creativity, innovativeness, innovation, novelty, newness, freshness, imagination, imaginativeness, break with tradition, resourcefulness, cleverness, daring, individuality, unusualness, unconventionality, unprecedentedness, uniqueness, distinctiveness.

originally ▶ adverb *the conference was originally scheduled for November* **at first**, first, in/at the beginning, to begin with, initially, in the first place, at the start, at the outset, in the first instance, from day one; informal from the word go.

originate ▶ verb 1 *the disease originates from East Africa* **arise**, have its origin, derive, begin, start, stem, spring, emerge, develop, grow, rise, flow, emanate, issue.
2 *Bill Levy originated the idea* **invent**, be the inventor of, create, initiate, devise, think up, dream up, coin, conceive, design, concoct, contrive, formulate, form, evolve, develop, generate, engender, produce, discover, set in motion, set up, inaugurate, launch, mastermind, pioneer, introduce, establish, institute, bring about, found, give birth to, be the father/mother of; literary beget.
OPPOSITES terminate, end.

originator ▶ noun **inventor**, creator, architect, author, prime mover, father, mother, maker, initiator, innovator, founder, pioneer, mastermind, discoverer, establisher, developer, designer; literary begetter.

ornament ▶ noun 1 *small tables covered with ornaments* **knick-knack**, trinket, bauble, piece of bric-a-brac, bibelot, gewgaw, gimcrack, furbelow, objet, accessory; informal whatnot, dingle-dangle; Brit. informal doobry, doodah; N. Amer. informal tchotchke, tsatske; dated folderol; archaic whim-wham, kickshaw, bijou.
2 *a cream silk dress that had no ornament at all* **decoration**, adornment, embellishment, ornamentation, trimming, accessories, frills, frippery, finery, enhancement, beautification, garnish, garnishing, garnishment, gingerbread.
▶ verb *the gold ring was exquisitely ornamented with tiny pearls* **decorate**, adorn, embellish, trim, garnish, bedeck, deck (out), festoon, enhance, beautify, grace, accessorize, dress up; literary bedizen, furbelow.

ornamental ▶ adjective *ornamental plasterwork* **decorative**, fancy, ornate, attractive, pretty, artistic, ornamented, showy, gingerbread, for show, non-functional.

ornamentation ▶ noun *she wore simple clothing with no ornamentation* **decoration**, adornment, embellishment, ornament, finery, frippery, frills, trimmings, accessories, embroidery, garnishing, garnishment, gingerbread; rare fallalery.

ornate ▶ adjective 1 *an ornate Venetian gilt mirror* **elaborate**, decorated, embellished, adorned, ornamented, fancy, over-elaborate, fussy, busy, ostentatious, showy, baroque, rococo, florid, wedding-cake, gingerbread; informal flash, flashy.
2 *ornate, metaphorical language* **elaborate**, over-elaborate, flowery, florid, flamboyant; **grandiose**, pompous, pretentious, affected, high-flown, high-sounding, orotund, fulsome, magniloquent, grandiloquent, rhetorical, oratorical, bombastic, laboured, strained, overwrought, overblown, overdone, convoluted, stilted, turgid, inflated; informal highfalutin, purple; rare tumid, pleonastic, euphuistic, aureate, Ossianic, fustian, hyperventilated.
OPPOSITES plain, austere, simple.

orotund ▶ adjective 1 *Halliwell's orotund voice* **deep**, sonorous, strong, powerful, full, full-toned, rich, fruity, clear, round, resonant, ringing, reverberating, loud, booming, imposing; rare canorous.
2 *the orotund rhetoric of his prose* **pompous**, pretentious, affected,

mannered, fulsome, grandiose, ornate, over-elaborate, overblown, flowery, florid, flamboyant, inflated, high-flown, high-sounding, magniloquent, grandiloquent, declamatory, rhetorical, oratorical, theatrical, rotund, bombastic, overwrought, overdone, convoluted, turgid; *informal* highfalutin, purple; *rare* tumid, euphuistic, aureate, Ossianic, fustian, hyperventilated.

orthodox ▶ adjective **1** *his views were orthodox in his time* **conventional**, mainstream, conformist, accepted, approved, received, recognized, correct, proper, established, well established, authorized, authoritative, traditional, traditionalist, prevailing, prevalent, common, popular, customary, usual, normal, regular, standard, canonical, doctrinal, unheretical, conservative, unoriginal; *French* bien pensant.
OPPOSITES unconventional, unorthodox, nonconformist.
2 *an orthodox Hindu* **conservative**, traditional, observant, conformist, devout, strict, true, true blue, of the faith, of the true faith.

orthodoxy ▶ noun **1** *a pillar of orthodoxy, he challenged the theological liberalism of his time* **conventionality**, conventionalism, conformism, conservatism, traditionalism, conformity, properness, propriety, correctness, doctrinalism, unoriginality.
2 *the prevailing aesthetic orthodoxies* **doctrine**, belief, conviction, creed, dogma, credo, theory, view, idea, tenet, teaching, practice, received wisdom, article of faith.

oscillate ▶ verb **1** *the pendulum started to oscillate* **swing**, sway, swing from side to side, swing back and forth, swing backwards and forwards, swing to and fro, vibrate; *N. Amer. informal* wigwag.
2 *he was oscillating between fear and bravery* **waver**, swing, fluctuate, alternate, see-saw, veer, yo-yo, sway, go from one extreme to the other, vary, vacillate, teeter, hover; *informal* wobble, blow hot and cold.

oscillation ▶ noun **1** *the oscillation of the pendulum* **swinging**, swing, swaying, swinging from side to side, swinging backwards and forwards, swinging back and forth, swinging to and fro, vibration.
2 *his oscillation between commerce and art* **wavering**, fluctuation, see-sawing, vacillation, yo-yoing, variation.

ossify ▶ verb **1** *these cartilages may ossify* **turn into bone**, become bony, harden, solidify, stiffen, rigidify, petrify, fossilize; *rare* indurate.
2 *past oligarchies have fallen from power because they ossified* **become inflexible**, become rigid, fossilize, harden, rigidify, stagnate, become unyielding/obdurate, become unprogressive, cease developing.

ostensible ▶ adjective *there are of course dangers in taking ostensible motives as real ones* **apparent**, seeming, outward, surface, superficial, professed, supposed, avowed, presumed, so-called, alleged, declared, claimed, purported, pretended, feigned, specious; *rare* ostensive.
OPPOSITES real, genuine.

ostensibly ▶ adverb *it is ostensibly a book about football* **apparently**, seemingly, on the face of it, to all appearances, on the surface, to all intents and purposes, outwardly, superficially, allegedly, professedly, supposedly, purportedly; *rare* pretendedly, ostensively.
OPPOSITES genuinely, really, truly.

ostentation ▶ noun *consumers abandoned the excess and ostentation of the 1980s* **showiness**, show, showing off, ostentatiousness; **pretentiousness**, pretension, vulgarity, conspicuousness, obtrusiveness, display, flamboyance, gaudiness, garishness, tinsel, brashness, loudness, extravagance, ornateness, theatricality, kitschness, affectation, bad taste, tastelessness, self-advertisement, exhibitionism, flaunting; *informal* flashiness, flash, flashness, glitz, glitziness, ritziness, swankiness, swank, splashiness.
OPPOSITES modesty, unpretentiousness.

ostentatious ▶ adjective *an ostentatious display of wealth* **showy**, **pretentious**, conspicuous, obtrusive, flamboyant, gaudy, garish, tinsel, tinselly, brash, vulgar, loud, extravagant, fancy, ornate, affected, theatrical, overdone, over-elaborate, kitsch, tasteless; *informal* flash, flashy, over the top, OTT, glitzy, ritzy, swanky, splashy; *N. Amer. informal* bling-bling, superfly; *US black English* dicty.
OPPOSITES plain, unobtrusive, restrained, modest.

ostracism ▶ noun *the threat of social ostracism* **exclusion**, rejection, repudiation, shunning, spurning, the cold shoulder, cold-shouldering, boycotting, blackballing, blacklisting, snubbing, avoidance, barring, banishment, exile, expulsion; *N. Amer.* disfellowship; *Christianity* excommunication.
OPPOSITES acceptance, welcome.

ostracize ▶ verb *individuals who took such action risked being ostracized by their fellow workers* **exclude**, shun, spurn, cold-shoulder, give someone the cold shoulder, reject, repudiate, boycott, blackball, blacklist, cast off, cast out, shut out, avoid, ignore, snub, cut dead, keep at arm's length, leave out in the cold, bar, ban, debar, banish, exile, expel; *Brit.* send to Coventry; *N. Amer.* disfellowship; *informal* freeze out, hand someone the frozen mitt; *Brit. informal* blank; *dated* cut; *Christianity* excommunicate.
OPPOSITES welcome, accept, befriend, include.

other ▶ adjective **1** *these homes use other fuels only because gas is unavailable* **alternative**, different, dissimilar, disparate, distinct, separate, contrasting, unlike, variant.
2 *are there any other questions?* **more**, further, additional, extra, added, supplementary, supplemental.

WORD LINKS
related prefix **hetero-** (e.g. ***heterosexual, heteropolar***)

otherwise ▶ adverb **1** *hurry up, otherwise we'll be late* **or else**, or, if not.
2 *she's exhausted, but otherwise she's fine* **in other respects**, in other ways, apart from that.
3 *he could not have acted otherwise* differently, in any other way.

other-worldly ▶ adjective *his face was lean with a distant, other-worldly look* **ethereal**, fey, dreamy, spiritual, mystic, mystical; unearthly, supernatural, preternatural, transcendental; unworldly.

ounce ▶ noun *it took every ounce of courage she possessed to board the plane* **particle**, scrap, bit, speck, iota, whit, jot, trace, atom, shred, crumb, fragment, grain, drop, spot, mite, tittle, jot or tittle, modicum; *Irish* stim; *informal* smidgen, smidge, tad; *archaic* scantling, scruple.

ourselves ▶ pronoun
□ **by ourselves**. *See* BY ONESELF *at* BY.

oust ▶ verb *armed forces ousted the new coalition government* **drive out**, expel, force out, throw out, remove, remove from office/power, eject, get rid of, depose, topple, unseat, overthrow, bring down, overturn, put out, drum out, thrust out, push out, turn out, purge, evict, dispossess, dismiss, dislodge, displace, supplant, disinherit, show someone the door; banish, deport, exile; *informal* boot out, kick out, give someone the boot; *Brit. informal* turf out; *dated* out.

out ▶ adjective & adverb **1** *I'm afraid she's out at the moment* **not here**, not at home, not in, gone away, away, elsewhere, absent, away from one's desk.
OPPOSITE in.
2 *the secret was soon out* **revealed**, in the open, out in the open, common knowledge, public knowledge, known, disclosed, divulged, exposed.
OPPOSITES unknown, secret.
3 *the roses are out* **in flower**, flowering, in bloom, in full bloom, blooming, in blossom, blossoming, open.
OPPOSITE in bud.
4 *the book should be out by the end of the month* **available**, obtainable, in the shops, published, in print, issued.
5 *the fire was nearly out* **not burning**, extinguished, no longer alight, quenched, doused, dead, defunct.
6 *grunge is out* **no longer in fashion**, out of fashion, unfashionable, out of style, dated, out of date, outdated, not in, behind the times; *French* démodé, passé; *informal* old hat, not with it.
OPPOSITE fashionable.
7 *smoking is out and so is too much alcohol* **forbidden**, not permitted, not allowed, proscribed, taboo, impermissible, unacceptable, not advisable; *informal* not on.
OPPOSITES permitted, ok.
8 *he was slightly out in his calculations* **mistaken**, inaccurate, incorrect, wide of the mark, wrong, in error, off.
OPPOSITES spot on, accurate.
□ **out cold unconscious**, knocked out, out for the count, KO'd, insensible, comatose, senseless; *informal* kayoed, dead to the world; *Brit. informal* spark out; *rare* soporose, soporous.
▶ verb (*informal*) *it was not our intention to out him* **expose**, unmask, uncover.

out-and-out ▶ adjective *he really is an out-and-out chauvinist* **utter**, downright, thoroughgoing, absolute, complete, thorough, through and through, total, unmitigated, outright, real, perfect, consummate, surpassing, sheer, rank, pure, unqualified, inveterate, positive, dyed-in-the-wool, true-blue, undiluted, unalloyed, unadulterated, in every respect, unconditional; blatant, flagrant, overt, naked, barefaced, brazen; *N. Amer.* full-bore; *informal* deep-dyed; *Brit. informal* right; *Austral./NZ informal* fair; *archaic* arrant; *rare* right-down.

outbreak ▶ noun **1** *an outbreak of legionnaires' disease | a fresh outbreak of sectarian killings* **eruption**, flare-up, upsurge, outburst, epidemic, breakout, sudden appearance, rash, wave, spate, flood, explosion, burst, blaze, flurry; *rare* recrudescence, ebullition, boutade.
2 *he was interned on the outbreak of war* **start**, beginning, onset, breaking out, opening, outset, day one, inception, dawn, genesis; *formal* commencement.

outburst ▶ noun *outbursts of emotion | a wild outburst of applause* **eruption**, explosion, burst, outbreak, flare-up, blow-up, blaze, attack, fit, spasm, paroxysm, access, rush, gale, flood, storm, hurricane, torrent, outpouring, surge, upsurge, spurt, effusion, outflow, outflowing, welling up; *informal* splurt; *rare* ebullition, boutade.

outcast ▶ noun *a social outcast* **pariah**, persona non grata, reject, leper, untouchable; foundling, waif, stray; exile, refugee, displaced person, DP, evacuee, expatriate, outsider, outlaw, castaway; *rare* Ishmael.
OPPOSITE insider.

outclass ▶ verb *he proceeded to win his next nine races, completely outclassing his rivals* **surpass**, be superior to, be better than, outshine, overshadow, eclipse, outdo, outplay, outmanoeuvre, outdistance, outstrip, outrun, outpace, out-think, get the better of, dwarf, put in the shade, upstage, transcend; top, cap, trump, trounce, beat, defeat, better, put to shame, exceed, leave behind, outrank; *informal* be a cut above, be head and shoulders above, run rings round, leave standing, walk away from; *archaic* outrival, outvie.

outcome ▶ noun *the future of the industry could hinge on the outcome of next month's election* **result**, end result, consequence, net result, upshot, effect, after-effect, aftermath, conclusion, sequel, follow-up, issue, product, end product, end, development, offshoot, outgrowth, wake, denouement; *Medicine* sequelae; *informal* pay-off; *archaic* success.

outcry ▶ noun **1** *an outcry of spontaneous passion* **shout**, exclamation, cry, yell, howl, whoop, roar, scream, shriek, screech; *informal* holler.
2 *the public outcry led to the closure of the bank* **protest(s)**, protestation(s), complaints, howls of protest, objections, indignation, furore, clamour, clamouring, fuss, commotion, uproar, hue and cry, row, outbursts, tumult, opposition, dissent, vociferation; *informal* hullabaloo, ballyhoo, ructions, stink.
OPPOSITE indifference.

outdated ▶ adjective *an outdated rail network* **old-fashioned**, out of date, outmoded, out of fashion, unfashionable, out of style, dated, out, outworn, old, former, musty, old-time, old-world, behind the times, behindhand, past, bygone, archaic, obsolescent, obsolete, ancient, antiquated, superannuated, defunct, medieval, prehistoric, antediluvian, old-fogeyish, old-fangled, backward-looking, quaint, anachronistic, crusted, feudal, fusty, moth-eaten, olde worlde; *French* passé, démodé, vieux jeu; *informal* old hat, square, not with it, out of the ark, creaky, mouldy; *N. Amer. informal* horse-and-buggy, clunky, rinky-dink, mossy; *archaic* square-toed.
OPPOSITES current, modern, fashionable.

outdistance ▶ verb **1** *the colt outdistanced the train at a canter* **outrun**, outstrip, run faster than, outpace, leave behind, get (further) ahead of, gain on, draw away from, overtake, pass, shake off, throw off, lose, put distance between oneself and someone else, widen the gap between oneself and someone else.
2 *the sugar mill at Torres outdistanced all its rivals in output* **surpass**, outshine, do better than, outclass, outdo, excel, exceed, transcend, top, cap, trump, beat, better, leave behind, lead; *informal* leave standing, walk away from; *archaic* outrival, outvie.

outdo ▶ verb *each lady tried to outdo the other in the number of coffee parties given* **surpass**, outshine, do better than; overshadow, eclipse, outclass, outmanoeuvre, out-think, get the better of, dwarf, put in the shade, upstage, put to shame; **excel**, exceed, transcend, top, cap, trump, beat, better, outdistance, outstrip, outrun, outpace, lead, leave behind, get (further) ahead of, gain on, draw away from, overtake, pass; *informal* be a cut above, be head and shoulders above, run rings round, leave standing, walk away from; *archaic* outrival, outvie.

O

CHOOSE THE RIGHT WORD

outdo, excel, surpass
See EXCEL.

outdoor ▶ adjective *a popular outdoor activity* **open air**, out-of-doors, outside, exterior, external; exposed to the elements, not under cover, field; *French* en plein air, plein-air; *Italian* al fresco.
OPPOSITES indoor, inside.

outer ▶ adjective **1** *the outer layer of a vegetable is often the most nutritious* **outside**, outermost, outward, exterior, external, surface, superficial.
2 *manufacturing industry has moved from inner cities to outer areas* **outlying**, distant, remote, faraway, furthest, peripheral, fringe, border, marginal, suburban, perimeter.
OPPOSITE inner.

outface ▶ verb *the Cabinet successfully outfaced the shop stewards' movement* **stand up to**, face down, cow, overawe, intimidate, browbeat, confront, beard, outstare, stare out/down, defy.

outfit ▶ noun **1** *I haven't had a chance to wear this outfit yet* **costume**, suit, uniform, ensemble, habit, attire, clothes, clothing, dress, garb; regalia, regimentals, rig, livery; accoutrements, trappings, disguise; *Brit.* kit, strip; *informal* get-up, gear, togs; *Brit. informal* rig-out; *formal* apparel; *literary* array, raiment.
2 *many photographers require an easy-to-use studio lighting outfit* **kit**, equipment, tools, utensils, implements, tackle, apparatus, paraphernalia, things, stuff; *Military* accoutrement; *rare* turnout.
3 *the company has no intention of setting up a local manufacturing outfit in the UK* **organization**, set-up, enterprise, company, firm, partnership, house, business, group, band, body, crew, team, coterie, clique; unit, formation, corps, commando, cadre, squad, squadron, patrol, troop, platoon, detachment.
▶ verb *there were enough swords and suits of armour to outfit an army* **equip**, kit out, fit out/up, rig out, supply, issue, furnish with, provide, provision, stock, arm; dress, attire, clothe, robe, costume, garb, deck out, drape, array, accoutre, get up, turn out, trick out/up; *informal* doll up; *literary* bedizen, caparison; *archaic* apparel, invest, habit, trap out.

outfitter ▶ noun **clothier**, **tailor**, **couturier**, couturière, stylist, costumier, dressmaker, garment maker, cutter, seamstress; corsetière, milliner, haberdasher; *dated* modiste; *rare* sartor.

outflow ▶ noun *the seabed was forced apart by the outflow of lava* **discharge**, outflowing, outpouring, outrush, rush, flood, deluge, issue, spurt, jet, cascade, stream, torrent, gush, outburst; flow, flux, welling, leakage, escape, drain, drainage, outflux, emanation, effluence, effluent, effusion; *technical* efflux.

outgoing ▶ adjective **1** *children who are outgoing and friendly* **extrovert**, **uninhibited**, unreserved, demonstrative, affectionate, warm, friendly, genial, cordial, affable, easy-going, easy, hail-fellow-well-met, approachable, sociable, convivial, lively, gregarious; communicative, responsive, open, forthcoming, frank, expansive; talkative, garrulous, loquacious.
OPPOSITES reserved, introverted, withdrawn.
2 *the outgoing president* **departing**, retiring, leaving.
OPPOSITE incoming.

outgoings ▶ plural noun *monthly outgoings* **expenses**, expenditure, spending, outlay, money spent, payments, disbursements, costs, overheads.

outgrowth ▶ noun **protuberance**, **swelling**, excrescence, growth, knob, lump, bump, bulge, eruption, protrusion, projection, prominence; tumour, cancer, boil, carbuncle, pustule, spot, pimple; *technical* process; *rare* tumescence.

outing ▶ noun **1** *they would go on family outings to the movies* **trip**, excursion, jaunt, expedition, pleasure trip, day trip, day out, tour, mystery tour, airing, drive, ride, run, turn, cruise, sally; *informal* junket, spin, tootle, joyride, tool; *Scottish informal* hurl.
2 *the outing of public figures by the gay press* **exposure**, unmasking, uncovering, revelation, exposé.

outlandish ▶ adjective *he wears outlandish clothes* **weird**, queer, offbeat, far out, freakish, grotesque, quirky, zany, eccentric, off-centre, idiosyncratic, unconventional, unorthodox, funny, bizarre, fantastic, unusual, extraordinary, strange, unfamiliar, unknown, unheard of, alien, foreign, peculiar, odd, curious; atypical, irregular, anomalous, deviant, abnormal, quaint, out of the way, ludicrous, preposterous; *French* outré; *informal* way-out, wacky, freaky, kooky, screwy, kinky, oddball, cranky; *N. Amer. informal* off the wall, in left field, bizarro; *dated* singular.
OPPOSITES ordinary, commonplace, conventional.

outlast ▶ verb *the buildings outlasted generations of occupants* **outlive**, survive, live after, remain alive after, live/last longer than, outwear; come through, ride out, weather, withstand, live through.

outlaw ▶ noun *bands of outlaws held up trains* **fugitive**, wanted criminal, outcast, exile, pariah, bandit, desperado, brigand, criminal, robber; *informal* villain.
▶ verb **1** *a county council has voted to outlaw fox-hunting on its land* **ban**, bar, prohibit, forbid, veto, embargo, boycott, make illegal, disallow, proscribe, interdict.
OPPOSITES permit, allow.
2 *she kept silent for fear that she would be outlawed* **banish**, exile, cast out, exclude, expel, shut out; repudiate, condemn, put a price on someone's head.

outlay ▶ noun *the project involved comparatively little financial outlay* **expenditure**, expenses, spending, outgoings, money spent, cost, price, charge, payment, disbursement, investment, injection of capital.

outlet ▶ noun **1** *fumes from someone's central-heating outlet* **vent**, vent hole, way out, exit, egress; **outfall**, opening, channel, trench, culvert, cut, conduit, ditch, mouth, valve, safety valve, blow-off; blowhole; orifice, pore, duct.
2 *ensuring that farmers have an outlet for their crops* **market**, retail outlet, marketplace, selling place, shop, store.
3 *childless women find an outlet for their mothering instincts through other channels* **means of expression**, release, means of release, release mechanism, safety valve, vent, avenue, way of harnessing, channel.

outline ▶ noun **1** *he could see the rectangular outline of the building* **silhouette**, **profile**, figure, shape, contour, form, line, lineaments, delineation; configuration, perimeter, circumference, tracing, layout, framework, skeleton, diagram, sketch.
2 *the statement gives an outline of public expenditure for each department* **rough idea**, thumbnail sketch, (quick) rundown, abbreviated version, summary, synopsis, résumé, precis, abridgement, abstract, reduction, digest; epitome, essence, storyline, storyboard, main points, gist, bones, bare bones, skeleton, draft, plan, sketch, scheme.
▶ verb **1** *she could see the budgie outlined against the sky* **silhouette**, define, demarcate, delimit, mark off; sketch, delineate, trace, pencil.
2 *students can apply some of the techniques outlined in this chapter* **rough out**, sketch out, block out, indicate, touch on, draft, give a thumbnail sketch of, give a rough idea of, give a quick rundown on, summarize, precis.

outlive ▶ verb *she outlived her husband by nearly thirty years* **live on after**, live longer than, outlast, remain alive after, survive; outwear, come through, ride out, weather, withstand, live through.

outlook ▶ noun **1** *the two men were wholly different in character and outlook* **point of view**, viewpoint, views, slant, angle, interpretation, opinion, thinking, way of thinking, perspective, attitude, standpoint, stance, position, frame of mind.
2 *the house has a lovely open outlook over the golf course* **view**, vista, prospect, panorama, scene, aspect, exposure, surroundings.
3 *low interest rates had improved the outlook for the economy* **prospects**, expectations, expectancy, hopes, likely improvement, lookout, future, chances, chances of success.

outlying ▶ adjective *customers from outlying areas will be able to contact the main centres by telephone* **distant**, **remote**, outer, outermost, out of the way, faraway, far-flung, peripheral, provincial, inaccessible, obscure, off the beaten track, unfrequented, backwoods.
OPPOSITES central, metropolitan.

outmanoeuvre ▶ verb **1** *the English were almost outmanoeuvred by the French army* **outflank**, circumvent, bypass, shake/throw off, get around.
2 *he hoped to outmanoeuvre his critics* **outwit**, outsmart, out-think, outplay, be cleverer than, steal a march on, trick, make a fool of, get the better of; *informal* outfox, pull a fast one on, put one over on, run/make rings round; *dated* outjockey.

outmoded ▶ adjective *an exercise in junking outmoded policies* **out of date**, **old-fashioned**, outdated, out of fashion, outworn, dated, behind the times, ancient, archaic, antiquated, obsolescent, dead, obsolete, disused, defunct, abandoned, tired, exhausted, stale, hackneyed, superannuated; *French* passé; *informal* old hat, out of the ark.
OPPOSITES fashionable, modern.

out of date ▶ adjective **1** *the precinct is out of date as a modern shopping centre* **old-fashioned**, outmoded, out of fashion, unfashionable, frumpish, frumpy, out of style, outdated, dated, out, outworn, old, former, musty, old-time, old-world, behind the times, behindhand, past, bygone, archaic, obsolescent, obsolete, ancient, antiquated, superannuated; defunct, medieval, prehistoric, antediluvian, old-fogeyish, old-fangled, backward-looking, quaint, anachronistic, crusted, feudal, fusty, moth-eaten, olde worlde; *French* démodé, vieux jeu, passé; *informal* old hat, square, not with it, out of the ark, creaky, mouldy; *N. Amer. informal* horse-and-buggy, clunky, rinky-dink, mossy; *archaic* square-toed.
OPPOSITES modern, fashionable.
2 *many of the facts in the book are now out of date* **superseded**, obsolete, no longer current/topical, stale, expired, extinct, lapsed, elapsed, run out, invalid, void, null and void.
OPPOSITE current.

out of the way ▶ adjective **1** *out-of-the-way places* **outlying**, outer, outermost; **distant**, remote, faraway, far-flung, peripheral, isolated, sequestered, lonely, godforsaken, secluded, inaccessible, obscure, off the beaten track, unfrequented, backwoods.
OPPOSITES accessible, near, handy.
2 *I don't find his methods out of the way* **strange**, unusual, peculiar, odd, funny, curious, bizarre, weird, uncanny, queer, unexpected, unfamiliar, abnormal; atypical, anomalous, untypical, different, out of the ordinary, foreign, exceptional, rare, extraordinary, remarkable, puzzling, mystifying, mysterious, perplexing, baffling, unaccountable, incongruous, uncommon, irregular, singular, deviant, aberrant, freak, freakish; suspicious, dubious, questionable; eerie, unnatural; *Scottish* unco; *French* outré; *informal* fishy, creepy, spooky; *Brit. informal* rum; *N. Amer. informal* bizarro.
OPPOSITE run-of-the-mill.

out of work ▶ adjective **unemployed**, jobless, out of a job, workless, redundant, laid off, idle, between jobs; *Brit. informal* on the dole, signing on, 'resting'; *Austral. informal* on the wallaby track.

outpouring ▶ noun *these countries have not significantly curbed the outpouring of sewage* **outflow**, outflowing, outrush, rush, flood, deluge, discharge, issue, spurt, jet, cascade, stream, torrent, gush, outburst, flow, flux, welling, leakage, escape, drain, drainage, outflux, emanation, effluence, effluent, effusion; *technical* efflux.

output ▶ noun *industrial output fell by 2.8% in the year to November* **production**, product, amount/quantity produced, yield, harvest, return, volume, gross national product, gross domestic product, out-turn, achievement, accomplishment; works, writings, creation, oeuvre.

outrage ▶ noun **1** *there was widespread public outrage at the proposal* **indignation**, fury, anger, rage, disapproval, wrath, shock, resentment, horror, disgust, amazement.
2 *that young children are starving to death is an outrage* **affront**, **scandal**, offence, insult, injustice, disgrace, infamy.
3 *no group has yet claimed responsibility for the bomb outrage* **atrocity**, act of violence/brutality/savagery, evil, abomination, obscenity, act of wickedness, crime, wrong, horror, enormity, violation, brutality, barbarism, barbarity, inhumane act, villainy, disgrace.
▶ verb *his remarks outraged his female parishioners* **enrage**, infuriate, incense, anger, scandalize, offend, give offence to, make indignant, affront, be an affront to, shock, horrify, disgust, revolt, repel, appal, displease.

outrageous ▶ adjective **1** *the outrageous burden of taxation* **shocking**, disgraceful, scandalous, atrocious, appalling, abhorrent, monstrous, heinous; evil, wicked, abominable, terrible, horrible, horrid, horrendous, dreadful, hideous, foul, nauseating, sickening, vile, villainous, nasty, ghastly, odious, loathsome, shameful, infamous, nefarious, iniquitous, unspeakable, intolerable, insufferable, insupportable, unendurable, unbearable; impossible, exasperating, offensive, maddening, distressing; immoderate, exorbitant, unreasonable; *Brit. informal* over the top, OTT, steep, beastly.
OPPOSITES acceptable, mild, moderate.
2 *we can all sneer at people who are caught out by outrageous offers* **far-fetched**, unlikely, highly unlikely, doubtful, dubious, questionable, implausible, unconvincing, unbelievable, incredible, ridiculous, preposterous, extravagant, elaborate, high-flown, overdramatic, overdone, sensationalized, excessive, overstated, inflated, highly coloured.
OPPOSITES realistic, credible.
3 *pop stars wearing outrageous clothes* **eye-catching**, startling, striking, flamboyant, showy, flashy, gaudy, ostentatious, dazzling; saucy, shameless, brazen, brash, unspeakable, adventurous, bold, daring, audacious, swashbuckling, defiant, daredevil, shocking.
OPPOSITE inconspicuous.

outré ▶ adjective *the composer's more outré harmonies* **weird**, queer, outlandish, offbeat, far out, freakish, grotesque, quirky, zany, eccentric, off-centre, idiosyncratic, unconventional, unorthodox, funny, bizarre, fantastic, unusual, extraordinary, strange, unfamiliar, unknown, unheard of, alien, foreign, peculiar, odd, curious, atypical, irregular, anomalous, deviant, abnormal, quaint, out of the way, ludicrous, preposterous; *informal* way-out, wacky, freaky, kooky, screwy, kinky, oddball, cranky; *N. Amer. informal* off the wall, in left field, bizarro; *dated* singular.
OPPOSITES ordinary, normal.

outright ▶ adverb **1** *he rejected the proposal outright* **completely**, entirely, wholly, fully, totally, categorically, absolutely, altogether, utterly, flatly, in every respect, unreservedly, without reservation, without exception, thoroughly, quite.
OPPOSITES in part, partially.
2 *I can't bring myself to tell her outright* **explicitly**, straightforwardly, directly, forthrightly, openly, frankly, candidly, honestly, truly, sincerely, bluntly, plainly, in plain language, unreservedly, without constraint, truthfully, without dissembling, to someone's face, straight from the shoulder, without beating about the bush, with no holds barred, man to man, woman to woman; *informal* on the level; *Brit. informal* straight up.
3 *the passengers were killed outright* **instantly**, instantaneously, immediately, at once, straight away, there and then, then and there, on the spot.
4 *houses could be paid off gradually, but paintings had to be bought outright* **all at once**, at/in one fell swoop, in one go.
▶ adjective **1** *it was an outright lie* **out-and-out**, absolute, complete, utter, downright, sheer, stark, thorough, thoroughgoing, categorical, unequivocal, undeniable, unqualified, unmodified, unrestricted, unmitigated, unconditional, positive, simple, wholesale, all-out, rank, consummate, pure; *archaic* arrant.
2 *the outright winner* **definite**, unequivocal, clear, unqualified, incontestable, undeniable, unmistakable, categorical, straightforward.

outrun ▶ verb *an antelope could easily outrun a lion* **run faster than**, outstrip, outdistance, outpace, leave behind, get (further) ahead of, gain on, draw away from, overtake, pass, shake off, throw off, lose, put distance between oneself and one's pursuer(s), widen the gap between oneself and one's pursuer(s); *informal* leave standing, walk away from.

outset ▶ noun *it must be stressed at the outset that correct identification is the chief problem* **start**, starting point, beginning, arrival, (first) appearance, dawn, birth, origin, inception, conception, opening, launch, inauguration, institution, initiation, debut, creation, day one, the first; *informal* kick-off, the word go; *formal* commencement.
OPPOSITES end, conclusion.

outshine ▶ verb *a single large house plant can outshine any number or ornaments* **surpass**, be superior to, overshadow, eclipse, outclass, dwarf, tower above/over, put in the shade, upstage, put to shame, excel, exceed, transcend, top, cap, trump, beat, better, outstrip, outrun; *informal* be a cut above, be head and shoulders above, run rings round, leave standing, walk away from; *archaic* outrival, outvie.

outside ▶ noun **1** *the outside of the building is decorated in fine style* **outer/external surface**, surface, exterior, outer side, case, skin, shell, crust, husk, covering, outer layer, sheath, facade, elevation, front, frontage.
2 *the outside of the bend* **outer/longer edge**, edge, the long way round.
▶ adjective **1** *go and put the outside lights on* **exterior**, external, outer, outermost, outward, outdoor, out-of-doors.
2 *this work is to be carried out by outside contractors* **independent**, consultant, consulting, hired, temporary, freelance, casual, visiting, non-resident, external, extramural, peripatetic; extraneous, extrinsic, outward, alien, foreign.
3 *an outside chance* **slight**, slender, slim, small, tiny, faint, negligible,

O

marginal, remote, distant, vague, unlikely, improbable; little.
▶ **adverb** *they went outside | shall we eat outside?* **outdoors**, out of doors, out of the house, on the outside, externally, exteriorly.
OPPOSITE inside.

WORD LINKS
related prefixes **ecto-** (e.g. ***ectoderm, ectoplasm***), **exo-** (e.g. ***exoskeleton, exocrine***), **extra-** (e.g. ***extramural, extravehicular***)

outsider ▶ **noun** *to an outsider the scene would have appeared normal* **stranger**, visitor, non-member, odd man out; foreigner, alien, outlander, immigrant, emigrant, émigré; incomer, newcomer, parvenu, arriviste, interloper, intruder, gatecrasher; outcast, misfit, individualist, nonconformist, free spirit, unorthodox person, original, bohemian, eccentric, maverick, rebel, dissenter, dissident.

outsize ▶ **adjective 1** *she started searching in her outsize handbag* **huge**, oversized, enormous, gigantic, very big, very large, great, giant, colossal, massive, mammoth, vast, immense, tremendous, monumental, prodigious, mountainous, monstrous, elephantine, king-sized, king-size, gargantuan, Herculean, Brobdingnagian, substantial, extensive, hefty, bulky, weighty, heavy, gross; *informal* mega, monster, whopping, whopping great, thumping, thumping great, humongous, jumbo, hulking, bumper, astronomical; *Brit. informal* whacking, whacking great, ginormous.
2 *an outsize and very grand Welsh actor* **very large**, big, massive, fat, corpulent, gross, obese, overweight, stout, fleshy, heavy, plump, portly, chubby, rotund, podgy, roly-poly, paunchy, pot-bellied, beer-bellied, ample, well upholstered, broad in the beam, bulky, bloated, flabby, Falstaffian; *informal* porky, pudgy, tubby, blubbery, poddy; *Brit. informal* fubsy; *N. Amer. informal* lard-assed; *archaic* pursy; *rare* abdominous.

outskirts ▶ **plural noun** *a house on the outskirts of the town* **outlying districts**, edges, fringes, suburbs, suburbia; purlieus, borders, periphery, margin, boundary; surrounding area/district, environs; *French* faubourg, banlieue; *Spanish* barrio.

outsmart ▶ **verb** *buyers and sellers attempt to outsmart each other* **outwit**, out-think, outmanoeuvre, outplay, be cleverer than, steal a march on, trick, make a fool of, get the better of; *informal* outfox, pull a fast one on, put one over on, run/make rings round; *dated* outjockey.

outspoken ▶ **adjective** *an outspoken critic of the government* **forthright**, direct, candid, frank, straightforward, honest, open, straight, straight from the shoulder, plain, plain-spoken, vociferous, vocal; explicit, point-blank, round, blunt, abrupt, bluff, brusque, unequivocal, free, unreserved, uninhibited, unceremonious; *archaic* free-spoken.
OPPOSITES diplomatic, reticent, evasive.

CHOOSE THE RIGHT WORD
outspoken, candid, frank, forthright, blunt
See CANDID.

O

outspread ▶ **adjective** *the kestrels were soaring with outspread wings* **fully extended**, outstretched, stretched out, spread out, fanned out, splayed out, expanded, unfolded, unfurled, open, open wide, wide open, opened out.

outstanding ▶ **adjective 1** *an outstanding painter* **excellent**, marvellous, magnificent, superb, fine, wonderful, superlative, exceptional, formidable, first-class, first-rate, virtuoso, skilful, masterful, masterly; *informal* great, terrific, tremendous, super, smashing, amazing, fantastic, sensational, fabulous, fab, ace, crack, A1, mean, awesome, magic, bad, wicked, out of this world; *Brit. informal* brilliant, brill; *N. Amer. informal* neat, badass, boss; *Austral. informal* bonzer; *Brit. informal, dated* wizard, spiffing, ripping, topping, champion, capital, top-hole; *N. Amer. informal, dated* swell, keen; *vulgar slang* shit-hot.
OPPOSITE mediocre.
2 *the most outstanding decorative element of the Mausoleum* **remarkable**, extraordinary, exceptional, striking, eye-catching, vivid, arresting, impressive, distinctive, unforgettable, catchy, haunting, indelible, not/never to be forgotten, memorable, signal, special, momentous, monumental, significant, historic, notable, noteworthy, important, consequential, distinguished, pre-eminent, eminent, well known, famous, famed, celebrated, renowned, notorious, illustrious; *informal* out of this world.
OPPOSITE unexceptional.
3 *how much work is still outstanding?* **to be done**, undone, not done, neglected, omitted, unattended to, unfinished, incomplete, left, remaining, pending, ongoing.
OPPOSITES complete, finished.
4 *outstanding debts* **unpaid**, unsettled, owing, owed, to be paid, payable, receivable, due, overdue, undischarged, in arrears, in the red; *N. Amer.* delinquent, past due.
OPPOSITES paid, settled.

outstrip ▶ **verb 1** *speeding at 90 mph, he outstripped police cars for an hour* **go faster than**, outrun, outdistance, outpace, leave behind, get (further) ahead of, gain on, draw away from, overtake, pass, shake off, throw off, lose, put distance between oneself and someone else, widen the gap between oneself and someone else; *informal* leave standing, walk away from.
2 *demand far outstrips supply* **surpass**, exceed, be more than, go beyond, better, beat, top, overshadow, eclipse, put to shame.

outward ▶ **adjective** *she put on an outward appearance of sadness* **external**, outer, outside, outermost, exterior; extrinsic, surface, superficial, visible, observable, noticeable, perceptible, discernible, seeming, apparent, ostensible, evident, obvious.
OPPOSITES inward, inner, internal.

outwardly ▶ **adverb** *the house is outwardly no different from any of the others* **externally**, on the outside, on the surface, superficially, on the face of it, at first sight/glance, to/from all appearances, to the casual eye/observer, as far as one can see/tell/judge, to all intents and purposes, apparently, ostensibly, seemingly, evidently.
OPPOSITE inwardly.

outweigh ▶ **verb 1** *Dixon was outweighed by nearly two stone and was knocked down twice in the second round* **be heavier than**.
2 *the costs outweigh the benefits* **be greater than**, exceed, be superior to, take precedence/priority over, prevail over, have the edge on/over, preponderate over, override, tip/turn the scales/balance against, supersede, offset, cancel out, (more than) make up for, outbalance, overbalance, compensate for, redress.

outwit ▶ **verb** *constant vigilance is needed to outwit enemy infiltrators* **outsmart**, out-think, outmanoeuvre, outplay, be cleverer than, steal a march on, trick, gull, make a fool of, get the better of; *informal* outfox, pull a fast one on, put one over on, run/make rings round; *dated* outjockey.

outworn ▶ **adjective** *many of his doctrines are outworn today* **out of date**, outdated, old-fashioned, out of fashion, outmoded, dated, behind the times, ancient, archaic, antiquated, obsolescent, dead, obsolete, disused, defunct, tired, exhausted, stale, hackneyed, superannuated; *French* passé; *informal* old hat, out of the ark.
OPPOSITES up to date, fresh, original.

oval ▶ **adjective** **egg-shaped**, ovoid, ovate, oviform, elliptical, ellipsoidal; *technical* obovate.

ovation ▶ **noun** *the show ended with an ovation from the audience* **round of applause**, applause, handclapping, clapping, cheering, cheers, bravos, acclaim, standing ovation, acclamation, praise, plaudits, laurels, tribute, accolade, bouquets; *informal* (big) hand; *rare* laudation, extolment.

oven ▶ **noun** **stove**, kitchen stove, microwave (oven), (kitchen) range; roaster, kiln; *Indian* tandoor; *NZ* hangi; *archaic* caboose.

over ▶ **preposition 1** *there will be cloud over most of the country* **above**, on top of, higher than, higher up than, atop.
OPPOSITES under, below.
2 *a view over the lake | he walked over the grass* **across**, on to, around, throughout, all through, throughout the extent of, everywhere in, in all parts of.
3 *he has three people over him at work* **superior to**, above, higher up than, more powerful than, in charge of, responsible for, commanding.
4 *over 200,000 people now live in the area* **more than**, above, in excess of, exceeding, upwards of, beyond, greater than.
5 *this led to further discussion over what constitutes success* **on the subject of**, about, concerning, apropos of, with reference to, speaking of, with regard/respect to, regarding, as regards, relating to, respecting, in connection with, as for, re; *Latin* in re.
□ **over and above** *she had an allowance from her father over and above her paltry salary* **in addition to**, on top of, over and beyond, plus, as well as, besides, not to mention, along with, let alone.
▶ **adverb 1** *a flock of geese flew over* **overhead**, above, on high, aloft, past, by.
2 *the relationship is over* **at an end**, finished, concluded, terminated, no more, ended, extinct, gone, dead, a thing of the past, ancient history.
3 *he paid all his bills and still had some money over* **left over**, left, remaining, unused, surplus, superfluous, in excess, extra, in addition.
□ **over and over** *he is a crashing bore who tells the same old jokes over and over* **repeatedly**, again and again, over and over again, time and again, time and time again, many times over, on many/several occasions, often, frequently, recurrently, constantly, continually, persistently, regularly, habitually, ad nauseam.

WORD LINKS
related prefixes **super-** (e.g. ***superstructure, superlunary***), **sur-** (e.g. ***surtitle, surtax***), **supra-** (e.g. ***suprarenal, supranational***), **hyper-** (e.g. ***hypersonic, hyperlink***)

overact ▶ **verb** *she's a weepy actress with a strong tendency to overact* **exaggerate**, overdo it, overplay it; *informal* **ham it up**, camp it up, pile it on, lay it on thick, lay it on with a trowel.

overall ▶ **adjective** *the overall cost of a project* **all-inclusive**, general, comprehensive, universal, all-embracing, gross, net, final, inclusive; master, ruling, sweeping, wholesale, complete, blanket, across the board,

umbrella, global, worldwide, international, pandemic, nationwide, countrywide, coast-to-coast, company-wide.
▶ adverb *overall, things have improved* **generally**, in general, generally speaking, altogether, all in all, on balance, on average, for the most part, mostly, in the main, on the whole, largely, by and large, to a large extent, to a great degree; predominantly, mainly, chiefly, as a rule, principally, basically, substantially.

overawe ▶ verb *Jane was often overawed by her landlady* **intimidate**, daunt, cow, take someone's breath away, awe, disconcert, blind someone with something, unnerve, discourage, subdue, abash, dismay, frighten, alarm, scare, deter, terrify, terrorize, browbeat, bully; *informal* psych out; *N. Amer. informal* buffalo.

overbalance ▶ verb *she turned round so fast that she almost overbalanced* **fall over**, topple over, lose one's balance, lose one's footing, tip over, keel over, capsize, overturn, turn turtle; **push over**, upend, upset.

overbearing ▶ adjective *he was at the mercy of his overbearing wife* **domineering**, dominating, autocratic, tyrannical, despotic, heavy-handed, oppressive, high-handed, bullying, high and mighty, lordly, lording it, officious, masterful, dictatorial, bossy, imperious, pontifical, pompous, peremptory, arrogant, cocksure, proud, over-proud, overweening, presumptuous, opinionated, dogmatic; *informal* pushy, throwing one's weight about, cocky.

overblown ▶ adjective *an overblown piece of writing* **overwritten**, extravagant, florid, grandiose, pompous, over-elaborate, flowery, overwrought, pretentious, high-flown, turgid, bombastic, oratorical, grandiloquent, magniloquent, orotund; *informal* highfalutin, over the top, OTT; *rare* euphuistic, fustian, aureate, hyperventilated.
OPPOSITES simple, plain.

overcast ▶ adjective *the sky was murky and overcast* **cloudy**, clouded, clouded over, overclouded, sunless, darkened, dark, grey, black, leaden, heavy, dull, murky, dirty, misty, hazy, foggy, louring, threatening, menacing, promising rain, dismal, dreary, cheerless, sombre.
OPPOSITES bright, clear.

overcharge ▶ verb **1** *clients feel that they are being overcharged for an inadequate service* **swindle**, charge too much, cheat, defraud, gazump, fleece, short-change, surcharge; *informal* rip off, sting, screw, soak, rob, diddle, do, rook, clip; *N. Amer. informal* gouge; *Brit. informal, dated* rush.
OPPOSITE undercharge.
2 *the decoration is overcharged with statues and other accessories* **overstate**, overdo, exaggerate, over-colour, over-embroider, over-embellish, embroider, embellish; overwrite, overdraw; *informal* pile it on, lay it on thick, lay it on with a trowel.

overcoat ▶ noun. *See centre pages for list of* **Coats, Cloaks, and Jackets**

overcome ▶ verb **1** *neither team was strong enough to overcome the other* **defeat**, beat, best, conquer, trounce, thrash, rout, vanquish, overwhelm, overpower, destroy, drub, get the better of, triumph over, prevail over, gain a victory over, win over/against, outdo, outclass, outstrip, surpass, excel, worst, subdue, quash, crush; *informal* slaughter, murder, kill, clobber, hammer, whip, lick, paste, crucify, demolish, tank, wipe the floor with, make mincemeat of, blow out of the water, take to the cleaners, walk (all) over, run rings around; *Brit. informal* stuff; *N. Amer. informal* shellac, skunk.
2 *a one-day course which helps people overcome their fear of flying* **get the better of**, prevail over, control, get control of, get/bring under control, master, gain mastery over, deal with, conquer, defeat, vanquish, beat, triumph over, best, worst, overpower, overwhelm; get over, get a grip on, curb, subdue, subjugate, repress, quell, quash; *informal* lick.
▶ adjective *I was overcome, half-suffocated by the sadness* **overwhelmed**, emotional, moved, affected, struck, choky, speechless, at a loss for words, shaken, disturbed; *informal* bowled over.

overconfident ▶ adjective *her downfall came through being overconfident* **cocksure**, smug, conceited, self-assured, self-assertive, unabashed, brash, swaggering, blustering, overbearing, overweening, presuming, presumptuous, riding/heading for a fall, foolhardy; *informal* cocky, too big for one's boots; *rare* hubristic.
OPPOSITES diffident, shy, unsure of oneself.

overcritical ▶ adjective *overcritical parents* **fault-finding**, hypercritical, captious, carping, cavilling, quibbling, hair-splitting, hard to please, over-censorious, over-particular; fussy, finicky, fastidious, meticulous, pedantic, over-exacting, overscrupulous, punctilious, perfectionist; *informal* nit-picking, pernickety; *archaic* overnice.
OPPOSITE uncritical.

overcrowded ▶ adjective *pupils are forced to share textbooks in overcrowded classrooms* **overfull**, overflowing, full to overflowing/bursting, crammed full, cram-full, jammed, packed like sardines, congested, choked, overloaded, overpopulated, overpeopled, overrun, crowded, thronged, swarming, teeming; *informal* bursting/bulging at the seams, full to the gunwales, jam-packed, like the Black Hole of Calcutta.
OPPOSITES deserted, empty, vacant.

overdo ▶ verb **1** *if you overdo the atmosphere, the effect is likely to be comic* **exaggerate**, overstate, do to death, overemphasize, overplay, go overboard with, dramatize, overdramatize; colour, embroider, embellish, inflate, amplify, magnify, make a mountain out of a molehill, blow up, blow up out of all proportion; *informal* ham up, camp up, make a (big) thing of/about, pile on, lay it on thick, lay it on with a trowel, make a production of, make a big deal out of; *archaic* pull the longbow.
OPPOSITES understate, play down.
2 *don't overdo the drink* **have/do/use/drink too much ...**, overindulge in, have/use/do/eat/drink to excess, carry too far, carry to extremes, not know when to stop, be intemperate.
3 *they always overdid beef* **overcook**, overbake, burn, burn to a cinder/crisp; *informal* burn to a frazzle.
□ **overdo it work too hard**, overwork, do too much, work like a Trojan/horse/slave, work day and night, burn the midnight oil, burn the candle at both ends, strain oneself, sweat, sweat blood, overtax oneself, overtax one's strength, overburden oneself, overload oneself, drive/push oneself too hard, work/run oneself into the ground, wear oneself to a shadow, work one's fingers to the bone, wear oneself out, have too many irons in the fire, have too many balls in the air, burn oneself out, bite off more than one can chew; *informal* kill oneself, knock oneself out; *vulgar slang* work/sweat one's balls off.

overdone ▶ adjective **1** *the flattery was overdone* **excessive**, too much, undue, immoderate, inordinate, disproportionate, inflated, beyond the pale, overstated, overworked, laboured, exaggerated, over-elaborate, overemphasized, extravagant, over-enthusiastic, effusive, over-effusive, gushing, fulsome, highly coloured, sensationalistic, forced, affected; theatrical, melodramatic, stagy; *informal* a bit much, over the top, OTT, hyped up, laid on with a trowel, camp.
OPPOSITE understated.
2 *overdone food* **overcooked**, overbaked, dried out, burnt, burnt to a cinder/crisp; *informal* burnt to a frazzle.
OPPOSITE underdone.

overdue ▶ adjective **1** *the ship is overdue* **late**, not on time, behind schedule, behindhand, behind time, delayed, belated, tardy, unpunctual.
OPPOSITES early, punctual, on time.
2 *an automatic right to claim interest on overdue payments* **unpaid**, unsettled, owing, owed, to be paid, payable, receivable, due, outstanding, undischarged, in arrears, in the red; *N. Amer.* delinquent, past due.

overeat ▶ verb *most of us are inclined to overeat occasionally* **eat too much**, be greedy, eat like a horse, gorge (oneself), overindulge, overindulge oneself, surfeit, guzzle, feast; *informal* binge, stuff one's face, stuff oneself, pack it away, put it away, make a pig of oneself, pig oneself, pig out; *N. Amer. informal* scarf out; *rare* gourmandize, gluttonize.
OPPOSITES fast, diet.

overemphasize ▶ verb *the importance of appropriate design methods cannot be overemphasized* **overstress**, exaggerate, attach too much importance/weight to, make too much of, overplay, overdo, overdramatize, belabour, labour, dwell on, harp on, make something out of nothing, make a mountain out of a molehill; *informal* make a big thing about/of, blow up out of all proportion.
OPPOSITES understate, play down.

overflow ▶ verb *cream overflowed the edges of the shallow dish* **spill over**, flow over, run over, brim over, well over, slop over, slosh over, pour forth, stream forth, flood, discharge, surge, debouch.
▶ noun **1** *a ball valve failure would lead to tank overflow in the loft* **overspill**, spill, spillage, flood, flooding, inundation, excess water.
2 *to accommodate the overflow, five more offices have been built* **surplus**, excess, additional people/things, extra people/things, remainder, overabundance, overspill.

overflowing ▶ adjective *the floods were caused by overflowing rivers* **overfull**, full to overflowing/bursting, spilling over, running over, crammed full, cram-full, jammed, overcrowded, packed like sardines, congested, choked, overloaded, overpopulated, overpeopled, overrun, crowded, thronged, swarming, teeming; *informal* bursting/bulging at the seams, full to the gunwales, jam-packed, like the Black Hole of Calcutta.

overhang ▶ verb *the shrubs overhang the lawn | the crag below us overhung* **stick out (over)**, stand out (over), extend (over), project (over), protrude (over), jut (over), jut out (over), poke out (over), beetle (over), bulge out (over), loom (over), hang over, cantilever out (over); *archaic* be imminent; *rare* impend, protuberate.

overhaul ▶ verb **1** *I've been overhauling the gearbox* **service**, maintain, repair, mend, fix up, patch up, rebuild, renovate, revamp, recondition, remodel, refit, refurbish, modernize; regulate, adjust; check, check out, check over, check up on, give something a check-up, investigate, inspect, examine, survey; revise, update, reconsider, rework, restructure, realign, shake up; *N. English* fettle; *informal* do up.
2 *Kenyon was the only man who could have overhauled him in the world title race* **overtake**, pass, get past, go past, go by, go faster than, get/pull ahead of, outdistance, outstrip; gain on, catch up with, draw level with.

overhead ▶ adverb *another burst of thunder erupted overhead* **above**, up above, high up, (up) in the sky, on high, above/over one's head, in flight, aloft.

▶ adjective *the proposed 400,000-volt overhead line and its pylons* **aerial**, elevated, raised, suspended, projecting, overhanging.
OPPOSITE underground.

overheads ▶ plural noun **running costs**, operating costs, fixed costs, budget items, costs, expenses; *Brit.* oncosts.
OPPOSITES variable costs, cost of sales.

overindulge ▶ verb **1** *it's all too easy to overindulge at Christmas* **drink/eat too much**, overeat, drink like a fish, overdrink, be greedy, be immoderate, be intemperate, overindulge oneself, overdo it, not know when to stop, drink/eat/go to excess, gorge (oneself), surfeit, guzzle, feast; *informal* binge, go on a binge, stuff one's face, stuff oneself, pack it away, put it away, paint the town red, push the boat out, go overboard, live it up, make a pig of oneself, pig oneself; *N. Amer. informal* scarf out; *archaic* tope; *rare* gourmandize, gluttonize.
2 *his mother had overindulged him* **spoil**, give in to, indulge, humour, pander to, cosset, pamper, mollycoddle, baby, spoon-feed, feather-bed; *informal* spoil rotten.

overindulgence ▶ noun *overindulgence in food and drink* **intemperance**, immoderation, excess, overeating, overdrinking, prodigality, lack of restraint, gorging, surfeit, debauch, debauchery, dissipation, dissoluteness, greed, gluttony, orgy; *informal* binge.
OPPOSITE temperance.

overjoyed ▶ adjective *Ms Bailey was overjoyed at the birth of her daughter* **ecstatic**, euphoric, thrilled, elated, delighted, on cloud nine/seven, walking/treading on air, in seventh heaven, jubilant, rapturous, beside oneself with joy, jumping for joy, exultant, transported, delirious, enraptured, blissful, in raptures, as pleased as Punch, cock-a-hoop, as happy as a sandboy, as happy as Larry, like a child with a new toy; *informal* over the moon, on top of the world, on a high, tickled pink; *N. English informal* made up; *N. Amer. informal* as happy as a clam; *Austral. informal* wrapped.
OPPOSITES dejected, depressed; impassive, unmoved.

overlay ▶ verb *the area was concreted and overlaid with green, red, and white mosaic marble* **cover**, face, surface, veneer, inlay, laminate; carpet, blanket, swathe, cloak, veil, shroud; overspread, encrust, smear, daub, bedaub, coat, plaster, plate, varnish, glaze, wash, suffuse.

▶ noun *the joists must be protected with an overlay of glass-fibre insulation* **covering**, layer, face, surface, veneer, lamination, encrustation, carpet, blanket, sheet, curtain, canopy, cover, cloak, veil, pall, shroud, screen, mask, cloud, envelope; coat, smear, daub, plating, varnish, glaze, wash.
OPPOSITES underlay, base.

overload ▶ verb **1** *iron has to be carried in alternate holds to avoid overloading the ship* **overburden**, put too much in, overcharge, encumber, burden, weigh down; *rare* surcharge.
2 *you should take care not to overload the electrical wiring* **strain**, impose excessive strain on, overtax, stretch, overwork, overuse; deluge, swamp, oversupply, overwhelm, clog, snow under, beset.

▶ noun *there was an overload of demands on government* **excess**, overabundance, superabundance, profusion, glut, surfeit, surplus, superfluity, more than enough, too many, too much; avalanche, deluge, flood, abundance, plethora, overkill, backlog.

overlook ▶ verb **1** *he overlooked a mistake on the first page* **miss**, fail to notice, fail to observe, fail to spot, fail to see, leave, leave unnoticed; *informal* slip up on.
OPPOSITES spot, notice.
2 *his work has been overlooked by modern authors* **disregard**, neglect, ignore, pay no attention/heed to, turn a blind eye, turn a deaf ear to, pass over, omit, skip (over), gloss over, leave out, leave undone, forget.
3 *it is a shortcoming that many are willing to overlook* **deliberately ignore**, not take into consideration, disregard, take no notice of, take no account of, make allowances for, let pass, turn a blind eye to, wink at, blink at, connive at, excuse, pardon, forgive, condone, let someone off with, let go, sink, bury, let bygones be bygones; *informal* let something ride.
OPPOSITE punish.
4 *the breakfast room overlooks a peaceful garden* **have a view of**, afford a view of, look over/across, look on to, look out on/over, face, front on to, give on to, give over, open out over, command a view of, command, dominate.

overly ▶ adverb *these guitars aren't cheap, but they're not overly expensive either* **unduly**, excessively, inordinately, too, to too great an extent/degree, immoderately, exceedingly; wildly, absurdly, ridiculously, outrageously, unreasonably, exorbitantly, impossibly.

overpower ▶ verb **1** *the prisoners might rebel and overpower the crew* **gain control over**, overwhelm, prevail over, get the better of, get the upper hand over, gain mastery over, master, control, overthrow, overturn, upset, subdue, suppress, subjugate, repress, quell, quash, crush, finish, bring someone to their knees, break, conquer, defeat, vanquish, beat, be victorious over, gain a victory over, triumph over, best, worst, trounce, rout; *informal* thrash, lick, clobber, whip, wipe the floor with, drub, tank, blow out of the water.
2 *he was overpowered by grief* **overcome**, overwhelm, sweep over, move, stir, affect, touch, impress, sweep someone off their feet, strike, stun, shake, disturb, devastate, take aback, daze, leave speechless, spellbind, dazzle, floor; *informal* bowl over, blow away, knock/hit for six, knock sideways, get to.

overpowering ▶ adjective **1** *overpowering grief* **overwhelming**, burdensome, oppressive, weighty, unbearable, unendurable, intolerable, shattering, intimidating, overbearing, dominating; *informal* mind-blowing.
2 *an overpowering smell* **stifling**, suffocating, pervasive, penetrating, strong, pungent, powerful; nauseating, nauseous, sickly, offensive, acrid, astringent, sharp, bitter, fetid, cloying, mephitic; heady, aromatic.
3 *overpowering evidence* **irrefutable**, undeniable, unquestionable, indisputable, incontestable, incontrovertible, compelling, conclusive, forceful, telling.
OPPOSITES mild, slight.

overrate ▶ verb *it is easy to overrate what Frederick achieved* **assess too highly**, overestimate, overvalue, rate/prize too highly, think too much of, exaggerate the worth of, attach too much importance to; praise too highly, exaggerate the merits of, over-praise, oversell, glorify, magnify; *informal* blow up; *rare* over-prize.
OPPOSITES underrate, underestimate.

overreach ▶ verb
□ **overreach oneself** *he waited for his opponents to overreach themselves* **try to do too much**, overestimate one's ability, overdo it, overstretch oneself, strain oneself, wear/burn oneself out, go too far, try to be too clever/smart, bite off more than one can chew, be too clever by half, have too many irons in the fire, have too many balls in the air, defeat one's own ends, have one's scheme backfire on one, have one's scheme boomerang on one, be hoist with one's own petard.

overreact ▶ verb *parents should set children a good example rather than overreact* **get upset over nothing**, react disproportionately, get overexcited, go too far, act irrationally, lose one's sense of proportion, exaggerate, make something out of nothing, make a mountain out of a molehill, blow something up out of all proportion; *informal* press/push/hit the panic button; *Brit. informal* go over the top.
OPPOSITES be impassive, be cool.

override ▶ verb **1** *the court could not override her decision* **disallow**, overrule, countermand, veto, set aside, quash, overturn, overthrow; cancel, reverse, rescind, rule against, revoke, withdraw, retract, take back, repeal, repudiate, recant, annul, nullify, declare null and void, invalidate, negate, void, abrogate; *Law* vacate; *archaic* recall.
OPPOSITES allow, accept.
2 *the government can override all opposition* **disregard**, pay no heed to, take no account of, close one's mind to, turn a deaf ear to, discount, ignore, ride roughshod over, trample on.
OPPOSITES listen to, take notice of.
3 *such a positive attitude will override any negative thoughts* **outweigh**, supersede, take precedence over, take priority over, be more important than, tip/turn the scales/balance against, offset, cancel out, (more than) make up for, outbalance, overbalance, compensate for, redress.

overriding ▶ adjective *safety was the overriding consideration* **most important**, of greatest importance, of prime importance, of supreme importance, of greatest significance, uppermost, top, supreme, first, first and foremost, highest, pre-eminent, outstanding, predominant, dominant, prevailing, preponderant, principal, leading, primary, paramount, chief, main, major, most prominent, cardinal, foremost, central, key, focal, pivotal, essential; *informal* number-one.
OPPOSITES insignificant, irrelevant.

overrule ▶ verb *this ban was overruled by a federal court* **countermand**, cancel, reverse, rescind, repeal, revoke, retract, withdraw, take back, rule against, disallow, override, veto, set aside, quash, overturn, overthrow, repudiate, recant, annul, nullify, declare null and void, invalidate, negate, void, abrogate; *Law* vacate; *archaic* recall.
OPPOSITES allow, accept.

overrun ▶ verb **1** *guerrillas overran the principal military barracks* **invade**, storm, march into, occupy, infest, swarm over, surge over, flow over, inundate, swamp, overwhelm, permeate, penetrate, spread over, spread like wildfire over, run riot over, overgrow, grow over.
2 *the talks overran the deadline for an agreement* **exceed**, go beyond, go over, last longer than, overshoot, run over.

oversee ▶ verb *it was decided to appoint a project manager to oversee the building work* **supervise**, superintend, be in charge of, be responsible for, run, look after, keep an eye on, inspect, administer, organize, manage, direct, guide, control, be in control of, preside over, head (up), lead, chair, umpire, referee, judge, adjudicate, moderate, govern, rule, command.

overseer ▶ noun **supervisor**, foreman, forewoman, chargehand, team leader, controller, manager, manageress, line manager; boss, head, head of department, superintendent, captain; *Scottish* grieve; *informal* chief, head honcho, governor, super; *Brit. informal* gaffer, guv'nor; *N. Amer. informal* straw boss; *Austral. informal* pannikin boss; *Mining* overman.

overshadow ▸ verb **1** *a massive hill overshadows the town* **shade**, darken, conceal, obscure, block out, obliterate, eclipse, screen, shroud, veil, mantle, cloak, mask; dominate, command, overlook.
2 *it is easy to let this feeling of tragedy overshadow his story* **cast gloom over**, blight, take the pleasure out of, bring a note of sadness to, take the edge off, mar, spoil, ruin.
3 *he was always overshadowed by his brilliant elder brother* **outshine**, eclipse, put in the shade, surpass, exceed, excel, be superior to, outclass, outstrip, outdo, top, cap, trump, transcend, tower above/over, dwarf, upstage, shame, put to shame, outdistance, lead; *informal* be head and shoulders above, be a cut above; *archaic* extinguish.

oversight ▸ noun **1** *I must apologize for this stupid oversight* **mistake**, error, fault, failure, omission, lapse, inaccuracy, slip, blunder, faux pas, miscalculation; *informal* slip-up, boo-boo; *Brit. informal* boob; *N. Amer. informal* goof.
2 *the omission was not due to oversight or ignorance* **carelessness**, inattention, neglect, negligence, forgetfulness, inadvertence, laxity, dereliction, neglectfulness.
3 *school governors have oversight of the curriculum* **supervision**, surveillance, superintendence, inspection, charge, care, administration, management, government, direction, control, command, handling, custody.

overstate ▸ verb *he admitted that he had perhaps overstated his case* **exaggerate**, overdo, overemphasize, overplay, dramatize, colour, embroider, embellish, enhance, magnify, inflate, amplify, make a mountain out of a molehill; *informal* make a big thing out of, blow up, blow up out of all proportion; *archaic* draw the long bow.
OPPOSITE understate.

overstatement ▸ noun *it is not an overstatement to say that a crisis is imminent* **exaggeration**, overemphasis, magnification, amplification, overplaying, dramatization, colouring, embroidery, embellishment, enhancement, inflation, extravagance, hyperbole, excessiveness, overestimation, overvaluation, aggrandizement.
OPPOSITE restraint.

overt ▸ adjective *there was little overt opposition to parliamentary government* **undisguised**, unconcealed, plain to see, plainly seen, plain, clear, apparent, conspicuous, unmistakable, obvious, noticeable, observable, visible, manifest, patent, open, public, above board; blatant, glaring, shameless, brazen.
OPPOSITES covert, hidden.

overtake ▸ verb **1** *a green car overtook the taxi* **pass**, get past, go past, go by, overhaul, get/pull ahead of, leave behind, outdistance, outstrip; gain on, catch up with, draw level with, go faster than.
2 *tourism overtook coffee as the main earner of foreign currency* **outstrip**, surpass, overshadow, eclipse, outshine, outclass; dwarf, put in the shade, put to shame, excel, exceed, transcend, top, cap, trump, beat, better; *informal* leave standing, walk away from; *archaic* outrival, outvie.
3 *the calamity which overtook us* **befall**, happen to, come upon, hit, strike, fall on, overwhelm, overpower, overcome, be visited on, engulf, sweep over, take by surprise, surprise, catch unawares, catch unprepared, catch off guard; *literary* betide, whelm.

overthrow ▸ verb **1** *the President was overthrown in a bloodless coup* **remove (from office/power)**, bring down, bring about the downfall of, topple, bring low, undo, depose, oust, displace, supplant, unseat, subvert, dethrone, disestablish, dissolve.
2 *an attempt to overthrow Soviet rule* **put an end to**, defeat, conquer, displace, break up, subvert, annihilate, dissolve.
▸ noun **1** *the overthrow of the Shah of Iran* **removal (from office/power)**, downfall, fall, collapse, toppling, undoing, deposition, ousting, displacement, supplanting, unseating, subversion, dethronement, disestablishment, dissolution.
2 *their aim was the overthrow of capitalism* **ending**, defeat, displacement, fall, rout, collapse, downfall, demise, break-up, subversion, annihilation, dissolution.

overtone ▸ noun **connotation**, hidden meaning, secondary meaning, implication, association, undercurrent, undertone, echo, vibrations, hint, suggestion, insinuation, intimation, flavour, colouring, smack, suspicion, feeling, aura, atmosphere, nuance, trace, murmur, touch, vein; *rare* subcurrent.

overture ▸ noun **1** *the overture to Don Giovanni* **prelude**, introduction, opening, introductory movement, voluntary; *rare* verset.
2 *the talks were no more than the overture to a long debate* **preliminary**, prelude, curtain-raiser, introduction, lead-in, precursor, forerunner, harbinger, herald, start, beginning; *informal* opener.
3 *the enemy were making peace overtures* **opening move**, conciliatory move, move, approach, advances, feeler, signal, proposal, proposition, pass, offer, tender, suggestion.

overturn ▸ verb **1** *the boat overturned* **capsize**, turn turtle, keel over, tip over, topple over, turn over, overbalance, turn topsy-turvy; *Nautical* pitchpole.
2 *I overturned a full supermarket trolley on to my leg* **upset**, tip over, topple over, turn over, throw over, overthrow, knock over, upend, invert, turn topsy-turvy; *informal* roll; *archaic* overset.
3 *the Senate may yet overturn this ruling* **cancel**, reverse, rescind, repeal, revoke, retract, countermand, withdraw, take back, rule against, disallow, override, overrule, veto, set aside, quash, overthrow, repudiate, recant, annul, nullify, declare null and void, invalidate, negate, void, abrogate; *Law* vacate; *archaic* recall.
OPPOSITES allow, accept.

overused ▸ adjective **hackneyed**, overworked, worn out, time-worn, worn, tired, played out, stereotyped, clichéd, threadbare, stale, trite, banal, stock, hack, unoriginal, derivative, platitudinous.
OPPOSITES fresh, original.

overweening ▸ adjective **overconfident**, conceited, cocksure, cocky, smug, haughty, supercilious, disdainful, lofty, patronizing, arrogant, proud, vain, vainglorious, self-important, egotistical, high-handed, magisterial, cavalier, imperious, domineering, dictatorial, overbearing, presumptuous, lordly, peremptory, pompous, officious, blustering, boastful, self-assertive, opinionated, bold, forward, insolent; *informal* high and mighty, throwing one's weight about/around, uppish; *rare* hubristic.
OPPOSITES modest, diffident, unassuming.

overweight ▸ adjective *Allen was in his early fifties and somewhat overweight* **fat**, obese, stout, corpulent, gross, fleshy, plump, portly, chubby, rotund, podgy, roly-poly, paunchy, pot-bellied, beer-bellied, bloated, flabby, Falstaffian, big, large, ample, well fed, well upholstered, well padded, broad in the beam, bulky, outsize, massive, heavy; *informal* porky, pudgy, tubby, blubbery, poddy; *Brit. informal* fubsy; *N. Amer. informal* lard-assed; *archaic* pursy; *rare* abdominous.
OPPOSITES skinny, scrawny, thin, undernourished.

overwhelm ▸ verb **1** *advancing sand dunes could overwhelm built-up areas | they were overwhelmed with work* **swamp**, submerge, engulf, bury, deluge, flood, inundate; clog, saturate, glut, overload, beset, overburden, snow under.
2 *Spain overwhelmed Russia in the hockey* **defeat (utterly/heavily/easily)**, trounce, rout, beat, beat hollow, conquer, vanquish, be victorious over, gain a victory over, prevail over, get the better of, triumph over; best, worst, gain mastery over, master, overpower, overcome, overthrow, subdue, suppress, subjugate, repress, quell, quash, crush, finish, bring someone to their knees, break; *informal* thrash, lick, clobber, whip, wipe the floor with, drub, tank, blow out of the water.
3 *she was overwhelmed by a sense of tragedy* **overcome**, move, stir, affect, touch, impress, sweep someone off their feet, strike, stun, make emotional, dumbfound, shake, disturb, devastate, take aback, daze, spellbind, dazzle, floor, leave speechless, take someone's breath away, stagger; *informal* bowl over, blow away, knock/hit for six, knock sideways, blow someone's mind, get to.

overwhelming ▸ adjective **1** *an overwhelming number of players declared themselves unavailable for the competition* **very large**, profuse, enormous, immense, inordinate, massive, huge, formidable, stupendous, prodigious, fantastic, staggering, shattering, devastating, sweeping; *informal* mind-boggling, mind-blowing.
OPPOSITE small.
2 *we have overwhelming public support* **very strong**, forceful, profound, uncontrollable, irrepressible, irresistible, unbearable, overpowering, oppressive, unutterable, compelling, irrefutable.

overwork ▸ verb **1** *the school doctor says that we should work hard, but not overwork* **work too hard**, work like a Trojan/horse/slave, work/run oneself into the ground, wear oneself to a shadow, work one's fingers to the bone, drive oneself into the ground, sweat, sweat blood, work day and night, burn the candle at both ends, burn the midnight oil, overtax oneself, overtax one's strength, kill oneself, burn oneself out, do too much, overdo it, strain oneself, overburden oneself, overload oneself, drive/push oneself too hard; *informal* knock oneself out, work one's tail off; *vulgar slang* work/sweat one's balls off.
OPPOSITE be idle.
2 *my colleagues did not want to overwork me* **exploit**, drive (too hard), drive into the ground, tax, overtax, sweat, overburden, put upon, impose on, oppress; be a slave driver, be a hard taskmaster.

overworked ▸ adjective **1** *a mistake on the part of overworked staff* **stressed**, under stress, stressed out, stress-ridden, strained, overtaxed, overburdened, overloaded, exhausted, fatigued, worn out.
2 *'new' must be one of the most overworked words in an advertising agency* **hackneyed**, overused, worn out, worn, tired, played out, stereotyped, clichéd, threadbare, stale, trite, banal, platitudinous, stock, hack, unoriginal.

overwrought ▸ adjective **1** *this must have been a shock, and you're overwrought* **tense**, agitated, nervous, on edge, edgy, keyed up, worked up, highly strung, neurotic, overexcited, beside oneself, distracted, distraught, under a strain, frantic, frenzied, hysterical, panicky, restless, jittery, fidgety, jumpy; *Brit.* nervy; *informal* in a state, in a tizzy, uptight, twitchy, wound up, wired, het up; *Brit. informal* throwing a wobbly, strung up.
OPPOSITES calm, cool, laid-back.
2 *the painting is technically brilliant but overwrought* **excessively ornate**,

over-ornate, over-elaborate, over-embellished, overblown, exaggerated, overdone, florid, busy, fussy, contrived, overworked, strained, laboured, baroque, rococo.
OPPOSITES plain, understated.

owe ▶ verb *I still owe him £200* **be in debt (to)**, be indebted (to), be in arrears (to), be under an obligation (to), be obligated (to), be beholden to; be in debit, be overdrawn (by), be in the red; *informal* be in debt to the tune of.
OPPOSITE settle up.

owing ▶ adjective *no rent was owing* **unpaid**, unsettled, to be paid, payable, receivable, due, overdue, undischarged, owed, outstanding, in arrears, in the red; *N. Amer.* delinquent, past due.
OPPOSITES paid, settled.

□ **owing to** *our train was halted owing to an air raid in the region* **because of**, as a result of, on account of, on grounds of, due to, as a consequence of, thanks to, through, by reason of, by/in virtue of, for the sake of, in view of, after, following, in the wake of.

own ▶ adjective *he has his own reasons* **personal**, individual, particular, private, personalized, idiosyncratic, characteristic, unique; *rare* especial.
OPPOSITES shared, common.

▶ pronoun

□ **get one's own back** *we'll get our own back on them for the way they have treated us* **have/get/take one's revenge (on)**, be revenged (on), revenge oneself (on), hit back, get back at, get, get even (with), even the score (with), settle a/the score, settle accounts (with), give as good as one gets, play tit for tat, repay, pay someone back, give someone their just deserts, reciprocate, retaliate (against/on), take reprisals (against), exact retribution (on), let someone see how it feels, give someone a taste of their own medicine.

□ **hold one's own** *Britain has begun to hold its own in world markets* **stand firm**, stand one's ground, maintain/keep one's position, keep one's end up, keep one's head above water, compete, survive, manage, cope, get through, get on, get along, get by.
OPPOSITE go under.

□ **on one's own 1** *she's not here now and I am all on my own* **alone**, all alone, (all) by oneself, in a solitary state, single, solitary, unaccompanied, companionless, partnerless, unattended, unescorted, unchaperoned, solo; *informal* by one's lonesome; *Brit. informal* on one's tod, on one's lonesome, on one's jack, on one's Jack Jones.
OPPOSITE in company.
2 *she works well with tasks she has to achieve on her own* **unaided**, unassisted, without help, without assistance, (all) by oneself, (all) alone, by one's own efforts, under one's own steam, independently, single-handed(ly), standing on one's own two feet, off one's own bat, on one's own initiative.
OPPOSITES jointly, with help.

▶ verb **1** *I own this house* **be the owner of**, possess, be the (proud) possessor of, have in one's possession, have to one's name, count among one's possessions, have, keep, retain, maintain, hold, be blessed with, enjoy, boast.
2 *she had to own that she felt a little that way herself* **admit**, allow, concede, grant, accept, accede, acknowledge, recognize, agree, confess.

□ **own up** *we so often feel guilty and are afraid to own up | he still couldn't own up to the lie* **confess (to)**, admit to, admit guilt, plead guilty, accept blame/responsibility, acknowledge (that), tell the truth (about), make a clean breast of it, tell all; *informal* come clean (about), spill the beans, get something off one's chest.
OPPOSITES hush up, conceal.

WORD LINKS
related prefix **idio-** (e.g. ***idiolect, idiotype***)

owner ▶ noun **possessor**, holder, proprietor/proprietress, homeowner, freeholder, landlord, landlady, master/mistress, keeper; *rare* proprietrix.

WORD LINKS
relating to an owner **proprietary**

ownership ▶ noun **possession**, right of possession, holding, freehold, proprietorship, proprietary rights, title.

ox *See centre pages for list of* **Cattle**

▶ noun bull, bullock, steer, beef; beast of burden, draught animal.

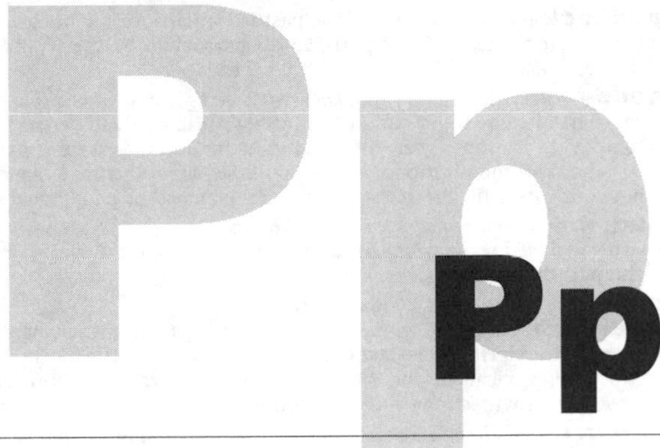

pace ▶ **noun 1** *he stepped back a pace* **step**, stride, footstep.
2 *they continued their steady slow pace* **gait**, stride, walk, tread, march; rhythm.
3 *he had driven home at a furious pace* **speed**, rate, swiftness, quickness, rapidity, velocity, tempo, momentum; *informal* clip, lick.
▶ **verb** *she paced up and down | the chauffeur paced the forecourt anxiously* **walk**, stride, tread, march, pound, patrol, walk up and down, walk back and forth, cross, traverse.

pacific ▶ **adjective 1** *there were demonstrations in the normally pacific community* **peace-loving**, peaceable, pacifist, non-violent, non-aggressive, non-belligerent, non-combative, mild, gentle, equable, dovelike, dovish; *rare* pacifistic.
OPPOSITES hostile, aggressive, belligerent.
2 *he raised his right hand, palm forward, as a sign of his pacific intentions* **conciliatory**, peacemaking, placatory, placating, propitiatory, appeasing, mollifying, calming, mediatory, mediating, diplomatic; *rare* irenic.
OPPOSITE warmongering.
3 *pacific waters* **calm**, still, motionless, smooth, tranquil, placid, waveless, unruffled, undisturbed, like a millpond; quiet, peaceful, at peace.
OPPOSITE stormy.

pacifism ▶ **noun** **peacemaking**, conscientious objection(s), passive resistance, love of peace, peace-mongering; dovishness, non-violence; *rare* satyagraha.

pacifist ▶ **noun** **peace-lover**, conscientious objector, passive resister, peacemaker, peace-monger, appeaser, pacifier; *informal* dove, peacenik; *Brit. informal* conchie; *rare* satyagrahi.
OPPOSITE warmonger.

pacify ▶ **verb** *Gregory tried to think of a way of pacifying his wife* **placate**, appease, calm, calm down, conciliate, propitiate, assuage, mollify, soothe, tranquillize, content, still, quieten, silence, relax, compose.
OPPOSITES provoke, enrage, inflame.

pack ▶ **noun 1** *a pack of cigarettes* **packet**, container, package, box, crate, carton, parcel.
2 *a 60km yomp with a 45lb pack, rifle, and webbing* **backpack**, rucksack, knapsack, kitbag, duffel bag, bag, satchel, load, luggage.
3 *a pack of wolves* **group**, herd, troop.
4 *a pack of youngsters who spent all their time together* **crowd**, mob, group, band, troupe, party, set, club, clique, coterie, gang, rabble, horde, throng, huddle, multitude, mass, assembly, gathering, collection, host, contingent; *informal* crew, bunch.
▶ **verb 1** *she helped pack the hamper* **fill**, fill up, put things in, load, stuff, cram.
2 *it took only a few minutes to pack their belongings* **stow**, put away, store, box up, crate; put in a case/trunk.
3 *the glasses were packed tightly in straw* **wrap (up)**, package, parcel, tie (up), swathe, swaddle, encase, enfold, envelop, cloak, bale, bundle, cover (up), protect.
4 *Christmas shoppers packed the store* **throng**, crowd (into), fill (to overflowing), cram full, mob, cram, jam, press into, squash into, squeeze into.
5 *wet the cloth and pack it against the wall* **compress**, **press**, squash, squeeze, jam, tamp, ram, thrust, force, wedge, crush, flatten.
□ **pack something in** (*informal*) **1** *one of the models has packed in her day job* **resign from**, **leave**, give up, drop, abandon, renounce, relinquish; *informal* quit, chuck, jack in.
2 *he might have to pack in smoking* **give up**, abstain from, drop, desist from, refrain from, steer clear of, give a wide berth to, reject, eschew, forswear, avoid, discontinue; *informal* quit, leave off, kick; *archaic* forsake.
□ **pack someone off** (*informal*) *the best thing is to pack the kiddies off to Grandma* **send off**, **dispatch**, dismiss, bundle off; *informal* send packing.
□ **pack up** (*informal*) **1** *something electrical is bound to pack up over Christmas* **break down**, **stop working**, cease to work/function, fail, give out, stall, come to a halt, develop a fault, malfunction, go wrong, break, act up, be defective/faulty, crash; *informal* conk out, go kaput, go phut; *Brit. informal* play up.
2 *there's no point worrying—if you do, it's time to pack up* **stop**, call it a day, break off, quit, desist, not continue, halt, finish, cease; *informal* leave off, knock off, pack/jack it in.
□ **pack something up** *in the morning, she packed up her belongings* **put away**, tidy up/away, clear up/away, store, stow.

package ▶ **noun 1** *69,000 packages of asparagus* **parcel**, **packet**, container, box, carton.
2 *an annual subscription charge for a complete package of services* **collection**, bundle, lot; combination, conglomeration, raft, package deal.
▶ **verb** *goods packaged in recyclable materials* **wrap**, wrap up, gift-wrap; pack, pack up, parcel, parcel up, box, case, encase, bundle, bundle up.

packaging ▶ **noun** *avoid products with excessive packaging* **wrapping**, wrappers, packing, cover, covering.

packed ▶ **adjective** *an audience of 500 in the packed conference hall* **crowded**, **full**, filled, filled to capacity, thronged, mobbed, loaded, crammed, jammed, solid, packed like sardines, overcrowded, overfull, overloaded, brimful, alive, teeming, seething, swarming; *informal* jam-packed, chock-full, chock-a-block, wall-to-wall, full to the gunwales, bursting/bulging at the seams.

packet ▶ **noun 1** *a packet of cigarettes* **pack**, **carton**, box, cardboard box, container, case, package, parcel, padded bag; *trademark* Jiffy bag.
2 (**a packet**) (*informal*) *that must have cost a packet* **a fortune**, a considerable/vast/large sum of money, a king's ransom; *informal* a small fortune, millions, billions, lots/pots/heaps of money, a mint, a bundle, a wad, a pile, a stack, a heap, a tidy sum, a killing, a pretty penny, telephone numbers; *Brit. informal* a bomb, loadsamoney, a shedload, shedloads; *N. Amer. informal* big bucks, big money, gazillions; *Austral. informal* big bickies, motser, motza.

pact ▶ **noun** *the guerrilla group made a peace pact with the government* **agreement**, **treaty**, entente, protocol, deal, contract, settlement, arrangement, bargain, compact, obligation, understanding, covenant, bond, concord, concordat, convention; armistice, truce; alliance, league.

pad[1] ▶ **noun 1** *Sister will put a pad over your eye for the time being* **dressing**, compress, pack, padding, wadding, wad, stuffing.
2 *the chair comes with a loose seat pad* **cushion**, squab, pillow, bolster; filling, stuffing, upholstery.
3 *he was making notes on a pad* **notebook**, notepad, writing pad, memo pad, jotter, tablet, block, sketch pad, sketchbook; *N. Amer.* scratch pad.
▶ **verb** *a quilted jacket padded with duck feathers for extra warmth* **stuff**, fill, pack, line, wad, upholster, cushion.
□ **pad something out** *don't pad out your answer to make it seem impressive* **spin out**, fill out, augment, amplify, increase, add to, stretch out, eke out, flesh out, lengthen, overdo, protract, elaborate.
OPPOSITES tighten up; condense.

pad[2] ▶ **verb** *I make no noise as I pad along towards the bedroom* **walk quietly**, tread softly, walk barefoot, walk in stockinged feet, walk in slippers, shuffle, soft-shoe.

padding ▶ **noun 1** *the boots have padding around the ankle* **wadding**, cushioning, stuffing, packing, upholstery, filling, filler, lining.
2 *write in a concise manner with no padding* **verbiage**, verbosity, verboseness, wordiness, prolixity, prolixness; *Brit. informal* waffle, wittering, flannel; *rare* logorrhoea.

paddle[1] ▶ **noun** *use the paddles to row ashore* **oar**, scull, sweep, blade, spoon, spade.
▶ **verb** *we paddled out another hundred yards* **row gently**, pull, scull.

paddle[2] ▶ **verb** *a few children were paddling in the shallow water* **splash about**, wade; dabble, slop, squelch.

paddock ▶ **noun** **field**, meadow, pasture; enclosure for horses, yard, pen, pound, stockade; *N. English* park; *Scottish* parrock; *N. Amer.* corral; *French* parc fermé; *S. African* kraal; (*in S. America*) potrero.

paddy ▶ **noun** (*Brit. informal*) *you know what Bert's like when he's in a paddy* **rage**, fit of rage/anger/temper, fit of bad/ill temper, towering rage, temper, bad temper, pet, fit of pique, tantrum, fury, frenzy, paroxysm, passion, bad mood, mood; *informal* state; *Brit. informal* strop; *N. Amer. informal* blowout, hissy fit; *Brit. informal, dated* bate, wax; *archaic* paddywhack.

padlock *See centre pages for list of* **Locks**
▶ **verb** *you should padlock ladders to something secure* **lock**, lock up, fasten, chain, bolt; secure.

padre *See centre pages for list of* **Priests**
▶ **noun** **priest**, chaplain, minister (of religion), pastor, father, parson, clergyman, cleric, ecclesiastic, man of God, man of the cloth, churchman, vicar, rector, curate, curé, divine, evangelist, preacher; *Scottish* kirkman; *informal* reverend, Holy Joe, sky pilot; *Austral. informal* josser.

paean ▶ **noun** *Moses leads the people in a great paean of triumph | paeans of praise for everybody's wisdom* **song of praise**, hymn, psalm, anthem, shout of praise, alleluia; praise, plaudit, exaltation, glorification, eulogy, tribute, testimonial, extolment, encomium, panegyric, accolade, acclamation, commendation, compliment, bouquet.

pagan ▶ **noun** *the early Christians believed that the pagans worshipped trees* **heathen**, infidel, idolater/idolatress, atheist, irreligious person, agnostic, sceptic, heretic, apostate; *archaic* paynim.
OPPOSITE believer.
▶ **adjective** *the great pagan festival of the solar solstice* **heathen**; ungodly, irreligious, infidel, idolatrous, atheistic, agnostic, sceptical, faithless, impious; *rare* paganistic, paganish, apostatical, nullifidian, heathenish, heathenistic.

page[1] ▶ **noun 1** *a book of 672 pages* **folio**, sheet, side, leaf; recto, verso.
2 *a glorious page in this distinguished writer's life* **period**, time, episode, stage, phase, epoch, era, chapter; event, incident, point.

page[2] ▶ **noun 1** *a page in a hotel* **errand boy**, pageboy, messenger boy; *N. Amer.* bellboy, bellhop; *Brit. informal, dated* Buttons.
2 *a page at a wedding* **attendant**, pageboy, train-bearer.
▶ **verb** *could you please page Mr Johnson in the dining room?* **call (for)**, ask for, broadcast for, summon, send for.

pageant ▶ **noun** *the Queen attended a 1,000-horse pageant and re-creation of the coronation parade* **parade**, procession, cavalcade, scene, play, representation, tableau, tableau vivant; display, spectacle, extravaganza, show.

pageantry ▶ **noun** *the Trooping of the Colour brings Londoners out for a historic day of military pageantry* **spectacle**, display, ceremony, ceremoniousness, magnificence, pomp, glory, splendour, grandeur, glamour, flourish, glitter, theatricality, drama, show, showiness; *informal* pizzazz, razzle-dazzle, razzmatazz; *rare* grandezza.

pain ▶ **noun 1** *it seemed impossible that anyone could endure such pain for so long* **suffering**, agony, affliction, torture, torment, discomfort, soreness.
2 *she had a dull pain in her stomach* **ache**, aching, soreness, hurt, throb, throbbing, smarting, pricking, sting, stinging, twinge, shooting pain, stab, pang, spasm; stitch, cramp; discomfort, irritation, stiffness, tenderness.
3 *the pain of losing a loved one* **sorrow**, grief, heartache, heartbreak, sadness, unhappiness, distress, desolation, misery, wretchedness, despair, desperation, mental suffering, emotional suffering, trauma; bitterness, anguish, affliction, tribulation, vexation, woe, agony, torment, torture.
4 *that child is a pain* **nuisance**, pest, bother, vexation, irritant, source of irritation/annoyance, worry, problem, inconvenience, trial, tribulation, plague, source of aggravation, bore, thorn in the flesh, the bane of one's life; *informal* pain in the neck, drag; *vulgar slang* pain in the arse.
5 (**pains**) *he took great pains to hide his feelings* **care**, effort, bother, trouble, labour, exertion, strain, struggle.
□ **be at pains** *they were at pains to put him at ease* **try hard**, make a great effort, make an effort, make every effort, spare no effort, take (great) pains, take care, put oneself out, apply oneself, exert oneself; strive, endeavour, try, struggle, battle, labour, toil, strain, work, aim; do one's best, do all one can, do one's utmost, give (it) one's all, go all out; *informal* bend/fall/lean over backwards, give it one's best shot.
▶ **verb 1** *her foot is still paining her* **hurt**, cause pain, be painful, be sore, ache, throb, smart, burn, prickle, sting, pinch, twinge, cause discomfort, be tender; *informal* kill; *Brit. informal* play up.
2 *the memory of the event still pains her* **sadden**, grieve, distress, make miserable/wretched, trouble, worry, bother, perturb, disturb, oppress, harrow, cause anguish to, afflict; cut to the quick, mortify, torment, torture, wound, sting, gnaw at.

WORD LINKS

pain in a part of the body	**-algia (e.g. *neuralgia*)**
medicine for reducing pain	**analgesic**
drug making one unable to feel pain	**anaesthetic**
branch of medicine concerning insensitivity to pain	**anaesthesiology**

pained ▶ **adjective** *she stared at Hebden with a pained expression on her face* **upset**, hurt, wounded, injured, insulted, offended, aggrieved, affronted, displeased, distressed, disgruntled, put out, annoyed, angered, angry, cross, exasperated, indignant, irritated, vexed, piqued, irked, stung, galled, nettled, needled, peeved, ruffled, resentful, in a huff, huffy, in high dudgeon, fed up; *informal* riled, miffed, rattled, aggravated, peed off, hacked off; *Brit. informal* narked, eggy, cheesed off, browned off, brassed off; *N. Amer. informal* teed off, ticked off, sore; *dated* miffy, snuffy; *vulgar slang* pissed off.

painful ▶ **adjective 1** *a painful arm* **sore**, hurting, hurt, tender, aching, throbbing, smarting, burning, irritating, agonizing, excruciating; *informal* gut-wrenching.
2 *a painful experience* **distressing**, unpleasant, nasty, bitter, awful, disquieting, disturbing, upsetting, traumatic, miserable, wretched, sad, heartbreaking, heart-rending, agonizing, harrowing, mortifying; unendurable, unbearable, torturous, cruel, uncomfortable, disagreeable; *rare* distressful.
OPPOSITES pleasant, agreeable.

painfully ▶ **adverb** *the whole affair had been painfully embarrassing* **distressingly**, worryingly, upsettingly, disturbingly, sadly, pitifully, unfortunately, agonizingly, harrowingly, excruciatingly, chillingly, alarmingly, insufferably, unendurably, unbearably, torturously, cruelly, uncomfortably, embarrassingly, disconcertingly, unenviably, unpleasantly; woefully, dreadfully, terribly, awfully, horribly; *dated* frightfully.

painkiller ▶ **noun** **analgesic**, pain reliever, anodyne, anaesthetic, narcotic, embrocation, liniment; *rare* palliative, demulcent.

painless ▶ **adjective 1** *any killing of animals should be painless* **pain-free**, under anaesthetic.
OPPOSITE painful.
2 *getting rid of him proved painless* **easy**, trouble-free, effortless, undemanding, unexacting, simple, uncomplicated, smooth, plain sailing; *informal* as easy as pie, as easy as falling off a log, as easy as ABC, a piece of cake, child's play, a cinch; *dated* a snip.
OPPOSITES difficult, demanding.

painstaking ▶ **adjective** **careful**, meticulous, thorough, assiduous, sedulous, attentive, diligent, industrious, laborious, hard-working, conscientious, ultra-careful, punctilious, scrupulous, demanding, exacting, searching, close, elaborate, minute, accurate, correct, studious, rigorous, particular; religious, strict; pedantic, fussy.
OPPOSITES careless, negligent, slapdash.

paint *See centre pages for list of* **Paints**
▶ **noun** **colouring**, colourant, tint, dye, stain, pigment, wash, colour; varnish.
▶ **verb 1** *simply paint the ceiling* **colour**, apply paint to, decorate, tint, dye, stain, distemper, whitewash, emulsion, gloss, spray, spray-paint, airbrush, roller, coat, cover.
2 *soldiers arrested three men who had been painting slogans on a wall* **daub**, smear, plaster, spray, spray-paint, airbrush.
3 *he was twelve when Modigliani painted him* **portray**, picture, paint a picture of, depict, delineate, draw, sketch, represent, catch (a likeness of); reproduce, illustrate, render.
4 *you paint a very stark picture of the suffering* **tell**, recount, narrate, set forth/out, outline, sketch, detail, unfold, describe, depict, characterize, evoke, conjure up.
□ **paint the town red** **celebrate**, carouse, enjoy oneself, make merry, have a good/wild time, party, have a party; *N. Amer.* step out; *informal* go out on the town, whoop it up, make whoopee, have a night on the tiles, live it up, have a ball, push the boat out; *dated* go on a spree.

painting *See centre pages for lists of* **Painting Types** **Painting Techniques and Methods**
▶ **noun** **picture**, illustration, portrayal, depiction, delineation, representation, likeness, image, sketch, cartoon, artwork; oil painting, oil, watercolour, canvas.

pair ▶ **noun 1** *a pair of gloves* **set of two**, set, matching set, matched set, two of a kind.
2 *the pair were arrested on Saturday | a pair of pheasants* **two**, couple, duo, brace, twosome; twins; *archaic* twain; *rare* duplet, dyad, duad, doubleton.
3 *a pair of lines in Chaucer's first fabliau* **couplet**, distich.
4 *a coach and pair* **two horses**, team, yoke, span.
5 *they drank a toast of long life and many babies to the happy pair* **couple**, man and wife, husband and wife, partners, lovers.
▶ **verb** *a cardigan paired with a matching skirt* **match**, put together, couple, twin, partner, marry up.
□ **pair off/up** *Rachel paired up with Tommy* **get together**, join up, link up, team up, unite, form a partnership, form a couple, make a twosome.

pal (*informal*) ▶ **noun** **friend**, companion, comrade, intimate, familiar, confidant, alter ego, second self; playmate, classmate, schoolmate, workmate; *informal* chum, buddy, bosom pal, sidekick, cully, spar, crony, mucker, butty, main man; *Brit. informal* mate, oppo, china; *N. English informal* marrow, marrer, marra; *N. Amer. informal* amigo, compadre, paisan; *N. Amer. &*

S. African informal homeboy, homegirl; *S. African informal* gabba; *archaic* compeer; *rare* fidus Achates.
▶ **verb**
□ **pal up** *I palled up with Alan* **become friendly**, make friends, become friends, form a friendship; *informal* get in; *N. Amer. informal* buddy up; *informal, dated* chum up.

palace ▶ **noun** **royal/official residence**, castle, mansion, stately home; (*in France*) château; (*in Italy*) palazzo; (*in German-speaking countries*) schloss; (*in Spain*) alcazar; (*in Turkey, historical*) seraglio.

WORD LINKS
like a palace **palatial**

palatable ▶ **adjective 1** *a very palatable local red wine | palatable meals* **tasty**, appetizing, pleasant-tasting; eatable, edible, drinkable, flavourful, flavoursome, savoury, delicious, delectable, enjoyable, mouth-watering, luscious, toothsome, succulent, dainty; *informal* scrumptious, finger-licking, yummy, scrummy, nummy, moreish, delish, yum-yum; *literary* ambrosial; *rare* comestible, flavorous, ambrosian, sapid, nectarean, nectareous.
OPPOSITES tasteless, insipid, unpalatable.
2 *he gives us the truth—not all of it is palatable* **pleasant**, acceptable, satisfactory, pleasing, agreeable, easy to take, to one's liking, pleasurable, nice; *rare* sapid.
OPPOSITES disagreeable, unpalatable, unpleasant.

palate ▶ **noun 1** *the tea was so hot it burned her palate* **roof of the mouth**; hard palate, soft palate.
2 *the spicy menus have been toned down to suit the tourist palate* **sense of taste**, taste, taste buds; appetite, stomach.
3 *a wine with a zingy, peachy palate* **flavour**, taste, savour; *rare* goût.

WORD LINKS
repair of cleft palate **palatoplasty**

palate or palette?
These words may be confused because of their similar pronunciation, but they are in fact unrelated. A person's **palate** is their sense of taste and discrimination (*this dish may be too exotic for the British palate*). Literally, the word denotes the roof of the mouth. **Palette**, on the other hand, literally denotes an artist's board for mixing colours, but is also used to refer to the range of colours used (*gold, burnt orange, stone, and mink are used to create a warm palette*).

palatial ▶ **adjective** *a palatial five-star hotel* **luxurious**, de luxe, magnificent, sumptuous, splendid, grand, opulent, lavishly appointed, lavish, lush, grandiose, rich, imposing, impressive, fine, stately, regal, majestic; fancy, upmarket, exclusive; spacious, large-scale; *informal* plush, plushy, swanky, posh, ritzy, swish; *rare* palatian.
OPPOSITES humble, modest.

palaver ▶ **noun 1** *what was all that palaver about?* **fuss**, fuss and bother, bother, commotion, trouble, rigmarole, folderol, ado; *informal* song and dance, performance, to-do, carry-on, carrying-on, kerfuffle, hoo-ha, hullabaloo, ballyhoo, business, pantomime, hoopla; *NZ informal* bobsy-die.
2 (*dated*) *you can tell him that, when you are having one of your little palavers with him* **conversation**, chat, discussion, talk, meeting, conference, get-together, tête-à-tête, head-to-head, session, dialogue, colloquy; *informal* parley, powwow, confab, chinwag; *N. Amer. informal* rap, skull session; *formal* confabulation.
▶ **verb** *don't stand there palavering all day* **chatter**, gossip, prattle, prate, babble, blather, blether, blither, maunder, gabble, jabber, tittle-tattle; *Scottish & Irish* slabber; *informal* chit-chat, jaw, gas, gab, yak, yackety-yak, yabber, yatter; *Brit. informal* natter, rabbit, witter, chunter, waffle, chinwag; *archaic* twaddle, clack.

pale[1] ▶ **noun 1** *the pales of a fence* **stake**, post, pole, paling, picket, upright; palisade.
2 *a woman who stands outside the pale of family and community life* **boundary**, confines, bounds, limits.
□ **beyond the pale** *his behaviour was beyond the pale* **unacceptable**, unseemly, improper, indiscreet, unsuitable, irregular, unreasonable, intolerable, disgraceful, deplorable, outrageous, scandalous, shocking, insupportable, objectionable, offensive, distasteful; *informal* not on, not the done thing, out of order, out of line; *dated* not quite the thing; *Austral./NZ informal* over the fence; *rare* exceptionable.

pale[2] ▶ **adjective 1** *his pale skin | she looked pale and drawn* **white**, pallid, pasty, pasty-faced, wan, colourless, anaemic, bloodless, washed out, peaky, peakish, ashen, ashen-faced, ashy, chalky, chalk-white, grey, whitish, white-faced, whey-faced, waxen, waxy, blanched, drained, pinched, green, ghastly, sickly, sallow, as white as a sheet, as white as a ghost, deathly pale, cadaverous, corpse-like, looking as if one had seen a ghost; milky, creamy, cream, ivory, milk-white, alabaster; *informal* like death warmed up; *Scottish informal* peely-wally; *rare* etiolated, lymphatic.
OPPOSITES flushed, rosy.
2 *pale colours* **light**, light-coloured, pastel, neutral, light-toned, muted, subtle, soft, low-key, restrained; faded, bleached, dusty, whitish, washed out, insipid.
3 *the pale light of morning* **dim**, faint, weak, feeble, thin, watery, wan.
OPPOSITES dark; bright.
4 *a pale imitation of the real thing* **inferior**, poor, feeble, weak, insipid, wishy-washy, vapid, bland, puny, flat, inadequate, ineffectual, ineffective, half-hearted; lame, tame, uninspired, unimaginative, lacklustre, spiritless, lifeless, anaemic, bloodless; *informal* pathetic; *rare* etiolated.
▶ **verb 1** *his face paled* **go/turn white**, grow/turn/become pale, blanch, blench, lose colour; whiten, lighten.
2 *everything else pales by comparison* **decrease in importance**, lose significance, pale into insignificance; fade, dwindle, diminish, lessen, dim, lose lustre.

palisade ▶ **noun** **fence**, paling, enclosure, defence, barricade, stockade, fortification, bulwark.

pall[1] ▶ **noun 1** *the coffin lay under a rich velvet pall* **funeral cloth**, coffin covering.
2 *a pall of black smoke hung over the quarry* **cloud**, covering, cloak, mantle, veil, shroud, layer, blanket, sheet, curtain, canopy.
□ **cast a pall over** *the news cast a pall over the occasion* **spoil**, take the fun/enjoyment/pleasure out of, cast a shadow over, overshadow, envelop in gloom, darken, cloud, put a damper on, mar, blight.

pall[2] ▶ **verb** *two years of pandering to bloated businessmen began to pall* **become/grow tedious**, become/grow boring, become/grow tiresome, lose its/their interest, lose attraction, wear off, cloy; bore, tire, fatigue, weary, sicken, nauseate; irritate, irk.

palliate ▶ **verb 1** *the treatment works by palliating symptoms* **alleviate**, ease, relieve, soothe, take the edge off, assuage, allay, dull, soften, lessen, moderate, temper, mitigate, diminish, decrease, blunt, deaden, abate; *rare* lenify.
2 *if only there were some way to palliate his dirty deed* **disguise**, hide, gloss over, conceal, whitewash, cover, cover up, camouflage, cloak, mask, paper over, varnish over; excuse, justify, extenuate, minimize, mitigate, make light of, tone down, play down, downplay.

palliative ▶ **adjective** *the role of these drugs is essentially palliative* **soothing**, alleviating, sedative, calmative, calming; *rare* alleviative, alleviatory, lenitive, demulcent, assuasive, mitigatory, mitigative, paregoric.
▶ **noun** *antibiotics and palliatives* **painkiller**, analgesic, pain reliever, sedative, tranquillizer, anodyne, calmative, opiate, bromide; *rare* lenitive, demulcent, mitigative, paregoric.

pallid ▶ **adjective 1** *his skin was damp and pallid | a pallid child* **pale**, white, pasty, pasty-faced, wan, colourless, anaemic, bloodless, washed out, peaky, peakish, peaked, whey-faced, ashen, ashen-faced, ashy, chalky, chalk-white, grey, whitish, white-faced, waxen, waxy, blanched, drained, pinched; green, ghastly, sickly, sallow, deathly pale, cadaverous, corpse-like; *informal* like death warmed up; *Scottish informal* peely-wally; *rare* etiolated, lymphatic.
OPPOSITES flushed, rosy.
2 *pallid watercolours of the better-known beauty spots of Norfolk* **insipid**, uninspired, colourless, uninteresting, feeble, dull, boring, tedious, tired, unexciting, unimaginative, lifeless, spiritless, sterile, anaemic, bloodless, bland, vapid, wishy-washy.
OPPOSITES vivid, lively.

pallor ▶ **noun** *her dark hair accentuated her pallor* **paleness**, pallidness, lack of colour, whiteness, colourlessness, wanness, ashen hue, pastiness, peakiness, greyness, sickliness, sallowness; *rare* etiolation.

pally ▶ **adjective** **friendly**, on good terms, close, familiar, affectionate, intimate; *informal* as thick as thieves, thick, matey, buddy-buddy, palsy-walsy, chummy.

palm[1] ▶ **verb**
□ **palm something off** *they palmed off their shoddiest products on the tourists* **foist**, fob off, offload, get rid of, dispose of; *informal* unload.
▶ **noun**
□ **grease someone's palm** **bribe**, buy off, buy, corrupt, suborn, give an inducement to; *informal* give a backhander to, give a sweetener to, square.
□ **have someone in the palm of one's hand** **have control over**, have power over, have influence over, have someone at one's mercy, have someone in one's clutches, have someone eating out of one's hand, have someone on a string; *N. Amer.* have someone in one's hip pocket.

WORD LINKS
relating to the palm of the hand **volar**

palm[2] ▶ **noun** *she holds the palm for absent-mindedness* **prize**, trophy, award, crown, wreath, laurel wreath, laurels, bays; honour, glory, fame, victory, triumph, success, accolade.

palmist ▶ **noun** *she was told by a palmist that she would die in her thirties* **fortune teller**, palm-reader, clairvoyant, chiromancer; *rare* chirosophist, palmister.

palmistry ▶ **noun** **fortune telling**, palm-reading, clairvoyancy, chiromancy; *rare* chirosophy, chirognomy.

palmy ▶ **adjective** *the palmy days of the 1960s* **happy**, fortunate, glorious, prosperous, halcyon, golden, flourishing, successful, thriving, rosy, roaring, booming, triumphant.

palpable ▶ adjective **1** *a palpable bump at the bridge of the nose* **tangible**, touchable, noticeable, detectable, solid, concrete, material, substantial, real.
2 *his reluctance was palpable* **perceptible**, perceivable, visible, noticeable, appreciable, discernible, detectable, observable, tangible, recognizable, notable, unmistakable, transparent, indisputable, self-evident, incontrovertible, incontestable, undeniable; **obvious**, clear, plain, plain to see, evident, apparent, manifest, patent, marked, conspicuous, pronounced, striking, distinct; as plain as a pikestaff, as plain as the nose on one's face, standing/sticking out like a sore thumb, standing/sticking out a mile, right under one's nose, staring one in the face, writ large, beyond doubt, beyond question, written all over someone, as clear as day, blinding, inescapable, overt, open, undisguised, unconcealed, glaring, blatant, flagrant, barefaced, gross, stark.
OPPOSITES intangible, imperceptible.

CHOOSE THE RIGHT WORD

palpable, perceptible, noticeable, appreciable
See PERCEPTIBLE.

palpitate ▶ verb **1** *her heart began to palpitate* **beat rapidly**, pound, throb, pulsate, pulse, thud, thump, hammer, flutter, pitter-patter, go pit-a-pat, quiver, pump, race, pant, thrill; *rare* quop.
2 *she was palpitating with terror* **tremble**, quiver, quake, shake, shake like a leaf, shiver, shudder; *rare* quave.

paltry ▶ adjective **1** *a paltry sum of money | a paltry 41p* **small**, meagre, trifling, insignificant, negligible, inadequate, insufficient, scant, scanty, derisory, pitiful, pitiable, pathetic, miserable, sorry, wretched, puny, trivial, niggardly, beggarly, mean, ungenerous, inappreciable, mere; *informal* measly, piddling, piffling, mingy, poxy, dinky; *rare* exiguous.
OPPOSITES considerable, substantial.
2 *naval glory struck him as paltry* **worthless**, petty, trivial, unimportant, insignificant, inconsequential, of little account/consequence, meaningless, negligible, nugatory, minor, footling, contemptible; *informal* penny-ante; *Brit. informal* twopenny, twopenny-halfpenny; *N. Amer. informal* nickel-and-dime, picayune.
OPPOSITES important, significant, valuable.

pamper ▶ verb *Trevor's big sister pampered him* **spoil**, **indulge**, overindulge, cosset, mollycoddle, coddle, baby, pet, wait on someone hand and foot, cater to someone's every whim, feather-bed, wrap in cotton wool; humour, pander to; *archaic* cocker.

pamphlet ▶ noun **brochure**, leaflet, booklet, circular, flyer, handbill, handout, bill, notice, tract; *N. Amer.* mailer, folder; *N. Amer. & Austral.* dodger.

pan¹ ▶ noun **1** *heat the olive oil in a heavy pan* saucepan, frying pan, pot, casserole, wok, skillet, bain-marie, fish kettle, pressure cooker, poacher, chafing dish; container, cooking utensil; *Indian* karahi.

2 *the evaporation of sea water in salt pans* **hollow**, pit, basin, depression, dip, indentation, crater, cavity, concavity.
▶ verb **1** (*informal*) *the movie was panned by the critics* **criticize**, censure, attack, lambaste, condemn, find fault with, give a bad press to, flay, savage, shoot down, bring under fire; *informal* knock, take to pieces, take/pull apart, crucify, hammer, slam, bash, give something a battering; roast, skewer, maul, throw brickbats at; *Brit. informal* slate, rubbish, slag off; *N. Amer. informal* trash, pummel; *Austral./NZ informal* bag, monster.
OPPOSITES praise, commend, applaud.
2 *prospectors panned for gold* **sift for**, search for, look for.
□ **pan out 1** *Harold's idea had been a good one even if it hadn't panned out* **succeed**, be successful, work, turn out well, work out; *informal* do the trick.
2 *the deal panned out badly* **turn out**, work out, conclude, end (up), result, come out, fall out, develop, evolve; *rare* eventuate.

pan² ▶ verb *the camera panned to the building* **swing (round)**, sweep, track, move, turn, circle.

panacea ▶ noun *a panacea for the country's economic problems* **universal cure**, cure-all, cure for all ills, universal remedy, sovereign remedy, heal-all, nostrum, elixir, wonder drug, perfect solution, magic formula, magic bullet; *rare* catholicon, diacatholicon, panpharmacon.

panache ▶ noun *they played with panache and authority* **flamboyant confidence**, flamboyance, confidence, self-assurance, style, stylishness, flair, elan, dash, flourish, verve, zest, spirit, brio, éclat, vivacity, vigour, gusto, animation, liveliness, vitality, enthusiasm, energy; *informal* pizzazz, oomph, zip, zing.

pancake ▶ noun **crêpe**, drop scone, galette, waffle, griddle cake, batter cake, flannel cake; *N. Amer.* flapjack, slapjack; *Russian* blini; *Mexican* tortilla, tostada; *Indian* chapatti, dosa; *Jewish* latke, blintze.

pandemic ▶ adjective *the disease is pandemic in Africa* **widespread**, prevalent, pervasive, rife, rampant, epidemic; universal, global.

pandemonium ▶ noun *we heard a massive bang and then there was complete pandemonium* **bedlam**, **chaos**, mayhem, uproar, madness, havoc, turmoil, tumult, commotion, confusion, disorder, anarchy, furore, frenzy, clamour, din, hubbub, hue and cry, babel, rumpus, fracas, hurly-burly, maelstrom; *W. Indian* bangarang; *informal* hullabaloo, all hell breaking loose, madhouse.
OPPOSITES silence, peace.

pander ▶ verb
□ **pander to** *David was always there to pander to her every whim* **indulge**, gratify, satisfy, cater to, give in to, fulfil, yield to, bow to, humour, please, accommodate, comply with, go along with.

pane ▶ noun **sheet of glass**, panel, windowpane.

panegyric ▶ noun *he finished up with a panegyric on the Vice-Chancellor* **eulogy**, **speech of praise**, paean, accolade, tribute, testimonial; commendation, acclamation.

panel ▶ noun **1** *a control panel* **console**, instrument panel, fascia, board, dashboard; instruments, controls, dials.
2 *a panel of judges* **group**, advisory group, team, body, committee, jury, council, board, commission.

pang ▶ noun **1** *hunger pangs* **pain**, sharp pain, shooting pain, twinge, stab, spasm, ache, cramp.
2 *Melissa felt a pang of remorse* **qualm**, misgiving, scruple, twinge, prick, dart, twitch, gnawing.

panic ▶ noun *she felt a wave of panic | he ran outside in a panic* **alarm**, anxiety, nervousness, fear, fright, trepidation, dread, terror, horror, agitation, hysteria, consternation, perturbation, dismay, disquiet, apprehension, apprehensiveness; *informal* flap, fluster, state, cold sweat, funk, tizzy, tizz; *N. Amer. informal* swivet.
OPPOSITES calm, calmness.
▶ verb **1** *there's no need to panic* **be alarmed**, be scared, be nervous, be afraid, overreact, become panic-stricken, take fright, be filled with fear, be terrified, be agitated, be hysterical, lose one's nerve, be perturbed, get overwrought, get worked up, go/fall to pieces, lose control, fall apart; *informal* flap, get in a flap, lose one's cool, get the jitters, get into a tizzy/tizz, run around like a headless chicken, freak, freak out, get in a stew, get the willies, get the (screaming) heebie-jeebies; *Brit. informal* get the wind up, go into a (flat) spin, have kittens, lose one's bottle, throw a wobbly, have an attack of the wobblies.
2 *talk of love panicked her* **frighten**, alarm, scare, unnerve, fill with panic, agitate, horrify, terrify; *informal* throw into a tizzy/tizz, freak, freak out, spook; *Brit. informal* put the wind up.
OPPOSITE relax.

panic-stricken ▶ adjective **alarmed**, frightened, scared, scared stiff, frightened/scared out of one's wits, frightened/scared to death, terrified, terror-stricken, terror-struck, petrified, horrified, horror-stricken, horror-struck, fearful, afraid, aghast, panicky, panic-struck, frenzied, frantic, in a frenzy, nervous, agitated, hysterical, beside oneself, perturbed, dismayed, disquieted, worked up, overwrought; *informal* in a cold sweat, in a (blue) funk, in a flap, in a fluster, in a state, in a tizzy/tizz, jumpy, jittery; *Brit. informal* in a flat spin, funky; *dialect* frit.
OPPOSITES calm, relaxed.

panoply ▶ noun **1** *the full panoply of America's military might* **array**, range, collection.
2 *all the panoply of Western religious liturgy* **trappings**, regalia, apparatus; splendour, spectacle, show, display; ceremony, ritual.

panorama ▶ noun **1** *stopping the car, he surveyed the panorama* **view**, vista, wide view, aerial view, bird's-eye view, scenic view, prospect, perspective, outlook, aspect, scene, scenery, landscape, seascape.
2 *a panorama of the contemporary art scene* **overview**, overall picture, survey, review, perspective, presentation, appraisal.

panoramic ▶ adjective **1** *a panoramic view of Manhattan* **sweeping**, wide, extensive, bird's-eye, scenic, commanding.
2 *a panoramic look at 20th century German art* **wide-ranging**, extensive, broad, far-reaching, overall, comprehensive, sweeping, all-encompassing, all-embracing, inclusive, general.
OPPOSITES restricted, narrow, limited.

pant ▶ verb **1** *the Brigadier was panting a little as they reached the top of the slope* **breathe heavily**, breathe hard, breathe quickly, puff, huff and puff, puff and blow, gasp, wheeze, heave, blow.
2 *the track has the sort of subtle start that makes you pant for more* **yearn for**, long for, crave, hanker after/for, pine for, ache for, hunger for, thirst for, be hungry for, be greedy for, be thirsty for, itch for, sigh for, be dying for, cry out for, wish for, desire, be consumed with desire for, want, covet; *informal* have a yen for; *archaic* be athirst for, suspire for.
▶ noun *Robyn was breathing in shallow pants* **gasp**, puff, wheeze, breath.

panting ▶ adjective **out of breath**, breathless, short of breath, puffed out, puffing, huffing and puffing, puffing and blowing, gasping, gasping for breath, wheezing, wheezy, winded, short-winded; *informal* out of puff.

pantry ▶ noun **larder**, storage room, store, storeroom; *Brit.* buttery, butlery, still room; *archaic* spence.

pants *See centre pages for lists of* **Underwear** **Trousers**
▶ **plural noun 1** (Brit.) **underpants**, briefs, Y-fronts, boxer shorts, boxers, long johns, knickers, French knickers, bikini briefs; G-string, thong; Brit. tanga briefs, camiknickers; N. Amer. shorts, undershorts; informal panties, undies, frillies; Brit. informal kecks, smalls; dated drawers, bloomers; N. Amer. dated step-ins; historical pantalettes, Directoire drawers.
2 (N. Amer.) **trousers**.

pap ▶ **noun 1** *a plateful of tasteless pap* **soft food**, mush, semi-liquid food, baby food, slop, slush, swill, pulp, purée, mash, paste; informal goo, gloop, gook; N. Amer. informal glop.
2 *an aspiring writer sees his profound drama turned into commercial pap by Hollywood* **trivia**, pulp, pulp fiction, rubbish, trash, nonsense, froth; Brit. candyfloss; informal dreck, drivel, twaddle, rot; rare pabulum, pablum.

paper *See centre pages for list of* **Newspapers**
▶ **noun 1** *a sheet of paper* writing paper, notepaper.
2 *the story made the front page of the local paper* **newspaper**; informal print, rag.
3 *the paper was peeling off the walls* **wallpaper**, wallcovering; Brit. woodchip; trademark Anaglypta, Lincrusta.
4 *toffee papers* **wrapper**, wrapping.
5 *we had to sit a three-hour paper* **exam**, examination, test.
6 *he published a paper which proved to be a landmark in the evolution of macroeconomic ideas* **essay**, article, composition, monograph, thesis, work, dissertation, treatise, study, report, analysis, tract, critique, exegesis, review, disquisition, discourse, piece of writing; N. Amer. theme.
7 (**papers**) *the personal papers of major political figures* **documents**, certificates, forms, letters, files, deeds, records, dossiers, diaries, archives, legal papers, paperwork, documentation; informal treeware; rare muniments, instruments, assignments.
8 (**papers**) *two men stopped us and asked us for our papers* **identification papers**, identification documents, identity card, ID, credentials, bona fides.
□ **on paper 1** *he's putting a few thoughts down on paper* **in writing**, written down, in black and white, in print, on record; recorded, documented, printed.
2 *the combatants were, on paper at least, evenly matched* **in theory**, theoretically, hypothetically, in the abstract, supposedly.
▶ **verb** *we papered the walls and put up curtains to match* **wallpaper**, hang wallpaper on, line; decorate.
□ **paper over something** *the unions tried to paper over their differences* **cover up**, hide, conceal, disguise, camouflage, gloss over, whitewash, varnish over, draw a veil over.

papery ▶ **adjective** *papery leaves | dry, papery skin* **thin**, paper-thin, gossamer-thin, ultra-thin, flimsy, delicate, insubstantial, fragile, frail, light, lightweight; rare papyraceous, chartaceous.

par ▶ **noun**
□ **below par 1** *the team's performances have been consistently below par* **substandard**, inferior, not up to standard, not up to scratch, under par, below average, lacking, wanting, second-rate, mediocre, middling, poor, bad, inadequate, unsatisfactory, uninspired, undistinguished; informal not up to snuff; N. Amer. informal bush-league.
2 *I'm feeling a bit below par this evening* **slightly unwell**, not (very) well, not oneself, not in good shape, out of sorts; ill, ailing, unwell, poorly, indisposed; unhealthy, unfit, washed out, run down, tired, fatigued, peaky, liverish; sick, queasy, nauseous; Brit. off, off colour; informal under the weather, not up to snuff, funny, peculiar, crummy, lousy, rough; Brit. informal ropy, grotty; Scottish informal wabbit; Austral./NZ informal crook; dated seedy, queer.
□ **on a par with** *his writings are held to be on a par with those of Marx, Lenin, and Mao* **as good as**, comparable with, in the same class/league as, equivalent to, much the same as, equal to, a match for, on a level with, on an equal footing with, of the same standard as.
□ **par for the course** *long hours are par for the course in catering* **normal**, typical, standard, usual, predictable, what one would expect, only to be expected.
□ **up to par** *those students whose grades are up to par* **good enough**, up to the mark, satisfactory, acceptable, adequate, passable, up to scratch, all right; informal OK, up to snuff.

parable ▶ **noun** *the parable of the prodigal son* **allegory**, moral story, moral tale, fable, lesson, exemplum; Judaism Haggadah; rare apologue.

parade ▶ **noun 1** *a St George's Day parade | a military parade* **procession**, march, cavalcade, motorcade, cortège, ceremony, spectacle, display, pageant, concours, file, train, column; array, review, muster, dress parade, tattoo; Brit. march past; Indian jatha, yatra, rath yatra; W. Indian mas.
2 *his daughter made a great parade of doing the housework* **exhibition**, show, display, performance, production, spectacle, demonstration; fuss, bother, to-do, commotion, ado; informal hoo-ha.
3 *she walked along the parade as far as the pier* **promenade**, walk, walkway, esplanade, mall; N. Amer. boardwalk; Brit. informal prom; Spanish alameda.
▶ **verb 1** *the teams will parade through the city with a police escort* **march**, process, file, troop, go in columns, pass in formation, promenade.
2 *she paraded up and down her office* **strut**, swagger, swank, stride, stalk, prance; N. Amer. informal sashay.
3 *he was keen to parade his knowledge* **display**, exhibit, make a show of, flaunt, show, show off, demonstrate, draw attention to, air.

> **CHOOSE THE RIGHT WORD**
>
> **parade, strut, swagger**
>
> *See* STRUT.

paradigm ▶ **noun** *the institutional arrangements of a particular society cannot serve as a paradigm for all others* **model**, pattern, example, standard, prototype, archetype; ideal, gauge, criterion, paragon, exemplar.

paradisal ▶ **adjective heavenly**, idyllic, blissful, divine, sublime, Elysian, perfect; literary Arcadian; rare paradisiacal, paradisical.

paradise ▶ **noun 1** *the pagan belief that the soul of a murdered person never entered paradise* **heaven**, the kingdom of heaven, the promised land, the heavenly kingdom, the City of God, the celestial city, the abode of God, the abode of the saints, Zion, Abraham's bosom; Christianity the New Jerusalem; Classical Mythology Elysium, the Elysian Fields, the Islands of the Blessed; Scandinavian Mythology Valhalla; Arthurian Legend Avalon.
2 *Adam and Eve's expulsion from Paradise* **the Garden of Eden**, Eden.
3 *Bali is a lush tropical paradise* **Utopia**, fairyland, Shangri-La, heaven, idyll, nirvana; literary Arcadia.
4 *the sun rising slowly above the mountains—sheer paradise!* **bliss**, heaven, ecstasy, rapture, delight, joy, happiness, nirvana, seventh heaven, heaven on earth.
OPPOSITE hell.

paradox ▶ **noun** *the apparent paradox of simultaneous unemployment and skilled-labour shortages* **contradiction**, contradiction in terms, self-contradiction, inconsistency, incongruity, anomaly, conflict; absurdity, oddity, enigma, puzzle, mystery, conundrum; rare oxymoron, antinomy.

paradoxical ▶ **adjective** *it was paradoxical that a government dedicated to privatization should produce a bill to nationalize the legal profession* **contradictory**, self-contradictory, inconsistent, incongruous, anomalous, conflicting; improbable, impossible, odd, illogical, confusing, absurd, puzzling, baffling, bewildering, incomprehensible, inexplicable; rare oxymoronic.

paragon ▶ **noun** *a paragon of fortitude and cheerfulness | your cook is a paragon* **perfect example**, shining example, good example, model, epitome, archetype, ideal, exemplar, nonpareil, paradigm, embodiment, personification, quintessence, standard, prototype, apotheosis, the crème de la crème, the beau idéal, acme; jewel, gem, flower, angel, treasure; a perfect example of its kind; informal one in a million, the bee's knees, something else, the tops; archaic a nonsuch.

paragraph ▶ **noun 1** *the letter's concluding paragraph* **section**, subdivision, part, subsection, division, portion, segment, bit, passage, clause.
2 *appointments which rate a paragraph in the more serious newspapers* **report**, article, item, piece, notice, write-up, note, mention.

parallel ▶ **adjective 1** *parallel lines* **side by side**, aligned, collateral, equidistant.
2 *problems parallel to those we discussed earlier* **similar**, analogous, comparable, corresponding, like, resembling, much the same, of a kind, akin, related, kindred, equivalent, correspondent, homologous, analogical, cognate, coequal, matching, duplicate.
3 *a parallel universe* **coexisting**, coexistent, concurrent; contemporaneous, simultaneous, synchronous.
OPPOSITES different, dissimilar, divergent.
▶ **noun 1** *it is difficult to find an exact parallel* **counterpart**, analogue, equivalent, likeness, correspondent, match, twin, duplicate, equal, coequal, mirror; rare homologue.
2 *there is an interesting parallel between these figures and those of 1994* **similarity**, likeness, resemblance, analogy, correspondence, equivalence, correlation; comparison, relation, symmetry, parity, parallelism, similitude, coequality.
▶ **verb 1** *his experiences parallel mine in many ways* **resemble**, be similar to, be like, bear a resemblance to; correspond to, be analogous to, be comparable/equivalent to, compare with, equate with/to, correlate with, imitate, echo, remind one of, duplicate, mirror, repeat, recreate, follow, match, be in harmony with, chime (in) with; coincide with, keep pace with.
2 *her performance has never been paralleled* **equal**, match, rival, emulate, touch.

paralyse ▶ **verb 1** *both of his legs were temporarily paralysed* **disable**, cripple, immobilize, render/make powerless, incapacitate, lame, debilitate, numb, deaden, benumb, dull; rare obtund, torpefy.
2 *Maisie seemed to have been paralysed by the sight of him* **immobilize**, transfix, become rooted to the spot, freeze, stun, render motionless, become horror-struck/horror-stricken, petrify; rare gorgonize.
3 *the regional capital was paralysed by a general strike* **bring to a standstill**, immobilize, bring to a (grinding) halt, halt, stop, freeze, cripple, disable,

P

put out of action/commission, render inoperative, deactivate; *rare* disenable.

paralysed ▶ adjective **disabled**, crippled, handicapped, incapacitated, paralytic, lame; dead, numb, benumbed, powerless, immobilized, helpless, useless; *Medicine* paraplegic, quadriplegic, tetraplegic, monoplegic, hemiplegic, paretic, paraparetic; *dated* palsied.

paralysis ▶ noun **1** *the disease can cause paralysis* **immobility**, powerlessness, lack of sensation, numbness, deadness, incapacity, debilitation; *Medicine* paraplegia, quadriplegia, tetraplegia, monoplegia, hemiplegia, diplegia, paresis, paraparesis; *dated* palsy.
2 *strike leaders claimed an almost complete paralysis of the ports* **shutdown**, immobilization, stoppage, halt, standstill, stopping.

paralytic ▶ adjective **1** *her hands became paralytic* **paralysed**, crippled, disabled, incapacitated, dead, numb, benumbed, powerless, immobilized; helpless, useless. *See also* PARALYSED.
2 (*Brit. informal*) *a leaving party which left everyone paralytic. See* DRUNK.
OPPOSITE sober.

parameter ▶ noun *they set the parameters of the debate* **framework**, variable, limit, boundary, limiting factor, limitation, restriction, specification, criterion, guideline; *technical* constant.

paramount ▶ adjective *the safety of the staff is paramount | children's needs should be of paramount importance* **most important**, of greatest importance, of prime importance, of supreme importance; uppermost, supreme, chief, overriding, predominant, cardinal, foremost, first and foremost, prime, primary, principal, pre-eminent, highest, utmost, main, key, central, leading, major, top, topmost, dominant; *informal* number-one.

paramour ▶ noun *his stepfather's paramour* **lover**, beloved, significant other; mistress, girlfriend, kept woman, other woman, inamorata; boyfriend, other man, inamorato, gigolo; *informal* fancy woman, fancy man, toy boy, sugar daddy, bit on the side, bit of fluff; *historical* hetaera, odalisque; *archaic* concubine, doxy, leman, courtesan, cicisbeo.

paranoia ▶ noun **persecution complex**, delusions, obsession, megalomania, monomania; psychosis.

paranoid ▶ adjective *they probably don't mean me at all—I'm probably just being paranoid* **irrationally anxious**, over-suspicious, paranoiac, suspicious, mistrustful, distrustful, fearful, insecure; *Brit. informal* para.

parapet ▶ noun **1** *Marian leaned over the parapet of the bridge* **balustrade**, barrier, wall, railing, fence.
2 *the sandbags that made up the parapet had been blown away* **barricade**, rampart, bulwark, bank, embankment, fortification, defence, breastwork, earthwork, bastion; battlement, castellation; *rare* bartizan.

paraphernalia ▶ plural noun *the paraphernalia necessary for home improvements* **equipment**, stuff, things, apparatus, tackle, kit, implements, tools, utensils, material(s), appliances, rig, outfit, accoutrements, appurtenances, impedimenta, miscellaneous articles, odds and ends, bits and pieces, bits and bobs, trappings, accessories; *informal* gear, junk, rubbish, the necessary, dunnage, traps; *Brit. informal* clobber, gubbins, odds and sods; *archaic* equipage.

P

paraphrase ▶ verb *you can either quote or paraphrase literary texts* **reword**, rephrase, put/express in other words, put/express in one's own words, express differently, rewrite, restate, rehash, interpret, gloss.
▶ noun *this paraphrase of St Paul's words* **rewording**, rephrasing, rewriting, rewrite, restatement, restating, rehash, rendition, rendering, version, interpretation, gloss; *rare* paraphrasis.

parasite ▶ noun *Sam was a parasite with no interest in anything but drink and gambling* **hanger-on**, cadger, leech, passenger, drone; *informal* bloodsucker, sponger, sponge, scrounger, freeloader; *Brit. informal* ligger; *N. Amer. informal* moocher, mooch; *Austral./NZ informal* bludger.

WORD LINKS
fear of parasites **parasitophobia**
branch of medicine concerning parasitic organisms **parasitology**

parasitic ▶ adjective *the parasitic behaviour of some bureaucrats* **exploitative**, parasitical; *informal* bloodsucking, sponging, freeloading.

parcel ▶ noun **1** *a parcel of food and clothes* **package**, packet; pack, carton, bundle, box, case, bale; *archaic* fardel.
2 *a 21-acre parcel of land* **plot**, piece, patch, tract, area, section, allotment; *N. Amer.* lot, plat.
3 *a parcel of rogues* **group**, band, pack, gang, crowd, mob, company, collection, horde, party, troop; *informal* crew, bunch.
▶ verb **1** *she parcelled up the papers* **pack**, pack up, package, wrap, wrap up, gift-wrap, tie up, do up, box, box up, bundle up, fasten together.
2 *parcelling out commercial farmland in small plots will reduce productivity* **divide up**, portion out, distribute, share out, allocate, allot, apportion, hand out, give out, deal out, dole out, mete out, dispense, split up, carve up; *informal* divvy up, dish out.

parched ▶ adjective **1** *the parched earth* **dry**, as dry as a bone, bone dry, dried up, dried out, arid, waterless, desiccated, dehydrated, sun-baked, baked, burned, scorched, seared, withered, shrivelled; *literary* sear, adust; *rare* exsiccated.
OPPOSITES wet, soaking.
2 *Can I have a drink, please? I'm parched* **thirsty**, dehydrated, dry; *informal* gasping; *Austral./NZ informal* spitting chips; *archaic* athirst; *rare* thirstful, droughty, sitient.

parching ▶ adjective *the parching southern sun* **searing**, scorching, blistering, flaming, blazing (hot), baking (hot), burning, fiery, torrid, withering; *informal* boiling, boiling hot, sizzling, roasting, sweltering.

pardon ▶ noun **1** *he obtained pardon for his sins* **forgiveness**, absolution, remission, clemency, mercy, lenience, leniency, condonation; *historical* indulgence.
2 *he offered a full pardon to the five convicted men* **reprieve**, free pardon, general pardon, amnesty, exoneration, exculpation, release, acquittal, discharge; *rare* oblivion.
▶ verb **1** *I know she will pardon me* **forgive**, absolve, have mercy on, be merciful to, deal leniently with; **excuse**, condone, overlook; *rare* remit.
OPPOSITE blame.
2 *the convicted men were subsequently pardoned* **exonerate**, acquit, amnesty, exculpate; **let off**, grant a pardon to, reprieve, release, free, spare.
OPPOSITE punish.
▶ exclamation *'Pardon?' I said, cupping a hand to my ear* **what did you say**, what, eh, I beg your pardon, beg pardon, sorry, excuse me, say again; *N. Amer.* pardon me; *informal* come again.

CHOOSE THE RIGHT WORD
pardon, forgive, excuse, condone
See FORGIVE.

pardonable ▶ adjective *a pardonable error* **excusable**, forgivable, allowable, condonable, understandable, minor, slight, venial, not serious, permissible.
OPPOSITE inexcusable.

pare ▶ verb **1** *pare 4 strips of zest from the lemon | pare the mangoes* **cut (off)**, trim (off), peel (off), shave (off), strip (off), clip (off), skin; *technical* decorticate, excoriate.
2 *the company's domestic operations have been pared down* **reduce**, diminish, decrease, cut, cut back/down, make cutbacks in, whittle away/down, trim, slim down, prune, lower, lessen, retrench, curtail.

parent ▶ noun **1** *her parents divorced when she was seven* **mother**, **father**; birth/biological parent, adoptive mother/father, surrogate mother, foster-parent, foster-mother, foster-father, step-parent, stepmother, stepfather, guardian; single parent, lone parent, co-parent; *informal* one's old man, one's old woman, one's old lady; *rare* begetter, procreator, progenitor, progenitress, progenitrix, genitor, pater.
2 *rhythm and blues, the parent of rock and roll* **source**, origin, genesis, originator, root, fountain, cause, author, architect; **precursor**, forerunner, predecessor, antecedent, forebear, ancestor; *literary* wellspring; *rare* radix.
▶ verb *all children are special to those who parent them* **bring up**, be the parent of, look after, take care of, rear, raise, nurture.

WORD LINKS
killing of one's parent **parricide**

parentage ▶ noun *a young woman of African parentage* **origins**, extraction, birth, family, ancestry, lineage, heritage, pedigree, descent, line of descent, line, blood, bloodline, stock, paternity, roots, derivation; *rare* filiation, stirps.

parenthetical ▶ adjective *parenthetical remarks* **incidental**, supplementary, by-the-way, by-the-by, in parentheses, parenthetic, in brackets; explanatory, qualifying, inserted, interposed, extraneous.

parenthetically ▶ adverb **incidentally**, **by the way**, by the by(e), in passing, en passant, by way of explanation, in parenthesis; *informal* BTW.

parenthood ▶ noun **childcare**, child-rearing, motherhood, fatherhood, parenting, mothering, fathering.

pariah ▶ noun *they were treated as social pariahs* **outcast**, persona non grata, leper, reject, untouchable, undesirable; *rare* unperson.

parings ▶ plural noun **peelings**, clippings, peel, rind, cuttings, trimmings, shavings, strips, pieces, slivers, fragments, shreds.

parish ▶ noun **1** *the parish of Poplar in East London* **district**, community.
2 *a vicar must do nothing that would scandalize the parish* **parishioners**, churchgoers, church, congregation, flock, fold, community.

WORD LINKS
relating to a parish **parochial**

parity ▶ noun *parity of incomes between rural workers and those in industrial occupations* **equality**, equivalence, uniformity, sameness, consistency, correspondence, congruity, congruence, levelness, unity, coequality, parallelism, evenness.

park ▶ noun **1** *Yvonne and her friends were playing in the park* **public garden**, recreation ground, playground, play area, public/municipal park.
2 *a property set in fifty acres of park* **parkland**, grassland, woodland, garden(s), lawns, grounds, estate; *literary* greensward.

3 *he was the liveliest player on the park* **playing field**, football field, field, pitch.
▶ **verb 1** *he parked his car outside Emma's house* **leave**, station, position; stop, pull up.
2 *park your bag by the door* **put**, put down, place, deposit, set, set down, leave, stick, shove, dump, plump; *informal* plonk, plunk; *Brit. informal* bung.
□ **park oneself** *he parked himself in the seat opposite* **sit down**, seat oneself, settle (oneself), install oneself, plant oneself, ensconce oneself, plump oneself, plop oneself, flump, perch; *informal* plonk oneself.

parlance ▶ **noun** *a Munro, in climbing parlance, is a Scottish mountain exceeding 3000 feet in height* **jargon**, language, phraseology, idiom, -speak, talk, speech, way/manner of speaking, vocabulary, vernacular, tongue, idiolect, patter, argot, patois, cant; *French* façon de parler; *informal* lingo.

parley ▶ **noun** *a peace parley* **negotiation**, talk(s), meeting, conference, summit, discussion, dialogue, conclave, consultation, deliberation, colloquy; *informal* confab, powwow; *formal* confabulation; *dated* palaver.
▶ **verb** *the two parties were willing to parley* **discuss terms**, talk, hold talks, speak to each other, confer, consult with each other, negotiate, deliberate; *informal* powwow.

parliament ▶ **noun 1** *the Queen's speech to Parliament* **the Houses of Parliament**, Westminster, the House of Commons, the House of Lords, the Commons, the Lords, the House, the Lower House, the Upper House, the Mother of Parliaments.
2 *the Russian parliament* **legislature**, legislative assembly, congress, senate, chamber, house, upper house, lower house, upper chamber, lower chamber, second chamber, convocation, diet, council, assembly, Chamber of Deputies.

parliamentary ▶ **adjective** *parliamentary assemblies* **legislative**, law-making, lawgiving, deliberative, governmental, congressional, senatorial, democratic, elected, representative; *rare* legislatorial.

parlour ▶ **noun 1** *they had tea in the parlour* **sitting room**, living room, lounge, front room, best room, drawing room, morning room, salon; *Brit.* reception room.
2 *a beauty parlour* **salon**, shop, establishment, store.

parlous ▶ **adjective** (*archaic or humorous*) *the parlous state of the industry* **bad**, dire, dreadful, awful, terrible, appalling, frightful, grave, serious, desperate, precarious, uncertain, touch-and-go, difficult, unsafe, perilous, dangerous, risky; pitiful, wretched, sorry, poor, lamentable, woeful, hopeless; *informal* dicey, hairy, lousy; *Brit. informal* dodgy, chronic.

parochial ▶ **adjective** *parochial attitudes* **narrow-minded**, small-minded, provincial, insular, narrow, small-town, inward-looking, limited, restricted, localist, conservative, conventional, short-sighted, petty, close-minded, blinkered, myopic, introverted, illiberal, hidebound, intolerant; *Brit.* parish-pump; *N. Amer. informal* jerkwater, hick.
OPPOSITES cosmopolitan, broad-minded, liberal.

parochialism ▶ **noun** **narrow-mindedness**, **localism**, provincialism, insularity, narrowness, small-mindedness.

parody ▶ **noun 1** *a parody of the gothic novel* **satire**, burlesque, lampoon, pastiche, caricature, take-off, skit, imitation, mockery; *informal* spoof, send-up; *W. Indian informal* pappyshow; *Brit. vulgar slang* piss-take; *rare* pasquinade, pasticcio.
2 *an appalling parody of the truth* **distortion**, travesty, poor imitation, caricature, mockery, misrepresentation, perversion, corruption, debasement; apology for.
▶ **verb** *his speciality was parodying schoolgirl fiction* **satirize**, burlesque, lampoon, caricature, mimic, imitate, ape, copy, do, do an impression of, make fun of, travesty, take off; *informal* send up; *Brit. vulgar slang* take the piss out of.

paroxysm ▶ **noun** *violent paroxysms of coughing | a paroxysm of rage* **spasm**, attack, fit, burst, bout, convulsion, seizure, outburst, outbreak, eruption, explosion, flare-up, access; throes; *rare* ebullition, boutade.

parrot ▶ **verb** *they parroted slogans without appreciating their significance* **repeat mindlessly**, repeat, repeat mechanically, echo, say again.
WORD LINKS
relating to parrots **psittacine**

parrot-fashion ▶ **adverb** *his wife had just repeated the phrase parrot-fashion* **mechanically**, by rote, mindlessly, without thinking, unthinkingly, automatically.

parry ▶ **verb 1** *Sharpe parried the blow* **ward off**, fend off, stave off, turn aside; **deflect**, hold off, block, avert, counter, rebuff, repel, repulse, hold/keep at bay.
2 *I parried her constant questions about my job-hunting activities* **evade**, sidestep, avoid, dodge, answer evasively, field, fend off, deflect, circumvent, steer clear of, fight shy of; *informal* duck.

parsimonious ▶ **adjective** **mean**, miserly, niggardly, close-fisted, penny-pinching, cheese-paring, ungenerous, penurious, illiberal, close, grasping, Scrooge-like, stinting, sparing, frugal; *informal* tight-fisted, stingy, tight, mingy, money-grubbing, skinflinty; *N. Amer. informal* cheap; *Brit. vulgar slang* tight-arsed, tight as a duck's arse; *archaic* near.
OPPOSITES generous, extravagant, lavish.

parsimony ▶ **noun** **meanness**, miserliness, parsimoniousness, niggardliness, close-fistedness, closeness, penuriousness, penny-pinching, cheese-paring, illiberality, frugality; *informal* stinginess, minginess, tightness, tight-fistedness; *N. Amer.* cheapness; *archaic* nearness.
OPPOSITE generosity.

parson *See centre pages for list of* **Priests**
▶ **noun** **vicar**, rector, clergyman, member of the clergy, cleric, chaplain, pastor, curate, churchman, man of the cloth, man of God, ecclesiastic, minister, priest, preacher, divine; *French* curé; *informal* reverend, padre, Holy Joe, sky pilot; *Austral. informal* josser.

part ▶ **noun 1** *the last part of the cake | a large part of life is spent at the workplace* **bit**, slice, chunk, lump, hunk, wedge, fragment, scrap, segment, piece; portion, share, proportion, percentage, fraction, division, section.
OPPOSITES whole, entirety.
2 *some car parts are now assembled by people working at home* **component**, bit, constituent, element, unit, module, ingredient.
3 *some of pigs' body parts are very much like ours* organ, limb, member, biological structure.
4 *this chapter links the second and third parts of the book* **section**, division, component, volume, chapter, passage, act, scene, episode, instalment.
5 *her parents lived in another part of the country* **district**, neighbourhood, quarter, section, area, region, sector, zone, belt, territory, locality; *informal* neck of the woods.
6 *one of the boy actors played the part of Juliet* **role**, theatrical role, character, persona, representation, portrayal, depiction.
7 *I don't care how long he's had to learn the part* **lines**, words, script, dialogue, speech, libretto, book, lyrics, score.
8 *he was jailed for his part in the affair* **involvement**, role, function, hand, job, task, work, responsibility, capacity, post, position, office, participation, bit, contribution, concern, province.
□ **for the most part**. *See* MOST.
□ **in part** *inflation is caused in part by indirect tax increases* **to a certain extent/degree**, to a limited extent/degree, to some extent/degree, partly, partially, half, in some measure, relatively, comparatively, moderately, (up) to a point, a little, somewhat; not totally, not wholly, not entirely, not fully, incompletely; slightly, fractionally.
OPPOSITE completely.
□ **on the part of** *there is increased interest in these coins on the part of collectors* **by**, made by, done by, carried out by, caused by, from, in, of; for which someone is responsible.
□ **in good part**. *See* GOOD.
□ **take part** *anyone interested is welcome to take part* **participate**, join in, get involved, enter, go in for something, throw oneself into something, share in something, play a part, play a role, be a participant, partake, contribute, be associated, associate oneself, have a hand, have something to do with something, be (a) party to something, cooperate, help, assist, lend a hand; *informal* get in on the act, pitch in.
□ **take part in** *the cadets are obliged to take part in adventurous training* **participate in**, engage in, enter into, join in, get involved in, go in for, throw oneself into, share in, play a part in, play a role in, be a participant in, partake in, contribute to, be associated with, associate oneself with, have a hand in, have something to do with, be (a) party to.
□ **take someone's part** *an attack would drive Count William to take his son's part* **support**, give one's support to, take the side of, side with, be on the side of, stand by, stand up for, stick up for, be supportive of, encourage, back, back up, give one's backing to, uphold, be loyal to, defend, come to the defence of, champion, ally (oneself) with, associate oneself with, favour, abet, aid and abet.
OPPOSITE turn against.
▶ **verb 1** *the curtains parted and the show began | he knelt down and parted the heather with his hands* **separate**, **divide**, divide in two, split, split in two, break up; move apart; *rare* disjoin.
OPPOSITE join.
2 *if we part like this I may never see him again* **leave**, take one's leave, say goodbye/farewell/adieu, say one's goodbyes, say/make one's farewells, separate, break up, go one's (separate) ways, take oneself off, set off, be on one's way, go, go away, get going, depart, be off; *informal* split, push off, hit the road, skedaddle, scram, shove off.
OPPOSITES arrive; meet.
□ **part with** *she had no wish to part with any of her land* **give up**, relinquish, forgo, surrender, hand over, deliver up, let go of, renounce, give away, dispose of, discard, abandon, sacrifice, yield, cede.
OPPOSITE acquire.
▶ **adjective** *a part payment is refundable* **incomplete**, partial, half, semi-, demi-, near, moderate, limited, slight, inadequate, insufficient, unfinished.
OPPOSITE complete.
▶ **adverb** *the engine components can be supplied part finished* **to a certain extent/degree**, to a limited extent/degree, to some extent/degree, partly, partially, in part, half, in some measure, relatively, comparatively, moderately, (up) to a point, a little, somewhat; not totally, not wholly, not entirely, not fully, incompletely, nearly, very nearly, almost, just about, all but; slightly, barely, scarcely, fractionally, inadequately,

insufficiently, not nearly.
OPPOSITE completely.

partake ▶ verb **1** *video conferencing allows executives to **partake in** negotiations abroad* **participate in**, take part in, engage in, enter into, join in, get involved in, share in, play a part in, contribute to, have a hand in, have something to do with.
2 *she had **partaken** of a cheese sandwich and a cup of coffee* **consume**, have, eat, drink, take, devour, polish off, ingest; *informal* tuck into, wolf down, dispose of, get outside of, get one's laughing gear round.
3 *Bohemia is where eastern and western Europe meet, **partaking of** both, part of neither* **have the qualities/attributes of**, suggest, evoke, be characterized by, hint at, evince, manifest.

partial ▶ adjective **1** *the partial recovery of the economy* **incomplete**, limited, qualified, restricted, imperfect, fragmentary, unfinished.
OPPOSITES complete, total, whole.
2 *the paper gave a distorted and very partial view of the situation* **biased**, prejudiced, partisan, one-sided, slanted, skewed, coloured, interested, parti pris, discriminatory, preferential, jaundiced; unjust, unfair, inequitable, unbalanced.
OPPOSITES unbiased, impartial, disinterested.
□ **be partial to** *Celeste was partial to bacon sandwiches* **like**, love, enjoy, have a liking for, be fond of, be keen on, have a fondness for, have a weakness for, have a soft spot for, have a taste for, be taken with, care for, have a predilection/proclivity/penchant for, be enamoured of; *informal* adore, be mad about/on, have a thing about, be crazy about, be potty about, be nutty about; *N. Amer. informal* cotton to, be nutso over/about; *Austral./NZ informal* be shook on.

> **CHOOSE THE RIGHT WORD**
>
> **partial, biased, prejudiced**
> *See* BIASED.

partiality ▶ noun **1** *the president had shown partiality towards the group's cause* **bias**, prejudice, favouritism, favour, partisanship, unfair preference, discrimination, unjustness, unfairness, inequity.
2 *his partiality for brandy and soda was notorious* **liking**, love, fondness, taste, weakness, soft spot, keenness, inclination, predilection, predisposition, proclivity, penchant, fancy, relish, passion.

partially ▶ adverb *the plan was only partially successful* **to a limited extent/degree**, partly, to a certain extent/degree, to some extent/degree, in part, not totally, not wholly, not entirely, not fully, relatively, moderately, (up) to a point, half, somewhat, in some measure, comparatively, fractionally, slightly, incompletely.

participant ▶ noun **participator**, contributor, sharer, party, member, partaker; entrant, competitor, player, contestant, contender, candidate.

participate ▶ verb *400,000 people **participated in** the peaceful demonstration* **take part**, engage, join, get involved, share, play a part, play a role, be a participant, partake; cooperate, help, assist, lend a hand; go in for, contribute to, be associated with, associate oneself with, have a hand in, have something to do with, be (a) party to; *informal* get in on the act, pitch in.

participation ▶ noun *the government's participation in the peace talks* **involvement**, taking part, part, engagement, contribution; sharing, association, partaking, joining in.

particle *See centre pages for lists of* **Particles** **Quarks**
▶ noun **1** *minute particles of rock* **bit**, tiny bit, piece, tiny piece, speck, spot, fleck, dot, atom, molecule; mote, fragment, sliver, splinter.
2 *he never showed a particle of sympathy for her* **iota**, jot, whit, bit, scrap, shred, crumb, morsel, mite, atom, drop, hint, touch, trace, suggestion, whisper, suspicion, scintilla, grain, tittle, jot or tittle; any; *Irish* stim; *informal* smidgen, smidge, tad; *archaic* scantling, scruple.

particular ▶ adjective **1** *the action seems to discriminate against a particular group of companies* **specific**, certain, distinct, separate, isolated; single, individual, peculiar, discrete, definite, express, precise.
OPPOSITE general.
2 *an issue of particular importance* **special**, extra special, especial, exceptional, unusual, marked, singular, uncommon, notable, noteworthy, remarkable, outstanding, unique; *formal* peculiar.
OPPOSITE ordinary.
3 *he was particular about what he ate* **fussy**, fastidious, meticulous, punctilious, discriminating, selective, painstaking, exacting, demanding, critical, over-particular, over-fastidious, finicky, faddish, finical, dainty; *informal* pernickety, choosy, picky; *Brit. informal* faddy; *archaic* nice.
OPPOSITES careless, easy-going, laid-back.
4 *he gave a long and particular account of his journey* **detailed**, blow-by-blow, itemized, item-by-item, thorough, minute, exact, explicit, precise, faithful, close, circumstantial, painstaking, meticulous, punctilious, particularized.
▶ noun *the two contracts will be the same in every particular* **detail**, item, point, fine point, specific, specification, element, aspect, respect, regard, particularity, fact, feature, circumstance, thing.
□ **in particular 1** *she wasn't talking about anyone in particular* **specific**, special.
2 *beer drinkers in particular were hit by prices rising faster than inflation* **particularly**, specifically, to be specific, especially, specially.

particularity ▶ noun **1** *the particularity of each human being* **individuality**, distinctiveness, uniqueness, singularity, originality, peculiarity.
2 *parties must present their case with some degree of particularity* **detail**, precision, exactness, accuracy, thoroughness, scrupulousness, meticulousness.
3 *local and personal particularities* **feature**, trait, characteristic, idiosyncrasy, peculiarity, quirk, detail, item, circumstance, point, property.

particularize ▶ verb *the indictment particularized several incidents* **specify**, detail, itemize, list, enumerate, spell out, be specific about, cite, stipulate, instance, distinguish; *rare* individuate.

particularly ▶ adverb **1** *the acoustics in the church are particularly good* **especially**, specially, very, extremely, exceptionally, singularly, peculiarly, distinctly, unusually, extraordinarily, extra, uncommonly, uniquely, remarkably, strikingly, outstandingly, amazingly, incredibly, awfully, terribly, really, notably, markedly, decidedly, surprisingly, conspicuously; *N. English* powerful, right; *informal* seriously, majorly, mucho; *Brit. informal* jolly, dead, well; *informal, dated* devilish, frightfully.
2 *he particularly asked that I should help you* **specifically**, explicitly, expressly, in particular, especially, specially.

parting ▶ noun **1** *it was an emotional parting* **farewell**, leave-taking, goodbye, adieu, departure, leaving, going (away); valediction.
2 *he and his wife kept their parting quiet from the press* **separation**, **break-up**, splitting up, split, split-up, breaking up, divorce, rift, breach, parting of the ways, estrangement, rupture; *Brit. informal* bust-up.
3 *the parting of the Red Sea* **division**, dividing, separation, separating, splitting, breaking up/apart, severance, disjoining, detachment, partition, partitioning.
▶ adjective *a parting kiss* **farewell**, goodbye, departing, leaving, last, final, closing, concluding, valedictory; deathbed, dying.

partisan ▶ noun **1** *Conservative partisans claimed that television news was biased against their party* **supporter**, follower, adherent, devotee, champion, backer, upholder, promoter, fanatic, fan, enthusiast, stalwart, zealot, disciple, votary; *N. Amer.* booster, cohort; *N. Amer. informal* rooter; *rare* janissary, sectary.
2 *the partisans opened fire from the woods* **guerrilla**, freedom fighter, resistance fighter, member of the resistance, underground fighter, irregular soldier, irregular; terrorist.
▶ adjective *the government had adopted a blatantly partisan attitude* **biased**, prejudiced, one-sided, coloured, discriminatory, preferential, partial, interested, parti pris, bigoted, sectarian, factional, unjust, unfair, inequitable, unbalanced.
OPPOSITES impartial, unbiased.

partisanship ▶ noun **bias**, prejudice, one-sidedness, discrimination, favouritism, favour, unfair preference, partiality, sectarianism, factionalism; injustice, unfairness, inequity.

partition ▶ noun **1** *the partition of Palestine in 1947* **dividing up**, partitioning, separation, division, dividing, subdivision, splitting, splitting up, split-up, breaking up, break-up, parting, segregation, severance; *rare* partitionment.
2 *the room was divided by partitions* **screen**, **divider**, room divider, dividing wall, barrier, wall, fence, panel, separator.
▶ verb **1** *the resolution partitioned Palestine into two states* **divide**, divide up, subdivide, separate, split, split up, cut up, carve up, break up, sever, segregate; share, share out, parcel out, portion, portion out.
2 *the huge halls and corridors have been partitioned* **subdivide**, **separate**, divide, divide up; separate off, section, section off, screen off, wall off, fence off.

partly ▶ adverb *the book is partly autobiographical* **to a certain extent/degree**, to some extent/degree, to a limited extent/degree, in part, partially, a little, somewhat, not totally, not wholly, not entirely, not fully, relatively, moderately, (up) to a point, half, in some measure, comparatively, slightly.
OPPOSITES completely, wholly.

partner ▶ noun **1** *two former business partners* **colleague**, associate, co-worker, fellow worker, co-partner, collaborator, ally, comrade, companion, teammate; *French* confrère; *Brit. informal* oppo; *Austral./NZ informal* offsider; *archaic* compeer; *rare* consociate.
2 *his partner in crime* **accomplice**, confederate, accessory, collaborator, fellow conspirator, right hand, right-hand man/woman, helper, abetter; *N. Amer.* cohort; *informal* sidekick.
3 *are you worried about your relationship with your partner?* **spouse**, husband, wife, consort, helpmate, helpmeet; **lover**, girlfriend, boyfriend, fiancé, fiancée, significant other, live-in lover, cohabitee, common-law husband/wife, man, woman, mate; *Italian* inamorato, inamorata; *informal* hubby, old man, old lady, old woman, missus, missis, better half, other half, POSSLQ

(person of the opposite sex sharing living quarters); *Brit. informal* dutch, her indoors; *Brit. rhyming slang* trouble and strife; *dated* beau, young man, lady; *informal, dated* intended.

partnership ▶ **noun 1** *the close partnership between Britain and the US* **cooperation**, association, collaboration, coalition, alliance, union, compact, league, confederation, co-partnership, affiliation, relationship, fellowship, connection; *rare* consociation.
2 *the partnership now owns twenty-two department stores* **company**, firm, business, corporation, organization, association, consortium, establishment, house, cooperative, concern, operation, undertaking, conglomerate, combine, syndicate; *informal* outfit, set-up.

parturition ▶ **noun childbirth**, giving birth, birth, birthing, delivery, labour; *archaic* confinement, childbed, accouchement, travail.

party ▶ **noun 1** *150 people attended the party* **social gathering**, gathering, social occasion, social event, social function, function, get-together, celebration, reunion, festivity, jamboree, reception, at-home, soirée, social; dance, ball, ceilidh, frolic, carousal, carouse; *N. Amer.* fête, hoedown, shower, bake, cookout, levee; *Austral./NZ* corroboree; *W. Indian* bashment; *Hawaiian* luau; *Spanish* tertulia; *Jewish* simcha; *informal* bash, shindig, shindy, rave, blowout, beer-up, disco, do, shebang, bop, hop, whoopee, after-party; *Brit. informal* rave-up, thrash, knees-up, beanfeast, beano, bunfight, jolly, lig; *Irish informal* hooley, crack; *N. Amer. informal* blast, wingding, kegger; *Austral./NZ informal* shivoo, rage, ding, jollo, rort; *S. African informal* jol; *dated* squash, squeeze, ding-dong.
2 *a party of British tourists arrived* **group**, company, body, gang, band, crowd, pack, contingent; *informal* bunch, crew, gaggle, posse, load.
3 *left-wing parties were highly critical of the proposals* **faction**, political party, group, grouping, side, alliance, affiliation, association, coalition, movement, cabal, junta, bloc, camp, set, caucus, sect.
4 *a certain party's name is not to be mentioned* **person**, individual, human being, somebody, someone; *informal* character.
5 *the trial judge must apportion blame between the parties* **litigant**, plaintiff, defendant; participant.
□ **be a party to** *I am not going to be a party to their plan for nabbing you* **get involved in/with**, be associated with, concern/involve oneself in, be a participant in, touch, handle.
▶ **verb** *let's party!* **celebrate**, have fun, enjoy oneself, have a party, have a good/wild time, rave it up, carouse, make merry; *informal* go out on the town, paint the town red, whoop it up, let one's hair down, make whoopee, have a night on the tiles, live it up, have a ball, go on a bender, push the boat out, go on a spree; *S. African informal* jol.

parvenu ▶ **noun upstart**, social climber, arriviste, vulgarian; the nouveau riche, the new rich.

pass[1] ▶ **verb 1** *the traffic passing through the village* **go**, **proceed**, move, progress, make one's way, travel, drive, fly; run, flow, course, stream, roll, drift, sweep.
OPPOSITES halt, stop.
2 *every time a car passed him, he worried it might be the police* **overtake**, go past, move past, go by, get ahead of, pull ahead of, go ahead of; outstrip, outdistance, lap, leave behind; *Brit.* overhaul.
3 *as time passed, my feelings towards him slowly changed* **elapse**, go by, go past, proceed, progress, advance, wear on, slip by, slip away, roll by, glide by, tick by.
4 *he passed the time writing letters* **occupy**, spend, fill, use (up), employ, devote, take up, while away, beguile; kill, waste, fritter, dissipate.
5 *pass me the salt, please* **hand**, let someone have, give, hand over, hand round, reach; transfer, convey, deliver; throw, toss; *informal* chuck, bung.
6 *he passed the ball back to the goalkeeper* **kick**, hit, throw, head, lob, loft.
7 *on her death in 1865, the estate passed to her grandson* **be transferred**, be made over, be turned over, be signed over, go, devolve, be left, be bequeathed, be handed down/on, be given, be consigned, be passed on.
8 *his death passed almost unnoticed* **happen**, occur, take place, come about, transpire; *literary* befall; *rare* eventuate.
9 *the storm passed as quickly as it had begun* **come to an end**, cease to exist, fade, fade away, melt away, blow over, run its course, ebb, die out, evaporate, vanish, peter out, draw to a close, disappear, finish, end, cease, terminate; *rare* evanish.
10 *God's peace passes all human understanding* **surpass**, exceed, go beyond, transcend, outdo, surmount, outstrip.
11 *he passed the entrance exam* **be successful in**, succeed in, gain a pass in, get through, come through, meet the requirements of, pass muster in; qualify, graduate; *informal* come up to scratch in, come up to snuff in, sail through, scrape through.
OPPOSITE fail.
12 *the Senate passed the defence bill by seventy votes to sixteen* **approve**, vote for, accept, ratify, adopt, carry, agree to, authorize, sanction, endorse, validate, legalize, put into effect, enact; *informal* OK.
OPPOSITE reject.
13 *there was no way she could let that comment pass* **go unnoticed**, go unheeded, stand, go, be accepted, go unremarked, go undisputed, go uncensored.
14 *I'm hardly in a position to pass judgement on her* **declare**, pronounce, utter, express, deliver, issue, set forth.
15 *he felt a stinging sensation every time he passed urine* **discharge**, excrete, eliminate, evacuate, expel, emit, void, release, let out.
□ **come to pass** *such a moment came to pass one fateful Saturday back in 1985* **happen**, come about, occur, transpire, arise; *literary* befall.
□ **pass away/on** *she passed away peacefully in her sleep.* See DIE.
□ **pass as/for** *she could easily pass for someone half her age* **be mistaken for**, be taken for, be regarded as, be accepted as.
□ **pass off 1** *the rally passed off peacefully* **take place**, go off, happen, occur, be carried though, be completed, be brought to a conclusion, be accomplished; turn out, fall out, pan out; *N. Amer.* go down.
2 *when the dizziness passed off he sat up and looked at his watch* **wear off**, come to an end, fade, fade away, pass, disappear, vanish, die down, ebb.
□ **pass someone off** *he added Natasha's name to his passport, passing her off as his daughter* **misrepresent**, falsely represent, give a false identity to; disguise, dress up.
□ **pass out** *she probably banged her head when she passed out* **faint**, collapse, lose consciousness, black out, keel over; *informal* flake out, conk out; *literary* swoon.
□ **pass something over** *the court cannot possibly pass over these offences* **disregard**, overlook, ignore, avoid considering, not take into consideration, forget, pay no attention to, let pass, let go, gloss over, take no notice of, pay no heed to, take no account of, close one's eyes to, turn a deaf ear to, turn a blind eye to, omit, skip; *archaic* overleap.
□ **pass something up** *I can't pass up a bargain like this, can I?* **fail to take advantage of**, turn down, reject, refuse, decline, deny oneself, give up, forgo, let go by, let pass, miss, miss out on, ignore, brush aside, dismiss, waive, spurn, neglect, abandon; *informal* give something a miss.
▶ **noun 1** *you can only get in if you have a pass* **permit**, warrant, authorization, licence; passport, visa, safe conduct, exeat; free ticket, free admission, complimentary ticket; *rare* laissez-passer.
2 *a cross-field pass* **kick**, hit, throw, shot, header.
□ **come to a pretty pass** *things have come to a pretty pass if the tabloids are influencing England's selection policy* **reach a regrettable/bad state (of affairs)**, be in a worrying state, be in a sad plight, be in troubled circumstances, be in dire straits; *informal* be in a pickle/hole.
□ **make a pass at** *I bet he made a pass at Elizabeth* **make sexual advances to**, make advances to, make sexual overtures to, proposition, make a sexual approach to; *informal* come on to, make a play for; *N. Amer. informal* hit on, make time with, put the make on; *dated* make love to.

pass[2] ▶ **noun** *a pass through the mountains* **route**, way, road, narrow road, passage, cut, gap, gorge, canyon, ravine, gully, defile, col, couloir; *Scottish* bealach; *N. Amer.* notch.

passable ▶ **adjective 1** *the beer was passable* **adequate**, all right, fairly good, acceptable, sufficiently good, sufficient, satisfactory, moderately good, not (too) bad, average, tolerable, fair, decent, respectable, presentable, admissible, allowable; mediocre, middling, ordinary, run-of-the-mill, workaday, indifferent, unremarkable, undistinguished, unexceptional; *informal* OK, so-so, fair-to-middling, nothing to write home about, no great shakes, not up to much, not much cop, bog-standard, vanilla, plain vanilla; *NZ informal* half-pie.
OPPOSITES unacceptable; excellent.
2 *the road is still passable* **navigable**, traversable, negotiable, crossable, able to be travelled on/along, unblocked, unobstructed, open, clear, usable.
OPPOSITE impassable.

passably ▶ **adverb** *a passably good dinner* **quite**, rather, somewhat, fairly, reasonably, moderately, comparatively, relatively, after a fashion, to a limited extent/degree, to a certain degree, to some extent, tolerably; adequately, satisfactorily; *informal* pretty.

passage ▶ **noun 1** *only one incident marred their passage through the country* | *the passage of sound through water* **transit**, progress, passing, movement, moving, motion, going, crossing, travelling, traversal, traverse.
2 *the passage of time* **passing**, advance, course, march, moving on, flow.
3 *they obtained a passage to Ajaccio from the French Minister of Culture* **safe conduct**, entry, admission, access; permission/authorization to travel through, leave to travel in; warrant, visa.
4 *the overnight passage to Aberdeen was wild and stormy* **voyage**, crossing, trip, cruise, sail; journey, tour, trek.
5 *police officers cleared a passage to the front door* **way**, way through, route, path, course.
6 *a small passage led to the kitchen* **corridor**, passageway, hall, hallway, entrance hall, entrance, walkway, aisle, gangway.
7 *a passage between the buildings* **alley**, alleyway, lane, path, pathway, way, footpath, track, trackway, road, thoroughfare; *Scottish & N. English* ginnel, snicket, vennel, wynd, twitten; *N. Amer.* areaway; *W. Indian & US* trace; *Indian* gully.
8 *food and air passages* | *the nasal passages* **duct**; orifice, opening, aperture, hole, channel; inlet, outlet.
9 *an abrupt passage from the darkness of the Middle Ages to the light of the Renaissance* **transition**, development, progress, progression, move, change, shift, conversion, metamorphosis.

10 *the passage of a Private Member's Bill* **enactment**, passing, ratification, acceptance, approval, adoption, authorization, sanction, validation, legalization, endorsement.
11 *a passage from 'Macbeth'* **extract**, excerpt, quotation, quote, citation, cite, reading, section, piece, selection, part, snippet, fragment, portion; text, paragraph, verse, stanza, canto, line, sentence, phrase.

passageway ▶ noun **1** *the house was full of secret passageways* **corridor**, hall, passage, hallway, walkway, gangway, aisle.
2 *her hotel was at the end of a narrow passageway off the main street* **alley**, alleyway, lane, path, pathway, way, footpath, track, trackway, road, thoroughfare; *Scottish & N. English* ginnel, snicket, vennel, wynd, twitten; *N. Amer.* areaway; *W. Indian & US* trace; *Indian* gully.

passé ▶ adjective (*French*) *this type of film has long been denounced as passé* **out of date**, outdated, out, dated, unfashionable, out of fashion, old-fashioned, outmoded, out of style, behind the times, outworn, archaic, obsolescent, obsolete, ancient, antiquated, superannuated, defunct, dead, old-fogeyish, old-fangled, quaint, anachronistic, olde worlde, medieval; *French* démodé; *N. Amer.* horse-and-buggy; *informal* old hat, square, not with it, out of the ark, creaky, mouldy, square-toed; *N. Amer. informal* clunky, rinky-dink, mossy.
OPPOSITE fashionable.

passenger ▶ noun **1** *more than fifty passengers escaped injury when the train was derailed* **traveller**, commuter, voyager, rider, fare payer, fare; deck passenger, foot passenger.
2 *all departments have their share of passengers* **hanger-on**, drone, idler, parasite; *informal* freeloader.

passing ▶ adjective **1** *his death was of only passing interest* **fleeting**, transient, transitory, ephemeral, evanescent, brief, short-lived, short, temporary, momentary, fading, impermanent; *rare* fugacious.
OPPOSITES permanent, lasting.
2 *the sculpture is worth more than a passing glance* **hasty**, rapid, hurried, brief, quick; **cursory**, superficial, casual, perfunctory, desultory, incidental, summary, glancing.
OPPOSITE careful.
▶ noun **1** *the passing of time has done little to improve the situation* **passage**, course, progress, advance, process, flow.
2 *it was with much regret that I learned of Jack's passing | the passing of 'traditional' art* **death, demise**, passing away, passing on, end, expiry, loss, expiration, decease; disappearance, vanishing, dying out; *rare* quietus.
3 *the passing of the government's new Heritage Bill* **enactment**, passage, ratification, acceptance, approval, adoption, authorization, sanction, validation, legalization, endorsement.
□ **in passing** *he mentioned in passing that you had a lot of female visitors* **incidentally**, by the by, by the way, as it happens, in the course of conversation, en passant, parenthetically.

passion ▶ noun **1** *the passion with which voters attach themselves to a particular political party* **fervour**, ardour, intensity, enthusiasm, eagerness, zeal, zealousness, vehemence, vigour, avidity, avidness, feeling, emotion, fire, heat, fieriness, fierceness, excitement, energy, animation, gusto, zest, zestfulness, spirit, spiritedness, commitment, fanaticism, violence; *rare* fervency, ardency, passionateness.
OPPOSITES indifference, apathy.
2 *he gradually worked himself up into a passion* **rage**, blind rage, fit of rage/anger/temper, temper, towering rage, outburst of anger, tantrum, fury, frenzy, paroxysm, fever; *Brit. informal* paddy; *Brit. informal, dated* wax, bate, paddywhack.
3 *Roman's deep voice was husky with passion* **love**, desire, sexual love, sexual desire, lust, ardour, hunger, yearning, longing, craving, adoration, infatuation, lasciviousness, lustfulness; *French* amour fou; *rare* concupiscence, nympholepsy.
4 *his passion for football* **enthusiasm**, love, mania, keen interest, fascination, obsession, fanaticism, fixation, predilection, compulsion, appetite, relish, partiality, liking, interest, weakness, penchant, addiction, fondness; *informal* thing, yen; *rare* appetency.
5 *English literature is something of a passion with me* **obsession**, preoccupation, craze, mania, rage, hobby horse.
6 *the Passion of Christ* **crucifixion**, pain, suffering, agony, martyrdom; *rare* martyrization.

passionate ▶ adjective **1** *a passionate entreaty | passionate hatred* **intense**, impassioned, ardent, fervent, zealous, vehement, fiery, heated, feverish, emotional, heartfelt, eager, excited, animated, spirited, vigorous, strong, energetic, messianic, fanatical, frenzied, wild, fierce, consuming, violent, tumultuous, flaming, raging, burning, uncontrollable, ungovernable; *rare* perfervid, fervid, passional.
OPPOSITES apathetic, half-hearted.
2 *McGregor is **passionate about** sport* **very keen on**, very enthusiastic about, addicted to, devoted to, infatuated with; *informal* mad about, crazy about, hooked on, nuts about, nutty about, gone on; *N. Amer. informal* nutso over; *Austral./NZ informal* shook on.
3 *a passionate lover | a passionate kiss* **amorous**, ardent, hot-blooded, red-blooded, warm-blooded, aroused, loving, on fire, sexy, sensual, erotic, lustful, sultry, torrid; *informal* steamy, sizzling, hot, red-hot, turned on.
OPPOSITES cold, passionless.
4 *Christina was passionate and given to terrible tantrums* **excitable**, emotional, intense, fiery, volatile, mercurial, quick-tempered, hot-headed, highly strung, hot-blooded, impulsive, temperamental, tempestuous, dramatic, melodramatic.
OPPOSITES phlegmatic, placid.

passionless ▶ adjective **1** *he was not as passionless as they made out* **unemotional**, cold, cold-blooded, emotionless, frigid, cool, unfeeling, unloving, unresponsive, undemonstrative, impassive, withdrawn, unapproachable, aloof, detached, distant, dispassionate, remote.
OPPOSITE passionate.
2 *the whole movie seems oddly passionless* **dull**, boring, lacking in vitality, spiritless, lifeless, soulless, wooden, dry, desiccated, flat, uninspired, unimpassioned, insipid, lacklustre, colourless, anaemic, bloodless, vapid.
OPPOSITE exciting.

passive ▶ adjective **1** *he played only a passive role in the proceedings* **inactive**, non-active, non-participative, non-participating, uninvolved, dormant, quiescent, inert.
2 *the women were portrayed as passive victims* **submissive**, acquiescent, unresisting, yielding, unassertive, non-resistant, compliant, complaisant, pliant, resigned, obedient, docile, tractable, malleable, pliable, meek, subdued, deferential, forbearing, long-suffering, patient, lamblike, non-violent, supine; non-aggressive; *archaic* resistless.
OPPOSITES active, assertive.
3 *the woman's face was passive* **emotionless**, impassive, indifferent, unemotional, unmoved, unconcerned, dispassionate, passionless, detached, unresponsive, undemonstrative, remote, aloof, calm, apathetic, phlegmatic, lifeless.

passport ▶ noun **1** **travel document**, travel papers, papers, travel permit, visa, identity card, ID, laissez-passer.
2 *good qualifications are the passport to success* **key**, path, way, route, avenue, means of access, door, doorway, entry, entrée, admission, admittance, open sesame.

password ▶ noun **word of identification**, sign, signal, word; open sesame; *Military, archaic* watchword, countersign, parole.

past ▶ adjective **1** *memories of times past | writers from past centuries* **gone by**, over, over and done with, no more, gone, done, dead and buried, finished, ended, forgotten, bygone, former, old, of old, earlier, long-ago, ancient, defunct, extinct; *literary* of yore, olden, foregone.
2 *the past few months* **last**, recent, preceding, latter.
3 *a past chairman of the society* **previous**, former, prior, foregoing, late, erstwhile, one-time, sometime, ex-; *formal* quondam; *archaic* whilom.
OPPOSITES present; future.
▶ noun *she gave little away about her past* **history**, background, life story, life, experience, career to date, biography.
□ **in the past** *some of the shelters may have been habitation sites in the past* **formerly**, previously, in days/years/times gone by, in bygone days, back in the day, in former times, in the (good) old days, at one time, in days of old, in the olden days, in olden times; before, hitherto, once, once upon a time, time was when, in auld lang syne, long ago, in antiquity; *literary* in days of yore, of yore, in yesteryear.
▶ preposition **1** *she walked past the cafe* **in front of**, by, beyond.
2 *he's well past retirement age* **beyond**, beyond the limits of, in excess of.
▶ adverb *they averted their eyes and hurried past* **along**, by, on.

pasta ▶ noun. *See centre pages for list of types of* **Pasta**

paste ▶ noun **1** *blend the ingredients to a paste* **purée**, mixture, pulp, mush, pap, blend; *informal* goo.
2 *wallpaper paste* **adhesive**, glue, gum, fixative; *N. Amer.* mucilage.
3 *fish paste* **spread**, pâté.
▶ verb *a notice was pasted on the door* **glue**, stick, fasten, gum, fix, affix.

pastel ▶ adjective *pastel colours* **pale**, soft, delicate, light, light-coloured, light-toned, muted, subtle, subdued, faint, soft-hued, low-key, understated.
OPPOSITES dark; bright, vivid.

pastiche ▶ noun **1** *a pastiche of literary models and sources* **mixture**, blend, medley, melange, miscellany, mixed bag, pot-pourri, mosaic, patchwork, mix, compound, composite, collection, motley collection, assortment, conglomeration, hotchpotch, hodgepodge, jumble, ragbag, mishmash, farrago, hash; *rare* gallimaufry, olio, olla podrida, salmagundi, omnium gatherum, macédoine, motley.
2 *the operetta is a pastiche of 18th century style* **imitation**, parody, take-off; *rare* pasticcio.

pastille ▶ noun **lozenge**, sweet, gumdrop, drop, gum; tablet, pill; *rare* dragée, jujube, troche.

pastime ▶ noun **hobby**, leisure activity/pursuit, sport, game, recreation, amusement, avocation, diversion, divertissement, distraction, relaxation, pleasure, entertainment, fun, interest, sideline, enthusiasm, passion, fad, craze, mania, obsession; *informal* bug, thing.

past master ▶ noun *the manager was a past master at recharging faltering spirits* **expert**, virtuoso, master, wizard, genius, artist, old hand, adept, professional, doyen, veteran, maestro, connoisseur, authority, grandmaster, master hand, skilled person; *informal* ace, buff, pro, star, whizz, hotshot; *Brit. informal* dab hand; *N. Amer. informal* maven, crackerjack.

pastor *See centre pages for list of* **Priests, Religious Officials and Members of Religious Orders**
▶ noun **priest**, minister (of religion), parson, clergyman, cleric, chaplain, padre, father, ecclesiastic, man of God, man of the cloth, churchman, preacher; *Scottish* kirkman; *N. Amer.* dominie; *informal* reverend, Holy Joe, sky pilot; *Austral. informal* josser.

pastoral ▶ adjective **1** *a pastoral scene* **rural**, country, countryside, countrified, outdoor, rustic, agricultural, agrarian, provincial, grassy, green, verdant; simple, innocent, idyllic, unspoilt; *literary* bucolic, sylvan, Arcadian; *rare* exurban, georgic.
OPPOSITE urban.
2 *his pastoral duties* **priestly**, clerical, ecclesiastical, ministerial; *rare* hieratic, sacerdotal, vicarial, parsonical, rectorial, churchly, prelatic, apostolic.

pastry *See centre pages for list of* **Cakes, Puddings, and Desserts**
▶ noun **1** *I've come to get some pastries for tea* **tart**, tartlet, pie, pasty, patty, turnover, slice.
2 *seal the two layers of pastry together* puff pastry, choux pastry, flaky pastry, shortcrust pastry, filo pastry; *N. Amer.* piecrust.

pasture ▶ noun **grazing land**, grazing, grassland, grass, pastureland, pasturage, range, ley, paddock, croft; meadow, field, water meadow, sheepwalk; *Scottish & N. English* shieling, bent; *literary* lea, mead, greensward, sward; *Irish & Canadian* bawn; *Austral./NZ* run; *S. African* veld; (*in Switzerland*) alp; (*in France*) bocage; (*in S. America*) potrero.

WORD LINKS
relating to pasture **pastoral**

pasty ▶ adjective *people with pasty faces* **pale**, pallid, wan, colourless, anaemic, bloodless, ashen, white, white as a ghost/sheet, grey, jaundiced, waxen, chalky, chalk-white, milky, pasty-faced, whey-faced, peaky, sickly, tired-looking, washed out, sallow, drained, drawn, sapped, ghostly, deathly, deathlike; *rare* etiolated.

pat[1] ▶ verb *Brian patted her absent-mindedly on the shoulder* **tap**, slap lightly, clap, dab; touch, stroke, pet, caress, fondle, rub.
□ **pat someone on the back congratulate**, praise, sing the praises of, express approval of, take one's hat off to; **commend**, compliment, applaud, acclaim, give someone a pat on the back, throw bouquets at.
□ **pat oneself on the back boast**, brag, crow, swagger, swank, blow one's own trumpet, congratulate oneself; preen oneself, pride oneself; *informal* talk big.
▶ noun **1** *a pat on the cheek* **tap**, light blow, clap, dab; caress, stroke, fondle, touch.
2 *a pat of butter* **piece**, dab, lump, portion, knob, mass, cake, chunk, wedge, hunk, gobbet, ball, curl; *rare* clod, gob.

pat[2] ▶ adjective *up to now, he has given pat, perfunctory answers* **glib**, simple, simplistic, facile, slick, smooth, unconvincing, perfunctory.
▶ adverb *his reply came rather pat* **opportunely**, conveniently, advantageously, at just/exactly the right moment, expediently; usefully, beneficially, favourably, profitably, appropriately, fittingly, suitably, aptly, timely, auspiciously, luckily, happily, providentially, felicitously, seasonably, propitiously.
□ **off pat** *in time he'll have the jargon off pat* **word-perfect**, by heart, by rote, word for word, parrot-fashion, verbatim, by memory, memorized.
□ **get something off pat memorize**, commit to memory, remember, retain, learn by heart, learn, learn by rote, impress on the memory, become word-perfect in; *archaic* con.

patch ▶ noun **1** *an old jacket with patches on the elbows* **piece of cloth/material/fabric/leather**, reinforcement; piece sewn on.
2 *he had a patch over one eye* **cover**, eyepatch, covering, pad, shield.
3 *a small reddish patch on her wrist* **blotch**, mark, spot, smudge, dot, speck, speckle, smear, stain, streak, stripe, blemish; birthmark, port wine stain, strawberry mark; *informal* splodge, splotch; *technical* naevus.
4 *a patch of ground* **plot**, area, piece, strip, row, lot, tract, parcel; bed, border, allotment.
5 *Adam and his wife are going through a difficult patch* **period**, time, spell, phase, stretch, interval; stint, run, term, span, extent; *Brit. informal* spot.
▶ verb *her jeans were neatly patched* **mend**, repair, put a patch on, cover, sew, sew up, stitch, stitch up.
□ **patch something up 1** *the remaining houses were either being patched up or demolished* **repair**, mend, fix hastily, do a makeshift repair on, repair/fix temporarily; cobble, botch; *Nautical* jury-rig.
2 *he's trying to patch things up with his wife* **reconcile**, make up, settle, conciliate; **remedy**, put to rights, rectify, clear up, set right, heal, mend, cure, make good, resolve, square, harmonize.

patchwork ▶ noun *work that was a patchwork of different styles* **assortment**, miscellany, mixture, melange, medley, blend, variety, mixed bag, mix, diversity, collection, selection, assemblage, combination, motley collection, pot-pourri, conglomeration, jumble, mess, confusion, mishmash, hotchpotch, hodgepodge, ragbag, pastiche, farrago, hash; *informal* scissors-and-paste job; *rare* gallimaufry, omnium gatherum, olio, salmagundi, macédoine.

patchy ▶ adjective **1** *a stretch of patchy grass | their first aid teaching has been patchy* **uneven**, bitty, varying, variable, variegated, dappled, mottled, speckled, multicoloured; intermittent, fitful, occasional, fluctuating, sporadic, erratic, irregular, random.
OPPOSITES uniform, constant.
2 *we have only patchy evidence* **fragmentary**, deficient, inadequate, insufficient, lacking, rudimentary, limited, sketchy.
OPPOSITES complete, comprehensive.

patent ▶ noun *a company has since taken out a patent on the chemical* **copyright**, licence, legal protection, right, performing right, permit, privilege, charter, franchise, registered trademark.
▶ adjective **1** *the idea is patent nonsense* **obvious**, clear, plain, evident, apparent, manifest, self-evident; distinct, definite, transparent, overt, discernible, visible, conspicuous, blatant, downright, barefaced, flagrant, palpable, glaring, glaringly obvious, undisguised, unconcealed, unmistakable, unequivocal, unquestionable, undeniable.
OPPOSITES unobtrusive, inconspicuous.
2 *patent medicines* **proprietary**, patented, licensed, protected, branded, brand-name, own-brand, own-label, designer-label.

paternal ▶ adjective **1** *some employers felt paternal concern for their workers* **fatherly**, fatherlike, patriarchal; protective, vigilant, concerned, solicitous, kindly, warm, friendly, benevolent, compassionate, sympathetic.
2 *his paternal grandfather* **on one's father's side**, patrilineal, patrimonial.
OPPOSITE maternal.

paternity ▶ noun *he refused to admit paternity of the child* **fatherhood**; *rare* fathership.

path ▶ noun **1** *a much-trodden path led down to the beach* **footpath**, pathway, footway, pavement, track, jogging track, trail, trackway, bridleway, bridle path, ride, riding, towpath, walk, walkway, promenade, esplanade, avenue, lane, alley, alleyway, passage, passageway, byway, sidetrack, berm, causeway, right of way; cycle path, cycle track, cycleway; *N. Amer.* sidewalk, bikeway; *W. Indian & US* trace; *French* pavé.
2 *dozens of journalists blocked his path* **route**, way, course, approach, road; direction, bearing, line, track, beat, round, run; orbit, trajectory.
3 *good quality consultation may be one path to consider* **course of action**, route, road, avenue, procedure, direction, line, approach, tack, method, system, scheme, strategy, tactic, plan, formula.

pathetic ▶ adjective **1** *he made a small, pathetic groan* **pitiful**, pitiable, piteous, to be pitied, moving, touching, poignant, plaintive, stirring; affecting, distressing, disquieting, disturbing, upsetting, miserable, heartbreaking, heart-rending, agonizing, harrowing, mortifying, sad, wretched, poor, forlorn, tragic, doleful, mournful, woeful; *rare* distressful.
OPPOSITES comical; cheerful.
2 (*informal*) *he made some pathetic excuse about the train being delayed* **feeble**, woeful, sorry, poor, pitiful, lamentable, deplorable, miserable, wretched, contemptible, despicable, inadequate, meagre, paltry, insufficient, negligible, insubstantial, unsatisfactory, worthless.
OPPOSITES admirable, excellent.

pathfinder ▶ noun *she sees herself as a pathfinder for her daughter's generation* **pioneer**, trailblazer, groundbreaker, experimenter, trendsetter, front runner, leader, leading light, guiding light, torch-bearer, pacemaker, originator, instigator, initiator, innovator, avant-gardist, developer, creator, discoverer, founder, founding father, architect.

pathological ▶ adjective **1** *a pathological condition* **morbid**, diseased.
2 (*informal*) *a pathological liar* **compulsive**, obsessive, inveterate, habitual, persistent, chronic, clinical, hardened, confirmed, unreasonable, irrational, illogical.

pathos ▶ noun *the pathos of Antoine's predicament* **poignancy**, tragedy, sadness, pitifulness, piteousness, pitiableness, plaintiveness, sorrowfulness.

patience ▶ noun **1** *she tried everyone's patience to the limit* **forbearance**, tolerance, restraint, self-restraint, resignation, stoicism, fortitude, sufferance, endurance; calmness, composure, even temper, even-temperedness, equanimity, equilibrium, serenity, tranquillity, imperturbability, unexcitability, understanding, indulgence, lenience, kindness, consideration; *rare* longanimity, inexcitability.
2 *a task requiring patience* **perseverance**, persistence, endurance, tenacity, diligence, assiduity, application, staying power, indefatigability, doggedness, determination, resolve, resolution, resoluteness, obstinacy, insistence, singleness of purpose, purposefulness, pertinacity.
OPPOSITE impatience.

patient ▶ adjective **1** *I must ask you to be patient with my navigation* **forbearing**, uncomplaining, tolerant, long-suffering, resigned, stoical; calm, composed, serene, even-tempered, tranquil, imperturbable, unexcitable, accommodating, understanding, indulgent, kind, considerate; *informal* unflappable, cool; *rare* longanimous, equanimous, inexcitable.
2 *a good deal of dogged, patient work* **persevering**, persistent, tenacious,

P

diligent, assiduous, indefatigable, dogged, determined, resolved, resolute, obstinate, insistent, single-minded, purposeful, pertinacious.
▶ noun *the trust between doctor and patient* **sick person**, case, sufferer, victim; **invalid**, convalescent, outpatient, day patient, inpatient, hospital patient; the sick, the infirm; *rare* valetudinarian.

patio ▶ noun **terrace**, courtyard, veranda, loggia, court, plaza, quadrangle, quad, cloister; *N. Amer.* sun deck, deck, porch; *Austral./NZ* sleepout; *S. African* stoep; *Hawaiian* lanai; *technical* peristyle.

patois ▶ noun **vernacular**, dialect, local parlance, local speech/talk/usage/idiom/slang/tongue, local variety, regional language, non-standard language/variety, jargon, argot, patter, cant, -speak; *informal* (local) lingo.

patriarch ▶ noun *the respected patriarch of the household* **senior figure**, father, paterfamilias, leader, elder, grandfather; guiding light, guru.

patrician ▶ noun *the great patricians of the Empire* **aristocrat**, grandee, noble, nobleman, noblewoman, lord, lady, peer, peeress, peer of the realm, titled man/woman/person, landowner; landowning class, landed gentry/aristocracy; *informal* top person; *Brit. informal* nob, chinless wonder.
▶ adjective *the patrician families of Bordeaux* **aristocratic**, noble, noble-born, of noble birth, titled, blue-blooded, high-born, well born, upper-class, elite, landowning, landed, born with a silver spoon in one's mouth; *Brit.* county, upmarket; *informal* upper-crust, top-drawer, {huntin', shootin', and fishin'}; *archaic* gentle, of gentle birth.

patrimony ▶ noun *constant wars and invasions have destroyed the country's cultural patrimony* **heritage**, inheritance, birthright; property, riches, wealth, possessions; legacy, bequest, endowment, estate, bequeathal; *Law* devise, hereditament.

patriot ▶ noun *a great patriot who had died for his country* **nationalist**, loyalist; chauvinist, jingoist, jingo, flag-waver, isolationist, xenophobe.
OPPOSITE traitor.

patriotic ▶ adjective **nationalist**, nationalistic, loyalist, loyal; chauvinistic, jingoistic, jingo, flag-waving, isolationist, xenophobic; *N. Amer. dated* spreadeagle.
OPPOSITE traitorous.

patriotism ▶ noun *a national flag or anthem has the power to instil patriotism* **nationalism**, patriotic sentiment, allegiance/loyalty to one's country, loyalism; chauvinism, jingoism, flag-waving, isolationism, xenophobia.
OPPOSITE treachery.

patrol ▶ noun **1** *anti-poaching patrols have ceased* **vigil**, guard, watch, monitoring, policing, beat, beat-pounding, patrolling, round, sentry duty; reconnoitre, surveillance, survey, examination; *informal* recce.
2 *at 2.20 the patrol reached the jeeps* **patrolman/patrolwoman**, sentinel, sentry, garrison, defender; detail, scout, scouting party, task force, escort, convoy.
▶ verb *a security guard was attacked patrolling a housing estate | they patrolled behind enemy lines* **keep guard (on)**, guard, keep watch (on); police, walk the beat (of), pound the beat (of), make the rounds (of), walk along/round, range (over), perform sentry duty (on); picket, stand guard (over), keep a vigil (on), keep a lookout (over), cover, monitor, defend, safeguard; cruise, pound, prowl, rove, roam.

P

patron ▶ noun **1** *a patron of the arts* **sponsor**, backer, financier, subsidizer, underwriter, guarantor, benefactor/benefactress, contributor, subscriber, donor; philanthropist, promoter, friend, helper, supporter, upholder, advocate, champion, protector; *informal* angel; *rare* Maecenas.
2 *patrons of shops, restaurants, and clubs* **customer**, client, frequenter; shopper, buyer, purchaser, consumer, diner, user, visitor, guest, member of the audience/crowd; (**patrons**) clientele; *informal* regular.

patronage ▶ noun **1** *art patronage does not come cheap* **sponsorship**, backing, funding, financing, philanthropy, promotion, furtherance, help, aid, assistance, support, guaranty, encouragement, championship, advocacy, defence, protection, guardianship, aegis, auspices.
2 *the abuse of political patronage* **power of appointment**, right of appointment, favouritism, nepotism, partisanship, partiality, preferential treatment; the old boy network.
3 *that form of address implies slight patronage* **condescension**, patronizing, deigning, stooping, disdain, disrespect, scorn, contempt, mockery; snobbery, snobbishness; *rare* patronization.
4 *bus patronage was declining* **custom**, trade, business, commerce, trafficking; shopping, buying, purchasing.

patronize ▶ verb **1** *don't patronize me!* **treat condescendingly**, treat with condescension, condescend to, look down on, talk down to, put down, humiliate, treat like a child, treat as inferior, treat with disdain, treat scornfully/contemptuously, be snobbish to, look down one's nose at.
2 *they patronized the local tradesmen* **do business with**, buy from, shop at, be a customer of, be a client of, bring trade/custom to, deal with, trade with; frequent, haunt, attend, visit; subscribe to, join, become a member of, support; *informal* hang out at.
3 *Joseph Bonaparte patronized a national museum of painting* **sponsor**, back, fund, finance, be a patron of, promote, further, foster, help, aid, assist, support, encourage, champion, protect.

patronizing ▶ adjective **condescending**, supercilious, superior, imperious, haughty, lofty, lordly, magisterial, disdainful, scornful, contemptuous, cavalier, snobbish, pompous; *informal* uppity, high and mighty, snooty, stuck-up; *Brit. informal* toffee-nosed.
OPPOSITES friendly; humble.

patter[1] ▶ verb **1** *raindrops pattered against the wooden shutters* **pitter-patter**, tap, drum, clatter, beat, pound, rattle, throb, pulsate, rat-a-tat, go pit-a-pat, pit-a-pat, clack, click-clack, thrum; *archaic* bicker, clacket.
2 *she pattered across the floor* **scurry**, scuttle, skip, trip, tiptoe, walk lightly, walk on tiptoe.
▶ noun *the rain had stopped its vibrating patter above him* **pitter-patter**, tapping, pattering, drumming, drumbeat, clatter, beat, beating, tattoo, pounding, throb, pulsation, rat-a-tat, pit-a-pat, clack, click-clack, clacketing, thrum, thrumming.

patter[2] ▶ noun **1** *this witty gentleman's patter is now issued on a cassette* **rambling(s)**, **prattle**, prating, blather, blither, drivel, chatter, jabber, gabble, babble, glib talk, monologue; *Scottish* blether; *informal* gab, yak, yackety-yak, yabbering, yatter; *Brit. informal* rabbiting, wittering, waffle, chuntering; *archaic* twaddle, clack.
2 *the salesmen's patter was good* **(sales) pitch**, sales talk, line, spiel.
3 *the patter of the local peasantry* **way/manner of speaking**, speech, language, idiom, vocabulary, jargon, parlance, argot, patois, cant, -speak, dialect, vernacular, idiolect, phraseology, terminology; *French* façon de parler; *informal* lingo.
▶ verb *she pattered on incessantly* **prattle**, ramble, prate, blather, blether, blither, drivel, rattle, chatter, jabber, gabble, babble; *informal* gab, yak, yackety-yak, yabber, yatter; *Brit. informal* rabbit, witter, waffle, natter, chunter; *Austral. informal* mag; *archaic* twaddle, clack.

pattern See centre pages for lists of **Patterns** **Shapes**
▶ noun **1** *the pattern on the wallpaper* **design**, decoration, motif, marking, ornament, ornamentation, device, figure.
2 *the ants' behaviour pattern* **system**, order, arrangement, method, sequence, structure, scheme, plan, form, format, framework, composition, constitution, shape, make-up, configuration.
3 *such a step would set the pattern for at least a generation* **model**, example, criterion, standard, basis, point of reference, gauge, norm, formula, guide, scale, guideline, yardstick, touchstone, benchmark, ideal, exemplar, paradigm, canon; blueprint, archetype, prototype, original, design; template, mould, cast, matrix, last, layout, outline, sketch, draft, stencil, sample, specimen, specification, shape, plan, style, source, type.
4 *a book of textile patterns* **sample**, specimen, swatch.
▶ verb *there is a dread that someone else is patterning your life* **shape**, influence, form, model, fashion, mould, style; affect, determine, direct, control, guide, lead.

patterned ▶ adjective **decorated**, ornamented, figured, tessellated, mosaic; goffered, crimped, watered, moiré, fancy, adorned, embellished, intricate.
OPPOSITE plain.

paucity ▶ noun *a paucity of evidence* **scarcity**, sparseness, sparsity, dearth, shortage, rarity, rareness, poverty, insufficiency, deficiency, inadequacy, famine, lack, want, meagreness, limitedness, scantiness, skimpiness, paltriness, restrictedness, deficit, shortfall; *rare* exiguity.
OPPOSITE abundance.

paunch ▶ noun **pot belly**, fat/protruding stomach/belly/abdomen, beer belly, stomach, belly, middle, midriff, waist, waistline; *informal* beer gut, gut, tummy, tum, pot, breadbasket; *dated, humorous* corporation.

pauper ▶ noun **poor person**, indigent, bankrupt, insolvent; beggar, mendicant, down-and-out; *informal* have-not. *See also* POOR.

pause ▶ noun *there was a pause in the conversation* **stop**, **cessation**, break, halt, stoppage, standstill, interruption, check, lull, respite, stay, breathing space, discontinuation, discontinuance, hiatus, gap, lapse (of time), interlude, intermission, interval, entr'acte; adjournment, suspension, moratorium, interregnum; rest, time out, stopover, delay, hold-up, wait; hesitation, beat, caesura; *informal* let-up, breather.
▶ verb *Hannah paused for a moment before answering* **stop**, cease, halt, discontinue, break off, take a break, take a breath; adjourn, desist, rest, hold back, wait, delay, hesitate, hang back, pull up, mark time, falter, waver; *informal* let up, take a breather.
OPPOSITES continue, proceed.

pave ▶ verb *the centre of the garden was to be paved* **cover**, surface, floor, top, finish, concrete (over), asphalt, flag, tile, tar, tarmac, metal.
□ **pave the way for** *a consultative document that could pave the way for legislation* **prepare for**, prepare the way for, clear the way for, open the way for, make preparations for, make provision for, get ready for, lay the foundations for, do the groundwork for, work round/up to, approach/introduce the subject of, put things in order for, set the scene for, smooth the path of, usher in, herald, show in, harbinger, precede, be the forerunner/precursor of.

pavement ▶ noun *I had parked blocking the pavement* **footpath**, paved path, pedestrian way, walkway, footway; *N. Amer.* sidewalk.

paw ▶ noun **foot**, pad; forepaw, hind paw.
▶ verb **1** *their offspring were yammering and pawing each other* **poke**, handle

roughly/carelessly/clumsily, finger, thumb, pull, grab, maul, manhandle, mangle, mess up.
2 *some Casanova had tried to paw her* **fondle**, feel, maul, molest; *informal* grope, feel up, touch up, goose.

pawn¹ ▶ **verb** *he pawned his watch to buy some clothes* **pledge**, deposit with a pawnbroker, put in pawn, give as security, put up as security/collateral, use as collateral, mortgage; *informal* hock, put in hock; *Brit. informal* pop.

pawn² ▶ **noun** *she was a pawn in the battle for the throne* **puppet**, dupe, hostage, counter, cog; tool, cat's paw, instrument; *informal* stooge.

pay ▶ **verb 1** *I must pay him for his work* **reward**, reimburse, recompense, give payment to, settle up with, remunerate, tip, indemnify.
2 *the public would prefer to pay a few pounds more council tax* **spend**, expend, pay out, lay out, part with, disburse, hand over, remit, render; *informal* dish out, shell out, fork out, cough up; *N. Amer. informal* ante up, pony up.
3 *the company was unable to pay its debts* **discharge**, settle, pay off, pay in full, meet, clear, square, defray, honour, satisfy, make good, liquidate.
4 *our reputation for quality and service will pay dividends* **yield**, pay out, return, produce, bring in; *informal* rake in.
5 *he has made the buses pay* **be profitable**, make money, make a profit, be remunerative, make a return, provide a living.
6 *it may pay you to drop all your sails while you anchor* **be advantageous to**, **benefit**, be of advantage to, be of benefit to, be beneficial to, be profitable to, be worthwhile to, repay, serve.
7 *he had always found it difficult to pay Martha compliments* **bestow**, present, grant, give, hand out, extend, offer, proffer, render, afford.
8 *I'll make him pay for his mistakes* **suffer**, suffer the consequences, be punished, pay a penalty, atone, make atonement, pay the price, get one's deserts, take one's medicine; *informal* get one's comeuppance.
□ **pay someone back** *I'll pay you back for what you've done!* **get one's revenge on**, be revenged on, revenge oneself on, give someone their just deserts, reciprocate, punish, avenge oneself on, hit back at, get back at, get, get even with, settle a/the score with, settle accounts with, pay someone out, retaliate against, take reprisals against, exact retribution on; let someone see how it feels, give someone a taste of their own medicine.
□ **pay something back** *they did eventually pay me back the money* **repay**, pay off, give back, return, remunerate, compensate, make restitution/amends to, reimburse, recoup, refund, restore, make good, indemnify, requite.
□ **pay for** *he had just enough money to pay for the meal* **defray the cost of**, settle up for; **finance**, endow, donate/leave money for; support, back, stake, fund, capitalize, provide finance/capital for, furnish credit for, subsidize, sponsor; treat someone to; *informal* foot the bill for, shell out for, fork out for, cough up for; *N. Amer. informal* ante up for, pony up for.
□ **pay someone off 1** *the taxi had gone before Tunney could pay off the driver* **pay what one owes**; dismiss, discharge.
2 *arrangements were made to pay off the police and hush it all up* **bribe**, suborn, buy, buy off, get at, induce, lure, entice, grease someone's palm, oil someone's palm/hand.
□ **pay something off 1** *you use the proceeds to pay off your loan* **pay in full**, pay, settle, discharge, meet, clear, square, honour, satisfy, make good, liquidate.
□ **pay off** *his hard work paid off* **meet with success**, be successful, succeed, be effective, work, get results, be profitable.
□ **pay someone out** *this was to pay Emma out, to make her feel guilty* **get one's revenge on**, be revenged on, revenge oneself on, repay, give someone their just deserts, reciprocate, punish, avenge oneself on, hit back at, get back at, get, get even with, settle a/the score with, settle accounts with, pay someone back, retaliate on/against, take reprisals against, exact retribution on; let someone see how it feels, give someone a taste of their own medicine.
□ **pay something out** *she had to pay out £300 for treatment* **spend**, expend, pay, lay out, put up, part with, hand over, remit, furnish, supply, disburse, contribute, give, donate, invest, advance, pledge; *informal* dish out, shell out, fork out/up, cough up.
□ **pay up** *he has been allowed a week to pay up* **make payment**, pay, settle up, pay in full, meet one's obligations, come up with the money; *informal* fork out/up, come across, cough up; *Brit. informal* stump up.
OPPOSITE withhold.
▶ **noun** *equal pay for women* **salary**, **wages**, wage, take-home pay, gross/net pay, payment; earnings, fee(s), remuneration, stipend, emolument(s), honorarium, allowance, handout(s), recompense, compensation, reimbursement, reward, income, revenue, profit(s), proceeds, takings, gain, lucre.

payable ▶ **adjective** *capital gains tax is payable if the shares are sold* **due**, to be paid, owed, owing; outstanding, unpaid, unsettled, receivable, overdue, undischarged, in arrears, in the red; *N. Amer.* delinquent, past due.

payment ▶ **noun 1** *a seller may offer discounts for early payment* **remittance**, remission, settlement, discharge, clearance, liquidation, reckoning.
2 *twelve monthly payments* **instalment**, premium, amount, remittance; deposit, retainer, subscription.
3 *they offer extra payment for good performance* **salary**, **wages**, wage, pay, earnings, fee(s), remuneration, take-home pay, gross/net pay; rate, price, hire, stipend, emolument(s), honorarium, allowance, handout, recompense, compensation, reimbursement, reward, income, revenue, profit(s), proceeds, takings, gain, lucre.

pay-off ▶ **noun** (*informal*) **1** *the lure of enormous pay-offs in hard currency could prove irresistible* **payment**, payout, reward, recompense, consideration; **bribe**, inducement, 'incentive', enticement; *N. Amer.* payola; *informal* kickback, sweetener, carrot, backhander, hush money, slush fund, cut, graft; *Brit. informal* bung, dropsy; *N. Amer. informal* plugola, schmear; *Austral. informal* sling; *rare* douceur, drop.
2 *sales are forecast to produce a pay-off of £160,000* **return**, return on investment, yield, payback, reward, profit, gain, income, revenue, interest, dividend, percentage.
3 *the murderer is finally unmasked in a dramatic pay-off* **outcome**, **denouement**, culmination, conclusion, development, result, consequence, out-turn, end result, upshot, aftermath; *archaic* success.

pea ▶ **noun**. *See centre pages for list of* **Beans, Pulses, and Peas**

peace ▶ **noun 1** *can't a man get any peace around here?* **tranquillity**, **calm**, calmness, restfulness, peace and quiet, peacefulness, quiet, quietness, quietude, silence, soundlessness, hush, noiselessness, stillness, still; privacy, privateness, seclusion, solitude, isolation, retirement, lack of disturbance/interruption, freedom from interference.
OPPOSITES noise; irritation.
2 *those who have guilty secrets rarely enjoy true peace of mind* **serenity**, peacefulness, tranquillity, equanimity, calm, calmness, composure, placidity, placidness, rest, repose, ease, comfort, contentment, content, contentedness, security; bliss, joy, nirvana.
OPPOSITES agitation, distress.
3 *we pray for peace in the province* **law and order**, lawfulness, order, peacefulness, peaceableness, harmony, harmoniousness, accord, concord, amity, amicableness, goodwill, friendship, cordiality, non-aggression, non-violence; ceasefire, respite, lull.
OPPOSITE conflict.
4 *the envoy hopes to set the seal on a lasting peace today* **treaty**, **truce**, ceasefire, armistice, end/cessation/suspension of hostilities, moratorium, agreement, alliance, concord, appeasement, reconciliation.
OPPOSITE war.

WORD LINKS
intended to bring about peace **irenic**

peaceable ▶ **adjective 1** *a calm, quiet, and peaceable man* **peace-loving**, unwarlike, non-belligerent, non-violent, non-combative, non-aggressive, easy, easy-going, placid, gentle, meek, mild, inoffensive, good-natured, even-tempered, amiable, amicable, friendly, affable, genial, civil, cooperative, conciliatory, pacific, pacifist, dovelike, dovish; *rare* irenic, pacifistic.
OPPOSITES aggressive, belligerent.
2 *a peaceable society* **peaceful**, **strife-free**, harmonious, amicable, amiable, friendly, cordial; well behaved, law-abiding, disciplined, orderly, civilized; *archaic* ruly.
OPPOSITES unruly, warring.

peaceful ▶ **adjective 1** *the cottage is in a peaceful setting* **tranquil**, **calm**, restful, pleasant, quiet, still, relaxing, soothing, sleepy, silent, soundless, hushed, noiseless, undisturbed, untroubled, private, secluded, solitary, isolated, free from disturbance/interruption/interference.
OPPOSITES bustling, noisy.
2 *his peaceful, contemplative mood vanished* **serene**, calm, tranquil, composed, placid, at peace, at rest, at ease, in repose, reposeful, undisturbed, untroubled, unworried, unruffled, anxiety-free, content, blissful, secure.
OPPOSITE agitated.
3 *peaceful conditions between the two countries* **harmonious**, at peace, strife-free, peaceable, on good terms, amicable, friendly, cordial, non-violent, unwarlike; orderly, disciplined.
OPPOSITES hostile, warring.

CHOOSE THE RIGHT WORD

peaceful, calm, serene, tranquil, placid
See CALM.

peacemaker ▶ **noun** **arbitrator**, arbiter, mediator, negotiator, conciliator, go-between, middleman, intermediary, moderator, intervenor, interceder, intercessor, reconciler, broker, honest broker, liaison officer, pacifier, appeaser; umpire, referee, adjudicator, judge; peace-monger, pacifist, conscientious objector, passive resister, peace-lover, dove; *informal* peacenik; *rare* satyagrahi.

peak ▶ **noun 1** *there was snow on the very peaks of the mountains* **summit**, top, crest, pinnacle, spire, heights, brow, apex, crown, tip, cap, vertex, acme, zenith, apogee.
2 *the highest unclimbed peak in the Karakoram* **mountain**, hill, height, alp, aiguille, serac, puy, crag, tor, inselberg; bluff, scarp, escarpment,

P

eminence, prominence, elevation; ridge, range, massif, sierra, cordillera; *Scottish* ben, Munro; *S. African* berg; *Arabic* jebel; *archaic* mount.
3 *the peak of a cap* **brim**, visor.
4 *he is at the peak of his career as a singer* **height**, high point/spot, pinnacle, summit, top, highlight, climax, culmination, consummation, epitome, apex, zenith, ascendancy, crowning point, peak of perfection; acme, meridian, apogee, prime, heyday, ne plus ultra, nonpareil, best part, perfection, top form, highest level.
OPPOSITES bottom, nadir, trough.
▶ **verb** *Labour support may have peaked last week* **reach its highest point**, reach the high point; **climax**, reach a climax, come to a climax, culminate, reach the zenith, come to a head.
▶ **adjective** *storage capacity has to be adequate to meet peak loads* **maximum**, maximal, top, greatest, highest, utmost, uttermost, extreme; ultimate, best, optimum.
OPPOSITE minimum.

peaky ▶ **adjective** *you're looking a bit peaky* **pale**, **pasty-faced**, pasty, wan, drained, washed out, drawn, pallid, colourless, anaemic, bloodless, whey-faced, ashen, ashen-faced, ashy, grey, pinched, sickly, sallow, as white as a sheet/ghost, deathly pale, cadaverous, corpse-like, ill-looking, sickly-looking; ill, unwell, poorly, bad, out of sorts, indisposed, not oneself, sick, queasy, nauseous, nauseated, liverish, green about the gills, run down; *Brit.* off, off colour; *informal* under the weather, below par, not up to par, funny, peculiar, rough, lousy, rotten, awful, terrible, dreadful, crummy, seedy; *Brit. informal* grotty, ropy; *Scottish informal* wabbit, peely-wally; *Austral./NZ informal* crook; *rare* peaked, peakish, etiolated.

peal ▶ **noun 1** *just then, a peal of bells rings out* **chime**, carillon, ring, ringing, knell, toll, tolling, sound, sounding, death knell, clang, boom, resounding, reverberation, change, touch; *archaic* tocsin; *rare* tintinnabulation.
2 *Ross burst into peals of laughter* **shriek**, shout, scream, howl, gale, fit, eruption, ripple, roar, hoot.
3 *a peal of thunder crashed directly overhead* **rumble**, roar, boom, rumbling, crash, clap, crack, resounding, reverberation.
▶ **verb 1** *the bell pealed again* **ring**, ring out, chime, chime out, clang, toll; sound, clash, bong, clink, ding, jingle; boom, resound, reverberate.
2 *the lightning flashed and the thunder pealed* **rumble**, roar, boom, crash, resound, reverberate.

peasant ▶ **noun 1** *the peasants were driving their cows to market* **agricultural worker**, **small farmer**, rustic, son of the soil, countryman, countrywoman, farmhand, swain, villein, serf; *French* paysan; *Russian* muzhik, kulak; *Spanish* campesino, paisano; *Italian* contadino; *Egyptian* fellah; *Indian* ryot; *archaic* carl, cottier, kern, hind.
2 *he refused to sit with people he called peasants* **lout**, boor, oaf, clown, churl, yokel, bumpkin, country bumpkin, village idiot, provincial, barbarian; *Irish* culchie, bosthoon, bogman; *informal* clod, clodhopper, yahoo; *N. Amer. informal* hayseed, hick, rube, hillbilly; *Austral. informal* ocker; *rare* bucolic.

peccadillo ▶ **noun** **misdemeanour**, minor offence, petty offence, delinquency; indiscretion, lapse, misdeed, infraction, error, slip; *informal* slip-up.

P

peck ▶ **verb 1** *the cockerel tried to peck my heel* **bite**, nip, strike, hit, tap, rap, jab, poke, prick.
2 *he pecked her on the cheek* **kiss**, plant a kiss, give someone a peck; *informal* give someone a smacker.
3 (*informal*) *the old lady* **pecked at** *her food* **nibble**, pick at, pick over, take very small bites from, eat listlessly, toy with, play with, eat like a bird, show no appetite for, eat sparingly of.

peculiar ▶ **adjective 1** *something even more peculiar began to happen* **strange**, unusual, odd, funny, curious, bizarre, weird, uncanny, queer, unexpected, unfamiliar, abnormal, atypical, anomalous, untypical, different, out of the ordinary, out of the way; exceptional, rare, extraordinary, remarkable; puzzling, mystifying, mysterious, perplexing, baffling, unaccountable, incongruous, uncommon, irregular, singular, deviant, aberrant, freak, freakish; suspicious, dubious, questionable; eerie, unnatural; *Scottish* unco; *French* outré; *informal* fishy, creepy, spooky; *Brit. informal* rum; *N. Amer. informal* bizarro.
OPPOSITES normal, ordinary.
2 *his peculiar behaviour at the airport* **bizarre**, eccentric, strange, odd, weird, queer, funny, unusual, abnormal, idiosyncratic, unconventional, outlandish, offbeat, freakish, quirky, quaint, droll, zany, off-centre; *informal* wacky, freaky, kooky, screwy, kinky, oddball, cranky; *N. Amer. informal* off the wall, wacko; *Austral./NZ informal, dated* dilly.
3 (*informal*) *I still feel a bit peculiar* **unwell**, ill, poorly, bad, out of sorts, indisposed, not oneself, sick, queasy, nauseous, nauseated, peaky, liverish, green about the gills, run down, washed out; *Brit.* off, off colour; *informal* under the weather, below par, not up to par, funny, rough, lousy, rotten, awful, terrible, dreadful, crummy, seedy; *Brit. informal* grotty, ropy; *Scottish informal* wabbit, peely-wally; *Austral./NZ informal* crook; *rare* peaked, peakish.
4 *attitudes and mannerisms* **peculiar to** *the islanders* **characteristic of**, typical of, representative of, belonging to, indicative of, symptomatic of, suggestive of, exclusive to, like, in character with.
5 *Elena added her own peculiar contribution* **distinctive**, characteristic, distinct, different, individual, individualistic, distinguishing, typical, special, specific, representative, unique, idiosyncratic, personal, private, essential, natural; identifiable, unmistakable, conspicuous, notable, remarkable; *rare* singular.

> **CHOOSE THE RIGHT WORD**
> **peculiar, strange, odd, curious**
> *See* STRANGE.

peculiarity ▶ **noun 1** *the problems arise from a legal peculiarity* **oddity**, anomaly, abnormality, twist, quirk, eccentricity, trick.
2 *it was a strange physical peculiarity of his* **idiosyncrasy**, mannerism, quirk, foible, caprice, whimsy; *rare* singularity.
3 *a peculiarity of Phaistos is its two sets of royal apartments* **characteristic**, feature, (essential) quality, nature, property, trait, particularity, aspect, attribute, mark, badge, stamp, hallmark, trademark, distinction, point.
4 *he points out the peculiarity of this notion* **strangeness**, peculiarness, oddness, bizarreness, weirdness, queerness, abnormality, unexpectedness, unfamiliarity, atypicality, anomalousness, curiosity, mystery, incongruity, uncommonness, irregularity, deviancy, aberrance, aberrancy, freakishness, suspiciousness, dubiousness, questionableness; eeriness, unnaturalness; *informal* fishiness, creepiness, spookiness; *rare* dubiety, singularity.
5 *I see you have noticed a certain peculiarity about my appearance* **outlandishness**, **bizarreness**, unconventionality, idiosyncrasy, weirdness, oddness, eccentricity, unusualness, abnormality, queerness, peculiarness, strangeness; grotesqueness, freakishness, quirkiness, quaintness, drollness, zaniness; *informal* wackiness, freakiness, kookiness, kinkiness, crankiness; *N. Amer. informal* screwiness.

pecuniary ▶ **adjective** *he was free from all pecuniary anxieties* **financial**, monetary, money, fiscal, economic, capital, commercial, budgetary.

pedagogic ▶ **adjective** **educational**, educative, edifying, pedagogical, teaching, instructional, instructive, didactic, informative, informational; academic, scholastic, tuitional; *rare* propaedeutic.

pedagogue (*archaic or humorous*) ▶ **noun** **teacher**, schoolteacher, schoolmaster, schoolmistress, master, mistress, tutor; coach, lecturer, academic, don, professor, reader, instructor, educator, educationalist, educationist, guru, mentor; *Scottish* dominie; *Brit. informal* beak; *Austral./NZ informal* chalkie, schoolie.

pedant ▶ **noun** *pedants insist that the 21st century starts with 2001* **dogmatist**, purist, literalist, formalist, doctrinaire; precisionist, perfectionist; quibbler, hair-splitter, casuist, sophist, fault-finder, caviller, carper; *informal* nit-picker; *archaic* pettifogger; *rare* precisian, Dryasdust.

pedantic ▶ **adjective 1** *a pedantic interpretation of the rules* **overscrupulous**, scrupulous, precise, exact, over-exacting, perfectionist, precisionist, punctilious, meticulous, fussy, fastidious, finical, finicky; dogmatic, purist, literalist, literalistic, formalist, scholastic; casuistic, casuistical, sophistic, sophistical; captious, hair-splitting, quibbling, pettifogging, fault-finding, hypercritical, cavilling, carping; *informal* nit-picking, pernickety; *archaic* overnice.
2 *pedantic words like 'irriguous'* **learned**, cerebral, didactic, bookish, pedagogic, donnish, highbrow, ivory-tower, pretentious, pompous; intellectual, academic, scholastic, scholarly, literary; *informal* egghead.

pedantry ▶ **noun 1** *keeping the two distinct is more than mere pedantry* **dogmatism**, purism, literalism, formalism; overscrupulousness, scrupulousness, precision, exactness, perfectionism, fastidiousness, punctiliousness, meticulousness, finickiness, finicality; captiousness, quibbling, hair-splitting, fault-finding, cavilling, carping, casuistry, sophistry; *informal* nit-picking; *archaic*, pettifogging, pettifoggery.
2 *the book lacks the creaking pedantry of many such works* **pretentiousness**, pomposity, pompousness, dullness, tedium; intellectualism, academicism, scholasticism, scholarliness, erudition, studiousness, didacticism, bookishness, pedagogism, donnishness.

peddle ▶ **verb 1** *they are peddling water filters* **sell**, sell from door to door, hawk, tout, vend, offer for sale; carry, stock, offer, market, merchandise, trade, trade in, deal in, traffic in; *informal* push; *Brit. informal* flog.
2 *the unorthodox views peddled by independent research institutes* **advocate**, suggest, urge, recommend, champion; preach, present, put forward, advance, offer, introduce, spread, proclaim, propound, promote.

pedestal ▶ **noun** *a bust of Shakespeare on a pedestal* **plinth**, base, support, bottom, bed, foot, substructure, mounting, platform, stand, foundation, pillar, column, pier; *Architecture* podium, socle.
□ **put someone on a pedestal** *at an early age one puts one's father on a pedestal* **idealize**, exalt, lionize, heroize, aggrandize; look up to, respect, hold in high regard, think highly of, have a high opinion of, hold in admiration, admire; esteem, revere, glorify, adulate, worship, hero-worship, adore, reverence, venerate, deify.

pedestrian ▶ **noun** *a collision between a pedestrian and a car* **walker**,

person on foot, hiker, rambler, stroller, wayfarer, footslogger; *rare* foot traveller.
OPPOSITE driver.

▶ **adjective** *the cup final was a pedestrian affair* **dull**, plodding, boring, tedious, monotonous, uneventful, unremarkable, tiresome, wearisome, uninspired, uncreative, unimaginative, unexciting, uninteresting, lifeless, dry; unvarying, unvaried, repetitive, repetitious, routine, commonplace, average, workaday; ordinary, everyday, unoriginal, mediocre, run-of-the-mill, flat, prosaic, matter-of-fact, turgid, stodgy, mundane, humdrum; *informal* OK, so-so, bog-standard, vanilla, plain vanilla, nothing to write home about, not so hot, not up to much; *Brit. informal* common or garden; *NZ informal* half-pie.
OPPOSITES inspired, exciting.

pedigree ▶ **noun** *Hereford cattle have a long pedigree* **ancestry**, descent, lineage, line, line of descent, genealogy, family tree, extraction, derivation, origin, heritage, parentage, paternity, birth, family, dynasty, house, race, strain, stock, breed, blood, bloodline, history, background, roots; *rare* stirps, filiation, stemma.

▶ **adjective** *a pedigree cat* **pure-bred**, thoroughbred, pure, pure-blooded, full-blooded.

pedlar, **peddler** ▶ **noun 1** *we saw pedlars of watches and compact discs* **travelling salesman**, door-to-door salesman; street trader; *Brit.* barrow boy; *W. Indian* higgler; *Brit. informal* fly-pitcher; *dated* hawker; *archaic* chapman, packman; *rare* huckster, crier, colporteur.
2 *a drug pedlar* **trafficker**, dealer; *informal* pusher.

peek ▶ **verb 1** *one of the models had peeked at the audience from behind the curtains* **peep**, have a peep, have a peek, take a secret look, spy, take a sly/stealthy look, sneak a look, glance, cast a brief look, look hurriedly, look, peer; *Scottish* keek; *informal* take a gander, have a look-see, give someone/something a/the once-over, have a squint; *Brit. informal* have a dekko, have/take a butcher's, take a shufti.
2 *the deer's antlers peeked out from a clump of aspen trees* **appear (slowly/partly)**, show, come into view/sight, make an appearance, put in an appearance, present oneself/itself, become visible, emerge, issue, peep, peer out, surface, loom, show one's/its face, come to light, spring up, pop up.

▶ **noun** *she sneaked a peek at the map* **secret look**, sly look, stealthy look, sneaky look, peep, glance, glimpse, brief/hurried/quick look, look, peer; *Scottish* keek; *informal* gander, look-see, squint, eyeful; *Brit. informal* dekko; butcher's, shufti.

peel ▶ **verb 1** *peel and core the fruit* **pare**, skin, take the skin/rind off, strip, shave, trim, flay; hull, shell, husk, shuck; *technical* decorticate.
2 *a long knife peels the veneer from a round log* **trim (off)**, peel off, pare, strip (off), shave (off), remove, take off, flay; *technical* excoriate.
3 *the paper on the ceiling had started to peel* **flake (off)**, peel off, come off in layers/strips; blister; *technical* exfoliate, desquamate.

□ **keep one's eyes peeled** *keep your eyes peeled for bandits* **keep a (sharp) lookout**, be on the lookout, look out, keep one's eyes open, keep an eye out/open, observe, watch (closely), keep watch, be watchful, be on the watch, be alert, be on the alert, be on the qui vive, be on guard; beware, mind out, be vigilant, be wary, be careful, pay attention, take heed; *Brit.* keep one's eyes skinned; *informal* keep one's peepers peeled.

□ **peel something off** *he peeled off his wet clothes* **take off**, strip off, cast off, remove, discard, throw off; *dated* doff, divest oneself of.

▶ **noun** *orange peel* **rind**, **skin**, covering, zest; hull, pod, crust, shuck, capsule, outer layer; *technical* epicarp, pericarp, exocarp; *rare* integument.

peep[1] ▶ **verb 1** *I peeped through the keyhole* **look quickly**, cast a brief look, take a secret look, spy, take a sly/stealthy look, sneak a look, peek, have a peek, glance, peer; *Scottish* keek; *informal* take a gander, have a look-see, give someone/something a/the once-over, have a squint; *Brit. informal* have a dekko, have/take a butcher's, take a shufti.
2 *the moon peeped through a chink in the clouds* **appear (slowly/partly)**, show, come into view/sight, make an appearance, put in an appearance, present oneself/itself, become visible, emerge, issue, peek, peer out, surface, loom, show one's/its face, come to light, spring up, pop up.

▶ **noun** *I'll just take a peep at it* **quick look**, brief look, sly look, stealthy look, sneaky look, peek, glance, glimpse, look, peer; *Scottish* keek; *informal* gander, look-see, squint, eyeful; *Brit. informal* dekko, butcher's, shufti.

peep[2] ▶ **noun 1** *one morning I heard a telltale peep* **cheep**, chirp, chirrup, tweet, twitter, chirr, pipe, piping, warble, squeak, chatter.
2 *there's been not a peep out of the children* **sound**, noise, cry, utterance, word; *informal* cheep.
3 *a looted painting was sold without a peep* **complaint**, grumble, moan, mutter, murmur, grouse, objection, protest, protestation, outcry, demur, argument, remonstrance, remonstration, exception, grievance, cavil, quibble, word, sound; *informal* niggle, gripe, grouch, beef.

▶ **verb** *the fax peeped and began to flutter out the papers* **cheep**, chirp, chirrup, tweet, twitter, chirr, squeak.

peephole ▶ **noun opening**, gap, cleft, spyhole, slit, crack, chink, keyhole, aperture, orifice, crevice, cranny, fissure; *Architecture* arrow slit, embrasure, squint; *rare* judas (hole).

peer[1] ▶ **verb** *he swivelled his head to peer in our direction* **squint**, look closely/earnestly, try to see, look through narrowed eyes, narrow one's eyes, screw up one's eyes; peep, peek, pry, spy, look, gawp, gaze, stare, gape; scrutinize, survey, examine, view, eye, scan, observe, study, regard, contemplate; *informal* snoop; *rare* squinny.

peer[2] *See centre pages for list of* **Nobles**

▶ **noun 1** *hereditary and life peers* **aristocrat**, lord, lady, peer of the realm, peeress, noble, nobleman, noblewoman, titled man/woman/person, patrician, member of the aristocracy/nobility/peerage.
2 *the quality of medical work can only be reviewed by a doctor's peers* **equal**, fellow, co-worker, match, like, rival; *French* confrère; *rare* compeer, co-equal.
3 *he looks older than his peers* **contemporary**, person of the same age; *rare* coeval.

peerage ▶ **noun aristocracy**, nobility, peers and peeresses, lords and ladies, the House of Lords, the Lords, titled nobility/class, titled men/women/people, landed gentry; *rare* patriciate.

peerless ▶ **adjective** *a peerless performance* **incomparable**, matchless, unrivalled, inimitable, beyond compare, unparalleled, unequalled, without equal, unmatched, beyond comparison, second to none, unsurpassed, unsurpassable, nonpareil; unique, consummate, perfect, rare, exquisite, transcendent, surpassing, superlative, supreme; *rare* unexampled.

peeve ▶ **verb** (*informal*) *the surprise early closing of the bar peeved more than one punter* **irritate**, annoy, anger, vex, bother, provoke, displease, upset, exasperate, agitate, gall, irk, get/put someone's back up, disgruntle, put out, pique, rankle with, nettle, bait, goad, needle, get on someone's nerves, ruffle, ruffle someone's feathers, make someone's hackles rise, raise someone's hackles; drive to distraction; *Brit.* rub up the wrong way; *informal* aggravate, miff, rile, get under someone's skin, get in someone's hair, get up someone's nose, hack off, get someone's goat, get, get to, bug; *Brit. informal* nark, get on someone's wick, give someone the hump, wind up, get across; *N. Amer. informal* tick off, rankle, ride, gravel; *vulgar slang* piss off; *rare* exacerbate, hump, rasp.

CHOOSE THE RIGHT WORD

peeve, annoy, irritate, aggravate, vex

See ANNOY.

peeved ▶ **adjective** (*informal*) *she was peeved that he had succeeded* **irritated**, annoyed, cross, angry, angered, furious, enraged, in a temper, bothered, vexed, displeased, disgruntled, dissatisfied, indignant, upset, exasperated, galled, irked, put out, aggrieved, offended, affronted, resentful, piqued, nettled, ruffled, in high dudgeon; *informal* aggravated, miffed, riled, hacked off, peed off, *Brit. informal* narked, eggy, cheesed off, browned off, brassed off; *N. Amer. informal* teed off, ticked off, sore, steamed; *vulgar slang* pissed off.

peevish ▶ **adjective** *the remark came out sounding peevish and sensitive* **irritable**, irascible, fractious, fretful, cross, petulant, pettish, crabbed, crabby, crotchety, cantankerous, curmudgeonly, disagreeable, miserable, morose, peppery, on edge, edgy, impatient, complaining, querulous; bitter, moody, in a bad mood, grumpy, huffy, scratchy, out of sorts, out of temper, ill-tempered, bad-tempered, ill-natured, ill-humoured, sullen, surly, sulky, sour, churlish, touchy, testy, tetchy, snappish, waspish, prickly, crusty, bilious, liverish, dyspeptic, splenetic, choleric; *N. English* mardy; *informal* snappy, chippy, grouchy, cranky, whingeing, whingy; *Brit. informal* narky, ratty, eggy, like a bear with a sore head; *N. Amer. informal* sorehead, soreheaded, peckish; *Austral./NZ informal* snaky; *dated* miffy.
OPPOSITES affable, easy-going.

peg ▶ **noun spike**, pin, nail, dowel, skewer, rivet, brad, screw, bolt, hook, stick, nog, spigot; *Nautical* fid; *Curling* hack; *Quoits* hob; *Mountaineering* piton; *Golf* tee; *Rowing* thole (pin); *rare* knag, spile.

□ **take someone down a peg or two humble**, humiliate, mortify, bring/take down, bring low, demean, show up, shame, put to shame, make ashamed, discomfit, disgrace, discredit, downgrade, debase, degrade, devalue, dishonour, embarrass, put someone in their place, make a fool of, chasten, subdue, get the better of, have the last laugh on, abash, abase, crush, squash, quash, deflate, flatten, make someone eat humble pie; *informal* put down, settle someone's hash, cut down to size; *N. Amer. informal* make someone eat crow.

▶ **verb 1** *the flysheet is draped over and pegged to the ground* **fix**, pin, attach, fasten, secure, make fast.
2 *we decided to peg our prices* **hold down**, keep down, fix, set, hold, control, freeze, limit.

□ **peg away** (*informal*) *I am going to peg away with this novel* **work hard**, work away, hammer away, grind away; persevere, persist, exert oneself, apply oneself, keep at it, plod, soldier on; *informal* slog, beaver (away), plug (away), stick at, stick with it; *Brit. informal* graft, get one's head down.

pejorative ▶ **adjective disparaging**, derogatory, denigratory, deprecatory, defamatory, slanderous, libellous, abusive, insulting, slighting, vituperative, disapproving, contemptuous; *informal* bitchy; *rare* invective, contumelious.

P

OPPOSITES complimentary, approbatory.

pellet ▶ noun **1** *millions of blind worker ants each carry a tiny pellet of mud* **little ball**, little piece; *technical* prill.
2 *pellet wounds inflicted by shotguns* **bullet**, shot, lead shot, buckshot.
3 (usually **pellets**) *rabbit pellets* **excrement**, excreta, dropping, faeces, dung, stool, dirt, mess, motion.

pell-mell ▶ adverb **1** *the sparrows fly pell-mell up the hedgerow* **helter-skelter**, headlong, (at) full tilt, hotfoot, post-haste, hurriedly, hastily; wildly, impetuously, recklessly, rashly, precipitately, impulsively; *informal* slap bang; *archaic* hurry-scurry.
2 *the words slipped pell-mell into one another* **in disorder**, in confusion, in a muddle/jumble, in disarray, in a disorganized manner, untidily, in a mess, in a heap, anyhow; *informal* all over the place, every which way; *Brit. informal* all over the shop, shambolically; *N. Amer. informal* all over the map, all over the lot.

pellucid ▶ adjective **1** *the pellucid Caribbean waters | a pellucid singing tone* **translucent**, transparent, clear, crystal clear, crystalline, bright, glassy, limpid, unclouded.
2 *pellucid prose* **easily understood**, easily grasped, comprehensible, understandable, intelligible, articulate, coherent, lucid, clear, crystal clear, crystalline; graspable, fathomable, digestible, straightforward, direct, simple, plain, well constructed, graphic, explicit, unambiguous, user-friendly.

pelt[1] ▶ verb **1** *they pelted him with snowballs* **bombard**, shower, attack, assail, batter, pepper, strafe, rake, sweep, enfilade, blitz; throw at, rain something down on, fire a broadside at; *archaic* cannonade, fusillade.
2 *the rain was now **pelting down*** **pour**, teem, stream; rain cats and dogs, rain hard; *Brit. informal* bucket down, come down in stair rods, rain stair rods.
3 (*informal*) *they pelted into the factory* **run**, race, leap, sprint, dash, rush, speed, streak, shoot, whizz, whoosh, buzz, zoom, flash, blast, charge, stampede, chase, career, bustle, hare, fly, wing, kite, skite, dive, jump, skip, scurry, scud, scutter, scramble, hurry, hasten; *informal* belt, scoot, scorch, tear, zap, zip, whip; *Brit. informal* bomb, bucket, shift; *N. Amer. informal* boogie, hightail, clip; *N. Amer. vulgar slang* drag/tear/haul ass; *informal, dated* cut along.

pelt[2] ▶ noun *a man who used to hunt otters for their pelts* **skin**, hide, fleece, coat, fur, fell.

pen[1] *See centre pages for list of* **Writing Implements**
▶ verb *he penned a great number of articles* **write**, write down, jot down, note, set down, take down, inscribe, scribble, scrawl, pencil, compose, draft, formulate, draw up, dash off, put in writing, put down on paper, commit to paper, put in black and white.

pen[2] ▶ noun *the sheep in the pen behind the barn* **enclosure**, fold, sheepfold, pound, compound, paddock, stockade, sty, coop, cage, stall, lock-up; *N. Amer.* corral; *Scottish* parrock; *S. African* kraal; (*in S. America*) potrero.
▶ verb *Norman had the camel **penned up** in his yard* **confine**, enclose, impound, shut in, fence in; hurdle, rail in, coop (up), immure, mew up, box up/in, lock up/in, cage, imprison, intern, hold captive, incarcerate; encircle, surround, ring, encompass, hem in, close in, hedge in, trap; *N. Amer.* corral.

penal ▶ adjective **1** *a penal institution* **disciplinary**, punitive, corrective, correctional, retributive.
2 *he avoided borrowing at penal rates of interest* **exorbitant**, extortionate, excessive, outrageous, preposterous, immoderate, unreasonable, inordinate, iniquitous, inflated, sky-high, expensive, gross.

penalize ▶ verb **1** *he promised to penalize parents whose children missed school* **punish**, discipline, inflict a penalty on, exact a penalty from, deal with, mete out punishment to, sentence, impose a sentence on, chastise, castigate, correct, chasten.
OPPOSITE reward.
2 *an enterprise culture penalizes those at the bottom of the income pile* **handicap**, inflict a handicap on, unfairly disadvantage, put at an unfair disadvantage, put in an unfavourable position, cause to suffer, put a stumbling block in the way of, put a hindrance/impediment in the way of.
OPPOSITES favour, help.
3 *Section 18 penalizes the possession of a firearm with intent to commit a crime* **prohibit**, forbid, ban, outlaw, bar, veto, embargo, declare something a punishable offence, make something punishable, make illegal, disallow, proscribe, interdict.
OPPOSITE legalize.

penalty ▶ noun **1** *increased penalties for dumping oil at sea* **punishment**, sanction, punitive action, retribution, penance; **fine**, forfeit, sentence; *rare* mulct.
OPPOSITE reward.
2 *for some, the economic penalties of motherhood outweigh its attractions* **disadvantage**, difficulty, drawback, handicap, snag, downside, minus, detriment, unpleasant aspect; trial, torment, bane, tribulation, affliction, suffering, burden, trouble, worry; deprivation, cost, undesirable consequence.
OPPOSITE advantage.

penance ▶ noun *self-awareness is the necessary ingredient for penance | penances for a variety of sins* **atonement**, expiation, self-punishment, self-mortification, self-abasement, reparation, amends, penalty, punishment.
□ **do penance** *you must do penance for the crimes in your life* **atone**, make amends/reparation/recompense/restitution, make up, redeem oneself, pay the penalty, pay, recompense, pay the price, expiate, redress, compensate.

penchant ▶ noun *he has a penchant for champagne* **liking**, fondness, preference, taste, relish, appetite, partiality, soft spot, love, passion, desire, fancy, whim, weakness, inclination, bent, bias, proclivity, predilection, predisposition, affinity.

pencil ▶ noun **1** *a sharpened pencil* lead pencil, propelling pencil; pencil crayon; *Brit.* chinagraph pencil; *historical* slate pencil.
2 *a pencil of light* **beam**, ray, shaft, finger, gleam.
▶ verb **1** *she pencilled slogans on an envelope* **write**, write down, jot down, note, set down, take down, inscribe; **scribble**, rough out, write roughly, scrawl, pen, compose, draft; formulate, draw up, dash off, put in writing, put down on paper, commit to paper, put in black and white.
2 *pencil a line along the top of the moulding* **draw**, trace, plot, chart, sketch, outline.
□ **pencil something in** *they have pencilled in 1 May for a family day out* **arrange provisionally**, make as a provisional arrangement, arrange subject to confirmation, forecast tentatively.

pendant ▶ noun *he slipped the pendant over his neck* locket, medallion, drop, stone; necklace, chain.

pendent ▶ adjective *pendent catkins* **hanging**, suspended, supported from above, dangling, pendulous, drooping, droopy, flaccid, swinging, swaying, trailing, flowing, falling, tumbling; *rare* pendant, pensile.

pending ▶ adjective **1** *dismissal of all other litigation pending between them* **unresolved**, undecided, unsettled, unconcluded, uncertain, awaiting decision, awaiting action, undetermined, (still) open, hanging fire, (up) in the air, in limbo, in the balance, on ice, in reserve, in abeyance, ongoing, awaiting attention, outstanding, to be done, undone, not done, unattended to, unfinished, incomplete, left, remaining; *informal* on the back burner.
2 *her rumoured pending marriage* **imminent**, impending, about to happen/be, forthcoming, upcoming, on the way, coming, approaching, looming, gathering, prospective, near, nearing, close, close at hand, in the offing, in the wind, to come, -to-be, anticipated, expected.
▶ preposition **1** *the two boys were released on bail pending another hearing next week* **awaiting**, waiting for, until, till, before, until there is/are.
2 *they were freed on police bail pending further inquiries* **during**, throughout, in the course of, for the time/duration of.

pendulous ▶ adjective *this magnolia produces large, white, pendulous flowers* **drooping**, dangling, droopy, sagging, saggy, floppy; hanging, suspended, supported from above, pendent; swinging, swaying, falling, tumbling, trailing, flowing, loose, relaxed; *rare* pensile.

penetrable ▶ adjective **1** *vines grow best in a penetrable subsoil* **permeable**, pervious, porous, open; honeycombed, cellular, holey; sieve-like, leaky; pierceable; accessible.
OPPOSITES impervious; impenetrable.
2 *their sing-song creole was only **penetrable by** aficionados* **understandable**, fathomable, graspable, approachable; easy to understand; comprehensible to, intelligible to, accessible to.
OPPOSITE incomprehensible.

penetrate ▶ verb **1** *the sharp point of the spear did not penetrate his throat* **pierce**, puncture, make a hole in, perforate, stab, prick, probe, gore, spike, stick, impale, transfix, bore (through), drill (through), lance.
2 *the oil has penetrated into the stones* **seep**, soak, percolate, filter, infiltrate, spread, diffuse; enter, make one's way into/through, pass/move/flow into, get into.
3 *they penetrated the enemy territory via a gap cut in the fence* **infiltrate**, slip into, sneak into, creep into, insinuate oneself into, worm one's way into, make inroads into, invade, intrude on, overrun.
4 *I am allowing the healing energy to penetrate my digestive organs* **permeate**, pervade, fill, spread throughout, imbue, suffuse, diffuse through, seep through, steep, impregnate, inform, infuse, saturate, charge, drench, inundate; influence, infect, excite, stimulate, inspire.
5 *humans' efforts to penetrate the enigma of their beginnings* **understand**, comprehend, apprehend, fathom, grasp, perceive, discern, get to the bottom of, solve, resolve, make out, make sense of, interpret, puzzle out, work out, figure out, unravel, decipher, make head or tail of; *informal* crack, get, tumble to, latch on to, cotton on to; *Brit. informal* suss out, twig.
6 *Douglas was at the door before Jamieson's words penetrated* **be understood**, be comprehended, be taken in, be grasped, become clear; **register**, make an impression, get through, sink in, fall into place, dawn, come home; *informal* click.
7 *I don't think the implication penetrated my mind all that quickly* **get through to**, be understood/comprehended by, register on, make an impression on, have an impact on.

penetrating ▶ adjective **1** *a penetrating wind* **piercing**, cutting, stinging, biting; **keen**, sharp, acute, numbing, harsh, fierce, raw; frosty, freezing, frigid, chill, chilling, glacial, arctic, wintry, cold, bitterly/intensely cold, nippy; *Brit. informal* parky; *rare* nipping.
OPPOSITES gentle, mild.
2 *a penetrating voice* **shrill**, strident, piercing, carrying, clearly audible, loud, strong, high, high-pitched, piping, ear-piercing, ear-splitting, screechy, intrusive.
OPPOSITES mellow, soft.
3 *a penetrating smell* **pungent**, pervasive, strong, powerful, suffocating, stifling; sharp, acrid, acid, sour, biting, stinging, burning, smarting, irritating, nauseating, nauseous, sickly, offensive, astringent, bitter, fetid, cloying; heady, aromatic, flowery, fragrant; *literary* mephitic.
OPPOSITE mild.
4 *penetrating eyes* **observant**, searching, intent, alert, shrewd, perceptive, probing, piercing, sharp, keen.
5 *a penetrating analysis* **perceptive**, insightful, keen, sharp, sharp-witted, quick-witted, intelligent, clever, smart, incisive, piercing, knife-like, razor-edged, trenchant, astute, shrewd, subtle, quick, ready, clear, acute, discriminating, percipient, perspicacious, discerning, sensitive, thoughtful, penetrative, deep, profound.
OPPOSITE dull.
6 *penetrating questions* **enquiring**, searching, sharp, incisive, probing, deep, inquisitive, analytic, in-depth.

CHOOSE THE RIGHT WORD

penetrating, keen, acute

See KEEN.

penetration ▶ noun **1** *skin penetration by infective larvae* **perforation**, piercing, puncturing, puncture, riddling, stabbing, prick, pricking, probing, goring, spiking, sticking, impaling, impalement, transfixing, transfixion, boring, drilling, lancing, tapping.
2 *rot that is attributable to rain penetration* **infiltration**, entry, inflow, spread, spreading, diffusion, percolation, filtering, seepage, soaking, soakage.
3 *remarks of great penetration* **insight**, **discernment**, perception, perceptiveness, intelligence, sharp-wittedness, quick-wittedness, cleverness, smartness, incisiveness, keenness, sharpness, trenchancy, astuteness, shrewdness, acuteness, subtlety, clarity, acuity, discrimination, sensitivity, thoughtfulness, profundity, percipience, perspicacity, perspicuity, sagacity.
OPPOSITE dullness.

peninsula ▶ noun **cape**, promontory, point, head, headland, foreland, ness, horn, bill, bluff, limb; *Scottish* mull; *archaic* half-island, half-isle, demi-island.

penis ▶ noun **phallus**, (male) member, (male) organ, sex, erection; *N. Amer. informal* pee-pee; *Irish informal* mickey; *humorous* lunch box; *vulgar slang* cock, dick, prick, knob, chopper, tool, equipment, dipstick, ding-a-ling, dong, (one-eyed) trouser snake, shaft, ramrod, root, boner, length, meat, pudding, pego, John Thomas, Johnson, machine, manhood, thing, winkle, middle leg, third leg, old man, joystick, pencil, pisser, prong, putz, rig, rod, Roger, stalk, stiffy, tonk, tube, weapon, yard; *Brit. vulgar slang* willy, horn, how's your father, peter, plonker, todger; *N. Amer. vulgar slang* dork, pecker, weenie, wiener, schlong, whang, whanger; *technical* intromittent organ; *archaic* membrum virile, virile member, nerve, person, propagator, tarse, verge, pizzle; *archaic, vulgar slang* loom, needle, pillicock, pintle, runnion.

penitence ▶ noun *the writer prays to God in penitence* **repentance**, contrition, compunction, regret, remorse, remorsefulness, ruefulness, pangs of conscience, self-reproach, contriteness, self-accusation, shame, sorrow, guilt.

penitent ▶ adjective *she stood with her hands joined below her waist like a penitent child* **repentant**, contrite, regretful, remorseful, sorry, apologetic, conscience-stricken, rueful, ashamed, shamefaced, abject.
OPPOSITES impenitent, unrepentant.

pen-name ▶ noun **pseudonym**, assumed name, incognito, alias, stage name, professional name, false name, sobriquet, nickname; *French* nom de plume, nom de guerre; *rare* allonym, anonym.

pennant ▶ noun *pennants fly from the towers* **banner**, banderole, streamer, flag, standard, ensign, jack, pennon, colour(s); *Brit.* pendant; *Nautical* burgee; *rare* gonfalon, guidon, labarum.

penniless ▶ adjective *Van Gogh died penniless* **poor**, indigent, impoverished, penurious, impecunious, in penury, moneyless, without a sou, as poor as a church mouse, poverty-stricken, destitute, necessitous; bankrupt, bust, insolvent; needy, in need/want, badly off, in reduced circumstances, in straitened circumstances, hard up, on one's beam-ends, unable to make ends meet, underprivileged; *Brit.* on the breadline, without a penny (to one's name); *informal* broke, flat broke, cleaned out, strapped for cash, strapped, on one's uppers, without two pennies/(brass) farthings to rub together; *Brit. informal* stony broke, skint, in Queer Street; *N. Amer. informal* stone broke; *rare* pauperized, beggared.
OPPOSITES wealthy, affluent.

penny ▶ noun
□ **a pretty penny** (*informal*) *I bet this costs a pretty penny* **a lot of money**, a fortune, a considerable/vast sum of money, millions, billions, a king's ransom, a killing, a windfall, a bonanza; *informal* a small fortune, lots/pots/heaps of money, a mint, a bundle, a packet, a wad, a pile, a stack, a heap, a tidy sum; telephone numbers; *Brit. informal* a bomb, shedloads, a shedload; *N. Amer.* big bucks, big money, gazillions; *Austral. informal* big bickies, motser, motza.
□ **two/ten a penny** *nursing homes are two a penny in Devon* **numerous**, abundant, thick on the ground, profuse, plentiful, prolific, copious, legion, innumerable, countless, infinite, numberless; in large numbers, by the gross, in strength, by the yard; very common, widespread, popular, universal, ubiquitous; *literary* myriad, innumerous, manifold.

penny-pincher ▶ noun **skinflint**, miser, Scrooge, niggard, cheese-parer; *informal* meanie, money-grubber, cheapskate; *N. Amer. informal* tightwad; *vulgar slang* tight-arse.
OPPOSITES spendthrift; philanthropist.

penny-pinching ▶ adjective **mean**, miserly, niggardly, parsimonious, close-fisted, cheese-paring, penurious, scrimping, grasping, greedy, avaricious, Scrooge-like, ungenerous, illiberal, close; *informal* stingy, mingy, tight, tight-fisted, money-grubbing, money-grabbing; *vulgar slang* tight-arsed; *archaic* near.
OPPOSITES generous, liberal, munificent.

pension ▶ noun **1** *they will get a pension when they retire* **annuity**, superannuation; retirement pension, old-age pension, state pension, company pension, occupational pension, employer's pension, contributory pension, non-contributory pension, supplementary pension, graduated pension, earnings-related pension, index-linked pension, personal pension, private pension, portable pension.
2 *a disability pension* **welfare payment**, allowance, benefit, support, welfare, assistance; widow's pension, war pension, disablement/disability pension, invalidity pension.

pensioner ▶ noun **retired person**, old-age pensioner, OAP, senior citizen; *N. Amer.* senior, retiree; *rare* retirer, pensionary.

pensive ▶ adjective **thoughtful**, thinking, reflective, contemplative, musing, meditative, introspective, prayerful, philosophical, cogitative, ruminative, absorbed, engrossed, rapt, preoccupied, deep/immersed/lost in thought, in a brown study, broody, serious, studious, solemn, dreamy, dreaming; wistful, brooding, melancholy, sad; *rare* ruminant.

CHOOSE THE RIGHT WORD

pensive, wistful, plaintive

See WISTFUL.

pent-up ▶ adjective *a release of pent-up emotion* **repressed**, suppressed, stifled, smothered, restrained, constrained, confined, bottled up, held in/back, kept in check, curbed, bridled.

penurious ▶ adjective **1** *a penurious student* **poor**, as poor as a church mouse, poverty-stricken, destitute, necessitous, in penury, impecunious, impoverished, indigent, needy, in need/want, badly off, in reduced circumstances, in straitened circumstances, hard up, on one's beam-ends, unable to make ends meet, underprivileged, penniless, without a sou, moneyless, bankrupt, bust, insolvent; *Brit.* on the breadline, without a penny (to one's name); *informal* broke, flat broke, cleaned out, strapped for cash, strapped, on one's uppers; *Brit. informal* stony broke, skint, without two pennies/(brass) farthings to rub together, in Queer Street; *N. Amer. informal* stone broke; *rare* pauperized, beggared.
OPPOSITE wealthy.
2 *a penurious old skinflint* **mean**, miserly, niggardly, parsimonious, penny-pinching, close-fisted, cheese-paring, scrimping, grasping, greedy, avaricious, Scrooge-like, ungenerous, illiberal, close; *informal* stingy, mingy, tight, tight-fisted, money-grubbing, money-grabbing; *vulgar slang* tight-arsed; *archaic* near.
OPPOSITE generous.

penury ▶ noun **extreme/dire poverty**, pennilessness, impecuniousness, impoverishment, indigence, need, neediness, want, destitution, privation, deprivation, hardship, beggary, bankruptcy, insolvency, ruin, reduced circumstances, straitened circumstances; *rare* pauperism, pauperdom, mendicity.
OPPOSITES wealth, affluence.

people ▶ noun **1** *crowds of people* **human beings**, persons, individuals, humans, mankind, humankind, the human race, Homo sapiens, humanity, the human species, mortals, (living) souls, personages, {men, women, and children}; *informal* folk, peeps.
2 *the British people have not been told the truth* **citizens**, subjects, electors, voters, taxpayers, residents, inhabitants, (general) public, citizenry, nation, population, populace, community, society.

P

3 *a man of the people* **the proletariat**, the common people, the masses, the populace, the multitude, the rank and file, the commonality, the commonalty, the third estate, the plebeians, the crowd; *derogatory* the hoi polloi, the common herd, the rabble, the mob, the riff-raff, the canaille, the great unwashed, the ragtag (and bobtail), the proles, the plebs.
4 *her people don't live far away* **family**, parents, relatives, relations, folk, kinsmen, kin, kith and kin, next of kin, one's (own) flesh and blood, blood relatives/relations, nearest and dearest; *informal* folks; *formal* kinsfolk, kinfolk.
5 *the peoples of Africa* **race**, tribe, clan, (ethnic) group, strain, stock, caste, nation, country, population, populace; *archaic* breed, folk, seed.
▶ **verb** *the Indians who once peopled Newfoundland* **populate**, settle (in), colonize, establish oneself in, inhabit, live in, occupy; *formal* be, reside in, domiciled in, dwell in.

WORD LINKS

relating to (ordinary) people	**demotic, plebeian**
related prefix	**demo-** (e.g. ***democratic, demography***)
relating to a people	**ethnic**
study of people	**anthropology**
study of different peoples	**ethnology**
fear of people	**anthropophobia**
killing of a people	**ethnocide**

pep (*informal*) ▶ **noun** *full of pep after the holidays* **dynamism**, life, go, energy, spirit, liveliness, animation, bounce, sparkle, effervescence, fizz, verve, spiritedness, ebullience, high spirits, enthusiasm, initiative, vitality, vivacity, fire, dash, panache, elan, snap, zest, zeal, exuberance, vigour, gusto, drive, push, brio; *informal* feistiness, get-up-and-go, gumption, oomph, pizzazz, vim, zing, zip.
▶ **verb**
□ **pep something up** *the turbocharger is designed to pep up performance* **improve, enliven**, animate, liven up, put some/new life into, invigorate, vitalize, revitalize, vivify, ginger up, energize, electrify, galvanize, put some spark into, stimulate, get something going, add zest to, perk up, brighten up, cheer up; season, spice, add spice to, pepper, leaven, flavour, add flavouring to; *informal* buck up.
OPPOSITE subdue.

pepper ▶ **verb 1** *salt and pepper the potatoes* season, flavour, spice, spice up.
2 *a sprinkle of stars peppered the desert skies* **sprinkle**, fleck, intersperse, dot, spot, bespatter, dab, bestud, stipple, pock, freckle, scatter; *literary* befleck, bestrew.
3 *another burst of enemy bullets peppered the tank* **bombard**, pelt, shower, rain down on, attack, assail, batter, fire a broadside at, strafe, rake, sweep, enfilade, blitz, hit; *archaic* cannonade, fusillade.

peppery ▶ **adjective 1** *this salami is very peppery* **spicy**, spiced, peppered, hot, highly seasoned, pungent, fiery, gingery, piquant, sharp.
OPPOSITES mild, bland.
2 *retired generals are expected to be peppery* **irritable**, peevish, cross, crabbed, crabby, crotchety, cantankerous, hot-tempered, irascible, fiery, quick-tempered, impatient, complaining, querulous, curmudgeonly, bitter, acerbic, sour, caustic, moody, grumpy, huffy, brusque, surly, curt, gruff, scratchy, ill-tempered, bad-tempered, short-tempered, ill-natured, ill-humoured, touchy, sharp-tongued, testy, tetchy, snappish, snarling, waspish, prickly, crusty, bilious, liverish, dyspeptic, splenetic, choleric; *informal* snappy, chippy, grouchy, cranky; *Brit. informal* narky, ratty, eggy, like a bear with a sore head; *N. Amer. informal* peckish, sorehead, soreheaded; *Austral./NZ informal* snaky; *informal, dated* miffy.
OPPOSITE easy-going.

perceive ▶ **verb 1** *Belinda immediately perceived the flaws in her story* **discern**, recognize, become cognizant of, become aware of, become conscious of, get/come to know, tell, distinguish, grasp, understand, take in, make out, find, identify, hit on, comprehend, apprehend, figure out, deduce, conclude, see, discover, learn, appreciate, realize, ascertain, sense, divine, intuit; *informal* catch on to; *Brit. informal* twig; *rare* cognize.
2 *sharks and rays cannot perceive colour* **see**, make out, pick out, discern, detect, catch sight of, spot, observe, glimpse, notice, recognize, identify; hear, smell, sniff (out), scent, nose out, feel, taste, sense.
3 *he was perceived as too negative* **look on**, view, regard, consider, think of, judge, deem, appraise, assess, adjudge, figure (out), size up, value, rate, suppose, think, sum up, weigh up.

perceptible ▶ **adjective noticeable**, perceivable, detectable, discernible; appreciable, visible, observable, recognizable; obvious, evident, manifest, patent, clear, distinct, plain, overt, conspicuous, distinguishable, unmistakable, unconcealed, transparent, apparent; significant, measurable, tangible, palpable.
OPPOSITES imperceptible, inconspicuous.

perception ▶ **noun 1** *our perception of our own limitations | his perception of the world* **discernment**, appreciation, recognition, realization, cognizance; **awareness**, consciousness, knowledge, acknowledgement, grasp, understanding, comprehension, interpretation, apprehension; impression, sense, sensation, feeling, observation, picture, notion, thought, belief, conception, idea, judgement, estimation.

CHOOSE THE RIGHT WORD

perceptible, palpable, appreciable, noticeable

- What is **perceptible** can be noticed, but only just (*there was a slight but perceptible air of neglect*). The word is commonly used, in conjunction with *barely, hardly*, or *scarcely*, to convey that a phenomenon is so slight or insignificant that it is difficult to notice (*she gave a barely perceptible nod*). It can also be used to emphasize that something is noticeable, even though slight (*the smell was not strong but easily perceptible, like a large zoo passed at a distance*).
- Something that is **palpable** impinges far more forcefully on our consciousness. A more literary word, literally meaning 'able to be touched or felt', *palpable* is used to describe an intense feeling or atmosphere (*there was a palpable sense of excitement*) or something that is intellectually self-evident (*they sometimes stooped to making public statements that were palpable nonsense*).
- Something **appreciable** is large or important enough to be easily perceived, and typically a measurable amount, quantity, change, or process (*tea and coffee both contain appreciable amounts of caffeine | there has been no appreciable improvement in their relative economic performance*).
- Something described as **noticeable** is typically quite conspicuous (*a noticeable difference between school and university teaching is the lack of personal attention*). It is commonly used to express relative conspicuousness, with *less, more, very*, etc. (*road noise tends to be more noticeable in certain weather conditions*), and with the impersonal subject *it* and a *that*-clause (*it is noticeable that all these graves are found near the Pilgrims' Way*).

2 *he talks with great perception on all matters theatrical* **insight**, perceptiveness, percipience, perspicacity, perspicuity, understanding, keenness, sharpness, sharp-wittedness, quick-wittedness, intelligence, intuition, cleverness, incisiveness, trenchancy, wit, astuteness, shrewdness, acuteness, acuity, subtlety, clarity, discrimination, discernment, sensitivity, penetration, thoughtfulness, profundity.

perceptive ▶ **adjective insightful**, discerning, responsive, sensitive, observant; piercing, penetrating, percipient, perspicacious, penetrative, intelligent, clever, canny, keen, sharp, sharp-witted, quick-witted, astute, shrewd, subtle, quick, ready, clear, acute, discriminating; intuitive, thoughtful, deep, profound.
OPPOSITES obtuse, unobservant, dull.

perch ▶ **noun** *the budgerigar shuffled along its perch* **pole**, rod, branch, roost, rest, resting place.
▶ **verb 1** *three swallows perched on the telegraph wire* **roost**, sit, rest; **alight**, settle, land, come to rest.
2 *she perched a pair of pince-nez on her nose* **put**, place, set, rest, balance.
□ **be perched** *the church is perched on a hill above Florence* **be located**, be situated, be positioned, be sited, stand.

perchance ▶ **adverb** (*literary*) **1** *if perchance he arrives on time* **by chance**, by any chance, by some chance, as it may be, as it may happen, as things may turn out.
2 *perchance the outlook is not as bleak as she imagines* **maybe**, perhaps, possibly, for all one knows, it could be (that), it is possible (that), conceivably; *N. English* happen; *literary* peradventure, mayhap, haply; *rare* percase.

percipience ▶ **noun perceptiveness**, perception, discernment, astuteness, shrewdness, insight, penetration, perspicacity, perspicaciousness, sharpness, sharp-wittedness, quick-wittedness, keen-wittedness, acuteness, acuity, discrimination, clear-sightedness, far-sightedness, intelligence, cleverness, canniness, wit, intuition, intuitiveness, alertness, judiciousness, judgement, wisdom, sagacity, sageness, understanding, sensitivity; *N. Amer. informal* savvy; *rare* sapience, arguteness.

percipient ▶ **adjective** *a percipient political commentator* **astute**, perceptive, shrewd, discerning, perspicacious, sharp, sharp-witted, acute, penetrating, discriminating, clear-sighted, clear-eyed, far-sighted, intelligent, clever, canny, intuitive, quick, alert, sensible, judicious, wise, sagacious, sage, incisive, sharp-sighted, far-seeing, open-eyed, understanding, responsive, sensitive; *informal* on the ball, smart, downy; *Brit. informal* suss; *Scottish & N. English informal* pawky; *N. Amer. informal* heads-up; *dated* long-headed; *rare* argute.
OPPOSITES obtuse, stupid.

percolate ▶ **verb 1** *water that has percolated through the soil* **filter**, drain, drip, ooze, seep, trickle, dribble, strain, leak, leach; *rare* filtrate, transude.
2 *a few of these technological marvels began to slowly percolate into the countryside* **spread**, be disseminated, filter, pass, go; penetrate, permeate, pervade, infiltrate.
3 *he put some coffee on to percolate* **brew**; *informal* perk.

percussion *See centre pages for list of* **Percussion Instruments**
▸ noun *the clattering percussion of objects striking the walls and the shutters* **crash**, bang, smash, clash, bump, thump, thwack, whack; impact, collision, striking, beating, shock, knock.

perdition ▸ noun **damnation**, eternal punishment; **hell**, hellfire, spiritual destruction, doom, ruin, ruination, condemnation, destruction, downfall.

peregrinations ▸ plural noun *his European peregrinations* **travels**, wanderings, journeys, voyages, expeditions, explorations, perambulations, odysseys, trips, treks, excursions; globetrotting, travelling, wandering, journeying, roving, roaming, wayfaring, trekking.

peremptory ▸ adjective **1** *'Just do it!' came the peremptory reply* **brusque**, imperious, high-handed, brisk, abrupt, summary, commanding, authoritative, overbearing, dogmatic, autocratic, dictatorial, bossy, domineering, arbitrary, arrogant, overweening, lordly, tyrannical, despotic, imperial, magisterial, authoritarian; emphatic, firm, insistent, imperative, positive.
2 *a peremptory order of the court* **incontrovertible**, irreversible, binding, absolute, final, conclusive, decisive, definitive, categorical, irrefutable, unconditional, unchallengeable; *Law* unappealable.

perennial ▸ adjective *the perennial fascination with crime* **everlasting**, perpetual, eternal, continuing, unending, never-ending, endless, undying, ceaseless, abiding, enduring, lasting, persisting, permanent, constant, continual, unfailing, unchanging, never-changing.

perfect ▸ adjective (stress on the first syllable) **1** *she strove to be the perfect wife* **ideal**, model, without fault, faultless, flawless, consummate, quintessential, exemplary, best, best-example, ultimate, copybook.
2 *it was a perfect holiday* **superb**, exquisite, superlative, excellent, wonderful, marvellous, beautiful, sublime, magnificent, idyllic, blissful, Utopian; unrivalled, unequalled, matchless, unparalleled, beyond compare, without equal, second to none, too good to be true, unmatched, incomparable, nonpareil, peerless, inimitable, unexcelled, unsurpassed, unsurpassable; *informal* out of this world, terrific, fantastic, fabulous, great, super, heavenly, glorious, gorgeous, divine, phenomenal, sensational, brilliant, dreamy, fab, fabby, fantabulous, brill, awesome, to die for, magic, ace; *rare* unexampled, indefectible.
3 *an E-type Jaguar in perfect condition* **flawless**, mint, as good as new, pristine, impeccable, immaculate, superb, superlative, optimum, prime, optimal, peak, excellent, faultless, as sound as a bell, unspoilt, unblemished, undamaged, spotless, unmarred, unimpaired; *informal* tip-top, A1.
4 *a perfect copy* **exact**, precise, accurate, faithful, correct, unerring, right, close, true, strict; *Brit. informal* spot on; *N. Amer. informal* on the money.
OPPOSITES imperfect, faulty, defective.
5 *the perfect Christmas present for golfers everywhere* **ideal**, just right, right, appropriate, fitting, fit, suitable, apt, made to order, tailor-made; very; *Brit. informal* spot on, just the job.
6 *she felt a perfect idiot* **absolute**, complete, total, real, out-and-out, thorough, thoroughgoing, downright, utter, sheer, consummate, unmitigated, unqualified, veritable, in every respect, unalloyed; *Brit. informal* right; *Austral./NZ informal* fair; *archaic* arrant.
▸ verb (stress on the second syllable) *he's busy perfecting his bowling technique* **improve**, make perfect, bring to perfection, better, polish (up), burnish, hone, refine, consummate, put the finishing/final touches to, ameliorate, brush up, fine-tune; *rare* meliorate.

perfection ▸ noun **1** *the satiny perfection of her skin* **flawlessness**, **excellence**, superbness, sublimity, exquisiteness, magnificence, perfectness, faultlessness, impeccability, immaculateness, exemplariness.
2 *for her, he was still perfection* **the ideal**, a paragon, the ne plus ultra, the beau idéal, a nonpareil, the crème de la crème, the last word, the ultimate, a dream; *informal* one in a million, the tops, the best/greatest thing since sliced bread, the bee's knees; *archaic* a nonsuch.
3 *the perfection of new mechanisms of economic management* **improvement**, betterment, refinement, refining, perfecting, polishing, amelioration; *rare* melioration.

perfectionist ▸ noun **purist**, stickler for perfection, idealist, pedant, precisionist, formalist; *archaic* precisian.

perfectly ▸ adverb **1** *a perfectly cooked meal | things have worked out perfectly* **superbly**, superlatively, excellently, flawlessly, faultlessly, to perfection, without fault, ideally, wonderfully, marvellously, magnificently, sublimely, admirably, inimitably, incomparably, impeccably, immaculately, exquisitely, consummately; *N. Amer.* to a fare-thee-well; *informal* like a dream, to a T, terrifically, fantastically.
OPPOSITE badly.
2 *I think we understand each other perfectly* **absolutely**, utterly, completely, altogether, entirely, wholly, totally, thoroughly, fully, quite, in every respect.
3 *you know perfectly well that is not what I meant* **very**, quite, full; *informal* damn, damned; *Brit. informal* jolly, bloody; *N. Amer. informal* darned; *archaic or N. English* right.

perfidious ▸ adjective *a perfidious lover* **treacherous**, duplicitous, deceitful, disloyal, faithless, unfaithful, traitorous, treasonous, false, untrue, double-dealing, dishonest, two-faced, untrustworthy; *rare* false-hearted, double-faced, truthless, Punic.
OPPOSITES faithful, loyal.

perfidy ▸ noun *the perfidy of her lover* **treachery**, duplicity, deceit, perfidiousness, deceitfulness, disloyalty, infidelity, faithlessness, unfaithfulness, betrayal, treason, falseness, falsity, double-dealing, dishonesty, two-facedness, untrustworthiness, breach of trust; *rare* false-heartedness, Punic faith.
OPPOSITES faithfulness, loyalty.

perforate ▸ verb *fragments of an explosive bullet perforated his intestines* **pierce**, penetrate, enter, puncture, prick, bore through, riddle, hole, make/punch/put holes in.

perforce ▸ adverb (*formal*) *amateurs, perforce, have to settle for less expensive solutions* **necessarily**, of necessity, inevitably, unavoidably, by force of circumstances, needs must; *Latin* nolens volens; *informal* like it or not.

perform ▸ verb **1** *I have my duties to perform | your agent cannot perform miracles for you* **carry out**, do, execute, discharge, bring about, bring off, accomplish, achieve, fulfil, complete, conduct, effect, dispatch, work, implement; *informal* pull off; *archaic* acquit oneself of; *rare* effectuate.
OPPOSITES neglect, omit.
2 *the car performs well at low speeds* **function**, work, operate, run, go, respond, behave, act, acquit oneself/itself.
3 *the play has already been performed in Britain* **stage**, put on, present, mount, enact, act, represent, do, produce.
4 *the band will be performing live in Hyde Park* **appear**, play, be on stage.

performance ▸ noun **1** *there are two evening performances* **show**, production, showing, presentation, entertainment, staging, act; concert, recital; *Brit.* house; *informal* gig.
2 *their performance of Mozart's concerto in E flat was beautifully judged* **rendition**, rendering, interpretation, account, playing, acting, representation, staging.
3 *the continual performance of a single task reduces a man to the level of a machine* **carrying out**, execution, discharge, conducting, conduct, effecting, accomplishment, achievement, completion, fulfilment, dispatch, implementation; *rare* effectuation.
4 *the tests assess the performance of the processor* **functioning**, working, operation, running, behaviour, capabilities, capability, capacity, power, potential.
5 *he made a great performance of telling her about it* **fuss**, fuss and bother, production, palaver, parade, scene, display, exhibition; *informal* song and dance, to-do, hoo-ha, ballyhoo, business, pantomime, hoopla; *Brit. informal* carry-on; *NZ informal* bobsy-die.

performer *See centre pages for lists of* **Actors** **Entertainers** **Musicians** **Singers**
▸ noun **actor, actress**, thespian, artiste, artist, entertainer, trouper; star, superstar; *rare* executant; (**performers**) troupe, company, cast.

perfume ▸ noun **1** *a bottle of perfume* **scent**, fragrance, eau de toilette, toilet water, eau de cologne, cologne, spray, aftershave.
2 *the heady perfume of lilacs* **smell**, odour, aroma, scent, fragrance, bouquet, redolence.

perfumed ▸ adjective *perfumed soap* **sweet-smelling**, sweet-scented, scented, fragrant, aromatic, sweet; *rare* fragranced, aromatized, perfumy.

perfunctory ▸ adjective *the guards gave a perfunctory look up and down the carriage* **cursory**, desultory; **quick**, brief, hasty, hurried, rapid, passing, fleeting, summary; token, casual, superficial, uninterested, careless, half-hearted, unthinking, sketchy, mechanical, automatic, routine, offhand, indifferent, inattentive; dismissive.
OPPOSITES careful, thorough.

perhaps ▸ adverb *perhaps he'll come tomorrow* **maybe**, for all I know, for all you know, it could be (that), it may be (that), it is possible (that), possibly, conceivably, feasibly; *N. English* happen; *literary* peradventure, perchance, mayhap, haply; *rare* percase.

peril ▸ noun *a situation fraught with peril | the perils of alcohol abuse* **danger**, jeopardy, risk, riskiness, hazard, insecurity, uncertainty, menace, threat, perilousness; pitfall, problem.
OPPOSITES safety, security.

> **CHOOSE THE RIGHT WORD**
> **peril, danger, hazard, risk**
> *See* DANGER.

perilous ▸ adjective *a perilous journey through the mountains | the economy remained in a perilous state* **dangerous**, fraught with danger, hazardous, risky, unsafe, treacherous; precarious, vulnerable, uncertain, insecure, critical, desperate, exposed, at risk, in jeopardy, in danger, touch-and-go; problematic, difficult; *informal* hairy, dicey; *N. Amer. informal* gnarly; *archaic or humorous* parlous.
OPPOSITES safe, secure.

perimeter ▸ noun **1** *the perimeter of a circle* **circumference**, outside, outer edge.

P

2 *the perimeter of the vast estate* **boundary**, border, frontier, limits, outer limits, bounds, confines, edge, margin, fringe(s), periphery, borderline, verge; *literary* bourn, marge, skirt; *rare* ambit.
OPPOSITES centre, middle, heart.

period *See centre pages for list of* **Geological Ages**
▶ noun 1 *he had long periods of depression | a six-week period* **time**, spell, interval, stretch, term, span, phase, session, bout, run, space, duration, chapter, stage; while; *Brit. informal* patch.
2 *the post-war period | the period of the French Revolution* **era**, age, epoch, time, days, years, aeon; generation, date.
3 *a double maths period* **lesson**, class, session.
4 *women who suffer from painful periods* **menstruation**, menstrual flow; *informal* the curse, monthlies, time of the month; *technical* menses; *archaic* time; *rare* flowers.
5 (*N. Amer.*) *a comma instead of a period* **full stop**, full point, point, stop.
6 *it's a hard job, period* **and that's that**, and that is the end of the matter, full stop, finis.

periodic ▶ adjective *Michael had to make periodic visits to the hospital* **regular**, periodical, at fixed intervals, recurrent, recurring, repeated, cyclical, cyclic, seasonal; occasional, infrequent, intermittent, sporadic, spasmodic, odd.

periodical ▶ noun *articles in specialist periodicals* **journal**, publication, magazine, newspaper, paper, review, digest, gazette, newsletter, organ, serial, annual, quarterly, monthly, bimonthly, fortnightly, weekly, biweekly; *informal* mag, book, glossy.
▶ adjective. *See* PERIODIC.

peripatetic ▶ adjective *his peripatetic way of life* **nomadic**, itinerant, travelling, wandering, roving, roaming, migrant, migratory, ambulatory, unsettled, vagabond, vagrant.

peripheral ▶ adjective 1 *some of the city's peripheral housing estates* **outlying**, outer, on the edge/outskirts, outermost, fringe, border, surrounding; *rare* circumferential, perimetric.
2 *fund raising by the school is peripheral to the main business of teaching | peripheral issues* **secondary**, **subsidiary**, incidental, tangential, marginal, minor, unimportant, lesser, inessential, non-essential, immaterial, superficial, ancillary, borderline; irrelevant, beside the point, of little account, extraneous.
OPPOSITES central, vital.

periphery ▶ noun *rambling estates on the periphery of the city* **edge**, outer edge, margin, fringe, boundary, border, perimeter, circumference, rim, verge, borderline; outskirts, outer limits/regions/reaches, bounds; *literary* bourn, marge, skirt; *rare* ambit.
OPPOSITES centre, middle, heart.

periphrastic ▶ adjective *the periphrastic nature of legal syntax* **circumlocutory**, circuitous, roundabout, indirect, tautological, prolix, verbose, wordy, long-winded, rambling, wandering, tortuous, diffuse, discursive; *rare* pleonastic, circumlocutionary, ambagious.

P

perish ▶ verb 1 *millions of young British soldiers perished* **die**, lose one's life, be killed, fall, expire, meet one's death, be lost, lay down one's life, breathe one's last, draw one's last breath, pass away, go the way of all flesh, give up the ghost, go to glory, meet one's maker, go to one's last resting place, cross the great divide; *informal* bite the dust, kick the bucket, cash in one's chips, croak, turn up one's toes, shuffle off this mortal coil, go the way of the dinosaurs, conk out, buy it; *Brit. informal* snuff it, peg out, pop one's clogs, hop the twig/stick; *N. Amer. informal* bite the big one, buy the farm, check out, hand in one's dinner pail; *Austral./NZ informal* go bung; *literary* exit; *archaic* decease, depart this life.
2 *must these hopes perish so soon?* **come to an end**, die (away), be destroyed, cease to exist, disappear, vanish, fade, dissolve, evaporate, melt away, pass into oblivion, wither.
OPPOSITES live, survive.
3 *the potatoes had all perished | an abandoned tyre whose rubber had perished* **go bad**, go off, spoil, rot, go mouldy, moulder, putrefy, decay, decompose; deteriorate, disintegrate, fall apart, crumble.

perishable ▶ adjective **liable to rot**, easily spoilt, decomposable, biodegradable; *rare* putrescible, decayable, putrefiable.

perjure ▶ verb
□ **perjure oneself** *Colum had tried to make her perjure herself to give him an alibi* **lie under oath**, lie, commit perjury, give false evidence/testimony, forswear oneself, be forsworn, bear false witness/testimony, swear falsely.

perjury ▶ noun *the jury found him guilty of theft, perjury, and fraudulent trading* **lying under oath**, violation of an oath, giving false evidence/testimony, bearing false witness/testimony, forswearing oneself, making false statements, wilful falsehood; mendacity, mendaciousness.

perk[1] ▶ verb
□ **perk up** *as he thought about the evening ahead he perked up slightly | the economy has been slow to perk up* **cheer up**, brighten (up), become more cheerful, become livelier, feel happier, take heart, be heartened, liven up, revive; improve, get better, recover, rally, take a turn for the better, look up, pick up, bounce back, be on the mend; *informal* buck up.

□ **perk someone/something up** *you look as though you could do with something to perk you up* **cheer up**, liven up, brighten up, make more cheerful/lively, make happier, raise someone's spirits, give someone heart, give someone a boost/lift, revitalize, invigorate, energize, enliven, ginger up, put new life/heart into, add some zest to, put some spark into, rejuvenate, refresh, vitalize, vivify, wake up; *informal* buck up, pep up; *rare* inspirit.

perk[2] ▶ noun *your contract may offer a variety of perks, such as private health care* **fringe benefit**, additional benefit, benefit, advantage, bonus, dividend, extra, plus, premium, consideration, reward; *N. Amer.* lagniappe; *informal* freebie; *Brit. informal* golden hello; *formal* perquisite; *rare* appanage.

perky ▶ adjective *I felt much more perky after I put the phone down* **cheerful**, lively, vivacious, animated, bubbly, effervescent, bouncy, bouncing, spirited, high-spirited, in high spirits, cheery, merry, buoyant, ebullient, exuberant, jaunty, frisky, sprightly, spry, bright, sunny, jolly, full of the joys of spring, sparkly, pert; *informal* full of beans, bright-eyed and bushy-tailed, chirpy, chipper; *N. Amer. informal* sassy, saucy, peppy; *dated* gay; *archaic* perk, as merry/lively as a grig, wick.

permanence ▶ noun *our craving for some sense of permanence in a rapidly changing world* **stability**, durability, persistence, permanency, fixity, fixedness, changelessness, immutability, endurance, dependability, constancy, continuance, continuity, immortality, indestructibility, perpetuity, endlessness; *rare* lastingness, everlastingness, eternalness, eternality, perdurability, perenniality, imperishability, inalterability, unchangeableness, unchangeability.

permanent ▶ adjective 1 *a permanent ban on the dumping of nuclear waste at sea | permanent brain damage* **lasting**, enduring, indefinite, continuing, perpetual, everlasting, eternal, abiding, constant, persistent, irreparable, irreversible, lifelong, indissoluble, indelible, standing, perennial, unending, endless, never-ending, immutable, unchangeable, unalterable, invariable, unchanging, changeless, undying, imperishable, indestructible, ineradicable; *rare* perdurable.
2 *a permanent job* **long-term**, long-lasting, lasting, stable, fixed, established, sound, secure, solid, firm, continuing, durable.
OPPOSITES temporary, fleeting, ephemeral.

permanently ▶ adverb 1 *the attack left her permanently disabled* **for all time**, forever, for good, for always, for good and all, for ever and ever, (for) evermore, in perpetuity, lastingly, indelibly, immutably, inalterably, invariably, until the end of time, everlastingly, enduringly, abidingly; *N. Amer.* forevermore; *informal* for keeps, until the cows come home, until hell freezes over, until doomsday, until kingdom come; *archaic* for aye.
OPPOSITE temporarily.
2 *I was permanently hungry* **continually**, constantly, perpetually, perennially, always, forever, ever, invariably, eternally, persistently.

permeable ▶ adjective **porous**, pervious, penetrable, spongy, absorbent, absorptive.
OPPOSITES impermeable, watertight.

permeate ▶ verb 1 *the delicious smell emanating from the kitchen permeated the entire flat* **pervade**, spread through, fill, filter through, diffuse through, imbue, penetrate, pass through, percolate through, perfuse, extend throughout, be disseminated through, flow through, charge, suffuse, run through, steep, impregnate, inform, infiltrate.
2 *these resins are able to permeate partly decayed timber* **soak through**, **penetrate**, seep through, saturate, percolate through, leach through, pass through, spread through.

permissible ▶ adjective *permissible levels of atmospheric pollution* **permitted**, allowable, allowed, acceptable, legal, lawful, legitimate, admissible, licit, authorized, sanctioned, within accepted bounds, tolerated, tolerable, proper, all right, in order; excusable, pardonable, venial; *informal* legit, OK.
OPPOSITES forbidden, unacceptable.

permission ▶ noun *you must get permission from your manager for all absences* **authorization**, consent, leave, authority, sanction, licence, dispensation, assent, acquiescence, agreement, approval, seal of approval, approbation, endorsement, blessing, imprimatur, clearance, acceptance, allowance, tolerance, sufferance, empowerment, freedom, liberty; *informal* the go-ahead, the thumbs up, the OK, the green light, say-so; *rare* permit. *See 'Choose the Right Word' below.*

permissive ▶ adjective *the permissive society of the 1960s* **liberal**, broad-minded, open-minded, non-restrictive, free, free and easy, easy-going, live-and-let-live, latitudinarian, laissez-faire, libertarian, unprescriptive, unrestricted, tolerant, forbearing, indulgent, lenient; overindulgent, lax, soft.
OPPOSITES intolerant, strict.

permit ▶ verb (stress on the second syllable) *no company would permit an unqualified accountant to audit its books* **allow**, let, authorize, give someone permission/authorization/leave, sanction, grant, grant someone the right, license, empower, enable, entitle, qualify; **consent to**, assent to, give one's consent/assent to, give one's blessing to, give someone/something the nod, acquiesce in, agree to, accede to, approve of, tolerate, countenance, suffer, brook, admit of; legalize, legitimatize,

CHOOSE THE RIGHT WORD

permission, authorization, consent, leave

- **Permission** is generally given by someone wielding power by reason of position, authority, or ownership, who does not usually intend to participate in the activity for which it is sought (*they are seeking planning permission for a supermarket on the site | he has permission to leave school early*).
- Superiors within some institution or system give **authorization**, which often involves an actual delegation of authority (*authorization of credit card transactions in the UK typically takes about 3 to 5 seconds | authorization to attend courses must be obtained from the education chairman*).
- **Consent** is typically used when what is at issue is not a difference in power, but whether someone is able or allowed to make a free choice that is informed by at least some knowledge of possible alternatives and consequences (*in English law, a woman may not be given in marriage without her consent*). *Consent*, constituting agreement, has acquired two special uses in relation to the law regarding sexual intercourse and medical procedures (*the raising or lowering of the age of consent | you should not be tested without your consent, except in cases of extreme medical emergency*). *Consent* can also be used for official permission (*the absence of planning consent*).
- In legal or parliamentary contexts, **leave** denotes permission to inaugurate an official procedure (*an application for leave to appeal*). Elliptically, it is used for permission to be absent from military duty (*shore leave*) or from any job (*25 days' annual leave*).

legitimate; *informal* give the go-ahead to, give the thumbs up to, OK, give the OK to, give the green light to, say the word.
OPPOSITES ban, forbid, prohibit.
▶ **noun** (stress on the first syllable) *I need to see your permit* **authorization**, licence, pass, voucher, ticket, warrant, document, certification; passport, visa; *rare* triptyque, carnet, laissez-passer, firman.

permutation ▶ **noun** *all the possible permutations were explored* **variation**, alteration, modification, change, shift, transformation, transposition, transmutation, mutation; *Brit. informal* perm; *humorous* transmogrification.

pernicious ▶ **adjective** *a pernicious influence on society* **harmful**, damaging, destructive, injurious, hurtful, detrimental, deleterious, dangerous, adverse, inimical, unhealthy, unfavourable, bad, evil, baleful, wicked, malign, malevolent, malignant, noxious, poisonous, cancerous, corrupting, ruinous, deadly, lethal, fatal; *literary* malefic, maleficent; *archaic* pestilent, pestilential, baneful, pestiferous.
OPPOSITES beneficial, benign, favourable.

pernickety ▶ **adjective** (*informal*) **fussy**, difficult to please, difficult, finicky, over-fastidious, fastidious, over-particular, particular, faddish, finical, dainty, punctilious, hair-splitting, exacting, demanding, critical, overcritical; *informal* nit-picking, choosy, picky; *Brit. informal* faddy; *N. Amer. informal* persnickety; *archaic* nice, overnice.
OPPOSITES easy-going, laid-back.

peroration ▶ **noun 1** *the blazing peroration with which the speech ended* **closing remarks**, conclusion, ending, close, final section, summation, summing-up, recapitulation, reiteration; *informal* recap, recapping.
2 *a perfectly dreadful hour-long peroration* **speech**, lecture, talk, address, oration, sermon, disquisition, discourse, declamation, harangue, diatribe; *informal* spiel.

perpendicular ▶ **adjective 1** *the shadows of the perpendicular stones lay parallel to one another* **upright**, vertical, erect, plumb, straight (up and down), on end, standing, upended.
OPPOSITE horizontal.
2 *lines perpendicular to each other* **at right angles**, at 90 degrees, square.
3 *the perpendicular hillside* **steep**, sheer, precipitous, abrupt, bluff, vertiginous; *rare* scarped, acclivitous, declivitous.

perpetrate ▶ **verb** *right-wing elements perpetrated a series of attacks and assaults* **commit**, carry out, perform, execute, do, effect, bring about, be guilty of, be to blame for, be responsible for, accomplish, inflict, wreak; *informal* pull off, pull; *rare* effectuate.

perpetual ▶ **adjective 1** *deep caves in perpetual darkness* **everlasting**, never-ending, eternal, permanent, unending, endless, without end, lasting, long-lasting, constant, abiding, enduring, perennial, timeless, ageless, deathless, undying, immortal; unfailing, unchanging, never-changing, changeless, unvarying, unfading, invariable, immutable, indissoluble, indestructible, imperishable; *rare* sempiternal, perdurable.
OPPOSITES transitory, temporary.
2 *they lived in a perpetual state of fear* **constant**, permanent, uninterrupted, continuous, unremitting, unending, unceasing, persistent, unbroken.
OPPOSITE intermittent.
3 *Clara could recall her mother's perpetual nagging at her father* **interminable**, incessant, ceaseless, endless, without respite, relentless, unrelenting, persistent, frequent, continual, continuous, non-stop, never-ending, recurrent, repeated, unremitting, sustained, round-the-clock, habitual, chronic, unabating; *informal* eternal.

perpetuate ▶ **verb** *a monument to perpetuate the memory of those killed in the war* **keep alive**, keep going, keep in existence, preserve, conserve, sustain, maintain, continue, extend, carry on, keep up, cause to continue, prolong; immortalize, commemorate, memorialize, eternalize; *literary* eternize.

perpetuity ▶ **noun**
□ **in perpetuity** *the complete archive will be preserved in perpetuity as a unified collection* **forever**, permanently, for always, for good, for good and all, perpetually, (for) evermore, for ever and ever, for all (future) time, until the end of time, eternally, for eternity, everlastingly; *N. Amer.* forevermore; *informal* for keeps, until hell freezes over, until doomsday; *archaic* for aye.

perplex ▶ **verb 1** *she was perplexed by her husband's moodiness* **puzzle**, baffle, mystify, bemuse, bewilder, confound, confuse, nonplus, disconcert, dumbfound, throw, throw/catch someone off balance, get, exercise, worry, befuddle, fuddle, addle, fog; *informal* flummox, be all Greek to, discombobulate, stump, bamboozle, floor, beat, faze, make someone scratch their head, fox; *archaic* wilder, distract, gravel, maze, pose, cause to be at a stand.
2 (*dated*) *it is possible to perplex the question* **complicate**, make complicated/complex, confuse, make obscure/unclear, obscure, obfuscate, cloud, befog, blur, muddle, mix up; muddy the waters; *rare* ravel.

CHOOSE THE RIGHT WORD

perplex, puzzle, mystify, baffle

See PUZZLE.

perplexed ▶ **adjective** *her perplexed expression* **puzzled**, baffled, mystified, bemused, bewildered, confused, nonplussed, disconcerted, dumbfounded, worried, at a loss, at sea, befuddled, fuddled, addled; *informal* flummoxed, bamboozled, discombobulated, stumped, fazed, beaten; *Canadian & Austral./NZ informal* bushed; *archaic* wildered, distracted, mazed.

perplexing ▶ **adjective** **puzzling**, baffling, mystifying, mysterious, bewildering, confusing, disconcerting, worrying, unaccountable, difficult to understand, inexplicable, impenetrable, unfathomable, paradoxical, peculiar, funny, strange, weird, odd, beyond one; complex, complicated, difficult, hard, taxing, knotty, thorny, ticklish, involved, intricate, convoluted, labyrinthine, Byzantine; *informal* spiny, mind-bending; *archaic* wildering.

perplexity ▶ **noun 1** *he scratched his head in perplexity* **confusion**, bewilderment, puzzlement, bafflement, incomprehension, lack of comprehension, mystification, bemusement, befuddlement; quandary, nonplus; *informal* bamboozlement, discombobulation; *rare* disconcertion, disconcertment.
2 *the perplexities of international relations* **complexity**, complication, intricacy, problem, difficulty, dilemma, mystery, puzzle, enigma, paradox, obscurity; obfuscation.

perquisite ▶ **noun** (*formal*). *See* PERK[2].

per se ▶ **adverb** *possessing a knife was not per se an unlawful act* **in itself**, of itself, by itself, as such, intrinsically; by its very nature, in essence, by definition, essentially.

persecute ▶ **verb 1** *no one should be persecuted for their religious beliefs* **oppress**, abuse, victimize, ill-treat, mistreat, maltreat, discriminate against, punish, inflict pain/suffering on, tyrannize, afflict, torment, torture, martyr.
2 *she complained of being persecuted by the press* **harass**, hound, plague, badger, harry, bait, intimidate, pick on, trouble, molest, tease, pester, bother, worry, annoy, bedevil, bully, victimize, terrorize; *N. Amer.* devil; *informal* hassle, give someone a hard time, get on someone's back, make it/things hot for someone, get/stick the knife into; *Austral. informal* heavy; *US black slang* vamp on.

persecution ▶ **noun 1** *victims of religious persecution* **oppression**, victimization, maltreatment, ill-treatment, mistreatment, abuse, ill-usage, discrimination, tyranny, tyrannization, punishment, torment, torture; pogrom; *informal* witch hunt; *N. Amer. informal* red-baiting.
2 *the persecution I endured at school got worse as I got older* **harassment**, hounding, harrying, badgering, teasing, bullying, molestation.

perseverance ▶ **noun** *medicine is a field which requires dedication and perseverance* **persistence**, tenacity, determination, resolve, resolution, resoluteness, staying power, purposefulness, firmness of purpose; patience, endurance, application, diligence, sedulousness, dedication, commitment, doggedness, pertinacity, assiduity, assiduousness, steadfastness, tirelessness, indefatigability, stamina; intransigence, obstinacy; *German* Sitzfleisch; *informal* stickability; *N. Amer. informal* stick-to-it-iveness; *archaic* continuance; *rare* perseveration.

persevere ▶ **verb** *she always perseveres in spite of discouraging setbacks* **persist**, continue, carry on, go on, keep on, keep going, not give up,

P

struggle on, hammer away, be persistent, be determined, see/follow something through, keep at it, show determination, press on/ahead, stay with something, not take no for an answer, be tenacious, be pertinacious, be patient, stand one's ground, stand fast/firm, hold on, hold out, go the distance, stay the course, plod on, plough on, grind away, stop at nothing, leave no stone unturned; *informal* soldier on, hang on, plug away, peg away, stick to one's guns, stick at it, stick it out, hang in there, bash on.
OPPOSITES give up, stop, quit.

persist ▶ verb **1** *Corbett persisted with his questioning* **persevere**, continue, carry on, go on, keep at it, keep on, keep going, keep it up, not give up, be persistent, be determined, see/follow something through, show determination, press on/ahead, plod on, plough on, stay with something, not take no for an answer; be tenacious, be pertinacious, insist, be patient, be diligent, stand one's ground, stand fast/firm, hold on, hold out, go the distance, stay the course, grind away, struggle on, hammer away, stop at nothing, leave no stone unturned; *informal* plug away, peg away, stick at it, soldier on, hang on, stick to one's guns, stick it out, hang in there, bash on.
OPPOSITES abandon, stop.
2 *if dry weather persists, water the lawn thoroughly* **continue**, hold, carry on, last, keep on, keep up, remain, linger, stay, endure, survive.

persistence ▶ noun *he had risen to his present position by dint of hard work and sheer persistence* **perseverance**, tenacity, determination, resolve, resolution, resoluteness, staying power, purposefulness, firmness of purpose, patience, endurance, application, diligence, sedulousness, dedication, commitment, doggedness, persistency, pertinacity, assiduity, assiduousness, steadfastness, tirelessness, indefatigability, stamina; intransigence, obstinacy; *German* Sitzfleisch; *informal* stickability; *N. Amer. informal* stick-to-it-iveness; *archaic* continuance; *rare* perseveration.

persistent ▶ adjective **1** *he's a very persistent man* **tenacious**, persevering, determined, resolute, purposeful, dogged, single-minded, tireless, indefatigable, pertinacious, patient, diligent, assiduous, sedulous, unflagging, untiring, unwavering, insistent, importunate, relentless, unrelenting; stubborn, intransigent, obstinate, obdurate.
OPPOSITE irresolute.
2 *persistent rain will affect many areas* **continuing**, constant, continual, continuous, non-stop, lasting, never-ending, steady, uninterrupted, unbroken, interminable, incessant, unceasing, endless, unending, perpetual, unremitting, unrelenting, relentless, unrelieved, sustained.
OPPOSITES intermittent, occasional.
3 *a persistent cough* **chronic**, permanent, lingering, nagging, frequent, repeated, habitual.

person ▶ noun *you were probably the last person to see Glynn alive | he's an aggressive person* **human being**, individual, man/woman, human, being, living soul, soul, mortal, creature; figure, personage; *informal* character, type, sort, beggar, cookie, customer; *Brit. informal* bod; *Austral. informal* bastard; *informal, dated* body, dog, cove; *Brit. vulgar slang* sod, bugger; *archaic* wight.
□ **in person** *the Queen was unable to be there in person* **physically**, in the flesh, personally, bodily, actually; oneself; *Latin* in propria persona; *informal* as large as life; *archaic* in one's own person.

WORD LINKS
killing of a person **homicide**

persona ▶ noun *his brash public persona is a facade for a very vulnerable man* **image**, face, public face, character, personality, identity, self, front, facade, mask, guise, exterior, role, part.

personable ▶ adjective *a personable young man* **pleasant**, agreeable, likeable, nice, amiable, affable, charming, congenial, genial, good-natured, engaging, pleasing; attractive, presentable, good-looking, nice-looking, pretty, appealing; *Scottish* couthy; *Scottish & N. English* bonny, canny; *dated* taking; *archaic* comely.
OPPOSITES unpleasant, disagreeable, unattractive.

personage ▶ noun *a succession of Hollywood personages* **important person**, VIP, luminary, celebrity, personality, name, famous name, household name, public figure, star, mogul, leading light, dignitary, notable, notability, person of note, worthy, panjandrum; person; *informal* celeb, somebody, big shot, big noise, big gun, hotshot, big cheese, bigwig, big fish; *Brit. informal* nob; *N. Amer. informal* big wheel, kahuna, macher, high muckamuck, high muckety-muck.

personal ▶ adjective **1** *a highly personal style* **distinctive**, characteristic, unique, individual, one's own, particular, private, peculiar, exclusive, idiosyncratic, individualized, personalized; *rare* especial.
OPPOSITES public, general.
2 *the President made personal campaign appearances* **in person**, in the flesh, actual, live, physical.
3 *our manager will give personal attention to your enquiry* **individual**, particular, special, in person.
4 *I'm sick of you prying into my personal life!* **private**, confidential, one's own business, intimate, secret.
5 *I count him as a personal friend* **intimate**, close, dear, great, bosom.
6 *they have personal knowledge of the situation* **direct**, empirical, first-hand, immediate, experiential.
7 *how dare you make personal remarks!* **derogatory**, disparaging, belittling, insulting, critical, rude, slighting, disrespectful, offensive, pejorative.

personal or personnel?
Despite their similar spelling, these words are quite different in meaning. The adjective **personal** denotes things relating or belonging to an individual (*personal belongings should be clearly marked*). One's *personal life* is private; the expression generally denotes a person's emotions and relationships as distinct from their career. **Personnel**, on the other hand, is a noun denoting the staff employed by an organization (*no major salary increases for personnel are likely*).

personality ▶ noun **1** *her cheerful and vibrant personality* **character**, nature, disposition, temperament, make-up, persona, psyche, identity.
2 *she's always had loads of personality* **charisma**, magnetism, strength of personality, force of personality, character, powers of attraction, charm, presence, individuality, attractiveness.
3 *an official opening by a famous personality* **celebrity**, VIP, star, superstar, name, famous name, household name, big name, somebody, leading light, notable, personage, luminary, notability, worthy; *informal* celeb, televisionary.

personalize ▶ verb **1** *all these products can be personalized to the client's exact requirements* **customize**, individualize, give a personal touch to, make distinctive, make to order.
2 *attempts to personalize God* **personify**, humanize, anthropomorphize.

personally ▶ adverb **1** *I will deal personally with any queries* **in person**, oneself.
2 *personally, I think he made a very sensible move* **for my (own) part**, for myself, according to my way of thinking, to my mind, in my estimation, as far as I am concerned, in my (own) view/opinion, from my own point of view, from where I stand, from my standpoint, as I see it, if you ask me, for my money, in my book; privately.
□ **take something personally** *don't take it personally if they turn you down* **take something as an insult**, regard something as a slight, take something amiss, take offence at, be offended by; **be upset**, be aggrieved, be affronted, take umbrage, take exception, be indignant, feel insulted, feel hurt.

personification ▶ noun *he was the very personification of British pluck and diplomacy* **embodiment**, incarnation, epitome, quintessence, essence, type, symbol, soul, picture, model, symbolization, exemplification, exemplar, image, representation, likeness, manifestation; *rare* avatar.

personify ▶ verb **1** *in the poem, the oak trees are personified* **humanize**, anthropomorphize, personalize.
2 *you personify every foreigner's image of the perfect English gentleman* **epitomize**, embody, be the embodiment/incarnation of, typify, exemplify, represent, symbolize, stand for, give human form/shape to, body forth, incarnate, be representative of, encapsulate, manifest; *rare* image.

personnel ▶ noun *sales personnel* **staff**, employees, workforce, workers, labour force, manpower, human resources, people, men and women; crew, team, force, organization; *informal* liveware.

personnel or personal?
See PERSONAL.

perspective ▶ noun **1** *her perspective on everything had been changing* **outlook**, view, viewpoint, point of view, standpoint, position, stand, stance, angle, slant, attitude, frame of mind, frame of reference, approach, way of looking/thinking, vantage point, interpretation.
2 *a perspective of the whole valley* **view**, vista, panorama, prospect, bird's-eye view, sweep, outlook, aspect; *archaic* lookout.

perspicacious ▶ adjective *his more perspicacious advisers recommended caution* **discerning**, shrewd, perceptive, astute, penetrating, observant, percipient, sharp-witted, sharp, quick, quick-witted, keen-witted, alert, clear-sighted, sharp-sighted, clear-eyed, far-sighted, far-seeing, acute, clever, canny, intelligent, insightful, judicious, wise, sagacious, sage, sensitive, intuitive, understanding, open-eyed, aware, thinking, discriminating; *informal* on the ball, smart, downy; *Brit. informal* suss; *N. Amer. informal* heads-up; *rare* sapient, long-headed, argute.
OPPOSITES inattentive, dull, stupid.

perspicacity ▶ noun *Adam was surprised at the perspicacity of Mary's comments* **perceptiveness**, shrewdness, astuteness, discernment, perception, penetration, percipience, perspicaciousness, sharpness, sharp-wittedness, quick-wittedness, keen-wittedness, clear-sightedness, sharp-sightedness, far-sightedness, acuteness, acuity, cleverness, canniness, intelligence, insight, wit, judiciousness, sound judgement, acumen, sagacity, wisdom, sageness, sensitivity, intuition, intuitiveness, understanding, discrimination, keenness; *informal* smartness; *N. Amer. informal* smarts; *rare* sapience, arguteness.

perspicuous ▸ adjective *a detailed and perspicuous explanation* **clear**, **lucid**, crystal clear, limpid, pellucid, unambiguous, plain, understandable, transparent, comprehensible, intelligible, clearly expressed; *rare* luminous, luculent.

perspiration ▸ noun **sweat**, moisture, dampness, wetness; a lather; sweating; *informal* a muck sweat; *technical* diaphoresis, hidrosis.

perspire ▸ verb **sweat**, be dripping/pouring with sweat, glow, be damp, be wet, break out in a sweat; *informal* be in a muck sweat; *rare* sudate.

persuadable ▸ adjective **easily persuaded**, amenable, adaptable, accommodating, cooperative, malleable, pliable, compliant, flexible, acquiescent, tractable, pliant, yielding, biddable, complaisant, like putty in one's hands, impressionable, manageable, manipulable, influenceable, suggestible, susceptible; *rare* persuasible, suasible, convincible, susceptive.

persuade ▸ verb **1** *he tried to persuade her to come with him* **prevail on**, talk someone into, coax, convince, make, get, press someone into, induce, win someone over, bring someone round, argue someone into, pressure someone into, pressurize someone into, coerce, influence, sway, prompt, inveigle, entice, tempt, lure, cajole, wheedle someone into, get round, blarney, prod someone into, reason someone into; *Law* procure; *informal* sweet-talk, smooth-talk, soft-soap, twist someone's arm.
OPPOSITES dissuade, discourage, deter.
2 *shortage of money persuaded them to abandon the scheme* **cause**, lead, move, dispose, incline, motivate, induce.

CHOOSE THE RIGHT WORD

persuade, convince, induce

See CONVINCE.

persuasion ▸ noun **1** *Monica needed plenty of persuasion before she actually left* **coaxing**, persuading, coercion, inducement, convincing, blandishment, encouragement, urging, prompting, inveiglement, temptation, cajolery, enticement, wheedling, pressure, moral pressure; *informal* sweet-talking, smooth-talking, soft-soaping, arm-twisting; *rare* suasion.
2 *varying political and religious persuasions* **group**, grouping, sect, denomination, party, camp, side, faction, religion, cult, affiliation, school of thought, belief, creed, credo, faith, philosophy.
3 *she entertained a strong persuasion that her brother would one day return* **belief**, opinion, conviction, faith, certainty, certitude, view.

persuasive ▸ adjective *a persuasive argument | he was so persuasive* **convincing**, effective, cogent, compelling, potent, forceful, eloquent, impressive, weighty, influential, sound, valid, powerful, strong, effectual, efficacious, winning, telling, plausible, credible; silky, smooth-tongued, silver-tongued, slick, glib, not taking no for an answer; *informal* smooth-talking; *rare* suasive, assuasive, suasory.
OPPOSITES unconvincing, weak.

pert ▸ adjective **1** *a pert little hat with a feather* **jaunty**, neat, trim, stylish, smart, spruce, perky, rakish; *informal* natty; *N. Amer.* saucy.
2 *a young girl with dark hair and a pert manner* **impudent**, impertinent, cheeky, irreverent, forward, insolent, disrespectful, flippant, familiar, presumptuous, audacious, bold, bold as brass, brazen, cocky, out of line, shameless; *informal* fresh, flip, lippy, mouthy, smart-arsed; *Brit. informal* saucy; *N. Amer. informal* sassy, nervy, smart-assed; *archaic* malapert; *rare* tossy.

pertain ▸ verb **1** *developments pertaining to the economy* **concern**, relate to, be related to, be connected with, be relevant to, have relevance to, apply to, be pertinent to, have reference to, refer to, have a bearing on, appertain to, bear on, affect, involve, cover, touch; *archaic* regard.
2 *the shop premises and stock and all assets pertaining to the business* **belong to**, be a part of, be an adjunct of, go along with, be included in.
3 *salaries which are much lower than those that pertain in Western Europe* **exist**, be the order of the day, obtain, be in effect, be the case, be prevalent, prevail, be current, be established.

pertinacious ▸ adjective *she was very pertinacious in her questions* **determined**, tenacious, persistent, persevering, assiduous, purposeful, resolute, dogged, indefatigable, insistent, single-minded, unrelenting, relentless, implacable, uncompromising, unyielding, tireless, unshakeable, importunate, stubborn, stubborn as a mule, mulish, obstinate, obdurate, strong-willed, headstrong, inflexible, unbending, intransigent, intractable, pig-headed, bull-headed, stiff-necked, with one's toes/feet dug in, wilful, refractory, contrary, perverse; *Brit. informal* bloody-minded; *rare* indurate.
OPPOSITES irresolute, tentative.

pertinent ▸ adjective *she asked me a lot of very pertinent questions* **relevant**, to the point, apposite, appropriate, suitable, fitting, fit, apt, applicable, material, germane, to the purpose, apropos; *Latin* ad rem; *rare* appurtenant.
OPPOSITES irrelevant, inappropriate.

pertness ▸ noun *a Liverpool-born lass renowned for pertness* **impudence**, impertinence, cheek, cheekiness, sauciness, effrontery, irreverence, insolence, disrespect, disrespectfulness, flippancy, presumption, presumptuousness, audacity, audaciousness, boldness, brazenness, forwardness, cockiness, shamelessness; *informal* mouth, neck, brass neck, nerve; *Brit. informal* sauce; *Scottish informal* snash; *N. Amer. informal* sassiness, sass, chutzpah, a smart mouth; *archaic* malapertness; *rare* procacity.

perturb ▸ verb *David's appearance perturbed his parents* **worry**, upset, unsettle, disturb, concern, trouble, make anxious, make uneasy, make fretful, disquiet; discompose, disconcert, discomfit, unnerve, alarm, bother, distress, dismay, gnaw at, agitate, fluster, ruffle, discountenance, exercise; *informal* rattle, faze; *archaic* pother.
OPPOSITE reassure.

perturbed ▸ adjective *she didn't seem perturbed at the noises around her* **upset**, worried, unsettled, disturbed, concerned, troubled, anxious, ill at ease, uneasy, fretful, disquieted; disconcerted, discomposed, unnerved, alarmed, bothered, distressed, dismayed, apprehensive, nervous, restless, agitated, flustered, ruffled, shaken, flurried, discountenanced, uncomfortable; *informal* twitchy, rattled, fazed, discombobulated; *N. Amer. informal* antsy; *rare* unquiet.
OPPOSITES unperturbed, calm, composed.

perusal ▸ noun *I continued my perusal of the instructions* **reading**, scrutiny, inspection, examination, study, scanning, review; read, look, scan, glance, skim, browse.

peruse ▸ verb *as he sipped his coffee, he perused the newspaper* **read**, study, scrutinize, inspect, examine, wade through, look through; browse through, leaf through, scan, run one's eye over, glance through, flick through, skim through, thumb through, dip into; *archaic* con.

pervade ▸ verb *a strong smell of floor polish pervaded the house | her whole being seemed pervaded by a dreamy languor* **spread through**, permeate, fill, suffuse, be diffused through, diffuse through, imbue, penetrate, pass through, filter through, percolate through, infuse, perfuse, extend throughout, be disseminated through, flow through, run through; charge, steep, saturate, impregnate, inform, infiltrate, invade, affect.

pervasive ▸ adjective *a pervasive smell of staleness | ageism is pervasive in our society* **prevalent**, penetrating, pervading, permeating, extensive, ubiquitous, omnipresent, present everywhere, rife, widespread, general, common, universal, pandemic, epidemic, endemic, inescapable, insidious; immanent; *rare* permeative, suffusive, permeant.

perverse ▸ adjective **1** *he is being deliberately perverse* **awkward**, contrary, difficult, unreasonable, uncooperative, unhelpful, obstructive, disobliging, unaccommodating, troublesome, tiresome, annoying, vexatious, obstreperous, disobedient, unmanageable, uncontrollable, recalcitrant, refractory, rebellious; wilful, headstrong, self-willed, capricious, wayward, cross-grained, stubborn, obstinate, obdurate, pertinacious, mulish, pig-headed, bull-headed, intractable, intransigent, inflexible; *Scottish* thrawn; *informal* cussed; *Brit. informal* **bloody-minded**, bolshie, stroppy; *N. Amer. informal* balky; *archaic* froward, contumacious; *rare* contrarious.
OPPOSITES accommodating, cooperative.
2 *juries often come up with a verdict that is manifestly perverse* **illogical**, irrational, unreasonable, contradictory, wrong, wrong-headed, incorrect, irregular, inappropriate, unorthodox.
OPPOSITE reasonable.
3 *an evil life dedicated to perverse pleasure* **perverted**, depraved, unnatural, abnormal, deviant, degenerate, immoral, warped, twisted, corrupt; wicked, base, evil; *informal* kinky, sick, pervy, sicko.

perversion ▸ noun **1** *a twisted perversion of the truth* **distortion**, misrepresentation, falsification, travesty, misinterpretation, misconstruction, twisting, corruption, subversion, misuse, misapplication, debasement.
2 *his book revolutionized ideas about sexual perversion* **deviance**, deviancy, deviation; unnaturalness, corruption, depravity, degeneracy, debauchery, vice, wickedness, immorality, aberration, abnormality, perversity, irregularity; *informal* kinkiness.

perversity ▸ noun **1** *some streak of perversity made her refuse his offer* **contrariness**, perverseness, awkwardness, unreasonableness, difficultness, waywardness, capriciousness, wilfulness, refractoriness, stubbornness, obstinacy, obduracy, mulishness, pig-headedness; *informal* cussedness; *Brit. informal* **bloody-mindedness**; *archaic* frowardness.
2 *the perversity of the decision* **unreasonableness**, irrationality, illogicality, wrong-headedness, irregularity, inappropriateness.

pervert ▸ verb (stress on the second syllable) **1** *people who attempt to pervert the rules for their own gain* **distort**, warp, corrupt, subvert, twist, bend, abuse, divert, deflect, misapply, misuse, misrepresent, misinterpret, misconstrue, falsify, garble.
2 *potentially great men can be perverted and destroyed by power* **corrupt**, lead astray, deprave, make degenerate, debauch, debase, warp, vitiate, pollute, poison, contaminate; *archaic* demoralize.
▸ noun (stress on the first syllable) *a sexual pervert* **deviant**, degenerate, debauchee, perverted person, depraved person; *informal* perv, perve, dirty old man, sicko, weirdo.

P

perverted ▶ adjective *it's impossible to understand the perverted mentality of someone who could do such a thing* **unnatural, deviant**, warped, corrupt, twisted, abnormal, unhealthy, depraved, perverse, aberrant, distorted, immoral, corrupted, debauched, debased, degenerate, sadistic, evil, wicked, vile, amoral, rotten, wrong, bad; informal sick, kinky, pervy, sicko.

pessimism ▶ noun *formerly he had been prone to pessimism, full of gloomy predictions about the future* **defeatism**, negative thinking, negativity, expecting the worst, doom and gloom, gloom, gloominess; **hopelessness**, lack of hope, cynicism, fatalism, depression, despair, melancholy, despondency, dejection, angst, distrust, doubt; German Weltschmerz; informal looking on the black side.

pessimist ▶ noun *pessimists attempted to paint a picture of a nation in decline* **defeatist**, fatalist, alarmist, prophet of doom, cynic, doomsayer, doomster, gloom-monger, doom-monger, doomwatcher, Cassandra; sceptic, doubter, doubting Thomas; misery, killjoy, worrier, Job's comforter; informal doom and gloom merchant, wet blanket; N. Amer. informal gloomy Gus.
OPPOSITE optimist.

pessimistic ▶ adjective *a pessimistic outlook on life* **gloomy**, negative, defeatist, downbeat, gloom-ridden, cynical, bleak, fatalistic, dark, black, despairing, despondent, depressed, dejected, demoralized, hopeless, melancholy, glum, lugubrious, suspicious, distrustful, doubting, alarmist; informal given to looking on the black side.
OPPOSITES optimistic, hopeful, cheerful.

pest ▶ noun *that child is a real pest* **nuisance**, bother, annoyance, irritation, irritant, thorn in one's flesh/side, vexation, trial, the bane of one's life, menace, curse, problem, trouble, worry, inconvenience, bore, gadfly; informal pain, pain in the neck, aggravation, headache, cuss; Scottish informal nyaff, skelf; N. Amer. informal nudnik, pain in the butt; Austral./NZ informal nark; Brit. informal, dated blighter, blister; Brit. vulgar slang pain in the arse.

pester ▶ verb *I've been pestered by reporters for days* **badger**, hound, annoy, bother, harass, trouble, plague, irritate, irk, chivvy, keep after; persecute, torment, molest, bedevil, besiege, harry, worry, beleaguer, nag, dun, importune; informal hassle, bug, aggravate, give someone a hard time, get on someone's nerves, drive round the bend, drive up the wall, get in someone's hair, get up someone's nose, get at, get on someone's back; N. English mither; N. Amer. informal ride, devil.

pestilence ▶ noun *Londoners fled in time of pestilence* **plague**, bubonic plague, the Black Death; disease, contagious disease, contagion, infection, sickness, epidemic, pandemic; archaic the pest, lues.

pestilential ▶ adjective **1** *pestilential fever* **plague-like**, contagious, communicable, epidemic, pestilent, dangerous, injurious, harmful, destructive, virulent, pernicious; toxic, venomous; malign, fatal, deadly; informal catching; literary pestiferous.
2 *what a pestilential man!* **annoying**, irritating, infuriating, exasperating, maddening, troublesome, bothersome, tiresome, irksome, vexing, vexatious; informal aggravating, pesky, infernal, pestiferous, plaguy, pestilent.

P

pet[1] ▶ noun *the others teased him and called him teacher's pet* **favourite**, darling, the apple of one's eye, idol; Brit. informal blue-eyed boy/girl; N. Amer. informal fair-haired boy/girl.
▶ adjective **1** *a pet lamb* **tame**, domesticated, domestic, tamed; Brit. house-trained; N. Amer. housebroken.
2 *his pet theory* **favourite**, favoured, cherished, prized, dear to one's heart, preferred, particular, special, chosen, personal, treasured, precious.
□ **pet name affectionate name**, term of endearment, endearment, nickname, diminutive; rare hypocorism, hypocoristic.
▶ verb **1** *the cats came to be petted* **stroke**, caress, fondle, pat.
2 *an only child, she had always been petted by her parents* **pamper**, spoil, mollycoddle, coddle, cosset, baby, indulge, overindulge, dote on, wrap in cotton wool; archaic cocker.
3 *she watched the couples petting in their cars* **kiss and cuddle**, kiss, cuddle, embrace, caress; informal canoodle, neck, smooch, bill and coo; Brit. informal snog; N. Amer. informal make out, get it on, play kissy-face; informal, dated spoon.

pet[2] ▶ noun *Mum's in a pet* **bad mood**, mood, bad temper, temper, sulk, fit of the sulks, ill temper, ill humour, fit of pique, huff, tantrum; informal grump; Brit. informal paddy, strop; N. Amer. informal blowout, hissy fit; Brit. informal, dated bate, wax; archaic paddywhack, miff, the pouts.

peter ▶ verb
□ **peter out** *the economic recovery is in danger of petering out* **fizzle out**, fade (away), die away/out, dwindle, diminish, taper off, tail off, trail away/off, wane, ebb, melt away, evaporate, disappear, come to nothing, fail, fall through, come to a halt, come to an end, run out, give out; decrease, subside.

petite ▶ adjective *she was dark, petite, and sophisticated* **small**, dainty, diminutive, slight, little, tiny, elfin, delicate, small-boned; Scottish wee; informal pint-sized; Brit. informal dinky.

petition ▶ noun **1** *about 7,000 people signed a petition objecting to the scheme* **appeal**, round robin, list of signatures/protesters.
2 *a steady stream of petitions to Allah were audible* **entreaty**, supplication, plea, prayer, appeal, request, application, invocation, suit; archaic orison; rare imploration.
▶ verb *human rights activists petitioned the king to release the hunger strikers* **appeal to**, request, ask, call on, entreat, beg, implore, beseech, plead with, make a plea to, pray, apply to, solicit, press, urge, adjure, present one's suit to, importune; rare obsecrate.

petrified ▶ adjective **1** *she looked absolutely petrified* **terrified**, terror-stricken, terror-struck, horrified, horror-stricken, horror-struck, scared/frightened out of one's wits, scared witless, scared/frightened to death, aghast, appalled; paralysed, stunned, stupefied, transfixed, benumbed, frozen.
2 *the petrified remains of prehistoric animals* ossified, fossilized; rare lapidified.

petrify ▶ verb *the thought of speaking in public petrified her* **terrify**, horrify, frighten, scare, scare to death, scare someone out of their wits, scare witless, scare the living daylights out of, frighten the life out of, strike terror into, fill with fear, put the fear of God into, make someone's blood run cold, chill someone's blood, panic, throw into a panic, alarm, appal; paralyse, stun, stupefy, transfix; informal scare the pants off; Brit. informal throw into a blue funk, put the wind up; Irish informal scare the bejesus out of; archaic affright.

petrol ▶ noun **fuel**; unleaded, superunleaded, diesel; N. Amer. gasoline, gas; informal juice.

petticoat ▶ noun **slip**, underskirt, half-slip, underslip, undergarment; historical crinoline, farthing, hoop petticoat; archaic kirtle.

petty ▶ adjective **1** *a maze of petty regulations* **trivial**, trifling, minor, small, slight, unimportant, insignificant, inessential, inconsequential, inconsiderable, negligible, paltry, footling, fiddling, niggling, pettifogging, nugatory, of little account; informal piffling, piddling, penny-ante; Brit. informal twopenny-halfpenny; N. Amer. informal nickel-and-dime, picayune; N. Amer. vulgar slang chickenshit.
OPPOSITES important, serious, major.
2 *they took other forms of revenge which were no less petty* **small-minded**, narrow-minded, mean, ungenerous, grudging, shabby, spiteful.
OPPOSITES magnanimous, generous.

petulance ▶ noun **peevishness**, bad temper, ill temper, pettishness, pique, impatience, irritability, moodiness, sulkiness, snappishness, touchiness, waspishness, irascibility, tetchiness, testiness, querulousness, fractiousness, cantankerousness, grumpiness, grouchiness, crabbiness, ill humour, spleen; sullenness, surliness, sourness, churlishness, ungraciousness; N. English mardiness; informal whinginess; N. Amer. informal crankiness, a sore head.

petulant ▶ adjective *he sounded as petulant as a spoiled child* **peevish**, bad-tempered, ill-tempered, pettish, cross, impatient, irritable, moody, in a bad mood, sulky, snappish, crotchety, touchy, waspish, irascible, tetchy, testy, querulous, fractious, captious, cantankerous, grumpy, complaining, whiny, fretful, huffish, huffy, pouty, disgruntled, crabbed, crabby, ill-humoured; sullen, surly, sour, churlish, ungracious; splenetic, choleric; informal snappy, chippy, grouchy, cranky; Brit. informal ratty, narky, eggy, whingy, miffy, mumpish; N. English informal mardy; N. Amer. informal soreheaded, sorehead, peckish.
OPPOSITES good-humoured, easy-going, affable.

phantasmagorical ▶ adjective *phantasmagorical figures and landscapes* **dreamlike**, phantasmagoric, psychedelic, kaleidoscopic, surreal, unreal, illusory, visionary, hallucinatory, fantastic, fantastical, chimerical, nightmarish, Kafkaesque; ghostly, spectral, wraithlike, unearthly, other-worldly, ghastly, eerie, weird, uncanny; informal spooky; rare phantasmal, phantasmic.

phantom ▶ noun **1** *a phantom who haunts lonely roads* **ghost**, apparition, spirit, spectre, wraith, shadow; Scottish & Irish bodach; W. Indian duppy; informal spook; literary phantasm, shade, revenant, wight; rare eidolon, manes.
2 *he tried to clear the phantoms from his head and grasp reality* **figment of the imagination**, delusion, hallucination, illusion, chimera, vision, fantasy, mirage; rare phantasm.

Pharisaic ▶ adjective *a mean-spirited, Pharisaic bunch of suburbanites* **self-righteous**, sanctimonious, Pharisaical, holier-than-thou, pietistic, moralizing, priggish, self-satisfied, smug, hypocritical, insincere, Pecksniffian, canting; Scottish unco guid; informal preachy, goody-goody.

phase ▶ noun **1** *the final phase of the election campaign* **stage**, period, chapter, episode, part, step, point, time, juncture.
2 *he's going through a difficult phase* **period**, stage, time, spell; Brit. informal patch.
3 *the phases of the moon* **aspect**, shape, form, appearance, state, condition.
▶ verb
□ **phase something in introduce gradually**, incorporate by stages, begin using, ease in, start using.
□ **phase something out eliminate gradually**, withdraw/remove/replace gradually, discontinue, get rid of by stages, stop using, ease off, run down, wind down, wind up, deactivate, finish, end.

phenomenal ▸ adjective *sales growth has been nothing short of phenomenal* **exceptional**, extraordinary, remarkable, outstanding, amazing, astonishing, astounding, stunning, staggering, marvellous, magnificent, wonderful, sensational, breathtaking, miraculous, singular; incredible, unbelievable, inconceivable, unimaginable, uncommon, unheard of; unique, unparalleled, unprecedented, unusual, unusually good, too good to be true, superlative, prodigious, surpassing, rare; *informal* fantastic, fabulous, stupendous, out of this world, terrific, tremendous, brilliant, mind-boggling, mind-blowing, awesome, stellar; *literary* wondrous.
OPPOSITES ordinary, usual, run-of-the-mill.

phenomenon ▸ noun **1** *war was not a rare phenomenon in the 18th century* **occurrence**, event, happening, fact, situation, circumstance, experience, case, incident, episode, sight, appearance, thing.
2 *the band was a pop phenomenon* **marvel**, sensation, wonder, prodigy, miracle, rarity, nonpareil, curiosity, spectacle; *informal* something else, something to write home about, something to shout about; *N. Amer. informal* standout; *rare* oner.

philander ▸ verb *he had no time or inclination to philander* **womanize**, have affairs/an affair, flirt, trifle/toy/dally with someone's affections; *informal* play around, carry on, play the field, sleep around; *N. Amer. informal* fool around; *vulgar slang* screw around; *rare* be a carpet knight, coquet.

philanderer ▸ noun *everyone warned me he was a philanderer* **womanizer**, Casanova, Don Juan, Lothario, flirt, ladies' man, playboy, Romeo, seducer, rake, roué, libertine, debauchee; *informal* stud, skirt-chaser, ladykiller, wolf; *informal, dated* gay dog.

philanthropic ▸ adjective *a philanthropic desire to improve the lot of other people | a philanthropic millionaire* **charitable**, generous, benevolent, humanitarian, public-spirited, altruistic, socially concerned, magnanimous, munificent, open-handed, bountiful, liberal, ungrudging, unstinting, generous to a fault, beneficent, benignant, caring, compassionate, solicitous, unselfish, selfless, humane, kind, kind-hearted, big-hearted; *literary* bounteous; *rare* eleemosynary.
OPPOSITES selfish, mean, miserly.

philanthropist ▸ noun *the trust was founded by an American philanthropist* **benefactor**, benefactress, humanitarian, patron, patroness, donor, contributor, giver, sponsor, backer, helper, altruist, good Samaritan; do-gooder, Lady Bountiful; *archaic* almsgiver; *rare* philanthrope, Maecenas.

philanthropy ▸ noun *he acquired a considerable fortune and was noted for his philanthropy* **benevolence**, generosity, humanitarianism, public-spiritedness, altruism, social conscience, social concern, charity, charitableness, brotherly love, fellow feeling, magnanimity, munificence, liberality, largesse, open-handedness, bountifulness, beneficence, benignity, unselfishness, selflessness, humanity, kindness, kind-heartedness, big-heartedness, compassion, humaneness; patronage, sponsorship, backing, help; *historical* almsgiving; *literary* bounty, bounteousness.

philippic ▸ noun *Viscount Castlereagh was the butt of Shelley's philippic* **tirade**, diatribe, invective, denunciation, rant, polemic, broadside, harangue, verbal onslaught, reviling, railing, decrying, condemnation, brickbat(s), flak, criticism, attack, censure, lecture, berating, admonishment, admonition, reprimand, rebuke, abuse, stream of abuse, battering, stricture, tongue-lashing; denouncement, vituperation, obloquy, fulmination, vilification, castigation, reproof, reproval, upbraiding; *informal* knocking, bashing, blast; *Brit. informal* slating.

philistine ▸ noun *she was no philistine, but an artist herself* **lowbrow**, anti-intellectual, materialist, bourgeois; **boor**, ignoramus, lout, oaf, barbarian, primitive, savage, brute, yahoo, vulgarian.
▸ adjective *a philistine effort to destroy culture* **crass**, **tasteless**, uncultured, uncultivated, uneducated, untutored, unenlightened, unread, commercial, materialist, bourgeois, unsophisticated, unrefined; boorish, barbarian, barbarous, barbaric, primitive, savage, brutish, loutish, oafish, uncivilized, uncouth, vulgar, coarse, rough.

philosopher ▸ noun **thinker**, theorist, theorizer, theoretician, philosophizer, metaphysicist, metaphysician, epistemologist, dialectician, logician; speculator, hypothesizer, seeker after truth, dreamer; scholar, intellect, intellectual, learned person, sage, wise man, Solomon, guru, pundit.

philosophical ▸ adjective **1** *a philosophical question* **theoretical**, **analytical**, rational, metaphysical, logical, reasoned, esoteric, scholarly, erudite.
2 *in a philosophical mood* **thoughtful**, thinking, reflective, pensive, meditative, musing, contemplative, introspective, prayerful, cogitative, ruminative, brooding, broody, serious, studious, solemn, dreamy, dreaming; *rare* ruminant.
OPPOSITES active, practical.
3 *training officers have learnt to be philosophical about such mishaps* **calm**, composed, cool, collected, {cool, calm, and collected}, self-possessed, serene, tranquil, placid, stoical, impassive, sober, dispassionate, detached, unemotional, phlegmatic, unperturbed, imperturbable, equable, unruffled, patient, forbearing, long-suffering, tolerant, accommodating, indulgent, easy-going, even-tempered, restrained, fatalistic, unexcitable, resigned, rational, logical, realistic, practical; *informal* unflappable.
OPPOSITES emotional, upset.

philosophize ▸ verb *he paused for a while to philosophize on racial equality* **theorize**, moralize, sermonize, pontificate, preach.

philosophy *See centre pages for list of branches of* **Philosophy**
▸ noun **1** *a lecturer in philosophy* **thinking**, **reasoning**, thought, wisdom, knowledge.
2 *I'd like to see your philosophy in action* **beliefs**, credo, faith, convictions, ideology, ideas, thinking, notions, theories, doctrine, tenets, values, principles, ethics, attitude, line, view, viewpoint, outlook, world view, school of thought; *German* Weltanschauung.

phlegm ▸ noun **1** **mucus**, catarrh, mucous secretion.
2 *British phlegm and perseverance carried them through many difficult situations* **self-control**, calmness, calm, coolness, composure, sangfroid, level-headedness; **equanimity**, serenity, tranquillity, placidity, placidness, impassivity, self-possession, self-confidence, self-assurance, stolidity, stolidness, imperturbability, impassiveness, dispassionateness; *informal* cool, unflappability.

phlegmatic ▸ adjective *a phlegmatic attitude to every crisis* **self-controlled**, calm, cool, composed, {cool, calm, and collected}, cool-headed, controlled, serene, tranquil, placid, impassive, self-possessed, self-confident, self-assured, stolid, imperturbable, unruffled, poised, level-headed, dispassionate, philosophical; *informal* unflappable; *rare* equanimous.
OPPOSITES excitable, quick-tempered.

phobia *See centre pages for list of* **Phobias**
▸ noun **abnormal fear**, irrational fear, obsessive fear, fear, dread, horror, terror, dislike, hatred, loathing, detestation, distaste, aversion, antipathy, revulsion, repulsion; spectre, bugbear, bogey, nightmare, bête noire; complex, fixation, preoccupation, idée fixe, mania, neurosis, anxiety, obsession; *informal* thing, hang-up.

phone ▸ noun **1** *she spent hours on the phone* **telephone**, mobile phone, mobile, cellphone, car phone, radio-telephone, cordless phone, videophone, extension; *N. Amer.* speakerphone; *Brit. informal* blower; *Brit. rhyming slang* dog and bone.
2 *pick up the phone and dial 999* **handset**, earpiece, receiver.
3 *give me a phone sometime* **phone call**, telephone call, call, ring; *informal* buzz; *Brit. informal* tinkle, bell.
▸ verb *maybe I should phone the police* **telephone**, call, call up, give someone a call/ring, ring, ring up, get someone on the phone, get on the phone to, get, reach, dial, make/place a call (to); *informal* buzz, give someone a buzz; *Brit. informal* bell, give someone a bell/tinkle, get on the blower to; *N. Amer. informal* get someone on the horn.

phoney ▸ adjective *he gave a phoney address* **bogus**, not genuine, sham, false, fake, fraudulent, forged, feigned, counterfeit, so-called, spurious, pseudo; imitation, man-made, mock, ersatz, artificial, synthetic, manufactured, simulated, reproduction, replica, facsimile, dummy, model, toy; make-believe, pretended, contrived, affected, insincere; *informal* pretend, put-on; *Brit. informal, dated* cod.
OPPOSITES authentic, genuine.
▸ noun **1** *the doctor's a phoney* **impostor**, sham, fake, fraud, mountebank, quack, cheat, swindler, fraudster, confidence trickster, defrauder, hoaxer, bluffer, pretender, masquerader, charlatan, rogue, scoundrel; *informal* con man, con artist; *dated* confidence man.
2 *the diamond's a phoney* **counterfeit**, fake, forgery, sham, hoax, imitation, copy, reproduction, replica, facsimile, dummy, model, toy.

photocopy ▸ noun *he sent me a photocopy of the article* **reproduction**, copy, mimeograph, mimeo, facsimile, fax, duplicate; *trademark* Xerox, photostat.
▸ verb *you can photocopy the entry form* **copy**, mimeograph, mimeo, xerox, photostat, fax, duplicate, reproduce, make a Xerox of.

photograph ▸ noun *a photograph of her father* **picture**, photo, shot, snap, snapshot, likeness, image, portrait, study, print, slide, transparency, negative, positive, plate, film, bromide, frame, exposure, still, proof, enlargement; *Brit.* enprint.
▸ verb *the Princess was photographed leaving the castle* **take someone's picture/photo**, take/get a picture of, take/get a snapshot/snap of, take, snap, shoot, take/get a shot of, take a likeness of, record, film, capture/record on film/celluloid.

photographer ▸ noun lensman, paparazzo, documentarian; cameraman; *informal* snapper; *N. Amer. informal* shutterbug; *rare* photographist.

photographic ▸ adjective **1** *a photographic display* **in photographs**, pictorial, graphic; cinematic, filmic.
2 *a photographic memory* **detailed**, graphic, exact, precise, accurate, minute, faithful, lifelike, vivid, realistic, naturalistic, cinematic, filmic.

phrase ▸ noun *the man who coined the phrase 'desktop publishing'* **expression**, group of words, word group, construction, clause, locution, wording, term, turn of phrase, idiom, idiomatic expression, set phrase, phrasal idiom, phrasal verb; remark, comment, saying, utterance, witticism, tag; quotation, quote, citation; line, sentence.
▸ verb *how could I phrase the question?* **express**, put into words, put, word,

P

style, formulate, couch, frame, set forth, utter, say, tell, articulate, verbalize, communicate, convey, get/put across.

phraseology ▸ noun **wording**, choice of words, phrasing, usage, idiom, diction, parlance, words, language, vocabulary, terminology; jargon, patter, cant, -speak, dialect, vernacular, argot, patois, style, way of speaking/writing, manner of speaking/writing, style of speech/writing, mode of speech/writing; French façon de parler; informal lingo; rare idiolect.

physical ▸ adjective **1** *mental and physical well-being* **bodily**, corporeal, corporal, fleshly, in the flesh; rare somatic.
OPPOSITE mental.
2 *hard physical work* **manual**, labouring, blue-collar.
OPPOSITES clerical; intellectual.
3 *our spiritual relationship affects our physical relationship* **earthly**, worldly, terrestrial, earthbound, non-spiritual, unspiritual, material; carnal, fleshly, sensual; mortal, human, temporal; brutish, bestial, animal, base, sordid; secular, lay, mundane.
OPPOSITE spiritual.
4 *everything physical in the universe* **material**, substantial, solid, concrete, tangible, palpable, visible, real, actual.
OPPOSITES abstract, intangible.

physician *See centre pages for list of* **Doctors and Dentists**
▸ noun **doctor**, doctor of medicine, MD, medical practitioner, medical man/woman/person; Navy surgeon; informal doc, medic, medico, quack; archaic leech, sawbones.

physiognomy ▸ noun *his physiognomy was European* **face**, features, countenance, profile; expression, facial expression, look; informal mug, kisser, clock; Brit. informal mush, dial, phizog, phiz; Brit. rhyming slang boat race; Scottish & Irish informal coupon; N. Amer. informal puss, pan; formal mien; literary visage, lineaments; archaic front.

physique ▸ noun **body**, build, figure, frame, anatomy, constitution, shape, form, proportions, (physical) make-up, physical/body structure, physical development, muscles, musculature, skeleton, flesh; informal vital statistics, bod, carcass, chassis; rare soma.

pick ▸ verb **1** *he lives on a fruit farm and helps to pick apples* **harvest**, gather (in), collect, take in, pluck, pull, dig, crop, reap, bring home; literary glean, garner, cull.
2 *pick the time that suits you best* **choose**, select, pick out, single out, include, hand-pick, decide on, settle on, fix on; sift out, sort out, take, prefer, favour, opt for, plump for, vote for, elect, name, nominate, adopt, designate, assign, appoint, allot, identify, specify, mention, cite.
OPPOSITES reject, discard.
3 *Beth only* **picked at** *her food* **nibble**, peck, eat listlessly, toy with, play with, take very small bites from, push one's food around (on) one's plate, eat like a bird, show no appetite for, eat sparingly of.
4 *people were singing and picking guitars* **strum**, twang, thrum, pluck, finger.
5 *he had taught them how to pick a lock* **force open**, break open, prise open, open without a key, break into; informal jemmy, crack.
6 *she was trying to pick a fight with him* **provoke**, start, cause, incite, invite, foment, stir up, whip up, encourage, kindle, instigate, excite, prompt, bring about.

P

□ **pick someone/something off** *the soldiers were picked off by a sniper* **shoot (down)**, gun down, fire at, hit, put a bullet in; fell, bring down, take out, kill, bag, wound, injure; informal pot, zap, plug; literary slay.
□ **pick on** *why don't you pick on somebody else?* **bully**, victimize, tyrannize, torment, persecute; criticize, grumble at, discriminate against; badger, bait, goad, tease; informal get at, have it in for, have a down on, be down on, needle.
□ **pick something out 1** *it's impossible to pick out any single painting for praise* **choose**, select, pick, single out, hand-pick, decide on, settle on, fix on; sift out, sort out, take, prefer, favour, opt for, plump for, vote for, elect, name, nominate, adopt, designate, assign, appoint, allot, identify, specify, mention, cite.
2 *it was difficult to pick out anything in the torrential rain* **see**, discern, spot, distinguish, perceive, make out, detect, notice, observe, recognize, identify, catch sight of, glimpse, discover; literary espy, behold, descry.
□ **pick up 1** *the Japanese economy will soon pick up again* **improve**, get better, recover, mend, be on the road to recovery, rally, make a comeback, bounce back, perk up, look up, take a turn for the better, turn the/a corner, be given/take on a new lease of life, be on the mend, develop, make headway, progress, make progress, advance.
2 *the wind began to pick up* **get stronger**, strengthen, become more powerful, blow up.
□ **pick someone/something up 1** *bend at the knees to pick up a bulky object* **lift**, take up, raise, hoist, scoop up, gather up, seize, snatch up, grab.
□ **pick someone up 1** *be sure to pick up Kirsty from school* **fetch**, **collect**, go to get, go/come and get, call for, go/come for; give someone a lift, give someone a ride.
2 (informal) *he was picked up by the police for questioning* **arrest**, apprehend, detain, take into custody, take prisoner, seize, capture, catch, take in; informal collar, nab, run/pull in, nick, pinch, bust, nail, do, feel someone's collar.
3 (informal) *he thought of going to a nightclub and picking up a girl* strike up a casual acquaintance/relationship with, take up with; make advances to; informal get off with, pull, cop off with.
□ **pick something up 1** *not the most obvious place to pick up a bargain* **find**, discover, locate, come across, stumble across, happen on, chance on, unearth, obtain, come by, come to have, get, receive, procure; secure, take/get possession of, acquire; purchase, buy; informal get hold of, get/lay one's hands on, get one's mitts on, bag, land, net.
2 *he picked up the story in the 1950s* **begin again**, begin, take up, start again, start, resume, recommence, carry on, go on, continue.
3 *Georgiana began picking up Spanish* **learn**, get to know, acquire (a knowledge of), acquire skill in, become competent/proficient in, master; digest, imbibe, assimilate, absorb, take in; informal get the hang of.
4 *she has picked up a virus* **catch**, contract, get, become infected with, become ill with, go/come down with.
5 *he was full of gossip picked up from the ships he visited* **hear**, hear tell, find out, get to know, get wind of, be informed of, be told, learn, be made aware of, be given to understand; glean, discern, become conscious/aware of, observe, notice, perceive.
6 *we've picked up a distress signal* **receive**, detect, get, hear.
▸ noun **1** *please take your pick* **choice**, selection, option, decision; preference, favourite.
2 *the pick of the crop* **best**, finest, top, choice, choicest, prime, cream, flower, prize, treasure, pearl, gem, jewel, the jewel in the crown, the crème de la crème, elite, elect; informal the tops.

picket ▸ noun **1** *forty pickets were arrested* **striker**, **demonstrator**, protester, objector, picketer; strike picket, flying picket.
2 *they decided to organize a picket* **demonstration**, picket line, blockade, boycott; picketing, secondary picketing.
3 *a glider can be secured by tying it down with pickets* **stake**, **peg**, post, paling; upright, stanchion, pier, piling, palisade.
▸ verb *over 200 people picketed the factory* **demonstrate at**, form a picket at, man the picket line at, launch a demonstration at, protest at, form a protest group at; blockade, isolate, surround, cordon off.

pickle ▸ noun **1** *cheese and pickle sandwiches* **relish**, chutney, chow chow, piccalilli, sauerkraut; Indian achar; Japanese tsukemono.
2 *steep the vegetables in pickle* **marinade**, brine, vinegar.
3 (informal) *they got into an awful pickle* **plight**, predicament, mess, difficulty, trouble, crisis, dire/desperate straits, ticklish/tricky situation, problem, quandary, dilemma; informal tight corner, tight spot, jam, fix, stew, scrape, bind, hole, hot water, pretty/fine kettle of fish; Brit. informal spot of bother.
▸ verb *the olives are ready for pickling* **preserve**, souse, marinate, conserve; bottle, tin, can, pot.

pick-me-up ▸ noun **1** *we have grown accustomed to using tea or coffee as a pick-me-up* **tonic**, restorative, energizer, stimulant, antidepressant, refresher; informal pep pill, upper, reviver, bracer; Medicine analeptic, roborant.
2 *his winning goal was a perfect pick-me-up* **boost**, boost to the spirits, fillip, uplift, reviver, stimulant, stimulus, invigoration; informal shot in the arm.

pickpocket ▸ noun **thief**, petty thief, sneak thief; bag-snatcher, purse-snatcher; archaic cutpurse, pickpurse, pocket-picker, purse-picker, finger, dipper, reefer.

pickup ▸ noun **1** *David brought the wardrobe home in his pickup* pickup truck, utility vehicle/truck; monster truck; S. African bakkie; Austral./NZ informal ute.
2 *a pickup in the housing market* **improvement**, recovery, revival, upturn, upswing, rally, comeback, resurgence, renewal, reinvigoration, advancement, betterment; a turn for the better.
OPPOSITES slump, downturn.

picnic ▸ noun **1** *a picnic on the beach* **outdoor meal**, alfresco meal, barbecue; garden party; informal barbie; French fête champêtre, déjeuner sur l'herbe; N. Amer. clambake, cookout, burgoo; NZ hangi; S. African braaivleis.
2 (informal) *diving in the North Sea has never been a picnic* **easy task**, easy job, child's play, five-finger exercise, gift, walkover, nothing, sinecure, gravy train; informal doddle, piece of cake, money for old rope, money for jam, cinch, breeze, sitter, kids' stuff, cushy job/number, doss, cakewalk, pushover; N. Amer. informal duck soup, snap; Austral./NZ informal bludge, snack; S. African informal a piece of old tackie; Brit. vulgar slang a piece of piss; dated snip.

pictorial ▸ adjective *a pictorial history of Gateshead* **illustrated**, with illustrations, with pictures, with drawings, with sketches; in pictures, in picture form, in photographs, photographic, graphic; representational, depictive, illustrative, drawn.

picture *See centre pages for lists of types and forms of* **Painting**
▸ noun **1** *one of his pictures stood on an easel in the centre of the room* **painting**, **drawing**, sketch, print, canvas, delineation, cartoon, portrait, portrayal, illustration, artwork, depiction, likeness, representation, image, icon.
2 *I would not let the photographer take the picture* **photograph**, photo, shot, snap, snapshot, image, portrait, study; print, slide, transparency, negative, positive, plate, film, bromide, frame, exposure, still, proof, enlargement; Brit. enprint.
3 *they have a picture of the sort of person the child should be* **concept**, idea, impression, mental picture, view, (mental) image, vision, visualization,

notion, theory, abstraction.
4 *the picture of health* **personification**, embodiment, epitome, essence, perfect example, soul, model; *rare* exemplar, archetype, quintessence.
5 *a picture starring Robert De Niro* **film**, movie, feature film; *Brit.* cinema film; *N. Amer.* motion picture; *informal* flick; *dated* moving picture.
6 (**the pictures**) *Julie took me to the pictures on Saturday* **the cinema**, the movies, the silver screen, the big screen; *N. Amer.* a motion picture house; *informal* the flicks.
□ **get the picture understand the situation**, work out what's going on, see the light, see daylight, get the point; fathom, grasp, understand, follow, see, take in, realize, perceive, apprehend; *informal* understand/see what's what, catch on, latch on, get the drift, get the message, get it.
□ **put someone in the picture inform**, fill in, give details to, explain the situation to, give information to, explain the circumstances to, describe the state of affairs to, bring up to date, update, brief, keep posted; *informal* clue in, bring up to speed.
▶ **verb 1** *this child was pictured at a feeding centre* **photograph**, take/get a photograph/photo of, take someone's picture/photo, take/get a picture of, take/get a snapshot/snap of, take, snap, shoot, take/get a shot of; record, film, capture/record on film/celluloid.
2 *in the drawing they were pictured against a snowy background* **paint**, **draw**, paint a picture of, sketch, depict, delineate, portray, catch (a likeness of), show, illustrate, reproduce, render, represent.
3 *Anne still pictured Richard as he had been* **visualize**, see in one's mind, see in one's mind's eye, conjure up a picture of, conjure up an image of, imagine, conceive, call to mind, image, see, evoke; fantasize about, dream about; *rare* envision.

picturesque ▶ **adjective 1** *a picturesque maze of narrow streets* **attractive**, **pretty**, beautiful, lovely, scenic, charming, quaint, pleasing, delightful, romantic.
OPPOSITES ugly, drab.
2 *a picturesque description* **vivid**, graphic, colourful, impressive, striking.
OPPOSITE dull.

piddling ▶ **adjective** (*informal*) *a piddling little incident | they were bought for piddling sums* **trivial**, trifling, petty, footling, slight, small, insignificant, unimportant, inconsequential, inconsiderable, of little account, peripheral, subsidiary, negligible, worthless, useless; meagre, inadequate, insufficient, paltry, scant, scanty, derisory, pitiful, pitiable, miserable, sorry, wretched, puny, niggardly, beggarly, mean, ungenerous, inappreciable, mere; *informal* measly, pathetic, piffling, mingy, poxy; *N. Amer. informal* nickel-and-dime, dinky; *rare* exiguous.
OPPOSITE significant.

pie *See centre pages for lists of* **Cakes, Puddings, and Desserts** *and savoury* **Pies**
▶ **noun pastry**, tart, tartlet, quiche, pasty, patty, turnover.
□ **pie in the sky** (*informal*) *their dreams of travel are pie in the sky* **false hope**, illusion, delusion, unrealizable dream, fantasy, pipe dream, daydream, reverie, mirage, castle in the air, castle in Spain.

piebald ▶ **adjective black and white**, brown and white, pied, skewbald; dappled, brindled, brindle, spotted, marked, mottled, speckled, flecked, patchy, blotchy, blotched, variegated, multicoloured, multicolour, particoloured, tabby; *N. Amer.* pinto; *rare* marled, jaspé.

piece ▶ **noun 1** *a piece of cheese | a piece of wood* **bit**, section, slice, chunk, segment, lump, hunk; wedge, slab, knob, block, cake, bar, tablet, brick, cube, stick, length; offcut, sample, particle, fragment, flake, sliver, splinter, wafer, chip, crumb, grain, speck, scrap, remnant, shred, shard, snippet, mite; mouthful, morsel; *Brit. informal* wodge.
2 *his ability to take a clock to pieces* **component**, part, bit, section, segment, constituent, element; unit, module.
3 *a piece of furniture | a vital piece of evidence* **example**, specimen, sample, instance, illustration, occurrence, case.
4 *he gets $16 million plus a piece of the profit* **share**, slice, portion, quota, part, bit, percentage, amount, quantity, ration, fraction, division, subdivision; allocation, allotment, measure, apportionment; *informal* cut, whack, rake-off; *rare* quantum, moiety.
5 *one of the finest pieces is a Tuscan vase | a piece of music* **work of art**, work; musical work, composition, creation, production, opus.
6 *the reporter who wrote the piece* **article**, item, story, report, essay, study, review, composition, paper, column.
7 *the pieces on a chess board* **token**, counter, man, disc, chip, marker.
□ **in one piece 1** *I checked my camera to see if it was still in one piece* **unbroken**, entire, whole, intact, undamaged, unharmed, unmarked, untouched, unspoilt.
2 *I'll bring her back in one piece* **unhurt**, uninjured, unscathed, safe, safe and sound.
□ **in pieces 1** *the dish lay in pieces on the floor* **broken**, in bits, shattered, smashed, in smithereens; *informal* bust.
2 *this man's only ambition appeared to be to cut him in pieces* **apart**, up, to pieces; *literary* asunder.
□ **go/fall to pieces** *he went to pieces when his wife died* **have a (mental/nervous) breakdown**, break down, go out of one's mind, crack, snap, lose control, lose one's head, fall apart; *informal* crack up, come/fall apart at the seams, disintegrate, freak, freak out, get in a stew; *Brit. informal* go into a (flat) spin.
□ **tear/pull someone/something to pieces** *theatre critics would tear the production to pieces* **criticize**, attack, censure, condemn, denigrate, find fault with, give a bad press to, pillory, maul, lambaste, flay, savage; *informal* knock, slam, pan, bash, take apart, crucify, hammer, lay into, roast, skewer; *Brit. informal* slate, rubbish, slag off; *N. Amer. informal* pummel, cut up; *Austral./NZ informal* bag, monster; *rare* excoriate.
▶ **verb**
□ **piece something together** *it might be possible to piece the photographs together | investigators are now trying to piece together what happened* **put together**, assemble, compose, construct, join up, fit together, join, unite, reassemble, reconstruct, put back together, mend, repair, patch up, sew (up); build up a picture/impression of.

pièce de résistance ▶ **noun** (*French*) **masterpiece**, magnum opus, masterwork, tour de force, showpiece, prize, gem, jewel, jewel in the crown, speciality, special, claim to fame, forte; *French* chef-d'œuvre.

piecemeal ▶ **adverb** *the reforms were implemented piecemeal* **a little at a time**, piece by piece, bit by bit, gradually, slowly, in stages, in steps, step by step, little by little, by degrees, in/by fits and starts, in bits; bittily, irregularly, erratically, unevenly, discontinuously, disjointedly, unsystematically; *rare* inchmeal.

pied ▶ **adjective** *pied horses* **multicoloured**, variegated, particoloured, tabby, black and white, brown and white, piebald, skewbald, dappled, brindled, brindle, spotted, marked, mottled, speckled, flecked, patchy, blotchy, blotched; *N. Amer.* pinto; *rare* marled, jaspé.

pier ▶ **noun 1** *I left my boat tied up to the pier* **jetty**, quay, wharf, dock, landing, landing stage, landing place, slipway, marina, waterfront, breakwater, mole, groyne, dyke, sea wall, embankment.
2 *the piers of the bridge* **support**, cutwater, pile, piling, plinth, pedestal, foot, footing, abutment, buttress, stanchion, prop, stay, upright, pillar, post, column.

pierce ▶ **verb 1** *be careful not to pierce the skin | pierce a hole with a skewer* **make a hole in**, penetrate, puncture, punch, perforate, riddle, stab, prick, probe, gore, spike, stick, impale, transfix, bore (through), drill (through), lance, tap.
2 *her father's anguish had pierced her to the quick* **hurt**, wound, pain, grieve, sadden, distress, make miserable/wretched, upset, trouble, harrow, cause anguish to, afflict, perturb, disturb; cut to the quick; affect, move, sting, mortify, sear, torment, torture, gnaw at, vex, gall.
3 *shafts of bright sunlight pierced the smoke* **penetrate**, pass through, burst through, percolate, pervade, permeate, filter through, light up.

piercing ▶ **adjective 1** *a piercing shriek* **shrill**, ear-piercing, ear-splitting, high-pitched, air-rending, penetrating, shattering, strident, loud, strong; sharp, intrusive, screechy, squawky.
2 *the piercing cold* **freezing**, frosty, frigid, chill, chilling, glacial, arctic, wintry, sharp, keen, biting, stinging, cutting, penetrating, numbing, harsh, fierce, raw, bitter; *Brit. informal* parky; *rare* nipping.
3 *a piercing pain* **intense**, excruciating, agonizing, sharp, stabbing, shooting, stinging, severe, extreme, fierce, harrowing, searing, penetrating, racking, insufferable, unbearable, unendurable, torturous; *rare* exquisite.
4 *a piercing glance* **shrewd**, discerning, perceptive, probing, searching, observant, penetrating, penetrative, sharp, keen, alert, intent, inquisitive.
5 *a piercing intelligence* **perceptive**, percipient, perspicacious, penetrating, discerning, discriminating, intelligent, quick-witted, sharp, sharp-witted, shrewd, insightful, keen, acute, astute, clever, smart, incisive, knife-like, razor-edged, trenchant, subtle, quick, ready, clear, sensitive, thoughtful, deep, profound.

piety ▶ **noun 1** *the piety of a saint* **devoutness**, devotion, piousness, religiousness, religion, holiness, godliness, sanctity, sanctitude, saintliness, devotion to God, veneration, reverence, faith, religious duty, spirituality, sacredness, religious zeal, fervour, pietism, religiosity.
2 *the strict code of filial piety* **dutifulness**, obedience, deference, duty, respect, respectfulness, compliance, acquiescence, tractability, tractableness; submissiveness, submission, subservience.
OPPOSITE impiety.

piffle ▶ **noun** (*informal*) *you don't actually believe this piffle, do you?* **nonsense**, rubbish, garbage, claptrap, balderdash, blather, blether, moonshine; foolishness, silliness; *informal* rot, tripe, hogwash, baloney, drivel, bilge, bosh, bull, bunk, guff, eyewash, poppycock, phooey, hooey, malarkey, twaddle, dribble; *Brit. informal* cobblers, codswallop, stuff and nonsense, tosh, cack; *Scottish & N. English informal* havers; *Irish informal* codology; *N. Amer. informal* flapdoodle, blathers, applesauce, wack, bushwa; *informal, dated* bunkum, tommyrot, cod, gammon, toffee; *vulgar slang* bullshit, crap, balls; *Brit. vulgar slang* bollocks; *Austral./NZ vulgar slang* bulldust.

piffling ▶ **adjective** *Mummy gives me such a piffling allowance* **inadequate**, insufficient, tiny, small, minimal, trifling, paltry, pitiful; miserly, miserable; negligible, token, nominal; insulting, derisory, contemptible, outrageous; ridiculous, laughable, ludicrous, risible, preposterous, absurd; *informal* measly, stingy, lousy, pathetic, piddling, mingy, poxy;

P

N. Amer. informal nickel-and-dime.

pig *See centre pages for list of* **Pigs**

▶ **noun 1** *she decided to keep pigs* **hog**, boar, sow, porker, swine, piglet; *children's word* piggy; *rare* baconer, cutter, grunter.
2 (*informal*) *he's eaten the lot, the pig* **glutton**, guzzler, gobbler, gorger, gourmand, gourmandizer; *informal* greedy pig, hog, greedy guts, guts; *Brit. informal* gannet.
3 (*informal*) *what an absolute pig he was this evening* **brute**, monster, devil; scoundrel, rogue, wretch; *informal* **bastard**, beast, louse, swine, rat, son of a bitch, s.o.b., low life; *Brit. informal* toerag; *Scottish informal* scrote; *informal, dated* bounder, rotter, heel, stinker, blighter; *dated* cad; *vulgar slang* shit, sod, bugger.

WORD LINKS

male	**boar**
female	**sow**
young	**piglet**
relating to pigs	**porcine**
home	**sty**

pigeon ▶ **noun** squab, homing pigeon, homer, carrier pigeon; dove.

WORD LINKS

young **squab**

pigeonhole ▶ **noun 1** *there was a note in my pigeonhole* **cubbyhole**, compartment, slot, locker, niche.
2 *he had to supply information about his identity so he could be put in the right bureaucratic pigeonhole* **category**, categorization, compartment, class, classification, group, grouping, grade, grading, designation, set, section, division.
▶ **verb 1** *people everywhere wish to pigeonhole you* **categorize**, compartmentalize, classify, characterize, label, brand, tag, designate, grade, codify, sort, rank, rate.
2 *a plan for new intercity trains was pigeonholed last year* **postpone**, put off, put back, defer, shelve, delay, hold over, put on one side, lay aside, adjourn, suspend, put on ice, mothball, put in cold storage; *N. Amer.* table; *informal* put on the back burner.

pig-headed ▶ **adjective** **obstinate**, stubborn, stubborn as a mule, mulish, bull-headed, obdurate, headstrong, self-willed, wilful, perverse, contrary, recalcitrant, refractory, stiff-necked; tenacious, dogged, single-minded, inflexible, uncompromising, adamant, intractable, intransigent, unyielding, unmalleable, unpersuadable.

pigment ▶ **noun** **colouring matter**, colouring agent, colouring, colourant, colour, tint, dye, dyestuff, stain.

pile[1] ▶ **noun 1** *a pile of stones* **heap**, stack, mound, pyramid, mass, quantity, bundle, clump, bunch, jumble; collection, accumulation; assemblage, store, stockpile, aggregation; hoard, load, tower, rick; *N. Amer.* cold deck; *Scottish, Irish, & N. English* rickle; *Scottish* bing.
2 *I've a pile of work to do* **great deal**, lot, great/large amount, large quantity, abundance, superabundance, cornucopia, plethora, wealth, profusion, mountain; quantities, reams, plenty; *informal* load, heap, mass, ocean, stack, ton; *Brit. informal* shedload; *N. Amer. informal* slew; *Austral./NZ informal* swag; *vulgar slang* shitload.
3 (*informal*) *he wants to make his pile as quickly as possible* **fortune**, considerable/vast/large sum of money, millions, billions; *informal* small fortune, mint, lots/pots/heaps/stacks of money, bomb, packet, killing, bundle, wad, tidy sum, pretty penny, telephone numbers; *Brit. informal* shedloads, loadsamoney; *N. Amer. informal* big bucks, big money, gazillions; *Austral. informal* big bickies, motser, motza.
4 *his recently inherited stately pile* **mansion**, stately home, hall, manor, big house, manor house, country house, castle, palace; edifice, impressive building/structure, residence, abode, seat; *French* château, manoir; *Italian* palazzo.
▶ **verb 1** *he piled up brushwood* **heap (up)**, stack (up), make a heap/pile/stack of; accumulate, assemble, put together.
2 *he piled his plate with the fried eggs* **load**, heap, fill (up), lade, pack, stack, charge, stuff, cram; smother, stock.
3 *news was meanwhile piling up* **increase**, grow, rise, mount, escalate, soar, spiral, leap up, shoot up, rocket, climb, accumulate, accrue, build up, multiply, intensify, swell; *literary* wax.
4 *they piled up the points* **amass**, accumulate, collect, gather (in), pull in, assemble, stockpile, heap up, store up, garner, lay by/in, put by; bank, deposit, husband, save (up), squirrel away, salt away; *informal* stash away.
5 *half a dozen of us piled into an old station wagon* **crowd**, climb, charge, tumble, stream, flock, flood, pack, squeeze, push, shove, jostle, elbow, crush, jam.
□ **pile it on** (*informal*) *it was a sad case but he really piled it on* **exaggerate**, overstate the case, make a mountain out of a molehill, overdo, overplay, dramatize, overdramatize; *informal* lay it on thick, lay it on with a trowel, ham it up, blow up out of all proportion, give someone a sob story.

pile[2] ▶ **noun** *a wall supported by timber piles* **post**, rod, pillar, column, support, foundation, piling; plinth, pedestal, foot, footing, base, substructure, underpinning, bed, subfloor, abutment, pier, cutwater, buttress, stanchion, prop, stay, upright; *rare* underprop.

pile[3] ▶ **noun** *a carpet with a short pile* **fibres**, threads, loops; nap, velvet, shag, plush; fur, hair; soft surface, surface.

pile-up ▶ **noun** *a pile-up on the motorway* **crash**, multiple crash, car crash, collision, multiple collision, smash, car smash, accident, car accident, road accident, traffic accident; bump; *Brit.* RTA (road traffic accident); *N. Amer.* wreck; *informal* smash-up; *Brit. informal* shunt, prang.

pilfer ▶ **verb** *the gun was part of a cache pilfered from the air force three years ago* **steal**, thieve, rob, take, snatch, purloin, loot, rifle, abscond with, carry off, pillage; *informal* walk off/away with, run away/off with, swipe, nab, rip off, lift, liberate', borrow', filch, snaffle, snitch; *Brit. informal* pinch, half-inch, nick, whip, knock off, nobble, bone; *N. Amer. informal* heist, glom; *Austral. informal* snavel; *W. Indian informal* tief; *archaic* crib, hook.

pilgrim ▶ **noun** **visitor to a shrine**, worshipper, devotee, believer, traveller, wayfarer, crusader; *Islam* haji, alhaji; *historical* palmer.

pilgrimage ▶ **noun** **religious journey**, holy expedition, crusade, mission, trip, journey, excursion; *Indian* yatra; *Islam* hajj.

pill ▶ **noun** *a sleeping pill* **tablet**, capsule, caplet, pellet, lozenge, pastille; *rare* jujube, bolus, troche, pilule.

pillage ▶ **verb 1** *the abbey was pillaged* **ransack**, steal from, plunder, rob, raid, loot, rifle, sack; dispossess, strip, deprive, denude, devastate, lay waste, ravage, harry, maraud; *literary* despoil; *archaic* spoil, reave, rape; *rare* depredate, spoliate, forage.
2 *windows and columns pillaged from a more ancient town* **steal**, pilfer, thieve, rob, take, snatch, purloin, loot, rifle, abscond with, carry off; *informal* walk off/away with, run away/off with, swipe, nab, rip off, lift, 'liberate', 'borrow', filch, snaffle, snitch; *Brit. informal* pinch, half-inch, nick, whip, knock off, nobble, bone; *N. Amer. informal* heist, glom; *Austral. informal* snavel; *W. Indian informal* tief; *archaic* crib, hook, reave.
▶ **noun** *they believed the rebellious peasants to be intent on pillage* **robbery**, robbing, raiding, pillaging, plunder, plundering, looting, sacking, sack, ransacking, ravaging, laying waste, devastation, depredation, rape, harrying, marauding; *literary* despoiling, rapine; *archaic* spoliation, reaving.

pillar ▶ **noun 1** *eight stone pillars supported a dome* **column**, post, pole, support, upright, vertical, baluster, pier, pile, piling, pilaster, stanchion, standard, prop, buttress; rod, shaft, leg, mast, tower, pylon; obelisk, monolith; *technical* newel, caryatid, telamon, herm.
2 *he was a pillar of his local community* **stalwart**, mainstay, strength, tower of strength, bastion, rock; leading light, worthy, backbone, support, upholder, champion, torch-bearer.

pillory ▶ **noun** *offenders were punished by being put in the pillory* **stocks**.
▶ **verb 1** *he was savagely pilloried by the press* **attack**, criticize, censure, condemn, denigrate, find fault with, give a bad press to, lambaste, flay, savage, brand, stigmatize, cast a slur on, denounce; *informal* knock, slam, pan, bash, take to pieces, take apart, crucify, hammer, lay into, slate, rubbish, slag off, roast, skewer; *N. Amer. informal* pummel; *Austral./NZ informal* bag, monster; *archaic* slash; *rare* excoriate.
2 *his children were pilloried at school and his wife humiliated* **ridicule**, jeer at, sneer at, deride, show up, hold up to shame, mock, hold up to ridicule, heap scorn on, treat with contempt, scorn, make fun of, poke fun at, laugh at, make jokes about, scoff at, be sarcastic about, tease, taunt, rag, chaff, jibe at, twit; *informal* kid, rib, josh, wind up, take the mickey out of, make a monkey of; *N. Amer. informal* goof on, rag on, razz, pull someone's chain; *Austral./NZ informal* chiack, poke mullock at, sling off at; *Brit. vulgar slang* take the piss (out of); *archaic* quiz, flout (at).

pillow ▶ **noun** *his head rested on the pillow* **cushion**, **bolster**, headrest, pad, support, rest.
▶ **verb** *she pillowed her head on folded arms* **lay**, cushion, cradle, rest, support, prop (up).

pilot ▶ **noun 1** *a fighter pilot* **airman/airwoman**, flyer, aeronaut; captain, commander, co-pilot, first/second officer, wingman; aircrew; *informal* skipper; *dated* aviator, aviatrix; *N. Amer. informal* jock, fly boy.
2 *a harbour pilot* **navigator**, helmsman, guide, steersman, coxswain; leader, director, usher, escort, attendant.
3 *a pilot for a possible TV series* **trial episode**, pilot episode, pilot programme; sample, experiment.
▶ **adjective** *the scheme will begin with a pilot project* **experimental**, exploratory, trial, test, sample, model, tentative, speculative, preliminary.
▶ **verb 1** *he piloted the crippled jet to safety* **fly**, be at the controls of, control, handle, manoeuvre, drive, operate, steer, regulate, monitor, direct, captain; *informal* skipper; *rare* aviate.
2 *he had piloted the ship through the night* **navigate**, guide, steer, direct, sail, usher, shepherd, show the way to, lead, conduct, escort, convoy.
3 *the enclosed questionnaire has been piloted in a number of institutions* **test**, trial, put to the test, try out, carry out trials on, experiment with, assess, investigate, examine, appraise, evaluate, check out.

pimp ▶ **noun** *the pimp forced the girl back on to the streets* **procurer**, procuress; go-between; brothel-keeper, madam; *French* souteneur; *Brit. informal* ponce; *Austral. informal* hoon; *rare* pander, panderess, mack, bawd, fancy man.

pimple ▶ **noun** **spot**, pustule, blackhead, boil, swelling, eruption, carbuncle, wen, cyst, abscess, blister; acne; *informal* whitehead, zit; *Scottish*

P

informal plook; *technical* comedo; *rare* papule, bleb, blain, whelk.

pin ▶ noun **1** *fasten the hem with a pin* **tack**, safety pin, nail, staple, skewer, spike, brad, fastener.
2 *a broken pin in the machine* **peg**, **bolt**, rivet, dowel, screw, set screw; *rare* thole.
3 *they wore pins that read 'Kindness to all animals'* **badge**, brooch, sticker.
▶ verb **1** *she pinned the brooch to her dress* **attach**, fasten, affix, fix, stick, tack, nail, staple, clip, join, link, secure.
2 *they had to pin me to the ground* **hold**, restrain, press, pinion, constrain, hold fast, hold down, immobilize.
3 *he was scared they'd* **pin** *the crime* **on** *him* **blame for**, lay the blame for something on, hold responsible for something, attribute something to, impute something to, ascribe something to, lay something at someone's door; *informal* stick something on.
□ **pin someone/something down 1** *your supporting troops can just as easily pin down the enemy from a distance* **confine**, **trap**, hem in, corner, close in, shut in, hedge in, pen in, restrain, entangle, enmesh, immobilize.
2 *she tried to pin him down to something definite* **make someone commit themselves**, constrain, force, compel, pressure, put pressure on, pressurize, tie down, nail down.
3 *it evoked some distant memory but he couldn't quite pin it down* **define**, put one's finger on, put into words, put words to, express in words, express, designate, name, specify, identify, pinpoint, place, home in on.

pinch ▶ verb **1** *he pinched my arm harder* **nip**, **tweak**, squeeze, compress, grasp.
2 *my new shoes pinch my big toe* **hurt**, cause pain to, pain; **squeeze**, crush, cramp, chafe, confine; be uncomfortable, cause discomfort, be painful.
3 *if I scraped and pinched a bit, I might manage* **economize**, be economical, scrimp, scrimp and save, cut corners, reduce wastage, skimp, stint, be sparing, be frugal, cut back, tighten one's belt, draw in one's horns, retrench, cut expenditure, cut one's coat according to one's cloth; be niggardly, be tight-fisted, be close; *informal* be stingy, be tight, be mingy.
4 (*informal*) *he was pinched for drink-driving* **arrest**, take into custody, apprehend, take prisoner, detain, seize, capture, catch, lay hold of, take in, haul in; *informal* collar, nab, pick up, run/pull in, nick, bust, nail, do, feel someone's collar.
5 (*Brit. informal*) *you shouldn't have pinched his biscuits* **steal**, thieve, rob, take, snatch, pilfer, purloin, loot, rifle, abscond with, carry off; embezzle, misappropriate; *informal* walk off/away with, run away/off with, swipe, nab, rip off, lift, 'liberate', 'borrow', filch; *Brit. informal* nick, half-inch, whip, knock off, nobble, bone; *N. Amer. informal* heist, glom; *Austral. informal* snavel; *W. Indian informal* tief; *archaic* crib, hook.
▶ noun **1** *he gave her arm a pinch* **nip**, **tweak**, squeeze.
2 *a pinch of salt* **small quantity**, bit, touch, dash, spot, trace, soupçon, speck, taste; *informal* smidgen, smidge, tad.
□ **at a pinch** *there's room for four adults, five at a pinch* **if necessary**, **with difficulty**, in case of necessity, if need be, in an emergency, just possibly; *N. Amer.* in a pinch; *Brit. informal* at a push.
□ **feel the pinch** *the recession hit us hard and many of our customers have been feeling the pinch* **suffer hardship**, have less money, be short of money, be poor, be impoverished, suffer poverty, suffer adversity.
□ **if it comes to the pinch if things get bad**, if it comes to the push, in an emergency, in a crisis, in times of hardship, if one is in difficulty, in time of need, in case of necessity, if necessary.

pinched ▶ adjective *their pale, pinched faces, dulled with years of lost endeavour* **strained**, stressed, fraught, tense, taut, tired, worn, drained, sapped; wan, peaky, pale, pallid, pasty, pasty-faced, colourless, anaemic, washed out, ashen, ashen-faced, grey, blanched; thin, drawn, haggard, gaunt, wizened, cadaverous, hollow-cheeked, hollow-eyed, emaciated.
OPPOSITES healthy, glowing, chubby.

pine ▶ verb **1** *she thinks I am pining away from love* **languish**, decline, go into a decline, lose strength, weaken, waste away, dwindle, wilt, wither, fade, flag, sicken, droop, brood, mope, moon; *archaic* peak.
2 *Leopold was clearly* **pining for** *his son* **yearn**, long, ache, sigh, hunger, thirst, itch, languish, carry a torch; miss, mourn, lament, grieve over, cry/weep over, fret about, shed tears for, bemoan, rue, regret the loss/absence of, hanker for/after, eat one's heart out over, cry out for.

> **CHOOSE THE RIGHT WORD**
>
> **pine, yearn, long, hanker**
> *See* YEARN.

pinion ▶ verb *he was pinioned to the ground* **hold down**, pin down, press down, restrain, constrain, hold fast, immobilize; **tie**, bind, rope, fasten, secure, shackle, fetter, tether, lash, truss (up), chain (up), hobble, manacle, handcuff; *informal* cuff.

pink ▶ adjective **rosy**, rose, rose-coloured, rosé, pale red, salmon, salmon-pink, shell-pink; flesh-coloured, flushed, blushing.
▶ noun *those who are in the pink of condition* **prime**, perfection, best, finest, top form, height, highest level, upper limit, limit; utmost, peak of perfection, uttermost, greatest, extreme, extremity, ceiling; epitome, apex, zenith, acme, bloom, blossoming, flowering, full flowering; *Latin* ne plus ultra.
□ **in the pink in good health**, in perfect health, very healthy, very well, hale and hearty, bursting with health, in rude health; blooming, flourishing, thriving, vigorous, strong, lusty, robust, bounding, in fine fettle, fit, (as) fit as a flea, (as) fit as a fiddle, in tip-top condition, in excellent shape.

pinnacle ▶ noun **1** *soaring pinnacles of rock* **peak**, needle, crag, tor, summit, top, crest, apex, tip, vertex; *French* aiguille, serac, puy; *N. Amer.* hoodoo; *technical* inselberg.
2 *the intricate pinnacles of the clock tower* **turret**, minaret, spire, belfry, obelisk, needle, pyramid, cone, finial, shikara, mirador; *rare* bartizan.
3 *the brothers have reached the pinnacle of the sport* **highest level**, peak, height, high point/spot, summit, top, climax, crowning point, peak of perfection, apex, vertex, zenith, apogee, ascendancy, upper limit, acme, meridian.
OPPOSITES nadir, trough.

pinpoint ▶ noun *a pinpoint of light from a torch* **point**, spot, speck, dot, fleck; dapple, speckle; source.
▶ adjective *pinpoint accuracy was necessary* **precise**, strict, rigorous, meticulous, scrupulous, punctilious; scientific, mathematical, exact, accurate, correct, careful, unerring.
▶ verb *pinpoint the cause of the trouble* **identify**, discover, determine, distinguish, find, locate, detect, track down, run to earth, spot, diagnose, recognize, name, single out, pick out, pin down, home in on, zero in on, nail down, put one's finger on.

pioneer ▶ noun **1** *the pioneers of the Wild West* **settler**, colonist, colonizer, frontiersman/frontierswoman, explorer, trailblazer, discoverer.
2 *a pioneer of motoring* **developer**, innovator, groundbreaker, trailblazer, pathfinder, front runner, founder, founding father, architect, experimenter, instigator, avant-gardist, creator; avant-garde, spearhead.
▶ verb *he pioneered the sale of motor insurance through high-street shops* **develop**, **introduce**, evolve, start, begin, launch, instigate, initiate, take the initiative in, take the lead in, spearhead, institute, establish, found, give birth to, be the father/mother of, originate, set in motion, create, open up, lay the groundwork for, lead the way for, prepare the way for, lay the foundations of; blaze a trail, set the ball rolling, break new ground, make the first move.

pious ▶ adjective **1** *a pious family* **religious**, devout, devoted, dedicated, reverent, God-fearing, churchgoing, spiritual, prayerful, holy, godly, saintly, faithful, dutiful, righteous.
OPPOSITES impious, irreligious.
2 *a pious platitude* **sanctimonious**, hypocritical, insincere, self-righteous, holier-than-thou, pietistic, churchy; for form's sake, to keep up appearances; *informal* goody-goody, pi; *rare* religiose, Pharisaic, Pharisaical.
OPPOSITE sincere.
3 *a pious hope* **sincere**, **forlorn**, vain, desperate, despairing, doomed, hopeless, lost; unlikely, unduly optimistic, unrealistic.

> **CHOOSE THE RIGHT WORD**
>
> **pious, religious, devout**
> *See* RELIGIOUS.

pip ▶ noun *grapes with the pips removed* **seed**, stone, pit.

pipe ▶ noun **1** *a central-heating pipe* **tube**, conduit, hose, main, duct, line, channel, canal, conveyor, pipeline, drain, tubing, piping, siphon, cylinder; *Medicine* fistula.
2 *he smokes a pipe* **tobacco pipe**, briar (pipe), meerschaum, clay pipe; *Brit.* churchwarden; *Scottish & N. English* cutty; *Anglo-Irish* dudeen; *rare* calabash, calumet, chibouk, hookah, narghile, calean, hubble-bubble, bong, chillum.
3 *someone was playing a pipe* **whistle**, penny whistle, flute, recorder, fife; chanter, drone; wind instrument.
4 (**pipes**) *Scottish regimental pipes and drums* **bagpipes**; pan pipes; *Irish* uillean pipes.
▶ verb **1** *the beer is piped into barrels* **convey**, channel, siphon, run, feed, lead, bring.
2 *the programmes will be piped in from London* **transmit**, feed, lead, patch.
3 *he heard a tune being piped* **play on a pipe**; play the pipes, tootle, whistle; *literary* flute.
4 *outside a curlew piped | a voice piping away in French* **chirp**, cheep, chirrup, twitter, chatter, warble, trill, peep, sing, shrill, squeal, squeak.
□ **pipe down** (*informal*) **be quiet**, quieten down, be silent, fall silent, hush, stop talking, hold one's tongue; *informal* shut up, shut one's face/mouth/trap/gob, button up, button it/one's lip, belt up, wrap up, wrap it up, put a sock in it.

pipe dream ▶ noun **fantasy**, false hope, illusion, delusion, daydream, unrealizable dream, reverie, mirage, castle in the air, castle in Spain, chimera; *informal* pie in the sky.

pipeline ▶ noun *a gas pipeline* **pipe**, conduit, main, line, duct, channel, tube, conveyor.
□ **in the pipeline** *there are more changes in the pipeline* **on the way**, in preparation, being prepared, in production, under way, coming, forthcoming, upcoming, imminent, about to happen, near, close, brewing, in the offing, in the wind, anticipated, expected.

pipsqueak ▶ noun (informal) *I won't have some nineteen-year-old pipsqueak telling me what to do* **insignificant person**, nobody, nonentity, non-person, gnat, insect, cipher, pygmy; upstart; informal squirt, stripling; Brit. informal nerk, johnny, squit, whippersnapper; Scottish informal nyaff; N. Amer. informal bozo, picayune, pisher, snip; dated puppy, pup; archaic, informal dandiprat.
OPPOSITE somebody.

piquancy ▶ noun **1** *when added to certain dishes, the herb gives a tantalizing piquancy* **spiciness**, tang, spice, tastiness, savouriness, pungency, edge, sharpness, tartness, pepperiness, saltiness, bite, zest; informal zing, kick, punch; archaic relish.
2 *the play retains much of its original piquancy* **interest**, fascination, excitement, vigour, vitality, liveliness, spirit, colour, sparkle, zest, spice, spiciness, sharpness, raciness, saltiness, provocativeness, bite, edge; informal zing, pizzazz.

piquant ▶ adjective **1** *a piquant sauce of tamarind, chillis, and garlic* **spicy**, tangy, spiced, peppery, hot; tasty, flavoursome, flavourful, appetizing, highly seasoned, savoury, pungent, sharp, tart, zesty, strong, salty; rare sapid, flavorous.
2 *a particularly piquant story* **intriguing**, stimulating, interesting, fascinating, colourful, exciting, arresting, lively, sparkling, spirited, witty, spicy, provocative, racy, salty; informal juicy.
OPPOSITES bland, insipid, dull.

pique ▶ noun *he left in a fit of pique* **irritation**, annoyance, resentment, anger, displeasure, indignation, temper, bad temper, wounded/hurt pride, wounded/hurt feelings, petulance, ill humour, peevishness, offence, umbrage, vexation, exasperation, disgruntlement, discontent, discontentment.
▶ verb **1** *his scientific curiosity was piqued* **stimulate**, arouse, rouse, provoke, whet, awaken, excite, kindle, stir, spur, intrigue, galvanize.
2 *she was piqued by Stephen's neglect of her* **irritate**, annoy, bother, vex, provoke, displease, upset, offend, affront, anger, exasperate, infuriate, gall, irk, get someone's back up, disgruntle, nettle, needle, ruffle, get on someone's nerves, ruffle someone's feathers, make someone's hackles rise, rub up the wrong way; informal peeve, aggravate, miff, rile, get, get to, bug, get under someone's skin, get in someone's hair, get up someone's nose, hack off, get someone's goat, wind up; Brit. informal nark, get on someone's wick, give someone the hump, get across; N. Amer. informal tick off, rankle, ride, gravel; vulgar slang piss off; rare exacerbate, hump, rasp.

piracy ▶ noun **1** *piracy on the high seas* **robbery at sea**, freebooting; historical buccaneering.
2 *software companies are reluctant to say how much piracy costs them* **illegal reproduction**, plagiarism, illegal copying, copyright infringement, bootlegging, stealing, theft.

pirate ▶ noun **1** *pirates boarded the ship* **freebooter**; marauder, raider; historical buccaneer, privateer; archaic corsair, rover, sea rover; rare picaroon, filibuster, sea thief, sea robber, water thief, sea wolf, sea rat, water rat, marooner.
2 *software pirates* **copyright infringer**, plagiarist, plagiarizer.
▶ verb *designers may pirate good ideas* **reproduce illegally**, infringe the copyright of, copy illegally, plagiarize, poach, steal, appropriate, bootleg; informal crib, lift, rip off; Brit. informal nick, pinch.

pirouette ▶ noun *Sandra performed a little pirouette* **spin**, twirl, whirl, turn, gyration, revolution.
▶ verb *she pirouetted before the wardrobe mirror* **spin round**, twirl, whirl, turn round, gyrate, revolve, pivot.

pistol ▶ noun **revolver**, gun, handgun, side arm; automatic pistol, six-shooter, thirty-eight, derringer, Browning automatic; informal gat; N. Amer. informal piece, shooting iron, Saturday night special, rod, roscoe; trademark Colt, Webley, Luger.

pit[1] ▶ noun **1** *a rectangular pit dug in the ground* **hole**, ditch, trench, trough, hollow, shaft, mineshaft, excavation, cavity, pothole, rut; abyss, chasm, gulf, crater.
2 *controversy over plans for pit closures* **coal mine**, colliery, quarry, workings, diggings.
3 *the ugly pits stood out on her skin* **pockmark**, pock, mark, hollow, indentation, depression, dent, dint, concavity, dimple.
□ **the pits** (informal) *this place really is the pits* **the worst**, the lowest of the low; rock-bottom, extremely bad, awful, terrible, dreadful, wretched, unspeakable, deplorable; informal appalling, lousy, abysmal, dire; Brit. informal chronic, grotty, pants, a load of pants.
▶ verb **1** *his skin had been pitted by acne* **mark**, pockmark, scar, blemish, disfigure.
2 *rain poured down, pitting the bare earth* **make holes in**, make hollows in, hole, dent, indent, depress, dint, pothole.
□ **pit someone/something against** *a chance to pit your wits against the world champions* **set against**, match against, put in opposition to, put in competition with, measure against; compete with/against, contend with, vie with, grapple with, wrestle with; informal pitch against.

pit[2] ▶ noun *cherry pits* **stone**, pip, seed.

pitch[1] ▶ noun **1** *the umpires declared the pitch unfit for first-class cricket* **playing field**, field, ground, sports field; stadium, arena; Brit. close, park.
2 *her voice rose in pitch* **tone**, timbre, sound, key, tonality, modulation, frequency.
3 *the pitch of the roof* **steepness**, angle, gradient, slope, slant, tilt, incline, cant, rake, dip, inclination.
4 *her frustration reached such a pitch that she screamed* **level**, intensity, point, degree, height, extent.
5 *a pitch of the ball* **throw**, cast, fling, hurl, toss, delivery, lob; informal chuck, heave.
6 *his sales pitch* **patter**, talk; informal spiel, line.
7 *the street traders had already reserved their pitches* **site**, place, spot, station; Scottish stance; Brit. informal patch.
8 *the pitch of the ship* **lurch**, pitching, lurching, roll, rolling, plunging, reeling, swaying, rocking, list, wallowing, labouring; rare keeling.
□ **make a pitch for** *he made a clear pitch for the support of the left of the party* **try to obtain**, try to acquire, try to get, bid for, make a bid for.
▶ verb **1** *he crumpled the page up and pitched it into the fireplace* **throw**, toss, fling, hurl, cast, lob, launch, flip, shy, dash, aim, direct, propel, bowl; informal chuck, sling, heave, buzz, whang, bung; N. Amer. informal peg; Austral. informal hoy; NZ informal bish.
2 *he pitched overboard* **fall**, fall headlong, tumble, topple, plunge, plummet, dive, take a nosedive, nosedive.
3 *they pitched their tents for the night* **put up**, set up, erect, raise, position, fix in position, place, locate; set up camp.
4 *the boat pitched sharply* **lurch**, toss (about), plunge, roll, reel, sway, rock, flounder, keel, list, wallow, labour; Nautical pitchpole.
□ **pitch in** *everyone pitched in to complete the task* **help out**, help, assist, lend a hand, join in, participate, play a part, contribute, do one's bit, chip in, cooperate, collaborate, put one's shoulder to the wheel; Brit. informal muck in, get stuck in.
□ **pitch into** *he pitched into the youths with such fury that they ran off* **attack**, turn on, lash out at, set upon, assault, fly at, lunge at, let fly at, tear into, weigh into, belabour; informal lay into, sail into, lace into, let someone have it, take a pop at; N. Amer. informal light into.

pitch[2] ▶ noun *the cement is coated with pitch* bitumen, asphalt, tar.
WORD LINKS
relating to pitch **piceous**

pitch-black ▶ adjective *the sky was pitch-black | her pitch-black hair* **black**, dark, pitch-dark, black as pitch; inky, pitchy, starless, moonless, unilluminated, unlighted; jet-black, coal-black, jet, ebony, raven, sooty; literary sable, Stygian; rare Cimmerian.

pitcher ▶ noun *a pitcher of iced water* **jug**, ewer, jar, crock; N. Amer. creamer; historical jorum.

piteous ▶ adjective *a piteous cry/sight* **sad**, pitiful, to be pitied, pitiable, pathetic, distressing, heart-rending, heartbreaking, moving, affecting, touching, plaintive, poignant, forlorn, poor, wretched, abject, miserable, tragic, lamentable, grievous; rare distressful.

pitfall ▶ noun *the pitfalls of setting up an office at home* **hazard**, danger, risk, peril, difficulty, catch, snag, stumbling block, drawback; informal banana skin.

pith ▶ noun **1** *the pith of the argument* **essence**, essential part, main point, fundamental point, heart, substance, heart of the matter, nub, core, quintessence, point, crux, gist, salient point, focal point, nucleus, meat, kernel, marrow, burden; informal nitty-gritty.
2 *he writes with a combination of pith and exactitude* **succinctness**, conciseness, concision, pithiness, economy of language, brevity; vigour, cogency, weight, depth, force, forcefulness, power, strength.

pithy ▶ adjective *pithy comments* **succinct**, terse, concise, compact, short, short and sweet, brief, condensed, compendious, to the point, summary, epigrammatic, crisp, laconic, pointed, thumbnail, significant, meaningful, expressive, incisive, forceful, telling, trenchant, finely honed, aphoristic, sententious.
OPPOSITES verbose, long-winded.

pitiful ▶ adjective **1** *two children in a very pitiful state* **distressing**, sad, piteous, to be pitied, pitiable, pathetic, disturbing, heart-rending, heartbreaking, saddening, moving, affecting, touching, tear-jerking, plaintive, poignant, forlorn, poor, sorry, wretched, abject, miserable, tragic, woeful, lamentable, grievous; rare distressful.
2 *they earn a pitiful $50 a month* **paltry**, miserable, meagre, beggarly, insufficient, insignificant, trifling, negligible, pitiable, derisory; informal pathetic, measly, piddling, piffling, mingy; Brit. informal poxy; N. Amer. informal dinky.
3 *his performance was pitiful* **dreadful**, awful, terrible, lamentable, hopeless, wretched, sorry, poor, bad, feeble, well below par, pitiable,

woeful, inadequate, contemptible, deplorable, despicable, laughable, worthless; *informal* pathetic, useless, rotten, appalling, lousy, abysmal, dire, the pits; *Brit. informal* chronic, pants, a load of pants.

pitiless ▶ adjective *a pitiless executioner* **merciless**, ruthless, cruel, heartless; **relentless**, remorseless, hard-hearted, hard, stony-hearted, stony, with a heart of stone, cold-blooded, cold-hearted, harsh, callous, severe, unmerciful, unrelenting, unsparing, unforgiving, unfeeling, uncaring, unsympathetic, uncharitable, lacking compassion, unbending, unmoved, inflexible, inexorable, implacable, unpitying, unremitting, brutal, inhuman, inhumane, barbarous, barbaric, savage, sadistic; *archaic* inclement.
OPPOSITES merciful, compassionate, kind.

CHOOSE THE RIGHT WORD

pitiless, relentless, remorseless, ruthless
See RELENTLESS.

pittance ▶ noun *the musicians were paid a pittance* **a very small amount**, a tiny amount, an insufficient amount, next to nothing, very little; *informal* peanuts, chicken feed, slave wages, a shoestring; *N. Amer. informal* chump change.

pitted ▶ adjective **1** *his skin was sallow and pitted* **pockmarked**, pocked, scarred, blemished, marked; *archaic* pocky.
OPPOSITE smooth.
2 *the pitted lane* **potholed**, rutted, rutty, holey, bumpy, rough, uneven, eaten away; dented, indented.

pity ▶ noun **1** *her voice was full of pity* **compassion**, commiseration, condolence, sorrow, regret, sadness, distress, sympathy, fellow feeling, understanding, feeling, emotion; *archaic* ruth, rue.
OPPOSITES indifference, cruelty.
2 *it's a pity he never had any children of his own* **shame**, crying shame, cause for regret/disappointment, source of regret, sad thing, unfortunate thing, bad luck, misfortune; *informal* crime, bummer, sin.
□ **take pity on** *Amanda looked so upset that Jean took pity on her* **feel sorry for**, relent, show sympathy for, show compassion towards, be compassionate towards, be sympathetic/charitable towards, have mercy on, show mercy to, help, help out, put someone out of their misery.
▶ verb *I could see from their faces that they pitied me* **feel sorry for**, feel pity for, feel for, feel sympathy for, sympathize with, be sympathetic towards, empathize with, commiserate with, have compassion for, be compassionate towards, take pity on, be moved by, bleed for, have one's heart go out to, condole with, weep for, grieve for.

pivot ▶ noun **1** *the machine turns on a pivot* **central shaft**, fulcrum, axis, axle, swivel, pin, hub, spindle, hinge, pintle, kingpin, gudgeon, trunnion.
2 *his financial methods became the pivot of government policy* **centre**, focal point, focus, central point, hub, heart, nucleus, raison d'être, crux, keystone, cornerstone, linchpin, kingpin.
▶ verb **1** *a large panel in the side pivots inwards* **rotate**, turn, revolve, spin, swivel, twirl, whirl, wheel, oscillate.
2 *the government's reaction* **pivoted on** *the response of the prime minister* **depend**, hinge, turn, centre, hang, rely, rest, be contingent; revolve around.

pivotal ▶ adjective *Japan's pivotal role in the world economy* **central**, crucial, vital, critical, focal, essential, key, significant, important, determining, decisive, deciding.

pixie ▶ noun **elf**, fairy, sprite, imp, brownie, puck, leprechaun, hobgoblin, peri; *literary* faerie, fay; *rare* nix, nixie, elfin, hob.

placard ▶ noun *placards with slogans that read 'Stop the War'* **notice**, poster, public notice, sign, bill, sticker, advertisement; banner; *French* affiche; *informal* ad; *Brit. informal* advert.

placate ▶ verb *John did his best to placate her* **pacify**, calm, calm down, appease, mollify, soothe, win over, quiet, conciliate, propitiate, make peace with, humour; pour oil on troubled waters; *Brit.* quieten (down); *Austral.* square someone off.
OPPOSITES provoke, anger.

placatory ▶ adjective *a placatory gesture* **conciliatory**, pacifying, appeasing, calming, mollifying, propitiatory, peacemaking; *rare* pacificatory, placative, propitiative, irenic.

place ▶ noun **1** *the hotel is an ideal place to have pre-dinner cocktails* **location**, site, spot, scene, setting, position, point, situation, area, region, whereabouts, locale; venue; *technical* locus.
2 *she gets to visit millions of foreign places every year* **town**, **city**, village, hamlet; country, state, area, region; **locality**, district, neighbourhood, quarter, section; *literary* clime.
3 *at last she had a place of her own* **home**, house, flat, apartment, a roof over one's head; accommodation, establishment, property; rooms, quarters, lodgings; *French* pied-à-terre; *informal* pad, digs; *Brit. informal* gaff; *formal* residence, abode, dwelling, dwelling place, domicile, habitation.
4 *I think if I were in your place, I'd agree* **situation**, position, circumstances, condition; *informal* shoes.
5 *a place was reserved for her in the front row* **seat**, chair, position, space.
6 *I offered him a place in the company* **job**, position, post, appointment, situation, office; employment; *informal* berth; *archaic* employ.
7 *I know my place* **status**, position, station, standing, grade, rank, footing, niche; *dated* estate.
8 *she decided it was not her place to make such suggestions* **responsibility**, duty, job, task, role, function, part, concern, affair, mission, charge; right, privilege, prerogative.
□ **in place 1** *the full length veil was held in place by a band of pearls* **in position**, in situ.
2 *contingency plans should be in place* **ready**, set up, established, arranged, in order, all set.
□ **in place of** *use lemon juice in place of salt | maybe Newman can go in my place* **instead of**, as an alternative for, rather than, as a substitute for, as a replacement for, in exchange for, in lieu of; in someone's stead.
□ **out of place 1** *I never saw her with a hair out of place* **out of position**, out of order, in disorder, disarranged, in disarray, disorganized, in a mess, messy, topsy-turvy, muddled.
2 *he has never said anything to me that was out of place* **inappropriate**, unsuitable, unseemly, improper, untoward, inapposite, out of keeping, unbecoming, unfit, misplaced, wrong.
3 *such a glamorous woman seemed out of place in a launderette* **incongruous**, out of one's element, like a fish out of water, uncomfortable, ill at ease, uneasy.
□ **put someone in his/her place humiliate**, take down a peg or two, deflate, crush, squelch, squash, humble, mortify, make someone eat humble pie, take the wind out of someone's sails; *informal* cut down to size, settle someone's hash; *N. Amer. informal* make someone eat crow.
□ **take place** *people laid flowers at the spot where the crash took place* **happen**, occur, come about, transpire, crop up, materialize, arise, chance, fall out; *N. Amer. informal* go down; *literary* come to pass, befall, betide.
□ **take the place of** *Lucy stepped in at very short notice to take Joan's place* **replace**, stand in for, be a substitute for, substitute for, act for, fill in for, cover for; take over from, relieve.
▶ verb **1** *newspapers and magazines were placed on the table* **put down**, **put**, set, set down, lay down, deposit, position, plant, rest, stand, sit, settle, station, situate, leave, stow, prop, lean; arrange, set out, array; *informal* stick, dump, bung, park, plonk, pop; *N. Amer. informal* plunk.
2 *I would never betray the trust you placed in me* **put**, lay, set, pin, invest.
3 *a survey placed the company 13th for achievement* **rank**, order, put in order, grade, group, arrange, sort, class, classify, categorize; put, set, assign.
4 *she seemed familiar, but Joe couldn't quite place her* **identify**, recognize, remember, put one's finger on, put a name to, pin down, locate, pinpoint.
5 *the agency had placed 3,000 people in work | the children were placed with foster-parents* **find employment for**, find a job for; **find a home for**, accommodate, find accommodation for; allocate, assign, appoint.

placement ▶ noun **1** *the placement of the chairs around the fire* **positioning**, placing, putting in place, arrangement, position, arranging, deployment, location, disposition, disposal, emplacement, installation, stationing.
2 *teaching practice placements* **job**, assignment, posting, position, appointment, engagement.

placid ▶ adjective **1** *she's normally very placid* **even-tempered**, **calm**, equable, tranquil, imperturbable, unexcitable, peaceable, peaceful, serene, mild, gentle, quiet, cool, cool-headed, collected, {cool, calm, and collected}, composed, self-possessed, poised, easy-going, temperate, level-headed, steady, unruffled, unmoved, undisturbed, unperturbed, unemotional, phlegmatic, stolid, bovine; *informal* unflappable; *rare* equanimous.
OPPOSITES excitable, temperamental.
2 *the placid waters of a small lake | a placid village* **quiet**, calm, tranquil, still, peaceful, motionless, smooth, waveless, pacific, unruffled, undisturbed, like a millpond; restful, sleepy.
OPPOSITES stormy, rough.

CHOOSE THE RIGHT WORD

placid, peaceful, calm, serene, tranquil
See CALM.

plagiarism ▶ noun *there were accusations of plagiarism* **copying**, infringement of copyright, piracy, theft, stealing, poaching, appropriation; *informal* cribbing.

plagiarize ▶ verb *he was fined for plagiarizing a song* **copy**, **pass off as one's own**, infringe the copyright of, pirate, steal, poach, borrow, appropriate; *informal* rip off, lift, crib; *Brit. informal* pinch, nick.

plague ▶ noun **1** *an outbreak of plague | they died of the plague* **disease**, sickness; bubonic plague, pneumonic plague, the Black Death; contagious disease, contagion, epidemic, pandemic; *archaic* pestilence, the pest, murrain.
2 *another hot summer has produced a plague of cat fleas* **huge number**,

infestation, epidemic, invasion, influx, swarm, multitude, host.
3 *staff theft is usually the plague of restaurants* **bane**, curse, scourge, affliction, blight, cancer, canker.
▶ **verb 1** *he has been plagued by poor health* **afflict**, bedevil, cause suffering to, torture, torment, trouble, beset, dog, curse, rack.
2 *he was plaguing her with questions* **pester**, harass, badger, bother, torment, persecute, bedevil, harry, hound, disturb, trouble, be a nuisance to, keep after, irritate, worry, nag, annoy, vex, molest; *N. English* mither; *informal* hassle, bug, aggravate, give someone a hard time, drive up the wall, drive round the bend; *N. Amer. informal* devil, ride.

plain ▶ **adjective 1** *it was plain that something was very wrong* **obvious**, clear, crystal clear, as clear as crystal, evident, apparent, manifest, patent, visible, discernible, perceptible, perceivable, noticeable, detectable, recognizable, observable, unmistakable, transparent, palpable, distinct, pronounced, marked, striking, conspicuous, overt, self-evident, indisputable; as plain as a pikestaff, staring someone in the face, writ large, written all over someone, as plain as day, plain to see, beyond (a) doubt, beyond question; *informal* as plain as the nose on one's face, standing/sticking out like a sore thumb, standing/sticking out a mile.
2 *put it in plain English* **intelligible**, comprehensible, understandable, coherent, accessible, uncomplicated, lucid, perspicuous, unambiguous, clear, simple, straightforward, clearly expressed, clear-cut, direct, digestible, user-friendly.
OPPOSITES unclear, obscure.
3 *there were indrawn breaths at such plain speaking* **candid**, frank, outspoken, forthright, plain-spoken, direct, honest, truthful, blunt, downright, unvarnished, bald, straight from the shoulder, explicit, unequivocal; *informal* upfront; *archaic* round, free-spoken.
4 *her plain black dress* **simple**, ordinary, unadorned, undecorated, unembellished, unornamented, unpretentious, unostentatious, unfussy, homely, homespun, basic, modest, unsophisticated, penny plain, without frills; stark, severe, spartan, austere, chaste, bare, uncluttered, restrained, muted, unpatterned, patternless, everyday, workaday.
OPPOSITES fancy, elaborate.
5 *a rather plain girl* **unattractive**, unprepossessing, as plain as a pikestaff, ugly, ill-favoured, unlovely, ordinary-looking; *N. Amer.* homely; *informal* not much to look at; *Brit. informal* no oil painting.
OPPOSITES attractive, beautiful, good-looking.
6 *a plain, honest man with no nonsense about him* **straightforward**, unpretentious, simple, ordinary, average, unassuming, unaffected, honest-to-goodness, ingenuous, artless, guileless, sincere; *N. Amer.* cracker-barrel.
OPPOSITES pretentious, affected.
7 *it was plain bad luck* **sheer**, pure, downright, out-and-out, unmitigated, rank, nothing other than.
▶ **adverb** *this is just plain stupid* **downright**, utterly, absolutely, completely, totally, really, thoroughly, positively, profoundly, categorically, simply, incontrovertibly, unquestionably, undeniably; *informal* plumb.
▶ **noun** *the vast treeless plains of North America* **grassland**, **flatland**, lowland, pasture, meadowland, open country, prairie, savannah, steppe; (*in S. America*) tableland, tundra, pampas, campo, llano, vega; (*in southern Africa*) veld; *Geology* pediplain; *literary* champaign.

P

plain-spoken ▶ **adjective** *he was well known for being plain-spoken* **candid**, frank, outspoken, forthright, plain-speaking, direct, honest, truthful, open, bluff, blunt, not afraid to call a spade a spade, speaking straight from the shoulder, downright, straightforward, explicit, unequivocal, unambiguous, undiplomatic; *informal* upfront; *archaic* round, free-spoken.
OPPOSITES evasive, guarded, reticent.

plaintive ▶ **adjective** *a plaintive cry* **mournful**, sad, wistful, doleful, pathetic, pitiful, piteous, melancholy, melancholic, sorrowful, unhappy, wretched, woeful, grief-stricken, broken-hearted, heartbroken, desolate, heart-rending, forlorn, woebegone, disconsolate; *literary* plangent, heartsick, dolorous.

CHOOSE THE RIGHT WORD
plaintive, wistful, pensive
See WISTFUL.

plan ▶ **noun 1** *he had a new plan for raising money* **scheme**, plan of action, idea, master plan, game plan, proposal, proposition, ploy, suggestion, project, programme, system, method, procedure, strategy, stratagem, formula, recipe, scenario, arrangement, schedule, agenda; way, means, measure, tactic, tack, plot, device, manoeuvre, ruse; *archaic* shift.
2 *her plan was really just to find the hotel* **intention**, aim, idea, intent, objective, object, goal, target, hope, aspiration, ambition.
3 *plans for the clubhouse have been drawn up by a local architect* **blueprint**, drawing, scale drawing, diagram, sketch, chart, map, layout; illustration, representation, delineation; *N. Amer.* plat.
▶ **verb 1** *plan your route in advance | oil workers were planning strike action* **organize**, arrange, work out, think out, design, line up, outline, sketch out, map out, chalk out, draft, prepare, schedule, programme, formulate, frame, project, develop, set up, fix up, shape, build, devise, concoct, contrive; plot, scheme, cook up, hatch, brew, mastermind, orchestrate, choreograph; *N. Amer.* slate; *rare* excogitate.
2 *he plans to buy an apartment in the city* **intend**, make plans, aim, propose, mean, be resolved, have in mind, hope, want, wish, desire, contemplate, envisage, foresee, envision, expect; *formal* purpose.
3 *there are many things to bear in mind when planning a new garden* **design**, draw up a plan of, make a drawing of, draw up a layout of, sketch out, make a map of, map out, make a representation of; *N. Amer.* plat.

plane¹ ▶ **noun 1** *a horizontal plane* **flat surface**, level surface; the flat, horizontal.
2 *trying to reach a higher plane of achievement* **level**, stage, degree, standard, stratum; position, rung, echelon, footing.
▶ **adjective** *a plane surface* **flat**, level, horizontal, even, flush, levelled, true; smooth, regular, uniform; *technical* planar; *rare* homaloidal.
▶ **verb 1** *seagulls swooped and planed overhead* **soar**, glide, float, drift, wheel.
2 *boats planing across the water* **skim**, glide.

plane² *See centre pages for list of* **Aircraft**
▶ **noun** *the plane crashed close to the airport* **aircraft**, craft, flying machine; *Brit.* aeroplane; *N. Amer.* airplane, ship; *informal* bird; *Brit. informal, dated* kite.

WORD LINKS
science of flight **aeronautics**

plangent ▶ **adjective** (*literary*) *from somewhere outside came a plangent keening* **melancholy**, mournful, plaintive; sonorous, reverberant, reverberating, resonant, loud.

plank ▶ **noun** *rough wooden planks* **board**, floorboard, beam, timber, stave, deal.

planning ▶ **noun** *the planning should be every bit as enjoyable as the event itself* **preparation(s)**, organization, arrangement, forethought, design, designing, drafting, working out, setting up, groundwork.

plant¹ *See centre pages for lists of* **Flowering Plants and Shrubs** **Fruit** **Fungi, Mushrooms, and Toadstools** **Grasses, Sedges, and Rushes** **Nuts** **Plant Types** **Plant Parts** **Poisonous Plants and Fungi** **Trees and Shrubs** **Vegetables**
▶ **noun 1** *a pot plant | garden plants* flower, vegetable, herb, shrub, weed; (**plants**) greenery, flora, vegetation, undergrowth; *rare* herbage, verdure.
2 *we thought he was a CIA plant spreading disinformation* **spy**, informant, informer, undercover agent, secret agent, agent, mole, infiltrator, operative; *N. Amer. informal* spook.
▶ **verb 1** *plant the seeds this autumn and they will flower next summer* **sow**, scatter, seed, put in the ground; bed out, set out, transplant.
2 *he planted his feet more firmly on the ground* **put**, **place**, set, position, station, situate, settle, stick, fix; *informal* plonk.
3 *someone had planted the idea in Alexander's mind* **insert**, impress, imprint, instil, put, place; implant, introduce, sow the seeds of, fix, establish, embed, root, lodge.
4 *the letters might have been planted there to embarrass the government* **hide**, place secretly, conceal, secrete.

WORD LINKS

related prefix	**phyto-** (e.g. ***phytoplankton***)
related suffix	**-phyte** (e.g. ***epiphyte***)
study of plants	**botany**
plant-eating	**herbivorous**
substance used to kill plants	**herbicide**

plant² *See centre pages for list of* **Factories and Workshops**
▶ **noun 1** *the plant commenced production in June* **factory**, works, foundry, mill, workshop, shop, yard, industrial unit.
2 *there has been inadequate investment in new plant* **machinery**, machines, equipment, apparatus, appliances, gear.

plaque ▶ **noun** *a commemorative plaque* **memorial tablet**, plate, stone plate, metal plate, tablet, panel, sign, brass, medallion, plaquette, cartouche.

plaster ▶ **noun 1** *he stripped away the plaster to expose the bare brick* **plasterwork**, stucco; *trademark* Artex; *rare* pargeting, parging.
2 *a statuette made of plaster* **plaster of Paris**, gypsum.
3 *waterproof plasters* **sticking plaster**, adhesive dressing, dressing, bandage; *trademark* Elastoplast, Band-Aid.
▶ **verb 1** *home-made bread plastered with butter* **cover thickly**, smother, spread, smear, cake, coat, daub, bedaub, overlay; *literary* besmear.
2 *he arrived late, his hair plastered down with sweat* **flatten (down)**, smooth down, slick down, sleek down.

plastic ▶ **adjective 1** *at very high temperatures, rocks may become plastic* **malleable**, mouldable, shapable, pliable, pliant, ductile, flexible, soft, workable, supple, bendable; *informal* bendy; *rare* fictile.
OPPOSITE rigid.
2 *the plastic minds of young children* **impressionable**, malleable, easily influenced, responsive, receptive, mouldable, pliable, pliant, flexible, compliant, tractable, manageable, controllable, docile, biddable, persuadable, susceptible, manipulable, influenceable; unformed, inexperienced; *rare* ductile, persuasible, suasible.
OPPOSITE intractable.

3 *she smiled a little plastic smile* **artificial**, false, synthetic, fake, superficial, pseudo, sham, bogus, ersatz, assumed, spurious, specious, unnatural, insincere; *informal* phoney, pretend.
OPPOSITE genuine.

plasticity ▶ noun *the plasticity of the clay* **malleability**, softness, pliancy, pliability, flexibility, suppleness, ductility.

plate ▶ noun 1 *he pushed his empty plate to one side* **dish**, platter, bowl, salver; dinner plate, side plate, soup plate; *Scottish & N. English* ashet; *archaic* trencher, charger; *rare* paten.
2 *a plate of spaghetti* **plateful**, helping, portion, serving, platter.
3 *the ship's hull was made of overlapping steel plates* **panel**, sheet, layer, lamina, leaf, pane, slab.
4 *a brass plate on the door* **plaque**, nameplate, door plate, tablet, sign, brass, medallion, plaquette, cartouche.
5 *the book contains sixty colour plates* **picture**, print, illustration, photograph, photo, engraving, lithograph; *rare* vignette.
▶ verb *the roof was plated with steel* **cover**, coat, overlay, laminate, veneer; electroplate, anodize, galvanize, gild, platinize, silver, tin, nickel.

plateau ▶ noun 1 *a windswept plateau* **upland**, tableland, elevated plain, mesa, highland, table.
2 *house prices have reached a plateau* period of little change, quiescent period, levelling off period; let-up, break, respite, lull.

platform ▶ noun 1 *another official climbed on the platform and spoke to the crowd* **stage**, **dais**, stand, rostrum, podium, soapbox; *Indian* mandapam.
2 *the Democratic Party's platform* **policy**, **programme**, party line, manifesto, plan, plan of action, principles, tenets, objectives, aims.

platitude ▶ noun *a string of empty platitudes* **cliché**, truism, commonplace, hackneyed/trite/banal/overworked saying, banality, old chestnut; bromide, inanity, tag.

platitudinous ▶ adjective *politicians delivering platitudinous sound bites* **hackneyed**, overworked, overused, clichéd, banal, trite, commonplace, stock, stereotyped, stereotypical, set, well worn, stale, tired, vapid, inane, unimaginative, unoriginal, vieux jeu, dull, flat, conventional; *informal* corny, old hat; *rare* truistic, bromidic.
OPPOSITES original, fresh.

platonic ▶ adjective *our relationship is purely platonic* **non-sexual**, non-physical, chaste; spiritual, intellectual, friendly.
OPPOSITES physical, sexual.

platoon ▶ noun *a platoon of British Royal Marines* **unit**, patrol, troop, squad, team, squadron, company, group, corps, division, outfit, detachment, contingent.

platter ▶ noun *the meat was arranged on silver platters* **plate**, dish, serving plate, serving dish, salver, tray; *Scottish & N. English* ashet; *archaic* charger, trencher; *rare* paten.

plaudits ▶ plural noun *the president will win plaudits from most economists if he carries through his plans* **praise**, acclaim, acclamation, commendation, congratulations, encomiums, approval, approbation, accolades, compliments, cheers, tributes, salutes, bouquets; a pat on the back, kudos, good press; applause, a round of applause, a standing ovation; *informal* a (big) hand; *rare* laudation.
OPPOSITES condemnation, criticism.

plausible ▶ adjective *a plausible explanation* **credible**, reasonable, believable, likely, feasible, probable, tenable, possible, conceivable, imaginable, within the bounds of possibility, convincing, persuasive, cogent, sound, rational, logical, acceptable, thinkable; smooth-talking, smooth-tongued, smooth, glib, specious; *rare* verisimilar, colourable.
OPPOSITES unlikely, improbable.

play *See centre pages for list of* **Plays**
▶ verb 1 *the children were playing with toys on the floor* **amuse oneself**, entertain oneself, enjoy oneself, have fun, have a good time, relax, rest, be at leisure, occupy oneself, divert oneself, play games, frolic, frisk, gambol, romp, cavort, caper; *informal* mess about/around, lark (about/around); *dated* sport; *archaic or humorous* disport oneself.
2 *I used to play football* **take part in**, participate in, engage in, be involved in, join in, compete in, do.
3 *Liverpool play Sheffield United on Wednesday* **compete against**, contend against, oppose, take on, challenge, vie with, rival.
4 *he was about to play Macbeth* **act the part of**, play the part of, act, take the role of, enact, represent, perform, appear as, portray, depict, impersonate, pretend to be, execute, render, interpret; *rare* personate.
5 *he never learned to play a musical instrument* **perform on**, make music on; blow, sound, strum.
6 *his hair gleamed as the sunlight played on it* **move lightly**, dance, flit, dart, ripple, lick, touch.
□ **play around** (*informal*) *I played around a bit but now I've settled down* **womanize**, philander, have affairs/an affair, flirt, dally, trifle/toy with someone's affections; *informal* carry on, mess about/around, play the field, play away, sleep around, swing, be a maneater; *N. Amer. informal* fool around; *vulgar slang* screw around; *rare* coquet.
□ **play at** *like a dictator he will play at being kind and good* **pretend to be**, give the appearance of, assume/affect the role of, pass oneself off as, masquerade as, profess to be, pose as, impersonate, make out, fake, feign, simulate, affect, go through the motions of; *N. Amer. informal* make like.
□ **play ball** (*informal*) *if you play ball, I can help you* **cooperate**, collaborate, play along, play the game, go along with the plan, show willing, be willing, help, lend a hand, assist, be of assistance, contribute, reciprocate, respond; *informal* pitch in.
□ **play something down** *ministers sought to play down the extent of the damage* **make light of**, make little/nothing of, set little/no store by, gloss over, de-emphasize, underemphasize, downplay, understate, underplay, minimize, shrug off; soft-pedal, tone down, diminish, downgrade, trivialize, detract from, underrate, underestimate, undervalue, think little of, disparage, decry, deprecate, talk down, belittle, slight, scoff at, sneer at; *informal* pooh-pooh; *rare* derogate.
OPPOSITE exaggerate.
□ **play for time use delaying tactics**, stall, temporize, gain time, hang back, hang fire, hold back, procrastinate, beat about the bush, drag one's feet, delay, filibuster, stonewall.
□ **play it by ear improvise**, extemporize, rise to the occasion, ad lib; take it as it comes; *Latin* ad libitum; *informal* busk it, wing it.
□ **play on** *it is despicable to play on the fears of ordinary people* **exploit**, take advantage of, use, make use of, turn to (one's) account, profit by, capitalize on, impose on, trade on, milk, abuse, misuse; *informal* walk all over.
□ **play the fool clown about/around**, act the clown, act the fool, fool about/around, mess about/around, monkey about/around, footle about/around, joke, play pranks, indulge in horseplay; *informal* horse about/around, screw around, puddle about/around, act the goat, lark about/around; *Brit. informal* muck about/around, fanny about/around; *Brit. vulgar slang* piss about/around, arse about/around; *dated* play the giddy goat.
□ **play the game** *I don't trust them—they don't always play the game* **play fair**, be fair, play by the rules, abide by the rules, follow the rules, conform, be a good sport, toe the line, keep in step.
□ **play up** 1 *there were some boys that really did play up* **misbehave**, be misbehaved, behave badly, be bad, be naughty, be mischievous, get up to mischief, be disobedient, be awkward, give/cause/make trouble; *Brit. informal* be stroppy, be bolshie.
2 (*Brit. informal*) *the boiler's playing up again* **not work properly**, be defective, be faulty, malfunction, act up, give trouble; *informal* be/go on the blink.
3 (*Brit. informal*) *his injured leg was playing up* **be painful**, hurt, ache, be sore, cause pain, cause discomfort, cause trouble, annoy; *informal* kill someone, give someone gyp.
□ **play something up** *the press has played up the problems* **emphasize**, put/lay emphasis on, accentuate, bring/draw/call attention to, focus attention on, point up, underline, underscore, highlight, spotlight, foreground, feature, give prominence to, bring to the fore, heighten, stress, accent.
□ **play up to** *he's been playing up to her the whole time* **ingratiate oneself with**, seek the favour of, try to get on the good side of, curry favour with, court, fawn on/over, make up to, keep someone sweet, toady to, crawl to, grovel to, pander to, be obsequious towards, truckle to, flatter; *informal* soft-soap, suck up to, butter up, be all over, lick someone's boots; *N. Amer. informal* brown-nose; *vulgar slang* lick/kiss someone's arse.
▶ noun 1 *one must strike a balance between work and play* **amusement**, entertainment, relaxation, recreation, enjoyment, pleasure, diversion, distraction, leisure, fun, games, fun and games; playfulness, horseplay, skylarking, larks, a good time, jollification, junketing, merrymaking, revelry; *informal* living it up; *dated* sport.
OPPOSITE work.
2 *a play by Shakespeare* **drama**, stage play, stage show, theatrical work, theatrical piece, radio play, television play, teleplay, screenplay, comedy, tragedy, farce, sketch; production, performance, spectacle, show.
3 *they have understood the play of the real world* **action**, activity, operation, movement, motion, agency, employment, working, function, functioning, exercise, interaction, interplay.
4 *the steering rack was loose, and there was a little play* **movement**, freedom of movement, free motion, slack, give; room to manoeuvre, room to operate, scope, latitude, elbow room, space, margin.
5 *we enable people to give full play to their energy and abilities* **scope**, range, latitude, liberty, licence, freedom, indulgence, free rein, release.

playboy ▶ noun *Nigel isn't the marrying type—he's just a playboy* **socialite**, pleasure seeker, sybarite; ladies' man, womanizer, philanderer, rake, roué; rich man about town; *informal* ladykiller, gay dog; *W. Indian informal* saga boy.

player *See centre pages for lists of* **Actors** **Cricket Roles and Positions** **Musicians** **Rugby Players**
▶ noun 1 *a tournament enjoyed by both players and spectators* **participant**, **contestant**, competitor, contender, team member; sportsman, sportswoman, sportsperson, athlete.
2 *the younger players in the orchestra* **musician**, performer, instrumentalist, soloist, virtuoso, artist, artiste.
3 *the players of the Royal Shakespeare Company* **actor**, **actress**, performer, thespian, entertainer, artist, artiste, trouper.

playful ▶ adjective 1 *she was in a playful mood* **frisky**, jolly, fun-loving,

P

lively, full of fun, high-spirited, spirited, in high spirits, exuberant, perky, skittish, coltish, kittenish; mischievous, impish, devilish, puckish, roguish, rascally, tricksy, prankish; *informal* full of beans, frolicky; *dated* gay; *archaic* frolicsome, gamesome, sportive; *rare* ludic.
OPPOSITE solemn.
2 *a playful remark* **light-hearted**, in fun, in jest, joking, jokey, teasing, humorous, jocular, jesting, good-natured, tongue-in-cheek, facetious, frivolous, flippant, arch, waggish, flirtatious, whimsical; *rare* jocose.
OPPOSITE serious.

playground ▶ noun play area, park, playing field, recreation ground, amusement park; *Brit.* adventure playground.

playmate ▶ noun **friend**, playfellow, companion; *informal* chum, pal, buddy; *Brit. informal* mate.

plaything ▶ noun *a child's plaything* **toy**, game, amusement.

playwright ▶ noun **dramatist**, writer, tragedian; scriptwriter, screenwriter, scenarist; *rare* dramaturge, dramaturgist, comedist.

plea ▶ noun **1** *a desperate plea for aid* **appeal**, entreaty, supplication, petition, prayer; request, call, solicitation, invocation, suit; *rare* imploration, adjuration.
2 *her plea of a headache was not entirely false* **claim**, explanation, defence, justification, vindication; excuse, pretext.

plead ▶ verb **1** *he had pleaded with her to stay* **beg**, entreat, beseech, implore, appeal to, petition, supplicate, importune, pray to, request, ask earnestly, call on, adjure; apply to, solicit; *rare* obsecrate.
2 *his accomplice pleaded ignorance | she pleaded her case to no avail* **claim**, use as an excuse, assert, allege; **argue**, state, present, put forward.

pleasant ▶ adjective **1** *a very pleasant evening* **enjoyable**, pleasing, pleasurable, nice, agreeable, satisfying, gratifying, welcome, good, acceptable, to one's liking; entertaining, amusing, diverting; delightful, charming, inviting, attractive, beautiful; fine, balmy, salubrious; *Scottish* bonny, couthy; *informal* lovely, great; *N. Amer. informal* neat; *S. African informal* lekker, mooi.
2 *the staff are always pleasant* **friendly**, agreeable, amiable, affable, nice, genial, likeable, amicable, lovely, good-humoured, personable, congenial, hospitable, approachable, good-natured, companionable; gracious, courteous, polite, cordial, obliging, helpful, considerate; cheerful, warm, charming, engaging, winning, delightful, sweet, as nice as pie, sympathetic; *German* gemütlich; *N. English & Scottish* canny; *Scottish* couthy; *archaic* fair-spoken.
OPPOSITES unpleasant, disagreeable, nasty.

pleasantry ▶ noun **1** (usually **pleasantries**) *we exchanged the usual pleasantries* **banter**, badinage; inconsequential remark, friendly/good-natured remark, polite remark, casual remark; *N. Amer. informal* josh.
2 *he laughed at his own pleasantry* **joke**, **witticism**, quip, jest, gag, witty remark, sally; *French* bon mot; *informal* wisecrack, crack.

please ▶ verb **1** *he'd do anything to please her* **make happy**, give pleasure to, make someone pleased/glad/content, make someone feel good, delight, charm, amuse, divert, entertain, be agreeable to, gladden, cheer up; satisfy, gratify, humour, oblige, content, suit; *informal* tickle pink.
OPPOSITES displease, annoy.
2 *guests are urged to do as they please* **like**, want, wish, desire, see/think fit, choose, be inclined, will, prefer, opt.
▶ adverb *let me know as soon as possible, please | please sit down* **if you please**, if you wouldn't mind, if you would be so good; kindly, have the goodness to, pray; *archaic* prithee.

pleased ▶ adjective *Edward seemed really pleased to see me* **happy**, glad, delighted, gratified, grateful, thankful, content, contented, satisfied, well pleased, thrilled, elated, as pleased as Punch, overjoyed, cock-a-hoop, like a dog with two tails, like a child with a new toy; *informal* over the moon, tickled pink, on cloud nine/seven; *Brit. informal* chuffed; *N. English informal* made up; *Austral. informal* wrapped; *derogatory* complacent, smug; *humorous* gruntled.
OPPOSITES unhappy, dissatisfied.

pleasing ▶ adjective **1** *a very pleasing day* **nice**, **agreeable**, pleasant, pleasurable, satisfying, gratifying, welcome, good, acceptable, to one's liking, enjoyable, entertaining, amusing, delightful, fine; *informal* lovely. *See also* PLEASANT *sense* 1.
2 *her pleasing manner* **friendly**, **amiable**, pleasant, agreeable, affable, nice, genial, likeable, good-humoured, charming, engaging, winning, delightful; *informal* lovely. *See also* PLEASANT *sense* 2.

pleasurable ▶ adjective *a pleasurable experience* **pleasant**, enjoyable, delightful, nice, pleasing, agreeable, to one's liking, congenial, gratifying; fun, entertaining, amusing, diverting; *informal* lovely, great, wonderful; *S. African* lekker, mooi.
OPPOSITES disagreeable, unpleasant.

pleasure ▶ noun **1** *she smiled with pleasure* **happiness**, delight, joy, gladness, rapture, glee, satisfaction, gratification, fulfilment, contentment, contentedness, enjoyment, amusement; *humorous* delectation.
2 *watercolour painting is one of his greatest pleasures* **joy**, delight, source of pleasure, enjoyment, amusement, diversion, recreation, pastime, divertissement; treat, thrill.
3 *he doesn't believe in mixing business and pleasure* **enjoyment**, fun, entertainment, amusement, diversion, recreation, leisure, relaxation; *informal* jollies; *Brit. informal* beer and skittles.
4 *they were indolent and addicted to a life of pleasure* **sensual gratification**, **hedonism**, indulgence, self-indulgence, self-gratification, lack of self-restraint, lotus-eating; *rare* sybaritism.
5 *what's your pleasure?* **wish**, **desire**, preference, will, inclination, choice, option.
□ **take pleasure in** *even the youngest children take pleasure in music* **enjoy**, delight in, love, like, adore, be entertained by, be amused by, be pleased by, appreciate, relish, savour, revel in, glory in; *informal* get a kick out of, get a thrill out of.
□ **with pleasure** *'Would you mind telling me the way to the station?' 'With pleasure.'* **gladly**, willingly, happily, readily, cheerfully, by all means, of course; *archaic* fain.
OPPOSITES displeasure, sorrow, pain.

WORD LINKS
pursuit of pleasure **hedonism**

pleat ▶ noun *a pleat at the edge of the curtain* **fold**, tuck, crease, gather, pucker, crimp; *rare* plication.
▶ verb *the garment is softly pleated at the front* **fold**, tuck, crease, gather, pucker, crimp; *rare* plicate.

plebeian ▶ noun *the hostility towards him was shared by plebeians and gentry alike* **proletarian**, **commoner**, common person, man/woman/person in the street, working-class person, worker, working person; peasant; *informal, derogatory* pleb, prole.
OPPOSITES aristocrat, noble, patrician.
▶ adjective **1** *people of plebeian descent* **lower-class**, low-class, working-class, proletarian, common, peasant, mean, humble, lowly, low, of low birth, low-born, low-ranking, ignoble, undistinguished; *archaic* baseborn.
OPPOSITES aristocratic, noble, patrician.
2 *a man of plebeian tastes* **uncultured**, uncultivated, unrefined, lowbrow, philistine, uneducated, unpolished, provincial, rustic; coarse, uncouth, crass, common, vulgar, base, boorish, gross; *informal* plebby; *Brit. informal* non-U; *rare* illiberal.
OPPOSITES refined, cultivated, sophisticated.

plebiscite ▶ noun *a plebiscite for the approval of constitutional reforms* **vote**, referendum, ballot, poll.

pledge ▶ noun **1** *he fulfilled his election pledge to end the war* **promise**, undertaking, vow, word, word of honour, commitment, assurance, oath, covenant, bond, agreement, guarantee, warrant.
2 *he had given the object as a pledge to a creditor* **surety**, **bond**, security, collateral, guarantee, deposit, pawn; *archaic* gage, earnest.
3 *take this as a pledge of my sincerity* **token**, **symbol**, sign, mark, testimony, proof, evidence, badge.
▶ verb **1** *the president had publicly pledged that he would root out corruption* **promise**, give one's word, vow, swear, give an assurance, give an undertaking, undertake, take an oath, swear an oath, engage, contract, commit oneself, bind oneself, declare, affirm, avow, state; *rare* asseverate.
2 *Japan pledged $100 million in aid* **undertake to give**, promise (to give), donate, contribute, give, make a gift of, put oneself down for, put up; *Brit.* covenant.
3 *even his home is pledged as security against the loans* **mortgage**, put up as collateral, guarantee, pawn; *archaic* gage, plight.

plenary ▶ adjective **1** *the council has plenary powers to administer the agreement* **unconditional**, unlimited, unrestricted, unqualified, absolute, complete, sweeping, comprehensive; plenipotentiary.
2 *a plenary session of the European Parliament* **full**, fully constituted, general, complete, entire, open.

plenipotentiary ▶ noun *his last posting was as plenipotentiary in Paris* **diplomat**, representative; ambassador, minister, emissary, chargé d'affaires, chargé, envoy, legation; *archaic* legate.

plenitude ▶ noun *Croft Farm boasts a plenitude of animals and birds* **abundance**, lot, large number, wealth, profusion, quantity, cornucopia, plethora, superabundance; *informal* load, heap, mass, stack, ton; *Brit. informal* shedload; *N. Amer. informal* slew; *Austral./NZ informal* swag.

plenteous ▶ adjective (*literary*). *See* PLENTIFUL.

plentiful ▶ adjective *a plentiful supply of food* **abundant**, copious, ample, profuse, rich, lavish, liberal, generous, bountiful, large, huge, great, bumper, flush, overflowing, superabundant, infinite, inexhaustible, opulent, prolific, teeming; *informal* a gogo, galore; *S. African informal* lank; *literary* bounteous, plenteous.
OPPOSITES scarce, meagre.
□ **be plentiful be abundant**, abound, be numerous, exist in abundance, proliferate, be thick on the ground; *informal* grow on trees; *Brit. informal* be two/ten a penny.

plenty ▶ noun *we live in times of plenty* **prosperity**, affluence, wealth, opulence, comfort, well-being, luxury; plentifulness, abundance, fruitfulness, profusion; *literary* plenteousness.
▶ pronoun *there are plenty of books available on the subject* **a lot of**, many, a

P

great deal of, a good deal of, a large number/amount of, a plethora of, quantities of, enough, more than enough, enough and to spare, no lack of, sufficient, a wealth of, a feast of, a cornucopia of; *informal* loads of, lots of, heaps of, bags of, stacks of, piles of, masses of, tons of, oodles of, oceans of, a raft of, a hatful of, more ... than one can shake a stick at; *Brit. informal* lashings of; *N. Amer. informal* scads of, a slew of, gobs of, gazillions of; *Austral./NZ informal* a swag of; *vulgar slang* a shitload of, shitloads of; *archaic* a deal of, a mickle of, a peck of.

plethora ▶ noun *a plethora of newspaper opinion polls* **excess**, **abundance**, overabundance, superfluity, surfeit, profusion, more than enough, too many, too much, enough and to spare, superabundance, surplus, glut, flood, torrent, deluge, embarrassment; *informal* more ... than one can shake a stick at; *rare* nimiety.
OPPOSITES dearth, lack.

pliability ▶ noun *the pliability of leather* **flexibility**, pliancy, elasticity, whippiness, suppleness, malleability, plasticity, springiness, ductility, bendability.

pliable ▶ adjective **1** *quality leather is pliable* **flexible**, easily bent, bendable, pliant, elastic, supple, stretchable, malleable, workable, plastic, whippy, springy, limber, ductile, tensile; *informal* bendy; *archaic* flexile.
OPPOSITE rigid.
2 *pliable teenage minds* **malleable**, easily influenced, impressionable, flexible, adaptable, pliant, compliant, docile, biddable, tractable, like putty in one's hands, yielding, manageable, governable, controllable, amenable, accommodating, susceptible, suggestible, influenceable, persuadable, manipulable, responsive, receptive; *rare* persuasible, suasible, susceptive.
OPPOSITES intractable, obdurate.

pliant ▶ adjective **1** *the tsar had replaced him with a more pliant successor* **compliant**, biddable, docile, tractable, yielding, malleable, manageable, governable, controllable, amenable, accommodating, susceptible, suggestible, easily influenced, influenceable, persuadable, manipulable, like putty in one's hands, responsive, receptive; *rare* persuasible, suasible, susceptive.
2 *memories of Isabelle lying pliant in his arms* **supple**, soft, loose-limbed, willowy, lissom, lithe, limber.

plight ▶ noun *an attempt to highlight the plight of the homeless* **predicament**, unfortunate/difficult situation, sorry condition, sad state, trouble, difficulty, mess, dire straits, extremity, bind; circumstances, situation, condition, case, state; *informal* dilemma, tight corner/spot, hole, pickle, jam, fix, scrape.

plod ▶ verb **1** *Melissa plodded wearily up the stairs* **trudge**, walk heavily, clump, stomp, stump, tramp, drag oneself, lumber, slog; *Brit. informal* trog.
2 *I suppose I'll just have to plod through the whole book* **work one's way**, wade, plough, toil, trawl, soldier (on), proceed laboriously, labour; *informal* slog.

plot ▶ noun **1** *a plot to overthrow the government* **conspiracy**, intrigue, secret plan/scheme, stratagem; machinations; *rare* cabal, complot, covin.
2 *the plot of her next novel* **storyline**, story, chain of events, scenario, action, thread; *rare* diegesis, mythos.
3 *a three-acre plot* **piece of ground**, patch, area, location, parcel, tract, allotment, acreage; *N. Amer.* lot, plat; *N. Amer. & Austral./NZ* homesite; *S. African* stand, yard, erf.
▶ verb **1** *he was found guilty of plotting the downfall of the government* **plan**, scheme, arrange, organize, lay, hatch, concoct, devise, frame, think up, dream up, cook up, brew, conceive.
2 *the president's brother was accused of plotting against him* **conspire**, scheme, participate in a conspiracy, intrigue, collude, connive, manoeuvre; *rare* machinate, cabal, complot.
3 *the position of the fifty-three sites was plotted* **mark**, chart, map, indicate, represent, graph.

plotter ▶ noun *the plotters had intended to assassinate the president* **conspirator**, co-conspirator, schemer, intriguer; planner; *rare* machinator, conspirer, Machiavellian, cabalist.

plough ▶ verb **1** *the fields had been ploughed* **cultivate**, till, work, furrow, harrow, ridge, break up, turn up.
2 *the car overturned and ploughed into a lamp post* **career**, plunge, crash, smash, bulldoze, hurtle, cannon, lurch, drive, run, careen; *N. Amer. informal* barrel.
3 *they ploughed their way through deep snow* **trudge**, plod, toil, clump, push one's way, wade, flounder, press, move laboriously; *informal* slog; *Brit. informal* trog.

ploy ▶ noun *perhaps this had been a ploy to revive her husband's fading interest* **ruse**, **tactic**, move, device, stratagem, scheme, trick, gambit, cunning plan, manoeuvre, contrivance, expedient, dodge, subterfuge, game, wile; *Brit. informal* wheeze; *archaic* shift.

pluck ▶ verb **1** *Jane plucked a thread from the lapel of his coat* **remove**, **pick off**, pick, pull, pull off/out, extract, take, take off.
2 *she plucked at his T-shirt* **pull (at)**, tug (at), clutch (at), snatch (at), take hold of, grab, seize, catch (at), tweak, twitch, jerk; *informal* yank.
3 *the turkeys are plucked and cleaned* remove the feathers from, strip of feathers; *rare* deplume, displume.
4 *he picked up the guitar and began to pluck the strings* **strum**, pick, thrum, twang, plunk, finger; play pizzicato.
▶ noun *it must have taken a lot of pluck to go there alone* **courage**, bravery, nerve, pluckiness, boldness, courageousness, braveness, backbone, spine, daring, spirit, intrepidness, intrepidity, fearlessness, mettle, determination, fortitude, resolve, resolution, stout-heartedness, hardihood, dauntlessness, valour, doughtiness, heroism, audacity; *informal* grit, guts, spunk, gutsiness, gumption; *Brit. informal* bottle, ballsiness; *N. Amer. informal* moxie, cojones, sand; *vulgar slang* balls.

plucky ▶ adjective *plucky staff defeat armed raiders* **brave**, courageous, bold, daring, fearless, intrepid, spirited, game, valiant, valorous, lionhearted, heroic, gallant, stout-hearted, stout, dauntless, resolute, determined, gritty, stalwart, undaunted, indomitable, unflinching, audacious, unafraid, doughty, mettlesome; *informal* gutsy, ballsy, spunky, have-a-go, feisty.
OPPOSITES cowardly, timid, timorous.

plug ▶ noun **1** *she pulled out the plug and the liquid drained away* **stopper**, bung, cork, seal, spigot, spile; *N. Amer.* stopple.
2 *a plug of tobacco* **wad**, quid, twist, chew; *N. Amer. informal* chaw; *rare* pigtail, cud, cake.
3 (*informal*) *he put in a plug for his new book* **piece of publicity**, favourable mention, advertisement, promotion, recommendation, mention, good word, commercial; *informal* hype, push, puff, ad, boost, ballyhoo; *Brit. informal* advert.
▶ verb **1** *plug the holes with dowels* **stop (up)**, seal (up/off), close (up/off), cork, stopper, bung, block (up/off), dam (up), fill (up), pack, stuff; *N. Amer.* stopple.
2 (*informal*) *he plugged his new film* **publicize**, promote, give publicity to, advertise, mention, give a mention to, write up, build up, beat/bang the drum for, commend, draw attention to; *informal* hype, hype up, push, puff, boost.
3 (*informal*) *don't say a word or I'll plug you* **shoot**, hit, shoot down, gun down, pick off; *informal* blast, pump full of lead.
□ **plug away** (*informal*) *he plugged away at his writing* **toil**, labour, toil away, plod away, work away, slave away, soldier on with, persevere with, persist with, keep on with, plough on with, hammer away, grind away; *informal* slog away, beaver away, peg away; *archaic* drudge away.

plum ▶ adjective *a plum job* **excellent**, very good, wonderful, marvellous, choice, best, prize, first-class; *informal* great, terrific, cushy; *Brit. informal* plummy.

plumb[1] ▶ verb *the actor's attempt to plumb the twisted psyche of Richard III* **explore**, probe, delve into, search, examine, investigate, scrutinize, inspect, sound out, go into, understand, fathom, get to the bottom of, penetrate, unravel.
□ **plumb the depths** *she had* **plumbed the depths of** *depravity* **find**, reach the lowest possible level, reach the lowest point, get down to the bottom, reach the nadir, experience the worst extremes, reach rock bottom.
▶ adverb **1** *the bullets went plumb through the middle of the screen* **right**, exactly, precisely, directly, dead, straight, without interruption; *informal* bang, slap, slap bang, smack.
2 *they must both be plumb crazy* **utterly**, absolutely, completely, downright, totally, entirely, wholly, quite, altogether, thoroughly, stark.
3 *the bell hangs plumb within the tower of the church* **vertically**, perpendicularly, straight up, straight up and down.
▶ adjective *the bird's flight ends with a plumb drop* **vertical**, perpendicular, straight.

plumb[2] ▶ verb *he had* **plumbed in** *a washing machine* **install**, put in, fit, put/set in place.

plume ▶ noun *black ostrich plumes* **feather**, crest, quill; *technical* plumule; *literary* pinion.
▶ verb
□ **plume oneself** *he plumed himself on his latest innovation* **congratulate oneself**, pat oneself on the back, pride oneself, preen oneself, feel proud about, feel self-satisfied about, boast about; *archaic* pique oneself.

plummet ▶ verb **1** *the plane plummeted to the ground* **plunge**, fall headlong, hurtle, nosedive, dive, drop, crash, descend rapidly.
2 *share prices plummeted* **fall steeply/sharply**, plunge, tumble, drop/decrease rapidly, go down, sink, slump; *informal* crash, nosedive, take a nosedive.

plummy ▶ adjective (*Brit. informal*) *a plummy voice* **upper-class**, refined, aristocratic, affected, Home Counties, fruity, grand; *Scottish* Kelvinside, Morningside; *Brit. informal* posh, Sloaney; *S. African informal* larney.

plump[1] ▶ verb **1** *exhausted, Jack plumped down on to a chair* **flop**, **collapse**, sink, fall, drop, slump, plop oneself; *informal* plonk oneself; *N. Amer. informal* plank oneself.
2 *she plumped her bag on the table* **put**, put down, set, set down, deposit, dump, stick, place; *informal* plonk; *Brit. informal* bung; *N. Amer. informal* plunk.
3 *I* **plumped for** *a fixed-rate mortgage* **choose**, decide on, go for, opt for, pick, pick out, settle on, select, take, elect, fix on, come down in favour of, vote for, single out, prefer; *Brit.* pitch on.

P

plump[2] ▶ adjective *a plump, rosy-faced girl* **chubby**, **fat**, stout, rotund, buxom, well upholstered, well covered, well padded, of ample proportions, ample, roly-poly, round, rounded, well rounded, full, fattish, dumpy, chunky, broad in the beam, portly, overweight, fleshy, paunchy, bulky, corpulent; *informal* tubby, pudgy, beefy, porky, blubbery, poddy; *Brit. informal* podgy, fubsy; *N. Amer. informal* zaftig, corn-fed, lard-assed; *archaic* pursy; *rare* abdominous.
OPPOSITES thin, slender, skinny.

plumpness ▶ noun *his wife was inclined to plumpness* **fat**, fatness, chubbiness, stoutness, dumpiness, portliness, fleshiness, corpulence; *informal* tubbiness, pudginess, porkiness; *Brit. informal* podginess; *rare* embonpoint.

plunder ▶ verb **1** *the invaders plundered the countryside* **pillage**, loot, rob, raid, ransack, strip, fleece, ravage, lay waste, devastate, maraud, sack, rape; *literary* despoil; *archaic* spoil, pirate, reave; *rare* depredate, spoliate, forage.
2 *millions of pounds plundered from pension funds* **steal**, take illegally, purloin, seize, thieve, rob, pillage, carry off; make off with, misappropriate, embezzle.
▶ noun **1** *the plunder of the villages* **looting**, pillaging, plundering, robbery, robbing, raiding, ransacking, devastation, depredation, laying waste, sacking, marauding; *literary* despoiling, rapine, ravin; *rare* spoliation.
2 *the army sacked the city and carried off huge quantities of plunder* **booty**, **loot**, stolen goods, spoils, prizes, ill-gotten gains, haul, takings, pickings; *informal, dated* swag, boodle.

plunge ▶ verb **1** *Joy stripped her clothes off and plunged into the sea* **jump**, **dive**, hurl oneself, throw oneself, fling oneself, launch oneself, catapult oneself, cast oneself, pitch oneself.
2 *the aircraft plunged to the ground* **crash**, **plummet**, pitch, drop, fall, fall headlong, tumble, nosedive, take a nosedive, crash-dive, descend.
3 *the car turned, plunging down a bumpy alley* **charge**, **hurtle**, career, plough, cannon, lurch, careen, rush, dash, tear; *N. Amer. informal* barrel.
4 *world oil prices plunged in the 1980s* **fall steeply/sharply**, plummet, drop rapidly, go down, tumble, sink, slump; *informal* crash, nosedive, take a nosedive.
5 *he plunged the dagger into the man's back* **thrust**, stick, ram, drive, jab, stab, push, shove, force, sink.
6 *plunge the pears into a bowl of cold water* **immerse**, submerge, sink, dip, dunk, douse, duck.
7 *the room was plunged into darkness* **throw**, cast, pitch.
8 *the boat plunged* **lurch**, pitch, roll, reel, toss about, keel, list, wallow, labour, flounder, make heavy weather; *Nautical* pitchpole.
▶ noun **1** *a plunge into the deep end of the pool* **jump**, **dive**; nosedive, fall, pitch, drop, plummet, descent, tumble; *archaic* plump.
2 *the bank declared a 76% plunge in its profits* **fall**, **drop**, tumble, slump; *informal* nosedive, crash.
□ **take the plunge** *he decided to take the plunge and become a full-time professional musician* **commit oneself**, go for it, throw caution to the wind(s), give it one's all, give it all one has, go all out; *informal* jump in at the deep end, go for broke.

P

plurality ▶ noun *a plurality of religious traditions* **wide variety**, large number, lot, diversity, range; multitude, multiplicity, galaxy, wealth, profusion, abundance, quantity, quantities, score, plethora, host; *informal* load, stack, heap, pile, mass, ton; *Brit. informal* shedload; *N. Amer. informal* slew; *Austral./NZ informal* swag.

plus ▶ preposition **1** *three plus three makes six* **and**, **added to**, increased by, with the addition of.
2 *he wrote forty-seven novels plus various other books* **as well as**, together with, along with, in addition to, added to, and, not to mention, besides, coupled with, with.
OPPOSITE minus.
▶ noun *one of the pluses of the job is having really supportive colleagues* **advantage**, good point, plus point, asset, pro, benefit, added advantage, additional benefit, fringe benefit, bonus, extra, added extra, perk, dividend, attraction, attractive feature, beauty; *formal* perquisite.
OPPOSITES disadvantage, drawback, minus.

plush ▶ adjective *a plush hotel in the south of France* **luxurious**, luxury, de luxe, sumptuous, palatial, lavish, lavishly appointed, gorgeous, opulent, splendid, magnificent, lush, rich, costly, expensive, upmarket, fancy, stylish, grandiose; *informal* posh, ritzy, swanky, plushy, classy, glitzy; *Brit. informal* swish; *N. Amer. informal* swank; *rare* palatian, Lucullan.
OPPOSITES plain, austere, cheap.

plutocrat ▶ noun *champagne-swilling plutocrats* **rich person**, capitalist, tycoon, magnate, nabob, millionaire, billionaire, multimillionaire, nouveau riche, person of means; *informal* fat cat, moneybags, zillionaire; *rare* Midas, Croesus, Dives.

ply[1] ▶ verb **1** *the gondolier plied his single oar* **use**, wield, work, work with, employ, operate, utilize, manipulate, handle.
2 *for three years he plied a profitable export trade* **engage in**, carry on, be engaged in, pursue, conduct, follow, practise, work at, occupy oneself with, busy oneself with; *archaic* prosecute.
3 *ferry boats ply between all the resorts on the lake* **go regularly**, travel regularly, make regular journeys, travel, go back and forth, shuttle, commute.
4 *she plied me with tea and scones* **provide**, supply, keep supplying, lavish, shower, regale, load, heap.
5 *he plied her with questions about her visit* **bombard**, assail, besiege, beset, pester, plague, harass, importune; *informal* hassle.

ply[2] ▶ noun *tiles that have a black PVC ply in the lamination* **layer**, thickness, strand, sheet, leaf, fold, insertion.

poach ▶ verb **1** *old Hector's been poaching salmon again* **hunt illegally**, catch/trap/kill illegally, plunder.
2 *employers risk having their newly trained workers poached by other firms* **steal**, appropriate, purloin, misappropriate, take; *informal* nab, swipe; *Brit. informal* nick, pinch.
3 *they resented foreign film-makers trying to poach on their territory* **encroach on**, trespass on, invade, infringe on, intrude on.

pocket ▶ noun **1** *a roomy, padded bag with pockets on either side* **compartment**, pouch, receptacle, sack, cavity.
2 *all the jewellery was far beyond her pocket* **means**, budget, resources, financial resources, finances, funds, money, capital, assets, wherewithal; *N. Amer.* pocketbook.
3 *there were pockets of disaffection in parts of the country* **area**, **patch**, small area, isolated area, district, region, island, cluster, centre.
▶ adjective *a pocket dictionary* **small**, little, miniature, mini, compact, concise, abridged, potted, portable; *N. Amer.* vest-pocket; *informal* pint-sized.
▶ verb *he was arrested and charged with pocketing $900,000 of his followers' money* **steal**, take for oneself, help oneself to, appropriate, misappropriate, thieve, purloin, embezzle, expropriate; *informal* filch, swipe, snaffle, lift, rip off, skim; *Brit. informal* pinch, nick, half-inch, whip, nobble; *rare* peculate, defalcate.

pockmark ▶ noun *his face was covered with pockmarks* **scar**, **pit**, pock, pitted scar, mark, blemish.

pod ▶ noun *pea pods* **shell**, husk, hull, case, seed vessel; *N. Amer.* shuck; *technical* pericarp, capsule, legume.

podgy ▶ adjective *she's a bit podgy* **chubby**, plump, fat, fattish, stout, rotund, buxom, well upholstered, well covered, well padded, of ample proportions, ample, roly-poly, round, rounded, well rounded, full, chunky, broad in the beam, dumpy, portly, overweight, fleshy, paunchy, bulky; *informal* tubby, pudgy, porky, blubbery, poddy; *Brit. informal* fubsy; *N. Amer. informal* zaftig, corn-fed, lard-assed; *archaic* pursy, abdominous.
OPPOSITES thin, skinny, slender.

podium ▶ noun **platform**, stage, dais, rostrum, stand, soapbox; *Indian* mandapam.

poem *See centre pages for lists of* **Poems** **Verse Forms** **Verse Metres and Metrical Feet**
▶ noun **verse**, song, rhyme, piece of poetry, verse composition, metrical composition; *rare* verselet.

poet *See centre pages for list of* **Writers**
▶ noun **verse writer**, versifier, verse-maker, rhymester, rhymer, sonneteer, lyricist, lyrist, elegist; laureate; *literary* bard, swan; *derogatory* poetaster; *historical* troubadour, balladeer; *archaic* rhymist; *rare* metricist, ballad-monger, idyllist, Parnassian, poeticule.

poetic ▶ adjective **1** *poetic compositions* **in verse**, verse, metrical, rhythmical; poetical, lyrical, lyric, elegiac, rhapsodic; *rare* Parnassian.
2 *his rather poetic language* **expressive**, figurative, symbolic, flowery, moving, aesthetic, artistic, tasteful, graceful, elegant, elevated, fine, beautiful; sensitive, imaginative, creative.

poetry *See centre pages for lists of* **Poems** **Verse Forms** **Verse Metres and Metrical Feet**
▶ noun **poems**, **verse**, verses, versification, metrical composition, rhythmical composition, rhymes, rhyming, balladry; *Welsh* penillion; *literary* poesy, Parnassus.

WORD LINKS
Muses of poetry **Calliope, Erato, Terpsichore**

pogrom ▶ noun **massacre**, slaughter, wholesale slaughter, mass slaughter, mass killing, mass murder, mass homicide, mass execution, night of the long knives, annihilation, extermination, decimation, carnage, bloodbath, bloodletting, butchery, genocide, holocaust, Shoah, ethnic cleansing, megadeath; persecution, witch-hunt, destruction, victimization.

poignancy ▶ noun *the fact that he was soon to die gave his words a special poignancy* **pathos**, **sadness**, pitifulness, piteousness, sorrow, mournfulness, wretchedness, misery, bitterness, pain, painfulness, distress, tragedy.

poignant ▶ adjective *the father of the murder victim bade a poignant farewell to his son* **touching**, moving, sad, saddening, affecting, pitiful, piteous, pitiable, pathetic, sorrowful, mournful, tearful, wretched, miserable, bitter, painful, distressing, disturbing, heart-rending, heartbreaking, tear-jerking, plaintive, upsetting, tragic.

point[1] ▶ noun **1** *the point of a knitting needle* **tip**, sharp end, tapered end, end, extremity; prong, spike, tine, nib, barb.
2 *the dark surface of the ocean was studded with points of light* **pinpoint**, dot,

spot, speck, fleck, mark.
3 *a prearranged meeting point* **place**, position, location, site, spot, area, locality, locale; *technical* locus.
4 *at this point in her life, what she needs is a bit of romance* **time**, stage, juncture, period, phase; moment in time, moment, instant.
5 *when it came to the point he would probably do what was expected of him* **decisive moment**, critical moment, moment of truth, point of no return, crunch, crux, zero hour.
6 *tension between them had reached such a point that they barely spoke* **level**, degree, stage, pitch, extent, height.
7 *you have ignored a number of important points* **detail**, item, particular, fact, thing, piece of information, idea, argument, consideration, factor, element, aspect, regard, respect; subject, issue, topic, question, matter.
8 *it took her a long time to get to the point* **most important fact**, main point, central point, essential point, essence, nub, focal point, salient point, heart of the matter, keynote, core, pith, marrow, meat, crux; meaning, significance, signification, import, gist, substance, drift, thrust, burden, theme, sense, moral, relevance, tenor; *informal* brass tacks, nitty-gritty.
9 *what's the point of telling me this?* **purpose**, aim, object, objective, goal, intention, end, design, reason, use, utility, sense, motive, value, advantage.
10 *she had to admit he had his good points* **attribute**, characteristic, feature, trait, quality, property, aspect, facet, side; streak, peculiarity, idiosyncrasy.
□ **beside the point** *his comments seem to me to be beside the point* **irrelevant**, immaterial, unimportant, not to the point, neither here nor there, nothing to do with it, not pertinent, not germane, off the subject, inapposite, inconsequential, incidental, pointless, out of place, wide of the mark, unconnected, peripheral, tangential, extraneous, extrinsic.
□ **in point of fact** *in point of fact nothing at all has been laid on* **in fact**, as a matter of fact, actually, in actual fact, really, in reality, as it happens, in truth, to tell the truth, truly.
□ **make a point of** *he made a point of reading all the reviews* **make an effort to**, go out of one's way to, put/place emphasis on.
□ **on the point of** *she was on the point of saying something, but changed her mind* **just about to, on the verge of**, about to, going to, on the brink of, ready to, all set to.
□ **point of view 1** *they expressed different points of view* **opinion**, view, belief, attitude, feeling, sentiment, way of thinking, way of looking at it, thoughts, ideas.
2 *try and see things from his point of view* **position**, perspective, viewpoint, standpoint, angle, slant, outlook, stand, stance, vantage point, side, frame of reference.
□ **to the point** *his observations were concise and to the point* **relevant**, pertinent, apposite, germane, applicable, apropos, appropriate, apt, fitting, suitable, material, connected, related, linked; *Latin* ad rem; *rare* appurtenant.
□ **up to a point** *this is true, but only up to a point* **partly, to some extent**, to a certain extent, to some degree, to a certain degree, in part, somewhat, partially, not totally, not entirely, not wholly.
▶ **verb 1** *she drew a revolver and pointed it at him* **aim**, direct, level, train; *N. Amer.* draw/get a bead on.
2 *all the evidence* **pointed to** *his guilt* **indicate**, suggest, be evidence of, evidence, signal, signify, denote, be symptomatic of, be a sign/symptom of, reveal, manifest; *literary* bespeak, betoken.
□ **point something out** *the flaws in the plan have already been pointed out* **identify**, show, designate, draw/call attention to, direct attention to, indicate, specify, detail, mention, refer to, allude to, touch on.
□ **point something up** *studies are pointing up the value of specific vitamins* **emphasize, highlight**, draw attention to, accentuate, underline, underscore, turn the spotlight on, spotlight, foreground, put/lay emphasis on, stress, give prominence to, play up, focus attention on, accent, bring to the fore.

point² ▶ **noun** *the ship rounded the point* **promontory**, headland, head, foreland, cape, peninsula, bluff, ness, horn, bill.

point-blank ▶ **adverb 1** *Waxman fired the pistol point-blank at Clyde* **at very close range**, at point-blank range, close up, close to.
2 *she couldn't say so point-blank to Alison* **bluntly, directly**, straight, straightforwardly, frankly, candidly, forthrightly, openly, explicitly, unequivocally, unambiguously, unmistakably, plainly, clearly, flatly, positively, certainly, decisively, categorically, outright.
▶ **adjective** *a point-blank refusal* **blunt, direct**, straight, straightforward, straight from the shoulder, frank, candid, forthright, open, explicit, unequivocal, unambiguous, unmistakable, plain, clear, clear-cut, crystal clear, well defined, flat, positive, certain, decisive, unqualified, categorical, outright, downright.

pointed ▶ **adjective 1** *the pointed end of the stick* **sharp**, spear-like, needle-like, spear-shaped, V-shaped, tapering, tapered, cone-shaped, conic, conical, acute, sharp-cornered, wedge-shaped, sharp-edged, edged, jagged, spiky, spiked, barbed; *informal* pointy; *technical* acicular, lanceolate, acuminate, subulate, mucronate, aculeate; *rare* cuspidate, cusped, conoid.
2 *a pointed remark* **cutting**, trenchant, biting, incisive, acid, acerbic, tart, caustic, scathing, mordant, razor-edged, venomed, venomous, piercing, penetrating; *N. Amer. informal* snarky; *rare* acidulous, mordacious.

pointer ▶ **noun 1** *the pointer moved to 'start engines'* **indicator**, needle, arrow, hand.
2 *the met officer used a pointer on the chart* **stick**, rod, cane, pole, laser pointer, cursor.
3 *the politicians' mood is a pointer to the outcome of the election* **indication**, indicator, clue, hint, lead, sign, signal, evidence, symptom, implication, intimation, inkling, suggestion.
4 *perhaps I can give a few pointers to anyone just starting up* **tip**, hint, piece of advice, suggestion, guideline, recommendation, warning.

pointless ▶ **adjective senseless, futile**, hopeless, fruitless, useless, needless, wasted, in vain, unavailing, aimless, idle, to no purpose, purposeless, worthless, valueless, unproductive, unprofitable; absurd, insane, nonsensical, stupid, silly, irrelevant, footling, fatuous, foolish, hollow, inane, ridiculous.
OPPOSITES useful, valuable.

> **CHOOSE THE RIGHT WORD**
>
> **pointless, futile, fruitless, vain**
>
> *See* FUTILE.

poise ▶ **noun 1** *poise and good deportment can be cultivated* **balance**, equilibrium, control, grace, gracefulness, presence.
2 *in spite of this setback she retained her poise* **composure**, equanimity, self-possession, aplomb, presence of mind, assurance, self-assurance, self-control, nerve, calmness, coolness, sangfroid, countenance, collectedness, serenity, dignity, imperturbability, suaveness, urbanity, elegance; *informal* cool, unflappability.
▶ **verb 1** *the dancer was poised on one foot | a world poised between peace and war* **balance**, hold (oneself) steady, steady oneself, be suspended, hang suspended, remain motionless, hang in mid-air, hang, hover.
2 *the president was poised for decisive action* **position oneself**, ready oneself, prepare oneself, brace oneself, get into position, gear oneself up, stand by; balance, steady.

poised ▶ **adjective** *a very poised young woman* **self-possessed**, self-assured, composed, assured, self-controlled, cool-headed, calm, cool, {cool, calm, and collected}, at ease, tranquil, serene, unperturbed, unruffled, impassive, nonchalant, confident, self-confident, dignified, equable, imperturbable, suave, urbane, elegant; *informal* together, unfazed, unflappable; *rare* equanimous.
OPPOSITES excited, flustered; inelegant.

poison *See centre pages for lists of* **Poisonous Plants and Fungi** **Poisonous Substances and Gases**
▶ **noun 1 toxin**, venom; *archaic* bane; *rare* toxicant.
2 *Marianne would waste no time in spreading her poison* **malice**, maliciousness, ill will, hate, malevolence, malignity, malignancy, balefulness, embitterment, embitteredness, spite, spitefulness, venom, acrimony, acrimoniousness, rancour; bad influence, blight, bane, contagion, cancer, canker, corruption, pollution.
▶ **verb 1** *her stepmother poisoned her* **administer poison to**, give poison to; murder.
2 *a blackmailer had been poisoning baby foods* **contaminate**, put poison in, adulterate, tamper with, spike, lace, doctor.
3 *the Amazon basin is being poisoned by mercury* **pollute**, contaminate, taint, foul, befoul, dirty, blight, spoil.
4 *his mind was poisoned against her* **prejudice**, bias, jaundice, colour, embitter, sour, envenom, warp, corrupt, subvert.

WORD LINKS

related prefixes	**toxi-** (e.g. ***toxigenic***), **toxico-** (e.g. ***toxicodendron***), **toxo-** (e.g. ***toxocariasis***)
study of poisons	**toxicology**

poisonous ▶ **adjective 1** *a poisonous snake* **venomous**, deadly.
OPPOSITE harmless.
2 *a poisonous chemical* **toxic**, deadly, fatal, lethal, mortal, death-dealing, virulent, noxious.
OPPOSITES harmless, non-toxic.
3 *he shot a poisonous glance towards Rickie* **malicious**, malevolent, hostile, vicious, spiteful, bitter, venomous, evil-intentioned, ill-natured, vindictive, vengeful, vitriolic, rancorous, malign, malignant, pernicious, mean, nasty, harmful, hurtful, wounding; slanderous, libellous, defamatory; *informal* bitchy, catty; *literary* malefic, maleficent.
OPPOSITE benevolent.

poke ▶ **verb 1** *they poked him in the ribs | he poked the baton hard into the man's stomach* **prod**, jab, dig, nudge, tap, butt, ram, shove, punch, prick, jolt; thrust, stab, push, plunge, stick, insert, drive, lunge.
2 *leave the cable* **poking out** *of the wall* **stick out**, jut out, stand out, protrude, project, extend, loom; *rare* protuberate.
□ **poke about/around** *you've no right to go poking around in that cupboard*

search, hunt, rummage (around), forage, scrabble, grub, root about/around, scavenge, fish about/around, rake around, feel around, grope around, nose around, ferret (about/around); pry into, ransack, rake through, sift through, go through, shuffle through, rifle through, scour, comb, explore, probe; *Brit. informal* rootle (around).

□ **poke fun at** *they giggled and poked fun at Eleanor* **mock**, make fun of, laugh at, make jokes about, ridicule, jeer at, sneer at, deride, treat with contempt, treat contemptuously, scorn, laugh to scorn, scoff at, pillory, be sarcastic about, satirize, lampoon, burlesque, parody, tease, taunt, rag, make a monkey of, chaff, jibe at; *informal* send up, kid, rib, josh; *Brit. informal* wind up, take the mickey out of; *N. Amer. informal* goof on, rag on, razz, pull someone's chain; *Austral./NZ informal* poke mullock at, sling off at, chiack; *Brit. informal, dated* twit, rot; *Brit. vulgar slang* take the piss (out of); *dated* make sport of; *archaic* joke, quiz, flout.

□ **poke one's nose into** *she was poking her nose into something that did not concern her* **pry into**, **interfere in**, nose around in, intrude on, butt into, meddle with, tamper with; *informal* snoop into.

▶ **noun 1** *Carrie gave him a poke* **prod**, jab, dig, elbow, nudge, tap, butt.
2 *a poke in the eye with a stick* **thrust**, push, jab, shove, plunge, insertion.

poker ▶ **noun.** *See centre pages for list of* **Poker Hands**

poky ▶ **adjective** *a poky room* **small**, little, tiny; **cramped**, confined, restricted, narrow, tight, uncomfortable, cell-like, boxy; *informal* with no room to swing a cat; *euphemistic* 'compact', 'bijou', 'easy to maintain/clean', 'well planned'; *archaic* strait; *rare* incommodious.
OPPOSITES spacious, roomy, palatial.

polar ▶ **adjective 1** *polar weather conditions* **Arctic**, **Antarctic**; **cold**, frozen, freezing, frigid, chill, chilling, icy, icy-cold, glacial, gelid, Siberian; *rare* boreal, hyperborean, circumpolar, brumal, borean, hyperboreal.
2 *the two polar types of interview* **opposite**, opposed, opposing, oppositional, diametrically opposed, extreme, contrary, contradictory, antithetical, antagonistic, conflicting, counterbalancing; *rare* antitypical, antonymous, antipodal, contrarious, dichotomous, oppositive.

polarity ▶ **noun** *the polarity between social and biological explanations* **difference**, separation, opposition, contradiction, contradictoriness, antithesis, duality, antagonism, conflict, dichotomy; *rare* contrariety, antonymy.

pole[1] ▶ **noun** *the notice was pinned on a wooden pole* **post**, pillar, stanchion, standard, paling, pale, stake, stick, picket, palisade, support, prop, batten, mast, bar, shaft, rail, rod, beam, spar, crosspiece, upright, vertical; staff, stave, cane, spike, baton, truncheon.

pole[2] ▶ **noun** *our points of view are at opposite poles* **extremity**, extreme, limit; *rare* antipode.

□ **poles apart** *our views are poles apart* **completely different**, as different as they could be, widely separated, directly opposed, antithetical, incompatible, irreconcilable, miles/worlds apart, at opposite extremes/poles, like night and day; *Brit.* like chalk and cheese; *rare* antipodal.

WORD LINKS
relating to both the North and South Poles **bipolar**

P

polemic ▶ **noun 1** *this is not just a polemic against injustice* **diatribe**, invective, denunciation, denouncement, rant, tirade, broadside, attack, harangue, verbal onslaught; condemnation, brickbats, criticism, admonishment, admonition, abuse, stream of abuse, stricture, tongue-lashing, castigation, reprimand, rebuke, reproof, reproval, upbraiding; *informal* knocking, blast; *Brit. informal* slating; *rare* philippic.
2 (**polemics**) *skilled in polemics* **argumentation**, argument, debate, contention, dispute, disputation, discussion, controversy, altercation, faction, wrangling; *formal* contestation.

▶ **adjective.** *See* POLEMICAL.

polemical ▶ **adjective** *Brunner published a polemical tract against Barth* **critical**, hostile, bitter, polemic, virulent, vitriolic, venomous, waspish, corrosive, biting, caustic, trenchant, cutting, acerbic, sardonic, sarcastic, scathing, acid, sharp, keen, tart, pungent, stinging, astringent, incisive, devastating, piercing; *rare* acidulous, mordacious.

police *See centre pages for list of* **Police Officers and Forces**

▶ **noun** the police force, police officers, policemen, policewomen, officers of the law, the forces of law and order, law-enforcement officers, law-enforcement agency; *Brit.* constabulary; *Scottish & Irish* polis; *French* gendarmerie; *German* Polizei; *Italian* carabinieri; *historical* watch; *informal* the cops, the fuzz, the law, the Man, the boys in blue, the long arm of the law; *Brit. informal* the (Old) Bill; coppers, rozzers, bobbies, busies, bizzies, the force, plod, PC Plod; *N. Amer. informal* the heat, ...'s finest; *informal, derogatory* pigs, the filth; *black English, derogatory* Babylon.

▶ **verb 1** *it would not be possible to police the area effectively* **maintain law and order in**, keep the peace in, keep guard over, keep watch on, watch over, guard, protect, defend, patrol, make the rounds of.
2 *the cost of policing the demonstration* **control**, keep in order, keep under control, regulate.
3 *the regulations will be policed by Environmental Health officers* **enforce**, regulate, implement, oversee, check (up on), supervise, monitor, observe, watch.

police officer *See centre pages for list of* **Police Officers and Forces**

▶ **noun policeman**, **policewoman**, officer of the law, law-enforcement officer/agent, officer; *Brit.* constable; *N. Amer.* patrolman, trooper, roundsman, peace officer; *Indian* kotwal, jawan; *French* gendarme; *informal* cop, jack, uniform; *Brit. informal* copper, bobby, rozzer, busy, bizzy, plod, PC Plod; *N. Amer. informal* bear; *Austral./NZ informal* walloper, demon; *French informal* flic; *informal, derogatory* pig; *informal, dated* flatfoot, bogey, flattie, woodentop; *archaic* peeler, runner, bluebottle, finger.

policy ▶ **noun 1** *government policy on international trade* **plans**, **strategy**, proposed action, blueprint, approach, scheme, stratagem, programme, schedule, code, system, guidelines, intentions, notions, theory, line, position, stance, attitude.
2 *it was good policy to listen politely* **practice**, custom, procedure, wont, way, tack, routine, matter of course, style, pattern, convention, mode, rule.

polish ▶ **verb 1** *I polished his shoes* **shine**, wax, buff, rub up, rub down; gloss, burnish, brighten, smooth; varnish, oil, glaze, lacquer, enamel, japan, shellac; *archaic* furbish.
2 *it's time to polish up your essay* **perfect**, refine, improve, hone, embellish, enhance, put the finishing/final touches to; brush up, revise, copy-edit, correct, emend, rewrite, rephrase, go over, touch up, finish off; *informal* clean up.

□ **polish something off 1** *he had polished off an apple pie and a strawberry milkshake* **eat up**, **finish**, consume, devour, eat greedily, guzzle, feast on, wolf down, down, bolt; drink up, empty, drain, quaff, gulp (down); *informal* binge on, stuff one's face with, stuff oneself with, get outside of, murder, pack away, put away, scoff (down), shovel down, pig oneself on, pig out on, sink, swill, knock back, get one's laughing gear round; *Brit. informal* shift, gollop, bevvy; *N. Amer. informal* scarf (down/up), snarf (down/up), inhale; *rare* ingurgitate, bib.
2 *a third enemy plane tried to polish him off* **destroy**, put an end to, finish off, dispatch, dispose of, do away with, eliminate, kill, liquidate; *informal* bump off, knock off, do in, blow away, take out; *N. Amer. informal* rub out.
3 *I'll polish off the last few pages* **complete**, finish, deal with, wrap up, accomplish, execute, discharge, do, get done, fulfil, achieve, attain, end, conclude, close, bring to a conclusion/end/close, finalize, stop, cease, terminate, round off, wind up; *informal* sew up, have something sewn up.

▶ **noun 1** *shoe polish | nail polish* **wax**, **varnish**, glaze, lacquer, enamel, japan, shellac.
2 *this process achieves a good surface polish* **shine**, gloss, lustre, sheen, sparkle, patina, finish, smoothness.
3 *he had changed, with all his polish and scholarship* **sophistication**, refinement, urbanity, suavity, suaveness, elegance, style, grace, finish, accomplishment, finesse, subtlety, distinction, taste, cultivation, culture, politeness, civility, gentility, breeding, courtesy, courteousness, (good) manners; *informal* class.

polished ▶ **adjective 1** *a polished table* **shiny**, shining, bright, glossy, gleaming, lustrous; smooth, level, glassy, slippery; waxed, buffed, burnished, sanded, ground, varnished, glazed, lacquered, enamelled, japanned, shellacked; *archaic* furbished.
OPPOSITES dull, tarnished; rough.
2 *a polished performance of Mozart's Divertimento in D* **expert**, accomplished, masterly, masterful, skilful, skilled, clever, proficient, adept, deft, adroit, dexterous, impeccable, flawless, faultless, perfect, consummate, exquisite, outstanding, excellent, superb, superlative, remarkable, first-rate, fine, talented, gifted; *informal* ace, class.
OPPOSITE inexpert.
3 *polished manners* **refined**, cultivated, civilized, civil, well bred, polite, courteous, well mannered, genteel, decorous, proper, respectable, courtly, urbane, suave, sophisticated, seemly.
OPPOSITES gauche, ill-bred.

polite ▶ **adjective 1** *we were too polite to comment* **well mannered**, civil, courteous, respectful, deferential, well behaved, well bred, gentlemanly, ladylike, chivalrous, gallant, genteel, cultivated, gracious, urbane, well brought up; tactful, considerate, thoughtful, discreet, diplomatic; *dated* mannerly.
OPPOSITES rude, impolite.
2 *the picture outraged polite society* **civilized**, refined, cultured, sophisticated, genteel, well bred, urbane, elegant, courtly.
OPPOSITES savage, uncivilized. *See 'Choose the Right Word' below*

politeness ▶ **noun** *I have been treated with great politeness* **courtesy**, civility, respect, deference, good breeding, manners, good manners, chivalry, gallantry, gentility, cultivation, grace, urbanity; tact, tactfulness, consideration, considerateness, thoughtfulness, discretion, diplomacy; *dated* mannerliness.
OPPOSITE rudeness.

politic ▶ **adjective** *I did not think it politic to express my reservations* **wise**, prudent, sensible, judicious, canny, well judged, sagacious, expedient, shrewd, astute, discreet, tactful, diplomatic; recommended, advantageous, beneficial, profitable, gainful, desirable, advisable; appropriate, suitable, fitting, apt, timely, opportune, propitious, provident.
OPPOSITES inadvisable, injudicious, unwise.

CHOOSE THE RIGHT WORD

polite, civil, courteous

These three adjectives all describe people or actions that are considerate and exhibit good manners.

- **Polite** is the most common word and is used in general social rather than commercial settings (*he was always polite on the phone | I only asked a polite question*); compare *courteous* below. Sometimes *polite* actions are just the minimum required or done purely for sake of good manners (*I tried to make polite conversation*). It can also mean 'civilized and cultured' since politeness can involve glossing over subjects that are socially unacceptable because they are coarse or embarrassing (*this is not what passes for humour in polite society*).
- **Civil** behaviour is formal and rather reserved and may be only the absolute minimum required to avoid actually being rude (*his replies were civil, but scarcely welcoming*).
- **Courteous** either suggests a particularly graceful and charming politeness (*a courteous regard for the lady's feelings*) or is used in commercial contexts (*friendly and courteous staff*).

political ▶ adjective **1** *the political affairs of the nation* **governmental**, government, local government, ministerial, parliamentary, party political, diplomatic, legislative, policy-making, constitutional, public, civic, state, administrative, bureaucratic.
2 *he certainly wasn't a political animal* **activist**, active, militant, factional, partisan, party, party political.

politician ▶ noun **legislator**, Member of Parliament, MP, representative, minister, statesman, stateswoman, political leader, lawmaker, public servant, elected official, office-bearer; (*in the US*) senator, congressman, congresswoman; *informal* politico; *N. Amer. informal* pol.

politics *See centre pages for lists of* **Political Philosophies and Systems** *and* **Governments**
▶ noun **1** *a career in politics* **government**, local government, affairs of state, public affairs, diplomacy, party politics.
2 *he studies politics* **political science**, civics, statecraft, statesmanship; *rare* polity.
3 *what are his politics?* **political views/beliefs/leanings/sympathies**, party politics, political alliance.
4 *office politics* **power struggle**, manipulation, machination(s), manoeuvring, jockeying for position, wheeler-dealing, machiavellianism, opportunism, realpolitik.

poll ▶ noun **1** *the electoral rules provided for a second-round poll* **vote**, **ballot**, show of hands, straw vote/poll, referendum, plebiscite, election.
2 *apathy might cause the poll to be unduly low* **voting figures**, vote, returns, count, tally.
3 *they may conduct a poll to investigate whether people enjoyed their holidays* **survey**, opinion poll, canvass, market research, sampling, census.
▶ verb **1** *57% of the people polled supported his action* **canvass**, **survey**, ask, question, interview, ballot, sample.
2 *she polled 119 votes* **get**, gain, register, record, return.

pollute ▶ verb **1** *fish farms will pollute the lake* **contaminate**, adulterate, taint, poison, befoul, foul, dirty, soil, blight, make filthy, infect.
OPPOSITES clean, purify.
2 *the propaganda that polluted this nation* **corrupt**, poison, warp, pervert, deprave, defile, blight, debauch, sully, besmirch, desecrate, violate.
OPPOSITE purify.

pollution ▶ noun **1** *pollution caused by vehicle emissions* **contamination**, contaminating, adulteration, adulterating, tainting, impurity, fouling, befouling, foulness, dirtiness, dirtying, soiling, filthiness, infection, infecting.
OPPOSITE purity.
2 *research into the pollution of young minds* **defilement**, **corruption**, corrupting, poison, poisoning, blight, warping, depravation, depravity, sullying, besmirching, desecration, violation.

pomp ▶ noun *the pomp and popular jubilation accompanying his arrival* **ceremony**, ceremoniousness, ceremonial, solemnity, ritual, display, spectacle, pageantry, pageant; show, showiness, ostentation, splendour, grandeur, grandness, magnificence, majesty, stateliness, glory, gloriousness, sumptuousness, opulence, lavishness, richness, brilliance, radiance, dazzle, theatricality, drama, flourish, glitter, style, éclat, resplendence, splendidness; *informal* pizzazz, razzle-dazzle, razzmatazz.
OPPOSITE simplicity.

pomposity ▶ noun **1** *Musgrave was inclined to pomposity* **self-importance**, imperiousness, pompousness, sententiousness, grandiosity, affectation, stiffness, airs, pretentiousness, pretension, arrogance, vanity, haughtiness, pride, conceit, egotism, superciliousness, condescension, affectedness; *informal* snootiness, uppishness, uppitiness.
OPPOSITES modesty, humility.
2 *he seems to equate pomposity with profundity* **bombast**, loftiness, pompousness, turgidity, grandiloquence, magniloquence, ornateness, portentousness, pedantry, boastfulness, boasting, bragging, sonorousness, windiness; *rare* fustian, euphuism, orotundity.

pompous ▶ adjective **1** *a pompous official who kept quoting the rules* **self-important**, imperious, overbearing, domineering, magisterial, pontifical, sententious, grandiose, affected, stiff, pretentious, puffed up, arrogant, vain, haughty, proud, conceited, egotistic, supercilious, condescending, patronizing; *informal* snooty, uppity, uppish.
OPPOSITES modest, humble, self-effacing.
2 *pompous language* **bombastic**, high-sounding, high-flown, lofty, turgid, grandiloquent, magniloquent, ornate, overblown, inflated, rhetorical, oratorical, declamatory, sonorous, portentous, pedantic, boastful, boasting, bragging, braggart, Falstaffian; *informal* highfalutin, windy; *rare* fustian, euphuistic, orotund.

pond ▶ noun **pool**, puddle, lake, tarn, reservoir, waterhole, lagoon, inland sea, swim; *Brit.* stew; *Scottish* loch, lochan; *Anglo-Irish* lough; *N. Amer.* pothole, bayou, tank; *NZ* moana; *literary* mere, plash.

ponder ▶ verb *she had plenty of time to ponder over the incident* **think about**, give thought to, consider, review, reflect on, mull over, contemplate, study, meditate on, muse on, deliberate about, cogitate on, dwell on, brood on/over, ruminate about/on, chew over, puzzle over, speculate about, weigh up, turn over in one's mind; be in a brown study; *informal* put on one's thinking cap about; *archaic* pore on; *rare* cerebrate.

ponderous ▶ adjective **1** *a mechanical doll performed a ponderous dance* **clumsy**, **slow**, heavy, awkward, lumbering, slow-moving, cumbersome, heavy-footed, ungainly, graceless, maladroit, uncoordinated, blundering, like a bull in a china shop; *informal* clodhopping, clunky; *archaic* lubberly; *rare* cumbrous.
OPPOSITES light, graceful, elegant.
2 *his ponderous sentences* **laboured**, laborious, dull, awkward, clumsy, forced, stilted, unnatural, artificial, turgid, stodgy, stolid, lifeless, plodding, pedestrian, boring, uninteresting, solemn, serious, tedious, monotonous, dry, dreary, pedantic; ornate, elaborate, over-elaborate, intricate, convoluted, verbose, long-winded, windy, prolix.
OPPOSITE lively.

pontifical ▶ adjective *such explanations were greeted with pontifical disdain* **pompous**, cocksure, self-important, arrogant, superior; **opinionated**, dogmatic, doctrinaire, dictatorial, authoritarian, domineering; intolerant, prejudiced, biased, bigoted; adamant, obstinate, stubborn, pig-headed, bull-headed, obdurate, of fixed views, headstrong, wilful, single-minded, rigid, inflexible, uncompromising, unyielding.
OPPOSITES open-minded; humble.

pontificate ▶ verb *he began to pontificate about life and art* **hold forth**, expound, declaim, preach, lay down the law, express one's opinion (pompously), sound off, spout (off), dogmatize, sermonize, moralize, pronounce, lecture, expatiate; *informal* preachify, mouth off, spiel; *rare* perorate.

pooh-pooh ▶ verb (*informal*) *this idea was pooh-poohed by the scientific community* **dismiss**, reject, brush aside, play down, spurn, rebuff, repudiate, disregard, discount, wave aside, make light of, make little of, belittle, treat with contempt, ridicule, deride, mock, hold up to scorn, scoff at, sneer at; *N. Amer. informal* slam-dunk; *Austral./NZ informal* wipe.

pool[1] ▶ noun **1** *pools of water in the fields after the rain* **puddle**, pond.
2 *the hotel has its own pool* **swimming pool**, baths, lido, piscina, plunge pool; *Brit.* swimming bath(s); *N. Amer. rare* natatorium.

pool[2] ▶ noun **1** *a car pool | a pool of skilled labour* **supply**, common supply, reserve(s), store, reservoir, stock, stockpile, accumulation, storehouse, hoard, cache, fund, backlog.
2 *the cash would come from the pool of money set aside for such incidents* **fund**, reserve, kitty, pot, bank, purse; jackpot, ante, stakes.
▶ verb *the members pool their skills and their grants* **combine**, put together, amalgamate, group, join, unite, lump together, merge; fuse, conglomerate, agglomerate, coalesce, integrate; share.

poor ▶ adjective **1** *a poor family* **poverty-stricken**, impoverished, necessitous, beggarly, in penury, penurious, impecunious, indigent, needy, needful, in need/want, badly off, in reduced circumstances, in straitened circumstances, destitute, hard up, short of money, on one's beam-ends, unable to make ends meet, underprivileged, deprived, penniless, without a sou, as poor as a church mouse, moneyless; bankrupt, bust, insolvent, in debt, in the red; *Brit.* on the breadline, without a penny (to one's name); *informal* broke, flat broke, cleaned out, strapped for cash, strapped, on one's uppers, without two pennies/(brass) farthings to rub together; *Brit. informal* stony broke, skint, in Queer Street; *N. Amer. informal* stone broke; *rare* pauperized, beggared.
OPPOSITES rich, wealthy.
2 *poor workmanship* **substandard**, below standard, below par, bad, deficient, defective, faulty, imperfect, inferior, mediocre; abject, appalling, abysmal, atrocious, awful, terrible, dismal, dreadful, unsatisfactory, low-grade, second-rate, third-rate, jerry-built, shoddy, crude, tinny, trashy, rubbishy, miserable, wretched, lamentable, deplorable, pitiful, inadequate, insufficient, unacceptable, execrable,

P

frightful; *informal* crummy, dire, bum, diabolical, rotten, sad, tatty, tenth-rate; *Brit. informal* ropy, duff, rubbish, pants, a load of pants, grotty; *vulgar slang* crap, crappy; *archaic* direful; *rare* egregious.
OPPOSITE superior.
3 *a poor crop of apples* **meagre**, scanty, scant, paltry, limited, disappointing, restricted, reduced, modest, insufficient, inadequate, sparse, spare, deficient, negligible, insubstantial, skimpy, short, little, lean, small, slight, slender; miserable, lamentable, pitiful, puny, niggardly, beggarly; *informal* measly, stingy, pathetic, piddling; *rare* exiguous.
OPPOSITES satisfactory, good.
4 *poor soil* **unproductive**, barren, unyielding, unfruitful, uncultivatable; depleted, exhausted, bare, arid, sterile; *rare* infecund; *N. Amer. rare* hardscrabble.
OPPOSITES fertile, productive.
5 *tropical oceanic waters are generally* **poor in** *nutrients* **deficient in**, lacking (in), wanting (in), short of/on, low on, missing, with an insufficiency of, with too few/little ....
OPPOSITE rich in.
6 *you poor thing* **unfortunate**, unlucky, luckless, unhappy, hapless, ill-fated, ill-starred, pitiable, pitiful, wretched.
OPPOSITE lucky.

poorly ▶ **adverb** *the text is poorly written* **badly**, deficiently, defectively, faultily, imperfectly, unsuccessfully, incompetently, inexpertly, abjectly, appallingly, abysmally, atrociously, awfully, terribly, dismally, dreadfully; crudely, shoddily, inadequately, unsatisfactorily, unacceptably, execrably, frightfully; *informal* crummily, diabolically.
▶ **adjective** (*Brit.*) *she felt poorly yesterday* **ill**, unwell, indisposed, ailing, not (very) well, not oneself, not in good shape, out of sorts, not up to par, under/below par, peaky, liverish; sick, queasy, nauseous; *Brit.* off, off colour; *informal* under the weather, not up to snuff, funny, peculiar, crummy, lousy, rough; *Brit. informal* ropy, grotty; *Scottish informal* wabbit; *Austral./NZ informal* crook; *dated* queer, seedy.

pop ▶ **verb 1** *champagne corks were popping* **go bang**, go off with a bang, go off, crack, snap, burst, explode.
2 *I'm just popping upstairs* **go**, drop by/in/into/round, stop by, visit; *informal* tootle, whip; *Brit. informal* nip.
3 *pop a clear polythene bag over the pot* **put**, place, slip, slide, push, stick, rest, deposit, set, lay, settle, locate, install, drop, shove, hang, position, arrange.
□ **pop up** *many familiar faces pop up during the twenty-six episodes* **appear**, appear suddenly/unexpectedly/abruptly, occur suddenly/abruptly, come into view/sight, materialize, arrive, make/put in an appearance; come along, happen, emerge, arise, crop up, turn up, present itself, come on the scene, come to light, manifest itself; *informal* show up.
▶ **noun 1** *the balloons burst with a pop* **bang**, crack, snap, boom, explosion, report.
2 (*informal*) *a bottle of pop* **fizzy drink**, soft drink, carbonated drink; *N. Amer.* soda; *Scottish informal* scoosh.

pope ▶ **noun pontiff**, sovereign/supreme pontiff, Bishop of Rome, Holy Father, Vicar of Christ, His Holiness.
WORD LINKS
relating to a pope **papal, pontifical**
position of pope **papacy**

pop music *See centre pages for list of* **Musical Genres**
▶ **noun pop**, popular music, chart music.

poppycock ▶ **noun** (*informal*) *Tory MPs dismissed Labour's claims as poppycock* **nonsense**, rubbish, garbage, claptrap, balderdash, blather, blether, moonshine; foolishness, silliness; *informal* rot, tripe, hogwash, baloney, drivel, bilge, bosh, bull, bunk, guff, eyewash, piffle, phooey, hooey, malarkey, twaddle, dribble; *Brit. informal* cobblers, codswallop, stuff and nonsense, tosh, cack; *Scottish & N. English informal* havers; *N. Amer. informal* flapdoodle, blathers, applesauce, wack, bushwa; *informal, dated* bunkum, tommyrot, cod, gammon, toffee.

populace ▶ **noun population**, inhabitants, residents, natives, occupants, occupiers; community, country, public, people, nation; common people, general public, man/woman in the street, masses, multitude, rank and file, commonality, commonalty, third estate, plebeians, proletariat, crowd; *N. Amer.* man/woman on the street; *informal* folk, common folk; *Brit. informal* Joe Public, Joe Bloggs; *N. Amer. informal* John Doe; *humorous* denizens; *derogatory* the hoi polloi, common herd, rabble, mob, riff-raff, the canaille, the great unwashed, ragtag (and bobtail), proles, plebs; *rare* indigenes.

popular ▶ **adjective 1** *the most popular boy around | the restaurant is very popular* **well liked**, liked, favoured, in favour, well received, approved, admired, accepted, welcome, sought-after, in demand, desired, wanted; commercial, marketable, saleable, fashionable, in fashion, in vogue, voguish, all the rage, hot; *informal* in, cool, big; *Brit. informal, dated* all the go.
OPPOSITE unpopular.
2 *popular science | the popular press* **non-specialist**, non-technical, non-professional, amateur, lay, lay person's, general, middle-of-the-road; accessible, approachable, simplified, plain, simple, easy, straightforward, understandable, readily understood, easy to understand, intelligible; mass-market, middlebrow, lowbrow, pop, bland, cheap.
OPPOSITE highbrow.
3 *policy-makers should listen to popular opinion* **widespread**, general, common, current, prevalent, prevailing, customary, universal, standard, stock, shared, in circulation, rife; **ordinary**, usual, accepted, established, acknowledged, recognized, conventional, orthodox, conformist.
4 *a popular movement for independence* **mass**, general, communal, collective, social, societal, collaborative, group, civil, public, civic; democratic, representative.

popularity ▶ **noun 1** *the growing popularity of the city as a holiday destination* **fashionableness**, vogue, stylishness; approval, favour, admiration, regard, acceptance, acclaim, welcome, demand; commerciality, marketability, saleability; adoration, adulation, idolization, lionization; *informal* coolness, trendiness.
2 *the new popularity of collectivist ideas* **currency**, prevalence, commonness, universality, recognition.

popularize ▶ **verb 1** *tobacco-smoking was popularized by Sir Walter Raleigh* **make popular/fashionable**, bring into vogue, create a fashion for; market, publicize, hype.
2 *he popularized the subject, writing fourteen books for the layman* **simplify**, make accessible, give mass-market appeal to, familiarize; vulgarize.
3 *the report popularized the notion that the world was running out of oil* **give currency to**, spread, propagate, give credence to, universalize, generalize.

popularly ▶ **adverb 1** *it was popularly believed that every strange old woman was a witch* **widely**, generally, universally, commonly, by many/most/all, usually, regularly, customarily, habitually, conventionally, ordinarily, traditionally, as a rule.
2 *the Carboniferous is popularly known as the 'Age of Amphibians'* **informally**, unofficially, simply, non-technically; by lay people, by non-specialists.
3 *the President is popularly elected for a five-year term* **democratically**, by the people, universally, by universal suffrage.

populate ▶ **verb 1** *the island is populated by some 40,000 people* **inhabit**, live/reside in, occupy, people; *formal* dwell in.
2 *we are trying to populate a land which has been derelict* **settle (in)**, colonize, people, move into, occupy, take up residence in, make one's home in, open up, pioneer, overrun.

population ▶ **noun inhabitants**, residents, people, citizens, citizenry, public, community, populace, society, natives, occupants, occupiers; *informal* folk, common folk; *humorous* denizens.
WORD LINKS
related prefix **demo-** (e.g. ***demography, democracy***)

populous ▶ **adjective** *the country's second most populous city* **densely populated**, heavily populated, thickly populated, heavily settled, crowded, congested, packed, jammed, crammed, teeming, swarming, seething, crawling, full; *informal* jam-packed.
OPPOSITES uninhabited, deserted.

porcelain ▶ **noun.** *See centre pages for list of* **Pottery and Porcelain**

porch ▶ **noun vestibule**, foyer, entrance, entrance hall, entry, portal, portico, lobby, anteroom; *N. Amer.* ramada, stoop; *Austral./NZ* sleepout; *Indian* mandapam; *Architecture* lanai, narthex, galilee, peristyle, stoa, colonnade, porte cochère, tambour.

pore[1] ▶ **noun** *sweat poured from every pore in his body* opening, orifice, aperture, hole, outlet, inlet, vent; *technical* stoma, hydathode, ostiole, ostium, foramen.

pore[2] ▶ **verb** *they* **pored over** *a map of Eastern Europe* **study**, read intently, peruse, be absorbed in, scrutinize, scan, examine, go over/through.

pornographic ▶ **adjective obscene**, indecent, improper, indelicate, crude, lewd; **erotic**, titillating, arousing, suggestive, sexy, risqué; coarse, vulgar, gross, dirty, ribald, smutty, filthy, bawdy, earthy, corrupting, exploitative, prurient, salacious, immoral; off-colour, adult, X-rated, hard-core, soft-core; *informal* porn, porno, blue, skin; *rare* rank.
OPPOSITES decent, pure, wholesome.

pornography ▶ **noun erotica**, pornographic material, pornographic literature/films/videos, hard-core pornography, soft-core pornography, dirty books; smut, filth, vice; *informal* porn, hard porn, soft porn, porno, skin/girlie magazines, cheesecake, pornies; *dated, rare* facetiae; curiosa.

porous ▶ **adjective permeable**, penetrable, pervious; absorbent, sponge-like, spongy, sieve-like, leaky, honeycombed, cellular, open, holey; *technical* absorptive; *rare* percolative, cavernulous, leachy, porose, poriferous, spongiose, foraminous, pory.
OPPOSITE impermeable.

port[1] ▶ **noun 1** *the German port of Kiel* **seaport**, port city/town; *French* entrepôt.
2 *shells exploded down by the port* **harbour**, dock, docks, haven, mooring, jetty, pier, marina; anchorage, roads; *archaic* hithe; *rare* moorage, harbourage, roadstead.

port[2] ▶ **noun** *push the water supply pipes into the correct ports in the shower* **aperture**, **opening**, outlet, inlet, socket, vent, passage, porthole, trap, embrasure, door, gate.

portable ▶ adjective **transportable**, movable, mobile, transferable, easily carried, easy to carry, conveyable, travelling, travel; lightweight, compact, handy, convenient, manageable; *rare* portative.

portal ▶ noun *he walked up to the portal of the palazzo* **doorway**, gateway, entrance, way in, way out, exit, egress, opening; door, gate, threshold; *N. Amer.* entryway.

portend ▶ verb *the sound of the death-watch beetle was thought to portend the death of someone in the house* **presage**, augur, foreshadow, foretell, prophesy; **be a sign of**, be a warning of, warn of, be an omen of, be an indication of, be a harbinger of; indicate, herald, signal, bode, announce, promise, threaten, point to, mean, signify, spell, denote; *literary* betoken, foretoken, forebode, harbinger.

portent ▶ noun **1** *here was a striking portent of things to come* **omen**, sign, indication, presage, warning, forewarning, harbinger, augury, signal, promise, threat, menace, ill omen, forecast, prediction, prognostication, prophecy, straw in the wind, writing on the wall, hint, auspice; premonition, presentiment, feeling, vague feeling, funny feeling, feeling in one's bones, foreboding, misgiving; *literary* foretoken.
2 *the word 'plague' carries terrifying portent* **significance**, importance, import, consequence, meaning, meaningfulness, moment, momentousness, weight, weightiness, cruciality.

portentous ▶ adjective **1** *portentous signs had been seen* **ominous**, warning, foreshadowing, predictive, premonitory, prognosticatory, momentous, fateful; threatening, menacing, foreboding, sinister, ill-omened, inauspicious, unpropitious, unpromising, gloomy, unfavourable.
2 *Dr Chen muttered some portentous dialogue* **pompous**, bombastic, self-important, pontifical, ponderous, solemn, sonorous, grandiloquent, declamatory, overblown, inflated, rhetorical, oratorical.

porter[1] ▶ noun *she asked a porter to help with their bags* **carrier**, bearer, baggage carrier, baggage bearer; Sherpa; stretcher bearer; *N. Amer.* redcap, skycap; *Indian* khalasi; *Spanish* cargador.

porter[2] ▶ noun (*Brit.*) *some elegant blocks of flats have a full-time porter on the front door* **doorman**, doorkeeper, door attendant, commissionaire, gatekeeper; caretaker, janitor, concierge.

portion ▶ noun **1** *the upper portion of the chimney | he could repeat large portions of Shakespeare* **part**, piece, bit, section, chunk, segment, slice, fragment; wedge, lump, slab, hunk, parcel, tranche; *Brit. informal* wodge.
2 *she wanted the right to decide how her portion of the allowance should be spent* **share**, slice, quota, part, bit, percentage, amount, quantity, ration, piece, fraction, division, subdivision, allocation, allotment, measure, apportionment; *informal* cut, whack, rake-off; *rare* quantum, moiety.
3 *a generous portion of chips* **helping**, serving, amount, quantity, piece; plateful, bowlful.
4 *disease and hopeless poverty were certain to be his portion* **destiny**, lot, fate, fortune, luck, kismet; what is written in the stars; *archaic* dole, cup, heritage.
▶ verb *her mother portioned out the food* **share out**, allocate, apportion, distribute, hand out, deal out, dole out, give out, dish out, parcel out, divide out, allot, dispense, measure out, mete out; *informal* divvy up.

portly ▶ adjective *a portly, florid-faced man* **stout**, plump, fat, overweight, heavy, corpulent, fleshy, paunchy, pot-bellied, beer-bellied, of ample build, ample, well upholstered, well padded, broad in the beam, rotund, roly-poly, round, rounded, stocky, bulky, Falstaffian; *informal* tubby, beefy, porky, pudgy, blubbery, poddy; *Brit. informal* podgy, fubsy; *N. Amer. informal* lard-assed, corn-fed; *archaic* pursy; *rare* abdominous.
OPPOSITES slim, thin.

portrait ▶ noun **1** *a portrait of King George III* **painting**, picture, drawing, sketch, likeness, image, study, representation, portrayal, depiction, canvas; miniature, self-portrait, kit-cat portrait; *informal* oil; *formal* portraiture.
2 *she turned to photography, taking portraits for the Sunday Times* **photograph**, photo, studio portrait, picture, shot, study, still, snap, snapshot, vignette; *historical* daguerreotype, carte de visite.
3 *the book paints a vivid portrait of contemporary Italy* **description**, portrayal, representation, depiction, impression, account, story, chronicle; thumbnail sketch, vignette, profile, characterization.

portray ▶ verb **1** *many artists choose to portray Windermere in sunny weather* **paint**, draw, paint/draw a picture of, picture, sketch, depict, represent, illustrate, present, show, render; *literary* limn.
2 *the ineffectual Oxbridge dons portrayed by Evelyn Waugh* **describe**, depict, characterize, represent, delineate, present, show, paint in words, evoke.
3 *an article which portrays her as the victim of a loveless marriage* **represent**, depict, characterize, describe, present.
4 *the actor portrays a spy* **play the part of**, play, act the part of, take the role of, act, represent, appear as; *rare* personate.

portrayal ▶ noun **1** *a portrayal of an Imperial Amazon parrot* **painting**, picture, drawing, portrait, sketch, representation, depiction, study, rendering.
2 *her acute and witty portrayal of adolescence* **representation**, characterization, depiction, description, delineation, presentation, study, evocation.
3 *Brando's famous portrayal of Vito Corleone in 'The Godfather'* **performance as**, acting, playing, enacting, representation, interpretation; *rare* personation.

pose ▶ verb **1** *pollution levels pose a threat to people's health* **constitute**, present, create, cause, produce, give rise to, lead to, result in.
2 *the question posed in Chapter 1 remains unanswered* **put forward**, raise, ask, put, set, submit, advance, propose, propound, posit, broach, suggest, postulate, moot.
3 *he asked her to come to his studio and pose for him* **be a model**, model, sit, take up a position, assume an attitude, strike a pose.
4 *he posed her on the sofa* **position**, place, put, arrange, lay out, set out, dispose, locate, situate; *archaic* posture.
5 *a bunch of fashion victims stood posing at the bar* **behave affectedly**, strike an attitude, strike a pose, posture, attitudinize, put on airs, put on an act; *informal* show off; *N. Amer. informal* cop an attitude.
□ **pose as** *a gang posing as police officers hijacked the lorry* **pretend to be**, impersonate, pass oneself off as, be disguised as, masquerade as, profess to be, purport to be, set oneself up as, assume/feign the identity of, pass for, represent oneself as; *rare* personate.
▶ noun **1** *a photograph of a glamorous brunette in a sexy pose* **posture**, position, stance, attitude, bearing.
2 *she found her pose of aggrieved innocence hard to keep up* **pretence**, act, affectation, facade, show, front, display, masquerade, posture; play-acting, attitudinizing, dissimulation.

poser[1] ▶ noun *'How are we going to get there?' This was a bit of a poser* **difficult question**, awkward problem, knotty problem, vexed question, tough one, puzzle, mystery, conundrum, puzzler, enigma, riddle; *informal* dilemma, facer, toughie, tough/hard nut to crack, brain-teaser, stumper, cruncher.

poser[2] ▶ noun *he's such a poser* **exhibitionist**, poseur, poseuse, self-publicist; *informal* show-off, pseud; *rare* attitudinizer, posturer.

poseur ▶ noun. See POSER[2].

posh ▶ adjective **1** (*informal*) *a posh Beverly Hills hotel* **smart**, stylish, upmarket, fancy, high-class, fashionable, chic, luxurious, luxury, de luxe, exclusive, select, sumptuous, opulent, lavish, grand, rich, elegant, ornate, ostentatious, showy; *N. Amer.* high-toned; *informal* classy, swanky, snazzy, plush, plushy, ritzy, flash, la-di-da; *Brit. informal* swish; *N. Amer. informal* swank, tony; *S. African informal* larney; *US black English* dicty; *Brit. informal, dated* swagger; *derogatory* chichi; *archaic* swell; *rare* sprauncy.
2 (*Brit. informal*) *her posh accent* **upper-class**, aristocratic, upmarket, Home Counties; *informal* upper-crust, top-drawer; *Brit. informal* plummy, Sloaney, U.

posit ▶ verb *there are those who posit a purely biological basis for this phenomenon* **postulate**, put forward, advance, propound, submit, predicate, hypothesize, take as a hypothesis, set forth, propose, pose, assert; presuppose, assume, presume.

position ▶ noun **1** *radars determine the aircraft's position* **location**, place, situation, spot, site, locality, locale, scene, setting, area, point; whereabouts, bearings, orientation; *Austral./NZ slang* possy; *technical* locus.
2 *she levered herself into a standing position* **posture**, stance, attitude, pose; set, arrangement, disposition, placement.
3 *the company's financial position is dire* **situation**, state, condition, circumstances, set of circumstances, state of affairs, case; predicament, plight, pass, strait(s).
4 *all the political parties were jockeying for position* **advantage**, pole position, advantageous position, favourable position, the upper hand, the edge, the whip hand, primacy; *N. Amer. informal* the catbird seat; *Austral./NZ informal* the box seat.
5 *people's awareness of their position in society* **status**, place, level, rank, grade, grading, rating, standing, station, footing; stature, prestige, influence, reputation, repute, importance, consequence, class.
6 *I'm looking for a secretarial position* **job**, post, situation, appointment, role, occupation, employment; office, capacity, duty, function; opening, vacancy, niche, opportunity, placement; *informal* berth; *Austral. informal* grip; *archaic* employ.
7 *the chancellor was asked to clarify the government's position on the matter* **point of view**, viewpoint, opinion, way of thinking, outlook, attitude, stand, standpoint, stance, posture, angle, perspective, approach, slant, thinking, policy, thoughts, ideas, sentiments, feelings.
▶ verb *he pulled out a chair and positioned it between them* **put**, place, locate, situate, set, site, stand, station; lay, lie, rest, prop, plant, stick, install, settle; arrange, dispose, array, range, lay out, deploy; orient, orientate; *informal* plonk, park; *rare* posit.

positive ▶ adjective **1** *I am confident of getting a positive response from the commission* **affirmative**, favourable, approving, in the affirmative, good, constructive, enthusiastic, supportive, reassuring, encouraging, corroborative.
OPPOSITE negative.
2 *the results of the blood test were positive* showing a reaction, affirmative.
OPPOSITE negative.
3 *do something positive about your problems* **constructive**, practical, useful, pragmatic, productive, helpful, worthwhile, beneficial, effective, efficacious.

P

4 *she seems a lot more positive these days* **optimistic**, hopeful, confident, forward-looking, cheerful, sanguine, buoyant, assured; *informal* upbeat.
OPPOSITE pessimistic.
5 *in spite of these positive signs, economists are not predicting a recovery* **favourable**, good, pleasing, welcome, promising, encouraging, heartening, propitious, auspicious.
OPPOSITE negative.
6 *positive proof of identification must be produced* **definite**, conclusive, certain, categorical, unequivocal, incontrovertible, indisputable, undeniable, incontestable, unmistakable, unambiguous, indubitable, unquestionable, irrefutable, beyond question, beyond a doubt, absolute, reliable, persuasive, convincing, concrete, tangible, clear, clear-cut, precise, direct, explicit, express, firm, decisive, real, actual; *informal* as sure as eggs is eggs.
OPPOSITES doubtful, disputable.
7 *I am positive that he's not coming back* **certain**, sure, convinced, confident, satisfied, free from doubt, assured, persuaded.
OPPOSITES uncertain, unsure.
8 *the journey was a positive nightmare* **utter**, complete, sheer, absolute, real, total, perfect, out-and-out, pure, outright, thoroughgoing, thorough, downright, unmitigated, unqualified, consummate, veritable, rank, unalloyed; *Brit. informal* right, bloody; *Austral./NZ informal* fair.

CHOOSE THE RIGHT WORD

positive, sure, certain, convinced, definite
See SURE.

positively ▶ adverb **1** *this is positively my last word on the matter* **emphatically**, confidently, firmly, categorically, definitely, with certainty, conclusively, without qualification, certainly, beyond question, unquestionably, undoubtedly, indisputably, unmistakably, indubitably, assuredly.
2 *he looked positively livid* **absolutely**, really, downright, simply, thoroughly, completely, utterly, totally, perfectly, extremely, to a marked degree, decidedly, fairly; *informal* plain, plumb.

possess ▶ verb **1** *the hat was the only one she possessed* **own**, have, be the owner of, have in one's possession, be in possession of, be the possessor of, have to one's name, hold.
2 *he did not possess a sense of humour* **have**, be blessed with, be endowed with, be gifted with, be possessed of, be born with; enjoy, boast, benefit from; *archaic* participate of.
3 *it was almost as though some supernatural force had possessed him* **take control of**, have power over, take over, have mastery over, cast a spell over, bewitch, enchant, enthral, control, dominate, influence; madden, drive mad; *rare* bedevil.
4 *she was possessed by a burning need to talk to him* **obsess**, dominate, haunt, preoccupy, consume; eat someone up, prey on one's mind, become an obsession with, be uppermost in one's mind, take control of.
□ **possess oneself of** *he possessed himself of a loaded shotgun* **acquire**, obtain, get, get hold of, procure, secure, take, seize, take/gain possession of, get one's hands on; *informal* get one's mitts on.

possessed ▶ adjective *he ran towards the door like a man possessed* **mad**, demented, insane, crazed, maddened, berserk, out of one's mind; bewitched, enchanted, under a spell, obsessed, haunted; *rare* bedevilled.

possession ▶ noun **1** *the estate came into the possession of the Heslerton family* **ownership**, proprietorship, control, hands, keeping, care, custody, charge, hold, title, guardianship.
2 *an attempt to drive the tenant out of her possession of the premises* **occupancy**, tenure, occupation, holding, tenancy.
3 *that photograph was Bert's most precious possession* **asset**, thing, article, item owned, chattel.
4 (**possessions**) *he loaded Francesca and all her possessions into his car* **belongings**, things, property, worldly goods, goods, personal effects, effects, stuff, assets, accoutrements, paraphernalia, impedimenta, bits and pieces, luggage, baggage, bags and baggage, chattels, movables, valuables; *Law* goods and chattels; *informal* gear, junk, dunnage, traps; *Brit. informal* clobber; *S. African informal* trek; *vulgar slang* shit, crap.
5 *France's former colonial possessions* **colony**, dependency, territory, holding, dominion, protectorate.
□ **take possession of seize**, appropriate, impound, expropriate, sequestrate, sequester, confiscate; take, get, acquire, obtain, secure, procure, possess oneself of, get hold of, get one's hands on, help oneself to; occupy, conquer, capture, commandeer, requisition; *Law* distrain, attach, disseize; *Scottish Law* poind; *informal* get one's mitts on.

possessive ▶ adjective **1** *he was very possessive—he wanted me to spend every minute with him* **proprietorial**, overprotective, clinging, controlling, dominating, jealous.
2 *one of those possessive women who wants to grab everything within reach* **grasping**, greedy, acquisitive, covetous, selfish; *N. Amer. informal* grabby.

possibility ▶ noun **1** *there was still a possibility that he might be found alive* **chance**, likelihood, probability, prospect, hope; risk, hazard, danger, fear.
2 *they discussed the possibility of launching a major research project on the theme* **feasibility**, practicability, chances, odds, attainability, achievability, potentiality, conceivability, probability; opportunity, scope; *rare* workableness.
3 *buying a smaller house is one possibility* **option**, alternative, choice, course of action, solution, recourse; *informal* bet.
4 (**possibilities**) *he had distinct possibilities as a player* **potential**, potentiality, promise, prospects; capability, ability, aptitude, capacity; *informal* what it takes.

possible ▶ adjective **1** *it's not possible to check the accuracy of the figures* **feasible**, able to be done, practicable, viable, within the bounds/realms of possibility, attainable, achievable, realizable, within reach, workable, manageable; *informal* on, doable.
OPPOSITE impossible.
2 *there was another possible reason for his disappearance* **conceivable**, plausible, imaginable, thinkable, believable, likely, potential, probable, credible, tenable, odds-on; *informal* on the cards.
OPPOSITE unlikely.
3 *he was a possible future leader of the party* **potential**, prospective, likely, probable, could-be, would-be, aspiring.

possibly ▶ adverb **1** *possibly he took the boy with him* **perhaps**, maybe, it may/could be, it is possible, it is conceivable, for all one knows, feasibly, very likely; hopefully, God willing; *N. English* happen; *literary* peradventure, perchance, mayhap, haply; *rare* percase.
2 *you can't possibly refuse* **conceivably**, under any circumstances, by any means, at all, in any way.
3 *could you possibly spare me a few moments?* **please**, kindly, be so good as to; by any chance, if possible.

post[1] ▶ noun *a high roof supported by wooden posts* **pole**, stake, upright, shaft, prop, support, picket, strut, pillar, pale, paling, column, piling, standard, stanchion, pylon, stave, rod, newel, baluster, jamb, bollard, mast; fence post, gatepost, finger post, king post; *N. Amer. & Austral.* milepost; *historical* palisade; *technical* puncheon, shore.
▶ verb **1** *he studied the notice posted on the wall* **affix**, attach, fasten, hang, display, pin (up), put up, stick (up), tack (up), nail (up).
2 *the group posted a net profit of $1.1 million* **announce**, report, make known, advertise, publish, publicize, circulate, broadcast.

post[2] ▶ noun (*Brit.*) **1** *the winners will be notified by post* **mail**, the postal service/system; airmail, surface mail, registered mail, special delivery; *informal* snail mail; *N. Amer. & W. Indian* the mails; *Indian* dak, tappal.
2 *did we get any post?* **letters**, cards, correspondence; parcels, packages, packets; mail, junk mail, direct mail.
3 *what time is the last post?* **postal delivery/collection**, mail delivery/collection.
▶ verb **1** (*Brit.*) *post the order form today* **send**, send off, mail, put in the post/mail, get off, send/dispatch by post, transmit, remit, convey, consign, forward, redirect; airmail.
2 *post the transaction in the second column* **record**, **write in**, enter, fill in, register, note, list.
□ **keep someone posted** *I'll keep you posted about his progress* **keep informed**, inform, keep up to date, keep in the picture, keep briefed, brief, give someone the latest information, update, fill in, let someone know, advise, notify, apprise, report to; *informal* clue in, keep up to speed.

post[3] ▶ noun **1** *there were seventy candidates for the post* **job**, position, appointment, situation, place, office, assignment, employment, placing; vacancy, opening; *informal* berth; *Austral. informal* grip; *archaic* employ.
2 *'Back to your posts!' he commanded* **assigned position**, area of duty; position, place, location, station, observation post, base, beat.
▶ verb **1** *he'd been posted to Berlin* **send**, send to take up an appointment, assign to a post, dispatch.
2 *armed guards were posted beside the exit door* **put on duty**, station, position, put, situate, set, locate, install, establish, base, garrison.

poster ▶ noun *a poster advertising his latest film* **notice**, placard, public notice, bill, sign, advertisement, announcement, affiche, playbill, sticker; *Brit.* fly-poster; *China* dazibao; *informal* ad; *Brit. informal* advert.

posterior ▶ adjective **1** *the posterior part of the skull* **rear**, hind, back, hinder, rearward; *technical* dorsal, caudal, posticous.
OPPOSITES anterior, front.
2 (*formal*) *a date posterior to the first Reform Bill* **later than**, subsequent to, following, succeeding, after.
OPPOSITE previous.
▶ noun (*humorous*) *her plump posterior* **buttocks**, **behind**, backside, rear, rear end, rump, seat, haunches, hindquarters, cheeks; *Brit.* bottom; *French* derrière; *German* Sitzfleisch; *informal* sit-upon, stern, BTM; *Brit. informal* bum, botty, prat, jacksie, tochus; *N. Amer. informal* butt, fanny, tush, tushie, tail, duff, buns, booty, caboose, heinie, patootie, keister, tuchis; *W. Indian informal* batty; *black English* rass, rusty dusty; *Brit. vulgar slang* arse; *N. Amer. vulgar slang* ass; *technical* nates; *humorous* fundament; *archaic* breech.

posterity ▶ noun **1** *the names of those who died are recorded for posterity on a framed scroll* **future generations**, succeeding generations, those who come after us; the future.
2 *God appeared to Abraham with a promise that his posterity should inhabit the*

land **descendants**, heirs, successors, offspring, children, family, progeny, scions; *Law* issue; *archaic* seed.

post-haste ▶ adverb *he departed post-haste for Venice* **as quickly as possible**, without delay, (very) quickly, speedily, swiftly, without further/more ado, with all speed, promptly, immediately, at once, straight away, right away, directly, forthwith; *informal* double quick, p.d.q. (pretty damn quick), pronto, before you can say Jack Robinson, straight off; *archaic* straight, instanter.

postman, postwoman ▶ noun **postal worker**; *N. Amer.* mailman, letter carrier, mail carrier; *Brit. informal* postie.

post-mortem ▶ noun **1** *the hospital will want to carry out a post-mortem* **autopsy**, post-mortem examination, PM, dissection, necropsy.
2 *the very last thing she needed was a post-mortem of her failed relationship* **analysis**, evaluation, assessment, appraisal, examination, review, investigation, breakdown, critique, study; *rare* anatomization.

postpone ▶ verb *he had to postpone his scheduled trip to South Africa* **put off**, delay, defer, put back, hold over/off, carry over, reschedule, adjourn, stay, shelve, stand over, pigeonhole, keep in abeyance, suspend, mothball; *N. Amer.* put over, table, take a rain check on; *N. Amer. Law* continue; *informal* put on ice, put on the back burner, put in cold storage; *rare* remit, respite.
OPPOSITES advance, bring forward.

postponement ▶ noun *a further postponement of the trial* **deferral**, deferment, delay, putting off/back, rescheduling, adjournment, shelving, suspension; stay, respite; *Law* moratorium; *N. Amer. Law* continuance; *rare* put-off.

postscript ▶ noun **1** *handwritten at the bottom of the letter was a postscript* **afterthought**, PS, additional remark; *rare* subscript.
2 *he translated, reprinted, or edited works, adding postscripts of his own* **addendum**, supplement, appendix, codicil, afterword, addition, adjunct; *rare* postlude, subscript.

postulate ▶ verb *such hypotheses have been postulated by highly reputable geologists* **put forward**, **suggest**, advance, posit, hypothesize, take as a hypothesis, propose, assume, presuppose, suppose, presume, predicate, take for granted, theorize.

posture ▶ noun **1** *the priest quietly resumed his kneeling posture* **position**, pose, attitude, stance.
2 *she took ballet lessons to improve her posture* **bearing**, carriage, comportment, way of standing/sitting, stance; *Brit.* deportment.
3 *trade unions adopted a more militant posture in wage negotiations* **attitude**, stance, stand, standpoint, view, point of view, viewpoint, opinion, position, way of thinking, frame of mind, outlook, angle, slant, perspective.
▶ verb *Keith postured, flexing his biceps for Douglas to see* **pose**, strike an attitude, put on airs, attitudinize, behave affectedly, strut; *informal* show off; *N. Amer. informal* cop an attitude, hot-dog.

posy ▶ noun *a posy of snowdrops and violets* **bouquet**, bunch, bunch of flowers, spray, nosegay, corsage; buttonhole, boutonnière; *rare* tussie-mussie.

pot ▶ noun **1** *from below came the rattling of pots in the kitchen* **cooking utensil**, container, receptacle, vessel; pan, saucepan, casserole, stewpot, stockpot, skillet, dixie, chafing dish, cauldron, crucible, crock, basin, bowl; *S. African* potjie; *Indian* lota, surahi; *archaic* pipkin, cruse, pottle, Dutch oven, gallipot.
2 *glazed earthenware pots filled with geraniums and petunias* **flowerpot**, planter, jardinière.
3 *Jim raked in half the pot* **bank**, kitty, pool, purse, stakes, ante, jackpot.
4 (*informal*) *a man with a florid face and a big pot.* See POT BELLY.
□ **go to pot** *the foundry was allowed to go to pot in the seventies* **deteriorate**, decline, degenerate, go to (rack and) ruin, go downhill, go to seed, decay, fall into disrepair, become dilapidated, run down, rot, slide; *informal* go to the dogs, go down the tubes, hit the skids; *Austral./NZ informal* go to the pack.

pot-bellied ▶ adjective **paunchy**, beer-bellied, portly, rotund, roly-poly, stout, overweight, corpulent, Falstaffian; *informal* porky, tubby.

pot belly ▶ noun **paunch**, belly, beer belly, gut, fat/protruding stomach; *informal* beer gut, pot, tummy, spare tyre, middle-aged spread; *N. Amer. informal* bay window; *informal, dated* corporation.

potency ▶ noun **1** *the sheer potency of poetry* **power**, powerfulness, vigour, strength, might, mightiness, force, forcefulness; influence, dominance, energy, potential; *literary* puissance.
2 *the potency of his words* **forcefulness**, force, effectiveness; **persuasiveness**, cogency, impressiveness, strength, authoritativeness, authority; power, powerfulness.
3 *the potency of the drugs* **strength**, powerfulness, power; headiness; **efficacy**, effectiveness, efficaciousness; *informal* kick.

potent ▶ adjective **1** *the party could be a potent political force in the future* **powerful**, strong, vigorous, mighty, formidable, influential, commanding, dominant, forceful, dynamic, redoubtable, overpowering, overwhelming; *literary* puissant.
OPPOSITES weak, impotent.
2 *one of the most potent arguments was marshalled by defence contractors* **forceful**, **convincing**, cogent, compelling, persuasive, powerful, strong, effective, effectual, eloquent, impressive, telling, sound, well founded, valid, weighty, authoritative, irresistible.
3 *two doses of a very potent drug* | *a potent alcoholic brew* **strong**, powerful, effective, efficacious; **intoxicating**, heady, hard, stiff, spiritous.
OPPOSITE weak.

potentate ▶ noun *diplomatic missions to foreign potentates* **ruler**, head of state, monarch, sovereign, king, queen, emperor, empress, prince, tsar, crowned head, mogul, dynast, overlord, leader.

potential ▶ adjective *a potential source of conflict* **possible**, likely, prospective, future, probable, budding, in the making; latent, embryonic, developing, dormant, inherent, unrealized, undeveloped.
▶ noun *the economic potential of the area* | *he obviously has great potential* **possibilities**, potentiality, prospects; promise, capability, capacity, ability, power; aptitude, talent, flair; *informal* what it takes.

WORD LINKS
measurement of electrical potential **potentiometry**

potion ▶ noun *Dotty concocted strange potions from the herbs in her tiny garden* **concoction**, mixture, brew, elixir, philtre, drink, decoction; medicine, tincture, tonic; *archaic* potation; *literary* draught.

pot-pourri ▶ noun *this book is a pot-pourri of curious animal stories* **mixture**, assortment, collection, selection, assemblage, medley, miscellany, melange, mix, variety, motley collection, mixed bag, patchwork, pastiche, blend; smorgasbord, ragbag, hotchpotch, hodgepodge, mishmash, jumble, farrago; *rare* gallimaufry, omnium gatherum, olio, olla podrida, salmagundi, pasticcio, macédoine, motley.

potter ▶ verb *we pottered down to the library* **amble**, wander, meander, stroll, saunter, maunder; *informal* mosey, tootle, toddle; *Brit. informal* mooch; *N. Amer. informal* putter.
□ **potter about/around** *I spent Monday at home, just pottering about* **do nothing much**, amuse oneself, tinker about/around, fiddle about/around, footle about/around, do odd jobs; *informal* mess about/around, piddle about/around, puddle about/around; *Brit. informal* muck about/around, fanny about/around; *N. Amer. informal* putter about/around, lollygag.

pottery *See centre pages for list of* **Pottery and Porcelain**
▶ noun **china**, crockery, ceramics, ware.

WORD LINKS
relating to pottery **ceramic, fictile**

potty ▶ adjective **1** *I must be going potty* **mad**, insane, out of one's mind, deranged, demented, not in one's right mind; *informal* crazy, mental, off one's head, nuts, off one's rocker, round the bend, bats, bonkers; *Brit. informal* barmy, crackers.
OPPOSITE sane.
2 *she's potty about you* **infatuated with**, very keen on, devoted to, in love with, smitten with, enamoured of, addicted to; enthusiastic about, passionate about; *informal* mad about, crazy about, nuts about.
OPPOSITE indifferent.

pouch ▶ noun **1** *he took a small leather pouch from his pocket* **bag**, purse, wallet, sack, sac, pocket, container, receptacle; *Scottish* poke, sporran; *historical* reticule.
2 *a kangaroo's pouch* **abdominal pouch**; *technical* marsupium.

poultry ▶ noun. *See centre pages for list of* **Fowl**

pounce ▶ verb *two men pounced on him, demanding cash* **jump on**, spring on, leap on, swoop (down) on, dive at, drop down on, lunge at, bound at, fall on, set on, make a grab for, take by surprise, take unawares, catch off-guard, attack suddenly; ambush, mug; *informal* jump.
▶ noun *with a sudden pounce, the cheetah's jaws fastened on the gazelle's throat* **leap**, spring, jump, swoop, dive, lunge, bound.

pound[1] ▶ verb **1** *the two bigger men pounded him with their fists* **beat**, strike, hit, batter, thump, pummel, punch, rain blows on, belabour, hammer, thrash, set on, tear into, weigh into, bang, crack, drub, welt, thwack; *informal* bash, clobber, wallop, beat the living daylights out of, give someone a (good) hiding, whack, biff, bop, lay into, pitch into, lace into, let someone have it, knock into the middle of next week, sock, lam, whomp; *Brit. informal* stick one on, slosh; *N. Amer. informal* boff, bust, slug, light into, whale; *Austral./NZ informal* dong, quilt; *literary* smite, swinge.
2 *40ft waves pounded the seafront* **beat against**, crash against, batter, dash against, crack into/against, lash, strike, hit, buffet.
3 *US gunships pounded the capital* **bombard**, bomb, shell, blitz, strafe, torpedo, pepper, fire on, attack; *archaic* cannonade.
4 *pound the cloves with salt and pepper until smooth* **crush**, grind, pulverize, beat, mill, pestle, mash, pulp, bruise, powder, granulate; *technical* triturate, comminute; *archaic* bray, levigate; *rare* kibble.
5 *I heard him pounding along the gangway* **walk/run heavily**, stomp, lumber, clomp, clump, tramp, trudge; thunder; *N. Amer.* tromp.
6 *she leaned weakly against the door, her heart pounding* **throb**, thump, thud,

P

hammer, pulsate, pulse, pump, palpitate, race, beat heavily, go pit-a-pat, pitter-patter, vibrate, drum; *literary* pant, thrill; *rare* quop.

pound² ▶ noun **1** *a pound of apples* **pound weight**, pound avoirdupois, lb, pound troy.
2 *every Christmas she sent the girls ten pounds each* **pound sterling**, £; *Brit. informal* **quid**, smacker, smackeroo, nicker, oner, oncer; *Brit. historical* sovereign.

pound³ ▶ noun *the dog ended up in the local pound* **enclosure**, compound, pen, yard; *Brit.* greenyard; *historical* pinfold.

pour ▶ verb **1** *blood was pouring from his nose* **stream**, flow, run, gush, cascade, course, spout, jet, spurt, flood, surge, spill, rush, well, spew, discharge; *Brit. informal* sloosh; *rare* disembogue.
2 *Amy poured more wine into his glass* **tip**, let flow, dribble, drizzle, splash, spill, decant, discharge; *informal* slosh, glug, slop; *archaic* circumfuse.
3 *the sky was black and it was pouring with rain* **rain heavily/hard**, teem down, pelt down, tip down, beat down, lash down, sheet down, come down in torrents/sheets, rain cats and dogs; *informal* be chucking it down; *Brit. informal* bucket down, come down in buckets/bucketloads, come down by the bucketful, come down in stair rods, tipple down; *N. Amer. informal* rain pitchforks; *Brit. vulgar slang* piss down.
4 *people poured off the train* **throng**, crowd, swarm, stream, flood, gush, teem.

pout ▶ verb *'But everyone else is going,' said Crystal, pouting* **look petulant**, pull a face, look sulky, purse one's lips, make a moue, turn the corners of one's mouth down; scowl, glower, sulk; *rare* mop and mow.
▶ noun *a childish pout* **petulant expression**, sulky expression, moue, face, scowl, glower.

poverty ▶ noun **1** *they experienced years of relentless poverty* **penury**, destitution, indigence, pennilessness, privation, deprivation, impoverishment, neediness, need, want, hardship, impecuniousness, impecuniosity, hand-to-mouth existence, beggary, pauperism, straitened circumstances, bankruptcy, insolvency; *Economics* primary poverty; *rare* pauperdom.
OPPOSITE wealth.
2 *the poverty of choice meant that many left-wing voters read right-wing papers* **scarcity**, deficiency, dearth, shortage, paucity, insufficiency, inadequacy, absence, lack, want, deficit, meagreness, limitedness, restrictedness, sparseness, sparsity; *rare* exiguity.
OPPOSITE abundance.
3 *the poverty of her imagination* **inferiority**, mediocrity, poorness, barrenness, aridity, sterility.

WORD LINKS
fear of poverty **peniaphobia**

poverty-stricken ▶ adjective *his family was poverty-stricken and starving* **extremely poor**, impoverished, destitute, penniless, on one's beam-ends, as poor as a church mouse, without a sou, dirt poor, in penury, penurious, impecunious, indigent, needy, needful, in need/want, unable to make ends meet, down and out, necessitous, beggarly, moneyless, bankrupt, in straitened circumstances; *Brit.* on the breadline, without a penny (to one's name); *informal* broke, flat broke, cleaned out, strapped for cash, strapped, on one's uppers; *Brit. informal* stony broke, skint, without two pennies/farthings to rub together, in Queer Street; *N. Amer. informal* stone broke; *rare* pauperized, beggared.

powder ▶ noun fine particles, fine grains, dust; talcum powder, talc; *archaic* pulvil, pulvilio; *rare* pounce.
▶ verb **1** *give lipstick staying power by lightly powdering your lips first* **dust**, sprinkle/dredge/cover with powder, talc.
2 *the rose petals are dried and powdered* **crush**, grind, pulverize, pound, mill, granulate; *technical* comminute, triturate; *archaic* bray, levigate.

powdered ▶ adjective *powdered milk* dried, freeze-dried, dehydrated; *technical* lyophilized.

powder room ▶ noun **lavatory**, toilet; *Brit.* the Ladies, cloakroom, (public) convenience; *N. Amer.* ladies' room, restroom, bathroom, washroom, comfort station; *Brit. informal* loo.

powdery ▶ adjective **1** *a powdery residue* **fine**, dry, fine-grained, powder-like, dusty, chalky, floury, mealy, sandy, crumbly, friable, granulated, granular; ground, crushed, pulverized; *rare* pulverulent, levigated.
2 *her pale powdery cheeks* **powder-covered**, powdered.

power ▶ noun **1** *my mother suffered a stroke and lost the power of speech | I'll do everything within my power to help* **ability**, capacity, capability, potential, potentiality, faculty, property, competence, competency.
OPPOSITES inability, incapacity.
2 *the unions wield enormous power in party affairs* **control**, authority, influence, dominance, mastery, domination, rule, command, ascendancy, supremacy, dominion, sovereignty, jurisdiction, sway, weight, leverage, hold, grasp, say; *informal* clout, pull, beef, teeth; *N. Amer. informal* drag; *literary* puissance.
3 *police do not have the power to stop and search* **authority**, right, authorization, warrant, licence, prerogative, faculty; *informal* say-so.
4 *in the eighteenth century Russia became a major European power* **state**, country, nation, world power, superpower.
5 *he hit the ball with as much power as he could | the sheer physical power of the man* **strength**, powerfulness, might, force, forcefulness, mightiness, weight, vigour, energy, intensity, potency; brawn, brawniness, muscle; *informal* punch; *Brit. informal* welly; *literary* thew.
6 *the power of his arguments* **forcefulness**, powerfulness, potency, strength, force, eloquence, effectiveness, cogency, persuasiveness, impressiveness, authoritativeness; *informal* punch.
OPPOSITES weakness, impotence.
7 *the new engine has more power* **driving force**, horsepower, hp, acceleration; *informal* poke, oomph; *N. Amer. informal* grunt.
8 *generating power from waste* **energy**, electrical power, nuclear power, solar power, steam power, water power; *informal* juice.
9 (*informal*) *the holiday in Tenerife did him* **a power of** *good* **a great deal of**, a lot of, much; *informal* lots of, loads of, heaps of, masses of, tons of; *dated* a deal of.
□ **have someone in/under one's power have control over**, have influence over, have under one's thumb, have at one's mercy, have in one's clutches, have in the palm of one's hand, have eating out of one's hand, have on a string, have one's claws into; *N. Amer.* have in one's hip pocket; *informal* have over a barrel.
□ **the powers that be** *the powers that be did nothing to diffuse the situation* **the authorities**, the people in charge, the establishment, the government, the administration, the men in (grey) suits.

WORD LINKS
obsession with power **megalomania**

powerful ▶ adjective **1** *his powerful shoulders bulged under his suit* **strong**, muscular, muscly, sturdy, strapping, robust, mighty, hefty, brawny, burly, husky, athletic, manly, well built, Herculean, tough, solid, substantial, lusty; *informal* beefy, hunky; *dated* stalwart; *literary* stark, thewy.
OPPOSITE weak.
2 *a powerful local aperitif* **intoxicating**, heady, hard, strong, stiff; *rare* spirituous, intoxicant.
3 *a powerful blow across the face* **violent**, forceful, heavy, hard, mighty, vigorous, hefty, thunderous.
OPPOSITE gentle.
4 *he felt a powerful desire to kiss her* **intense**, keen, acute, fierce, violent, passionate, ardent, burning, consuming, strong, irresistible, overpowering, overwhelming, fervent, fervid.
5 *a powerful nation* **influential**, strong, high-powered, important, controlling, dominant, commanding, potent, forceful, vigorous, dynamic, formidable, redoubtable; *informal* big, high-octane; *literary* puissant.
OPPOSITES weak, powerless.
6 *a powerful and detailed critique of current thinking in social research* **cogent**, compelling, convincing, persuasive, eloquent, impressive, striking, telling, influential; forceful, strong, effective; dramatic, passionate, graphic, vivid, moving, potent, authoritative, great, weighty, vigorous, forcible, irresistible, substantial.
OPPOSITE ineffective.

powerless ▶ adjective *we felt intimidated and powerless | police are powerless to prosecute the offenders* **impotent**, helpless, without power, ineffectual, inadequate, ineffective, with no say, useless, defenceless, vulnerable, weak, feeble, paralysed; unable, not able, incapable; *literary* impuissant; *archaic* resistless.
OPPOSITES powerful, strong.

practicability ▶ noun *we expressed doubts about the practicability of the scheme* **feasibility**, viability, practicality, possibility, workability, workableness, achievability, attainability; usefulness, use, utility, value.

practicable ▶ adjective *it is important that all practicable steps be taken to prevent violence breaking out* **realistic**, **feasible**, possible, within the bounds/realms of possibility, within reason, viable, reasonable, sensible, workable, achievable, attainable; *informal* doable; *rare* accomplishable.
OPPOSITES impracticable, impossible.

practical ▶ adjective **1** *they have practical experience of language-teaching methods* **empirical**, hands-on, pragmatic, real, actual, active, applied, experiential, experimental, non-theoretical, in the field; *informal* how-to; *technical* heuristic; *rare* empiric.
OPPOSITE theoretical.
2 *the opposition have failed to put forward any practical alternatives* **feasible**, practicable, realistic, viable, workable, possible, within the bounds/realms of possibility, reasonable, sensible, useful, helpful, constructive; *informal* doable; *rare* accomplishable.
3 *do you want your clothes to be practical or frivolous?* **functional**, serviceable, sensible, useful, utilitarian, utility, everyday, workaday, ordinary; suitable, appropriate.
4 *I'm just being practical—we must find a ground-floor flat* **realistic**, sensible, down-to-earth, pragmatic, businesslike, matter-of-fact, reasonable, rational, commonsensical, hard-headed, no-nonsense, with one's/both feet on the ground; *informal* hard-nosed.
OPPOSITE impractical.

5 *it was a practical certainty that he would try to raise more money* **virtual**, effective, in effect.

practicality ▶ **noun 1** *we asked an architect to consider the practicality of cleaning the stonework* **feasibility**, possibility, practicability, viability, workability; utility, usefulness, use, value.
2 *the table is a masterpiece of elegance and practicality* **functionalism**, functionality, serviceability; usefulness, utility.
3 *he spoke with calm practicality* **common sense**, sense, realism, pragmatism, matter-of-factness.
4 *the practicalities of army life* **practical details**, mechanics; *informal* nitty gritty, nuts and bolts.

practical joke ▶ **noun trick**, joke, prank, jape, hoax; *informal* leg-pull; *N. Amer. informal* dido; *Austral. informal* goak; *dated* cutup, rag; *archaic* quiz.

practically ▶ **adverb 1** *the cinema was practically empty* **almost**, nearly, very nearly, virtually, just about, all but, more or less, not far from, close to, in effect, as good as, to all intents and purposes, approaching, verging on, bordering on, next to, essentially, basically; *informal* pretty much, pretty nearly, pretty well; *literary* well-nigh.
2 *'You can't afford it,' he pointed out practically* **realistically**, sensibly, reasonably, pragmatically, matter-of-factly, rationally, with common sense.

practice ▶ **noun 1** *the principles and practice of radiotherapy* **application**, exercise, use, operation, implementation, execution, enactment, action, doing.
2 *it has become common practice to employ women lawyers for the defence in rape trials* **custom**, procedure, policy, convention, tradition, fashion, habit, wont, method, system, routine, institution, way, rule; *Latin* modus operandi; *formal* praxis.
3 *it takes lots of practice to get this technique right | the team's final practice on Friday evening* **training**, rehearsal, repetition, preparation, exercise, drill, study; practice session, dummy run, run-through, try-out, warm-up; *informal* dry run.
4 *such was his disillusionment that he gave up the practice of medicine* **profession**, career, business, work, pursuit, occupation, following.
5 *small legal practice seeks reliable receptionist/secretary* **business**, firm, office; partnership; company, enterprise; *informal* outfit.
□ **in practice** *your proposal is all very well in theory, but in practice it will not work* **in reality**, actually, in real life, realistically, practically, effectively.
□ **out of practice rusty**, unpractised.
□ **put something into practice** *I wondered if I would ever be able to put my professional training into practice* **use**, make use of, put to use, utilize, apply, employ, exercise, put into effect/operation, draw on, bring into play.

practise ▶ **verb 1** *once they'd selected the songs he practised them every day* **rehearse**, run through, go through, go over, work on, work at, repeat; polish, refine, perfect.
2 *performers were practising for the air show* **train**, rehearse, prepare, exercise, drill, work out, warm up, go through one's paces, keep one's hand in, get into shape, do exercises, study; *Brit. informal* knock up.
3 *we still practise some of these rituals today* **carry out**, perform, do, observe, put into practice, execute, follow, exercise.
4 *she practised medicine for three years* **work at**, pursue a career in, have a career in, go in for, engage in, specialize in, ply, follow; *N. Amer.* hang out one's shingle; *archaic* prosecute.

practised ▶ **adjective** *Sam was a practised judge of character* **expert**, **experienced**, seasoned, skilled, skilful, accomplished, proficient, talented, able, capable, adept, adroit, consummate, master, masterly, veteran; trained, qualified, well trained, well versed; *informal* crack, ace, mean, demon, wizard; *N. Amer. informal* crackerjack; *archaic or humorous* compleat.

pragmatic ▶ **adjective** *my father was entirely pragmatic in his response to difficult situations* **practical**, matter of fact, realistic, sensible, down-to-earth, commonsensical, hard-headed, expedient, businesslike, with both/one's feet on the ground, rational, reasonable, no-nonsense, unsentimental, unidealistic; *informal* hard-nosed.
OPPOSITES impractical, unrealistic; idealistic.

praise ▶ **verb 1** *the police praised Parveen for her courage* **commend**, express approval of, express admiration for, applaud, pay tribute to, speak highly of, eulogize, compliment, congratulate, celebrate, sing the praises of, praise to the skies, rave about, go into raptures about, heap praise on, wax lyrical about, say nice things about, make much of, pat on the back, take one's hat off to, throw bouquets at, lionize, admire, hail, cheer, flatter; *N. Amer. informal* ballyhoo; *black English* big someone/something up; *dated* cry someone/something up; *rare* laud, panegyrize.
OPPOSITES criticize, condemn.
2 *we praise God for past blessings* **worship**, glorify, honour, exalt, adore, pay tribute to, pay homage to, give thanks to, venerate, reverence, hallow, bless; *archaic* magnify; *rare* laud.
▶ **noun 1** *James was full of praise for the medical teams | he left Washington with the President's praises ringing in his ears* **approval**, acclaim, admiration, approbation, acclamation, plaudits, congratulations, commendation, applause, flattery, adulation; tribute, accolade, cheer, compliment, a pat on the back, eulogy, encomium, panegyric, ovation, bouquet, laurels; *N. Amer.* puffery; *rare* laudation, eulogium.
2 *give praise to God* **honour**, **thanks**, glory, glorification, worship, devotion, exaltation, adoration, veneration, reverence, tribute.

WORD LINKS
expressing praise **laudatory**

praiseworthy ▶ **adjective** *the government's praiseworthy efforts to improve efficiency in health and education* **commendable**, **laudable**, admirable, creditable, worthy, worthy of admiration, meritorious, deserving, honourable, estimable, exemplary, excellent, sterling, fine; *rare* applaudable.
OPPOSITES blameworthy, disgraceful.

pram ▶ **noun** (*Brit.*) pushchair; *N. Amer.* baby carriage, stroller, pushcart; *Brit. trademark* baby buggy; *formal* perambulator.

prance ▶ **verb** *he was prancing around in his underpants* **cavort**, dance, jig, trip, caper, jump, leap, spring, bound, skip, hop; parade, strut, swagger, swank; frisk, gambol, romp, frolic, curvet; *N. Amer. informal* sashay, cut a/the rug; *rare* peacock, rollick, capriole.

prank ▶ **noun** *a silly student prank* **practical joke**, trick, mischievous act, piece of mischief, joke, escapade, stunt, caper, jape, game, hoax, antic; *informal* lark, leg-pull; *N. Amer. informal* dido; *Austral. informal* goak; *informal, dated* rag, cutup; *archaic* quiz; *rare* frolic, freak, gambado, gambade, rig, prat.

prattle ▶ **verb** *he loved to prattle on about his friends' affairs* **chatter**, babble, prate, blather, blether, ramble, gabble, jabber, twitter, go on, run on, rattle on/away, blither, maunder, drivel, patter, gossip, tittle-tattle, tattle, yap, jibber-jabber, cackle; *Scottish & Irish* slabber; *informal* chit-chat, jaw, gas, gab, blabber, yak, yackety-yak, yabber, yatter, shoot one's mouth off; *Brit. informal* witter, rabbit, chunter, natter, waffle; *N. Amer. informal* run off at the mouth; *Austral./NZ informal* mag; *archaic* twaddle, clack, twattle.
▶ **noun** *do you intend to keep up this childish prattle?* **chatter**, babble, talk, prating, blather, blether, rambling, gabble, jabber, drivel, palaver, tattle; *informal* gab, yak, yackety-yak, yabbering, yatter, twaddle; *Brit. informal* wittering, waffle, waffling, natter, chuntering; *archaic* clack, twattle.

pray ▶ **verb 1** *let us pray | he prayed to God* **say one's prayers**, be at prayer, make one's devotions; offer a prayer/prayers, commune with.
2 *she prayed God to give her enlightenment | I prayed for forgiveness* **invoke**, call on, implore, appeal to, entreat, beseech, beg, ask/request earnestly, plead, crave, petition, solicit, supplicate, importune; *rare* obsecrate.

prayer *See centre pages for list of* **Prayers**
▶ **noun 1** *she stood in the chapel listening to the priest's murmured prayers* invocation, intercession, devotion; *archaic* orison.
2 *Shannon sent up a quick prayer that she wouldn't bump into him en route* **appeal**, plea, entreaty, petition, solicitation, supplication, request, suit, invocation; *rare* obsecration, imploration, adjuration.
□ **not have a prayer** (*informal*) **have no hope**, **not have/stand a chance**, have/stand no chance, not have/stand the ghost of a chance; *informal* not have a hope in hell, not have a cat in hell's chance, not have a dog's chance, not have/stand an earthly, not have a snowball's chance (in hell); *Austral./NZ informal* not have Buckley's (chance).

prayer book ▶ **noun service book**; *Church of England* Book of Common Prayer; *Roman Catholic Church* missal, breviary; *Judaism* Machzor, Siddur; *historical* ordinal, primer; *rare* formulary, euchologion, euchology.

preach ▶ **verb 1** *he preached to a large congregation* **give a sermon**, deliver a sermon, sermonize, spread the gospel, evangelize, address, speak; *rare* gospelize.
2 *a church that preaches the good news of Jesus* **proclaim**, teach, spread, propagate, expound, explain, make known.
3 *my parents have always preached toleration* **advocate**, recommend, advise, urge, exhort, teach, counsel, champion, inculcate, instil.
4 *who are you to preach at me?* **moralize**, be moralistic, sermonize, pontificate, lecture, harangue; *informal* preachify; *rare* ethicize.

WORD LINKS
relating to preaching **homiletic**
art of preaching **homiletics**

preacher *See centre pages for list of* **Priests, Religious Officials, and Members of Religious Orders**
▶ **noun minister (of religion)**, parson, clergyman, clergywoman, member of the clergy, priest, man/woman of the cloth, man/woman of God, cleric, churchman, churchwoman, evangelist, apostle, missionary, revivalist, evangelical, gospeller, sermonizer, spreader of the faith, crusader, proselytizer, moralizer; *Scottish* kirkman; *N. Amer.* televangelist, dominie; *informal* reverend, padre, Holy Joe, sky pilot, hot gospeller; *N. Amer. informal* preacher man, preach; *Austral. informal* josser; *rare* predicant, pulpiteer, homilist.

preaching ▶ **noun** *large crowds came to hear his preaching* **religious teaching**, instruction, message; sermons, sermonizing, homilies, evangelism, homiletics; *rare* pulpitry, kerygma.

preachy ▶ **adjective** (*informal*) *her speeches can sometimes sound preachy* **moralistic**, moralizing, sanctimonious, self-righteous, holier-than-thou, priggish, sententious, pietistic, didactic, dogmatic; *Scottish* unco guid; *rare*

Pharisaic, Pharisaical.

preamble ▶ noun *Lord Denning's preamble to the report* **introduction**, preliminary/preparatory/opening remarks, preliminary/preparatory/opening statement, preliminaries, preface, lead-in, overture, prologue; foreword, prelude, front matter, forward matter; *informal* intro, prelims; *rare* proem, prolegomenon, exordium, prolusion, prodrome.

prearranged ▶ adjective *they met at prearranged meeting points in the city* **arranged beforehand/in advance**, arranged, agreed, predetermined, pre-established, pre-planned, set, fixed.

precarious ▶ adjective *the club's precarious financial position* **uncertain**, insecure, unreliable, unsure, unpredictable, undependable, risky, hazardous, dangerous, unsafe, hanging by a thread, hanging in the balance, perilous, treacherous, on a slippery slope, on thin ice, touch-and-go, built on sand, doubtful, dubious, delicate, tricky, problematic; unsettled, unstable, unsteady, shaky, rocky, wobbly; *informal* dicey, chancy, hairy, iffy; *Brit. informal* dodgy; *archaic or humorous* parlous.
OPPOSITES safe, secure.

precaution ▶ noun **1** *have your car regularly serviced as a precaution against mechanical breakdowns* **safeguard**, preventative/preventive measure, safety measure, insurance, defence, provision; *informal* backstop.
2 (dated) *I groped my way forward with infinite precaution* **caution**, cautiousness, circumspection, care, vigilance, watchfulness, attentiveness, attention, wariness, chariness; prudence.

precautionary ▶ adjective *keeping him in overnight was just a precautionary measure* **preventative**, preventive, safety, protective; *rare* precautional.

precede ▶ verb **1** *a clever advertising campaign preceded the film* **go/come before**, go in advance of, lead up to, lead to, pave the way for, prepare the way for, set the scene for, herald, introduce, usher in, antecede, predate, antedate; *archaic* forgo, prevene.
OPPOSITES follow, succeed.
2 *he opened the door and allowed Catherine to precede him into the studio* **go ahead of**, go in front of, go before; go first, lead the way.
3 *he preceded the book with a collection of poems* **preface**, prefix, introduce, begin, open, launch.

precedence ▶ noun *quarrels over precedence among the Bonaparte family* **priority**, pre-eminence, rank, seniority, superiority, primacy, first place, pride of place, eminence, supremacy, ascendancy, preference.
□ **take precedence over** *artistic integrity should take precedence over economic considerations* **take priority over**, be considered more important/urgent than, outweigh, supersede, prevail over, come before.

precedent ▶ noun *there are few precedents for this sort of legislation | we hope to set a legal precedent* **model**, exemplar, example, pattern, previous case, prior case, previous instance/example, prior instance/example; paradigm, criterion, yardstick, standard, lead, guide.

preceding ▶ adjective *this discussion amplifies many of the issues raised in the preceding chapters* **foregoing**, previous, prior, former, precursory, earlier, above, above-mentioned, aforementioned, above-stated, above-named, antecedent; *rare* anterior, prevenient, precedent, precursive, supra.

precept ▶ noun **1** *the precepts of Orthodox Judaism* **principle**, rule, tenet, canon, code, doctrine, guideline, working principle, law, ordinance, statute, command, order, decree, mandate, dictate, dictum, directive, direction, instruction, injunction, prescription, commandment; *Judaism* mitzvah; *rare* prescript.
2 *precepts that her grandmother used to quote* **maxim**, saying, adage, axiom, aphorism, saw, proverb, motto; *rare* apophthegm.

precinct ▶ noun **1** *the main pedestrian precinct* **area**, zone, sector, district, section, quarter, region.
2 (**precincts**) *within the hallowed precincts of the City of London* **bounds**, boundaries, limits, confines; surrounding area, environs, surroundings, purlieus, surrounds, neighbourhood, vicinity, locality.
3 *they entered the cathedral precinct* **enclosure**, close, quadrangle, court, courtyard; *informal* quad.

precious ▶ adjective **1** *precious works of art* **valuable**, costly, expensive, high-priced, dear; invaluable, priceless, beyond price, of incalculable value/worth; rare, choice, fine, exquisite, irreplaceable, inestimable.
2 *the photograph album was her most precious possession* **valued**, cherished, treasured, prized, favourite, dear, dearest, beloved, darling, adored, loved, special, esteemed, worth its weight in gold, revered, venerated, hallowed.
OPPOSITES worthless, cheap.
3 *his exaggerated, precious manners* **affected**, over-refined, artificial, studied, pretentious, chichi, flowery, mannered, contrived, effete; *informal* twee, la-di-da; *Brit. informal* poncey; *rare* alembicated.

precipice ▶ noun **cliff face**, steep cliff, rock face, sheer drop, cliff, crag, bluff, height, escarpment, scarp, escarp, scar; *Scottish* linn; *S. African* krantz; *literary* steep.

precipitate ▶ verb **1** *the incident precipitated a political crisis* **bring about**, bring on, cause, lead to, occasion, give rise to, trigger, spark, touch off, provoke, hasten, accelerate, expedite, speed up, advance, quicken, push forward, further, instigate, induce.
2 *the crampon failed, precipitating them both down the mountain* **hurl**, catapult, throw, plunge, launch, project, fling, cast, heave, propel.
▶ adjective **1** *we should not make precipitate cuts to our conventional forces* **hasty**, overhasty, rash, hurried, rushed; **impetuous**, impulsive, spur-of-the-moment, precipitous, incautious, imprudent, injudicious, ill-advised, heedless, reckless, hare-brained, foolhardy; *informal* harum-scarum, previous; *rare* temerarious.
2 *a precipitate decline in the party's fortunes.* See PRECIPITOUS *sense 2.*

> **CHOOSE THE RIGHT WORD**
> **precipitate, headlong, impetuous, impulsive**
> See IMPETUOUS.

precipitous ▶ adjective **1** *the road became narrower, the drop on each side more precipitous* **steep**, sheer, high, perpendicular, abrupt, sharp, dizzy, vertiginous, vertical, bluff; *rare* acclivitous, declivitous.
2 *his fall from power was precipitous* **sudden**, **rapid**, swift, abrupt, meteoric, headlong, speedy, quick, fast, hurried, breakneck, violent, precipitate, unexpected, without warning, unanticipated, unforeseen; *rare* precipitant.
3 *he was arguably too precipitous.* See PRECIPITATE *adjective sense 1.*

precis ▶ noun *a precis of the report* **summary**, synopsis, résumé, abstract, outline, summarization, summation; **abridgement**, digest, condensation, abbreviation, survey, overview, rundown, run-through, sketch; *French* tour d'horizon; *N. Amer.* wrap-up; *Law* headnote, brief; *rare* conspectus, summa, epitome, compendium.
▶ verb *another strategy for improving your writing skills is to precis a passage* **summarize**, sum up, give a summary/synopsis/precis of, give the main points of; **abridge**, condense, shorten, synopsize, abstract, outline, compress, abbreviate; *rare* epitomize.

precise ▶ adjective **1** *precise measurements* **exact**, **accurate**, correct, error-free, pinpoint, specific, detailed, explicit, clear-cut, unambiguous, meticulous, close, strict, definite, particular, express; minute, faithful.
OPPOSITES imprecise, inaccurate.
2 *at that precise moment the car stopped* **exact**, **particular**, very, specific, actual, distinct.
3 *the attention to detail is very precise* **meticulous**, careful, exact, scrupulous, punctilious, conscientious, particular, exacting, methodical, strict, rigorous; mathematical, scientific.
OPPOSITES loose, careless.

> **CHOOSE THE RIGHT WORD**
> **precise, accurate, exact**
> See ACCURATE.

precisely ▶ adverb **1** *at 2 o'clock precisely, the phone rang | she lives precisely in the centre of Canada* **exactly**, sharp, on the dot; **promptly**, prompt, dead (on), on the stroke of ..., on the dot of ...; right, directly, squarely; *informal* bang (on), spot on, smack, slap, slap bang, plumb; *N. Amer.* on the button, on the nose, smack dab.
2 *Toby is precisely the kind of man I have been looking for* **exactly**, absolutely, just, in all respects, in every way, entirely, altogether; *informal* to a T.
3 *fertilization can be timed precisely* **accurately**, exactly, carefully, to a nicety; clearly, distinctly, strictly.
4 *'You mean it was a conspiracy?' 'Precisely'* **yes**, exactly, quite, absolutely, right, that's right, just so, quite so, indubitably, without a doubt, definitely; *informal* you bet, I'll say.

precision ▶ noun *the deal was planned and executed with military precision* **exactness**, exactitude, accuracy, accurateness, correctness, preciseness, clarity, clearness, distinctness; faithfulness, fidelity; care, carefulness, meticulousness, scrupulousness, punctiliousness, particularity, methodicalness, perfection, rigour, rigorousness, nicety.

preclude ▶ verb *his difficulties preclude him from leading a normal life* **prevent**, make it impossible for, make it impracticable for, rule out, put a stop to, stop, prohibit, debar, interdict, block, bar, hinder, impede, inhibit, exclude, disqualify, forbid; *Law* estop.

precocious ▶ adjective *some of the boys were extremely precocious* **advanced**, old beyond one's years, forward, ahead of one's peers, mature, prematurely developed, ahead, gifted, talented, clever, intelligent, quick; *informal* smart; *rare* rathe-ripe.
OPPOSITES backward, slow.

preconceived ▶ adjective *some people tend to have preconceived ideas about us* **predetermined**, prejudged; prejudiced, biased.

preconception ▶ noun *they had no preconceptions about his personality or his politics* **preconceived idea/notion**, presupposition, assumption, presumption, prejudgement, expectation, prepossession; prejudice, bias; *French* parti pris.

precondition ▶ noun *political stability is a precondition for economic revival* **prerequisite**, necessary condition, obligatory condition, essential condition, condition, requirement, necessity, essential, necessary thing, imperative, stipulation, proviso; *Latin* sine qua non; *informal* must.

precursor ▶ noun **1** *the precursors of the Expressionist movement | a three-stringed precursor of the guitar* **forerunner**, predecessor, forefather, father, parent, antecedent, ancestor, forebear, progenitor; pioneer, trailblazer.
2 *lapses in form are often a precursor of disasters to come* **harbinger**, herald, prelude, sign, signal, indication, portent, omen.

precursory ▶ adjective *a precursory version of 'Lolita' | precursory seismic activity* **preliminary**, prior, previous, antecedent, preceding, introductory, preparatory, prefatory; warning, premonitory; *rare* anterior, precursive, preludial, prelusive, prevenient.

predatory ▶ adjective **1** *predatory birds* **predacious**, carnivorous, hunting, raptorial, ravening; of prey; *rare* raptatorial.
2 *I could see a predatory gleam in his eyes* **exploitative**, wolfish, rapacious, greedy, acquisitive, avaricious, vulturine; *rare* vulturous.
3 *a warlike and predatory clan* **marauding**, plundering, pillaging, ravaging, looting, robbing, thieving, rapacious; *rare* plunderous.

predecessor ▶ noun **1** *the Prime Minister learned from his predecessor's mistakes* **former/previous holder of the post**, forerunner, precursor, antecedent.
OPPOSITE successor.
2 *our Victorian predecessors* **ancestor**, forefather, forebear, progenitor, antecedent.
OPPOSITE descendant.

predestined ▶ adjective *some people claim that everything is predestined* **preordained**, ordained, foreordained, destined, predetermined, fated; *rare* predestinated.

predetermined ▶ adjective **1** *they are expected to manage their departments with a predetermined budget* **prearranged**, arranged/established in advance, set, fixed, preset, pre-agreed, pre-established, pre-planned, pre-decided, agreed, settled.
2 *the notion of a predetermined, God-given order to the world* **predestined**, preordained, foreordained, fated.

predicament ▶ noun *I really cannot understand how you could have allowed yourself to get into such a predicament* **difficult situation**, **awkward situation**, mess, difficulty, problematic situation, plight, quandary, trouble, muddle, mare's nest, crisis; *informal* hole, fix, jam, sticky situation, pickle, scrape, bind, tight spot/corner, spot, corner, dilemma, hot/deep water, kettle of fish, how-do-you-do.

predicate ▶ verb *all the social sciences are predicated on the notion that individuals are not isolated* **base**, **be dependent**, found, establish, rest, build, ground, premise.

predict ▶ verb *it is difficult to predict what the outcome will be* **forecast**, foretell, foresee, prophesy, divine, prognosticate, anticipate, see, say, tell in advance, project, speculate, envision, envisage, imagine, picture, estimate, conjecture, guess, hazard a guess; *archaic* augur, previse, presage, foreshow; *Scottish archaic* spae; *rare* vaticinate, auspicate.

predictable ▶ adjective *Guido's reaction was predictable | a novel described as 'drearily predictable'* **foreseeable**, (only) to be expected, expected, par for the course; **unsurprising**, anticipated, probable, likely, foreseen; formulaic, formularized, obvious; *informal* inevitable, on the cards.

prediction ▶ noun *seven months later, his prediction came true* **forecast**, prophecy, divination, prognosis, prognostication, augury; bet, projection, conjecture, guess; *rare* vaticination, prognostic, auspication.

predilection ▶ noun *her predilection for married men* **liking**, fondness, preference, partiality, taste, penchant, weakness, soft spot, fancy, inclination, leaning, bias, propensity, bent, proclivity, proneness, predisposition, tendency, affinity, appetite, love; *archaic* gusto.
OPPOSITES dislike, disinclination.

predispose ▶ verb **1** *lack of exercise may predispose an individual to high blood pressure* **make susceptible**, make liable, make prone, lay open, make vulnerable, put at risk of, leave open, make subject.
2 *attitudes and opinions which predispose people to behave in a certain way* **lead**, incline, move, persuade, influence, sway, induce, prompt, dispose, make, make of a mind to; bias, prejudice.

predisposed ▶ adjective *the audience were young and predisposed to like the film* **inclined**, prepared, ready, of a mind, disposed, minded, willing, not unwilling, in the mood, liable, susceptible; biased, prejudiced.

predisposition ▶ noun **1** *those who have a hereditary predisposition to heart disease* **susceptibility**, proneness, tendency, liability, inclination, disposition, vulnerability, weakness; *Homeopathy* miasm.
2 *differences in public perceptions of the news were associated with people's political predispositions* **preference**, predilection, inclination, leaning, propensity, bent, proclivity, penchant, liking; bias, prejudice; *rare* velleity.

predominance ▶ noun **1** *there are other reasons for the predominance of women carers* **prevalence**, dominance, greater number/amount, preponderance, majority, bulk; *rare* predomination.
2 *Stalin's military predominance in eastern Europe* **supremacy**, mastery, control, power, ascendancy, dominance, sway, pre-eminence, superiority, leadership, hegemony, sovereignty; upper hand, edge; *rare* predomination, paramountcy, prepotence, prepotency, prepollency.

predominant ▶ adjective **1** *the predominant objectives of the organization* **main**, chief, principal, most important, of greatest importance, primary, prime, overriding, uppermost, central, cardinal, leading, foremost, key, paramount, preponderant, prevailing; most obvious, most noticeable, most prominent; *informal* number-one, top-priority.
OPPOSITES subsidiary, minor.
2 *the predominant political forces* **controlling**, in control, dominant, predominating, more/most powerful, more/most important, pre-eminent, ascendant, superior, in the ascendancy, ruling, leading, principal, chief, main, supreme, prevalent; *rare* prepotent, prepollent.

predominantly ▶ adverb *although predominantly a disease of older men, it is not unknown in people of his age* **mainly**, mostly, for the most part, chiefly, principally, primarily, predominately, preponderantly, in the main, on the whole, largely, by and large, to a large extent, to a great degree, typically, in general, generally, usually, commonly, as a rule.

predominate ▶ verb **1** *small-scale producers predominate in the south* **be in the majority**, preponderate, be predominant, be greater/greatest in amount/number, be prevalent, prevail, dominate, reign, be the order of the day; be most prominent, be most noticeable, stand out, stick out.
2 *private interest was not allowed to* **predominate over** *the public good* **prevail**, dominate, be dominant, hold sway, have/get the upper hand, carry most weight, be in control, rule; override, overshadow, outweigh.

pre-eminence ▶ noun *his pre-eminence as a historian* **superiority**, supremacy, greatness, excellence, distinction, prominence, predominance, eminence, peerlessness, transcendence, importance, prestige, stature, fame, renown, celebrity; *rare* supereminence.

pre-eminent ▶ adjective *the country's pre-eminent environmentalist* **greatest**, leading, foremost, best, finest, chief, outstanding, excellent, distinguished, prominent, eminent, important, major, star, top, topmost, famous, renowned, celebrated, illustrious, towering, supreme, superior, exceptional, unrivalled, unsurpassed, unequalled, inimitable, incomparable, matchless, peerless, unmatched, arch-, transcendent; *N. Amer.* marquee; *rare* supereminent.
OPPOSITES unknown, undistinguished; inferior.

pre-eminently ▶ adverb *the novel is pre-eminently a realistic genre | he was pre-eminently qualified to act as peace broker* **primarily**, principally, above all, chiefly, mostly, mainly, in particular; particularly, par excellence, especially, manifestly, eminently, supremely, conspicuously, notably, signally, singularly, emphatically, uniquely, outstandingly, incomparably, inimitably.

pre-empt ▶ verb **1** *his action may have pre-empted Soviet military intervention* **forestall**, prevent; steal a march on, anticipate, get in before; *informal* get one's retaliation in first.
2 *many tables were already pre-empted by family parties* **commandeer**, take possession of, occupy, seize, arrogate, appropriate, take over, take, acquire, secure, reserve.

preen ▶ verb **1** *a robin sat on a low branch, preening its feathers* **clean**, **tidy**, groom, smooth, arrange; *archaic* plume, prink.
2 *his wife preened before the mirror* **admire oneself**, primp oneself, primp, prink oneself; pretty oneself, prettify oneself, smarten oneself, beautify oneself, make oneself pretty/smart/beautiful, groom oneself, tidy oneself, spruce oneself up; *informal* titivate oneself, doll oneself up; *Brit. informal* tart oneself up; *N. Amer. informal* gussy oneself up; *archaic* plume oneself, trig oneself.
□ **preen oneself** *he's busy preening himself on acquiring such a pretty girlfriend* **congratulate oneself**, be pleased with oneself, pride oneself, be proud of oneself, pat oneself on the back, give oneself a pat on the back, feel self-satisfied; *archaic* pique oneself.

preface ▶ noun *Sartre's famous preface to de Beauvoir's first novel* **introduction**, foreword, preamble, prologue, prelude, preliminary/prefatory/opening remarks; front matter, forward matter; *informal* prelims, intro; *rare* proem, exordium, prolegomenon, prolusion, prodrome.
▶ verb *the catalogue is prefaced by a memoir of the artist* **precede**, introduce, prefix, begin, open, start, launch, lead up to, lead into; *rare* prologue, premise.

prefatory ▶ adjective *three further prefatory remarks are necessary* **introductory**, preliminary, opening, initial, preparatory, explanatory, lead-in, initiatory, precursory, prior, antecedent; *rare* prefatorial, precursive, prodromal, prodromic, preambular, preambulatory, preludial, prelusive, prelusory, exordial, proemial, prolegomenal.
OPPOSITES final, closing.

prefect ▶ noun (*Brit.*) *a school prefect* **monitor**; *Brit.* praepostor, prepostor.

prefer ▶ verb **1** *I prefer white wine to red | those who prefer to travel by rail* **like better**, would rather (have), would sooner (have), favour, be more partial to, lean/incline towards, think preferable; choose, select, pick, opt for, go for, vote for, plump for, single out, elect, wish, desire, want; *informal* fancy.
2 (*formal*) *do you want to prefer charges?* **bring**, press, file, lodge, tender, present, place, lay, submit, put forward, proffer, offer, propose.
3 (*archaic*) *he was preferred to the post in 1589* **promote**, upgrade, advance, raise, move up, elevate, aggrandize.

P

preferable ▸ adjective *personal pension plans may be preferable if you change jobs frequently* **better**, best, more desirable, more suitable, more advisable, advantageous, superior, preferred, recommended, favoured, nicer, more expedient; *rare* predilect.
OPPOSITE undesirable.

preferably ▸ adverb *applicants should be graduates, preferably with some relevant experience* **ideally**, if possible, for preference, by preference, from choice, by choice, as a matter of choice, much rather, rather; much sooner, sooner.

preference ▸ noun **1** *my mother was a little put out by my preference for boys' games* **liking**, partiality, predilection, proclivity, fondness, taste, inclination, leaning, bias, bent, penchant, predisposition, desire, wish.
2 *I like most types of music, but my preference is rock* **favourite**, first choice, top of the list, choice, selection, pick; *informal* cup of tea, bag, thing; *N. Amer. informal* druthers.
3 *preference will be given to applicants with some proficiency in Japanese* **priority**, favour, precedence, advantage, preferential treatment, favoured treatment, favouritism.
□ **in preference to** *the thief chose their home in preference to others* **rather than**, instead of, in place of, sooner than, above, before, over.

preferential ▸ adjective *regular blood donors do not received preferential treatment when they themselves need a transfusion* **special**, **better**, privileged, superior, favoured, advantageous, favourable; partial, discriminatory, partisan, biased.

preferment ▸ noun *superior qualifications were by no means a guarantee of preferment* **promotion**, advancement, advance, elevation, being upgraded, a rise, betterment, moving up, a step up, a step up the ladder; aggrandizement; *informal* a kick upstairs.
OPPOSITE demotion.

prefigure ▸ verb *his work prefigures that of the magic realists* **foreshadow**, be an early indication of, presage, be a presage of, be a harbinger of, herald, suggest, indicate, point to; *literary* foretoken.

pregnancy ▸ noun gestation; *rare* gravidity, parturiency.

WORD LINKS
relating to pregnancy **antenatal, prenatal, gestational, gestatory**

pregnant ▸ adjective **1** *when I told Chris I was pregnant, I expected him to panic* **expecting a baby**, having a baby, with a baby on the way, having a child, expectant, carrying a child; *French* enceinte; *informal* expecting, in the family way, expecting a happy event, preggers, preggy, with a bun in the oven, with one in the oven, up the pole; *Brit. informal* in the club, up the duff, in the pudding club, up the spout, up the stick; *N. Amer. informal* knocked up, having swallowed a watermelon seed; *Austral. informal* preggo, clucky, with a joey in the pouch; *informal, dated* in trouble, in pod; *archaic* with child, heavy/big with child, in a delicate condition, in an interesting condition, childing, on the way; *technical* gravid, parturient; *rare* impregnate; *N. Amer. rare* infanticipating, storked; (**be pregnant with**) expect, carry, bear.
2 *a sacred rite, pregnant with religious significance* **filled**, charged, heavy, fraught, replete, teeming; full of, abounding in, rich in.
3 *there was a pregnant pause* **meaningful**, significant, eloquent; **suggestive**, expressive, loaded, meaning, charged, pointed, telling, revealing, weighty.

P

prehistoric ▸ adjective **1** *prehistoric times* **primitive**, primeval, primordial, primal, earliest, ancient, early, antediluvian; *rare* pristine, primigenial.
2 *the special effects in the film now look prehistoric* **out of date**, outdated, outmoded, old-fashioned, passé, ancient, antiquated, archaic, antique, superannuated, anachronistic, outworn, behind the times, primitive, medieval, quaint, old-fangled, obsolescent, obsolete, antediluvian, fossilized; *informal* out of the ark, old hat, creaky, mouldy; *N. Amer. informal* horse-and-buggy, mossy, clunky.
OPPOSITE modern.

WORD LINKS
related prefixes **archaeo-** (e.g. *archaeology, archaeopteryx*), **palaeo-** (e.g. *Palaeolithic, palaeography*)

prejudge ▸ verb *it is wrong to prejudge an issue on the basis of speculation* **judge prematurely**, anticipate; jump to conclusions about; *rare* forejudge, prejudicate.

prejudice ▸ noun **1** *male prejudices about women* **preconceived idea**, preconception, preconceived notion; prejudgement.
2 *he claimed that his opponents were motivated by prejudice* **bigotry**, **bias**, partisanship, partiality, intolerance, discrimination, a jaundiced eye, preference, one-sidedness, unfairness, inequality, inequity; racism, racialism, anti-Semitism, chauvinism, sexism, ageism, heterosexism, classism, fattism; *US* Jim Crowism.
3 *without prejudice to the interests of other countries* **detriment**, harm, disadvantage, damage, injury, hurt, impairment, loss.
▸ verb **1** *it was felt that the article would prejudice the jury* **bias**, influence, sway, predispose, make biased, make partial, make partisan, colour, poison, jaundice, warp, twist, slant, distort; *rare* prepossess.
2 *this could prejudice his chances of victory in the November election* **damage**, be detrimental to, be prejudicial to, be disadvantageous to, injure, harm, hurt, mar, spoil, impair, undermine, be deleterious to, hinder, compromise.

prejudiced ▸ adjective *his prejudiced views* **biased**, bigoted, discriminatory, partisan, partial, one-sided, jaundiced, intolerant, narrow-minded, unfair, unjust, inequitable, non-objective, unobjective, blinkered, parti pris, coloured, distorted, warped, loaded, weighted; racist, racialist, anti-Semitic, chauvinistic, chauvinist, sexist, heterosexist, ageist, disablist, classist, fattist.
OPPOSITES unbiased, impartial, fair.

CHOOSE THE RIGHT WORD
prejudiced, biased, partial
See **BIASED**.

prejudicial ▸ adjective *disclosure of the information would be prejudicial to the interests of the company* **detrimental**, damaging, injurious, harmful, disadvantageous, unfavourable, hurtful, inimical, deleterious, counterproductive; *rare* prejudicious.
OPPOSITES beneficial, advantageous.

preliminary ▸ adjective **1** *the discussions are still at a preliminary stage* **preparatory**, introductory, initial, opening, prefatory, prior, preceding, lead-in, initiatory, precursory; early, advance, exploratory, pilot, test, trial, experimental, explorative; *rare* precursive, prodromal, prodromic, preludial, prelusive, prelusory.
OPPOSITE concluding.
2 *the preliminary rounds of the European Cup* **qualifying**, eliminating.
OPPOSITES closing, final.
□ **preliminary to** *the geese gather in the estuaries, preliminary to their flight southwards* **in preparation for**, before, in advance of, prior to, ahead of, preparatory to.
▸ noun **1** *without any preliminaries, he began interrogating me* **introduction**, preamble, opening, opening/prefatory remarks, formalities.
2 *political activity was seen as a necessary preliminary to the resumption of the military campaign* **prelude**, preparation, preliminary/preparatory measure, preliminary action, overture, groundwork, first round.

prelims ▸ plural noun (*informal*) *the publisher usually provides the prelims and the jacket copy* **front matter**, introductory material, preliminary material, prefatory material, forward matter, introduction, foreword, preface, preamble; *informal* intro; *rare* proem, prolegomenon, exordium.

prelude ▸ noun **1** *a ceasefire was agreed as a prelude to full peace negotiations* **preliminary**, overture, opening, preparation, introduction, start, beginning, curtain-raiser, lead-in, precursor, forerunner, harbinger, herald; *informal* opener; *formal* commencement; *rare* prolusion.
2 *the piece begins with an orchestral prelude* **overture**, introductory movement, introduction, opening, voluntary; *rare* verset.
3 *the whole passage forms a prelude to Part III* **introduction**, preface, prologue, foreword, preamble; *informal* intro; *rare* proem, exordium, prolegomenon, prodrome.
OPPOSITES conclusion, postscript.

premature ▸ adjective **1** *Jenks' term of office was cut short by his premature death* **untimely**, early, unseasonable, too soon, too early, before time.
OPPOSITE overdue.
2 *a premature baby* preterm; *informal* prem; *N. Amer. informal* preemie.
OPPOSITES overdue, late.
3 *she felt that such a step would be premature* **rash**, overhasty, hasty, too soon, precipitate, precipitous, impulsive, impetuous, ill-timed, ill-considered; *informal* jumping the gun, previous.

prematurely ▸ adverb **1** *Sam was born three months prematurely* **too soon**, too early, before the usual time, ahead of time, before one's time; preterm.
2 *his main concern was not to act prematurely* **rashly**, overhastily, hastily, too soon, too early, precipitately, precipitously; *informal* at half-cock, half-cocked; *archaic* untimely.

premeditated ▸ adjective *premeditated murder* **planned**, intentional, intended, deliberate, pre-planned, calculated, cold-blooded, conscious, done on purpose, wilful, prearranged, preconceived, considered, studied, purposive; *Law, dated* prepense.
OPPOSITES accidental, unintentional; spontaneous.

premeditation ▸ noun *it looks as if he wore gloves and that would point to premeditation* **planning**, intent, forethought, pre-planning, advance planning, prearrangement, deliberation; criminal intent, malice aforethought, scheming, plotting; *Law* mens rea.

premier ▸ adjective *one of Britain's premier chefs* **leading**, foremost, chief, principal, head, top-ranking, top, prime, primary, first, highest, second to none, pre-eminent, main, senior, outstanding, master; *N. Amer.* ranking; *informal* top-notch, crack.
▸ noun *the Italian premier* **head of government**, prime minister, PM, president, chief minister, chancellor.

premiere ▸ noun *the new musical is having its world premiere at the Haymarket Theatre tonight* **first performance**, first showing, first night, opening, opening night, debut, launch.

premise ▶ noun *a philosophy based on the premise that human life consists of a series of choices* **proposition**, assumption, hypothesis, thesis, presupposition, postulation, postulate, supposition, presumption, surmise, conjecture, speculation, datum, argument, assertion, belief, thought; *Brit.* premiss.

▶ verb *one school of thought premised that the cosmos is indestructible* **postulate**, hypothesize, conjecture, posit, theorize, suppose, presuppose, surmise, assume, predicate, argue, state, assert; *rare* hypothecate.

premises ▶ plural noun *the company has moved to new premises in Gloucester* **building(s)**, property, site, establishment, office, place.

premiss ▶ noun (*Brit.*). *See* PREMISE.

premium ▶ noun **1** *a 25-year policy with monthly premiums of £30* **insurance charge**, insurance payment, regular payment, instalment.
2 *customers are reluctant to pay a premium for organic fruit* **surcharge**, additional payment, extra amount/charge, additional fee.
3 *you may receive a foreign service premium and a cost of living allowance* **bonus**, extra, percentage, perk, recompense, remuneration, prize, reward; incentive, inducement; *formal* perquisite; *historical* bounty.

□ **at a premium** *parking space is at a premium in Japanese cities* **scarce, in great demand**, like gold dust, hard to come by, in short supply, thin on the ground, few and far between, not to be had, rare, rare/scarce as hen's teeth; *informal* not to be had for love or money.

□ **put/place a premium on 1** *I place a high premium on the historic relationship between the United States and Britain* **value greatly**, attach great/special importance to, set great store by, regard as particularly valuable/important, put a high value on, hold in high regard, appreciate greatly.
2 *the huge increase in the price of oil put a premium on the coal industry* **make valuable**, make invaluable, put a high value on, make essential, make important.

▶ adjective *the quality of premium American table wines improves every year* **superior**, premier, high-end, top-end, exclusive, elite, top, select, choice, de luxe, luxurious, classy, prime, first-rate, high-quality, top-quality, high-grade, five-star, fine, finest; *Brit.* upmarket.
OPPOSITE inferior.

premonition ▶ noun **foreboding**, presentiment, intuition, feeling, hunch, suspicion, sneaking suspicion, feeling in one's bones, funny feeling, vague feeling, inkling, idea, sixth sense; misgiving, worry, anxiety, apprehension, apprehensiveness, fear, dread; *archaic* presage.

preoccupation ▶ noun **1** *in spite of my preoccupation I enjoyed the journey* **pensiveness**, concentration, engrossment, absorption, self-absorption, musing, thinking, thinking of other things, deep thought, brown study, brooding; abstraction, absent-mindedness, absence of mind, distraction, forgetfulness, inattentiveness, wool-gathering, inadvertence, heedlessness, dream, reverie, daydreaming, oblivion, obliviousness.
2 *their main preoccupation is providing winter feed for their cattle* **obsession**, concern, fixation; fascination, passion, enthusiasm, hobby horse, pet subject, compulsion, fetish, complex, neurosis, mania; *French* idée fixe; *informal* bee in one's bonnet, hang-up, thing, bug.

preoccupied ▶ adjective **1** *officials preoccupied with their careers* **obsessed**, concerned; passionate about, absorbed in, engrossed in, interested in, intent on, involved in, wrapped up in, sunk in, immersed in, taken up.
2 *she looked worried and preoccupied* **lost in thought**, deep in thought, immersed in thought, in a brown study, pensive, brooding, absent-minded, distracted, abstracted, distrait, heedless, far away, oblivious.

preoccupy ▶ verb *the issues which currently preoccupy environmentalists* **engross**, concern, absorb, dominate, take up someone's whole attention, take up all of someone's time, distract, obsess, occupy, grip, enthral, consume, haunt, prey on someone's mind, become an obsession with, be uppermost in someone's mind, take control of.

preordain ▶ verb *he believes that everything we do is preordained* **predestine**, destine, foreordain, ordain, fate, doom, foredoom, predetermine, determine, mark out, prescribe.

preparation ▶ noun **1** *the preparation of contingency plans* **devising**, putting together, thinking up, drawing up, construction, composing, composition, editing, fashioning, concocting, production, getting ready, making ready, arrangement, development, assembling, assembly.
2 (**preparations**) *preparations for the conference will begin almost immediately* **arrangements**, planning, plans, provision, preparatory measures, preliminaries, necessary steps, groundwork, spadework, foundation, gearing up.
3 *too much of the curriculum was taken up with preparation for exams* **instruction**, teaching, education, coaching, training, tutoring, inculcation, grooming, disciplining, drilling, priming, briefing, guiding, direction.
4 *a preparation such as benzyl benzoate is needed to kill off the mites* **mixture**, compound, concoction, composition, blend, amalgam, solution, suspension, emulsion, tincture, medicine, potion, cream, ointment, lotion.

preparatory ▶ adjective *there is much preparatory work to be done* **preliminary**, initial, prior, introductory, prefatory, opening, basic, elementary, fundamental, rudimentary, preparative, precursory, initiatory.

□ **preparatory to** *she touched up her make-up preparatory to leaving* **in preparation for**, in advance of, before, prior to, previous to, in anticipation of, in expectation of, leading up to.

prepare ▶ verb **1** *I want you to prepare a plan of action for me* **make ready**, get ready, put together, draw up, produce, arrange, develop, assemble, construct, compose, edit, devise, work out, think up, conceive, formulate, concoct, fashion, work up, lay.
2 *the meal was easy to prepare* **cook**, make, get, put together, assemble, muster, dish up, concoct, blend, infuse, brew; *informal* fix, rustle up; *Brit. informal* knock up.
3 *if you want peace, prepare for war* **get ready**, make preparations, arrange things, make provision, get everything set, take the necessary steps, do the necessary, lay the groundwork, do the spadework, gear oneself up, gird up one's loins, fit oneself out, kit oneself out, rig oneself out, provide, arm oneself; face up to; *informal* psych oneself up.
4 *the top teams prepare for such an event all year* **train**, get into shape, practise, exercise, warm up; get ready, get set.
5 *we enable employees to prepare for exams* **study**, work, do preparation, revise, do homework; *Brit. informal* swot.
6 *this course is written specifically to prepare students for these exams* **instruct**, teach, educate, coach, train, tutor, inculcate, groom, discipline, drill, prime, brief, guide, direct, put in the picture.
7 *you must prepare yourself for a shock* **brace**, make ready, tense, steel, steady, buttress, strengthen, fortify; *literary* gird.

prepared ▶ adjective **1** *he will need to be well prepared for the task* **ready**, set, all set, equipped, primed, in a fit state; waiting, available, on hand, fixed, poised, in position.
2 *you've got to be prepared to cut your price* **willing**, ready, disposed, predisposed, inclined, favourably inclined, of a mind, minded, in the mood, agreeable.

preponderance ▶ noun **1** *the preponderance of women among older people* **prevalence**, predominance, dominance.
2 *the preponderance of evidence indicates that such is likely to be the case* **bulk, majority**, greater quantity, larger part, best/better part, main part, most, almost all, more than half, mass, weight, (main) body, lion's share, predominance, generality.
3 *many members were dissatisfied with the preponderance of the trade unions* **predominance**, dominance, ascendancy, leadership, mastery, supremacy, control, sway, power; advantage, upper hand, edge; *rare* paramountcy.

preponderant ▶ adjective *the Western states remained militarily preponderant in the region* **dominant**, predominant, prevalent, in control, more/most powerful, superior, supreme, ascendant, in the ascendancy; controlling, more/most important, pre-eminent, predominating, ruling, leading, principal, chief, main; *rare* prepotent, prepollent.

prepossessing ▶ adjective **attractive**, beautiful, pretty, handsome, good-looking, fetching, striking, pleasing, pleasant, agreeable, appealing, likeable, lovable, amiable, charming, delightful, engaging, inviting, alluring, magnetic, winning, enchanting, captivating, bewitching, fascinating; *dated* taking; *archaic* fair.
OPPOSITES ugly, unprepossessing.

preposterous ▶ adjective **absurd**, ridiculous, foolish, stupid, ludicrous, farcical, laughable, comical, risible, hare-brained, asinine, inane, nonsensical, pointless, senseless, insane, unreasonable, irrational, illogical; outrageous, shocking, astonishing, monstrous, unbelievable, incredible, unthinkable; *informal* crazy.
OPPOSITES reasonable, sensible.

prerequisite ▶ noun *training is a prerequisite for competence* **necessary condition**, precondition, condition, essential, requirement, requisite, necessity, proviso, qualification, imperative, basic, rudiment, obligation, duty; *Latin* sine qua non; *informal* must.
OPPOSITE non-essential.

▶ adjective *the student must have the prerequisite knowledge* **necessary**, needed, required, called for, essential, requisite, vital, basic, of the essence, indispensable, imperative, obligatory, mandatory, compulsory; *French* de rigueur; *rare* needful.
OPPOSITES unnecessary, non-essential.

prerogative ▶ noun **entitlement**, right, privilege, advantage, due, birthright; liberty, authority, authorization, power, licence, permission, dispensation, leave, consent, warrant, charter, franchise, sanction; exemption, immunity, indemnity; *French* carte blanche; *Law, historical* droit.

presage ▶ verb *the owl's hooting was thought to presage death* **portend**, augur, foreshadow, foretell, prophesy, be an omen of, herald, be a sign of, be the harbinger of, be a warning of, give a warning of, warn of, be an indication of, indicate, be a presage of, signal, bode, announce, promise, threaten; point to, mean, signify, spell, denote, add up to, amount to; *literary* betoken, foretoken, forebode, harbinger.

▶ noun *these symptoms were a sombre presage of his final illness* **omen**, sign, indication, portent, warning, forewarning, harbinger, foreshadowing, augury, signal, promise, threat, ill omen, forecast, prediction, prognostication, prophecy, straw in the wind, writing on the wall, hint;

literary foretoken; *archaic* auspice.

prescience ▶ **noun** *with the uncanny prescience of children, they had divined that he was a fake* **far-sightedness**, foresight, foreknowledge; psychic powers, clairvoyance; prediction, prognostication, divination, prophesy, augury; insight, vision, intuition, perception, percipience; *Hinduism & Buddhism* third eye; *rare* vaticination, haruspication, pythonism, prevision, psychism, adumbration.

prescient ▶ **adjective** *much of what happened was predicted in Leonard's prescient article* **prophetic**, predictive, visionary; psychic, clairvoyant; far-seeing, far-sighted, with foresight, prognostic, divinatory, oracular, sibylline, apocalyptic, fateful, revelatory; insightful, intuitive, perceptive, percipient; *rare* foreknowing, previsional, vatic, mantic, vaticinal, vaticinatory, prognosticative, augural, adumbrative, fatidic, fatidical, haruspical, pythonic.

prescribe ▶ **verb 1** *your doctor may prescribe an antibiotic* **order**, advise, authorize, direct.
2 *traditional values prescribe a life of domesticity* **advise**, recommend, advocate, commend, urge, suggest, subscribe to, endorse, support, back, champion, argue for, promote.
3 *two rules prescribe the nature of that duty* **stipulate**, lay down, dictate, specify, impose, set down, determine, establish, fix, formulate, appoint, decree, order, command, pronounce, ordain, require, direct, enjoin, make provision for, promulgate.

prescribe or proscribe?

Prescribe is sometimes confused with **proscribe**, but their meanings are totally different. *Prescribe* is a much commoner word and means either 'issue a medical prescription' or 'recommend with authority', as in *the doctor prescribed antibiotics. Proscribe*, on the other hand, is a formal word meaning 'condemn or forbid', as in *gambling was strictly proscribed by the authorities.*

prescription ▶ **noun 1** *the doctor wrote her a prescription for more sedatives* **instruction**, order, direction, authorization; *informal* script; *archaic* recipe.
2 *he was asked to fetch a prescription from the chemist* **medicine**, drug, medication, remedy, cure, dose, treatment, preparation, mixture; *archaic* physic; *rare* medicament, medicinal, nostrum.
3 *a painless prescription for improvement* **method**, measure; **recommendation**, suggestion, advice, recipe, formula, direction.

prescriptive ▶ **adjective** *guidelines must avoid being too prescriptive* **dictatorial**, authoritarian, tyrannical, despotic; arbitrary, oppressive, repressive, coercive; insistent, dogmatic, pontifical; binding, enforceable; limiting, narrow, rigid; *informal* bossy.
OPPOSITES free and easy; optional.

presence ▶ **noun 1** *presence of a train on a section of track was indicated electrically* **existence**, being there.
OPPOSITE absence.
2 *I would like to request the presence of an adjudicator* **attendance**, attending, appearance, residence, occupancy; company, companionship; *informal* turning up, showing, showing up.
OPPOSITE absence.
3 *he was impressed by her presence* **bearing**, carriage, stance, deportment, comportment, attitude, posture, manner, air, guise; **demeanour**, mien, behaviour, conduct, dignified air/demeanour, dignified bearing, dignity.
4 *a woman of presence* **aura**, charisma, personality, strength/force of personality, individuality, magnetism, attraction; poise, self-assurance, self-possession, self-confidence.
5 *she felt a presence in the castle* **ghost**, spirit, spectre, phantom, vision, wraith, shadow, poltergeist, manifestation, apparition, supernatural being; *Scottish & Irish* bodach; *W. Indian* duppy; *informal* spook; *literary* shade, visitant, revenant; *archaic* eidolon.
□ **presence of mind composure**, equanimity, self-possession, level-headedness, aplomb, poise, assurance, self-assurance, self-control, nerve, calmness, sangfroid, countenance, collectedness, imperturbability; alertness, quickness, quick-wittedness; *informal* cool, unflappability.

present[1] (stress on the first syllable) ▶ **adjective 1** *a doctor must be present at the ringside* **in attendance**, attending, here, there, near, nearby, at hand, close/near at hand, adjacent, available, ready; accounted for.
OPPOSITE absent.
2 *organic compounds are present in the waste* **in existence**, existing, existent, extant.
OPPOSITE absent.
3 *in the present climate jobs are hard to come by* **current**, present-day, existing, contemporary, immediate; *archaic* instant.
OPPOSITES past; future.
▶ **noun** (**the present**) *forget the past and think about the present* **now**, today, the present time, the here and now, this day and age, the present moment, the time being.
OPPOSITES past; future.
□ **at present** *at present he is very angry* **at the moment**, just now, right now, at this time, at the present time, currently, presently, at this moment in time; in this day and age, nowadays.
□ **for the present** *for the present she stayed where she was* **for the time being**, for now, for the moment, for a while, in the meanwhile, in the meantime, provisionally, temporarily, pro tem; *rare* for the nonce.
□ **the present day modern times**, the present age/time, nowadays, now.

present[2] (stress on the second syllable) ▶ **verb 1** *Eddy will present the cheque to the winner* **hand over**, give, give out, dispense, hand out, confer, bestow, award, grant, donate, gift, accord, extend, entrust, furnish.
2 *the committee finally presented its report* **submit**, set forth, put forward, put up, proffer, offer, show, tender, advance, propose, propound, suggest, venture, bring up, broach, moot, air, ventilate, table, register, lay, lodge, introduce, move, volunteer.
3 *may I present my wife?* **introduce**, make known, acquaint someone with, make acquainted with.
4 *I called to present my warmest compliments* **offer**, give, express, extend.
5 *they presented their new product at an exhibition last month* **demonstrate**, show, put on show/display/view, exhibit, display, introduce, launch, unveil; parade, flaunt.
6 *they have a reputation for presenting good quality opera* **stage**, put on, put before the public, produce, mount, organize; perform, render, act.
7 *she is to present a breakfast TV show* **host**, introduce, announce, compère, anchor, be the presenter of; *N. Amer. informal* emcee.
8 *the authorities sought to present him as a common criminal* **represent**, describe, portray, depict, characterize.
□ **present oneself 1** *he was ordered to present himself at the office at ten* **be present**, make an appearance, appear, attend, turn up, arrive.
2 *make the most of opportunity when it presents itself* **occur**, arise, happen, transpire, emerge, come about, appear, materialize, come up, crop up, pop up, turn up.

present[3] (stress on the first syllable) ▶ **noun** *I got him this tie as a birthday present* **gift**, donation, offering, contribution, handout, presentation, bestowal; largesse, alms, charity, bonus, award, premium, bounty, boon, favour; bequest, legacy, settlement; subsidy, grant, endowment, benefaction; tip, gratuity; (*in the Middle and Far East*) baksheesh; *French* pourboire; *informal* prezzie, freebie, perk, sweetener; *formal* perquisite; *archaic* conferment.

presentable ▶ **adjective 1** *I'm trying to make the place look presentable* **tidy**, **neat**, fit to be seen, orderly, straight, clean, spick and span, in good order, shipshape (and Bristol fashion), in apple-pie order.
2 *you'd better make yourself presentable* **smartly dressed**, tidily dressed, smart, tidy, of smart appearance, well groomed, dapper, elegant, trim, spruce; *informal* natty.
3 *they have produced one or two quite presentable videos* **fairly good**, passable, decent, respectable, adequate, all right, satisfactory, moderately good, not (too) bad, average, tolerable, fair; *informal* OK.

presentation ▶ **noun 1** *the presentation of his certificate took place at the conference* **awarding**, presenting, giving, handing over, dispensing, handing out, conferral, bestowal, granting, donation, award, according, extending, entrusting, furnishing.
2 *the presentation of foods in the supermarket* **appearance**, arrangement, organization, packaging, exposition, disposition, display, layout.
3 *let's decide what you're going to wear for your presentation to the Queen* **introduction**, making known, acquainting; *dated* debut, coming out.
4 *the presentation of drastic proposals for economic reform* **submission**, proffering, offering, tender, tendering, advancing, proposal, propounding, suggestion, venturing, broaching, mooting, airing, ventilating, tabling, registering, introduction, moving, volunteering.
5 *a sales presentation* **demonstration**, talk, lecture, address, speech, show, exhibition, display, introduction, launch, launching, unveiling, parading.
6 *a Radio 4 presentation of his latest play* **staging**, production, performance, mounting, organizing, showing, show, representation, rendition.

present-day ▶ **adjective current**, present, contemporary, latter, latter-day, present-time, twenty-first-century, modern, latest, existing, extant, recent; up to date, up to the minute, fashionable, trendsetting, voguish, modish, the latest, new, newest, newfangled, new-fashioned; *informal* mod, trendy, cool, now.
OPPOSITES past; future.

presentiment ▶ **noun** *I understood that you had some sort of presentiment of disaster* **premonition**, foreboding, intuition, feeling, hunch, suspicion, sneaking suspicion, feeling in one's bones, funny feeling, vague feeling, inkling, idea, sixth sense; misgiving, worry, anxiety, apprehension, apprehensiveness, fear, dread; *archaic* presage.

presently ▶ **adverb 1** *I shall see you presently* **soon**, shortly, directly, quite soon, in a short time, in a short/little while, at any moment/minute/second, in a moment/minute/second, in less than no time (at all), in next to no time, before long, by and by; *N. Amer.* momentarily; *S. African* just now; *informal* pretty soon, any moment now, before you know it, before you can say Jack Robinson, in a jiffy, in two shakes of a lamb's tail; *Brit. informal* in a mo; *archaic or informal* anon; *literary* ere long.
2 *he is presently abroad* **at present**, currently, at the/this moment, at the present moment/time, now, nowadays, these days, today, in this day and age; *Brit. informal* at the minute.

preservation ▸ noun **1** *waste tar was used in wood preservation* **conservation**, protection, maintenance, care, safeguarding, keeping.
2 *the ruling classes were bent on preservation of the status quo* **continuation**, conservation, keeping up, keeping alive, keeping going, maintenance, upholding, sustaining, prolongation, perpetuation.
3 *the preservation of food | the preservation of dead bodies* **conserving**, bottling, tinning, canning, potting, chilling, freezing, freeze-drying, quick-freezing, drying, desiccation, dehydration; curing, smoking, kippering, salting, pickling, marinating, sousing, corning, jellying, candying; embalming, mummification.

preserve ▸ verb **1** *the oil helps to preserve the wood* **conserve**, protect, maintain, care for, take care of, look after, save, safeguard, keep.
OPPOSITES damage; neglect.
2 *the employers wished to preserve the status quo* **continue**, conserve, keep up, keep alive, keep going, maintain, continue with, uphold, sustain, prolong, perpetuate.
OPPOSITES discontinue, abandon.
3 *she wanted to preserve him from harassment* **guard**, protect, keep, defend, safeguard, secure, shelter, shield, screen, watch over.
4 *spices enabled us to preserve food | I preserved the worm in alcohol* **conserve**, bottle, tin, can, pot, chill, freeze, freeze-dry, quick-freeze, dry, desiccate, dehydrate; cure, smoke, kipper, salt, pickle, marinate, souse, corn, jelly, candy; embalm, mummify.
OPPOSITES consume, use.
▸ noun **1** *strawberry preserve* **jam**, jelly, marmalade, conserve, confection; N. Amer. dulce; French confiture.
2 *high culture remains the preserve of an educated middle-class minority* **domain**, area, field, sphere, orbit, arena, realm, province, speciality, specialism, territory, department; informal thing, turf, bailiwick.
3 *an animal preserve* **sanctuary**, reserve, reservation, game reserve.

preside ▸ verb *a chairman has to be elected to **preside at** the meeting* **chair**, take the chair, be chairman/chairwoman/chairperson, officiate (at); conduct, run, lead, guide, moderate.
□ **preside over be in charge of**, be responsible for, be accountable for, be at the head/helm of, head, be head of, manage, administer, organize, be in control of, control, direct, lead, run, govern, rule, be boss of, head up, conduct, command, supervise, superintend, oversee, handle; informal be in the driving/driver's seat, be in the saddle, pull the strings, call the shots/tune.

president ▸ noun **1** *terrorists have assassinated the president* **head of state**, chief of state, elected head of a country.
2 *the president of the society* **head**, chief, director, leader, governor, principal, master, chancellor, vice-chancellor, dean, rector, warden, provost, captain, figurehead; N. Amer. informal prexy, prex.
3 *the president of the company* **chairman**, chairwoman; managing director, MD, chief executive (officer), CEO, director.

press ▸ verb **1** *press the paper firmly on to the type* **push (down)**, press down, thumb, depress, bear down on, lean on, lower, pin, pinion, hold down, force, ram, thrust, cram, squeeze, compress, wedge.
2 *the brown suit had been brushed and pressed* **smooth**, iron, smooth out, remove creases from, put creases in; steam, calender.
3 *tips on how to press flowers* **flatten**, make flat, smooth out.
4 *friends come in to help us gather and press the grapes* **crush**, squeeze, squash, compress, mash, pulp, reduce, clamp, pack down, tamp, condense, compact, trample, stamp, tread, grind, mill, pound, pulverize, macerate.
5 *she pressed the child to her bosom* **clasp**, hold close, hug, cuddle, squeeze, crush, enfold, clutch, grasp, embrace.
6 *Winnie pressed his hand* **squeeze**, give something a squeeze, grip, clutch, pinch.
7 *the crowd **pressed round** for a better view* **cluster**, gather; converge, congregate, flock, push forward, swarm, throng, crowd, seethe, surge, rush.
8 *the government was able to press its claim for recognition* **plead**, urge, advance insistently, file, prefer, lodge, tender, present, place, lay, submit, put forward.
9 *you should **press** him **to** undertake the most careful inquiry* **urge**, pressure, put pressure on, pressurize, force, drive, impel, push, coerce, nag; lean on, prevail on; dragoon into, steamroller into, browbeat into, use strong-arm tactics on, have someone do something; informal put the heat on, put the screws on, twist someone's arm, railroad into, bulldoze into.
10 *workers were pressed into accepting new contracts* **pressurize**, pressure, push, goad, dragoon, steamroller, browbeat, importune, wheedle, cajole, sway, argue, talk; informal railroad, bulldoze.
11 *our campaigns include **pressing for** a ban on the ivory trade* **call**, ask, clamour, push, make a claim, campaign; insist on, demand.
□ **be pressed for** *you should never need to arrange interviews when you are pressed for time* **have too little**, be short of, have barely enough, have an insufficiency of, have insufficient, lack, be lacking (in), be wanting, be deficient in, be deprived of, be low on, need, be/stand in need of; informal be strapped for.
□ **press on** *the team regrouped and pressed on* **proceed**, **keep going**, continue, carry on, move forward, move along, advance, make progress, make headway, press ahead, forge on/ahead, push on, go on, keep on, not give up, struggle on, hammer away, be persistent, be pertinacious, persevere, persist, keep at it, be determined, show determination, stay with it, be tenacious, go the distance, stay the course, plod on, plough on, grind away, see/follow something through; informal soldier on, hang on, plug away, peg away, stick at it, stick it out, hang in there.
▸ noun **1** *he printed his poems on his own press* **printing press**, printing machine.
2 *a private press prints solely what it chooses to print* **publishing house**, publishing company, printing establishment/firm/business/house.
3 (**the press**) *rumours began to appear in the press | the freedom of the press* **the media**, **the newspapers**, the papers, the news media, journalism, the newspaper world, the newspaper business, the print media, the fourth estate; journalists, newspapermen, newsmen, newspaper women, reporters, columnists, commentariat, pressmen, presswomen; informal journos, hacks, hackettes, news hounds; N. Amer. informal newsies; dated publicists; Brit. dated Fleet Street.
4 *the company has had its share of bad press* **reports**, press treatment, press coverage, press reporting, press articles, press reviews, press write-ups.

pressing ▸ adjective **1** *a pressing problem* **urgent**, critical, crucial, acute, desperate, serious, grave, dire, drastic, burning, extreme, life-and-death.
OPPOSITE non-urgent.
2 *I have a pressing engagement* **important**, of the utmost importance, high-priority, pivotal, critical, crucial, compelling, demanding, necessary, key, vital; imperative, essential, of the essence; inescapable.
OPPOSITE unimportant.
3 *a pressing invitation to dinner* **insistent**, persistent, determined, resolute, tenacious, obstinate, dogged, unrelenting, importunate; repeated, unremitting, continuous, incessant, demanding, entreating, clamorous; rare exigent.

pressure ▸ noun **1** *a confined gas exerts a constant pressure on the wall of its container* **(physical) force**, load, stress, thrust; compression, compressing, squeezing, crushing, weight, heaviness.
2 *we shall not put pressure on you to borrow money* **coercion**, force, compulsion, constraint, duress, oppression, enforcement, insistence, demand, entreaty, goading, pestering, provocation, harassment, nagging, harrying, badgering, intimidation, arm-twisting, pressurization, persuasion, influence.
3 *she had a lot of pressure from work* **strain**, stress, tension, heat, burden, load, weight, drain, trouble, care, adversity, difficulty; informal hassle.
▸ verb *it might be possible to **pressure** him **into** resigning* **coerce**, pressurize, press, push, persuade, influence, force, squeeze, bulldoze, hound, harass, nag, harry, badger, goad, prod, pester, browbeat, brainwash, bully, bludgeon, intimidate, dragoon, twist someone's arm, strong-arm; bring pressure to bear on, use pressure on, put pressure on, lean on; N. Amer. blackjack; informal railroad, put the screws/squeeze on; N. Amer. informal hustle, fast-talk.

WORD LINKS

related prefix	**baro-** (e.g. ***barotrauma***)
device for measuring atmospheric pressure	**barometer, barograph**
instrument for measuring blood pressure	**sphygmomanometer**

pressurize ▸ verb *he never tried to **pressurize** Buffy **into** buying the apple* **coerce**, pressure, press, push, persuade, influence, force, squeeze, bulldoze, hound, harass, nag, harry, badger, goad, prod, pester, browbeat, brainwash, bully, bludgeon, intimidate, dragoon, twist someone's arm, strong arm; use pressure on, put pressure on, lean on, prevail on; N. Amer. blackjack; informal railroad, put the screws/squeeze on; N. Amer. informal hustle, fast-talk.

prestige ▸ noun *he experienced a tremendous increase in prestige following his victory* **status**, standing, stature, prestigiousness, reputation, repute, regard, fame, note, renown, honour, esteem, estimation, image, account, rank, celebrity, importance, prominence, consequence, class, distinction, influence, weight, authority, supremacy, eminence, superiority; laurels, kudos, cachet; NZ mana; Indian izzat; informal clout, brownie points.

prestigious ▸ adjective **1** *his work appeared in prestigious journals of physics* **reputable**, distinguished, respected, esteemed, estimable, eminent, august, honoured, of high standing, of note, highly regarded, well thought of, acclaimed, authoritative, well known, in the public eye, celebrated, illustrious, leading, renowned, famed, famous.
OPPOSITES disreputable; obscure.
2 *a prestigious job* **impressive**, conferring prestige, important, prominent, exalted, high-ranking, influential, imposing, powerful, glamorous; well paid, high-end, expensive; Brit. upmarket.
OPPOSITES minor, humble, lowly.

presumably ▸ adverb *presumably he'll get the job* **I assume**, I expect, I believe, I presume, I take it, I suppose, I imagine, I dare say, I would have thought, it is to be presumed, I guess, in all probability, probably, in all likelihood, all things being equal, all things considered, as likely/like as not, doubtless, undoubtedly, no doubt, without doubt; on the face of it, apparently, seemingly.

presume ▸ verb **1** *I presume that it had once been an attic* **assume**, suppose,

P

dare say, imagine, take it, expect, believe, think, surmise, guess, judge, trust, conjecture, speculate, postulate, posit, hypothesize, deduce, divine, infer, conclude, presuppose, take for granted, take as read.
2 *let me **presume to** give you a word of advice* **venture**, dare, have the temerity, have the audacity, have the effrontery, be so bold as, make so bold as, go so far as; take the liberty of.

□ **presume on** *he was wary of presuming on their friendship* **take advantage of**, take unfair advantage of, exploit, take liberties with; rely on, depend on, count on, bank on, reckon on, place reliance on, trust.

presumption ▶ noun **1** *this presumption may be easily rebutted* **assumption**, supposition, presupposition, belief, thought, guess, expectation, judgement, surmise, conjecture, speculation, hypothesis, postulation, premise, generalization, inference, deduction, conclusion.
2 *he apologized for his presumption in arriving without warning* **brazenness**, audacity, boldness, audaciousness, temerity, arrogance, egotism, front, presumptuousness, pertness, forwardness; cockiness, shamelessness, insolence, impudence, bumptiousness, impertinence, effrontery, face, cheek, cheekiness, gall; rudeness, incivility, impoliteness, disrespect, disrespectfulness, familiarity, freshness; *informal* nerve, neck, brass neck, chutzpah; *N. Amer. informal* sass, sassiness; *archaic* assumption.

presumptive ▶ adjective **1** *dating of these structures can only be presumptive* **conjectural**, speculative, tentative, suppositional, notional, hypothetical; theoretical, academic, unproven, unconfirmed.
OPPOSITE definitive.
2 *the heir presumptive* **probable**, likely, prospective, assumed, supposed, expected, predictable, awaited, anticipated; odds-on, plausible, foreseeable.

presumptuous ▶ adjective *it's rather presumptuous to judge my character on such short acquaintance* **brazen**, **overconfident**, arrogant, egotistical, overbold, bold, audacious, pert, forward, familiar, impertinent, fresh, free, insolent, impudent, cocksure; cheeky, rude, impolite, uncivil, bumptious; **overhasty**, hasty, premature, previous, precipitate, impetuous; *informal* cocky; *N. Amer. informal* sassy; *archaic* presumptive, assumptive.
OPPOSITES timid, unassuming.

presuppose ▶ verb **1** *the following course of action presupposes the existence of a policy-making group* **require**, necessitate, imply, entail, mean, involve, assume, suppose, have as a necessary condition, have as a precondition.
2 *I had presupposed that theme parks make people happy* **presume**, assume, take it for granted, take it, take it as read/given, suppose, surmise, think, accept, consider, postulate, posit.

presupposition ▶ noun *he challenged the presupposition that all enzymes are proteins* **presumption**, assumption, preconception, preconceived idea/notion, supposition, hypothesis, surmise, speculation, guess, prediction, thesis, theory, premise, belief, suspicion, thought, argument, postulation, prejudgement.

pretence ▶ noun **1** *cease this pretence and be true to yourself* **make-believe**, act, putting on an act, acting, dissembling, shamming, sham, faking, feigning, simulation, falsification, dissimulation, invention, imagination, self-deception, play-acting, posturing, posture, posing, pose, cant, attitudinizing; deception, deceit, deceitfulness, fraud, hoax, fraudulence, fabrication, duplicity, artifice, subterfuge, treachery, trickery, dishonesty, hypocrisy, falsity, lying, mendacity, lack of veracity; *Brit.* false colours; *informal* kidology; *rare* simulacrum.
OPPOSITES reality; honesty.
2 *he made a pretence of being unconcerned* **false show**, show, semblance, affectation, false appearance, appearance, outward appearance, impression, image, front, false front, guise, colour, facade, display, posture, pose, masquerade, mask, cloak, veil, veneer, smokescreen, camouflage, cover, travesty, parody, charade; *archaic* snivel.
3 *she herself had long since dropped any pretence to faith* **claim**, aspiration, purporting, profession.
4 *he was absolutely without pretence* **pretentiousness**, display, ostentation, affectation, showiness, flaunting, posturing, posing, humbug.
5 *he abducted the queen on the pretence of seeking to protect her* **pretext**, false excuse, guise, sham, ruse, wile, trickery; lie, falsehood.

pretend ▶ verb **1** *they just **pretend to** listen* **make as if**, profess, affect; dissimulate, dissemble, pose, posture, put it on, put on a false front, go through the motions, sham, fake it; *informal* kid.
2 *if you like, I'll pretend to be the dragon* **put on an act**, make believe, play at, act, play-act, pass oneself off as, bluff, impersonate.
3 *it was useless to pretend innocence* **feign**, sham, fake, simulate, put on, counterfeit, affect.
4 *he did not even **pretend to** a crushing burden of work* **claim**, lay claim to, make a claim to, purport to have, profess to have, go through the motions of having.
▶ adjective (*informal*) *she picked up the phone and had a pretend conversation* **imaginary**, imagined, pretended, make-believe, made-up, fantasy, fantasized, fancied, dream, dreamed-up, unreal, fanciful, invented, fictitious, fictive, mythical, feigned, fake, mock, imitative, sham, simulated, artificial, ersatz, dummy, false, faux, spurious, bogus, counterfeit, fraudulent, forged, pseudo; *informal* phoney; *S. African informal* play-play.

pretended ▶ adjective *her eyes widened in pretended astonishment* **fake**, faked, affected, assumed, professed, purported, spurious, ostensible, quasi-, contrived, in name only; insincere, hypocritical, mock, imitation, simulated, so-called, make-believe, pseudo, sham, false, bogus; counterfeit, fraudulent, forged; *informal* pretend, phoney.

pretender ▶ noun *a pretender to the throne* **claimant**, aspirant, claimer.

pretension ▶ noun **1** *the author firmly denies any pretension to exhaustive coverage | literary pretensions* **aspiration**, claim, assertion, pretence, profession, purporting.
2 *I dislike the pretension of her style* **pretentiousness**, affectation, affectedness, ostentation, ostentatiousness, artificiality, attitudinizing, airs, posing, posturing, showing off, hypocrisy, snobbery, show, flashiness; pomposity, pompousness, floweriness, grandiosity, grandness, grandiloquence, magniloquence, elaborateness, extravagance, heroics, flamboyance, ornateness, bombast, turgidity, rhetoric, pedantry; *informal* la-di-da; *Brit. informal* side; *Austral./NZ informal* guyver; *rare* fustian, flatulence.

pretentious ▶ adjective *Clytemnestra is a pretentious name for a dog* **affected**, ostentatious, chichi, showy, flashy, tinselly, conspicuous, flaunty, tasteless, kitschy; overambitious, pompous, artificial, flatulent, inflated, overblown, fustian, hyperventilated, mannered, high-flown, high-sounding, flowery, grandiose, big, grand, elaborate, extravagant, heroic, flamboyant, ornate, grandiloquent, magniloquent, bombastic, turgid, orotund, rhetorical, oratorical; *N. Amer.* sophomoric; *informal* highfalutin, la-di-da, posey, pseud, pseudo; *Brit. informal* poncey, toffee-nosed; *US black English* dicty.
OPPOSITES natural, unaffected.

preternatural ▶ adjective *autumn had arrived with preternatural speed* **extraordinary**, out of the ordinary, exceptional, unusual, uncommon, rare, singular, signal, peculiar, unprecedented, outstanding, remarkable, phenomenal, abnormal, anomalous, inexplicable, unaccountable; supernatural, paranormal, mystical, unearthly, unworldly, other-worldly, fantastic, magical, prodigious, wonderful, wondrous, miraculous; strange, mysterious, odd, weird.

pretext ▶ noun *he called at her house on the pretext of enquiring after Mr Bradshaw* **excuse**, false excuse, ostensible reason, alleged reason, plea, supposed grounds; guise, ploy, pretence, ruse, semblance, show, blind, pose, masquerade, mask, cloak, veil, veneer, smokescreen, camouflage, cover, travesty, parody, charade.

prettify ▶ verb *the landscape had been tamed and weakened by man's attempts to prettify nature* **beautify**, make attractive, make pretty, pretty up, titivate, dress up, adorn, ornament, embellish, trick out, decorate, smarten (up), glamorize, prink, preen, primp; *informal* doll up, do up, give something a facelift; *Brit. informal* tart up.
OPPOSITE uglify.

pretty ▶ adjective *a pretty child* **attractive**, lovely, good-looking, nice-looking, fetching, prepossessing, appealing, charming, delightful, nice, engaging, pleasing; darling, sweet, dear, adorable, lovable; winning, winsome, cute, as pretty as a picture, dainty, graceful; handsome, well favoured, personable, beautiful, glamorous, gorgeous, ravishing, stunning, bewitching, alluring; chocolate-box; *Scottish & N. English* bonny; *informal* easy on the eye; *literary* beauteous; *archaic* fair, comely.
OPPOSITES plain; ugly.
▶ adverb *a pretty large sum of money* **quite**, rather, somewhat, fairly, reasonably, moderately, comparatively, relatively, tolerably, passably, adequately, satisfactorily, decently, respectably; *informal* kind of, sort of.
▶ verb *she's prettying herself* **beautify**, make attractive, make pretty, prettify, pretty up, adorn, ornament, embellish, smarten, glamorize, prink, preen, primp; put make-up on; *informal* do oneself up; *Brit. informal* tart oneself up.

prevail ▶ verb **1** *we can only hope that common sense will prevail* **win**, win out, win through, triumph, be victorious, be the victor, gain the victory, carry the day, carry all before one, finish first, come out ahead, come out on top, succeed, prove superior, conquer, overcome, gain/achieve mastery, gain ascendancy; take the crown, gain the palm, rule, reign.
2 *the excellent conditions that prevailed in the 1950s* **exist**, be in existence, be present, be the case, hold, obtain, occur, be prevalent, be current, be rife, be rampant, be the order of the day, be customary, be established, be common, be widespread, be in force, be in effect; abound, hold sway, predominate, preponderate; endure, survive, persist.

□ **prevail on/upon** *Jane had prevailed on Dorothy to come* **persuade**, induce, talk someone into, coax, convince, make, get, press someone into, win someone over, sway, bring someone round, argue someone into, urge, pressure someone into, pressurize someone into, bring pressure to bear on, coerce, influence, prompt; inveigle, entice, tempt, lure; cajole, wheedle someone into, get round, prod someone into, reason someone into; *Law* procure; *informal* sweet-talk, soft-soap, twist someone's arm, smooth-talk.

prevailing ▶ adjective *a research project examined prevailing attitudes in the classroom* **current**, existing, prevalent, usual, common, most usual, commonest, most frequent, general, mainstream; widespread, rife, in circulation; set, recognized, established, customary, acknowledged, accepted, ordinary; popular, fashionable, in fashion, in style, in vogue.

prevalence ▶ noun *the prevalence of smoking among teenagers* **commonness**, currency, widespread presence, generality, pervasiveness, universality, extensiveness, ubiquity, ubiquitousness; rampancy, rifeness; frequency, regularity; familiarity, acceptance; popularity, fashionableness.

prevalent ▶ adjective *the work attitudes still prevalent in the UK* **widespread**, prevailing, frequent, usual, common, general, universal, pervasive, extensive, ubiquitous, ordinary; endemic, rampant, rife; recognized, established, accepted; current, popular, fashionable, in fashion, in style, in vogue.
OPPOSITES uncommon, rare.

prevaricate ▶ verb *he seemed to prevaricate when journalists asked pointed questions about his involvement* **be evasive**, beat about the bush, hedge, fence, shilly-shally, shuffle, dodge (the issue), sidestep (the issue), pussyfoot, equivocate, be non-committal, parry questions, be vague, vacillate, quibble, cavil, lie; temporize, stall, stall for time; *Brit.* hum and haw; *informal* duck the issue; *archaic* palter; *rare* tergiversate.

prevent ▶ verb **stop**, put a stop to, avert, nip in the bud, fend off, turn aside, stave off, ward off, head off, shut out, block, intercept, halt, arrest, check, stay; hinder, impede, hamper, obstruct, baulk, foil, thwart, obviate, cheat, frustrate, forestall, counteract, inhibit, hold back, curb, restrain, preclude, pre-empt, save, help, suppress; disallow, prohibit, forbid, proscribe, exclude, debar, bar, deter; *archaic* let.
OPPOSITES allow; cause; encourage.

preventive, **preventative** ▶ adjective **1** *preventive maintenance is the key to dependability* **inhibitory**, deterrent, pre-emptive, obstructive; **precautionary**, protective.
2 *preventive medicine* **prophylactic**, disease-preventing, precautionary, protective.
▶ noun **1** *a preventive against crime* **precautionary measure**, deterrent, preventive/protective measure, safeguard, security, protection, defence, hindrance, block, check, impediment, curb, restraint, obstruction.
2 *substances that have value as disease preventives* **prophylactic**, prophylactic device, prophylactic medicine, preventive drug.

previous ▶ adjective **1** *the previous five years | her previous boyfriend* **foregoing**, preceding, precursory, antecedent, above; old, earlier, prior, former, ex-, past, last, sometime, one-time, erstwhile; *formal* quondam; *archaic* whilom; *rare* anterior.
OPPOSITES following, next.
2 (*informal*) *I admit I may have been previous* **overhasty**, hasty, premature, precipitate, impetuous, too early, too soon, untimely, presumptuous; *informal* ahead of oneself.
□ **previous to** *previous to this everything was fine* **before**, prior to, until, till, up to, earlier than, preceding, leading up to, in advance of, ahead of, ante-, pre-; *rare* anterior to.
OPPOSITES after, as a result of.

previously ▶ adverb **formerly**, earlier, earlier on, before, until now/then, hitherto, once, at one time, in the past, in days gone by, in years gone by, in times gone by, in bygone days, in times past, in former times, time was when; in advance, in readiness, ahead of time, sooner, already, beforehand; *formal* heretofore.

prey ▶ noun **1** *lions tend to kill prey their own size* **quarry**, game, kill.
OPPOSITES predator, hunter.
2 *an opposing Counsel will find you easy prey in his cross-examination* **victim**, target, dupe, fool, innocent, gull; *informal* sucker, soft/easy touch, pushover, chump; *Brit. informal* muggins, charlie; *N. Amer. informal* patsy, sap, schlemiel, pigeon, mark; *Austral./NZ informal* dill; *Brit. informal, dated* juggins.
▶ verb
□ **prey on 1** *most hoverfly larvae prey on aphids* **hunt**, catch, seize; eat, devour, feed on, live on, live off.
2 *it is a callous thing to do, to prey on a vulnerable elderly woman* **exploit**, victimize, molest, pick on, intimidate, harass, hound, take advantage of; trick, swindle, cheat, hoodwink, fleece; attack, terrorize; blackmail, bleed; *informal* con.
3 *the unfinished Requiem had begun to prey on his mind* **oppress**, weigh on, weigh heavily on, lie heavy on, burden, be a burden on/to, hang over, gnaw at; **trouble**, worry, beset, disturb, depress, distress, haunt, nag, torment, plague, obsess, take over, take control of.

price ▶ noun **1** *the purchase price of a car* **cost**, asking price, selling price, charge, fee, terms, payment, rate, fare, levy, toll, amount, sum, total, figure; worth, (monetary) value; outlay, expense, expenses, expenditure, bill; valuation, quotation, estimate; *informal* damage.
2 *she accepted spinsterhood as the price of her career* **consequence**, result, cost, toll, penalty, sacrifice, forfeit, forfeiture; downside, snag, drawback, disadvantage, minus; trial, torment, bane, tribulation, affliction, suffering, burden, trouble, worry, deprivation, undesirable consequence.
OPPOSITES reward; advantage.
3 *he had a price on his head* **reward**, bounty, premium; recompense, compensation.
□ **at a price** *the software is available, but at a price* **at a high price/cost**, at considerable cost, for a great deal of money.
□ **at any price** *it's not for sale at any price | my father was a gentle person, wanting peace at any price* **whatever the price**, whatever the cost, at whatever cost, no matter (what) the cost, cost what it may, regardless.
□ **beyond price** *the Crown Jewels are of course beyond price* **of incalculable value/worth**, of inestimable value/worth, of immeasurable value/worth, invaluable, priceless, without price, worth its weight in gold, worth a king's ransom; irreplaceable, incomparable, unparalleled, expensive, costly, high-priced, at a premium, rich, dear, rare, choice, fine, exquisite, precious, treasured, prized, cherished.
▶ verb *a family day ticket is priced at £5.00* **fix/set the price of**, put a price on, cost, value, rate, evaluate, assess, estimate, appraise, assay.

priceless ▶ adjective **1** *a fabulous house full of priceless works of art* **of incalculable value/worth**, of inestimable value/worth, of immeasurable value/worth, invaluable, beyond price, without price, worth its weight in gold, worth a king's ransom; rare, irreplaceable, incomparable, unparalleled, expensive, costly, high-priced, at a premium, rich, dear, choice, fine, exquisite, treasured, prized, precious, cherished.
OPPOSITES worthless, cheap.
2 (*informal*) *Jim thought this was priceless and laughed loudly* **hilarious**, extremely amusing, very funny, comic, comical, riotous, uproarious, screamingly/hysterically funny, too funny for words, side-splitting, rib-tickling, absurd, ridiculous; *informal* a scream, a hoot; *dated* killing, killingly funny.

pricey ▶ adjective (*informal*) **expensive**, dear, costly, high-priced, high-cost, high-end; overpriced, exorbitant, excessive, extortionate, outrageous, inflated; lavish, extravagant; *Brit.* upmarket, over the odds; *informal* steep.
OPPOSITE cheap.

prick ▶ verb **1** *prick the potatoes all over with a fork* **pierce**, puncture, make/put a hole in, stab, perforate, rupture, riddle, penetrate, nick, spear, slit, incise, knife, bore, spike, skewer, spit, stick, punch, pin, needle, jag, jab; *rare* pink, transpierce.
2 *his eyes began to prick in the smoke* **sting**, smart, burn, tingle, prickle, itch; hurt, be sore, be irritated.
3 *his conscience began to prick him* **trouble**, worry, distress, cause someone distress, perturb, disturb, oppress, harrow, harass, cause someone anguish, afflict, torment, plague, prey on, gnaw at, cut, touch, stab, pain, cause someone pain.
4 *ambition pricked him on to greater effort* **goad**, prod, incite, provoke, urge, spur, sting, whip, prompt, stimulate, encourage, inspire, motivate, push, propel, impel.
5 *the horse pricked up its ears* **raise**, erect, point.
□ **prick up one's ears listen carefully**, pay attention, become attentive, begin to take notice, attend, concentrate on hearing, lend an ear, pin one's ears back; *informal* be all ears; *literary* hark.
▶ noun **1** *the patient will feel a prick in the back* **jab**, sting, pinprick, stab, nick, jag.
2 *he could still see the prick of that vanished drawing pin in the plaster* **hole**, puncture, perforation, pinhole; nick, wound, cut, gash.
3 *Juliet felt the prick of tears behind her eyelids* **sting**, stinging, smart, smarting, burning, tingle, tingling, itch, itching, soreness, irritation.
4 *the prick of conscience* **pang**, pricking, twinge, stab, gnawing.

prickle ▶ noun **1** *the cactus is covered with prickles* **thorn**, needle, barb, spike, point, spine, quill, spur, bristle, prong, tine; *technical* spicule.
2 *Willie felt a cold prickle crawl up his back* **tingle**, tingling sensation, tingling, prickling sensation, chill, thrill, itching, creeping sensation, gooseflesh, goose pimples, pins and needles; *Medicine* paraesthesia; *rare* formication.
▶ verb **1** *the thought made her prickle with excitement* **tingle**, itch, have a creeping sensation, have goose pimples, have gooseflesh, have goosebumps, have pins and needles.
2 *its tiny spikes prickled his skin* **make something tingle**, make something smart, make something itch; sting, prick.

prickly ▶ adjective **1** *the hedgehog curled up into a prickly ball* **spiky**, spiked, thorny, barbed, spiny, pronged, bristled, bristly; briary, brambly, burry, rough, scratchy, sharp; *technical* spiculate, spicular, aculeate, barbellate, spinose, spinous, muricate, setaceous.
2 *my skin feels all prickly* **tingly**, tingling, prickling, stinging, smarting, itching, itchy, creeping, crawling.
3 *Mr Griffith was a prickly character* **irritable**, irascible, peevish, fractious, fretful, cross, crabbed, crabby, crotchety, cantankerous, curmudgeonly, disagreeable, miserable, morose, petulant, pettish, peppery, on edge, edgy, impatient, complaining, querulous, bitter, moody, huffy, grumpy, scratchy, ill-tempered, bad-tempered, ill-natured, ill-humoured, sullen, surly, sulky, sour, churlish, touchy, testy, tetchy, grouchy, snappish, waspish, crusty, bilious, liverish, dyspeptic, splenetic, choleric; *informal* snappy, chippy, cranky, whingeing, whingy; *Brit. informal* narky, ratty, eggy, stroppy, shirty; *N. Amer. informal* peckish, soreheaded; *Austral./NZ informal* snaky; *informal, dated* miffy, waxy.
OPPOSITES affable, easy-going.
4 *the prickly question of the refugees* **problematic**, awkward, ticklish, tricky, delicate, sensitive, difficult, hard, baffling, perplexing, knotty, thorny,

P

tough, troublesome, bothersome, trying, taxing, irksome, vexatious, worrying; complicated, complex, intricate, convoluted, involved; *informal* sticky; *Brit. informal* dodgy.

pride ▶ noun **1** *the triumphs of war were a source of pride to them* **self-esteem**, dignity, honour, self-respect, ego, self-worth, self-image, self-identity, self-regard, pride in oneself, pride in one's abilities, belief in one's worth, faith in oneself; *French* amour propre.
OPPOSITE shame.
2 *many craftsmen take pride in a good job well done* **pleasure**, joy, delight, gratification, fulfilment, satisfaction, sense of achievement; comfort, content, contentment.
3 *he refused her offer out of sheer pride* **arrogance**, vanity, self-importance, hubris, self-conceit, conceit, conceitedness, self-love, self-glorification, self-adulation, self-admiration, narcissism, egotism, presumption, superciliousness, haughtiness, snobbery, snobbishness; disdain, disdainfulness, condescension, pretentiousness; *French* hauteur; *informal* big-headedness, swollen-headedness; *literary* vainglory.
OPPOSITES modesty, humility.
4 *the six-year-old bull is the pride of the herd* **best**, finest, top, cream, pick, choice, choicest, most select, elite, prize, jewel, the jewel in the crown, flower, gem, pearl, treasure, paragon, leading light, glory; *French* crème de la crème.
OPPOSITE dregs.
5 *the large vegetable garden was the pride of the hospital gardener* **source of satisfaction**, pride and joy, darling, apple of someone's eye, treasured possession, admiration, object of admiration, joy, delight, marvel.
▶ verb
□ **pride oneself on** *she prided herself on her sincerity* **be proud of**, be proud of oneself for, take pride in, take satisfaction in, congratulate oneself on, flatter oneself on, preen oneself on, pat oneself on the back for, revel in, glory in, delight in, exult in, rejoice in, triumph over; feel self-satisfied about, vaunt, boast about, brag about, crow about, gloat over; *archaic* pique oneself on/in.

priest *See centre pages for list of* **Priests**
▶ noun **clergyman**, **clergywoman**, minister (of religion), cleric, ecclesiastic, pastor, parson, churchman, churchwoman, man/woman of the cloth, man/woman of God, father; *Scottish* kirkman; *N. Amer.* dominie; *informal* reverend, padre, Holy Joe, sky pilot; *Austral. informal* josser.

WORD LINKS
relating to priests **clerical, hieratic, sacerdotal**
fear of priests **hierophobia**

priestly ▶ adjective **clerical**, pastoral, priestlike, canonical, ecclesiastical; *archaic* vicarial; *rare* sacerdotal, hieratic, Aaronic, rectorial, presbyteral.

prig ▶ noun prude, puritan, killjoy, Mrs Grundy, Grundy, pedant, old maid, schoolmarm, Pharisee, hypocrite, pietist, priggish person; *N. Amer.* bluenose; *informal* goody-goody, Goody Two-Shoes, holy Joe, holy Willie, Miss Prim, stuffed shirt; *literary* Tartuffe; *archaic* precisian.

priggish ▶ adjective **self-righteous**, holier-than-thou, smug, sanctimonious, moralistic, sententious, prudish, puritanical, prim, strait-laced, tight-laced, stuffy, starchy, prissy, Victorian, schoolmarmish, schoolmistressy, old-maidish, narrow, narrow-minded, censorious, Pecksniffian, Pharisaic, hypocritical; *informal* goody-goody; *rare* Grundyish.
OPPOSITES broad-minded, permissive.

prim ▶ adjective *a prim, fastidious woman* **demure**, proper, prim and proper, formal, stuffy, strait-laced, prudish; prissy, mimsy, priggish, puritanical, niminy-piminy, Victorian, old-maid, old-maidish, schoolmistressy, schoolmarmish, governessy; *Brit.* po-faced; *informal* starchy; *archaic* square-toed; *rare* Grundyish.
OPPOSITES uninhibited; informal.

primacy ▶ noun *the primacy of industry over agriculture* **greater importance**, priority, precedence, pre-eminence, preference, superiority, first place, pride of place, weighting, supremacy, ascendancy, sovereignty, dominance, dominion, leadership; *rare* paramountcy.

prima donna ▶ noun **1** *this solo was added to give the prima donna another aria* **leading soprano**, leading lady, diva, (opera) star, protagonist, heroine, principal singer, female lead.
2 *the sport's overpaid prima donnas would throw tantrums on court* **temperamental person**, unpredictable person, self-important person.

primal ▶ adjective **1** *they ignore their primal masculine instincts* **basic**, fundamental, essential, elemental, primary, vital, central, intrinsic, indispensable, inherent, cardinal; characteristic.
OPPOSITE peripheral.
2 *the sea is the primal source of all living things on earth* **original**, initial, early, earliest, first, primitive, primeval, primary.
OPPOSITES subsequent; derivative.

primarily ▶ adverb **1** *the bishop was primarily a leader of the local community* **first and foremost**, first, firstly, essentially, in essence, fundamentally, in the first place, most importantly, principally, predominantly, predominately, basically, elementally, above all, especially, particularly.
2 *such work is undertaken primarily for large institutional clients* **mostly**, for the most part, chiefly, mainly, in the main, on the whole, largely, by and large, to a large extent, to a great degree, substantially, overall, in general, effectively, especially, generally, usually, typically, commonly, as a rule.

primary ▶ adjective **1** *the police believe that crime detection is their primary role* **main**, chief, key, prime, central, principal, foremost, first, most important, predominant, paramount, overriding, major, ruling, dominant, master, supreme, cardinal, pre-eminent, ultimate; *informal* number-one.
OPPOSITES secondary, subordinate.
2 *you must start by removing the primary cause of the trouble* **original**, earliest, initial, beginning, first; **essential**, fundamental, basic.
OPPOSITE secondary.

prime[1] ▶ adjective **1** *his prime reason for going to America* **main**, chief, key, primary, central, principal, foremost, first, most important, paramount, major, dominant, supreme, overriding, cardinal, pre-eminent, ultimate; *informal* number-one.
OPPOSITES secondary, subordinate.
2 *deforestation is the prime cause of flooding* **fundamental**, basic, essential, elemental, primary, vital, central.
OPPOSITE secondary.
3 *extensive areas of prime agricultural land* **top-quality**, highest quality, top, best, first-class, first-rate, high-grade, grade A, superior, supreme, flawless, choice, select, finest, superlative, peak, optimal, model; excellent, marvellous, magnificent, superb, fine, wonderful, exceptional, formidable; *informal* tip-top, A1, top-notch.
OPPOSITE inferior.
4 *the NHS remains the prime example of a public health service* **archetypal**, prototypical, typical, classic, ideal, excellent, standard, stock, conventional, characteristic, quintessential.
▶ noun *he was, in his prime, the most famous man in the world* **heyday**, best days/years, day, time, prime of one's life, maturity; youth, springtime, salad days, bloom, flowering, full flowering, perfection; peak, pinnacle, height, high point/spot, zenith, ascendancy.

prime[2] ▶ verb **1** *he grabbed a gun from a nearby rack and primed it* **prepare**, load, set up, ready, make ready, get ready, equip, gear up.
2 *Mischa knew what to say, as Lucy had primed him carefully* **brief**, give information to, fill in, prepare, supply with facts, put in the picture, inform, advise, notify, tell, instruct, coach, drill; *informal* clue in, give someone the low-down; *Brit. informal* gen up.

prime minister ▶ noun **premier**, first minister, head of the government; *Brit.* First Lord of the Treasury.

primeval ▶ adjective **1** *one of Europe's last areas of primeval forest* **ancient**, earliest, first, prehistoric, antediluvian, antique, primordial, primitive, primal; pristine, original, untouched by humans; aboriginal, indigenous; *rare* autochthonous, autochthonic, primigenial.
OPPOSITE modern.
2 *all sorts of primeval fears* **instinctive**, primitive, basic, primal, primordial, intuitive, intuitional, involuntary, inborn, innate, inherent, inbred, natural, congenital, hereditary, inherited, in the blood, ingrained.

primitive ▶ adjective **1** *primitive times | some of these primitive insects learned to fly* **ancient**, earliest, first, prehistoric, antediluvian, antique, primordial, primeval, primal, primary, lower, original, proto-, ur-; aboriginal, indigenous; *rare* autochthonous, autochthonic, primigenial.
OPPOSITES modern, recent; developed.
2 *idealization of the way of life of primitive peoples must be avoided* **preliterate**, non-industrial; simple, unsophisticated.
OPPOSITES advanced, literate, industrial.
3 *the quarrier worked with primitive tools* **crude**, simple, rough, basic, elementary, rough-hewn, rudimentary, undeveloped, unrefined, unsophisticated, rude, rough and ready, makeshift; old-fashioned, obsolete, archaic.
OPPOSITES sophisticated, advanced.
4 *primitive art* **simple**, natural, unsophisticated, naive, unaffected, undeveloped, childlike, innocent, artless, unpretentious; untaught, untrained, untutored.
OPPOSITES sophisticated, refined.

primordial ▶ adjective **1** *these primordial chunks of dust and ice lie in the very fringes of the solar system* **ancient**, earliest, first, prehistoric, antediluvian, antique, primeval, primitive, primal; *rare* autochthonous, autochthonic, primigenial.
OPPOSITE modern.
2 *the primordial desire for earthly happiness* **instinctive**, primitive, basic, primal, primeval, intuitive, intuitional, involuntary, inborn, innate, inherent, inbred, natural, congenital, hereditary, inherited, in the blood, ingrained.

primp ▶ verb *Fran primped her hair | they passed a few women primping at the mirrors* **groom**, tidy, arrange, brush, comb, smooth; smarten (up), spruce up, freshen (up), beautify, pretty, preen, prink (up); *informal* titivate, doll up; *Brit. informal* tart up; *N. Amer. informal* gussy up; *archaic* plume, trig (up).

prince ▶ noun *the prince of a neighbouring state* **ruler**, **sovereign**, lord, overlord, dynast, leader, monarch, crowned head; royal duke, king, emperor, tsar, grand duke, elector, potentate, suzerain, crown prince, princeling, prince regent, mogul, baron, liege (lord); emir, sheikh, sultan, maharaja, raja; *historical* atheling.

princely ▶ adjective **1** *the Cathedral is flanked by princely buildings* **magnificent**, grand, impressive, imposing, splendid, superb, majestic, glorious, striking, spectacular, awe-inspiring, breathtaking; sumptuous, opulent, fine, luxurious, de luxe, lavish, resplendent; monumental, palatial, august, distinguished, noble, proud, stately, dignified, exalted, great, royal, regal, kingly, imperial; rich, brilliant, beautiful, elegant, gorgeous; *informal* splendiferous, ritzy, posh; *rare* splendacious, magnolious.
2 *this will cost the Treasury the princely sum of £11m* **huge**, enormous, generous, handsome, massive, gigantic, very big, very large, great, giant, colossal, mammoth, vast, immense, tremendous, mighty, stupendous, monumental, prodigious, mountainous, monstrous, substantial; *informal* mega, monster, whopping, whopping great, thumping, thumping great, humongous, jumbo, hulking, bumper, astronomical; *Brit. informal* whacking, whacking great, ginormous.

principal ▶ adjective *vehicle emissions are the principal cause of bad air* **main**, chief, primary, leading, foremost, first, most important, predominant, dominant, (most) prominent; key, crucial, vital, essential, basic, staple, critical, pivotal, salient, prime, central, focal; premier, paramount, major, ruling, master, supreme, overriding, cardinal, capital, pre-eminent, ultimate, uppermost, highest, utmost, top, topmost, arch-; *informal* number-one.
OPPOSITES minor, subordinate, subsidiary.
▶ noun **1** *the principal of the firm of contractors* **boss**, chief, chief executive (officer), CEO, chairman, chairwoman, managing director, MD, president, director, manager, employer, head, leader, ruler, controller; *informal* head honcho; *Brit. informal* gaffer, governor, guv'nor.
2 *the school's principal* **head teacher**, head, headmaster, headmistress, director; dean, rector, warden, chancellor, vice-chancellor, president, provost, governor; *N. Amer. informal* prexy, prex.
3 *she is currently a principal in a soap opera* **leading actor/actress**, leading player/performer, leading man/lady, lead, star; protagonist, hero, heroine, leading role, title role; prima donna, diva, prima ballerina.
4 *no repayment of the loan's principal is required for the first few years* **capital sum**, capital, capital funds, working capital, financial resources; money, debt, loan.

> **principal or principle?**
> *See* PRINCIPLE.

principally ▶ adverb *the decline is principally due to overfishing* **mainly**, mostly, chiefly, for the most part, in the main, on the whole, largely, by and large, to a large extent, to a great degree, predominantly, predominately, above all, first and foremost, basically, substantially, overall, in general, effectively, especially, particularly, primarily, generally, usually, typically, commonly, as a rule.

principle ▶ noun **1** *the most elementary principles of physics* **truth**, proposition, concept, idea, theory, postulate; assumption, basis, fundamental, essence, essential; philosophy.
2 *they stuck to the principle of laissez-faire* **doctrine**, belief, creed, credo, attitude, rule, golden rule, guideline, formula, standard, criterion, tenet, truism, code, ethic, maxim, motto, axiom, aphorism, notion, dictum, dogma, canon, law.
3 *a woman of principle | he was applauded for sticking to his principles* **morals**, morality, moral standards, moral values, ethics, code of ethics, beliefs, credo, ideals, standards, integrity, uprightness, high-mindedness, righteousness, virtue, probity, rectitude, sense of honour, honour, decency, conscience, sense of duty, scruples.
□ **in principle 1** *there is no reason, in principle, why we couldn't work together* **in theory**, theoretically, on paper, in an ideal world; *French* en principe.
2 *he has accepted the idea in principle* **in general**, **on balance**, generally, in essence, by and large, on the whole, all in all, in the main, all things considered, taking everything into consideration.

> **principle or principal?**
> Although the words **principle** and **principal** are pronounced in the same way, they do not have the same meaning. *Principle* is a noun meaning 'a fundamental basis of a system of thought or belief', as in *this is one of the basic principles of democracy. Principal*, on the other hand, is normally an adjective meaning 'main or most important', as in *one of the country's principal cities. Principal* can also be a noun, where it is used to refer to the most senior or most important person in an organization or other group (*the deputy principal*).

principled ▶ adjective *she took a principled feminist stance* **moral**, ethical, good, virtuous, righteous, upright, upstanding, high-minded, right-minded, proper, correct, honourable, honest, just, noble, incorruptible, scrupulous, conscientious, respectable, decent.
OPPOSITE unprincipled.

prink ▶ verb *he prinked himself in front of the mirror* **groom**, tidy, arrange, brush, comb, smooth, smarten (up), spruce up, freshen (up), beautify, pretty, preen, primp; *informal* titivate, doll up; *Brit. informal* tart up; *N. Amer. informal* gussy up; *archaic* plume, trig (up).

print *See centre pages for list of* **Printing Processes**
▶ verb **1** *four newspapers are printed in the town* **set in print**, send to press, run off, preprint, reprint, pull, proof, copy, reproduce; *Computing* list, dump; *informal* put to bed, litho.
2 *patterns of birds, flowers, and trees were printed on the cloth* **imprint**, impress, stamp, mark.
3 *they printed 30,000 copies of the offending magazine* **publish**, issue, release, disseminate, circulate, propagate, purvey.
4 *one particular incident is indelibly printed on her memory* **register**, record, note, impress, imprint, engrave, etch, stamp, mark, brand, set, ingrain.
▶ noun **1** *the print was very small* **type**, printing, letters, lettering, characters, type size, typeface, face, font; *Brit.* fount.
2 *there were fresh prints of the deceased's left hand on the bottle* **impression**, fingerprint, mark; footprint.
3 *the picture was supposed to be a print of the Coventry tapestry* **reproduction**, copy, replica, imitation, facsimile, duplicate.
4 *there was a print of a hunting scene on one wall* **picture**, design, engraving, etching, lithograph, silk screen, linocut, monoprint, plate, cut, woodcut, vignette.
5 *the processor sends you the prints and negatives* **photograph**, photo, snap, snapshot, shot, picture; positive, still, proof, enlargement; *Brit.* enprint.
6 *our room was luxuriously furnished with soft floral prints* **printed material/cloth/fabric**, patterned material/cloth/fabric, chintz.
□ **in print 1** *he looks forward to seeing his work in print* **printed**, in black and white, on paper; published, out, on the streets.
2 *they continued to keep the book in print and supply it* **published**, printed, available in bookshops, obtainable in the shops, in circulation, on the market, on the shelves.
□ **out of print** *this volume is now out of print* **no longer available**, unavailable, unobtainable, o.p., no longer published/printed, not on the market.

prior ▶ adjective *visitors can tour the mill by prior arrangement* **earlier**, previous, preceding, foregoing, antecedent, advance, preparatory, preliminary, initial; *rare* anterior, precedent.
OPPOSITES later, subsequent.
□ **prior to** *prior to the seventeenth century clocks were made by blacksmiths* **before**, until, till, up to, previous to, earlier than, preceding, leading up to, in advance of, ahead of, ante-, pre-; *rare* anterior to.
OPPOSITES after, following.

priority ▶ noun **1** *pioneering new forms of surgery should be a priority for the National Health Service* **prime concern**, first concern, most important consideration, most pressing matter, matter of greatest importance, primary issue.
2 *the government's commitment to give priority to primary education* **precedence**, greater importance, preference, precedency, pre-eminence, first/highest place, predominance, primacy, the lead, weighting, weight.
3 *traffic already on the roundabout has priority* **right of way**.

priory ▶ noun **religious house**, religious community, abbey, cloister; monastery, friary; convent, nunnery; *rare* coenobium, coenoby, beguinage.

prise ▶ verb **1** *Joe was trying to prise the cap off a bottle of painkillers* **lever**, **force**, wrench, pull, wrest, twist; jemmy; *N. Amer.* pry, jimmy.
2 *it shouldn't have been necessary to prise information from them* **extract/obtain with difficulty**, worm out; *Brit.* winkle out.

prison ▶ noun **jail**, penal institution, place of detention, lock-up, place of confinement, guardhouse, detention centre; *Brit.* young offender institution; *N. Amer.* penitentiary, correctional facility, jailhouse, boot camp, stockade, house of correction; *informal* the clink, the slammer, inside, stir, the jug, the big house, the brig, the glasshouse; *Brit. informal* the nick; *N. Amer. informal* the can, the pen, the cooler, the joint, the pokey, the slam, the skookum house, the calaboose, the hoosegow; *Brit. informal, dated* the chokey, bird, quod; *historical* pound, roundhouse; *Brit. historical* youth custody centre, approved school, borstal, bridewell; *Scottish historical* tollbooth; *French, historical* bastille; *N. Amer. historical* reformatory.
WORD LINKS
relating to prison **carceral, custodial**

prison cell ▶ noun cell, police cell, cage, condemned cell, dungeon; *informal* sweatbox; *rhyming slang* flowery dell, flowery; *N. Amer. informal* bullpen, tank, drunk tank; *Austral./NZ informal* peter.

prisoner ▶ noun **1** *a prisoner serving a life sentence* **convict**, inmate; trusty; *informal* jailbird, con, lifer; *Brit. informal* (old) lag; *N. Amer. informal* yardbird; *archaic* transport.
2 *the army took several hundred prisoners* **prisoner of war**, POW; hostage, captive, detainee, internee.

prissy ▶ adjective *he hated it when she swore, but he didn't like to sound prissy* **prudish**, priggish, prim, prim and proper, niminy-piminy, strait-laced; formal, proper, stuffy, mimsy, namby-pamby, Victorian, old-maidish,

P

schoolmistressy, schoolmarmish, governessy; *Brit.* po-faced; *informal* goody-goody, starchy; *rare* square-toed, Grundyish.
OPPOSITE broad-minded.

pristine ▶ adjective *a pristine white handkerchief* **immaculate**, in perfect condition, perfect, in mint condition, as new, unspoilt, spotless, flawless, clean, fresh, new, virgin, pure, unused; unmarked, unblemished, untarnished, untouched, unsullied, undefiled.
OPPOSITES dirty, sullied.

privacy ▶ noun *a walled garden ensures complete privacy* **seclusion**, privateness, solitude, isolation, retirement, peace, peace and quiet, peacefulness, quietness, lack of disturbance, lack of interruption, freedom from interference; *rare* sequestration, reclusion.

private ▶ adjective **1** *his private plane* **personal**, **one's own**, individual, particular, special, exclusive, privately owned.
OPPOSITE public.
2 *his private talks with the UK prime minister* **confidential**, strictly confidential, secret, top secret, classified, unofficial, off the record, not for publication, not to be made public, not to be disclosed, closet; backstage, offstage, privileged, one-on-one, tête-à-tête; covert, clandestine, surreptitious; *Latin* in camera; *informal* hush-hush.
OPPOSITES open, public.
3 *their private thoughts on the subject* **intimate**, personal, secret; innermost, inward, unspoken, undeclared, undisclosed, unvoiced, sneaking, hidden.
4 *he was a very private man* **reserved**, introvert, introverted, self-contained, reticent, discreet, uncommunicative, non-communicative, unforthcoming, secretive, retiring, ungregarious, unsocial, unsociable, withdrawn, solitary, insular, reclusive, hermit-like, hermitic.
OPPOSITE extrovert.
5 *he hustled her away, searching for some private spot* **secluded**, secret, quiet, undisturbed, concealed, hidden, remote, isolated, out of the way, sequestered.
OPPOSITES busy, crowded.
6 *we can phone from the library—we'll be private in there* **undisturbed**, uninterrupted, without disturbance, without interruption; alone, by ourselves.
7 *the president was visiting China in a private capacity* **unofficial**, **personal**, non-official, non-public.
OPPOSITE official.
8 *80 per cent of the funding came from private industry* **independent**, non-state-controlled, non-state-run, privatized, denationalized, non-public, commercial, private-enterprise.
OPPOSITES public, nationalized, state-controlled.
▶ noun *a private in the army* **private soldier**, common soldier; infantryman, foot soldier, trooper; *Brit.* sapper, ranker; (*in the US*) GI, enlisted man; *French* poilu; *Indian* jawan; *Brit. informal* Tommy, squaddie, Tommy Atkins; *N. Amer. informal* grunt, buck private; *Austral./NZ informal* digger; *S. African informal* troopie; *archaic* swad, swaddy.
□ **in private** *the inquiry will be held in private* **in secret**, secretly, in secrecy, privately, behind closed doors, in camera, with no one else present; in confidence, confidentially, between ourselves, off the record; *Latin* sub rosa; *French* entre nous, à huis clos.
OPPOSITE in public.

P

private detective ▶ noun **private investigator**, detective, operative; *Brit.* enquiry agent; *informal* private eye, PI, sleuth, snoop; *N. Amer. informal* private dick, peeper, shamus, gumshoe; *informal, dated* hawkshaw, sherlock; *N. Amer. dated* Pinkerton.

privately ▶ adverb **1** *I wanted the opportunity to talk to you privately* **in private**, with no one else present, behind closed doors, between ourselves, confidentially, in confidence, discreetly, in secret, secretly; *French* entre nous; *Latin* in camera.
OPPOSITE publicly.
2 *privately, MPs were disturbed by the news* **secretly**, inwardly, deep down, personally, unofficially.
3 *they lived their lives very privately* **out of the public eye**, out of public view, in seclusion, in solitude, alone, without being disturbed, without being interrupted.

private parts ▶ plural noun **genitals**, genitalia, sexual organs, reproductive organs, pudenda, nether regions, crotch groin; *informal* privates, bits, naughty bits, dangly bits.

privation ▶ noun *years of rationing and privation* **deprivation**, hardship, poverty, penury, indigence, destitution, impoverishment, want, need, neediness; disadvantage, austerity; suffering, affliction, distress, misery; *rare* impecuniousness, impecuniosity.
OPPOSITES plenty; luxury.

privilege ▶ noun **1** *he sought to reduce the legal privileges of the unions* **advantage**, right, benefit, prerogative, entitlement, birthright, due; concession, freedom, liberty.
2 *it was a privilege to meet her* **honour**, pleasure, source of pleasure/pride/satisfaction.
3 *a breach of parliamentary privilege* **immunity**, exemption, dispensation.

privileged ▶ adjective **1** *she comes from a privileged background* **wealthy**, rich, affluent, prosperous; **lucky**, fortunate, special, elite, favoured, select; advantaged, socially advantaged.
OPPOSITES underprivileged, disadvantaged.
2 *he accused me of giving away privileged information* **confidential**, private, secret, top secret, restricted, classified, not for publication, off the record, inside; *informal* hush-hush; *archaic* privy.
3 *the MP is privileged but the reporter and the publisher could face civil action* **immune (from prosecution)**, protected, exempt, excepted.

privy ▶ adjective **1** *she was not privy to any information contained in those letters* **aware of**, acquainted with, in on, informed of, advised of, apprised of, in the know about, cognizant of; *informal* genned up on, clued in on, clued up on, wise to, hip to.
2 (*archaic*) *a privy place* **secret**, hidden; concealed, secluded.
▶ noun **lavatory**, toilet, latrine, water closet, WC, urinal; outhouse, earth closet, jakes; *Brit.* cloakroom, convenience, the Gents, the Ladies, powder room; *N. Amer.* restroom, bathroom, men's room, ladies' room, washroom, comfort station; *French* pissoir; *informal* little boys' room, little girl's room, smallest room; *Brit. informal* loo, bog, khazi, lav, throne, thunderbox, cottage; *N. Amer. informal* john, can, honey bucket, head, tea room; *Austral./NZ informal* dunny, little house, dyke; *S. African informal* long drop; *N. English informal* netty; *vulgar slang* pisser, crapper, shithouse; *archaic* closet, garderobe, necessary house.

prize ▶ noun **1** *Britain's most prestigious prize for contemporary art | a £2,500 cash prize* **award**, reward, premium; trophy, cup, medal, plate, shield; honour, accolade, crown, laurels, bays, palm; jackpot, bonanza, purse, winnings, sweepstake; *informal* pot; *dated* garland; *archaic* guerdon; *Biblical* prey.
2 *the prizes of war* **spoils**, booty, plunder, loot, pickings, profits, takings.
▶ adjective **1** *a prize bull can father thousands of cows* **champion**, award-winning, prize-winning, winning, top, top-class, first-class, first-rate, choice, quality, select, best.
OPPOSITE second-rate.
2 *a prize example of how well organic farming can function* **outstanding**, excellent, superlative, superb, supreme, very good, prime, fine, magnificent, marvellous, wonderful; *informal* great, terrific, tremendous, fantastic, top-notch, A1.
3 *you must think I'm a prize idiot* **utter**, complete, total, absolute, real, perfect, positive, veritable; *Brit. informal* right, bloody; *Austral./NZ informal* fair; *archaic* arrant.
▶ verb *this was the era when honesty was prized above all other virtues* **value**, set/place a high value on, set great store by, rate highly, attach great importance to, esteem, hold in high regard, think highly of, treasure, cherish, hold dear, appreciate greatly.

prized ▶ adjective *his prized collection of soccer memorabilia* **treasured**, precious, valued, cherished, much loved, beloved.

prizewinner ▶ noun **champion**, winner, medallist, cup winner, prizeman, victor; *Brit.* victor ludorum; *informal* champ.

probability ▶ noun **1** *the probability of higher mortgage rates* **likelihood**, likeliness, prospect, expectation, chance, chances, odds, possibility.
2 *relegation back to the Second Division looks like a distinct probability* **probable event**, prospect, possibility, good/fair/reasonable bet.

probable ▶ adjective *it is probable that the economic situation will deteriorate further* **likely**, most likely, odds-on, expected, to be expected, anticipated, predictable, foreseeable, ten to one, presumed, potential, credible, quite possible, possible, feasible; *informal* on the cards, a good/fair/reasonable bet.
OPPOSITES improbable, unlikely.

probably ▶ adverb *I knew I would probably never see her again* **in all likelihood**, **in all probability**, as likely as not, very likely, most likely, likely, as like as not, ten to one, the chances are, doubtless, no doubt, all things considered, taking all things into consideration, all things being equal, possibly, perhaps, maybe, it may be, presumably, on the face of it, apparently; *archaic* like enough, belike.

probation ▶ noun *clerks were only paid a proper salary after the first three years of probation* **trial period**, test period, experimental period, trial; apprenticeship, traineeship, training, novitiate.

probationer ▶ noun **trainee**, novice, apprentice, inexperienced worker, new recruit, learner, beginner, tyro, neophyte; *informal* rookie, greenhorn; *N. Amer. informal* probie.

probe ▶ noun *a probe into alleged financial irregularities at the club* **investigation**, inquiry, enquiry, examination, scrutiny, inquest, exploration, study, research, analysis, scrutinization.
▶ verb **1** *hands probed his body from top to bottom* **examine**, feel, feel around, explore, prod, poke, check.
2 *a lengthy public enquiry probed the cause of the disaster* **investigate**, conduct an investigation into, inquire/enquire into, look into, study, conduct an inquiry/enquiry into, examine, scrutinize, go into, carry out an inquest into, research, analyse, dissect, search into, delve into, dig into; sound, plumb.

probity ▶ noun *the chancellor exuded competence and fiscal probity* **integrity**, honesty, uprightness, decency, morality, rectitude, goodness, virtue,

right-mindedness, trustworthiness, truthfulness, honour, honourableness, justice, fairness, equity; principles, ethics.
OPPOSITE untrustworthiness.

problem ▶ noun **1** *he's been under increasing stress due to business and personal problems | they ran into a problem* **difficulty**, trouble, worry, complication, difficult situation, mess, muddle, mix-up; snag, hitch, drawback, stumbling block, obstacle, hurdle, hiccup, setback, catch; catch-22, vexed question, quandary, the rub; predicament, plight, can of worms, hornets' nest, Gordian knot; misfortune, mishap, misadventure; informal dilemma, headache, prob, hassle, pickle, fix, tight spot, fly in the ointment, how-do-you-do, job, gremlin, facer; N. Amer. informal katzenjammer; rare nodus.
2 *'I don't want to be a problem,' Lucy said* **nuisance**, source of difficulty, bother, pest, source of trouble, irritant, thorn in one's side/flesh, vexation; informal drag, pain, pain in the neck; vulgar slang pain in the arse.
3 *arithmetical problems* **puzzle**, question, poser, enigma, riddle, conundrum; informal teaser, brain-teaser.
▶ adjective *a problem child* **troublesome**, difficult, unmanageable, unruly, disobedient, uncontrollable, ungovernable, intractable, recalcitrant, intransigent, refractory; delinquent, maladjusted, disturbed.
OPPOSITES well behaved, manageable.

problematic ▶ adjective *the piece is among the most problematic of all his major works* **difficult**, hard, problematical, taxing, troublesome, tricky, awkward, controversial, ticklish, complicated, complex, knotty, thorny, prickly, involved, intricate, vexed; paradoxical, puzzling, baffling, perplexing; informal sticky; Brit. informal dodgy.
OPPOSITES easy, simple, straightforward.

procedure ▶ noun *the council agreed a procedure for dealing with future breaches of the law* **course of action**, line of action, plan of action, policy, series of steps, plan, method, system, strategy, stratagem, way, approach, formula, mechanism, methodology, MO (modus operandi), SOP (standard operating procedure), technique, means, measure, process, proceeding, operation, agenda; routine, drill, practice.

proceed ▶ verb **1** *after almost six weeks, she was still uncertain how to proceed* **begin**, make a start, get going, move, set something in motion; **take action**, act, go on, take steps, take measures, go ahead, make progress, make headway.
2 *he turned off the road and proceeded down the long drive* **go**, **make one's way**, advance, move, move forward, move along, progress, carry on, press on, push on.
OPPOSITE stop.
3 *the government confirmed its decision to* **proceed with** *the investigations* **go ahead**, carry on, go on, continue, keep on, get on, get ahead; pursue, prosecute.
4 *there is not enough evidence to* **proceed against** *him* **take to court**, start proceedings against, take proceedings against, begin an action against, start an action against, sue.
5 *his claim that all power proceeded from God* **originate**, have its origin, spring, stem, come, derive, arise, issue, flow, emanate, descend, result, follow, ensue, begin, emerge, start.

proceeding ▶ noun **1** *have they any idea of the danger of such a proceeding?* **course of action**, action, step, measure, move, operation, manoeuvre, procedure, process, act, deed, undertaking, initiative, venture, transaction.
2 (**proceedings**) *she began to enjoy the evening's proceedings* **events**, activities, business, affairs, happenings, goings-on, doings.
3 (**proceedings**) *the proceedings of the meeting are to be published later* **report(s)**, transactions, minutes, account(s), record(s), business; annals, archives; French procès-verbal.
4 (**proceedings**) *in 1989 he began libel proceedings against the paper* **legal action**, legal proceedings, judicial proceedings, lawsuit, suit, case, action, litigation.

proceeds ▶ plural noun *the event starts at 1pm and all proceeds will go to Animal Welfare* **profits**, takings, earnings, receipts, returns, income, revenue, gain, yield; Sport gate, gate money, gate receipts; N. Amer. take.

process (stress on the first syllable) ▶ noun **1** *faxing a seventy page document is an expensive process* **procedure**, operation, action, activity, exercise, affair, business, job, task, undertaking, proceeding.
2 *the development of a new canning process* **method**, procedure, system, technique, means, practice, way, approach.
3 *they may find themselves, in the process of time, caring for their elderly parents* **course**, advance, progress, progression, unfolding, evolution.
4 (Law) *the person on whom the process is to be served* **summons**, writ, subpoena; N. Amer. citation.
□ **in the process of** *the company is in the process of moving into new premises in Palo Alto* **in the course of**, in the middle of, in the midst of.
▶ verb *I'll make sure that your application is processed quickly* **deal with**, attend to, see to, sort out, handle, take care of, action, organize, manage.

procession ▶ noun **1** *a ceremonial procession through the town* **parade**, march, cavalcade, motorcade, cortège; column, file, train; march past; Indian jatha, yatra; W. Indian mas.
2 *he employed a procession of nubile young secretaries* **series**, succession, stream, steady stream, string, sequence, chain, run.

proclaim ▶ verb **1** *four of the five men arrested proclaimed their innocence* **declare**, announce, pronounce, state, make known, give out, advertise, publish, broadcast, promulgate, trumpet, blazon, blaze, shout something from the rooftops; profess, assert, maintain, protest.
2 *he proclaimed himself president* **declare**, pronounce, announce.
3 *the very shape and design of the new schools proclaimed acceptance of a new way of thinking* **demonstrate**, indicate, show, signify, reveal, testify to, manifest, betray.

proclamation ▶ noun **1** *the rector issued a proclamation forbidding such practices* **decree**, order, edict, command, rule, ruling, announcement, declaration, pronouncement, statement; (in Spanish-speaking countries) pronunciamento.
2 *the shooting resulted in the proclamation of a state of emergency* **announcement**, declaration, pronouncement, notification, advertisement, publishing, broadcasting, promulgation; literary blazoning.

proclivity ▶ noun *his sexual proclivities are none of your business* **liking**, inclination, tendency, leaning, disposition, propensity, bent, bias, penchant, predisposition, predilection, partiality, preference, taste, fondness, weakness, proneness; rare velleity.

procrastinate ▶ verb *fear of failure is often the reason why people procrastinate* **delay**, put off doing something, postpone action, defer action, be dilatory, use delaying tactics, stall, temporize, play for time, play a waiting game, dally, drag one's feet/heels, take one's time; hesitate, vacillate, dither, be indecisive, be undecided, waver; Brit. haver, hum and haw; Scottish swither; informal dilly-dally, shilly-shally.

procrastination ▶ noun **dithering**, delaying tactics, dilatoriness, stalling, temporizing, hesitation, vacillation; Brit. humming and hawing; informal dilly-dallying, shilly-shallying.

procreate ▶ verb *the biological imperative to procreate* **produce offspring**, reproduce, multiply, propagate, breed; bring young into the world, father offspring, sire offspring; literary beget offspring.

procure ▶ verb **1** *vegetables and fruit were not easy to procure* **obtain**, acquire, get, find, come by, secure, pick up, get possession of; buy, purchase; informal get hold of, get one's hands on, get one's mitts on.
2 (archaic or Law) *his uncle procured his death by means of a poisoned drink* **bring about**, cause, contrive, effect.
3 *the police found that he was procuring* **be a pimp**, be pimping; Brit. informal ponce; N. Amer. informal hustle.

prod ▶ verb **1** *Cassie prodded him in the chest* **poke**, jab, dig, nudge, elbow, butt, push, stab.
2 *the campaign was intended to prod the government into action* **spur**, stimulate, stir, rouse, prompt, drive, push, galvanize, move, motivate, encourage, persuade, urge, chivvy, impel, actuate; incite, goad, egg on, provoke.
▶ noun **1** *a sharp prod in the ribs* **poke**, jab, dig, nudge, butt, push, shove, thrust.
2 *you need a gentle prod to remind you that life is only what you make it* **stimulus**, push, prompt, reminder, prompting, spur, motivation; incitement, goad.
3 *an electric cattle prod* **goad**, stick, spike.

prodigal ▶ adjective **1** *prodigal habits die hard* **wasteful**, extravagant, spendthrift, improvident, imprudent, immoderate, profligate, thriftless, excessive, intemperate, irresponsible, self-indulgent, reckless, wanton.
OPPOSITES thrifty, economical; parsimonious.
2 *a composer who is prodigal with his talents* **generous**, **lavish**, liberal, unstinting, unsparing, bountiful; copious, profuse; abundant in, abounding in, rich; literary bounteous.
OPPOSITE mean.

prodigious ▶ adjective **1** *prodigious quantities of food | his prodigious talent* **enormous**, huge, colossal, immense, vast, great, massive, gigantic, mammoth, tremendous, considerable, substantial, large, sizeable, inordinate, monumental, mighty, gargantuan; amazing, astonishing, astounding, staggering, stunning, marvellous, remarkable, wonderful, phenomenal, terrific, miraculous, impressive, striking, startling, sensational, spectacular, extraordinary, exceptional, breathtaking, incredible, unbelievable, unusual; informal humongous, stupendous, fantastic, fabulous, fantabulous, mind-boggling, mind-blowing, flabbergasting, mega, awesome; Brit. informal ginormous; literary wondrous.
OPPOSITES small; unexceptional.
2 *prodigious apparitions were seen* **unnatural**, monstrous, grotesque, abnormal.

prodigy ▶ noun **1** *he was a child prodigy, giving his first concert at the age of nine* **child genius**, genius, wonder child, mastermind, virtuoso; German wunderkind; informal whizz-kid, whizz, wizard, Einstein.
2 *Germany seemed a prodigy of industrial discipline* **model**, classic example, paragon, paradigm, epitome, exemplar, ideal, prototype, archetype, type.

produce ▶ verb (stress on the second syllable) **1** *the plant is currently scheduled to produce 1,100 cars a day* **manufacture**, make, construct, build, fabricate, put together, assemble, turn out, bring out, process, create; mass-produce; informal churn out.

P

2 *the vineyards in the Val d'Or produce excellent wines* **yield**, grow, give, supply, provide, furnish, bear, bring forth.
3 *she produced a litter of ten puppies* **give birth to**, bear, breed, bring into the world, give life to, spawn.
4 *the garden where the artist produced many of his flower paintings* **create**, compose, originate, develop, fashion, turn out.
5 *she dug into her bag and produced her card | no evidence was produced to support the allegation* **present**, offer, proffer, show, display, exhibit; pull out, bring out, draw out, fish out, extract; provide, furnish, advance, put forward, bring forward, come up with, set forth, bring to light.
6 *direct communication between the two countries will produce greater understanding* **give rise to**, bring about, cause, occasion, generate, engender, lead to, result in, effect, induce, initiate, start, set off; contribute to, make for, be conducive to, foster, promote; provoke, precipitate, breed, spark off, trigger; *literary* beget.
7 *a group of young women committed to producing quality drama* **stage**, put on, mount, present, put before the public, show, perform.
▶ **noun** (stress on the first syllable) *organically grown produce* **food**, foodstuff(s); crops, fruit, vegetables, greens; goods, products, commodities, staples, wares; *Brit.* greengrocery; *N. Amer. rare* truck.

WORD LINKS
suffixes meaning '-producing' **-facient (e.g. *abortifacient*), -fic (e.g. *soporific*), -genic (e.g. *hallucinogenic*)**

producer ▶ **noun 1** *the company is the largest European car producer* **manufacturer**, maker, builder, fabricator, creator.
2 *Tanzanian coffee producers* **grower**, farmer.
3 *a producer and director of musical films* **impresario**, manager, administrator, promoter, regisseur.

product ▶ **noun 1** *new electronic products | household products* **artefact**, commodity, manufactured item/article/thing; creation, invention; goods, wares, merchandise, produce.
2 *her fear was a product of her emotional insecurity* **result**, consequence, outcome, effect, upshot, fruit, by-product, spin-off, legacy, issue.

production ▶ **noun 1** *the production of nuclear weapons* **manufacture**, manufacturing, making, producing, construction, building, fabrication, assembly, creation; mass production.
2 *the production of literary works* **creation**, composition, origination, development, fashioning.
3 *literary productions of the 1980s* **work**, publication, book, novel, composition, piece, creation, opus; work of art, painting, picture.
4 *areas affected by acid rain had seen a fall in agricultural production* **output**, yield, fruits; productivity.
5 *ticket concessions are available to students on production of suitable identification* **presentation**, offering, proffering, showing, display, exhibition.
6 *a new production of 'The Merchant of Venice'* **performance**, staging, mounting.
7 *she took a starring role in a recent production by the St Albans Theatrical Society* **play**, drama, film, concert, musical; show, performance, presentation, piece.

productive ▶ **adjective 1** *few small towns can have had so productive a group of artists* **prolific**, inventive, creative; dynamic, energetic, vigorous, effective.
OPPOSITE unproductive.
2 *the talks were said to have been long and productive* **useful**, constructive, profitable, fruitful, gainful, valuable, effective, worthwhile, beneficial, helpful, rewarding, gratifying.
OPPOSITE unproductive.
3 *productive agricultural land* **fertile**, fruitful, rich, fecund, high-yielding.
OPPOSITES sterile, barren.

productivity ▶ **noun 1** *workers have boosted productivity by 30 per cent* **efficiency**, production, productiveness, work rate, output, yield, capacity, productive capacity.
2 *the productivity of the soil* **fruitfulness**, fertility, productiveness, fecundity, richness.

profane ▶ **adjective 1** *a talk that tackled subjects both sacred and profane* **secular**, lay, non-religious, non-church, temporal, worldly, earthly; unsanctified, unconsecrated, unhallowed; *rare* laic.
OPPOSITES religious, sacred.
2 *a profane, unprincipled man* **irreverent**, ungodly, godless, impious, disrespectful, irreligious, unbelieving, disbelieving, sacrilegious, idolatrous.
3 *he was famous for his wildly profane language* **obscene**, **blasphemous**, foul, vulgar, crude, filthy, dirty, smutty, coarse, rude, offensive, scurrilous, off colour, indecent, indecorous; *rare* Fescennine, Cyprian.
OPPOSITE decorous.
▶ **verb** *it was a serious matter to profane a tomb* **desecrate**, violate, defile, treat with disrespect, debase, degrade, contaminate, pollute, taint.

profanity ▶ **noun 1** *he led her away, hissing profanities in her ear | an outburst of profanity* **oath**, swear word, expletive, curse, obscenity, four-letter word, dirty word, execration, imprecation; blasphemy, swearing, foul language, bad language, cursing; *informal* cuss, cuss word.
2 *some traditional festivals were irremediably tainted with profanity* **idolatry**, sacrilege, irreligiousness, ungodliness, impiety, unholiness, profaneness, blasphemy, irreverence, disrespectfulness, disrespect.

profess ▶ **verb 1** *he professed his undying love for her* **declare**, announce, proclaim, assert, state, affirm, avow, maintain, protest, aver, vow; *rare* asseverate.
2 *she thrived on the publicity she professed to loathe* **claim**, pretend, purport, allege, make a pretence of, lay claim, make out that; *informal* let on that.
3 *in 325 the Emperor himself professed Christianity* **state/affirm one's faith in**, affirm one's allegiance to, make a public declaration of, declare publicly, avow, confess, acknowledge publicly.

professed ▶ **adjective 1** *their professed commitment to human rights* **supposed**, ostensible, alleged, claimed, so-called, soi-disant, self-styled, apparent, pretended, purported, would-be.
2 *a professed and active Christian* **declared**, self-acknowledged, self-confessed, confessed, sworn, avowed, confirmed, certified.

professedly ▶ **adverb** *the government is threatening to break one of its professedly sacred principles* **supposedly**, ostensibly, allegedly, apparently, avowedly, purportedly, by one's own account.

profession ▶ **noun 1** *his chosen profession of teaching | the legal profession* **career**, occupation, calling, vocation, line of work, line of employment, line, métier; business, trade, craft, walk of life, sphere; job, position; *Scottish* way; *informal* racket; *archaic* employ.
2 *a profession of allegiance* **declaration**, affirmation, statement, announcement, proclamation, assertion, avowal, vow, claim, allegation, protestation; acknowledgement, admission, confession; *rare* asseveration, averment.

professional ▶ **adjective 1** *people in professional occupations* **white-collar**, executive, non-manual.
OPPOSITE manual.
2 *a professional tennis player* **paid**, salaried, non-amateur, full-time.
OPPOSITE amateur.
3 *I think we gave a thoroughly professional performance* **expert**, accomplished, skilful, adept, masterly, masterful, excellent, fine, polished, finished, skilled, proficient, competent, capable, able, efficient, experienced, practised, trained, seasoned, slick, businesslike, deft, dexterous; *informal* ace, crack, top-notch.
OPPOSITES amateurish, incompetent, inept.
4 *it's really not professional of me to comment on these things* **appropriate**, ethical, fitting, in order, correct; *French* comme il faut.
▶ **noun 1** *affluent young professionals* **white-collar worker**, professional worker, office worker.
2 *it's his first season as a professional* **professional player**, non-amateur, paid player; *informal* pro.
3 *she was a real professional on stage* **expert**, master, maestro, past master, trouper, adept, virtuoso, old hand, skilled person, authority; *informal* pro, ace, whizz, hotshot; *Brit. informal* dab hand, wizard; *N. Amer. informal* maven, crackerjack; *rare* proficient.
OPPOSITE amateur.

professor ▶ **noun** *a former professor of French at Oxford University* holder of a chair, chair, head of faculty, head of department; Regius professor, emeritus professor; don, academic; *N. Amer.* full professor, academician; *informal* prof.

proffer ▶ **verb** *Coleman proffered his resignation* **offer**, tender, present, extend, give, submit, volunteer, suggest, propose, put forward; hold out.
OPPOSITES refuse, withdraw.

proficiency ▶ **noun** *her proficiency was obvious to everyone who sailed with her* **skill**, skilfulness, expertise, experience, ability, capability, capacity, competence, competency, adeptness, adroitness, excellence, mastery, prowess, professionalism, aptitude, deftness, dexterity, finesse, facility, effectiveness, accomplishment, aptness, expertness, talent; *informal* know-how.
OPPOSITE incompetence.

proficient ▶ **adjective** *a proficient horsewoman* **skilled**, skilful, expert, accomplished, experienced, practised, trained, seasoned, well versed, adept, adroit, deft, dexterous, able, capable, competent, professional, effective, apt, handy, talented, gifted, masterly, consummate, master; good, great, excellent, brilliant; *informal* crack, ace, mean, wicked; *Brit. informal* wizard; *N. Amer. informal* crackerjack; *vulgar slang* shit-hot; *archaic or humorous* compleat.
OPPOSITES inept, inexpert, incompetent.

profile ▶ **noun 1** *she looked up at his handsome profile silhouetted against the dark sky* **side view**, outline, silhouette, contour, shape, form, figure, lines.
2 *she wrote a profile of Martin Luther King* **description**, account, study, portrait, portrayal, depiction, rundown, sketch, outline.
□ **keep a low profile lie low**, keep quiet, keep out of the public eye, avoid publicity, keep oneself to oneself, keep out of sight.
▶ **verb** *he was profiled in the Irish Times* **describe**, write about, write an article about, give an account of, characterize, portray, depict, outline, sketch.

profit ▶ **noun 1** *no one can guarantee a profit on stocks and shares* **financial**

gain, gain, return(s), payback, dividend, interest, yield, surplus, excess; gross profit, net profit, operating profit; N. Amer. take; informal killing, pay dirt, bottom line; Brit. informal bunce.
OPPOSITE loss.
2 *Stevenson decided that there was little profit in going on* **advantage**, benefit, value, use, gain, good, avail, worth, usefulness; informal mileage, percentage; archaic behoof.
OPPOSITE disadvantage.
▶ **verb 1** *many local people believe that the development will profit them* **benefit**, be beneficial to, be of benefit to, be advantageous to, be of advantage to, be of use to, be of value to, do someone good, help, be helpful to, be of service to, serve, assist, aid, stand someone in good stead, further the interests of, advance, promote.
2 *certain sectors of society had visibly profited* **make money**, make a killing, make a profit; informal rake it in, clean up, make a packet, make a bundle, line one's pockets; N. Amer. informal make big bucks, make a fast/quick buck.
□ **profit from** *loopholes in the law allowed landlords to profit from the situation* **benefit from**, **take advantage of**, obtain an advantage from, derive benefit from, reap the benefit of, capitalize on, make the most of, turn to one's advantage, put to good use, do well out of, utilize, exploit, make capital out of, maximize, gain from; informal cash in on, milk.

profitable ▶ **adjective 1** *a profitable venture* **moneymaking**, profit-making, commercial, successful, commercially successful, money-spinning, sound, solvent, in the black, cost-effective, fruitful, gainful, remunerative, financially rewarding, paying, lucrative, bankable.
OPPOSITES unprofitable, loss-making.
2 *working with Kelly had been a profitable experience for him* **beneficial**, useful, advantageous, helpful, of use, of service, valuable, productive, worthwhile; rewarding, fruitful, enriching, illuminating, informative, well spent, salutary.
OPPOSITES fruitless, useless.

profiteer ▶ **verb** *the companies are thus removed from the common temptation to profiteer* **overcharge**, racketeer, make an excessive/illegal profit; informal make a fast/quick buck, make a quick killing.
▶ **noun** *letters in the paper denounced capitalist profiteers* **extortionist**, extortioner, racketeer, exploiter, black marketeer; (in Japan) yakuza; informal bloodsucker; Austral. informal urger.

profiteering ▶ **noun** **extortion**, racketeering, exploitation; Brit. Rachmanism.

profitless ▶ **adjective** *further argument would be profitless* **pointless**, useless, to no purpose, (of) no use, unprofitable, futile, vain, in vain, to no avail, to no effect, fruitless, senseless, unproductive, purposeless, idle, worthless, valueless, ineffective, unavailing, unrewarding, thankless; archaic bootless.

profligate ▶ **adjective 1** *profligate local authorities* **wasteful**, extravagant, spendthrift, improvident, prodigal, immoderate, excessive, thriftless, imprudent, reckless, irresponsible.
OPPOSITES thrifty, frugal.
2 *he succumbed to drink and a profligate lifestyle* **dissolute**, degenerate, dissipated, debauched, corrupt, depraved, reprobate, unprincipled, immoral; promiscuous, loose, wanton, licentious, lascivious, lecherous, libertine, lewd, decadent, rakish, shameless, abandoned, unrestrained, fast; sybaritic, voluptuary.
OPPOSITES moral, upright.
▶ **noun 1** *an out-and-out profligate, darting from one partner to the next* **libertine**, debauchee, degenerate, reprobate, roué, lecher, rake, loose liver, dissolute person; sybarite, voluptuary, sensualist; informal lech; dated rip.
2 *he's a gambler and a drunkard—a profligate in every way* **spendthrift**, prodigal, squanderer; informal waster; archaic wastrel.

profound ▶ **adjective 1** *a sigh of profound relief* **heartfelt**, intense, keen, great, very great, extreme, sincere, earnest, deep, deepest, deeply felt, wholehearted, acute, overpowering, overwhelming, deep-seated, deep-rooted, fervent, ardent.
OPPOSITES superficial; mild.
2 *the silence was so profound that I could hear my heart beating* **complete**, utter, total, absolute, extreme, pronounced.
3 *the implications of this discovery are profound* **far-reaching**, radical, extensive, exhaustive, thoroughgoing, sweeping.
4 *a profound analysis of the problems* **wise**, learned, clever, intelligent, with/showing great knowledge, knowledgeable, intellectual, scholarly, sage, sagacious, erudite, discerning, penetrating, perceptive, astute, thoughtful, full of insight, insightful, percipient, perspicacious, philosophical, deep; rare sapient.
OPPOSITES superficial, stupid.
5 *expressing profound truths in simple language* **complex**, abstract, deep, weighty, serious, difficult; **abstruse**, recondite, esoteric, metaphysical, impenetrable, unfathomable, mysterious, obscure, dark.

profoundly ▶ **adverb 1** *she was profoundly grateful that none of her colleagues could see her* **extremely**, very, deeply, exceedingly, greatly, immensely, enormously, terribly, tremendously, awfully, intensely, heartily, keenly, acutely, from the bottom of one's heart, painfully, thoroughly, sincerely, so; informal well, jolly, seriously, majorly, oh-so; informal, dated devilish; N. Amer. informal mighty, plumb; S. African informal lekker; literary sore, thrice.
2 *he spoke profoundly on the subject* **discerningly**, penetratingly, wisely, sagaciously, thoughtfully, philosophically, weightily, seriously, learnedly, eruditely.

profundity ▶ **noun 1** *the simplicity and profundity of the message* **wisdom**, **(deep) insight**, intelligence, sagacity, acuity, depth, profoundness, perceptiveness, penetration, perception, percipience, perspicuity, discernment, thoughtfulness; rare sapience.
2 *the profundity of her misery* **intensity**, depth, extremity, severity, keenness, profoundness, strength.

profuse ▶ **adjective 1** *she telephoned me with profuse apologies for the misunderstanding* **copious**, prolific, abundant, ample, extravagant, lavish, liberal, unstinting, fulsome, effusive, gushing, immoderate, unrestrained, excessive, inordinate; informal over the top, gushy.
2 *so profuse are the flowers that you could imagine you were in a tropical garden* **luxuriant**, plentiful, copious, abundant, lush, rich, exuberant, riotous, teeming, overabundant, superabundant, rank, rampant; informal jungly.
OPPOSITES meagre, sparse.

profusion ▶ **noun** *a profusion of shrubs and flowers* **abundance**, lot, mass, host, plenitude, cornucopia, riot; plethora, superfluity, superabundance, glut, surplus, surfeit; quantities, scores, millions, multitude; informal sea, wealth; lots, heaps, masses, stacks, piles, loads, bags, mountains, tons, oodles; Brit. informal shedload; Austral./NZ informal swag; rare nimiety.

progenitor ▶ **noun 1** *he was the progenitor of an illustrious family* **ancestor**, forefather, forebear, parent; archaic begetter; rare primogenitor, procreator, stirps.
2 *the progenitor of modern jazz* **originator**, founder, instigator, source; forerunner, predecessor, precursor, antecedent.

progeny ▶ **noun 1** *physical characteristics are passed on from parents to their progeny by genes* **offspring**, children, young, family, brood; Law issue; derogatory spawn; rare progeniture, quiverful.
2 *the progeny of the Scottish settlers who settled there in the mid-1800s* **descendants**, successors, heirs, stock, scions, lineage; archaic seed, posterity.

prognosis ▶ **noun** *it is very difficult to make an accurate prognosis* **forecast**, prediction, projection, prognostication, prophecy; rare prognostic.

prognosticate ▶ **verb** *the economists were prognosticating financial Armageddon* **forecast**, predict, prophesy, foretell, divine; archaic presage, augur, previse; Scottish archaic spae; rare vaticinate, auspicate.

prognostication ▶ **noun** *their prognostications had proved remarkably accurate* **prediction**, forecast, prophecy, divination, prognosis, projection; rare vaticination, auspication, prognostic.

program ▶ **noun.** *See centre pages for list of types of computer* **Program**

programme ▶ **noun 1** *an action-packed programme of events* **schedule**, **agenda**, calendar, timetable; order of events, list of events, order of the day, line-up, list, listing; bill, menu, bill of fare.
2 *a government programme to rescue the ailing economy* **scheme**, plan, plan of action, series of measures, project, strategy.
3 *the programme attracted an audience of almost twenty million* **broadcast**, production, show, presentation, transmission, performance, telecast, simulcast; documentary, play, comedy, film, docudrama, newscast, chat show, magazine (programme), phone-in; episode, instalment; informal prog.
4 *a programme of study* **course**, syllabus, curriculum.
5 *shall I buy a programme?* **guide**, list of performers/players/artistes; N. Amer. playbill.
▶ **verb 1** *she tried to programme her day into housework and study* **arrange**, **organize**, schedule, plan, map out, lay out, timetable, line up, prearrange; N. Amer. slate.
2 *some hotels programme their canned music in 24-hour cycles* **set**, fix, arrange.

progress ▶ **noun** (stress on the first syllable) **1** *ceaseless rain made further progress impossible* **forward movement**, onward movement, progression, advance, advancement, headway, passage; going.
2 *the progress of medical science | little progress was reported during the peace talks* **development**, advance, advancement, headway, step(s) forward, progression, improvement, betterment, growth; breakthrough.
□ **in progress** *a game of cricket was in progress* **under way**, **going on**, ongoing, happening, occurring, taking place, proceeding, being done, being performed, continuing, in operation; awaiting completion, not finished, not completed, on the stocks; N. Amer. in the works.
▶ **verb** (stress on the second syllable) **1** *they progressed slowly back along the grass* **go**, make one's way, move, move forward, go forward, proceed, continue, advance, go on, make progress, make headway, press on, gain ground, push forward, go/forge ahead, work one's way.
OPPOSITE return.
2 *the practice has a strong commercial base and has progressed steadily* **develop**, make progress, advance, make headway, take steps forward, make strides, get better, come on, come along, move on, get on, gain ground, shape up, improve, thrive, prosper, blossom, flourish; grow, expand, increase, mature, evolve; informal be getting there.

P

OPPOSITES regress, deteriorate.

progression ▶ noun **1** *a progression of calm, still days and nights* **succession**, series, sequence, string, stream, parade, chain, concatenation, train, row, order, course, flow, cycle.
2 *antiviral drugs appear to halt progression of the disease* **development**, progress, process, continuation, continuance, advance, advancement, movement, forward movement, onward movement, passage, career, march; evolution, growth, evolvement.

progressive ▶ adjective **1** *the progressive deterioration of the social conditions of farm labourers* **continuing**, continuous, increasing, growing, developing, ongoing, intensifying, accelerating, escalating; gradual, step by step, cumulative.
2 *a teacher with progressive views on primary education* **modern**, liberal, advanced, forward-looking, forward-thinking, go-ahead, enlightened, enterprising, innovative, up-and-coming, new, dynamic, avant-garde, modernistic; radical, left-wing, reforming, reformist, revolutionary, revisionist, progressivist.
OPPOSITES conservative, reactionary.
▶ noun *people present themselves as progressives or traditionalists* **innovator**, reformer, reformist, liberal, libertarian, progressivist, progressionist, leftist, left-winger.

prohibit ▶ verb **1** *a law to prohibit the dumping of nuclear waste at sea* **forbid**, ban, bar, interdict, veto, proscribe, make illegal, place an embargo on, embargo, disallow, outlaw; taboo; *Law* enjoin, restrain.
OPPOSITES permit, authorize.
2 *severe physical disabilities prohibited him from entering regular school* **prevent**, stop, rule out, preclude, make impossible, hinder, impede, hamper, obstruct, restrict, constrain.
OPPOSITES allow, facilitate.

> **CHOOSE THE RIGHT WORD**
> **prohibit, forbid, ban**
> *See* FORBID.

prohibited ▶ adjective *smoking is prohibited in many public places in Britain* **forbidden**, banned, not allowed, not permitted, illegal, illicit, against the law, barred, vetoed, proscribed, embargoed, disallowed, outlawed, contraband; taboo; *Latin* non licet; *German* verboten; *Islam* haram; *NZ* tapu; *informal* no go.

prohibition ▶ noun **1** *the prohibition of cannabis* **banning**, forbidding, prohibiting, barring, debarment, vetoing, proscription, disallowing, disallowance, interdiction, outlawing, making illegal.
2 *a prohibition on the sale of food containing pesticide residues* **ban**, bar, interdict, veto, embargo, injunction, proscription, boycott, moratorium.

prohibitive ▶ adjective **1** *production costs have been prohibitive* **excessively high**, extortionate, excessive, exorbitant, sky-high, preposterous, outrageous, scandalous, out of the question, beyond one's means, more than one can afford, unreasonable, impossible, overinflated; *informal* steep, criminal.
2 *prohibitive regulations* **proscriptive**, prohibitory, restrictive, suppressive, repressive, restraining, inhibitory.

project ▶ noun (stress on the first syllable) **1** *a project to reforest the country's coastal areas* **scheme**, plan, plan of action, programme, enterprise, undertaking, venture, activity, operation, campaign; proposal, proposition, idea, conception.
2 *he's doing some sort of history project* **assignment**, piece of work, homework, piece of research, task.
▶ verb (stress on the second syllable) **1** *substantial growth of over six per cent is projected for 1993 and 1994* **forecast**, predict, estimate, calculate, gauge, reckon, expect, extrapolate.
2 *his projected book on Greenland was never completed* **intend**, plan, propose, map out, devise, design, outline.
3 *balconies projected over the lake* **stick out**, jut out, jut, protrude, extend, stand out, hang over, overhang, bulge out, poke out, lap over, ride over, thrust out, obtrude, cantilever; *archaic* be imminent, protuberate.
4 *they projected missiles at each other from behind their barricades* **throw**, cast, fling, hurl, toss, lob, launch, discharge, propel, shoot; *informal* chuck, sling, bung, heave.
5 *the one light projected azure shadows on the wall* **cast**, throw, send, shed, let fall, reflect, shine.
6 *he projected an unassuming and non-threatening image* **convey**, put across, put over, communicate, present, promote; present oneself as.
7 *it's not me who's unhappy—she's projecting her own problems on to me!* **attribute**, ascribe, impute, assign; externalize.

projectile *See centre pages for lists of* **Bombs and Mines** **Bullets and Shot** **Projectiles and Projectile Weapons**
▶ noun **missile**; *rare* trajectile.

projecting ▶ adjective *she had projecting teeth | a projecting bay window* **sticking out**, protuberant, protruding, prominent, jutting, jutting out, overhanging, standing out, proud, bulging, bulbous; *technical* obtrusive, extrusive; *rare* protrusive, protrudent, excrescent, exsertile.

projection *See centre pages for list of* **Map Types and Projections**
▶ noun **1** *the company claims it has exceeded its initial sales projection* **estimate**, forecast, prediction, calculation, prognosis, prognostication, reckoning, expectation; forecasting, estimation, computation; extrapolation.
2 *tiny projections on the chalk face of the cliffs* **protuberance**, protrusion, sticking-out bit, overhang, ledge, shelf, ridge, prominence, spur, outcrop, outgrowth, jut, bulge, jag, snag; flange, eminence.

proletarian ▶ adjective *those from less privileged, proletarian backgrounds* **working-class**, plebeian, cloth-cap, common, ordinary.
▶ noun *a growing mass of disaffected proletarians* **working-class person**, worker, working person, plebeian, commoner, ordinary person, man/woman/person in the street; *informal* Joe Bloggs; *derogatory* prole.

proletariat ▶ noun **the workers**, working-class people, wage-earners, the labouring classes, the common people, the ordinary people, the lower classes, the masses, the commonalty, the rank and file, the third estate, the plebeians; *derogatory* the hoi polloi, the plebs, the proles, the great unwashed, the mob, the rabble, the canaille.
OPPOSITES aristocracy, nobility.

proliferate ▶ verb *the debate continued and articles in the media proliferated* **increase rapidly**, grow rapidly, multiply, become more numerous, mushroom, snowball, burgeon, escalate, rocket, run riot.
OPPOSITES decrease, dwindle.

proliferation ▶ noun *the proliferation of missiles and missile technology* **rapid increase**, growth, multiplication, spread, escalation, expansion, build-up, buildout, burgeoning, snowballing, mushrooming.
OPPOSITE decrease.

prolific ▶ adjective **1** *the plant bears a prolific crop of large, firm tomatoes* **plentiful**, abundant, bountiful, profuse, copious, luxuriant, rich, lush, proliferative; fertile, fruitful, fecund; rife, rank; *literary* plenteous, bounteous; *rare* proliferous.
2 *he was enormously prolific, writing 263 solo cantatas and arias* **productive**, creative, inventive, fertile.

prolix ▶ adjective *his prolix speeches could often be tiresome* **lengthy**, long-winded, long-drawn-out, overlong, prolonged, protracted, interminable, laborious, ponderous, endless, unending, verbose, wordy, full of verbiage, verbal, diffuse, discursive, digressive, rambling, wandering, circuitous, meandering, maundering, periphrastic, circumlocutory; *informal* windy; *rare* ambagious, pleonastic, circumlocutionary, logorrhoeic.

prologue ▶ noun *the prologue to his book on the harrowing contemporary history of Cambodia* **introduction**, foreword, preface, preamble, prelude, preliminary; *informal* intro; *rare* exordium, proem, prolegomenon, prooemium, prooemion.
OPPOSITE epilogue.

prolong ▶ verb *unwilling to prolong the conversation, Kate said her goodbyes* **lengthen**, make longer, extend, extend the duration of, draw out, drag out, protract, spin out, stretch out, string out, elongate; carry on, continue, keep up, keep something going, go on with, perpetuate, sustain; *archaic* wire-draw.
OPPOSITE shorten.

promenade ▶ noun **1** *they strolled along the tree-lined promenade* **esplanade**, front, seafront, parade, walk, boulevard, avenue, walkway, mall; *N. Amer.* boardwalk; (*in Spanish-speaking countries*) alameda; *Brit. informal* prom.
2 *our nightly promenade up and down the road* **walk**, stroll, saunter, turn, wander, amble, breather, airing; *N. Amer.* paseo; *Italian* passegiata; *informal* mosey; *dated* constitutional; *rare* perambulation.
▶ verb *people were promenading along the pavements and down the pier* **walk**, stroll, saunter, wander, amble, stretch one's legs, take a walk/stroll, go for a walk/stroll, take the air; *informal* mosey; *rare* perambulate.

prominence ▶ noun **1** *his rise to prominence was meteoric* **fame**, celebrity, eminence, pre-eminence, importance, distinction, greatness, note, notability, prestige, stature, standing, position, rank, renown, repute, illustriousness, acclaim, influence, account, consequence, visibility.
2 *the US and UK press gave prominence to the reports* **good coverage**, close attention, importance, precedence, weight, a high profile, top billing, noticeability.
3 *the steep rocky prominence resembled a snow-capped mountain* **hillock**, hill, hummock, mound, outcrop, spur, rise, tor, ridge, peak, pinnacle, elevation; promontory, cliff, crag, headland, height; *French* arête.
4 *bony prominences in the arm and leg* **protuberance**, projection, swelling, bump, bulge, lump; *technical* process, bulla.

prominent ▶ adjective **1** *a prominent member of the Royal College of Surgeons* **important**, **well known**, leading, eminent, pre-eminent, distinguished, notable, noteworthy, noted, public, outstanding, foremost, of mark, illustrious, celebrated, famous, renowned, acclaimed, famed, honoured, esteemed, respected, well thought of, influential, prestigious, big, top, great, chief, main; *N. Amer.* major-league.

OPPOSITES unimportant, obscure, unknown.
2 *his cheekbones were high and prominent* **protuberant**, protruding, projecting, jutting, jutting out, standing out, sticking out, proud, bulging, bulbous; raised, elevated; *rare* protrusive, protrudent, excrescent.
3 *the rectangular fields and straight lanes that are now such a prominent feature of the landscape* **conspicuous**, noticeable, easily seen, obvious, evident, discernible, recognizable, distinguishable, unmistakable, eye-catching, pronounced, salient, striking, outstanding, dominant, predominant; obtrusive.
OPPOSITE inconspicuous.

promiscuity ▶ noun *allegations of alcoholism and sexual promiscuity* **licentiousness**, lack of sexual discrimination, promiscuousness, immorality, wantonness, debauchery, dissoluteness, dissipation, libertinism, profligacy, incontinence; *informal* sleeping around; *dated* looseness.
OPPOSITES chastity, celibacy.

promiscuous ▶ adjective **1** *despite what you seem to think, I have never been promiscuous* **licentious**, sexually indiscriminate, immoral, unchaste, debauched, dissolute, dissipated, profligate, of easy virtue, fast; libertine, wanton, abandoned, unrestrained, uncontrolled, incontinent; *informal* easy, swinging; *N. Amer. informal* roundheeled; *W. Indian informal* slack; *informal, derogatory* sluttish, whorish, tarty, slaggy; *dated* loose; *archaic* light; *rare* riggish.
OPPOSITES chaste; moral, pure.
2 *the promiscuous popping of antibiotics hasn't helped his T-cell count* **indiscriminate**, undiscriminating, unselective, random, irresponsible, haphazard, thoughtless, unthinking, unconsidered, casual, careless.
OPPOSITES careful, selective.

promise ▶ noun **1** *if I don't go I'll be breaking my promise* **word of honour**, word, assurance, pledge, vow, guarantee, oath, bond, undertaking, agreement, commitment, contract, covenant, compact.
2 *Derek showed considerable promise in a number of sports* **potential**, ability, aptitude, capability, capacity, potentiality; talent, flair.
3 *dawn came with a promise of fine weather* **indication**, hint, suggestion, sign.
▶ verb **1** *she promised to keep it a secret* **give one's word**, swear, pledge, vow, undertake, guarantee, assure, contract, engage, give an undertaking, give an assurance, commit oneself, bind oneself, cross one's heart (and hope to die), swear/take an oath, covenant; *archaic* plight.
2 *the skies promised a blissful day of warm summer sunshine* **indicate**, give an/every indication of, lead one to expect, give good grounds for expecting, point to, denote, signify, be a sign of, be evidence of, show signs of, hint at, suggest, give hope of, hold out hopes of, bespeak, presage, be a presage of, augur, herald, bode, foreshadow, portend; *literary* betoken, foretoken, forebode; *rare* harbinger.

promising ▶ adjective **1** *he made a promising start to his cricketing career* **good**, encouraging, favourable, hopeful, full of promise, auspicious, propitious, optimistic, positive, bright, rosy, likely-looking, heartening, reassuring.
OPPOSITES unfavourable, inauspicious, ominous.
2 *a promising young actor* **with potential**, budding, up-and-coming, rising, coming, in the making; talented, gifted, able, apt.

promontory ▶ noun **headland**, point, cape, head, foreland, horn, spit, hook, bill, ness, naze, peninsula; bluff, cliff, precipice, prominence, projection, overhang, height, ridge, spur; *Scottish* mull.

promote ▶ verb **1** *she's been promoted—she's head of her department now* **advance**, upgrade, give promotion to, give a higher position to, elevate, move up, raise, improve the position/status of, aggrandize; *informal* kick upstairs; *archaic* prefer.
OPPOSITE demote.
2 *an organization promoting racial equality* **encourage**, further, advance, assist, aid, help, contribute to, foster, nurture, develop, boost, stimulate, forward; advocate, recommend, urge, support, back, endorse, champion, speak for, proselytize, sponsor, espouse, push for, work for.
OPPOSITES obstruct, impede.
3 *she went over to America to promote her new book* **advertise**, publicize, give publicity to, beat/bang the drum for, popularize, sell, market, merchandise; *informal* push, plug, give a plug to, hype, hype up, give a puff to, puff, puff up, boost, flog; *N. Amer. informal* ballyhoo, flack, huckster.

promoter ▶ noun *promoters of alternative tourism point to its contribution to economic growth* **advocate**, champion, supporter, backer, upholder, proponent, exponent, protagonist, campaigner; *N. Amer.* booster.

promotion ▶ noun **1** *his promotion to the rank of Brigadier* **preferment**, upgrading, move up, elevation, advancement, advance, step up, step up the ladder, aggrandizement; *informal* kick upstairs.
2 *the promotion of competition in our domestic economy* **encouragement**, furtherance, furthering, advancement, assistance, aid, help, contribution to, fostering, boosting, stimulation, development; advocacy, recommendation, urging, support, backing, endorsement, championship, sponsoring, espousal; *N. Amer. informal* boosterism.
3 *two tiring weeks of promotion for his first English-language movie* **advertising**, publicity, marketing, selling, advertising/publicity campaign, propaganda, publicization; *informal* hard sell, hype, plugging, puff, puffery; *N. Amer. informal* ballyhoo.

prompt ▶ verb **1** *a sense of alarm prompted her to knock again* **induce**, make, move, cause, motivate, lead, dispose, persuade, incline, encourage, stimulate, prod, impel, spur on, urge, inspire; provoke, incite.
OPPOSITE discourage.
2 *the move could prompt a rise in UK base lending rates* **give rise to**, bring about, cause, occasion, result in, lead to, elicit, produce, bring on, engender, induce, call forth, evoke, precipitate, trigger, spark off, provoke, instigate.
OPPOSITES deter, restrain.
3 *the bridegroom could not follow the marriage service and had to be prompted by the impatient clergyman* **remind**, cue, give someone a cue, help out, coach, feed; jog someone's memory, refresh someone's memory.
▶ adjective *I should be grateful for a prompt reply* **quick**, swift, rapid, speedy, fast, direct, immediate, instant, instantaneous, expeditious, early, punctual, in good time, on time, timely; ready, willing, eager, unhesitating; *archaic* rathe.
OPPOSITES slow, late; unwilling.
▶ adverb *he set off at 3.30 prompt* **exactly**, precisely, sharp, on the dot, dead, dead on, promptly, punctually, on the nail; *informal* bang on, spot on; *N. Amer. informal* on the button, on the nose; *Austral./NZ informal* on the knocker.
▶ noun *he stopped, and Julia supplied a prompt* **reminder**, cue, feed.

prompting ▶ noun *Gilbert needed no prompting and moved quickly towards her* **encouragement**, reminder(s), reminding, cue(s), prodding, pushing, persuasion, hint(s), advice, suggestion(s), assistance, inducement.

promptly ▶ adverb **1** *William arrived promptly at 7.30* **punctually**, on time, on the dot, on the nail; *informal* bang on, spot on; *N. Amer. informal* on the button; *Austral./NZ informal* on the knocker.
2 *I expect the matter to be dealt with promptly* **quickly**, swiftly, rapidly, speedily, fast, as soon as possible, expeditiously; at once, immediately, straight away, right away, now, without delay, without hesitation, forthwith, directly, instantly, instantaneously, by return, unhesitatingly; *N. Amer.* momentarily; *informal* pronto, a.s.a.p., p.d.q. (pretty damn quick), in double quick time.

promptness ▶ noun *he acted with commendable promptness* **speed**, swiftness, speediness, rapidity, promptitude, alacrity, dispatch, quickness, expeditiousness, expedition, immediacy, instantaneousness, readiness, willingness, eagerness; punctuality.

promulgate ▶ verb **1** *ideas which Ruskin had been the first to promulgate* **make known**, make public, publicize, spread, communicate, propagate, disseminate, circulate, broadcast, promote, announce, proclaim; *literary* bruit about.
2 *the new law was promulgated on December 19* **put into effect**, enact, implement, enforce, pass.

prone ▶ adjective **1** *tired, malnourished people are prone to infection* **susceptible**, vulnerable, liable, inclined, given, subject, disposed, predisposed, open; likely to have/get, apt to get, with a tendency to get, at risk of, in danger of getting.
OPPOSITES resistant, immune.
2 *he was stretched prone on the ground* **(lying) face down**, face downwards, on one's stomach, on one's front; **lying flat**, lying down, flat, horizontal, prostrate; *rare* procumbent.
OPPOSITE upright; supine.

proneness ▶ noun *her proneness to anxiety* **susceptibility**, liability, tendency, inclination, disposition, predisposition, vulnerability, openness, propensity, proclivity; *Homeopathy* miasm.

prong ▶ noun **tine**, point, tip, spike, projection.

pronounce ▶ verb **1** *his name is difficult to pronounce* **say**, enunciate, articulate, utter, express, voice, vocalize, get one's tongue round, sound; *rare* enounce.
2 *the judge pronounced that he would be sentenced to sixteen years' imprisonment* **announce**, proclaim, declare, rule, decree, ordain, adjudicate, lay down, affirm, assert, state, judge; *rare* asseverate.

pronounced ▶ adjective *a strong voice with a pronounced German accent* **noticeable**, marked, strong, conspicuous, striking, distinct, decided, definite, prominent, notable, unmistakable, inescapable, obvious, evident, plain, clear, recognizable, identifiable; broad, thick.
OPPOSITES faint, inconspicuous, indefinite.

pronouncement ▶ noun *his public pronouncements were brilliantly timed and phrased* **announcement**, proclamation, declaration, formal statement, assertion, judgement, ruling, adjudication, decree, edict, ordinance, dictum, promulgation, deliverance; (*in Tsarist Russia*) ukase; (*in Spain & Spanish-speaking countries*) pronunciamento; *Latin* ipse dixit; *rare* asseveration.

pronunciation ▶ noun *her Merseyside pronunciation | the dictionary includes*

P

a guide to the pronunciation of difficult and foreign words **accent**, manner of speaking, speech pattern, speech, diction, delivery, elocution, intonation, modulation; articulation, enunciation, saying, uttering, utterance, sounding, voicing, vocalization; *rare* orthoepy.

WORD LINKS
study of correct pronunciation **orthoepy**

proof ▶ noun **1** *the last thing she wanted was proof of Luke's betrayal* **evidence**, verification, corroboration, authentication, confirmation, certification, validation, attestation, demonstration, substantiation, witness, testament; documentation, facts, data, testimony; ammunition.
2 *a desk strewn with the proofs of a book he was correcting* **page proof**, galley proof, galley, pull, slip, trial print; revise.
▶ adjective *their battle armour is proof against most weapons* **resistant**, impenetrable, impervious, repellent; proofed, treated; waterproof, windproof, rainproof, leakproof, damp-proof, weatherproof, bulletproof, bombproof, fireproof, soundproof, childproof, tamper-proof; *rare* imperviable.

prop ▶ noun **1** *steel props support the 1.5 km long underpass construction* **pole**, post, beam, support, upright, brace, buttress, stay, shaft, strut, stanchion, shore, pier, vertical, pillar, pile, piling, bolster, truss, column, rod, stick; *French* point d'appui; *Mining* sprag.
2 *he found himself becoming the emotional prop of the marriage* **mainstay**, pillar, anchor, rock, backbone, support, cornerstone; supporter, upholder, sustainer.
▶ verb **1** *he propped his bike against the garage wall* **lean**, rest, set, stand, position, place, lay, balance, steady.
2 *the longest branches were initially* **propped up** *with planks* **hold up**, shore up, bolster up, buttress, support, brace, underpin, reinforce, strengthen; *archaic* underprop.
3 *the government's attempt to* **prop up** *their loss-making state airline* **subsidize**, underwrite, fund, finance, maintain; **support**, give support to, bolster (up), shore up, buttress; help, aid, assist, revitalize.

propaganda ▶ noun *regulations restricting political propaganda were relaxed* **information**, promotion, advertising, advertisement, publicity, advocacy; spin, newspeak, agitprop, disinformation, counter-information, brainwashing, indoctrination, the big lie; *informal* info, hype, plugging.

propagandist ▶ noun *an enthusiastic propagandist for the government's reforms* **advocate**, champion, supporter, promoter, proponent, exponent, campaigner, crusader, publicist, evangelist, apostle, proselytizer, indoctrinator; *informal* plugger, spin doctor.

propagandize ▶ verb **1** *political concepts propagandized by the West* **advocate**, champion, support, promote, publicize, propagate, promulgate, campaign for, proclaim, preach.
2 *they should not be propagandized into spending beyond their means* **persuade**, convince, brainwash, indoctrinate, proselytize.

propagate ▶ verb **1** *the plant can be easily propagated by taking leaf cuttings* **breed**, grow, cultivate, generate; *technical* layer, pipe.
2 *the wild flowers and herbs get cut before they have a chance to flower and propagate* **reproduce**, multiply, proliferate, breed, procreate, increase, spawn; self-seed, self-sow.
3 *the advanced ideas drawn from the West or propagated by other leading democrats* **spread**, disseminate, communicate, pass on, put about, make known, promulgate, circulate, transmit, distribute, broadcast, publish, publicize, proclaim, preach, promote; propagandize.

propel ▶ verb **1** *a long fishing boat propelled by six oars* **push/move forwards**, move, set in motion, get moving, drive.
2 *he propelled the ball vertically into the air* **throw**, thrust, toss, fling, hurl, lob, let fly, launch, pitch, project, send, shoot; *informal* chuck, sling, bung.
3 *confusion propelled her into action* **spur**, drive, prompt, precipitate, catapult, motivate, force, impel.

propeller ▶ noun rotor, screw, airscrew, vane, propulsor; *informal* prop.

propensity ▶ noun *her propensity to jump to conclusions | his propensity for accidents* **tendency**, inclination, predisposition, proneness, proclivity, readiness, susceptibility, liability, disposition; aptness, penchant, leaning, predilection, bent, habit, weakness.

proper ▶ adjective **1** *Dan hadn't had a proper job for over ten years* **real**, genuine, actual, true, bona fide; *informal* kosher.
2 *they didn't apply through the proper channels* **right**, correct, accepted, orthodox, conventional, established, official, formal, regular, acceptable; appropriate, suitable, fitting, apt, due; *French* de règle; *archaic* meet.
OPPOSITES inappropriate, wrong.
3 *her parents' view of what was proper for a well-bred girl | Sally-Anne was very prim and proper* **respectable**, decorous, seemly, decent, refined, ladylike, gentlemanly, genteel; formal, conventional, correct, orthodox, polite, punctilious, sedate, modest, demure, virtuous; becoming, befitting, fit, done; *French* comme il faut.
OPPOSITES improper, unconventional.
4 (*Brit. informal*) *you've made a proper fool of yourself* **complete**, absolute, real, perfect, total, thorough, thoroughgoing, utter, out-and-out, positive, unmitigated, consummate; *Brit. informal* right; *Austral./NZ informal* fair; *archaic* arrant.
5 *the formalities* **proper to** *her age and position* **belonging**, relating, pertaining, related, relevant, unique, peculiar; associated with.

CHOOSE THE RIGHT WORD

proper, fitting, suitable, appropriate
See APPROPRIATE.

property ▶ noun **1** *a widower who left all his property to his housekeeper* **possessions**, belongings, things, goods, worldly goods, effects, personal effects, stuff, chattels, movables; resources, assets, valuables, fortune, capital, riches, wealth, holdings, securities, patrimony; *Law* personalty, goods and chattels; *informal* gear; *S. African informal* trek.
2 *a growing number of Germans are buying property in Denmark | empty council properties* **building(s)**, premises, house(s), land, estates, acres, acreage; freehold, leasehold; *Law* real property, realty; *N. Amer.* real estate.
3 *garlic has been known for its healing properties for more than 5,000 years* **quality**, attribute, characteristic, feature, power, trait, mark, hallmark.

prophecy ▶ noun **1** *her prophecy is coming true* **prediction**, forecast, prognostication, prognosis, divination, augury; *rare* prognostic.
2 *the gift of prophecy* **foretelling the future**, forecasting the future, fortune telling, crystal-gazing, prediction, second sight, clairvoyance, prognostication, divination, soothsaying; *rare* vaticination, augury, sortilege, auspication.

prophesy ▶ verb *many commentators prophesied disaster* **predict**, foretell, forecast, foresee, forewarn of, prognosticate, divine; *archaic* augur, presage, previse, foreshow, croak; *Scottish archaic* spae; *rare* vaticinate, auspicate.

prophet, prophetess ▶ noun **seer**, soothsayer, forecaster of the future, fortune teller, clairvoyant, prognosticator, prophesier, diviner; oracle, augur, sibyl; *Scottish* spaewife, spaeman; *rare* haruspex, vaticinator, oracler.
□ **prophet of doom pessimist**, doom-monger, doom merchant, Cassandra, Jeremiah, doomster, doomsayer; *informal* doom and gloom merchant.

prophetic ▶ adjective *his words proved prophetic—in less than a week he was dead* **prescient**, predictive, prophetical, far-seeing, prognostic, divinatory, oracular, sibylline, apocalyptic, fateful, revelatory, inspired; *rare* vatic, mantic, vaticinal, vaticinatory, prognosticative, augural, adumbrative, fatidic, fatidical.

prophylactic ▶ adjective *prophylactic measures should be taken* **preventive**, preventative, precautionary, protective, disease-preventing, pre-emptive, counteractive, preclusive, anticipatory, inhibitory, deterrent.
▶ noun **1** *vaccination remains one of the greatest prophylactics the world has ever known* **preventive measure**, precaution, safeguard, safety measure; preventive medicine.
2 (*N. Amer.*) *a packet of prophylactics* **condom**, sheath; female condom; *Brit. trademark* Durex, Femidom; *informal* Frenchy; *Brit. informal* johnny, something for the weekend; *N. Amer. informal* rubber, safe, safety, skin; *Brit. informal, dated* French letter; *dated* protective.

prophylaxis ▶ noun *the use of HRT as a prophylaxis against osteoporosis* **preventive treatment**, prevention, protection.

propinquity ▶ noun **1** *discussion of family support often seems to assume geographical propinquity* **proximity**, closeness, nearness, adjacency; *rare* contiguity, contiguousness, vicinity, vicinage.
2 *propinquity of descent* **close kinship**, close relationship, family connection, blood ties, consanguinity.

propitiate ▶ verb *George's attempt to propitiate his father did not succeed* **appease**, placate, mollify, pacify, make peace with, conciliate, make amends to, soothe, calm, humour, win over, satisfy; pour oil on troubled waters; *Austral.* square someone off.

propitious ▶ adjective *the timing for such a meeting seemed propitious* **favourable**, auspicious, promising, providential, advantageous, fortunate, lucky, optimistic, bright, happy, rosy, full of promise, heaven-sent, hopeful, beneficial; opportune, suitable, apt, fitting, timely, well timed.
OPPOSITES inauspicious, unfortunate.

proponent ▶ noun *a radical Roman Catholic priest and outspoken proponent of liberation theology* **advocate**, supporter, upholder, exponent, promoter, adherent, endorser, champion, defender, backer, subscriber, patron, espouser, friend, apostle, apologist, pleader, proposer, propounder, spokesperson, spokesman, spokeswoman; enthusiast, propagandist.

proportion ▶ noun **1** *only a small proportion of the land can be farmed* **part**, portion, amount, quantity, bit, piece, percentage, section, segment, share, quota, division, fraction, measure.
2 *the proportion of water to alcohol* **ratio**, distribution, relative amount/number; relationship.
3 *serious photographers interested in line and proportion should find the exhibition instructive* **balance**, symmetry, harmony, correspondence, correlation, congruity, agreement, concord.

4 (**proportions**) *men of huge proportions | an achievement of quite extraordinary proportions* **size, dimensions**, magnitude, measurements; mass, volume, bulk; expanse, extent, width, breadth, scale, scope, range.

proportional ▶ adjective *an increase in working hours unaccompanied by a proportional increase in wages* **corresponding**, proportionate, comparable, in proportion, pro rata, commensurate, equivalent, consistent, relative, correlated, correlative, analogous, analogical; *rare* commensurable.
OPPOSITE disproportionate.

proposal ▶ noun **1** *the Select Committee gave the proposal a very mixed reception* **scheme**, plan, project, programme, manifesto, motion, bid, proposition, presentation, submission, approach, suggestion, overture, draft, recommendation, tender, terms; *rare* proffer.
2 *the proposal of a flexible school leaving age* **putting forward, suggesting**, proposing, advancing, offering, presentation, submitting, submission, preferring, filing, lodging, tabling, introduction, initiation, tendering, bidding, projecting, recommendation, advocacy, propounding, proffering, positing.
OPPOSITE withdrawal.

propose ▶ verb **1** *we could propose a simpler system* **put forward, suggest**, advance, offer, present, move, submit, prefer, file, lodge, table, initiate, bring, bring forward, come up with, tender, bid, project, recommend, advocate, propound, proffer, posit.
OPPOSITE withdraw.
2 *how do you propose to raise the money?* **intend**, have the intention, mean, plan, have plans, set out, have in mind/view, resolve, be resolved, aim, purpose, contemplate, think of, aspire, desire, want, wish, expect.
3 *it is premature to propose Mr Lang for canonization* **nominate**, put forward, put up, name, suggest, submit, present, recommend.
OPPOSITE withdraw.
4 *first he must propose to Emily* **ask someone to marry you**, make an offer of marriage, offer marriage, ask for someone's hand in marriage; *informal* pop the question.

proposition ▶ noun **1** *they advanced the proposition that investors prefer high earnings growth* **theory, hypothesis**, thesis, argument, premise, postulation, theorem, concept, idea, statement.
2 *I have a business proposition to put to you* **proposal, scheme**, plan, project, programme, manifesto, motion, bid, presentation, submission, suggestion, recommendation, approach.
3 *I'm not in the market for your sort of proposition* **sexual advance**, sexual overture, indecent proposal, improper suggestion, soliciting; *informal* pass, come-on.
4 *getting cold water into the attic is no problem, but hot water is a different proposition* **task**, job, undertaking, venture, activity, problem, affair.
▶ verb *he never dared proposition her* **propose sex with**, make sexual advances to, make sexual overtures to, make an indecent proposal to, make an improper suggestion to; *informal* give someone the come-on.

propound ▶ verb *the theory of relativity was first propounded by Albert Einstein in 1905* **put forward**, advance, offer, present, set forth, submit, tender, suggest, come up with, broach, moot, bring up, mention, introduce, postulate, propose, pose, discuss, hypothesize, peddle, spread, promote, advocate, proffer, posit.

proprietor, proprietress ▶ noun **owner**, possessor, holder, keeper, freeholder, landowner, squire, landlord/landlady, master/mistress; innkeeper, hotel-keeper, hotelier, licensee, patron, shopkeeper; title-holder, deed-holder; *rare* proprietrix.

propriety ▶ noun **1** *he always behaves towards me with the utmost propriety* **decorum**, respectability, decency, correctness, appropriateness, good manners, courtesy, politeness, rectitude, civility, modesty, demureness; sobriety, refinement, decorousness, seemliness, becomingness, discretion, gentility, etiquette, breeding, conventionality, orthodoxy, formality, protocol; *formal* probity; *archaic* tenue.
OPPOSITE impropriety, indecorum.
2 (**proprieties**) *he was careful to preserve the proprieties in public* **etiquette**, social conventions, social grace(s), social niceties, one's Ps and Qs, protocol, decorum, standards, civilities, ceremony, formalities, rules of conduct, accepted behaviour, conventionalities, good manners, good form, the done thing, the thing to do, punctilio, attention to detail; *archaic* convenance(s).
3 *they question the propriety of certain investments made by the council* **correctness**, rightness, fitness, suitability, suitableness, appropriateness, aptness, morality, ethicality.
OPPOSITE impropriety.

propulsion ▶ noun *these seabirds use their wings for propulsion under water* **thrust, motive force**, propelling force, impelling force, impetus, impulse, drive, driving force, actuation, push, surge, pressure, momentum, power.

prosaic ▶ adjective **1** *flowers are given variously poetic or prosaic names* **unimaginative**, uninspired, matter-of-fact, dull, dry, humdrum, mundane, pedestrian, heavy, plodding, lifeless, dead, spiritless, lacklustre, undistinguished, stale, jejune, bland, insipid, vapid, vacuous, banal, hackneyed, trite, literal, factual, unpoetic, unemotional, unsentimental, clear, plain, unadorned, unembellished, unvarnished, monotonous, deadpan, flat.
OPPOSITES imaginative, inspired.
2 *Bloomwater's present owner was a more prosaic figure* **ordinary**, everyday, usual, common, conventional, straightforward, routine, humdrum, commonplace, run-of-the-mill, workaday, businesslike, pedestrian, tame, mundane, dull, dreary, tedious, boring, ho-hum, uninspiring, monotonous.
OPPOSITE interesting.

proscribe ▶ verb **1** *gambling was proscribed* **forbid**, prohibit, ban, bar, disallow, rule out, embargo, veto, make illegal, interdict, outlaw, taboo.
OPPOSITES allow, permit.
2 *a case was made for precisely the sort of intervention which the Report proscribed* **condemn**, denounce, attack, criticize, censure, denigrate, damn, reject.
OPPOSITES authorize, accept.
3 (*historical*) *the Chilean Communist Party was proscribed from 1927 to 1931* **outlaw**, boycott, black, blackball, exclude, ostracize; exile, expel, expatriate, evict, deport; *Christianity* excommunicate.

> **proscribe or prescribe?**
> *See* PRESCRIBE.

proscription ▶ noun **1** *the proscription of the sale of alcohol on Sundays* **prohibition**, prohibiting, forbidding, banning, ban, barring, bar, disallowing, ruling out, embargo, embargoing, vetoing, veto, making illegal, interdicting, interdict, outlawing, tabooing.
OPPOSITE allowing.
2 *composers began to find ways of circumventing the proscription on opera* **condemnation**, denunciation, attack, criticism, censure, denigration, damning, rejection.

prosecute ▶ verb **1** *they were going to prosecute the offender* **take to court**, bring/institute legal proceedings against, bring an action against, take legal action against, accuse, cite, summons, sue, try, bring to trial, put on trial, put in the dock, bring a charge against, bring a criminal charge against, charge, prefer charges against, bring a suit against, indict, arraign; *N. Amer.* impeach; *informal* have the law on, do; *N. Amer. informal* jug; *rare* implead.
OPPOSITES defend; let off, pardon.
2 *we have to prosecute this war to a successful conclusion* **pursue**, carry on, conduct, direct, engage in, work at, proceed with, continue, continue with, keep on with, go ahead with; fight, wage.
OPPOSITE give up.

proselyte ▶ noun **convert**, new believer, catechumen, recruit, neophyte, newcomer, initiate, tyro, novice.

proselytize ▶ verb **1** *I'm not here to proselytize* **evangelize**, convert, seek/make converts, bring to God/Christ, bring into the fold, spread the gospel/word (to), propagandize, preach (to), win over, recruit; brainwash.
2 *they are preoccupied with proselytizing a liberal view* **promote**, present, spread, proclaim, peddle, propound, preach, back, urge, suggest, support, advocate, endorse, champion, sponsor, espouse, advance, further, assist, aid, help, contribute to, foster, boost.

prosimian ▶ noun. *See centre pages for list of* **Lemurs and Other Prosimians**

prospect ▶ noun (stress on the first syllable) **1** *there is little prospect of success* **likelihood**, hope, expectation, anticipation, (good/poor) chance, chances, odds, probability, possibility, likeliness, promise, lookout; dream; fear, danger, hazard.
2 (**prospects**) *she would have better job prospects with a postgraduate qualification* **possibilities**, potential, promise, expectations, outlook, future, scope.
3 *finding schools abroad may be a daunting prospect for employees* **vision, thought**, idea, contemplation; task, undertaking.
4 *Jimmy, who plays in midfield, is an exciting prospect* **candidate**, possibility; *informal* catch.
5 *guests are greeted with a pleasant prospect from the ground-floor lounge* **view**, vista, outlook, perspective, panorama, aspect, scene; scenery, sweep, landscape, seascape, townscape, cityscape, surroundings; picture, spectacle, sight; *archaic* lookout.
□ **in prospect** *further job losses are in prospect* **coming soon**, on the way, in the pipeline, likely to happen, to come, coming up, at hand, close/near at hand, near, imminent, in the offing, in view, in store, on the horizon, in the wings, just around the corner, in the air, in the wind, brewing, upcoming, forthcoming, impending, approaching; *informal* on the cards.
▶ verb (stress on the second syllable) **1** *the mining companies never got to prospect the area* **inspect**, survey, make a survey of, explore, search, scout, reconnoitre, examine, check out.
2 *he obtained rights to prospect for minerals* **search**, look, seek, hunt, go after, dowse.

prospective ▶ adjective *the prospective buyer should always endeavour to* *negotiate* **potential**, possible, probable, likely, future, eventual, -to-be, soon-to-be, in the making, destined, intended; **intending**, aspiring, would-be; forthcoming, approaching, coming, imminent; presumptive, designate.

prospectus ▶ noun *a school or company prospectus* **brochure**, description, announcement, advertisement; syllabus, curriculum, catalogue, programme, list, scheme, particulars, schedule, outline, synopsis; pamphlet, literature.

prosper ▶ verb *the European personal computer market continued to prosper* **do well**, get on well, go well, fare well; **thrive**, flourish, flower, bloom, blossom, burgeon, grow vigorously, shoot up; boom, expand, spread, pick up, improve, come on; succeed, be successful, make it, do all right for oneself, get ahead, progress, make progress, make headway, advance, get on in the world, go up in the world, arrive, fly high, make one's mark, make good, become rich, strike gold/oil, be in clover; *informal* go places, go great guns, make the big time, be in the pink, be fine and dandy, be on easy street, live the life of Riley; *archaic* make good speed.
OPPOSITES fail, collapse, crash.

CHOOSE THE RIGHT WORD

prosper, flourish, thrive
See FLOURISH.

prosperity ▶ noun *Britain's prosperity depends on its exports* **wealth**, **success**, profitability, affluence, riches, opulence, the good life, (good) fortune, ease, plenty, welfare, comfort, security, well-being; luxury, life of luxury, milk and honey, a bed of roses; prosperousness, successfulness; *archaic* speed, Godspeed.
OPPOSITES hardship; failure.

prosperous ▶ adjective *a prosperous family shipping firm* **thriving**, doing well, prospering, buoyant, expanding, flourishing, successful, strong, vigorous, productive, profitable, booming, burgeoning, fruitful, roaring, golden, palmy; **affluent**, wealthy, rich, moneyed, with deep pockets, well off, well-to-do, opulent, substantial, fortunate, lucky, in clover; *informal* on a roll, on the up and up, rolling in it, rolling in money, in the money, loaded, stinking rich, well heeled, flush, made of money, on easy street; *Brit. informal* quids in; *informal, dated* oofy.
OPPOSITES depressed; poor.

prostitute ▶ noun **whore**, sex worker, call girl, white slave; male prostitute, rent boy, call boy, gigolo; *euphemistic* model, escort, masseuse; *Brit.* tom; *French* fille de joie; *Spanish* puta; *N. Amer.* sporting girl/woman/lady, chippy; *informal* tart, pro, moll, tail, brass nail, grande horizontale, woman on the game, working girl, member of the oldest profession, renter, toy boy; *N. Amer. informal* hooker, hustler; *black English* ho; *vulgar slang* bumboy; *dated* streetwalker, woman of the streets, lady/woman of the night, scarlet woman, cocotte; *archaic* courtesan, strumpet, harlot, trollop, woman of ill repute, lady of pleasure, Cyprian, doxy, drab, quean, trull, wench; *rare* sing-song girl, succubus.
▶ verb *they couldn't bring themselves to prostitute their art by copying others* **betray**, sacrifice, profane, sell, sell out, debase, degrade, demean, devalue, cheapen, lower, misapply, misemploy, misuse, pervert, squander, waste; abandon one's principles, be untrue to oneself.

prostitution ▶ noun **whoring**, the sex industry, streetwalking, Mrs Warren's profession, white slavery, sex tourism; *informal* the oldest profession, the game, the trade; rough trade; *N. Amer. informal* hooking, hustling, the life; *dated* whoredom; *archaic* courtesanship, harlotry, Magdalenism, the social evil.

prostrate ▶ adjective (stress on the first syllable) **1** *they surged forward around the prostrate figure on the ground* **prone**, **lying flat**, lying down, flat, stretched out, spreadeagled, sprawling, horizontal, recumbent, on one's front; *rare* procumbent.
OPPOSITE upright.
2 *his wife was prostrate with shock* **overwhelmed**, overcome, overpowered, brought to one's knees, crushed, stunned, dazed; speechless, helpless, paralysed, laid low, impotent; *informal* knocked/hit for six.
3 *the fever which had just left me prostrate* **worn out**, exhausted, fatigued, tired out, overtired, weary, sapped, dog-tired, spent, drained, played out, debilitated, enervated, low; *informal* all in, done (in/up), dead, dead beat, dead tired, dead on one's feet, ready to drop, fagged out, bushed, whacked, worn to a frazzle, burnt-out; *Brit. informal* knackered; *N. Amer. informal* pooped.
OPPOSITE fresh.
▶ verb (stress on the second syllable) *she expected to find Kathleen prostrated by the tragedy in her family* **overwhelm**, overcome, overpower, bring to one's knees, crush, devastate, make helpless, paralyse, lay low, make powerless, debilitate, incapacitate, weaken, enfeeble, devitalize, enervate, handicap, immobilize, hamstring, make impotent, wear out, exhaust, tire out, fatigue, weary, make weary, drain, sap, wash out, take it out of, tax, overtax, undermine; *informal* knacker, whack, frazzle, do in, knock out, fag out; *N. Amer. informal* poop.
□ **prostrate oneself** *he prostrated himself on the altar mat* **throw oneself flat**, throw oneself down, lie down, stretch oneself out, bow low, throw oneself at someone's feet; *dated* measure one's length.

prostration ▶ noun *he was left exhausted, sometimes near to prostration* **collapse**, weakness, debility, lassitude, exhaustion, fatigue, tiredness, enervation, emotional exhaustion; paralysis; desolation, despair, despondency, dejection, depression, helplessness.

protagonist ▶ noun **1** *the very first line of the play is spoken by the protagonist* **chief character**, central/principal/main/leading character, chief/central/principal/main/leading participant, principal, hero/heroine, leading man/lady, title role, lead, star, (leading/key) player, (leading) figure, leading light.
OPPOSITE minor character.
2 *the EC is a great protagonist of deregulation* **supporter**, upholder, adherent, backer, proponent, advocate, promoter, champion, exponent, standard-bearer, torch-bearer, prime mover, moving spirit, mainstay, spokesman/spokeswoman/spokesperson.
OPPOSITE opponent.

protean ▶ adjective **1** *the diverse and protean nature of mental disorders* **ever-changing**, **variable**, changeable, mutable, kaleidoscopic, erratic, quicksilver, inconstant, inconsistent, unstable, unsteady, shifting, uneven, unsettled, fluctuating, chameleon-like, chameleonic; fluid, wavering, vacillating, mercurial, volatile, unpredictable, wayward, unreliable, undependable; *technical* labile; *rare* stayless, changeful.
OPPOSITES constant, consistent.
2 *Shostakovich was a remarkably protean composer* **versatile**, adaptable, flexible, all-round, multifaceted, multitalented, many-sided, resourceful, malleable.
OPPOSITE limited.

protect ▶ verb *the men fought hand-to-hand to protect their women and children* **keep safe**, keep from harm, save, safeguard, shield, preserve, defend, cushion, shelter, screen, secure, fortify, guard, mount/stand guard on; watch over, look after, take care of, care for, tend, keep, mind, afford protection to, harbour, house, hedge, inoculate, insulate.
OPPOSITES expose, neglect; attack, harm.

protection ▶ noun **1** *physical fitness provides considerable protection against stress* **defence**, shielding, shelter, preservation, conservation, safe keeping, safeguarding, safety, security, sanctuary, refuge, lee, immunity, insurance, indemnity.
2 *he remains in hiding under the protection of the United States* **safe keeping**, care, charge, keeping, protectorship, guidance, aegis, auspices, umbrella, guardianship, support, patronage, championship, providence.
3 *a good education is not a protection against the hazards of life* **barrier**, buffer, shield, screen, hedge, cushion, preventive, preventative, armour, safeguard; refuge, bulwark, bastion, wall.

protective ▶ adjective **1** *firefighters wear special protective clothing* **preservative**, protecting, safeguarding, shielding, defensive, safety, precautionary, preventive, preventative, covering; waterproof, fireproof, heatproof, insulating; shatterproof, toughened, armoured.
2 *he felt protective towards the girl* **solicitous**, **caring**, mindful, careful, wary, watchful, vigilant, warm, paternal/maternal, fatherly/motherly, gallant, chivalrous; overprotective, possessive, jealous, clinging.

protector ▶ noun **1** *his wife was always his chief protector* **defender**, preserver, bodyguard, minder, guardian, guard, champion, watchdog, ombudsman, knight in shining armour, guardian angel, patron, chaperone, escort, keeper, custodian; *informal* hired gun.
2 *I encounter men drilling the roads without wearing ear protectors* **guard**, shield, pad, buffer, cushion, screen; protection.

protégé, fem. **protégée** ▶ noun **pupil**, student, trainee, apprentice; **disciple**, follower, discovery, ward, dependant, charge; *archaic* fosterling.

protest ▶ noun (stress on the first syllable) **1** *voters humiliated the government as a protest against high public spending* **objection**, exception, complaint, disapproval, disagreement, opposition, challenge, dissent, demurral, remonstration, expostulation, fuss, outcry; railing, inveighing, fulmination, protestation.
OPPOSITES support, approval.
2 *women staged a protest outside the gates* **demonstration**, march, protest march, peace camp, rally, sit-in, human chain, occupation, sleep-in, dirty protest, write-in, non-cooperation; work-to-rule, industrial action, stoppage, strike, walkout, mutiny, picket, boycott; *Indian* morcha, gherao, hartal; *informal* demo.
▶ verb (stress on the second syllable) **1** *people began to protest at the development of nuclear power* **express opposition**, raise objections, object, make a protest, dissent, take issue, make/take a stand, put up a fight, kick, take exception, complain, express disapproval, disagree, express disagreement, demur, remonstrate, expostulate, make a fuss; cry out, speak out, rail, inveigh, fulminate; oppose, challenge, denounce; *informal* kick up a fuss/stink.
OPPOSITE acquiesce.
2 *two dozen people protested outside the cathedral* **demonstrate**, march, hold a rally, sit in, form a human chain, occupy somewhere, sleep in, stage a dirty protest, refuse to cooperate; work to rule, take industrial action,

stop work, down tools, strike, go on strike, walk out, mutiny, picket somewhere; boycott something.
3 *Richardson has always protested his innocence* **insist on**, claim, maintain, declare, announce, profess, proclaim, assert, affirm, argue, vow, avow, aver, pledge, swear, swear to, testify to; *rare* asseverate.

protestation ▶ **noun 1** *police poured scorn on the bombers' protestations of regret* **declaration**, announcement, statement, profession, assertion, insistence, claim, affirmation, assurance, attestation, oath, vow, pledge, avowal; *rare* maintenance, asseveration.
2 *no amount of protestations will make you change your mind* **objection**, protest, statement of opposition, exception, complaint, disapproval, opposition, challenge, dissent, demurral, remonstration, fuss, outcry; railing, inveighing, fulmination; *informal* stink.

protester ▶ **noun 1** *a spokesman for the council admitted losing protesters' letters* **objector**, opposer, opponent, complainer, dissenter, dissident, nonconformist; *rare* dissentient.
2 *sixty protesters were arrested for wire-cutting* **demonstrator**, protest marcher, human chain; striker, mutineer, picket.

protocol ▶ **noun 1** *he was always a stickler for protocol* **etiquette**, conventions, formalities, customs, rules of conduct, procedure, ritual, code of behaviour, accepted behaviour, conventionalities, propriety, proprieties, one's Ps and Qs, decorum, manners, courtesies, civilities, good form, the done thing, the thing to do, punctilio; *French* politesse.
2 *the two countries signed a protocol on defence and security* **agreement**, treaty, entente, concord, concordat, convention, deal, pact, contract, compact, settlement, arrangement; armistice, truce; *rare* engagement.

prototype ▶ **noun** *he was working on the prototype of an inexpensive but effective ventilator* **original**, first example, first model, master, mould, template, framework, mock-up, pattern, type; **design**, guide, blueprint; sample, example, paradigm, archetype, exemplar.

protract ▶ **verb** *the Opposition will try to protract the discussion* **prolong**, extend, extend the duration of, stretch out, draw out, lengthen, make longer, elongate, drag out, spin out, string out, carry on, continue, keep up, keep something going, go on with, perpetuate, sustain; *archaic* wire-draw.
OPPOSITES curtail, shorten.

protracted ▶ **adjective** *his appointment followed weeks of protracted negotiations* **prolonged**, extended, stretched out, drawn out, long-drawn-out, lengthened, lengthy, long, overlong, dragged out, spun out, strung out, sustained, marathon; interminable, never-ending, endless, lingering; slow, time-consuming; long-winded, verbose, prolix, wordy, rambling.

protrude ▶ **verb** *a handle protrudes from the motor housing* **stick out**, jut, jut out, poke out, project, stand out, come through, peek, poke, stick up, hang out, loom (out), extend, obtrude; balloon, bulge (out), swell (out), pouch (out); *N. Amer. informal* pooch (out); *rare* protuberate.

protruding ▶ **adjective** *he had protruding teeth* **sticking out**, jutting, jutting out, standing out, prominent, protuberant, proud, obtrusive; overhanging, projecting; bulging, bulbous, swollen, distended; *informal* goofy; *rare* protrusive, outjutting, excrescent, gibbous.
OPPOSITES sunken; inconspicuous.

protrusion ▶ **noun 1** *the neck vertebrae have short vertical protrusions* **bump**, lump, knob, hump, jut, projection, prominence, protuberance, overhang, eminence, ledge, shelf, ridge; swelling, bulge, excrescence, outgrowth, growth, carbuncle; *technical* process; *rare* tumescence, intumescence, tumefaction.
2 *a phonetician would comment on protrusion of the lips* **sticking out**, jutting, projection, projecting, obtrusion, obtruding, prominence, protuberance; swelling, bulging; *rare* tumescence, tumefaction.

protuberance ▶ **noun 1** *some of the duck-billed dinosaurs evolved protuberances on top of their heads* **bump**, lump, knob, hump, jut, projection, prominence, protrusion, overhang, eminence, ledge, shelf, ridge, swelling, bulge, excrescence, outgrowth, growth, carbuncle; *rare* tumescence, intumescence, tumefaction.
2 *the protuberance of the incisors in the species suggests that they were extremely important* **sticking out**, jutting, projection, projecting, obtrusion, obtruding, prominence, protrusion; swelling, bulging; *rare* tumescence, tumefaction.

protuberant ▶ **adjective** *his eyes are a little protuberant* **bulging**, bulbous, popping, swelling, swollen, distended, sticking out, jutting, jutting out, protruding; projecting, prominent, proud, humped, obtrusive; *informal* goggle; *rare* protrusive, outjutting, excrescent, gibbous.
OPPOSITE sunken.

proud ▶ **adjective 1** *Moira was a delight to her proud parents | we are very proud of our herb garden* **pleased (with)**, glad (about/at), happy (about/at/with), delighted (about/at/with), joyful (at), overjoyed (at/over), thrilled (at/about/by/with), well pleased (with), satisfied (with), gratified (at), content (at), appreciative (of).
OPPOSITE ashamed.
2 *it's a proud day for all of our workers* **pleasing**, gratifying, satisfying, fulfilling, rewarding, cheering, heart-warming; happy, good, memorable, notable, red-letter, glorious, splendid, wonderful, marvellous.
OPPOSITE shameful.
3 *they were poor but proud* **self-respecting**, dignified, noble, worthy; independent.
OPPOSITE humble.
4 *he is too proud to admit to being in the wrong* **arrogant**, conceited, vain, self-important, full of oneself, narcissistic, egotistical, puffed up, jumped-up, boastful, smug, complacent, disdainful, condescending, pretentious, scornful, supercilious, snobbish, imperious, pompous, overbearing, bumptious, lordly, presumptuous, overweening, haughty, high and mighty, high-handed; *informal* cocky, big-headed, swollen-headed, too big for one's boots, stuck-up, uppity, snooty, toffee-nosed, highfalutin; *informal, dated* too big for one's breeches; *literary* vainglorious; *rare* hubristic.
OPPOSITES modest, humble.
5 *she took a final look down the proud granite staircase* **magnificent**, splendid, resplendent, grand, noble, stately, imposing, dignified, distinguished, august, illustrious, striking, impressive, majestic, glorious, sumptuous, marvellous, awe-inspiring, awesome, monumental, palatial, statuesque, heroic; superb, regal, royal, kingly, queenly, princely, imperial.
OPPOSITE unimpressive.
6 *fill the holes slightly proud to allow for sanding smooth* **projecting**, sticking out/up, jutting, jutting out, protruding, prominent, raised, convex, elevated.
OPPOSITES concave; flush.

prove ▶ **verb 1** *you cannot prove that they are wrong* **demonstrate**, show, show beyond doubt, show to be true, manifest, produce/submit proof, produce/submit evidence, establish evidence, evince; witness to, give substance to, determine, demonstrate the truth of, substantiate, corroborate, verify, ratify, validate, authenticate, attest, certify, document, bear out, confirm.
OPPOSITE disprove.
2 *the rumour proved to be correct* **turn out**, be found, happen.
□ **prove oneself demonstrate one's abilities/qualities/courage**, show one's (true) mettle, show what one is made of.

provenance ▶ **noun** *the police were suspicious about the provenance of the paintings* **origin**, source, place of origin; birthplace, spring, wellspring, fount, roots, history, pedigree, derivation, root, etymology; *N. Amer.* provenience; *rare* radix.

proverb ▶ **noun** **saying**, adage, saw, maxim, axiom, motto, aphorism, epigram, gnome, dictum, precept; words of wisdom; catchphrase, slogan, byword, watchword; truism, platitude, cliché; *French* bon mot; *rare* apophthegm.

proverbial ▶ **adjective** *the pirate's greed was as proverbial as his cowardice* **well known**, famous, famed, renowned, traditional, time-honoured, legendary, acknowledged, accepted; notorious, infamous.

provide ▶ **verb 1** *the government refused to provide money for the project* **supply**, give, issue, furnish, lay out, come up with, dispense, bestow, impart, produce, yield, bring forth, bear, deliver, donate, contribute, pledge, advance, spare, part with, allocate, distribute, allot, assign, put forward, put up, proffer, present, extend, render; *informal* fork out; *N. Amer. informal* ante up, pony up.
OPPOSITES refuse; withhold.
2 *please provide her with the necessary documents* **equip**, furnish, issue, supply, outfit; fit out, rig out, kit out, arm, array, attire, accoutre, provision, stock, purvey, accommodate, bestow, favour, endow, present; *informal* fix up.
OPPOSITE deprive.
3 *the work at least enabled him to* ***provide for*** *his family* **feed**, nurture, nourish, give food to, provide board for; **support**, maintain, keep, sustain, provide sustenance for, fend for, finance, endow; take care of, care for, look after.
OPPOSITE neglect.
4 *this procedure can provide an opportunity for testing opinion* **make available**, present, offer, afford, accord, give, add, bring, yield, impart, bestow, confer, lend.
5 *we have* ***provided for*** *further restructuring* **prepare**, allow, make provision, make preparations, be prepared, anticipate, arrange, make arrangements, get ready, plan, make plans, cater.
6 *the bunkers were to* ***provide against*** *future Chinese attacks* **take precautions**, take steps/measures, guard, forearm oneself; make provision for.
7 *the contract provides that the tenants are responsible for house repairs* **stipulate**, lay down, have as a condition, make it a condition, require, order, ordain, demand, prescribe, state, set out, specify.

provided ▶ **conjunction** *the clove-pink needs no special cultivation, provided it has well-drained soil* **if, on condition that**, providing (that), provided that, presuming (that), assuming (that), on the assumption that, as long as, given (that), with the provision/proviso that, with/on the understanding that, if and only if, contingent on, in the event that, allowing that.

providence ▶ **noun 1** *her life was mapped out for her by providence* **fate**, destiny, nemesis, kismet, God's will, divine intervention, predestination, predetermination; astral influence, the stars; fortune, fortuity,

serendipity, chance, luck, accident, circumstances, coincidence; one's lot (in life); *archaic* one's portion.
2 *it was considered a duty to encourage providence* **prudence**, **foresight**, forethought, far-sightedness, judgement, judiciousness, shrewdness, circumspection, wisdom, sagacity, common sense, precaution, caution, care, carefulness; good management, careful budgeting, thrift, thriftiness, economy; *N. Amer.* forehandedness.

provident ▶ **adjective** **prudent**, far-sighted, judicious, shrewd, circumspect, forearmed, wise, sagacious, sensible, commonsensical, politic, cautious, careful, thrifty; *N. Amer.* forehanded; *rare* forethoughtful.
OPPOSITE improvident.

providential ▶ **adjective** **1** *the battle was won with the aid of a providential wind* **opportune**, advantageous, favourable, auspicious, propitious, heaven-sent, welcome, golden, good, right, lucky, happy, fortunate, benign, felicitous, timely, well timed, ripe, seasonable, convenient, expedient.
OPPOSITE inopportune.
2 *shooting stars are not providential signs* **divine**, heaven-sent, miraculous.

provider ▶ **noun** *the state is still the main provider of welfare* **supplier**, donor, giver, contributor, source, mainstay.

providing ▶ **conjunction** *the public are admitted to the galleries, providing they make a small donation* **if**, **on condition that**, provided (that), providing that, presuming (that), assuming (that), on the assumption that, as long as, given (that), with the provision/proviso that, with/on the understanding that, if and only if, contingent on, in the event that, allowing that.

province *See centre pages for list of* **Districts**
▶ **noun** **1** *Egypt was still a province of the Ottoman Empire* **territory**, region, state, department, canton, area, district, sector, zone, division, administrative district/division/unit/area; colony, settlement, dominion, fief, protectorate, mandate, dependency, possession, holding, satellite state.
2 (**the provinces**) *wages were higher in London than in the provinces* **non-metropolitan areas/counties**, the rest of the country, middle England/America, rural areas/districts, the countryside, the backwoods, the wilds, the wilderness, the back of beyond; *informal* the sticks, the middle of nowhere; *N. Amer. informal* the boondocks.
3 *that's outside my province, I'm afraid* **area of responsibility**, area of activity, area of interest, area of knowledge, area, department, responsibility, sphere, world, realm, field, discipline, domain, territory, orbit, preserve, business, affair, line of business, line, speciality, forte, line of country, charge, concern, worry, duty, jurisdiction, authority; *informal* pigeon, bailiwick, turf.

provincial ▶ **adjective** **1** *the provincial government* **regional**, state, territorial, district, local; sectoral, zonal, cantonal, county, parochial; colonial.
OPPOSITE national.
2 *both the London and provincial press* **non-metropolitan**, small-town, non-city, non-urban, outlying, rural, country, rustic, backwoods, backwater; *informal* one-horse; *N. Amer. informal* hick, freshwater.
OPPOSITES national; metropolitan; cosmopolitan.
3 *pompous bankers and their dull, provincial wives* **unsophisticated**, **narrow-minded**, parochial, small-town, suburban, insular, parish-pump, inward-looking, limited, restricted, localist, conservative, narrow; small-minded, petty, blinkered, illiberal, inflexible, bigoted, prejudiced, intolerant; *N. Amer. informal* jerkwater, corn-fed.
OPPOSITES sophisticated; broad-minded.
▶ **noun** *those who did not know what it took were dismissed as provincials* **(country) bumpkin**, country cousin, rustic, yokel, village idiot, peasant, churl, lout, boor, oaf, clown, barbarian, yahoo; *Irish, derogatory* culchie, bogman; *informal* clod, clodhopper; *Brit. informal* yob, yobbo, plonker; *N. Amer. informal* schlub, hayseed, hick, rube, hillbilly; *Austral. informal* ocker; *rare* bucolic.

provision ▶ **noun** **1** *the President condemned the provision of weapons to guerrillas* **supplying**, supply, providing, purveying, delivery, furnishing, equipping, giving, donation, allocation, distribution, presentation.
2 *there has been limited provision for gifted children in the past* **facilities**, services, amenities, resource(s), equipment, arrangements; means, offering, funds, benefits, assistance, allowance(s), concession(s), opportunities.
3 (**provisions**) *the English troops were tired and running out of provisions* **supplies**, food and drink, food, stores, stocks, groceries, foodstuff(s), rations, iron rations, eatables, edibles, fare, daily bread, staples; *Scottish* vivers; *informal* grub, bread, eats, chow, nosh, scoff; *N. Amer. informal* chuck; *archaic* victuals, vittles, viands, commons, meat; *rare* sustenance, provender, comestibles, aliment, viaticum, commissariat.
4 *he never made any sort of provision for the future* **preparations**, plans, planning, prearrangement, arrangements, precautions, precautionary steps/measures, contingency.
5 *nearly everyone will be covered by the provisions of the Act* **term**, clause, requirement, specification, stipulation; proviso, condition, rider, qualification, restriction, reservation, caveat, limitation.

provisional ▶ **adjective** *a provisional government | provisional results from the election* **interim**, temporary, pro tem; transitional, changeover, stopgap, short-term, fill-in, make-do, acting, caretaker, TBC (to be confirmed), subject to confirmation; pencilled in, working, conditional, qualified, tentative, contingent, makeshift, improvised, preliminary, unfinished; *Latin* pro tempore; *rare* provisory, interregnal, provisionary.
OPPOSITES permanent; definite.

provisionally ▶ **adverb** *he was appointed provisionally for one year* **subject to confirmation**, in an acting capacity, as a fill-in, short-term, pro tem, temporarily, for the interim, for the present, for the time being, for now, for the nonce; conditionally, tentatively; *Latin* ad interim, pro tempore; *rare* contingently, provisorily.

proviso ▶ **noun** *he let his house out for the year, with the proviso that his own staff should remain to run it* **condition**, stipulation, provision, clause, rider, qualification, restriction, reservation, caveat, limitation; strings.

provocation ▶ **noun** **1** *he remained calm despite severe provocation* **goading**, prodding, egging on, incitement, rousing, stirring, stimulation, prompting, inducement, encouragement, urging, inspiration, stimulus, pressure; **annoyance**, irritation, nettling, agitation, vexation, being rubbed up the wrong way; harassment, plaguing, molestation; teasing, taunting, torment; affront, insults; *informal* hassle, aggravation.
2 *without provocation, Jones punched Mr Cartwright* **justification**, excuse, pretext, occasion, call, motivation, motive, cause, grounds, reason, purpose, need.

provocative ▶ **adjective** **1** *he was making provocative remarks guaranteed to drive her into a fury* **annoying**, irritating, exasperating, infuriating, provoking, maddening, goading, vexing, galling; affronting, insulting, offensive, inflaming, rousing, arousing, inflammatory, incendiary, controversial; *informal* aggravating, in-your-face; *rare* instigative, agitative.
OPPOSITES soothing, calming.
2 *provocative dress does not constitute an invitation to sexual assault* **sexy**, sexually arousing, sexually exciting, alluring, seductive, tempting, suggestive, inviting, tantalizing, titillating; indecent, pornographic, indelicate, immodest, shameless; erotic, sensuous, slinky, passionate, sexual, piquant, racy, juicy, risqué, raunchy, steamy, coquettish, amorous, flirtatious, come-hither; *informal* kinky, tarty; *vulgar slang* fuck-me.
OPPOSITES modest, decorous.

provoke ▶ **verb** **1** *a planned golf course has provoked anger among locals* **arouse**, produce, evoke, cause, give rise to, occasion, call forth, draw forth, elicit, induce, inspire, excite, spark off, touch off, kindle, generate, engender, instigate, result in, lead to, bring on, contribute to, make for, foster, promote, breed, precipitate, prompt, trigger; *literary* beget, enkindle.
OPPOSITE allay.
2 *he might be provoked into making remarks he'd regret* **goad**, spur, prick, sting, prod, egg on, hound, badger, incite, rouse, stir, move, stimulate, motivate, excite, inflame, work/fire up, impel, pressure, pressurize, prompt, induce, encourage, urge, inspire.
OPPOSITE deter.
3 *he thought that I was trying to provoke him* **annoy**, make angry, anger, incense, enrage, send into a rage, irritate, infuriate, exasperate, exacerbate, madden, pique, nettle, get/take a rise out of, bother, upset, agitate, vex, irk, gall, get/put someone's back up, get on someone's nerves, ruffle, ruffle someone's feathers, make someone's hackles rise, raise someone's hackles, make someone's blood boil, rub up the wrong way, put someone out; harass, harry, plague, molest; tease, taunt, torment; affront, insult, offend; *informal* peeve, aggravate, hassle, miff, rile, needle, get, get to, bug, hack off, get under someone's skin, get in someone's hair, get up someone's nose, get someone's goat, get across someone; *Brit. informal* get on someone's wick, give someone the hump, wind up, nark; *N. Amer. informal* rankle, ride, gravel; *vulgar slang* piss off; *Brit. vulgar slang* get on someone's tits.
OPPOSITES pacify, appease.

provoking ▶ **adjective** *really, you can be most provoking* **annoying**, irritating, exasperating, infuriating, provocative, maddening, goading, vexing, galling, affronting, insulting, offensive; inflaming, inflammatory, incendiary, controversial; *informal* aggravating, in-your-face; *rare* instigative, agitative.

prow ▶ **noun** *the prow of a ship* **bow**, bows, stem, fore, forepart, front, head, nose, cutwater; *informal* sharp end; *rare* fore-end, stem-post, beak, beak-head.

prowess ▶ **noun** **1** *his prowess as a winemaker* **skill**, skilfulness, expertise, effectiveness, mastery, facility, ability, capability, capacity, talent, genius, adroitness, adeptness, aptitude, dexterity, deftness, competence, competency, professionalism, excellence, accomplishment, experience, proficiency, expertness, finesse, know-how; *French* savoir faire.
OPPOSITES inability, ineptitude.
2 *the knights were famed for their prowess in battle* **courage**, bravery, gallantry, valour, heroism, intrepidness, intrepidity, nerve, pluck, pluckiness, doughtiness, hardihood, braveness, courageousness, dauntlessness, gameness, manfulness, boldness, daring, audacity, spirit, fearlessness; mettle, determination, fortitude, steadfastness, stoutness,

resolve, resolution, backbone, spine, stout-heartedness; *informal* bottle, grit, guts, spunk, gutsiness, gumption, ballsiness; *N. Amer. informal* moxie, cojones, sand; *vulgar slang* balls; *archaic* valiance.
OPPOSITE cowardice.

prowl ▶ verb *youths have been prowling around the back of the flats* **move stealthily**, slink, skulk, steal, nose, pussyfoot, sneak, sidle, stalk, creep; roam, range, rove, cruise, hunt, scavenge; *informal* snoop.

proximity ▶ noun *their minds were concentrated by the proximity of the enemy* **closeness**, nearness, presence, juxtaposition, propinquity, adjacency; accessibility; *rare* contiguity, vicinity, vicinage.

proxy ▶ noun *any member is entitled to appoint another person as his proxy to attend and vote instead of him* **deputy**, representative, substitute, delegate, agent, surrogate, stand-in, attorney, ambassador, emissary, go-between, envoy; *rare* factor, procurator.

prude ▶ noun **puritan**, prig, killjoy, moral zealot/fanatic, moralist, Mrs Grundy, Grundy, old maid, schoolmarm, pietist, Victorian, priggish person; *N. Amer.* bluenose; *informal* goody-goody, Goody Two-Shoes, holy Joe, holy Willie, Miss Prim.

prudence ▶ noun **1** *foresters argue about the prudence of drastic thinning* **wisdom**, judgement, good judgement, judiciousness, sagacity, shrewdness, advisability, common sense, sense.
OPPOSITE folly.
2 *an elder counselled prudence* **caution**, cautiousness, care, carefulness, canniness, chariness, wariness, circumspection; far-sightedness, foresight, forethought; discretion.
OPPOSITE recklessness.
3 *thanks to his father's prudence, a fortune was made* **thrift**, thriftiness, providence, good management, careful budgeting, economy, canniness, frugality, abstemiousness; *N. Amer.* forehandedness; *rare* sparingness.

prudent ▶ adjective **1** *it is not always prudent to approach strangers found in desolate spots* **wise**, well judged, judicious, sagacious, sage, shrewd, advisable, well advised, politic, sensible, commonsensical.
OPPOSITES unwise, imprudent.
2 *a prudent approach to borrowing* **cautious**, careful, canny, chary, wary, circumspect, far-sighted, forearmed; *N. Amer.* forehanded; *rare* forethoughtful.
OPPOSITES incautious, imprudent.
3 *Phyllis was a prudent shopper* **thrifty**, provident, economical, canny, sparing, frugal, abstemious, scrimping.
OPPOSITES extravagant, imprudent.

prudish ▶ adjective *his grandmother was a rather prudish woman* **puritanical**, puritan, priggish, prim, prim and proper, formal, moralistic, strait-laced, prissy, mimsy, stuffy, niminy-piminy, Victorian, old-maid, old-maidish, schoolmistressy, schoolmarmish, governessy; *informal* goody-goody, starchy; *rare* Grundyish.
OPPOSITES permissive, liberal, broad-minded.

prune ▶ verb **1** *it will soon be time to prune the apple trees* **cut back**, trim, thin, thin out, pinch back, crop, clip, shear, pollard, top, dock; shape, even up, neaten, tidy (up).
2 *prune lateral shoots of wisteria* **cut off**, lop (off), chop off, hack off, clip, snip (off), nip off, dock, sever, detach, remove.
3 *companies are pruning their headquarters teams in an attempt to save money* **reduce**, cut, cut back, cut down, cut back on, pare, pare down, slim down, make reductions in, make cutbacks in, trim, whittle away/down, decrease, diminish, axe, shrink, minimize; eliminate, get rid of, do away with; *informal* slash.

prurient ▶ adjective *obscene material deals with sex in a manner appealing to prurient interest* **salacious**, licentious, voyeuristic, lascivious, lecherous, lustful, lewd, libidinous, lubricious; depraved, debauched, degenerate, dissolute, dissipated; *rare* concupiscent.

pry ▶ verb *she might start prying into his private affairs | I don't mean to pry* **enquire impertinently into**, investigate impertinently, be inquisitive about, be curious about, poke about/around in, ferret (about/around) in, delve into, eavesdrop on, listen in on; mind someone else's business, be a busybody, tap someone's phone; spy on, interfere in, meddle in, intrude on; scrutinize, probe; *informal* stick/poke one's nose in/into, be nosy (about), nose into, snoop about/around/round in; *Austral./NZ informal* stickybeak.
OPPOSITE mind one's own business.

prying ▶ adjective *their prying neighbours* **inquisitive**, curious, busybody, probing, spying, eavesdropping, impertinent, interfering, meddling, meddlesome, intrusive; *informal* **nosy**, snooping, snoopy; *rare* busy.

psalm ▶ noun **sacred song**, hymn, song of praise, religious song, anthem, carol, chant, plainsong, canticle, antiphon, introit, prayer; psalmody, psalter; *rare* paean, lay, miserere.

pseud ▶ noun *what a pseud to tell her she had a Pre-Raphaelite face!* **pretentious person**, poser, poseur, show-off, sham, fraud; *informal* phoney.

pseudo ▶ adjective *there is something pseudo about him | a pseudo science* **bogus**, sham, phoney, imitation, artificial, mock, ersatz, quasi-, fake, feigned, pretended, false, faux, spurious, counterfeit, fraudulent, deceptive, misleading, assumed, contrived, affected, insincere; *informal* pretend, put-on; *Brit. informal* cod.
OPPOSITE genuine.

pseudonym ▶ noun *Hanbury wrote a novel under the pseudonym of James Aston* **pen-name**, assumed name, incognito, alias, false name, professional name, sobriquet, stage name, nickname; *French* nom de plume, nom de guerre; *rare* allonym, anonym.

psych ▶ verb (*informal*)
□ **psych someone out unsettle**, upset, agitate, disturb, make nervous, put off, put off balance, put someone off their stroke, intimidate; outstare, stare down, outface, stand up to, daunt, cow, deter, awe, disconcert, unnerve, discourage, subdue, abash, dismay; frighten, alarm, scare, terrify, terrorize, browbeat, pressure, pressurize; *N. Amer. informal* buffalo.
□ **psych oneself up** *we had to psych ourselves up for the race* **nerve oneself**, steel oneself, summon/gather/screw up one's courage, prepare, prepare oneself, gear oneself up, arm oneself, brace oneself, get ready, urge oneself on, gird (up) one's loins, get in the mood, get in the right frame of mind.

psyche ▶ noun *Laura saw clearly the effect of beautiful surroundings on the psyche* **soul**, spirit, (inner) self, innermost self, (inner) ego, true being, essential nature, life force, vital force, inner man/woman, persona, identity, personality, individuality, make-up, subconscious, mind, intellect; *technical* anima, pneuma; *Ancient Egypt* ka; *Hinduism* atman.
OPPOSITE body.

psychiatrist ▶ noun **psychoanalyst**, **psychologist**, psychopathologist, psychotherapist, therapist, counsellor; mind doctor, head doctor; *N. Amer.* alienist; *informal* **shrink**, headshrinker, trick cyclist; men in white coats.

psychic ▶ adjective **1** *there may be psychic effects, such as poltergeist activity* **supernatural**, paranormal, other-worldly, supernormal, preternatural, metaphysical, extrasensory, transcendental, magic, magical, mystical, mystic, occult; *rare* necromantic.
2 *you have to tell me—I'm not psychic* **clairvoyant**, telepathic, telekinetic, spiritualistic, with second sight, with a sixth sense.
3 *psychoanalysts argue that motherhood is important for psychic development* **emotional**, spiritual, inner; cognitive, psychological, intellectual, mental, psychiatric, psychogenic; *rare* psychical, mindly, phrenic.
▶ noun *the planchette is used by psychics and mediums* **clairvoyant**, fortune teller, prophet, seer, soothsayer, forecaster of the future, crystal-gazer, astrologer, prognosticator, prophesier, oracle, augur, sibyl, Cassandra, mind-reader, palmist, palm-reader, chiromancer, medium, telepathist, spiritualist, spiritist; *rare* necromancer, chirosophist, palmister.

psychological ▶ adjective **1** *other drugs can do much more psychological damage* **mental**, emotional, intellectual, inner, non-physical, cerebral, brain, rational, cognitive, abstract, conceptual, theoretical; *rare* psychical, mindly, phrenic.
2 *it was concluded that her pain was psychological* **(all) in the mind**, psychosomatic, emotional, irrational, subjective, subconscious, subliminal, unconscious; imaginary, unreal.
OPPOSITE physical.

psychology *See centre pages for list of branches of* **Psychology**
▶ noun **1** *she has a degree in psychology* **study of the mind**, science of the mind, science of the personality, study of the mental processes.
2 *research on the psychology of the road user* **mindset**, mind, mental processes, thought processes, way of thinking, cast of mind, frame of mind, turn of mind, mentality, persona, psyche, (mental) attitude(s), make-up, character, disposition, temperament, temper, behaviour; *informal* what makes someone tick.

psychopath ▶ noun *Rick was a dangerous psychopath who might kill again* **madman/madwoman**, mad person, deranged person, maniac, lunatic, psychotic, sociopath; *informal* loony, fruitcake, nutcase, nut, nutter, psycho, schizo, head case, headbanger, sicko, crank, crackpot; *N. Amer. informal* screwball, crazy, kook, meshuggener, nutso.

psychopathic ▶ adjective *could she have been attacked by some psychopathic killer?* **severely mentally ill**, mentally ill, insane, mad, certifiable, deranged, demented, of unsound mind, out of one's mind, not in one's right mind, not together, crazed, maniac, maniacal, lunatic, unbalanced, unhinged, unstable, disturbed, distracted, stark mad, manic, frenzied, raving, distraught, frantic, hysterical, delirious, mad as a hatter, mad as a March hare; *Latin* non compos mentis; *informal* crazy, mental, off one's head, out of one's head, off one's nut, nuts, nutty, nutty as a fruitcake, off one's rocker, not (quite) right in the head, round the bend, stark staring/raving mad, raving mad, bats, batty, bonkers, cuckoo, loopy, loony, bananas, loco, dippy, screwy, with a screw loose, schizoid, touched, gaga, up the pole, not all there, not right upstairs, away with the fairies, foaming at the mouth; *Brit. informal* barmy, crackers, barking, barking mad, round the twist, off one's trolley, daft, as daft as a brush, not the full shilling; *N. Amer. informal* buggy, off the wall, nutsy, nutso, out of one's tree, meshuga, squirrelly, wacko; *Canadian & Austral./NZ informal* bushed; *NZ informal* porangi; *technical* psychotic, sociopathic, psychopathological.

psychosomatic ▶ adjective *a diagnosis of psychosomatic illness should not be made lightly* **(all) in the mind**, psychological, irrational, stress-related, stress-induced, subjective, subconscious, unconscious.

psychotic ▶ adjective *he was attacked by his psychotic cell mate* **severely mentally ill**, insane, mad, certifiable, deranged, demented, of unsound mind, out of one's mind, not in one's right mind, not together, crazed, lunatic, unbalanced, unhinged, unstable, disturbed, distracted, stark mad, maniac, maniacal, manic, frenzied, raving, distraught, frantic, hysterical, delirious, mad as a hatter, mad as a March hare; Latin non compos mentis; informal crazy, mental, off one's head, out of one's head, off one's nut, nuts, nutty, nutty as a fruitcake, off one's rocker, not (quite) right in the head, round the bend, raving mad, bats, batty, bonkers, cuckoo, loopy, loony, bananas, loco, screwy, with a screw loose, touched, gaga, up the pole, not all there, not right upstairs, away with the fairies, foaming at the mouth; Brit. informal barmy, crackers, barking, barking mad, round the twist, off one's trolley, daft, as daft as a brush, not the full shilling; N. Amer. informal buggy, off the wall, nutsy, nutso, out of one's tree, meshuga, squirrelly, wacko; Canadian & Austral./NZ informal bushed; NZ informal porangi; technical psychopathic, psychopathological, sociopathic.

pub ▶ noun (Brit.) **bar**, wine bar, inn, tavern, hostelry, taproom, roadhouse; Brit. public house, free house, tied house; Scottish howff; N. Amer. cafe; Canadian beer parlour; Austral./NZ hotel; Spanish cantina; German Bierkeller, Weinstube; informal watering hole; Brit. informal local, boozer; N. Amer. informal gin mill; historical alehouse, pot-house, taphouse, beerhouse; N. Amer. historical saloon.

puberty ▶ noun *the onset of puberty may occur as early as eleven or twelve* **adolescence**, pubescence, sexual maturity, growing up; youth, young adulthood, teenage years, teens, the awkward age; rare juvenescence.

public ▶ adjective **1** *the public sector of the economy* **state**, national, federal, government; constitutional, democratic, civic, civil, official, social, municipal, community, local; communal, nationalized; urban, metropolitan.
OPPOSITE private.
2 *there is a great public demand for information on food* **popular**, general, common, communal, collective, shared, joint, universal, widespread.
3 *Stukeley was already a well-known physician and public figure* **prominent**, well known, in the public eye, leading, important, eminent, pre-eminent, recognized, distinguished, notable, noteworthy, noted, outstanding, foremost, of mark; illustrious, celebrated, famous, renowned, acclaimed, famed, honoured, esteemed, respected, well thought of, influential, prestigious.
OPPOSITES obscure, unknown.
4 *plans are afoot to ban smoking in public places* **open (to the public)**, **communal**, not private, not exclusive, accessible to all, available, free, unrestricted, community.
OPPOSITES private, restricted.
5 *he never made his views public* **known**, widely known, overt, plain, obvious, in circulation, published, publicized, exposed.
OPPOSITE secret.
▶ noun **1** *the opinion polls do not reflect the true opinions of the British public* **people**, citizens, subjects, general public, electors, electorate, voters, taxpayers, ratepayers, residents, inhabitants, citizenry, population, populace, community, society, country, nation, world; everyone.
2 *he was adored by his public and his pupils* **audience**, spectators, followers, following, fans, devotees, aficionados, admirers; patrons, clientele, market, consumers, buyers, customers, readers; informal buffs, freaks.
□ **in public publicly**, in full view of people/the public, openly, in the open, for all to see, undisguisedly, blatantly, flagrantly, brazenly, with no attempt at concealment, overtly, boldly, audaciously, unashamedly, shamelessly, unabashed, wantonly, immodestly; Latin coram populo.
OPPOSITE secretly.

WORD LINKS
fear of public places **agoraphobia**

publication ▶ noun **1** *he is the author of numerous publications* **book**, volume, hardback, paperback, title, work, tome, opus, treatise, manual, register, almanac, yearbook, compendium; newspaper, paper, magazine, periodical, part-work, newsletter, gazette, bulletin, journal, report, daily, weekly, fortnightly, monthly, quarterly, annual, comic, organ, booklet, brochure, catalogue, magalogue; informal glossy, rag, mag, 'zine, fanzine.
2 *she was in England for the publication of her new book* **issuing**, announcement, publishing, printing, notification, reporting, declaration, communication, proclamation, broadcasting, publicizing, advertising, distribution, spreading, dissemination, promulgation, issuance, appearance, emergence.

publicity ▶ noun **1** *the blaze of publicity surrounding him vanished overnight* **public attention**, public interest, public notice, media attention/interest, exposure, glare, limelight, fuss, commotion; fame, renown, celebrity, stardom, notability, notoriety; informal to-do.
2 *clever publicity has created a wave of enthusiasm* **promotion**, advertising, propaganda; boost, push, fanfare; informal hype, ballyhoo, puff, puffery, build-up, razzmatazz; plug.

publicize ▶ verb **1** *the king's itinerary was normally publicized in advance* **make known**, make public, bring to public notice/attention, announce, report, communicate, impart, disclose, reveal, divulge, leak, publish, broadcast, transmit, issue, put out, distribute, spread, unfold, disseminate, circulate, air, blazon, herald, proclaim, promulgate.
OPPOSITES conceal, suppress.
2 *they promised to publicize the book in China* **advertise**, promote, build up, talk up, push, beat the drum for, boost, merchandise; informal hype, plug, puff (up).

public-spirited ▶ adjective *the debris was left for public-spirited citizens to remove* **community-minded**, socially concerned, philanthropic, charitable, helpful to others; **altruistic**, humanitarian, generous, unselfish, selfless.

publish ▶ verb **1** *we want to publish good-quality literary works* **issue**, bring out, produce, print.
2 *it would be useful to publish his comments* **make known**, make public, publicize, bring to public notice/attention, announce, report, declare, post, communicate, impart, broadcast, transmit, issue, put out, distribute, spread, promulgate, propagandize, disseminate, circulate, air, blazon, herald, proclaim; disclose, reveal, divulge, leak.

pucker ▶ verb *I find a zigzag stitch tends to pucker the fabric* **wrinkle**, crinkle, cockle, crumple, rumple, ruck up, scrunch up, corrugate, ruffle, screw up, crease, shrivel, furrow, crimp, gather, draw, tuck, pleat; Brit. rare ruckle.
▶ noun *cotton thread can produce a pucker in the sewing with shrinkage* **wrinkle**, fold, crinkle, crumple, corrugation, furrow, line, gather, tuck, pleat.

puckish ▶ adjective *he had very a puckish sense of humour* **mischievous**, naughty, impish, elfin, roguish, playful, sly, arch, waggish, teasing, prankish, pixieish.

pudding *See centre pages for list of* **Cakes, Puddings, and Desserts**
▶ noun *Pete had given up on the stew and was eating the pudding* **dessert**, sweet, sweet course/dish, second course, last course; Brit. informal afters, pud.

puddle ▶ noun *puddles of water* **pool**, spill, splash; literary plash.

puerile ▶ adjective *it was the cause of many a puerile pub argument* **childish**, immature, infantile, juvenile, adolescent, babyish; silly, inane, fatuous, jejune, asinine, foolish, petty.
OPPOSITES mature; sensible.

puff ▶ noun **1** *a puff of wind* **gust**, blast, rush, squall, gale, whiff, breath, flurry, draught, waft, breeze, blow; literary zephyr.
2 *he took a puff at his cigar* **pull**; informal drag.
3 (informal) *the publishers expected a puff in our literary column* **favourable mention**, piece of publicity, favourable review, advertisement, promotion, recommendation, commendation, mention, good word, commercial; informal push, ad, boost; Brit. informal advert.
4 (informal) *extravagant statements are accepted as part of a salesman's puff* **publicity**, advertising, promotion, marketing, propaganda, push, puffery, build-up, boosting; patter, line, pitch, sales talk, presentation; informal **spiel**, hype, ballyhoo.
▶ verb **1** *he reached the top of the stairs, puffing a little* **breathe heavily**, breathe loudly/rapidly/quickly, pant, puff and pant, puff and blow, blow; **gasp**, fight for breath, catch one's breath.
2 *Hauser* ***puffed at*** *his cigarette* **smoke**, draw on, pull on, drag on, suck at/on.
3 (informal) *the royal family may not be used to puff commercial products* **advertise**, promote, give publicity to, publicize, push, recommend, commend, endorse, put in a good word for, beat the drum for; informal give a puff to, hype (up), plug; rare merchandise.
□ **puff out/up** *if she went for a walk her ankles puffed up* **bulge**, swell (out), stick out, distend, belly (out), balloon (up/out), expand, inflate, enlarge; rare tumefy, intumesce,
□ **puff something out/up** *he puffed out his cheeks* **distend**, stick out, cause to swell, cause to bulge, belly (out), balloon (up/out), expand, dilate, inflate, blow up, pump up, enlarge, bloat.

puffed ▶ adjective **1** *I'll be too puffed to dance properly* **out of breath**, breathless, short of breath, puffed out, panting, puffing, huffing and puffing, puffing and blowing, gasping, gasping for breath, wheezing, wheezy, winded, short-winded; informal out of puff.
2 *he was just another* ***puffed-up*** *tinpot dictator* **self-important**, conceited, arrogant, bumptious, self-assertive, full of oneself, pompous, overbearing, (self-)opinionated, cocky, presumptuous, forward, imperious, domineering, magisterial, pontifical, sententious, grandiose, affected, stiff, vain, haughty, proud, egotistic; supercilious, condescending, patronizing; informal snooty, uppity, uppish.

puffy ▶ adjective *her eyes were puffy from crying* **swollen**, puffed up, distended, enlarged, full, inflated, dilated, bloated, engorged, bulging, baggy; rare tumid, turgescent, tumescent, tumefied, oedematous, ventricose.

pugilism ▶ noun **boxing**, prizefighting, bare-knuckle boxing/fighting, fisticuffs, sparring; the ring; archaic the noble art/science (of self-defence).

pugilist ▶ noun **boxer**, fighter, prizefighter, sparring partner; informal

P

bruiser, pug; *rare* ringster.

pugnacious ▶ adjective *the bouncer that night was a pugnacious 42-year-old from East London* **combative**, **aggressive**, antagonistic, belligerent, bellicose, warlike, quarrelsome, argumentative, contentious, disputatious, defiant, hostile, threatening, truculent; irascible, fiery, hot-tempered, ill-tempered, bad-tempered, rough.
OPPOSITES peaceable; friendly.

puke ▶ verb *he sank to his knees and puked again* **vomit**, throw up, retch; cough up, bring up, regurgitate; heave, gag; *Brit.* be sick; *N. Amer.* get sick; *informal* chunder, chuck up, hurl, spew, do the technicolor yawn, keck; *Brit. informal* honk, sick up; *Scottish informal* boke; *N. Amer. informal* spit up, barf, upchuck, toss one's cookies.

pukka ▶ adjective **1** *it wouldn't be considered the pukka thing to do* **respectable**, decorous, proper, genteel, formal, polite, conventional, right, correct, accepted, presentable, decent, smart; *French* comme il faut; *Brit. informal* posh, top-notch, tip-top.
OPPOSITE improper.
2 *their old van was up against pukka racing cars* **genuine**, authentic, proper, actual, real, true, bona fide, veritable, original, not copied, legitimate; *informal* kosher, the real McCoy.
OPPOSITE imitation.

pull ▶ verb **1** *he pulled a small plastic box towards him* **tug**, haul, drag, draw, trail, tow, heave, lug, strain at, jerk, lever, prise, wrench, wrest, twist; *N. Amer.* pry; *informal* yank.
OPPOSITE push.
2 *I'll let you pull the next bad tooth* **pull out**, draw out, take out, extract, remove, root out.
3 *he still feels pain in his back where he has pulled a muscle* **strain**, sprain, turn, wrench, rick, stretch, tear; dislocate, put out of joint, damage.
4 *before World War II, race days here pulled big crowds* **attract**, draw, pull in, bring in, lure, charm, engage, enchant, captivate, bewitch, seduce, catch the eye of, entice, tempt, beckon, interest, fascinate.
OPPOSITE repel.
□ **pull something apart** *it is wise to pull the gearbox apart only when absolutely necessary* **dismantle**, disassemble, take/pull to pieces, take/pull to bits, take apart, strip down; demolish, destroy, break up.
OPPOSITES build, assemble.
□ **pull back** *the army was forced to pull back behind the canal* **withdraw**, retreat, draw back, fall back, retire, disengage, pull out, back off, give way/ground; flee, take flight, turn tail, beat a (hasty) retreat.
OPPOSITE advance.
□ **pull something down** *several old buildings were pulled down* **demolish**, knock down, take down, tear down, dismantle, raze, raze to the ground, level, flatten, bulldoze, destroy, lay waste.
OPPOSITES build, erect.
□ **pull in** *a police car pulled in behind* **stop**, halt, come to a stop/halt, park, arrive, pull over, draw in, draw up.
□ **pull someone/something in 1** *comedies continued to pull in the biggest audiences* **attract**, draw, pull, bring in, lure, charm, engage, enchant, captivate, bewitch, seduce, catch the eye of, entice, tempt, beckon, interest, fascinate.
2 (*informal*) *the police pulled him in for questioning* **arrest**, apprehend, detain, take into custody, take prisoner, seize, capture, catch, take in; *informal* collar, nab, nick, pinch, pick up, run in, bust, nail, do, feel someone's collar.
OPPOSITE release.
3 (*informal*) *the company has pulled in £70m from disposals* **earn**, be paid, make, get, bring in, rake in, clear, collect, net, gross, pocket, take home.
□ **pull someone's leg tease**, fool, play a trick on, make fun of, joke with, rag, chaff, twit, pull the wool over someone's eyes; *informal* kid, bamboozle, lead up the garden path, take for a ride, rib, take the mickey out of, get/take a rise out of; *Brit. informal* wind up, have on.
□ **pull something off** *they pulled off a daring crime* **achieve**, fulfil, succeed in, accomplish, bring off, bring about, carry out, carry off, execute, perform, perpetrate, discharge, complete, conduct, negotiate, clinch, work out, fix, effect, establish, engineer.
□ **pull out 1** *one of their star players has pulled out with stomach trouble* **withdraw**, resign, leave, retire, step down, get out, quit, back out, bow out.
2 *the French pulled out of the agreement* **retreat from**, leave, quit, abandon, give up, stop participating in, get out of, back out of, bow out of, renege on.
OPPOSITES join, engage in.
□ **pull something out** *Goetz pulled out a gun and fired* **take out**, draw, pull, draw out, bring out, get out, withdraw, fish out, produce.
□ **pull over** *I decided to pull over on to the hard shoulder* **stop**, halt, come to a stop/halt, pull in, pull off the road, draw in, park, arrive, draw up.
□ **pull through** *she has serious injuries, but we are all praying for her to pull through* **get better**, get well again, improve, recover, rally, survive, come through, recuperate; get over something; be all right.
□ **pull something to pieces 1** *can I trust you not to pull my radio to pieces?* **dismantle**, disassemble, take to pieces, take/pull to bits, take/pull apart, strip down, demolish, destroy, break up.
2 *we should look at those draft guidelines and be prepared to pull them to pieces* **criticize**, attack, censure, condemn, denigrate, find fault with, pillory, maul, lambaste, flay, savage; *informal* knock, slam, pan, bash, take apart, crucify, hammer, lay into, roast, skewer; *Brit. informal* slate, rubbish, slag off; *N. Amer. informal* pummel, cut something up; *Austral./NZ informal* bag, monster; *archaic* slash; *rare* excoriate.
□ **pull oneself together regain one's composure**, regain one's self-control, regain control of one's emotions, recover, get a grip/hold on oneself, get over it, become one's old self; *informal* snap out of it, get one's act together, buck up.
□ **pull up** *a van pulled up with six men inside* **stop**, draw up, come to a stop/halt, halt, come to a standstill, brake, park; arrive.
□ **pull someone up** *he grinned unabashedly when his mother pulled me up* **reprimand**, rebuke, scold, chide, chastise, upbraid, berate, castigate, reprove, reproach, censure, take to task, tear into, admonish, lecture, lambaste, read someone the Riot Act, haul over the coals; *informal* tell off, give someone a telling-off, bawl out, dress down, give someone hell, give someone a talking-to, give someone a dressing-down, give someone an earful, give someone a piece of one's mind, blow up, give someone a roasting, give someone a rocket, give someone a rollicking, give someone a row; *Brit. informal* tick off, carpet, give someone a mouthful; *N. Amer. informal* chew out; *Austral. informal* monster; *rare* reprehend, excoriate.
▶ noun **1** *give the chain one sharp downward pull* **tug**, haul, jerk, heave; *informal* yank.
2 *she took a huge pull on her beer* **gulp**, draught, drink, swallow, mouthful, sip, sup; *informal* swill, swig, slug.
3 *he took a long pull on the cigarette* **puff**; *informal* drag.
4 *she felt the pull of the tranquillity of the place* **attraction**, lure, allurement, enticement, drawing power, draw, magnetism, influence, enchantment, magnet, temptation, invitation, fascination, appeal.
5 *he could get you a job–he has a lot of pull* **influence**, sway, strength, power, authority, say, prestige, standing, weight, leverage, muscle, teeth; *informal* clout, beef.

pullover ▶ noun. *See centre pages for list of* **Pullovers**

pulp ▶ noun **1** *he kneaded the fungus into a pulp* **mash**, mush, purée, cream, pressé, pap, slop, paste, slush, mulch, swill, slurry, semi-liquid, semi-fluid, mess; baby food; *informal* gloop, goo, gook; *N. Amer. informal* glop; *technical* triturate; *rare* pomace.
2 *monkeys suck the sweet pulp off cocoa seeds* **flesh**, soft part, fleshy part, marrow, meat.
▶ verb *then pulp the gooseberries through a sieve* **mash**, purée, cream, crush, press, smash, liquidize, liquefy, sieve, shred, squash, pound, beat, macerate, mill, grind, mince, soften, mangle; *technical* comminute, triturate; *archaic* levigate, bray, powderize.
▶ adjective *perhaps pulp fiction is your métier rather than poetry?* **trashy**, rubbishy, cheap, sensational, lurid, tasteless, kitschy; *informal* tacky.

pulpit ▶ noun **stand**, lectern, platform, podium, stage, staging, dais, rostrum; soapbox, stump; box, dock; *Islam* minbar; *rare* ambo, tribune.

pulpy ▶ adjective *cook the rhubarb slowly until it is soft and pulpy* **mushy**, soft, semi-liquid, pappy, slushy, sloppy, spongy, squashy, squelchy, squishy; succulent, juicy; *informal* gooey, gloopy; *Brit. informal* squidgy; *rare* pulpous.

pulsate ▶ verb *the flesh of the clam pulsates gently as water is pumped through it* **palpitate**, pulse, throb, vibrate, pump, undulate, surge, heave, rise and fall, ebb and flow; beat, pound, thud, thump, hammer, drum, thrum, oscillate, reverberate; tick, flutter, pitter-patter, go pit-a-pat, quiver; *rare* quop.

pulse[1] ▶ noun **1** *she could feel the pulse at the base of her neck* **heartbeat**, pulsation, pulsing, throb, throbbing, vibration, pounding, thudding, thud, thumping, thump, drumming.
2 *the pulse of the train wheels* **rhythm**, beat, rhythmical flow/pattern, measure, metre, tempo, cadence.
3 *a dolphin emits short pulses of ultrasound* **burst**, blast, spurt, eruption, impulse, surge; *informal* splurt.
▶ verb *loud music pulsing throughout the building* **throb**, pulsate, vibrate, palpitate, beat, pound, thud, thump, hammer, drum, thrum, oscillate, reverberate; pitter-patter, go pit-a-pat, quiver; *rare* quop.

WORD LINKS

related prefix	**sphygmo-**
study of the pulse	**sphygmology**
instrument for recording the pulse	**sphygmograph**

pulse[2] ▶ noun. *See centre pages for list of* **Beans, Pulses, and Peas**

pulverize ▶ verb **1** *mustard seeds may be pulverized into flour* **grind**, crush, pound, crumble, powder, turn to dust; mill, crunch, squash, press, pulp, mash, sieve, mince, mangle, chew, shred, macerate; *technical* comminute, triturate; *archaic* levigate, bray, powderize.
2 (*informal*) *he could have pulverized the opposition* **defeat utterly**, annihilate, beat hollow, trounce, rout, crush, smash, break, overwhelm, vanquish; *informal* hammer, clobber, thrash, whip, lick, paste, pound, crucify, demolish, destroy, drub, tank, take to the cleaners, wipe the floor with, make mincemeat of, blow out of the water, murder, slaughter, massacre,

P

flatten, turn inside out; *Brit. informal* stuff, marmalize; *N. Amer. informal* blow out, cream, skunk.

pummel ▶ verb *he felt like a boxer who had been pummelled mercilessly* **batter**, pound, rain blows on, belabour, drub, hammer; punch, beat, strike, hit, thump, thrash, bang, welt, crack, whack, thwack; *informal* bash, clobber, wallop, beat the living daylights out of, give someone a (good) hiding/beating/drubbing, belt, tan, biff, bop, lay into, pitch into, lace into, let someone have it, knock into the middle of next week, sock, lam, whomp; *Brit. informal* stick one on, slosh; *N. Amer. informal* boff, bust, slug, light into, whale; *Austral./NZ informal* dong, quilt; *literary* smite, swinge.

pump ▶ verb **1** *an engine pumped air out of the tube* **force**, drive, push, send, transport, raise, inject; suck, draw, tap, milk, siphon, withdraw, expel, extract, bleed, drain.
2 *I fetched the bike and* ***pumped up*** *the back tyre* **inflate**, blow up; swell, aerate, fill up, enlarge, distend, expand, dilate, bloat, puff up; *rare* tumefy.
OPPOSITE deflate.
3 *one man was still alive, with blood pumping from his leg* **spurt**, spout, squirt, jet, surge, spew, gush, stream, flow, flood, pour, spill, rush, well, cascade, run, course, discharge; *Brit. informal* sloosh; *rare* disembogue.
4 (*informal*) *I started pumping them for information* **ask**, question (persistently/intensely), quiz, interrogate, probe, put questions to, sound out, cross-examine, catechize; *informal* grill, put the screws on, give someone the third degree, put someone through the third degree, put someone through the wringer/mangle, worm something out of someone.

pun ▶ noun **play on words**, wordplay, double entendre, double meaning, innuendo, witticism, quip; *French* bon mot, jeu de mots; *rare* paronomasia, equivoque, amphibology, pivot, calembour, carriwitchet, clench, clinch, conundrum, nick, pundigrion, whim, quibble.

punch[1] ▶ verb *Jimmy punched him in the face* **hit**, strike, knock, thump, thwack, jab, cuff, clip, smash, slam, welt; batter, buffet, thrash, pound, pummel, rain blows on, drub, box someone's ears; *informal* sock, slug, biff, bop, wallop, clobber, bash, whack, clout, crown, poke, lick, let someone have it, knock into the middle of next week, lam, whomp, deck, floor; *Brit. informal* stick one on, dot, slosh; *N. Amer. informal* boff, bust, whale; *Austral./NZ informal* dong, quilt, king-hit; *literary* smite, swinge.
▶ noun **1** *he landed a punch on Lorrimer's nose* **blow**, hit, knock, thump, thwack, box, jab, fist, cuff, clip, smash, slam, welt, straight, uppercut, hook, body blow; *informal* sock, slug, biff, bop, wallop, bash, whack, clout, poke, lick, belt; *N. Amer. informal* boff, bust, whale; *Austral./NZ informal* dong, king-hit, stoush; *dated* buffet; *archaic* plug.
2 *strong and full of punch, this album is one of their best* **vigour**, vigorousness, liveliness, vivacity, vitality, force, forcefulness, drive, strength, zest, animation, verve, panache, enthusiasm, impact, bite, kick, effectiveness, influence; *informal* oomph, pizzazz, zing, zip.

punch[2] ▶ verb *Flora handed him her ticket, which he punched* **make a hole in**, put/punch holes in, perforate, puncture, pierce, prick, hole, riddle, spike, skewer, spit, stick, pin, needle; *rare* pink, transpierce.

punch-up ▶ noun *Mark quit the band after a punch-up at a Beverly Hills party* **fight**, scuffle, fracas, brawl, struggle, tussle, fist fight, fisticuffs, melee, scrimmage, free-for-all, free fight, affray, fray, riot, skirmish, exchange, clash, encounter; quarrel, commotion, disorder, tumult, breach of the peace, disturbance; *Irish, N. Amer., & Austral.* donnybrook; *informal* scrap, set-to, ruction, shindy, shindig, stand-up, dust-up, tangle, tiff; *informal, dated* mill; *Brit. informal* bust-up, ding-dong; *Scottish informal* stooshie, swedge; *N. Amer. informal* rough house, rumble; *Austral./NZ informal* stoush; *archaic* broil; *rare* bagarre.

punchy ▶ adjective *passionate, punchy acting* **forceful**, incisive, strong, powerful, vigorous, vivacious, zestful, animated, dynamic, enthusiastic, effective, impressive, striking, telling, influential, cogent, compelling, convincing, persuasive, eloquent, dramatic, passionate, graphic, vivid, moving, potent, authoritative, great, forcible, aggressive, irresistible, effectual; *informal* zappy, in-your-face.
OPPOSITES feeble, ineffectual.

punctilio ▶ noun **1** *a relaxation of the extreme punctilio of earlier generations was now to be seen* **conformity**, scrupulousness, meticulousness, conscientiousness, punctiliousness, exactitude, precision, strictness, nicety; **etiquette**, protocol, ceremony, conventions, formalities, customs, rules of conduct, procedure, ritual, code of behaviour, accepted behaviour, propriety, proprieties, one's Ps and Qs, decorum, manners, courtesies, civilities, conventionalities, good form, the done thing, the thing to do; *French* politesse.
OPPOSITE informality.
2 *both counsel and judges follow the punctilios of court procedure* **detail**, finer point, nicety, particular, subtlety, nuance, refinement, distinction.

punctilious ▶ adjective *his punctilious implementation of orders impressed the King* **meticulous**, conscientious, careful, diligent, attentive, ultra-careful, scrupulous, painstaking, exact, precise, accurate, correct, thorough, studious, rigorous, mathematical, detailed, perfectionist, methodical, particular, religious, strict; **fussy**, fastidious, hair-splitting, finicky, finical, demanding, exacting, pedantic; *informal* nit-picking, pernickety; *N. Amer. informal* persnickety; *archaic* nice, overnice, laborious.
OPPOSITES careless, easy-going, slapdash.

punctual ▶ adjective *Mrs Marsh liked her guests to be punctual* **on time**, prompt, to/on schedule, in good time, in time, when expected, timely, well timed; *informal* on the dot; *Brit. informal* bang/spot on time.
OPPOSITES late, early.

punctually ▶ adverb *please arrive punctually | Edward arrived there punctually at nine* **promptly, on time**, at the proper time, at the right time, dead on time; prompt, sharp, exactly, precisely, to the minute, to the second, dead; *Brit. informal* bang on time, spot on time, bang on, spot on.

punctuate ▶ verb **1** *pupils should be shown how to set out and punctuate direct speech* **add punctuation to**, put punctuation marks in, dot; *archaic* point, apostrophize, accentuate.
2 *slides were used to punctuate the talk* **break up**, interrupt, intersperse, pepper, sprinkle, scatter, strew, dot.

punctuation *See centre pages for list of* **Punctuation Marks**
▶ noun **punctuation marks**, points.

puncture ▶ noun **1** *the back offside tyre developed a puncture* **hole**, perforation, prick, rupture, cut, nick, slit, leak.
2 *my bike has got a puncture* **flat tyre**; *informal* flat.
▶ verb **1** *he deliberately punctured another child's bicycle tyre* **make a hole in**, pierce, penetrate, rupture, perforate, riddle, stab, cut, nick, slit, prick, spike, stick, impale, transfix, bore (through), drill (through), lance, tap; decompress, depressurize, deflate.
2 *she knows how to puncture the wordiness of his speeches* **put an end to**, cut short, reverse, prick, deflate, flatten, reduce.

pundit ▶ noun *a leading pundit predicts a further interest-rate cut this year* **expert**, authority, adviser, member of a think tank, member of a policy unit, specialist, consultant, doyen, master, mentor, guru, sage, savant; *informal* buff, whizz, boffin.

pungent ▶ adjective **1** *the pungent smell of the horses* **strong**, powerful, pervasive, penetrating, suffocating, stifling; **sharp**, acrid, acid, sour, biting, stinging, burning, smarting, irritating; nauseating, nauseous, sickly, offensive, astringent, bitter, fetid, cloying; *literary* mephitic.
OPPOSITES bland, mild.
2 *the marinade is more pungent than soy sauce* **sour**, acid, biting, bitter, tart, vinegary, tangy; highly flavoured, aromatic, spicy, spiced, piquant, peppery, hot, fiery.
OPPOSITES bland, mild.
3 *pungent remarks* **caustic**, biting, trenchant, cutting, acerbic, sardonic, sarcastic, scathing, acrimonious, pointed, barbed, acid, sharp, keen, tart, stinging, astringent, incisive, devastating, piercing, penetrating, rapier-like, razor-edged, critical, bitter, polemic, virulent, vitriolic, venomous, waspish, corrosive, mordant, stringent; *rare* acidulous, mordacious.
OPPOSITES bland, mild.

punish ▶ verb **1** *some parents punish their children harder than they should* **penalize, discipline**, mete out punishment to, bring someone to book, teach someone a lesson, make an example of; tan/whip someone's hide; *informal* get, scalp, murder, wallop, thump, give it to someone, throw the book at, come down on (like a ton of bricks), have someone's guts for garters, skin alive; *Brit. informal* drop on, give someone what for; *N. Amer. informal* tear down; *dated* chastise; *archaic* chasten, recompense, visit.
OPPOSITES pardon, exonerate.
2 *Boro's in-form strikers will be quick to punish any mistakes by United's defence* **exploit**, take advantage of, put to advantage, use, make use of, turn to (one's) account, profit by/from, capitalize on, cash in on, trade on; *informal* walk all over.
3 *a new rise in prescription charges would punish the poor* **treat harshly/unfairly**, be unfair to, unfairly disadvantage, put at an unfair disadvantage, put in an unfavourable position, handicap, do a disservice to, make someone suffer, hurt, wrong, ill-use, maltreat.

punishable ▶ adjective *money-laundering is a punishable offence* **illegal**, unlawful, illegitimate, criminal, felonious, actionable, prosecutable, indictable, penal, blameworthy, dishonest, fraudulent, unauthorized, unsanctioned, outlawed, banned, forbidden, barred, prohibited, interdicted, proscribed.

punishing ▶ adjective *she went on a punishing schedule of visits to the US* **arduous**, demanding, taxing, onerous, burdensome, strenuous, rigorous, stressful, trying, severe, cruel, stiff, heavy, hard, difficult, uphill, tough, exhausting, fatiguing, wearying, enervating, debilitating, prostrating, sapping, wearing, draining, tiring, gruelling, grinding, back-breaking, crippling, relentless, unsparing, inexorable; *informal* killing, murderous.
OPPOSITES easy, effortless.

punishment *See centre pages for lists of* **Punishments** **Torture Instruments**
▶ noun **1** *judicial ideology stresses the punishment of the guilty* **penalizing**, punishing, disciplining; retribution, damnation; *dated* chastising, chastisement.
2 *the teacher may impose reasonable punishments* **penalty**, discipline, correction, retribution, penance, sentence, reward, one's just deserts, medicine, the price, the rap, requital, vengeance, justice, judgement, sanction; *informal* comeuppance; *Brit., Military* jankers; *dated* chastisement.

3 *both boxers gave and took punishment* **battering**, thrashing, beating, thumping, pounding, pummelling, hammering, buffeting, drubbing; *informal* walloping, bashing, roughing up, hiding, belting.
4 *domestic ovens are not constructed to take continual punishment* **maltreatment**, mistreatment, ill-treatment, abuse, ill-use, rough handling, mishandling, manhandling; injury, damage, harm.

WORD LINKS
relating to punishment **punitive, penal**
study of punishment **penology**
fear of punishment **poinephobia**

punitive ▶ **adjective 1** *truancy rates would decline if tougher punitive measures against parents were taken* **penal**, disciplinary, corrective, correctional, retributive; in retaliation, in reprisal; *rare* penitentiary, punitory, castigatory.
2 *the government plans to announce punitive taxes on imports* **harsh**, severe, stiff, austere, cruel, savage, stringent, burdensome, demanding, draconian, drastic, swingeing, crushing, crippling; high, sky-high, inflated, exorbitant, extortionate, excessive, outrageous, inordinate, iniquitous, immoderate, unreasonable.

punter ▶ **noun** (*Brit. informal*) **1** *each punter has a 1:39 chance of a win* **gambler**, backer, staker, speculator; *N. Amer.* bettor; *informal* plunger; *N. Amer. informal* high roller; *Austral./NZ informal* spieler.
2 *you have to get the punters to pack in* **customer**, client, patron; buyer, purchaser, shopper, consumer, user, visitor, guest; member of the audience/crowd; (**punters**) clientele, patronage, audience, following, trade, business, market; *Brit. informal* bums on seats.
3 *imagine her pimp sending her a punter at this time of day* **customer**, client, kerb-crawler; *informal* john, trick, score.

puny ▶ **adjective 1** *we grew up puny, with bad chests* **undersized**, underdeveloped, undernourished, underfed, stunted, slight, small, little, diminutive, dwarfish, pygmy; **weak**, feeble, weakly, sickly, delicate, frail, fragile; *informal* weedy, pint-sized.
OPPOSITES strong, sturdy.
2 *the men were jeering at the villagers' puny efforts to save their homes* **pitiful**, pitiable, inadequate, negligible, insufficient, scant, scanty, derisory, miserable, sorry, wretched, meagre, paltry, trifling, trivial, insignificant, inconsequential, petty; *informal* pathetic, measly, piddling, piffling, mingy, poxy, dinky; *rare* exiguous.
OPPOSITES significant, sizeable, substantial.

pupil ▶ **noun 1** *they are former pupils of the school* **student**, schoolchild, schoolboy, schoolgirl, scholar.
2 *will you take me on as your pupil?* **disciple**, follower, learner, student, protégé, apprentice, trainee, probationer, novice, recruit, beginner, tyro, neophyte.

puppet ▶ **noun 1** *a puppet show* **marionette**, glove puppet, hand puppet, finger puppet, rod puppet, shadow puppet.
2 *the US believed Ho Chi Minh to be a puppet of the Chinese* **pawn**, tool, instrument, cat's paw, poodle, creature, hostage, counter, cog, dupe; mouthpiece, minion, figurehead; *informal* flunkey, lackey, stooge.

purchase ▶ **verb** *the school decided to purchase the software* **buy**, acquire, obtain, pick up, snap up, take, secure, procure, come by, pay for, shop for, invest in, put money into; *informal* get hold of, get one's hands on, get one's mitts on, score.
OPPOSITES sell, market.
▶ **noun 1** *if you are not delighted with your purchase, we will give you a full refund* **acquisition**, investment, buy, order, deal, bargain, property, asset, possession, holding; shopping, goods.
OPPOSITE sale.
2 *his hand fought for purchase on the smooth wall* **grip**, firm contact, attachment, hold, foothold, footing, toehold, fingerhold, anchorage, support, grasp; resistance, friction, leverage, advantage.

purchaser ▶ **noun buyer**, shopper, customer, consumer, client, patron, investor, user; clientele, patronage, public, trade, market; *Law* vendee; *rare* emptor.

pure ▶ **adjective 1** *every coin was of pure gold* **unmixed**, unalloyed, unadulterated, unblended, uncontaminated, sterling, solid, refined, one hundred per cent, 100%; clarified, clear, filtered, distilled, processed, neat, straight, undiluted; flawless, perfect, genuine, authentic, real, actual, bona fide, veritable, pukka, true.
OPPOSITES impure, adulterated.
2 *they have their health because the air is so pure* **clean**, clear, fresh, crisp, refreshing, sparkling, unpolluted, untainted, unadulterated, uncontaminated; wholesome, natural, healthy, health-giving, healthful, good for you; salubrious, sanitary, uninfected, disinfected, germ-free, sterile, sterilized, pasteurized, aseptic.
OPPOSITES impure, dirty, polluted.
3 *she did so want to be pure in body and mind* **virtuous**, moral, ethical, good, righteous, angelic, saintly, pious, honourable, reputable, wholesome, clean, honest, upright, upstanding, exemplary, above reproach, irreproachable, innocent; chaste, pure as the driven snow, virginal, maidenly; decent, worthy, noble, blameless, guiltless, sinless, stainless, spotless, unsullied, unblemished, unspoilt, unaffected, uncorrupted, undefiled; *informal* squeaky clean; *Christianity* immaculate, impeccable.
OPPOSITE immoral.
4 *a system that emphasized practical rather than pure research* **theoretical**, abstract, conceptual, academic, hypothetical, philosophical, speculative, conjectural, non-practical, non-technical; *informal* blue-sky.
OPPOSITES applied, practical.
5 *three hours of pure magic—a show not to be missed* **sheer**, utter, simple, absolute, downright, out-and-out, rank, complete, thorough, total, perfect, consummate, unmitigated, unqualified, palpable, patent; *archaic* arrant.

pure-bred ▶ **adjective** *only pure-bred dogs can take part in shows* **pedigree**, thoroughbred, full, full-bred, pure-blooded, blooded, pedigreed, pure, genuine.
OPPOSITES hybrid, mixed, mongrel.

purely ▶ **adverb** *he seemed to regard the exchange purely as a joke* **entirely**, completely, absolutely, totally, wholly, exclusively, uniquely, solely, only, simply, just, merely; no more than.

purgative *See centre pages for list of* **Laxatives**
▶ **adjective** *I took some purgative medicine* **laxative**, aperient, lenitive, cathartic, evacuant, purging; *archaic* eccoprotic.
▶ **noun** *orris root was once used medicinally as a purgative* **laxative**, enema, aperient, lenitive, cathartic, evacuant; *dated* purge; *archaic* eccoprotic.

purgatory ▶ **noun** *the pre-med year was a necessary term of purgatory* **torment**, torture, misery, suffering, affliction, anguish, agony, wretchedness, woe, tribulation, hell, hell on earth; an ordeal, a nightmare, a hellhole, an abyss; trials and tribulations.
OPPOSITES paradise, bliss.

purge ▶ **verb 1** *the experience has purged them of the desire to doubt* **cleanse**, clear, purify, wash, shrive, absolve, free someone from; make someone pure; *rare* lustrate.
2 *the party was purged of the so-called 'capitalist roaders'* **rid**, clear, cleanse, empty, strip, scour, void; *rare* depurate.
3 *human rights violators would be purged from the army* **remove**, get rid of, clear out, sweep out, expel, eject, exclude, evict, dismiss, sack, oust, axe, depose, eradicate, root out, weed out, scour.
▶ **noun** *the purge of the dissidents from the party* **removal**, expulsion, ejection, exclusion, eviction, clearance, clear-out, discharge, dismissal, sacking, ousting, deposition, eradication, rooting out, weeding out; *rare* deposal.

purify ▶ **verb 1** *trees help purify the air* **clean**, make pure, refine, cleanse, decontaminate; filter, sieve, strain, sift, clarify, clear, freshen, deodorize; boil, distil, sanitize, disinfect, sterilize, pasteurize, fumigate; *technical* autoclave, liquate, rectify; *rare* depollute, filtrate.
OPPOSITES pollute, contaminate.
2 *for months he lived there purifying himself* **purge**, cleanse, clear, free, unburden, deliver, relieve; redeem, shrive, exorcize, sanctify; *rare* lustrate.
OPPOSITES corrupt, defile.

WORD LINKS
relating to ceremonial purification **lustral**

purist ▶ **noun** *the purist will point out that every aircraft accident results from human error of some kind* **pedant**, precisionist, perfectionist, formalist, literalist, stickler, traditionalist, doctrinaire, quibbler, hair-splitter, dogmatist, casuist, sophist, fault-finder, caviller, carper, pettifogger; *informal* nit-picker; *rare* precisian, Dryasdust.

puritan ▶ **noun** *today's puritans impede frank talk about sexuality* **moralist**, pietist, prude, prig, moral zealot/fanatic, killjoy, Mrs Grundy, Grundy, old maid, schoolmarm, Victorian, priggish person, ascetic; *informal* goody-goody, Goody Two-Shoes, holy Joe, holy Willie, Miss Prim; *N. Amer. informal* bluenose.

puritanical ▶ **adjective** *the region's farmers are insular and puritanical* **moralistic**, pietistic, strait-laced, tight-laced, stuffy, starchy, prissy, prudish, puritan, prim, priggish, Victorian, schoolmarmish, schoolmistressy, old-maidish, narrow-minded, censorious, sententious; austere, severe, spartan, ascetic, hair-shirt, abstemious; *informal* goody-goody; *rare* Grundyish.
OPPOSITES permissive, broad-minded.

purity ▶ **noun 1** *the purity of our tap water* **cleanness**, clearness, clarity, freshness, freedom from adulteration/contamination, lack of pollution, untaintedness; wholesomeness, naturalness, healthiness, healthfulness, salubrity; sterility, salubriousness.
OPPOSITES impurity, pollution.
2 *perhaps in a foul world these men were seeking purity* **virtue**, virtuousness, lack of corruption, morality, goodness, righteousness, rectitude, saintliness, piety, honour, honesty, integrity, uprightness, decency, worthiness, nobility of soul/spirit, ethicality; blamelessness, guiltlessness, innocence, chastity, sinlessness, stainlessness, spotlessness, irreproachableness, immaculateness, impeccability.
OPPOSITE immorality.

purloin ▶ **verb** *they crash cars through storefronts to purloin merchandise* **steal**, thieve, rob, take, snatch, pilfer, loot, abscond with, carry off,

P

appropriate; *informal* walk off/away with, run away/off with, swipe, nab, rip off, lift, 'liberate', 'borrow', filch, snaffle, snitch; *Brit. informal* pinch, half-inch, nick, whip, knock off, nobble, bone; *N. Amer. informal* heist, glom; *Austral. informal* snavel; *W. Indian informal* tief; *archaic* crib, hook.

purport ▶ verb (stress on the second syllable) *this work purports to be authoritative* **claim**, lay claim, profess, pretend; set oneself up (as), appear, seem; allege/maintain/assert/proclaim/imply that one is, be apparently, be ostensibly, pose as, impersonate, pass oneself off as, be disguised as, masquerade as, feign the identity of, pass for, represent oneself as; *rare* personate.

▶ noun (stress on the first syllable) **1** *the purport of his remarks is already familiar* **gist**, substance, drift, implication, intention, meaning, significance, signification, sense, essence, import, tenor, thrust, message, spirit.
2 *the purport of the attack was to prove him wrong* **intention**, purpose, intent, object, objective, aim, goal, target, end, plan, scheme, design, idea, ambition, desire, wish, hope.

purpose ▶ noun **1** *the main purpose of his visit* **motive**, motivation, grounds, cause, impetus, occasion, reason, point, basis, justification.
2 *the trade unions insisted that their purpose was not to subvert the market economy* **intention**, aim, object, objective, goal, end, plan, scheme, target; ambition, aspiration, desire, wish, hope.
3 *I cannot see any purpose in just saying no* **advantage**, benefit, good, use, usefulness, value, merit, worth, gain, profit, avail, result, outcome, effect; *informal* mileage, percentage; *archaic* behoof, boot.
4 *the original purpose of this large porch was to shelter pilgrims* **function**, role; *French* raison d'être.
5 *Middlesbrough had started the game with more purpose and menace* **determination**, resoluteness, resolution, resolve, firmness (of purpose), steadfastness, backbone, drive, push, thrust, enthusiasm, ambition, initiative, enterprise, motivation, single-mindedness, commitment, conviction, dedication; *informal* get-up-and-go.

□ **on purpose** *her mother made a terrible clatter with the plates on purpose* **deliberately**, intentionally, purposely, by design, wilfully, calculatedly, premeditatedly, wittingly, knowingly, consciously; in cold blood, of one's own volition; **expressly**, explicitly, specifically, especially, specially.

▶ verb (*formal*) *they purposed to reach the summit that night* **intend**, mean, aim, plan, design, have the intention, have in mind, have a mind; **decide**, resolve, determine, propose, have plans, set out, aspire, desire, want, wish, expect, hope; set one's sights on, have in view, contemplate, think of.

purposeful ▶ adjective *I sense a more purposeful attitude towards clients* **determined**, resolute, resolved, firm, steadfast, single-minded; enthusiastic, ambitious, enterprising, motivated, committed, dedicated, persistent, persevering, tenacious, dogged, unfaltering, unwavering, unshakeable.
OPPOSITES aimless, irresolute.

purposely ▶ adverb *Whitlock purposely fired wide | had Amanda done that purposely to horrify them?* **deliberately**, intentionally, on purpose, by design, wilfully, calculatedly, premeditatedly, wittingly, knowingly, consciously, in cold blood, of one's own volition; **expressly**, explicitly, specifically, especially, specially, just; *Law* with malice aforethought; *rare* purposefully.
OPPOSITE accidentally.

purse ▶ noun **1** *Mother opened her handbag and fished for her purse* **wallet**, pouch, money bag; *N. Amer.* change purse, pocketbook.
2 (*N. Amer.*) *the many things that go into a woman's purse* **handbag**, bag, clutch bag, shoulder bag, evening bag, pochette; *N. Amer.* pocketbook; *historical* reticule, scrip.
3 *the cost of running the schools is borne by the public purse* **fund**, funds, resources, money, kitty, pool, coffers, bank, treasury, exchequer, finances, wealth, reserves, cash, capital, assets; *N. Amer.* fisc.
4 *the fight in Berlin will net him a $75,000 purse* **prize**, award, reward; prize money, winnings, stake(s).

▶ verb *the doctor pursed his lips in thought* **press together**, compress, contract, tighten, pucker, screw up, wrinkle, pout.

pursuance ▶ noun **1** *he has been arrested in pursuance of section 7 of this Act* **execution**, discharge, implementation, performance, carrying out, conducting, conduct, effecting, doing, accomplishment, achievement, completion, fulfilment, dispatch, pursuing, prosecution, enforcement, following.
2 *their pursuance of militant expansion* **seeking of**, search for, pursuit of; quest for, hunt for, mission to acquire.

pursue ▶ verb **1** *I pursued him down the garden* **go after**, run after, follow, chase, give chase to; hunt, stalk, track, trail, trace, shadow, dog, hound, course; *informal* tail.
OPPOSITES avoid, flee.
2 *it would be unprofitable to pursue the goal of political union* **strive for**, push towards, work towards, try for, seek, search for, quest (after), be intent on, aim at/for, have as a goal, have as an objective, aspire to.
OPPOSITE eschew.
3 *he was desperate to impress a woman he had been pursuing for weeks* **woo**, court, pay court to, pay suit to, chase after, chase, run after; *informal* make up to; *dated* make love to, romance, set one's cap at, seek the hand of, pay addresses to.
4 *she also pursued a political career* **engage in**, be engaged in, be occupied in, participate in, take part in, work at, practise, follow, prosecute, conduct, ply, apply oneself to, go in for, take up.
OPPOSITE shun.
5 *the appointee will be encouraged to pursue his or her own research* **conduct**, undertake, follow, carry on, devote oneself to, go on with, proceed with, go ahead with, keep/carry on with, continue with, continue, take further, prosecute, persist in, stick with/at.
6 *he decided not to pursue the matter* **investigate**, research, inquire into, look into, examine, study, review, check, scrutinize, analyse, delve into, dig into, probe.
OPPOSITE give up.

pursuit ▶ noun **1** *the police are even-handed in their pursuit of terrorists* **chasing**, pursuing, stalking, tracking, trailing, shadowing, dogging, hounding; chase after, hunt for; *informal* tailing.
2 *the organization is devoted to the pursuit of profit* **striving towards**, push towards, aspiration for, quest after/for, search for; aim of, goal of, objective of, dream of.
3 *redirect your energies to a worthwhile pursuit* **activity**, leisure activity, leisure pursuit, leisure interest, hobby, pastime, diversion, avocation, recreation, relaxation, divertissement, sideline, entertainment, amusement, sport, game; **occupation**, trade, calling, vocation, craft, business, line, work, job, employment.

purvey ▶ verb **1** *he had acquired a massive fortune purveying a health drink* **sell**, supply, provide, furnish, cater, retail, deal in, trade, carry, handle, stock, offer, auction, have for sale, put on the market, peddle, hawk, tout, traffic in; *informal* flog.
2 *the majority of newspapers purvey typically right-wing attitudes* **pass on**, transmit, broadcast, disseminate, spread, put round, put about, circulate, communicate, make known, publicize, publish; provide, supply, furnish, make available, peddle.

purveyor ▶ noun *a local purveyor of gourmet sandwiches* **seller**, vendor, trader, retailer, supplier, provider, stockist, tout, trafficker; *dated* pedlar, hawker.

pus ▶ noun *the boil may be lanced to drain the pus* **matter**, suppuration, discharge, secretion; *rare* sanies.

WORD LINKS
relating to pus **purulent**
related prefix **pyo- (e.g. *pyogenic*)**

push ▶ verb **1** *she tried to push him away* **shove**, thrust, propel, impel; send, press, drive, plunge, stick, force, shoot, ram, bump, knock, strike, hit, jolt, butt, prod, poke, nudge, elbow, shoulder; bulldoze, sweep, jostle, bundle, hustle, hurry, rush, manhandle.
OPPOSITE pull.
2 *he tried to push his way into the flat* **force (one's way)**, shove, thrust, squeeze, jostle, elbow, shoulder; thread, wind, work, inch.
3 *he managed to push a silent panic button* **press (down)**, push down, depress, exert pressure on, bear down on, hold down, squeeze; **operate**, activate, actuate.
4 *don't push her to join in if she doesn't want to* **urge**, press, pressure, put pressure on, pressurize, force, drive, impel, coerce, nag; lean on, prevail on; dragoon into, steamroller into, browbeat into, use strong-arm tactics on; *informal* put the heat on, put the screws on, twist someone's arm, railroad into, bulldoze into.
5 *the manufacturers of each fuel push their own products* **advertise**, publicize, promote, give publicity to, beat/bang the drum for, popularize; sell, market, merchandise; *informal* plug, give a plug to, hype, hype up, give a puff to, puff, puff up, boost, flog; *N. Amer. informal* ballyhoo, flack, huckster.

□ **push someone around bully**, domineer, boss about/around, ride roughshod over, trample on, tread on, bulldoze, abuse, mistreat, maltreat, kick around/about, browbeat, lean on, tyrannize, intimidate, threaten, torment, terrorize, victimize, pick on.

□ **push for** *the trade unions will be likely to push for wage increases* **demand**, insist on, clamour for, ask/call for, request, press for, campaign for, work for, lobby for, speak for, drum up support for, sponsor, urge, promote, advocate, recommend, champion, espouse.

□ **push off** (*informal*) *push off, will you—I'm busy* **go away**, depart, leave, take oneself off, take off, get out, get out of my sight; go, go your way, get going, get moving, be off, take your leave, decamp, absent yourself; be off with you, shoo; *informal* hit the road, fly, skedaddle, split, vamoose, scat, scram, make yourself scarce, be on your way, run along, beat it, get, get lost, shove off, buzz off, clear off, skip off, pop off, go (and) jump in the lake; on your bike, go and chase yourself; *Brit. informal* get stuffed, sling your hook, hop it, bog off, naff off; *N. Amer. informal* bug off, light out, haul off, haul ass, take a powder, hit the trail, take a hike; *Austral./NZ informal* rack off, nick off; *S. African informal* voetsak, hamba; *vulgar slang* bugger off, piss off, fuck off; *Brit. vulgar slang* sod off; *literary* begone, avaunt.
OPPOSITES stay, remain.

□ **push on** *I decided to push on towards the coast* **continue one's journey**, continue on one's way, carry on, advance, press on, progress, make progress, proceed, go on, make headway, gain ground, push forward, go/forge ahead; resume one's journey, start off again.

▶ **noun 1** *I felt a push in the back* **shove**, thrust, ram, bump, knock, hit, jolt, butt, prod, poke, elbow, nudge, shoulder, jostle.

2 *the enemy's eastward push had overrun Dutch positions* **advance**, drive, thrust, charge, attack, assault, onslaught, onrush, offensive, sortie, foray, raid, sally, invasion, incursion, blitz, campaign; *archaic* onset.

□ **at a push** (*Brit. informal*) *at a push, you could use a disk editor to recover files* **if necessary**, in case of necessity, if need be, if needs must, if forced, if all else fails, in an emergency.

pushing ▶ **adjective** *I don't want to seem pushing or jealous* **assertive**, thrusting, pushy, ambitious, aggressive, forceful, forward, obtrusive, bold, brash, bumptious, arrogant, officious, bossy, presumptuous, full of oneself, self-assertive, over-assertive, overbearing, domineering, confident, overconfident, cocksure; loud, obnoxious, offensive; *informal* cocky; *rare* pushful.

OPPOSITE retiring.

pushover ▶ **noun 1** *if the panel withdrew its report, word would soon get about that it was a pushover* **weakling**, not a force to be reckoned with, feeble opponent, unworthy opponent, man of straw; easy meat, easy game; *informal* soft/easy touch, easy mark.

2 *this course is no pushover, even for experts* **easy task**, easy job, five-finger exercise, gift, walkover, sinecure, gravy train; child's play, nothing; *informal* doddle, piece of cake, picnic, money for old rope, money for jam, cinch, breeze, sitter, kids' stuff, cushy job/number, doss, cakewalk; *N. Amer. informal* duck soup, snap; *Austral./NZ informal* bludge, snack; *S. African informal* a piece of old tackie; *Brit. vulgar slang* a piece of piss; *dated* snip.

pushy ▶ **adjective** *behind every successful child there is a pushy parent* **assertive**, thrusting, pushing, ambitious, aggressive, forceful, forward, obtrusive, bold, brash, bumptious, arrogant, officious, bossy, presumptuous, full of oneself, self-assertive, overbearing, domineering, confident, overconfident, cocksure; loud, obnoxious, offensive; *informal* cocky; *rare* pushful.

OPPOSITE retiring.

pusillanimous ▶ **adjective** *the President's increasingly pusillanimous stance on social issues* **cowardly**, timorous, timid, fearful, faint-hearted, lily-livered, chicken-hearted, pigeon-hearted, spineless, craven, base, shrinking, trembling, quaking, cowering, weak-kneed; *informal* wimpish, sissy, yellow, yellow-bellied, chicken, gutless; *archaic* poor-spirited, recreant.

OPPOSITES brave, fearless, plucky.

pussyfoot ▶ **verb 1** *you can't pussyfoot around with children's welfare* **equivocate**, be evasive, be non-committal, evade/dodge/sidestep/fudge the issue, prevaricate, quibble, parry questions, hedge, fence, vacillate, shuffle about, beat about the bush; *Brit.* hum and haw; *informal* duck the question, sit on the fence, shilly-shally, blow hot and cold; *rare* tergiversate.

2 *I had to pussyfoot over the crunchy gravel* **creep**, move stealthily, tiptoe, pad, soft-shoe, steal, sneak, nose, sidle, stalk, prowl, slink, skulk, tread warily.

pustule ▶ **noun pimple**, spot, blackhead, boil, swelling, eruption, carbuncle, wen, cyst, abscess, blister; *informal* whitehead, zit; *Scottish informal* plook; *technical* comedo; *rare* papule, bleb, blain, whelk.

put ▶ **verb 1** *she put the parcel on a chest in the hall* **place**, set, put down, set down, lay, lay down, deposit, situate, position, settle; leave, stow, prop, lean, plant, pose; *informal* stick, dump, bung, park, plonk, pop; *N. Amer. informal* plunk; *rare* posit.

2 *Preston didn't see that he could be* **put in** *either category* **assign to**, consign to, allocate to, place in; classify with, categorize with, bracket with.

3 *don't try and* **put** *the blame* **on** *me* **lay**, pin, place, impose, fix; attribute to, impute to, attach to, assign to, allocate to, ascribe to.

4 *the proposals* **put to** *the Finance Committee on 9 December* **submit**, present, tender, offer, proffer, advance, suggest, propose; set before, lay before.

5 *to put it bluntly, he gets on my nerves* **express**, word, phrase, frame, formulate, render, convey, couch; state, say, utter, voice, speak, articulate, pronounce.

6 *legal experts put the cost of bringing the case to court at more than £8,000* **estimate**, calculate, reckon, gauge, assess, evaluate, value, judge, measure, compute, establish, fix, set, guess; *informal* guesstimate.

□ **put something about** *the rumour had been deliberately put about by the authorities* **spread (about/around)**, circulate, make public, make known, disseminate, broadcast, publicize, pass on, propagate, announce, give out, bandy about; *literary* bruit abroad.

□ **put about** *the ship put about* **turn round**, change direction, come/go about, change course, alter course.

□ **put something across/over** *the party needs to put across its message more efficiently and effectively* **communicate**, get across/over, convey, explain, make clear, make understood, express, spell out, clarify; bring something home to someone, get through to someone.

□ **put something aside 1** *we've got a little bit put aside in the bank* **save**, put/lay by, put away, set/lay aside, put to one side, deposit, reserve, keep in reserve, keep, store, stockpile, hoard, stow away, cache; *informal* salt away, squirrel away, stash away.

2 *politicians put aside their differences in pursuit of a peaceful political solution* **disregard**, set aside, ignore, pay no heed to, forget, discount, shrug off, bury, consign to oblivion.

□ **put someone away** (*informal*) **1** *they've got enough on him to put him away for life* **put in prison**, put behind bars, imprison, jail, lock up/away, shut up/away, incarcerate, confine; *informal* cage; *Brit. informal* bang up, send down; *N. Amer. informal* send up, jug.

2 *you're trying to convince me I'm senile—you want me put away!* **commit**, certify, section, hospitalize, institutionalize.

□ **put something away 1** *I put away some money every week* **save**, put aside, put/lay by, set/lay aside, put to one side, reserve, keep in reserve, deposit, keep, store, stockpile, hoard, stow away, cache; *informal* salt away, squirrel away, stash away.

2 *she doesn't seem to put anything away—there are clothes everywhere* **replace**, put back, return to its place, tidy away, tidy up, clear away.

3 (*informal*) *did you see how much food she put away?* **eat**, consume, devour, down, gobble up, bolt, wolf down, guzzle; **drink**, gulp down; *informal* polish off, tuck away, demolish, get outside of, pack away, scoff (down), shovel down, pig out on, sink, knock back, get one's laughing gear round; *Brit. informal* shift, gollop, bevvy; *N. Amer. informal* scarf (down/up), snarf (down/up), inhale; *rare* ingurgitate, bib.

□ **put something back 1** *he put the books back carefully* **replace**, return to its place, restore, put away, tidy away.

2 *they have put back the film's release date to September* **postpone**, defer, delay, put off, adjourn, hold over, reschedule, table; *N. Amer.* put over, lay something on the table.

□ **put someone down 1** (*informal*) *he put me down in front of my own staff* **criticize**, belittle, disparage, deprecate, denigrate, take down a peg or two, slight, humiliate, show up, mortify, shame, crush, squash, deflate; *informal* have a go at, cut down to size, settle someone's hash; *N. Amer. informal* make someone eat crow.

2 *I put him down as shy* **consider to be**, judge to be, reckon to be, take to be; regard, categorize, mark down, have down, take for.

□ **put something down 1** *he put his ideas down on paper* **write down**, put in writing, note down, make a note of, jot down, take down, set down, put in black and white, list, record, register, log, enter.

2 *security forces put down the rebellion* **suppress**, put an end to, crush, quash, quell, overthrow, stamp out, squash, repress, check, subdue.

3 *the horse's condition deteriorated and he had to be put down* **destroy**, put to sleep, put out of its misery, put to death, kill; *N. Amer.* euthanize.

4 *I can't imagine what came over me—put it down to the heat* **attribute**, ascribe, set down, chalk up, impute, assign; blame on.

□ **put something forward** *recently, another explanation has been put forward | he put himself forward for the post* **propose**, offer, advance, submit, present, tender, move, introduce, proffer, set forth, table; suggest, nominate, put up, name, recommend.

□ **put something in** *Dr Kailey put in a claim for compensation* **submit**, present, make, file, enter, lodge.

□ **put in for** *some people put in for voluntary redundancy* **apply for**, put in an application for, request, seek, ask for, try for.

□ **put someone off 1** *the smell put Lisa off* **deter**, discourage, dishearten, demoralize, dissuade, daunt, unnerve, intimidate, scare off; offend, repel, disgust, revolt, repulse, sicken, nauseate; *informal* turn off.

2 *the players weren't put off by the disturbance* **distract**, put someone off their stroke, disturb someone's concentration, cause someone to lose their concentration, divert someone's attention, sidetrack.

□ **put something off** *it's very easy to put off difficult decisions* **postpone**, defer, delay, put back, adjourn, hold over, reschedule, shelve, table; *N. Amer.* put over, lay on the table, take a rain check on; *informal* put on ice, put on the back burner.

□ **put it on** *he laughed but Olivia thought he was putting it on* **pretend**, put on an act, play-act, make believe, fake it, go through the motions.

□ **put something on 1** *she put on jeans and a black T-shirt* **get dressed in**, dress in, don, clothe oneself in, pull on, climb into, fling on, throw on, pour oneself into, slip into, change into, rig oneself out in; *informal* tog oneself up/out in, doll oneself up in.

2 *I put the landing light on* **switch on**, turn on, flick on, power up; activate.

3 *the obvious solution was for the company to put on an additional train* **provide**, lay on, supply, furnish, make available, run; *informal* sort out, fix up.

4 *the museum is putting on an exhibition of Monet's paintings* **organize**, stage, mount, present, produce; perform.

5 *Adam put on an American accent* **feign**, fake, sham, simulate, affect, assume.

6 *he put a fiver on Thetford Queen and it won* **bet**, gamble, stake, wager, place, lay, risk, chance, hazard.

□ **put one over on** (*informal*) *they've been trying to put one over on us and they won't get away with it* **deceive**, trick, hoodwink, mislead, lead astray, delude, fool, take in, dupe, outwit, steal a march on, throw off the scent, put on the wrong track; *informal* pull a fast one on, pull the wool over someone's eyes, take for a ride, con, bamboozle, lead up the garden path, slip something over on, sell a pup to; *N. Amer. informal* give someone a

P

bum steer; *Austral. informal* pull a swifty on.

□ **put someone out 1** *Maria was put out by the slur on her character* **annoy**, anger, irritate, offend, affront, displease, exasperate, infuriate, provoke, irk, vex, pique, nettle, gall, upset; *informal* rile, miff, peeve, aggravate, hack off; *Brit. informal* nark; *vulgar slang* piss off.
2 *I'm sure she wouldn't want to put you out, especially when you're feeling unwell* **inconvenience**, trouble, bother, impose on, cause inconvenience to, create difficulties for, put someone to any trouble, disoblige; *informal* put someone on the spot; *rare* discommode, incommode.

□ **put something out 1** *firemen put out the blaze* **extinguish**, quench, douse, stamp out, smother, beat out; blow out, snuff out; *Scottish* dout.
2 *he put out a press release explaining his decision* **issue**, publish, release, bring out, broadcast, circulate, make known, make public, publicize, post.

□ **put someone up 1** *we're going to put him up for a few days* **give accommodation to**, provide with accommodation, accommodate, house, take in, give a roof to, give a bed to, lodge, quarter, billet.
2 *the SDLP are expected to put up a candidate* **nominate**, propose, put forward, recommend.

□ **put something up 1** *the building was put up about 100 years ago* **build**, construct, erect, raise, set up.
2 *she put up a poster advertising the concert* **display**, pin up, stick up, hang up, nail up, post.
3 *they asked local architects to put up alternative schemes* **propose**, put forward, present, submit, recommend, suggest, tender.
4 *unless the economy recovers, they will be forced to put up taxes* **increase**, raise, lift; *informal* jack up, hike, bump up.
5 *union leaders put up 90% of the funding* **provide**, supply, furnish, give, come up with, contribute, donate, pledge, pay, advance; *informal* fork out, cough up, shell out, dish out; *N. Amer. informal* ante up, pony up.

□ **put upon** (*informal*) *his eagerness to please ensured that he was put upon* **take advantage of**, impose on, take for granted, exploit, use, misuse; *informal* walk all over.

□ **put someone up to** (*informal*) *Is this some kind of seduction scene? Did Shirley put you up to it?* **persuade to**, encourage to, urge to, spur on to, egg on to, incite to, goad to.

□ **put up with** *Harriet told him she was not prepared to put up with such behaviour* **tolerate**, take, stand (for), accept, stomach, swallow, endure, bear, brook, support, submit to, take something lying down; *informal* stick, abide, lump it; *Brit. informal* wear, be doing with; *archaic* suffer.

putative ▶ adjective *the putative father of her child* **supposed**, assumed, presumed; acknowledged, accepted, recognized; commonly believed, commonly regarded, presumptive, alleged, reputed, reported, rumoured; *rare* reputative.

put-down ▶ noun *he was still smarting from the put-down* **snub**, **disparaging remark**, insult, slight, affront, rebuff, sneer, disparagement, humiliation, slap in the face, barb, jibe, criticism; *informal* dig, brush-off.

putrefy ▶ verb **decay**, rot, decompose, go bad, go off, perish, spoil, deteriorate, fester, moulder; gangrene, mortify; *rare* necrose, sphacelate.

putrescent ▶ adjective **decaying**, rotting, putrefying, decomposing, festering, going bad, going off; *rare* putrefactive, putrefacient.

putrid ▶ adjective *putrid meat | a putrid smell* **decomposing**, decomposed, decaying, decayed, rotting, rotten, bad, off, putrefied, putrescent, rancid, mouldy, spoilt; foul, fetid, stinking, rank; *rare* putrefacient, putrefactive, olid.

puzzle ▶ verb **1** *Isabelle's apparent change of heart puzzled me* **perplex**, **confuse**, bewilder, bemuse, baffle, mystify, confound, nonplus, throw, set someone thinking; *informal* flummox, discombobulate, faze, stump, beat, make someone scratch their head, fog; *archaic* wilder, gravel, maze, pose; *rare* obfuscate.
2 *she lay awake for some time, **puzzling over** the problem* **think hard about**, give much thought to, rack one's brains about, mull over, muse over, ponder, brood about, contemplate, meditate on, consider, reflect on, deliberate on, chew over, turn over in one's mind, cogitate on, wonder about, ask oneself about; *archaic* pore on.
3 *Amanda was trying to **puzzle out** what her father had meant* **work out**, understand, comprehend, think out, think through, sort out, reason out, solve, make sense of, get to the bottom of, make head or tail of, unravel, untangle, decipher, decode, find the key to, piece together; *informal* figure out, suss out, crack.
▶ noun *the meaning of the poem has always been a puzzle* **enigma**, mystery, paradox, conundrum, poser, riddle, question, question mark, problem; *informal* stumper.

CHOOSE THE RIGHT WORD

puzzle, perplex, mystify, baffle

These four verbs describe different degrees of puzzlement. All are commonly used as participial adjectives (*puzzling*, *puzzled*, etc.).

- **Puzzle** is used of relatively mild problems that typically do not cause serious worries or are likely to be resolved. It is a fairly neutral word (*one remark he made puzzled me | that was the most puzzling aspect of the whole affair*).
- **Perplex** is a more literary word than *puzzle* and can be used of more difficult or intractable problems (*Ruth was perplexed by her husband's moodiness | he was in a very perplexing situation*).
- **Mystify** describes even greater puzzlement, with the suggestion that the cause is likely to remain a mystery (*the disease that is mystifying doctors and spreading rapidly | the figure melted into thin air, leaving the foreman completely mystified*).
- **Baffle** is the most emphatic word, suggesting extreme puzzlement (*skincare products bearing baffling scientific claims*). It is also beloved of journalists (*police are baffled after a gang stole 150 T-shirts*).

puzzled ▶ adjective *Fiona looked puzzled* **perplexed**, **confused**, bewildered, bemused, baffled, mystified, confounded, nonplussed, at a loss, at sea; *informal* flummoxed, discombobulated, stumped, fazed, clueless, without a clue; *Canadian & Austral./NZ informal* bushed; *archaic* wildered, gravelled, mazed.

puzzling ▶ adjective *his explanation was rather puzzling* **difficult**/**hard to understand**, baffling, perplexing, mystifying, bewildering, confusing, complicated, unclear, beyond one, above one's head, mysterious, enigmatic, ambiguous, paradoxical, obscure, abstruse, unfathomable, inexplicable, incomprehensible, impenetrable, cryptic, oracular; *archaic* wildering.
OPPOSITES clear, straightforward; comprehensible.

pygmy ▶ noun **1 very small person**, person of restricted growth, midget, dwarf, Tom Thumb, runt; *informal* shrimp, pint-sized person; *rare* homunculus, manikin, Lilliputian, fingerling, thumbling.
2 *he saw his brother as a poetic giant among literary pygmies* **insignificant person**, lightweight, mediocrity, nobody, gnat, insect, cipher; (**pygmies**) small fry; *informal* pipsqueak, squirt; *Brit. informal* nerk, johnny, squit, whippersnapper; *Scottish informal* nyaff; *N. Amer. informal* bozo, picayune, pisher, snip; *archaic, informal* dandiprat; *N. Amer. vulgar slang* pissant.
OPPOSITE giant.

pyromaniac ▶ noun **arsonist**, incendiary, firebomber; *Brit.* fire-raiser; *informal* firebug, pyro; *N. Amer. informal* torch.

quack ▸ noun **1** *the man is a quack selling fake medicines* **swindler**, charlatan, mountebank, confidence trickster, fraud, fraudster, impostor, trickster, racketeer, hoaxer, sharper, rogue, villain, scoundrel; *informal* con man, shark, flimflammer, sharp; *Brit. informal* twister; *N. Amer. informal* grifter, bunco artist, chiseller; *Austral. informal* shicer, magsman, illywhacker; *dated* confidence man; *rare* defalcator.
2 *get the quack to examine you* **doctor**, physician, medical practitioner, medical man/woman/person; *Navy* surgeon; *informal* doc, medic, medico; *archaic* leech, sawbones.
▸ adjective *a quack doctor | a quack cancer therapy* **bogus**, false, fraudulent, unqualified, not genuine; spurious, sham, imitation, mock, fake, feigned, simulated, dummy, make-believe, so-called, forged, counterfeit, pseudo, pretended; *informal* phoney, pretend; *Brit. informal* cod.

quadrangle ▸ noun **courtyard**, quad, court, cloister, precinct, square, plaza, piazza, enclosure, close.

quaff ▸ verb *Suzy quaffed glass after glass of white wine | miners quaffed from decorated pottery beakers* **drink**, swallow, gulp (down), guzzle, slurp, attack, down, drink up/down, force down, get down, finish off, polish off, drain, empty, imbibe, have, take, partake of, ingest, consume, sup, sip, lap; take alcohol, indulge, tipple, carouse, overdrink, overindulge, tope; *informal* booze, sink, kill, glug, swig, swill, slug, hit, knock back, dispose of, toss off, get one's laughing gear round; take a drop, wet one's whistle, hit the bottle, take to the bottle, crack a bottle, drink like a fish, get tanked up; *Brit. informal* get outside (of), shift, murder, neck, bevvy; *N. Amer. informal* bend one's elbow, chug, snarf (down), scarf (down); *archaic* bib, sot.

quagmire ▸ noun **1** *the rains arrived and the area was transformed into a red quagmire* **swamp**, morass, bog, peat bog, marsh, mire, quag, marshland, fen, slough, quicksand; *Scottish & N. English* moss; *Irish* corcass; *N. Amer.* bayou, pocosin, moor; *archaic* marish, carr.
2 *the case has become a judicial quagmire* **muddle**, mix-up, mess, predicament, unfortunate/difficult/awkward situation, mare's nest, quandary, entanglement, tangle, jumble, imbroglio; trouble, confusion, difficulty; corner, tight corner/spot; *informal* sticky situation, pickle, hole, stew, dilemma, fix, bind, jam, scrape, kettle of fish, how-do-you-do, hot/deep water; *W. Indian* comess.

quail ▸ verb *his supporters quailed at the size of the army ranged against them* **cower**, cringe, waver, falter, get cold feet; flinch, shrink, recoil, start, shy (away), pull back, back away, draw back; shudder, shiver, tremble, shake, quake, blench, blanch.

quaint ▸ adjective **1** *narrow streets lead to a quaint bridge over the river* **picturesque**, charming, sweet, attractive, pleasantly old-fashioned, old-fashioned, old-world, toytown; *N. Amer.* cunning; *Brit. informal* twee, arty-crafty; *pseudo-archaic* olde, olde worlde.
OPPOSITES modern; ugly.
2 *Polybius comments on the quaint customs of the Romans* **unusual**, different, out of the ordinary, out of the way, unfamiliar, curious, eccentric, quirky, bizarre, zany, whimsical, fanciful, idiosyncratic, unconventional, outlandish, offbeat, off-centre; *French* outré.
OPPOSITES normal, ordinary.

quake ▸ verb **1** *the ground quaked as they walked on it* **shake**, tremble, quiver, shiver, shudder, sway, rock, wobble, move, heave, convulse.
2 *we quaked every time we saw police or soldiers* **tremble**, shake, shake with fear, shake like a leaf, shudder, shiver; blench, blanch, flinch, shrink, recoil, start, shy (away), pull back, back away, draw back, cower, cringe, waver, falter, get cold feet.

CHOOSE THE RIGHT WORD

quake, shake, tremble, shiver, quiver
See SHAKE.

qualification ▸ noun **1** *a professional teaching qualification | qualification for the pension was to be determined by a committee* **certificate**, diploma, degree, licence, document, warrant; **eligibility**, acceptability, adequacy, suitableness, suitability, preparedness, fitness; proficiency, skill, ability, quality, skilfulness, adeptness, capability, capacity, aptitude.
2 *I have difficulty in accepting that submission without some qualification* **modification**, limitation, restriction, reservation, stipulation, allowance, adaptation, alteration, adjustment, amendment, revision, refinement, moderation, tempering, softening, lessening, reduction, mitigation; condition, proviso, provision, caveat, rider.

qualified ▸ adjective **1** *he was a fully qualified engineer* **certified**, certificated, chartered, licensed, professional; **trained**, fit, equipped, prepared, competent, knowledgeable, accomplished, proficient, skilled, skilful, adept, practised, experienced, expert, seasoned, capable, able.
2 *the report received qualified approval from the colleges* **limited**, conditional, restricted, bounded, contingent, circumscribed, reserved, guarded, cautious, hesitant, tentative, equivocal; modified, adapted, amended, adjusted, moderated, refined, tempered, lessened, reduced.

qualify ▸ verb **1** *you may qualify for free prescriptions* **be eligible**, meet the requirements; be entitled to, be allowed, be permitted.
2 *ninety per cent of new arrivals are unlikely to qualify as refugees* **count**, be counted, be considered, be designated, be characterizable, be eligible; meet the requirement of.
3 *despite her disability she managed to qualify as a solicitor* **gain qualifications**, gain certification, be certified, be licensed, be authorized; pass, graduate, make the grade, succeed, get through, come through with flying colours, pass muster.
4 *the students had taken a course which qualified them to teach children* **authorize**, allow, permit, license, empower, fit, equip, prepare, arm, make ready, train, educate, coach, teach.
OPPOSITE disqualify.
5 *the authors later qualified their findings* **modify**, limit, make conditional, restrict, add reservations to, add to, make additions to, add a rider to; moderate, temper, soften, tone down, modulate, mitigate, reduce, lessen, decrease, diminish, lower, abate.

quality ▸ noun **1** *the system will compress digital TV signals while retaining most of the original quality | a poor quality of life* **standard**, grade, class, classification, calibre, status, condition, character, nature, constitution, make-up, form, rank, worth, value, level; sort, type, kind, variety.
2 *work of such quality remains a rarity* **excellence**, superiority, merit, worth, value, virtue, calibre, eminence, pre-eminence, supremacy, transcendence, distinction, refinement, incomparability, account; talent, skill, skilfulness, virtuosity, expertise, brilliance, craftsmanship, flair, finish, mastery.
3 *they have many good qualities* **feature**, trait, attribute, characteristic, point, aspect, facet, side, streak, property, peculiarity, idiosyncrasy, quirk; mark, badge, stamp, hallmark, trademark.

qualm ▸ noun **1** *I have no qualms about going to Japan* **misgiving**, doubt, reservation, second thought, worry, concern, anxiety; (**qualms**) hesitation, hesitance, hesitancy, demur, reluctance, disinclination, apprehension, trepidation, disquiet, disquietude, unease, uneasiness.
OPPOSITE confidence.
2 *the terrorists showed no qualms about shooting down the crowds* **scruple**, pang of conscience, twinge of conscience/remorse; (**qualms**) compunction, remorse.

quandary ▸ noun *George was in a quandary* **dilemma**, plight, predicament, state of uncertainty, state of perplexity, unfortunate situation, difficult situation, awkward situation; trouble, muddle, mix-up, mare's nest, mess, confusion, difficulty, impasse, stalemate; *Brit.* cleft stick; *informal* sticky situation, pickle, hole, stew, fix, bind, jam.

quantity ▸ noun **1** *the quantity of food collected | the quantity of animals killed was quite dramatic* **amount**, **number**, total, aggregate, sum, quota, group,

size, mass, weight, volume, bulk, load, consignment, expanse, extent, length, area; quantum, proportion, portion, part; dose, dosage.
2 *police divers recovered a quantity of ammunition | quantities of empty drinks cans have been found in the building* **an amount**, **a number**, a good number/few, a lot, a large amount, a good/great deal; quite a number, scores, many, considerable amounts, plenty; several, numerous, countless, innumerable, ample, copious, abundant, plentiful, considerable, substantial; *informal* a pile, piles, oodles, tons, lots, loads, heaps, masses, stacks, scads, bags, more … than one can shake a stick at; *Brit. informal* lashings, a shedload, shedloads; *N. Amer. informal* gobs; *vulgar slang* a shitload.

quark ▶ noun. *See centre pages for list of flavours and colours of* **Quarks and Antiquarks**

quarrel ▶ noun *there was a quarrel about how much my father was paid* **argument**, row, fight, disagreement, difference of opinion, dissension, falling-out; **dispute**, disputation, contention, squabble, contretemps, clash, altercation, exchange, brawl, tussle, disturbance, conflict, affray, brouhaha, commotion, uproar, tumult, war of words, shouting match, fracas, feud; wrangle, tangle, misunderstanding; *Irish, N. Amer., & Austral.* donnybrook; *informal* tiff, set-to, shindig, shindy, stand-up, run-in, spat, scrap, dust-up, ruction; *Brit. informal* barney, bunfight, ding-dong, bust-up, ruck, slanging match; *Scottish informal* rammy; *N. Amer. informal* hassle; *archaic* broil, miff; *French archaic* tracasserie(s).
OPPOSITES reconciliation, agreement.
▶ verb *I should be sorry to quarrel over it* **argue**, have a row/fight, row, fight, disagree, fail to agree, differ, be at odds, have a misunderstanding, be at variance, fall out; dispute, bicker, squabble, brawl, chop logic; wrangle, spar, bandy words, cross swords, lock horns, be at each other's throats, be at loggerheads; *informal* scrap, argufy, spat; *archaic* altercate.
□ **quarrel with** *it is difficult to quarrel with the verdict* **find fault with**, fault, criticize, argue with/against, object to, be hostile to, censure, condemn, be against, be anti, oppose, be in opposition to, take exception to, attack, take issue with, find lacking, pick holes in, impugn, contradict, dispute, rebut, complain about, cavil at, carp at; *informal* knock; *formal* gainsay; *rare* controvert.
OPPOSITE agree with.

CHOOSE THE RIGHT WORD

quarrel, argue, wrangle, dispute, bicker

- **Quarrel** is used of people having an angry argument (*he married her for her money, so now they're always quarrelling*). One may also dispassionately *quarrel with* something in the sense of disagreeing with or objecting to it (*there was nothing in this document with which he could quarrel*).
- **Arguing** involves two people staunchly, possibly also acrimoniously, defending two different and incompatible points of view (*he and Martin used to argue for hours about the paranormal*).
- **Wrangle** suggests a long, complex, and sometimes intense debate or argument, often a legal or political one (*the party is facing internal wrangling and a cash crisis | after considerable wrangling a compromise was reached*).
- People who **dispute** are expected to show more reasoned argument than if they are merely quarrelling. *Dispute* is mainly used of denying or arguing against a specified view, and the matter of contention is typically a direct object (*people who dispute the official interpretation of their rights*).
- **Bicker** represents an argument as childish, on account of either the logic employed or the triviality of the issue disputed (*those who had fought together for the overthrow of Charles I now bickered amongst themselves | there was no point in bickering over trifles*).

Q

quarrelsome ▶ adjective *he was pleased to be leaving his quarrelsome neighbours behind* **argumentative**, disputatious, disputative, contentious, confrontational, captious, factious, cavilling, pugnacious, combative, ready for a fight, defiant, hostile, antagonistic, bellicose, belligerent, militant, warring, fighting, battling; threatening, litigious; irascible, cantankerous, irritable, petulant, truculent, fiery, quick-tempered, hot-tempered, ill-tempered, bad-tempered, choleric; bickering, wrangling; *Brit. informal* stroppy; *N. Amer. informal* scrappy.
OPPOSITE peaceable.

quarry ▶ noun *he had no intention of allowing his quarry to elude him* **prey**, victim; the hunted; prize, object, goal, target, kill; wild fowl, game, big game.

quarter ▶ noun **1** *the Latin quarter of Paris* **district**, area, region, part, side, neighbourhood, precinct, locality, sector, section, zone, tract, belt; ghetto, community, colony; pocket, enclave, territory, province, parish, ward.
2 *help came from an unexpected quarter* **source**, direction, place, point, spot, location; person.
3 (**quarters**) *rooms that had once been servants' quarters* **accommodation**, lodgings, rooms, chambers, place of residence, home, shelter; *French* pied-à-terre; *Brit. informal* digs; *informal, dated* pad, billet; *formal* abode, dwelling, dwelling place, residence, domicile, habitation.
4 *the riot squads gave no quarter, using their batons liberally* **mercy**, leniency, clemency, lenity, compassion, pity, charity, forbearance, indulgence, kindness, sympathy, tolerance.
▶ verb **1** *they were quartered in a sumptuous villa* **accommodate**, house, board, lodge, give accommodation to, provide with accommodation, put up, take in, give a bed to, install, give a roof to, put a roof over someone's head, shelter; *informal, dated* billet.
2 *I started to quarter the streets, eyes peeled for the car* **patrol**, range over, tour, reconnoitre, traverse, survey, inspect, spy out, scout; *Brit. informal* recce.

quash ▶ verb **1** *the Court of Appeal may quash the sentence* **cancel**, reverse, rescind, repeal, revoke, retract, countermand, withdraw, take back, rule against, disallow, overturn, override, overrule, veto, set aside, overthrow, repudiate, annul, nullify, declare null and void, invalidate, render invalid, negate, void, abrogate; *Law* vacate; *archaic* recall.
OPPOSITE validate.
2 *we want to quash these horrible suggestions* **put an end to**, stamp out, put a stop to, end, finish, get rid of, crush, put down, check, crack down on, curb, nip in the bud, thwart, frustrate, squash, quell, subdue, suppress, repress, quench, extinguish, stifle, abolish, terminate; beat, overcome, defeat, rout, destroy, demolish, annihilate, wipe out; *informal* squelch, put the kibosh on, clobber; *rare* extirpate.
OPPOSITES bring about, prompt.

quasi- ▶ combining form **1** *she had problems with drugs, alcohol, and a quasi-religious cult* **supposedly**, seemingly, apparently, allegedly, reportedly, professedly, ostensibly, on the face of it, to all appearances, on the surface, to all intents and purposes, outwardly, superficially, purportedly, nominally, by one's/its own account, on paper; pseudo-; *rare* pretendedly, ostensively.
2 *diplomacy was then a quasi-profession, in which family connections counted for much* **supposed**, seeming, apparent, alleged, reported, ostensible, purported, nominal, so-called, would-be, pseudo-; bogus, sham, phoney, imitation, artificial, mock, ersatz, fake, forged, feigned, pretended, simulated, false, spurious, counterfeit, fraudulent, deceptive; *informal* pretend, put-on; *Brit. informal* cod; *rare* ostensive.
3 *a quasi-autonomous non-governmental organization* **partly**, partially, in part, part, to a certain extent/degree, to a limited extent/degree, to some extent/degree, half, in some measure, relatively, comparatively, moderately, (up) to a point, a little, somewhat; **almost**, nearly, very nearly, just about, all but, not totally, not wholly, not entirely, not fully, incompletely.

quaver ▶ verb *his voice quavered with emotion* **tremble**, quiver, shake, flutter, vibrate, pulsate, oscillate, fluctuate, waver, ripple, falter, trill, twitter, warble.

quay ▶ noun **dock**, wharf, pier, harbour, berth, jetty, landing, landing stage, landing place, slipway, marina, waterfront, sea wall, embankment.

queasy ▶ adjective *he still felt queasy and he was grateful for the fresh air* **nauseous**, nauseated, bilious, sick; seasick, carsick, trainsick, airsick, travel-sick, suffering from motion sickness, suffering from altitude sickness; ill, unwell, poorly, bad, out of sorts, dizzy, peaky, liverish, green about the gills; *Brit.* off, off colour; *N. Amer.* sick to one's stomach; *informal* funny, peculiar, rough, lousy, rotten, awful, terrible, dreadful, crummy; *Austral./NZ informal* crook; *rare* peakish.

queen ▶ noun **1** *the Queen waved and smiled* **monarch**, sovereign, head of state, ruler, Crown, Her Majesty; king's consort, queen consort, queen mother.
2 (*informal*) *the queen of soul music* **doyenne**, star, leading light, celebrity, big name, superstar, top dog, queen bee, mistress, prima donna, idol, heroine, favourite, darling; goddess, belle, pin-up.
3 (*informal*) **homosexual man**, homosexual, gay; *informal* **pansy**, nancy, nelly, limp-wristed man, effeminate man, camp man, queer, homo, a friend of Dorothy; *Brit. informal* poof, poofter, ponce, jessie, woofter; *N. Amer. informal* cupcake, swish, twinkie; *Austral. informal* wonk; *S. African informal* moffie.
OPPOSITE heterosexual.

queer ▶ adjective **1** *it seemed queer to see the windows all dark* **odd**, strange, unusual, funny, peculiar, curious, bizarre, weird, outlandish, eccentric, unconventional, unorthodox, uncanny, unexpected, unfamiliar, abnormal, anomalous, atypical, untypical, different, out of the ordinary, out of the way, extraordinary, remarkable, puzzling, mystifying, mysterious, perplexing, baffling, unaccountable, incongruous, uncommon, irregular, outré, offbeat, singular, deviant, aberrant, freak, freakish; suspicious, dubious, questionable; eerie, unnatural; *Scottish* unco; *informal* fishy, creepy, spooky, freaky; *Brit. informal* rum; *N. Amer. informal* off the wall; bizarro.
OPPOSITES ordinary, conventional, normal.
2 *there's something queer going on up there* **suspicious**, suspect, irregular, questionable, dubious, doubtful, funny, mysterious, murky, dark, criminal, dishonest, corrupt, nefarious, crafty, deceitful, shifty,

underhand, dishonourable, unscrupulous, unprincipled, fraudulent, illegal, unlawful; *informal* fishy, shady, bent.
3 (*Brit. informal, dated*) *you just feel queer because you're packed full of drugs* **ill**, unwell, poorly, bad, out of sorts, indisposed, not oneself, sick, queasy, nauseous, nauseated, peaky, liverish, green about the gills, run down, washed out, faint, dizzy, giddy; *Brit.* off, off colour; *informal* under the weather, below par, not up to par, funny, peculiar, rough, lousy, rotten, awful, terrible, dreadful; *Brit. informal* grotty, ropy; *Scottish informal* wabbit, peely-wally; *Austral./NZ informal* crook; *dated* seedy; *rare* peaked, peakish.
OPPOSITE well.
4 (*informal*) *lots of their friends were queer* **homosexual**, gay, lesbian, sapphic; *informal* homo, pink, lavender, camp, swinging the other way, limp-wristed, queeny, dykey; *Brit. informal* bent, poofy; *N. Amer. informal* fruity; *rare* homophile, Uranian.
OPPOSITE heterosexual.
▶ **noun** (*informal*) *the queers are all coming out of the closet* **homosexual**, gay, lesbian; *informal* pansy, nancy, nelly, queen, a friend of Dorothy, homo, les, lezzy, lesbo, femme, dyke, butch; *Brit. informal* poof, poofter, ponce, jessie, woofter; *N. Amer. informal* cupcake, swish, twinkie; *Austral. informal* wonk; *S. African informal* moffie; *W. Indian informal* zami, batty boy, batty man; *rare* tribade, homophile, Uranian.
OPPOSITE heterosexual.
▶ **verb** *trying to crash the party would probably queer the whole deal* **spoil**, damage, impair, harm, be detrimental to, mar, wreck, destroy, devastate, smash, shatter, scupper, scotch, disrupt, undo, thwart, hinder, foil, ruin, blight, injure, cripple, hurt, jeopardize, endanger, imperil, threaten, put at risk, undermine, prejudice, be prejudicial to, be disadvantageous to, play havoc with, be deleterious to, compromise; *informal* botch, blow, put the kibosh on.

quell ▶ **verb 1** *troops were called in to quell the unrest* **put an end to**, stamp out, put a stop to, end, finish, get rid of, crush, put down, check, crack down on, curb, nip in the bud, thwart, frustrate, squash, quash, subdue, suppress, repress, quench, extinguish, stifle, abolish, terminate, beat, overcome, defeat, rout, destroy, demolish, annihilate, wipe out, extirpate; *informal* squelch, put the kibosh on, clobber.
OPPOSITES bring about, prompt.
2 *he managed to quell his initial misgivings* **calm**, soothe, pacify, settle, quieten, quiet, put at rest, lull, silence, put behind one, rise above, allay, appease, stay, assuage, abate, deaden, dull, tranquillize, mitigate, moderate, palliate.
OPPOSITE succumb to.

quench ▶ **verb 1** *they quenched their thirst with local wine and spring water | his answer had not quenched my curiosity at all* **satisfy**, slake, sate, satiate, gratify, relieve, assuage, take the edge off, appease, meet, fulfil, indulge; **lessen**, deaden, decrease, lower, reduce, diminish, curb, check, still, damp; **suppress**, extinguish, smother, stifle, overcome.
2 *the flames were quickly quenched with buckets of water* **extinguish**, put out, snuff out, smother, douse, dampen down.

querulous ▶ **adjective** *there'll be no rest for me with a querulous adolescent* **petulant**, complaining, pettish, touchy, testy, tetchy, waspish, prickly, crusty, peppery, fractious, fretful, irritable, cross, crabbed, crabby, crotchety, cantankerous, curmudgeonly, disagreeable, miserable, morose, on edge, edgy, impatient, bitter, moody, in a bad mood, grumpy, huffy, scratchy, out of sorts, out of temper, ill-tempered, bad-tempered, ill-natured, ill-humoured, sullen, surly, sulky, sour, churlish, bilious, liverish, dyspeptic, splenetic, choleric; *informal* snappish, snappy, chippy, grouchy, cranky, whingeing, whingy; *Brit. informal* narky, ratty, eggy, like a bear with a sore head, peckish; *N. Amer. informal* sorehead, soreheaded; *Austral./NZ informal* snaky; *informal, dated* miffy.

query ▶ **noun 1** *we are happy to answer any queries about our products* **question**, enquiry; interrogation, examination; *Brit. informal* quiz, quizzing.
2 *there was a query as to who actually owned the hotel* **doubt**, uncertainty, question, question mark, reservation, suspicion; scepticism.
▶ **verb 1** *'Why do they all wear yellow?' queried Isabel* **ask**, enquire, question; *Brit. informal* quiz.
2 *folk may query the authenticity of this* **question**, call in/into question, doubt, raise/entertain doubts about, throw doubt on, have/harbour/express suspicions about, suspect, feel uneasy about, have/harbour/express reservations about, challenge, dispute, cast aspersions on, object to, raise objections to.

quest ▶ **noun 1** *nothing will stop their quest for her killer* **search**, hunt, pursuit; pursuance of, investigation into.
2 *Sir Galahad was nearing the end of his quest* **expedition**, adventure, journey, voyage, trek, travels, odyssey, wandering, journeying, exploration, venture, search, undertaking; crusade, mission, pilgrimage, errand; *rare* peregrination.
□ **in quest of** *I telephoned Downing Street in quest of the Prime Minister* **searching for**, after, seeking, looking for, on the lookout for, in search of, in pursuit of, chasing after.
▶ **verb** (*literary*) *his eyes quested to left and right* **search**, seek, look, hunt, pursue, investigate, explore, probe, inspect.

question ▶ **noun 1** *you didn't answer my question* **enquiry**, query; interrogation, examination; *Brit. informal* quiz, quizzing.
OPPOSITES answer, response.
2 *there is no question that he is ill* **doubt**, dispute, argument, debate, uncertainty, dubiousness, controversy, reservation; *rare* dubiety.
OPPOSITE certainty.
3 *it is a question of trust | he wrote essays on the principal political questions of the day* **issue**, matter, business, problem, point at issue, point, concern, subject, topic, theme, item, case, proposal, proposition, debate, argument, dispute, bone of contention, controversy.
□ **beyond question 1** *her loyalty is really beyond question* **undoubted**, beyond doubt, without doubt, certain, indubitable, indisputable, irrefutable, incontestable, incontrovertible, unquestionable, undeniable, unmistakable, clear, patent, manifest, obvious, palpable.
OPPOSITE in doubt.
2 *the results demonstrated beyond question that gas accumulated in some quantity* **indisputably**, irrefutably, incontestably, incontrovertibly, unquestionably, undeniably, undoubtedly, beyond doubt, without doubt, certainly, indubitably, unmistakably, clearly, patently, manifestly, obviously, palpably.
□ **in question** *the matter in question* **at issue**, being discussed, under discussion, under consideration, on the agenda, for debate, to be discussed, to be decided.
□ **out of the question** *going back to the railway station was out of the question* **impossible**, beyond the bounds of possibility, impracticable, unattainable, unachievable, not feasible, not worth considering, unworkable, unobtainable, inconceivable, unthinkable, unimaginable, unrealizable, unsuitable; beyond one, hopeless, absurd, ridiculous, preposterous, outrageous, ludicrous, beyond the realm of reason; *informal* not on.
▶ **verb 1** *the magistrate may question the suspect and other witnesses* **interrogate**, ask questions of, put questions to, cross-examine, cross-question, quiz, probe, canvass, catechize, interview, debrief, sound out, examine, give the third degree to; *informal* grill, pump.
2 *she should question his motives* **query**, call in/into question, doubt, raise/entertain doubts about, throw doubt on, have/harbour/express suspicions about, suspect, feel uneasy about, have/harbour/express reservations about, challenge, dispute, cast aspersions on, object to, raise objections to.

WORD LINKS
relating to questions **interrogative**

questionable ▶ **adjective 1** *it is questionable whether such an attack could be effective | he indulges in jokes of questionable taste* **controversial**, contentious, open to question, open to doubt, in doubt, doubtful, dubious, uncertain, unsure, debatable, in dispute, in question, arguable, problematic, problematical; unverified, unprovable, unresolved, unsettled, undecided, equivocal, unconvincing, implausible, improbable, not definite, unclear, not obvious, apocryphal, spurious, borderline, marginal, moot; *informal* iffy; *Brit. informal* dodgy.
OPPOSITES certain, indisputable.
2 *some of his questionable financial dealings have been investigated* **suspicious**, suspect, under suspicion, irregular, dubious, doubtful, odd, queer, strange, not quite right, mysterious, murky, dark, shifty, unsavoury, disreputable, potentially dishonest, potentially illegal; *informal* funny, fishy, shady, iffy; *Brit. informal* dodgy.

questionnaire ▶ **noun** **question sheet**, set of questions, survey form, form, test, exam, examination, quiz, opinion poll; *technical* questionary, personality inventory.

queue ▶ **noun 1** *there was a queue of people waiting for the bus* **line**, row, column, file, chain, string, stream; procession, train, succession, progression, cavalcade, sequence, series; waiting list, reserve list; *N. Amer.* breadline, wait list, backup, waiting line; *Brit. informal* crocodile.
2 *he was sitting in taxi, stuck in a queue along Knightsbridge* **traffic jam**, jam, tailback, line, stream, gridlock; *informal* snarl-up, traffic snarl.
▶ **verb** *we queued for ice creams* **line up**, stand in a queue, form a queue, queue up, wait in line, form a line, form lines, get into rows/columns, fall in, file, walk/move in line; *Brit. informal* form a crocodile.

quibble ▶ **noun 1** *apart from that quibble, it was fine* **minor criticism**, trivial objection, trivial complaint, adverse comment, protest, query, argument, exception, moan, grumble, grouse, cavil; *informal* niggle, gripe, beef, grouch, nit-picking; *archaic* pettifogging, amphibology.
2 *I ignored his ridiculous quibbles about interest rates* **evasion**, dodge; (**quibbles**) avoidance, equivocation, prevarication, hedging, fudging.
▶ **verb 1** *no one would* ***quibble with*** *the subtitle* **find fault with**, raise trivial objections to, complain about, object to, cavil at, carp about; split hairs, chop logic; criticize, query, fault, pick, holes in; *informal* nit-pick; *archaic* pettifog.
2 *he's always quibbling, so that it is difficult to get a straight answer out of him* **be evasive**, equivocate, avoid the issue, prevaricate, hedge, fudge, be ambiguous; *informal* beat about the bush.

quick ▶ **adjective 1** *John was generally a quick worker* **fast**, swift, rapid, speedy, high-speed, expeditious; brisk, lively, sprightly, nimble, prompt; lightning, meteoric, overnight, whirlwind, fast-track, whistle-stop,

breakneck, smart; *informal* nippy, zippy; *Brit. informal* cracking; *literary* fleet; *rare* tantivy, alacritous, volant.
OPPOSITE slow.
2 *she took a quick look behind her* **hasty**, hurried, cursory, perfunctory, superficial, desultory, incidental, summary, glancing; **brief**, short, fleeting, passing, transient, transitory, short-lived, flying, lightning, momentary, temporary.
OPPOSITES long, careful.
3 *there was no quick end to the recession* **sudden**, instantaneous, immediate, instant, abrupt, sharp, precipitate, breakneck, headlong.
4 *she isn't as quick as the others, but she works hard* **intelligent**, bright, clever, gifted, able, brilliant, astute, quick-witted, sharp-witted, ready, quick off the mark; observant, alert, sharp, wide awake, receptive, perceptive; *informal* brainy, smart, on the ball, on one's toes, quick on the uptake.
OPPOSITE stupid.

quicken ▶ **verb 1** *his pulse quickened | she unconsciously quickened her pace* **speed up**, accelerate, step up, hasten, hurry, hurry up; *informal* gee up.
OPPOSITE slow.
2 *the film quickened his interest in wild life* **stimulate**, excite, stir up, arouse, rouse, waken, animate, activate, incite, galvanize, instigate, whet, inspire, kindle, fan, refresh, strengthen, invigorate, reanimate, reactivate, revive, revitalize, resuscitate, revivify; titillate, tempt.
OPPOSITE dull.

quickly ▶ **adverb 1** *he began to walk quickly* **fast**, swiftly, rapidly, speedily, at high speed, with all speed, at (full) speed, at the speed of light, at full tilt, as fast as one's legs can carry one, at a gallop, briskly, at the double, post-haste, with all possible haste, like a whirlwind, like an arrow from a bow, at breakneck speed, expeditiously, madly, hotfoot, with dispatch; *informal* double quick, in double quick time, p.d.q. (pretty damn quick), nippily, like (greased) lightning, hell for leather, like mad, like crazy, like blazes, like the wind, like a bomb, like nobody's business, like a scalded cat, like the deuce, a mile a minute, like a bat out of hell, like a bullet out of a gun; *Brit. informal* like the clappers, at a rate of knots, like billy-o; *N. Amer. informal* lickety-split; *literary* apace.
OPPOSITE slowly.
2 *sensing her discomfort, he quickly went on | the apartments were sold quite quickly* **immediately**, directly, at once, now, straight away, right away, instantly, forthwith, as soon as possible, shortly, without delay, without further/more ado, instantaneously, expeditiously, suddenly, abruptly; soon, soon after, promptly, early; *N. Amer.* momentarily; *informal* like a shot, a.s.a.p. (as soon as possible), pronto, before you can say Jack Robinson, before the ink is dry on the page, before you can say knife, straight off; *archaic* straight, instanter.
3 *he calmed the animal and quickly inspected it* **briefly**, fleetingly, briskly; **hastily**, in haste, precipitately, hurriedly, in a hurry, cursorily, perfunctorily, superficially, desultorily.

quick-tempered ▶ **adjective** *they tend to be impulsive and quick-tempered* **irritable**, irascible, hot-tempered, short-tempered, fiery, touchy, volatile; peevish, cross, crabbed, crabby, crotchety, cantankerous, impatient, grumpy, huffy, brusque, ill-tempered, bad-tempered, ill-natured, ill-humoured, testy, tetchy, snarling, waspish, prickly, crusty, peppery, bilious, liverish, dyspeptic, splenetic, choleric; *informal* snappish, snappy, chippy, cranky, grouchy, on a short fuse; *Brit. informal* narky, ratty, eggy, like a bear with a sore head; *N. Amer. informal* peckish, soreheaded; *Austral./NZ informal* snaky; *informal, dated* miffy.
OPPOSITES placid, calm.

quick-witted ▶ **adjective** **alert**, astute, perceptive, quick, quick-thinking, sharp-witted, sharp, shrewd, penetrating, discerning, perspicacious; wide awake, ready, quick off the mark, observant; intelligent, bright, clever, gifted, able, brainy, brilliant; *informal* smart, on the ball, on one's toes, quick on the uptake.
OPPOSITES stupid, slow.

quid pro quo ▶ **noun** *a congressman's support for the president on a particular issue may not represent a straightforward quid pro quo* **exchange**, trade, trade-off, swap, switch, barter, substitute, substitution, reciprocity, reciprocation, return, payment, remuneration, amends, compensation, indemnity, recompense, restitution, reparation, satisfaction; *rare* requital.

quiescent ▶ **adjective** *the volcano is in a quiescent state* **inactive**, inert, latent, fallow, passive, idle, at rest, inoperative, deactivated, in abeyance, quiet; still, motionless, immobile, stagnant, dormant, asleep, slumbering, sluggish, lethargic, torpid.
OPPOSITE active.

quiet ▶ **adjective 1** *the whole pub went quiet* **silent**, still, hushed, noiseless, soundless; mute, dumb, speechless, voiceless, unspeaking.
2 *she spoke in a quiet voice* **soft**, low, lowered, muted, muffled, faint, indistinct, inaudible, dull; hushed, whispered, stifled, suppressed.
OPPOSITE loud.
3 *a quiet village | he liked the quiet life* **peaceful**, sleepy, tranquil, calm, still, relaxing, soothing, pleasant, restful, undisturbed, free from disturbance, free from interruption, free from interference, untroubled; unfrequented, private, secluded, sequestered, retired, isolated, out of the way, off the beaten track, solitary.
OPPOSITE busy.
4 *I thought we'd better have a quiet word together before the kids come* **private**, confidential, secret, discreet, unofficial, off the record, between ourselves, between you and me (and the bedpost/gatepost/doorpost/wall).
OPPOSITE public.
5 *he's a very quiet, private person* **calm**, equable, serene, composed, {cool, calm, and collected}, placid, untroubled, peaceful, peaceable, tranquil, gentle, mild, phlegmatic, imperturbable, unexcitable; moderate, reserved, uncommunicative, unresponsive, taciturn, secretive, withdrawn, silent; meek, mousy, retiring, reticent, unforthcoming, shy, self-effacing, diffident, modest, temperate, restrained, unassuming, unassertive, unemotional; *informal* unflappable; *rare* equanimous.
6 *I've always preferred quiet colours* **unobtrusive**, unostentatious, unpretentious, restrained, reserved; soft, pale, pastel, muted, understated, subdued, subtle, low-key, conservative, sober, plain, ordinary.
OPPOSITE loud.
7 *you can't keep a mass murder quiet for long* **secret**, top secret, confidential, strictly confidential, classified, unrevealed, undisclosed, unpublished, untold, unknown, uncommunicated, under wraps, unofficial, off the record, not for publication/circulation, not to be made public, not to be disclosed, clandestine, surreptitious; *Latin* sub rosa; *informal* hush-hush, mum.
OPPOSITE public.
8 *business is quiet today* **slow**, slow-moving, stagnant, slack, sluggish, inactive, not busy, idle.
▶ **noun** *after London, the quiet of the country was almost tangible* **peacefulness**, peace and quiet, peace, restfulness, calm, calmness, tranquillity, serenity; silence, quietness, stillness, still, quietude, hush, noiselessness, soundlessness; privacy, privateness, seclusion, solitude, isolation, retirement, lack of disturbance/interruption, freedom from interference.

quieten ▶ **verb 1** *the teacher had to stop to quieten the children down* **silence**, make quieter, hush, shush, quiet, still; *informal* shut up.
2 *her travelling companions had quietened* **fall silent**, stop talking, break off, become quiet, quieten down, grow silent, shush, hold one's tongue; *informal* shut up, clam up, shut it, pipe down, shut one's mouth/face/trap, put a sock in it, button one's lip, button it, cut the cackle; *Brit. informal* wrap up; *N. Amer. informal* save it.
3 *he tried using lithium salts to quieten manic patients* **calm**, calm down, pacify, soothe, subdue, tranquillize, cool, content, silence, relax, comfort, compose.
4 *Dexter yearned for a cigarette and could not quieten the urge* **allay**, appease, assuage, mollify, palliate, ease, lessen, reduce, abate, mitigate, moderate, stifle, dull, deaden, lull, temper, subjugate, repress, quell, quash, overcome, rise above.

quietly ▶ **adverb 1** *she quietly absorbed the lovely surroundings* **silently**, in silence, noiselessly, soundlessly, inaudibly; mutely, dumbly, tacitly; *literary* stilly.
2 *he spoke quietly so as not to disturb anyone* **softly**, making little noise, in a low voice, in low/hushed/muted/subdued tones, in a whisper/murmur/mumble, murmuringly, under one's breath, in an undertone, sotto voce, gently, faintly, weakly, feebly.
OPPOSITES loudly, audibly.
3 *some bonds were sold quietly to Club members* **discreetly**, privately, confidentially, secretly, unofficially, off the record, between ourselves, between you and me (and the bedpost/gatepost/doorpost/wall).
OPPOSITE publicly.
4 *Mrs Wilson dressed quietly in grey or black* **unobtrusively**, unostentatiously, unpretentiously, with restraint, with reserve, conservatively, soberly, modestly, demurely, plainly.
OPPOSITE loudly.
5 *she is quietly confident* **calmly**, patiently, placidly, serenely, undemonstratively, unemotionally, unassumingly.

quietness ▶ **noun** *she was glad of the quietness of her surroundings* **peacefulness**, peace and quiet, peace, restfulness, calm, calmness, tranquillity, serenity; silence, stillness, still, quiet, quietude, hush, noiselessness, soundlessness.

quilt ▶ **noun** **duvet**, continental quilt, counterpane, bedspread, cover, coverlet, Durham quilt; *Brit.* eiderdown; *Scottish, trademark* downie; *French* plumeau; *N. Amer.* comforter, puff; *Austral./NZ trademark* Doona; *Indian* rezai; *Turkish* yorgan; *archaic* counterpoint, pourpoint.

quintessence ▶ **noun 1** *Wemmick's cottage is the quintessence of the Victorian home* **perfect example**, exemplar, prototype, stereotype, picture, epitome, embodiment, personification, paragon, ideal; best, cream, elite, flower, jewel, gem, pick, prime, last word, acme of perfection; *French* crème de la crème, beau idéal.
2 *they wanted to know how our brains function and thereby discover the quintessence of intelligence* **essence**, soul, spirit, ethos, nature, core, heart, centre, crux, nub, nucleus, kernel, marrow, pith, substance, sum and substance; *informal* nitty-gritty; *Philosophy* quiddity, esse.

quintessential ▶ **adjective** *skiing was the quintessential 1980s yuppie holiday*

typical, prototypical, stereotypical, archetypal, classic, model, essential, standard, stock, representative, true to type, conventional; ideal, consummate, exemplary, best, ultimate, supreme, absolute.

quip ▸ noun *the quip failed to provoke a smile* **joke**, witty remark, witticism, jest, pun, sally, pleasantry, epigram, aphorism; (**quips**) repartee, banter; *French* bon mot; *informal* one-liner, gag, crack, wisecrack, funny.
▸ verb *'There's no accounting for taste,' I quipped* **joke**, jest, pun, sally, banter; *informal* gag, wisecrack.

quirk ▸ noun **1** *he likes working with people he knows because they know his quirks* **idiosyncrasy**, peculiarity, oddity, eccentricity, foible, whim, whimsy, notion, conceit, vagary, caprice, fancy, kink, crotchet, mannerism, habit, characteristic, trait, feature, obsession, fad; *French* idée fixe; *informal* hang-up, thing; *rare* singularity.
2 *by a quirk of history they were related to seven American presidents* **chance**, **fluke**, freak, anomaly, unusual occurrence, turn, peculiar turn of events, twist, twist of fate.

quirky ▸ adjective *he had this quirky sense of humour* **eccentric**, **idiosyncratic**, unconventional, unorthodox, unusual, strange, bizarre, weird, peculiar, odd, freakish, outlandish, offbeat, out of the ordinary, Bohemian, alternative, zany; *French* outré; *informal* wacky, freaky, kinky, way-out, far out, kooky, oddball, off the wall; *N. Amer. informal* in left field; bizarro.
OPPOSITE conventional.

> CHOOSE THE RIGHT WORD
> **quirky, eccentric, unconventional, idiosyncratic**
> *See* ECCENTRIC.

quisling ▸ noun **collaborator**, fraternizer, colluder, sympathizer; **traitor**, turncoat, betrayer, informer, back-stabber, double-crosser, double-dealer, renegade, defector, deserter, apostate, Judas, snake in the grass, fifth columnist; *informal* two-timer; *Austral. informal* dog.

quit ▸ verb **1** *let us assume he quit the lay-by at about 12.30* **leave**, go away from, depart from, vacate, evacuate, move out of, exit from, withdraw from, abandon, desert.
OPPOSITES arrive at; occupy.
2 (*informal*) *he's decided to quit his job | this defeat will increase the calls for the manager to quit* **resign (from)**, leave, hand in one's notice, give notice, stand down (from), give up, bow out, relinquish, depart from, vacate, walk out (on), retire (from), abdicate; *informal* chuck, pack in.
OPPOSITE take up.
3 (*informal*) *she has to quit living in the past | the best advice to smokers is to quit* **give up**, stop, finish, cease, discontinue, not continue, drop, leave off, break off, abandon, abstain from, renounce, desist (from), refrain (from), eschew, forbear from, avoid, forgo, do without; call it a day; *informal* pack (it) in.
OPPOSITES start; continue.

quite ▸ adverb **1** *there are in fact two quite different types* **completely**, fully, entirely, totally, wholly, absolutely, utterly, outright, thoroughly, altogether, in every respect, in all respects, without reservation, without exception.
2 *it was quite common in the last century* **fairly**, rather, somewhat, a bit, a little, slightly, relatively, comparatively, moderately, after a fashion, reasonably, to some extent/degree, to a certain extent; *informal* pretty, kind of, sort of.

quiver ▸ verb **1** *I sat quivering with terror until dawn* **tremble**, shake, shiver, quaver, quake, shudder, convulse.
2 *the bird runs along, quivering its wings* **flutter**, agitate, vibrate, flap, beat.
▸ noun *Mr Beckenham could hear a quiver in her voice* **tremor**, tremble, shake, shaking, shakiness, shiver, frisson, chill, vibration, quaver, quake, shudder, flutter, oscillation, fluctuation, waver, ripple, falter.

> CHOOSE THE RIGHT WORD
> **quiver, shake, quake, tremble, shiver**
> *See* SHAKE.

quixotic ▸ adjective *the 1000-storey building is a vast, exciting and perhaps quixotic project* **idealistic**, unbusinesslike, romantic, extravagant, starry-eyed, visionary, Utopian, perfectionist, unrealistic, unworldly; **impracticable**, unworkable, impossible, non-viable, inoperable, unserviceable; useless, ineffective, ineffectual, inefficacious.

quiz ▸ noun **1** *the talk was followed by a gardening quiz* **test of knowledge**, competition, panel game, quiz game, quiz show.
2 *jockey faces new quiz over pub killings* **interrogation**, questioning, cross-examination, cross-questioning, interview, catechism, examination; *informal* grilling, pumping, the third degree.
▸ verb *a man was being quizzed by police last night* **question**, interrogate, put questions to, probe, sound out, interview, examine, cross-examine, catechize; *informal* grill, put the screws on, pump, give someone the third degree, put someone through the third degree, put someone through the wringer/mangle, worm something out of someone.

quizzical ▸ adjective *'To do what?' he asked with a cool, quizzical look* **puzzled**, perplexed, baffled, questioning, enquiring, mystified, curious, sceptical; **amused**, sardonic, supercilious, mocking, teasing.

quota ▸ noun *he rarely took his full quota of holiday* **allocation**, share, allowance, limit, ration, portion, apportionment, assignment, dispensation, slice, slice of the cake; percentage, commission, measure, proportion, part, piece, fraction, division, subdivision, bit, amount, number, range, quantity; *informal* cut, whack, rake-off.

quotation ▸ noun **1** *a quotation from Dryden* **citation**, quote, reference, mention, allusion, excerpt, extract, selection, passage, line, cutting, clip, clipping, snippet, reading, section, piece, part, fragment, portion, paragraph, verse, stanza, canto, sentence, phrase; *N. Amer.* cite; *informal, dated* gobbet.
2 *the company will then give you a quotation for the work* **estimate**, estimated price, price, quote, tender, bid, cost, charge, rate, figure.

quote ▸ verb **1** *he quoted a sentence from a speech by Lord Denning* **recite**, repeat, say again, reproduce, restate, retell, echo, iterate, parrot; take, extract, excerpt, derive; misquote; *archaic* ingeminate.
2 *Russell quoted one case in which a person had died in a fire* **cite**, mention, refer to, make reference to, give, name, instance, specify, identify; relate, recount, enumerate, list, itemize, spell out, allude to, adduce, exemplify, put forward, point out, call attention to, present, offer, advance, propose.
3 *he quoted £45 for building a staircase* **estimate**, state, set, tender, bid, offer; price something at.

quotidian ▸ adjective **1** *the car sped off through the quotidian traffic* **daily**, everyday, occurring each/every day, day-to-day; *rare* diurnal, circadian.
2 *they took me home in Gillian's dreadfully quotidian motor car* **ordinary**, average, normal, run-of-the-mill, everyday, standard, typical, middle-of-the-road, common, conventional, mainstream, unremarkable, unexceptional, unpretentious, modest, plain, simple, workaday, undistinguished, nondescript, characterless, colourless, commonplace, humdrum, mundane, unmemorable; pedestrian, prosaic, uninteresting, uneventful, dull, boring, uninspiring, homely, homespun, *Brit.* common or garden; *N. Amer.* garden-variety; *informal* OK, so-so, bog-standard, nothing to write home about, a dime a dozen, no great shakes, not up to much; *N. Amer. informal* ornery.
OPPOSITES unusual, exciting.

rabbit *See centre pages for list of* **Rabbits and Hares**
▶ **noun** buck, doe; *Brit.* coney; *children's word* bunny (rabbit).
WORD LINKS
home **warren, burrow, hutch**

rabble ▶ **noun 1** *a rabble of noisy, angry youths* **mob**, (disorderly) crowd, throng, gang, swarm, host, horde, pack, press, crush, jam, gathering, assemblage, multitude, mass, body, group; *archaic* rout.
2 *democracy was often taken to mean rule by* ***the rabble*** **the common people**, the masses, the populace, the public, the multitude, the rank and file, the commonality, the commonalty, the third estate, the plebeians, the proletariat, the peasantry, the crowd, the hoi polloi, the lower classes, the common herd, the riff-raff, the canaille, the great unwashed, the dregs of society, the ragtag (and bobtail), the proles, the plebs.
OPPOSITES aristocracy, nobility.

rabble-rouser ▶ **noun** *a Communist rabble-rouser* **agitator**, troublemaker, instigator, agent provocateur, mischief-maker, incendiary, firebrand, revolutionary, demagogue.

Rabelaisian ▶ **adjective** *a Rabelaisian novel* **ribald**, racy, bawdy, vulgar, coarse, earthy, risqué, lewd, blue, spicy; **exuberant**, uninhibited, vigorous, lively; satirical, parodic, irreverent, disrespectful; *informal* raunchy.
OPPOSITES boring, tame, strait-laced.

rabid ▶ **adjective 1** *a rabid anti-royalist* **extreme**, fanatical, overzealous, over-enthusiastic, extremist, violent, maniacal, wild, passionate, fervent, diehard, uncompromising; intolerant, unreasonable, illiberal, bigoted, prejudiced, biased, partisan, one-sided; *informal* raving, gung-ho; *literary* perfervid.
OPPOSITES moderate, liberal, half-hearted.
2 *she was bitten by a rabid dog* **rabies-infected**, mad, foaming at the mouth, hydrophobic.

race[1] ▶ **noun 1** *Dave won the race and Andy came second* **contest**, competition; relay, event, fixture, heat, rally, trial, time trial, head-to-head.
2 *the race for naval domination accelerated* **competition**, contest, rivalry, contention, quest.
3 *the brook was diverted into the mill race* **channel**, waterway, watercourse, conduit, sluice, spillway, aqueduct.
▶ **verb 1** *Jimmy will race in the semi-finals* **compete**, take part in a race, run, contend.
2 *dogs would race the train furiously* **compete against**, have a race with, run against, be pitted against, try to beat.
3 *Cally raced after him* **hurry**, dash, run, rush, sprint, bolt, dart, gallop, career, charge, shoot, hurtle, hare, bound, fly, speed, zoom, go hell for leather, pound, streak, scurry, scuttle, scamper, scramble, make haste, hasten, lose no time, spank along, really move; *informal* tear, belt, pelt, scoot, zap, zip, whip, step on it, get a move on, hotfoot it, leg it, steam, put on some speed, go like a bat out of hell, burn rubber; *Brit. informal* bomb, bucket, put one's foot down; *Scottish informal* wheech; *N. Amer. informal* boogie, hightail it, clip, barrel, get the lead out; *informal, dated* cut along; *N. Amer. vulgar slang* drag/tear/haul ass; *literary* fleet; *archaic* post, hie, haste.
4 *she tried to calm herself, but her heart was racing* **beat rapidly**, pound, throb, pulsate, pulse, thud, thump, hammer, palpitate, flutter, pitter-patter, go pit-a-pat, quiver, vibrate, pump, pant, thrill; *rare* quop.

race[2] ▶ **noun 1** *the school has pupils of many different races* **ethnic group**, racial type, (ethnic) origin.
2 *we Scots were a bloodthirsty race then* **people**, nation.
3 *a new race of novelists had appeared* **group**, type, sort, class, kind, variety, ilk, genre, cast, style, brand, vintage, order, breed, species, generation.
4 (*literary*) *a prince of the race of Solomon* **family**, line, lineage, house, dynasty, stock, blood, folk, clan, tribe; ancestry, descent, bloodline; progeny, offspring, issue.
WORD LINKS
killing of a race **ethnocide, genocide**

racial ▶ **adjective** *he suggests that modern racial differences have a long evolutionary history* **ethnic**, race-related, ethnological; cultural, national, tribal, folk.

racism ▶ **noun racial discrimination**, racialism, racial prejudice/bigotry, xenophobia, chauvinism, bigotry, bias, intolerance; anti-Semitism; (*in S. Africa, historical*) apartheid.

racist ▶ **noun** *the party organizer was exposed as a racist* **racial bigot**, racialist, xenophobe, chauvinist; anti-Semite.
▶ **adjective** *a racist society* **(racially) discriminatory**, racialist, prejudiced, bigoted, biased, intolerant, illiberal; anti-Semitic.
OPPOSITES multicultural, tolerant.

rack ▶ **noun** *turn the cake out on to a wire rack to cool* **framework**, frame, stand, holder, shelf, form, trestle, support, bin, box, bunker, container, structure.
□ **on the rack under pressure**, under stress, under a strain, in distress; suffering, going through torture, in agony, in pain, racked with pain; in trouble, in difficulties, having problems.
▶ **verb** *she was racked with guilt | the pain racked his whole body* **torment**, afflict, torture, pain, agonize, cause agony/suffering/pain to, harrow, pierce, stab, wound, crucify; plague, bedevil, persecute, harass, distress, trouble, worry; convulse; *literary* rend.
□ **rack one's brains** *she racked her brains, but there was nothing she could tell him* **think hard**, put one's mind to something, give much thought to something, concentrate, try to remember, puzzle over something, cudgel one's brains, furrow one's brow; *informal* scratch one's head.

racket ▶ **noun 1** *the engine makes the most incredible racket* **noise**, din, hubbub, clamour, row, uproar, hullabaloo, tumult, commotion, rumpus, fracas, pandemonium, clangour, brouhaha, disturbance; crash, clatter, clash, babble, shouting, yelling, babel; *W. Indian* bangarang.
2 (*informal*) *he was accused of masterminding a gold-smuggling racket* **criminal activity**, illegal scheme/enterprise, fraud, fraudulent scheme, swindle, bit of sharp practice; *informal* game, scam, rip-off; *Brit. informal* ramp; *N. Amer. informal* shakedown.

raconteur ▶ **noun storyteller**, teller of tales, spinner of yarns, narrator, relater, recounter; *Austral. informal* magsman; *rare* anecdotist, anecdotalist.

racy ▶ **adjective** *the show included a rather racy striptease revue* **risqué**, sexy, naughty, spicy, juicy, suggestive, ribald, indelicate, indecorous, indecent, immodest, off colour, dirty, rude, smutty, crude, bawdy, vulgar, salacious, coarse; lively, entertaining, stimulating, exciting; *N. Amer.* gamy; *informal* raunchy, blue, close to the bone, near the bone; *Brit. informal* fruity, near the knuckle, saucy; *euphemistic* adult.
OPPOSITES dull, prim.

raddled ▶ **adjective** *he had begun to look quite raddled* **haggard**, gaunt, hollow-eyed, drawn, with sunken cheeks, pinched, tired, fatigued, drained, exhausted, worn out, washed out; unwell, unhealthy, below/under par, on one's last legs; *informal* the worse for wear.
OPPOSITE healthy.

radiance ▶ **noun 1** *the radiance of the sun* **light**, shining, brightness, brilliance, luminosity, radiation, beams, rays, illumination, blaze, glow, luminousness, gleam, lustre, glitter, sparkle, flash, dazzle, shimmer, glare; luminescence, incandescence, fluorescence, phosphorescence; *rare* irradiance, lucency, lambency, effulgence, refulgence, coruscation.
OPPOSITE darkness.
2 *her face flooded with radiance as she saw him* **joy**, joyfulness, elation,

jubilance, ecstasy, rapture, euphoria, delirium, happiness, delight, pleasure.
OPPOSITES gloom, misery.
3 *her skin had the unmistakable radiance of youth* **splendour**, resplendence, magnificence, brilliance, dazzle, beauty, vividness, glory, gloriousness.

radiant ▶ **adjective 1** *the radiant moon* **shining**, bright, illuminated, lit, lighted, brilliant, gleaming, glowing, ablaze, luminous, luminescent, lustrous, incandescent, glittering, sparkling, dazzling, flashing, shimmering; *literary* irradiant, lucent, lambent, splendent; *rare* effulgent, refulgent, coruscating.
OPPOSITES dark, dull.
2 *flushed and radiant, she smiled up at him* **joyful**, elated, thrilled, overjoyed, jubilant, in raptures, enraptured, rapturous, ecstatic, beside oneself with joy, euphoric, deliriously happy, blissfully happy, in seventh heaven, on cloud nine/seven, delighted, joyous, pleased, happy, beaming, glowing, transported, in transports of joy/pleasure/delight; *informal* on top of the world, over the moon, blissed out; *Austral. informal* wrapped.
OPPOSITE gloomy.
3 *the opening chorus is another radiant piece* **splendid**, magnificent, brilliant, dazzling, scintillating, vivid, intense, beautiful, gorgeous, transcendent, resplendent, impressive, spectacular, striking, stunning, glorious, superb, majestic, great, breathtaking, ravishing, sumptuous, fine; *informal* splendiferous; *rare* splendacious, magnolious.

radiate ▶ **verb 1** *the hot stars radiate energy* **emit**, give off/out, send out/forth, discharge, scatter, diffuse; shed, cast, beam out.
2 *a faint light radiated from the cage* **shine**, be diffused, beam, emanate.
3 *their faces radiate interest and hope* **display**, show, exhibit, demonstrate; transmit, emanate, breathe, be a/the picture of.
4 *four spokes radiate from the hub* **spread out**, fan (out), ray (out), branch (out/off), diverge, extend, separate, split off, issue; *technical* divaricate, ramify.

radiation ▶ **noun.** *See centre pages for list of* **Radiation Types**

radical ▶ **adjective 1** *radical reform is long overdue* **thoroughgoing**, thorough, complete, total, entire, absolute, utter, comprehensive, exhaustive, root-and-branch, sweeping, far-reaching, wide-ranging, extensive, profound, drastic, severe, serious, major, desperate, stringent, violent, forceful, rigorous, draconian.
OPPOSITE superficial.
2 *the apparently radical differences between logic and natural language* **fundamental**, basic, essential, quintessential; inherent, innate, structural, deep-seated, intrinsic, organic, constitutive, root.
OPPOSITE minor.
3 *a radical political movement* **revolutionary**, progressive, reforming, reformist, revisionist, progressivist; leftist, left-wing, socialist; extreme, extremist, fanatical, militant, diehard; *informal* red; *derogatory* Bolshevik.
OPPOSITES conservative, reactionary; moderate.
▶ **noun** *he was by no means a radical* **revolutionary**, progressive, reformer, revisionist; leftist, left-winger, socialist; militant, zealot, extremist, fanatic, diehard; *informal* ultra, red; *derogatory* Bolshevik, Bolshevist.
OPPOSITES conservative, reactionary; moderate.

raffish ▶ **adjective** *his cosmopolitan, raffish air* **rakish**, jaunty, dapper, dashing, sporty, flashy; unconventional, bohemian; devil-may-care, casual, careless; louche, disreputable, dissolute, dissipated, debauched, decadent; *informal* flash.

raffle ▶ **noun** *she won the car in a raffle* **lottery**, (prize) draw, sweepstake, sweep, tombola, ballot; *Brit. trademark* Instants; *N. Amer.* lotto, numbers game/pool/racket; *Austral./NZ* tote, pakapoo.

rag[1] ▶ **noun 1** *he wiped his hands on an oily rag* **piece of cloth**, bit/scrap/fragment of cloth, cloth; *N. Amer. informal* schmatte; *archaic* clout.
2 (**rags**) *a man dressed in rags* **tattered clothes**, torn clothing, tatters, old clothes, cast-offs, hand-me-downs.

rag[2] ▶ **noun** (*Brit.*) *students caused a ninety-minute traffic jam during their rag week* **fund-raising event**, charity event, charitable event, collection.
▶ **verb** (*informal*) *the President is now ragged mercilessly on national television. See* TEASE.

ragamuffin ▶ **noun urchin**, guttersnipe, waif; *informal* scarecrow; *dated* gamin, gamine; *historical* mudlark; *archaic* street Arab, wastrel, tatterdemalion.

ragbag ▶ **noun** *a ragbag of products of all shapes and sizes* **jumble**, hotchpotch, hodgepodge, mishmash, mess, confusion, hash, pastiche, farrago; **assortment**, mixture, miscellany, medley, motley, motley collection, mixed bag, melange, mix, blend, variety, diversity, collection, selection, assemblage, combination, conglomeration, pot-pourri; *rare* mingle-mangle, gallimaufry, omnium gatherum, olio, salmagundi, macédoine.

rage ▶ **noun 1** *Keith's rage is caused by frustration* **fury**, anger, wrath, outrage, indignation, passion, hot temper, spleen, resentment, pique, annoyance, vexation, exasperation, displeasure, bitterness, rancour, antagonism, hostility; *literary* ire, choler.
OPPOSITE calmness.
2 *Toby flew into a rage at this remark* **temper**, fit of rage/fury/anger/temper, fit of bad/ill temper, towering rage, bad temper, pet, fit of pique, tantrum, fury, frenzy of rage/anger, rampage, paroxysm of rage/anger, passion, bad mood, mood; *informal* grump, strop, state; *N. Amer. informal* blowout, hissy fit; *Brit. informal, dated* bate, wax, skid; *archaic* paddywhack.
3 *the current rage for portable computing* **craze**, passion, fashion, taste, desire, craving, appetite, trend, vogue, fad, enthusiasm, love, obsession, compulsion, weakness, fondness, fixation, fetish, mania, fascination, preoccupation; *informal* thing, yen; *rare* cacoethes.
□ **(all) the rage** *for today's children, video and computer games are all the rage* **very popular**, in fashion, in style, in vogue, (all) the fashion, the (latest) craze, the (latest) thing, (all) the vogue, in (great) demand, much sought-after, ultra-fashionable; *French* le dernier cri; *informal* in, the in thing, cool, big, trendy, hot, hip; *Brit. informal, dated* all the go.
▶ **verb 1** *she raged silently all the way back to the cottage* **be angry**, be furious, be enraged, be incensed, be infuriated, seethe, be beside oneself, have a fit, boil, be boiling over, rant, rave, rant and rave, storm, fume, spit, breathe fire, burn; *informal* be livid, be wild, jump up and down, froth/foam at the mouth, be steamed up, have steam coming out of one's ears; *Brit. informal* do one's head/nut in.
2 *he **raged against** the carving-up of the land* **protest strongly at**, complain vociferously about, disagree violently with, oppose strongly, denounce; **fulminate**, storm, inveigh, rail, kick, expostulate, make a fuss about; *informal* kick up a fuss/stink about.
3 *a tropical storm was raging* **be violent**, be at its height, be turbulent, be tempestuous, be uncontrollable, thunder, rampage.

ragged ▶ **adjective 1** *a pair of ragged jeans* **tattered**, in tatters, torn, ripped, split, in holes, holey, moth-eaten, frayed, worn, worn out, well worn, worn to shreds, falling to pieces, threadbare, the worse for wear, patched, scruffy, shabby, decrepit, old; *informal* tatty; *literary* rent.
2 *a ragged child* **dressed in rags**, shabby, unkempt; *Brit.* down at heel.
OPPOSITE smart.
3 *a ragged coastline* **jagged**, craggy, rugged, uneven, rough, irregular, broken; serrated, sawtooth, saw-edged, notched, nicked, indented; *technical* crenulate, crenulated, denticulate, denticulated, dentate, crenate, crenated, serrate, serrulate.
4 *the ragged remnants of an expedition sought refuge in the village* **disorganized**, **in disarray**, confused, in confusion, disordered, disorderly; muddled, jumbled, in a muddle/jumble, straggling, straggly, fragmented.

raging ▶ **adjective 1** *a raging mob* **angry**, furious, enraged, incensed, infuriated, irate, wrathful, seething, fuming, blazing, flaming mad, blazing mad, mad, ranting, raving, beside oneself; *informal* livid, wild; *Brit. informal, dated* waxy.
OPPOSITES calm, placid.
2 *raging seas* | *a raging storm* **stormy**, violent, strong, wild, turbulent, tempestuous, blustery.
OPPOSITE calm.
3 *a raging headache* **excruciating**, agonizing, very painful, searing, harrowing, throbbing, acute, very bad, sharp.
4 *her raging thirst* **severe**, extreme, huge, excessive, very great, inordinate.

raid ▶ **noun 1** *the raid on Dieppe* **surprise attack**, hit-and-run raid, tip-and-run raid, assault, descent, blitz, incursion, foray, sortie; sally, inroad, onslaught, onrush, storming, charge, thrust, offensive, invasion; *German* blitzkrieg; *Italian* razzia.
2 *clothing worth £40,000 has been stolen in a raid on a shop in Bond Street* **robbery**, burglary, hold-up, break-in; mugging, robbing, pillaging, looting, plunder, plundering, ransacking, sack, sacking, marauding; *informal* snatch, smash-and-grab; *Brit. informal* blag; *N. Amer. informal* heist, stick-up.
3 *police discovered stolen ammunition during a raid on the flat* **swoop**, surprise search; *N. Amer. informal* bust, takedown.
▶ **verb 1** *the aim was to raid shipping in Benghazi harbour* **attack**, make a raid on, assault, set upon, descend on, swoop on, harass, harry, blitz, make inroads on, assail, storm, rush, charge.
2 *they live as outlaws, raiding villages and towns for food and clothing* **plunder**, steal from, pillage, loot, rifle, maraud, strip, ransack, sack; *literary* despoil; *archaic* reave, spoil; *rare* depredate, spoliate, forage.
3 *they had raided the electrical store next door* **rob**, steal from, hold up, break into, make a raid on; *N. Amer. informal* stick up.
4 *homes and offices in Merseyside were raided by police* **search**, make a search of, swoop on, make a raid on; *N. Amer. informal* bust.

raider ▶ **noun** *armed raiders escaped with several thousand pounds of jewellery* **attacker**, assailant; **robber**, burglar, thief, housebreaker; plunderer, pillager, looter, marauder, ransacker, sacker, invader; *archaic* reaver.

rail ▶ **verb** *Johnson **rails against** injustice and oppression* **protest strongly at**, make a protest against, fulminate against, inveigh against, rage against, thunder against, declaim against, remonstrate about, expostulate about, make a fuss about, speak out against, express disapproval of, criticize severely, denounce, censure, condemn; **object to**, raise objections to, take issue with, oppose strongly, complain vociferously/bitterly about, disagree violently with, kick against, take great exception to, make/take a stand against, put up a fight against, challenge; *informal* kick up a fuss/stink about.

railing ▶ noun **fence**, fencing, rail(s), paling, palisade, balustrade, banister, hurdle, barrier, parapet.

raillery ▶ noun *the affectionate raillery from her fellow workers* **teasing**, good-humoured mockery, chaff, banter, ragging, badinage, japing; *informal* leg-pulling, ribbing, joshing, kidding, kidology; *N. Amer. informal* josh; *rare* persiflage.

rain ▶ noun **1** *the rain had almost stopped* rainfall, precipitation, raindrops, rainwater, wet weather; the wet, a fall of rain; sprinkle, drizzle, mizzle, Scotch mist, shower, rainstorm, cloudburst, torrent, downpour, deluge, squall, thunderstorm.
2 *a rain of hot ash | a rain of blows* **shower**, deluge, flood, torrent, spate, avalanche, outpouring, rush, flurry; volley, storm, hail, barrage, broadside, salvo.
▶ verb **1** *it was raining heavily* **pour (down)**, pelt down, tip down, teem down, beat down, lash down, sheet down, come down, come down in torrents/sheets, rain cats and dogs; fall, shower, drizzle, spit; *informal* be chucking it down; *Brit. informal* bucket down, come down in buckets/bucketloads, come down in stair rods, tipple down; *Brit. vulgar slang* piss down.
2 *bombs rained on the city's crowded streets* **fall**, pour/rain down, drop, shower.
3 *guerrillas rained mortar bombs on the capital* **shower**, pour, drop; bombard someone with, pepper someone with, pelt someone with.

WORD LINKS
relating to rain **pluvial, pluvious, hyetal**

rainbow ▶ noun. *See centre pages for list of colours of the* **Rainbow**

rainy ▶ adjective *rainy weather* **wet**, showery, drizzly, damp, inclement.
OPPOSITE dry.

raise ▶ verb **1** *Arthur raised a hand in greeting | the remains of the ship were eventually raised* **lift**, lift up, raise aloft, elevate; uplift, upraise, hoist, haul up, heave up, lever up, hitch up, take up; *Brit. informal* hoick up; *rare* upheave, uprear, upthrust.
2 *he raised the child to a sitting position* **set upright**, place vertical, set up, put up, stand (up), upend, stand on end; pitch.
OPPOSITES knock over, lay down.
3 *there was no alternative but to raise prices* **increase**, put up, push up, up, mark up, step up, lift, augment, escalate, inflate, swell, add to; *informal* hike (up), jack up, bump up.
OPPOSITES lower, reduce.
4 *I really hope they can raise their game* **improve**, boost, lift, enhance, make better, ameliorate, upgrade.
5 *he raised the volume of his voice slightly | they were able to raise public awareness of the issues involved* **increase**, heighten, make higher, lift, augment, amplify, magnify, intensify, boost, step up, turn up, add to; make louder, louden.
OPPOSITE lower.
6 *the temple was raised in about 900 BC* **build**, construct, erect, assemble, put up.
OPPOSITES demolish, raze.
7 *the yeast created enough gas to raise the thick bread dough* **cause to rise**, make rise, leaven, ferment; puff up, dilate, inflate.
8 *how do you propose to raise the money?* **get**, obtain, acquire; accumulate, amass, scrape together, collect; fetch, realize, yield, net, make.
OPPOSITES distribute, spend.
9 *the city had raised troops to fight for the Government* **recruit**, enlist, sign up, conscript, call to arms, call up, muster, mobilize, levy, rally, press, get/gather together, collect, assemble, call together; *N. Amer.* draft.
OPPOSITES stand down, demobilize.
10 *stamp duty is a tax raised on transfers of ownership* **levy**, impose, exact, demand, charge.
11 *he raised one objection after another* **bring up**, introduce, advance, broach, mention, allude to, touch on, suggest, moot, put forward, bring forward, pose, present, table, propose, submit; air, ventilate.
OPPOSITES withdraw, keep quiet about.
12 *the disaster raised doubts about the safety of nuclear power* **give rise to**, occasion, cause, bring into being, bring about, produce, engender, draw forth, elicit, create, set going, set afoot, result in, lead to, prompt, awaken, arouse, excite, summon up, activate, evoke, induce, kindle, incite, stir up, trigger, spark off, provoke, instigate, foment, whip up; *literary* beget, enkindle.
OPPOSITES allay, end.
13 (*N. Amer.*) *most parents manage to raise their children successfully* **bring up**, rear, nurture, look after, care for, take care of, provide for, mother, parent, tend, protect, cherish; educate, train, foster.
14 *he raised cattle in Nebraska* **breed**, rear, nurture, keep, tend.
15 *wheat is also raised in considerable quantity* **grow**, farm, cultivate, produce, propagate, bring on; plant.
16 *he was raised to the peerage* **promote**, advance, upgrade, elevate, prefer, ennoble, aggrandize, exalt, give a higher rank to, give advancement to; *informal* kick upstairs.
OPPOSITE demote.
17 *raids across the border raised the spectre of civil war* **cause to appear**, call up, call forth, invoke, summon (up), conjure up.
OPPOSITE lay.
18 *Alfonso at once raised the siege of Saragossa* **end**, stop, bring to an end, put an end to, terminate, abandon, lift.
OPPOSITES start, impose.
19 (*Brit. informal*) *see if you can raise them on the radio* **contact**, get in touch with, get hold of, reach, communicate with; phone, radio, call; *Brit.* get on to.
□ **raise hell** (*informal*). See **HELL**.
▶ noun (*N. Amer.*) *he wanted a raise and some extra holiday* **rise**, pay/wage/salary increase, increment.

raised ▶ adjective *the plate bears an inscription in raised letters* **embossed**, relief, relievo, cameo, die-stamped, thermographed, ribbed.
OPPOSITE engraved.

rake[1] ▶ verb **1** *another man was raking the clippings into a sack* **scrape up/together**, collect, gather.
2 *she raked the gravel meticulously* **smooth**, smooth out, level, even out, flatten, comb.
3 *the cat raked his face with its claws* **scratch**, lacerate, scrape, rasp, graze, abrade, grate, bark; *technical* excoriate.
4 *she raked a hand through her hair* **drag**, pull, scrape, draw, tug.
5 *Dempster raked through his pockets* **rummage**, search, hunt, sift, rifle; ransack, comb, turn upside down, scour, go through with a fine-tooth comb.
6 *machine-gun fire raked the streets* **sweep**, enfilade, pepper, strafe; *archaic* cannonade, fusillade.
7 *her eyes raked the room* **search**, scan, look around/round/over, survey, study, inspect, scour, scrutinize, examine, explore; *N. Amer. informal* scope.
□ **rake something in** (*informal*) *the movie raked in over $300 million* **earn**, make, get, gain, get paid, obtain, acquire, accumulate, bring in, gather in, pull in, haul in, pocket, realize, make a profit of, fetch, return, yield, raise, clear, net, gross.
□ **rake something up** *I was afraid that someone had raked up the past* **remind people of**, revive the memory of, recollect, remember, call to mind; drag up, dredge up, speak out about.

rake[2] ▶ noun *the third earl had the reputation of being something of a rake* **playboy**, libertine, profligate; degenerate, roué, debauchee, dissolute man, loose-liver; lecher, seducer, ladies' man, womanizer, philanderer, adulterer, Don Juan, Lothario, Casanova; *informal* ladykiller, lech; *dated* gay dog, rip, blood; *archaic* rakehell; *rare* dissolute.

rake-off ▶ noun (*informal*) *he demanded a 10 per cent rake-off* **share**, cut, percentage, dividend, commission; portion, part, half, ration, allocation, allotment, measure, apportionment; *informal* whack, slice of the cake, piece of the action.

rakish ▶ adjective *his moustache gave him a slightly rakish look* **dashing**, debonair, sporty, jaunty, devil-may-care, breezy; stylish, fashionable, dapper, spruce; raffish, disreputable, louche; *informal* sharp.

rally ▶ verb **1** *the hard-pressed French troops rallied and held their position* **reassemble**, regroup, re-form, reunite, gather together again, get together again; round up.
OPPOSITE disperse.
2 *the exiled monarch rallied an Irish Catholic army* **muster**, marshal, mobilize, raise, call up, call to arms, recruit, enlist, conscript, draft; assemble, bring together, call together, summon, gather, gather together, round up, mass, collect; *formal* convoke; *archaic* levy.
OPPOSITES demobilize, disband.
3 *ministers rallied in a concerted effort to denounce rumours of the rift* **come/get together**, band together, assemble, group, join, join together, join forces, link (up), combine, unite, ally, collaborate, cooperate, work together, act together, pull together.
OPPOSITES separate, split up.
4 *he tried to rally support for more radical policies* **gather**, accumulate, collect, assemble, amass, muster, marshal, organize, round up, garner, harvest; get up, raise, mobilize, whip up.
5 *the shock grew less and her spirits rallied | share prices have rallied* **recover**, improve, get better, pick up, revive, come back, make a comeback, rebound, bounce back, perk up, look up, take a turn for the better, turn the/a corner, be given a new lease of life, take on a new lease of life; emerge from something, get over something, shake something off; *informal* come up smiling.
OPPOSITE deteriorate.
▶ noun **1** *there was a rally in support of the strike* **meeting**, mass meeting, gathering, assembly; **demonstration**, march, protest march, parade; *informal* get-together, demo.
2 *blizzards caused a short-lived rally in oil prices* **recovery**, upturn, improvement, revival, comeback, rebound, resurgence, renewal, a turn for the better, reaction; *technical* dead cat bounce.
OPPOSITE slump.

ram ▶ verb **1** *he rammed his sword back into its sheath* **force**, thrust, plunge, stab, push, sink, dig, stick, cram, jam, stuff, pack, compress, squeeze,

wedge, press, tamp, pound, drive, hammer, bang.
2 *a stolen van was used to ram the police car* **hit**, strike, crash into, collide with, be in collision with, meet head-on, run into, slam (into), smash into, dash against, crack into/against, bump (into), bang (into), knock into, butt; *N. Amer.* impact.

ramble ▶ **verb 1** *we rambled around the Cornwall countryside* **walk**, take a walk, go for a walk, hike, tramp, backpack, trek; wander, stroll, saunter, amble, drift, roam, range, rove, traipse, jaunt; *Scottish & Irish* stravaig; *informal* mosey, tootle; *Brit. informal* pootle; *rare* vagabond, perambulate, peregrinate.
2 *I'm not going to ramble on about environmental issues* **chatter**, babble, prattle, prate, blather, blether, gabble, jabber, twitter, go on, run on, rattle on/away, blither, maunder, drivel; *informal* jaw, gas, gab, yak, yackety-yak, yabber, yatter, shoot one's mouth off; *Brit. informal* witter, rabbit, chunter, natter, waffle; *N. Amer. informal* run off at the mouth; *Austral./NZ informal* mag; *archaic* twaddle, clack, twattle.
▶ **noun** *I had looked forward to a leisurely ramble amongst the hills* **walk**, hike, trek; wander, stroll, saunter, amble, roam, traipse, jaunt, promenade, trip, excursion, tour; *informal* mosey, tootle; *Brit. informal* pootle; *rare* perambulation, peregrination.

rambler ▶ **noun walker**, hiker, stroller, saunterer, wanderer, roamer, rover, drifter, traveller, wayfarer.

rambling ▶ **adjective 1** *a long, rambling speech* **long-winded**, garrulous, verbose, wordy, prolix; digressive, wandering, maundering; roundabout, circuitous, diffuse, discursive, circumlocutory, oblique, periphrastic; disconnected, disjointed, ill-thought-out, incoherent, illogical.
OPPOSITES concise, pithy.
2 *a maze of narrow, rambling streets* **winding**, twisting, twisty, labyrinthine; **sprawling**, spreading, straggling.
3 *a rambling rose* **trailing**, creeping, straggling, vining, prostrate.

ramification ▶ **noun** *the political ramifications of shutting the factory would be immense* **consequence**, result, aftermath, outcome, effect, upshot, issue, sequel; complication, development, implication; product, by-product, outgrowth, spin-off.

ramp ▶ **noun** *there was a ramp down to a double garage on basement level* **slope**, sloping surface, bank, incline, inclined plane, gradient, grade, tilt, angle; rise, ascent, acclivity; drop, descent, declivity.

rampage ▶ **verb** *stone-throwing mobs rampaged through the streets* **rush wildly/madly**, riot, run riot, go on the rampage, run amok, go berserk, storm, charge, tear; rave; *informal* steam.
▶ **noun**
▫ **on the rampage** *a sacked chef went on the rampage in his kitchen* **berserk**, out of control, wild, violent, frenzied, running amok, rioting, riotous, destructive, rampaging; *N. Amer. informal* postal.

rampant ▶ **adjective 1** *the rampant inflation of the mid-1970s* **uncontrolled**, unrestrained, unchecked, unbridled, widespread, pandemic, epidemic, pervasive; out of control, out of hand, rife, spreading like wildfire.
OPPOSITES controlled, under control.
2 *that first interested glance had been replaced by one of rampant dislike* **vehement**, strong, violent, forceful, raging, wild, intense, fanatical, passionate.
OPPOSITE mild.
3 *rampant vegetation* **luxuriant**, exuberant, lush, rank, rich, riotous, profuse, lavish, vigorous, productive; *informal* jungly.
4 (*Heraldry*) *two large stone pillars surmounted by rampant lions* **upright**, standing (up), erect, rearing, vertical, perpendicular, upended, on end.

rampart ▶ **noun defensive wall**, embankment, earthwork, parapet, breastwork, battlement, stockade, palisade, bulwark, bastion, barbican, outwork, fortification; *Latin* vallum; *rare* bartizan, circumvallation.

ramshackle ▶ **adjective** *a ramshackle cottage* **tumbledown**, dilapidated, derelict, ruinous, falling to pieces, decrepit, neglected, gone to rack and ruin, run down, crumbling, decaying, disintegrating, rickety, shaky, unsteady, broken down, unsound, unsafe; *informal* shambly, geriatric; *N. Amer. informal* shacky.
OPPOSITES well maintained, sturdy.

rancid ▶ **adjective** *the smell of rancid butter* **sour**, stale, turned, rank, putrid, foul, rotten, bad, off, old, tainted; gamy, high, fetid, stinking, malodorous, foul-smelling, evil-smelling; unpleasant, noxious, revolting, nasty, sickening, offensive; *literary* noisome, mephitic; *rare* miasmic, miasmal, olid.
OPPOSITE fresh.

rancorous ▶ **adjective** *the campaign became increasingly rancorous as it progressed* **bitter**, spiteful, hateful, resentful, acrimonious, malicious, malevolent, malign, malignant, hostile, antipathetic, venomous, poisonous, vindictive, evil-intentioned, ill-natured, baleful, vengeful, vitriolic, virulent, pernicious, mean, nasty; *informal* bitchy, catty; *literary* malefic, maleficent.
OPPOSITE amicable.

rancour ▶ **noun** *an atmosphere of festering rancour and distrust* **bitterness**, spite, hate, hatred, resentment, malice, ill will, malevolence, malignancy, animosity, antipathy, enmity, hostility, acrimony, venom, poison, vindictiveness, balefulness, vengefulness, vitriol, virulence, perniciousness, meanness, nastiness; *informal* bitchiness, cattiness; *literary* maleficence.
OPPOSITE amicability.

random ▶ **adjective** *random spot checks | a random sample of eighty-six people* **unsystematic**, arbitrary, unmethodical, haphazard, unarranged, unplanned, undirected, casual, indiscriminate, non-specific, stray, erratic; chance, accidental, hit-and-miss; serendipitous, fortuitous, contingent, adventitious; non-linear, entropic, fractal; *rare* aleatory, stochastic.
OPPOSITES systematic, planned.
▫ **at random** *five schools were chosen at random* **unsystematically**, arbitrarily, randomly, without prearrangement, without method, unmethodically, haphazardly, without conscious choice, leaving things to chance; out of a hat, by lot.
OPPOSITE systematically.

range ▶ **noun 1** *it was beyond his range of vision | the age range of all patients was 39–97* **span**, scope, compass, radius, scale, gamut, reach, sweep, extent, area, field, orbit, ambit, province, realm, domain, horizon, latitude; limits, bounds, confines, parameters.
2 *a range of mountains* **row**, chain; **sierra**, cordillera, ridge, massif; line, file, rank, string, series.
3 *the toucan eats a very wide range of fruits | a new range of quality foods* **assortment**, variety, diversity, mixture, collection, array, set, selection, choice, pick; kind, sort, type, class, rank, order, genus, species.
4 *Bertha put the dish into the range to cook* **stove**, cooking stove, kitchen stove; *trademark* Aga.
5 *cows grazed on open range* **pasture**, pasturage, pastureland, grass, grassland, grazing land, ley, paddock, croft; *literary* lea, mead, greensward, sward; *Scottish & N. English* shieling, bent; *Irish & Canadian* bawn; *Austral./NZ* run; *S. African* veld; (*in Switzerland*) alp; (*in France*) bocage; (*in S. America*) potrero.
▶ **verb 1** *annual charges range from 0.5% to 1%* **vary**, fluctuate, differ; extend, stretch, reach, cover, go, run, pass.
2 *on the long stalls are ranged all sorts of fresh farm products* **line up**, align, draw up, put/set in order, order, place, position, arrange, dispose, set out, array, rank.
3 *herdsmen ranged over the steppes* **roam**, rove, traverse, travel, journey, wander, stray, drift, ramble, meander, amble, stroll, traipse, walk, hike, trek, backpack; *rare* peregrinate.
4 *the pupils were ranged according to ability* **classify**, class, categorize, type, rank, order, sort, bracket, group, rate, grade, size, graduate, pigeonhole, designate; break down, codify, catalogue, file, list, label, tabulate, index.

> **CHOOSE THE RIGHT WORD**
> **range, wander, roam, rove, stray**
> *See* WANDER.

rangy ▶ **adjective** *his rangy figure* **long-legged**, long-limbed, leggy, tall, slender, slim, lean; thin, gangling, gangly, lanky, spindly, skinny, spare, scrawny, bony, gaunt.
OPPOSITE stocky.

rank[1] *See centre pages for lists of* **Police Officers** *and military* **Ranks**
▶ **noun 1** *a former civil servant elevated to ministerial rank* **position**, **grade**, level, echelon, gradation, point on the scale, rung on the ladder; class, stratum, status, station, standing.
2 *the girl must come from a family of rank* **high standing**, nobility, aristocracy, blue blood, high birth, eminence, distinction, prestige; prominence, influence, importance, consequence, power.
3 *the first rank of riflemen was instructed to lie down* **row**, line, file, column, series, succession, string, train, procession; queue.
▫ **the rank and file 1** *both the officers and the rank and file* **other ranks**, soldiers and NCOs, lower ranks; common/ordinary/private soldiers, soldiers, men, troops.
2 *the rank and file of the organization* **ordinary members**; grass roots.
3 *a speech redolent with phrases designed to warm the hearts of the rank and file* **the people**, the proletariat, the common people, the masses, the populace, the multitude, the commonality, the commonalty, the third estate, the plebeians, the crowd; *derogatory* the hoi polloi, the common herd, the rabble, the mob, the riff-raff, the canaille, the great unwashed, the ragtag (and bobtail), the proles, the plebs.
▶ **verb 1** *the plant is ranked as endangered* **classify**, class, categorize, rate, grade, type, order, sort, bracket, group, pigeonhole, designate; codify, catalogue, file, list, tabulate.
2 *Swainson felt that an illustrator ranked below a real man of science* **have a rank**, **be graded**, be placed, be positioned, have a status, be classed, be classified, be categorized; belong.
3 *rows of tulips were ranked like guardsmen* **line up**, align, draw up, put/set in order, order, place, position, arrange, dispose, set out, array, range.

rank[2] ▶ **adjective 1** *rank vegetation* **abundant**, lush, luxuriant, dense, profuse, flourishing, exuberant, vigorous, productive, spreading, overgrown; *informal* jungly.
OPPOSITE sparse.

R

2 *a rank smell* **offensive**, unpleasant, nasty, disagreeable, revolting, sickening, obnoxious, noxious; foul-smelling, evil-smelling, fetid, smelly, stinking, reeking, reeky, high, off, rancid, putrid, malodorous, ill-smelling, fusty, musty, stale; *Brit. informal* niffy, pongy, whiffy, humming; *literary* noisome, mephitic; *rare* miasmic, miasmal, olid.
OPPOSITE pleasant.
3 *rank stupidity* **downright**, utter, outright, out-and-out, absolute, complete, sheer, stark, thorough, thoroughgoing, categorical, unequivocal, undeniable, unqualified, unmodified, unrestricted, unmitigated, unconditional, positive, simple, wholesale, all-out, perfect, consummate, patent, pure, total, entire, flat, direct, dead, final, conclusive; *archaic* arrant; *rare* right-down.

rankle ▶ verb *their insults still rankle with Martin* **cause resentment to**, cause annoyance to, annoy, upset, anger, irritate, offend, affront, displease, exasperate, infuriate, provoke, irk, vex, pique, nettle, gall, gnaw at, eat away at, grate on; fester; *informal* rile, miff, peeve, aggravate, hack off; *Brit. informal* nark; *N. Amer. informal* tick off; *vulgar slang* piss off.

ransack ▶ verb **1** *burglars had ransacked the place* **plunder**, pillage, steal from, raid, rob, loot, rifle, sack, strip, denude; ravage, maraud, lay waste, devastate; *literary* despoil; *archaic* reave; *rare* depredate, spoliate.
2 *she ransacked the wardrobe for something to wear* **rummage through**, hunt through, search (through), rake through, scour, rifle, look all round, go through, comb, scrabble around in, poke around in, rummage around in, hunt around in, explore, turn inside out, turn over.

ransom ▶ noun **1** *the kidnappers demanded a huge ransom* **pay-off**, payment, price.
2 *the ransom of the prisoners* **release**, freedom, setting free, deliverance, liberation, rescue, redemption, restoration.
▶ verb *the girl was subsequently ransomed for £4 million* **obtain the release of**, exchange for a ransom, buy the freedom of, release, free, deliver, liberate, rescue, redeem, restore to freedom.

rant ▶ verb *she was still ranting on about the unfairness of it all* **hold forth**, go on and on, deliver a tirade, rant and rave, fulminate, sound off, spout, pontificate, trumpet, bluster, declaim; shout, yell, roar, bellow; *informal* mouth off; *rare* vociferate.
▶ noun *he went into a rant about the people who were annoying him* **tirade**, harangue, diatribe, broadside, verbal onslaught; *rare* philippic.

rap[1] ▶ verb **1** *he stood up and rapped the table | she rapped his fingers with a ruler* **hit**, strike, bang, thump, knock; *informal* whack, thwack, bash, wallop; *literary* smite.
2 *I rapped on the open door of his office* **knock**, tap; bang, hammer, batter, pound.
3 (*informal*) *banks are to be rapped for delaying interest rate cuts*. See REBUKE.
▶ noun **1** *a rap on the knuckles* **blow**, hit, knock, bang, crack, thump; *informal* whack, thwack, bash, wallop.
2 *there was a rap at the door* **knock**, knocking, tap, bang, banging, hammering, battering, pounding, rat-tat.
□ **take the rap** (*informal*) *I don't want him to take the rap for something he didn't do* **be punished**, **be blamed**, take the blame, pay, suffer, suffer the consequences, pay the price; answer for something; *informal* be for it; *Brit. informal* carry the can.
OPPOSITE get off scot-free.

rap[2] ▶ noun *they didn't care a rap about me* **whit**, iota, jot, hoot, scrap, bit, fig; one bit, even a little bit, two hoots, the smallest amount, the tiniest bit; *informal* damn, tinker's cuss/curse, brass farthing, monkey's.

rapacious ▶ adjective *rapacious landlords* **grasping**, **greedy**, avaricious, acquisitive, covetous, mercenary, materialistic, insatiable, predatory, voracious, usurious, extortionate; *informal* money-grubbing; *N. Amer. informal* grabby.
OPPOSITE generous.

rapacity ▶ noun **greed**, avarice, rapaciousness, acquisitiveness, covetousness, materialism, predatoriness, voracity, voraciousness, graspingness, mercenariness, usury, extortion.
OPPOSITE unselfishness.

rape ▶ noun **1** *the man was charged with rape* **sexual assault**, sexual abuse; date rape, gang rape; *N. Amer.* acquaintance rape; *informal* gang bang; *archaic or humorous* a fate worse than death; *archaic* ravishment, defilement.
2 *people everywhere decry the rape of rainforest* **destruction**, violation, vandalizing, ravaging, pillaging; **plundering**, raiding, desecration, defilement; marauding, ransacking, sacking, sack; *literary* despoilment, rapine; *rare* despoliation, spoliation.
3 (*archaic*) *the rape of the Sabine women* **abduction**, carrying off, kidnapping, seizure, capture.
▶ verb **1** *he raped her at knifepoint* **sexually assault**, violate, force oneself on, abuse sexually; date-rape, gang-rape; *informal* gang-bang; *euphemistic* have one's (evil) way with; *archaic* ravish, defile, dishonour.
2 *they raped our country* **ravage**, plunder, pillage, violate, desecrate, defile; lay waste, ransack, sack; maraud over, raid; *literary* despoil; *archaic* spoil, reave; *rare* depredate, spoliate.
3 (*archaic*) *the Romans raped the Sabine women* **abduct**, carry off, kidnap, seize, capture, make off with.

rapid ▶ adjective *his rapid rise to stardom | they made a rapid exit* **quick**, fast, swift, speedy, high-speed, expeditious, express, brisk, lively, prompt, flying, fleeting, lightning, meteoric, overnight, whirlwind, fast-track, whistle-stop; sudden, instantaneous, immediate, instant, hurried, hasty, abrupt, sharp, precipitate, breakneck, headlong; *informal* p.d.q. (pretty damn quick); *literary* fleet; *rare* alacritous, volant.
OPPOSITES slow, leisurely.

rapidity ▶ noun **quickness**, swiftness, speed, speediness, briskness, expeditiousness, alacrity, dispatch, velocity, promptness, promptitude; suddenness, immediacy, instantaneousness, hurriedness, haste, hastiness, abruptness, precipitateness; *literary* fleetness, celerity.

rapidly ▶ adverb *he drove rapidly to the scene of the accident* **quickly**, fast, swiftly, speedily, at (full) speed, at the speed of light, post-haste, hotfoot, at full tilt, as fast as one's legs can carry one, at a gallop, expeditiously, briskly, promptly; hurriedly, in a hurry, fast and furious, hastily, in haste, in a rush, precipitately, abruptly; *informal* like a shot, double quick, p.d.q. (pretty damn quick), before one can say Jack Robinson, in a flash, hell for leather, pronto, at the double, like a bat out of hell, like (greased) lightning, like a madman/madwoman, like mad, like crazy, like blazes, like a streak, like the wind, like a bomb, like nobody's business, like a scalded cat, like the deuce, a mile a minute, before the ink is dry on the page, before one can say knife; *Brit. informal* like the clappers, at a rate of knots, like billy-o; *N. Amer. informal* lickety-split; *literary* apace.
OPPOSITE slowly.

rapport ▶ noun *she had established an amazing rapport with Ben* **affinity**, close/special relationship, (mutual) understanding, bond, empathy, harmony, sympathy, link, accord.

rapprochement ▶ noun *growing political and diplomatic rapprochement between the two countries* **reconciliation**, increased understanding, détente, restoration of harmony, agreement, cooperation, harmonization, softening.

rapt ▶ adjective **1** *the rapt teenage audience* **fascinated**, enthralled, spellbound, captivated, riveted, gripped, mesmerized, enchanted, entranced, charmed, bewitched, transported, enraptured; thrilled, ecstatic, rapturous; *informal* blissed out.
OPPOSITES uninterested, inattentive.
2 *she stood motionless for a second, as if rapt in thought* **engrossed**, absorbed, lost, preoccupied, in a brown study, intent.

rapture ▶ noun *she gazed up at him in rapture* **ecstasy**, bliss, euphoria, elation, exaltation, joy, joyfulness, joyousness, cloud nine, seventh heaven, transport, rhapsody, enchantment, delight, exhilaration, happiness, pleasure, ravishment; *informal* the top of the world; *humorous* delectation.
OPPOSITES boredom, indifference.
□ **go into raptures** *the critics went into raptures about her performance* **enthuse**, rhapsodize, rave, gush, wax lyrical, express intense pleasure/enthusiasm; heap praise on, praise to the skies, make much of; *informal* go wild/mad/crazy.

rapturous ▶ adjective *he was given a rapturous reception by a flag-waving crowd* **ecstatic**, joyful, joyous, elated, euphoric, enraptured, on cloud nine, in seventh heaven, transported, in transports, in raptures, beside oneself with joy/happiness, rhapsodic, ravished, enchanted, enthusiastic, delighted, thrilled, overjoyed, blissful, happy; *informal* over the moon, on top of the world, blissed out; *Austral. informal* wrapped.
OPPOSITES bored, indifferent.

rara avis ▶ noun (*Latin*) *a man of integrity in high office is something of a rara avis* **rarity**, rare person/thing, rare bird, wonder, marvel, nonpareil, nonsuch, one of a kind, find; anomaly, curiosity, oddity, aberration, freak; *Brit. informal* one-off, oner.

rare ▶ adjective **1** *their rare moments of privacy* **infrequent**, few and far between, scarce, sparse, scattered, thin on the ground, golden, like gold dust, as scarce as hen's teeth; occasional, limited, odd, isolated, sporadic, intermittent, unaccustomed, unwonted; *Brit.* out of the common.
OPPOSITES common, frequent.
2 *a collector of rare stamps and coins | one of Britain's rarest birds* **unusual**, uncommon, unfamiliar, out of the ordinary, atypical, singular, remarkable, recherché, special, precious.
OPPOSITES ordinary, commonplace.
3 *he's a man of rare talent* **exceptional**, outstanding, unparalleled, peerless, matchless, unique, unequalled, incomparable, unrivalled, inimitable, beyond compare, beyond comparison, without equal, second to none, unsurpassed, surpassing, exquisite, superb, consummate, superior, superlative, first-class, first-rate, special, choice, excellent, very fine; *informal* A1, top-notch; *rare* unexampled.
OPPOSITES common, everyday.

rarefied ▶ adjective *the academic or rarefied nature of much of their work* **esoteric**, exclusive, select, private, cliquish; elevated, exalted, lofty.
OPPOSITE commonplace.

rarely ▶ adverb *she rarely mentions her late husband* **seldom**, infrequently, on rare occasions, hardly ever, scarcely ever, hardly, scarcely, almost never, once in a while, only now and then, not often, only occasionally, sporadically; *informal* once in a blue moon.

R

OPPOSITES often, frequently.

raring ▶ adjective *he was raring to get back in the ring* **eager**, keen, enthusiastic, full of enthusiasm, impatient, longing, champing/chafing at the bit, desperate; ready, willing; *informal* dying, itching, gagging.

rarity ▶ noun **1** *the rarity of earthquakes there has lulled people into a false sense of security* **infrequency**, rareness, unusualness, uncommonness, singularity, uniqueness; scarcity, scarceness, sparseness.
2 *steam locomotives are now becoming something of a rarity* **collector's item**, rare person/thing, rare bird, marvel, wonder, nonpareil, one of a kind, find, conversation piece; curiosity, oddity, anomaly, freak; *Latin* rara avis; *Brit. informal* one-off, oner.

rascal ▶ noun **1** *what's the little rascal been up to now?* **scallywag**, scamp, devil, imp, monkey, mischievous person, mischief-maker, wretch; *informal* horror, monster; *Brit. informal* perisher; *Irish informal* spalpeen; *N. English informal* tyke, scally; *N. Amer. informal* varmint, hellion; *dated* rip; *archaic* rapscallion, scapegrace.
2 *a double-dealing rascal* **scoundrel**, rogue, ne'er-do-well, good-for-nothing, reprobate; *informal* villain, rat; *Scottish informal* scrote; *informal, dated* rotter, bounder; *dated* cad; *archaic* miscreant, blackguard, knave, vagabond, varlet, wastrel.

rash[1] ▶ noun **1** *next day, he broke out in a rash* **spots**, skin eruption, breakout; hives, heat rash, nettle rash, nappy rash; *technical* erythema, exanthema, urticaria, papules, roseola, purpura, pompholyx; *rare* efflorescence.
2 *the incident provoked a rash of articles in the press* **series**, succession; **spate**, wave, flood, deluge, torrent; outbreak, plague, epidemic, explosion, run, flurry; *rare* boutade.

rash[2] ▶ adjective *he cursed himself for being so rash | a rash decision* **reckless**, impetuous, impulsive, hasty, overhasty, foolhardy, incautious, precipitate, precipitous, premature, careless, heedless, thoughtless, imprudent, foolish, headstrong, adventurous, over-adventurous, hot-headed, daredevil, devil-may-care, overbold, audacious, indiscreet; ill-considered, unconsidered, unthinking, ill-advised, injudicious, ill-judged, misguided, spur-of-the-moment, unthought-out, hare-brained, unwary, unguarded, wild, madcap; *informal* harum-scarum; *rare* temerarious.
OPPOSITES careful, cautious, prudent.

CHOOSE THE RIGHT WORD

rash, reckless, foolhardy

All these adjectives are used to criticize actions or people for a lack of proper caution.

- **Rash** suggests an overhasty judgement that one might regret (*now isn't the time for us to make rash statements | he would be rash to expect everyone to obey him all the time*).
- **Reckless** typically describes something more serious: a *reckless* act is that of a person who simply does not care what damage they cause to themselves or others (*reckless consumption of the earth's resources | he could be convicted of causing death by reckless driving*).
- **Foolhardy**, as the word suggests, refers to foolish daring, and a *foolhardy* act is most likely to harm the *foolhardy* person themselves (*old mines were not to be left open as an invitation to any foolhardy visitor*).

rasp ▶ verb **1** *enamel is rasped off the edges of the horse's teeth* **scrape**, file, rub, abrade, grate, sand, sandpaper, scratch, scour; *technical* excoriate.
2 *'What's going on?' he rasped* **croak**, say/utter hoarsely, squawk, shrill, caw.
3 *her hard, metallic voice rasped his nerves* **grate on**, jar on, irritate, irk; get on someone's nerves, set someone's teeth on edge; *Brit. informal* rub up the wrong way.
▶ noun *the rasp of the engine* **grinding**, grating, scraping, scrape, scratching, scratch.

rasping ▶ adjective *a dry, rasping sound | his father's rasping voice* **harsh**, grating, jarring, raspy, discordant, dissonant, scratchy, creaky; hoarse, rough, gravelly, croaky, croaking, gruff, husky, throaty, guttural; *rare* stridulant.

rat *See centre pages for list of* **Rodents**
▶ noun **1** *her rat of a husband cheated on her* **scoundrel**, wretch, rogue; *informal* beast, pig, swine, bastard, creep, louse, snake, snake in the grass, bum, lowlife, scumbag, heel, skunk, dog, weasel; *Brit. informal* rotter, bounder; *N. Amer. informal* rat fink; *Irish informal* sleeveen; *Austral. informal* dingo; *dated* cad; *vulgar slang* shit.
2 *the most famous rat in mob history* **informer**, betrayer, stool pigeon; *informal* snitch, finger, squealer, nose; *Brit. informal* grass, supergrass, nark, snout; *Scottish & N. Irish informal* tout; *N. Amer. informal* fink, stoolie; *Austral. informal* fizgig, pimp, shelf; *archaic* intelligencer, beagle.
▶ exclamation *Rats! I've lost my ticket!* **damn**, damnation, blast, hell, heck, Gordon Bennett; *Brit.* bother; *informal* drat, sugar, botheration, flip, flipping heck/hell; *Brit. informal* dash, blooming heck/hell, blinking heck/hell; *N. Amer. informal* doggone it, shucks, shoot, tarnation; *Indian informal* arré; *dated* confound it, pish.
▶ verb (*informal*)
□ **rat on 1** *we may have been poor but ratting on our friends was something we didn't do* **inform on/against**, betray, be disloyal to, be unfaithful to, break one's promise to, break faith with, sell out, stab someone in the back; *informal* tell on, sell down the river, blow the whistle on, squeal on, stitch up, peach on, do the dirty on; *Brit. informal* grass on, shop; *N. Amer. informal* rat out, finger, drop a/the dime on; *Austral. informal* pimp on, pool, put someone's pot on.
2 *he accused the government of ratting on an earlier pledge* **break**, renege on, go back on, back out of, default on, welsh on; break one's word.

rate ▶ noun **1** *a fixed rate of interest | the maximum rate of taxation* **percentage**, ratio, proportion, scale, standard.
2 *boats can be hired for a reasonable daily rate | an hourly rate of $30* **charge**, price, cost, tariff, hire, fare, figure, amount, outlay; tax, duty, levy, toll; fee, remuneration, pay, payment, wage, allowance; *informal* damage.
3 *the rate of change was very fast* **speed**, pace, tempo, velocity, momentum; gait; *informal* clip, lick.
▶ verb **1** *they were asked to rate their ability at different driving manoeuvres* **assess**, evaluate, appraise, weigh up, judge, estimate, calculate, compute, gauge, measure, adjudge, value, put a value on; grade, rank, classify, class, categorize, position, place.
2 *the scheme was rated as no more than moderately effective* **consider to be**, judge to be, reckon to be, think to be, hold to be, deem to be, find to be; regard, account, esteem, mark down as, look on, count.
3 *his statement rated only a brief mention near the end of the report* **merit**, deserve, warrant, be worthy of, be worth, be entitled to, be deserving of, have a claim to, have a right to.
4 (*informal*) *I think he's okay, but Benny doesn't rate him* **think highly of**, have a high opinion of, admire, think much of, set much store by, hold in esteem, esteem, value, hold in high regard.
□ **at any rate** *at any rate, I think I'm in with a chance* **in any case**, anyhow, anyway, at all events, in any event, nevertheless; whatever happens, no matter what happens, come what may, regardless, notwithstanding.

rather ▶ adverb **1** *I'd rather you went* **by preference**, sooner, preferably, from/by choice, more willingly, more readily; *N. Amer.* if I had my druthers.
2 *it all sounds rather complicated* **quite**, a bit, a little, fairly, slightly, somewhat, relatively, to some degree/extent, comparatively, moderately; *informal* pretty, sort of, kind of, kinda.
3 *she was finally forced to confront her true feelings for him—or rather, her lack of feelings* **more precisely**, to be precise, to be exact, strictly speaking, correctly speaking.
4 *she seemed indifferent* ***rather than*** *angry* **more**, more truly; as opposed to, instead of.
5 *the judgement was not impulsive, but rather a carefully thought-out decision* **on the contrary**, quite the opposite, instead.

ratify ▶ verb *both countries were due to ratify the treaty by the end of the year* **confirm**, approve, sanction, endorse, agree to, accept, consent to, assent to, affirm, uphold, corroborate, authorize, formalize, certify, validate, recognize; sign, countersign, put one's name to.
OPPOSITES reject, revoke.

rating ▶ noun *the hotel's four-star rating* **grade**, classification, class, grading, ranking, rank, category, categorization, designation, position, standing, status, placing; assessment, evaluation, appraisal; mark, score.

ratio ▶ noun **proportion**, comparative number/extent, quantitative relation, correlation, relationship, correspondence, balance; percentage, fraction, quotient.

ration ▶ noun **1** *she allowed herself a daily ration of chocolate* **allowance**, allocation, quota, fixed amount, amount, quantity, share, portion, helping, allotment, measure, part, lot, proportion, percentage; *rare* apportionment, quantum, moiety.
2 (**rations**) *the garrison had run out of rations* **supplies**, provisions, food, food and drink, foodstuffs, eatables, edibles; necessaries, necessities, stores; *Scottish* vivers; *informal* grub, eats; *N. Amer. informal* chuck; *archaic* victuals, vittles, viands, meat, commons; *rare* comestibles, provender, aliment, viaticum.
▶ verb **1** *coal and petrol were also rationed* **control**, limit (to a fixed amount), restrict (the consumption of), conserve, budget.
2 *they* ***rationed out*** *the water* **distribute**, share out, measure out, divide out/up, apportion, give out, deal out, issue, allocate, allot, dispense, hand out, pass out, dole out, parcel out; *rare* admeasure.

rational ▶ adjective **1** *a rational approach to the problem* **logical**, reasoned, well reasoned, sensible, reasonable, cogent, coherent, intelligent, wise, judicious, sagacious, astute, shrewd, perceptive, enlightened, clear-eyed, clear-sighted, commonsensical, common-sense, well advised, well grounded, sound, sober, prudent, circumspect, politic; down-to-earth, practical, pragmatic, matter-of-fact, hard-headed, with both one's feet on the ground, unidealistic; *informal* joined-up.
OPPOSITES irrational, illogical.
2 *she was not fully rational at the time of signing the agreement* **lucid**,

coherent, sane, in one's right mind, able to think/reason clearly, of sound mind, in possession of all one's faculties; normal, balanced, well balanced, clear-headed; *Latin* compos mentis; *informal* all there.
OPPOSITE insane.
3 *man is a self-conscious, rational being* **intelligent**, thinking, discriminating, reasoning; cognitive, mental, cerebral, logical, analytical, conceptual; *rare* ratiocinative.

rationale ▶ **noun** *the government's rationale for introducing such radical legislation* **reason(s)**, reasoning, thinking, (logical) basis, logic, grounds, sense; principle, theory, philosophy, hypothesis, thesis, argument, case; motive, motivation, the whys and wherefores, explanation, justification, excuse, vindication; *French* raison d'être.

rationalize ▶ **verb 1** *as soon as Mary had gone he began to rationalize his behaviour* **justify**, explain (away), account for, defend, vindicate, excuse, make excuses for, make allowances for, give an explanation for, provide a rationale for, make acceptable; *rare* extenuate.
2 *they embarked on a series of attempts to rationalize the industry* **streamline**, make more efficient, improve the running of, trim, slim down, hone, make economies in, reduce wastage in, simplify; make cutbacks in, cut back on, prune, retrench on; reorganize, modernize, update.
3 *Parliament should seek to rationalize the country's court structure* **reorganize**; clarify, make consistent, apply logic/reasoning to; *rare* pragmatize.

rattle ▶ **verb 1** *we were awakened by the sound of stones rattling against the window* **clatter**, bang, clang, clank, clink, clunk.
2 *he put his hand in his pocket and rattled his small change* **jingle**, jangle, clink, tinkle.
3 *the bus rattled along the bumpy streets* **jolt**, bump, bounce, shake, vibrate, jar; *Brit.* judder; *rare* jounce.
4 *the government were clearly rattled by the campaign* **unnerve**, disconcert, disturb, fluster, shake, perturb, discompose, discomfit, discountenance, make nervous, put off, throw off balance, ruffle, agitate, put off one's stroke, upset, frighten, scare; *informal* faze, throw, get to.
▶ **noun 1** *the rattle of bottles as he stacked the crates* **clatter**, clattering, clank, clanking, clink, clinking, clanging; jingle, jingling, jangle, jangling.
2 *there was a choking rattle in his throat* death rattle; *technical* rale.
□ **rattle something off** *she rattled off the names of films he had directed* **reel off**, **recite**, list rapidly, fire off, run through, enumerate; *informal* spiel off.
□ **rattle on/away** *she found herself rattling on about the meaning of life* **prattle**, babble, chatter, gabble, prate, go on, run on, jabber, jibber-jabber, gibber, blether, blather, blither, ramble, maunder, drivel, twitter; *informal* gab, yak, yackety-yak, yap, yabber, yatter; *Brit. informal* witter, rabbit, chunter, waffle; *Scottish & Irish informal* slabber; *N. Amer. informal* run off at the mouth; *archaic* twaddle, clack, twattle.

ratty ▶ **adjective** (*Brit. informal*) *'don't bother!' he repeated, sounding ratty.* See IRRITATED.

raucous ▶ **adjective 1** *outbursts of raucous laughter* **harsh**, strident, screeching, squawky, squawking, sharp, grating, discordant, dissonant, inharmonious, unmelodious, jarring, brassy; rough, rasping, husky, hoarse, scratchy; noisy, loud, piercing, shrill, ear-splitting, penetrating, clamorous, cacophonous.
OPPOSITES soft, dulcet.
2 *a hilariously raucous hen night* **rowdy**, noisy, boisterous, roisterous, unruly, disorderly, wild.
OPPOSITES peaceful, quiet, restrained.

R

raunchy ▶ **adjective** (*informal*) *the show went on for a long time and it was fairly raunchy* **sexually explicit**, sexy, suggestive, erotic, racy, risqué, provocative, spicy, juicy, bawdy, ribald, uninhibited, unrestrained, earthy; coarse, rude, smutty, vulgar, crude; *informal* steamy, naughty; *Brit. informal* saucy, fruity; *N. Amer. informal* gamy; *euphemistic* adult.

ravage ▶ **verb** *the inhabitants of the country had been decimated, their land ravaged* **lay waste**, **devastate**, ruin, leave in ruins, destroy, wreak havoc on, leave desolate, level, raze, demolish, wipe out, wreck, damage; pillage, plunder, harry, maraud, ransack, sack, loot; *literary* despoil, rape; *archaic* spoil, havoc; *rare* depredate, spoliate.

ravaged ▶ **adjective** *a ravaged landscape* **devastated**, ruined, wrecked, desolate; war-torn, battle-scarred.

ravages ▶ **plural noun 1** *skin that showed the ravages of time* **damaging effects**, ill effects, scars.
2 *few places these days are untouched by the ravages of man* **acts of destruction**, destruction, damage, devastation, ruin, havoc, depredation(s), wreckage; *literary* rape.

rave ▶ **verb 1** *the old man was raving about Armageddon and the fires of hell* **talk wildly**, babble, jabber, ramble, maunder; talk incoherently, be delirious.
2 *I was angry as hell—I raved and swore at them* **rant**, rant and rave, rage, explode in anger, lose one's temper, be beside oneself, storm, fulminate, deliver a tirade/harangue, go into a frenzy, lose control; shout, roar, thunder, bellow; be very angry, be furious, be enraged, be incensed, fume; *informal* fly off the handle, flip one's lid, blow one's top, go up the wall, blow a fuse, go off the deep end, hit the roof, go through the roof, be livid, have a fit, lose one's cool, go mad, go bananas, go wild, freak out, have steam coming out of one's ears, foam/froth at the mouth, go ape, be fit to be tied; *Brit. informal* go spare, go crackers; *N. Amer. informal* flip one's wig; *vulgar slang* go apeshit.
3 *he raved about her talent and predicted she'd win all the Oscars* **praise enthusiastically**, go into raptures about/over, wax lyrical about, sing the praises of, praise to the skies, heap praise on, rhapsodize over, enthuse about/over, gush about/over, throw bouquets at, express delight over, acclaim, eulogize, extol; *informal* go wild about, be mad about, go on about; *N. Amer. informal* ballyhoo; *black English* big someone/something up; *dated* cry someone/something up; *rare* laud, panegyrize.
OPPOSITES criticize, condemn.
▶ **noun** (*informal*) **1** *the imaginative menu won raves from the local food critics* **enthusiastic/lavish praise**, a rapturous reception, tribute, plaudits, encomiums, bouquets; acclaim, applause.
OPPOSITES criticism, condemnation.
2 *their annual fancy-dress rave.* See PARTY.
3 *TV news reports have depicted raves as all-night drug parties* warehouse party, acid house party; *informal* all-nighter.
▶ **adjective** (*informal*) *his big break came when a critic gave him a rave review* **very enthusiastic**, rapturous, glowing, ecstatic, full of praise, rhapsodic, laudatory, eulogistic, panegyrical, excellent, highly favourable.

raven ▶ **adjective** *her thick raven hair* **black**, glossy black, jet-black, coal-black, ebony, inky, sooty; *literary* sable.

WORD LINKS
relating to ravens **corvine**
collective noun **unkindness**

ravenous ▶ **adjective 1** *I'm absolutely ravenous—I missed lunch* **very hungry**, starving, starved, famished; *informal* with one's stomach cleaving to one's backbone; *rare* sharp-set, esurient.
OPPOSITE full.
2 *her ravenous appetite* **voracious**, insatiable, ravening, wolfish; greedy, gluttonous, gannet-like; *literary* insatiate; *rare* edacious.

rave-up ▶ **noun** (*Brit. informal*) *festive rave-ups.* See PARTY.

ravine ▶ **noun gorge**, canyon, gully, pass, defile, couloir, gap; chasm, abyss, gulf; *S. English* chine, bunny; *N. English* clough, gill, thrutch; *Scottish* cleuch, heugh; *N. Amer.* gulch, coulee, flume; *American Spanish* arroyo, barranca, quebrada; *Indian* nullah, khud; *S. African* sloot, kloof, donga; *rare* khor.

raving ▶ **adjective 1** *she's raving mad.* See MAD.
2 *she'd never been a raving beauty* **very great**, considerable, remarkable, extraordinary, singular, striking, outstanding, stunning.

ravings ▶ **plural noun** *he dismissed her words as the ravings of a hysterical woman* **gibberish**, rambling, babbling, wild talk, incoherent talk.

ravish ▶ **verb 1** *I'm sorry I kissed you, but I swear I've no intention of ravishing you* **rape**, sexually assault/abuse, violate, force oneself on, molest; seduce; *euphemistic* take advantage of, have one's (wicked) way with; *archaic* dishonour, defile.
2 *those who adore the steely, mineral style of Chablis will be ravished by this wine* **enrapture**, send into raptures, enchant, fill with delight, delight, charm, entrance, enthral, captivate, bewitch, spellbind, fascinate, transport, overjoy; *informal* blow away; *rare* rapture.
3 (*archaic*) *her infant child was ravished from her breast* **seize**, snatch, carry off/away, steal, kidnap, abduct, take by force; *literary* rape.

ravishing ▶ **adjective** *you look utterly ravishing* **very beautiful**, gorgeous, stunning, wonderful, exquisite, lovely, striking, magnificent, dazzling, radiant, delightful, charming, enchanting, entrancing, captivating, bewitching; *informal* incredible, amazing, sensational, fantastic, fabulous, terrific, smashing, heavenly, divine, out of this world, fab, drop-dead gorgeous, knockout, delectable, scrumptious; *N. Amer. informal* babelicious, bodacious.
OPPOSITE hideous.

raw ▶ **adjective 1** *a piece of raw carrot | raw fish* **uncooked**, fresh; underdone.
OPPOSITE cooked.
2 *the cost of raw materials is likely to rise | raw silk* **unprocessed**, untreated, unrefined, crude, natural, unmilled, unprepared, unfinished; green.
OPPOSITES refined, processed.
3 *a group of raw recruits* **inexperienced**, new, lacking experience, untrained, unskilled, unpractised, untried, untested, unseasoned, untutored, unschooled; callow, immature, green, ignorant, naive, unsophisticated; *informal* wet behind the ears.
OPPOSITES experienced, skilled.
4 *his skin was raw in places* **sore**, red, inflamed, painful, sensitive, tender; abraded, chafed, skinned, open, exposed, unhealed, bloody; *technical* excoriated.
5 *it was a raw morning with a bitter east wind* **bleak**, cold, chilly, chilling, chill, freezing, icy, icy-cold, wintry, bitter, biting, piercing, penetrating, sharp, keen, damp, wet; *informal* nippy; *Brit. informal* parky.
OPPOSITES warm, balmy.
6 *the raw emotions depicted in such stories* **strong**, intense, passionate, fervent, vehement, powerful, violent, acute; **undisguised**, unconcealed,

unrestrained, uninhibited.
7 *raw, contemporary images of Latin America* **realistic**, true to life, unembellished, unvarnished, gritty, naked, bare, brutal, harsh; **frank**, candid, honest, forthright, straightforward, direct, blunt, outspoken; *informal* warts and all.
OPPOSITES unrealistic, idealized.
8 *raw but authentic artistic power* **unsophisticated**, crude, rough, unpolished, unrefined, undeveloped.
□ **in the raw** (*informal*) *I slept in the raw.* See NAKED.

raw-boned ▶ adjective **thin**, as thin as a rake, lean, gaunt, bony, angular, skinny, spare, lanky, scrawny, scraggy, hollow-cheeked; underfed, underweight, emaciated, skeletal, half-starved; *dated* spindle-shanked.
OPPOSITES plump, well padded.

ray ▶ noun **1** *misty rays of light shone through the trees* **beam**, shaft, streak, bar, pencil, finger, stream, gleam, flash, glint, glimmer, flicker, twinkle, shimmer.
2 *there was just one small ray of hope* **glimmer**, flicker, spark, glint, trace, hint, indication, suggestion, sign, scintilla, whisper.
▶ verb *Fran leaned forward, her fair hair raying out in the water* **spread out**, fan out, radiate out.

raze ▶ verb *during the campaign, 80,000 people were killed and 440 villages razed* **destroy**, demolish, raze to the ground, tear down, pull down, knock down, knock to pieces, level, flatten, bulldoze, fell, wipe out, lay waste, ruin, wreck.

re ▶ preposition *correspondence re the formation of neighbourhood watch schemes* **about**, concerning, regarding, with regard to, relating to, apropos (of), on the subject of, respecting, in respect of, with respect to, with reference to, as regards, in the matter of, in connection with, referring to, touching on; *Scottish* anent.

reach ▶ verb **1** *Travis reached out a hand and pulled her towards him* **stretch out**, hold out, extend, outstretch, thrust out, stick out; *literary* outreach.
2 (*informal*) *reach me that book* **pass**, hand, give, let someone have.
3 *by the time she reached Helen's house she was exhausted* **arrive at**, get to, get as far as, come to, make it to, gain; end up at, land up at, set foot on; *informal* make, hit.
4 *the temperature reached 94°F | his political popularity had reached a new low* **attain**, get to, amount to; **rise to**, climb to; **fall to**, sink to, drop to; run to; *informal* hit.
5 *the two governments failed to reach an agreement* **achieve**, attain, gain, accomplish; work out, draw up, put together, strike, negotiate, thrash out, hammer out.
6 *one of their solicitors has been trying to reach you all day* **get in touch with**, contact, get through to, get, communicate with, make contact with; speak to, talk to; *informal* get hold of; *Brit. informal* raise.
7 *their central concern is to reach more people at all levels of society* **influence**, sway, carry weight with, get through to, get to, make an impression on, have an effect on, have an impact on, register with.
▶ noun **1** *Bobby moved out of his reach* **grasp**, range.
2 *set yourself small goals which are within your reach* **capabilities**, capacity.
3 *they may be beyond the reach of the law* **jurisdiction**, authority, sway, control, command, influence; **scope**, range, compass, ambit, orbit, latitude; sphere, area, field, territory.

react ▶ verb **1** *Ginny wondered how he would react if she told him the truth* **behave**, act, take it, conduct oneself, proceed; **respond**, reply, answer; retaliate; *rare* comport oneself.
2 *it was perhaps no wonder that he reacted against this spartan, puritanical environment* **rebel against**, oppose, revolt against, rise up against.

reaction ▶ noun **1** *his reaction had bewildered her | the reaction from listeners was encouraging* **response**; answer, reply, rejoinder, retort, riposte; feedback; *informal* comeback.
2 *during the 1960s there was a reaction against this kind of sociology* **backlash**, counteraction, recoil.
3 *the forces of reaction which spring up in the face of change* **conservatism**, ultra-conservatism, the right, the right wing, the extreme right; counter-revolution, revanchism.

reactionary ▶ adjective *government policy became increasingly reactionary* **right-wing**, conservative, rightist, ultra-conservative; blimpish, diehard; traditionalist, conventional, traditional, old-fashioned, unprogressive; *N. Amer.* Birchite.
OPPOSITES radical, progressive.
▶ noun *he was later to become an extreme reactionary* **right-winger**, conservative, rightist, diehard, Colonel Blimp; traditionalist, conventionalist; *N. Amer.* Birchite; *informal* stick-in-the-mud.
OPPOSITE radical.

read ▶ verb **1** *he sat reading the evening newspaper* **peruse**, study, scrutinize, look through; pore over, devour, be absorbed in, bury oneself in; wade through, plough through; run one's eye over, cast an eye over, leaf through, scan, glance through, flick through, skim through, thumb through, flip through, browse through, dip into; *archaic* con.
2 *'Listen to this,' he said and read a passage of the letter* **read out**, read aloud, say aloud, recite, declaim.
3 *I can't read my own writing* **decipher**, make out, make sense of, interpret, understand, comprehend.
4 *his remark could be read as a dig at Forsyth* **interpret**, take, take to mean, construe, see, explain, understand.
5 *the thermometer read 0°C* **indicate**, register, record, display, show, have as a reading, measure.
6 *I can't read your future, you know* **foresee**, predict, forecast, foretell, prophesy, divine, prognosticate; *archaic* augur, presage.
7 *he went on to read modern history at Oxford* **study**, do, take; *N. Amer. & Austral./NZ* major in.
□ **read something into something** *officials cautioned against reading too much into the statistics* **infer from**, interpolate from, assume from, attribute to; read between the lines, get hold of the wrong end of the stick.
□ **read up on** *Chris had read up on this particular method of teaching children to write* **study**, get up; *informal* bone up on; *Brit. informal* mug up on, swot; *archaic* con.
▶ noun *I settled down for a read of 'The Irish Press'* **perusal**, study, scan, scrutiny; look (at), browse (through), glance (through), leaf (through), flick (through), skim (through).

WORD LINKS

readable	**legible**
unreadable	**illegible**
ability to read	**literacy**
inability to read	**illiteracy**

readable ▶ adjective **1** *the inscription is still perfectly readable* **legible**, easy to read, decipherable, easily deciphered, clear, intelligible, understandable, comprehensible, easy to understand.
OPPOSITES illegible, indecipherable.
2 *her novels are immensely readable* **enjoyable**, entertaining, interesting, absorbing, engaging, gripping, enthralling, engrossing, compulsive, stimulating; worth reading, well written; *informal* unputdownable.
OPPOSITES boring, unreadable.

readily ▶ adverb **1** *Durkin readily offered to drive him* **willingly**, without hesitation, unhesitatingly, gladly, happily, cheerfully, with pleasure, with good grace, without reluctance, ungrudgingly, voluntarily; eagerly, promptly, quickly; freely.
OPPOSITE reluctantly.
2 *the island is readily accessible from the mainland* **easily**, with ease, without difficulty, effortlessly.
OPPOSITE with difficulty.

readiness ▶ noun **1** *their readiness to accept new technology* **willingness**, inclination, enthusiasm, eagerness, keenness, gameness; promptness, quickness, alacrity; ease, facility; *dated* address.
2 *we need to maintain our forces in a state of readiness* **preparedness**, preparation, fitness.
3 *I was surprised at the readiness of his reply* **promptness**, quickness, rapidity, swiftness, speed, speediness, punctuality, timeliness; **cleverness**, sharpness, astuteness, shrewdness, keenness, discernment, aptness, adroitness, deftness, skill, skilfulness.
□ **in readiness** *there were candles in readiness, and Anne quickly lit them | the troops were in readiness for a possible battle* **ready**, at the ready, available, on hand, accessible, handy, at one's fingertips; **prepared**, primed, on standby, standing by, on stand-to, on call, on full alert; *informal* on tap.

reading ▶ noun **1** *a cursory reading of the financial pages* **perusal**, study, scan, scanning, scrutiny; browse (through), look (through), glance (through), leaf (through), flick (through), skim (through).
2 *a man of wide reading* **learning**, book learning, scholarship, education, erudition, knowledge (of literature).
3 *readings from the Bible* **passage**, lesson; section, piece, selection; recital, recitation.
4 *a one-sided reading of the situation* **interpretation**, construal, understanding, account, explanation, analysis, construction; version; *informal* take.
5 *the reading on the gas meter* **record**, figure, indication, read-out, display, measurement.

ready ▶ adjective **1** *are you ready to go now? | she'd gone too far—he wasn't ready for this* **prepared**, all set, set, organized, in a fit state, equipped, primed; *informal* fit, psyched up, geared up, up for it, hot to trot.
OPPOSITES unprepared, taken by surprise.
2 *supper's ready | at last everything was ready* **completed**, finished, prepared, organized, done, arranged, fixed, in readiness; ripe; *informal* done and dusted.
OPPOSITES incomplete, in preparation.
3 *he's always ready to help* **willing**, prepared, pleased, inclined, agreeable, disposed, predisposed, minded, of a mind, in the mood, apt, prone, given, likely; **eager**, keen, happy, glad; *informal* game.
OPPOSITES reluctant, unwilling.
4 *she looked ready to collapse* **about to**, on the point of, on the verge of, on the brink of, close to, as if one is going to, in danger of, liable to, likely to.
5 *the early settlers found a ready supply of flints in the chalk cliffs* **easily**

R

available, available, accessible; **handy**, close at hand, at hand, to hand, on hand, near at hand, convenient, within reach, at the ready, near, at one's fingertips, at one's disposal; on call; *informal* on tap.
6 *she had a ready answer to this challenge | Sir Vivien is blessed with great charm and a ready wit* **prompt**, quick, rapid, swift, speedy, fast, immediate, unhesitating; timely; **clever**, sharp, astute, shrewd, keen, acute, perceptive, discerning, resourceful, smart, bright, alert, apt, adroit, deft, agile, skilful; *archaic* rathe.
□ **at the ready** *a group of parents stood on the sidelines, camcorders at the ready* **in position**, poised, ready for use, ready for action, waiting; all systems go; *N. Amer.* on deck.
□ **make ready** *the crew were busily making ready for the departure* **prepare**, make preparations, make provisions, get everything ready, take the necessary steps, do the necessary, gear up for; gear oneself up.
▶ **verb** *seven other vessels were readied and armed | he wanted time to ready himself* **prepare**, get ready, make ready, organize, equip, put together, fix; prime, set; gear oneself up, arm oneself; *informal* psych oneself up; *literary* gird oneself, gird up one's loins.

ready-made ▶ **adjective 1** *ready-made clothing* **ready to wear**, off the shelf; *Brit.* off the peg; *N. Amer.* off the rack.
OPPOSITES bespoke, tailor-made.
2 *ready-made meals* **pre-cooked**, oven-ready, TV, frozen, convenience.

real ▶ **adjective 1** *she treats fictional characters as if they were real people* **actual**, existent, non-fictional, non-fictitious, factual; historical; material, physical, tangible, concrete, palpable, corporeal, substantial; *rare* unimaginary, veridical.
OPPOSITES unreal, imaginary.
2 *do you think it could be real gold?* **genuine**, authentic, bona fide, pukka; *informal* honest-to-goodness, your actual, kosher.
OPPOSITES imitation, fake.
3 *it's not my real name* **true**, actual.
4 *there were tears of real grief in his eyes* **sincere**, genuine, true, unfeigned, unpretended, heartfelt, from the heart, unaffected, earnest, wholehearted, fervent, honest, truthful.
OPPOSITE false.
5 *he was a real man with manly pursuits* **proper**, true, rightly so called; *informal* regular; *archaic* very.
6 *you made me look a real idiot* **complete**, utter, thorough, absolute, total, prize, perfect, veritable; *Brit. informal* right, proper; *Austral./NZ informal* fair; *archaic* arrant.
▶ **adverb** (*N. Amer. informal*) *that was real good of you.* See **VERY**.

realism ▶ **noun 1** *his optimism was tinged with realism* **pragmatism**, practicality, matter-of-factness, common sense, level-headedness, clear-sightedness.
2 *both stories show life in a mining town with some degree of realism* **authenticity**, fidelity, verisimilitude, truthfulness, faithfulness, naturalism; *informal* telling it like it is.

realistic ▶ **adjective 1** *you've got to be realistic and accept what has happened* **practical**, pragmatic, matter-of-fact, down-to-earth, sensible, commonsensical; rational, logical, reasonable, level-headed, clear-sighted, hard-headed, businesslike, sober, unromantic, unsentimental, unidealistic, tough-minded, robust, hard-boiled, unemotional; *informal* with both/one's feet on the ground, hard-nosed, no-nonsense.
OPPOSITES unrealistic, idealistic.
2 *a regional settlement remains an important and realistic aim* **achievable**, attainable, feasible, practicable, within the bounds of possibility, viable, reasonable, sensible, logical, workable; *informal* doable.
OPPOSITE impracticable.
3 *the film was not intended to be a realistic portrayal of the war* **true to life**, lifelike, true, truthful, faithful, real-life, close, naturalistic, authentic, genuine, representational, graphic, convincing; *French* vérité; *informal* kitchen-sink, warts and all; *rare* verisimilar, veristic, speaking.
OPPOSITES imaginative, fictional.

reality ▶ **noun 1** *he is unable to distinguish between fantasy and reality* **the real world**, real life, actuality; truth; physical existence, corporeality, substantiality, materiality.
OPPOSITE fantasy.
2 *the harsh realities of life* **fact**, actuality, truth, verity.
3 *the reality of Marryat's detail* **verisimilitude**, authenticity, realism, fidelity, faithfulness.
OPPOSITE idealism.
□ **in reality** *she sounded sympathetic but in reality she was furious* **in fact**, in actual fact, in point of fact, as a matter of fact, actually, really, in truth, if truth be told; in practice; *archaic* in sooth.

realization ▶ **noun 1** *the growing realization that many of these diseases were intimately related to people's lifestyles* **awareness**, understanding, comprehension, consciousness, apprehension, cognizance, appreciation, recognition, perception, discernment.
2 *the realization of our dreams surpassed our wildest expectations* **actualization**, **fulfilment**, achievement, accomplishment, attainment, bringing to fruition, bringing into being, consummation, effecting; *rare* effectuation, reification.

realize ▶ **verb 1** *it took him a moment to realize what she meant | I realized someone was watching me* **register**, perceive, discern, be/become aware of (the fact that), be/become conscious of (the fact that), notice; understand, grasp, take in, comprehend, see, recognize, work out, fathom (out), appreciate, ascertain, apprehend, be/become cognizant of, know, conceive; discover, find; see the light; *informal* latch on to, cotton on to, catch on to, tumble to, get, figure out, get a fix on, wrap one's mind around, get the message, get the picture; *Brit. informal* twig, suss; *N. Amer. informal* savvy; *rare* cognize.
2 *he realized a 15-year dream by restoring the castle to its original glory* **fulfil**, achieve, accomplish, make real, make a reality, make happen, make concrete, bring to fruition, bring about, bring off, consummate, perform, carry out, carry through, execute, actualize, effect; *rare* effectuate, reify.
3 *he had been able to realize significant trading profits for his companies* **make**, obtain, clear, acquire, gain, bring in, reap; earn, return, produce.
4 *when the goods were put up for sale by auction, they realized £3000* **be sold for**, sell for, fetch, go for, get, make, net.
5 *he realized other assets and used the money to subsidize the business* **cash in**, convert into cash; liquidate, capitalize.

really ▶ **adverb 1** *although he lived in a derelict house, he was really very wealthy* **in fact**, in actual fact, actually, in reality, in point of fact, as a matter of fact, in truth, if truth be told, to tell the truth, in actuality; *archaic* in sooth.
2 *he really likes her | I really appreciate what you've done* **genuinely**, truly, honestly; undoubtedly, without a doubt, indubitably, certainly, surely, assuredly, unquestionably, undeniably; indeed; *archaic* verily.
3 *I bet this place is really spooky late at night | they were really kind to me* **very**, extremely, thoroughly, decidedly, awfully, terribly, frightfully, dreadfully, fearfully, exceptionally, exceedingly, immensely, uncommonly, remarkably, eminently, extraordinarily, most, positively, downright; heartily; *Scottish* unco; *N. Amer.* quite; *French* très; *informal* terrifically, tremendously, right, devilishly, ultra, too … for words, mucho, mega, seriously, majorly, oh-so, stinking; *Brit. informal* jolly, ever so, dead, well, fair; *N. Amer. informal* real, mighty, awful, plumb, powerful, way, bitching; *S. African informal* lekker; *informal, dated* devilish; *archaic* exceeding, sore.
4 *his career is really over* **for all practical purposes**, to all intents and purposes, virtually, just about, almost.
▶ **exclamation** *'Apparently they've split up.' 'Really?'* is that so, is that a fact, well I never, well I never did; go on, you don't say; *informal* well knock/blow me down with a feather; *Brit. informal* well I'll be blowed; *N. Amer. informal* well what do you know about that; *archaic* go to.

realm ▶ **noun 1** *his prime concern was to promote peace in the realm* **kingdom**, sovereign state, monarchy; empire, principality, palatinate, duchy; country, land, domain, dominion, nation, province.
2 *the realm of academic research* **domain**, sphere, area, field, department, arena; world, region, province, territory, zone, orbit.

reap ▶ **verb 1** *the corn was reaped in two stages* **harvest**, garner, gather in, bring in, take in; cut, crop.
2 *it may be some time before the company reaps the benefits of its current investments* **receive**, obtain, get, acquire, secure, bring in, realize, derive, procure.

rear[1] ▶ **verb 1** *I was born and reared in Newcastle* **bring up**, care for, look after, nurture, parent; educate, train, instruct; *N. Amer.* raise.
2 *he reared cattle and sheep* **breed**, raise, keep, tend.
3 *laboratory-reared plantlets* **grow**, cultivate.
4 *Harry stiffened and reared his head* **raise**, lift (up), hold up, uplift, upraise.
5 *Creagan Hill reared up before them* **rise**, rise up, tower, soar, loom.
6 (*archaic*) *her family reared a sumptuous mausoleum over her remains* **build**, erect, put up, construct.

rear[2] ▶ **noun 1** *a door at the rear of the building* **back**, back part, hind part, back end, other end; *Anatomy* occiput; *Nautical* stern.
OPPOSITE front.
2 *Sophie and I brought up the rear of the queue* **end**, tail end, rear end, back end, tail; *N. Amer.* tag end; *Nautical* aft, after.
OPPOSITES front, vanguard; bow.
3 *he slapped her on the rear* **buttocks**, backside, behind, rear end, rump, seat, haunches, hindquarters, cheeks; *Brit.* bottom; *French* derrière; *German* Sitzfleisch; *informal* sit-upon, stern, BTM, tochus; *Brit. informal* bum, botty, prat, jacksie; *N. Amer. informal* butt, fanny, tush, tushie, tail, duff, buns, booty, caboose, heinie, patootie, keister, tuchis; *W. Indian informal* batty; *humorous* posterior, fundament; *black English* rass, rusty dusty; *Brit. vulgar slang* arse; *N. Amer. vulgar slang* ass; *technical* nates.
▶ **adjective** *the car's rear bumper* **back**, end, rearmost, endmost; hind, hinder, hindmost; *technical* posterior, caudal.
OPPOSITES front, foremost.

rearrange ▶ **verb 1** *the curtains had been drawn, the furniture rearranged* **reposition**, move round, change round, arrange differently, regroup, switch round, swap round.
2 *Tony had rearranged his work schedule* **reorganize**, alter, adjust, change (round), reorder, reschedule, rejig, reshuffle; *informal* jigger.

reason ▶ **noun 1** *he cited a lack of funds as the main reason for his decision* **cause**, grounds, ground, basis, rationale; **motive**, motivation, purpose,

R

point, aim, intention, objective, goal, occasion, impetus, inducement, incentive; **explanation**, justification, case, argument, defence, apology, vindication, excuse, pretext, rationalization; warrant; the whys and wherefores; *Latin* apologia.
2 *a rising crescendo of postmodern voices today rail against reason and science* **rationality**, logic, logical thought, scientific thinking, reasoning, thought, cognition; the mind, intellect, intelligence, intellectuality; *Philosophy* nous; *rare* ratiocination.
OPPOSITES emotion, feeling.
3 *he was afraid of losing his reason* **sanity**, mind, mental faculties, mental health, soundness of mind; senses, wits; *informal* marbles.
4 *he continues, against reason, to love the woman passionately* **good sense**, good judgement, common sense, sense, judgement, understanding, wisdom, sagacity; reasonableness, moderation, propriety; practicality, practicability, advisability.
□ **by reason of** *those incapable of supporting themselves by reason of age, infirmity, or disease* **because of**, on account of, as a result of, as a consequence of, owing to, due to, by virtue of, thanks to, through.
□ **with reason** *he was anxious, with reason, about his own political survival* **justifiably**, justly, legitimately, rightly, properly, reasonably.
▶ **verb 1** *such a child, left to himself, grows up unable to express himself and unable to reason* **think rationally**, think logically, think straight, use one's mind, use one's common sense, use one's head, use one's brain, think things through, cogitate; intellectualize; *informal* put on one's thinking cap; *rare* cerebrate, ratiocinate, logicize.
2 *Scott reasoned that if Annabel were having a heart attack, she wouldn't be able to talk on the telephone* **calculate**, come to the conclusion, conclude, reckon, think, consider, be of the opinion, be of the view, judge, deduce, infer, surmise; *N. Amer. informal* figure.
3 *she was growing too tired to* ***reason it out*** **work out**, find an answer/solution to, think through, come to a conclusion about, sort out, make sense of, get to the bottom of, puzzle out, solve; *informal* figure out.
4 *her husband tried to* ***reason with*** *her, but she refused to listen* **talk round**, bring round, win round, persuade, coax, prevail on, convince; show someone the error of their ways, make someone see the light.

WORD LINKS
relating to reason **rational**

reasonable ▶ **adjective 1** *a reasonable man | it seemed a reasonable explanation* **sensible**, rational, open to reason, full of common sense, logical, fair, fair-minded, just, equitable, decent; intelligent, wise, level-headed, practical, realistic; based on good sense, sound, judicious, well thought out, well grounded, reasoned, well reasoned, valid, commonsensical, advisable, well advised; tenable, plausible, feasible, credible, acceptable, admissible, believable, viable.
OPPOSITES unreasonable, illogical.
2 *you must take all reasonable precautions to ensure the safety of your property* **within reason**, practicable, sensible; appropriate, suitable, fitting, proper.
OPPOSITES excessive, obsessional.
3 *most hire cars are in reasonable condition* **fairly good**, acceptable, satisfactory, average, adequate, respectable, fair, decent, all right, not bad, tolerable, passable; *informal* OK, fair-to-middling.
OPPOSITES bad, poor.
4 *good hot food at reasonable prices* **inexpensive**, moderate, low, low-cost, low-priced, modest, within one's means, economical, cheap, budget, bargain; competitive.
OPPOSITES expensive, inflated.

reasoned ▶ **adjective** *reasoned argument* **logical**, rational, well thought out, clear, lucid, coherent, cogent, systematic, methodical, organized, well organized, well expressed, well presented, considered, sensible, intelligent.
OPPOSITES illogical, unsystematic.

reasoning ▶ **noun** *I can't quite follow your reasoning | the reasoning behind their decisions* **thinking**, line of thought, train of thought, thought, thought process, logic, reason, rationality, analysis, interpretation, explanation, deduction, rationalization, argumentation; reasons, rationale, arguments, premises, case; supposition, hypothesis, thesis; *Philosophy* dialectics; *rare* cerebration, ratiocination, mentation.

reassure ▶ **verb** *Daniel patted his wife's arm and tried to reassure her* **put/set someone's mind at rest**, dispel someone's fears, restore/bolster someone's confidence, raise someone's spirits, put someone at ease, encourage, hearten, buoy up, cheer up; comfort, soothe; *rare* inspirit.
OPPOSITES alarm, unnerve.

rebate ▶ **noun** *you will be entitled to a 20 per cent rebate* **refund**, partial refund, repayment; discount, deduction, reduction, decrease; allowance, concession.

rebel ▶ **noun** (stress on the first syllable) **1** *the rebels took control of the capital* **revolutionary**, insurgent, revolutionist, mutineer, agitator, subversive, guerrilla, anarchist, terrorist; freedom fighter, resistance fighter; traitor, renegade; (*in Mexico, historical*) Zapatista; (*in S. America, historical*) Montonero; *rare* insurrectionist, insurrectionary.
2 *the modernist concept of the artist as a rebel, challenging society's norms* **nonconformist**, dissenter, dissident, iconoclast, maverick; heretic, recusant, apostate, schismatic.
▶ **verb** (stress on the second syllable) **1** *the citizens of the town rebelled* **revolt**, mutiny, riot, rise up, rise up in arms, take up arms, stage/mount a rebellion, take to the streets, defy the authorities, refuse to obey orders, be insubordinate.
2 *his stomach rebelled at the mere thought of food* **recoil**, show/feel repugnance; shrink (from), flinch (from), shy away (from), pull back (from).
3 *most teenagers go through a stage of* ***rebelling against*** *their parents* **defy**, disobey, refuse to obey, flout, kick against, challenge, oppose, resist, be at odds with, refuse to accept the authority of, repudiate; dissent; fly in the face of, kick over the traces.
OPPOSITES obey, conform.
▶ **adjective** (stress on the first syllable) **1** *the rebel officers who led the abortive coup* **insurgent**, revolutionary, mutinous, rebellious, mutinying; traitorous, renegade; *rare* insurrectionary, insurrectionist.
2 *rebel MPs | rebel clergymen* **rebellious**, defiant, disobedient, insubordinate, subversive, disaffected, malcontent, resistant, dissentient, recalcitrant, unmanageable, ungovernable; nonconformist, maverick, iconoclastic; heretical, recusant, apostate, schismatic; *archaic* contumacious.
OPPOSITES obedient, compliant.

rebellion ▶ **noun 1** *troops were sent into the area to suppress the rebellion* **uprising**, revolt, insurrection, mutiny, revolution, insurgence, insurgency, rising, rioting, riot; civil disobedience, civil disorder, unrest, anarchy, fighting in the streets; coup; *French* coup d'état, jacquerie; *German* putsch.
2 *he joined the Communist Party, more as an act of rebellion than anything else* **defiance**, disobedience, rebelliousness, insubordination, mutinousness, subversion, subversiveness, resistance, dissent, nonconformity; heresy, apostasy, schism, recusancy; *archaic* contumacy.
OPPOSITE obedience.

rebellious ▶ **adjective 1** *rebellious troops* **rebel**, insurgent, mutinous, disorderly, lawless, out of control, mutinying, rebelling, rioting, riotous, revolutionary, seditious, subversive; breakaway, traitorous, renegade; *rare* insurrectionary, insurrectionist.
OPPOSITES obedient, law-abiding.
2 *a rebellious adolescent* **defiant**, **disobedient**, insubordinate, unruly, ungovernable, unmanageable, uncontrollable, turbulent, mutinous, wayward, obstreperous, recalcitrant, refractory, intractable, resistant, dissentient, disaffected, malcontent; nonconformist; *Brit. informal* bolshie; *archaic* contumacious.
OPPOSITES conformist, compliant.

rebirth ▶ **noun** *the rebirth of black nationalism | his spiritual rebirth* **revival**, renaissance, renascence, resurrection, reawakening, renewal, resurgence, regeneration, restoration, new beginning; revitalization, rejuvenation, revivification; reincarnation.

rebound ▶ **verb 1** *the ball rebounded off the wall* **bounce**, bounce back, spring back, ricochet, boomerang, glance, recoil; *N. Amer.* carom; *rare* resile.
2 *sterling rebounded and closed half a pfennig higher* **recover**, rally, bounce back, pick up, make a recovery, make a comeback.
3 *Thomas's tactics* ***rebounded on*** *him* **backfire on**, misfire on, boomerang on, have an adverse effect on, have unwelcome repercussions for, come back on, be self-defeating for, cause one to be hoist with one's own petard; *informal* score an own goal; *archaic* redound on.

R

rebuff ▶ **verb** *his offer was immediately rebuffed | she rebuffed the prince on several occasions* **reject**, turn down, spurn, refuse, decline, repudiate, disdain; snub, slight, repulse, repel, dismiss, brush off, turn one's back on; give someone the cold shoulder, cold-shoulder, ignore, cut (dead), look right through; *informal* give someone the brush-off, tell someone where to get off, put down, freeze out, stiff-arm; *Brit. informal* knock back; *N. Amer. informal* give someone the bum's rush, give someone the brush; *Austral. informal* snout; *informal, dated* give someone the go-by.
OPPOSITES accept, welcome.
▶ **noun** *the rebuff did little to dampen his ardour* **rejection**, snub, slight, repulse, cut; refusal, spurning, repudiation, repulsion, cold-shouldering, discouragement; *informal* brush-off, knock-back, put-down, kick in the teeth, slap in the face, smack in the face, smack in the eye.

rebuild ▶ **verb** *they must have spent a colossal amount rebuilding the stadium* **reconstruct**, renovate, restore, refashion, remodel, revamp, remake, reassemble; recondition; *N. Amer. informal* rehab.
OPPOSITE demolish.

rebuke ▶ **verb** *however much she hated seeing him drink, she never rebuked him in front of others* **reprimand**, reproach, scold, admonish, reprove, remonstrate with, chastise, chide, upbraid, berate, take to task, pull up, castigate, lambaste, read someone the Riot Act, give someone a piece of one's mind, haul over the coals, criticize, censure; *informal* tell off, give someone a talking-to, give someone a telling-off, dress down, give someone a dressing-down, give someone an earful, give someone a roasting, give someone a rocket, rap, rap over the knuckles, slap

someone's wrist, let someone have it, bawl out, give someone hell, come down on, blow up, pitch into, lay into, lace into, give someone a caning, slap down, blast, rag, keelhaul; *Brit. informal* tick off, have a go at, carpet, give someone a mouthful, tear someone off a strip, give someone what for, give someone a rollicking, wig, give someone a wigging, give someone a row, row; *N. Amer. informal* chew out, ream out; *Austral. informal* monster; *Brit. vulgar slang* bollock, give someone a bollocking; *N. Amer. vulgar slang* chew someone's ass, ream someone's ass; *dated* call down, rate, give someone a rating, trim; *rare* reprehend, objurgate.
OPPOSITES praise, compliment, commend.

▶ **noun** *Damian sat down, completely silenced by the rebuke* **reprimand**, reproach, reproof, scolding, admonishment, admonition, reproval, remonstration, lecture, upbraiding, castigation, lambasting, criticism, censure; *informal* telling-off, rap, rap over the knuckles, dressing-down, earful, roasting, bawling-out, caning, blast, row; *Brit. informal* ticking-off, carpeting, rollicking, wigging; *Brit. vulgar slang* bollocking; *dated* rating.
OPPOSITES praise, compliment, commendation.

rebut ▶ **verb** *the shadow chancellor rebutted the prime minister's allegations* **refute**, deny, disprove, prove wrong, prove false; invalidate, negate, contradict, counter, discredit, give the lie to, drive a coach and horses through, quash, explode, shoot down, destroy; *informal* shoot full of holes, blow sky-high; *rare* controvert, confute, negative.
OPPOSITE confirm.

rebuttal ▶ **noun** *a point-by-point rebuttal of the accusations* **refutation**, denial, disproving, counter-argument, countering, invalidation, negation, contradiction; *Law* counterstatement, surrejoinder, rebutter, surrebutter, replication; *rare* confutation, disproval.
OPPOSITE confirmation.

recalcitrant ▶ **adjective** *a class of recalcitrant fifteen-year-olds* **uncooperative**, obstinately disobedient, intractable, unmanageable, ungovernable, refractory, insubordinate, defiant, rebellious, mutinous, wilful, wayward, headstrong, self-willed, contrary, perverse, difficult, awkward, obdurate; *Brit. informal* bloody-minded, bolshie, stroppy; *archaic* contumacious, froward; *rare* renitent, pervicacious.
OPPOSITES amenable, docile, compliant.

recall ▶ **verb 1** *he recalled his student days at Harvard* **remember**, recollect, call to mind, think of; think back on/to, look back on, cast one's mind back to, reminisce about, hark back to; *Scottish* mind.
OPPOSITE forget.
2 *their daring exploits and the nobility of their spirit recall the legendary days of chivalry* **bring to mind**, call to mind, put one in mind of, call up, summon up, conjure up, evoke, echo, allude to.
3 *the Panamanian ambassador was recalled from Peru* **summon back**, order back, call back, bring back.
OPPOSITES dissolve, prorogue.
4 (*formal*) *he sent another note to Lord Grey, recalling his earlier communication* **revoke**, rescind, cancel, retract, countermand, take back, withdraw, repeal, veto, overrule, override, abrogate; annul, invalidate, nullify, declare null and void, void; *rare* disannul, negate.
OPPOSITES ratify, confirm.

▶ **noun 1** *the recall of the ambassador* **summoning back**, ordering back, calling back; summons.
2 *most people find they can improve their recall of dreams with practice* **recollection**, memory, remembrance; *technical* anamnesis.
3 (*formal*) *the Chancery Division may possess power to order the recall of probate* **revocation**, rescinding, cancellation, cancelling, retraction, retracting, countermanding, withdrawal, abrogation, repeal, vetoing, veto; annulment, invalidation, nullification; *rare* rescission.

recant ▶ **verb 1** *a Hungarian Marxist who was forced to recant his political beliefs* **renounce**, forswear, disavow, deny, repudiate, renege on, abjure, relinquish, abandon; *archaic* forsake.
OPPOSITE reaffirm.
2 *he was charged with heresy, refused to recant, and was put to death* **change one's mind**, be apostate, defect, renege; *rare* apostatize, tergiversate.
3 *he recanted his testimony* **retract**, take back, withdraw, disclaim, disown, recall, unsay.

recantation ▶ **noun** **renunciation**, renouncement, disavowal, denial, repudiation, retraction, withdrawal; apostasy; *rare* abjuration, retractation.

recapitulate ▶ **verb** *I will recapitulate some of the main points of the argument* **summarize**, sum up; **restate**, state again, repeat, reiterate, go over, run over, run through, review; enumerate, recount, list; *informal* recap; *rare* epitomize.

recede ▶ **verb 1** *the flood waters receded | her footsteps receded down the stairs* **retreat**, go back, move back, move further off, move away, withdraw; ebb, subside, go down, abate, fall back, sink; *rare* retrocede.
OPPOSITES advance, approach.
2 *I stood on the deck watching the harbour lights recede into the distance* **disappear from view**, gradually disappear, fade into the distance, be lost to view, pass from sight, grow less visible.
3 *by May 23, fears of widespread violence had receded* **diminish**, lessen, grow less, decrease, dwindle, fade, abate, subside, ebb, wane, fall off, taper off, peter out, shrink; *rare* de-escalate.
OPPOSITES grow, intensify.

receipt ▶ **noun 1** *the receipt of his letter threw Clara into ecstasy* **receiving**, reception, getting, obtaining, gaining; acceptance; arrival, delivery; *rare* recipience.
2 *always make sure you get a receipt* **proof of purchase**, sales slip, sales ticket, till receipt; stub, counterfoil, voucher, slip, docket; *Law, dated* acquittance.
3 (**receipts**) *receipts from council house sales* **proceeds**, takings, money/payment received, income, revenue, earnings, turnover; gate; profits, gains, financial return(s), return(s); *N. Amer.* take.

receive ▶ **verb 1** *Tony received his award at a gala lunch in London | they received £650 in damages* **be given**, be presented with, be awarded, collect, accept, have conferred on one; get, obtain, gain, acquire, secure, come by, pick up, be provided with, take; derive; win, be paid, earn, gross, net, accrue; inherit, come into; *informal* cop.
OPPOSITES give, present.
2 *she received a letter from the council threatening court action* **be sent**, be in receipt of; accept delivery of, accept, take into one's possession.
OPPOSITE send.
3 *Alec received the news on Monday afternoon* **be told**, be informed of, be notified of, be made aware of, hear, discover, find out (about), learn, gather, get wind of.
4 *he received her suggestion with a complete lack of interest* **hear**, listen to; respond to, react to, take; meet, greet.
5 *she received a serious head injury* **experience**, sustain, undergo, meet with, encounter, go through, be subjected to, come in for; **suffer**, bear, endure.
6 *the young couple looked radiant as they received their guests* **greet**, welcome, say hello to, show in, usher in, admit, let in.
7 *she's not receiving visitors* **entertain**, be at home to.

receiver ▶ **noun 1** *the receiver of a gift* **recipient**, beneficiary, donee; legatee; *Law* grantee, devisee.
OPPOSITE donor.
2 *a telephone receiver* **handset**, apparatus; headset, earpiece.

recent ▶ **adjective 1** *recent research* **new**, the latest, late, current, fresh, modern, contemporary, present-day, up to date, up to the minute, latter-day, latter; *rare* neoteric.
OPPOSITE old.
2 *his recent visit* **not long past**, occurring/appearing recently; immediate, just gone.
OPPOSITE former.

recently ▶ **adverb** *Kate recently published her first novel* **not long ago**, a short time ago, in the last few days/weeks/months, in the past few days/weeks/months, a little while back; lately, of late, latterly; just now; newly, freshly.

receptacle ▶ **noun** **container**, holder, vessel, repository; box, tin, bin, can, canister, drum, case, chest, casket, crate, tank; basin, pan, pot, dish, bowl; bag, pouch, purse, basket; *archaic* reservatory.

reception ▶ **noun 1** *the reception of the goods* **receipt**, receiving, getting, acceptance; *rare* recipience.
2 *the reception of foreign diplomatic representatives* **greeting**, welcome, welcoming, entertaining.
3 *they met with a chilly reception from my mother* **response**, reaction, treatment; acknowledgement, recognition.
4 *there was a small reception after the preview* **(formal) party**, function, social occasion, social event, entertainment, soirée, gathering, get-together, celebration; *N. Amer.* levee; *informal* do, bash; *Brit. informal* rave-up, thrash, knees-up, jolly, beanfeast, bunfight, beano.

receptive ▶ **adjective** *a receptive audience* **open-minded**, ready/willing to consider new ideas, open to new ideas, open to suggestions, open, responsive, amenable, sympathetic, well disposed, interested, attuned, flexible, willing, favourable, approachable, accessible, friendly, welcoming; susceptible, impressionable, suggestible, pliable, pliant; *rare* susceptive, acceptive, acceptant.
OPPOSITES resistant, unresponsive.

recess ▶ **noun 1** *two recesses fitted with floor-to-ceiling bookshelves* **alcove**, bay, niche, nook, corner, inglenook; hollow, cavity; apse; *Japanese* tokonoma; *technical* oriel, aumbry, exedra; *archaic* tabernacle.
2 (**recesses**) *the deepest recesses of Broadcasting House* **innermost parts/reaches**, remote/secret places, dark corners, heart, inner sanctum, interior; depths, bowels; *informal* innards; *rare* penetralia.
3 *the Commons rises for the Christmas recess on Thursday* **adjournment**, break, interlude, interval, rest, intermission, respite, temporary closure, temporary cessation of business; holiday, vacation, time off; *informal* breather, time out.

▶ **verb** *we'll recess for lunch and reconvene at 2 pm* **adjourn**, suspend proceedings, take a recess, break, stop, take a break; *informal* knock off, take five, take time out.

recession ▶ **noun** *the country is in the depths of a recession* **economic decline**, downturn, depression, slump, slowdown, trough, stagnation;

stagflation; hard times.
OPPOSITES boom, upturn.

recherché ▶ adjective *most of the titles are recherché and long out of stock* **obscure**, **rare**, esoteric, abstruse, arcane, recondite, little known; exotic, strange, unusual, unfamiliar, out of the ordinary.
OPPOSITE commonplace.

recipe ▶ noun **1** *try our quick and tasty recipe for beef goulash* cooking instructions/procedure/directions; archaic receipt.
2 *low local taxes are not always a **recipe for** electoral success* **means/way of achieving**, means/way of ensuring; **prescription**, formula, method, technique, system, procedure, plan; likely cause of, source of; MO, process, means, way; blueprint; Latin modus operandi.

recipient ▶ noun *the recipient of the prize* receiver, beneficiary, donee, legatee; Law grantee, devisee.
OPPOSITE donor.

reciprocal ▶ adjective **1** *reciprocal, passionate love* **given/felt in return**, corresponding; **requited**, returned, reciprocated.
2 *reciprocal obligations and duties* **mutual**, common, shared, joint, corresponding, correlative, give-and-take, exchanged, complementary; rare reciprocatory, reciprocative, commutual.

reciprocate ▶ verb **1** *Karen had done her bit for me, and I was more than happy to reciprocate* **do the same (in return)**, respond in kind, return the favour; give as good as one gets, give tit for tat.
2 *a hopeless love that could not possibly be reciprocated* **requite**, return, feel/give in return, repay, give back; match, equal.

recital ▶ noun **1** *he gave his first recital at the age of 16* **concert**, performance, musical performance, public performance, solo performance, solo, show; informal gig.
2 *her recital of Adam's failures and shortcomings | his recital of the events of the night* **enumeration**, list, litany, catalogue, listing, detailing, itemizing, specification; **account**, report, description, narrative, narration, record, story, tale, chronicle, history; recapitulation, rehearsal, run through; recounting, telling, relation; rare recountal.
3 *a recital of the Lord's Prayer in French* **recitation**, saying aloud, reading aloud, repetition, declaiming, declamation, rendition, rendering.

recitation ▶ noun **1** *the recitation of his poem* **recital**, saying aloud, reading aloud, declaiming, declamation, rendering, rendition, delivery, performance.
2 *do not respond to the question with a recitation of your life story* **account**, description, narration, narrative, story, tale, history; recapitulation, rehearsal, run through; rare recountal.
3 *those who could do so entertained the others with songs and recitations* **reading**, passage, piece, something known off by heart; poem, verse, monologue; informal one's party piece.

recite ▶ verb **1** *he began to recite verses of the Koran in a sing-song voice* **repeat from memory**, say aloud, read aloud, declaim, quote, speak, deliver, render; intone, chant; spout, parrot, say parrot fashion; Judaism daven; rare cantillate, intonate, bespout.
2 *sometimes, if he got bored, he would just stand up and start reciting* **give a recitation**, say a poem, perform; informal do one's party piece.
3 *once again, Sir John recited the facts they knew* **enumerate**, list, detail, itemize, reel off, rattle off; **recount**, relate, describe, narrate, give an account of, run through, recapitulate, repeat, rehearse, specify, particularize, spell out.

reckless ▶ adjective *he was angry with himself and that made him reckless* **rash**, careless, thoughtless, incautious, heedless, unheeding, inattentive, hasty, overhasty, precipitate, precipitous, impetuous, impulsive, daredevil, devil-may-care, hot-headed; **irresponsible**, wild, foolhardy, headlong, over-adventurous, over-venturesome, audacious, death-or-glory; ill-advised, injudicious, misguided, hare-brained, madcap, imprudent, unwise, ill-considered, unconsidered, ill-conceived, unthinking, indiscreet, mindless, negligent; Brit. tearaway; informal harum-scarum, bull-in-a-china-shop; rare temerarious.
OPPOSITES careful, cautious, prudent.

> **CHOOSE THE RIGHT WORD**
> **reckless, rash, foolhardy**
> See **RASH**.

reckon ▶ verb **1** *the cost to the company was reckoned at £6,000 | Pat reckoned up the cost* **calculate**, compute, work out, put a figure on, figure, number, quantify; **count (up)**, add up, total, tally; Brit. tot up.
2 *Anselm reckoned Hugh among his friends* **include**, count, number; consider to be, deem to be, regard as, look on as, take to be.
3 (informal) *I reckon she had her eye on him from the start* **believe**, think, be of the opinion, be of the view, be convinced, suspect, dare say, have an idea, have a feeling, imagine, fancy, guess, suppose, assume, surmise, conjecture, consider; N. Amer. informal figure; archaic ween.
4 *category A prisoners are reckoned the most dangerous* **regard as**, consider, judge, hold to be, view, think of as, look on as; deem, rate, evaluate, gauge, count, estimate; repute.
5 *when I spend that much I **reckon to** get good value for money* **expect**, anticipate, hope to, be looking to; **count on**, rely on, depend on, bank on, calculate on, be sure of, trust in, take for granted, take as read; N. Amer. informal figure on.
□ **to be reckoned with** *Michael Ryan was still a force to be reckoned with* **important**, of considerable importance, not to be ignored, significant, considerable; influential, powerful, strong, potent, formidable, redoubtable, dominant, commanding; informal a hard nut to crack.
□ **reckon with 1** *it's her mother you'll have to reckon with* **deal with**, cope with, contend with, handle, face, face up to.
2 *they hadn't reckoned with her burning ambition to win* **take into account**, take into consideration, bargain for, bargain on, allow for, anticipate, foresee, be prepared for, plan for; bear in mind, consider, take cognizance of, take note of.
□ **reckon without** *unfortunately he had reckoned without sniffer dogs* **overlook**, ignore, fail to take account of, fail to anticipate, disregard, lose sight of, fail to notice.
OPPOSITE take into account.

reckoning ▶ noun **1** *by the judge's reckoning, this comes to close on $2 million* **calculation**, estimation, computation, working out, summation, counting; addition, total, tally, score.
2 *by her reckoning, it was high time her luck changed* **opinion**, view, judgement, evaluation, way of thinking, estimate, estimation, appraisal, consideration.
3 *the terrible reckoning that he deserved* **retribution**, fate, doom, nemesis, judgement, punishment, what is coming to someone.
□ **day of reckoning judgement day**, day of judgement, day of retribution, final accounting, final settlement; Christianity doomsday.

reclaim ▶ verb **1** *travelling expenses can be reclaimed* **get back**, claim back, have returned, recover, take back, regain, retrieve, recoup; rare recuperate.
OPPOSITE forfeit.
2 *Henrietta had reclaimed him from a life of vice* **save**, rescue, redeem, win back; reform.
OPPOSITE abandon.

recline ▶ verb *his mother was reclining on the sofa* **lie**, lie down, lie back, lean back; be recumbent, be prone; **rest**, relax, repose; **loll**, lounge, sprawl, stretch out, drape oneself over; literary couch.
OPPOSITES stand; sit up.

recluse ▶ noun **1** *a religious recluse* **hermit**, ascetic; monk, nun; Islam marabout, santon; rare eremite, anchorite, anchoress, stylite, coenobite.
2 *a natural recluse who found all human relationships difficult* **loner**, solitary, lone wolf; introvert, misanthrope; rare solitudinarian, solitaire, solitarian, isolate.

reclusive ▶ adjective *she lived a reclusive life and was hardly ever seen* **solitary**, secluded, isolated, hermit-like, cloistered, sequestered, withdrawn, retiring, shut away; introverted, unsociable, antisocial, misanthropic; rare seclusive, eremitic, eremitical, hermitic, anchoritic.
OPPOSITES gregarious, sociable.

recognition ▶ noun **1** *he stared at her, but there was no sign of recognition on his face* **identification**, recollection, recall, remembrance.
2 *his recognition of his lack of political experience* **acknowledgement**, acceptance, admission, conceding, concession, granting; realization, awareness, consciousness, knowledge, perception, appreciation, understanding, apprehension, cognizance.
3 *the organization will seek recognition by the International Rugby Board* **official approval**, certification, accreditation, endorsement, sanctioning, validation, ratification.
4 *the team deserve recognition for the tremendous job they are doing* **appreciation**, gratitude, thanks, congratulations, a pat on the back, credit, commendation, acclaim, acclamation; tributes, acknowledgement, reward, honour, homage, applause, a round of applause, accolades; a mention; informal bouquets, brownie points.

recognizable ▶ adjective *he spoke with a faint but recognizable Irish lilt* **identifiable**, noticeable, perceptible, discernible, appreciable, detectable, distinguishable, observable, perceivable; visible, notable, measurable; **distinct**, marked, conspicuous, unmistakable, clear, apparent, evident; archaic sensible.
OPPOSITE imperceptible.

recognize ▶ verb **1** *Hannah recognized him at once* **identify**, place, know, know again, pick out, put a name to; **remember**, recall, recollect, call to mind; know by sight; Scottish & N. English ken; rare agnize.
OPPOSITE forget.
2 *he had never liked Marler, though he recognized his ability* **acknowledge**, **accept**, admit, concede, allow, grant, confess, own; **realize**, be aware of, be conscious of, perceive, discern, appreciate, understand, apprehend, see, be cognizant of; informal take on board; rare cognize.
OPPOSITE overlook.
3 *psychotherapists recognized by the British Psychological Society* **officially approve**, certify, accredit, endorse, sanction, put the seal of approval on; **acknowledge**, validate, accept as valid, ratify, uphold, support.

R

4 *the Trust recognized the hard work of those involved in the project* **pay tribute to**, show appreciation of, appreciate, give recognition to, show gratitude to, be grateful for, acclaim, commend, salute, applaud, take one's hat off to, reward, honour, pay homage to.

recoil ▶ verb (stress on the second syllable) **1** *as he leaned towards her, she instinctively recoiled* **draw back**, jump back, spring back, jerk back, pull back; **flinch**, shy away, shrink (back), blench, start, wince, cower, quail.
2 *he pictured them in his mind and* ***recoiled from*** *the thought* **feel revulsion at**, feel disgust at, feel abhorrence at, be unable to bear, be unable to stomach, shrink from, shy away from, baulk at, hesitate at.
3 *his rifle recoiled* **kick (back)**, jerk back, spring back, fly back, jump back.
4 *his attempts to discredit them will eventually* ***recoil on*** *him* **rebound on**, come back on, affect badly; misfire, backfire, boomerang, go wrong, fail to work out, be unsuccessful, go amiss, come to grief, meet with disaster; *archaic* redound on.
▶ noun (stress on the first syllable) *the recoil of the gun* **kickback**, kick.

recollect ▶ verb *he grimaced as he recollected the incident* **remember**, recall, call to mind, think of; think back to, cast one's mind back to, look back on; reminisce about, hark back to, summon up, revive the memory of; *Scottish* mind; *archaic* bethink oneself of.
OPPOSITE forget.

recollection ▶ noun *Leonard's recollections of his early childhood are vague* **memory**, remembrance, mental image, impression, reminiscence; *technical* anamnesis.

recommend ▶ verb **1** *his former employer recommended him for the post* **advocate**, endorse, commend, approve, suggest, put forward, propose, advance, nominate, put up, mention; speak favourably of, speak well of, put in a good word for, beat the drum for, vouch for, look with favour on; *informal* push, plug; *black English* big something up.
OPPOSITES reject, veto.
2 *the committee recommended a cautious approach* **advise**, counsel, urge, exhort, enjoin, prescribe, speak in favour of, speak for, argue for, back, support, offer as one's opinion; suggest, advocate, propose.
OPPOSITE argue against.
3 *however little else there was to recommend her, she could at least cook* **have in one's favour**, render appealing/attractive/desirable, endow with appeal/attraction, give an advantage to; *informal* have going for one.

recommendation ▶ noun **1** *the government accepted the advisory group's recommendations* **advice**, counsel, guidance, direction, exhortation, enjoinder, advocacy; suggestion, proposal, submission; *Law, Brit.* rider.
2 *a personal recommendation is best when you are looking for an agent* **commendation**, endorsement, good word, favourable mention, special mention, testimonial; suggestion, tip; praise, words of approval/approbation; *informal* plug.
3 *some forsaken place whose only recommendation is that it has lots of men and very few women* **advantage**, good point/feature, thing in one's/its favour, appealing/favourable aspect, benefit, blessing, asset, boon, attraction, appeal, selling point.

recompense ▶ verb **1** *the Home Secretary contended that offenders should recompense their victims* **compensate**, indemnify, repay, reimburse, pay money to, make reparation to, make restitution to, make amends to.
2 *she wanted to recompense him in some way* **reward**, pay, pay back; *archaic* guerdon.
3 *she still hadn't received much to recompense her loss* **make up for**, compensate for, make amends for, make restitution for, make reparation for, redress, make good, satisfy.
▶ noun *substantial damages were paid in recompense* **compensation**, reparation, restitution, indemnification, indemnity; reimbursement, repayment, reward, redress, satisfaction; *Latin* quid pro quo; *archaic* guerdon, meed; *rare* solatium.

reconcilable ▶ adjective *I believe the two sets of findings are reconcilable* **compatible**, consistent, congruous, congruent, consonant.

reconcile ▶ verb **1** *the news reconciled us* **reunite**, bring (back) together (again), restore friendly relations between, restore harmony between, make peace between, resolve differences between, bring to terms; pacify, appease, placate, propitiate, mollify; *rare* conciliate.
OPPOSITES estrange, alienate.
2 *it wasn't easy trying to reconcile his religious beliefs with his career* **make compatible**, harmonize, square, make harmonious, synthesize, make congruent, cause to be in agreement, cause to sit happily/easily with; adjust, balance, attune; *rare* syncretize.
3 *the quarrel was reconciled* **settle**, resolve, patch up, sort out, smooth over, iron out, put to rights, mend, remedy, heal, cure, rectify.
4 *the creditors had to* ***reconcile themselves to*** *drastic losses of income and capital* **accept**, come to accept, resign oneself to, come to terms with, learn to live with, get used to, make the best of, submit to, accommodate oneself to, adjust oneself to, become accustomed to, acclimatize oneself to; grin and bear it; *informal* like it or lump it.

reconciliation ▶ noun **1** *the reconciliation of the disputants* **reuniting**, reunion, bringing (back) together (again), conciliation, reconcilement; pacification, appeasement, placating, propitiation, mollification.
OPPOSITES estrangement, alienation.
2 *a reconciliation of their differences* **resolution**, settlement, rectification; settling, resolving, mending, remedying.
3 *there was little hope of reconciliation between the two groups* **restoration of friendly relations**, restoration of harmony, agreement, compromise, understanding, peace, an end to hostilities, amity, concord; *French* rapprochement, détente; *informal* fence-mending.
OPPOSITE feud.
4 *the reconciliation of scientific philosophy with clinical practice* **harmonizing**, harmonization, synthesis, squaring, adjustment, balancing; *rare* syncretization.
OPPOSITE incompatibility.

recondite ▶ adjective *the recondite realms of Semitic philology* **obscure**, abstruse, arcane, esoteric, little known, recherché, abstract, deep, profound, cryptic, difficult, complex, complicated, involved; over/above one's head, incomprehensible, unfathomable, impenetrable, opaque, dark, mysterious, occult, cabbalistic, secret, hidden; *rare* Alexandrian.
OPPOSITES straightforward, simple, familiar.

CHOOSE THE RIGHT WORD

recondite, obscure, abstruse, esoteric, arcane
See OBSCURE.

recondition ▶ verb *the engine had been completely reconditioned* **overhaul**, rebuild, renovate, restore, repair, fix up, reconstruct, remodel, renew, refit, refurbish, make over; *informal* do up, revamp, vamp up.

reconnaissance ▶ noun *he took some marines to make a reconnaissance of the island* **preliminary survey**, survey, exploration, observation, investigation, examination, inspection, probe, scrutiny, scan; patrol, search, expedition; reconnoitring, scouting (out), spying out; *informal* recce; *Brit. informal* shufti; *N. Amer. informal* recon.

reconnoitre ▶ verb *a survey plane was dispatched to reconnoitre the area* **survey**, make a reconnaissance of, explore, scout (out), make a survey of, make an observation of; find out the lie of the land, see how the land lies; investigate, examine, spy out, scrutinize, scan, inspect, observe, take a look at, take stock of; patrol; *informal* recce, make a recce of, case, case the joint, check out; *Brit. informal* take a shufti round, suss out; *N. Amer. informal* recon.

reconsider ▶ verb *the government might be forced to reconsider its decision* **rethink**, review, revise, re-examine, re-evaluate, reassess, reappraise, think better of, think over, take another look at, look at in a different light, have another think about; change, alter, modify; think again, think twice, have second thoughts, review one's position, come round, change one's mind.

reconsideration ▶ noun *a reconsideration of the case* **review**, re-examination, reassessment, re-evaluation, reappraisal, rethink, another look, a fresh look.

reconstruct ▶ verb **1** *the building had to be substantially reconstructed | a pressing need to reconstruct the war-damaged economy* **rebuild**, restore, renovate, recreate, remake, reassemble, remodel, refashion, revamp, recondition, refurbish; regenerate, breathe new life into, reform, make over, overhaul, re-establish, reorganize; *N. Amer. informal* rehab.
2 *an effort to reconstruct the events of that day* **recreate**, build up a picture/impression of, form a picture/impression of, piece together, re-enact, build up; see in one's mind's eye.

record ▶ noun (stress on the first syllable) **1** *written records of the past | fraud squad officers want to examine his bank records* **account(s)**, document(s), documentation, data, file(s), dossier(s), information, evidence, report(s); annal(s), archive(s), chronicle(s); note(s), minutes, transactions, proceedings, transcript(s); certificate(s), deed(s), instrument(s); diary, journal, memoir; register, log, logbook; yearbook, almanac; inventory, list, catalogue; case history, case study, casebook; *French* procès-verbal; *dated* act(s); *rare* muniment(s).
2 *I spent a lot of time listening to records* album; vinyl; tape, cassette, disc, compact disc, CD; recording, release; *dated* gramophone record, LP, long-player, single, forty-five, twelve-inch (single), EP (extended-play); seventy-eight, 78; *Brit. dated* black disc; *N. Amer. dated* phonograph record.
3 *Cameron would have faced a High Court sentence had it not been for his good record* **previous conduct/performance**, track record, previous achievements/accomplishments, career to date, history, past, life history, background; reputation; *Latin* curriculum vitae.
4 *he's got a record as long as my arm* **criminal record**, police record, list of offences, list of previous convictions; previous; history of crime; *Military* crime sheet; *Brit. informal* form; *N. Amer. informal* rap sheet.
5 *it was my greatest race and a British record* **best performance**, highest achievement, star performance; best time, fastest time, furthest distance; personal best; world record.
6 *a personal and lasting record of what they have achieved* **reminder**, memorial, souvenir, memento, token, token of remembrance,

R

remembrance, keepsake, testimony, testament, testimonial, witness, monument.

□ **off the record 1** *he was at pains to emphasize that his comments were off the record* **unofficial, confidential**, in (strict) confidence, not for publication, not for public consumption, not to be made public, not for circulation, not to be disclosed, not to be mentioned, private, secret, classified, (to be kept) under wraps.
OPPOSITE official.
2 *senior opposition figures are beginning to admit, off the record, that they made a mistake* **unofficially, privately**, in (strict) confidence, confidentially, between ourselves; *Latin* sub rosa; *Italian* in petto; *French* entre nous; *informal* between you, me, and the bedpost/gatepost; *archaic* under the rose.
OPPOSITES officially, publicly.

▶ **adjective** (stress on the first syllable) *the company announced record pre-tax profits* **record-breaking**, best ever, its/one's best, optimum, unbeaten, unsurpassed, unparalleled, unequalled, superlative, second to none, never previously achieved.
OPPOSITE worst.

▶ **verb** (stress on the second syllable) **1** *the doctor recorded her blood pressure on a chart* **write down**, set down, put in writing, put down, take down, note, make a note of, jot down, put down on paper, commit to paper; **document**, put on record, post; enter, minute, register, chronicle, file, put on file, chart, docket, log; inscribe, transcribe; list, catalogue, make an inventory of; *rare* diarize.
2 *the thermometer recorded a temperature of 99°F* **indicate**, register, read, show, display.
3 *the team recorded their fourth away win of the season* **achieve**, accomplish, gain, earn, chalk up, notch up, turn in; *informal* clock up.
4 *the recital was recorded live at the Schleswig-Holstein Music Festival* **make a record/recording of**, tape, tape-record; video-record, videotape, video, audiotape; telerecord.
5 *he took time out from working with the band to record a new solo album* **make**, produce, cut, put on disc/tape; *informal* lay down, put on wax.

recorder ▶ **noun 1** tape recorder, cassette recorder, video cassette recorder, VCR, video recorder, videotape recorder, video.
2 keeper of records, record keeper; registrar, archivist, annalist, diarist, chronicler, historian; scribe, clerk; *rare* chronologer, chronologist, chronographer.
3 woodwind instrument, fipple flute, flute; descant recorder.

recount ▶ **verb** *she listened incredulously to the chain of events recounted by her sister* **tell**, relate, narrate, give an account of, describe, portray, depict, paint, unfold, set forth, present, report, outline, delineate, retail, recite, repeat, rehearse, relay, convey, communicate, impart; detail, enumerate, list, specify, itemize, cite, particularize, catalogue.

recoup ▶ **verb** *the club managed to recoup £300* **get back**, regain, recover, win back, retrieve, repossess, redeem, make good; *rare* recuperate.

recourse ▶ **noun** *surgery may be the only recourse* **option**, possibility, alternative, possible course of action, resort, way out, place/person to turn to, source of assistance, available resource, hope, remedy, choice, expedient; refuge.

□ **have recourse to** *all three countries had recourse to the IMF for standby loans* **resort to**, make use of, use, avail oneself of, utilize, employ, turn to, call on, draw on, bring into play, bring into service, look to, appeal to; fall back on, run to.

recover ▶ **verb 1** *he's still recovering from a heart attack* **recuperate**, get better, get well, convalesce, regain one's strength, regain one's health, get stronger, get back on one's feet, feel oneself again, get back to normal, return to health; be on the mend, be on the road to recovery, pick up, rally, respond to treatment, make progress, improve, heal, take a turn for the better, turn the corner, get out of the woods, get over something, shake something off, pull through, bounce back, revive; *Brit.* pull round; *informal* perk up.
OPPOSITES deteriorate, worsen, go downhill.
2 *the FTSE 100 share index recovered to end the day down 30.5 points* **rally**, improve, pick up, make a recovery, rebound, bounce back, come back, make a comeback.
3 *around £385,000-worth of the stolen material had now been recovered* **retrieve**, regain (possession of), get back, win back, take back, recoup, reclaim, repossess, recapture, retake, redeem; find (again), track down, trace; claw back; *Law* replevin, replevy; *rare* recuperate.
OPPOSITE lose.
4 *gold coins and bars recovered from the wreck of a seventeenth-century galleon* **salvage**, save, rescue, retrieve, reclaim, redeem.

□ **recover oneself** *she recovered herself, grateful that he had not noticed how nervous she had been* **pull oneself together**, regain one's composure/self-control, regain control of oneself, take a hold of oneself, steady oneself; *informal* get a grip (on oneself), get one's act together, snap out of it.

recovery ▶ **noun 1** *she could face lengthy physiotherapy and her recovery may be slow* **recuperation**, convalescence, return to health, process of getting better, rehabilitation, healing, rallying.
OPPOSITE relapse.
2 *the Polish economy was beginning to show signs of recovery* **improvement**, rallying, picking up, betterment, amelioration; rally, upturn, upswing, comeback, revival, renewal, a turn for the better.
OPPOSITE deterioration.
3 *the recovery of the stolen works of art* **retrieval**, regaining, repossession, getting back, recapture, reclamation, recouping, retaking, redemption; *Law* replevin; *rare* recoupment, recuperation.
OPPOSITE loss.

recreation ▶ **noun 1** *cycling is becoming more popular, both for recreation and for travel to work* **pleasure**, leisure, relaxation, fun, enjoyment, entertainment, amusement, refreshment, restoration, distraction, diversion; play, sport; *informal* R and R, jollies; *Brit. informal* beer and skittles; *N. Amer. informal* rec; *archaic* disport.
OPPOSITE work.
2 *his favourite recreations were skating and fishing* **pastime**, hobby, leisure activity, leisure pursuit, leisure interest, entertainment, diversion, divertissement, distraction, avocation.

recrimination ▶ **noun** *tears and bitter recriminations followed | she told herself that nothing was to be gained by recrimination* **accusation(s)**, mutual accusation(s), counter-accusation(s), countercharge(s), counterattack(s), retaliation(s); quarrelling, squabbling, bickering; *Brit. informal* rowing.

recruit ▶ **verb 1** *a special unit of Portuguese-speaking soldiers was recruited* **enlist**, sign up, enrol, engage, take on, round up; call up, conscript; *N. Amer.* draft, muster in, induct; *historical* press, press-gang, shanghai; *archaic* levy, impress, list, conscribe, crimp, attest.
2 *a king's power depended on his capacity to recruit armies and to lead them* **muster**, form, raise, gather/bring together, assemble, mobilize, marshal, round up, call to arms.
OPPOSITES demobilize, disband.
3 *the company is planning to recruit a thousand new staff* **hire**, employ, take on, take into one's employ; **enrol**, sign up, get, obtain, acquire.
OPPOSITES dismiss, lay off.
4 (*archaic*) *he was staying at Madeira to recruit his health* **restore**, build up, fortify, strengthen, reinvigorate, revive, revitalize, refresh, replenish; *archaic* renovate.

▶ **noun 1** *thousands of recruits had been enlisted* conscript, new soldier; *N. Amer.* draftee, inductee; *Brit. informal* sprog; *N. Amer. informal* plebe, buck private, yardbird.
OPPOSITE veteran.
2 *the profession continues to attract a flow of top-quality recruits* **new member**, new entrant, newcomer, new boy/girl, initiate; **trainee**, apprentice; beginner, novice, learner, tyro, neophyte, proselyte; *N. Amer.* tenderfoot, hire; *informal* rookie, new kid, newbie, cub; *N. Amer. informal* greenhorn.

rectify ▶ **verb** *mistakes made now cannot be rectified later* **correct**, put/set/make right, right, put to rights, sort out, deal with, amend, revise, remedy, repair, fix, cure, heal, make good, reform, harmonize, retrieve, improve, better, ameliorate, adjust, resolve, settle, redress, square; *informal* patch up.

rectitude ▶ **noun** *local worthies rarely challenged the rectitude of the chief constable* **righteousness**, goodness, virtue, moral virtue, morality, honour, honourableness, integrity, principle, probity, honesty, right-mindedness, trustworthiness, truthfulness, uprightness, upstandingness, good character, scrupulousness, decency, fairness, equity, justice; principles, ethics.
OPPOSITES infamy, dishonesty.

rectum ▶ **noun**
WORD LINKS
related prefix **procto-** (e.g. ***proctology***)

recumbent ▶ **adjective** *he stepped over the recumbent body* **lying**, flat, horizontal, stretched out, sprawled, spreadeagled, reclining, resting, lounging, prone, prostrate, supine; lying down, lying flat, (flat) on one's back, on one's stomach/front, (flat) on one's face; *rare* procumbent.
OPPOSITES erect, standing, upright.

recuperate ▶ **verb 1** *he fell ill that summer and travelled to the south of France to recuperate* **get better**, recover, convalesce, get back to normal, get well, regain one's strength/health, get back on one's feet, get over something; be on the road to recovery, be on the mend, improve, mend, pick up, rally, revive, perk up, pull through, bounce back.
2 *he won an appeal and recuperated the money* **get back**, regain, recover, win back, recoup, retrieve, reclaim, repossess, have something returned, be reunited with, find, redeem, rescue.

recur ▶ **verb** *they cannot guarantee that the problem will not recur* **happen again**, reoccur, occur again, be repeated, repeat (itself); happen repeatedly, come and go; come back (again), return, come round (again); reappear, appear again, flare up; *rare* recrudesce.

recurrent ▶ **adjective** *the waking of life is a recurrent theme in this poem* **repeated**, recurring, repetitive, reiterative, periodic, happening at intervals, cyclical, cyclic, seasonal, perennial, regular, habitual, chronic, continual, frequent; intermittent, sporadic, spasmodic, odd.
OPPOSITES isolated, single, unique.

recycle ▶ **verb** *all our stores now collect and recycle cardboard boxes* **reuse**, reprocess, convert into something, reclaim, recover; salvage, save.

R

red ▸ adjective **1** *a red dress* scarlet, vermilion, ruby, ruby-red, ruby-coloured, cherry, cherry-red, cerise, cardinal, carmine, wine, wine-red, wine-coloured, claret, claret-red, claret-coloured, blood-red; flame, flaming, coral, cochineal, rose, rosy; brick-red, maroon, rusty, foxy, rufous; reddish; *literary* damask, vermeil; *Heraldry* sanguine, gules; *rare* rufescent.
2 *he was somewhat red in the face from his exertions* **flushed**, reddish, pink, pinkish, florid, high-coloured, rubicund, roseate; ruddy, healthy-looking, rosy, glowing; burning, flaming, feverish; embarrassed, shamefaced; *archaic* sanguine; *rare* erubescent, rubescent.
3 *the chlorine in the water made his eyes red* **bloodshot**, red-rimmed, inflamed; swollen, sore.
4 *the lady with the red hair* reddish, flaming red, flame-coloured, auburn, Titian, chestnut, carroty, ginger, sandy, foxy.
▸ noun (*informal, derogatory*) *in this film the war is against drug barons rather than Reds* **Communist**, Marxist, socialist, left-winger, leftist, Bolshevik, revolutionary; *informal* Commie, lefty.
□ **in the red** *his account is still in the red* **overdrawn**, in debt, in debit, in deficit, owing money, in arrears, showing a loss.
OPPOSITE in the black.
□ **see red** (*informal*) *she saw red and hit him with the hammer* **become very angry**, become enraged, go into a rage, lose one's temper; *informal* go/get mad, go crazy, go wild, go bananas, hit the roof, go through the roof, go up the wall, go off the deep end, fly off the handle, blow one's top, blow a fuse/gasket, lose one's rag, go ape, flip, flip one's lid, go non-linear, go ballistic, go psycho; *Brit. informal* go spare, go crackers, do one's nut; *N. Amer. informal* flip one's wig, blow one's lid/stack; *vulgar slang* go apeshit.
WORD LINKS
related prefixes **rhodo- (e.g. *Rhodophyta*), erythro- (e.g. *erythrocyte*)**

red-blooded ▸ adjective *like any attractive red-blooded man he's had his share of romances* **manly**, masculine, all-male, virile, macho; strong, strapping, rugged, robust, powerful, vigorous; *informal* hunky.

redden ▸ verb **1** *the rain and cold reddened our faces* **make/colour red**; *rare* mantle.
2 *Sean felt his cheeks redden* **go/turn red,** go/turn pink/crimson/scarlet, blush, flush, colour, colour up, crimson, burn; *rare* mantle.

redeem ▸ verb **1** *one feature alone redeems the book* **save**, compensate for the defects of, rescue, justify, vindicate.
2 *he fell in that race but fully redeemed himself next time out* **vindicate**, save/free from blame, absolve, remove guilt from.
3 *he had decided to stop trying to redeem the sins of America* **atone for**, make amends for, make restitution for.
4 *she committed herself to redeeming sinners* **save**, free/save/deliver from sin, turn from sin, convert, purge/absolve of sin.
5 *Billy has to redeem his drums from the pawnbrokers* **retrieve**, regain, recover, get back, reclaim, repossess, have something returned, rescue; buy back, repurchase.
6 *this voucher can be redeemed at any branch of the shop* **exchange**, give in exchange, swap, barter, cash in, convert, turn in, return, trade in.
7 *Parliament absolved the King from all obligation to redeem this debt* **pay off**, pay back, clear, discharge, square, honour, make good.
8 *the government made no effort to redeem this promise* **fulfil**, carry out, discharge, make good, execute; keep, keep to, stick to, hold to, adhere to, abide by, heed, obey, be faithful to, honour, meet, satisfy.

redeeming ▸ adjective *his work is not without redeeming features* **compensating**, compensatory, extenuating, offsetting, qualifying, redemptive; *rare* extenuatory.

redemption ▸ noun **1** *God's redemption of his people* **saving**, saving/freeing from sin, vindication, absolution.
2 *cash must be available for the redemption of possessions* **retrieval**, recovery, reclamation, repossession, recoupment, return, rescue; repurchase.
3 *the redemption of credit vouchers* **exchange**, swapping, bartering, cashing in, conversion, return, trade-in.
4 *the redemption of the mortgage* **paying off**, paying back, discharge, clearing, squaring, honouring; *archaic* quittance.
5 *the redemption of his obligations* **fulfilment**, carrying out, discharge, making good, execution, performing, accomplishment, achievement, observance, honouring, meeting, satisfying, adherence to.

red-handed ▸ adjective *the thief was caught red-handed* **in the act**, with one's fingers/hand in the till; *Latin* in flagrante delicto; *informal* dead to rights; *Brit. informal* bang to rights; with one's trousers down; *N. Amer. informal* with one's pants down.

redolent ▸ adjective **1** *an old village church is redolent of everything that is England* **evocative**, suggestive, reminiscent, remindful.
2 *the air was redolent of patchouli* **smelling of**, reeking of; scented with, fragrant with, perfumed with.

redoubtable ▸ adjective *he had already proved himself a redoubtable commander of troops* **formidable**, awe-inspiring, fearsome, daunting, alarming; impressive, commanding, tremendous, indomitable, invincible, resolute, doughty, mighty, strong, powerful.

redound ▸ verb **1** (*formal*) *he must hope that his diplomatic effort will still redound to his credit* **contribute to**, be conducive to, result in, lead to, effect; have an effect on, affect; *formal* conduce to.
2 (*archaic*) *the unimagined consequences of the detonation* **redounded upon** *them* **rebound on**, have an adverse effect on, come back on, recoil on; misfire, backfire.

redress ▸ verb **1** *people no longer take to the barricades to redress wrongs* **rectify**, correct, put/set/make right, right, put to rights, compensate for, sort out, deal with, amend, remedy, repair, fix, cure, heal, make good, reform, harmonize, retrieve, improve, better, ameliorate, adjust, resolve, settle, square; *informal* patch up.
2 *bad news is drowning out the good news, but we aim to redress the balance* **even up**, regulate, adjust, equalize, make level, regularize, correct.
▸ noun *their best hope of redress lay in court action* **compensation**, reparation, restitution, recompense, repayment, damages, indemnity, indemnification; requital, retribution, satisfaction, remedy, comeback; justice, atonement, amends.

reduce ▸ verb **1** *the aim is to reduce pollution* **lessen**, make less, make smaller, lower, bring down, decrease, turn down, diminish, take the edge off, minimize; shrink, narrow, contract, shorten, foreshorten, truncate, taper, close, abbreviate, condense, concentrate, abridge; deplete, axe, cut, cut back/down, make cutbacks in, scale down, trim, slim (down), prune, chop, curtail, limit; moderate, lighten, ease, dilute, mitigate, commute, qualify, alleviate, relax, abate; *Finance* amortize.
OPPOSITES increase, enlarge.
2 *he succeeded in reducing her to tears* **bring to**, bring to the point of, force into, drive into.
3 *he was jailed for five years and reduced to the ranks* **demote**, downgrade, lower, lower in rank/status; abase, humble, demean, belittle, humiliate, bring low; *N. Amer. informal* bust.
OPPOSITE promote.
4 *ribs of beef have been reduced to £1.88 a pound* **make cheaper**, lower the price of, lower/cut in price, cheapen, cut, mark down, discount, put on sale, offer at a giveaway price; *informal* slash, knock down.
OPPOSITE put up.
□ **in reduced circumstances impoverished**, in straitened circumstances, ruined, bankrupt, bankrupted, bust, insolvent; **poor**, indigent, penurious, impecunious, in penury, moneyless, without a sou, as poor as a church mouse, poverty-stricken, destitute, necessitous; needy, in need/want, badly off, hard up, on one's beam-ends, unable to make ends meet, underprivileged; *Brit.* on the breadline, without a penny (to one's name); *informal* broke, flat broke, cleaned out, strapped for cash, strapped, on one's uppers; *Brit. informal* stony broke, skint, without two pennies/(brass) farthings to rub together, in Queer Street; *N. Amer. informal* stone broke; *rare* pauperized, beggared.

reduction ▸ noun **1** *a reduction in pollution* **lessening**, lowering, decrease, diminution, minimizing.
OPPOSITES increase, enlargement.
2 *the closure of those offices led to a reduction in staff* **depletion**, cut, cutting, cutback, scaling down, trimming, slimming (down), pruning, axing, chopping, curtailment, limiting.
3 *there will be some reduction in the pressure to keep costs down* **easing**, lightening, moderation, dilution, mitigation, commuting, qualification, alleviation, relaxation, abatement.
4 *a reduction in status* **demotion**, downgrading, lowering; abasement, humbling, demeaning, belittling, humiliation, bringing low.
OPPOSITE promotion.
5 *substantial reductions on children's clothes* **discount**, markdown, deduction, (price) cut, pullback, concession, allowance; *informal* slash.
OPPOSITE increase.

redundancy ▸ noun **1** *there is a great deal of redundancy in language* **superfluity**, unnecessariness, expendability, uselessness, excess.
2 *they know redundancy is in the offing | a hospital has announced 300 redundancies* **sacking**, dismissal, lay-off, discharge, notice; unemployment; *Brit.* one's cards; *informal* marching orders.

redundant ▸ adjective **1** *many churches have become redundant over the last twenty years* **unnecessary**, not required, inessential, unessential, needless, unneeded, uncalled for, dispensable, disposable, expendable, unwanted, useless; **surplus**, surplus to requirements, superfluous, too much/many, supernumerary, excessive, in excess, extra, additional, spare; *French* de trop; *informal* needed like a hole in the head.
OPPOSITES essential, necessary.
2 *2,000 workers were* **made redundant sacked**, dismissed, laid off, discharged; **unemployed**, idle, jobless, out of work, out of a job; *rare* disemployed.
OPPOSITES in work, employed.

reef ▸ noun *waves crashed over the reef* **shoal**, bar, sandbar, sandbank, spit; ridge, ledge, shelf, atoll, key; barrier reef, fringing reef; *Scottish* skerry; (*in Spanish America*) cay.

reek ▸ verb *the whole place reeked of cheap perfume* **stink**, smell, smell bad/disgusting, give off a bad smell, stink/smell to high heaven.
▸ noun *the reek of cattle dung* **stink**, bad smell, foul smell, stench, taint, effluvium; *Brit. informal* niff, pong, whiff, hum; *Scottish informal* guff; *N. Amer.*

informal, dated funk; *rare* miasma, mephitis, malodour, fetor.

reel ▶ verb **1** *Cormack reeled as the ship began to roll* **stagger**, lurch, sway, rock, stumble, totter, wobble, falter, waver, swerve, pitch, roll.
2 *the Government was still **reeling from** the currency crisis* **be shaken by**, be stunned by, be in shock after, be shocked by, be numb from, be dazed by, be taken aback by, be staggered by, be aghast at, be dumbfounded at, be dumbstruck at, be upset by, be bowled over by, feel giddy/dizzy from, feel confused by.
3 *she closed her eyes and the room reeled* **go round**, go round and round, whirl, spin, revolve, gyrate, swirl, twirl, turn, wheel, swim.
□ **reel something off** *he reeled off a choice string of unpleasant epithets* **recite**, rattle off, loose off, fire off, list rapidly, run through, enumerate, detail, itemize; *informal* spiel off.

refer ▶ verb **1** *he **referred to** errors in the article* **mention**, make mention of, make reference to, allude to, touch on, speak of/about, talk of/about, write about, cite, name, comment on, deal with, go into, treat (of), note, point out, call attention to, bring up, raise, broach, introduce; *rare* advert to, moot.
2 *the matter has been referred to my insurers* **pass**, hand on, send on, transfer, remit, direct, leave, commit, entrust, assign, hand over.
3 *these figures **refer** only to 2001* **apply to**, **be relevant to**, have relevance to, concern, relate to, belong to, be about, have to do with, be connected with, have reference to, pertain to, appertain to, be pertinent to, have a bearing on, bear on, affect, involve, cover, touch, touch on; *archaic* regard.
4 *the name is an ancient word **referring** to a Saxon village* **denote**, describe, indicate, mean, depict, symbolize, signify, designate, stand for, represent.
5 *the constable **referred to** his notes | please **refer to** your manager for the correct password* **consult**, turn to, look at, look up (in), seek information from, search in, have recourse to, call on; seek advice from, call in, take counsel from, ask.

referee ▶ noun **1** *the referee blew his whistle for a penalty* **umpire**, judge, adjudicator, arbitrator, arbiter, mediator; *informal* ref.
2 *applications should include a curriculum vitae and the names of two referees* **supporter**, character witness, backer, advocate.
▶ verb **1** *he refereed the Scotland v Spain game* **umpire**, judge, adjudicate, run, be in control of.
2 *they asked him to referee in the dispute* **arbitrate**, mediate, act as arbitrator/arbiter/mediator/negotiator.

reference ▶ noun **1** *his journal contains many **references to** railways* **mention of**, allusion to, comment on, remark about; citation of, instance of.
2 *some references are given in the bibliography to this chapter* **source**, information source, citation, authority, credit; note, footnote; bibliographical data, bibliography.
3 *this was an appropriate case for a reference to the European Court of Justice* **referral**, transfer, passing on, handover, direction, remission.
4 *his employer gave him a glowing reference* **testimonial**, character reference, recommendation, good word, backing; credentials; *dated* character.
□ **with reference to apropos**, with regard to, regarding, as regards, with respect to, on the subject of, in the matter of, re; in relation to, relating to, in connection with.

referendum ▶ noun *he called for a referendum on the death penalty* **public vote**, **plebiscite**, popular vote, ballot, poll.

refine ▶ verb **1** *we were losing this valuable fibre by refining our cereal foods and sugar* **purify**, clarify, clear, cleanse, strain, sift, filter, rarefy, distil, concentrate, process, treat; *technical* rectify.
OPPOSITE adulterate.
2 *the supporting documents help students to refine their English language skills* **improve**, perfect, polish (up), hone, temper, fine-tune, elaborate, touch up, revise, edit, copy-edit; complete, finish, finish off, put the final/finishing touches to, crown, consummate; *informal* tweak.
OPPOSITE lose.

refined ▶ adjective **1** *refined sugar* **purified**, pure, clarified, clear, strained, sifted, filtered, rarefied, distilled, concentrated, processed, treated, polished; *technical* rectified.
OPPOSITE crude, raw.
2 *a refined lady* **cultivated**, cultured, polished, civilized, stylish, elegant, sophisticated, urbane; civil, polite, gracious, courtly, well mannered, well bred, gentlemanly, ladylike, genteel; *informal* couth.
OPPOSITES boorish, coarse.
3 *she is a woman of refined taste* **discriminating**, discerning, selective, fastidious, sensitive, perceptive; sophisticated, cultured, educated, enlightened; exquisite, impeccable, delicate, fine.

refinement ▶ noun **1** *the refinement of sugar* **purification**, refining, clarifying, clarification, cleansing, straining, sifting, filtering, filtration, rarefaction, distillation, concentration, processing, treatment, treating; *technical* rectification.
OPPOSITE adulteration.
2 *all programs have bugs and need endless refinement* **improvement**, perfection, polishing, honing, fine-tuning, touching up, revision, editing, copy-editing; completion, finishing, finishing off, the final/finishing touches, crowning, consummation; *informal* tweaking.
3 *a woman who spoke with self-conscious refinement* **style**, elegance, finesse, polish, finish, sophistication, urbanity; civility, politeness, grace, graciousness, courtliness, good manners, good breeding, gentility; cultivation, culture, taste, discrimination; *French* politesse.

reflect ▶ verb **1** *the snow reflects a great deal of light* **send back**, throw back, cast back, give back, bounce back, shine back, return, mirror.
OPPOSITE absorb.
2 *their facial expressions reflected their feelings* **indicate**, show, display, demonstrate, be evidence of, register, reveal, betray, evince, disclose, exhibit, manifest; express, bespeak, communicate, bear out, attest, prove, evidence; result from.
3 *he **reflected on** his responsibilities as a teacher* **think about**, give thought to, consider, give consideration to, review, mull over, contemplate, study, cogitate about/on, meditate on, muse on, deliberate about/on, ruminate about/on/over, dwell on, brood on/over, agonize over, worry about, chew over, puzzle over, speculate about, weigh up, revolve, turn over in one's mind, be in a brown study; *informal* put on one's thinking cap; *archaic* pore on; *rare* cerebrate.
□ **reflect badly on** *the incident reflected badly on the government* **discredit**, do discredit to, be a discredit to, disgrace, shame, put in a bad light, damage, damage/tarnish/blemish the reputation of, give a bad name to, bring into disrepute, become a stain/blot of the escutcheon of, detract from.

reflection ▶ noun **1** *the colours seen in soap bubbles are caused by reflection of light* **sending back**, throwing back, casting back, mirroring, backscattering.
OPPOSITE absorption.
2 *she glanced at her own reflection in the mirror* **image**, mirror image, likeness; echo.
3 *your hands and nails are a reflection of your well-being* **indication**, display, demonstration, manifestation; expression, attestation, proof, evidence.
4 *the sale is not any reflection on the business* **slur**, aspersion, imputation, censure, reproach, shame, criticism, source of discredit, derogation.
5 *after some reflection, he turned the offer down* **thought**, thinking, consideration, contemplation, study, deliberation, pondering, meditation, musing, rumination, cogitation, brooding, agonizing; *rare* cerebration.
6 *write down your reflections on the subject* **opinion**, thought, view, viewpoint, belief, feeling, idea, impression, conclusion, judgement, assessment, estimation; **comment**, observation, remark, statement, utterance, pronouncement, declaration.

reflex ▶ adjective *sneezing is a reflex action* **instinctive**, automatic, mechanical, involuntary, knee-jerk, reflexive, impulsive, intuitive, spontaneous, unconscious, subliminal, unthinking, unpremeditated, unconditioned, untaught, unlearned, unintentional, unwitting, inadvertent, accidental.
OPPOSITES conscious, voluntary, learned.

reform ▶ verb **1** *a comprehensive plan to reform the health-care system* **improve**, make better, better, ameliorate, refine, mend, rectify, correct, rehabilitate; **alter**, make alterations to, change, adjust, make adjustments to, adapt, amend, revise, recast, reshape, refashion, redesign, restyle, revamp, renovate, rework, redo, remake, rebuild, reconstruct, remodel, make over, remould, reorganize, revolutionize, reorient, reorientate, vary, transform, convert; customize, tailor; *technical* permute; *rare* permutate.
OPPOSITES preserve, maintain.
2 *after his marriage he reformed* **mend one's ways**, change for the better, change completely, make a fresh start, turn over a new leaf, become a new person, reconstruct oneself, improve, go straight, get back on the straight and narrow.
OPPOSITE worsen.
▶ noun *the reform of the prison system* **improvement**, betterment, amelioration, refinement, rectification, correction, rehabilitation; **alteration**, change, adjustment, adaptation, amendment, revision, recasting, reshaping, refashioning, redesigning, restyling, revamp, revamping, renovation, reworking, redoing, remake, rebuilding, reconstruction, remodelling, makeover, remoulding, reorganizing, reorganization, reorienting, reorientation, transformation, conversion; customizing, tailoring.

refractory ▶ adjective *a refractory child* **obstinate**, stubborn, stubborn as a mule, mulish, bull-headed, pig-headed, obdurate, headstrong, self-willed, wayward, wilful, perverse, contrary, recalcitrant, obstreperous, disobedient, insubordinate, rebellious, mutinous, defiant, stiff-necked, intractable, intransigent, unyielding, unmalleable, unmanageable, ungovernable, unpersuadable; *Scottish* thrawn; *informal* cussed; *Brit. informal* **bloody-minded**, bolshie, stroppy; *N. Amer. informal* balky; *archaic* contumacious, froward; *rare* contrarious.
OPPOSITES obedient, manageable.

refrain ▶ verb *he appealed to the protestors to **refrain from** violence* **abstain**, desist, hold back, stop oneself, withhold; forbear, forgo, do without, dispense with, resist the temptation to, avoid, steer clear of, give a wide berth to, have nothing to do with, fight shy of, eschew, shun, renounce,

R

forswear, abjure, leave alone, not touch, reject; stop, cease, finish, discontinue, give up, break off, drop; *informal* quit, leave off, kick, swear off; *Brit. informal* jack in; *archaic* forsake.

refresh ▶ **verb 1** *the cool air will refresh me* **reinvigorate**, revitalize, revive, restore, brace, fortify, strengthen, give new strength to, enliven, perk up, stimulate, freshen, energize, exhilarate, reanimate, wake up, resuscitate, revivify, rejuvenate, regenerate, renew, breathe new life into; blow away the cobwebs; *informal* buck up, pep up; *rare* inspirit.
OPPOSITE weary.
2 *let me refresh your memory* **jog**, stimulate, prompt, prod, activate, rouse, arouse; cue, help out, give someone a cue.
3 (*N. Amer.*) *I refreshed his glass* **refill**, top up, replenish, recharge.

refreshing ▶ **adjective 1** *a refreshing drink | a refreshing breeze* **invigorating**, revitalizing, reviving, restoring, bracing, fortifying, enlivening, stimulating, freshening, energizing, exhilarating, reanimating, revivifying, rejuvenating; thirst-quenching; *rare* inspiriting.
2 *these latest proposals are a refreshing change of direction* **welcome**, **stimulating**, new, novel, creative, fresh, imaginative, original, different, innovative, innovatory, innovational, inventive, ingenious, inspired, resourceful, unusual, unconventional, unorthodox, unfamiliar, unprecedented, groundbreaking, pioneering, avant-garde, unique, individual, individualistic, distinctive; not just another.

refreshment ▶ **noun 1** *the hotel provided refreshment at reasonable prices | refreshments will be available in the interval* **food and drink**, sustenance, fare, liquid refreshment; snacks, titbits, eatables, a bite, drinks; *informal* nibbles, eats, grub, bread, nosh, chow, booze; *Brit. informal* scoff; *N. Amer. informal* chuck; *formal* comestibles, provender; *archaic* victuals, vittles, viands, meat, commons; *rare* aliment, pabulum.
2 *spiritual refreshment* **invigoration**, revitalizing, revival, restoring, strengthening, enlivening, perking up, stimulation, freshening, energizing, reanimation, resuscitation, revivification, rejuvenation, regeneration, renewal.

refrigerate ▶ **verb** *refrigerate the dough for an hour* **keep cold**, cool, cool down, chill; freeze, deep-freeze, ice.
OPPOSITES heat; defrost.

refuge ▶ **noun 1** *many homeless people were seeking refuge in subway stations* **shelter**, protection, safety, security, asylum, sanctuary; preservation, safe keeping.
2 *the park serves as a refuge for mountain gorillas* **sanctuary**, place of shelter, shelter, place of safety, haven, safe haven, sanctum, safe house, harbour, port in a storm, ark; retreat, bolt-hole, foxhole, hiding place, hideaway, hideout, fastness; *Spanish* querencia.

refugee ▶ **noun** *she had fled to England as a refugee* **displaced person**, DP, escapee, fugitive, asylum seeker, runaway, exile, émigré, stateless person, outcast, returnee; *Austral. informal* reffo.

refund ▶ **verb** (stress on the second syllable) **1** *we guarantee to refund your money if you're not entirely satisfied with your order* **repay**, **give back**, return, pay back, restore; replace, make good.
2 *there was no alternative but to refund the subscribers* **reimburse**, compensate, recompense, square accounts with, settle up with, make restitution/amends to, recoup, remunerate, indemnify.
▶ **noun** (stress on the first syllable) *if you are not entirely satisfied, return the goods within 14 days for a full refund* **repayment**, reimbursement, restitution, reparation; rebate, indemnity, indemnification.

R

refurbish ▶ **verb** *millions of pounds are needed to refurbish the conference and exhibition halls* **renovate**, recondition, rehabilitate, revamp, make over, overhaul, restore, renew, develop, redevelop, rebuild, reconstruct, remodel; redecorate, brighten up, freshen up, spruce up; improve, upgrade, refit, fix up, re-equip; modernize, update, bring up to date, bring into the twenty-first century; *N. Amer.* bring up to code; *informal* do up; *N. Amer. informal* rehab.

refusal ▶ **noun 1** *we have had only one refusal to our invitation* **non-acceptance**, no, dissent, demurral, negation, rebuff, turndown; regrets; *informal* knock-back, brush-off; *rare* declinature.
OPPOSITE acceptance.
2 *you can have first refusal* **option**, choice, consideration, opportunity to purchase.
3 *the Council's refusal of planning permission* **withholding**, failure to grant, denial, veto, turndown; *informal* the thumbs down.
OPPOSITE granting.

refuse[1] (stress on the second syllable) ▶ **verb 1** *he refused their invitation to lunch* **decline**, **turn down**, say no to; reject, spurn, scorn, rebuff, disdain, repudiate, dismiss, repulse; shake one's head, send one's regrets; baulk at, demur at, protest at, jib at, draw the line at; *informal* pass up; *Brit. informal* knock back.
OPPOSITE accept.
2 *the Council refused planning permission* **withhold**, not grant, disapprove, deny, discountenance; *informal* give the thumbs down to.
OPPOSITE grant.

refuse[2] (stress on the first syllable) ▶ **noun** *dogs nosed around in piles of refuse* **rubbish**, waste, debris, litter, garbage, discarded matter, detritus, dross, landfill, scrap, rubble, slag, spoilage, sullage, sewage, slop; dregs, lees, leavings, leftovers, sweepings; *N. Amer.* trash; *Austral./NZ* mullock; *informal* dreck, junk; *Brit. informal* gash; *Archaeology* debitage; *rare* draff, raffle, raff.

CHOOSE THE RIGHT WORD

refuse, decline, reject, spurn

These words all share the basic meaning of saying 'no' to something, but they can also convey how or why it was said.

- **Refuse** is the most neutral word for simply saying 'no' to a request, suggestion, or offer (*I refused to answer their questions | he must refuse any food offered him*). *Refuse* is the only one of these words that can have two objects (*the USA had refused him an entry visa*).
- To **decline** something is to refuse it politely and rather formally (*I am sorry to have to decline your offer*). *Decline* and *refuse* are the only two of these words that can followed by an infinitive (*he declined to speculate about a cancer cure*).
- **Reject** suggests that what is on offer is felt to be not good enough (*an article which her editor had rejected*). It is also used, especially in official contexts, when a request is not granted (*the coroner rejected a request to submit a technical report*). *Reject* is also used of the body's immune system response to a transplanted organ.
- **Spurn** suggests disdain or contempt (*the opposition spurned an invitation to participate in a coalition government | she cut herself off from us and spurned our forgiveness*), although nowadays journalists often use it in a weaker sense (*pensions managers may spurn equities*). Both *spurn* and *reject* are also used of refusing affection to someone who used to be or might be expected to be the object of it (*a spurned lover | he was reared on the bottle, having been completely rejected by his mother*).

refute ▶ **verb 1** *attempts to refute Einstein's theory of relativity* **disprove**, prove wrong/false, show/prove to be wrong/false, rebut, confute, give the lie to, demolish, explode, debunk, drive a coach and horses through, discredit, invalidate; *informal* shoot full of holes, shoot down (in flames), blow sky-high; *rare* controvert, negative.
OPPOSITE confirm.
2 *a spokesman totally refuted the allegation of bias* **deny**, reject, repudiate, rebut, declare to be untrue; contradict; *formal* gainsay.
OPPOSITE accept.

refute or deny?

The core meaning of **refute** is 'prove (a statement or theory) to be wrong', as in *attempts to refute Einstein's theory*. In the second half of the 20th century, a sense developed in which *refute* is treated as synonymous with **deny**, as in *I absolutely refute the charges made against me*, where no evidence or argument to show that the charges are untrue is given. Traditionalists object to the second use, but it is now widely accepted in standard English.

regain ▶ **verb 1** *government troops regained control of the area | he did not regain consciousness* **recover**, get back, win back, recoup, retrieve, reclaim, repossess, have something returned, be reunited with, rescue, salvage; take back, retake, recapture, reconquer.
2 *it would be easier to regain the glacier by traversing the mountain* **return to**, get back to, find one's way back to, reach again, reattain, rejoin.

regal ▶ **adjective 1** *a regal feast was laid before him* **majestic**, fit for a king/queen/prince/princess, grand, impressive, imposing, splendid, superb, magnificent, noble, proud, stately, dignified, exalted, glorious, striking, spectacular, awe-inspiring, breathtaking, sumptuous, opulent, fine, luxurious, de luxe, lavish, resplendent, monumental, palatial, august, distinguished, great; *informal* splendiferous, ritzy, posh; *rare* splendacious, magnolious.
2 *his regal forebears* **royal**, kingly, queenly, princely, sovereign, crowned.
OPPOSITE plebeian.

regale ▶ **verb 1** *the carol-singers were regaled with refreshment at most houses* **supply lavishly**, entertain lavishly/sumptuously, ply, wine and dine, fête, feast, cater for, serve, feed.
2 *he regaled her with a colourful account of that afternoon's meeting* **entertain**, amuse, divert, delight, fascinate, captivate, beguile; treat to.

regard ▶ **verb 1** *we regard these results as encouraging* **consider**, look on, view, see, hold, think, think of, contemplate, count, judge, deem, estimate, evaluate, interpret, appraise, assess, make of, find, put down as, take for, account, reckon, treat, adjudge, size up, value, rate, gauge, sum up, weigh up.
2 *he regarded her with a cold stare* **look at**, contemplate, eye, gaze at, stare at; watch, observe, view, survey, scan; examine, inspect, study, scrutinize; *literary* behold.

3 (archaic) *he seldom regards her advice* **heed**, pay heed to, pay attention to, attend to, listen to, mind, take notice of, take into consideration, take into account.
▶ **noun 1** *he has no regard for human life* **consideration**, care, concern, sympathy, thought, mind, notice, heed, attention, interest.
2 *doctors are held in high regard by society* **esteem**, respect, high opinion, acclaim, admiration, approval, approbation, popularity, appreciation, estimation, favour, deference, reverence, veneration, liking, affection, love.
3 (**regards**) *Jamie sends his regards* **best wishes**, good wishes, greetings, kind/kindest regards, felicitations, salutations, respects, compliments, best, love; archaic remembrances, devoirs.
4 *she was aware of his steady regard* **look**, gaze, stare, fixed look, intent look; observation, contemplation, examination, inspection, study, scrutiny.
5 *in this regard I disagree with you* **respect**, aspect, facet, consideration, point, item, characteristic, particular, detail, specific, particularity, fact; matter, issue, topic, question, circumstance.
□ **with regard to** *I am writing with regard to an article in your November edition.* See REGARDING.

regarding ▶ **preposition** *further details regarding this scheme are available from the Council* **concerning**, as regards, with regard to, in regard to, with respect to, in respect of, with reference to, relating to, respecting, as for, as to, re, about, apropos, on the subject of, in connection with; French vis-à-vis; Latin in re.

regardless ▶ **adverb** *he decided to go, regardless* **anyway**, anyhow, in any case, nevertheless, nonetheless, notwithstanding, despite everything, in spite of everything, for all that, after everything, no matter what, even so, just the same, all the same, be that as it may, in any event, come what may, (come) rain or shine, whatever the cost; informal still and all, irregardless.
□ **regardless of** *the Commission should promote equal opportunities for people regardless of age* **irrespective of**, without regard to, without reference to, disregarding, unmindful of, heedless of, careless of/about, indifferent to, unconcerned about, without consideration of, negligent of, setting aside, discounting, ignoring, notwithstanding, no matter, despite, in spite of, for all; informal irregardless of.
OPPOSITES mindful of, heedful of.

regenerate ▶ **verb** *government grants have helped to regenerate many of our inner-city areas* **revive**, **revitalize**, renew, restore, breathe new life into, revivify, rejuvenate, reanimate, resuscitate, reawaken, rekindle, kick-start, uplift, change radically, improve, amend; reorganize, reconstruct, renovate, overhaul; informal give a shot in the arm to.

regime ▶ **noun 1** *the former Communist regime of East Germany* **government**, authorities, system of government, rule, reign, dominion, sovereignty, jurisdiction, authority, control, command, administration, establishment, direction, management, leadership.
2 *a favourable tax regime | many people who start a health regime stop it too early* **system**, arrangement, scheme, code; apparatus, mechanism; order, pattern, method, procedure, routine, policy, practice, course, plan, programme; diet, regimen.

regiment ▶ **noun** *the regiment was fighting somewhere in France* **unit**, outfit, force; army, group, corps, division, brigade, battalion, squadron, company, commando, battery, platoon, section, crew, detachment, contingent, band, legion, cohort.
▶ **verb** *every aspect of their life is strictly regimented* **organize**, order, systematize, control, manipulate, regulate, manage, discipline, keep a tight rein on, bring into line, rule with a rod of iron; rare methodize.

regimented ▶ **adjective** *the regimented environment of the ward* **strict**, strictly regulated, organized, disciplined, controlled, ordered, systematic, neat, tidy, orderly; uniform, unvarying, unvaried, unchanging, even, unbroken, monotonous, dull.
OPPOSITES free, varied.

region *See centre pages for list of* **Districts**
▶ **noun** *the western region of the country* **district**, province, territory, division, area, section, sector, zone, belt, tract, stretch, expanse, terrain, part, quarter, locality, locale; informal parts; Brit. informal patch.
□ **in the region of** *a population in the region of 1,400* **approximately**, about, around, roughly, in the neighbourhood of, in the area of, of the order of, something like, some, round about, close to, near to, just about, practically, more or less; or so, or thereabouts, there or thereabouts, give or take a few, plus or minus a few, give or take a bit, in round numbers; not far off, nearly, almost, approaching; Brit. getting on for; Latin circa; informal as near as dammit to; N. Amer. informal in the ballpark of.

regional ▶ **adjective 1** *there was considerable regional variation* **geographical**, topographical, zonal, territorial, topical; by region, from one region to another.
2 *a regional parliament* **local**, localized, devolved; state, territorial, provincial, sectoral, zonal, cantonal, county, district, parochial; native, vernacular.
OPPOSITE national.

register ▶ **noun 1** *the register of electors* **official list**, listing, roll, roster, index, directory, catalogue, schedule, inventory, tally, calendar.
2 *her death was recorded in the parish register* **record**, chronicle, diary, journal, log, logbook, ledger, archive; annals, files.
3 *the lower register of the piano* **range**, area, region, reaches, sweep; voice, notes, octaves.
▶ **verb 1** *the car is registered in his name | I wish to register a complaint* **record**, put on record, enter, file, lodge, post, set down, inscribe, write down, put in writing, submit, report, take down, note, minute, list, log, catalogue.
2 *it is not too late to* **register for** *the conference* **enrol**, put one's name down, enlist, enter, sign on, sign up, apply; go in for; check in.
3 *the dial registered much more than half an ounce* **indicate**, read, record, show, display.
4 *her face registered gathering anger* **display**, show, express, exhibit, evince, betray, disclose, evidence, reveal, manifest, demonstrate, reflect, bespeak, testify to; literary betoken.
5 *the content of her statement did not register* **make an impression**, get through, sink in, fall into place, penetrate, have an effect, dawn, strike home, be understood; strike someone.

regress ▶ **verb** *he regressed to his former state of madness* **revert**, retrogress, relapse, lapse, backslide, go backwards, slip back, drift back, subside, sink back; **deteriorate**, decline, worsen, degenerate, get worse, fall, fall off, fall away, drop, ebb, wane, slump; informal go downhill, go to pot, go to the dogs; rare recidivate, retrograde.
OPPOSITES progress, improve.

regret ▶ **verb 1** *they may come to regret their decision* **be sorry about**, feel contrite about, feel apologetic about, feel remorse about/for, be remorseful about, rue, repent (of), feel repentant about, be regretful at/about, have a conscience about, blame oneself for.
OPPOSITES applaud, welcome.
2 *it made him regret the passing of his youth* **mourn**, grieve for/over, feel grief at, weep over, sigh over, fret about, pine over; feel sad about, be regretful at/about, lament, feel sorrow at, sorrow for, be upset/disappointed about, deplore.
▶ **noun 1** *it was an injudicious action, and both players later expressed regret* **remorse**, sorrow, contrition, contriteness, repentance, penitence, pangs of conscience, guilt, compunction, remorsefulness, ruefulness, shame, self-reproach, self-accusation, self-condemnation; rare sorriness.
OPPOSITE satisfaction.
2 (**regrets**) *please give your grandmother my regrets as I have to leave* **apology**, apologies, expression of regret; refusal, non-acceptance.
3 *the family left London with genuine regret* **sadness**, sorrow, disappointment, dismay, unhappiness, dejection, lamentation, grief, mourning, mournfulness.
OPPOSITES happiness, gladness.

regretful ▶ **adjective 1** *she sounded genuinely regretful* **sorry**, remorseful, contrite, repentant, rueful, penitent, conscience-stricken, apologetic, abject, guilty, guilt-ridden, ashamed, shamefaced, sheepish, in sackcloth and ashes, afraid; rare compunctious.
OPPOSITE unrepentant.
2 *there was no time to feel regretful when Greg and his family left* **sad**, unhappy, sorrowful, dejected, depressed, downcast, miserable, downhearted, down, despondent, despairing, disconsolate, out of sorts, desolate, wretched, glum, gloomy, dismal, blue, melancholy, melancholic, low-spirited, mournful, woeful, woebegone, doleful, forlorn, crestfallen; informal down in the mouth, down in the dumps.
OPPOSITE glad.

regrettable ▶ **adjective** *a regrettable lack of foresight was at the root of it* **undesirable**, unfortunate, unwelcome, sad, sorry, woeful, disappointing, distressing, too bad; deplorable, lamentable, reprehensible, shameful, disgraceful, blameworthy, ill-advised, dreadful, terrible, awful; rare egregious.
OPPOSITES desirable, welcome.

regular ▶ **adjective 1** *he had to plant the flags at regular intervals* **uniform**, even, consistent, constant, unchanging, unvarying, orderly, systematic, fixed; symmetrical.
OPPOSITES irregular, erratic.
2 *a poem with a very regular beat* **rhythmic**, steady, even, uniform, constant, unchanging, unvarying; smooth.
OPPOSITES irregular, unsteady.
3 *the reprocessing plant has been the subject of regular protests* **frequent**, repeated, continual, recurrent, periodic, habitual, constant, perpetual, oft repeated, repetitive, numerous.
OPPOSITE occasional.
4 *in their haste to be rich they deviated from safe and regular methods of business* **established**, conventional, orthodox, proper, formal, official, fixed, stated, approved, sanctioned, bona fide, standard, usual, traditional, classic, time-honoured, tried and tested, tried and trusted.
OPPOSITES irregular, experimental.
5 *you should have a regular procedure for taking and recording attendance* **methodical**, systematic, structured, well ordered, well organized, orderly, efficient, smooth-running, streamlined, well regulated,

R

disciplined, planned, well planned, businesslike, meticulous, punctilious. OPPOSITE haphazard.
6 *his regular route to work* **usual**, normal, customary, habitual, routine, typical, everyday, accustomed, established, expected, wonted, ordinary, daily, common.
OPPOSITE unusual.
7 (*informal, dated*) *he's a regular charmer* **utter**, real, absolute, complete, thorough, thoroughgoing, total, unmitigated, outright, out-and-out, perfect, consummate, surpassing, sheer, rank, pure, unqualified, inveterate, positive, dyed-in-the-wool, true-blue, undiluted, unalloyed, unadulterated, in every respect; *N. Amer.* full-bore; *informal* deep-dyed; *Brit. informal* right, proper; *Austral./NZ informal* fair; *archaic* arrant; *rare* right-down.

regulate ▶ verb **1** *the flow of the river has been regulated with sluices* **control**, adjust, manage, balance, set, synchronize, modulate, tune.
2 *businesses that are regulated under the Financial Services Act* **supervise**, oversee, police, superintend, monitor, check (up on), keep an eye on, inspect, administer, be responsible for; **control**, manage, direct, guide, govern, rule, order; *informal* keep tabs on, keep a tab on, keep a beady eye on.

regulation ▶ noun **1** *EC regulations regarding health and safety in the workplace* **rule**, ruling, order, directive, act, law, by-law, statute, edict, canon, ordinance, pronouncement, mandate, dictate, dictum, decree, fiat, proclamation, command, injunction, procedure, requirement, prescription, precept, guideline; (*in Tsarist Russia*) ukase; (*in Spanish-speaking countries*) pronunciamento.
2 *chromium is thought to play a very important part in the regulation of blood sugar* **adjustment**, control, management, balancing, setting, synchronization, modulation, tuning.
3 *the regulation of financial services* **supervision**, **policing**, overseeing, superintendence, monitoring, inspection, administration; **control**, management, responsibility for, direction, guidance, government, rule, ordering.
▶ adjective *regulation dress went by the board in such extreme conditions* **official**, prescribed, set, fixed, required, mandatory, compulsory, obligatory; correct, acceptable, appropriate, proper, fitting, standard, normal, usual, customary.
OPPOSITES non-standard, unofficial, informal.

regurgitate ▶ verb **1** *a ruminant continually regurgitates food from its stomach* **vomit**, bring up, disgorge; *archaic* regorge.
2 *I knew how to regurgitate facts for examinations* **repeat**, say again, restate, recapitulate, iterate, reiterate, recite, rehearse, parrot; *informal* trot out.

rehabilitate ▶ verb **1** *efforts are made to rehabilitate patients after treatment* **restore to health/normality**, reintegrate, readapt, retrain; *N. Amer. informal* rehab.
2 *with the fall of the government, many former dissidents were rehabilitated* **reinstate**, reinstall, restore, bring back, re-establish; **pardon**, absolve, exonerate, exculpate, forgive.
3 *the authority has an excellent reputation for rehabilitating vacant housing* **recondition**, restore, renew, renovate, refurbish, revamp, make over, make fit for habitation/use, overhaul, develop, redevelop, convert, rebuild, reconstruct, remodel; redecorate, brighten up, freshen up, spruce up; improve, upgrade, refit, fix up, re-equip; modernize, update, bring up to date, bring into the twenty-first century; *N. Amer.* bring something up to code, rehab; *informal* do up.

R

rehearsal ▶ noun **1** *we've got a rehearsal for the school concert* **practice**, practice session, try-out, trial performance, read-through, sing-through, walk-through, run-through, going-over, drill; *informal* dry run.
2 *they would interrupt speakers with lengthy rehearsals of facts and figures* **enumeration**, listing, itemization, detailing, spelling out, setting out, specification, naming, cataloguing, recitation, rattling off, presentation; list, catalogue.

rehearse ▶ verb **1** *I had rehearsed this role for years* **prepare**, practise, try out, read through, sing through, walk through, run through/over, go over; *N. Amer. informal* run down.
2 *he was rehearsing with the rest of the band* **practise**, have a practice session, prepare, have a trial performance, go through one's paces.
3 *I recall him rehearsing the Vienna Philharmonic in two works by Tchaikovsky* **train**, drill, prepare, coach, tutor, groom, put someone through their paces, teach, instruct, school, direct, guide, inculcate.
4 *this carefully worded document rehearsed the arguments for making the joint award* **enumerate**, list, itemize, detail, spell out, set out, present, specify, name, give, describe, delineate, catalogue, recite, rattle off; **restate**, repeat, reiterate, recapitulate, recount, go over, run through, review; *informal* recap.

reign ▶ verb **1** *Robert II reigned for nineteen years* **be king/queen**, be monarch, be sovereign, sit on the throne, occupy the throne, wear the crown, wield the sceptre, hold sway, rule, govern, be in power.
2 *chaos reigned for a few moments* **prevail**, exist, be in existence, be present, be the case, hold, obtain, occur, be prevalent, be current, be rife, be rampant, be the order of the day, be customary, be established, be common, be widespread, be in force, be in effect; abound, predominate, preponderate, be supreme, hold sway; endure, survive, persist.
▶ noun **1** *the later years of Henry's reign* **rule**, sovereignty, monarchy.
2 *during his reign as manager* **period in office**, incumbency, tenancy, managership, leadership; period as champion.

WORD LINKS
relating to a reign **regnal**

reigning ▶ adjective **1** *the reigning monarch* **ruling**, regnant; on the throne.
2 *the reigning world champion* **incumbent**, current, in office, presiding, in power.
3 *the reigning legal conventions* **prevailing**, existing, extant, contemporary, present, current, modern, latest; usual, common, set, recognized, established, accepted, ordinary, popular, fashionable; general, pervasive, ubiquitous, widespread, rampant, universal; in force, in fashion, in style, in vogue.

reimburse ▶ verb **1** *it is usual for companies to reimburse travel costs* **repay**, refund, return, pay back, give back, restore, replace, make good.
2 *we'll reimburse you out of petty cash* **compensate**, recompense, refund, repay, square accounts with, settle up with.

rein ▶ noun *he has no rein on his own behaviour* **restraint**, check, curb, constraint, restriction, limitation, control, bridle, brake.
▶ verb *he reined in his horse | he made no attempt to rein back costs* **restrain**, check, curb, constrain, hold back, keep in check, keep under control, hold in, regulate, restrict, control, bridle, put the brakes on, slow down, curtail, limit, stop, arrest.
□ **free rein** *you'd be given free rein to run the show how you wanted it* **freedom**, scope, a free hand, leeway, latitude, elbow room, space, room, flexibility, liberty, independence, play, slack, free play, leisure, licence, room to manoeuvre, scope for initiative, freedom of action, freedom from restriction, indulgence, laxity, margin; *French* carte blanche.
□ **keep a tight rein on exercise strict control over**, keep on a tight rein, allow little freedom to, regulate, manage, discipline, regiment, keep in line, rule with a rod of iron.

reincarnation ▶ noun **rebirth**, transmigration of the soul, metempsychosis; *Hinduism & Buddhism* samsara; *rare* transanimation.

reinforce ▶ verb **1** *experts constructed a new stone wall to reinforce the dam* **strengthen**, fortify, bolster up, shore up, buttress, prop up, underpin, brace, stiffen, toughen, support, hold up; *archaic* underprop.
2 *the scheme reinforces the links between colleges and companies* **strengthen**, fortify, bolster up, shore up, buttress, prop up, underpin, support; cement, uphold, defend, maintain, back (up), buoy up; boost, give a boost to, aid, assist, help, promote, encourage, deepen, broaden, enrich, enhance, intensify, improve; underline, heighten, emphasize, stress.
3 *the USA would have as little as two weeks to reinforce NATO troops* **augment**, increase, add to, supplement, boost, swell, build up, top up.

reinforcement ▶ noun **1** *the proposed directive would require reinforcement of the landing gear* **strengthening**, fortification, bolstering, shoring up, propping up, buttressing, underpinning, bracing, stiffening, supporting, holding up.
2 *reinforcement of the heavy bomber force was continuing* **augmentation**, increase, supplementing, boosting, swelling, building up, build-up, topping up.
3 (**reinforcements**) *they were forced into a temporary retreat but returned later with reinforcements* **additional troops**, fresh troops, additional police, supplementaries, auxiliaries, reserves; support, backup, help; *archaic* succours.

reinstate ▶ verb *he was reinstated as President on 21 August* **restore**, return to a former position, return to power, put back, replace, bring back, reinstitute, reinstall, rehabilitate, re-establish.

reinstatement ▶ noun *the reinstatement of the legitimate government* **restoration**, return to a former position, return to power, bringing back, reinstitution, reinstallation, rehabilitation, re-establishment.

reiterate ▶ verb *he reiterated his opposition to abortion* **repeat**, say again, restate, retell, recapitulate, go over (and over), iterate, rehearse, belabour, dwell on, harp on, hammer away at; *N. Amer. informal* do over; *archaic* ingeminate.

reject ▶ verb (stress on the second syllable) **1** *the miners rejected the government's offer to negotiate their demands* **turn down**, refuse, decline, say no to; dismiss, spurn; *informal* give the thumbs down to, give the red light to, give something a miss; *Brit. informal* knock back; *rare* negative.
OPPOSITE accept.
2 *she had been deeply in love with Jamie, but he rejected her* **rebuff**, spurn, repudiate, cut off, cast off, cast aside, discard, jettison, abandon, desert, turn one's back on, have nothing (more) to do with, wash one's hands of, cast out, shut out, exclude, shun, cold-shoulder, give someone the cold shoulder; ostracize, blackball, blacklist, avoid, give a wide berth to, ignore, snub, cut dead, keep at arm's length, leave out in the cold; *Brit.* send to Coventry; *N. Amer.* disfellowship; *informal* give someone the brush-off, kick someone in the teeth, freeze out, hand someone the frozen mitt; *informal, dated* give someone the go-by; *Brit. informal* blank; *dated* cut; *Christianity* excommunicate; *archaic* forsake.

OPPOSITE welcome.

▸ **noun** (stress on the first syllable) **1** *I got it cheap—it is only a reject* **substandard article**, discard, second; (**rejects**) substandard goods.
2 *even a reject like him could be of use in such a godforsaken spot* **failure**, loser, incompetent; (**rejects**) flotsam.

> **CHOOSE THE RIGHT WORD**
>
> **reject, refuse, decline, spurn**
> See REFUSE

rejection ▸ **noun 1** *the chairman is expected to issue a rejection of the offer* **refusal**, non-acceptance, declining, turning down, no, dismissal, spurning, rebuff; *informal* knock-back.
OPPOSITE acceptance.
2 *it took a long while before he got over Madeleine's rejection of him* **repudiation**, rebuff, spurning, abandonment, forsaking, desertion, shutting out, exclusion, shunning, cold-shouldering, ostracizing, ostracism, blackballing, blacklisting, avoidance, ignoring, snubbing, snub, cutting dead; *Brit.* sending to Coventry; *informal* brush-off, a kick in the teeth; *Christianity* excommunication.
OPPOSITE welcome.

rejoice ▸ **verb 1** *palaeontologists rejoiced when they discovered a complete dinosaur skeleton* **be joyful**, be happy, be pleased, be glad, be delighted, be elated, be ecstatic, be euphoric, be overjoyed, be as pleased as Punch, be cock-a-hoop, be jubilant, be rapturous, be in raptures, be transported, be beside oneself with joy, be delirious, be thrilled, jump for joy, be on cloud nine, be walking/treading on air, be in seventh heaven, exult, glory, triumph; celebrate, cheer, revel, make merry; *informal* be over the moon, be on top of the world, be blissed out, whoop it up; *Austral. informal* be wrapped; *archaic* joy, jubilate.
OPPOSITES mourn, lament.
2 *he rejoiced in his success* **take delight in**, find/take pleasure in, find/take satisfaction in, feel satisfaction at, find joy in, enjoy, appreciate, revel in, glory in, bask in, delight in, exult in, triumph over, relish, savour, luxuriate in, wallow in; **be/feel proud of**, feel proud about, be proud of oneself for, congratulate oneself on, flatter oneself on, preen oneself on, pat oneself on the back for, give oneself a pat on the back for; **crow about**, feel self-satisfied about, vaunt, boast about, brag about, gloat over; *archaic* pique oneself on/in.

rejoicing ▸ **noun** *this should be an occasion for rejoicing* **happiness**, pleasure, joy, gladness, delight, elation, cheer, jubilation, euphoria, delirium, ecstasy, rapture, transports of delight, exuberance, exultation, glory, triumph, celebration, revelry, merrymaking, festivity, feasting.
OPPOSITE mourning.

rejoin[1] ▸ **verb** *the side road rejoins the main road further on* **return to**, be reunited with, come/get/go back to, join again, find one's way back to, reach again, regain, reattain.

rejoin[2] ▸ **verb** *Eugene rejoined that you couldn't expect to see him in the dark* **answer**, reply, respond, return, retort, riposte, come back, counter.

rejoinder ▸ **noun** *the smart rejoinder to a put-down usually occurs to me on the bus on the way home* **answer**, reply, response, retort, riposte, counter, sally; *informal* comeback.

rejuvenate ▸ **verb** *the leadership change was seen as an attempt to rejuvenate the party* **revive**, revitalize, renew, regenerate, restore, breathe new life into, make someone feel young again, revivify, reanimate, resuscitate, refresh, reawaken, rekindle, put new life into, put new heart into, add some zest to, put some spark into, kick-start, uplift; reorganize, reconstruct, renovate, overhaul, revamp, modernize; *informal* give a shot in the arm to, pep up, buck up.

relapse ▸ **verb 1** *although most children remain well after this procedure, a few relapse* **get ill/worse again**, have/suffer a relapse, worsen, deteriorate, degenerate, take a turn for the worse, sicken, weaken, fail, sink.
OPPOSITES recover, improve.
2 *the old woman relapsed into silence* **revert**, lapse; regress, retrogress, backslide, fall back, go backwards, slip back, slide back, drift back, degenerate; *rare* recidivate, retrograde.

▸ **noun 1** *one of the patients later suffered a relapse* **deterioration**, worsening of someone's condition, turn for the worse, setback, weakening; **recurrence**, repetition.
OPPOSITES recovery, improvement.
2 *he foresaw a relapse into an excessively objective kind of theology* **decline**, lapse, deterioration, worsening, degeneration, backsliding, recidivism, reversion, regression, retrogression, downturn, fall, falling, falling away, slipping, drop, descent, sinking, slide.

relate ▸ **verb 1** *he goes on to relate many other such stories* **tell**, recount, narrate, give an account of, describe; portray, depict, paint, unfold, set forth, present, report, chronicle, outline, delineate, retail, recite, repeat, rehearse, relay, convey, communicate, impart, spin; detail, enumerate, list, specify, itemize, cite, particularize, catalogue.
2 *they found that mortality is* **related to** *unemployment levels | the infant cannot yet relate cause and effect* **connect (with)**, associate (with), link (with), correlate (with), ally (with), couple (with), bracket (with); bring together, find/establish a connection between, find/establish a relationship between, find/establish a link between, find/establish an association between, find/establish a correspondence between.
3 *the charges* **relate to** *offences allegedly committed on 4 August* **apply to**, be relevant to, have relevance to, concern, refer to, have reference to, belong to, pertain to, be pertinent to, have to do with, bear on, have a bearing on, appertain to, affect, involve, cover, touch; *archaic* regard.
4 *many adolescents find it hard to* **relate to** *a stepfather* **have a rapport with**, get on (well) with, respond to, sympathize with, feel sympathy with, feel for, identify with, empathize with, connect with, understand, speak the same language as, be in tune with, be on the same wavelength as; *informal* hit it off with.

related ▸ **adjective 1** *an amalgam of several related ideas* **connected**, interconnected, associated, linked, coupled, correlated, allied, affiliated, accompanying, concomitant, corresponding, analogous, kindred, parallel, comparable, equivalent, homologous, incidental.
OPPOSITES unconnected, separate.
2 *are you two related?* **of the same family**, kin, akin, kindred, of the same blood, with a common ancestor/forebear, connected; *rare* agnate, consanguineous, cognate.
OPPOSITE unrelated.

relation *See centre pages for list of* **Relatives**

▸ **noun 1** *he understood the* **relation between** *religion and life* **connection**, relationship, association, link, correlation, correspondence, parallel, tie-in, tie-up, alliance, bond, interrelation, interconnection; interdependence of.
2 *such information had no* **relation to** *national security* **relevance**, applicability, application, reference, pertinence, bearing on, regard.
3 *are you a relation of his?* **relative**, member of someone's/the family, one's (own) flesh and blood, next of kin; (**relations**) family, kin, kith and kin, kindred; *formal* kinsman, kinswoman.
4 (**relations**) *he sought to improve relations with India* **dealings**, associations, communication, relationship, connections, contact, interaction, intercourse.
5 (**relations**) (*formal*) *all thought of* **sexual relations** *was abhorrent to her. See* SEX.

relationship ▸ **noun 1** *the relationship between diet and diabetes* **connection**, relation, association, link, correlation, correspondence, parallel, tie-in, tie-up, alliance, bond, interrelation, interconnection; interdependence of.
2 *we have evidence here of some direct relationship with the Marquesses of Bath* **family ties**, family connections, blood relationship, blood ties, kinship, affinity, consanguinity, common ancestry, common lineage, connection; *technical* propinquity.
3 *he reacted badly to the end of his relationship with his girlfriend* **romance**, love affair, affair, affair of the heart, love, amorous entanglement, flirtation, liaison; *French* affaire de/du cœur, amour.

relative *See centre pages for list of* **Relatives**

▸ **adjective 1** *the relative importance of each factor* **comparative**, respective, comparable, correlative, parallel, corresponding, reciprocal.
OPPOSITE absolute.
2 *a kitten requires three times more nourishment,* **relative to** *body weight, than a fully grown cat* **proportionate**, proportional, in proportion, commensurate, corresponding, dependent on, based on.
OPPOSITE disproportionate.
3 *Semtex was able to be smuggled with relative ease* **moderate**, reasonable, a fair degree of, considerable, some; comparative, qualified, modified; in/by comparison.
OPPOSITES great, complete.

▸ **noun** *he's a relative of mine* **relation**, member of someone's/the family, one's (own) flesh and blood, next of kin; *formal* kinsman, kinswoman; (**relatives**) **family**, kin, kith and kin, kindred; *informal* folks; *formal* kinsfolk; *dated* people.

> **WORD LINKS**
> *killing of a near relative* **parricide**

relatively ▸ **adverb** *the roads were still relatively clear* **comparatively**, in comparison, by comparison, proportionately; **quite**, fairly, reasonably, rather, somewhat, to a limited extent/degree, to a certain extent/degree, to some extent/degree, to an extent, to a degree, within reason, within limits, tolerably, passably, adequately, satisfactorily; *informal* pretty, kind of, sort of.

relax ▸ **verb 1** *yoga or meditation may be helpful in learning to relax* **unwind**, loosen up, ease up/off, let up, slow down, de-stress, unbend, rest, repose, put one's feet up, take it easy, take time off, take time out, slack off, be at leisure, take one's leisure, take one's ease, laze, luxuriate, do nothing, sit back, lounge, loll, slump, flop, idle, loaf, enjoy oneself, amuse oneself, play, entertain oneself; *informal* let it all hang out, let one's hair down, unbutton, veg out; *N. Amer. informal* hang loose, stay loose, chill out, kick back.
OPPOSITES be tense, psych oneself up.
2 *a walk will relax you* **calm**, calm down, unwind, loosen up, make less

R

tense/uptight, quieten, tranquillize, soothe, pacify, compose.
OPPOSITE psych someone up.
3 *he relaxed his grip on the mug* **loosen**, loose, slacken, unclench, weaken, lessen, let up, reduce, diminish.
OPPOSITE tighten.
4 *she felt her tense muscles relax* **become less tense**, become less stiff/rigid, loosen, slacken, ease, unknot.
OPPOSITES tighten, contract.
5 *the ministry relaxed some of the restrictions* **moderate**, modify, temper, make less strict/formal, ease, ease up on, loosen, lessen, lighten, slacken; alleviate, mitigate, qualify, dilute, weaken, reduce, diminish, decrease; *informal* let up on.
OPPOSITE tighten up.

relaxation ▸ **noun 1** *a state of relaxation* **mental repose**, composure; calm, tranquillity, peacefulness, calming oneself, loosening up, unwinding, winding down.
OPPOSITE anxiety.
2 *I just play for relaxation nowadays* **recreation**, enjoyment, amusement, entertainment, diversion, distraction, fun, pleasure, rest, refreshment, relief, respite, leisure, leisure activity/pursuit; *informal* R and R.
3 *skills for coping with anxiety include muscle relaxation* **loosening**, slackening, loosing, easing.
OPPOSITES tightening, contraction.
4 *relaxation of censorship rules* **moderation**, modification, easing, loosening, lessening, lightening, slackening; alleviation, mitigation, qualification, dilution, weakening, diminution, reduction; *informal* letting up.
OPPOSITE tightening up.

relay ▸ **noun** *an uninterrupted relay of the performance* **broadcast**, transmission, programme, communication, telecast, show, feed.
▸ **verb** *it is better for individuals to talk directly to each other rather than relay messages through a third party* **pass on**, hand on, transfer, repeat, retail, impart, communicate, send, transmit, broadcast, feed, disseminate, make known, publish, spread, circulate.

release ▸ **verb 1** *the government released some 150 prisoners* **free**, set free, let go, allow to leave, set/let/turn loose, let out, liberate, set at liberty, deliver, rescue, ransom, emancipate; *historical* manumit.
OPPOSITE imprison.
2 *Burke released the animal* **untie**, undo, loose, let go, unhand, unloose, unbind, unchain, unleash, unfetter, unclasp, unshackle, unmanacle, extricate, unhitch, unbridle, detach, disentangle.
OPPOSITE tie up.
3 *this enabled vast numbers of troops to be released for the other front* **make available**, free, free up; contribute, put at someone's disposal, supply, furnish, provide; deploy.
OPPOSITE detain.
4 *Stephen was released from his promise* **let off**, excuse, exempt, discharge, deliver; clear, exculpate, absolve, acquit, exonerate.
OPPOSITE hold someone to.
5 *police released news of his arrest yesterday* **make public**, make known, bring to public notice/attention, issue, break, announce, declare, report, post, reveal, divulge, disclose, publish, publicize, print, broadcast, air, transmit, put out, circulate, communicate, impart, disseminate, distribute, spread, propagate, purvey.
OPPOSITES suppress, withhold.
6 *another series has just been released on video cassette* **launch**, put on the market, market, put on sale, offer for sale, bring out, unveil, present, make available, distribute.
▸ **noun 1** *the government ordered the release of 106 political prisoners* **freeing**, liberation, deliverance, ransom, emancipation; freedom, liberty; *historical* manumission.
2 *continuous consultation took place regarding the release of the news* **issuing**, breaking, announcement, declaration, reporting, posting, revealing, divulging, disclosure, publishing, publication, printing, broadcasting, airing, transmission, putting out, circulation, communication, imparting, dissemination, distribution, spreading, propagation, purveying.
3 *a press release* **announcement**, bulletin, newsflash, briefing, dispatch, publication, proclamation.
4 *the group's last release was a big seller* CD, disc, record, single, album; video, film; book.
5 *the next release of the network operating system* **version**, edition, issue, model, mark, draft, form, impression, publication.

relegate ▸ **verb** *she was relegated to the status of mere spokesperson* **downgrade**, lower, lower in rank/status, put down, move down; consign, banish, exile; demote, degrade, declass, strip someone of their rank, reduce to the ranks, disrate, drum out; *N. Amer.* bust.
OPPOSITES upgrade, promote.

relent ▸ **verb 1** *the Government considered making everybody pay the tax but relented* **change one's mind**, do a U-turn, back-pedal, back down, give way, give in, capitulate, yield, accede, come round, acquiesce; soften, melt, weaken, unbend, become merciful, become lenient, have/show pity, have/show mercy, give quarter; agree to something, allow something, concede something, admit something; *Brit.* do an about-turn.
OPPOSITE harden.
2 *by early evening the rain relented* **ease off**, slacken, let up, ease, ease up, relax, abate, drop, fall off, die down, lessen, decrease, diminish, moderate, subside, weaken, tail off.
OPPOSITES strengthen, worsen.

relentless ▸ **adjective 1** *their relentless pursuit of quality* **persistent**, continuing, constant, continual, continuous, non-stop, lasting, never-ending, steady, uninterrupted, unabated, unabating, unbroken, interminable, incessant, unstoppable, unceasing, endless, unending, perpetual, unremitting, unrelenting, unrelieved, sustained; **unfaltering**, unflagging, untiring, unwavering, unswerving, undeviating, persevering, determined, resolute, purposeful, dogged, single-minded, tireless, indefatigable, patient, diligent, assiduous, sedulous, tenacious, pertinacious, insistent, importunate; stubborn, intransigent, obstinate, obdurate.
OPPOSITES short-lived, irresolute, intermittent.
2 *a relentless taskmaster* **harsh**, grim, fierce, cruel, severe, strict, punishing, remorseless, merciless, pitiless, ruthless, unmerciful, unsparing, heartless, hard-hearted, hard, stony-hearted, stony, with a heart of stone, cold-blooded, cold-hearted, unforgiving, unfeeling, uncaring, unsympathetic, uncharitable, lacking compassion, unpitying; **inflexible**, unbending, uncompromising, obdurate, unyielding, unmoved, inexorable, implacable.
OPPOSITES lenient, merciful.

CHOOSE THE RIGHT WORD

relentless, remorseless, ruthless, pitiless

These words all apply to people or processes that are not affected by anyone's wishes or entreaties. They differ chiefly in the extent to which they emphasize continuing activity or the attitude with which it is carried out.

- A **relentless** action or process cannot be stopped (*the relentless march of rainforest destruction*) and is unvaryingly intense or severe (*the ships were subjected to relentless air attack*). When applied to a person, it means 'inflexible or uncompromising' but does not necessarily imply a lack of pity or humanity (*a patient but relentless taskmaster*).
- **Remorseless** is used of a process that will not be stopped or deflected however great the suffering or distress it causes (*the company continued the remorseless cost-cutting drive*). When used of a person, the word marks them out as having no regret or guilt about the distress they have caused (*a remorseless killer*).
- A **ruthless** person has no pity or compassion for others (*ruthless terrorists murdered a child yesterday*) and is usually determined to continue regardless (*Lenin was an astute and ruthless political operator*).
- Whereas a *ruthless* person is generally ruthless in pursuit of some goal, the emphasis of **pitiless**, a rarer word, is on a more intrinsic absence of pity itself (*his cold pitiless voice*).

relevant ▸ **adjective** *make a note of the relevant page numbers* **pertinent**, applicable, apposite, material, apropos, to the point, to the purpose, germane, admissible; appropriate, apt, fitting, suitable, proper; connected, related, linked; *Latin* ad rem; *rare* appurtenant.
OPPOSITE irrelevant.

reliable ▸ **adjective 1** *reliable evidence* **dependable**, good, well founded, well grounded, authentic, definitive, attested, valid, genuine, from the horse's mouth, sound, true; *Brit.* copper-bottomed.
OPPOSITE unreliable.
2 *a reliable friend* **trustworthy**, dependable, good, true, faithful, devoted, steady, steadfast, staunch, unswerving, unwavering, constant, loyal, trusty, dedicated, committed, unfailing, infallible, certain, sure; truthful, honest.
OPPOSITES unreliable, untrustworthy.
3 *the new bikes have reliable V-brakes* **dependable**, **safe**, fail-safe, tried and tested, well built, well engineered, good.
OPPOSITE unreliable.
4 *a reliable firm* **reputable**, dependable, trustworthy, honest, responsible, established, proven, stable, sound, solid, secure, safe, safe as houses.
OPPOSITES unreliable, dodgy.

reliance ▸ **noun 1** *saving for a pension reduces* **reliance on** *the state* **dependence**, dependency; seeking support from, leaning on.
2 *he displayed a lack of* **reliance on** *his own judgement* **trust in**, confidence in, faith in, credence in, belief in, conviction in; credit.

relic ▸ **noun 1** *a Viking relic which was more than a thousand years old* **artefact**, historical object, ancient object, antiquity, antique, heirloom, object of virtu, curio; fossil.
2 (**relics**) *a shrine containing the saint's relics* **remains**, body parts, bones; corpse, dead body, cadaver; holy/sacred objects; *Latin* reliquiae.

relief ▸ **noun 1** *it was such a relief to share my secret worries with her | I found relief in desperately scribbling poetry* **reassurance**, **consolation**, comfort,

R

solace, calmness, relaxation, repose, ease.
2 *the relief of pain* **alleviation**, alleviating, relieving, mitigation, mitigating, assuagement, assuaging, palliation, allaying, appeasement, soothing, easing, dulling, lessening, reduction, abatement.
OPPOSITE intensification.
3 *she just needed relief from her burden of bags* **freedom**, release, liberation, deliverance, exemption, discharge.
4 *how she needed a little light relief!* **respite**, remission, lightening, brightening; amusement, diversion, entertainment, jollity, jollification, recreation; interruption, break; *informal* let-up.
OPPOSITES seriousness, solemnity.
5 *the coming of the rains brought no physical relief to the besieged* **help**, aid, assistance, succour, care, sustenance; subsidy, benefit, charity, gifts, donations, financial assistance, debt remission; a helping hand, a leg up.
6 *his relief arrived to take over* **replacement**, substitute, deputy, reserve, standby, stopgap, cover, stand-in, supply, fill-in, locum, locum tenens, understudy, proxy, surrogate.
□ **throw something into relief** *this brief account throws into sharp relief the differences between the rival theories* **highlight**, spotlight, give prominence to, foreground; set off, point up, throw up, show up; emphasize, bring out, stress, accent, underline, underscore, accentuate; heighten, intensify, increase, enhance.
OPPOSITES mask, play down.

relieve ▸ verb **1** *a battery-powered device which helps relieve pain* **alleviate**, mitigate, assuage, allay, soothe, soften, palliate, appease, ease, dull, reduce, lessen, diminish.
OPPOSITE aggravate.
2 *his studies helped to relieve the boredom* **counteract**, reduce, alleviate, mitigate, brighten, lighten, sweeten, bring respite to, make something bearable; interrupt, punctuate, vary, break up, stop, bring an end to, cure, dispel; prevent.
OPPOSITES exacerbate, emphasize.
3 *there was no shortage of helpers to relieve us for breaks* **replace**, take over from, take the place of, stand in for, act as stand-in for, fill in for, substitute for, act as a substitute for, deputize for, be a proxy for, cover for, provide cover for, act as locum for, hold the fort for, do something in someone's place/stead.
4 *this **relieves** the teacher **of** a heavy load of formal teaching* **free of/from**, set free from, release from, liberate from, exempt from, excuse from, absolve from, let off, extricate from, discharge from, unburden of, disburden of, disencumber of; deliver from, rescue from, save from; *rare* disembarrass of.
OPPOSITE put an extra burden on.
□ **relieve oneself**. *See* URINATE, DEFECATE.

relieved ▸ adjective *I'll be relieved when it's all over* **glad**, thankful, grateful, pleased, happy; put at one's ease, easy/easier in one's mind, comforted, cheered, reassured.
OPPOSITES worried, anxious.

religion *See centre pages for lists of* **Religions and Sects** **Christian Denominations** **Christian Doctrinal Movements** **Christian Religious Orders**
▸ noun *the right to freedom of religion | what religion are you?* **faith**, belief, divinity, worship, creed, teaching, doctrine, theology; **sect**, cult, religious group, faith community, church, denomination, body, following, persuasion, affiliation.

WORD LINKS
study of religion **divinity, theology**

CHOOSE THE RIGHT WORD

religious, devout, pious

- **Religious** basically means 'relating to a religion' (*the patriotic and religious duty of any Jew*) or 'believing in a religion' (*the word is regarded by many religious people with considerable disapproval*), and both senses are neither critical nor approving. Only in the second sense can *religious* be used after the verb *to be*, or be qualified by an adverb, to express the degree of someone's commitment (*he wasn't a churchgoer, but very religious*). Sometimes it is used in an extended sense to suggest that someone attaches particular importance to a secular object or pursuit; there may be a critical suggestion that such devotion is misplaced (*he always had a religious obsession with fame*).
- **Devout** is used to indicate a deep and genuine religious commitment (*he was a devout Quaker and would not allow a pub in the village*), and is an approving word. It is also used to convey total or uncritical enthusiasm for or commitment to a secular object (*a devout soccer fan*).
- **Pious**, too, can convey religious commitment (*donations to the Church from pious laymen*) but is now mainly used pejoratively to denote hypocritical religiosity (*I know what's under that pious face of yours*).

religious ▸ adjective **1** *he was a very religious person* **devout**, pious, reverent, believing, godly, God-fearing, dutiful, saintly, holy, prayerful, churchgoing, practising, faithful, devoted, committed.
OPPOSITES atheistic, irreverent.
2 *it was against her religious beliefs | religious music* **spiritual**, theological, scriptural, doctrinal, church, churchly, ecclesiastical, holy, divine, celestial, heavenly, sacred, devotional, sanctified, consecrated, dedicated, hallowed; schismatic, sectarian.
OPPOSITES secular, civil.
3 *pay religious attention to detail* **scrupulous**, conscientious, meticulous, sedulous, punctilious, zealous, strict, rigid, rigorous, exact, close, unfailing, unswerving, undeviating; **fussy**, pedantic, fastidious, nit-picking, finicky, finical.
OPPOSITE slapdash.

relinquish ▸ verb **1** *he relinquished control of the company to his sons* **renounce**, give up, part with, give away; **hand over**, turn over, lay down, let go of, waive, resign, abdicate, yield, cede, surrender, sign away.
OPPOSITES keep, retain.
2 *he offered to relinquish his post as acting President* **leave**, resign from, stand down from, bow out of, walk out of, retire from, give up, depart from, vacate, pull out of, abandon, abdicate; *informal* quit, chuck, jack in; *archaic* forsake.
3 *he relinquished his pipe-smoking* **discontinue**, stop, cease, give up, drop, desist from; avoid, steer clear of, give a wide berth to; reject, eschew, forswear, refrain from, abstain from, forbear from, forgo; *informal* quit, leave off, kick; *archaic* forsake.
OPPOSITE continue.
4 *she relinquished her grip on the door* **let go**, release, loose, unloose, loosen, relax.

relish ▸ noun **1** *he dug into his plate of food with relish* **enjoyment**, gusto, delight, pleasure, glee, rapture, satisfaction, contentment, contentedness, gratification, happiness, exhilaration, excitement, titillation, appreciation, liking, fondness, enthusiasm, appetite, zest; *humorous* delectation.
OPPOSITE dislike.
2 *the sauce is ideal served as hot relish with beefburgers* **condiment**, accompaniment, sauce, dressing, flavouring, seasoning, dip.
▸ verb **1** *he was relishing his moment of glory* **enjoy**, delight in, love, like, adore, be pleased by, take pleasure in, rejoice in, appreciate, savour, revel in, luxuriate in, glory in; **gloat over**, feel self-satisfied about, crow about; *informal* get a kick out of, get a thrill out of.
OPPOSITE dislike.
2 *I don't relish the drive, but we could go by train* **look forward to**, fancy, anticipate with pleasure, await with pleasure, lick one's lips over, be unable to wait for, count the days until, long for, hope for.
OPPOSITE dread.

reluctance ▸ noun *she sensed his reluctance to continue* **unwillingness**, disinclination, lack of enthusiasm; hesitation, hesitance, hesitancy, diffidence, timidity, timorousness, trepidation, backwardness (in coming forward); demurral, wavering, vacillation, foot-dragging, resistance; doubts, second thoughts, scruples, qualms, pangs of conscience, misgivings; *archaic* disrelish.
OPPOSITES willingness, eagerness.

reluctant ▸ adjective **1** *she persuaded her reluctant parents to buy her a cat* **unwilling**, disinclined, unenthusiastic, grudging, resistant, resisting, opposed, antipathetic; hesitant.
OPPOSITES willing, eager.
2 *Hilary gave a reluctant smile* **shy**, bashful, coy, retiring, diffident, reserved, restrained, withdrawn, shrinking, timid, timorous, sheepish, unconfident, insecure, unsure, suspicious, unassertive; apprehensive, fearful; *rare* costive.
OPPOSITES eager, ready.
3 *the man was **reluctant to** leave* **loath**, unwilling, disinclined, not in the mood, indisposed, sorry, averse, slow; chary of, not in favour of, against, opposed to; hesitant about, diffident about, bashful about, shy about, coy about; ashamed to, afraid to.
OPPOSITES willing, eager, ready.

rely ▸ verb **1** *I think we can **rely on** his discretion* **depend**, count, bank, place reliance, bargain, plan, reckon; anticipate, expect, pin one's hopes on, hope for, take for granted, take on trust, trust; be confident of, have (every) confidence in, be sure of, believe in, have faith in, pin one's faith on, trust in, cling to, swear by; *N. Amer. informal* figure on.
OPPOSITE distrust.
2 *law centres have had to **rely on** government funding to keep going* **be dependent**, depend, lean, hinge, turn, hang, rest, pivot, be contingent; be unable to manage without, have recourse to, resort to, fall back on.

remain ▸ verb **1** *unless that is sorted out, the problem will remain* **continue to exist**, endure, last, abide, go on, carry on, persist, hang in the air, stay around/round, stand, be extant, hold out, prevail, survive, live on.
OPPOSITE cease to exist.
2 *he would have to remain in hospital for around a month* **stay**, stay behind,

R

stay put, wait, wait around, linger, be left, hold on, hang on, rest, stop; *informal* hang around/round; *Brit. informal* hang about; *formal* sojourn; *dated* tarry; *archaic* bide.
OPPOSITES go, depart, leave.
3 *union leaders remain sceptical* **continue to be**, stay, keep, persist in being, carry on being, go on being.
4 *I think we should leave them alone for the few minutes that remain* **be left**, be left over, be still available, be unused; have not yet passed, have not yet expired.

remainder ▶ **noun** *eighty-seven members are elected directly, and the remainder by proportional representation* **residue**, **balance**, remaining part/number/quantity, part/number/quantity (that is) left over, rest, others, those left, remnant, remnants, rump, surplus, difference, extra, excess, superfluity, overflow, overspill, additional people/material/things, extra people/material/things; *technical* residuum.

remaining ▶ **adjective 1** *the cutbacks will help protect the jobs of the remaining 160 workers | he still had 4,300 pounds of fuel remaining* **residual**, surviving, left, left over, unused; extra, surplus, spare, superfluous, excess, in excess, in addition.
2 *he settled his remaining debts* **unsettled**, outstanding, unresolved, unfinished, incomplete, to be done, undone, not done, unattended to; unpaid.
3 *those are my only remaining memories of my first five years* **surviving**, **lasting**, enduring, continuing, persisting, lingering, abiding, long-lived, (still) existing, extant, in existence, living, lifelong, long-term, perennial.
OPPOSITE short-lived.

remains ▶ **plural noun 1** *she downed the remains of her drink in one go* **remainder**, residue, remaining part/number/quantity, part/number/quantity (that is) left over, rest, remnant, remnants; leftovers, leavings, scraps, debris, detritus; *technical* residuum.
2 *Pula's Roman remains include the public baths and a triumphal arch* **antiquities**, relics; inheritance, heritage; *Latin* reliquiae.
3 *Saint Ubaldo's remains are housed in the basilica* **corpse**, dead body, body, cadaver, carcass; body parts, bones, skeleton.

remark ▶ **verb 1** *'You're very quiet,' he remarked, breaking into her thoughts* **comment**, say, observe, mention, reflect, state, declare, announce, pronounce, assert; interpose, interject; come out with; *formal* opine.
2 *many critics remarked on the rapport between the two stars* **comment on**, mention, refer to, speak of, pass comment on, say something about, touch on.
3 *he remarked the absence of policemen* **note**, notice, observe, take note of, mark, perceive, discern.
▶ **noun 1** *Soanes claimed that his remarks had been misinterpreted* **comment**, statement, utterance, observation, declaration, pronouncement; reflection, thought, opinion; **(remarks)** words.
2 *these discrepancies were thought worthy of remark* **attention**, notice, comment, mention, observation, consideration, heed, acknowledgement, recognition.

remarkable ▶ **adjective** *a remarkable coincidence | the remarkable achievements of modern medicine* **extraordinary**, exceptional, amazing, astonishing, astounding, marvellous, wonderful, sensational, stunning, incredible, unbelievable, miraculous, phenomenal, prodigious; **striking**, outstanding, momentous, impressive, singular, signal, pre-eminent, memorable, unforgettable, never to be forgotten, unique, arresting, eye-catching, conspicuous, noteworthy, notable, great, considerable, distinctive, important, distinguished, prominent; out of the ordinary, unusual, uncommon, rare, surprising, curious, strange, odd, peculiar, uncanny; *Scottish* unco; *informal* fantastic, terrific, tremendous, stupendous, awesome, out of this world, unreal; *literary* wondrous.
OPPOSITES ordinary, commonplace, run-of-the-mill.

remediable ▶ **adjective** *surgically remediable diseases* **curable**, treatable, medicable, operable; able to be put right, capable of solution, solvable, soluble, reparable, repairable, rectifiable, resolvable, retrievable; *rare* corrigible.
OPPOSITES irremediable, incurable.

remedy ▶ **noun 1** *traditional herbal remedies* **treatment**, cure, medicine, medication, medicament, drug, restorative; antidote, prophylactic; nostrum, panacea, cure-all; therapy; *archaic* physic, specific.
2 *marriage is sometimes prescribed as a remedy for all kinds of life problems* **solution**, answer, cure, antidote, corrective, curative, nostrum, panacea, cure-all, heal-all, palliative, balm, magic formula; countermeasure; *informal* magic bullet.
3 *the company is not liable and he has no effective remedy against them* **(means of) redress**, (means of) reparation, comeback.
▶ **verb 1** *little has been done to remedy the situation* **put right**, set right, set to rights, put to rights, right, rectify, retrieve, solve, fix, sort out, put in order, straighten out, resolve, deal with, correct, repair, mend, redress, make good; improve, amend, ameliorate, make better, better.
2 *anaemia can be remedied by iron tablets* **cure**, treat, heal, make better, counteract, control; relieve, ease, alleviate, soothe, palliate.

remember ▶ **verb 1** *she smiled wistfully, remembering happy times* **recall**, call to mind, recollect, think of; put a name to, place; reminisce about, think back to, look back on, hark back to, cast one's mind back to, summon up, muse on; take a trip down memory lane; *Scottish* mind; *archaic* bethink oneself of.
OPPOSITE forget.
2 *do you think you can remember all that or shall I write it down?* **memorize**, commit to memory, retain; learn off by heart, get off pat.
OPPOSITE forget.
3 *you must remember that she's still only five years old* **bear in mind**, keep in mind, not lose sight of the fact, not forget, be mindful of the fact; take into account, take into consideration.
OPPOSITE overlook.
4 *remember to feed the cat* **don't forget**, be sure, be certain; mind that you, make sure that you.
OPPOSITE neglect.
5 *please remember me to Alice* **send one's best wishes to**, send one's regards to, give one's love to, send greetings from, send one's compliments to, say hello to; *archaic* commend oneself to.
6 *yesterday the nation remembered those who gave their lives in times of conflict* **commemorate**, pay tribute to, honour, salute, celebrate, pay homage to, pay one's respects to, memorialize, keep alive the memory of; spare a thought for.
7 *she had remembered them in her will* **bequeath something to**, leave something to, make someone a gift, give something to, bestow something on.

remembrance ▶ **noun 1** *his face took on a faint expression of remembrance* **recollection**, reminiscence, nostalgia; remembering, recalling, recollecting, reminiscing; *technical* anamnesis.
2 *she smiled at the remembrance* **memory**, recollection, reminiscence, echo from the past, mental image, thought.
3 *we sold poppies in remembrance of all those who died* **commemoration**, memory, recognition.
4 *take this ring as a remembrance of my father* **memento**, reminder, keepsake, souvenir, token, commemoration, memorial, relic, something to remember someone by; *archaic* remembrancer.
5 (**remembrances**) (*archaic*) *he sent his affectionate remembrances to his sister* **greetings**, regards, kindest regards, best wishes, good wishes, compliments, salutations, felicitations, respects; love, best; *French* devoirs.

remind ▶ **verb 1** *I left a note on the cooker to remind him* **jog someone's memory**, refresh someone's memory, help someone remember, cause someone to remember; prompt, nudge, give someone a cue.
2 *the song* **reminded** *me of my ex-wife* **make one think of**, cause one to remember, put one in mind of, take one back to, bring/call to mind, awake one's memories of, evoke, call up, conjure up, summon up.

reminder ▶ **noun** *Granny sometimes needed the odd reminder* **prompt**, prompting, cue, nudge; aide-memoire, mnemonic.

reminisce ▶ **verb** *Duncan and I reminisced about the last time we'd worked together* **remember (with pleasure)**, cast one's mind back to, think back to, look back on, be nostalgic about, hark back to, recall, recollect, reflect on, call to mind, review; exchange memories, take a trip down memory lane, indulge in reminiscence, dwell on the past.

reminiscences ▶ **plural noun** *her reminiscences of a wartime childhood* **memories**, recollections, reflections, remembrances, anecdotes; memoirs.

reminiscent ▶ **adjective** *a highly sophisticated style* **reminiscent of** *Italian art of the same period* **similar to**, comparable with, inviting/bearing comparison with, tending to make one think of; **evocative of**, suggestive of, redolent of; *rare* remindful of.

remiss ▶ **adjective** *I can see that I have been very remiss* **negligent**, neglectful, irresponsible, careless, thoughtless, heedless, unthinking, unmindful, lax, slack, slipshod, lackadaisical, forgetful, inattentive, unheeding; lazy, dilatory, indolent; *N. Amer.* derelict; *informal* sloppy; *formal* delinquent; *Maritime Law* barratrous; *archaic* disregardful, oscitant.
OPPOSITES careful, diligent, painstaking.

remission ▶ **noun 1** *the remission of all taxation on export sales for ten years* **cancellation**, setting aside, suspension, revocation, repeal, rescinding, abrogation.
2 (*Brit.*) *he was released within three years after remission for good behaviour* **reduction in sentence**, reduced sentence; allowance, deduction.
3 *spontaneous remission of acute leukaemia is unusual* **respite**, abeyance, **diminution of intensity**, diminution of severity, period of temporary recovery.
4 *the wind howled that night without remission* **respite**, lessening, abatement, easing, moderation, decrease, reduction, diminution, slackening, dying down, dwindling, lull, ebbing, waning; *informal* let-up.
5 *the remission of sins* **forgiveness**, pardoning, absolution, exoneration, exculpation; *historical* indulgence.
6 *the remission of the matter to a subcommittee* **referral**, passing on, transfer, redirection.

remit ▶ **verb** (stress on the second syllable) **1** *the fines imposed on the Earl of Lancaster were remitted* **cancel**, set aside, revoke, repeal, rescind, abrogate, suspend.
2 *they refused to remit customs duties to the federal authorities* **send**, dispatch,

forward, transmit, convey; **pay**, hand over, make payment of.
3 *the case was remitted to the Court of Appeal* **pass (on)**, refer, send on, transfer, hand on, direct, assign, commit, entrust.
4 *we remitted all further discussion until he sent me a copy of his letter* **postpone**, defer, put off, put back, shelve, delay, hold over/off, stand over, suspend, prorogue, reschedule, keep in abeyance; *N. Amer.* put over, lay on the table, table; *N. Amer. Law* continue; *informal* put on the back burner, put on ice, put in cold storage; *rare* respite.
5 *God's act of remitting the sins of guilty men* **pardon**, forgive; excuse, overlook, pass over.
6 *the fever remitted* **diminish**, lessen, decrease, ease (up), abate, moderate, dwindle, wane, ebb, subside.
7 *she remitted her efforts* **slacken**, relax, reduce, decrease, diminish, lessen; cease, stop, halt, desist from.
▶ **noun** (stress on the first syllable) *his remit includes administering the consumer credit licensing system* **area of responsibility**, area of activity, sphere, orbit, scope, ambit, province, territory, realm, department, turf; brief, instructions, orders; *informal* bailiwick.

remittance ▶ **noun 1** *complete the booking form and send it together with your remittance* **payment**, settlement, money, fee; cheque, money order, transfer of funds; *technical* negotiable instrument; *formal* monies.
2 *he gets a remittance once every three months* **allowance**, sum of money, consideration.

remnant ▶ **noun 1** *they cleared up the remnants of the picnic* **remains**, remainder, leftovers, leavings, residue, rest; stub, butt, end, tail end; dregs, lees; *technical* residuum.
2 *remnants of cloth* **scrap**, piece, bit, fragment, shred, offcut, oddment.

remonstrate ▶ **verb 1** *'I'm not a child!' he remonstrated | I* **remonstrated with** *him but he just laughed in my face* **protest**, complain, expostulate; argue with, take issue with, take to task, make a protest to; reprimand, reproach, reprove, upbraid, berate, scold; *rare* reprehend, objurgate.
2 *pro-reform deputies* **remonstrated against** *this proposal* **object strongly to**, complain vociferously about, protest against, lodge a protest against, argue against, take a stand against, oppose strongly, take exception to, take issue with, make a fuss about, challenge, raise objections to, express disapproval of, express disagreement with, speak out against; deplore, condemn, denounce, criticize; *informal* kick up a fuss/stink about.
OPPOSITE accept.

remorse ▶ **noun** *he was filled with remorse* **contrition**, deep regret, repentance, penitence, guilt, feelings of guilt, bad/guilty conscience, compunction, remorsefulness, ruefulness, contriteness, sorrow, shame, self-reproach, self-accusation, self-condemnation; pangs of conscience.
OPPOSITE indifference.

remorseful ▶ **adjective** *many parents feel very remorseful after punishing their children* **sorry**, full of regret, regretful, sad, contrite, repentant, penitent, guilt-ridden, conscience-stricken, guilty, ashamed, chastened, shamefaced, self-reproachful, rueful, apologetic; *rare* compunctious.
OPPOSITE unrepentant.

remorseless ▶ **adjective 1** *a remorseless killer* **heartless**, pitiless, merciless, ruthless, callous, cruel, hard-hearted, stony-hearted, with a heart of stone, cold-hearted, harsh, inhumane, unmerciful, unforgiving, unfeeling, unpitying, uncompromising, unkind; *rare* marble-hearted.
OPPOSITES merciful, compassionate.
2 *the company continued its remorseless cost-cutting drive* **relentless**, unrelenting, unremitting, unabating, inexorable, implacable, unstoppable.

> **CHOOSE THE RIGHT WORD**
> **remorseless, relentless, ruthless, pitiless**
> *See* RELENTLESS.

remote ▶ **adjective 1** *doctors who practise in areas remote from hospitals | the remote past* **faraway**, **distant**, far, far off, far removed; dim and distant.
OPPOSITES close, near.
2 *a remote mountain village* **isolated**, out of the way, outlying, off the beaten track, secluded, in the depths of ..., hard to find, lonely, in the back of beyond, in the hinterlands, off the map, in the middle of nowhere, godforsaken, obscure, inaccessible, cut-off, unreachable; faraway, far-flung; *N. Amer.* in the backwoods, lonesome; *S. African* in the backveld, in the platteland; *Austral./NZ* in the backblocks, in the booay; *informal* unget-at-able, in the sticks; *N. Amer. informal* jerkwater, in the tall timbers; *Austral./NZ informal* Barcoo, beyond the black stump; *literary* lone; *archaic* unapproachable.
OPPOSITE central.
3 *the parables may seem somewhat* **remote from** *modern times* **irrelevant to**, unrelated to, unconnected to, unconcerned with, not pertinent to, inapposite to, immaterial to, unassociated with, inappropriate to; foreign to, alien to; *rare* extrinsic to.
OPPOSITE relevant.
4 *up to now, the possibility had seemed so remote as not to need consideration* **unlikely**, improbable, implausible, doubtful, dubious, far-fetched; faint, slight, slim, small, slender, minimal, marginal, negligible, insignificant, inconsiderable.
OPPOSITES likely, strong.
5 *when I was a child, she wasn't so remote* **aloof**, distant, detached, impersonal, withdrawn, reserved, uncommunicative, unforthcoming, unapproachable, unresponsive, indifferent, unconcerned, preoccupied, abstracted; unfriendly, unsociable, stand-offish, cool, chilly, cold, haughty; introspective, introvert, introverted.
OPPOSITES friendly, approachable.

> **CHOOSE THE RIGHT WORD**
> **remote, distant, faraway, far-off**
> *See* DISTANT.

removal ▶ **noun 1** *the removal of heavy artillery from towns and villages* **taking away**, moving, carrying away, shifting, transfer, transporting; confiscation.
OPPOSITE installation.
2 *opposition parties demanded his immediate removal from office* **dismissal**, eviction, ejection, expulsion, throwing out, ousting, dislodgement, displacement, purging, unseating, deposition; dethronement, dethroning; *N. Amer.* ouster; *informal* sacking, firing.
OPPOSITE appointment.
3 *the removal of customs barriers within the EC* **withdrawal**, **abolition**, elimination, doing away with, taking away.
OPPOSITES introduction, bringing in.
4 *the removal of errors* **deletion**, elimination, erasing, rubbing out, erasure, effacing, obliteration.
5 *removal of weeds is important* **uprooting**, eradication, destruction.
6 *regular removal of old branches from the base will encourage newer growth* **cutting off**, chopping off, hacking off, amputation, excision.
7 *her removal to France* **move**, transfer, relocation; *Scottish & N. English* flit, flitting.
8 *the removal of a gang member by a rival* **killing**, murder, disposal, elimination, termination, assassination; *informal* liquidation.

remove ▶ **verb 1** *switch off the power and remove the plug* **detach**, unfasten, separate; **pull out**, take out, disconnect.
OPPOSITE attach.
2 *he took the box and removed the lid* **take off**, undo, unfasten.
OPPOSITE put on.
3 *he pulled out his wallet and removed a twenty dollar bill* **take out**, **produce**, bring out, get out, draw out, withdraw, extract, pull out, fish out.
OPPOSITE insert.
4 *police searched his flat, removing fifteen bags of clothing* **take away**, carry away, move, shift, convey, transport; confiscate, take possession of; *informal* cart off.
OPPOSITES replace, put back.
5 *in the bathroom, Sheila soon removed the mud* **clean off**, wash off, wipe off, rinse off, scrub off, sponge out.
6 *Henry removed his coat* **take off**, pull off, peel off, shrug off, discard, divest oneself of, shed, fling off, fling aside, climb out of, slip out of; undo, unfasten, unbutton, unzip; *dated* doff.
OPPOSITES don, put on.
7 *he was removed from his post as head of the security department* **dismiss**, discharge, get rid of, dislodge, displace, throw out, evict, eject, expel, oust, purge, unseat, depose, topple, supplant; dethrone; *informal* sack, fire, kick out, boot out, give someone the boot, give someone their marching orders, show someone the door; *Brit. informal* turf out; *dated* out.
OPPOSITES install, appoint.
8 *tax relief on life assurance premiums was removed* **withdraw**, **abolish**, eliminate, get rid of, do away with, take away, stop, put an end to, cut; *informal* axe.
OPPOSITES introduce, bring in.
9 *Gabriel carefully removed the last two words* **delete**, erase, rub out, cross out, strike out, ink out, score out, block out, blue-pencil, cut out, eliminate, efface, obliterate.
OPPOSITE add.
10 *weeds have to be removed and a good general weedkiller applied* **uproot**, take out, pull out, eradicate, destroy.
11 *sometimes it may be necessary to remove branches of the tree* **cut off**, chop off, lop off, hack off, amputate, excise.
12 (*dated*) *in 1800 he removed to Edinburgh* **move**, move house, move away, relocate, transfer, decamp; migrate, emigrate; *Scottish & N. English* flit; *Brit. informal* up sticks; *N. Amer. informal* pull up stakes.
13 *mobsters like that could simply have you removed if they didn't like you* **kill**, murder, put to death, get rid of, dispose of, assassinate, eliminate, execute, wipe out; *informal* bump off, do away with, do in, do for, knock off, take out, top, stiff, croak, liquidate, blow away, give someone the works, wipe off the face of the earth; *N. Amer. informal* rub out, waste, smoke, ice, off; *N. Amer. euphemistic* terminate with extreme prejudice.
▶ **noun** *it is almost impossible, at this remove, to reconstruct the impact of the incident* **distance**, space of time, interval.

R

removed ▶ adjective *the programme was described as a fairy story completely removed from reality* **distant**, remote, disconnected, different; unrelated to, unconnected to, foreign to, alien to.

remunerate ▶ verb *lawyers should be fairly remunerated for work done* **pay**, reward, reimburse, recompense, give payment to; *rare* fee.

remuneration ▶ noun *it's a demanding job which deserves adequate remuneration* **payment**, pay, salary, wages; earnings, fee(s), stipend, emolument(s), honorarium, remittance, consideration, reward, recompense, reimbursement, repayment.

remunerative ▶ adjective *he left to take up a more remunerative post elsewhere* **lucrative**, **well paid**, financially rewarding, financially worthwhile, moneymaking, paying, gainful; profitable.

renaissance ▶ noun *the renaissance of Byzantine art and scholarship* **revival**, renewal, resurrection, reawakening, re-emergence, reappearance, resurgence, rejuvenation, regeneration, rebirth, new birth, new dawn, new beginning; *rare* renascence, recrudescence, rejuvenescence.

rend ▶ verb *a crisis which threatened to rend the Atlantic alliance apart* **tear/rip apart**, tear/rip in two, tear/rip to pieces, split, rupture, sever, separate; *literary* cleave, tear/rip asunder, sunder, rive; *rare* dissever.

render ▶ verb **1** *her fury rendered her temporarily speechless* **make**, cause to be/become, leave.
2 *Burcham was quickly surrounded by people anxious to render assistance* **give**, provide, supply, furnish, make available, contribute; **offer**, extend, proffer.
3 *the invoices rendered by the accountants amounted to £11,690* **send in**, present, tender, submit.
4 *it was about an hour before the jury rendered their verdict* **deliver**, return, hand down, bring in, give, announce, pronounce, proclaim.
5 *a sailor was bound to render instant obedience to a midshipman* **show**, display, exhibit, evince, manifest.
6 *her paintings are rendered in wonderfully vivid colours* **paint**, draw, depict, portray, represent, reproduce, execute; *literary* limn.
7 *the French songstress had just rendered all three verses of the Marseillaise* **perform**, play, sing, execute, interpret.
8 *the film's Jewish characters are vividly rendered* **act**, perform, play, depict; interpret.
9 *the phrase is almost impossible to render into English* **translate**, put, express, transcribe, convert; rephrase, reword; transliterate; *dated* construe.
10 *he was called upon to* **render up** *the stolen money* **give back**, return, restore, pay back, repay, hand over, give up, surrender, relinquish, deliver, turn over, yield, cede.
11 *the fat can be rendered and used for cooking* **melt down**, clarify, purify.

rendezvous ▶ noun **1** *Edward turned up late for their rendezvous* **meeting**, appointment, engagement, assignation; *informal* date; *literary* tryst.
2 *you'd be welcome to use my place as a rendezvous* **meeting place**, venue, place of assignation; *literary* trysting place.
▶ verb *at seven o'clock she reached the wine bar where they had agreed to rendezvous* **meet**, come together, get together, gather, assemble.

rendition ▶ noun **1** *a muted rendition of Beethoven's Fifth* **performance**, rendering, interpretation, presentation, execution, delivery; playing, singing, reading, recitation, recital.
2 *the artist's rendition of Adam and Eve mourning the dead Abel* **depiction**, portrayal, representation, delineation.
3 *the flatbread is my rendition of the classic Italian focaccia* **version**, variation, take on.
4 *an interpreter's rendition of a message* **translation**, transliteration, transcription; interpretation, version, reading, construction.

renegade ▶ noun **1** *he was denounced as a renegade* **traitor**, defector, deserter, turncoat, betrayer; rebel, mutineer; quisling, fifth columnist; *rare* renegado, tergiversator.
OPPOSITE follower.
2 (*archaic*) *he had become what all religions fear most, a renegade* **apostate**, heretic, dissenter; *archaic* recreant.
OPPOSITES adherent, disciple.
▶ adjective **1** *350 army mutineers led by a renegade colonel* **treacherous**, traitorous, disloyal, perfidious, treasonous, rebel, mutinous, rebellious.
OPPOSITES loyal, faithful.
2 *a renegade monk* **apostate**, heretic, heretical, dissident; *archaic* recreant.

renege ▶ verb *he reneged on a campaign promise to keep taxes down* **default on**, fail to honour, go back on, break, back out of, pull out of, withdraw from, retreat from, welsh on, backtrack on; repudiate, retract; go back on one's word, break one's word, break one's promise, do an about-face; *informal* cop out of, rat on.
OPPOSITES keep, honour.

renew ▶ verb **1** *I renewed my search for Frankie* **resume**, return to, pick up again, take up again, come back to, reopen, begin again, start again, restart, recommence; continue (with), carry on (with), proceed with; re-establish.
2 *they renewed their vows at a cathedral service in Chicago* **reaffirm**, reassert, confirm; repeat, reiterate, restate, say again, iterate; *rare* ingeminate.
3 *she needed something to renew her interest in life* **revive**, regenerate, revitalize, reinvigorate, restore, breathe new life into, resurrect, resuscitate, awaken, wake up, rejuvenate, stimulate; *archaic* renovate.
4 *the hotel was completely renewed in 1990* **renovate**, restore, modernize, redecorate, refurbish, revamp, make over, improve, recondition, rehabilitate, overhaul, redevelop, rebuild, reconstruct, remodel; update, bring up to date; refit, re-equip, refurnish; *N. Amer.* bring something up to code; *informal* do up, fix up, give something a facelift, vamp up; *Brit. informal* tart up; *N. Amer. informal* rehab.
5 *the station renewed Jackie's contract after three months* **extend**, prolong.
6 *I had to run to the store to renew my supply of toilet paper* **replenish**, stock up, restock, resupply, refill, top up; replace.

renewal ▶ noun **1** *the renewal of our friendship* **resumption**, recommencement; continuation; re-establishment.
2 *the landscapes of the Lake District were a lifelong source of spiritual renewal* **regeneration**, restoration, revival, reinvigoration, revitalization, rejuvenation; *archaic* renovation.
3 *the comprehensive renewal of older urban areas* **renovation**, restoration, modernization, improvement, reconditioning, rehabilitation, regeneration, overhauling, redevelopment, rebuilding, reconstruction; gentrification; repair, mending.

renounce ▶ verb **1** *Edward renounced his claim to the French throne* **give up**, relinquish, abandon, resign, abdicate, surrender, sign away, waive, forego; *Law* disclaim; *rare* abnegate, demit.
OPPOSITES assert, reassert.
2 *Hungary renounced the 1977 agreement on environmental grounds* **reject**, refuse to abide by, refuse to recognize, repudiate.
OPPOSITES accept, abide by.
3 *she had renounced her family* **repudiate**, deny, discard, reject, give up, forswear, abandon, wash one's hands of, turn one's back on, have nothing more to do with, have done with; disown, cast off, cast aside, disinherit, cut off, throw off, spurn, shun; *archaic* forsake.
OPPOSITE embrace.
4 *by renouncing champagne, Eliot felt that he was exercising a measure of self-denial* **abstain from**, give up, go without, do without, desist from, refrain from, swear off, keep off, eschew, reject, cease to indulge in; *informal* quit, leave off, pack in, kick, lay off.
OPPOSITE turn to.
□ **renounce the world become a recluse**, become a hermit, turn one's back on society, retreat, withdraw, cloister oneself, hide oneself away, shut oneself off/away, cut oneself off.

renovate ▶ verb *the hotel has been completely renovated* **modernize**, restore, redecorate, refurbish, revamp, make over, recondition, rehabilitate, overhaul, repair, redevelop, rebuild, reconstruct, remodel; update, bring up to date, improve; upgrade, gentrify; refit, re-equip, refurnish; *N. Amer.* bring something up to code; *informal* do up, fix up, give something a facelift, vamp up; *Brit. informal* tart up; *N. Amer. informal* rehab.

renovation ▶ noun *the renovation of council properties* **modernization**, restoration, redecoration, refurbishment, revamping, makeover, reconditioning, rehabilitation, overhauling, repair, redevelopment, rebuilding, reconstruction, remodelling, updating, improvement; gentrification, upgrading; refitting; *informal* facelift.

renown ▶ noun *a number of them achieved political renown* **fame**, distinction, eminence, pre-eminence, prominence, repute, reputation, prestige, acclaim, celebrity, note, notability, mark, consequence, standing, stature, account; glory, illustriousness.
OPPOSITES obscurity, anonymity.

renowned ▶ adjective *Satyajit Ray, the renowned Indian film maker* **famous**, celebrated, famed, eminent, distinguished, acclaimed, illustrious, pre-eminent, prominent, great, esteemed, well thought of, of note, of consequence, of repute, of high standing; well known, much publicized, noted, notable, prestigious; fabled, legendary, proverbial; *informal* on the map.
OPPOSITES unknown, obscure, unsung.

CHOOSE THE RIGHT WORD

renowned, famous, celebrated, well known

See FAMOUS.

rent[1] ▶ noun *I can't afford to pay the rent* **hire charge**, rental; fee, cost, price, rate, tariff.
▶ verb **1** *she rented a car at the airport* **hire**, lease, charter.
2 *I'm hoping to rent a house in Hampstead for a few weeks* **occupy temporarily**, live in temporarily; take.
3 *if you don't want to sell it, why don't you rent it out?* **let (out)**, lease (out), hire (out); sublet, sublease.

rent[2] ▶ noun **1** *his knee poked through the rent in his trousers* **rip**, tear, split, hole, gash, slash, slit, opening, perforation.
2 *a vast rent in the Andes, about 2000 feet deep* **gorge**, chasm, fault, rift, fissure, crevasse; cleft, crack, breach; break, fracture, rupture.

renunciation ▶ **noun 1** *Henry III's renunciation of his rights to Normandy* **relinquishment**, giving up, abandonment, resignation, abdication, surrender, signing away, waiving, foregoing; *Law* disclaimer; *rare* abnegation, demission.
OPPOSITES assertion, reassertion.
2 *he claimed that only complete* ***renunciation of*** *sex can lead to the realization of God* **abstention from**, refraining from, going without, doing without, giving up of, eschewal of, rejection of.
3 *France called on them to prove their renunciation of terrorism* **repudiation**, rejection, abandonment, forsaking, forswearing, disavowal, denial; *rare* abjuration.

reorganize ▶ **verb** *the company reorganized its manufacturing and distribution operations* **restructure**, change, make alterations to, make adjustments to, alter, adjust, transform, shake up, rationalize, reshuffle, redeploy, rearrange, reshape, refashion, recast, overhaul, rebuild, reconstruct; reschedule, rejig, reorder.

repair[1] ▶ **verb 1** *the car was taken to a garage to be repaired* **mend**, fix (up), put right, set right, restore, restore to working order, make as good as new, patch up, put back together, overhaul, service, renovate, recondition, rehabilitate, rebuild, reconstruct, refit, adjust, regulate; *N. English* fettle; *informal* see to.
2 *an army of seamstresses repaired costumes and cut new ones* **mend**, darn, sew up, stitch up, patch up; *archaic* clout.
3 *the government repaired relations with several other countries* **put/set right**, put to rights, patch up, mend, fix, sort out, straighten out, make better, improve, right, heal, cure, remedy, retrieve.
OPPOSITES wreck, worsen, destroy.
4 *she sought to repair the wrong she had done* **rectify**, make good, put right, correct, right, redress, make up for, make amends for, make reparation for, compensate for.
OPPOSITE compound.
▶ **noun 1** *the building is in urgent need of repair* **restoration,** fixing (up), renovation, rebuilding, reconstruction; mending, servicing; improvement, adjustment; *archaic* reparation.
2 *a virtually invisible repair* **mend**; darn, patch.
3 *are the tools in good repair?* **condition**, working order, state, shape, form, fettle; *Brit. informal* nick.
□ **beyond repair** *their relationship may well be beyond repair* **irreparable**, irreversible, past mending, irretrievable, hopeless, past hope, beyond hope, irremediable, irrecoverable, incurable, beyond cure; written off.
OPPOSITES reparable, rectifiable.

repair[2] ▶ **verb** (*formal*) *relax in the stylish bar before* ***repairing to*** *the dining room* **go to**, adjourn to, head for, wend one's way to; retire to, withdraw to, retreat to; set off for, take off for, leave for, depart for; *formal* remove to; *literary* betake oneself to.

reparable ▶ **adjective** *I think the situation is still reparable* **rectifiable**, remediable, able to be put/set right, curable, restorable, recoverable, retrievable, salvageable; *rare* corrigible.
OPPOSITE beyond repair.

reparation ▶ **noun** *there is a range of ways in which offenders may make reparation to their victims* **amends**, restitution, redress, compensation, recompense, repayment, atonement; indemnification, indemnity, damages; *rare* solatium.

repartee ▶ **noun** *an evening of wit and repartee* **banter**, badinage, witty conversation, bantering, raillery, witticism, crosstalk, wordplay, patter; witty remarks, witticisms, ripostes, sallies, quips; joking, jesting, teasing, chaff, chaffing, drollery; *French* bons mots; *rare* persiflage.

repast ▶ **noun** (*formal*) *they sat down to a sumptuous repast* **meal**, feast, banquet; snack; *informal* spread, feed, bite, bite to eat; *Brit. informal* nosh, nosh-up; *formal* collation, refection.

repay ▶ **verb 1** *I'm making an effort to repay customers who have been cheated* **reimburse**, refund, pay back, recompense, compensate, remunerate, square accounts with, settle up with, indemnify, pay off; *rare* recoup.
2 *community care grants do not have to be repaid* **pay back**, return, refund, reimburse, give back.
3 *I'd like to be able to repay her generosity* **reciprocate**, return, requite, recompense, reward; return the favour, return the compliment; *archaic* guerdon.
4 *there are a number of interesting books on this subject that would repay further study* **be well worth**; be worth one's while, be worthwhile, be useful, be advantageous.

repayment ▶ **noun 1** *without that certificate, the charity cannot obtain the repayment of the basic rate tax* **refund**, reimbursement, paying back.
2 *I would prefer them to keep this as some repayment for all they have done* **recompense**, reward, compensation, reparation, restitution.

repeal ▶ **verb** *the Act was repealed in 1990* **revoke**, rescind, cancel, reverse, abrogate, annul, nullify, declare null and void, make void, void, invalidate, render invalid, quash, abolish, set aside, countermand, retract, withdraw, overrule, override; *Law* vacate, avoid; *archaic* recall; *rare* disannul.
OPPOSITES introduce, enact, ratify.
▶ **noun** *the repeal of Protective Custody Law* **revocation**, rescinding, cancellation, reversal, annulment, nullification, voiding, invalidation, quashing, abolition, abrogation, setting aside, countermanding, retraction, withdrawal, rescindment, overruling, overriding; *archaic* recall; *rare* rescission, disannulment.
OPPOSITES introduction, enactment, ratification.

repeat ▶ **verb 1** *she repeated her story in a flat monotone* **say again**, restate, reiterate, go through again, go over again, run through again, iterate, rehearse, recapitulate; *informal* recap; *rare* reprise, ingeminate.
2 *children can remember and repeat large chunks of text* **recite**, quote, reproduce; **echo**, parrot, regurgitate; say again, restate; *informal* trot out.
3 *Steele had been invited to repeat his work in a scientific environment* **do again**, redo, replicate, duplicate, perform again.
4 *the episodes from the first two series were constantly repeated* **rebroadcast**, rerun, reshow, replay.
□ **repeat itself** *now history has repeated itself* **reoccur**, occur again, happen again, recur, reappear.
▶ **noun 1** *the ladies' final was a repeat of the previous year's fixture* **repetition**, duplication, replication, rerun; duplicate, replica, copy; echo; *rare* ditto.
2 *he's the highest-paid US showbiz star, thanks to repeats of his TV show* **rerun**, replay, rebroadcast, reshowing.

repeated ▶ **adjective** *he made repeated complaints about the noise* **recurrent**, frequent, persistent, unremitting, sustained, continual, incessant, constant, ceaseless; regular, periodic, many, numerous, a great many, very many, countless; *informal*, more ... than one can shake a stick at.
OPPOSITES occasional, sporadic.

repeatedly ▶ **adverb** *she tried repeatedly to bring up the subject of money* **frequently**, often, again and again, over and over (again), time and (time) again, time after time, many times, on many occasions, many a time, many times over; {day in, day out}, day after day, {week in, week out}, night and day, all the time; persistently, recurrently, constantly, continually, regularly; *N. Amer.* oftentimes; *Latin* ad nauseam; *informal* 24-7; *literary* many a time and oft, oft, oft-times.
OPPOSITES never, seldom.

repel ▶ **verb 1** *the rebels were repelled by army units* **fight off**, repulse, drive back/away, put to flight, force back, beat back, push back, thrust back; hold off, ward off, fend off, stand off, stave off, parry, keep at bay, keep at arm's length; foil, check, frustrate; *Brit.* see off; *informal* send packing; *archaic* rebut.
2 *the polypropylene cover will repel water* **be impervious to**, be impermeable to, keep out, be resistant to, resist.
OPPOSITE attract; absorb; let through.
3 *the thought of kissing him repelled me* **revolt**, disgust, repulse, sicken, nauseate, make someone feel sick, turn someone's stomach, be repulsive to, be extremely distasteful to, be repugnant to, make shudder, make someone's flesh creep, make someone's skin crawl, make someone's gorge rise, put off, offend, horrify; *informal* turn off, give someone the creeps, give someone the heebie-jeebies, make someone want to throw up; *N. Amer. informal* gross out.
OPPOSITE delight.
4 (*archaic*) *Hester repelled the offered medicine* **reject**, decline, turn down, spurn; rebuff.
OPPOSITE welcome.

repellent ▶ **adjective 1** *a repellent stench | critics found the film pretentious and repellent* **revolting**, repulsive, disgusting, repugnant, sickening, nauseating, stomach-turning, stomach-churning, nauseous, emetic, vile, nasty, foul, appalling, abominable, hideous, horrible, awful, dreadful, terrible, obnoxious, loathsome, offensive, objectionable, off-putting, distasteful, disagreeable, uninviting; abhorrent, despicable, reprehensible, contemptible, odious, heinous, obscene, hateful, execrable; gruesome, grisly; *N. Amer.* vomitous; *informal* sick-making, ghastly, putrid, horrid, God-awful, gross, gut-churning, yucky, icky, cringe-making; *Brit. informal* beastly; *literary* noisome; *archaic* disgustful, loathly; *rare* rebarbative.
OPPOSITES delightful, lovely.
2 *the detergent forms a repellent coating | water-repellent leather* **impermeable**, impervious, resistant; -proof; *rare* imperviable.

repent ▶ **verb** *he later* ***repented of*** *what he had done | her stubbornness and pride would not allow her to repent* **feel remorse for**, regret, be sorry for, rue, reproach oneself for, be ashamed of, feel contrite about, wish that one had not done something; be penitent, see the error of one's ways, be regretful, be remorseful, be repentant, be conscience-stricken, be guilt-ridden, wear sackcloth and ashes.

repentance ▶ **noun** *her apparent lack of repentance made me even angrier* **remorse**, contrition, contriteness, penitence, sorrow, sorrowfulness, regret, ruefulness, remorsefulness, pangs of conscience, prickings of conscience, shame, guilt, self-reproach, self-condemnation, compunction; *Christianity* conversion; *archaic* rue; *rare* sorriness.

repentant ▶ **adjective** *Nancy looked suitably repentant and said she was sorry* **penitent**, contrite, regretful, full of regret, sorrowful, rueful, remorseful, apologetic, conscience-stricken, ashamed, guilt-ridden, chastened, self-reproachful, shamefaced, guilty; *rare* compunctious.

OPPOSITES unrepentant, impenitent.

repercussion ▶ noun **1** *the political repercussions of the scandal were devastating* **consequence**, result, effect, outcome, by-product; reverberation, backlash, ripple, shock wave; aftermath, fallout.
2 (archaic) *the bomb went off, a jarring thud followed by a vicious repercussion* **reverberation**, recoil, kickback, rebound, echo.

repertoire ▶ noun *his repertoire of quotes and quips* **collection**, stock, range, repertory; reserve, store, repository, supply, stockpile.

repetition ▶ noun **1** *statistics have already been quoted and they bear repetition* **reiteration**, repeating, restatement, retelling, iteration, recapitulation; recital, rehearsal; informal recap; rare reprise, iterance.
2 *the repetition of words just heard* **repeating**, echoing, parroting, quoting, copying; Psychiatry echolalia.
3 *she drew back, fearful of a repetition of the scene in the kitchen* **recurrence**, reoccurrence, repeat, rerun, replication, duplication; echo.
4 *there is some repetition, but not enough to detract from the valuable information the book contains* **repetitiousness**, repetitiveness, redundancy, superfluity, tautology.

repetitious ▶ adjective *boring, repetitious work.* See REPETITIVE.

repetitive ▶ adjective *he spent day after day doing the same repetitive tasks* **monotonous**, tedious, boring, uninteresting, humdrum, mundane, tiresome, wearisome, dreary, soul-destroying, mind-numbing; **unvaried**, unchanging, unvarying, undiversified, lacking variety, recurrent, recurring, repeated, repetitious, routine, mechanical, automatic, clockwork; Brit. informal samey.
OPPOSITES varied, interesting.

rephrase ▶ verb *perhaps I should rephrase the question* **reword**, put differently, put another way, put in other words, express differently, recast; paraphrase.

repine ▶ verb (literary) *even if I die, I doubt that he'll repine* **fret**, be/feel unhappy, mope, languish, eat one's heart out, be/feel miserable, be/feel upset, be/feel despondent, brood; lament, grieve, mourn, sorrow, pine, agonize.

replace ▶ verb **1** *Adam replaced the receiver thoughtfully* **put back**, return, return to its place, restore.
OPPOSITE remove.
2 *a new chairman was brought in to replace him* **take the place of**, succeed, be a replacement for, take over from, supersede, follow after, come after; supplant, oust; stand in for, substitute for, act as stand-in for, deputize for, act for, stand in lieu of, fill in for, cover for, relieve, act as locum for, understudy; step into the breach, hold the fort; informal fill someone's shoes/boots, step into someone's shoes/boots, sub for.
3 *she took away his empty cereal bowl and* **replaced** *it* **with** *a plate piled high with toast* **substitute**, **exchange**, change; give in place of, give as a replacement for, give in return/exchange for, swap for.

> **CHOOSE THE RIGHT WORD**
>
> **replace, supersede, supplant**
>
> All three words are used when one person or thing takes the place of another, but each has different connotations.
>
> - **Replace** is the most neutral term. One person or thing may replace another as part of a normal process (*the interim government was replaced by an elected one*) or in an emergency (*Heslop replaces Underwood, who has a broken jaw*).
> - Something that has been **superseded** has had its place taken by something more up to date or otherwise preferable (*the older mainframes are being superseded by more powerful, more compact systems*); the emphasis is on the fact of being replaced rather than on the new person or thing, since the word is typically used in the passive, and it is common not to mention the replacement (*current models may be superseded in due course*).
> - There is emphasis on the person or thing that **supplants** another, as they are mentioned more often than with *supersede* or *replace*, and *supplant* is normally used in the active (*the communist or socialist society which Marx believed would eventually supplant capitalism*). There may be a sense of injustice if the new person or thing is seen as a poor substitute (*vast, impersonal motorways supplanted the agreeably irregular network of real roads*).

replacement ▶ noun **1** *the nanny was taken ill and we had barely a week to find a replacement* **successor**, someone else; **substitute**, stand-in, fill-in, locum, understudy, proxy, surrogate; relief, cover, stopgap; Latin locum tenens.
OPPOSITE predecessor.
2 *the wiring was in urgent need of replacement* **renewal**, replacing; substitution.

replenish ▶ verb **1** *she went to the drinks cabinet to replenish their glasses* **refill**, top up, fill up, recharge, reload; N. Amer. freshen; Scottish plenish.
OPPOSITE empty.
2 *the organization's supplies were replenished by a new airlift of weaponry* **stock up**, restock, restore, fill up, make up; replace, renew.
OPPOSITES exhaust, use up.

replete ▶ adjective **1** *the guests, replete with roast lamb and chocolate mousse, lingered over coffee* **well fed**, **sated**, satiated, full, full up, full to bursting, satisfied; glutted, gorged; informal stuffed; archaic satiate, surfeited.
2 *a sumptuous environment replete with European antiques* **filled**, full, well stocked, well supplied, well provided, crammed, crowded, packed, jammed, stuffed, teeming, overflowing, bursting, brimful, brimming, loaded, overloaded, thick, solid, charged, abounding; informal jam-packed, chock-a-block, chock-full, chocker.

replica ▶ noun **1** *I cannot confirm whether it is a replica or a real firearm at this stage* **copy**, **model**, duplicate, reproduction, replication; **dummy**, imitation; carbon copy, facsimile; informal knock-off, dupe.
OPPOSITES original, genuine article.
2 *Amelie was physically a replica of her mother* **perfect likeness**, exact likeness, double, lookalike, living image, mirror image, image, picture, twin, clone; German Doppelgänger; informal spitting image, dead ringer, ringer, dead spit, spit and image.

replicate ▶ verb *the technology would be very hard to replicate* **copy**, reproduce, duplicate, make a copy of, make a replica of; recreate, repeat, perform again; clone.

reply ▶ verb **1** *Rachel didn't bother to reply* **answer**, respond; acknowledge, write back; take the bait, rise to the bait, come back.
2 *'No, I didn't,' he replied, defensively* **respond**, answer, say in response, rejoin, return; retort, counter, fling back, hurl back, retaliate, come back; rare riposte.
▶ noun *he did not wait for a reply* **answer**, response, acknowledgement, rejoinder, return, reaction; retort, riposte; informal comeback.

report ▶ verb **1** *the government reported the biggest fall in manufacturing output since 1981* **announce**, describe, give an account of, tell of, detail, delineate, outline; communicate, pass on, relay; divulge, disclose, reveal; make public, publish, circulate, set out, set forth, put out, post, broadcast; blazon, herald, proclaim, declare, publicize, promulgate; document, record, chronicle; formal adumbrate.
2 *many magazines happily* **report on** *the titillating activities of the stars* **investigate**, look into, inquire into, survey, research, study; **write about**, write an account of, broadcast details of, cover, describe, give details of, write up; commentate on.
3 *I reported him to the police* **make a complaint against**, make a charge against, inform on, tattle on, accuse; informal blow the whistle on, grass on, shop, tell on, squeal on, rat on, split on, peach on; rare delate on.
4 *Juliet reported for duty at 8.30* **present oneself**, arrive, appear, turn up, clock in, sign in; make oneself known, announce oneself, come, be present; Brit. clock on; N. Amer. punch in, punch the (time) clock; informal show up.
▶ noun **1** *I've asked James for a full report of the meeting* **account**, review, record, description, exposition, statement, delineation; transactions, proceedings, transcripts, minutes; French compte rendu, procès-verbal; Military, informal sitrep.
2 *police received reports of drug dealing in the area* **news**, **information**, word, intelligence, intimation; literary tidings; archaic advices.
3 *I followed his progress through television and newspaper reports* **story**, account, description; **article**, piece, item, column, feature, write-up, exposé; **bulletin**, communiqué, dispatch, communication.
4 (Brit.) *his last school report had been good* **assessment**, evaluation, appraisal; marks; N. Amer. report card, grades.
5 *reports of his imminent resignation circulated* **rumour**, whisper, piece of gossip, piece of hearsay; French on dit; informal buzz; rare bruit.
6 (dated) *according to report, he had been dismissed from the Navy for drunkenness* **rumour**, **hearsay**, talk, gossip, tittle-tattle, word of mouth; informal the grapevine; N. Amer. informal scuttlebutt; archaic fame.
7 (archaic) *those who are true, and honest, and of good report* **reputation**, repute, regard, character, name, standing, stature.
8 *they heard the report of a gun* **bang**, blast, crack, pop, shot, gunshot; explosion, detonation, boom; crash, noise, sound, echo, reverberation.

reporter ▶ noun **journalist**, correspondent, newspaperman, newspaperwoman, newsman, newswoman, columnist, writer, blogger; broadcaster, newscaster, news commentator, announcer, presenter; investigative journalist, photojournalist, war correspondent, lobby correspondent; Brit. pressman; N. Amer. legman, wireman; Austral. roundsman; informal news hound, hack, hackette, stringer, journo, talking head; N. Amer. informal newsy, thumbsucker.

repose ▶ noun **1** *in repose, her face still showed signs of the strain she had been under* **rest**, **relaxation**, inactivity, restfulness, stillness, idleness; sleep, slumber.
OPPOSITES work, activity.
2 *true repose can never be found in that house* **peace**, peace and quiet, peacefulness, quiet, quietness, quietude, calm, calmness, tranquillity, stillness; leisure, ease, respite, time off, breathing space.
OPPOSITES stress, strain.

3 *such a depth of repose in so young a man* **composure**, calmness, serenity, tranquillity, equanimity, peace of mind; poise, self-possession, aplomb, self-assurance, dignity.
OPPOSITE agitation.
▶ **verb 1** *the diamond reposed on a bed of plum velvet* **lie**, be placed, be set, be situated, be positioned, be supported, rest.
2 (*literary*) *perhaps Jessica had not realized how much trust he had reposed in her* **put**, place, lay, lodge, set, consign, invest, entrust.
3 *the beds on which we were to repose* **lie**, lie down, recline, stretch out; **rest**, relax, sleep, slumber, take one's ease; *literary* couch.

repository ▶ **noun** *a permanent repository for spent nuclear fuel | he's a veritable repository of musical knowledge* **store**, storing place, storehouse, depository; reservoir, bank, cache, treasury, treasure house, treasure trove, fund, mine, archive, repertory; warehouse, depot, storeroom, safe; container, receptacle.

reprehensible ▶ **adjective** *his conduct was morally reprehensible* **deplorable**, disgraceful, discreditable, disreputable, despicable, blameworthy, culpable, wrong, bad, shameful, dishonourable, ignoble, erring, errant, objectionable, odious, opprobrious, repugnant, inexcusable, unpardonable, unforgivable, insufferable, indefensible, unjustifiable, regrettable, unacceptable, unworthy, remiss; criminal, sinful, scandalous, iniquitous; condemnable, reprovable, blameable, reproachable, censurable; *rare* exceptionable.
OPPOSITES creditable, praiseworthy, good.

represent ▶ **verb 1** *many of Dickens' characters represent a single idea or quality* **symbolize**, **stand for**, personify, epitomize, typify, be symbolic of; embody, be the embodiment/incarnation of, give human form/shape to, body forth, illustrate, incorporate, reflect; *rare* incarnate, image.
2 *the initials which represent her myriad qualifications* **stand for**, correspond to; designate, denote, mean; *literary* betoken.
3 *Hathor, the Egyptian sky goddess, is represented as a woman with cow's horns* **depict**, portray, render, picture, delineate, show, illustrate, characterize, paint, draw, sketch; exhibit, display; *literary* limn.
4 *she sacked him for* **representing** *himself* **as** *the owner of the factory* **describe as**, present as, profess to be, purport to be, claim to be, set oneself up as, pass oneself off as, pose as, pretend to be, masquerade as.
5 *for many people, ageing represents a threat to their independence* **constitute**, be, amount to, mean, be regarded as.
6 *a fifteen-member panel was chosen to represent a cross section of the public* **be a typical sample of**, be representative of, typify, stand for.
7 *Rachel will represent Hampshire at Havant this Saturday* **play for**, appear for; be a member of the team.
8 *MPs representing Scottish constituencies* **be elected by**, be the councillor/MP for, have the vote of.
9 *his solicitor represented him in court* **appear for**, act for, speak for, act/speak on behalf of, be spokesperson for, be the representative of.
10 *the Queen was represented by Lord Lewin* **deputize for**, act as a substitute for, substitute for, stand in for, take the place of, replace.
11 *I represented the case to him as I saw it* **point out**, state, indicate, present, set forth, put forward.
12 *the vendors have represented that such information is accurate* **claim**, maintain, state, say, affirm, allege, contend; *rare* asseverate.

representation ▶ **noun 1** *Rossetti's representation of women* **portrayal**, **depiction**, delineation, presentation, rendition, rendering, characterization, description.
2 *the earliest representations of the human form* **likeness**, **painting**, **drawing**, picture, portrait, illustration, sketch, diagram; image, model, figure, figurine, statue, statuette, bust, head, effigy, icon; simulacrum, reproduction.
3 *anyone who wishes to make representations to the council should make them in writing* **statement**, deposition, allegation, claim; declaration, account, exposition, report, argument; protestation, remonstrance, expostulation.

representative ▶ **adjective 1** *a representative sample of British society* **typical**, prototypical, characteristic, illustrative, indicative; archetypal, paradigmatic, exemplary.
OPPOSITES atypical, unrepresentative.
2 *Britannia, a female figure allegorically representative of Britain* **symbolic**, emblematic, evocative.
3 *a system of representative government* **elected**, elective, chosen, democratic, popular, nominated, appointed, commissioned; delegated, authorized, accredited, official.
OPPOSITE totalitarian.
▶ **noun 1** *a representative of the Royal Pharmaceutical Society* **spokesperson**, spokesman, spokeswoman, agent; officer, official; mouthpiece.
2 *a sales representative* **commercial traveller**, travelling salesman, salesman, saleswoman, agent, traveller; *informal* rep, knight of the road; *N. Amer. informal* drummer; *Brit. archaic* commercial.
3 *the Cambodian representative at the UN* **delegate**, commissioner, ambassador, attaché, envoy, emissary, chargé, chargé d'affaires, commissary, deputy, aide; *Scottish* depute; *Canadian & Austral.* agent general; *Roman Catholic Church* nuncio; *archaic* legate, factor.
4 *our representatives in parliament* **Member of Parliament**, MP, Member; councillor; *N. Amer.* Member of Congress, congressman, congresswoman, senator.
5 *he acted as his father's representative* **deputy**, substitute, stand-in, proxy, surrogate.
6 *fossil representatives of lampreys and hagfishes* **example**, **specimen**; exemplar, exemplification, type, archetype, illustration.

repress ▶ **verb 1** *the rebellion was successfully repressed* **suppress**, quell, quash, subdue, put down, put an end to, crush, squash, extinguish, stamp out, put a stop to, stop, end, nip in the bud; defeat, conquer, rout, overpower, overwhelm, triumph over, trounce, vanquish, get the better of; contain, gain control over, gain mastery over; *informal* squelch.
2 *a ruling class which repressed and exploited workers and peasants* **oppress**, subjugate, hold down, keep down, rule with a rod of iron, rule with an iron hand, dominate, intimidate, master, domineer over, tyrannize, subject, crush, overpower, overcome.
3 *in later childhood these emotions may well be repressed* **restrain**, hold back, keep back, hold in, bite back, suppress, fight back, keep in check, check, control, keep under control, curb, rein in, contain, silence, muffle, stifle, smother, swallow, choke back, strangle, gag; conceal, hide, bottle up, inhibit, frustrate; *informal* button up, keep the lid on, cork up.
OPPOSITES release, express.

repressed ▶ **adjective 1** *a repressed country* **oppressed**, subjugated, subdued, tyrannized, ground down, downtrodden.
OPPOSITES free, democratic.
2 *repressed feelings of hostility* **restrained**, suppressed, held back, held in, kept in check, muffled, stifled, smothered, pent up, bottled up; concealed, hidden, subconscious, unconscious; unfulfilled, latent.
OPPOSITES overt, expressed.
3 *a reclusive, emotionally repressed man* **inhibited**, frustrated, restrained, self-restrained, withdrawn, introverted; *informal* uptight, hung up.
OPPOSITES uninhibited, relaxed.

repression ▶ **noun 1** *the brutal repression of the peaceful protests* **suppression**, quelling, quashing, subduing, crushing, squashing, stamping out; *informal* squelching.
2 *20 years of militarism and political repression* **oppression**, subjugation, suppression, domination, tyranny, subjection, despotism, dictatorship, authoritarianism; censorship.
OPPOSITES freedom, liberty.
3 *the repression of sexual urges* **restraint**, restraining, holding back, keeping back, biting back, suppression, keeping in check, control, keeping under control, stifling, smothering, bottling up; inhibition, frustration.
OPPOSITE expression.

repressive ▶ **adjective** *a repressive military regime* **oppressive**, authoritarian, despotic, tyrannical, tyrannous, dictatorial, fascist, autocratic, totalitarian, dominating, coercive, draconian, iron-fisted, harsh, severe, strict, tough, cruel, brutal; undemocratic, illiberal; *rare* suppressive.
OPPOSITES democratic, liberal.

reprieve ▶ **verb 1** *she was sentenced to death, but was reprieved* **grant a stay of execution to**, cancel/postpone/commute/remit someone's punishment; pardon, spare, acquit, grant an amnesty to, amnesty; *informal* let off, let off the hook; *archaic* respite.
OPPOSITES charge, punish.
2 *the accident and emergency unit has also been reprieved* **save**, rescue, grant a stay of execution to, give a respite to; *informal* take off the hit list.
▶ **noun** *he was saved by a last-minute reprieve* **stay of execution**, cancellation of punishment, postponement of punishment, remission, suspension of punishment, respite; pardon, amnesty, acquittal; *N. Amer. Law* continuance; *informal* let-off.

reprimand ▶ **verb** *he was publicly reprimanded for his behaviour* **rebuke**, admonish, chastise, chide, upbraid, reprove, reproach, scold, remonstrate with, berate, take to task, pull up, castigate, lambaste, read someone the Riot Act, give someone a piece of one's mind, haul over the coals, lecture, criticize, censure; *informal* tell off, give someone a talking-to, give someone a telling-off, dress down, give someone a dressing-down, give someone an earful, give someone a roasting, give someone a rocket, give someone a rollicking, rap, rap over the knuckles, slap someone's wrist, send someone away with a flea in their ear, let someone have it, bawl out, give someone hell, come down on, blow up, pitch into, lay into, lace into, give someone a caning, put on the mat, slap down, blast, rag, keelhaul; *Brit. informal* tick off, have a go at, carpet, give someone a mouthful, tear somone off a strip, give someone what for, give someone some stick, wig, give someone a wigging, give someone a row, row; *N. Amer. informal* chew out, ream out; *Austral. informal* monster; *Brit. vulgar slang* bollock, give someone a bollocking; *N. Amer. vulgar slang* chew someone's ass, ream someone's ass; *dated* call down, rate, give someone a rating, trim; *rare* reprehend, objurgate.
OPPOSITES praise, commend, compliment.
▶ **noun** *they received a severe reprimand from the Office of Fair Trading* **rebuke**, reproof, admonishment, admonition, reproach, reproval, scolding,

remonstration, upbraiding, castigation, lambasting, lecture, criticism, censure; *informal* telling-off, rap, rap over the knuckles, slap on the wrist, flea in one's ear, dressing-down, earful, roasting, tongue-lashing, bawling-out, caning, blast; *Brit. informal* ticking-off, carpeting, wigging, rollicking, rocket, row; *Austral./NZ informal* serve; *Brit. vulgar slang* bollocking; *dated* rating.
OPPOSITES praise, commendation.

reprisal ▶ **noun** *he declined to be named for fear of reprisal* **retaliation**, counterattack, counterstroke, comeback; revenge, vengeance, retribution, requital, recrimination, an eye for an eye, a tooth for a tooth, tit for tat, getting even, redress, repayment, payback; *Latin* lex talionis; *informal* a taste of one's own medicine; *rare* ultion, a Roland for an Oliver.

reproach ▶ **verb** *Albert reproached him for being late* **rebuke**, reprove, scold, chide, reprimand, admonish, chastise, upbraid, remonstrate with, berate, take to task, pull up, castigate, lambaste, read someone the Riot Act, give someone a piece of one's mind, haul over the coals, lecture, criticize, find fault with, censure, express disapproval of; *informal* tell off, give someone a talking-to, give someone a telling-off, dress down, give someone a dressing-down, give someone an earful, give someone a roasting, give someone a rocket, give someone a rollicking, rap, rap someone over the knuckles, slap someone's wrist; *Brit. informal* tick off, have a go at, carpet, give someone a mouthful, tear someone off a strip, give someone what for, give someone some stick, wig, give someone a wigging, give someone a row, row; *dated* call down, rate, give someone a rating, trim; *rare* reprehend, objurgate, reprobate.
OPPOSITES praise, commend.

▶ **noun 1** *he reddened in acknowledgement of her reproach* **rebuke**, reproof, reproval, admonishment, admonition, scolding, reprimand, remonstration, lecture, upbraiding, castigation, lambasting, criticism, censure, disapproval, disapprobation; *informal* telling-off, rap, rap over the knuckles, slap on the wrist, dressing-down, earful, roasting, rollicking; *Brit. informal* ticking-off, carpeting, wigging; *Austral./NZ informal* serve; *dated* rating.
OPPOSITES praise, commendation.
2 *this party is a reproach to the British political system* **disgrace**, discredit, source of shame, outrage; blemish on, stain on, blot on, blot on the escutcheon of, slur on; scandal, stigma; *literary* smirch.
OPPOSITE credit.

□ **beyond/above reproach** *her public image had to be beyond reproach* **perfect**, beyond criticism, blameless, above suspicion, without fault, faultless, flawless, irreproachable, exemplary, unimpeachable, impeccable, immaculate, unblemished, spotless, untarnished, stainless, unstained, pure, as pure as the driven snow, whiter than white, sinless, guiltless, unsullied; *informal* squeaky clean.
OPPOSITE blameworthy.

reproachful ▶ **adjective** *Angela gave him a reproachful look but he persisted* **disapproving**, reproving, full of reproof, critical, censorious, disparaging, disappointed, withering, accusatory, admonitory, condemnatory, castigatory, fault-finding.
OPPOSITE approving.

reprobate ▶ **noun** *even a hardened reprobate like myself has some standards to adhere to* **rogue**, rascal, scoundrel, good-for-nothing, villain, wretch, unprincipled person, rake, profligate, degenerate, debauchee, libertine; troublemaker, mischief-maker, wrongdoer, evil-doer, transgressor, sinner; *French* roué, vaurien; *informal* scallywag, bad egg; *N. Amer. informal* scofflaw, hellion; *informal, dated* rotter, bounder; *dated* cad, ne'er-do-well; *archaic* miscreant, blackguard, knave, rapscallion, varlet, wastrel, rakehell, scapegrace.

▶ **adjective** *reprobate behaviour* **unprincipled**, roguish, bad, wicked, rakish, shameless, immoral, profligate, degenerate, dissipated, debauched, depraved, corrupt; incorrigible, hardened, unregenerate; *informal* scoundrelly, rascally; *archaic* knavish.
OPPOSITES upright, virtuous, principled.

▶ **verb** (*archaic*) *they reprobated his conduct* **criticize**, condemn, censure, denounce, express strong disapproval of; *rare* reprehend.
OPPOSITES praise, commend.

reproduce ▶ **verb 1** *each artwork is reproduced in full colour on a single page* **copy**, produce a copy of, make a facsimile of, duplicate, replicate; photocopy, xerox, photostat, mimeograph, mimeo, print; transcribe; clone; forge, counterfeit; *trademark* make a Xerox of.
2 *this work has not been reproduced in other laboratories* **repeat**, replicate, recreate, redo, perform again, reconstruct, remake; simulate, imitate, emulate, mirror, parallel, match, echo, mimic, ape, follow.
3 *some forms of animals and plants reproduce prolifically* **breed**, produce offspring, bear young, procreate, propagate, multiply, proliferate, give birth, spawn, increase.

reproduction ▶ **noun 1** *the reproduction of copyrighted material* **copying**, duplication, duplicating, replication, replicating; photocopying, xeroxing, photostatting, printing; transcription, cloning, forging, counterfeiting.
2 *a photostatic reproduction of the original* **print**, **copy**, reprint, duplicate, replica, facsimile, carbon copy; photocopy, mimeograph, mimeo; imitation, fake, forgery, counterfeit; *informal* dupe; *trademark* Xerox, photostat; *rare* ectype.
OPPOSITE original.
3 *marine invertebrates are not always restricted to one method of reproduction* **breeding**, producing young, procreation, multiplying, propagation, proliferation, spawning.

reproductive ▶ **adjective** *reproductive organs | reproductive ability* **generative**, procreative, propagative; **sexual**, genital, sex; *rare* progenitive, procreant, conceptive.

reproof ▶ **noun** *he muttered a reproof | he clicked his tongue at her in mock reproof* **rebuke**, reprimand, reproach, admonishment, admonition, reproval, remonstration; **disapproval**, disapprobation, criticism, censure, blame, condemnation, fault-finding; *informal* telling-off, rap over the knuckles, slap on the wrist, dressing down, blast; *Brit. informal* ticking-off, wigging; *Austral./NZ informal* serve; *Brit. vulgar slang* bollocking; *dated* rating; *rare* reprehension.
OPPOSITES approval, praise.

reprove ▶ **verb** *he annoyed the new chauffeur by reproving him for grinding the gears* **reprimand**, rebuke, reproach, scold, admonish, remonstrate with, chastise, chide, upbraid, berate, take to task, pull up, castigate, lambaste, read someone the Riot Act, give someone a piece of one's mind, haul over the coals, criticize, censure; *informal* tell off, give someone a talking-to, give someone a telling-off, dress down, give someone a dressing-down, give someone an earful, give someone a roasting, give someone a rocket, give someone a rollicking, rap, rap over the knuckles, slap someone's wrist, let someone have it, send someone away with a flea in their ear, bawl out, give someone hell, come down on, pitch into, lay into, lace into, give someone a caning, put on the mat, slap down, blast, rag, keelhaul; *Brit. informal* tick off, have a go at, carpet, give someone a mouthful, tear someone off a strip, give someone what for, give someone some stick, wig, give someone a wigging, give someone a row, row; *dated* call down, rate, give someone a rating, trim; *rare* reprehend, objurgate.
OPPOSITES praise, compliment.

reptile *See centre pages for lists of* **Reptiles** **Snakes**

WORD LINKS

related suffixes	**-saur (e.g. *ichthyosaur*), -saurus (e.g. *stegosaurus*)**
study of reptiles and amphibians	**herpetology**

reptilian ▶ **adjective 1** *reptilian species* reptile-like, reptile; cold-blooded; saurian, ophidian, crocodilian; *technical* poikilothermic; *rare* reptiloid, reptiliform, reptant, repent.
2 *a reptilian smirk twisted his features | the reptilian young reception clerk* **unpleasant**, distasteful, nasty, disagreeable, unappealing, unattractive, off-putting, horrible, horrid; unctuous, ingratiating, fulsome, oily, oleaginous; untrustworthy, devious, sly, underhand, crafty; *informal* smarmy, slimy, creepy, sneaky.
OPPOSITES nice, pleasant, attractive.

repudiate ▶ **verb 1** *in 1924 she repudiated communism | they have repudiated the founder of the party* **reject**, renounce, abandon, forswear, give up, turn one's back on, have nothing more to do with, wash one's hands of, have no more truck with, abjure, disavow, recant, desert, discard, disown, cast off, lay aside, cut off, rebuff; *archaic* forsake; *rare* disprofess.
OPPOSITE embrace.
2 *Cranham repudiated the allegations* **deny**, refute, contradict, rebut, dispute, disclaim, disavow; dismiss, brush aside; *formal* gainsay; *rare* controvert, negate.
OPPOSITES confirm, acknowledge.
3 *Egypt repudiated the treaty* **cancel**, set aside, revoke, rescind, reverse, retract, overrule, override, overturn, invalidate, nullify, declare null and void, abrogate; refuse to fulfil, disregard, ignore, disobey, dishonour, renege on, go back on, backtrack on; *Law* disaffirm, avoid, vacate.
OPPOSITES ratify, accept, abide by.
4 *he repudiated his first wife* **divorce**, end one's marriage to.
OPPOSITE marry.

repudiation ▶ **noun 1** *the repudiation of one's religious heritage* **rejection**, renunciation, renouncement, abandonment, forsaking, forswearing, giving up, disavowal, recantation, desertion, discarding, disowning, casting aside; *rare* abjuration.
2 *his repudiation of the allegations* **denial**, refutation, contradiction, rebuttal, rejection, disclaimer, disavowal; dismissal; *rare* negation.
OPPOSITES confirmation, acknowledgement.
3 *a repudiation of the contract* **cancellation**, revocation, rescindment, reversal, abrogation, retraction, invalidation, nullification; *Law* disaffirmation, disaffirmance, defeasance, avoidance; *rare* rescission.
OPPOSITES ratification, acceptance.

repugnance ▶ **noun** *a look of repugnance crossed Michael's features* **revulsion**, **disgust**, abhorrence, repulsion, nausea, loathing, horror, hatred, detestation, aversion, abomination, distaste, antipathy, dislike, contempt, odium; *archaic* disrelish; *rare* repellency, repellence.
OPPOSITES delight, liking.

repugnant ▶ **adjective 1** *the idea of cannibalism may seem repugnant to us*

abhorrent, revolting, repulsive, repellent, disgusting, offensive, objectionable, vile, foul, nasty, loathsome, sickening, nauseating, nauseous, hateful, detestable, execrable, abominable, monstrous, appalling, reprehensible, deplorable, insufferable, intolerable, unacceptable, despicable, contemptible, beyond the pale, unspeakable, noxious, obscene, base, hideous, grisly, gruesome, horrendous, heinous, atrocious, awful, terrible, dreadful, frightful, obnoxious, unsavoury, unpalatable, unpleasant, disagreeable, distasteful, dislikeable, off-putting, displeasing; *informal* ghastly, horrible, horrid, gross, putrid, sick-making, yucky, God-awful; *Brit. informal* beastly; *N. Amer. informal* skanky; *literary* noisome; *archaic* disgustful, scurvy, loathly; *rare* rebarbative.
OPPOSITES attractive, agreeable, pleasant.
2 (*formal*) *the restriction is* **repugnant to** *the nature of the tenancy* **incompatible with**, in conflict with, contrary to, at variance with, contradictory to, inconsistent with, alien to, opposed to; *rare* oppugnant to.

repulse ▶ verb **1** *the rebels made another assault on the Secretariat and were again repulsed* **repel**, **drive back**, drive away, fight back, fight off, put to flight, force back, beat off, beat back, push back, thrust back; ward off, hold off, stave off, fend off; foil, check, frustrate; *Brit.* see off; *informal* send packing; *archaic* rebut.
2 *she tried to show him affection, but was repulsed* **rebuff**, reject, spurn, snub, disdain, give someone the cold shoulder, cold-shoulder; *informal* give someone the brush-off, freeze out, stiff-arm; *Brit. informal* knock back; *N. Amer. informal* give someone the bum's rush, give someone the brush; *Austral. informal* snout; *informal, dated* give someone the go-by.
OPPOSITE welcome.
3 *his bid for the company was repulsed* **reject**, turn down, refuse, decline, say no to; *informal* give the thumbs down to.
OPPOSITE accept.
4 *the concept of being with a man repulsed her* **revolt**, disgust, repel, sicken, nauseate, make someone feel sick, turn someone's stomach, be repulsive to, be extremely distasteful to, make shudder, be repugnant to, make someone's flesh creep, make someone's skin crawl, make someone's gorge rise, offend, horrify; *informal* turn off, give someone the creeps, make someone want to throw up; *N. Amer. informal* gross out.
OPPOSITE delight.
▶ noun **1** *the repulse of the Austrian attack* **repelling**, driving back, putting to flight; warding off, holding off; **defeat**, check, foiling, frustration; *rare* repulsion.
2 *he was, no doubt, mortified by this repulse* **rebuff**, rejection, snub, slight, repudiation, spurning, cold-shouldering, discouragement; *informal* brush-off, knock-back, kick in the teeth, slap/smack in the face, smack in the eye.

repulsion ▶ noun *she shuddered with repulsion* **disgust**, revulsion, abhorrence, repugnance, nausea, loathing, horror, hatred, detestation, aversion, abomination, distaste, antipathy, dislike, contempt, odium; *archaic* disrelish; *rare* repellency, repellence.
OPPOSITES delight, liking.

repulsive ▶ adjective *Gleeson was so repulsive that surely no one would be interested in him* **revolting**, disgusting, abhorrent, repellent, repugnant, offensive, objectionable, vile, foul, nasty, loathsome, sickening, nauseating, stomach-churning, stomach-turning, hateful, detestable, execrable, abominable, monstrous, appalling, reprehensible, deplorable, insufferable, intolerable, despicable, contemptible, beyond the pale, unspeakable, noxious, horrendous, heinous, atrocious, awful, terrible, dreadful, frightful, obnoxious, unsavoury, unpleasant, disagreeable, distasteful, dislikeable, off-putting, uninviting, displeasing; ugly, as ugly as sin, hideous, grotesque, gruesome, unsightly, reptilian; *N. Amer.* vomitous; *informal* ghastly, horrible, horrid, God-awful, gross, putrid, sick-making, sick, yucky, icky; *Brit. informal* beastly; *N. Amer. informal* skanky; *literary* noisome; *archaic* disgustful, scurvy, loathly; *rare* rebarbative.
OPPOSITES delightful, pleasant, attractive.

reputable ▶ adjective *if you decide to have an alarm fitted, make sure it is done by a reputable company* **well thought of**, highly regarded, well respected, respected, respectable, with a good reputation, of repute, of good repute, creditable, esteemed, prestigious, estimable; established, well known; reliable, dependable, trusted, trustworthy, tried and trusted, honest, honourable, principled, above board, legitimate, upright, virtuous, irreproachable, worthy, good, excellent, conscientious; *informal* legit; *Brit. informal* copper-bottomed; *archaic* of good report.
OPPOSITES disreputable, untrustworthy.

reputation ▶ noun *her reputation has been seriously damaged by the scandal* **name**, **good name**, character, repute, standing, stature, status, position, rank, station; fame, celebrity, renown, esteem, eminence, prestige; image, stock, credit; *Indian* izzat; *N. Amer. informal* rep, rap; *archaic* honour, report; *rare* reputability.

repute ▶ noun **1** *a woman of ill repute | Ramsay knew her only by repute* **reputation**, name, character; *archaic* report.
2 *a firm of international repute* **fame**, renown, celebrity, distinction, high standing, stature, eminence, prominence, note, prestige, account; good reputation, good name.
OPPOSITES obscurity, infamy.

reputed ▶ adjective **1** *they are reputed to be amongst the richest men in France* **thought**, said, reported, rumoured, believed, held, considered, regarded, deemed, judged, estimated; alleged, purported.
OPPOSITE known.
2 *his reputed father | the reputed flatness of the Middle West* **supposed**, putative; apparent, ostensible; *rare* suppositious; *rare* reputative.
OPPOSITE actual.
3 *he had been elevated from obscurity to the status of reputed naturalist* **well thought of**, well respected, respected, highly regarded, with a good reputation, of good repute; well known, widely known.
OPPOSITES unknown, obscure.

reputedly ▶ adverb *the yew trees are reputedly the oldest in Europe* **supposedly**, by all accounts, according to popular belief, so the story goes, so I'm told, so people say, by repute, allegedly, putatively, apparently, seemingly, ostensibly; *rare* reputatively, putatitiously.

request ▶ noun **1** *we received several urgent requests for assistance* **appeal**, entreaty, plea, petition, solicitation, supplication, prayer, invocation; application; demand, call, summons, requisition; *literary* behest; *rare* imploration, adjuration, obtestation, impetration, obsecration.
2 *Charlotte insisted, at Ursula's request, on driving him to the station* **bidding**, asking, entreaty, pleading, solicitation, petitioning, supplication, begging; demand, instance.
3 *please indicate your requests on the booking form* **requirement**, wish, want, desire; choice; *Latin* desideratum.
▶ verb *the government requested foreign military aid | I requested him to inform Charles immediately* **ask for**, appeal for, call for, seek, solicit, plead for, put in a plea for, pray for, petition, sue for, supplicate for; apply for, put in an application for, put in for, place an order for, put in an order for, order; demand, require, requisition; **call on**, beg, beseech, entreat, implore, importune, adjure; invite, bid; *rare* obtest, impetrate, obsecrate.

require ▶ verb **1** *the youngest child required further hospital treatment* **need**, be in need of, stand in need of, have need of; be crying out for.
2 *it was a situation that required patience* **necessitate**, demand, call for, involve, entail, take.
3 *unquestioning faith and obedience is required* **demand**, insist on, call for, ask for, request, order, command, decree; exact; expect, look for.
4 *she was required to pay over £10,000 in costs* **order**, instruct, command, enjoin, oblige, bid, compel, constrain, charge, make, force.
5 *do you require anything else, sir?* **want**, wish, wish to have, desire; lack, be short of, be without, find oneself in need of.

required ▶ adjective **1** *the book is required reading for everyone interested in philosophical thought* **essential**, vital, indispensable, necessary, needed, called for, requisite, prerequisite; compulsory, obligatory, mandatory, prescribed, statutory; recommended, set; *French* de rigueur.
OPPOSITES optional, inessential.
2 *cut the cable to the required length* **desired**, preferred, chosen, selected; **correct**, proper, right.

requirement ▶ noun *it's essential to assess your requirements carefully before you buy* **need**, wish, demand, want, necessity, essential, necessary/essential item; prerequisite, requisite, precondition, condition, stipulation, specification; *Latin* desideratum, sine qua non; *informal* must.

requisite ▶ adjective *he lacks the requisite communication skills* **necessary**, **required**, prerequisite, essential, indispensable, vital, needed, needful; compulsory, obligatory, mandatory, stipulated, demanded, called-for, imperative; *French* de rigueur.
OPPOSITES optional, unnecessary, non-essential.
▶ noun **1** *she sold all sorts of goods, from vegetables to toilet requisites* **requirement**, need, necessity, essential, want, necessary/essential item.
2 *a university degree has become a requisite for any successful career in this field* **necessity**, essential requirement, prerequisite, essential, precondition, specification, stipulation; qualification; *Latin* desideratum, sine qua non; *informal* must.
OPPOSITE non-essential.

CHOOSE THE RIGHT WORD

requisite, necessary, essential, indispensable

See NECESSARY.

requisition ▶ noun **1** *in mid-1946, the Air Ministry placed its first requisition for an atomic bomb* **order**, purchase order, request, call, application; claim, demand, summons; *Brit.* indent.
2 *the illegal requisition of cultural treasures* **appropriation**, commandeering, possession, takeover, taking over, occupation; seizure, confiscation, expropriation, sequestration.
▶ verb **1** *the house was requisitioned by the army* **commandeer**, appropriate, take, take over, take possession of, occupy; seize, confiscate, expropriate, sequestrate, sequester.
2 *she requisitioned statements and demanded the material that was missing* **request**, order, call for, apply for, put in a claim for, put in for; demand.

R

requital ▶ noun **1** *take this from me in requital of your kindness* **repayment**, reward, return, payment, recompense, reparation.
2 *punishment ought not to be inflicted by the victim as a means of personal requital* **revenge**, vengeance, retribution, retaliation, redress, satisfaction; *Latin* quid pro quo.

requite ▶ verb **1** *the king promised to requite his hospitality* **return**, reciprocate, match; reward, repay, recompense; *archaic* guerdon.
2 *Drake had requited the wrongs inflicted on them* **avenge**, exact revenge for, revenge, retaliate for, pay someone back for; get/have/take one's revenge, take reprisals, settle old scores, settle the score with someone, take an eye for an eye (and a tooth for a tooth), give tit for tat, get even, give someone their just deserts, give someone a dose/taste of their own medicine, give as good as one gets, give like for like.
3 *she did not requite his love* **reciprocate**, return, feel/give in return.

rescind ▶ verb *the court has the power to rescind a bankruptcy order* **revoke**, repeal, cancel, reverse, abrogate, overturn, overrule, override, annul, nullify, declare null and void, make void, void, invalidate, render invalid, quash, abolish, set aside, countermand, retract, withdraw; *Law* vacate, avoid; *archaic* recall; *rare* disannul.
OPPOSITES enforce, enact.

rescission ▶ noun *the rescission of the contract* **revocation**, repeal, cancellation, rescindment, reversal, abrogation, annulment, nullification, invalidation, voiding, setting aside, retraction; *archaic* recall; *rare* disannulment.
OPPOSITE enforcement.

rescue ▶ verb **1** *an attempt was made to rescue the hostages* **save**, save from danger, save the life of, come to the aid of; **set free**, free, release, liberate, extricate, get someone out; deliver, redeem, ransom, emancipate, relieve; bail someone out; *Nautical* bring someone off; *informal* save someone's bacon, save someone's neck, save someone's skin.
OPPOSITES endanger, jeopardize; imprison; abandon.
2 *Boyd bent hastily to rescue his papers* **retrieve**, recover, salvage, get back; pick up, gather up, scoop up.
▶ noun *the rescue of 10 crewmen from a ship which had run aground on the Shetland Isles* **saving**, rescuing; release, freeing, liberation, extrication; deliverance, delivery, redemption, ransom, emancipation, relief.
□ **come to someone's rescue help**, assist, aid, lend a helping hand to, lend a hand to, bail out; be someone's knight in shining armour; *informal* save someone's bacon, save someone's neck, save someone's skin, get someone out of a tight spot.

research ▶ noun **1** *a group set up to oppose the use of animals in medical research* **investigation**, experimentation, testing, exploration, analysis, fact-finding, examination, scrutiny, scrutinization, probing; groundwork; *rare* indagation.
2 (**researches**) *he could no longer afford to continue his researches* **experiments**, experimentation, tests, inquiries, studies, analyses, work.
▶ verb **1** *the phenomenon has been widely researched* **investigate**, conduct investigations into, study, inquire into, make inquiries into, look into, probe, explore, analyse, examine, scrutinize, inspect, review, assess.
2 *I researched all the available material on the subject* **study**, read, read up on, pore over, delve into, dig into, sift through; *informal* check out.

resemblance ▶ noun *any resemblance between their reports is purely coincidental* **similarity**, likeness, alikeness, similitude; correspondence, congruity, congruence, coincidence, concurrence, conformity, agreement, equivalence; comparability, comparableness, comparison, parallelism, parity, analogy, affinity, closeness, nearness; sameness, identicalness, uniformity; *archaic* semblance.
OPPOSITE dissimilarity.

resemble ▶ verb *the woman resembled Jackie Kennedy | her views resemble those of the right-wing tabloid press* **look like**, be similar to, be like, bear a resemblance to, remind one of, put one in mind of, take after, favour, have a look of, make one think of; approximate to, smack of, have (all) the hallmarks of, correspond to, be not dissimilar to, be not unlike; echo, mirror, duplicate, parallel; *Zoology & Botany* mimic; *archaic* bear semblance to.
OPPOSITE differ from.

resent ▶ verb *the girls resented the fact that Peter got so much attention* **begrudge**, feel aggrieved at/about, feel bitter about, grudge, be annoyed at/about, be angry at/about, be resentful of, dislike, be displeased at/about, take exception to, object to, be offended by, take amiss, take offence at, take umbrage at; envy, feel envious of, feel jealous of; bear/harbour a grudge about; *archaic* take something ill.
OPPOSITES like, welcome, be pleased by.

resentful ▶ adjective *constant criticism will make your partner feel resentful* **aggrieved**, indignant, irritated, exasperated, piqued, put out, in high dudgeon, displeased, dissatisfied, disgruntled, discontented, malcontent, offended, bitter, hostile, acrimonious, rancorous, spiteful, jaundiced; envious, jealous, grudging, begrudging; sullen, sulky, sour, fed up, huffy, in a huff, irked; *informal* miffed, miffy, peeved, mad, aggravated; *Brit. informal* narked; *N. Amer. informal* sore; *W. Indian informal* vex; *vulgar slang* pissed off; *archaic* snuffy, wroth.
OPPOSITES satisfied, contented.

resentment ▶ noun *the proposal aroused deep resentment among many party members* **bitterness**, **indignation**, irritation, pique, displeasure, dissatisfaction, disgruntlement, discontentment, discontent, resentfulness, bad feelings, hard feelings, ill feelings, acrimony, rancour, animosity, hostility, jaundice, antipathy, antagonism, enmity, hatred, hate; envy, jealousy, malice, ill will; grudge, grievance, a chip on one's shoulder; *literary* ire.
OPPOSITES contentment, happiness.

reservation ▶ noun **1** *the British government expressed grave reservations about the proposals* **doubt**, qualm, scruple; **misgivings**, scepticism, unease, hesitation, hesitancy, demur, reluctance; objection; *Law* demurrer.
OPPOSITE confidence.
2 *groups of ten or more should make reservations* **advance booking**, booking, prior arrangement; charter/hire arrangements; *dated* engagement.
3 *Ms Jones wrote, confirming the reservation of the room* **booking**, ordering, arrangement, prearrangement, securing; charter, hire; *dated* engagement, engaging.
4 *the Yanomami Indian reservation* **reserve**, preserve, enclave, sanctuary, area, territory; homeland.
□ **without reservation** *Mr McNeill apologized without reservation* **wholeheartedly**, **unreservedly**, without qualification, without reserve, without demur, fully, completely, categorically, totally, entirely, wholly, in every respect; implicitly, unconditionally; *informal* all the way; *N. Amer. informal* flat out.

reserve ▶ verb **1** *ask your newsagent to reserve you a copy* **put to one side**, put aside, set aside, lay aside, keep back; **keep**, save, hold, keep in reserve, hold back, retain, conserve, preserve, put away, withhold, earmark; *informal* hang on to.
OPPOSITE use up.
2 *that evening, he reserved a table at Chez Jacques* **book**, make a reservation for, order, arrange in advance, arrange for, prearrange for, secure; charter, hire; *informal* bag; *dated* engage; *rare* bespeak.
3 *the management reserves the right to alter the advertised programme if necessary* **retain**, keep, hold, secure.
4 *I'd advise you to reserve your judgement on him until you get to know him a little better* **defer**, postpone, put off, delay, withhold; *N. Amer.* take something under advisement.
▶ noun **1** *Harriet had used up some of her precious reserves of petrol for this journey* **stock**, store, supply, stockpile, reservoir, pool, fund, bank, accumulation; hoard, cache.
2 *the men were stationed as a central reserve ready to be transported wherever necessary* **backup**; (**reserves**) **reinforcements**, extras, auxiliaries.
3 *a 2,500 acre nature reserve* **national park**, **animal sanctuary**, preserve, reservation, conservation area; safari park.
4 *Carrie found it very difficult to penetrate his reserve* **reticence**, self-restraint, restraint, self-containment; uncommunicativeness, unwillingness to open up, unapproachability, detachment, distance, remoteness, coolness, lack of warmth, aloofness, stand-offishness, constraint, formality, guardedness, unresponsiveness, secretiveness, taciturnity, silence; shyness, diffidence, timidity, self-effacement, inhibitedness, inhibition; coldness, frigidity; *French* froideur.
OPPOSITES friendliness, openness, approachability.
5 *she trusted him without reserve* **reservation**, qualification, condition, limitation, proviso; hesitation, doubt, qualm, scruple.
□ **in reserve** *the army had only one fresh regiment in reserve* **available**, at hand, to hand, on hand, on call, ready, in readiness, for use when needed, set aside; obtainable, accessible, at one's disposal, on tap; spare.
▶ adjective *United's reserve goalkeeper* **substitute**, stand-in, second-string, relief, replacement, fallback, emergency; in reserve, spare, extra, auxiliary, secondary.

reserved ▶ adjective **1** *as a young man, Sewell was rather reserved* **reticent**, self-restrained, restrained, quiet, private, self-contained; uncommunicative, unforthcoming, undemonstrative, unsociable, formal, constrained, cool, aloof, stand-offish, detached, distant, remote, unapproachable, unfriendly, withdrawn, guarded, secretive, close, silent, taciturn, close-mouthed; shy, retiring, diffident, timid, demure, self-effacing, shrinking, inhibited, introverted; unemotional, cold, chilly, frigid; *archaic* retired; *rare* Olympian.
OPPOSITES outgoing, open.
2 *the corner table is reserved, I'm afraid* **booked**, taken, spoken for, prearranged; chartered, hired; *dated* engaged; *rare* bespoken.
OPPOSITE free.

reservoir ▶ noun **1** *large numbers of birds frequent the reservoir* lake, pool, pond; water supply, water source, store of water; *technical* waterbody; *Scottish* loch; *Indian & Austral./NZ* tank; *Mexican Spanish* cenote.
2 *the toner reservoir is housed within a single-piece cartridge* **receptacle**, container, holder, repository, tank; sump.
3 *companies that fail to promote women are cutting their reservoir of managerial talent by half* **stock**, store, stockpile, reserve(s), supply, accumulation, bank, pool, fund; cache, hoard.

reshuffle ▶ verb (stress on the second syllable) *the prime minister reshuffled* *his cabinet* **reorganize**, restructure, change, change around, change the line-up of, shake up, rearrange, interchange, shuffle, regroup, rejig, redistribute, realign; *informal* jigger.

▶ **noun** (stress on the first syllable) *the company announced a management reshuffle* **reorganization**, restructuring, upheaval, change, rearrangement, regrouping, redistribution; *informal* shake-up.

reside ▶ **verb 1** *a number of students* ***reside in*** *flats and other lodgings in Coleraine* **live in**, occupy, inhabit, have one's home in, be settled in, have taken up residence in, have established oneself in; stay in, lodge in; *informal* hang out in; *N. Amer. informal* hang one's hat in; *formal* dwell in, be domiciled in, sojourn in; *archaic* bide in.
OPPOSITE visit.
2 *the Lewis Papers now reside in an air-conditioned vault in the suburbs of Chicago* **be situated**, be placed, be found, be located, lie, repose.
3 *a unitary state in which executive power* ***resides in*** *the president* **belong to**, be vested in, be bestowed on, be conferred on, be entrusted to, be in the hands of.
4 *the distinctive qualities that* ***reside within*** *each individual* **be inherent in**, be intrinsic to, be present in, inhere in; **exist in**, rest in, lie in, dwell in, abide in; consist in, subsist in; *rare* indwell.

residence ▶ **noun 1** (*formal*) *his private residence* **home**, house, flat, apartment, place of residence, address, accommodation, place; quarters, lodgings; seat; *French* pied à terre; *informal* pad, digs; *formal* dwelling, dwelling place, domicile, abode, habitation.
2 *his last known place of residence* **occupancy**, habitation, residency, inhabitation, tenancy, stay; *formal* abode, sojourn; *rare* inhabitancy, inhabitance, domiciliation, habitancy.

resident ▶ **noun 1** *the residents of New York City* **inhabitant**, local; householder, homeowner, houseowner; citizen, native, townsman, townswoman, taxpayer; occupant, occupier, tenant; *humorous* denizen, burgher; *formal* dweller; *rare* residentiary, indweller.
2 (*Brit.*) *at present, the hotel bar is open to residents only* **guest**, person staying, boarder, lodger, client.
OPPOSITE non-resident.
3 *residents at a nursing home near Middleton St George* **patient**, inmate.

▶ **adjective 1** *trustees resident in the UK* **living**, residing, in residence, staying, remaining; *formal* dwelling; *archaic* biding; *rare* residentiary.
2 *a resident nanny* **live-in**, living in.
3 *the resident registrar in obstetrics and gynaecology* **permanent**, incumbent; *French* en poste.
OPPOSITE visiting.
4 *the health-care needs of the resident population* **local**, neighbourhood.

residential ▶ **adjective** *a residential area* **suburban**; commuter, dormitory; *rare* exurban.

residual ▶ **adjective 1** *this machine has five programmes, and uses the residual heat to dry the dishes* **remaining**, leftover, unused, unconsumed; surplus, extra, excess, superfluous; *technical* residuary, remanent.
2 *she still seemed to feel some residual affection for her errant husband* **lingering**, lasting, enduring, abiding, persisting, surviving, vestigial.

residue ▶ **noun** *the residue of his estate was divided equally among them* **remainder**, remaining part, part leftover, rest, remnant, remnants; surplus, extra, excess, balance; remains, leftovers, leavings, dregs, lees, sediment, grounds, settlings; *technical* residuum, precipitate, sublimate; *Commerce* overage.

resign ▶ **verb 1** *the senior management resigned after the losses were announced* **leave**, go, hand in one's notice, give in one's notice, give notice, stand down, step down, bow out, walk out; *informal* **quit**, call it a day.
2 *19 MPs resigned their parliamentary seats* **give up**, leave, vacate, stand down from, retire from; *informal* quit, pack in, jack in; *archaic* demit.
OPPOSITE take up.
3 *he had resigned his right to the title* **renounce**, relinquish, give up, abandon, surrender, forego, cede, abdicate, sign away; *Law* disclaim; *archaic* forsake.
OPPOSITES claim, assert, keep.
4 *we* ***resigned ourselves to*** *a long wait* **reconcile oneself to**, become resigned to, become reconciled to, have no choice but to accept, come to terms with, learn to live with, get used to the idea of; give in to the inevitable, grin and bear it.
OPPOSITE refuse to accept.

resignation ▶ **noun 1** *his resignation from his government post | the resignation of his ministerial portfolio* **departure**, leaving, standing down, stepping down, retirement; giving up, vacating, relinquishment, renunciation, surrender, abdication; *informal* quitting; *archaic* demission.
2 *she toyed with the idea of handing in her resignation* **notice**, notice to quit, letter of resignation.
3 *he confronted the indignities of old age with his usual resignation* **patience**, forbearance, tolerance, stoicism, endurance, fortitude, sufferance, lack of protest, lack of complaint, acceptance of the inevitable, fatalism, acceptance, acquiescence, compliance, passivity, passiveness, non-resistance, submission, docility, phlegm; *rare* longanimity.
OPPOSITE resistance.

resigned ▶ **adjective** *'What time?' he asked, with a resigned sigh* **patient**, long-suffering, uncomplaining, forbearing, tolerant, stoical, philosophical, unprotesting, reconciled, fatalistic; **acquiescent**, compliant, unresisting, non-resistant, passive, submissive, subdued, docile, phlegmatic; *rare* longanimous.
OPPOSITE resistant.

resilience ▶ **noun 1** *he uses different types of vertical and cross strings in his rackets for added resilience* **flexibility**, pliability, suppleness, plasticity, elasticity, springiness, spring, give; **durability**, ability to last, strength, sturdiness, toughness.
OPPOSITES rigidity; fragility.
2 *she displayed an indomitable resilience in the face of misfortune* **strength of character**, strength, toughness, hardiness; **adaptability**, ability to bounce back, buoyancy, flexibility.
OPPOSITES vulnerability, weakness.

resilient ▶ **adjective 1** *remember that the more resilient the underlay, the more it will prolong the life of your carpet* **flexible**, pliable, pliant, supple, plastic, elastic, springy, rubbery; **durable**, hard-wearing, stout, strong, sturdy, tough.
OPPOSITES inflexible, rigid; fragile.
2 *he was still young and resilient* **strong**, tough, hardy; **quick to recover**, quick to bounce back, buoyant, difficult to keep down, irrepressible; **adaptable**, flexible.
OPPOSITES vulnerable, sensitive.

resist ▶ **verb 1** *the vine's hard wood helps it resist cold winters* **withstand**, be proof against, hold out against, combat, counter; weather, endure, outlast; repel, be resistant to, be impervious to, be impermeable to, keep out.
OPPOSITES be harmed by, be susceptible to.
2 *the old Marxists were already resisting his attempts to change the way things were done* **oppose**, fight against, refuse to accept, be hostile to, object to, be anti, take a stand against, defy, go against, set one's face against, kick against, baulk at; **obstruct**, impede, hinder, block, thwart, frustrate, inhibit, restrain; stop, halt, prevent, check, stem, curb; dig in one's heels; *archaic* reluct.
OPPOSITES accept, welcome.
3 *I resisted the urge to retort* **refrain from**, abstain from, keep from, forbear from, desist from, forgo, avoid; not give in to, restrain oneself from, prevent oneself from, stop oneself from, check oneself.
OPPOSITES succumb to, give in to.
4 *she tried to resist him, but she hadn't the strength* **struggle with/against**, fight (against), put up a fight against, battle against, stand up to, withstand, stand one's ground against, hold one's ground against, hold off, hold out against, contend with, confront, face up to; fend off, keep at bay, ward off, keep at arm's length.
OPPOSITES submit, yield.

□ **cannot resist** *he is a man who cannot resist a challenge* **love**, adore, relish, be addicted to, have a weakness for, be very partial to, be very keen on, be very fond of, like; delight in, enjoy, take great pleasure in; *informal* have a thing about, be mad about, be hooked on, get a kick out of, get a thrill out of.
OPPOSITE hate.

resistance ▶ **noun 1** *they displayed a narrow-minded* ***resistance to*** *change* **opposition to**, hostility to, aversion to, refusal to accept, unwillingness to accept, disinclination to accept, reluctance to accept, lack of enthusiasm for.
OPPOSITES acceptance, receptivity.
2 *James put up a spirited resistance* **opposition**, fight, battle, stand, struggle, confrontation, defiance.
OPPOSITES submission, surrender.
3 *tobacco lowers the body's* ***resistance to*** *disease* **ability to fight off**, ability to counteract, ability to withstand, immunity from, defences against; resilience.
4 *he joined the resistance* resistance movement, freedom fighters, underground, partisans, guerrillas; (*in France, historical*) Maquis.

resistant ▶ **adjective 1** *a reinforced PVC membrane which is* ***resistant to*** *water | people are more* ***resistant to*** *infection if they have an adequate diet* **impervious to**, proof against, unaffected by, repellent of; unsusceptible to, immune to, invulnerable to; water-resistant, waterproof, impenetrable; *rare* imperviable to.
OPPOSITE susceptible to.
2 *she is very* ***resistant to*** *change* **opposed to**, averse to, hostile to, inimical to, against, anti, unwilling to accept, disinclined to accept, reluctant to accept, unenthusiastic about.
OPPOSITE receptive to.

resolute ▶ **adjective** *France's resolute defence of Verdun* **determined**, purposeful, purposive, resolved, decided, adamant, single-minded, firm, unswerving, unwavering, undaunted, fixed, set, intent, insistent; steadfast, staunch, stalwart, earnest, manful, deliberate, unfaltering, unhesitating, unflinching, persevering, persistent, pertinacious, indefatigable, tenacious, bulldog, strong-minded, strong-willed, unshakeable, unshaken, steely, four-square, dedicated, committed,

R

constant; stubborn, dogged, obstinate, obdurate, inflexible, relentless, intransigent, implacable, unyielding, unbending, immovable, unrelenting; spirited, brave, bold, courageous, plucky, stout, stout-hearted, mettlesome, indomitable, strenuous, vigorous, gritty, stiff; N. Amer. rock-ribbed; informal gutsy, spunky; rare perseverant, indurate.
OPPOSITES irresolute, half-hearted.

resolution ▶ noun **1** *despite her resolution to remain calm, Shannon could feel her temper rising* **intention**, resolve, decision, intent, aim, aspiration, design, purpose, object, plan; commitment, pledge, promise, undertaking.
2 *the committee passed the resolution by 26 votes to 12* **motion**, proposal, proposition, plan; ruling, verdict, judgement, finding, adjudication, decision, declaration, decree; N. Amer. resolve; Law determination.
3 *she handled the work with resolution* **determination**, purpose, purposefulness, resolve, resoluteness, single-mindedness, strength of will, strength of character, will power, firmness, firmness of purpose, fixity of purpose, intentness, decision, decidedness; steadfastness, staunchness, manfulness, perseverance, persistence, indefatigability, tenacity, tenaciousness, staying power, strong-mindedness, backbone, dedication, commitment, constancy, the bulldog spirit, pertinacity, pertinaciousness; stubbornness, doggedness, obstinacy, obdurateness, obduracy, inflexibility; spiritedness, braveness, bravery, boldness, courage, pluck, courageousness, pluckiness, stout-heartedness; German Sitzfleisch; informal guts, spunk, grit, stickability; N. Amer. informal stick-to-it-iveness; archaic intension; rare perseveration.
OPPOSITES irresolution, half-heartedness.
4 *it is hoped that the proposals will pave the way for a satisfactory* **resolution** *of the problem* **solution to**, answer to, end to, explanation to; resolving, settlement, settling, solving, sorting out, working out, rectification, unravelling, disentanglement, clarification, conclusion, ending; informal cracking.
OPPOSITES continuation, prolonging.

resolve ▶ verb **1** *the government seems to think that the matter can be resolved overnight* **settle**, sort out, solve, find a solution to, find an answer to, fix, work out, straighten out, deal with, put right, set right, put to rights, rectify, iron out, reconcile; answer, explain, fathom, unravel, disentangle, clarify, clear up, throw light on; informal sew up, hammer out, thrash out, patch up, crack, figure out.
2 *Charity resolved not to think about him any longer* **determine**, decide, make up one's mind, take a decision, reach a decision, conclude, come to the conclusion; settle on a plan of action.
3 *the committee resolved that the council should proceed* **vote**, pass a resolution, rule, move, decide formally, agree, undertake.
4 *these compounds can be resolved into their active constituents by various methods* **break down**, break up, separate, reduce, decompose, divide; disintegrate, dissolve.
OPPOSITE combine.
5 *one of the most important of a lawyer's accomplishments is the ability to resolve facts into their legal categories* **analyse**, dissect, break down, anatomize.
6 *the shore came closer, the grey smudge* **resolving into** *green fields and a sandy beach* **turn into**, **be transformed into**, become clearly visible as, change into, metamorphose into, be transmuted into.
7 *all my doubts were resolved* **dispel**, remove, allay, dissipate, clear up, banish, put an end to.
OPPOSITE reinforce.

R

▶ noun **1** *attempts to intimidate him merely strengthened his resolve* **determination**, resolution, firmness of purpose, fixity of purpose, purpose, purposefulness, resoluteness, single-mindedness, strength of will, strength of character, will power, firmness, intentness, decision, decidedness; steadfastness, staunchness, manfulness, perseverance, persistence, indefatigability, tenacity, tenaciousness, staying power, strong-mindedness, backbone, dedication, commitment, constancy, the bulldog spirit, pertinacity, pertinaciousness; stubbornness, doggedness, obstinacy, obdurateness, obduracy, inflexibility; spiritedness, braveness, bravery, boldness, courage, courageousness, pluck, pluckiness, stout-heartedness; German Sitzfleisch; informal guts, spunk, grit, stickability; N. Amer. informal stick-to-it-iveness; archaic intension; rare perseveration.
OPPOSITE indecision.
2 *he made a resolve not to go there alone next time* **decision**, resolution, commitment, intention; conclusion.

CHOOSE THE RIGHT WORD

resolve, decide, determine

See DECIDE.

resolved ▶ adjective *he was resolved to marry her* **determined to**, bent on, hell bent on, set on, intent on, insistent on, committed to the idea of.

resonant ▶ adjective **1** *a resonant voice with an attractive Welsh lilt* **deep**, low, sonorous, full, full-bodied, vibrant, rich, clear, ringing, orotund; bass, baritone, basso; loud, carrying, booming, thunderous, thundering; plangent; rare pear-shaped, canorous.
OPPOSITES faint, thin, weak.
2 *alpine valleys resonant with the sound of church bells* **reverberating**, ringing, resounding, echoing, filled; vibrating, pulsating.
3 *that most resonant of all English four-letter words—home* **evocative**, suggestive, expressive, redolent, moving, poignant, haunting.

resort ▶ noun **1** *a English seaside resort* **holiday destination**, holiday centre, tourist centre, centre, spot, retreat, haunt; spa, watering place; informal tourist trap, honeypot.
2 *it is desirable that the matter be settled without* **resort** *to legal proceedings* **recourse to**, turning to, the use of, utilizing; application to, appealing to, looking to.
3 *strike action should only be used as a last resort* **expedient**, measure, possible course of action, step, recourse, alternative, option, choice, source of help, source of assistance, someone/something to turn to, possibility, hope, remedy.
□ **in the last resort ultimately**, in the end, at the end of the day, finally, in the long run, eventually; when all is said and done; informal when push comes to shove.
▶ verb
□ **resort to** *I don't have to resort to such underhand tricks* **have recourse to**, fall back on, turn to, look to, make use of, use, utilize, avail oneself of, employ, bring into play/service, press into service, call on; adopt, exercise; stoop to, descend to, sink to.

resound ▶ verb **1** *an explosion of thunder resounded round the silent street* **echo**, re-echo, reverberate, ring out, fill the air, boom, peal, thunder, rumble.
2 *a large building resounding with the clang of hammers* **reverberate**, echo, re-echo, resonate, ring; vibrate, pulsate.
3 *whatever they do next will not resound in the way their earlier achievements did* **be acclaimed**, be celebrated, be renowned, be famed, be noted, be glorified, be proclaimed, be trumpeted, be talked about, be on everyone's lips.
OPPOSITE sink into obscurity.

resounding ▶ adjective **1** *a resounding bass voice* **reverberant**, reverberating, resonant, resonating, echoing, vibrant, ringing, sonorous, deep, rich, clear; loud, booming, thunderous, deafening.
OPPOSITE faint.
2 *the show was a resounding success* **enormous**, huge, massive, very great, tremendous, terrific, colossal; **emphatic**, decisive, conclusive, striking, impressive, outstanding, unmistakable, notable, noteworthy, memorable, remarkable, phenomenal, monumental; informal whopping, thumping, fantastic; Brit. informal ginormous.

resource ▶ noun **1** (usually **resources**) *is the company using its resources efficiently?* **assets**, funds, wealth, money, riches, capital; staff, people; supplies, materials, store(s), stock(s), reserve(s), holding(s); supply, reservoir, pool, fund, stockpile, accumulation, hoard.
2 *your tutor is there as a resource* **facility**, amenity, aid, help, service, support; convenience, advantage, benefit.
3 *so often her only resource is tears* **expedient**, resort, means, measure, method, course, way, scheme, plan, plot, stratagem, manoeuvre, machination, agency, trick, ruse, artifice, device, tool.
4 *a person of resource* **initiative**, resourcefulness, enterprise, imagination, imaginativeness, ingenuity, inventiveness; quick-wittedness, cleverness, native wit, talent, ability, capability; spirit, spiritedness, enthusiasm, drive, zest, dash, ambition, energy, vigour, vitality; informal gumption, get-up-and-go, go, push, oomph, pizzazz, pep, zip, vim.

resourceful ▶ adjective *somebody proved how resourceful they were by organizing the help of three local firemen* **ingenious**, imaginative, inventive, creative; quick-witted, clever, bright, sharp, talented, gifted, able, capable; spirited, enthusiastic, ambitious, energetic, vigorous.
OPPOSITE unimaginative.

respect ▶ noun **1** *the respect due to a great artist* **esteem**, regard, high regard, high opinion, acclaim, admiration, approbation, approval, appreciation, estimation, favour, popularity, recognition, veneration, awe, reverence, deference, honour, praise, homage.
OPPOSITE contempt.
2 *he speaks to the old lady with respect* **due regard**, consideration, thoughtfulness, attentiveness, politeness, courtesy, civility, deference.
OPPOSITE disrespect.
3 (**respects**) *it was normal to pay one's respects to the local military commander on arriving* **regards**, kind/kindest regards, compliments, greetings, best wishes, good wishes, felicitations, salutations; archaic remembrances; French archaic devoirs.
4 *the report turned out to be accurate in every respect* **aspect**, regard, facet, feature, way, sense, characteristic, particular, point, detail, question, matter, connection.
□ **with respect to/in respect of concerning**, regarding, as regards, in/with regard to, with reference to, relating to, respecting, as for, as to, re, about, apropos, on the subject of, in the matter of, in connection with; French vis-à-vis; Latin in re.
▶ verb **1** *as a teacher he was highly respected for his industry and patience* **esteem**, admire, think highly of, have a high opinion of, hold in high regard,

hold in (high) esteem, think much of, approve of, appreciate, cherish, value, set (great) store by, prize, treasure, look up to, pay homage to, venerate, revere, reverence, adulate, worship, idolize, put on a pedestal, lionize, hero-worship, honour, applaud, praise, favour.
OPPOSITE despise.
2 *at least they respect your privacy* **show consideration for**, show regard for, take into consideration, take into account, make allowances for, take cognizance of, observe, pay heed/attention to, bear in mind, be mindful of, be heedful of, remember; *archaic* regard.
OPPOSITE scorn.
3 *her father respected her wishes | democrats must respect the law* **abide by**, comply with, follow, adhere to, conform to, act in accordance with, acquiesce to, assent to, consent to, accord to, yield to, submit to, defer to, bow to, obey, observe, hold to, keep (to), stick to, stand by, heed.
OPPOSITES ignore, disobey.

respectable ▶ **adjective 1** *she came from a highly respectable middle-class background* **reputable**, of good repute, upright, honest, honourable, trustworthy, above board, worthy, decent, good, virtuous, admirable, well bred, clean-living, proper, decorous; genteel, accepted, presentable; *French* comme il faut.
OPPOSITES disreputable, unworthy.
2 *he earns a respectable salary* **fairly good**, passable, decent, fair, reasonable, presentable, moderately good, not bad; **substantial**, considerable, ample, sizeable; *informal* not to be sneezed at, OK.
OPPOSITES paltry, small.

respectful ▶ **adjective** *a uniformed attendant gave them a respectful salute* **deferential**, reverent, admiring, humble, reverential, dutiful, subservient; **polite**, well mannered, civil, courteous, chivalrous, gallant, gracious, considerate, obliging, solicitous, thoughtful, attentive; *dated* mannerly; *rare* regardful.
OPPOSITES disrespectful, rude.

respective ▶ **adjective** *the girls had gone back to their respective boarding schools* **separate**, personal, own, particular, individual, specific, special, corresponding, relevant, appropriate, different, various, several.

respite ▶ **noun 1** *the thought of a brief respite was tempting* **rest**, break, breathing space, interval, intermission, interlude, recess, lull, pause, time out, hiatus, halt, stop, stoppage, cessation, discontinuation, standstill; relief, relaxation, repose; *informal* breather, let-up.
2 *granting respite from debts was a means of encouraging men to serve in the army* **postponement**, deferment, delay, stay, stay of execution, reprieve, remission, suspension, adjournment, moratorium; *N. Amer. Law* continuance.

resplendent ▶ **adjective** *the General was resplendent in his uniform and military ribbons* **splendid**, magnificent, brilliant, dazzling, glittering, glowing, radiant, gorgeous, transcendent, impressive, imposing, spectacular, striking, stunning, glorious, superb, majestic, great, awe-inspiring, breathtaking, fine; *informal* splendiferous; *rare* splendacious, magnolious.

respond ▶ **verb 1** *they do not* **respond to** *questions* **answer**, reply to, say something in response to; acknowledge, greet, counter; make a response, make a rejoinder, make a riposte, make reply, come back.
OPPOSITES ask; ignore.
2 *'No,' she responded* **say in response**, answer, reply, rejoin, retort, return, riposte, counter, fling back, hurl back, retaliate, come back.
3 *Western countries have been slow to* **respond to** *appeals* **react to**, act in response to, make a response; hit back at, take the bait, rise to the bait, reciprocate, return the favour, retaliate, give as good as one gets, give tit for tat.
OPPOSITES make, ignore.

response ▶ **noun 1** *there was laughter at his response to the question* **answer**, reply, acknowledgement, rejoinder, retort, return, riposte, sally, counter; *informal* comeback.
OPPOSITE question.
2 *the Chancellor's move drew an angry response from opposition MPs* **reaction**, reply, reciprocation, retaliation; feedback; *informal* comeback.

responsibility ▶ **noun 1** *it was his responsibility to find witnesses* **duty**, task, function, job, role, place, charge, business, onus, burden, liability, accountability, answerability, province; *Brit. informal* pigeon.
2 *the organization denied responsibility for the bomb attack at the airport* **blame**, fault, guilt, culpability, blameworthiness, liability.
3 *teenagers may not be showing enough sense of responsibility to be safely granted privileges* **trustworthiness**, level-headedness, rationality, sanity, reason, reasonableness, sense, common sense, stability, maturity, adultness, reliability, dependability, competence.
4 *we train those staff who show an aptitude for managerial responsibility* **authority**, control, power, leadership, management, influence; duty.

responsible ▶ **adjective 1** *the Home Office is* **responsible for** *prisons* **in charge of**, in control of, at the helm of, accountable for, liable for, charged with; (**be responsible for**) **manage**, oversee, superintend, supervise, conduct, run, look after, organize, produce, see to.
2 *those* **responsible for** *the mistake have been dealt with* **accountable**, answerable, to blame; behind, at the bottom of, guilty of, culpable of; blameworthy, at fault, in the wrong.
OPPOSITE guiltless.
3 *Margaret holds a responsible position in marketing* **important**, powerful, authoritative, executive, decision-making, high.
OPPOSITE lowly.
4 *he is* **responsible to** *the president* **answerable**, accountable; supervised by, managed by.
5 *Mr Smith is likely to prove a respectable and responsible tenant* **trustworthy**, capable of being trusted, trusty, level-headed, rational, sane, reasonable, sensible, sound, stable, mature, adult; reliable, dependable, conscientious.
OPPOSITES irresponsible, untrustworthy.

responsive ▶ **adjective** *the industry must become more responsive to consumer needs* **quick to react**, reactive, receptive, open to suggestions, amenable, flexible, accessible, approachable, forthcoming, sensitive, perceptive, sympathetic, well disposed, susceptible, impressionable, open, alive, awake, aware.
OPPOSITES apathetic, insensitive.

rest[1] ▶ **verb 1** *he needed to rest and think* **relax**, take a rest, ease up/off, let up, slow down, pause, have/take a break, unbend, repose, laze, idle, loaf, do nothing, take time off, slack off, unwind, recharge one's batteries, be at leisure, take it easy, sit back, sit down, stand down, lounge, luxuriate, loll, slump, flop, put one's feet up, lie down, go to bed, have/take a nap, nap, catnap, doze, have/take a siesta, drowse, sleep; *informal* de-stress, take five, have/take a breather, veg out, snooze, snatch forty winks, get some shut-eye; *Brit. informal* kip, have a kip, get some kip; *N. Amer. informal* chill out, kick back, catch some Zs; *literary* slumber.
2 *his hands rested on the small rucksack he carried* **lie**, be laid, recline, repose, be, be placed, be positioned; be supported by, be propped up by.
3 *she rested her basket on the ground* **support**, prop (up), steady, balance, lean, lay, set, sit, stand, position, place, put.
4 *the film script* **rests on** *an improbable premise* **be based on**, be grounded in, be founded on, depend on, be dependent on, rely on, hinge on, turn on, hang on, pivot on, be contingent on, revolve around, centre on.
▶ **noun 1** *get some rest, or you won't be fit for tomorrow | Robbie was ready for a rest and some food* **repose**, relaxation, leisure, ease, inactivity, respite, time off, time out, breathing space; **sleep**; **period of relaxation**, period of repose, nap, doze, siesta; *informal* shut-eye, snooze, lie-down, forty winks; *Brit. informal* kip; *literary* slumber.
2 *I was in need of a short rest from work* **holiday**, vacation, recess; break, breathing space, pause, interval, interlude, intermission; time off, time out; *informal* breather.
3 *she took the poker from its rest* **stand**, base, holder, support, stay, prop, brace, rack, hook, frame, shelf, bracket, trestle, tripod, plinth, pedestal, foundation, bed, foot, substructure.
4 *our landing was cushioned by the snow, and we came to rest 100 metres lower* **a standstill**, a halt, a stop; stationary.

rest[2] ▶ **noun** *only the chairman has been elected—the rest are appointees* **remainder**, residue, balance, remaining part/number/quantity, part/number/quantity (that is) left over, others, those left, remains, remnant, remnants, rump, surplus, difference, extra, excess, superfluity, overflow, overspill, additional people/material/things, extra people/material/things; *technical* residuum.
▶ **verb** *you may rest assured that he is there* **remain**, continue to be, stay, keep, persist in being, carry on being, go on being.

restaurant *See centre pages for list of* **Restaurants**
▶ **noun** **eating place**, eating house; *informal* eatery.

restful ▶ **adjective** *I hope you have had a restful weekend* **relaxed**, relaxing, quiet, calm, calming, tranquil, soothing, peaceful, placid, reposeful, comfortable, leisurely, easy-going, undisturbed, free from disturbance/interruption/interference, untroubled, unhurried.
OPPOSITES exciting, noisy.

restitution ▶ **noun 1** *the claims were for restitution of land allegedly seized by the occupying power* **return**, restoration, handing back, replacement, surrender, yielding, recovery.
OPPOSITES seizure, occupation.
2 *he was ordered to pay $50,000 in restitution for the damage caused* **compensation**, recompense, reparation, damages, indemnification, indemnity, reimbursement, repayment, remuneration, reward, redress, satisfaction; quid pro quo; *archaic* guerdon, meed; *rare* solatium.

restive ▶ **adjective 1** *I haven't done anything about supper—Edward will be getting restive* **restless**, fidgety, edgy, on edge, tense, uneasy, ill at ease, worked up, nervous, agitated, anxious, on tenterhooks, keyed up, apprehensive, unquiet, impatient; *Brit.* nervy; *informal* jumpy, jittery, twitchy, uptight, wired, like a cat on a hot tin roof; *Brit. informal* like a cat on hot bricks.
OPPOSITE calm.
2 *the organization's militant wing has become increasingly restive* **unruly**, disorderly, out of control, uncontrollable, unmanageable, ungovernable, unbiddable, disobedient, defiant, up in arms, wilful, recalcitrant, refractory, insubordinate, disaffected, dissentious, riotous; **rebellious**,

R

mutinous, seditious, insurgent, insurrectionary, insurrectionist, revolutionary; *Brit. informal* bolshie; *archaic* contumacious.
OPPOSITES biddable, peaceable.

restless ▶ adjective **1** *she was restless, moving uneasily about the hut* **uneasy**, ill at ease, restive, fidgety, edgy, on edge, tense, worked up, nervous, agitated, anxious, on tenterhooks, keyed up, apprehensive, unquiet, impatient; *Brit.* nervy; *informal* jumpy, jittery, twitchy, uptight, wired, like a cat on a hot tin roof; *Brit. informal* like a cat on hot bricks.
OPPOSITE calm.
2 *he had spent a restless night* **sleepless**, wakeful, insomniac; fitful, broken, disturbed, troubled, unsettled, uncomfortable; tossing and turning; *archaic* watchful; *rare* insomnolent.
OPPOSITE peaceful.

restlessness ▶ noun **1** *at lunch there was an odd restlessness among his pupils* **unease**, restiveness, fidgetiness, edginess, tenseness, nervousness, agitation, anxiety, fretfulness, discomposure, jitteriness, apprehension, unquietness, disquiet, disquietude, impatience.
OPPOSITE calm.
2 *a walk outside might help night restlessness* **sleeplessness**, insomnia, wakefulness; *archaic* watchfulness.
OPPOSITES repose, sleep.

restoration ▶ noun **1** *an opposition rally demanded the restoration of democracy* **reinstatement**, reinstitution, re-establishment, reimposition, reinstallation, rehabilitation, return, putting back, replacing.
OPPOSITE abolition.
2 *the restoration of derelict housing* **repair**, repairing, fixing, mending, refurbishment, reconditioning, rehabilitation, rebuilding, reconstruction, remodelling, redecoration, revamping, revamp, makeover, overhaul; redevelopment, renovation, modernization, updating, bringing up to date; upgrading, gentrification; *informal* facelift; *N. Amer. informal* rehab.
OPPOSITE neglect.

restore ▶ verb **1** *his aim was to restore democracy in the country* **reinstate**, put back, replace, bring back, reinstitute, reimpose, reinstall, rehabilitate, re-establish, return to a former position/state.
OPPOSITE abolish.
2 *we'll try to restore it to its rightful owner* **return**, give back, hand back, take back, remit.
OPPOSITE keep.
3 *the building has been carefully restored* **repair**, fix, mend, refurbish, recondition, rehabilitate, rebuild, reconstruct, remodel, redecorate, revamp, make over, overhaul; put back into its original condition; redevelop, renovate, modernize, update, bring up to date; upgrade, gentrify; refit, re-equip, refurnish; *N. Amer.* bring up to code; *informal* do up, fix up, give a facelift to; *N. Amer. informal* rehab.
OPPOSITE neglect.
4 *sleep can be just as effective in restoring us physically* **reinvigorate**, revitalize, revive, refresh, energize, reanimate, resuscitate, brace, fortify, strengthen, give new strength to, build up, revivify, rejuvenate, regenerate, renew, breathe new life into, enliven, stimulate, freshen.

restrain ▶ verb **1** *Charles restrained his anger* **control**, keep under control, check, hold/keep in check, curb, suppress, repress, contain, keep within bounds, limit, regulate, restrict, moderate, dampen, put a brake on, subdue, smother, choke back, stifle, bridle, leash, bit, muzzle, bottle up, cork, rein back, rein in, keep in; *informal* keep the lid on.
OPPOSITES provoke, encourage.
2 *she had to* ***restrain*** *herself* ***from*** *slamming the receiver down* **prevent**, stop, keep, hold back; hinder, impede, hamper, restrict, constrain, obstruct; *archaic* hold.
OPPOSITE force.
3 (*Law*) *a court could* ***restrain*** *a doctor* ***from*** *continuing treatment* **prohibit**, ban, bar, disallow, interdict; forbid, veto, proscribe; *Law* enjoin.
OPPOSITES compel, encourage.
4 *the insane used to be restrained with straitjackets* **tie up**, bind, strap, truss, pinion, lash, tether, chain (up), fetter, shackle, manacle, put in irons, handcuff.

R

restrained ▶ adjective **1** *compared with her exuberant father, Julie was quite restrained* **self-controlled**, controlled, self-restrained, moderate, not given to excesses, sober, steady, phlegmatic, unemotional, inhibited, undemonstrative, unassuming, quiet, calm, thoughtful, reticent, discreet, guarded.
OPPOSITES immoderate, emotional.
2 *the restrained elegance of their new floral wallpapers* **muted**, soft, pale, subdued, discreet, subtle, quiet, unobtrusive, unostentatious, understated, artistic, tasteful, graceful.
OPPOSITES garish, loud, extravagant.

restraint ▶ noun **1** *he acts as a restraint on their impulsiveness* **constraint**, check, control, restriction, limitation, curtailment; rein, bridle, brake, damper, deterrent, hindrance, impediment, obstacle, retardant, inhibition; *informal* clampdown, wet blanket.
OPPOSITE incitement.
2 *the customary restraint of the British police* **self-control**, self-restraint, self-discipline, control, moderation, temperateness, abstemiousness, non-indulgence, prudence, judiciousness.
OPPOSITE abandon.
3 *the dining room has been decorated with commendable restraint* **subtlety**, mutedness, understatedness, taste, tastefulness, delicacy, delicateness, discretion, discrimination.
OPPOSITES excess, indulgence.
4 *her restraint puts people off* **reserve**, self-restraint, self-control, self-possession, lack of emotion, sobriety, coldness, formality, aloofness, detachment, reticence, uncommunicativeness.
OPPOSITES forwardness, outspokenness.
5 *a warrant for the release of the person under restraint* **confinement**, captivity, custody, detention, imprisonment, internment, incarceration, constraint, committal, quarantine, arrest; *archaic* duress; *rare* detainment.
6 *children must wear an approved child restraint* **belt**, harness, strap.

restrict ▶ verb **1** *a busy working life restricted his leisure activities* **limit**, set/impose limits on, keep within bounds, keep under control, regulate, control, moderate, cut down on.
2 *the cuff supports the ankle without restricting movement* **hinder**, interfere with, impede, hamper, obstruct, block, slow, check, curb, retard, handicap, straitjacket, tie, cramp.
3 *he managed to* ***restrict himself*** *to a 15-minute speech* **confine**, limit; make do with only, be happy with.

restricted ▶ adjective **1** *this may be the result of cramming so much into a restricted space* **cramped**, confined, constricted, small, narrow, compact, tight, poky, minimal, sparse, inadequate; *archaic* strait; *rare* incommodious.
OPPOSITE roomy.
2 *people on a restricted calorie intake* **limited**, controlled, regulated; reduced, curbed; moderate, modest; deficient.
OPPOSITES unlimited, unrestricted.
3 *she parked in a restricted zone* **out of bounds**, off limits; private, closed off, regulated; secret, top secret, privy, classified; exclusive, reserved, privileged; *informal* hush-hush.
OPPOSITES unrestricted, public.

restriction ▶ noun **1** *there will be no restriction on the number of places available* **limitation**, limit, constraint, control, check, curb; regulation, condition, provision, proviso, stipulation, requirement, qualification, demarcation, rider, strings.
2 *the practice of socialism involves the restriction of personal freedom* **reduction**, limitation, diminution, curtailment, cutback, cut, scaling down.
3 *the infection led to restriction of eye movement* **hindrance**, impediment, hampering, blocking, slowing, handicapping, straitjacket, reduction, limitation; interference with.

result ▶ noun **1** *stress is often the result of overwork* **consequence**, outcome, upshot, out-turn, sequel, effect, reaction, repercussion, reverberation, ramification, end, conclusion, termination, culmination, corollary, concomitant, aftermath, fruit(s), product, produce, by-product; *Medicine* sequelae; *informal* pay-off; *dated* issue; *archaic* success.
OPPOSITE cause.
2 *the result of this addition* **answer**, solution, calculation; sum, total, aggregate, product, quotient.
3 *his exam results* **mark**, score, percentage, grade, grading, rating, place, placing, position, rank, ranking; assessment, appraisal, evaluation.
4 *he was dissatisfied with the result of the recent trial* **verdict**, decision, outcome, conclusion, opinion, determination, judgement, adjudication, arbitration, findings, ruling, pronouncement, decree, settlement, order.
▶ verb **1** *differences between species could result from differences in their habitat* **follow**, ensue, develop, stem, spring, arise, derive, evolve, proceed, emerge, emanate, issue, flow; occur, happen, take place, come about, supervene; be caused by, be brought about by, be produced by, originate in, attend, accompany, be consequent on; *Philosophy* supervene on.
OPPOSITE cause.
2 *the shooting* ***resulted in*** *the deaths of five people* **end in**, culminate in, finish in, terminate in, involve, lead to, prompt, elicit, precipitate, trigger, spark off, provoke; **cause**, bring about, occasion, effect, bring to pass, create, give rise to, produce, engender, generate, induce; *formal* redound to; *literary* beget.

resume ▶ verb **1** *the government agreed to resume negotiations* **restart**, recommence, begin again, start again, reopen; take up again, renew, reinstitute, return to, continue with, carry on with; proceed with, go on with, push on with, pick up where one left off.
OPPOSITES suspend, abandon.
2 *the priest quietly resumed his kneeling posture* **return to**, come back to, take up again, reoccupy, occupy again.
OPPOSITE leave.
3 *the seller can resume possession of the goods* **take back**, recover, take up again, assume again, re-establish.
OPPOSITE renounce.

résumé ▶ noun **1** *this is a brief résumé of the problems* **summary**, precis, synopsis, abstract, outline, summarization, summation; abridgement, digest, condensation, abbreviation, survey, overview, rundown, run-through, review, sketch; *French* tour d'horizon; *N. Amer.* wrap-up; *Law* headnote, brief; *rare* conspectus, summa, epitome, compendium.

2 (*N. Amer.*) *a few Saturdays in a veterinary hospital might look great on her résumé* **CV**, life history, biography, details; *Latin* **curriculum vitae**; *N. Amer.* vita, bio.

resumption ▸ **noun** *the minister called for a resumption of negotiations* **restart**, restarting, recommencement, reopening, reinstitution; continuation, carrying on, taking up again, renewal, return to.
OPPOSITES suspension, abandonment.

resurgence ▸ **noun** *there has been a resurgence of interest in jazz* **renewal**, revival, recovery, rally, upturn, comeback, reinvigoration, reawakening, resurrection, reappearance, re-emergence, rejuvenation, regeneration, new birth, rebirth, renaissance, new dawn, new beginning; **resumption**, recommencement, continuation, re-establishment; *Italian* risorgimento; *rare* renascence, recrudescence, rejuvenescence.

resurrect ▸ **verb 1** *on the third day Jesus was resurrected* **raise from the dead**, restore to life, bring back to life, revive.
2 *it gives him a chance to resurrect his career* **revive**, restore, regenerate, revitalize, breathe new life into, give the kiss of life to, give a new lease of life to, reinvigorate, renew, resuscitate, awaken, wake up, rejuvenate, stimulate, re-establish, relaunch; *archaic* renovate.

resurrection ▸ **noun 1** *the resurrection of Jesus* **raising from the dead**, restoration to life; rising from the dead, return from the dead.
2 *the promised resurrection of the cottage hospital* **revival**, restoration, regeneration, revitalization, reinvigoration, renewal, resuscitation, awakening, rejuvenation, stimulation, re-establishment, relaunch, reintroduction, reinstallation, reappearance, rebirth, renaissance, renascence, comeback.

resuscitate ▸ **verb 1** *medics tried to resuscitate him* **bring round**, revive, bring back, bring (back) to life, bring someone (back) to their senses, bring back to consciousness, rescue, save, bring back from the edge of death; give artificial respiration to, give the kiss of life to, give cardiac massage to, defibrillate.
2 *measures to resuscitate the economy* **revive**, resurrect, restore, regenerate, revitalize, breathe new life into, give the kiss of life to, give a new lease of life to, reinvigorate, renew, awaken, wake up, rejuvenate, stimulate, re-establish, relaunch; *archaic* renovate.

retain ▸ **verb 1** *the government retained a minority share in the privatized industries* **keep**, keep possession of, keep hold of, hold on to, hold fast to, keep back, hang on to, cling to; *literary* cleave to.
OPPOSITES give up, lose.
2 *existing footpaths are to be retained* **maintain**, keep, continue, preserve, reserve, conserve, perpetuate, cherish.
OPPOSITES abolish, discontinue, alter.
3 *some students retain facts easily* **remember**, memorize, keep in one's mind, keep in one's memory; **learn**, learn by heart, get by heart, commit to memory, get off pat, learn by rote, impress on the memory, become word-perfect in; **recall**, call to mind, recollect, think of, succeed in remembering; *archaic* con.
OPPOSITE forget.
4 *the solicitor will retain a barrister when necessary* **employ**, commission, contract, pay, keep on the payroll, have in employment; **hire**, engage, appoint, recruit, put on the payroll, secure the services of, sign on, sign up, take on, take into one's employ.
OPPOSITE dismiss.

retainer ▸ **noun 1** *you're paid a retainer every month to keep me informed* **retaining fee**, fee, periodic payment, partial payment, deposit, advance, subscription, standing charge.
2 *a faithful family retainer* **attendant**, follower, servant, hireling, hanger-on, escort, minion, lackey, flunkey, vassal, dependant, domestic, valet, footman.

retaliate ▸ **verb** *they could torment him without his being able to retaliate* **fight back**, strike back, hit back, respond, react, reply, reciprocate, counterattack, return fire, return the compliment, put up a fight, take the bait, rise to the bait, return like for like, get back at someone, get, give tit for tat, give as good as one gets, let someone see how it feels, give someone a dose/taste of their own medicine; **have/get/take one's revenge**, take/exact/wreak revenge, be revenged, revenge oneself, avenge oneself, take reprisals, get even, even the score, settle a/the score, settle accounts, pay someone back (in their own coin), pay someone out, repay someone, exact retribution, take an eye for an eye (and a tooth for a tooth); *informal* give someone their comeuppance; *Brit. informal* get one's own back; *rare* give someone a Roland for an Oliver.
OPPOSITE turn the other cheek.

retaliation ▸ **noun** *the bombing was in retaliation for a rebel raid on two border villages* **revenge**, vengeance, reprisal, retribution, requital, recrimination, an eye for an eye (and a tooth for a tooth), getting even, redress, repayment, payback; **response**, reaction, reply, reciprocation, counterattack, counterstroke, comeback, tit for tat, measure for measure, blow for blow; *Latin* lex talionis; *rare* ultion, a Roland for an Oliver.

retard ▸ **verb** *the worst thing that governments can do is to retard this admittedly painful process* **delay**, **slow down**, slow up, hold back, set back, keep back, hold up, postpone, put back, detain, decelerate, put a brake on; **hinder**, hamper, obstruct, inhibit, impede, handicap, hamstring, curb, check, restrain, restrict, arrest, interfere with, interrupt, encumber, clog; *Brit. informal* throw a spanner in the works of; *N. Amer. informal* throw a monkey wrench in the works of; *literary* stay, trammel, cumber.
OPPOSITES accelerate, expedite.

retch ▸ **verb 1** *he was sick in the road and stayed there for several minutes, retching* **gag**, heave, dry-heave, reach, convulse, almost vomit, have nausea, feel nauseous; *informal* keck.
2 *he retched all over the table* **vomit**, cough up, bring something up, regurgitate; *Brit.* be sick; *N. Amer.* get sick; *informal* puke (something up), chunder, chuck up, hurl, spew, do the technicolor yawn; *Brit. informal* honk, sick something up; *Scottish informal* boke; *N. Amer. informal* spit up, barf, upchuck, toss one's cookies.

reticence ▸ **noun** *she overcame her usual reticence and talked about their married life* **reserve**, introversion, restraint, inhibition, diffidence, shyness, modesty, distance, undemonstrativeness; **uncommunicativeness**, unresponsiveness, quietness, taciturnity, silence, secretiveness, secrecy.
OPPOSITE expansiveness.

reticent ▸ **adjective** *Smith was extremely reticent about his personal affairs* **reserved**, withdrawn, introverted, restrained, inhibited, diffident, shy, modest, unassuming, shrinking, distant, undemonstrative, wouldn't say boo to a goose; **uncommunicative**, unforthcoming, unresponsive, tight-lipped, close-mouthed, close-lipped, quiet, taciturn, silent, guarded, secretive, private, playing one's cards close to one's chest; *informal* mum.
OPPOSITES expansive, garrulous.

retinue ▸ **noun** *Sir James ordered one of his retinue to stable the horses* **entourage**, escort, company, court, attendant company, staff, personnel, household, cortège, train, suite, following, bodyguard; aides, associates, members of court, companions, attendants, servants, retainers, followers, camp followers, hangers-on; *informal* groupies; *archaic* rout.

retire ▸ **verb 1** *he retired two years ago* **give up work**, stop working, stop work; reach retirement age.
2 *we've retired him on full pension* **pension off**, force to retire, force to give up work; *informal* put out to grass.
3 *Gillian retired to her own office* **go off**, **withdraw**, go away, go out, exit, make an exit, take oneself off, depart, decamp, adjourn, leave for; shut oneself away in, absent oneself; *literary* betake oneself; *formal* repair.
4 *every diplomatic effort was made to get him and his army to retire* **retreat**, withdraw, pull back, fall back, pull out, disengage, back off, give way, give ground, flee, take flight, turn tail, beat a (hasty) retreat.
OPPOSITE advance.
5 *everyone retired early that night* **go to bed**, go to one's room, call it a day, go to sleep; *informal* turn in, hit the hay, hit the sack.

retired ▸ **adjective** *Thomas is a retired schoolteacher* **former**, ex-, emeritus, past, in retirement, pensioned, pensioned off; superannuated, elderly.
▸ **noun** (**the retired**) *a development of apartments for the retired* **retired people**, pensioners, old-age pensioners, OAPs, senior citizens, old people, the elderly; *N. Amer.* seniors, retirees; *rare* retirers, pensionaries.

retirement ▸ **noun 1** *they are just coming up to retirement* **giving up work**, stopping working, stopping work; *Scottish* retiral.
2 *he spent nearly the whole of his retirement there* **life after one retires**, retired years, post-work years.
3 *life in retirement in an English village* **seclusion**, retreat, solitude, loneliness, isolation, privacy, obscurity.

retiring ▸ **adjective 1** *a cut-glass bowl was presented to the retiring president* **departing**, outgoing.
OPPOSITE incoming.
2 *he was such a quiet, retiring man* **shy**, diffident, bashful, self-effacing, shrinking, unassuming, unassertive, reserved, reticent, quiet, timid, timorous, nervous, modest, demure, coy, meek, humble; private, secret, secretive, withdrawn, reclusive, unsociable; *rare* seclusive, eremitic, eremitical, hermitic, anchoritic.
OPPOSITES bold, outgoing.

retort ▸ **verb** *'Oh, sure,' she retorted* **answer**, reply, respond, say in response, acknowledge, return, counter, rejoin, riposte, retaliate, hurl back, fling back, snap back; round on someone, come back.
▸ **noun** *he wanted to make some sarcastic retort about her being bossy* **answer**, reply, response, acknowledgement, return, counter, rejoinder, riposte, sally, retaliation; *informal* comeback.

retract ▸ **verb 1** *the sea otter can retract the claws on its front feet* **pull in**, draw in, pull back, sheathe, put away.
OPPOSITE extend.
2 *he apologized and retracted his allegation* **take back**, withdraw, unsay, recant, disown, disavow, disclaim, abjure, repudiate, renounce, reverse, revoke, rescind, annul, cancel, go back on, backtrack on, do a U-turn on; eat one's words; *Brit.* do an about-turn on.
OPPOSITES assert, confirm.

retreat ▸ **verb 1** *the army retreated* **withdraw**, retire, draw back, pull back, pull out, fall back, give way, give ground, recoil, flee, take flight, beat a retreat, beat a hasty retreat, run away, run off, make a run for it, run for

R

it, make off, take off, take to one's heels, make a break for it, bolt, make a quick exit, clear out, make one's getaway, escape, head for the hills; *informal* beat it, vamoose, skedaddle, split, cut and run, leg it, show a clean pair of heels, turn tail, scram, hook it, fly the coop, skip off, do a fade; *Brit. informal* do a runner, scarper, do a bunk; *N. Amer. informal* light out, bug out, cut out, peel out, take a powder, skidoo; *Austral. informal* go through, shoot through; *archaic* fly, levant.
OPPOSITES advance; dig in.
2 *the tide was retreating* **go out**, ebb, recede, flow out, fall, go down.
OPPOSITE come in.
3 *the government had to retreat over the plan* **change one's decision**, change one's mind, change one's attitude, change one's plans; **back down**, climb down, do a U-turn, backtrack, back-pedal, retract, reconsider, eat one's words, eat humble pie, give in, concede defeat, shift one's ground; *Brit.* do an about-turn.
▶ **noun 1** *a counteroffensive caused the retreat of the imperial army* **withdrawal**, pulling back, flight; *rare* katabasis.
OPPOSITE advance.
2 *Democrats welcomed the President's retreat on the tax issue* **climbdown**, backdown, retraction, concession, about-face, U-turn; *Brit.* about-turn.
3 *she invited us to her retreat in rural Sweden* **refuge**, haven, resort, asylum, sanctuary, sanctum sanctorum; hideaway, hideout, hiding place; cottage, dacha, shelter, cabin, den, lair, nest; *informal* hidey-hole.
4 *a period of retreat from the world for spiritual regeneration* **seclusion**, withdrawal, retirement, solitude, isolation, hiding, privacy, sanctuary; *rare* sequestration, reclusion.

retrench ▶ **verb 1** *not all the directors wanted to retrench* **economize**, cut back, make cutbacks, make savings, make economies, reduce expenditure, be economical, be sparing, be frugal, budget, tighten one's belt, husband one's resources, draw in one's horns, save, scrimp and save, cut corners.
2 *welfare services will have to be retrenched* **reduce**, cut, cut back, cut down, cut back on, pare, pare down, slim down, bring down, make reductions in, make cutbacks in, trim, prune, whittle away/down, take off, decrease, lower, lessen, shorten, curtail, truncate, shrink, diminish, minimize; *informal* slash, axe.

retribution ▶ **noun** *the assassins were cornered, awaiting inevitable retribution* **punishment**, penalty, nemesis, fate, doom, one's just deserts, due reward, just reward, wages; **justice**, retributive justice, poetic justice, judgement, reckoning; **revenge**, reprisal, requital, retaliation, payback, vengeance, an eye for an eye (and a tooth for a tooth), tit for tat, measure for measure; **redress**, reparation, restitution, recompense, repayment, damages, satisfaction, remedy, comeback, atonement, amends; *informal* one's comeuppance; *archaic* measure.

retrieve ▶ **verb 1** *we made a laborious descent to retrieve our skis* **get back**, recover, regain (possession of), win back, recoup, reclaim, repossess, redeem, have returned; salvage, rescue, fetch, bring back; *Law* replevy; *rare* recuperate.
2 *they were working hard to retrieve the situation* **put right**, set right, set to rights, put to rights, rectify, remedy, restore, solve, sort out, straighten out, resolve, deal with, correct, repair, mend, fix, redress, make good; improve, amend, ameliorate, make better, better.

retro ▶ **adjective** *a retro restaurant with a Fifties-style lunch counter* **in period style**, period, nostalgic, evocative, of yesteryear, olde worlde; dated, old-fashioned, backward-looking, retrogressive, out of date, passé.

R

retrograde ▶ **adjective 1** *the closure of the factory is a retrograde step* **for the worse**, regressive, negative, downhill, unwelcome, unprogressive; worsening, deteriorating, degenerate, declining.
OPPOSITES positive, forward-looking.
2 *the retrograde motion of the planets* **backward**, backwards, reverse, rearward, directed backwards, retreating, retrogressive.
OPPOSITE forward.

retrospect ▶ **noun**
▫ **in retrospect looking back**, thinking back, on reflection, on re-examination, in/with hindsight.

retrospective ▶ **adjective** *the Government introduced retrospective legislation to change the rules* **backdated**, retroactive, ex post facto, backward-looking.

return ▶ **verb 1** *he returned to London* **go back**, **come back**, get back, arrive back, arrive home, come home, come again.
OPPOSITES depart, set out.
2 *the symptoms returned after a few days* **happen again**, recur, reoccur, occur again, be repeated, repeat (itself), come round (again); **reappear**, appear again, flare up; *rare* recrudesce.
OPPOSITE disappear.
3 *he would have to return the money he had been given* **give back**, send back, hand back, take back, carry back; pay back, repay, remit.
OPPOSITES keep; throw away.
4 *Peter returned the book to its place on the shelf* **restore**, put back, replace, reinstate, reinstall.
5 *he just managed to return the volley* **hit back**, send back; throw back.
OPPOSITE miss.
6 *the party faithful welcomed her, and she returned the compliment* **reciprocate**, requite, feel/give in return, repay, send/give in response, give back; match, equal; wish someone the same.
OPPOSITE ignore.
7 *'Later,' returned Isabel coldly* **answer**, reply, respond, say in response; acknowledge, counter, rejoin, riposte, retort, retaliate, hurl back, fling back, snap back; round on someone; *N. Amer.* come back.
8 *the jury returned a unanimous verdict* **deliver**, bring in, hand down, render, submit, announce, pronounce, proclaim.
9 *the club returned a small profit* **yield**, bring in, earn, make, realize, secure, net, gross, clear, pay out, fetch, pocket.
10 *the official Labour candidate was returned with 53% of the vote* **elect**, vote in, put in power, choose, opt for, select, pick, adopt.
▶ **noun 1** *failing health forced his* **return** *to Paris* homecoming, travel back to.
OPPOSITE departure.
2 *a buffer against the return of hard times* **recurrence**, reoccurrence, repeat, rerun, repetition; reappearance, flare-up; revival, rebirth, renaissance, resurrection, reawakening, re-emergence, resurgence; *rare* recrudescence, renascence.
OPPOSITE disappearance.
3 *I displayed notices requesting the return of books* **giving back**, handing back, replacement, restoration, reinstatement, reinstallation, restitution; *rare* reinstalment.
4 *it might be worth checking with the box office for returns* **returned item**, unsold item, unwanted item/ticket, reject, exchange.
5 *two returns to London, please* **return ticket/fare**; *N. Amer.* round trip ticket/fare.
OPPOSITE single.
6 *the company hoped for a quick return on its investment* **yield**, profit, returns, gain, income, revenue, interest, dividend, percentage; *Brit. informal* bunce.
7 *a census return* **statement**, report, submission, account, paper, record, file, dossier, write-up, data, information, log, journal, diary, register, summary; document, form.
▫ **in return for** *they were offered a reduction of their prison sentences in return for confessions to crimes* **in exchange for**, in consideration of; in response to, as a reward for, against, as a compensation for.

revamp ▶ **verb** *they plan to revamp the kitchen* **renovate**, redecorate, refurbish, recondition, rehabilitate, rebuild, reconstruct, overhaul, make over; **modernize**, update, bring up to date, renew; improve, upgrade; refit, re-equip, refurnish; brighten up, freshen up, spruce up; remodel, refashion, redesign, restyle, rejig, rework, redo, remould, reorganize; *N. Amer.* bring up to code; *informal* do up, fix up, give something a facelift, vamp up; *Brit. informal* tart up; *N. Amer. informal* rehab.

reveal ▶ **verb 1** *for operational reasons the police can't reveal his whereabouts* **divulge**, disclose, tell, let out, let slip, let drop, let fall, give away, give the game/show away, blurt (out), babble, give out, release, leak, betray, open up, unveil, bring out into the open; go public on/with, make known, make public, bring to public notice/attention, broadcast, air, publicize, publish, circulate, disseminate, pass on, report, declare, post, communicate, impart, unfold, vouchsafe; **confess**, admit, lay bare; *informal* let on, spill, blab, let the cat out of the bag, dish the dirt, take/blow the lid off, blow wide open, come clean about; *Brit. informal* cough, blow the gaff; *archaic* discover.
OPPOSITES hide, conceal.
2 *he let the garage door slide up to reveal a new car* **show**, display, exhibit, disclose, uncover, expose to view, allow to be seen, put on display, put on show, put on view, bare; *literary* uncloak, unclothe; *rare* unclose.
OPPOSITE hide.
3 *the data can be used to reveal a good deal about the composition of Anglo-Norman households* **bring to light**, uncover, turn up, expose to view, lay bare, unearth, dig up, excavate, unveil, unmask, detect, betray, be evidence of, indicate, demonstrate, manifest, evince, make clear, make plain; *literary* uncloak.

revel ▶ **verb 1** *with their exams out of the way they revelled all night* **celebrate**, make merry, have a party, party, feast, {eat, drink, and be merry}, carouse, roister, have fun, have a good time, enjoy oneself, go on a spree; *informal* live it up, whoop it up, have a fling, have a ball, make whoopee, rave, paint the town red; *Brit. informal* push the boat out; *dated* spree.
OPPOSITE mourn.
2 *he* **revelled in** *the applause which greeted him* **enjoy**, delight in, love, like, adore, be entertained by, be amused by, be pleased by, take pleasure in, appreciate, relish, lap up, savour, luxuriate in, bask in, wallow in, glory in; **gloat over**, feel self-satisfied about, crow about; *informal* get a kick out of, get a thrill out of.
OPPOSITE hate.
▶ **noun** *there are a few spots in town for night revels* **celebration**, festivity, jollification, merrymaking, carousal, carouse, spree, debauch, bacchanal; **party**, jamboree; *informal* rave, shindig, bash, jag; *Brit. informal* do, rave-up, knees-up, jolly, thrash, beano, beanfeast; *Irish informal* hooley, crack; *N. Amer. informal* wingding, blast; *Austral. informal* shivoo, rage, ding, jollo.

revelation ▶ **noun 1** *Washington has been rocked by the further revelation that the alleged killer is a respected economist* **disclosure**, surprising fact,

divulgence, declaration, utterance, announcement, report, news, leak, avowal; acknowledgement, admission, confession.
2 *the plot hinges on the revelation of a secret* **divulging**, divulgence, telling, disclosure, disclosing, letting slip, letting out, letting drop, giving away, giving out, leaking, leak, betrayal, unveiling, making known, making public, bringing to public notice/attention, broadcasting, airing, publicizing, publication, publishing, circulation, dissemination, passing on, proclamation, announcing, announcement, reporting, report, declaring, declaration, posting, communication, imparting, unfolding, vouchsafing; admission, confession; *rare* divulgation.
OPPOSITE keeping.
3 *new revelations of government corruption* **uncovering**, turning up, exposure, exposing, bringing to light, unearthing, digging up, unveiling, unmasking, smoking out, detecting, detection.
OPPOSITE covering up.

reveller ▶ **noun** *residents feared disturbances from late-night revellers* **merrymaker**, partygoer, carouser, roisterer, good-time boy/girl, pleasure seeker; *archaic* wassailer; *rare* celebrator, bacchanal, bacchant.

revelry ▶ **noun** *a night of beer-swilling revelry* **celebration(s)**, partying, parties, revels, festivity/festivities, jollification, merrymaking, carousing, carousal, roistering, debauchery, frolics; *informal* junketing.

revenge ▶ **noun 1** *she is seeking revenge for the murder of her husband* **vengeance**, retribution, retaliation, reprisal, requital, recrimination, an eye for an eye (and a tooth for a tooth), tit for tat, measure for measure, getting even, redress, satisfaction, repayment, payback; *Latin* lex talionis; *rare* ultion.
2 *they were so filled with revenge that they shot his father* **vengefulness**, vindictiveness, vitriol, virulence, spite, spitefulness, malice, maliciousness, malevolence, malignancy, ill will, animosity, antipathy, enmity, hostility, acrimony, venom, poison, hate, hatred, rancour, bitterness; *literary* revengefulness, maleficence.
▶ **verb 1** *he was determined to revenge his brother's murder* **avenge**, take/exact revenge for, make retaliation for, retaliate for, exact retribution for, take reprisals for, get redress for, get satisfaction for; requite.
2 *I'll* **be revenged on** *the whole pack of you* **take revenge on**, exact/wreak revenge on, get one's revenge on, avenge oneself on, take vengeance on, get even with, settle a/the score with, get, pay back, pay out, retaliate on/against, take reprisals against, exact retribution on, let someone see how it feels, give someone their just deserts, give someone a dose/taste of their own medicine, give as good as one gets; give/return like for like, give tit for tat, take an eye for an eye (and a tooth for a tooth); *informal* give someone their comeuppance; *Brit. informal* get one's own back on; *archaic* recriminate; *rare* give someone a Roland for an Oliver.

revenue ▶ **noun** *15% of all revenue is generated by a single product* **income**, takings, receipts, proceeds, earnings; **profit**, profits, returns, return, rewards, yield, interest, gain; *Brit. informal* bunce.
OPPOSITES outgoings, expenditure.

reverberate ▶ **verb** *her voice reverberated around the classroom* **resound**, echo, re-echo, repeat, resonate, pulsate, vibrate, ring, peal, boom, rumble, roll, pound, thump, drum, thrum.

reverberation ▶ **noun 1** *electronic musical instruments are totally free from any natural reverberation* **resonance**, echo, echoing, re-echoing, resounding, pulsation, vibration, ringing, peal, boom, booming, rumble, rumbling, roll, pound, pounding, thump, thumping, drumming, thrumming.
2 (usually **reverberations**) *the scandal's political reverberations* **repercussions**, ramifications; **consequence**, result, effect, upshot, outcome, out-turn, by-product; aftermath, fallout, backlash, ripple, shock wave.

revere ▶ **verb** *the president is revered as a national hero* **respect**, **admire**, think highly of, have a high opinion of, hold in high regard, esteem, hold in (high) esteem, think much of, approve of, appreciate, cherish, value, set (great) store by, prize, treasure, look up to; **worship**, pay homage to, venerate, reverence, adulate, hold in awe, idolize, put on a pedestal, lionize, hero-worship, honour, love.
OPPOSITE despise.

reverence ▶ **noun** *reverence for the countryside runs deep in this intensely respectful country* **high esteem**, high regard, great respect, acclaim, admiration, approbation, approval, appreciation, estimation, favour, recognition; **worship**, veneration, awe, homage, adoration, deference, honour, praise; liking, affection, love; *Roman Catholic Church* dulia.
OPPOSITE scorn.
▶ **verb** *they reverence modern jazz* **revere**, respect, admire, think highly of, have a high opinion of, hold in high regard, esteem, hold in (high) esteem, think much of, approve of, appreciate, cherish, value, set (great) store by, prize, treasure, look up to; **worship**, pay homage to, venerate, adulate, hold in awe, idolize, put on a pedestal, lionize, hero-worship, honour, love.
OPPOSITE despise.

reverent ▶ **adjective** *there was a reverent silence* **respectful**, reverential, worshipping, worshipful, adoring, loving, admiring, devoted, devout, dutiful, awed; deferential, submissive, humble, meek.
OPPOSITES irreverent, cheeky.

reverie ▶ **noun** *she was startled out of her reverie by a loud crash* **daydream**, daydreaming, trance, fantasy, vision, fancy, hallucination, musing; inattention, inattentiveness, wool-gathering, preoccupation, obliviousness, engrossment, absorption, self-absorption, absent-mindedness, abstraction, lack of concentration, lack of application; *Scottish* dwam.

reversal ▶ **noun 1** *there was to be no reversal of the British attitude* **turnaround**, turnround, turnabout, about-face, volte-face, change of heart, U-turn, sea change, swing, shift, swerve, backtracking; *Brit.* about-turn; *rare* tergiversation.
2 *there will have to be a reversal of roles* **swap**, **exchange**, change, swapping, trade, trading, interchange, transposition, inversion.
3 *the reversal of the decision followed intense public criticism* **alteration**, changing; **countermanding**, undoing, setting aside, upsetting, overturning, overthrow, disallowing, overriding, overruling, veto, vetoing, repudiation, revocation, repeal, abrogation, cancellation, rescinding, rescindment, annulment, nullification, voiding, invalidation, negation, quashing; withdrawal, recanting, retraction; *archaic* recall; *rare* rescission, disannulment.
4 *a late penalty was the only reversal suffered by the New Zealanders* **setback**, reverse, upset, check, non-success, failure, misfortune, mishap, misadventure, accident, disaster, tragedy, catastrophe, blow, disappointment, adversity, hardship, affliction, vicissitude, defeat, rout; ill luck, bad luck, distress, tribulation, woe, hard times.

reverse ▶ **verb 1** *the car reversed into a lamp post* **back**, go back/backwards, drive back/backwards, move back/backwards, send back/backwards; back-pedal.
OPPOSITE go forwards.
2 *you can reverse the bottle in the ice bucket to cool the wine in the neck first* **turn upside down**, turn over, upend, upturn, put bottom up, flip over, turn topsy-turvy, invert, capsize; *archaic* overset.
3 *when climbing on rough rock I reverse the jacket to protect the outer layer* **turn inside out**; *technical* evert, introvert, evaginate, invaginate.
4 *it may be a good idea to reverse the roles* **swap**, swap round, change, change round, exchange, interchange, switch, switch round, trade, transpose, invert, turn about/around.
OPPOSITE keep to.
5 *the crowd were clamouring for the umpire to reverse the decision* **alter**, change; **countermand**, undo, set aside, upset, overturn, overthrow, rule against, disallow, override, overrule, veto, repudiate, revoke, repeal, cancel, rescind, annul, nullify, declare null and void, void, invalidate, negate, abrogate, quash; withdraw, take back, recant, retract, back-pedal on, backtrack on, do a U-turn on; eat one's words; *Brit.* do an about-turn on; *Law* vacate; *archaic* recall.
OPPOSITES uphold, stick to.
▶ **adjective 1** *I would probably have a completely reverse opinion* **opposite**, contrary, converse, counter, inverse, obverse, opposing, contrasting, antithetical.
OPPOSITE same.
2 *here are the results in reverse order* **backward**, backwards, reversed, inverted, transposed, from bottom to top.
OPPOSITE forwards.
▶ **noun 1** *the reverse is the case* **opposite**, contrary, converse, inverse, obverse, antithesis, opposite/other extreme.
2 *a varied picture of successes and reverses* **setback**, reversal, upset, check, non-success, failure, misfortune, mishap, misadventure, accident, disaster, tragedy, catastrophe, blow, disappointment, adversity, hardship, affliction, vicissitude, defeat, rout; ill luck, bad luck, distress, tribulation, woe, hard times.
OPPOSITE success.
3 *the deadlines are listed on the reverse of this page* **other side**, reverse side, back, rear, underside, wrong side, flip side, B-side, verso.
OPPOSITES front, recto.

revert ▶ **verb 1** *life will soon* **revert to** *normal* **return**, go back, come back, change back, retrogress, regress, default; fall back into, relapse into, lapse into, drift back into; *archaic* retrograde.
2 *at the end of the lease the property reverts to the landlord* **be returned**; *Law* fall, escheat.

review ▶ **noun 1** *the Council is to undertake a review of its property portfolio* **analysis**, evaluation, assessment, appraisal, examination, investigation, scrutiny, inquiry, exploration, probe, inspection, study, audit; *rare* anatomization.
2 *the rent is due for review* **reconsideration**, re-examination, reassessment, re-evaluation, reappraisal, moderation, rethink, another look, a fresh look; **change**, alteration, modification, revision.
3 *he began to write reviews of local stage plays* **criticism**, critique, write-up, notice, assessment, evaluation, judgement, rating, commentary; piece, article, column; *Brit. informal* crit.
4 *a recent scientific review contained the following article* **journal**, periodical, magazine, organ, publication, proceedings, annual, quarterly, monthly.

5 *the authority's latest annual review of the local economy* **survey**, report, study, account, record, description, exposition, statement, delineation, overview, rundown, breakdown, overall picture; *French* compte rendu, procès-verbal; *Law* summing-up; *Military, informal* sitrep.
6 *in a traditional military review, the visiting leader inspects the soldiers up close* **inspection**, parade, display, demonstration, field day, tattoo, array, muster, procession; *Brit.* march past.
▶ **verb 1** *I shall first review the empirical evidence* **survey**, study, research, consider, take stock of, analyse, audit, examine, scrutinize, inquire into, make inquiries into, explore, look into, probe, investigate, conduct investigations into, inspect, assess, appraise, size up; *Law* sum up; *rare* anatomize.
2 *the referee reviewed the decision he'd made* **reconsider**, re-examine, reassess, re-evaluate, reappraise, moderate, rethink, think over, take another look at, take a fresh look at, look at in a different light, have another think about; **change**, alter, modify, revise.
OPPOSITE stick by.
3 *once in bed, he reviewed the day* **remember**, recall, recollect, reflect on, think through, go over in one's mind, cast one's mind back to, think back on, look back on; hark back to, call to mind, summon up, evoke.
4 *the Commander-in-Chief reviewed his troops* **inspect**, view, scrutinize; parade, muster, march past.
5 *John Daly reviewed the novel for the Times* **comment on**, discuss, evaluate, assess, appraise, judge, weigh up, rate, write up, critique, criticize.

reviewer ▶ **noun** *one reviewer remarked on the production's 'refreshing spontaneity'* **critic**, **commentator**, connoisseur, judge, observer, pundit, analyst, arbiter.

revile ▶ **verb** *he was arrested and reviled as a traitor* **criticize**, censure, condemn, attack, inveigh against, rail against, lambaste, flay, savage, brand, stigmatize, denounce; blacken someone's reputation, defame, smear, slander, libel, traduce, cast aspersions on, cast a slur on, malign, vilify, calumniate, besmirch, run down, abuse; *informal* knock, slam, pan, bash, take to pieces, take apart, crucify, hammer, lay into, slate, roast, skewer, rubbish, slag off, bad-mouth; *N. Amer. informal* pummel; *Austral./NZ informal* bag, monster; *rare* vituperate against, excoriate.
OPPOSITES praise, extol.

revise ▶ **verb 1** *she wasn't about to revise her opinion* **reconsider**, review, re-examine, reassess, re-evaluate, reappraise, rethink, think over, take another look at, take a fresh look at, look at in a different light, have another think about; **change**, alter, modify, disconfirm.
OPPOSITES retain, confirm.
2 *the editor has completely revised the text* **amend**, emend, correct, alter, change, adapt, edit, copy-edit, rewrite, redraft, recast, rephrase, rework, update, revamp.
OPPOSITE preserve.
3 (*Brit.*) *revise your lecture notes | he's revising for his exams* **go over**, reread, run through, study, memorize; cram; *informal* bone up on; *Brit. informal* swot up (on), mug up (on), swot.

revision ▶ **noun 1** *the conference called for revision of the Prayer Book* **emendation**, correction, alteration, changing, adaptation, editing, copy-editing, rewriting, redrafting, recasting, rephrasing, reworking, updating, revamping.
2 *this revision is much more readable* **version**, corrected version, edition, rewrite, reworking; variant, form, update, reading, rendition, adaptation.
OPPOSITES first edition, first draft.
3 *a major revision of the system* **reconsideration**, review, re-examination, reassessment, re-evaluation, reappraisal, rethinking, rethink, thinking over; **change**, alteration, modification.
4 *he was doing some revision for his exam* **rereading**, studying, memorizing, cramming; *Brit. informal* swotting.

revitalize ▶ **verb** *the plan would reduce inflation and revitalize the economy* **reinvigorate**, re-energize, brace, fortify, strengthen, give new strength to, give a boost to, build up, bolster, prop up, help, renew, regenerate, restore, revive, revivify, rejuvenate, reanimate, resuscitate, refresh, reawaken, rekindle, put new life into, breathe new life into, enliven, stimulate, put some spark into, kick-start, uplift; *informal* give a shot in the arm to, pep up, buck up, get going again.
OPPOSITE depress.

revival ▶ **noun 1** *a revival in the economy* **improvement**, rallying, picking up, betterment, amelioration, turn for the better; advance, rally, upturn, upswing, comeback, resurgence, renewal.
OPPOSITE downturn.
2 *new interest has resulted in the revival of old traditional crafts* **comeback**, bringing back, re-establishment, reintroduction, restoration, reappearance, resurrection, resuscitation, relaunch, reinstallation, regeneration, revitalization, reinvigoration, awakening, rejuvenation, stimulation, rebirth, renaissance, renascence.
OPPOSITE disappearance.

revive ▶ **verb 1** *attempts to revive the woman failed* **resuscitate**, bring round, bring to life, bring back, bring someone (back) to their senses, bring back to consciousness, bring back from the edge of death; rescue, save; give artificial respiration to, give the kiss of life to, give cardiac massage to, defibrillate.
2 *the man soon revived* **regain consciousness**, recover consciousness, come round, come to life, come to one's senses, recover, awake, wake up.
3 *a cup of tea revived her* **reinvigorate**, revitalize, refresh, energize, reanimate, resuscitate, brace, fortify, strengthen, revivify, rejuvenate, regenerate, renew, breathe new life into, enliven, stimulate, freshen.
OPPOSITE torpefy.
4 *the man who revived the Orient Express* **reintroduce**, re-establish, restore, resurrect, relaunch, bring back, reinstall, regenerate, revitalize, resuscitate, breathe new life into, give a new lease of life to; reinvigorate, renew, awaken, wake up, rejuvenate, stimulate; *archaic* renovate.
OPPOSITE abolish.

revoke ▶ **verb** *the Board has the power to revoke the licence of a bank* **cancel**, repeal, rescind, reverse, abrogate, annul, nullify, declare null and void, make void, void, invalidate, render invalid, quash, abolish, set aside, countermand, retract, withdraw, overrule, override; *Law* vacate, avoid; *archaic* recall; *rare* disannul.
OPPOSITES introduce, enact; ratify.

revolt ▶ **verb 1** *the people revolted against colonial rule* **rebel**, rise up, rise, take to the streets, take up arms, riot, mutiny, take part in an uprising, show resistance; resist/oppose authority, disobey/defy authority, refuse to obey orders, be insubordinate.
2 *the sight and smell revolted him* **disgust**, sicken, nauseate, make someone sick, make someone feel sick, make someone's gorge rise, turn someone's stomach, upset, be repugnant to, repel, repulse, be repulsive to, make someone's flesh crawl, make someone shudder, put off, offend, be offensive to, cause offence to, shock, horrify; *informal* turn off; *N. Amer. informal* gross out.
▶ **noun** *there was an armed revolt in progress* **rebellion**, revolution, insurrection, mutiny, uprising, riot, rioting, rising, insurgence, insurgency, coup, overthrow, seizure of power, subversion, sedition, anarchy, disorder, protest, strike, act of resistance, act of defiance; *French* coup d'état, jacquerie; *German* putsch.

revolting ▶ **adjective** *the sink was covered in a revolting green scum* **disgusting**, sickening, nauseating, stomach-turning, stomach-churning, repulsive, repellent, repugnant, appalling, abominable, hideous, horrible, awful, dreadful, terrible, obnoxious, nauseating, vile, nasty, foul, loathsome, offensive, objectionable, off-putting, distasteful, disagreeable, uninviting; abhorrent, despicable, reprehensible, contemptible, odious, heinous, obscene, hateful, execrable; gruesome, grisly; *N. Amer.* vomitous; *informal* sick-making, ghastly, putrid, horrid, God-awful, gross, gut-churning, yucky, icky, cringe-making; *Brit. informal* beastly; *N. Amer. informal* skanky; *literary* noisome; *archaic* disgustful, loathly; *rare* rebarbative.
OPPOSITES attractive, pleasant.

revolution ▶ **noun 1** *the French Revolution* **rebellion**, revolt, insurrection, mutiny, uprising, riot, rioting, rising, insurgence, insurgency, coup, overthrow, seizure of power; subversion, sedition, anarchy, disorder, protest, strike, act of resistance, act of defiance; *French* coup d'état; *German* putsch; *rare* jacquerie.
2 *there has been a revolution in printing techniques* **dramatic change**, radical change, drastic/radical alteration, complete shift, sea change, metamorphosis, transformation, conversion, innovation, breakaway; reorganization, restructuring, reformation, remodelling, rearrangement, reorientation, regrouping, redistribution; upheaval, upset, disruption, convulsions, cataclysm; *informal* shake-up; *N. Amer. informal* shakedown; *humorous* transmogrification.
3 *the prop shaft turns 4.7 times for one revolution of a road wheel* **single turn**, turn, rotation, circle, whirl, twirl, spin, wheel, roll, round, cycle, circuit, lap.
4 *the rate of revolution of the earth* **turning**, gyration, rotation, circumrotation, wheeling, turning around, circling, whirling, twirling, spinning, swivelling, rolling, orbital motion, orbiting, orbit; *rare* circumgyration.

revolutionary ▶ **adjective 1** *revolutionary troops* **rebellious**, rebel, insurgent, rioting, mutinous, mutinying, renegade, insurrectionary, seditious, factious, insubordinate, subversive; rabble-rousing, inflammatory, extremist, anarchic; *rare* revolting, insurrectionist.
OPPOSITES moderate, law-abiding.
2 *a society undergoing revolutionary change* **thoroughgoing**, thorough, complete, total, entire, absolute, utter, comprehensive, exhaustive, sweeping, far-reaching, wide-ranging, extensive, profound; drastic, severe, serious, major, desperate, stringent, violent, forceful, rigorous, draconian.
3 *a revolutionary kind of wheelchair* **new**, novel, original, unusual, unfamiliar, unconventional, unorthodox, different, fresh, imaginative, creative, innovative, innovatory, innovational, inventive, ingenious, modern, ultra-modern, state-of-the-art, advanced, avant-garde, futuristic, pioneering, groundbreaking, trailblazing; rare, unique, singular, unprecedented, uncommon; experimental, untested, untried, unknown, surprising, strange, exotic, out of the ordinary, newfangled; *N. Amer.* left-

field; *rare* unhackneyed, new-fashioned, neoteric.
OPPOSITES conventional, orthodox.
▸ noun *his actions were not those of a revolutionary* **rebel**, insurgent, revolutionist, Bolshevik, mutineer, insurrectionary, agitator, subversive, guerrilla, anarchist; freedom fighter, resistance fighter; *rare* insurrectionist; *French rare* frondeur.

revolutionize ▸ verb *aerial photography revolutionized archaeology* **transform**, alter dramatically, transfigure, make far-reaching changes in, shake up, stir up, turn upside down, restructure, reorganize, rejig, reform, recast, reshape, remould, transmute, metamorphose; *humorous* transmogrify.

revolve ▸ verb **1** *overhead, the fan revolved slowly* **go round**, turn round, rotate, spin, whirl, pirouette, wheel.
2 *the moon revolves around the earth* **circle**, go, travel, orbit, gyrate, circulate, loop, wheel; *rare* encircle.
3 *a man whose life* **revolves around** *cars* **be concerned with**, be preoccupied with, be absorbed in, focus on, concentrate on, centre around, hang on, rely on, rest on, pivot on.
4 *they were revolving various thoughts in their minds* **think about**, give thought to, consider, reflect on, mull over, contemplate, study, meditate on, muse on, think over, think on, deliberate about/on, cogitate about/on, dwell on, brood on/over, agonize over, worry about, ruminate about/on/over, chew over, puzzle over, speculate about, weigh up, review, turn over; *archaic* pore on.

revulsion ▸ noun *he spoke of the country's revulsion at the bombing* **disgust**, repulsion, abhorrence, repugnance, nausea, loathing, horror, hatred, detestation, aversion, abomination, distaste, antipathy, dislike, contempt, odium; *archaic* disrelish; *rare* repellency, repellence.
OPPOSITES delight, liking.

reward ▸ noun **1** *the dog's owners have offered a reward for its safe return* **recompense**, prize, prize money, winnings, purse, award, honour, decoration, profit, advantage, benefit, bonus, plus, premium; **bounty**, price; present, gift, tip, gratuity, inducement, carrot, payment, consideration, return, requital; *informal* pay-off, cut, perk; *formal* perquisite; *archaic* guerdon, meed.
2 *he thought his reward cruel after such loyal service* **treatment**, handling, service, reception.
▸ verb *they were to be well rewarded for their work* **recompense**, pay, remunerate, give a bounty to, give a present to, make something worth someone's while, tip, honour, decorate, give an award to, recognize, requite; *archaic* guerdon.
OPPOSITE punish.

rewarding ▸ adjective *pilgrims found their journey a highly rewarding experience* **satisfying**, gratifying, pleasing, fulfilling, enriching, edifying, beneficial, illuminating, informative, worthwhile, advantageous, productive, fruitful, valuable.
OPPOSITE unrewarding.

reword ▸ verb *the rules were reworded in 1986* **rewrite**, rephrase, recast, put differently, put another way, put in other words, express differently, redraft, rework, revise, edit; paraphrase.

rewrite ▸ verb *pupils are asked to rewrite a document from an opposite point of view* **revise**, recast, rework, reword, rephrase, redraft.

rhetoric *See centre pages for list of* **Rhetorical Devices and Figures of Speech**
▸ noun **1** *he was considered to excel in this form of rhetoric* **oratory**, eloquence, power of speech, command of language, expression, way with words, delivery, diction.
2 *there is a good deal of rhetoric in this field* **bombast**, loftiness, turgidity, grandiloquence, magniloquence, ornateness, portentousness, pomposity, boastfulness, boasting, bragging, heroics, hyperbole, extravagant language, purple prose, pompousness, sonorousness; windiness, wordiness, verbosity, prolixity; *informal* hot air; *rare* tumidity, fustian, euphuism, orotundity.

rhetorical ▸ adjective **1** *the skilful use of such rhetorical devices like metaphor* **stylistic**, oratorical, linguistic, verbal.
2 *he had a tendency to engage in rhetorical hyperbole* **extravagant**, grandiloquent, magniloquent, high-flown, high-sounding, sonorous, lofty, orotund, bombastic, grandiose, pompous, pretentious, overblown, oratorical, turgid, flowery, florid, declamatory, Ciceronian; *informal* highfalutin; *rare* tumid, epideictic, fustian, euphuistic, aureate, Demosthenic, Demosthenean.

rhyme ▸ noun *the words of a famous rhyme were going through her head* **poem**, piece of poetry, verse, ditty, ode, limerick, song, jingle, verse composition, metrical composition; (**rhymes**) poetry, versification, rhyming, doggerel; *rare* verselet.

rhythm ▸ noun **1** *the rhythm of the rock music thumped relentlessly* **beat**, cadence, tempo, time, pace, pulse, throb, lilt, swing; *technical* periodicity.
2 *poetic features such as rhythm, rhyme, and alliteration* **metre**, measure, pattern, stress, accent, pulse, time, flow, cadence.
3 *part of the normal rhythm of daily life* **pattern**, flow, tempo, regular features, recurrent nature.

rhythmic ▸ adjective *a rhythmic orchestral accompaniment* **pulsing**, with a steady pulse, rhythmical, metrical, measured, throbbing, beating, pulsating, cadenced, lilting, repeated, periodic, regular, steady, even, paced.
OPPOSITES smooth, irregular.

rib ▸ noun

WORD LINKS
relating to ribs **costal**
between ribs **intercostal**

ribald ▸ adjective *the more ribald the men's remarks, the faster she walked* **bawdy**, indecent, risqué, rude, racy, broad, earthy, Rabelaisian, spicy, suggestive, titillating, improper, naughty, indelicate, indecorous, off colour, locker-room; vulgar, dirty, filthy, smutty, crude, offensive, salacious, coarse, obscene, lewd, pornographic, X-rated; *informal* blue, raunchy; *Brit. informal* fruity, near the knuckle, saucy; *N. Amer. informal* gamy; *euphemistic* adult.

ribaldry ▸ noun *not for him the slightly raucous ribaldry with which most of the chaps used to greet us* **bawdy remarks/jokes/songs**, **bawdiness**, indecency, rudeness, raciness, broadness, earthiness, spiciness, suggestiveness, titillation, impropriety, naughtiness, indelicacy, indecorousness; **obscenity**, vulgarity, dirt, filth, filthiness, smut, smuttiness, crudeness, salaciousness, coarseness, lewdness, pornography; *informal* blueness, raunchiness; *Brit. informal* fruitiness, sauciness; *rare* bawdry, salacity.

rich ▸ adjective **1** *rich people pay higher rates of tax* **wealthy**, affluent, moneyed, well off, well-to-do, with deep pockets, prosperous, opulent, substantial, propertied; *N. Amer.* silk-stocking; *informal* rolling in money, rolling in it, in the money, loaded, stinking rich, filthy rich, well heeled, flush, made of money, quids in, worth a packet, worth a bundle, on easy street; *informal, dated* oofy.
OPPOSITE poor.
2 *the castle houses rich furnishings and tapestries* **sumptuous**, opulent, luxurious, luxury, de luxe, palatial, lavish, lavishly appointed, gorgeous, splendid, magnificent, resplendent, lush, plush, costly, expensive, upmarket, fancy, stylish, elegant, exquisite, grandiose; *informal* posh, ritzy, swanky, plushy, classy, glitzy; *Brit. informal* swish; *N. Amer. informal* swank; *rare* palatian, Lucullan.
OPPOSITES plain, austere, cheap.
3 *the walled garden was already* **rich in** *spring flowers* **abounding in**, well provided with, well supplied with, well stocked with, replete with, abundant in, rife with, crammed with, crowded with, packed with, jammed with, stuffed with, teeming with, swarming with, overflowing with, bursting with, brimful with, brimming with, loaded with, overloaded with, thick with, solid with; *informal* jam-packed with, chock-a-block with, chock-full of; *Austral./NZ informal* chocker with.
4 *the town offers a rich supply of coffee shops and restaurants* **plentiful**, abundant, copious, ample, profuse, lavish, liberal, generous, bountiful, large, huge, great, bumper, overflowing, superabundant, infinite, inexhaustible, prolific; *S. African informal* lank; *literary* bounteous, plenteous.
OPPOSITES meagre, poor.
5 *blackcurrant bushes require fairly rich soil* **fertile**, productive, fecund, fruitful, lush, arable.
OPPOSITE barren.
6 *mussels should not be bathed in a rich sauce* **creamy**, fatty, buttery, heavy, full-flavoured.
OPPOSITES light, delicate.
7 *a lovely, rich, oaky wine* **full-bodied**, heavy, luscious, robust, opulent, big, fruity, fat.
OPPOSITE light.
8 *the rich colours of autumn* **strong**, deep, full, intense, vivid, brilliant, warm, vibrant, graphic.
OPPOSITES delicate, pastel.
9 *her rich contralto voice* **sonorous**, full, resonant, ringing, vibrant, deep, clear, mellow, mellifluous, melodious, full-bodied, strong, booming, fruity; *rare* mellifluent.
OPPOSITES thin, reedy.
10 (*informal*) *that's rich, coming from you* **preposterous**, outrageous, unreasonable, absurd, ironic, ridiculous, ludicrous, laughable, risible; *informal* a bit much, a joke, a laugh, priceless; *Brit. informal* over the top, OTT, a bit thick.

riches ▸ plural noun **1** *he may decide to invest some of his new-found riches here* **money**, wealth, finance(s), funds, cash, hard cash, (filthy) lucre, wherewithal, means, assets, liquid assets, capital, resources, reserves; opulence, gold, property, treasure, affluence, substance, prosperity; *informal* dough, bread, loot, the ready, readies, shekels, moolah, the necessary, boodle, dibs, gelt, ducats, rhino, gravy, scratch, stuff, oof; *Brit. informal* dosh, brass, lolly, spondulicks, wonga, ackers; *N. Amer. informal* greenbacks, simoleons, bucks, jack, mazuma, dinero; *Austral./NZ informal* Oscar; *informal, dated* splosh, green, tin; *Brit. dated* l.s.d.; *N. Amer. informal, dated* kale, rocks, shinplasters; *archaic* pelf.
2 *we were able to see many of the underwater riches of the island* **resources**,

R

treasure(s), bounty, jewels, gems, valuables, masterpieces, pride, cornucopia.

richly ▶ adverb **1** *he gazed round the richly furnished audience chamber* **sumptuously**, opulently, luxuriously, palatially, lavishly, gorgeously, splendidly, magnificently, resplendently, plushly, expensively, fancily, stylishly, elegantly, exquisitely, grandiosely; *informal* poshly, ritzily, swankily, classily, glitzily; *Brit. informal* swishly.
OPPOSITES meanly, shabbily.
2 *Anne is finding the joy that she richly deserves* **fully**, thoroughly, in full measure, well, completely, wholly, totally, entirely, absolutely, altogether, amply, utterly, perfectly, quite, in every respect, in all respects.

rickety ▶ adjective *we went carefully up the rickety stairs* **shaky**, unsteady, unsound, unsafe, tottering, crumbling, decaying, disintegrating, tumbledown, broken-down, dilapidated, ramshackle, derelict, ruinous, falling to pieces, decrepit; *informal* shambly, geriatric; *N. Amer. informal* shacky.

rid ▶ verb *they had rid the building of all asbestos* **clear**, free, make free, cleanse, purge, purify, empty, strip, scour, void, relieve, deliver.
□ **get rid of 1** *we'll have to get rid of some of our stuff* **dispose of**, do away with, throw away, throw out, toss out, clear out, discard, scrap, remove, dispense with, lose, dump, bin, unload, jettison, dismiss, expel, eject, weed out, root out; *informal* chuck (away), ditch, junk, get shut of; *Brit. informal* get shot of, see the back of; *N. Amer. informal* shuck off.
2 *hawks were introduced to get rid of the rats* **destroy**, abolish, eliminate, banish, annihilate, obliterate, wipe out, kill; *N. Amer. informal* nuke.

riddle[1] ▶ noun *they hope for an answer to the riddle of why he was killed* **puzzle**, conundrum, brain-teaser, Chinese puzzle, problem, unsolved problem, question, poser, enigma, mystery, quandary, paradox; *Zen Buddhism* koan; *informal* stumper.

riddle[2] ▶ verb **1** *his car was riddled by sniper fire* **perforate**, hole, make/put/punch holes in, pierce, penetrate, puncture, honeycomb, pepper; prick, gore, bore through, transfix.
2 *he died eight months later, riddled with cancer* **permeate**, **suffuse**, fill, pervade, spread through, imbue, inform, charge, saturate, overrun, take over, overspread, infiltrate, run through, filter through, be diffused through, invade, beset, pester, plague.
3 *when sowing small seeds, the soil must be riddled* **sieve**, sift, strain, screen, filter, purify, refine, winnow; *archaic* bolt, griddle.

ride ▶ verb **1** *she can ride a horse* **sit on**, mount, be mounted on, bestride; **manage**, handle, control, steer.
2 *two men were riding round the town on stolen motor bikes* **travel**, go, move, progress, proceed, make one's way; drive, cycle; trot, canter, gallop.
▶ noun *he took us for a ride in his car* **trip**, journey, drive, run, expedition, excursion, outing, jaunt, tour, airing, turn, sally; lift; *informal* junket, spin, tootle, joyride, tool; *Scottish informal* hurl.

ridicule ▶ noun *he was subjected to ridicule by his colleagues* **mockery**, derision, laughter, scorn, scoffing, contempt, jeering, sneering, sneers, jibes, jibing, joking, teasing, taunts, taunting, ragging, chaffing, twitting, raillery, sarcasm, satire, lampoon, burlesque, caricature, parody; *informal* kidding, kidology, ribbing, joshing; *Brit. informal* winding up, taking the mickey; *N. Amer. informal* goofing, razzing, pulling someone's chain; *Austral./NZ informal* chiacking; *archaic* sport; *Brit. vulgar slang* taking the piss.
OPPOSITES praise, respect.
▶ verb *it was easy to ridicule him in his battered old hat* **deride**, mock, laugh at, heap scorn on, hold up to shame, hold up to ridicule, expose to ridicule, jeer at, jibe at, sneer at, show up, treat with contempt, scorn, make fun of, poke fun at, make jokes about, laugh to scorn, scoff at, pillory, be sarcastic about, satirize, lampoon, burlesque, caricature, parody, tease, taunt, rag, chaff, twit; *informal* kid, rib, josh, wind up, take the mickey out of; *N. Amer. informal* goof on, rag on, razz, pull someone's chain; *Austral./NZ informal* chiack, poke mullock at, sling off at; *Brit. vulgar slang* take the piss (out of); *dated* make sport of; *archaic* quiz, flout (at).
OPPOSITE praise.

CHOOSE THE RIGHT WORD

ridicule, mockery, derision

See MOCKERY.

ridiculous ▶ adjective **1** *the car looked ridiculous with a yellow child's cot strapped to the roof* **laughable**, absurd, comical, funny, hilarious, humorous, risible, derisory, droll, amusing, entertaining, diverting, farcical, slapstick, silly, facetious, ludicrous, hysterical, riotous, side-splitting; *informal* crazy, priceless; *dated* killing; *rare* derisible.
OPPOSITE serious.
2 *it was a ridiculous suggestion* **pointless**, senseless, silly, foolish, foolhardy, stupid, inane, nonsensical, fatuous, childish, puerile, half-baked, hare-brained, scatterbrained, feather-brained, ill-thought-out, ill-conceived, crackpot, idiotic, brainless, mindless, witless, vacuous, asinine, moronic; *informal* half-witted.
OPPOSITE sensible.
3 *this is a ridiculous exaggeration* **absurd**, preposterous, stupid, ludicrous, farcical, laughable, comical, risible, nonsensical, pointless, senseless, insane, unreasonable, irrational, illogical, outrageous, shocking, astonishing, monstrous, unbelievable, incredible, unthinkable; *informal* crazy.
OPPOSITE reasonable.

rife ▶ adjective **1** *violence is rife in our cities* **widespread**, general, common, universal, extensive, ubiquitous, global, omnipresent, everywhere, present everywhere, pandemic, epidemic, endemic, inescapable, insidious, prevalent, penetrating, pervading, pervasive, permeating, immanent; *rare* permeative, suffusive, permeant.
OPPOSITES scarce, unknown.
2 *the village was rife with gossip* **overflowing**, bursting, alive, swarming, teeming, seething, lousy; **abounding in**, abundant in, overrun by, full of.
OPPOSITE devoid of.

riff-raff ▶ noun (*informal*) *she said that she thought my friends were riff-raff* **rabble**, scum, refuse, garbage, rubbish, trash, vermin, the lowest of the low, in the underclass, the dregs of society, good-for-nothings, undesirables; *informal* peasants; *Brit. informal* as common as muck.
OPPOSITES elite, high-class.

rifle ▶ verb **1** *she rifled through the contents of her wardrobe* **rummage**, search, hunt, forage, sift, rake; ransack, comb, turn upside down, scour.
2 *the man kept her talking while an accomplice rifled her home* **burgle**, rob, steal from, loot, raid, plunder, sack, ransack, pillage.

rift ▶ noun **1** *a deep rift in the Antarctic ice* **crack**, fault, flaw, split, break, breach, fissure, fracture, cleft, crevice, gap, cranny, slit, chink, interstice, cavity, opening, space, hole, aperture.
2 *a rift between the government and the presidency* **breach**, division, split; quarrel, squabble, disagreement, difference of opinion, falling-out, fight, row, altercation, argument, war of words, dispute, conflict, contretemps, clash, wrangle, tussle, feud, battle royal; estrangement, alienation, schism; *informal* run-in, spat, scrap; *Brit. informal*, ding-dong, bust-up.

rig[1] ▶ verb **1** *these vessels were rigged with a single square sail* **equip**, kit out, fit out/up, supply, outfit, furnish, accoutre, array, provide, provision, stock, arm.
2 *I rigged myself out in all-American gear* **dress**, attire, clothe, robe, garb, array, deck out, drape, accoutre, outfit, costume, get up, turn out, trick out/up; *informal* doll up; *literary* bedizen, caparison; *archaic* apparel, invest, habit, trap out.
3 *Alfred will rig up a bit of shelter* **set up hastily**, erect hastily, assemble hastily, throw together, cobble together, put together, whip up, improvise, devise, contrive, jury-rig; *Brit. informal* knock up.
▶ noun **1** *he had left his CB radio rig switched on* **apparatus**, appliance, piece of equipment, tool, machine, device, tackle, gear, mechanism, outfit, plant, kit, implement, utensil, instrument, contraption, contrivance, gadget, structure, system; *informal* gizmo.
2 *an officer in the rig of the American Army Air Corps* **uniform**, costume, ensemble, outfit, suit, livery, attire, clothes, clothing, garments, dress, garb, regimentals, accoutrements, regalia, finery, trappings, disguise; *Brit.* kit, strip; *informal* get-up, gear, togs; *Brit. informal* rig-out; *formal* apparel; *archaic* array, raiment, habit, habiliments, vestments.

rig[2] ▶ verb *he will not need to rig the election or buy voters* **manipulate**, arrange fraudulently, interfere with, influence, gerrymander, juggle, massage, distort, misrepresent, pervert, manoeuvre, tamper with, tinker with, doctor; **falsify**, forge, fake, engineer, trump up; *informal* fix, cook; *Brit. informal* fiddle.

rigging ▶ noun. *See centre pages for lists of* **Rigging** **Sails**

right ▶ adjective **1** *I do not believe that it would be right to reverse this decision* **just**, fair, equitable, good, upright, righteous, virtuous, proper, moral, morally justified, ethical, honourable, honest, principled; lawful, legal.
OPPOSITES wrong, unjust.
2 *he was first to give the right answer | you haven't gone about it the right way* **correct**, accurate, without error, unerring, exact, precise; accepted, proper, valid, orthodox, conventional, established, official, formal, regular; *informal* on the mark; *Brit. informal* spot on; *French* de règle; *archaic* meet.
OPPOSITES wrong, inaccurate.
3 *the right person for the job* **suitable**, appropriate, acceptable, fitting, fit, correct, proper, desirable, preferable, ideal; well suited, well qualified.
OPPOSITES wrong, unsuitable.
4 *you've come at just the right moment* **opportune**, advantageous, favourable, auspicious, propitious, promising, heaven-sent, golden, good, lucky, happy, fortunate, benign, providential, felicitous, timely, well timed, ripe, seasonable, convenient, expedient, suitable, appropriate, apt, fitting.
OPPOSITES wrong, inopportune.
5 *unfortunately he is not quite right in the head* **sane**, in one's right mind, of sound mind, in possession of all one's faculties, able to think/reason clearly, lucid, rational, coherent, balanced, well balanced; *Latin* compos mentis; *informal* all there.
OPPOSITES insane, of unsound mind.

6 *John's face does not look right* **healthy**, in good health, fine, hale, in good shape, in trim, in good trim, well, fit, fighting fit, normal, sound, up to par; *informal* up to scratch, in the pink.
OPPOSITES wrong, unhealthy.
7 *my right hand* **right-hand**; *Nautical* port; *Heraldry* dexter.
OPPOSITES left; starboard; sinister.
8 (*informal*) *the library is a right mess* **absolute**, complete, total, real, out-and-out, thorough, thoroughgoing, downright, perfect, utter, sheer, consummate, unmitigated, unqualified, veritable, in every respect, unalloyed; *Austral./NZ informal* fair; *archaic* arrant.

▶ **adverb 1** *she was right at the limit of her patience* **completely**, fully, entirely, totally, wholly, absolutely, altogether, utterly, thoroughly, quite; all the way, to the maximum extent, to the hilt, in all respects, in every respect.
2 *the hotel is right in the middle of the village* **exactly**, precisely, directly, immediately, just, squarely, square, dead; *informal* bang, slap bang, smack, slap, plumb; *N. Amer. informal* smack dab.
3 *keep going* **right on** *till you come to a blue house* **straight**, directly, in a straight line, as the crow flies.
OPPOSITE indirectly.
4 (*informal*) *he'll be right down* **straight**, **immediately**, instantly, at once, straight away, right away, now, right now, this/that (very) minute, this/that instant, in/like a flash, directly, on the spot, forthwith, without further/more ado, promptly, quickly, without delay, then and there, there and then, here and now, a.s.a.p., as soon as possible, as quickly as possible, with all speed; *N. Amer.* in short order; *French* tout de suite; *informal* straight off, toot sweet, double quick, in double quick time, p.d.q. (pretty damn quick), pronto, before you can say Jack Robinson; *N. Amer. informal* lickety-split; *Indian informal* ekdam; *archaic* straightway, instanter, forthright.
OPPOSITES sometime, later, not now.
5 *I think I heard right* **correctly**, accurately, properly, exactly, precisely, aright, rightly, perfectly, unerringly, faultlessly, truly.
OPPOSITES wrong, imperfectly.
6 *you get treated right there* **justly**, fairly, equitably, impartially, well, properly, morally, ethically, honourably, honestly, lawfully, legally.
OPPOSITE unjustly.
7 *things usually turn out right in the end* **well**, for the better, for the best, favourably, happily, advantageously, to one's advantage, beneficially, profitably, providentially, luckily, opportunely, conveniently, to one's satisfaction.
OPPOSITES badly, for the worse.

□ **right away** *I'll go and find them right away* **at once**, straight away, now, right now, this/that (very) minute, this/that instant, immediately, instantly, in/like a flash, directly, on the spot, forthwith, without further/more ado, promptly, quickly, without delay, then and there, there and then, here and now, a.s.a.p., as soon as possible, as quickly as possible, with all speed; *N. Amer.* in short order; *French* tout de suite; *informal* straight off, toot sweet, double quick, in double quick time, p.d.q. (pretty damn quick), pronto, before you can say Jack Robinson, from the word go; *N. Amer. informal* lickety-split; *Indian informal* ekdam; *archaic* straight, straightway, instanter, forthright.
OPPOSITES sometime, later, not now, in due course.

▶ **noun 1** *the difference between right and wrong* **goodness**, rightness, righteousness, virtue, virtuousness, integrity, rectitude, uprightness, principle, propriety, morality, truth, truthfulness, honesty, honour, honourableness, justice, justness, fairness, equity, equitableness, impartiality; lawfulness, legality.
OPPOSITE wrong.
2 *everyone has the right to say no* **entitlement**, prerogative, privilege, advantage, due, birthright, liberty, authority, authorization, power, licence, permission, dispensation, leave, consent, warrant, charter, franchise, sanction, exemption, immunity, indemnity; *French* carte blanche; *Law, historical* droit.

□ **by rights** *by rights, these young people should have been destined for college or university* **properly**, in fairness, correctly, legally, technically, in (all) conscience; *Law* de jure.
OPPOSITE unfairly.

□ **in the right** *technically he is in the right* **justified**, vindicated, borne out, with right on one's side, with the law on one's side, right.
OPPOSITE in the wrong.

□ **put something to rights remedy**, put right, set right, set to rights, rectify, retrieve, solve, fix, resolve, sort out, put in order; **straighten out**, deal with, correct, repair, mend, redress, make good; **improve**, amend, ameliorate, make better, better.

□ **within one's rights** *she was within her rights to do this* **entitled**, permitted, allowed, at liberty, empowered, authorized, qualified, licensed, justified.

▶ **verb 1** *you must be able to right a capsized dinghy* **turn the right way up again**, turn back over, set upright again, stand upright again.
OPPOSITES invert, capsize.
2 *he would do what was necessary to right the situation* **remedy**, put right, set right, put to rights, set to rights, rectify, retrieve, solve, fix, resolve, sort out, put in order; **straighten out**, deal with, correct, repair, mend, redress, make good; **improve**, amend, ameliorate, make better, better.
OPPOSITE worsen.
3 *my bill seeks to right this serious wrong* **rectify**, correct, put right, set right, make right, sort out, deal with, remedy, repair, fix, cure, resolve, settle, square, make amends for; avenge, vindicate.

WORD LINKS

relating to the right-hand side	**dextral**
related prefix	**dextro-** (e.g. ***dextrorotatory***)

righteous ▶ **adjective 1** *the scriptures contain rules for righteous living* **good**, virtuous, upright, upstanding, decent, worthy; **ethical**, **principled**, moral, high-minded, law-abiding, just, honest, innocent, faultless, honourable, blameless, guiltless, irreproachable, sinless, uncorrupted, saintly, angelic, pure, noble, noble-minded, pious, God-fearing.
OPPOSITES wicked, sinful.
2 *a look of righteous anger came over his face* **justifiable**, justified, legitimate, defensible, supportable, just, rightful; well founded, sound, valid, admissible, allowable, understandable, excusable, acceptable, reasonable, sensible.
OPPOSITE unjustifiable.

righteousness ▶ **noun** *the successful are always tempted to regard their success as a reward for righteousness* **goodness**, virtue, virtuousness, uprightness, decency, integrity, worthiness, rectitude, probity, morality, ethicalness, high-mindedness, justice, honesty, honour, honourableness, innocence, blamelessness, guiltlessness, irreproachability, sinlessness, saintliness, purity, nobility, noble-mindedness, piety, piousness.
OPPOSITES wickedness, sinfulness.

rightful ▶ **adjective 1** *I intend to return it to its rightful owner* **legal**, lawful, licit, sanctioned; **real**, true, proper, correct, recognized, genuine, warranted, authentic, acknowledged, approved, licensed, statutory, constitutional, valid; *Latin* bona fide; *Law* de jure; *informal* legit, kosher.
OPPOSITE wrongful.
2 *women have long been denied their rightful place in society* **deserved**, well deserved, merited, earned, well earned; **due**, just, right, fair, proper, fitting, appropriate, apt, suitable, reasonable.
OPPOSITE undeserved.

right-wing ▶ **adjective** *the right-wing opposition party* **conservative**, rightist, ultra-conservative; blimpish, diehard, reactionary, traditionalist, conventional, traditional, old-fashioned, unprogressive; *N. Amer.* Birchite.
OPPOSITES left-wing, radical.

rigid ▶ **adjective 1** *sandwiches are best packed in a rigid container* **stiff**, hard, firm, inflexible, non-flexible, unbending, unyielding, inelastic; taut, tight; *rare* impliable, unmalleable.
OPPOSITES flexible, plastic.
2 *many dog owners establish a rigid routine for feeding* **fixed**, set, firm, inflexible, unalterable, unchangeable, immutable, unvarying, invariable, hard and fast, cast-iron.
OPPOSITE flexible.
3 *poorer nations warned against a rigid approach to IMF funding* **strict**, severe, stern, stringent, rigorous, inflexible, uncompromising, resolute, determined, immovable, unshakeable; unrelenting, intransigent, unyielding, unwavering, unswerving, obdurate, unadaptable, adamant.
OPPOSITES flexible, lenient.

rigmarole ▶ **noun 1** *she went through all the rigmarole of dressing and making up* **lengthy process**, **fuss**, fuss and bother, bother, commotion, trouble, folderol, ado, pother; *informal* palaver, song and dance, performance, to-do, carry-on, carrying-on, kerfuffle, hoo-ha, hullabaloo, ballyhoo, business, pantomime, hassle, hoopla; *NZ informal* bobsy-die.
2 *that rigmarole about the house being haunted was just to keep people away* **lengthy story/explanation**, saga, yarn, recitation, burble, burbling, maundering, shaggy-dog story; *informal* spiel, banging on, palaver.

rigorous ▶ **adjective 1** *their rigorous attention to detail paid off* **meticulous**, punctilious, conscientious, careful, diligent, attentive, ultra-careful, scrupulous, painstaking, exact, precise, accurate, correct, thorough, studious, exhaustive, mathematical, detailed, perfectionist, methodical, particular, religious, strict; **fussy**, fastidious, hair-splitting, finicky, finical, demanding, exacting, pedantic; *informal* nit-picking, pernickety; *N. Amer. informal* persnickety; *archaic* nice, overnice, laborious.
OPPOSITE slapdash.
2 *the rigorous enforcement of minor school rules* **strict**, severe, stern, stringent, austere, spartan, tough, hard, harsh, rigid, cruel, savage, relentless, unsparing, inflexible, authoritarian, despotic, draconian, intransigent, uncompromising, demanding, exacting.
OPPOSITE lax.
3 *rigorous yachting conditions* **harsh**, severe, bad, bleak, extreme, inclement; unpleasant, disagreeable, foul, nasty, filthy; stormy, blustery, squally, wild, tempestuous, storm-tossed, violent, heavy, heaving, raging, choppy, agitated.
OPPOSITES gentle, mild.

rigour ▶ **noun 1** *the mines were operated under conditions of some rigour* **strictness**, severity, sternness, stringency, austerity, toughness, hardness, harshness, rigidity, inflexibility; cruelty, savagery, relentlessness,

unsparingness, authoritarianism, despotism, intransigence.
OPPOSITE laxness.
2 *a speech noted for its intellectual rigour* **meticulousness**, thoroughness, carefulness, attention to detail, diligence, scrupulousness, exactness, exactitude, precision, accuracy, correctness, strictness, punctiliousness, conscientiousness; *archaic* nicety.
OPPOSITE carelessness.
3 (**rigours**) *she could not face the rigours of the journey* **hardship**, harshness, severity, adversity, suffering, privation, ordeal, misery, distress, trial; discomfort, inconvenience.
OPPOSITE pleasures.

rig-out ▶ noun (*Brit. informal*) *some of her rig-outs are gorgeous.* See OUTFIT *sense 1.*

rile ▶ verb (*informal*) *he had a sceptical air guaranteed to rile Ursula* **irritate**, annoy, bother, vex, provoke, displease, upset, offend, affront, anger, exasperate, infuriate, gall, irk, get/put someone's back up, disgruntle, pique, rankle with, nettle, needle, ruffle, get on someone's nerves, ruffle someone's feathers, make someone's hackles rise, raise someone's hackles, rub up the wrong way; *informal* peeve, aggravate, miff, get, get to, bug, get under someone's skin, get in someone's hair, get up someone's nose, hack off, get someone's goat; *Brit. informal* nark, get on someone's wick, give someone the hump, wind up, get across; *N. Amer. informal* tick off, rankle, ride, gravel; *vulgar slang* piss off; *Brit. vulgar slang* get on someone's tits; *rare* exacerbate, hump, rasp.
OPPOSITES conciliate, soothe.

rim ▶ noun **1** *she stared at him over the rim of her cup* **brim**, edge, lip.
2 *the limestone formed a jagged rim along the lake* **edge**, **border**, side, verge, margin, brink, fringe, boundary, perimeter, circumference, limits, periphery, bound, extremity; *literary* marge, bourn, skirt.

rind ▶ noun *add the grated rind of one lemon* **skin**, peel, covering, zest; hull, pod, shell, husk, crust, shuck, capsule, outer layer, bark; hide; *technical* epicarp, pericarp, exocarp; *rare* integument.

ring[1] ▶ noun **1** *a ring round the moon means rain* **circle**, circlet, band, round, loop, hoop, circuit, halo, disc.
2 *she wasn't wearing a ring* **wedding ring**, band of gold, marriage token.
3 *a circus ring | a boxing ring* **arena**, enclosure, area, field, ground, platform; amphitheatre, colosseum, stadium.
4 *a ring of onlookers forms around them* **circle**, group, knot, cluster, bunch, band, gathering, throng, crowd, flock, assemblage, mob, pack.
5 *a large spy ring existed right under their noses* **gang**, syndicate, cartel, mob, band, organization, confederation, confederacy, federation, union, association, circle, society, combine, consortium, alliance, league, cabal, cell, coterie, crew, junta.
▶ verb *riot police ringed the building* **circle**, encircle, circumscribe, encompass, loop, gird, girdle, enclose, surround, embrace, form a ring round, go around, hem in, fence in, confine, seal off.

WORD LINKS
ring-shaped **annular**

ring[2] ▶ verb **1** *the vicar arranged to ring the church bells | she rang the doorbell* **toll**, sound, strike, peal; press, set off; *rare* tintinnabulate.
2 *church bells rang all day* **chime**, ring out, chime out, toll, peal, knell; sound, clang, bong, clink, ding, jingle, tinkle.
3 *the whole cellar rang with laughter* **resound**, reverberate, resonate, echo, re-echo; vibrate, pulsate.
4 *I'll ring you tomorrow* **telephone**, phone, call, call up, ring up, give someone a ring, give someone a call, get someone on the phone, get on the phone to, get, reach, dial, make/place a call (to); *informal* buzz, give someone a buzz; *Brit. informal* bell, give someone a bell, give someone a tinkle, get on the blower to; *N. Amer. informal* get someone on the horn.
□ **ring something in** *the bells were beginning to ring in the new year* **herald**, signal, announce, proclaim, usher in, introduce, launch, celebrate, mark, signify, indicate, give notice of; *literary* betoken, harbinger, knell.
▶ noun **1** *there was the sharp ring of a bell from the gate* **ringing**, chime, carillon, toll, tolling, peal, knell; sound, sounding, clang, clanging, clink, clinking, ding, dinging, jingle, jingling, tinkle, tinkling; *archaic* tocsin; *rare* tintinnabulation.
2 *I'll give Chris a ring* **call**, telephone call, phone call; *informal* buzz; *Brit. informal* bell, tinkle.

rinse ▶ verb *he* **rinsed out** *a couple of mugs | Jean rinsed the crumbs off the plates* **wash**, wash out, wash lightly, clean, cleanse, bathe, dip, drench, splash, hose down, swill, sluice; flush out/away, wash off.

riot ▶ noun **1** *there was a riot when he was arrested* **uproar**, rampage, furore, tumult, commotion, upheaval, disturbance, street fight, melee, row, scuffle, fracas, fray, affray, brawl, free-for-all; violent disorder, violence, mob violence, street fighting, vandalism, frenzy, mayhem, turmoil, lawlessness, anarchy; *N. Amer. informal* wilding.
2 *the garden was a riot of colour* **mass**, sea, lavish display, splash, extravagance, extravaganza, flourish, show, exhibition.
□ **run riot 1** *family rooms are useful for letting noisier children run riot* **go on the rampage**, rampage, riot, run amok, go berserk, get out of control, run free, go undisciplined; *informal* raise hell.
2 *in rainforest, the daily downpours let vegetation run riot* **grow profusely**, spread uncontrolled, increase rapidly, grow rapidly, luxuriate, spread like wildfire, burgeon, prosper; multiply, mushroom, snowball, escalate, rocket.
▶ verb *the miners rioted and attacked the local Party HQ* **rampage**, go on the rampage, run riot, take to the streets, fight in the streets, start a fight, raise an uproar, cause an affray, run/go wild, run amok, go berserk, fight, brawl, scuffle; *informal* raise hell.

riotous ▶ adjective **1** *the match was abandoned after a demonstration in the National Stadium turned riotous* **unruly**, rowdy, disorderly, disruptive, out of control, rioting, uncontrollable, ungovernable, unmanageable, unbiddable, insubordinate, undisciplined, turbulent, uproarious, tumultuous; violent, wild, ugly, brawling, lawless, anarchic.
OPPOSITES law-abiding, peaceable, calm.
2 *a riotous party* **boisterous**, lively, loud, noisy, rip-roaring, unrestrained, uninhibited, roisterous, uproarious, unruly, rollicking; abandoned, orgiastic, debauched, depraved; *Brit. informal* rumbustious; *N. Amer. informal* rambunctious; *archaic* robustious.
OPPOSITES restrained, quiet.

rip ▶ verb **1** *the man threatened to rip the posters down* **tear**, snatch, jerk, tug, wrench, wrest, prise, force, heave, haul, drag, pull, twist, peel, pluck, grab, seize; *informal* yank.
2 *she ripped Leo's note into tiny pieces* **tear**, slit, cut, gash, cleave, slash, claw, savage, mangle, mutilate, hack; *literary* rend.
▶ noun *a green corduroy jacket with a rip in the sleeve* **tear**, slit, split, rent, laceration, cut, gash, slash.

ripe ▶ adjective **1** *a ripe tomato* **mature**, ripened, fully developed, full grown, ready to eat, soft, lush, juicy, tender; luscious, sweet, full-flavoured, mellow.
OPPOSITES unripe, green.
2 *the former dock is ripe for development* **ready**, fit, suitable, right.
OPPOSITES unready, unsuitable.
3 *he lived to the ripe old age of ninety* **advanced**, hoary, venerable, old.
OPPOSITES young, early.
4 *the time is ripe for his return* **opportune**, advantageous, favourable, auspicious, propitious, promising, heaven-sent, good, right, fortunate, benign, providential, felicitous, well timed, seasonable, convenient, expedient, suitable, appropriate, apt, fitting.
OPPOSITE unsuitable.

ripen ▶ verb **1** *tomatoes ripen faster when placed on a window ledge* **become ripe**, mature, come to maturity, mellow; become tender.
2 *to ripen melons, keep them at room temperature for a few days* **make ripe**, mature, bring to maturity, mellow.

rip-off ▶ noun (*informal*) *another victim of the pension rip-off* **fraud**, swindle, fraudulent scheme, confidence trick, mare's nest; overcharging; *informal* con, con trick, scam, flimflam, gyp, kite; *Brit. informal* ramp, twist, swizz, daylight robbery; *N. Amer. informal* rip, shakedown, hustle, grift, bunco, boondoggle; *Austral. informal* rort; *Brit. archaic, informal* do, flanker, have.

riposte ▶ noun *his mother forestalled his indignant riposte by replacing the receiver* **retort**, counter, rejoinder, sally, return, retaliation, answer, reply, response; *informal* comeback.
▶ verb *'And heaven help you,' riposted Sally* **retort**, counter, rejoin, return, retaliate, hurl back, fling back, snap back, answer, reply, respond, say in response; round on someone, come back.

ripple ▶ noun *he blew ripples in the surface of his coffee* **wavelet**, wave, undulation, ripplet, ridge, crease, wrinkle, ruffle, pucker.
▶ verb *before her the sea rippled placidly | a breeze rippled the surface of the lake* **form ripples (on)**, flow in wavelets, undulate, popple, lap, purl, babble; form something into ridges, crease, wrinkle, ruffle, pucker.

rise ▶ verb **1** *the sun rose across the bay* **move up**/**upwards**, come/go up, make one's/its way up, arise, ascend, climb, climb up, mount, soar.
OPPOSITES fall, descend, set.
2 *the mountains rising above us* **loom**, tower, soar, rise up, rear (up), stand high, reach high.
3 *prices rose by over 3%* **go up**, get higher, increase, grow, advance, soar, shoot up, surge (up), leap, jump, rocket, escalate, spiral.
OPPOSITE drop.
4 *living standards have risen substantially* **improve**, get better, advance, go up, get higher, soar, shoot up.
OPPOSITE worsen.
5 *his voice rose in anger* **get higher**, grow, increase, become louder, swell, intensify.
OPPOSITE drop.
6 *he rose from his chair* **stand up**, get/rise to one's feet, get up, jump up, leap up, spring up; become erect, straighten up; *literary* arise.
OPPOSITE sit.
7 *he rises every day at dawn* **get up**, get out of bed, rouse oneself, stir, bestir oneself, be up and about; *informal* rise and shine, shake a leg, surface; *literary* arise.

OPPOSITES go to bed, retire.
8 *the court rose at midday* **adjourn**, recess, be suspended, suspend proceedings, pause, break off, take a break; *informal* knock off, take five.
OPPOSITES continue, resume.
9 *he rose through the ranks to become managing director* **make progress**, make headway, make strides, forge ahead, come on, climb, advance, get on, make/work one's way, be promoted.
10 *he refused to* **rise to** *the bait* **react to**, respond to, take.
11 *Christ rose again on the third day* **come back to life**, be raised from the dead, come back from the dead, be resurrected, be restored to life, revive, be revived.
OPPOSITE die.
12 *the dough was starting to rise* **swell**, expand, enlarge, puff up; ferment.
13 *the nation would eventually rise against its oppressors* **rebel**, revolt, mutiny, riot, rise up (in arms), take up arms, stage/mount a rebellion, take to the streets.
OPPOSITE kowtow.
14 *the River Rhine rises in the Swiss Alps* **originate**, begin, start, emerge, appear; issue from, spring from, flow from, emanate from; *formal* commence.
OPPOSITE disgorge.
15 *the sickness lightened a little and her spirits rose* **lift**, improve, cheer up, grow buoyant, become optimistic/hopeful, brighten, take a turn for the better; *informal* buck up.
16 *the ground rose gently away from the river* **slope upwards**, slant upwards, go uphill, incline, climb, get higher.
OPPOSITES shelve, drop away.
▶ **noun 1** *a price rise* **increase**, hike, advance, growth, leap, upsurge, upswing, ascent, climb, jump, escalation, spiralling.
2 *the managing director got a rise of 11.3%* **pay increase**, salary/wage increase, hike, increment; *N. Amer.* raise.
3 *a rise in standards* **improvement**, amelioration, advance, upturn, leap, jump.
4 *they were alarmed by Hitler's rise to power* **progress**, climb, progression, advancement, promotion, elevation, aggrandizement.
5 *we began to walk up the rise* **(upward) slope**, incline, elevation, acclivity, rising ground, eminence, hillock, hill.

risible ▶ **adjective** *their irresponsibility would be risible were it not so dangerous* **laughable**, **ridiculous**, absurd, comical, comic, amusing, funny, hilarious, humorous, droll, entertaining, diverting, farcical, slapstick, silly, facetious, ludicrous, hysterical, uproarious, riotous, side-splitting, zany, grotesque; *informal* rib-tickling, crazy, priceless; *dated* killing; *rare* derisible.
OPPOSITE serious.

risk ▶ **noun 1** *to publish the story was indeed a risk | there is a certain amount of risk involved* **chance**, **uncertainty**, unpredictability, precariousness, instability, insecurity, perilousness, riskiness, gamble, venture.
OPPOSITE safety.
2 *do not use the stove inside a tent because of the risk of fire* **possibility**, chance, probability, likelihood, danger, peril, threat, menace, fear, prospect.
OPPOSITE impossibility.
3 *they're putting their own lives at risk* **danger**, peril, jeopardy, hazard, threat, menace.
▶ **verb 1** *a father risked his life to save his twin babies from a fire* **endanger**, put at risk, put in danger, expose to danger, put on the line, take a chance with, imperil, jeopardize, put in jeopardy, hazard, gamble (with), bet, wager, chance, venture.
2 *in a tweed coat you risk getting cold and wet* **chance**, venture, take the risk of, stand a chance of.

CHOOSE THE RIGHT WORD

risk, danger, peril, hazard noun
See DANGER.

risk, endanger, imperil, jeopardize verb
See ENDANGER.

risky ▶ **adjective** *risky sports like skindiving and hang-gliding are not covered* **dangerous**, fraught with danger, high-risk, hazardous, perilous, unsafe, insecure, exposed, defenceless, precarious, touch-and-go, tricky, treacherous; uncertain, unpredictable, speculative; *informal* chancy, dicey, sticky, hairy; *Brit. informal* dodgy; *N. Amer. informal* gnarly; *archaic or humorous* parlous.
OPPOSITE safe.

risqué ▶ **adjective** *the girls would giggle and tell risqué stories* **bawdy**, indecent, ribald, rude, racy, broad, earthy, Rabelaisian, spicy, suggestive, titillating, improper, naughty, indelicate, indecorous, off colour, locker-room; vulgar, dirty, filthy, smutty, crude, offensive, salacious, coarse, obscene, lewd, pornographic, X-rated; *informal* blue, raunchy; *Brit. informal* fruity, near the knuckle, saucy; *N. Amer. informal* gamy; *euphemistic* adult.

rite ▶ **noun** *coronation has long been a religious rite* **ceremony**, ritual, ceremonial, observance, service, sacrament, liturgy, worship, office, celebration; performance, act, practice, order, custom, tradition, convention, institution, procedure.

ritual ▶ **noun** *the official thanksgiving was an elaborate civic ritual* **ceremony**, rite, ceremonial, observance; service, sacrament, liturgy, worship; office, celebration, performance, act, practice, order, custom, tradition, convention, institution, formality, procedure, protocol.
▶ **adjective** *the ritual burial was to ward off evil spirits* **ceremonial**, ritualistic, prescribed, set, formal, stately, solemn, dignified, celebratory, sacramental, liturgical; customary, traditional, conventional, routine, usual, habitual.

ritzy ▶ **adjective** (*informal*) *his ritzy $4 million oceanside mansion* **luxurious**, luxury, de luxe, plush, sumptuous, palatial, lavish, lavishly appointed, gorgeous, opulent, splendid, magnificent, lush, glamorous, glittering, rich, costly, expensive, upmarket, fancy, stylish, grandiose; *informal* posh, swanky, plushy, classy, glitzy; *Brit. informal* swish; *N. Amer. informal* swank; *rare* palatian, Lucullan.
OPPOSITES plain, austere.

rival ▶ **noun 1** *his chief rival for the nomination* **competitor**, **opponent**, contestant, contender, challenger; adversary, antagonist, enemy, foe; *rare* corrival, vier.
OPPOSITES partner, ally.
2 *in terms of versatility the tool has no rival* **equal**, match, peer, equivalent, fellow, counterpart, like; *rare* compeer.
▶ **verb** *few countries can rival Slovakia for mountain scenery* **compete with**, vie with, match, be a match for, equal, emulate, measure up to, come up to, compare with, bear comparison with, be comparable to/with, parallel, be in the same league as, be in the same category as, be on a par with, be on a level with, touch, keep pace with, keep up with; challenge; *informal* hold a candle to.
▶ **adjective** *the rival candidates* **competing**, in competition, opposing, opposed, in opposition, contending, conflicting, in conflict; *rare* corrival.

rivalry ▶ **noun** *the growing rivalry between the two groups* **competitiveness**, competition, contention, vying; opposition, conflict, struggle, strife, feuding, dissension, discord, antagonism, friction, enmity; *informal* keeping up with the Joneses.

riven ▶ **adjective** *the country was riven by civil war* **torn apart**, split, rent, ripped apart, ruptured, severed; *literary* cleft, torn asunder, ripped asunder; *rare* dissevered.

river ▶ **noun 1** **watercourse**, waterway, stream, tributary, brook, inlet, rivulet, rill, runnel, streamlet, freshet; canal, channel; *Scottish & N. English* burn; *N. English* beck; *S. English* bourn; *N. Amer. & Austral./NZ* creek; *Austral.* billabong; *rare* rillet.
2 *a river of molten lava* **stream**, torrent, flood, deluge, cascade; spate, wave.
□ **sell someone down the river** (*informal*) **cheat**, trick, swindle, defraud, dupe, hoodwink; double-cross, betray, deceive, sell out, stab in the back; exploit, take advantage of; *informal* do, con, take for a ride, sell, diddle, bamboozle, finagle, bilk, rip off, fleece.

WORD LINKS

relating to rivers	**fluvial, potamic, riparian, riverine**
related prefixes	**fluvio- (e.g. *fluviometer, fluvioglacial*), potamo- (e.g. *potamoplankton*)**
study of rivers	**potamology**
fear of rivers	**potamophobia**

riveted ▶ **adjective 1** *he walked away, leaving her riveted to the spot* **fixed**, rooted, frozen; unable to move, motionless, unmoving, immobile, stock-still, as still as a statue, as if turned to stone.
2 *he was riveted by the newsreels* **fascinated**, engrossed, gripped, captivated, enthralled, intrigued, spellbound, rapt, mesmerized, transfixed.
OPPOSITES bored, uninterested.
3 *the children's eyes were* **riveted on** *the headmistress* **fixed on**, fastened on, focused on, concentrated on, pinned on, locked on, directed at.

riveting ▶ **adjective** *a riveting book* **fascinating**, gripping, engrossing, very interesting, very exciting, thrilling, absorbing, captivating, enthralling, intriguing, compelling, compulsive, spellbinding, mesmerizing, hypnotic, transfixing; *informal* unputdownable.
OPPOSITES boring, dull.

road *See centre pages for list of* **Roads**
▶ **noun 1** *the roads were crowded with holiday traffic* **highway**, thoroughfare, roadway; road surface, *N. Amer.* pavement.
2 *a key step on the road to economic recovery* **way**, path, route, direction, course.
3 *there seemed an almost endless queue of freighters and tankers waiting in the roads* **anchorage**, channel, haven; *rare* roadstead.
□ **on the road** *the band have been on the road all year* **on tour**, touring, travelling, doing the rounds, on the circuit.

roam ▶ **verb** *a tramp who had roamed the country for nine years* **wander**, rove,

R

ramble, meander, drift, maunder; walk, traipse; prowl; range, travel, tramp, traverse, trek through; *Scottish & Irish* stravaig; *Irish* streel; *informal* knock about/around, cruise, mosey, tootle; *Brit. informal* pootle, swan; *rare* perambulate, peregrinate, circumambulate, vagabond.

> **CHOOSE THE RIGHT WORD**
>
> **roam, wander, rove, range, stray**
>
> See WANDER.

roar ▶ noun **1** *the roars of the crowd increased in intensity* **shout**, bellow, yell, cry, howl, shriek, scream, screech; clamour, clamouring; *N. Amer. informal* holler; *rare* vociferation, ululation.
OPPOSITE whisper.
2 *the deafening roar of the wind and the sea* **loud noise**, boom, booming, crash, crashing, rumble, rumbling, roll, thundering, peal, crack, clap, thunderclap.
3 *his claims were greeted with roars of laughter* **guffaw**, howl, hoot, shriek; gale, peal.
▶ verb **1** *'Get out!' roared Angus* **bellow**, yell, shout, bawl, howl, cry, shriek, scream, screech; *N. Amer. informal* holler; *rare* vociferate, ululate.
OPPOSITE whisper.
2 *thunder roared and lightning flashed* **boom**, rumble, crash, roll, thunder, peal.
3 *the movie has left preview audiences roaring* **guffaw**, laugh heartily, roar/howl/shriek with laughter, laugh hysterically, laugh uproariously, be convulsed with laughter, burst out laughing, hoot; *informal* split one's sides, be rolling in the aisles, be doubled up, crack up, laugh like a drain, be in stitches, die laughing; *Brit. informal* crease up, fall about.
OPPOSITE weep.
4 *a motorbike roared past* **speed**, zoom, whizz, flash; *informal* belt, tear, vroom, scorch, zap, zip, burn rubber; *Brit. informal* bomb.

roaring ▶ adjective **1** *a roaring fire* **blazing**, burning, red-hot.
2 (*informal*) *last week's 70s night was a roaring success* **enormous**, huge, massive, (very) great, tremendous, terrific; complete, unqualified, out-and-out, thorough, unmitigated; *informal* rip-roaring, whopping, thumping, fantastic.

roast ▶ verb **1** *potatoes roasted in olive oil* **cook**, bake, grill; spit-roast, pot-roast; *N. Amer.* broil.
2 (*informal*) *they roasted Lavelle for eating at exclusive restaurants at the company's expense.* See CRITICIZE.

roasting (*informal*) ▶ adjective *a roasting day in London* **extremely hot**, baking (hot), blazing (hot), sweltering, scorching, blistering, searing, torrid; *informal* sizzling, boiling (hot).
▶ noun *the manager hauled him in and gave him a roasting.* See LECTURE *sense* 2.

rob ▶ verb **1** *the gang were convicted of robbing Barclays Bank in Kelvedon* **burgle**, steal from, hold up, break into; raid, loot, ransack, plunder, pillage, sack; *N. Amer.* burglarize; *informal* do, turn over, steam, knock off, stick up; *archaic* spoil, reave.
2 *police are hunting a man who robbed an old woman at gunpoint last night* **steal from**; *informal* **mug**, jump, roll; *N. Amer. informal* clip.
3 *he was robbed of his savings* **cheat**, swindle, defraud, fleece, dispossess; *informal* bilk, do out of, con out of, rook out of, skin, steal someone blind; *N. Amer. informal* stiff; *rare* mulct.
4 (*informal*) *my suit cost £70, and he thinks I was robbed* **overcharge**, charge too much; *informal* rip off, screw, sting, do, diddle; *N. Amer. informal* gouge; *Brit. informal, dated* rush.
5 *defeat robbed him of his chance of regaining the world No 1 ranking* **deprive**, strip, divest; deny.
6 (*informal*) *I didn't buy it—I robbed it.* See STEAL.

robber ▶ noun **burglar**, thief, housebreaker, cat burglar, sneak thief, mugger, shoplifter, stealer, pilferer; raider, looter, plunderer, pillager, marauder; bandit, brigand, pirate, highwayman; *Indian* dacoit; *informal* crook, cracksman, steamer; *Brit. informal, dated* drummer; *N. Amer. informal* yegg, second-story man/worker; *W. Indian informal* tief; *Brit. rhyming slang* tea leaf.

robbery ▶ noun **1** *they were arrested for robbery | a spate of robberies* **burglary**, theft, thievery, stealing, breaking and entering, housebreaking, larceny, shoplifting, pilfering, filching, embezzlement, misappropriation, swindling, fraud; hold-up, break-in, raid; looting, pillage, plunder; *informal* mugging, smash-and-grab, steaming, snatch; *Brit. informal* blag; *N. Amer. informal* heist, stick-up.
2 *Six quid? That's robbery* daylight robbery; *informal* a rip-off.

robe ▶ noun **1** *the women were draped from head to toe in heavy black robes* cloak, wrap, mantle, cape, kaftan; *N. Amer.* wrapper; *Arabic* dishdasha, djellaba; *Turkish* dolman; *African* kanzu; *Hawaiian* muumuu.
2 (**robes**) *coronation robes* **garb**, regalia, costume, livery, finery, trappings; garments, clothes; *formal* apparel; *archaic* raiment, habiliments, vestments, vesture, habit.
3 *his priestly robes* **vestment**, surplice, cassock, rochet, alb, dalmatic, chasuble; canonicals, pontificals.
4 *a short towelling robe* **dressing gown**, bathrobe, housecoat, negligee, kimono; *French* peignoir, robe de chambre; *N. Amer.* wrapper.
▶ verb *I went into the vestry and robed for the Mass* **dress oneself**, dress, get dressed, attire oneself, enrobe; *archaic* apparel oneself.

robot ▶ noun **automaton**, android, machine, golem; *informal* bot, droid.

robust ▶ adjective **1** *a large and robust man* **strong**, vigorous, sturdy, tough, powerful, powerfully built, solidly built, as strong as a horse/ox, muscular, sinewy, rugged, hardy, strapping, brawny, burly, husky; **healthy**, fit, fighting fit, as fit as a fiddle/flea, bursting with health, hale and hearty, hale, hearty, lusty, in fine fettle, in good health, in good shape, in trim, in good trim, able-bodied; *Brit.* in rude health; *informal* beefy, hunky; *dated* stalwart; *literary* thewy, stark.
OPPOSITES weak, frail.
2 *these knives are more robust and better at cutting* **durable**, resilient, tough, hard-wearing, long-lasting, well made; **sturdy**, strong, strongly made.
OPPOSITE fragile.
3 *Libby took her usual robust view of the matter* **down-to-earth**, hard-headed, sensible, practical, realistic, pragmatic, common-sense, commonsensical, matter-of-fact, businesslike, level-headed, unromantic, unsentimental, unidealistic; tough-minded, forceful, vigorous; *informal* no-nonsense, hard-nosed.
OPPOSITES impractical, romantic.
4 *a robust red wine* **strong**, full-bodied, flavourful, full-flavoured, flavoursome, full of flavour, rich; *rare* sapid.
OPPOSITES insipid, tasteless.

rock[1] ▶ verb **1** *the ship rocked on the water* **move to and fro**, move backwards and forwards, move back and forth, sway, swing, see-saw; roll, pitch, plunge, toss, lurch, reel, list; wobble, undulate, oscillate; *Nautical* pitchpole.
2 *the building began to rock on its foundations* **shake**, vibrate, quake, tremble.
3 *Wall Street was rocked by the news and shares fell 4.3 per cent* **stun**, shock, stagger, astound, astonish, amaze, startle, surprise, dumbfound, daze, shake, shake up, set someone back on their heels, take aback, throw, unnerve, disconcert.

rock[2] *See centre pages for lists of* **Gems** **Minerals** **Rocks**
▶ noun **1** *a narrow gully strewn with rocks* **boulder**, stone; *Austral. informal* goolie.
2 *a castle built on a rock* **crag**, cliff, tor, outcrop, outcropping.
3 *he was the rock on which his whole family relied* **foundation**, cornerstone, support, prop, mainstay, backbone; tower of strength, pillar of strength, bulwark, anchor, source of protection, source of security.
4 (*informal*) *she was wearing a massive rock on her fourth finger* **diamond**, precious stone, jewel.
□ **on the rocks** (*informal*) **1** *Sue's marriage was on the rocks* **in difficulty**, in trouble, breaking down, practically over, heading for divorce, heading for the divorce courts; in tatters, in pieces, destroyed, shattered, ruined, beyond repair.
2 *he ordered a Scotch on the rocks* **with ice**, on ice.

WORD LINKS

related prefixes	**litho-** (e.g. ***lithography***), **petro-** (e.g. ***petroleum***)
related suffix	**-lite** (e.g. ***hyalite***)
study of rocks	**lithology, petrology, petrography**

rocket *See centre pages for lists of* **Projectiles** **Fireworks**
▶ noun **1** *guerrillas fired five rockets at the capital yesterday* **missile**, projectile; *rare* trajectile.
2 (*Brit. informal*) *he got a rocket from the director.* See LECTURE *sense* 2.
▶ verb **1** *prices have rocketed during the last ten years* **shoot up**, soar, increase rapidly, rise rapidly, escalate, spiral upwards; *informal* go through the ceiling, go through the roof, skyrocket.
OPPOSITES fall, plummet.
2 *they rocketed into the alley ahead of the police car* **speed**, zoom, shoot, roar, whizz, career, go hell for leather; *informal* scorch, tear, go like a bat out of hell; *Brit. informal* bomb; *N. Amer. informal* barrel, hightail it.

rocky[1] ▶ adjective *damp leaves covered the rocky path | Malta is naturally rocky and treeless* **stony**, rock-strewn, pebbly, shingly, rough, bumpy, rugged, hard; craggy, mountainous.
OPPOSITES smooth, flat.

rocky[2] ▶ adjective **1** *that table's a bit rocky* **unsteady**, shaky, unstable, wobbly, tottery, rickety, flimsy; *Irish* bockety.
OPPOSITE steady.
2 *the couple had a rocky marriage* **difficult**, up and down, problematic, precarious, unsteady, unstable, uncertain, unsure, unreliable, undependable, built on sand; *informal* iffy.
OPPOSITES solid, stable.

rococo ▶ adjective *rococo Victorian wrought ironwork | his rococo diction* **ornate**, fancy, very elaborate, curlicued, over-elaborate, extravagant, baroque, fussy, busy, ostentatious, showy, wedding-cake, gingerbread; flowery, florid, flamboyant, high-flown, high-sounding, magniloquent, grandiloquent, orotund, rhetorical, oratorical, bombastic, overwrought, overblown, overdone, convoluted, turgid, inflated; *informal* highfalutin,

purple; *rare* tumid, pleonastic, euphuistic, aureate, Ossianic, fustian, hyperventilated.
OPPOSITES plain, simple.

rod ▶ **noun 1** *an iron rod* **bar**, stick, pole, baton, staff; shaft, strut, rail, spoke; cane, birch, switch; *historical* knout.
2 *the ceremonial rod of the House of Commons* **staff**, wand, mace, sceptre; *Greek Mythology* caduceus.
3 (**the rod**) *instruction in these subjects was brisk and accompanied by the rod* **corporal punishment**, the cane, the lash, the birch, the belt, the strap; beating, flogging, caning, birching.
WORD LINKS
rod-shaped **rhabdoid**

rodent ▶ **noun.** *See centre pages for lists of* **Rodents** **Squirrels**
WORD LINKS
substance used to kill rodents **rodenticide**

rogue ▶ **noun 1** *you are a rogue, Colin, without ethics or scruples* **scoundrel**, villain, reprobate, rascal, good-for-nothing, wretch; *Spanish* picaro; *informal* rat, bastard, son of a bitch, s.o.b., nasty piece of work, dog, cur, louse, crook; *Scottish informal* scrote; *Irish informal* spalpeen; *N. Amer. informal* slicker; *W. Indian informal* scamp; *informal, dated* rotter, bounder, hound, blighter, vagabond; *dated* cad, ne'er-do-well; *archaic* miscreant, blackguard, dastard, knave, varlet, wastrel, mountebank, picaroon.
2 *we were at school together—he was a right little rogue* **scamp**, rascal, imp, devil, monkey, mischief-maker; *informal* scallywag, monster, horror, terror, holy terror; *Brit. informal* perisher; *N. English informal* tyke, scally; *N. Amer. informal* hellion, varmint; *archaic* scapegrace, rapscallion.

roguish ▶ **adjective 1** *a roguish and untrustworthy character* **unprincipled**, dishonest, deceitful, unscrupulous, untrustworthy, reprobate, shameless, wicked, villainous; incorrigible, unregenerate; *informal* shady, scoundrelly, rascally; *archaic* knavish.
OPPOSITES honest, honourable.
2 *a roguish grin* **mischievous**, playful, teasing, cheeky, naughty, wicked, impish, puckish, devilish, arch, waggish, rakish, raffish; *rare* ludic.
OPPOSITE serious.

roister ▶ **verb** *the mansions in which the nobility of the city had once roistered* **enjoy oneself**, celebrate, revel, carouse, frolic, romp, have fun, have a good time, make merry, have a party, party, {eat, drink, and be merry}, go on a spree; *informal* live it up, whoop it up, have a fling, have a ball, make whoopee, paint the town red; *dated* spree; *rare* rollick.

role *See centre pages for list of* **Roles in the Theatre**
▶ **noun 1** *he had a small role in Coppola's 'Dracula'* **part**, character; title role; bit part, walk-on part, non-speaking part.
2 *his success in his role as President of the European Community* **capacity**, position, job, post, office, task, duty, responsibility, mantle, place, situation; **function**, part, contribution, hand.

roll *See centre pages for list of* **Bread and Bread Rolls**
▶ **verb 1** *the empty bottle rolled down the pavement* **turn round and round**, go round and round, turn over and over, spin, rotate; bowl.
2 *waiters rolled in trolleys laden with food* **wheel**, push, trundle.
3 *we rolled past endless rows of shacks* **travel**, go, move, pass, cruise, be carried, be conveyed, sweep.
4 *the months rolled by* **pass**, go by/past, slip by/past, slide by/past, sail by/past, glide by/past, fly by/past, elapse, wear on, steal by/past, march on.
5 *tears were rolling down her cheeks* **flow**, run, course, stream, pour, spill, trickle.
6 *mist rolled here and there in thick white clouds* **billow**, undulate, rise and fall, toss, tumble; *literary* welter.
7 *he rolled his handkerchief into a ball* **wind**, coil, furl, fold, curl; twist.
8 *roll out the pastry on a floured surface* **flatten**, level, smooth; even out.
9 *they were rolling about with laughter* **stagger**, lurch, reel, sway, pitch, totter, teeter, wobble.
10 *the ship began to roll* **lurch**, toss, rock, pitch, plunge, sway, reel, list, keel, wallow, labour, make heavy weather.
11 *the sky had darkened and thunder rolled in the west* **rumble**, reverberate, echo, re-echo, resound, boom, peal, roar, grumble.
□ **roll in** (*informal*) **1** *since the appeal, money has been rolling in* **pour in**, flood in, flow in, stream in; *informal* arrive by the truckload.
2 *he rolled in about 9.00* **arrive**, turn up, appear, walk in, make/put in an appearance, show one's face; *informal* show up, pitch up, fetch up, roll up, blow in.
OPPOSITE leave.
□ **rolling in it** (*informal*) **rich**, wealthy, affluent, moneyed, well off, well-to-do, prosperous, substantial, propertied; *informal* in the money, loaded, stinking rich, filthy rich, well heeled, flush, made of money, quids in, worth a packet, worth a bundle, on easy street; *informal, dated* oofy.
OPPOSITE penniless.
□ **roll something out** *she rolled out her towel* **unroll**, spread out, unfurl, unfold, open (out), unwind, uncoil, lay out.
OPPOSITE roll up.
□ **roll something up** *she rolled up her pyjamas* **fold (up)**, furl, wind up, coil (up), bundle up.
OPPOSITES unroll, roll out.
□ **roll up** (*informal*) *at that moment, the police rolled up* **arrive**, come, turn up, appear, make/put in an appearance, show one's face; *informal* show up, pitch up, fetch up, roll in, blow in.
OPPOSITE leave.
▶ **noun 1** *a roll of wrapping paper* **cylinder**, tube, scroll; bolt.
2 *a roll of film* **reel**, spool.
3 *a thick roll of notes* **wad**, bundle.
4 *a roll of the dice* **throw**, toss; turn, rotation, revolution, spin.
5 *the roll of the ship* **rocking**, tossing, lurching, pitching, plunging, swaying.
6 *the parish has just 100 people on its electoral roll* **list**, register, listing, directory, record, file, index, catalogue, inventory; census.
7 *a roll of thunder | a roll of drums* **rumble**, reverberation, echo, boom, thunder, thunderclap, clap, crack, roar, grumble; tattoo, rataplan.

rollicking[1] ▶ **noun** (*Brit. informal*) *I got a rollicking for turning up late. See* LECTURE *sense* 2.

rollicking[2] ▶ **adjective** *a rollicking party* **lively**, boisterous, exuberant, frisky, spirited; riotous, noisy, rip-roaring, wild, unrestrained, uninhibited, rowdy, roisterous, unruly; *Brit. informal* rumbustious; *N. Amer. informal* rambunctious; *archaic* frolicsome, robustious.
OPPOSITES restrained, quiet.

rolling ▶ **adjective** *the rolling waves* **undulating**, surging, heaving, tossing, rippling, rising and falling, swelling; billowing, billowy; *rare* undulant.
OPPOSITE flat.

roly-poly ▶ **adjective** *a roly-poly man with a walrus moustache* **chubby**, plump, fat, stout, rotund, buxom, well upholstered, well covered, well padded, of ample proportions, ample, round, rounded, well rounded, full, fattish, dumpy, chunky, broad in the beam, portly, overweight, fleshy, paunchy, bulky, corpulent; *informal* tubby, pudgy, beefy, porky, blubbery, poddy; *Brit. informal* podgy, fubsy; *N. Amer. informal* zaftig, corn-fed, lard-assed; *archaic* pursy; *rare* abdominous.
OPPOSITES thin, slender, skinny.

romance ▶ **noun 1** *despite the age gap, romance blossomed* **love**, passion, ardour, adoration, devotion; affection, fondness, intimacy, attachment.
2 *he's had his share of romances* **love affair**, affair, affair of the heart, relationship, liaison, courtship, amorous/romantic entanglement, intrigue, attachment; flirtation, dalliance; *French* amour, affaire, affaire de/du cœur.
3 *a best-selling author of historical romances* **love story**; novel; romantic fiction, light fiction, sentimental fiction; *informal* tear jerker.
4 *the romance of the Far East* **mystery**, **glamour**, excitement, colourfulness, colour, exoticism, mystique; appeal, allure, fascination, charm.
▶ **verb 1** (*dated*) *I heard he was romancing Meg* **woo**, chase, pursue, run after; go out with; *informal* see, go steady with, date; *Austral. informal* track with, track square with; *dated* court, pay court to, pay suit to, seek the hand of, pay one's addresses to, set one's cap at; *archaic* make love to.
2 *to a certain degree, I am romancing the past* **romanticize**, idealize, be unrealistic about, look at something through rose-tinted/rose-coloured spectacles, paint a rosy picture of.

romantic ▶ **adjective 1** *he's very handsome, and so romantic* **loving**, amorous, passionate, tender, tender-hearted, fond, affectionate; *informal* lovey-dovey.
2 *the disc jockey kept the romantic records for the end of the night* **sentimental**, hearts-and-flowers; mawkish, over-sentimental, cloying, sickly, saccharine, sugary, syrupy; *informal* slushy, mushy, sloppy, schmaltzy, weepy, cutesy, gooey, drippy, sloshy, soupy, treacly, cheesy, corny, icky, sick-making, toe-curling; *Brit. informal* soppy; *N. Amer. informal* cornball, sappy, hokey, three-hankie; *trademark* Mills and Boon.
OPPOSITES unsentimental, gritty.
3 *a beautiful cottage in a romantic setting* **idyllic**, picturesque, fairy-tale; beautiful, lovely, charming, delightful, pretty.
4 *romantic notions of rural communities* **idealistic**, idealized, unrealistic, head-in-the-clouds, out of touch with reality; starry-eyed, optimistic, hopeful, visionary, utopian, fairy-tale, fanciful, dreamy, ivory-towered; impractical, unpractical, unworkable, improbable, unlikely; *rare* Micawberish, Panglossian.
OPPOSITES realistic, practical, down-to-earth.
5 *she found him an intensely romantic figure* **fascinating**, **glamorous**, attractive, interesting, mysterious, exotic, exciting, quixotic.
▶ **noun** *the guy is an incurable romantic* **idealist**, sentimentalist, romanticist; dreamer, visionary, utopian, Don Quixote, fantasist, fantasizer; *archaic* fantast.
OPPOSITE realist.

Romeo ▶ **noun** *no Italian Romeo with an over-active libido was going to catch her* **ladies' man**, Don Juan, Casanova, Lothario, womanizer, playboy, lover, seducer, philanderer, flirt; gigolo; *informal* wolf, ladykiller, stud, skirt-chaser; *informal, dated* gay dog; *archaic* gallant.

romp ▶ **verb 1** *two fox cubs romped playfully on the bank* **play**, frolic, frisk, gambol, jump about/around, spring about/around, bound about/around,

R

skip, prance, caper, sport, cavort; *rare* rollick, curvet.
2 *South Africa romped to a six-wicket win over India* **sweep**, sail, coast; win easily, win hands down, run away with it; *informal* win by a mile, walk it.

roof ▶ **noun**
□ **hit the roof** (*informal*) *Ron will hit the roof when he sees this* **be very angry**, be furious, lose one's temper, go into a rage, breathe fire; *informal* go mad, go crazy, be hopping mad, be livid, go wild, go bananas, have a fit, blow one's top, blow a fuse, blow a gasket, do one's nut, go through the roof, go up the wall, go off the deep end, go ape, flip, flip one's lid, lose one's rag, be fit to be tied, go non-linear; *Brit. informal* go spare, go crackers, get one's knickers in a twist; *N. Amer. informal* flip one's wig.
WORD LINKS
roof-shaped **tectiform**

rook ▶ **verb** (*informal*) *police files are overflowing with complaints from people who've been rooked.* See SWINDLE.

room *See centre pages for list of* **Rooms**
▶ **noun 1** *there isn't much room* **space**, free space; headroom, legroom; area, territory, expanse, extent, volume; *informal* elbow room.
2 *there's always room for improvement* **scope**, capacity, margin, leeway, latitude, freedom; occasion, opportunity, chance.
3 *he wandered around the room* *archaic* chamber.
4 (**rooms**) *he had rooms in the Pepys building, overlooking the River Cam* **lodgings**, quarters; accommodation, a place, a place to stay, a billet; suite, apartments; *Brit. informal* digs; *formal* abode.
▶ **verb** *he had roomed there since September* **lodge**, board, have rooms; live, stay; be quartered, be housed, be billeted; *formal* dwell, reside, be domiciled, sojourn.

roomy ▶ **adjective** *the accommodation was roomy and warm | a roomy coat* **spacious**, commodious, capacious, sizeable, generous, big, large, broad, wide, extensive; voluminous, ample, loose-fitting; *rare* spacey.
OPPOSITES cramped, tiny, poky; tight-fitting.

root ▶ **noun 1** *the fungus attacks a plant's roots* radicle, rhizome, rootstock, tuber, tap root, rootlet; *rare* radicel.
2 *the root of the problem* **source**, origin, starting point, seed, germ, beginnings, genesis; **cause**, reason; base, basis, foundation, bottom, seat, fundamental; core, nucleus, heart, kernel, nub, essence; *Latin* fons et origo; *literary* fountainhead, wellspring, fount; *rare* radix.
3 (**roots**) *he has rejected his roots* **origins**, beginnings, family, ancestors, predecessors; heritage; birthplace, native land, motherland, fatherland, homeland, native country, native soil.
□ **put down roots** *they married and put down roots in Britain* **settle**, become established, establish oneself, make one's home, set up home.
□ **root and branch 1** *the whole ghastly superstructure should be brought down and got rid of, root and branch* **completely**, entirely, wholly, totally, utterly, thoroughly; radically.
2 *the party wanted a root-and-branch reform of the electoral system* **complete**, total, entire, utter, thorough; radical.
□ **take root 1** *leave the plants to take root over the next couple of weeks* **begin to germinate**, begin to sprout, establish, strike, take.
2 *Christianity had taken root in Persia and Syria earlier than in Rome* **become established**, establish itself, become fixed, take hold; develop, thrive, flourish.
▶ **verb 1** *give the shoot a gentle tug to see if it has rooted* **take root**, grow roots, become established, establish, strike, take.
2 *June is a good month to begin rooting cuttings* **plant**, bed out, sow.
3 *he rooted around in the cupboard and brought out a packet of biscuits* **rummage**, hunt, search, rifle, delve, forage, dig, nose, poke; *Brit. informal* rootle.
□ **root for** (*informal*) *the clamour of baseball fans rooting for their team* **cheer**, applaud, cheer on, support, encourage, urge on, shout for.
□ **root something out 1** *the hedge was rooted out* **uproot**, tear something up by the roots, pull something up, grub something out; *rare* deracinate.
OPPOSITE plant.
2 *his main purpose was to root out corruption in the judiciary* **eradicate**, get rid of, eliminate, weed out, remove, destroy, put an end to, do away with, wipe out, stamp out, extirpate, abolish, extinguish.
OPPOSITE establish.
3 *are you hoping to root out some dark secret from Joseph's past?* **unearth**, dig up, dig out, turn up, bring to light, uncover, discover, dredge up, ferret out, hunt out, nose out, expose.
WORD LINKS
relating to roots **radical**
related prefix **rhizo- (e.g. *rhizomorph*)**

rooted ▶ **adjective 1** *such views are rooted in Indian culture* **embedded**, fixed, firmly established, implanted; deep-rooted, entrenched, ingrained, ineradicable.
2 *Nell was rooted to the spot* **unable to move from**, frozen to, riveted to, paralysed to, glued to, fixed to; stock-still, as still as a statue, as if turned to stone, motionless, unmoving.

rootless ▶ **adjective** *once she had been proud of being rootless* **itinerant**, unsettled, drifting, roving, footloose; **homeless**, without family ties, of no fixed abode, without a settled home, vagabond.

rope *See centre pages for list of* **Ropes**
▶ **noun cord**, cable, line, strand, hawser; string.
□ **know the ropes** (*informal*) **know what to do**, know the procedure, know the routine, know one's way around, know one's stuff, know what's what, understand the set-up, be experienced, be an old hand, know all the ins and outs; *informal* know the drill, know the score.
OPPOSITE be a beginner.
▶ **verb** *his feet were roped together* **tie**, bind, lash, truss, pinion; secure, moor, fasten, make fast, attach; hitch, tether, lasso.
□ **rope someone in/into** *they tried to rope me into helping out* **persuade to/into**, talk into, inveigle into; enlist, engage; *informal* drag in/into.
WORD LINKS
relating to ropes **funicular**

ropy ▶ **adjective 1** (*Brit. informal*) *I feel a bit ropy, actually.* See ILL.
2 (*Brit. informal*) *the Italians were helped by some ropy defending from the home team.* See SUBSTANDARD.
3 *ropy strands of sticky lava* **viscous**, gelatinous, viscid, sticky, glutinous, mucilaginous, thick; **stringy**, thready, fibrous, filamentous.

roster ▶ **noun** *according to the roster, he was due to work today* **list**, listing, register, schedule, agenda, calendar, roll, directory, table; *Brit.* **rota**.

rostrum ▶ **noun dais**, platform, podium, stage; soapbox; *Indian* mandapam; *rare* tribune.

rosy ▶ **adjective 1** *her rosy cheeks | a rosy complexion* **pink**, pinkish, rose-pink, rose-coloured, roseate, red, reddish, rose-red; glowing, healthy-looking, fresh, radiant, blooming; blushing, flushed; ruddy, high-coloured, rubicund, florid; *rare* erubescent, rubescent.
OPPOSITES pale, pallid, sallow.
2 *Ian's future looks rosy* **promising**, full of promise, optimistic, auspicious, hopeful, full of hope, encouraging, favourable, bright, sunny, golden, cheerful, happy; *informal* upbeat.
OPPOSITES bleak, dismal, depressing.

rot ▶ **verb 1** *the floorboards in the centre of the room had rotted* **decay**, decompose, disintegrate, crumble, become rotten; corrode, perish.
2 *the meat was beginning to rot* **go bad**, go off, spoil; go sour, moulder, go mouldy, taint; putrefy, fester, become gangrenous, mortify; *rare* necrose, sphacelate.
3 *poor city neighbourhoods have been left to rot for years* **deteriorate**, degenerate, decline, decay, fall into decay, go to rack and ruin, become dilapidated, go to seed, go downhill, languish, moulder; *informal* go to pot, go to the dogs, go down the toilet.
OPPOSITES recover, improve.
▶ **noun 1** *the leaves were turning black with rot* **decay**, decomposition; corrosion; mould, mouldiness, mildew, blight, canker; putrefaction, putrescence; wet rot, dry rot.
2 *staunch defenders of traditionalism argued that the rot set in with Van Gogh and Gauguin* **deterioration**, decline; corruption, canker, cancer.
3 (*informal*) *stop talking rot* **nonsense**, rubbish, balderdash, gibberish, claptrap, blarney, blather, blether; *informal* hogwash, baloney, tripe, drivel, bilge, bosh, bull, bunk, hot air, eyewash, piffle, poppycock, phooey, hooey, malarkey, twaddle, guff, dribble; *Brit. informal* cobblers, codswallop, cock, stuff and nonsense, tosh; *Scottish & N. English informal* havers; *N. Amer. informal* garbage, flapdoodle, blathers, wack, bushwa, applesauce; *informal, dated* bunkum, tommyrot, cod, gammon.
OPPOSITE sense.
WORD LINKS
related prefix **sapro- (e.g. *saprogenic*)**

rota ▶ **noun** (*Brit.*) **roster**, list, schedule, register, timetable, calendar.

rotary ▶ **adjective** *rotary motion* **rotating**, rotatory, rotational, revolving, turning, spinning, gyrating, gyratory, whirling.

rotate ▶ **verb 1** *the wheels had to rotate continually to provide power* **revolve**, go round, turn, turn round, move round, spin, gyrate, wheel, whirl, twirl, swivel, circle, pirouette, pivot, reel.
2 *many nurses rotate between high risk and low risk areas during the course of their work* **alternate**, take turns, take it in turns, work/act in sequence, trade places, change, switch, interchange, exchange, swap; pass from one to another in rotation, move around.

rotation ▶ **noun 1** *the rotation of the wheels* **revolving**, turning, spinning, gyration, wheeling, whirling, twirling, swivelling, circling.
2 *one rotation of the Earth* **turn**, revolution, spin, whirl, orbit.
3 *each member state acts as president of the council for six months in rotation* **sequence**, succession; alternation, cycle.
WORD LINKS
related prefix **gyro- (e.g. *gyroscope, gyrocompass*)**

rote ▶ **noun**
□ **by rote** *they were able to recite Newton's laws by rote* **mechanically**, automatically, without thinking, unthinkingly, parrot-fashion, mindlessly; **from memory**, by heart.

rotten ▶ adjective **1** *the smell of rotten meat* **decaying**, decayed, rotting, bad, off, decomposed, decomposing, putrid, putrescent, spoiled, spoilt, tainted, perished, mouldy, mouldering, mildewy, sour, rancid, rank, festering, fetid, stinking, smelly, unfit for human consumption; addled; maggoty, worm-eaten, wormy, flyblown.
OPPOSITE fresh.
2 *the wooden floor was rotten in places* **disintegrating**, crumbling, falling to pieces, decomposing, decaying; corroding.
OPPOSITE sound.
3 *he had the most disgusting rotten teeth* **decaying**, decayed, crumbling, carious, black; *rare* caried.
4 *a New York detective who's rotten to the core* **corrupt**, unprincipled, dishonest, dishonourable, unscrupulous, untrustworthy, immoral, villainous, bad, wicked, evil, sinful, iniquitous, vicious, base, amoral, debauched, degenerate, dissolute, dissipated, depraved, perverted, wanton; venal; *informal* crooked, warped; *Brit. informal* bent.
OPPOSITES honourable, decent, incorruptible.
5 (*informal*) *it was a rotten thing to do* **nasty**, unkind, unpleasant, foul, bad, obnoxious, vile, contemptible, despicable, wretched, shabby; spiteful, mean, malicious, poisonous, mean-spirited, cruel, hateful, hurtful; unfair, uncharitable, uncalled for, below the belt, unacceptable, unwarranted; *informal* dirty, filthy, dirty rotten, low-down, off; *Brit. informal* beastly, out of order; *vulgar slang* shitty.
OPPOSITES nice, pleasant, kind.
6 (*informal*) *he was a rotten journalist* **bad**, poor, dreadful, awful, terrible, frightful, atrocious, hopeless, inadequate, inferior, unsatisfactory, laughable, substandard; *informal* crummy, pathetic, useless, lousy, appalling, abysmal, dire; *Brit. informal* duff, chronic, poxy, rubbish, pants, a load of pants; *N. Amer. vulgar slang* chickenshit.
OPPOSITES good, accomplished.
7 (*informal*) *you can keep your rotten job for all I care!* **wretched**, horrible, unspeakable; *informal* damn, damned, blasted, blessed, flaming, precious, confounded; *Brit. informal* flipping, blinking, blooming, bloody, bleeding, effing, chuffing; *N. Amer. informal* goddam; *Austral./NZ informal* plurry; *Brit. informal, dated* bally, ruddy, deuced; *vulgar slang* fucking, frigging; *Brit. vulgar slang* sodding; *Irish vulgar slang* fecking.
8 (*informal*) *she's had a pretty rotten time* **unpleasant**, disagreeable, miserable, awful, dreadful, terrible, frightful, bad, vile, grim, horrid, horrible, ghastly; disappointing, regrettable, unfortunate, unlucky; *informal* lousy, beastly, diabolical; *Brit. informal* shocking.
OPPOSITES delightful, good, nice.
9 (*informal*) *I feel rotten about it—I've ruined his life* **guilty**, conscience-stricken, remorseful, guilt-ridden, ashamed, chastened, contrite, sorry, full of regret, regretful, repentant, penitent, shamefaced, self-reproachful, apologetic.
10 (*Brit. informal*) *I felt rotten and couldn't eat for two days* **ill**, unwell, poorly, bad, out of sorts, indisposed, not oneself, sick, queasy, nauseous, nauseated, peaky, liverish, green about the gills, run down, washed out, faint, dizzy, giddy, light-headed; *Brit.* off, off colour; *informal* under the weather, below par, not up to par, funny, peculiar, rough, lousy, awful, terrible, dreadful, crummy; *Brit. informal* grotty, ropy; *Scottish informal* wabbit, peely-wally; *Austral./NZ informal* crook; *dated* queer, seedy; *rare* peaked, peakish.
OPPOSITES well, okay.
▶ adverb (*informal*) *he fancies you something rotten* **very much**, **a lot**, a great deal; really.

rotter ▶ noun (*informal*) *we had decided that all men were rotters* **scoundrel**, rogue, villain, wretch, reprobate; *informal* beast, pig, swine, rat, creep, bastard, louse, snake, snake in the grass, skunk, dog, weasel, scumbag, heel, stinker, stinkpot, bad lot, nasty piece of work; *Scottish informal* scrote; *Irish informal* spalpeen; *N. Amer. informal* rat fink, fink; *Austral. informal* dingo; *informal, dated* hound, bounder, blighter; *vulgar slang* son of a bitch, s.o.b., shit; *dated* cad; *archaic* blackguard, dastard, vagabond, knave, varlet.

rotund ▶ adjective **1** *a small, rotund man in his late thirties* **plump**, chubby, fat, stout, roly-poly, fattish, portly, dumpy, chunky, broad in the beam, overweight, heavy, pot-bellied, beer-bellied, paunchy, Falstaffian; buxom, well upholstered, well covered, well padded, of ample proportions, ample, round, rounded, well rounded, full; flabby, fleshy, bulky, corpulent, obese; *informal* tubby, pudgy, beefy, porky, blubbery, poddy; *Brit. informal* podgy, fubsy; *N. Amer. informal* zaftig, corn-fed, lard-assed; *archaic* pursy; *rare* abdominous.
OPPOSITES thin, slender, skinny.
2 *huge stoves bearing rotund cauldrons* **round**, bulbous, spherical; *rare* rotundate, spheral, spheric, spherular, orbicular.
3 *his splendidly rotund tone* **sonorous**, full-toned, full-bodied, round, rich, deep, mellow, resonant, reverberant; magniloquent, grandiloquent, orotund; *rare* pear-shaped, canorous.
OPPOSITES thin, reedy.

roué ▶ noun *he had lived the life of a roué in the fleshpots of London and Paris* **libertine**, rake, debauchee, dissolute man, loose-liver, degenerate, profligate; lecher, seducer, ladies' man, womanizer, philanderer, adulterer, Don Juan, Lothario, Casanova, playboy; sensualist, sybarite, voluptuary; *informal* ladykiller, lech, dirty old man, goat, wolf, skirt-chaser; *dated* gay dog, rip, blood; *archaic* rakehell; *rare* dissolute.

rough ▶ adjective **1** *she stumbled on the rough ground* **uneven**, irregular, bumpy, stony, rocky, broken, rugged, jaggy, craggy; rutted, pitted, rutty.
OPPOSITES flat, smooth.
2 *the terrier's coat is rough and thick* **coarse**, bristly, scratchy, prickly; **shaggy**, hairy, hirsute, bushy, fuzzy.
OPPOSITES smooth, sleek.
3 *the tree has a rough, purplish-brown bark* **gnarled**, knotty, lumpy, knobbly, nodular; *rare* nodulous, nodose.
4 *the cream brings immediate relief to rough skin* **dry**, leathery, weather-beaten; **chapped**, chafed, calloused, scaly, scabrous; *technical* furfuraceous.
OPPOSITE smooth.
5 *his voice was rough with barely controlled anger* **gruff**, hoarse, harsh, rasping, raspy, husky, throaty, gravelly, guttural.
OPPOSITE soft.
6 *down the hall, a noise of rough laughter and shouting could be heard* **raucous**, discordant, cacophonous, grating, jarring, strident, harsh, dissonant, unmusical, inharmonious, unmelodious.
OPPOSITE dulcet.
7 *a bottle of rough red wine* **sharp-tasting**, sharp, sour, acidic, acid, vinegary; *rare* acidulous.
OPPOSITES sweet, mellow.
8 *he tends to get rough when he's drunk* **violent**, brutal, vicious; **aggressive**, belligerent, pugnacious, thuggish; **boisterous**, rowdy, disorderly, unruly, unrestrained, wild, riotous, undisciplined, unmanageable; *informal* ugly.
OPPOSITES gentle, passive.
9 *a robust machine, able to withstand rough handling* **careless**, clumsy, inept, unskilful.
OPPOSITE careful.
10 *Sophie disliked his rough manners* **boorish**, loutish, oafish, brutish, coarse, crude, uncouth, rough-hewn, roughcast, vulgar, unrefined, unladylike, ungentlemanly, uncultured, ill-bred, ill-mannered, unmannerly, impolite, churlish, discourteous, uncivil, ungracious, rude, brusque, blunt, curt.
OPPOSITES cultured, civilized, refined.
11 *rough seas* **turbulent**, stormy, storm-tossed, tempestuous, violent, heavy, heaving, raging, choppy, agitated.
OPPOSITE calm.
12 *the weather was really rough* **stormy**, wild, tempestuous, squally, wet, rainy, windy, blustery; foul, filthy, nasty, inclement, unpleasant, disagreeable.
OPPOSITE fine.
13 (*informal*) *they gave him a very rough time* **difficult**, hard, tough, bad, unpleasant, demanding, arduous.
OPPOSITES easy, pleasant.
14 (*Brit. informal*) *you were a bit rough on her* **harsh**, hard, tough, stern, sharp, abrasive, severe, unfair, unjust, unrelenting, unfeeling, insensitive, nasty, cruel; **unkind**, unsympathetic, inconsiderate, brutal, heartless, savage, merciless, extreme.
OPPOSITES kind, gentle.
15 (*informal*) *'How are you feeling?' 'Pretty rough'* **ill**, unwell, poorly, bad, out of sorts, indisposed, not oneself, sick, queasy, nauseous, nauseated, peaky, liverish, green about the gills, run down, washed out, faint, dizzy, giddy, light-headed; *Brit.* off, off colour; *informal* under the weather, below par, not up to par, funny, peculiar, lousy, rotten, awful, terrible, dreadful, crummy; *Brit. informal* grotty, ropy; *Scottish informal* wabbit, peely-wally; *Austral./NZ informal* crook; *dated* seedy; *rare* peaked, peakish.
OPPOSITES well, okay.
16 *she cobbled together a rough draft and then rewrote it* **preliminary**, hasty, quick, sketchy, cursory, basic, crude, rudimentary, rough and ready, raw, unpolished, unrefined; incomplete, unfinished, uncompleted.
OPPOSITES finished, perfected.
17 *this is only a rough estimate* **approximate**, inexact, estimated, imprecise, vague, general, hazy; *N. Amer. informal* ballpark.
OPPOSITES exact, accurate, precise.
18 *I'm afraid the accommodation is rather rough* **plain**, **basic**, simple, rough and ready, rustic, rude, crude, primitive, spartan, uncomfortable.
OPPOSITE luxurious.
▶ noun **1** *the artist's initial roughs are very important* **preliminary sketch**, draft, outline, mock-up, model.
2 (*Brit.*) *a bunch of roughs attacked him* **ruffian**, thug, lout, hooligan, hoodlum, rowdy, bully boy, brawler; *Austral.* larrikin; *informal* tough, roughneck, bruiser, gorilla, yahoo; *Brit. informal* yob, yobbo, bovver boy, lager lout; *Scottish & N. English informal* keelie, ned; *Austral./NZ informal* roughie.
▶ verb *rough the surface with sandpaper* **roughen**, make rough.
□ **rough something out draft**, sketch out, outline, block out, mock up; suggest, delineate, give a brief idea of; *formal* adumbrate.
□ **rough someone up** (*informal*) **beat up**, beat, attack, assault, knock about/around, maltreat, mistreat, abuse, batter, manhandle; *informal* do over, bash up, work over, beat the living daylights out of; *Brit. informal* duff up; *N. Amer. informal* beat up on.

rough and ready ▶ adjective *a somewhat rough and ready solution to the problem* **basic**, simple, crude, unrefined, unpolished, unsophisticated;

makeshift, make-do, thrown together, cobbled together, provisional, stopgap, improvised, extemporary; hurried, sketchy; *Latin* ad hoc.
OPPOSITE sophisticated.

rough and tumble ▶ noun **1** *the row started a real rough and tumble* **scuffle**, struggle, fight, brawl, fracas, rumpus, melee, free-for-all, scrimmage; *Irish, N. Amer., & Austral.* donnybrook; *Law, dated* affray; *informal* scrap, dust-up, punch-up, shindy; *N. Amer. informal* rough house.
2 *the boisterous rough and tumble of four three-year-olds* **fun and games**, horseplay, play, high jinks, romping.

roughly ▶ adverb **1** *he shoved her roughly away from him* **violently**, forcefully, forcibly, abruptly, unceremoniously.
OPPOSITE gently.
2 *they treated him roughly* **harshly**, unkindly, severely, unsympathetically; brutally, violently, savagely, inhumanly, mercilessly, cruelly, heartlessly.
OPPOSITES kindly, gently.
3 *a deal worth roughly £2.4 million* **approximately**, about, around, round about, in the region of, something like, in the area of, in the neighbourhood of, of the order of, or so, or thereabouts, there or thereabouts, more or less, give or take a few, plus or minus a few; nearly, close to, as near as dammit, not far off, approaching; *Brit.* getting on for; *S. African* plus-minus; *Latin* circa; *N. Amer. informal* in the ballpark of.
OPPOSITES exactly, precisely.

roughneck ▶ noun (*informal*). *See* RUFFIAN.

round ▶ adjective **1** *a small round window | a round glass ball* **circular**, disc-shaped, disk-like; ring-shaped, hoop-shaped, hoop-like, annular; **spherical**, globular, ball-shaped, globe-shaped, orb-shaped, orb-like, cylindrical, bulbous, bulb-shaped, balloon-like; convex, curved, curvilinear, rounded, rotund; *technical* cycloidal, discoid, discoidal, spheroid, spheroidal; *rare* globate, globose, orbicular, orbiculate.
2 *a short round man with a loud voice* **plump**, chubby, fat, stout, rotund, roly-poly, fattish, portly, dumpy, chunky, broad in the beam, overweight, heavy, pot-bellied, beer-bellied, paunchy, Falstaffian; buxom, well upholstered, well covered, well padded, of ample proportions, ample, rounded, well rounded, full; flabby, fleshy, bulky, corpulent, obese; *informal* tubby, pudgy, beefy, porky, blubbery, poddy; *Brit. informal* podgy, fubsy; *N. Amer. informal* zaftig, corn-fed, lard-assed; *archaic* pursy; *rare* abdominous.
OPPOSITES thin, slender, skinny.
3 *his deep, round voice went down well with the listeners* **sonorous**, resonant, rich, full, full-toned, full-bodied, mellow, mellifluous, rounded, reverberant, orotund; *rare* pear-shaped, canorous.
OPPOSITES harsh, thin, reedy.
4 *a round dozen* **complete**, entire, whole, full, undivided, unbroken.
5 (*archaic*) *she berated him in round terms* **candid**, frank, direct, honest, truthful, straightforward, plain, plain-spoken, blunt, outspoken, forthright, downright, unvarnished, bald, straight from the shoulder, explicit, unequivocal; *informal* upfront, not pulling any punches, not beating about the bush; *archaic* free-spoken.
OPPOSITE evasive.
▶ noun **1** *divide the dough into 2 oz pieces and mould into rounds* **circle**, disc, circlet; **ring**, hoop, band; **ball**, sphere, globe, orb, bead; *technical* annulus.
2 *the local policeman was on his rounds* **circuit**, beat, course, route; tour, turn.
3 *the first round of the World 500cc championship* **stage**, level; **heat**, game, lap, bout, contest.
4 *an endless round of late-night parties* **succession**, sequence, series, cycle.
5 *the gun can fire 30 rounds a second* **bullet**, cartridge, shell, shot.
▶ preposition & adverb **1** *there's a maze of alleys round the station* **around**, about, encircling, enclosing; near, in the neighbourhood of, in the vicinity of, in the area of; orbiting.
2 *casinos dotted round the south of France* **throughout**, all over, here and there in, everywhere in.
□ **round about** *he earns round about £40,000 a year* **approximately**, about, around, roughly, in the neighbourhood of, in the area of, of the order of, just about, something like, more or less, as near as dammit, to, close to, near to, practically; or so, or thereabouts, there or thereabouts, give or take a few, plus or minus a few, give or take a bit, in round numbers; not far off, nearly, almost, approaching; *Brit.* getting on for; *S. African* plus-minus; *Latin* circa; *N. Amer. informal* in the ballpark of.
OPPOSITES precisely, exactly.
□ **round the bend** (*informal*) **mad**, insane, out of one's mind, deranged, demented, not in one's right mind, certifiable, of unsound mind, crazed, lunatic, unbalanced, unhinged, unstable, disturbed, frenzied, raving, distraught, mad as a hatter, mad as a March hare; *Latin* non compos mentis; *informal* crazy, mental, off one's head, out of one's head, off one's nut, nuts, nutty, nutty as a fruitcake, off one's rocker, not (quite) right in the head, raving mad, bats, batty, bonkers, cuckoo, loopy, loony, bananas, loco, dippy, screwy, touched, gaga, doolally, up the pole, not all there, out to lunch, not right upstairs, away with the fairies; *Brit. informal* barmy, crackers, barking, barking mad, round the twist, off one's trolley, as daft as a brush, not the full shilling, two sandwiches short of a picnic; *N. Amer. informal* buggy, off the wall, nutsy, nutso, out of one's tree, meshuga, squirrelly, wacko, gonzo; *Canadian & Austral./NZ informal* bushed; *NZ informal* porangi.
OPPOSITE sane.
□ **round the clock 1** *I've got a team working round the clock* **day and night**, night and day, all the time, {morning, noon, and night}, the entire time, continuously, non-stop, uninterruptedly, without interruption, without a break, steadily, unremittingly; *informal* all the hours God sends, 24-7.
OPPOSITE intermittently.
2 *she needs round-the-clock supervision* **continuous**, constant, non-stop, continual, uninterrupted, without interruption, unbroken, steady.
OPPOSITE intermittent.
▶ verb *the ship rounded the point* **go round**, move round, travel round, sail round, circumnavigate; orbit; skirt.
□ **round something off 1** *the square edges were rounded off* **smooth off**, plane off, sand off, level off.
2 *the annual Christmas party rounded off a hugely successful year for the company* **complete**, finish off, crown, cap, top off, conclude, close, bring to a close/end, end.
OPPOSITE begin.
□ **round on** *Guido rounded on Rosie, as though she were to blame* **snap at**, attack, turn on, set upon, weigh into, fly at, let fly at, lash out at, hit out at, lambaste; *informal* bite someone's head off, jump down someone's throat, lay into, wade into, lace into, pitch into, tear into; *Brit. informal* have a go at; *N. Amer. informal* light into.
□ **round someone/something up gather together**, herd together, drive together, bring together, muster, marshal, rally, assemble, collect, group; *N. Amer.* corral, wrangle.
OPPOSITES disperse, scatter.

roundabout ▶ adjective **1** *the bus took a very long and roundabout route to Linby* **circuitous**, indirect, meandering, winding, serpentine, tortuous; *rare* anfractuous.
OPPOSITE straight.
2 *I did ask him, in a roundabout sort of way* **indirect**, oblique, circuitous, circumlocutory, periphrastic; meandering, discursive, digressive, long-winded; evasive; *rare* circumlocutionary, ambagious.
OPPOSITE direct.
▶ noun (*Brit.*) **1** *go straight on at the roundabout* *N. Amer.* rotary, traffic circle.
2 *an old-fashioned roundabout with painted wooden horses* **merry-go-round**, carousel; *archaic* whirligig.

roundly ▶ adverb **1** *the 13 per cent pay increase was roundly condemned* **vehemently**, emphatically, fiercely, forcefully, sharply, bitterly, severely; **bluntly**, outspokenly, forthrightly, baldly, plainly, frankly, candidly.
OPPOSITES mildly, gently.
2 *she was roundly defeated by a ratio of two votes to one* **utterly**, completely, totally, thoroughly, decisively, conclusively, heavily, soundly.
OPPOSITE narrowly.

round-up ▶ noun **1** *a cattle round-up* **gathering together**, collecting up, collection, assembly, assembling, rally, rallying, muster, mustering, marshalling; herding together; *N. Amer.* rodeo, corralling, wrangling.
OPPOSITE dispersal.
2 *the Monday sports round-up* **summary**, synopsis, overview, review, survey, outline, summarization, digest, recapitulation; *French* precis, tour d'horizon; *N. Amer.* wrap-up; *informal* recap.

rouse ▶ verb **1** *he roused Ralph at dawn* **wake**, wake up, awaken, waken, arouse; call, get up; *informal* give someone a shout, knock up.
2 *she roused and looked around* **wake up**, wake, awaken, come to, get up, get out of bed, rise, bestir oneself; *formal* arise.
OPPOSITE go to sleep.
3 *he roused the crowd with a speech* **stir up**, excite, galvanize, electrify, stimulate, inspire, move, fire up, fire the enthusiasm of, fire the imagination of, get going, whip up, inflame, agitate, goad, provoke; incite, egg on, spur on; *N. Amer.* light a fire under; *rare* inspirit.
OPPOSITE calm.
4 *he's got quite a nasty temper when he's roused* **provoke**, **annoy**, anger, make angry, infuriate, send into a rage, madden, incense, vex, irk, work up, exasperate; *informal* aggravate.
OPPOSITES pacify, appease.
5 *the letter's disappearance roused my suspicions* **arouse**, awaken, give rise to, prompt, provoke, stimulate, pique, stir up, trigger, spark off, touch off, kindle, elicit; *literary* beget, enkindle.
OPPOSITE allay.

rousing ▶ adjective *Mr Edmonds made a rousing speech* **stirring**, inspiring, exciting, stimulating, moving, electrifying, invigorating, enlivening, animating, energizing, exhilarating; **enthusiastic**, vigorous, hearty, energetic, lively, spirited, animated; inflammatory; *N. Amer. informal* stem-winding; *rare* anthemic, inspiriting.
OPPOSITES dull; half-hearted.

rout ▶ noun **1** *the army's offensive turned into an ignominious rout* **disorderly retreat**, retreat, flight, headlong flight.
2 *Newcastle scored 13 tries in the 76–4 rout* **crushing defeat**, overwhelming defeat, defeat, trouncing, annihilation; debacle, fiasco; *informal* licking, hammering, clobbering, thrashing, pasting, drubbing, hiding, caning,

demolition, going-over, pounding, massacre; *N. Amer. informal* shellacking. OPPOSITE victory.

▶ **verb 1** *his army was routed at the Battle of Milvian Bridge* **put to flight**, put to rout, drive off, dispel, scatter; defeat, beat, conquer, vanquish, crush, overpower, overwhelm, overthrow, subjugate.
2 *the German star routed the defending champion* **beat hollow**, trounce, defeat utterly, annihilate, triumph over, win a resounding victory over, be victorious over, best, get the better of, worst, bring someone to their knees; *informal* lick, hammer, clobber, thrash, paste, pound, pulverize, crucify, demolish, destroy, drub, give someone a drubbing, cane, wipe the floor with, walk all over, give someone a hiding, take to the cleaners, blow out of the water, make mincemeat of, murder, massacre, slaughter, flatten, turn inside out, tank; *Brit. informal* stuff, marmalize; *N. Amer. informal* blow out, cream, shellac, skunk, slam.
OPPOSITE lose.

route ▶ **noun** *he walked back by a different route* **way**, **course**, road, path, avenue, direction; circuit, round, beat; passage, journey, flight path.
▶ **verb** *the system will ensure that specialist enquiries are routed to the most appropriate staff* **direct**, send, convey, dispatch, forward.

routine ▶ **noun 1** *his early morning routine never varied* **procedure**, practice, pattern, drill, regime, regimen, groove; programme, schedule, plan; formula, method, system, order; ways, customs, habits, usages; wont; *Latin* modus operandi; *formal* praxis.
2 *his stand-up routine depends heavily on improvisation* **act**, performance, number, turn, piece, line; *informal* shtick, spiel, patter.
▶ **adjective 1** *a routine health check* **standard**, regular, customary, accustomed, normal, usual, ordinary, established, natural, unexceptional, typical; everyday, common, commonplace, conventional, day-to-day, habitual, wonted, familiar.
OPPOSITE unusual.
2 *a routine urban-action movie* **boring**, tedious, tiresome, wearisome, monotonous, humdrum, run-of-the-mill, prosaic, dreary, pedestrian, menial; unvarying, unchanging; predictable, workaday, hackneyed, stock, unexciting, uninteresting, uninspiring, unimaginative, unoriginal, banal, trite; uneventful.
OPPOSITE exciting.

rove ▶ **verb** *for ten years I roved about* **wander**, roam, ramble, drift, meander, go hither and thither, maunder; range, travel about; gallivant; *Scottish* stravaig; *Irish* streel; *rare* vagabond, circumambulate, peregrinate.

CHOOSE THE RIGHT WORD

rove, wander, roam, range, stray

See WANDER.

rover ▶ **noun** **wanderer**, traveller, globetrotter, drifter, bird of passage, roamer, itinerant, transient; nomad, gypsy, Romany; tramp, vagrant, vagabond; *N. Amer.* hobo; *informal* gadabout; *Scottish archaic* landloper.

row[1] (rhymes with 'go') ▶ **noun 1** *rows of small children* **line**, **column**, file, cordon, queue; procession, chain, string, series, succession; *informal* crocodile.
2 *the middle row of seats* **tier**, line, rank, bank.
□ **in a row** *three days in a row* **consecutively**, one after the other, in succession; running, straight; *informal* on the trot.

row[2] (rhymes with 'cow') (*Brit. informal*) ▶ **noun 1** *have you and Peter had a row?* **argument**, quarrel, squabble, fight, contretemps, disagreement, difference of opinion, dissension, falling-out, dispute, disputation, contention, clash, altercation, shouting match, exchange, war of words; *informal* tiff, set-to, run-in, spat; *Brit. informal* barney, slanging match, bunfight, ding-dong, bust-up; *N. Amer. informal* rhubarb; *archaic* broil, miff; *Scottish archaic* threap, collieshangie; *French archaic* tracasserie(s).
OPPOSITES reconciliation, agreement.
2 *Zach could hardly hear because of the row the crowd was making* **din**, noise, racket, clamour, uproar, tumult, hubbub, commotion, disturbance, brouhaha, ruckus, rumpus, pandemonium, babel; *informal* ruction, hullabaloo; *N. Amer. informal* foofaraw.
3 *if Ted spotted you at it, he'd give you a row* **reprimand**, rebuke, reproof, admonition, reproach, reproval, scolding, remonstration, upbraiding, castigation, lambasting, lecture, criticism, censure; *informal* rap, rap over the knuckles, telling-off, slap on the wrist, flea in one's ear, dressing-down, roasting, tongue-lashing, bawling-out, caning, blast; *Brit. informal* ticking-off, carpeting, wigging, rollicking, rocket; *Austral./NZ informal* serve; *Brit. vulgar slang* bollocking; *dated* rating.
▶ **verb** *lots of couples row about money* **argue**, quarrel, squabble, bicker, have a row/fight, fight, fall out, disagree, fail to agree, differ, be at odds, have a misunderstanding, be at variance, have words, dispute, spar, wrangle, bandy words, cross swords, lock horns, be at each other's throats, be at loggerheads; *informal* scrap, go at it hammer and tongs, argufy; *archaic* altercate, chop logic; *Scottish archaic* fratch.

rowdy ▶ **adjective** *gangs of rowdy youths* **unruly**, disorderly, badly behaved, obstreperous, riotous, unrestrained, undisciplined, ill-disciplined, unmanageable, uncontrollable, ungovernable, uncontrolled, disruptive, out of hand, out of control, rough, wild, turbulent, lawless; boisterous, irrepressible, uproarious, rollicking, roisterous, rackety, noisy, loud, clamorous; *Brit. informal* rumbustious; *N. Amer. informal* rambunctious; *archaic* rampageous.
OPPOSITES peaceful, quiet, restrained.
▶ **noun** *the pub was filling up with rowdies* **ruffian**, troublemaker, lout, hooligan, thug, bully boy, hoodlum, brawler; *Brit.* tearaway; *Scottish & N. English* keelie, ned; *Austral.* larrikin; *informal* tough, bruiser, yahoo; *Brit. informal* rough, yob, yobbo, bovver boy, lager lout; *Austral./NZ informal* roughie.

royal ▶ **adjective 1** *a royal wave | the royal prerogative* **regal**, kingly, queenly, kinglike, queenlike, princely; sovereign, monarchical.
2 *tourists can expect a royal welcome* **excellent**, fine, marvellous, magnificent, splendid, superb, wonderful, first-rate, first-class; *informal* fantastic, terrific, great, tremendous, grand.
3 (*informal*) *she's a royal pain in the neck* **complete**, utter, total, real, absolute, thorough, veritable; *informal* flaming, damn, damned, blasted, blessed, confounded; *Brit. informal* proper, right, flipping, blinking, blooming, bloody, bleeding, effing, chuffing; *Austral./NZ informal* plurry; *Brit. informal, dated* bally, ruddy; *vulgar slang* fucking, frigging.

rub ▶ **verb 1** *Polly rubbed the back of her neck* **massage**, knead; stroke, pat.
2 *Rodney was rubbing suntan lotion on Sophie's back* **apply**, put on, smear, smooth, spread, work in, cream in.
3 *badly fitting shoes can rub painfully* **chafe**, pinch, scrape, abrade; hurt, be sore, be painful.
□ **rub along** (*Brit. informal*) *we rubbed along as best as we could* **manage**, cope, get along/on, make do, be/fare/do all right, muddle along/through, shift; *informal* make out, get by.
□ **rub something down** *the horses were unsaddled and rubbed down* **clean**, sponge, wash; dry; groom; smooth.
□ **rub it in** (*informal*) **emphasize**, stress, underline, highlight; **keep going on about**, harp on, dwell on, make an issue of; *informal* rub someone's nose in it.
□ **rub off on** *my father had a strong contempt for science which rubbed off on me* **be transferred to**, be passed on to, be transmitted to, be communicated to; affect, influence, have an effect on.
OPPOSITES have no effect on; be water off a duck's back to.
□ **rub someone out** (*N. Amer. informal*). *See* KILL.
□ **rub something out** **erase**, delete, scrub out, wipe off, remove, efface, obliterate, expunge.
OPPOSITES add, leave.
□ **rub shoulders with** **associate with**, mingle with, fraternize with, socialize with, mix with, keep company with, consort with; *N. Amer.* rub elbows with; *informal* hang around/out with, hobnob with, run around with, knock about/around with, pal around with, chum around with; *Brit. informal* hang about.
□ **rub something up** *the top of the stove was rubbed up every day* **polish**, buff up, burnish, shine, wax; clean, wipe, scrub, scour.
□ **rub someone up the wrong way** (*informal*) **irritate**, annoy, irk, vex, provoke, displease, exasperate, infuriate, get on someone's nerves, get/put someone's back up, put out, pique, upset, nettle, needle, ruffle someone's feathers, make someone's hackles rise, try someone's patience; jar on, grate on; *informal* aggravate, get, get to, bug, miff, peeve, rile, get under someone's skin, get in someone's hair, get up someone's nose, hack off, get someone's goat; *Brit. informal* nark, get on someone's wick, give someone the hump, wind up, get across; *N. Amer. informal* rankle, ride, gravel; *vulgar slang* piss off; *Brit. vulgar slang* get on someone's tits; *rare* exacerbate, hump, rasp.
OPPOSITE charm.
▶ **noun 1** *she gave my back a rub* **massage**, rub-down.
2 *I gave my shoes a final rub* **polish**, buffing; wipe, clean.
3 *that's the rub—will busy managers contemplate reading such a large amount of material?* **problem**, **difficulty**, trouble, drawback, hindrance, obstacle, obstruction, impediment; snag, hitch, catch.

WORD LINKS
related prefix **tribo-** (e.g. ***triboelectricity***)
study of friction **tribology**

rubbish ▶ **noun 1** *a more environmentally friendly way of disposing of rubbish* **refuse**, waste, garbage, litter, discarded matter, debris, detritus, scrap, dross; flotsam and jetsam, lumber; sweepings, leavings, leftovers, scraps, dregs, offscourings, odds and ends; muck; *N. Amer.* trash; *Austral./NZ* mullock; *informal* dreck, junk; *Brit. informal* grot, gash; *Archaeology* debitage; *rare* draff, raffle, raff, cultch, orts.
2 *she's talking a load of rubbish* **nonsense**, balderdash, gibberish, claptrap, blarney, blather, blether, moonshine; *informal* hogwash, baloney, tripe, drivel, bilge, bosh, bull, bunk, rot, hot air, eyewash, piffle, poppycock, phooey, hooey, malarkey, twaddle, guff, dribble; gobbledegook; *Brit. informal* codswallop, cock, cobblers, stuff and nonsense, tosh, taradiddle, cack; *Scottish & N. English informal* havers; *Irish informal* codology; *N. Amer. informal* garbage, flapdoodle, blathers, wack, bushwa, applesauce; *informal, dated* bunkum, tommyrot, cod, gammon, toffee; *vulgar slang* shit, crap, bullshit, balls; *Austral./NZ vulgar slang* bulldust.
OPPOSITE sense.

R

▶ **verb** (*Brit. informal*) *he seems to spend a lot of his time rubbishing trade unions.* See CRITICIZE.
▶ **adjective** (*Brit. informal*) *they're a rubbish team.* See HOPELESS sense 4.

rubbishy ▶ **adjective** (*informal*) *a crop of delightfully named but rubbishy books* **worthless**, valueless, trashy, inferior, unsatisfactory, substandard, second-rate, third-rate, poor-quality, low-quality, low-grade, cheap, shoddy, tawdry, gimcrack, twopenny-halfpenny; **bad**, poor, dreadful, awful, terrible, frightful, atrocious; *informal* crummy, appalling, abysmal, lousy, dire, tacky; *Brit. informal* duff, chronic, rubbish, poxy, pants, a load of pants; *vulgar slang* crap, crappy, chickenshit.
OPPOSITE high-quality.

rubble ▶ **noun** *at the moment we are still trying to dig people out of the rubble* **debris**, remains, ruins, wreckage; broken bricks.

ruction ▶ **noun** (*informal*) *what's that ruction going on outside?* | *the painting caused ructions at the National Gallery* **disturbance**, noise, racket, din, commotion, fuss, pother, uproar, furore, hue and cry, rumpus, ruckus, fracas; altercation, quarrel; (**ructions**) an outcry, trouble, the devil to pay, hell to pay; *informal* to-do, carry-on, hullabaloo, hoo-ha, ballyhoo, stink; *Brit. informal* row, kerfuffle; *N. Amer. informal* foofaraw.

ruddy ▶ **adjective 1** *he was tall and fair with a ruddy complexion* **reddish**, red, rosy, rosy-cheeked, pink, pinkish, roseate, rubicund; healthy-looking, glowing, fresh; flushed, blushing; florid, high-coloured; *archaic* sanguine; *rare* erubescent, rubescent.
OPPOSITES pale, unhealthy.
2 *the ruddy glow of the low sun* **red**, reddish, scarlet, vermilion, crimson, blood-red, rose-red, pink, roseate.
3 (*Brit. informal*) *you ruddy idiot!* **complete**, total, utter; *informal* damn, damned, blasted, blessed, flaming, confounded, blithering; *Brit. informal* flipping, blinking, blooming, bloody, bleeding, effing, chuffing; *N. Amer. informal* goddam, doggone; *Austral./NZ informal* plurry; *Brit. informal, dated* bally; *vulgar slang* fucking, frigging; *Irish vulgar slang* fecking.

rude ▶ **adjective 1** *a rude, arrogant young man* **ill-mannered**, bad-mannered, impolite, discourteous, impertinent, insolent, impudent, cheeky, audacious, presumptuous, uncivil, disrespectful, unmannerly, ill-bred, churlish, crass, curt, brusque, blunt, ungracious, graceless, brash, unpleasant, disagreeable, offhand, short, sharp; **offensive**, insulting, derogatory, disparaging, abusive; tactless, undiplomatic, uncomplimentary, uncharitable, unchivalrous, ungallant, ungentlemanly, unladylike; *archaic* malapert, contumelious; *rare* underbred, mannerless.
OPPOSITES polite, civil, chivalrous.
2 *some of the boys made rude jokes about her shapely figure* **vulgar**, coarse, smutty, dirty, filthy, crude, lewd, obscene, offensive, indelicate, improper, indecorous, salacious, off colour, tasteless, in bad taste; risqué, naughty, ribald, bawdy, racy, broad, spicy, colourful, suggestive; *informal* blue, raunchy, nudge-nudge; *Brit. informal* fruity, near the knuckle, saucy; *N. Amer. informal* gamy; *euphemistic* adult.
OPPOSITE clean.
3 *if they expected a friendly atmosphere, they were in for a rude awakening* **abrupt**, sudden, sharp, startling; **unpleasant**, disagreeable, nasty, harsh.
4 *everything in the rude cabin was filthy* **primitive**, crude, rudimentary, rough, rough-hewn, rough and ready, simple, basic, makeshift.
OPPOSITES sophisticated, classy.
5 (*archaic*) *a rude and barbarous people* **uneducated**, ignorant, untutored, illiterate, uncultured, uncultivated, uncivilized, unrefined, rough, coarse, uncouth, boorish, oafish, loutish.
OPPOSITES educated, civilized.

R

rudeness ▶ **noun** *I wanted to apologize for my rudeness the other day* **discourteousness**, discourtesy, lack of manners, bad manners, impoliteness, impertinence, impudence, insolence, effrontery, audacity, presumptuousness, cheek, cheekiness, incivility, disrespect, disrespectfulness, churlishness, crassness, curtness, brusqueness, bluntness, ungraciousness, brashness, sharpness, abusiveness; tactlessness, lack of tact, lack of diplomacy, ungentlemanly behaviour, unladylike behaviour, boorishness, uncouthness; *informal* lip; *Brit. informal* sauce, backchat; *N. Amer. informal* back talk, smart mouth, sass; *archaic* malapertness, contumely.
OPPOSITES politeness, good manners.

rudimentary ▶ **adjective 1** *a simple device which can be constructed by anyone with rudimentary carpentry skills* **basic**, elementary, introductory, early, primary, initial, first; fundamental, essential; *rare* rudimental.
OPPOSITE advanced.
2 *the equipment in all the workshops was rudimentary* **primitive**, **crude**, simple, unsophisticated, rough, rough and ready, makeshift, rude.
OPPOSITE sophisticated.
3 *spider monkeys have four long fingers, but only a rudimentary thumb* **vestigial**, undeveloped, incomplete, embryonic, immature; non-functional; *technical* abortive, primitive, obsolete.
OPPOSITE developed.

rudiments ▶ **plural noun** *the rudiments of statistics and probability theory* **basic principles**, basics, fundamentals, elements, essentials, first principles; beginnings, foundation; *informal* nuts and bolts, ABC.

rue ▶ **verb** *she might live to rue this impetuous decision* **regret**, be sorry about, feel apologetic/remorseful about, feel remorse for, repent of; reproach oneself for, kick oneself for; deplore, lament, bemoan, bewail.

rueful ▶ **adjective** *'I've been pretty stupid, haven't I?' Harry said, with a rueful smile* **sorrowful**, regretful, apologetic, sorry, remorseful, shamefaced, sheepish, hangdog, contrite, repentant, penitent, conscience-stricken, self-reproachful; woebegone, woeful, sad, melancholy, mournful; *rare* compunctious.
OPPOSITES happy; unrepentant.

ruffian ▶ **noun** *she was set upon by a gang of young ruffians* **thug**, scoundrel, villain, rogue, rascal, lout, hooligan, hoodlum, vandal, delinquent, rowdy, bully boy, bully, brute; *Austral.* larrikin; *informal* tough, bruiser, heavy, gorilla, yahoo; *Brit. informal* rough, yob, yobbo, bovver boy, lager lout; *Scottish & N. English informal* keelie, ned; *N. Amer. informal* hood, goon; *Austral./NZ informal* roughie; *archaic* miscreant; *rare* myrmidon.

ruffle ▶ **verb 1** *Patrick kissed her on the cheek and ruffled her hair* **disarrange**, tousle, dishevel, rumple, run one's fingers through, make untidy, tumble, riffle, disorder; mess up, make a mess of, tangle; *N. Amer. informal* muss, muss up.
OPPOSITE smooth.
2 *a light wind ruffled the water* **make ripples in**, ripple, riffle, roughen.
OPPOSITE smooth.
3 *'Keep calm,' she told herself, 'don't let him ruffle you'* **annoy**, irritate, irk, vex, nettle, needle, anger, exasperate; **disconcert**, unnerve, fluster, flurry, agitate, harass, upset, disturb, discomfit, put off, put someone off their stroke, throw off balance, make nervous, discompose, discountenance, cause someone to lose their composure, perturb, unsettle, bother, affect, ruffle someone's feathers, worry, disquiet, trouble, confuse; *informal* rattle, faze, throw, get to, put into a flap, throw into a tizz, rile, niggle, aggravate, bug, miff, peeve, discombobulate, shake up; *Brit. informal* wind up, nark, get across.
OPPOSITES soothe, calm.
▶ **noun** *a very full shirt with ruffles down the front* **frill**, flounce, ruff, ruche, jabot, furbelow.

rug See centre pages for list of **Carpets and Rugs**
▶ **noun 1** *Charles and Elaine were sitting on the rug in front of the fire* **mat**, carpet; *N. Amer.* floorcloth.
2 *his legs were wrapped in a tartan rug* **blanket**, coverlet, throw, wrap; travelling rug; *N. Amer.* lap robe, steamer rug.
3 (*informal*) *he's still wearing that ridiculous rug* **toupee**, wig, hairpiece; *rare* merkin.

Rugby ▶ **noun**. See centre pages for list of **Rugby Players**

rugged ▶ **adjective 1** *the rugged coast path meanders among tall cliffs* **rough**, uneven, bumpy, rocky, stony, irregular, pitted, broken up, jagged, craggy, precipitous.
OPPOSITE smooth.
2 *the sort of conditions which could tear a wheel off a less rugged vehicle* **durable**, robust, sturdy, strong, strongly made, hard-wearing, built to last, tough, resilient.
OPPOSITES flimsy, fragile.
3 *up on the scaffolding, two rugged manly types whistled at her* **well built**, burly, strong, big and strong, muscular, muscly, brawny, strapping, chunky, husky, hulking, broad-shouldered, powerfully built, muscle-bound; tough, hardy, robust, sturdy, vigorous, hale and hearty, lusty, solid, mighty; *informal* hunky, beefy; *dated* stalwart; *literary* thewy, stark.
OPPOSITES frail, weedy, skinny.
4 *Drew's rugged features* **strong**, craggy, rough-hewn, rough-textured, manly, masculine; irregular; weather-beaten, weathered.
OPPOSITES delicate, pretty.
5 *a rugged outdoor life* **austere**, tough, harsh, spartan, exacting, taxing, demanding, difficult, hard, arduous, rigorous, strenuous, onerous.
OPPOSITE easy.
6 *the region is a bastion of rugged individualism* **uncompromising**, unwavering, unflinching, firm, tenacious, determined, resolute.
OPPOSITES ineffectual, feeble.

ruin ▶ **noun 1** *these handsome red-brick buildings may now be saved from ruin* **disintegration**, decay, disrepair, dilapidation, falling to pieces, decrepitude, ruination; **destruction**, devastation, damage, demolition, wreckage.
OPPOSITES reconstruction, preservation.
2 (**ruins**) *the ruins of an ancient church* **remains**, remnants, fragments, relics, remainder, rubble, debris, detritus, wreckage; wreck.
3 *the situation was thought to spell electoral ruin for Labour* **downfall**, collapse, defeat, overthrow, undoing, fall, failure, breakdown, break-up, disintegration, devastation, ruination; Waterloo; *rare* labefaction.
OPPOSITES triumph, success.
4 *despite extra sales, many shopkeepers are facing ruin* **bankruptcy**, insolvency, penury, poverty, destitution, impoverishment, indigence, beggary, financial failure; disaster, catastrophe, calamity; *rare* pauperism, pauperdom, mendicity.
OPPOSITES wealth, success.

□ **in ruins 1** *today, the abbey is in ruins* **derelict**, ruined, gone to rack and

ruin, in disrepair, falling to pieces, falling apart, dilapidated, tumbledown, ramshackle, broken-down, decrepit, decaying, ruinous; neglected, uncared-for.
OPPOSITE intact.
2 *he was a bitter man, his career in ruins* **destroyed**, ruined, in pieces, in ashes, falling down about one's ears; over, finished, at an end; *informal* in tatters, in shreds, on the rocks, done for.
OPPOSITE flourishing.
▶ **verb 1** *a confrontation now would ruin all my plans* **wreck**, destroy, devastate, wreak havoc on, reduce to nothing, damage, spoil, mar, injure, blast, blight, smash, shatter, dash, torpedo, scotch, make a mess of, mess up; sabotage, poison; *informal* louse up, screw up, foul up, put the kibosh on, banjax, do for, blow a hole in, nix, queer; *Brit. informal* scupper, cock up, dish; *Austral. informal* euchre, cruel; *vulgar slang* fuck up; *archaic* bring to naught.
OPPOSITES restore, save.
2 *the bank's collapse was believed to have ruined nearly 2,000,000 people* **bankrupt**, make bankrupt, cause to go bankrupt, make insolvent, impoverish, reduce to penury/destitution, bring to ruin, bring someone to their knees, wipe out, break, cripple; *rare* pauperize, beggar.
3 *a country that was ruined by decades of civil war* **destroy**, devastate, lay waste, leave in ruins, wreak havoc on, ravage, leave desolate; raze, demolish, blast, wreck, wipe out, flatten, level, crush; *archaic* waste.
OPPOSITES rebuild, repair.

ruined ▶ **adjective** *a fascinating medieval town with a ruined castle* **derelict**, in ruins, gone to rack and ruin, dilapidated, ruinous, tumbledown, ramshackle, broken-down, decrepit, in disrepair, falling to pieces, falling apart, crumbling, decaying, disintegrating; neglected, uncared-for; *informal* shambly; *N. Amer. informal* shacky; *literary* blasted.
OPPOSITES intact, well maintained.

ruinous ▶ **adjective 1** *the spectre of a ruinous trade war loomed* **disastrous**, devastating, catastrophic, calamitous, cataclysmic, crippling, crushing, dire, injurious, damaging, destructive, harmful; costly.
OPPOSITE beneficial.
2 *lending money at ruinous interest rates* **extortionate**, exorbitant, excessively high, sky-high, outrageous, inflated, more than can be afforded; *Brit.* over the odds; *informal* criminal, steep.
3 *a little to the west of the house is an old, ruinous chapel* **derelict**, in ruins, ruined, gone to rack and ruin, dilapidated, tumbledown, ramshackle, broken-down, decrepit, in disrepair, falling to pieces, falling apart, crumbling, decaying, disintegrating; neglected, uncared-for; *informal* shambly; *N. Amer. informal* shacky.
OPPOSITES intact, well maintained.

rule ▶ **noun 1** *you should follow any health and safety rules which apply to your workplace* **regulation**, ruling, directive, order, court order, act, law, by-law, statute, edict, canon, ordinance, pronouncement, mandate, command, dictate, dictum, decree, fiat, proclamation, injunction, commandment, prescription, stipulation, requirement, precept, guideline, direction; (*in Tsarist Russia*) ukase; (*in Spain & Spanish-speaking countries*) pronunciamento.
2 *the general rule is that problems are referred upwards through the organization* **procedure**, practice, protocol, convention, standard, norm, form, routine, custom, habit, wont; *formal* praxis.
3 *moderation in all things—that's the golden rule* **precept**, principle, standard, axiom, truth, truism, maxim, aphorism.
4 *Punjab came under British rule in 1849* **control**, jurisdiction, command, power, sway, dominion, government, administration, sovereignty, leadership, ascendancy, supremacy, authority, direction, mastery, hegemony, regime, influence; *Indian* raj; *archaic* regiment.
□ **as a rule usually**, generally, in general, normally, ordinarily, customarily, almost always, for the most part, on the whole, by and large, in the main, mainly, mostly, more often than not, commonly, typically, on average, in most cases.
▶ **verb 1** *El Salvador was ruled by Spain until 1821* **govern**, preside over, control, have control of, be in control of, lead, be the leader of, dominate, run, head, direct, administer, manage, regulate; *literary* sway.
2 *Mary ruled for only six years* **be in power**, be in control, hold sway, be in authority, be in command, be in charge, govern, be at the helm; **reign**, sit on the throne, wear the crown, wield the sceptre, be monarch, be sovereign.
3 *a High Court judge ruled that the children should be sent back to their father* **decree**, order, direct, pronounce, make a judgement, judge, adjudge, adjudicate, lay down, ordain; decide, find, determine, resolve, settle, establish, hold; *rare* asseverate.
4 *up in the shanty towns, subversion ruled* **prevail**, obtain, be the order of the day, predominate, hold sway, be supreme.
□ **rule something out exclude**, eliminate, reject, dismiss, disregard; preclude, prohibit, prevent, obviate, disallow.

WORD LINKS
related suffixes **-cracy (e.g. *democracy*), -archy (e.g. *oligarchy*)**

ruler *See centre pages for lists of* **Nobles** **Rulers' Titles**
▶ **noun leader**, **sovereign**, monarch, potentate, crowned head, head of state; overlord, chief, chieftain, lord; dynast; despot, dictator, tyrant, autocrat; *rare* tetrarch, ethnarch, autarch.
OPPOSITE subject.

ruling ▶ **noun** *the judge's ruling was slammed by medical experts and union leaders* **decision**, pronouncement, resolution, decree, determination, injunction; **judgement**, adjudication, finding, verdict; sentence.
▶ **adjective 1** *the ruling monarch* **reigning**, sovereign, on the throne; *rare* regnant.
2 *the secretary general of Japan's ruling party* **governing**, in charge, leading, dominant, controlling, commanding, supreme, most powerful, ascendant, in the ascendancy; *rare* prepotent, prepollent.
3 *in the early 1950s football remained the ruling passion of working men* **main**, chief, principal, major, prime, most important, dominating, foremost; prevalent, predominant, widespread, general, popular; central, focal; *informal* number-one; *rare* regnant.
OPPOSITES subsidiary, minor.

rum ▶ **adjective** (*Brit. informal*) *she's a rum one, and no mistake* **odd**, strange, peculiar, unusual, funny, bizarre, queer, weird, curious, abnormal, singular; suspicious, suspect, dubious, questionable; *Scottish* unco; *informal* funny peculiar.
OPPOSITES ordinary, normal.

rumble ▶ **verb** *thunder rumbled high above us* **boom**, thunder, roll, roar, resound, reverberate, echo, grumble, growl.

rumbustious ▶ **adjective** (*Brit. informal*) *rumbustious football fans* **boisterous**, unrestrained, irrepressible, exuberant, uproarious, rollicking, roisterous, rackety, noisy, loud, clamorous; **unruly**, disorderly, rowdy, badly behaved, riotous, undisciplined, ill-disciplined, unmanageable, uncontrollable, ungovernable, uncontrolled, obstreperous, disruptive, wild, rough; *N. Amer. informal* rambunctious; *archaic* rampageous; *rare* robustious.
OPPOSITES restrained, quiet.

ruminate ▶ **verb 1** *we sat ruminating on the nature of existence* **think about**, contemplate, consider, give thought to, give consideration to, mull over, meditate on, muse on, ponder on/over, deliberate about/on, cogitate about/on, dwell on, brood on/over, agonize over, worry about, chew over, puzzle over; turn over in one's mind; *archaic* pore on.
2 *cows emit more methane when they are ruminating* **chew the cud**.

rummage ▶ **verb** *Nancy rummaged in her bag for her cigarettes* **search (through)**, hunt through, scrabble about/around in, root about/around in, ferret (about/around) in, fish about/around in, poke around in, dig in, grub about in, delve in, go through, explore, sift through, rifle through, scour, ransack, turn over; *Brit. informal* rootle around in; *Austral./NZ informal* fossick through; *rare* roust around in.

rumour ▶ **noun 1** *rumour has it that they have been dabbling in the black arts* **gossip**, hearsay, talk, tittle-tattle; *informal* the grapevine, the word on the street; *N. Amer. informal* scuttlebutt, poop; *archaic* fame.
2 *she had already heard rumours about the couple's problems* **piece of gossip**, report, story, whisper, canard; speculation; information, word, news; *French* on dit; *informal* buzz; *rare* bruit.
OPPOSITE hard facts.

rumoured ▶ **adjective** *the pop singer Elton John is rumoured to be among the customers* **said to be**, reported to be; reportedly, reputedly, allegedly, apparently, by all accounts, so the story goes.

rump ▶ **noun 1** *he removed his hand from Shirley's rump* **buttocks**, behind, backside, rear, rear end, seat, haunches, cheeks; hindquarters, croup; *Brit.* bottom; *French* derrière; *German* Sitzfleisch; *informal* sit-upon, stern, BTM, tochus; *Brit. informal* bum, botty, prat, jacksie; *N. Amer. informal* butt, fanny, tush, tushie, tail, duff, buns, booty, caboose, heinie, patootie, keister, tuchis; *W. Indian informal* batty; *humorous* fundament, posterior; *black English* rass, rusty dusty; *Brit. vulgar slang* arse; *N. Amer. vulgar slang* ass; *technical* nates; *archaic* breech.
2 *the rump of the army* **remainder**, remaining part/number, rest, remnant, remnants, remains; those left.

rumple ▶ **verb 1** *one bed was empty, the sheet rumpled* **crumple**, crease, wrinkle, tumble, crush, crinkle, ruck, ruck up, scrunch up, disorder; *Brit. rare* ruckle.
OPPOSITE smooth (out).
2 *Ian rumpled her hair* **ruffle**, disarrange, tousle, dishevel, run one's fingers through, riffle; make untidy, mess up, make a mess of; *N. Amer. informal* muss, muss up.
OPPOSITE smooth.

rumpus ▶ **noun** (*informal*) *there's a terrible rumpus going on outside* **disturbance**, commotion, uproar, confusion, furore, brouhaha, hue and cry, ruckus, fuss, fracas, melee, tumult, riot, brawl, free-for-all, scuffle, struggle, altercation, quarrel; noise, racket, din, outcry; *Irish, N. Amer., & Austral.* donnybrook; *informal* to-do, carry-on, ruction, shindig, shindy, hullabaloo, hoo-ha, ballyhoo, dust-up, scrap, stink; *Brit. informal* row, kerfuffle; *Scottish informal* stooshie; *N. Amer. informal* foofaraw, rough house; *Law, dated* affray; *archaic* broil; *rare* bagarre.

run ▶ **verb 1** *she jumped out of her car and ran across the road* **sprint**, race, dart, rush, dash, hasten, hurry, scurry, scuttle, scamper, hare, bolt,

R

bound, fly, gallop, career, charge, pound, shoot, hurtle, speed, streak, whizz, zoom, sweep, go like lightning, go hell for leather, go like the wind, flash, double; jog, lope, trot, jogtrot, dogtrot; *informal* tear, pelt, scoot, hotfoot it, leg it, belt, zip, whip, go like a bat out of hell, step on it, get a move on, get cracking, put on some speed, stir one's stumps; *Brit. informal* hop it, bomb; *N. Amer. informal* boogie, hightail it, barrel, get the lead out; *informal, dated* cut along; *archaic* post, hie.
OPPOSITE dawdle.
2 *the other three men turned and ran* **flee**, run away, run off, make a run for it, run for it, take flight, make off, take off, take to one's heels, make a break for it, bolt, beat a (hasty) retreat, make a quick exit, make one's getaway, escape, head for the hills, do a disappearing act; *informal* beat it, clear off, clear out, vamoose, skedaddle, split, cut and run, leg it, show a clean pair of heels, turn tail, scram; *Brit. informal* do a runner, scarper, do a bunk; *N. Amer. informal* light out, bug out, cut out, peel out, take a powder, skidoo; *Austral. informal* go through, shoot through; *vulgar slang* bugger off; *archaic* fly.
OPPOSITE stay.
3 *he decided to run in the marathon* **compete**, take part, participate; enter, be in.
4 *my horse ran second to Suave Dancer in this race last year* **finish**, come in, come.
5 *a shiver ran down my spine | the ball ran towards the green* **go**, pass, move, travel; roll, coast.
6 *Grant ran his eye down the column of figures* **cast**, pass, skim, flick, slide.
7 *a narrow, twisting road which runs the length of the Duddon valley* **extend**, stretch, reach, range, continue, go.
8 *rainwater ran from the eaves* **flow**, pour, stream, gush, flood, glide, cascade, spurt, jet, issue; roll, course, slide, spill, trickle, seep, drip, dribble, leak; *Brit. informal* sloosh.
9 *the walls were* **running with** *condensation* **stream with**, drip with, be covered with, be wet with; be flooded by.
10 *my nose was running* **stream**, drip, exude/secrete/ooze liquid.
11 *a courtesy bus runs to Sorrento three times a day* **travel**, **ply**, shuttle, go, make a regular journey.
12 *I'll run you back to your hotel* **drive**, give someone a lift, take, bring, ferry, chauffeur; transport, convey.
13 *he runs a transport company* **be in charge of**, manage, administer, direct, control, be in control of, be the boss of, boss, head, lead, govern, supervise, superintend, oversee, look after, organize, coordinate, regulate; operate, conduct, carry on, own; preside over, officiate at.
14 *he could no longer afford to run a car* **maintain**, keep, own, possess, have, drive.
15 *they ran a series of tests* **carry out**, do, perform, fulfil, execute.
16 *he left the engine running | her car runs well* **operate**, function, work, go, be in operation; tick over, idle; perform, behave.
17 *the lease runs for twenty years* **be valid**, last, be in effect, operate, be in operation, be operative, be current, continue, be effective, have force, have effect.
18 *the show ran in the West End for two years* **be staged**, be presented, be performed, be on, be put on, be produced; be mounted; be screened; last.
19 *he first* **ran for** *president in 1984* **stand for**, stand for election as, stand as a candidate for, be a contender for, put oneself forward for, put oneself up for.
20 *the Guardian ran the story on Friday* **publish**, print, feature, carry, put out, release, issue.
21 *they run drugs for the cocaine cartels* **smuggle**, traffic in, deal in.
22 *they were run out of town* **chase**, drive, hunt, hound, put to flight.

□ **run across** *we ran across David when we were playing in LA* **meet (by chance)**, come across, run into, chance on, stumble on/across, happen on; *informal* bump into; *archaic* run against.

□ **run after** (*informal*) *ever since his school days, girls have been running after him* **pursue**, chase, make romantic advances to, flirt with; *informal* make up to, make eyes at, give the come-on to, come on to, be all over; *N. Amer. informal* vamp; *dated* set one's cap at.

□ **run along** (*informal*) *run along now, can't you see I'm busy?* **go away**, be off with you, shoo, on your way, make yourself scarce; *informal* scram, buzz off, skedaddle, scat, beat it, get lost, shove off, clear off; *Brit. informal* hop it; *S. African informal* hamba, voetsak; *literary* begone, avaunt.

□ **run away 1** *she screamed and the men ran away* **flee**, run off, make a run for it, run for it, take flight, make off, take off, take to one's heels, make a break for it, bolt, beat a (hasty) retreat, make a quick exit, make one's getaway, escape, head for the hills; *informal* beat it, clear off, clear out, vamoose, skedaddle, split, cut and run, leg it, show a clean pair of heels, turn tail, scram, hook it, fly the coop, skip off, do a fade; *Brit. informal* do a runner, scarper, do a bunk; *N. Amer. informal* light out, bug out, cut out, peel out, take a powder, skidoo; *Austral. informal* go through, shoot through; *archaic* fly, levant.
OPPOSITE stay.
2 *the administration has tried to* **run away from** *its responsibilities* **evade**, dodge, get out of, shirk; avoid, disregard, ignore, take no notice of, pay no attention to, turn one's back on; *informal* shut one's eyes to, duck, cop out of.
OPPOSITES face up to, deal with.
3 *Doyle* **ran away with** *another man's wife* **run off with**, elope with.
4 *Mario Andretti ran away with the championship* **win easily**, win hands down; *informal* win by a mile, walk it, romp home.

□ **run down** *he was dismayed to discover how much the farm had run down* **decline**, degenerate, go downhill, become dilapidated, go to seed, fall into decay, decay, go to rack and ruin; *informal* go to pot, go to the dogs.
OPPOSITES recover, improve.

□ **run someone/something down 1** *the boy was run down by joyriders* **run over**, knock down, knock over, knock to the ground; hit, strike.
2 *she began to run him down in front of other people* **criticize**, denigrate, belittle, disparage, deprecate, speak badly off, speak ill of, find fault with; revile, vilify; *informal* put down, knock, bad-mouth, have a go at; *Brit. informal* rubbish, slag off; *rare* derogate, asperse.
OPPOSITE praise.

□ **run something down 1** *she finally ran a copy of the book down in Covent Garden* **find**, discover, locate, track down, trace, run to earth, unearth, hunt out, ferret out.
2 *employers should run down their labour forces gradually* **reduce**, cut back on, cut, downsize, decrease, pare down, trim; phase out, wind down, wind up.
OPPOSITE increase.

□ **run for it flee**, make a run for it, run away, run off, take flight, make off, take off, take to one's heels, make a break for it, bolt, beat a (hasty) retreat, make a quick exit, make one's getaway, escape, head for the hills, take oneself off, decamp, abscond, do a disappearing act; *informal* beat it, clear off, clear out, vamoose, skedaddle, split, cut and run, leg it, show a clean pair of heels, scram, hook it, fly the coop, do a fade; *Brit. informal* do a runner, scarper, do a bunk, have it away (on one's toes); *N. Amer. informal* light out, bug out, cut out, peel out, take a powder, skidoo.

□ **run high** *patriotic fervour was running high* **be strong**, be vehement, be fervent, be passionate, be intense.

□ **run in** *he has a history of heart disease, which runs in the family* **be common in**, be frequently found in, be inherent in.

□ **run someone in** (*informal*) **arrest**, take into custody, apprehend, detain, take in, take prisoner, put in jail, throw in jail; *informal* pick up, pull in, haul in, pinch, bust, nab, nail, do, collar, feel someone's collar; *Brit. informal* nick.

□ **run into 1** *the plane was badly damaged when it ran into a parked aircraft* **collide with**, be in collision with, hit, strike, crash into, smash into, knock into, plough into, barge into, meet head-on, ram; *N. Amer.* impact.
OPPOSITE miss.
2 *I ran into Hugo the other day* **meet (by chance)**, run across, chance on, stumble on/across, happen on; *informal* bump into; *archaic* run against.
3 *the negotiators immediately ran into a problem* **experience**, encounter, meet with, be faced with, run up against, be confronted with, come face to face with.
4 *Peter had been left with debts running into six figures* **reach**, extend to, be as high/much as.

□ **run low** *food supplies were running low* **dwindle**, diminish, become depleted, get less, be used up, become exhausted, be short, be in short supply, be tight.
OPPOSITE be plentiful.

□ **run off 1** *three youths scrambled out of the car and ran off* **flee**, run away, make a run for it, run for it, take flight, make off, take off, take to one's heels, make a break for it, bolt, beat a (hasty) retreat, make a quick exit, make one's getaway, escape, head for the hills, make oneself scarce, decamp, abscond, do a disappearing act; *informal* beat it, clear off, clear out, vamoose, skedaddle, split, cut and run, leg it, show a clean pair of heels, scram, hook it, skip off; *Brit. informal* do a runner, scarper, do a bunk, have it away (on one's toes); *N. Amer. informal* light out, bug out, cut out, peel out, take a powder, skidoo; *Austral. informal* go through, shoot through; *vulgar slang* bugger off; *archaic* fly, levant.
OPPOSITE stay.
2 (*informal*) *his wife* **ran off with** *one of the doctors* **run away with**, elope with, go off with.
3 (*informal*) *he* **ran off with** *the £1000 in the appeal fund* **steal**, take, snatch, purloin, abscond with, help oneself to; **pilfer**, embezzle, misappropriate; *informal* walk off/away with, swipe, nab, rip off, lift, 'liberate', 'borrow', filch, snaffle, snitch; *Brit. informal* pinch, half-inch, whip, knock off, nobble; *N. Amer. informal* heist, glom; *Austral. informal* snavel; *W. Indian informal* tief.

□ **run something off 1** *Sophie, would you just run off a list of all the outstanding accounts, please?* **copy**, photocopy, xerox, duplicate, print, photostat, mimeograph; make, produce, do.
2 *run off some of the water that has been standing in the pipes* **drain**, drain off, bleed off, draw off, pump out.

□ **run on 1** *the call ran on for two and a quarter hours* **continue**, go on, carry on, last, keep going, extend, stretch.
2 *your mother does run on, doesn't she?* **talk incessantly**, talk a lot, rattle on, go on, chatter on, gabble on, ramble on; *informal* yak, gab, yackety-yak, yap, yabber, yatter; *Brit. informal* rabbit on, witter on, natter on, chunter on,

R

talk the hind leg off a donkey; *Scottish & Irish* slabber on; *N. Amer. informal* run off at the mouth; *Austral./NZ informal* mag; *archaic* twaddle, twattle, clack.
3 *my thoughts ran too much on death* **be preoccupied with**, be concerned with, dwell on, focus on, be focused on, revolve around, centre around, be dominated by, be fixated with.

□ **run out 1** *food supplies were running out* **be used up**, dry up, be exhausted, be finished, give out, peter out, fail; exhaust.
OPPOSITE be plentiful.
2 *they've run out of cash* **have none left**, have no more of, be out of; use up, exhaust one's supply of, consume, eat up; sell out of; *informal* be fresh out of, be cleaned out of.
3 *her contract was due to run out* **expire**, come to an end, end, terminate, finish; lapse, be no longer valid.

□ **run out on someone** (*informal*) **desert**, abandon, leave in the lurch, jilt, leave high and dry, discard, cast aside, throw over, turn one's back on; *informal* walk out on, dump, ditch, leave someone holding the baby, leave flat; *archaic* forsake.

□ **run over 1** *the bathwater's running over* **overflow**, spill over, spill, brim over; *rare* overbrim.
2 *the project ran wildly over budget* **exceed**, go over, go beyond, overshoot, overreach.

□ **run someone/something over run down**, knock down, knock over, knock to the ground, hit, strike.

□ **run something over** *he quickly ran over the story* **recapitulate**, repeat, run through, go over, go through, reiterate, review; **look through**, look over, read through; *informal* recap.

□ **run the show** (*informal*) **be in charge**, be in control, be the boss, be at the helm, be in the driving seat, be in the driver's seat, be at the wheel, be in the saddle, pull the strings, be responsible; *informal* call the shots.

□ **run through 1** *her husband had long ago run through their money* **squander**, fritter away, spend, spend like water, throw away, dissipate, waste, go through, consume, use up; *informal* blow.
2 *the markedly sceptical attitude that runs through his writings* **pervade**, permeate, suffuse, imbue, inform, go through.
3 *he ran through his notes again* **go over**, go through, look over, look through, cast one's eye over, take a look at, run over; read, study, scan, peruse, review, examine, inspect; *informal* give something a/the once-over.
4 *okay, let's run through scene three again* **rehearse**, practise, go through, go over, repeat, do again; recapitulate; *N. Amer.* run down; *informal* recap.

□ **run someone through** *Campbell threatened to run him through with his sword* **stab**, pierce, transfix, impale.

□ **run to 1** *the original bill ran to £22,000* **reach**, extend to, be as high as, be as much as; **amount to**, add up to, total, come to, equal.
2 *sorry, we can't run to champagne* **afford**, stretch to, manage, have money for.
3 *he was running to fat* **tend to**, show a tendency to; become, get, grow.

▶ **noun 1** *his early morning run along the Embankment* **sprint**, race, dash, gallop, rush, spurt; **jog**, trot.
2 *she volunteered to do the school run* **route**, way, course, journey; circuit, round, beat.
3 *we went out for a run in the car* **drive**, ride, turn; **trip**, excursion, outing, jaunt, short journey, airing; *informal* spin, joyride, tootle; *Scottish informal* hurl.
4 *the current run of unseasonably hot weather | an unbeaten run of eleven home victories* **period**, spell, stretch, spate, bout; patch, interval, time; **series**, succession, sequence, string, chain, streak.
5 *the budget accelerated a run on sterling* **demand for**, rush for, sudden request for, clamour for.
6 *Margaret gave them* **the run** *of her home* **unrestricted/free use of**, unrestricted access to; a free hand in, a free rein in.
7 *it's certainly different from the usual run of East European cafes* **type**, kind, sort, variety, class, category, order.
8 *against the run of play, Mytchett scored a second goal* **trend**, tendency, course, direction, movement, drift, tide, current; tenor.
9 *the wire mesh of a chicken run* **enclosure**, pen, coop, compound.
10 *a steep run with 10 cm of fresh snow* **slope**, piste, track; bump run; *N. Amer.* trail.
11 *she had a run in her nylons* **ladder**, rip, tear, snag, hole.

□ **in the long run eventually**, in the end, ultimately, when all is said and done, in the final analysis, in the fullness of time; *Brit. informal* at the end of the day.

□ **on the run 1** *a con man on the run* **on the loose**, at large, loose; **running away**, fleeing, in flight, fugitive; *informal* AWOL; *N. Amer. informal* on the lam.
2 *I've been on the run all day* **busy**, rushing about, rushed off one's feet, dashing about, hurrying about, in a rush, in a hurry, on the move, active; *informal* on the go.

□ **the runs** (*informal*). *See* DIARRHOEA.

WORD LINKS
place for running or racing **-drome**

runaway ▶ **noun** *a 16-year-old runaway* **fugitive**, escaper, escapee; refugee; truant; absconder, deserter; *archaic* runagate.
▶ **adjective 1** *a runaway horse* **out of control**, escaped, loose, on the loose; riderless.
2 *a runaway 6–3 victory* **easy**, effortless; *informal* as easy as pie.
3 *prices were heavily increased by runaway inflation* **rampant**, out of control, uncontrolled, unchecked, unbridled, unsuppressed.
OPPOSITE controlled.

rundown ▶ **noun 1** *let me give you a brief rundown of the situation* **analysis**, review, overview, briefing, brief, sketch, thumbnail sketch, outline, rough idea; **summary**, résumé, synopsis, precis, recapitulation, run-through, summarization, summation; *French* tour d'horizon; *informal* low-down, recap; *rare* conspectus, summa.
2 *the rundown of NATO forces in the area* **reduction**, cut, cutback, decrease, curtailment, drop, decline, diminution.

run down ▶ **adjective 1** *a run-down area of East London* **dilapidated**, tumbledown, ramshackle, derelict, ruinous, falling to pieces, decrepit, gone to rack and ruin, in ruins, broken-down, crumbling, decaying, disintegrating; **neglected**, uncared-for, unmaintained, depressed, down at heel, seedy, shabby, dingy, slummy, insalubrious, squalid; *informal* shambly, crummy; *Brit. informal* grotty; *N. Amer. informal* shacky.
OPPOSITE smart.
2 *by eating more leafy green vegetables you can avoid feeling run down and tense* **unwell**, ill, poorly, out of sorts, unhealthy, peaky, not oneself, below par, in bad shape; **tired**, debilitated, drained, exhausted, fatigued, enervated, weak, worn out, washed out; *Brit.* off, off colour; *informal* under the weather, crummy; *Brit. informal* not (feeling) up to snuff, ropy, knackered; *Scottish informal* wabbit; *Austral./NZ informal* crook; *dated* seedy, queer; *rare* peaked, peakish.
OPPOSITES healthy, well.

run-in ▶ **noun** (*informal*) *his latest run-in with the authorities* **disagreement**, argument, dispute, difference of opinion, altercation, confrontation, contretemps, quarrel; brush, encounter, tangle; fight, clash, skirmish, tussle; *informal* set-to, dust-up, shindig, shindy, spat, scrap; *Brit. informal* row; *Scottish informal* rammy.

runner ▶ **noun 1** *seven runners were limbering up* **athlete**; sprinter, hurdler, racer, long-distance runner, cross-country runner; jogger; competitor, contender, participant, entrant; *informal* miler.
2 *a strawberry runner* **shoot**, offshoot, sprout, tendril, sprig, sucker; *technical* stolon, flagellum.
3 *bookmakers employed runners who ran round picking up bets* **messenger**, courier, errand boy, messenger boy; scout; agent, collector; *N. Amer. informal* gofer.

□ **do a runner** (*Brit. informal*). *See* RUN AWAY *at* RUN.

running ▶ **noun 1** *it was his running between the wickets that really caught the eye* **sprinting**, sprint, racing; jogging, jog.
2 *the day-to-day running of the school* **administration**, management, managing, organization, coordination, orchestration, handling, direction, conduct, overseeing, controlling, control, regulation, supervision, charge.
3 *the smooth running of her department* **operation**, working, functioning, performance.

□ **in the running** *he's in the running for a Nobel Prize* **likely to win/get/receive**, in contention for, a candidate for, in line for, on the shortlist for, being considered for, up for.

□ **out of the running** *Downpatrick are out of the running for championship honours this season* **out of contention**, out of the competition, out of the contest, no longer a candidate for.

▶ **adjective 1** *the sound of running water* **flowing**, streaming, gushing, rushing, moving.
2 *a running argument* **continuous**, ongoing, sustained, unceasing, incessant, ceaseless, uninterrupted, constant, perpetual, unbroken; **recurrent**, recurring, perennial.
3 *I'm not going to wear the same thing two days running* **in succession**, in a row, in sequence, one after the other, consecutively; straight, together; *informal* on the trot.

runny ▶ **adjective** *runny egg yolk* **liquefied**, liquid, fluid, melted, molten, flowing; thin, watery, diluted; *S. African* slap.
OPPOSITES solid, viscous.

run-of-the-mill ▶ **adjective** *the match was a pretty run-of-the-mill affair* **ordinary**, average, standard, middle-of-the-road, unremarkable, unexceptional, undistinguished, unmemorable, forgettable, commonplace, humdrum, mundane, nondescript, characterless, colourless, conventional, normal, pedestrian, prosaic, uninspired, uninspiring, quotidian, uninteresting, uneventful, dull, boring, routine, bland, lacklustre, tame, mediocre, middling, indifferent, unimpressive; *N. Amer.* garden-variety; *informal* OK, so-so, bog-standard, vanilla, plain vanilla, nothing to write home about, nothing to get excited about, nothing special, a dime a dozen, no great shakes, not up to much; *Brit. informal* common or garden; *N. Amer. informal* ornery; *NZ informal* half-pie.
OPPOSITES remarkable, extraordinary, exceptional.

rupture ▶ **noun 1** *a recent series of pipeline ruptures* **break**, fracture, crack; **burst**, split, fissure, blowout.
2 *the rupture was due more to personal than to intellectual differences* **rift**, estrangement, break-up, breach, split, severance, separation, parting, division, alienation; disagreement, quarrel, feud; schism; *informal* falling-out, bust-up; *Brit. informal* row.

3 *ruptures are most common in the very young or very old* **hernia**.
▶ **verb 1** *the steel drum enclosing the reactor core might rupture* **break**, fracture, crack, breach; **burst**, split, tear, puncture; *informal* bust.
2 *the situation threatened to rupture their relationships* **sever**, break, cut off, break off, breach, disrupt; separate, divide; *literary* tear asunder, cleave, rend, sunder, rive; *rare* dissever.

rural ▶ **adjective** *an idealized view of rural life | rural areas of Britain* **country**, countryside, pastoral, rustic, bucolic; agricultural, farming, agrarian; *literary* Arcadian, sylvan; *rare* georgic, agrestic, exurban.
OPPOSITES urban, city, town.

ruse ▶ **noun** *a ruse to throw would-be pursuers off the scent* **ploy**, stratagem, tactic, move, device, scheme, trick, gambit, cunning plan, manoeuvre, contrivance, expedient, dodge, subterfuge, machination, game, wile, smokescreen, red herring, blind; the oldest trick in the book; *Brit. informal* wheeze; *archaic* shift.

rush ▶ **verb 1** *Simone rushed back into the house* **hurry**, dash, run, race, sprint, bolt, dart, gallop, career, charge, shoot, hurtle, hare, bound, fly, speed, zoom, go hell for leather, pound, plunge, dive, whisk, streak, scurry, scuttle, scamper, scramble, make haste, hasten, bustle, bundle; stampede; *informal* tear, belt, pelt, scoot, zap, zip, whip, step on it, get a move on, hotfoot it, leg it, steam, put on some speed, go like a bat out of hell; *Brit. informal* bomb, bucket; *Scottish informal* wheech; *N. Amer. informal* boogie, hightail it, clip, barrel, get the lead out; *informal, dated* cut along; *N. Amer. vulgar slang* drag/tear/haul ass; *literary* fleet; *archaic* post, hie, haste.
OPPOSITE dawdle.
2 *the noise of water rushing along gutters* **flow**, pour, gush, surge, stream, cascade, shoot, swirl, run, course; spout, spurt, pump, jet; *Brit. informal* sloosh.
3 *the tax was rushed through parliament* **send rapidly**, pass rapidly, hurry, push, hasten, speed, hustle, press, steamroller, force; *informal* railroad.
4 *some demonstrators rushed the cordon of tanks and troops* **attack**, charge, run at, fly at, assail; storm, attempt to capture.
▶ **noun 1** *the men made a rush for the exit* **dash**, run, sprint, dart, bolt, charge, scramble, bound, break; stampede.
2 *the lunchtime rush gathered pace* **hustle and bustle**, commotion, bustle, hubbub, hurly-burly, flurry of activity, stir; *archaic* hurry scurry.
3 *travel agents say there's been a last minute rush for holidays abroad* **demand**, clamour, call, request, run (on).
4 *Peacock was in no rush to leave Tyneside* **hurry**, haste, dispatch; urgency.
5 *a rush of adrenalin | he felt a rush of excitement* **surge**, flow, gush, stream, flood, spurt; dart, thrill, flash, flush, blaze, stab.
6 *a rush of cold night air* **gust**, draught, flurry.
7 *I made a sudden rush at him* **charge**, onslaught, attack, sortie, sally, assault, onrush.
▶ **adjective** *a rush job* **urgent**, high-priority, top-priority, emergency; hurried, hasty, fast, quick, rapid, swift; *N. Amer. informal* hurry-up.

rushed ▶ **adjective 1** *a rushed divorce from his wife was arranged* **hasty**, fast, speedy, quick, swift, rapid, hurried, brisk, expeditious; precipitate.
2 *he had been too rushed in Rome to enjoy his stay* **in a hurry**, running about, run off one's feet, rushing about, dashing about, pushed for time, pressed for time; **busy**, hectic, frantic.

rust ▶ **verb** *the pipe is wrapped with special tape to prevent it from rusting* **corrode**, oxidize, become rusty, tarnish; crumble away, decay, rot.
WORD LINKS
containing rust **ferruginous**

rust-coloured ▶ **adjective** *his rust-coloured hair and beard* **reddish-brown**, tawny, chestnut, russet, coppery, copper, auburn, Titian, reddish, ginger, gingery, rusty, rufous; brick-red, brick; *rare* rufescent.

rustic ▶ **adjective 1** *a rustic setting* **rural**, country, countryside; countrified; pastoral, bucolic; agricultural, agrarian; *literary* Arcadian, sylvan; *rare* georgic, agrestic, exurban.
OPPOSITES urban, city, town.
2 *rustic wooden tables* **plain**, simple, homely, unsophisticated, homespun; peasant; rough and ready, rough, rude, crude.
OPPOSITES fancy, elaborate.
3 *rustic peasants* **unsophisticated**, uncultured, unrefined, uncultivated, simple, plain, homely, artless, unassuming, guileless, naive, ingenuous; coarse, rough, uncouth, graceless, awkward, cloddish, boorish, lumpen; *N. Amer.* backwoods, hillbilly, hick; *archaic* clownish.
OPPOSITES sophisticated, cultured, urbane.
▶ **noun** *they paused to watch the rustics dancing and carousing* **countryman**, **countrywoman**, peasant, son/daughter of the soil, country bumpkin, bumpkin, yokel, country cousin; *French* paysan; *Spanish* campesino; *Italian* contadino, paisano; *Russian* muzhik, kulak; *Egyptian* fellah; *Indian* ryot; *Irish informal* culchie, bogman; *N. Amer. informal* hillbilly, hayseed, hick, rube; *Austral./NZ informal* bushy; *archaic* clown, villein, swain, hind, carl, cottier; *rare* bucolic.

rustle ▶ **verb 1** *the wind rustled lightly through the cottonwoods | her dress of white satin rustled as she walked* **swish**, whisper, sigh, whoosh; *rare* susurrate.
2 *he was making a lucrative living rustling cattle* **steal**, thieve, take, abduct, kidnap.
□ **rustle something up** (*informal*) **prepare hastily**, produce, make, put together; *informal* fix; *Brit. informal* knock up.
▶ **noun** *he could hear the soft rustle of her skirt* **swish**, swishing, whisper, whispering, rustling; *rare* susurration, susurrus.

rusty ▶ **adjective 1** *rusty barbed wire* **rusted**, rust-covered, corroded, oxidized; tarnished, discoloured; *rare* aeruginous.
2 *his hair was a vibrant rusty colour* **reddish-brown**, chestnut, auburn, tawny, russet, coppery, copper, Titian, rust-coloured, reddish, rufous; brick-red, brick; *rare* rufescent.
3 *my French is a little rusty* **out of practice**, not as good as it used to be, below par; unpractised, not what it was, neglected, deficient, impaired, weak.

rut ▶ **noun 1** *the Land Rover bumped across the ruts* **wheel track**, furrow, groove, track, trough, ditch, trench, gutter, gouge, crack, hollow, hole, pothole, cavity, crater.
2 *Julian felt he was stuck in a rut* **boring routine**, humdrum existence, routine job, same old round, groove, grind, daily grind, treadmill, dead end, assembly line.

ruthless ▶ **adjective** *a ruthless killer | his ruthless determination* **merciless**, pitiless, cruel, heartless, hard-hearted, hard, stony-hearted, stony, with a heart of stone, cold-blooded, cold-hearted, harsh, callous, severe, unmerciful, unrelenting, unsparing, unforgiving, unfeeling, uncaring, unsympathetic, uncharitable, lacking compassion; **relentless**, remorseless, unbending, inflexible, inexorable, implacable, unpitying, unremitting, steely; brutal, inhuman, inhumane, barbarous, barbaric, savage, bloodthirsty, sadistic, vicious, fierce, ferocious, cut-throat, dog-eat-dog; *archaic* inclement, fell; *rare* marble-hearted.
OPPOSITES merciful, compassionate, gentle.

CHOOSE THE RIGHT WORD

ruthless, remorseless, pitiless, relentless
See RELENTLESS.

sable ▶ **adjective** *a sable curtain starred with gold* **black**, jet-black, jet, pitch-black, pitch-dark, pitch, black as pitch, pitchy, ebony, raven, sooty, dusky, ink-black, inky, black as ink, coal-black, black as coal, black as night; *literary* ebon.

sabotage ▶ **noun 1** *the fire may have been an act of sabotage* **wrecking**, deliberate damage, vandalism, destruction, obstruction, disruption, crippling, impairment, incapacitation; *rare* ecotage.
2 *this procedure is open to sabotage by an awkward participant* **disruption**, spoiling, ruining, wrecking, undermining, filibustering, impairment, damage, subversion; *Brit. informal* a spanner in the works; *N. Amer. informal* a monkey wrench in the works.
▶ **verb 1** *a guerrilla group sabotaged the national electricity grid* **wreck**, deliberately damage, vandalize, destroy, obstruct, disrupt, cripple, impair, incapacitate.
2 *it would be very easy for me to sabotage your plans* **disrupt**, spoil, ruin, wreck, undermine, filibuster, impair, damage, threaten, subvert; *Brit. informal* throw a spanner in the works of; *N. Amer. informal* throw a monkey wrench in the works of.

sac ▶ **noun** *cephalopods have an ink sac* **bag**, pouch, bladder, blister; *technical* bursa, acinus, follicle, cyst, saccule, utricle, vesicle, vesica, vesicula, theca, liposome.

saccharine ▶ **adjective** *some saccharine love songs* **sentimental**, over-sentimental, over-emotional, mawkish, cloying, sickly, sugary, syrupy, sickening, nauseating, maudlin, lachrymose, banal, trite; *informal* mushy, slushy, sloppy, schmaltzy, weepy, cutesy, lovey-dovey, gooey, drippy, sloshy, soupy, treacly, cheesy, corny, icky, sick-making, toe-curling; *Brit. informal* soppy, twee; *N. Amer. informal* cornball, sappy, hokey, three-hankie.

sack[1] ▶ **noun 1** *a sack full of flour* **bag**, pack, pouch, pocket; *N. Amer. & Indian* gunny; *Scottish* poke.
2 (**the sack**) (*informal*) *I'd better get on with my work now or I'll get the sack* **dismissal**, discharge, redundancy, termination of employment, one's marching orders; *informal* the boot, the bullet, the axe, the (old) heave-ho, the elbow, the push, the bounce; *Brit. informal* one's cards, the chop.
3 (**the sack**) (*informal*) *you don't stay long in the sack* **bed**; *Scottish* kip; *Brit. informal* pit.
□ **hit the sack** (*informal*) **go to bed**, retire, go to one's room, call it a day, go to sleep; *informal* turn in, hit the hay.
OPPOSITE get up.
▶ **verb** (*informal*) *she was sacked for refusing to work on Sundays* **dismiss**, give someone their notice, throw out, get rid of, lay off, make redundant, let go, discharge, cashier; *informal* fire, kick out, boot out, give someone the sack, give someone the boot, give someone the bullet, give someone the (old) heave-ho, give someone the elbow, give someone the push, give someone their marching orders, show someone the door, send packing; *Brit. informal* give someone their cards, turf out; *dated* out.
OPPOSITES hire, take on.

sack[2] ▶ **verb** *Edward I sacked the town in 1296* **ravage**, lay waste, devastate, ransack, strip, fleece, plunder, pillage, loot, rob, raid; *literary* despoil; *archaic* spoil, reave; *rare* depredate, spoliate, forage.
▶ **noun** *after the sack of the city the cathedral fell into decay* **laying waste**, ransacking, plunder, plundering, sacking, looting, ravaging, pillage, pillaging, devastation, depredation, stripping, robbery, robbing, raiding; *literary* despoiling, rape, rapine, ravin; *rare* spoliation.

sackcloth ▶ **noun 1** *both clergy and laity wore an extremely uncomfortable black sackcloth* **hessian**, sacking, hopsack, hopsacking, burlap; *N. Amer. & Indian* gunny; *East Indies* tāt; *historical* poldavy, stramin, sugarsack.
2 *she walked through the town barefoot in the frost, clad in sackcloth* **penitential garb**, hair shirt; **mourning clothes**, mourning, funeral clothes.
□ **in/wearing sackcloth and ashes penitent**, contrite, regretful, full of regret, sorrowful, rueful, remorseful, apologetic, conscience-stricken, ashamed, guilt-ridden, chastened, shamefaced, self-reproachful, guilty; *rare* compunctious.
OPPOSITE unrepentant.

sacred *See centre pages for lists of* **Sacred Texts** **Bible**
▶ **adjective 1** *only the priest was allowed to approach this most sacred place* **holy**, hallowed, blessed, blest, consecrated, sanctified, dedicated, venerated, revered.
OPPOSITES unconsecrated, cursed.
2 *sacred music* **religious**, spiritual, devotional, church, churchly, ecclesiastical.
OPPOSITES secular, profane.
3 *Coronation Hill was sacred to an Aboriginal group* **sacrosanct**, inviolable, inviolate, unimpeachable, invulnerable, untouchable, inalienable, protected, defended, secure, safe, unthreatened.

WORD LINKS
related prefix **hiero-** (**e.g.** ***hierogram, hierocracy***)

CHOOSE THE RIGHT WORD

sacred, holy, hallowed, blessed

- Something that is **sacred** is set apart by its own divine power or its association with a divine being (*they built shrines round sacred trees | horses were sacred beasts*). The word conveys the respect or awe with which such things are regarded; it can be applied by extension to something regarded as supremely important though not for religious reasons (*one's dreams are too sacred to be shattered*). Occasionally it carries a note of dry amusement at someone who attaches undue importance to an undeserving object (*WAAFs were never allowed within the sacred portals of the men's quarters*). It has a separate sense of 'religious' in *sacred music*, as opposed to *profane* or *secular*.
- **Holy** emphasizes intrinsic divinity; hence it is used in Christian theology as an epithet of God (*the Holy Spirit | the Holy Trinity*). It has a sense which *sacred* does not: 'morally or spiritually excellent' (*he was known as a holy man and canonized in 1401*).
- **Hallowed** is used of something that has been declared sacred, typically a place (*everyone wished to set up a cenotaph on hallowed ground | Sikhism's most hallowed shrine*). It is in fact more commonly used, often humorously, of secular objects regarded with great reverence (*Wembley's hallowed turf*).
- Something described as **blessed** has been consecrated to a holy purpose (*the blessed bread is distributed at the end of the service*), as contrasted with the *sacred* and the *holy*, which may be intrinsically associated with the divine. Applied to people, *blessed* can convey both the divine favour and happiness that has been bestowed on them and the virtue or holiness which has earned it (*she joined her blessed mother in heaven*); with these connotations, it is a title given to a person who has been beatified as the first stage in the Roman Catholic process of canonization (*a statue of the Blessed Oliver Plunkett*). In secular contexts, *blessed* denotes people or things that bring welcome pleasure or relief (*the air-conditioned cabin is a blessed relief from the streets of Freetown*).

sacrifice ▶ **noun 1** *initiation ceremonies include the sacrifice of animals* **ritual slaughter**, hecatomb, immolation, offering, oblation; self-sacrifice, self-immolation.
2 *Abraham set out to offer Isaac as a sacrifice* **(votive) offering**, gift, oblation, victim, burnt offering.
3 *the agreement has been achieved without any sacrifice of sovereignty* **giving up**, abandonment, surrender, foregoing, renouncing, renunciation, renouncement, forfeiture, loss, relinquishment, resignation, abdication,

signing away, yielding, ceding, waiving.
4 *many parents make sacrifices to send their children to independent schools* **renunciation**, relinquishment, loss, self-sacrifice; sacrifice something, give up things.
▶ **verb 1** *an ox and two goats were sacrificed* **offer up**, immolate, slaughter.
2 *he hadn't sacrificed his humanitarian principles* **give up**, abandon, surrender, forgo, renounce, forfeit, relinquish, resign, abdicate, sign away, yield, cede, waive; prostitute, betray.

sacrificial ▶ **adjective** *the altar may have been used for sacrificial offerings* **votive**, atoning, expiatory, oblatory, oblational, propitiatory.

sacrilege ▶ **noun** *the sacrilege of committing a murder on holy ground* **desecration**, profanity, profaneness, profanation, blasphemy, impiety, impiousness, sin, irreverence, irreligion, irreligiousness, godlessness, unholiness, disrespect.
OPPOSITES piety, respectfulness.

sacrilegious ▶ **adjective** *he condemned the book as a vicious, sacrilegious attack on their faith* **profane**, blasphemous, impious, sinful, irreverent, irreligious, godless, ungodly, unholy, disrespectful.
OPPOSITES pious, respectful.

sacrosanct ▶ **adjective** *the rights of parents are sacrosanct for this government* **sacred**, hallowed, respected, inviolable, inviolate, unimpeachable, unchallengeable, invulnerable, untouchable, inalienable, set apart, protected, defended, secure, safe, unthreatened.

sad ▶ **adjective 1** *every one of us felt sad at having to part company* **unhappy**, sorrowful, dejected, regretful, depressed, downcast, miserable, downhearted, down, despondent, despairing, disconsolate, out of sorts, desolate, bowed down, wretched, glum, gloomy, doleful, dismal, blue, melancholy, melancholic, low-spirited, mournful, woeful, woebegone, forlorn, crestfallen, broken-hearted, heartbroken, inconsolable, grief-stricken; *informal* down in the mouth, down in the dumps.
OPPOSITES happy, cheerful.
2 *people who knew her sad story have helped her* **tragic**, unhappy, unfortunate, awful, sorrowful, miserable, cheerless, wretched, sorry, pitiful, pitiable, grievous, traumatic, upsetting, depressing, distressing, dispiriting, heartbreaking, heart-rending, agonizing, harrowing; *rare* distressful.
OPPOSITES cheerful, amusing, comic.
3 *this is a sad state of affairs* **unfortunate**, regrettable, sorry, wretched, deplorable, lamentable, pitiful, pitiable, pathetic, shameful, disgraceful.
OPPOSITE fortunate.

sadden ▶ **verb** *I was saddened by the number of casualties* **depress**, dispirit, dishearten, grieve, desolate, discourage, upset, get down, bring down, cast down, dash, dampen someone's spirits, cast a gloom on, bring tears to someone's eyes, break someone's heart, make someone's heart bleed; *archaic* deject.
OPPOSITE cheer up.

saddle ▶ **verb** *they were unwilling to be saddled with children* **burden**, encumber, lumber, hamper, weigh down, land, charge; inflict something on, impose something on, thrust something on, unload something on, fob something off on to.

sadism ▶ **noun** *these incidents displayed a streak of sadism* **schadenfreude**; **callousness**, barbarity, bestiality, perversion, viciousness, brutality, cruelty, savagery, fiendishness, cold-bloodedness, inhumanity, ruthlessness, heartlessness, mercilessness, pitilessness.

sadistic ▶ **adjective** *we learned that a sadistic killer was on the loose in the area* **callous**, barbarous, bestial, perverted, vicious, brutal, cruel, savage, fiendish, cold-blooded, inhuman, ruthless, heartless, merciless, pitiless.

S

sadness ▶ **noun** *there will be great sadness at this news* **unhappiness**, sorrow, dejection, regret, depression, misery, cheerlessness, downheartedness, despondency, despair, desolation, wretchedness, glumness, gloom, gloominess, dolefulness, melancholy, low spirits, mournfulness, woe, broken-heartedness, heartache, grief; *informal* down; *rare* disconsolateness, disconsolation, dismalness.
OPPOSITE happiness.

safe ▶ **adjective 1** *the children are safe in bed | the jewels are safe in the bank* **protected from harm/danger**, shielded, sheltered, guarded, defended, secure, safe and sound, out of harm's way, all right.
OPPOSITES unsafe, insecure, at risk.
2 *the missing children are all safe* **unharmed**, all right, alive and well, well, unhurt, uninjured, unscathed, in one piece, undamaged, out of danger, out of the wood(s); *informal* OK.
OPPOSITE in danger.
3 *the building is quite safe | it was a safe place to hide* **secure**, sound, risk-free, riskless, impregnable, unassailable, invulnerable.
OPPOSITE dangerous.
4 *he's a safe person to be with* **trustworthy**, capable of being trusted, trusty, faithful, reliable, dependable, responsible; level-headed, rational, sane, reasonable, sensible, sound, stable, mature, discreet, adult; capable, competent, conscientious; reputable, upright, honest, honourable.
OPPOSITE unreliable.
5 *he's a safe driver | on the safe side* **cautious**, circumspect, prudent, chary, attentive; **timid**, unadventurous, conservative, unenterprising; *informal* leery.
OPPOSITE reckless.
6 *the makers of the drug say it is safe for most people* **harmless**, innocuous, non-toxic, non-poisonous, non-irritant, benign, wholesome, mild.
OPPOSITE harmful.
▶ **noun** *I'm proud of my medal and keep it in a safe* **strongbox**, safety-deposit box, safe-deposit box, coffer, casket, money chest, cash box, repository, depository, locker; strongroom, vault.

safe conduct ▶ **noun 1** *UN inspectors had been guaranteed safe conduct* **freedom of movement**, freedom to travel, free access; immunity.
2 *the Scottish envoys had safe conducts to travel to Nottingham* **(travel) permit**, pass, passport, transit visa, authority, authorization, credentials; *French* laissez-passer.

safeguard ▶ **noun** *early warning provides a safeguard against operational crises* **protection**, defence, guard, shelter, screen, buffer, preventive, precaution, prophylactic, provision, security, safety measure, surety, cover, insurance, indemnity.
▶ **verb** *the contract will safeguard about 1000 jobs* **protect**, afford protection to, shield, screen, defend, guard, keep safe, shelter; **preserve**, conserve, look after, save, secure.
OPPOSITE jeopardize.

safe keeping ▶ **noun** *the document was deposited in the bank vaults for safe keeping | the cash is placed in the safe keeping of the head teacher* **protection**, **preservation**, safety; custody, care, charge, keeping, surveillance, supervision, guardianship, trusteeship, tutelage, wardship.

safety ▶ **noun 1** *she is still driving too fast for the safety of local residents* **welfare**, well-being, protection, security.
OPPOSITE danger.
2 *research into the safety of roll-on roll-off ferries* **security**, soundness, secureness, dependability, reliability, impregnability.
3 *they had to reach the safety of open water* **shelter**, sanctuary, refuge.
4 *the safety of medicines* **harmlessness**, lack of side effects.

sag ▶ **verb 1** *he sagged back in his chair* **sink**, **subside**, slump, crumple, loll, flop.
2 *the house is very old and the floors all sag* **curve down**, hang down, dip, droop, swag, bulge, bag.
3 *his spirits sagged as the team suffered yet another defeat* **falter**, weaken, languish, flag, fade, wilt, shrivel, wither, fail, fall.
4 *industrial production has sagged* **decline**, fall, go down, drop, drop/fall off, turn down, decrease, diminish, reduce, sink; slump, plummet, tumble; *informal* crash, take a nosedive, nosedive.

saga ▶ **noun 1** *the Celts' tribal sagas abound with mythical figures* **epic**, chronicle, legend, folk tale, romance, traditional story, history, narrative, adventure, fairy story, myth; *French* roman-fleuve.
2 *the embarrassed staff related the sorry saga of how the seats had been removed* **rigmarole**, **story**, lengthy story/statement/explanation; chain of events, catalogue of disasters; *informal* spiel, palaver.

sagacious ▶ **adjective** *the President sent his most sagacious aide to help Republican candidates* **wise**, clever, intelligent, with/showing great knowledge, knowledgeable, sensible, sage; discerning, judicious, canny, penetrating, perceptive, acute, astute, shrewd, prudent, politic, thoughtful, full of insight, insightful, percipient, perspicacious, philosophical, profound, deep; *informal* streetwise; *rare* sapient.
OPPOSITES stupid, foolish.

sagacity ▶ **noun** *a man of great sagacity* **wisdom**, **(deep) insight**, intelligence, understanding, judgement, acuity, astuteness, insight, sense, canniness, sharpness, depth, profundity, profoundness, perceptiveness, penetration, perception, percipience, perspicuity, discernment, erudition, learning, knowledgeability, thoughtfulness; *rare* sapience.
OPPOSITE stupidity.

sage ▶ **noun** *the Chinese sage Confucius* **wise man/woman**, learned man/woman, man/woman of letters, philosopher, scholar, thinker, savant, Solomon, Nestor, Solon; pandit, authority, expert, guru, maharishi, mahatma, elder, teacher, guiding light, mentor.
OPPOSITE fool.
▶ **adjective** *he makes some very sage comments in his book* **wise**, learned, clever, intelligent, with/showing great knowledge, knowledgeable, sensible, intellectual, scholarly, sagacious, erudite; discerning, judicious, canny, penetrating, perceptive, acute, astute, shrewd, prudent, politic, thoughtful, full of insight, insightful, percipient, perspicacious, philosophical, profound, deep; *rare* sapient.
OPPOSITE foolish.

sail *See centre pages for list of* **Sails**
▶ **noun** *the upright rig means more sail is presented to the wind* canvas.
▶ **verb 1** *we sailed across the Atlantic* **go by water**, go by sea, go on a sea voyage, voyage, steam, navigate, cruise, ride the waves.
2 *you can learn to sail here* yacht, boat, go sailing; crew, helm, skipper a boat.
3 *we sail tonight* **set sail**, **put to sea**, put out (to sea), leave port, leave

dock, leave harbour, hoist sail, raise sail, weigh anchor, put off, shove off.
4 *he is sailing the ship* **steer**, captain, pilot, skipper, navigate, con, helm.
5 *untidy grey clouds were sailing past a pale moon* **glide**, drift, float, flow, slide, slip, sweep, skim, coast, skate, breeze, flit.
6 *a pencil sailed past his ear* **whizz**, speed, streak, shoot, whip, whoosh, buzz, zoom, flash, blast, career, fly, wing, kite, skite, scud; *informal* scorch, tear, zap, zip.
7 *the ball sailed high into the air* **soar**, wing, wing its way, take to the air, fly, ascend, mount, climb, arc, curve.
□ **sail into** *he really sailed into the driver of the other car* **attack**, set upon, set about, fall on, assault, assail, tear into, weigh into, lay into, light into, pitch into, turn on, lash out at, hit out at, strike out at, (let) fly at, lash, round on, drub, thump, batter, hammer, pummel, beat, paste, thrash, belabour, lambaste, berate, abuse; *informal* let someone have it; *Brit. informal* have a go at.
□ **sail through** *she sailed through GCSE | he sailed through the Royal Grammar School* **succeed easily at**, gain success in easily, pass easily, romp through, walk through.
OPPOSITES fail, scrape through.

sailing ship ▶ noun. *See centre pages for list of* **Sailing Ships and Boats**

sailor ▶ noun *I want to be a sailor and go to sea* **seaman**, seafarer, seafaring man, mariner; boatman, yachtsman, yachtswoman; hand, crew member; *informal* (old) salt, sea dog, bluejacket; *Brit. informal* matelot, matlow, matlo; *informal, dated* tar, Jack Tar, hearty; **(sailors) crew**, complement.

saint ▶ noun
WORD LINKS
related prefix **hagio- (e.g. *hagiography*)**
fear of saints **hagiophobia**

saintliness ▶ noun *one could only admire the bishop's courage and saintliness* **holiness**, godliness, piety, devoutness, spirituality, blessedness; **virtue**, righteousness, purity, goodness, morality, sanctity, unworldliness, innocence, lack of corruption, ethicality, blamelessness, stainlessness, spotlessness, irreproachableness, guiltlessness, sinlessness.
OPPOSITES ungodliness, sinfulness.

saintly ▶ adjective *he was a saintly but somewhat ineffective archbishop* **holy**, godly, pious, God-fearing, religious, devout, spiritual, prayerful, blessed; **virtuous**, righteous, good, moral, ethical, unworldly, innocent, sinless, blameless, guiltless, irreproachable, stainless, spotless, uncorrupted, pure, sainted, saintlike, angelic.
OPPOSITES unholy, sinful.

sake ▶ noun **1** *some parts of the mechanism are omitted from the diagram for the sake of clarity* **cause**, purpose, reason, aim, end, objective, object, goal, motive; **for purposes of**, for, in the interests of, in the cause of, in the furtherance of, in order to achieve, with something in mind.
2 *she knew she had to be brave for the sake of her daughter* **benefit**, advantage, good, well-being, welfare, interest, gain, profit; in someone's interests, to someone's advantage.

salacious ▶ adjective **1** *a piece of salacious writing* **pornographic**, obscene, indecent, improper, indelicate, crude, lewd, erotic, titillating, arousing, suggestive, sexy, risqué, coarse, vulgar, gross, dirty, ribald, smutty, filthy, bawdy, earthy; corrupting, exploitative, prurient, immoral; off colour, nasty, adult, X-rated, low, hard-core, soft-core; *informal* porn, porno, blue, skin; *rare* rank.
2 *our father told us to stay away from salacious women* **lustful**, lecherous, licentious, lascivious, libidinous, prurient, lewd; lubricious, debauched, dissolute, wanton, loose, fast, impure, unchaste, intemperate, dissipated, degenerate, sinful, depraved, crude, goatish; sensual, libertine, promiscuous, carnal; *informal* randy, horny, raunchy, pervy, naughty; *rare* concupiscent, lickerish.

salary ▶ noun *his annual salary was £35,000* **pay**, earnings, remuneration, fee(s), emolument(s), stipend, honorarium, hire, wages, wage, gross pay, payment, earned income; take-home pay, net pay.

sale ▶ noun **1** *a law to curb the sale of firearms* **selling**, vending, disposal; dealing, trading, bargaining.
OPPOSITE purchase.
2 *they chalk up a sale every two seconds* **deal**, **transaction**, bargain, disposal.
OPPOSITE purchase.
□ **for sale** *is that picture for sale?* **on the market**, on sale, on offer, available for purchase, able to be bought/purchased, purchasable, obtainable, in the shops.

salesperson ▶ noun *she worked as a salesperson for a time* **salesman**, **saleswoman**, sales assistant, assistant, shop assistant, saleslady, salesgirl, seller, negotiator, representative, sales representative, agent; reseller, auctioneer, travelling salesperson/salesman/saleswoman, shopkeeper, trader, merchant, dealer; *N. Amer.* sales clerk; *informal* counter-jumper, rep, knight of the road; *dated* shop boy, shop girl, shopman, traveller, commercial traveller, pedlar, hawker.

salient ▶ adjective *the salient points stuck out clearly in her mind* **important**, main, principal, major, chief, primary, notable, noteworthy, outstanding, arresting, conspicuous, striking, noticeable, obvious, remarkable, signal, prominent, pronounced, predominant, dominant, key, crucial, vital, essential, basic, staple, critical, pivotal, prime, central, focal, paramount.
OPPOSITES unimportant, inconspicuous.

saliva ▶ noun *saliva ran down his chin* **spit**, spittle, dribble, drool, slaver, slobber, sputum.

sallow ▶ adjective *his lips were blue with the cold and his cheeks sunken and sallow* **yellowish**, jaundiced, pallid, wan, pale, waxen, anaemic, bloodless, colourless, pasty, pasty-faced; unhealthy-looking, sickly, sickly-looking, washed out, peaky, peakish, peaked; *informal* like death warmed up; *Scottish informal* wabbit, peely-wally; *rare* etiolated, lymphatic.
OPPOSITES rosy, glowing.

sally ▶ noun **1** *a week later the garrison made a sally against us* **charge**, sortie, foray, thrust, drive, offensive, attack, raid, assault, descent, blitz, incursion, invasion, onset, inroad, onslaught, rush, onrush; *German* blitzkrieg; *Italian* razzia.
2 *he sent a dutiful report on his fruitless sally into North Wales* **expedition**, excursion, trip, outing, jaunt, run, visit, tour, escapade, airing.
3 *he looked round, delighted with his sally* **witticism**, witty remark, smart remark, quip, barb, pleasantry, epigram, aphorism; joke, pun, jest; **retort**, riposte, counter, rejoinder, return, retaliation; *French* bon mot; *informal* one-liner, gag, wisecrack, crack, funny, comeback.

salon ▶ noun **1** *a hairdressing salon* **shop**, parlour, establishment, place, premises, building, place of business, boutique, store.
2 *the famous mirrored salon in the Chateau de Chavigny* **reception room**, drawing room, morning room, sitting room, living room, lounge, front room, best room, parlour.

salt ▶ noun **1** *the temptation to add more salt to food should be resisted* **sodium chloride**; table salt, sea salt, marine salt, rock salt.
2 (*literary*) *he described danger as the salt of pleasure* **zest**, spice, spiciness, sharpness, raciness, saltiness; flavour, piquancy, pungency, tang, bite, edge; liveliness, vigour, vitality, spirit, colour, sparkle; *informal* zing, zip, punch, pizzazz.
3 (*informal*) *the bay was angry, as old salts would say. See* SEAMAN.
□ **with a pinch of salt** *you have to take what she says with a pinch of salt* **with reservations**, with misgivings, with a grain of salt, sceptically, cynically, mistrustfully, doubtfully, doubtingly, suspiciously, disbelievingly, questioningly, quizzically, incredulously.
OPPOSITES credulously, as gospel.
▶ adjective *salt water* **salty**, salted, saline, briny, brackish.
OPPOSITE fresh.
▶ verb
□ **salt something away** (*informal*) *she had salted money away in Brazil* **save**, **put aside**, put away, put by, lay by, set aside, lay aside, put to one side, reserve, keep in reserve, deposit, keep, store, stockpile, hoard, stow away, cache; *informal* squirrel away, stash away.

salty ▶ adjective **1** *salty water | the bacon was quite salty* **salt**, salted, saline, briny, brackish; piquant, tangy; over-salted.
OPPOSITES fresh, bland.
2 *the Princess has a salty sense of humour* **lively**, vigorous, spirited, colourful, sparkling; zesty, zestful, spicy, sharp; **racy**, piquant, pungent, tangy, biting; *informal* punchy.

salubrious ▶ adjective **1** *I anticipate that I shall find the climate eminently salubrious* **healthy**, health-giving, healthful, beneficial, good for one's health, wholesome, salutary.
OPPOSITE unhealthy.
2 *we managed to move to a more salubrious area of London* **pleasant**, agreeable, nice, select, upmarket, high-class, leafy, fashionable, expensive, luxurious, grand, fancy; *informal* posh, swanky, plushy, classy, glitzy; *Brit. informal* swish; *N. Amer. informal* swank.
OPPOSITES unpleasant, downmarket.

salutary ▶ adjective **1** *those incidents are a salutary reminder of the dedication of police officers* **beneficial**, good, good for one, advantageous, profitable, productive, helpful, useful, of use, of service, valuable, worthwhile, practical; relevant, timely.
OPPOSITES unwelcome; irrelevant.
2 *the salutary Atlantic air* **healthy**, health-giving, healthful, salubrious, beneficial, good for one's health, wholesome.
OPPOSITES unhealthy, unwholesome.

salutation ▶ noun *her early morning salutation was delivered with chilly sangfroid* **greeting**, salute, address, hail, welcome, toast, tribute, homage, obeisance.

salute ▶ noun **1** *he gave the Brigadier a smart salute* **gesture of respect**, greeting, salutation, address, hail, welcome, tribute, wave; homage, obeisance, acknowledgement.
2 *the awards were described as an American salute to British courage* **tribute**, testimonial, honour, homage, toast, compliment, bouquet, eulogy; recognition of, celebration of, acknowledgement of.
▶ verb **1** *the Emperor saluted the assembled ambassadors* **greet**, address, hail,

S

welcome, acknowledge, pay one's respects to, toast, make obeisance to, wave to, accost.
2 *we salute a truly great photographer* **pay tribute to**, pay homage to, honour, recognize, celebrate, acknowledge, take one's hat off to.

salvage ▶ verb **1** *all attempts to salvage the Danish cargo vessel have been called off* **rescue**, save, recover, retrieve, raise, reclaim, get back, restore, reinstate.
2 *his first goal salvaged a precious point for his club* **retain**, preserve, conserve; **regain**, win back, recoup, recapture, redeem, snatch.
▶ noun **1** *the salvage operation is taking place 400 miles off the coast of Newfoundland* **rescue**, saving, recovery, raising, reclamation, restoration, salvation.
2 *I bought an old car from a salvage dealer* **scrap**, waste, waste material, waste paper, remains.

salvation ▶ noun **1** *we are here to bring you to salvation by way of repentance* **redemption**, deliverance, saving, help, reclamation.
OPPOSITES damnation, downfall, destruction.
2 *she clung to that conviction, knowing it was her salvation* **lifeline**, preservation, conservation, means of escape.

salve ▶ noun *lip salve* **ointment**, cream, balm, unction, unguent, balsam, pomade, rub, embrocation, emollient, liniment.
▶ verb *she promised him lunch to salve her conscience* **soothe**, lighten, alleviate, assuage, comfort, ease, allay, dull, mollify, mitigate, palliate.

salver ▶ noun *he offered her caviar from a silver salver* **platter**, plate, dish, tray; *Scottish & N. English* ashet; *archaic* trencher, charger; *rare* paten.

same ▶ adjective **1** *it turned out that we were staying at* ***the same*** *hotel* **the identical**, the very same, selfsame, one and the same, the very.
OPPOSITES another, different.
2 *all three patients had* ***the same*** *symptoms* **matching**, identical, alike, duplicate, carbon-copy, twin, paired, coupled, double, indistinguishable, interchangeable, corresponding, equivalent, parallel, (all) of a piece, like, like (two) peas in a pod, comparable, similar, correlative, congruent, tallying, agreeing, concordant, consonant.
OPPOSITES different, dissimilar.
3 *the Allied landings took place that same month* **selfsame**, aforesaid, aforementioned.
OPPOSITE another.
4 *international hotels tend to provide* ***the same*** *menu worldwide* **unchanging**, unchanged, changeless, unvarying, unvaried, invariable, constant, consistent, uniform, regular.
OPPOSITES different, varying.
▶ noun *Louise would have said* ***the same*** **the same thing**, the aforementioned, the aforesaid, the above-mentioned.
□ **all the same 1** *I was frightened all the same* **in spite of that/everything**, nevertheless, nonetheless, even so, however, but, still, yet, though, be that as it may, for all that, despite that/everything, after everything, having said that, just the same, at the same time, in any event, come what may, at any rate, notwithstanding, regardless, anyway, anyhow; *informal* still and all; *archaic* howbeit, withal, natheless.
2 *it's all the same to me—see if I care* **immaterial**, of no importance, of no consequence, inconsequential, unimportant, of no matter/moment, of little account, irrelevant, insignificant, trivial, petty, slight, inappreciable.
OPPOSITE of great importance.

WORD LINKS
related prefix **hom(e)o-** (e.g. ***homosexual, homeopathy***)

S

sameness ▶ noun **1** *a tyranny of sameness is sweeping the earth* **similarity**, **uniformity**, resemblance, likeness, alikeness, similitude, closeness, comparability, correspondence, indistinguishability, consistency, equality, equalness, parity, equivalence, interchangeability, parallelism; **monotony**, changelessness, invariability, standardization, lack of variety, tedium, tediousness, routine, routineness, humdrum, predictability, repetition, duplication; *archaic* semblance.
OPPOSITES variety, difference, contrast.
2 *the sameness of the force on two electrons explains why they accelerate at the same rate* **identity**, identicalness, oneness, selfsameness, congruity, congruence.
OPPOSITE difference.

sample ▶ noun **1** *they each sent a sample of the soil from their district* **specimen**, example, bit, snippet, illustration, demonstration, exemplification, instance, selection, representative piece; model, prototype, pattern, dummy, swatch, test piece, pilot, trailer, trial, indication, foretaste, taste, taster, tester, smear; *archaic* scantling.
2 *the survey was carried out on a sample of 10,000 people nationwide* **cross section**, variety, sampling, test.
▶ verb *plenty of people turned up to sample the culinary offerings* **try out**, try, taste, sip, nibble, test, put to the test, dip into, experiment with, experience, inspect, examine, check out, appraise, evaluate.
▶ adjective **1** *the sample group is very small* **representative**, illustrative, selected, specimen, test, trial, typifying, typical.
2 *a sample copy can be obtained at a special price of £2.50* **specimen**, test, trial, pilot, dummy.

sanatorium ▶ noun *he spent long periods in the sanatorium undergoing treatment* **infirmary**, clinic, sickbay, sickroom, medical centre, hospital, hospice, nursing home, convalescent home, rest home; *N. Amer.* sanitarium; *informal* san.

sanctify ▶ verb **1** *a small shrine was built to sanctify the site* **consecrate**, make holy, make sacred, bless, hallow, set apart, dedicate to God, anoint, ordain, canonize, beatify.
2 *they felt obliged to fulfil God's purpose by sanctifying themselves and doing his will* **purify**, cleanse, free from sin, absolve, unburden, redeem, exculpate, wash someone's sins away; *rare* lustrate.
3 *we must not sanctify this outrageous state of affairs* **approve**, sanction, give the stamp of approval to, underwrite, condone, justify, vindicate, endorse, support, back, ratify, confirm, warrant, permit, allow, accredit, authorize, legitimize, legitimatize.

sanctimonious ▶ adjective *one tries to set a bit of an example, if that's not too sanctimonious* **self-righteous**, holier-than-thou, churchy, pious, pietistic, moralizing, unctuous, smug, superior, priggish, mealy-mouthed, hypocritical, insincere, for form's sake, to keep up appearances; *informal* goody-goody, pi; *rare* religiose, Pharisaic, Pharisaical, Tartuffian.

sanction ▶ noun **1** (usually **sanctions**) *codes of practice should be accompanied by sanctions for offenders | trade sanctions* **penalty**, punishment, deterrent; punitive action, discipline, penalization, correction, retribution; **embargo**, ban, prohibition, boycott, barrier, restriction, tariff.
OPPOSITE reward.
2 *the scheme is to receive the sanction of the court* **authorization**, consent, leave, permission, authority, warrant, licence, dispensation, assent, acquiescence, agreement, approval, seal/stamp of approval, approbation, recognition, endorsement, accreditation, confirmation, ratification, validation, blessing, imprimatur, clearance, acceptance, allowance; *informal* the go-ahead, the thumbs up, the OK, the green light, say-so; *rare* permit.
OPPOSITES prohibition, ban.
▶ verb **1** *the rally was sanctioned by the government* **authorize**, consent to, permit, allow, give leave for, give permission for, warrant, accredit, license, give assent to, endorse, agree to, approve, accept, give one's blessing to, back, support; *informal* give the thumbs up to, give the green light to, OK; *N. Amer. rare* approbate.
OPPOSITES prohibit, ban.
2 *the penalties for water pollution are frail in comparison with those available to sanction traditional crime* **punish**, discipline someone for.

sanctity ▶ noun **1** *few could attain the sanctity of St Francis* **holiness**, godliness, sacredness, blessedness, saintliness, sanctitude, spirituality, piety, piousness, devoutness, devotion, righteousness, goodness, virtue, virtuousness, purity.
OPPOSITE wickedness.
2 *gone is the sanctity of the family meal* **sacrosanctity**, ultimate importance, inviolability; *rare* paramountcy.

sanctuary ▶ noun **1** *the sanctuary at Delphi was dedicated to Apollo* **holy place**, temple, shrine, tabernacle, altar, sanctum, inner sanctum, holy of holies, sacrarium, bema, naos, adytum; *Latin* sanctum sanctorum; *Architecture* presbytery.
2 *the island was a sanctuary, untouched by the mad modern world* **refuge**, haven, harbour, port in a storm, oasis, shelter, retreat, bolt-hole, foxhole, hideout, hiding place, hideaway, den, asylum, safe house, fastness; *Spanish* querencia.
3 *he was given sanctuary in the US Embassy in Beijing* **safety**, safe keeping, protection, shelter, security, immunity, asylum.
4 *a bird sanctuary* **reserve**, park, wildlife reserve, nature reserve, reservation, preserve, home, shelter.

sanctum ▶ noun **1** *the carving is done in that portion of the temple designed to be the sanctum* **holy place**, shrine, sanctuary, altar, inner sanctum, holy of holies; *Latin* sanctum sanctorum.
2 *the inner bar remained a private sanctum for the regulars* **refuge**, retreat, bolt-hole, foxhole, hideout, hiding place, hideaway, study, den; *Spanish* querencia.

sand ▶ noun *she came bounding across the sand* **beach**, sands, shore, seaside, seashore, foreshore, (sand) dunes, sandhills, desert; *literary* strand.

sane ▶ adjective **1** *an accused person is presumed to be sane until they can prove the contrary* **of sound mind**, right in the head, in one's right mind, in possession of all one's faculties, able to think/reason clearly, lucid, clear-headed, rational, coherent, balanced, well balanced, stable, normal; *Latin* compos mentis; *informal* all there.
OPPOSITES insane, mad.
2 *who would think it sane to use nuclear weapons?* **sensible**, practical, advisable, responsible, realistic, full of common sense, prudent, circumspect, pragmatic, wise, reasonable, rational, mature, level-headed, commonsensical, judicious, politic, sound, balanced, sober.
OPPOSITE foolish.

sangfroid ▶ noun *he recovered his usual sangfroid* **composure**, equanimity, self-possession, level-headedness, equilibrium, aplomb, poise, assurance, self-assurance, self-control, nerve, calmness, coolness, countenance, collectedness, imperturbability, presence of mind; *informal* cool, unflappability.

sanguine ▶ adjective 1 *he is sanguine about the remorseless advance of information technology* **optimistic**, bullish, hopeful, buoyant, positive, disposed to look on the bright side, confident, cheerful, cheery, bright, assured; *informal* upbeat; *archaic* of good cheer.
OPPOSITES pessimistic, gloomy.
2 (*archaic*) *a sanguine complexion.* See FLORID.

> **CHOOSE THE RIGHT WORD**
> **sanguine, confident, optimistic, hopeful**
> See CONFIDENT.

sanitary ▶ adjective *improvements in health are also the result of more sanitary conditions* **hygienic**, clean, germ-free, antiseptic, aseptic, sterile, sterilized, uninfected, disinfected, unpolluted, uncontaminated, salubrious, healthy, pure, wholesome.
OPPOSITE insanitary.

sanitize ▶ verb 1 *the best way to sanitize a chiller is to let boiling water flow through it* **sterilize**, disinfect, clean, cleanse, cauterize, purify, fumigate, pasteurize, decontaminate; *technical* autoclave; *rare* depollute.
2 *sometimes she would depart from her official schedule and visit some village that had not been sanitized in advance* **make presentable**, make acceptable, make palatable, clean up; **purge**, expurgate, bowdlerize, censor, emasculate, blue-pencil, water down.

sanity ▶ noun 1 *she wondered if she was losing her sanity* **soundness of mind**, mental health, mental faculties, balance, balance of mind, stability, reason, rationality, saneness, lucidity, lucidness, sense, senses, wits, normality, right-mindedness.
OPPOSITE insanity.
2 *we are delighted that sanity has prevailed* **sense**, common sense, good sense, wisdom, prudence, judiciousness, practicality, reasonableness, rationality, soundness, sensibleness.
OPPOSITE insanity.

sap[1] ▶ noun 1 *these insects suck the sap from the roots of trees* **plant fluid**, vital fluid, life fluid, juice, secretion, liquor, liquid.
2 *people full of sap and ready to go* **vigour**, energy, gusto, drive, push, brio, dynamism, life, go, spirit, liveliness, animation, bounce, sparkle, effervescence, fizz, verve, spiritedness, ebullience, high spirits, enthusiasm, initiative, vitality, vivacity, fire, dash, panache, elan, snap, zest, zeal, exuberance; *informal* feistiness, get-up-and-go, gumption, oomph, pizzazz, vim, zing, zip.
▶ verb 1 *the great loss of life had sapped the will of the troops to attack* **erode**, wear away, wear down, deplete, reduce, lessen, lower, attenuate, undermine, exhaust, impair, drain, bleed, consume.
2 *the confirmation of his friend's guilt sapped him of all energy* **drain**, empty, exhaust, deprive, milk.

sap[2] ▶ noun (*informal*) *he realized that he'd just made a sap of himself.* See IDIOT sense 1.

sarcasm ▶ noun *his voice was heavy with sarcasm* **derision**, mockery, ridicule, satire, irony, scorn, sneering, scoffing, gibing, taunting; trenchancy, mordancy, acerbity; *rare* causticity, mordacity.

sarcastic ▶ adjective *I've had enough of your sarcastic comments* **sardonic**, ironic, ironical, satirical; derisive, scornful, contemptuous, mocking, ridiculing, sneering, jeering, scoffing, taunting, snide; caustic, scathing, trenchant, mordant, cutting, sharp, stinging, acerbic, tart, acid; *Brit. informal* sarky; *rare* mordacious, acidulous.

> **CHOOSE THE RIGHT WORD**
> **sarcastic, sardonic, ironic, caustic**
> - A **sarcastic** comment expresses the opposite of what it literally means, thus mocking the person on the receiving end, while possibly entertaining others (*'That's nice,' Broomhead said in his most sarcastic manner | the youngsters gave a sarcastic cheer*).
> - **Sardonic** suggests a grimmer, more cynical amusement. It is used of actual utterances less frequently than the other three words, so people typically give a *sardonic smile* or *grin*, display *sardonic amusement*, or *raise a sardonic eyebrow*.
> - As with *sarcasm*, **ironic** remarks convey the opposite of their literal meaning, but more subtly and with an effect of wry amusement rather than blatant mockery (*Annie Lennox's first solo LP 'Diva', which she claims is an ironic title*).
> - A **caustic** remark is cruellest of all; it is straightforward, but scathing or bitter (*she longed to hurl some caustic retort at him*).

sardonic ▶ adjective *his sardonic wit* **mocking**, satirical; **sarcastic**, ironical, ironic, cynical, scornful, contemptuous, derisive, derisory, sneering, jeering, scoffing, taunting; scathing, caustic, trenchant, mordant, cutting, sharp, stinging, acerbic, tart, acid; wry, dry; *Brit. informal* sarky; *rare* mordacious, acidulous.

> **CHOOSE THE RIGHT WORD**
> **sardonic, sarcastic, ironic, caustic**
> See SARCASTIC.

sash ▶ noun **belt**, cummerbund, waistband, girdle; *Japanese* obi; *archaic* cincture, zone.

satanic ▶ adjective *how could ordinary people have committed such satanic atrocities?* **diabolical**, fiendish, devilish, demonic, demoniac, demoniacal, Mephistophelian; hellish, infernal, accursed, wicked, evil, sinful, iniquitous, nefarious, vile, foul, abominable, unspeakable, loathsome, monstrous, atrocious, heinous, hideous, odious, horrible, horrifying, shocking, appalling, dreadful, awful, terrible, ghastly, abhorrent, despicable, damnable, villainous, depraved, perverted, ungodly, dark, black, black-hearted, immoral, amoral; vicious, cruel, savage, brutish, bestial, barbaric, barbarous; *rare* cacodemonic, egregious, flagitious, facinorous.

sate ▶ verb 1 *he rested, his passion temporarily sated* **satiate**, fully satisfy; slake, quench, take the edge off.
OPPOSITES starve, deprive, dissatisfy.
2 *the children were sated with blackberries* **gorge**, stuff, fill, overfill, overfeed, surfeit, glut, cloy.

satellite ▶ noun 1 *the European Space Agency's ERS-1 satellite* **space station**, space capsule, spacecraft; artificial satellite, communications satellite, weather satellite, television satellite; sputnik, COBE, IRAS; *informal* Comsat.
2 *the two small satellites of Mars* **moon**, secondary planet.
3 *Bulgaria was then a Russian satellite* **dependency**, colony, protectorate, dominion, possession, holding; *historical* fief, tributary.
4 *many were Hollywood people, writers and actors and their satellites* **acolyte**, follower, camp follower, disciple, hanger-on, shadow; henchman, sidekick, lackey, flunkey, minion, underling, hireling, vassal; puppet, stooge, creature; toady, sycophant, parasite; dependent, dependant; *Brit.* poodle; *N. Amer.* cohort; *informal* yes-man, bootlicker; *N. Amer. informal* gofer, suck-up, brown-nose; *Indian informal* chamcha; *Brit. vulgar slang* arse-licker, bum-sucker; *N. Amer. vulgar slang* ass-kisser; *archaic* retainer, client.
▶ adjective *a satellite state* **dependent**, subordinate, subsidiary, ancillary; puppet, vassal; *historical* tributary.

satiate ▶ verb *he leaned back against the cushions, satiated by the Christmas fare* **fill**, fully satisfy, sate; slake, quench; gorge, stuff, overfill, overfeed, surfeit, glut, cloy; sicken, nauseate.
OPPOSITES starve, deprive, dissatisfy.

satiety ▶ noun *a commercial culture that exhorted one to consume to the point of satiety and well beyond* **satiation**, satisfaction, sufficiency, repleteness, repletion, fullness; over-fullness, surfeit.
OPPOSITE hunger.

satiny ▶ adjective *the satiny, honey-coloured wood* **smooth**, shiny, glossy, shining, gleaming, lustrous, sleek, silky, sheeny; polished, patinated; slippery, glassy; *rare* nitid.

satire ▶ noun 1 *a stinging satire on American politics* **parody**, burlesque, caricature, lampoon, skit, take-off, squib, travesty; *informal* spoof, send-up; *Brit. vulgar slang* piss-take; *rare* pasquinade, pasticcio.
2 *in recent years, the phenomenon has become the subject of satire* **mockery**, ridicule, derision, scorn, caricature; irony, sarcasm.

satirical ▶ adjective *a collection of satirical essays on English social life* **mocking**, ironic, ironical, satiric, sarcastic, sardonic, scornful, derisive, ridiculing, taunting; caustic, trenchant, mordant, biting, cutting, sharp, pointed, keen, stinging, acerbic, pungent, cynical; critical, irreverent, disparaging, disrespectful, Rabelaisian; *rare* Hudibrastic, mordacious.

satirize ▶ verb *a strip cartoon satirizing middle-aged, middle-class liberals* **mock**, ridicule, hold up to ridicule, deride, make fun of, poke fun at, parody, lampoon, burlesque, caricature, take off, travesty; criticize, censure, pillory; *informal* send up; *Brit. informal* take the mickey out of; *Brit. vulgar slang* take the piss out of; *archaic* squib; *rare* pasquinade.

satisfaction ▶ noun 1 *he smiled with satisfaction* **contentment**, contentedness, content, pleasure, gratification, fulfilment, happiness, sense of well-being, pride, sense of achievement, delight, joy, enjoyment, relish, triumph; self-satisfaction, smugness, complacency; *archaic* self-content.
OPPOSITES dissatisfaction, displeasure, discontent.
2 *the satisfaction of consumer needs and wants* **fulfilment**, gratification; appeasement, assuagement.
3 *investors may have to turn to the courts for satisfaction* **compensation**, recompense, reparation, restitution, repayment, payment, settlement, reimbursement, indemnification, indemnity, damages; redress, amends, atonement; justice; requital, retribution; *Latin* quid pro quo.
OPPOSITE loss.

S

satisfactory ▶ adjective *David Kerslake made a satisfactory debut for Leeds* **adequate**, all right, acceptable, good enough, sufficient, sufficiently good, fine, in order, up to scratch, up to the mark, up to standard, up to par, competent, reasonable, quite good, fair, decent, not bad, average, tolerable, passable, middling, moderate; presentable; suitable, convenient; informal OK, so-so, fair-to-middling; N. Amer. & Austral./NZ informal jake.
OPPOSITES unsatisfactory, inadequate, unacceptable, poor.

satisfied ▶ adjective **1** *Henry felt satisfied with the day's work | there was a satisfied smile on her face* **pleased**, well pleased, happy, content, contented; proud, triumphant; smug, self-satisfied, pleased with oneself, complacent; Brit. informal like the cat that's got the cream; N. Amer. vulgar slang shit-eating; humorous gruntled.
OPPOSITES dissatisfied, unhappy.
2 *the pleasure of satisfied desire* **fulfilled**, gratified, appeased, assuaged; archaic satiate.
OPPOSITE unfulfilled.
3 *I am quite satisfied that most of my staff are happy with their conditions of employment* **convinced**, certain, sure, positive, free from doubt, persuaded, easy in one's mind.
OPPOSITES uncertain, unconvinced.

satisfy ▶ verb **1** *he wanted one last chance to satisfy his hunger for romance* **fulfil**, gratify, meet, fill, serve, provide for, supply; indulge, cater to, pander to; appease, assuage; quench, slake, satiate, sate, take the edge off; rare satisfice.
OPPOSITE frustrate.
2 *his role was a creative one, and it satisfied him up to a point* **please**, content, make happy.
OPPOSITES dissatisfy, frustrate.
3 *she satisfied herself that it had been an accident* **convince**, persuade, assure, make certain; reassure, put someone's mind at rest, dispel someone's doubts.
4 *products which satisfy the EC's criteria will be awarded a special eco label* **comply with**, meet, fulfil, answer, conform to; match up to, measure up to, come up to; suffice, be good enough, fit/fill the bill; Law perfect; informal make the grade, cut the mustard.
5 *there was insufficient collateral to satisfy the loan* **repay**, pay, pay off, pay in full, settle, make good, discharge, square, liquidate, clear.

satisfying ▶ adjective **1** *it's hard work, but very satisfying* **fulfilling**, rewarding, gratifying, pleasing, enjoyable, pleasurable, to one's liking; worthwhile, constructive, productive, valuable, beneficial.
OPPOSITES dissatisfying, frustrating, pointless.
2 *potatoes are satisfying and provide good value for money* **filling**.
3 *a satisfying explanation* **satisfactory**, reasonable, acceptable; convincing, persuasive; reassuring.
OPPOSITE unsatisfactory.

saturate ▶ verb **1** *heavy autumn rain saturated the ground* **soak**, drench, waterlog, wet through, wet; souse, steep, douse, impregnate; technical ret; Scottish & N. English drouk; archaic sop.
OPPOSITE dry out.
2 *the air was saturated with the stench of joss sticks* **permeate**, impregnate, suffuse, imbue, pervade, steep, charge, infuse, inform, fill, spread throughout.
3 *Japan's electronics industry began to saturate the world markets* **flood**, glut, swamp, oversupply, overfill, overload.
OPPOSITE starve.

saturated ▶ adjective **1** *his trousers were saturated* **soaked**, soaking, soaking wet, wet through, sopping, sopping wet, sodden, dripping, dripping wet, wringing wet, drenched, streaming wet; soaked to the skin, like a drowned rat.
OPPOSITE bone dry.
2 *the saturated ground* **waterlogged**, soggy, squelchy, heavy, muddy, swampy, boggy.

saturnine ▶ adjective **1** *he was a rather saturnine individual who never spoke an unnecessary word* **gloomy**, sombre, melancholy, melancholic, moody, miserable, lugubrious, dour, glum, unsmiling, humourless, grumpy, bad-tempered; taciturn, uncommunicative, unresponsive.
OPPOSITES cheerful, jovial.
2 *his saturnine good looks* **swarthy**, dark, dark-skinned, dark-complexioned; mysterious, mercurial, moody.

sauce *See centre pages for list of* **Sauces and Dips**
▶ noun **1** *serve with a piquant sauce and redcurrant jelly* condiment, relish, ketchup, flavouring; dip, dressing; French jus, coulis.
2 (Brit. informal) *'I'll have less of your sauce,' said Aunt Edie* **impudence**, impertinence, cheek, cheekiness, effrontery, irreverence, sauciness, pertness, freshness, flippancy, insolence, rudeness, disrespect, disrespectfulness, familiarity, presumption, presumptuousness, audacity, audaciousness, boldness, brazenness, forwardness, cockiness, shamelessness; informal mouth, lip, neck, brass neck, nerve, face; Brit. informal backchat; Scottish informal snash; N. Amer. informal sassiness, sass, chutzpah, smart mouth, back talk; archaic malapertness, contumely; rare procacity.
OPPOSITES politeness, respectfulness.
3 (N. Amer. informal) *she's been on the sauce for years* **alcohol**, liquor, alcoholic drink, strong drink, intoxicating drink, spirits; informal booze, the bottle, the hard stuff, mother's milk, hooch; Brit. informal wallop; N. English & Irish informal sup; N. Amer. informal juice; Austral./NZ informal grog.

saucepan ▶ noun **cooking utensil**, pan, pot, casserole, skillet, stockpot, stewpot; steamer, double boiler; billy, billycan, dixie; N. Amer. trademark Crockpot; Provençal tian; S. African potjie.

saucy ▶ adjective (informal) **1** *saucy seaside postcards* **suggestive**, titillating, risqué, rude, bawdy, racy, ribald, spicy; informal raunchy, smutty; Brit. informal fruity; N. Amer. informal gamy.
OPPOSITES demure, prim.
2 *you saucy little minx!* **cheeky**, impudent, impertinent, irreverent, forward, insolent, disrespectful, flippant, familiar, presumptuous, audacious, bold, bold as brass, brazen, cocky, out of line, shameless; informal fresh, flip, lippy, mouthy, smart-arsed; N. Amer. informal sassy, nervy, smart-assed; archaic malapert; rare tossy.
OPPOSITES polite, respectful.
3 *her cap sat at a saucy angle on her black hair* **jaunty**, rakish, sporty, raffish; pert, perky, stylish, dashing, dapper; informal natty, snazzy, snappy; N. Amer. informal spiffy, sassy; dated gay.

saunter ▶ verb *they sauntered back to the car* **stroll**, amble, wander, meander, drift, maunder, potter, walk, promenade, ramble; go for a walk, go for a stroll, take a walk, stretch one's legs, take the air; Scottish & Irish stravaig; Irish streel; informal mosey, tootle; Brit. informal pootle; rare perambulate.
▶ noun *a quiet saunter down the road* **stroll**, amble, wander, meander, walk, turn, constitutional, ramble, airing, promenade, breather; N. Amer. paseo; Italian passegiata; informal mosey, tootle; Brit. informal pootle.

> **CHOOSE THE RIGHT WORD**
>
> **saunter, stroll, amble**
>
> See STROLL.

sausage *See centre pages for list of* **Sausages**
▶ noun Brit. informal banger; Austral. informal snag.

savage ▶ adjective **1** *packs of savage dogs roamed the streets* **ferocious**, fierce; **wild**, untamed, undomesticated, feral; predatory, ravening.
OPPOSITE tame.
2 *James died after a savage assault at his home near Blackpool* **vicious**, brutal, cruel, sadistic, ferocious, fierce, violent, bloody, murderous, homicidal, bloodthirsty, bestial, brutish, barbaric, barbarous, merciless, ruthless, pitiless, heartless, inhuman, harsh, callous, cold-blooded; archaic fell, sanguinary.
3 *Calvert launched a savage attack on European free-trade policy* **fierce**, blistering, scathing, searing, stinging, devastating, mordant, trenchant, caustic, cutting, biting, withering, virulent, vitriolic.
OPPOSITES mild, gentle.
4 *a savage race* **primitive**, uncivilized, unenlightened, non-literate, in a state of nature, heathen; wild, barbarian, barbarous, barbaric; archaic rude.
OPPOSITE civilized.
5 *the most savage landscape you are likely to see in the Pyrenees* **rugged**, rough, wild, inhospitable, uninhabitable.
6 *the decision was a savage blow for the town* **severe**, crushing, devastating, crippling, terrible, awful, dreadful, dire, catastrophic, calamitous, ruinous; mortal, lethal, fatal.
▶ noun **1** *Sheila had expected mud huts and savages* **barbarian**, wild man, wild woman, primitive, heathen; cannibal; Caliban.
2 *the mother of one of the victims has described his assailants as savages* **brute**, beast, monster, barbarian, ogre, demon, sadist, animal.
▶ verb **1** *11-year-old Kelly was savaged by two Rottweilers* **maul**, attack, tear to pieces, lacerate, claw, bite, mutilate, mangle; worry.
2 *British critics savaged the film* **criticize severely**, attack, lambaste, condemn, flay, shoot down, pillory, revile; informal jump on, tear to pieces, take to pieces, take/pull apart, lay into, pitch into, hammer, slam, bash, do a hatchet job on, crucify, give something a battering, roast, skewer, throw brickbats at, knock; Brit. informal slate, rubbish, slag off; N. Amer. informal bad-mouth, pummel; Austral./NZ informal trash, bag, monster, give someone bondi; archaic excoriate, slash.
OPPOSITES praise, commend, applaud.

savagery ▶ noun *the appalling savagery of the attack* **brutality**, ferocity, fierceness, violence, viciousness, cruelty, sadism, barbarity, barbarousness, murderousness, bloodthirstiness, brutishness, mercilessness, ruthlessness, pitilessness, inhumanity, heartlessness; rare ferity.
OPPOSITES mildness, gentleness.

savant ▶ noun *Sir Isaiah Berlin, the Oxford savant* **intellectual**, scholar, sage, philosopher, thinker, learned person, wise person, Solomon; guru,

S

master, authority; *Indian* mahatma, maharishi, pandit.
OPPOSITES ignoramus, fool.

save ▶ verb **1** *the captain was saved by his crew when a windscreen blew out during the flight* **rescue**, come to someone's rescue, save someone's life, come to someone's aid; set free, free, liberate, deliver, extricate, snatch; bail out; *Nautical* bring off; *informal* save someone's bacon, save someone's neck, save someone's skin.
OPPOSITE endanger.
2 *the fifteenth century farmhouse has been saved from demolition* **preserve**, keep safe, keep, protect, safeguard, guard, conserve; salvage, retrieve, reclaim, rescue.
3 *we've saved enough for a deposit on a house | start saving newspapers to use for wrapping china* **put aside**, set aside, lay aside, put by, put to one side, lay by, keep, retain, reserve, keep in reserve, conserve, stockpile, store, hoard, save for a rainy day, keep for future use, put in a safe place; collect, amass; *N. Amer.* set by; *informal* salt away, squirrel away, stash away, hang on to.
OPPOSITES waste, fritter away, use up.
4 *I suppose I'll have to start saving* **economize**, be (more) economical, make economies, scrimp, scrimp and scrape; be thrifty, be frugal, tighten one's belt, cut back, make cutbacks, budget, retrench, husband one's resources, cut costs, cut expenditure, draw in one's horns, watch one's pennies; *N. Amer.* pinch the pennies; *black English* rake and scrape.
OPPOSITES spend, be extravagant.
5 *if I'd known this a few days ago, it would have saved a lot of trouble* **prevent**, obviate, forestall, spare; stop; avoid, avert; make unnecessary, rule out.
OPPOSITE cause.
▶ preposition & conjunction *no one needed to know save herself | the kitchen was empty save for Boris* **except (for)**, apart from, but (for), other than, besides, aside from, with the exception of, bar, barring, excluding, omitting, leaving out, saving; *informal* outside of.

saving ▶ noun **1** *this resulted in a considerable saving in development costs* **reduction**, cut, decrease, economy.
2 *after five years of scrimping and saving we bought a modest house* **economizing**, economy, frugality, thrift, thriftiness, retrenchment, cutting back, belt-tightening, penny-pinching; carefulness, prudence.
3 (**savings**) *he wanted to know how to invest his savings* **nest egg**, money put by for a rainy day, life savings; capital, assets, funds, resources, reserves.

saving grace ▶ noun *the bungalow's only saving grace was a room with spectacular views of the sea* **redeeming feature**, compensating feature, good point, thing in its/one's favour, appealing/attractive aspect, advantage, asset, selling point; mitigating/extenuating feature.

Saviour ▶ noun *in the centre of the mosaic, the Saviour is depicted, attended by two archangels* **Christ**, Jesus, Jesus Christ, the Redeemer, the Messiah, Our Lord, the Lamb of God, the Son of God, the Son of Man, the Prince of Peace, the King of Kings, Emmanuel.

saviour ▶ noun *to many Frenchmen, de Gaulle appeared to be the saviour of France | luckily my saviour, Larry, was on hand to help me* **rescuer**, liberator, deliverer, emancipator; champion, knight in shining armour, friend in need, Good Samaritan; salvation.

savoir faire ▶ noun (*French*) *he had been faced with a situation that even his charm and savoir faire were unable to resolve* **social skill**, social grace(s), urbanity, urbaneness, suaveness, suavity, finesse, sophistication, poise, aplomb, grace, adroitness, accomplishment, polish, style, smoothness, tact, tactfulness, diplomacy, discretion, delicacy, sensitivity; assurance, confidence, knowledge, know-how; *French* savoir vivre; *informal* savvy.
OPPOSITES awkwardness, gaucheness.

savour ▶ verb **1** *I savoured each delicious mouthful | she wanted to savour every moment of the evening* **relish**, enjoy, enjoy to the full, taste to the full, appreciate, delight in, take pleasure in, revel in, smack one's lips over, luxuriate in, bask in, drool over; *informal* smack one's chops over.
2 *such a declaration would savour of immodesty* **suggest**, smack of, have the hallmarks of, have all the signs of, give the impression of, seem like, have the air of, have a suggestion of, be indicative of, hint at, have overtones of.
▶ noun **1** *the subtle savour of wood smoke* **taste**, flavour, tang, smack; **smell**, aroma, fragrance, scent, perfume, bouquet, odour, whiff; *archaic* relish; *rare* sapidity.
2 *a savour of bitterness seasoned my feelings towards him* **trace**, hint, suggestion, touch, smack.
3 *her usual diversions had lost their savour* **piquancy**, interest, attraction, fascination, flavour, spice, zest, excitement, enjoyment, joy; *informal* zing.

savoury ▶ adjective **1** *cloves can be used to flavour both sweet and savoury dishes* **salty**, **spicy**, piquant, tangy.
OPPOSITE sweet.
2 *a rich, savoury aroma was wafting from the kitchen* **appetizing**, mouth-watering, delicious, delectable, aromatic, luscious; tasty, flavoursome, flavourful, palatable, toothsome; *informal* scrumptious, finger-licking, yummy, scrummy, nummy, moreish, delish, yum-yum; *literary* ambrosial; *rare* flavorous, ambrosian, sapid, nectarean, nectareous.
OPPOSITES unappetizing, unpalatable.
3 *everyone knew it was a front for less savoury operations* **acceptable**, pleasant, palatable, wholesome, respectable, honourable, proper, seemly, creditable.
OPPOSITES unpleasant, unacceptable, dishonourable.
▶ noun *a tray of cocktail savouries* **canapé**, hors d'oeuvre, appetizer, titbit; *French* amuse-gueule.

savvy (*informal*) ▶ noun *much will depend on his political savvy* **shrewdness**, astuteness, sharp-wittedness, sharpness, acuteness, acumen, acuity, intelligence, wit, canniness, common sense, discernment, insight, understanding, penetration, perception, perceptiveness, perspicacity, perspicaciousness, knowledge, sagacity, sageness; *informal* nous, horse sense; *rare* sapience, arguteness.
OPPOSITES inexperience, ignorance.
▶ verb *he knew she had been making a fool of him, but he didn't quite savvy how* **realize**, understand, comprehend, grasp, see, know, apprehend; *informal* get, get a fix on, catch on, latch on, cotton on; *Brit. informal* twig, suss.
▶ adjective *Bob is a savvy veteran who knows all the tricks* **shrewd**, astute, sharp-witted, sharp, acute, intelligent, clever, canny, perceptive, perspicacious, sagacious, sage; *informal* on the ball, smart, streetwise; *Scottish & N. English informal* pawky; *N. Amer. informal* heads-up; *rare* long-headed, sapient, argute.
OPPOSITES stupid, gullible.

saw[1] ▶ noun. *See centre pages for list of* **Saws** (*tools*)

saw[2] ▶ noun *spare me the old saw about eggs and omelettes* **saying**, maxim, proverb, aphorism, axiom, adage, motto, epigram, dictum, gnome; expression, phrase; platitude, cliché, truism; *rare* apophthegm.

say ▶ verb **1** *she felt her stomach flutter as he said her name* **speak**, utter, voice, pronounce, give utterance to, give voice to, vocalize.
2 *'I must go,' she said* **declare**, state, announce; **remark**, observe, mention, comment, note, add; reply, respond, answer, rejoin; whisper, mutter, mumble, mouth; *informal* come out with.
3 *Newall says he's innocent* **claim**, maintain, assert, hold, insist, contend, aver, affirm, avow; allege, profess; *formal* opine; *rare* asseverate.
4 *I can't conjure up the words to say how I feel | what are you trying to say, Inspector?* **express**, put into words, phrase, articulate, communicate, make known, get across, put across, convey, verbalize, render, tell; reveal, divulge, impart, disclose; imply, suggest, signify, denote, mean.
5 *they sang hymns and said a prayer* **recite**, repeat, utter, deliver, perform, declaim, orate.
6 *the lighted dial of her watch said one twenty* **indicate**, show, read.
7 *I'd say about 90 per cent of my stories are off the top of my head* **estimate**, judge, guess, hazard a guess, dare say, predict, speculate, surmise, conjecture, venture; imagine, think, believe; *informal* reckon.
8 *let's say you'd just won a million pounds* **suppose**, assume, imagine, presume, take as a hypothesis, hypothesize, postulate, posit.
9 *she determined to find something to say in his favour* **adduce**, propose, advance, bring forward, offer, plead.
□ **be said** *it is said that she lived to be over a hundred | his widow was said to be inconsolable* **be reported**, be thought, be believed, be alleged, be rumoured, be reputed, be put about; be described, be asserted; apparently, seemingly, it seems that, it appears that, (so) they say, (so) the story goes, by all accounts, rumour has it, the rumour is.
□ **that is to say** *people emigrated for economic reasons—that is to say, because they were poor* **in other words**, to put it another way, to rephrase it; i.e., that is, to wit, viz., namely, sc.; *Latin* id est, scilicet, videlicet.
□ **to say the least** *his performance was disappointing to say the least* **to put it mildly**, putting it mildly, without any exaggeration, at the very least, as an understatement.
▶ noun **1** *Miss Honey was determined to have her say* **right/chance/turn to speak**, right/chance/turn to express one's opinion, vote, opinion, view, voice; *informal* one's twopence worth, one's twopenn'orth.
2 *don't I have any say in the matter?* **influence**, sway, weight, authority, voice, input, share, part; *informal* clout.

saying ▶ noun *you know the old saying about all work and no play?* **proverb**, maxim, aphorism, axiom, adage, saw, tag, motto, precept, epigram, epigraph, dictum, gnome, pearl of wisdom; expression, phrase, formula; slogan, catchphrase; platitude, cliché, commonplace, truism; *rare* apophthegm.
□ **it goes without saying of course**, naturally, needless to say, it is taken for granted, it is understood/assumed, it is taken as read, it is accepted, it is unquestionable, it is an accepted fact; obviously, self-evidently, manifestly; *informal* natch.

say-so ▶ noun *Kathleen ran things around here and nothing could be done without her say-so* **authorization**, approval, seal of approval, agreement, consent, assent, permission, endorsement, sanction, ratification, approbation, acquiescence, confirmation, blessing, leave; *informal* OK, the go-ahead, the green light, the thumbs up.
OPPOSITES refusal, denial.

scald ▶ verb *the boiling water scalded his skin* **burn**, scorch, sear; *technical* cauterize.

scalding ▶ adjective *a jet of scalding water* **extremely hot**, burning, blistering, searing, red-hot; piping hot; *informal* **boiling (hot)**, sizzling.

S

scale[1] ▶ noun **1** *all reptiles have scales covering the skin* **plate**; *technical* lamella, lamina, squama, scute, scutum.
2 *the disease causes scales on the skin* **flake**; (**scales**) scurf, dandruff; *technical* furfur.
3 *scale is bad enough in kettles, but can have a disastrous effect on the insides of boilers* **limescale**; deposit, encrustation, coating; *Brit.* fur.

scale[2] *See centre pages for list of* **Tonic Sol-Fa Notes**
▶ noun **1** *the Celsius scale of temperature* **calibrated system**, calibration, graduated system, system of measurement, measuring system, register.
2 *two men at opposite ends of the social scale* **hierarchy**, ladder, ranking, pecking order, order, spectrum, progression, succession, sequence, series.
3 *the number of points needed to represent the line will depend on the scale of the map* **ratio**, proportion, relative size.
4 *no one foresaw the scale of the disaster* **extent**, **size**, scope, magnitude, dimensions, range, breadth, compass, degree, reach, spread, sweep.
▶ verb *thieves scaled an 8ft high fence* **climb**, ascend, go up, go over, clamber up, shin (up), scramble up, mount; *N. Amer.* shinny (up); *rare* escalade.
□ **scale something down** *manufacturing capacity has been scaled down* **reduce**, cut down, cut back, cut, make cutbacks in, decrease, lessen, lower, trim, slim down, prune, curtail.
□ **scale something up** *the departments intend to scale up their activities* **increase**, expand, augment, build up, add to; step up, boost, escalate.

scales ▶ plural noun **weighing machine**, balance, pair of scales; steelyard.

scaly ▶ adjective **1** *the dragon's scaly hide* *technical* squamate, squamose, squamous, lamellate, lamellar, lamelliform, lamellose; *rare* squamulose.
2 *scaly patches of dead skin* **dry**, **flaky**, flaking, peeling, scurfy, rough, scabrous, mangy, scabious; *technical* furfuraceous, lepidote.

scam ▶ noun (*informal*) *the scam involved a series of bogus reinsurance deals* **fraud**, swindle, fraudulent scheme, racket, trick, diddle; *informal* con, con trick, flimflam, gyp, kite; *Brit. informal* ramp, twist; *N. Amer. informal* hustle, grift, shakedown, bunco, boondoggle; *Austral. informal* rort.

scamp ▶ noun *he was a little scamp in those days* **rascal**, monkey, devil, imp, rogue, wretch, mischief-maker, troublemaker, prankster; *informal* scallywag, horror, monster, terror, holy terror; *Brit. informal* perisher, pickle; *Irish informal* spalpeen; *N. English informal* tyke, scally; *N. Amer. informal* varmint, hellion; *dated* rip; *archaic* rapscallion, scapegrace.

scamper ▶ verb *the boy scampered off | his dogs scampered around the yard* **scurry**, scuttle, dart, run, rush, dash, race, sprint, hurry, hasten, make haste; romp, frolic, gambol; *Brit.* scutter; *informal* scoot, beetle.

scan ▶ verb **1** *Adam scanned the horizon | his eyes were scanning her face* **study**, **examine**, scrutinize, inspect, survey, search, scour, sweep, rake; look at, look someone/something up and down, stare at, gaze at, eye, watch, contemplate, regard; take stock of; *Hunting* glass; *informal* check out, recce; *N. Amer. informal* scope; *archaic* con.
2 *he pulled out a leather-bound diary and scanned the pages* **glance through/over**, look through/over, have a look at, run/pass/cast one's eye over, skim, flick through, flip through, riffle through, leaf through, thumb through, read quickly, browse through; peruse.
OPPOSITE pore over.
▶ noun **1** *a careful scan of the terrain* **inspection**, scrutiny, examination, survey, search.
2 *a quick scan through the 'For Sale' pages* **glance**, look, flick, browse, skim.
3 *a brain scan* **examination**, screening; ultrasound (scan).

scandal ▶ noun **1** *he was forced out of office because of a sex scandal* **outrageous wrongdoing**, outrageous behaviour, immoral behaviour, unethical behaviour, discreditable behaviour, shocking incident/series of events, impropriety, misconduct, wrongdoing; offence, transgression, crime, sin; skeleton in the closet; *informal* business, affair, -gate.
2 *unmarried motherhood at that time was fraught with scandal* **shame**, dishonour, disgrace, disrepute, discredit, infamy, ignominy, embarrassment; odium, opprobrium, censure, obloquy; stigma.
3 *it's a scandal that the disease is not yet being adequately treated* **disgrace**, outrage, injustice; shame, pity, crying shame; affront, insult, reproach.
4 *you know what scandals were spread about me* **malicious gossip**, malicious rumour(s), slander, libel, scandalmongering, calumny, defamation, aspersions, muckraking, smear campaign; *informal* dirt.

scandalize ▶ verb *Henry is said to have been scandalized by William's conduct* **shock**, appal, outrage, horrify, disgust, revolt, repel, sicken, nauseate; offend, give offence to, affront, insult, cause raised eyebrows.
OPPOSITE impress.

scandalmonger ▶ noun **gossip**, muckraker, tattler; *rare* quidnunc, calumniator.

scandalous ▶ adjective **1** *it is scandalous that elderly patients should be treated in that way* **disgraceful**, shocking, outrageous, monstrous, criminal, wicked, sinful, shameful, atrocious, appalling, terrible, dreadful, disgusting, abhorrent, despicable, deplorable, reprehensible, obscene, iniquitous, inexcusable, intolerable, insupportable, unforgivable, unpardonable; *rare* egregious.
OPPOSITES acceptable, praiseworthy.
2 *a series of scandalous liaisons* **discreditable**, disreputable, dishonourable, improper, unseemly, sordid.
OPPOSITES seemly, proper.
3 *she loved to spread scandalous rumours* **scurrilous**, malicious, slanderous, libellous, defamatory; *rare* calumnious, calumniatory, aspersive.

scant ▶ adjective *he paid scant attention to these wider issues | there is only scant evidence to support this hypothesis* **little**, little or no, minimal, hardly any, limited, negligible, barely sufficient, meagre; insufficient, too little, not enough, inadequate, deficient; *rare* exiguous.
OPPOSITES abundant, ample, sufficient.

scanty ▶ adjective **1** *they paid whatever they could out of their scanty wages to their families | details of his life are scanty* **meagre**, scant, minimal, limited, modest, restricted, sparse; tiny, small, paltry, negligible, insufficient, inadequate, deficient, sketchy, too small/little/few, not enough, poor; thin, thinning; scarce, in short supply, thin on the ground, few and far between; *informal* measly, piddling, mingy, pathetic; *rare* exiguous.
OPPOSITES abundant, ample, plentiful.
2 *her ridiculously scanty nightdress threatened to fall off altogether* **skimpy**, revealing, short, brief; low, low-cut; indecent.
OPPOSITE modest.

CHOOSE THE RIGHT WORD

scanty, sparse, meagre
See MEAGRE.

scapegoat ▶ noun **whipping boy**, victim, Aunt Sally; *N. Amer.* goat; *informal* fall guy; *N. Amer. informal* patsy.

scar ▶ noun **1** *a tall dark man with a scar on his left cheek* **cicatrix**; **mark**, blemish, disfigurement, discoloration, defacement; pockmark, pock, pit; wound, lesion, burn; birthmark, naevus; (**scars**) *Christianity* stigmata.
2 *behind the smile there were deep psychological scars* **trauma**, damage, shock, injury, suffering, upset.
▶ verb **1** *Antony lost a lot of blood and is likely to be scarred for life* **disfigure**, mark, blemish, blotch, discolour; pockmark, pit; *Christianity* stigmatize.
2 *the scenic red-rock vistas have been scarred by strip mining* **damage**, spoil, mar, deface, injure; *rare* disfeature.
3 *she was profoundly scarred by her father's suicide* **traumatize**, damage, injure, wound; distress, disturb, upset.

scarce ▶ adjective **1** *the drought means that the crops have failed and food is scarce | scarce financial resources* **in short supply**, short, scant, scanty, meagre, sparse, hard to find, hard to come by, not enough, too little, insufficient, deficient, inadequate, lacking, wanting; at a premium, like gold dust, not to be had, scarcer than hen's teeth; paltry, negligible, thin; *informal* not to be had for love nor money; *rare* exiguous.
OPPOSITES plentiful, abundant.
2 *birds that prefer dense forest interiors are becoming scarcer* **rare**, few and far between, thin on the ground, seldom seen/found; uncommon, unusual, infrequent; *Brit.* out of the common.
OPPOSITE common.

scarcely ▶ adverb **1** *she could scarcely hear what he was saying* **hardly**, barely, only just; almost not.
2 *I scarcely ever see him* **rarely**, seldom, infrequently, not often, hardly ever, almost never, on rare occasions, every once in a while; *informal* once in a blue moon.
OPPOSITE often.
3 *this could scarcely be accidental* **surely not**, not, hardly, certainly not, definitely not, not at all, on no account, under no circumstances, by no means; *N. Amer.* noway.

scarcity ▶ noun **1** *the scarcity of affordable housing* **shortage**, dearth, lack, want, undersupply, insufficiency, paucity, scarceness, scantness, meagreness, sparseness, scantiness, poverty; deficiency, inadequacy, limitedness; unavailability, absence; *rare* exiguity, exiguousness.
OPPOSITES abundance, excess, surplus.
2 *the bird's current scarcity is the result of a lack of appropriate food* **rarity**, rareness, infrequency, sparseness, uncommonness, unusualness.
OPPOSITE commonness.

scare ▶ verb *the thought of what might happen scared her* **frighten**, make afraid, make fearful, make nervous, panic, throw into a panic; terrify, petrify, scare/frighten to death, scare/frighten someone out of their wits, scare stiff, scare witless, scare/frighten the living daylights out of, scare/frighten the life out of, scare the hell out of, strike terror into, fill with fear, put the fear of God into, make someone jump (out of their skin), make someone's hair stand on end, give someone goose pimples, make someone's blood run cold, chill someone's blood, send into a cold sweat, make someone shake in their shoes; **startle**, alarm, give someone a fright, give someone a turn; shock, appal, horrify; intimidate, daunt, unnerve; *informal* give someone the heebie-jeebies, scare the pants off, scarify, make someone's hair curl; *Brit. informal* throw into a blue funk, put the wind up; *Irish informal* scare the bejesus out of; *N. Amer. informal* spook; *vulgar slang* scare shitless, scare the shit out of; *archaic* fright, affright.
OPPOSITE reassure.

S

▶ **noun** *you gave me a scare—how did you get here?* **fright**, shock, start, turn, jump; *informal* the heebie-jeebies.

> **CHOOSE THE RIGHT WORD**
>
> **scare, frighten, startle**
>
> *See* FRIGHTEN.

scared ▶ **adjective** *it was growing dark and she began to feel scared* **frightened**, afraid, fearful, nervous, panicky, agitated, alarmed, worried, intimidated; terrified, petrified, horrified, panic-stricken, scared stiff, frightened/scared out of one's wits, scared witless, frightened/scared to death, terror-stricken, terror-struck, horror-stricken, horror-struck, frantic, hysterical, beside oneself; with one's heart in one's mouth, shaking in one's shoes, shaking like a leaf, shaky; *Scottish* feart; *informal* in a cold sweat, in a (blue) funk, jumpy, jittery; *Brit. informal* funky, windy; *N. Amer. informal* spooked; *vulgar slang* scared shitless, shit scared, shitting bricks, bricking oneself; *dialect* frit; *archaic* afeared, affrighted.
OPPOSITES confident, laid-back, calm.

scaremonger ▶ **noun** **alarmist**, prophet of doom, Cassandra, voice of doom, doom-monger; pessimist; *informal* doom and gloom merchant.

scarf ▶ **noun** **muffler**; headscarf, headsquare, square; stole, tippet; neckerchief, kerchief, cravat, bandanna; *N. Amer.* babushka; *dated* comforter; (*in Spanish-speaking countries*) mantilla, rebozo.

scarper ▶ **verb** (*Brit. informal*) *they left the stuff where it was and scarpered.* See RUN AWAY *at* RUN.

scary ▶ **adjective** (*informal*) *we set off for the graveyard—it was really scary* **frightening**, scaring, hair-raising, terrifying, petrifying, spine-chilling, blood-curdling, chilling, horrifying, alarming, appalling, daunting, formidable, fearsome, nerve-racking, unnerving; eerie, sinister; *informal* creepy, spine-tingling, spooky, hairy.

scathing ▶ **adjective** *the shadow trade and industry spokesman launched a scathing attack on the government* **devastating**, withering, blistering, extremely critical, searing, scorching, fierce, ferocious, savage, severe, stinging, biting, cutting, mordant, trenchant, virulent, caustic, vitriolic, scornful, sharp, bitter, acid, harsh, unsparing; *rare* mordacious.
OPPOSITES mild, gentle; complimentary.

scatter ▶ **verb 1** *he broke the slices of bread into pieces and scattered them over the lake | scatter the seeds as evenly as possible* **throw**, strew, toss, fling; **sprinkle**, spread, distribute, sow, broadcast, intersperse, disseminate; shower, spatter, spray; *literary* bestrew.
OPPOSITES collect, gather.
2 *the police fired over their heads and the crowd scattered | he spurred his horse forward, scattering onlookers in all directions* **disperse**, break up, disband, separate, move/go in different directions, go separate ways; dissipate, disintegrate, dissolve; drive, send, put to flight, chase.
OPPOSITES assemble, converge, congregate.
3 *the sky above them was scattered with stars* **fleck**, stud, dot, cover, sprinkle, stipple, spot, pepper; litter; *literary* bestud.

> **CHOOSE THE RIGHT WORD**
>
> **scatter, disperse, dissipate**
>
> These words all describe the spreading out or elimination of something or a group of things that originally formed a concentrated or closely knit whole.
>
> - **Scatter** emphasizes the random distribution of something over a wide area (*the occupants had scattered far and wide | sow thinly in rows, rather than scattering the seeds randomly*).
> - With **disperse**, the emphasis is primarily on the parting and spreading out of people or things rather than on where they all go (*troops were deployed to disperse the protesters*), but the result will probably be more even or organized than with *scatter.* Unlike *scatter, disperse* can refer to the thinning of mist, cloud, and similar concentrations of small particles (*the blanket of fog above their heads began to disperse*).
> - With **dissipate**, the emphasis is more on the actual loss of a commodity, substance, or form of energy than on the manner of its going: something that is *dissipated* is spread out so thinly that it is no longer detectable or usable (*the semiconductor has low power requirements, thereby dissipating little heat*). *Dissipate* can also describe the thinning of mist or cloud; unlike *disperse*, it is extended to the fading away of emotions, especially unpleasant ones (*she waited a moment for her exasperation to dissipate*). If money or resources are *dissipated*, they are squandered on something or other (*he turned out to be a waster and dissipated his fortune*).

scatterbrained ▶ **adjective** *a scatterbrained young woman* **absent-minded**, forgetful, with a mind like a sieve, disorganized, unsystematic; dreamy, wool-gathering, with one's head in the clouds, feather-brained, feather-headed, birdbrained, empty-headed, erratic, giddy; *informal* scatty, dizzy, dippy, not with it.
OPPOSITES organized, together.

scattering ▶ **noun** *a scattering of freckles across the bridge of her nose* **handful**, few, one or two, not many, a small number; **sprinkling**, dusting, smattering, smatter.

scavenge ▶ **verb** *pigs and poultry scavenged for food around the farm* **rummage**, search, hunt, look, forage, root about/around, scratch about/around, grub about/around; *rare* mudlark.

scenario ▶ **noun 1** *Walt wrote scenarios for a major Hollywood studio* **plot**, outline, storyline, framework, structure, scheme, plan, layout; screenplay, script; synopsis, summary, precis; *technical* schema; *rare* diegesis.
2 *every possible scenario must be explored* **sequence of events**, course of events, chain of events, series of developments, situation.
3 *this film has a more contemporary scenario* **setting**, background, context, scene, milieu.

scene ▶ **noun 1** *others were treated at the scene of the accident for cuts and bruises* **location**, site, place, position, point, spot; locale, whereabouts; arena, stage, set; *technical* locus.
2 *tapestries and shields adorned the wall, setting the scene for the conference | the scene is London, in the late 1890s* **background**, setting, context, milieu, backdrop; *French* mise en scène.
3 *there had been terrible scenes of violence in Europe* **incident**, event, episode, happening, moment.
4 *an impressive mountain scene* **view**, vista, outlook, panorama, prospect, sight; landscape, scenery; picture, tableau, spectacle.
5 *she made an embarrassing scene outside the bank* **fuss**, exhibition of oneself, performance, tantrum, outburst, commotion, disturbance, row, upset, contretemps, furore, brouhaha; *informal* song and dance, to-do; *Brit. informal* carry-on.
6 *Michael never joined in—I don't think it was his scene | the Irish music scene* **area of interest**, field of interest, field, interest, speciality, territory, province, preserve; sphere, world, milieu, realm, domain; *informal* thing.
7 *the last scene of the play* **subdivision**, division, section, segment.
8 *a scene from a Laurel and Hardy film* **section**, segment, part, clip, sequence.

□ **behind the scenes 1** *informal discussions continued behind the scenes* **secretly**, in secret, privately, in private, behind closed doors, clandestinely, surreptitiously; confidentially, off the record; *informal* on the quiet, on the q.t.
OPPOSITE publicly.
2 *behind-the-scenes diplomatic activity* **secret**, private, clandestine, surreptitious; confidential.
OPPOSITE public.

scenery ▶ **noun 1** *the beautiful scenery of central and west Wales* **landscape**, countryside, country, terrain, topography, setting, surroundings, environment; view, vista, panorama, prospect, outlook; cityscape, townscape, roofscape, riverscape, seascape, waterscape, snowscape.
2 *we had all helped with the scenery and costumes* **stage set**, set, flats, backdrop, drop curtain; setting, background, decor; *Brit.* backcloth; *French* coulisse, mise en scène.

scenic ▶ **adjective** *the most scenic route from Florence to Siena* **picturesque**, pretty, pleasing, attractive, lovely, beautiful, charming, pretty as a picture, easy on the eye; impressive, striking, spectacular, breathtaking; panoramic.
OPPOSITES dreary, unattractive.

scent ▶ **noun 1** *the scent of freshly cut hay* **smell**, fragrance, aroma, perfume, redolence, savour, odour, whiff; bouquet, nose.
OPPOSITES stink, stench.
2 *she brushed her hair and sprayed scent over her body* **perfume**, fragrance, toilet water, lavender water, cologne; *French* parfum, eau de toilette, eau de cologne; *informal* scoosh.
3 *the hounds picked up the scent of a hare* **spoor**, trail, track; *Hunting* foil, wind.
4 *the day was gloomy and cold with a scent of rain on the air* **hint**, suggestion, trace, whiff.

▶ **verb 1** *a shark can scent blood from well over half a kilometre away* **smell**, detect the smell of, pick up the smell of, get a whiff of.
2 *Rose looked at him, scenting a threat* **sense**, become aware of, become conscious of, detect, discern, perceive, recognize, get wind of, sniff out, nose out.

scented ▶ **adjective** *scented soap | scented pine woods* **perfumed**, fragranced, perfumy; **sweet-smelling**, fragrant, aromatic; *rare* aromatized.
OPPOSITES smelly, malodorous.

sceptic ▶ **noun 1** *sceptics said the marriage wouldn't last* **cynic**, doubter, questioner, scoffer; pessimist, prophet of doom; *rare* Pyrrhonist, minimifidian.
2 *empowered by that Spirit, sceptics have found faith* **agnostic**; atheist, unbeliever, non-believer, disbeliever, doubting Thomas; rationalist; *rare* nullifidian.
OPPOSITE believer.

S

sceptical ▶ adjective *they were sceptical about the Treasury's forecast of inflation dropping to 3 per cent* **dubious**, doubtful, having reservations, taking something with a pinch of salt, doubting, questioning; cynical, distrustful, mistrustful, suspicious, disbelieving, misbelieving, unconvinced, incredulous, hesitant, scoffing; pessimistic, defeatist; informal iffy; rare Pyrrhonist, minimifidian.
OPPOSITES certain, convinced; optimistic.

scepticism ▶ noun **1** *members of the organization greeted his ideas with scepticism* **doubt**, doubtfulness, dubiousness, a pinch of salt, lack of conviction; **disbelief**, cynicism, distrust, mistrust, suspicion, misbelief, incredulity; pessimism, defeatism; rare dubiety, Pyrrhonism, scepsis, minimifidianism.
OPPOSITE conviction.
2 *a vague kind of scepticism is one of the commonest spiritual diseases in this generation* **agnosticism**, doubt; atheism, unbelief, non-belief; rationalism.
OPPOSITES belief, faith.

schedule ▶ noun **1** *until that decision is made we cannot begin to draw up an engineering schedule* **plan**, programme, timetable, scheme.
2 *I have a very busy schedule for the next few days* **timetable**, agenda, diary, calendar, appointment book, list of appointments, social calendar; itinerary.
3 *ring us for a schedule of all our courses* **list**, catalogue, inventory; syllabus.
□ **behind schedule** *the project is three months behind schedule* **late**, running late, overdue, behind time, not on time, behind, behindhand, behind target.
▶ verb *another meeting was scheduled for April 20* **arrange**, organize, plan, programme, timetable, fix a time for, make arrangements for, book, set up, line up, slot in, time; N. Amer. slate.

schematic ▶ adjective **1** *this concept is shown in schematic form in Figure 1* **simplified**; **diagrammatic**, representational, illustrative, graphic, delineative; symbolic.
2 *his rather schematic notions of what marriage can be* **simplistic**, oversimplified, oversimple, formulaic, formularized, unimaginative; facile, shallow.

scheme ▶ noun **1** *adventurous fund-raising schemes* **plan**, project, plan of action, programme, strategy, stratagem, game plan; enterprise, venture, measure, move, course of action, line of action; system, procedure, design, formula, recipe; device, tactic, contrivance; proposal, proposition, suggestion, idea, blueprint; Brit. informal wheeze; Austral. informal lurk; archaic shift.
2 *police uncovered a scheme to steal paintings worth more than $250,000* **plot**, intrigue, conspiracy, secret plan; ruse, ploy, stratagem, manoeuvre, subterfuge; machinations; informal game, racket, scam, dodge; S. African informal schlenter.
3 *the sonnet's rhyme scheme* **arrangement**, system, organization, configuration, pattern, format, layout, disposition; technical schema.
▶ verb *he schemed to bring about the collapse of the government* **plot**, hatch a plot, conspire, take part in a conspiracy, intrigue, connive, manoeuvre, plan, lay plans; rare machinate, cabal, complot.

schemer ▶ noun **plotter**, conspirator, intriguer, intrigant, intrigante, conniver; tactician, strategist, planner; rare machinator, conspirer, Machiavellian, cabalist.

scheming ▶ adjective *at long last he had seen his scheming wife for what she really was* **cunning**, crafty, calculating, devious, designing, conniving, wily, sly, tricky, artful, guileful, slippery, slick; **manipulative**, Machiavellian, unscrupulous, disingenuous; duplicitous, deceitful, underhand, treacherous; informal foxy; S. African informal slim; archaic subtle.
OPPOSITES ingenuous, honest, artless.

schism ▶ noun *the widening schism between church leaders and politicians* **division**, **split**, rift, breach, rupture, break, separation, severance, estrangement, alienation, detachment; chasm, gulf; discord, disagreement, dissension, disunion; rare scission.

schismatic ▶ adjective *the proliferation of schismatic religious movements over the previous few years* **separatist**, heterodox, dissident, dissentient, dissenting, heretical; **breakaway**, splinter.
OPPOSITES mainstream, orthodox.

schmaltzy ▶ adjective (informal) *the record's schmaltzy love songs* **sentimental**, over-sentimental, mawkish, cloying, sickly, saccharine, sugary, syrupy; Brit. twee; informal **slushy**, sloppy, mushy, weepy, cutesy, lovey-dovey, gooey, drippy, sloshy, soupy, treacly, cheesy, corny, icky, sick-making, toe-curling; Brit. informal soppy; N. Amer. informal cornball, sappy, hokey, three-hankie.

scholar ▶ noun **1** *a leading French biblical scholar* **academic**, intellectual, learned person, professor, man of letters, woman of letters, mind, intellect, savant, polymath, highbrow, bluestocking; authority, expert, pundit, mastermind; Hindu pandit; Jewish rabbi; informal egghead; N. Amer. informal pointy-head; archaic bookman.
2 (archaic) *after two or three months there were 28 scholars* **pupil**, student, schoolchild, schoolboy, schoolgirl, learner.

scholarly ▶ adjective **1** *an earnest, scholarly man* **learned**, erudite, academic, well read, widely read, intellectual, literary, lettered, well educated, knowledgeable, cultured, cultivated, highbrow; studious, bookish, donnish, bluestocking, cerebral; informal egghead; N. Amer. informal pointy-headed; archaic clerkly.
OPPOSITES uneducated, illiterate, ignorant.
2 *a young woman aspiring to a scholarly career* **academic**, educational, scholastic, professorial, pedagogic, pedagogical.
3 *a scholarly account of the period* **well researched**, painstaking, studious, thorough, detailed, thoroughgoing, comprehensive, exhaustive; well argued, well informed, well reasoned, authoritative.

scholarship ▶ noun **1** *Prague became one of the centres of medieval scholarship | a woman of great scholarship* **learning**, book learning, knowledge, erudition, education, letters, culture, academic study, academic achievement, intellectual attainment; wisdom, lore.
2 *a scholarship of £200 per term* **grant**, award, endowment, payment; fellowship; Brit. bursary, bursarship, exhibition.

scholastic ▶ adjective **1** *Walter's scholastic achievements* **academic**, educational, school, scholarly.
2 *scholastic attempts to distinguish between the various religious denominations* **scholarly**, learned, academic, erudite, donnish; pedantic, over-subtle, over-precise, hair-splitting, precisionist; informal nit-picking; archaic overnice.

school *See centre pages for list of* **Schools**
▶ noun **1** *the school caters for children with learning difficulties* **educational institution**, centre of learning; academy, college; Latin alma mater; rare phrontistery.
2 *the University's School of English* **department**, faculty, division.
3 *he painted in oils, in a manner strongly reminiscent of the Barbizon School* **group**, set, circle, clique, faction, sect; followers, following, disciples, apostles, pupils, students, admirers, devotees, votaries; proponents, adherents, imitators, copiers, emulators; rare epigones.
4 *the school of linguistics associated with his ideas* **way of thinking**, school of thought, persuasion, creed, credo, doctrine, belief, faith, outlook, opinion, point of view; denomination; **approach**, method, style; informal ism.
▶ verb **1** *he was born in Paris and schooled in Lyon* **educate**, teach, instruct.
2 *he schooled her in horsemanship | she had schooled herself to be patient* **train**, teach, tutor, coach, instruct, drill, discipline, direct, guide, prepare, groom, mould, shape, form; prime, verse; indoctrinate, inculcate.

WORD LINKS
relating to schools **scholastic**

schooling ▶ noun **1** *his parents paid for his schooling* **education**, teaching, tuition, instruction, tutoring, tutelage; lessons; learning, book learning.
2 *the schooling of horses* **training**, coaching, instruction, drill, drilling, discipline, disciplining; preparation, guidance.

schoolteacher ▶ noun **teacher**, schoolmaster, schoolmistress, instructor, tutor, educationist; Brit. master, mistress; Scottish informal dominie; N. Amer. informal schoolmarm; Austral./NZ informal chalkie, schoolie; rare preceptor, pedagogue.

science *See centre pages for lists of branches of* **Science** **Engineering** **Geography** **Mathematics** **Medicine** **Psychology**
▶ noun *the science of criminology* **branch of knowledge**, body of knowledge/information/facts, area of study, discipline, field.

scientific ▶ adjective **1** *scientific research | the scientific establishment in Britain* technological, technical; research-based, factual, knowledge-based, empirical; chemical, biological, medical.
2 *you need to approach it in a more scientific way* **systematic**, **methodical**, organized, well organized, ordered, orderly, meticulous, rigorous, exact, precise, accurate, mathematical, regulated, controlled; analytical, rational.
OPPOSITES unsystematic, random.

scientist *See centre pages for lists of branches of* **Science** **Engineering** **Geography** **Mathematics** **Medicine** **Psychology** *and a list of* **Doctors and Dentists**
▶ noun **researcher**, technologist; Brit. informal boffin.

scintilla ▶ noun *there is not the faintest scintilla of truth in it* **particle**, iota, jot, whit, atom, speck, bit, trace, ounce, shred, crumb, morsel, fragment, grain, drop, spot, mite, tittle, jot or tittle, modicum, hint, touch, suggestion, whisper, suspicion; informal smidgen, smidge, tad; Irish informal stim; archaic scantling, scruple.

scintillate ▶ verb *the brilliant stones scintillated in the sunlight* **sparkle**, shine, gleam, glitter, flash, shimmer, twinkle, glint, glisten, wink, blink; literary glister; rare coruscate, fulgurate, effulge, luminesce, phosphoresce, incandesce.

scintillating ▶ adjective **1** *a scintillating diamond necklace* **sparkling**, shining, bright, brilliant, gleaming, glittering, twinkling, flashing, shimmering, shimmery; rare scintillant.
OPPOSITES dull, matte.
2 *his scintillating closing speech | the team produced a scintillating second-half performance* **brilliant**, dazzling, exciting, exhilarating, stimulating, invigorating; vivacious, sparkling, effervescent, lively, vibrant, animated,

ebullient, bright; witty, clever; *rare* coruscating.
OPPOSITES boring, dull, pedestrian.

scion ▶ noun **1** *the process involves grafting a scion of the chosen tree on to rootstock of the same species* **cutting**, graft, slip; shoot, offshoot, twig.
2 *the scion of an aristocratic Massachusetts family* **descendant**, offshoot; heir, successor; child, issue, offspring.
OPPOSITES ancestor, predecessor.

scoff[1] ▶ verb *she told Jack it was a bad omen, but he* **scoffed at** *her superstitions* **mock**, deride, ridicule, sneer at, be scornful about, treat contemptuously, jeer at, jibe at, make fun of, poke fun at, laugh at, scorn, laugh to scorn, dismiss, pooh-pooh, make light of, belittle; taunt, tease, make a fool of, rag; *informal* thumb one's nose at, take the mickey out of; *Austral./NZ informal* poke mullock at; *Brit. vulgar slang* take the piss out of; *dated* make sport of; *rare* fleer at, bite one's thumb at, scout at.

scoff[2] (*Brit. informal*) ▶ verb *I bet he's scoffed all the chips* **eat**, devour, consume, guzzle, gobble, wolf down, polish off, finish off, gulp down, bolt; *informal* put away, nosh, get outside of, pack away, demolish, shovel down, stuff (down), stuff one's face with, stuff oneself with, pig oneself on, pig out on, sink, get one's laughing gear round; *Brit. informal* gollop, shift; *N. Amer. informal* scarf (down/up), snarf (down/up), inhale; *rare* ingurgitate.
▶ noun *ice cream was seen as suitable scoff to keep the under-tens quiet* **food**, fare, eatables, refreshments; *informal* grub, nosh, chow, eats, feed; *Brit. informal* tuck; *N. Amer. informal* chuck; *archaic* victuals, vittles, meat.

scold ▶ verb *Mum took Anna away, scolding her for her bad behaviour* **rebuke**, reprimand, reproach, reprove, admonish, remonstrate with, chastise, chide, upbraid, berate, take to task, pull up, castigate, lambaste, read someone the Riot Act, give someone a piece of one's mind, go on at, haul over the coals, criticize, censure; *informal* tell off, give someone a talking-to, give someone a telling-off, dress down, give someone a dressing-down, give someone an earful, give someone a roasting, give someone a rocket, give someone a rollicking, rap, rap over the knuckles, slap someone's wrist, let someone have it, send someone away with a flea in their ear, bawl out, give someone hell, come down on, blow up, pitch into, lay into, lace into, give someone a caning, put on the mat, slap down, blast, rag, keelhaul; *Brit. informal* tick off, have a go at, carpet, give someone a mouthful, tear someone off a strip, give someone what for, give someone some stick, wig, give someone a wigging, give someone a row, row; *N. Amer. informal* chew out, ream out, take to the woodshed; *Austral. informal* monster; *Brit. vulgar slang* bollock, give someone a bollocking; *N. Amer. vulgar slang* chew someone's ass, ream someone's ass; *dated* call down, rate, give someone a rating, trim; *rare* reprehend, objurgate.
OPPOSITES praise, compliment.
▶ noun (*archaic*) *she is turning into a scold* **nag**, nagger, shrew, fishwife, harpy, termagant, harridan; complainer, moaner, grumbler, fault-finder, carper; *N. Amer. informal* kvetch; *rare* Xanthippe.

scolding ▶ noun *Joe meekly accepted her scolding* **rebuke**, reprimand, reproach, reproof, admonishment, admonition, reproval, remonstration, lecture, upbraiding, castigation, lambasting, criticism, censure; *informal* telling-off, rap, rap over the knuckles, dressing-down, earful, roasting, bawling-out, caning, blast, row; *Brit. informal* ticking-off, carpeting, rollicking, wigging; *Brit. vulgar slang* bollocking; *dated* rating.
OPPOSITES praise, compliment, commendation.

scoop ▶ noun **1** *a measuring scoop is provided* **spoon**, ladle, dipper; bailer.
2 *add a scoop of vanilla ice cream* **spoonful**, ladleful, portion, lump, ball; *informal* dollop.
3 (*informal*) *reporters at the three tabloid papers competed for scoops* **exclusive (story)**, inside story, exposé, revelation; coup; the latest.
▶ verb **1** *a hole was* **scooped out** *in the floor* **hollow out**, gouge out, dig, excavate, cut out.
2 *halve the potatoes,* **scoop out** *the flesh and mash it with the yogurt mixture* **remove**, take out, spoon out, scrape out, ladle out; bail out.
3 *she* **scooped up** *armfuls of clothes and dumped them on the bed* **pick up**, gather up, lift, sweep up, catch up, take up; snatch up, grab; remove, clear away.
OPPOSITE drop.

scoot ▶ verb (*informal*) *Hilary panicked and scooted down the corridor* **dash**, dart, run, sprint, race, rush, hurry, hasten, hare, hurtle, bolt, shoot, charge, career, speed, fly, whizz, zoom; scuttle, scurry, scamper, skip, skitter, trot; *Brit.* scutter; *informal* tear, pelt, zip, belt, beetle; *archaic* post, hie; *rare* skirr.
OPPOSITES amble, stroll.

scope ▶ noun **1** *we widened the scope of our investigation | a study of the subject is beyond the scope of this book* **extent**, range, breadth, width, reach, sweep, purview, span, stretch, spread, horizon; area, sphere, field, realm, compass, orbit, ambit, terms of reference, field of reference, jurisdiction, remit; confine, limit; gamut, competence.
2 *the scope for major change is always limited by political realities* **opportunity**, freedom, latitude, leeway, capacity, liberty, room, room to manoeuvre, elbow room, play; possibility, chance.

scorch ▶ verb **1** *the buildings around us were scorched by the fire* **burn**, sear, singe, char, blacken, discolour; *rare* torrefy.
2 *grass scorched by the sun* **dry up**, desiccate, parch, wither, shrivel; burn, bake, roast.
3 (*informal*) *to get to New York you have to scorch along sixteen-lane highways* **speed**, zoom, whizz, blast; *informal* zap, zip, burn, burn rubber, belt, vroom; *Brit. informal* bomb, bucket, put one's foot down, blind; *N. Amer. informal* barrel, lay rubber.

scorching ▶ adjective **1** *the scorching July sun* **extremely hot**, red-hot, unbearably hot, baking (hot), blazing, flaming, fiery, burning, blistering, searing, sweltering, torrid, tropical, like an oven, like a furnace, like a blowtorch; parching, withering; *N. Amer.* broiling; *informal* boiling (hot), sizzling.
OPPOSITE freezing.
2 *he faced scorching criticism* **fierce**, savage, scathing, withering, blistering, searing, devastating, stringent, severe, harsh, stinging, biting, mordant, trenchant, caustic, virulent, vitriolic.
OPPOSITE mild.

score ▶ noun **1** *the final score was 4–3* **result**, outcome; **number of goals/runs/points**, total, sum total, tally, count.
2 *an IQ score of 161* **rating**, grade, mark, percentage.
3 *check the shaft for rust, scores, and any other types of damage* **scratch**, nick, notch, snick, scrape, groove, chip, cut, gouge, incision, slit, gash; mark; *archaic* scotch.
4 *I've got a score to settle with you* **grievance**, bone to pick, axe to grind, grudge, complaint; dispute, bone of contention; *rare* crow to pluck.
5 (**the score**) (*informal*) *he knew the score before he got here* **the situation**, the position, the facts, the truth of the matter, the (true) state of affairs, the picture, the story, how things stand, the lie of the land; *Brit.* the state of play; *N. Amer.* the lay of the land; *informal* the set-up, what's what.
6 *he had resigned on the score of ill health* **grounds**, reason, basis, count; cause, motive, rationale.
7 (*archaic*) *the week's score at the public house was paid up* **bill**, account, tally, reckoning, amount due; debt; *N. Amer.* check; *informal* tab.
8 (**scores**) *police have received scores of complaints | scores of people attended his funeral* **a great many**, a lot, a great/good deal, a large/great number/amount, great quantities, plenty, a host, hosts, a crowd, crowds, droves, a bevy, bevies, an army, armies, a horde, hordes, a flock, flocks, herds, a throng, throngs, legions, a multitude, multitudes, a swarm, swarms; copious, abundant, profuse, an abundance, a profusion; *informal* lots, umpteen, loads, masses, stacks, scads, heaps, piles, bags, tons, oodles, dozens, hundreds, thousands, millions, billions, zillions, more ... than one can shake a stick at; *Brit. informal* shedloads, a shedload; *N. Amer. informal* a slew, a bunch, gazillions, gobs, bazillions; *Austral./NZ informal* a swag; *vulgar slang* a shitload; *literary* myriad, divers.
OPPOSITE few.
□ **on this/that score** *there were no complaints on that score* **on this/that subject**, as/so far as this/that is/was concerned, in this/that respect, about this/that, on this/that matter, as regards this/that.
□ **pay off/settle old scores** *he can't resist settling old scores—the book is full of retaliatory digs and sneers* **take (one's) revenge**, hit back at someone, get back at someone, retaliate, get even, get one's own back, pay someone back, give someone a dose/taste of their own medicine, pay someone back in their own coin.
▶ verb **1** *he has already scored 13 goals for Aston Villa this season* **get**, gain, chalk up, win, achieve, attain, make; record; *informal* notch up, bag, knock up, rack up.
2 *when I was your age I spent every summer weekend scoring for my father's village cricket team* **keep (the) score**, keep count, keep a record, keep a tally.
3 (*informal*) *his new movie really scored* **be successful**, be a success, achieve success, win, triumph, make an impression, have an impact, go down well, get an enthusiastic reception; *informal* be a hit, be a winner, be a sell-out, go down a storm.
4 *the Quartet Suite was scored for flute, violin, viola da gamba, and continuo* **orchestrate**, arrange, set, adapt; write, compose; *rare* instrument.
5 *score the wood in criss-cross patterns* **scratch**, cut, make a notch/notches in, make a groove/grooves in, notch, incise, scrape, nick, snick, chip, gouge, slit, gash; mark; cross-hatch; carve, engrave; *archaic* scotch.
□ **score points off** *Harry was continually seeking ways to score points off Sam* **get the better of**, gain an advantage over, outdo, best, worst, have the edge over; have the last laugh on, make a fool of, humiliate; *informal* get/be one up on, get one over on.
□ **score something out/through** *she scored out the last word* **cross out**, strike out, put a line through, ink out, blue-pencil, scratch out; **delete**, obliterate, expunge.

scorn ▶ noun *he was unable to hide the scorn in his voice* **contempt**, derision, contemptuousness, disdain, derisiveness, scornfulness, mockery, sneering, scoffing; *archaic* contumely, despite.
OPPOSITES admiration, respect.
▶ verb **1** *critics scorned the painting, but it was very popular with those who attended the exhibition | his father was a man who scorned tradition* **deride**, be contemptuous about, hold in contempt, treat with contempt, pour/heap scorn on, be scornful about, look down on, look down one's nose at,

S

disdain, curl one's lip at, mock, scoff at, sneer at, sniff at, jeer at, laugh at, laugh out of court; disparage, slight; dismiss, cock a snook at, spit in the eye/face of, spit on, thumb one's nose at; *informal* turn one's nose up at, blow raspberries at; *N. Amer. informal* give the Bronx cheer to; *Brit. vulgar slang* piss on/over; *archaic* contemn; *rare* misprize, scout.
OPPOSITES admire, respect.
2 *'I am a woman scorned,' she thought* **spurn**, rebuff, reject, ignore, shun, snub.
3 *even at her lowest ebb, she would have* **scorned to** *stoop to such tactics* **refuse to**, refrain from, not lower oneself to; be above, consider it beneath one.

scornful ▸ adjective *Isabel ignored his scornful remarks* **contemptuous**, full of contempt, derisive, derisory, withering, mocking, scoffing, sneering, jeering, scathing, snide, disparaging, slighting, supercilious, disdainful, superior, dismissive; *informal* sniffy, snotty; *archaic* contumelious.
OPPOSITES admiring, respectful.

scornfully ▸ adverb *'How would she know?' said Anne scornfully* **contemptuously**, with contempt, derisively, witheringly, mockingly, with a sneer, scathingly, snidely, disparagingly, superciliously, disdainfully, dismissively; *informal* sniffily, snottily.
OPPOSITES admiringly, respectfully.

Scotch ▸ noun. See centre pages for list of **Whiskies**

scotch ▸ verb *their plans were scotched by the Pentagon* **put an end to**, put a stop to, bring to an end, nip in the bud, put the lid on; ruin, wreck, scupper, destroy, devastate, smash, shatter, demolish, queer; frustrate, thwart; *informal* put paid to, blow, put the kibosh on, clobber; *Brit. informal* dish.

scot-free ▸ adverb *the real criminals behind the racket are getting away scot-free* **unpunished**, without punishment, unreprimanded; unscathed, unhurt, unharmed, without a scratch, uninjured, undamaged, safe; *rare* scatheless.

Scotland ▸ noun *Brit.* north of the border; *Scottish* the land o' the leal; *Latin* Caledonia; *informal* the land of cakes.

scoundrel ▸ noun *the lying scoundrel admitted that he was married to another woman* **rogue**, rascal, good-for-nothing, reprobate, unprincipled person; cheat, swindler, fraudster, trickster, charlatan; *informal* villain, bastard, beast, son of a bitch, s.o.b., rat, louse, swine, dog, hound, skunk, heel, snake, snake in the grass, wretch, scumbag, bad egg, stinker; *Scottish informal* scrote; *Irish informal* sleeveen, spalpeen; *N. Amer. informal* rat fink; *informal, dated* rotter, bounder, blighter; *vulgar slang* shit, bugger; *N. Amer. vulgar slang* motherfucker, mother, mofo; *dated* cad, ne'er-do-well; *archaic* blackguard, miscreant, knave, dastard, vagabond, varlet, wastrel, rapscallion, whoreson.

scour[1] ▸ verb *she scoured the cooker and cleaned out the kitchen cupboards* **scrub**, rub, clean, wash, cleanse, wipe; polish, buff (up), shine, burnish; abrade; *Scottish & N. English* dight; *archaic* furbish.

scour[2] ▸ verb *Christina scoured the antique shops until she found the perfect piece* **search**, comb, hunt through, rummage through, sift through, go through with a fine-tooth comb, root through, rake through, leave no stone unturned, mine, look all over, look high and low in; ransack, turn upside-down, turn over; drag; *Austral./NZ informal* fossick through.

scourge ▸ noun **1** (*historical*) *he was beaten with a scourge* **whip**, horsewhip, lash, strap, birch, switch, flail; *N. Amer.* bullwhip, rawhide; *historical* cat-o'-nine-tails, knout; *rare* flagellum, quirt, blacksnake.
2 *inflation was the scourge of the mid-1970s | the scourge of war* **affliction**, bane, curse, plague, menace, evil, misfortune, burden, cross to bear, thorn in one's flesh/side, bitter pill, trial, nuisance, pest; torment, torture, misery, suffering; blight, cancer, canker; punishment, penalty, visitation.
OPPOSITES blessing, godsend.
▸ verb **1** (*historical*) *he was publicly scourged* **flog**, whip, beat, horsewhip, lash, flagellate, flail, strap, birch, cane, thrash, belt, leather; *N. Amer.* bullwhip; *informal* give someone a hiding, tan someone's hide, lather, take a strap to, beat the living daylights out of; *N. Amer. informal* whale; *archaic* switch, stripe, thong; *rare* quirt.
2 *scurvy was a disease which scourged the English for centuries* **afflict**, plague, torment, torture, curse, cause suffering to, oppress, burden, bedevil, beset; devastate; punish.

S

scout ▸ noun **1** *scouts reported that the enemy were massing at two points ahead* **lookout**, lookout man/woman, outrider, advance guard, vanguard, spy; *French* avant-courier.
2 *I returned from a lengthy scout round the area* **reconnaissance**, reconnoitre; exploration, search, expedition; *informal* recce; *Brit. informal* shufti; *N. Amer. informal* recon.
3 *Brock slid the ball in from 14 yards, impressing watching scouts* **talent spotter**, talent scout, recruiter; *N. Amer. informal* bird dog.
▸ verb **1** *I scouted around for some logs* **search**, look, hunt, cast about/around/round, ferret (about/around), root about/around.
2 *a night patrol was sent to* **scout out** *the area* **reconnoitre**, explore, take a look at, make a reconnaissance of, inspect, investigate, spy out, survey, make a survey of; examine, scan, study, observe; see how the land lies, find out the lie of the land; *informal* recce, make a recce of, check out, case, case the joint; *Brit. informal* take a shufti round, suss out; *N. Amer. informal* recon.

scowl ▸ noun *she stamped into the room with a scowl on her face* **frown**, glower, glare, grimace, black look; *informal* dirty look; *Scottish archaic* glunch.
OPPOSITES smile, grin.
▸ verb *she* **scowled at** *him defiantly* **glower**, frown, glare, lour, look daggers at, look angrily at, give someone a black look; make a face, pull a face, turn the corner's of one's mouth down, pout; *informal* give someone a dirty look; *archaic* mop and mow, glout; *Scottish archaic* glunch.
OPPOSITES smile, grin, beam.

scrabble ▸ verb *she scrabbled around in the sandy earth* **scratch**, grope, rummage, root, pole, grub, scavenge, fumble, feel, clamber, scramble; *archaic* grabble.

scraggy ▸ adjective *a scraggy mongrel* **scrawny**, thin, thin as a rake, skinny, skin-and-bones, gaunt, bony, angular, gawky, rangy, raw-boned, skeletal, emaciated, pinched; lean, slim, slender, lanky, spindly, gangly, gangling; *dated* spindle-shanked.
OPPOSITES fat, plump.

scram ▸ verb (*informal*) *scram or I'll call the police* **go away**, depart, leave, take yourself off, take off, get out, get out of my sight; go, go your way, get going, get moving, move off, be off, set off, set out, start out, make a start, take your leave, decamp, duck out, take wing, walk out, walk off, absent yourself; be off with you!, shoo!; *informal* hit the road, fly, skedaddle, split, vamoose, scat, make yourself scarce, be on one's way, run along, beat it, get, get lost, push off, shove off, buzz off, clear off, skip off, pop off, go (and) jump in the lake; on your bike!, go and chase yourself!; *Brit. informal* get along, push along, get stuffed, sling your hook, hop it, hop the twig/stick, bog off, naff off; *N. Amer. informal* bug off, light out, haul off, haul ass, take a powder, hit the trail, take a hike; *Austral. informal* nick off; *Austral./NZ informal* rack off; *S. African informal* voetsak, hamba; *vulgar slang* bugger off, piss off, fuck off; *Brit. vulgar slang* sod off; *literary* begone, avaunt.

scramble ▸ verb **1** *we scrambled over the boulders to inspect the rapids below* **clamber**, climb, crawl, claw one's way, scrabble, grope one's way; *N. Amer.* shinny.
2 *he scrambled for shelter behind a heap of rubble* **struggle**, **hurry**, scurry, scud, scutter, hasten, rush, race, run.
3 *the children scrambled for new pennies thrown down from the tower* **jostle**, scuffle, scrimmage, tussle, battle, struggle, strive, compete, contend, vie, jockey.
4 *his stage fright scrambled the lines in his head* **muddle**, confuse, mix up, jumble (up), disarrange, disorganize, disorder, disturb, throw into disorder, throw into confusion, get into a tangle, mess up.
▸ noun **1** *a short scramble over the rocks takes you to our secret spot* **clamber**, climb, ascent, trek.
2 *it was a scramble to get there on time* **struggle**, **hurry**, rush, race, scurry.
3 *I lost Tommy in the scramble for a seat* **tussle**, jostle, scrimmage, scuffle, battle, struggle, free-for-all, competition, contention, vying, jockeying; **muddle**, confusion, melee.

scrap[1] ▸ noun **1** *he scribbled Pamela's address on a scrap of paper* **fragment**, piece, bit, offcut, oddment, snippet, snip, tatter, wisp, shred, remnant.
2 *there wasn't a scrap of evidence to link him with the body* **bit**, speck, iota, particle, ounce, whit, jot, atom, shred, crumb, morsel, fragment, grain, drop, hint, touch, trace, suggestion, whisper, suspicion, scintilla, spot, mite, tittle, jot or tittle, modicum; *Irish* stim; *informal* smidgen, smidge, tad; *archaic* scantling, scruple.
3 (**scraps**) *between jobs he slept rough and lived on scraps* **leftovers**, uneaten food, leavings, crumbs, scrapings, slops, dregs, scourings, offscourings, remains, remnants, residue, odds and ends, bits and pieces, bits and bobs; pieces, bits.
4 *the whole thing was made from bits of scrap* **waste**, refuse, garbage, rubbish, litter, discarded matter, debris, detritus, dross; flotsam and jetsam, lumber; *N. Amer.* trash; *Austral./NZ* mullock; *informal* dreck, junk; *Brit. informal* grot, gash; *rare* draff, raffle, raff, cultch, orts.
▸ verb **1** *the government intended to scrap sixty-two naval ships* **throw away**, throw out, dispose of, get rid of, do away with, toss out, throw on the scrap heap, clear out, discard, remove, dispense with, lose, eliminate, dump, bin, jettison, shed, dismiss, expel, eject, weed out, root out; decommission, recycle, break up, demolish, write off; **destroy**, annihilate, obliterate; *informal* chuck (away/out), ditch, junk, get shut of; *Brit. informal* get shot of, see the back of; *N. Amer. informal* trash, shuck off, wreck.
OPPOSITES keep, preserve.
2 *campaigners are calling for the plans to be scrapped* **abandon**, drop, abolish, withdraw, throw out, do away with, give up, stop, put an end to, cancel, eliminate, cut, jettison; *informal* axe, ditch, dump, junk, chuck in.
OPPOSITES keep, restore.

scrap[2] (*informal*) ▸ noun *he would always win a scrap with Stephen* **quarrel**, argument, row, fight, disagreement, difference of opinion, dissension, falling-out, dispute, disputation, contention, squabble, contretemps, clash, altercation, exchange, brawl, tussle, conflict, affray, war of words, shouting match, fracas, wrangle, tangle, misunderstanding, passage of/at arms, battle royal; *Irish, N. Amer., & Austral.* donnybrook; *informal* tiff, set-to, run-in, shindig, shindy, stand-up, spat, dust-up, ruction; *Brit. informal* barney, bunfight, ding-dong, bust-up, ruck, slanging match; *Scottish informal* rammy; *N. Amer. informal* hassle; *archaic* broil, miff; *Scottish archaic* threap, collieshangie; *French archaic* tracasserie(s).

▶ **verb** *the older boys started scrapping with me* **quarrel**, argue, have a row/fight, row, fight, disagree, fail to agree, differ, be at odds, have a misunderstanding, be at variance, fall out, dispute, squabble, brawl, bicker, chop logic, spar, wrangle, bandy words, cross swords, lock horns, be at each other's throats, be at loggerheads; *informal* argufy; *archaic* altercate.

scrape ▶ **verb 1** *the men only had to scrape the ship and overhaul her rigging* **abrade**, grate, sand, sandpaper, scour, scratch, rub, file, rasp.
2 *she scraped the earth back and saw something blue buried there* **rake**, drag, push, brush, sweep.
3 *their boots scraped along the floor* **grate**, creak, grind, jar, rasp, scratch, drag, rub, squeak, screech, grit, set someone's teeth on edge.
4 *the stag first scrapes a hole in the ground* **scoop out**, hollow out, dig out, dig, excavate, gouge out, quarry, make.
5 *Ellen had scraped her shins on the wall* **graze**, scratch, abrade, scuff, rasp, skin, rub raw, cut, lacerate, bark, chafe, strip, flay, wound; *technical* excoriate.

□ **scrape by** *students have to scrape by on an inadequate grant* **manage**, cope, survive, muddle through/along, scrape along, make ends meet, get by/along, make do, manage to live with difficulty, barely/scarcely manage to live, barely/scarcely have enough to live on, keep the wolf from the door, keep one's head above water, scrimp, scrape a living; *informal* make out.

□ **scrape through** *he managed to scrape through the exam* **just pass**, pass and no more, pass by a narrow margin, just succeed in, narrowly achieve.

□ **scrape something together** *we scraped together enough coins to buy some tea* **collect**, amass, gather, rake together, rake up, dredge up, get hold of, raise, muster, accumulate, build up.

▶ **noun 1** *he heard the scrape of a stool being dragged across the floor* **grate**, grating, creak, creaking, grind, grinding, jar, jarring, rasp, rasping, scratch, scratching, rub, rubbing, squeak, squeaking, screech, screeching.
2 *the shopkeeper sustained scrapes to his knee and hand in the struggle* **graze**, scratch, abrasion, cut, laceration, wound.
3 (*informal*) *he's always getting into scrapes because he trusts the wrong people* **predicament**, plight, tight corner, tight spot, ticklish/tricky situation, problem, quandary, dilemma, crisis, mess, muddle; *informal* jam, fix, stew, bind, hole, hot water, a pretty/fine kettle of fish; *Brit. informal* spot of bother; (**scrapes**) trouble, difficulty, straits, dire/desperate straits, distress.

scrappy ▶ **adjective** *the match was a scrappy affair* **disorganized**, untidy, disjointed, unsystematic, thrown together, uneven, bitty, sketchy, superficial, perfunctory, slipshod, inadequate, imperfect, incoherent, piecemeal; fragmentary, incomplete, unfinished, unpolished, deficient, defective.

scratch ▶ **verb 1** *take care not to scratch the surface on plastic baths* **score**, abrade, scrape, roughen, scuff (up), lacerate, groove, gash, engrave, incise, gouge.
2 *thorns scratched her tender skin* **graze**, scrape, abrade, rasp, skin, rub raw, cut, lacerate, bark, chafe, strip, flay, wound; *technical* excoriate.
3 *he scratched the back of his neck* **rub**, claw (at), scrape, tear at.
4 *many names had been scratched out or overwritten* **cross out**, strike out, score out, delete, erase, remove, strike off, eliminate, cancel, expunge, obliterate.
5 *due to a knee injury she was forced to scratch from the race* **withdraw**, pull out (of), back out (of), bow out (of), stand down, give up, leave, quit.

□ **scratch about/around** *the authority had scratched around for every spare penny over the years* **search**, hunt (around), cast about/around/round, rummage (around), forage (about), poke around/about, scrabble, grub about/around, root (around), scavenge, fish about/around, rake around, feel around, grope (around), nose around/about/round, ferret (about/around).

▶ **noun 1** *he had two scratches on his cheek* **graze**, scrape, abrasion, cut, laceration, wound.
2 *there was a large dent in the panel and a scratch in the paint* **score**, mark, line, abrasion, scrape, scuff, laceration, groove, gash, gouge.

□ **up to scratch** *the workmanship once again is up to scratch* **good enough**, up to the mark, up to standard, up to par, satisfactory, acceptable, adequate, passable, sufficient, competent, all right; *informal* OK, up to snuff.
OPPOSITES below standard, unacceptable.

scrawl ▶ **verb** *he scanned the page, then scrawled his name at the bottom* **scribble**, write hurriedly, write untidily, write illegibly, scratch, doodle, dash off, jot (down).

▶ **noun** *you might wonder how pharmacists decipher a doctor's scrawl* **scribble**, hurried handwriting, untidy handwriting, illegible handwriting, squiggle(s); *archaic* cacography.

scrawny ▶ **adjective** *he was small, scrawny, and hairless* **skinny**, thin, thin as a rake, skin-and-bones, gaunt, bony, angular, gawky, scraggy, rangy, raw-boned, skeletal, emaciated, pinched; lean, slim, slender, lanky, spindly, gangly, gangling; *dated* spindle-shanked.
OPPOSITES plump, fat.

scream ▶ **verb** *he screamed in pain* **shriek**, screech, yell, howl, shout, bellow, bawl, cry out, call out, yawp, yelp, squeal, wail, squawk, squall, caterwaul, whoop; *N. Amer. informal* holler.
OPPOSITE whisper.

▶ **noun 1** *a scream of pain* **shriek**, screech, yell, howl, shout, bellow, bawl, cry, yawp, yelp, squeal, wail, squawk, squall, caterwaul, whoop; *N. Amer. informal* holler.
OPPOSITE whisper.
2 (*informal*) *the whole thing's a scream* **laugh**; hoot, comedy; *informal* gas, giggle, lark, riot, bundle of fun, bundle of laughs; *informal, dated* yell. *See also* FUNNY.
3 (*informal*) *he's an absolute scream* **wit**, hoot, comedian, comic, entertainer, joker, clown, buffoon; *informal* character, gas, giggle, riot; *Austral./NZ informal* hard case; *informal, dated* caution, case, card, yell.
OPPOSITE bore.

screech ▶ **verb** *'Look what you've made me do!' she screeched | the car screeched to a halt* **shriek**, squeal, squawk, howl, shout, yell, bellow, bawl, cry out, call out, yawp, yelp, wail, squall, caterwaul, whoop; *N. Amer. informal* holler.
OPPOSITE whisper.

▶ **noun** *the wailing rose in pitch to an awful screech* **shriek**, squeal, squawk, howl, shout, yell, bellow, bawl, cry, yawp, yelp, wail, squall, caterwaul, whoop; *N. Amer. informal* holler.
OPPOSITE whisper.

screen ▶ **noun 1** *he dressed hurriedly behind the screen* **partition**, (room) divider, dividing wall, separator, curtain, arras, blind, awning, shade, shutter, canopy, windbreak.
2 *the computer comes with a 15-inch screen* **display**, monitor, visual display unit, VDU, cathode-ray tube, CRT.
3 *every window has a screen here because of the mosquitoes* **mesh**, net, netting.
4 *the hedge acts as a screen against the wind* **buffer**, protection, shield, shelter, guard, safeguard.
5 *the earth must be put through a screen* **sieve**, riddle, sifter, strainer, colander, filter, winnow; *archaic* griddle.

▶ **verb 1** *the far end of the hall had been screened off as a waiting room* **partition off**, divide off, separate off, curtain off.
2 *during the experiment the speaker was screened from the children's view* **conceal**, hide, mask, shield, shelter, shade, protect, guard, safeguard, veil, cloak, camouflage, disguise.
3 *the security is excellent and the staff are very tightly screened* **vet**, check, check up on, check out, evaluate, assess, scrutinize, test.
4 *health-care workers who had had contact with the patient were screened for diphtheria* **check**, test, examine, investigate, scan.
5 *coal used to be screened by hand* **sieve**, riddle, sift, strain, filter, sort, winnow; *archaic* bolt, griddle.
6 (*informal*) *the programme is screened on Thursday evenings at 7.30* **show**, present, air, broadcast, transmit, televise, put out, put on the air, telecast, relay.

screw ▶ **noun 1** *fit the shelf to its supports with the screws provided* **bolt**, fastener; nail, pin, tack, spike, rivet, brad.
2 *the handle needs a couple of screws to tighten it* **turn**, twist, wrench, lever, heave.
3 *the ship's twin screws* **propeller**, rotor.

□ **put the screws on** (*informal*) **pressurize**, put pressure on, use pressure on, pressure, press, bring force to bear on, force, drive, impel, coerce, urge, push, nag; lean on, prevail on; dragoon, steamroller, browbeat, use strong-arm tactics on, have someone do something; hold/put a gun/pistol to someone's head; *informal* put the heat on, put the squeeze on, twist someone's arm, railroad, bulldoze.

▶ **verb 1** *he screwed the lid back on the jar* **tighten**, turn, twist, wind, work.
2 *I screwed the boards down tightly* **fasten**, secure, fix, attach, clamp, bolt, rivet, batten.
3 *she intended to screw money out of them* **extort**, force, extract, wrest, wring, squeeze; *informal* bleed someone of something.
4 (*informal*) *they screwed him at least once, so now he doesn't trust them at all* **cheat**, swindle, defraud, gazump, fleece; overcharge, short-change; *informal* rip off, bilk, diddle, do, sting, soak, rob, clip, gyp, skin; *N. Amer. informal* stiff, gouge; *Brit. informal, dated* rush; *archaic* cozen; *rare* mulct.

□ **screw something up 1** *Christina screwed up her face in disgust* **wrinkle (up)**, pucker, crumple, crease, furrow, contort, distort, twist, purse.
2 (*informal*) *they'll screw up the whole economy* **wreck**, ruin, destroy, devastate, wreak havoc on, reduce to nothing, damage, spoil, mar, injure, blast, blight, smash, shatter, dash, torpedo, scotch, make a mess of, mess up; *informal* louse up, foul up, put the kibosh on, banjax, do for, blow a hole in, nix, queer; *Brit. informal* scupper, cock up, dish; *Austral. informal* euchre, cruel; *vulgar slang* fuck up; *archaic* bring to naught.
OPPOSITE sort out.

screwy ▶ adjective (*informal*) *are the cases you work on always this screwy?* See STRANGE, CRAZY.

scribble ▶ verb *he scribbled a few lines on a scrap sheet* **write hurriedly**, write untidily, write illegibly, scratch, scrawl, doodle, dash off, jot (down).
▶ noun *the postman would never have been able to decipher your scribble* **illegible handwriting**, hurried handwriting, untidy handwriting, squiggle(s), jottings; *rare* cacography.

scribe ▶ noun 1 (*historical*) *if he wished to send a letter he would have to get a scribe to write it for him* **clerk**, secretary, copyist, transcriber, amanuensis, recorder, record keeper; (*in Africa*) mallam; *informal* pen-pusher; *N. Amer. informal* pencil-pusher; *archaic* penman, scrivener, writer.
2 (*informal*) *he'd been corresponding with a local cricket scribe before the trip* **writer**, author, penman, journalist, reporter; *informal* hack.

scrimmage ▶ noun *seventeen hecklers were thrown out after terrific scrimmages in the audience* **fight**, battle, struggle, tussle, brawl, fracas, rumpus, melee, free-for-all, rough and tumble; *Irish, N. Amer., & Austral.* donnybrook; *Law, dated* affray; *informal* scrap, dust-up, punch-up, set-to, shindy; *Brit. informal* scrum; *N. Amer. informal* rough house.

scrimp ▶ verb *she scrimped for six months to buy a pair of evening gloves* **economize**, skimp, be (more) economical, make economies, scrimp and scrape, save; be thrifty, be frugal, tighten one's belt, cut back, make cutbacks, budget, retrench, husband one's resources, cut costs, cut expenditure, draw in one's horns, watch one's pennies, look after the pence; *N. Amer.* pinch the pennies; *black English* rake and scrape.
OPPOSITE spend.

script ▶ noun 1 *it was written in a careful script* **handwriting**, writing, hand, autograph, pen, letters, longhand, penmanship, calligraphy, chirography; scribble, scrawl; *informal* fist.
2 *the script of the play* **text**, book, screenplay, libretto, lyrics, score, lines, parts, dialogue, words, manuscript.

scripture *See centre pages for lists of* **Sacred Texts and Holy Books** *and Books of the* **Bible**
▶ noun *he appeals solely to scripture for his authority* **sacred text**, Holy Writ, the Bible, the Holy Bible, the Gospel, the Good Book, the Word of God, the Book of Books.

Scrooge ▶ noun *he is depicted as a Scrooge keeping tight hold of the purse strings* **miser**, penny-pincher, pinchpenny, niggard, cheese-parer, hoarder, saver; *informal* skinflint, meanie, money-grubber, cheapskate; *N. Amer. informal* tightwad; *vulgar slang* tight-arse.
OPPOSITES spendthrift; philanthropist.

scrounge ▶ verb *they were always scrounging food from the tourists* **beg**, borrow; *informal* cadge, sponge, bum, touch someone for; *Brit. informal* scab; *Scottish informal* sorn on someone for; *N. Amer. informal* mooch; *Austral./NZ informal* bludge.

scrounger ▶ noun *the unemployed are often depicted as scroungers* **beggar**, borrower, parasite, scrounge, cadger; *informal* sponger, freeloader; *Scottish informal* sorner; *N. Amer. informal* mooch, moocher, schnorrer; *Austral./NZ informal* bludger.

scrub[1] ▶ verb 1 *he scrubbed the kitchen floor* **scour**, rub, brush, sponge, swab, clean, cleanse, wash, wipe.
2 (*informal*) *you could only save that much by scrubbing the Navy* **abolish**, scrap, throw out, abandon, drop, do away with, give up, discontinue, take away, stop, put an end to, cancel, call off, eliminate, cut, jettison, discard, forget (about), abort; *informal* axe, ditch, dump, junk.
OPPOSITES keep, restore.

S

scrub[2] ▶ noun *there the buildings ended and the scrub began* **brush**, brushwood, scrubland, undergrowth, coppice, copse, thicket.

scruffy ▶ adjective *he wore scruffy jeans* **shabby**, worn, down at heel, shoddy, ragged, tattered, mangy, sorry, run down, disreputable; **untidy**, unkempt, bedraggled, messy, dishevelled, ungroomed, ill-groomed, sleazy, seedy, slatternly, slovenly; **dirty**, squalid, filthy; *informal* tatty, the worse for wear, scuzzy, grungy, yucky; *Brit. informal* grotty; *N. Amer. informal* raggedy.
OPPOSITES smart, tidy, clean.

scrumptious ▶ adjective (*informal*) *a piece of scrumptious gateau* **delicious**, gorgeous, tasty, good, mouth-watering, appetizing, inviting, palatable, delectable, delightful, succulent, rich, sweet, choice, dainty, savoury, flavoursome, flavourful, piquant, luscious, toothsome; *informal* delish, scrummy, yummy, yum-yum; *Brit. informal* moreish; *N. Amer. informal* finger-licking, nummy; *literary* ambrosial; *rare* ambrosian, nectareous, nectarean.
OPPOSITES inedible, unpalatable.

scrunch ▶ verb *I had* **scrunched up** *the pages and stuffed them into the gaps* **crumple (up)**, crunch (up), crush, rumple, screw up, squash (up), twist (up), mash (up), squeeze, compress, chew (up); *informal* squidge.

scruple ▶ verb *they would not scruple to cut his throat* **hesitate**, be reluctant, be loath, have qualms about, have scruples about, have misgivings about, have reservations about, stick at, think twice about, baulk at, demur about/from, mind doing something; recoil from, shrink from, hang back from, shy away from, flinch from, drag one's feet/heels over, waver about, vacillate about; *informal* boggle at; *archaic* disrelish something.
OPPOSITE jump at the chance.

scruples ▶ plural noun 1 *he had no scruples about eavesdropping* **qualms**, twinge of conscience, compunction, hesitation, reservations, second thoughts, doubt(s), misgivings, pangs of conscience, uneasiness, reluctance.
2 *I respect your scruples* **principles**, standards, values, morals, morality, moral concern, ethics, conscience, creed, beliefs.

scrupulous ▶ adjective 1 *the research has been carried out with scrupulous attention to detail* **careful**, meticulous, painstaking, thorough, assiduous, sedulous, attentive, diligent, conscientious, ultra-careful, punctilious, searching, close, elaborate, minute, studious, rigorous, particular; religious, strict; pedantic, fussy.
OPPOSITES careless, slapdash.
2 *the finances were in the hands of one of our most scrupulous colleagues* **honest**, honourable, upright, upstanding, high-minded, righteous, right-minded, moral, ethical, good, virtuous, principled, proper, correct, just, noble, incorruptible, conscientious, respectable, decent.
OPPOSITES dishonest, unscrupulous.

scrutinize ▶ verb *Basil scrutinized the painting* **examine carefully**, **inspect**, survey, scan, study, look over, peruse; search, investigate, explore, probe, research, inquire into, go over, go over with a fine-tooth comb, check, audit, review, sift, analyse, dissect.
OPPOSITE glance at.

scrutiny ▶ noun *Frick continued his scrutiny of the room* **careful examination**, **inspection**, survey, scan, study, perusal; search, investigation, exploration, research, probe, inquiry, check, audit, review, analysis, dissection; *informal* going-over, look-see, once-over.
OPPOSITES glance, cursory look.

scud ▶ verb *a few dark clouds scudded across the sky* **speed**, race, sail, streak, shoot, sweep, skim, whip, whizz, whoosh, buzz, zoom, flash, blast, career; hare, fly, wing, kite, skite, scurry, flit, scutter, hurry, hasten, rush; *informal* belt, scoot, scorch, tear, zap, zip; *Brit. informal* bomb, bucket, shift; *N. Amer. informal* boogie, hightail, clip; *N. Amer. vulgar slang* drag/tear/haul ass; *informal, dated* cut along.

scuff ▶ verb *the girl scuffed the toe of her shoe in the gravel* **scrape**, rub, drag, brush, scratch, graze, abrade, rasp, lacerate, chafe, roughen.

scuffle ▶ noun *there was a scuffle outside the pub* **fight**, struggle, tussle, brawl, fracas, rumpus, melee, free-for-all, rough and tumble, scrimmage, disturbance, brouhaha, commotion; *Irish, N. Amer., & Austral.* donnybrook; *Law, dated* affray; *informal* scrap, dust-up, punch-up, set-to, shindy; *N. Amer. informal* rough house.
▶ verb *tempers flared as the supporters scuffled with other passengers* **fight**, struggle, tussle, exchange blows, come to blows, brawl, grapple, clash, scrimmage; *informal* scrap, have a dust-up, have a punch-up, have a set-to; *N. Amer. informal* rough-house.

sculpt ▶ verb *the Minoans were adept at sculpting human figures from ivory* **carve**, **model**, chisel, sculpture, fashion, form, shape, cast, cut, hew; *rare* sculp.

sculptor ▶ noun *a bronze statue by the fifth-century sculptor Polyclitus* **carver**, modeller.

sculpture ▶ noun *a Michelangelo sculpture of the Madonna* **carving**, **model**, statue, statuette, figure, figurine, effigy, bust, head, image, likeness.
▶ verb *the west doorway is richly decorated with sculptured figures* **sculpt**, carve, chisel, model, fashion, form, shape, cast, cut, hew; *rare* sculp.

scum ▶ noun 1 *it is important that the scum on the surface is not disturbed* **film**, layer, covering, froth, foam, suds, dross, dirt.
2 (*informal*) *the glorious traditions of the Service meant nothing to scum like that* **despicable person/people**, rabble, riff-raff, refuse, garbage, trash, vermin, good-for-nothing(s), undesirable(s), the lowest of the low, the dregs of society; *Brit.* trog(s); *informal* dirt, dirty dog(s), rat(s), louse(s), toad(s), worm(s), scumbag(s), crud(s), cur(s), no-good(s); *N. Amer. informal* pond scum, scuzzball(s), sleazeball(s); *archaic* dastard(s).

scupper ▶ verb 1 *the captain decided to scupper the ship* **sink**, scuttle, submerge, send to the bottom, open the seacocks in.
OPPOSITES float, raise.
2 (*informal*) *he denied trying to scupper the agreement* **ruin**, wreck, destroy, devastate, wreak havoc on, damage, spoil, mar, injure, blast, blight, smash, shatter, dash, torpedo, scotch, mess up; sabotage, poison; *informal* louse up, screw up, foul up, put the kibosh on, banjax, do for, blow a hole in, nix, queer; *Brit. informal* cock up, dish; *Austral. informal* euchre, cruel; *vulgar slang* fuck up; *archaic* bring to naught.
OPPOSITES further, promote.

scurrility ▶ noun *this scurrility is aimed at provoking controversy* **abuse**, scurrilousness, disparagement, denigration, deprecation, insult, defamation, slander, libel, scandal, calumny, aspersions, invective, opprobrium, vituperation, vitriol, venom; *informal* bitchiness; *archaic* contumely; *dated* billingsgate.

scurrilous ▶ adjective *a scurrilous attack on her character* **abusive**, vituperative, derogatory, disparaging, denigratory, pejorative, deprecatory, insulting, offensive, defamatory, slanderous, libellous, scandalous, opprobrious, vitriolic, venomous; **unfounded**, ill-founded, groundless, baseless, unsubstantiated, unwarranted, unsupported, insupportable, uncorroborated, unjustified, unjustifiable; *informal* bitchy; *rare* contumelious, calumnious, calumniatory, aspersive, invective.

scurry ▶ verb *waiters scurry to and from their cafes* **scamper**, scuttle, bustle, skip, trot, hurry, hasten, make haste, rush, race, dash, run, sprint; *Brit.* scutter; *informal* scoot, beetle.
OPPOSITES amble, stroll.
▶ noun **1** *there was a scurry to get out* **rush**, race, dash, run, sprint; scamper, scampering, scuttle, scuttling, scramble, scrambling, bustle, bustling, trot, hurry; *Brit.* scutter, scuttering.
OPPOSITE stroll.
2 *none of these people speak a word of English, hence the scurry of interpreters* **swarm**, cloud, flock, horde, throng, bustle, maelstrom, turmoil, flurry, whirl, flood.

scurvy ▶ noun

WORD LINKS
preventing scurvy **antiscorbutic**

scuttle ▶ verb *there were men scuttling across the upper deck* **scamper**, scurry, scramble, bustle, skip, trot, hurry, hasten, make haste, rush, race, dash, run, sprint; *Brit.* scutter; *informal* scoot, beetle.
▶ noun *there was the soft scuttle of rats* **scamper**, scampering noise, scurry, scurrying; bustle, bustling, trot, hurry, haste, rush, race, dash, run, sprint; rustle, rasp, scratching noise; *Brit.* scutter, scuttering.

sea ▶ noun **1** *the sea sparkled in the sun* **(the) ocean**, the waves; *informal* the drink; *Brit. informal* the briny; *N. Amer. informal* salt chuck; *literary* the deep, the main, the foam; *NZ rare* moana.
OPPOSITES land, dry land; fresh water.
2 *there were very heavy seas and the boat overturned* **wave**, breaker, roller, comber, billow; *Austral.* bombora; *informal* boomer; *N. Amer. informal* kahuna; (**seas**) **swell**, white horses, white caps.
3 *the ground was now a sea of glutinous mud | I saw a sea of roofs and turrets* **expanse**, stretch, span, area, tract, sweep, blanket, sheet, carpet, mass; multitude, host, profusion, abundance, plethora.
□ **at sea** *as teachers we may leave our students completely at sea* **confused**, perplexed, puzzled, baffled, mystified, bemused, bewildered, nonplussed, disconcerted, disoriented, dumbfounded, at a loss, at sixes and sevens, adrift; *informal* flummoxed, bamboozled, discombobulated, stumped, fazed, beaten; *Canadian & Austral./NZ informal* bushed; *archaic* wildered, distracted, mazed.
OPPOSITES clear, enlightened.
▶ adjective *a fine sea view | sea creatures* **marine**, ocean, oceanic; salt, saltwater, seawater, watery, pelagic; ocean-going, seagoing, seafaring, afloat; maritime, naval, nautical; *rare* thalassic, pelagian.
OPPOSITES land, shore; freshwater.

WORD LINKS
relating to the sea	**marine, maritime, nautical**
under the sea	**submarine**
surveying of the sea	**hydrography**
fear of the sea	**thalassophobia**

seafaring ▶ adjective *an ancient seafaring people* **maritime**, nautical, naval, seagoing, pelagic, sea; *rare* pelagian.

seal[1] ▶ noun **1** *the seal round the bath has come unstuck* **sealant**, sealer, adhesive.
2 *the king put his seal on the letter* **emblem**, symbol, insignia, device, badge, crest, coat of arms, token, mark, monogram, stamp.
3 *the Energy Minister gave his* **seal of approval** *to the project* **ratification**, assurance, attestation, confirmation, guarantee, authentication, warrant, warranty; charter, licence, imprimatur, validation; **blessing**, stamp of approval, approval, consent, agreement, permission, sanction, authority, endorsement, clearance, approbation.
□ **set the seal on** *parliament assembled at York to set the seal on the royalist victory* **endorse**, confirm, guarantee, ratify, validate; **authorize**, certify, warrant, authenticate, seal, put the seal on, cap, clinch, wind up, close; *informal* sew up.
▶ verb **1** *he read the letter and sealed the envelope | she quietly sealed the door behind her* **fasten**, secure, shut, close up, lock, bolt, board up.
2 *seal each bottle while it is hot* **stop up**, seal up, make airtight, make watertight, close, shut, cork, stopper, stop, plug, block, block up, bung up, clog, clog up, choke, occlude, fill.
3 *police* **sealed off** *the High Street* **close off**, shut off, cordon off, fence off, form a ring around, put a cordon sanitaire round, isolate, quarantine, segregate.
4 *he held out his hand to seal the bargain* **clinch**, secure, settle, conclude, complete, establish; set the seal on, cap, wind up, close; *informal* sew up.

seal[2] ▶ noun. *See centre pages for list of* **Seals, Sea Lions, and Sea Cows**

WORD LINKS
male	**bull**
female	**cow**
young	**pup, calf**
collective noun	**rookery**
relating to seals	**phocine**

seam ▶ noun **1** *I use small stitches so that the seam is not obvious* **join**, stitching, joint, junction, closure, line; *Surgery* suture.
2 *a seam of coal* **layer**, stratum, vein, lode, deposit.
3 *the seams of his face* **furrow**, crease, corrugation, fold, groove, crinkle, pucker, line, ridge, wrinkle, crow's foot, scar.

seaman ▶ noun *Captain Bligh was a superb seaman | he joined a cargo ship as a mere seaman* **sailor**, seafarer, seafaring man, mariner, boatman, hand, crew member, rating; *informal* (old) salt, sea dog, bluejacket; *Brit. informal* matelot, matlow, matlo; *informal, dated* tar, Jack Tar, hearty; (**seamen**) **crew**, complement.
OPPOSITE landlubber.

seamy ▶ adjective *he seemed very knowledgeable about the seamy side of life* **sordid**, disreputable, seedy, sleazy, corrupt, shameful, low, dark, squalid, unwholesome, unsavoury, rough, mean, nasty, unpleasant.
OPPOSITE salubrious.

sear ▶ verb **1** *the heat of the muzzle blast seared the side of his face* **scorch**, burn, singe, scald, char; **dry up/out**, parch, desiccate, dehydrate, wither, shrivel; discolour, brown, blacken, carbonize; *Medicine* cauterize; *rare* exsiccate.
2 *sear the meat before adding the rest of the ingredients* **flash-fry**, seal, brown, fry/grill quickly, toast.
3 *his betrayal had seared her terribly* **distress**, grieve, sadden, make miserable/wretched, upset, trouble, harrow, cause anguish to, afflict, perturb, disturb; hurt, wound, pain, cut to the quick; affect, move, sting, mortify, torment, torture, gnaw at, vex, gall.

search ▶ verb **1** *we* **searched for** *clues* **hunt**, look, explore, forage, fish about/around, look high and low, cast about/around/round, ferret (about/around), root about/around, rummage about/around; seek, scout out, pursue.
2 *he searched the house thoroughly* **look around/round**, explore, probe, hunt through, look through, scrabble about/around in, root about/around in, ferret (about/around) in, rummage about/around in, rummage in/through, forage through, fish about/around in, poke around in, dig in, grub about/around in, delve in, go through, sift through, rifle through, scour, comb, ransack, turn over, go through with a fine-tooth comb; turn upside down, turn inside out, leave no stone unturned in; *Brit. informal* rootle around in; *Austral./NZ informal* fossick through; *rare* roust around in.
3 *these statutes enable the police to stop and search suspects* **examine**, inspect, check, frisk; *informal* give someone a/the once-over.
□ **search me!** (*informal*) **I don't know**, how should I know?, why ask me?, it's a mystery, I haven't an inkling/clue, I haven't the least idea, I've no idea; *informal* dunno, don't ask me, I haven't the faintest/first/foggiest (idea/notion), it beats me, ask me another.
▶ noun *we continued our* **search for** *a hotel* **hunt**, look, exploration, scout, probe, dig, digging, forage, foraging, scavenge, scavenging, ferreting (about/around), rummage, rummaging about/around, rooting about/around, rifling, scouring, quest, pursuit of, seeking after.
□ **in search of** *they are forced to travel in search of food* **searching for**, hunting for, after, seeking, looking for, on the lookout for, in quest of, in pursuit of, on the track of, questing after, chasing after.

searching ▶ adjective **1** *a searching look* **observant**, penetrating, piercing, probing, curious, discerning, incisive, keen, alert, perceptive, shrewd, sharp, intent, minute, thorough.
OPPOSITE casual.
2 *searching questions* **penetrating**, probing, incisive, inquisitive, analytic, deep, in-depth, inquiring.
OPPOSITES cursory, vague.

searing ▶ adjective **1** *the searing heat of the flames* **scorching**, blistering, flaming, blazing (hot), baking (hot), burning, fiery, torrid, parching, withering; *informal* boiling, boiling hot, sizzling, roasting, sweltering.
2 *she winced with the searing pain* **intense**, excruciating, agonizing, sharp, stabbing, shooting, stinging, severe, extreme, fierce, harrowing, piercing, penetrating, racking, insufferable, unbearable, unendurable, torturous; *rare* exquisite.
3 *she made national headlines with her searing attack on the President* **fierce**, savage, blistering, scathing, stinging, devastating, mordant, trenchant, caustic, cutting, biting, withering, virulent, vitriolic.

seashell ▶ noun. *See centre pages for list of* **Shells**

seaside ▶ noun *a day out at the seaside* **coast**, shore, coastal region, seashore, seaboard, sea coast, waterside; beach resort, beach, sand, sands, foreshore; *technical* littoral; *literary* strand.

season ▶ noun *the rainy season | the opera season* **period**, active period, time, time of year, spell, term, phase, stage.
□ **in season** *strawberries are in season* **available**, obtainable, readily

available/obtainable, to be had, on offer, on the market, growing, common, plentiful, abundant.
OPPOSITE out of season.
▶ verb **1** *remove the bay leaves and season the casserole to taste* **flavour**, add flavouring to, add salt/pepper to, spice, add spices/herbs to; *informal* pep up, add zing to.
2 *his albums include standard numbers seasoned with a few of his own tunes* **enliven**, leaven, add spice to, enrich, liven up, animate, augment; *informal* pep up, add zest/zing to.
3 *oak should be well seasoned* **mature**, age, mellow, condition, acclimatize, temper, prepare, prime, ripen.

seasonable ▶ adjective **1** *seasonable weather* **usual**, expected, predictable, normal for the time of year, appropriate to the time of year.
OPPOSITE unseasonable.
2 (*dated*) *seasonable advice* **timely**, opportune, well timed, appropriate, expedient, suitable, apt, fitting.
OPPOSITE ill-timed.

seasonable or seasonal?

Something **seasonable** is appropriate to a particular occasion or time of year (*surprise your Christmas guests with variations on seasonable recipes*). **Seasonal** is a more common word, and means 'varying with or determined by the time of year' (*a seasonal climate | seasonal employment*). A *seasonal crop*, ripening at a particular time of year, might also be seen as *seasonable* in the sense of being characteristic of that time; and from this connection, together with the similarity between the words, a use of *seasonal* in the sense 'appropriate to the time of year' has developed (*there's not much seasonal goodwill in evidence*).

seasoned ▶ adjective *seasoned travellers* **experienced**, practised, well versed, expert, knowledgeable, sophisticated, established, habituated, long-serving, time-served, veteran, hardened, battle-scarred, consummate, well trained.
OPPOSITES inexperienced, callow, green.

seasoning ▶ noun *stir in the bean sprouts, garlic, soy sauce, and seasoning* **flavouring**, salt and pepper, herbs, spices, condiments, dressing, relish.

seat *See centre pages for list of* **Chairs and Stools**
▶ noun **1** *enough seats for the audience/spectators* **chair**, place, space; (**seats**) seating, seating accommodation, room.
2 *the patient can then move his seat or legs* **buttocks**, behind, backside, rear, rear end, rump, haunches, hindquarters, cheeks; *Brit.* bottom; *French* derrière; *German* Sitzfleisch; *informal* sit-upon, stern, BTM, tochus; *Brit. informal* bum, botty, prat, jacksie; *N. Amer. informal* butt, fanny, tush, tushie, tail, duff, buns, booty, caboose, heinie, patootie, keister, tuchis; *W. Indian informal* batty; *humorous* fundament, posterior; *black English* rass, rusty dusty; *Brit. vulgar slang* arse; *N. Amer. vulgar slang* ass; *technical* nates; *archaic* breech.
3 *the seat of government* **headquarters**, location, site, whereabouts, place, base, centre, nerve centre, nucleus, centre of operations/activity, hub, focus, focal point, heart.
4 *the family had a country seat in Surrey* **residence**, ancestral home, mansion, stately home, abode.
▶ verb **1** *they seated themselves round the table | he was seated next to Margaret* **position**, put, place, stand, station; install, settle, arrange, dispose, array, range, deploy; *informal* plonk, park; *rare* posit.
2 *the hall seats 500* **have room for**, contain, take, sit, hold, accommodate.

seating ▶ noun *the theatre has seating for 600* **seats**, room, places, chairs, seating accommodation, accommodation.

seaweed ▶ noun
WORD LINKS
related prefix **phyco-** (e.g. ***phycocyanin***)
study of seaweed **phycology**

secede ▶ verb *the Southern states seceded from the Federal Union* **withdraw from**, break away from, break with, separate (oneself) from, sever relations with, leave, quit, split with, split off from, disaffiliate from, defect from, resign from, pull out of, drop out of, have nothing more to do with, turn one's back on, repudiate, reject, renounce, desert; form a splinter group.
OPPOSITE join.

secession ▶ noun *the republic's secession from the Soviet Union* **withdrawal**, break, breakaway, separation, severance, schism, apostasy, leaving, quitting, split, splitting, disaffiliation, resignation, pulling out, dropping out, desertion, defection.
OPPOSITES joining; unification.

secluded ▶ adjective *the house overlooks a quiet, secluded garden* **sheltered**, **private**, concealed, hidden, undisturbed, unfrequented, sequestered, tucked away.
OPPOSITES public, busy, accessible.

seclusion ▶ noun *he spends much of his time in seclusion at his mountain cottage* **isolation**, solitude, retreat, privacy, privateness, retirement, withdrawal, purdah, an ivory tower, concealment, hiding, secrecy, peace, peace and quiet, peacefulness, quietness, lack of disturbance, lack of interruption, freedom from interference; *rare* sequestration, reclusion.

second¹ (stress on the first syllable) ▶ adjective **1** *the second day of the trial* **next**, following, after the first, subsequent, ensuing, succeeding, coming.
OPPOSITES first, preceding.
2 *would you like a second helping?* **additional**, extra, fresh, another, further, repeat, supplementary, supplemental.
OPPOSITE first.
3 *he keeps a second pair of glasses in his office* **spare**, extra, additional, alternative, another, backup, relief, fallback, substitute, auxiliary, ancillary; redundant, surplus, superfluous; *N. Amer.* alternate.
OPPOSITES primary, principal.
4 *Malcolm is dropping down to captain the second team* **secondary**, lower, subordinate, subsidiary, lesser, minor, subservient, supporting, lower-grade, inferior.
OPPOSITES first, top.
5 *there was a fear that the conflict would turn into a second Vietnam* **another**, duplicate, reproduction, twin, double, new, replicate, matching; repeat of, copy of, carbon copy of.
OPPOSITE original.
□ **second to none** *the hotel offers a level of service that is second to none* **incomparable**, matchless, unrivalled, inimitable, beyond compare, unparalleled, without parallel, unequalled, without equal, unmatched, in a class of its own, beyond comparison, peerless, unsurpassed, unsurpassable, nonpareil, unique; **perfect**, consummate, rare, exquisite, transcendent, surpassing, superlative, supreme; *rare* unexampled.
▶ noun **1** *Eva had been working as his second* **assistant**, attendant, helper, aide, supporter, backer, auxiliary, right-hand man/woman, girl/man Friday, second in command, number two, deputy, vice-, understudy, subordinate, adjutant, subaltern, henchman; *informal* sidekick.
2 (**seconds**) (*informal*) *he enjoyed the pie so much he asked for seconds* **a second helping**, a further helping, more.
3 (**seconds**) *sometimes factory shops sell seconds* **imperfect goods**, faulty goods, defective goods, flawed goods, inferior goods, rejects, export rejects, discards.
▶ verb *George Beale seconded the motion* **formally support**, give one's support to, announce one's support for, vote for, back, back up, approve, give one's approval to, endorse, promote, commend.
WORD LINKS
related prefix **deuter(o)- (e.g. *deuterium, Deuteronomy*)**

second² (stress on the first syllable) ▶ noun *I'll only be gone for a second* **moment**, bit, little while, short time, instant, split second; *informal* sec, jiffy, jiff; *Brit. informal* mo, tick, two ticks.
□ **in a second** *you'll see in a second* **(very) soon**, in a minute, in a moment, in a trice, in a flash, shortly, any minute, any minute now, in a short time, in an instant, in the twinkling of an eye, in (less than) no time, in no time at all, before you know it, before long; *N. Amer.* momentarily; *informal* in a jiffy, in two shakes, in two shakes of a lamb's tail, before you can say Jack Robinson, in the blink of an eye, in a blink, in the wink of an eye, in a wink, before you can say knife; *Brit. informal* in a tick, in two ticks, in a mo; *N. Amer. informal* in a snap.

second³ (stress on the second syllable) ▶ verb *personnel are sometimes seconded to charities* **assign temporarily**, lend; transfer, move, shift, relocate, assign, reassign, send, attach, allocate, detail, appoint.

secondary ▶ adjective **1** *'women's issues' have often been seen as secondary* **subordinate**, lesser, lower, lower-level, minor, peripheral, incidental, tangential, marginal, ancillary, subsidiary, subservient, non-essential, inessential, of little account, unimportant, less important.
OPPOSITES primary, central.
2 *primary sources are not necessarily more accurate than secondary sources* **indirect**, non-primary, derived, derivative, resulting, resultant, concomitant, accompanying, consequential, contingent, second-hand.
OPPOSITES primary, direct.
3 *they bombed their secondary target instead* **alternative**, spare, extra, additional, another, backup, supporting, relief, fallback, substitute, auxiliary; *N. Amer.* alternate.
OPPOSITES primary, main.

second-class ▶ adjective *we were treated like second-class citizens* **second-rate**, second-best, low-class, inferior, lesser, unimportant.

second-hand ▶ adjective **1** *a second-hand car* **used**, old, nearly new, worn, pre-owned, handed-down, cast-off; *informal* hand-me-down, reach-me-down.
OPPOSITE new.
2 *they shouldn't have to rely on second-hand information* **indirect**, secondary, derivative, derived, vicarious.
OPPOSITE first-hand.
▶ adverb *the information was invariably gathered second-hand* **indirectly**, at second hand, on the bush/jungle telegraph; *informal* on the grapevine.
OPPOSITE directly.

second in command ▶ noun *he left it to his second in command to sort out the details* **deputy**, number two, subordinate, assistant, right-hand man/woman, vice-, understudy, lieutenant, adjutant, subaltern; *informal* sidekick.

secondly ▶ adverb *firstly it is wrong and secondly it is difficult to implement* **furthermore**, also, moreover; second, in the second place, next; secondarily.

second-rate ▶ adjective *he replied tetchily that he never made second-rate films* **substandard**, below standard, below par, bad, deficient, defective, faulty, imperfect, inferior, mediocre; abject, poor, appalling, abysmal, atrocious, awful, terrible, dismal, dreadful, unsatisfactory, low-grade, third-rate, jerry-built, shoddy, crude, tinny, trashy, rubbishy, miserable, wretched, lamentable, deplorable, pitiful, inadequate, insufficient, unacceptable, execrable, frightful; *informal* crummy, dire, bum, diabolical, rotten, sad, tatty, tacky, tenth-rate; *Brit. informal* ropy, duff, rubbish, pants, a load of pants, grotty; *vulgar slang* crap, crappy; *archaic* direful; *rare* egregious.
OPPOSITES first-rate, excellent.

secrecy ▶ noun **1** *there is no guarantee that the secrecy of the material will be maintained* **confidentiality**, classified nature, privateness.
2 *you must make him understand the need for secrecy* **clandestineness**, furtiveness, surreptitiousness, secretiveness, stealth, stealthiness, covertness, cloak and dagger, mystery.
3 *in the secrecy of that room, her eyes now betrayed all* **seclusion**, privacy, concealment, shelter, solitariness, loneliness, retirement, isolation, remoteness, privateness; *rare* sequestration.

secret ▶ adjective **1** *they have a secret plan* **confidential**, strictly confidential, top secret, classified, restricted, unrevealed, undisclosed, unpublished, untold, unknown, uncommunicated, behind someone's back, under wraps, unofficial, off the record, not for publication/circulation, not to be made public, not to be disclosed; *Latin* sub rosa; *informal* hush-hush, mum.
OPPOSITES known, public.
2 *there is a secret drawer in the table* **hidden**, concealed; camouflaged, disguised; unnoticeable, invisible, inconspicuous.
OPPOSITE visible.
3 *a secret operation to infiltrate terrorist groups* **clandestine**, covert, undercover, underground, hidden, shrouded, conspiratorial, surreptitious, stealthy, cloak-and-dagger, hole-and corner, closet; sneaky, sly, underhand, shifty, furtive; *informal* hush-hush.
OPPOSITE overt.
4 *a secret message | a secret code* **cryptic**, encoded, coded, enciphered, hidden, mysterious, abstruse, recondite, arcane, esoteric, cabbalistic.
OPPOSITE open.
5 *a secret place* **secluded**, **private**, concealed, hidden, sheltered, undisturbed, unfrequented, solitary, lonely, sequestered, out of the way, remote, isolated, off the beaten track, tucked away, cut-off.
OPPOSITES known about, public.
6 *he's a very secret person* **uncommunicative**, secretive, unforthcoming, reticent, taciturn, silent, non-communicative, quiet, tight-lipped, close-mouthed, close, playing one's cards close to one's chest, clamlike, reserved, introvert, introverted, self-contained, discreet.
OPPOSITES open, communicative, chatty.
▶ noun **1** *he just can't keep a secret* **confidential matter**, confidence, private affair, skeleton in the cupboard.
OPPOSITE public knowledge.
2 *the secrets of the universe* **mystery**, enigma, problem, paradox, puzzle, conundrum, poser, riddle, question, question mark.
OPPOSITE known fact.
3 *the secret of their success* **recipe**, formula, blueprint, magic formula, key, answer, solution.
□ **in secret** *groups of MPs met in secret over the summer* **secretly**, without anyone knowing, in private, privately, in confidence, confidentially, behind closed doors, behind the scenes, behind someone's back, under cover, under the counter, discreetly, unobserved, quietly, furtively, stealthily, on the sly, on the quiet, privily, conspiratorially, covertly, clandestinely, on the side; *Latin* sub rosa, in camera; *informal* on the q.t.
OPPOSITE openly.

WORD LINKS
denoting something secret **crypto- (e.g. *cryptogram*)**

secret agent ▶ noun *his tutor might have been a British secret agent* **spy**, agent, double agent, counterspy, field agent, undercover agent, operative, plant, infiltrator, mole; *N. Amer. informal* spook; *archaic* intelligencer.

secretary ▶ noun *he asked his secretary to place a call through to England* **assistant**, personal assistant, PA, administrator, clerk, clerical assistant, amanuensis, girl/man Friday; typist, shorthand typist, copyist, keyboarder, stenographer.

secrete[1] ▶ verb *the gland can become enlarged and secrete excess levels of the hormone* **produce**, **discharge**, emit, excrete, exude, ooze, leak, leach, emanate, give off, release, send out; *Medicine* extravasate.
OPPOSITE absorb.

secrete[2] ▶ verb *Bert and I were to secrete ourselves behind the curtains* **conceal**, hide, cover up, veil, shroud, disguise, screen, bury, stow away, sequester, cache; *informal* stash away.
OPPOSITES reveal, show.

secretion ▶ noun *histamine promotes the secretion of gastric acid | a secretion produced by the thoracic gland* **production**, **discharge**, emission, excretion, exudation, ooze, oozing, leakage, leaching, emanation, giving off, release, sending out; *Medicine* extravasation.

secretive ▶ adjective *a secretive person* **uncommunicative**, secret, unforthcoming, reticent, taciturn, silent, non-communicative, quiet, tight-lipped, close-mouthed, close, playing one's cards close to one's chest, clamlike, reserved, introvert, introverted, self-contained, discreet.
OPPOSITES open, communicative, chatty.

secretly ▶ adverb **1** *the microphones had been used for secretly recording conversations* **covertly**, without anyone knowing, in secret, in private, privately, in confidence, confidentially, behind closed doors, behind the scenes, behind someone's back, under cover, under the counter, discreetly, unobserved, quietly, furtively, stealthily, on the sly, on the quiet, privily, conspiratorially, clandestinely, on the side; *Latin* sub rosa, in camera; *informal* on the q.t.
OPPOSITE publicly.
2 *I think he was secretly jealous of Bartholomew* **privately**, in one's heart, in one's heart of hearts, in one's innermost thoughts.
OPPOSITE openly.

sect *See centre pages for lists of* **Religions and Sects**
▶ noun *he joined a rather weird religious sect* **(religious) cult**, religious group, faith community, denomination, persuasion, religious order; splinter group, faction, schism, schismatic group/religion/church, heretical movement.

sectarian ▶ adjective *this party should offer the voters a real alternative to sectarian politics* **factional**, schismatic, cliquish, clannish, partisan, parti pris; denominational; **doctrinaire**, dogmatic, extreme, fanatical, rigid, inflexible, bigoted, hidebound, narrow-minded.
OPPOSITES tolerant, liberal, broad-minded.
▶ noun *the Church is split between the dogmatism of the sectarians and the tolerance of the more open-minded* **separatist**, dissenter, dissident, nonconformist, free thinker, renegade, recusant, schismatic, revisionist; unbeliever, sceptic, agnostic, atheist; zealot, Young Turk, extremist, radical, activist, militant; bigot, dogmatist, partisan, devotee.

section ▶ noun **1** *I unscrewed every section of the copper pipe* **segment**, part, component, division, piece, portion, length, element, module, unit, constituent, bit, slice, fraction, fragment.
2 *this last section of the questionnaire relates solely to training* **subdivision**, part, chapter, subsection, division, portion, component, bit, passage, clause, act, scene, episode, instalment.
3 *the reference section of your local library* **department**, part, division, branch, sector, wing, compartment.
4 *a residential section of the capital* See SECTOR sense 2.

sectional ▶ adjective *there are universal principles that transcend sectional interests* **individual**, **group**, separate, divided, special, personal, private, exclusive, local, provincial, regional, national, sectarian, factional, party, party political, class, racial, partisan, partial, selfish.
OPPOSITES collective, universal.

sector ▶ noun **1** *every sector of the industry is affected* **part**, branch, arm, division, subdivision, area, department, category, field, sphere, layer, stratum, corner.
2 *the north-eastern sector of the town* **district**, quarter, part, section, zone, precinct, borough, locality, neighbourhood, side; province, territory, division, region, area, belt, tract, locale; *N. Amer. informal* hood.

secular ▶ adjective *secular music | a secular building* **non-religious**, lay, non-church, temporal, worldly, earthly, profane; unsanctified, unconsecrated, unhallowed; *rare* laic.
OPPOSITES holy, religious, sacred.

secure ▶ adjective **1** *check to ensure that all nuts and bolts are secure* **tight**, firm, taut, fixed, secured, done up; closed, shut, locked, sealed.
OPPOSITES loose, unlocked.
2 *make sure that the ladder you are working on is secure* **stable**, fixed, secured, fast, safe, steady, immovable, unshakeable, dependable; anchored, moored, jammed, rooted, braced, cemented, riveted, nailed, tied; strong, sturdy, solid, sound.
OPPOSITES precarious, rocky.
3 *jars kept secure in a pantry may survive for several generations | children need an environment in which they can feel secure* **protected from harm/danger**, free from danger, sheltered, shielded, guarded, unharmed, undamaged, safe and sound, safe, out of harm's way, in a safe place, in safe hands, invulnerable, immune, impregnable, unassailable; **at ease**, unworried, reassured, relaxed, happy, comfortable, confident.
OPPOSITES vulnerable, threatened, unsettled.
4 *few young people face a secure future* **certain**, assured, reliable, dependable, settled, fixed, established, solid, sound.
OPPOSITES uncertain, insecure.
▶ verb **1** *pins secure the handle to the main body* **fix**, attach, fasten, affix, link, hitch, join, connect, couple, bond, append, annex, stick, pin, tack, nail, staple, clip.

S

2 *the doors had not been properly secured* **fasten**, **close**, shut, lock, bolt, chain, seal, board up.
3 *Athens was seeking to secure herself from a lightning invasion from the west* **protect**, make safe, make sound, make invulnerable, make immune, make impregnable, fortify, strengthen, shelter, shield, guard.
4 *he killed the engine, then leapt out to secure the boat* **tie up**, moor, make fast, lash, hitch, berth; anchor.
5 *a written constitution would secure the rights of the individual* **assure**, ensure, insure, guarantee, warrant, protect, indemnify, confirm, establish.
6 *the company has already secured two million pounds' worth of business* **obtain**, acquire, gain, get, find, come by, pick up, procure, get possession of; buy, purchase; informal get hold of, land, get one's hands on, lay one's hands on, get one's mitts on.
OPPOSITES lose, let slip.

security ▸ noun **1** *the security of the nation's citizens is our highest responsibility* **safety**, freedom from danger; protection, safe keeping, shielding, guarding, care; invulnerability, impregnability, unassailability.
OPPOSITES vulnerability, danger.
2 *he could give her the security she needed* **feeling of safety**, feeling of ease, absence of worry/anxiety, peace of mind, freedom from doubt, certainty, happiness, comfort, confidence.
OPPOSITE disquiet.
3 *employees have an interest in the security of their jobs* **certainty**, safe future, assured future, safety, reliability, dependability, solidness, soundness.
4 *the two accused men appeared in court amid tight security* **safety measures**, safeguards; guards, surveillance, defence, protection.
5 *additional security for your loan may be required* **guarantee**, collateral, surety, pledge, bond; hostage, pawn, backing, bail; archaic gage, earnest.

sedate[1] ▸ verb *the patient had to be sedated heavily* **tranquillize**, give a sedative to, put under sedation, calm down, quieten, pacify, soothe, relax, dope, drug, administer drugs/narcotics/opiates to, knock out, anaesthetize; stupefy.
OPPOSITES invigorate, energize.

sedate[2] ▸ adjective **1** *sedate suburban domesticity* **calm**, tranquil, placid, composed, serene, steady, unruffled, imperturbable, unflappable; **dignified**, serious, serious-minded, formal, decorous, proper, prim, demure, sober, earnest, staid, stiff, stuffy, boring; informal starchy, stick-in-the-mud.
OPPOSITES exciting, wild.
2 *they continued at a more sedate pace* **slow**, unhurried, relaxed, leisurely, unrushed, slow-moving, slow-going, slow and steady, easy, easy-going, gentle, comfortable, restful, undemanding, lazy, languid, languorous, plodding, dawdling, leisured, measured, steady; informal laid-back.
OPPOSITE fast.

sedative ▸ adjective *he took a combination of sedative drugs* **tranquillizing**, calming, depressant, soothing, calmative, relaxing, soporific; Medicine neuroleptic.
▸ noun *the doctor gave him a sedative* **tranquillizer**, calmative, depressant, sleeping pill, soporific, narcotic, opiate; Medicine neuroleptic; informal trank, sleeper, downer.

sedentary ▸ adjective *a sedentary job* **sitting**, seated, desk-bound, desk, inactive, still, stationary.
OPPOSITES active, mobile.

sediment ▸ noun *there is a thick layer of sediment on the bottom* **dregs**, lees, deposit, grounds, settlings, residue, remains, accumulation, silt, sludge, alluvium; technical precipitate, sublimate, residuum; rare draff, grouts.

sedition ▸ noun *advocating multiparty democracy is considered sedition* **incitement (to riot/rebellion)**, agitation, rabble-rousing, fomentation (of discontent), troublemaking, provocation, inflaming; **rebellion**, revolt, insurrection, rioting, mutiny, insurgence, insurgency, subversion, civil disorder, insubordination, disobedience, resistance, defiance.

seditious ▸ adjective **1** *a seditious speech* **rabble-rousing**, inciting, agitating, fomenting, troublemaking, provocative, inflammatory.
2 *the interior minister issued a decree outlawing seditious groups* **revolutionary**, rebellious, insurrectionist, mutinous, insurgent, subversive, insubordinate, civil disobedience, dissident, defiant, disloyal, treasonous.

seduce ▸ verb **1** *he took her to his tent where he seduced her* **persuade someone to have sexual intercourse**, take away someone's innocence; rape, violate, debauch; lead astray, corrupt, deprave; informal bed, pop someone's cherry, tumble; euphemistic have one's (wicked) way with, take advantage of; literary ravish, deflower; archaic dishonour, ruin.
2 *people are seduced by the packaging of inferior products* **attract**, allure, lure, tempt, entice, beguile, cajole, wheedle, ensnare, charm, captivate, enchant, hypnotize, mesmerize, tantalize, titillate, bewitch, ravish, inveigle, lead astray, trap; manoeuvre, deceive, dupe.

seducer ▸ noun *the man was an accomplished seducer* **womanizer**, philanderer, deceiver, adulterer, Romeo, Don Juan, Lothario, Casanova, playboy, lecher, ladies' man; informal ladykiller, lech, dirty old man, goat, wolf, skirt-chaser.

seduction ▸ noun **1** *he had engaged in gambling, drinking, and the seduction of women* **persuading someone to have sexual intercourse**, taking away someone's innocence; rape, violation, debauching, corruption; informal bedding, tumbling; archaic dishonouring, ruin; dated ravishment, defloration.
2 *the seduction of ambition | the more cerebral seductions of art and literature* **temptation**, **attraction**, lure, allure, call, pull, draw, charm, bait, decoy, magnet; (**seductions**) **appeal**, attractiveness, fascination, interest, glamour, drawing power, magnetism, enchantment, enticement; informal come-on.

seductive ▸ adjective **1** *she appears in the guise of a seductive temptress* **sexy**, sexually arousing, sexually exciting, alluring, tempting, suggestive, tantalizing, fascinating, ravishing, captivating, bewitching, immodest, shameless, erotic, sensuous, sultry, slinky, passionate, raunchy, steamy, coquettish, amorous, flirtatious, provocative, come-hither; informal come-to-bed, tarty; vulgar slang fuck-me.
OPPOSITE repulsive.
2 *she crept towards the seductive warmth of the stove* **attractive**, appealing, inviting, alluring, tempting, enticing, beguiling, engaging, winning, irresistible.
OPPOSITES repellent, off-putting.

seductress ▸ noun *the story of an innocent art student who becomes a wanton seductress* **temptress**, siren, femme fatale, enchantress, sorceress, Delilah, Circe, Lorelei, Mata Hari; **flirt**, coquette, Lolita, loose woman; informal tart; N. Amer. informal vamp; archaic fizgig, wanton, strumpet.

sedulous ▸ adjective *he picked a spine from his leg with sedulous care* **diligent**, careful, meticulous, thorough, assiduous, attentive, industrious, laborious, hard-working, conscientious, ultra-careful, punctilious, scrupulous, painstaking, searching, close, elaborate, minute, studious, rigorous, particular; religious, strict; pedantic, fussy.
OPPOSITE nonchalant.

see[1] ▸ verb **1** *I can see the house* **discern**, perceive, glimpse, catch/get a glimpse of, spot, notice, catch sight of, sight; **make out**, pick out, spy, distinguish, identify, recognize, detect, note, mark; informal clap/lay/set eyes on, clock; literary behold, descry, espy.
2 *they saw a television programme on Hong Kong* **watch**, look at, view, observe, catch.
3 *would you like to see over the house?* **inspect**, view, see round, look around/round, look through, have a look around/round, have a tour of, go on a tour of, tour, survey, scrutinize; informal give something a/the once-over.
4 *I can't see how this helps us* **understand**, grasp, comprehend, follow, take in, realize, appreciate, recognize, work out, get the drift of, make out, conceive, perceive, fathom (out), become cognizant of; informal get, latch on to, cotton on to, catch on to, tumble to, figure out, get the hang of, get a fix on, get one's head round/around, get the message, get the picture; Brit. informal twig, suss; N. Amer. informal savvy; rare cognize.
5 *I must go and see what Victor is up to* **find out**, discover, learn, ascertain, get to know, determine, establish; ask, enquire, make enquiries as to, investigate; Brit. informal suss out.
6 *let me see* **think**, consider, contemplate, reflect, deliberate, have a think, meditate, muse, ponder, cogitate, brood, agonize; give it some thought, mull it over, chew it over, puzzle over it, turn it over in one's mind, revolve it in one's mind; rare cerebrate.
7 *he checked to see that all of his desk drawers were locked | see that you do it now* **make sure**, make certain, see to it, check, verify, take care, mind, satisfy oneself, ensure; remember to, be/make sure to, not forget to.
8 *I see trouble ahead* **foresee**, predict, forecast, prophesy, prognosticate, anticipate, envisage, envision, picture, visualize; archaic augur, previse, presage, foreshow.
9 *about a year later, I saw a friend in town* **meet (by chance)**, encounter, run into, run across, stumble on/across, happen on, chance on, come across; informal bump into; archaic run against.
10 *they see each other from time to time* **meet (by arrangement)**, meet up with, get together with, have a meeting, have meetings, meet socially, make a date with.
11 *I'd better see a doctor about it* **consult**, confer with, talk to, speak to, seek advice/information from, take counsel from, have recourse to, call on, call in, turn to, ask.
12 *the doctor will see you now* **interview**, give an interview to, give a consultation to, give an audience to, give a hearing to, receive, talk to; examine, treat.
13 *he's seeing someone else now* **go out with**, **be dating**, take out, be someone's boyfriend/girlfriend, keep company with, go with, be with, court, have a fling with, have an affair with, dally with; informal go steady with; Brit. informal, dated walk out with; N. Amer. informal, dated step out with.
14 *he saw her to her car* **escort**, accompany, show, walk, conduct, lead, take, usher, guide, shepherd, attend.

□ **see about** *I'll go and see about fixing a meal* **arrange**, make arrangements for, see to, deal with, take care of, look after, attend to, sort out; organize, be responsible for, take responsibility for, be in charge of, direct.

□ **see through** *I can see right through your little plot | I saw through you from the start* **not be deceived by**, not be taken in by, be wise to, get/have the measure of, read like a book, fathom, penetrate, realize, understand; *informal* not fall for, have someone's number, know someone's (little) game.
OPPOSITE be hoodwinked by.

□ **see someone through** *it was Francine's devotion which saw him through* **sustain**, encourage, buoy up, cheer along, keep going, keep someone's head above water, tide over; **support**, give strength to, be a source of strength to, be a tower of strength to, comfort, help (out), assist.
OPPOSITE let someone down.

□ **see something through** *I want to see the job through* **bring to completion**, continue to the end, bring to a finish; **persevere with**, persist with, continue (with), carry on with, go on with, keep at, keep on with, keep going with, keep up, not give up with, follow through, press on/ahead with, plod on through, plough on through, stay with; not take no for an answer; *informal* plug away at, peg away at, stick at, soldier on with, stick something out, stick to one's guns, hang in there.
OPPOSITE give up (on).

□ **see to** *I'll go and see to the sitting-room fire* **attend to**, deal with, see about, take care of, look after, sort out, fix up, get together, organize, arrange, be responsible for, be in charge of, direct, run, manage, conduct, administer, administrate.

WORD LINKS
fear of being seen **scopophobia**

see[2] ▶ noun *a bishop's see* **diocese**, bishopric.

seed ▶ noun **1** *sow the seeds in trays or pots* pip, stone, pit, nut, kernel, germ; *technical* ovule.
2 *the male of the species supplies the seed for reproduction* **semen**, sperm, spermatic fluid, seminal fluid, milt, ejaculate, emission; *Biology* spermatozoa; *vulgar slang* come, cum, jism, jissom, jizz; *Brit. vulgar slang* spunk.
3 *each war contains within it the seeds of a fresh war* **genesis**, source, origin, root, starting point, germ, beginnings, potential (for); **cause**, reason, motivation, motive; base, basis, foundation, bottom, seat, fundamental; core, nucleus, heart, kernel, nub, essence; *Latin* fons et origo; *literary* fountainhead, wellspring, fount.
4 (*archaic*) *Abraham and his seed* **descendants**, heirs, successors, scions; **offspring**, children, sons and daughters, progeny, family, youngsters, babies, brood; *Law* issue; *informal* kids, quiverful; *derogatory* spawn; *archaic* fruit, fruit of someone's loins.

□ **go to seed** *with the ferry gone and the road traffic diverted the place has gone to seed* **deteriorate**, degenerate, decline, decay, fall into decay, run to seed, go to rack and ruin, become dilapidated, go downhill, break down, waste away, wither away, languish, moulder, rot; *informal* go to pot, go to the dogs, go down the toilet.

WORD LINKS
relating to seeds **seminal**

seedy ▶ adjective **1** *he began hanging out at a seedy bar* **sordid**, disreputable, seamy, sleazy, corrupt, shameful, low, dark, squalid, unwholesome, unsavoury, rough, mean, nasty, unpleasant.
OPPOSITE classy.
2 *the live-in caretaker of a seedy block of flats* **dilapidated**, tumbledown, ramshackle, derelict, ruinous, falling to pieces, decrepit, gone to rack and ruin, in ruins, broken-down, crumbling, decaying, disintegrating; **neglected**, uncared-for, unmaintained, depressed, run down, down at heel, shabby, dingy, slummy, insalubrious, squalid; *informal* shambly, crummy; *Brit. informal* grotty; *N. Amer. informal* shacky.
OPPOSITES high-class, fashionable.
3 (*dated*) *feeling rather seedy* **ill**, unwell, poorly, bad, out of sorts, indisposed, not oneself, sick, queasy, nauseous, nauseated, peaky, liverish, green about the gills, run down, washed out, faint, dizzy, giddy, light-headed; *Brit.* off, off colour; *informal* under the weather, below par, not up to par, funny, peculiar, lousy, rotten, rough, awful, terrible, dreadful, crummy; *Brit. informal* grotty, ropy; *Scottish informal* wabbit, peely-wally; *Austral./NZ informal* crook; *rare* peaked, peakish.
OPPOSITES fit, well.

seek ▶ verb **1** *six bombers took off and flew southwards to seek the enemy* **search for**, try to find, look for, look about/around/round for, cast about/around/round for, be on the lookout for, be after, hunt for, be in quest of, quest (after), be in pursuit of.
2 *the new regime sought his extradition* **try to obtain**, pursue, go after, strive for, go for, push towards, work towards, be intent on, aim at/for, have as a goal, have as an objective.
3 *you may need to seek the advice of a specialist* **ask for**, request, solicit, call on, invite, entreat, beg for, petition for, appeal for, apply for, put in for.
4 *we constantly seek to improve the service* **try**, attempt, endeavour, strive, work, aim, aspire, do one's best, set out; *formal* essay.

seem ▶ verb *she seemed annoyed at this* **appear**, appear to be, have the appearance/air of being, give the impression of being, look, look like, look as though one is, look to be, have the look of, show signs of; come across as, strike someone as, give someone the feeling that one is, sound.

seeming ▶ adjective **1** *there is a seeming contradiction here* **apparent**, outward, surface.
OPPOSITES actual, real.
2 *you can't simply kill him, even with a seeming accident* **pretended**, feigned, specious, professed, supposed, presumed, avowed, so-called, alleged, declared, claimed, purported, ostensible; *rare* ostensive.
OPPOSITE genuine.

seemingly ▶ adverb *he stared down the seemingly endless corridor* **apparently**, on the face of it, to all appearances, as far as one can see/tell, on the surface, to all intents and purposes, outwardly, evidently, superficially, supposedly, avowedly, allegedly, professedly, purportedly; *rare* pretendedly, ostensively.
OPPOSITE genuinely.

seemly ▶ adjective *it was not thought seemly to look in a mirror in those days* **decorous**, proper, decent, becoming, fitting, suitable, appropriate, apt, apposite, meet, in good taste, genteel, polite, conventional, the done thing, right, correct, acceptable; *French* comme il faut.
OPPOSITES unseemly, unbecoming, unsuitable.

seep ▶ verb *oil continued to seep out of the sunken vessel* **ooze**, trickle, exude, drip, dribble, flow, issue, discharge, excrete, escape, leak, drain, bleed, sweat, well, leach, filter, percolate, permeate, soak; *Medicine* extravasate; *rare* filtrate, transude, exudate.

seepage ▶ noun *the clay soil has slowed down the seepage of radioactive material into the groundwater* **oozing**, seeping, trickle, trickling, drip, dribble, flow, issuance, discharge, excretion, escape, leak, leakage, drainage, bleeding, sweating, welling, leaching, filtration, percolation, secretion; *Medicine* extravasation; *archaic* transudation, exudation.

seer ▶ noun *a seer had foretold that the earl would assume the throne* **prophet**, **prophetess**, sibyl, augur, soothsayer, wise man, wise woman, sage, oracle, prognosticator, prophesier, forecaster of the future, diviner, fortune teller, crystal-gazer, clairvoyant, psychic, spiritualist, medium; *Scottish* spaeman, spaewife; *rare* haruspex, vaticinator, oracler.

see-saw ▶ verb *the market see-sawed as rumours spread* **fluctuate**, swing, go from one extreme to the other, go up and down, rise and fall, oscillate, alternate, yo-yo, teeter, be unstable, be unsteady, vary, shift, sway, ebb and flow.

seethe ▶ verb **1** *the brew foamed and seethed* **boil**, bubble, simmer, foam, froth, rise, ferment, fizz, effervesce.
2 *the shallow water seethed with creatures* **teem**, swarm, boil, bubble, foam, ferment, swirl, convulse, churn, whirl, surge.
3 *I was still seething at the injustice of it* **be angry**, be furious, be enraged, be incensed, be infuriated, be beside oneself, have lost one's temper, have/throw a fit, boil, simmer, be boiling over, chafe, rage, be in a rage, rant, rave, rant and rave, storm, fume, smoulder, spit, breathe fire, burn; *informal* be livid, be wild, jump up and down, froth/foam at the mouth, be steamed up, be hot under the collar, have steam coming out of one's ears; *Brit. informal* do one's head/nut in, throw a wobbly.

see-through ▶ adjective *a see-through plastic map pouch | a dress with see-through sleeves* **transparent**, translucent, clear, limpid, crystal clear, crystalline, pellucid, glassy; thin, light, lightweight, flimsy, sheer, diaphanous, filmy, gossamer, gossamer-like, gossamer-thin, chiffony, cobwebby, gauzy, gauze-like, ultra-fine.
OPPOSITES opaque, substantial.

segment ▶ noun (stress on the first syllable) **1** *arrange the orange segments on top of the filling* **piece**, part, bit, section, chunk, division, portion, slice, fragment, component, wedge, lump, slab, hunk, parcel, tranche; *Brit. informal* wodge.
OPPOSITE whole.
2 *economic growth would bring benefits to all segments of society* **subdivision**, division, fraction, part, portion, section, constituent, element, unit, module, ingredient, slice, department, compartment, sector; branch, wing.
OPPOSITE whole.
▶ verb (stress on the second syllable) *they plan to segment the company's 22% market share into four sections* **divide**, divide up, subdivide, separate, split, split up, cut up, carve up, slice up, break up, dismember; sever, segregate, divorce, partition, section, compartment; **share out**, portion out, distribute.
OPPOSITE amalgamate.

segregate ▶ verb *he campaigns for routes which segregate cycles from motor vehicles* **separate**, set apart, keep apart, sort out; isolate, quarantine, insulate, exclude, closet, protect, shield, partition; **divide**, detach, disconnect, sever, divorce, dissociate, cut off; sequester.
OPPOSITE amalgamate.

segregation ▶ noun *they recommend the full segregation of vehicles and pedestrians in the town centre* **separation**, setting apart, keeping apart, sorting out; isolation, quarantine, insulation, exclusion, closeting, protection, shielding, partitioning; **division**, detachment, disconnection, dissociation; sequestration, partition; (*in S. Africa, historical*) apartheid.
OPPOSITE integration.

seize ▶ verb **1** *a protester broke through the security cordon and seized the*

S

microphone **grab**, grasp, snatch, seize hold of, grab hold of, take hold of, lay hold of, lay (one's) hands on, get one's hands on, take a grip of, grip, clutch, take, pluck.
OPPOSITE let go of.
2 *army rebels seized an air force base* **capture**, take, overrun, annex, occupy, take possession of, conquer, take over, subjugate, subject, colonize.
OPPOSITES relinquish, retreat from; liberate.
3 *the drugs were seized by customs officers at Kennedy Airport* **confiscate**, impound, commandeer, requisition, appropriate, expropriate, take possession of, sequester, sequestrate, take away, take over, take; *Law* distrain, attach, disseize; *Scottish Law* poind.
OPPOSITE release.
4 *terrorists have seized his wife and children* **kidnap**, abduct, take captive, take prisoner, take hostage, hold to ransom; hijack; *informal* snatch; *Brit. informal* nobble, nab.
OPPOSITES release, ransom.
□ **seize on** *governments have seized on recycling as the best way to reduce rubbish* **grasp**, grasp with both hands, grab (at), leap at, snatch, jump at, pounce on, exploit.
OPPOSITES overlook, fail to take advantage of.

seizure ▶ **noun 1** *Napoleon's seizure of Spain* **capture**, occupation, takeover, overrunning, annexation, annexing, invasion, conquering, subjugation, subjection, colonization.
OPPOSITES restitution; liberation.
2 *the authorities resorted to the seizure of defaulters' property* **confiscation**, impounding, commandeering, requisitioning, appropriation, expropriation, sequestration; *Law* distraint, distrainment, attachment, disseizin; *Scottish Law* poind.
OPPOSITE restitution.
3 *the rumoured seizure of UN observers by guerrillas* **kidnapping**, kidnap, abduction, hostage-taking; hijacking; *informal* snatching; *Brit. informal* nobbling.
OPPOSITES release, ransoming.
4 *the baby suffered a seizure on the plane* **convulsion**, spasm, paroxysm, collapse, sudden illness, attack, fit, bout; stroke, apoplexy; *Medicine* ictus.

WORD LINKS
relating to a seizure **ictal** (*Medicine*)

seldom ▶ **adverb** *he was seldom absent* **rarely**, infrequently, on rare occasions, hardly ever, scarcely ever, hardly, scarcely, almost never, (every) once in a while, only now and then, not often, only occasionally, sporadically; *informal* once in a blue moon.
OPPOSITES often, frequently.

select ▶ **verb** *the important thing is to select the correct tool for the job* **choose**, pick, hand-pick, single out, pick out, sort out, take, opt for, decide on, settle on, set, fix, fix on, adopt, determine, designate, name, nominate, appoint, elect, specify, stipulate, prefer, favour.
▶ **adjective 1** *a small and select group of SAS members* **choice**, hand-picked, carefully chosen, prime, first-rate, first-class, high-grade, grade A, superior, finest, best, high-quality, top-quality, top-class, supreme, superb, excellent, rare, prize, prize-winning, award-winning; *informal* tip-top, A1, top-notch.
OPPOSITES inferior, mediocre.
2 *the concert was a very fashionable occasion with a select audience* **exclusive**, elite, favoured, limited, rarefied, privileged, cliquish, private; *informal* posh.
OPPOSITE common.

selection ▶ **noun 1** *Jed had made his selection of toys* **choice**, pick, option, preference, election.
2 *we offer a wide selection of dishes* **range**, array, diversity, display, variety, assortment, mixture, line-up, set, repertoire.
3 *the publication of a selection of his poems* **anthology**, assortment, choice, miscellany, medley, pot-pourri, collection, assemblage.

selective ▶ **adjective** *he is very selective in his reading* **discriminating**, discriminatory, discerning, critical, exacting, demanding, particular, hard to please; fussy, fastidious, faddish, careful, cautious; *informal* **choosy**, pernickety, picky; *Brit. informal* faddy; *archaic* nice.
OPPOSITE indiscriminate.

self ▶ **noun** *these whispers come from our inner self* **ego**, I, oneself, persona, person, identity, character, personality, psyche, soul, spirit, mind, intellect, inner man/woman/person, inner self, one's innermost feelings, one's heart of hearts.
OPPOSITE other.

WORD LINKS
related prefixes **auto-** (e.g. ***autobiography, automobile***), **ego-** (e.g. ***egosurfing***)
obsession with oneself **egomania, egotism, egocentrism**
killing oneself **suicide**

self-assembly ▶ **noun** *the artist can buy easel kits for self-assembly* **do-it-yourself**, DIY, self-build.
▶ **adjective** *self-assembly furniture* **flat-pack**, in kit form, kit, do-it-yourself, DIY, self-build.

self-assurance ▶ **noun** *such courses provide them with the training and self-assurance they need* **self-confidence**, confidence, belief in oneself, positiveness, assertiveness, assurance, self-reliance, self-possession, composure, nerve, poise, presence, aplomb.
OPPOSITES diffidence, unsureness.

self-assured ▶ **adjective** *a stubborn and self-assured lady* **self-confident**, confident, believing in oneself, positive, assertive, assured, authoritative, commanding, self-reliant, self-possessed, composed, poised.
OPPOSITES diffident, unsure.

self-centred ▶ **adjective** *your father's too self-centred to care what you do* **egocentric**, egotistic, egotistical, egomaniacal, self-regarding, self-absorbed, self-obsessed, self-seeking, self-interested, self-serving, wrapped up in oneself, inward-looking, introverted, selfish, self-loving, narcissistic, vain; **inconsiderate**, thoughtless, unthinking, uncaring, uncharitable, unkind; *informal* looking after number one.
OPPOSITE considerate.

self-confidence ▶ **noun** *she took care to build up his self-confidence by involving him in the planning* **morale**, confidence, self-assurance, belief in oneself, positiveness, assertiveness, assurance, self-reliance, self-possession, composure, nerve, poise, presence, aplomb.
OPPOSITES diffidence, unsureness.

self-confident ▶ **adjective** *they were now the self-confident, responsible young ladies they had been trained to be* **self-assured**, confident, believing in oneself, positive, assertive, assured, authoritative, commanding, self-reliant, self-possessed, composed, poised.
OPPOSITES diffident, unsure.

self-conscious ▶ **adjective** *he gave me a self-conscious grin* **embarrassed**, uncomfortable, ill at ease, uneasy, nervous, tense, edgy; unnatural, inhibited, gauche, awkward, strained; modest, shy, diffident, bashful, blushing, timorous, timid, retiring, shrinking.
OPPOSITES confident, natural.

self-contained ▶ **adjective 1** *each train was a self-contained unit* **complete**, independent, separate, free-standing, enclosed.
OPPOSITE linked.
2 *a very self-contained child* **independent**, standing on one's own two feet, self-sufficient, self-reliant, introverted, undemonstrative, quiet, private, aloof, insular, reserved, unemotional, uncommunicative, reticent, secretive.
OPPOSITES dependent; forthcoming, outgoing.

self-control ▶ **noun** *he had recovered his self-control* **self-discipline**, self-restraint, restraint, control, self-mastery, self-possession, will power, strength of will, composure, coolness; moderation, temperateness, temperance, abstemiousness, abstention, non-indulgence; *informal* cool; *rare* countenance.
OPPOSITES loss of control, indiscipline.

self-denial ▶ **noun** *a farm built up over the years by hard work and self-denial* **self-sacrifice**, selflessness, unselfishness, altruism, self-discipline, asceticism, abnegation, self-abnegation, self-deprivation, abstemiousness, abstinence; moderation, austerity, temperance, abstention, renunciation; celibacy, chastity; teetotalism; *rare* continence.
OPPOSITE self-indulgence.

self-discipline ▶ **noun** *his observance of his diet was a show of tremendous self-discipline* **self-control**, self-mastery, control; restraint, self-restraint; will power, strength of will, firmness, firmness of purpose, purposefulness, strong-mindedness, resolution, resolve, moral fibre; doggedness, persistence, determination, tenacity; *informal* grit.

self-employed ▶ **adjective** *a self-employed painter and decorator* **freelance**, independent, one's own boss, working for oneself, casual; consultant, consulting; temporary, part-time, jobbing, visiting, non-resident, outside, external, extramural, peripatetic.
OPPOSITES staff, in-house, employed.

self-esteem ▶ **noun** *assertiveness training for those with low self-esteem* **self-respect**, self-regard, pride in oneself/one's abilities, faith in oneself, pride, dignity, morale, self-confidence, confidence, self-assurance, assurance; *French* amour propre.
OPPOSITES lack of self-confidence, self-deprecation.

self-evident ▶ **adjective** *the reason for this is self-evident* **obvious**, clear, plain, evident, apparent, manifest, patent; distinct, definite, transparent, overt, discernible, visible, conspicuous, palpable, glaringly obvious, undisguised, unconcealed, unmistakable, unequivocal, unquestionable, undeniable.
OPPOSITE unclear.

self-explanatory ▶ **adjective** *this paragraph is largely self-explanatory* **easily understood**, readily comprehensible, intelligible, straightforward, unambiguous, unproblematic, accessible, clearly expressed, user-friendly, simple, self-evident, obvious, clear, crystal clear.
OPPOSITE impenetrable.

self-governing ▶ **adjective** *Singapore became a self-governing state in 1959* **independent**, sovereign, autonomous, non-aligned, free; self-legislating, self-determining.

S

OPPOSITES dependent, subservient.

self-government ▶ noun *Senegal achieved self-government in 1958* **independence**, self-rule, home rule, self-legislation, self-determination, sovereignty, autonomy, non-alignment, freedom.
OPPOSITES hegemony, colonialism.

self-important ▶ adjective *he was given the nickname Colonel because he was so self-important* **conceited**, arrogant, bumptious, self-assertive, full of oneself, puffed up, swollen-headed, pompous, overbearing, (self-)opinionated, cocky, swaggering, strutting, presumptuous, forward, imperious, domineering, magisterial, pontifical, sententious, grandiose, vain, haughty, overweening, proud, egotistic, egotistical; supercilious, condescending, patronizing; *informal* snooty, uppity, uppish.
OPPOSITE humble.

self-indulgence ▶ noun *there is also the chance for some self-indulgence, such as taking breakfast in bed* **hedonism**, indulgence, pursuit of pleasure, pleasure-seeking, luxury, lotus-eating, epicureanism, self-gratification; lack of self-restraint, intemperance, intemperateness, immoderation, overindulgence, excess, extravagance, the high life, high living, licence, licentiousness, sensualism, voluptuousness, dissipation, dissoluteness, decadence; *rare* sybaritism.
OPPOSITES abstemiousness, restraint.

self-indulgent ▶ adjective *it was regarded as an ailment contracted by women who led an idle, self-indulgent life* **pleasure-seeking**, **hedonistic**, sybaritic, indulgent, luxurious, lotus-eating, epicurean; unrestrained, intemperate, immoderate, overindulgent, excessive, extravagant, licentious, sensual, voluptuous, dissipated, dissolute, decadent.
OPPOSITES abstemious, restrained.

self-interest ▶ noun *laissez-faire is an economic system based on individualism and self-interest* **self-seeking**, self-serving, self-obsession, self-absorption, self-regard, egocentrism, egotism, egomania, introversion, selfishness; **lack of consideration**, inconsiderateness, thoughtlessness, unthinkingness; *informal* looking after number one.
OPPOSITES altruism; generosity

self-interested ▶ adjective *it is necessary for people to think and act not simply as self-interested individuals* **self-seeking**, self-serving, self-obsessed, self-absorbed, self-regarding, wrapped up in oneself, egocentric, egotistic, egotistical, egomaniacal, inward-looking, introverted, selfish; **inconsiderate**, thoughtless, unthinking, uncaring; *informal* looking after number one.
OPPOSITES altruistic, considerate; generous.

selfish ▶ adjective *he is just selfish by nature* **egocentric**, egotistic, egotistical, egomaniacal, self-centred, self-regarding, self-absorbed, self-obsessed, self-seeking, self-serving, wrapped up in oneself, inward-looking, introverted, self-loving; **inconsiderate**, thoughtless, unthinking, uncaring, heedless, unmindful, regardless, insensitive, tactless, uncharitable, unkind; mean, miserly, grasping, greedy, mercenary, money-grubbing, acquisitive, opportunistic, out for what one can get; *informal* looking after number one, on the make.
OPPOSITES unselfish, selfless, altruistic, considerate, generous.

selfishness ▶ noun *selfishness is one of the biggest problems in marriages* **egocentrism**, egotism, egomania, introversion, self-seeking, self-serving, self-obsession, self-absorption, self-regard, self-interest, self-love; **lack of consideration**, inconsiderateness, thoughtlessness, unthinkingness, heedlessness, regardlessness, insensitivity, insensitiveness, tactlessness, uncharitableness, unkindness; **meanness**, miserliness, greed, acquisitiveness, opportunism; *informal* looking after number one.
OPPOSITES unselfishness, altruism; generosity.

selfless ▶ adjective *an act of selfless devotion* **unselfish**, altruistic, self-sacrificing, self-denying; **considerate**, compassionate, kind, decent, noble, public-spirited; **generous**, magnanimous, ungrudging, unstinting, charitable, benevolent, liberal, open-handed, philanthropic.
OPPOSITES selfish, egoistic, inconsiderate, mean.

self-possessed ▶ adjective *a girl who has been shy or awkward can become quite self-possessed as she cares for her new baby* **assured**, self-assured, calm, cool, {cool, calm, and collected}, composed, at ease, tranquil, serene, unperturbed, unruffled, impassive, nonchalant, confident, self-confident, sure of oneself, poised, dignified, equable, imperturbable, suave, urbane, elegant; *informal* together, unfazed, unflappable; *rare* equanimous.
OPPOSITES unsure, nervous.

self-possession ▶ noun *she had recovered her usual self-possession* **composure**, assurance, self-assurance, self-control, calmness, coolness, cool head; ease, tranquillity, serenity, imperturbability, impassivity, equanimity, nonchalance, confidence, self-confidence, sureness, poise, dignity, aplomb, presence of mind, nerve, sangfroid, countenance, collectedness, suaveness, urbanity, elegance; *informal* cool, unflappability.
OPPOSITE nervousness.

self-reliance ▶ noun *a commitment to greater European self-reliance in defence matters* **self-sufficiency**, self-support, self-sustenance, self-standing, independence; *rare* autarky.
OPPOSITE dependence.

self-reliant ▶ adjective *ineligible for social security, they have to be entirely self-reliant* **self-sufficient**, self-supporting, self-sustaining, self-standing, able to stand on one's own two feet, living on one's hump; self-contained, independent, self-made; *rare* autarkic, autarkical.
OPPOSITE dependent.

self-respect ▶ noun *she lost her self-respect when her husband was attracted to her colleague* **self-esteem**, self-regard, pride in oneself/one's abilities, faith in oneself, pride, dignity, morale, self-confidence, confidence, self-assurance, assurance; *French* amour propre.
OPPOSITE self-deprecation.

self-restraint ▶ noun *with great self-restraint, he did not grab the rod from his friend's hand* **self-control**, restraint, control, self-discipline, self-mastery, self-possession, will power, strength of will, moderation, temperateness, temperance, abstemiousness, abstention, non-indulgence; *informal* cool; *rare* countenance.
OPPOSITE self-indulgence.

self-righteous ▶ adjective *you're too self-righteous to see your own frailties* **sanctimonious**, holier-than-thou, self-satisfied, smug, priggish, complacent, too good to be true, pious, pietistic, moralizing, unctuous, superior, mealy-mouthed, hypocritical; *informal* goody-goody; *rare* Pharisaic, Pharisaical, Tartuffian.
OPPOSITE humble.

self-righteousness ▶ noun *his diary records the incident in a tone of self-righteousness* **sanctimoniousness**, sanctimony, self-satisfaction, smugness, superiority, priggishness, complacency, piety, unctuousness, hypocrisy; *rare* pietism, Pharisaism, Tartufferie.
OPPOSITE humility.

self-sacrifice ▶ noun *self-sacrifice involved giving up her fine mansion and living in cheap lodgings* **self-denial**, selflessness, unselfishness, altruism, self-discipline, asceticism, abnegation, self-abnegation, self-deprivation, abstemiousness, abstinence, moderation, austerity, temperance, abstention, renunciation; celibacy, chastity, teetotalism; *rare* continence.

self-satisfaction ▶ noun *the cosy self-satisfaction of the educated classes* **complacency**, self-congratulation, smugness, superiority, self-approval, self-approbation.
OPPOSITE humility.

self-satisfied ▶ adjective *Janice climbed into the Mercedes and looked around her with a self-satisfied smile* **complacent**, self-congratulatory, smug, superior, puffed up, pleased with oneself, self-approving, well pleased, proud of oneself; *informal* goody-goody, I'm-all-right-Jack; *Brit. informal* like the cat that's got the cream; *N. Amer. informal* wisenheimer; *N. Amer. vulgar slang* shit-eating.
OPPOSITE humble.

self-seeking ▶ adjective *Duncan was far from being a self-seeking assassin* **self-interested**, self-serving, self-obsessed, self-absorbed, self-regarding, wrapped up in oneself, egocentric, egotistic, egotistical, egomaniacal, inward-looking, introverted, selfish; **inconsiderate**, thoughtless, unthinking, uncaring; *informal* looking after number one.
OPPOSITE altruistic.

self-styled ▶ adjective *the self-styled 'General' is in fact the biggest obstacle to peace in the region* **would-be**, **self-appointed**, so-called, self-titled, professed, self-confessed, confessed, sworn, avowed; *French* soi-disant; *rare* self-named.

self-sufficiency ▶ noun *the drought undermined the country's self-sufficiency in rice* **independence**, self-reliance, self-support, self-sustenance, self-standing; *rare* autarky.
OPPOSITE dependence.

self-sufficient ▶ adjective *the economy became nearly self-sufficient in many foodstuffs* **independent**, self-supporting, self-sustaining, self-reliant, self-standing, able to stand on one's own two feet, living on one's hump; self-contained, self-made; *rare* autarkic, autarkical.
OPPOSITE dependent.

self-supporting ▶ adjective *the remaining one third of Pomeranian farmers had rather larger, self-supporting farms* **self-sufficient**, self-sustaining, self-reliant, self-standing, able to stand on one's own two feet, living on one's hump; self-contained, independent, self-made, autarkic, autarkical.
OPPOSITE dependent.

self-willed ▶ adjective *she was a bossy, self-willed creature* **wilful**, contrary, perverse, uncooperative, wayward, headstrong, stubborn, stubborn as a mule, obstinate, obdurate, pig-headed, mulish, intransigent, recalcitrant, refractory, stiff-necked, intractable, unpersuadable, ungovernable, difficult, disobedient, insubordinate, naughty; *informal* cussed; *Brit. informal* bloody-minded; *archaic* contumacious.
OPPOSITES obedient, easily led.

sell ▶ verb **1** *they are trying to sell their house* **dispose of**, get rid of, vend, auction (off); put up for sale, offer for sale, put on sale; trade, barter, exchange, part-exchange, give in part-exchange.
OPPOSITE buy.
2 *he sells fruit and vegetables* **trade in**, deal in, be in the business of, traffic in, stock, carry, offer for sale, handle, peddle, hawk, retail, market, advertise, promote.

S

3 *the book should sell well* **be bought**, be purchased, go; sell like hot cakes, move, be in demand.
4 *the kit sells for £79.95* **be priced at**, sell at, retail at, go for, be, be found for, be trading at, cost.
5 *the President still has to sell the deal to Congress* **persuade someone to accept**, convince someone of the merits of, talk someone into, bring someone round to, win someone over to, get acceptance for, win approval for, get support for, get across, promote.

□ **sell someone down the river** (*informal*). *See* RIVER.

□ **sell out 1** *the garage had sold out of petrol* **have none left**, be out of stock of, have run out of, have sold all one's ...; *informal* be fresh out of, be cleaned out of.
OPPOSITE have plenty of.
2 *the English edition sold out very quickly* **be bought up**, be depleted, be exhausted.
OPPOSITE flop.
3 *he does not see himself as having sold out* **abandon one's principles**, prostitute oneself, sell one's soul, betray one's cause/ideals, be untrue to oneself, go over to the other side, play false, sacrifice oneself, debase oneself, degrade oneself, demean oneself.

□ **sell someone out** *you sold me out to the cops, didn't you?* **betray**, inform on/against; be disloyal to, be unfaithful to, desert, break one's promise to, double-cross, break faith with, stab in the back; *informal* tell on, sell down the river, blow the whistle on, squeal on, stitch up, peach on, do the dirty on; *Brit. informal* grass on, shop; *N. Amer. informal* rat out, finger, drop a/the dime on; *Austral. informal* pimp on, pool, put someone's pot on.

□ **sell someone short 1** *she is always selling herself short* **undervalue**, underrate, underestimate, disparage, deprecate, belittle; *rare* derogate.
2 *shopkeepers were selling people short* **swindle**, cheat, give short measure to, defraud, fleece; short-change, overcharge.

seller *See centre pages for list of* **Sellers of Goods**
▶ **noun** *sellers of fruit and vegetables* **vendor**, **retailer**, purveyor, shopkeeper, supplier, stockist, trader, merchant, dealer; salesperson, salesman, saleswoman, sales assistant, assistant, shop assistant, travelling salesperson/salesman/saleswoman, representative, sales representative, agent, negotiator, reseller, auctioneer; *N. Amer.* sales clerk; *informal* counter-jumper, rep, knight of the road; *dated* saleslady, salesgirl, shop boy, shop girl, shopman, pedlar, hawker, traveller, commercial traveller; *archaic* chapman.
OPPOSITE buyer.

selling ▶ **noun 1** *the selling of property* **vending**, selling off, auctioning, trading, trade (in); traffic, trafficking, barter, bartering, exchange, exchanging, part-exchange, part-exchanging.
2 *a career in selling* **salesmanship**, sales, marketing, merchandising, promotion, advertising.

semblance ▶ **noun** *there remained at least a semblance of discipline* **appearance**, outward appearance, approximation, show, air, guise, pretence, facade, front, veneer.

semen ▶ **noun** *the rapist was identified by a semen sample* **sperm**, spermatic fluid, seminal fluid, seed, milt, ejaculate, emission; *technical* spermatozoa; *vulgar slang* come, cum, jism, jissom, jizz; *Brit. vulgar slang* spunk.

WORD LINKS
relating to semen **seminal**

seminal ▶ **adjective 1** *her paper is still considered a seminal work on the subject* **influential**, formative, groundbreaking, pioneering, original, creative, innovative; imaginative, productive, major, important.
OPPOSITES irrelevant, unimportant.
2 *seminal fluid* **spermatic**, sperm, seed; *technical* spermatozoal, spermatozoan.

seminar ▶ **noun 1** *these suggestions were discussed at a seminar attended by education authority officials* **discussion**, symposium, meeting, conference, congress, convention, forum, convocation, colloquy, summit, synod, conclave, consultation.
2 *teaching is usually in the form of seminars* **study group**, workshop, tutorial, lecture, session, class, lesson, period.

seminary ▶ **noun** *he went to a seminary to study for the priesthood* **theological college**, rabbinical college, Talmudical college, academy, training college, training institute, school, high school, conservatory.

send ▶ **verb 1** *she said she'd send me a letter* **dispatch**, post, mail, put in the post/mail, address, get off, convey, consign, direct, forward, redirect, send on, remit, airmail.
OPPOSITE receive.
2 *they sent a message to headquarters* **transmit**, convey, communicate; telephone, phone, broadcast, televise, telecast, radio, fax, email, upload, ISDN, FTP; *dated* telegraph, wire, cable.
OPPOSITE receive.
3 *we have sent for a doctor* **call**, call for, call in, summon, ask to come, request, request the presence/attendance of, order, contact, fetch.
4 *I squeezed the plastic bottle and sent a jet of petrol out of it* **propel**, project, send forth, eject, deliver, discharge, spout, fire, shoot, blast, catapult, launch, release, force, push, impel, ram; throw, fling, toss, lob, hurl, shy, cast, let fly; *informal* chuck, sling, bung.
5 *the empty barrels send off evil-smelling fumes* **emit**, give off, discharge, exude, send out, send forth, eject, release, leak.
6 *it's enough to send one mad* **make**, drive, cause to be/become.
7 (*informal*) *it's the spectacle and music that send us, not the words* **excite**, stimulate, move, rouse, stir, thrill, electrify, intoxicate, enrapture, enthral, grip, ravish, charm, delight, give pleasure to, titillate; *informal* turn on, blow away, give someone a buzz/kick, stoke.

□ **send someone down 1** (*Brit.*) *she was sent down from Cambridge* **expel**, exclude; *Brit.* rusticate.
OPPOSITES admit; readmit.
2 *he pleaded guilty and was sent down for life* **send to prison**, sentence to imprisonment, imprison, jail, incarcerate, lock up, confine, detain, intern, immure; *informal* put away; *Brit. informal* bang up.
OPPOSITES release; let off.

□ **send someone off** (*Sport*) *Miller was sent off for a second bookable offence* **order off**, tell to leave the field, dismiss; show someone the red card; *informal* red-card, send for an early bath, give someone their marching orders, sin-bin.

□ **send someone/something up** (*informal*) *we used to send him up something rotten* **satirize**, **ridicule**, make fun of, parody, lampoon, mock, caricature, imitate, ape; *informal* take off, spoof, take the mickey out of; *archaic* monkey; *Brit. vulgar slang* take the piss out of.

send-off ▶ **noun** *she was given a rousing send-off at her retirement party* **farewell**, goodbye, adieu, leave-taking, valediction, going-away party; funeral; *Latin* vale.
OPPOSITE welcome.

send-up ▶ **noun** *a good-natured French send-up of the Hollywood private-eye film* **satire**, burlesque, lampoon, pastiche, caricature, take-off, skit, squib, imitation, impression, impersonation, mockery, mimicry, travesty; *informal* spoof, mickey-take; *W. Indian informal* pappyshow; *Brit. vulgar slang* piss-take; *rare* pasquinade, pasticcio.

senile ▶ **adjective** *she couldn't cope with her senile husband* **doddering**, doddery, decrepit, aged, long in the tooth, senescent, failing, declining, infirm, feeble, unsteady, in one's dotage, losing one's faculties, in one's second childhood, mentally confused, suffering from Alzheimer's (disease), suffering from senile dementia; *informal* past it, gaga, soft in the head; *rare* anile.
OPPOSITE in the prime of life.

senility ▶ **noun** *he was declared unfit for office on grounds of senility* **decrepitude**, infirmity, feebleness, unsteadiness, senescence, decline, old age, dotage, second childhood, confusion, Alzheimer's (disease), senile dementia; *informal* softening of the brain; *rare* caducity, anility.
OPPOSITE the prime of life.

senior ▶ **adjective 1** *senior school pupils* **older**, elder; more grown up.
OPPOSITES junior, younger.
2 *you mustn't say that to a senior officer* **higher-ranking**, highest-ranking, high-ranking, superior, top, chief, more/most important; *N. Amer.* ranking.
OPPOSITES junior, subordinate.
3 *Albert Saul Senior* **the Elder**; *Brit.* major; *N. Amer.* I, (the First).

senior citizen ▶ **noun** *a Christmas treat for the senior citizens of the village* **retired person**, (old-age) pensioner, OAP; old person, elderly person, elder, geriatric, old fogey, dotard, Methuselah, patriarch; *N. Amer.* senior, retiree, golden ager; *informal* old stager, old-timer, oldie, ancient, wrinkly, crock, crumbly; *Brit. informal* buffer, josser; *N. Amer. informal* oldster, woopie; *literary* senex; *rare* retirer, pensionary.

seniority ▶ **noun** *the Chief Clerk was next in seniority* **rank**, standing, primacy, superiority, precedence, priority, longer service, age; greater age, higher rank.

sensation ▶ **noun 1** *excessive pressure on the eyeball causes a sensation of light* **feeling**, sense, awareness, consciousness, perception, impression, tickle, tingle, prickle.
2 *I caused something of a sensation by announcing that this boat would cost £1m* **commotion**, stir, uproar, furore, outrage, scandal, impact; interest, excitement, agitation; *informal* splash, to-do, hullabaloo.
3 *the new cars were a sensation when they first appeared* **great success**, sell-out, triumph, star attraction, talking point; *informal* smash, smash hit, hit, box-office hit, show-stopper, winner, crowd-puller, wow, knockout, biggie.

sensational ▶ **adjective 1** *a sensational murder trial* **amazing**, startling, astonishing, staggering, shocking, appalling, horrifying, scandalous; stirring, exciting, thrilling, electrifying; fascinating, interesting, notable, noteworthy, important, significant, remarkable, momentous, historic, newsworthy.
OPPOSITE run-of-the-mill.
2 *the newspapers ran sensational stories about kids indulging in drugs* **overdramatized**, dramatic, melodramatic, exaggerated, sensationalist, sensationalistic, graphic, explicit, unrestrained, lurid; rubbishy, trashy, cheap, tasteless, kitschy, yellow, pulp, garish, full-frontal; *informal* shock-horror, tacky, juicy; *N. Amer. informal* whiz-bang.
OPPOSITES dull, understated.

S

3 (informal) *she looked sensational in her new evening dress* **gorgeous**, stunning, wonderful, exquisite, lovely, magnificent, dazzling, radiant, delightful, charming, enchanting, entrancing, captivating, bewitching; **striking**, spectacular, remarkable, outstanding, impressive, memorable, unforgettable, unique, arresting, eye-catching; marvellous, superb, excellent, exceptional, fine, superlative, formidable, first-class, first-rate, virtuoso, skilful, masterful, masterly; informal great, terrific, tremendous, super, smashing, fantastic, stupendous, fabulous, fab, heavenly, divine, drop-dead gorgeous, knockout, delectable, scrumptious, ace, A1, mean, awesome, magic, bad, wicked, out of this world, unreal; Brit. informal brilliant, brill; N. Amer. informal neat, babelicious, bodacious; Austral. informal bonzer; Brit. informal, dated wizard, spiffing, ripping, topping, champion, capital, top-hole; N. Amer. informal, dated swell, keen; vulgar slang shit-hot.
OPPOSITES ordinary, unremarkable.

sense ▶ noun **1** *the sense of touch* **sensory faculty**, feeling, sensation, perception; sight, hearing, touch, taste, smell, sixth sense; Zoology, dated sensibility.
2 *she felt a sense of guilt* **awareness**, **feeling**, sensation, consciousness, perception, recognition.
3 *a sense of humour* **appreciation**, awareness, understanding, comprehension, discernment, acknowledgement.
4 *the driver had the sense to press the panic button* **wisdom**, **common sense**, good sense, practicality, sagacity, sharpness, discernment, perception; native wit, mother wit, wit, level-headedness, intelligence, cleverness, astuteness, shrewdness, judgement, soundness of judgement, understanding, reason, logic, brain, brains; informal gumption, nous, horse sense, savvy; Brit. informal loaf, common; N. Amer. informal smarts.
OPPOSITES stupidity, mindlessness.
5 *I can't see the sense in leaving all the work to you* **purpose**, point, reason, aim, object, motive, use, utility, value, advantage, benefit.
6 *here there are two different senses of 'exist'* **meaning**, definition, import, denotation, signification, significance, purport, implication, intention, nuance, drift, gist, thrust, tenor, burden, theme, message, essence, spirit, substance.
▶ verb *she could sense their hostility to her | he sensed that disaster was imminent* **discern**, feel, observe, notice, get the impression of, recognize, pick up, be/become cognizant of, be/become aware of, be/become conscious of, get/come to know, tell, distinguish, make out, find, identify, comprehend, apprehend, see, discover, learn, appreciate, realize, suspect, have a funny feeling, have a hunch, just know, divine, intuit, conceive; informal catch on to; Brit. informal twig; rare cognize.

senseless ▶ adjective **1** *he was punched and kicked senseless by a gang of thugs* **unconscious**, out cold, out, cold, stunned, numb, numbed, insensible, insensate, comatose, knocked out, out for the count; informal KO'd, kayoed, laid out, dead to the world, out like a light; Brit. informal spark out; rare soporose, soporous.
OPPOSITES conscious, aware.
2 *a senseless waste of life* **pointless**, **futile**, hopeless, fruitless, useless, needless, wasted, in vain, unavailing, aimless, idle, to no purpose, purposeless, worthless, meaningless, valueless, unproductive, unprofitable; **absurd**, foolish, mad, insane, asinine, moronic, imbecilic, nonsensical, stupid, idiotic, silly, irrelevant, footling, fatuous, hollow, inane, ridiculous, ludicrous, mindless, unintelligent, unwise, irrational, illogical; informal daft.
OPPOSITES sensible, wise.

sensibility ▶ noun **1** *the study of literature leads to a growth of intelligence and sensibility* **sensitivity**, sensitiveness, finer feelings, delicacy, subtlety, taste, discrimination, discernment; understanding, insight, empathy, appreciation, awareness of the feelings of others; feeling, intuition, intuitiveness, responsiveness, receptivity, receptiveness, perceptiveness, awareness.
2 (**sensibilities**) *the wording was changed because it might offend people's sensibilities* **feelings**, emotions, finer feelings, delicate sensitivity, sensitivities, susceptibilities, moral sense, sense of outrage.

sensible ▶ adjective *isn't this the sensible thing to do? | she's a very sensible person* **practical**, realistic, responsible, full of common sense, reasonable, rational, logical, sound, circumspect, balanced, sober, no-nonsense, pragmatic, level-headed, serious-minded, thoughtful, commonsensical, down-to-earth, wise, prudent, mature; judicious, sagacious, sharp, shrewd, far-sighted, intelligent, clever.
OPPOSITE foolish.

sensitive ▶ adjective **1** *as people get older, their bodies often grow less sensitive to changes in external temperature* **responsive to**, quick to respond to, sensitized to, reactive to, sentient of; aware of, conscious of, alive to; susceptible to, easily affected by, vulnerable to; attuned to, tuned in to; rare susceptive of.
OPPOSITES unresponsive, impervious, insensitive.
2 *don't use facial scrubs if your skin is sensitive | his innocent words touched sensitive spots within her own heart* **delicate**, easily damaged, fragile; tender, sore, painful, raw.
OPPOSITES resilient, tough.
3 *these matters will need sensitive handling by the social services | a poignant, sensitive movie* **tactful**, careful, thoughtful, diplomatic, delicate, subtle, finely tuned, kid-glove; **sympathetic**, compassionate, understanding, empathetic, intuitive, feeling, responsive, receptive; perceptive, discerning, acute, insightful.
OPPOSITES insensitive, clumsy, like bull in a china shop.
4 *I didn't realize he was so sensitive | her father was sensitive about his bald patch* **easily offended**, easily upset, easily hurt, thin-skinned, touchy, oversensitive, hypersensitive, defensive; emotional, volatile, temperamental; paranoid, neurotic; informal twitchy, uptight; rare umbrageous.
OPPOSITE thick-skinned.
5 *a politically sensitive issue* **difficult**, delicate, tricky, awkward, problematic, ticklish, precarious; controversial, emotive; informal sticky.
OPPOSITE uncontroversial.

sensitivity ▶ noun **1** *many commonly prescribed drugs increase the sensitivity of the skin to ultraviolet light* **responsiveness**, sensitiveness, reactivity; susceptibility, vulnerability; rare reactiveness, susceptivity, susceptibleness.
OPPOSITE imperviousness.
2 *introducing change calls for patience and sensitivity* **consideration**, care, thoughtfulness, tact, diplomacy, delicacy, subtlety, finesse, finer feelings; understanding, empathy, awareness of the feelings of others, sensibility, feeling, intuition, intuitiveness, responsiveness, receptivity, receptiveness; perceptiveness, perception, discernment, insight; French savoir faire.
OPPOSITE insensitivity.
3 *Shiona's sensitivity on the subject of boyfriends* **touchiness**, oversensitivity, hypersensitivity, thin skin, defensiveness; informal twitchiness.
4 *the sensitivity of the issue* **delicacy**, trickiness, awkwardness, difficulty, ticklishness.

sensual ▶ adjective **1** *sensual pleasure* **physical**, physically gratifying, carnal, bodily, fleshly, animal; hedonistic, epicurean, sybaritic, voluptuary, Dionysiac; rare appetitive.
OPPOSITES spiritual, mental.
2 *a beautiful, sensual woman | his touch was warm and sensual* **sexually attractive**, sexy, voluptuous, sultry, seductive, passionate; sexually exciting/arousing, erotic, sexual.
OPPOSITES ascetic, frigid, passionless.

sensual or sensuous?

The words **sensual** and **sensuous** are frequently used interchangeably to mean 'gratifying the senses', especially in a sexual sense. Some people maintain a distinction according to which *sensuous* is a more neutral term, meaning 'relating to the senses rather than the intellect', as in *swimming is a beautiful, sensuous experience*, while *sensual* relates to gratification of the senses, especially sexually, as in *a sensual massage*. In practice, however, the connotations are such that it is difficult to distinguish the words in this way.

sensualist ▶ noun **hedonist**, pleasure lover, pleasure seeker, sybarite, voluptuary; epicure, epicurean, gastronome, gastronomist; French bon vivant, bon viveur.
OPPOSITE puritan.

sensuality ▶ noun *her heavy eyelids gave her face an air of sleepy sensuality* **sexiness**, sexual attractiveness, voluptuousness, sultriness, seductiveness, passion; sexuality, eroticism; physicality, carnality.
OPPOSITE asceticism.

sensuous ▶ adjective **1** *big, richly coloured, sensuous canvases | his sensuous love of music* **aesthetically pleasing**, aesthetic, pleasurable, gratifying, rich, sumptuous, luxurious; affective; sensory, sensorial.
2 *her full, sensuous lips* **sexually attractive**, sexy, seductive, voluptuous, luscious, lush.

sensuous or sensual?

See SENSUAL.

sentence ▶ noun **1** *Jones showed no emotion as the judge passed sentence* **judgement**, ruling, pronouncement, decision, determination, decree; verdict; punishment.
2 *her husband is serving a three-year sentence for fraud* **prison term**, prison sentence, jail sentence, penal sentence; life sentence, suspended sentence; informal time, stretch, stint; Brit. informal porridge; N. Amer. informal rap; rhyming slang bird.
▶ verb *the men will be sentenced at a later date | two of the accused were sentenced to death* **pass judgement on**, impose a sentence on, pronounce sentence on, mete out punishment to, punish, convict; condemn, doom.

sententious ▶ adjective *his sententious remarks were unbearable* **moralistic**, moralizing, sanctimonious, self-righteous, pietistic, pious, priggish,

S

Pecksniffian, judgemental, canting; pompous, pontifical, self-important; *Scottish* unco guid; *informal* preachy, preachifying; *Brit. informal* pi.

sentient ▶ adjective *I fail to see any sound moral justification for treating sentient creatures as mere commodities* **feeling**, capable of feeling, living, live; conscious, aware, responsive, reactive.
OPPOSITE insentient.

sentiment ▶ noun **1** *the comments in today's Daily Telegraph echo my own sentiments* **view**, point of view, way of thinking, feeling, attitude, thought, opinion, belief, idea.
2 *overpowered by an intense sentiment of horror, I leapt up* **feeling**, emotion.
3 *many of the appeals rely on treacly sentiment | there's no room for sentiment at the hard edge of professional sport* **sentimentality**, mawkishness, over-sentimentality, emotionalism, overemotionalism, sentimentalism; **emotion**, sensibility, finer feelings, tender feelings, tenderness, softness, soft-heartedness, tender-heartedness; *Brit.* tweeness; *informal* schmaltz, mush, slush, sob stuff, slushiness, sloppiness, slop, goo, corn, corniness, hokum, cheese; *Brit. informal* soppiness; *N. Amer. informal* sappiness, hokeyness.

sentimental ▶ adjective **1** *she felt a sentimental attachment to the place creep over her | I wanted to hold on to one of the vases for sentimental reasons* **nostalgic**, tender, emotional, dewy-eyed, misty-eyed, affectionate, loving.
OPPOSITES dispassionate, practical.
2 *the film is unfocused and sentimental* **mawkish**, over-sentimental, overemotional, cloying, sickly, saccharine, sugary, sugar-coated, syrupy; romantic, hearts-and-flowers, touching, pathetic; *Brit.* twee; *informal* slushy, sloppy, mushy, weepy, tear-jerking, schmaltzy, cutesy, lovey-dovey, gooey, drippy, sloshy, soupy, treacly, cheesy, corny, icky, sick-making, toe-curling; *Brit. informal* soppy; *N. Amer. informal* cornball, sappy, hokey, three-hankie; *trademark* Mills-and-Boon.
OPPOSITES gritty, unsentimental, realistic, hard-headed.
3 *Hannah had always been sentimental about animals* **soft-hearted**, tender-hearted, soft, soft-centred; *informal* soppy.

sentimentality ▶ noun *a romantic fiction of unashamed sentimentality* **mawkishness**, over-sentimentality, sentimentalism, emotionalism, overemotionalism; nostalgia, pathos; romanticism; kitsch; *Brit.* tweeness; *informal* schmaltz, mush, slush, sob stuff, slushiness, sloppiness, slop, corn, corniness, hokum, cheese; *Brit. informal* soppiness; *N. Amer. informal* sappiness, hokeyness.

sentry ▶ noun **guard**, sentinel, lookout, watch, watchman, patrol, picket; *historical* vedette.

separable ▶ adjective *body and soul are not separable* **divisible**, distinguishable, distinct, independent; detachable, removable, severable; *technical* scissile.

separate ▶ adjective **1** *he had kept his personal life quite separate from his job | they went their separate ways* **unconnected**, unrelated, different, discrete, distinct, disparate; detached, divorced, disconnected, independent, autonomous; respective, individual, particular, several.
OPPOSITES interdependent, connected; same.
2 *the infirmary was* ***separate from*** *the main building* **set apart from**, unattached to, not attached to, not joined to, disjoined from; fenced off from, cut off from, segregated from, isolated from, shut off from; free-standing, by itself, alone; self-contained, detached.
OPPOSITES attached, joined.
▶ verb **1** *police were trying to separate two rioting mobs | the twins were separated at birth* **part**, split (up), break up, move apart, divide; *archaic* sunder.
OPPOSITES unite, bring together.
2 *the connectors come in two parts, which can be easily separated* **disconnect**, pull apart, break apart, detach, disengage, uncouple, unyoke, disarticulate, disassemble, disunite, disjoin, disaffiliate; split in two, divide in two, sever; disentangle, unravel.
OPPOSITES join, connect, combine.
3 *the second stage of the rocket failed to separate* **become detached**, become disconnected, come apart, come away, uncouple, break off.
OPPOSITE link up with.
4 *he led Cleo through the kitchen gardens to the wall that separated the two estates* **divide**, partition, lie between, come between, stand between, keep apart; bisect, intersect.
OPPOSITES link, bridge.
5 *the west end of the south aisle was* ***separated off*** **isolate**, partition off, divide off, section off; close off, shut off, cordon off, fence off, curtain off, screen off.
6 *they separated at the airport* **part company**, part, go their separate ways, go different ways, split, split up, say goodbye/farewell/adieu, say one's goodbyes; disperse, disband, scatter.
OPPOSITE meet.
7 *the road separated and ran around both sides of the immense lawn* **fork**, divide, branch, bifurcate, diverge, go in different directions; *rare* divaricate.
OPPOSITES converge, merge.
8 *after her parents separated, she was brought up by her mother* **split up**, break up, part, stop living together, part company, reach a parting of the ways, become estranged; divorce, get divorced, get a divorce.
OPPOSITES get together; marry.
9 *the skins are separated from the juice before fermentation | we need to separate fact from fiction* **isolate**, set apart, put to one side, segregate; sort out, sift out, winnow out, filter out, remove, weed out; distinguish, differentiate, dissociate.
OPPOSITE mix.
10 *individuals who* ***separate themselves from*** *a society of which they have formerly been members* **break away from**, break with, secede from, sever relations with, withdraw from, delink from, leave, quit, split with, dissociate oneself from, disaffiliate oneself from, resign from, pull out of, drop out of, have nothing more to do with, repudiate, reject, desert.
OPPOSITE join.

separated ▶ adjective *his parents are separated* **living separately**, no longer together, apart, living apart, parted; estranged.
OPPOSITE together.

separately ▶ adverb *I'll have to interview you all separately | the passengers will be returning separately* **individually**, one by one, one at a time, singly; **apart**, not together, independently, alone, by oneself, on one's own, personally; *formal* severally.

separation ▶ noun **1** *according to tradition, death represents the separation of the soul from the body | the separation of BT from the Post Office in 1981* **disconnection**, detachment, severance, uncoupling, dissociation, disassociation, disjunction, disunion, disaffiliation, segregation; partition; *literary* sundering; *rare* disseverment.
OPPOSITE unification.
2 *presumably you were the cause of Rachel and Florian's separation* **break-up**, split, split-up, parting, estrangement, parting of the ways, rift, rupture, breach; divorce; legal separation, judicial separation; *Brit. informal* bust-up.
OPPOSITE marriage.
3 *the separation between art and life* **distinction**, difference, differentiation, division, dividing line; polarity; gulf, gap, chasm.
OPPOSITE connection.

September ▶ noun
WORD LINKS
birthstone **sapphire**

septic ▶ adjective *a septic finger | his leg went septic* **infected**, festering, suppurating, pus-filled, putrid, putrefying, putrefactive, purulent, poisoned, diseased; inflamed, angry, red, hot, swollen; *rare* pussy.

sepulchral ▶ adjective *'There's been an accident,' he said in sepulchral tones* **gloomy**, lugubrious, sombre, melancholy, melancholic, sad, sorrowful, mournful, doleful, mirthless, cheerless, joyless, funereal, dismal; *literary* dolorous.
OPPOSITES cheerful, happy.

sepulchre ▶ noun **tomb**, vault, burial place, burial chamber, crypt, catacomb, mausoleum, sarcophagus, pyramid; grave; *Archaeology* mastaba; *rare* undercroft.

sequel ▶ noun **1** *the film was successful enough to inspire a sequel* **follow-up**, continuation.
2 *the immediate sequel was an armed uprising in several cities* **consequence**, result, upshot, outcome, development, issue, end, conclusion, postscript; effect, after-effect, aftermath; *Medicine* sequelae; *informal* pay-off; *archaic* success; *rare* sequent.

sequence ▶ noun **1** *the sequence of events became clear* **succession**, order, course, series, chain, concatenation, train, string, cycle, progression; arrangement, pattern; chronology; flow.
2 *a sequence from his new film* **excerpt**, clip, scene, extract, episode, section, segment.

sequester ▶ verb **1** *he* ***sequestered himself*** *from the world* **isolate oneself**, hide oneself away, shut oneself away, seclude oneself, cut/shut oneself off, set oneself apart, segregate oneself; closet oneself, withdraw oneself, remove oneself, retire.
2 *the government sequestered all his property* **confiscate**, seize, sequestrate, take possession of, take, appropriate, expropriate, impound, commandeer, arrogate; *Law* distrain, attach, disseize; *Scottish Law* poind.

sequestered ▶ adjective *she wondered if she had been unwise to shut herself away in this sequestered spot* **secluded**, cloistered, hidden away, concealed, tucked away, hard to find; **isolated**, out of the way, off the beaten track, remote, cut off; unfrequented, lonely; quiet, private, secret; *archaic* retired.
OPPOSITES busy; central, public.

sequestrate ▶ verb *in November 1956 the property was sequestrated by the Egyptian authorities* **confiscate**, seize, take possession of, take, sequester, appropriate, expropriate, impound, commandeer, arrogate; *Law* distrain, attach, disseize; *Scottish Law* poind.

seraphic ▶ adjective *he listened with an expression of seraphic contentment on his face* **blissful**, beatific, sublime, rapturous, ecstatic, joyful, rapt; **serene**, ethereal; pure, innocent, cherubic, saintly, angelic; celestial, heavenly, holy, divine.
OPPOSITE demonic.

serendipitous ▶ adjective *their diligent efforts were coupled with the joys of serendipitous discovery* **chance**, accidental; **lucky**, fortuitous; unexpected, unanticipated, unforeseen, unlooked-for; coincidental; *informal* fluky.

S

serendipity ▸ noun *technical innovation may be the result of pure serendipity* **chance**, happy chance, accident, happy accident, fluke; **luck**, good luck, good fortune, fortuity, fortuitousness, providence; coincidence, happy coincidence.

serene ▸ adjective **1** *on the surface I might have seemed serene, but underneath I was panicking* **calm**, composed, collected, {cool, calm, and collected}, as cool as a cucumber, tranquil, peaceful, at peace, pacific, untroubled, relaxed, at ease, poised, self-possessed, unperturbed, imperturbable, undisturbed, unruffled, unworried, unexcitable, placid, equable, even-tempered; *N. Amer.* centered; *informal* together, unflappable.
OPPOSITES anxious, nervous, agitated.
2 *Trentino is a labyrinth of deep valleys and serene lakes* **peaceful**, tranquil, quiet, still, restful, relaxing, soothing, undisturbed, untroubled.
OPPOSITES turbulent, noisy.
3 *the serene western sky* **cloudless**, unclouded, clear, bright, sunny.
OPPOSITES cloudy, stormy.

> CHOOSE THE RIGHT WORD
>
> **serene, calm, tranquil, placid, peaceful**
>
> *See* CALM.

serenity ▸ noun **1** *she radiated an air of serenity* **calmness**, calm, composure, tranquillity, peacefulness, peace of mind, peace, peaceableness, collectedness, poise, aplomb, self-possession, sangfroid, imperturbability, equanimity, equableness, ease, placidity, placidness; *informal* togetherness, unflappability; *rare* ataraxy, ataraxia.
OPPOSITES anxiety, agitation.
2 *the garden is an oasis of serenity amidst the bustling city* **peace**, peace and quiet, peacefulness, tranquillity, calm, quiet, quietness, quietude, stillness, restfulness, repose.
OPPOSITE disruption.
3 *the serenity of the sky* **cloudlessness**, clearness, brightness, sunniness.
OPPOSITES cloudiness, storminess.

serf ▸ noun (*historical*) **bondsman**, slave, servant, menial, villein, thrall, helot, ceorl; vassal, liegeman.
OPPOSITES freeman, master.

series ▸ noun **1** *detectives are investigating a series of burglaries in the area | a series of lectures on modern art* **sequence**, succession, string, chain, concatenation, train, run, chapter, round, progression, procession; **spate**, wave, stream, rash, outbreak; set, course, cycle; row, line, bank, battery, arrangement, order.
2 *a new drama series* **set of programmes**, programme, production, serial; situation comedy, soap opera; *informal* sitcom, soap.

serious ▸ adjective **1** *he had a serious expression on his face | Prudence was a thin, pale, serious young woman* **solemn**, earnest, grave, sober, sombre, unsmiling, poker-faced, stern, grim, dour, humourless, stony-faced; **thoughtful**, preoccupied, deep in thought, pensive, meditative, ruminative, contemplative, introspective; staid, sedate, studious, bookish.
OPPOSITES light-hearted, cheerful, jovial.
2 *we have some serious decisions to make* **important**, significant, consequential, of consequence, momentous, of moment, key, grave, weighty, far-reaching, major; urgent, pressing, crucial, critical, vital, life-and-death, high-priority; no joke, no laughing matter.
OPPOSITES trivial, unimportant.
3 *the need to give serious consideration to other methods of dealing with terrorism* **careful**, detailed, in-depth, deep, profound, meaningful.
OPPOSITE superficial.
4 *a serious play about Art and Life* **intellectual**, **highbrow**, heavyweight, deep, profound, literary, learned, scholarly, cultured; classical; *informal* heavy.
OPPOSITES light, lowbrow, populist.
5 *four of the victims received serious injuries | he appealed for emergency foreign aid to combat the serious shortages of foodstuff and medicines* **severe**, grave, bad, critical, acute, alarming, worrying, grievous, dreadful, terrible, dire, extreme, dangerous, perilous, precarious; *archaic or humorous* parlous.
OPPOSITES minor, negligible.
6 *is the government serious about developing decent employment opportunities for women?* **in earnest**, earnest, sincere, wholehearted, genuine, meaning what one says; committed, firm, resolute, resolved, determined.
OPPOSITES uncommitted, half-hearted, flippant.
7 (*informal*) *she spends serious sums of money.* See CONSIDERABLE.

seriously ▸ adverb **1** *Faye nodded seriously, biting her lower lip* **solemnly**, earnestly, gravely, soberly, sombrely, without smiling, with a poker face, sternly, grimly, dourly, humourlessly; thoughtfully, pensively, meditatively, ruminatively, contemplatively.
OPPOSITES cheerfully, jovially.
2 *one woman died and another was seriously injured* **severely**, gravely, badly, critically, acutely, sorely, grievously, desperately, alarmingly, dangerously, perilously.
OPPOSITE slightly.
3 *do you seriously expect me to believe that?* **really**, actually, honestly.
4 *seriously, I'm very pleased that you're staying* **joking aside/apart**, to be serious, honestly, without joking, no joking, truthfully, truly, I mean it; *informal* Scout's honour; *Brit. informal* straight up; *dated* honest Injun.
5 (*informal*) *'I've handed in my notice.' 'Seriously?'* **really?** is that so? is that a fact? you're joking! well I never, well I never did, go on, you don't say; *informal* you're kidding! well knock/blow me down with a feather; *Brit. informal* well I'll be blowed; *N. Amer. informal* well what do you know about that?, *archaic* go to.
6 (*informal*) *he was seriously rich* **extremely**, very, really, dreadfully, terribly, awfully, fearfully, incredibly, amazingly, exceptionally, exceedingly, immensely, uncommonly, remarkably, extraordinarily; *Scottish* unco; *French* très; *informal* terrifically, tremendously, right, ultra, mega, mucho, stinking, majorly, oh-so, madly; *Brit. informal* jolly, ever so, dead, well; *N. Amer. informal* real, mighty, awful, powerful, way, bitching; *S. African informal* lekker; *informal, dated* devilish, frightfully; *archaic* exceeding.

seriousness ▸ noun **1** *in spite of the seriousness of his expression, Rostov was amused* **solemnity**, solemnness, earnestness, graveness, gravity, gravitas, soberness, sobriety, sombreness, sternness, grimness, dourness, humourlessness; **thoughtfulness**, preoccupation, pensiveness.
OPPOSITES cheerfulness, joviality.
2 *I stressed the seriousness of the matter* **importance**, significance, consequence, momentousness, moment, weightiness, weight; urgency, crucialness, vitalness.
OPPOSITES triviality, unimportance.
3 *he tried to play down the seriousness of his injuries* **severity**, severeness, gravity, graveness, acuteness, grievousness, extremity, danger, dangerousness, perilousness.
4 *I doubt his seriousness* **earnestness**, sincerity, wholeheartedness, genuineness; commitment, firmness, resolution, resolve, determination.

sermon ▸ noun **1** *he preached a sermon based on a text from the Book of Wisdom* **homily**, address, speech, talk, discourse, oration; lesson; preaching, teaching; *rare* peroration.
2 *he realized that if he said any more he would have to listen to another lengthy sermon* **lecture**, tirade, harangue, diatribe; speech, disquisition, monologue, declamation, exhortation; reprimand, reproach, reproof, scolding, admonishment, admonition, reproval, remonstration, upbraiding, castigation, lambasting, criticism, censure; *informal* spiel, telling-off, talking-to, rap over the knuckles, dressing-down, earful, roasting, bawling-out, blast, row; *Brit. informal* ticking-off, carpeting, rollicking, wigging; *Brit. vulgar slang* bollocking; *dated* rating.
OPPOSITES commendation, pat on the back.

WORD LINKS
relating to sermons **homiletic**
art of preaching sermons **homiletics**

serpentine ▸ adjective **1** *a narrow, serpentine path wound down through woods of cedar and pine* **winding**, windy, zigzag, zigzagging, twisting, twisty, turning, meandering, curving, sinuous, snaking, snaky, tortuous; *rare* anfractuous, flexuous, meandrous, serpentiform.
OPPOSITE straight.
2 *Labour's serpentine leadership election rules* **complicated**, intricate, complex, involved, tortuous, convoluted, tangled, elaborate, knotty, confusing, bewildering, baffling; inextricable, entangled, impenetrable, Byzantine, Daedalian, Gordian; *rare* involute, involuted.
OPPOSITES straightforward, simple.

serrated ▸ adjective *a ten-inch hunting knife with a serrated blade* **jagged**, sawtoothed, sawtooth, saw-edged, zigzag, notched, indented, toothed; *technical* serrate, serrulate, serrulated, serriform, serratiform, crenulated, crenate, denticulate, denticulated.
OPPOSITES smooth, straight.

serried ▸ adjective *the serried mass of dark conifers | serried ranks of soldiers* **close together**, packed together, close-set, dense, tight, compact; massed, assembled, tiered.
OPPOSITE scattered.

servant ▸ noun **1** *an army of servants were cleaning the hall after the previous night's banquet* **attendant**, retainer; domestic help, domestic worker, domestic, help, cleaner, cleaning woman/lady, helper; lackey, flunkey, minion; maid, housemaid, maidservant, lady's maid, handmaid, parlour maid, scullery maid, serving maid, girl, maid-of-all-work; footman, page, page boy, valet, butler, man, gentleman's gentleman, batman, manservant, houseman, houseboy, boy; housekeeper, steward, major domo; coachman, postilion, equerry; menial, drudge, hireling, slave; *N. Amer.* hired help; *S. African* jong; (*in Spanish-speaking countries*) mozo; *Indian* bearer, chokra, amah, bai; *Brit. dated* charwoman, charlady, char, boots; *Brit. informal* Mrs Mop, daily woman, daily, skivvy; *Brit. university slang* scout, bedder, gyp; *archaic* seneschal, abigail, servitor, scullion, tweeny, servingman, servingwoman, serving wench, turnspit, varlet, vassal, serf; *rare* famulus.
OPPOSITES master, mistress.
2 *he was a great servant of the Labour Party* **helper**, supporter, follower.

serve ▸ verb **1** *they have served their political masters faithfully for the past 40 years* **work for**, be in the service of, perform duties for, be employed by, have a job with; obey, be obedient to, carry out the wishes of.

S

2 *I decided that I wanted to work somewhere where I could serve the community* **be of service to**, be of use to, help, give help to, assist, give assistance to, aid, lend a hand to, give a helping hand to, do a good turn to, make a contribution to, do one's bit for, do something for, benefit; minister to, succour.
3 *altogether she had* **served on** *the committee for 11 years* **be a member of**, work on, be on, sit on, have/hold a place on, perform duties on, carry out duties on.
4 *California is limiting the number of terms a politician can serve in office | Lewis served his apprenticeship in Scotland* **carry out**, perform, do, fulfil, complete, discharge; spend, go through.
5 *serve the soup hot with lots of crusty bread | dinner is served at candlelit tables* **dish up/out**, give out, distribute, set out, plate up, spoon out, ladle out; present, provide, supply, make available.
6 *Elizabeth walked off to serve another customer* **attend to**, give one's attention to, attend to the requirements of, deal with, see to; **assist**, help, look after, take care of.
7 *the landlord's daughter served at table* **act as waiter/waitress**, wait, distribute food/refreshments; *N. Amer. informal* sling hash, sling plates.
8 *they were just about to* **serve** *him* **with** *a writ* **deliver to**, present with, give to, hand over to, cause to accept.
9 *she stabbed the cigarette out in a saucer* **serving as** *an ashtray* **act as**, function as, fulfil the function of, do duty as, do the work of, act as a substitute for.
10 *official forms are obtainable that, with minor adaptation, will serve in all but a few cases* **suffice**, be adequate, be good enough, be all right, fit/fill the bill, do, answer; be useful, serve a purpose, meet requirements, suit.
11 *Cornish householders wonder if they are being fairly served* **treat**, deal with, act towards, behave towards, conduct oneself towards, handle.

service ▶ **noun 1** *there has been an improvement in pay and conditions of service* **work**, employment, employ, labour, performance of one's duties.
2 *he has done us a great service | Josie offered her services as a babysitter* **act of assistance**, good turn, favour, kindness, helping hand; (**services**) **assistance**, help, aid, offices, ministrations.
3 *both the food and the service were excellent* **waiting**, waitressing, waiting at table, serving of food and drink, attendance, serving.
4 *high quality products which will give many years of reliable service* **use**, usage.
5 *he took his car in for a service* **overhaul**, servicing, maintenance check, routine check, check.
6 *he will be cremated tomorrow after a private funeral service | the first words of the marriage service* **ceremony**, ritual, rite, observance, ordinance; liturgy, sacrament, office.
7 *the provision of a wide range of local services | the national telephone service* **amenity**, facility, resource, utility; system.
8 (**the services**) *if you're about to leave the services, the prospect of Civvy Street can be daunting* **armed forces**, armed services, forces, military; army, navy, air force, marines.
□ **be of service** *a close liaison between mathematics and computer science can be of service to an archaeologist* **help**, assist, benefit, be helpful, be of assistance, be beneficial, be advantageous, be of benefit, serve, advantage, be useful, be of use, be profitable, profit, be valuable, be of worth, do someone a good turn.
□ **out of service** *one of the elevators is out of service* **out of order**, not working, not in working order, not functioning, broken, broken-down, out of commission, acting up, unserviceable, faulty, defective, non-functional, inoperative, in disrepair; down; *informal* conked out, bust, (gone) kaput, gone phut, on the blink, gone haywire, shot; *Brit. informal* knackered, jiggered, wonky; *N. Amer. informal* on the fritz, out of whack; *Brit. vulgar slang* buggered.
▶ **verb** *ensure that gas appliances are serviced regularly* **overhaul**, check, check over, go over, give a maintenance check to, maintain, keep in good condition; repair, mend, recondition.

serviceable ▶ **adjective 1** *an ageing but still serviceable water supply system* **in working order**, working, functioning, functional, operational, operative; usable, workable, viable, useful, of use.
OPPOSITES outworn, non-functioning, unusable.
2 *sturdy, serviceable lace-up shoes* **functional**, utilitarian, sensible, practical, non-decorative, plain, unadorned; **hard-wearing**, durable, lasting, long-lasting, tough, strong, robust, wear-resistant.
OPPOSITES decorative, impractical.

servile ▶ **adjective** *his attitude towards Mandeville can only be described as servile* **obsequious**, sycophantic, excessively deferential, subservient, fawning, toadying, ingratiating, unctuous, oily, oleaginous, greasy, grovelling, cringing, toadyish, slavish, abject, craven, humble, Uriah Heepish, self-abasing; *informal* slimy, bootlicking, smarmy, sucky, soapy, forelock-tugging; *N. Amer. informal* brown-nosing, apple-polishing; *Brit. vulgar slang* arse-licking, bum-sucking; *N. Amer. vulgar slang* kiss-ass, ass-kissing.
OPPOSITES bossy, assertive.

servility ▶ **noun** *Lovat was used to servility—he couldn't remember when anyone had last disagreed with him* **obsequiousness**, sycophancy, excessive deference, subservience, submissiveness, fawning, toadyism, toadying, grovelling, cringing, unctuousness, oiliness, abjectness, abjection, cravenness, slavishness, humility, self-abasement; *informal* smarminess, sliminess, bootlicking; *N. Amer. informal* apple-polishing; *Brit. vulgar slang* arse-licking, bum-sucking; *N. Amer. vulgar slang* ass-kissing.
OPPOSITES bossiness, assertiveness.

serving ▶ **noun** *a large serving of spaghetti* **portion**, helping, plateful, platter, plate, bowlful; amount, quantity, ration.

servitude ▶ **noun** *Indian slaves were bought and sold and kept in servitude* **slavery**, enslavement, bondage, subjugation, subjection, domination; *literary* thraldom; *historical* serfdom, vassalage.
OPPOSITES freedom, liberty.

session ▶ **noun 1** *a special session of the OECD Environment Committee* **meeting**, sitting, assembly, conclave, plenary; hearing; conference, discussion, forum, symposium; *Scottish* sederunt, diet; *N. Amer. & NZ* caucus.
2 *I'll arrange some training sessions* **period**, time, spell, stretch, bout.
3 (*informal*) *we had a bit of a session last night* **drinking bout**, binge; *informal* sesh, booze-up, beer-up, liquid lunch, drunk, blind, souse; *Scottish informal* skite; *N. Amer. informal* jag; *Brit. vulgar slang* piss-up; *archaic* fuddle, potation.
4 *the college is recognized by the Government and the next session begins on 1st August* **academic year**, school year; **term**, school term; *N. Amer.* semester, trimester.

set[1] ▶ **verb 1** *Beth set the two bags on the kitchen table* **put**, place, put down, lay, lay down, deposit, position, settle, station; leave, stow, prop, lean, stand, plant, pose, dispose; *informal* stick, dump, bung, park, plonk, plump, pop; *N. Amer. informal* plunk; *rare* posit.
2 (**be set**) *the cottage was set on a hill at the back of the village* **be situated**, be located, lie, stand, be sited, be perched; be found.
3 *the bright red benches were attached to the ground by bolts set in concrete | a huge square cut emerald set in platinum* **fix**, embed, insert; mount.
4 *an enamelled gold figurine set with precious stones* **adorn**, ornament, decorate, embellish, deck, bedeck; *literary* bejewel.
5 *I'll go and set the table* **lay**, prepare, arrange, make ready.
6 *to find out if attitudes really have changed, we set three couples five everyday tasks* **assign**, allocate, give, allot, deal, prescribe.
7 *anyone can lose weight if they set their mind to it* **apply**, address, direct, aim, turn, focus, concentrate.
8 *the government had still not set a date for the election* **decide on**, select, choose, arrange, schedule; fix, fix on, determine, designate, name, appoint, specify, stipulate; settle, resolve on, agree on, confirm.
9 *he spun round in surprise and then he set his horse towards her* **direct**, steer, orientate, point, aim, train.
10 *his time in the 25m freestyle set a national record* **establish**, set up, create, provide, institute.
11 *Mr Crump set his watch by the clock in the hall* **adjust**, regulate, synchronize, coordinate, harmonize; calibrate; put right, correct; *technical* collimate.
12 *have you set the alarm?* **programme**, activate; switch on, turn on.
13 *the adhesive will set hard in about an hour | pour the mixture on top of the jelly and leave it to set* **solidify**, harden, become solid, become hard, stiffen, thicken, gel; cake, congeal, coagulate, clot; freeze, crystallize; *rare* gelatinize.
OPPOSITE melt.
14 *the sun was setting and a warm, red glow filled the sky* **go down**, sink, dip below the horizon; vanish, disappear, subside, decline.
OPPOSITE rise.
□ **set about 1** *Mike set about raising £5000 to pay for the boy's medical treatment | she set about her task with vigour* **begin**, start, make a start on, go about, set to, get to work on, get down to, get going on, embark on, tackle, attack, address oneself to, buckle down to, undertake; put/set the wheels in motion, get down to business, get/set the ball rolling, put one's shoulder to the wheel, put one's hand to the plough, roll up one's sleeves, get things moving; *informal* get cracking, get one's finger out, get weaving; *formal* commence.
2 *he was pushed up against the wall as the youths set about him* **attack**, assail, assault, hit, strike, beat, give someone a beating, thrash, pound, pummel, wallop, hammer, tear into, set upon, fall on, turn on, let fly at; *informal* lay into, lace into, beat the living daylights out of, sail into, pitch into, let someone have it, get stuck into, paste, do over, work over, rough up, knock about/around; *Brit. informal* duff up, have a go at; *N. Amer. informal* beat up on, light into.
□ **set something against something else** *these figures need to be set against the incomes of the other social groups* **compare**, juxtapose, place side by side with; **offset**, set off against; contrast.
OPPOSITE take in isolation.
□ **set someone against someone else** *he wants to set you against me* **alienate from**, estrange from, cause to dislike; drive a wedge between, cause hostility between, sow dissension, set at odds.
OPPOSITE reconcile.
□ **set someone apart distinguish**, differentiate, mark off, mark out, single out, make different, separate, demarcate.
□ **set something apart** *one pew was set apart from the rest* **isolate**, separate, segregate, put to one side.
□ **set something aside 1** *set aside some money each month for emergencies*

save, put by, put aside, put away, lay aside, lay by, put to one side, keep, reserve, keep in reserve; store, stockpile, hoard, stow away, cache, put in a safe place, put down; earmark, withhold, keep for oneself; *N. Amer.* set by; *informal* salt away, squirrel away, stash away, hang on to.
OPPOSITES use, use up, spend.
2 *he set aside his half-empty cup and strode towards the door* **put down**, put to one side, discard, abandon, dispense with, cast aside, drop.
OPPOSITE pick up.
3 *can't you set aside your differences for now?* **disregard**, put aside, put to one side, ignore, forget, discount, shrug off, bury, consign to oblivion.
4 *the Court of Appeal set aside the High Court decision* **overrule**, overturn, reverse, revoke, countermand, rule against, nullify, render null and void, annul, cancel, quash, dismiss, reject, repudiate, abrogate, remit; *Law* vacate, disaffirm; *archaic* recall.
OPPOSITES uphold, confirm.
□ **set something at naught** (*archaic*) *her efforts were set at naught by those around her* **disregard**, dismiss, make light of, belittle, discount, ignore, brush aside, wave aside, play down, take no account of, laugh at, pooh-pooh, treat with contempt, sneer at, scoff at; *N. Amer. informal* slam-dunk.
OPPOSITES value, respect.
□ **set someone back** (*informal*) *that must have set you back a bit!* **cost**; *Brit. informal* knock back.
□ **set someone/something back** *we'll have to re-advertise the position, which will set us back another six months | the growth of American trade unionism was set back by the economic depression* **delay**, hold up, hold back, slow down, slow up, retard, put a brake on, check, decelerate; **hinder**, impede, obstruct, hamper, inhibit, interfere with, frustrate, thwart; *Brit. informal* throw a spanner in the works of; *N. Amer. informal* throw a monkey wrench in the works of; *archaic* stay.
OPPOSITES speed up, expedite.
□ **set something down 1** *that evening, he set down his thoughts* **write down**, put in writing, put down, put down on paper, put in black and white, jot down, note down, make a note of; record, register, log, catalogue, tabulate.
2 *the Association set down a code of practice for all members to comply with* **formulate**, draw up, establish, frame; **lay down**, determine, fix, stipulate, specify, codify, prescribe, impose, ordain.
3 *I set it down to the fact that he'd had no experience with girls* **attribute**, put down, ascribe, assign, chalk up; blame on, impute, lay at the door of.
□ **set forth** *accompanied by a large entourage, she set forth for Framlingham* **set out**, set off, start out, sally forth, begin one's journey, leave, depart, set sail; *archaic* set forward.
OPPOSITE arrive.
□ **set something forth** *the policy paper of March 2 sets forth the core of Labour's programme* **present**, describe, set out, detail, delineate, explain, expound, give an account of, rehearse, catalogue, particularize; state, declare, announce; submit, offer, put forward, advance, propose, propound.
□ **set free** *on 27 June he and other leading Communists were set free* **release**, free, let go, allow to leave, set/let/turn loose, let out, liberate, set at liberty, deliver, emancipate; *literary* disenthral; *historical* manumit.
OPPOSITE imprison.
□ **set in** *the pilot was winched to safety before bad weather set in* **begin**, start, arrive, come, develop, become established, get under way, settle in; *formal* commence.
□ **set something in motion**. See MOTION.
□ **set off** *on the appointed day, we set off for Heathrow* **set out**, start out, set forth, sally forth, begin one's journey, leave, depart, embark, set sail; *informal* hit the road; *archaic* set forward.
OPPOSITE arrive.
□ **set something off 1** *police don't know how the bomb was set off* **detonate**, explode, blow up, touch off, trigger; ignite, light.
OPPOSITE defuse.
2 *the announcement set off a wave of protest* **give rise to**, cause, lead to, set in motion, occasion, bring about, bring on, begin, start, initiate, precipitate, prompt, trigger (off), spark (off), touch off, provoke, incite, stimulate; *formal* commence.
OPPOSITE bring to an end.
3 *a velvet dress in a deep royal blue which set off her auburn hair* **enhance**, bring out, emphasize, show off, throw into relief, point up; complement; heighten, intensify, increase.
OPPOSITE clash with.
□ **set on** *he and his friends were set on by a gang* **attack**, assail, assault, hit, strike, beat, give someone a beating, thrash, pound, pummel, wallop, hammer, tear into, set about, set upon, fall on, turn on, let fly at; *informal* lay into, lace into, beat the living daylights out of, sail into, pitch into, let someone have it, get stuck into, paste, do over, work over, rough up, knock about/around; *Brit. informal* duff up, have a go at; *N. Amer. informal* beat up on, light into.
□ **set one's heart on** *Marilyn had set her heart on white satin and four bridesmaids* **want desperately**, wish for, desire, long for, yearn for, be consumed with desire for, hanker after/for, ache for, hunger for, thirst for, lust after/for, sigh for, burn for, itch for, be dying for, die for.
□ **set out 1** *he set out early next morning* **start**, make a start, start out, set off, set forth, begin one's journey; depart, leave, get under way, sally forth, embark, set sail; *informal* hit the road; *archaic* set forward.
OPPOSITE arrive.
2 *well, you've achieved what you set out to achieve* **aim**, intend, mean, seek, have in mind; hope, aspire, want; set one's sights on.
□ **set something out 1** *the gifts were set out on trestle tables* **arrange**, lay out, spread out, array, dispose, present, put out; display, exhibit.
2 *they set out a series of guidelines* **present**, describe, set forth, detail; **explain**, expound, delineate; state, declare, announce; submit, offer, put forward, advance, propose, propound.
□ **set someone up 1** *his father set him up in business* **establish**; finance, fund, back, subsidize.
2 *after my operation the doctor recommended a cruise to set me up again* **restore to health**, make better, make stronger, strengthen, build up, invigorate, energize, fortify; rehabilitate.
3 (*informal*) *suppose Lorton had set him up for Newley's murder?* **falsely incriminate**, frame, fabricate evidence against, trap, entrap; *Brit. informal* fit up.
□ **set something up 1** *a monument to her memory was set up in Gloucester Cathedral* **erect**, put up, construct, build, raise, elevate; **place**, put (in position).
2 *she set up the business with a £4,000 bank loan* **establish**, start, begin, get going, initiate, institute, found, create, bring into being, inaugurate, lay the foundations of.
3 *I'll ask my secretary to set up a meeting with him* **arrange**, organize, fix, fix up, fix a time for, schedule, timetable, sort out, line up.

set[2] ▶ **noun 1** *an envelope containing a set of colour postcards* **group**, **collection**, series, complete series; assortment, selection, compendium, batch, number, combination, grouping, assemblage; arrangement, array.
2 *it was a fashionable haunt of the literary set* **clique**, coterie, circle, crowd, group, lot, crew, band, company, pack, ring, camp, fraternity, school, clan, faction, party, sect, league, cabal; *informal* gang, bunch.
3 *a chemistry set* **kit**, **apparatus**, equipment, rig, outfit.
4 *a set of cutlery* **canteen**; box, case.
5 *a set of Coalport china* **service**.
6 *although he's in the bottom set, he's doing quite well* **class**, form, study group; **stream**, band.
7 *something in the set of his shoulders suggested that he was uneasy* **posture**, position, cast, attitude; bearing, carriage.
8 *her husband's brow furrowed as he noted the set of her face* **expression**, look; determined expression, fixed look.
9 *sponsorship was necessary to defray the costs of building and painting the set* **stage furniture**, stage set, stage setting, setting, scenery, backdrop, wings, flats; *French* mise en scène.

set[3] ▶ **adjective 1** *we have set procedures for dealing with such matters | a staid man with a set routine* **fixed**, established, hard and fast, determined, predetermined, arranged, prearranged, prescribed, scheduled, specified, defined, appointed, decided, agreed; unvarying, unchanging, invariable, unvaried, unchanged, rigid, inflexible, cast-iron, strict, settled, predictable; routine, standard, customary, regular, normal, usual, habitual, accustomed, wonted, conventional.
OPPOSITES changing, variable, unpredictable.
2 *she had set ideas about bringing up children* **inflexible**, rigid, fixed, firm, deep-rooted, deep-seated, ingrained, entrenched, unchangeable.
OPPOSITE flexible.
3 *he had a number of set speeches for such occasions* **stock**, standard, routine, rehearsed, well worn, formulaic, unspontaneous, unoriginal, conventional, stale, hackneyed, stereotyped, overused.
OPPOSITES fresh, original.
4 *I was all set for the evening | get set for a long, cold winter* **ready**, prepared, organized, equipped, primed; *informal* fit, geared up, psyched up, up for it.
OPPOSITE unprepared.
5 *he's set on marrying that girl* **determined to**, intent on, bent on, hell bent on, committed to the idea of, resolved to, resolute about, insistent about/on.
OPPOSITE uncertain.
6 *last night you were dead set against the idea* **opposed to**, averse to, hostile to, in opposition to, resistant to, antipathetic to, unsympathetic to; *informal* anti.

setback ▶ **noun** *Alexander was faced with one setback after another and most people would have given up* **problem**, difficulty, hitch, complication, upset, disappointment, misfortune, mishap, piece of bad luck, unfortunate development, reversal, reverse, reverse of fortune; blow, body blow, knock; stumbling block, hindrance, impediment, obstruction; delay, hold-up, check; *informal* glitch, hiccup, (double) whammy, kick in the teeth, knock-back, one in the eye; *archaic* foil.
OPPOSITES breakthrough, step forward.

settee ▶ **noun sofa**, couch, divan, chaise longue, love seat, chesterfield; sofa bed; *Brit.* put-you-up; *French* canapé, tête-à-tête; *N. Amer.* davenport, day bed, studio couch, sectional; *rare* squab.

setting ▶ **noun 1** *a converted barn in a beautiful rural setting | it was an*

unlikely setting for a marriage proposal **surroundings**, position, situation, environment, background, backdrop, milieu, environs; habitat; spot, place, location, locale, site, scene; context, frame; area, neighbourhood, region, district; *French* mise en scène; *technical* locus.
2 *a garnet in a heavy gold setting* **mounting**, mount, fixture, surround.

setting up ▶ noun *the setting up of a national information centre* **establishment**, establishing, organization, institution, creation, formation, foundation, founding, initiation, inauguration, inception, origination, constitution.
OPPOSITE abolition.

settle ▶ verb **1** *every effort was made to settle the dispute* **resolve**, sort out, reach an agreement about, find a solution to, find an answer to, solve, clear up, bring to an end, fix, work out, iron out, smooth over, straighten out, deal with, put right, set right, put to rights, rectify, remedy, reconcile; *informal* patch up; *archaic* compose.
OPPOSITE prolong.
2 *Joyce settled their affairs in London* **put in order**, sort out, straighten out, tidy up, order, arrange, organize, adjust, clear up, set to rights, regulate, systematize.
3 *they had not yet* **settled on** *a date for the wedding* **decide on**, set, fix, come to a decision about, agree on, name, determine, establish, arrange, arrive at, appoint, designate, assign; confirm; choose, select, pick.
4 *she went down to the lobby to settle her bill* **pay**, pay in full, settle up, discharge, square, clear, defray, liquidate, satisfy.
5 *the union* **settled for** *a 4.2% pay increase this autumn* **accept**, agree to, accede to, acquiesce in, assent to; compromise on.
6 *in 1863, the family* **settled in** *London* **make one's home**, set up home, take up residence, put down roots, establish oneself; go to live, move to, emigrate to; *N. Amer.* set up housekeeping in; *formal* become domiciled in.
OPPOSITE move away from.
7 *European immigrants settled much of Australia* **colonize**, establish a colony in, occupy; people, inhabit, populate.
8 *Catherine* **settled down to** *her work* **apply oneself to**, turn one's attention to, address oneself to, get down to, set about, set to work on, begin to tackle, attack; concentrate on, focus on, devote oneself to.
9 ***settle down**, all of you!* **calm down**, quieten down, be quiet, be still, relax.
10 *a small brandy had helped to settle her nerves* **calm**, calm down, quieten, quiet, soothe, compose, pacify, lull, subdue, quell; sedate, tranquillize.
OPPOSITES agitate, disturb.
11 *he settled into an armchair* **sit down**, seat oneself, install oneself, plant oneself, ensconce oneself, plump oneself, flump; *informal* park oneself, plonk oneself.
OPPOSITE stand up.
12 *come and read to Tom while I settle him* **make comfortable**, tuck in, bed down.
13 *a butterfly settled on the flower* **land**, come to rest, come down, alight, light, descend, perch.
OPPOSITE take off.
14 *sediment settles near the bottom of the tank* **sink**, subside, fall, gravitate; precipitate out.
OPPOSITE rise.

settlement ▶ noun **1** *unions succeeded in reaching a pay settlement* **agreement**, deal, arrangement, resolution, accommodation, bargain, understanding, pact; compromise; decision, conclusion, determination.
2 *the settlement of the dispute* **resolution**, sorting out, settling, solution, solving, bringing to an end, working out, smoothing over, reconciliation; successful arbitration/mediation/brokering; *informal* patching up; *archaic* composition.
3 *a remote frontier settlement* **community**, colony, outpost, encampment; trading post, post; village, hamlet; kibbutz, commune; *American Indian* pueblo, rancheria; *S. African* werf; *NZ* kainga; *Archaeology* terramare; *historical* plantation.
4 *the settlement of the area* **colonization**, settling, populating, peopling; *historical* plantation.
5 *the settlement of his debt* **payment**, discharge, defrayal, liquidation, settling, settling up, clearance, clearing, satisfaction; *archaic* reckoning.

settler ▶ noun **colonist**, colonizer, frontiersman, frontierswoman, pioneer; immigrant, newcomer; *Brit.* incomer; *N. Amer. historical* homesteader, habitant, redemptioner, squatter.
OPPOSITE native.

set-to ▶ noun (*informal*) *when he came on the scene, there was a right old set-to.* See ARGUMENT sense 1.

set-up ▶ noun **1** *their current telecommunications set-up* **system**, structure, organization, arrangement, framework, format, layout, configuration, composition; situation, conditions, circumstances.
2 *a set-up called Film International* **organization**, group, body, concern, agency, association, syndicate, operation, movement; company, firm; society, league, club; *informal* outfit.
3 (*informal*) *the whole thing was a set-up* **trick**, trap; conspiracy; *informal* put-up job, frame-up, frame.

seven ▶ cardinal number **septet**, septuplets; *Poetry* heptameter, septenarius; *technical* heptad; *rare* sevensome, septenary.

WORD LINKS

related prefixes	**hept(a)- (e.g. *heptathlon*), sept(i)- (e.g. *septivalent*)**
relating to seven	**septenary**
seven-sided figure	**heptagon**
relating to seven years	**septennial**

sever ▶ verb **1** *the head had been completely severed from the body* **cut off**, chop off, lop off, hack off, cleave, hew off, shear off, slice off, split; break off, tear off; divide, separate, part, detach, disconnect; amputate, dock; *literary* rend; *archaic* sunder; *rare* dissever.
OPPOSITES join, attach.
2 *she had died from a single knife wound which had severed the artery* **cut**, cut through, rupture, split, pierce, rip, tear.
3 *China severed diplomatic relations with Guinea-Bissau in June 1990* **break off**, discontinue, suspend; bring to an end, end, put an end to, terminate, stop, cease, conclude, dissolve.
OPPOSITES maintain, establish, initiate.

several ▶ adjective **1** *several people arrived early* **some**, a number of, a few, not very many, a handful of, a small group of, various, a variety of, assorted, sundry, diverse; *literary* divers.
OPPOSITES a lot, many.
2 *the two levels of government must sort out their several responsibilities* **respective**, individual, own, particular, specific; **separate**, different, diverse, disparate, divergent, distinct, discrete; various, sundry.
OPPOSITE joint.

severally ▶ adverb (*formal*) *a three-person board, the members of which would be severally nominated by the company* **separately**, individually, singly, discretely; respectively.
OPPOSITE jointly.

severe ▶ adjective **1** *severe shortages of basic foodstuffs | the victim sustained severe head injuries* **acute**, very bad, serious, grave, critical, dire, drastic, grievous, extreme, dreadful, terrible, awful, frightful, appalling, sore; alarming, worrying, distressing, dangerous, perilous, life-threatening; *Medicine* peracute, profound; *archaic or humorous* parlous.
OPPOSITES minor, negligible.
2 *the severe storms which battered Orkney earlier this year* **fierce**, violent, strong, wild, powerful, forceful, intense; tempestuous, turbulent, tumultuous.
OPPOSITE gentle.
3 *it was an exceptionally severe winter* **harsh**, hard, bitter, bitterly cold, cold, bleak, freezing, icy, arctic, polar, Siberian, extreme, nasty.
OPPOSITE mild.
4 *Maria complained of a severe headache* **excruciating**, agonizing, violent, intense, dreadful, awful, terrible, frightful, unbearable, intolerable, unendurable; stabbing, shooting; *informal* splitting, thumping, pounding.
OPPOSITE slight.
5 *their traumatic experiences meant that the further five-mile walk would be a severe test of their remaining stamina* **very difficult**, demanding, hard, tough, arduous, formidable, taxing, exacting, rigorous, punishing, onerous, gruelling, burdensome, heavy; back-breaking, uphill, stiff.
OPPOSITES easy, simple.
6 *the government's economic policies came in for severe criticism* **harsh**, scathing, sharp, strong, fierce, ferocious, stringent, savage, blistering, searing, stinging, scorching, devastating, mordant, trenchant, caustic, biting, cutting, withering, rigorous, unsparing; smart, sound.
OPPOSITE mild.
7 *a campaign against severe tax penalties* **extortionate**, excessive, unreasonable, inordinate, outrageous, sky-high, harsh, stiff; **punitive**, punishing, penal; *Brit.* swingeing.
8 *army service offered poor living conditions, low pay, and severe discipline | Ceauşescu singled out this minority for especially severe treatment* **strict**, stern, rigorous, harsh, hard, inflexible, uncompromising, inexorable, implacable, rigid, unbending, relentless, unrelenting, unyielding, merciless, pitiless, ruthless, draconian, oppressive, repressive, punitive, rough, nasty; tyrannical, iron-fisted, iron-handed, brutal, inhuman, cruel, savage; *Austral./NZ informal* solid.
OPPOSITES lenient, lax.
9 *his severe expression softened* **stern**, dour, grim, grim-faced, forbidding, disapproving, tight-lipped, unsmiling, unfriendly, sombre, grave, sober, serious, austere, stiff, flinty, stony, steely, glowering, frowning; cold, aloof, frosty, icy, frigid.
OPPOSITES genial, friendly.
10 *the severe style of early Classical Greek architecture* **plain**, simple, restrained, unadorned, undecorated, unembellished, unornamented, austere, chaste, spare, stark, ultra-plain, unfussy, without frills, spartan, ascetic, monastic, puritanical; functional, clinical, uncluttered; classic.
OPPOSITES ornate, fancy.

severely ▶ adverb **1** *Picher was severely injured* **very badly**, extremely badly, seriously, gravely, critically, grievously, acutely, sorely; dangerously; fatally.
OPPOSITE slightly.

2 *he was severely criticized by the chairman* **sharply**, roundly, soundly, fiercely, scathingly, savagely; *informal* like a ton of bricks.
OPPOSITE mildly.
3 *the view that rapists should be treated more severely was repeated in the editorial* **harshly**, strictly, sternly, rigorously, relentlessly, mercilessly, pitilessly, oppressively, repressively, roughly, sharply, with an iron hand, with a rod of iron; **brutally**, cruelly, savagely.
OPPOSITE leniently.
4 *she looked severely at Harriet* **sternly**, grimly, dourly, disapprovingly, sombrely, gravely, seriously, stiffly; coolly, coldly, frostily, icily.
OPPOSITE genially.
5 *a stout woman dressed severely in black* **plainly**, simply, austerely, without adornment, without frills, starkly, spartanly, monastically; classically.

severity ▶ noun **1** *the severity of the disease* **acuteness**, seriousness, gravity, graveness, severeness, grievousness, extremity; danger, dangerousness.
2 *global warming was blamed for an increase in the severity of storms | the pain increased in severity* **strength**, **intensity**, ferocity, fierceness, violence, power, powerfulness, force, forcefulness.
3 *the severity of the winter may have killed the grass* **harshness**, severeness, cold, coldness, bleakness, extremity.
OPPOSITE mildness.
4 *the Emperor was often on bad terms with his younger brothers, whom he treated with great severity | the severity of the sentence caused surprise* **harshness**, strictness, hardness, sternness, toughness, rigorousness, rigour, stringency, inflexibility, relentlessness, pitilessness, ruthlessness; **brutality**, inhumanity, cruelty, savagery.
OPPOSITE leniency.
5 *Robyn flinched at the severity of his expression* **sternness**, dourness, grimness, sombreness, unfriendliness, graveness, gravity, soberness, seriousness, austereness, austerity, stiffness, flintiness, stoniness, steeliness; coldness, frostiness, iciness, frigidity.
OPPOSITE geniality.
6 *a white, filmy gown that contrasted with the black severity of her own attire* **plainness**, simplicity, restraint, lack of adornment, lack of decoration, lack of ornament, lack of embellishment, austerity, spareness, starkness; functionalism.
OPPOSITE elaboration.

sew ▶ verb *her aunt sewed the last seams of the tunic | I sewed black armbands to their coats* **stitch**, machine stitch; embroider; seam, hem, tack, baste; attach, fasten.
OPPOSITES unpick, remove.
□ **sew something up 1** *no sooner was one tear sewn up than another appeared* **darn**, mend, repair, patch; *archaic* clout.
OPPOSITES rip, tear.
2 (*informal*) *last week, the company sewed up a deal with IBM* **secure**, clinch, pull off, bring off, settle, conclude, bring to a successful conclusion, complete, finalize, tie up, seal, set the seal on; *informal* swing.
OPPOSITE lose.

sewing *See centre pages for list of* **Sewing Techniques and Stitches**
▶ noun **needlework**, needlecraft, fancy-work, stitching.

WORD LINKS
relating to sewing **sutorial, sutorian**

sex ▶ noun **1** *a group of teenage boys sat around the table talking about sex* **sexual intercourse**, intercourse, lovemaking, making love, sex act, sexual relations, sexual/vaginal/anal penetration; mating; *informal* nooky; *Brit. informal* bonking, rumpy pumpy, a bit of the other, how's your father; *S. African informal* pata-pata; *vulgar slang* screwing, fucking; *Brit. vulgar slang* shagging; *formal* coitus, coition, copulation; *archaic* fornication, carnal knowledge, congress, commerce.
2 *you can learn how to teach your children about sex* **the facts of life**, sexual reproduction, reproduction; *informal* the birds and the bees.
3 *adults of both sexes* **gender**.
□ **have sex (with) have sexual intercourse (with)**, **make love (to)**, sleep with/together, go to bed with/together; mate (with); seduce, rape, ravish; *informal* do it, do the business, go all the way, make whoopee, have one's way with, bed, know in the biblical sense, tumble; *Brit. informal* bonk, get one's oats; *N. Amer. informal* boff, get it on (with); *euphemistic* be intimate (with); *vulgar slang* fuck, screw, bang, lay, get one's leg over, shaft, dick, frig, do, have, hump, poke, shtup, dip one's wick, ride, service, tup; *Brit. vulgar slang* have it away (with), have it off (with), shag, knob, get one's end away, knock someone off, give someone one, roger, grind, stuff; *Scottish vulgar slang* podger; *N. Amer. vulgar slang* ball, jump, jump someone's bones, bone, pork, diddle, nail; *Austral./NZ vulgar slang* root; *formal* copulate (with); *archaic* fornicate (with), possess, lie with/together, couple (with), swive, know.

WORD LINKS
relating to sex **carnal**
obsession with sex **erotomania, nymphomania**
fear of sex **erotophobia**

sex appeal ▶ noun *she just oozes sex appeal* **sexiness**, seductiveness, sexual attractiveness, desirability, sensuality, sexuality; magnetism, charisma; *informal* it, oomph, SA.

sexism ▶ noun *he admitted that the company had been accused of sexism* **chauvinism**, **discrimination**, prejudice, bias; machismo, laddishness.

sexless ▶ adjective *she's very thin, so thin that she looks almost sexless* **asexual**, non-sexual, neuter; **androgynous**, epicene; *technical* parthenogenetic.

sexual ▶ adjective **1** *the sexual organs* **reproductive**, genital, sex, procreative.
2 *sexual pleasure | sexual activity* **carnal**, erotic, coital, venereal; sensual.
3 *she's so sexual, don't you think?* **sexy**, sexually attractive, seductive, desirable, alluring, inviting, sensual, sultry, slinky, provocative, tempting, tantalizing; nubile, voluptuous, shapely, luscious, lush; feline; *informal* fanciable, beddable, come-hither, come-to-bed; *Brit. informal* fit; *N. Amer. informal* foxy, cute; *Austral. informal* spunky.

sexual intercourse ▶ noun. *See* **SEX**.

sexuality ▶ noun **1** *there was no doubting the fact that this woman had a powerful sexuality* **sensuality**, sexiness, seductiveness, desirability; **sexual appetite**, sexual instincts, sexual urges, passion, desire, lust; eroticism, physicality.
2 *I've always been pretty open about my sexuality* **sexual orientation**, orientation, sexual preference, leaning, persuasion; heterosexuality, homosexuality, lesbianism, bisexuality; transsexuality, omnisexuality, pansexuality.
3 *sexuality within holy matrimony was only justified as a necessary part of reproduction* **sexual activity**, reproductive activity, procreation, sexual intercourse, sex, intercourse, sexual relations.

sexy ▶ adjective **1** *she's so sexy | her dark, sexy eyes* **sexually attractive**, seductive, desirable, alluring, inviting, sensual, sultry, slinky, provocative, tempting, tantalizing; nubile, voluptuous, shapely, luscious, lush; feline; bedroom; flirtatious, coquettish; *informal* fanciable, beddable, come-hither, come-to bed; *Brit. informal* fit; *N. Amer. informal* foxy, cute, bootylicious; *Austral. informal* spunky; *vulgar slang* fuck-me.
OPPOSITE undesirable.
2 *a TV show featuring sexy home videos* **erotic**, arousing, exciting, stimulating, hot; **sexually explicit**, titillating, suggestive, racy, risqué, provocative, spicy, juicy, adult, X-rated; rude, coarse, smutty, pornographic, vulgar, crude, lewd, lubricious; *informal* raunchy, steamy, naughty, horny, porno, blue, skin; *Brit. informal* saucy, fruity; *N. Amer. informal* gamy.
OPPOSITE family.
3 *neither of them was feeling sexy* **aroused**, sexually excited, amorous, lustful, passionate; *informal* horny, hot, turned on, sexed up; *Brit. informal* randy; *N. Amer. informal* squirrelly; *rare* concupiscent.
4 *sales promotion is fast becoming an area that product managers see as sexy* **exciting**, stimulating, interesting, appealing, intriguing; fashionable; *informal* trendy.
OPPOSITES dull, boring.

shabby ▶ adjective **1** *a shabby little bar in Paddington* **run down**, down at heel, scruffy, uncared-for, neglected, dilapidated, in disrepair, ramshackle, tumbledown; **dingy**, seedy, slummy, insalubrious, squalid, sordid, mean, wretched, miserable; *informal* crummy, scuzzy, tacky, grungy, shambly, beat-up; *Brit. informal* grotty; *N. Amer. informal* shacky.
OPPOSITES smart, upmarket.
2 *an old lady in a shabby grey coat* **scruffy**, well worn, worn, old, worn out, threadbare, moth-eaten, mangy, ragged, frayed, tattered, battered, decrepit, unkempt, having seen better days, falling apart at the seams; faded, dowdy; dirty, grubby; *informal* tatty, ratty, the worse for wear; *N. Amer. informal* raggedy, raggedy-ass; *Austral. informal* warby; *rare* out at elbows.
OPPOSITES new, in good condition.
3 *it's pretty hard to come to terms with Angela's shabby treatment of Rick* **contemptible**, despicable, dishonourable, disreputable, discreditable, mean, mean-spirited, base, low, dirty, shameful, sorry, ignoble, unfair, unworthy, ungenerous, unkind, ungentlemanly, cheap, shoddy, unpleasant, nasty; *informal* rotten, low-down, hateful; *Brit. informal* beastly; *vulgar slang* shitty; *archaic* scurvy.
OPPOSITES decent, honourable.

shack ▶ noun **hut**, shanty, cabin, log cabin, lean-to, shed; hovel; *Scottish* bothy, shieling, shiel; *Canadian* tilt; *S. African* hok; *Austral.* gunyah, mia-mia, humpy; *NZ* whare; *American Indian* hogan, wickiup; (*in Brazil*) favela; *N. Amer. archaic* shebang.
▶ verb
□ **shack up with** (*informal*) *he's been shacking up with a girl for months* **cohabit**, live with, live together, share a house; *informal, dated* live in sin, live over the brush.

shackle ▶ verb **1** *the prisoner was shackled to the heavy steel chair in the centre of the room* **chain**, fetter, manacle; secure, tie (up), bind, tether, hobble; put in chains, put/clap in irons, handcuff; *archaic* gyve.
OPPOSITE free.
2 *investigative journalists could soon be shackled by a new European directive on data protection* **restrain**, restrict, limit, constrain; hamper, hinder, impede, obstruct, handicap, hamstring, encumber, inhibit, check, curb, tie down; tie someone's hands, cramp someone's style; *rare* trammel.
OPPOSITE give someone free rein.

S

shackles ▸ plural noun **1** *the men filed through their shackles and made a desperate bid for freedom* **chains**, fetters, irons, leg irons, manacles, handcuffs; bonds, tethers, ropes, restraints; *informal* cuffs, bracelets; *archaic* darbies, gyves, bilboes.
2 *the shackles of bureaucracy* **restrictions**, trammels, restraints, constraints, straitjacket; impediments, hindrances, obstacles, barriers, encumbrances, obstructions, checks, curbs; ball and chain.

shade ▸ noun **1** *they sat in the shade of a large oak tree* **shadow**, shadiness, shadows; coolness, cool; shelter, cover.
OPPOSITES light, glare.
2 *light rain began falling and* **the shades of evening** *drew on* **darkness**, gathering darkness, dimness, dusk, semi-darkness, twilight; gloom, gloominess, murkiness, murk; *literary* gloaming.
OPPOSITES sunlight, daylight.
3 *fabrics in autumnal shades | various shades of blue* **colour**, hue; **tone**, tint, tinge; intensity.
4 *a word with many shades of meaning* **nuance**, gradation, modulation, shading, degree, difference, variation, variety; nicety, subtlety; undertone, overtone.
5 *there was* **a shade** *of wistfulness in his tone | her skirt was* **a shade** *too short* **a little**, a bit, a trace, a touch, a dash, a modicum, a soupçon, a suspicion, a hint, a suggestion, a tinge, a smack; slightly, rather, somewhat; *informal* a tad, a smidgen.
6 (**shades**) *the film is about a celebrity being stalked by an obsessed man—shades of 'The Bodyguard'* **echoes**, a reminder, memories, intimations, suggestions, hints.
7 *she saw a crouching figure silhouetted against the window shade* **blind**, curtain, venetian blind; **screen**, shield, cover, covering, protection; awning, canopy.
8 (*informal*) *he was wearing shades and a string vest* **sunglasses**, dark glasses; *Austral. informal* sunnies; *trademark* Polaroids, Raybans.
9 (*literary*) *he confronted the shade of his lost love* **ghost**, spectre, phantom, apparition, spirit, wraith, phantasm, shadow; *Scottish & Irish* bodach; *informal* spook; *literary* revenant, wight; *rare* manes, eidolon.
□ **put someone/something in the shade** *stunts that put his previous daredevilry in the shade* **surpass**, outshine, outclass, overshadow, eclipse, exceed, excel, transcend, cap, top, outstrip, outdo, put to shame, make look pale by comparison, be better than, beat, outplay, outperform, upstage, dwarf; *informal* run rings around, be head and shoulders above, be a cut above, leave standing; *archaic* outrival, outvie.
▸ verb **1** *vines shaded a garden filled with fountains and citrus trees* **cast a shadow over**, shadow, shut out the light from, block off the light to; darken, dim; shelter, cover, screen.
2 *the shaded area of the diagram | she* **shaded in** *the outline of a chimney* **darken**, colour in, pencil in, block in, fill in; cross-hatch.
3 *the sky shaded from turquoise to night blue | at times, self-consciousness can shade into actual fear* **change gradually**, transmute, turn, go, become; **merge**, blend.

shadow ▸ noun **1** *a dim night light cast her shadow against the closed double doors* **silhouette**, outline, shape, contour, profile; penumbra, umbra.
2 *the north side of the cathedral was deep in shadow | a stranger slowly approached from the shadows* **shade**, shadowiness, darkness, gathering darkness, dimness, semi-darkness, twilight; gloom, gloominess, murkiness, murk, obscurity; *literary* gloaming; *rare* tenebrosity, umbrage.
3 *for years, unemployment has cast a dark shadow over the area | the shadow of war fell across Europe* **cloud**, black cloud, pall; gloom, gloominess, blight; threat.
4 *she knew without any shadow of doubt that he was lying* **slightest bit**, trace, scrap, shred, crumb, particle, ounce, atom, iota, scintilla, jot, whit, grain, tittle, jot or tittle; *Irish* stim; *informal* smidgen, smidge, tad; *archaic* scantling, scruple.
5 *a shadow of a smile creased her mouth* **trace**, hint, suggestion, suspicion, ghost, glimmer, flicker.
6 *he's a shadow of his former self | the band were a pale shadow of the Beatles* **inferior version**, poor imitation, apology, travesty; ghost, spectre, phantom; remnant.
7 *he had become her shadow, staying constantly by her side* **constant companion**, inseparable companion, alter ego, second self, Siamese twin; close friend, bosom friend, intimate; *informal* bosom pal; *rare* fidus Achates.
8 *no matter where Johnson went, his shadow stayed with him* follower; *informal* **tail**.
▸ verb **1** *the market is shadowed by St Margaret's church* **overshadow**, cast a shadow over, envelop in shadow, shade, block off the light to; darken, dim.
2 *he had been up all night shadowing a team of poachers* **follow**, trail, track, dog someone's footsteps, keep watch on; stalk, pursue, hunt; *informal* tail, keep tabs on, keep a tab on.

WORD LINKS
fear of shadows **sciophobia**

shadowy ▸ adjective **1** *a long shadowy corridor | the shadowy garden* **dark**, dim, gloomy, murky; shady, shaded, sunless; *literary* tenebrous, crepuscular; *rare* tenebrious, umbrageous, umbrose, umbriferous, umbrous, caliginous, Cimmerian.
OPPOSITES bright, sunny.
2 *a shadowy figure appeared through the mist* **indistinct**, hazy, indefinite, lacking definition, out of focus, vague, nebulous, ill-defined, faint, blurred, blurry, unclear, indistinguishable, unrecognizable, indeterminate, unsubstantial; ghostly, phantom, spectral, wraithlike; *rare* nebulose.
OPPOSITES distinct, clear.

shady ▸ adjective **1** *a shady corner of the garden* **shaded**, shadowy, dark, dim, sunless; sheltered, screened, covered, protected, shrouded; leafy, arboured; cool; *literary* bosky, bowery, tenebrous; *rare* umbrageous, tenebrious, umbrose, umbriferous, umbrous, caliginous, Cimmerian.
OPPOSITES bright, sunny.
2 *shady deals* **suspicious**, suspect, questionable, dubious, doubtful, of dubious character, disreputable, untrustworthy, dishonest, dishonourable, devious, slippery, tricky, underhand, unscrupulous, irregular, potentially illegal, unethical; *N. Amer.* snide; *informal* shifty, fishy, murky; *Brit. informal* dodgy; *Austral./NZ informal* shonky.
OPPOSITES reputable, honest.

shaft ▸ noun **1** *a wooden shaft about a yard long | the shaft of a golf club* **pole**, stick, rod, staff, shank, upright; **handle**, hilt, butt, stock, stem; *historical* pikestaff, thill; *rare* helve.
2 *the shaft of a feather* **quill**; *technical* rachis.
3 *shafts of early sunlight* **ray**, beam, gleam, streak, pencil, finger, bar; *literary* lance.
4 *shafts of criticism* **cutting remark**, barb, gibe, taunt, sting; *informal* dig.
5 *the main shaft was impassable | a ventilation shaft* **mineshaft**, tunnel, passage, pit, adit, downcast, upcast; **borehole**, bore; duct, air shaft, well, light well, flue, vent; *rare* winze.

shaggy ▸ adjective *his shaggy beard | a shaggy wolfhound lay in front of the fire* **hairy**, hirsute, bushy, thick, woolly, fleecy, long-haired, unshorn, uncut, shock-headed; tangled, tousled, unkempt, dishevelled, untidy, matted; *rare* crinose, hispid.
OPPOSITES sleek; close-cropped.

shake ▸ verb **1** *the whole building seemed to shake* **vibrate**, tremble, quiver, quake, shiver, shudder, judder, jiggle, wobble, rock, sway, swing, roll, oscillate; convulse.
2 *I was shaking with fear* **tremble**, quiver, quake, shiver, shudder, shake like a leaf; *rare* quave.
3 *she stood in the hall and shook her umbrella | I shook the sauce bottle* **jiggle**, joggle, wave from side to side; agitate; *informal* waggle.
4 *he shook his stick at the old man* **brandish**, wave, flourish, swing, wield; raise.
5 *it was the crazed look in his eyes that really shook her* **upset**, distress, disturb, unsettle, perturb, disconcert, discompose, disquiet, unnerve, trouble, take aback, throw off balance, agitate, fluster; shock, alarm, frighten, scare, worry, dismay; *informal* rattle, get to, do someone's head in; *N. Amer. informal* mess with someone's head.
OPPOSITES soothe, reassure.
6 *the escalation in costs is certain to shake the confidence of private investors* **weaken**, undermine, damage, impair, harm, hurt, injure, have a bad effect on; reduce, diminish, decrease, lessen.
OPPOSITE strengthen.
□ **shake a leg** (*informal*) **hurry up**, get a move on, be quick, speed up; *informal* get cracking, get moving, make it snappy, step on it, step on the gas, rattle one's dags; *Brit. informal* get one's skates on, stir one's stumps; *N. Amer. informal* get a wiggle on; *S. African informal* put foot; *dated* make haste.
□ **shake someone off** *Manville thought he had shaken off his pursuer* **get away from**, escape, elude, give someone the slip, leave behind, throw off, throw off the scent, dodge, lose, get rid of, rid oneself of; outdistance, outstrip; *Brit. informal* get shot of.
□ **shake something off** *he has shaken off his back trouble | Simon has finally shaken off her pernicious influence* **recover from**, get over, get better after; get rid of, free oneself from, lose; *Brit. informal* get shot of, see the back of; *N. Amer. informal* shuck off.
□ **shake someone/something up 1** *the accident really shook him up. See* SHAKE *sense 5.*
2 *he presented plans to shake up the legal profession* **reorganize**, restructure, revolutionize, alter dramatically, make far-reaching changes in, transform, reform, overhaul, update; reshuffle.
3 *I hired you because I thought you might shake the place up a bit* **put some life into**, enliven, put some spark into, liven up, stir up, rouse, get going.
▸ noun **1** *she removed his wet coat and gave it a shake* **jiggle**, joggle, jerk; *informal* waggle.
2 *a shake of his thick forefinger* **flourish**, brandish, wave.
3 (**the shakes**) *I had a bad case of the shakes | I wouldn't go in there, it gives me the shakes* **a fit of trembling**, delirium tremens, tremors; the horrors; *informal* the DTs, the jitters, the willies, the heebie-jeebies, the jim-jams, the jumps, the yips; *Austral. rhyming slang* Joe Blakes.
4 (*informal*) *police switchboards were flooded with requests for information on the*

shake **earthquake**, earth tremor, aftershock, convulsion; *informal* quake; *N. Amer. informal* tremblor.

□ **in two shakes (of a lamb's tail)** *(informal) I'll be back in two shakes* **in a moment**, in a second, in a flash, in a minute, shortly, any minute, any minute now, in a short time, (very) soon, in an instant, in the twinkling of an eye, in (less than) no time, in no time at all, before you know it, before long; *N. Amer.* momentarily; *informal* in a jiffy, before you can say Jack Robinson, in the blink of an eye, in a blink, in the wink of an eye, in a wink, before you can say knife; *Brit. informal* in a tick, in two ticks, in a mo; *N. Amer. informal* in a snap.

□ **no great shakes** *(informal) it's no great shakes as a piece of cinema* **not very good**, undistinguished, unmemorable, forgettable, unexceptional, uninspired, uninspiring, uninteresting, indifferent, unimpressive, lacklustre; *informal* nothing to write home about, nothing to get excited about, nothing special, not up to much; *NZ informal* half-pie.
OPPOSITE exceptional.

> **CHOOSE THE RIGHT WORD**
>
> **shake, tremble, shiver, quiver, quake**
>
> - **Shake** is the most general term (*buildings shook in Sacramento*): the others denote shaking of various degrees of intensity, and when used of a person, indicate more often than *shake* that it results from weakness or emotion. *Shake* and *quiver* are the only ones that can be used transitively (*a severe earthquake shook the area*).
> - To **tremble** is to shake uncontrollably with slight, rapidly repeated movements. Trembling is especially associated with fear or weakness (*the boy spoke cockily, but his voice trembled* | *she held the letter with trembling hands*).
> - **Shiver** denotes a similar slight and uncontrollable shaking, but, unlike *tremble*, it can be used only of bodies and other physical objects, not, for example, of voices (*the spectators shivered and drew their coats firmly about them*). Shivering is most commonly caused by cold or horror (*Katherine shivered and drew her coat more tightly round her* | *she shivered at the threat in his quiet voice*).
> - To **quiver** is to move lightly and rapidly and often results from strong emotion (*Anthea's eyelids quivered* | *'Don't you love me any more?' I asked, quivering my bottom lip*).
> - To **quake** is to shake violently (*the rumbling vibrations set the whole valley quaking*). Applied to people, *quake* indicates extreme fear and is typically used figuratively (*those words should have them quaking in their boots*).

shake-up ▶ **noun** *the company's boardroom shake-up followed a £365m pre-tax loss* **reorganization**, restructuring, rearrangement, change, reshuffle, regrouping, redistribution, overhaul, revamp, makeover; upheaval; *N. Amer. informal* shakedown.

shaky ▶ **adjective 1** *she walked over to him on shaky legs* **trembling**, shaking, tremulous, quivering, quivery, unsteady, wobbly, weak; quavery; *informal* trembly.
OPPOSITE steady.
2 *he levered himself to his feet and took a few shaky steps* **faltering**, unsteady, uncertain, tentative, wobbly, wobbling, tottering, tottery, teetering, doddering, doddery, shaking, staggering.
3 *I still feel a bit shaky* **faint**, dizzy, light-headed, giddy; weak, weak-kneed, weak at the knees, wobbly, quivery, unsteady, groggy, muzzy; *informal* trembly, all of a tremble, all of a quiver, with rubbery legs, woozy; *rare* vertiginous.
4 *a room furnished with two iron beds and a shaky table* **unsteady**, unstable, wobbly, precarious, rocky, rickety, flimsy, frail; decrepit, ramshackle, dilapidated, on its last legs; *informal* teetery; *Brit. informal* wonky, dicky.
OPPOSITE stable.
5 *the evidence against him is distinctly shaky* **unreliable**, untrustworthy, questionable, dubious, doubtful, tenuous, suspect, unsubstantial, flimsy, weak, nebulous, unsound, undependable, unsupported, unsubstantiated, ungrounded, unfounded; *informal* iffy; *Brit. informal* dodgy.
OPPOSITES sound, strong.

shallow ▶ **adjective** *a shallow analysis of contemporary society* **superficial**, facile, glib, simplistic, oversimplified, schematic, slight, flimsy, insubstantial, lightweight, empty, trivial, trifling; surface, skin-deep; frivolous, foolish, silly, unintelligent, unthinking, unscholarly, ignorant.
OPPOSITES profound, serious; in-depth.

sham ▶ **noun 1** *all the tenderness he had shown her had been nothing more than a sham* **pretence**, fake, act, fiction, simulation, imposture, fraud, feint, lie, counterfeit; putting on an act, faking, feigning, play-acting, dissembling; humbug; *informal* a put-up job.
OPPOSITES the real McCoy, the genuine article.
2 *he was a sham, totally unqualified for his job as a senior doctor* **charlatan**, fake, fraud, impostor, pretender, masquerader, dissembler, wolf in sheep's clothing; quack, mountebank; *informal* phoney.
▶ **adjective** *she didn't want any more pretend closeness, any more sham togetherness* **fake**, pretended, feigned, simulated, false, artificial, bogus, synthetic, spurious, ersatz, insincere, not genuine, manufactured, contrived, affected, plastic, make-believe, fictitious; imitation, mock, counterfeit, fraudulent; *informal* pretend, put-on, phoney, pseudo; *Brit. informal, dated* cod.
OPPOSITES real, genuine.
▶ **verb 1** *she shams indifference* **feign**, fake, pretend, put on, make a pretence of, simulate, counterfeit, affect, imitate.
2 *was he ill or was he shamming?* **pretend**, fake, dissemble; malinger; *informal* put it on; *Brit. informal* swing the lead.

shaman ▶ **noun medicine man**, medicine woman, healer; witch doctor; *North American Indian* powwow, pawaw; *South American Indian* peai, peaiman; *(in Hawaii)* kahuna; *(in Greenland)* angekok; *(in Malaysia & Indonesia)* pawang; *(in SE Asia)* dukun.

shamble ▶ **verb** *he shambled off down the corridor* **shuffle**, lumber, totter, dodder, stumble; scuff/drag one's feet; hobble, limp.
OPPOSITES run, sprint, bound.

shambles ▶ **plural noun 1** *he called an emergency summit of ED leaders to sort out the shambles* **chaos**, mess, muddle, confusion, disorder, disarray, disorganization, havoc, mare's nest; *Brit. informal* dog's dinner, dog's breakfast.
2 *the room was a shambles* **complete mess**, pigsty; *N. Amer.* pigpen; *informal* disaster area; *Brit. informal* tip.
3 *(archaic) blood ran down from the shambles where the animals were slaughtered* **slaughterhouse**, abattoir; *Brit.* butchery, knacker's yard; *archaic* butcher-row.

shambling ▶ **adjective** *a big, shambling bear of a man* **ungainly**, lumbering, shuffling, awkward, clumsy, uncoordinated, heavy-footed.
OPPOSITES dapper, neat, trim, petite.

shambolic ▶ **adjective** *(Brit. informal) he accused the party headquarters of running a shambolic campaign* **chaotic**, disorganized, muddled, confused, in (total) disarray, at sixes and sevens, unsystematic, haphazard, hit-or-miss, scrappy, fragmented, inefficient; *informal* all over the place; *Brit. informal* all over the shop; *N. Amer. informal* all over the map, all over the lot.
OPPOSITES efficient, organized.

shame ▶ **noun 1** *Lily walked in front of him, her face scarlet with shame* **humiliation**, mortification, chagrin, ignominy, loss of face, shamefacedness, embarrassment, indignity, abashment, discomfort, discomfiture, discomposure.
OPPOSITE pride.
2 *I felt a pang of shame at telling Alice a lie* **guilt**, remorse, contrition, compunction.
OPPOSITE indifference.
3 *the incident had brought shame on the family* **disgrace**, dishonour, discredit, degradation, ignominy, disrepute, ill-repute, infamy, scandal, odium, opprobrium, obloquy, condemnation, contempt; *rare* disesteem, reprobation, derogation.
OPPOSITES honour, glory.
4 *it's a shame she never married* **pity**, misfortune, crying shame, cause for regret, source of regret, sad thing, unfortunate thing; bad luck, ill luck; *informal* bummer, crime, sin.
5 *this situation is a shame to our country* **discredit to**, disgrace to, stain on, blemish on, blot on, blot on the escutcheon of, slur on, reproach to, bad reflection on; stigma, scandal, outrage; *literary* smirch on.
OPPOSITE credit.
□ **put someone/something to shame outshine**, outclass, overshadow, eclipse, surpass, excel, be superior to, outstrip, outdo, put in the shade, upstage, leave behind; show up, humble; *informal* run rings around, be head and shoulders above, leave standing, knock into a cocked hat; *Brit. informal* knock spots off; *archaic* outrival, outvie; *rare* put to the blush.
OPPOSITE not be a patch on.
▶ **verb 1** *you have shamed your family's name* **disgrace**, dishonour, discredit, bring into disrepute, degrade, debase, defame, stigmatize, taint, sully, tarnish, besmirch, stain, blacken, drag through the mud/mire, give a bad name to, put in a bad light.
OPPOSITES honour, do credit to, enhance the reputation of.
2 *he had been shamed in public* **humiliate**, mortify, make someone feel ashamed, chagrin, embarrass, abash, chasten, humble, put someone in their place, take down a peg or two, cut down to size, show up; *N. Amer. informal* make someone eat crow.

> **CHOOSE THE RIGHT WORD**
>
> **shame, ignominy, disgrace, dishonour**
>
> *See* DISGRACE.

shamefaced ▶ **adjective** *Giles looked shamefaced* **ashamed**, abashed, sheepish, guilty, conscience-stricken, guilt-ridden, contrite, sorry, remorseful, repentant, penitent, hangdog, regretful, rueful, apologetic; **embarrassed**, mortified, red-faced, chagrined, humiliated, uncomfortable, discomfited; in sackcloth and ashes; *informal* with one's tail between one's legs; *rare* compunctious.
OPPOSITES proud, unrepentant.

S

shameful ▶ adjective **1** *no one can justify such shameful behaviour* **disgraceful**, deplorable, despicable, contemptible, dishonourable, discreditable, reprehensible, base, mean, low, blameworthy, unworthy, ignoble, shabby, inglorious, infamous, unprincipled, shocking, scandalous, outrageous, abominable, atrocious, appalling, disgusting, vile, odious, monstrous, heinous, unspeakable, loathsome, sordid, bad, wicked, immoral, nefarious, indefensible, inexcusable, unforgivable; *informal* low-down, hateful; *archaic* knavish, dastardly, scurvy; *rare* egregious, flagitious.
OPPOSITES admirable, honourable, laudable.
2 *are you saying that my father had a shameful secret of some sort?* **embarrassing**, mortifying, shaming, humiliating, degrading, ignominious; *informal* blush-making.
OPPOSITE praiseworthy.

shameless ▶ adjective **1** *O'Brien marvelled at his shameless self-promotion* **flagrant**, blatant, barefaced, overt, brazen, brash, audacious, outrageous, undisguised, unconcealed, transparent; unabashed, unashamed, without shame, unembarrassed, unblushing, unrepentant; *archaic* arrant.
OPPOSITES reticent, diffident.
2 *I suppose you think me shameless for telling you I want you so much* **brazen**, bold, forward, immodest, indecorous, wanton, abandoned.
OPPOSITES demure, modest.

shanty ▶ noun **shack**, hut, cabin, lean-to, shed; hovel; *Scottish* bothy, shieling, shiel; *Canadian* tilt; *S. African* hok; (*in Brazil*) favela; *N. Amer. dated* shebang.

shape *See centre pages for lists of* **Curves** **Lens Shapes** **Patterns** **Shapes** **Triangles**
▶ noun **1** *the sweater was too big for her but did not disguise the shape of her body | the rectangular shape of the dining table* **form**, appearance, configuration, formation, structure; figure, build, physique, body; contours, lines, outline, silhouette, profile; design, format; cut, pattern, mould.
2 *a woman was drowned in the lough and now haunts the area in the shape of a fox* **guise**, likeness, semblance, form, appearance, image, aspect.
3 *you're in pretty good shape, Donald* **condition**, state, health, state of health, trim, fettle, order, repair; *Brit. informal* nick.
4 *dressmaking shapes* **pattern**, model.
□ **take shape** *a glorious idea began to take shape in her brain* **become clear**, become definite, become tangible, crystallize, gel, come together, fall into place.
▶ verb **1** *an alloy of two metals that could be shaped into knives and tools* **form**, fashion, make, create, mould, model, cast, frame, sculpt, sculpture, block; carve, cut, hew, whittle.
2 *current attitudes were shaped by Bowlby's influential report to the World Health Organization* **determine**, create, produce, form, fashion, mould, define, develop, build, construct; influence, affect.
□ **shape up 1** *the 20-year-old is shaping up nicely* **improve**, show improvement, get better, make headway, make progress, progress, show promise; develop, take shape, come on, come along, turn out, go.
2 *simple ideas to help you shape up while you're getting a tan* **get fit**, get into shape, tone up; slim, lose weight, get thinner.

WORD LINKS

related prefix	**morpho-** (e.g. *morphometry*)
related suffix	**-morph** (e.g. *polymorph, ectomorph*)
study of the shapes of things	**morphology**

shapeless ▶ adjective **1** *these shapeless lumps are called sea squirts* **formless**, amorphous, unformed, indefinite, nebulous; misshapen.
2 *Alison was wearing a shapeless grey woollen dress* **baggy**, badly cut, sack-like, tent-like, oversized, sagging, saggy, ill-fitting, ill-proportioned, inelegant, unshapely, formless.
OPPOSITE tailored.

shapely ▶ adjective *Katherine's shapely figure was swathed in blue silk* **well proportioned**, well formed, well shaped, attractive, clean-limbed; **curvaceous**, voluptuous, sexy, opulent, full-figured, Junoesque, rounded, buxom, full-bosomed; *informal* curvy; *archaic* comely; *rare* sightly, well turned, gainly.
OPPOSITE misshapen.

shard ▶ noun *shards of glass flew in all directions* **piece**, fragment, bit, sliver, splinter, shiver, chip, particle, scrap; paring, shaving.

share ▶ noun *her share of the profits from the original television show* **portion**, part, division, bit, quota, allowance, ration, allocation, allotment, lot, measure, due; percentage, commission; dividend; stake, interest, equity; helping, serving; *informal* cut, whack, slice, piece/slice of the cake, piece of the action, rake-off; *Brit. informal* divvy; *rare* apportionment, quantum, moiety.
▶ verb **1** *we were a real eighties couple—we shared the bills and the shopping* **split**, divide, go halves in/with; *informal* go fifty-fifty in, go Dutch.
2 *they shared out the peanuts* **apportion**, portion out, divide up, allocate, ration out, give out, distribute, dispense, hand out, dish out, deal out, dole out, parcel out, measure out; carve up; *informal* divvy up.
3 *a tutorial is an opportunity for a student to share in the learning process* **participate in**, take part in, play a part in, have a role in, be involved in, contribute to, have a hand in, have something to do with, partake in; have a share in, have a percentage of, have a stake in.
OPPOSITE be excluded from.

shark *See centre pages for list of* **Sharks**
▶ noun

WORD LINKS

relating to sharks **squaloid**

sharp ▶ adjective **1** *you will need a very sharp knife* **keen**, sharp-edged, razor-sharp, razor-edged; sharpened, honed, whetted; serrated, knife-like, cutting, edged; *rare* acute.
OPPOSITE blunt.
2 *he winced as a sharp pain shot through his left leg* **excruciating**, agonizing, intense, violent, piercing, stabbing, shooting, stinging, severe, acute, keen, fierce, searing; exquisite.
3 *Danish Blue has a distinctively sharp taste* **tangy**, piquant, strong; **acidic**, acid, acidy, sour, tart, vinegary, pungent, bitter; *N. Amer.* acerb; *rare* acidulous, acetic, acetous.
OPPOSITES mild, mellow, bland.
4 *the air still had a sharp sooty smell* **acrid**, burning, pungent.
OPPOSITE sweet.
5 *Isabel couldn't repress a sharp cry of pain | a sharp crack of thunder* **loud**, **piercing**, shrill, high-pitched, high, penetrating, harsh, strident; ear-splitting, deafening, thunderous, booming, head-splitting.
OPPOSITES quiet, soft.
6 *it was growing dark and a sharp wind was blowing off the sea* **cold**, chilly, chill, brisk, keen, piercing, penetrating, biting, cutting, icy, bitter, freezing, glacial, raw, harsh; *informal* nippy; *Brit. informal* parky.
OPPOSITES warm, balmy.
7 *some sharp words were exchanged* **harsh**, bitter, hard, cutting, scathing, caustic, biting, barbed, trenchant, mordant, acrimonious, acerbic, tart, acid, sarcastic, sardonic, ill-tempered, spiteful, venomous, malicious, vitriolic, vicious, hurtful, nasty, unkind, severe, cruel, wounding, abusive; curt, brusque, abrasive; *N. Amer.* acerb; *informal* bitchy, catty; *rare* mordacious, acidulous.
OPPOSITES kind, amicable.
8 *she was achingly aware of a sharp sense of loss* **intense**, acute, keen, strong, bitter, fierce, searing, piercing, heartfelt, very great, overpowering.
9 *her face was thin and her nose sharp | each leaf ends in a sharp point* **pointed**, tapering, tapered, needle-like, spiky; *informal* pointy; *technical* acicular, lanceolate, acuminate, subulate, mucronate, aculeate; *rare* cuspidate, cusped, conoid.
OPPOSITE rounded.
10 *the lens brings the rays of all the different colours into sharp focus | there was a sharp difference of opinion between them* **distinct**, clear-cut, clear, well defined, well focused, crisp; stark; obvious, marked, definite, pronounced, evident, manifest.
OPPOSITES blurred, indistinct.
11 *a sharp increase in interest rates* **sudden**, abrupt, rapid; steep, precipitous, precipitate.
OPPOSITE gradual.
12 *a large articulated lorry was turning the sharp corner* **hairpin**, tight, angular.
13 *Moore set off at a sharp pace* **brisk**, rapid, quick, fast, smart, swift, speedy, vigorous, spirited, lively; *informal* snappy.
OPPOSITE slow.
14 *the edge of the gully had a very sharp drop* **steep**, sheer, abrupt, precipitous, vertical, vertiginous; *rare* acclivitous, declivitous.
OPPOSITES gentle, gradual.
15 *his sharp eyes had seen a figure moving in the darkness* **keen**, perceptive, observant, acute, sharp-sighted, beady, hawklike.
OPPOSITE weak.
16 *his mind was as sharp as it had ever been | she was sharp and witty* **perceptive**, discerning, percipient, perspicacious, penetrative, piercing, penetrating, discriminating, sensitive, incisive, keen, keen-witted, acute, sharp-witted, quick, quick-witted, clever, shrewd, astute, intelligent, intuitive, bright, agile, nimble, nimble-witted, alert, quick off the mark, ready, apt, fine, finely honed, rapier-like, probing, searching, insightful, knowing; *informal* smart, on the ball, quick on the uptake, not missing a trick, savvy, with all one's wits about one, downy; *Brit. informal* suss, knowing how many beans make five; *Scottish & N. English informal* pawky; *N. Amer. informal* cute, heads-up; *rare* long-headed, argute.
OPPOSITES slow, dull, stupid.
17 *it sounds as if he's a sharp operator* **clever**, shrewd, canny, smart; **cunning**, wily, crafty, artful, guileful, unscrupulous, dishonest; *informal* slick; *Brit. informal* fly.
OPPOSITES naive, ingenuous.
18 *they were greeted by a young man in a sharp suit* **smart**, stylish, fashionable, chic, modish, elegant, spruce; *informal* trendy, cool, snazzy, classy, flash, snappy, natty, nifty, dressy; *N. Amer. informal* fly, spiffy, sassy, kicky; *archaic* trig.
OPPOSITES shabby, scruffy.
▶ adverb **1** *I'll pick you up at nine o'clock sharp* **precisely**, exactly, on the dot; **promptly**, prompt, punctually, dead on, on the stroke of …; *N. Amer. informal* on the button, on the nose; *Austral./NZ informal* on the knocker.

OPPOSITES approximately, roughly.
2 *the world stock market hiccup of October 1987 pulled people up sharp* **abruptly**, suddenly, sharply, all of a sudden, unexpectedly, without warning.

sharpen ▶ verb **1** *first sharpen the carving knife* **make sharp/sharper**, hone, whet, strop, grind, file; *rare* edge, acuminate.
OPPOSITE blunt.
2 *the world's top players are* **sharpening up** *their grass court skills before Wimbledon* **improve**, brush up, polish up, better, enhance; hone, refine, fine-tune, perfect.

sharp-eyed ▶ adjective *a sharp-eyed witness contacted the police with details of a car spotted nearby* **observant**, perceptive, sharp-sighted, eagle-eyed, with eyes like a hawk, hawk-eyed, keen-eyed, lynx-eyed, gimlet-eyed; watchful, vigilant, alert, on the alert, on the lookout, on the qui vive, with one's eyes/open/peeled/skinned; *informal* beady-eyed; *rare* Argus-eyed.
OPPOSITE unobservant.

sharpness ▶ noun **1** *the pain came again, with a sharpness that made her cry out* **intensity**, severity, acuteness, keenness, violence, fierceness, ferocity.
2 *she felt thankful for her jacket's protection against the sharpness of the wind* **chilliness**, chill, briskness, coldness, keenness, iciness, bitterness, harshness.
OPPOSITES warmth, balminess.
3 *he winced slightly at the sharpness in her voice* **harshness**, asperity, bitterness, acerbity, acidity, tartness, edge.
OPPOSITES kindness, friendliness.
4 *focusing needs to be done carefully to obtain maximum sharpness* **clarity**, definition, precision, crispness.
OPPOSITE blurriness.
5 *the sharpness of his mind* **acuity**, acuteness, keenness, sharp-wittedness, quick-wittedness, perceptiveness, discernment, percipience, penetration, discrimination, cleverness, shrewdness, astuteness, intelligence, intuitiveness, agility, nimbleness; *informal* savvy.
OPPOSITE dullness.

shatter ▶ verb **1** *one of the shots had shattered his windscreen | the wine spilt and the glasses shattered* **smash**, smash to smithereens, break, break into pieces, burst, blow out; explode, implode; splinter, crack, fracture, fragment, disintegrate; *informal* bust; *rare* shiver.
2 *the announcement shattered hopes of an early release for the foreign hostages* **destroy**, wreck, ruin, dash, crush, devastate, demolish, wreak havoc with, blast, blight, wipe out, overturn, torpedo, scotch; burst someone's bubble; *informal* put the kibosh on, banjax, do for, blow a hole in, nix, put paid to, queer; *Brit. informal* scupper, dish; *archaic* bring to naught.
3 *everyone was shattered by the news* **devastate**, shock, stun, daze, dumbfound, traumatize, crush, overwhelm, greatly upset, distress; *informal* knock for six, knock sideways, knock the stuffing out of.
OPPOSITES please, excite.

shattered ▶ adjective **1** *we couldn't believe how bad the reviews were—Michael was absolutely shattered* **devastated**, shocked, stunned, dazed, staggered, dumbfounded, traumatized, crushed, overwhelmed; heartbroken, broken-hearted; *informal* knocked/hit for six, knocked sideways.
OPPOSITES pleased, thrilled.
2 (*informal*) *I feel too shattered to do more than crawl into bed.* See EXHAUSTED.

shattering ▶ adjective *the death of her elder son from tuberculosis was a shattering blow* **devastating**, crushing, staggering, severe, savage, overwhelming, traumatic, very great, dreadful, terrible, awful.

shave ▶ verb **1** *he had* **shaved off** *his beard | his hair was closely shaved at the sides* **cut off**, snip off; crop, trim, barber, tonsure.
2 *the electric version can* **shave off** *excess wood quickly and easily* **plane off**, pare off, shear off, whittle off, scrape off.
3 *shave Parmesan over the top* **grate**, shred.
4 *he fought the seat at the last two elections, shaving the majority to 2,000 in 1992* **reduce**, cut, bring down, lessen, decrease, make smaller, prune, pare down, shrink, slim down, whittle down.
5 *Dad said the shortcut would* **shave** *at least 20 miles* **off** *the trip* **take off**, remove from, lop off, cut off.
6 *his shot shaved the post* **touch lightly**, brush, brush against, graze, glance off, kiss.

sheaf ▶ noun *he sat down at the table with a sheaf of papers* **bundle**, bunch, stack, pile, heap, mass, armful, collection; *informal* load, wodge.

sheath ▶ noun **1** *he slid the gleaming sword out of its sheath* **scabbard**, case.
2 *an optical fibre has a core and a cladding encased in a tough protective plastic sheath* **covering**, cover, case, casing, envelope, sleeve, wrapper; *technical* tunica, capsule, fascia, neurilemma, epimysium, perimysium, perineurium, sarcolemma; coleoptile, coleorhiza, ochrea.
3 *a barrier method of contraception such as a sheath* **condom**; contraceptive; *N. Amer.* prophylactic; *Brit. trademark* Durex; *Brit. informal* johnny, something for the weekend; *N. Amer. informal* rubber, safe, safety, skin; *Brit. informal, dated* French letter, Frenchy; *dated* protective.

shed[1] ▶ noun *guinea pigs and rabbits should be kept in sheds or garages* **hut**, lean-to, outhouse, outbuilding, shack; potting shed, woodshed; cattle shed, cow-house; *Brit.* lock-up; *N. Amer.* barn, smokehouse; *Austral./NZ* woolshed; *N. English* shippon; *S. English* linhay; *archaic* hovel.

shed[2] ▶ verb **1** *tall beech trees shed their leaves over a disused tennis court* **let fall**, let drop, drop; scatter, spill, shower.
2 *the caterpillar has to shed its skin four or five times to allow it to grow* **slough off**, cast, cast off, moult; *technical* exuviate.
OPPOSITE grow.
3 *we shed our jackets* **take off**, remove, pull off, peel off, shrug off, discard, divest oneself of, doff, fling off, fling aside, climb out of, slip out of; undo, unfasten, unbutton, unzip.
OPPOSITES don, put on.
4 *too much blood has been shed* **spill**, pour forth, let flow, discharge.
5 *the two firms are each to shed ten workers* **make redundant**, dismiss, let go, discharge, give someone their notice, get rid of, discard; *informal* sack, give someone the sack, fire, give someone their cards, give someone their marching orders, send packing, give someone the boot, give someone the bullet, give someone the push, give someone the (old) heave-ho, boot out.
OPPOSITES hire, take on.
6 *the revolutionaries must shed their populist illusions* **discard**, get rid of, dispose of, do away with, drop, abandon, throw out, jettison, lose, scrap, cast aside/off, dump, have done with, reject, repudiate; *informal* ditch, junk, get shut of; *Brit. informal* get shot of, see the back of; *N. Amer.* shuck off.
OPPOSITES adopt, keep.
7 *the moon shed a watery light on the scene* **cast**, send forth, send out, radiate, give out, diffuse, disperse, scatter.
□ **shed tears** *a number of the pupils shed tears as they read the many messages of sympathy* **weep**, cry, sob, blubber; lament, grieve, mourn, bewail, wail; *Scottish* greet; *informal* blub, boohoo; *literary* pule.

sheen ▶ noun *her hair, once so dark and lustrous, had lost its sheen* **shine**, lustre, gleam, patina, gloss, shininess, burnish, polish, shimmer, glimmer, sparkle, brightness, brilliance, radiance.
OPPOSITE dullness.

sheep *See centre pages for list of* **Sheep**
▶ noun ram, ewe, lamb, wether, bellwether; *Brit.* tup; *Austral. informal* jumbuck, woolly.

WORD LINKS

male	**ram**
female	**ewe**
young	**lamb**
relating to sheep	**ovine**
collective noun	**flock, herd**

sheepish ▶ adjective *Sam looked sheepish and apologetic* **embarrassed**, uncomfortable, hangdog, self-conscious; shamefaced, ashamed, abashed, mortified, chastened, chagrined; remorseful, contrite, rueful, regretful, penitent, repentant; shy, bashful, diffident.
OPPOSITE unabashed.

sheer[1] ▶ adjective **1** *he whistled at the sheer audacity of the plan* **utter**, complete, absolute, total, pure, perfect, downright, out-and-out, thorough, thoroughgoing, through and through, consummate, patent, surpassing, veritable, unqualified, unmitigated, unalloyed, unadulterated, unmixed; stark, rank; plain, simple, mere; *Brit. informal* proper; *Austral./NZ informal* fair; *archaic* arrant; *rare* right-down.
2 *there was a terrifying sheer drop to the sea* **precipitous**, very steep, perpendicular, vertical, abrupt, bluff, sharp, vertiginous; *rare* acclivitous, declivitous, scarped.
OPPOSITE gradual.
3 *a dress of sheer white silk chiffon* **diaphanous**, gauzy, filmy, floaty, very thin, translucent, transparent, see-through, gossamer, gossamer-like, chiffony, insubstantial, ultra-fine, fine.
OPPOSITES thick, heavy.

sheer[2] ▶ verb **1** *the boat sheered off to beach further along the coast* **swerve**, swing, veer, slew, skew, change course, drift, yaw.
OPPOSITE stay on course.
2 *her mind* **sheered away from** *images she didn't want to dwell on* **turn away**, flinch, recoil, shy away; refuse to contemplate, avoid, evade.
OPPOSITE face up to.

sheet ▶ noun **1** *she changed the sheets and tidied the room* (**sheets**) **bed linen**, linen, bedclothes.
2 *the lake was covered with a sheet of ice* **layer**, stratum; covering, blanket, coating, coat, overlay, lamina, lamination, veneer, film, skin, membrane.
3 *a sheet of glass* **pane**, panel, piece, plate; slab.
4 *she ripped out the paper and put in a fresh sheet* **piece of paper**, leaf, page, folio.
5 *the glistening sheet of water* **expanse**, area, stretch, sweep.

shelf ▶ noun **1** *she put Frank's card on the shelf* **ledge**, bracket, sill, rack; bookshelf, mantelshelf, mantelpiece; shelving; (*in a church or monastery*) predella, retable.
2 *the waters above the shelf* **sandbank**, sandbar, bank, bar, reef, shoal.
□ **on the shelf** *the tangled love life of a 30-year old woman who fears she will be left on the shelf* **unmarried**, single, without a partner/spouse, without a

S

husband/wife, unattached, on one's own; lonely, unloved, neglected; *archaic* sole.
OPPOSITE married.

shell *See centre pages for list of* **Shells (Seashells)**
▶ **noun 1** *the shell of a crab* **carapace**, outside, exterior; armour.
2 *peanuts roasted in their shells* **pod**, casing, case, husk, hull; integument, cover, covering; *N. Amer.* shuck.
3 *the sound of shells passing overhead* **projectile**, bomb; grenade; bullet, cartridge, shot; *rare* trajectile.
4 *the metal shell of the car* **framework**, frame, chassis, skeleton, basic structure; hull, exterior.
▶ **verb 1** *they were shelling peas* **extract**; husk, hull, pod; *N. Amer.* shuck.
2 *rebel artillery began to shell the city* **bombard**, fire on, open fire on, shoot at, attack, pound, bomb, blitz, strafe; *archaic* cannonade.
□ **shell something out** (*informal*) *they shelled out £3.3 million for the England striker. See* PAY.

WORD LINKS
related prefix **conch(o)-** (e.g. *conchometer*)
study or collection of shells **conchology**

shellfish *See centre pages for lists of* **Crustaceans Molluscs**
▶ **noun** **crustacean**, bivalve, mollusc.

shelter ▶ **noun 1** *the plants provide shelter for animals* **protection**, shield, cover, a roof, screen, shade; safety, security, defence, refuge, sanctuary, asylum, safe keeping, safeguarding.
OPPOSITES danger, exposure.
2 *she runs a shelter for battered cats* **sanctuary**, place of shelter, refuge, accommodation, housing, home, place of safety, haven, safe haven, sanctum, safe house; harbour, port in a storm, ark; retreat, bolt-hole, foxhole, hiding place, hideaway, hideout, fastness; *Spanish* querencia.
▶ **verb 1** *the hut sheltered him from the cold wind* **protect**, keep safe, shield, cover, screen, shade, keep from harm, afford protection to, provide protection for, save, safeguard, wrap, cover for, preserve, conserve, defend, cushion, secure, guard, hedge; inoculate, insulate.
OPPOSITES endanger, expose.
2 *the anchorage where convoys sheltered in bad weather* **take shelter**, take refuge, seek protection, seek refuge, seek sanctuary, take cover; *informal* hole up.

sheltered ▶ **adjective 1** *a sheltered stretch of water lying between the coast and the peninsula* **protected**, screened, shielded, covered, calm; shady, shaded, cool; cosy, snug, warm.
OPPOSITE exposed.
2 *their daughter had led a sheltered life* **secluded**, withdrawn, isolated, protected, immune, cloistered, unworldly, sequestered, retired, reclusive; privileged, secure, safe, quiet, cosy, comfortable.

shelve ▶ **verb** *plans to reopen the school have been shelved* **put to one side**, lay aside, pigeonhole, stay, stand over, keep in abeyance, suspend, mothball; **postpone**, put off, delay, defer, put back, hold over/off, carry over, reschedule, do later, adjourn; put off the evil day/hour; **abandon**, drop, abolish, withdraw, throw out, do away with, give up, take away, stop, put an end to, cancel, eliminate, cut, jettison; *N. Amer.* put over, table, lay on the table, take a rain check on; *N. Amer. Law* continue; *informal* put on ice, put on the back burner, put in cold storage, axe, ditch, dump, junk, chuck in; *rare* remit, respite.
OPPOSITES carry out, execute, implement; revive.

shepherd ▶ **noun** *he worked as a shepherd* shepherd boy, shepherdess, herdsman, herdswoman; *N. Amer.* sheepman.
▶ **verb** *police shepherded thousands of workers away from the area* **guide**, conduct, usher, convoy, marshal, steer, herd, lead, take, escort, accompany, walk; show, see, attend, chaperone.

S

sherry ▶ **noun.** *See centre pages for list of* **Sherries**

shield ▶ **noun 1** *using his shield to fend off blows* buckler, target; (*in Australia*) hielaman; *Heraldry* escutcheon; *Mythology* aegis; *archaic* targe.
2 *a protective coating of grease provides a shield against abrasive dirt* **protection**, guard, defence, cover, screen, shade, safety, security, shelter, safeguard, support, bulwark, protector.
▶ **verb** *he pulled his cap lower to shield his eyes from the glare | these people have been completely shielded from economic forces* **protect**, keep safe, cover, screen, shade, keep from harm, afford protection to, provide protection for, save, safeguard, wrap, preserve, conserve, defend, cushion, secure, guard, inoculate, insulate.
OPPOSITES expose, endanger.

shift ▶ **verb 1** *Lawton had already shifted some chairs to form a barricade* **move**, carry, transfer, transport, convey, take, bring, bear, lug, cart, haul, fetch, switch, move around, transpose, relocate, reposition, rearrange, displace.
2 *her foot began to tingle and she shifted her position | they cannot be trusted; they shift their position from day to day* **change**, alter, adjust, make adjustments to, adapt, amend, recast, vary, modify, revise, reverse, retract, do a U-turn on; eat one's words; *Brit.* do an about-turn on.
OPPOSITES keep, stick to.
3 *the cargo has shifted* **move**, slide, slip, move around, be displaced.
4 *the wind has shifted* **veer**, alter, change, back, vary, fluctuate, turn, swing, change direction.
5 (*Brit.*) *a small rubber brush with large prongs really shifts the dirt* **get rid of**, take out, get off, remove, budge, lift, expunge.
□ **shift for oneself** *the least and the most able being left to shift for themselves* **cope (on one's own)**, manage (by oneself), survive, manage without help/assistance, make it on one's own, fend for oneself, take care of oneself, make do, get by/along, scrape by/along, muddle through/along; make ends meet, keep the wolf from the door, stand on one's own two feet, keep one's head above water; *informal* paddle one's own canoe, make out.
▶ **noun 1** *the shift of people into south of the country has slowed substantially* **movement**, move, shifting, transference, transport, conveyance, switch, transposition; **relocation**, repositioning, rearrangement.
2 *a shift in public opinion* **change**, alteration, adjustment, adaptation, amendment, recasting, variation, modification, revision, reversal, retraction, sea change, U-turn; *Brit.* about-turn.
3 *they worked three shifts—morning, afternoon, and evening* **work period**, stint, spell of work, stretch.
4 *the night shift goes home at 8 a.m.* **group**, crew, gang, team, squad, patrol.
5 *he had to resort to dubious shifts to make enough money to live on* **stratagem**, scheme, subterfuge, expedient, dodge, trick, ruse, wile, artifice, deception, strategy, device, plan.

shiftless ▶ **adjective** *he thought the whole family shiftless and dishonest* **lazy**, idle, indolent, slothful, lethargic, lackadaisical; spiritless, apathetic, improvident, aimless, worthless, feckless, good-for-nothing, ne'er-do-well; inefficient, incompetent, inept, unambitious, unenterprising.
OPPOSITES enthusiastic, enterprising.

shifty ▶ **adjective** (*informal*) *he had a shifty look about him* **devious**, evasive, slippery, duplicitous, false, deceitful, underhand, untrustworthy, double-dealing, two-faced, dishonest, shady, wily, crafty, cunning, tricky, sneaky, furtive, treacherous, artful, sly, scheming, contriving; *N. Amer.* snide, snidey; *informal* foxy, iffy; *Austral./NZ informal* shonky.
OPPOSITES honest, open, trustworthy.

shilly-shally ▶ **verb** *the government shilly-shallied about the matter* **dither**, be indecisive/irresolute, be undecided, be uncertain, be unsure, be doubtful, vacillate, waver, teeter, hesitate, oscillate, fluctuate, falter, drag one's feet; *Brit.* haver, hum and haw; *Scottish* swither; *informal* dilly-dally, blow hot and cold, sit on the fence.

shimmer ▶ **verb** *the glow of the lanterns shimmered on the water* **glint**, glisten, flicker, twinkle, sparkle, flash, scintillate, flare, glare, gleam, glow, glimmer, glitter, dance, blink, wink; *rare* coruscate, fulgurate.
▶ **noun** *the wet streets reflected the shimmer of lights from never-ending traffic* **glint**, glistening, flicker, twinkle, sparkle, flash, scintillation, flare, glare, gleam, glow, glimmer, lustre, glitter, dancing, blinking, winking; *rare* coruscation, fulguration.

shin ▶ **verb** *he shinned up a tree | she shinned down the rope* **climb (up/down)**, clamber up/down, scramble up/down, scrabble up/down, swarm up/down, shoot up/down, go up/down; mount, ascend, scale, claw one's way up; descend, slide down, drop down; *N. Amer.* shinny.

shine ▶ **verb 1** *the sun shone through the window* **emit light**, give off light, beam, radiate, gleam, glow, glint, glimmer, sparkle, twinkle, flicker, glitter, glisten, shimmer, flash, dazzle, flare, glare, fluoresce; *literary* glister; *rare* coruscate, fulgurate, effulge, luminesce, incandesce, phosphoresce.
2 *she would even shine his shoes for him* **polish**, burnish, buff, wax, gloss, brighten, brush, smooth, rub up.
3 *they shone at university* **excel**, be outstanding, be brilliant, be excellent, be very good, be successful, be expert, stand out, be pre-eminent.
▶ **noun 1** *he flinched at the sight of the ravaged face now caught in the shine of the moon* **light**, brightness, gleam, glow, glint, glimmer, sparkle, twinkle, flicker, glitter, glisten, shimmer, flash, dazzle, beam, flare, glare, radiance, illumination, luminescence, luminosity, incandescence, phosphorescence, fluorescence; *rare* refulgence, lambency, effulgence, fulguration.
2 *linseed oil helps restore the shine to a dull surface* **polish**, burnish, gleam, gloss, lustre, sheen, patina.

shining ▶ **adjective 1** *a shining expanse of water* **gleaming**, bright, illuminated, lit, lighted, ablaze, brilliant, lustrous, glowing, glinting, sparkling, twinkling, flickering, glittering, glistening, shimmering, flashing, dazzling, glaring, luminous, luminescent, incandescent, phosphorescent, fluorescent; *literary* glistering, irradiant, lucent, lucid, lambent; *rare* effulgent, refulgent, coruscating, fulgurating.
OPPOSITE dark.
2 *she had an eager, shining face* **glowing**, beaming, radiant, blooming, healthy, happy.
OPPOSITE gloomy.
3 *a new folding chair made of shining chromium tubes* **shiny**, bright, polished, burnished, gleaming, glossy, glassy, satiny, sheeny, lustrous, smooth; *rare* nitid.
OPPOSITE matt.
□ **a shining example** *a shining example of British enterprise* **paragon**, model, epitome, archetype, ideal, exemplar, nonpareil, paradigm, embodiment,

personification, quintessence, standard, prototype, apotheosis, the crème de la crème, the beau idéal, acme, jewel, gem, flower, angel, treasure, an outstanding example, a perfect example of its kind; *informal* one in a million, the bee's knees, something else, the tops; *archaic* a nonsuch.
OPPOSITE poor example.

shiny ▶ adjective *a shiny red mackintosh* **glossy**, glassy, bright, polished, burnished, gleaming, satiny, sheeny, lustrous, smooth; *rare* nitid.
OPPOSITE matt.

ship *See centre pages for lists of* **Ships and Boats** **Ship Parts** **Sailing Ships and Boats**
▶ noun *a ship's hull* **vessel**, craft, boat.

WORD LINKS
relating to ships **marine, maritime, nautical, naval**

shirk ▶ verb **1** *she was brave and would not shirk any task* **evade**, dodge, avoid, get out of, sidestep, shuffle off, run away from, shrink from, shun, slide out of, play truant from, skip, miss, not attend; **neglect**, let slide, not attend to, pay little/no attention to, be remiss about, be lax about, leave undone, lose sight of, skimp on; *informal* duck, duck out of, cop out of; *Brit. informal* skive off, funk; *N. Amer. informal* cut; *Austral./NZ informal* duck-shove.
2 *discipline was strict and no one shirked* **evade one's duty**, be remiss, be negligent, skulk, play truant, malinger; *Brit. informal* skive (off), wag, dodge the column, swing the lead, scrimshank, slack; *N. Amer. informal* goof off, goldbrick, play hookey; *Austral./NZ informal* bludge, play the wag.

shirker ▶ noun **dodger**, truant, (habitual) absentee, malingerer, layabout, loafer, idler; *informal* slacker, cyberslacker; *Brit. informal* skiver, wag, scrimshanker; *Austral./NZ informal* duck-shover; *archaic* shirk.

shirt ▶ noun. *See centre pages for list of* **Shirts**

shiver[1] ▶ verb *she was shivering with fear* **tremble**, quiver, shake, shudder, quaver, quake, vibrate, palpitate, flutter, convulse.
▶ noun *she gave a shiver as the door opened* **tremble**, trembling, quiver, quivering, shake, start, shudder, shuddering, quaver, quake, vibration, tremor, palpitation, flutter, convulsion, twitch, jerk.

CHOOSE THE RIGHT WORD
shiver, shake, tremble, quiver, quake
See SHAKE.

shiver[2] ▶ noun *a shiver of glass* **splinter**, sliver, fragment, chip, shard, paring, shaving, shred, smithereen, particle, bit, piece.
▶ verb (*rare*) *the window shivered into thousands of pieces* **shatter**, splinter, smash, smash into smithereens, fragment, disintegrate, burst, explode, crack, break.

shivery ▶ adjective *she felt sick and shivery* **trembling**, trembly, quivering, quivery, shaking, shaky, shuddering, shuddery, quavering, quavery, quaking; **cold**, chilly, chilled.

shoal ▶ noun *three ships ran aground on the shoal* **sandbank**, bank, mudbank, bar, sandbar, tombolo, shallow, shelf, sands; (*in Latin America*) cay.

shock[1] ▶ noun **1** *the news of the murder came as a shock* **blow**, upset, disturbance, source of distress, source of amazement/consternation; **surprise**, revelation, a bolt from the blue, a bolt out of the blue, thunderbolt, bombshell, rude awakening, eye-opener; *informal* whammy.
2 *you really gave me a shock then* **fright**, scare, jolt, start, state of agitation/perturbation, distress, consternation, panic; *informal* turn.
3 *she was taken to hospital suffering from shock after the accident* **trauma**, a state of shock, traumatism, prostration, stupor, stupefaction, collapse, breakdown.
4 *the first shock of a great earthquake* **vibration**, shaking movement, reverberation, shake, jolt, jar, jarring, jerk; bump, impact, blow, collision, crash, clash.
▶ verb *her savage murder shocked the nation* **appal**, horrify, scandalize, outrage, repel, revolt, disgust, nauseate, sicken, offend, give offence to, traumatize, make someone's blood run cold, distress, upset, perturb, disturb, disquiet, unsettle, discompose, agitate; stun, rock, stagger, astound, astonish, amaze, startle, surprise, dumbfound, daze, shake, shake up, jolt, set someone back on their heels, take aback, throw, unnerve, disconcert, bewilder.

shock[2] ▶ noun *a shock of red hair* **mass**, mane, mop, thatch, head, crop, bush, cloud, frizz, fuzz, foam, curls, tangle, chaos, cascade, quiff, halo.

shocking ▶ adjective *it was the next day before they heard the shocking news* **appalling**, horrifying, horrific, dreadful, awful, frightful, terrible, horrible, scandalous, outrageous, disgraceful, vile, abominable, ghastly, foul, monstrous, unspeakable, abhorrent, hideous, atrocious, repellent, revolting, odious, repulsive, repugnant, disgusting, nauseating, sickening, grisly, loathsome, offensive, distressing, upsetting, perturbing, disturbing, disquieting, unsettling, agitating; stunning, staggering, amazing, astonishing, startling, stupefying, overwhelming, bewildering, unnerving, surprising.
OPPOSITES admirable, wonderful, delightful.

shoddy ▶ adjective **1** *we're not paying good money for shoddy goods* **poor-quality**, inferior, second-rate, third-rate, low-grade, cheap, cheapjack, tawdry, rubbishy, trashy, gimcrack, jerry-built, crude, tinny; *informal* tacky, tatty, junky; *Brit. informal* ropy, duff, rubbish, grotty.
OPPOSITE well made.
2 *shoddy workmanship* **careless**, slapdash, sloppy, slipshod, scrappy, untidy, messy, hasty, hurried, negligent, cursory.
OPPOSITE careful.

shoe ▶ noun. *See centre pages for list of* **Footwear**

shoemaker ▶ noun **cobbler**, bootmaker; *Scottish & N. English* souter; *archaic* cordwainer, snob, snab; *rare* broguer, clogger.

shoot ▶ verb **1** *he went out to shoot rabbits* **gun down**, shoot down, mow down, hit, wound, injure, cut down, bring down; put a bullet in, pick off, bag, fell, kill; execute, put before a firing squad; *informal* pot, blast, pump full of lead, plug, zap; *literary* slay.
2 *the men began to* **shoot at** *the enemy* **fire (at/on)**, open fire (at/on), aim at, snipe at, let fly (at), blaze away; bombard, shell.
3 *faster than a machine gun can shoot bullets* **discharge**, fire, launch, let off, loose off, let fly, send forth, emit.
4 *a police car shot past* **race**, hurry, hasten, flash, dash, dart, rush, speed, hurtle, streak, really move, spank along, whirl, whizz, go like lightning, go hell for leather, whoosh, buzz, zoom, swoop, blast, charge; stampede, gallop, chase, career, bustle, sweep, hare, fly, wing, scurry, scud, scutter; *informal* belt, scoot, scorch, tear, zap, zip, whip (along), get cracking, get a move on, step on it, burn rubber, go like a bat out of hell; *Brit. informal* bomb, bucket, shift, put one's foot down; *N. Amer. informal* clip, boogie, hightail, barrel, lay rubber; *literary* fleet; *N. Amer. vulgar slang* drag/tear/haul ass; *archaic* post, hie.
5 *some years one or other plant fails to shoot* **sprout**, put forth shoots, put forth buds, bud, burgeon, germinate; *technical* pullulate.
6 *the film was shot on location in Tunisia* **film**, photograph, take/get a photograph/photo of, take/get photographs of, take/get a picture of, take/get pictures of, take someone's picture/photo, take/get a snapshot/snap of, take, snap, capture/record on film/celluloid; make a film of, televise, video.
▶ noun *I nip off the new shoots to make the plant bush out* **sprout**, offshoot, scion, sucker, bud, spear, runner, tendril, sprig, cutting; *technical* stolon, flagellum, bine, ratoon.

shop *See centre pages for list of specialist* **Shops**
▶ noun **1** *a shop selling all sorts of goods* **store**, retail store, outlet, retail outlet, cash and carry; boutique, salon, parlour; establishment, emporium, department store, supermarket, hypermarket, superstore, warehouse club, warehouse, factory outlet, chain store, mall, shopping mall, shopping centre, retail centre, megastore, bargain basement, concession, market, mart, stall, stand, booth, counter, trading post; *Brit.* multiple (shop/store), lock-up; *N. Amer.* minimart, convenience store, mini-mall; *informal* shed.
2 *he works in the machine shop* **workshop**, workroom, plant, factory, works, manufacturing complex, industrial unit, mill, foundry, yard, garage, atelier, studio; *Brit.* shop floor; *archaic* manufactory.
▶ verb **1** *we shop twice a week | he was going to* **shop for** *spices in the market* **go shopping**, do the shopping, buy what one needs/wants, buy things, go to the shops; buy, purchase, get, acquire, obtain, pick up, snap up, procure, stock up on, get in supplies of, look to buy, be in the market for.
2 (*Brit. informal*) *the police got him to shop his fellow bank raiders* **inform on/against**, betray, sell out, tell tales on, be disloyal to, be unfaithful to, break one's promise to, break faith with, stab in the back; *informal* tell on, rat on, put the finger on, squeal on, stitch up, snitch on, peach on, sing about, sell down the river, blow the whistle on, do the dirty on; *Brit. informal* grass on, split on; *N. Amer. informal* rat out, finger, fink on, drop a/the dime on; *Austral./NZ informal* pimp on, pool, put someone's pot on.

shopkeeper *See centre pages for list of* **Sellers of Goods**
▶ noun *the shopkeeper was counting some change out on the counter* **shop-owner**, **shop manager**, shop proprietor, retailer, dealer, seller, trader, trafficker, wholesaler, broker, salesman, saleswoman, salesperson, tradesman, distributor, agent, vendor; *N. Amer.* storekeeper; *Brit. dated* shopman.

shopper ▶ noun *supermarkets helping the shopper to make more informed choices* **buyer**, purchaser, customer, consumer, client, patron; (**shoppers**) **clientele**, patronage, public, trade, market; *Law* vendee; *rare* emptor.

shopping centre ▶ noun *Florida's largest shopping centre has over 200 shops* **shopping precinct**, shopping complex, (shopping) mall, (shopping) arcade, galleria, (shopping) parade; marketplace, mart, flea market, fair, bazaar, piazza; *N. Amer.* plaza, strip mall; *Arabic* souk; *historical* agora; *archaic* emporium.

shore[1] ▶ noun *his friends swam out from the shore* **seashore**, seaside, beach, coast, coastal region, seaboard, sea coast, bank, lakeside, verge, edge, shoreline, waterside, front, shoreside, foreshore, sand, sands; *technical* littoral; *literary* strand.

WORD LINKS
relating to a shore **littoral**

S

shore[2] ▶ verb *rescue workers had to shore up the building* **prop up**, hold up, bolster up, support, brace, buttress, strengthen, fortify, reinforce, underpin, truss, stay; *archaic* underprop.

short ▶ adjective **1** *a short piece of string* small, little, tiny, minuscule; *informal* teeny, teeny-weeny.
OPPOSITE long.
2 *the problem for short people was to see them over the crowd* **small**, little, petite, tiny, squat, stocky, dumpy, stubby, elfin, dwarf, dwarfish, midget, pygmy, diminutive, Lilliputian, homuncular, minuscule, miniature; *Scottish* wee; *informal* pint-sized, teeny, teeny-weeny, pocket-sized, knee-high to a grasshopper; *Brit. informal* fubsy.
OPPOSITE tall.
3 *there is a female redwing in the short scrubby bushes* **low**, squat, stubby, miniature, dwarf; *Scottish* wee.
OPPOSITE tall.
4 *the Times published a short report of the affair* **concise**, brief, succinct, to the point, compact, terse, curt, summary, economical, crisp, short and sweet, pithy, epigrammatic, laconic, pointed, thumbnail, abridged, abbreviated, condensed, synoptic, compendious, summarized, contracted, curtailed, truncated.
OPPOSITES long, overlong, verbose.
5 *for a short time | a short look at the instruments* **brief**, momentary, temporary, short-lived, impermanent, short-term, cursory, fleeting, passing, fugitive, flying, lightning, transitory, transient, ephemeral, evanescent, fading, quick, meteoric; *rare* fugacious.
6 *let's take the short route* **direct**, straight.
OPPOSITE roundabout.
7 *money is a bit short at the moment | there is only a short supply of food* **scarce**, in short supply, scant, scanty, meagre, sparse, hard to find, hard to come by, not enough, too little, insufficient, deficient, inadequate, lacking, wanting; at a premium, like gold dust, not to be had, scarcer than hen's teeth; paltry, negligible, thin; *informal* not to be had for love nor money; *rare* exiguous.
OPPOSITE plentiful.
8 *he was rather short with her* **curt**, sharp, abrupt, blunt, brusque, terse, offhand, gruff, ungracious, graceless, surly, snappy, testy, tart, rude, discourteous, uncivil, impolite, ill-mannered, bad-mannered.
OPPOSITES patient, courteous.
9 *short pastry* **crumbly**, crispy, crisp, brittle, friable; shortcrust; fatty.

□ **in short** *in short, then, the government is being called to account for the economic disaster* **briefly**, to put it briefly/succinctly/concisely, in a word, in a nutshell, in a few words, in precis, in essence, to cut a long story short, to come to the point; in conclusion, summarizing, in summary, to sum up, in sum.
OPPOSITE in full.

□ **short of 1** *holidays or sickness may leave a ward short of nurses* **deficient in**, lacking (in), wanting (in), in need of, low on, short on, missing, with an insufficiency of, with too few/little ...; *informal* strapped for, pushed for, minus.
2 *short of interning suspects without trial, there is little the security forces can do* **apart from**, other than, in any other way than, aside from, besides, except (for), excepting, without, without going so far as, excluding, leaving out, not counting, disregarding, save (for).

> **CHOOSE THE RIGHT WORD**
>
> **shorten, abbreviate, abridge, truncate, curtail**
>
> - **Shorten** is the most general term for reducing the length of duration of something (*the reforms had made progress in shortening hospital waiting lists | we are not allowed to give drugs to shorten life*).
> - The most common thing to be **abbreviated** is a word or phrase (*Hybrid Perpetual, abbreviated to H.P.*). Something that does not last as long as was planned may be described as *abbreviated*, especially if the shortening is forced by circumstances and is seen as excessive or undesirable (*his abbreviated stay in Princeton*), and the word can also be used of clothes created shorter than usual (*tight or abbreviated shorts are unacceptable*).
> - A text or other work that has been **abridged** has been made shorter by cutting out details while preserving the proportions orbasic character of the original (*the editor reserves the right to abridge letters*).
> - To **truncate** something is to cut off one end (*a truncated pyramid*). There is usually a sense that the item is mutilated as a result (*Tolkien found that the Old English being dished up was in a grossly truncated form*), or that something has been brought to an end too soon (*further discussion was truncated by the arrival of tea*).
> - Something that is **curtailed** is typically restricted in scope, especially in freedom of action (*ill health probably curtailed his activities | contemporaries sought to curtail the influence of the Court*), but the word is also used for an unplanned shortening in time (*rain forced us to curtail our visit*).

▶ adverb *Iris headed for the kitchen, then stopped short* **abruptly**, suddenly, sharply, all of a sudden, all at once, unexpectedly, without warning, out of the blue.

shortage ▶ noun *the shortage of people with adequate training* **scarcity**, sparseness, sparsity, dearth, paucity, poverty, insufficiency, deficiency, inadequacy, famine, lack, want, meagreness, scantiness, limitedness, restrictedness, deficit, shortfall, rarity, rareness; *rare* exiguity.
OPPOSITE abundance.

shortcoming ▶ noun *he was fully aware of his own shortcomings* **defect**, fault, flaw, imperfection, deficiency, limitation, blemish, failing, drawback, weakness, weak point, foible, fallibility, frailty, vice, infirmity.
OPPOSITE strength.

shorten ▶ verb **1** *you can shorten your essay without losing its balance | an invention that helped shorten the war* **make shorter**, abbreviate, abridge, condense, precis, synopsize, contract, compress, reduce, lessen, shrink, decrease, diminish, cut, cut down, cut short, dock, trim, clip, crop, pare down, prune; **curtail**, truncate; turn up, take up.
OPPOSITES lengthen, extend, elongate.
2 *the days are shortening* **get shorter**, grow shorter, grow less, contract, compress, shrink.
OPPOSITE lengthen.

short-lived ▶ adjective *this was a short-lived setback* **brief**, short, momentary, temporary, impermanent, short-term, cursory, fleeting, passing, fugitive, flying, lightning, transitory, transient, ephemeral, evanescent, fading, quick, meteoric; *rare* fugacious.
OPPOSITE long-lived.

shortly ▶ adverb **1** *she will be with you shortly* **soon**, directly, presently, quite soon, in a short time, in a short/little while, at any moment/minute/second, in a moment/minute/second, in less than no time (at all), in next to no time, before long, by and by; *N. Amer.* momentarily; *S. African* just now; *informal* pretty soon, any time/day/minute/second/moment now, before one knows it, before one can say Jack Robinson, in a jiffy, in two shakes of a lamb's tail; *Brit. informal* in a mo, sharpish; *archaic or informal* anon; *literary* ere long.
2 *'I know that,' he replied shortly* **curtly**, sharply, abruptly, bluntly, brusquely, tersely, in an offhand manner, gruffly, ungraciously, gracelessly, surlily, snappily, testily, tartly, rudely, discourteously, uncivilly, impolitely.
OPPOSITES patiently, courteously.

short-sighted ▶ adjective **1** *a short-sighted neighbour asked me what the flowers were* **myopic**; *N. Amer.* nearsighted; *informal* as blind as a bat; *archaic* purblind.
OPPOSITES long-sighted; normal-sighted.
2 *short-sighted critics will no doubt dismiss this film as trash* **narrow-minded**, narrow, unimaginative, lacking foresight, improvident, unadventurous, small-minded, short-term, insular, parochial, provincial.
OPPOSITES far-sighted, imaginative.

short-staffed ▶ adjective *we're rather short-staffed what with Christmas and everything* **understaffed**, short-handed, undermanned, below strength.
OPPOSITE overstaffed.

short-tempered ▶ adjective *she found she was short-tempered with shop assistants* **irritable**, irascible, hot-tempered, quick-tempered, fiery, peevish, cross, crabbed, crabby, crotchety, cantankerous, impatient, grumpy, huffy, brusque, ill-tempered, bad-tempered, ill-natured, ill-humoured, touchy, volatile, testy, tetchy, snarling, waspish, prickly, crusty, peppery, bilious, liverish, dyspeptic, splenetic, choleric; *informal* snappish, snappy, chippy, grouchy, cranky, on a short fuse; *Brit. informal* narky, ratty, eggy, like a bear with a sore head; *N. Amer. informal* peckish, soreheaded; *Austral./NZ informal* snaky; *informal, dated* miffy.
OPPOSITES placid, calm, easy-going, phlegmatic.

shot[1] *See centre pages for list of* **Bullets and Shot**
▶ noun **1** *a shot rang out* report of a gun, crack, bang, blast, explosion, discharge of a gun; (**shots**) gunfire.
2 *the cannon have run out of shot* **ball**, bullet, cannonball, slug, projectile; pellets, ammunition.
3 *his partner pulled off a winning backhand shot* **stroke**, hit, strike; kick, throw, pitch, roll, bowl, lob, fling, hurl, shot-put.
4 *Mike was an excellent shot* **marksman**, markswoman, shooter, rifleman; *rare* shootist.
5 *here's a shot of us on holiday* **photograph**, photo, snap, snapshot, picture, likeness, image, portrait, study, print, slide, transparency, negative, positive, plate, film, bromide, frame, exposure, still, proof, enprint, enlargement.
6 (*informal*) *it's nice to get a shot at steering* **attempt**, try, effort, endeavour; turn, chance, opportunity; guess; *informal* go, stab, crack, bash, whack; *formal* essay.
7 *you need typhoid and cholera shots* **injection**, inoculation, immunization, vaccination, revaccination, booster; *Medicine* venepuncture; *informal* jab, fix, hype.

□ **a shot in the arm** (*informal*) *the improvements will provide a shot in the arm for thousands of small businesses* **boost**, fillip, pick-me-up, tonic, stimulus,

spur, push, impetus, encouragement.
OPPOSITE blow.

□ **a shot in the dark** *Cunliffe admitted that his figure was little more than a shot in the dark* **guess**, random guess, wild guess, surmise, supposition, conjecture, speculation, theorizing.

□ **like a shot** (*informal*) *he would take the job like a shot* **without hesitation**, unhesitatingly, very willingly, eagerly, enthusiastically, gladly; **immediately**, at once, right away, right now, quickly, straight away, instantly, instantaneously, directly, forthwith, promptly, without delay; *informal* in/like a flash, before one can say Jack Robinson, before one can say knife.

□ **not by a long shot** *he is not yet out of the woods, not by a long shot* **by no means**, by no manner of means, not at all, in no way, not in the least, not in the slightest, not the least bit, certainly not, absolutely not, definitely not, on no account, under no circumstances; *Brit.* not by a long chalk; *informal* no way.

shot[2] ▶ **adjective** *shot silk* **variegated**, mottled, watered, moiré; multicoloured, many-coloured, varicoloured; iridescent, opalescent, lustrous, shimmering.

shoulder ▶ **noun**

□ **give someone the cold shoulder** **snub**, shun, cold-shoulder, ignore, turn one's back on, cut, cut dead, look right through, rebuff, dismiss, reject, brush off, turn down, spurn, disdain, refuse, decline, repudiate, ostracize; *informal* give someone the brush-off, tell someone where to get off, put down, freeze out, stiff-arm; *Brit. informal* knock back, send to Coventry; *N. Amer. informal* give someone the bum's rush, give someone the brush; *Austral. informal* snout; *informal, dated* give someone the go-by.

□ **put one's shoulder to the wheel** **get (down) to work**, apply oneself, set to work, fall to, buckle down, get down to business, put one's hand to the plough, roll up one's sleeves, get things moving, start the ball rolling; work hard, make an effort, strive, be industrious/diligent/assiduous, exert oneself; *informal* give it one's best shot, get cracking, get one's finger out, get weaving, get the show on the road, get off one's backside; *Brit. informal* get stuck in; *dated* buckle to.

□ **shoulder to shoulder** **1** *the regiment lined up shoulder to shoulder in three columns* **side by side**, abreast, alongside (each other), level, beside each other, cheek by jowl.
2 *he fought off the attack on economic internationalism, shoulder to shoulder with City bankers* **united**, together, jointly, working together, in partnership, in collaboration, in cooperation, cooperatively, side by side, arm in arm, hand in hand, in unity, in unison, in alliance, in league, in concert, concertedly, conjointly, as one.

▶ **verb** **1** *Britain shouldered the primary responsibility for the stability of the area* **take on**, take on oneself, undertake, accept, assume; bear, carry, support, sustain, be responsible for.
2 *another lad shouldered him aside | he shouldered his way through the crowd* **push**, shove, thrust, propel, jostle, elbow, force, crowd, prod, poke, nudge, knock, ram, bulldoze, sweep, bundle, hustle, hurry, rush, manhandle.

shout ▶ **verb** *'Help,' he shouted* **yell**, cry, cry out, call, call out, roar, howl, bellow, bawl, call at the top of one's voice, clamour, bay, cheer, yawp, yelp, wail, squawk, shriek, scream, screech, squeal, squall, caterwaul, whoop; raise one's voice; *N. Amer. informal* holler; *rare* vociferate.
OPPOSITE whisper.

▶ **noun** *a shout of pain* **yell**, cry, call, roar, howl, bellow, bawl, clamour, bay, cheer, yawp, yelp, wail, squawk, shriek, scream, screech, squeal, squall, caterwaul, whoop; *N. Amer. informal* holler; *rare* vociferation.
OPPOSITE whisper.

shove ▶ **verb** **1** *she shoved him back into the chair* **push**, thrust, propel, impel; send, press, drive, plunge, stick, force, shoot, ram, barge, bump, knock, strike, hit, jolt, butt, prod, poke, nudge, elbow, shoulder; bulldoze, sweep, jostle, bundle, hustle, hurry, rush, manhandle.
2 *she shoved past him and ran off* **push (one's way)**, force one's way, barge (one's way), elbow (one's way), shoulder one's way, muscle, bludgeon one's way, plunge, crash, bulldoze, sweep, bundle, hustle, hurry, rush.

□ **shove off** (*informal*) *shove off—I don't want you here* **go away**, depart, leave, take off, get out, get out of my sight; go, go your way, get going, take oneself off, get moving, move off, be off, set off, set out, start out, make a start, take one's leave, decamp, duck out, take wing, walk out, walk off; be off with you!, shoo!; *informal* hit the road, fly, skedaddle, split, vamoose, scat, scram, make oneself scarce, be on one's way, run along, beat it, get, get lost, push off, buzz off, clear off, skip off, pop off, go (and) jump in the lake; on your bike!, go and chase yourself!; *Brit. informal* get along, push along, get stuffed, sling your hook, hop it, hop the twig/stick, bog off, naff off; *N. Amer. informal* bug off, light out, haul off, haul ass, take a powder, hit the trail, take a hike; *Austral. informal* nick off; *Austral./NZ informal* rack off; *S. African informal* voetsak, hamba; *vulgar slang* bugger off, piss off, fuck off; *Brit. vulgar slang* sod off; *literary* begone, avaunt.

▶ **noun** *she gave him a hefty shove* **push**, thrust, barge, ram, bump, bang, jolt, butt, knock, prod, poke, nudge, elbow, shoulder, jostle.

shovel ▶ **noun** *the turf had been dug up by vandals using a pick and shovel* spade, scoop; *Austral./NZ* banjo; *archaic* peel.

▶ **verb** *supporters tried to shovel snow off the pitch* **scoop (up)**, spade, dig, excavate, move, shift, heap, spoon, ladle, toss.

show ▶ **verb** **1** *the dropped stitches can be left if they do not show* **be visible**, be seen, be in view, manifest; appear, be revealed, be obvious.
OPPOSITE be invisible.
2 *he wouldn't show the picture* **display**, **exhibit**, put on show, put on display, put on view, expose to view, unveil, present; launch, introduce, air, demonstrate, set out, set forth, arrange, array, flaunt, parade, uncover, reveal.
OPPOSITE conceal.
3 *it was Frank's turn to show his frustration* **manifest**, make manifest, exhibit, reveal, convey, communicate, make known; indicate, express, proclaim, intimate, make plain, make obvious, signify, evince, evidence, disclose, betray, divulge, give away.
OPPOSITE suppress.
4 *I'll show you how to make a daisy chain* **demonstrate to**, point out to, explain to, describe to, expound to; clarify, make clear, illustrate, explicate, expound, elucidate; teach, instruct someone in, give instructions in, give an idea of, tutor someone in, indoctrinate someone in.
5 *recent events show this to be true* **prove**, demonstrate, confirm, show beyond doubt, manifest, produce/submit proof, produce/submit evidence, establish evidence, evince; witness to, give substance to, determine, demonstrate the truth of, convince someone, substantiate, corroborate, verify, establish, ratify, validate, authenticate, attest, certify, testify, document, bear out.
6 *a young woman showed them to their seats* **escort**, accompany, take, walk, conduct, lead, usher, bow, guide, direct, steer, shepherd, attend, chaperone.
7 (*informal*) *we were waiting for them, but they never showed* **appear**, arrive, come, get here, get there, be present, put in an appearance, make an appearance, materialize, turn up, present oneself, report, clock in, sign in; *Brit.* clock on; *N. Amer.* punch in, punch the (time) clock; *informal* show up.

□ **show off** (*informal*) *he was showing off, trying to make a really big impression* **behave affectedly**, put on airs, put on an act, give oneself airs, boast, brag, crow, trumpet, gloat, glory, swagger around, swank, bluster, strut, strike an attitude, strike a pose, posture, attitudinize; draw attention to oneself, blow one's own trumpet; *N. Amer. informal* cop an attitude; *Austral./NZ informal* skite, big-note oneself.

□ **show something off** *the easel was commonly used to show off a painting* **display**, show to advantage, exhibit, demonstrate; parade, make a show of, draw attention to, flaunt, wave, dangle, brandish, vaunt.

□ **show up** **1** *modern-day swabs do show up on X-rays* **be visible**, be obvious, be seen, be revealed, be conspicuous, stand out, catch the eye.
OPPOSITE be invisible.
2 (*informal*) *only two waitresses showed up for work.* See **SHOW** sense 7.

□ **show someone/something up** **1** *the sun showed up the faded shabbiness of the room* **expose**, reveal, bring to light, lay bare, make visible, make obvious, manifest, highlight, pinpoint, put the spotlight on.
OPPOSITE conceal.
2 *they showed him up in front of his friends* **humiliate**, humble, mortify, bring/take down, bring low, demean, expose, show in a bad light, shame, put to shame, discomfit, disgrace, discredit, downgrade, debase, degrade, devalue, dishonour, embarrass; put someone in their place, make a fool of, chasten, subdue, get the better of, have the last laugh on; abash, abase, crush, squash, quash, deflate, flatten, make someone eat humble pie; *informal* put down, settle someone's hash, cut down to size; *N. Amer. informal* make someone eat crow.
OPPOSITE put someone in a good light.

▶ **noun** **1** *a spectacular show of bluebells* **display**, array, arrangement, exhibition, presentation, exposition, spectacle.
2 *the Paris motor show* **exhibition**, demonstration, display, exposition, fair, presentation, extravaganza, spectacle, pageant; *N. Amer.* exhibit.
3 *they decided to take in a show while they were up in London* **performance**, public performance, theatrical performance, production, staging; play, drama, film, concert, musical, piece; *informal* gig.
4 *she's only doing it for show* **appearance**, display, impression, ostentation, affectation, image, window dressing.
5 *Drew made a show of looking around for firewood* **pretence**, outward appearance, false appearance, front, false front, air, guise, semblance, false show, illusion, pose, affectation, profession, parade.
6 (*informal*) *I don't run the show* **undertaking**, affair, operation, proceedings, enterprise, business, venture, organization, establishment.

showdown ▶ **noun** *the government was contemplating a future showdown with the miners* **confrontation**, deciding event, clash, face-off, moment of truth, crisis.

shower ▶ **noun** **1** *a shower of rain* **fall**, light fall, drizzle, flurry, sprinkling, mizzle; downpour, deluge.
2 *a shower of arrows* **volley**, cascade, hail, rain, storm, salvo, bombardment, barrage, fusillade, broadside, cannonade.
3 *he was pleased by the shower of awards* **avalanche**, **deluge**, rush, flood, spate, torrent, cluster, flurry, wave, outbreak, outpouring; **profusion**,

S

abundance, plethora, superabundance, glut; large number, large quantity, mass.
OPPOSITES trickle; dearth.

▶ **verb 1** *confetti showered down on us* **rain**, fall, drizzle, spray, mizzle, hail.
2 *she showered them with gifts* **deluge**, flood, inundate, swamp, submerge, engulf, bury; overwhelm, saturate, glut, overload, beset, overburden, snow under.
3 *Macmillan showered political honours on his backbenchers* **lavish**, pour, load, heap, bestow freely; give freely, give generously; waste, squander; *informal* blow.

showing ▶ **noun 1** *another showing of the three-part series* **presentation**, appearance, broadcast, airing, televising, staging, playing, production, demonstration, performance.
2 *on its present showing in the polls the party doesn't stand a chance* **performance**, track record, record, results, success, achievement, conduct, reputation.

showman ▶ **noun 1** *a travelling showman at a fair* **impresario**, stage manager, publicist; ringmaster, host, compère, master of ceremonies, MC; presenter, anchorman, anchorwoman, anchorperson; *N. Amer. informal* emcee.
2 *he is a great talker and showman* **entertainer**, performer, player, artist, artiste, trouper, star, virtuoso, extrovert, self-publicist, show-off.

show-off ▶ **noun** *he was a show-off, with a big flashy car* **exhibitionist**, extrovert, poser, poseur, poseuse, peacock, swaggerer, egotist, bragger, braggart, boaster, self-publicist; *informal* pseud, trendy, swanker; *N. Amer. informal* blowhard; *rare* attitudinizer, posturer.

showy ▶ **adjective** *showy costume jewellery* **ostentatious, conspicuous**, pretentious, obtrusive, flamboyant, gaudy, garish, brash, vulgar, loud, extravagant, fancy, ornate, affected, theatrical, overdone, over-elaborate, kitsch, tasteless; *informal* flash, flashy, over the top, OTT, glitzy, ritzy, swanky, splashy; *N. Amer. informal* superfly, bling-bling; *US black English* dicty.
OPPOSITES discreet, restrained, plain.

shred ▶ **noun 1** *her beautiful dress was torn to shreds* **tatter**, scrap, strip, ribbon, rag, snippet, snip, remnant, fragment, sliver, splinter, chip, bit, tiny bit, piece, tiny piece, wisp.
2 *we have not a shred of evidence to go on* **scrap**, bit, tiny amount, speck, iota, particle, ounce, whit, jot, atom, molecule, crumb, morsel, fragment, grain, drop, hint, touch, trace, suggestion, whisper, suspicion, scintilla, spot, mite, tittle, jot or tittle, modicum; *Irish* stim; *informal* smidgen, smidge.

▶ **verb** *you can use the grating blade of a food processor to shred the vegetables* **chop finely**, cut up, tear up, rip up, grate, rub into pieces, mince, mangle, chew, macerate, grind, granulate, pulverize.

shrew ▶ **noun** *Matilda has the reputation of being a shrew* **virago**, dragon, termagant, vixen, cat, fishwife, witch, hellcat, she-devil, tartar, spitfire, hag, gorgon, harridan, fury, ogress, harpy; *informal* battleaxe, old bag, old bat, bitch; *archaic* scold; *rare* Xanthippe.

shrewd ▶ **adjective** *a shrewd businessman | a shrewd career move* **astute**, sharp-witted, sharp, acute, intelligent, clever, alert, canny, perceptive, perspicacious, observant, discriminating, sagacious, sage, wise, far-seeing, far-sighted; cunning, artful, crafty, wily, calculating, disingenuous; *informal* on the ball, smart, savvy; *Brit. informal* suss; *Scottish & N. English informal* pawky; *N. Amer. informal* heads-up; *rare* long-headed, sapient, argute; (**be shrewd**) have all one's wits about one.
OPPOSITES stupid, unwise; ingenuous.

shrewdly ▶ **adverb** *she had invested the money shrewdly* **astutely**, acutely, intelligently, cleverly, smartly, alertly, with all one's wits about one, cannily, perceptively, perspicaciously, observantly, discriminatingly, sagaciously, sagely, wisely, far-sightedly; cunningly, artfully, craftily, wilily, calculatingly, disingenuously.
OPPOSITE unwisely.

shrewdness ▶ **noun** *his bombast concealed considerable political shrewdness* **astuteness**, sharp-wittedness, sharpness, acuteness, acumen, acuity, intelligence, cleverness, smartness, alertness, wit, canniness, common sense, discernment, insight, understanding, penetration, perception, perceptiveness, perspicacity, perspicaciousness, discrimination, knowledge, sagacity, sageness; cunning, artfulness, craftiness, wiliness, calculation, calculatedness; *informal* nous, horse sense, savvy; *rare* sapience, arguteness.
OPPOSITE stupidity.

shrewish ▶ **adjective** *orphaned at birth, he was brought up by his shrewish sister* **bad-tempered**, quarrelsome, nasty, mean, spiteful, sharp-tongued, scolding, nagging, peevish, catty, snappy, vindictive, aggressive; venomous, rancorous, bitchy, snide, backbiting, petulant, vixenish, cattish; complaining, grumbling, fault-finding, carping, cavilling, criticizing, captious.

shriek ▶ **verb** *she shrieked with laughter* **scream**, **screech**, squeal, squawk, roar, howl, bellow, bawl, shout, yell, cry, cry out, call, call out, call at the top of one's voice, clamour, bay, cheer, yawp, yelp, squall, caterwaul, whoop, wail; raise one's voice; *N. Amer. informal* holler.
OPPOSITES sigh, whisper.

▶ **noun** *a shriek of laughter* **scream**, **screech**, squeal, squawk, roar, howl, bellow, bawl, shout, yell, cry, call, clamour, bay, cheer, yawp, yelp, squall, caterwaul, whoop, wail; *N. Amer. informal* holler.

shrill ▶ **adjective** *a shrill scream rent the air* **high-pitched**, **piercing**, high, sharp, ear-piercing, ear-splitting, air-rending, penetrating, shattering, strident, loud, strong, intrusive, screeching, shrieking, screechy, squawky.
OPPOSITES low, soft, dulcet.

shrine ▶ **noun 1** *the shrine of St James* **holy place**, temple, church, chapel, tabernacle, altar, sanctuary, sanctum; *Buddhism* stupa, tope; *Islam* dargah, marabout; *Hinduism* tirtha; (*in Tibet*) chorten; (*in ancient Rome*) sacrarium, nymphaeum; *archaic* fane; *rare* martyry, ciborium, feretory.
2 *Davis has turned his home into a shrine to the jockey* **memorial**, monument, cenotaph, cairn, place dedicated to ....
3 *the abbey was built around the shrine of Saint Alban* **tomb**, burial chamber, sepulchre, mausoleum, crypt, vault, catacomb, reliquary, charnel house; *rare* feretory.

shrink ▶ **verb 1** *a sweater that shrank in the wash | the workforce has shrunk to less than a thousand* **get smaller**, become/grow smaller, contract, diminish, lessen, reduce, decrease, dwindle, narrow, shorten, slim, decline, fall off, drop off, condense, deflate, shrivel, wither.
OPPOSITES expand, increase.
2 *the summer sun had shrunk and dried the wood* **make smaller**, contract, lessen, reduce, decrease, narrow, shorten, truncate, abbreviate, condense, slim down, pare down, concentrate, abridge, compress, squeeze, deflate, shrivel, wither.
OPPOSITES expand, increase.
3 *he shrank back against the wall* **draw back**, recoil, jump back, spring back, jerk back, pull back, start back, back away, retreat, withdraw; **flinch**, shy away, blench, start, wince, cringe, cower, quail.
4 *he doesn't **shrink from** naming names* **recoil**, shy away, hang back, demur, flinch; **have scruples about**, scruple about, have misgivings about, have qualms about, be loath to, be reluctant to, be unwilling to, be disinclined to, be indisposed to, be sorry to, be averse to, be slow to; be chary of, fight shy of, not be in favour of, be against, be opposed to, be hesitant to, be diffident about, be bashful about, be shy about, be coy about, be ashamed to, be afraid to, hesitate to, hate to, not like to, not have the heart to, drag one's feet/heels over, waver about, vacillate about, think twice about, baulk at, quail at, mind doing something; *informal* boggle at; *archaic* disrelish something.
OPPOSITES confront, be eager to.

shrivel ▶ **verb** *full sun is likely to shrivel the leaves | the bark of affected trees turns black and shrivels* **wither**, wrinkle, pucker up, shrink; wilt; **dry up**, desiccate, dehydrate, parch, frazzle, scorch, sear, burn; *literary* blast; *rare* exsiccate.
OPPOSITE plump up.

shrivelled ▶ **adjective** *she was clutching the remnants of the shrivelled flowers* **withered**, dry, dried up, desiccated, dehydrated, wrinkled, puckered, wizened, faded; **parched**, frazzled, scorched, seared, burnt; *literary* blasted, sear; *rare* exsiccated.
OPPOSITES fresh, plump, juicy.

shroud ▶ **noun 1** *the Turin Shroud* **winding sheet**, grave clothes, burial clothes, cerements, chrisom.
2 *a shroud of mist | governments are cloaking the operation in a shroud of secrecy* **covering**, cover, pall, cloak, mask, mantle, blanket, sheet, layer, overlay, envelope, cloud, veil, screen, curtain, canopy.

▶ **verb** *a sea mist shrouded the jetties* **cover**, envelop, veil, cloak, curtain, swathe, wrap, blanket, screen, cloud, mantle, conceal, hide, disguise, mask, obscure, surround, overlay, clothe; *literary* enshroud.

shrub *See centre pages for lists of* **Flowering Plants and Shrubs**, **Trees and Shrubs**

▶ **noun** *this eucalyptus can be encouraged to grow as a shrub* **bush**, woody plant; (**shrubs**) undergrowth, shrubbery.

shrug ▶ **verb**

□ **shrug something off** *he shrugged off suggestions that he was keen to quit politics* **disregard**, dismiss, take no notice of, ignore, set aside, pay no heed to, forget, not trouble about, gloss over, play down, talk down, make light of, make little/nothing of, minimize, discount, diminish, downgrade, trivialize.

shudder ▶ **verb** *she still shuddered at the thought of him* **shake**, shiver, tremble, quiver, quaver, vibrate, palpitate, flutter, quake, heave, convulse.

▶ **noun** *another great shudder racked his body* **shake**, shiver, tremor, tremble, trembling, quiver, quivering, quaver, start, vibration, palpitation, flutter, convulsion, spasm, twitch, jerk.

shuffle ▶ **verb 1** *they shuffled along the passage towards the headmaster's study* **shamble**, drag one's feet, stumble, lumber; stagger, teeter, totter, dodder, reel, lurch; hobble, limp.
2 *she looked down and shuffled her feet inanely* **scrape**, drag, scratch, grind, scuffle, scuff.
3 *he shuffled the cards and began to deal* **mix**, mix up, mingle, intermix;

shift about, rearrange, reorganize, jumble.

shun ▶ verb *he shunned publicity | everyone seemed to shun her* **avoid**, evade, eschew, steer clear of, shy away from, fight shy of, recoil from, keep away from, keep one's distance from, give a wide berth to, have nothing to do with, leave alone, not touch; **snub**, give someone the cold shoulder, cold-shoulder, ignore, turn one's back on, cut, cut dead, look right through; **reject**, rebuff, dismiss, brush off, turn down, spurn, disdain, refuse, decline, repudiate, ostracize; *informal* give someone the brush-off, tell someone where to get off, put down, freeze out, stiff-arm; *Brit. informal* knock back, send to Coventry; *N. Amer. informal* give someone the bum's rush, give someone the brush; *Austral. informal* snout; *informal, dated* give someone the go-by.
OPPOSITES accept; seek; welcome.

shut ▶ verb *please shut the door* **close**, draw/pull/push to, slam, fasten; put the lid on, bar, lock, latch, padlock, secure, seal; put up the shutters.
OPPOSITES open, unlock.

□ **shut down** *the factory has shut down* **cease activity**, close, close down, cease production, cease operating, come to a halt, go on strike, cease trading, collapse, fail, crash, go under, go to the wall, go bankrupt, become insolvent, go into receivership, go into liquidation, be liquidated, be wound up, be closed (down), be shut (down); *informal* go bust, go bump, fold, flop, go broke, go belly up.

□ **shut something down 1** *they have shut down the factory* **close**, close down, discontinue, put into receivership, liquidate, put into liquidation.
OPPOSITES open, open up.
2 *the correct way to shut the machine down is to type 'exit'* **switch off**, power down, stop, halt.
OPPOSITES switch on, start.

□ **shut someone/something in** *she pushed the dogs into the breakfast room and shut them in* **confine**, enclose, impound, shut up, pen (in/up), fence in, hedge in; hurdle, rail in, coop (up), mew up, immure, box up/in, wall in/up, lock up/in, cage, imprison, intern, hold captive, incarcerate, encircle, surround, ring, encompass, hem in, close in, trap; *N. Amer.* corral; *rare* gird, compass.

□ **shut someone/something out 1** *he had accidentally shut me out of the house* **lock out**, keep out, exclude, leave out, refuse entrance to, deny admittance to.
OPPOSITE let in.
2 *she tried to shut out those memories* **block**, suppress, halt, stop, forget.
OPPOSITES call up, recall.
3 *the bamboo shut out the light as effectively as the forest canopy* **keep out**, block out, screen, cover up, hide, conceal, veil.
OPPOSITE let in.

□ **shut up** (*informal*) *just shut up and listen* **be quiet**, keep/stay quiet, be/keep/stay silent, hold one's tongue, keep one's lips sealed; **stop talking**, say no more, quieten (down), fall silent, dry up; *informal* keep mum, button one's lip, button it, cut the cackle, pipe down, clam up, shut it, shut your face/mouth/trap, keep your face/mouth/trap shut, belt up, put a sock in it, give it a rest; *Brit. informal* wrap up, wrap it up, shut your gob; *N. Amer. informal* save it.
OPPOSITE speak up.

□ **shut someone/something up 1** *I haven't shut the hens up yet* **confine**, enclose, impound, pen (in/up), fence in, hedge in; hurdle, rail in, coop (up), mew up, box up/in, wall in/up, immure, lock up/in, cage, imprison, intern, hold captive, incarcerate, encircle, surround, ring, encompass, hem in, close in, shut in, trap; *N. Amer.* corral; *rare* gird, compass.
2 (*informal*) *that should shut them up* **quieten (down)**, silence, hush, shush, quiet, still, gag, muzzle.

shutter ▶ noun *Ianthe went over to the window and flung open the shutters* blind, roller blind, venetian blind, louvre, shade, curtain, screen, awning, canopy; *French* jalousie, persiennes.

shuttle ▶ verb **1** *minibuses shuttle between the centre and the car park* **ply**, run, commute, alternate, come and go, go/travel back and forth, go/travel to and fro.
2 *he works as a pilot shuttling planes between a Greek island and the mainland* **ferry**, take/run back and forth, chauffeur.

shy[1] ▶ adjective *as a teenager I was painfully shy* **bashful**, **diffident**, timid, sheepish, reserved, reticent, introverted, retiring, self-effacing, shrinking, withdrawn, timorous, mousy, fearful, apprehensive, nervous, hesitant, reluctant, doubting, insecure, wary, suspicious, chary, unconfident, inhibited, constrained, repressed, self-conscious, embarrassed, coy, demure, abashed, modest, humble, meek.
OPPOSITES bold, brash, confident.
▶ verb
□ **shy away from** *don't shy away from saying what you think* **flinch**, demur, recoil, hang back; have scruples about, scruple about, have misgivings about, have qualms about, be averse to, be chary of, not be in favour of, be against, be opposed to, be diffident about, be bashful about, be shy about, fight shy of, be coy about; be loath to, scruple to, be reluctant to, be unwilling to, be disinclined to, not be in the mood to, be indisposed to, be sorry to, be slow to, be hesitant to, be ashamed to, be afraid to, hesitate to, hate to, not like to, not have the heart to, drag one's feet/heels over, waver about, vacillate about, think twice about, baulk at, quail at, mind doing something; *informal* be cagey about, boggle at; *archaic* disrelish.

CHOOSE THE RIGHT WORD

shy, bashful, diffident, timid

- A **shy** person lacks confidence and is uncertain how to behave or what to say in the presence of other people (*the British are supposed to be a staid, shy, retiring lot | I was inordinately shy of girls*). *Shy* is also used of people who try to avoid someone or something about which they feel uneasy (*people can be very shy about giving compliments | small investors remained shy of the stock market*).
- **Bashful** denotes a nervous reluctance to draw attention to oneself (*many men are bashful about discussing their feelings out in the open*). The word can have a faintly old-fashioned or humorous tinge to it.
- **Diffident** describes someone who is so modest or hesitant that they have difficulty in putting themselves forward (*'Aren't you Sergei Rozanov?' she enquired in a soft, diffident voice | he was very diffident about working with classical actors*).
- **Timid** means 'lacking normal confidence or courage'. It stems from fear, resulting in excessive nervousness in the presence of others (*I was too timid to ask for what I wanted | she gave him a timid smile*). It can also imply an unwillingness to take risks; thus a *timid* action is often inadequate, half-hearted, or piecemeal (*the history of the UN's peacekeeping operations shows what can go wrong when timid measures are tried*).

shy[2] ▶ verb *they began shying stones at him* **throw**, toss, fling, hurl, cast, lob, launch, flip, pitch, dash, aim, direct, propel, bowl; *informal* chuck, heave, sling, buzz, whang, bung; *N. Amer. informal* peg; *Austral. informal* hoy; *NZ informal* bish.

shyness ▶ noun *overcome with shyness, she looked down at her feet* **bashfulness**, **diffidence**, sheepishness, reserve, reservedness, introversion, reticence, timidity, timidness, timorousness, fearfulness, nervousness, mousiness, apprehension, hesitancy, hesitation, reluctance, doubt, insecurity, wariness, suspicion, chariness, lack of confidence, inhibitedness, constraint, repression, self-effacement, self-consciousness, embarrassment, coyness, demureness, modesty, humility, meekness.

sibling ▶ noun *the birth of a sibling is a stressful event in the life of a child* **brother or sister**; (**siblings**) brothers and/or sisters.

WORD LINKS
killing of a sibling, by an animal **siblicide**

sick ▶ adjective **1** *half of children in the class are sick* **ill**, unwell, poorly, ailing, indisposed, laid up, bad, out of sorts, not oneself; *Brit.* off, off colour; *informal* under the weather, on the sick list; *Austral./NZ informal* crook.
OPPOSITES well, healthy.
2 *he was starting to feel sick* **nauseous**, nauseated, queasy, bilious, sick to one's stomach, green, green about the gills; seasick, carsick, airsick, travel-sick, suffering from motion sickness, suffering from altitude sickness, suffering from radiation sickness; *informal* about to throw up; *N. Amer. informal* barfy; *rare* qualmish.
3 (*informal*) *we're sick about the closure plans* **disappointed**, miserable, depressed, dejected, despondent, downcast, disconsolate, unhappy, low-spirited, distressed; **angry**, cross, enraged, annoyed, disgusted, displeased, disgruntled, fed up, grumpy; *Brit. informal* cheesed off.
OPPOSITE glad.
4 *I'm thoroughly sick of this music* **fed up with**, bored with/by, tired of, weary of, jaded with/by, surfeited with/by, satiated with, glutted with/by; (**be sick of**) have had enough of; *informal* have had a basinful of, have had it up to here with; have had something up to here.
OPPOSITE fond.
5 *a sick joke* **macabre**, black, ghoulish, morbid, perverted, gruesome, sadistic, cruel, offensive.
OPPOSITE in good taste.

□ **be sick** (*Brit.*) *he was sick in a bucket* **vomit**, **throw up**, retch; cough up, bring up, regurgitate; heave, gag; *N. Amer.* get sick; *informal* chunder, chuck up, hurl, spew, do the technicolor yawn, keck, ralph; *Brit. informal* honk, sick up; *Scottish informal* boke; *N. Amer. informal* spit up, barf, upchuck, toss one's cookies.

sicken ▶ verb **1** *the stench of blood sickened him* **nauseate**, make someone feel nauseous, make someone sick, turn someone's stomach, make someone's gorge rise, make someone's stomach rise, revolt, disgust, appal, repel, repulse, be repugnant to, offend; *informal* make someone want to throw up; *N. Amer. informal* gross out.
2 *his little sister had sickened and died* **become ill**, fall ill, be taken ill, be taken sick, catch something; **relapse**, have/suffer a relapse, worsen, deteriorate, weaken, fail, sink.
OPPOSITE recover.
3 *I think I'm sickening for something* **become ill with**, fall ill with, be taken ill with, show symptoms of, become infected with, get, catch, develop,

S

pick up, contract, come down with, be struck down with, be stricken with; *Brit.* go down with; *informal* take ill with; *N. Amer. informal* take sick with.
OPPOSITES recover from, get over.
4 *they are afraid they will* **sicken of** *each other* **tire**, weary, become/get tired of, become/get fed up with, become/get bored with/by, become/get satiated with, feel jaded with, have had a surfeit of, have had a glut of; *informal* become/get bored of, have had something up to here.

sickening ▶ adjective *there were some sickening photographs of the dead boys* **nauseating**, stomach-turning, stomach-churning, repulsive, revolting, disgusting, repellent, repugnant, appalling, abominable, hideous, horrible, awful, dreadful, terrible, obnoxious, nauseous, vile, nasty, foul, loathsome, offensive, objectionable, off-putting, distasteful, disagreeable, uninviting; abhorrent, despicable, reprehensible, contemptible, odious, heinous, obscene, hateful, execrable; gruesome, grisly; *N. Amer.* vomitous; *informal* sick-making, ghastly, putrid, horrid, God-awful, gross, gut-churning, yucky, icky, cringe-making; *Brit. informal* beastly; *N. Amer. informal* skanky; *literary* noisome; *archaic* disgustful, loathly; *rare* rebarbative.
OPPOSITES wholesome, delightful.

sickle ▶ noun
WORD LINKS
sickle-shaped **falcate**

sickly ▶ adjective **1** *a sickly child* **unhealthy**, in poor health, chronically ill, often ill, always ill; **delicate**, frail, weak, feeble, puny.
OPPOSITES healthy, robust.
2 *the foul streets and the sickly faces he encountered* **pale,** wan, pasty, colourless, sallow, pallid, white, waxen, ashen; ashen-faced, anaemic, bloodless, peaky, peakish, languid, listless, washed out; *informal* like death warmed up; *Scottish informal* peely-wally; *rare* etiolated, lymphatic.
OPPOSITE healthy-looking.
3 *his hotel room had been repainted a sickly green* **insipid**, pale, faint, light, light-coloured, light-toned, milky, whitish, wan, washed out, faded, bleached, colourless, dusty, flat, feeble; muted, subtle, soft, pastel, low-key, restrained.
OPPOSITES bold, deep, lurid.
4 *sickly love songs* **sentimental**, over-sentimental, overemotional, mawkish, cloying, sugary, syrupy, saccharine, sickening, nauseating, maudlin, lachrymose, banal, trite; *Brit.* twee; *informal* mushy, slushy, sloppy, schmaltzy, weepy, cutesy, lovey-dovey, gooey, drippy, sloshy, soupy, treacly, cheesy, corny, icky, sick-making, toe-curling; *Brit. informal* soppy; *N. Amer. informal* cornball, sappy, hokey, three-hankie.

sickness *See centre pages for lists of* **Illnesses**
▶ noun **1** *she was absent through sickness | an incurable sickness* **illness**, disease, disorder, ailment, complaint, affliction, infection, malady, infirmity, indisposition; *informal* lurgy, bug, virus; *Austral. informal* wog.
2 *a wave of sickness swept over her* **nausea**, biliousness, queasiness.
3 *he suffered sickness and diarrhoea for five days* **vomiting**, retching, gagging, upset stomach, stomach upset; travel-sickness, seasickness, carsickness, airsickness, motion sickness, morning sickness, altitude sickness; *informal* throwing up, puking; *rare* qualms.

side ▶ noun **1** *at the side of the road | the eastern side of the lake* **edge**, border, verge, boundary, margin, fringe, fringes, flank, brink, bank, brim, rim, lip, perimeter, circumference, extremity, periphery, limit, outer limit, limits, bound, bounds; hand; *literary* marge, bourn, skirt.
OPPOSITES centre, heart; end.
2 *he was driving on the wrong side of the road | the left side of the brain* **half**, part; carriageway, lane; hemisphere.
3 *on the east side of the city* **district**, quarter, area, region, part, neighbourhood, precinct, locality, sector, section, zone, tract, belt, ghetto, community, colony, pocket, enclave, territory, province, parish, ward.
4 *manuscripts should be typed, on one side of the paper only* **surface**, face, plane, part, facet, aspect, facade.
5 *he felt he should put his side of the argument* **point of view**, viewpoint, view, perspective, opinion, way of thinking, mind, standpoint, stance, stand, position, attitude, posture, outlook, frame of reference, slant, aspect, angle, facet.
6 *his family was ruined by backing the losing side in the civil war* **faction**, camp, bloc, clique, caucus, entente, axis, ring, party, wing, splinter group, sect, clan, set.
7 *there was a mixture of old and young players in their side* **team**, squad, line-up, crew.
8 (*Brit. informal*) *she has all the money in the world, but there's absolutely no side about her* **pretension**, pretentiousness, affectation, affectedness, ostentation, ostentatiousness, artificiality, attitudinizing, airs, airs and graces, superciliousness, posing, posturing, showing off, boasting, boastfulness, hypocrisy, snobbery, show, flashiness; pomposity, pompousness, flatulence, grandiosity, grandness; *informal* snootiness; *Austral./NZ informal* guyver; *rare* fustian.
□ **side by side 1** *they cycled along side by side* **alongside (each other)**, beside each other, abreast, level, shoulder to shoulder, cheek by jowl, together, close together.
2 *most transactions proceed side by side* **at the same time**, at one and the same time, at the same instant/moment, simultaneously, contemporaneously; (all) together, as a group.
OPPOSITE in line.
□ **take the side of** *any who took the side of the enemy would be treated as enemies themselves* **support**, give one's support to, take the part of, side with, be on the side of, stand by, stand up for, stick up for, be supportive of, encourage, back, back up, give one's backing to, uphold, take to one's heart, be loyal to, defend, come to the defence of, champion, ally (oneself) with, associate oneself with, sympathize with, favour, prefer, abet, aid and abet.
OPPOSITE oppose.
▶ adjective **1** *the frame had elaborately carved side pieces* **lateral**, wing, flank, flanking.
OPPOSITE front.
2 *this is just a side issue* **subordinate**, lesser, lower, lower-level, secondary, minor, peripheral, incidental, tangential, marginal, ancillary, subsidiary, subservient, non-essential, inessential, immaterial, borderline, irrelevant, beside the point, of little account, extraneous, unimportant, less important.
OPPOSITES central, primary.
3 *a side look* **sidelong**, sideways, sideward, oblique, indirect.
OPPOSITE straight.
▶ verb *the British tend to* **side with** *the underdog. See* TAKE THE SIDE OF.
WORD LINKS
relating to the side of something **lateral**
figure with a given number of sides **-gon (e.g. *pentagon*)**

sideline ▶ noun *he founded the fast-food company as a sideline to his petrol station* **secondary occupation**, second job, subsidiary; **hobby**, leisure activity/pursuit, recreation, diversion, distraction.
□ **on the sidelines** *he is biding his time on the sidelines, ready to step in* **without taking part**, without getting involved.

sidelong ▶ adjective *he gave her a sidelong glance* **indirect**, oblique, sideways, sideward, side; **surreptitious**, furtive, covert, sly.
OPPOSITES straight, overt.
▶ adverb *he looked sidelong at her* **indirectly**, obliquely, sideways, out of the corner of one's eye; **surreptitiously**, furtively, covertly, slyly; *archaic* askance.

side-splitting ▶ adjective (*informal*) *side-splitting anecdotes* **hilarious**, extremely amusing, very funny, very humorous, comic, riotous, uproarious, screamingly/hysterically funny, too funny for words, rib-tickling, comical, absurd, ridiculous; *informal* a scream, a hoot, priceless; *dated* killing, killingly funny.

sidestep ▶ verb *he neatly sidestepped the questions about crime* **avoid**, evade, dodge, escape, elude, circumvent, skirt round, give a wide berth to, find a way round, bypass, steer clear of, get out of, shirk; *informal* duck.
OPPOSITES tackle, meet something head on.

sidetrack ▶ verb *he allows himself to be constantly sidetracked by minor problems* **distract**, divert, deflect, draw away, lead away, turn aside, head off.

sideways ▶ adverb **1** *I slid off the horse sideways* **to the side**, laterally, crabwise; athwart.
2 *the expansion slots are mounted sideways* **edgewise**, sidewards, side first, edgeways, end on.
3 *he looked sideways at her* **obliquely**, indirectly, sidelong; covertly, furtively, surreptitiously, slyly; *archaic* askance.
▶ adjective **1** *there is little sideways force on the mast* **lateral**, sideward, on the side, side to side.
2 *a sideways look* **oblique**, indirect, sidelong, side; covert, furtive, surreptitious, sly.

sidle ▶ verb *she sidled into the room apologetically* **creep**, sneak, slink, slip, slide, skulk, prowl, steal, edge, inch, ease, worm, nose, move furtively, move with stealth, tread warily.
OPPOSITES march, stride.

siege ▶ noun **blockade**, beleaguerment, encirclement; *archaic* investment; *rare* besiegement.
OPPOSITES relief, raising.

siesta ▶ noun *after lunch they would take a siesta* **afternoon sleep**, nap, catnap, doze, drowse, rest; *informal* snooze, lie-down, forty winks, a bit of shut-eye; *Brit. informal* kip, zizz; *literary* slumber.

sieve ▶ noun *use a sieve to strain the mixture* **strainer**, sifter, filter, colander, riddle, screen, muslin cloth; *archaic* griddle.
▶ verb **1** *sieve the mixture into a bowl* **strain**, sift, screen, filter, riddle; *archaic* bolt, griddle.
2 *a hoard of coins was carefully sieved from the ash* **separate out**, filter out, sift, sort out, isolate, divide, part, segregate, put to one side, weed out, remove, extract.

sift ▶ verb **1** *sift the flour into a large bowl* **sieve**, strain, screen, filter, riddle, purify, refine, winnow; *archaic* bolt, griddle.
2 *we first sift out those applications which are unlikely to succeed* **separate out**, filter out, sort out, isolate, divide, part, segregate, put to one side, weed

out, get rid of, remove.
3 *crash investigators have been **sifting through** the wreckage | until we sift the evidence ourselves, we can't comment objectively* **search through**, look through, rummage through, root about/around in, ferret (about/around) in, poke around in, go through, turn over, explore, examine, inspect, scrutinize, pore over, investigate, conduct investigations into, enquire into, conduct an inquiry into, delve into, go into, analyse, screen, sieve, probe, dissect, review, assess; *Brit. informal* rootle around in; *Austral./NZ informal* fossick through; *rare* roust around in.

sigh ▶ verb **1** *she sighed with relief* **breathe out**, exhale; groan, moan; *rare* suspire.
2 *the wind sighed in the trees* **rustle**, whisper, murmur, sough.
3 *he **sighed for** days gone by* **yearn**, long, pine, ache, languish, carry a torch; **grieve over**, cry/weep for/over, fret about, shed tears for; bemoan, rue, miss, mourn, lament, regret the loss/absence of, hanker for/after, eat one's heart out over, hunger/thirst for; cry out for, pant for, crave, have a yen for, dream of.

sight ▶ noun **1** *she has excellent sight* **eyesight**, vision, eyes, faculty of sight, power of sight, ability to see, visual perception, observation.
2 *her first sight of it gave her a severe shock* **view**, glimpse, seeing, glance at, look at.
3 *he was almost within sight of the enemy* **range of vision**, field of vision, view.
4 *we are all equal in the sight of God* **perception**, judgement, belief, opinion, point of view, view, viewpoint, outlook, observation; thought(s), thinking, way of thinking, mind, perspective, standpoint; verdict, estimation, feeling, sentiment, impression, idea, notion.
5 *the town's historic sights* **landmark**, place of interest, thing worth seeing, (distinctive/prominent) feature, monument, spectacle, scene, view, area, landscape, display, show, exhibition, curiosity, rarity, beauty, marvel, wonder, splendour; *informal* something to write home about.
6 (*informal*) *I changed so quickly into these clothes I must be a sight* **eyesore**, spectacle, monstrosity, horror, mess; *informal* fright, blot on the landscape.
□ **catch sight of** *they turned off the main road and caught sight of the cottage* **glimpse**, catch/get a glimpse of, see, spot, spy, notice, observe, make out, discern, pick out, sight, detect, have sight of; *informal* clap/lay/set eyes on; *literary* espy, behold, descry.
□ **set one's sights on** *she set her sights on a teaching career* **aspire to**, aim at/for, try for, strive for/towards, work towards, be after, want, seek, have in view, think of, hope for.
▶ verb *one of the helicopters has sighted wreckage in the area* **glimpse**, catch/get a glimpse of, catch sight of, see, spot, spy, notice, observe, make out, pick out, detect, have sight of; *informal* clap/lay/set eyes on; *literary* espy, behold, descry.

WORD LINKS
relating to sight **optical, visual**

sightseer ▶ noun **1** *a car park for sightseers to the estate* **tourist**, visitor, tripper, holidaymaker, traveller, globetrotter; *Brit. informal* emmet, grockle; *rare* excursionist.
2 *get those gawping sightseers off the bridge* busybody, gawker, ghoul; *informal* rubberneck; *Brit. informal* gawper.

sign ▶ noun **1** *flowers are often given as a sign of affection* **indication**, signal, symptom, hint, pointer, suggestion, intimation, mark, manifestation, demonstration; **token**, testimony, evidence, attestation, proof; *rare* sigil.
2 *it may have been a sign of things to come* **portent**, omen, warning, forewarning, augury, presage; promise, threat, hint.
3 *Sir Edmund made a sign, and the soldiers followed him* **gesture**, signal, wave, gesticulation, cue, nod; action, movement, motion; body language, kinesics.
4 *there were signs saying 'keep out'* **notice**, signpost, signboard, warning sign, road sign, traffic sign; placard, board, plate, pointer, arrow, marker, waymark, indicator; poster, bill, sticker, advertisement; *informal* ad; *Brit. informal* advert.
5 *the dancers were daubed with signs which I assumed were messages to their gods* **symbol**, mark, cipher, letter, character, numeral, figure, type, code, hieroglyph; signifier, ideogram, logogram, graph; rune, diacritic, representation, emblem, device, badge, insignia, arms, coat of arms, crest, logo; (**signs**) writing, hieroglyphics.
▶ verb **1** *he signed the letter and put it in the envelope* **autograph**, endorse, witness, initial, put one's mark on, countersign, re-sign; *Law* set one's hand to, subscribe; *archaic* underwrite, style; *rare* chirographate.
2 *the government was unwilling to sign the agreement* **endorse**, **validate**, certify, authenticate, authorize, sanction, legalize, put into effect, enact; **agree to**, approve, ratify, adopt, say yes to, give one's approval to, rubber-stamp; *informal* give something the go-ahead, give something the green light, OK, give something the OK, give something the thumbs up.
OPPOSITE repudiate.
3 *he merely signed his name at the bottom* **write**, inscribe, pen, pencil, scribble, scrawl, dash off, put, add; *archaic* underwrite.
4 *we have signed a very talented player* **recruit**, hire, engage, employ, take on, appoint, take into one's employ, take into employment, contract, put on the payroll, sign on/up, enrol, enlist; *dated* take into service.
OPPOSITE dismiss.
5 *she then signed to Susan to leave* **gesture**, signal, give a sign to, indicate, direct, motion, gesticulate; wave, beckon, nod.
□ **sign on/up** *he signed on for a permanent career in the Air Force* **enlist**, take a job, sign, join (up), join the forces/services, enrol, register, volunteer, put one's name down, become a member; *dated* take service, go into service; *archaic* take the King's/Queen's shilling.
OPPOSITE resign.
□ **sign someone on/up** *Chapman had signed on new players in July* **recruit**, hire, engage, employ, take on, appoint, take into one's employ, take into employment, contract, put on the payroll, sign, enrol, enlist; *dated* take into (one's) service.
OPPOSITE dismiss.
□ **sign something over** *they have signed over ownership of the animals to the RSPCA* **transfer**, turn over, make over, hand over, hand on, give, hand down, leave, bequeath, bestow, pass on, devolve, transmit, cede, deliver, assign, consign, convey, entrust.
OPPOSITES keep; accept.

signal[1] ▶ noun **1** *the policeman raised his hand as a signal to stop* **gesture**, sign, wave, gesticulation, cue, prompt, indicator, indication, communication, message; alert, warning, tip-off; action, movement, motion; body language, kinesics.
2 *the move by their rival was a clear signal that the company was in trouble* **indication**, sign, symptom, hint, pointer, suggestion, intimation, clue, manifestation, demonstration; token, testimony, evidence, attestation, proof.
3 *the encroaching dark is a signal for people to emerge to dump their trash* **cue**, prompt, occasion, green light, incentive, impetus, impulse, stimulus; *informal* go-ahead.
▶ verb **1** *a lorry driver signalled to her to cross the road* **gesture**, sign, give a sign to, indicate, direct, motion, gesticulate; wave, beckon, nod.
2 *the Community could signal displeasure by refusing to cooperate* **indicate**, show, express, communicate; announce, proclaim, declare, pronounce.
3 *his death signals the end of an era* **mark**, signify, mean, be a sign of, spell, add up to, amount to, be evidence of, denote, imply, be symptomatic of, be a symptom of, reveal, manifest, designate; **foretell**, herald, bode, announce, be an indication of, indicate, point to, warn of, be a warning of, give a warning of, be an omen of, promise, threaten, presage, augur, portend, foreshadow, prophesy; *literary* betoken, foretoken, forebode, harbinger.

signal[2] ▶ adjective *although a signal failure, the campaign produced one benefit for the Allies* **notable**, noteworthy, remarkable, striking, glaring, outstanding, significant, momentous, memorable, unforgettable, pronounced, marked, obvious, impressive, distinguished, uncommon, unusual, particular, special, extraordinary, exceptional, conspicuous, rare.

significance ▶ noun **1** *tourism is of considerable significance in this area* **importance**, import, noteworthiness, consequence, substance, seriousness, gravity, weight, weightiness, magnitude, moment, momentousness; memorableness, unforgettableness, pronounced nature, remarkableness, outstanding nature, markedness, obviousness, conspicuousness, strikingness, distinction, impressiveness, uncommonness, unusualness, rarity, extraordinariness, exceptionalness, specialness; *rare* cruciality.
OPPOSITE insignificance.
2 *the significance of his remarks was not lost on Scott* **meaning**, sense, signification, import, thrust, drift, gist, burden, theme, implication, tenor, message, essence, substance, relevance, purport, intention, spirit, point.

significant ▶ adjective **1** *a significant increase in sales* **notable**, noteworthy, worthy of attention, remarkable, outstanding, important, of importance, of consequence, consequential; serious, crucial, weighty, material, appreciable, momentous, of moment, memorable, unforgettable, pronounced, marked, considerable, obvious, conspicuous, striking, glaring, signal, impressive, uncommon, unusual, rare, extraordinary, exceptional, particular, special.
OPPOSITES insignificant, minor.
2 *he gave her a significant look* **meaningful**, expressive, eloquent, informative, revealing, indicative, suggestive, symbolic, relevant, pregnant, knowing, telling, pithy, valid, purposeful.
OPPOSITE meaningless.

significantly ▶ adverb **1** *this is a significantly better car than the old model* **notably**, remarkably, outstandingly, importantly, seriously, crucially, materially, appreciably; memorably, unforgettably, pronouncedly, markedly, considerably, obviously, conspicuously, strikingly, glaringly, signally, impressively, unusually, extraordinarily, exceptionally, particularly, specially.
OPPOSITE slightly.
2 *he paused significantly* **meaningfully**, expressively, eloquently, informatively, revealingly, indicatively, suggestively; relevantly, knowingly, tellingly, purposefully; pregnantly.
OPPOSITE meaninglessly.

signify ▶ verb **1** *this decision signified a fundamental change in their priorities* **be evidence of**, be a sign of, mark, signal, mean, spell, add up to, amount to, denote, be symptomatic of, be a symptom of, reveal, manifest, designate; announce, herald, be an indication of, indicate, point to; *literary* betoken.
2 *the symbol of an egg signifies life* **mean**, denote, designate, represent, symbolize, stand for, correspond to, be equivalent to, imply; *literary* betoken.
3 *signify your agreement by signing the letter below* **express**, indicate, show, communicate, intimate; announce, proclaim, declare, pronounce.
OPPOSITES withhold; keep secret.
4 *the locked door doesn't necessarily signify* **mean anything/something**, be of importance, be of consequence, be important, be significant, be of significance, carry weight, be of account, count, matter, be relevant; *informal* cut any ice.

silence ▶ noun **1** *the sound of falling stones broke the silence of the night* **quietness**, quiet, quietude, still, stillness, hush, tranquillity, noiselessness, soundlessness, peace, peacefulness, peace and quiet.
OPPOSITES sound, noise.
2 *she was reduced to silence* **speechlessness**, wordlessness, voicelessness, dumbness, muteness; taciturnity, reticence, uncommunicativeness, unresponsiveness.
OPPOSITES speech; loquacity.
3 *politicians keep their silence on the big issues* **secretiveness**, secrecy, reticence, taciturnity, uncommunicativeness, concealment.
OPPOSITES communication, communicativeness.
▶ verb **1** *he silenced her with a kiss | Barnes has failed to silence his critics* **quieten**, quiet, hush, shush, still; **gag**, muzzle, censor, stifle.
2 *the ventilator also silences outside noises* **muffle**, deaden, soften, mute, smother, dampen, damp down, tone down, mask, suppress, reduce, abate; extinguish, kill.
OPPOSITE amplify.
3 *cheap nuclear power would silence complaints from industry* **stop**, put an end to, put a stop to, cut short, suppress.
OPPOSITES occasion, encourage.

silent ▶ adjective **1** *the night was silent* **completely quiet**, still, hushed, inaudible, noiseless, soundless, peaceful, tranquil, so quiet you could hear a pin drop.
OPPOSITES audible, noisy.
2 *you have the right to remain silent* **speechless**, quiet, unspeaking, wordless, voiceless, dumb, mute, taciturn, reticent, uncommunicative, unforthcoming, tight-lipped, close-mouthed, untalkative, tongue-tied, saying nothing, at a loss for words, struck dumb; *informal* mum.
OPPOSITE loquacious.
3 *we gave silent thanks that no one else had the right money for the jukebox* **unspoken**, wordless, unsaid, unstated, undeclared, unexpressed, unmentioned, unpronounced, unvoiced, tacit, implicit, understood, implied, taken for granted.
OPPOSITE spoken.

silently ▶ adverb **1** *Nancy took off her shoes and crept silently up the stairs* **quietly**, inaudibly, noiselessly, soundlessly, in silence.
OPPOSITES audibly, noisily.
2 *they drove on silently for a few minutes* **without a word**, saying nothing, speechlessly, quietly, in silence, unspeakingly, wordlessly, voicelessly, dumbly, mutely, taciturnly, reticently, uncommunicatively.
OPPOSITES while talking, in conversation.
3 *I silently said goodbye* **without words**, wordlessly, in one's head, tacitly, implicitly; *rare* subvocally, unspokenly.
OPPOSITE aloud.

S

silhouette ▶ noun *the silhouette of St Peter's is dominated by Michelangelo's dome* **outline**, contour(s), profile, delineation, form, shape, figure, shadow, features, lines, curves, configuration.
▶ verb *the castle was silhouetted against the sky* **outline**, etch, delineate, define, demarcate, delimit, mark off, trace; (**be silhouetted**) stand out.

silky ▶ adjective *she had long, silky hair* **smooth**, soft, sleek, lustrous, fine, glossy, satiny, silken, velvety.

silly ▶ adjective **1** *don't be so silly* **foolish**, **stupid**, unintelligent, idiotic, brainless, mindless, witless, imbecilic, imbecile, doltish; imprudent, thoughtless, rash, reckless, foolhardy, irresponsible; mad, erratic, unstable, scatterbrained, feather-brained; flighty, frivolous, giddy, fatuous, inane, immature, childish, puerile, half-baked, empty-headed, half-witted, slow-witted, weak-minded; *informal* daft, crazy, dotty, scatty, loopy, screwy, soft, brain-dead, cretinous, thick, thickheaded, birdbrained, pea-brained, pinheaded, dopey, dim, dim-witted, dippy, pie-faced, fat-headed, blockheaded, boneheaded, lamebrained, chuckleheaded, dunderheaded, wooden-headed, muttonheaded, damfool; *Brit. informal* divvy; *Scottish & N. English informal* glaikit; *N. Amer. informal* dumb-ass, chowderheaded; *S. African informal* dof; *W. Indian informal* dotish; *dated* tomfool.
OPPOSITES sensible, rational.
2 *that was a silly thing to do* **unwise**, imprudent, thoughtless, foolish, stupid, idiotic, senseless, mindless, fatuous; rash, reckless, foolhardy, irresponsible, inadvisable, injudicious, ill-considered, misguided, inappropriate, illogical, irrational, unreasonable; hare-brained, absurd, ridiculous, ludicrous, laughable, risible, farcical, preposterous, asinine; *informal* daft, crazy.
OPPOSITES sensible, rational.
3 *he would brood about silly things* **trivial**, trifling, frivolous, footling, petty, niggling, small, slight, minor, insignificant, unimportant, inconsequential, of little account; *informal* piffling, piddling; *N. Amer. informal* small-bore.
OPPOSITE important.
4 *he often drank himself silly* **senseless**, insensible, unconscious, stupid, dopey, into a stupor, into oblivion, into senselessness, into a daze; numb, dazed, stunned, stupefied, groggy, muzzy.
▶ noun (*informal*) *come on, silly* **nincompoop**, dunce, simpleton; *informal* nitwit, ninny, dimwit, dope, dumbo, dummy, chump, goon, jackass, fathead, bonehead, chucklehead, knucklehead, lamebrain, clod, pea-brain, pudding-head, thickhead, wooden-head, pinhead, airhead, birdbrain, scatterbrain, noodle, donkey; *Brit. informal* silly billy, stupe, nit, clot, twit, berk, twerp; *Scottish informal* nyaff, sumph, gowk, balloon; *N. Amer. informal* bozo, boob, schlepper, goofball, goof, goofus, galoot, lummox, dip, simp, spud, coot, palooka, poop, yo-yo, dingleberry; *Austral./NZ informal* drongo, dill, hoon, alec, galah, nong, bogan, poon, boofhead; *S. African informal* mompara; *informal, dated* muttonhead, noddy; *archaic* clodpole, spoony, mooncalf.

silt ▶ noun *the annual flooding brought more silt* **sediment**, deposit, alluvium, mud, slime, ooze, sludge; sand, clay.
▶ verb *the old harbour had* ***silted up*** **become blocked**, become choked, become clogged, fill up (with silt), become filled, become dammed.

silver ▶ noun **1** *the table was laden with freshly polished silver* **silverware**, (silver) plate; dishes, plates, flatware; cutlery, {knives, forks, and spoons}.
2 *Fred reached into his pocket and took out a handful of silver* **coins**, coinage, specie; change, small change, loose change; *informal* shrapnel.
OPPOSITE notes.
3 *she won three silvers* **silver medal**, second prize.
▶ adjective **1** *a man with silver hair* **grey**, greyish, white, greyish-white, whitish-grey, light.
2 *the silver water* **silvery**, shining, lustrous, bright, gleaming; *literary* argent.
▶ verb *a silvered bracelet* **plate with silver**, coat with silver, overlay with silver, laminate with silver, back with silver; plate, electroplate.

similar ▶ adjective **1** *the two of you are very similar* **alike**, (much) the same, indistinguishable, close, near, almost identical, homogeneous, interchangeable; kindred, akin, related; *informal* much of a muchness.
OPPOSITES dissimilar, different.
2 *northern India and similar areas* **comparable**, like, corresponding, homogeneous, parallel, equivalent, analogous, matching.
3 *other parts of the region were* ***similar to*** *Wales* **like**, much the same as, comparable to, close to, near (to), in the nature of.
OPPOSITES dissimilar to, unlike.
□ **be similar to resemble**, look like, have the appearance of, correspond to, simulate, mimic.
OPPOSITE differ from.

similarity ▶ noun *the similarity between him and his daughter was startling* **resemblance**, likeness, sameness, similar nature, similitude, comparability, correspondence, comparison, analogy, parallel, parallelism, equivalence; interchangeability, closeness, nearness, affinity, homogeneity, agreement, indistinguishability, uniformity; community, kinship, relatedness; *archaic* semblance.
OPPOSITES dissimilarity, difference.

similarly ▶ adverb **likewise**, in similar fashion, in like manner, comparably, correspondingly, uniformly, indistinguishably, closely, analogously, homogeneously, in parallel, equivalently, in the same way, the same, identically, by the same token.
OPPOSITES differently, the opposite way.

similitude ▶ noun *Conrad uses a range of constructions which express or imply similitude* **resemblance**, similarity, likeness, sameness, similar nature, comparability, correspondence, comparison, analogy, parallel, parallelism, equivalence; interchangeability, closeness, nearness, affinity, homogeneity, agreement, indistinguishability, uniformity; community, kinship, relatedness; *archaic* semblance.
OPPOSITES dissimilarity, difference.

simmer ▶ verb **1** *a pan of vegetable soup was simmering on the stove | simmer the apple until it is tender* **boil gently**, not quite boil, cook gently, stew, poach; bubble; *rare* seethe.
2 *she was simmering with resentment* **be furious**, be enraged, be angry, be incensed, be infuriated, be beside oneself, have lost one's temper, have a fit, boil, seethe, be boiling over, chafe, rage, be in a rage, rant, rave, rant and rave, storm, fume, smoulder, spit, breathe fire, burn; *informal* be livid, be wild, jump up and down, froth/foam at the mouth, be steamed up, be hot under the collar, have steam coming out of one's ears; *Brit. informal* do one's head/nut in.
□ **simmer down** *he stormed out of the theatre in a rage but soon simmered down* **become less angry**, cool off, cool down, be placated, let someone smooth one's ruffled feathers, contain oneself, control oneself, become

calmer, calm down, become quieter, quieten down, loosen up, settle (down).
OPPOSITE get steamed up.

simper ▶ verb *she simpered, looking pleased with herself* **smile affectedly**, smile coquettishly, giggle, titter, smirk, look coy.

simple ▶ adjective **1** *it sounds difficult I know, but it's really pretty simple* **straightforward**, **easy**, uncomplicated, uninvolved, effortless, painless, manageable, undemanding, unexacting, elementary, child's play, plain sailing, a five-finger exercise, nothing; *informal* as easy as falling off a log, as easy as pie, as easy as ABC, a piece of cake, a cinch, a snip, easy-peasy, no sweat, a doddle, a pushover, money for old rope, money for jam, kids' stuff, a breeze, a doss, a cakewalk; *N. Amer. informal* duck soup, a snap; *Austral./NZ informal* a bludge, a snack; *S. African informal* a piece of old tackle; *Brit. vulgar slang* a piece of piss.
OPPOSITES difficult, hard, demanding, complicated.
2 *the chapter on finance explains in simple language how a profit and loss account is compiled* **clear**, plain, straightforward, clearly expressed, intelligible, comprehensible, uncomplicated, understandable, (words) of one syllable, lucid, coherent, unambiguous, direct, accessible, uninvolved; *informal* user-friendly.
OPPOSITE complex.
3 *a simple white blouse | a simple, square house in Bath stone* **plain**, unadorned, undecorated, unembellished, unornamented, without ornament/ornamentation, unelaborate, unpretentious, unostentatious, unfussy, no-nonsense, basic, modest, unsophisticated, penny plain, without frills, honest, homely, homespun, everyday, workaday; stark, severe, spartan, austere, chaste, spare, bare; muted, unpatterned, patternless; classic, understated, uncluttered, clean, restrained; *N. Amer.* homestyle; *informal* no-frills.
OPPOSITES fancy, elaborate.
4 *the simple fact is that stray dogs are a menace | she was overcome at last by simple exhaustion* **basic**, fundamental; **mere**, sheer, pure, pure and simple.
5 *she wondered how he would react if she told him the simple truth* **candid**, frank, honest, direct, sincere, plain, absolute, unqualified, bald, stark, naked, blunt, unadorned, unvarnished, unembellished.
6 *simple country people* **unpretentious**, unsophisticated, ordinary, unaffected, unassuming, natural, honest-to-goodness, modest, homely, wholesome, humble, quiet, lowly, rustic; innocent, artless, guileless, childlike, naive, ingenuous, gullible, inexperienced; *N. Amer.* cracker-barrel; *informal* green.
OPPOSITES pretentious, affected.
7 (*dated*) *he was a bit simple, but quite harmless* **with learning difficulties**, with a learning disability, with special (educational) needs; of low intelligence, unintelligent; *dated* backward, simple-minded, feeble-minded, slow-witted, dull witted, retarded, mentally retarded, subnormal, mentally subnormal, educationally subnormal, ESN, mentally handicapped, mentally impaired, mentally disabled, mentally defective.
OPPOSITE gifted.
8 *simple chemical substances* **non-compound**, non-complex, uncompounded, uncombined, unmixed, unblended, unalloyed, pure, basic, single, elementary, fundamental.
OPPOSITE compound.

simpleton ▶ noun *there will always be those in business who persist in treating their customers like simpletons* **fool**, nincompoop, dunce, dullard, ignoramus; *informal* idiot, imbecile, moron, cretin, halfwit, thicko, thickhead, nitwit, dope, dimwit, dumbo, dummy, donkey, stupid, stupe; *Brit. informal* twit, nit, twerp, clot, muggins, juggins, silly billy; *Scottish informal* nyaff, sumph, gowk; *Irish informal* gobdaw; *N. Amer. informal* sap, schmuck. *See also* FOOL.

simplicity ▶ noun **1** *recipes will be judged on taste, appearance, simplicity, and appeal* **straightforwardness**, ease, easiness, simpleness, lack/absence of complication, effortlessness, manageability.
OPPOSITE difficulty.
2 *the simplicity of the everyday language* **clarity**, clearness, plainness, simpleness, intelligibility, comprehensibility, understandability, lucidity, lucidness, coherence, directness, straightforwardness, accessibility; *informal* user-friendliness.
OPPOSITES complexity, intricacy.
3 *the charm of the building lies in its simplicity* **plainness**, lack/absence of adornment, lack/absence of decoration, lack/absence of ornament/ornamentation, lack/absence of embellishment, unpretentiousness; starkness, austereness, austerity, spareness, severity; classic lines, clean lines, lack/absence of clutter, restraint, purity.
OPPOSITES ornateness, fanciness.
4 *the simplicity of their lifestyle* **unpretentiousness**, ordinariness, lack of sophistication, lack of affectation, naturalness, modesty, homeliness, wholesomeness, quietness; innocence, guilelessness, naivety, ingenuousness.
OPPOSITES pretentiousness, affectation.

simplify ▶ verb *the government intends to simplify existing environmental legislation | this information is simplified in Figure 4.1* **make simple/simpler**, make easy/easier to understand/do, make plainer, clarify, make more comprehensible, make more intelligible, remove the complexities from, disentangle, untangle, unravel; paraphrase, put in words of one syllable, make more accessible, popularize; streamline, reduce to essentials, rationalize; *N. Amer. informal* dumb down.
OPPOSITE complicate.

simplistic ▶ adjective *the proposed solutions are far too simplistic | an irritatingly simplistic film* **facile**, superficial, oversimple, oversimplified, schematic, black and white; shallow, pat, glib, jejune, naive; *N. Amer. informal* dime-store, bubblegum.

simply ▶ adverb **1** *he spoke simply and forcefully* **straightforwardly**, directly; **clearly**, plainly, intelligibly, lucidly, unambiguously.
2 *she was dressed simply in a white blouse and dark skirt* **plainly**, without adornment, without decoration, without ornament/ornamentation, without embellishment, soberly, unfussily, unelaborately, unostentatiously, without frills; severely, austerely, starkly, with restraint, monastically; classically, without clutter.
3 *they lived simply* **unpretentiously**, modestly, naturally, quietly.
4 *people like her are accepted in society simply because they have enormous sums of money* **merely**, just, purely, solely, only, for no other reason.
5 *Mrs Marks was simply livid* **utterly**, absolutely, completely, positively, really, totally; *informal* plain, plumb.
6 *it's simply the best thing ever written on the subject* **without doubt**, unquestionably, undeniably, incontrovertibly, altogether, unreservedly, certainly, unconditionally, categorically, entirely, wholly; easily.

simulate ▶ verb **1** *it was impossible to force a smile, to simulate pleasure* **feign**, pretend, fake, sham, affect, put on, counterfeit, go through the motions of, give the appearance of.
2 *this stage aims to simulate the actual conditions on the production line* **imitate**, reproduce, replicate, duplicate, mimic, parallel, be a mock-up of.

simulated ▶ adjective **1** *she howled in simulated anguish* **feigned**, fake, mock, pretended, affected, assumed, counterfeit, sham, insincere, not genuine, false, bogus, spurious; *informal* pretend, put-on, phoney; *Brit. informal, dated* cod.
OPPOSITES genuine, real.
2 *a simulated leather handbag* **artificial**, imitation, fake, false, faux, mock, synthetic, man-made, manufactured, ersatz, plastic.
OPPOSITE real.

simultaneous ▶ adjective *officers carried out simultaneous raids on homes across the city* **concurrent**, happening at the same time, done at the same time, contemporaneous, concomitant, coinciding, coincident, synchronous, synchronized, synchronic; coexistent, parallel, side by side.
OPPOSITE asynchronous.

simultaneously ▶ adverb *Alison and Frank spoke simultaneously* **at the same time**, at one and the same time, at the same instant/moment, at once, concurrently, concomitantly; together, all together, in unison, in concert, in chorus, as a group; *rare* synchronously.
OPPOSITE singly.

sin *See centre pages for lists of* **Sins** **Virtues**
▶ noun **1** *a sin in the eyes of God* **immoral act**, wrong, wrongdoing, act of evil/wickedness, transgression, crime, offence, misdeed, misdemeanour, error, lapse, fall from grace; *archaic* trespass.
2 *the human capacity for sin* **wickedness**, wrongdoing, wrong, evil, evil-doing, sinfulness, ungodliness, unrighteousness, immorality, vice, transgression, crime, error, iniquity, irreligiousness, irreverence, profanity, blasphemy, impiety, impiousness, sacrilege, profanation, desecration.
OPPOSITES virtue, good.
3 (*informal*) *the way they spend money—it's a sin* **scandal**, crime, disgrace, outrage.
▶ verb *I sinned and brought down shame on us* **commit a sin**, offend against God, commit an offence, transgress, do wrong, commit a crime, break the law, misbehave, go astray, stray from the straight and narrow, go wrong, fall from grace; *archaic* trespass.

sincere ▶ adjective **1** *my wife and I would like to express our sincere gratitude for what you did* **heartfelt**, wholehearted, profound, deep, from the heart; **genuine**, real, unfeigned, unaffected, true, honest, bona fide, earnest, cordial, fervent, ardent, devout; *rare* full-hearted. *See 'Choose the Right Word' below.*
OPPOSITES perfunctory, token.
2 *Jean is such a sincere person* **honest**, genuine, truthful, unhypocritical, meaning what one says, straightforward, direct, frank, candid; artless, guileless, ingenuous; *informal* straight, upfront, on the level; *N. Amer. informal* on the up and up; *Austral./NZ informal* dinkum.
OPPOSITES insincere, hypocritical, disingenuous, two-faced.

sincerely ▶ adverb *I sincerely hope that this scheme will succeed* **genuinely**, honestly, really, with all sincerity, truly, truthfully, wholeheartedly, with all one's heart, from the bottom of one's heart, earnestly, fervently, seriously; without pretence, without feigning, in good faith.

CHOOSE THE RIGHT WORD

sincere, genuine, unfeigned, unaffected

These words are all used to indicate that someone or something can be trusted to be what they appear to be.

- **Sincere** is used of emotions that are free from pretence or deceit (*a sincere concern for the future of Britain*), and can also be used of a person (*a sincere and generous man*). It can also apply to the results of such genuine feelings (*very bad but sincere poems | please accept my sincere condolences*).
- A feeling described as **genuine** is truly that feeling and not a hypocritical imitation of it (*a man with a genuine love of his country*). When used of a person, *genuine* can have two quite different senses, depending on the noun and the context: 'truly what they are said or appear to be' (*no genuine police officers will demand cash on the spot for speeding offences*) or 'having emotions that are what they appear to be' (*most of the people in the regiment were hard-working, genuine people*).
- **Unfeigned** is a rarer, more literary word, used only for emotions, not people (*a broad smile of unfeigned delight*).
- **Unaffected** is used either of a person who behaves naturally and simply, without trying to impress with artificiality or insincerity (*what a pretty, unaffected girl she was, full of life and fun*) or of their emotions (*taking unaffected pleasure in his friend's good fortune*).

sincerity ▶ noun *there seems no reason to doubt the sincerity of her apology* **honesty**, **genuineness**, truthfulness, good faith, lack of deceit, integrity, probity, trustworthiness; wholeheartedness, seriousness, earnestness; straightforwardness, openness, candour, candidness, guilelessness, ingenuousness; *Latin* bona fides.
OPPOSITE insincerity.

sinecure ▶ noun *Connie's job was a sinecure that could be done by anyone* **easy job**, soft option; *informal* cushy number, money for old rope, money for jam, picnic, doddle, cinch, gravy train; *Austral. informal* bludge.

sinewy ▶ adjective *he was tall, blonde, and sinewy* **muscular**, well muscled, muscly, brawny, well built, powerfully built, burly, strapping, sturdy, rugged, strong, powerful, broad-shouldered, athletic, well knit, muscle-bound, Herculean, manly; *informal* hunky, beefy, husky; *dated* stalwart; *literary* thewy; *Physiology* mesomorphic.
OPPOSITES puny, weedy.

sinful ▶ adjective **1** *he warned her that such talk was sinful | sinful men* **immoral**, **wicked**, wrong, morally wrong, wrongful, evil, bad, iniquitous, corrupt, ungodly, godless, unholy, irreligious, unrighteous, sacrilegious, profane, blasphemous, impious, irreverent, criminal, nefarious, depraved, degenerate, perverted, erring, fallen, impure, sullied, tainted; *rare* peccable.
OPPOSITES sinless, virtuous, godly, innocent.
2 *a sinful waste of money* **reprehensible**, scandalous, disgraceful, deplorable, shameful, criminal, iniquitous.
OPPOSITE admirable.

sinfulness ▶ noun **immorality**, **wickedness**, sin, wrongdoing, evil, evilness, evil-doing, iniquitousness, corruption, turpitude, ungodliness, godlessness, unholiness, irreligiousness, sacrilegiousness, profanity, blasphemy, impiety, impiousness, irreverence, impurity, depravity, degeneracy, vice, perversion, pervertedness; *rare* peccability, peccancy.
OPPOSITE virtue.

S

sing ▶ verb **1** *Miguelito began to sing a traditional Spanish folk song* croon, carol, warble, trill, pipe, quaver; chant, intone; chorus; yodel; render, perform; *informal* belt out; *rare* troll.
2 *the birds were singing in the chestnut trees* **warble**, trill, twitter, chirp, chirrup, cheep, peep.
3 *he sang out a greeting* **call out**, call, cry, cry out, shout, yell, trumpet, bellow, roar; *informal* holler, cooee.
4 (*informal*) *maybe he's going to sing to the police* **inform (on someone)**, tell tales (on someone); *informal* squeal, rat on someone, blow the whistle on someone, peach (on someone), snitch (on someone), put the finger on someone, sell someone down the river; *Brit. informal* grass (on someone), shop someone; *N. Amer. informal* rat someone out, finger someone, fink on someone, drop a/the dime on someone; *Austral. informal* pimp on someone.

singe ▶ verb *sparks burnt holes in my shirt and the fire singed my sleeve* **scorch**, burn, sear, char, blacken.

singer *See centre pages for lists of types of* **Singer** *and* **Voice**
▶ noun **vocalist**, soloist, songster, songstress; *French* chanteuse.

single ▶ adjective **1** *a single red rose | the lobby was empty except for a single security guard* **one**, one only, sole, lone, solitary, isolated, by itself; unique, exclusive; unaccompanied, by oneself, alone, solo; odd.
OPPOSITES double, multiple.
2 *she wrote down every single word | alcohol is the single most important cause of violence* **individual**, separate, distinct, particular.
3 *is she single?* **unmarried**, unwed, unwedded, unattached, free, without a partner/husband/wife, wifeless, husbandless, spouseless, partnerless, a bachelor, a spinster; on the shelf; *archaic* sole.
OPPOSITE married.
▶ verb
□ **single someone/something out** *the prime minister singled him out for promotion when he was a junior whip* **select**, pick out, fix on, choose, decide on; target, earmark; mark out, distinguish, differentiate, separate out, set apart/aside, put aside; cull.

WORD LINKS

related prefixes	**uni-** (e.g. ***unicycle, unicuspid***), **mono-** (e.g. ***monochrome, monophagous***), **haplo-** (e.g. ***haplology, haplotype***)
obsession with a single thing	**monomania**

single-handed ▶ adverb *he's been running the place single-handed* **by oneself**, alone, on one's own, solo, unaided, unassisted, without help, by one's own efforts, independently; under one's own steam.
OPPOSITES jointly, with help.

single-minded ▶ adjective *I've never met anyone so ambitious and single-minded* **determined**, full of determination, hell-bent, committed, unswerving, unwavering, undeviating, resolute, purposeful, set, fixed, devoted, dedicated, uncompromising, persevering, tireless, tenacious, persistent, pertinacious, indefatigable; obsessive, fanatical, dogged, monomaniacal; obstinate, stubborn, unyielding, intransigent, pig-headed, inflexible, obdurate.
OPPOSITES half-hearted, lackadaisical.

singly ▶ adverb *we should interview people singly and discreetly* **one by one**, one at a time, one after the other, individually, separately, by oneself, on one's own; apart; independently; *Latin* seriatim; *formal* severally.
OPPOSITES together, simultaneously.

sing-song ▶ adjective *he began to recite in a sing-song voice* **chanting**, chant-like; **monotonous**, monotone, droning, toneless.

singular ▶ adjective **1** *the success of the appeal demonstrates the gallery's singular capacity to attract sponsors* **remarkable**, extraordinary, exceptional, outstanding, striking, signal, eminent, especial, particular, notable, noteworthy, conspicuous, distinctive, impressive; rare, unique, unparalleled, unprecedented, superior, superlative, amazing, astonishing, phenomenal, astounding, sensational, spectacular; *informal* tremendous, awesome, fantastic, fabulous, terrific, stupendous, unreal.
OPPOSITES ordinary, run-of-the-mill.
2 *Lydia wondered why on earth Betty was behaving in so singular a fashion* **strange**, unusual, odd, peculiar, funny, curious, extraordinary, bizarre, eccentric, weird, queer, outlandish, offbeat, unexpected, unfamiliar, abnormal, aberrant, atypical, unconventional, out of the ordinary, incongruous, unnatural, anomalous, untypical, puzzling, mystifying, mysterious, perplexing, baffling, unaccountable; *French* outré; *N. Amer. informal* off the wall.
OPPOSITES normal, unsurprising.

singularity ▶ noun **1** *the anthology communicates both the singularity and the universality of women's deepest concerns* **uniqueness**, distinctiveness, difference, individuality, particularity.
2 *his psychological singularities* **idiosyncrasy**, quirk, trait, foible, peculiarity, oddity, eccentricity, abnormality.

singularly ▶ adverb *I have to admit it was a singularly foolish thing to do* **remarkably**, extraordinarily, exceptionally, very, extremely, really, outstandingly, strikingly, signally, eminently, especially, particularly, incredibly, awfully, terribly, decidedly, supremely, peculiarly, distinctly, conspicuously; amazingly, astonishingly, phenomenally, astoundingly, spectacularly, prodigiously, unusually, uncommonly, extra; *N. English* right; *informal* tremendously, seriously, majorly, fantastically, terrifically, stupendously; *Brit. informal* jolly, dead, well; *N. Amer. informal* powerful.

sinister ▶ adjective **1** *there was a sinister undertone in his words* **menacing**, threatening, ominous, forbidding, baleful, frightening, eerie, alarming, disturbing, disquieting, dark, black, suggestive of evil, evil-looking; ill-omened, inauspicious, unpropitious, portentous; *Scottish* eldritch; *informal* spooky, scary, creepy; *rare* minatory, minacious, minatorial, bodeful, direful.
2 *we need not assume a sinister motive for these meetings* **evil**, wicked, bad, criminal, corrupt, nefarious, villainous, base, vile, malevolent, malicious, malign; underhand; *informal* shady.
OPPOSITES innocent, good.

sink ▶ verb **1** *he saw the coffin sink below the surface of the waves* **become submerged**, be engulfed, go down, drop, fall, descend; disappear, vanish.
OPPOSITES rise, float.
2 *500 passengers and crew were saved after the luxury cruise liner sank yesterday* **founder**, go under, submerge, capsize.
3 *they sank their ships, rather than let them fall into enemy hands* **scupper**, scuttle, send to the bottom, open the seacocks in.
4 *the Bank of England sank lingering hopes of an imminent recovery* **destroy**, ruin, wreck, put an end to, be the ruin/ruination of, wreak havoc on, demolish, devastate, blast, blight, smash, shatter, dash, torpedo, scotch,

sabotage; *informal* put the kibosh on, put the skids under, put paid to, banjax, do for, blow a hole in, nix; *Brit. informal* scupper, dish, throw a spanner in the works of; *N. Amer. informal* throw a monkey wrench in the works of; *Austral. informal* euchre, cruel; *archaic* bring to naught.
5 *they agreed to sink their differences* **ignore**, overlook, disregard, forget, put aside, set aside, put to one side, bury, consign to oblivion.
6 *I sank myself in the communal life of the place* **immerse oneself in**, plunge oneself into, lose oneself in, bury oneself in, absorb oneself, occupy oneself with.
7 *the plane sank towards the small airstrip* **descend**, drop, go down/downwards, come down/downwards, go lower; fall, plunge, plummet, pitch, fall headlong, nosedive.
OPPOSITE ascend.
8 *the sun was sinking in a red glow* **set**, go down/downwards, dip beneath the horizon, descend.
OPPOSITE rise.
9 *Loretta sank into an armchair* **lower oneself**, flop, collapse, drop down, slump, plump oneself; *informal* plonk oneself, plop oneself; *N. Amer. informal* plank oneself.
OPPOSITE stand up.
10 *her voice sank to a confidential whisper* **fall**, drop, become/get lower, become/get quieter, become/get softer.
OPPOSITE rise.
11 *whatever she is guilty of, she would never sink to your level* **stoop**, lower oneself, descend, be reduced; demean oneself, debase oneself.
12 *his breathing was laboured—he was clearly sinking fast* **deteriorate**, decline, fade, fail, weaken, grow weak, flag, languish, degenerate, decay, waste away; be at death's door, be on one's deathbed, be breathing one's last, be about to die, be approaching death, be slipping away, have one foot in the grave, be in extremis, become moribund; *informal* go downhill, be on one's last legs, be giving up the ghost.
OPPOSITES recover, improve.
13 *sink 3-inch pots of good soil into the ground | screws sunk beneath the surface of the wood* **embed**, insert; **drive**, place, put down, plant, position.
14 *they planned to sink a gold mine in Oklahoma* **dig**, excavate, bore, drill.
15 (*informal*) *after sinking five pints of lager, he decided it was time to leave* **drink**, quaff, gulp down; *informal* down, swill, knock back, polish off, dispose of, shift; *Brit. informal* get outside of, neck, bevvy; *N. Amer. informal* chug, scarf down.
16 *many investors sank their life savings into the company* **invest**, put, venture, risk, plough.
□ **sink in** *Peter read the letter twice before its meaning sank in* **register**, penetrate, be understood, be comprehended, be realized, be taken in, be grasped, become clear, get through.
▸ **noun** *he washed himself as best he could at the sink in the bathroom* **basin**, washbasin, handbasin, wash-hand basin; *dated* lavabo.

sinless ▸ **adjective** *she was asleep, looking as careless and sinless as a child* **innocent**, pure, virtuous, faultless, unsullied, undefiled, as pure as the driven snow, whiter than white, uncorrupted, unblemished, untainted, untarnished; irreproachable, blameless, guiltless; *informal* squeaky clean; *Theology*) immaculate, impeccable.
OPPOSITES sinful, wicked.

sinner ▸ **noun** **wrongdoer**, evil-doer, transgressor, offender, criminal; *archaic* miscreant, trespasser, reprobate.

sinuous ▸ **adjective 1** *a small town with a slow-moving, sinuous river* **winding**, windy, serpentine, curving, twisting, meandering, snaking, snaky, zigzag, zigzagging, turning, bending, curling, coiling, undulating; tortuous; *technical* sinuate, ogee; *rare* anfractuous, flexuous, meandrous, serpentiform.
OPPOSITE straight.
2 *she got to her feet in one sinuous movement* **lithe**, supple, agile, graceful, loose-limbed, limber, lissom, willowy; *informal* slinky; *literary* lithesome.
OPPOSITE clumsy.

sip ▸ **verb** *Amanda sipped her coffee* **drink slowly**, drink, taste, sample; *dated* sup.
▸ **noun** *he took another sip of whisky* **mouthful**, swallow, drink, drop, dram, nip; taste; *informal* slurp, swig; *dated* sup.

siren ▸ **noun 1** *the wail of an air-raid siren* **alarm**, alarm bell, warning bell, danger signal; whistle, horn; *Brit.* hooter; *archaic* tocsin.
2 *seamed stockings are the trademark of a true siren* **seductress**, temptress, femme fatale, Mata Hari, enchantress, Circe, Lorelei, Delilah; **flirt**, coquette, Lolita; *informal* mantrap; *N. Amer. informal* vamp.

sissy (*informal*) ▸ **noun** *I'd hate the other boys to think he was a sissy* **coward**, weakling, milksop, Milquetoast, namby-pamby, crybaby, baby; *informal* weed, softie, nancy, nancy boy, pansy, ponce, mollycoddle, chicken; *Brit. informal* wet, mummy's boy, big girl's blouse, jessie, yellow-belly, funk; *N. Amer. informal* pantywaist, cupcake, pussy; *Austral./NZ informal* sook; *S. African informal* moffie; *archaic* poltroon.
▸ **adjective** *he felt sure his father would think the whole idea was sissy* **cowardly**, weak, feeble, spineless, effeminate, effete, limp-wristed, womanish, unmanly, soft; *informal* wet, weedy, wimpish, wimpy, sissyish, sissified, swishy, yellow, yellow-bellied; *N. Amer. informal* candy-assed.

sister ▸ **noun 1** *I had nine brothers and sisters* **female sibling**; *informal* sis; *Brit. rhyming slang* skin and blister.
2 *working together with our European brothers and sisters in the struggle against fascism* **comrade**, friend, partner, associate, colleague.
3 *Mother Mary Bernadette is one of nine sisters in the convent* **nun**, novice, abbess, prioress, Mother Superior, Reverend Mother; bride of Christ, religious, conventual, contemplative; *Roman Catholic Church* canoness; *literary* vestal; *historical* anchoress, ancress; *rare* vowess.

WORD LINKS

relating to a sister	**sororal**
related prefix	**sorori-** (e.g. *sorority*)
killing of one's sister	**soriricide**; *Law* **fratricide**

sit ▸ **verb 1** *you'd better sit down | Lily sat on the window seat to read the letters* **take a seat**, seat oneself, settle down, be seated, take a chair; perch, install oneself, ensconce oneself, plant oneself, plump oneself, flop, collapse, sink down, flump; *informal* take the load/weight off one's feet, park oneself, plonk oneself; *Brit. informal* take a pew.
OPPOSITES stand, rise.
2 *she sat the package on the table* **put**, place, set, put down, set down, lay, deposit, rest, leave, stand; *informal* stick, bung, dump, park, plonk, pop, plant.
OPPOSITE lift.
3 *the chapel sat about 3,000 people* **hold**, seat, have seats for, have space for, have room for, accommodate, take.
4 *Walter Deverell asked her to sit for him* **pose**, model.
5 *an attractive hotel sitting on the west bank of the River Dee* **be situated**, be located, be positioned, be sited, be placed, perch, rest, stand.
6 *normally, the Appeals Committee sits on Saturday* **be in session**, meet, be convened, assemble.
7 *they were determined that women jurists should sit on the tribunal* **serve on**, have a seat on, hold a seat on, be a member of, carry out duties on, work on.
8 *his shyness doesn't sit easily with Hollywood tradition* **be harmonious**, go, fit in, harmonize, mesh.
9 *I wonder if she'll be able to get Mrs Hillman to sit* **babysit**, babymind, childmind.
□ **sit back** *sit back and enjoy the music* **relax**, unwind, lie back, loosen up; *informal* let it all hang out, lighten up, veg out; *N. Amer. informal* hang loose, stay loose, chill out, kick back.
□ **sit in for** *he's sitting in for the regular disc jockey* **stand in for**, fill in for, take the place of, cover for, substitute for, be a substitute for, act as stand-in for, deputize for, hold the fort; *informal* sub for; *N. Amer. informal* pinch-hit for.
□ **sit in on** *I sat in on a training session for therapists* **attend**, be present at, be an observer at, observe, watch; *N. Amer.* audit.
□ **sit tight** (*informal*) **1** *this shouldn't take long—just sit tight* **stay put**, stay there, wait there, remain in one's place.
2 *we're advising our clients to sit tight and neither buy nor sell* **take no action**, wait, hold back, hang back, be patient, bide one's time, play a waiting game; *informal* hold one's horses.

site ▸ **noun 1** *the site of the Battle of Flodden* **location**, place, position, situation, locality, whereabouts, locale, spot, scene, setting; *technical* locus.
2 *a building site* **plot**, lot, area; *N. Amer.* plat.
▸ **verb** *175 weapons have been dumped in bins sited at police stations* **place**, put, position, situate, locate, set, install.

sitting ▸ **noun** *all-night sittings of Parliament* **session**, meeting, assembly, plenary; hearing; consultation; *Scottish* sederunt, diet; *N. Amer. & NZ* caucus.
▸ **adjective** *a sitting position* **sedentary**, seated.
OPPOSITE standing.

sitting room ▸ **noun** **living room**, lounge, front room, drawing room, morning room, reception room, salon, family room; *S. African* sitkamer; *dated* parlour, withdrawing room.

situate ▸ **verb** *hypermarkets are usually situated on the outskirts of towns* **locate**, site, set, position, place, base; build, establish; install; station, post.

situation ▸ **noun 1** *the club's financial situation had deteriorated* **circumstances**, set of circumstances, state of affairs, affairs, state, condition, case; predicament, plight; *informal* kettle of fish, ball game.
2 *have a drink—it'll give me a chance to fill you in on the situation* **the facts**, the picture, how things stand, the lie of the land, what's going on; *Brit.* the state of play; *N. Amer.* the lay of the land; *informal* what's what, the score, the set-up.
3 *the hotel enjoys a pleasant situation on the south bank of the River Swale* **location**, place, position, spot, site, locality, locale; setting, environment; *Austral./NZ informal* possy; *technical* locus.
4 *he had recently been offered a situation in America* **job**, post, position, place, appointment; employment; *informal* berth; *Austral. informal* grip; *archaic* employ.
5 (*archaic*) *he was much above my sister's situation in life* **status**, station, position, standing, footing, rank, degree.

S

six ▶ cardinal number **sextet**, sextuplets; *Poetry* sestet, sestina, senarius, sixain; *technical* hexad; *rare* sixsome.

WORD LINKS

related prefixes	**hexa- (e.g. *hexameter*), sex(i)- (e.g. *sexivalent*)**
relating to six	**senary**
six-sided figure	**hexagon**
relating to six years	**sexennial**

size ▶ noun *the room was of medium size | she seemed slightly awed by the size of the building* **dimensions**, measurements, proportions, magnitude, largeness, bigness, bulk, area, expanse, square footage, footage, acreage; breadth, width, length, height, depth; extent, scope, range, scale; volume, capacity, mass, weight, avoirdupois; immensity, amplitude, hugeness, vastness.
▶ verb *the drills are sized in millimetres* **sort**, categorize, classify.
□ **size someone/something up** *having sized up the competition, I was confident that I had nothing to fear* **assess**, appraise, form an estimate of, measure up, take the measure of, weigh up, estimate, judge, take stock of, evaluate, gauge, rate; *Brit. informal* suss out.

sizeable ▶ adjective *sizeable sums of money* **fairly large**, substantial, considerable, respectable, significant, largish, biggish, decent, decent-sized, generous, handsome; *Scottish & N. English* bonny; *informal* tidy, not to be sneezed at, serious; *archaic* goodly.
OPPOSITES small, tiny.

sizzle ▶ verb *thick slabs of bacon sizzled in the pan* **crackle**, frizzle, sputter, hiss, spit, fry.

sizzling ▶ adjective (*informal*) **1** *the sizzling summer temperatures* **extremely hot**, red-hot, unbearably hot, baking (hot), blazing, flaming, fiery, burning, scorching, blistering, searing, sweltering, torrid, tropical, like an oven, like a furnace, like a blowtorch; parching, withering; *N. Amer.* broiling; *informal* boiling (hot).
OPPOSITE freezing.
2 *that was the start of a sizzling affair* **passionate**, torrid, amorous, ardent, sexy, lustful, erotic; *informal* steamy, hot, red-hot.

skedaddle ▶ verb (*informal*) *when he saw us, he skedaddled.* See **RUN AWAY** at **RUN**.

skeletal ▶ adjective **1** *a tall, skeletal man* **emaciated**, very thin, as thin as a rake, cadaverous, skin-and-bones, hollow-cheeked, scrawny, scraggy, skinny, bony, angular, stick-like, raw-boned, lantern-jawed, gaunt, haggard, wasted; starved, half-starved, undernourished, underfed; shrunken, wizened, fleshless; *informal* looking like a bag of bones, anorexic, anorectic; *dated* spindle-shanked; *archaic* starveling.
OPPOSITES fat, obese.
2 *a rather skeletal account of the phenomenon* **lacking in detail**, incomplete, outline, inadequate, insufficient, fragmentary, sketchy, patchy, bitty, scrappy, broad-brush, superficial, perfunctory; thumbnail.
OPPOSITES detailed, full, thorough.

skeleton See centre pages for lists of **Bones** **Vertebrae**
▶ noun **1** *she was no more than a skeleton at the end* **skin and bone**, stick, scrag; *informal* bag of bones; *Scottish informal* skinnymalinks; *archaic* starveling.
2 *the concrete skeleton of an unfinished building* **framework**, basic structure, frame, shell; chassis.
3 *the skeleton of a report* **outline**, draft, abstract, plan, blueprint; main points, bones, bare bones; sketch, rough draft.
▶ adjective *there was only a skeleton staff on duty* **minimum**, minimal, smallest possible, basic, reduced; essential.

WORD LINKS

study of the skeleton	**osteology**

S

sketch ▶ noun **1** *a quick sketch of the proposed design* **drawing**, preliminary drawing, outline; diagram, representation, delineation, design, plan; tracing; *informal* rough; *technical* underdrawing, cartoon, maquette, ébauche, esquisse, croquis.
2 *she slipped next door and gave May a rough sketch of what had happened* **outline**, brief idea, rundown, run-through, main points, thumbnail sketch, bones, bare bones, skeleton; **summary**, synopsis, brief description, recapitulation, summarization, abstract, precis, résumé; *French* tour d'horizon; *N. Amer.* wrap-up; *informal* recap.
3 *a biographical sketch* **description**, portrait, vignette, cameo, profile, portrayal, depiction; potted biography.
4 *a hilarious sketch from their latest BBC series* **skit**, scene, piece, performance, act, item, turn, routine, number; playlet.
▶ verb **1** *as they talked, he began to sketch the garden* **draw**, make a drawing of, draw a picture of, depict, portray, represent, delineate, pencil; rough out, outline.
2 *the company sketched out its plans for tackling the problem* **describe**, outline, give a brief idea of, give a rundown of, give a thumbnail sketch of, rough out, block out, trace out, chalk out, map out, delineate, indicate; **summarize**, give a summary of, give an abstract/precis/résumé of, precis, recapitulate.

sketchily ▶ adverb *this idea is only sketchily outlined in the prologue* **perfunctorily**, cursorily, superficially, scantily, skimpily; incompletely, imperfectly, patchily, scrappily; vaguely, imprecisely, roughly, crudely; hastily, hurriedly.
OPPOSITES thoroughly, exhaustively, fully.

sketchy ▶ adjective *he has only been able to provide the police with sketchy details of the youths* **incomplete**, inadequate, limited, patchy, scrappy, bitty, fragmentary, rudimentary; **superficial**, cursory, perfunctory, slight, scanty, skimpy, meagre, insufficient; **vague**, imprecise, fuzzy; hurried, hasty, provisional; *informal* on the back of an envelope.
OPPOSITES detailed, exhaustive, full.

skew-whiff ▶ adjective & adverb (*Brit. informal*) *his tie was skew-whiff.* See **CROOKED** *sense 4.*

skilful ▶ adjective *he was also a skilful diplomat* **expert**, accomplished, skilled, masterly, virtuoso, master, consummate, proficient, talented, gifted, adept, adroit, deft, dexterous, able, good, competent, capable, efficient, experienced, trained, practised, professional, polished, well versed, versed, smart, clever, ingenious, brilliant, ready, apt, handy, artful; *informal* great, mean, wicked, nifty, crack, ace, wizard; *Brit. informal* a dab hand at; *N. Amer. informal* crackerjack; *vulgar slang* shit-hot; *archaic or humorous* compleat; *rare* habile.
OPPOSITES incompetent, inept, amateurish.

skill ▶ noun **1** *once again, he demonstrated his skill as a politician* **expertise**, skilfulness, expertness, adeptness, adroitness, deftness, dexterity, ability, prowess, mastery, competence, competency, capability, efficiency, aptitude, artistry, art, finesse, flair, virtuosity, experience, professionalism, talent, cleverness, smartness, ingenuity, versatility, knack, readiness, handiness; *informal* know-how.
OPPOSITE incompetence.
2 *bringing up a family gives you many skills* **accomplishment**, strength, gift, forte.

skilled ▶ adjective *more than 170 skilled engineers are employed on the project* **experienced**, trained, qualified, professional, proficient, practised, seasoned, accomplished, expert, skilful, master, talented, gifted, adept, adroit, deft, dexterous, able, good, competent, capable, efficient, well versed, versed, smart, clever; *informal* crack; *N. Amer. informal* crackerjack.
OPPOSITES unskilled, inexperienced.

skim ▶ verb **1** *as the scum rises, skim it off* **remove**, take off, scoop off, spoon off, ladle off; cream.
2 *the boat skimmed over the waters of the loch* **glide**, move lightly, slide, sail, plane, scud, skate, float, coast; aquaplane, skid.
3 *he bent to pick up a small pebble, skimming it across the water* **throw**, toss, fling, cast, pitch; bounce, skip.
4 *she* ***skimmed through*** *the newspaper* **glance through**, flick through, flip through, leaf through, thumb through, read quickly, scan, look through, have a quick look at, run one's eye over, dip into, browse through.
OPPOSITE pore over.
5 *Hannah had* ***skimmed over*** *this part of the story as she told it to the policeman* **mention briefly**, make only brief mention of, pass over quickly, skate over, gloss over; skip.
OPPOSITE elaborate on.

skimp ▶ verb **1** *whatever fabric you buy, don't* ***skimp on*** *the amount* **stint on**, scrimp on, be sparing with, be economical with, economize on, be frugal with, cut back on; **be mean with**, be parsimonious with, be niggardly with; cut corners, pinch pennies; *informal* be stingy with, be mingy with, be tight with.
OPPOSITES squander, lavish.
2 *the process cannot be skimped* **do hastily**, do carelessly, dash off, cut corners with; *rare* scamp.

skimpy ▶ adjective **1** *Judy wriggled into a skimpy black dress* **revealing**, short, brief, scanty, insubstantial; low, low-cut; flimsy, thin, see-through, indecent.
OPPOSITE modest.
2 *the information on second-home ownership is rather skimpy* **meagre**, scanty, scant, sketchy, limited, restricted, inadequate, insufficient, paltry, deficient, negligible, insubstantial, small, sparse; *rare* exiguous.
OPPOSITES comprehensive, exhaustive.

skin ▶ noun **1** *these chemicals could damage the skin* **epidermis**, dermis; *technical* cuticle, cutis, corium, derma, derm, integument, tegument.
2 *Mary's fair skin* **complexion**, colouring, skin colour, skin tone, pigmentation.
3 *until recent years, leopard skins fetched high prices* **hide**, pelt, fleece; *Austral.* greenhide; *technical* crop, kip; *archaic* fell.
4 *a banana skin* **peel**, rind, outside; *technical* integument.
5 *the coffee was cold, with a skin on it | the water was covered by a thin skin of ice* **film**, coating, coat, layer, overlay; sheet; membrane; *technical* pellicle.
6 *the plane's skin was ripped apart by the force of the explosion* **casing**, cover, covering, exterior, pod.
□ **by the skin of one's teeth** *he won, but only by the skin of his teeth* **only just**, just, narrowly, by a hair's breadth, by a very small margin, by the narrowest of margins, barely, by a nose; *informal* by a whisker.
□ **get under someone's skin 1** *it was the sheer effrontery of them which got under my skin* **irritate**, annoy, gall, irk, get/put someone's back up, pique,

rankle with, nettle, needle, bother, vex, provoke, displease, upset, offend, affront, anger, exasperate, disgruntle, ruffle, get on someone's nerves, ruffle someone's feathers, make someone's hackles rise, raise someone's hackles, rub up the wrong way; *informal* peeve, aggravate, miff, get, get in someone's hair, get up someone's nose, hack off, get someone's goat; *Brit. informal* nark, get on someone's wick, give someone the hump, wind up, get across; *N. Amer. informal* tick off, rankle, ride, gravel; *vulgar slang* piss off; *Brit. vulgar slang* get on someone's tits; *rare* exacerbate, hump, rasp.
2 *she's got under my skin—I can't stop thinking about her* **obsess**, intrigue, captivate, interest greatly, charm; enthral, enchant, fill someone's mind, mesmerize, hypnotize, entrance.

□ **it's no skin off my nose** (*informal*) *it's no skin off my nose—I never wanted to go to Germany in the first place* **I don't care**, I don't mind, I'm not bothered, it doesn't bother me, it doesn't matter to me, it's of no concern to me, it's of no importance to me; *informal* I don't give/care a damn/hoot/toss/rap, I don't give a monkey's; *vulgar slang* I don't give a shit.

▶ **verb 1** *scald and skin the tomatoes* **peel**, pare, hull; *technical* decorticate.
2 *he slipped and skinned his knee* **graze**, scrape, abrade, bark, cut, rub something raw, chafe; *technical* excoriate.
3 (*informal*) *Dad would* **skin** *me* **alive** *if I forgot it* **punish severely**, tan/whip someone's hide; *informal* murder, scalp, thump, give it to someone, come down on someone (like a ton of bricks), have someone's guts for garters; *Brit. informal* give someone what for.

WORD LINKS

relating to the skin	**cutaneous**
related prefix	**dermato-**
under the skin	**subcutaneous**
branch of medicine concerning the skin	**dermatology**
study of skin markings	**dermatoglyphics**
surgical repair of skin	**dermatoplasty**

skin-deep ▶ **adjective** *their left-wing attitudes were only skin-deep* **superficial**, on the surface, surface, external, outward; shallow, empty, artificial, meaningless.
OPPOSITES deep, heartfelt.

skinflint ▶ **noun** (*informal*) *don't be such a skinflint—you earn more than she does* **miser**, penny-pincher, Scrooge, pinchpenny, niggard, cheese-parer; *informal* meanie, money-grubber, cheapskate; *N. Amer. informal* tightwad; *vulgar slang* tight-arse.
OPPOSITE spendthrift.

skinny ▶ **adjective** *a tall, skinny man* **thin**, scrawny, scraggy, bony, angular, raw-boned, hollow-cheeked, gaunt, as thin as a rake, skin-and-bones, stick-like, emaciated, skeletal, pinched, undernourished, underfed; **slim**, lean, slender, rangy; lanky, spindly, gangly, gangling, gawky; *informal* looking like a bag of bones, anorexic, anorectic; *dated* spindle-shanked; *rare* starveling, macilent.
OPPOSITES fat, plump, obese.

skip ▶ **verb 1** *she began to skip down the path* **caper**, prance, trip, dance, bound, jump, leap, spring, hop, bounce, gambol, frisk, romp, cavort, bob; *rare* curvet.
OPPOSITE trudge.
2 *if you don't mind, I'd rather we skipped the biographical stuff* **omit**, leave out, miss out, dispense with, do without, pass over, bypass, skim over, steer clear of, disregard, ignore; *informal* give something a miss.
OPPOSITE include.
3 *I skipped school to visit my mother* **fail to attend**, play truant from, miss, absent oneself from, take French leave from; *N. Amer.* cut; *Brit. informal* skive off, wag; *N. Amer. informal* play hookey from, goof off; *Austral./NZ informal* play the wag from.
OPPOSITE attend.
4 *I'll* **skip through** *the magazine first* **glance at**, have a quick look at, flick through, flip through, leaf through, scan, run one's eye over.
OPPOSITE pore over.
5 (*informal*) *I'm not giving them a chance to* **skip off** *again* **run off**, run away, do a disappearing act, make off, take off; *informal* beat it, clear off, vamoose, skedaddle, split, cut and run, fly the coop, do a fade; *Brit. informal* do a runner, do a bunk, scarper; *N. Amer. informal* light out, cut out, take a powder; *Austral. informal* go through, shoot through; *vulgar slang* bugger off.
OPPOSITES stay, stay put.

skirmish ▶ **noun 1** *the unit was caught up in several skirmishes* **fight**, battle, clash, conflict, encounter, confrontation, engagement, fray, contest, combat, tussle, scrimmage, fracas, affray, melee; *archaic* rencounter.
2 *there was a skirmish over the budget* **argument**, quarrel, squabble, contretemps, disagreement, difference of opinion, dissension, falling-out, dispute, disputation, contention, clash, altercation, exchange, war of words; *Irish, N. Amer., & Austral.* donnybrook; *informal* tiff, set-to, run-in, spat, dust-up; *Brit. informal* row, barney, ding-dong, bust-up, bit of argy-bargy, ruck; *Scottish informal* rammy; *archaic* broil, miff; *Scottish archaic* threap, collieshangie.

▶ **verb** *they* **skirmished** *briefly* **with** *soldiers from Fort Benton* **fight**, do battle with, battle with, engage with, close with, combat, clash with, come to blows with, exchange blows with, struggle with, tussle with; *informal* scrap with.

skirt *See centre pages for list of* **Skirts**
▶ **noun 1** *a black velvet skirt* long skirt, short skirt.
2 (*archaic*) *I marched until I came to the skirt of the wood* **edge**, perimeter, margin, fringe(s), rim, boundary, border; *literary* bourn, marge.
3 (*archaic*) *his low-roofed house on the skirts of the village* **outskirts**, outlying districts, purlieus, periphery.

▶ **verb 1** *he did not go through the city but skirted it* **go round**, move round, walk round, circle, circumnavigate.
2 *the fields that skirted the highway were full of cattle* **border**, edge, flank, fringe, line, lie alongside.
3 *he had carefully* **skirted round** *the subject of Elise* **avoid**, evade, steer clear of, sidestep, dodge, circumvent, bypass, pass over, fight shy of; ignore, overlook, gloss over, fail to mention; *informal* duck; *Austral./NZ informal* duck-shove.

skit ▶ **noun** *an old vaudeville skit | a skit on daytime magazine programmes* **comedy sketch**, act, piece, turn, item, routine, number; **parody**, take-off, pastiche, burlesque, satire, travesty, squib; *informal* spoof, send-up; *Brit. vulgar slang* piss-take; *rare* pasquinade.

skittish ▶ **adjective 1** *she joined in the drinking and afterwards grew skittish* **playful**, lively, high-spirited, frisky, coltish; flirtatious, kittenish, coquettish; *informal* flirty; *archaic* frolicsome, sportive, gamesome, frolic, wanton.
OPPOSITES solemn, staid.
2 *Cranston's mount was skittish* **restive**, excitable, nervous, easily frightened; skittery, jumpy, fidgety, highly strung.
OPPOSITE calm.

skive ▶ **verb** (*Brit. informal*) *they'll think I'm skiving | I skived off school* **malinger**, pretend to be ill, feign/fake illness; play truant, truant; **avoid work**, evade one's duty, shirk, skulk, idle; *N. Amer.* cut; *Brit. informal* bunk off, swing the lead, wag, scrimshank, dodge the column; *Irish informal* mitch off; *N. Amer. informal* goldbrick, play hookey, goof off; *Austral./NZ informal* play the wag.

skiver ▶ **noun** (*Brit. informal*) **malingerer**, shirker, work-dodger, idler, layabout; *informal* do-nothing, slacker, cyberslacker, passenger; *Brit. informal* lead-swinger, scrimshanker; *N. Amer. informal* gold brick, goof-off; *Austral./NZ informal* bludger; *French archaic* fainéant.

skulduggery ▶ **noun** *there is no evidence to support any allegations of skulduggery* **trickery**, swindling, fraudulence, double-dealing, sharp practice, unscrupulousness, underhandedness, chicanery, machinations; *informal* shenanigans, funny business, hanky-panky, monkey business; *Brit. informal* monkey tricks, jiggery-pokery; *N. Amer. informal* monkeyshines.

skulk ▶ **verb** *he spent most of his time skulking about the corridors* **lurk**, loiter, hide, conceal oneself, lie in wait, keep out of sight; **creep**, sneak, slink, move furtively, sidle, slope, pad, prowl, tiptoe, pussyfoot.

skull ▶ **noun**

WORD LINKS

relating to the skull	**cranial**
related prefix	**cranio-** (e.g. *craniotomy*)
study of skull shape as supposed indicator of character	**phrenology**
study of the skull	**craniology**
measurement of the skull	**craniometry**
incision into skull	**craniotomy**

sky ▶ **noun** *they lay on the grass, gazing up at* **the sky** the atmosphere, the stratosphere, the skies, airspace; *literary* **the heavens**, the firmament, the vault of heaven, the blue, the (wide) blue yonder, the welkin, the ether, the empyrean, the azure, the upper regions, the sphere.

□ **to the skies** *he wrote to his sister praising Lizzie to the skies* **effusively**, profusely, very highly, very enthusiastically, unreservedly, without reserve, ardently, fervently; fulsomely, extravagantly, inordinately, excessively, immoderately.

WORD LINKS

relating to the sky **celestial, supernal, empyrean**

slab ▶ **noun** *slabs of concrete | a chipped saucer containing a slab of soap* **piece**, block, hunk, chunk, lump; portion; cake, tablet, brick, wodge.

slack ▶ **adjective 1** *she heard a splash and the rope went slack* **loose**, limp, not taut, not tight, hanging, flapping; relaxed, flexible, pliant.
OPPOSITES tight, taut, stretched.
2 *try these tips to tone and tighten slack, unattractive skin* **flaccid**, flabby, loose, sagging, saggy, drooping, droopy, soft.
OPPOSITES taut, toned, firm.
3 *she was wearing a slack blue dress* **baggy**, loose-fitting, loose, not tight, generously cut, roomy; shapeless, sack-like, oversized, ill-fitting, bagging, hanging, flapping, saggy.
OPPOSITES tight, tailored.
4 *business had never been so slack* **sluggish**, slow, quiet, slow-moving, not busy, inactive, flat, depressed, stagnant.

S

OPPOSITES busy, thriving.

5 *the bank's slack accounting procedures | some slack defensive play by Villa* **lax**, negligent, neglectful, remiss, careless, slapdash, slipshod, lackadaisical, lazy, inefficient, incompetent, inattentive, offhand, casual, disorderly, disorganized; N. Amer. derelict; informal sloppy, slap-happy, do-nothing, asleep at the wheel; Brit. vulgar slang half-arsed; formal delinquent; rare otiose, poco-curante.

OPPOSITES meticulous, diligent.

▶ **noun 1** *the rope had just enough slack in it to allow her to reach him* **looseness**, play, give.

2 *as domestic demand starts to flag, foreign demand will help pick up the slack* **surplus**, excess, residue, spare capacity.

3 *he slept deeply, refreshed by a little slack in the daily routine* **lull**, pause, respite, spell of inactivity, interval, break, hiatus, breathing space; informal let-up, breather.

▶ **verb 1** *the horse slacked his pace* **reduce**, lessen, slacken, slow, ease up/off.

OPPOSITE increase.

2 (Brit. informal) *okay, carry on with this painting and no slacking* **idle**, shirk, be inactive, be lazy, be indolent, sit back and do nothing, waste time, lounge about; Brit. informal skive, bunk off; N. Amer. informal goof off.

OPPOSITE work hard.

□ **slack off 1** *the rain had slacked off to a soft drizzle* **decrease**, lessen, subside, get less, let up, ease off, abate, moderate, diminish, dwindle, die down, fall off, drop off, taper off, ebb, recede, wane.

OPPOSITE intensify.

2 *I told him to slack off a bit* **relax**, take things easy, let up, ease up/off, do less, loosen up, slow down, be less active; N. Amer. informal hang loose, stay loose, chill out.

OPPOSITE work harder.

□ **slack up** *the horse didn't slack up until he reached the trees* **slow down**, slow, decelerate, reduce speed, drop speed, put the brakes on.

OPPOSITES speed up, accelerate.

slacken ▶ **verb 1** *he slackened his grip | the straps can be slackened to allow greater freedom of movement* **loosen**, make looser, release, relax, loose; lessen, reduce, weaken; Nautical, dated veer.

OPPOSITE tighten.

2 *her footsteps slackened | he slackened his pace a little* **become/get/make slower**, slow down, slow, decelerate, reduce in speed, slack.

OPPOSITES speed up, quicken.

3 *I think the rain might just be slackening* **decrease**, lessen, subside, ease up/off, get less, let up, abate, moderate, become less intense, slack off, diminish, dwindle, die down, fall off, drop off, taper off, ebb, recede, wane.

slacker ▶ **noun** (informal) **layabout**, idler, shirker, loafer, malingerer, work-dodger, clock-watcher, good-for-nothing, sluggard, laggard; informal passenger, lazybones, slugabed, couch potato, cyberslacker; Brit. informal skiver, lead-swinger, scrimshanker; N. Amer. informal gold brick, goof-off; Austral./NZ informal bludger; French archaic fainéant.

OPPOSITE workaholic.

slag ▶ **verb** (Brit. informal)

□ **slag someone/something off**. See CRITICIZE.

slake ▶ **verb** *slake your thirst with a citron pressé* **quench**, satisfy, take the edge off, sate, satiate, relieve, assuage, gratify.

slam ▶ **verb 1** *he left the room, slamming the door behind him* **bang**, shut/close with a bang, shut/close noisily, shut/close with a crash, shut/close with force, fling shut.

OPPOSITES pull something to, close gently.

2 *the car mounted the pavement, slamming into a lamp post* **crash into**, smash into, smack into, collide with, be in collision with, hit, strike, ram, plough into, meet head-on, run into, bump into, crack into/against; N. Amer. impact.

OPPOSITE miss.

3 (informal) *he was slammed by the critics for his first-half performance. See* CRITICIZE.

slander ▶ **noun** *he'd sue me for slander if I made the accusation publicly* **defamation**, defamation of character, character assassination, misrepresentation of character, calumny, libel; scandalmongering, malicious gossip, muckraking, smear campaigning, disparagement, denigration, derogation, aspersions, vilification, traducement, obloquy, backbiting, scurrility; lie, slur, smear, untruth, false accusation, false report, insult, slight; informal mud-slinging; N. Amer. informal bad-mouthing; archaic contumely.

OPPOSITES acclamation, praise.

▶ **verb** *they were accused of slandering the head of state* **defame**, defame someone's character, blacken someone's name, give someone a bad name, tell lies about, speak ill/evil of, drag through the mud/mire, throw/sling/fling mud at, sully someone's reputation, libel, smear, run a smear campaign against, cast aspersions on, spread scandal about, besmirch, tarnish, taint, misrepresent; **malign**, traduce, vilify, calumniate, disparage, denigrate, decry, run down; N. Amer. slur; Brit. informal do a hatchet job on; rare derogate, asperse, vilipend.

OPPOSITES acclaim, praise.

> **CHOOSE THE RIGHT WORD**
>
> **slander, malign, libel, defame, traduce**
>
> See MALIGN.

slanderous ▶ **adjective** *you have no right to make such slanderous accusations* **defamatory**, denigratory, disparaging, derogatory, libellous, pejorative, false, untrue, lying, misrepresentative, damaging, injurious, scurrilous, scandalous, poisonous, vicious, opprobrious, malicious, abusive, insulting; informal dirty, mud-slinging; rare calumnious, calumniatory, aspersive, aspersory.

slang ▶ **noun** **informal language**, colloquialisms, idioms, patois, argot, cant, dialect; jargon, terminology; rhyming slang, back slang; informal lingo.

slanging match ▶ **noun** (Brit. informal) *the decision provoked a slanging match between all three major parties. See* QUARREL.

slant ▶ **verb 1** *he felt as though the floor was beginning to slant* **slope**, tilt, incline, be at an angle, angle, tip, cant, be askew, skew, lean, dip, pitch, shelve, list, bank, heel.

2 *it doesn't automatically follow that their findings will be slanted in favour of their own beliefs* **bias**, distort, twist, skew, colour, weight, spin, angle, orient, give a slant to, give a bias to.

▶ **noun 1** *the slant of the roof* **slope**, incline, tilt, ramp, gradient, pitch, angle, rake, cant, camber, skew, leaning, inclination, shelving, listing.

2 *some of the essays have a feminist slant* **point of view**, viewpoint, standpoint, stance, angle, perspective, approach, view, opinion, attitude, position, frame of reference; bias, leaning, partiality, prejudice, twist, bent; spin.

slanting ▶ **adjective** *the slanting angle of the deck* **oblique**, sloping, at an angle, angled, not straight, on an incline, inclined, tilting, tilted, atilt, slanted, aslant, slantwise, diagonal, canted, cambered, leaning, dipping, shelving, listing; crooked, askew, skew; Scottish squint; N. Amer. cater-cornered, catty-cornered, kitty-corner.

OPPOSITE straight.

slap ▶ **verb 1** *he slapped her hard across the face* **hit**, strike, smack, crack, clout, cuff, thump, punch, thwack, spank, rap, beat; informal whack, wallop, biff, swipe, clip, bop, belt, bash, sock; Brit. informal slosh; N. Amer. informal boff, slug, bust; Austral./NZ informal dong, quilt; archaic smite.

2 *he slapped a £10 note down on the table* **fling**, throw, toss, sling, slam, bang; informal bung, plonk.

3 *all you need to do is slap on a coat of paint* **daub**, plaster, spread; apply.

4 (informal) *the United States slapped a huge tax on European wine imports* **impose**, levy, put on, add.

□ **slap someone down** (informal) *Uncle Max was always slapping me down for being big-headed* **reprimand**, rebuke, reproach, scold, admonish, take to task; squash, squelch, put down, put someone in their place, take down a peg or two, deflate; informal tell off; Brit. informal tick off, have a go at.

▶ **noun** *he gave her a slap across the cheek* **smack**, blow, thump, cuff, clout, punch, crack, thwack; spank, rap, bang; informal whack, wallop, clip, biff, swipe, bop, belt, bash, sock.

□ **a slap in the face** *his remarks were a slap in the face for the local community* **rebuff**, rejection, snub, insult, affront, put-down, humiliation, a blow to one's pride.

OPPOSITE praise.

□ **a slap on the back** *they deserve a hearty slap on the back for their efforts* **congratulations**, commendation, approbation, approval, accolades, encomiums, compliments, tributes, a pat on the back, praise, acclaim, acclamation, a round of applause; informal a (big) hand; rare laudation.

OPPOSITES condemnation, criticism.

□ **a slap on the wrist** *this was not a question, but a slap on the wrist* **reprimand**, rebuke, reproof, scolding, admonition, admonishment, reproval; informal telling-off, rap over the knuckles, dressing-down; Brit. informal ticking-off, wigging; Austral./NZ informal serve; Brit. vulgar slang bollocking.

▶ **adverb** (informal) *the bypass goes slap through Oxford's green belt* **straight**, right, directly, squarely, dead, plumb, point-blank; **exactly**, precisely; informal smack, bang, slap bang; N. Amer. informal spang, smack dab.

slapdash ▶ **adjective** *this can lead to slapdash, irresponsible journalism* **careless**, slipshod, lackadaisical, hasty, hurried, disorganized, haphazard, unsystematic, untidy, messy, thrown together, last-minute, hit-or-miss, offhand, thoughtless, heedless, negligent, neglectful, remiss, cursory, perfunctory, lax, slack; informal sloppy, shambolic, all over the place, slap-happy; Brit. informal all over the shop.

OPPOSITES careful, meticulous, painstaking.

slap-happy ▶ **adverb** (*informal*) **1** *Drysdale's slap-happy friend* **happy-go-lucky**, devil-may-care, carefree, cheerful, breezy, easy-going, nonchalant, insouciant, blithe, airy, casual, irresponsible.
OPPOSITES serious, solemn.
2 *the slap-happy way the tests were carried out.* See SLAPDASH.
3 *she's a bit slap-happy after such a narrow escape* **dazed**, stupefied, punch-drunk, unsteady, wobbly.

slap-up ▶ **adjective** (*Brit. informal*) *a slap-up dinner* **lavish**, sumptuous, elaborate, expensive, no-expense-spared, fit for a king, princely; excellent, splendid, magnificent, marvellous, superb, first-class.
OPPOSITE meagre.

slash ▶ **verb 1** *her car had been scratched and the tyres slashed | she threatened to slash her wrists* **cut (open)**, gash, slit, split open, lacerate, knife, hack, make an incision in, score; rip, tear; *literary* rend.
2 (*informal*) *the company was forced to slash prices* **reduce**, cut, drop, bring down, mark down, lower, put down.
OPPOSITES raise, put up.
3 (*informal*) *they have threatened to slash 10,000 jobs worldwide* **get rid of**, axe, cut, shed, lose.
OPPOSITE create.
▶ **noun 1** *he staggered over with a crimson slash across his temple* **cut**, gash, laceration, slit, hack, score, incision; wound, injury; rip, tear, rent.
2 *sentence breaks are indicated by slashes* **solidus**, **oblique**, backslash, diagonal, virgule, slant.

slashing ▶ **adjective** (*informal*) *a slashing attack by the newspapers* **devastating**, withering, blistering, extremely critical, searing, scorching, fierce, ferocious, savage, severe, stinging, biting, cutting, incisive, mordant, trenchant, virulent, caustic, vitriolic, scornful, sharp, bitter, acid, harsh, unsparing; *rare* mordacious.
OPPOSITES mild, gentle; complimentary.

slate ▶ **verb** (*Brit. informal*) *his work was slated by the critics* **criticize harshly**, attack, pillory, lambaste, condemn, flay, savage, shoot down, revile, vilify; *informal* pan, knock, tear/pull/take to pieces, take/pull apart, crucify, hammer, slam, do a hatchet job on, bash, give something a battering, roast, skewer, maul, throw brickbats at; *Brit. informal* rubbish, slag off; *N. Amer. informal* trash, pummel; *Austral./NZ informal* bag, monster; *archaic* slash; *rare* excoriate.
OPPOSITES praise, commend, applaud.

slatternly ▶ **adjective** *a slatternly girl wearing cardigans and a thick scarf* **slovenly**, untidy, messy, scruffy, unkempt, ill-groomed, dishevelled, frowzy, blowsy; dirty, grubby; sluttish; *N. Amer. informal* raggedy, *archaic* draggle-tailed.

slaughter ▶ **verb 1** *the animals were slaughtered according to Islamic laws* **kill**, butcher.
2 *innocent civilians are being slaughtered* **massacre**, murder, butcher, kill, kill off, annihilate, exterminate, execute, liquidate, eliminate, destroy, decimate, wipe out, mow down, cut down, cut to pieces, put to the sword, put to death, send to the gas chambers; *literary* slay.
3 (*informal*) *the first team were slaughtered* **defeat utterly**, **trounce**, annihilate, beat hollow, drub, give a drubbing to, crush, rout; *informal* hammer, clobber, thrash, paste, pound, pulverize, massacre, crucify, demolish, destroy, wipe the floor with, take to the cleaners, make mincemeat of, murder, flatten, turn inside out; *Brit. informal* stuff, marmalize; *N. Amer. informal* shellac, blow out, cream, skunk.
▶ **noun 1** *the slaughter of 20 peaceful demonstrators* **massacre**, **murder**, murdering; mass murder, mass killing, wholesale killing, indiscriminate killing, mass homicide, execution, mass execution, destruction, mass destruction, annihilation, extermination, liquidation, decimation, carnage, butchery; pogrom, genocide, ethnic cleansing, holocaust, Shoah, night of the long knives; *literary* slaying; *rare* battue, hecatomb.
2 *a scene of slaughter* **carnage**, bloodshed, indiscriminate bloodshed, bloodletting; bloodbath.
3 (*informal*) *a desperate attempt to avoid their imminent electoral slaughter* **crushing defeat**, annihilation, drubbing, trouncing, rout; *informal* massacre, hammering, thrashing, caning, demolition, going-over, licking, pasting, pounding; *N. Amer. informal* shellacking.

slaughterhouse ▶ **noun** **abattoir**; *Brit.* butchery, knacker's yard; *archaic* shambles, butcher-row.

slave ▶ **noun 1** (*historical*) *most of the work on the land was done by slaves* bondsman, bondswoman, bondservant, bondslave, serf, vassal, thrall; *historical* helot, odalisque, blackbird, hierodule.
OPPOSITES freeman, master.
2 *Anna was attracted to him and within 24 hours was his willing slave* **drudge**, servant, general factotum, man/maid of all work, lackey, minion; *Brit. informal* skivvy, dogsbody, slavey, poodle, fag; *N. Amer.* gofer; *rare* slaveling.
▶ **verb** *I'm sick of slaving away for a pittance* **toil**, labour, grind, sweat, work one's fingers to the bone, work day and night, work like a Trojan/dog, keep one's nose to the grindstone, exert oneself, grub, plod, plough; *informal* work one's guts out, work one's socks off, kill oneself, sweat blood, knock oneself out, plug away, slog away; *Brit. informal* graft, fag; *Austral./NZ informal* bullock; *Brit. vulgar slang* work one's balls/arse/nuts off; *N. Amer. vulgar slang* work one's ass/butt off; *archaic* drudge, travail, moil.
OPPOSITES relax; skive.

WORD LINKS
like a slave **servile**

slave-driver ▶ **noun** **(hard) taskmaster**, (hard) taskmistress, tyrant.

slaver ▶ **verb** *the Labrador was slavering at the mouth* **drool**, slobber, dribble, salivate; *Scottish & Irish* slabber; *archaic* drivel.

slavery ▶ **noun 1** (*historical*) *thousands had been sold into slavery* **bondage**, enslavement, servitude, subjugation, thraldom, thrall, serfdom, vassalage, enthralment, yoke; captivity, bonds, chains, fetters, shackles; *US History* peculiar institution.
OPPOSITES freedom, liberty, emancipation.
2 *working here is sheer slavery* **drudgery**, toil, (hard) slog, hard labour, grind, sweated labour; *Austral./NZ informal* (hard) yakka; *archaic* travail, moil.
OPPOSITES sinecure, soft option, money for old rope.

slavish ▶ **adjective 1** *they were reviled as slavish lackeys of the government* **servile**, subservient, fawning, obsequious, sycophantic, excessively deferential, toadying, ingratiating, unctuous, grovelling, cringing, toadyish, sycophantish, abject, craven, humble, Uriah Heepish, self-abasing; *informal* slimy, bootlicking, sucky, soapy, forelock-tugging; *N. Amer. informal* brown-nosing, apple-polishing; *Brit. vulgar slang* arse-licking, bum-sucking; *N. Amer. vulgar slang* kiss-ass, ass-kissing, suckholing.
OPPOSITES independent, assertive.
2 *a slavish copying of medieval motifs* **unoriginal**, uninspired, unimaginative, uninventive, non-innovative, imitative, derivative.
OPPOSITES original, imaginative.

slay ▶ **verb 1** *8,000 men from the regiment were slain* **kill**, murder, put to death, do to death, put to the sword, butcher, cut down, cut to pieces, slaughter, massacre, shoot down, gun down, mow down, assassinate, execute, dispatch, destroy, eliminate, annihilate, exterminate, dispose of; *informal* wipe out, take out, bump off, do in, do for, rub out, top, wipe off the face of the earth, blow away, liquidate, stiff; *N. Amer. informal* waste, smoke, ice, off.
2 (*informal*) *you slay me, you really do* **amuse greatly**, convulse with mirth/laughter, entertain greatly, make someone laugh; *informal* have people rolling in the aisles, make someone crack up, kill, knock dead, be the death of, wow, be a hit with; *Brit. informal* crease up.

slaying ▶ **noun** *the gruesome slaying of eleven youngsters* **murder**, killing, homicide, putting to death, execution, butchery, slaughter, massacre, assassination, dispatch, destruction, extermination; *informal* liquidation; *rare* mactation.

sleazy ▶ **adjective 1** *a series of deals involving sleazy arms dealers and middlemen* **corrupt**, immoral, sordid, unsavoury, unpleasant, disreputable; *informal* shady, sleazoid, sleazo.
OPPOSITES reputable, principled.
2 *a sleazy tenpin bowling alley* **squalid**, seedy, seamy, sordid, slummy, insalubrious, unpleasant, unprepossessing, mean, cheap, low-class, run down, down at heel; *informal* scruffy, scuzzy, tacky, crummy, grungy, ratty; *Brit. informal* grotty; *N. Amer. informal* skanky.
OPPOSITES upmarket, smart.

sledge ▶ **noun** **toboggan**, bobsleigh, sleigh; *N. Amer.* sled; (*in Canada*) carriole; (*in Russia*) kibitka; (*in Labrador*) komatik; *historical* travois.

sleek ▶ **adjective 1** *his sleek dark hair* **smooth**, **glossy**, shiny, shining, gleaming, lustrous, silken, silky, satiny, velvety, sheeny; well brushed, polished, burnished.
OPPOSITES dull, rough.
2 *he ran his hand lingeringly over the car's sleek lines* **streamlined**, trim, aerodynamic; elegant, graceful, flowing, smooth.
3 *a group of sleek young men in city suits* **well groomed**, stylish, wealthy-looking, prosperous-looking.
OPPOSITES unkempt, slovenly.

sleep ▶ **noun** *why don't you go and lie down and have a sleep?* **nap**, doze, rest, siesta, drowse, catnap; beauty sleep; *informal* snooze, forty winks, a bit of shut-eye, power nap; *Brit. informal* kip, zizz; *children's language* bye-byes; *literary* slumber.
□ **go to sleep** *I went to sleep almost as soon as my head hit the pillow* **fall asleep**, get to sleep; *informal* drop off, nod off, go off, drift off, crash out, go out like a light, flake out, conk out; *N. Amer. informal* sack out, zone out.
□ **put something to sleep** *the horse's condition deteriorated and he was put to sleep* **put down**, destroy, put out of its misery.
▶ **verb** *she slept for about an hour* **be asleep**, doze, rest, take a siesta, nap, take a nap, catnap, drowse; sleep like a log/top; *informal* snooze, snatch

S

forty winks, get some shut-eye, be in the land of Nod; *Brit. informal* kip, have a kip, get one's head down, zizz, get some zizz, doss (down); *N. Amer. informal* catch some Zs; *literary* slumber, be in the arms of Morpheus.
OPPOSITE wake up.

WORD LINKS
related prefixes **hypno-** (e.g. ***hypnotherapy***), **narco-** (e.g. ***narcolepsy***), **somn-** (e.g. ***somnambulism***)
causing sleep **sedative, hypnotic, soporific**
fear of sleep **hypnophobia**

sleepiness ▶ noun **drowsiness**, tiredness, somnolence, languor, languidness, doziness; lethargy, sluggishness, inactivity, heaviness, lassitude, enervation, torpor, torpidity; *Medicine* narcosis, narcolepsy; *rare* somnolency, comatoseness, oscitancy, oscitation.

sleepless ▶ adjective *she spent a sleepless night agonizing over what had happened | he lay sleepless until dawn* **wakeful**, restless, disturbed, without sleep; **awake**, wide awake, unsleeping, tossing and turning; insomniac; *archaic* watchful; *rare* insomnolent.

sleeplessness ▶ noun *sleeplessness can lead to irritability and aggression* **insomnia**, wakefulness.

sleepwalker ▶ noun **somnambulist**, noctambulist; *rare* night-walker.

sleepwalking ▶ noun **somnambulism**, noctambulism; *rare* somnambulation, noctambulation, night-walking.

sleepy ▶ adjective **1** *it was a hot day and she felt very sleepy* **drowsy**, tired, somnolent, languid, languorous, heavy-eyed, dozy, nodding, asleep on one's feet, yawning; lethargic, sluggish, inactive, enervated, torpid, comatose; *informal* snoozy, dopey, yawny; *literary* slumberous; *rare* oscitant, slumbersome.
OPPOSITES awake, alert.
2 *the sleepy heat of the afternoon* **soporific**, sleep-inducing, somnolent, hypnotic.
OPPOSITES energizing, invigorating.
3 *a sleepy little fishing village* **quiet**, peaceful, tranquil, placid, slow-moving, inactive; dull, boring, backwater, backwoods; *informal* one-horse.
OPPOSITE busy.

sleight of hand ▶ noun **1** *she rolled a cigarette with impressive sleight of hand* **dexterity**, adroitness, deftness, nimbleness of fingers, skill.
2 *this is financial sleight of hand of the worst sort* **deception**, deceit, dissimulation, double-dealing, chicanery, trickery, sharp practice, legerdemain.

slender ▶ adjective **1** *her tall slender figure* **slim**, lean, willowy, sylphlike, svelte, lissom, graceful, snake-hipped, rangy; slight, slightly built, delicate; thin, skinny, spare, attenuated, lanky, spindly; *rare* gracile, attenuate.
OPPOSITES fat, plump.
2 *a notion based on slender evidence* **meagre**, limited, slight, modest, scanty, scant, sparse, small, little, paltry, inconsiderable, insubstantial, inadequate, insufficient, deficient, negligible, trifling; *rare* exiguous.
OPPOSITES considerable, substantial, abundant.
3 *the chances of recruiting enough people seemed slender* **faint**, remote, feeble, flimsy, tenuous, fragile, slim; outside, distant, unlikely, improbable.
OPPOSITES good, strong.

sleuth ▶ noun (*informal*) **private detective**, detective, private investigator, investigator; *Brit.* enquiry agent; *informal* private eye, PI, snoop, sleuth-hound; *N. Amer. informal* private dick, dick, peeper, shamus, gumshoe; *informal, dated* hawkshaw, sherlock; *N. Amer. dated* Pinkerton.

slice ▶ noun **1** *a slice of fruit cake | thick slices of chicken* **piece**, portion, wedge, chunk, hunk, lump, slab, segment; rasher, collop; sliver, wafer, shaving; helping; *Brit.* round; *Cookery* escalope, scallop, scaloppina, fricandeau; *Brit. informal* wodge; *rare* hunch.
2 *local authorities control a huge slice of public spending* **share**, part, portion, tranche, piece, bit, parcel, proportion, allotment, allocation, percentage; ration, quota; *informal* cut, whack, rake-off.
▶ verb **1** *slice the cheese as thinly as possible* **cut**, cut up, carve, divide, segment, section.
2 *one man had his ear* **sliced off** *in the fight* **cut off**, sever, chop off, hack off, shear off; separate; *rare* dissever.

slick ▶ adjective **1** *a slick advertising campaign* **efficient**, **smooth**, smooth-running, polished, well organized, well run, streamlined; skilful, deft, adroit, dexterous, masterly, professional, clever, smart, sharp, shrewd.
OPPOSITES amateurish, clumsy, inexpert.
2 *his slick and facile use of the written word* **glib**, smooth, fluent, plausible, neat, pat, superficial; disingenuous, insincere, specious, meretricious, shallow.
OPPOSITES profound, thoughtful.
3 *the slick manager of the Berkeley Chase Hotel* **suave**, urbane, sophisticated, polished, assured, self-assured, smooth-talking, smooth-spoken, smooth-tongued, silver-tongued, glib; unctuous, oily, ingratiating; *informal* smarmy.
OPPOSITES unsophisticated, gauche.
4 *her slick brown hair* **shiny**, glossy, shining, sleek, smooth, silky, silken; oiled, plastered down, Brylcreemed.
5 *the pavements were slick with rain* **slippery**, slithery, wet, greasy, oily, icy, glassy, smooth; *informal* slippy, skiddy; *rare* lubricious.
OPPOSITES dry, rough.
▶ verb *his black hair was slicked down* **smooth**, sleek, flatten; plaster, grease, oil, gel; *informal* smarm.

CHOOSE THE RIGHT WORD
slick, glib, smooth, urbane
See GLIB.

slide ▶ verb **1** *the glass slid across the table | the car slid across the road* **glide**, move smoothly, slip, slither, skim, skate, glissade, coast, plane; **skid**, slew, aquaplane.
2 *tears slid down her cheeks* **trickle**, run, flow, pour, stream, course, spill.
3 *four men slid out of the shadows* **creep**, steal, slink, slip, glide, tiptoe, sidle, ease, edge.
4 *the country is sliding into recession* **sink**, fall, drop, descend; decline, degenerate, deteriorate.
□ **let something slide neglect**, pay little/no attention to, not attend to, be remiss about, be lax about, shirk, skimp on, let something go downhill, let something go to seed.
▶ noun **1** *the current slide in house prices* **fall**, decline, drop, slump, tumble, downturn, downswing; *informal* nosedive.
OPPOSITE rise.
2 *David placed the slide back in its case* microscope slide; transparency, mount.

slight ▶ adjective **1** *the chance of success is slight* **small**, modest, little, tiny, minute, inappreciable, imperceptible, infinitesimal, hardly worth mentioning, negligible, inconsiderable, insignificant, minimal, marginal; remote, scant, slim, outside; faint, vague, subtle, gentle; *informal* minuscule; *rare* exiguous.
OPPOSITES big, considerable.
2 *the book is a slight work by his usual standards* **minor**, inconsequential, trivial, trifling, unimportant, lightweight, superficial, shallow, of little account, petty, paltry; *informal* penny-ante; *Brit. informal* twopenny-halfpenny; *N. Amer. informal* nickel-and-dime.
OPPOSITES major, substantial.
3 *Elizabeth's slight figure* **slim**, slender, slightly built, petite, diminutive, small, delicate, dainty, small-boned, elfin; thin, skinny, spare, puny, undersized, frail, weak; *Scottish* wee; *informal* pint-sized, pocket-size; *rare* gracile, attenuate.
OPPOSITES sturdy, burly, muscular.
4 *slight, flat-bottomed boats made only of timber* **flimsy**, insubstantial, fragile, frail, rickety, jerry-built.
OPPOSITES strong, robust.
▶ verb *he was convinced that he had been socially slighted* **insult**, **snub**, rebuff, repulse, spurn, treat disrespectfully, give someone the cold shoulder, cold-shoulder, brush off, turn one's back on, keep at arm's length, disregard, ignore, cut (dead), neglect, take no notice of, disdain, scorn; *informal* give someone the brush-off, freeze out, stiff-arm, knock back; *informal, dated* give someone the go-by; *rare* misprize, scout.
OPPOSITES respect, welcome.
▶ noun *she often started rows in response to what she saw as slights on Nicky's part* **insult**, affront, slur, disparaging remark; **snub**, rebuff, rejection; spurning, cold-shouldering, disregard, rudeness, disrespect, disdain, scorn; *informal* put-down, dig, brush-off, kick in the teeth, slap in the face.
OPPOSITE compliment.

slighting ▶ adjective *slighting references to foreigners* **insulting**, disparaging, belittling, derogatory, disrespectful, denigratory, uncomplimentary, pejorative, abusive, offensive, defamatory, slanderous, libellous, scurrilous; disdainful, scornful, contemptuous; *informal* bitchy; *archaic* contumelious.
OPPOSITE complimentary.

slightly ▶ adverb *she felt slightly ill at ease* **a little**, a bit, somewhat, rather, moderately, to some degree, to a certain extent, to a slight extent, faintly, vaguely, obscurely; marginally, a shade; *informal* sort of, kind of, kinda.
OPPOSITE very.

slim ▶ adjective **1** *she was tall and slim with long blonde hair* **slender**, lean, willowy, sylphlike, svelte, lissom, graceful, snake-hipped, rangy, clean-limbed, trim, slight, slightly built; thin, as thin as a reed, skinny, spare, attenuated, lanky, spindly; *rare* gracile, attenuate.
OPPOSITES fat, plump.
2 *a slim silver bracelet* **narrow**, slender, slimline.
OPPOSITE broad.
3 *there was only a slim chance of escape* **slight**, small, slender, faint, feeble, poor, flimsy, tenuous, fragile, negligible, marginal, minimal; outside, remote, distant, unlikely, improbable.
OPPOSITES good, strong.
▶ verb **1** *if you eat only wholefoods, it should be easy to slim* **lose weight**, get thinner, lose/shed some pounds, lose some inches, get into shape, shape

up, reduce, diet, go on a diet; *N. Amer.* slenderize.
OPPOSITE put on weight.
2 *the number of staff had been* ***slimmed down*** *from 32 to 24* **reduce**, cut, cut down/back, make cutbacks in, scale down, trim, decrease, diminish, pare down, whittle away, prune; rationalize, downsize.
OPPOSITE increase.

slime ▶ **noun** *the steps were covered in green and black slime* **ooze**, sludge, muck, mud, mire; mucus; *informal* goo, gunk, yuck, gook, gloop; *Brit. informal* gunge, grot; *N. Amer. informal* guck, glop.

slimy ▶ **adjective 1** *the floor was cold and slimy* **slippery**, slithery, greasy, oozy, muddy, mucky, sludgy, miry; clammy, wet; sticky, viscous, viscid, mucilaginous, glutinous, mucous, mucoid; *informal* slippy, gunky, gooey, gloopy, gummy.
2 *her slimy press agent* **obsequious**, sycophantic, excessively deferential, subservient, fawning, toadying, ingratiating, unctuous, oily, oleaginous, greasy, reptilian, grovelling, cringing, toadyish, sycophantish, slavish, abject, craven, humble, Uriah Heepish, self-abasing; *informal* bootlicking, smarmy, sucky, soapy, forelock-tugging; *N. Amer. informal* brown-nosing, apple-polishing; *Brit. vulgar slang* arse-licking, bum-sucking; *N. Amer. vulgar slang* kiss-ass, ass-kissing, suckholing.

sling ▶ **noun 1** *she had her arm in a sling* **support bandage**, support, bandage, strap.
2 *700 men armed only with slings* **catapult**, slingshot; *Austral./NZ* shanghai.
▶ **verb 1** *a hammock was slung between two trees | she noticed the binoculars slung round his neck* **hang**, suspend, string, dangle, swing, drape.
2 (*informal*) *she took off her jacket and slung it on the sofa* **throw**, toss, fling, hurl, cast, pitch, lob, launch, flip, shy, catapult, send flying, let fly with; *informal* chuck, bung, heave, buzz, whang; *N. Amer. informal* peg; *Austral. informal* hoy; *NZ informal* bish.

slink ▶ **verb** *she slunk past the open door of the living room* **creep**, sneak, steal, slip, slide, sidle, edge, move furtively, tiptoe, pussyfoot, pad; skulk, lurk; prowl.

slinky ▶ **adjective** (*informal*) **1** *a slinky black evening dress* **tight**, clinging, tight-fitting, close-fitting, figure-hugging, skintight, sheath-like; sexy; *informal* sprayed on.
OPPOSITE baggy.
2 *the outfit gave her a slinky, model-like elegance* **sinuous**, feline, willowy, graceful, sleek.

slip[1] ▶ **verb 1** *she slipped on the ice* **slide**, skid, slither, glide; **fall over**, fall, lose one's balance, lose/miss one's footing, stumble, tumble, trip.
2 *the envelope slipped through Luke's fingers* **fall**, drop, slide.
3 *we slipped out by a back door* **creep**, steal, sneak, slide, sidle, slope, slink, pad, tiptoe, pussyfoot, edge, move stealthily/quietly, insinuate oneself.
4 *many people feel standards have slipped* **decline**, deteriorate, degenerate, worsen, get worse, fall, fall off, drop, decay, backslide, regress; *informal* go downhill, go to the dogs, go to pot, go down the tube/tubes, go down the toilet, hit the skids.
OPPOSITE improve.
5 *the bank's shares slipped 1.5p to 227p* **drop**, go down, sink, slump, tumble, plunge, plummet, decrease, depreciate; *informal* crash, nosedive.
OPPOSITE rise.
6 *the hours* ***slipped by*** *so quickly that she had no time to brood* **pass**, elapse, go by/past, roll by/past, glide by/past, slide by/past, fly by/past, steal by/past, tick by/past, wear on.
7 *she slipped the map into her pocket* **put**, tuck, stow, insert; *informal* pop, stick, shove, stuff.
OPPOSITE remove.
8 *Sarah* ***slipped into*** *a black velvet skirt* **put on**, pull on, don, dress/clothe oneself in, get into, climb into, fling on, throw on; pour oneself into; change into; *informal* tog oneself up/out in, doll oneself up in.
OPPOSITE take off.
9 *in the bathroom she quickly* ***slipped out of*** *her clothes* **take off**, remove, pull off, peel off, shrug off, discard, shed, divest oneself of, doff, fling off, fling aside, climb out of; undo, unfasten, unbutton, unzip.
OPPOSITE put on.
10 *he was already slipping the knot of his tie* **untie**, unfasten, undo, loosen, disentangle, untangle, unsnarl.
OPPOSITES tie, do up.

□ **let something slip reveal**, disclose, divulge, let out, give away, come out with, blurt out, leak; give the game away; *informal* let on, blab, let the cat out of the bag, spill the beans; *Brit. informal* blow the gaff; *archaic* discover.
OPPOSITE keep something secret.

□ **slip away 1** *how did they manage to slip away?* **escape**, make one's escape, get away, break free, make one's getaway, abscond, decamp; disappear, vanish; *informal* fly the coop; *Brit. informal* do a bunk, do a runner; *N. Amer. informal* take a powder.
2 *she slipped away in her sleep at two o'clock in the morning* **die**, pass away, pass on, expire, breathe one's last, go, go to meet one's maker, shuffle off this mortal coil, go to one's last resting place, go the way of all flesh, cross the Styx; *informal* pop off, snuff it, croak, kick the bucket, give up the ghost, turn up one's toes, cash in one's chips, conk out, flatline; *Brit. informal* pop one's clogs, peg out, hop the twig/stick; *N. Amer. informal* check out, hand in one's dinner pail; *Austral./NZ informal* go bung; *archaic* decease, depart this life, exit.

□ **slip up** (*informal*) *we can't afford to slip up like that again* **make a mistake**, blunder, make a blunder, get something wrong, miscalculate, make an error, trip up, err, go wrong; *informal* make a bloomer, make a boo-boo, screw up, make a howler, muff something up; *Brit. informal* boob, cock something up, drop a clanger; *N. Amer. informal* goof up.

▶ **noun 1** *a single slip could send them plummeting down the mountainside* **false step**, misstep, slide, skid, fall, trip, tumble.
2 *the Chinese prime minister made a similar slip a couple of years ago* **mistake**, error, blunder, miscalculation, gaffe, faux pas, slip of the tongue/pen; oversight, omission; indiscretion, impropriety, lapse; inaccuracy, fault, defect; *informal* slip-up, boo-boo, boner, howler; *Brit. informal* boob, clanger, bloomer; *N. Amer. informal* goof, blooper, bloop; *Latin* lapsus linguae, lapsus calami.
3 *a silk slip* **underskirt**, petticoat, underslip, half-slip.

□ **give someone the slip** (*informal*) *we gave them the slip at the station* **escape from**, get away from, evade, dodge, elude, lose, shake off, throw off, throw off the scent, get clear of, get rid of, get free from, break away from, leave behind; *informal* ditch; *Brit. informal* get shot of; *archaic* bilk.

slip[2] ▶ **noun 1** *she wrote the number down on a slip of paper* **piece of paper**, scrap of paper, paper, sheet, note; chit, coupon, voucher; *informal* stickie; *trademark* Post-it (note).
2 *they took seeds or slips from rare and threatened plants* **cutting**, graft; scion, shoot, offshoot, sprout, sprig, runner.

□ **a slip of a ...** *it amazed him that such a slip of a girl could be so strong* **small**, slender, slim, slight, slightly built, petite, little, tiny, diminutive, elfin, dainty, delicate, frail; *Scottish* wee; *informal* pint-sized.

slipper ▶ **noun 1** *he slid out of bed and pulled on his slippers* carpet slipper, bedroom slipper, house shoe, mule, moccasin; *N. Amer.* slipperette; *rare* pantofle, pantable, panton.
2 *she wore a white organdie dress and high-heeled satin slippers* pump, mule.

slipperiness ▶ **noun 1** *the slipperiness of the path* **smoothness**, slickness, greasiness, oiliness, iciness, glassiness; sliminess, wetness; *informal* slippiness.
2 *his campaign has been hurt not so much by scandal, but by his slipperiness* **evasiveness**, unreliability, unpredictability; deviousness, craftiness, cunning, wiliness, trickiness, artfulness, guilefulness, slickness, untrustworthiness, duplicitousness, dishonesty, treachery, two-facedness; *informal* shadiness, shiftiness; *rare* tergiversation.

slippery ▶ **adjective 1** *heavy rain had made the roads slippery* **slithery**, greasy, oily, icy, glassy, smooth, slick; slimy, wet; *informal* slippy, skiddy; *rare* lubricious.
OPPOSITES dry, rough.
2 *Martin's a slippery customer* **evasive**, unreliable, unpredictable, hard to pin down; **devious**, crafty, cunning, wily, tricky, artful, guileful, slick, sly, sneaky, scheming, contriving, untrustworthy, deceitful, deceptive, duplicitous, dishonest, treacherous, false, two-faced; *N. Amer.* snide; *informal* shady, shifty, foxy, iffy; *Brit. informal* dodgy; *Austral./NZ informal* shonky.
OPPOSITES open, reliable, trustworthy.

slipshod ▶ **adjective** *he blamed unprofessionalism and a slipshod approach for the club's performance* **careless**, lackadaisical, slapdash, disorganized, unorganized, haphazard, hit-or-miss, last minute, untidy, messy, unsystematic, unmethodical, casual, offhand, thoughtless, heedless, negligent, neglectful, remiss, lax, slack, slovenly; *informal* sloppy, all over the place, slap-happy; *Brit. informal* all over the shop.
OPPOSITES careful, meticulous, painstaking.

slip-up ▶ **noun** (*informal*) *it was all down to a simple clerical slip-up* **mistake**, slip, error, blunder, miscalculation, oversight, omission, gaffe, faux pas, slip of the tongue/pen, lapse; inaccuracy, fault, defect; *informal* boo-boo, boner, howler; *Brit. informal* boob, clanger, bloomer, cock-up; *N. Amer. informal* goof, blooper, bloop; *Latin* lapsus linguae, lapsus calami.

slit ▶ **noun 1** *make three diagonal slits in each side of the trout and season generously* **cut**, incision, split, slash, gash, laceration; rip, tear, rent; vent, placket.
2 *Henry saw a face peeping through a slit in the curtains* **opening**, gap, chink, space, crack, cranny, aperture, slot; peephole.
▶ **verb** *he threatened to slit her throat* **cut**, slash, split open, slice open, gash, lacerate, make an incision in; tear, rip; pierce, knife, lance; *literary* rend.

slither ▶ **verb** *Ben and I slithered down the bank | a green snake slithered silently across the grass* **slide**, slip, glide, glissade; squirm, wriggle, snake, worm, slink, creep, crawl; skid.

sliver ▶ **noun** *slivers of glass | a sliver of cheese* **splinter**, shard, shiver, chip, flake, shred, scrap, slither, shaving, paring; slice, wafer; piece, fragment, bit; *Scottish* skelf; *technical* rove.

slob ▶ **noun** (*informal*) *her no-good slob of a husband* **layabout**, good-for-nothing, sluggard, laggard; lout, oaf; *informal* slacker, couch potato, pig; *Brit. informal* slummock, yob; *N. Amer. informal* schlump, bum, lardass; *archaic* sloven, lurdan.

slobber ▶ **verb drool**, slaver, dribble, salivate, water at the mouth; *Scottish*

& *Irish* slabber; *archaic* drivel.

slog ▶ verb **1** *they were slogging away to meet a deadline* **work hard**, toil, labour, work one's fingers to the bone, work like a Trojan/dog, work day and night, exert oneself, keep at it, keep one's nose to the grindstone, grind, slave, grub, plough, plod, peg; *informal* beaver, plug, put one's back into something, work one's guts out, work one's socks off, knock oneself out, sweat blood, kill oneself; *Brit. informal* graft, fag; *Austral./NZ informal* bullock; *Brit. vulgar slang* work one's balls/arse/nuts off; *N. Amer. vulgar slang* work one's ass/butt off; *archaic* drudge, travail, moil.
OPPOSITES skive, take it easy.
2 *the three of them slogged around the streets of the capital in the July heat* **trudge**, tramp, traipse, toil, plod, trek, footslog, drag oneself; *Brit. informal* trog, yomp; *N. Amer. informal* schlep.
▶ noun **1** *writing the book took 10 months' hard slog* **hard work**, toil, toiling, labour, struggle, effort, exertion, grind, {blood, sweat, and tears}, drudgery; Herculean task; *informal* sweat, elbow grease; *Brit. informal* graft; *Austral./NZ informal* (hard) yakka; *archaic* travail, moil.
OPPOSITES leisure, relaxation.
2 *a steady uphill slog* **trudge**, tramp, traipse, plod, trek, footslog; *Brit. informal* trog, yomp; *N. Amer. informal* schlep.

slogan ▶ noun *well-known advertising slogans* **catchphrase**, catchline, catchword, jingle, saying, formula, legend; watchword, motto, mantra, rallying cry; shibboleth; *N. Amer. informal* tag line.

slop ▶ verb *water slopped over the edge of the sink* **spill**, flow, overflow, run, slosh, splash, splatter, spatter.
□ **slop around/about** (*Brit. informal*) *at weekends he would slop about in his oldest clothes* **laze (around/about)**, lounge (around/about), do nothing, loll (around/about), loaf (around/about), slouch (about/around), vegetate; *informal* hang around, veg out; *Brit. informal* hang about, mooch about/around, slummock around; *N. Amer. informal* bum around, bat around/about, lollygag.

slope ▶ noun **1** *the roof should have a slope sufficient for proper drainage* **gradient**, incline, angle, slant, inclination, pitch, decline, ascent, declivity, acclivity, rise, fall, downward, upward, downslope, upslope, ramp, rake, tilt, tip, dip, camber, cant, bevel; *N. Amer.* grade, downgrade, upgrade.
2 *a steep, grassy slope* **hill**, hillside, hillock, bank, rise, escarpment, scarp; *Scottish* brae; *technical* glacis, versant, adret, ubac, bajada, piedmont; *literary* steep.
3 *a ten-minute cable-car ride delivers you to the slopes* **piste**, run, track; nursery slope, dry slope, dry-ski slope; *N. Amer.* trail.
▶ verb *the garden sloped down to a stream* **slant**, incline, tilt; drop away, fall away, decline, descend, sink, shelve, lean, dip; rise, ascend, climb.
□ **slope off** (*informal*) *they gathered up their belongings and sloped off* **leave**, go away, go, slip away, take oneself off, make oneself scarce, take one's leave, make off, steal away, slink off, creep off, sneak off; *informal* push off, clear off.
OPPOSITE arrive.

sloping ▶ adjective *a sloping floor* **at a slant**, on the slant, at an angle, not straight, slanting, slanted, slantwise, slant, oblique, leaning, inclining, inclined, angled, cambered, canted; askew, skew, lopsided, crooked, tilting, tilted, atilt, dipping, out of true, out of line; *Scottish* squint; *rare* declivitous, declivous, acclivitous, acclivous.
OPPOSITES level, straight.

sloppy ▶ adjective **1** *they sat round the table eating a sloppy chicken curry* **runny**, watery, thin, liquid, semi-liquid, mushy, soupy; wet, soggy, slushy, sludgy; *S. African* slap; *informal* gloopy.
OPPOSITES dry, solid.
2 *we gave away a goal through sloppy defending* **careless**, slapdash, slipshod, lackadaisical, disorganized, haphazard, unmethodical, unsystematic, hit-or-miss, untidy, messy, thoughtless, inattentive, heedless, hasty, hurried; thrown together, last-minute, cursory, perfunctory, negligent, neglectful, remiss, lax, slack, slovenly; amateurish, unprofessional; *informal* shambolic, all over the place, slap-happy; *Brit. informal* all over the shop.
OPPOSITES careful, meticulous.
3 *sloppy T-shirts* **baggy**, loose-fitting, loose, generously cut, not tight, roomy; shapeless, sack-like, slack, oversized, ill-fitting, bagging.
OPPOSITES tight, tailored.
4 *sloppy letters from a boy she had met on holiday* **sentimental**, mawkish, over-sentimental, overemotional, cloying, sickly, saccharine, sugary, sugar-coated, syrupy; romantic, hearts-and-flowers; *Brit.* twee; *informal* slushy, mushy, weepy, tear-jerking, schmaltzy, cutesy, lovey-dovey, gooey, drippy, sloshy, soupy, treacly, cheesy, corny, icky, sick-making, toe-curling; *Brit. informal* soppy; *N. Amer. informal* cornball, sappy, hokey, three-hankie; *trademark* Mills-and-Boon.
OPPOSITES unemotional, gritty.

slosh ▶ verb **1** *he slammed the glass on the table and beer sloshed over the side* **spill**, slop, splash, flow, overflow, splatter, spatter.
2 *workers sloshed round in rubber boots* **splash**, swash, squelch, wade; *informal* splosh.
3 *she sloshed more wine into her glass* **pour**, slop, splash; *informal* glug.
4 (*Brit. informal*) *Gary sloshed him* **hit**, strike, thump, slog, punch, cuff, smack, thwack, box someone's ears; *informal* whack, belt, bash, biff, bop, clout, wallop, swipe, sock, lam, crown, whomp, deck, floor; *Brit. informal* stick one on, dot; *N. Amer. informal* boff, bust, slug, whale; *Austral./NZ informal* dong, quilt; *literary* smite, swinge.

slot ▶ noun **1** *he slid a coin into the slot of the jukebox* **aperture**, slit, crack, hole, opening, groove, notch.
2 *the programme's mid-morning slot* **spot**, time, period; place, position, niche, space; *informal* window.
▶ verb *he slotted a cassette into the tape machine* **insert**, put, place, fit, slide, slip.

sloth ▶ noun *sloth and bad organization seem to be to blame* **laziness**, idleness, indolence, slothfulness, inactivity, inertia, sluggishness, apathy, accidie, listlessness, lassitude, passivity, lethargy, languor, torpidity, slowness, heaviness, dullness, shiftlessness; *French archaic* fainéance; *rare* hebetude.
OPPOSITES industriousness, energy.

slothful ▶ adjective *fatigue made him slothful* **lazy**, idle, indolent, work-shy, inactive, inert, sluggish, apathetic, lethargic, listless, languid, torpid, slow-moving, slow, heavy, dull, enervated, shiftless, lackadaisical; *informal* bone idle, do-nothing; *French archaic* fainéant; *rare* otiose.
OPPOSITES active, industrious, energetic.

slouch ▶ verb *Nicky slouched back in his chair* **slump**, hunch; loll, droop, sag, stoop.

slovenly ▶ adjective **1** *he was upbraided for his slovenly appearance* **scruffy**, untidy, messy, unkempt, ill-groomed, slatternly, dishevelled, bedraggled, tousled, rumpled, frowzy, blowsy, down at heel; dirty, grubby; sluttish; *informal* slobbish, slobby; *N. Amer. informal* raggedy, schlumpy, raunchy; *archaic* draggle-tailed.
OPPOSITES tidy, neat.
2 *his work is slovenly and his manners are unsatisfactory* **careless**, slapdash, slipshod, disorganized, unorganized, unsystematic, unmethodical, haphazard, hit-or-miss, untidy, messy, thoughtless, negligent, neglectful, lax, lackadaisical, slack; *informal* sloppy, slap-happy, couldn't-care-less.
OPPOSITES careful, meticulous, painstaking.

slow ▶ adjective **1** *a slow pace | their slow walk back to the village* **unhurried**, leisurely, measured, moderate, deliberate, steady, sedate, slow-moving, slow-going, easy, relaxed, unrushed, gentle, undemanding, comfortable; ponderous, plodding, laboured, dawdling, loitering, lagging, laggard, sluggish, sluggardly, snail-like, tortoise-like, leaden-footed, leaden, creeping; *N. Amer. informal* lollygagging.
OPPOSITES fast, rapid, brisk.
2 *a slow process* **long-drawn-out**, time-consuming, lengthy, long-lasting, protracted, prolonged, interminable; gradual, progressive.
OPPOSITES brief, short.
3 *he didn't guess—he can be so slow* **obtuse**, stupid, unperceptive, imperceptive, blind, uncomprehending, unimaginative, insensitive, bovine, stolid, slow-witted, dull-witted, unintelligent, doltish, witless, blockish; *informal* dense, dim, dim-witted, thick, slow on the uptake, dumb, dopey, not with it, boneheaded, blockheaded, lamebrained, wooden-headed, muttonheaded; *Brit. informal* dozy; *Scottish & N. English informal* glaikit; *N. Amer. informal* dumb-ass, chowderheaded; *S. African informal* dof.
OPPOSITES astute, bright, perceptive.
4 *the objectors were not **slow to** voice their opinions* **reluctant**, unwilling, disinclined, loath, averse, indisposed; hesitant about, afraid of, chary of, shy of.
5 *an attempt by the industry to boost sales in a slow season* **sluggish**, slack, quiet, slow-moving, not busy, inactive, flat, depressed, stagnant, dead; unproductive.
OPPOSITES busy, hectic.
6 *a slow and mostly aimless narrative* **dull**, boring, uninteresting, unexciting, uneventful, tedious, tiresome, wearisome, dry, as dry as dust, monotonous, plodding, tame, dreary, lacklustre; *informal* ho-hum.
OPPOSITES gripping, exciting, action-packed.
7 *Stratford's too small, too slow—I've got to get away* **quiet**, sleepy, unprogressive, behind the times, backward, backwoods, backwater; *informal* dead, one-horse, dead-and-alive; *N. Amer. informal* dullsville.
▶ verb **1** *the traffic forced him to **slow down*** **reduce speed**, go slower, decelerate, lessen one's speed, brake, put the brakes on, slack off.
OPPOSITES accelerate, speed up.
2 *Paula, you really need to **slow down*** **take it easy**, relax, ease up/off, take a break, take some time off, slack off; *informal* let up; *N. Amer. informal* chill out, hang loose, kick back.
OPPOSITE work harder.
3 *he'll only **slow us up** | such a development would **slow down** economic growth in Europe* **hold back**, hold up, keep back, delay, detain, retard, set back; restrict, restrain, limit, put the brakes on, check, curb, rein in, interfere with, inhibit, impede, obstruct, hinder, hamper, get in the way of, handicap; *archaic* stay.
OPPOSITE speed up.

WORD LINKS
abnormally slow heart action **bradycardia**

slowly ▶ adverb **1** *Rose walked off slowly* **unhurriedly**, without hurrying, at

a leisurely pace, at a slow pace, leisurely, steadily, taking one's time, in one's own good time; at a snail's pace, ploddingly, with heavy steps, with leaden steps, heavily; *Music* adagio, lento, largo, larghetto, adagietto.
OPPOSITES fast, quickly, rapidly.
2 *her health is improving slowly* **gradually**, bit by bit, by degrees, little by little, slowly but surely, step by step, inchmeal.
OPPOSITE by leaps and bounds.

sludge ▶ noun *the channel had become silted up with layer upon layer of sludge* **mud**, muck, mire, ooze, silt, alluvium, dirt, slime, slush, slurry; sediment, lees, dregs, deposit, grounds, settlings, precipitate, residue; *Scottish & N. English* clart; *Irish* slob; *informal* gunk, crud, gloop, grunge, gook, goo; *Brit. informal* gunge, grot; *N. Amer. informal* guck, glop; *rare* grouts.

sluggish ▶ adjective **1** *Alex woke late, feeling tired and sluggish* **lethargic**, listless, lacking in energy, unenergetic, lifeless, inert, inactive, slow, torpid, dull, languid, apathetic, passive, unresponsive, weary, tired, fatigued, sleepy, half asleep, drowsy, heavy-eyed, enervated, somnolent; lazy, idle, indolent, slothful, sluggardly; phlegmatic, bovine; *Medicine* asthenic, neurasthenic; *informal* dozy, dopey, yawny; *N. Amer. informal* logy; *archaic* lymphatic.
OPPOSITES vigorous, energetic, active.
2 *the sluggish global economy* **inactive**, quiet, slow, slow-moving, slack, flat, depressed, stagnant, static.
OPPOSITES busy, brisk.

sluggishness ▶ noun **1** *Rob put down his sluggishness to over-exuberant birthday celebrations* **lethargy**, inertia, listlessness, lack of energy, lifelessness, inactivity, inaction, slowness, languor, languidness, torpor, torpidity, dullness, heaviness, apathy, passivity, weariness, tiredness, lassitude, fatigue, sleepiness, drowsiness, enervation, somnolence, laziness, idleness, indolence, sloth, slothfulness; phlegm; *Medicine* asthenia, neurasthenia, anergia; *informal* doziness, dopeyness; *rare* hebetude.
OPPOSITES vigour, energy, animation.
2 *they are having difficulties exporting because of the sluggishness of other economies* **lack of activity**, quietness, slowness, slackness, flatness, stagnation.
OPPOSITE briskness.

sluice ▶ verb **1** *crews sluiced down the decks of their ship* **wash**, wash down, rinse, swill down, clean, cleanse, flush.
2 *the water sluiced out through the open door* **pour**, flow, run, gush, cascade, stream, course, spout, jet, spurt, flood, surge, spill, rush, well, spew, discharge; *Brit. informal* sloosh; *rare* disembogue.

slum ▶ noun **hovel**; **(slums)** ghetto, shanty town; *(in Brazil)* favela; *Indian* jhuggi, jhuggi jhopri, bustee; *Canadian informal* Cabbagetown; *rare* rookery.

slumber *(literary)* ▶ verb *the child slumbered fitfully against his chest* **sleep**, be asleep, doze, rest, take a siesta, nap, take a nap, catnap, drowse, sleep like a log/top; *informal* snooze, snatch forty winks, get some shut-eye, be in the land of Nod; *Brit. informal* kip, have a kip, get one's head down, zizz, get some zizz, doss (down); *N. Amer. informal* catch some Zs; *literary* be in the arms of Morpheus.
OPPOSITE wake up.
▶ noun *he drifted off into an uneasy slumber* **sleep**, nap, doze, rest, siesta, drowse, catnap; beauty sleep; *informal* snooze, forty winks, a bit of shut-eye; *Brit. informal* kip, zizz.

slummy ▶ adjective *a slummy area of town* **seedy**, insalubrious, squalid, sleazy, seamy, sordid, dingy, mean, wretched; **run down**, down at heel, shabby, dilapidated, in disrepair, neglected, uncared-for, unmaintained, depressed; *informal* crummy, scruffy, scuzzy, grungy; *Brit. informal* grotty; *N. Amer. informal* shacky, skanky.
OPPOSITES smart, upmarket.

slump ▶ verb **1** *he slumped into a chair* **sit heavily**, flop, flump, collapse, sink, fall, subside; sag, slouch; *informal* plonk oneself, plop oneself.
OPPOSITES stand up, sit up.
2 *houses prices slumped* **fall steeply**, plummet, plunge, tumble, drop, go down, slide, decline, decrease; reach a new low; *informal* crash, nosedive, take a nosedive, go into a tailspin.
OPPOSITES rise, soar.
3 *the reading standards of 7-year-olds have slumped* **decline**, deteriorate, degenerate, worsen, get worse, slip, lapse; *informal* go downhill, go to pot, go to the dogs, nosedive, take a nosedive.
OPPOSITE improve.
▶ noun **1** *a slump in annual profits* **steep fall**, plunge, drop, collapse, tumble, plummet, downturn, downswing, slide, decline, falling off, decrease, lowering, devaluation, depreciation; meltdown; *informal* nosedive.
OPPOSITE rise.
2 *higher interest rates would drive the country into a slump* **recession**, economic decline, depression, slowdown, trough; stagnation, stagflation; hard times.
OPPOSITES boom, upturn.

slur ▶ verb *she was slurring her words* **mumble**, speak unclearly, garble, stumble over, stammer; *rare* misarticulate.
OPPOSITE enunciate.
▶ noun *it is a gross slur on a highly respected and honest man* **insult**, slight, slander, slanderous statement, libel, libellous statement, misrepresentation, defamation, aspersion, calumny, smear; allegation, imputation, insinuation, innuendo.

slush ▶ noun **1** *he wiped the slush off his shoes* **melting snow**, wet snow; muck, mush, mud, sludge.
2 *(informal) the slush of Hollywood's romantic fifties films* **sentimentality**, mawkishness, over-sentimentality, emotionalism, overemotionalism, sentimentalism, banality, triteness; *Brit.* tweeness; *informal* schmaltz, mush, sob stuff, slushiness, sloppiness, slop, goo, corn, corniness, hokum, cheese; *Brit. informal* soppiness; *N. Amer. informal* sappiness, hokeyness.

slut ▶ noun **promiscuous woman**; prostitute, whore; slattern; *euphemistic* model, escort, masseuse; *French* poule; *informal* **tart**, floozie, bike, pro; *Brit. informal* scrubber, slag, slapper; *N. Amer. informal* tramp, hooker, hustler, roundheel, chippy, skank, puta; *black English* ho; *dated* scarlet woman, loose woman, hussy, woman of ill repute, streetwalker, trollop; *archaic* harlot, strumpet, wanton, drab, doxy, trull, sloven.

sly ▶ adjective **1** *she's getting sly in her old age* **cunning**, crafty, clever, wily, artful, guileful, tricky, conniving, scheming, devious, designing, deceitful, duplicitous, dishonest, disingenuous, underhand, sneaky, untrustworthy; manipulative, calculating, Machiavellian; *informal* foxy, shifty; *Brit. informal* fly; *Austral./NZ informal* shonky; *S. African informal* slim; *archaic* subtle; *rare* carny.
OPPOSITES honest, artless.
2 *he gave her a sly grin* **roguish**, mischievous, impish, puckish, playful, teasing, naughty, wicked, waggish; arch, knowing; *Scottish & N. English informal* pawky.
3 *she took a sly sip of water* **surreptitious**, furtive, stealthy, covert, secret.
▶ noun
□ **on the sly** *is she meeting some other guy on the sly?* **in secret**, secretly, furtively, stealthily, sneakily, slyly, surreptitiously, covertly, clandestinely, on the quiet, on the side, behind someone's back, under cover; under the counter; *informal* on the q.t.
OPPOSITE openly.

smack[1] ▶ noun **1** *she gave Mark a smack across the face* **slap**, blow, spank, cuff, clout, thump, punch, rap, swat, thwack, crack; *informal* whack, clip, biff, wallop, swipe, bop, belt, bash, sock.
2 *the parcel landed with a solid smack on the terrace below* **bang**, crash, thud, thump, wham.
3 *(informal) she gave him a quick smack on the cheek* **kiss**, peck; *informal* smacker.
□ **a smack in the face/eye** *this could only be seen as a smack in the face for the government* **rebuff**, rejection, repulse, snub, insult, affront, put-down, humiliation, blow to one's pride, slap in the face; *informal* brush-off.
▶ verb **1** *he lost his temper and smacked her* **slap**, hit, strike, spank, cuff, clout, thump, punch, rap, swat, thwack, crack; put someone over one's knee, make someone feel the back of one's hand, box someone's ears; *informal* whack, clip, wallop, biff, swipe, bop, belt, bash, sock, give someone a hiding, warm someone's bottom, give someone a hot bottom; *Brit. informal* slosh; *Scottish & N. English informal* skelp, scud; *N. Amer. informal* boff, slug, bust; *Austral./NZ informal* dong, quilt; *archaic* smite.
2 *the waiter smacked a plate on the table* **bang**, slam, crash, thump, sling, fling; *informal* bung, plonk; *N. Amer. informal* plunk.
▶ adverb *(informal) I ran smack into the back of a parked truck | our mother's house was smack in the middle of the city* **straight**, right, directly, squarely, headlong, dead, plumb, point-blank; **exactly**, precisely; *informal* slap, bang, slap bang, smack bang; *N. Amer. informal* spang, smack dab.

smack[2] ▶ verb
□ **smack of 1** *the tea smacked strongly of tannin* **taste of**, have the flavour of, have the savour of.
2 *I didn't want to engage in anything that smacked of self-promotion* **suggest**, hint at, have overtones of, have a suggestion of, have the air of, give the impression of, have the hallmark of, have the stamp of, resemble, seem like; smell of, reek of.
▶ noun **1** *anything with even a modest smack of hops dries the palate* **taste**, flavour, savour; *archaic* relish.
2 *there was more than a smack of bitterness in his words* **trace**, tinge, touch, suggestion, hint, scintilla, impression, overtone, air, suspicion, whisper, whiff.

small ▶ adjective **1** *a small flat in Fulham | he put his hand in his jacket and pulled out a small package* **little**, small-scale, compact, bijou; portable; tiny, miniature, mini, minute, microscopic, minuscule; toy, baby; poky, cramped, boxy; *Scottish* wee; *informal* tiddly, teeny, weeny, teeny-weeny, teensy, teensy-weensy, itsy-bitsy, itty-bitty, eensy, eensy-weensy, pocket-sized, half-pint, dinky, ickle, with no room to swing a cat; *Brit. informal* titchy; *N. Amer. informal* little-bitty, vest-pocket.
OPPOSITES big, large.
2 *he was a very small man* **short**, little, slight, slightly built, small-boned, petite, diminutive, elfin, tiny; puny, undersized, stunted; squat, stubby; dwarf, dwarfish, midget, pygmy, bantam, homuncular, Lilliputian; a slip of a ...; *Scottish* wee; *informal* teeny, teeny-weeny, pint-sized.
OPPOSITES heavily built, tall, large.
3 *we may have to make a few small changes* **slight**, minor, unimportant,

S

trifling, trivial, insignificant, inconsequential, inappreciable, inconsiderable, negligible, nugatory, paltry, infinitesimal; *informal* minuscule, piffling, piddling.
OPPOSITES major, substantial.
4 *small helpings of vegetables* **inadequate**, meagre, insufficient, ungenerous, not enough; *informal* measly, stingy, mingy, pathetic.
OPPOSITES generous, ample.
5 *they had succeeded in making him feel small* **foolish**, stupid, insignificant, unimportant; embarrassed, humiliated, uncomfortable, mortified, chagrined, ashamed; deflated, crushed.
OPPOSITE proud.
6 *the captain had been paying small attention* **hardly any**, not much, scant, little or no, little, minimal.
7 *a small farmer* **small-scale**, small-time; modest, unpretentious, humble, lowly, simple.
OPPOSITES large-scale, substantial.

WORD LINKS
related prefixes **micro-** (e.g. ***microscope, microbrewery***), **mini-** (e.g. ***minidisc, minibeast***), **nano-** (e.g. ***nanotechnology, nanosecond***)

small change ▶ noun **coins**, change, coppers, silver, cash; *formal* specie.

small-minded ▶ adjective *a bunch of small-minded bigots* **narrow-minded**, petty-minded, petty, mean, mean-spirited, mean-minded, uncharitable, ungenerous, grudging, close-minded, short-sighted, myopic, blinkered, inward-looking, narrow, conventional, unimaginative, parochial, provincial, insular, small-town, localist; intolerant, illiberal, reactionary, conservative, hidebound, dyed-in-the-wool, diehard, limited, restricted, set in one's ways, inflexible, dogmatic, rigid, entrenched, prejudiced, bigoted, biased, partisan; *Brit.* parish-pump, blimpish; *French* borné; *N. Amer. informal* jerkwater; *rare* claustral.
OPPOSITES broad-minded, tolerant, open-minded.

small-time ▶ adjective *small-time crooks | a small-time printer* **minor**, small-scale, small; petty, unimportant, insignificant, of no account, of no consequence, inconsequential; *N. Amer.* minor-league; *informal* penny-ante, piddling; *N. Amer. informal* two-bit, no-account, bush-league, picayune.
OPPOSITES major, important, big-time.

smarminess ▶ noun (*informal*) *I just can't bear his smarminess* **unctuousness**, smoothness, slickness, oiliness, greasiness, fulsomeness, obsequiousness; *informal* sliminess; *rare* unctuosity.

smarmy ▶ adjective (*informal*) *he's too smarmy* **unctuous**, ingratiating, smooth, slick, oily, greasy, fulsome, flattering, obsequious, sycophantic, fawning; *informal* slimy, sucky, soapy.

smart ▶ adjective **1** *you look very smart | a pair of smart black shoes* **well dressed**, well turned out, fashionably dressed, fashionable, stylish, chic, modish, elegant, neat, besuited, spruce, trim, dapper, debonair; shiny, gleaming, bright, spotless, clean, spick and span; *French* soigné; *informal* snazzy, natty, snappy, sharp, nifty, cool, with it; *N. Amer. informal* sassy, spiffy, fly, kicky; *dated* as if one had just stepped out of a bandbox; *Brit. informal, dated* swagger; *archaic* trig.
OPPOSITE scruffy.
2 *a smart restaurant* **fashionable**, stylish, high-class, exclusive, chic, fancy; *Brit.* upmarket; *N. Amer.* high-toned; *informal* trendy, posh, ritzy, plush, plushy, classy, swanky, glitzy; *Brit. informal* swish; *N. Amer. informal* swank, tony; *S. African informal* larney; *US black English* dicty; *derogatory* chichi.
OPPOSITES unfashionable, downmarket.
3 (*informal*) *Joey will know what to do—he's the smart one* **clever**, bright, intelligent, sharp, sharp-witted, quick-witted, nimble-witted, shrewd, astute, acute, apt, able; well educated, well read; perceptive, percipient, discerning; *informal* brainy, savvy, streetwise, on the ball, quick on the uptake.
OPPOSITE stupid.
4 *he set off at a smart pace* **brisk**, quick, fast, rapid, swift, lively, spanking, energetic, spirited, vigorous, jaunty; *informal* snappy, cracking, rattling.
OPPOSITE slow.
5 *he gave the animal a smart blow on the snout* **sharp**, severe, forceful, violent; painful.
OPPOSITE gentle.
□ **look smart** (*Brit.*) *come up here and look smart about it!* **be quick**, hurry up, speed up; *informal* make it snappy, get cracking, get moving, step on it, step on the gas, rattle one's dags; *Brit. informal* get one's skates on, stir one's stumps; *N. Amer. informal* get a wiggle on; *S. African informal* put foot.
▶ verb **1** *her eyes were smarting from the smoke* **sting**, burn, tingle, prickle; hurt, ache.
2 *she had smarted at Jenny's accusations* **feel annoyed**, feel upset, feel offended, take offence, feel aggrieved, feel indignant, feel put out, feel hurt, feel wounded, feel resentful.

smart alec ▶ noun *informal* **wise guy**, smarty-pants, smarty; *Brit. informal* **know-all**, clever clogs, clever Dick, smart-arse, smarty-boots; *N. Amer. informal* know-it-all, smart-ass; *archaic* wiseacre.

S

smarten ▶ verb **1** *the cottages had been smartened up* **spruce up**, make smarter, clean up, tidy up, make neater, make tidy, put in order; redecorate, refurbish, brighten up, modernize; *informal* do up; *Brit. informal* tart up, posh up; *N. Amer. informal* gussy up.
2 *Ellie smartened herself up* **groom oneself**, spruce oneself up, freshen oneself up, preen oneself, primp oneself, prink oneself, pretty oneself, beautify oneself; *informal* titivate oneself, doll oneself up; *Brit. informal* tart oneself up; *archaic* plume oneself, trig oneself.

smash ▶ verb **1** *one of the men smashed a window | drinks fell and glasses smashed* **break**, break to pieces, smash to smithereens, shatter; splinter, crack, disintegrate; *informal* bust; *rare* shiver.
2 *she's smashed the car* **crash**, wreck; *Brit.* write off; *Brit. informal* prang; *N. Amer. informal* total.
3 *the car smashed into a brick wall* **crash into**, collide with, be in collision with, hit, strike, ram, smack into, slam into, bang into, plough into, meet head-on, run into, drive into, bump into, crack into/against; dash against; *N. Amer.* impact.
4 *Donald smashed him over the head* **hit**, strike, thump, punch, cuff, smack, thwack; *informal* whack, belt, bash, biff, bop, clout, wallop, swipe, sock, lam, crown, whomp, deck, floor; *Brit. informal* stick one on, slosh, dot; *N. Amer. informal* boff, bust, slug, whale; *Austral./NZ informal* dong, quilt; *literary* smite, swinge.
5 *he smashed the club's hopes of FA Cup glory* **destroy**, wreck, ruin, shatter, dash, crush, devastate, demolish, blast, blight, wipe out, overturn, torpedo, scotch; burst someone's bubble; *informal* put the kibosh on, banjax, do for, blow a hole in, nix, put paid to, queer; *Brit. informal* scupper, dish; *archaic* bring to naught.
▶ noun **1** *he heard the smash of glass* **breaking**, shattering, crashing, crash.
2 *a motorway smash* **crash**, multiple crash, car crash, collision, multiple collision, accident, car accident, road accident, traffic accident, road traffic accident, bump; *Brit.* RTA; *N. Amer.* wreck; *informal* pile-up, smash-up; *Brit. informal* prang, shunt.
3 (*informal*) *a box-office smash* **great success**, sensation, sell-out, triumph; *French* succès fou; *informal* hit, smash hit, winner, crowd-puller, knockout, wow, biggie.

smashing ▶ adjective *tell Anna we had an absolutely smashing day* **wonderful**, **marvellous**, excellent, splendid, magnificent, superb, glorious, sublime, lovely, delightful; *informal* super, great, amazing, fantastic, terrific, tremendous, phenomenal, sensational, heavenly, gorgeous, dreamy, grand, fabulous, fab, fabby, fantabulous, awesome, magic, ace, cool, mean, bad, wicked, mega, crucial, mind-blowing, far out, A1, sound, out of this world, marvy, spanking; *Brit. informal* brilliant, brill; *N. Amer. informal* peachy, dandy, jim-dandy, neat, badass, boss, radical, rad, boffo, bully, bitching; *Austral./NZ informal* beaut, bonzer; *S. African informal* kif, lank; *black English* dope, def, phat; *informal, dated* groovy, divine; *Brit. informal, dated* capital, champion, wizard, corking, cracking, ripping, spiffing, top-hole, topping, beezer; *N. Amer. informal, dated* swell, keen; *archaic* goodly.

smattering ▶ noun *an audience with a smattering of classical education* **bit**, small amount, little, modicum, touch, soupçon; superficial knowledge, nodding acquaintance, passing acquaintance, rudiments, elements, basics; *informal* smidgen, smidge, tad.

smear ▶ verb **1** *the table was smeared with grease* **streak**, smudge, stain, mark, soil, dirty; blur; *informal* splotch, splodge; *literary* besmirch.
2 *smear the meat with olive oil* **cover**, coat, grease, lard; anoint; *literary* bedaub.
3 *she smeared sunblock on her skin* **spread**, rub, daub, slap, slather, smother, plaster, cream, slick; apply, put on, dab; *literary* besmear.
4 *it's a campaign by people who are trying to smear our reputation* **sully**, tarnish, besmirch, blacken, drag through the mud/mire, stain, taint, damage, defame, discredit, defile, vilify, malign, slander, libel, stigmatize, calumniate; *N. Amer.* slur; *informal* do a hatchet job on; *literary* smirch; *rare* asperse, vilipend.
▶ noun **1** *a smear of yellow paint | smears of blood* **streak**, smudge, daub, dab, spot, patch, blotch, blob; stain, mark; *informal* splotch, splodge.
2 *there were a number of press smears about some of his closest aides* **false accusation**, false report, false imputation, slander, libel, lie, untruth, slur, defamation, calumny, vilification; stain, taint.

smell ▶ noun **1** *there was a smell of burning in the air* **odour**, whiff.
2 *the smell of new-mown grass* **aroma**, fragrance, scent, perfume, redolence, tang, savour; bouquet, nose.
3 *27 cats lived there—you can imagine the smell* **stench**, stink, reek, fetidness, effluvium, miasma; *Brit. informal* pong, niff, whiff, hum; *Scottish informal* guff; *N. Amer. informal* funk; *rare* fetor, malodour, mephitis.
▶ verb **1** *Peter smelled her perfume* **get a whiff of**, scent, get a sniff of, detect the smell of.
2 *the dogs smelled each other* **sniff**, nose.
3 *the room was dirty and it smelled* **stink**, stink to high heaven, reek, have

a bad smell, be stinking, be malodorous; *Brit. informal* pong, hum.
4 *it smells like a hoax to me* **give the impression of**, smack of, savour of, have the hallmarks of, have all the signs of, seem/appear like, have the air of, suggest.

WORD LINKS
relating to smell **osmic**
measurement of intensity of a smell **odorimetry**
relating to the sense of smell **olfactory**

smelly ▶ **adjective** *the tunnel was damp and smelly | smelly fish* **foul-smelling**, evil-smelling, stinking, stinking to high heaven, reeking, fetid, malodorous, pungent, acrid, rank, putrid, noxious; off, gamy, high; musty, fusty; *Brit.* frowsty; *W. Indian* fresh; *informal* stinky, reeky; *Brit. informal* niffing, niffy, pongy, whiffy, humming; *N. Amer. informal* funky; *literary* noisome, mephitic; *rare* olid, miasmic, miasmal.

smile ▶ **verb** *Joseph looked up at her and smiled* **grin**, beam, grin like a Cheshire cat, grin from ear to ear, twinkle; *informal* be all smiles.
▶ **noun** *she gave him a warm smile* **grin**, beam; smirk, simper; leer.
OPPOSITES frown, scowl.

smirk ▶ **verb** *she turned and smirked at Edward* **smile smugly**, simper, snigger; leer; *Scottish archaic* smicker, smirtle.

smitten ▶ **adjective 1** *he was smitten with cholera* **struck down with**, laid low with, prostrated with, suffering from, affected by, afflicted by, plagued with; *archaic* stricken with.
2 *you know Jane's smitten with you?* **infatuated with**, besotted with, in love with, head over heels in love with, hopelessly in love with, obsessed with, enamoured of, very attracted to, very taken with, devoted to, charmed by, captivated by, enchanted by, enthralled by, bewitched by, beguiled by, under someone's spell; *informal* bowled over by, swept off one's feet by, struck on, crazy about, mad about, wild about, potty about, very keen on, gone on, sweet on, into; *literary* ensorcelled by.
OPPOSITE indifferent.

smog ▶ **noun** **exhaust fumes**, fumes, smoke, pollution, gas; fog, haze, vapour; *Brit. informal* pea-souper.

smoke ▶ **verb 1** *the peat fire was smoking* **smoulder**, emit smoke, emit fumes; *archaic* reek.
2 *Henry lay back in the chair and smoked his cigarette* **puff on**, draw on, pull on; inhale; light up; *informal* take a drag of, drag on.
3 *they smoke their own salmon* **cure**, preserve, dry.
▶ **noun** *the smoke from the bonfire* **fumes**, exhaust, gas, vapour; smog.

smoky ▶ **adjective 1** *the smoky atmosphere* **smoke-filled**, smoggy, hazy, foggy, murky, thick; smelly; *informal* reeky; *Brit. informal* fuggy.
OPPOSITES fresh, airy.
2 *the walls were smoky* **smoke-stained**, sooty, discoloured, grimy, dirty, begrimed.
OPPOSITE clean.
3 *her wide smoky eyes* **grey**, dark grey, slate grey, sooty, black, dark.

smooth ▶ **adjective 1** *they lay down to sunbathe on the smooth flat rocks* **even**, level, flat, horizontal, as flat as a pancake, plane, flush, unwrinkled, featureless; *rare* unrough.
OPPOSITES uneven, rough.
2 *his face was smooth and youthful* **clean-shaven**, smooth-shaven, hairless.
OPPOSITES rough, hirsute.
3 *a marble floor worn smooth over the centuries* **glossy**, shiny, shining, gleaming, glassy, sheeny, lustrous, bright, sleek, silky, satiny, polished, burnished; *rare* nitid.
OPPOSITE matt.
4 *a lovely smooth sauce* **creamy**, whipped, velvety, of an even consistency.
OPPOSITE lumpy.
5 *a smooth sea* **calm**, still, tranquil, placid, serene, undisturbed, unruffled, even, flat, glassy, mirror-like, waveless, dead calm, like a millpond.
OPPOSITES rough, choppy.
6 *electronic and other high-tech components ensure the smooth running of the equipment* **steady**, regular, rhythmic, uninterrupted, unbroken, flowing, frictionless, fluid, fluent.
OPPOSITES irregular, jerky.
7 *the smooth working of the world economy* **straightforward**, easy, effortless, trouble-free, untroubled, well ordered, simple; plain sailing.
OPPOSITE fraught.
8 *a smooth wine* **mellow**, mild, agreeable, pleasant, bland, soft, soothing.
OPPOSITES harsh, bitter.
9 *Mozart loved the smooth, resonant tone of the clarinet* **dulcet**, soft, soothing, mellow, sweet, sweet-sounding, sweet-toned, pretty, silvery, honeyed, mellifluous, melodious, musical, lilting, lyrical, harmonious, euphonious; *rare* mellifluent.
OPPOSITE raucous.
10 *Hogan was a smooth, confident Foreign Office man* **suave**, urbane, sophisticated, polished, debonair, courteous, gracious, smooth-tongued, glib, persuasive, slick, oily, ingratiating, unctuous; *informal* smarmy.
OPPOSITE gauche.
▶ **verb 1** *pour the mixture into the lined tin and smooth the surface | she stood up and smoothed out her dress* **flatten**, make flat, level, make level, level out, level off, make even, even off, even out, press (down), roll, steamroll, iron, plane, make uniform, make regular, regularize.
2 *the diplomats have apologized and made every effort to smooth over the situation* **settle**, resolve, patch up, sort out, iron out, put to rights, mend, remedy, heal, cure, rectify.
3 *a plan for smoothing the conversion of the power stations from coal to gas* **ease**, make easy, make easier, facilitate, clear the way for, pave the way for, smooth the way for, open the door for, expedite, assist, aid, help, help along, oil, oil the wheels of, lubricate.

CHOOSE THE RIGHT WORD
smooth, urbane, slick, glib
See GLIB.

smoothly ▶ **adverb 1** *her hair was combed smoothly back from her forehead* **evenly**, level, flat, flush, as flat as a pancake, horizontally.
OPPOSITE roughly.
2 *the door closed smoothly behind them* **steadily**, frictionlessly, fluidly, fluently, without bumping, without jerking; quietly; regularly, rhythmically.
OPPOSITE jerkily.
3 *he was happy that the day had gone smoothly* **without a hitch**, like clockwork, with no trouble, without difficulty, easily, effortlessly, as planned, (according) to plan, swimmingly, satisfactorily, very well; *informal* like a dream, like magic.
OPPOSITE disastrously.
4 *'All taken care of,' he said smoothly* **suavely**, urbanely, calmly, evenly, placidly; glibly, persuasively, slickly, ingratiatingly, unctuously; *informal* smarmily; *rare* oilily.
OPPOSITE abrasively.

smoothness ▶ **noun 1** *the smoothness of the road surfaces* **evenness**, levelness, flatness, plainness.
OPPOSITES unevenness, roughness.
2 *his dress shirt gleamed white against the tanned smoothness of his freshly shaved skin* **clean-shavenness**, smooth-shavenness, hairlessness.
OPPOSITES roughness, hirsuteness.
3 *the strength of glass is usually down to its surface smoothness* **glossiness**, gloss, shine, shininess, gleam, glassiness, sheen, lustre, brightness, sleekness, silkiness, polish, burnish.
OPPOSITE dullness.
4 *this fat substitute has the smoothness associated with fat* **creaminess**, even consistency.
OPPOSITE lumpiness.
5 *the smoothness of the sea* **calmness**, stillness, tranquillity, placidness, serenity, evenness, flatness, glassiness.
OPPOSITES roughness, choppiness.
6 *the engine has a V12-style smoothness* **steadiness**, smooth running, regularity, rhythm, rhythmicity, freedom from interruption, flow, frictionlessness, fluidity, fluency.
OPPOSITES irregularity, jerkiness.
7 *this system was cumbersome but worked with reasonable smoothness* **straightforwardness**, ease, easiness, effortlessness, simplicity.
OPPOSITE trouble.
8 *the strength of champagne is belied by its smoothness of flavour* **mellowness**, mildness, pleasantness, blandness, softness.
9 *the smoothness of the sounds* **softness**, mellowness, sweetness, sweet sound, sweet tone, prettiness, silveriness, mellifluousness, melodiousness, musicality, lilt, lyricism, harmony, euphony.
OPPOSITE raucousness.
10 *she was irritated by his smoothness* **suaveness**, urbaneness, urbanity, sophistication, polish, finish, courteousness, grace, smooth talking, glibness, persuasiveness, slickness, oiliness, ingratiation, unctuousness; *informal* smarminess.
OPPOSITE gaucheness.

smooth-talking ▶ **adjective** *a smooth-talking gang conned an elderly woman into giving her bank cash card away* **persuasive**, plausible, credible, silver-tongued, smooth-tongued, smooth-spoken, slick, glib, eloquent, fast-talking, suave, ingratiating, silky, unctuous, obsequious, fawning, sycophantic, flattering; *informal* smarmy.
OPPOSITES no-nonsense, blunt.

smother ▶ **verb 1** *a teenage mum tried to smother her baby in hospital* **suffocate**, stifle, asphyxiate, choke, throttle, strangle, strangulate.
2 *police officers tried to smother the flames with their jackets* **extinguish**, put out, snuff out, dampen, damp down, stamp out, douse, choke.
3 *we smothered the children with suncream* **smear**, daub, bedaub, spread, cover; *literary* besmear.
4 *it's time for you to leave the house—she'll smother you if you remain* **overwhelm**, inundate, envelop, trap, surround, cocoon.
5 *she smothered a sigh* **stifle**, muffle, strangle, gag, restrain, repress, suppress, hold back, keep back, fight back, choke back, bite back, swallow, contain, bottle up, conceal, hide; bite one's lip; *informal* button

up, keep the lid on, cork up.

smoulder ▶ verb **1** *the bonfire still smouldered* **burn slowly**, smoke, glow; *archaic* reek.

2 *she was smouldering with resentment* **seethe**, boil, fume, burn, simmer, be boiling over, be beside oneself; *informal* be livid, be wild, jump up and down, froth/foam at the mouth.

3 *discontent had been smouldering for years* **exist unseen**, burn, seethe, simmer, fester, lie dormant.

smudge ▶ noun *there was a thick smudge of blood on his car* **streak**, smear, mark, dirty mark, spot, fleck, speck, stain, blotch, stripe, dot, blot, blob, dab, blur, smut, fingermark; *informal* splotch, splodge; *literary* smirch.

▶ verb **1** *her face and arms were smudged with dust* **streak**, mark, dirty, spot, soil, muddy, fleck, speck, blotch, blacken, smear, stripe, dot, blot, blob, daub, bedaub, stain; *informal* splotch, splodge; *literary* besmirch.

2 *she dabbed her eyes, careful not to smudge her make-up* **smear**, streak, blur, mess up.

smug ▶ adjective *he was feeling smug after his win* **self-satisfied**, complacent, self-congratulatory, superior, puffed up, pleased with oneself, self-approving, well pleased, proud of oneself; *informal* goody-goody; *Brit. informal* like the cat that's got the cream, I'm-all-right-Jack; *N. Amer. informal* wisenheimer; *N. Amer. vulgar slang* shit-eating.

smuggle ▶ verb *they smuggled drugs into Britain* **bring/take illegally**, run, sneak.

smuggler ▶ noun *a convicted cocaine smuggler* **contrabandist**, runner, courier, bootlegger; *informal* mule; *N. Amer. informal* moonshiner.

smutty ▶ adjective *his humour is of the smutty adolescent variety* **vulgar**, dirty, rude, filthy, crude, offensive, salacious, coarse, obscene, indecent, lewd, pornographic, X-rated, risqué, racy, broad, earthy, bawdy, Rabelaisian, spicy, suggestive, titillating, improper, naughty, indelicate, indecorous, ribald, off colour, locker-room; *informal* blue, raunchy; *Brit. informal* fruity, near the knuckle, saucy; *N. Amer. informal* gamy; *euphemistic* adult.

OPPOSITE pure.

snack ▶ noun *this makes a snack for two or a substantial meal for one* **light meal**, something to eat, sandwich, supper, treat, refreshments, nibbles, canapés, titbit(s); *informal* bite, bite to eat, a little something; *Brit. informal* elevenses.

▶ verb *don't* ***snack on*** *sugary foods and drinks during the day* **eat between meals**, nibble, munch; *informal* graze.

snaffle ▶ verb (*informal*) *Ginny took a fancy to my gardening shorts and snaffled them* **steal**, thieve, rob, take, purloin, help oneself to, abscond with, run off with, carry off; pilfer, embezzle, misappropriate; *informal* walk off/away with, run away/off with, swipe, nab, rip off, lift, 'liberate', 'borrow', filch, snitch; *Brit. informal* nick, pinch, half-inch, whip, knock off, nobble, bone, scrump, blag; *N. Amer. informal* heist, glom; *Austral. informal* snavel; *W. Indian informal* tief; *archaic* crib, hook.

snag ▶ noun **1** *the snag is that a stronger economy might mean higher inflation* **obstacle**, difficulty, complication, catch, hitch, stumbling block, pitfall, unseen problem, problem, barrier, impediment, hindrance, inconvenience, setback, hurdle, disadvantage, downside, drawback, minus; *informal* hiccup.

2 *the wooden rails become smooth over time, with no snags or rough corners* **sharp projection**, jag, jagged bit; thorn, spur; *informal* sticky-out bit.

3 *she got a snag in her tights* **tear**, rip, rent, ladder, run, hole, gash, slash, slit.

▶ verb **1** *she wouldn't want cats' claws snagging her tights* **tear**, rip, ladder, gash.

2 *the zip runs freely and doesn't* ***snag on*** *the fabric* **catch (in)**, hook, jag; get caught in/on.

S

snake *See centre pages for list of* **Snakes**

▶ noun **1** *literary* serpent; *Zoology* ophidian; *Austral. rhyming slang* Joe Blake.

2 *that man is a cold-blooded snake* **traitor**, turncoat, betrayer, informer, back-stabber, double-crosser, double-dealer, quisling, Judas; **cheat**, swindler, fraudster, trickster, charlatan, viper, serpent, snake in the grass; *informal* two-timer, creep, rat, beast, pig, swine, skunk, dog, weasel, bastard; *Brit. informal* twister; *Brit. informal, dated* bounder, rotter; *N. Amer. informal* rat fink; *Irish informal* sleeveen; *Austral. informal* dingo; *vulgar slang* shit; *dated* heel, cad, blackguard.

▶ verb *the road snakes inland* **twist**, wind, twist and turn, meander, zigzag; curl, coil, wreathe, spiral, twine, loop, curve, corkscrew.

WORD LINKS

relating to snakes	**colubrine, ophidian, serpentine, anguine**
study of snakes	**ophiology**
fear of snakes	**ophidiophobia**

snap ▶ verb **1** *the safety rope snapped and Davis was sucked under the water* **break**, break in/into two, fracture, splinter, separate, come apart, part, split, crack; *informal* bust.

OPPOSITE hold.

2 *she claims she snapped after years of violence* **lose one's self-control**, crack, freak, freak out, get overwrought, go to pieces, get hysterical, get worked up, flare up; *informal* crack up, lose one's cool, blow one's top, fly off the handle; *Brit. informal* throw a wobbly.

3 *a white Range Rover passed, the Union flag snapping from a small mast on the bonnet* **crack**, flick, click, crackle; **flutter**, wave, flap, quiver, vibrate.

4 *a dog was* ***snapping at*** *his heels* **bite**, gnash its teeth; try to bite, try to nip.

5 *'I'm not that old!' Anna snapped | there's no need to* ***snap at*** *me—I'm only trying to help* **say/speak roughly**, say/speak brusquely, say/speak nastily, say/speak abruptly, say/speak angrily, bark, snarl, growl, fling, hurl; lash out at; retort, rejoin, riposte, retaliate, snap back; round on someone; *informal* jump down someone's throat, fly off the handle at.

6 *they could see photographers snapping the royal shooting party* **photograph**, take/get a photograph/photo of, take someone's picture/photo, take/get a picture of, picture, take/get a snapshot/snap of, take, shoot, take/get a shot of, take a likeness of, record, film, capture/record on film/celluloid.

□ **snap out of it** (*informal*) *you've had a bad time, and now you're snapping out of it* **recover**, recover/regain control of oneself, recover/regain control of one's emotions, recover/regain one's composure, recover/regain one's calm, recover/regain one's self-control, get/take a grip/hold on oneself, pull oneself together, get over it, become one's old self, get better, cheer up, become cheerful, perk up; *informal* get one's act together, buck up.

OPPOSITE mope.

□ **snap something up** *people are snapping up bargains all over the place* **buy eagerly/quickly**, jump at, accept eagerly, snatch at, take advantage of, grab (at), snatch, seize (on), grasp, grasp with both hands, pounce on, swoop down on.

OPPOSITE pass up.

▶ noun **1** *she closed her purse with a snap* **click**, crack, pop, clink, tick, report, smack, whack, crackle.

2 *there was a sudden cold snap immediately after Christmas* **period**, spell, time, interval, season, stretch, run; *Brit. informal* patch, spot.

3 *the snap of the dialogue* **dynamism**, life, go, energy, spirit, vigour, vigorousness, liveliness, sparkle, vivacity, vitality, sprightliness, force, forcefulness, drive, strength, animation, verve, panache, elan, enthusiasm, exuberance, gusto, brio, zest, bite; *informal* oomph, pizzazz, zing, zip, feistiness.

OPPOSITES inertia, lethargy.

4 *Mark showed me his holiday snaps of Barbados* **photograph**, picture, photo, shot, snapshot, likeness, image, portrait, study, print, slide, transparency, negative, positive, plate, film, bromide, frame, exposure, still, proof, enprint, enlargement.

snappy ▶ adjective (*informal*) **1** *he's in a snappy mood* **irritable**, irascible, short-tempered, hot-tempered, quick-tempered, fiery, peevish, cross, crabbed, crabby, crotchety, cantankerous, impatient, grumpy, huffy, brusque, ill-tempered, bad-tempered, ill-natured, ill-humoured, touchy, volatile, testy, tetchy, snarling, waspish, prickly, crusty, peppery, bilious, liverish, dyspeptic, splenetic, choleric; *informal* snappish, chippy, grouchy, cranky, on a short fuse; *Brit. informal* narky, ratty, eggy, like a bear with a sore head; *N. Amer. informal* peckish, soreheaded; *Austral./NZ informal* snaky; *informal, dated* miffy.

OPPOSITES good-natured, peaceable.

2 *a snappy catchphrase* **concise**, succinct, memorable, catchy, neat, clever, crisp, pithy, witty, incisive, brief, short, short and sweet, sharp, terse, curt, laconic, aphoristic, epigrammatic.

OPPOSITE long-winded.

3 *a snappy dresser* **smart**, well dressed, well turned out, besuited, fashionably dressed, fashionable, stylish, chic, modish, elegant, neat, spruce, trim, dapper, debonair; *French* soigné; *informal* snazzy, natty, sharp, nifty, cool, with it; *N. Amer. informal* sassy, spiffy, fly, kicky; *dated* as if one had just stepped out of a bandbox; *Brit. informal, dated* swagger; *archaic* trig.

OPPOSITE slovenly.

□ **make it snappy** *into bed with you, and make it snappy!* **hurry**, hurry (it) up, be quick (about it), get a move on, come along, look lively, speed up, move faster; *informal* get moving, get cracking, step on it, step on the gas, move it, buck up, shake a leg; *Brit. informal* get your skates on; *Brit. informal, dated* stir your stumps; *N. Amer. informal* get a wiggle on; *Austral./NZ informal* rattle your dags; *S. African informal* put foot; *dated* make haste.

OPPOSITE dilly-dally.

snare ▶ noun **1** *he came upon a hare struggling in an illegal snare* **trap**, gin, net, noose; *rare* springe.

2 *prudent people can avoid the snares of the Football Act by not walking on the pitch* **pitfall**, trick, trap, tangle, web, mesh, catch, danger, hazard, peril; *literary* toils.

▶ verb **1** *cats were snared by people who look after game birds* **trap**, catch, net, bag, ensnare, entrap; *rare* springe.

2 *Havvie had already managed to snare one Yankee heiress* **entrap**, ensnare, trap, catch, get hold of, seize, capture, bag, hook, land.

snarl[1] ▶ verb **1** *a pack of snarling wolves* growl, show its teeth.

2 *'Shut your mouth!' he snarled | I used to* ***snarl at*** *anyone I disliked* **say/speak roughly**, say/speak brusquely, say/speak nastily, say/speak angrily, bark, snap, growl, fling, hurl; lash out at; round on someone; *informal* jump down someone's throat, fly off the handle at.

snarl[2] ▶ verb

□ **snarl something up 1** *the trailing lead got snarled up in a bramble bush* **tangle**, entangle, entwine, enmesh, ravel, knot, twist, intertwine,

jumble, muddle, foul.
OPPOSITE untangle.
2 *a heavy backlog of cases has snarled up the court process* **complicate**, confuse, muddle, jumble, throw into disorder, embroil, make difficult; *informal* mess up.
OPPOSITES sort out, facilitate.

snarl-up ▶ **noun** (*informal*) **1** *Edinburgh's daily traffic snarl-ups* **traffic jam**, jam, tailback, line, stream, gridlock.
2 *the main cause of the brouhaha is a snarl-up in terminology* **muddle**, mess, tangle, jumble, entanglement, imbroglio; misunderstanding, misinterpretation, misconstruction, misapprehension, misconception, the wrong idea, false impression, confusion; mistake, error, mix-up, bungle; *W. Indian* comess; *informal* hash, mess-up, foul-up, screw-up; *N. Amer. informal* snafu; *vulgar slang* fuck-up; *Brit. vulgar slang* balls-up.

snatch ▶ **verb 1** *she snatched the last sandwich from the plate* **grab**, seize, seize hold of, grab hold of, take hold of, lay hold of, lay (one's) hands on, get one's hands on, take, pluck; take a grip of, grip, grasp, clutch.
2 (*informal*) *someone snatched my handbag on a bus* **steal**, thieve, rob, take, pilfer, purloin, loot, rifle, abscond with, carry off; embezzle, misappropriate; *informal* walk off/away with, run away/off with, swipe, nab, rip off, lift, 'liberate', 'borrow', filch, snaffle, snitch; *Brit. informal* pinch, half-inch, nick, whip, knock off, nobble, bone; *N. Amer. informal* heist, glom; *Austral. informal* snavel; *W. Indian informal* tief; *archaic* crib, hook.
3 (*informal*) *she posed as a childminder and snatched Julie from her home. See* ABDUCT.
4 *Fogdoe skied a brilliant second run to snatch victory in the men's slalom* **achieve**, secure, obtain, seize, pluck, wrest, scrape.
5 *I snatched at the chance* **accept eagerly**, jump at, take advantage of, grab (at), snap up, seize (on), grasp, grasp with both hands, pounce on, swoop down on; buy eagerly/quickly.
▶ **noun 1** *brief snatches of sleep* **period**, spell, time, fit, bout, interval, duration, season, term, stretch, span, phase, run; *Brit. informal* patch, spot.
2 *he heard a snatch of their conversation* **fragment**, snippet, smattering, bit, scrap, piece, part, extract, excerpt, portion, section, selection.
3 (*informal*) *her snatch of £3 million in used notes has been described as 'the perfect crime'. See* THEFT.

snazzy ▶ **adjective** *they look good in those snazzy little silk dresses* **stylish**, smart, attractive, lovely, glamorous, gorgeous, stunning; fashionable, dapper, debonair, dashing, jaunty, rakish, spruce; chic, modish, elegant, trim; *informal* trendy, cool, sharp, snappy, with it, swinging, nifty, natty, groovy; *N. Amer. informal* sassy, spiffy, fly, kicky; *dated* as if one had just stepped out of a bandbox, gay; *Brit. informal, dated* swagger; *archaic* trig.
OPPOSITE dowdy.

sneak ▶ **verb 1** *I sneaked out by the back exit* **creep**, slink, steal, slip, slide, sidle, edge, move furtively, tiptoe, pussyfoot, pad, prowl.
2 *someone sneaked a camera inside* **bring/take surreptitiously**, bring/take secretly, bring/take illicitly, smuggle, spirit, slip.
3 *she sneaked a glance at her watch | he sneaked a doughnut while no one was looking* **snatch**, take a furtive/stealthy/surreptitious ..., get furtively/stealthily/surreptitiously, steal.
4 (*Brit. informal*) *it felt wrong, like sneaking to an adult | a little squirt called Ollie Bogwhistle sneaked on me* **inform (on/against)**, act as an informer, tell tales (on), report, give someone away, be disloyal (to), sell someone out, stab someone in the back; *informal* squeal (on), rat (on), blow the whistle (on), peach (on), snitch (on), put the finger on, sell someone down the river, stitch someone up; *Brit. informal* grass (on), split (on), shop; *Scottish informal* clype (on); *N. Amer. informal* rat someone out, finger, fink on, drop a/the dime on; *Austral. informal* pimp on, pool, put someone's pot on.
▶ **noun** (*Brit. informal*) *Ethel was the form sneak and goody-goody* **informer**, betrayer, stool pigeon; *informal* snitch, finger, squealer, rat, whistle-blower, nose; *Brit. informal* grass, supergrass, nark, snout; *Scottish informal* clype; *Scottish & N. Irish informal* tout; *N. Amer. informal* fink, stoolie; *Austral. informal* fizgig, pimp, shelf; *archaic* intelligencer, beagle.
▶ **adjective** *a sneak thief | a sneak preview* **furtive**, secret, stealthy, sly, surreptitious, clandestine, covert; private, quick, surprise.

sneaking ▶ **adjective 1** *she had a sneaking admiration for him* **secret**, private, hidden, concealed, innermost, inward, unexpressed, unvoiced, undisclosed, undeclared, undivulged, unconfessed, unavowed.
2 *I have a sneaking feeling I may have broken a bone in my right hand* **niggling**, nagging, lurking, insidious, lingering, gnawing, unrelenting, persistent, worrying.

sneaky ▶ **adjective** *it was a sneaky trick and I fell for it* **sly**, crafty, cunning, wily, clever, artful, scheming, devious, guileful, tricky, conniving, designing, deceitful, duplicitous, dishonest, disingenuous, underhand, untrustworthy, unscrupulous, double-dealing; **furtive**, secretive, secret, stealthy, surreptitious, sneaking, skulking, slinking, clandestine, hidden, covert, cloaked, conspiratorial, under the table; *informal* dirty, foxy, shifty; *Brit. informal* fly; *Austral./NZ informal* shonky; *S. African informal* slim; *archaic* subtle; *rare* carny.
OPPOSITES honest, open.

sneer ▶ **noun 1** *I spent a lot of time watching daytime television with a sneer on my face* **curl of the/one's lip**, disparaging smile, contemptuous smile, smug smile, conceited smile, cruel smile, mirthless smile, smirk, snicker, snigger.
2 *I was oblivious to the sneers of others* **jibe**, barb, jeer, taunt, insult, cutting remark, slight, affront, slur, insinuation; (**sneers**) **scorn**, scoffing, contempt, disdain, mockery, ridicule, derision; *informal* dig.
▶ **verb 1** *he looked me right in the face and sneered* **curl one's lip**, smile disparagingly, smile contemptuously, smile smugly, smile conceitedly, smile cruelly, smile mirthlessly, smirk, snicker, snigger.
2 *it is easy to sneer at the credulous pilgrims* **scoff at**, scorn, be contemptuous of, treat with contempt, hold in contempt, disdain, mock, jeer at, gibe at, ridicule, deride, taunt, insult, make cutting remarks about, slight, affront; *N. Amer.* slur; *N. Amer. informal* jive.

sneeze ▶ **verb**
□ **not to be sneezed at** (*informal*) *the average saving of £550 was not be sneezed at* **worth having**, considerable, substantial, sizeable, fairly large, largish, biggish, significant; fairly good, passable, reasonable, moderately good, not bad, worth taking into account; *informal* OK.

snicker ▶ **verb** *she is a woman they all love to snicker at* **snigger**, sneer, smirk, simper; titter, giggle, chortle.
▶ **noun** *he could not evoke a snicker with his jokes* **snigger**, sneer, smirk, simper; titter, giggle, chortle.

snide ▶ **adjective** *I'm fed up with your snide remarks* **disparaging**, derogatory, deprecating, deprecatory, denigratory, insulting, vituperative, disapproving, contemptuous; mocking, taunting, ridiculing, sneering, jeering, scoffing; scornful, derisive, sarcastic, caustic, biting, bitchy, shrewish, spiteful, hurtful, nasty, mean; *Brit. informal* sarky; *rare* mordacious.
OPPOSITES complimentary, sympathetic.

sniff ▶ **verb 1** *Maria sniffed and wiped her nose | he sniffed the morning air* **inhale**, snuffle, breathe in, snuff (up).
2 *carefully she sniffed the fruit* **smell**, test the smell of, nose at; detect the smell of, pick up the smell of, catch the scent of, scent, get a whiff of.
□ **sniff at** *the working mothers were all sniffed at by the uniformed nannies* **scorn**, disdain, hold in disdain, show contempt for, be contemptuous of, treat/regard with contempt, hold in contempt, treat as inferior, be snobbish to, despise, look down on, pour/heap scorn on, sneer at, scoff at; *informal* turn one's nose up at, look down one's nose at.
□ **sniff something out** (*informal*) *journalists who sniff out sensation or scandal* **detect**, find, search out, discover, disclose, bring to light, track down, dig up, hunt out, ferret out, root out, uncover, unearth, disinter, smell out, nose out, follow the scent of, scent out, run to earth/ground.
▶ **noun 1** *she gave a loud sniff* **snuffle**.
2 *the sniff of lunch was everywhere | I haven't had a sniff of fresh air* **smell**, scent, whiff; lungful.
3 (*informal*) *they're off at the first sniff of trouble* **indication**, hint, intimation, whiff, inkling, suggestion, suspicion, whisper, trace, signal, sign, clue, gleam, wind.

sniffy ▶ **adjective** (*informal*) *some people are sniffy about tea bags* **contemptuous**, scornful, full of contempt, derisive, derisory, withering, mocking, scoffing, sneering, jeering, scathing, snide, disparaging, slighting, supercilious, disdainful, superior, dismissive; *informal* snotty; *archaic* contumelious.
OPPOSITES friendly, complimentary.

snigger ▶ **verb** *the boys at school were sure to snigger at him behind his back* **give a suppressed laugh**, snicker, sneer, smirk, simper; titter, giggle, chortle.
▶ **noun** *it was a good joke, but it got hardly a snigger* **suppressed laugh**, snicker, sneer, smirk, simper; titter, giggle, chortle.

snip ▶ **verb 1** *an usher neatly snips your ticket in two* **cut**, clip, cut into, slit, nick, gash, notch, incise, snick.
2 *always have your secateurs in hand to snip faded flowers* **cut off**, snip off, trim (off), clip, prune, hack off, chop off, saw off, lop (off), dock, crop, sever, separate, detach, remove, take off.
▶ **noun 1** *make snips along the length up to this line* **cut**, clip, trim; slit, nick, gash, notch, incision, snick.
2 *the collage consists of snips of wallpaper* **scrap**, cutting, shred, strip, ribbon, rag, snippet, remnant, fragment, sliver, splinter, chip, bit, tiny bit, piece, tiny piece, speck, crumb, spot, fleck, wisp.
3 (*Brit. informal*) *at £1 million, the goalkeeper has turned out to be* ***a snip*** **bargain**, good buy, cheap buy; (good) value for money, surprisingly cheap; *informal* giveaway, steal.
OPPOSITE rip-off.
4 (*informal*) *the job was* ***a snip*** **easy task**, **easy job**, child's play, five-finger exercise, gift, walkover, nothing, sinecure, gravy train; *informal* doddle, piece of cake, picnic, money for old rope, money for jam, cinch, breeze, sitter, kids' stuff, cushy job/number, doss, cakewalk, pushover; *N. Amer. informal* duck soup, snap; *Austral./NZ informal* bludge, snack; *S. African informal* a piece of old tackie; *Brit. vulgar slang* a piece of piss.

snippet ▶ **noun** *snippets of information* **piece**, bit, scrap, fragment, morsel, particle, shred, snatch, excerpt, extract.

snivel ▶ **verb 1** *they found him slumped in a chair, snivelling* **sniffle**, snuffle, run at the nose, have a runny/running nose; **whimper**, whine, weep, cry,

shed tears, sob, howl, mewl, bawl; *Scottish* greet; *informal* blub, blubber, boohoo; *Brit. informal* grizzle.
2 *if you get caught, you shouldn't snivel about what you get* **complain**, moan, mutter, grumble, grouse, groan, grouch, growl, carp, bleat, whine, object, make a fuss; *Scottish & Irish* gurn; *informal* gripe, beef, bellyache, bitch, whinge, sound off, go on; *Brit. informal* chunter, create, be on at someone; *N. English informal* mither; *N. Amer. informal* kvetch; *S. African informal* chirp; *Brit. dated* crib, natter.

snobbery ▶ **noun** *there was a complete lack of snobbery about staff mingling with guests* **affectation**, **pretentiousness**, condescension, affectedness, pretension, elitism, snobbishness, arrogance, pride, haughtiness, airs, airs and graces, disdain, disdainfulness, superciliousness, exclusiveness; *informal* snootiness, uppitiness; *Brit. informal* side.

snobbish ▶ **adjective** *the snobbish distinction between art and craft* **elitist**, snobby, superior, supercilious, exclusive; arrogant, proud, haughty, disdainful; patronizing, condescending; pretentious, affected; *informal* snooty, uppity, high and mighty, la-di-da, stuck-up, hoity-toity, snotty; *Brit. informal* toffee-nosed; *N. Amer. informal* high-hat, toplofty.

snoop (*informal*) ▶ **verb 1** *you shouldn't snoop into our affairs* **pry**, inquire impertinently, be inquisitive (about), inquire, do some detective work; be curious, poke about/around, mind someone else's business, be a busybody, nose into, stick/poke one's nose in/into; interfere (in/with), meddle (in/with), intrude (on); *informal* be nosy (about), nosy; *Austral./NZ informal* stickybeak.
2 *they decided to snoop around the building* **investigate**, explore, ferret (about/around) in, rummage in, search, delve into, peer into, prowl around, nose around/about/round, have a good look at.
▶ **noun 1** *White went off for a snoop around, as policemen do* **search**, nose, look, prowl, ferret, poke, exploration, investigation.
2 *the broadcast was intercepted by radio snoops.* See SNOOPER.

snooper ▶ **noun** *a snooper employed by her ex-husband's lawyer* **eavesdropper**, pryer, interferer, meddler, busybody; investigative journalist; **investigator**, detective, private detective, private investigator, operative; *Brit.* enquiry agent; *informal* snoop, nosy parker, Paul Pry, private eye, PI, sleuth; *N. Amer. informal* private dick, peeper, shamus, gumshoe; *Austral./NZ informal* stickybeak; *informal, dated* hawkshaw, sherlock; *N. Amer. dated* Pinkerton.

snooty ▶ **adjective** *they thought that I was too snooty to be friends with them* **arrogant**, proud, haughty, conceited, lofty, aloof, disdainful, superior, self-important, supercilious, exclusive; **snobbish**, patronizing, condescending, affected, pretentious, elitist, snobby; *informal* uppity, high and mighty, la-di-da, stuck-up, hoity-toity, snotty; *Brit. informal* toffee-nosed; *N. Amer. informal* high-hat, toplofty.
OPPOSITES friendly, modest.

snooze (*informal*) ▶ **noun** *a sandy bank looked a good place for a snooze* **sleep**, nap, doze, rest, siesta, drowse, catnap; beauty sleep; *informal* forty winks, a bit of shut-eye; *Brit. informal* kip, zizz; *literary* slumber.
▶ **verb** *her eyes finally stayed closed as she gently snoozed* **sleep**, be asleep, doze, rest, take a siesta, nap, take a nap, catnap, drowse; sleep like a log/top; *informal* snatch forty winks, get some shut-eye, be in the land of Nod; *Brit. informal* kip, have a kip, get one's head down, zizz, get some zizz, doss (down); *N. Amer. informal* catch some Zs; *literary* be in the arms of Morpheus, slumber.
OPPOSITE be awake.

snout ▶ **noun** *the spiny anteater has a long pointed snout* **muzzle**, face; nose, proboscis, trunk; mouth, jaws, maw; beak; *Scottish & N. English* neb.

snow *See centre pages for list of* **Snow Types and Conditions**
▶ **noun** **snowflakes**, flakes, snowdrift, snowfield, snowpack; snowfall, snowstorm, blizzard; sleet, hail, soft hail; avalanche; *N. Amer.* snowslide.
WORD LINKS
relating to snow **niveous, nival**
fear of snow **chionophobia**

snub ▶ **verb** *they were accused of snubbing their hosts by missing two official functions* **insult**, slight, affront, humiliate, treat disrespectfully; rebuff, spurn, repulse, cold-shoulder, brush off, disdain, scorn, give someone a slap in the face, give someone the cold shoulder, turn one's back on, keep someone at arm's length; cut (dead), ignore, take no notice of; *N. Amer.* stiff; *informal* give someone the brush-off, freeze out, stiff-arm, knock back, put down; *informal, dated* give someone the go-by; *rare* misprize, scout.
▶ **noun** *she was angry and humiliated at her very public snub* **rebuff**, **insult**, repulse, slight, affront, slap in the face, humiliation; *informal* brush-off, put-down.

snuff ▶ **verb** *a breeze snuffed out the candle* **extinguish**, put out, douse, smother, choke, stamp out, blow out, quench, stub out, turn out, dampen, damp down.
OPPOSITES light, ignite.

snug ▶ **adjective 1** *our tents were snug and dry* **cosy**, comfortable, warm, homely, cheerful, welcoming, friendly, congenial, hospitable, relaxed, restful, reassuring, intimate, sheltered, secure; *informal* comfy.
OPPOSITES bleak, unwelcoming.
2 *a snug black minidress* **tight**, close-fitting, figure-hugging, skintight, slinky, close, sheath; *informal* sprayed on.
OPPOSITE loose.

snuggle ▶ **verb** *I snuggled down in my sleeping bag | Tess snuggled up to him* **nestle**, curl up, huddle (up), cuddle up (to), nuzzle (up to), settle, ensconce oneself, lie close to; embrace, hug; *N. Amer.* snug down.

soak ▶ **verb 1** *soak the beans overnight in water* **immerse**, steep, submerge, submerse, dip, sink, dunk, bathe, wet, rinse, douse, marinate, souse, pickle, ret.
2 *we got soaked by the rain* **drench**, wet through, saturate, waterlog, deluge, inundate, submerge, drown, swamp; *archaic* sop.
3 *the sweat soaked through his clothes* **permeate**, penetrate, percolate, soak into, seep into/through, spread through, infuse, impregnate, imbue, pervade.
4 *use clean tissues to soak up any droplets of water* **absorb**, suck up, draw up/in, blot (up), mop (up), sponge up, sop up, take in/up.

soaking ▶ **adjective** *get your jacket off, it's soaking* **drenched**, soaked, soaked to the skin, like a drowned rat, wet through, soaked through, sodden, soggy, waterlogged, saturated, sopping (wet), dripping (wet), wringing (wet), streaming.
OPPOSITES parched, bone dry.

soap ▶ **noun**
WORD LINKS
relating to soap **saponaceous**

soar ▶ **verb 1** *the bird spread its wings and soared into the air* **fly up**, wing, wing its way; take off, take flight, take to the air; ascend, climb, rise, mount.
OPPOSITE plummet.
2 *the gulls soared on the summery winds* **glide**, plane, float, drift, wheel, hang, hover.
3 *the cost of living continued to soar* **increase rapidly**, shoot up, rise rapidly, escalate, spiral upwards; *informal* go through the ceiling, go through the roof, skyrocket.

sob ▶ **verb** *he broke down and sobbed like a child* **weep**, cry, shed tears, snivel, whimper, whine, howl, mewl, bawl; *Scottish* greet; *informal* blub, blubber, boohoo; *Brit. informal* grizzle.

sober ▶ **adjective 1** *they were drunk more often than sober* **not drunk**, not intoxicated, clear-headed, as sober as a judge; **teetotal**, abstinent, non-drinking; abstemious, temperate, moderate; *informal* on the wagon, dry.
OPPOSITE drunk.
2 *a sober view of life* **serious**, sensible, solemn, thoughtful, grave, sombre, severe, earnest, sedate, staid, dignified, steady, level-headed, serious-minded, businesslike, down-to-earth, commonsensical, pragmatic, self-controlled, restrained, conservative; strict, puritanical; *Scottish* douce.
OPPOSITES light-hearted, frivolous.
3 *a sober account of the trial* **unemotional**, dispassionate; factual, realistic, objective; low-key, matter-of-fact, prosaic, no-nonsense, rational, logical, straightforward, well considered, plain.
OPPOSITES sensational, emotional.
4 *a sober grey suit* **sombre**, **restrained**, subdued, severe, austere; conventional, traditional, staid, unadventurous; dark, dark-coloured, quiet, drab, plain.
OPPOSITE flamboyant.
▶ **verb 1** *I ought to sober up a bit* **become sober**, become clear-headed; *informal* dry out.
2 *that coffee sobered him up* **make sober**, clear someone's head; *informal* dry out.
3 *he smiled at her, but then his expression sobered* **become (more) serious**, settle (down), relax, soften, steady, cool.
4 *his expression sobered her* **make (more) serious**; subdue, calm down, quieten, steady; bring to, bring down to earth, make reflective/pensive, make someone stop and think, give someone pause for thought.

sobriety ▶ **noun 1** *he hated her more in his sobriety than when he was drunk* **soberness**, clear-headedness; **abstinence**, teetotalism, non-indulgence, non-drinking; abstemiousness, temperance, moderation, moderateness.
2 *his daughter had always been a model of sobriety* **seriousness**, solemnness, solemnity, thoughtfulness, gravity, graveness, sombreness, severity, earnestness, sedateness, staidness, dignity, dignified demeanour, steadiness, level-headedness, serious-mindedness, common sense, pragmatism, practicality, practicalness, self-control, self-restraint, conservatism, strictness, puritanism.

so-called ▶ **adjective** *many so-called critics are in fact told what to write* **inappropriately named**; supposed, alleged, presumed, ostensible, reputed, pretended, feigned, artificial, synthetic, counterfeit; nominal, in title/name only, titular; self-styled, self-titled, professed, would-be, self-appointed; *French* soi-disant; *rare* self-named.

soccer ▶ **noun** **Association Football**; *Brit.* football.

sociability ▶ **noun** **friendliness**, affability, amiability, amicability, cordiality, neighbourliness, companionability, gregariousness, conviviality, clubbability; warmness, warmth, warm-heartedness, good nature, niceness, pleasantness, geniality, civility, liveliness; communicativeness, responsiveness, forthcomingness, openness,

S

extroversion, approachability, accessibility; *informal* chumminess, clubbiness; *archaic* hospitableness, good-naturedness.
OPPOSITES unsociability, unfriendliness, uncommunicativeness, solitariness.

sociable ▶ adjective *being a sociable person, Eva loved entertaining* **friendly**, affable, amicable, cordial, neighbourly, hospitable, companionable, gregarious, convivial, clubbable; warm, warm-hearted, good-natured, genial, easy to get on/along with, lively; communicative, responsive, forthcoming, open, outgoing, extrovert, easy-going, easy, hail-fellow-well-met, approachable, accessible; *informal* chummy, clubby; *Brit. informal* matey; *N. Amer. informal* regular; *rare* conversable.
OPPOSITES unsociable, unfriendly; solitary.

social ▶ adjective **1** *alcoholism is a major social problem* **communal**, community, community-based, collective, group, general, popular, civil, civic, public, societal; endemic, pandemic.
OPPOSITE individual.
2 *a social club* **recreational**, entertainment, amusement, leisure.
3 *the mountain gorilla is a uniquely social animal | many venomous animals live in social groups* **gregarious**, organized, civilized, interactional.
▶ noun *the club has a social once a month* **party**, gathering, social gathering, social occasion, social event, social function, function, get-together, celebration, reunion, festivity, jamboree, reception, at-home, soirée; *informal* bash, shindig, shindy, do; *Brit. informal* rave-up, knees-up, beanfeast, beano, bunfight, jolly, thrash.

socialism ▶ noun **leftism**, Fabianism, syndicalism, consumer socialism, utopian socialism, welfarism; communism, Bolshevism; radicalism, militancy; progressivism, social democracy; labourism; Marxism, Leninism, Marxism–Leninism, neo-Marxism, Trotskyism, Maoism.
OPPOSITE conservatism.

socialist ▶ adjective *the socialist movement* **left-wing**, Fabian, syndicalist, utopian socialist; communist, communistic, Bolshevik, leftist; radical, revolutionary, militant, red; progressive, progressivist, reforming, social-democrat; Labour, Labourite, labourist; Marxist, Leninist, Marxist–Leninist, Trotskyite, Maoist; *informal, derogatory* lefty, pink, pinko, Bolshie, Commie.
OPPOSITE conservative.
▶ noun *she was a socialist* **left-winger**, Fabian, syndicalist, utopian socialist; communist, Bolshevik, leftist; radical, revolutionary, militant, red; progressive, progressivist, reformer, social democrat; Labourite, labourist; Marxist, Leninist, Marxist–Leninist, Trotskyite, Maoist; *informal, derogatory* lefty, pink, pinko, Bolshie, Commie.
OPPOSITE conservative.

socialize ▶ verb *guests can socialize in a real holiday atmosphere* **interact**, converse, be sociable, mix, mingle, get together, meet, keep company, fraternize, consort; entertain, have people round; get out (and about), go out, meet people; *informal* hobnob.
OPPOSITE keep oneself to oneself.

society ▶ noun **1** *drugs, crime, and other dangers to society* **the community**, the public, the general public, the people, the population; civilization, the world at large, humankind, mankind, humanity.
2 *a modern industrial society* **culture**, group, community, civilization, nation, population.
3 *Lady Angela will teach you all you need to know to enter society* **polite society**, high society, the aristocracy, the gentry, the nobility, the upper classes, the elite, the privileged classes, the county set; the smart set, the fashionable, the A-list, the wealthy, the beautiful people, the crème de la crème, the beau monde, the haut monde; *informal* the upper crust, the top drawer, the jet set; *Brit. informal* nobs, toffs; *informal, dated* swells.
4 *a local history society* **association**, club, group, band, circle, fellowship, body, guild, college, lodge, order, fraternity, confraternity, brotherhood, sisterhood, sorority, league, federation, union, alliance, affiliation, institution, coterie; *rare* sodality.
5 *she shunned the society of others* **company**, companionship, fellowship, friendship, comradeship, camaraderie, social intercourse.

WORD LINKS
related prefix **socio-** (e.g. ***socio-economic, sociopath***)
study of society **sociology**

sodden ▶ adjective **1** *his clothes were sodden* **soaking**, soaking wet, soaked, soaked through, wet through, saturated, drenched, sopping (wet), dripping (wet), wringing (wet), streaming.
2 *the sodden ground* **waterlogged**, soggy, saturated, sopping (wet); boggy, swampy, miry, fenny, oozy, marshy; heavy, squelchy, soft; *rare* quaggy.
OPPOSITES dry, arid.

sodomy ▶ noun **anal intercourse**, anal sex, buggery, pedication; *formal* intercourse per anum; *N. Amer. vulgar slang* reaming; *gay slang* a bit of ring.

sofa ▶ noun **settee**, couch, divan, chaise longue, love seat, chesterfield, Knole sofa; sofa bed; *Brit.* put-you-up; *French* canapé, tête-à-tête; *N. Amer.* davenport, day bed, studio couch, sectional; *rare* squab.

soft ▶ adjective **1** *soft margarine* **mushy**, squashy, pulpy, pappy, slushy, sloppy, squelchy, squishy, oozy, doughy, semi-liquid; *informal* gooey, gloopy; *Brit. informal* squidgy; *rare* pulpous.
OPPOSITE hard.
2 *soft ground* **swampy**, marshy, boggy, miry, fenny, oozy; heavy, squelchy; *rare* quaggy.
OPPOSITE firm.
3 *a soft cushion* **supple**, elastic, springy, pliable, pliant, squashy, resilient, cushiony, spongy, compressible, flexible, ductile, malleable, tensile, plastic.
OPPOSITE hard.
4 *soft fabric* **velvety**, smooth, cushiony, fleecy, downy, leathery, furry, silky, silken, satiny, suede-effect; *informal* like a baby's bottom.
OPPOSITES harsh, rough.
5 *a soft wind* **gentle**, light, mild, moderate, calm, balmy, delicate, zephyr-like.
OPPOSITE strong.
6 *soft light* **dim**, low, faint, shaded, subdued, muted, mellow.
OPPOSITE harsh.
7 *soft colours* **pale**, pastel, muted, washed out, understated, restrained, subdued, subtle.
OPPOSITE lurid.
8 *he spoke in soft tones* **quiet**, low, faint, muted, subdued, muffled, hushed, quietened, whispered, stifled, murmured, gentle, dulcet, indistinct, inaudible.
OPPOSITES strident, clear.
9 *the soft outlines of the trees* **blurred**, vague, hazy, misty, foggy, veiled, cloudy, clouded, nebulous, fuzzy, blurry, ill-defined, indistinct, unclear, flowing, fluid.
OPPOSITE sharp.
10 *he seduced her with soft words* **kind**, gentle, mild, sympathetic, soothing, tender, sensitive, affectionate, loving, warm, warm-hearted, sweet, sentimental, mushy, romantic; *informal* slushy, schmaltzy.
OPPOSITE harsh.
11 *many teachers are too soft with their pupils* **lenient**, easy-going, tolerant, forgiving, forbearing, indulgent, generous, clement, permissive, liberal, lax; **tender-hearted**, soft-hearted.
OPPOSITE strict.
12 (*informal*) *he must be going soft in the head* **foolish**, **stupid**, simple, brainless, mindless, witless, imbecilic, imbecile, mad; scatterbrained, feather-brained, giddy, inane, empty-headed, half-witted, slow-witted, weak-minded, feeble-minded; *informal* daft, crazy, dotty, scatty, loopy, screwy, dopey, dippy; *Brit. informal* divvy, soppy; *Scottish & N. English informal* glaikit; *S. African informal* dof; *W. Indian informal* dotish.
OPPOSITE sensible.

soften ▶ verb **1** *he could reduce interest rates to soften the blow of tax increases* **alleviate**, ease, relieve, soothe, take the edge off, assuage, allay, dull, cushion, lessen, moderate, temper, mitigate, palliate, diminish, decrease, blunt, deaden, abate, tone down; *rare* lenify.
2 *the winds softened* **die down**, abate, subside, moderate, let up, calm down, lessen, grow less, decrease, diminish, slacken, dwindle, weaken.
□ **soften someone up 1** *they used long-range shelling to soften up defensive positions* **weaken**, undermine someone's resistance, reduce someone's defensive capability.
2 *he would soften up potential buyers in the pub before a sale* **charm**, win over, persuade, influence, undermine someone's resistance, disarm, work on, sweeten, butter up, soft-soap; *Brit. informal* nobble.

soft-hearted ▶ adjective *you ought to have turned her away but you were always soft-hearted* **kind**, tender-hearted, kind-hearted, mild, tender, kindly, gentle, sympathetic, affectionate, generous, charitable, compassionate, indulgent, humane, lenient, merciful, beneficent, benign, benignant, benevolent.
OPPOSITE hard-hearted.

softly-softly ▶ adjective (*informal*) *we tried a softly-softly approach originally because we didn't want to push them too hard* **cautious**, circumspect, discreet, gentle, gradual, calm, restrained, patient, tactful, diplomatic.
OPPOSITE clumsy.

soft-pedal ▶ verb *the major candidates wish to soft-pedal the immigration issue* **play down**, make light of, make little/nothing of, set little/no store by, gloss over, de-emphasize, underemphasize, downplay, understate, underplay, minimize, shrug off.
OPPOSITES emphasize; exaggerate.

soft spot ▶ noun *Fabia had a soft spot for dogs* **liking**, love of, fondness, taste, weakness, keenness on, inclination, partiality, predilection, predisposition for/towards, proclivity for/towards, penchant, bias towards, fancy.
OPPOSITES dislike, aversion.

soggy ▶ adjective *the thick, soggy mass of fallen leaves* **soft and wet**, mushy, squashy, pulpy, pappy, slushy, sloppy, squelchy, squishy, oozy, doughy, semi-liquid, over-moist; swampy, marshy, boggy, miry, fenny; soaking, soaked, soaked through, wet through, saturated, drenched, sopping (wet), dripping (wet), wringing (wet); *informal* gooey, gloopy; *Brit. informal* squidgy; *rare* quaggy, pulpous.

soil[1] ▶ noun **1** *blueberries need very acid soil* **earth**, loam, sod, ground, dirt, clay, turf, topsoil, mould, humus, marl, dust.

S

2 *the existence of American bases on British soil* **territory**, land, space, terra firma; domain, dominion, orbit, jurisdiction, region, country.

soil² ▶ verb **1** *he might soil his expensive suit* **dirty**, get/make dirty, get/make filthy, blacken, grime, begrime, stain, muddy, splash, spot, spatter, splatter, smear, smudge, sully, spoil, defile, pollute, contaminate, foul, befoul; *informal* make mucky, muck up.
OPPOSITES keep clean; clean.
2 *the reputation of the company is being soiled by sinister elements* **damage**, **sully**, injure, stain, blacken, tarnish, taint, besmirch, blemish, defile, blot, smear, bring discredit to, dishonour, drag through the mud.

sojourn (*formal*) ▶ noun *his sojourn in France* **stay**, visit, stop, stopover, residence; holiday; *N. Amer.* vacation.
▶ verb *monks who had sojourned in Chinese monasteries* **stay**, live; put up, stop, stop over, break one's journey, lodge, room, board, have rooms, be quartered, be housed, be billeted; holiday; *N. Amer.* vacation; *dated* tarry; *archaic* bide, abide.

solace ▶ noun *they tried to find solace in pictures of their little girl as they wanted to remember her* **comfort**, consolation, cheer, support, relief.
▶ verb *Miss Wharton was driven home to be solaced with tea and sympathy* **comfort**, give solace to, console, cheer, support, relieve, soothe, calm.

soldier *See centre pages for lists of* **Soldiers** **Ranks**
▶ noun *thirty soldiers died during the operation* **fighter**, serviceman, servicewoman, fighting man, fighting woman, comrade-in-arms, warrior, trooper; (**soldiers**) cannon fodder; (*in the US*) GI, enlisted man; *Brit. informal* squaddie; *Brit. military slang* pongo; *archaic* man-at-arms.
▶ verb
□ **soldier on** (*informal*) *Graham wasn't enjoying this, but he soldiered on* **persevere**, persist, carry on doggedly, keep on, keep going, not give up, struggle on, hammer away, be persistent, be determined, see/follow something through, keep at it, show determination, press on/ahead, stay with something, not take no for an answer, be tenacious, be pertinacious, stand one's ground, stand fast/firm, hold on, hold out, go the distance, stay the course, plod on, plough on, grind away; *informal* hang on, plug away, peg away, stick to one's guns, stick at it, stick it out, hang in there, bash on.

WORD LINKS
relating to soldiers **military**

sole¹ ▶ noun
WORD LINKS
relating to the sole of the foot **plantar, volar**

sole² ▶ adjective *my sole aim was to contribute to the national team* **only**, one (and only), single, solitary, lone, unique, only possible, individual, exclusive, singular.

solecism ▶ noun **1** *the poems are marred by solecisms* **(grammatical) mistake**, error, blunder; *informal* howler, boob; *Latin* lapsus linguae, lapsus calami; *archaic* cacology.
2 *it would have been a solecism to answer the question* **faux pas**, gaffe, breach of etiquette, impropriety, piece of indecorum, social indiscretion, inappropriate behaviour, infelicity, slip, error, blunder, miscalculation, lapse; *French* gaucherie; *informal* slip-up, boo-boo; *Brit. informal* boob, clanger, bloomer; *Brit. informal, dated* floater; *N. Amer. informal* goof, blooper, bloop.

solely ▶ adverb *people are appointed solely on the basis of merit* **only**, simply, just, merely, uniquely, exclusively, entirely, completely, absolutely, totally, wholly, alone, no more than, to the exclusion of everything/everyone else.

solemn ▶ adjective **1** *a solemn occasion* **dignified**, ceremonious, ceremonial, stately, courtly, majestic, imposing, impressive, awe-inspiring, portentous, splendid, magnificent, grand, important, august, formal.
OPPOSITE frivolous.
2 *Tim looked very solemn* **serious**, earnest, grave, sober, sombre, unsmiling, poker-faced, stern, grim, dour, humourless, glum, gloomy, moody, stony-faced; **thoughtful**, preoccupied, deep in thought, pensive, meditative, ruminative, contemplative, introspective; staid, sedate, studious, bookish, owlish.
OPPOSITE light-hearted.
3 *a solemn promise* **sincere**, earnest, honest, genuine, firm, committed, unconditional, heartfelt, wholehearted, sworn, formal.
OPPOSITE insincere.

solemnity ▶ noun **1** *the solemnity of the occasion* **dignity**, ceremony, stateliness, courtliness, majesty, impressiveness, portentousness, splendour, magnificence, grandeur, importance, augustness, formality; solemnness.
2 *he paused and looked at Mike with great solemnity* **seriousness**, earnestness, gravity, sobriety, sombreness, sternness, grimness, dourness, humourlessness, glumness, gloominess, moodiness; **thoughtfulness**, preoccupation, pensiveness, meditativeness; staidness, sedateness, studiousness, bookishness, owlishness; solemnness.
3 (usually **solemnities**) *the law requires certain solemnities to make a contract binding* **formalities**, proceedings, business, rigmarole, ado, ceremony, rite, ritual, celebration, festivity; *informal* palaver, performance.

solemnize ▶ verb *their weddings were solemnized in the Dutch Reformed Church* **perform**, **celebrate**, ceremonialize; **formalize**, officiate at.

solicit ▶ verb **1** *Phil had been trying to solicit his help all morning* **ask for**, request, apply for, put in for, seek, beg, plead for, sue for, crave, canvass, call for, drum up, press for; *rare* impetrate.
2 *they are endlessly solicited for their opinions* **ask**, beg, beseech, implore, plead with, entreat, appeal to, apply to, lobby, petition, importune, canvass, supplicate, call on, press, pressure; *rare* obsecrate.
3 *prostitutes gather in the centre of the city to solicit* **work as a prostitute**, engage in prostitution, accost people, make sexual advances, tout (for business); *N. Amer. informal* hustle.

solicitor ▶ noun (*Brit.*) *they sued the company through their solicitor* **lawyer**, legal representative, legal practitioner, legal executive, notary (public), advocate, attorney; *Brit.* commissioner for oaths, articled clerk, Solicitor General, Attorney General, Official Solicitor; (*in England & Wales*) Recorder; (*in Scotland*) law agent; (*in Scotland, historical*) writer to the Signet; *informal* brief.

solicitous ▶ adjective *she was always solicitous about the welfare of her students* **concerned**, caring, attentive, mindful, interested, considerate, thoughtful; anxious, worried; *archaic* tender.

solicitude ▶ noun *it may be that their solicitude for the boy was slightly harmful* **concern**, care, attentiveness, mindfulness, consideration, considerateness, thoughtfulness, solicitousness, carefulness; **anxiety**, worry; *archaic* concernment.

solid ▶ adjective **1** *the stream was frozen solid* **hard**, rock-hard, rigid, firm, solidified, set, frozen, jellied, congealed, concrete.
OPPOSITES liquid, gaseous.
2 *a pendant made of solid gold* **pure**, 24-carat, unalloyed, unmixed, unadulterated, genuine, complete.
OPPOSITES alloyed; plated; hollow.
3 *a solid line of people | for a solid hour* **continuous**, uninterrupted, unbroken, non-stop, unremitting, incessant, constant, consecutive, undivided.
OPPOSITE broken.
4 *good solid houses* **well built**, well constructed, sound, substantial, strong, sturdy, stout, durable, stable.
OPPOSITE flimsy.
5 *a solid argument* **well founded**, well grounded, valid, sound, reasonable, logical, weighty, authoritative, convincing, cogent, plausible, credible, reliable.
OPPOSITES untenable, incoherent.
6 *a solid friendship* **dependable**, reliable, firm, unshakeable, trustworthy, stable, steadfast, unfailing, staunch, constant, unwavering.
OPPOSITE unreliable.
7 *the family have established themselves in this country as solid citizens* **sensible**, level-headed, dependable, trustworthy, down-to-earth, decent, law-abiding, upright, upstanding, worthy.
8 *the company is very solid and will come through the current recession* **financially sound**, secure, creditworthy, of good financial standing, in funds, profit-making, able to pay its debts, debt-free, solvent, in credit, not in debt, out of debt, in the black; *Finance* ungeared, unlevered; *rare* unindebted.
9 *they received solid support from their colleagues* **unanimous**, united, uniform, consistent, undivided; of one mind, of the same mind, in unison; *rare* consentient.
OPPOSITE divided.

solidarity ▶ noun *there was a great feeling of solidarity between us all* **unanimity**, unity, like-mindedness, agreement, accord, harmony, consensus, concord, concurrence, singleness of purpose, community of interest, mutual support, cooperation, cohesion, team spirit, camaraderie, esprit de corps.

solidify ▶ verb *these droplets of liquefied rock solidify rapidly* **harden**, go hard, set, freeze, ice over/up, gel, thicken, stiffen, congeal, clot, coagulate, curdle, cake, dry, bake, consolidate, ossify, fossilize, petrify; *rare* gelatinize.
OPPOSITES liquefy, melt, thaw, gasify.

soliloquy ▶ noun *Viola ends the scene with a soliloquy* **monologue**, speech, address, lecture, oration, sermon, homily, stand-up, aside; dramatic monologue, interior monologue; *informal* spiel.
OPPOSITE dialogue.

solitary ▶ adjective **1** *I live a pretty solitary life* **lonely**, companionless, unaccompanied, by oneself/itself, on one's/its own, (all) alone, friendless; **antisocial**, unsociable, withdrawn, reclusive, cloistered, introverted, hermitic; *N. Amer.* lonesome.
OPPOSITE sociable.
2 *solitary farmsteads were sparingly dotted about* **isolated**, remote, out of the way, outlying, off the beaten track, in the depths of …, hard to find, lonely, in the back of beyond, in the hinterlands, off the map, in the middle of nowhere, godforsaken, obscure, inaccessible, cut-off, tucked away, unreachable; faraway, far-flung; secluded, hidden, concealed, private, unfrequented, unvisited, undisturbed, sequestered, desolate; *N. Amer.* in the backwoods, lonesome; *S. African* in the backveld, in the

S

platteland; Austral./NZ in the backblocks, in the booay; informal unget-at-able, in the sticks; N. Amer. informal jerkwater, in the tall timbers, in the boondocks; Austral./NZ informal Barcoo, beyond the black stump; literary lone; archaic unapproachable.
OPPOSITES accessible, busy.
3 *we have not a solitary shred of evidence to go on* **single**, lone, sole, unique, only, one, individual; odd.
▶ **noun** *at school he remained a solitary* **loner**, lone wolf, introvert, recluse, hermit; rare eremite, anchorite, anchoress, stylite, coenobite.

solitude ▶ **noun 1** *she savoured her few hours of freedom and solitude* **loneliness**, solitariness, remoteness, isolation, seclusion, retirement, withdrawal, purdah, privacy, privateness, peace, peace and quiet, desolation; N. Amer. lonesomeness; rare sequestration, reclusion.
OPPOSITE company.
2 *solitudes like the area around the loch are becoming more and more precious* **wilderness**, undisturbed area, unspoilt area, rural area, wilds, backwoods, the back of beyond; desert, emptiness, wasteland, no-man's-land; (in Australia) the bush, the outback; N. Amer. & Austral./NZ backcountry; S. African the backveld; informal the sticks, the middle of nowhere; N. Amer. informal the boondocks; archaic retirement.

WORD LINKS
fear of solitude **eremophobia**

solo ▶ **adjective** *a solo flight* **unaccompanied**, single-handed, companionless, unescorted, unattended, unchaperoned, independent, lonely, solitary; alone, all alone, on one's own, by oneself/itself, without companions, in a solitary state; archaic single, sole.
OPPOSITE accompanied.
▶ **adverb** *she'd spent most of her life flying solo* **unaccompanied**, alone, all alone, on one's own, single-handed, single-handedly, by oneself/itself, without companions, companionless, unescorted, unattended, unchaperoned, unaided, by one's own efforts, independently, under one's own steam, in a solitary state.
OPPOSITES accompanied, in company, with help.

solution ▶ **noun 1** *there is no easy solution to this problem* **answer**, result, resolution, way out, panacea; key, formula, guide, clue, pointer, gloss; explanation, explication, clarification, interpretation, elucidation, exposition.
2 *a solution of ammonia in water* **mixture**, mix, blend, compound, suspension, tincture, infusion, emulsion, colloid, gel, fluid; Chemistry aerosol.

solve ▶ **verb** *that doesn't solve our immediate problem* **find an/the answer to**, find a/the solution to, answer, resolve, work out, puzzle out, fathom, find the key to, decipher, decode, break, clear up, interpret, translate, straighten out, get to the bottom of, make head or tail of, unravel, disentangle, untangle, unfold, piece together, explain, expound, elucidate; informal figure out, suss out, crack.
OPPOSITES encode, complicate, obfuscate.

solvent ▶ **adjective** *although the business was solvent, Chambers asked his bank for an overdraft facility* **financially sound**, able to pay one's debts, debt-free, not in debt, out of debt, in the black, in funds, in credit, creditworthy, of good financial standing, solid, secure, profit-making; Finance ungeared, unlevered; rare unindebted.
OPPOSITE in debt.

sombre ▶ **adjective 1** *it was the custom to wear very sombre clothes to a funeral* **dark**, dark-coloured, dull, dull-coloured, drab, dingy, shady; restrained, subdued, sober, funereal, severe, austere.
OPPOSITE bright.
2 *he looked at her with a sombre expression* **solemn**, earnest, serious, grave, sober, unsmiling, poker-faced, stern, grim, dour, humourless, stony-faced; **gloomy**, depressed, sad, melancholy, dismal, doleful, mournful, joyless, cheerless, lugubrious, funereal, sepulchral.
OPPOSITE cheerful.

somebody ▶ **noun** *nobody was going to stop her becoming a somebody* **important person**, VIP, personage, public figure, notable, notability, dignitary, pillar of society, pillar of the community, worthy; someone, name, big name, famous name, household name, personality, celebrity, leading light, star, superstar; lion, heavyweight, grandee, luminary, panjandrum; magnate, mogul; informal celeb, bigwig, big shot, big noise, big cheese, big gun, big fish, biggie, heavy, hotshot, megastar.
OPPOSITE nonentity.

some day ▶ **adverb** *some day I'll live in the countryside* **sometime**, one day, one of these days, at some time in the future, at some point in the future, at a future time/date, one of these fine days, sooner or later, by and by, in due course, in the fullness of time, in the long run.
OPPOSITES immediately; never.

somehow ▶ **adverb** *I knew that I had to be involved somehow* **by some means**, by any means (whatsoever), in some way, (in) one way or another, no matter how, somehow or other, by fair means or foul, by hook or by crook, come what may, come hell or high water.

sometime ▶ **adverb 1** *we must visit her sometime* **some day**, one day, one of these days, at some time/point in the future, at a future time/date, one of these fine days, sooner or later, by and by, in due course, in the fullness of time, in the long run.
OPPOSITES immediately; never.
2 *the break-in happened sometime on Sunday afternoon* **at some time**, at some point; during, in the course of.
▶ **adjective** *the sometime editor of the paper* **former**, past, previous, prior, foregoing, late, erstwhile, one-time, ex-; formal quondam; archaic whilom.

sometimes ▶ **adverb** *he sometimes talks nonsense* **occasionally**, from time to time, (every) now and then/again, every so often, (every) once in a while, on occasion, on occasions, on the odd occasion, at times, off and on, at intervals, periodically, sporadically, spasmodically, erratically, irregularly, intermittently, in/by fits and starts, fitfully, discontinuously, piecemeal; rare interruptedly.

somewhat ▶ **adverb 1** *matters have improved somewhat since then* **a little**, a bit, a little bit, to a limited extent/degree, to a certain degree, to some extent, to some degree, (up) to a point, in some measure, rather, quite, within limits; N. Amer. informal some; informal kind of, sort of.
OPPOSITES massively, hugely.
2 *a somewhat thicker book* **slightly**, relatively, comparatively, moderately, fairly, marginally, a shade, rather, quite, within limits.

somnolent ▶ **adjective 1** *he was feeling decidedly somnolent after his lunch* **sleepy**, drowsy, tired, languid, languorous, heavy-eyed, dozy, nodding, groggy, half asleep, asleep on one's feet, yawning; lethargic, sluggish, inactive, enervated, torpid, comatose; informal snoozy, dopey, yawny; literary slumberous; rare oscitant, slumbersome.
2 *the film's action took place in a somnolent northern village* **quiet**, restful, tranquil, calm, peaceful, pleasant, relaxing, soothing, undisturbed, untroubled, isolated.

somnolent or soporific?
See SOPORIFIC.

son ▶ **noun** **male child**, boy, son and heir; descendant, offspring; informal lad.

WORD LINKS
relating to a son **filial**
killing of one's son or daughter **filicide**

song *See centre pages for list of* **Musical Forms**
▶ **noun 1** *a beautiful song* air, strain, ditty, melody, tune, popular song, pop song, number, track; literary lay.
2 *all sounds were muffled except the song of the birds* **call(s)**, calling, chirp(s), chirping, cheep(s), cheeping, peep(s), peeping, chirrup(s), chirruping, warble(s), warbling, trill(s), trilling, twitter, twittering, whistling, piping, birdsong.
□ **song and dance** (informal) *she would be sure to make a song and dance about her aching feet* **fuss**, fuss and bother, bother, commotion, trouble, rigmarole, folderol, ado, pother; informal palaver, performance, to-do, carry-on, carrying-on, kerfuffle, hoo-ha, hullabaloo, ballyhoo, business, pantomime, hoopla; Indian tamasha; NZ informal bobsy-die.

songster *See centre pages for list of* **Singers**
▶ **noun** *talented songsters from all over Merseyside took pubs by storm* **singer**, vocalist, soloist, songstress, crooner, warbler, melodist, artiste; French chanteuse; informal popster, soulster, folkie.

sonorous ▶ **adjective 1** *he read aloud with a sonorous and musical voice* **resonant**, rich, full, round, ringing, booming, vibrant, deep, clear, mellow, mellifluous, melodious, full-toned, orotund, full-bodied, fruity, strong, resounding, reverberating, reverberant, vibrating, pulsating; rare canorous.
2 *he relished the sonorous words of condemnation* **impressive**, imposing, majestic, extravagant, grandiloquent, magniloquent, high-flown, high-sounding, lofty, rotund, orotund, bombastic, grandiose, pompous, pretentious, overblown, oratorical, rhetorical, turgid, flowery, florid, declamatory, Ciceronian; informal highfalutin; rare tumid, epideictic, fustian, euphuistic, aureate, Demosthenic, Demosthenean.

soon ▶ **adverb 1** *she'll be there soon* **in a short time**, shortly, presently, in the near future, before long, in a little while, in a minute, in a moment, in an instant, in a twinkling, in the twinkling of an eye, before you know it, any minute (now), any day (now), any time (now), by and by; informal pronto, in (less than) no time, in no time (at all), in a jiffy, in two shakes, in two shakes of a lamb's tail, before you can say Jack Robinson; Brit. informal sharpish, in a tick, in two ticks; dated directly; archaic or informal anon; literary ere long.
2 *how soon can you get here?* **early**, quickly, promptly, speedily, punctually; by when.

sooner ▶ **adverb 1** *he should have done it sooner* **earlier**, before, beforehand, in advance, in readiness, ahead of time, already.
2 *I would sooner stay* **rather**, by preference, preferably, from/by choice, more willingly, more readily; N. Amer. if I had my druthers.

soot ▶ noun
WORD LINKS
relating to soot **fuliginous**

soothe ▶ verb **1** *Rachel patted his hand to soothe him* **calm**, calm down, quiet, pacify, subdue, settle, settle down, comfort, hush, lull, tranquillize, appease, win over, conciliate, make peace with, mollify, propitiate; *Brit.* quieten (down).
OPPOSITES agitate, disturb.
2 *it contains a mild local anaesthetic to soothe the pain* **alleviate**, ease, relieve, take the edge off, assuage, allay, dull, soften, lessen, moderate, temper, palliate, mitigate, diminish, decrease, blunt, deaden, abate; *rare* lenify.
OPPOSITE aggravate.

soothing ▶ adjective **1** *soothing music* **relaxing**, restful, quiet, calm, calming, reassuring, tranquil, peaceful, placid, reposeful, tranquillizing, soporific.
2 *a soothing ointment* **palliative**, mild, calmative, alleviating; *rare* alleviative, alleviatory, lenitive, demulcent, assuasive, mitigatory, mitigative, paregoric.

soothsayer ▶ noun *a soothsayer had promised him he should die there* **prophet**, **prophetess**, seer, sibyl, augur, wise man, wise woman, sage, oracle, prognosticator, prophesier, forecaster of the future, diviner, fortune teller, crystal-gazer, clairvoyant, psychic, spiritualist, medium, palmist, palm-reader; *Scottish* spaeman, spaewife; *rare* haruspex, vaticinator, oracler.

sophisticated ▶ adjective **1** *sophisticated production techniques* **advanced**, highly developed, innovatory, trailblazing, revolutionary; modern, ultra-modern, futuristic, avant-garde, state of the art, the latest, new, the newest, up to the minute; complex, complicated, elaborate, intricate, subtle, delicate; gimmicky.
OPPOSITES crude, backward.
2 *a chic, sophisticated woman* **worldly**, worldly-wise, experienced, enlightened, cosmopolitan, knowledgeable; suave, urbane, cultured, cultivated, civilized, polished, smooth, refined, elegant, stylish; *informal* cool.
OPPOSITES naive, unsophisticated.

sophistication ▶ noun *despite his jeans, there was still an air of sophistication about him* **worldliness**, experience; suaveness, urbanity, urbaneness, culture, civilization, polish, smoothness, refinement, elegance, style, poise, finesse; *French* savoir faire; *informal* cool.
OPPOSITES naivety, uncouthness.

sophistry ▶ noun **1** *to claim that patients differ in any more fundamental way is pure sophistry* **specious reasoning**, the use of fallacious arguments, sophism, casuistry, quibbling, equivocation, fallaciousness.
2 *he went along with this sophistry, but his heart clearly wasn't in it* **fallacious argument**, sophism, fallacy, quibble; *Logic* paralogism.

soporific ▶ adjective *soporific drugs | soporific music* **sleep-inducing**, somnolent, sedative, calmative, tranquillizing, narcotic, opiate, drowsy, sleepy, somniferous; boring, dull, deadly dull, monotonous; *Medicine* hypnotic; *rare* somnific.
OPPOSITE invigorating.
▶ noun *she was given a soporific* **sleeping pill**, sleeping potion, sedative, calmative, tranquillizer, narcotic, opiate; *Medicine* hypnotic.
OPPOSITE stimulant.

soporific or somnolent?
Strictly speaking, these words apply to cause and effect. **Soporific** means 'causing sleepiness' (*the motion of the train had a soporific effect on Mr. Wishart*), while **somnolent** means 'inclined to sleep' (*the lunch had rendered some of the elders somnolent*).

soppy ▶ adjective (*Brit. informal*) **1** *I find love songs really soppy* **sentimental**, over-sentimental, overemotional, mawkish, cloying, sickly, saccharine, sugary, sugar-coated, syrupy; romantic, hearts-and-flowers; *Brit.* twee; *informal* slushy, sloppy, mushy, weepy, tear-jerking, schmaltzy, cutesy, lovey-dovey, gooey, drippy, sloshy, soupy, treacly, cheesy, corny, icky, sick-making, toe-curling; *N. Amer. informal* cornball, sappy, hokey, three-hankie; *trademark* Mills-and-Boon.
2 *my little sisters were too soppy for our adventurous games* **silly**, foolish, soft, feeble, namby-pamby, cowardly, spineless; *informal* sissy, sissified, drippy, wimpish, wimpy, weedy, daft; *Brit. informal* wet.

sorcerer, **sorceress** ▶ noun **wizard**, **witch**, (black) magician, warlock, diviner, occultist, voodooist, enchanter, enchantress, necromancer, magus, medicine man, medicine woman, shaman, witch doctor; (*in southern Africa*) sangoma; *Irish* pishogue; *N. Amer. & W. Indian* conjure woman; *rare* thaumaturge, thaumaturgist, theurgist, spell-caster, mage, magian.

sorcery ▶ noun **(black) magic**, the black arts, witchcraft, wizardry, the occult, occultism, enchantment, spell, incantation, necromancy, divination, voodooism, voodoo, hoodoo, witching, medicine, shamanism; *rare* thaumaturgy, theurgy, witchery, demonry.

sordid ▶ adjective **1** *I'm not interested in your sordid little affairs* **sleazy**, seedy, seamy, unsavoury, shoddy, vile, foul, tawdry, louche, cheap, base, low, low-minded, debased, degenerate, corrupt, dishonest, dishonourable, disreputable, despicable, discreditable, contemptible, ignominious, ignoble, shameful, wretched, abhorrent, abominable, disgusting; *informal* sleazoid.
OPPOSITES high-minded, respectable.
2 *the lane was a narrow, sordid little gully, chock-full of rubbish* **dirty**, filthy, mucky, grimy, muddy, grubby, shabby, messy, soiled, stained, smeared, smeary, scummy, slimy, sticky, sooty, dusty, unclean, foul, squalid, flea-bitten, slummy; *informal* cruddy, grungy, yucky, icky, crummy, scuzzy; *Brit. informal* manky, gungy, grotty; *Austral./NZ informal* scungy; *literary* besmirched.
OPPOSITE immaculate.

sore ▶ adjective **1** *a sore leg* **painful**, in pain, hurting, hurt, aching, throbbing, smarting, stinging, burning, irritating, irritated, agonizing, excruciating; inflamed, angry, red, reddened, sensitive, tender, delicate, chafed, raw, bruised, wounded, injured.
OPPOSITE healthy.
2 (*N. Amer. informal*) *I didn't even know they were sore at us* **upset**, **angry**, annoyed, cross, angered, furious, enraged, in a temper, bothered, vexed, displeased, disgruntled, dissatisfied, indignant, exasperated, irritated, galled, irked, put out, aggrieved, offended, affronted, resentful, piqued, nettled, ruffled, in high dudgeon; *informal* aggravated, miffed, peeved, riled, hacked off, peed off; *Brit. informal* narked, eggy, cheesed off, browned off, brassed off; *N. Amer. informal* teed off, ticked off, steamed; *vulgar slang* pissed off.
OPPOSITE happy.
3 *we are in sore need of you* **dire**, urgent, pressing, desperate, critical, crucial, acute, grave, serious, intense, crying, burning, compelling, drastic, extreme, life-and-death, great, very great, terrible; *archaic or humorous* parlous; *rare* exigent.
OPPOSITES some, slight.
▶ noun *a sore on his leg* **inflammation**, swelling, lesion; wound, scrape, abrasion, chafe, cut, laceration, graze, contusion, bruise; running sore, ulcer, ulceration, boil, abscess, carbuncle, canker.

sorrow ▶ noun **1** *he felt genuine sorrow at what had happened* **sadness**, unhappiness, dejection, regret, depression, misery, cheerlessness, downheartedness, despondency, despair, desolation, wretchedness, glumness, gloom, gloominess, heaviness of heart, dolefulness, melancholy, low spirits, mournfulness, woe, broken-heartedness, heartache, grief; *informal* down; *literary* dolorous; *rare* disconsolateness, disconsolation, dismalness.
OPPOSITE joy.
2 *the joys and sorrows of life* **trouble**, difficulty, problem, adversity, misery, woe, affliction, trial, tribulation, misfortune, reverse of fortune, misadventure, mishap, stroke of bad luck, setback, reverse, blow, failure, accident, disaster, tragedy, catastrophe, calamity.
▶ verb *they stood sorrowing over the grave of their niece* **be sad**, feel sad, be miserable, be despondent, despair, suffer, ache, agonize, anguish, be wretched, be dejected, be heavy of heart, pine, weep, shed tears, grieve, mourn, lament, wail.
OPPOSITE rejoice.

sorrowful ▶ adjective **1** *she looked at him with sorrowful eyes* **sad**, unhappy, dejected, regretful, depressed, downcast, miserable, downhearted, down, despondent, despairing, disconsolate, desolate, bowed down, wretched, glum, gloomy, doleful, dismal, blue, melancholy, melancholic, low-spirited, mournful, woeful, woebegone, forlorn, crestfallen, broken-hearted, heartbroken, inconsolable, grief-stricken; *informal* down in the mouth, down in the dumps.
OPPOSITES happy, cheerful.
2 *the sorrowful news of his father's death* **tragic**, sad, unhappy, awful, miserable, wretched, sorry, pitiful, pitiable, grievous, traumatic, upsetting, depressing, distressing, disturbing, disquieting, dispiriting, heartbreaking, heart-rending, agonizing, harrowing; *rare* distressful.
OPPOSITES cheerful, comic.

sorry ▶ adjective **1** *I was sorry to hear about his accident* **sad**, unhappy, sorrowful, distressed, upset, depressed, downcast, miserable, downhearted, disheartened, dejected, down, despondent, despairing, disconsolate, broken-hearted, heartbroken, inconsolable, grief-stricken.
OPPOSITE glad.
2 *he couldn't help feeling sorry for her* **full of pity**, sympathetic, pitying, compassionate, moved, commiserative, consoling, empathetic, caring, concerned, understanding.
OPPOSITE unsympathetic.
3 *I'm sorry if I was a bit brusque* **regretful**, remorseful, contrite, repentant, rueful, penitent, conscience-stricken, apologetic, abject, guilty, guilt-ridden, self-reproachful, bad, ashamed, shamefaced, sheepish, in sackcloth and ashes, afraid; *rare* compunctious.
OPPOSITE unrepentant.
4 *he looks a sorry sight | we keep quiet about the whole sorry business* **pitiful**, pitiable, heart-rending, distressing; **unfortunate**, wretched, unhappy, unlucky, disastrous, calamitous, regrettable, mortifying, shameful, awful; *rare* distressful.

S

sort ▶ noun **1** *what sort of book do you like reading?* **type**, kind, variety, class, category, classification, style; description, condition, calibre, quality, nature, manner, design, shape, form, pattern, group, set, bracket, genre, species, rank, genus, family, order, breed, race, strain, generation, vintage, make, model, brand, stamp, ilk, kidney, cast, grain, mould; *N. Amer. informal* stripe.
2 (*informal*) *he was a good sort* **person**, individual, soul, creature, human being; man, woman, boy, girl; *informal* fellow, chap, bloke, lad, guy, geezer, gent, kid, brat, character, type, beggar, cookie, customer; *Brit. informal* bod; *N. Amer. informal* dude, hombre; *Austral. informal* bastard; *informal, dated* body, dog, cove; *Brit. vulgar slang* sod, bugger; *archaic* wight.
□ **out of sorts 1** *she is feeling a bit out of sorts* **unwell**, ill, poorly, bad, indisposed, not oneself, sick, queasy, nauseous, nauseated, peaky, liverish, green about the gills, run down, washed out; *Brit.* off, off colour; *informal* under the weather, below par, not up to par, not up to the mark, funny, peculiar, rough, lousy, rotten, awful, terrible, dreadful, crummy; *Brit. informal* grotty, ropy; *Scottish informal* wabbit, peely-wally; *Austral./NZ informal* crook; *dated* seedy.
2 *she may have been out of sorts but she meant every word* **irritable**, irascible, peevish, fractious, fretful, cross, crabbed, crabby, crotchety, cantankerous, curmudgeonly, disagreeable, petulant, pettish; on edge, edgy, impatient, complaining, querulous, peppery, bitter, moody, grumpy, huffy, scratchy, ill-tempered, bad-tempered, ill-natured, ill-humoured, sullen, surly, sulky, sour, churlish, touchy, testy, tetchy, snappish, waspish, crusty, bilious, liverish, dyspeptic, splenetic, choleric; *informal* snappy, chippy, grouchy, cranky, whingeing, whingy; *Brit. informal* narky, ratty, eggy, stroppy, shirty; *N. Amer. informal* peckish, sorehead, soreheaded; *Austral./NZ informal* snaky; *informal, dated* miffy.
3 *Tim says you've been out of sorts and would like to have a chat* **unhappy**, dejected, sad, miserable, down, downhearted, downcast, depressed, blue, melancholy, morose, gloomy, glum, dispirited, discouraged, disheartened, despondent, disconsolate, with a long face, forlorn, crestfallen, woebegone, subdued, fed up, low, in low spirits, in the doldrums, heavy-hearted; *informal* down in the dumps, down in the mouth; *Brit. informal* brassed off, cheesed off, browned off, peed off; *N. Amer. informal* teed off, ticked off; *vulgar slang* pissed off.
□ **sort of** (*informal*) **1** *those people look sort of familiar* **slightly**, faintly, remotely, vaguely; **somewhat**, moderately, quite, rather, fairly, reasonably, comparatively, relatively, to a limited extent/degree, to a certain degree, to some extent; *informal* pretty, kind of, kinda.
OPPOSITE very.
2 *then he sort of pirouetted and fell over* **as it were**, in a (strange) kind of way, somehow.
▶ verb **1** *the children soon got the idea and sorted things of similar size and shape* **classify**, class, categorize, catalogue, grade, rank, group, divide, sort out; **organize**, arrange, order, put in order, marshal, assemble, collocate, codify, tabulate, systematize, systemize, structure, pigeonhole; *rare* methodize.
2 *the problem with the port engine was soon sorted* **resolve**, settle, sort out, solve, find a solution to, find an answer to, fix, work out, straighten out, deal with, put right, set right, put to rights, rectify, iron out; answer, explain, fathom, unravel, disentangle, clarify, clear up, throw light on; *informal* sew up, hammer out, thrash out, patch up, crack, figure out.
□ **sort something out 1** *she sorted out the clothes, some to be kept, some to be thrown away* **organize**, arrange, sort, put in order, set in order, straighten out, marshal, dispose, lay out, regulate; group, classify, categorize, catalogue, codify, systematize, systemize, tabulate; *rare* methodize.
2 *she started sorting out the lettuce from the spinach* **separate (out)**, pick out, divide, isolate, remove, segregate, sift, sieve, weed out, winnow; keep apart; put to one side.
3 *the teacher helps the children to sort out their problems. See* SORT *sense 2.*

sortie ▶ noun **1** *the inhabitants made several sorties against their besiegers* **foray**, sally, charge, offensive, attack; raid, thrust, drive, assault, onset, inroad, onslaught, rush, onrush; *German* blitzkrieg; *Italian* razzia.
2 *he was already a veteran of twelve bomber sorties* **raid**, flight, operational flight, mission, operation.

so-so ▶ adjective *he's only a so-so golfer* **mediocre**, indifferent, average, middle-of-the-road, middling, medium, moderate, everyday, workaday, ordinary, tolerable, passable, adequate, fair; **inferior**, second-rate, uninspired, undistinguished, unexceptional, unexciting, unremarkable, run-of-the-mill, not very good, pedestrian, prosaic, lacklustre, forgettable, amateur, amateurish; *informal* bog-standard, fair-to-middling, (plain) vanilla, nothing to write home about, no great shakes, not so hot, not up to much; *NZ informal* half-pie.
OPPOSITE outstanding.

soul ▶ noun **1** *painting is the art of reaching the soul through the eyes* **spirit**, psyche, (inner) self, innermost self, (inner) ego, inner being, true being, essential nature, animating principle, life force, vital force, inner man/woman; persona, identity, personality, individuality, make-up, subconscious; *technical* anima, pneuma; (*in ancient Egypt*) ka; *Hinduism* atman.
2 *he is the very soul of discretion* **embodiment**, personification, incarnation, epitome, quintessence, essence; type, symbol, picture, model, symbolization, exemplification, exemplar, image, representation, likeness, manifestation; *rare* avatar.
3 *there was not a soul in sight* **person**, human being, individual, man, woman, {man, woman, or child}, human, being, living soul, mortal, creature, body.
4 *their interpretation lacked soul* **inspiration**, feeling, emotion, passion, animation, intensity, fervour, ardour, enthusiasm, eagerness, warmth, energy, vitality, vivacity, spirit, spiritedness, commitment; *rare* fervency, ardency, passionateness.

soulful ▶ adjective *she gave him a soulful glance* **emotional**, deep, deeply felt, profound, fervent, heartfelt, sincere, passionate; meaningful, significant, eloquent, expressive; moving, inspiring, stirring, uplifting; sad, mournful, doleful.
OPPOSITE matter-of-fact.

soulless ▶ adjective **1** *the team quickly attempted to stamp its personality on the soulless office space* **characterless**, featureless, bland, dull, colourless, dreary, drab, uninspiring, unremarkable, unexceptional, undistinguished, unmemorable, grey, anaemic, insipid; ordinary, mundane, commonplace, average, mediocre, run-of-the-mill.
2 *it was soulless, non-productive work* **boring**, dull, deadly dull, tedious, dreary, routine, humdrum, ho-hum, tiresome, wearisome, uninteresting, uninspiring, unexciting, soul-destroying, mind-numbing, lifeless, dry; monotonous, unvarying, repetitive, repetitious, mechanical.
OPPOSITE exciting.

sound[1] ▶ noun **1** *she heard the sound of the car driving away* **noise**, note, din, racket, row, bang, report, hubbub, resonance, reverberation.
OPPOSITE silence.
2 *she did not make a sound* **utterance**, cry, word, noise, peep; *informal* cheep.
3 *the sound of the flute* **music**, tones, note, chord.
4 *they do not like the sound of her plans* **idea**, thought, concept, impression, prospect, description.
5 *the cemetery nestled beneath the cliffs, within sound of the sea* **hearing distance**, hearing, distance, earshot, range.
▶ verb **1** *the buzzer sounded* **go (off)**, **resonate**, resound, reverberate, blow, blare; ring, chime, peal, toll, ding, clang.
2 *engine drivers must sound their whistle* **operate**, set off; play, blow, blast, toot, blare; ring, chime, peal, toll, ding, clang; *literary* wind.
3 *do you sound the 'h' in 'Doha'?* **pronounce**, verbalize, voice, enunciate, articulate, vocalize, say; *rare* enounce.
4 *a Labour backbencher sounded a warning* **utter**, express, voice, speak, pronounce, declare, announce, deliver, put into words, intone.
5 *it sounds a crazy idea* **appear to be**, appear, look, look to be, look like, seem, seem to be, have the appearance/air of being, give/create the impression of being, strike someone as being, give every indication of being.
6 *you sound as though you really believe that* **appear**, look, seem; give/create the impression that, strike someone that, give every indication that; *informal* look like.

WORD LINKS
relating to sound **acoustic, sonic, aural, audio**
related prefixes **audio- (e.g. *audio-visual*), sono- (e.g. *sonogram*)**
fear of sound **acoustiphobia**

CHOOSE THE RIGHT WORD
sound, valid, cogent
See VALID.

sound[2] ▶ adjective **1** *your heart is as sound as a young man's | he was not of sound mind* **healthy**, in good condition, toned, fit, physically fit, hale and hearty, in good shape, in fine fettle, in trim, disease-free, undamaged, uninjured, unimpaired.
OPPOSITE unhealthy.
2 *it is a very sound building* **well built**, solid, well constructed, substantial, strong, sturdy, stout, durable, stable, intact, whole, undamaged, unimpaired.
OPPOSITES unsafe, flimsy.
3 *that is very sound advice* **well founded**, well grounded, valid, reasonable, logical, solid, weighty, authoritative, convincing, cogent, plausible, credible, reliable.
OPPOSITE unsound.
4 *a sound judge of character* **reliable**, dependable, trustworthy, fair; good, sensible, intelligent, wise, judicious, sagacious, astute, shrewd, perceptive, percipient.
OPPOSITE unreliable.
5 *lenders have to ensure that the company is financially sound* **solvent**, able to pay its debts, debt-free, not in debt, out of debt, in the black, in funds, in credit, creditworthy, of good financial standing, solid, secure; *rare* unindebted.
OPPOSITES insolvent, in debt; bankrupt.
6 *a sound sleep* **deep**, undisturbed, unbroken, uninterrupted, untroubled, peaceful.
OPPOSITES shallow, light, broken, fitful.

7 *such people should be given a sound thrashing* **thorough**, proper, real,regular, complete, total, veritable, without reserve, unqualified, out-and-out, thoroughgoing, downright, absolute, drastic, severe; *informal* damn, right, royal, right royal; *Austral./NZ informal* fair.
OPPOSITE slight.

sound[3] ▶ **verb** *he was sounding the depth of the river with a pole* **measure**, gauge, determine, test, investigate, survey, take a reading of, plumb, fathom, probe.

□ **sound someone out 1** *he sounded people out and found the responses favourable* **canvass**, test the opinions of, survey, poll, question, interview, sample; test the water, see how the land lies; *informal* pump.
2 *officials arrived to sound out public opinion* **investigate**, test, check, examine, probe, carry out an investigation of, conduct a survey of, research, research into, carry out research into, explore, look into, canvass, elicit.

sound[4] ▶ **noun** *he cast off and headed back across the sound* **channel**, (sea) passage, strait(s), neck, narrows, waterway, stretch of water; **inlet**, branch, arm (of the sea), fjord, creek, bay, voe; estuary, firth.

soup ▶ **noun**. *See centre pages for list of* **Soups**

sour ▶ **adjective 1** *too much pulp produces a sour wine* **acid**, acidy, acidic, acidulated, tart, bitter, sharp, acetic, vinegary, pungent, acrid, biting, stinging, burning, smarting, unpleasant, distasteful; *N. Amer.* acerb; *technical* acerbic; *rare* acidulous.
OPPOSITE sweet.
2 *milk bottles with traces of sour milk lingering in them* **(gone) bad**, (gone) off, turned, curdled, fermented, rancid; old, tainted, high, rank, foul, fetid, overripe; *N. Amer.* clabbered.
OPPOSITE fresh.
3 *a sour old man* **embittered**, **resentful**, nasty, spiteful, sharp-tongued, irritable, irascible, peevish, fractious, fretful, cross, crabbed, crabby, crotchety, cantankerous, curmudgeonly, disagreeable, petulant, pettish; complaining, querulous, bitter, moody, grumpy, huffy, scratchy, bad-tempered, ill-tempered, ill-natured, ill-humoured, sullen, surly, sulky, churlish, touchy, testy, tetchy, snappish, waspish, crusty, bilious, liverish, dyspeptic, splenetic, choleric; *informal* snappy, chippy, grouchy, cranky, whingeing, whingy; *Brit. informal* narky, ratty, eggy, stroppy, shirty; *N. Amer. informal* peckish, sorehead, soreheaded; *Austral./NZ informal* snaky; *informal, dated* miffy, waxy.
OPPOSITES pleasant, amiable.

▶ **verb 1** *five years of war had soured him* **embitter**, make bitter, make resentful, anger, exasperate, disillusion, disenchant, poison, envenom, disaffect, dissatisfy, frustrate, alienate.
2 *a dispute soured relations between the two countries for over a year* **spoil**, mar, damage, harm, impair, be detrimental to, wreck, upset, hurt, worsen, poison, colour, blight, tarnish.
OPPOSITE improve.

source ▶ **noun 1** *the source of the river* **spring**, origin, head, well head, headspring, headwater(s); *S. African* eye; *literary* wellspring.
2 *the source of the rumour* **origin**, place of origin; birthplace, spring, wellspring, fount; starting point, history, pedigree, provenance, derivation, root, etymology; beginning, genesis, start, rise, cause; author, originator, initiator, creator, inventor, architect, father, mother; *N. Amer.* provenience; *literary* fountainhead, begetter; *rare* radix.
3 *a historian will need to use both primary and secondary sources* **reference**, authority, informant; documentation.

sourpuss ▶ **noun** (*informal*) *Beth, who used to be such a sourpuss, made a very funny card for my birthday* **misery**, mope, dog in the manger, damper, dampener, spoilsport, pessimist, prophet of doom; **shrew**, curmudgeon, discontent, complainer, grumbler, moaner, fault-finder, carper; *N. Amer.* crank; *informal* crosspatch, grouch, grump, virago, grouser, whinger, wet blanket, party-pooper, doom merchant; *N. Amer. informal* kvetch; *rare* jade, melancholiac.

S

souse ▶ **verb** *a crunchy bruschetta soused in green olive oil* **drench**, soak, steep, douse, saturate, plunge, immerse, dip, submerge, sink, dunk.

soused ▶ **adjective 1** *a soused herring* **pickled**, marinated, soaked, steeped.
OPPOSITE fresh.
2 (*informal*) *he was well and truly soused. See* **DRUNK**.
OPPOSITE sober.

south ▶ **adjective** *the south coast of England | a south wind* **southern**, southerly, southwardly, meridional, Antarctic, polar; *technical* austral.
OPPOSITE north.

▶ **adverb** *I dawdled around for a while and then headed south* **to the south**, southward, southwards, southwardly.
OPPOSITE north.

souvenir ▶ **noun** *the recording provides a souvenir of a great production* **memento**, keepsake, reminder, remembrance, token, memorial; testimonial, trophy, relic; (**souvenirs**) memorabilia; *archaic* memorandum.

sovereign ▶ **noun ruler**, monarch, supreme ruler, Crown, crowned head, head of state, potentate, suzerain, overlord, dynast, leader; king, queen, emperor, empress, prince, princess, tsar, royal duke, grand duke, elector, crown prince, princeling, prince regent, mogul, baron, liege (lord), lord, emir, sheikh, sultan, maharaja, raja; *historical* atheling.

▶ **adjective 1** *he asserted that sovereign power belonged to the people* **supreme**, absolute, unlimited, unrestricted, unrestrained, unbounded, boundless, infinite, ultimate, total, unconditional, full, utter, paramount; **principal**, chief, dominant, predominant, ruling; **royal**, regal, kingly, monarchical.
2 *the Allies turned the western part of Germany into a sovereign state* **independent**, self-governing, autonomous, self-determining, self-legislating; non-aligned, free.
3 (*dated*) *a sovereign remedy for all ills* **effective**, efficient, powerful, potent, efficacious, effectual; practical, useful, productive, helpful, valuable, worthwhile; excellent, outstanding, reliable, unfailing; *informal* sure-fire.
OPPOSITES ineffective, useless.

sovereignty ▶ **noun 1** *the government renewed its claim to sovereignty over the islands* **jurisdiction**, supremacy, dominion, power, ascendancy, suzerainty, tyranny, hegemony, domination, sway, predominance, authority, control, influence, rule; *Indian* raj; *archaic* regiment.
OPPOSITES subservience, subjection.
2 *full West German sovereignty was achieved in 1955* **autonomy**, **independence**, self-government, self-rule, home rule, self-legislation, self-determination, non-alignment, freedom.
OPPOSITES hegemony, colonialism.

sow ▶ **verb 1** *sow the seeds in rows 30cm apart* scatter, spread, broadcast, disperse, strew, disseminate, distribute; drill, dibble, put in the ground; *literary* bestrew.
2 *large fields were sown with only cabbages or asparagus* **plant**, seed, reseed.
3 *the new policy has sown confusion and doubt* **cause**, bring about, occasion, create, give rise to, lead to, produce, engender, generate, induce, invite, implant, plant, lodge, prompt, evoke, elicit, initiate, precipitate, instigate, trigger, spark off, provoke; end in, culminate in, finish in, terminate in, involve, mean, entail, necessitate; promote, foster, foment; *formal* redound to; *literary* beget.

space ▶ **noun 1** *there was not enough space for them all* **room**, expanse, extent, capacity, area, volume, spaciousness, scope, latitude, expansion, margin, leeway, play, clearance; headroom, legroom, elbow room.
2 *the green spaces in and around London are under constant threat from developers* **area**, open space, open area, unoccupied area, empty area, expanse, stretch, sweep, tract.
3 *the space between the timbers was filled with mud and straw* **gap**, interval, opening, aperture, gulf, cavity, cranny, fissure, rift, crack, breach, break, split, flaw, crevasse, interstice, lacuna.
4 *make sure students have written their name in the appropriate space* **blank**, empty space, gap.
5 *after a space of seven years | within the space of three hours* **period**, span, time, duration, stretch, course, interval, season, term.
6 *Britain's first woman in space* **outer space**, deep space, the universe, the cosmos, the galaxy, the solar system, infinity.

▶ **verb** *the chairs should be* **spaced out** *round the table | the teams are spaced only a few metres apart* **place at intervals**, separate, place, position, arrange, line up, range, order, array, dispose, lay out, deploy, locate, settle, situate, set, stand, station.

WORD LINKS
study of space **cosmology, astronomy**

spaceman, **spacewoman** ▶ **noun astronaut**, cosmonaut, space traveller, space cadet; *N. Amer. informal* jock.

spacious ▶ **adjective 1** *a spacious house* **roomy**, commodious, capacious, palatial, airy, voluminous, high-ceilinged, sizeable, open, generous, large, big, vast, immense, rambling, ample.
OPPOSITES cramped, poky.
2 *spacious grounds* **extensive**, broad, wide, wide open, expansive, sweeping, rolling, rambling, open, ample, large, sizeable, substantial, vast, immense.

spadework ▶ **noun** *the politicians coming along have benefited from the spadework done for them* **preliminary work**, preparations, planning, groundwork, foundations, homework, preliminaries, provision, preparatory measures; hard work, donkey work, labour, drudgery, slog, toil, hard labour, sweated labour, hack work, chores, exertion; *informal* grind, sweat, elbow grease; *Brit. informal* graft; *archaic* travail, moil.

Spain ▶ **noun**

WORD LINKS
relating to Spain **Hispanic**
related prefix **Hispano-** (e.g. *Hispano-French*)
relating to Spain and Portugal **Iberian**

span ▶ **noun 1** *gannets have black tipped wings with a six-foot span* **(full) extent**, length, width, reach, stretch, spread, distance, compass, range.
2 *within the span of one working day* **period**, space, time, duration, stretch, course, interval, season, term.

▶ **verb 1** *a bridge spanned the mountain stream* **bridge**, cross, traverse, pass over, arch over, vault over.
2 *his career spanned twenty-five years | their interests span almost all the conventional disciplines* **extend over**, last, stretch across, spread over, cover,

range over, comprise, compass.

spank ▶ verb *she was spanked for spilling ink on the carpet* **smack**, slap, slipper, put someone over one's knee, thrash, cane, belt, leather, cuff; *informal* wallop, whack, lather, give someone a hiding, give someone a hot bottom, warm someone's bottom, give someone a licking; *Scottish* scud; *Scottish & N. English* skelp; *dated* tan, tan/whip someone's hide.

spar ▶ verb *the sight of husband and wife sparring in public* **quarrel**, argue, have a row/fight, row, fight, disagree, fail to agree, differ, be at odds, have a misunderstanding, be at variance, fall out, dispute, squabble, brawl, bicker, chop logic, wrangle, bandy words, cross swords, lock horns, be at each other's throats, be at loggerheads; *informal* scrap, argufy, spat, have a spat; *archaic* altercate.

spare ▶ adjective **1** *a spare set of keys* **extra**, supplementary, additional, second, another, alternative, emergency, reserve, backup, relief, fallback, substitute, fresh, auxiliary, ancillary; *N. Amer.* alternate.
OPPOSITE principal.
2 *the company proposes to sell off spare land* **surplus**, surplus to requirements, superfluous, too much/many, supernumerary, excessive, in excess, going begging; **redundant**, not required, unnecessary, inessential, unessential, needless, unneeded, uncalled for, dispensable, disposable, expendable, unwanted, useless; *French* de trop.
OPPOSITES useful, required.
3 *what do you do in your spare time?* **free**, leisure, unoccupied, own.
OPPOSITE occupied.
4 *a spare, bearded figure* **slender**, lean; willowy, sylphlike, svelte, lissom, graceful, snake-hipped, rangy, clean-limbed, trim, slight, slightly built, without an ounce of fat; thin, as thin as a reed, skinny, gaunt, attenuated, lanky, spindly; *informal* skin and bone; *rare* gracile, attenuate.
OPPOSITE fat.
□ **go spare** (*Brit. informal*) *he'll go spare if you're late* **become very angry**, become enraged, go into a rage, lose one's temper; *informal* go/get mad, go crazy, go wild, see red, go bananas, hit the roof, go through the roof, go up the wall, go off the deep end, fly off the handle, blow one's top, blow a fuse/gasket, lose one's rag, go ape, flip, flip one's lid, go non-linear, go ballistic, go psycho; *Brit. informal* go crackers, do one's nut; *N. Amer. informal* flip one's wig, blow one's lid/stack; *vulgar slang* go apeshit.
▶ verb **1** *he could not spare any money* **afford**, do without, manage without, get along without, dispense with, part with, give, let someone have, provide.
2 *animal lovers launched an appeal to spare the dog | few of the men were spared by their captors* **not harm**, leave uninjured, leave unhurt; **be merciful to**, show mercy to, have mercy on, be lenient to, deal leniently with, have pity on; pardon, grant a pardon to, excuse, leave unpunished, forgive, reprieve, release, free, let off, amnesty; *informal* go easy on.
□ **to spare** *we still have a few plants to spare* **left over**, left, over, remaining, unused, unneeded, not required, still available, surplus to requirements; superfluous, surplus, extra; *informal* going begging.

sparing ▶ adjective *he was more sparing with his admiration than with his criticism* **thrifty**, economical, frugal, canny, careful, prudent, cautious, abstemious, saving, scrimping, parsimonious; **mean**, miserly, niggardly, close-fisted, penny-pinching, cheese-paring, ungenerous, penurious, illiberal, close, grasping, Scrooge-like, stinting; *informal* stingy, tight-fisted, tight, mingy, money-grubbing, skinflinty; *N. Amer. informal* cheap; *archaic* near; *Brit. vulgar slang* tight-arsed, tight as a duck's arse.
OPPOSITES extravagant, lavish.

spark ▶ noun **1** *a spark of light* **flash**, flicker, flare, glint, twinkle, scintillation, streak, spot, pinprick.
2 *there was not a spark of truth in what he said* **particle**, iota, jot, whit, glimmer, flicker, atom, speck, bit, trace, vestige, ounce, shred, crumb, morsel, fragment, grain, drop, spot, mite, tittle, jot or tittle, modicum, hint, touch, suggestion, whisper, suspicion, scintilla; *informal* smidgen, smidge, tad; *Irish informal* stim; *archaic* scantling, scruple.
3 *we like to get new members for the group as it gives us more spark* **liveliness**, animation, life, bounce, sparkle, effervescence, fizz, verve, spirit, pep, spiritedness, ebullience, high spirits, enthusiasm, initiative, vitality, vivacity, fire, dash, go, panache, elan, snap, zest, zeal, exuberance; **vigour**, energy, gusto, drive, push, brio, dynamism; *informal* feistiness, get-up-and-go, gumption, oomph, pizzazz, vim, zing, zip.
▶ verb *the collapse of the trial sparked a furious row last night* **give rise to**, cause, lead to, set in motion, occasion, bring about, bring on, begin, start, initiate, precipitate, prompt, trigger (off), set off, touch off, provoke, incite, stimulate, stir up.
OPPOSITE bring to an end.

sparkle ▶ verb **1** *her earrings sparkled as she turned her head* **glitter**, glint, glisten, twinkle, flicker, flash, blink, wink, shimmer, dance, shine, gleam, glow; *literary* glister; *rare* coruscate, fulgurate, effulge.
2 *after a glass of wine, she began to sparkle* **be lively**, be vivacious, be animated, be ebullient, be exuberant, be bubbly, be effervescent, be sparkling, be witty, be brilliant, be enthusiastic, be full of life.
▶ noun **1** *I swim every day and I love the blue sparkle of the pool* **glitter**, glint, twinkle, twinkling, flicker, flickering, shimmer, flash, flashing, blinking, winking, dancing, shine, gleam, glow; *rare* coruscation, fulguration, effulgence.
2 *she reminded Melissa of champagne, full of fizz and sparkle* **vivacity**, animation, liveliness, vitality, life, verve, high spirits, exuberance, zest, buoyancy, effervescence, enthusiasm, ardour, energy, vigour, go, elan, gusto, brio, bounce, spirit, spiritedness, dynamism, activity, fire, panache, colour, dash, drive; *informal* oomph, pizzazz, pep, zing, zip, vim, get-up-and-go.

sparkling ▶ adjective **1** *sparkling silver jewellery* **glittering**, glinting, glistening, scintillating, twinkling, flickering, flashing, shimmering, shimmery, bright, brilliant, iridescent, opalescent, lustrous, dancing, shining, gleaming, glowing; *literary* glistering; *rare* coruscating, coruscant, fulgurating, effulgent, scintillant.
OPPOSITES dull, matte.
2 *sparkling wine* **effervescent**, fizzy, carbonated, aerated, gassy, bubbly, bubbling, fizzing, foaming, frothy; *French* mousseux, pétillant; *Italian* spumante, frizzante; *German* Schaum-, Perl-.
OPPOSITES still, flat.
3 *a sparkling performance* **brilliant**, dazzling, scintillating, exciting, exhilarating, stimulating, invigorating; vivacious, effervescent, lively, vibrant, animated, ebullient, bright; witty, clever; *rare* coruscating.
OPPOSITES boring, dull, pedestrian.

sparse ▶ adjective *areas of sparse population* **scanty**, scant, scattered, thinly distributed, scarce, infrequent, sporadic, few and far between; meagre, paltry, skimpy, limited, in short supply, at a premium, hard to come by; slight, thin.
OPPOSITES abundant, plentiful; thick.

> **CHOOSE THE RIGHT WORD**
>
> **sparse, scanty, meagre**
>
> *See* MEAGRE.

spartan ▶ adjective *a spartan life | spartan but adequate rooms* **austere**, harsh, hard, frugal, stringent, rigorous, arduous, strict, stern, severe, rigid; **ascetic**, abstemious, self-denying, hair-shirt; bleak, joyless, grim, bare, stark, uncomfortable, simple, plain.
OPPOSITES luxurious, opulent.

spasm ▶ noun **1** *Lee felt a muscle spasm in her back* **convulsion**, contraction, throes, cramp; **twitch**, jerk, tic, start, shudder, shiver, tremor, tremble.
2 *a spasm of coughing* **fit**, paroxysm, attack, burst, bout, seizure, outburst, outbreak, explosion, access; *informal* splurt; *rare* ebullition, boutade.

spasmodic ▶ adjective *spasmodic fighting continued* **intermittent**, fitful, irregular, sporadic, erratic, occasional, infrequent, scattered, patchy, isolated, odd, uneven, periodic, periodical, recurring, recurrent, on and off.

spate ▶ noun *a spate of burglaries* **series**, succession, run, cluster, string, outbreak, rash, epidemic, explosion, plague, wave, flurry, rush, flood, deluge, torrent, outpouring.

spatter ▶ verb *specks of blood spattered his face* **splash**, bespatter, splatter, spray, sprinkle, shower, speck, speckle, fleck, mottle, blotch, smear, stain, mark, dirty, soil, daub, cover; *informal* splotch, splodge; *Scottish & Irish informal* slabber; *literary* besprinkle, bedabble.

spawn ▶ verb *he wrote in a dry style that spawned hundreds of imitations* **give rise to**, bring about, occasion, generate, engender, originate, lead to, result in, effect, induce, initiate, start, set off; breed, bear, give birth to; provoke, precipitate, spark off, trigger; contribute to, make for, be conducive to, foster, promote; *literary* beget.

speak ▶ verb **1** *she refused to speak about the incident | he was speaking the truth* **talk**, say (anything/something); **utter**, state, declare, tell, voice, express, pronounce, articulate, enunciate, vocalize, verbalize; *rare* enounce.
2 *we spoke the other day* **have a conversation**, talk, have a talk, have a discussion, converse, communicate, chat, have a chat, pass the time of day, have a word, gossip, make conversation; *informal* have a confab, chew the fat/rag; *Brit. informal* natter, have a chinwag; *N. Amer. informal* shoot the breeze; *rare* confabulate.
3 *the Minister spoke for two hours* **give a speech**, give a talk, talk, lecture, give a lecture, deliver an address, give a sermon, hold forth, discourse, expound, expatiate, orate, harangue, sermonize, pontificate; *informal* spout, spiel, speechify, preachify, jaw, sound off, drone on.
4 *he was spoken of as a promising student* **mention**, make mention of, talk about, discuss, refer to, make reference to, bring in, introduce, remark on, comment on, allude to, advert to, deal with, treat.
5 *his expression spoke disbelief* **indicate**, mean, suggest, show, denote, display, demonstrate, be evidence of, register, reflect, reveal, betray, evince, disclose, exhibit, manifest; express, convey, signify, impart, bespeak, communicate, bear out, attest, testify to, prove, evidence; *literary* betoken.
6 *we really must speak to him about his rudeness* **reprimand**, rebuke, admonish, chastise, chide, upbraid, reprove, reproach, scold, remonstrate

with, berate, take to task, pull up, castigate, lambaste, read someone the Riot Act, give someone a piece of one's mind, haul over the coals, lecture, criticize, censure; *informal* tell off, give someone a talking-to, give someone a telling-off, dress down, give someone a dressing-down, give someone an earful, give someone a roasting, give someone a rocket, give someone a rollicking, rap, rap over the knuckles, slap someone's wrist, send someone away with a flea in their ear, let someone have it, bawl out, give someone hell, come down on, blow up, pitch into, lay into, lace into, give someone a caning, put on the mat, slap down, blast, rag, keelhaul; *Brit. informal* tick off, have a go at, carpet, give someone a mouthful, tear someone off a strip, give someone what for, give someone stick, wig, give someone a wigging, give someone a row, row; *N. Amer. informal* chew out, ream out; *Austral. informal* monster; *Brit. vulgar slang* bollock, give someone a bollocking; *N. Amer. vulgar slang* chew someone's ass, ream someone's ass; *dated* call down, rate, give someone a rating, trim; *rare* reprehend, objurgate.

□ **speak for 1** *the MP who speaks for the Liberal Democrats on education* **represent**, speak on behalf of, act for, act on behalf of, appear for, intercede for, express the views of, act as spokesman for, act as spokeswoman for, act as spokesperson for.
2 *who would like to speak for the motion?* **advocate**, champion, uphold, defend, stand up for, support, speak in support of, promote, recommend, urge, back, endorse, sponsor, espouse.
OPPOSITES speak against, oppose.

□ **speak out/up** *women have been speaking out on this issue for some time* **speak publicly**, speak openly, speak boldly, speak frankly, speak one's mind, sound off, spout off, go on, stand up and be counted.

□ **speak up** *you'll have to speak up to be heard* **speak (more) loudly**, speak out, speak clearly, raise one's voice, shout, yell, bellow, call at the top of one's voice; *N. Amer. informal* holler.

speaker ▸ noun *an accomplished speaker* **speech-maker**, public speaker, lecturer, talker, speechifier, expounder, orator, declaimer, rhetorician, haranguer; spokesman, spokeswoman, spokesperson, mouthpiece; reader, lector, commentator, broadcaster, narrator; *informal* tub-thumper, spieler, spin doctor; *historical* demagogue, rhetor; *rare* prolocutor.

spear ▸ noun. *See centre pages for lists of* **Projectiles** **Weapons**

spearhead ▸ noun **1** *a Bronze Age spearhead* **spear tip**, spear point.
2 *the Party became the spearhead of the struggle against Fascism* **leader(s)**, driving force; forefront, avant-garde, front runner(s), front line, vanguard, van, cutting edge.
▸ verb *she was to spearhead the inner-city campaign* **lead**, head, front, be the driving force behind; be in the forefront of, be in the front line of, lead the way in/for, be in the van of, be in the vanguard of.

special ▸ adjective **1** *they always make a special effort at Christmas | she's a very special person* **exceptional**, particular, extra special, unusual, marked, singular, uncommon, notable, noteworthy, remarkable, outstanding, unique.
OPPOSITE ordinary.
2 *we want to preserve our town's special character* **distinctive**, distinct, individual, particular, specific, certain, peculiar, definite, express, precise.
OPPOSITE general.
3 *a special occasion* **momentous**, significant, memorable, of moment, signal, important, historic, festive, gala, red-letter.
4 *this is a special tool used for recutting washer seats on taps* **specific**, particular, purpose-built, tailor-made, custom-built.

specialist ▸ noun *a specialist in electronics* **expert**, authority, pundit, professional, consultant, connoisseur, fancier, master, maestro, adept, virtuoso, old hand, skilled person; *informal* pro, buff, ace, whizz, wizard, hotshot; *Brit. informal* dab hand; *N. Amer. informal* maven, crackerjack; *rare* proficient.
OPPOSITES generalist; amateur; dunce.

speciality ▸ noun **1** *his speciality was watercolours* **forte**, strong point, strength, métier, long suit, strong suit, talent, skill, bent, gift, claim to fame, department, pièce de résistance; *informal* bag, thing, cup of tea.
2 *funding was agreed for specialities like psychiatry and anaesthesia* **area of specialization**, specialty, field of study, area, branch of knowledge, medical/surgical field.

species ▸ noun *there are several species of spadefoot toad* **type**, kind, sort; genus, family, order, breed, race, strain, variety, class, category, classification; style, manner, design, shape, form, pattern, group, set, bracket, genre, rank, generation, vintage, make, model, brand.

specific ▸ adjective **1** *I use this place for a specific purpose* **particular**, specified, certain, fixed, set, determined, distinct, separate, definite, single, individual, peculiar, discrete, express, precise.
OPPOSITE general.
2 *make sure you give very specific instructions* **exact**, **accurate**, precise, correct, error-free, pinpoint, detailed, explicit, express, clear-cut, well defined, unambiguous, unequivocal, meticulous, close, strict, definite.
OPPOSITE vague.

specification ▸ noun **1** *there was no clear specification of objectives* **statement**, stating, naming, identification, definition, defining, describing, description, setting out, setting down, framing, itemizing, designation, designating, detailing, listing, spelling out, enumeration, enumerating, particularizing, cataloguing, citing, instancing; stipulating, stipulation, prescribing, prescription, commanding, ordaining; *rare* individuation.
2 (usually **specifications**) *air-raid shelters built to government specifications were death traps* **instructions**, stipulations, requirements, conditions, provisions, restrictions, provisos, guidelines, parameters, order; description, details, delineation.

specify ▸ verb *the manufacturer would not specify the sums involved* **state**, name, identify, define, describe, set out, set down, draw up, frame, itemize, designate, detail, list, spell out, enumerate, particularize, catalogue, cite, instance, be specific about; stipulate, prescribe, order, command, ordain; *rare* individuate.

specimen ▸ noun *he was asked for a specimen of his handwriting* **sample**, example, bit, snippet, illustration, demonstration, exemplification, instance, selection, representative piece; model, prototype, pattern, dummy, swatch, test piece, pilot, trailer, trial, indication, foretaste, taste, taster, tester, smear; *archaic* scantling.

specious ▸ adjective *a specious argument* **plausible but wrong**, seemingly correct, misleading, deceptive, false, fallacious, unsound, casuistic, sophistic.

speck ▸ noun **1** *the figure in the distance had become a mere speck* **dot**, pinprick, spot, fleck, speckle, stain, mark, smudge, blemish.
2 *he brushed a speck of dust from his sleeve* **particle**, bit, tiny bit, piece, tiny piece, atom, molecule, grain, trace.

speckled ▸ adjective *a large speckled brown egg* **flecked**, speckly, specked, freckled, freckly, spotted, spotty, dotted, stippled, sprinkled, mottled, dappled, blotchy, brindled.
OPPOSITE plain.

spectacle ▸ noun **1** *the Queen's Birthday Parade is a spectacle fit for a monarch* **display**, show, performance, presentation, exhibition, pageant, parade, extravaganza.
2 *the four men did present rather an odd spectacle* **sight**, vision, view, scene, prospect, vista, outlook, picture.
3 *be careful, Your Highness, or you're liable to make a spectacle of yourself* **exhibition**, laughing stock, fool, curiosity.

spectacles *See centre pages for list of* **Glasses**
▸ plural noun **glasses**, eyewear; *N. Amer.* eyeglasses; *informal* specs.

spectacular ▸ adjective **1** *a spectacular victory* **impressive**, magnificent, splendid, dazzling, sensational, stunning, dramatic, remarkable, outstanding, memorable, unforgettable, never to be forgotten, unique.
OPPOSITE unimpressive.
2 *a spectacular view* **striking**, picturesque, eye-catching, breathtaking, arresting, glorious; *informal* out of this world.
OPPOSITE dull.
▸ noun *French history was represented in a spectacular for tourists* **extravaganza**, display, spectacle, exhibition, performance, presentation, show, pageant.

spectator ▸ noun *the game attracted about 40,000 spectators* **onlooker**, watcher, looker-on, fly on the wall, viewer, observer, witness, eyewitness, bystander, non-participant, sightseer; commentator, reporter, monitor, blogger; *informal* rubberneck; *literary* beholder.
OPPOSITES participant, player.

spectral ▸ adjective *four spectral shapes moved through the thick yellow mist* **ghostly**, wraithlike, shadowy, phantom, incorporeal, insubstantial, disembodied, unearthly, other-worldly; ghastly, eerie, weird, uncanny; *informal* spooky; *rare* phantasmal, phantasmic.

spectre ▸ noun **1** *the spectres of the murdered boys* **ghost**, phantom, apparition, spirit, wraith, shadow, presence, illusion; *Scottish & Irish* bodach; *German* doppelgänger; *W. Indian* duppy; *informal* spook; *literary* phantasm, shade, revenant, wight; *rare* eidolon, manes.
2 *the spectre of a ruinous trade war loomed* **threat**, menace, shadow, cloud, vision; prospect; danger, peril, fear, dread.

spectrum ▸ noun *a broad spectrum of opinion* **range**, gamut, sweep, scope, span; scale; variety; compass, orbit, ambit.

speculate ▸ verb **1** *my colleagues speculate about my private life* **conjecture**, theorize, form theories, hypothesize, make suppositions, postulate, guess, make guesses, surmise; think, wonder, muse.
2 *investors can make profits from speculating on the stock market* **gamble**, take a risk/chance, venture, take a venture, wager; invest, play the market; *Brit. informal* have a flutter, punt.

speculation ▸ noun **1** *his resignation fuelled speculation of an imminent cabinet reshuffle* **conjecture**, theorizing, hypothesizing, supposition, guesswork; talk; theory, hypothesis, thesis, postulation, guess, surmise, opinion, notion; prediction, forecast; *informal* guesstimate.
2 *a speculation on the stock market* **gamble**, venture, risk; gambling; investment; *informal* spec; *Brit. informal* flutter; *archaic* adventure.

speculative ▸ adjective **1** *any discussion of the question is largely speculative* **conjectural**, suppositional, theoretical, hypothetical, based on guesswork, putative, academic, notional, abstract; tentative, unproven,

untested, unfounded, groundless, unsubstantiated; *rare* ideational, suppositious, suppositive.
OPPOSITE proven.
2 *a speculative investment* **risky**, hazardous, unsafe, uncertain, unpredictable; *informal* chancy, dicey, iffy; *Brit. informal* dodgy.
OPPOSITE safe.

speech ▶ noun **1** *he was born deaf and without the power of speech* **speaking**, talking, verbal communication, verbal expression, articulation.
2 *her speech was slurred | Peter's speech was clearly cockney* **diction**, elocution, manner of speaking, articulation, enunciation, pronunciation; utterance, words, phraseology, talk; *rare* orthoepy.
3 *an after-dinner speech* **talk**, address, lecture, discourse, oration, disquisition, peroration, declamation, deliverance, presentation; valedictory; sermon, homily; harangue, diatribe, tirade, rant; monologue, soliloquy, recitation; effusion, outpouring; *N. Amer.* salutatory; *informal* spiel; *rare* allocution, predication, philippic.
4 *Spanish popular speech* **language**, tongue, parlance, idiom, dialect, idiolect, vernacular, patois; *French* façon de parler; *informal* lingo, patter, -speak.

WORD LINKS
relating to speech **lingual, oral, phonetic, phonic**
related suffixes **-phone (e.g. *Francophone*), -phasia (e.g. *dysphasia*)**

speechless ▶ adjective **1** *she was momentarily speechless* **lost for words**, at a loss for words, struck dumb, dumbstruck, bereft of speech, tongue-tied, unable to get a word out, inarticulate; mute, dumb, voiceless; dumbfounded, thunderstruck, shocked, astounded, aghast, amazed, dazed; *informal* flabbergasted, mum, knocked/hit for six; *Brit. informal* gobsmacked; *rare* dumbstricken, mumchance, obmutescent.
OPPOSITES loquacious, verbose.
2 *Lisa stared back at him in speechless misery* **silent**, unspoken, unexpressed, wordless, unsaid, unvoiced.
OPPOSITE vocal.

speed ▶ noun **1** *Lesley grew frustrated at the slow speed of their progress* **rate**, pace, tempo, momentum.
2 *we were grateful for the speed of the government's response* **rapidity**, swiftness, speediness, alacrity, quickness, fastness, celerity, velocity, dispatch, promptness, immediacy, expeditiousness, expedition, briskness, sharpness; haste, hurry, hurriedness, precipitateness; acceleration; *informal* lick, clip; *literary* fleetness; *rare* alacritousness.
OPPOSITES slowness, dilatoriness.
▶ verb **1** *I sped back home* **hurry**, race, run, sprint, dash, bolt, dart, rush, hasten, hurtle, career, streak, shoot, whizz, zoom, go like lightning, go hell for leather, spank along, bowl along, rattle along, whirl, whoosh, buzz, swoop, flash, blast, charge, stampede, gallop, sweep, hare, fly, wing, scurry, scud, scutter, scramble; *informal* belt, pelt, tear, hotfoot it, leg it, zap, zip, whip, scoot, scorch, burn rubber, go like a bat out of hell; *Brit. informal* bomb, bucket, shift, put one's foot down, go like the clappers; *Scottish informal* wheech; *N. Amer. informal* clip, boogie, hightail, barrel, lay rubber, get the lead out; *N. Amer. vulgar slang* drag/tear/haul ass; *literary* fleet; *archaic* post, hie; *rare* drive.
OPPOSITES amble, stroll.
2 *Cook was over the limit and he was speeding* **drive too fast**, exceed the speed limit, break the speed limit.
3 *a short holiday will speed his recovery* **hasten**, expedite, speed up, hurry up, accelerate, step up, advance, further, forward, promote, boost, give a boost to, stimulate, aid, assist, help along, facilitate; *informal* crank up.
OPPOSITES hinder, hold up, set back, slow down.
□ **speed up** *Smith shouted at them to speed up* **hurry up**, accelerate, move faster, go faster, drive faster, get a move on, put a spurt on, open it up, increase speed, pick up speed, gather speed; *Brit.* look smart; *informal* get cracking, get moving, step on it, step on the gas, shake a leg, rattle one's dags; *Brit. informal* get one's skates on, stir one's stumps; *N. Amer. informal* get a wiggle on; *S. African informal* put foot; *dated* make haste.
OPPOSITE slow down.
□ **speed something up** *the episode speeded up the process of political change.* See SPEED *sense* 3.

WORD LINKS
related prefixes **tacho- (e.g. *tachometer*), tachy- (e.g. *tachygraphy*)**
fear of speed **tachophobia**
measurement of speed **tachometry, velocimetry**

speedily ▶ adverb *you should ensure that complaints are handled speedily* **rapidly**, swiftly, quickly, fast, post-haste, at (full) speed, at the speed of light, at full tilt, as fast as one's legs can carry one, at a gallop; promptly, immediately, briskly; hastily, hurriedly, precipitately; *informal* p.d.q. (pretty damn quick), double quick, at a lick, hell for leather, pronto, at the double, a mile a minute, like the wind, like a bomb, like a bat out of hell, like a scalded cat, like the deuce, like nobody's business, like (greased) lightning, like a madman/madwoman; *Brit. informal* like the clappers, at a rate of knots, like billy-o; *N. Amer. informal* lickety-split; *literary* apace.
OPPOSITE slowly.

speedy ▶ adjective **1** *a speedy reply* **rapid**, swift, quick, fast, prompt, immediate, expeditious, express, brisk, sharp, unhesitating; whirlwind, lightning, meteoric, overnight, fast-track, whistle-stop; hasty, hurried, precipitate, precipitous, breakneck, summary, on-the-spot, rushed; *informal* p.d.q. (pretty damn quick), snappy, quickie; *rare* alacritous.
OPPOSITES slow, leisurely, dilatory.
2 *a speedy hatchback* **fast**, fast-moving, high-speed; *informal* nippy, zippy; *literary* fleet, fleet of foot, fleet-footed; *rare* volant.
OPPOSITES slow, plodding.

spell[1] ▶ verb *the drought could spell disaster for wildlife in some parts of the country* **lead to**, result in, bring about, bring on, cause, be the cause of; mean, amount to, add up to, constitute, signal, signify, point to; portend, augur, presage, herald, bode, promise; involve; *literary* betoken, harbinger, foretoken, forebode.
□ **spell something out** *Chapman spelled out his aims for the club* **explain**, make clear, make plain, elucidate, clarify; **specify**, set out, set forth, state precisely, be specific about, itemize, detail, enumerate, list, unfold, expound, particularize, delineate, catalogue, rehearse.

WORD LINKS
spelling system of a language **orthography**

spell[2] ▶ noun **1** *the witch recited a spell* **incantation**, charm, conjuration, rune, magic formula; abracadabra; (**spells**) **sorcery**, magic, witchcraft, witchery; *N. Amer.* hex, mojo; *NZ* makutu.
2 *Margaret surrendered to his spell* **irresistible influence**, fascination, magnetism, animal magnetism, charisma, allure, lure, charm, attraction, pull, draw, enticement, beguilement; magic, romance, mystique, glamour.
□ **cast a spell on** *everyone froze, as if a wizard had cast a spell on them* **bewitch**, enchant; curse, jinx, witch; *N. Amer.* hex; *Austral.* point the bone at; *literary* entrance.

spell[3] ▶ noun **1** *the current spell of dry weather* **period**, time, interval, season, stretch, run, course, round, span, streak; snap; *Brit. informal* patch, spot.
2 *his spells of dizziness* **bout**, fit, attack; dose.
3 *she did a spell at the tiller* **stint**, turn, stretch, session, term; shift, tour of duty, watch.

spellbinding ▶ adjective *a spellbinding tale of her life in the Far East* **fascinating**, enthralling, entrancing, bewitching, captivating, intriguing, riveting, transfixing, engrossing, gripping, very interesting, very exciting, thrilling, absorbing, compelling, compulsive, mesmerizing, mesmeric, hypnotic, magical; *informal* unputdownable.
OPPOSITES boring, dull.

spellbound ▶ adjective *the audience was spellbound* **enthralled**, fascinated, rapt, riveted, transfixed, gripped, entranced, captivated, bewitched, under someone's spell, enraptured, enchanted, mesmerized, hypnotized; *informal* hooked.
OPPOSITES bored, uninterested.

spend ▶ verb **1** *she spent £185 on a pair of shoes* **pay out**, lay out, expend, disburse; squander, go through, run through, waste, fritter away; lavish; *informal* fork out, shell out, dish out, cough up, blow, splash out, splurge, lash out; *Brit. informal* stump up, blue; *Austral./NZ informal* knock down; *archaic* spring; *N. Amer. informal* pony up.
OPPOSITES save, keep, hoard.
2 *the whole of the morning was spent gardening* **pass**, occupy, fill, take up, while away, use up.
3 *I've spent hours helping him* **put in**, devote, employ; waste.
4 *the storm of the previous evening had spent its force* **use up**, consume, exhaust, deplete, drain.

spendthrift ▶ noun *Christopher was a notorious spendthrift* **profligate**, prodigal, squanderer, waster; *informal* big spender; *archaic* wastrel.
OPPOSITES miser, skinflint, Scrooge.
▶ adjective *his spendthrift father* **profligate**, improvident, thriftless, wasteful, extravagant, free-spending, prodigal, squandering; irresponsible.
OPPOSITES miserly, thrifty, frugal.

spent ▶ adjective **1** *they wrote him off as a spent force* **used up**, consumed, exhausted, finished, depleted, drained, emptied; *informal* played out, burnt out.
2 *he stretched his stiff back, feeling old and spent* **exhausted**, tired, tired out, weary, wearied, worn out, dog-tired, bone-tired, bone-weary, on one's last legs, drained, fatigued, ready to drop, enervated, debilitated, limp; *informal* done in, all in, dead on one's feet, beat, dead beat, bushed, fagged out, knocked out, wiped out, zonked out, worn to a frazzle, frazzled, bushwhacked; *Brit. informal* knackered, whacked, jiggered; *Scottish informal* wabbit; *N. Amer. informal* pooped, tuckered out, fried, whipped; *Austral./NZ informal* stonkered; *Brit. vulgar slang* buggered, shagged out; *Austral./NZ vulgar slang* rooted; *archaic* toilworn; *rare* fordone.

sperm ▶ noun **semen**, seminal fluid, spermatic fluid, seed, ejaculate, emission; milt; *technical* spermatozoa; *informal* come, cum; *vulgar slang* jism, jissom, jizz; *Brit. vulgar slang* spunk.

spew ▶ verb **1** *factories and chemical plants were spewing out clouds of yellow smoke* **emit**, discharge, eject, expel, belch out, pour out, spout, disgorge.
2 *240 million cubic metres of lava spewed out of the volcano* **pour**, gush, spurt,

surge, spout, jet, rush; erupt.
3 (*informal*) *he felt faint and nauseous—he had to get out before he spewed* **vomit**, **throw up**, heave, retch, gag; cough up, bring up, regurgitate; *Brit.* be sick; *N. Amer.* get sick; *informal* puke, chunder, chuck up, hurl, do the technicolor yawn; keck; *Brit. informal* honk, sick up; *Scottish informal* boke; *N. Amer. informal* spit up, barf, upchuck, toss one's cookies.

sphere ▶ **noun 1** *a glass sphere* **globe**, ball, orb, spheroid, globule, round; bubble; *rare* spherule.
2 *Russia's sphere of influence* **area**, field, compass, orbit; range, scope, extent; jurisdiction, remit; *informal* bailiwick, turf, patch.
3 *he lacked experience in the sphere of foreign affairs* **domain**, realm, province, field, area, region, territory, arena, department; area of interest, area of study, discipline, speciality, specialty.
4 (*archaic*) *a higher sphere of society* **social stratum**, social class, class, rank, station, status, walk of life; caste.

spherical ▶ **adjective** *the electric light bulb hung in a spherical Japanese lantern* **round**, globular, ball-shaped, globe-shaped, orb-shaped, orb-like, bulbous, bulb-shaped, balloon-like; convex, curved, curvilinear, rounded, rotund; *technical* cycloidal, discoid, discoidal, spheroid, spheroidal, spheric; *rare* globate, globose, globoid, orbicular, orbiculate.

spice *See centre pages for lists of* **Herbs** **Spices**
▶ **noun 1** *they use 21 different spices to make their curry powder* **flavouring**, seasoning, herb; condiment, relish.
2 *the risk of detection had added spice to their affair* **excitement**, interest, colour, piquancy, spiciness, zest, savour, tang, sharpness, saltiness; bite, edge; *informal* zip, zing, zap, punch, kick; *literary* salt.
▶ **verb**
□ **spice something up** *spice up your life with this new seductive fragrance* **liven up**, make more exciting, enliven, revitalize, vitalize, perk up, put some/new life into, put some spark into, ginger up, stir up, get going, galvanize, electrify, add some zest to, give a boost to, add some colour to; *informal* pep up, jazz up, buck up, hot up.

spick and span ▶ **adjective** *the whole place was spick and span* **neat and tidy**, as neat as a new pin, orderly, well ordered, in (good) order, well kept, shipshape (and Bristol fashion), in apple-pie order, immaculate, uncluttered, straight, trim, spruce; spotless, as fresh as paint; *archaic* tricksy.
OPPOSITES disorderly, untidy.

spicy ▶ **adjective 1** *a spicy sausage casserole* **piquant**, tangy, peppery, hot, picante; spiced, seasoned, savoury; tasty, flavoursome, flavourful, well seasoned, strongly flavoured, zesty, strong, sharp, pungent; *rare* sapid, flavorous.
OPPOSITES bland, tasteless.
2 *he regaled them with spicy stories* **entertaining**, colourful, lively, spirited, exciting, piquant, zesty, zestful; **risqué**, racy, salty, scandalous, ribald, suggestive, titillating, bawdy, naughty, salacious, off colour, indelicate, immodest, dirty, smutty; *informal* raunchy, juicy; *Brit. informal* saucy, fruity; *N. Amer. informal* gamy.
OPPOSITES boring, dull, clean.

spider ▶ **noun.** *See centre pages for list of* **Spiders**
WORD LINKS
fear of spiders **arachnophobia**

spiel ▶ **noun** (*informal*) *he launched into a big spiel about the merits of the product* **speech**, line, patter, pitch, sales pitch; **monologue**, rigmarole, story, saga.

spike ▶ **noun 1** *a metal spike* **prong**, barb, point, skewer, stake, spit, projection; tine, nail, pin; spur; *Mountaineering* piton; *technical* fid; *historical* pricket.
2 *the prickly spikes of a cactus* **thorn**, spine, prickle, bristle; *technical* spicule.
▶ **verb 1** *she spiked another oyster* **impale**, spear, skewer; pierce, penetrate, perforate, stab, run through, stick, spit, transfix; *rare* transpierce.
2 (*informal*) *he claimed his drink had been spiked with drugs* **adulterate**, contaminate, drug; *informal* lace, slip a Mickey Finn into, dope, doctor, cut.
3 *the Assembly may well spike his tax-cut proposals* **put a stop to**, put an end to, put the lid on, scupper, scotch, derail; frustrate, foil, thwart, stymie, baulk, hinder, obstruct; *informal* put paid to, put the kibosh on, clobber; *Brit. informal* dish.

spill ▶ **verb 1** *everyone jumped and Kevin spilled his drink* **knock over**, tip over, upset, overturn.
2 *some of the wine spilled on to the floor* **overflow**, flow, pour, run, slop, slosh, splash, splatter; brim, well; leak, escape; *Brit. informal* splosh; *rare* overbrim.
3 *students began to spill out of the building* **stream**, pour, surge, swarm, flood, throng, crowd, mill.
4 *the horse was wrenched off course, spilling his rider* **unseat**, throw, dislodge, unhorse.
5 (*informal*) *she ought not to be spilling out his troubles to you* **reveal**, disclose, divulge, let out, leak, blurt out, babble, betray, make known, tell; *informal* let on, blab.
□ **spill the beans** (*informal*) *he gave me a look which made me wonder if Mavis had spilled the beans* **reveal everything**, tell all, give the game away, talk; *informal* let the cat out of the bag, blab, spill one's guts, come clean; *Brit. informal* blow the gaff.
OPPOSITE keep a secret.
▶ **noun 1** *a 25-tonne oil spill* **spillage**; **leak**, leakage, overspill, overflow, flood; *archaic* spilth.
2 *he decided to rest following his spill in the opening race* **fall**, tumble, accident; *informal* header, cropper, nosedive.

spin ▶ **verb 1** *the bike lay on the grass, wheels still spinning* **revolve**, rotate, turn, turn round, go round, whirl, gyrate, circle.
2 *Lisa spun round to face him* **whirl**, wheel, twirl, turn, swing, twist, swivel, pirouette, pivot, swirl; *Scottish* birl.
3 *her head was spinning* **reel**, go round, whirl, be in a whirl, swim, be giddy, be dizzy.
4 *she spun me a yarn about her husband running off to Poland* **tell**, recount, relate, narrate, unfold, weave; concoct, invent, fabricate, make up.
□ **spin something out** *the longer you can spin out the negotiations the better* **prolong**, protract, draw out, stretch out, drag out, string out, extend, extend the duration of, carry on, keep going, keep alive, continue; expand, enlarge, fill out, pad out, amplify, lengthen; *archaic* wire-draw.
OPPOSITES cut short, curtail.
▶ **noun 1** *a spin of the wheel* **rotation**, revolution, turn, whirl, twirl, gyration; pirouette, swirl; *Scottish* birl.
2 *the agency fought hard to put a positive spin on the campaign's progress* **slant**, angle, twist, bias.
3 *he took Lily for a spin in the car* **trip**, jaunt, outing, excursion, short journey, expedition, sally; **drive**, ride, run, turn, airing; *informal* tootle, joyride; *Scottish informal* hurl.
□ **in a flat spin** (*Brit. informal*) **agitated**, flustered, in a panic, worked up, beside oneself, overwrought, frantic; *informal* in a flap, in a fluster, in a state, in a dither, all of a dither, in a tizz/tizzy, in a tiz-woz; *Brit. informal* having kittens.
OPPOSITES calm, relaxed.

spindle ▶ **noun** pivot, pin, rod, axle; axis; *technical* gudgeon, mandrel, arbor, capstan, staff, fusee.

spindly ▶ **adjective 1** *he was pale, spindly, and ginger-haired* **tall**, **thin**, skinny, lean, lanky, spare, gangling, gangly, scrawny, scraggy, bony, raw-boned, gawky, rangy, angular; *informal* weedy; *dated* spindle-shanked.
OPPOSITES stocky, fat, thickset.
2 *spindly chairs* **rickety**, flimsy, wobbly, shaky, fragile, frail, insubstantial.

spine *See centre pages for list of* **Vertebrae**
▶ **noun 1** *the teenager injured his spine playing rugby* **backbone**, spinal column, vertebral column, vertebrae; back; *technical* dorsum, rachis.
2 *players of very high quality who will form the spine of our side* **mainstay**, backbone, cornerstone, foundation, basis.
3 *he has shown a great deal of spine this year* **strength of character**, strength of will, firmness of purpose, firmness, resolution, resolve, determination, fortitude, mettle, moral fibre, backbone, steel, nerve, spirit, pluck, pluckiness, courage, courageousness, bravery, braveness, valour, manliness; *informal* guts, grit, spunk; *Brit. informal* bottle; *vulgar slang* balls.
OPPOSITE weakness.
4 *the spines of a hedgehog | cactus spines* **needle**, quill, bristle, barb, spike, prickle; thorn; *technical* spicule, spicula, spiculum, spinule.
WORD LINKS
relating to the spine **vertebral**

spine-chilling ▶ **adjective** *a spine-chilling ghost story* **terrifying**, blood-curdling, petrifying, hair-raising, frightening, scaring, chilling, horrifying, fearsome; eerie, sinister; *informal* spine-tingling, scary, creepy, spooky.
OPPOSITES comforting, reassuring.

spineless ▶ **adjective** *Fiona could have smacked him for being so spineless* **weak**, weak-willed, weak-kneed, feeble, spiritless, soft, ineffectual, inadequate, irresolute, indecisive; **cowardly**, timid, timorous, fearful, faint-hearted, pusillanimous, craven, submissive, unmanly, namby-pamby, lily-livered, chicken-hearted, limp-wristed, afraid of one's shadow; *informal* wimpish, wimpy, sissy, sissified, chicken, yellow, yellow-bellied, gutless, pathetic; *Brit. informal* wet; *N. Amer. vulgar slang* candy-assed, chickenshit; *archaic* poor-spirited, recreant.
OPPOSITES bold, brave, strong-willed.

spiny ▶ **adjective** *spiny clumps of blackthorn* **prickly**, spiky, thorny, thistly, briary, brambly, bristly, bristled, spiked, barbed, pronged, scratchy, sharp; *technical* spiculate, spicular, spiniferous, aculeate, barbellate, spinose, spinous, muricate, setaceous.

spiral ▶ **adjective** *a spiral column of smoke* **coiled**, helical, helix-shaped, corkscrew, curling, winding, twisting, whorled, scrolled; *technical* cochlear, cochleate, voluted, helicoid, helicoidal.
▶ **noun** *a spiral of smoke* **coil**, helix, curl, corkscrew, twist, gyre, whorl, scroll, curlicue, convolution; *technical* volute, volution.
▶ **verb 1** *a wisp of smoke spiralled up from the trees* **coil**, wind, twirl, swirl, twist, wreathe, snake, gyrate.
2 *inflation continued to spiral* **soar**, shoot up, rocket, increase rapidly, rise

rapidly, leap up, escalate, climb, mount; *informal* skyrocket, go through the ceiling, go through the roof.
OPPOSITE fall.
3 *the economy is spiralling downward* **deteriorate**, decline, degenerate, worsen, get worse; *informal* go downhill, take a nosedive, go to pot, go to the dogs, hit the skids, go down the toilet, go down the tubes.
OPPOSITE improve.

spire ▶ **noun** *the spire of a nearby church* **steeple**, belfry; flèche; *Hinduism* shikara.

spirit ▶ **noun 1** *we seek a harmony between body and spirit* **soul**, psyche, inner self, inner being, essential being; *Philosophy* pneuma; *Psychology* anima, ego, id; (*in ancient Egypt*) ka; *Hinduism* atman.
OPPOSITES body, flesh.
2 *the spirit of nature | their spirit lives on* **life force**, animating principle, vital spark, breath of life; *French* élan vital.
3 *local people say that his spirit walks among the hills* **ghost**, phantom, spectre, apparition, wraith, shadow, presence; *Scottish & Irish* bodach; *German* Doppelgänger; *W. Indian* duppy; *informal* spook; *literary* phantasm, shade, revenant, visitant, wight; *rare* eidolon, manes.
4 *this thought dampened even my optimistic spirit* **temperament**, disposition, character, nature, personality, temper, make-up, humour, cast/turn of mind, complexion; mind, heart.
5 *she's got the right spirit* **attitude**, frame of mind, way of thinking, way of looking at it, state of mind, point of view, outlook, thoughts, ideas.
6 *the spirit of the team is high* **morale**, team spirit; *French* esprit de corps.
7 *the spirit of the nineteenth century* **ethos**, prevailing tendency, motivating force, animating principle, dominating characteristic, essence, quintessence; **atmosphere**, mood, feeling, temper, tenor, climate; **attitudes**, beliefs, principles, standards, ethics.
8 *though he was in considerable discomfort, his spirit never failed him* **courage**, bravery, courageousness, braveness, pluck, pluckiness, valour, strength of character, fortitude, backbone, spine, mettle, stout-heartedness, determination, firmness of purpose, resolution, resoluteness, resolve, fight, gameness; *informal* guts, grit, spunk; *Brit. informal* bottle; *N. Amer. informal* sand, moxie.
9 *they played with great spirit | she was full of spirit and raring to go* **animation**, **enthusiasm**, eagerness, keenness, liveliness, vivacity, vivaciousness, energy, verve, vigour, dynamism, zest, dash, elan, panache, sparkle, exuberance, gusto, brio, pep, go, sap, fervour, zeal, fire, passion; *informal* pizzazz, oomph, zing, zip, zap, vim, get-up-and-go.
10 *we must be seen to keep to the spirit of the law as well as the letter* **real/true meaning**, true intention, essence, substance.
▶ **verb**
□ **spirit someone/something away** *the girl was spirited away before we got anywhere near her* **abduct**, kidnap, make off with, run away with, whisk away, carry off, steal away with, snatch, seize; abscond with.

spirited ▶ **adjective** *an attractive and spirited young woman | the team produced a spirited performance* **lively**, vivacious, vibrant, full of life, vital, animated, high-spirited, sparkling, sprightly, energetic, active, vigorous, dynamic, dashing, enthusiastic, passionate, fiery; courageous, brave, plucky, bold, valiant, mettlesome, intrepid, determined, resolute, enterprising; *informal* feisty, spunky, have-a-go, gutsy, ballsy; *N. Amer. informal* peppy.
OPPOSITES timid, apathetic, lifeless.

spiritless ▶ **adjective** *Lilian was a pallid, spiritless woman | a spiritless performance* **apathetic**, passive, unenthusiastic, lifeless, listless, lacking in vitality, weak, feeble, spineless, droopy, limp, languid, bloodless, insipid, characterless, submissive, meek, irresolute, indecisive; **lacklustre**, flat, colourless, passionless, uninspiring, uninspired, wooden, dry, desiccated, unimpassioned, anaemic, vapid, dull, boring; *informal* wishy-washy; *Brit. vulgar slang* half-arsed.
OPPOSITES spirited, lively.

spirits *See centre pages for lists of* **Drinks** **Whiskies**
▶ **plural noun 1** *she was in good spirits when I left* **mood**, frame of mind, state of mind, emotional state, humour, temper.
2 *I don't usually drink spirits* **strong liquor**, liquor, strong drink; gin, vodka, whisky, brandy, rum; *informal* hard stuff, shorts, firewater, hooch.

spiritual ▶ **adjective 1** *the spiritual dimension of human experience* **non-material**, inner, psychic, psychical, psychological; **incorporeal**, intangible, other-worldly, unworldly, ethereal; transcendent, mystic, mystical, numinous, metaphysical; *rare* extramundane, immaterial.
OPPOSITES physical, material, corporeal, mundane.
2 *spiritual music* **religious**, sacred, divine, holy, non-secular, church, churchly, ecclesiastic, devotional.
OPPOSITE secular.

spit¹ ▶ **verb 1** *Cranston coughed and spat* **expectorate**, hawk; *Brit. informal* gob, hoick.
2 *'Go to hell', she spat* **snap**, say angrily, hiss, rasp, splutter.
3 *the bubbling fat began to spit* **sizzle**, hiss, crackle, sputter, frizzle, fizz.
4 (*Brit.*) *it began to spit* **rain lightly**, drizzle, spot; *N. English* mizzle; *N. Amer.* sprinkle.
▶ **noun** *he wiped the spit from his face* **spittle**, saliva, sputum, slaver, slobber, dribble, drool; phlegm; *Brit. informal* gob.
□ **the (very) spit** (*informal*) *Felix is the spit of Rosa's brother* **exact likeness**, living image, mirror image, very image, double, twin, lookalike, replica, clone, duplicate, copy; *German* doppelgänger; *informal* **spitting image**, spit and image, ringer, dead ringer.

spit² ▶ **noun** *chicken cooked on a spit* **skewer**, brochette, rotisserie; *rare* broach.

spite ▶ **noun** *he'd think I was saying it out of spite* **malice**, maliciousness, ill will, ill feeling, spitefulness, bitterness, animosity, hostility, antagonism, enmity, resentment, resentfulness, rancour, malevolence, venom, spleen, gall, malignance, malignity, evil intentions, envy, hate, hatred, vengeance, vengefulness, vindictiveness; nastiness, mean-spiritedness, meanness; *informal* bitchiness, cattiness; *literary* maleficence.
OPPOSITES benevolence, goodwill, affection.
□ **in spite of** *in spite of their mutual dislike, he had helped her* **despite**, notwithstanding, regardless of, for all; undeterred by, in defiance of, in the face of; even though, although.
▶ **verb** *I used to worry that you would make trouble, just to spite Martin* **upset**, hurt, wound, distress, injure; **annoy**, irritate, vex, displease, provoke, gall, peeve, pique, offend, put out; thwart, foil, frustrate; *informal* aggravate, rile, miff; *vulgar slang* piss off.
OPPOSITE please.

spiteful ▶ **adjective** *the other girls made spiteful remarks about Paula* **malicious**, mean, nasty, cruel, unkind, unfriendly, snide, hurtful, wounding, barbed, cutting, hateful, ill-natured, bitter, venomous, poisonous, acid, hostile, rancorous, malevolent, evil-intentioned, baleful, vindictive, vengeful, vitriolic, vicious, splenetic, malign, malignant, bilious; defamatory; *informal* bitchy, catty; *literary* malefic, maleficent; *rare* squint-eyed.
OPPOSITES benevolent, kind, friendly.

splash ▶ **verb 1** *splash your face with cool water* **sprinkle**, spray, shower, splatter, slosh, slop, squirt; daub; wet.
2 *his boots were splashed with mud* **spatter**, bespatter, splatter, speck, speckle, blotch, smear, stain, mark; *informal* splotch, splodge; *Scottish & Irish informal* slabber; *literary* bedabble.
3 *the Atlantic Ocean splashed against the pier* **swash**, wash, break, lap; **dash**, beat, lash, batter, crash, buffet, surge; *literary* plash.
4 *children splashed about gleefully in the shallow water* **paddle**, wade, slosh; wallow; *informal* splosh.
5 *the story was splashed across the front pages* **blazon**, display, spread, plaster, trumpet, publicize, broadcast, headline; *informal* splatter.
□ **be splashed with** *Lonnie's face was splashed with freckles* **be flecked with**, be dotted with, be stippled with, be studded with, be scattered with.
□ **splash out** (*Brit. informal*) *she splashed out on a Mercedes* **be extravagant**, go on a spending spree, splurge, spare no expense, spend lavishly, spend a lot of money; *informal* lash out, push the boat out, go mad, go on a shopping binge, indulge in some retail therapy.
▶ **noun 1** *the splash of the water against the rocks* **splashing**, swashing, dashing, beating, battering; *literary* plash, plashing; *archaic* swash.
2 *there was a splash of blood on his forehead* **spot**, blob, dab, daub, smudge, smear, speck, speckle, fleck; mark, stain; *informal* splotch, splosh, splodge.
3 *a splash of lemonade* **drop**, dash, bit, spot, soupçon, dribble, driblet; little, small amount; *Scottish informal* scoosh.
4 *add a red scarf to give a splash of colour* **patch**, burst, streak.
5 *a front-page splash* **feature**, story, article, piece; display; *N. Amer. informal* screamer.
□ **make a splash** (*informal*) **cause a sensation**, cause a stir, attract attention, draw attention to oneself/itself, get noticed, make an impression, make an impact, cut a dash.

spleen ▶ **noun** *obviously you're annoyed but that doesn't give you the right to vent your spleen on me* **bad temper**, bad mood, ill temper, ill humour, annoyance, anger, wrath, vexation, crossness, irritation, displeasure, dissatisfaction, irritability, irascibility, cantankerousness, peevishness, petulance, pettishness, pique, querulousness, crabbiness, testiness, tetchiness, snappishness, waspishness, touchiness, moodiness, sullenness, resentment, rancour, biliousness, sourness; **spite**, spitefulness, ill feeling, malice, maliciousness, bitterness, animosity, antipathy, hostility, malevolence, venom, gall, malignance, malignity, acrimony, bile, hatred, hate; *literary* ire, choler.
OPPOSITE good humour.

splendid ▶ **adjective 1** *a splendid palazzo on the Grand Canal | their splendid costumes* **magnificent**, sumptuous, grand, impressive, imposing, superb, spectacular, resplendent, opulent, luxurious, palatial, de luxe, rich, fine, costly, expensive, lavish, ornate, gorgeous, glorious, dazzling, elegant, handsome, beautiful; stately, majestic, kingly, princely, regal, noble, proud; *informal* plush, plushy, posh, swanky, ritzy, splendiferous; *Brit. informal* swish; *N. Amer. informal* swank; *literary* brave; *rare* splendacious, splendorous, magnolious, palatian.
OPPOSITES modest, unimpressive, ordinary.
2 *an MP with a splendid reputation* **distinguished**, glorious, glittering, illustrious, remarkable, outstanding, exceptional, celebrated, renowned, famous, impressive, notable, noted, eminent, noble, lofty, venerable, exemplary.

S

OPPOSITE undistinguished.
3 (*informal*) *we had a splendid holiday* **excellent**, **wonderful**, marvellous, magnificent, superb, glorious, sublime, lovely, delightful, first-class, first-rate; *informal* super, great, smashing, amazing, fantastic, terrific, tremendous, phenomenal, sensational, incredible, heavenly, gorgeous, dreamy, grand, fabulous, fab, fabby, fantabulous, awesome, magic, ace, cool, mean, bad, wicked, mega, crucial, mind-blowing, far out, A1, sound, out of this world, marvy, spanking; *Brit. informal*, brilliant, brill; *N. Amer. informal* peachy, dandy, jim-dandy, neat, badass, boss, radical, rad, boffo, bully, bitching, bodacious; *Austral./NZ informal* beaut, bonzer; *S. African informal* kif, lank; *black English* dope, def, phat; *informal, dated* groovy, divine; *Brit. informal, dated* capital, champion, wizard, corking, ripping, cracking, spiffing, top-hole, topping, beezer; *N. Amer. informal, dated* swell, keen; *archaic* goodly.
OPPOSITES dreadful, awful, horrible.

splendour ▶ noun **1** *a wedding long remembered for its splendour* **magnificence**, grandeur, sumptuousness, impressiveness, resplendence, opulence, luxury, luxuriousness, richness, fineness, lavishness, ornateness, glory, gloriousness, gorgeousness, splendidness, beauty, elegance; majesty, stateliness, nobility, pomp, pomp and circumstance, panoply, pageantry, spectacle; *informal* ritziness, poshness, splendiferousness.
OPPOSITES ordinariness, modesty.
2 (*literary*) *shafts of golden splendour burnished the leaves* **brightness**, radiance, brilliance, light, gleam, glow, lustre, shine, luminosity, luminousness; *rare* refulgence, effulgence.

splenetic ▶ adjective *he wrote a characteristically splenetic article* **bad-tempered**, ill-tempered, ill-humoured, angry, wrathful, cross, peevish, petulant, pettish, irritable, irascible, cantankerous, choleric, dyspeptic, testy, tetchy, snappish, waspish, crotchety, crabby, crabbed, querulous, resentful, rancorous, bilious, sour, bitter, acid, liverish; **spiteful**, malicious, ill-natured, hostile, acrimonious, malevolent, malignant, malign; *informal* bitchy; *rare* atrabilious, envenomed.
OPPOSITE good-humoured.

splice ▶ verb *it is easier to splice than any other rope of similar construction | a video splicing together bits from 63 interviews* **interweave**, braid, plait, entwine, intertwine, interlace, knit, mesh; join, unite, connect, bind, fasten, tie; *Nautical* marry.
□ **get spliced** (*informal*) *they paid £15,000 for a wedding package and ended up getting spliced in a car park* **get married**, marry, wed, get wed, become man/husband and wife, plight one's troth; *informal* tie the knot, get hitched, get yoked, take the plunge, say 'I do'; *archaic* become espoused.
OPPOSITES divorce, get divorced.

splinter ▶ noun *small splinters of wood | a splinter of glass* **sliver**, shiver, chip, shard, needle; fragment, piece, bit, shred, spell, spillikin; shaving, paring; (**splinters**) matchwood, flinders; *Scottish* skelf; *technical* gallet, spall.
▶ verb *the windscreen splintered* **shatter**, break into tiny pieces, break into fragments, smash, smash into smithereens, fracture, split, crack, disintegrate, crumble; *technical* spall; *rare* shiver.

split ▶ verb **1** *the bedside table had been split in two* **break**, chop, cut, hew, lop, cleave; snap, crack; *informal* bust.
2 *the ice cracked and split* **break apart**, fracture, rupture, fissure, snap, come apart, splinter.
3 *not only was her dress covered in mud, it was split* **tear**, rip, slash, slit; *literary* rend.
4 *it is an issue which could split the Party* **divide**, disunite, separate, sever; bisect, partition; *literary* tear asunder, cleave, rend; *archaic* sunder, rive; *rare* dichotomize, factionalize.
OPPOSITES unite, unify.
5 *the consortium plan to split the assets between them* **share (out)**, divide (up), apportion, allocate, allot, distribute, dole out, parcel out, measure out; carve up, slice up; halve; *informal* divvy up.
6 *soon afterwards the path splits* **fork**, divide in two, divide, bifurcate, go in different directions, diverge, branch; *rare* divaricate.
OPPOSITES converge, merge.
7 *they **split up** last year* **break up**, separate, part, part company, become estranged, reach a parting of the ways; divorce, get a divorce, get divorced; *Brit. informal* bust up.
OPPOSITES get together, marry.
8 (*informal*) *as soon as the gig ended, she split.* See LEAVE *sense* 1.
9 (*Brit. informal*) *I told him I wouldn't **split on** him* **inform on/against**, tell tales on, give away, sell out, stab in the back; *informal* tell on, squeal on, blow the whistle on, rat on, peach on, stitch up, do the dirty on, sell down the river; *Brit. informal* grass on, shop; *N. Amer. informal* rat out, drop a/the dime on, finger; *Austral. informal* pimp on, pool, put someone's pot on.
□ **split hairs**. *See* HAIR.
▶ noun **1** *a split in the rock face* **crack**, fissure, cleft, crevice, break, fracture, breach.
2 *light squeezed through a small split in the curtain* **rip**, tear, cut, rent, slash, slit.
3 *the accusations caused a split in the Party* **division**, **rift**, breach, schism, rupture, partition, separation, severance, break-up, alienation, estrangement; *rare* scission.
4 *he's been living in London since the acrimonious split with his wife* **break-up**, split-up, separation, parting, estrangement, parting of the ways, rift, rupture, breach; divorce; legal separation, judicial separation; *Brit. informal* bust-up.
OPPOSITE marriage.

WORD LINKS
easily split **fissile**
related prefix **schizo- (e.g. *schizocarp*)**

split-up ▶ noun *I was still getting over my split-up with Richard* **break-up**, separation, split, parting, estrangement, parting of the ways, rift, rupture; divorce; *Brit. informal* bust-up.

spoil ▶ verb **1** *too much sun spoils the complexion* **mar**, damage, impair, blemish, disfigure, blight, flaw, deface, scar, injure, harm; ruin, destroy, wreck; be a blot on the landscape; *rare* disfeature.
OPPOSITES improve, enhance.
2 *two days of rain spoiled all my plans* **ruin**, wreck, destroy, upset, undo, mess up, make a mess of, dash, sabotage, scupper, scotch, torpedo, blast, vitiate; cast a shadow over, cast a pall over, cloud, darken, take the shine off, put a damper on, take the enjoyment/pleasure out of, take the edge off; upset someone's apple cart, cook someone's goose; *informal* foul up, louse up, muck up, queer, screw up, put the kibosh on, banjax, blow a hole in, do for, nix; *Brit. informal* cock up, dish, queer someone's pitch, throw a spanner in the works of; *N. Amer. informal* rain on someone's parade, throw a monkey wrench in the works of; *Austral. informal* cruel, euchre; *vulgar slang* bugger up, fuck up, balls up; *archaic* bring to naught.
OPPOSITES further, help; enhance.
3 *his sisters spoil him and so does his mother* **overindulge**, pamper, indulge, mollycoddle, cosset, coddle, baby, spoon-feed, feather-bed, wait on hand and foot, cater to someone's every whim, wrap in cotton wool, kill with kindness; nanny, nursemaid; dote on; *archaic* cocker.
OPPOSITES neglect, treat harshly, be strict with.
4 *I've got some ham that will spoil if we don't eat it tonight* **go bad**, go off, go rancid, turn, go sour, sour, go mouldy, moulder, become addled, curdle, become rotten, rot, perish, decompose, decay, putrefy.
OPPOSITE keep.
□ **spoiling for** *Cooper was spoiling for a fight* **eager for**, itching for, looking for, keen to have, raring for, after, bent on, set on, on the lookout for, longing for.

spoils ▶ plural noun **1** *the looters carried their spoils away* **booty**, **loot**, stolen goods, plunder, ill-gotten gains, haul, pickings, takings; *informal, dated* swag, boodle.
2 *he did not have the slightest intention of sharing the spoils of office with Craigbarnet* **benefits**, advantages, perks; *formal* perquisites; *rare* appanages.

spoilsport ▶ noun **killjoy**, dog in the manger, misery, damper; *informal* wet blanket, party-pooper; *Austral./NZ informal* wowser.

spoken ▶ adjective *spoken communication* **verbal**, **oral**, uttered, voiced, expressed, stated; unwritten; by word of mouth; *Latin* viva voce.
OPPOSITES unspoken, written.
□ **spoken for 1** *some of the villas are already spoken for* **reserved**, booked, set aside; chosen, selected, claimed; chartered, hired; *rare* bespoke.
OPPOSITE free.
2 *he knows Claudine is spoken for* **attached**, going out with someone; **engaged**; *informal* going steady; *dated* betrothed.
OPPOSITES unattached, free.

spokesman, **spokeswoman** ▶ noun **spokesperson**, representative, agent, mouthpiece, voice; negotiator, arbitrator, mediator, intermediary, middleman, go-between, moderator, broker, honest broker; delegate; *informal* spin doctor; *rare* prolocutor, fugleman, negotiant.

sponge ▶ verb *a boy was **sponging down** the Daimler's windows* **wash**, clean, wipe, swab; mop, rinse, sluice, swill.
□ **sponge off/on** (*informal*) *she could not bear the thought of sponging on her parents* **scrounge off/from**, live off, be a parasite on, impose on, beg from, borrow from, be dependent on; *informal* freeload on, cadge from, bum off; *N. Amer. informal* mooch off; *Austral./NZ* bludge on.

sponger ▶ noun (*informal*) *many saw him as an easy touch and he was surrounded by an army of spongers* **parasite**, hanger-on, leech, scrounger, passenger, drone, beggar; *informal* freeloader, sponge, cadger, bum, bloodsucker; *Brit. informal* ligger; *N. Amer. informal* mooch, moocher, schnorrer; *Austral./NZ informal* bludger.

spongy ▶ adjective **1** *the material has a spongy texture* **soft**, cushiony, cushioned, squashy, compressible, yielding; springy, resilient, elastic; porous, absorbent, absorptive, permeable, pervious; light; *technical* spongiform; *Brit. informal* squidgy; *rare* spongiose.
OPPOSITES hard, solid.
2 *he felt the spongy soil drawing him downwards* **waterlogged**, wet, soft, heavy, muddy, boggy, marshy, squelchy.
OPPOSITES hard, compacted.

sponsor ▶ noun *the production cost £50,000, most coming from local sponsors* **backer**, **patron**, promoter, subsidizer, benefactor, benefactress, guarantor, underwriter, supporter, friend; *informal* angel; *rare* Maecenas.

▶ verb *Cathay Pacific sponsored the event* **finance**, put up the money for, fund, subsidize, underwrite, back, promote, lend one's name to, be a patron of, act as guarantor of, support; *informal* foot the bill for, pick up the tab for; *N. Amer. informal* bankroll.

sponsorship ▶ noun *the team would like to thank the Institute for its sponsorship* **backing**, support, patronage, funding, financing, promotion; aegis, auspices; help, aid, assistance.

spontaneous ▶ adjective **1** *a spontaneous display of affection* **unforced**, voluntary, unconstrained, unprompted, unbidden, unsolicited, unplanned, unpremeditated, unrehearsed, impulsive, impetuous, unstudied, impromptu, spur-of-the-moment, extempore, extemporaneous; unschooled, untaught, uninstructed; *informal* off-the-cuff.
OPPOSITES planned, forced, calculated.
2 *a spontaneous reaction to danger* **reflex**, automatic, knee-jerk, involuntary, unthinking, unconscious, instinctive, instinctual; *informal* gut.
OPPOSITE conscious.
3 *she seems friendly and spontaneous* **natural**, uninhibited, relaxed, unselfconscious, unaffected, easy, free and easy; impulsive, impetuous; open, genuine.
OPPOSITE inhibited.

spontaneously ▶ adverb **1** *the huge crowd spontaneously broke into applause* **without being asked**, of one's own accord, voluntarily, on impulse, impulsively, on the spur of the moment, extempore, extemporaneously; *informal* off the cuff.
2 *he'd reacted spontaneously, displaying the full force of his anger* **without thinking**, automatically, unthinkingly, involuntarily, instinctively.

spoof (*informal*) ▶ noun **1** *a rather bad Agatha Christie spoof* **parody**, pastiche, burlesque, take-off, skit, imitation; *informal* send-up; *Brit. vulgar slang* piss-take; *rare* pasquinade, pasticcio.
2 *word got out that the whole thing had been a spoof* **hoax**, trick, joke, game; *informal* leg-pull, con; *N. Amer. informal* dido; *archaic* quiz.
▶ verb *his quirky personality has been spoofed by several comedians* **parody**, take off, burlesque, pastiche, make fun of; *informal* send up; *Brit. vulgar slang* take the piss out of.

spooky ▶ adjective (*informal*) *the atmosphere was decidedly spooky* **eerie**, sinister, ghostly, uncanny, weird, unearthly, mysterious; **frightening**, spine-chilling, hair-raising, scaring, terrifying, petrifying, chilling; *informal* **creepy**, scary, spine-tingling.

sporadic ▶ adjective *we braved the sporadic showers | sporadic fighting broke out* **occasional**, infrequent, irregular, periodical, periodic, scattered, patchy, isolated, odd, uneven; **intermittent**, spasmodic, on and off, random, fitful, desultory, erratic, unpredictable.
OPPOSITES frequent, regular, steady, continuous.

sport *See centre pages for lists of* **Athletics Events** **Ball Games** **Cricket Roles and Positions** **Equestrian Sports** **Gymnastics Events** **Martial Arts** **Motor Sports** **Rugby Players** **Sports** **Swimming Strokes, Kicks, and Dives** **Tennis Strokes**
▶ noun **1** *he takes part in a variety of sports | we did a lot of sport* **(competitive) game(s)**, physical recreation, physical activity, physical exercise; pastime.
2 (*dated*) *the puzzle amuses them and it would be a pity to spoil their sport* **fun**, pleasure, enjoyment, entertainment, amusement, diversion, divertissement, play, recreation.
□ **in sport** *I have assumed the name was given more or less in sport* **as a joke**, in jest, jokingly, for fun, teasingly, playfully.
□ **make sport of** (*dated*) *the other boys made sport of him* **make fun of**, poke fun at, tease, taunt, chaff, make jokes about, make the butt of one's jokes, ridicule, mock, laugh at, rag, deride, scoff at, jeer at, jibe at; *informal* take the mickey out of, send up, wind up, make a monkey of; *N. Amer. informal* goof on, rag on, pull someone's chain, razz; *Austral./NZ informal* poke mullock at, sling off at; *Brit. informal, dated* rot, twit; *archaic* smoke, rally, quiz.
▶ verb **1** *he sported a gardenia in his buttonhole* **wear**, **display**, exhibit, have on show, show off, flourish, parade, flaunt.
2 (*dated*) *the children sported in the water* **play**, have fun, amuse oneself, entertain oneself, enjoy oneself, divert oneself, frolic, gambol, frisk, romp, cavort, caper; *informal* lark (about/around); *archaic or humorous* disport oneself; *archaic* wanton; *rare* rollick.

sporting ▶ adjective *it was jolly sporting of you to let me have first go* **sportsmanlike**, sportsmanly, generous, gentlemanly, considerate, good; fair, just, honourable; *Brit. informal* decent.
OPPOSITES unsporting, unfair.

sportive ▶ adjective (*archaic*) *a group of sportive children* **playful**, lively, full of fun, fun-loving, high-spirited, spirited, in high spirits, jolly, merry, light-hearted, blithe, gleeful, frisky, exuberant, perky, skittish, sprightly, coltish, jaunty, prankish, frolicking, romping, capering; *informal* full of beans, frolicky; *archaic* frolicsome, gamesome, blithesome, frolic, wanton; *rare* ludic.
OPPOSITES solemn, staid.

sporty ▶ adjective (*informal*) **1** *two sporty types wearing jogging suits* **athletic**, fit, active, energetic, outdoor; hearty; *N. Amer. informal* outdoorsy.
OPPOSITES unfit; lazy.
2 *his spring collection combines a sporty feel with fresh colours* **stylish**, smart, jaunty; **casual**, informal; *informal* trendy, sharp, natty, snazzy, snappy; *N. Amer. informal* sassy, spiffy.
OPPOSITES formal, dressy.
3 *the sporty 1.5 litre coupe* **fast**, speedy; *informal* nippy, zippy.
OPPOSITE slow.

spot ▶ noun **1** *the dog was white with black spots | there were a few spots of blood on the pavement* **mark**, patch, dot, speck, speckle, fleck, smudge, smear, stain, blotch, blot, splash, daub; *technical* petechia; *informal* splotch, splosh, splodge; *rare* macule, macula.
2 *this cream will improve the appearance of wrinkles, brown spots, and uneven skin tone* **discoloration**; freckle; liver spot, age spot, mole; birthmark, port wine stain, strawberry mark; *technical* naevus.
3 *he had an angry spot on the side of his nose* **pimple**, pustule, blemish, blackhead, boil, swelling, eruption, wen, sty; pock, pockmark; **(spots) acne**, rash; *technical* comedo; *informal* zit, whitehead; *Scottish informal* plook; *N. Amer. informal* hickey; *rare* papule, bleb, whelk, blain.
4 (*archaic*) *this was a black spot upon my character* **stain**, blemish, blot on the escutcheon, blot, taint, defect, flaw, brand, stigma.
5 *there are miles of footpaths and plenty of secluded spots* **place**, location, site, position, point, situation, scene, setting, locale, locality, area, neighbourhood, region; venue; *technical* locus.
6 *social policy has a regular spot on the agenda* **position**, place, niche, slot, space; *informal* window.
7 (*Brit. informal*) *would you like a spot of brandy?* **bit**, little, some, small amount, morsel, modicum, bite; drop, splash; *informal* smidgen, smidge, tad; *Scottish informal* scoosh.
8 (*informal*) *you're in a* ***tight spot*** **difficult situation**, awkward situation, tricky situation, predicament, mess, difficulty, trouble, plight, corner, quandary, dilemma; *informal* fix, jam, hole, sticky situation, pickle, scrape, pretty/fine kettle of fish, hot water, how-do-you-do.
□ **on the spot** *any official found to be involved in such incidents will be sacked on the spot* **immediately**, there and then, then and there, straight away, right away, forthwith, instantly, summarily, without delay, without hesitation, at once, that instant, directly; outright; *N. Amer.* in short order; *archaic* straight, straightway, instanter, forthright.
▶ verb **1** *she spotted Iris hovering by the door* **notice**, see, observe, discern, detect, perceive, make out, pick out, distinguish, recognize, identify, locate; catch sight of, glimpse, sight; mark, remark; *Brit. informal* clock; *literary* descry, espy.
2 *her clothes were spotted with grease* **stain**, mark, fleck, speckle, blotch, mottle, smudge, streak, splash, spatter, bespatter; dirty, soil; *informal* splotch, splosh, splodge; *literary* besmirch, smirch.
3 (*archaic*) *his soul was spotted with sin* **sully**, stain, tarnish, blacken, taint, blemish.
4 *it was still spotting with rain* **rain lightly**, drizzle; *Brit.* spit; *N. English* mizzle; *N. Amer.* sprinkle.

spotless ▶ adjective **1** *the kitchen was spotless | a spotless white shirt* **perfectly clean**, ultra-clean, pristine, immaculate, shining, shiny, gleaming, spick and span; freshly laundered, snowy, snowy-white, snow-white, whiter than white; unsoiled, unmarked, unstained; *rare* speckless.
OPPOSITES dirty, filthy.
2 *a spotless reputation* **unblemished**, unsullied, untarnished, untainted, unstained, pure, as pure as the driven snow, whiter than white, lily-white, flawless, immaculate, impeccable, faultless, blameless, guiltless, sinless, unimpeachable, irreproachable, above reproach; innocent, untouched, undefiled, uncorrupted; *informal* squeaky clean.
OPPOSITES impure, tarnished.

spotlight ▶ noun (**the spotlight**) *she was constantly in the spotlight* **the public eye**, the glare of publicity, the limelight; the focus of public attention/interest, the focus of media attention/interest.
▶ verb *the conference spotlighted the strength of his conservative opponents* **focus attention on**, highlight, point up, draw/call attention to, foreground, accentuate, accent, make conspicuous, underline, underscore, give prominence to, throw into relief, turn the spotlight on, bring to the fore, bring home; focus on, zero in on, stress, emphasize.
OPPOSITE play down.

spot on ▶ adjective (*Brit. informal*) *Evert's prediction was spot on* **accurate**, **correct**, right, perfect, exact, unerring, so as to hit the nail on the head; *informal* bang on; *N. Amer. informal* on the money, on the nose.
OPPOSITES wrong, incorrect.

spotted ▶ adjective **1** *the spotted leaves* **mottled**, dappled, dapple, pied, piebald, brindled, brindle, speckled, speckly, flecked, specked, stippled; *informal* splodgy, splotchy; *technical* macular, maculate, maculated, foxed, guttate.
2 *a black-and-white spotted dress* **polka-dot**, spotty, dotted; *informal* dotty.

spotty ▶ adjective **1** (*Brit.*) *his spotty face* **pimply**, pimpled, acned, poor-complexioned; pockmarked, pocky; blotchy, blotched; *informal* zitty; *Scottish informal* plooky.
OPPOSITE clear-complexioned.
2 *a spotty dog | spotty, purply-pink flowers* **spotted**, mottled, speckled, speckly, flecked, specked, stippled; *informal* splodgy, splotchy; *technical*

S

macular, maculate, maculated, foxed, guttate.
3 *a spotty dress* **polka-dot**, spotted, dotted; *informal* dotty.
4 *on the whole the standard of football was spotty* **patchy**, uneven, inconsistent, erratic, fluctuating, irregular, non-uniform.
OPPOSITES consistent, uniform.

spouse ▶ noun **husband**, **wife**, partner, mate, consort; *informal* better half, other half, old man, old woman, old lady, hubby, missis, missus, wifey; *Brit. informal* dutch, trouble and strife, her indoors; *dated* lady; *archaic* helpmate, helpmeet.

spout ▶ verb **1** *lava was spouting from the crater* **spurt**, gush, spew, pour, stream, rush, erupt, surge, shoot, pump, squirt, spray, flow, issue; disgorge, discharge, emit, belch forth.
2 *he began to spout off about the decline of the welfare state* **hold forth**, sound off, go on, talk at length, expatiate, pontificate, declaim, orate, rant, sermonize; *informal* mouth off, speechify, spiel; *rare* perorate.
▶ noun *a tough metal can with a handy pouring spout* **nozzle**, lip, rose; *technical* sparkler, spile.
□ **up the spout** (*Brit. informal*) **1** *my computer's up the spout.* See BROKEN sense 3.
2 *his daughter's up the spout.* See PREGNANT.

sprawl ▶ verb **1** *he sprawled on a sofa in the living room* **stretch out**, lounge, loll, lie, lie down, lie back, recline, drape oneself, be recumbent, be prostrate, be supine, slump, flop, slouch.
2 *gorse and hawthorn sprawled over the hillside* **spread**, stretch, straggle, ramble, trail, spill.

spray[1] ▶ noun **1** *a fine spray of water* **shower**, sprinkling, sprinkle, jet, mist, drizzle, droplets; spume, spindrift; foam, froth; *rare* spoondrift.
2 *Mary took a perfume spray from her handbag* **atomizer**, vaporizer, aerosol, sprinkler; nebulizer; spray gun.
▶ verb **1** *water was sprayed over the ground | spray the plants with sugar water* **sprinkle**, shower, spread in droplets, spatter; scatter, disperse, diffuse; mist; douche; *literary* besprinkle.
2 *water sprayed into the air* **spout**, jet, gush, spurt, shoot, squirt, stream.

spray[2] ▶ noun **1** *a spray of honeysuckle* **sprig**, small stem, twig, branch; *rare* branchlet.
2 *a small spray of yellow roses* **bouquet**, bunch, posy, nosegay, corsage; wreath, garland; buttonhole; flower arrangement; *French* boutonnière; *rare* tussie-mussie.

spread ▶ verb **1** *he fetched the map and spread it out on the table* **lay out**, open out, unfurl, unroll, roll out, shake out; straighten out, fan out; stretch out, extend; *literary* outspread.
OPPOSITE fold up.
2 *the spectacular landscape spread out below* **extend**, stretch, open out, be displayed, be exhibited, be on show; sprawl.
3 *Harry gestured at the untidy papers spread all over his desk* **scatter**, strew, disperse; *literary* bestrew.
4 *disaffection with his policies is spreading* **grow**, increase, escalate, advance, develop, broaden, expand, widen, proliferate, mushroom; *Medicine* metastasize.
5 *Ballard started to spread rumours about him* **disseminate**, circulate, pass on, put about, communicate, diffuse, make public, make known, purvey, broadcast, publicize, propagate, promulgate; repeat; *literary* bruit about/abroad.
OPPOSITE suppress.
6 *she spread cold cream on her face* **smear**, daub, plaster, slather, lather, apply, put; smooth, rub.
7 *a thick slice of bread liberally spread with butter* **cover**, coat, layer, daub, smother; butter.
8 *a row of candles spread a brilliant pool of light* **cast**, diffuse, shed, radiate.
9 (*archaic*) *will you make the dinner while we spread the table?* **set**, lay, arrange.
▶ noun **1** *the spread of learning* **expansion**, proliferation, extension, growth, mushrooming, increase, escalation, buildout, advance, advancement, development; dissemination, diffusion, transmission, propagation.
2 *the male's antlers can attain a spread of six feet* **span**, width, extent, stretch, reach.
3 *the immense spread of the heavens* **expanse**, area, sweep, stretch.
4 *papers on a wide spread of subjects* **range**, span, spectrum, sweep; variety.
5 (*N. Amer.*) *a patchwork spread* **bedspread**, bedcover, cover, coverlet, throw, afghan; *Brit.* eiderdown; *N. Amer.* comforter; *dated* counterpane.
6 (*informal*) *his mother laid on a huge spread* **large**/**elaborate meal**, feast, banquet, repast; *informal* blowout, nosh.

spree ▶ noun **1** *a shopping spree* **unrestrained bout**, orgy; *informal* binge, splurge.
2 *it may stop after one or two drinks or it may go on into a spree* **drinking bout**, debauch; *informal* binge, bender, session, sesh, booze-up, beer-up, souse, drunk, blind; *Scottish informal* skite; *N. Amer. informal* jag, toot; *NZ informal* boozeroo; *Brit. vulgar slang* piss-up; *literary* bacchanal, bacchanalia; *archaic* wassail, fuddle, potation.

sprig ▶ noun *a sprig of lilac* **small stem**, spray, twig, branch; *rare* branchlet.

sprightly ▶ adjective *she was quite sprightly for her age* **lively**, spry, energetic, active, full of life, full of energy, vigorous, spirited, animated, vivacious, playful, jaunty, perky, frisky, agile, nimble; *informal* chipper, sparkly, zippy, zappy, full of vim and vigour, bright-eyed and bushy-tailed, full of beans; *N. Amer. informal* peppy, peart; *N. English informal* wick; *archaic* frolicsome, sportive, as lively/merry as a grig.
OPPOSITES doddering, sluggish, lethargic, inactive.

spring ▶ verb **1** *Gina sprang to her feet | the cat sprang off her lap* **leap**, jump, bound, vault, hop.
2 *the branch sprang back* **fly back**, recoil; kick back; *rare* resile.
3 *some of these feelings spring from fears about death and ageing* **originate from**, have its origins in, derive from, arise from, stem from, emanate from, proceed from, start from, issue from, evolve from, come from.
4 *about fifty men sprang from nowhere and surrounded them* **appear suddenly**, appear unexpectedly, materialize; *informal* pop up.
5 *I'm sorry to spring the news on you like this* **announce suddenly**/**unexpectedly**, present suddenly/unexpectedly, introduce suddenly/unexpectedly, reveal suddenly/unexpectedly.
6 *hotels are springing up all along the coast* **appear**, develop quickly, shoot up, sprout up, come into being, come into existence; proliferate, mushroom.
▶ noun **1** *we're getting married next spring* **springtime**, Eastertide; *literary* springtide, Maytime.
2 *with a sudden spring he leapt on to the table* **leap**, jump, bound, vault, hop; pounce; *rare* saltation.
3 *the mattress has lost its spring* **springiness**, bounciness, bounce, resilience, elasticity, flexibility, stretch, stretchiness, give; *rare* tensility.
4 *there was a new spring in his step* **buoyancy**, bounce, bounciness, energy, liveliness, light-heartedness, jauntiness, sprightliness, confidence.
5 *a mineral spring* **well head**; source; spa, geyser, hot spring, thermal spring, sulphur spring; *literary* well, wellspring, fount.
6 *the springs of his own emotions* **origin**, source, fountainhead, root, roots, basis.
▶ adjective *two days of warm spring weather* **springlike**, vernal.
WORD LINKS
relating to the season of spring **vernal**

springy ▶ adjective **1** *the turf was springy beneath her feet* **elastic**, stretchy, whippy, stretchable, tensile; flexible, bouncy, resilient, cushiony, spongy, rubbery; *rare* tensible.
OPPOSITES hard, stiff, rigid.
2 *he left the room with a springy step* **buoyant**, bouncy, lively, light, light-hearted, carefree, jaunty, sprightly, confident.
OPPOSITE heavy.

sprinkle ▶ verb **1** *he sprinkled water over the towel* **splash**, trickle, spray, shower; spatter.
2 *sprinkle sesame seeds over the top* **scatter**, strew; drizzle; *literary* bestrew.
3 *when the cake is cool, sprinkle it with icing sugar* **dredge**, dust, powder.
4 *the sky was sprinkled with stars* **dot**, stipple, stud, bestud, fleck, speckle, bespeckle, spot, pepper; scatter, cover; *literary* besprinkle.

sprinkling ▶ noun **1** *serve with a sprinkling of nutmeg* **scattering**, sprinkle, scatter, dusting; pinch, dash.
2 *a sprinkling of elderly ladies were making their way to church* **few**, one or two; **handful**, small number, trickle, smattering.

sprint ▶ verb *she sprinted across the square* **run**, race, dart, rush, dash, hasten, hurry, scurry, scuttle, scamper, hare, bolt, bound, fly, gallop, career, charge, pound, shoot, hurtle, speed, streak, whizz, zoom, go like lightning, go hell for leather, go like the wind, flash; *informal* tear, pelt, scoot, hotfoot it, leg it, belt, zip, whip, go like a bat out of hell, step on it, get a move on, get cracking, put on some speed, stir one's stumps; *Brit. informal* hop it, bomb, go like the clappers; *N. Amer. informal* boogie, hightail it, barrel, get the lead out; *informal, dated* cut along; *archaic* post, hie.
OPPOSITE walk.

sprite ▶ noun **fairy**, **elf**, pixie, imp, brownie, puck, peri, goblin, hobgoblin, kelpie, leprechaun; nymph, dryad, sylph, naiad; *literary* faerie, fay; *rare* hob, nix, nixie, elfin.

sprout ▶ verb **1** *the weeds began to sprout* **germinate**, put forth shoots, bud; *rare* burgeon, vegetate, pullulate.
2 *many black cats sprout a few white hairs* **grow**, develop; send forth, put forth.
3 *crocuses sprouted up from the grass | forms of nationalism sprouted as the system collapsed* **spring up**, shoot up, come up, grow, burgeon, develop, appear, mushroom, proliferate.

spruce ▶ adjective *the Captain appeared on deck looking very spruce* **neat**, **well groomed**, well turned out, well dressed, besuited, smart, trim, dapper, elegant, chic; *French* soigné; *informal* natty, snazzy; *N. Amer. informal* spiffy; *dated* as if one had just stepped out of a bandbox; *archaic* trig.
OPPOSITES scruffy, untidy, dishevelled.
▶ verb **1** *the cottage had been spruced up since her last visit* **smarten up**, make smarter, tidy up, make tidy, make neater, neaten up, put in order, clean up; *informal* do up; *Brit. informal* tart up, posh up; *N. Amer. informal* gussy up.
2 *Sarah had spruced herself up* **groom oneself**, tidy oneself, smarten oneself up, freshen oneself up, preen oneself, primp oneself, prink oneself, pretty oneself, beautify oneself; *Brit.* have a wash and brush-up; *informal* titivate oneself, doll oneself up; *Brit. informal* tart oneself up; *archaic*

S

plume oneself, trig oneself.

spry ▶ adjective *he's remarkably spry for a man of his age* **sprightly**, lively, energetic, active, full of life, full of energy, vigorous, spirited, animated, vivacious, playful, jaunty, perky, frisky, agile, nimble; *informal* chipper, sparkly, zippy, zappy, full of vim and vigour, full of beans; *N. Amer. informal* peppy, peart; *N. English informal* wick; *archaic* frolicsome, sportive, as lively as a grig.
OPPOSITES doddery, inactive.

spume ▶ noun *the spume of the white-capped waves | the cork popped and Charles caught the spume in a tall glass* **foam**, froth, surf, spindrift, spray; fizz, effervescence, bubbles, head; lather, suds.

spunk ▶ noun (*informal*) *your sister's got more spunk than you* **courage**, bravery, pluck, pluckiness, courageousness, braveness, valour, mettle, gameness, daring; **determination**, spirit, backbone, strength of character, fortitude, nerve; *informal* guts, grit; *Brit. informal* bottle, ballsiness; *N. Amer. informal* cojones, sand, moxie; *vulgar slang* balls.

spur ▶ noun **1** *he dug his spurs into the horse's flanks* rowel, spike.
2 *the outcome of the election added a further spur to the reform movement* **stimulus, incentive**, encouragement, stimulant, stimulation, inducement, impetus, prod, prompt; incitement, goad; fillip; motive, motivation; *informal* kick up the backside, shot in the arm.
OPPOSITES disincentive, discouragement.
3 *the doctor took an X-ray which showed a spur of bone on the heel* **projection**, spike; protuberance, protrusion; *technical* process.
□ **on the spur of the moment** *his decision had been made on the spur of the moment* **impulsively**, on impulse, impetuously, without thinking, without planning, without premeditation, unpremeditatedly, impromptu, spontaneously, on the spot; suddenly, all of a sudden, unexpectedly, out of the blue.
▶ verb **1** *she spurred her horse towards the hedge* dig one's spurs into, rowel.
2 *the confrontation spurred him into writing a letter of resignation | desperation spurred her on* **stimulate**, give the incentive to, act as a stimulus/incentive to, encourage, prompt, propel, prod, induce, impel, motivate, move, galvanize, inspire, urge, drive, egg on, stir; incite, goad, provoke, prick, sting; *N. Amer. informal* root on, light a fire under.

spurious ▶ adjective *it was possible to arrange retirements on spurious medical grounds* **bogus**, fake, not genuine, specious, false, factitious, counterfeit, fraudulent, trumped-up, sham, mock, feigned, pretended, contrived, fabricated, manufactured, fictitious, make-believe, invalid, fallacious, meretricious; artificial, imitation, simulated, ersatz; *informal* phoney, pseudo, pretend; *Brit. informal* cod; *rare* adulterine.
OPPOSITES authentic, genuine, real.

spurn ▶ verb *he spurned the offer of a drink* **refuse**, decline, say no to, reject, rebuff, scorn, turn down, turn away, repudiate, treat with contempt, disdain, look down one's nose at, despise; snub, slight, disown, jilt, repulse, repel, dismiss, brush off, turn one's back on; give someone the cold shoulder, cold-shoulder, ignore, cut (dead), look right through; *informal* turn one's nose up at, give someone the brush-off, tell someone where to get off, put down, freeze out, stiff-arm, kick in the teeth; *Brit. informal* knock back; *N. Amer. informal* give someone the bum's rush, give someone the brush; *Austral. informal* snout; *informal, dated* give someone the go-by.

CHOOSE THE RIGHT WORD

spurn, reject, refuse, decline
See REFUSE.

spurt ▶ verb *he cut his finger, and blood spurted over the sliced potatoes | Mount Pinatubo spurted clouds of steam and ash into the air* **squirt**, shoot, spray, fountain, jet, erupt; gush, pour, stream, rush, pump, surge, spew, spill, flow, course, well, spring, burst, issue, emanate; disgorge, discharge, emit, belch forth, expel, eject; *Brit. informal* sloosh.
▶ noun **1** *the sudden spurt of water scared the bird away* **squirt**, spray, fountain, jet, spout; gush, outpouring, stream, rush, surge, burst, spill, flow, flood, cascade, torrent.
2 *I felt a spurt of pleasure* **burst**, outburst, fit, bout, attack, rush, spate, surge, flurry, access.
3 *Daisy put on a spurt to hurry down to the river* **burst of speed**, turn of speed, increase of speed, burst of energy, sprint, rush.

spy ▶ noun *the government had planted two spies in the organization* **secret agent**, undercover agent, enemy agent, foreign agent, secret service agent, intelligence agent, double agent, counterspy, industrial spy, fifth columnist, mole, plant, scout; control, handler; *N. Amer.* spook; *informal* snooper; *archaic* intelligencer; *archaic, informal* beagle.
▶ verb **1** *she spied some asparagus on a stall* **notice**, observe, see, spot, sight, catch sight of, glimpse, catch/get a glimpse of, make out, discern, pick out, detect, have sight of; *informal* clap/lay/set eyes on; *literary* espy, behold, descry.
2 *the couple were* **spied on** *by reporters* **observe furtively**, keep under surveillance, watch, keep a watch on, keep an eye on, keep under observation, follow, shadow, trail; *informal* tail; *rare* surveil.
3 *he agreed to spy for the West* **be a spy**, be engaged in spying, gather intelligence, work for the secret service; *informal* snoop.

spying ▶ noun *he was charged with spying for a foreign power* **espionage**, undercover work, cloak-and-dagger activities, surveillance, reconnaissance, intelligence, eavesdropping, infiltration, counter-espionage, counter-intelligence; (*in Japan*) ninjutsu; *informal* bugging, wiretapping, recon.

squabble ▶ noun *there was a squabble over which way they should go* **quarrel**, row, argument, fight, contretemps, disagreement, difference of opinion, dissension, falling-out, dispute, disputation, contention, clash, altercation, shouting match, exchange, war of words; tussle, conflict, fracas, affray, wrangle, tangle, passage of/at arms, battle royal; *Irish, N. Amer., & Austral.* donnybrook; *informal* tiff, set-to, run-in, shindig, shindy, stand-up, spat, scrap, dust-up; *Brit. informal* barney, slanging match, bunfight, ding-dong, bust-up, ruck; *Scottish informal* rammy; *N. Amer. informal* rhubarb; *archaic* broil, miff; *Scottish archaic* threap, collieshangie; *French archaic* tracasserie(s).
▶ verb *the boys were squabbling over a ball* **quarrel**, row, argue, bicker, have a row/fight, fight, fall out, disagree, fail to agree, differ, be at odds, have a misunderstanding, be at variance, have words, dispute, spar, wrangle, bandy words, cross swords, lock horns, be at each other's throats, be at loggerheads; *informal* scrap, go at it hammer and tongs, argufy; *archaic* altercate, chop logic; *Scottish archaic* threap.

squad ▶ noun **1** *an assassination squad* **group**, gang, band, body, crew, team, mob, crowd, outfit, force.
2 *a firing squad* **detachment**, detail, platoon, battery, troop, patrol, squadron, cadre, commando; unit, formation.

squalid ▶ adjective **1** *the squalid, overcrowded prison* **dirty**, filthy, grubby, grimy, mucky, slummy, slum-like, foul, vile, low, poor, sorry, wretched, dismal, dingy, miserable, mean, nasty, seedy, shabby, sordid, sleazy, insalubrious, slovenly, repulsive, disgusting; **neglected**, uncared-for, unmaintained, broken-down, run down, down at heel, dilapidated, ramshackle, tumbledown, gone to rack and ruin, crumbling, decaying; *informal* scruffy, scuzzy, crummy, shambly, grungy, ratty, tacky; *Brit. informal* grotty; *N. Amer. informal* shacky.
OPPOSITES clean, pleasant.
2 *a squalid attempt to save themselves from electoral embarrassment* **improper**, **sordid**, unseemly, unsavoury, sleazy, seedy, seamy, shoddy, vile, foul, tawdry, louche, cheap, base, low, low-minded, nasty, debased, degenerate, depraved, corrupt, dishonest, dishonourable, disreputable, despicable, discreditable, disgraceful, contemptible, ignominious, ignoble, shameful, wretched, abhorrent, odious, abominable, disgusting; *informal* sleazoid.
OPPOSITES proper, decent.

squall ▶ noun *squalls of driving rain* **gust**, storm, blast, flurry, shower, gale, blow, rush, puff, scud; windstorm, thunderstorm.

squally ▶ adjective *conditions were still wintry with squally showers of rain* **stormy**, gusty, gusting, blustery, blustering, windy, breezy, blowy; wild, violent, turbulent, tempestuous, rough, boisterous.

squalor ▶ noun *they lived in squalor* **dirt**, dirtiness, squalidness, filth, filthiness, grubbiness, grime, griminess, muck, muckiness, slumminess, foulness, vileness, poverty, wretchedness, dinginess, meanness, nastiness, seediness, shabbiness, sordidness, sleaziness, insalubrity, slovenliness, repulsiveness; **neglect**, decay, dilapidation; *informal* scruffiness, scuzziness, crumminess, grunge, grunginess, rattiness, tackiness; *Brit. informal* grottiness.
OPPOSITE cleanliness.

S

squander ▶ verb *entrepreneurs squander their profits on expensive cars* **waste**, misspend, misuse, throw away, dissipate, fritter away, run through, lose, lavish, spend recklessly, spend unwisely, make poor use of, be prodigal with, spend money like water; *informal* blow, splurge, pour/throw money down the drain, spend money as if it grows on trees, spend money as if there were no tomorrow, spend money as if it were going out of style; *Brit. informal* blue, splash out.
OPPOSITES manage, make good use of; save.

square ▶ noun **1** *I got it at a shop in the square* town square, village square, market square, marketplace, close, quadrangle, quad, courtyard; arcade, mall, galleria, precinct, forum; (*in Spain*) plaza; (*in Italy*) piazza.
2 (*informal*) *you're such an old square!* **(old) fogey**, conservative, traditionalist, conventionalist, diehard, conformist, bourgeois, museum piece, fossil, dinosaur, troglodyte; *informal* stick-in-the-mud, fuddy-duddy, back number, stuffed shirt; *N. Amer. informal* sobersides.
▶ adjective **1** *a square table* quadrilateral, rectangular, oblong, right-angled, at right angles, perpendicular; straight, straight on, level, parallel, horizontal, upright, vertical, true, plane; cubic.
2 *the sides were square at half-time* **level**, even, drawn, equal, all square, tied, balanced, on a level, in a position of equality; close together, neck and neck, level pegging, nip and tuck, side by side, on a par, evenly matched, with nothing to choose between them; *informal* even-steven(s).
OPPOSITE uneven.

3 *she'd been as square with him as anybody could be* **fair**, **honest**, just, equitable, straight, true, upright, above board, ethical, decent, proper, right and proper, honourable, genuine; *informal* on the level.
OPPOSITE underhand.
4 (*informal*) *children actually prefer their parents to be square* **old-fashioned**, behind the times, out of date, conservative, traditionalist, conventional, diehard, conformist, bourgeois, strait-laced, fogeyish, stuffy, unadventurous, boring; *informal* stick-in-the-mud, fuddy-duddy.
OPPOSITE trendy.
▶ **verb 1** *do those announcements really square with the facts?* **agree**, tally, be in agreement, be consistent, match up, correspond, fit, coincide, accord, conform, be in harmony, harmonize, be consonant, be compatible, be congruous.
2 *his goal squared the match 1–1* **level**, even, make equal.
3 *would you* **square up** *the bill?* **pay**, pay in full, settle, settle up, discharge, clear; defray, liquidate, satisfy, meet, account for, make good.
4 *they were accused of trying to square the press* **bribe**, buy off, buy, corrupt, suborn, give an inducement to; *informal* grease someone's palm, give a backhander to, give a sweetener to.
5 *I'd like you to come, if only to square certain things with your dad* **resolve**, sort out, settle, reach an agreement about, find a solution to, find an answer to, solve, clear up, fix, work out, iron out, smooth over, straighten out, deal with, put right, set right, put to rights, rectify, remedy; *informal* patch up; *archaic* compose.

squash ▶ **verb 1** *wash and squash the cans before depositing them* **crush**, squeeze, flatten, compress, press, smash, distort, mangle, pound, tamp down, trample (down), stamp on; pulp, mash, cream, liquidize, beat, pulverize, macerate.
2 *she squashed some of her clothes inside the bag* **force**, ram, thrust, plunge, push, stick, cram, jam, stuff, pack, compress, squeeze, wedge, press, tamp, pound, drive, hammer, bang.
3 *the proposal was immediately squashed by the Heritage Department* **put an end to**, put a stop to, bring to an end, nip in the bud, scotch, put the lid on; ruin, wreck, scupper, destroy, devastate, smash, shatter, demolish, queer; frustrate, thwart; *informal* put paid to, blow, put the kibosh on, clobber; *Brit. informal* dish.
4 *there was no need to squash him in front of his friends* **humiliate**, humble, mortify, show up, bring down, take down, bring low, demean, expose, show in a bad light, shame, put to shame, make ashamed, discomfit, disgrace, discredit, downgrade, debase, degrade, devalue, dishonour, embarrass, put someone in their place, make a fool of, chasten, subdue, get the better of, have the last laugh on, abash, abase, crush, quash, deflate, flatten, make someone eat humble pie; *informal* put down, settle someone's hash, cut down to size; *N. Amer. informal* make someone eat crow.

squashy ▶ **adjective 1** *a squashy pillow* **springy**, resilient, spongy, soft, pliant, pliable, yielding, supple, elastic, cushiony, compressible, tender, flexible, ductile, malleable, tensile, plastic.
OPPOSITE firm.
2 *the pears have gone a bit squashy* **mushy**, pulpy, pappy, slushy, sloppy, squelchy, squishy, oozy, doughy, semi-liquid, soft; *informal* gooey, gloopy; *Brit. informal* squidgy; *rare* pulpous.

squat ▶ **verb** *I let my back slide down the pillar until I was squatting on the floor* **crouch (down)**, hunker (down), sit on one's haunches, sit on one's heels, sit, bend down, bob down, duck down, hunch, cower, cringe.
▶ **adjective 1** *he was muscular and squat* **stocky**, dumpy, stubby, stumpy, short, thickset, heavily built, sturdy, sturdily built, heavyset, chunky, solid; burly, beefy; cobby; *technical* mesomorphic, pyknic; *Austral./NZ* nuggety; *Brit. informal* fubsy.
2 *a two-storey classical building with a squat tower* **low**, stumpy, short, small, stocky, stunted.

squawk ▶ **verb 1** *the geese flew upriver, squawking* **screech**, squeal, shriek, scream, croak, crow, caw, cluck, clack, cackle, hoot, cry, call.
2 (*informal*) *he is well known for squawking about price-fixing* **complain**, protest, object, express disapproval, raise objections, make/take a stand, put up a fight, kick, take exception, grouse, grouch, grumble, whine, wail, moan, carp, squeal; *informal* kick up a fuss, kick up a stink, gripe, bellyache, bitch, beef, whinge; *N. English informal* mither.
▶ **noun 1** *with a startled squawk the rook flew off* **screech**, squeal, shriek, scream, croak, crow, caw, cluck, clack, cackle, hoot, cry, call.
2 (*informal*) *her plan provoked a loud squawk from her friends* **complaint**, protest, objection, fuss, grouse, grouch, grumble, whine, wail, moan, carp, squeal; *informal* stink, gripe, bellyache, bitch, beef, whinge.

squeak ▶ **noun 1** *the dying squeak of a captured vole or bird* **peep**, cheep, pipe, piping, squeal, tweet, warble, yelp, whimper.
2 *Clare heard the squeak of the garden gate hinge* **screech**, creak, scrape, grate, rasp, jar, groan.
▶ **verb 1** *the rat squeaked* **peep**, cheep, pipe, squeal, tweet, yelp, whimper.
2 *the hinges of the gate squeaked as she opened it* **screech**, creak, scrape, grate, rasp, jar, groan.

squeal ▶ **noun** *they drew up with a squeal of brakes | the harsh squeal of a fox* **screech**, scream, shriek, squawk, howl, cry, wail, squall, yawp, yelp, shrill.
▶ **verb 1** *the taxi squealed to a halt | a dog squealed* **screech**, scream, shriek, squawk, howl, cry, wail, squall, yawp, yelp, shrill.
2 *the bookies only squealed because we beat them* **complain**, protest, object, express disapproval, raise objections, make/take a stand, put up a fight, kick, take exception, grouse, grouch, grumble, whine, wail, moan, carp, squawk; *informal* kick up a fuss, kick up a stink, gripe, bellyache, bitch, beef, whinge; *N. English informal* mither.
3 (*informal*) *who squealed to the police? | drug traffickers get lighter sentences in return for* **squealing on** *their colleagues* **inform (on/against)**, act as an informer, tell tales (on), sneak (on), report, give away, be disloyal (to), sell out, stab in the back; *informal* rat (on), blow the whistle (on), peach (on), snitch (on), put the finger on, sell down the river, stitch up; *Brit. informal* grass (on), split (on), shop; *Scottish informal* clype (on); *N. Amer. informal* rat out, finger, fink on, drop a/the dime on; *Austral. informal* pimp on, pool, put someone's pot on.

squeamish ▶ **adjective 1** *some of us ate the monkey, but the squeamish ones had a tin of corned beef | my husband was always squeamish about nappies* **easily nauseated**, nervous; **(be squeamish about) be put off by**, cannot stand the sight of, … makes one feel sick.
2 *less squeamish nations will not hesitate to sell them arms* **scrupulous**, principled, conscientious, fastidious, particular, punctilious, finicky, fussy, prissy, prudish, strait-laced, honourable, upright, upstanding, high-minded, righteous, right-minded, moral, ethical; *informal* pernickety.

squeeze ▶ **verb 1** *I squeezed the plastic bottle and sent a jet of water out of it* **compress**, press, crush, squash, pinch, nip, grasp, grip, clutch, flatten, knead; mash, pulp; wring, screw.
2 *squeeze the juice from both oranges* **extract**, press, force, express.
3 *Sally squeezed her feet into the sandals* **force**, thrust, stick, cram, ram, jam, stuff, pack, compress, wedge, press, squash, tamp, drive.
4 *we all squeezed into Steve's van* **crowd**, crush, cram, pack, jam, squash, wedge oneself, shove, push, jostle, force one's way, thrust.
5 *the headmaster flung his arms round Robert and squeezed him warmly* **hug**, embrace, cuddle, clasp, crush, clutch, press, enfold, envelop, enclasp, wrap, encircle, fold, take in one's arms, hold tight, hold close, cling to; *archaic* strain.
6 *councils will want to* **squeeze** *as much money* **out of** *taxpayers as they can* **extort**, force, extract, wrest, wring, tear from, milk; *informal* bleed someone of something.
7 (*informal*) *she used the opportunity to squeeze him for information* **pressurize**, pressure, bring pressure to bear on, strong-arm; suck dry, milk, fleece, wring, exploit, impose on; *informal* put the squeeze on, lean on, bleed, put the screws on; *N. Amer. & Austral. informal* put the bite on.
▶ **noun 1** *a squeeze of the trigger | he gave her hand a squeeze* **press**, pinch, nip; grasp, grip, clutch; compression.
2 *Jimmy put an arm around her shoulders and gave her a squeeze* **hug**, embrace, cuddle, clasp, hold.
3 *it was a tight squeeze in the tiny hall* **crush**, jam, squash, press, huddle, tightly packed crowd; congestion.
4 *a squeeze of lemon juice* **drop**, few drops, dash, splash, dribble, trickle, spot, hint, touch, bit.

squint ▶ **verb 1** *the bright sun made them squint* **screw up one's eyes**, narrow one's eyes, look with/through narrowed eyes, peer, blink; *rare* squinny.
2 *he'll need an operation because he squints* **be cross-eyed**, have a squint; *Scottish* be skelly; *technical* suffer from strabismus, be strabismic; *Brit. informal* be boss-eyed.
▶ **noun 1** (*informal*) *we must have another squint at his record card* **look**, glance, peep, peek, glimpse; view, examination, study, inspection, scan, sight; *informal* eyeful, dekko, butcher's, gander, look-see, once-over, shufti, recce; *Austral./NZ informal* geek, squiz.
2 *does he have a squint?* **cross-eyes**; *Brit. informal* boss-eye; *technical* strabismus.

squire ▶ **noun 1** *a country squire* **landowner**, landholder, landlord, lord of the manor, country gentleman.
2 (*historical*) *before him went his squire carrying a banner* **attendant**, courtier, equerry, aide, companion, steward, page boy, servant boy, serving boy, cup-bearer, train-bearer.

squirm ▶ **verb** *I tried to squirm away | he squirmed as he recalled the phrases he had used* **wriggle**, wiggle, writhe, twist, slide, slither, turn, shift, fidget, jiggle, twitch, thresh, flounder, flail, toss and turn; agonize.

squirrel *See centre pages for list of* **Squirrels**
▶ **verb**
□ **squirrel something away** *try to squirrel a little cash away for a rainy day* **save**, put aside, put by, lay by, set aside, lay aside, put to one side, reserve, keep in reserve, preserve, deposit, keep, store, stockpile, accumulate, collect, stock up with/on, heap up, hoard, stow away, cache, garner; *informal* salt away, stash away.

WORD LINKS
relating to squirrels **sciurine**
home **drey**

S

squirt ▶ **verb 1** *this mollusc can squirt a cloud of purple ink into the water | a jet of ink squirted out of the tube* **spurt**, shoot, spray, fountain, jet, erupt; gush, pour, stream, rush, pump, surge, spew; spill, flow, course, well, spring, burst, issue, emanate; disgorge, discharge, emit, belch forth, expel, eject; *Brit. informal* sloosh.
2 *she squirted me with scent* **splash**, wet, spray, shower, spatter, bespatter, splatter, sprinkle; *Scottish & Irish informal* slabber; *literary* besprinkle.
▶ **noun 1** *a squirt of water* **spurt**, jet, spray, fountain, gush, stream, surge, flow.
2 (*informal*) *a little squirt called Ollie Bogwhistle sneaked on me* **impudent person, insignificant person**, gnat, insect; *informal* **pipsqueak**, twerp; *Brit. informal* nerd, johnny, squit, whippersnapper, git, plonker; *Scottish informal* nyaff; *N. Amer. informal* bozo, picayune, pisher, snip, smart mouth; *archaic* malapert, quean; *archaic, informal* dandiprat; *N. Amer. vulgar slang* pissant; (**squirts**) small fry.

stab ▶ **verb 1** *he stabbed him in the stomach* **knife**, run through, skewer, spear, bayonet, gore, spike, stick, impale, transfix, pierce, prick, puncture, penetrate, perforate, gash, slash, cut, tear, scratch, wound, injure; *rare* transpierce.
2 *she stabbed at the earth with a fork* **lunge**, thrust, jab, poke, prod, dig.
□ **stab someone in the back betray**, be disloyal to, be unfaithful to, desert, break one's promise to, double-cross, break faith with, sell out, play false, inform on/against; *informal* tell on, sell down the river, blow the whistle on, squeal on, stitch up, peach on, do the dirty on; *Brit. informal* grass on, shop; *N. Amer. informal* rat out, finger, drop a/the dime on; *Austral. informal* pimp on, pool, put someone's pot on.
▶ **noun 1** *a stab in the leg* **knife wound**, puncture, gash, slash, incision, prick, cut, perforation, wound, injury.
2 *they gesticulated to us using violent stabs into the air* **lunge**, thrust, jab, poke, prod, dig, punch.
3 *little stabs of pain shot through her* **twinge**, pang, ache, throb, spasm, cramp, dart, blaze, prick, flash, thrill, gnawing.
4 (*informal*) *Meredith made a feeble stab at joining in* **attempt**, try, effort, endeavour; guess; *informal* go, shot, crack, bash, whack; *formal* essay.

stability ▶ **noun 1** *parents should check the stability of play equipment* **firmness**, solidity, steadiness, secureness, strength, fastness, stoutness, sturdiness, security, safety.
2 *doubts were raised regarding his mental stability* **balance**, balance of mind, mental health, soundness, rationality, reason, lucidity, lucidness, sense, sanity, saneness, right-mindedness.
3 *the stability of their relationship | price stability* **steadiness**, firmness, sureness, secureness, solidity, strength, durability, lasting nature, enduring nature, constancy, permanence, changelessness, invariability, immutability, indestructibility, reliability, dependability; *rare* lastingness, perdurability, perenniality, imperishability, inalterability, unchangeableness, unchangeability.

stable ▶ **adjective 1** *a very stable tent* **firm**, solid, steady, secure, fixed, strong, fast, stout, sturdy, safe, moored, anchored, stuck down, immovable, well built, well constructed, substantial.
OPPOSITES unstable, rickety.
2 *a stable person* **well balanced**, balanced, sound, mentally sound, of sound mind, sane, normal, right in the head, in possession of all one's faculties, able to think/reason clearly, lucid, clear-headed, rational, coherent, steady, reasonable, sensible, sober, down-to-earth, matter-of-fact, with both one's feet on the ground; *Latin* compos mentis; *informal* all there.
OPPOSITES unstable, unbalanced.
3 *a stable relationship | prices have remained relatively stable* **secure**, solid, strong, steady, firm, sure, steadfast, level, unwavering, unvarying, unfaltering, unfluctuating, unswerving; established, long-lasting, long-lived, deep-rooted, well founded, well grounded, abiding, durable, enduring, lasting, constant, permanent, reliable, dependable, true.
OPPOSITES unstable, rocky, lasting, changeable.

stack ▶ **noun 1** *a stack of boxes* **heap**, pile, mound, mountain, pyramid, mass, store, stockpile, hoard, load, tower, drift, clamp, hack; *N. Amer.* cold deck; *Scottish, Irish, & N. English* rickle; *Scottish* bing.
2 *a good stack of hay* **haystack**, rick, hayrick, stook, mow, haymow, barleymow; *rare* ruck, shock, cock.
3 *there's a stack of cinemas in Leicester Square | there's stacks of work to be done* **a great deal**, a lot, a great/large amount, a large quantity, quantities, plenty, abundance, superabundance, plethora, cornucopia, a wealth, profusion, a mountain, reams; *informal* lots, load, loads, heap, heaps, mass, masses, pile, piles, ocean, oceans, oodles, ton, tons; *Brit. informal* lashings, shedload; *N. Amer. informal* slew, gobs, scads; *Austral./NZ informal* swag; *vulgar slang* shitload.
OPPOSITES few; little.
4 *the main stack belches out clouds of black smoke* **chimney**, factory chimney, chimney stack, smokestack, funnel, exhaust pipe.
5 *Devil's Chimney is actually a sea stack* **pillar**, column; tor, dome, plug, stalagmite; *French* puy.
▶ **verb 1** *Shirley began to stack the plates* **heap (up)**, pile (up), make a heap/pile/stack of; assemble, put together, collect, hoard, store, stockpile.
2 *he spent most of the time stacking shelves* **load**, fill (up), lade, pack, charge, stuff, cram; stock.
OPPOSITE empty.

stadium ▶ **noun arena**, field, ground, pitch; bowl, amphitheatre, coliseum, colosseum, enclosure, ring, dome, astrodome, manège; track, course, racetrack, racecourse, speedway, velodrome; (*in ancient Rome*) circus; *W. Indian* gayelle; *rare* cirque.

staff ▶ **noun 1** *there is a reluctance to take on new staff* **employees**, workers, workforce, personnel, hands, hired hands, labourers, human resources, manpower, labour; office workers, white-collar workers, assistants, secretaries; teachers, lecturers; doctors, nurses; *N. Amer.* interns; *humorous* liveware.
2 *a tall man with a cowboy hat and a walking staff* **stick**, walking stick, cane, crook, crutch, prop.
3 *the miller's wife strikes her husband over the head with a staff* **club**, stick, cudgel, bludgeon, life preserver, shillelagh, baseball bat; truncheon, baton; *N. Amer.* blackjack; *Indian* lathi, danda; *S. African* kierie, knobkerrie, sjambok; *Brit. informal* cosh.
4 *a staff of office* **rod**, tipstaff, mace, wand, sceptre, crozier, verge; *Greek Mythology* caduceus.
▶ **verb** *the departments are staffed by professional civil servants* **man**, people, crew, work, operate, occupy.

stage ▶ **noun 1** *a stage in the development* **phase**, period, juncture, step, point, time, moment, instant, division, level.
2 *the last stage of a race/journey* **part**, section, portion, stretch, phase; leg, lap, circuit.
3 *stand on a stage in the theatre* **platform**, dais, stand, grandstand, staging, apron, rostrum, podium, soapbox, stump; pulpit, box, dock; *Indian* mandapam; *rare* tribune.
4 (**the stage**) *she has written for the stage, television, and film* **(the) theatre**, drama, dramatics, dramatic art, show business, the play, the footlights; *informal* the boards, rep; *rare* thespianism.
5 *Britain is playing a leading role on the international stage* **scene**, setting, context, frame, sphere, field, realm, forum, site, arena, background, backdrop; affairs.
▶ **verb 1** *they recently staged 'The Magic Flute' in a car factory* **put on**, put before the public, present, produce, mount, direct; perform, act, render, give.
2 *the Residents' Association staged a protest march* **organize**, arrange, make arrangements for, coordinate, lay on, put together, fix up, get together; orchestrate, choreograph, be responsible for, be in charge of, direct, run, manage, stage-manage, conduct, administrate, administer, set up, mastermind, engineer; *rare* concert.

stagger ▶ **verb 1** *Sonny took the blow on the temple and staggered sideways* **lurch**, walk unsteadily, reel, sway, teeter, totter, stumble, wobble, move clumsily, weave, flounder, falter, pitch, roll.
2 *I was staggered to find it was six o'clock* **astonish**, amaze, nonplus, startle, astound, surprise, bewilder, stun, flabbergast, shock, shake, stop someone in their tracks, stupefy, leave open-mouthed, take someone's breath away, dumbfound, daze, benumb, confound, disconcert, shatter, take aback, jolt, shake up; *informal* bowl over, knock for six, floor, blow someone's mind, strike dumb.
3 *meetings are staggered throughout the day* **spread (out)**, space (out), time at intervals, overlap.
4 *stagger the screws at each joint* **alternate**, step, arrange in a zigzag.

staggered ▶ **adjective** *she was staggered to hear she had a rival* **astonished**, astounded, amazed, stunned, thunderstruck, shattered, flabbergasted, nonplussed, taken aback, startled, surprised, bewildered, shocked, shaken, stupefied, open-mouthed; dumbfounded, dumbstruck, speechless, at a loss for words; dazed, benumbed, confounded, disconcerted, shaken up; *informal* bowled over, knocked for six, floored, flummoxed, caught on the hop, caught on the wrong foot, unable to believe one's eyes/ears; *Brit. informal* gobsmacked.

stagnant ▶ **adjective 1** *stagnant water* **still**, motionless, immobile, inert, lifeless, dead, standing, slack, static, stationary; **foul**, stale, dirty, filthy, putrid, putrefied, brackish.
OPPOSITES flowing, running; fresh.
2 *a stagnant economy* **inactive**, sluggish, slow, slow-moving, lethargic, static, flat, depressed, quiet, dull, declining, moribund, dying, dead, dormant, stagnating.
OPPOSITES active, vibrant.

stagnate ▶ **verb 1** *there should be no points in the system where cleaning solutions can stagnate* **stop flowing**, become stagnant, become trapped; stand; become foul, become stale; fester, putrefy.
OPPOSITE flow.
2 *imports rose while exports stagnated* **become stagnant**, do nothing, stand still, be sluggish, lie dormant, be inert, languish, decline, deteriorate, fall.
OPPOSITES rise, boom.

staid ▶ **adjective** *staid old ladies* **sedate**, respectable, quiet, serious, serious-minded, steady, conventional, traditional, unadventurous, unenterprising, set in one's ways; grave, solemn, severe, sombre, sober, proper, decorous, formal; stuffy, prim, demure, prissy, stiff; *informal*

S

starchy, uptight, stick-in-the-mud.
OPPOSITES frivolous, daring, informal.

stain ▶ verb **1** *her clothing was stained with blood* **discolour**, blemish, soil, mark, muddy, spot, spatter, splatter, smear, splash, smudge, blotch, blacken; dirty, get/make dirty, get/make filthy, sully, spoil, defile, pollute, contaminate, foul, befoul, grime, begrime; *literary* besmirch.
2 *the awful events would unfairly stain the city's reputation* **damage**, injure, harm, sully, soil, blacken, tarnish, taint, besmirch, blemish, defile, blot, smear, bring discredit to, dishonour, drag through the mud.
3 *wood can always be stained to a darker shade* **colour**, tint, dye, tinge, shade, pigment; varnish, paint, colour-wash.
▶ noun **1** *there were mud stains on my shoes* **mark**, spot, spatter, splatter, blotch, blemish, smudge, smear; dirt, foxing.
2 *he has been discharged without a stain on his character* **blemish**, injury, taint, blot, blot on one's escutcheon, slur, smear, discredit, dishonour, stigma; damage.
3 *an exterior type of wood stain* **tint**, colour, dye, tinge, shade, pigment, colourant; varnish, paint, colour wash.

stake[1] ▶ noun *he was replacing broken stakes in a barbed-wire fence* **post**, pole, stick, spike, upright, support, prop, strut, stave, pale, paling, picket, pile, piling, stanchion, shaft, cane, beanpole, rod, mast; *historical* palisade.
▶ verb **1** *the plants have to be staked* **prop up**, tie up, tether, support, hold up, bolster up, brace, buttress, reinforce, truss, stay.
2 *British governments staked their claim to disputed areas by formalizing imperial control* **assert**, declare, proclaim, state, make, lay, establish, put on record, put in.
□ **stake something out 1** *the slaves were made to stake out canefields in the rainforest* **mark off**, mark out, demarcate, mark the boundaries/limits of, outline, measure out, define, delimit, fence off, section off, close off, shut off, cordon off, bound, circumscribe.
2 (*informal*) *they'd staked out Culley's flat for half a day* **observe**, watch, keep an eye on, keep under observation, keep watch on, keep under surveillance, survey, monitor, keep under scrutiny, watch like a hawk, keep a weather eye on, spy on, check out; *informal* keep tabs on, keep a tab on, case, keep a beady eye on; *rare* surveil.

stake[2] ▶ noun **1** *if the horse wins, you get five times your stake back* **bet**, wager, ante, pledge, hazard.
2 *they are racing for record stakes this year* **prize money**, purse, pot, winnings.
3 *he had just knocked another competitor out of the promotion stakes* **competition**, contest, battle, challenge, rivalry, race, running, struggle, scramble.
4 *he retains a 40% stake in the business* **share**, interest, financial interest, investment, involvement, concern.
▶ verb *one gambler staked everything he'd got and lost* **bet**, wager, place a bet of, lay, put on, gamble, pledge, chance, venture, risk, hazard.

stale ▶ adjective **1** *stale bread | stale cheese* **dry**, dried out, hard, hardened, old, past its best, past its sell-by date; off, mouldy, rotten, decayed, unfresh, rancid, rank.
OPPOSITE fresh.
2 *stale air* **stuffy**, close, musty, fusty, unfresh, stagnant, frowzy; *Brit.* frowsty, fuggy.
3 *stale beer* **flat**, sour, insipid, tasteless, turned, spoiled, off.
4 *the jokes are a bit stale for real belly laughs* **hackneyed**, tired, worn out, overworked, threadbare, warmed-up, banal, trite, stock, stereotyped, clichéd, run-of-the-mill, commonplace, platitudinous, unoriginal, unimaginative, uninspired, flat; out of date, outdated, outmoded, passé, archaic, obsolete, defunct, antiquated; *N. Amer.* warmed-over; *informal* old hat, corny, out of the ark, played out, past their sell-by date.
OPPOSITE original.

CHOOSE THE RIGHT WORD

stale, trite, hackneyed
See TRITE.

stalemate ▶ noun *the talks had reached a stalemate* **deadlock**, impasse, standstill, dead end, stand-off, draw, tie, dead heat.

stalk[1] ▶ noun *the stalk of a plant* **stem**, shoot, trunk, stock, cane, bine, bent, haulm, straw, reed; branch, bough, twig; *technical* pedicel, peduncle, petiole, phyllode, scape, seta, stipe, caudex, axis.

WORD LINKS
relating to stalks **cauline**

stalk[2] ▶ verb **1** *he noticed a stoat stalking a rabbit* **creep up on**, trail, follow, shadow, track down, go after, be after, dog, hound, course, hunt, pursue, chase, give chase to, run after; *informal* tail.
2 *without another word she turned and stalked out* **strut**, stride, march, flounce, storm, stomp, sweep, swagger, prance.

stall ▶ noun **1** *a market stall* **stand**, table, counter, booth, kiosk, compartment.
2 *he hauled the animal out of the stall* **pen**, coop, sty, corral, enclosure, compartment, cubicle.
3 (**stalls**) (*Brit.*) *they sat in the stalls of the empty theatre N. Amer.* orchestra, parterre.
▶ verb **1** *the launching of the agency has been stalled for more than a year* **obstruct**, impede, interfere with, hinder, hamper, block, interrupt, hold up, hold back, stand in the way of, frustrate, thwart, baulk, inhibit, hamstring, sabotage, encumber, restrain, slow, slow down, retard, delay, stonewall, forestall, arrest, check, stop, halt, stay, derail, restrict, limit, curb, put a brake on, bridle, fetter, shackle; *informal* stymie; *N. Amer. informal* bork; *rare* trammel.
2 *quit stalling and give me the money* **use delaying tactics**, play for time, temporize, gain time, hang back, hang fire, hold back, procrastinate, hedge, beat about the bush, drag one's feet, delay, filibuster, stonewall.
3 *stall him until I've had time to take a look* **delay**, divert, distract; **hold off**, stave off, fend off, keep off, ward off, keep at bay, keep at arm's length.

stalwart ▶ adjective *a stalwart supporter of the cause* **staunch**, loyal, faithful, committed, devoted, dedicated, dependable, reliable, steady, constant, trusty, hard-working, vigorous, stable, firm, steadfast, redoubtable, resolute, unswerving, unwavering, unhesitating, unfaltering.
OPPOSITES disloyal, unfaithful, unreliable.

stamina ▶ noun *rowing is ideal for building stamina* **endurance**, staying power, indefatigability, tirelessness, resistance, resilience, fortitude, strength, vigour, energy, staunchness, steadfastness, robustness, toughness, determination, tenacity, perseverance; *informal* grit.

stammer ▶ verb *he always began to stammer when he was under pressure* **stutter**, speak haltingly, stumble over one's words, hesitate, falter, fumble for words, pause, halt, mumble, splutter.
▶ noun *a rather insecure young man with a slight stammer* **stutter**, speech impediment, speech defect.

stamp ▶ verb **1** *he threw his cigarette down and* ***stamped on*** *it* **trample**, step, tread, tramp; **crush**, squash, flatten.
2 *John stamped off, muttering* **stomp**, stump, clomp, clump, tramp, thunder, lumber, trudge.
3 *the binder would stamp his name on the inside edge of a front or back cover* **imprint**, print, impress, punch, inscribe, engrave, chase, etch, carve, emboss, brand, frank, mark, label.
4 *the date was stamped indelibly on his memory* **fix**, inscribe, etch, carve, imprint, impress, register.
5 *his style stamps him as a player to watch* **identify**, characterize, brand, distinguish, mark out, set apart, single out, designate, categorize, classify.
□ **stamp something out** *urgent action is required to stamp out corruption* **put an end to**, put a stop to, end, finish, get rid of, crush, put down, check, crack down on, weed out, curb, nip in the bud, scotch, squash, quash, quell, subdue, suppress, repress, quench, extinguish, stifle, abolish, eliminate, eradicate, terminate, beat, overcome, defeat, destroy, demolish, annihilate, wipe out, extirpate; *informal* squelch, put the kibosh on, clobber.
OPPOSITES bring in, introduce.
▶ noun **1** *the whole project has the stamp of authority* **mark**, hallmark, indication, label, brand, tag, badge, characteristics, peculiarity, attribute, sign, seal, sure sign, telltale sign, quality, smack, smell, savour, air.
2 *the new prior was of a very different stamp from his predecessor* **type**, kind, sort, variety, class, category, classification, style, description, condition, calibre, status, quality, nature, manner; design, shape, form, pattern, group, set, bracket, genre, species, rank, genus, family, order, breed, race, strain, generation, vintage, make, model, brand, ilk, kidney, cast, grain, mould; *N. Amer.* stripe.

stamp collecting ▶ noun **philately**; *archaic* timbrophily, timbromania.

stampede ▶ noun *she didn't dare ride fast in case she startled the cows into a stampede* **charge**, panic, rush, flight, rout, scattering.
▶ verb *the nearby sheep stampeded as if they sensed impending danger* **bolt**, charge, rush, flee, take flight, dash, race, career, sweep, run.

stance ▶ noun **1** *the kick is performed by starting from a natural stance and bringing up the right leg* **posture**, body position, pose, attitude, bearing.
2 *it is possible for individual teachers to take a more liberal stance* **attitude**, stand, point of view, viewpoint, opinion, way of thinking, outlook, standpoint, posture, position, angle, perspective, approach, slant, thinking, line, policy, thoughts, ideas, sentiments, feelings.

stand ▶ verb **1** *Lionel stood in the doorway* **be on one's feet**, be upright, be erect, be vertical.
OPPOSITES sit, lie.
2 *the two men* ***stood up*** *and shook hands* **rise**, rise to one's feet, get to one's feet, get up, straighten up, pick oneself up, find one's feet, be upstanding; *literary* arise.
OPPOSITES sit down, lie down.
3 *a village once stood there* **be**, be situated, be located, be positioned, be set, be found, be sited, be established, be perched, sit, perch, nestle.
4 *he stood the book on edge* **put**, set, set up, erect, upend, place, position, locate, situate, prop, lean, plant, stick, install, arrange, dispose, deposit; *informal* plonk, park.

5 *my decision stands* **remain in force**, remain valid, remain effective, remain operative, remain in operation, hold, hold good, obtain, apply, prevail, reign, rule, hold sway, be the case, exist, be in use.
6 *his heart could not stand the strain* **withstand**, endure, bear, put up with, take, cope with, handle, sustain, resist, stand up to.
7 (informal) *I can't stand brandy* **endure**, tolerate, bear, put up with, take, abide, suffer, support, brook, countenance, face; informal stick, swallow, stomach, hack, wear.

□ **stand by** *two battalions were on their way, and a third was standing by* **wait**, be prepared, be in (a state of) readiness, be ready for action, be on full alert, be at battle stations, wait in the wings.
OPPOSITE stand down.

□ **stand by someone/something 1** *she had stood by him during his years in prison* **remain/be loyal to**, stand up for, support, give one's support to, be supportive of, back, back up, give one's backing to, uphold, defend, come to the defence of, stick up for, champion, take someone's part, take the side of, side with.
OPPOSITE abandon.
2 *the government must stand by its pledges* **abide by**, keep (to), adhere to, hold to, stick to, observe, heed, comply with, act in accordance with.
OPPOSITE go back on.

□ **stand down** *no further action was required and all units stood down* **relax**, stand easy, come off full alert.
OPPOSITE stand by.

□ **stand for 1** *BBC stands for British Broadcasting Corporation* **mean**, be an abbreviation of, represent, signify, denote, indicate, correspond to, be equivalent to, symbolize; literary betoken.
2 (informal) *I won't stand for any nonsense* **put up with**, endure, tolerate, allow, accept, take, abide, suffer, support, brook, countenance; informal stick, swallow, stomach, hack, wear.
3 *we stand for animal welfare* **advocate**, champion, uphold, defend, stand up for, support, be in favour of, promote, recommend, urge, back, endorse, sponsor, espouse, push for, work for, campaign for.
OPPOSITE oppose.

□ **stand in** *I'll stand in as coach | Brown* **stood in for** *the injured Simpson* **deputize**, act, act as deputy, substitute, act as substitute, act as stand-in, fill in, sit in, do duty, take over, act as understudy, act as locum, do a locum, be a proxy, cover, provide cover, hold the fort, step into the breach; take the place of, do something in someone's place/stead, replace, relieve, take over from, understudy; informal sub, fill someone's shoes/boots, step into someone's shoes/boots; N. Amer. pinch-hit.

□ **stand out 1** *the veins in his neck stood out* **project**, stick out, bulge (out), protrude, jut out, jut, extend, poke out, obtrude; archaic protuberate.
OPPOSITE lie flat.
2 *in that dress she stood out in the crowd* **be noticeable**, be noticed, be visible, be seen, be obvious, be conspicuous, stick out, be striking, be distinctive, be prominent, attract attention, catch the eye, leap out, show up; informal stick/stand out a mile, stick/stand out like a sore thumb.
OPPOSITE be inconspicuous.

□ **stand up** *he has no proof that would stand up in court* **remain/be valid**, be sound, be plausible, hold water, hold up, stand questioning, survive investigation, bear examination, be verifiable, be provable, ring true, be convincing.
OPPOSITE fall down.

□ **stand someone up** *she threw eggs over his car after he stood her up* **fail to keep a date with**, fail to meet, fail to keep an appointment with, fail to turn up for, jilt, let down.

□ **stand up for someone/something** *we should stand up for our great tradition of parliamentary democracy* **remain/be loyal to**, stand by, support, give one's support to, be supportive of, back, back up, give one's backing to, uphold, defend, come to the defence of, stick up for, champion, take someone's part, take the side of, side with.
OPPOSITE abandon.

□ **stand up to someone/something 1** *she had the courage of her convictions and stood up to her parents* **defy**, confront, challenge, oppose openly, resist, show resistance to, brave, take on, put up a fight against, take a stand against.
OPPOSITE give in to.
2 *the old house has stood up to the war* **withstand**, survive, come through (unscathed), outlast, outlive, weather, ride out.
OPPOSITE succumb to.

▶ **noun 1** *the party's tough stand on immigration* **attitude**, stance, point of view, viewpoint, opinion, way of thinking, outlook, standpoint, posture, position, angle, perspective, approach, slant, thinking, policy, line, thoughts, ideas, sentiments, feelings.
2 *he maintained his stand against tyranny* **opposition to**, resistance to, objection to, defensive position against, hostility to, animosity towards, disapproval of.
3 *a large mirror on a stand* **base**, support, mounting, platform, rest, plinth, bottom; tripod, rack, trivet, bracket, frame, case, shelf, gripper.
4 *a beer stand* **stall**, booth, kiosk.
5 *a taxi stand* **rank**, station, park, parking place, place, bay.
6 *the train drew to a stand by the signal box* **stop**, halt, standstill, dead stop.
7 *a stand of trees* **copse**, spinney, thicket, grove, coppice, wood; rare boscage.

standard ▶ **noun 1** *the standard of work is very good* **quality**, level, grade, degree, worth, calibre, merit, excellence.
2 *half the beaches fail to comply with European standards* **guideline**, norm, yardstick, benchmark, gauge, measure, criterion, guide, touchstone, model, pattern, example, exemplar, paradigm, ideal, archetype, specification, requirement, rule, principle, law, canon.
3 *offenders against society's standards are punished* **principle**, rule of living; (**standards**) code of behaviour, code of honour, morals, scruples, ethics, ideals.
4 *the raising of the regiment's standard will be a particularly poignant moment* **flag**, banner, pennant, pennon, streamer, ensign, colour(s), banderole; Brit. pendant; Nautical burgee; (in ancient Rome) vexillum; rare gonfalon, guidon, labarum.
▶ **adjective 1** *the standard rate of income tax* **normal**, usual, typical, stock, common, ordinary, customary, conventional, habitual, accustomed, expected, wonted, everyday, regular, routine, day-to-day, daily, established, settled, set, fixed, traditional, quotidian, prevailing.
OPPOSITES unusual, special.
2 *this book will certainly become the standard work on the subject* **definitive**, established, classic, recognized, approved, accepted, authoritative, most reliable, most complete, exhaustive, official.

standardize ▶ **verb** *they attempted to standardize the names of the plants they were growing* **systematize**, make consistent, make uniform, make comparable, regulate, normalize, bring into line, equalize; homogenize, assimilate, regiment, mass-produce, stereotype; rare methodize.

stand-in ▶ **noun** *Davies is the obvious stand-in for the injured Cartwright* **substitute**, replacement, reserve, representative, deputy, surrogate, lieutenant, second, second string, proxy, understudy, double, locum, supply, fill-in, cover, relief, stopgap, standby; informal temp; Latin locum tenens; N. Amer. informal pinch-hitter.
▶ **adjective** *a stand-in goalkeeper* **substitute**, replacement, reserve, deputy, second-string, fill-in, stopgap, supply, surrogate, relief, acting, temporary, provisional, caretaker; N. Amer. informal pinch-hitting.

standing ▶ **noun 1** *his standing in the community* **status**, rank, ranking, position, social position, station, level, footing, place; repute, reputation, estimation, stature; archaic condition, degree, report.
2 *the departmental records officer was a person of some standing* **seniority**, rank, eminence, prominence, prestige, reputation, good reputation, repute, stature, esteem, illustriousness, importance, account, consequence, influence, weight, sway, distinction, renown, note, notability, noteworthiness; informal clout; dated mark.
3 *a squabble of long standing* **duration**, existence, continuance, endurance, length of time, life, validity.
▶ **adjective 1** *standing stones* **upright**, erect, vertical, plumb, upended, on end, rearing, straight (up and down), perpendicular; on one's feet; not yet reaped; Heraldry rampant.
OPPOSITES flat, lying down, seated.
2 *standing water* **stagnant**, still, motionless, immobile, inert, lifeless, dead, slack, static, stationary.
OPPOSITE flowing.
3 *a standing invitation* **permanent**, perpetual, everlasting, continuing, abiding, constant, fixed, indefinite, open-ended; regular, repeated.
OPPOSITES temporary, occasional.

stand-off ▶ **noun** *Europe has shown that it is possible to live with a nuclear stand-off* **deadlock**, stalemate, impasse, standstill, dead end, draw, tie, dead heat.

stand-offish ▶ **adjective** (informal) *an arrogant, stand-offish prig* **aloof**, distant, remote, detached, impersonal, withdrawn, reserved, uncommunicative, unforthcoming, unapproachable, unfriendly, unsociable, cool, chilly, cold, haughty, disdainful, uninvolved, unresponsive, indifferent, unconcerned, preoccupied, abstracted; introspective, introvert, introverted; rare Olympian.
OPPOSITES friendly, approachable, sociable.

standpoint ▶ **noun** *she writes on religion from the standpoint of a believer* **point of view**, viewpoint, vantage point, attitude, stance, stand, view, opinion, position, way of thinking, frame of mind, outlook, perspective, angle, slant.

standstill ▶ **noun** *the traffic came to a standstill* **halt**, stop, dead stop, stand.

staple ▶ **adjective** *rice was the staple crop grown in most villages* **main**, principal, chief, major, primary, leading, foremost, first, most important, predominant, dominant, (most) prominent, key, crucial, vital, indispensable, essential, basic, fundamental, standard, critical, pivotal, prime, central, premier; informal number-one.

star *See centre pages for list of* **Star Types**
▶ **noun 1** *the sky was full of stars* **celestial body**, heavenly body, sun; asteroid, planet, planetoid; literary orb.
2 (**stars**) *what do my stars say?* **horoscope**, forecast, augury; dated nativity.
3 *the stars of the film* **principal**, leading lady, leading man, lead, female

S

lead, male lead, hero, heroine.
OPPOSITE extra.
4 *a star of the world of chess* **celebrity**, superstar, name, big name, famous name, household name, somebody, someone, lion, leading light, public figure, important person, VIP, personality, personage, notability, dignitary, worthy, grandee, luminary, panjandrum; *informal* celeb, bigwig, big shot, big noise, big cheese, big gun, big fish, biggie, heavy, megastar; *Brit. informal* nob; *N. Amer. informal* kahuna, macher, high muckamuck, high muckety-muck.
OPPOSITE nobody.
▶ **adjective 1** *Elinor was a star pupil* **brilliant**, talented, gifted, able, bright, brainy, clever, masterly, consummate, precocious.
OPPOSITE poor.
2 *the star attraction* **top**, leading, best, greatest, foremost, major, pre-eminent, champion.
OPPOSITE insignificant.

WORD LINKS

relating to stars	**astral, sidereal, stellar**
related prefixes	**astro- (e.g. *astrophysics*), sidero- (e.g. *siderostat*)**
study of stars	**astronomy**
measurement of stars	**astrometry**
describing and mapping of stars	**uranography**

starchy ▶ **adjective** (*informal*) *the chairman of the area board had a rather starchy personality* **staid**, sedate, sober, stiff, reserved, impersonal, formal, pompous, prim, priggish, fogeyish, strait-laced, conformist, conventional, conservative, old-fashioned, of the old school; stodgy, stuffy, boring, dull, dreary, uninteresting; *informal* square, straight, fuddy-duddy, stick-in-the-mud, uptight.

stare ▶ **verb** *he stared at her in amazement* **gaze**, gape, goggle, gawk, glare, ogle, leer, peer, look fixedly, look vacantly; study, survey, observe, watch closely, eyeball, outstare; *informal* rubberneck; *Brit. informal* gawp.
□ **stare someone in the face** *the solution was staring him in the face* **be obvious**, be clear, be plain, be plain to see, be crystal clear, be evident, be apparent, be manifest, be patent, be conspicuous, be prominent, be transparent, be clear-cut, be palpable, be unmistakable, be indisputable, be self-evident, be undeniable, be as plain as a pikestaff, be writ large, be written all over one, be as clear as day, be blinding, be inescapable; *informal* be as plain as the nose on one's face, be standing/sticking out like a sore thumb, be standing/sticking out a mile, be right under one's nose.

stark ▶ **adjective 1** *the ridge formed a stark silhouette against the sky | the crisp white shirt was a stark contrast to his weather-beaten tan* **sharply delineated**, sharp, sharply defined, well focused, crisp, distinct, obvious, evident, clear, clear-cut, graphic, striking.
OPPOSITES fuzzy, indistinct.
2 *a stark landscape* **desolate**, bare, barren, arid, vacant, empty, forsaken, godforsaken, bleak, dreary, gloomy, sombre, depressing, cheerless, joyless, uninviting, miserable, grim, harsh, oppressive, merciless; *literary* drear.
OPPOSITE pleasant.
3 *an upright chair was the only furniture in the stark room* **austere**, severe, bleak, plain, simple, bare, unadorned, unembellished, undecorated, uncomfortable.
OPPOSITES comfortable; ornate.
4 *he came running back in stark terror* **sheer**, utter, complete, absolute, total, pure, perfect, positive, downright, out-and-out, outright; thorough, thoroughgoing, through and through, consummate, surpassing, veritable, rank, unequivocal, undeniable, unqualified, unmitigated, unalloyed, unadulterated, unmixed.
5 *the stark fact is that the societies simply do not have the funds* **blunt**, bald, bare, simple, straightforward, basic, plain, unadorned, unembellished, unvarnished, harsh, grim.
OPPOSITE disguised.
▶ **adverb** *he was stark naked | have you gone stark staring mad?* **completely**, totally, utterly, absolutely, downright, dead, entirely, wholly, fully, quite, altogether, simply, thoroughly, truly.

start ▶ **verb 1** *the meeting starts at 7.45* **begin**, get under way, go ahead, get going; *informal* kick off; *formal* commence.
OPPOSITE finish.
2 *this was how her illness had started* **come into being**, begin, be born, come into existence, appear, arrive, come forth, emerge, erupt, burst out, arise, originate, break, unfold, develop, crop up, first see the light of day; *formal* commence.
OPPOSITES end, clear up.
3 *I'm starting a campaign to get the law changed* **establish**, set up, found, lay the foundations of, lay the cornerstone of, lay the first stone of, sow the seeds of, create, bring into being, institute, initiate, inaugurate, introduce, open, begin, launch, float, kick-start, get something off the ground, get something going, get something moving, get something working, get something functioning, activate, originate, pioneer, organize, mastermind, embark on, make a start on, tackle, set about; *informal* kick something off.
OPPOSITES end, wind up.
4 *we had better start now if we are going to finish the job in time* **make a start**, begin, make a beginning, take the first step, lay the first stone, make the first move, get going, go ahead, set things moving, buckle to/down, turn to, put one's shoulder to the wheel, put one's hand to the plough, start/get/set the ball rolling; *informal* get moving, get cracking, get stuck in, get down to it, get to it, get down to business, get one's finger out, get the show on the road, take the plunge, kick off, pitch in, get off one's backside, fire away; *Brit. informal* get weaving; *formal* commence.
OPPOSITES stop; hang about; give up.
5 *Yanto started out across the sand at a brisk pace* **set off**, set out, start out, set forth, begin one's journey, get on the road, depart, leave, get under way, make a start, sally forth, embark, sail; *informal* hit the road, hit the trail, push off; *archaic* set forward.
OPPOSITES arrive; stay.
6 *you can start up the machine with the footswitch* **activate**, set in motion, switch on, turn on, fire up; energize, actuate, set off, start off, get/set something going/moving, start something functioning, start something operating, kick-start.
OPPOSITES stop, close down.
7 *the machine started up* **begin working**, start functioning, get going, start operating.
OPPOSITE stop.
8 *'Oh my!' she said, starting* **flinch**, **jerk**, jump, twitch, recoil, shrink, blench, wince, shy.
9 (*literary*) *she had seen Meg start suddenly from the thicket* **jump**, leap, spring, bound, dash, charge, pounce, dive, rush, dart.
▶ **noun 1** *we were present at the start of the event* **beginning**, inception, onset, emergence, (first) appearance, arrival, eruption, dawn, birth; establishment, foundation, institution, origination, inauguration, induction, creation, opening, launch, float, floating; *informal* kick-off; *formal* commencement.
2 *that was the start of the trouble* **origin**, source, root, starting point, germ, seeds, beginning, genesis; **cause**, reason, motivation, motive; *Latin* fons et origo; *literary* fountainhead, wellspring, fount.
3 *I gave them a quarter of an hour's start* **lead**, head start, advantage, advantageous position.
4 *they have worked hard to give their children a start in life* **advantageous beginning**, flying start, opening, opportunity, chance, helping hand, encouragement, lift, assistance, support, boost, kick-start; *informal* break, leg up.
5 *she awoke with a start* **jerk**, twitch, flinch, wince, spasm, convulsion, jump.

startle ▶ **verb** *a sudden sound in the doorway startled her | he was startled to see a column of smoke* **surprise**, **frighten**, scare, alarm, give someone a shock, give someone a fright, give someone a jolt, make someone jump; **perturb**, unsettle, agitate, disturb, disconcert, disquiet; *informal* give someone a turn, make someone jump out of their skin, flabbergast.
OPPOSITE put at ease.

CHOOSE THE RIGHT WORD

startle, frighten, scare
See FRIGHTEN.

startling ▶ **adjective** *startling news awaited him at Naples* **surprising**, astonishing, amazing, unexpected, unforeseen, staggering, shocking, stunning; extraordinary, remarkable, dramatic; **disturbing**, unsettling, perturbing, disconcerting, disquieting; **frightening**, alarming, scary.
OPPOSITES predictable, ordinary.

starvation ▶ **noun** *half of the country's people face starvation as a result of the civil war* **extreme hunger**, lack of food, famine, want, undernourishment, malnourishment, fasting; deprivation of food; death from lack of food.

starving ▶ **adjective** *she devotes her energies to helping the world's starving children | I'm usually starving by lunchtime* **dying of hunger**, dying from lack of food, faint from lack of food, deprived of food, undernourished, malnourished, starved, half-starved, unfed; very hungry, ravenous, famished, empty, hollow; fasting; (**be starving**) be hungry; *informal* could eat a horse.
OPPOSITES well fed, full.

stash (*informal*) ▶ **verb** *he gathered up his things and stashed them away | he had money stashed away in overseas accounts* **store**, stow, pack, load, cache, garner, hide, conceal, secrete; hoard, put aside, set aside, put by, lay by, lay aside, save, stockpile, keep in reserve, reserve, deposit, keep, put by for a rainy day; *informal* salt away, squirrel away.
▶ **noun** *the thieves had never found my small stash of money* **cache**, hoard, stock, stockpile, store, supply, accumulation, collection, reserve, fund, pool; *rare* amassment.

state[1] ▶ **noun 1** *the current state of the UK economy* **condition**, shape, situation, circumstances, state of affairs, position; predicament, plight.
2 *she is in no state to make decisions* **mood**, humour, temper, disposition,

S

spirits, morale, state of mind, emotional state, frame of mind, attitude; condition, shape.
3 *don't get into a state* **fluster**, flutter, frenzy, fever, fret, panic, state of agitation, state of anxiety, nervous state, distressed state; *informal* flap, tizzy, tiz-woz, twitter, dither, stew, sweat; *N. Amer. informal* twit.
4 (*informal*) *your room is in a state* **untidiness**, **mess**, untidy state, chaos, disorder, disarray, disorganization, confusion, clutter, muddle, heap, shambles, tangle, mishmash; turmoil; *informal* muck.
5 *the states that comprise the EC* **country**, nation, land, sovereign state, nation state, kingdom, empire, republic, confederation, federation, body politic, commonwealth, power, world power, superpower, polity, domain, territory; fatherland, motherland; *Law* realm; *Latin* res publica.
6 *a federation of six states* **province**, federal state, region, territory, canton, department, county, area, district, sector, zone; *Brit.* shire.
7 *the power of the state should not be used to curtail individual liberty* **government**, parliament, the administration, the regime, the authorities, the council, the Establishment.
▶ **adjective** *the President made a state visit to China* **ceremonial**, official, formal, governmental, national, public.
OPPOSITES unofficial, private, informal.

state[2] ▶ **verb** *people will be invited to state their views* **express**, voice, utter, say, tell, declare, affirm, assert, aver, announce, make known, communicate, reveal, disclose, divulge, give out, give voice to, pronounce, articulate, enunciate, proclaim, present, expound, preach, promulgate, publish, broadcast; set out, set down, frame, formulate, spell out, be specific about; *informal* come out with; *rare* asseverate.

stated ▶ **adjective** *routine health checks at stated intervals | the stated aim of the programme* **set**, fixed, settled, agreed, declared, determined, approved, authorized, accredited, ruled, ordained, designated, laid down; **claimed**, official, supposed, professed, alleged.
OPPOSITES undefined, irregular; tacit; actual.

stately ▶ **adjective** *a stately procession* **dignified**, **majestic**, ceremonious, courtly, imposing, impressive, solemn, awe-inspiring, regal, imperial, elegant, grand, glorious, splendid, magnificent, resplendent, important, august, formal; slow-moving, measured, deliberate.

statement ▶ **noun** *do you agree with this statement?* **declaration**, expression of views/facts, affirmation, assertion, announcement, utterance, communication; revelation, disclosure, divulgence, pronouncement, recitation, articulation, proclamation, presentation, expounding, explanation, promulgation; account, testimony, evidence, report, bulletin, communiqué; *rare* asseveration, averment.

state-of-the-art ▶ **adjective** *the studio boasted the finest state-of-the-art recording equipment* **modern**, ultra-modern, futuristic, avant-garde, the latest, new, the newest, up to the minute; advanced, highly developed, innovatory, trailblazing, revolutionary; sophisticated, complex, complicated, elaborate, intricate, subtle, delicate; gimmicky.

statesman, **stateswoman** ▶ **noun** **senior politician**, respected political figure, elder statesman, political leader, national leader, grand old man, GOM; *French* éminence grise.

static ▶ **adjective 1** *they are to keep prices static for the rest of the year* **unchanged**, fixed, stable, steady, unchanging, changeless, unvarying, invariable, constant, consistent, uniform, undeviating.
OPPOSITE variable.
2 *a static display of aircraft* **stationary**, motionless, immobile, unmoving, still, stock-still, at a standstill, at rest, halted, stopped, parked, immobilized, not moving, not moving a muscle, like a statue, rooted to the spot, unstirring, frozen, inactive, inert, lifeless, inanimate.
OPPOSITES mobile, active, dynamic.

station ▶ **noun 1** *calling at all stations to Oxford* **stopping place**, stop, halt, station stop, stage; terminus, terminal, depot; railway station, train station, passenger station; bus station, coach station.
2 *a research station in the rainforest | a naval station* **establishment**, base, base camp, camp; post, depot; mission; site, facility, installation, yard; (*in India, historical*) cantonment.
3 *a police station* **office**, depot, base, headquarters, centre; *N. Amer.* precinct, station house, substation; *Indian* kotwali, thana; *informal* cop shop; *Brit. informal* nick.
4 *a radio station* **channel**, broadcasting organization; wavelength.
5 (*Austral./NZ*) *as a youngster he was sent out to Australia to work as a jackaroo on a sheep station* **ranch**, range; farm.
6 *the lookout resumed his station in the bow* **assigned position**, post, area of duty, place, situation, location.
7 (*dated*) *Karen was getting ideas above her station* **rank**, place, status, position in society, social class, level, grade, standing; caste; *archaic* condition, degree.
▶ **verb** *a flagman was stationed at the road crossing* **put on duty**, post, position, place, set, locate, site; establish, install; deploy, base, garrison.

stationary ▶ **adjective 1** *a stationary vehicle* **motionless**, parked, halted, stopped, immobilized, immobile, unmoving, still, static, stock-still, at a standstill, at rest, not moving; like a statue, rooted to the spot, unstirring, frozen, inactive, inert, lifeless, inanimate.
OPPOSITE moving.
2 *a stationary population* **unchanging**, unvarying, invariable, constant, consistent, uniform, unchanged, changeless, fixed, stable, steady, undeviating.
OPPOSITE shifting.

> **stationary or stationery?**
> Owing to their similarity in spelling, **stationary** and **stationery** are often confused; but their meanings have nothing in common. *Stationary* is an adjective meaning 'motionless' (*the car ploughed into a stationary van*). *Stationery* is a noun denoting writing and office materials (*bills for stamps and stationery*).

statue ▶ **noun** **sculpture**, figure, effigy, statuette, figurine, idol; carving, bronze, representation, likeness, image, graven image, model; bust, head.

statuesque ▶ **adjective** *the headmistress was statuesque* **tall and dignified**, imposing, striking, stately, majestic, noble, magnificent, splendid, impressive, regal, well proportioned, handsome, beautiful.

stature ▶ **noun 1** *she was small in stature* **height**, tallness, loftiness; size, build, physical make-up.
2 *an architect of international stature* **reputation**, repute, standing, status, position, prestige, distinction, illustriousness, eminence, pre-eminence, prominence, importance, import, influence, weight, consequence, account, note, fame, celebrity, renown, acclaim.

status ▶ **noun 1** *an improvement in the status of women* **standing**, rank, ranking, position, social position, station, level, footing, place; repute, reputation, estimation, stature; *archaic* condition, degree, report.
2 *those who enjoy wealth and status* **prestige**, kudos, cachet, standing, stature, prestigiousness, reputation, repute, (good) name, regard, fame, note, renown, honour, esteem, estimation, image, account, rank, character, celebrity, importance, prominence, consequence, class, distinction, laurels, influence, weight, authority, supremacy, eminence, superiority; *NZ* mana; *Indian* izzat; *informal* clout.

statute ▶ **noun** *the statute in question gave rise to an action for damages* **law**, regulation, enactment, act, bill, decree, edict, rule, ruling, resolution, promulgation, measure, motion, dictum, command, order, stipulation, commandment, directive, pronouncement, ratification, proclamation, dictate, diktat, fiat, covenant, demand, by-law; *N. Amer.* ordinance; (*in Tsarist Russia*) ukase; (*in Spain & Spanish-speaking countries*) pronunciamento.

staunch[1] ▶ **adjective** *a staunch supporter of the cause* **stalwart**, loyal, faithful, trusty, committed, devoted, dedicated, dependable, reliable, steady, constant, hard-working, vigorous, stable, firm, steadfast, redoubtable, resolute, unswerving, unwavering, unhesitating, unfaltering.
OPPOSITES disloyal, unfaithful, unreliable.

staunch[2] ▶ **verb** *he bound his thigh firmly, staunching the flow of blood* **stem**; **hold back**, stop, halt, check, block, dam; restrict, restrain, control, contain, curb, slow, lessen, reduce, diminish, retard; *N. Amer.* stanch; *archaic* stay.

stave ▶ **verb 1** *the ship had been driven aground, her hull staved in* **break in**, smash in, put a hole in, push in, kick in, cave in, splinter, shiver, fracture.
2 *the government is introducing emergency measures to stave off a crisis* **avert**, prevent, avoid, preclude, rule out, counter, forestall, nip in the bud; ward off, fend off, head off, keep off, keep at bay.

stay[1] ▶ **verb 1** *the man told her to stay where she was* **remain (behind)**, stay behind, stay put; **wait**, wait around, linger, stick, continue, be left, hold on, hang on, lodge, rest, delay, pause, stop; *informal* hang around/round; *Brit. informal* hang about; *dated* tarry; *archaic* bide.
OPPOSITE leave.
2 *we can't stay hidden any longer* **continue to be**, remain, keep, continue, persist in being, carry on being, go on being, rest.
3 *the girls have come to stay with us* **visit**; spend some time, put up, stop, stop off, stop over, break one's journey; holiday; lodge, room, board, have rooms, be housed, be accommodated, be quartered, be billeted; take up residence, take a room, settle; *N. Amer.* vacation; *formal* sojourn; *archaic* bide, abide.
4 *legal proceedings in such cases would be either stayed or dropped completely* **postpone**, put off, delay, defer, put back, hold over/off, carry over, reschedule, do later, shelve, stand over, pigeonhole, put/hold in abeyance, mothball; adjourn, suspend, prorogue; put off the evil day/hour; *N. Amer.* put over, table, lay on the table, take a rain check on; *N. Amer. Law* continue; *informal* put on ice, put on the back burner, put in cold storage; *rare* remit, respite.
OPPOSITE advance.
5 (*literary*) *he tries to stay the progress of barbarism* **delay**, **slow down**, slow up, hold back, set back, keep back, hold up, postpone, put back, detain, decelerate, put a brake on, retard; **hinder**, hamper, obstruct, inhibit,

S

impede, handicap, hamstring, curb, check, restrain, restrict, arrest, interfere with, interrupt, encumber, clog; *Brit. informal* throw a spanner in the works of; *N. Amer. informal* throw a monkey wrench in the works of; *rare* trammel, cumber.
OPPOSITE promote.
▸ noun **1** *a brief stay at a hotel* **visit**, stop, stop-off, stopover, break, holiday, rest; *N. Amer.* vacation; *formal* sojourn.
2 *a stay of judgement* **postponement**, putting off, delay, deferment, deferral, putting back, carrying over, rescheduling, shelving, pigeonholing, mothballing; adjournment, suspension, prorogation; *N. Amer.* tabling.

stay² ▸ noun *the mast was raised and the stays rigged* **strut**, **wire**, brace, tether, prop, beam, rod, support, truss, buttress, pier, shaft, shore, stanchion, stake, stick, spike, post; *Nautical* shroud.
▸ verb *her masts were stayed with lengths of telephone wire* **brace**, tether, strut, wire, prop, support, truss, buttress, shore up, stake, stick.

staying power ▸ noun (*informal*) *she won't have to rough it on this trip, but she still needs staying power.* See STAMINA.

steadfast ▸ adjective **1** *he was a steadfast friend* **loyal**, faithful, committed, devoted, dedicated, dependable, reliable, steady, true, constant, staunch, trusty.
OPPOSITE disloyal.
2 *a steadfast policy of internationalism* **firm**, determined, resolute, steady, staunch, stalwart, stout, relentless, implacable, single-minded; unchanging, unwavering, unhesitating, unfaltering, unswerving, unyielding, unflinching, inflexible, uncompromising.
OPPOSITE irresolute.

steady ▸ adjective **1** *the base was not steady, and the model fell over* **stable**, balanced, firm, fixed, secure, secured, fast, safe, immovable, unshakeable, dependable; anchored, moored, jammed, rooted, braced, cemented, riveted, nailed, tied.
OPPOSITES unstable, loose.
2 *press the button again, keeping the camcorder as steady as you can* **motionless**, still, unshaking, static, stationary, unmoving, sure.
OPPOSITE shaky.
3 *a steady gaze* **fixed**, intent, immovable, immobile, unwavering, unfaltering.
OPPOSITE darting.
4 *a solid, steady young man* **sensible**, level-headed, well balanced, balanced, rational, settled, mature, down-to-earth, full of common sense, stolid, calm, equable, imperturbable, reliable, dependable, sound, sober, serious-minded, responsible, serious.
OPPOSITES flighty, impulsive, airy-fairy, immature.
5 *a fixed-interest bond is used to provide a steady income* **constant**, unchanging, changeless, unvarying, invariable, undeviating; uniform, even, regular, consistent; continuous, continual, unceasing, ceaseless, perpetual, unremitting, unwavering, unfaltering, unfluctuating, undying, unending, endless, round-the-clock, all-year-round; reliable, dependable.
OPPOSITES fluctuating, intermittent, sporadic.
6 *a steady boyfriend* **regular**, unchanging, habitual, usual, customary, established, settled, firm, devoted, faithful.
OPPOSITES occasional, on-off.
▸ verb **1** *he propped his elbow on his knee to steady the rifle* **stabilize**, make steady, hold steady; secure, fix, make fast; brace, support; balance, poise.
2 *I took a deep breath to steady my nerves* **calm**, calm down, soothe, quieten, quiet, compose, settle, pacify, lull; subdue, quell, control, get a grip on; sedate, tranquillize.

steal ▸ verb **1** *the raiders stole a fax machine* **purloin**, thieve, take, take for oneself, help oneself to, loot, pilfer, abscond with, run off with, appropriate, abstract, carry off, shoplift; embezzle, misappropriate; have one's fingers/hand in the till; *informal* walk off/away with, run away/off with, rob, swipe, nab, rip off, lift, 'liberate', 'borrow', filch, snaffle, snitch, souvenir; *Brit. informal* nick, pinch, half-inch, whip, knock off, nobble, bone, scrump, blag; *N. Amer. informal* heist, glom; *Austral. informal* snavel; *W. Indian informal* tief; *archaic* crib, hook; *rare* peculate, defalcate; (**be stolen**) *informal* walk, go walkies.
2 *he alleged that his work was stolen by his tutor* **plagiarize**, copy, pass off as one's own, infringe the copyright of, pirate, poach, borrow, appropriate; *informal* rip off, lift, pinch, nick, crib.
3 *she was a beauty, and he'd often wanted to steal a kiss* **snatch**, sneak, obtain stealthily, get surreptitiously.
4 *he stole out of the room* **creep**, sneak, slink, slip, slither, slide, glide, sidle, slope, edge, move furtively, tiptoe, pussyfoot, pad, prowl.
□ **steal the show be the centre of attention**, get all the attention, attract the most attention, be the focus of attention, be the main attraction, be the outstanding feature, put the others in the shade, be the high point/spot, be the best part, have all eyes on one, be the cynosure; (**steal the show from someone**) outshine, put in the shade, upstage, overshadow, eclipse, outclass, dwarf, tower above/over, put to shame.
▸ noun **1** (*N. Amer.*) *New York's biggest art steal* **theft**, robbery, raid, ram raid, burglary, larceny, thievery, break-in, hold-up; embezzlement, misappropriation, swindle, fraud; (*in India or Burma*) dacoity; *informal* snatch, pinch, smash-and-grab (raid), stick-up, mugging, job; *Brit. informal* blag; *N. Amer. informal* heist; *rare* peculation, defalcation.
2 (*informal*) *at £30 it's a steal.* See BARGAIN.

WORD LINKS
compulsion to steal **kleptomania**

stealing ▸ noun *he was convicted of stealing* **theft**, thieving, thievery, robbery, larceny, burglary, shoplifting, pilfering, pilferage, looting, appropriation, misappropriation; embezzlement; *rare* peculation, defalcation.

WORD LINKS
compulsive stealing **kleptomania**
fear of stealing **kleptophobia**

stealth ▸ noun *what they could not accomplish by violence or chicanery they would have to accomplish by stealth* **furtiveness**, secretiveness, secrecy, surreptitiousness, sneakiness, slyness, covertness, stealthiness, clandestineness.
OPPOSITE openness.

stealthy ▸ adjective *there was a good deal of stealthy coming and going within the building* **furtive**, secretive, secret, surreptitious, sneaking, sly, skulking, slinking, clandestine, hidden, covert, cloaked, conspiratorial, under the table.
OPPOSITE open.

steam ▸ noun **1** *steam gushed from the spout of the kettle* **water vapour**, condensation, mist, haze, fog, exhalation, moisture, dampness; *rare* fume, smoke.
2 *he starts fast but tends to run out of steam* **energy**, vigour, vigorousness, vitality, stamina, enthusiasm; **momentum**, impetus, power, force, strength, thrust, impulse, push, drive, driving power; speed, pace, velocity.
□ **let off steam** (*informal*) **give vent to one's feelings**, speak one's mind, sound off, lose one's inhibitions, let oneself go; use up energy, release surplus energy.
OPPOSITE bottle things up.
□ **under one's own steam unaided**, unassisted, without help, without assistance, independently, by oneself, by one's own efforts, on one's own two feet.
OPPOSITE with help.
▸ verb (*informal*) *he bounced out of the car and steamed into the shop.* See RUN.
□ **get steamed up** (*informal*) **1** *he got really steamed up about forgetting his papers* **become agitated**, get worked up, get overwrought, get flustered, panic, become panic-stricken; *informal* get het up, get into a state, get into a tizzy, get uptight, get into a stew, get the willies, get the heebie-jeebies, go into a flat spin; *Brit. informal* have kittens, have an attack of the wobblies.
OPPOSITE calm down.
2 *they get steamed up about the media* **become very angry**, become enraged, go into a rage, lose one's temper; *informal* go/get mad, go crazy, go wild, see red, go bananas, hit the roof, go through the roof, go up the wall, go off the deep end, fly off the handle, blow one's top, blow a fuse/gasket, lose one's rag, go ape, flip, flip one's lid, go non-linear, go ballistic, go psycho; *Brit. informal* go crackers, go spare, do one's nut; *N. Amer. informal* flip one's wig, blow one's lid/stack; *vulgar slang* go apeshit.
□ **steam up** *glass lenses are more likely to steam up than plastic* **mist (up)**, fog (up), become misty/misted, become covered with condensation.

steamy ▸ adjective **1** *the hot, steamy jungle* **humid**, muggy, sticky, dripping, moist, damp, clammy, sultry, sweltering, boiling, sweaty, steaming, like a Turkish bath, like a sauna.
2 (*informal*) *the steamy love scenes have been cut* **erotic**, sexy, sexually explicit, suggestive, racy, risqué, provocative, spicy, juicy, bawdy, ribald, uninhibited, unrestrained, earthy; *informal* raunchy, naughty; *Brit. informal* saucy, fruity; *N. Amer. informal* gamy; *euphemistic* adult.
3 (*informal*) *Mac was having this steamy affair with Caroline* **passionate**, torrid, amorous, ardent, loving, hot-blooded, sexy, lustful, erotic; *informal* sizzling, zipless, hot, red-hot.

steel ▸ verb
□ **steel oneself** *his team were steeling themselves for disappointment* **brace oneself**, nerve oneself, summon/gather/screw up/muster one's courage, screw one's courage to the sticking place, gear oneself up, prepare oneself, get in the right frame of mind, make up one's mind; fortify oneself, harden oneself, bolster oneself; *informal* psych oneself up; *literary* gird (up) one's loins.

steely ▸ adjective **1** *the steely predawn light* **blue-grey**, grey, steel-coloured, steel-grey, iron-grey; harsh.
OPPOSITE soft.
2 *his steely pectoral muscles* **hard**, firm, toned, rigid, stiff, tense, tensed, taut, stretched.
OPPOSITE flabby.
3 *he would stare hard at you with steely eyes* **cruel**, unfeeling, merciless, ruthless, pitiless, heartless, hard-hearted, hard, stony, cold-blooded, cold-hearted, harsh, callous, severe, unmerciful, unrelenting, relentless,

unpitying, unsparing, unforgiving, uncaring, unsympathetic, uncharitable, lacking compassion, remorseless, unbending, unmoved, inflexible, inexorable, implacable, unremitting; *literary* adamantine; *rare* marble-hearted.
OPPOSITE kind.
4 *she had a steely determination that had made her a success in a man's world* **resolute**, firm, fixed, steadfast, dogged, single-minded; bitter, burning, fiery, ferocious, fierce, fanatical, furious; ruthless, inflexible, iron, granite, stony, grim, gritty, gutsy; unquenchable, unflinching, unswerving, unfaltering, untiring, unwavering, unyielding, undaunted.
OPPOSITE half-hearted.

steep[1] ▶ adjective **1** *steep limestone cliffs* **precipitous**, sheer, abrupt, sharp, perpendicular, vertical, bluff, vertiginous, dizzy; *rare* declivitous, acclivitous, scarped.
OPPOSITE gentle.
2 *a steep rise in unemployment* **sharp**, sudden, precipitate, precipitous, rapid.
OPPOSITE gradual.
3 (*informal*) *the prices are a bit steep* **expensive**, dear, costly, high, stiff; unreasonable, excessive, overpriced, exorbitant, extortionate, outrageous, prohibitive; *Brit.* over the odds; *informal* pricey, over the top, OTT, criminal.
OPPOSITE reasonable.

steep[2] ▶ verb **1** *the ham is then steeped in brine for three or four days* **marinade**, marinate, soak, souse, macerate; pickle, brine.
2 *winding sheets were steeped in mercury sulphate as a disinfectant* **soak**, saturate, immerse, submerge, wet through, drench; *technical* ret.
3 *a city* **steeped in** *history* **imbue with**, fill with, permeate with, pervade with, suffuse with, infuse with, perfuse with, impregnate with, soak in; *rare* stew in.

steeple ▶ noun *the steeple of St Bride's church* **spire**, church tower, tower, bell tower, belfry; minaret; *Italian* campanile.

steer ▶ verb **1** *he steered the boat slowly towards the busy quay* **guide**, direct, manoeuvre; navigate, pilot, drive, be in the driver's seat of, be at the wheel of; *Nautical* con, helm.
2 *Luke steered her down the path towards his car* **guide**, conduct, direct, lead, take, usher, escort, shepherd, marshal, herd.
□ **steer clear of** *you'd best steer clear of him—he's a nasty piece of work* **keep away from**, keep one's distance from, keep at arm's length, give a wide berth to, avoid, avoid dealing with, have nothing to do with, shun, eschew; sidestep, evade, dodge, skirt round, circumvent, fight shy of; *informal* duck.
OPPOSITES seek out, confront.

stem[1] ▶ noun **1** *with any shrub or tree, look for firm healthy roots and a sturdy straight stem* **trunk**, **stalk**, stock, cane; *technical* peduncle.
2 *the rose has dark foliage and purplish stems* **stalk**, shoot, twig; *technical* bine, pedicel, petiole, peduncle, axis.
▶ verb
□ **stem from** *her depression stems from domestic difficulties* **have its origins in**, arise from, originate from, spring from, derive from, come from, be rooted in, emanate from, issue from, flow from, proceed from, result from, be consequent on; **be caused by**, be brought on/about by, be produced by.
OPPOSITES cause, give rise to; be independent of.

WORD LINKS
relating to stalks **cauline**

stem[2] ▶ verb *paramedics tried to stem the flow of blood* **staunch**, stop, halt, check, hold back, restrain, restrict, control, contain, curb; block, dam; slow, lessen, reduce, diminish, retard; *N. Amer.* stanch; *archaic* stay.

stench ▶ noun *the stench made me feel sick* **stink**, bad smell, foul smell, reek, miasma, effluvium; *Brit. informal* niff, pong, whiff, hum; *Scottish informal* guff; *N. Amer. informal* funk; *rare* mephitis, malodour, fetor, noisomeness.

stentorian ▶ adjective *a bulky man was holding forth in stentorian tones* **loud**, booming, thundering, thunderous, trumpeting, blaring, roaring, ear-splitting, deafening; ringing, resonant, sonorous, carrying, vibrant, powerful, strong, full; strident; *rare* stentorious.
OPPOSITES quiet, soft.

step ▶ noun **1** *Frank took another step forward* **pace**, footstep, stride.
2 *she heard Ellis's step on the stairs* **footstep**, footfall, tread, tramp.
3 *she left the room with a springy step* **gait**, walk, way of walking, tread, bearing, carriage.
4 *the market is only a step from the end of the pier* **short distance**, stone's throw, spitting distance; *informal* {a hop, skip, and a jump}.
5 *Susan sat on the top step | Maureen ran down the steps* **stair**, tread, tread board; (**steps**) **stairs**, staircase, stairway; *N. Amer.* stoop.
6 *there was a pint of milk on the step* **doorstep**, sill.
7 *the steps of a ladder* **rung**, tread.
8 *calling in the bailiffs is a very serious step* **course of action**, measure, move, act, action, procedure, proceeding, initiative; manoeuvre, tactic, strategy, stratagem, operation; *French* démarche.
9 *a significant step towards a ceasefire* **advance**, progression, development, step in the right direction, step forward, move, movement; breakthrough.
10 *the first step on the managerial ladder* **stage**, level, grade, rank, degree; phase; notch.
□ **in step** *he is utterly in step with mainstream American thinking* **in accord**, in harmony, in agreement, in tune, in line, in keeping, in conformity, in accordance, in consensus, in consilience.
OPPOSITE out of step.
□ **mind/watch one's step be careful**, take care, step carefully/cautiously, walk carefully/cautiously, tread carefully/cautiously, exercise care/caution, mind how one goes, look out, watch out, watch oneself, be wary, be circumspect, be chary, take heed, be attentive, be on one's guard, have/keep one's wits about one, be on the qui vive.
□ **out of step** *the paper was often out of step with public opinion* **at odds**, at variance, in disagreement, out of tune, out of line, not in keeping, out of harmony, at loggerheads, in opposition, at outs.
OPPOSITE in step.
□ **step by step one step at a time**, bit by bit, gradually, in stages, by degrees, slowly, steadily, slowly but surely; *rare* gradatim.
□ **take steps** *the government must take steps to discourage age discrimination* **take action**, take measures, act, take the initiative, move.
▶ verb **1** *she stepped off the gangway* **walk**, move, tread, pace, stride.
2 *the bull had stepped on his hat* **tread**, stamp, trample, tramp; squash, crush, flatten.
□ **step down resign**, stand down, give up one's post/job, bow out; retire, abdicate; *informal* quit, call it a day.
OPPOSITE take up office.
□ **step in intervene**, intercede, become/get involved, act, take action, take measures, take a hand; mediate, arbitrate, intermediate.
□ **step on it** (*informal*) **hurry up**, get a move on, speed up, go faster, be quick; *informal* get cracking, get moving, step on the gas, rattle one's dags; *Brit. informal* get one's skates on, stir one's stumps; *N. Amer. informal* get a wiggle on; *S. African informal* put foot; *dated* make haste.
□ **step something up 1** *the army stepped up its offensive in the north* **increase**, intensify, strengthen, augment, escalate, scale up, boost; *informal* up, crank up.
2 *I stepped up my pace* **speed up**, increase, accelerate, quicken, hasten.
OPPOSITE decrease.

stepmother ▶ noun
WORD LINKS
relating to a stepmother **novercal**

stereotype ▶ noun *the stereotype of the alcoholic as a down-and-out vagrant* **standard/conventional image**, received idea, cliché, hackneyed idea, formula.
▶ verb *the city is too easily stereotyped as an industrial wasteland* **typecast**, pigeonhole, conventionalize, standardize, categorize, compartmentalize, label, tag.

stereotyped ▶ adjective *stereotyped images of village life* **stock**, conventional, stereotypical, conventionalized, standardized, standard, formulaic, predictable; hackneyed, clichéd, cliché-ridden, banal, trite, platitudinous, unoriginal, overused, overworked, well worn, stale, tired; typecast; *informal* corny, old hat.
OPPOSITES unconventional, original, fresh.

sterile ▶ adjective **1** *the treatment left her sterile* **infertile**; childless; *technical* infecund; *archaic* barren.
OPPOSITES fertile, fecund.
2 *vast tracts of sterile desert land* **unproductive**, infertile, unfruitful, uncultivatable; arid, dry, barren, lifeless, desert.
OPPOSITES rich, fertile, productive.
3 *a sterile debate* **pointless**, profitless, unproductive, unfruitful, fruitless, unrewarding, abortive, unsuccessful, ineffectual, ineffective, worthless, useless, unprofitable, futile, vain, idle; *archaic* bootless; *rare* unfructuous.
OPPOSITE fruitful.
4 *sterile academicism* **unimaginative**, uninspired, uninspiring, unoriginal, stale, lifeless, musty.
OPPOSITES creative, original.
5 *the cells can be propagated in sterile conditions* **aseptic**, sterilized, germ-free, antiseptic, disinfected, uninfected, uncontaminated, unpolluted, pure, clean; sanitary, hygienic.
OPPOSITE septic.

sterility ▶ noun **1** *these compounds have successfully been used in the treatment of sterility* **infertility**; childlessness; *technical* infecundity; *archaic* barrenness.
OPPOSITES fertility, fecundity.
2 *the sterility of the soil* **unproductiveness**, unfruitfulness, infertility, sterileness, non-productivity; aridness, aridity, barrenness, lifelessness.
OPPOSITES richness, fertility, productiveness.
3 *the sterility of the debate | he contemplated the sterility of his life* **pointlessness**, unproductiveness, unfruitfulness, fruitlessness, uselessness, futility, profitlessness, worthlessness, abortiveness; emptiness, barrenness, aridity; *archaic* bootlessness.
OPPOSITE fruitfulness.
4 *a temperature of 121°C is the minimum needed to achieve sterility* **asepsis**,

S

freedom from germs, lack of infection/contamination/pollution, disinfection, purity, cleanliness.
OPPOSITE contamination.

sterilize ▶ verb **1** *the wards had been thoroughly sterilized* **disinfect**, purify, fumigate, decontaminate, sanitize; pasteurize; clean, cleanse; *technical* autoclave; *rare* depurate, depollute.
OPPOSITE contaminate.
2 *in the last half of the year, over 6.5 million people were sterilized* hysterectomize, vasectomize; *rare* ovariectomize, oophorectomize, eunuchize.
3 *she launched a campaign to have France's 30 million cats and dogs sterilized* **castrate**, geld, neuter, cut, caponize, emasculate; **spay**; *N. Amer. & Austral.* alter; *informal* fix, doctor.

sterling ▶ adjective (*Brit.*) *the sterling work of the social services department* **excellent**, first-rate, first-class, exceptional, outstanding, splendid, superlative, of the first order, of the highest order, of the first water, magnificent, wonderful, fine, great, praiseworthy, laudable, admirable; *informal* A1, top-notch.
OPPOSITES poor, unexceptional.

stern[1] ▶ adjective **1** *Nick's expression was stern* **serious**, **unsmiling**, frowning, poker-faced, severe, forbidding, grim, unfriendly, sombre, grave, sober, austere, dour, stony, flinty, steely, unrelenting, unyielding, unforgiving, unbending, unsympathetic, disapproving; *rare* Rhadamanthine.
OPPOSITES genial, friendly.
2 *the stern measures taken by the government added to its unpopularity* **strict**, severe, stringent, harsh, drastic, hard, tough, fierce, extreme, rigorous, rigid, exacting, demanding, uncompromising, unsparing, inflexible, authoritarian, draconian; *Austral./NZ informal* solid.
OPPOSITES lenient, lax.

stern[2] ▶ noun *the stern of the ship* **rear end**, rear, back, tail, poop.
OPPOSITE bow.

stew *See centre pages for list of* **Stews**
▶ noun *a beef stew* **casserole**.
▫ **in a stew** (*informal*) *she's in a right old stew* **agitated**, anxious, in a state of nerves, nervous, in a state of agitation, in a panic, worked up, keyed up, overwrought, wrought up, flustered, flurried, in a pother; *informal* in a flap, in a state, all of a dither, in a sweat, in a tizz/tizzy, in a tiz-woz, all of a lather, het up, in a twitter; *Brit. informal* strung up, windy, having kittens, all of a doodah; *N. Amer. informal* in a twit; *Austral./NZ informal* toey; *dated* overstrung.
OPPOSITES cool, calm, relaxed, laid-back.
▶ verb **1** *stew the meat for an hour or so* **braise**, casserole, fricassée, simmer, boil; jug; *S. African* smoor; *archaic* seethe.
2 (*informal*) *there's no point stewing over it* **worry**, fret, agonize, be anxious, be nervous, be agitated, get in a panic, get worked up, get in a fluster, get overwrought; *informal* get in a flap, get in a state, get in a tizz/tizzy, get in a tiz-woz, get in a sweat, get steamed up, get in a lather.
3 (*informal*) *the girls sat stewing in the heat* **swelter**, be very hot, perspire, sweat; *informal* roast, bake, be boiling.

steward ▶ noun **1** *an air steward* **flight attendant**, cabin attendant, member of the cabin staff; stewardess, air hostess; *N. Amer. informal* stew.
2 *the race stewards did not uphold my protest* **official**, marshal, organizer.
3 *the steward of the Carewscourt estate* **(estate) manager**, agent, overseer, custodian, caretaker; *Brit.* land agent, bailiff; *Scottish* factor; *historical* reeve.
4 (*Brit. historical*) *the steward of the household* **major-domo**, seneschal, manciple; butler.

stick[1] ▶ noun **1** *he gathered sticks and lit a fire* **piece of wood**, twig, small branch.
2 *Roger still walked with a stick* **walking stick**, cane, staff; malacca, alpenstock, blackthorn, ashplant, rattan, thumb stick; crook; crutch; *Austral./NZ* waddy.
3 *the stems require adequate support—sticks or netting can be used* **cane**, pole, beanpole, post, stake, upright, rod.
4 *he had beaten her with a stick* **club**, cudgel, bludgeon, shillelagh; truncheon, baton; cane, birch, switch, rod; *Indian* lathi, danda; *S. African* kierie, knobkerrie; *Brit. informal* cosh.
5 (*Brit. informal*) *he's going to get some stick for this* **criticism**, flak, censure, reproach, reproof, condemnation, castigation, chastisement, blame, abuse; punishment; *informal* a bashing, a roasting, a caning, an earful, a bawling-out; *Brit. informal* verbal, a rollicking, a wigging, a rocket, a row; *Brit. vulgar slang* a bollocking; *rare* animadversion.
OPPOSITES praise, commendation.
▫ **the sticks** (*informal*) *you should stop living in the sticks and move to London* **the country**, the countryside, the provinces, rural districts, the backwoods, the back of beyond, the wilds, the hinterland, a backwater; *N. Amer.* the backcountry, the backland; *Austral./NZ* the backblocks, the booay; *S. African* the backveld, the platteland; *informal* the middle of nowhere; *N. Amer. informal* the boondocks, the boonies, the tall timbers; *Austral./NZ informal* Woop Woop, beyond the black stump.

stick[2] ▶ verb **1** *he stuck his fork into the sausage* **thrust**, push, insert, jab, dig, plunge, ram, force; poke, prod.
2 *the bristles stuck into his skin* **pierce**, penetrate, puncture, prick, spike, stab.
3 *his front teeth stuck out* **protrude**, jut out, project, stand out, extend, poke out, obtrude; bulge; overhang, beetle; *informal* be goofy; *rare* protuberate, impend.
4 *the shabbiness of the surroundings stuck out* **stand out**, be noticeable, be conspicuous, be obvious, catch the eye, be obtrusive.
5 *the plastic seats stuck to my skin* **adhere**, cling, be fixed, be glued.
6 *a message was stuck to his computer screen* **affix**, attach, fasten, fix; paste, glue, gum, tape, sellotape, pin, tack; weld, solder.
7 *he drove into a bog, where his wheels stuck fast* **become trapped**, become jammed, jam, catch, become wedged, become lodged, become fixed, become embedded, become immobilized, become unable to move, get bogged down.
8 *one particular incident sticks in his mind* **remain**, stay, linger, dwell, persist, continue, last, endure.
OPPOSITE be forgotten.
9 *the authorities couldn't make the charges stick* **be upheld**, hold, be believed, gain credence, be regarded as valid; *informal* hold water.
10 (*informal*) *just stick that sandwich on my desk* **put**, place, set, put down, set down, lay, lay down, deposit, situate, position; leave, stow; *informal* dump, bung, park, plonk, pop; *N. Amer. informal* plunk.
11 (*informal*) *I don't think I can stick it any longer* **tolerate**, put up with, take, stand (for), accept, stomach, swallow, endure, bear, support, brook, submit to, take something lying down; *Scottish* thole; *informal* abide; *Brit. informal* wear, be doing with; *archaic* suffer.
12 (*archaic*) *if I had my knife here I would stick him* **stab**, run through, transfix, impale, spit, spear.
▫ **stick at** *if you wish to learn a language, you must stick at it* **persevere with**, persist with, keep at, work at, continue with, carry on with, go on with, not give up with, hammer away at, stay with, see/follow through, go the distance, stay the course; *informal* soldier on with, stick it out, hang in there, put one's back into.
OPPOSITE give up.
▫ **stick by** *whatever happens I'll stick by him* **support**, stand by, be loyal to, remain faithful to, be supportive of, be on someone's side, side with, back, defend.
OPPOSITES turn against, turn one's back on, let down.
▫ **stick it out** *I decided to stick it out for another couple of months* **put up with it**, grin and bear it, keep at it, keep going, stay with it, see it through, see it through to the end; persevere, persist, carry on, struggle on; *informal* hang in there, soldier on, tough it out, peg away, plug away, bash on.
OPPOSITE give up.
▫ **stick to** *the government stuck to their election pledges* **abide by**, keep, adhere to, hold to, fulfil, make good.
OPPOSITE break.
▫ **stick up for** *I don't know anyone else who would stick up for me the way you do* **support**, give one's support to, take the side of, side with, be on the side of, stand by, stand up for, take someone's part, be supportive of, be loyal to, defend, come to the defence of, champion, speak up for, fight for.
OPPOSITES turn against, turn one's back on.

stick-in-the-mud ▶ noun (*informal*) **(old) fogey**, conservative, museum piece, fossil, dinosaur, troglodyte; *informal* fuddy-duddy, square, back number, stuffed shirt; *N. Amer. informal* sobersides.

sticky ▶ adjective **1** *sticky tape | a sticky label* **adhesive**, adherent, gummed; *rare* tenacious.
2 *too much water made the clay sticky and difficult to work* **glutinous**, viscous, viscid; **gluey**, tacky, gummy, treacly, syrupy; mucilaginous; *Brit.* claggy; *Scottish & N. English* clarty; *informal* gooey, gloopy, cloggy, gungy, icky; *N. Amer. informal* gloppy; *rare* viscoid.
OPPOSITE dry.
3 *an unusually hot and sticky summer* **humid**, muggy, close, sultry, sweltering, steamy, oppressive, airless, stifling, suffocating, sweaty, soupy, like a Turkish bath, like a sauna.
OPPOSITES fresh, cool.
4 *thanks for getting me out of a very sticky situation* **awkward**, difficult, tricky, ticklish, problematic, delicate, touch-and-go, embarrassing, sensitive, uncomfortable; *informal* hairy.
OPPOSITE easy.

stiff ▶ adjective **1** *a sheet of stiff black cardboard* **rigid**, hard, firm, hardened, inelastic, non-flexible, inflexible, ungiving; *rare* impliable, unmalleable.
OPPOSITES flexible, plastic; limp.
2 *mix to a stiff paste* **semi-solid**, viscous, viscid, thick, stiffened; firm, compact, dense; *rare* viscoid.
OPPOSITE runny.
3 *her muscles were stiff | his stiff legs* **aching**, achy, painful; arthritic, rheumatic; taut, tight; *informal* creaky, rheumaticky, rusty; *archaic* stark.
OPPOSITES supple, limber.
4 *she greeted him with stiff politeness* **formal**, reserved, unfriendly, chilly, cold, frigid, icy, austere, unrelaxed, brittle, stand-offish, wooden, forced, constrained, strained, stilted; prim, punctilious, stuffy; *informal* starchy, uptight.

OPPOSITES relaxed, informal.
5 *they face stiff fines and a possible jail sentence* **harsh**, severe, hard, punitive, punishing, stringent, swingeing, crippling, rigorous, drastic, strong, heavy, draconian.
OPPOSITES lenient, mild.
6 *the army had put up a stiff resistance* **vigorous, determined**, full of determination, strong, spirited, resolute, tenacious, steely, four-square, unflagging, unyielding, dogged, stubborn, obdurate; N. Amer. rock-ribbed.
OPPOSITE half-hearted.
7 *a long, stiff climb up the bare hillside* **difficult**, hard, arduous, tough, strenuous, laborious, uphill, exacting, demanding, formidable, challenging, punishing, back-breaking, gruelling, Herculean; tiring, fatiguing, exhausting; informal killing, hellish; Brit. informal knackering; archaic toilsome.
OPPOSITE easy.
8 *a stiff breeze* **strong**, vigorous, powerful, brisk, fresh, gusty; howling.
OPPOSITE gentle.
9 *you need a stiff drink* **strong**, potent, alcoholic, spirituous, intoxicant.
OPPOSITE weak.

stiffen ▸ verb **1** *stir until the mixture stiffens* **become stiff**, thicken; set, become solid, solidify, harden, gel, congeal, coagulate, clot.
2 *she stiffened her muscles | without exercise, joints will stiffen* **make/become stiff/rigid**, tense (up), tighten, tauten; rigidify; technical ankylose.
OPPOSITE relax.
3 *attempts to intimidate them have only stiffened their resolve* **strengthen**, harden, toughen, fortify, give strength to, reinforce, brace, steel, give a boost to.
OPPOSITE weaken.

stiff-necked ▸ adjective *he was stiff-necked and argumentative* **stubborn**, obstinate, mulish, as stubborn as a mule, pig-headed, bull-headed, unyielding, inflexible, unbending, intractable, uncompromising, obdurate; self-willed, wilful, opinionated, strong-minded, strong-willed, refractory; N. Amer. informal balky; archaic contumacious; rare indurate.
OPPOSITES compliant, tractable.

stifle ▸ verb **1** *people in the streets were stifled by the fumes | Hester had stifled her husband with a bolster* **suffocate**, choke, asphyxiate; smother.
2 *Eleanor stifled a giggle* **suppress**, smother, restrain, keep back, hold back, hold in, fight back, choke back, gulp back, withhold, check, keep in check, swallow, muffle, quench, curb, silence, contain, bottle up; bite one's lip, cork up.
OPPOSITE let out.
3 *high taxes were stifling private enterprise | public debate is being stifled* **constrain**, hinder, hamper, impede, hold back, curb, check, restrain, prevent, inhibit; put an end/stop to, stop, quash, squash, stamp out, destroy, crush, extinguish, deaden, damp down, subdue, suppress, repress; silence, muffle, mute, gag.
OPPOSITE encourage.

stifling ▸ adjective *in summer, Venice is often stifling* **very hot**, sweltering; **airless**, suffocating, oppressive, humid, close, muggy, sticky, soupy; informal boiling.
OPPOSITES cold, chilly.

stigma ▸ noun *the stigma of bankruptcy* **shame**, disgrace, dishonour; stain, taint, blot, blot on one's escutcheon, blemish, brand, mark, slur; literary smirch.
OPPOSITES honour, credit.

stigmatize ▸ verb *trade unionism was stigmatized as inimical to the interests of society* **condemn**, denounce; brand, label, mark out; disparage, vilify, pillory, pour scorn on, cast a slur on, defame, discredit.

still ▸ adjective **1** *Polly lay quite still* **motionless**, unmoving, without moving, without moving a muscle, stock-still, immobile, like a statue, as if turned to stone, as if rooted to the spot, unstirring, stationary; at rest, at a standstill; inert, lifeless.
OPPOSITES moving, active.
2 *the night was dark and still | the still waters of the lake* **quiet**, silent, hushed, soundless, noiseless, undisturbed, sound-free; **calm**, tranquil, peaceful, serene, windless, wind-free, halcyon; flat, even, smooth, placid, pacific, waveless, glassy, like a millpond, unruffled; stagnant, standing; literary stilly.
▸ noun *the still of the night* **quietness**, quiet, quietude, silence, stillness, hush, soundlessness, noiselessness; calmness, calm, tranquillity, peace, peacefulness, peace and quiet, serenity.
OPPOSITES noise, disturbance, hubbub.
▸ adverb **1** *I understand he's still married to her* **up to this time**, up to the present time, until now, even now, yet.
OPPOSITE no longer.
2 *I'm afraid he's crazy. Still, he's harmless* **nevertheless**, however, in spite of that, despite that, notwithstanding, for all that, all the same, even so, be that as it may, having said that, nonetheless, but; informal still and all; archaic withal, natheless, howbeit.
▸ verb **1** *he stilled the clamour with a wave of his hand* **quieten**, quiet, silence, hush; calm, settle, pacify, soothe, lull, allay, assuage, appease, subdue.
OPPOSITE stir up.
2 *the wind stilled* **abate**, die down, grow less, lessen, subside, ease up/off, let up, moderate, slacken, weaken, fade away.
OPPOSITES get stronger, get up.

stilted ▸ adjective *after a few minutes of stilted conversation, she retreated* **strained**, forced, contrived, constrained, laboured, laborious, stiff, self-conscious, awkward, unnatural, wooden, unrelaxed; artificial, mannered.
OPPOSITES natural, effortless, spontaneous.

stimulant ▸ noun **1** *a stimulant that has a direct effect on the nervous system* **tonic**, restorative, reviver, energizer, refresher; antidepressant; informal pep pill, upper, pick-me-up, bracer; technical excitant, analeptic.
OPPOSITES sedative, downer.
2 *population growth is a major stimulant to industrial development* **stimulus**, incentive, encouragement, impetus, inducement, fillip, boost, spur, prompt, prod, jog; provocation, goad, incitement; informal shot in the arm, kick up the backside.
OPPOSITE deterrent.

stimulant or stimulus?

While both these words have meanings relating to something's effect on activity, they are distinct. A **stimulant** is a substance that increases or speeds up bodily activity (*tisanes may appeal to people who find ordinary tea too much of a stimulant | a heart and respiratory stimulant*). **Stimulus**, on the other hand, denotes something that causes a particular physical response (*the syndrome causes bizarre responses to any stimulus to the hemiplegic side*), or something that acts as an incentive to activity or development (*the authorities are convinced of the value of investment as a stimulus to growth*).

stimulate ▸ verb *his passionate interest in the music stimulated Mozart to study Bach's fugues | I want to stimulate their imaginations* **encourage**, act as a stimulus/incentive/impetus/fillip/spur to, prompt, prod, move, motivate, trigger, spark, spur on, galvanize, activate, kindle, fire, fire with enthusiasm, fuel, whet, nourish; inspire, rouse, arouse, excite, animate, quicken, ginger up, pique, electrify; stir up, whip up, instigate, foment, fan, incite, provoke, sting, inflame, goad; N. Amer. light a fire under; literary inspirit, spirit someone up; rare incentivize, fillip.
OPPOSITE discourage.

stimulating ▸ adjective **1** *plant extracts which have a stimulating effect on the circulation* **restorative**, tonic, invigorating, bracing, energizing, restoring, reviving, refreshing, vitalizing, revitalizing, vivifying, revivifying; informal pick-me-up; technical analeptic, trophic.
OPPOSITE sedative.
2 *a stimulating lecture by Professor Battersby* **thought-provoking**, interesting, fascinating, inspiring, inspirational, lively, sparkling, entertaining, exhilarating, exciting, stirring, rousing, intriguing, stimulative, giving one food for thought, piquant, refreshing; provocative, challenging; informal sexy; rare exalté.
OPPOSITES uninspiring, uninteresting, boring.

stimulus ▸ noun *cheap energy provided a major stimulus to economic development in western Europe* **spur**, stimulant, encouragement, impetus, boost, prompt, prod, incentive, inducement, inspiration, fillip; motive, motivation, impulse; provocation, goad, incitement; informal shot in the arm, kick up the backside; technical precipitant.
OPPOSITES deterrent, discouragement.

stimulus or stimulant?

See STIMULANT.

S

sting ▸ noun **1** *the herb is said to relieve the pain of wasp and bee stings* **prick**, wound, injury; bite, nip, puncture.
2 *to soothe the sting of a cut or burn use aloe juice* **smarting**, smart, stinging, tingling, tingle, pricking; pain, soreness, hurt, irritation.
3 *I recalled the sting of his betrayal* **heartache**, heartbreak, agony, torture, torment, hurt, pain, anguish, distress, desolation, misery.
4 *she smiled to take the sting out of her words* **sharpness**, severity, bite, edge, pointedness, asperity, pungency, mordancy, acerbity, acidity, tartness; **sarcasm**, acrimony, malice, spite, venom; rare causticity, mordacity.
5 (informal) *that little sting netted him the Bentley and a £350,000 house* **swindle**, fraud, piece of deception, trickery, cheat, bit of sharp practice; informal rip-off, con, con trick, diddle, fiddle; N. Amer. informal bunco.
▸ verb **1** *she was stung by a scorpion* **prick**, wound, injure, hurt; bite, nip, penetrate; poison; rare urticate.
2 *her eyes were stinging from all the smoke* **smart**, tingle, burn, be painful, hurt, be irritated, be sore, ache.
3 *in the past she had been stung by his criticism of her* **upset**, wound, distress, make miserable, cut to the quick, sear, grieve, hurt, pain, torment, mortify.
4 *he was stung into action by an article in the paper* **provoke**, goad, incite, spur, prick, prod, rouse, stir up, drive, move, motivate, galvanize, stimulate.

OPPOSITE deter.
5 (*informal*) *an elaborate fraud which stung the bank for thousands* **swindle**, defraud, cheat, fleece, gull; *informal* rip off, screw, do, rook, diddle, take for a ride, skin, clip, gyp; *N. Amer. informal* chisel, gouge, bunco; *Brit. informal, dated* rush.

stingy ▶ **adjective** (*informal*) *Colin was notoriously stingy* **mean**, miserly, parsimonious, niggardly, close-fisted, penny-pinching, cheese-paring, penurious, Scrooge-like, ungenerous, illiberal, close; *informal* mingy, tight, tight-fisted; *N. Amer. informal* cheap; *vulgar slang* tight-arsed; *archaic* near.
OPPOSITES generous, liberal, magnanimous.

stink ▶ **verb 1** *his clothes stank of sweat* **reek**, smell foul/bad/disgusting, stink/smell to high heaven, give off a bad smell.
2 (*informal*) *the whole idea stinks* **be very unpleasant**, be abhorrent, be despicable, be contemptible, be disgusting, be vile, be foul; *N. Amer. informal* suck.
3 (*informal*) *the whole affair* **stinks of** *a set-up* **strongly suggest**, have all the hallmarks of, smack of, give the impression of; reek of, smell of.
▶ **noun 1** *the stink of the place hit me as I went in* **stench**, reek, foul smell, bad smell, fetidness, effluvium, malodour, malodorousness, miasma; *Brit. informal* pong, niff, hum; *Scottish informal* guff; *Brit. rhyming slang* pen and ink; *N. Amer. informal* funk; *rare* fetor, mephitis, noisomeness.
2 (*informal*) *she kicked up a tremendous stink* **fuss**, commotion, rumpus, ruckus, trouble, outcry, uproar, brouhaha, furore; *informal* song and dance, to-do, carry-on, hoo-ha; *Brit. informal* row, kerfuffle; *N. Amer. informal* foofaraw.

stinker ▶ **noun** (*informal*) **1** *he's a real stinker* **unpleasant person**; *informal* swine, beast, pig, rat, creep, bastard, louse, snake, snake in the grass, skunk, dog, weasel, lowlife, scumbag, heel, stinkpot, bad lot, son of a bitch, s.o.b., nasty piece of work; *Scottish informal* scrote; *Irish informal* spalpeen; *N. Amer. informal* rat fink, fink, dirtbag; *Austral. informal* dingo; *NZ informal* kuri; *informal, dated* rotter, hound, bounder, blighter; *vulgar slang* shit, sod; *dated* cad; *archaic* blackguard, dastard, knave, varlet, whoreson.
2 *it's been a stinker of a day* **nightmare**, horror; *informal* beast, pig, swine, bummer, bastard, bitch; *Austral./NZ informal* cow; *vulgar slang* bugger, sod.

stinking ▶ **adjective 1** *a mountain of stinking rubbish* **foul-smelling**, evil-smelling, stinking to high heaven, reeking, fetid, malodorous, pungent, acrid, rank, putrid, noxious; *W. Indian* fresh; *informal* smelly, stinky, reeky; *Brit. informal* niffing, niffy, pongy, whiffy, humming; *N. Amer. informal* funky; *literary* noisome, mephitic; *rare* olid, miasmic, miasmal.
OPPOSITES sweet-smelling, aromatic.
2 (*informal*) *I've got a stinking cold and a sore throat* **dreadful**, awful, terrible, frightful, ghastly, nasty, appalling, vile, very bad; *Brit. informal* rotten, shocking.
OPPOSITES mild, slight.

stint ▶ **verb** *he doesn't stint on wining and dining* **skimp on**, scrimp on, be economical with, economize on, be sparing with, hold back on, be frugal with; **be mean with**, be parsimonious with, be niggardly with; limit, restrict; pinch pennies, spoil the ship for a ha'porth of tar; *informal* be stingy with, be mingy with, be tight-fisted with, be tight with.
▶ **noun** *his six-month stint on the surgical wards* **spell**, stretch, period, time, turn, run, session, term; shift, tour of duty, watch.

stipulate ▶ **verb** *he stipulated certain conditions before their marriage* **specify**, set down, set out, lay down, set forth, state clearly; demand, require, insist on, make a condition of, make a precondition/proviso of, prescribe, impose; *Law* provide.

stipulation ▶ **noun** *the only stipulation was that Edwards should retain his job as chairman for three years* **condition**, precondition, proviso, provision, prerequisite, requisite, specification; demand, requirement, non-negotiable point; rider, caveat, qualification; clause; terms.

S

stir ▶ **verb 1** *use a wooden spoon to stir the mixture | stir the ingredients together* **mix**, blend, agitate; beat, whip, whisk, fold in; *N. Amer.* muddle.
2 *Travis stirred in his sleep* **move slightly**, change one's position, twitch, quiver, tremble.
3 *a gentle breeze stirred the leaves* **disturb**, **rustle**, shake, move, flutter, agitate, swish.
4 *when Ruth eventually stirred, it was nearly lunchtime* **get up**, get out of bed, rouse oneself, bestir oneself, rise, show signs of life, be up and about, be active; **wake up**, awaken, waken; *informal* be up and doing, rise and shine, surface; *literary* arise.
OPPOSITES go to bed, retire.
5 *you won't even have to* **stir out of** *your office* **leave**, depart from, go out of; **move from**, budge from, make a move from, shift from.
OPPOSITES stay, stay put.
6 *her imagination was stirred by the thought* **arouse**, rouse, kindle, inspire, stimulate, excite, awaken, waken, quicken, animate, activate, galvanize, fire, electrify, whet; *literary* enkindle.
OPPOSITE stultify.
7 *the outbreak of the war stirred him to action* **spur**, drive, rouse, prompt, propel, prod, move, motivate, encourage; urge, impel, induce; provoke, goad, prick, sting, incite, inflame; *N. Amer.* light a fire under.
□ **stir something up** *his remarks stirred up a furore* **whip up**, work up, foment, fan the flames of, trigger, spark off, excite, provoke, instigate, incite; cause, precipitate, produce, generate, give rise to.
OPPOSITES stifle, suppress.
▶ **noun** *the event caused quite a stir* **commotion**, disturbance, fuss, ado, excitement, flurry, uproar, ferment, brouhaha, furore, turmoil, sensation; *informal* to-do, hoo-ha, hullabaloo, flap, song and dance, splash; *Brit. informal* kerfuffle.

stirring ▶ **adjective** *stirring accounts of our heroic history* **exciting**, thrilling, action-packed, gripping, riveting, dramatic, rousing, spirited, stimulating, moving, inspiring, inspirational, electrifying, passionate, impassioned, emotive, emotional, emotion-charged, heady, soul-stirring; *N. Amer.* stem-winding; *rare* inspiriting, anthemic.
OPPOSITES boring, pedestrian.

stitch *See centre pages for list of* **Sewing Techniques and Stitches**
▶ **noun** *he was panting and had a stitch* **sharp pain**, stabbing pain, shooting pain, stab of pain, pang, twinge, spasm.
▶ **verb** *the seam on her skirt needs stitching* **sew**, baste, tack, seam, hem; **sew up**, repair, mend, darn.
□ **stitch someone up** (*Brit. informal*) *I've been stitched up by the Richardson gang* **falsely incriminate**, get someone into trouble; *informal* frame, set up; *Brit. informal* fit someone up, drop someone in it.

stock ▶ **noun 1** *cash-and-carry outlets rely on a rapid turnover of stock* **merchandise**, **goods**, wares, items/articles for sale, commodities; *rare* vendibles.
2 *a stock of fuel | he had a good stock of jokes* **store**, supply, stockpile, reserve, hoard, cache, reservoir, accumulation, quantity, pile, heap, load; fund, bank, pool, mine, repertoire, repertory, inventory; collection, selection, assortment, variety, range; *rare* amassment.
3 *all the stock were housed and fed in sheds* **livestock**, **farm animals**, cattle, beasts; cows, sheep, pigs, horses, oxen, goats; flocks, herds.
4 *the railway's in-service stock is being repainted* **rolling stock**, trains, locomotives, carriages, wagons; machinery, equipment, apparatus, appliances, implements.
5 *the value of the company's stock rose by 86 per cent* **capital**, funds, assets, property.
6 *stock owned by foreign investors | blue-chip stocks* **investments**, shares, holdings, securities, equities, bonds; portfolio.
7 *I felt I was right but my stock was low with this establishment* **reputation**, standing, status, repute, position.
8 *he sighed and threw up his hands in a way that betrayed his French stock* **descent**, **ancestry**, origin(s), parentage, pedigree, lineage, line, line of descent, heritage, birth, extraction, background, family, blood, bloodline, genealogy, beginnings; *rare* filiation, stirps.
9 *a pint of chicken stock* **broth**; *French* bouillon.
10 *the stock of a tree* **trunk**, tree trunk, stem, stalk; *technical* caudex.
11 *the stock of a weapon* **handle**, butt, haft, grip, shaft, shank, helve.
□ **in stock** *we can order a book for you if we don't have it in stock* **for sale**, on sale, available, on the shelf.
□ **take stock of** *you need to take stock of the situation first* **review**, assess, reassess, weigh up, appraise, evaluate, re-evaluate, look carefully at, make an appraisal of; see how the land lies; *informal* size up.
▶ **adjective 1** *the rug comes in six stock sizes* **standard**, regular, ordinary, average; readily available, widely available; staple.
OPPOSITE non-standard.
2 *that has been the stock response to previous economic slowdowns* **usual**, routine, predictable, set, standard, staple, customary, familiar, conventional, traditional, stereotyped, clichéd, hackneyed, unoriginal, formulaic, ready-made, well worn, overused, overworked, worn out, banal, trite, platitudinous, tired, run-of-the-mill, commonplace.
OPPOSITES original, unusual.
▶ **verb 1** *most supermarkets now stock a range of organic produce* **sell**, market; supply, keep, keep in stock, have, have for sale, carry, handle; offer, provide; trade in, deal in.
2 *the bathroom was stocked with a variety of expensive toilet articles* **supply**, provide, equip, furnish, provision.
3 *I must* **stock up** *the fridge* **fill**, fill up, load, restock, replenish.
4 *you'd better* **stock up with** *fuel* **amass supplies of**, obtain a store of, buy up, stockpile, lay in, put away, put aside, put down, store up, collect, gather, accumulate, hoard, cache; *informal* squirrel away, salt away, stash away.

stockings ▶ **plural noun** nylons, stay-ups; tights; hosiery, hose; *N. Amer.* pantyhose.

stockpile ▶ **noun** *a stockpile of weapons* **stock**, store, supply, accumulation, collection, reserve, hoard, cache; bank, pool, fund, mine, reservoir; arsenal; *rare* amassment.
▶ **verb** *food and ammunition had been stockpiled* **store up**, amass, accumulate, hoard, cache, collect, gather, pile up, heap up, lay in, put away, put/set aside, put down, put by, put away for a rainy day, stow away, keep, keep in reserve, save; *informal* squirrel away, salt away, stash away.

stock-still ▶ **adverb** *he stood stock-still* **motionless**, completely still, unmoving, without moving, immobile, without moving a muscle, as if rooted to the spot, like a statue, as if turned to stone, unstirring; immobilized, inert.
OPPOSITE moving.

stocky ▶ adjective *a short, stocky man* **thickset**, heavily built, sturdy, sturdily built, heavyset, bull-necked, chunky, solid, dumpy, stubby, stumpy, squat; burly, beefy, meaty, hulking, strapping, hefty; cobby; *technical* mesomorphic, pyknic; *Austral./NZ* nuggety; *Brit. informal* fubsy.
OPPOSITES slender, skinny.

stodgy ▶ adjective **1** *rich, stodgy puddings* **indigestible**, starchy, filling, heavy, solid, substantial, lumpy, leaden.
OPPOSITES light, fluffy.
2 *a stodgy young man* **boring**, **dull**, uninteresting, dreary, deadly; prosaic, staid, sedate; **stuffy**, pompous, conventional; *informal* fuddy-duddy, square.
3 *he used to write rather stodgy plays* **boring**, **dull**, deadly dull, dull as ditchwater, uninteresting, dreary, turgid, tedious, dry, wearisome, heavy-going, unimaginative, uninspired, unexciting, unoriginal, monotonous, humdrum; laboured, wooden, ponderous, plodding, pedantic, banal, verbose.
OPPOSITES interesting, lively.

stoical ▶ adjective *my mother was more stoical and scorned such self-pity* **long-suffering**, uncomplaining, patient, forbearing, accepting, stoic, with the patience of Job, resigned, impassive, unemotional, phlegmatic, philosophical, fatalistic, imperturbable, calm, cool, unexcitable, stolid; *informal* unflappable; *rare* longanimous.

stoicism ▶ noun *she accepted her sufferings with remarkable stoicism* **patience**, forbearance, resignation, lack of protest, lack of complaint, fortitude, endurance, acceptance, acceptance of the inevitable, fatalism, philosophicalness, impassivity, dispassion, phlegm, imperturbability, calmness, coolness, cool; stolidness; *informal* unflappability; *rare* longanimity.

stoke ▶ verb *Dad returned to his chair while I stoked the fire* **add fuel to**, mend, keep burning, tend, fuel.

stole ▶ noun **shawl**, scarf, wrap, boa, tippet, cape.

stolid ▶ adjective *a stolid, slow-speaking man* **impassive**, phlegmatic, unemotional, calm, placid, unexcitable; apathetic, uninterested, unimaginative, indifferent; dull, bovine, lumpish, wooden, slow, lethargic, torpid, stupid.
OPPOSITES emotional, lively, imaginative.

stomach ▶ noun **1** *she had pains in her stomach* **abdomen**, belly, gut, middle; *informal* tummy, tum, breadbasket, insides; *Austral. informal* bingy.
2 *his fat stomach* **paunch**, pot belly, beer belly, girth; *informal* beer gut, pot, tummy, spare tyre, middle-aged spread; *Scottish informal* kyte; *N. Amer. informal* bay window; *dated, humorous* corporation.
3 *she had no stomach for food | he had little stomach for a fight* **appetite**, taste, hunger; **inclination**, desire, thirst, liking, fondness, relish, fancy, mind.
▶ verb **1** *if you cannot stomach orange juice, try apple juice* **digest**, keep down, find palatable, manage to eat/consume, swallow.
2 *I've had just about all I can stomach of your malicious slanders* **tolerate**, put up with, take, stand, endure, accept, swallow, bear, support, brook, submit to, countenance; *Scottish* thole; *informal* stick, hack, abide; *Brit. informal* wear, be doing with; *archaic* suffer.

WORD LINKS

relating to the stomach	**gastric**
branch of medicine concerning the stomach	**gastroenterology**
inflammation of the stomach	**gastritis**
inflammation of the stomach and intestines	**gastroenteritis**
removal of the stomach	**gastrotomy**
repair of the stomach	**gastroplasty**
opening of the stomach	**gastrostomy**
incision of the stomach	**gastrotomy**

stomach ache ▶ noun **indigestion**, dyspepsia; colic, gripe; *informal* bellyache, tummy ache, collywobbles.

stone *See centre pages for lists of* **Birthstones** **Gems** **Rocks**
▶ noun **1** *a gang of youths threw stones and missiles at police officers* **rock**, pebble, boulder; (**stones**) cobbles, gravel, scree; *rare* concretion.
2 *a memorial stone had been erected in place of the wooden cross* **gravestone**, headstone, tombstone; tablet, monument, monolith, obelisk.
3 *cracked paving stones* **slab**, flagstone, flag, sett.
4 *a gold ring with a small red stone* **gem**, gemstone, jewel, precious stone, semi-precious stone, brilliant; *informal* rock, sparkler; *archaic* bijou.
5 *cut the fruit in half and remove the stones* **kernel**, seed, pip, pit; *technical* endocarp.

WORD LINKS

relating to stone	**lithic, lapidary**
related prefix	**litho- (e.g. *lithography*)**
study of precious stones	**gemmology**

stony ▶ adjective **1** *a stony path* **rocky**, rock-strewn, pebbly, gravelly, shingly, gritty; rough, hard, rugged.
OPPOSITE smooth.
2 *his questions were met with a stony stare* **unfriendly**, cold, chilly, frosty, icy, frigid; hard, flinty, steely, stern, severe; fixed, expressionless, blank, poker-faced, deadpan; unfeeling, uncaring, unsympathetic, lacking compassion, insensitive, unmoved, indifferent, unresponsive, cold-hearted, callous, heartless, tough, hard-hearted, stony-hearted, inflexible, unbending, unyielding, uncompromising, merciless, pitiless, ruthless, unforgiving, hostile; *literary* adamantine; *rare* indurate, marble-hearted, Rhadamanthine.
OPPOSITES friendly, sympathetic.

stony broke ▶ adjective (*Brit. informal*). *See* PENNILESS.

stooge ▶ noun **1** *a government stooge* **underling**, minion, lackey, subordinate, assistant; henchman, myrmidon; **puppet**, pawn, cat's paw, instrument, tool, creature; *informal* sidekick, skivvy; *Brit. informal* dogsbody, poodle.
2 *a comedian's stooge* **butt**, foil, straight man.

stool ▶ noun. *See centre pages for list of* **Chairs and Stools**

stoop ▶ verb **1** *Linda stooped to pick up the bottles* **bend down**, bend, lean over, lean down, kneel, crouch down, squat down, hunker down, hunch down.
2 *he stooped his head* **lower**, bend, incline, bow, duck.
3 *he tends to stoop when he walks* **hunch one's shoulders**, walk with a stoop, be round-shouldered.
4 *are you suggesting that I would stoop to blackmail?* **lower oneself**, sink, descend, resort; be reduced, go as far as, sink as low as.
5 (*archaic*) *she wouldn't stoop to let any man marry her* **condescend**, deign, lower oneself, humble oneself, demean oneself, debase oneself.
▶ noun *a tall, thin man with a stoop* **hunch**, droop/sag of the shoulders; round-shoulderedness; *technical* curvature of the spine, kyphosis.

stop ▶ verb **1** *drastic measures are needed to stop the decline* **put an end to**, put a stop to, bring to an end, end, bring to a stop, halt, bring to a halt; finish, bring to a close, terminate, bring to a standstill, wind up, discontinue, cut short, interrupt, nip in the bud; immobilize, paralyse, deactivate, shut down.
OPPOSITES start, begin; continue.
2 *you really should stop smoking* **cease**, discontinue, refrain from, desist from, forbear from, break off, call a halt to, call it a day; give up, abandon, abstain from, cut out; *Nautical* belay; *informal* quit, leave off, knock off, pack in, lay off, give over, jack in.
3 *the car stopped outside a terraced house* **pull up**, draw up, come to a stop, come to a halt, come to rest, pull in, pull over; park; *Austral.* prop.
4 *the music stopped | work stopped at the mine in 1948* **come to an end**, come to a stop, cease, end, finish, draw to a close, be over, conclude, terminate, come to a standstill; pause, break off; peter out, fade away.
5 *she pressed a pad against his side to stop the flow of blood* **stem**, staunch, hold back, check, dam, slow, restrict, restrain; *N. Amer.* stanch; *archaic* stay.
6 *he tried to stop her leaving the house* **prevent**, hinder, obstruct, impede, block, bar, preclude; dissuade from.
OPPOSITE encourage.
7 *a court action brought by protesters attempting to stop the road plan* **thwart**, baulk, foil, frustrate, stand in the way of, forestall; scotch, derail; *informal* put paid to, put the stopper on, put the kibosh on, do for, stymie; *Brit. informal* scupper.
OPPOSITE expedite.
8 *talks broke down, and the employers stopped the strikers' wages* **withhold**, suspend, keep back, hold back, refuse to pay, cut off, discontinue.
9 *he tried to stop the hole with the heel of his boot* **block (up)**, plug, close (up), fill (up); seal, caulk; bung up, clog (up), jam (up), choke (up); occlude.
□ **stop off/over** *he decided to stop over in Paris* **break one's journey**, take a break, pause; stay, remain, put up, lodge, rest; *formal* sojourn; *dated* tarry.
▶ noun **1** *all business came to a stop* **halt**, end, finish, close, standstill; cessation, conclusion, termination, stoppage, discontinuation, discontinuance; pause.
OPPOSITES start, beginning, continuation.
2 *a brief stop at the small town of Kenora* **break**, stopover, stop-off, stay, rest; *formal* sojourn.
3 *she got off the bus at the last stop* **bus stop**, stopping place, halt; terminus, terminal, depot, station; *Brit.* fare stage, stage.
4 *a stop at the end of a sentence* **full stop**, full point, point; punctuation mark; *N. Amer.* period.
□ **put a stop to** *new legislation could well put a stop to this practice* **bring to an end**, halt, put an end to, end, bring to a stop, bring to a halt; finish, bring to a close, terminate, bring to a standstill, wind up, discontinue, nip in the bud, put a/the lid on; quell, quash, subdue, suppress, stifle; *informal* put paid to, put the kibosh on, put the stopper on, do for.

stopgap ▶ noun *such tissue transplants are only a stopgap until more sophisticated alternatives can be found* **temporary solution**, improvisation, expedient, makeshift, last resort; substitute, stand-in.
▶ adjective *a stopgap solution | a stopgap prime minister* **temporary**, provisional, interim, pro tem, short-term, working, makeshift, improvised, emergency, impromptu, rough and ready; caretaker, acting, stand-in, fill-in; *Nautical* jury-rigged, jury; *rare* expediential.
OPPOSITE permanent.

stopover ▶ noun *a brief stopover in the United Kingdom en route to the US* **stay**, stop, break, stop-off, visit; *formal* sojourn.

stoppage ▶ noun **1** *the stoppage of grain exports* **discontinuation**, discontinuance, stopping, halting, halt, cessation, termination, end, finish; interruption, suspension, breaking off.

S

OPPOSITES start, beginning, continuation.
2 *a two-day stoppage by workers in the hotel industry* **strike**, walkout, shutdown, closure; industrial action.
3 *the stoppage of the blood supply* **obstruction**, blocking; *technical* occlusion, arrest, stasis, suppression.
4 *a stoppage in the petrol supply* **blockage**, obstruction, block; airlock.
5 (*Brit.*) *she was paid £3.40 an hour before stoppages* **deduction**, subtraction.

stopper ▶ **noun** *a cologne bottle with a cork and chrome stopper* **cork**, lid, cap, top; **plug**, bung, spigot, spile; *N. Amer.* stopple.

store ▶ **noun 1** *a store of food | her vast store of knowledge* **supply**, stock, stockpile, reserve, cache, hoard, accumulation, cumulation, quantity, pile, heap, load; fund, bank, pool, mine, wealth, deposit, reservoir, inventory, repertoire, repertory; *rare* amassment.
2 *a grain store* **storeroom**, storehouse, warehouse, repository, depository, entrepôt; granary, silo; larder, pantry; arsenal, armoury; *Brit. historical* still room; *archaic* garner, spence.
3 (**stores**) *there was a vital need to recruit fresh men and to replenish the stores* **supplies**, provisions, stocks, rations, food, foodstuffs; *formal* comestibles, provender.
4 *a DIY store* **shop**, retail outlet, department store, chain store, emporium; supermarket, hypermarket, superstore; mart.
□ **set store by** *Gwen set great store by good manners* **value**, attach great importance to, put a high value on, put a premium on; **think highly of**, hold in (high) regard, have a high opinion of, admire, appreciate, respect, prize, esteem; *informal* rate.
▶ **verb 1** *the animals need a place to store food for the winter* **keep**, keep in reserve, stow, stockpile, lay in/aside, set aside, put away, put down, put to one side, deposit, save, hoard, cache; stock up with/on, get in supplies of, collect, gather, accumulate, cumulate, amass; husband, reserve, preserve; *informal* put away for a rainy day, squirrel away, salt away, stash.
OPPOSITE use.
2 *furniture that had been stored in the attic for thirty years* **put into storage**, put in store, stow (away), put away; warehouse.
OPPOSITE discard.

storehouse ▶ **noun** **warehouse**, depository, repository, store, storeroom, depot, entrepôt; granary, silo; treasury, vault, strongroom; arsenal, armoury; (*in India & Malaysia*) godown; *archaic* garner.

storey ▶ **noun** *a small flat on the second storey* **floor**, level, tier; flight, deck; piano nobile, mezzanine, entresol.

storm ▶ **noun 1** *the severe storms that battered Orkney earlier this year* **tempest**, squall; gale, hurricane, tornado, cyclone, typhoon; thunderstorm, cloudburst, downpour, rainstorm, hailstorm, deluge, monsoon, tropical storm, electrical storm; snowstorm, blizzard; dust storm, dust devil; *N. Amer.* williwaw, ice storm, windstorm; (*in central Asia*) buran. *See also* **WIND**.
2 *he's at the centre of a drugs storm in Germany* **uproar**, commotion, furore, brouhaha, trouble, disturbance, hue and cry, upheaval; controversy, scandal, argument, fracas, fight, war of words; *informal* to-do, hoo-ha, rumpus, hullabaloo, ballyhoo, ructions, stink; *Brit. informal* row.
3 *the decision provoked a storm of protest* **outburst**, outbreak, explosion, eruption, outpouring, surge, upsurge, avalanche, torrent, flood, deluge; blaze, flare-up.
4 *a storm of bullets* **volley**, salvo, fusillade, barrage, discharge, shower, spray, hail, rain.
5 *an attempt at a storm on the castle was beaten back by defenders* **assault**, attack, onslaught, offensive, charge, raid, foray, sortie, rush, descent, incursion, thrust, push, blitz, blitzkrieg, aggression; *archaic* onset.
▶ **verb 1** *she snatched up her coat and stormed out of the kitchen* **stride angrily**, stomp, march, charge, stalk, flounce, stamp, fling.
2 *police stormed the building* **attack**, charge, rush, conduct an offensive on, make an onslaught on, make a raid/foray/sortie on, descend on, take by storm, attempt to capture.
3 *his mother stormed at him and ordered him to go to bed* **rant**, rave, rant and rave, shout, bellow, roar, thunder, rage, explode.

S

stormy ▶ **adjective 1** *the weather was wet and stormy | a stormy wind was blowing* **blustery**, squally, wild, tempestuous, turbulent, windy, gusty, blowy, rainy, thundery, rough, choppy; angry, dirty, foul, nasty, inclement; howling, roaring, raging, furious; *rare* boisterous.
OPPOSITES calm, fine.
2 *the votes came after a long and stormy debate | their relationship had been stormy* **angry**, heated, fiery, fierce, impassioned, passionate, 'lively'; **tempestuous**, turbulent, tumultuous, explosive, volatile, violent, intense.
OPPOSITE peaceful.

story *See centre pages for list of* **Stories** (*Types of Story and Novel*)
▶ **noun 1** *an adventure story* **tale**, narrative, account, recital; anecdote; chronicle, history; *informal* yarn, spiel.
2 *the novel has a good story* **plot**, storyline, scenario, chain of events; *technical* diegesis.
3 *the story appeared in the papers in the usual tabloid style* **news item**, news report, article, feature, piece; exclusive, exposé; spoiler; *informal* scoop.
4 *there have been a lot of stories going round, as you can imagine* **rumour**, piece of gossip, piece of hearsay, whisper; speculation; *French* on dit; *informal* kidology; *Austral./NZ informal* furphy.
5 *Harper changed his story about how the fire started* **testimony**, statement, report, account, version, description, representation.
6 *Ellie never told stories—she had always believed in the truth* **lie**, fib, falsehood, untruth, fabrication, fiction, piece of fiction; white lie; *Irish* pishogue; *W. African* nancy story; *informal* tall story, fairy story, fairy tale, cock and bull story, shaggy-dog story, whopper, terminological inexactitude, fish story; *Brit. informal* pork pie, porky pie, porky.
OPPOSITE the truth.

storyteller ▶ **noun** **narrator**, teller of tales, taleteller, spinner of yarns; raconteur, raconteuse; writer, author, novelist, chronicler, fabulist; (*in Africa*) griot; (*in India*) kathak; *Austral. informal* magsman; *rare* anecdotist, anecdotalist.

stout ▶ **adjective 1** *a short stout man* **fat**, fattish, plump, portly, rotund, roly-poly, pot-bellied, round, dumpy, chunky, broad in the beam, overweight, fleshy, paunchy, corpulent; buxom, well upholstered, well covered, well padded, of ample proportions, ample, rounded, well rounded; stocky, burly, bulky, hulking, hefty, meaty, heavily built, solidly built, thickset, heavyset, sturdy, well built; *informal* tubby, pudgy, beefy, porky, blubbery, poddy; *Brit. informal* podgy, fubsy; *N. Amer. informal* zaftig, corn-fed, lard-assed; *archaic* pursy; *rare* abdominous.
OPPOSITES thin, slender.
2 *Billy had armed himself with a stout stick | stout leather shoes* **strong**, sturdy, heavy, solid, substantial, robust, tough, strongly made, durable, hard-wearing; thick.
OPPOSITES flimsy, fragile.
3 *the garrison put up a stout resistance* **determined**, full of determination, vigorous, forceful, spirited, stout-hearted; **staunch**, steadfast, stalwart, firm, resolute, unyielding, unbending, unfaltering, unswerving, unwavering, unflinching, stubborn, dogged; **brave**, bold, plucky, courageous, valiant, valorous, gallant, fearless, undaunted, dauntless, doughty, mettlesome, unafraid, intrepid, manly, heroic, lionhearted; *N. Amer.* rock-ribbed; *informal* gutsy, spunky.
OPPOSITES half-hearted, feeble, cowardly.

stout-hearted ▶ **adjective** *a stout-hearted man who was not easily deterred* **brave**, **determined**, full of determination, courageous, bold, plucky, spirited, valiant, valorous, gallant, fearless, undaunted, dauntless, doughty, unafraid, intrepid, manly, heroic, lionhearted; **stalwart**, staunch, steadfast, firm, resolute, unfaltering, unswerving, unwavering, unflinching; *N. Amer.* rock-ribbed; *informal* gutsy, spunky.
OPPOSITES cowardly, feeble.

stove ▶ **noun** **oven**, range; charcoal burner, furnace; *Brit.* cooker; *Indian* tandoor; *trademark* Aga, Primus.

stow ▶ **verb** *Barney began stowing her luggage into the boot* **pack**, load, store; place, put, put away, deposit; bundle, cram, jam, wedge, stash; *informal* stuff, shove.
OPPOSITES unload, remove.
□ **stow away** *he stowed away on a ship bound for South Africa* **hide**, conceal oneself, secrete oneself; travel secretly.

straddle ▶ **verb 1** *she straddled the motorbike and revved it up* **sit/stand astride**, bestride, bestraddle; mount, get on.
2 *a mountain range straddling the Franco-Swiss border* **lie on both sides of**, be situated on both sides of, extend across; span.
3 *a man who had straddled the issue of taxes* **be equivocal about**, be undecided about, be non-committal about, equivocate about, vacillate about, waver about; *Brit.* hum and haw; *informal* sit on the fence.

strafe ▶ **verb** *military aircraft strafed the village* **bomb**, shell, bombard, fire on, open fire on, machine-gun, rake with gunfire, blitz, enfilade, pound, rake, pepper; attack; *archaic* fusillade.

straggle ▶ **verb 1** *a few of the men were straggling some half a mile behind the rest* **trail**, lag, dawdle, amble, wander, walk slowly, meander, drift; fall behind, bring up the rear; be strung out.
2 *his thin grey hair straggled over the collar of his coat* **grow untidily**, be messy, be dishevelled, be unkempt.
3 *copses of beech and alder straggled along the banks* **spread irregularly**, sprawl, be scattered, be dispersed.

straggly ▶ **adjective** *a thin woman with straggly hair* **untidy**, messy, unkempt, straggling, dishevelled, bedraggled; *informal* ratty.

straight ▶ **adjective 1** *the aircraft continued on a straight course | a long, straight road* **unswerving**, undeviating, linear, direct, as straight as an arrow, uncurving, unbending.
OPPOSITES winding, zigzag.
2 *one of us must have knocked that picture—it's not straight* **level**, even, true, in line, aligned, square, plumb, properly positioned; symmetrical; vertical, upright, perpendicular; horizontal.
OPPOSITES crooked, askew.
3 *it'll take a long time to get the place straight* **in order**, tidy, neat and tidy, neat, shipshape (and Bristol fashion), in apple-pie order, orderly, spick and span, organized, arranged, sorted out, straightened out, trim, spruce; *informal* together.
OPPOSITES untidy, messy.

4 *a straight answer* **honest**, direct, frank, candid, truthful, sincere, forthright, straightforward, plain-spoken, plain-speaking, plain, blunt, downright, outspoken, straight from the shoulder, no-nonsense, unequivocal, unambiguous, unqualified, unvarnished; *informal* upfront; *archaic* round, free-spoken.
OPPOSITES indirect, evasive.
5 *action is never effective without straight thinking* **logical**, rational, clear, lucid, sound, coherent, unemotional, dispassionate.
OPPOSITES irrational, illogical.
6 *three straight wins* **successive**, in succession, consecutive, in a row, one after the other; running, uninterrupted, solid, unbroken; *informal* on the trot.
7 *straight brandy* **undiluted**, neat, unmixed, unadulterated, pure, unblended, uncut; *N. Amer. informal* straight up.
OPPOSITE diluted.
8 (*informal*) *she won't stand for anything like that—she's too straight* **respectable**, upright, upstanding, honourable, honest, on the level, decent, right-minded, law-abiding; **conventional**, conservative, traditional, conformist, old-fashioned, strait-laced, unadventurous; *informal* stuffy, square, fuddy-duddy.
▶ **adverb 1** *he looked me straight in the eyes | the ball hit him straight on the head* **right**, directly, squarely, full, plumb; *informal* smack, bang, slap bang; *N. Amer. informal* spang, smack dab.
2 *she drove straight home* **directly**, right, by a direct route, without deviating, in a beeline; as the crow flies, by the shortest route.
3 *I'll call you straight back* **right away**, straight away, without delay, immediately, directly, at once, as soon as possible, a.s.a.p.; *French* tout de suite; *informal* toot sweet, before you can say Jack Robinson, before you can say knife; *archaic* straightway, instanter.
OPPOSITES later, eventually.
4 *I told her straight that it was over* **frankly**, directly, straight out, candidly, honestly, forthrightly, outspokenly, plainly, point-blank, bluntly, flatly, roundly, straight from the shoulder, with no holds barred, without beating about the bush, without mincing words, unequivocally, unambiguously, in plain English, to someone's face; *informal* pulling no punches; *Brit. informal* straight up.
5 *he's so wound up over you he can't think straight* **logically**, rationally, clearly, lucidly, coherently, cogently, unemotionally, dispassionately; properly, correctly.
□ **go straight reform**, mend one's ways, turn over a new leaf, make a fresh start; *informal* get back on the straight and narrow.
OPPOSITE reoffend.
□ **straight away** *okay, I'll get on to it straight away* **at once**, right away, now, right now, this/that (very) minute, this/that instant, immediately, instantly, in/like a flash, directly, on the spot, forthwith, without further/more ado, promptly, quickly, without delay, then and there, there and then, here and now, a.s.a.p., as soon as possible, as quickly as possible, with all speed; *N. Amer.* in short order; *French* tout de suite; *informal* straight off, toot sweet, double quick, in double quick time, p.d.q. (pretty damn quick), pronto, before you can say Jack Robinson, from the word go; *N. Amer. informal* lickety-split; *Indian informal* ekdam; *archaic* straight, straightway, instanter, forthright.
OPPOSITES later, eventually.
□ **straight from the shoulder** *he spoke straight from the shoulder* **frankly**, candidly, honestly, directly, forthrightly, bluntly, plainly, roundly, explicitly, outspokenly, unequivocally, unambiguously, with no holds barred, without beating about the bush, without mincing words, man to man, woman to woman; *informal* pulling no punches.
OPPOSITE evasively.

WORD LINKS
related prefix **ortho-**
straightening of teeth **orthodontics**

straighten ▶ **verb 1** *Rory straightened his tie | she brushed her hair and straightened her clothing* **make straight**, align; adjust, arrange, rearrange, tidy, make tidy, neaten, spruce up; uncoil, unkink, uncurl.
2 *he didn't know how to* ***straighten things out*** *with Viola* **put/set right**, sort out, iron out, clear up, settle, resolve, find a solution to, put in order, tidy up, regulate, regularize, rectify, repair, remedy; disentangle, unravel, unsnarl, untangle; *informal* patch up.
OPPOSITES confuse, complicate.
3 *he* ***straightened up***, *using the bedside table for support* **stand up**, stand up straight, stand upright, straighten one's back.
OPPOSITE bend over.

straightforward ▶ **adjective 1** *the process was remarkably straightforward* **uncomplicated**, simple, easy, effortless, painless, undemanding, unexacting; elementary, plain sailing, a five-finger exercise, child's play; routine; *informal* as easy as falling off a log, as easy as pie, as easy as ABC, a piece of cake, a cinch, a snip, easy-peasy, no sweat, a doddle, money for old rope, money for jam, kids' stuff, a breeze, a doss, a cakewalk; *N. Amer. informal* duck soup, a snap; *Austral./NZ informal* a bludge, a snack; *S. African informal* a piece of old tackle.
OPPOSITES complicated, difficult.
2 *a straightforward man* **honest**, **frank**, candid, open, truthful, sincere, on the level, honest-to-goodness; **forthright**, plain-speaking, direct, unambiguous, straight from the shoulder, downright, not afraid to call a spade a spade; *informal* upfront, on the square; *N. Amer. informal* two-fisted, on the up and up; *archaic* free-spoken, round.
OPPOSITES evasive, guarded, disingenuous.

strain[1] ▶ **verb 1** *take care that you don't strain yourself* **overtax**, overwork, overburden, overextend, overreach, overtask, make too many demands on, run/work oneself into the ground, exert excessively, drive too far, exert to the limit, push to the limit; exhaust, wear out, fatigue, tire, tax; overdo it, work too hard; *informal* knacker, knock oneself out.
2 *on cold days you are more likely to strain a muscle* **injure**, hurt, damage, impair; pull, wrench, tear, twist, sprain, rick, crick.
3 *we strained to haul the guns up an almost perpendicular slope* **struggle**, labour, toil, make a supreme effort, make every effort, spare no effort, strain every nerve, try very hard, strive, break one's back, push/drive oneself to the limit, do one's best; *informal* pull out all the stops, go all out, give it one's all, bend/lean over backwards, give it one's best shot, bust a gut, break one's neck, do one's damnedest, kill oneself; *Austral. informal* go for the doctor.
4 *the flood of refugees is straining the relief services* **make severe demands on**, make excessive demands on, overtax, be too much for; exceed the limits of, drain, sap, use up, exceed the range/scope of, overstep; test, tax, put a strain on, fray.
5 *the bear strained at the chain around its neck* **pull**, tug, heave, haul, jerk; push; *informal* yank.
6 (*archaic*) *she strained the infant to her bosom* **clasp**, press, clutch, squeeze, hold tight; **embrace**, hug, enfold, fold, envelop.
7 *strain the mixture to remove the seeds* **sieve**, sift, filter, screen, riddle, separate; percolate; leach; *rare* filtrate, griddle.
▶ **noun 1** *the rope snapped under the strain* **tension**, tightness, tautness, shear, distension; *rare* tensity.
2 *a severe stomach muscle strain* **injury**; sprain, wrench, twist, rick.
3 *the overwhelming strain of her job* **pressure**, demands, burdens, exertions; stress, tension; *informal* hassle.
4 *Melissa was showing signs of strain* **stress**, tension, nervous tension, anxiety; exhaustion, fatigue, tiredness, weariness, pressure of work, overwork, duress.
OPPOSITE relaxation.
5 (**strains**) *the soothing strains of Brahms's lullaby* **sound**, music; melody, tune, air, song.

strain[2] ▶ **noun 1** *a different strain of flu | a strain of mice* **variety**, kind, type, sort; breed, genus.
2 *Hawthorne was of Puritan strain* **descent**, **ancestry**, stock, origin(s), parentage, pedigree, lineage, line, heritage, birth, extraction, derivation, background, family, blood, bloodline, genealogy, roots; *rare* filiation, stirps.
3 *there was a* ***strain of*** *insanity on her mother's side of the family* **tendency to**, susceptibility to, propensity to, proneness to, proclivity to, inclination to; trait, characteristic, disposition.
4 *they have injected a strain of solemnity into a genre of film renowned for its irreverence* **element**, strand, streak, vein, note, trace, touch, dash, tinge, suggestion, hint, suspicion; *French* soupçon.
5 (*archaic*) *he continued in the same strain for over an hour* **tone**, spirit, vein, tenor, temper; manner, way, style.

strained ▶ **adjective 1** *a strained silence | relations between the two countries were strained* **awkward**, **tense**, uneasy, uncomfortable, fraught, edgy, difficult, troubled, embarrassed, unrelaxed, stilted.
OPPOSITES relaxed, friendly.
2 *Jean's pale, strained face* **drawn**, careworn, worn, pinched, tired, exhausted, weary, fatigued, drained; haggard, hollow-cheeked.
3 *he gave her a strained smile* **forced**, constrained, laboured, wooden, stiff, self-conscious, hollow, unnatural; **artificial**, insincere, false, affected, put-on.
OPPOSITE natural.

strainer ▶ **noun sieve**, colander, filter, sifter, riddle, screen; *archaic* griddle.

strait ▶ **noun 1** *the island is separated from the mainland by a strait about six miles wide* **channel**, sound, narrows, inlet, stretch of water, arm of the sea, sea passage, neck; *Scottish* kyle.
2 (**straits**) *by Christmas, the company was in* ***desperate straits*** **a bad/difficult situation**, a sorry condition, difficulty, trouble, crisis, a mess, a predicament, a plight, a tight corner; *informal* a pretty/fine kettle of fish, hot water, deep water, a jam, a hole, a bind, a fix, a scrape.

straitened ▶ **adjective** *he died in 1886, leaving the family* ***in straitened circumstances*** **impoverished**, poverty-stricken, poor, destitute, penniless, on one's beam-ends, as poor as a church mouse, without a sou, dirt poor, in penury, penurious, impecunious, indigent, needy, needful, in need/want, unable to make ends meet, down and out, necessitous, beggarly, moneyless, bankrupt, in reduced circumstances; *Brit.* on the breadline, without a penny (to one's name); *informal* broke, flat broke, cleaned out, strapped for cash, strapped, on one's uppers; *Brit. informal* stony broke, skint, without two pennies/farthings to rub together, in Queer Street;

S

N. Amer. informal stone broke; *rare* pauperized, beggared.

strait-laced ▶ adjective *his strait-laced parents were horrified* **prim and proper**, prim, proper, prudish, priggish, puritanical, moralistic, prissy, mimsy, niminy-piminy, shockable, Victorian, old-maidish, schoolmistressy, schoolmarmish, governessy; conventional, conservative, old-fashioned, stuffy, staid, of the old school, narrow-minded; *informal* goody-goody, starchy, square, fuddy-duddy, stick-in-the-mud; *rare* Grundyish, Pecksniffian.
OPPOSITES permissive, broad-minded.

strand[1] ▶ noun **1** *strands of wool* **thread**, filament, fibre; length, piece, string; ply; *technical* fibril.
2 *a few strands of blonde hair* **lock**, tress, wisp, tendril; curl, ringlet.
3 *his introduction draws the ideological strands of this ambitious work together* **element**, component, factor, ingredient, aspect, feature; theme, strain.

strand[2] ▶ noun (*literary*) *they'd gone for a walk along the strand* **seashore**, shore, beach, sands, foreshore, shoreline; coast, seaside, seaboard, waterfront, front, waterside, water's edge; *technical* littoral; *French* plage.

stranded ▶ adjective **1** *the stranded ship* **beached**, grounded, run aground, high and dry, stuck; shipwrecked, wrecked; marooned, cast away.
2 *she was left stranded in a city she hardly knew* **helpless**, without help/assistance, without resources, in difficulties; in the lurch, abandoned, forsaken, deserted; trapped, cut off.

strange ▶ adjective **1** *suddenly, I heard a strange noise | strange things have been happening round here* **unusual**, odd, curious, peculiar, funny, bizarre, weird, uncanny, queer, unexpected, unfamiliar, abnormal, atypical, anomalous, untypical, different, out of the ordinary, out of the way, extraordinary, remarkable, puzzling, mystifying, mysterious, perplexing, baffling, unaccountable, inexplicable, incongruous, uncommon, irregular, singular, deviant, aberrant, freak, freakish, surreal; suspicious, dubious, questionable; eerie, unnatural; *French* outré; *Scottish* unco; *informal* fishy, creepy, spooky; *Brit. informal* rum; *N. Amer. informal* bizarro.
OPPOSITES ordinary, usual.
2 *he's a very strange man | their strange clothes and hairstyles* **weird**, **eccentric**, odd, peculiar, funny, bizarre, unusual, abnormal; **unconventional**, idiosyncratic, outlandish, offbeat, freakish, quirky, quaint, zany, off-centre; *informal* wacky, way out, freaky, kooky, kinky, oddball, like nothing on earth, cranky; *N. Amer. informal* screwy, off the wall, wacko; *Austral./NZ informal, dated* dilly.
OPPOSITES normal, conventional.
3 *when children visit a strange house, they are often a little shy* **unfamiliar**, unknown, new, alien, previously unencountered.
OPPOSITE familiar.
4 *Jean was beginning to feel a little strange* **ill**, unwell, poorly, indisposed, not (very) well, not oneself, out of sorts, not up to par, under/below par, peaky, liverish, sick, queasy, nauseous; *Brit.* off, off colour; *informal* under the weather, not up to snuff, funny, peculiar, crummy, lousy, rough; *Brit. informal* ropy, grotty; *Scottish informal* wabbit; *Austral./NZ informal* crook; *dated* queer, seedy.
OPPOSITE well.
5 *it had been a long time since she'd seen him and she felt strange* **ill at ease**, uneasy, edgy, uncomfortable, awkward, self-conscious, embarrassed; out of place, like a fish out of water, disorientated.
OPPOSITE relaxed.
6 (*archaic*) *I am strange to the work.* See A STRANGER TO.

CHOOSE THE RIGHT WORD

strange, odd, curious, peculiar

These words are all applied to things that are unusual or unfamiliar; they generally also suggest that something is in some way surprising.

- **Strange** is the most neutral term for something that is not expected or is hard to understand or explain (*this is strange behaviour for a left-wing party | he looked at her with a strange expression*). This is the only word of the four that can be used in the expression *strange to say*, as in *I went to see 'Fallen Angels', which, strange to say, is a hit.*
- **Odd** gives a stronger sense that the speaker or writer is perplexed (*do you think it odd that I pay her bills? | they were an odd family*).
- Describing something as **curious** implies that one finds it not only strange or puzzling but also interesting or appealing (*the church has a curious history | the room is filled with a curious mixture of people*). It rarely has the connotation of deviance that the other words can have.
- Something described as **peculiar** is felt to be very strange, even disturbingly so (*he was struck by the peculiar appearance of a group of birds | whoever thought up that joke has a peculiar sense of humour*).

S

strangeness ▶ noun *the strangeness of Eliot's behaviour* **oddity**, **eccentricity**, oddness, peculiarity, curiousness, bizarreness, weirdness, queerness, unexpectedness, unusualness, abnormality, atypicality, unfamiliarity, unaccountability, inexplicability, incongruity, incongruousness, outlandishness, irregularity, singularity; freakishness, surrealness.
OPPOSITES ordinariness, conventionality.

stranger ▶ noun **1** *the man standing beside her was a complete stranger* **unknown person**; *Scottish* unco.
2 *he was a stranger in the town* **newcomer**, new arrival, incomer; visitor; foreigner, outsider, alien; *N. English* offcomer; *Austral. informal* blow-in.

□ **a stranger to** *Harker was a stranger to self-doubt* **unaccustomed to**, unfamiliar with, unused to, unacquainted with, new to, fresh to, inexperienced in, unpractised in, unversed in, unconversant with; *archaic* strange to.

strangle ▶ verb **1** *the victim was strangled with a scarf* **throttle**, choke, garrotte; asphyxiate, stifle; *informal* strangulate.
2 *she strangled a sob* **suppress**, smother, stifle, repress, restrain, hold back, hold in, fight back, bite back, gulp back, swallow, choke back, check.
OPPOSITE let out.
3 *too much security is strangling commercial activity in the town* **hamper**, hinder, impede, restrict, interfere with, inhibit, hold back, curb, check, restrain, constrain; prevent, put an end/stop to, stop, quash, squash, stamp out, destroy, crush, extinguish, deaden, damp down, subdue, suppress, repress; silence, muffle, mute, gag.
OPPOSITES encourage, promote.

strap ▶ noun *he undid the thick leather straps* **thong**, tie, cord, band, belt, tape; leash, lead.
▶ verb **1** *a leather bag was strapped on to the bicycle frame* **fasten**, secure, tie, bind, make fast, lash; buckle; truss, pinion.
2 *the goalkeeper's knee was strapped up* **bandage**, bind.
3 *his father had strapped him* **beat**, flog, whip, leather, belt, thrash, lash, horsewhip, birch, cane, strike, hit, clout; *informal* wallop, whack, tan someone's hide, give someone a (good) hiding, beat the living daylights out of, lather, larrup; *N. Amer. informal* whale; *archaic* stripe, thong.

strapping ▶ adjective *they had three strapping sons* **big**, **strong**, well built, sturdily built, sturdy, brawny, burly, broad-shouldered, muscular, muscly, well muscled, robust, rugged, lusty, Herculean; *informal* hunky, beefy, husky; *dated* stalwart; *literary* thewy, stark.
OPPOSITES puny, weedy.

stratagem ▶ noun *he deployed various cunning stratagems* **plan**, scheme, tactic, manoeuvre, move, course/line of action, ploy, gambit, device, wile; trick, ruse, plot, machination, subterfuge, artifice, contrivance, expedient, dodge, deception, deceit; *Brit. informal* wheeze; *Austral. informal* lurk; *archaic* shift.

strategic ▶ adjective **1** *a strategic move towards their long-term goal of gaining international recognition* **planned**, calculated, deliberate; tactical, politic, judicious, prudent, clever, shrewd, well thought out.
OPPOSITE random.
2 *Russia's retention of strategic bases in the region* **essential**, key, vital, crucial, critical, important.
OPPOSITE unimportant.

strategy ▶ noun **1** *the government's economic strategy* **master plan**, grand design, game plan, plan of action, plan, policy, proposed action, scheme, blueprint, programme, procedure, approach, schedule; tactics, set of tactics.
2 *the process could revolutionize military strategy* **the art of war**, military science, military tactics; generalship.

strategy or tactics?

Both these words denote approaches adopted after reasoning about the best way to achieve one's aims. In military usage, **strategy** denotes the overall planning of operations, while **tactics** applies to the deployment of troops in battle, contributing towards the achievement of a larger *strategy*. More generally, *strategy* denotes planning, usually long-term, towards a major goal (*rethinking sales strategy | the tourist board has launched a major review of its strategy for tourism in Wales*), while *tactics* refers to the adoption of plans in response to a more immediate problem (*the player should be free to concentrate on the tactics of the game*).

stratum ▶ noun **1** *a stratum of flint* **layer**, vein, seam, lode, bed; stratification, thickness, sheet, lamina.
2 *a particular stratum of society* **level**, class, echelon, rank, grade, station, gradation; group, set, bracket; caste; *archaic* estate, sphere.

stray ▶ verb **1** *a young gazelle which had strayed from the herd* **wander off**, go astray, drift, get separated; get lost, lose one's way.
2 *we appeared to have strayed a long way from our original topic* **digress**, deviate, wander, drift, get sidetracked, go off at a tangent; get off the subject, lose the thread; *rare* divagate.
3 *the younger the men were, the more likely they were to stray* **be unfaithful**, have affairs, philander; *informal* play around, carry on, play the field.
4 *he had strayed from the path of righteousness* **sin**, transgress, err, go astray,

go wrong, do wrong, stray from the straight and narrow, go down the primrose path, fall from grace; *archaic* trespass.
5 (*archaic*) *you are too young to be straying about in a strange place* **roam**, rove, wander, ramble, meander, drift, range, stroll, amble; *Scottish* stravaig.
▶ **adjective 1** *a stray dog* **homeless**, lost, strayed, gone astray; abandoned, unclaimed; wandering, vagrant.
2 *she was killed by a stray bullet* **random**, chance, accidental, freak, unexpected, casual, haphazard; odd, isolated, lone, single; scattered, occasional, incidental.
▶ **noun** *the council employs two wardens to deal with strays* **homeless animal**, stray dog/cat; homeless person, waif, foundling; (*in Asia*) pye-dog.

CHOOSE THE RIGHT WORD
stray, wander, roam, rove, range
See WANDER.

streak ▶ **noun 1** *a streak of orange light appeared in the east* **band**, line, strip, stripe, vein, slash, bar; ray, finger, pencil, stroke; trace, touch, fleck, dash; *technical* stria, striation, lane.
2 *the damp grass had left green streaks on her legs* **mark**, smear, smudge, stain, blotch; *informal* splodge, splotch.
3 *a streak of lightning* **bolt**, shaft, flash, beam.
4 *Tammy had a streak of self-destructiveness* **element**, vein, trace, touch, dash, strain; trait, characteristic.
5 *I suppose my winning streak had to come to an end eventually* **period**, spell, stretch, run, time; series; *Brit. informal* patch.
▶ **verb 1** *the sky was streaked with red* **stripe**, band, bar, fleck; *technical* striate; *archaic* freak.
2 *overalls streaked with maroon paint* **mark**, daub, smear, smudge, stain; *informal* splodge, splotch.
3 *Miranda streaked across the road* **race**, dash, rush, run, sprint, bolt, dart, gallop, career, charge, shoot, hurtle, hare, bound, fly, speed, zoom, go hell for leather, plunge, dive, whisk, scurry, scuttle, scamper, scramble; *informal* tear, belt, pelt, scoot, zap, zip, whip, step on it, get a move on, hotfoot it, leg it, steam, put on some speed, go like a bat out of hell, burn rubber; *Brit. informal* bomb, go like the clappers, bucket, put one's foot down; *Scottish informal* wheech; *N. Amer. informal* boogie, hightail it, clip, barrel, get the lead out; *informal, dated* cut along; *N. Amer. vulgar slang* drag/tear/haul ass; *literary* fleet; *archaic* post, hie, haste.

streaky ▶ **adjective** *a songbird with streaky brown plumage* **striped**, stripy, streaked, banded, barred; veined; brindle, brindled; *technical* striate, striated.

stream ▶ **noun 1** *a mountain stream* **brook**, rivulet, rill, runnel, streamlet, freshet; river, watercourse; tributary; *Brit.* winterbourne; *Scottish & N. English* burn; *N. English* beck; *S. English* bourn; *N. Amer. & Austral./NZ* creek; *Austral.* billabong, anabranch; *technical* influent, confluent; *rare* rillet, brooklet, runlet.
2 *he was scalded by a stream of boiling water* **jet**, **flow**, rush, gush, surge, spurt, spout, torrent, flood, cascade, fountain, outpouring, outflux, outflow, effusion; current; *technical* efflux.
3 *a steady stream of visitors | a stream of questions* **succession**, series, string, chain; barrage, volley, battery; flood, avalanche, torrent, tide, spate.
OPPOSITE trickle.
▶ **verb 1** *tears were streaming down her face | rain streamed off the roof* **flow**, **pour**, course, run, gush, surge, spurt, flood, cascade, sluice; slide, spill, slip, glide, trickle; well.
2 *children streamed out of the classrooms* **pour**, surge, flood, swarm, pile, crowd, throng.
3 *a flag streamed from the mast* **flutter**, float, flap, fly, blow, waft; wave, swing, undulate, ripple.
OPPOSITE dangle.

streamer ▶ **noun** **pennant**, pennon, flag, banderole, banner, standard, ensign, gonfalon, burgee; ribbon; *rare* vexillum.

streamlined ▶ **adjective 1** *streamlined cars* **aerodynamic**; smooth, sleek, trim, elegant, graceful; *technical* faired.
2 *a streamlined organization* **efficient**, smooth-running, well run, well organized, slick; modernized, up to date, rationalized, simplified; time-saving, labour-saving.
OPPOSITE inefficient.

street ▶ **noun** *Amsterdam's narrow cobbled streets* **road**, thoroughfare, way; avenue, drive, row, crescent, terrace, close, parade; side street, side road, lane, alley; *French* boulevard; *N. Amer.* highway, strip, blacktop. *See also* ROAD.
□ **the man/woman in the street** **an ordinary person**, an average person, Mr/Mrs Average, John Citizen; *Brit. informal* Joe Bloggs, Joe Public, the man on the Clapham omnibus; *N. Amer. informal* John Doe, Joe Sixpack; *derogatory* pleb, plebeian.
□ **on the streets** *the number of people who are on the streets is growing* **homeless**, living rough, sleeping rough, without a roof over one's head, of no fixed abode, down and out, vagrant.

strength ▶ **noun 1** *a man of enormous physical strength* **power**, brawn, brawniness, muscle, muscularity, burliness, sturdiness, robustness, toughness, hardiness, lustiness; vigour, energy, force, might, forcefulness, mightiness; *informal* beef; *Brit. informal* welly; *literary* thew, thewiness.
OPPOSITES weakness, puniness, frailty.
2 *Oliver began to regain his strength* **health**, fitness, healthiness, vigour; stamina.
OPPOSITE infirmity.
3 *she'd always prided herself on her inner strength* **fortitude**, resilience, backbone, spirit, strength of character, toughness of spirit, firmness, steadfastness, strong-mindedness, stoicism; courage, bravery, pluck, pluckiness, courageousness, braveness; *informal* guts, grit, spunk.
OPPOSITE vulnerability.
4 *they were taking no chances with the strength of the retaining wall* **robustness**, sturdiness, firmness, toughness, soundness, solidity, solidness, durability, stability; impregnability, resistance.
OPPOSITE weakness.
5 *the political and military strength of European governments* **power**, influence, dominance, ascendancy, supremacy; leverage; *informal* clout, beef; *literary* puissance.
OPPOSITES weakness, impotence.
6 *street protests demonstrated the strength of feeling against the president* **intensity**, vehemence, force, forcefulness, depth, ardour, fervour, violence; degree, level; *rare* fervency, ardency.
OPPOSITE half-heartedness.
7 *the strength of the argument for property taxation* **cogency**, forcefulness, force, weight, power, potency, persuasiveness, effectiveness, efficacy, soundness, validity.
OPPOSITES weakness, ineffectiveness.
8 *what do you regard as your strengths?* **strong point**, advantage, asset, forte, strong suit, long suit, aptitude, talent, gift, skill; virtue; speciality, specialty; *French* métier.
OPPOSITES failing, fault, flaw; limitation.
9 (*literary*) *he was my closest friend, my strength and shield* **support**, tower/pillar of strength, rock, mainstay, anchor.
10 *the peacetime strength of the army was 415,000* **size**, extent, magnitude, largeness, greatness; complement.
□ **on the strength of** *she got into Princeton on the strength of her essays* **because of**, by virtue of, on account of, on the basis of, based on, on the grounds of.

strengthen ▶ **verb 1** *calcium helps strengthen growing bones* **make strong/stronger**, build up, give strength to, make healthy, nourish.
OPPOSITE weaken.
2 *engineers strengthened the walls* **reinforce**, make stronger, buttress, brace, shore up, underpin; *rare* underprop.
3 *strengthened glass* **toughen**, temper, anneal.
4 *the wind had strengthened* **become strong/stronger**, gain strength, intensify, pick up, heighten.
OPPOSITES die down, ease off.
5 *his insistence strengthened her determination* **fortify**, bolster, make stronger, give strength to, give a boost to, boost, reinforce, harden, stiffen, toughen, steel, cement; increase, add to, fuel, add fuel to; renew, vitalize, give new energy to, buoy up, hearten.
OPPOSITES sap, weaken.
6 *the organization strengthened its efforts to expand such programmes* **step up**, increase, heighten, escalate, scale up; *informal* up, crank up, beef up.
OPPOSITES relax, decrease.
7 *the argument is strengthened by evidence from clinical data* **reinforce**, make more forceful, lend more weight to; support, back up, bolster, confirm, bear out, substantiate, corroborate, authenticate; consolidate.
OPPOSITE undermine.

strenuous ▶ **adjective 1** *it's a pretty strenuous climb* **arduous**, difficult, hard, tough, taxing, demanding, exacting, uphill, stiff, formidable, heavy, exhausting, tiring, fatiguing, gruelling, back-breaking, murderous, punishing; *informal* no picnic, killing; *Brit. informal* knackering; *archaic* toilsome.
OPPOSITES easy, effortless.
2 *the college has made strenuous efforts to attract overseas students* **vigorous**, energetic, active, enthusiastic, keen, zealous, forceful, strong, Herculean, spirited, dynamic, intense, determined, resolute, tenacious, tireless, stout, indefatigable, unremitting, dogged, pertinacious.
OPPOSITES half-hearted, feeble.

stress ▶ **noun 1** *he's obviously under a lot of stress* **strain**, pressure, tension, nervous tension, worry, anxiety, nervousness; trouble, difficulty, distress, trauma, suffering, pain, grief; *informal* hassle.
OPPOSITE relaxation.
2 *he has started to lay greater stress on the government's role in education* **emphasis**, importance, weight, force, insistence.
3 *normally, the stress falls on the first syllable* **emphasis**, accent, accentuation; beat; *Prosody* ictus.
4 *the distribution of stress is uniform across the bar* **pressure**, **tension**, strain, tightness, tautness; *rare* tensity.
▶ **verb 1** *they stressed the need for reform* **emphasize**, draw attention to, focus attention on, underline, underscore, point up, place emphasis on, lay

S

stress on, highlight, spotlight, turn the spotlight on, bring to the fore, foreground, accentuate, press home, impress on someone, make a point of, dwell on, harp on, belabour, insist on, rub in.
OPPOSITES play down, understate.
2 *in French, the last syllable is usually stressed* **place the emphasis on**, give emphasis to, emphasize, place the accent on.
3 *the staff were stressed by the demands he made upon them* **overstretch**, overtax, push to the limit, pressurize, pressure, burden, make tense, cause to feel mental/emotional strain; worry, upset, distress, harass; *informal* hassle.

stressful ▶ **adjective** *he had had a particularly stressful day* **demanding**, trying, exacting, taxing, difficult, hard, tough; **fraught**, traumatic, pressured, tense, frustrating; worrying, nerve-racking, anxious, anxiety-ridden; wearing, tiring, exhausting, draining.
OPPOSITES relaxing, easy.

stretch ▶ **verb 1** *the material stretches* **be elastic**, be stretchy, be stretchable, be tensile.
2 *he stretched the elastic until it snapped* **pull**, pull out, draw out, extend, lengthen, elongate; expand, distend.
3 *stretch your weekend into a mini summer vacation* **prolong**, lengthen, make longer, extend, extend the duration of, draw out, spin out, protract.
OPPOSITE shorten.
4 *my budget won't* **stretch to** *a weekend at a health farm* **be sufficient for**, be enough for, cover, reach to; afford, have the money for.
5 *the cost of the court case has stretched their finances* **put a strain on**, put great demands on, overtax, overextend, be too much for; drain, sap.
6 *Owen was stretching the truth a little* **bend**, strain, distort; exaggerate, overstate, embellish, overdraw; *informal* lay it on thick.
7 *she* **stretched out** *her hand to him* **reach out**, hold out, put out, extend, outstretch, thrust out, stick out; proffer, offer; *literary* outreach.
OPPOSITE withdraw.
8 *he stood up and stretched his arms* **extend**, straighten, straighten out, unbend.
9 *she* **stretched out** *on the sofa* **lie down**, recline, lean back, be recumbent, be prostrate, be prone, sprawl, drape oneself, lounge, loll.
10 *the desert* **stretches for** *miles* **extend**, spread, continue, range, unfold, unroll, be unbroken; cover, span.
▶ **noun 1** *magnificent stretches of forest* **expanse**, area, tract, belt, sweep, extent, spread, reach; length, distance.
2 *a four-hour stretch* **period**, time, spell, term, run, stint, session; tour of duty, shift.
3 (*informal*) *he's served six years of a ten-year stretch* **prison sentence**, sentence, prison term; *N. Amer. informal* rap.
▶ **adjective** *today's popular stretch fabrics* **stretchy**, stretchable, elastic, elasticated.

strew ▶ **verb** *his room was strewn with books and papers* **scatter**, spread, disperse, distribute, litter, toss, sprinkle, sow, broadcast; *literary* bestrew, besprinkle.
OPPOSITE gather.

stricken ▶ **adjective** *Raymond was stricken with grief | she looked at Anne's stricken face* **troubled**, affected, deeply affected, afflicted, struck, hit, injured, wounded.
OPPOSITE unaffected.

strict ▶ **adjective 1** *a strict interpretation of the new law* **precise**, exact, literal, close, faithful, true, accurate, unerring, scrupulous, careful, meticulous, rigorous, stringent; conscientious, punctilious, painstaking, thorough; *informal* spot on, on the mark, on the beam, on the nail, on the button.
OPPOSITES imprecise, loose.
2 *strict controls on public spending* **stringent**, rigorous, severe, harsh, hard, rigid, tough, extreme.
OPPOSITE liberal.
3 *their parents were too strict* **stern**, **severe**, harsh, uncompromising, authoritarian, firm, austere, illiberal, inflexible, unyielding, unbending, no-nonsense; *Austral./NZ informal* solid.
OPPOSITE lenient.
4 *the information will be treated in strict confidence* **absolute**, utter, complete, total, perfect.
5 *her father was a strict Roman Catholic* **orthodox**, fundamentalist, conservative, traditional; devout, conscientious, true, religious.
OPPOSITES moderate, liberal.

strictness ▶ **noun 1** *the strictness of the gun control laws* **severity**, harshness, rigidity, rigidness, stringency, rigorousness, austerity; authoritarianism, sternness.
OPPOSITE flexibility.
2 *the provision has been interpreted with some strictness* **precision**, preciseness, accuracy, exactness, exactitude, correctness, faithfulness, closeness, correspondence; meticulousness, scrupulousness, thoroughness.
OPPOSITE imprecision.

stricture ▶ **noun 1** *guilt was induced by the constant strictures of the nuns* **criticism**, censure, blame, condemnation, reproof, reproach, admonishment, disparagement, flak; *informal* knocking; *Brit. informal* stick, slating.
OPPOSITE praise.
2 *the strictures on Victorian women* **constraint**, restriction, limitation, control, restraint, straitjacket, curb, check, impediment, bar, barrier, obstacle.
OPPOSITE freedom.
3 *a small intestinal stricture* **narrowing**, constriction, strangulation, tightness.
OPPOSITE dilatation.

stride ▶ **verb** *she came striding down the garden path* **march**, stalk, pace, tread, step, walk.
▶ **noun** *he walked with long swinging strides* **step**, long step, large step, pace, footstep.
□ **take something in one's stride deal with easily**, cope with easily, think nothing of, accept as quite usual/normal, not bat an eyelid.
OPPOSITE be fazed by.

strident ▶ **adjective** *a strident voice interrupted the consultation* **harsh**, raucous, rough, grating, rasping, jarring, loud, stentorian, shrill, screeching, piercing, ear-piercing; unmelodious, unmusical, discordant, dissonant, unharmonious; *rare* stridulous, stridulant, stridulatory, stentorious.
OPPOSITES soft, dulcet.

strife ▶ **noun** *the history of the Empire is full of strife* **conflict**, friction, discord, disagreement, dissension, variance, dispute, argument, quarrelling, wrangling, bickering, controversy, contention; disharmony, ill feeling, bad feeling, bad blood, hostility, animosity; *informal* falling-out.
OPPOSITES harmony, peace, cooperation.

strike ▶ **verb 1** *the teacher actually struck and hurt Mary* **hit**, slap, smack, beat, thrash, spank, thump, thwack, punch, cuff, crack, swat, knock, rap; pummel, pound, batter, pelt, welt, assault, box someone's ears; cane, lash, whip, club, cudgel; *Austral./NZ informal* quilt; *informal* **clout**, wallop, belt, whack, bash, clobber, bop, biff, sock, deck, slug, plug, knock about/around, knock into the middle of next week, lay into, do over, rough up; *literary* smite.
2 *at seven sharp he struck the gong* **bang**, beat, hit, pound; *informal* bash, wallop.
3 *the stolen car struck a tree* **crash into**, collide with, be in collision with, hit, run into, knock into, bang into, bump into, smash into, slam into, crack into/against, dash against; *N. Amer.* impact.
4 *Jennifer struck the ball into the back of the net* **hit**, drive, propel, force; *informal* clout, wallop, slam, swipe.
5 *he struck a match and lit the oil lamp* **ignite**, light.
OPPOSITE extinguish.
6 *she was counting the day's takings when the killer struck* **attack**, make an attack/assault, set upon someone, fall on someone, assault someone.
7 *the disease is striking 3,000 people a year* **affect**, afflict, attack, hit, come upon, smite.
8 *democratic societies must strike a balance between order and freedom* **achieve**, reach, arrive at, find, attain, effect, establish.
9 *we have struck a satisfactory bargain* **agree**, agree on, come to an agreement on, settle on, sign, endorse, ratify, sanction; *informal* clinch.
10 *the picture showed him striking a heroic pose* **assume**, adopt, take on, take up, affect, feign, put on; *N. Amer. informal* cop.
11 *the engineers had struck oil* **discover**, find, come upon, light on, chance on, happen on, stumble on/across, unearth, uncover, turn up.
12 *a thought suddenly struck her* **occur to**, come to, dawn on one, hit; come to mind, spring to mind, enter one's head, present itself, come into one's consciousness.
13 *you strike me as an intelligent young woman* **seem to**, appear to, look to; give someone the impression of being; impress, affect, have an impact on.
14 *our drivers are striking and demanding guarantees of their safety* **take industrial action**, go on strike, down tools, walk out, work to rule; mutiny, rebel, revolt.
15 *they are about to strike the big tent* **take down**, pull down, bring down; take apart.
OPPOSITE pitch.
16 *Lord Bridport struck his flag* **lower**, take down, let down, bring down.
OPPOSITE hoist.
17 *he ordered the driver to strike south towards the Thames* **go**, make one's way, set out, head, direct one's footsteps, move towards.
□ **strike something out delete**, cross out, erase, rub out, obliterate.
□ **strike something up 1** *the accompanist struck up 'Land of Hope and Glory'* **begin to play**, start to play, begin/start/commence playing, embark on.
2 *we struck up a friendship* **begin**, start, embark on, set going, initiate, instigate, establish; *formal* commence.
▶ **noun 1** *staff held a 48-hour strike* **industrial action**, walkout.
2 *an imminent military strike* **attack**, air strike, air attack, assault, bombing, blitz.
3 *a lucky strike in 1848 gave rise to the term 'gold rush'* **find**, discovery, unearthing, uncovering.

striking ▶ adjective **1** *Lizzie bears a striking resemblance to her sister* **noticeable**, obvious, conspicuous, evident, salient, visible, distinct, prominent, marked, clear-cut, notable, manifest, unmistakable, distinctive, strong; rare, uncommon, out of the ordinary; significant, remarkable, extraordinary, incredible, amazing, astounding, astonishing, surprising, staggering, phenomenal.
OPPOSITES inconspicuous; unremarkable.
2 *an opportunity to see Kenya's striking landscape* **impressive**, imposing, grand, splendid, magnificent, spectacular, breathtaking, superb, marvellous, wonderful, outstanding, dazzling, stunning, staggering, sensational, dramatic, awesome, awe-inspiring, eye-catching, picturesque; *informal* great, fabulous, fab, smashing; *archaic* splendent.
OPPOSITES ordinary, unimpressive.
3 *a former bunny girl with striking looks* **stunning**, attractive, good-looking, beautiful, glamorous, gorgeous, prepossessing, comely, captivating, enchanting, arresting, ravishing, alluring, handsome, pretty, bonny; *informal* drop-dead gorgeous, smashing, fabulous, fab, out of this world, knockout.
OPPOSITES unattractive, unremarkable.

string *See centre pages for list of* **Stringed Instruments**
▶ noun **1** *a ball of string* **twine**, cord, yarn, thread, strand, fibre; rope, cable, line, wire, ligature, thong, hawser; *rare* fillis.
2 *they lease their pubs to a string of brewers* **chain**, series, group, firm, company.
3 *a string of convictions* **series**, succession, chain, sequence, concatenation, run, streak; pattern.
4 *a long winding string of wagons and horses* **queue**, **procession**, line, row, file, column, rank, convoy, train, cavalcade, stream, succession, sequence; *informal* crocodile.
5 *a string of priceless pearls* **strand**, rope, necklace, rosary, chaplet.
6 *I broke a string on my guitar* guitar string, violin string; piano wire; drone; *literary* chord.
7 (**strings**) *an instrumental piece for horns and strings* **stringed instruments.**
8 (**strings**) *a guaranteed loan with no strings attached* **conditions**, qualifications, provisions, provisos, caveats, stipulations, riders, contingencies, prerequisites, limitations, limits, constraints, restrictions, reservations, requirements, obligations; *informal* catches.
▶ verb **1** *lights were strung across the promenade* **hang**, suspend, sling, stretch; thread, loop, festoon.
2 *wire mesh was strung from one catwalk to the other* **stretch**, sling, run, fasten, tie, secure, link.
3 *a necklace of wooden beads strung on a silver chain* **thread**, loop, link, join.
□ **string along** *with my name I could always string along with the Irish gang* **go along**, go too, come too, join in; accompany, join, join up with, take up with.
□ **string someone along mislead**, deceive, take in, take advantage of, dupe, hoax, fool, make a fool of, bluff; make use of, play with, toy with, dally with, trifle with, play fast and loose with; *informal* lead up the garden path, take for a ride, put one over on, kid.
□ **string something out 1** *these journalists certainly know how to string a story out* **protract**, spin out, draw out, drag out, lengthen, stretch, stretch out.
OPPOSITE shorten.
2 *enemy airfields are strung out along the Gulf* **spread out**, space out, set apart, place at intervals, distribute, extend, fan out, scatter, straggle.
□ **string someone up** (*informal*) **hang**, lynch, gibbet; *informal* make swing.

stringent ▶ adjective *the safety regulations are very stringent* **strict**, firm, rigid, rigorous, severe, harsh, tough, tight, exacting, demanding, inflexible, stiff, hard and fast, uncompromising, draconian, extreme.
OPPOSITES lenient, flexible.

stringy ▶ adjective **1** *the girl is small with stringy hair* **straggly**, straggling, lank, thin.
OPPOSITE luxuriant.
2 *a stringy brunette* **lanky**, gangling, gangly, rangy, wiry, angular, bony, reedy; spindly, spindling, skinny, scrawny, thin, thin as a rake, spare, gaunt, emaciated, skeletal, raw-boned.
OPPOSITE plump.
3 *he had to chew the stringy meat* **fibrous**, gristly, sinewy, chewy, ropy, tough, leathery, leather-like, hard.
OPPOSITES tender, succulent.

strip[1] ▶ verb **1** *he stripped and got into bed* **undress**, strip off, take one's clothes off, remove one's clothes, shed one's clothes, unclothe, disrobe, strip naked, denude oneself, expose oneself, reveal oneself, uncover oneself; *informal* peel off; *dated* divest oneself of one's clothes.
OPPOSITE dress.
2 *you'll have to strip off the paint* **peel**, remove, take off, flake, scrape, scratch, shave, abrade, rub, clear, clean; pare, skin, flay; *technical* excoriate, decorticate.
3 *the university stripped him of his doctorate* **take away from**, dispossess, deprive, confiscate, divest, relieve, deny, rob.
4 *the mechanics are stripping down my engine* **dismantle**, disassemble, take to pieces, take to bits, take apart, break up, demolish.
OPPOSITES construct, assemble.
5 *the house had been stripped of everything of value* **empty**, clear, clean out, plunder, rob, burgle, loot, rifle, pillage, ransack, gut, lay bare, devastate, sack, ravage, raid; *literary* despoil; *archaic* spoil, reave.
▶ noun *he led out an England team sporting a new strip* **outfit**, clothes, clothing, garments, costume, suit, dress, garb; *Brit.* **kit**; *informal* gear, get-up; *Brit. informal* rig-out.

strip[2] ▶ noun *cut a strip of paper 12cm wide* **narrow piece**, piece, bit, band, belt, ribbon, sash, stripe, bar, swathe, slip, fillet, shred.

stripe ▶ noun *green tracksuit bottoms with a yellow stripe on the side* **line**, band, strip, belt, bar, swathe, streak, striation, vein, thread; chevron, flash, blaze, marking; *technical* stria.

striped ▶ adjective *a blue and white striped shirt* **banded**, stripy, barred, lined; streaky, striated, variegated.

stripling ▶ noun *a thin, blonde boy—a mere stripling* **youth**, adolescent, youngster, boy, schoolboy, lad, child, teenager, juvenile, minor, junior, young man, whippersnapper, fledgling; *Scottish* laddie, bairn; *informal* kid, young 'un, nipper, shaver, tot; *derogatory* brat, urchin, guttersnipe; *archaic* hobbledehoy.
OPPOSITE old man.

stripy ▶ adjective *he wore stripy skintight trousers* **striped**, barred, lined, banded; streaky, striated, variegated.

strive ▶ verb **1** *I shall strive to be virtuous* **try**, try hard, attempt, endeavour, aim, aspire, venture, undertake, seek, make an effort, make every effort, spare no effort, exert oneself, do one's best, do all one can, do one's utmost, give one's all, labour, work, toil, strain, struggle, apply oneself; have a go at; *informal* bend/fall/lean over backwards, go all out, give it one's best shot, give it a whirl, have a crack at, have a stab at, pull out all the stops; *formal* essay.
2 *scholars must strive against this bias* **struggle**, fight, battle, combat, contend, grapple; campaign, war, crusade.

stroke ▶ noun **1** *the rebel Duke had suffered five strokes of the axe* **blow**, hit, thump, thwack, punch, slap, smack, welt, cuff, box, knock, rap, buffet; *informal* wallop, clobber, clout, whack, bash, belt, sock, bop, biff, swipe, slug; *archaic* smite.
2 *Anwar was playing cricket strokes* **shot**, hit, strike.
3 *Mick swam a couple of strokes* **movement**, action, motion, move.
4 *it was a stroke of genius by the Prime Minister* **feat**, accomplishment, achievement, attainment, coup, master stroke, stratagem.
5 *the flat pencil can be used for broad strokes* **mark**, line, slash, solidus, virgule.
6 *the budget was full of bold strokes* **detail**, touch, bit, point, item.
7 *I counted the strokes of the church clock* **peal**, ring, knell, striking, ding-dong, boom.
8 *he had recently suffered a small stroke* **thrombosis**, embolism, cerebral vascular accident, CVA, cerebral haemorrhage, ictus, seizure; *archaic* apoplexy.
▶ verb *she reached out and stroked the cat* **caress**, fondle, pat, pet, touch, brush, rub, massage, knead, soothe; manipulate, finger, handle, feel, maul, tickle; *informal* paw.

stroll ▶ verb *they strolled along the gravelled paths* **saunter**, amble, wander, meander, ramble, dawdle, promenade, walk, go for a walk, take a walk, roam, traipse, stretch one's legs, get some exercise, get some air, take the air; *Scottish & Irish* stravaig; *informal* mosey, tootle; *Brit. informal* pootle, mooch, swan; *N. Amer. informal* putter; *rare* perambulate, peregrinate.
▶ noun *a stroll in the park* **saunter**, amble, wander, walk, turn, promenade, airing, breather; outing, excursion, jaunt; *informal* mosey, tootle; *Brit. informal* pootle; *dated* constitutional; *rare* perambulation.

CHOOSE THE RIGHT WORD

stroll, saunter, amble

These words have in common the idea of relaxed and unhurried movement.

- People who are **strolling** are typically walking for pleasure, at a relaxed pace which allows them to enjoy their surroundings or company, or both (*a day for lovers to stroll through leafy woods*). They are definitely under no pressure to exert themselves. As a noun, a *stroll* is typically *a gentle stroll*.
- **Saunter** can be used in the same way, but it may also suggest a more self-conscious or conspicuous freedom from hurry or anxiety. Someone may saunter to emphasize their lack of concern when they might be expected to be nervous (*Jasper was sauntering past the police station*), or their feeling that they have privileged access to a place (*Dana sauntered into Claudia's office*).
- Someone who is **ambling** is walking in a particularly casual way, giving the impression that they have no definite destination or objective (*he ambled down the corridor, whistling*). *Amble* is more commonly used of animals (such as a *bear* or a *horse*) than the other two words are.

strong ▶ adjective **1** *a big strong farmer's lad* **powerful**, **muscular**, brawny, well built, powerfully built, strapping, sturdy, hefty, burly, meaty, robust, fit, athletic, vigorous, tough, rugged; stalwart, staunch, mighty, hardy; lusty, Herculean, strong as an ox/horse/lion; *informal* beefy, hunky, husky.
OPPOSITES weak, puny.
2 *she hasn't been strong since Father's death* **well**, healthy, in good health, fit, fighting fit, robust, vigorous, blooming, thriving, bursting with health, in rude health, hale, hale and hearty, hearty, in good shape, in excellent shape, in good condition, in good trim, in fine fettle, sound, sound in body and limb; *informal* in the pink, fit as a fiddle, in tip-top condition.
OPPOSITE frail.
3 *a lady of strong character* **forceful**, determined, spirited, dynamic, self-assertive, tough, tenacious, high-powered, formidable, aggressive, redoubtable, zealous, firm, resolute, strong-minded; *informal* gutsy, feisty.
OPPOSITE weak.
4 *a strong fortress surrounded by a moat* **secure**, well built, indestructible, well fortified, well defended, well protected, impregnable, impenetrable, inviolable, unassailable; solid.
5 *strong cotton bags* **durable**, hard-wearing, heavy-duty, tough, sturdy, well made, substantial, solid, rugged; resistant, resilient, imperishable, indestructible, long-lasting, enduring.
OPPOSITE weak.
6 *a strong breeze | the current is too strong* **forceful**, powerful, vigorous, fierce, intense, extreme.
OPPOSITE gentle.
7 *a strong interest in literary activities* **keen**, eager, deep, acute, dedicated, passionate, fervent, zealous.
8 *he still retained strong feelings for the woman* **intense**, forceful, vehement, passionate, ardent, fervent, profound, deep-seated; consuming, extreme, acute, fierce; *rare* fervid, perfervid, passional.
9 *a strong supporter of the women's movement* **keen**, eager, enthusiastic, earnest, dedicated, staunch, loyal, steadfast, passionate, fierce, fervent.
10 *there are strong arguments for introducing grants* **compelling**, cogent, forceful, powerful, potent, weighty, convincing, plausible, effective, efficacious, sound, valid, well founded, telling; impressive, persuasive, influential, authoritative.
OPPOSITES weak, unconvincing.
11 *there was a need to take strong action* **firm**, forceful, severe, strict, drastic, extreme, draconian.
12 *she bore a very strong resemblance to Vera* **marked**, noticeable, pronounced, distinct, definite, clear-cut, obvious, evident, unmistakable, notable.
OPPOSITE slight.
13 *a strong voice* **loud**, powerful, forceful, lusty, stentorian, resonant, sonorous, orotund, full, rich, deep, booming, penetrating, carrying, clear; strident; *informal* fruity; *rare* canorous.
OPPOSITES quiet, weak.
14 *he didn't like strong language* **bad**, foul, obscene, profane, blasphemous.
15 *strong blues and yellows* **intense**, deep, rich, warm, bright, brilliant, vivid, striking, colourful, graphic.
OPPOSITE pale.
16 *the strong lights of the studio* **bright**, brilliant, intense, radiant, gleaming, dazzling, glaring.
17 *strong black coffee* **concentrated**, undiluted, highly flavoured.
OPPOSITES weak, mild.
18 *slices of strong cheese* **highly flavoured**, strongly flavoured, flavourful, flavoursome, savoury, pungent, aromatic, piquant, tangy, sharp, biting, zesty, spicy, hot; *rare* flavorous, sapid.
OPPOSITE mild.
19 *he would have blown his money on horses and strong drink* **alcoholic**, intoxicating, inebriating, hard, heady, potent, stiff, spirituous, vinous, intoxicant.
OPPOSITES non-alcoholic, soft.

S

strong-arm ▶ adjective *strong-arm tactics were deployed by both sides* **aggressive**, forceful, bullying, coercive, oppressive, threatening, intimidatory, terrorizing, thuggish, violent; *informal* bully-boy.

strongbox ▶ noun *she would rob her father's strongbox* **safe**, safety-deposit box, safe-deposit box, coffer, cash box, money box, money chest, locker, repository; vault, bank.

stronghold ▶ noun **1** *they charged towards the enemy stronghold* **fortress**, fort, castle, citadel, garrison, keep, tower, hold, donjon, bunker; fastness.
2 *the seat appeared to be an impregnable Tory stronghold* **bastion**, centre, refuge, hotbed.

strong-minded ▶ adjective *a strong-minded social reformer* **determined**, firm, resolute, resolved, purposeful, purposive, sure, self-disciplined, strong-willed, uncompromising, unyielding, unbending, unwavering, unswerving, unfaltering, unshakeable, inexorable, forceful, persistent, persevering, tenacious, dogged, stubborn; dedicated, committed, stalwart; *N. Amer.* rock-ribbed; *informal* gutsy, spunky; *rare* perseverant, indurate.
OPPOSITES weak-willed, half-hearted.

strong point ▶ noun *arithmetic had never been her strong point* **strength**, strong suit, long suit, forte, aptitude, bent, speciality, specialty, métier, claim to fame, skill; *informal* thing, bag, line, cup of tea.
OPPOSITE weakness.

strong-willed ▶ adjective *he was strong-willed and independent* **determined**, iron-willed, resolute, stubborn, stubborn as a mule, mulish, obstinate, wilful, headstrong, strong-minded, self-willed, inflexible, unbending, unyielding, intransigent, intractable, obdurate, recalcitrant, refractory; forceful, domineering; *informal* pushy; *rare* indurate.
OPPOSITES weak-willed, spineless.

stroppy ▶ adjective (*informal*) *I won't push it unless he gets stroppy* **bad-tempered**, ill-tempered, irritable, grumpy, cantankerous, truculent, sulky, sullen, awkward, uncooperative, unhelpful, recalcitrant, refractory, difficult, perverse, contrary, confrontational, argumentative, quarrelsome, obstreperous, choleric; *Scottish* thrawn; *informal* pig-headed, cussed; *Brit. informal* shirty, ratty, narky, bolshie, bloody-minded; *N. Amer. informal* balky, scrappy; *archaic* contumacious, froward; *rare* contrarious.

structural ▶ adjective *the effects of structural changes in the industry | earth tremors caused structural damage* **constructional**, organizational, systemic, constitutional, configurational, formational; *technical* tectonic.

structure ▶ noun **1** *a vast Gothic structure with strange ornamental spirelets* **building**, edifice, construction, erection, pile, complex, assembly.
2 *the structure of local government | the plant's structure is simple* **construction**, form, formation, shape, composition, fabric, anatomy, make-up, constitution; organization, system, arrangement, layout, design, frame, framework, configuration, conformation, pattern, plan, mould; *informal* set-up.
▶ verb *the programme is structured around periods of residential study* **arrange**, organize, order, design, shape, give structure to, assemble, construct, build, put together.

struggle ▶ verb **1** *they struggled to make sense of the words* **strive**, try hard, endeavour, make every effort, spare no effort, exert oneself, do one's best, do all one can, do one's utmost, battle, labour, toil, strain, bend over backwards, put oneself out; *informal* go all out, give it one's best shot, put one's back into it, plug away, peg away; *Brit. informal* graft; *formal* essay.
2 *James was hit in the mouth as he struggled with the raiders* **fight**, grapple, wrestle, scuffle, brawl, spar, exchange blows, come to blows; *informal* scrap; *Scottish informal* swedge.
3 *research teams struggle to be first to the finish* **compete**, contend, contest, vie, fight, battle, clash, wrangle, jockey, lock horns, cross swords, war, wage war, feud.
4 *she struggled over the dunes* **scramble**, flounder, stumble; make one's way with difficulty, drag oneself, fight/battle one's way, battle, labour.
▶ noun **1** *the continuing struggle for justice* **endeavour**, striving, effort, exertion, labour, work, toiling, pains; **campaign**, battle, crusade, drive, push, movement; *Brit. informal* graft.
2 *we were able to apprehend the gang without a struggle* **fight**, scuffle, brawl, tussle, wrestling match, sparring match, wrestling bout, bout, skirmish, fracas, melee, affray, encounter, disturbance, breach of the peace; *informal* scrap, barney, set-to, dust-up, punch-up, ruction, free-for-all, argy-bargy; *Brit. informal* bust-up, ding-dong; *Scottish informal* swedge.
3 *a third of the population perished in the struggle* **conflict**, fight, battle, armed conflict, combat, confrontation, clash, skirmish, encounter, engagement; **hostilities**, fighting, war, warfare, campaign, crusade.
4 *an unresolved struggle within the leadership* **contest**, competition, battle, fight, clash, feud; contention, vying, rivalry, strife, friction, feuding, conflict.
5 *life has been a struggle for me* **effort**, labour, problem, trial, trouble, stress, strain, bother, battle; *informal* grind, hassle, pain.

strumpet ▶ noun (*archaic*) *a strumpet from a house of ill fame* **prostitute**, whore, call girl, sex worker; *euphemistic* model, escort, masseuse; *French* fille de joie, demi-mondaine; *Spanish* puta; *N. Amer.* hustler, sporting girl/woman/lady, chippy; *informal* tart, pro, hooker, moll, tail, brass nail, grande horizontale, woman on the game, working girl, member of the oldest profession; *black English* ho; *dated* woman of the streets, lady/woman of the night, scarlet woman, cocotte; *archaic* courtesan, harlot, trollop, woman of ill repute, lady of pleasure, Cyprian, doxy, drab, quean, trull, wench; *rare* sing-song girl.

strung up ▶ adjective *he was strung up and unable to relax* **tense**, nervous, on edge, edgy, overwrought, jumpy, keyed up, worked up, agitated, restive; anxious, worried, apprehensive, ill at ease, uneasy, unquiet; *Brit.* nervy; *informal* uptight, wound up, twitchy, jittery, wired, a bundle of nerves, like a cat on a hot tin roof.
OPPOSITES relaxed, laid-back.

strut ▶ verb *he strutted around his vast office* **swagger**, swank, parade, prance, flounce, stride, sweep; walk confidently, walk arrogantly; *N. Amer. informal* sashay; *rare* peacock. *See* 'Choose the Right Word' *below*.

stub ▶ noun **1** *he ground his cigar stub into the ashtray* **butt**, end, tail end, remnant; *informal* dog-end, fag end.
2 *please retain your ticket stub* **counterfoil**, ticket slip, detachable portion, coupon, tab, receipt.
3 *he found a stub of pencil* **stump**, remnant, end, tail end, remains.

CHOOSE THE RIGHT WORD

strut, swagger, parade

These words all refer to types of ostentatious movement.

- **Strut** refers to a stiff, erect movement suggesting aggressive self-importance (*he strutted around his vast office like a peacock*). There is often a suggestion that this self-importance is combined with other qualities that the writer or speaker finds obnoxious (*a strutting Nazi*), or that it is used to conceal feelings of inadequacy (*a small man's strutting arrogance | he strutted angrily and aimlessly off*). It is frequently also used of birds such as *peacocks, pheasants, cockerels*, and *chickens*.
- To **swagger** is to walk with an easier, more expansive and swinging movement, reflecting arrogant self-confidence (*he swaggered around the room in his new uniform*).
- Someone who is **parading** is walking in a way that is calculated to draw attention (*I've seen her parading round the village in her fur coat and jewellery*).

stubble ▸ noun **1** *a field of stubble* **stalks**, straw.
2 *a weather-beaten face covered in grey stubble* **bristles**, whiskers, designer stubble, hair, facial hair, beard; *informal* five o'clock shadow.

stubbly ▸ adjective *he scratched his stubbly chin* **bristly**, unshaven, fuzzy, whiskery, whiskered, hairy, bearded; prickly, rough, coarse, scratchy, spiky.
OPPOSITES smooth; clean-shaven.

stubborn ▸ adjective **1** *you're too stubborn to admit it* **obstinate**, stubborn as a mule, mulish, headstrong, wilful, strong-willed, self-willed, pig-headed, bull-headed, obdurate, awkward, difficult, contrary, perverse, recalcitrant, refractory; firm, adamant, resolute, dogged, persistent, pertinacious, inflexible, iron-willed, uncompromising, uncooperative, unaccommodating, intractable, unbending, unyielding, unmalleable, unadaptable; *N. Amer.* rock-ribbed; *informal* stiff-necked; *Brit. informal* bolshie, bloody-minded; *N. Amer. informal* balky; *archaic* contumacious, froward.
OPPOSITES compliant, docile.
2 *stubborn stains* **indelible**, permanent, lingering, persistent, tenacious, fast, resistant.

CHOOSE THE RIGHT WORD

stubborn, obstinate, headstrong, wilful

See OBSTINATE.

stubby ▸ adjective **1** *a small stubby man with glasses* **dumpy**, stocky, chunky, chubby, thickset, sturdy, heavyset, squat, solid; **short**, stumpy, dwarfish, midget, pygmy, diminutive, undersized; *Austral./NZ* nuggety; *Brit. informal* fubsy; *technical* mesomorphic, pyknic.
OPPOSITES slender; tall.
2 *a stubby pencil* **short**, stumpy, small, little; *Scottish* wee.

stuck ▸ adjective **1** *there was a message stuck to his computer screen* **fixed**, fastened, attached, glued, pinned.
2 *the iron gate looked rusted and stuck* **immovable**, stuck fast, jammed, immobile, unbudgeable, fast, stiff, fixed, rooted.
3 *if you get stuck, leave a blank and come back to it* **baffled**, beaten, lost, at a loss, puzzled, muddled, perplexed, nonplussed, bewildered, at one's wits' end; *informal* stumped, up against a brick wall, bogged down, clueless, flummoxed, fazed, bamboozled.

□ **get stuck into** (*Brit. informal*) *Walsh got stuck into the project* **get down to**, make a start on, embark on, set about, go about, get to work at, get to grips with, tackle, set one's hand to, throw oneself into; *informal* have a crack at, have a go at; *formal* commence.

□ **stuck on** (*informal*) *you're still stuck on her, aren't you?* **infatuated with**, besotted with, smitten with, in love with, head over heels in love with, hopelessly in love with, obsessed with, enamoured of, very attracted to, very taken with, devoted to, charmed by, captivated by, enchanted by, enthralled by, bewitched by, beguiled by, under someone's spell; *informal* bowled over by, swept off one's feet by, struck on, crazy about, mad about, wild about, potty about, very keen on, gone on, sweet on, into, carrying a torch for.
OPPOSITE indifferent to.

□ **stuck with** *he was stuck with her for two months* **lumbered with**, left with, made responsible for, hampered by.

stuck-up ▸ adjective *a bunch of stuck-up executives* **conceited**, proud, arrogant, haughty, condescending, disdainful, patronizing, snobbish, snobby, supercilious, imperious, above oneself, self-important, overweening, lordly; *informal* high and mighty, snooty, uppity, uppish, big-headed, swollen-headed, hoity-toity, la-di-da, too big for one's boots; *Brit. informal* toffee-nosed, posh; *literary* vainglorious.
OPPOSITES modest, unassuming.

studded ▸ adjective *a gold cigarette box studded with jewels* **dotted**, scattered, spotted, sprinkled, covered, flecked, peppered, spangled; *literary* bespangled, bejewelled.

student ▸ noun **1** *a student at Edinburgh University* **undergraduate**, postgraduate, scholar, tutee; freshman, freshwoman, finalist; *N. Amer.* sophomore, coed; *Brit. informal* fresher; *N. Amer. informal* frosh.
2 *a former student of Whitby School* **pupil**, schoolchild, schoolboy, schoolgirl, scholar; infant, junior, senior.
3 *a first-year nursing student* **trainee**, apprentice, probationer, recruit, novice, learner, beginner; *Christianity* postulant, novitiate; *informal* greenhorn, rookie.

studied ▸ adjective *the words were said with studied politeness* **deliberate**, careful, thoughtful, considered, conscious, calculated, intentional, volitional, designed, mannered, measured, studious, knowing, purposeful; guarded, contrived, affected, forced, strained, laboured, feigned, artificial, overworked, overdone, self-conscious.
OPPOSITES natural, spontaneous.

studio ▸ noun *he had worked hard on the dramatic murals in the studio* **workshop**, workroom, atelier; workplace, place of work, office, study.

studious ▸ adjective **1** *a studious and enquiring nature* **scholarly**, academic, bookish, book-loving, intellectual, erudite, learned, donnish, serious, earnest, thoughtful, cerebral; *informal* brainy; *Brit. informal* swotty.
2 *he gave studious attention to the question* **diligent**, careful, attentive, industrious, assiduous, painstaking, thorough, meticulous, punctilious, zealous, sedulous, heedful; *archaic* nice.
OPPOSITES careless, negligent.
3 *they noted his studious absence from public view* **deliberate**, wilful, conscious, calculated, intentional, volitional, designed, mannered, measured, studied, knowing, purposeful, contrived, artificial.
OPPOSITES natural, spontaneous.

study ▸ noun **1** *two years of study in the sixth form* **learning**, education, schooling, work, academic work, book work, scholarship, tuition, research; *informal* swotting, cramming.
2 *a study of manufacturing in the UK* **investigation**, enquiry, research, examination, analysis, review, survey, scrutiny, evaluation, interpretation.
3 *Father was shut up in his study* **office**, workroom, workplace, place of work, studio, library; den, cubbyhole, sanctum.
4 *this study concentrates mainly upon attitudes to death* **essay**, article, piece, work, review, report, paper, dissertation, commentary, discourse, critique, disquisition.

□ **in a brown study lost in thought**, lost in contemplation, in a reverie, thinking, reflecting, musing, pondering, contemplating, deliberating, ruminating, cogitating, dreaming, daydreaming; *informal* miles away.

▸ verb **1** *Anne studied hard at school* **work**, apply oneself, read up, revise, burn the midnight oil; *informal* swot, cram, mug up, bone up; *archaic* con.
2 *he studied electronics and accountancy* **learn**, read, read up on, work at, be taught, be tutored in; *informal* mug up on.
3 *Thomas was studying the effects of business re-engineering* **investigate**, inquire into, research, conduct research into, look into, examine, analyse, explore, probe, monitor, review, appraise, survey, conduct a survey of, scrutinize, dissect, delve into; *informal* check out, suss out.
4 *she studied her friend thoughtfully* **scrutinize**, examine, inspect, consider, regard, look at, eye, observe, watch, survey, keep an eye on, keep under surveillance; *informal* clock, check out; *N. Amer. informal* eyeball.

WORD LINKS

study of something	**-ology (e.g. *biology*)**
person who studies something	**-ologist (e.g. *biologist*)**

stuff ▸ noun **1** *suede is tough, resilient stuff* **material**, fabric, cloth, textile; matter, substance, medium.
2 *the village shop sells first-aid stuff* **items**, articles, objects, goods; *informal* **things**, bits and pieces, bits and bobs, odds and ends; *Brit. informal* odds and sods, gubbins.
3 *we stuck all my stuff in the suitcase* **belongings**, possessions, personal possessions, effects, property, goods, goods and chattels; paraphernalia, accoutrements, appurtenances, trappings; *informal* gear, things, tackle, kit; *Brit. informal* clobber, gubbins.
4 *he knows his stuff* **facts**, information, data, subject, discipline; *informal* onions.

□ **stuff and nonsense rubbish**, nonsense, twaddle, balderdash, claptrap, gibberish, drivel; *informal* poppycock, tripe, bunk, piffle, bosh, bilge, hot air, hogwash, hooey, baloney, mumbo-jumbo; *Brit. informal* cobblers, codswallop, tosh; *Scottish & N. English informal* havers; *Irish informal* codology; *N. Amer. informal* garbage, flapdoodle, blathers, wack, bushwa, applesauce; *informal, dated* tommyrot, rot, bunkum; *vulgar slang* bullshit, crap, bollocks, balls; *Austral./NZ vulgar slang* bulldust.

▸ verb **1** *flowers were used to stuff pillows and mattresses* **fill**, pack, pad, line, wad, upholster.
2 *Robyn stuffed clothes frantically into an overnight bag* **shove**, thrust, push, ram, cram, squeeze, press, force, compress, jam, wedge; pack, crowd, stow, pile, stick.
3 *pregnant mums* ***stuff themselves with*** *such strange food* **fill**, cram, gorge, overindulge, satiate; gobble, devour, wolf, guzzle; *informal* pig, pig out, make a pig of oneself, stuff oneself to the gills.

4 *my nose was stuffed up and my throat sore* **block**, stop, bung; congest, obstruct, choke.
5 (Brit. informal) *Town got stuffed every week.* See TROUNCE.

stuffing ▶ noun **1** *the stuffing is coming out of the armchair* **padding**, wadding, lining, filling, quilting, cushioning, upholstery, packing, filler; down, duck down, flock, kapok.
2 *sage and onion stuffing* **filling**, forcemeat, farce, salpicon; N. Amer. dressing.
□ **knock the stuffing out of** *Mike's death knocked the stuffing out of me* **devastate**, shatter, crush, shock, stun, distress, upset, traumatize; demoralize; informal knock for six, knock sideways.

stuffy ▶ adjective **1** *a stuffy atmosphere* **airless**, close, muggy, sultry, heavy, musty, stale, frowzy; stifling, suffocating, oppressive; Brit. frowsty; Brit. informal fuggy.
OPPOSITE airy.
2 *a stuffy young man* **staid**, sedate, sober, stiff, reserved, impersonal, formal, pompous, prim, priggish, fogeyish, strait-laced, conformist, conventional, conservative, old-fashioned, of the old school; stodgy, boring, dull, dreary, uninteresting; informal square, straight, starchy, fuddy-duddy, stick-in-the-mud, uptight.
OPPOSITES relaxed, informal; modern.
3 *a stuffy nose* **blocked**, stuffed up, bunged up.
OPPOSITE clear.

stultify ▶ verb **1** *free market forces had been stultified by the welfare state* **hamper**, impede, obstruct, thwart, frustrate, foil, suppress, smother, repress.
2 *he stultifies her with too much gentleness* **bore**, make bored, dull, numb, benumb, stupefy, deaden; informal bore rigid, bore stupid, bore to death; rare hebetate.
OPPOSITE excite.

stumble ▶ verb **1** *he stumbled on a brick and fell heavily* **trip**, trip over, trip up, lose one's balance, lose/miss one's footing, founder, slip, pitch.
2 *he stumbled back to his hotel room* **stagger**, totter, teeter, dodder, lurch, lumber, blunder, reel, flounder, bumble, shamble, hobble, wobble, move clumsily.
3 *the Consul had stumbled through his speech* **stammer**, stutter, hesitate, falter, speak haltingly, fumble for words; flounder, blunder, muddle; informal fluff one's lines.
□ **stumble across/on** *the scientists stumbled across the vaccine by chance* **come across**, come upon, chance on, happen on, light on, hit on, come up with; discover, encounter, find, unearth, uncover, locate, bring to light; informal dig up, put one's finger on.

stumbling block ▶ noun *the language problem is a fundamental stumbling block* **obstacle**, hurdle, barrier, bar, hindrance, impediment, handicap, disadvantage, restriction, limitation; snag, hitch, catch, drawback, difficulty, problem, weakness, defect, pitfall, complication; informal fly in the ointment, hiccup, facer; Brit. informal spanner in the works; N. Amer. informal monkey wrench in the works.
OPPOSITES advantage, benefit.

stump ▶ noun *a tree stump | a stump of candle* **stub**, end, tail end, remnant, remains, remainder, butt; piece, part, segment; informal fag end, dog end.
▶ verb **1** *education chiefs were stumped by some of the exam questions* **baffle**, perplex, puzzle, confuse, confound, bewilder, mystify, nonplus, defeat; be too much for, put at a loss, bring up short; informal flummox, fox, be all Greek to, throw, floor, discombobulate; archaic wilder, gravel, maze; rare obfuscate.
2 *she stumped along the landing to the bathroom* **stomp**, stamp, clomp, clump, lumber, trudge, plod; thump, thud, bang, thunder.
□ **stump something up** (Brit. informal) *the banks would be willing to stump up the extra money* **pay**, pay up, hand over, part with, give, put in, contribute, donate; informal **fork out**, shell out, lay out, come across with, cough up, chip in; N. Amer. informal ante up, pony up.

stumpy ▶ adjective *a little stumpy man | Ben cranked his bike with his stumpy legs* **short**, stubby, squat, stunted; **stocky**, sturdy, chunky, heavily built, heavyset, solid, thickset, bull-necked; informal beefy; Brit. informal fubsy.
OPPOSITES long, thin.

stun ▶ verb **1** *a glancing blow stunned Gary* **daze**, stupefy, knock senseless, knock unconscious, knock out, lay out; informal knock for six.
2 *she was quite stunned by her own success* **astound**, amaze, astonish, startle, take someone's breath away, dumbfound, stupefy, overwhelm, stagger, shock, confound, take aback, shake up; informal flabbergast, knock for six, knock sideways, hit like a ton of bricks, bowl over, floor, blow away.

stunner ▶ noun (informal) *the girl was a stunner* **beauty**, belle, goddess, Venus, siren, charmer, seductress; dream, vision, sensation; informal looker, good-looker, lovely, knockout, cracker, smasher, bobby-dazzler, dish, sight for sore eyes, eye-catcher, eyeful, peach, honey.

stunning ▶ adjective **1** *a stunning 4–0 win in the League Cup final* **remarkable**, extraordinary, staggering, incredible, impressive, outstanding, amazing, astonishing, marvellous, phenomenal, splendid, imposing, breathtaking, thrilling; informal mind-boggling, mind-blowing, out of this world, fabulous, fab, super, fantastic, tremendous; literary wondrous.
OPPOSITES ordinary, run-of-the-mill.
2 *she was looking particularly stunning* **beautiful**, handsome, attractive, lovely, good-looking, comely, pretty, sexy; sensational, radiant, ravishing, striking, dazzling, devastating, wonderful, marvellous, magnificent, glorious, breathtaking, captivating, bewitching, charming, alluring, exquisite, impressive, splendid; Scottish & N. English bonny; informal gorgeous, drop-dead gorgeous, out of this world, fabulous, fab, smashing, super, easy on the eye, knockout; N. Amer. informal bootylicious; literary beauteous; rare pulchritudinous.
OPPOSITES ordinary, unattractive.

stunt[1] ▶ verb *a rare disease that stunts growth* **inhibit**, impede, hamper, hinder, restrict, retard, slow, curb, arrest, check, stop.
OPPOSITES promote, encourage.

stunt[2] ▶ noun *he performed stunts in circuses* **feat**, exploit, trick, antic, caper; coup, act, action, deed; French tour de force.

stunted ▶ adjective *a clump of stunted trees* **small**, little, tiny, undersized, undersize, diminutive, dwarf, dwarfish, pygmy; baby; Scottish wee.

stupefaction ▶ noun **1** *she has retreated into alcoholic stupefaction* **oblivion**, obliviousness, unconsciousness, insensibility, senselessness, numbness, lack of sensation/feeling, blankness; stupor, daze, blackout, coma, collapse.
2 *Don shook his head in stupefaction* **bewilderment**, confusion, perplexity, bafflement, wonder, wonderment, amazement, astonishment; shock, devastation.

stupefy ▶ verb **1** *the blow had stupefied her* **stun**, daze, befuddle, knock senseless, knock unconscious, knock out, lay out, benumb, numb.
2 *they became stupefied by some narcotic* **drug**, sedate, anaesthetize, give anaesthetic to, tranquillize, narcotize; intoxicate, inebriate; knock out, render unconscious; informal dope.
3 *the amount they spend on clothes would stupefy their grandparents* **shock**, stun, astound, dumbfound, overwhelm, stagger, amaze, astonish, startle, confound, take aback, shake up, leave open-mouthed, take someone's breath away; informal flabbergast, knock for six, knock sideways, hit like a ton of bricks, bowl over, floor, blow away.

stupendous ▶ adjective **1** *truly stupendous achievements* **amazing**, astounding, astonishing, extraordinary, remarkable, wonderful, prodigious, phenomenal, staggering, breathtaking; informal fantastic, mind-boggling, mind-blowing, great, terrific, awesome, unreal; literary wondrous.
OPPOSITES run-of-the-mill, ordinary.
2 *a roc was an imaginary bird of stupendous size* **colossal**, immense, vast, giant, gigantic, massive, monumental, mammoth, elephantine, gargantuan, prodigious, huge, very large, great, enormous, mighty, titanic, Herculean, Brobdingnagian; informal jumbo, bumper, monster, humongous, whopping, astronomical, mega; Brit. informal ginormous.
OPPOSITES minute, tiny.

stupid ▶ adjective **1** *they're not as stupid as they look* **unintelligent**, ignorant, dense, brainless, mindless, foolish, dull-witted, dull, slow-witted, witless, slow, dunce-like, simple-minded, empty-headed, vacuous, vapid, half-witted, idiotic, moronic, imbecilic, imbecile, obtuse, doltish; gullible, naive; informal thick, thick as two short planks, dim, dumb, dopey, dozy, crazy, barmy, cretinous, birdbrained, pea-brained, pig-ignorant, bovine, slow on the uptake, soft in the head, brain-dead, boneheaded, lamebrained, thickheaded, chuckleheaded, dunderheaded, wooden, wooden-headed, fat-headed, muttonheaded; Brit. informal daft, not the full shilling; N. Amer. vulgar slang dumb-ass.
OPPOSITES intelligent, clever, astute.
2 *I promised never to make the same stupid mistake again* **foolish**, silly, unintelligent, idiotic, brainless, mindless, scatterbrained, crackbrained, nonsensical, senseless, irresponsible, unthinking, ill-advised, ill-considered, inept, witless, damfool, unwise, injudicious, indiscreet, short-sighted; inane, absurd, ludicrous, ridiculous, laughable, risible, fatuous, asinine, pointless, meaningless, futile, fruitless, mad, insane, lunatic; informal crazy, dopey, cracked, half-baked, cock-eyed, hare-brained, nutty, potty, dotty, batty, barmy, gormless, cuckoo, loony, loopy, zany, screwy, off one's head, off one's trolley, out to lunch; Brit. informal daft; Scottish & N. English informal glaikit; N. Amer. vulgar slang half-assed.
OPPOSITES sensible, prudent.
3 *all he'd do was sit and drink himself stupid* **into a stupor**, into a daze, into a state of unconsciousness, into oblivion; stupefied, dazed, groggy, sluggish, semi-conscious, unconscious.
OPPOSITE alert.

stupidity ▶ noun **1** *he cursed the older man's stupidity* **lack of intelligence**, unintelligence, foolishness, denseness, brainlessness, ignorance, mindlessness, dull-wittedness, dull-headedness, dullness, slow-wittedness, doltishness, slowness, vacancy; gullibility, naivety; informal thickness, dimness, dumbness, dopiness, doziness, craziness.
OPPOSITE genius.
2 *she blushed at the stupidity of the question* **foolishness**, folly, silliness, idiocy, brainlessness, senselessness, irresponsibility, injudiciousness,

S

ineptitude, inaneness, inanity, irrationality, absurdity, ludicrousness, ridiculousness, fatuousness, fatuity, asininity, pointlessness, meaninglessness, futility, fruitlessness, madness, insanity, lunacy; *informal* craziness; *Brit. informal* daftness.
OPPOSITE sagacity.

stupor ▶ **noun** *they left him slumped in a drunken stupor* **daze**, state of stupefaction, state of senselessness, state of unconsciousness; inertia, torpor, insensibility, numbness, blankness, oblivion, coma, blackout; *Scottish* dwam; *rare* sopor.

sturdy ▶ **adjective 1** *the boy had grown sturdy and handsome* **strapping**, well built, well made, muscular, athletic, strong, hefty, brawny, powerfully built, powerful, solidly built, solid, burly, stocky, thickset, rugged, substantial, robust, vigorous, tough, hardy, mighty, lusty, Herculean; fit, able-bodied, healthy, in good health, hale and hearty, hearty, hale, in good shape, in good condition, sound, sound in body and limb; *informal* husky, beefy, meaty, chunky, fit as a fiddle; *dated* stalwart; *literary* thewy, stark.
OPPOSITES puny; frail.
2 *the boat was small but it was sturdy* **robust**, strong, strongly made, well built, well made, solid, substantial, stout, sound, serviceable, stable; tough, resilient, durable, long-lasting, built to last, hard-wearing, imperishable, indestructible, resistant; *dated* staunch.
OPPOSITES weak, ramshackle.
3 *nature is offering a sturdy resistance to man* **vigorous**, strong, stalwart, firm, determined, resolute, tenacious, staunch, steadfast, unyielding, unwavering, uncompromising.
OPPOSITE weak.

stutter ▶ **verb** *he stuttered over a word* **stammer**, stumble, speak haltingly, falter, speak falteringly, flounder, hesitate, pause, halt; blunder, splutter; *informal* fluff one's lines.
▶ **noun** *the editor had a bad stutter* **stammer**, speech impediment, speech defect; hesitancy, faltering.

WORD LINKS
fear of stuttering **lalophobia**

Stygian ▶ **adjective** (*literary*) *Paris was plunged after dark into Stygian gloom* **dark**, black, pitch-black, pitch-dark, inky, sooty, dusky, dim, murky, shadowy, unlit; gloomy, sombre, dismal, dreary, hellish, infernal, Hadean; *literary* crepuscular, tenebrous, Cimmerian, Tartarean, caliginous.

style ▶ **noun 1** *notice the differing styles of these two writers* **manner**, way, technique, method, methodology, approach, system, mode, form, practice; *Latin* modus operandi; *informal* MO.
2 *a non-directive style of counselling* **type**, kind, manner, variety, sort, nature, genre, vein, species, ilk, vintage, school, brand, quality, calibre, kidney; design, pattern, stamp, model, cast, grain; *N. Amer.* stripe.
3 *they wear their clothes with style* **flair**, stylishness, smartness, elegance, grace, gracefulness, poise, polish, suaveness, sophistication, urbanity, chic, dash, finesse, panache, elan, taste; *informal* class, pizzazz, ritziness, oomph, zing.
4 *Laura travelled in style* **comfort**, **luxury**, elegance, chic; affluence, wealth, opulence, lavishness.
5 *the groovy styles portrayed in the magazine* **fashion**, trend, vogue, mode, latest thing; fad, craze, rage.
6 *candidates are asked to criticize both the content and style of the novel* **phraseology**, mode of expression, wording, language.
▶ **verb 1** *winter sportswear styled by Karl and Derrick* **design**, fashion, tailor, make, produce.
2 *by 1300 there were about eighty men styled 'knight'* **call**, name, title, entitle, dub, designate, term, address, label, tag; christen, baptize, nickname; *archaic* clepe; *rare* denominate.

stylish ▶ **adjective** *a stylish gown | they are incredibly stylish people* **fashionable**, modish, voguish, modern, ultra-modern, contemporary, up to date, up to the minute, trendsetting; smart, sophisticated, elegant, chic, polished, dapper, debonair, dashing, fine, fancy, flashy, designer; *French* à la mode; *informal* trendy, with it, all the rage, bang up to date, in, now, hip, cool, big, natty, classy, nifty, dressy, ritzy, snazzy, snappy, flash, sharp; *N. Amer. informal* fly, kicky, tony, spiffy.
OPPOSITES unfashionable, dowdy.

stylus ▶ **noun** **needle**, pointer, probe, style; pen, hand; *rare* graphium.

stymie ▶ **verb** *NHS changes must not be allowed to stymie new medical treatments* **impede**, interfere with, hamper, hinder, obstruct, inhibit, frustrate, thwart, foil, spoil, stall, shackle, fetter, stop, check, block, cripple, handicap, scotch; *informal* put paid to, put the kibosh on, snooker; *Brit. informal* scupper, throw a spanner in the works of; *N. Amer. informal* throw a monkey wrench in the works of.
OPPOSITES assist, help.

suave ▶ **adjective** *a suave middle-aged man* **charming**, sophisticated, debonair, urbane, worldly, worldly-wise, polished, refined, poised, self-possessed, dignified, civilized, gentlemanly, gallant; smooth, smooth-talking, smooth-tongued, silver-tongued, glib, bland, polite, well mannered, civil, courteous, affable, tactful, diplomatic, slick; *informal* cool; *dated* mannerly.
OPPOSITES unsophisticated, rude.

suavity ▶ **noun** *he was somewhat shaken from his confident suavity* **charm**, sophistication, polish, urbanity, suaveness, worldliness, refinement, confidence, poise, aplomb, dignity, gentility, style; smoothness, politeness, courtesy, courteousness, civility, tact, tactfulness, diplomacy, subtlety; *French* savoir faire.

subconscious ▶ **adjective** *dreams reflect a person's subconscious desires* **unconscious**, latent, suppressed, repressed, subliminal, unfulfilled, dormant, hidden, concealed, underlying, innermost, deep, intuitive, instinctive, innate, involuntary; *informal* bottled up.
OPPOSITES conscious, expressed.
▶ **noun** *the creative powers of the subconscious* **unconscious mind**, mind, imagination, inner self, innermost self, self, inner man/woman, psyche, ego, superego, id, true being, essential nature.
OPPOSITE conscious mind.

subdue ▶ **verb 1** *he is said to have slain or subdued all those who had plotted against him* **conquer**, defeat, vanquish, get the better of, overpower, overcome, overwhelm, crush, quash, quell, beat, trounce, subjugate, master, suppress, gain the upper hand over, triumph over, tame, bring someone to their knees, hold in check, humble, chasten, cow; *informal* lick, thrash, wipe the floor with, clobber, demolish, hammer, make mincemeat of, walk all over.
2 *she could not subdue her longing for praise* **curb**, restrain, hold back, constrain, contain, inhibit, repress, suppress, stifle, smother, check, keep in check, arrest, bridle, rein in; control, govern, master, quash, quell; moderate, tone down, diminish, lessen, damp; *informal* lick, nip in the bud, keep a/the lid on.

subdued ▶ **adjective 1** *Lewis's subdued air had changed to one of high good humour* **sombre**, low-spirited, downcast, sad, dejected, depressed, low, gloomy, despondent, dispirited, disheartened, forlorn, woebegone; restrained, repressed, inactive, spiritless, lifeless, dull, unresponsive, withdrawn, pensive, thoughtful, preoccupied, quiet; *informal* down in the mouth, down in the dumps, out of sorts, in the doldrums, with a long face; *Brit. informal* brassed off, cheesed off, browned off; *N. Amer. informal* teed off, ticked off.
OPPOSITES lively, cheerful.
2 *they chatted in subdued tones* **hushed**, muted, quiet, low, soft, gentle, whispered, murmured, faint, muffled, indistinct, inaudible; noiseless, soundless, silent, still, calm.
OPPOSITES loud, noisy.
3 *the subdued light made Mary appear pale* **dim**, muted, toned down, softened, soft, lowered, shaded, low-key, subtle, unobtrusive, understated; sombre, dreary, dark.
OPPOSITE bright.

subject ▶ **noun** (stress on the first syllable) **1** *the structure of the economy is the subject of this chapter* **theme**, subject matter, topic, issue, question, concern, text, thesis, content, point, motif, thread; substance, essence, gist, matter. *See 'Choose the Right Word' below.*
2 *there were cuts in funding for popular university subjects* **branch of knowledge**, branch of study, course of study, course, discipline, field, area, specialism, speciality, specialty.
3 *six subjects did trials of the short-term memory tasks* **participant**, volunteer; case, client, patient; *informal* guinea pig.
4 *Soviet and British subjects* **citizen**, national, native, resident, inhabitant; taxpayer, voter.
5 *Santerre is a loyal subject of the king* **liege**, liegeman, vassal, subordinate, underling; henchman, retainer, follower.
▶ **verb** (stress on the second syllable) *they have been* **subjected to** *physical violence* **put through**, treat with; expose to, lay open to, submit to.
▶ **adjective** (stress on the first syllable)
□ **subject to 1** *the position is subject to budgetary approval* **conditional on**, contingent on, dependent on, depending on, controlled by; hingeing on, resting on, hanging on.
2 *horses are subject to a cough resembling the human common cold* **susceptible to**, liable to, prone to, vulnerable to, predisposed to, disposed to, apt/likely to suffer from, easily affected by, in danger of, at risk of, open to, wide open to; *rare* susceptive of.
OPPOSITE resistant.
3 *most people were subject to authority for a large part of their lives* **bound by**, constrained by, answerable to, accountable to, liable to, under the control of, at the mercy of.

subjection ▶ **noun** *the subjection of aboriginal peoples* **subjugation**, domination, oppression, control, mastery, repression, suppression, bondage, slavery, enslavement, persecution, exploitation, abuse.

subjective ▶ **adjective** *standards can be judged on quantitative data rather than on subjective opinion* **personal**, personalized, individual, internal, emotional, instinctive, intuitive, impressionistic; biased, prejudiced, bigoted, idiosyncratic, irrational; *informal* gut, gut reaction.
OPPOSITES objective, impartial.

subjugate ▶ **verb** *Norman leaders had subjugated most of Ireland's Gaelic population* **conquer**, vanquish, defeat, crush, quell, quash, gain mastery

S

CHOOSE THE RIGHT WORD

subject, topic, theme

- **Subject** is the most general term for something that is or could be written, talked, or thought about (*his mind was no longer on the subject of politics | please send questions on any subjects you would like discussed*). A *subject* also means a branch of knowledge studied at school, college, or university. (*sixth-form classes in less popular A-level subjects*).
- When distinguished from *subject*, **topic** can refer to a smaller and more specific area for discussion (*from this very complex subject, two topics concerning government grants have been selected for discussion in this section*). It is also the most common word for something discussed in speech (*her sole topic of conversation nowadays was the baby*).
- A **theme** is typically associated with a relatively long work or discussion and tends to be an underlying idea, recurring throughout it and unifying it (*she deals delicately with the themes of love and jealousy*). A *theme* is generally *developed* or *elaborated* rather than *discussed* or *debated*.

over, gain ascendancy over, gain control of, bring under the yoke, bring to heel, bring someone to their knees, overcome, overpower; enslave, tyrannize, oppress, repress, subdue, colonize, suppress; tame, break, humble; *informal* lick, clobber, hammer, wipe the floor with, walk all over.
OPPOSITE liberate.

sublimate ▶ verb *work can serve as a means of sublimating rage* **channel**, control, divert, transfer, redirect, convert, refine, purify, transmute.

sublime ▶ adjective **1** *a sublime vision of human potential* **exalted**, elevated, noble, lofty, awe-inspiring, awesome, majestic, magnificent, imposing, glorious, supreme; grand, great, outstanding, excellent, first-rate, first-class, superb, perfect, ideal, wonderful, marvellous, splendid, delightful, blissful, rapturous; *informal* fantastic, fabulous, fab, super, smashing, terrific, heavenly, divine, mind-blowing, too good to be true, out of this world.
OPPOSITES poor, lowly, ordinary.
2 *the sublime confidence of youth* **supreme**, total, complete, utter, consummate, extreme; arrogant.

subliminal ▶ adjective *the screen flashed subliminal messages* **subconscious**, unconscious; hidden, concealed.
OPPOSITE explicit.

submerge ▶ verb **1** *the U-boat would have had time to submerge* **go under water**, dive, sink, plunge, plummet, drop, go down.
OPPOSITE surface.
2 *half submerge the bowl in a large saucepan of hot water* **immerse**, dip, plunge, duck, dunk, sink.
3 *when the farmland was submerged many sheep were lost* **flood**, inundate, deluge, engulf, swamp, immerse, drown; overflow, pour over.
4 *her husband helped her to resist becoming completely submerged in work* **overwhelm**, inundate, deluge, swamp, bury, engulf, swallow up, consume, snow under, overload, overburden.
5 *a healthy return to old values which had been submerged* **hide**, conceal, veil, cloak, repress, suppress.

submission ▶ noun **1** *an instinctive submission to authority* **yielding**, capitulation, agreement, acceptance, consent, accession, compliance.
OPPOSITE defiance.
2 *Tim raised his hands in mock submission* **surrender**, yielding, capitulation, resignation, succumbing, defeat, fall; laying down one's arms, giving in, humbling oneself, knuckling under.
3 *he wanted to gain her total submission* **compliance**, submissiveness, yielding, malleability, acquiescence, tractability, tractableness, manageability, unassertiveness, non-resistance, passivity, obedience, biddability, dutifulness, duteousness, docility, meekness, tameness, patience, resignation, humility, self-effacement, deference, subservience, servility, subjection, self-abasement, obsequiousness, obeisance; *informal* bootlicking.
OPPOSITES defiance, resistance.
4 *you are required to write a report for submission to the Board* **presentation**, presenting, proffering, tendering, proposal, proposing, tabling, introduction, suggestion, venturing, broaching, airing, lodgement, positing.
5 *the plan was put forward by Stirling in his original submission* **proposal**, suggestion, proposition, recommendation, presentation, tender, bid, offer; motion, entry, advance, approach, overture; attempt, try, effort, draft; proffer.
6 *the trial judge rejected his submission* **argument**, assertion, contention, statement, claim, allegation, protestation, declaration.

submissive ▶ adjective *Mary was far from being a timidly submissive woman* **compliant**, yielding, malleable, acquiescent, accommodating, amenable, tractable, manageable, unassertive, non-resisting, passive, obedient, biddable, dutiful, duteous, docile, ductile, pliant, meek, timid, mild, patient, resigned, forbearing, subdued, humble, self-effacing, spiritless, deferential, obsequious, servile, slavish, self-abasing, spineless, grovelling, lamblike, supine; *informal* bootlicking, under someone's thumb; *archaic* resistless; *rare* longanimous.
OPPOSITES domineering, obstinate, intractable.

submissiveness ▶ noun *he could exhibit a saint-like submissiveness* **compliance**, submission, subservience, yielding, acquiescence, deference, assent, meekness, obedience, dutifulness, duteousness, biddableness, malleability, tractableness, tractability, tameness, docility, passiveness, passivity, humility, resignation, forbearance; obsequiousness, sycophancy, servility, self-abasement; *informal* bootlicking.
OPPOSITE assertiveness.

submit ▶ verb **1** *the countess had submitted under duress | you are* ***submitting*** *to male domination* **give in**, yield, give way, back down, cave in, bow, capitulate, relent, defer, agree, consent, accede, conform, acquiesce, comply, accept; surrender, lay down one's arms, raise/show/wave the white flag, knuckle under, humble oneself, bend the knee, kowtow, fall; *informal* throw in the towel/sponge.
OPPOSITE defy.
2 *he refused to* ***submit to*** *censorship* **be governed by**, abide by, be regulated by, comply with, observe, heed, accept, tolerate, endure, brook, put up with, stomach, adhere to, be subject to, agree to, consent to, conform to; *informal* keep in step, play by the rules, play it by the book, take it lying down, lump it; *Brit. informal* wear; *archaic* suffer.
OPPOSITES defy, resist.
3 *we submitted an unopposed bid for the franchise* **put forward**, present, set forth, offer, proffer, tender, advance, propose, suggest, volunteer, table, lodge, introduce, come up with, raise, air, moot; put in, send in, hand in, enter, register.
OPPOSITE withdraw.
4 *the appellant submitted that a community service order was inappropriate* **contend**, assert, argue, state, claim, aver, propound, posit, postulate, adduce, move, advocate, venture, volunteer; *formal* opine.

subnormal ▶ adjective **1** *years of subnormal trade activity* **below average**, below normal, too low, very low, below par, under par, poor, inferior, inadequate; *informal* not up to snuff.
OPPOSITES normal, average.
2 (*dated*) *the education of severely subnormal children* **with learning difficulties**, with special (educational) needs, of low intelligence, mentally disabled; educationally challenged, different; *dated* ESN, retarded, mentally handicapped, mentally defective, slow, backward, simple, simple-minded, feeble-minded, slow-witted, dull-witted.
OPPOSITES normal, gifted.

subordinate ▶ adjective **1** *she kept her distance from subordinate staff* **lower-ranking**, junior, lower, lesser, inferior, lowly, minor, supporting; second-fiddle.
OPPOSITES superior, senior.
2 *a subordinate rule* **secondary**, lesser, minor, subsidiary, subservient, ancillary, auxiliary, attendant, peripheral, marginal, of little account/importance; second-class, second-rate, second-fiddle; supplementary, accessory, additional, extra.
OPPOSITES central, major, chief.
▶ noun *the manager and his or her subordinate jointly review performance* **junior**, assistant, second, second in command, number two, right-hand man/woman, deputy, aide, adjutant, subaltern, apprentice, underling, flunkey, minion, lackey, mate, inferior; *informal* sidekick, henchman, second fiddle, man/girl Friday.
OPPOSITES superior, senior.

subordination ▶ noun *she could not tolerate a life of subordination* **inferiority**, inferior status/position, secondary status/position, lowliness; **subjection**, subservience, submission, dependence, servitude.
OPPOSITE superiority.

sub rosa ▶ adverb (*Latin*) *the committee is accustomed to operate sub rosa* **in secret**, secretly, in private, privately, in confidence, confidentially, behind closed doors, surreptitiously, discreetly, furtively, clandestinely, on the quiet, on the sly, unofficially, off the record, between ourselves; *Latin* in camera; *French* à huis clos; *Italian* in petto; *informal* on the q.t., between you, me, and the gatepost/bedpost; *archaic* under the rose.
OPPOSITES openly, publicly.

subscribe ▶ verb **1** *How many magazines do you* ***subscribe to****?* **pay a subscription**, buy regularly, take, take regularly, read, read regularly, contract to buy; be a member of, support.
2 *his release was secured by friends* ***subscribing to*** *a ransom fund* **donate**, make a donation, make a subscription, give, give money, make a contribution, pay, pledge; contribute towards, sponsor, finance, back, subsidize, underwrite; *informal* chip into, pitch into; *N. Amer. informal* kick in.
3 *I'm afraid I can't* ***subscribe to*** *the theory* **agree with**, be in agreement with, accede to, consent to, accept, believe in, endorse, back, support, advocate, champion.
4 *the names of signatories are subscribed* **sign**, write, inscribe, initial, autograph, countersign, witness, put one's mark on; add, append; *Law* set one's hand to; *archaic* underwrite, style, side-sign; *rare* chirographate.

S

subscriber ▸ noun *the journal has 10,000 subscribers* **reader**, regular reader, regular customer, follower, member, patron, supporter, backer, benefactor, sponsor, donor, contributor.

subscription ▸ noun **1** *a subscription to a London club* **membership fee**, dues, annual payment, charge, levy, retainer.
2 *the charity put every penny of your subscription to good use* **donation**, contribution, offering, gift, present, grant, bestowal, endowment, subsidy, benefaction, handout; *historical* alms; *rare* donative.
3 *he wanted to beat up anyone who flaunted their* ***subscription to*** *capitalism* **agreement with**, subscribing to, acceding to, consent to, acceptance of, belief in, endorsement of, backing for, support of.
4 *the subscription of the document was attested by at least one witness* **signature**, initials; addition, appendage.

subsequent ▸ adjective *he was a caring and stalwart friend to her during the subsequent months* **following**, ensuing, succeeding, successive, later, future, coming, upcoming, to come, next.
OPPOSITES previous, prior, former.
□ **subsequent to** *a record would be published subsequent to the meetings* **following**, after, in the wake of, at the close/end of, later than; *rare* posterior to.
OPPOSITE prior to.

subsequently ▸ adverb *he made a bid for the remaining shares and subsequently acquired them* **later**, later on, at a later date, at some time/point in the future, at a subsequent time, afterwards, in due course, following this/that, eventually, then, next, by and by; *informal* after a bit; *formal* thereafter, thereupon.
OPPOSITE previously.

subservient ▸ adjective **1** *women were expected to be decorative and subservient* **submissive**, deferential, acquiescent, compliant, accommodating, obedient, dutiful, duteous, biddable, yielding, meek, docile, ductile, pliant, passive, unassertive, spiritless, subdued, humble, timid, mild, lamblike; servile, slavish, grovelling, truckling, self-effacing, self-abasing, downtrodden, snivelling, cowering, cringing; *informal* under someone's thumb; *archaic* resistless; *rare* longanimous.
OPPOSITES domineering; independent.
2 *the rights of the individual are being made* ***subservient to*** *the interests of the state* **subordinate**, secondary, subsidiary, peripheral, marginal, ancillary, auxiliary, supplementary, inferior, immaterial; less important than, of lesser importance than, lower than.
OPPOSITE superior.
3 *the whole narration is* ***subservient to*** *the moral plan of exemplifying twelve virtues* **ancillary**, subordinate, secondary, supportive; instrumental, contributory, conducive, helpful, useful, advantageous, beneficial, valuable.

subside ▸ verb **1** *I'll wait a few minutes until the storm subsides | his anger subsided and he smiled* **abate**, let up, moderate, quieten down, calm, lull, slacken (off), ease (up), relent, die down, die out, peter out, taper off, recede, lessen, soften, alleviate, attenuate, remit, diminish, decline, dwindle, weaken, fade, wane, ebb, still, cease, come to a stop, come to an end, terminate.
OPPOSITES intensify, worsen.
2 *the ground was still waterlogged after the flood had subsided* **recede**, ebb, fall back, flow back, fall away, fall, go down, get lower, sink, sink lower; abate, diminish; *rare* retrocede.
OPPOSITE rise.
3 *the molten core of a volcano subsides into the earth* **sink**, sink back, settle, cave in, fall in, collapse, crumple, give way, drop down, sag, slump.
4 *Sarah subsided into a chair* **slump**, flop, sink, sag, slouch, loll, fall back, collapse, settle; *informal* flump, plonk oneself, plop oneself.
OPPOSITE rise.

subsidence ▸ noun *subsidence due to coal mining is a notorious problem* **collapse**, caving in, falling in, giving way, sinking, settling.

subsidiary ▸ adjective *a subsidiary company | monetary policy should be subsidiary to fiscal policy* **subordinate**, secondary, ancillary, auxiliary, lesser, minor, subservient, supplementary, supplemental, additional, extra, attendant, peripheral; second-fiddle, second-class, lower-level, lower-grade.
OPPOSITES central, principal, major.
▸ noun *he is a director of the company's two major subsidiaries* **subordinate company**, wholly owned company; **branch**, division, subdivision, section, part, dependency, peripheral, derivative, satellite, offshoot, wing, attachment, adjunct, appendage; *archaic* tributary.
OPPOSITE parent company.

subsidize ▸ verb *they were unwilling to subsidize the poorer southern republics* **give money to**, pay a subsidy to, give a grant to, contribute to, make a contribution to, invest in, sponsor, fund, finance, provide finance/capital for, capitalize, underwrite; back, support, give support to, keep, help, aid, assist, shore up, prop up, buttress; *informal* pick up the tab for, foot the bill for, shell out for, fork out for, cough up for, chip in for; *N. Amer. informal* bankroll, pony up for.

subsidy ▸ noun *the theatre receives a subsidy of 1.7 million pounds a year* **grant**, allowance, endowment, contribution, donation, bursary, gift, present, investment, bestowal, benefaction, allocation, allotment, handout; backing, support, aid, assistance, charity, relief, sponsorship, finance, funding, subvention; *informal* helping hand, leg up; *historical* alms; *rare* donative.

subsist ▸ verb **1** *he subsisted on a university pension | the birds cannot subsist on fruit alone* **survive**, live, stay alive, exist, eke out an existence, endure; **support oneself**, cope, manage, fare, get along, get by, get through, make (both) ends meet, make the grade, keep body and soul together, depend, rely for nourishment, feed; *informal* keep the wolf from the door, keep one's head above water, make out, hang on.
2 *the tenant's right of occupation subsists* **continue**, last, persist, endure, prevail, hold out, carry on, live on, live, survive, be in existence, exist, be alive, remain, abide, linger.
3 *the effect of genetic maldevelopment may* ***subsist in*** *chromasomal mutation* **lie**, reside, have its being, be inherent, rest, dwell, abide, be present, inhere; be attributable to, be ascribable to, be intrinsic to; *rare* indwell.

subsistence ▸ noun **1** *they depend for subsistence on fish and game* **survival**, existence, living, life; sustenance, nourishment, diet.
2 *he raised a total of £2,000 towards his own travel and subsistence* **maintenance**, keep, upkeep, support, livelihood, living, board, board and lodging; sustenance, nourishment, nutriment, provisions, supplies, food, food and drink, fare, bread; *Scottish* vivers; *informal* eats, nosh, chow, grub, scoff, bread and butter; *formal* comestibles, provender; *archaic* meat, vittles, commons, victuals, viands; *rare* aliment.

substance ▸ noun **1** *an organic substance* **material**, matter, stuff, medium, fabric.
2 *he saw ghostly figures with no substance* **solidity**, body, corporeality, reality, actuality, materiality, concreteness, tangibility; density, mass, weight, shape, structure.
3 *none of the objections put forward has any substance* **meaningfulness**, significance, importance, import, moment, power, soundness, validity, content, pith, marrow, core; basis, foundation; *informal* clout.
4 *the substance of the tale is too thin and familiar by far* **content**, subject matter, subject, theme, topic, text, message, material, burden, tenor, essence, quintessence, heart, meat, gist, drift, sense, import.
5 *Rangers are a team of substance and skill* **character**, backbone, mettle, strength of character; consequence, import, importance, significance, moment, magnitude, prominence; *informal* clout.
6 *the proprietors were independent men of substance* **wealth**, fortune, riches, affluence, prosperity, money, capital, means, resources, assets, property, estates, possessions.

substandard ▸ adjective *children were being educated in substandard buildings* **inferior**, second-rate, low-quality, low-grade, poor, poor-quality, inadequate, imperfect, faulty, defective, jerry-built, shoddy, shabby, crude, unsound, unacceptable, unsatisfactory, unworthy, disappointing; *informal* below par, not up to scratch, not up to snuff, tenth-rate, crummy, lousy; *Brit. informal* duff, ropy, rubbish; *vulgar slang* crap, crappy; *N. Amer. vulgar slang* chickenshit.

substantial ▸ adjective **1** *spirits are shadowy, human beings substantial* **real**, true, actual, existing; **physical**, solid, material, concrete, corporeal, tangible, non-spiritual; *rare* unimaginary.
OPPOSITES incorporeal, abstract.
2 *substantial progress had been made* **considerable**, real, material, weighty, solid, sizeable, meaningful, significant, important, notable, major, marked, valuable, useful, worthwhile.
OPPOSITES insubstantial, worthless.
3 *the plaintiff is unlikely to recover substantial damages* **sizeable**, considerable, significant, large, ample, appreciable, goodly, decent; *informal* tidy.
4 *a row of substantial Victorian villas* **sturdy**, solid, stout, strong, well built, well constructed, durable, long-lasting, hard-wearing, imperishable, impervious.
OPPOSITES insubstantial, jerry-built.
5 *the food is fit for substantial country gentlemen* **hefty**, stout, sturdy, strapping, large, big, solid, bulky, burly, well built, weighty, portly, tubby, chubby, beefy.
OPPOSITES slight, gaunt.
6 *substantial City companies* **successful**, buoyant, booming, doing well, profit-making, profitable, prosperous, wealthy, affluent, moneyed, well-to-do, rich, large; *informal* in the money, rolling in it, loaded, stinking rich, quids in.
OPPOSITE paltry.
7 *he is in substantial agreement with Lomax* **fundamental**, essential, basic.

substantially ▸ adverb **1** *the cost of oil imports has fallen substantially* **considerably**, significantly, greatly, a great deal, to a great extent, to a large extent, to a marked extent, markedly, appreciably.
OPPOSITE slightly.
2 *the draft statement was substantially accepted by the executive* **largely**, for the most part, by and large, on the whole, almost entirely, in the main, mainly, in effect, in essence, essentially, materially, basically, fundamentally, to all intents and purposes, to a great degree.

substantiate ▸ verb *none of the allegations were ever substantiated* **prove**,

S

give proof of, show to be true, give substance to, support, uphold, back up, bear out, justify, vindicate, validate, corroborate, verify, authenticate, confirm, endorse, give credence to, lend weight to, establish, demonstrate; vouch for, attest to, testify to, stand by, bear witness to.
OPPOSITES disprove, refute.

substitute ▶ noun *the casual workers might be substitutes for agency workers* **replacement**, deputy, relief, proxy, reserve, surrogate, cover, fill-in, stand-in, standby, locum, locum tenens, understudy, stopgap, alternative, ancillary; informal sub; N. Amer. informal pinch-hitter.
▶ adjective *a substitute teacher* **acting**, replacement, deputy, relief, reserve, surrogate, fill-in, stand-in, temporary, caretaker, alternative, locum, standby, backup, stopgap, interim, provisional, pro tem, proxy, ancillary; Latin pro tempore; informal second-string; N. Amer. informal pinch-hitting.
OPPOSITE permanent.
▶ verb 1 *low-fat cheese can be **substituted** for full-fat cheese* **exchange**, use as a replacement, switch; replace with, use instead of, use as an alternative to, use in place of, use in preference to; N. Amer. trade; informal swap.
2 *the Senate was empowered to **substitute** for the President* **deputize**, act as deputy, act as a substitute, fill in, sit in, stand in, act as stand-in, cover, act as locum, be a proxy, hold the fort; take the place of, replace, relieve, understudy, take over from, represent, act in someone's stead; informal sub, fill someone's boots/shoes, step into someone's boots/shoes; N. Amer. informal pinch-hit.

substitution ▶ noun *the substitution of a steam locomotive for horsepower* **exchange**, change, interchange; **replacement**, replacing, swapping, switching; swap, switch, trade-off, barter; N. Amer. trade.

subterfuge ▶ noun 1 *journalists should not use subterfuge to gain admission to people's homes* **trickery**, intrigue, deviousness, evasion, deceit, deception, dishonesty, cheating, duplicity, guile, cunning, craft, craftiness, slyness, chicanery, bluff, pretence, fraud, fraudulence, sophistry, sharp practice; informal monkey business, funny business, hanky-panky, jiggery-pokery, kidology, every trick in the book; Irish informal codology.
OPPOSITES honesty, openness.
2 *a disreputable subterfuge* **trick**, hoax, ruse, wile, ploy, stratagem, artifice, dodge, bluff, manoeuvre, machination, pretext, pretence, expedient, tactic, intrigue, scheme, deception, fraud, masquerade, blind, smokescreen, sleight, stunt, game; informal con, racket, scam, caper; Brit. informal wheeze; Austral. informal lurk; archaic shift.

subtle ▶ adjective 1 *the colours are soft and subtle | the dish had a very subtle flavour* **understated**, low-key, muted, toned down, subdued; **delicate**, faint, pale, soft, indistinct, indefinite, vague, washed out.
OPPOSITES lurid; obvious.
2 *subtle distinctions are of little value* **fine**, fine-drawn, ultra-fine, nice, overnice, minute, precise, narrow, tenuous; **hair-splitting**, indistinct, indefinite, elusive, abstruse; informal minuscule.
OPPOSITE crude.
3 *a robust and subtle mind* **astute**, keen, quick, fine, acute, sharp, razor-like, razor-sharp, rapier-like, canny, shrewd, aware, perceptive, discerning, sensitive, discriminating, penetrating, sagacious, wise, clever, intelligent, skilful, artful; sapient, percipient, perspicacious; informal on the ball, savvy; archaic politic.
OPPOSITE slow-witted.
4 *the plan was simple yet subtle* **ingenious**, clever, skilful, adroit, cunning, crafty, wily, artful, devious.
OPPOSITES crude, artless.

subtlety ▶ noun 1 *they prefer the cheese for its subtlety and depth of flavour* **delicacy**, delicateness, subtleness, elusiveness, faintness; **understatedness**, understatement, mutedness, softness.
2 *classification is fraught with subtlety* **fineness**, subtleness, precision, preciseness, niceness, nicety, nuance, shade, detail, slightness, minuteness, narrowness, tenuousness, indistinctness, indefiniteness, lack of definition, elusiveness.
3 *the subtlety of the human mind* **astuteness**, keenness, acuteness, fineness, sharpness, razor-sharpness, sharp-wittedness, canniness, shrewdness, perceptiveness, perception, discernment, sensitivity, discrimination, penetration, percipience, perspicacity, perspicuity, acuity, sagacity, wisdom, cleverness, intelligence, skilfulness, skill, artfulness, dexterity, brightness, finesse; informal savvy; rare sapience.
OPPOSITES slow-wittedness, dullness.
4 *the employers' tactics varied in their subtlety* **ingenuity**, cleverness, skilfulness, expertise, adroitness, complexity, intricacy, cunning, guile, craftiness, wiliness, artfulness, deviousness.
OPPOSITE crudeness.

subtract ▶ verb *the value of their child benefit is subtracted from their total welfare payments* **take away**, take from, take off, deduct, debit, abstract, discount, dock, remove, withdraw; informal knock off, minus.
OPPOSITE add.

suburb ▶ noun *a densely populated suburb of Amsterdam* **outlying district**, residential area, dormitory area/town, commuter belt, conurbation; suburbia, fringes, outskirts, purlieus; Brit. garden suburb; N. Amer. bedroom area; French faubourg, banlieue; Spanish barrio; rare exurb.

suburban ▶ adjective 1 *a suburban area* **residential**, commuter, dormitory; N. Amer. bedroom; rare exurban.
2 *he brought some much-needed glamour to Karen's drab suburban existence* **dull**, boring, uninteresting, conventional, ordinary, commonplace, average, unremarkable, undistinguished, unexceptional, pedestrian; **provincial**, unsophisticated, small-town, parochial, parish-pump, insular, inward-looking, limited, blinkered, bourgeois, middle-class, conservative; informal bog-standard, nothing to write home about, no great shakes, not up to much; Brit. informal common or garden.
OPPOSITES sophisticated, cosmopolitan.

subversive ▶ adjective *he was arrested and charged with subversive activities* **disruptive**, troublemaking, inflammatory, insurgent, insurrectionary, insurrectionist, rabble-rousing; **seditious**, revolutionary, treasonous, treacherous, mutinous, rebellious, rebel, renegade, unpatriotic, dissident, disloyal, perfidious, insubordinate, underground, undermining, corrupting, discrediting, destructive, harmful.
▶ noun *she was designated as a dangerous subversive* **troublemaker**, dissident, agitator, revolutionary, revolutionist, insurgent, insurrectionist, insurrectionary, renegade, rebel, mutineer, traitor.

subvert ▶ verb 1 *a plot to subvert the state* **destabilize**, unsettle, overthrow, overturn; bring down, bring about the downfall of, topple, depose, oust, supplant, unseat, dethrone, disestablish, dissolve; disrupt, wreak havoc on, sabotage, ruin, upset, destroy, annihilate, demolish, wreck, undo, undermine, undercut, weaken, impair, damage.
2 *he declared that Western intelligence services were attempting to subvert Soviet youth* **corrupt**, pervert, warp, deprave, defile, debase, distort, contaminate, poison, embitter; vitiate.

subway ▶ noun 1 *he walked through the subway* **underpass**, underground passage, pedestrian tunnel, tunnel.
2 *a ride on Tokyo's subway* **underground railway**, underground, metro; Brit. informal tube.

succeed ▶ verb 1 *Darwin succeeded where earlier evolutionists had failed* **triumph**, be victorious, achieve success, be successful, be a success, do well, make good, prosper, flourish, thrive, advance; informal make it, make the grade, cut it, crack it, make a name for oneself, make one's mark, get somewhere, do all right for oneself, arrive, find a place in the sun.
OPPOSITE fail.
2 *the plan would have succeeded but for an important factor* **be successful**, turn out well, work, work out, go as planned, get results, be effective, be profitable; informal come off, pay off, pan out, do the trick.
OPPOSITES fail, flop.
3 *Rosebery had succeeded Gladstone as Prime Minister* **replace**, take the place of, take over from, come after, follow, supersede, supplant, displace, oust, remove, unseat, usurp; informal step into someone's shoes, fill someone's shoes/boots.
OPPOSITE precede.
4 *he succeeded to his title in 1543* **inherit**, accede to, assume, take over, come into, acquire, attain, be elevated to.
OPPOSITES renounce, abdicate.
5 *their age of learning was succeeded by an age of superstition* **follow**, come after, follow after; take the place of, replace.
OPPOSITE precede.

succeeding ▶ adjective *strands of DNA are reproduced through succeeding generations* **subsequent**, successive, following, ensuing, later, future, next, coming.
OPPOSITES preceding, previous.

success ▶ noun 1 *we are very encouraged by the success of the scheme* **favourable outcome**, successfulness, favourable result, successful outcome, positive result, victory, triumph.
OPPOSITE failure.
2 *the modern-day trappings of success* **prosperity**, prosperousness, successfulness, affluence, wealth, riches, fortune, opulence, luxury, comfort, life of ease, the good life, milk and honey.
OPPOSITES failure, poverty.
3 *a West End musical success | the book was a far greater success than I'd expected* **triumph**, best-seller, box-office success, sell-out, coup, master stroke; informal **hit**, box-office hit, smash hit, smash, crowd-puller, winner, knockout, sensation, wow, biggie.
OPPOSITES failure, flop, disaster.
4 *her performance might well have made her a success* **star**, superstar, celebrity, big name, household name, somebody, important person, VIP, personality, public figure, dignitary, luminary, leading light; informal celeb, bigwig, big shot, big noise, big cheese, big fish, megastar; Brit. informal nob; N. Amer. informal kahuna, macher, high muckamuck.
OPPOSITES failure, nobody.

successful ▶ adjective 1 *he reported the particulars of his successful campaign to General Cass* **victorious**, triumphant; fortunate, lucky.
OPPOSITE unsuccessful.
2 *she is a very successful designer* **prosperous**, affluent, wealthy, rich, well-to-do, doing well, moneyed; famous, eminent, at the top, top; informal on the up and up, well heeled, flush, rolling in it, in the money, made of money, loaded, stinking rich, quids in.
OPPOSITE unsuccessful.

S

3 *successful companies know how to handle the occasional failure* **flourishing**, thriving, booming, buoyant, burgeoning, doing well, profitable, profit-making, moneymaking, lucrative, gainful, fruitful, solvent, bankable; productive, efficient, effective; *informal* going strong, on the up and up, rolling in it, in the money, loaded, quids in.
OPPOSITES unsuccessful, unprofitable, poor.

succession ▶ noun **1** *a succession of exciting events* **sequence**, series, progression, course, chain, cycle, round, string, train, line, line-up, run, continuation, flow, stream; concatenation.
2 *she produced a male heir and thus deprived him of the* ***succession to*** *the throne* **accession**, elevation; inheritance of, assumption of.
3 *he left behind him a disputed succession between his kinsmen* **line of descent**, line, descent, ancestral line, blood line, ancestry, dynasty, lineage, genealogy, heritage, pedigree, extraction, derivation, stock, strain, background.
□ **in succession** *he drank six pints of beer in rapid succession* **one after the other**, in a row, consecutively, one behind the other, successively, in sequence; running, straight, solid, uninterrupted; *informal* on the trot.

successive ▶ adjective *the team have made a great start with three successive wins* **consecutive**, in a row, straight, solid, sequential, succeeding, in succession, following, serial, running, continuous, unbroken, uninterrupted; *informal* on the trot; *rare* seriate.

successor ▶ noun *Mary was the rightful successor to the English throne* **heir**, heir apparent, inheritor, next-in-line, descendant, beneficiary; replacement, incomer, substitute.
OPPOSITE predecessor.

succinct ▶ adjective *he gave a succinct résumé of the economic situation* **concise**, short, brief, compact, condensed, crisp, laconic, terse, tight, to the point, economic, pithy, thumbnail, summary, short and sweet, in a few well-chosen words, compendious, epigrammatic, synoptic, aphoristic, gnomic.
OPPOSITES lengthy, long-winded, verbose.

> **CHOOSE THE RIGHT WORD**
>
> **succinct, concise**
>
> *See* CONCISE.

succour ▶ noun *they provide shelter and succour in times of need* **aid**, help, a helping hand, assistance; ministration, comfort, ease, relief, support, guidance, backing; *rare* easement.
▶ verb *the Navy was unable to succour colonies in Africa* **help**, aid, bring aid to, give help to, give/render assistance to, assist, lend a (helping) hand to, be of service to; **minister to**, care for, comfort, bring comfort to, bring relief to, support, be supportive of, sustain, protect, take care of, look after, attend to, serve, wait on.

succulent ▶ adjective *heaps of succulent black grapes | a succulent fillet of beef* **juicy**, moist, luscious, lush, fleshy, pulpy, soft, tender, fresh, ripe; choice, mouth-watering, appetizing, flavoursome, flavourful, tasty, delicious, delectable, palatable, toothsome; *informal* scrumptious, scrummy, yummy, moreish, finger-licking, delish; *literary* ambrosial; *rare* ambrosian, nectareous, nectarean, comestible, flavorous, sapid.
OPPOSITES dry, shrivelled; unappetizing.

succumb ▶ verb **1** *she* ***succumbed to*** *temptation* **yield**, give in, give way, submit, surrender, capitulate, cave in; be overcome by, be overwhelmed by, be conquered by, be beaten by.
OPPOSITES resist, conquer.
2 *he* ***succumbed to*** *an obscure lung complaint* **die from**, die of, pass away as a result of, be a fatality of; catch, develop, contract, pick up, get, become infected with, suffer from, fall victim to, fall ill with; *informal* come/go down with.
OPPOSITE withstand.

suck ▶ verb **1** *they sucked mint juleps through straws* **sip**, sup, siphon, slurp, draw, drink, gulp, lap, guzzle, quaff, swill, swallow, imbibe.
2 *Fran* ***sucked in*** *a deep breath* **draw**, pull, breathe, gasp, sniff, gulp; inhale, inspire, respire.
3 *the mud had* ***sucked*** *him* ***in*** *up to his waist* **draw**, pull; engulf, swallow up, swamp.
4 *young children can get* ***sucked into*** *a world of petty crime* **implicate in**, involve in, draw into; *informal* mix up in.
5 (*N. Amer. informal*) *I love your country but your weather sucks* **be very bad**, be awful, be terrible, be dreadful, be horrible, be very unpleasant, be abhorrent, be despicable, be contemptible, be vile, be foul; *Brit. informal* be pants, be a load of pants; *informal* **stink**.
□ **suck up** *they suck up to him, hanging on to his every word* **grovel**, creep, toady, be obsequious/servile/sycophantic, kowtow, bow and scrape, play up, truckle; fawn on, curry favour with, dance attendance on; *informal* bootlick, lick someone's boots, be all over, fall all over, butter up, rub up the right way, keep sweet; *Brit. vulgar slang* lick/kiss someone's arse.

suckle ▶ verb *they employed a wet nurse to suckle their babies* **breastfeed**, feed, nurse; *archaic* give suck to.

sudden ▶ adjective *a sudden downpour took us by surprise* **unexpected**, unforeseen, unanticipated, unlooked-for, without warning, without notice, not bargained for; immediate, instantaneous, instant, precipitous, precipitate, abrupt, rapid, swift, lightning, quick, hurried, sharp, without delay.
OPPOSITE gradual.

suddenly ▶ adverb *she suddenly began to laugh* **immediately**, instantaneously, instantly, in an instant, straight away, all of a sudden, at once, all at once, promptly, abruptly, in a trice, swiftly; **unexpectedly**, without warning, without notice, on the spur of the moment; *informal* straight off, out of the blue, in a flash, like a shot, before you can say Jack Robinson, before you can say knife, in two shakes (of a lamb's tail).
OPPOSITE gradually.

suds ▶ plural noun *Aunt Margaret was up to her elbows in suds* **lather**, foam, froth, bubbles, soap, soapiness; fizz, effervescence; *literary* spume.

sue ▶ verb **1** *he is likely to sue the contractor for negligence* **take legal action against**, take to court, bring an action against, bring a suit against, proceed against; charge, prosecute, prefer/bring charges against, bring to trial, summons, indict, arraign; *N. Amer.* impeach; *informal* have the law on, do.
2 *Richard was in no mood to* ***sue for*** *peace* **appeal**, petition, ask, beg, plead, entreat, implore, supplicate; solicit, request, seek; *rare* obtest, impetrate, obsecrate.

suffer ▶ verb **1** *I loved him too much to want to see him suffer* **hurt**, ache, be in pain, feel pain, be racked with pain, endure agony, agonize, be distressed, be in distress, experience hardship, be upset, be miserable, be wretched, be handicapped.
2 *he* ***suffered from*** *asthma for many years* **be afflicted by**, be affected by, be troubled with, have, have trouble with.
3 *England suffered a humiliating defeat* **undergo**, experience, be subjected to, receive, encounter, meet with, endure, face, live through, go through, sustain, bear.
4 *the school's reputation has suffered* **be impaired**, be damaged, deteriorate, fall off, decline, get worse.
5 *he was obliged to suffer intimate proximity with the man he detested* **tolerate**, put up with, bear, brook, stand, abide, endure, support, accept, weather; *informal* stick, stomach; *Brit. informal* wear, hack.
6 *my conscience would not suffer me to accept any more* **allow**, permit, let, give leave to, give assent to, sanction, give one's blessing to; *informal* give the green light to, give the go ahead to, give the thumbs up to, give someone/something the nod, OK.

suffering ▶ noun *the war caused widespread civilian suffering* **hardship**, distress, misery, wretchedness, adversity, tribulation; **pain**, agony, anguish, trauma, torment, torture, hurt, hurting, affliction, sadness, unhappiness, sorrow, grief, woe, angst, heartache, heartbreak, stress; *informal* hell, hell on earth; *literary* dolour.

suffice ▶ verb *their wages only suffice for the necessities | a simple yes or no will suffice* **be enough**, be sufficient, be adequate, do, serve, meet requirements, satisfy demands, answer/fulfil/meet one's needs, answer/serve the purpose, pass muster; *informal* fit/fill the bill, make the grade, cut the mustard, hit the spot.

sufficient ▶ adjective & determiner *they had secured sufficient evidence to justify a charge* **enough**, adequate, plenty of, ample, abundant; *informal* plenty.
OPPOSITES insufficient, inadequate.

suffocate ▶ verb **1** *she suffocated her victim after a furious row* **smother**, asphyxiate, stifle; choke; strangle, throttle, strangulate.
2 *two people suffocated in the crowd* **be smothered**, asphyxiate, be stifled.
3 *she felt as though she was suffocating in the heat* **be breathless**, be short of air, struggle for air; **be too hot**, swelter; *informal* roast, bake, boil.

suffrage ▶ noun *the congress is elected for five years by universal adult suffrage* **franchise**, right to vote, voting rights, the vote, enfranchisement, ballot; voice, say, option, choice.

suffuse ▶ verb *the room was suffused with soft, pink light | a feeling of relief suffused her* **permeate**, spread over, spread throughout, cover, bathe, pervade, wash, saturate, imbue, fill, load, charge, impregnate, inform, steep, colour; *literary* mantle.

·**sugar** *See centre pages for lists of edible and biochemical* **Sugars**

WORD LINKS
relating to sugar **saccharine**
related prefix **glyco-** (e.g. ***glycogen***)

sugary ▶ adjective **1** *go easy on sugary snacks* **sweet**, sugared, oversweet, sickly, sickly sweet.
OPPOSITES sour, tart.
2 *a sugary piano score* **sentimental**, over-sentimental, mawkish, cloying, sickly, sickly sweet, gushing, saccharine, oversweet, syrupy, slushy; *informal* soppy, schmaltzy, mushy, sloppy, cutesy, drippy, cheesy, corny.
OPPOSITES spare, stark.

suggest ▶ verb **1** *Ruth suggested a card-playing evening* **propose**, put forward, submit, recommend, advocate; advise, propound, urge, encourage, counsel; move, table.

S

2 *evidence suggests that teenagers are more responsive to price increases than adults* **indicate**, lead to the belief, give the impression, give the idea, argue, point to, demonstrate, show, evince.
3 *government sources suggested that the Prime Minister would not necessarily change his cabinet* **hint**, insinuate, imply, intimate, drive at, indicate; *informal* get at.
4 *the seduction scenes have enough ambivalence to suggest his guilt and her loneliness* **convey**, express, impart, imply, intimate, connote, smack of; put one in mind of, bring to mind, remind one of, evoke, evince, conjure up, summon up, call up; refer to, allude to, signify.

suggestion ▶ noun **1** *there are some suggestions for tackling this problem* **proposal**, proposition, motion, submission, recommendation; advice, counsel, exhortation, hint, tip, clue, tip-off, idea, piece of advice.
2 *I leaned back in my chair with just the suggestion of a smirk on my face* **hint**, trace, touch, suspicion, tinge, modicum, dash, soupçon; ghost, semblance, shadow, glimmer, impression, breath, whiff, undertone, whisper, nuance, undertone, connotation.
3 *there is no suggestion that the Secretary of State was party to a conspiracy* **insinuation**, hint, implication, intimation, innuendo, imputation.

> CHOOSE THE RIGHT WORD
> **suggestion, hint, innuendo, insinuation**
> *See* HINT.

suggestive ▶ adjective **1** *he was leering and making suggestive remarks* **indecent**, indelicate, improper, unseemly, titillating, provocative, sexual, sexy, off colour, smutty, dirty, ribald, bawdy, racy, blue, risqué, juicy, lewd, vulgar, coarse, salacious, prurient; *informal* naughty, near the knuckle, spicy.
2 *an odour suggestive of a brewery* **redolent**, evocative, reminiscent; **characteristic**, indicative, symptomatic, typical; peculiar to, exclusive to.

suicide ▶ noun *she committed suicide* **self-destruction**, taking one's own life, self-murder, self-slaughter, felo de se; self-immolation; *Hinduism, historical* suttee; *Japanese, historical* hara-kiri, suppuku; *informal* topping oneself, ending it all.

suit *See centre pages for list of* **Suits of Cards**
▶ noun **1** *a pinstriped suit* **outfit**, set of clothes, costume, ensemble; clothing, dress, attire, finery; habit, garb, livery; *informal* get-up, gear, togs, duds; *Brit. informal* kit, clobber; *rhyming slang* whistle (and flute); *formal* apparel; *archaic* vestments.
2 (*informal*) *they hated being messed around by suits in faraway boardrooms* **businessman**, **businesswoman**, business person, executive, bureaucrat, administrator, manager, director.
3 *he's been an expert witness in some important medical malpractice suits* **legal action**, lawsuit, suit at law, case, court case, action, cause, legal proceeding/process, proceedings, judicial proceedings, litigation, trial, legal dispute/contest, bringing to book, bringing of charges, indictment, prosecution.
4 (*archaic*) *he sought a passage to Christian lands, but they spurned his suit* **entreaty**, request, plea, appeal, petition, supplication, application, claim, solicitation, demand.
5 *he could not compete with John in Marian's eyes and his suit came to nothing* **courtship**, wooing, courting, addresses, attentions, homage, pursuit; respects, blandishments.
▶ verb **1** *blue really suits you* **look attractive on**, enhance the appearance of, look right on, look good on, become, flatter, show to advantage, set off, enhance, ornament, grace; *informal* do something for.
2 *we offer savings schemes to suit all pockets* **be convenient for**, be acceptable to, be suitable for, meet the requirements of, satisfy the demands of, be in line with the wishes of; befit, match, complement, go with; *informal* fit the bill.
3 *the recipes are ideally* **suited** *to students* **make appropriate to/for**, make fitting to/for, tailor, fashion, accommodate, adjust, adapt, modify, fit, gear, equip, design; (**be suited to**) be cut out for.
4 *the best way to construct a healthy diet is to find out which foods suit you* **be agreeable to**, agree with, be good for, be healthy for.

suitable ▶ adjective **1** *there was a dearth of suitable employment opportunities in the islands* **acceptable**, satisfactory, fit, worthy, fitting; *informal* right up someone's street.
OPPOSITES unsuitable, inappropriate.
2 *a drama serial suitable for all age groups* **appropriate**, fitting, fit, fitted, acceptable, apt, right.
OPPOSITES unsuitable, inappropriate.
3 *the music's more* **suitable for** *a lively dinner party* **appropriate to**, suited to, befitting, congruous with, in keeping with, in character with, tailor-made, custom-made; *informal* cut out for.
OPPOSITES unsuitable, unfit.
4 *they treated him with suitable respect* **proper**, **seemly**, decent, apt, appropriate, fitting, befitting, becoming, right, correct, due, worthy, decorous; *French* comme il faut.
OPPOSITE unsuitable.
5 *suitable candidates are expected to hold a PhD in chemistry* **well qualified**, well suited, competent, capable, able; right, appropriate, fitting, apt; desirable, preferable, ideal.
OPPOSITES unsuitable, unfit.

> CHOOSE THE RIGHT WORD
> **suitable, appropriate, proper, fitting**
> *See* APPROPRIATE.

suitcase ▶ noun *he carried a small battered suitcase* **travelling bag**, travel bag, case, grip, valise, overnight case, portmanteau, vanity case, holdall; briefcase, attaché case, Gladstone bag; trunk, chest; (**suitcases**) luggage, baggage.

suite ▶ noun **1** *a penthouse suite* **apartment**, flat, set of rooms, suite of rooms; living quarters, rooms, chambers.
2 *the Royal Saloon was built for the use of the Queen and her suite* **retinue**, entourage, train, escort, cortège, royal household, court, company, following, staff; attendants, retainers, followers, companions, servants.

suitor ▶ noun **1** *she decided to marry her suitor* **admirer**, beau, wooer, boyfriend, sweetheart, lover, inamorato, escort; *literary* swain, follower.
2 *the colonies became rival suitors for the location of the capital of the state* **petitioner**, supplicant, beseecher, suppliant, plaintiff, pleader, appellant, applicant; *rare* pretendant.

sulk ▶ verb *Dad was sulking in his room* **mope**, brood, pout, be sullen, have a long face, be in a bad mood, be put out, be out of sorts, be out of humour, be grumpy, be despondent, be moody, be resentful, pine, harbour a grudge, eat one's heart out, moon about/around; *informal* be in a huff, be down in the dumps, be miffed, glower.
OPPOSITE be cheerful.
▶ noun *he sank into a deep sulk and nursed his hurt pride* **bad mood**, fit of bad humour, fit of ill humour, fit of pique, pet, mood, pout, temper, bad temper, the sulks, the doldrums, the blues; *informal* huff, grump; *Brit. informal* strop, paddy.
OPPOSITE good mood.

sulky ▶ adjective *with sulky faces the students turned to go* **sullen**, surly, moping, pouting, moody, sour, piqued, petulant, disgruntled, ill-humoured, in a bad mood, having a fit of the sulks, out of humour, fed up, put out, out of sorts, mopey, mopish; bad-tempered, fractious, grumpy, huffy, scowling, glowering, resentful, dark, glum, gloomy, morose; angry, cross, peeved; *informal* chippy, mumpish, grouchy, stroppy; *N. English informal* mardy.
OPPOSITES cheerful, amiable.

sullen ▶ adjective *a bunch of sullen, spoilt brats* **surly**, sulky, pouting, sour, morose, resentful, glum, moody, gloomy, joyless, frowning, glowering, grumpy, touchy, peevish, indignant, embittered; bad-tempered, ill-tempered, cross, angry, testy; unresponsive, uncommunicative, unsociable, uncivil, unmannerly, unfriendly; *informal* stroppy.
OPPOSITES cheerful, sociable.

sully ▶ verb *he never sullied his lips with swear words* **taint**, defile, soil, tarnish, stain, blemish, besmirch, befoul, contaminate, pollute, spoil, mar, spot, make impure, disgrace, dishonour, injure, damage.
OPPOSITE purify.

sultry ▶ adjective **1** *a sultry, sweltering day* **humid**, close, airless, stuffy, stifling, suffocating, oppressive, muggy, sticky, sweltering, tropical, torrid, steamy, heavy; **hot**, warm, boiling, roasting.
OPPOSITES cool, cold, refreshing.
2 *a sultry film star* **passionate**, **attractive**, sensual, sexy, voluptuous, luscious, erotic, seductive, provocative, alluring, tempting.

sum ▶ noun **1** *a large sum of money* **amount**, quantity, volume.
2 *he handed over a smaller sum to creditors* **amount of money**, price, charge, fee, cost, tariff.
3 *the sum of two prime numbers* **total**, sum total, grand total, tally, aggregate, summation, gross; answer.
OPPOSITE difference.
4 *a belief in making your own way through life seems to be the sum of his wisdom* **entirety**, totality, total, whole, aggregate, summation, beginning and end, alpha and omega, be-all and end-all; *informal* whole shebang, whole caboodle, whole shooting match, {lock, stock, and barrel}.
5 *we did sums at school today* **arithmetical problem**, problem, calculation, reckoning, tally, question; (**sums**) **arithmetic**, mathematics, figures, numbers, computation; *Brit. informal* maths; *N. Amer. informal* math.
▶ verb
□ **sum up** *he was summing up on day two of a historic test case* **summarize the evidence**, review the evidence, give a summing-up, summarize the argument.
□ **sum someone/something up 1** *one reviewer summed it up as 'the most compelling performance recorded in the past few years'* **evaluate**, assess, appraise, value, rate, weigh up, gauge, judge, deem, adjudge, estimate, form an opinion of, form an impression of, make one's mind up about,

get the measure of, form a judgement of, make something of; *informal* size up.
2 *in a subsequent article he sums up the reasons for deindustrialization* **summarize**, make/give a summary of, precis, give an abstract of, encapsulate, outline, give an outline of, recap, recapitulate, review, put in a nutshell, condense, abridge, digest, synopsize, compress, give the gist.
OPPOSITE elaborate.

summarily ▶ adverb *he was accused of conspiracy and summarily executed* **immediately**, instantly, right away/off, straight away, at once, on the spot, directly, forthwith, promptly; speedily, swiftly, rapidly, expeditiously, without delay, without hesitation, suddenly, abruptly; **arbitrarily**, without formality, without notice, without warning, peremptorily, without discussion, without due process.

summarize ▶ verb *he summarized these ideas in a single phrase* **sum up**, abridge, condense, encapsulate, outline, give an outline of, put in a nutshell, recap, recapitulate, digest, give/make a summary of, give a synopsis of, synopsize, precis, give a precis of, give a résumé of, give an abstract of, abstract, sketch, give the main points of, give a rundown of, give the gist of, review; *rare* epitomize.
OPPOSITES elaborate, expand on.

summary ▶ noun *a summary of the team's findings was released in August* **synopsis**, precis, résumé, abstract, abridgement, digest, compendium, condensation, encapsulation, abbreviated version; outline, sketch, rundown, review, summing-up, survey, overview, run-through, notes, recapitulation, recap; *French* tour d'horizon; *N. Amer.* wrap-up; *rare* epitome, conspectus, summa.
▶ adjective **1** *a summary financial statement* **abridged**, abbreviated, shortened, condensed, concise, succinct, thumbnail, compact, terse, short, compressed, cursory, compendious, synoptic; brief, crisp, pithy, to the point.
OPPOSITES lengthy, in full.
2 *many collaborators faced summary execution* **immediate**, instant, instantaneous, on-the-spot, direct, forthwith, prompt; speedy, swift, rapid, expeditious, without delay, without hesitation, sudden, hasty, abrupt; arbitrary, without formality, without notice, without warning, peremptory, without discussion.
OPPOSITES dilatory, slow.

summer ▶ noun

WORD LINKS
relating to summer **aestival**

summer house ▶ noun *one of her favourite haunts as a child was the old summer house on the river bank* **gazebo**, pavilion, belvedere, arbour, bower, pergola; *archaic, Turkey & Iran* kiosk.

summit ▶ noun **1** *the summit of Mont Blanc* **top**, peak, crest, crown, apex, vertex, apogee, tip, cap; ridge, brink, brow, needle, crag, tor; mountain top, hilltop; *French* aiguille, serac.
OPPOSITES bottom, base.
2 *they consider the dramas of Aeschylus, Sophocles, and Euripides to form one of the summits of world literature* **acme**, peak, height, pinnacle, zenith, culmination, climax, high point, high spot, optimum, highlight, crowning glory, crowning point; best, finest, nonpareil; *Latin* ne plus ultra.
OPPOSITE nadir.
3 *it was agreed that the treaty would be signed at the next superpower summit* **meeting**, negotiation, conference, talk(s), discussion, conclave, consultation, deliberation, dialogue, parley, colloquy; *informal* confab, powwow; *formal* confabulation.

summon ▶ verb **1** *he was summoned to the American Embassy* **send for**, call for, ask for, request the presence of, demand the presence of; ask, invite; *archaic* bid.
2 *the court announced its decision to summon them as witnesses* **serve with a summons**, summons, cite, serve with a citation, serve with a writ, subpoena.
3 *the official receiver must summon a meeting* **convene**, assemble, order, call, muster, rally, levy, round up; announce, declare; *formal* convoke.
4 *he was unable to summon the courage to move closer to where the dogs were tied | people could still* **summon up** *energy and enthusiasm* **muster**, gather, collect, rally, call into action, mobilize, screw up.
5 *emigrants would* **summon up** *their memories of home* **call to mind**, bring to mind, call up/forth, conjure up, evoke, recall, revive, invoke, raise, arouse, kindle, awaken, excite, stir up, spark (off), provoke.
6 *their spirits may be summoned and used for either good or evil* **conjure up**, call up, invoke, rouse up.

summons ▶ noun **1** *the court issued a summons* **writ**, **subpoena**, warrant, arraignment, indictment, court order, process; *N. Amer.* citation; *Latin* subpoena ad testificandum.
2 *she had received a summons to go to the boss's office* **order**, directive, command, instruction, dictum, demand, decree, injunction, fiat, edict, direction, charge, bidding, call, request, invitation, plea, appeal.
▶ verb *he had been summonsed to appear in court* **serve with a summons**, summon, cite, serve with a citation, serve with a writ, subpoena.

sumptuous ▶ adjective *a sumptuous palace* **lavish**, luxurious, de luxe, opulent, magnificent, resplendent, gorgeous, splendid, grand, extravagant, lush, lavishly appointed, palatial, princely, rich, costly, expensive, impressive, imposing; *informal* plush, ritzy, swanky; *Brit. informal* swish.
OPPOSITES humble, plain, cheap.

sun ▶ noun **1** *he watched the sun go down over the sea | suns in other galaxies* **star**; *Roman Mythology* Sol; *Greek Mythology* Helios, Phoebus, Apollo; *Egyptian Mythology* Ra.
2 *she could feel the sun on her face* **sunshine**, sunlight, daylight, light, warmth; beams, rays.
▶ verb
□ **sun oneself** *he's been sunning himself on the golden shores of Bali* **sunbathe**, bask, bake, get a tan, tan, brown.

WORD LINKS
relating to the sun **solar**
related prefix **helio-** (e.g. ***heliograph, heliotrope***)
fear of the sun **heliophobia**

sunbathe ▶ verb *she lay sunbathing on the hot sand* **sun oneself**, bask, bake, get a tan, tan oneself, brown oneself; *Austral./NZ* sunbake; *informal* catch some rays.

sunburned, **sunburnt** ▶ adjective **1** *his scarlet, sunburned shoulders* **burnt**, peeling, inflamed, red, scarlet, blistered, blistering.
2 *a handsome sunburned face* **tanned**, suntanned, brown, bronzed, bronze, browned, weather-beaten.
OPPOSITE pale.

Sunday ▶ noun **the Lord's Day**, the Sabbath.

WORD LINKS
relating to Sunday **dominical**

sunder ▶ verb (*archaic*) *his father and he were sundered by religious differences* **divide**, split, cleave, separate, rend, rive, sever, break open/apart.

sundry ▶ adjective *wings, radiators, and sundry other items were sent out to various workshops* **various**, varied, miscellaneous, assorted, mixed, diverse, diversified, motley, random; several, numerous, many, manifold, multifarious, multitudinous, legion; *literary* divers; *rare* farraginous.

sunken ▶ adjective **1** *he was very gaunt, with sunken eyes* **hollowed**, hollow, depressed, deep-set, concave, dented, indented, caved in, drawn, haggard.
2 *a sunken garden* **below ground level**, at a lower level, lowered, recessed.

sunless ▶ adjective **1** *a cold sunless day* **dark**, overcast, cloudy, grey, gloomy, dismal, dreary, murky, hazy, louring, lowering.
2 *the sunless north-facing side of the house* **shady**, shadowy, dark, dim, dingy, gloomy, dull, ill-lit.

sunlight ▶ noun *the plane was gleaming in the winter sunlight* **daylight**, sun, sunshine, light of day, sun's rays, sunbeam, natural light, light.

sunny ▶ adjective **1** *a sunny spring afternoon* **bright**, sunshiny, sunlit, brilliant, clear, fine, fair; balmy, summery, clement; cloudless, unclouded, without a cloud in the sky.
OPPOSITES dull, shady.
2 *she has a sunny disposition* **cheerful**, cheery, happy, light-hearted, bright, glad, merry, joyful, bubbly, blithe, jolly, jovial, animated, buoyant, ebullient, upbeat, vivacious, sparky, perky, rosy; warm, friendly, outgoing, genial, benign, agreeable, pleasant; *dated* gay.
OPPOSITES miserable, introverted.
3 *the sunny side of life* **optimistic**, rosy, bright, cheerful, hopeful, auspicious, favourable, good.
OPPOSITES sad, pessimistic.

sunrise ▶ noun *the infantry advanced at sunrise* **dawn**, crack of dawn, daybreak, break of day, first light, first thing in the morning, early morning, cockcrow, morning; *N. Amer.* sunup; *literary* peep of day, aurora, dayspring.

sunset ▶ noun *strolling along the beach at sunset* **nightfall**, close of day, twilight, dusk, evening, half-light; *N. Amer.* sundown; *literary* eventide, gloaming, vesper.

sunshine ▶ noun **1** *we'll relax in the sunshine for a while* **sunlight**, sun, sun's rays, sunbeams, daylight, light of day, natural light, light.
2 *his smile was all sunshine* **happiness**, cheerfulness, cheer, gladness, laughter, gaiety, merriment, joy, joyfulness, glee, blitheness, bliss, sparkle, joviality, jollity.
3 (*Brit. informal*) *don't go telling me lies, sunshine* my friend, man; *Brit. informal* **mate**, matey, cock, squire, mush; *informal* pal, chum, buddy; *N. Amer. informal* bud, buster, amigo, Mac, bro; *Brit. informal, dated* old fellow, old bean, old boy, old chap, old fruit.

super ▶ adjective (*informal*) *win a super day out at York* **excellent**, superb, superlative, first-rate, first-class, superior, outstanding, remarkable, dazzling, marvellous, magnificent, wonderful, splendid, fine, exquisite, exceptional, glorious, sublime, peerless, perfect, of the first water; *informal* brilliant, great, fantastic, fabulous, terrific, awesome, ace, divine, smashing, A1, tip-top, top-notch, neat, mega, wicked, cool, banging,

crucial; *Brit. informal* brill, cracking.
OPPOSITES rotten, lousy.

superannuated ▶ adjective **1** *a superannuated civil servant* **pensioned off**, retired, pensioned; elderly, old; *informal, derogatory* over the hill, long in the tooth, past it, put out to grass.
2 *the old terminus was converted into a goods station, a common fate for superannuated passenger stations* **old**, old-fashioned, antiquated, out of date, outmoded, anachronistic, broken-down, outworn; **obsolete**, disused, fallen into disuse, no longer used, defunct, moribund; *informal* clapped out.

superb ▶ adjective **1** *he scored a superb goal* **excellent**, superlative, first-rate, first-class, superior, supreme, outstanding, remarkable, dazzling, marvellous, magnificent, wonderful, splendid, admirable, noteworthy, impressive, fine, exquisite, exceptional, glorious, sublime, perfect, of the first order, of the first water; *informal* great, fantastic, fabulous, terrific, super, awesome, ace, cool, A1, tip-top; *Brit. informal* brilliant, brill, smashing.
OPPOSITES poor, inferior.
2 *a superb diamond necklace* **magnificent**, majestic, splendid, grand, impressive, imposing, awe-inspiring, breathtaking; gorgeous, choice, resplendent, stately; sumptuous, opulent, lavish, luxurious, de luxe; *informal* plush, ritzy.
OPPOSITES poor, inferior.

supercilious ▶ adjective *a supercilious young minister* **arrogant**, haughty, conceited, disdainful, overbearing, pompous, condescending, superior, patronizing, imperious, proud, lofty, lordly, snobbish, snobby, overweening, smug; pretentious, affected; scornful, mocking, sneering, scoffing; *informal* hoity-toity, high and mighty, uppity, snooty, stuck-up, toffee-nosed, snotty, jumped up, too big for one's boots.
OPPOSITES humble, modest.

superficial ▶ adjective **1** *his face was blotched with superficial burns* **surface**, exterior, external, outer, outside, outermost, peripheral, slight.
OPPOSITES deep, thorough.
2 *she made no attempt to be friendly on anything but the most superficial level* **shallow**, surface, on the surface, skin-deep, minimal, artificial; insignificant, unimportant, empty, hollow, meaningless.
OPPOSITES deep, significant.
3 *a superficial investigation* **cursory**, perfunctory, casual, sketchy, desultory, unconsidered, token, slapdash, slipshod, offhand, inadequate, imperfect, slight; rushed, hasty, hurried, rapid, fleeting, passing.
OPPOSITES thorough, comprehensive.
4 *its spines give it a superficial resemblance to a hedgehog* **apparent**, **specious**, seeming, outward, ostensible, cosmetic, slight.
OPPOSITES genuine, authentic.
5 *I think there is too much superficial cricket autobiography available* **trivial**, lightweight, sketchy, slight, insignificant.
OPPOSITE profound.
6 *I suppose Michael was quite a superficial person, but to me he represented excitement* **facile**, shallow, glib, flippant, thoughtless, empty-headed, trivial, frivolous, silly, inane, without depth, fatuous.
OPPOSITE thoughtful.

superficially ▶ adverb *some reptiles and amphibians are superficially very alike | superficially, it was an obvious statement to make* **apparently**, **seemingly**, ostensibly, outwardly, on the surface, on the face of it, to all appearances, to all intents and purposes, at first glance, at face value, to the casual eye; externally, visibly, trivially.

superfluity ▶ noun *California has always had a superfluity of fresh crab* **surplus**, excess, overabundance, glut, surfeit, profusion, plethora, embarrassment, avalanche, deluge, flood, overload.
OPPOSITES lack, shortage.

S

superfluous ▶ adjective **1** *a tool for removing superfluous material* **surplus**, redundant, unneeded, not required, excess, extra, spare, to spare, remaining, unused, left over; useless, unproductive, undue, in excess, surplus to requirements; expendable, disposable, dispensable, unwanted, waste.
OPPOSITES necessary, essential.
2 *Charlie gave him a look that made words superfluous* **unnecessary**, needless, unneeded, inessential, pointless, redundant, uncalled for, unwarranted, unjustified, gratuitous.
OPPOSITES necessary, essential.

superhuman ▶ adjective **1** *their madness gives them superhuman strength* **extraordinary**, phenomenal, prodigious, stupendous, exceptional, great, immense, enormous, heroic, godlike, Herculean, remarkable.
OPPOSITES average, unremarkable.
2 *the superhuman power which raised Christ from the dead* **divine**, holy, spiritual, heavenly, godlike.
3 *superhuman agencies and powers* **supernatural**, preternatural, paranormal, other-worldly, unearthly, extramundane, magical, occult.
OPPOSITE mundane.

superintend ▶ verb *he was expected to superintend a grand banquet* **supervise**, oversee, be in charge of, be in control of, preside over, direct, administer, manage, run, look after, be responsible for, govern, operate, conduct, handle, steer, pilot.

superintendent ▶ noun **1** *he became superintendent of the university museum* **manager**, director, administrator, supervisor, overseer, controller, boss, chief, head, governor, organizer, conductor, foreman; *informal* honcho, gaffer.
2 (*N. Amer.*) *the building's superintendent* **caretaker**, **janitor**, warden, porter, custodian, keeper, watchman, steward.

superior ▶ adjective **1** *a superior officer had never apologized to him before* **higher-ranking**, higher-level, senior, higher, higher-up, upper-level, upper, loftier.
OPPOSITES inferior, junior.
2 *the superior candidate* **better**, more expert, more skilful, more advanced; worthier, fitter, preferred, predominant, prevailing, surpassing.
OPPOSITES inferior, worse.
3 *they recognized the value of superior workmanship* **finer**, better, higher-grade, higher-calibre, surpassing, of higher quality, greater, grander; **supreme**, accomplished, expert, consummate.
OPPOSITES inferior, low-quality.
4 *a very superior chocolate* **good-quality**, high-quality, first-class, first-rate, top-quality, high-grade, of the first water, of the first order; choice, select, exclusive, rare, singular, unique, prime, prize, upmarket, fine, excellent, superb, distinguished, exceptional, outstanding, marvellous, superlative, special; best, choicest, finest, matchless, peerless, unequalled, perfect, flawless; *French* par excellence.
OPPOSITES inferior, low-quality.
5 *a superior hotel* **high-class**, upper-class, select, exclusive, elite; *Brit.* upmarket; *informal* classy, posh, snobby.
OPPOSITES inferior, downmarket.
6 *Jake regarded her with superior amusement* **condescending**, supercilious, patronizing, haughty, disdainful, lofty, lordly, pompous, snobbish, snobby; *informal* high and mighty, hoity-toity, uppity, snooty, stuck-up, toffee-nosed, jumped up, too big for one's boots, uppish.
OPPOSITES humble, modest.
▶ noun *my immediate superior in the department* **manager**, boss, chief, supervisor, senior, controller, headman, foreman.
OPPOSITES inferior, subordinate, assistant.

superiority ▶ noun *despite the military superiority of the government forces, the rebels continued to hold on to territory in the south* **supremacy**, advantage, lead, dominance, primacy, ascendancy, leadership, precedence, edge, whip hand, better quality; excellence, eminence, distinction, greatness.
OPPOSITE inferiority.

superlative ▶ adjective *he is without doubt a superlative photographer* **excellent**, magnificent, wonderful, glorious, marvellous, brilliant, supreme, consummate, outstanding, prodigious, dazzling, remarkable, formidable, fine, choice, sterling, first-rate, first-class, of the first water, of the first order, of the highest order, premier, prime, unsurpassed, unequalled, unparalleled, unrivalled, unbeatable, peerless, matchless, singular, unique, transcendent, best, greatest, worthiest, pre-eminent, perfect, faultless, flawless; *informal* crack, ace, wicked.
OPPOSITES poor, unexceptional, mediocre.

supernatural ▶ adjective **1** *supernatural powers* **paranormal**, psychic, magic, magical, occult, mystic, mystical, miraculous, superhuman, supernormal, hypernormal, extramundane; inexplicable, uncanny, unaccountable, unbelievable, non-rational, weird, mysterious, arcane.
OPPOSITES natural, normal.
2 *stories about a supernatural hound* **ghostly**, phantom, spectral, magical, mystic, other-worldly, unearthly, unnatural, unreal, mysterious, fabulous; *informal* spooky.

supersede ▶ verb *I found myself superseded by much younger men | the tutorial has, in most colleges, been superseded by the lecture* **replace**, supplant, take the place of, take over from, substitute for, displace, oust, overthrow, remove, unseat, override; succeed, come after, step into the shoes of; *informal* crowd out, fill someone's boots.

> **CHOOSE THE RIGHT WORD**
> **supersede, supplant, replace**
> *See* REPLACE.

superstition ▶ noun **1** *Mungo remembered the old superstition that seagulls were the souls of dead sailors* **myth**, belief, old wives' tale, notion; legend, story.
2 *medicine was riddled with superstition and ignorance* **unfounded belief**, credulity; magic, sorcery, witchcraft; fallacy, delusion, illusion.
OPPOSITE science.

superstitious ▶ adjective **1** *superstitious beliefs* **mythical**, irrational, illusory, groundless, unfounded, unprovable; traditional.
OPPOSITES rational, factual, scientific.
2 *Joe is incredibly superstitious* **credulous**, prone to superstition; naive, gullible.
OPPOSITE sceptical.

supervise ▸ verb **1** *he left early to supervise the loading of the lorries* **superintend**, oversee, be in charge of, be in control of, preside over, direct, administer, manage, run, look after, be responsible for, govern, operate, conduct, organize, handle, guide, steer, pilot.
2 *you may also need to supervise the patient, in case he forgets what he is doing* **watch**, oversee, keep an eye on, observe, monitor, inspect, be responsible for, guide, mind.

supervision ▸ noun **1** *one of the Bank of England's functions is the supervision of the banking system* **administration**, management, direction, control, charge; overseeing, superintendence, regulation, government, governance, operation.
2 *there is a sign telling parents to keep their children under supervision* **observation**, inspection, guidance, custody, charge, safe keeping, care, guardianship, wardship, leadership.

supervisor ▸ noun *she exchanged a few words with the shift supervisor* **manager**, director, administrator, overseer, controller, boss, chief, superintendent, inspector, head, governor, superior, organizer, conductor, steward, foreman, ganger; *informal* honcho, gaffer.

supine ▸ adjective **1** *she lay supine on the fine white sand* **flat on one's back**, prone, recumbent, prostrate, stretched out, spreadeagled; lying, sprawling, horizontal, flat as a pancake.
OPPOSITES erect, vertical.
2 *a supine and cowardly press has allowed itself to be intimidated into censoring the truth* **weak**, spineless, yielding, enervated, effete; docile, acquiescent, pliant, submissive, servile, inactive, passive, inert, spiritless, apathetic, indifferent.
OPPOSITES strong, assertive.

supper ▸ noun **1** *the Rileys invited me to a formal supper* **dinner**, evening meal, main meal; feast, banquet, repast; *Brit.* tea.
2 *a bowl of soup with some crusty bread makes an ideal supper* **evening snack**; *informal* bite, bite to eat; *formal* collation, refection.

supplant ▸ verb **1** *vast impersonal motorways supplanted the agreeably irregular network of real roads* **replace**, displace, supersede, take the place of, take over from, substitute for, undermine, override.
2 *he was asking the man he supplanted as Prime Minister for help* **oust**, usurp, overthrow, remove, topple, unseat, depose, dethrone, eject, dispel; succeed, come after, step into the shoes of; *informal* fill someone's boots, crowd out.

> **CHOOSE THE RIGHT WORD**
> **supplant, supersede, replace**
> See REPLACE.

supple ▸ adjective **1** *he watched the movements of her supple body* **lithe**, limber, nimble, lissom, flexible, loose-limbed, loose-jointed, agile, acrobatic, fit, deft, willowy, graceful, elegant.
OPPOSITES stiff, unfit.
2 *supple leather* **pliant**, pliable, flexible, soft, bendable, workable, malleable, stretchy, stretchable, elastic, springy, yielding, rubbery, plastic, resilient.
OPPOSITES rigid, inflexible.

supplement ▸ noun **1** *a mouse is not a replacement for a keyboard, merely a supplement* **addition**, supplementation, additive, extra, companion, add-on, accessory, adjunct, appendage, appurtenance; *Computing* peripheral.
2 *the single room supplement is £16* **surcharge**, addition, increase.
3 *a supplement to the essays* **appendix**, addendum, end matter, tailpiece, codicil, rider, postscript, addition, extension, coda, sequel.
4 *our special supplement is packed with ideas for healthy hair* **magazine section**, pull-out, insert, special-feature section.
▸ verb *most of the families in the village supplemented their incomes by working in the wool-spinning mills* **augment**, increase, add to, boost, swell, amplify, enlarge, make larger/bigger/greater; top up, complement, round off, complete; widen, broaden, expand.

supplementary ▸ adjective **1** *many MPs feel the need to seek supplementary income* **additional**, extra, supplemental, increased, further, more; add-on, complementary, subsidiary, accessory, auxiliary, ancillary, supportive, reserve.
2 *a supplementary index* **appended**, attached, added, extra, accompanying, annexed, adjunct.

suppliant ▸ noun *she and the others who addressed high-ranking officials were not mere suppliants* **petitioner**, pleader, beseecher, supplicant, beggar, appellant, suitor, applicant, claimant.
▸ adjective *the faces around her were suppliant* **pleading**, begging, beseeching, imploring, entreating, supplicating, craving, on bended knee.

supplicate ▸ verb *he supplicated the emperor for the pardon of those who had supported the uprising* **entreat**, beseech, beg, plead with, implore, petition, appeal to, solicit, call on, urge, enjoin, importune, pray, invoke, sue, ask, request.

supplication ▸ noun *she made one last supplication to Sally* **entreaty**, plea, appeal, petition, solicitation, exhortation, urge, prayer, invocation, suit, request, application; beseeching, begging, pleading; *archaic* orison; *rare* imploration, obsecration.

supplies ▸ plural noun **1** *next time you go to a supermarket for your supplies, consider your shopping habits* **provisions**, stores, stocks, rations, food, food and drink, foodstuffs, eatables, subsistence, produce, necessities; *informal* eats, grub, nosh; *formal* comestibles, provender; *archaic* viands, victuals, vittles.
2 *they carried vital supplies to the trenches* **equipment**, apparatus, paraphernalia, wares, trappings, stuff, tackle, things; *Military* materiel.

supply ▸ verb **1** *they supplied money and professional assistance to rebels at by-elections* **give**, contribute, provide, furnish, donate, bestow, grant, endow, afford, impart, lay on, come up with, make available, proffer; dispense, allocate, allot, assign, disburse; lavish, shower, regale; *informal* fork out, shell out; *archaic* minister.
2 *Lake Cachuma supplies the city of Santa Barbara with water* **provide**, furnish, endow, serve, confer; equip, kit out, rig out, outfit, clothe, fit, arm; *rare* endue.
3 *small communities have just a few well-designed windmills to supply all their power needs* **satisfy**, meet, fulfil, fill, be adequate for, cater for.
▸ noun **1** *we've only a limited supply of food and water* **stock**, store, reserve, reservoir, stockpile, heap, pile, mass, hoard, cache, collection, storehouse, repository; fund, crop, mine, bank, arsenal.
2 *premises for the sale and supply of alcoholic liquor* **provision**, providing, supplying, furnishing, dissemination, distribution, laying on, sending out, serving, accommodation.
▸ adjective *a supply teacher* **substitute**, stand-in, fill-in, locum, temporary, stopgap.

support ▸ verb **1** *the roof was supported by massive stone pillars* **hold up**, bear, carry, prop up, keep up, bolster up, brace, shore up, underpin, buttress, reinforce.
2 *he was struggling to support his family* **provide for**, provide sustenance for, maintain, sustain, keep, take care of, look after.
3 *Martha lovingly supported him to the end* **give moral support to**, give strength to, be a source of strength to, comfort, bring comfort to, sustain, encourage, buoy up, hearten, fortify, console, solace, give sympathy to, reassure, succour, soothe; *informal* buck up.
OPPOSITES neglect, abandon.
4 *there seems to be evidence to support both of these arguments* **substantiate**, back up, give force to, give weight to, bear out, corroborate, confirm, attest to, verify, prove, validate, authenticate, endorse, ratify, document.
OPPOSITES contradict, undermine.
5 *all the money we receive will be used to support charitable projects in Africa* **help**, aid, assist; **contribute to**, give a donation to, give money to, back, underwrite, subsidize, fund, finance, succour; *N. Amer. informal* bankroll.
6 *he obtained 773 votes as an independent candidate supported by a residents' association* **back**, champion, give help to, help, assist, aid, be on the side of, side with, favour, prefer, abet, aid and abet, encourage; vote for, ally oneself with, stand behind, fall in with, stand up for, defend, take someone's part, take up the cudgels for; sponsor, vouch for, second, promote, endorse, sanction, approve of, give one's blessing to, smile on; *informal* stick up for, throw one's weight behind.
OPPOSITE oppose.
7 *a bold initiative to support human rights around the world* **advocate**, **promote**, further, champion, back, be on the side of, espouse, espouse the cause of, be in favour of, recommend, defend, subscribe to.
8 *at work during the day I could support the grief* **endure**, bear, put up with, tolerate, stand, abide, suffer, stomach, brook, sustain, shoulder, weather.
▸ noun **1** *one of the bridge supports had developed a six inch crack* **pillar**, post, prop, underprop, underpinning, base, substructure, foundation; brace, buttress, abutment, bolster, upright, stay, stand, trestle, crutch, plinth.
2 *he can't be forced to pay support for a wife abroad* **maintenance**, keep, sustenance, subsistence; food and accommodation.
3 *I was lucky to have my family's support during this difficult time* **moral support**, friendship, strengthening, strength, encouragement, buoying up, heartening, fortification, consolation, solace, succour, relief, easement; *informal* bucking up.
4 *he was a great support when her father died* **comfort**, help, assistance, tower of strength, prop, backbone, mainstay.
5 *we will provide support for essential community services* **contributions**, backing, donations, money, subsidy, funding, funds, finance, capital.
6 *many stars openly voiced their support for one candidate or another* **backing**, help, assistance, aid, votes, endorsement, sanction, approval, blessing, patronage.
7 *there has been a surge in support for decentralization* **advocacy**, backing, promotion, championship, espousal, defence, recommendation, recommending, argument for, arguing for.

> **CHOOSE THE RIGHT WORD**
> **support, help, aid, assist**
> See HELP.

S

supporter ▶ noun **1** *supporters of gun control* **advocate**, backer, adherent, promoter, champion, defender, upholder, votary, partisan, crusader, proponent, campaigner, believer, apologist.
OPPOSITE opponent.
2 *potential Labour supporters* **backer**, helper, adherent, follower, ally, voter, disciple, comrade, apologist, fanatic; member, card-carrying member, insider.
OPPOSITES opponent, adversary.
3 *the society is a charity that relies on its members and supporters for its income* **contributor**, donor, benefactor, sponsor, backer, patron, subscriber, friend, well-wisher; *informal* angel.
4 *the end of the match was greeted by cheers from both sets of supporters* **fan**, follower, enthusiast, devotee, lover, admirer, zealot, aficionado; *informal* buff, freak, nut.

supportive ▶ adjective **1** *a supportive head teacher* **encouraging**, caring, sympathetic, reassuring, understanding, concerned, helpful, nurturing, sensitive; protective, benevolent, kind, kindly, maternal, paternal.
OPPOSITE discouraging.
2 *local societies were largely* ***supportive of*** *the proposal* **in favour**, approving, pro, on the side of; favourable to, sympathetic to, in sympathy with, encouraging of, well disposed to, favourably disposed to, receptive to, responsive to.
OPPOSITE opposed to.

suppose ▶ verb **1** *I suppose he's used to this kind of work* **assume**, dare say, take for granted, take as read, presume, expect, take it; believe, think, fancy, be of the opinion, suspect, have a sneaking suspicion, sense, trust; guess, surmise, reckon, conjecture, theorize, deduce, infer, gather, glean, divine; *formal* opine.
2 *suppose your spacecraft had a two-stage rocket* **hypothesize**, postulate, theorize, posit, speculate, (let's) say, assume, imagine.
3 *the classical theory supposes rational players* **require**, presuppose, imply, assume; call for, need.

supposed ▶ adjective **1** *we have no viable theory to account for the supposed phenomena* **apparent**, seeming, alleged, putative, reputed, rumoured, claimed, purported, ostensible, specious; professed, declared, believed, assumed, presumed; *French* soi-disant.
2 *computers are* ***supposed to*** *make their lives easier | I'm* ***supposed to*** *meet him at 8.30* **meant**, intended, expected; ought, required, obliged.

supposition ▶ noun *there is a widespread supposition that there is nothing of any value in these techniques* **belief**, surmise, idea, notion, suspicion, conjecture, speculation, view, inference, theory, thesis, hypothesis, postulation, guess, guesswork, feeling, hunch, assumption, presumption.

suppress ▶ verb **1** *the government proved incapable of suppressing the rebellion by force* **subdue**, defeat, conquer, vanquish, triumph over, repress, crush, quell, quash, squash, stamp out, overpower, extinguish, put down, put out, crack down on, clamp down on, cow, drive underground; end, put an end to, stop, discontinue, terminate, halt, arrest.
OPPOSITES incite, encourage.
2 *she only just managed to suppress her irritation* **conceal**, **restrain**, stifle, smother, bottle up, keep a rein on, hold back, keep back, fight back, choke back, control, keep under control, check, keep in check, curb, contain, bridle, inhibit, put a lid on, deaden, muffle.
3 *the government denied that the report had been suppressed* **censor**, keep secret, conceal, hide, keep hidden, hush up, gag, keep silent about, withhold, cover up, smother, stifle, muzzle, ban, not disclose, not breathe a word of; mute, proscribe, outlaw, sweep under the carpet.
OPPOSITES publicize, disclose.

suppression ▶ noun **1** *the suppression of subversive activities* **subduing**, defeat, conquering, vanquishing, repression, crushing, quelling, quashing, squashing, stamping out, crackdown, clampdown, cowing, prevention, extinction; elimination, end, stopping, discontinuation, termination, halting, arrest.
OPPOSITES incitement, encouragement.
2 *the British seem to take great pride in the suppression of emotion* **concealment**, **restraint**, stifling, smothering, holding back, keeping back, choking back, control, keeping under control, checking, curbing, containing, bridling, inhibition, deadening, muffling.
3 *nobody's interest is served by the suppression of the truth* **censorship**, keeping secret, concealment, hiding, keeping hidden, hushing up, gagging, withholding, covering up, smothering, stifling, muzzling, banning, non-disclosure, proscription, outlawing, restriction.
OPPOSITES publication, disclosure.

suppurate ▶ verb *a suppurating sore* **fester**, form pus, swell up, gather, discharge, rot, run, weep, ooze, come to a head; *Medicine* maturate; *rare* matter.

supremacy ▶ noun **1** *they asserted the supremacy of the people over parliament* **ascendancy**, predominance, primacy, dominion, hegemony, authority, mastery, control, power, sway, rule, sovereignty, lordship, leadership, influence; *rare* predomination, paramountcy, prepotence, prepotency, prepollency.
2 *the battle for supremacy in the cellular radio market* **dominance**, superiority, pre-eminence, ascendancy, advantage; the upper hand, the whip hand, the edge; incomparability, inimitability, matchlessness, peerlessness, greatness, distinction.

supreme ▶ adjective **1** *the supreme commander of NATO forces* **highest ranking**, highest, leading, chief, head, top, foremost, principal, superior, premier, first, cardinal, prime, sovereign; directing, governing; greatest, dominant, predominant, pre-eminent, overriding, prevailing.
OPPOSITES subordinate, inferior.
2 *the race makes supreme demands on competitors | a supreme achievement* **extraordinary**, remarkable, incredible, extreme, intense, great, phenomenal, rare, surpassing, exceptional, outstanding, incomparable, inimitable, unparalleled, unrivalled, peerless, greatest, utmost, uttermost, maximum; severe, acute.
OPPOSITES minimum, mild.
3 *he was prepared to make the supreme sacrifice* **final**, last, ultimate; **utmost**, extreme, total, unconditional, greatest, highest; **fatal**, lethal, mortal.
OPPOSITE insignificant.

sure ▶ adjective **1** *I am sure that they did not have an affair* **certain**, positive, convinced, definite, confident, decided, assured, secure, satisfied, persuaded, easy in one's mind, free from doubt; unhesitating, unwavering, unfaltering, unvacillating, unshakeable, unshaken.
OPPOSITES unsure, uncertain, doubtful.
2 *he was* ***sure of*** *finding a way around the difficulties* **confident**, certain, assured; with no doubts about.
3 *someone was sure to cop it before the day was out* **bound**, destined, fated, predestined, very likely.
OPPOSITE unlikely.
4 *this is a very attractive way of presenting fruit and is a sure winner with the children* **guaranteed**, unfailing, infallible, unerring, assured, certain, inevitable, incontestable, irrevocable; *informal* sure-fire, in the bag, as sure as eggs is eggs.
5 *he could have thrown his servant into the street in the sure knowledge that it would be put down to robust good humour* **unquestionable**, indisputable, incontestable, irrefutable, incontrovertible, undeniable, indubitable, beyond question, beyond doubt; undoubted, absolute, categorical, true, certain, well grounded, well founded, proven, settled, decided; obvious, evident, plain, clear, conclusive, final, definite, unmistakable, manifest, patent.
6 *he chewed his beard restlessly, a sure sign that he's worried* **reliable**, dependable, trustworthy, unfailing, infallible, never-failing, certain, unambiguous, tested, tried and true, true, foolproof, established, effective, efficacious; *informal* sure-fire.
7 *the sure hand of the soloist provides an atmospheric foil for the orchestra* **firm**, steady, stable, secure, confident, solid, steadfast, unhesitating, unfaltering, unwavering, unswerving.
□ **be sure to** *be sure to send your press releases to the news desk* **remember to**, don't forget to, make sure to, see that you, mind that you, take care to, be certain to, be careful to.
OPPOSITES neglect to, forget to.
□ **for sure** (*informal*) *she's guilty for sure* **definitely**, surely, certainly, without doubt, without question, beyond any doubt, undoubtedly, indubitably, positively, absolutely, undeniably, unmistakably.
□ **make sure** *make sure that the pushchair you choose is covered in easy-clean fabrics* **check**, confirm, make certain, ensure; assure, verify, corroborate, validate, substantiate, guarantee.
▶ exclamation *'Can I ask you something?' 'Sure.'* **yes**, all right, of course, indeed, certainly, absolutely, agreed; *informal* OK, yeah, yep, uh-huh, you bet, I'll say, sure thing.

CHOOSE THE RIGHT WORD

sure, certain, convinced, positive, definite

These words are all used to describe a person who is confident that their belief is well founded and, in this sense, are all used after a verb such as *be*, *become*, or *remain*.

- **Sure**, **certain**, and **convinced** all have very similar meanings, but *sure* is the most common in this sense. They can all be followed by *of* (*one thing we were sure of: we couldn't go back*), *about* (*are you absolutely certain about this?*), or a clause, with or without *that* (*he was convinced that his theory was correct*). *Convinced* is the word most typically used with *of* in this sense (*everyone seems very convinced of his guilt*); *sure of* and *certain of* also mean 'confident of receiving or doing something' (*you are always sure of a welcome | he's not certain of his place in the Liverpool line-up*).
- **Positive** is typically used in speech or reported speech, with no following construction (*'Are you sure she won't want to pursue the issue?' 'Positive.'*). It can, however, be followed by a clause (*Columbus was positive that Japan lay just over the horizon*).
- If someone is **definite** about something, they are not only confident that it is true but are also stating their belief very firmly (*'Not a chance.' Jean was definite.*). *Definite*, in this sense, can be followed by a clause (*Sidney Knowles also saw the body and was quite definite that it was not Crabb*).

surely ▶ adverb **1** *surely you remembered to pack a toothbrush?* **it must be the case that**, I believe that, assuredly, without question; *informal* don't tell me that … not ….
2 *give me some water, or I shall surely die* **certainly**, for certain, for sure, to be sure, definitely, undoubtedly, without doubt, doubtless, beyond any/the shadow of a doubt, indubitably, unquestionably, incontestably, irrefutably, incontrovertibly, undeniably, without fail, inevitably, unavoidably; *informal* sure.
3 *their real achievement lay in slowly but surely creating and manipulating public opinion* **firmly**, steadily, confidently, solidly, securely, unhesitatingly, unfalteringly, unswervingly, determinedly, doggedly, assuredly.

surety ▶ noun **1** *these are all cases in which a wife has become a surety for her husband's obligations* **guarantor**, sponsor.
2 *he was released on bail of $100,000 with a further $100,000 surety* **pledge**, **collateral**, guaranty, guarantee, bond, assurance, insurance, bail, deposit; security, indemnity, indemnification; *archaic* gage, earnest.

surface ▶ noun **1** *the paint on the metal surface of the door began to blister* **outside**, exterior; **top**, **side**, facet, plane, aspect; **finish**, veneer.
OPPOSITES inside, interior.
2 *the report managed to get beneath the surface of police culture* **outward appearance**, superficial appearance, facade.
3 *lightly knead the dough on a floured surface* **worktop**, top, working top, work surface, counter, table, stand, horizontal surface.
□ **on the surface** *it sounded plausible enough on the surface* **at first glance**, to the casual eye, outwardly, to all appearances, apparently, ostensibly, superficially, externally, visibly.
OPPOSITES at root, fundamentally.
▶ adjective *lead news stories are concerned with surface appearances rather than underlying processes* **superficial**, external, exterior, outward, seeming, ostensible, apparent, cosmetic, skin deep.
OPPOSITE fundamental.
▶ verb **1** *a submarine surfaced in the fjord* **come to the surface**, come to the top, come up, rise.
OPPOSITE dive.
2 *the idea of road pricing first surfaced in the early sixties* **emerge**, arise, appear, come to light, come up, come into sight, come into view, come out, crop up, materialize, become visible, spring up, loom.
3 (*informal*) *our daughter eventually surfaces and has some breakfast* **get up**, get out of bed, appear, rise, wake, awaken.

surfeit ▶ noun *he had tummy trouble resulting from a surfeit of apples and vegetables* **excess**, surplus, abundance, oversupply, superabundance, superfluity, overdose, glut, avalanche, deluge; too much, more than enough; overindulgence, satiety, satiation; *informal* bellyful.
OPPOSITES lack, dearth.
▶ verb *we'll all be surfeited with food and fuddled with wine* **satiate**, gorge, overfeed, overfill, glut, cram, stuff, overindulge, fill; sicken, nauseate.

surge ▶ noun **1** *a surge of water* **gush**, rush, outpouring, stream, flow, sweep; *technical* efflux.
2 *a surge in oil production* **sudden increase**, rise, growth, upswing, upsurge, escalation, jump, leap, boost.
3 *he felt a sudden surge of anger* **rush**, blast, storm, torrent, blaze, outburst, eruption.
4 *he took one look at the surge of sea and lowered clouds* **swell**, swelling, heaving, billowing, rolling, roll, bulging, eddying, swirling, tide.
▶ verb **1** *contaminated water surged into people's homes | the crowd surged forward* **gush**, rush, stream, flow, burst, pour, cascade, spill, overflow, brim over, well, sweep, spout, spurt, jet, spew, discharge, roll, whirl; seethe, swarm, crowd.
2 *the Dow Jones index surged 47.63 points* **increase suddenly**, rise, grow, escalate, jump, leap, boost.
3 *the sea surged in the storm* **rise**, swell, heave, billow, roll, eddy, swirl.

surgery *See centre pages for lists of* **Operations** **Surgical Instruments**

surly ▶ adjective *a surly shop assistant* **bad-tempered**, ill-natured, grumpy, glum, crotchety, prickly, cantankerous, irascible, testy, ill-tempered, short-tempered, ungracious, splenetic, choleric, dyspeptic, bilious, crusty, abrupt, brusque, curt, gruff, blunt, churlish, ill-humoured, crabbed, crabby, uncivil, morose, dour, sullen, sulky, moody, moping, sour, unfriendly, unpleasant, scowling, unsmiling; humourless, disrespectful; *informal* chippy, grouchy.
OPPOSITES good-natured, friendly, pleasant.

surmise ▶ verb *she surmised that he was keen to leave* **guess**, conjecture, suspect, deduce, infer, come to the conclusion, conclude, theorize, speculate, glean, divine; assume, presume, suppose, understand, gather, feel, have a sneaking suspicion, hazard a guess, sense, be of the opinion, think, believe, imagine, judge, fancy, reckon; *formal* opine.
OPPOSITE know.

surmount ▶ verb **1** *his reputation is worldwide, and surmounts language barriers* **overcome**, conquer, get over, prevail over, triumph over, get the better of, beat, vanquish, master; clear, cross, make one's way round/past/over, make it round/past/over, pass over, be unstoppable by; deal with, cope with, resist, endure.
OPPOSITE be beaten by.
2 *the four surmount a ridge and see, in the valley below, a deserted city* **climb to the top of**, climb over, ascend, scale, mount.
OPPOSITES descend, climb down.
3 *its copper dome is surmounted by a bronze statue of Justice* **cap**, top, crown, tip.
4 *a funnel surmounted the structure* **rise above**, tower above, overtop, dominate.
OPPOSITE be dominated by.

surname ▶ noun *his surname was Jennings* **family name**, last name, patronymic.

surpass ▶ verb *radio far surpasses the press as a source of news* **excel**, be better than, be superior to, be greater than, exceed, transcend; **outdo**, outshine, outstrip, outclass, overshadow, put in the shade, eclipse; improve on, top, trump, cap, beat, better, outperform.

> **CHOOSE THE RIGHT WORD**
>
> **surpass, excel, outdo**
>
> *See* EXCEL.

surpassing ▶ adjective *a picture of surpassing beauty* **exceptional**, extraordinary, remarkable, outstanding, striking, phenomenal, rare, great, supreme, sublime, pre-eminent, consummate, incomparable, inimitable, incredible, unrivalled, unparalleled, matchless, unmatched, unequalled, peerless, unsurpassed, superlative, beyond words, beyond description; *informal* fabulous, fantastic, stupendous, out of this world, terrific, tremendous, awesome, stellar; *literary* wondrous.
OPPOSITES mediocre; poor.

surplus ▶ noun *a surplus of grain* **excess**, surfeit, overabundance, superabundance, superfluity, oversupply, oversufficiency, glut, profusion, plethora; remainder, residue, remnant; remains, leftovers.
OPPOSITES dearth, shortage, lack.
▶ adjective *clean off any surplus adhesive* **excess**, excessive, in excess, leftover, left, unused, remaining, extra, additional, reserve, spare; superfluous, redundant, unwanted, unneeded, not required, uncalled for, dispensable, disposable, expendable, useless; *French* de trop.
OPPOSITES necessary; insufficient.

surprise ▶ noun **1** *Kate looked at me in surprise* **astonishment**, amazement, incredulity, bewilderment, stupefaction, wonder, confusion, disbelief; consternation.
2 *the test was supposed to come as a big surprise* **shock**, bolt from/out of the blue, thunderbolt, bombshell, revelation, source of amazement, rude awakening, eye-opener; *informal* start; turn up for the books, shocker, whammy.
▶ verb **1** *I was so surprised when I got the letter telling me about the award that I burst into tears* **astonish**, amaze, nonplus, startle, astound, stun, flabbergast, stagger, shock, stop someone in their tracks, stupefy, leave open-mouthed, take someone's breath away, dumbfound, daze, benumb, confound, take aback, jolt, shake up; *informal* bowl over, knock for six, floor, blow someone's mind, strike dumb.
2 *it seems that she surprised a burglar and he attacked her* **take by surprise**, catch unawares, catch off guard, catch red-handed, catch in the act, catch napping, catch out, burst in on, catch someone with their trousers/pants down, catch in flagrante delicto; *Brit. informal* catch on the hop.

surprised ▶ adjective *he was surprised at the news* **astonished**, amazed, in amazement, nonplussed, taken aback, startled, astounded, stunned, flabbergasted, staggered, shocked, stupefied, open-mouthed, dumbfounded, dumbstruck, speechless, at a loss for words, thunderstruck, dazed, benumbed, confounded, agape, goggle-eyed, wide-eyed, jolted, shaken up; *informal* bowled over, knocked for six, floored, flummoxed, caught on the hop, caught on the wrong foot, unable to believe one's eyes/ears.

surprising ▶ adjective *he moves with surprising speed* **unexpected**, unanticipated, unforeseen, unpredictable, unpredicted; **astonishing**, amazing, startling, astounding, striking, staggering, incredible, extraordinary, dazzling, breathtaking, remarkable, wonderful, unusual; *informal* mind-blowing.
OPPOSITES unsurprising, predictable.

surrender ▶ verb **1** *the government surrendered to the Allied forces* **capitulate**, give in, give (oneself) up, yield, concede, submit, climb down, give way, defer, acquiesce, back down, cave in, relent, succumb, quit, crumble; be beaten, be overcome, be overwhelmed, fall victim; lay down one's arms, raise/show the white flag, throw in the towel/sponge, accept defeat, concede defeat.
OPPOSITES resist, withstand.
2 *the republics agreed to surrender certain powers to the central government* **give up**, relinquish, renounce, forgo, forswear, cede, abdicate, waive, forfeit, sacrifice; **hand over**, turn over, deliver (up), yield (up), resign, transfer, commit, grant; part with, let go of; *archaic* forsake.
OPPOSITE seize.

S

3 *to abandon the past is to surrender all purposeful hope of changing the world* **abandon**, leave behind, cast aside, turn one's back on, give up, lose.

▶ **noun 1** *the ordeal ended with the peaceful surrender of the hijackers* **capitulation**, submission, yielding, giving in, succumbing, acquiescence, laying down of arms, quitting; fall, defeat.

2 *a surrender of power to the shop floor* **relinquishment**, surrendering, renunciation, forgoing, forsaking, ceding, cession, abdication, waiving, resignation; handing over, giving up, yielding up, transfer, abandonment.

surreptitious ▶ **adjective** *Rory tried to sneak a surreptitious glance at Adam's wristwatch* **secret**, stealthy, clandestine, secretive, sneaky, sly, furtive, concealed, hidden, undercover, covert, veiled, under the table, cloak-and-dagger, backstair, indirect.

OPPOSITES blatant, open, honest.

surrogate ▶ **noun** *some argue that modern commerce is a surrogate for warfare* **substitute**, proxy, replacement; agent, deputy, representative, factor, stand-in, standby, stopgap, fill-in, relief, understudy.

surround ▶ **verb** *the next thing we knew we were surrounded by cops* **encircle**, enclose, encompass, ring, gird, girdle, go around; fence in, wall in, hedge in, hem in, close in, confine, ring (round), bound, circumscribe, delimit, cut off; besiege, siege, beset, beleaguer, throng, trap; *rare* environ, enwreathe.

▶ **noun** *a tiled fireplace with a wood surround* **border**, edging, edge, perimeter, boundary, margin, skirting, skirt, fringe.

surrounding ▶ **adjective** *the surrounding countryside* **neighbouring**, nearby, near, neighbourhood, local; adjoining, adjacent, bordering, abutting; encircling, encompassing; *rare* circumambient, circumjacent.

surroundings ▶ **plural noun** *a family-run hotel in exotic surroundings* **environment**, setting, milieu, background, backdrop, frame, element; conditions, circumstances, situation, context; vicinity, locality, habitat; ambience, atmosphere.

surveillance ▶ **noun** *leading members of the party were to be kept under surveillance* **observation**, scrutiny, watch, view, inspection, monitoring, supervision, superintendence; **spying**, espionage, intelligence, undercover work, infiltration, reconnaissance; *informal* bugging, wiretapping, phone-tapping, recon.

survey ▶ **verb** (stress on the second syllable) **1** *Jack stood back to survey his work* **look at**, look over, take a look at, observe, view, contemplate, regard, see, gaze at, stare at, eye, get a bird's-eye view of; **scrutinize**, examine, inspect, scan, study, consider, review, vet, weigh up, take stock of; *informal* size up; *literary* behold.

2 *the BBC surveyed four thousand drug users and their families* **interview**, question, canvass, poll, cross-examine, investigate, research, study, probe, sample.

3 *a structural engineer should be asked to survey the house* **make a survey of**, value, carry out a valuation of, estimate the value of; appraise, assess, prospect; triangulate.

▶ **noun** (stress on the first syllable) **1** *there is now a need for a survey of the current literature* **study**, consideration, review, overview; **scrutiny**, scrutinization, examination, inspection, exploration, appraisal, synopsis, outline, overall picture.

2 *a survey of sexual behaviour* **poll**, review, investigation, inquiry, study, probe, questionnaire, opinion poll, sampling, census, cross-examination, quiz, research.

3 *make a thorough survey of the property* **valuation**, **appraisal**, assessment, estimate, estimation, pricing.

survive ▶ **verb 1** *one passenger survived by escaping through a hole in the fuselage* **remain alive**, live, sustain oneself, cling to life, pull through, get through, hold on, hold out, make it, keep body and soul together.

2 *they're determined to ensure the theatre survives* **continue**, remain, last, persist, endure, live on, persevere, abide, go on, keep on, carry on, stay around, linger, be extant, exist, be.

3 *he was survived by Alice and their six sons* **outlive**, outlast, live (on) after, live longer than, remain alive after.

S

susceptibility ▶ **noun 1** *his susceptibility to flattery* **vulnerability**, sensitivity, openness, defencelessness, receptiveness, responsiveness.

OPPOSITES immunity, resistance.

2 *old age brings with it an increased susceptibility to illness* **liability**, vulnerability, inclination; **predisposition**, proneness, propensity, weakness; likelihood.

OPPOSITES immunity, resistance.

susceptible ▶ **adjective 1** *aggressive TV advertising aimed at susceptible children* **impressionable**, credulous, gullible, innocent, ingenuous, easily taken in, naive, defenceless, vulnerable, easily led, manageable, acquiescent, adaptable, persuadable, tractable; **sensitive**, responsive, tender, thin-skinned, highly strung, emotional.

OPPOSITES sceptical, streetwise.

2 *people susceptible to blackmail* **open to**, receptive to, vulnerable to, defenceless against; an easy target for; *rare* susceptive to.

3 *some people are more* **susceptible** *to ulcers than others* **liable to**, prone to, subject to, inclined to, predisposed to, disposed to, given to, easily affected by, in danger of, at risk of, at the mercy of.

OPPOSITES immune, resistant.

4 *the resulting database will be* **susceptible** *of commercial exploitation* **capable of**, admitting of, receptive of, open to, responsive to; allowing, permitting; *rare* susceptive of.

OPPOSITES incapable of, not open to.

suspect ▶ **verb** (stress on the second syllable) **1** *I began to suspect that she had made a mistake* **have a suspicion**, have a feeling, feel, be inclined to think, fancy, reckon, guess, surmise, conjecture, think, think it probable/likely, have a sneaking feeling, have a hunch; be of the opinion, suppose, conclude, expect, presume, consider, deduce, infer, glean, sense, imagine; be afraid, fear, have a foreboding; *formal* opine.

OPPOSITE know.

2 *he is suspected of cheating* **regard as guilty**, think to be guilty, regard as a wrongdoer.

3 *a broker whose honesty he had no reason to suspect* **doubt**, distrust, mistrust, have doubts about, harbour suspicions about, have misgivings about, be sceptical about, have qualms about, be suspicious of, be wary of, feel chary about, feel uneasy about, have/harbour reservations about, have a funny feeling about; *informal* smell a rat about.

▶ **noun** (stress on the first syllable) *a murder suspect* **suspected person**, accused, defendant.

▶ **adjective** (stress on the first syllable) *a suspect package* **suspicious**, dubious, untrustworthy, questionable, doubtful, odd, queer, potentially dangerous, potentially false, under suspicion, not quite right; *informal* fishy, funny, shady, not kosher; *Brit. informal* dodgy.

suspend ▶ **verb 1** *protestors had forced the legislative session to be suspended for three hours* **adjourn**, interrupt, break off, postpone, delay, defer, shelve, arrest, put off, intermit, prorogue, hold over, put aside, pigeonhole, put/hold/keep in abeyance; reschedule; cut short, bring to an end, cease, discontinue, dissolve, disband, terminate, call a halt to; *N. Amer.* table; *informal* put on ice, put on the back burner, mothball; *N. Amer. informal* take a rain check on.

OPPOSITES continue, resume.

2 *the treasurer was suspended from his duties pending an external investigation* **exclude**, debar, shut out, keep out, remove, eliminate, reject, expel, eject, evict, rusticate.

3 *two long fluorescent tubes were suspended from the ceiling* **hang**, sling, drape, string, put up; swing, dangle.

suspense ▶ **noun** *I can't bear the suspense a moment longer!* **tension**, uncertainty, doubt, doubtfulness, anticipation, expectation, expectancy, excitement, anxiety, nervousness, apprehension, apprehensiveness, strain.

□ **in suspense** *we now wait in suspense for the banker to turn the cards over* **eagerly**, agog, all agog, with bated breath, on tenterhooks, avid, excited, on edge, open-mouthed, anxious, edgy, jittery, jumpy, keyed up, overwrought, uneasy, worried; *informal* uptight, waiting for the axe to fall.

suspension ▶ **noun 1** *the government announced the suspension of army operations* **adjournment**, interruption, postponement, delay, deferral, deferment, shelving, stay, moratorium, arrest, intermission, interlude, prorogation, tabling, abeyance; rescheduling; hiatus, lacuna, lull, rest, break, pause, respite; armistice; cessation, end, halt, stoppage, cutting short, dissolution, disbandment, termination.

OPPOSITES continuation, resumption.

2 *his suspension from school* **exclusion**, debarment, removal, temporary removal, elimination, rejection, expulsion, ejection, eviction, rustication.

suspicion ▶ **noun 1** *she had a strong suspicion that he did not like her* **intuition**, feeling, impression, inkling, surmise, guess, conjecture, speculation, hunch, fancy, notion, supposition, view, belief, idea, conclusion, theory, thesis, hypothesis; presentiment, premonition; *informal* gut feeling, feeling in one's bones, funny feeling, sixth sense.

OPPOSITE certainty.

2 *I confronted him with my suspicions and he admitted everything* **misgiving**, doubt, qualm, wariness, chariness, reservation, hesitation, scepticism, lack of faith, uncertainty, question, question mark, leeriness, distrust, mistrust.

3 *it tasted like wine with a suspicion of bitters* **trace**, touch, suggestion, hint, soupçon, tinge, shade, whisper, whiff, bit, trifle, drop, dash, tincture, sprinkling, breath, taste, scent, shadow, glimmer, scintilla, speck, smack, jot, mite, iota, tittle, whit.

suspicious ▶ **adjective 1** *he was suspicious of all educational innovations | Dolly gave him a suspicious look* **doubtful**, unsure, dubious, wary, chary, sceptical, distrustful, mistrustful, disbelieving, having reservations, apprehensive, cynical, jaundiced; *informal* iffy.

OPPOSITES trustful, trusting.

2 *I think he's a highly suspicious character* **disreputable**, unsavoury, dubious, suspect, guilty-looking, dishonest-looking, strange-looking, queer-looking, funny-looking, slippery; *informal* shifty, shady; *Brit. informal* dodgy.

OPPOSITE upright.

3 *his wife disappeared in suspicious circumstances* **questionable**, odd, strange, dubious, irregular, queer, funny, doubtful, not quite right, under suspicion, mysterious, murky, dark, criminal, dishonest, corrupt; *informal* fishy, shady, dodgy.

OPPOSITES ordinary, innocent.

sustain ▶ verb **1** *they were concerned that the balcony might not be able to sustain the weight* **bear**, support, carry, stand, keep up, prop up, shore up, bolster, underpin, buttress.
OPPOSITE collapse under.
2 *she had lived life to the full, but now had only the memories of such times to sustain her* **comfort**, help, assist, encourage, succour, support, give strength to, be a source of strength to, be a tower of strength to, buoy up, carry, cheer up, hearten, see someone through; *informal* buck up.
OPPOSITES torment, plague.
3 *they were unable to sustain a coalition* **continue**, carry on, keep up, keep going, keep alive, keep in existence, keep, maintain, prolong, preserve, conserve, protract, perpetuate, bolster up, prop up, retain, extend.
4 *she had a slab of bread and cheese to sustain her | Britain sustained a much lower population than did Italy* **maintain**, continue, preserve, keep, keep alive, keep going, provide for; **nourish**, feed, nurture, provide board for.
5 *six Marines sustained slight injuries* **undergo**, experience, go through, suffer, endure.
6 *the allegation was not sustained by any court* **uphold**, validate, ratify, vindicate, confirm, endorse, approve; verify, corroborate, substantiate, bear out, prove, authenticate, attest to, back up, evidence, justify.

sustained ▶ adjective *a sustained attack on environmentalism* **continuous**, ongoing, steady, continual, continuing, constant, running, prolonged, persistent, non-stop, perpetual, unfaltering, unremitting, unabating, unrelenting, relentless, unrelieved, unbroken, never-ending, unending, incessant, unceasing, ceaseless, round the clock.
OPPOSITES intermittent, sporadic.

sustenance ▶ noun **1** *without sustenance the creature will die* **nourishment**, food, nutriment, nutrition, fare, diet, daily bread, provisions, rations, means of keeping body and soul together; *informal* grub, chow, scoff; *formal* comestibles, provender; *archaic* victuals, vittles, viands, meat; *rare* aliment.
2 *he kept two or three cows for the sustenance of his family* **support**, maintenance, keep, means of support, means, living, livelihood, subsistence, income, source of income.

swagger ▶ verb **1** *we swaggered into the arena dressed in our costumes* **strut**, parade, stride, roll, prance; walk confidently, walk arrogantly; *N. Amer. informal* sashay; *archaic* swash.
2 *he likes to swagger about his goodness to people* **boast**, brag, bray, bluster, crow, gloat, parade, strut, posture, pose, blow one's own trumpet, lord it; *informal* show off, swank, play to the gallery; *literary* rodomontade.
▶ noun **1** *there was a slight swagger in his stride* **strut**, parading, roll, prancing; confidence, arrogance, self-assurance, show, ostentation.
2 *Singleton was full of swagger now* **boasting**, bragging, bluster, bumptiousness, brashness, swashbuckling, vainglory, puffery; *informal* showing off, swank; *literary* braggadocio, rodomontade, gasconade.

CHOOSE THE RIGHT WORD

swagger, strut, parade
See STRUT.

swallow ▶ verb **1** *she had great difficulty swallowing food* **eat**, gulp down, consume, devour, eat up, put away, gobble (up), bolt (down), wolf down, stuff down, gorge oneself on, feast on, polish off; ingest, assimilate; *informal* scoff, get outside of.
2 *he swallowed the last of his drink* **drink**, gulp down, guzzle, quaff, imbibe, sup, slurp, suck, sip; *informal* swig, swill down, slug, down, toss off.
3 *I've no intention of swallowing any more of your insults* **tolerate**, endure, stand, put up with, bear, suffer, abide, submit to, countenance, stomach, brook, take, accept; *informal* stick, hack; *Brit. informal* wear.
4 *the magistrate swallowed my story and gave me a year's conditional discharge* **believe**, credit, accept, trust, put confidence in, give credit to, have faith in; *informal* fall for, buy, go for, {swallow something hook, line, and sinker}, take as gospel.
5 *last night she had swallowed her pride and rung his flat twice* **restrain**, repress, hold back, choke back, keep back, hold in, bite back, suppress, fight back; **overcome**, check, conquer, control, keep under control, keep in check, curb, rein in, contain; silence, muffle, stifle, smother, strangle, gag, hide, bottle up, inhibit, frustrate; bite one's lip; *informal* keep the lid on, button up, cork up.
□ **swallow someone/something up 1** *he watched them till the darkness swallowed them up* **engulf**, swamp, devour, flood over, overwhelm, overcome, bury, drown, inundate.
2 *a number of art colleges were swallowed up by polytechnics* **take over**, engulf, absorb, assimilate, incorporate, overrun, overwhelm, swamp.

WORD LINKS
fear of swallowing **phagophobia**

swamp ▶ noun *heavy rain turned the road into a swamp* **marsh**, bog, quagmire, mire, morass, fen, quag, sump; swampland, marshland, fenland, wetland; saltings; quicksand; *N. Amer.* salina, bayou, moor.
▶ verb **1** *the rain was driving down with great force, swamping the dry ground* **flood**, inundate, deluge, wash out, soak, drench, saturate, immerse.
2 *he was swamped by media attention* **overwhelm**, inundate, flood, deluge, engulf, snow under, bury, overload, overburden, overpower, weigh down, besiege, beset, consume.

swampy ▶ adjective *the swampy ground* **marshy**, boggy, fenny, miry; soft, soggy, muddy, spongy, heavy, squelchy, waterlogged, sodden, slimy, watery, wet, unstable; *technical* paludal; *rare* quaggy, uliginose.
OPPOSITES firm, dry.

swap ▶ verb **1** *I'd swapped some toy cars for a set of dice in a leather case* **exchange**, interchange, trade, barter, trade off, bargain, traffic; switch, change, replace.
2 *the players swapped jokes and drank pints in the clubhouse* **bandy**, exchange, trade, reciprocate, pass back and forth, give and take.
▶ noun *he was on the lookout for a job swap* **exchange**, interchange, trade, barter, switch, trade-off, substitution.

swarm ▶ noun **1** *a swarm of bees* **hive**, flight, flock, covey.
2 *there was the usual swarm of gendarmes rushing around* **crowd**, multitude, horde, host, mob, gang, throng, stream, mass, body, band, army, troop, legion, flock, herd, pack, drove, sea, array, myriad, pile; knot, cluster, group.
▶ verb *reporters and photographers were swarming all over the place* **flock**, crowd, throng, stream, surge, flood, seethe, pack, crush.
□ **be swarming with** *the field was swarming with sightseers* **be crowded with**, be thronged with, be overrun with, be full of, abound in, be teeming with, be bristling with, bristle with, be alive with, be crawling with, be infested with, overflow with, brim with, be prolific in, be abundant in; *informal* be thick with, be lousy with.

swarthy ▶ adjective *the tanned, swarthy skin of his face* **dark**, dark-coloured, dark-skinned, dark-complexioned, dusky, tanned, black, saturnine, olive-skinned; sallow; *rare* nigrescent, swart.
OPPOSITES pale, fair.

swashbuckling ▶ adjective *a band of swashbuckling young crusaders* **daring, romantic**, heroic, daredevil, swaggering, dashing, adventurous, rakish, bold, valiant, valorous, fearless, lionhearted, stout-hearted, dauntless, doughty, devil-may-care, gallant, chivalrous, dazzling, macho, ostentatious.
OPPOSITES timid, unadventurous.

swathe ▶ verb *his hands were swathed in bandages* **wrap**, envelop, bind, swaddle, bandage, bundle up, muffle up, cover, cloak, shroud, drape, wind, enfold, bedeck, overlay, encase, sheathe.

sway ▶ verb **1** *the curtains were swaying in the breeze | they smiled at him and swayed their hips* **swing**, shake, oscillate, rock, undulate, move from side to side, move to and fro, move back and forth.
2 *she swayed on her feet and the doctor put out a hand to steady her* **stagger**, wobble, rock, lurch, reel, roll, list, stumble, pitch, keel, veer, swerve.
3 *his thoughts sway constantly between the desire to go on and the desire to settle down* **waver**, fluctuate, vacillate, oscillate, alternate, vary, see-saw, yo-yo, equivocate, hesitate, shilly-shally, go from one extreme to the other; *Brit.* hum and haw; *informal* wobble, blow hot and cold.
4 *a lot of people are swayed by the media* **influence**, affect, bias, persuade, prevail on, bring round, talk round, win over, convert; manipulate, bend, mould; *informal* nobble.
5 *she mustn't allow herself to be swayed by emotion* **rule**, govern, dominate, control, direct, guide.
▶ noun **1** *the slow, easy sway of her hips* **swing**, sweep, wave, roll, shake, movement, oscillation, undulation.
2 *the province passed under the sway of the Franks* **jurisdiction**, rule, government, sovereignty, dominion, control, command, power, authority, ascendancy, domination, mastery.
3 *parliament is increasingly under the sway of dogmatists* **control**, domination, power, authority, supremacy, influence, leadership, direction, leverage; *informal* pull, clout.
□ **hold sway** *they had held sway in France for a quarter of a century* **hold power**, wield power, exercise power, rule, be most powerful, be in power, be in control, predominate, have the ascendancy, have the greatest influence, have the upper hand, have the edge, have/hold the whip hand; *informal* run the show, be in the driving seat, be in the saddle.

swear ▶ verb **1** *the godparents will then swear that they believe in the creed and the commandments | they swore to marry each other* **promise**, vow, promise under oath, solemnly promise, pledge oneself, give one's word, take an oath, swear an oath, swear on the Bible, give an undertaking, undertake, affirm, warrant, state, assert, declare, aver, proclaim, pronounce, profess, attest, guarantee; *Law* depose, make a deposition, bind oneself; *rare* asseverate.
2 *she swore that she would never go back to her aunt's house* **insist**, avow, be emphatic, pronounce, declare, assert, maintain, contend, aver, emphasize, stress.
3 *Kate spilled wine on her jeans and swore* **curse**, blaspheme, utter profanities, utter oaths, be foul-mouthed, use bad/foul language, be blasphemous, take the Lord's name in vain, swear like a trooper, damn; *informal* cuss, turn the air blue, eff and blind; *archaic* execrate.
□ **swear by 1** *I swear by the Blessed Virgin that it fell into the sea* **invoke**,

S

appeal to, call as one's witness.
2 (*informal*) *many of the locals swear by these computers* **express confidence in**, have faith in, put one's faith in, trust, have every confidence in, believe in; set store by, value; *informal* rate.
□ **swear off** *he swore off drink, tobacco, and gambling* **renounce**, forswear, forgo, abjure, abstain from, go without, shun, avoid, eschew, steer clear of, give a wide berth to, have nothing to do with; **give up**, dispense with, stop, cease, finish, discontinue, break off, drop; *informal* kick, quit, jack in.
OPPOSITE take up.

swearing ▶ noun *sixty per cent thought there was too much swearing on TV* **bad language**, foul language, strong language; **profanity**, obscenity, cursing, blaspheming, blasphemy, vilification, imprecation, curses, oaths, expletives, swear words, profanities, insults; *technical* coprolalia; *informal* cussing, effing and blinding, four-letter words.

swear word ▶ noun *in those days men did not use swear words in front of girls* **expletive**, obscenity, oath, curse, imprecation, epithet, dirty word, four-letter word; *N. Amer. informal* cuss word; (**swear words**) bad language, foul language, profanity, blasphemy, swearing.

sweat ▶ noun **1** *he was drenched with sweat* **perspiration**, moisture, dampness, wetness, lather; sweating; *informal* muck sweat; *technical* sudor, diaphoresis, hidrosis.
2 (*informal*) *I was in a sweat to get away* **fluster**, flutter, fret, fuss, panic, frenzy, fever, pother, state of anxiety, state of agitation, state of nervousness, nervous state, state of worry; *informal* state, flap, tizzy, tiz-woz, dither, stew, lather, twitter; *N. Amer. informal* twit.
3 (*informal*) *they made their money from the sweat of the working classes* **labour**, hard work, toil(s), effort(s), exertion(s), industry, industriousness, drudgery, slog, the sweat of one's brow; back-breaking task, labour of Hercules; *informal* graft, grind, elbow grease.
▶ verb **1** *the coat had made her so hot that she was sweating heavily* **perspire**, swelter, exude perspiration, drip with perspiration/sweat, be pouring with sweat, break out in a sweat, glow, be damp, be wet, secrete; *informal* be in a muck sweat, sweat buckets, sweat like a pig; *rare* sudate.
2 *I've sweated over this for the last six months, and I'm not going to see that work wasted* **work hard**, work, work like a Trojan, labour, toil, slog, slave, work one's fingers to the bone, keep one's nose to the grindstone; *informal* grind, graft, plug away, put one's back into something; *archaic* drudge.
3 *I sweated over my mistakes* **worry**, agonize, fuss, panic, fret, dither, lose sleep, be on tenterhooks, be in a state of anxiety, be in a state of agitation, be in a state of nervousness; *informal* be on pins and needles, be in a state, be in a flap, be in a tiz-woz, be in a stew, be in a lather, bite one's nails, torture oneself, torment oneself.
WORD LINKS
relating to sweat **sudatory, sudorific**

sweater ▶ noun. *See centre pages for list of* **Pullovers**

sweaty ▶ adjective *he rubbed his sweaty palms on his socks* **perspiring**, sweating, clammy, sticky, glowing, moist, damp, slimy, soggy, dripping, drenched.
OPPOSITES dry, cool.

sweep ▶ verb **1** *she swept the kitchen floor* **brush**, clean, scrub, wipe, mop, dust, scour, scrape, rake, buff; vacuum, hoover; *informal* do.
2 *I swept the crumbs off the floor* **remove**, wash away, expel, dispose of, eliminate, get rid of; brush, clean, clear, whisk.
3 *he was swept out to sea* **carry**, pull, drag, drive.
4 *riots swept the country* **engulf**, overwhelm, flood, flow across, surge over.
5 *he had swept down the stairs with his arm about John's shoulders* **glide**, sail, stride, breeze, stroll, sally, swagger, drift, flit, flounce.
6 *a flotilla of limousines swept past* **glide**, sail, dash, charge, rush, streak, speed, fly, zoom, swoop, whizz, hurtle; *informal* tear.
7 *fire swept through the building* **race**, hurtle, streak, spread like lightning; *informal* tear, whip.
8 *police had swept the conference room at 6am and 8am* **search**, probe, check, explore, hunt through, look through, delve in, go through, sift through, scour, comb, go through with a fine-tooth comb, leave no stone unturned in.
□ **sweep something aside** *they can sweep aside any criticism by declaring that they are rewarding the loyalty of dedicated fans* **disregard**, ignore, take no notice of, think no more of, dismiss, shrug off, forget about, brush aside.
□ **sweep something under the carpet** *their grievances became clearly visible and could no longer be conveniently swept under the carpet* **hide**, conceal, keep hidden, suppress, keep quiet about, hush up, not disclose, not breathe a word of, censor, gag, withhold, cover up, smother, stifle, muzzle, ban.
OPPOSITES disclose, publicize.
▶ noun **1** *with a great sweep of his hand, he bowed* **gesture**, movement, move, action, stroke, wave.
2 *both men were arrested in a nationwide security sweep* **search**, hunt, exploration, probe, forage, pursuit, quest.
3 *she looked out into the grey sweep of road* **curve**, curvature, bend, arc, arch, bow, turn.
4 *this is a modern resort featuring a long sweep of golden sand* **expanse**, tract, stretch, space, plain, extent, vastness, vista.
5 *the broad sweep of our business interests* **range**, span, scope, compass, reach, spread, ambit, remit, gamut, orbit, spectrum, sphere, purview, limit, extent.

sweeping ▶ adjective **1** *there will be more sweeping changes in education* **extensive**, wide-ranging, global, broad, wide, comprehensive, all-inclusive, all-embracing, far-reaching, across the board, worldwide, catholic, exhaustive, pervasive; thorough, in-depth, radical; *informal* wall-to-wall.
OPPOSITES narrow, restricted, limited.
2 *a sweeping victory for the Republican Party* **overwhelming**, decisive, thorough, complete, total, absolute, out-and-out, thoroughgoing, unconditional, unlimited, unrestricted, unqualified, plenary.
OPPOSITE narrow.
3 *there are dangers in making sweeping statements based on this research* **wholesale**, blanket, over-general, general, inclusive, all-inclusive, unqualified, indiscriminate, universal, oversimplified, imprecise.
OPPOSITES focused, narrow.
4 *a sweeping curved roof* **broad**, extensive, expansive, vast, spacious, roomy, boundless, panoramic.
OPPOSITES small, narrow.

sweet *See centre pages for lists of* **Cakes, Puddings, and Desserts** **Sweets and Confectionery**
▶ adjective **1** *a packet of sweet biscuits* **sugary**, **sweetened**, saccharine; sugared, honeyed, candied, glacé; syrupy, treacly, sickly, cloying.
OPPOSITES sour, sharp; savoury.
2 *the fresh sweet perfume of roses* **fragrant**, aromatic, sweet-smelling, perfumed, balmy, scented; *literary* ambrosial, redolent.
3 *she sang the tune in her sweet silvery voice* **musical**, tuneful, dulcet, melodious, lyrical, mellifluous, soft, harmonious, euphonious, silvery, honeyed, liquid, mellow, rich, smooth, sweet-sounding, sweet-toned, silver-toned, bell-like, golden.
OPPOSITES harsh, discordant.
4 *life was still sweet, despite Father's mean ways* **pleasant**, pleasing, agreeable, delightful, nice, satisfying, gratifying, welcome, good, acceptable, to one's liking, entertaining, charming, inviting, attractive, fine; *informal* lovely, great.
OPPOSITES harsh, disagreeable.
5 *she breathed in the sweet March air* **pure**, wholesome, fresh, uncontaminated, clean, clear, not sour, not rotten.
OPPOSITES harsh, rotten.
6 *she had such a sweet nature* **likeable**, appealing, engaging, amiable, pleasant, agreeable, genial, friendly, nice, good-natured, kind, kindly, kind-hearted, thoughtful, considerate; charming, winning, enchanting, captivating, delightful, lovely, as nice as pie; *Italian & Spanish* simpatico; *dated* taking.
OPPOSITE nasty.
7 *she looks quite sweet all tucked up* **cute**, lovable, adorable, endearing, charming, attractive, dear.
8 *my sweet little sister* **dear**, dearest, darling, beloved, loved, cherished, precious, treasured, prized, worshipped, idolized.
□ **sweet on** (*informal*) *he had been sweet on a couple of local girls* **fond of**, taken with, attracted to, charmed by, captivated by, enchanted by, in love with, enamoured of, infatuated with, keen on, devoted to, smitten with, head over heels in love with; *informal* gone on, mad about, struck on, daft about, into, bowled over by, swept off one's feet by.
OPPOSITE indifferent to.
▶ noun **1** *I got some sweets for the children* **piece of confectionery**, chocolate, bonbon, fondant, toffee; *N. Amer.* candy; *informal* sweetie; *archaic* sweetmeat, confection.
2 *you can whip up this delicious sweet in five minutes* **dessert**, pudding, sweet course, second course, last course; *Brit. informal* afters, pud.
3 *happy birthday my sweet!* **dear**, darling, dearest, dear one, love, sweetheart, beloved, honey, pet, treasure, angel.

sweeten ▶ verb **1** *sweeten the milk with a little sugar* **make sweet**, add sugar to, sugar, sugar-coat, add honey to, add sweetener to.
2 *he chewed coriander seeds to sweeten his breath* **freshen**, refresh, fresh, purify, deodorize, perfume.
3 *there is no way to sweeten the bad news* **soften**, ease, alleviate, make agreeable, relieve, mitigate, make less painful, mellow, temper, cushion; embellish, embroider, dress up.
4 (*informal*) *the dividend has been increased to sweeten shareholders* **mollify**, placate, soothe, soften, soften up, mellow, pacify, appease, win over.

sweetheart ▶ noun **1** *you look lovely, sweetheart* **darling**, dear, dearest, love, beloved, dear one, sweet; *informal* honey, sweetie, sugar, baby, babe, doll, poppet; *archaic* sweeting.
2 *my high-school sweetheart* **girlfriend**, **boyfriend**, lover, beloved, love, significant other, darling, true love, woman friend, man friend, lady friend, lady love, beau, loved one, suitor, admirer, paramour, inamorato, inamorata; *informal* steady, flame; *literary* swain; *dated* follower.

swell ▶ verb **1** *she felt her top lip swell up as she tasted blood* **expand**, bulge, distend, become distended, inflate, become inflated, dilate, become

S

bloated, bloat, blow up/out, puff up, balloon, fatten, fill out, tumefy, intumesce.
OPPOSITES shrink, contract.
2 *peasant hunger grew more acute as the population swelled* **grow larger**, grow greater, grow, enlarge, increase, expand, rise, wax, mount, escalate, accelerate, step up, accumulate, surge, multiply, proliferate, snowball, mushroom, skyrocket.
OPPOSITES decrease, wane.
3 *she felt herself* ***swell with*** *pride* **be filled**, be full of, be bursting, brim, overflow, be overcome.
4 *the graduate entry scheme has swelled the numbers entering the profession* **make larger**, make greater, enlarge, increase, increase in size/scope, expand, augment, boost, top up, build up, accelerate, step up, multiply.
OPPOSITE decrease.
5 *he passed a pub, the sound of loud music swelling from inside* **grow loud**, grow louder, become louder, amplify, intensify, heighten.
OPPOSITE quieten.
▶ **noun 1** *there was a brief swell in the volume of conversation* **increase**, rise, growth, expansion, escalation, acceleration, surge, stepping-up, proliferation, snowballing, mushrooming, skyrocketing.
OPPOSITES decrease, dip.
2 *a heavy swell on the sea* **billow**, billowing, undulation, surge, surging, wave, roll, rolling, bulge, bulging, rush, deluge, movement.
3 (dated) *his friend was an elegant Boston swell* **dandy**, fop, beau, poseur; archaic dude, blade, coxcomb, popinjay; informal fashion plate, trendsetter, nob, peacock, toff.
▶ **adjective 1** (N. Amer. informal, dated) *that's a swell idea* **excellent**, marvellous, wonderful, splendid, magnificent, superb, first-rate; informal super, great, amazing, fantastic.
OPPOSITES bad, poor.
2 (N. Amer. informal, dated) *a swell hotel* **luxurious**, de luxe, fashionable, elegant, expensive, grand, smart, stylish, exclusive; informal posh, plush, ritzy, swanky.
OPPOSITE cheap.

swelling ▶ **noun** *he had a great swelling under his eye* **bump**, lump, bulge, inflammation, protuberance, excrescence, enlargement, distension, prominence, protrusion, tumour, node, nodule; boil, blister, bunion, carbuncle, wen, sty, welt; rare tumescence.

sweltering ▶ **adjective** *a sweltering afternoon* **hot**, **stifling**, suffocating, humid, steamy, sultry, sticky, muggy, close, stuffy, airless, oppressive, tropical, torrid, burning, searing, parching, like an oven, like a Turkish bath, jungle-like; informal boiling, baking, roasting, blistering, sizzling.
OPPOSITES cold, chilly, cool.

swerve ▶ **verb** *a car swerved into her path* **veer**, change direction, go off course, deviate, skew, diverge, sheer, curve, twist, weave, zigzag, turn aside, branch off, sidetrack; Sailing tack; rare divagate.
▶ **noun** *the bowler must regulate his swerve so that the ball hits the wicket* **curve**, curl, bend, deviation, twist, change of direction; N. Amer., Pool & Billiards English.

swift ▶ **adjective 1** *Ramsay made a swift decision* **prompt**, rapid, sudden, immediate, instant, instantaneous, without delay, ready, punctual; abrupt, unhesitating, hasty, hurried, precipitate, headlong; informal p.d.q. (pretty damn quick).
OPPOSITE unhurried.
2 *most of them are swift runners* **fast**, rapid, quick, speedy, fleet-footed, fleet, swift as an arrow, like the wind, like lightning; literary winged, flying; informal nippy, supersonic.
OPPOSITES slow, sluggish.
3 *pupils are expected to make swift progress* **rapid**, quick, brisk, lively, speedy, fast, high-speed, expeditious, express, breakneck, meteoric, whirlwind; informal spanking, nippy.
OPPOSITES slow, leisurely.

swiftly ▶ **adverb 1** *the police reacted swiftly* **promptly**, immediately, instantly, instantaneously, without delay, post-haste, in a flash, in a trice, in the wink of an eye, in an instant, in no time (at all); readily, punctually, meteorically; suddenly, abruptly, unhesitatingly, hastily, hurriedly, precipitately, headlong; informal before you can say Jack Robinson, before you can say knife, like a shot, like greased lightning, p.d.q. (pretty damn quick), lickety-split, in a jiff/jiffy, pronto, in less than no time.
OPPOSITES unhurriedly, in due course.
2 *he went swiftly through the house* **rapidly**, quickly, fast, speedily, briskly, at high speed, at full tilt, like the wind, like lightning, at breakneck speed, as fast as one's legs can carry one, as swift as an arrow; informal double quick, nippily, like the clappers; literary apace.
OPPOSITE slowly.

swiftness ▶ **noun 1** *the children had the swiftness of weasels* **speed**, speediness, quickness, velocity, celerity, fleetness, fastness, rapidity, rapidness, liveliness; informal nippiness.
OPPOSITES slowness, sluggishness.
2 *bankruptcy can happen with surprising swiftness* **suddenness**, abruptness, instantaneity, rapidity, rapidness, haste, hastiness, briskness, hurriedness, hurry.
3 *the answer came with unwanted swiftness* **promptness**, immediateness, immediacy, instantaneousness, rapidity, rapidness, dispatch, punctuality; alacrity, expeditiousness, readiness, willingness.
OPPOSITES lateness, tardiness.

swill ▶ **verb 1** *she was swilling pints of bitter with the lads* **drink**, quaff, swallow, down, gulp down, drain, guzzle, imbibe, sup, slurp, consume; informal swig, swill (down), slug, knock back, knock off, toss off, put away, get one's laughing gear round, bend one's elbow; Brit. informal bevvy; N. Amer. informal chug, scarf down.
2 *with a clatter of buckets and bowls, we started to* ***swill down*** *the yard | she* ***swilled out*** *a glass* **wash**, sluice, clean out, flush, rinse, bathe, cleanse, drench.
▶ **noun 1** *he took a noisy swill of coffee* **gulp**, drink, swallow, draught, mouthful; informal swig, slug.
2 *if a regular source of swill is available, pig keeping can be profitable* **pigswill**, hogwash, pigwash, wash, mash; **slops**, scraps, refuse, scourings, leftovers, waste matter, waste, remains, detritus.

swim ▶ **verb 1** *when it rained they played squash or swam in the indoor pool* **bathe**, go swimming, take a dip, dip, splash around; float, tread water; dive, plunge; snorkel.
2 *Pip's food was* ***swimming in*** *gravy* **be saturated in**, be drenched in, be soaked in, be steeped in, be immersed in, be covered in, be full of.

swimming ▶ **noun.** *See centre pages for list of* **Swimming Strokes, Kicks, and Dives**

swimmingly ▶ **adverb 1** *everything was going swimmingly* **smoothly**, easily, effortlessly, very well, like clockwork, without a hitch, with no trouble, without difficulty, as planned, to plan; informal like a dream, like magic.
2 *Tommy and I got on swimmingly* **well**; informal famously, like a house on fire.

swimming pool ▶ **noun pool**, baths, leisure pool, lido, piscina; Brit. swimming bath(s); N. Amer. rare natatorium.

swimsuit ▶ **noun swimwear**, bathing dress, bathing suit; (swimming) trunks; bikini; Brit. swimming costume, bathing costume; informal swimming togs, cossie; Austral./NZ informal bathers.

swindle ▶ **verb** *the museum has been swindled out of a large sum of money* **defraud**, cheat, trick, fleece, dupe, deceive, rook, exploit, squeeze, milk, bleed; fool, take advantage of, mislead, delude, hoax, hoodwink, bamboozle, string along; embezzle; informal do, con, sting, diddle, fiddle, swizzle, swizz, rip off, take for a ride, pull a fast one on, pull the wool over someone's eyes, put one over on, sell a pup to, take to the cleaners, bilk, gull, finagle, gazump; N. Amer. informal stiff, euchre, bunco, hornswoggle; archaic cozen, sharp; rare mulct.
▶ **noun** *an insurance swindle* **fraud**, trick, deception, deceit, trickery, chicanery, exploitation, cheat, imposture, sham, sharp practice, artifice; ruse, dodge, racket, wile; informal con trick, con, sting, diddle, rip-off, fiddle, flimflam, swizzle, swizz; N. Amer. informal bunco.

swindler ▶ **noun** *more than 10,000 farmers have fallen victim to the swindlers* **fraudster**, fraud, confidence trickster, confidence man, cheat, trickster, rogue, mountebank, exploiter, pretender, charlatan, sham, impostor, hoaxer, embezzler; informal con man, con artist, shark, sharp, hustler, bilker, flimflam man, phoney, chiseller, crook, quack, bunco artist.

swing ▶ **verb 1** *the basket was swinging in the wind* **sway**, oscillate, move back and forth, move to and fro, wave, wag, dangle, rock, flutter, flap, vibrate, quiver.
2 *Helen swung the bottle, clubbing Goldman at the base of the skull* **brandish**, wave, flourish, wield, raise, shake, wag, twirl.
3 *this road swings off to the north* **curve**, bend, veer, turn, bear, wind, twist, deviate, slew, skew, sheer off, change course, drift, head.
4 *Penny swung down the drive* **stride**, march, sweep; stroll; N. Amer. informal sashay.
5 *the balance had once more swung from centralization to decentralization* **change**, fluctuate, oscillate, waver, alternate, see-saw, yo-yo, vary, shift, alter, undulate, ebb and flow, rise and fall, go up and down, go back and forth.
6 *what finally swung it for him was that his family kept writing to the State Governor* **accomplish**, achieve, obtain, acquire, get, secure, net, win, earn, attain, bag, capture, grab, hook; manoeuvre, sort out; informal wangle, land, fix (up), work, get hold of, nab, collar, pull down, knock off.
□ **swing the lead** (Brit. informal) *nearly a fifth of working time was wasted through workers swinging the lead.* See MALINGER.
▶ **noun 1** *a giant swing of the pendulum | the swing of her hips* **swaying**, oscillation, undulation; wagging, toing and froing, wobble; Astronomy libration.
2 *the swing to the Conservatives was 6 per cent* **change**, move; turnaround, turnround, turnabout, reversal, about turn, about face, volte face, change of heart, change of loyalties, U-turn, sea change, swerve, backtracking; rare tergiversation.
3 *there's been a swing towards plain food* **trend**, tendency, drift, movement, current, course.

S

4 *there was a sudden swing in her mood* **fluctuation**, change, shift, switch, variation, oscillation.
OPPOSITE stability.
5 *it's all soft swing and mellow music until the chorus* **rhythm**, beat, pulse, cadence, pace, rhythmical flow/pattern, measure, metre, tempo, lilt; *informal* groove.

swingeing ▶ **adjective** *swingeing cuts in public expenditure* **severe**, extreme, serious, substantial, drastic, harsh, punishing, excessive, oppressive, draconian, heavy.
OPPOSITES minor, mild.

swipe (*informal*) ▶ **verb 1** *without warning his right hand swiped at her mouth* **strike**, swing, hit, slap, cuff, lash out; *informal* belt, wallop, sock, biff, clout.
2 *they're always swiping sweets from the other kids* **steal**, thieve, take, pilfer, purloin, snatch, help oneself to, appropriate, abstract, shoplift; *informal* filch, lift, snaffle, rob, nab; *Brit. informal* nick, pinch, whip, half-inch, blag; *N. Amer.* glom.
▶ **noun** *she took a playful swipe at his face* **strike**, stroke, swing, hit, slap, brush, cuff, clip; *informal* belt, wallop.

swirl ▶ **verb** *the snow swirled around them | the water swirled over her ankles* **whirl**, eddy, billow, spiral, wind, churn, swish, agitate, circulate, revolve, spin, twist, gyrate; **flow**, ripple, stream, surge, seethe, foam, froth, boil, ferment.

switch ▶ **noun 1** *he pressed the switch on top of the telephone console* **button**, handle, lever, key, control, controller, disc, dial, joystick; circuit-breaker.
2 *we observed a switch from direct to indirect taxation* **change**, change of direction, move, shift, transition, transformation, diversion; reversal, turnaround, swerve, U-turn, changeover, transfer, conversion, substitution, exchange, interchange; *Brit.* about-turn.
3 *somebody pulled the old twenty-dollar bill switch on me* **exchange**, swap, trade, substitution, interchange, replacement, rotation.
4 *a switch of willow* **branch**, twig, shoot, stick, rod.
▶ **verb 1** *people in traditional employment might be encouraged to switch to agency working | he switched sides at the last moment* **change**, shift, convert, divert, redirect; reverse; *informal* chop and change.
2 *he managed to switch envelopes so that an empty one was sent instead* **exchange**, **swap**, interchange, trade, substitute, cause to change places, replace, rotate.
□ **switch something on** *he switched the kettle on* **turn on**, put on, flick on, activate, power up, start off, set going, get going, trigger off, set in motion, operate, initiate, actuate, boot up, initialize, energize.
□ **switch something off** *she was so shocked she'd switched the TV off* **turn off**, shut off, flick off, stop working, cut, power down, stop, halt, deactivate; extinguish.

swivel ▶ **verb** *she swivelled round in her seat* **turn**, spin, swing, rotate, revolve, pivot, twirl, whirl, wheel, gyrate, pirouette.
▶ **noun** *attached to the wall is a small television on a swivel* **pivot**, axle, spindle, hinge, axis, fulcrum, pin, hub, kingpin, gudgeon, trunnion.

swollen ▶ **adjective** *swollen glands* **expanded**, **distended**, bulging, inflamed, inflated, enlarged, dilated, bloated, blown-up, puffed up, puffy, ballooning, protruding, prominent, stretched, tumescent; *rare* tumid, oedematous, dropsical.
OPPOSITES shrunken, shrivelled.

swoop ▶ **verb 1** *the pigeons **swooped down** after the grain* **dive**, descend, sweep, pounce, drop, plummet, plunge, pitch, nosedive; rush, dart, speed, zoom.
2 *armed police **swooped on** a flat in east London* **raid**, search; pounce, make a raid; attack, assault, assail, charge; *N. Amer. informal* bust.
▶ **noun** *police arrested them in an early morning swoop* **raid**, surprise search; attack, assault; *N. Amer. informal* bust, takedown.

sword *See centre pages for list of* **Weapons**
▶ **noun** *a ceremonial sword* **blade**, steel; *literary* brand.
□ **cross swords quarrel**, disagree, have a dispute, wrangle, bicker, be at odds, be at loggerheads, lock horns, lock antlers; fight, do battle, engage in conflict, contend; challenge; *informal* have a dust-up, have a scrap, have a barney.
□ **put someone to the sword kill**, execute, put to death, murder, butcher, slaughter, annihilate, massacre, cut down, mow down; *literary* slay.

sybarite ▶ **noun hedonist**, sensualist, voluptuary, libertine, pleasure seeker, playboy, epicure, glutton, gourmand, gastronome; *French* bon vivant, bon viveur.
OPPOSITE puritan.

sybaritic ▶ **adjective** *the brothers' opulent and sybaritic lifestyle* **luxurious**, extravagant, pampered, lavish, self-indulgent, pleasure-seeking, sensual, voluptuous, hedonistic, epicurean, lotus-eating, libertine, debauched, dissolute, decadent, unrestrained.
OPPOSITES abstemious, ascetic.

sycophant ▶ **noun** *he was surrounded by flatterers and sycophants* **toady**, creep, crawler, fawner, flatterer, flunkey, truckler, groveller, doormat, lickspittle, kowtower, obsequious person, minion, hanger-on, leech, puppet, spaniel, Uriah Heep; *informal* bootlicker, yes-man; *vulgar slang* arse-licker, arse-kisser, brown-nose; *N. Amer. vulgar slang* suckhole.

sycophantic ▶ **adjective** *his clique of sycophantic friends* **obsequious**, servile, subservient, deferential, grovelling, toadying, fawning, flattering, ingratiating, cringing, unctuous, oily, slimy, creeping, crawling, truckling, slavish, bowing and scraping, Uriah Heepish, gushing; *informal* bootlicking, smarmy; *vulgar slang* arse-licking, arse-kissing, brown-nosing; *N. Amer. vulgar slang* suckholing.

syllabus ▶ **noun** *the A-level chemistry syllabus* **curriculum**, course, course of study, programme of study, educational programme, course outline; timetable, schedule.

symbol ▶ **noun 1** *the lotus is the symbol of purity* **emblem**, token, sign, representation, figure, image, type; metaphor, allegory.
2 *the chemical symbol for helium is He* **sign**, character, mark, letter, hieroglyph, ideogram.
3 *the Red Cross symbol* **logo**, emblem, badge, stamp, trademark, crest, insignia, coat of arms, seal, figure, device, rune, logotype, logogram, monogram, hallmark, tag, flag, motto, token, motif, colophon, ideogram.
WORD LINKS
study of written symbols **graphology**

symbolic ▶ **adjective 1** *few buildings can be as symbolic of the Roman Empire as the mighty Colosseum* **emblematic**, representative, typical, characteristic, distinctive, symptomatic; meaningful, significant.
2 *religious language is mostly used in symbolic or metaphorical ways* **figurative**, representative, illustrative, emblematic, allegorical, parabolic, non-literal, allusive, denotative, connotative, suggestive, mnemonic.
OPPOSITE literal.

symbolize ▶ **verb** *the wheel symbolizes the power of peaceful change* **represent**, be a symbol of, stand for, be a sign of, exemplify; denote, signify, mean, communicate, indicate, convey, express, imply, suggest, allude to; embody, epitomize, encapsulate, personify, typify; *literary* betoken; *archaic* symbol.

symmetrical ▶ **adjective 1** *the idea was that the library would be symmetrical, with the entrance and stairs in the centre* **regular**, uniform, consistent; evenly shaped, aligned, in line, congruous, equal; mirror-image, mirror-like.
OPPOSITES asymmetrical, disproportionate.
2 *the sturdy elegance and symmetrical beauty of the viaduct* **well balanced**, balanced, well proportioned, proportional, in proportion, regular, even, harmonious.
OPPOSITES asymmetrical, uneven.

symmetry ▶ **noun 1** *the garden is neat, laid out with perfect symmetry* **regularity**, evenness, uniformity, equilibrium, consistency, congruity, conformity, agreement, correspondence, orderliness, equality.
OPPOSITES asymmetry, irregularity.
2 *the remarkable symmetry of the poem* **balance**, proportions, regularity, evenness of form, harmony, harmoniousness, consonance, concord, coordination.
OPPOSITE asymmetry.

sympathetic ▶ **adjective 1** *a sympathetic listener | the dreaded bank manager often turns out to be highly sympathetic* **commiserating**, commiserative, pitying, condoling, consoling, comforting, supportive, encouraging; **compassionate**, caring, concerned, solicitous, empathetic; considerate, kindly, kind, kind-hearted, soft-hearted, tender-hearted, warm, warm-hearted; understanding, sensitive.
OPPOSITES unsympathetic, unfeeling.
2 *Rudy is the most sympathetic male character in the book* **likeable**, pleasant, agreeable, congenial, friendly, genial, companionable, easy to get along with; *Italian & Spanish* simpatico.
OPPOSITES unsympathetic, unfriendly.
3 *we got along well because I was **sympathetic to** his cause* **in favour of**, in sympathy with, approving of, pro, on the side of, supportive of, supporting of, favourable, encouraging of; well disposed to, favourably disposed to, receptive to, responsive to.
OPPOSITES unsympathetic, indifferent, opposed.

sympathize ▶ **verb 1** *he **sympathized with** his tearful wife* **pity**, feel/be sorry for, show sympathy for, be sympathetic towards, show compassion for, be compassionate towards, commiserate, offer condolences to, feel for, show concern, show interest; **console**, offer consolation to, comfort, solace, soothe, succour; be supportive of, support, encourage; **empathize with**, identify with, understand, relate to, be en rapport with, care for, weep for, grieve for, bleed for.
OPPOSITE disregard.
2 *they **sympathize with** feminist critiques of traditional theory* **agree**, support, be in sympathy, be sympathetic towards, be in favour of, go along, favour, be well disposed to, approve of, commend, back, side with, align, encourage.
OPPOSITE disapprove.

sympathizer ▶ **noun** *a Nazi sympathizer* **supporter**, advocate, backer, well-wisher, ally, partisan, fellow traveller; collaborator, fraternizer, conspirator, quisling, accomplice.

S

sympathy ▶ noun **1** *Sarah touched his arm in sympathy | he shows commendable sympathy for the world's poor* **commiseration**, pity, condolence, consolation, comfort, solace, support, encouragement; **compassion**, caring, concern, solicitude, solicitousness, empathy; consideration, kindness, kind-heartedness, tender-heartedness, tenderness, warmth, warm-heartedness.
OPPOSITE indifference.
2 *they might publicize John's case out of sympathy with a fellow journalist* **rapport**, fellow feeling, affinity, empathy, harmony, accord, compatibility; closeness, friendship, fellowship, togetherness, camaraderie, communion.
OPPOSITE hostility.
3 *their sympathy with the Republicans* **agreement**, harmony, favour, approval, approbation, support, encouragement, goodwill, commendation, partiality; association, alignment, affiliation.
OPPOSITE disapproval.

symptom ▶ noun **1** *he described the symptoms of the disease* **manifestation**, indication, indicator, sign, mark, feature, trait; *Medicine* prodrome.
2 *these bookshops are a symptom of the country's present turmoil* **expression**, sign, indication, mark, token, manifestation; omen, augury, portent, warning, testimony, evidence, proof, clue, hint.

symptomatic ▶ adjective *such incidents were symptomatic of tensions within the socialist movement* **indicative**, signalling, warning, characteristic, suggestive, typical, representative, symbolic; *rare* indicatory.

synopsis ▶ noun *a basic synopsis of the play* **summary**, precis, résumé, abstract, outline, condensation, digest, summarization, summing-up, rundown, round-up, abridgement, review, sketch, compendium; *rare* conspectus.

synthesis ▶ noun *this painting is a synthesis of elements derived from a variety of different types of ancient art* **combination**, union, amalgam, blend, mixture, compound, fusion, coalescence, composite, concoction, conglomerate, alloy; combining, unification, uniting, merging, amalgamation, conglomeration, weaving, interweaving, reconciliation, marrying.

synthetic ▶ adjective *synthetic leather* **artificial**, fake, false, faux, imitation, mock, simulated, ersatz, substitute; pseudo, sham, bogus, spurious, counterfeit, forged, pretended, so-called, plastic; man-made, manufactured, unnatural, fabricated; replica, reproduction, facsimile; *informal* phoney.
OPPOSITES real, genuine, natural.

> **CHOOSE THE RIGHT WORD**
>
> **synthetic, artificial, man-made**
> *See* ARTIFICIAL.

syrupy ▶ adjective **1** *a few teaspoons of syrupy medicine* **oversweet**, sweet, sickly sweet, sugary, treacly, honeyed, saccharine; **thick**, sticky, slimy, gluey, viscid, glutinous; *informal* gooey.
2 *syrupy romantic drivel* **sentimental**, over-sentimental, mawkish, cloying, sickly, sickly sweet, gushing, saccharine, maudlin, emotional, trite; *informal* soppy, schmaltzy, mushy, slushy, sloppy, weepy, cutesy, lovey-dovey, drippy, cheesy, corny.

system ▶ noun **1** *the legal system | a system of canals* **structure**, organization, order, arrangement, complex, apparatus, network; administration, institution; *informal* set-up.
2 *a system for regulating medical products* **method**, methodology, technique, process, procedure, approach, practice, line, line of action, line of attack, attack, means, way, manner, mode, framework, modus operandi; scheme, plan, policy, programme, regimen, set of principles, set of procedures, set of guidelines, formula, routine, tactic, tack.
3 *there was no system at all in the company* **methodicalness**, orderliness, systematization, planning, logic, routine.
4 (**the system**) *how do you give youngsters who have already been victimized faith in the system?* **the establishment**, the authorities, the powers that be, the ruling class, the regime, bureaucracy, officialdom; the status quo, the prevailing political/social order; *archaic* the regimen.

systematic ▶ adjective *these interviews were conducted in a systematic way* **structured**, methodical, organized, orderly, well ordered, planned, systematized, regular, routine, standardized, standard, formal, logical, coherent, consistent, efficient, businesslike, practical, careful, fastidious, meticulous; *informal* joined-up.
OPPOSITES disorganized, chaotic.

tab ▶ noun **1** *Joe knew it was his jacket, he'd seen his name stencilled on the tab* **tag**, flap, loop, lappet, label; strap, handle.
2 (*informal*) *the company will pick up the tab for any moving expenses* **bill**, invoice, account, statement, note/list of charges, charge, reckoning, tally; expense, cost; *N. Amer.* check; *archaic* score.

table *See centre pages for list of* **Tables and Desks**
▶ noun **1** *she put the plates on the table* board, work surface, worktop, counter, desk, bar, buffet, stand, bench, workbench, work table, top, horizontal surface, surface.
2 *he was reputed to provide an excellent table* **meal**, food, fare, diet, board, menu, nourishment, nutriment; eatables, rations, provisions; *informal* spread, grub, chow, eats, nosh; *archaic* victuals, vittles, viands.
3 *the text is accompanied by numerous tables* **list**, chart, diagram, figure, graph, plan; catalogue, inventory, digest, enumeration, tabulation, index, directory, register, itemization, record; *Computing* graphic.
▶ verb *an opposition MP had tabled a question in parliament* **submit**, put forward, bring forward, propose, suggest, move, enter, lodge, file, introduce, air, moot, lay.

tableau ▶ noun **1** *the sun and moon frequently appear in a symbolic role in mythic tableaux* **picture**, painting, representation, portrayal, illustration, image.
2 *in the first act the action is represented in a series of tableaux* **pageant**, tableau vivant, human representation, parade, diorama, scene.
3 *our entrance disturbed the domestic tableau around the fireplace* **scene**, arrangement, grouping, group; picture, spectacle, image, view, vignette.

tablet ▶ noun **1** *a carved stone tablet* **slab**, panel, plaque, plate, sign; stone, gravestone, headstone, tombstone, memorial.
2 *a headache tablet* **pill**, capsule, lozenge, caplet, pastille, pellet, drop, ball; *informal* tab; *rare* jujube, bolus, troche, pilule.
3 *a tablet of soap* **bar**, cake, slab, brick, block, chunk, piece.

taboo ▶ noun *the taboo against healing on the sabbath* **prohibition**, proscription, veto, interdiction, interdict, ban, restriction, boycott, non-acceptance, anathema.
OPPOSITES acceptance; encouragement.
▶ adjective *drinking, smoking, and gambling in his father's house were all taboo | taboo language* **forbidden**, prohibited, banned, proscribed, vetoed, ruled out, interdicted, outlawed, not permitted, not allowed, illegal, illicit, unlawful, impermissible, not acceptable, restricted, frowned on, beyond the pale, off limits, out of bounds; unmentionable, unspeakable, unutterable, ineffable, censored; rude, impolite, indecorous, dirty; *German* verboten; *Islam* haram; *NZ* tapu; *informal* no go; *rare* non licet.
OPPOSITES permitted, acceptable; encouraged.

tabulate ▶ verb *the survey results are tabulated in the appendix* **arrange**, order, organize, set out, chart; systematize, systemize, catalogue, list, sort, index, classify, class, codify, compile, group, range, dispose, file, log, grade, rate; *archaic* assort.

tacit ▶ adjective *the bargaining relies on informal agreements and tacit understandings* **implicit**, understood, implied, inferred, hinted, suggested, insinuated; **unspoken**, unstated, undeclared, unsaid, unexpressed, unmentioned, unvoiced, silent, mute, wordless, not spelt out; taken for granted, taken as read.
OPPOSITES explicit, stated.

> **CHOOSE THE RIGHT WORD**
>
> **tacit, unspoken, implicit**
> *See* IMPLICIT.

taciturn ▶ adjective *a shy, taciturn man* **untalkative**, uncommunicative, reticent, unforthcoming, quiet, unresponsive, secretive, silent, tight-lipped, close-mouthed, mute, dumb, inarticulate; reserved, withdrawn, introverted, retiring, antisocial, unsociable, distant, aloof, stand-offish, cold, detached, dour, sullen.
OPPOSITES talkative, loquacious.

tack ▶ noun **1** *tacks held the carpet to the floor* **pin**, drawing pin, nail, tin tack, staple, spike, rivet, stud; *N. Amer.* thumb tack.
2 (*Sailing*) *the brig bowled past on the opposite tack* **heading**, bearing, direction, course, track, path, line.
3 *he changed tack and began to play in a different style* **approach**, way, method, process; policy, procedure, technique, tactic, plan, strategy, stratagem, programme, line of attack; course of action, line of action, path, line, angle, direction, course.
▶ verb **1** *a photo was tacked to the wall* **pin**, nail, staple, fix, fasten, attach, secure, affix, put up, put down.
2 *when the dress was roughly tacked together she tried it on* **stitch**, baste, sew, bind, hem.
3 (*Sailing*) *the yachts tacked back and forth across the lake* **change course**, change direction, change heading; swerve, zigzag; veer off/away; *Nautical* go about, come about, beat, sail into the wind.
4 *he answered, but she had tacked and was already following a different line of questioning* **alter one's approach**, change course, change direction, do a U-turn, change one's mind, change one's attitude, have a change of heart; *Brit.* do an about-turn.
5 *there are some poems* **tacked on** *at the end of the book* **attach**, add, append, join, tag, annex.

tackle ▶ noun **1** *fishing tackle* **gear**, equipment, apparatus, outfit, kit, rig, hardware; tools, implements, instruments, accoutrements, paraphernalia, trappings, contrivances, appurtenances, utensils; *informal* things, stuff, clobber, bits and pieces; *archaic* equipage.
2 *they attached lifting tackle to it, and hauled it on deck* **system of pulleys**, hoisting gear, pulley, hoist, block and tackle, crane, winch, davit, windlass, sheave.
3 *his run was brought to a halt by the scrum half's tackle* **interception**, challenge, block, attack.
▶ verb **1** *we welcome the Government's determination to tackle environmental problems* **get to grips with**, apply oneself to, address oneself to, address, set about, go about, get to work at, busy oneself with, set one's hand to, grapple with, approach, take on, attend to, see to, throw oneself into, try to solve, try to deal with, try to cope with, try to sort out; deal with, take measures about, take care of, pursue, handle, manage; start on, embark on; *informal* get stuck into, have a crack at, have a go at, have a shot at.
2 *when I tackled Nina about it, she admitted that she'd bribed one of the chambermaids* **confront**, speak to, face (up to), initiate a discussion with, discuss something with, interview, question, cross-examine; accost, waylay; remonstrate with.
3 *he was stabbed in the chest after he tackled a masked intruder* **confront**, face up to, take on, contend with, challenge; **seize**, grab, take hold of, grapple with, obstruct, intercept, block, stop; knock/throw/bring down, floor, fell; *informal* have a go at.
4 *the winger got tackled* **intercept**, challenge, block, stop, attack.

tacky[1] ▶ adjective *the paint on the frame was still tacky* **sticky**, wet, gluey, gummy, glutinous, adhesive, viscous, viscid, treacly, syrupy, runny, clinging, sticking; *informal* gooey.

tacky[2] ▶ adjective *a tacky game show* **tawdry**, tasteless, kitsch, vulgar, crude, garish, gaudy, showy, loud, trashy, cheap, cheap and nasty, nasty, common, second-rate, Brummagem; *informal* flash, flashy, tatty, naff.
OPPOSITES tasteful, refined.

tact ▶ noun *the Inspector broke the news to me with tact and consideration* **sensitivity**, understanding, thoughtfulness, consideration, delicacy, diplomacy, discretion, discernment, judgement, prudence, judiciousness, perception, subtlety, wisdom, tactfulness; etiquette, courtesy, cordiality, politeness, decorum, mannerliness, polish, respect, respectfulness; *French* savoir faire, politesse; *informal* savvy.

OPPOSITES indiscretion, rudeness, tactlessness.

tactful ▶ adjective *a tactful little cough* **considerate**, sensitive, understanding, thoughtful, delicate, diplomatic, discreet, discerning, judicious, politic, perceptive, subtle, careful, treating someone/something with kid gloves; courteous, cordial, polite, decorous, seemly, respectful; *informal* savvy; *dated* mannerly.
OPPOSITES tactless, indiscreet, gauche.

tactic ▶ noun **1** *tax-saving tactics* **strategy**, scheme, stratagem, plan, set of tactics, manoeuvre, course/line of action; method, programme, expedient, gambit, move, approach, tack, path, road; device, trick, ploy, dodge, ruse, game, machination, contrivance, stunt; (**tactics**) means, wiles, artifice, subterfuge; *informal* wangle, caper; *archaic* shift.
2 (**tactics**) *the larger French fleet was decimated by superior tactics* **battle plans**, plans, game plans; **moves**, manoeuvres, logistics; strategy, policy, campaign; generalship, military science; organization, planning, arrangement, administration, direction, masterminding, orchestration, handling, running.

tactics or strategy?
See **STRATEGY**.

tactical ▶ adjective *this appeared to be a tactical move to try to force the CDF to agree to a coalition* **calculated**, planned, plotted, prudent, strategic, politic, diplomatic, judicious, shrewd, skilful, adroit, clever, smart, cunning, artful, wily; *informal* foxy.
OPPOSITES unwise; spontaneous.

tactless ▶ adjective *it was a cruel, tactless thing to say* **insensitive**, inconsiderate, thoughtless, unthinking, indelicate, undiplomatic, impolitic, indiscreet, unsubtle, clumsy, heavy-handed, graceless, awkward, unpolished, inept, bungling, maladroit, gauche, undiscerning, unsophisticated; blunt, straightforward, frank, plain-spoken, outspoken, abrupt, precipitate; gruff, bluff, rough, crude, coarse, speaking as one finds, calling a spade a spade, like a bull in a china shop; imprudent, injudicious, unwise, foolhardy; rude, impolite, uncouth, discourteous, crass, tasteless, impertinent, disrespectful, ungentlemanly, unladylike, boorish, uncivilized, uncivil; unkind, uncaring, uncalled for, callous, hurtful, thick-skinned, uncharitable, cruel.
OPPOSITES tactful, diplomatic, discreet.

tag ▶ noun **1** *a price tag* **label**, ticket, badge, mark, marker, tab, tally, sticker, docket, stub, chit, chitty, counterfoil, flag, stamp.
2 *his jacket was hung up by its tag* **tab**, flap, loop, lappet, label; strap, handle.
3 *he has vowed to throw off his 'bad boy' tag* **designation**, denomination, label, description, characterization, identification, identity; nickname, name, epithet, title, soubriquet, pet name, byname; *informal* handle, moniker; *formal* appellation, cognomen.
4 *his writing is full of tags from the Bible and Shakespeare* **quotation**, stock phrase, platitude, cliché, epithet, quote, extract, excerpt, passage, allusion, phrase; saying, proverb, maxim, axiom, adage, saw, aphorism, motto, epigram, epigraph, dictum, formula, truism, slogan, catchphrase; *informal, dated* gobbet.
▶ verb **1** *the bottles were tagged with colour-coded labels* **label**, attach tags to, put a label on, mark, ticket, earmark, identify, docket, flag, indicate.
2 *he became tagged as a 'thinking' actor* **designate**, describe, identify, classify, label, class, categorize, characterize; mark, stamp, brand, pigeonhole, stereotype, typecast, compartmentalize, typify; name, call, nickname, title, entitle, dub, term, style, christen, baptize.
3 *their heads were so large that the rest of their bodies seemed* ***tagged on*** *as an afterthought* **add**, tack, join; attach, append, affix, annex.
4 *her little boy was* ***tagging along*** *behind her* **follow**, trail; come after, go after, tread on the heels of, shadow, dog; go with, accompany, attend, escort; *informal* tail.

tail ▶ noun **1** *the dog's tail began to wag frantically* **hindmost part**, back end, appendage; brush, scut, dock; tailpiece, tail feathers; hind part, hindquarters; *technical* cauda, uropygium.
OPPOSITES front, head.
2 *new items are added on to the tail of the queue* **rear**, end, back, extremity, conclusion; bottom, lowest part; *Brit. informal* fag end.
OPPOSITES head, front.
3 *the tail of the hunting season* **close**, end, conclusion, termination, tail end.
OPPOSITES beginning, start.
4 (*informal*) *I can't put a tail on him, I don't know where he's gone* **detective**, investigator, private investigator, shadow; *informal* sleuth, private eye, tec; *N. Amer. informal* gumshoe, bogey, dick, private dick, shamus.
5 (*N. Amer. informal*) *the coach kicked Ryan in his tail. See* **BUTTOCKS**.
□ **on someone's tail** *a police car stayed on his tail for half a mile* **close behind someone**, following someone closely, (hard) on someone's heels, tailing someone.
□ **turn tail** *I was so shocked I just turned tail and ran home as fast as I could* **run away**, flee, bolt, make off, take to one's heels, show someone a clean pair of heels, cut and run, beat a (hasty) retreat; *informal* scram, scarper, skedaddle, vamoose.
OPPOSITE stand one's ground.
▶ verb (*informal*) *a flock of paparazzi had tailed them all over London* **follow**, shadow, stalk, trail, track, hunt, hound, dog, trace, pursue, chase, give chase to, run after, keep under surveillance.
□ **tail back** *traffic tailed back fourteen miles* **become congested**, form a tailback, jam.
□ **tail off/away** *the old lady's voice tailed off* **fade**, wane, ebb, dwindle, decrease, lessen, get less, diminish, decline, subside, abate, drop off, drop away, fall away, peter out, taper off; let up, ease off, die away, die out, die down, go into decline, waste away, recede, relent, desist, weaken, come to an end.
OPPOSITES increase, get more intense.

WORD LINKS
relating to a tail **caudal, cercal**

tailback ▶ noun **traffic jam**, queue, line, file; congestion.

tailor ▶ noun **outfitter**, dressmaker, garment-maker, couturier, fashion designer; clothier, costumier, seamstress; *dated* modiste.
▶ verb *both services can be tailored to customer requirements* **customize**, adapt, adjust, modify, change, convert, alter, attune, fashion, style, mould, gear, fit, cut, trim, suit, shape, reshape, tune.

WORD LINKS
relating to tailoring **sartorial**

taint ▶ noun *free from the taint of corruption* **trace**, touch, suggestion, hint, tinge, tincture; **smear**, stain, blot, blemish, slur, stigma, tarnish, scar, black mark, spot, imperfection, flaw, fault, defect, blot on one's escutcheon; discredit, dishonour, disgrace, shame.
▶ verb **1** *the world's last great wilderness is being tainted by pollution* **contaminate**, pollute, adulterate, infect, blight, befoul, spoil, soil, ruin, destroy.
OPPOSITE clean.
2 *fraudulent firms need to be weeded out, lest they taint the reputation of all firms* **tarnish**, sully, blacken, stain, besmirch, smear, blot, blemish, stigmatize, mar, corrupt, defile, soil, muddy, foul, dirty, damage, injure, harm, hurt, debase, infect, poison, vitiate, drag through the mud, blot one's copybook; brand.
OPPOSITE improve.

take ▶ verb **1** *Anna smiled as she took his hand* **lay hold of**, take hold of, get hold of, get into one's hands; grasp, grip, clasp, clutch, grab.
OPPOSITE give.
2 *he took an envelope from his inside pocket* **remove**, pull, draw, withdraw, extract, fish; confiscate, take possession of.
OPPOSITE give.
3 *the following passage is taken from my book 'Managing Stress'* **extract**, quote, cite, excerpt, derive, abstract, reproduce, copy, cull, choose.
4 *she took a little wine with her dinner* **drink**, imbibe; **consume**, swallow, eat, ingest.
5 *many thousands of prisoners were taken* **capture**, seize, catch, take captive, arrest, apprehend, take into custody; carry off, abduct, lay hold of; trap, snare.
OPPOSITES free, liberate.
6 *these thieving toerags have taken my car* **steal**, remove, appropriate, misappropriate, make off with, pilfer, purloin, abstract, dispossess someone of; *informal* filch, pinch, swipe, nick, snaffle, walk off with; *rare* peculate.
OPPOSITE give.
7 *take the bottom number from the total* **subtract**, deduct, remove, take away/off; discount; *informal* knock off, minus.
OPPOSITE add.
8 *all the seats had been taken* **occupy**, use, utilize, fill, hold; reserve, engage; *informal* bag.
9 *I have just taken a room in a nearby house* **rent**, lease, hire, charter; **reserve**, book, make a reservation for, arrange for, engage.
10 *I decided to take the job* **accept**, take up, take on, undertake.
OPPOSITE refuse.
11 *I'd take childbirth today over what my grandmother had to go through* **pick**, **choose**, select, decide on, settle on, fix on, single out; **prefer**, favour, opt for, plump for, vote for, elect.
OPPOSITES refuse, turn down.
12 *take, for instance, the English word 'one'* **consider**, ponder, contemplate, think about, weigh up, give thought to, mull over, deliberate over, examine, study, cogitate about, chew over, meditate over, ruminate over.
13 *he takes 'The Observer'* **subscribe to**, pay a subscription to, buy regularly, read regularly, read every day/week/month.
14 *a nurse took his temperature* **ascertain**, determine, establish, measure, find out, discover; calculate, compute, count, quantify, evaluate, rate, assess, appraise, gauge.
15 *she started to take notes* **write**, note (down), make a note of, set down, jot (down), scribble, scrawl, take down, record, register, document, minute, put in writing, commit to paper.
16 *I took it back to London with me* **bring**, **carry**, bear, transport, convey, move, transfer, shift, haul, drag, lug, cart, ferry; *informal* tote.

T

17 *she let the priest take her home* **escort**, accompany, help, assist, show, lead, show someone the way, lead the way, conduct, guide, see, usher, steer, pilot, shepherd, convey.
18 *he took the North London line to Acton* **travel on**, travel by, journey on, go via; use, make use of, utilize.
19 *the station takes its name from the nearby lake* **derive**, get, obtain, come by, acquire, pick up, be given.
20 *she took the prize for best individual speaker* **receive**, obtain, gain, get, acquire, collect, accept, be given, be presented with, be awarded, have conferred on one; secure, procure, come by, win, earn, pick up, walk away/off with, carry off; *informal* land, bag, net, scoop, cop.
21 *she feared that I might take the chance to postpone the ceremony* **act on**, take advantage of, capitalize on, use, exploit, make the most of, leap at, jump on, pounce on, seize (on), grasp, grab, snatch, accept, put to advantage, profit from, turn to account, cash in on.
OPPOSITES miss, ignore.
22 *he took great pleasure in creating his own individual style* **derive**, draw, acquire, obtain, get, gain, extract, procure; experience, undergo, feel, encounter, know, come into contact with, face.
23 *Elizabeth took the news of my sacking badly* **receive**, respond to, react to, meet, greet; deal with, cope with.
24 *do you take me for a fool?* **regard as**, consider to be, view as, look on as, see as, believe to be, think of as, reckon to be, imagine to be, deem to be, hold to be, judge to be.
25 *I* **take it** *that you are George Tenison* **assume**, presume, suppose, imagine, expect, believe, reckon, think, be of the opinion, gather, dare say, trust, surmise, deduce, guess, conjecture, fancy, suspect; take for granted, take as read.
26 *I take your point* **understand**, grasp, get, comprehend, apprehend, see, follow, take in; **accept**, appreciate, accept/acknowledge/admit the validity of, recognize, sympathize with, agree with.
27 *Shirley was rather taken with this idea* **captivate**, enchant, charm, delight, attract, win over, fascinate, bewitch, beguile, enthral, entrance, lure, infatuate, seduce, dazzle, hypnotize, mesmerize; please, amuse, divert, entertain, gladden, satisfy, gratify; *informal* tickle someone pink, tickle someone's fancy.
28 *I can't take much more of this business* **endure**, bear, suffer, tolerate, stand, put up with, stomach, brook, abide, carry, submit to, accept, permit, allow, admit, countenance, support, shoulder; *Scottish* thole.
29 *applicants may be asked to take a test* **perform**, **execute**, effect, discharge, carry out, accomplish, fulfil, complete, conduct, implement, do, make, have; *rare* effectuate.
30 *I went on to take English, History, and French* **study**, learn, be taught, have lessons in; read up on, work at, apply oneself to, acquire a knowledge of, gain an understanding of, grasp, master; take up, pursue; *Brit.* read; *informal* do.
31 *the journey should take a little over six hours* **last**, continue for, go on for, carry on for, keep on for, run on for, endure for; require, call for, need, necessitate, entail, involve.
32 *it would take an expert marksman with a high-powered rifle to hit him* **require**, need, necessitate, demand, call for, entail, involve.
33 *I take size 3 in shoes* **wear**, habitually wear, use; require, need, be fitted by, fit.
34 *we tried to bring the children up to think this way, but somehow it did not take* **be effective**, have/take effect, take hold, take root, be efficacious, be productive, be in force, be in operation, be efficient, be effectual, be useful; work, operate, succeed, function.

□ **take after** *Jenny takes after her mother* **resemble**, look like, be like, be similar to, bear a resemblance to, have the look of; remind one of, put one in mind of, make one think of, cause one to remember, recall, conjure up, suggest, evoke, call up; *informal* favour, be a chip off the old block, be the spitting image of.

□ **take a chair/seat** *take a seat, I'll be with you in a second* **sit down**, sit, seat oneself, settle (oneself), install oneself, plant oneself, ensconce oneself, plump oneself down, plop oneself down; flump, perch; *informal* take a pew, plonk oneself down.

□ **take against** *Bernard soon took against the idea* **take a dislike to**, feel hostile towards, view with disfavour, look askance on, become unfriendly towards.

□ **take something apart** *we took the machines apart several times* **dismantle**, pull/take to pieces, pull/take to bits, pull apart, disassemble, break up; tear down, demolish, destroy, pulverize, wreck, smash, shatter.
OPPOSITES put together, assemble.

□ **take someone/something apart** (*informal*) *she was relishing the sight of me being taken apart by the director* **criticize**, attack, censure, condemn, denigrate, find fault with, pillory, maul, lambaste, flay, savage; *informal* knock, slam, pan, bash, crucify, hammer, lay into, roast, skewer.
OPPOSITE lavish praise on.

□ **take someone back 1** *a dream which took me back to my first year in Vienna* **evoke**, awaken/evoke one's memories of, remind one of, put one in mind of, conjure up, summon up, call up; echo, suggest, smack of.
2 *if she apologizes I will take her back* **be reconciled to**, forgive, pardon, excuse, exonerate, absolve; accept back, welcome, receive; let bygones be bygones, forgive and forget, bury the hatchet.

□ **take something back 1** *I take back every word I said* **retract**, withdraw, renounce, disclaim, disown, unsay, disavow, recant, abjure, repudiate, override; back-pedal.
OPPOSITE stand by.
2 *I must take the keys back to the steward* **return**, carry back, bring back, fetch back, give back, hand back, send back, restore, remit.
OPPOSITES keep, hang on to.
3 *I'd damaged the box so the shop wouldn't take it back* **accept back**, give a refund for, exchange, trade, swap.
4 *in 1997 the Chinese took back Hong Kong* **regain**, repossess, reclaim, retrieve, recover, recoup, restore, get back; recapture, reconquer.
OPPOSITES give away, cede.

□ **take someone down a peg or two**. *See* PEG.

□ **take something down 1** *the policeman took down her particulars* **write down**, note down, make a note of, jot down, set down, mark down, record, put on record, commit to paper, put in black and white, register, draft, document, minute, pen.
2 *we took down the lighting rig at the end of the shoot* **remove**, dismantle, disassemble, unfasten, separate, take apart, take to pieces, take out, disconnect; demolish, tear down, level, raze.
OPPOSITE leave in place.
3 *they insisted he take down the flag* **pull down**, let down, haul down, move down, lower, drop, let fall, let sink.
OPPOSITES pull up, haul up.

□ **take someone in 1** *Mrs Smith took in paying guests* **accommodate**, board, house, feed, put up, take care of, admit, let in, receive, welcome, take, billet, harbour.
OPPOSITE turn someone away.
2 *you were taken in by an elaborate trick* **deceive**, delude, hoodwink, mislead, trick, dupe, fool, cheat, defraud, swindle, outwit, gull, humbug, bluff, hoax, bamboozle; *informal* con, bilk, pull the wool over someone's eyes, put one over on; *archaic* cozen.

□ **take something in 1** *at first she could hardly take in the news* **comprehend**, understand, grasp, follow, absorb, soak in, assimilate, make out; *informal* get.
2 *this route takes in some of the most dramatic cliffs in Britain* **include**, encompass, embrace, contain, comprise, cover, incorporate, embody, comprehend, subsume, envelop; digest, assimilate; admit, hold.

□ **take someone in hand** *someone has to take him in hand* **control**, have authority over, be in charge of, direct, preside over, lead, dominate, master; **reform**, improve, correct, change, make better, rehabilitate.

□ **take something in hand** *the time has come to take matters in hand* **deal with**, apply oneself to, address oneself to, get to grips with, get stuck into, busy oneself with, set one's hand to, grapple with, take on, attend to, see to, sort out, take care of, pursue, handle, manage; start on, embark on; *formal* commence.

□ **take it out of** *I'd had no idea how much hauling one of those things around would take it out of you* **exhaust**, drain, enervate, tire, fatigue, wear out, weary, debilitate, jade; *informal* fag out, whack, bush, knacker, poop.

□ **take off 1** *I walked up to the horse, but he took off at a great speed* **run away**, run off, flee, abscond, take flight, decamp, disappear, leave, go, depart, make off, bolt, make a run/break for it, take to one's heels, beat a hasty retreat, make a quick exit, make one's getaway, escape, head for the hills; *informal* split, beat it, clear off, clear out, skedaddle, vamoose, hightail it, light out.
OPPOSITE stay put.
2 *the plane took off* **become airborne**, leave the ground, take to the air, take wing; be launched, lift off, blast off.
OPPOSITES land, touch down.
3 *the idea really took off* **succeed**, do well, become popular, catch on, progress, prosper, flourish, thrive, boom, turn out well, work (out).
OPPOSITES fail, flop.

□ **take someone off** *he takes off the Prime Minister very well* **mimic**, impersonate, imitate, ape, parody, mock, caricature, satirize, burlesque, lampoon, ridicule; *informal* spoof, do, send up.

□ **take oneself off** *I took myself off to the office* **withdraw**, retire, take one's leave, make one's departure, leave, exit, depart, go away, pull out, quit, make oneself scarce; *informal* clear off, clear out.
OPPOSITE stay put.

□ **take something off 1** *they'd put a tinned steak and kidney pudding in the oven and forgotten to take its lid off* **detach**, remove, pull off; cut off, clip off, hack off, chop off, prune off, nip off; extract, sever, separate.
OPPOSITE leave on.
2 *she took off her clothes and folded them carefully* **remove**, doff, discard, strip off, peel off, throw off, divest oneself of.
OPPOSITE put on.
3 *it might help to take a pound or two off the price* **deduct**, subtract, take away, remove.

□ **take on** (*Brit. informal*) *don't take on so!* **get upset**, make a fuss, break down, get excited, go too far, lose one's sense of proportion, overreact; *informal* lose one's cool, get in a tizzy.
OPPOSITE keep calm.

□ **take someone on 1** *they could find no major challenger to take him on* **compete against**, oppose, challenge, confront, face, fight, pit/match oneself against, vie with, contend with/against, battle with/against, struggle against, take up cudgels against, stand up to, go head to head against.
2 *the Home Office took on extra staff* **engage**, hire, employ, enrol, enlist, sign up, take into employment, put on the payroll; *informal* take on board.
OPPOSITES fire, dismiss.

□ **take something on 1** *he took on additional responsibility* **undertake**, accept, take on oneself, tackle, turn one's hand to, adopt, assume, shoulder, embrace, acquire, carry, bear, support; *informal* have a go at.
2 *in this polarized society, even the narrowest psychological study took on political meaning* **acquire**, assume, come to have, come by.
OPPOSITES abandon, give up.

□ **take someone out** *the very first night he took her out, Frank proposed to her* **go out with**, escort, partner, accompany, go with; romance, court, woo, go courting with; *informal* date, see, go steady with.

□ **take someone/something out** (*informal*) *they were taken out by a sniper* **kill**, murder, assassinate, put to death, do away with, put an end to, get rid of, dispatch, execute, finish off, eliminate, exterminate, terminate; **destroy**, obliterate, annihilate; *informal* do in, bump off, rub out, wipe out, hit, mow down, top; *literary* slay.

□ **take something out** *that tooth will need to be taken out* **extract**, remove, pull (out), yank out, tug out, pluck out, prise out, separate, detach, draw; *Brit. informal* hoick out.
OPPOSITE put in.

□ **take something over** *she took over the editorship in 1989* **assume control of**, take control of, gain control of, take charge of, take command of, assume responsibility for; assume, acquire, gain, appropriate, be elevated to.

□ **take one's time** *he took his time going through the papers* **go slowly**, not hurry, be leisurely, proceed in a leisurely fashion, dally, dawdle, delay, linger, go at a snail's pace, drag one's feet, waste time, while away time, kill time; *informal* dilly-dally; *dated* tarry.
OPPOSITES hurry, rush.

□ **take to 1** *after being mugged a few months back, he had taken to carrying his money in different parts of his clothing* **make a habit of**, resort to, turn to, have recourse to, begin, start; *formal* commence.
OPPOSITE stop.
2 *Ruth took to Mrs Taylor the moment she opened the door* **develop a liking for**, like, get on with, become friendly with; *informal* take a shine to.
OPPOSITE dislike.
3 *the dog has really taken to hurdles racing* **become good at**, develop an ability/aptitude for, be suitable for; develop a liking for, like, enjoy, become interested in.

□ **take something up 1** *we took up our bags and left* **pick up**, grab, scoop up, gather up, snatch up, swoop up; carry; lift up, raise, uplift, heft, heave, elevate.
OPPOSITES put down, drop.
2 *in the thirties he took up abstract painting* **become involved in**, become interested in, engage in, participate in, take part in, practise, follow; begin, start; *formal* commence.
OPPOSITES give up, drop.
3 *she found that the meetings took up all her time* **consume**, fill, absorb, use, use up, occupy; cover, extend over; waste, squander, go through.
4 *her cousin took up the story* **resume**, recommence, restart, begin again, carry on, continue, carry on with, pick up, return to.
5 *he had decided to take up their offer of employment* **accept**, say yes to, agree to, accede to, adopt, get, gain.
OPPOSITE refuse.
6 *you'll need to take the skirt up an inch or two* **shorten**, make shorter, turn up; raise, lift, make higher.

□ **take up with** *she took up with a middle-aged art historian* **become friendly with**, become friends with, go around with, go along with, fall in with, join up with, string along with, get involved with, start seeing; *informal* knock about/around with, hang around/out with; *Brit. informal* hang about with.

▶ **noun 1** *the whalers' commercial take* **catch**, haul, bag, yield, net.
2 *he is determined to increase the state's tax take* **revenue**, income, gain, profit, money received, payments received; takings, proceeds, returns, receipts, profits, winnings, pickings, earnings, spoils; *Sport* gate money, purse; *Brit. informal* bunce.
3 *you need someone with a clapperboard at the start of each take* **scene**, sequence, filmed sequence, clip, part, segment.
4 *her wry and knowing take on sex and gender issues* **view of**, reading of, version of, interpretation of, understanding of, account of, explanation of, analysis of, approach to.

take-off ▶ **noun 1** *a chartered plane crashed soon after take-off* **departure**, **lift-off**, launch, blast-off, taking off; leaving, going; ascent, climbing, mounting, flight, flying, soaring.
OPPOSITES landing, touchdown.
2 *a take-off of a television talent show* **parody**, pastiche, mockery, caricature, travesty, satire, lampoon, mimicry, imitation, impersonation, impression, aping; *informal* send-up, spoof.

takeover ▶ **noun** *the takeover of a building society* **gaining of control**, change of ownership, purchase, acquisition, buying; buyout, coup, merger, amalgamation, incorporation, combination.

taking ▶ **adjective** (*dated*) *he was not a very taking person, she felt* **charming**, captivating, enchanting, beguiling, bewitching, alluring, fascinating, delightful, irresistible, magnetic, compelling, charismatic, pleasing, engaging, entrancing; personable, pleasant, agreeable, affable, congenial, genial, attractive, winning, lovable, sweet, prepossessing, fetching.
OPPOSITES unpleasant, repulsive.

takings ▶ **plural noun** *the day's takings* **proceeds**, returns, receipts, earnings, winnings, pickings, spoils; profit, gain, income, revenue, money received, payments received; *Sport* gate money, gate, purse.

tale ▶ **noun 1** *a tale of witches and warlocks* **story**, short story, narrative, anecdote, report, account, record, history; legend, fable, myth, romance, parable, allegory, epic, saga; *informal* yarn.
2 *Otto told me some shocking tales about Jean-Claude* **rumour**, gossip, hearsay, slander, talk, allegation, tittle-tattle, libel, story.
3 *they were exchanging racy stories and tall tales* **lie**, fib, falsehood, story, untruth, fabrication, fiction, piece of fiction; *informal* tall story, fairy story/tale, cock and bull story, shaggy-dog story, yarn.

talent ▶ **noun** *she demonstrated her talent for modelling with clay* **flair**, aptitude, facility, gift, knack, technique, touch, bent, ability, expertise, capacity, power, faculty; strength, strong point, forte, genius, brilliance; dexterity, adroitness, skill, cleverness, virtuosity, artistry.
OPPOSITES inability, clumsiness.

talented ▶ **adjective** *a talented musician* **gifted**, skilful, skilled, accomplished, brilliant, expert, consummate, master, masterly, first-rate, polished, artistic, adroit, dexterous, able, competent, capable, apt, deft, adept, proficient; *informal* crack, top-notch, top-drawer, ace, wizard.
OPPOSITES inept, talentless.

talisman ▶ **noun** **lucky charm**, charm, fetish, amulet, mascot, totem, idol, juju, phylactery; *archaic* periapt.

talk ▶ **verb 1** *I was talking to a friend who lives in the next town* **speak**, give voice, chat; chatter, gossip, prattle, prate, babble, rattle on, blather, blether, orate; *informal* yak, gab, jaw, go on, chew the fat; *Brit. informal* natter, rabbit, witter, chunter; *N. Amer. informal* rap, run off at the mouth; *Austral./NZ informal* mag.
2 *you're talking rubbish* **utter**, speak, say, voice, express, articulate, pronounce, enunciate, verbalize, vocalize.
3 *the music was quieter in here, and they were able to talk* **converse**, communicate, speak to each other, discuss things, have a talk, have a chat, have a tête-à-tête, confer, consult each other; negotiate, have negotiations, parley, palaver; *informal* have a confab, chew the fat/rag, jaw, rap; *formal* confabulate.
4 *he had been depressed, but had never talked of suicide* **mention**, make mention of, refer to, make reference to, speak about, discuss.
5 *I was able to talk English* **speak**, speak in, talk in, communicate in, converse in, express oneself in, discourse in, use.
6 *nothing would make her talk* **confess**, speak out, speak up, reveal all, inform, tell tales, tell, divulge information, tell the facts, give the game away, open one's mouth; *informal* come clean, blab, squeal, let the cat out of the bag, spill the beans, spill one's guts, grass, sing, rat.
7 *we mustn't keep meeting like this—people will talk* **gossip**, spread rumours, pass comment, make remarks, criticize.

□ **talk back** *he was always talking back to Dad* **answer back**, answer defiantly, be impertinent, answer impertinently, be cheeky, be rude, contradict, argue with, disagree with.

□ **talk big** (*informal*) *Henry was new to the job but he was already talking big* **brag**, boast, crow, bluster, exaggerate; *informal* blow one's own trumpet, shoot one's mouth off, swank, show off; *Austral./NZ informal* skite, big-note oneself.

□ **talk something down 1** *people constantly talk down the coal industry* **denigrate**, depreciate, deprecate, disparage, belittle, diminish, criticize; *informal* knock, pan, put down.
2 *the last Lancaster bomber was talked down to safety after the raid* **give landing instructions to**, bring to land, help to land.

□ **talk down to** *students on the course were talked down to as though they were children* **condescend to**, patronize, treat condescendingly, speak condescendingly to, speak haughtily to, look down one's nose at, look down on, put down, be snobbish to.

□ **talk someone into something** *he talked her into parting with an art collection worth £30,000* **persuade someone to**, convince someone to, argue someone into, cajole someone into, coax someone into, bring someone round to, talk someone round to, inveigle someone into, wheedle someone into, sweet-talk someone into, influence someone to, prevail on someone to; *informal* hustle, fast-talk.

□ **talk someone out of something** *I quickly talked him out of staying in Britain* **dissuade from**, persuade against, discourage from, deter from, stop, put off, advise against, urge against, divert from, argue out of.

▶ **noun 1** *he was bored with all this talk* **chatter**, chatting, chattering, gossiping, prattling, prating, gibbering, jabbering, babbling, gabbling,

rattling on, speaking, talking; *informal* yakking, gabbing; *Brit. informal* nattering, rabbiting, wittering.
2 *Polly felt in need of a talk with Vi, the person she turned to in an emergency* **conversation**, chat, discussion, tête-à-tête, heart-to-heart, dialogue, colloquy, parley, powwow, consultation, conference, meeting; *informal* confab, jaw, chit-chat, rap, gossip; *formal* confabulation.
3 (**talks**) *he held peace talks with his United Kingdom counterpart* **negotiations**, discussions; conference, summit, meeting, consultation, dialogue, symposium, seminar, conclave, colloquy, palaver, parley; bargaining, haggling, wheeling and dealing; mediation, arbitration, intercession, conciliation; *informal* powwow; *formal* confabulation.
4 *a firefighter giving a talk on her personal experiences* **lecture**, speech, address, discourse, oration, presentation, report, sermon, disquisition, dissertation, symposium; *informal* spiel.
5 *there was talk of a takeover* **gossip**, rumour, hearsay, tittle-tattle, news, report.
6 *the talk was of what their grandchildren were up to* **chat**, conversation, discussion, gossip; subject, theme, topic; information, news.
7 *baby talk* **speech**, language, dialect, jargon, cant, slang, idiom, idiolect, patois, accent; words; *informal* lingo.

talkative ▶ adjective *a talkative cab driver* **chatty**, **loquacious**, garrulous, voluble, conversational, gossipy, gossiping, chattery, chattering, babbling, blathering, gibbering, communicative; long-winded, wordy, verbose, profuse, prolix, rambling, gushing, effusive; *informal* gabby, mouthy, big-mouthed, with the gift of the gab, having kissed the blarney stone, yakking, gassy; *Brit. informal* able to talk the hind legs off a donkey; *rare* multiloquent, multiloquous.
OPPOSITES taciturn, reticent.

CHOOSE THE RIGHT WORD

talkative, chatty, loquacious, garrulous

- **Talkative** describes someone who enjoys talking and has more to say than the minimum required by circumstances or politeness (*a lively, talkative, intelligent man | he was the worse for drink, talkative and boastful*). It may be used approvingly or critically according to the situation—and whether the person in question has anything interesting to say.
- **Chatty** is used to describe both a person and what they say or write, and is typically approving. It tells us more about their informal, friendly *style* (*she is growing in confidence and is lively and chatty | she wrote a chatty letter to her mother*), although a *chatty* person usually has a lot to say.
- **Loquacious** is a more formal and less positive term, and often implies a tendency to talk excessively (*the Colonel was getting loquacious, relating his part in the campaign two years back*).
- **Garrulous** can be still more disapproving, implying that a person is loud or brash, but is by no means always so (*you're getting garrulous—what you need is sleep | everybody loved Harry, the garrulous comedian who could dominate any gathering*).

talker ▶ noun **1** *he's a good and persuasive talker* **conversationalist**, speaker, communicator.
2 *I think it's better to be a doer than a talker* **chatterer**, chatterbox, gossip; someone who is all talk.

talking-to ▶ noun (*informal*) *they gave Peter a talking-to about solving problems with words, not fists* **reprimand**, lecture, rebuke, scolding, reproof, reproach, rap on the knuckles, slap on the wrists, chiding, remonstration, upbraiding, berating, castigation, tirade, diatribe, admonition, admonishment, lambasting, censure, criticism, obloquy; *informal* telling-off, ticking-off, wigging, carpeting, tongue-lashing, dressing-down, rocket.
OPPOSITES commendation, pat on the back.

tall ▶ adjective **1** *a tall, thin man* **big**, **high**, large, huge, towering; colossal, gigantic, giant, monstrous, giant-size, Brobdingnagian; lanky, rangy, gangling, leggy, long-legged; *informal* long.
OPPOSITES short, small.
2 *tall buildings* **high**, big, lofty, towering, soaring, elevated, sky-high, sky-scraping; multi-storey.
OPPOSITE low.
3 *he's about 5 foot 8 inches tall* **in height**, high, from head to toe/foot.
OPPOSITE wide.
4 *a tall tale* **unlikely**, improbable, exaggerated, far-fetched, implausible, dubious, overblown, unbelievable, incredible, preposterous, outrageous, absurd; embroidered, dishonest, untrue; *informal* cock and bull.
OPPOSITES believable, credible.
5 *they thought that the deadline was a tall order* **demanding**, exacting, difficult, unreasonable, exorbitant, impossible.
OPPOSITE easy.

tally ▶ noun **1** *an officer keeps a tally of the amount due to each man* **running total**, count, record, reckoning, enumeration, register, account, roll, itemization, listing; census, poll.
2 *his tally of 1,816 wickets is still a county record* **total**, score, count, sum, result.
3 *the key is so cut as to form a tally with interior machinery* **counterpart**, match, mate, duplicate.
▶ verb **1** *these statistics tally fairly well with government figures* **correspond**, agree, accord, concur, coincide, match, fit, be in agreement, be consistent, conform, equate, harmonize, suit, be in tune, dovetail, correlate, parallel; *informal* square; *N. Amer. informal* jibe.
OPPOSITES disagree, differ.
2 *votes were being tallied with abacuses* **count**, calculate, add up, total, enumerate, compute; figure out, work out, reckon, measure, quantify, rate; *Brit.* tot up.

tame ▶ adjective **1** *a tame elephant* **domesticated**, domestic, not wild, docile, tamed, disciplined, broken, broken-in, trained, not fierce, gentle, mild, used to humans; pet; *Brit.* house-trained; *N. Amer.* housebroken.
OPPOSITES wild, fierce.
2 *a bunch of demoralized, tame civil servants always looking over their shoulders* **docile**, submissive, compliant, meek, obedient, tractable, acquiescent, amenable, manageable, unresisting, passive, mild, subdued, under someone's control/thumb, suppressed, unassertive, ineffectual.
OPPOSITE independent.
3 *every businessman needs a tame lawyer at his elbow* **amenable**, biddable, cooperative, available, willing.
OPPOSITE uncooperative.
4 *network TV on Saturday night is a pretty tame affair* **unexciting**, uninteresting, uninspired, uninspiring, dull, bland, flat, insipid, spiritless, pedestrian, vapid, lifeless, dead, colourless, run-of-the-mill, mediocre, ordinary, prosaic, humdrum, boring, tedious, tiresome, wearisome; **harmless**, safe, unobjectionable, inoffensive, mainstream; *informal* wishy-washy.
OPPOSITES exciting, adventurous.
▶ verb **1** *wild rabbits can be kept in captivity and eventually tamed* **domesticate**, break, train, master, subdue, subjugate, bring to heel, enslave.
2 *Christine had learned to tame her bad temper* **subdue**, curb, control, calm, master, bring to heel, tone down, water down, moderate, mitigate, tranquillize, overcome, discipline, suppress, repress, mollify, humble, cow, pacify, mellow, mute, temper, soften, bridle, get the better of, get a grip on; *informal* lick.

tamper ▶ verb **1** *she saw youths* ***tampering with*** *her neighbour's car* **interfere**, **monkey around**, meddle, tinker, fiddle (about/around), fool about/around, play about/around, toy, trifle, dabble; do mischief to, doctor, alter, change, adjust, damage, do damage to, harm, deface, vandalize, ruin; *informal* mess about/around; *Brit. informal* muck about/around.
2 *there's evidence that the defendant* ***tampered with*** *the jury* **influence**, get at, rig, manipulate, bribe, corrupt, bias, pervert; *informal* fix.

tan ▶ adjective *a tan waistcoat* **yellowish-brown**, brownish-yellow, light brown, pale brown, tawny.
▶ verb **1** *using a sunscreen means that you won't burn before you tan* **become suntanned**, take a suntan/tan, brown, go/become brown, bronze.
2 (*informal*) *if Mickey so much as touches a fishing net, I'll tan his hide* **thrash**, beat, wallop, belt, strap, spank, whip, lash, leather, cane, flog, flail, flagellate, horsewhip, birch, switch, flay; *informal* give someone a hiding, lam, larrup.

tang ▶ noun **1** *liven up your cooking with the tang of fresh lemons* **flavour**, taste, savour; **sharpness**, zest, zestiness, bite, edge, smack, piquancy, spice, spiciness, relish, tastiness; *informal* zip, punch, ginger, kick, pep.
2 *Caroline could smell the tang of the sea* **smell**, odour, aroma, fragrance, perfume, redolence.
3 *I wore a tang of aftershave* **trace**, touch, hint, whiff, suggestion, dab, smack, smattering.

tangible ▶ adjective **1** *if you purchase a tangible object, rather than a service, VAT is usually included in the price* **touchable**, palpable, tactile, material, physical, real, substantial, corporeal, solid, concrete; visible, noticeable.
OPPOSITE intangible.
2 *organizations want to see tangible benefits from their investment in technology* **real**, actual, solid, concrete, substantial, hard, well defined, definite, well documented, clear, clear-cut, distinct, manifest, evident, obvious, striking, indisputable, undoubted, unmistakable, positive, perceptible, verifiable, appreciable, measurable, discernible, intelligible.
OPPOSITES abstract, theoretical.

tangle ▶ verb **1** *Miles found himself tangled in coils of rope | the wool got* ***tangled up*** *in a big knot* **entangle**, snarl, catch, entwine, intertwine, intertwist, twist, ravel, knot, enmesh, coil, mat, jumble, muddle.
OPPOSITES untangle, disentangle, unravel.
2 *he was suffering from minor injuries after tangling with his old rival* **come into conflict**, become involved, have a dispute, dispute, argue, quarrel, fight, row, wrangle, squabble, contend, cross swords, lock horns.
▶ noun **1** *a tangle of branches* **snarl**, mass, mat, cluster, knot, mesh, disorder, thatch, web.
2 *the home team's defence got into an awful tangle* **muddle**, jumble, mix-up, confusion, entanglement, mishmash, shambles, scramble.

T

tangled ▶ adjective **1** *her tangled hair* **ravelled**, entangled, snarled (up), entwined, intertwisted, twisted, knotted, knotty, enmeshed, coiled, matted, tangly, messy, muddled; tousled, uncombed, unkempt, ratty; *informal* mussed up.
2 *a tangled bureaucratic mess* **confused**, jumbled, mixed up, messy, chaotic, scrambled, complicated, involved, convoluted, complex, intricate, knotty, tortuous, devious, maze-like, labyrinthine; *rare* involute, involuted.
OPPOSITES simple, straightforward.

tangy ▶ adjective *a tangy orange cake* **sharp-flavoured**, sharp, zesty, acid, acidic, tart, sour, bitter, harsh, biting, piquant, spicy, tasty, flavoursome, pungent.
OPPOSITES sweet; bland.

tank ▶ noun **1** *a hot water tank* **container**, receptacle, vat, cistern, barrel, storage chamber, repository, reservoir, holder, basin.
2 *a tank full of small fish* **aquarium**, bowl.
3 *they made use of tanks, artillery, and heavy weapons* **armoured vehicle**, armoured car, combat vehicle; *German* Panzer.

tantalize ▶ verb *I was tantalized by the mysterious secrets of her diary* **tease**, torment, torture, bait; tempt, entice, lure, titillate, intrigue, allure, beguile; flirt with, excite, fascinate, make someone's mouth water, lead on, keep hanging on.
OPPOSITES gratify, satisfy.

tantamount ▶ adjective
□ **tantamount to** *launching an attack would be tantamount to committing suicide* **equivalent to**, equal to, amounting to, as good as, more or less, synonymous with, virtually the same as, much the same as, comparable to, on a par with, commensurate with, along the lines of, as serious as, identical to.

tantrum ▶ noun *she throws a tantrum when she can't get the toy she wants* **fit of temper**, fit of rage, fit of pique, fit, outburst, flare-up, blow-up, pet, paroxysm, frenzy, bad mood, mood, huff, scene; *informal* paddy, wax, wobbly; *Brit. informal, dated* bate; *N. Amer. informal* blowout, hissy fit.

tap¹ ▶ noun **1** *she turned the cold tap on full* **valve**, spout, stopcock, cock, spile; *N. Amer.* faucet, spigot.
2 *they were found attempting to place a phone tap in the embassy* **listening device**, wiretap, wire, bug, bugging device, hidden microphone, receiver.
□ **on tap 1** *there are about half a dozen beers on tap* **on draught**, cask-conditioned, real-ale, from barrels, not bottled/canned.
2 (*informal*) *trained staff are on tap from 9 a.m. to 9 p.m.* **on hand**, to hand, at hand, available, ready, handy, accessible, obtainable, in reserve, standing by.
▶ verb **1** *several barrels had been tapped to celebrate* **draw liquid from**, drain, bleed, milk; **broach**, open, pierce, puncture.
2 *in the cellar, butlers were tapping ale* **pour (out)**, draw off, siphon off, pump out, decant, extract, withdraw, remove.
3 *the party leaders say that their telephones are tapped* **listen in on/to**, wiretap, eavesdrop on, spy on, monitor, overhear; *informal* **bug**, snoop on, get on record.
4 *its resources were to be tapped for the benefit of all mankind* **draw on**, exploit, milk, make use of, put to use, use, utilize, open up, mine, turn to account.

tap² ▶ verb **1** *she tapped on Lucy's door* **knock**, rap, strike, beat, drum, peck.
2 *Dad leant forward and tapped me on the knee* **touch**, pat, nudge, strike lightly, slap lightly, jab, poke, dig, shove, hit.
▶ noun **1** *there was a sharp tap at the door* **knock**, rap, strike, beat, peck; knocking, tapping, rapping, drumming, patter, pattering.
2 *Jack was startled by a tap on the shoulder* **touch**, pat, nudge, light blow, light slap, jab, poke, dig, shove, pressure.

tape ▶ noun **1** *she produced a package wrapped in white linen, tied with tape* **band**, strip, strap, belt, binding, string, ribbon, stripe, braid.
2 *secure the bandage with tape* **adhesive tape**, sticky tape, insulating tape, masking tape, parcel tape; *trademark* Sellotape.
3 *they listened to tapes throughout the journey* **recording**, **cassette**, tape recording; audiotape, audio cassette; reel, spool; videotape, video cassette, video.
▶ verb **1** *there was a card taped to the box* **bind**, tie, strap, fasten, stick, seal, secure, fix, join, attach, tether; *trademark* Sellotape.
2 *they taped off an area around the scene of the explosion* **cordon**, seal, close, shut, mark, fence; form a ring around, put a cordon sanitaire around, isolate, segregate; quarantine.
3 *police taped his confession* **record**, make a recording of, tape-record, video-record, video, put on tape/video/cassette.
□ **have someone taped** *I had him taped from the start* **understand fully**, know all about, have all the details of, know the ins and outs of; *informal* have someone's number.

taper ▶ verb **1** *it has roundish leaves which taper at the tip* **narrow**, thin (out), become narrow, become narrower, become thin, become thinner, come to a point, attenuate.
OPPOSITES thicken, swell.
2 *at first there was a flurry of meetings, but these soon tapered off* **decrease**, lessen, dwindle, diminish, reduce, subside, decline, die off, die away, die down, fade, peter out, wane, ebb, abate, wind down, slacken (off), fall off, drop off, trail off/away, let up, thin out; weaken, wilt, slump, plummet.
OPPOSITE increase.
▶ noun *a lighted taper* **candle**, spill, wick, night light; *archaic* dip, glim, rushlight, wax light.

tardiness ▶ noun *the tardiness of the company's response* **belatedness**, unpunctuality, lateness, delay, retardation, dilatoriness.
OPPOSITES punctuality, timeliness.

tardy ▶ adjective *I was fired for being tardy too often* **late**, unpunctual, behind time, behind schedule, behind, behindhand, not on time, overdue, belated, delayed, running late; slow; dilatory.
OPPOSITES punctual, early, on time.

target ▶ noun **1** *the competitor must shoot targets at ranges of 75 to 200 yards* **mark**, bullseye, goal, aim.
2 *eagles can spot their targets from half a mile* **prey**, quarry, game, kill, bag.
3 *they exceeded their profit target last year* **objective**, goal, object, aim, end, desired result; plan, purpose, intention, intent, design, aspiration, ambition, ideal, hope, desire, wish, holy grail.
4 *they were the target for a wave of abuse from the press* **victim**, butt, scapegoat, dupe, recipient, focus, object, subject, fair game, Aunt Sally.
□ **on target 1** *the Arsenal striker was bang on target* **accurate**, precise, unerring, sure, true, on the mark; *informal* spot on.
2 *the project was back on target* **on schedule**, on time, on track, on course.
▶ verb **1** *the two men were targeted by a gunman* **pick out**, single out, select, choose, decide on, earmark, fix on; **attack**, aim at, fire at.
2 *each product is targeted at a specific market* **aim**, direct, level, intend, focus, position.

tariff ▶ noun **1** *the reduction of trade barriers and import tariffs* **tax**, duty, toll, excise, levy, assessment, imposition, impost, charge, rate, fee, exaction; (**tariffs**) customs (duties), dues.
2 *make certain that you understand the tariff for calls* **price list**, schedule, list of charges, rate.

tarnish ▶ verb **1** *gold does not tarnish easily* **become discoloured**, discolour, stain, rust, oxidize, corrode, deteriorate; become dull, lose its shine, lose its lustre, blacken, become black.
OPPOSITES brighten, polish.
2 *detergents and scouring powder can tarnish metal* **dull**, make dull, dim, blacken, make black, discolour, stain, rust, oxidize, corrode.
OPPOSITES brighten, polish.
3 *he thought such rash actions would tarnish his reputation as a scholar* **sully**, besmirch, blacken, smirch, stain, blemish, blot, taint, soil, befoul, spoil, ruin, dirty, disgrace, mar, damage, defame, calumniate, injure, harm, hurt, undermine, debase, degrade, denigrate, dishonour, stigmatize, vitiate, drag through the mud.
OPPOSITE enhance.
▶ noun **1** *he was removing tarnish from the candlesticks* **discoloration**, oxidation, rust, tarnishing, blackening, film, patina.
2 *this won't overcome the tarnish on Alan's personal reputation* **smear**, black mark, slur, stain, blemish, blot, taint, stigma, smirch, flaw.

tarry ▶ verb (*dated*) *they were not allowed to tarry, but were taken upstairs immediately* **linger**, loiter, procrastinate, pause, delay, wait, lag, dawdle; *informal* hang around/round; *Brit. informal* hang about; *archaic* bide.
OPPOSITES hurry, rush.

tart¹ ▶ noun *a jam tart* **pastry**, flan, tartlet, quiche, strudel; **pie**, patty, pasty.

tart² (*informal*) ▶ noun (*derogatory*) *she was a tart I had picked up on a street corner.* See **PROSTITUTE**.
▶ verb **1** *she came back to tart herself up for the evening* **dress oneself up**, make oneself up, smarten oneself up, preen oneself, beautify oneself, groom oneself; *informal* doll oneself up, titivate oneself.
2 *we must tart this place up a bit* **decorate**, renovate, refurbish, redecorate, retouch, modernize; smarten up; *informal* do up, do over, fix up, give something a facelift.

tart³ ▶ adjective **1** *cook a few tart apples* **sour**, sharp, sharp-tasting, tangy, bitter, acid, acidic, zesty, piquant, pungent, strong, harsh, unsweetened, vinegary, lemony, citrus, burning, acrid, acetic; *rare* acidulous, acetous.
OPPOSITE sweet.
2 *she regretted her rather tart reply* **acerbic**, sharp, biting, cutting, keen, stinging, mordant, astringent, caustic, trenchant, incisive, pointed, piercing, bitter, barbed, scathing, sarcastic, sardonic, acrimonious, nasty, rude, vicious, spiteful, venomous, wounding.
OPPOSITE kind.

task ▶ noun *he set himself the daunting task of writing a full-length book* **job**, duty, chore, charge, labour, piece of work, piece of business, assignment, function, commission, mission, engagement, occupation, undertaking, exercise, business, responsibility, errand, detail, endeavour, enterprise, venture, quest, problem, burden.
□ **take someone to task** *he took some experts to task for their optimistic predictions* **rebuke**, reprimand, reprove, reproach, remonstrate with,

upbraid, scold, berate, lecture, castigate, censure, criticize, admonish, chide, chasten, lambaste, nag, blame, arraign, call to account, haul over the coals, read someone the Riot Act; *informal* tell off, give someone a dressing-down, give someone a talking-to; *Brit. informal* tick off, carpet; *N. Amer. informal* bawl out, chew out.
OPPOSITES praise, commend.

CHOOSE THE RIGHT WORD

task, job, chore, duty

These words all apply to activities that people are obliged to do, whether they want to or not. See also **WORK**.

- **Task** is the broadest term, meaning 'a piece of work to be done' (*caring for dependent older people can be a daunting task | a new team manager was given the task of harnessing the club's talent*).
- A **job** is primarily the occupation by which someone earns their living, in the course of which they may regularly have to perform a number of *tasks* (*Father landed a job as a technical engineer | 200 jobs are at risk*). A single piece of work for which someone is paid may also be referred to as a *job* (*the mechanic quoted him £50 for the job*), as can the responsibility to do something (*it's your job to know what's going on*).
- **Chores** are tedious routine tasks (*help with everyday chores like shopping or housework*) or tasks that are felt to be unpleasant but unavoidable (*financial planning is seen as a nasty chore*).
- **Duties** are tasks that one has to do as part of one's job, especially continuing ones (*your duties will include operating the switchboard*). In the singular, *duty* is usually service performed because of legal or moral obligation (*military duty | I came because I considered it to be my duty*). It can also describe such a feeling of obligation itself (*a sense of filial duty*).

taste ▶ noun **1** *a blue cheese with a distinctive sharp taste* **flavour**, savour, relish, tang, smack.
2 *would you care for a taste of brandy?* **mouthful**, drop, bit, spoonful, sample, sip, nip, swallow, touch, sprinkle, trickle, soupçon; dash, pinch, morsel, bite, nibble, titbit, shred, modicum.
3 *it was a bit sweet for my taste* **palate**, sense of taste, taste buds, appetite, stomach.
4 *a millionairess with a taste for adventure* **liking**, love, fondness, fancy, desire, preference, penchant, predilection, inclination, partiality, leaning, bent, disposition, proneness; **hankering**, appetite, thirst, hunger, relish, soft spot, weakness.
OPPOSITE dislike.
5 *it was then that I had my first* **taste of** *prison* **experience**, impression, sample; exposure to, contact with, involvement with, familiarity with, participation in.
6 *the house was furnished with taste* **judgement**, discrimination, discernment, tastefulness, cultivation, culture, refinement, polish, finesse, elegance, grace, style, stylishness.
OPPOSITE tastelessness.
7 *we may reject advertisements on grounds of taste* **decorum**, propriety, correctness, etiquette, politeness, tact, tactfulness, diplomacy, delicacy, nicety, sensitivity, discretion, tastefulness; *French* politesse.
▶ verb **1** *Adam tasted the wine and nodded to the waiter* **sample**, test, try, check, examine, savour; sip, sup, nibble.
2 *he could taste the blood in his mouth* **perceive**, discern, make out, distinguish, differentiate.
3 *a kind of beer that* **tasted of** *cashews* **have a flavour**, savour, smack, be reminiscent; suggest.
4 *it'll be good to taste real coffee again* **consume**, drink, eat, partake of, devour.
5 *he tasted defeat for the first time* **experience**, undergo, encounter, meet, come face to face with, come up against; know, have knowledge of, sample, try.
WORD LINKS
relating to the sense of taste **gustative, gustatory**

tasteful ▶ adjective **1** *the decor throughout the house is simple and tasteful* **in good taste**, discriminating, fastidious, refined, cultured, cultivated, sensitive, restrained, harmonious, fitting, fit, becoming, pleasing, elegant, graceful, stylish, smart, chic, attractive, beautiful, pretty, charming, handsome, exquisite, aesthetic, artistic.
OPPOSITES tasteless, tacky.
2 *this video is artistic, tasteful, but powerfully erotic* **decorous**, proper, seemly, correct, polite, tactful, respectable, restrained, appropriate, modest; *French* comme il faut.
OPPOSITE improper.

tasteless ▶ adjective **1** *the vegetables were watery and tasteless* **flavourless**, bland, insipid, unappetizing, unflavoured, savourless, watered-down, watery, weak, thin, vapid, uninspired; mild, boring, dull, uninteresting.
OPPOSITES tasty, appetizing.
2 *his suite is lined with tasteless leather burgundy panelling* **vulgar**, crude, tawdry, garish, gaudy, loud, trashy, showy, ostentatious, cheap, cheap and nasty, gross, meretricious, inelegant; *informal* flash, flashy, tatty, tacky, kitsch, naff.
OPPOSITES tasteful, refined.
3 *a tasteless remark* **crude**, vulgar, low, gross, indelicate, uncouth, crass, tactless, undiplomatic, indiscreet, inappropriate, offensive, unacceptable.
OPPOSITES seemly, tasteful.

tasty ▶ adjective *a tasty meal* **delicious**, palatable, luscious, mouth-watering, delectable, toothsome, succulent, juicy, dainty; appetizing, inviting, tempting; piquant, pungent, spicy, flavoursome, flavourful, full-flavoured; *informal* scrumptious, yummy, scrummy, finger-licking, delish, yum-yum, moreish; *dated* flavorous; *literary* ambrosial.
OPPOSITES bland, insipid.

tatters ▶ plural noun *he was forced to wear tatters a beggar would scorn* **rags**, scraps, shreds, bits, pieces, bits and pieces, torn pieces, ragged pieces, ribbons, clippings, fragments.
□ **in tatters 1** *his clothes were in tatters* **ragged**, torn, ripped, frayed, split, tattered, in shreds, in bits, in pieces, worn down, worn out, worn to shreds, moth-eaten, falling to pieces, threadbare.
2 *her marriage was in tatters* **ruined**, in ruins, on the rocks, destroyed, finished, shattered, demolished, devastated, in disarray.

tattle ▶ verb **1** *they were tattling about him over their teacups* **gossip**, tittle-tattle, chatter, chat, chit-chat, prattle, prate, babble, blabber, jabber, gabble, rattle on, spread rumours, spread gossip, circulate rumours, spread stories; *informal* chinwag, jaw, yak, gab; *Brit. informal* natter, rabbit on, witter on; *N. Amer. informal* run off at the mouth.
2 *I would tattle on her if I had any hard evidence* **inform**, report, talk, tell all, spill the beans; accuse; *informal* squeal, sing, let the cat out of the bag.
▶ noun *that's a load of tabloid tattle* **gossip**, rumour, tittle-tattle, hearsay, prattle, scandal, small talk, chit-chat.

taunt ▶ noun *he would play truant rather than face the taunts of his classmates* **jeer**, gibe, sneer, insult, barb, catcall, brickbat, scoff, slap in the face; (**taunts**) teasing, taunting, provocation, goading, ridiculing, derision, mockery, sarcasm; *informal* dig, put-down.
▶ verb *the crowd taunted him about his marriage split* **jeer at**, gibe at, sneer at, scoff at, poke fun at, make fun of, get at, insult, tease, chaff, torment, provoke, goad, ridicule, deride, mock, heckle; *N. Amer.* ride; *informal* rib, needle, put down, hassle, rag, guy; *dated* make sport of.

taut ▶ adjective **1** *the rope went taut* **tight**, tightly stretched, stretched, rigid, stressed, not slack, not loose.
OPPOSITES slack, loose.
2 *his muscles remained hard and taut* **flexed**, tensed, tightened, hard, solid, firm, rigid, stiff, unyielding.
OPPOSITE relaxed.
3 *he glared at her with a taut expression* **fraught**, strained, stressed, tense, drawn, drained, sapped, fatigued, tired; *informal* uptight.
4 *a taut, pacy, absorbing tale of gang life* **concise**, controlled, crisp, pithy, sharp, succinct, compact, terse.
OPPOSITE verbose.
5 *he ran a taut ship* **orderly**, in order, in good order, in good condition, tight, trim, neat, well ordered, well regulated, well disciplined, tidy, spruce, smart, shipshape (and Bristol fashion).

tautology ▶ noun *his speeches are notable for tautology, such as 'safe haven'* **repetition**, repetitiveness, repetitiousness, reiteration, redundancy, superfluity, periphrasis, iteration, duplication; wordiness, long-windedness, prolixity, verbiage, verbosity; *rare* pleonasm, perissology.

tavern ▶ noun (*archaic*) **pub**, inn, public house, bar, hostelry, taphouse, alehouse; *informal* watering hole; *Brit. informal* local, boozer; *N. Amer. historical* saloon.

tawdry ▶ adjective *she had cheap, tawdry rings on her fingers* **gaudy**, flashy, showy, garish, loud; **tasteless**, vulgar, brash, crass, rubbishy, trashy, junky, cheap, cheap and nasty, cheapjack, paltry, worthless, shoddy, shabby, meretricious, plastic, tinselly, gimcrack, Brummagem; *informal* flash, tatty, tacky, kitsch; *Brit. informal* twopenny-halfpenny.
OPPOSITES tasteful, refined.

tax *See centre pages for list of* **Taxes**
▶ noun **1** *they will have to pay tax on interest earned by savings* **levy**, tariff, duty, toll, excise, impost, contribution, assessment, tribute, tithe, charge, fee; liability; customs, dues; *Scottish, Irish, & Indian* cess.
OPPOSITE rebate.
2 *a heavy tax on the reader's attention* **burden**, load, weight, encumbrance, demand, strain, pressure, stress, drain, imposition; responsibility, duty, onus, obligation, care, worry.
▶ verb **1** *the president pledged to tax foreign companies more harshly* **levy a tax on**, impose a toll on, charge duty on, exact a tax on, demand a tax on; assess, charge, tithe; *rare* mulct.
2 *Basil's constant whining and struggling was taxing her strength* **strain**, stretch, put a strain on, make demands on, weigh heavily on, weigh down; burden, load, overload, encumber, push, push too far; overwhelm, try, task, wear out, exhaust, sap, drain, empty, enervate, fatigue, tire,

T

weary, weaken, overwork.
3 *Curzon taxed him with starting a revolution* **confront**, accuse, call to account, charge, blame, censure, condemn, denounce; prosecute, bring charges against, indict, arraign, incriminate; *N. Amer.* impeach; *informal* point the finger at.
OPPOSITES clear, exonerate.

WORD LINKS
relating to tax **fiscal**

taxing ▶ **adjective** *it's quite a taxing job she has* **demanding**, exacting, challenging, burdensome, arduous, onerous, difficult, hard, tough, heavy, laborious, back-breaking, strenuous, rigorous, uphill, stringent; tiring, exhausting, enervating, draining, sapping, stressful, wearing, trying, punishing, crushing; *informal* murderous; *rare* exigent.
OPPOSITES easy, gentle.

tea ▶ **noun.** *See centre pages for list of* **Teas**

teach ▶ **verb 1** *she teaches children with special needs | I started teaching in 1961* **educate**, instruct, school, tutor, give lessons to, coach, train, ground, enlighten, illuminate, verse, edify, prepare, din something into, indoctrinate, brainwash; drill, discipline, put someone through their paces; *N. Amer.* teach school.
2 *I was teaching English in a boy's school* **give lessons in**, lecture in, give instructions in, inform someone about, familiarize someone with, acquaint someone with, instil, inculcate, explicate, explain, expound.
3 *teaching your teenager how to negotiate is implicit in the process of formulating a contract* **train**, show, guide, instruct, demonstrate to, give someone an idea, make clear; *informal* learn.

WORD LINKS
relating to teaching **didactic, pedagogic, educational, educative**

teacher ▶ **noun** *a history teacher* **educator**, tutor, instructor, pedagogue, schoolteacher, schoolmaster, schoolmistress, master, mistress, governess, educationalist, educationist; supply teacher; coach, trainer; lecturer, professor, don, fellow, reader, academic; guide, mentor, guru, counsellor; sophist; *Scottish* dominie; *Indian* pandit; *N. Amer., chiefly derogatory* schoolmarm; *informal* teach; *Brit. informal* beak; *Austral./NZ informal* chalkie, schoolie; *archaic* doctor, schoolman, usher; *rare* preceptor.

team ▶ **noun 1** *the village cricket team | the company's sales team* **group**, **squad**, side, band, bunch, company, party, gang, selection, crew, troupe, set, line-up, array; body, corps, cadre, partnership, alliance, working party, posse.
2 *a team of horses* **pair**, span, yoke, duo, set, rig, tandem.
▶ **verb 1** *the horses are teamed in pairs* **harness**, yoke, saddle, bridle, hitch up, couple.
2 *for the long, lean look, team a loose-fitting T-shirt with a pair of matching shorts* **match**, coordinate, complement, pair up.
3 *you could* **team up** *with another artist to produce a larger exhibition* **join (up)**, join forces, collaborate, get together, come together, band together, work together; unite, combine, cooperate, merge, link, ally, associate, amalgamate, integrate, fraternize, form an alliance, pool resources, club together.

tear[1] (rhymes with 'bear') ▶ **verb 1** *I* **tore up** *the letter* **rip up**, rip in two, pull apart, pull to pieces, shred.
2 *her tights were torn by the rough concrete* **rip**, ladder, snag.
3 *his flesh was torn* **lacerate**, cut (open), cut to pieces, cut to ribbons, gash, slash, scratch, claw, mangle, mutilate, hack, pierce, stab; injure, wound.
4 *the traumas have* **torn** *her family* **apart** **divide**, split, split down the middle, sever, break apart, disunite, rupture; *literary* rend, rip asunder, cleave; *rare* sunder, rive, dissever.
OPPOSITES unite, unify.
5 *Gina tore the book from his hands* **snatch**, grab, seize, rip, wrench, wrest, pull, pluck; *informal* yank.
6 *I was torn by guilt* **torment**, torture, rack, harrow, wring, lacerate; *literary* rend.
7 (*informal*) *Jack tore down the street* **sprint**, race, run, dart, rush, dash, hasten, hurry, scurry, scuttle, scamper, hare, bolt, bound, fly, gallop, career, charge, pound, shoot, hurtle, speed, streak, flash, whizz, zoom, sweep, go like lightning, go hell for leather, go like the wind; *informal* pelt, scoot, hotfoot it, leg it, belt, zip, whip, go like a bat out of hell, step on it, get a move on, get cracking, put on some speed, stir one's stumps; *Brit. informal* go like the clappers, bomb, bucket; *Scottish informal* wheech; *N. Amer. informal* boogie, hightail it, barrel, get the lead out; *informal, dated* cut along; *archaic* post, hie.
OPPOSITES stroll, amble.
□ **tear something down** *they tore down the old barn* **demolish**, knock down, pull down, raze, raze to the ground, flatten, level, bulldoze; take down, dismantle, disassemble.
OPPOSITES build, erect.
▶ **noun** *there was a tear in her dress* **rip**, hole, split, rent, cut, slash, slit; ladder, run, snag.

tear[2] (rhymes with 'fear') ▶ **noun 1** *tears ran down her cheeks* **teardrop**.
2 *tears of perspiration* **drop**, droplet, bead, globule.
□ **in tears** *he was so hurt by her attitude he was nearly in tears* **crying**, weeping, sobbing, wailing, howling, bawling, whimpering; tearful, upset; *Scottish* greeting; *informal* weepy, teary, blubbing, blubbering.

WORD LINKS
relating to tears **lachrymal**
inducing tears **lachrymose**

tearaway ▶ **noun** **hooligan**, hoodlum, ruffian, lout, rowdy, roughneck; *Austral.* larrikin; *informal* tough, bruiser, yahoo; *Brit. informal* rough, yob, yobbo, bovver boy, lager lout; *Scottish & N. English informal* keelie, ned; *Austral./NZ informal* roughie.

tearful ▶ **adjective 1** *Georgina was tearful* **in tears**, crying, weeping, sobbing, wailing, snivelling, whimpering; close to tears, on the verge of tears, with tears in one's eyes; emotional, upset, distressed, sad, unhappy; *Scottish* greeting; *informal* weepy, teary, blubbering, blubbing; *rare* lachrymose, larmoyant.
OPPOSITES happy, smiling, laughing.
2 *a tearful farewell* **emotional**, upsetting, distressing, sad, heartbreaking, heart-rending, sorrowful; poignant, moving, touching, tear-jerking, affecting, pathetic; *literary* dolorous.
OPPOSITE cheerful.

tease ▶ **verb** *the other girls teased her about her accent* **make fun of**, poke fun at, chaff, make jokes about, rag, mock, laugh at, guy, satirize, be sarcastic about; **deride**, ridicule, scoff at, jeer at, jibe at; taunt, bait, goad, pick on; *informal* take the mickey out of, send up, rib, josh, wind up, have on, pull someone's leg, make a monkey of; *N. Amer. informal* goof on, rag on, put on, pull someone's chain, razz, fun, shuck; *Austral./NZ informal* poke mullock at, poke borak at, sling off at, chiack; *Brit. vulgar slang* take the piss out of; *Brit. informal, dated* rot; *dated* make sport of, twit; *archaic* quiz, smoke, flout at, rally.

technical ▶ **adjective 1** *an important technical achievement* **practical**, scientific, applied, applying science, non-theoretical; technological, high-tech, hi-tech; engineering.
2 *at first sight this might seem very technical* **specialist**, specialized, scientific; complex, complicated, esoteric.
3 *a technical fault* **mechanical**.

technique ▶ **noun 1** *different techniques were developed for dealing with the problem* **method**, approach, procedure, process, system, method of working, MO, operating procedure, course of action, plan of action, plan of attack, way, manner, mode, fashion, style; means, strategy, tack, tactic, line; routine, practice; *Latin* modus operandi.
2 *I was very impressed with his technique* **skill**, skilfulness, ability, capability, proficiency, expertise, expertness, mastery, talent, genius, artistry, art, craftsmanship, craft; aptitude, adroitness, adeptness, deftness, dexterity, dexterousness, knack, facility, competence; execution, performance, delivery; *informal* know-how; *dated* address.

tedious ▶ **adjective** *the work was tedious and physically demanding* **boring**, monotonous, dull, deadly dull, uninteresting, unexciting, unvaried, unvarying, lacking variety, mind-numbing, mindless, soul-destroying, soulless, humdrum, dreary, ho-hum, mundane, wearisome, wearying, tiresome, soporific, dry, as dry as dust, arid, lifeless, colourless, monochrome, uninspired, uninspiring, flat, plodding, slow, banal, vapid, insipid, bland, lacklustre, prosaic, run-of-the-mill, pedestrian, jejune, leaden, heavy; long drawn-out, overlong, long-winded, prolix, laborious, ponderous, endless, interminable; mechanical, routine; *Scottish* dreich; *informal* deadly, draggy; *Brit. informal* samey; *N. Amer. informal* dullsville.
OPPOSITES exciting, interesting.

CHOOSE THE RIGHT WORD

tedious, boring, monotonous, dull

See BORING.

tedium ▶ **noun** *to relieve the tedium of the days, they sang or told stories* **monotony**, monotonousness, tediousness, dullness, boredom, ennui, uneventfulness, lack of variety, lack of variation, lack of interest, lack of excitement, sameness, unchangingness, uniformity, routineness, humdrumness, dreariness, mundaneness, wearisomeness, tiresomeness, dryness, aridity, lifelessness, colourlessness, featurelessness, slowness, banality, vapidity, insipidity, blandness, prosaicness, jejuneness; long-windedness, prolixity, laboriousness, ponderousness, endlessness, interminableness; *informal* deadliness; *Brit. informal* sameyness.
OPPOSITES variety, excitement.

teem[1] ▶ **verb**
□ **teem with** *the pool was teeming with fish* **be full of**, be filled with, be alive with, be brimming with, be overflowing with, abound in, be swarming with, be bursting at the seams with; be packed with, be crowded with, be thronged with, be crawling with, be overrun by, bristle with, seethe with, be thick with, be crammed with, be cram-full of, be choked with, be congested with; *informal* be jam-packed with, be chock-a-block with, be chock-full with, be lousy with; *rare* pullulate with.

teem[2] ▶ **verb** *the rain was teeming down* **pour (down)**, pelt down, tip down, beat down, lash down, sheet down, come down in torrents/sheets, rain cats and dogs; *informal* be chucking it down; *Brit. informal* bucket down, come down in buckets/bucketloads, come down in stair rods, tipple down.

teenage ▸ adjective **adolescent**, teenaged, youthful, young, juvenile; *informal* teen.

teenager ▸ noun **adolescent**, youth, young person, boy, girl, minor, juvenile; *informal* teen, teeny-bopper.

teeny ▸ adjective (*informal*) *a teeny bedsit* **tiny**, minuscule, microscopic, very small, little, diminutive; micro, miniature, baby, toy, midget, dwarf, pygmy, Lilliputian; *Scottish* wee; *informal* teeny-weeny, teensy, teensy-weensy, weeny, itsy-bitsy, itty-bitty, eensy, eensy-weensy, tiddly, pint-sized, bite-sized, knee-high to a grasshopper; *Brit. informal* titchy, ickle; *N. Amer. informal* little-bitty.
OPPOSITES huge, big.

teeter ▸ verb **1** *Daisy teetered towards them in her high-heeled boots* **totter**, walk unsteadily, wobble, toddle; sway, rock, try to keep one's balance; stagger, stumble, reel, roll, lurch, pitch; *Scottish* stot.
2 *the situation teetered between tragedy and farce* **see-saw**, veer, fluctuate, oscillate, swing, yo-yo, alternate; waver, wobble; *N. Amer.* teeter-totter.

teeth *See centre pages for lists of* **Tooth Parts** **Tooth Types**
▸ plural noun. *See* TOOTH.

teetotal ▸ adjective *he's strictly teetotal these days* **abstinent**, abstemious; sober, avoiding alcohol; *informal* on the wagon, off the booze, off the sauce, dry.
OPPOSITES bibulous, boozy.

teetotalism ▸ noun **temperance**, abstinence, abstention, sobriety; *rare* Rechabitism, nephalism.

teetotaller ▸ noun **non-drinker**, abstainer; *Austral./NZ informal* wowser; *rare* Rechabite, nephalist, pussyfoot, white ribboner.
OPPOSITES drunk, lush.

telegram ▸ noun (*dated*) **telemessage**, cable, cablegram, telex; radiogram, radio-telegraph; *informal* wire.

telepathic ▸ adjective *as though he were telepathic, he glanced up at her* **psychic**, clairvoyant, with second sight, with a sixth sense.

telepathy ▸ noun **mind-reading**, thought transference; extrasensory perception, ESP; clairvoyance, sixth sense; psychometry.

telephone ▸ noun *Sophie picked up the telephone* **phone**, handset, receiver; *informal* blower; *N. Amer. informal* horn.
▸ verb *he telephoned me last night* **phone**, call, get someone on the phone, get on the phone to, get, reach, dial, make/place a call to; *Brit.* **ring up**, ring, give someone a ring; *informal* call up, give someone a call, give someone a buzz, buzz; *Brit. informal* give someone a bell, bell, give someone a tinkle, get on the blower to; *N. Amer. informal* get someone on the horn.

telescope *See centre pages for list of* **Telescopes**
▸ noun spyglass, glass; *informal* scope.
▸ verb **1** *the five steel sections telescope into one another* **slide together**, collapse.
2 *there was a grinding crunch of metal as the front of the car was telescoped* **crush**, concertina, squash, compact, compress.
3 *less recent employment experience can be telescoped into a short sentence or two* **condense**, shorten, reduce, abbreviate, abridge, summarize, precis, abstract, boil down, shrink, encapsulate; cut, truncate, curtail, trim; consolidate, conflate; *rare* capsulize.
OPPOSITE amplify.

televise ▸ verb *the BBC are televising the Cup Final* **broadcast**, screen, air, telecast, simulcast; transmit, relay.

television *See centre pages for list of* **Television Components**
▸ noun **TV**, television set; *informal* small screen; *Brit. informal* telly, the box, the gogglebox; *N. Amer. informal* the tube, the boob tube, the idiot box.

T

tell ▸ verb **1** *why didn't you tell me about this before?* **inform**, let know, notify, apprise, make aware, mention something to, acquaint with, advise, put in the picture, brief, fill in, break the news to; alert, warn, forewarn; *informal* clue in.
2 *I hope you are telling the truth | she was crying as she told the story* **speak**, utter, say, voice, state, declare; **communicate**, make known, impart, divulge, announce, proclaim, broadcast; **relate**, recount, narrate, give an account of, set forth, unfold, retail, report, chronicle, recite, rehearse, describe, portray, sketch, delineate, depict, paint, weave, spin.
3 *Corbett told him to leave* **instruct**, order, give orders, command, direct, charge, enjoin, call on, require; *literary* bid.
4 *I tell you, I did nothing wrong* **assure**, promise, give someone one's word, swear, guarantee; *dated* warrant.
5 *the figures tell a different story* **reveal**, show, be/give evidence of, disclose, indicate, convey, signify; display, exhibit.
6 *promise you won't tell?* **give the game away**, talk, tell tales, open one's mouth, tattle; *informal* spill the beans, let the cat out of the bag, blab; *Brit. informal* blow the gaff.
OPPOSITE keep a secret.
7 *he was afraid she would tell on him* **inform on/against**, tell tales on, give away, denounce, sell out, stab someone in the back; *informal* split on, blow the whistle on, rat on, peach on, squeal on, squeak on, stitch up, do the dirty on, sell down the river; *Brit. informal* grass on, sneak on, shop; *N. Amer. informal* rat out, drop a/the dime on, finger; *Austral./NZ informal* dob on, pimp on, pool, shelf, put someone's pot on; *rare* delate.
8 *it was hard to tell what he was thinking* **ascertain**, decide, determine, work out, make out, deduce, discern, perceive, see, identify, recognize, understand, comprehend; be sure, be certain; *informal* figure out, get a fix on; *Brit. informal* suss out.
9 *he didn't look as if he could tell a Renoir from a Renault* **distinguish**, differentiate, tell apart, discriminate.
10 *the strain of supporting the family was beginning to tell on him* **take its toll on**, leave its mark on, have an adverse effect on, affect.
□ **tell someone off** (*informal*) *my parents told me off for coming home late* **reprimand**, rebuke, reproach, scold, admonish, reprove, remonstrate with, chastise, chide, upbraid, berate, take to task, pull up, castigate, lambaste, read someone the Riot Act, give someone a piece of one's mind, haul over the coals, criticize, censure; *informal* give someone a talking-to, give someone a telling-off, dress down, give someone a dressing-down, give someone an earful, give someone a roasting, give someone a rocket, give someone a rollicking, rap, rap someone over the knuckles, slap someone's wrist, let someone have it, bawl out, give someone hell, come down on, blow up, pitch into, lay into, lace into, give someone a caning, blast, rag, keelhaul; *Brit. informal* tick off, have a go at, carpet, give someone a mouthful, tear someone off a strip, give someone what for, wig, give someone a wigging, give someone a row, row; *N. Amer. informal* chew out, ream out; *Austral. informal* monster; *Brit. vulgar slang* bollock, give someone a bollocking; *N. Amer. vulgar slang* chew someone's ass, ream someone's ass; *dated* call down, rate, give someone a rating, trim; *rare* reprehend, objurgate.
OPPOSITE praise.

teller ▸ noun **1** *a bank teller* **cashier**, bank clerk, clerk.
2 *a teller of tales* **narrator**, raconteur, raconteuse; storyteller; *Austral. informal* magsman; *rare* anecdotist, anecdotalist.

telling ▸ adjective *a telling critique of the military mind* **revealing**, significant; **convincing**, persuasive, forceful, striking, potent, powerful, strong, cogent, compelling; trenchant, weighty, important, meaningful, influential; effective, effectual.
OPPOSITES unimportant, insignificant.

telling-off ▸ noun (*informal*) *I've already had one telling off from Dad today* **reprimand**, rebuke, reproof, admonishment, admonition, reproach, reproval, scolding, remonstration, upbraiding, castigation, lambasting, lecture, criticism, censure; *informal* rap, rap over the knuckles, slap on the wrist, flea in one's ear, talking-to, dressing-down, earful, roasting, tongue-lashing, bawling-out, caning, blast, blowing up; *Brit. informal* ticking-off, carpeting, wigging, rollicking, rocket, row; *Austral./NZ informal* serve; *Brit. vulgar slang* bollocking; *dated* rating.

telltale ▸ adjective *a telltale blush spread over her face* **revealing**, revelatory, suggestive, meaningful, significant, meaning, indicative; unmistakable; *informal* giveaway.
▸ noun *'Steve did it, miss,' said a telltale* *N. Amer.* tattletale; *informal* **blabbermouth**, blabber, loud mouth, snitch, squealer; *Brit. informal* sneak; *Scottish informal* clype; *Austral./NZ informal* pimp; *dated* talebearer.

temerity ▸ noun *I doubt anyone will have the temerity to print these accusations* **audacity**, boldness, audaciousness, nerve, effrontery, impudence, impertinence, cheek, barefaced cheek, gall, presumption, presumptuousness, brazenness, forwardness, front, rashness; daring; *informal* face, neck, brass neck, brass; *N. Amer. informal* chutzpah; *informal, dated* hide; *Brit. informal, dated* crust; *rare* procacity, assumption.
OPPOSITES shyness, bashfulness.

temper ▸ noun **1** *Drew had walked out in a temper* **fit of rage**, rage, fury, fit of bad/ill temper, bad temper, tantrum, passion, paroxysm; fit of pique, bad mood, mood, pet, sulk; *informal* grump, huff, snit; *Brit. informal* strop, paddy; *Brit. informal, dated* bate, wax, skid; *N. Amer. informal* blowout, hissy fit; *archaic* paddywhack, miff.
2 *an uncharacteristic display of temper* **anger**, fury, rage, annoyance, vexation, crossness, irascibility, irritation, irritability, ill humour, ill temper, dyspepsia, spleen, pique, petulance, peevishness, pettishness, testiness, tetchiness, snappishness, crabbiness, resentment, surliness, churlishness; *Brit. informal* stroppiness; *literary* ire, choler.
OPPOSITE good humour.
3 *she struggled to keep her temper* **composure**, equanimity, self-control, self-possession, sangfroid, coolness, calm, calmness, tranquillity, good humour; *informal* cool.
4 *he was of a placid temper* **temperament**, disposition, nature, character, personality, make-up, constitution, mind, spirit, stamp, mettle, mould; mood, frame of mind, cast of mind, habit of mind, attitude; *archaic* humour, grain.
□ **lose one's temper** *suddenly, Maria lost her temper* **become very angry**, fly into a rage, explode, blow up, erupt, lose control, go berserk, breathe fire, begin to rant and rave, flare up, boil over; *informal* go mad, go crazy, go wild, go bananas, have a fit, see red, fly off the handle, blow one's top, blow a fuse, blow a gasket, do one's nut, hit the roof, go through

the roof, go up the wall, go off the deep end, lose one's cool, go ape, flip, flip one's lid, lose one's rag, lose it, freak out, be fit to be tied, be foaming at the mouth, burst a blood vessel, get one's dander up, go non-linear; *Brit. informal* go spare, go crackers, throw a wobbly, get one's knickers in a twist; *N. Amer. informal* flip one's wig; *Austral./NZ informal* go crook; *vulgar slang* go apeshit.

▶ **verb 1** *the steel is tempered by heat treatment* **harden**, strengthen, toughen, fortify; *technical* anneal.
2 *their idealism is tempered with realism* **moderate**, modify, modulate; tone down, mitigate, palliate, alleviate, allay, assuage, lessen, reduce, weaken, lighten, soften, cushion; qualify.

temperament ▶ **noun 1** *it was a particularly appealing prospect for a man of his temperament* **disposition**, nature, character, personality, make-up, constitution, complexion, temper, mind, spirit, stamp, mettle, mould; mood, frame of mind, cast of mind, bent, tendency, attitude, outlook; *archaic* grain, humour.
2 *he had begun to show signs of temperament* **volatility**, excitability, emotionalism, mercurialness, capriciousness, hot-headedness, quick-temperedness, hot-temperedness, irritability, impatience, petulance; moodiness, touchiness, sensitivity, oversensitivity, hypersensitivity.
OPPOSITES placidity, phlegm.

temperamental ▶ **adjective 1** *a temperamental chef* **volatile**, excitable, emotional, overemotional, mercurial, capricious, erratic, unpredictable, changeable, inconsistent, unstable, hot-headed, fiery, explosive, hot-tempered, short-tempered, quick-tempered, irritable, irascible, impatient, petulant, prima donna-ish, melodramatic; touchy, moody, sensitive, oversensitive, hypersensitive, highly strung, neurotic, easily upset; *informal* on a short fuse.
OPPOSITES calm, placid, phlegmatic.
2 *he had a temperamental dislike of all conflict* **inherent**, innate, natural, inborn, constitutional, deep-rooted, ingrained, congenital.

temperance ▶ **noun 1** *Davies was a devout Methodist and a strict advocate of temperance* **teetotalism**, abstinence, abstention, non-drinking, sobriety; prohibition; *rare* Rechabitism, nephalism.
OPPOSITES bibulousness, crapulence.
2 *the temperance of her lifestyle* **self-restraint**, restraint, moderation, self-control, self-discipline, lack of indulgence; abstemiousness, abstinence, self-denial, austerity, asceticism; *rare* continence.
OPPOSITES intemperance, excess, overindulgence.

temperate ▶ **adjective 1** *temperate climates* **mild**, clement, pleasant, agreeable, benign; gentle, balmy, fair.
OPPOSITE extreme.
2 *Charles was temperate in his consumption of both food and drink* **self-restrained**, restrained, moderate, self-controlled, controlled, disciplined; abstemious, self-denying, austere, ascetic; teetotal, abstinent.
OPPOSITES intemperate, immoderate.
3 *a lucid and temperate study* **balanced**, dispassionate, level-headed, sensible, rational, sober, sober-minded; *N. Amer.* sobersided.

tempest ▶ **noun 1** *the screaming tempest raged round the house* **storm**, gale, squall, hurricane, tornado, whirlwind, cyclone, typhoon. *See also* STORM.
2 *the tempest of World War II* **turmoil**, tumult, turbulence, ferment, disturbance, disorder, chaos, upheaval, disruption, commotion, uproar, storm, furore.
OPPOSITE tranquillity.

tempestuous ▶ **adjective 1** *the fine weather had broken and the day was tempestuous* **stormy**, blustery, squally, wild, turbulent, windy, gusty, blowy, rainy, thundery, rough, choppy; angry, dirty, foul, nasty, inclement; howling, roaring, raging, furious; *rare* boisterous.
OPPOSITES calm, fine.
2 *the increasingly tempestuous political environment* **turbulent**, stormy, tumultuous, violent, wild, 'lively', heated, explosive, uncontrolled, unrestrained, feverish, hysterical, frenetic, frenzied, frantic.
OPPOSITE peaceful.
3 *he was finding it harder and harder to live with such a tempestuous woman* **emotional**, passionate, intense, impassioned, fiery, temperamental; **volatile**, excitable, mercurial, capricious, unpredictable, erratic, hot-tempered, quick-tempered.
OPPOSITES placid, calm.

temple ▶ **noun**. *See centre pages for list of* **Places of Worship**

tempo ▶ **noun 1** *the tempo of the music quickened* **cadence**, speed, rhythm, beat, time, pulse; measure, metre.
2 *the tempo of life in Western society* **pace**, rate, speed, velocity.

temporal ▶ **adjective 1** *the temporal aspects of church government* **secular**, non-spiritual, worldly, profane, material, mundane, earthly, terrestrial; non-religious, lay; carnal, fleshly, mortal, corporeal; *rare* sublunary, terrene.
OPPOSITE spiritual.
2 *spatial and temporal boundaries* **of time**, time-related.

temporarily ▶ **adverb** *the girl was temporarily placed with a foster family* **for the time being**, for the moment, for now, for the present, in the interim, for the nonce, in/for the meantime, in the meanwhile; for a short time, for a short/little while, briefly, momentarily, fleetingly; provisionally, pro tem; *Latin* pro tempore, ad interim; *French* en attendant.
OPPOSITE permanently.

temporary ▶ **adjective 1** *temporary accommodation | the temporary captain* **non-permanent**, short-term, interim; **provisional**, pro tem, makeshift, stopgap; acting, fill-in, stand-in, caretaker; *Latin* ad interim, pro tempore.
OPPOSITE permanent.
2 *a temporary loss of self-control* **brief**, short-lived, momentary, fleeting, passing, impermanent, here today and gone tomorrow, transient, transitory, ephemeral, evanescent, fugitive; *rare* fugacious.
OPPOSITE lasting.

temporize ▶ **verb** *he'd been temporizing for weeks, hoping the problem would go away* **equivocate**, procrastinate, play for time, play a waiting game, stall, use delaying tactics, avoid committing oneself, avoid making a decision, delay, hang back, beat about the bush, be evasive, prevaricate, be indecisive, hesitate; *Brit.* hum and haw; *archaic* palter; *rare* tergiversate, use Fabian tactics.

tempt ▶ **verb 1** *they were not able to tempt any investors to bankroll the organization* **entice**, persuade, convince, inveigle, induce, cajole, coax, woo; *informal* sweet-talk, smooth-talk.
OPPOSITES discourage, deter, dissuade.
2 *vegetarian dishes unusual enough to tempt even the staunchest of meat-eaters* **allure**, attract, appeal to, whet the appetite of, make someone's mouth water; lure, seduce, beguile, tantalize, intrigue, captivate, draw.
OPPOSITES repel, put off.

□ **tempt fate** *to bale out at 250 feet was tempting fate* **run a risk**, live dangerously, play with fire, sail close to the wind, risk it.

CHOOSE THE RIGHT WORD

tempt, entice, lure

All these words are used of persuading someone to do something by offering them the prospect of something attractive.

- **Tempt** can imply that the person being persuaded knows that the attractive thing is wrong or unwise (*a large rucksack could tempt you to carry too much | a wealth of shops, bars, cafes, and restaurants have sprung up to tempt the visitor*). In the passive, it often means simply 'to be inclined' (*looking at the book one is tempted to ask what all the fuss is about*). The participial adjective *tempting* is common (*it's a very tempting offer*).
- **Entice** lacks the sense of persuading somone to do something that they know is wrong, and it typically has the sense of attracting someone in a particular direction (*the new crossing might entice drivers back onto the motorway*). It is often used in commercial or sexual contexts (*rival ferry companies cut fares to entice cross-Channel shoppers | she was busy laying plans to entice him away from his steady girlfriend*). The adjective *enticing* is common (*this is an enticing introduction to the subject*).
- To **lure** someone is typically to persuade them to go somewhere (*it would take more than Hollywood stardom to lure him away from his Sussex cottage*), and often with bad intentions (*he twice lured young women into his car*).

temptation ▶ **noun 1** *Mary resisted the temptation to answer her mother back* **desire**, urge, itch, impulse, inclination.
2 *he had no intention of exposing her to the temptations of London* **lure**, allurement, enticement, seduction, attraction, draw, pull, invitation; bait, decoy, snare, trap, siren song; *informal* come-on.
3 *the temptation of travel to exotic locations* **allure**, appeal, attraction, attractiveness, fascination.

tempting ▶ **adjective 1** *the tempting shops of the Via Nazionale* **enticing**, alluring, attractive, appealing, inviting, captivating, seductive; beguiling, fascinating, intriguing, tantalizing; irresistible.
OPPOSITES off-putting, uninviting.
2 *a plate of tempting cakes* **appetizing**, mouth-watering, delicious, succulent, luscious, toothsome; *informal* scrummy, scrumptious, yummy, finger-licking, delish; *Brit. informal* moreish; *N. Amer. informal* nummy.
OPPOSITE unappetizing.
3 *you look very tempting lying there* **seductive**, sexy, desirable, sexually attractive, provocative; nubile; *informal* beddable.
OPPOSITES undesirable, unattractive.

temptress ▶ **noun** *she'd behaved like a temptress in a fifties movie* **seductress**, siren, femme fatale, Mata Hari, Delilah, enchantress, sorceress, Circe, Lorelei; **flirt**, coquette, Lolita; *N. Amer. informal* vamp, mantrap.

ten ▶ **cardinal number** **decade**; *Music* decad, decuplet; *rare* tensome.

WORD LINKS

related prefixes	**deca-** (e.g. ***decathlon***), **dec(i)-** (e.g. ***decibel***)
relating to ten	**decimal, denary**
ten-sided figure	**decagon**
relating to ten years	**decennial**

T

tenable ▶ adjective *this politically convenient view is no longer tenable* **defensible**, justifiable, defendable, supportable, sustainable, maintainable, arguable, able to hold water, reasonable, rational, sound, viable, workable, plausible, credible, believable, conceivable, acceptable, imaginable.
OPPOSITES indefensible, untenable.

tenacious ▶ adjective **1** *he paused for a moment, but without releasing his tenacious grip* **firm**, tight, fast, clinging; strong, forceful, powerful, unshakeable, immovable, iron.
OPPOSITES loose, weak.
2 *he had a reputation for being a tenacious man | a tenacious battle to secure compensation* **persevering**, **persistent**, pertinacious, determined, dogged, single-minded, strong-willed, tireless, indefatigable, resolute, patient, purposeful, diligent, assiduous, sedulous, unflagging, staunch, steadfast, untiring, unwavering, unswerving, unshakeable, unyielding, uncompromising, insistent, importunate, relentless, unrelenting, inexorable, implacable; stubborn, intransigent, obstinate, obdurate, stiff-necked; *N. Amer.* rock-ribbed.
OPPOSITE irresolute.
3 *he had a tenacious memory* **retentive**, good; photographic.
4 *she struggled to free herself from the tenacious mud* **sticky**, adhesive, clinging, gluey, gummy, glutinous, viscid, viscous, mucilaginous; *Brit.* claggy; *Scottish & N. English* clarty.

tenacity ▶ noun *the tenacity with which he stuck to his story* **persistence**, pertinacity, determination, perseverance, doggedness, tenaciousness, single-mindedness, strength of will, firmness of purpose, strength of purpose, fixity of purpose, bulldog spirit, tirelessness, indefatigability, resolution, resoluteness, resolve, firmness, patience, purposefulness, staunchness, steadfastness, constancy, staying power, application, diligence, assiduity, sedulousness, insistence, relentlessness, inexorability, inexorableness, implacability, inflexibility; stubbornness, intransigence, obstinacy, obduracy, obdurateness; *German* Sitzfleisch; *informal* stickability; *N. Amer. informal* stick-to-it-iveness; *rare* continuance, perseveration.
OPPOSITES irresolution, lack of resolve.

tenancy ▶ noun *his tenancy of the property* **occupancy**, period of occupancy, occupation, period of occupation, residence, habitation, holding, possession; **tenure**, lease, rental, leasing, leasehold, renting; *rare* inhabitance, inhabitancy.
OPPOSITE freehold.

tenant ▶ noun **occupant**, resident, inhabitant; **leaseholder**, lessee, renter, holder; addressee; lodger, boarder; *Brit.* occupier, sitting tenant; *N. Amer.* roomer; *formal* dweller; *historical* feodary.
OPPOSITES owner, freeholder.

tend[1] ▶ verb **1** *I tend to get very involved in my work* **be inclined**, be apt, be disposed, be prone, be liable, have/show a tendency, be likely, have a propensity.
2 *younger voters tended towards the tabloid press* **incline**, lean, swing, veer, be drawn, gravitate, move; favour; show a preference for, be biased; *N. Amer.* trend.

tend[2] ▶ verb *his family had tended the sick for three generations | a well-tended garden* **look after**, take care of, care for, minister to, attend to, see to, wait on, cater to; watch over, keep an eye on, mind, protect, watch, guard; nurse, nurture, cherish; maintain, cultivate, keep, manage.
OPPOSITE neglect.

tendency ▶ noun **1** *his tendency to take the law into his own hands* **propensity**, proclivity, proneness, aptness, likelihood, inclination, disposition, predisposition, bent, leaning, penchant, predilection, susceptibility, liability; readiness; habit.
2 *this tendency towards cohabitation* **trend**, movement, drift, swing, gravitation; orientation, bias; direction, course, tide, turn.

T

tender[1] ▶ adjective **1** *he looked a gentle, tender man* **caring**, kind, kindly, kind-hearted, soft-hearted, tender-hearted, compassionate, sympathetic, warm, warm-hearted, feeling, fatherly, motherly, maternal, gentle, mild, benevolent, generous, giving, humane; susceptible, vulnerable; *informal* touchy-feely.
OPPOSITES hard-hearted, callous, unsympathetic.
2 *he placed a tender kiss on Fabia's brow* **affectionate**, fond, loving, emotional, warm, gentle, soft; amorous, adoring, amatory; *informal* lovey-dovey.
3 *tender love songs* **romantic**, sentimental, emotional, emotive, touching, moving, poignant, evocative; *Brit. informal* soppy.
4 *simmer for 25–30 minutes until the meat is tender* **easily chewed**, not tough, chewable, soft, edible, eatable; succulent, juicy, ripe; tenderized.
OPPOSITES tough, leathery.
5 *these flowers are tender* **delicate**, easily damaged, fragile, breakable, frail.
OPPOSITE hardy.
6 *her ankle was swollen and tender* **sore**, painful, sensitive, inflamed, raw, red, chafed; hurting, aching, throbbing, smarting, stinging, burning, irritated, bruised, wounded, injured.
7 *at the tender age of fifteen* **young**, youthful; early; impressionable, inexperienced, immature, unsophisticated, unseasoned, juvenile, callow, green, raw; *informal* wet behind the ears.
OPPOSITE advanced.
8 *the issue of conscription was a particularly tender one* **difficult**, delicate, tricky, awkward, problematic, troublesome, ticklish; controversial, emotive; *informal* sticky.
OPPOSITES uncontroversial, straightforward.

tender[2] ▶ verb **1** *she tendered her resignation* **offer**, proffer, present, put forward, propose, suggest, advance, submit, set before someone, extend, give, render; hand in.
2 *firms of interior decorators have been tendering for the work* **bid**, put in a bid, quote, give an estimate, propose a price.
▶ noun *six contractors were invited to submit tenders* **bid**, offer, quotation, quote, estimate, estimated price, price; proposal, submission.

tender-hearted ▶ adjective *a loyal and tender-hearted friend* **kind**, kindly, kind-hearted, tender, caring, compassionate, sympathetic, warm, warm-hearted, feeling, gentle, mild, benevolent, generous, giving, humane; fond, loving, affectionate, sensitive, soft-hearted, sentimental, soft-centred; *informal* touchy-feely.
OPPOSITES hard-hearted, callous, unfeeling.

tenderness ▶ noun **1** *I felt an enormous tenderness for her* **affection**, fondness, love, devotion, loving kindness, emotion, sentiment, sentimentality, emotionalism.
OPPOSITE dislike.
2 *with unexpected tenderness, Sven told her what had happened* **kindness**, kindliness, kind-heartedness, soft-heartedness, softness, tender-heartedness, compassion, compassionateness, care, concern, sympathy, warmth, warm-heartedness, fatherliness, motherliness, gentleness, benevolence, generosity, humaneness.
OPPOSITE callousness.
3 *meat of great flavour and tenderness* **succulence**, juiciness, softness.
OPPOSITE toughness.
4 *symptoms include abdominal tenderness and a high temperature* **sensitivity to pain**, soreness, painfulness, inflammation, rawness; ache, aching, smarting, throbbing, irritation, bruising.

tenet ▶ noun *this fundamental tenet of Marxism* **principle**, belief, doctrine, precept, creed, credo, article of faith, dogma, canon, rule; theory, component of a theory, thesis, conviction, persuasion, idea, view, opinion, position, hypothesis, postulation, presumption; (**tenets**) ideology, code of belief, teaching(s).

tennis ▶ noun. *See centre pages for list of* **Tennis Strokes**

tenor ▶ noun **1** *the general tenor of his speech* **sense**, meaning, theme, drift, thread, tendency, import, purport, intent, intention, burden, thrust, significance, message; gist, essence, substance, spirit; mood, character, vein, flavour; *archaic* strain.
2 *the even tenor of life in the village* **course**, direction, movement, drift, current, trend.

tense ▶ adjective **1** *the tense muscles of his neck* **taut**, stretched tight, tight, rigid, stretched, strained, stiff.
OPPOSITES slack, loose.
2 *by five o'clock, Loretta was feeling tense and irritable* **anxious**, **nervous**, on edge, edgy, strained, stressed, under a strain, under pressure, agitated, ill at ease, unrelaxed, in a state of nerves, in a state of agitation, fretful, uneasy, restless, worked up, keyed up, overwrought, highly strung, wrought up, strung out, jumpy, on tenterhooks, on pins and needles, with one's stomach in knots, fidgety, worried, apprehensive, upset, disturbed, panicky; *Brit.* nervy; *informal* with butterflies in one's stomach, a bundle of nerves, jittery, twitchy, in a state, uptight, wired, het up, stressed out, white-knuckled; *Brit. informal* strung up, windy; *N. Amer. informal* spooky, squirrelly; *Austral./NZ informal* toey; *dated* overstrung.
OPPOSITES calm, cool, relaxed.
3 *it was a tense moment for everyone* **nerve-racking**, stressful, anxious, worrying, fraught, charged, strained, nail-biting, worrisome, difficult, uneasy, uncomfortable; exciting, cliffhanging, knife-edge, dramatic, volatile, explosive; *informal* hairy, anxious-making, white-knuckle.
OPPOSITE relaxing.
▶ verb *Hebden tensed his cheek muscles* **tighten**, tauten, tense up, flex, contract, brace, stiffen; screw up, knot, strain, stretch; *N. Amer.* squinch up.
OPPOSITE relax.

tension ▶ noun **1** *the tension of the rope* **tightness**, tautness, tenseness, rigidity; pull, traction, stress, strain, straining, stretching; *rare* tensity.
OPPOSITES slackness, looseness.
2 *the tension was unbearable* **mental/emotional strain**, stress, anxiety, anxiousness, pressure; worry, apprehensiveness, apprehension, agitation, nerves, nervousness, jumpiness, edginess, restlessness; suspense, uncertainty, anticipation, excitement; *informal* butterflies (in one's stomach), collywobbles, jitteriness, twitchiness, the jitters, the willies, the heebie-jeebies, the shakes, the jumps, jim-jams, the yips; *Brit. informal* the (screaming) abdabs/habdabs; *Austral. rhyming slang* Joe Blakes.
OPPOSITE relaxation.
3 *the coup followed months of tension between the military and the government*

strained relations, strain, unease; ill feeling, friction, antagonism, antipathy, hostility, enmity.
OPPOSITE harmony.

tent ▶ noun. *See centre pages for list of* **Tents**

tentative ▶ adjective **1** *a tentative arrangement | this can only be a tentative conclusion* **provisional**, unconfirmed, unsettled, indefinite, pencilled in, preliminary, to be confirmed, TBC, subject to confirmation; **speculative**, conjectural, untried, unproven, unsubstantiated; exploratory, experimental, trial, test, pilot; *rare* provisory, provisionary.
OPPOSITE definite.
2 *he eventually tried a few tentative steps around his hospital room* **hesitant**, uncertain, cautious, unconfident, timid, hesitating, faltering, shaky, unsteady, halting; wavering, unsure, doubtful, diffident; *informal* iffy.
OPPOSITE confident.

tenterhooks ▶ plural noun
□ **on tenterhooks** *she had been on tenterhooks all night, waiting for Joe to return* **in suspense**, waiting with bated breath; **anxious**, nervous, nervy, apprehensive, worried, worried sick, on edge, edgy, tense, strained, stressed, agitated, in a state of nerves, in a state of agitation, fretful, restless, worked up, keyed up, overwrought, wrought up, strung out, jumpy, with one's stomach in knots, with one's heart in one's mouth, like a cat on a hot tin roof, fidgety, on pins and needles; *informal* with butterflies in one's stomach, jittery, twitchy, in a state, uptight, wired, in a stew, in a dither, all of a dither, in a sweat, in a flap, in a tizz/tizzy, all of a lather, het up, in a twitter, waiting for the axe to fall; *Brit. informal* strung up, windy, having kittens, all of a doodah; *N. Amer. informal* spooky, squirrelly, in a twit; *Austral./NZ informal* toey; *Brit. vulgar slang* shitting bricks, bricking oneself; *dated* overstrung.

tenuous ▶ adjective **1** *evidence that greenhouse warming had started was at best tenuous* **slight**, insubstantial, flimsy, negligible, weak, fragile, shaky, sketchy, doubtful, dubious, questionable, suspect; vague, nebulous, hazy, unspecific, indefinite, indeterminate.
OPPOSITES convincing, substantial, strong.
2 *a tenuous thread* **fine**, thin, slender, attenuated, delicate, gossamer, fragile.
OPPOSITE thick.

tenure ▶ noun **1** *they have a right to a fair rent and security of tenure* **tenancy**, occupancy, holding, occupation, residence; possession, title, ownership, proprietorship.
2 *his tenure as Secretary of State for Industry* **incumbency**, **term of office**, term, period of/in office, time, time in office.

tepid ▶ adjective **1** *tepid water* **lukewarm**, warmish, slightly warm; at room temperature; *French* chambré.
OPPOSITES hot; cold.
2 *his speech received a tepid response* **unenthusiastic**, apathetic, half-hearted, indifferent, cool, lukewarm, uninterested, unconcerned, offhand, perfunctory, desultory, limp, listless; *informal* unenthused; *Brit. vulgar slang* half-arsed.
OPPOSITES enthusiastic, passionate.

term ▶ noun **1** *a dictionary of current scientific and technical terms* **word**, expression, phrase, turn of phrase, idiom, locution; name, title, denomination, designation, label; *formal* appellation.
2 (**terms**) *a protest in the strongest possible terms* **language**, mode of expression, manner of speaking, phraseology, terminology; words, phrases, expressions.
3 (**terms**) *a legal document which sets out the terms of the contract* **conditions**, stipulations, specifications, provisions, provisos; restrictions, qualifications; particulars, details, points, clauses, articles.
4 (**terms**) *a policy offering the same cover and benefits on more favourable terms* **rates**, prices, charges, costs, fees; tariff.
5 *the President is elected for a single four-year term* **period**, period of time, time, length of time, spell, stint, duration; interval, stretch, run, phase; term of office, period of office, incumbency, administration.
6 (*archaic*) *the whole term of your natural life* **duration**, length, span.
7 *the summer term* **session**; *N. Amer.* semester, trimester, quarter.
□ **come to terms 1** *Charles V and Charles of Navarre came to terms* **reach (an) agreement/understanding**, come to an agreement/understanding, make a deal, reach a compromise, meet each other halfway, establish a middle ground, be reconciled.
2 *Philippa eventually* **came to terms with** *her situation* **accept**, come to accept, become reconciled to, reconcile oneself to, reach an acceptance (of), get used to, become accustomed to, adjust to, accommodate oneself to, acclimatize oneself to; learn to live with, become resigned to, make the best of; face up to.
□ **in terms of** *replacing the printers is difficult to justify in terms of cost* **with regard to**, as regards, regarding, concerning, as to, in respect of, with reference to, in the matter of, in connection with.
□ **on ... terms** *the two families were on friendly terms* **in a ... relationship (with)**, having ... relations (with), on a ... footing (with).
▶ verb *he has been termed the father of modern theology* **call**, name, entitle, title, style, designate, describe as, dub, label, tag; nickname; *rare* denominate.

terminal ▶ adjective **1** *a terminal illness* **incurable**, untreatable, inoperable; **fatal**, mortal, deadly, lethal, killing.
2 *terminal patients* **dying**, near death; incurable.
3 *the terminal tip of the probe* **end**, extreme.
OPPOSITES initial, first.
4 *a terminal bonus may be payable when a policy matures* **final**, last, concluding, closing, ultimate, finishing, terminating.
5 (*informal*) *you're making a terminal ass of yourself* **complete**, utter, absolute, total, real, thorough, out-and-out, downright, consummate, perfect, veritable; *Brit. informal* right, proper; *Austral./NZ informal* fair; *archaic* arrant.
▶ noun **1** *a railway terminal* **station**, last stop, end of the line; depot; *Brit.* terminus.
2 *the screen of a computer terminal* **workstation**, VDU, visual display unit, PC, input/output device; monitor, console, keyboard.

terminate ▶ verb **1** *treatment was terminated* **bring to an end**, end, bring to a close/conclusion, close, conclude, finish, stop, put an end to, put a stop to, wind up, discontinue, break off, cease, cut short, bring to an untimely end, abort; axe; *informal* pull the plug on.
OPPOSITES begin, start, commence, continue.
2 *the train will terminate in Stratford* **end its journey**, finish up, stop.
3 *the consultant assumed I would terminate the pregnancy* **abort**, end.

termination ▶ noun **1** *the termination of a contract* **ending**, end, closing, close, conclusion, finish, stop, stopping, stoppage, winding up, discontinuance, discontinuation, breaking off, cessation, cutting short; cancellation, dissolution; *Law* cesser, lapse; *informal* wind-up.
OPPOSITES start, beginning.
2 *she never considered having a termination* **abortion**; *rare* feticide.

terminology ▶ noun *medical terminology* **phraseology**, terms, expressions, words, language, parlance, vocabulary, nomenclature; usage, idiom, choice of words; jargon, cant, argot, patter, patois; *French* façon de parler; *informal* lingo, -speak, vernacular; *rare* idiolect.

terminus ▶ noun (*Brit.*) *the bus terminus* **station**, last stop, end of the line, terminal; depot, garage.

terrain ▶ noun *the rough, rocky terrain* **land**, ground, territory; topography, landscape, countryside, country.

terrestrial ▶ adjective *the idea of terrestrial events being driven by asteroids seems like science fiction* **earthly**, worldly, mundane, earthbound; *rare* tellurian, terrene, sublunary, subastral.
OPPOSITES cosmic, heavenly.

terrible ▶ adjective **1** *a terrible crime | he suffered terrible head injuries* **dreadful**, awful, appalling, horrific, horrifying, horrible, horrendous, atrocious, abominable, abhorrent, frightful, fearful, shocking, hideous, ghastly, grim, dire, hateful, unspeakable, gruesome, monstrous, sickening, heinous, vile; serious, grave, acute, desperate, grievous, distressing, lamentable; *rare* egregious.
OPPOSITES minor, negligible, insignificant.
2 *there was a terrible smell in the room* **nasty**, disgusting, very unpleasant, awful, dreadful, ghastly, horrid, horrible, vile, foul, abominable, frightful, loathsome, revolting, repulsive, odious, sickening, nauseating, nauseous, repellent, repugnant, horrendous, hideous, appalling, offensive, objectionable, obnoxious; noxious, evil-smelling, foul-smelling, smelly, stinking, rank, rancid, fetid, malodorous, acrid; *informal* gruesome, putrid, diabolical, yucky, sick-making, God-awful, gross, from hell, icky, stinky; *Brit. informal* beastly, grotty, whiffy, pongy, niffy; *N. Amer. informal* hellacious, lousy, skanky, funky; *Austral. informal* on the nose; *literary* noisome, mephitic; *archaic* disgustful, loathly; *rare* miasmal, olid.
OPPOSITES nice, delightful, lovely, pleasant.
3 *Blake was in terrible pain* **severe**, extreme, intense, excruciating, agonizing, unbearable, intolerable, unendurable, insufferable.
OPPOSITE slight.
4 *that's a terrible thing to say about anyone* **unkind**, nasty, unpleasant, foul, obnoxious, vile, contemptible, despicable, wretched, shabby; spiteful, mean, malicious, poisonous, mean-spirited, cruel, hateful, hurtful; unfair, uncharitable, uncalled for, below the belt, unacceptable, unwarranted; *informal* dirty, filthy, dirty rotten, low-down, beastly, off; *Brit. informal* out of order; *vulgar slang* shitty.
OPPOSITES kind, nice.
5 *I'm terrible at maths | Tom was a terrible father* **very bad**, dreadful, awful, frightful, atrocious, hopeless, poor, inadequate, inferior, unsatisfactory, laughable, substandard; *informal* crummy, pathetic, pitiful, useless, lousy, appalling, abysmal, dire; *Brit. informal* duff, chronic, poxy, rubbish, pants, a load of pants; *N. Amer. vulgar slang* chickenshit.
OPPOSITE brilliant.
6 (*informal*) *you're a terrible flirt | the place was in a terrible mess* **incorrigible**, outrageous, great, extreme; real, awful, dreadful, frightful, shocking; *informal* impossible, fearful; *Brit. informal* right, proper.
OPPOSITE a bit of a.
7 *I feel terrible—I've been in bed all day* **ill**, unwell, poorly, bad, indisposed, sick, queasy, nauseous, nauseated, peaky, liverish, out of sorts, green about the gills; faint, dizzy, giddy, light-headed; *Brit.* off, off colour; *informal* under the weather, rough, lousy, awful, dreadful, crummy; *Brit. informal* grotty, ropy; *Scottish informal* wabbit, peely-wally; *Austral./NZ informal* crook; *dated* queer, seedy; *rare* peaked, peakish.

OPPOSITE well.

8 *he still feels terrible about what he did to John* **guilty**, conscience-stricken, remorseful, guilt-ridden, ashamed, chastened, contrite, sorry, full of regret, regretful, repentant, penitent, shamefaced, self-reproachful, apologetic.

OPPOSITES untroubled, easy in one's mind.

terribly ▶ adverb **1** *she's terribly upset | that's terribly good of you* **very, extremely**, awfully, dreadfully, really, frightfully, exceptionally, exceedingly, immensely, thoroughly, uncommonly, remarkably, eminently, extraordinarily, incredibly, most, positively, decidedly, downright; heartily, profoundly; *Scottish* unco; *N. Amer.* quite; *informal* terrifically, tremendously, fearfully, desperately, seriously, devilishly, hugely, fantastically, madly, ultra, too ... for words, mucho, mega, majorly, oh-so, stinking; *Brit. informal* jolly, ever so, dead, well, fair, right; *N. Amer. informal* real, mighty, awful, plumb, powerful, way, bitching; *S. African informal* lekker; *informal, dated* devilish; *archaic* exceeding, sore.

2 *he played terribly* **very badly**, atrociously, awfully, dismally, dreadfully, appallingly, execrably, poorly, incompetently, inexpertly; *informal* abysmally, pitifully, crummily, diabolically, rottenly; *rare* egregiously.

3 *I shall miss you terribly* **very much**, greatly, a great deal, a lot, mightily; *informal* loads.

terrific ▶ adjective **1** *there was a terrific bang* **tremendous**, huge, massive, gigantic, colossal, mighty, great, very great, very big, prodigious, formidable, sizeable, considerable; intense, extreme, extraordinary, excessive, inordinate; *informal* mega, whopping, whopping great, humongous; *Brit. informal* whacking, whacking great, ginormous.

OPPOSITES slight, imperceptible.

2 (*informal*) *a terrific game of top-quality football | you look terrific!* **excellent, wonderful**, marvellous, magnificent, superb, splendid, glorious, sublime, lovely, delightful, first-class, first-rate, outstanding; consummate, perfect; *informal* super, great, smashing, amazing, fantastic, tremendous, phenomenal, sensational, incredible, heavenly, divine, gorgeous, dreamy, grand, fabulous, fab, fabby, fantabulous, brill, awesome, magic, ace, crack, cool, mean, bad, wicked, mega, crucial, mind-blowing, far out, A1, sound, out of this world, marvy, spanking; *Brit. informal*, brilliant; *N. Amer. informal* peachy, dandy, jim-dandy, neat, badass, boss, radical, rad, boffo, bully, bitching, bodacious, crackerjack; *Austral./NZ informal* beaut, bonzer; *S. African informal* kif, lank; *black English* dope, def, phat; *informal, dated* groovy; *Brit. informal, dated* capital, champion, wizard, corking, cracking, ripping, spiffing, top-hole, topping, beezer; *N. Amer. informal, dated* swell, keen; *vulgar slang* shit-hot; *archaic* goodly.

OPPOSITES dreadful, awful, horrible.

3 (*archaic*) *terrific scenes of slaughter and destruction* **dreadful**, terrible, appalling, awful, horrific, horrible, horrendous, horrifying, hideous, grim, ghastly, gruesome, frightful, fearful.

terrified ▶ adjective *it was the worst moment of my life—I was absolutely terrified* **petrified**, scared stiff, frightened/scared out of one's wits, scared witless, frightened/scared to death, terror-stricken, terror-struck, horror-stricken, horror-struck, paralysed with fear, horrified, panic-stricken, with one's heart in one's mouth, shaking in one's shoes, shaking like a leaf, frantic, hysterical, beside oneself; scared, frightened, afraid; *Scottish* feart; *informal* in a cold sweat, in a (blue) funk; *Brit. informal* funky, windy; *N. Amer. informal* spooked; *vulgar slang* scared shitless, shit scared, shitting bricks, bricking oneself; *dialect* frit; *archaic* afeared, affrighted.

OPPOSITES confident, unafraid.

terrify ▶ verb *the unspoken threat terrified her* **petrify**, scare stiff, scare/frighten someone out of their wits, scare witless, scare/frighten to death, scare/frighten the living daylights out of, scare/frighten the life out of, scare the hell out of, strike terror into, fill with fear, put the fear of God into, make someone's blood run cold, chill someone's blood, paralyse with fear, make someone's flesh creep, give someone goose pimples, make someone's hair stand on end, send into a cold sweat, make someone shake in their shoes; horrify, alarm, appal, panic, throw into a panic; frighten, scare; *informal* scare the pants off, make someone's hair curl, scarify; *Brit. informal* throw into a blue funk; *Irish informal* scare the bejesus out of; *N. Amer. informal* spook; *vulgar slang* scare shitless, scare the shit out of; *archaic* affright.

territory ▶ noun **1** *a tiny British territory on the outskirts of eastern Polynesia* **area of land**, area, region, enclave; country, state, land, dependency, colony, dominion, protectorate, fief, possession, holding; domain, county, district, zone, sector, quarter; soil; *archaic* demesne.

2 *mountainous territory* **terrain**, land, tract of land, ground, countryside.

3 *practically everyone else has been muscling in on my territory lately* **domain**, area of concern/interest/knowledge, province, department, field, preserve, sphere, arena, realm, world; *informal* bailiwick, turf.

4 *Sheffield was his territory* **sphere of operations**, area, section, stamping ground; haunts, purlieus; *informal* turf; *Brit. informal* patch, manor.

terror ▶ noun **1** *Ruth screamed in terror* **extreme fear**, dread, horror, fear and trembling, fright, trepidation, alarm, panic, shock; *informal* funk.

2 *she plunged into everyday activity to save herself from the terrors of her own mind* **demon**, fiend, devil, monster; horror, nightmare.

3 (*informal*) *he turned out to be a right little terror* **rascal**, devil, imp, monkey, wretch, scamp, mischief-maker, troublemaker; *informal* horror, holy terror; *Brit. informal* perisher; *Irish informal* spalpeen; *N. English informal* tyke, scally; *N. Amer. informal* varmint, hellion; *archaic* scapegrace, rapscallion.

terrorist ▶ noun bomber, arsonist, incendiary; gunman, assassin, desperado; hijacker; revolutionary, radical, guerrilla, urban guerrilla, subversive, anarchist, freedom fighter; *rare* insurrectionist, insurrectionary.

terrorize ▶ verb *families terrorized by racist thugs* **strike terror in/into**, fill with terror, scare, frighten, terrify, petrify; **persecute**, victimize, torment, tyrannize; **intimidate**, menace, threaten, oppress, bully, browbeat, cow; *Brit. informal* put the frighteners on, make it/things hot for someone; *N. Amer. informal* mau-mau.

terse ▶ adjective *he issued a terse warning* **curt**, brusque, abrupt, clipped, blunt, gruff, short, brief, concise, succinct, to the point, compact, crisp, pithy, incisive, short and sweet, economical, laconic, epigrammatic, summary, condensed.

OPPOSITES long-winded, verbose, rambling; polite.

> **CHOOSE THE RIGHT WORD**
>
> **terse, brusque, abrupt, curt**
>
> *See* BRUSQUE.

test ▶ noun **1** *we'll be conducting a series of scientific tests* **trial**, experiment, pilot study, try-out; check, examination, assessment, evaluation, appraisal, investigation, inspection, analysis, scrutiny, scrutinization, study, probe, exploration; screening; audition, screen test; *technical* assay.

2 *candidates may be required to take a test* **exam**, examination; paper, set of questions; *N. Amer.* quiz.

3 *the test of a good sparkling wine is the length of time the bubbles last in the glass* **criterion**, proof, indication, yardstick, touchstone, standard, measure, litmus test, barometer.

▶ verb **1** *during the summer, a small-scale prototype was tested | all donated blood is tested for antibodies* **try out**, trial, carry out trials on, put to the test, put through its paces, experiment with, pilot; **check**, examine, assess, evaluate, appraise, investigate, analyse, scrutinize, study, probe, explore; sample; screen; *technical* assay.

2 *such behaviour would severely test any marriage* **put a strain on**, strain, tax, try, make demands on, stretch; drain, sap; challenge.

testament ▶ noun *it is a testament to a decade of technological achievement* **testimony**, witness, evidence, proof, attestation; demonstration, indication, exemplification; **monument**, tribute.

testicles ▶ plural noun gonads; *N. Amer. informal* cojones; *vulgar slang* **balls**, knackers, nuts, rocks; *Brit. vulgar slang* bollocks, goolies.

testify ▶ verb **1** *you may be required to testify in court* **give evidence**, bear witness, be a witness, give one's testimony, attest; *technical* make a deposition; *Scottish archaic* depone.

2 *he testified that he had been threatened by a fellow officer* **attest**, swear, state on oath, state, declare, assert, affirm, avow, aver, certify; allege, profess, submit, claim; *technical* depose; *rare* asseverate.

OPPOSITE deny.

3 *the exhibits* **testify to** *the talents and versatility of the local sculptors* **be evidence/proof of**, attest to, confirm, evidence, prove, corroborate, substantiate, bear out; show, demonstrate, witness to, establish, indicate, reveal, bespeak; vouch for.

OPPOSITE belie.

testimonial ▶ noun **1** *Sir Hans drafted a glowing testimonial for him* **reference**, character reference, recommendation, letter of recommendation, commendation, endorsement, certificate of competence; *dated* character.

2 *in 1848 Airy received a testimonial from the Royal Astronomical Society* **tribute**, presentation, gift, trophy; memento, souvenir.

testimony ▶ noun **1** *Smith was in court to hear her testimony* **evidence**, sworn statement, attestation, affidavit; statement, declaration, assertion, affirmation, avowal, protestation; allegation, submission, claim; *technical* deposition; *rare* asseveration.

2 *the work is a testimony to his professional commitment* **testament**, proof, evidence, attestation, witness; confirmation, verification, corroboration; demonstration, indication, manifestation.

testing ▶ adjective *it was a particularly testing time for the organization* **difficult**, challenging, tough, hard; **stressful**, trying, wearing, taxing, demanding, exacting, onerous, arduous.

OPPOSITE easy.

testy ▶ adjective *he was testy, arrogant, and hard to get on with* **bad-tempered**, grumpy, ill-tempered, ill-natured, ill-humoured, dyspeptic, irritable, tetchy, irascible, peevish, crotchety, cantankerous, cross, fractious, disagreeable, pettish, crabbed, crabby, waspish, prickly, peppery, impatient, touchy, scratchy, volatile, crusty, liverish, splenetic, short-tempered, hot-tempered, quick-tempered, choleric; *informal* snappish, snappy, chippy, grouchy, cranky, on a short fuse; *Brit. informal* shirty, stroppy, narky, ratty, eggy, like a bear with a sore head; *N. Amer. informal*

peckish, soreheaded; *Austral./NZ informal* snaky; *informal, dated* miffy.
OPPOSITE good-humoured.

tetchy ▶ adjective *he can be very tetchy first thing in the morning* **irritable**, irascible, peevish, crotchety, cantankerous, cross, fractious, disagreeable, pettish, crabbed, crabby, waspish, prickly, testy, peppery, impatient, grumpy, bad-tempered, ill-tempered, ill-natured, ill-humoured, touchy, scratchy, volatile, crusty, dyspeptic, splenetic, liverish, short-tempered, hot-tempered, quick-tempered, choleric; *informal* snappish, snappy, chippy, grouchy, cranky, on a short fuse; *Brit. informal* shirty, narky, ratty, eggy, like a bear with a sore head; *N. Amer. informal* peckish, soreheaded; *Austral./NZ informal* snaky; *informal, dated* miffy.
OPPOSITE good-humoured.

tête-à-tête ▶ noun **conversation**, chat, cosy chat, talk, heart-to-heart, one-on-one, one-to-one; discussion, dialogue, duologue, consultation, colloquy, parley, powwow; *informal* confab, jaw, chit-chat, chinwag, gossip; *Brit. informal* natter; *N. Amer. informal* rap; *formal* confabulation.
▶ adverb *his business was conducted tête-à-tête* **privately**, in private; face to face, heart-to-heart; secretly, in secret, confidentially; *French* à deux.

tether ▶ verb *the horse had been tethered to a post* **tie**, tie up, hitch, rope, chain; fasten, secure; bind, fetter, shackle, restrain.
OPPOSITES unleash, release.
▶ noun **rope**, **chain**, cord, lead, leash; fetter, restraint; halter; *archaic* lyam.
□ **at the end of one's tether** *the poor man was clearly at the end of his tether* **at one's wits' end**, desperate, not knowing which way to turn, unable to cope; *N. Amer.* at the end of one's rope.

text ▶ noun **1** *a text which explores pain and grief* **written work**, book, work, printed work, narrative.
2 *the pictures are clear and relate well to the text* **words**, wording; subject matter, content, contents, body, main body, main matter.
3 *he sent all enquirers the text of Sir Derek's speech* **transcript**, script.
4 *academic texts* **textbook**, book; set book, set text.
5 *the text is taken from the First Book of Samuel* **passage**, extract, quotation, verse, line; reading, lesson.
6 *he took as his text the fact that Australia is a paradise* **theme**, subject, topic, issue, point, motif; thesis, argument.

textiles *See centre pages for list of* **Fabrics and Fibres**
▶ plural noun *hand-printed textiles* **fabrics**, cloths, materials.

texture ▶ noun *the quality and texture of the fabric* **feel**, touch; appearance, finish, surface, grain; quality, character; consistency; weave, nap.

thank ▶ verb **1** *the superintendent thanked him for his help* **express (one's) gratitude to**, express one's thanks to, offer/extend thanks to, say thank you to, show appreciation to.
2 *you have only yourself to thank for the plight you are in* **blame**, hold responsible.

thankful ▶ adjective **1** *Merrill closed the door, thankful that the evening was over* **relieved**, pleased, glad, grateful.
OPPOSITE disappointed.
2 *he was really thankful to her for coming to his aid* **grateful**, filled with gratitude, indebted, obliged, under an obligation, obligated, beholden.
OPPOSITE ungrateful.

> **CHOOSE THE RIGHT WORD**
> **thankful, grateful, appreciative**
> *See* GRATEFUL.

thankless ▶ adjective **1** *a thankless task* **unappreciated**, unrecognized, unrewarded, unacknowledged; unenviable, difficult, unpleasant, unrewarding, unprofitable, profitless, useless, fruitless, vain, futile; *archaic* bootless.
OPPOSITES rewarding, worthwhile.
2 *her thankless children* **ungrateful**, unappreciative, unthankful.
OPPOSITE grateful.

thanks ▶ plural noun *they expressed their thanks and wished her well* **gratitude**, gratefulness, appreciation; acknowledgement, recognition, credit.
□ **thanks to** *thanks to foreign loans, the economy was showing signs of recovery* **as a result of**, owing to, due to, because of, through, by reason of, as a consequence of, in consequence of, on account of, by virtue of, by dint of.
▶ exclamation *thanks for being so helpful* **thank you**, many thanks, thanks very much, thanks a lot, thank you kindly, much obliged, much appreciated, bless you; *informal* cheers, thanks a million; *Brit. informal* ta.

thaw ▶ verb **1** *the ice was beginning to thaw* **melt**, unfreeze, soften, liquefy, dissolve; *N. Amer.* unthaw.
OPPOSITES freeze, solidify.
2 *a frozen turkey may take up to two days to thaw* **defrost**.
OPPOSITE freeze.
3 *since I've been here, he's begun to thaw* **become friendlier**, become more genial, become more sociable, loosen up, relax, become more relaxed.

theatre *See centre pages for lists of parts of a* **Theatre** *and* **Plays** *(Types of Play and Drama)*
▶ noun **1** *there's a good play on at the theatre* **playhouse**, auditorium, amphitheatre, hippodrome, coliseum.
2 (**the theatre**) *what made you want to go into the theatre?* **acting**, performing; **drama**, the dramatic arts, dramaturgy, the thespian art, stagecraft, theatricals, theatrics; **show business**, the stage; *informal* the boards, show biz; *rare* thespianism, histrionics.
3 *the lecture theatre* **hall**, room, auditorium.
4 *over 200,000 American personnel were in the theatre of war by October* **scene**, arena, field/sphere/place of action; setting, site.

theatrical ▶ adjective **1** *a theatrical career* **stage**, dramatic, thespian, dramaturgical; **show-business**; *informal* showbiz; *rare* histrionic, theatric.
2 *Henry looked over his shoulder with theatrical caution* **exaggerated**, ostentatious, actressy, stagy, showy, melodramatic, overacted, overdone, histrionic, affected, mannered, artificial, stilted, unreal, forced; *informal* hammy, ham, campy.
OPPOSITES natural, unaffected.

theft ▶ noun *he was convicted of theft* **robbery**, stealing, thieving, larceny, thievery, robbing, pilfering, pilferage, purloining; shoplifting, burglary; raid, hold-up; appropriation, expropriation, misappropriation, embezzlement; (*in India*) dacoity; *informal* rip-off, smash and grab, snatch; *N. Amer. informal* heist, stick-up; *rare* peculation, defalcation.

WORD LINKS
compulsive theft **kleptomania**

theme ▶ noun **1** *a short speech on a theme of your choice* **subject**, topic, subject matter; matter, issue, question, concern; idea, concept, thread, motif, keynote, message; thesis, argument, text; gist, essence, core, substance, burden, thrust.
2 *the first violin takes up the theme* **melody**, tune, air, motif, leitmotif.
3 (*N. Amer.*) *students writing themes in French* **essay**, composition, paper, dissertation.

> **CHOOSE THE RIGHT WORD**
> **theme, subject, topic**
> *See* SUBJECT.

themselves ▶ pronoun
□ **by themselves**. *See* BY ONESELF *at* BY.

then ▶ adverb **1** *I was living in Cairo then* **at that time**, at that point, in those days; at that point in time, at that moment, on that occasion.
2 *she won the first and then the second game* **next**, after that, afterwards, subsequently, later.
3 *I'm paid a generous salary, and then there's the money I make at the races* **in addition**, also, besides, as well, additionally, on top of that, over and above that, moreover, furthermore, what's more, to boot; too.
4 *well, if that's what he wants, then he should leave* **in that case**, that being the case, that being so, under those circumstances, it follows that.

theological ▶ adjective *his theological writings* **religious**, scriptural, ecclesiastical, doctrinal; divine, holy; *rare* hierological.

theorem ▶ noun **proposition**, hypothesis, postulate, thesis, assumption, deduction, statement; rule, formula, principle.

theoretical ▶ adjective **1** *theoretical physics* **not practical**, conceptual, abstract, pure.
OPPOSITES practical, applied.
2 *a theoretical possibility* **hypothetical**, conjectural, academic, suppositional, speculative, notional, postulatory, conjectured, imagined, assumed, presumed, untested, unproven, unsubstantiated; *rare* suppositious, suppositive, ideational.
OPPOSITES concrete, actual, real.

theorize ▶ verb *Darwin theorized that the atolls marked the sites of vanished volcanoes* **speculate**, conjecture, hypothesize, take as a hypothesis, postulate, form/formulate a theory, propose, posit, surmise, suppose, guess; philosophize; *rare* hypothecate.

theory ▶ noun **1** *I reckon that confirms my theory* **hypothesis**, thesis, conjecture, supposition, speculation, postulation, postulate, proposition, premise, surmise, assumption, presumption, presupposition, notion, guess, hunch, feeling, suspicion; opinion, view, belief, thinking, thought(s), judgement, contention.
2 *the theory of quantum physics* **principles**, ideas, concepts; principled explanations; laws; philosophy, ideology, system of ideas, science.
□ **in theory** *in theory this method is ideal—in practice it is unrealistic* **in principle**, on paper, in the abstract, all things being equal, in an ideal world; hypothetically; *French* en principe.
OPPOSITES in practice, in reality.

therapeutic ▶ adjective *the therapeutic effects of acupuncture* **healing**, curative, curing, remedial, medicinal, restorative, health-giving, tonic, sanative, reparative, corrective, ameliorative, beneficial, good, salubrious, salutary; *technical* analeptic; *rare* iatric.
OPPOSITES harmful, detrimental.

therapist ▶ noun **psychologist**, psychotherapist, analyst, psychoanalyst, psychiatrist, mind doctor, head doctor; counsellor; healer; *N. Amer.* alienist; *informal* shrink, trick cyclist, head shrinker.

therapy *See centre pages for lists of* **Therapies** *and Branches of* **Medicine**
▸ **noun 1** *a wide range of complementary therapies* **treatment**, remedy, cure, remedial treatment, method of healing.
2 *he's currently in therapy* **psychotherapy**, psychoanalysis, analysis.

thereabouts ▸ **adverb 1** *all the land thereabouts was once in possession of the Vachel family* **near there**, around there, about there.
2 *they sold it for five million or thereabouts* **approximately (that number/ quantity)**, or so, or something like that, give or take a few, plus or minus a few, give or take a bit, in round numbers, not far off; *Brit.* getting on for; *Latin* circa; *N. Amer. informal* in the ballpark of.

thereafter ▸ **adverb** *thereafter their fortunes suffered a steep decline* **after that (time)**, following that, afterwards, subsequently, then, next.

therefore ▸ **adverb** *he was injured and therefore unable to play* **for that reason**, **consequently**, so, as a result, as a consequence, hence, thus, accordingly, then, that being so, that being the case, on that account; *Latin* ergo; *formal* whence; *archaic* wherefore, thence.

thesaurus ▸ **noun wordfinder**, wordbook, synonym dictionary/lexicon; *rare* synonymy.

thesis ▸ **noun 1** *the central thesis of his lecture* **theory**, contention, argument, line of argument, proposal, proposition, premise, assumption, presumption, hypothesis, postulation, surmise, supposition; belief, idea, notion, opinion, view; theme, subject, topic, text, matter; theorem.
2 *a doctoral thesis* **dissertation**, essay, paper, treatise, disquisition, composition, monograph, study, piece of writing; *N. Amer.* theme.

thick ▸ **adjective 1** *the walls are five feet thick* **in extent/diameter**, across, wide, broad, deep.
2 *his short, thick legs* **stocky**, sturdy, chunky, dumpy, hefty, thickset, beefy, meaty, broad, large, big, bulky, solid, substantial; fat, stout, plump.
OPPOSITES thin, slender.
3 *a thick Aran sweater* **chunky**, bulky, heavy, cable-knit, heavyweight; woollen, woolly.
OPPOSITES thin, light, lightweight.
4 *the station was* ***thick with*** *people* **crowded**, filled, packed, teeming, seething, swarming, crawling, crammed, thronged, bursting at the seams, solid, overflowing, choked, jammed, congested; covered; **full of**, cram-full of, overrun by, abounding in; *informal* jam-packed, chock-a-block, stuffed, chock-full of; *Austral./NZ informal* chocker; *rare* pullulating.
5 *the thick summer vegetation* **plentiful**, abundant, profuse, luxuriant, bushy, rich, riotous, exuberant; rank, rampant; **dense**, close-packed, concentrated, crowded, condensed, compact, impenetrable, impassable; serried; *informal* jungly.
OPPOSITES meagre, sparse.
6 *a thick paste* **semi-solid**, firm, stiff, stiffened, heavy; clotted, coagulated, viscid, viscous, gelatinous, mucilaginous, ropy; concentrated; *rare* inspissated, viscoid.
OPPOSITE runny.
7 *a motorway pile-up in thick fog* **dense**, heavy, opaque, impenetrable, soupy, murky, smoggy.
8 (*informal*) *he's a bit thick* **stupid**, unintelligent, ignorant, dense, brainless, mindless, foolish, dull-witted, dull, slow-witted, witless, doltish, slow, dunce-like, simple-minded, empty-headed, vacuous, vapid, half-witted, idiotic, moronic, imbecilic; obtuse, insensitive; gullible, naive; *informal* as thick as two short planks, thickheaded, dim, dumb, dopey, dippy, dozy, cretinous, birdbrained, pea-brained, pinheaded, pig-ignorant, bovine, slow on the uptake, soft in the head, brain-dead, boneheaded, lamebrained, chuckleheaded, dunderheaded, wooden-headed, fat-headed, thick-skulled, muttonheaded; *Brit. informal* daft, not the full shilling; *S. African informal* dof; *W. Indian informal* dotish; *N. Amer. vulgar slang* dumb-ass.
OPPOSITE clever.
9 *Guy's voice was thick with desire* **husky**, hoarse, throaty, guttural, gravelly, rough, raspy, rasping, croaky, croaking; indistinct, muffled.
OPPOSITES clear, shrill.
10 *a thick Scottish accent* **obvious**, pronounced, marked, broad, strong, rich, decided, distinct, conspicuous, noticeable, identifiable.
OPPOSITES faint, vague.
11 *she's very* ***thick with*** *him* **friendly**, intimate, familiar, on friendly/good terms, on the best of terms, hand in glove; close to, devoted to, inseparable from; *informal* pally, palsy-walsy, chummy, matey, buddy-buddy, as thick as thieves, well in.
OPPOSITE unfriendly.
□ **a bit thick** (*Brit. informal*) *I thought this was a bit thick and tried to defend myself* **unreasonable**, unfair, unjust, unjustified, uncalled for, unwarranted, unnecessary, excessive; *informal* below the belt, a bit much, off; *Brit. informal* out of order; *Austral./NZ informal* over the fence.
▸ **noun** *in the thick of the crisis* **midst**, centre, hub, middle, core, heart; focus.

thicken ▸ **verb 1** *stir over a gentle heat until the mixture thickens* **become thick/thicker**, stiffen, become firmer; condense, become more concentrated; solidify, set, gel, congeal, clot, coagulate, cake; *rare* inspissate, gelatinize.
2 *the plot thickened* **become more complicated**, become more involved, become more intricate, become more mysterious, deepen.

thicket ▸ **noun copse**, coppice, dense growth, grove, brake, covert, tangle, clump; wood; *Brit.* spinney; *archaic* hurst.

thickhead ▸ **noun** (*informal*) *this is no book for thickheads. See* FOOL.

thickheaded ▸ **adjective** (*informal*) *you thickheaded moron! See* STUPID.

thickness ▸ **noun 1** *the gateway is several feet in thickness* **width**, breadth, depth, diameter, extent.
2 *the immense thickness of the walls* **breadth**, broadness, width, wideness, largeness, bigness, bulkiness, solidness.
OPPOSITE thinness.
3 *several thicknesses of limestone* **layer**, stratum, stratification, seam, vein, band; sheet, film, lamina; ply; coat, coating.
4 *the thickness of the fog* **density**, denseness, heaviness, opacity, opaqueness, impenetrability, soupiness, murkiness.
5 *Cara could tell by the thickness of Susan's voice that she had been crying* **huskiness**, hoarseness, throatiness, gravelliness, roughness, raspiness, croakiness, indistinctness.

thickset ▸ **adjective 1** *a thickset man with a florid complexion* **heavily built**, stocky, bull-necked, sturdy, sturdily built, well built, chunky, burly, strapping, brawny, muscular, solid, heavy, hefty, beefy, meaty, hulking; cobby; *Austral./NZ* nuggety; *technical* mesomorphic, pyknic; *archaic* squabby.
OPPOSITES slight, lanky.
2 (*archaic*) *a thickset patch of elder trees* **dense**, thick, close-packed, crowded, compact.

thick-skinned ▸ **adjective** *I suppose you have to be pretty thick-skinned to be an MP* **tough**, impervious, unsusceptible, invulnerable, armour-plated, with a hide like an elephant, hardened, case-hardened, insensitive, unfeeling, uncaring; obtuse, stolid; *informal* hard-boiled; *rare* pachydermatous.
OPPOSITES sensitive, touchy, thin-skinned.

thief ▸ **noun robber**, burglar, housebreaker, cat burglar, shoplifter, pickpocket, sneak thief, mugger, larcenist, stealer, pilferer, poacher; embezzler, swindler; criminal, villain; kleptomaniac; raider, looter, plunderer, pillager, marauder; bandit, brigand, pirate, highwayman; *Indian* dacoit; *informal* crook, cracksman, steamer; *N. Amer. informal* yegg, second-story man/worker; *W. Indian informal* tief; *Brit. rhyming slang* tea leaf; *archaic* cutpurse, pickpurse, footpad, lurcher; *rare* peculator, defalcator.

thieve ▸ **verb** *he claimed it was the first time he had thieved anything* **steal**, take, purloin, help oneself to, snatch, pilfer, abscond with, run off with, appropriate, abstract, carry off, shoplift; embezzle, misappropriate; have one's fingers/hand in the till; *informal* walk off/away with, rob, swipe, nab, rip off, lift, 'liberate', 'borrow', filch, snaffle, snitch; *Brit. informal* nick, pinch, half-inch, whip, knock off, nobble, bone, scrump, blag; *N. Amer. informal* heist, glom; *Austral. informal* snavel; *W. Indian informal* tief; *archaic* crib, hook; *rare* peculate, defalcate.

thievery ▸ **noun.** *See* THIEVING.

thieving ▸ **noun** *some are drawn into a life of crime and petty thieving* **theft**, **stealing**, thievery, robbery, larceny, pilfering, pilferage; burglary, shoplifting, looting; misappropriation, expropriation, embezzlement; *rare* peculation, defalcation.
▸ **adjective** *Harry was a thieving, foul-mouthed old man* **light-fingered**, thievish, larcenous; dishonest; *informal* sticky-fingered, crooked, bent; *rare* furacious, kleptic, theftuous.
OPPOSITE honest.

thimbleful ▸ **noun** *a thimbleful of brandy* **bit**, spot, dram, nip, drop, splash; little, some, small amount; *Scottish informal* scoosh; *rare* toothful.

thin ▸ **adjective 1** *a thin white line* **narrow**, fine, pencil-thin, thread-like, attenuated; *rare* attenuate.
OPPOSITES thick, broad.
2 *thin, crisp pancakes* **wafer-thin**, paper-thin, papery.
OPPOSITE thick.
3 *the thin cotton of her nightdress* **lightweight**, light, fine, delicate, floaty, flimsy, diaphanous, gossamer, insubstantial; sheer, gauzy, filmy, chiffony, transparent, see-through, translucent.
OPPOSITES heavy, thick.
4 *a tall, thin woman dressed all in black* **slim**, lean, slender, rangy, willowy, svelte, sylphlike, spare, slight; **skinny**, underweight, scrawny, scraggy, bony, angular, raw-boned, hollow-cheeked, gaunt, as thin as a rake, as thin as a reed, like a matchstick, stick-like, skin-and-bones, emaciated, skeletal, cadaverous, like a skeleton, wasted, pinched, undernourished, underfed; lanky, spindly, stringy, gangly, gangling, reedy, weedy; *informal* looking like a bag of bones, anorexic, anorectic; *dated* spindle-shanked; *rare* gracile, starveling, macilent.
OPPOSITES fat, plump, overweight.
5 *he ran a hand over his thin grey hair* **sparse**, scanty, wispy, thinning.
OPPOSITES abundant, thick.
6 *attendance on the Conservative back benches was thin to say the least* **meagre**, paltry, poor, inadequate, insufficient, sparse, scanty, scattered.
7 *a bowl of thin soup* **watery**, watered down, weak, dilute, diluted, thinned down; runny, sloppy; *S. African* slap.
OPPOSITE thick.

T

8 *her thin voice trailed off* **weak**, faint, feeble, small, soft, low; reedy, high-pitched.
OPPOSITES strong, loud.
9 *the thin cold air of the mountains* **rarefied**.
10 *the plot is very thin* **insubstantial**, flimsy, slight, feeble, lame, poor, weak, shallow, tenuous, threadbare, inadequate, insufficient; **unconvincing**, unbelievable, implausible.
OPPOSITES meaty, convincing.
▶ **verb 1** *some paint must be* **thinned down** *before use* **dilute**, water down, weaken.
2 *the crowds were beginning to* **thin out** **become less dense/numerous**, decrease, diminish, dwindle, lessen, become less in number; disperse, dissipate, scatter.
3 *a beautiful shrub which becomes rather dense if not* **thinned out** *after flowering* **prune**, cut back, trim; *technical* single.

thing ▶ **noun 1** *the room was full of strange things* **object**, article, item, artefact, commodity; device, gadget, contrivance, instrument, utensil, tool, implement; entity, body; *informal* whatsit, what-d'you-call-it, what's-its-name, what's-it, whatchamacallit, thingummy, thingy, thingamabob, thingamajig, oojamaflip, oojah, gizmo; *Brit. informal* doodah, doobry, gubbins; *N. Amer. informal* doodad, doohickey, doojigger, dingus.
2 (**one's things**) *I'll come back tomorrow to collect my things* **belongings**, possessions, stuff, property, worldly goods, goods, personal effects, effects, paraphernalia, impedimenta, bits and pieces, bits and bobs; luggage, baggage, bags, bags and baggage, chattels, movables, valuables; **clothes**, garments; *Law* goods and chattels; *informal* gear, junk, togs, dunnage, traps; *Brit. informal* clobber; *S. African informal* trek; *vulgar slang* shit, crap.
3 (**things**) *her father's gardening things* **equipment**, apparatus, gear, kit, tackle, stuff; implements, tools, utensils; accoutrements.
4 *I've got several things to do this morning | his asthma stops him from doing things like swimming and running* **activity**; act, action, deed, undertaking, exploit, feat; task, job, chore, piece of business.
5 *I've got other things on my mind just now* **thought**, notion, idea, concept, conception; concern, matter, worry, preoccupation.
6 *I keep remembering things he said* **remark**, statement, comment, utterance, observation, declaration, pronouncement.
7 *quite a few odd things had happened in the last few days* **incident**, episode, event, happening, occurrence, eventuality, phenomenon.
8 (**things**) *how are things with you?* **matters**, affairs, circumstances, conditions, relations; state of affairs, situation, life.
9 *one of the things I like about you is your optimism* **characteristic**, quality, attribute, property, trait, feature, point, aspect, facet, element.
10 *there's another thing you should know* **fact**, piece of information, point, detail, particular, factor.
11 (**the thing**) *the thing is, I'm not sure if it's what I want* **fact of the matter**, fact, point, issue, problem.
12 *you lucky thing!* **person**, soul, creature, wretch; *informal* devil, beggar, bunny, bastard; *Brit. vulgar slang* sod, bugger.
13 *Dora developed a thing about noise* **phobia**, fear, horror, terror; dislike, aversion, hatred, detestation, loathing; obsession, fixation; complex, neurosis; *informal* hang-up, bee in one's bonnet.
14 *she had a* **thing about** *men who wore glasses* **penchant for**, preference for, taste for, inclination for, partiality for, predilection for, soft spot for, weakness for, fancy for, fondness for, liking for, love for, passion for; **fetish**, obsession, fixation.
15 (**one's thing**) *books aren't really my thing* **what one likes**, what interests one; *informal* one's cup of tea, one's bag, what turns one on, what floats one's boat.
16 (**the thing**) *cosmetic contact lenses are the thing on the catwalk* **fashionable**, in fashion, in vogue, popular, all the rage; *French* le dernier cri; *informal* trendy, cool, in, the in thing, big, with it, hip, happening, now.

think ▶ **verb 1** *do you think Isobel will come? | we thought he must have gone home* **believe**, be of the opinion, have as one's opinion, be of the view, be under the impression; expect, imagine, anticipate; surmise, suppose, conjecture, guess, fancy; conclude, determine, reason; *informal* reckon; *N. Amer. informal* figure; *formal* opine; *archaic* ween.
2 *his family was* **thought to be** *enormously rich* **deem**, judge, hold, reckon, consider, presume, estimate; regard as, view as.
3 *Jack thought for a moment* **ponder**, reflect, deliberate, meditate, contemplate, muse, cogitate, ruminate, be lost in thought, be in a brown study, brood; concentrate, rack one's brains, cudgel one's brains; *informal* put on one's thinking cap, sleep on it; *rare* cerebrate.
OPPOSITES act, leap into action.
4 *he began* **thinking about** *a career in politics* **consider**, contemplate, give thought to, entertain the idea of, deliberate about, weigh up, turn over in one's mind, mull over, chew over, reflect on, ruminate about, muse on; *N. Amer.* think on.
5 *she* **thought of** *all the visits she had made to her father* **recall**, remember, recollect, call to mind, bring to mind, think back to, review.
6 *she forced herself to think of how he must be feeling* **imagine**, picture, visualize, envisage, envision; dream about, fantasize about.
7 (*archaic*) *he thought to better his circumstances by marrying her* **intend**, aim, mean, plan, have in mind, purpose, propose; hope.
□ **think better of** *Lisa was about to say no, but then she thought better of it* **have second thoughts about**, think twice about, think again about, change one's mind about; reconsider, decide against; *informal* get cold feet about.
□ **think nothing of** *he thinks nothing of getting up at two or three o'clock in the morning* **consider normal**, consider usual, consider routine, take in one's stride, not think twice about; have no problems with, have no compunction about, have no hesitation about.
□ **think something over** *she went home to think over his offer* **consider**, contemplate, deliberate about, weigh up, consider the pros and cons of, mull over, ponder, reflect on, muse on, ruminate on.
□ **think something up** *the idea was thought up by one of my technology students* **devise**, dream up, come up with, invent, create, concoct, contrive, improvise, make up; hit on.
▶ **noun** *why don't you have a think about it?* **ponder**, muse, spell/period of deliberation/reflection/contemplation.

thinkable ▶ **adjective** *there is no thinkable alternative* **conceivable**, feasible, reasonable, acceptable, imaginable, possible, within the bounds of possibility; likely; *rare* cogitable.
OPPOSITES unthinkable, inconceivable.

thinker ▶ **noun** *one of the most influential economic thinkers of the century* **theorist**, theoretician, ideologist, philosopher, scholar, savant, sage, intellectual, intellect, mind, learned person, Solomon, Nestor; pundit, expert, mastermind; *informal* brain.
OPPOSITES doer, man/woman of action.

thinking ▶ **adjective** *he seemed a thinking man* **intelligent**, sensible, reasonable, rational, reasoning; logical, analytical; thoughtful, reflective, meditative, contemplative, pensive, philosophical; *rare* ratiocinative.
OPPOSITES stupid, irrational.
▶ **noun** *the agency explained the thinking behind the campaign* **reasoning**, idea(s), theory, thoughts, line of thought, philosophy, beliefs; conclusions; **opinion(s)**, view(s), point(s) of view, viewpoint(s), position, outlook, judgement, assessment, evaluation.

thin-skinned ▶ **adjective** *he was notoriously thin-skinned and disliked criticism* **sensitive**, oversensitive, hypersensitive, supersensitive, easily offended, quick to take offence, easily hurt, easily upset, touchy, defensive; paranoid, neurotic; *rare* umbrageous.
OPPOSITES insensitive, unfeeling, thick-skinned.

third-rate ▶ **adjective** *a third-rate hotel* **substandard**, below standard, bad, inferior, poor, poor-quality, low-grade; appalling, abysmal, atrocious, abject, awful, terrible, dismal, dreadful, execrable, frightful, miserable, wretched, lamentable, deplorable, pitiful, inadequate, insufficient, unsatisfactory, unacceptable; jerry-built, shoddy, tinny, trashy, rubbishy; *Brit.* cheap and nasty; *N. Amer.* cheapjack; *informal* lousy, not much cop, not up to much, crummy, bum, diabolical, rotten, sad, tatty, tacky, dire, tenth-rate; *Brit. informal* ropy, duff, naff, rubbish, pants, a load of pants, grotty; *vulgar slang* crap, crappy, shitty, chickenshit; *rare* direful, egregious.
OPPOSITES first-rate, excellent.

thirst ▶ **noun 1** *I need a drink—I'm dying of thirst* **thirstiness**, dryness; dehydration; *technical* polydipsia; *archaic* drought.
2 *his thirst for knowledge* **craving**, strong desire, longing, yearning, avidity, hunger, voracity, keenness, eagerness, lust, appetite, passion, love; itch, fancy, hankering; *informal* yen; *archaic* appetency, appetence.
OPPOSITES aversion, distaste.
▶ **verb** *she* **thirsted for** *power* **crave**, want, covet, desire, hunger for/after, lust for/after, hanker for/after, have one's heart set on; wish, long, have a longing, yearn, be hungry, be itching, pant, be desperate, be consumed with desire; *informal* have a yen, be dying; *archaic* be athirst.
OPPOSITE be averse to.

thirsty ▶ **adjective 1** *the boys were hot and thirsty* **longing for a drink**, in need of a drink, dry, dehydrated; *informal* parched, gasping; *Brit. informal* spitting feathers; *Austral./NZ informal* spitting chips; *rare* athirst, thirstful, droughty, sitient.
2 *the thirsty soil* **dry**, arid, dried up/out, as dry as a bone, parched, baked, desiccated, waterless, moistureless; *rare* droughty.
OPPOSITE waterlogged.
3 *his wife was thirsty for power* **eager**, hungry, greedy, thirsting, consumed with desire, avid, craving, longing, yearning, lusting, burning, desirous, hankering, itching; *informal* dying.

thong ▶ **noun** *the seals were worn on leather thongs round the owner's neck* **strip**, band, cord, string, lash, tie, belt, strap, tape, rope, tether.

thorn ▶ **noun** **prickle**, spike, barb, spine, bristle; *technical* spicule.

thorny ▶ **adjective 1** *he had to scramble through dense thorny undergrowth* **prickly**, spiky, barbed, spiny, spined, bristly, briary, sharp, pointed; *technical* spinose, spinous.
2 *the thorny subject of confidentiality* **problematic**, tricky, ticklish, delicate, controversial, awkward, prickly; **difficult**, knotty, tough, taxing, trying, troublesome, irksome, vexatious, bothersome, worrying, upsetting; **complicated**, complex, involved, convoluted, intricate, vexed; *informal*

sticky; *Brit. informal* dodgy.
OPPOSITES easy, uncomplicated.

thorough ▶ adjective **1** *a thorough investigation* **rigorous**, in-depth, exhaustive, thoroughgoing, minute, detailed, close, meticulous, scrupulous, assiduous, conscientious, painstaking, methodical, careful, sedulous, complete, comprehensive, elaborate, full, intensive, extensive, widespread, sweeping, searching, all-embracing, all-inclusive.
OPPOSITES superficial, cursory, partial.
2 *he is slow but thorough* **meticulous**, scrupulous, assiduous, conscientious, painstaking, punctilious, methodical, careful, attentive, diligent, industrious, persevering, laborious, hard-working.
OPPOSITE careless.
3 *the child is being a thorough nuisance* **utter**, downright, thoroughgoing, absolute, complete, total, out-and-out, outright, real, perfect, profound, proper, consummate, all-out, wholesale, surpassing, sheer, rank, pure, unqualified, unmitigated; *N. Amer.* full-bore; *Brit. informal* right; *Austral./NZ informal* fair; *rare* arrant, right-down.

thoroughbred ▶ adjective **1** *a thoroughbred horse* **pure-bred**, pedigree, pure, pure-blooded, full-blooded, pedigreed.
OPPOSITE hybrid.
2 (*informal*) *with its terrific handling and accurate steering, it feels like a thoroughbred coupé* **top-quality**, high-quality, first-class, first-rate, high-grade, of the first water, of the first order; choice, select, exclusive, rare, singular, unique, prime, prize, upmarket, fine, excellent, superb, distinguished, exceptional, outstanding, marvellous, superlative, special; best, choicest, finest, matchless, peerless, unequalled, perfect, flawless; *French* par excellence.

thoroughfare ▶ noun **1** *a scheme to stop the park being used as a thoroughfare* **through route**, access route, way, passage; *Brit. informal* rat run.
2 *the teeming thoroughfares of central London* **street**, road, roadway, avenue, boulevard, way; main road, high road, A road, B road, trunk road, arterial road, artery, broadway; *Brit.* dual carriageway, clearway, motorway; *French* autoroute; *Italian* autostrada; *German* Autobahn; *N. Amer.* highway, freeway, parkway, crossway, turnpike, pike, throughway, expressway, superhighway, interstate; *S. African* national road; *Austral.* beef road; *informal* main drag.

thoroughly ▶ adverb **1** *we will investigate every complaint thoroughly* **rigorously**, in depth, exhaustively, from top to bottom, minutely, closely, in detail, meticulously, scrupulously, assiduously, conscientiously, painstakingly, methodically, carefully, sedulously, completely, comprehensively, fully, to the fullest extent, intensively, extensively.
2 *she is thoroughly spoilt* **utterly**, downright, absolutely, completely, totally, entirely, really, perfectly, profoundly, properly, consummately, surpassingly, positively, simply, unconditionally, unreservedly, categorically, incontrovertibly, unquestionably, undeniably, in every respect, through and through, outright; *informal* plain, clean.

though ▶ conjunction *though Scott was not particularly interested in early editions he did own several* **although**, even though/if, in spite of the fact that, despite the fact that, notwithstanding the fact that, notwithstanding that, for all that, while, whilst, granted that, even supposing, despite the possibility that, albeit, however, yet, but.
▶ adverb *You can't always do that. You can try, though.* **nevertheless**, nonetheless, even so, however, be that as it may, for all that, in spite of that/everything, despite that/everything, after everything, having said that, just the same, all the same, at the same time, in any event, come what may, at any rate, notwithstanding, regardless, anyway, anyhow; *informal* still and all; *archaic* howbeit, withal, natheless.

thought ▶ noun **1** *a thought came to me as to how we should proceed* **idea**, notion, line of thinking, belief, concept, conception, conviction, opinion, view, impression, image, perception, mental picture; assumption, presumption, hypothesis, theory, supposition, postulation, abstraction, apprehension, understanding, conceptualization; feeling, funny feeling, suspicion, sneaking suspicion, hunch.
2 *the mere thought of being confined made her breathless* **anticipation**, expectation, prospect, contemplation, likelihood, possibility, fear.
3 *he gave up any thought of taking a degree* **hope**, aspiration, ambition, dream; **intention**, idea, plan, design, purpose, aim.
4 *it only took a moment's thought* **thinking**, reasoning, contemplation, musing, pondering, consideration, reflection, introspection, deliberation, study, rumination, cogitation, meditation, brooding, mulling over, reverie, brown study, concentration, debate, speculation; *rare* cerebration.
5 *I'll give the matter some thought* **attention**, consideration, heed, regard, notice, scrutiny, care.
6 *have you no thought for others?* **compassion**, sympathy, caring, concern, regard, solicitude, solicitousness, empathy; consideration, kindness, kindliness, kind-heartedness, tender-heartedness, tenderness, warmth, warm-heartedness; understanding, sensitivity, thoughtfulness, charity, charitableness, benignity, benevolence, philanthropy, altruism, magnanimity.

thoughtful ▶ adjective **1** *Uncle Albert paused, looking thoughtful* **pensive**, thinking, reflective, contemplative, musing, meditative, introspective, prayerful, philosophical, cogitative, ruminative, absorbed, engrossed, rapt, preoccupied, deep/immersed/lost in thought, in a brown study, brooding, broody, serious, studious, solemn, dreamy, dreaming, wistful, melancholy, sad; *rare* ruminant.
OPPOSITE vacant.
2 *how very thoughtful of you!* **considerate**, attentive, caring, understanding, sympathetic, solicitous, concerned, helpful, friendly, obliging, accommodating, neighbourly, unselfish, kind, kindly, compassionate, tender, charitable, benevolent.
OPPOSITES inconsiderate, self-centred.
3 *her work is thoughtful and provocative* **profound**, deep, intelligent, studious, philosophical, sensitive, pithy, serious, meaty, weighty.
OPPOSITE superficial.

thoughtless ▶ adjective **1** *I'm so sorry—how thoughtless of me* **inconsiderate**, uncaring, heedless, unmindful, regardless, insensitive, uncharitable, unkind; tactless, undiplomatic, indiscreet, careless, selfish, impolite, rude.
OPPOSITE considerate.
2 *to think a few minutes of thoughtless pleasure could end in such a terrible way* **unthinking**, heedless, careless, unmindful, absent-minded, injudicious, ill-advised, ill-considered, imprudent, unwise, foolish, silly, stupid, reckless, rash, precipitate, negligent, neglectful, remiss.
OPPOSITE careful.

> **CHOOSE THE RIGHT WORD**
> **thoughtless, careless, heedless**
> *See* CARELESS.

thousand ▶ cardinal number *informal* K, thou; *rare* chiliad.

WORD LINKS

related prefixes	**kilo- (e.g. *kilometre*), milli- (e.g. *milligram*)**
relating to a thousand	**millenary**
thousandth anniversary	**millennium**

thrall ▶ noun (*literary*) *he held us in his evil thrall* **power**, clutches, hands, control, grip, grasp, yoke; enslavement, bondage, slavery, subjection, subjugation, servitude, tyranny, oppression, domination, hegemony, supremacy.

thrash ▶ verb **1** *she thrashed him across the head and shoulders* **hit**, **beat**, flog, whip, horsewhip, scourge, lash, flagellate, flail, strap, birch, cane, belt, leather; *N. Amer.* bullwhip; *informal* give someone a hiding, tan someone's hide, lather, paste, take a strap to, beat the living daylights out of; *N. Amer. informal* whale; *archaic* switch, stripe, thong; *rare* quirt.
2 (*informal*) *Newcastle were thrashed 8–1 by the Czech team* **trounce**, beat hollow, defeat utterly, rout, annihilate, triumph over, win a resounding victory over, be victorious over, crush, overwhelm, best, get the better of, worst, bring someone to their knees; *informal* lick, hammer, clobber, paste, pound, pulverize, crucify, demolish, destroy, drub, give someone a drubbing, cane, walk all over, wipe the floor with, give someone a hiding, take to the cleaners, blow someone out of the water, make mincemeat of, murder, massacre, slaughter, flatten, turn inside out, tank; *Brit. informal* stuff, marmalize; *N. Amer. informal* blow out, cream, shellac, skunk, slam.
3 *he lay on the ground thrashing around in pain* **flail**, thresh, flounder, toss and turn, jerk, toss, squirm, writhe, twist, wriggle, wiggle, twitch.
□ **thrash something out 1** *it is essential that conflicting views are heard and thrashed out* **resolve**, settle, sort out, straighten out, iron out, reconcile, disentangle, clarify, clear up, talk through, confer about, debate, exchange views on/about, chew over, air, ventilate, argue out, argue the pros and cons of; go into, deal with, handle, pursue, examine, explore, review, study, scrutinize, analyse, weigh up, sift; *informal* kick around/about, bat around/about.
2 *they spent much of the weekend trying to thrash out an agreement* **produce**, come to a decision on, work out, form a resolution about, negotiate, agree on, bring about, complete, accomplish, carry through, effect.

thrashing ▶ noun **1** *what he needs is a good thrashing* **beating**, flogging, whipping, horsewhipping, scourging, lashing, flagellation, caning, belting, leathering; the strap, the birch, the cane, the belt; *N. Amer.* bullwhipping; *informal* hiding, tanning, lathering, pasting, going-over.
2 (*informal*) *the home side received their biggest thrashing ever* **crushing defeat**, overwhelming defeat, beating, trouncing, walloping, thumping, battering, rout; *informal* hiding, licking, pasting, caning, going-over, drubbing, hammering, pounding, clobbering, demolition, slaughter, massacre, annihilation; *N. Amer. informal* shellacking.

thread ▶ noun **1** *he sewed it up with needle and thread* **yarn**, **cotton**, filament, fibre, strand, string, twine, line; ply.
2 (*literary*) *the Thames was a thread of silver below them* **streak**, strand, stripe, line, striation, strip, seam, vein, belt, bar, swathe.
3 *she lost the thread of the conversation* **train of thought**, drift, direction, sense, theme, subject matter, motif, tenor, strain, thrust, subject, gist, burden, action; plot, storyline, scenario.
▶ verb **1** *he threaded the rope through a pulley* **pass**, string, weave, work, ease,

inch, move, push, poke, thrust.
2 *a little girl sat threading minute beads* **string**.
3 *she* ***threaded her way*** *through the tables* **weave (one's way)**, inch (one's way), wind (one's way), file, work (one's way), push (one's way), squeeze (one's way), shoulder (one's way), elbow (one's way), make one's way; progress, pass.

threadbare ▶ adjective **1** *a threadbare carpet* **worn**, well worn, old, thin, worn out, holey, moth-eaten, mangy, ragged, frayed, tattered, battered; decrepit, shabby, scruffy, unkempt; having seen better days, falling apart at the seams, in shreds, in tatters, falling to pieces; *informal* tatty, ratty, the worse for wear; *N. Amer. informal* raggedy, raggedy-ass; *Austral. informal* warby; *rare* out at elbows.
OPPOSITE pristine.
2 *his threadbare pontifications* **hackneyed**, trite, banal, vapid, platitudinous, clichéd, cliché-ridden, stock, conventional, unoriginal, overused, overworked, worn out, tired, stale, dull, pedestrian, run-of-the-mill, routine, humdrum, stereotyped; *informal* old hat, corny, played out; *rare* truistic, bromidic.
OPPOSITES original, fresh.
3 *their knowledge of pollutants was threadbare* **limited**, **sketchy**, restricted, basic, rudimentary, patchy, minimal, slight, slender, finite, bounded, narrow, lean, in short supply, short, meagre, scanty, sparse, insubstantial, deficient, lacking, inadequate, insufficient, paltry, poor, miserly, feeble.
OPPOSITES impressive, full; adequate.

threat ▶ noun **1** *the general had made threats against UN personnel* **threatening remark**, warning, ultimatum, intimidating remark; *rare* commination; (**threats**) menaces, menacing.
2 *the ash from the volcano poses a possible threat to aircraft* **danger**, peril, hazard, menace, risk.
3 *the company faces the threat of liquidation proceedings* **possibility**, chance, probability, likelihood, risk, danger, peril, menace, fear, prospect.

threaten ▶ verb **1** *how dare you threaten me?* **menace**, intimidate, browbeat, bully, cow, pressurize, lean on, terrorize, frighten, scare, alarm; make threats against, issue threats to, threaten to harm/kill.
2 *the rise of nationalism could threaten the stability of Europe* **endanger**, be a danger to, be a threat to, menace, imperil, put at risk, make vulnerable, expose to danger, put in jeopardy, jeopardize; *archaic* peril.
3 *the air was raw and threatened rain* **warn of**, be a warning of, give a warning of, promise, presage, augur, portend, foreshadow, prophesy, be an omen of; **foretell**, herald, bode, announce, be a harbinger of, be an indication of, indicate, point to; **be a sign of**, signal, signify, mean, spell, add up to, amount to, be evidence of; *literary* betoken, foretoken, forebode, harbinger.
4 *as rain threatened, the party was moved indoors* **be likely (to happen)**, be imminent, be (close) at hand, be near, be close, be approaching, be on the horizon, be just around the corner, be brewing, be gathering, be looming, be coming (soon), be coming up, be on the way, be expected, be anticipated, be in prospect, be in the wind, be in the air, be forthcoming, be impending; hang over someone; *informal* be on the cards.

CHOOSE THE RIGHT WORD

threaten, menace, intimidate

- When one person **threatens** another they indicate or say that they will do something harmful or unpleasant if that person does not comply with their wishes. They can *threaten* the person (*robbers were threatening the shop assistant with a gun*), or they can *threaten* the thing that will happen (*the general threatened an assault on the city | his attackers threatened to kill him*). *Threaten* can also be used of something that constitutes a danger (*the Amazonian forest is being threatened by a major oil extraction project*) and of undesirable events that are thought to be likely (*the slick threatens to become the world's largest*).
- **Menace** typically occurs as the adjective *menacing* and, compared to *threaten*, is less often used of active threats made by one person to another than of an impression, attitude, or more general danger (*he was a menacing, attacking centre-forward | pristine Amazonian forest is being menaced by an oil extraction project*).
- To **intimidate** someone is to behave in such a way as to frighten them into submission or inaction (*one witness had disappeared and two more had been intimidated*). A person or thing may also unintentionally *intimidate* someone by appearing so formidable that the other loses confidence (*I was intimidated by the whole idea of Cambridge*); this sense is often conveyed by the adjectival form *intimidating* (*she was tall, with a most intimidating manner*).

threatening ▶ adjective **1** *her mother had received a threatening letter* **menacing**, intimidating, bullying, frightening, terrifying, scary, fearsome, alarming, forbidding, baleful; warning, admonitory, cautionary; *rare* minacious, minatory, minatorial, comminatory.
2 *banks of threatening clouds were building up* **ominous**, glowering, brooding, sinister, menacing, black, thunderous, dark, wintry, gloomy, heavy, dire, ill, evil, baleful, forbidding, doomy, ugly, unpromising, portentous, foreboding, unpropitious, pessimistic, inauspicious, unfavourable, unlucky, ill-fated, dangerous; *archaic* direful; *rare* minacious.

three ▶ cardinal number **trio**, threesome, triad, troika, triumvirate, trilogy, triptych, trefoil, three-piece, triplets; *Poetry* tercet; *Music* triplet; *rare* tern, triunity, triune, triplicity.

WORD LINKS

related prefixes	**ter-** (e.g. ***tervalent***), **tri-** (e.g. ***trimaran***)
relating to three	**triple, treble, ternary**
three-sided figure	**triangle**
group of three powerful people	**triumvirate**
relating to three years	**triennial**
three-hundredth anniversary	**tercentenary**

three-dimensional ▶ adjective *a three-dimensional image* **solid**, concrete, having depth, sculptural, rounded; stereoscopic, stereographic, stereo-, virtual, holographic, perspective, pop-up; *technical* axonometric, orthorhombic.
OPPOSITE flat.

threesome ▶ noun *we planned excursions as a threesome* **trio**, triplet(s), triumvirate, triad, trinity, troika, triunity, triangle, triplex; *technical* trilogy, triptych, tercet; *Music* terzetto, pas de trois; *rare* trine.

threnody ▶ noun (*rare*) *a threnody for Chernobyl* **lament**, dirge, requiem, elegy, funeral song/chant, burial hymn, dead march, keen, plaint, knell; *Scottish* coronach; *rare* monody, epicedium, exequy.
OPPOSITE hymn.

threshold ▶ noun **1** *they stood on the threshold of the church* **doorstep**, sill, doorsill, doorway, entrance, entry, way in, door, gate, gateway, portal, approach.
2 *these young people are at the threshold of their careers* **start**, starting point, beginning, brink, verge, edge, dawn, birth, origin, inception, conception, opening, launch, inauguration, institution, initiation, debut, creation, day one; *informal* kick-off; *formal* commencement.
OPPOSITE end.
3 *100 dB is close to the human threshold of pain* **lower limit**, starting point, minimum, margin; *Psychology* limen.

WORD LINKS

relating to a threshold **liminal**

thrift ▶ noun *thrift and hard work led to betterment* **providence**, prudence, thriftiness, canniness, carefulness, good management, good husbandry, careful budgeting, economy, economizing, saving, scrimping and saving, scrimping, frugality, abstemiousness, parsimony, penny-pinching, miserliness; *N. Amer.* forehandedness; *rare* sparingness, frugalness.
OPPOSITES profligacy, extravagance.

thriftless ▶ adjective *he is a generous, often thriftless fellow* **extravagant**, profligate, spendthrift, unthrifty, improvident, wasteful, free-spending, prodigal, squandering, lavish; immoderate, excessive, imprudent, reckless, irresponsible.
OPPOSITE thrifty.

thrifty ▶ adjective *Gran brought me up to be thrifty and never to get into debt* **careful with money**, **provident**, prudent, canny, economical, frugal, sparing, scrimping, abstemious, parsimonious, penny-pinching, miserly; *N. Amer.* forehanded.
OPPOSITES profligate, extravagant.

thrill ▶ noun **1** *the thrill of jumping out of an aeroplane* **(feeling of) excitement**, thrilling experience, stimulation, sensation, glow, tingle, titillation; fun, enjoyment, amusement, delight, joy, pleasure, treat, adventure; *informal* buzz, kick; *N. Amer. informal* charge.
2 *a thrill of excitement ran through her* **tremor**, wave, rush, surge, flash, flush, blaze, stab, dart, throb, tremble, quiver, flutter, shudder, vibration; flow, gush, stream, flood, torrent.
▶ verb **1** *even though he couldn't read, the sight of books thrilled him* **excite**, stimulate, arouse, rouse, inspire, give joy to, delight, give pleasure to, stir (up), exhilarate, intoxicate, electrify, galvanize, move, motivate, fire (with enthusiasm), fire someone's imagination, fuel, brighten, animate, lift, quicken; *informal* give someone a buzz, give someone a kick; *N. Amer. informal* give someone a charge.
OPPOSITE bore.
2 *he* ***thrilled at*** *the sound of her voice* **be/feel excited**, tingle, feel joy; *informal* get a buzz out of, get a kick out of; *N. Amer. informal* get a charge out of.
3 *the shock of alarm thrilled through her* **rush**, race, surge, cascade, course, flood, flow, gush, wash, well up, sweep, flash, blaze, throb, quiver, shiver, flutter, shudder, vibrate.

thrilling ▶ adjective *racegoers are in for a thrilling contest today* **exciting**, stirring, action-packed, rip-roaring, gripping, riveting, fascinating, dramatic, hair-raising, rousing, lively, animated, spirited, stimulating, moving, inspiring, inspirational, electrifying, passionate, impassioned, emotive, emotional, emotion-charged, heady, soul-stirring; *N. Amer.* stem-winding; *rare* inspiriting, anthemic.
OPPOSITE boring.

thrive ▶ verb *there are several foliage plants that thrive in a window box*

T

flourish, prosper, grow vigorously, develop well, burgeon, bloom, blossom, do well, advance, make strides, succeed; shoot up; boom, profit, expand, go well, grow rich.
OPPOSITES decline, wither, fail, stagnate, die.

CHOOSE THE RIGHT WORD

thrive, flourish, prosper

See FLOURISH.

thriving ▶ adjective *a thriving business* **flourishing**, prosperous, prospering, growing, developing, burgeoning, blooming, healthy, successful, advancing, progressing; luxuriant, lush, prolific; booming, profitable, expanding; *informal* going strong.
OPPOSITES moribund, dying, unhealthy.

throat ▶ noun gullet, oesophagus; windpipe, trachea; crop, craw, maw; neck; *technical* pharynx, oropharynx, fauces, gorget; *informal, dated* the red lane; *archaic* throttle, gorge, gula.

WORD LINKS

relating to the throat	**guttural, jugular**
branch of medicine concerning the ear and throat	**otolaryngology**
branch of medicine concerning the ear, nose, and throat	**otorhinolaryngology**

throaty ▶ adjective *a low throaty voice* **gravelly**, husky, rough, guttural, deep, thick, gruff, growly, growling, hoarse, croaky, croaking; rasping, raspy, harsh, grating, jarring, discordant, dissonant, scratchy, creaky; *rare* stridulant.
OPPOSITE high-pitched.

throb ▶ verb *her arms and legs throbbed with tiredness* **pulsate**, beat, pulse, palpitate, pound, thud, thump, hammer, drum, thrum, reverberate, vibrate, pitter-patter, go pit-a-pat, quiver; *rare* quop.
▶ noun *the throb of the ship's engines* **pulsation**, beat, beating, pulse, pulsating, palpitation, pounding, thud, thudding, thump, thumping, hammering, drumming, thrum, thrumming, reverberation, vibration, pit-a-pat, pitter-patter, quivering.

throes ▶ plural noun *the throes of childbirth* **agony**, pain, paroxysm, pangs, suffering, torture, torment, anguish, distress, hardship, struggle; *archaic* travail; *rare* excruciation.
□ **in the throes of** *she was in the throes of her by-election campaign* **struggling with**, wrestling with, grappling with, tackling, toiling at/with, labouring at, slaving at, working at/on; **having to cope with**, enduring, living with, weathering, braving, facing, confronting; **in the middle of**, in the process of, in the course of, in the midst of, busy with, occupied in/with, taken up with/by, employed in, involved in, participating in, taking part in, absorbed in, engrossed in, immersed in, preoccupied with, carrying on, conducting, pursuing, following, practising.

thrombosis ▶ noun *he died from a thrombosis* **blood clot**, embolism, embolus, infarction; stroke, ictus, seizure; heart attack, coronary thrombosis, coronary; *archaic* apoplexy.

throne ▶ noun **1** *a golden throne* **seat of state**, royal seat.
2 *the tsar risked losing his throne* **sovereign power**, sovereignty, rule, command, dominion.

throng ▶ noun *he pushed his way through the throng* **crowd**, mass, multitude, horde, host, mob, assemblage, gathering, congregation, crush, press, body, band, army, troop, legion, gang, stream, swarm, flock, bevy, herd, pack, drove, array, sea, myriad, pile; knot, cluster, group.
▶ verb **1** *a crowd thronged the station* **pack (into)**, cram (into), jam, fill, press into, squeeze into; *N. Amer.* mob.
2 *people thronged to see the play* **rush**, stream, flock, troop, crowd, swarm, surge, flood, flow, spill, teem.
3 *a large crowd* **thronged round** *to listen | visitors* **thronged around** *him* **crowd round**, press round, mill around/round; congregate round, converge round, hem in, mob, jostle.

T

throttle ▶ verb **1** *there was a pair of hands round her throat, throttling her* **choke**, strangle, strangulate, garrotte, asphyxiate, smother, suffocate, stifle.
2 *attempts to throttle the criminal supply of drugs* **suppress**, inhibit, stifle, control, restrain, check, contain, put a/the lid on; crack down on, clamp down on, drive underground; **stop**, put an end to, bring to an end, end, stamp out, bring to a stop, halt, bring to a halt; *informal* put paid to, put the kibosh on, put the stopper on, do for.

through ▶ preposition **1** *it takes about twenty-five minutes to get through the tunnel | delicious smells wafted through the house* **into and out of**, to the other/far side of, from one side of ... to the other, from end to end of, between, past, by, down, along, across, by way of, via; throughout, around in, all over.
2 *he got the job through an advertisement* **by means of**, by way of, by dint of, through the agency of, via, using, with the help of, with the aid of, with the assistance of, thanks to, under the aegis of, by virtue of, as a result of, as a consequence of, on account of, owing to, because of.
3 *he worked through the night* **throughout**, all through, for the duration of, until/to the end of, during.
4 (*N. Amer.*) *the exhibition is open Tuesday through Sunday* **up to and including**, (from ...) to ... inclusive.
▶ adverb **1** *cosmic rays strike against atoms in the atmosphere as they pass through* **from one side to the other**, from one end to another, from end to end, from side to side, from top to bottom, in and out the other end/side.
2 *Victoria woke up, but Anthony slept through* **the whole time**, all the time, from start to finish, without a break, without an interruption, uninterrupted, non-stop, continuously, constantly, throughout.
3 *it was a struggle but we got through* **to the end**, to the finish, to the termination, to the completion, to the culmination, to a successful conclusion.
□ **through and through** *he was obviously a city kid through and through | I know you through and through* **in every respect**, to the core; **thoroughly**, utterly, downright, absolutely, completely, totally, wholly, fully, entirely, really, perfectly, profoundly, properly, consummately, surpassingly, positively, simply, unconditionally, unreservedly, categorically, incontrovertibly, unquestionably, undeniably, altogether, out-and-out.
▶ adjective **1** *are you through? | we're* **through with** *you here* **finished**, done, reached the end, completed, terminated; no longer involved with, no longer wanting anything to do with, tired of.
2 *a through train* **direct**; non-stop; without changes.

WORD LINKS

related prefix **dia-** (e.g. ***diameter, diachronic***)

throughout ▶ preposition & adverb **1** *it had repercussions throughout Europe | the house is in good order throughout* **all over**, all round, in every part (of), everywhere (in), all through, right through, here and there (in), round.
2 *Rose had generally been very fit throughout her life | both MPs retained a smiling dignity throughout* **all through**, through, for the duration (of), for the whole of, until the end (of), the whole time, all the time.

throw ▶ verb **1** *she threw their ball back* **hurl**, toss, fling, pitch, cast, lob, launch, flip, catapult, shy, dash, aim, direct, project, propel, send, bowl; *informal* chuck, heave, sling, buzz, whang, bung; *N. Amer. informal* peg; *Austral. informal* hoy; *NZ informal* bish.
OPPOSITES catch, hold.
2 *he threw the door open* **move quickly/suddenly**, push suddenly/violently, thrust, fling, propel, shoot, slam, smack, bang, crash, thump, push, force; *informal* plonk.
3 *a chandelier threw its bright light over the walls* **project**, cast, send, give off, emit, radiate.
4 *Cheryl drew back her fist and threw another punch* **deliver**, give, land.
OPPOSITE pull.
5 *she threw a withering glance at him* **direct**, cast, send, dart, shoot, bestow on, give.
6 *he was thrown twice in the final round* **fell**, throw to the ground, hurl to the ground, unbalance, bring down, floor, prostrate.
7 *the horse threw his rider* **unseat**, dislodge, upset, bring down.
8 *his question threw me* **disconcert**, unnerve, fluster, ruffle, flurry, agitate, harass, upset, disturb, discomfit, put off, put someone off their stroke, throw off balance, make nervous, discompose, discountenance, cause someone to lose their composure; perturb, unsettle, bother, affect, worry, disquiet, trouble, confuse; *informal* rattle, faze, put into a flap, throw into a tizz, discombobulate, shake up.
9 *if only he could find the switch to throw* **operate**, switch on, click on, engage, move.
10 *the pots were thrown on a wheel* **shape**, form, mould, fashion.
11 *he threw a farewell party for them* **give**, **host**, hold, have, provide, put on, lay on, arrange, organize.
□ **throw something away 1** *he decided to throw away his textbooks and get some practical experience* **discard**, throw out, dispose of, get rid of, do away with, toss out, scrap, throw on the scrap heap, clear out, remove, dispense with, lose, eliminate, dump, unload, jettison, shed, dismiss, expel, eject, weed out, root out; recycle, break up, demolish, write off; *informal* chuck (away/out), ditch, bin, junk, get shut of; *Brit. informal* get shot of, see the back of; *N. Amer. informal* trash, shuck off, wreck.
OPPOSITE keep.
2 *Cambridge threw away a 15–0 lead* **squander**, waste, fritter away, dissipate, run through, fail to exploit, make poor use of, lose, let slip; *informal* blow, pour/chuck something down the drain.
OPPOSITE exploit.
□ **throw someone off** *she thought she had thrown off her pursuer* **shake off**, get away from, escape, elude, give someone the slip, leave behind, throw off the scent, dodge, lose, get rid of, rid oneself of; outdistance, outstrip; *Brit. informal* get shot of.
□ **throw something off** *he shrugged, trying to throw off the pain* **get rid of**, cast off, discard, shake off, drop, jettison, free/rid oneself of.
□ **throw something on** *she threw on her clothes* **put on quickly**, pull on, drag on, don quickly, slip into.
□ **throw someone out** *Jim was thrown out when he climbed on to the stage | the government was thrown out after only eight months* **expel**, eject, evict, drive out, force out, oust, remove; remove from office/power, get rid of, depose, topple, unseat, overthrow, bring down, overturn, put out, drum out, thrust out, push out, turn out; dismiss, dislodge, displace, supplant, show someone the door; banish, deport, exile; *informal* boot out, kick out,

give someone the boot; *Brit. informal* turf out.

□ **throw something out 1** *I was continually having to throw out mouldy furniture.* See **THROW SOMETHING AWAY**.
2 *his case was thrown out because an industrial tribunal was not entitled to deal with it* **reject**, dismiss, turn down, say 'no' to, refuse, disallow, veto, squash; *informal* give the thumbs down to, give the red light to.
3 *a thermal light bulb throws out a lot of heat* **radiate**, emit, give off, send out, diffuse, disseminate, disperse.

□ **throw someone over** *he's going to throw you over for your sister* **abandon**, leave, desert, discard, turn one's back on, cast aside, cast off; **jilt**, break up with, finish with, leave in the lurch, leave high and dry, leave stranded; *informal* dump, ditch, chuck, drop, walk out on, run out on, rat on, leave flat, give someone the push, give someone the elbow, give someone the big E; *archaic* forsake.

□ **throw up** (*informal*) *she threw up in the gutter* **vomit**, retch; cough up, bring up, regurgitate; heave, gag; *Brit.* be sick; *N. Amer.* get sick; *informal* puke, chunder, chuck up, hurl, spew, do the technicolor yawn, keck; *Brit. informal* honk, sick up; *Scottish informal* boke; *N. Amer. informal* spit up, barf, upchuck, toss one's cookies.

□ **throw something up** *throwing up his career would have meant the end of financial support* **give up**, abandon, relinquish, resign (from), leave, eschew, abdicate; *informal* quit, chuck, pack in, jack in.

▶ **noun 1** *we were allowed two throws each* **lob**, pitch, flip, shy, go; bowl, ball; hurl, toss, fling, cast; *informal* chuck, heave, sling.
2 (*informal*) *drinks are only £1* ***a throw*** **each**, apiece, per item, for one.

throwaway ▶ **adjective 1** *more and more products are displayed without throwaway packaging* **disposable**, expendable, one-use, non-returnable, one-way, single-trip; cheap, ephemeral, obsolescent; paper, plastic, biodegradable, photodegradable.
2 *a million viewers had heard my throwaway remarks* **casual**, passing, careless, unthinking, unstudied, unconsidered, ill-considered, parenthetical; nonchalant, offhand.

thrust ▶ **verb 1** *she thrust her hands into her pockets | he tried to thrust his way past her* **shove**, push, propel, impel; send, press, drive, plunge, stick, force, shoot, ram, barge, bump, knock, strike, hit, jolt, butt, prod, poke, nudge, elbow, shoulder; bulldoze, sweep, jostle, bundle, hustle, hurry, rush, manhandle.
2 *he felt that fame had been thrust upon him* **impose**, force, foist, push, unload, inflict, obtrude, press, urge; (**thrust something on someone**) saddle someone with, land someone with, burden someone with, lumber someone with.

▶ **noun 1** *he gave the gate a hard thrust* **shove**, push, ram, prod, poke, stab, jab, lunge, drive, barge, bump, bang, jolt, butt, knock, nudge.
2 *a sudden armoured thrust into the city* **advance**, push, drive, charge, attack, assault, onslaught, onrush, offensive, sortie, foray, raid, sally, invasion, incursion, blitz, campaign; *archaic* onset.
3 *he countered this verbal attack with some choice thrusts of his own* **barbed remark**, verbal attack/assault, barb, hostile remark, insult; criticism, censure, vitriol.
4 *only one engine is producing thrust* **force**, motive force, propulsive force, propulsion, drive, driving force, actuation, impetus, impulse, impulsion, momentum, push, pressure, power.
5 *they failed to grasp the thrust of the speech* **gist**, substance, drift, implication, intention, burden, meaning, significance, signification, sense, essence, thesis, import, purport, tenor, message, spirit.

thrusting ▶ **adjective** *a thrusting young salesman* **aggressive**, **ambitious**, assertive, pushy, pushing, insistent, forceful, forward, energetic, determined, obtrusive, bold, brash; bumptious, presumptuous, full of oneself, self-assertive, overbearing, domineering, cocksure, loud, obnoxious; *informal* full of get-up-and-go; *rare* pushful.
OPPOSITES meek, unambitious.

thud ▶ **noun** *Jean heard the thud of the closing door* **thump**, clunk, clonk, crash, smash, smack, bang, boom, thunder, wallop; stomp, stamp, clump, clomp; *informal* wham, whump.

▶ **verb** *bullets thudded into the dusty ground* **thump**, clunk, clonk, crash, smash, smack, bang, thunder; stomp, stamp, clump, clomp; *informal* wham, whump.

thug ▶ **noun** **ruffian**, hoodlum, bully boy, bully, bandit, mugger, gangster, terrorist, gunman, murderer, killer, hit man, assassin, hooligan, vandal, Yardie; *informal* tough, bruiser, hired gun; *Brit. informal* rough, bovver boy, lager lout; *Scottish & N. English informal* ned; *N. Amer. informal* hood, goon; *Austral./NZ informal* roughie; *dated* cut-throat, desperado; *rare* myrmidon.

thumb ▶ **noun** (first) digit, opposable digit; *technical* pollex.

□ **all thumbs** (*Brit. informal*) **clumsy**, awkward, maladroit, inept, bungling, bumbling, incompetent, unskilful, heavy-handed, ungainly, inelegant, inexpert, graceless, ungraceful, gauche, unhandy, uncoordinated, gawky, cloddish, clodhopping; *informal* butterfingered, cack-handed, ham-fisted, ham-handed; *Brit. informal* all fingers and thumbs.
OPPOSITE dexterous.

□ **thumbs down** (*informal*) *moves to demolish a historic former engine shed have been given the thumbs down* **rejection**, refusal, veto, no, negation, rebuff, disapproval, turning down, turndown, non-acceptance, declining, dismissal, spurning, cold shoulder, cold-shouldering, snub, snubbing; *informal* red light, knock-back, kick in the teeth, smack in the face/eye.
OPPOSITES approval, welcome, thumbs up.

□ **thumbs up** (*informal*) *staff gave our police officers a resounding thumbs up* **approval**, seal of approval, approbation, endorsement, welcome, encouragement; **permission**, liberty, authorization, consent, yes, leave, authority, sanction, ratification, licence, dispensation, nod, assent, acquiescence, agreement, blessing, imprimatur, rubber stamp, clearance, acceptance; *informal* go-ahead, the OK, green light, say-so; *rare* permit.
OPPOSITES rejection, thumbs down.

▶ **verb 1** *as soon as she thumbed the button, the door slid open* **press**, push (down), depress, lean on.
2 *the man* ***thumbed through*** *his notebook* **leaf**, flick, flip, skim, browse, glance, look, riffle; read, scan, dip into, run one's eye over, have a look at; peruse.
3 (usually **thumbed**) *his dictionaries were thumbed and ink-stained* **make dog-eared**, mark, soil, mess up, handle roughly, maul, paw.
4 *thumb a lift | he was thumbing his way across France* **hitch-hike**, **ask for**, request, signal for; get, obtain; *informal* hitch, hitch a lift.

thumbnail ▶ **adjective** *a thumbnail sketch of the social and political climate* **concise**, short, brief, succinct, to the point, compact, terse, curt, summary, outline, crisp, short and sweet, quick, rapid, pithy, epigrammatic, laconic, pointed, abridged, abbreviated, condensed, synoptic, compendious, summarized, contracted, curtailed, truncated, potted.
OPPOSITES extensive, prolix.

thump ▶ **verb 1** *someone thumped him in the back | he thumped on the cottage door* **hit**, strike, beat, batter, pound, attack, assault, knock, rap, smack, thwack, slap, pummel, punch, rain blows on, belabour, hammer, cudgel, thrash, bang, drub, welt, cuff, crack, buffet, box someone's ears; *informal* bash, clobber, clout, clip, wallop, beat the living daylights out of, give someone a (good) hiding/beating/drubbing, whack, belt, tan, biff, bop, lay into, pitch into, lace into, let someone have it, knock into the middle of next week, sock, lam, whomp; *Brit. informal* stick one on, slosh; *N. Amer. informal* boff, bust, slug, light into, whale; *Austral./NZ informal* dong, quilt; *literary* smite, swinge.
2 *her heart thumped with fright* **throb**, pound, thud, hammer, pulsate, pulse, pump, palpitate, race, beat heavily, go pit-a-pat, pitter-patter, vibrate, drum; *literary* pant, thrill; *rare* quop.

▶ **noun 1** *your father would give you a good thump if you did that* **blow**, hit, punch, smack, thwack, slap, thrashing, bang, hiding, drubbing, lambasting, welt, cuff, box, crack; *informal* bash, clobber, clout, clip, wallop, whack, belt, tan, biff, bop, sock, lam, whomp; *Brit. informal* slosh; *N. Amer. informal* boff, bust, slug, whale; *Austral./NZ informal* dong; *dated* buffet.
2 *she heard a thump like a ball thrown against a wall* **thud**, clunk, clonk, crash, smash, smack, bang, boom, thunder, wallop; stomp, stamp, clump, clomp; *informal* wham, whump.

thumping ▶ **adjective 1** *he could hear a thumping noise* **thudding**, pounding, banging, throbbing, hammering, drumming, clunking, clonking, crashing.
2 (*informal*) *a thumping majority | his party's thumping victory in the election* **enormous**, huge, massive, vast, very great, tremendous, substantial, goodly, prodigious, gigantic, giant, terrific, fantastic, colossal, immense, mammoth, monumental, stupendous, gargantuan, elephantine, titanic, mountainous, monstrous; **emphatic**, roaring, decisive, conclusive, striking, impressive, outstanding, unmistakable, notable, noteworthy, memorable, remarkable, extraordinary, resounding, phenomenal; complete, unqualified, out-and-out, thorough; *informal* whopping, whopping great, thundering, mega, jumbo, humongous, monster, astronomical, dirty great, rip-roaring; *Brit. informal* whacking, whacking great, ginormous.

▶ **adverb** *a thumping good read* **extremely**, very, really, thoroughly, exceedingly, immensely, incredibly, amazingly, remarkably, exceptionally, uncommonly, extraordinarily, perfectly, truly, simply, positive, positively, downright; *Scottish* unco; *French* très; *informal* terrifically, tremendously, seriously, majorly, dreadfully, terribly, awfully, fearfully, screamingly, thundering, right, ultra, mega, mucho, stonking, socking, oh-so, madly; *Brit. informal* damn, damned, blasted, flaming, confoundedly, jolly, hellish, bloody, blooming, dead, well, dirty; *N. Amer. informal* real, mighty, awful, powerful, way, bitching; *S. African informal* lekker; *informal, dated* devilish, frightfully, dashed; *vulgar slang* fucking, frigging; *archaic* exceeding, thrice.

thunder ▶ **noun 1** *thunder and lightning* **thunderclap**, thunder crack, thunder roll, roll of thunder, peal of thunder, rumble of thunder, crack of thunder, crash of thunder, rumbling, crashing, roar; *literary* thunderbolt.
2 *she heard the thunder of hooves behind her* **rumble**, rumbling, boom, booming, roar, roaring, pounding, thud, thudding, thump, thumping, crash, crashing, bang, banging, ring, ringing, grumble, growl, resounding, reverberation, echo; tattoo, drumbeat, rataplan.

▶ **verb 1** *below me the surf thrashed and thundered* **rumble**, **boom**, roar, blast,

T

pound, thud, thump, bang, ring, grumble, growl, resound, reverberate, echo, beat.
2 *he* ***thundered*** *on about Italy's invasion of Abyssinia* **protest strongly at**, make a protest against, fulminate against, inveigh against, rail against, rage against, declaim against, remonstrate about, expostulate about, make a fuss about, speak out against, express disapproval of; object to, raise objections to, take issue with, oppose strongly, complain vociferously/bitterly about, disagree violently with, kick against, take exception to, make/take a stand against, put up a fight against, challenge, curse; **condemn**, criticize severely, denounce, censure; *informal* kick up a fuss/stink about.
3 *'Answer me,' he thundered* **roar**, bellow, bark, yell, shout, bawl, howl, cry, clamour, bay, scream, screech; growl, yowl; *N. Amer. informal* holler; *rare* vociferate, ululate.

WORD LINKS
fear of thunder **brontophobia/tonitrophobia/keraunophobia**

thundering ▶ **adjective** *he knocked Garber to the floor with two thundering rights to the chin. See* THUMPING.
▶ **adverb** *a thundering good read. See* THUMPING.

thunderous ▶ **adjective** *thunderous applause* **very loud**, tumultuous, booming, rumbling, roaring, blaring, resounding, reverberating, reverberant, echoing, vibrant, ringing, carrying, deafening, ear-splitting, ear-piercing, noisy.

thunderstruck ▶ **adjective** *Charles was so thunderstruck that his voice sounded faint* **astonished**, astounded, amazed, nonplussed, taken aback, startled, bewildered, stunned, flabbergasted, staggered, shocked, stupefied, open-mouthed, dumbfounded, dumbstruck, speechless, at a loss for words, dazed, benumbed, perplexed, confounded, agape, goggle-eyed, wide-eyed, dismayed, disconcerted, jolted, shaken up; *informal* bowled over, knocked for six, floored, flummoxed, caught on the hop, caught on the wrong foot, unable to believe one's eyes; *Brit. informal* gobsmacked.

thus ▶ **adverb 1** *the alloy is highly reflective and was thus widely used for mirrors* **consequently**, as a consequence, in consequence, so, that being so, therefore, accordingly, hence, as a result, for this/that reason, because of this/that, on this/that account; *Latin* ergo.
2 *legislation forbids such data being held thus* **like this/that**, in this/that way, in this/that manner, in this/that fashion, so, like so; as follows, as shown, as demonstrated; *informal* thusly; *archaic* in/on this/that wise.
□ **thus far** *thus far they had found nothing* **so far**, until now/then, up until now/then, till now/then, up to now/then, up to this/that point, hitherto; *rare* thitherto.

thwack ▶ **verb** *Pedro thwacked the backs of the man's legs with his crutch* **hit**, strike, beat, batter, pound, attack, assault, knock, rap, smack, slap, pummel, thump, punch, cudgel, thrash, bang, drub, welt, cuff, crack, buffet, box someone's ears; *informal* bash, clobber, clout, clip, wallop, whack, belt, tan, biff, bop, lay into, pitch into, lace into, let someone have it, knock into the middle of next week, sock, lam, whomp; *Brit. informal* stick one on, slosh; *N. Amer. informal* boff, bust, slug, light into, whale; *Austral./NZ informal* dong, quilt; *literary* smite, swinge.
▶ **noun** *he was given a painful thwack with a rolled-up magazine* **blow**, hit, punch, thump, smack, slap, bang, welt, cuff, box, crack; *informal* bash, clobber, clout, clip, wallop, whack, belt, tan, biff, bop, sock, lam, whomp; *Brit. informal* slosh; *N. Amer. informal* boff, bust, slug, whale; *Austral./NZ informal* dong; *dated* buffet.

thwart ▶ **verb** *the move was intended to thwart peace negotiations* **foil**, frustrate, baulk, stand in the way of, forestall; scotch, derail, smash, dash; stop, check, block, prevent, defeat, impede, obstruct, snooker, oppose, hinder, hamper; upset the apple cart, spike someone's guns; *informal* put paid to, put the stopper on, put the kibosh on, do for, stymie, cook someone's goose; *Brit. informal* scupper, put the mockers on, nobble, queer someone's pitch; *Austral./NZ & Irish vulgar slang* root; *archaic* traverse.
OPPOSITES assist, facilitate.

tic ▶ **noun** *he had a nervous tic around his left eye* **twitch**, spasm, jerk, convulsion, contraction, tremor, tremble.

tick ▶ **noun 1** *all that was required was a tick in the 'Yes' or 'No' column* **mark**, stroke, dash, line; *N. Amer.* check, check mark.
2 *the tick of his watch* **clicking**, click, clack, clacking, click-clack, ticking, tick-tock, snick, snicking, plock, plocking, beat, tap, tapping.
3 (*Brit. informal*) *I won't be a tick* **moment**, second, minute, bit, little while, short time, instant, split second; *informal* sec, jiffy, jiff; *Brit. informal* mo, two ticks.
OPPOSITE a long time.
□ **in a tick** (*Brit. informal*) *I'll be with you in a tick* **(very) soon**, in a second, in a minute, in a moment, in a trice, in a flash, shortly, any second, any minute, any minute now, in a short time, in an instant, in the twinkling of an eye, in (less than) no time, in no time at all, before you know it, before long; *N. Amer.* momentarily; *informal* in a jiffy, in two shakes, in two shakes of a lamb's tail, before you can say Jack Robinson, in the blink of an eye, in a blink, in the wink of an eye, in a wink, before you can say knife; *Brit. informal* in two ticks, in a mo; *N. Amer. informal* in a snap.
▶ **verb 1** *he should have ticked the box for no publicity | make a list of the animals and* ***tick off*** *the ones that you see* **mark**, mark off, check off, indicate.
2 *I could hear the clock ticking* **click**, clack, tick-tock, snick, plock, beat, tap.
□ **tick someone off 1** (*Brit. informal*) *she ticked the children off for being late. See* REPRIMAND.
2 (*N. Amer.*) *he is seen as an outsider, and that really ticks me off* **annoy**, irritate, infuriate, anger, incense, inflame, enrage, vex, irk, chagrin, exasperate, madden, pique, provoke, nettle, disturb, upset, perturb, discompose, put out, try, try someone's patience, get on someone's nerves, bother, trouble, worry, agitate, ruffle, hound, rankle with, nag, torment, pain, distress, tease, frustrate, chafe, grate, fret, gall, outrage, displease, offend, disgust, dissatisfy, disquiet; *Brit.* rub up the wrong way; *N. English* mither; *informal* peeve, miff, bug, bite, eat, hassle, aggravate, rile, get to, hack off, make someone's blood boil, make someone see red, get someone's goat, get someone's hackles up, make someone's hackles rise, get someone's back up, get someone's dander up, drive up the wall, drive bananas, needle, be a thorn in someone's side/flesh, be a pain in the neck, ruffle someone's feathers, get in someone's hair, get up someone's nose, get under someone's skin, give someone a hard time; *Brit. informal* nark, get on someone's wick, give someone the hump, wind up, get across; *N. Amer. informal* rankle, ride, gravel; *vulgar slang* piss off; *Brit. vulgar slang* get on someone's tits.
□ **tick over** *the engine was just ticking over* **idle**, run slowly in neutral.

ticket ▶ **noun 1** *a railway ticket* **pass**, warrant, authorization, licence, permit; token, coupon, voucher; carnet, season ticket, rover, complimentary ticket, chit, slip, card, stub, counterfoil; *N. Amer.* rain check; *informal* comp, ducat; *Brit. informal* chitty; *rare* laissez-passer, firman.
2 *a parking ticket* **notice**, notification, warning, certificate.
3 *a price ticket* **label**, tag, sticker, slip, tally, tab, marker, docket.

tickle ▶ **verb 1** *he tried to tickle her under the chin* **stroke**, pet, lightly touch, lightly prod, chuck; *archaic* titillate.
2 *he found something that tickled his imagination* **stimulate**, interest, appeal to, excite, arouse, captivate.
3 *he is tickled by the idea* **amuse**, entertain, divert, please, delight, gladden, cheer up, satisfy, gratify; *informal* tickle someone pink.
OPPOSITE bore.
▶ **noun** *Dad gave my chin a little tickle* **stroke**, pet, light prod, chuck; *archaic* titillation.

ticklish ▶ **adjective** *policy-makers are considering the ticklish question* **problematic**, tricky, delicate, sensitive, controversial, awkward, prickly, thorny; **difficult**, knotty, tough, taxing, trying, troublesome, irksome, vexatious, bothersome, worrying, upsetting; **complicated**, complex, involved, convoluted, intricate, vexed; *informal* sticky; *Brit. informal* dodgy.

tide ▶ **noun 1** *ships come up the river with the tide* **tidal flow**, ebb and flow, flood, water, tidewater, tide race, ebb, surge, current, stream, movement.
2 *the whole tide of history seemed to be quickening* **course**, movement, direction, trend, current, drift, run, turn, tendency, tenor, swing.
▶ **verb**
□ **tide someone over** *she needed a small loan to tide her over* **sustain**, keep someone going, keep someone's head above water, see someone through; keep the wolf from the door, bridge the gap, keep someone in funds; **help out**, assist, aid.

tidings ▶ **plural noun** (*literary*) *the bearer of good tidings* **news**, information, intelligence, reports, advice, notification, word, talk, the latest; notice, communication, message, dispatch, communiqué, bulletin, account, story; rumour, gossip, tittle-tattle, intimation, scandal, exposé; *informal* info, low-down, dope; *Brit. informal* gen.

tidy ▶ **adjective 1** *a tidy room* **neat**, neat and tidy, as neat as a new pin, orderly, well ordered, in (good) order, well kept, shipshape (and Bristol fashion), in apple-pie order, immaculate, spick and span, uncluttered, organized, well organized, well arranged, sorted out, straight, straightened out, trim, spruce; *archaic* tricksy.
OPPOSITES untidy, messy.
2 *he's a very tidy person* **smart**, spruce, dapper, trim, neat, well groomed, well turned out; organized, well organized, methodical, systematic, efficient, meticulous; fastidious; *informal* natty; *dated* as if one had just stepped out of a bandbox; *archaic* trig.
OPPOSITES scruffy; disorganized.
3 (*informal*) *a tidy sum* **large**, sizeable, considerable, substantial, significant, appreciable, handsome, generous, ample, respectable, largish, biggish, fair, decent, decent-sized, healthy; *Scottish & N. English* bonny; *informal* not to be sneezed at, serious; *archaic* goodly.
OPPOSITES small, tiny.
▶ **verb 1** *I'd better* ***tidy up*** *the living room* **put in order**, clear up, sort out, put to rights, straighten (out), make shipshape, clean, clean up, spruce up; *informal* dejunk.
2 *she wanted to* ***tidy herself up*** *before her appointment* **groom oneself**, spruce oneself up, freshen oneself up, preen oneself, primp oneself, prink oneself, pretty oneself, beautify oneself; *informal* titivate oneself, doll oneself up; *Brit. informal* tart oneself up; *archaic* plume oneself, trig oneself.

tie *See centre pages for list of* **Ties** *(Neckties)*

T

▶ **verb 1** *they tied Max to a chair* **bind**, tie up, tether, hitch, strap, truss, fetter, rope, chain, make fast, moor, lash, attach, fasten, fix, secure, join, connect, link, couple.
OPPOSITE untie.
2 *Renwick bent to tie his shoelace* **do up**; knot, make a knot in, make a bow in, lace.
3 *women who do paid work at home feel themselves tied by childcare responsibilities* **restrict**, restrain, limit, constrain, confine, cramp; hamper, hinder, impede, tie down, interfere with, slow, obstruct, block, handicap, hamstring, shackle, encumber, inhibit, check, curb; tie someone's hands, cramp someone's style; *rare* cumber, trammel.
4 *a pay deal tied to a productivity agreement* **link**, couple, connect, relate, join, marry, wed; make conditional on, bind up with, bundle with.
5 *they tied for second place* **draw**, be equal, be even, be level, be neck and neck.
□ **tie someone down** *they didn't marry because she was afraid of being tied down. See* TIE *sense 3.*
□ **tie in** *you haven't seen how all this* **ties in with** *their long-term aims* **be consistent**, tally, correlate, agree, be in agreement, accord, concur, coincide, conform, fit in, harmonize, be in tune, dovetail; correspond to, match, parallel, reflect, mirror; *informal* square; *N. Amer. informal* jibe.
□ **tie something in** *her husband is able to tie in his shifts with hers at the hospital* **fit in**, harmonize, dovetail, match, mirror, make something consistent, make something correspond, make something tally, make something correlate, make something agree, make something accord, make something coincide, make something conform; *informal* square.
□ **tie someone/something up 1** *Gabriel tied up his pony* **bind**, tie, tether, hitch, strap, truss, fetter, rope, chain, make fast, moor, lash, attach, fasten, fix, secure; join, connect, link.
OPPOSITE untie.
2 *do not tie your money up if you think you may need it quickly* **commit**, make unavailable, invest long-term.
3 *he is tied up in meetings all morning* **occupy**, engage, busy, keep busy, book, reserve, commit.
4 *they were anxious to tie up the contract* **finalize**, conclude, bring to a conclusion, wind up, wrap up, complete, finish off, seal, set the seal on, settle, secure, clinch.
▶ **noun 1** *a sleeveless jacket fastened at the back with ties* **lace**, string, cord, ligature, wire, bond, fetter, link, fastening, fastener.
2 *he was wearing a collar and tie* **necktie**; neckwear.
3 *it is important that we keep family ties strong* **bond**, connection, link, liaison, attachment, association, kinship, affiliation, allegiance, friendship, cords, union, relationship, relatedness, interdependence.
4 *pets can be a tremendous tie* **restriction**, curb, limitation, constraint, obligation, commitment, restraint, hindrance, check, obstruction, encumbrance, impediment, handicap.
5 *there was a tie for first place* **draw**, dead heat, deadlock, stalemate.
6 (*Brit.*) *Turkey's World Cup tie against Holland* **contest**, fixture, match, game, event, trial, test, test match, meeting; bout, fight, prizefight, duel; quarter-final, semi-final, final; friendly, derby, local derby; play-off, replay, rematch; *Canadian & Scottish* playdown; *N. Amer.* split; *archaic* tourney.

tie-in ▶ **noun** *there's a tie-in to another case I'm working on* **connection**, association, link, correlation, correspondence, parallel, tie-up, interrelation, relationship, relation, relatedness, interconnection, interdependence, analogy, similarity.

tier ▶ **noun 1** *rising tiers of empty seats* **row**, rank, bank, line; **layer**, level, plane, floor, storey, deck.
2 *the most senior tier of management* **grade**, gradation, step, echelon, point on the scale, rung on the ladder; *archaic* degree.

tie-up ▶ **noun** *the Bombay-based firm is contemplating tie-ups with software houses abroad* **link**, link-up, association, relationship, liaison; deal, bargain, contract, (business) arrangement, covenant, accommodation, understanding, settlement, protocol, accord, entente, compact, bond; alliance, coalition, federation, axis; *N. Amer.* trust.

tiff ▶ **noun** (*informal*) *she had had a tiff with Mr Carson* **quarrel**, squabble, row, argument, fight, contretemps, disagreement, difference of opinion, dissension, falling-out, dispute, disputation, contention, clash, altercation, shouting match, exchange, war of words; tussle, conflict, fracas, affray, wrangle, tangle; *Irish, N. Amer., & Austral.* donnybrook; *informal* set-to, run-in, shindig, shindy, stand-up, spat, scrap, dust-up; *Brit. informal* barney, slanging match, bunfight, ding-dong, bust-up, ruck; *Scottish informal* rammy; *N. Amer. informal* rhubarb; *archaic* broil, miff; *Scottish archaic* threap, collieshangie; *French archaic* tracasserie(s).

tight ▶ **adjective 1** *he took a tight grip on her arm* **firm**, fast, secure, fixed, clenched, clinched.
OPPOSITES relaxed, insecure.
2 *the rope was pulled tight* **taut**, rigid, stiff, tense, stretched, strained, stressed.
OPPOSITE slack.
3 *tight jeans* **tight-fitting**, close-fitting, narrow, figure-hugging, skintight, sheath-like; *informal* sprayed on.
OPPOSITE loose.
4 *a tight mass of fibres* **compact**, compacted, compressed, dense, hard, unyielding, solid.
OPPOSITE loose.
5 *rather a tight space* **small**, tiny, narrow, compact, poky, limited, restricted, confined, cramped, constricted, uncomfortable, minimal, sparse, inadequate; *rare* strait, incommodious.
OPPOSITES generous, roomy.
6 *the joint will be perfectly tight against petrol leaks* **impervious**, impenetrable, sealed, sound, hermetic; watertight, waterproof, airtight.
OPPOSITE leaking.
7 *security was tight at yesterday's ceremony* **strict**, rigorous, stringent, tough, rigid, firm, uncompromising, exacting, systematic, meticulous, painstaking, scrupulous.
OPPOSITE lax.
8 *he's in a tight spot* **problematic**, tricky, delicate, sensitive, controversial, awkward, prickly, thorny; **difficult**, knotty, tough, taxing, trying, troublesome, irksome, vexatious, bothersome, worrying, upsetting; *informal* sticky; *Brit. informal* dodgy.
OPPOSITE problem-free.
9 *there's no substitute for tight writing* **succinct**, economic, pithy, crisp, straightforward, concise, condensed, well structured, laconic, terse, to the point, summary, short and sweet, in a few well-chosen words; *rare* compendious, epigrammatic, synoptic, aphoristic, gnomic.
OPPOSITE verbose.
10 *it was a tight race* **close**, even, evenly matched, well matched; hard-fought, neck and neck.
OPPOSITE open.
11 *money is a bit tight just now* **scarce**, scanty, scant, skimpy, meagre, sparse; reduced, depleted, diminished, low, in short supply, limited; deficient, inadequate, insufficient.
OPPOSITES plentiful, abundant.
12 *he's tight with his money* **mean**, miserly, parsimonious, niggardly, close-fisted, penny-pinching, cheese-paring, penurious, Scrooge-like, ungenerous, illiberal, close; *informal* stingy, mingy, tight-fisted; *N. Amer. informal* cheap; *vulgar slang* tight-arsed; *archaic* near.
OPPOSITE generous.
13 (*informal*) *he came home tight from the pub. See* DRUNK.

tighten ▶ **verb 1** *when the structure is flat,* **tighten up** *the fixing screws* **secure**, make fast, make more secure, screw up, give an extra turn to.
OPPOSITE loosen.
2 *he tightened his grip on her arm* **strengthen**, make stronger, reinforce, harden, consolidate.
OPPOSITE loosen.
3 *she tightened the rope about his ankles* **tauten**, make/draw taut, make/draw tight, stretch, strain, extend, make rigid, rigidify, stiffen, tense.
OPPOSITE slacken.
4 *my throat tightened | he tightened his lips* **narrow**, become narrow/narrower, become tight/tighter, become pinched; constrict, contract, brace, draw in, compress, screw up, pucker, purse; *N. Amer.* squinch; *rare* constringe.
OPPOSITE relax.
5 *councillors have asked supermarkets to* **tighten up** *car park security* **increase**, make stricter, make more rigorous, make more stringent, make more rigid, stiffen, toughen (up), heighten, escalate, scale up; *informal* up, crank up, beef (up).
OPPOSITE relax.

tight-fisted ▶ **adjective** *being tight-fisted individuals, we bypassed the fee-paying nature trail* **mean**, **miserly**, parsimonious, niggardly, close-fisted, penny-pinching, cheese-paring, penurious, Scrooge-like, ungenerous, illiberal, close; *informal* stingy, mingy, tight; *N. Amer. informal* cheap; *vulgar slang* tight-arsed; *archaic* near.
OPPOSITES generous, liberal.

tight-lipped ▶ **adjective** *the company remains tight-lipped about the launch date* **reticent**, taciturn, uncommunicative, unforthcoming, unresponsive, close-mouthed, close-lipped; silent, quiet, unspeaking; guarded, secretive, private, withdrawn, playing one's cards close to one's chest, of few words, untalkative; *informal* mum.
OPPOSITES forthcoming, chatty.

till[1] ▶ **preposition & conjunction 1** *he stayed in bed till 7 | I will look after you till you die* **until**, up to, up till, up until, as late as, up to the time of/that, until such time as, pending; *N. Amer.* through.
OPPOSITES beyond, after.
2 *ownership is not transferred till delivery* **before**, prior to, previous to, up to, until, up until, up till, earlier than, in advance of, ante-, pre-.
OPPOSITE after.

till[2] ▶ **noun** *she counted the money in the till | there were queues at the till* **cash register**, cash box, cash drawer, strongbox; **checkout**, cash desk, pay desk, counter.
□ **have one's fingers/hand in the till** *he was caught with his fingers in the till and sacked* **steal**, thieve, rob one's employer, help oneself, embezzle, misappropriate funds; *rare* peculate, defalcate.

till[3] ▶ **verb** *he went back to tilling the land* **cultivate**, work, farm, plough, dig,

T

spade, turn over, turn up, break up, loosen, harrow, prepare, fertilize, plant; *literary* delve.

tilt ▶ **verb 1** *his hat tilted forward a little | they tilted their chairs back on two legs* **lean**, tip, list, slope, camber, bank, slant, incline, pitch, dip, cant, bevel, angle, cock, heel, careen, bend, be at an angle.
OPPOSITES level, right; be/come level, be/come upright.
2 *he tilts at his prey* **charge**, rush, run; **lunge**, prod, poke, jab, thrust.
3 (*historical*) *like a knight tilting at a wayside tournament* **joust**, tourney, enter the lists; contend, spar, fight, clash.
▶ **noun 1** *Mum's cup was on a tilt* **slope**, list, camber, gradient, bank, slant, incline, pitch, dip, cant, bevel, angle, heel; *N. Amer.* grade, downgrade, upgrade.
2 *a tilt of the head* **nod**, dip, tip, inclination, cock, bob.
3 (*historical*) *knights would take part in a tilt* **joust**, tournament, tourney, lists, combat, contest, fight, duel.
4 *a tilt at the European Cup* **attempt on**, bid for; *informal* go, crack, shot.
□ **(at) full tilt 1** *they charged full tilt down the side of the dell* **(at) full speed**, (at) full pelt, as fast as one's legs can carry one, at a gallop, helter-skelter, headlong, hotfoot, post-haste, hurriedly, hastily, wildly, pell-mell, impetuously, recklessly, rashly, at breakneck speed, precipitately, impulsively; *informal* p.d.q. (pretty damn quick), double quick, at a lick, hell for leather, pronto, at the double, a mile a minute, like the wind, like a bomb, like a bat out of hell, like a scalded cat, like the deuce, like nobody's business, like (greased) lightning, like a madman/madwoman; *Brit. informal* like the clappers, at a rate of knots, like billy-o; *N. Amer. informal* lickety-split; *literary* apace; *archaic* hurry-scurry.
2 *the marketing blitz has raged at full tilt for some time now* **with great force**, (with) full force, full blast, with a will, for all one is worth, with might and main, with all the stops out, all out, with a vengeance, vigorously, energetically, strongly, powerfully, madly; *informal* hammer and tongs, going great guns, like crazy, like mad; *Brit. informal* like billy-o.

timber ▶ **noun 1** *tenants had the right to cut standing timber* **wood**, logs, firewood; planks, wood products; forest, woodland, woods; *N. Amer.* lumber.
2 *the timbers of wrecked ships* **(wooden) beam**, spar, pole, plank, batten, lath, board, joist, rafter.

timbre ▶ **noun** *the Czech orchestra have just the right timbre for Smetana* **tone**, sound, sound quality, voice, voice quality, colour, tone colour, tonality, resonance, ring.

time ▶ **noun 1** *what time is it?* **hour**; *dated* o'clock.
2 *late at night was the best time to leave* **moment**, point, point in time, occasion, hour, minute, second, instant, juncture, stage, phase.
3 *he worked there for a time* **while**, spell, stretch, stint, span, season, interval, period, period of time, length of time, duration, run, space, phase, stage, term; *Brit. informal* patch.
4 *in the time of the dinosaurs* **era**, age, epoch, period, aeon, years, days; generation, date.
5 *I've known a lot of women in my time* **lifetime**, life, life span, allotted span, days, time on earth, existence, threescore years and ten; this mortal coil; *informal* born days.
6 *he had been a professional actor in his time* **heyday**, day, hour, prime, best days/years, youth, vigour, springtime, salad days, maturity.
7 *he would have a hard time in prison* **situation**, state of affairs, experience, life, way of life; **conditions**, circumstances, affairs, surroundings, environment, context, background, ambience, atmosphere.
8 *tunes in waltz time* **rhythm**, tempo, beat, pulse, flow; metre, measure, cadence, pattern; accent, stress.
□ **ahead of time** *the bridge was declared ready seven months ahead of time* **early**, earlier than expected, earlier than required, in good time, with time to spare, timely, in advance, sooner, in readiness, already.
OPPOSITES behind time, late.
□ **ahead of one's/its time** *he broke all the rules and achieved an effect that was way ahead of its time* **revolutionary**, avant-garde, futuristic, innovatory, innovative, innovational, trailblazing, pioneering, groundbreaking; ultra-modern, advanced, highly developed, the latest, new, the newest, up to the minute.
OPPOSITE behind the times.
□ **all the time** *he works all the time* **constantly**, the entire time, around the clock, day and night, night and day, {morning, noon, and night}, {day in, day out}, at all times, always, without a break, ceaselessly, endlessly, incessantly, perpetually, permanently, interminably, unceasingly, continuously, continually, eternally, unremittingly, remorselessly, relentlessly; *informal* 24-7; *archaic* without surcease.
OPPOSITES never; intermittently.
□ **at one time 1** *she was a nurse at one time* **formerly**, previously, once, in the past, at one point, at some point, once upon a time, time was when, in days/times gone by, in times past, in the (good) old days, back in the day, long ago; *literary* in days/times of yore, of yore; *archaic* sometime, erst, erstwhile, whilom.
OPPOSITE never.
2 *several matches were going on at one time* **simultaneously**, at once, at the same time, at one and the same time, at the same instant/moment, concurrently, concomitantly; together, all together, alongside each other, in unison, in concert, in chorus, as a group; *rare* synchronously.
OPPOSITES separately, consecutively.
□ **at the same time 1** *they arrived at the same time* **simultaneously**, at the same instant/moment, together, all together, as a group, at once, at one and the same time, at one time, concurrently, concomitantly, alongside each other, in unison, in concert, in chorus; *rare* synchronously.
OPPOSITES separately, consecutively.
2 *I can't really explain it, but at the same time I'm not convinced* **nevertheless**, nonetheless, even so, however, but, still, yet, though, be that as it may, for all that, in spite of that/everything, despite that/everything, after everything, having said that, just the same, all the same, in any event, come what may, at any rate, notwithstanding, regardless, anyway, anyhow; *informal* still and all; *archaic* howbeit, withal, natheless.
□ **at times** *she is at times cruel and ruthless* **sometimes**, occasionally, from time to time, (every) now and then/again, every so often, (every) once in a while, on occasion, on occasions, on the odd occasion, off and on, at intervals, periodically, sporadically, spasmodically, erratically, irregularly, intermittently, in/by fits and starts, fitfully, discontinuously, piecemeal; *rare* interruptedly.
OPPOSITE constantly.
□ **behind time** *she was behind time and had to rush* **late**, not on time, behind, behind schedule, behind target, behindhand, delayed, running late, overdue, belated, tardy, unpunctual; slow, dilatory.
OPPOSITES ahead of time, early.
□ **behind the times** *the children considered Dad to be behind the times* **old-fashioned**, outmoded, out of fashion, out of date, unfashionable, frumpish, frumpy, out of style, outdated, dated, out, outworn, old, former, dead, musty, old-time, old-world, behindhand, past, bygone, archaic, obsolescent, obsolete, ancient, antiquated, superannuated; defunct, medieval, prehistoric, antediluvian, old-fogeyish, old-fangled, conservative, backward-looking, quaint, anachronistic, crusted, feudal, fusty, moth-eaten, olde worlde; *French* démodé, vieux jeu, passé; *informal* old hat, square, not with it, out of the ark, creaky, mouldy; *N. Amer. informal* horse-and-buggy, clunky, rinky-dink, mossy; *archaic* square-toed.
OPPOSITES up to date; ahead of one's time.
□ **for the time being** *the sale has been cancelled for the time being* **for now**, for the moment, for the present, in the interim, for the nonce, in/for the meantime, in the meanwhile; for a short time, for a short/little while, briefly, momentarily, fleetingly; temporarily, provisionally, pro tem; *informal* for the minute; *Latin* pro tempore, ad interim; *French* en attendant.
OPPOSITE permanently.
□ **from time to time** *all children act up from time to time* **sometimes**, occasionally, (every) now and then/again, every so often, (every) once in a while, on occasion, on occasions, on the odd occasion, off and on, at times, at intervals, periodically, sporadically, spasmodically, erratically, irregularly, intermittently, in/by fits and starts, fitfully, discontinuously, piecemeal; *rare* interruptedly.
OPPOSITE constantly.
□ **in no time** *you'll have perfect-looking skin in no time | I can run there and back in no time* **(very) soon**, in a second, in a minute, in a moment, in a trice, in a flash, shortly, any second, any minute, any minute now, in a short time, in an instant, in less than no time, in no time at all, in next to no time, before you know it, before long; **(very) quickly**, rapidly, swiftly, at the speed of light; **suddenly**, immediately, instantly, instantaneously, promptly, without delay, post-haste; *N. Amer.* momentarily; *informal* in a jiffy, in two shakes, in two shakes of a lamb's tail, before you can say Jack Robinson, before you can say knife, in the twinkling of an eye, in a twinkling, in the blink of an eye, in a blink, in the wink of an eye, in a wink; *Brit. informal* in a tick, in two ticks, in a mo; *N. Amer. informal* in a snap.
OPPOSITES not for a while; slowly.
□ **in good time** *we'll be there in good time* **punctual(ly)**, prompt(ly), on time; early, with time to spare, ahead of time, before the appointed time, ahead of schedule.
OPPOSITE late.
□ **in time 1** *I came back in time for Molly's party* **early enough**, in good time, punctually, promptly, on time, not too late, with time to spare, at the appointed/right time, on schedule.
OPPOSITE late.
2 *the attraction of the uniform palled, and, in time, she left the service* **eventually**, ultimately, finally, in the end, as time goes on/by, by and by, one day, some day, sooner or later, in a while, after a bit, in the long run, in the fullness of time, when all is said and done, at a later time, at a later date, at length, at a future time/date, at some point in the future, in the future, in time to come, in due course.
OPPOSITE never.
□ **many a time** *many a time they had gone to bed hungry* **frequently**, often, repeatedly, again and again, over and over (again), time and (time) again, time after time, many times, on many occasions, many times over; {day in, day out}, day after day, {week in, week out}, night and day, all the time; persistently, recurrently, constantly, continually, regularly; *N. Amer.* oftentimes; *Latin* ad nauseam; *literary* many a time and oft, oft, oft-times.
OPPOSITE occasionally.

T

□ **on time** *the train was on time | we paid our bills on time* **punctual(ly)**, prompt(ly), in time, in good time, to/on schedule, when expected, timely, well timed; *informal* on the dot; *Brit. informal* bang/spot on time.
OPPOSITE late.

□ **time after time** *the camera produces excellent results time after time* **repeatedly**, again and again, over and over (again), time and (time) again, frequently, often, many times, many a time, on many occasions, many times over; {day in, day out}, day after day, {week in, week out}, night and day, all the time; persistently, recurrently, constantly, continually, regularly; *N. Amer.* oftentimes; *Latin* ad nauseam; *literary* many a time and oft, oft, oft-times.
OPPOSITES sporadically, never.

▶ **verb 1** *his meeting had been timed for three o'clock* **schedule**, set, set up, arrange, organize, fix, fix up, fix a time for, book, line up, slot in, prearrange, timetable, bill, programme, plan; *N. Amer.* slate.
2 *I had timed my arrival just about perfectly* **regulate**, adjust, calculate, set, synchronize.
3 *he timed it—it took two minutes and forty-three seconds* **measure**, put a stopwatch on, meter, count; *informal* clock.

WORD LINKS

relating to time	**chronological, horological, temporal**
related prefix	**chrono- (e.g. *chronograph*)**
study of time	**horology**
measurement of time	**chronometry, horology**
fear of time	**chronophobia**

time-honoured ▶ **adjective** *the barley is spread out and turned by hand in the time-honoured fashion* **traditional**, established, long-established, long-standing, long-lived, old-time, historic, age-old, folk, old-world, ancestral, enduring, lasting; **respected**, tried and tested, proven; **customary**, conventional, familiar, classic, ritual, ritualistic, habitual, set, fixed, routine, usual, wonted.

timeless ▶ **adjective** *this pretty wall clock has timeless good looks* **lasting**, **classic**, enduring, ageless, permanent, perpetual, perennial, abiding, unfailing, unchanging, never-changing, changeless, unvarying, unfading, invariable, unending, without end, ceaseless, never dying, undying, deathless, immortal, eternal, everlasting, immutable, indestructible, imperishable; *rare* sempiternal, perdurable.
OPPOSITES ephemeral, fleeting.

timely ▶ **adjective** *a timely warning* **opportune**, well timed, at the right time, prompt, punctual, convenient, appropriate, suitable, apt, fitting, expedient, seasonable, felicitous.
OPPOSITES inopportune, ill-timed, inappropriate, late.

CHOOSE THE RIGHT WORD

timely, opportune, auspicious
See OPPORTUNE.

timepiece ▶ **noun**. *See centre pages for list of* **Clocks and Watches**

time-server ▶ **noun** *the party is filling key state posts with its own loyal time-servers* **equivocator**, trimmer, Vicar of Bray; **hypocrite**, Janus, double-dealer, snake in the grass; **sycophant**, toady, crawler, fawner, truckler, groveller, kowtower, minion, hanger-on, leech, puppet, spaniel; *informal* bootlicker, yes-man; *rare* tergiversator.

time-serving ▶ **adjective** *they left the field to their more time-serving and less scrupulous brethren* **equivocating**, shifting, trimming, temporizing, shuffling; **hypocritical**, two-faced, double-dealing, treacherous, perfidious; **sycophantic**, servile, subservient, deferential, obsequious, grovelling, toadying; *rare* tergiversating.

timetable ▶ **noun 1** *a bus timetable | do you have a hectic timetable and feel you just don't have the time to exercise?* **schedule**, programme, agenda, calendar, diary, appointment book/diary, engagement diary, social life; list, rota, roster; itinerary.
2 *there was little place on the timetable for music, dance, and art* **syllabus**, curriculum, course, programme of instruction, teaching programme.
▶ **verb** *German lessons were timetabled on Wednesday and Friday* **schedule**, set, set up, arrange, organize, sort out, fix, fix up, fix a time for, time, book, line up, slot in, prearrange, bill, programme, plan; *N. Amer.* slate.

time-worn ▶ **adjective 1** *the carpet was old and time-worn* **worn out**, worn, well worn, old; thin, holey, moth-eaten, mangy, ragged, frayed, tattered, battered, dog-eared; decrepit, shabby, scruffy, unkempt; having seen better days, falling apart at the seams, in shreds, in tatters, falling to pieces, broken-down, ruined, damaged; *informal* tatty, ratty, the worse for wear; *N. Amer. informal* raggedy, raggedy-ass; *Austral. informal* warby; *rare* out at elbows.
OPPOSITES pristine, new.
2 *time-worn faces* **old**, aged, ancient, weathered, lined, wrinkled, hoary.
OPPOSITES unlined, fresh.
3 *unimaginative and time-worn presentations* **hackneyed**, trite, banal, vapid, platitudinous, clichéd, cliché-ridden, stock, conventional, unoriginal, overused, overworked, worn out, threadbare, tired, stale, dull, pedestrian, run-of-the-mill, routine, humdrum, stereotyped; *informal* old hat, corny, played out; *rare* truistic, bromidic.
OPPOSITES imaginative, fresh.

timid ▶ **adjective** *I was too timid to ask for what I wanted* **easily frightened**, lacking courage, fearful, apprehensive, afraid, frightened, scared, faint-hearted; trembling, quaking, cowering, weak-kneed; **shy**, diffident, bashful, self-effacing, shrinking, unassuming, unassertive, reserved, retiring, reticent, quiet, timorous, nervous, modest, demure, coy, meek, humble; **cowardly**, pusillanimous, lily-livered, pigeon-hearted, spineless, craven; *informal* wimpish, sissy, yellow, yellow-bellied, chicken, gutless; *archaic* poor-spirited, recreant.
OPPOSITES bold, forthcoming, brazen.

CHOOSE THE RIGHT WORD

timid, shy, bashful, diffident
See SHY.

timorous ▶ **adjective** *she was no helpless, timorous female* **easily frightened**, lacking courage, fearful, apprehensive, faint-hearted; trembling, quaking, cowering, weak-kneed; **shy**, diffident, bashful, self-effacing, shrinking, unassuming, unassertive, reserved, retiring, reticent, quiet, timid, nervous, modest, demure, coy, meek, humble; *informal* wimpish, sissy, yellow, yellow-bellied, chicken, gutless, trepidatious; *archaic* poor-spirited, recreant.
OPPOSITES bold, forthcoming, brazen.

tincture ▶ **noun 1** *tincture of iodine* **solution**, suspension, infusion, potion, elixir, extract, essence, quintessence, concentrate.
2 *she could not keep a tincture of bitterness out of her voice* **trace**, note, tinge, touch, dash, suggestion, hint, bit, scintilla, impression, air, savour, flavour, element, strand, streak, vein, overtone, suspicion, soupçon, whisper, whiff.

tinge ▶ **verb 1** *a mass of white blossom tinged with pink* **tint**, colour, dye, stain, shade, suffuse, flush, imbue, wash, overlay, bathe, saturate, steep, impregnate, permeate, penetrate, pervade, run through.
2 *his optimism is tinged with realism* **influence**, affect, touch, flavour, colour, suffuse, imbue, modify, magnify, distort, poison, sour, spice up, enliven.
▶ **noun 1** *the light had a blue tinge to it* **tint**, colour, shade, tone, hue, tincture, cast, flush, blush.
2 *a tinge of cynicism appeared in his writing* **trace**, note, touch, dash, suggestion, hint, bit, scintilla, impression, air, savour, flavour, element, strand, streak, vein, overtone, suspicion, soupçon, whisper, whiff, tincture.

tingle ▶ **verb 1** *her flesh still tingled from the shock* **prickle**, sting, smart, prick, itch, be itchy, be irritated, have a creeping sensation, have goose pimples, have gooseflesh, have pins and needles; *N. Amer.* have goosebumps.
2 *she was tingling with excitement* **tremble**, quiver, quaver, shiver, quake, twitch, wiggle, throb, shudder, pulsate, vibrate.
▶ **noun 1** *she felt a tingle in the back of her neck* **prickling**, tingling, sting, stinging, smart, smarting, pricking, itch, creeping sensation, goose pimples, gooseflesh, pins and needles; *N. Amer.* goosebumps.
2 *she felt another tingle of excitement* **tremor**, wave, rush, surge, flash, flush, blaze, stab, dart, throb, tremble, quiver, shiver, flutter, shudder, vibration; flow, gush, stream, flood, torrent.

tinker ▶ **verb** *he spent hours* **tinkering with** *the car | these proposals will do no more than* **tinker with** *the existing laws* **try to mend/improve**, work amateurishly on, fiddle with, play (about/around) with, toy with, trifle with, dally with, dabble with, potter about with, fool about/around with; tamper with, interfere with, meddle with; tinker at/with the edges of, adjust slightly; *informal* mess about/around with, rearrange the deckchairs on the Titanic; *Brit. informal* muck about/around with.

tinkle ▶ **verb 1** *a bell tinkled as he went into the shop* **ring**, jingle, jangle, chime, peal, ding, ping, clink, chink; *rare* tintinnabulate.
2 *cool water tinkled in the stone fountain* **splash**, purl, babble, burble; *literary* plash.
▶ **noun 1** *the tinkle of the doorbell* **ring**, chime, peal, ding, ping, clink, chink, jingle, jangle; *rare* tintinnabulation.
2 *the faint tinkle of water* **splash**, purl, babble, burble; *literary* plash.
3 (*Brit. informal*) *I'll give them a tinkle* **telephone call**, phone call, call; *informal* buzz; *Brit. informal* ring, bell.

tinny ▶ **adjective 1** *tinny music played in the background* **jangling**, jangly, jingling, jingly, plinky, thin, metallic.
OPPOSITES full, round, deep.
2 *a tinny little car* **flimsy**, thin, insubstantial, cheap, cheapjack, shoddy, poor-quality, inferior, low-grade, tawdry, rubbishy, trashy, gimcrack, jerry-built; *informal* tacky, tatty.
OPPOSITES solid, stout, well made.

tinpot ▶ adjective (*informal*) *some tinpot little dictatorship* **inferior**, second-rate, third-rate, gimcrack; *informal* Mickey Mouse, poxy; *Brit. informal* twopenny-halfpenny, pathetic; *N. Amer. informal* two-bit, dime-store; *N. Amer. vulgar slang* chickenshit.

tinsel ▶ noun **1** *fairy lights and tinsel hung from the ceiling* **spangle**, glitter, metallic yarn; *rare* clinquant.
2 *his taste for the tinsel of the art world* **ostentation**, showiness, show, showing off, ostentatiousness, pretentiousness, pretension, vulgarity, conspicuousness, obtrusiveness, display, flamboyance, gaudiness, garishness, tawdriness, meretriciousness, brashness, loudness, extravagance, ornateness, theatricality; kitschness, affectation, bad taste, tastelessness, self-advertisement, exhibitionism, flaunting; *informal* flashiness, flash, flashness, glitz, glitziness, ritziness, swankiness, swank, splashiness.
▶ adjective *Hollywood and its tinsel stardom* **ostentatious**, pretentious, showy, conspicuous, obtrusive, flamboyant, gaudy, garish, tawdry, meretricious, trashy, brash, vulgar, loud, extravagant, fancy, ornate, affected, theatrical, overdone, over-elaborate; kitsch, tasteless; *informal* flash, flashy, over the top, OTT, glitzy, ritzy, swanky, splashy; *N. Amer. informal* superfly, bling-bling, dicty.

tint ▶ noun **1** *the sky was taking on an apricot tint* **shade**, colour, tone, hue, tinge, cast, tincture, flush, blush.
2 *a hair tint* **dye**, colourant, colouring, wash; streaking, highlights, lowlights.

tiny ▶ adjective *a tiny person | a tiny sum* **minute**, small-scale, scaled-down, mini, baby, toy, pocket, petite, midget, dwarf, dwarfish, pygmy, knee-high, miniature, minuscule, microscopic, infinitesimal, micro, diminutive, pocket-sized, reduced, Lilliputian; trivial, trifling, negligible, insignificant, unimportant, minor, of no account, of no consequence, of no importance, not worth bothering about, not worth mentioning, inconsequential, minimal, inappreciable, imperceptible, nugatory, petty; token, nominal; **paltry**, inadequate, insufficient, meagre, derisory, pitiful, pathetic, miserable; *Scottish* wee; *N. Amer.* vest-pocket; *informal* teeny, teeny-weeny, teensy, teensy-weensy, weeny, itsy-bitsy, itty-bitty, eensy, eensy-weensy, tiddly, pint-sized, bite-sized, piddling, piffling, measly, mingy, poxy; *Brit. informal* titchy; *N. Amer. informal* little-bitty, nickel-and-dime.
OPPOSITES huge, significant.

tip[1] ▶ noun **1** *the tip of the spear* **point**, end, extremity, head, sharp end, spike, prong, tine, nib.
2 *the tips of the Glencoe mountains* **peak**, point, top, summit, apex, crown, crest, pinnacle, heights, brow, cap; spire; vertex, acme, zenith, apogee.
3 *the sticks have tips fitted to protect them* **cap**, cover, ferrule.
▶ verb *mountains tipped with snow* **cap**, top, crown, surmount, finish.

tip[2] ▶ verb **1** *the hay caught fire when the candle **tipped over** | the boat **tipped over*** **overturn**, turn over, topple (over), fall (over), tumble (over), overbalance; keel over, pitch (over), turn topsy-turvy, capsize, turn turtle; *Nautical* pitchpole.
OPPOSITE right itself.
2 *a whale could **tip over** a small boat* **upset**, overturn, topple over, turn over, throw over, knock over, push over, knock down, upend, invert, capsize, turn topsy-turvy; *informal* roll; *archaic* overset.
OPPOSITES level, right.
3 *I tipped my seat back | the car had tipped to one side* **lean**, tilt, list, slope, camber, bank, slant, incline, pitch, dip, cant, bevel, angle, cock, heel, careen, bend, be at an angle.
OPPOSITES level, right; be/become level, be/become upright.
4 *she tipped the contents of the bucket into the trough* **pour**, empty, drain, unload, dump, discharge, jettison, offload, drop, decant; *informal* slosh, slop.
▶ noun (*Brit.*) *you will have to take your own rubbish to the tip* **dump**, rubbish/refuse dump, rubbish/refuse heap, rubbish/refuse tip, dumping ground, dustheap, slag heap; midden, dunghill, dung heap; *Brit.* scrapyard; *N. Amer.* junkyard, nuisance grounds.

tip[3] ▶ noun **1** *he left the waiter a generous tip* **gratuity**, baksheesh, bonus, little extra, bit extra, present, gift, reward, inducement; *French* pourboire; *S. African* bonsella; *W. Indian* smalls; *informal* sweetener; *Brit. informal* dropsy.
2 *lots of useful tips to help you make the right choice* **hint**, suggestion, piece of advice, word, word of advice, pointer, cue, clue, guideline, recommendation, maxim; warning, word of warning; tip-off, forecast; advice, counsel, guidance, inside information; *Brit.* nap; *informal* how-to, wrinkle.
▶ verb **1** *it was customary to tip taxi drivers* **give a tip to**, reward, remunerate; *informal* sweeten.
2 (*Brit.*) *she is being tipped as an Oscar nominee* **predict**, back, recommend, think of, expect; *Brit.* nap.

tip[4] ▶ verb *sometimes the other player will fool you by just tipping a weak shot over your head* **strike/hit lightly**, touch, tap, flick, flip, lob, kiss, brush, pat, nudge.

tip-off ▶ noun (*informal*) *arrests came after a tip-off from a member of the public* **piece of information**, message, alert, prompt, warning, forewarning; hint, idea, cue, clue, lead; information received, evidence, advice, information, notification.

tipple ▶ verb **1** *boys discovered tippling were punished* **drink alcohol**, drink, have a drink; *informal* indulge, imbibe, booze, take a drop, wet one's whistle, knock something back, hit the bottle, take to the bottle, crack a bottle; *Brit. informal* bevvy; *N. Amer. informal* bend one's elbow; *archaic* wassail, tope.
2 *he tippled some extra rum ration* **drink**, swallow, gulp (down), guzzle, quaff, attack, down, drink up/down, get down, finish off, polish off, drain, empty, wash something down with, have, take, partake of, ingest, consume, sup, sip, lap; *informal* sink, kill, imbibe, swig, glug, slug, slurp, swill, hit, knock back, dispose of, toss off, get one's laughing gear round; *Brit. informal* get outside (of), shift, murder, neck, bevvy; *N. Amer. informal* snarf, chug, scarf (down); *archaic* bib.
▶ noun (*informal*) *their favourite tipple was claret* **alcoholic drink**, strong drink, drink, liquor, intoxicant; beverage, liquid refreshment; drop, dram, draught, swallow, sip, gulp, nip, tot, bracer, chaser; *informal* booze, hard stuff, hooch, poison, tincture, libation, swig, slug, glug, swill, snifter; *informal, dated* quaff.

tippler ▶ noun *Londoners are the country's top tipplers, according to official figures* **drinker**, serious drinker, hard drinker, problem drinker, alcoholic; drunk, drunkard, dipsomaniac, inebriate, sot; *informal* **boozer**, imbiber, alky, lush, barfly, sponge, souse, dipso, tosspot, wino, soak; *Austral./NZ informal* hophead; *archaic* toper; *vulgar slang* piss artist.
OPPOSITE teetotaller.

tipsy ▶ adjective *Alison had probably been drinking on the plane and was already a bit tipsy* **merry**, mellow, slightly drunk; *Brit. informal* tiddly, squiffy.
OPPOSITE sober.

tirade ▶ noun *she rounded on Nathan with a devastating tirade* **diatribe**, invective, polemic, denunciation, rant, broadside, attack, harangue, verbal onslaught; reviling, railing, decrying, condemnation, brickbats, flak, criticism, censure, lecture, berating, admonishment, admonition, reprimand, rebuke, reproof, reproval, upbraiding, abuse, stream of abuse, battering, stricture, tongue-lashing, vilification, castigation, denouncement, vituperation, obloquy, fulmination; *informal* knocking, blast; *Brit. informal* slating; *rare* philippic.

tire ▶ verb **1** *the ascent grew steeper and he began to tire* **get/grow/become tired**, become fatigued, weaken, grow weak, lose one's strength, flag, droop, drop.
OPPOSITE stay fresh.
2 *the journey had tired him* **fatigue**, tire out, wear out, overtire, weary, exhaust, drain, sap, wash out, tax, overtax, enervate, debilitate, enfeeble, jade, incapacitate, devitalize, prostrate; *informal* whack, shatter, bush, knacker, frazzle, wear to a frazzle, poop, take it out of, fag out, do in, knock out.
OPPOSITE refresh.
3 *they tired of his difficult behaviour* **weary**, become/get tired, become/get weary, become/get fed up, become/get fed to death, become/get bored, become/get satiated, become/get jaded, become/get sick, become/get sick to death, sicken; have had a surfeit, have had enough, have had a glut; *informal* have had something up to here.
4 *their constant boasting tires me* **bore**, weary, make someone fed up, sicken, nauseate; irk, irritate, exhaust someone's patience, annoy, exasperate, get on someone's nerves; *informal* get to.
OPPOSITES stimulate, excite.

tired ▶ adjective **1** *you're just tired from travelling* **worn out**, exhausted, fatigued, tired out, overtired, weary, sleepy, drowsy, wearied, sapped, dog-tired, spent, drained, jet-lagged, played out, debilitated, prostrate, enervated, jaded, low; *informal* all in, done (in/up), dead, dead beat, dead tired, dead on one's feet, asleep on one's feet, ready to drop, fagged out, bushed, worn to a frazzle, shattered, burnt out; *Brit. informal* knackered, whacked; *N. Amer. informal* pooped.
OPPOSITES energetic, fresh, wide awake.
2 *are you **tired of** having him here?* **fed up with**, bored with/by, weary of, sick of, sick and tired of, jaded with/by, surfeited with/by, satiated by, glutted with/by; (**be tired of**) have had enough of; *informal* have had a basinful of, have had it up to here with, have had something up to here.
3 *there were tired jokes about buckets and spades* **hackneyed**, worn out, stale, overworked, threadbare, warmed-up, banal, trite, stock, stereotyped, clichéd, run-of-the-mill, commonplace, platitudinous, unoriginal, unimaginative, uninspired, flat; out of date, outdated, outmoded, passé, archaic, obsolete, defunct, antiquated; *N. Amer.* warmed-over; *informal* old hat, corny, out of the ark, played out, past their sell-by date.
OPPOSITES fresh, lively.

tiredness ▶ noun *her eyes were heavy with tiredness* **fatigue**, weariness, exhaustion, prostration, overtiredness, collapse, jet lag; **sleepiness**, drowsiness, somnolence, doziness; **lethargy**, lassitude, languor, languidness, debility, enervation, listlessness, sluggishness, lifelessness, torpor, inertia.
OPPOSITES energy, vigour.

tireless ▸ adjective *a tireless worker for the party* **vigorous**, energetic, industrious, determined, resolute, enthusiastic, keen, zealous, forceful, strong, Herculean, spirited, dynamic, intense, dogged, tenacious, persevering, stout, pertinacious; **untiring**, unwearied, unflagging, unremitting, indefatigable, unshakeable, unrelenting, unswerving.
OPPOSITES lazy, half-hearted.

tiresome ▸ adjective **1** *a rather tiresome meeting of the Faculty Committee* **boring**, dull, tedious, monotonous, humdrum, wearisome, laborious, wearing, prosaic, unexciting, uninteresting, uneventful, unvarying, unvaried, unremarkable, repetitive, repetitious, routine, ordinary, everyday, day-to-day, quotidian, run-of-the-mill, commonplace, common, workaday, usual, pedestrian; *rare* banausic.
OPPOSITES interesting, exciting.
2 *an exceedingly tiresome man to deal with* **annoying**, irritating, infuriating, exasperating, maddening, trying, troublesome, bothersome, irksome, vexing, vexatious; *informal* aggravating, pesky, infernal, pestiferous, plaguy, pestilent.
OPPOSITE pleasant.

tiring ▸ adjective *it was very tiring work* **exhausting**, wearying, fatiguing, enervating, draining, sapping, stressful, wearing, trying, crushing; demanding, exacting, taxing, challenging, burdensome, arduous, gruelling, punishing, grinding, onerous, difficult, hard, tough, heavy, laborious, back-breaking, crippling, strenuous, rigorous, uphill, stringent, strict; *informal* killing, murderous, hellish; *rare* exigent.

tissue ▸ noun **1** *X-rays were accidentally found to penetrate living tissue* **matter**, material, substance, stuff; flesh, the body.
2 *the flowers are wrapped with tissue and bound with ribbon | a box of tissues* **tissue paper**, wrapping paper; **paper handkerchief**, disposable handkerchief, facial tissue, toilet tissue, toilet paper, wipe, paper towel, kitchen towel; *trademark* Kleenex.
3 *modern roofing felt is based on glass tissue reinforced with polyester* **gauze**, gossamer, chiffon; netting, mesh, lattice, web, webbing, screen, mat; fabric, material, textile, fibre.
4 *a tissue of lies* **web**, network, nexus, maze, tangle, knot, complex, mass, conglomeration, set, series, chain.

WORD LINKS
relating to organic tissue **histo-** (e.g. ***histopathology***)

titanic ▸ adjective *Blackburn Rovers were overcome in a titanic struggle with Liverpool* **colossal**, gigantic, monumental, massive, enormous, terrific, tremendous, fantastic, towering, immense, vast, giant, mammoth, elephantine, gargantuan, prodigious, huge, very large, great, substantial, mighty, Herculean, Brobdingnagian; *informal* jumbo, bumper, monster, stupendous, humongous, whopping, whopping great, thumping, thumping great, astronomical, mega; *Brit. informal* whacking, whacking great, ginormous.

titbit ▸ noun **1** *when the puppy comes to you, reward it with a titbit* **delicacy**, tasty morsel, dainty, fancy, confection, bonne bouche, luxury, treat; snack, nibble, savoury, appetizer; *informal* goody, bite, little something; *N. Amer.* tidbit; *archaic* sweetmeat.
2 *I'll tell you one titbit that should cheer you up* **piece of gossip**, bit of scandal, juicy bit of gossip, juicy bit of news, scrap of information, morsel of information, item of information.

tit for tat ▸ noun *the routine diplomatic tit for tat when countries expel each other's envoys* **retaliation**, reprisal, counterattack, counterstroke, comeback; revenge, vengeance, retribution, requital, recrimination, an eye for an eye, a tooth for a tooth, as good as one gets, getting even, redress, repayment, payback; *Latin* lex talionis; *informal* a taste of someone's own medicine; *rare* ultion, a Roland for an Oliver.

titillate ▸ verb *the lurid sensationalism designed to titillate local audiences* **arouse**, rouse, excite, stimulate, stir, thrill, interest, attract, please, fascinate; **tantalize**, lead on, seduce, tempt, ravish, inflame, kindle, provoke, quicken; *informal* turn on, send.
OPPOSITES bore, turn off.

titillate or titivate?
The verbs **titillate** and **titivate** sound alike but do not have the same meaning. *Titillate*, the commoner word, means 'stimulate or excite', often with sexual overtones, as in *the press are paid to titillate the public* or *a titillating account of the prostitution trade. Titivate*, on the other hand, means no more than 'smarten up with small changes', as in *she titivated her hair.*

titillating ▸ adjective *he had deliberately chosen a titillating title to help sales* **sexually arousing**, sexually exciting, sexually stimulating, provocative, salacious, lurid, sexy, sensual, erotic, pornographic; **suggestive**, seductive, tantalizing, tempting, interesting, fascinating, captivating; *Brit. informal* saucy.
OPPOSITES boring, off-putting.

titivate ▸ verb (*informal*) *she titivated her hair* **groom**, tidy, arrange, brush, comb, smooth, smarten (up), spruce up, freshen (up), beautify, pretty, preen, primp, prink (up); *informal* doll up, tart up; *N. Amer. informal* gussy up; *archaic* trig, plume.

titivate or titillate?
See TITILLATE.

title *See centre pages for lists of* **Nobles** **Rulers' Titles**
▸ noun **1** *the author and title of the book* **name**, subtitle; subject.
2 *the cartoon title and ensuing caption* **caption**, legend, inscription, label, heading, subheading, head, motto, slogan, device, wording, rubric; credit.
3 *the company publishes 400 titles a year* **publication**, work, offering; book, newspaper, paper, magazine, periodical, organ.
4 *he will inherit the title of Duke of Marlborough* **designation**, name, denomination, label, rank, status, office, position; **form of address**, epithet, style; *informal* moniker, handle; *formal* appellation.
5 *the fifth British woman athlete to win an Olympic title* **championship**, first place, crown, belt, medal, prize, trophy, cup, shield, plate; laurels, bays, palm, honour, accolade.
6 *the vendor is obliged to prove his title to the land* **ownership of**, proprietorship of, freehold of, entitlement to, right to, proprietary rights to, claim to; possession of, holding of, hold of, tenure of, control of, keeping of, charge of, custody of, guardianship of.
▸ verb *a policy paper titled 'Law and Order'* **call**, entitle, name, dub, give something the title of, designate, label, tag, describe something as, style, term, christen, baptize; *rare* clepe, denominate.

titter ▸ verb *several of his class began to titter* **giggle**, snigger, snicker, tee-hee, give a half-suppressed laugh, chuckle; smirk, sneer, simper.
▸ noun *she caused a few titters* **giggle**, snigger, snicker, tee-hee, half-suppressed laugh, chuckle; smirk, sneer, simper.

tittle ▸ noun *he had passed the night without a tittle of sleep* **bit**, tiny amount, scrap, shred, speck, iota, particle, ounce, whit, jot, jot or tittle, atom, crumb, morsel, fragment, grain, drop, hint, touch, trace, suggestion, whisper, suspicion, scintilla, spot, mite, modicum; *Irish* stim; *informal* smidgen, smidge.

tittle-tattle ▸ noun *she would never listen to tittle-tattle* **gossip**, rumour, tattle, idle talk, scandal, hearsay; whispers, stories, tales, canards, titbits; *French* bavardage, on dit; *German* Kaffeeklatsch; *W. Indian* labrish, shu shu; *informal* buzz; *Brit. informal* goss; *N. Amer. informal* scuttlebutt; *S. African informal* skinder; *rare* bruit.
OPPOSITES confirmed facts, the truth.
▸ verb *he was tittle-tattling all over the village* **gossip**, spread rumours, spread gossip, circulate rumours, spread stories, talk, whisper, tattle, tell tales; *S. African informal* skinder; *literary* bruit something about.

titular ▸ adjective **1** *the chancellor is the titular head of a university* **nominal**, in title/name only, formal, official, ceremonial; token, puppet; theoretical, purported, supposed, ostensible.
2 *the work's titular song* **eponymous**, identifying; after whom/which something is named; *rare* designative, appellative, denominative.

toad *See centre pages for list of* **Amphibians**
▸ noun (*informal*) *you're an arrogant little toad* **wretch**; *informal* beast, pig, swine, rat, creep, bastard, louse, snake, skunk, dog, weasel, lowlife, scumbag, heel, stinkpot, stinker, bad lot, no-good, son of a bitch, s.o.b., nasty piece of work; *Scottish informal* scrote; *Irish informal* spalpeen; *N. Amer. informal* rat fink, fink, schmuck; *Austral. informal* dingo; *NZ informal* kuri; *informal, dated* rotter, hound, bounder, cad, blighter; *black English* rass; *vulgar slang* shit, sod, prick; *archaic* blackguard, dastard, knave, varlet, whoreson.

WORD LINKS
relating to toads **batrachian, anural**

toadstool ▸ noun. *See centre pages for list of* **Fungi, Mushrooms, and Toadstools**

toady ▸ noun *a conniving little toady with an eye for the main chance* **sycophant**, obsequious person, creep, crawler, fawner, flatterer, flunkey, lackey, truckler, groveller, doormat, lickspittle, kowtower, minion, hanger-on, leech, puppet, stooge, spaniel, Uriah Heep; *informal* bootlicker, yes-man; *vulgar slang* arse-licker, arse-kisser; *Brit. vulgar slang* bum-sucker; *N. Amer. vulgar slang* brown-nose, suckhole.
OPPOSITES independent, one's own master.
▸ verb *she imagined him toadying to his rich clients* **be obsequious towards**, be servile towards, be sycophantic towards, grovel to, kowtow to, abase oneself to, demean oneself to, bow and scrape to, prostrate oneself to, truckle to, make up to, play up to, dance attendance on, fawn on, ingratiate oneself with, rub up the right way, curry favour with, flatter, court; *informal* suck up to, crawl to, creep to, be all over, lick someone's boots, fall all over, butter up, keep someone sweet; *N. Amer.* brown-nose; *vulgar slang* lick/kiss someone's arse.
OPPOSITE defy.

toast ▸ noun **1** *he raised his glass in a toast* **tribute**, salute, salutation;

honour, health; compliments, best wishes, greetings; *archaic* pledge.
2 *he was the toast of the West End* **darling, celebrity**, favourite, pet, heroine, hero, talk; apple of someone's eye, the focus of attention; *Brit. informal* blue-eyed boy/girl; *N. Amer. informal* fair-haired boy/girl.
▶ **verb 1** *meanwhile, split and toast the muffins* brown, crisp (up), grill, barbecue, bake, singe, sear; *N. Amer.* broil, charbroil.
2 *she toasted her hands in front of the fire* **warm**, warm up, heat, heat up, roast, bring back to life.
OPPOSITE cool down.
3 *we toasted the couple with champagne* **pay tribute to**, drink (to) the health of, drink to, salute, honour; *archaic* pledge.

today ▶ **adverb 1** *the work must be finished today* **this day**, this very day, before tomorrow, this morning, this afternoon, this evening.
2 *the complex tasks demanded of computers today* **nowadays**, at the present time, these days, in these times, at this time, in this day and age, now, just now, right now, currently, at present, at the present moment, at this moment in time; in the present climate, in the present circumstances, things being what they are; *N. Amer.* presently; *rare* contemporarily.
▶ **noun 1** *today is a rest day* **this day**, this very day.
2 *policies relevant to the society of today* **the present**, the present day, the present time, now, the here and now, this moment, this time, this period, this age.
WORD LINKS
relating to today **hodiernal**

toddle ▶ **verb 1** *he watched the child who toddled towards him* **totter**, teeter, wobble, falter, stagger, dodder, waddle, reel, lurch; shuffle, shamble, drag one's feet, stumble, lumber; *rare* doddle.
2 (*informal*) *every afternoon, Matilda would toddle down to the library* **amble**, wander, meander, stroll, saunter, maunder; *informal* mosey, tootle; *Brit. informal* mooch; *N. Amer. informal* putter.

to-do ▶ **noun** (*informal*) *Sally-Anne thought all this a great to-do about nothing* **commotion**, fuss, fuss and bother, bother, trouble, ado, disturbance, flurry, excitement, uproar, ferment, tumult, turmoil, hurly-burly, brouhaha, furore, storm, palaver, pantomime, production, hoopla, folderol, hue and cry, bustle, hustle and bustle, pother; *informal* hoo-ha, hullabaloo, flap, song and dance, business, rumpus, ballyhoo, splash; *Brit. informal* kerfuffle, carry-on; *NZ informal* bobsy-die.

together ▶ **adverb 1** *friends who work together* **with each other**, in conjunction, jointly, conjointly, in cooperation, cooperatively, in collaboration, in partnership, in combination, as one, in unison, in concert, concertedly, with one accord, in league, in alliance, in collusion, side by side, hand in hand, hand in glove, shoulder to shoulder, cheek by jowl; *informal* in cahoots.
OPPOSITE separately.
2 *they both spoke together* **simultaneously**, at the same time, at the same instant, at the same moment, all together, as a group, at once, at one and the same time, at one time, concurrently, concomitantly, alongside each other, in unison, in concert, in chorus; *rare* synchronously.
OPPOSITES separately, consecutively.
3 *I was not able to get up for days together* **in succession**, in a row, at a time, successively, consecutively, running, straight, on end, one after the other, continuously, without a break, without interruption; *informal* on the trot.
▶ **adjective** (*informal*) *she looks a very together young woman* **level-headed**, well balanced, well adjusted, balanced, sensible, practical, realistic, with one's feet on the ground, prudent, circumspect, pragmatic, wise, reasonable, rational, mature, stable, sane, even-tempered, commonsensical, full of common sense, judicious, sound, sober, businesslike, reliable, dependable; **well organized**, well ordered, orderly, efficient, neat, tidy, methodical, no-nonsense; **calm**, cool, collected, composed, {cool, calm, and collected}, serene, relaxed, at ease, equable, moderate, unworried, unmoved, unemotional, cool-headed, imperturbable; **self-confident**, confident, self-possessed, assured, self-assured, assertive; *informal* unflappable.
OPPOSITES unbalanced, flustered, disorganized.

toil ▶ **verb 1** *she rolled up her sleeves and toiled all night* **work hard**, labour, work one's fingers to the bone, work like a Trojan, work like a dog, work day and night, exert oneself, keep at it, keep one's nose to the grindstone, grind away, slave away, grub away, plough away, plod away; *informal* slog away, peg away, beaver away, plug away, put one's back into something, work one's guts out, work one's socks off, knock oneself out, sweat blood, kill oneself; *Brit. informal* graft away, fag; *Austral./NZ informal* bullock; *Brit. vulgar slang* work one's balls/arse/nuts off; *N. Amer. vulgar slang* work one's ass/butt off; *archaic* drudge, travail, moil.
OPPOSITES rest, relax, laze.
2 *she began to toil up the cliff path* **struggle**, move with difficulty, labour, trudge, tramp, traipse, slog, plod, trek, footslog, sweat, drag oneself, fight (one's way), push; *Brit. informal* trog, yomp; *N. Amer. informal* schlep.
▶ **noun** *a life of toil* **hard work**, toiling, labour, slaving, struggle, effort, exertion, application, industry, grind, slog, {blood, sweat, and tears}, drudgery; *informal* sweat, elbow grease; *Brit. informal* graft; *Austral./NZ informal* (hard) yakka; *archaic* travail, moil.

CHOOSE THE RIGHT WORD
toil, work, labour
See **WORK**.

toilet ▶ **noun 1** *he had to go to the toilet* **lavatory**, WC, water closet, (public) convenience, facilities, urinal, privy, latrine, outhouse, earth closet, jakes; *Brit.* cloakroom, the Ladies, the Gents, powder room; *N. Amer.* restroom, bathroom, washroom, men's room, ladies' room, comfort station; *French* pissoir; *informal* little girls' room, little boys' room, smallest room; *Brit. informal* loo, bog, khazi, lav, throne, thunderbox, cottage; *N. English informal* netty; *N. Amer. informal* can, john, honey bucket, tea room; *Austral./NZ informal* dunny, little house, dyke; *vulgar slang* pisser, crapper, shithouse; *Nautical* head; *archaic* closet, garderobe, necessary house.
2 *she had always taken a long time over her toilet* **washing**, bathing, showering; wash, bath, shower; grooming, dressing, make-up; *formal or humorous* ablutions; *dated* toilette; *rare* lavation, lustration.

toils ▶ **plural noun** (*literary*) *Henry had become caught in the toils of his own deviousness* **trap**, net, snare.

token ▶ **noun 1** *a token of our appreciation* **symbol**, sign, emblem, badge, representation, indication, mark, index, manifestation, expression, pledge, demonstration, recognition; evidence, attestation, proof.
2 *he kept the menu as a token of their golden wedding* **memento**, souvenir, keepsake, reminder, record, trophy, relic, remembrance, memorial; *archaic* memorandum.
3 *a book token* **voucher**, coupon, chit, docket, stamp, order, credit note, IOU; *Brit. informal* chitty.
4 *a telephone token* **counter**, disc, substitute coin, jetton, chip, piece, man.
▶ **adjective 1** *the union is balloting its members for a one-day token strike* **symbolic**, emblematic, indicative; peppercorn.
2 *the practice now meets only token resistance* **perfunctory**, slight, nominal, minimal, insignificant, minor, trivial, mild, hollow, unimportant, trifling, of no account, of no consequence, of no importance, not worth bothering about, not worth mentioning, inconsequential, superficial, small, tiny, minute, inappreciable, imperceptible, infinitesimal, nugatory, petty; paltry, inadequate, insufficient, meagre, derisory, pitiful, pathetic, miserable; *informal* minuscule, piddling, piffling, measly, mingy, poxy; *N. Amer. informal* nickel-and-dime; *rare* exiguous.

tolerable ▶ **adjective 1** *did you have a tolerable journey?* **bearable**, endurable, sufferable, supportable, brookable; admissible, manageable, pardonable, excusable, forgivable.
OPPOSITE intolerable.
2 *he had a tolerable voice* **fairly good**, passable, adequate, all right, acceptable, good enough, sufficiently good, sufficient, satisfactory, moderately good, not (too) bad, average, fair, decent, respectable, presentable; admissible, allowable; mediocre, middling, ordinary, run-of-the-mill, workaday, indifferent, unremarkable, undistinguished, unexceptional, amateur, amateurish; *informal* OK, so-so, fair-to-middling, nothing to write home about, no great shakes, not up to much, not much cop, bog-standard, vanilla, plain vanilla; *NZ informal* half-pie.
OPPOSITES unacceptable; exceptional; appalling.

tolerance ▶ **noun 1** *an advocate of religious tolerance* **forbearance**, toleration, sufferance, liberality, open-mindedness, lack of prejudice, lack of bias, broad-mindedness, liberalism; patience, long-suffering, magnanimity, sympathy, understanding, charity, lenience, leniency, lenity, indulgence, clemency, permissiveness, complaisance, laxness.
OPPOSITE intolerance.
2 *tolerance to alcohol decreases with age* **endurance of**, acceptance of; **resistance to**, immunity to, non-susceptibility to, resilience to.
OPPOSITE intolerance.
3 *a 1% maximum tolerance in measurement* **deviation**, fluctuation, variation, allowance, play, clearance, leeway; **inaccuracy**, imprecision, inexactness.

tolerant ▶ **adjective** *a more tolerant attitude towards other religions* **open-minded**, forbearing, liberal, unprejudiced, unbiased, unbigoted; broad-minded, catholic, patient, long-suffering, magnanimous, sympathetic, understanding, charitable, lenient, indulgent, permissive, free and easy, easy-going, complaisant, lax.
OPPOSITES intolerant, narrow-minded.

tolerate ▶ **verb 1** *their leader would not tolerate serious dissent | how was it that she could tolerate such noise?* **allow**, permit, authorize, sanction, condone, indulge, agree to, accede to, approve of; **endure**, put up with, bear, take, stand, support, submit to, stomach, undergo; **accept**, swallow, brook, countenance, admit of, recognize, acknowledge; **ignore**, turn a blind eye to, wink at; *Scottish* thole; *informal* stick, hack, abide; *Brit. informal* wear, be doing with; *archaic* suffer.
OPPOSITE ban.
2 *his wife could not tolerate eggs* **consume**, take, stomach, digest, eat,

T

receive, be subjected to, withstand subjection to, be treated with.

toleration ▸ **noun 1** *scant toleration is shown to individuals who do not conform* **forbearance**, liberality, open-mindedness, lack of prejudice, lack of bias, broad-mindedness, liberalism; patience, long-suffering, magnanimity, sympathy, charity, lenience, leniency, lenity, indulgence, sufferance, clemency, permissiveness, condoning, condonation, complaisance, laxness.
2 *the church's toleration of the other great religions* **acceptance**, tolerance, approval, understanding, endurance, putting up with, ignoring.
3 *countries which do not practise religious toleration* **freedom of worship**, religious freedom, freedom of conscience.

toll[1] ▸ **noun 1** *a motorway toll* **charge**, fee, payment, levy, tariff, dues, tax, duty, impost.
2 *the toll of dead and injured mounted* **number**, count, tally, total, running total, sum total, grand total, sum, score, reckoning, enumeration, register, record, inventory, list, listing, account, roll, roster, index, directory.
3 *the toll of addictive disease is still terrible* **adverse effect(s)**, undesirable consequence(s), detriment, harm, damage, injury, hurt; cost, price, loss, disadvantage, suffering, penalty.

toll[2] ▸ **verb** *I had heard the bell toll | the old prison bell was tolled when executions took place* **ring (out)**, chime (out), strike, peal, knell; sound, clash, clang, bong, boom, resound, reverberate.

tomb ▸ **noun burial chamber**, burial place, sepulchre, mausoleum, vault, crypt, undercroft, catacomb, pyramid, charnel house, shrine, ossuary, reliquary; last/final resting place, grave, barrow, burial mound, burial pit; monument, memorial, cenotaph, marker; *Archaeology* mastaba; *rare* feretory.

WORD LINKS
relating to a tomb **sepulchral**

tombstone ▸ **noun gravestone**, headstone, stone, grave marker, memorial, monument, obelisk.

tome ▸ **noun volume**, book, work, opus, writing, publication, title.

tomfool ▸ **adjective** (*dated*) *she was destined to take part in some tomfool caper.* See SILLY sense 1.

tomfoolery ▸ **noun** *the tomfoolery of MPs at question time* **silliness**, fooling, clowning, capering, capers, antics, pranks, tricks, buffoonery, skylarking, nonsense, horseplay, mischief, foolishness, foolery, stupidity; *informal* messing about/around, larking about/around, larks, shenanigans; *Brit. informal* monkey tricks; *dated* harlequinade.

tone ▸ **noun 1** *bassoons add considerably to the tone of the tuba* **timbre**, sound, sound quality, voice, voice quality, colour, tone colour, tonality, resonance, ring.
2 *'So there you are!' he called in a friendly tone* **intonation**, tone of voice, mode of expression, expression, inflection, pitch, modulation, accentuation.
3 *the somewhat impatient tone of his letter* **mood**, quality, feel, style, note, air, attitude, character, spirit, flavour, grain, temper, humour, effect; **tenor**, vein, drift, gist.
4 *the dialling tone* **note**, beep, bleep, whine, buzz, warble, burr, signal.
5 *old-fashioned tones of primrose, lavender, and rose* **tint**, shade, colour, hue, tinge, cast, tincture.
▸ **verb** *the rich orange colour of the wood* **tones** *beautifully* **with** *the yellow roses* **harmonize**, go, go well, blend, fit, coordinate, team, accord; match, suit, complement.
▫ **tone something down 1** *he has had to tone down his gaudy garments to get them into department stores* **subdue**, make less garish, soften, lighten, dim, mute.
2 *the newspapers refused to tone down their criticism of the government* **moderate**, modify, modulate, mitigate, temper, dampen, soften, lighten; subdue, restrain, stifle, bridle, bottle up, contain; qualify; *informal* keep the lid on.

tongue ▸ **noun 1** *a foreign tongue* **language**, dialect, patois, vernacular, mother tongue, native tongue, jargon, argot, cant, pidgin, creole, lingua franca; speech, parlance; *informal* lingo, patter.
2 *when would she learn to censor her impetuous tongue?* **way/manner of speaking**, way/manner of talking, form/mode of expression, choice of words, verbal expression; conversation, vocabulary, phraseology, style, parlance, speech; *French* façon de parler.

WORD LINKS
relating to the tongue **lingual, glossal**
inflammation of the tongue **glossitis**
surgical removal of tongue **glossectomy**

tongue-tied ▸ **adjective** *usually he was tongue-tied with strangers* **lost for words**, at a loss for words, struck dumb, dumbstruck, bereft of speech, speechless, wordless, unable to get a word out, inarticulate; mute, dumb, voiceless, silent; *informal* mum; *rare* dumbstricken, mumchance, obmutescent.
OPPOSITES loquacious, articulate.

tonic ▸ **noun 1** *for over five thousand years ginseng has been used as a natural tonic* **stimulant**, restorative, refresher, cordial; *Medicine* analeptic, roborant; *informal* pick-me-up, bracer, livener.
2 *we found the change of scene a tonic* **boost**, stimulant, fillip, pleasure; stimulus, spur, push; *informal* shot in the arm, pick-me-up, reviver.

tonic sol-fa ▸ **noun.** *See centre pages for list of* **Tonic Sol-Fa Notes**

too ▸ **adverb 1** *invasion would be too risky* **excessively**, overly, over, unduly, immoderately, inordinately, unreasonably, ridiculously, to too great an extent/degree, extremely, very; *informal* too-too.
2 *Simons wanted his coffee black, too* **also**, as well, in addition, additionally, into the bargain, besides, furthermore, moreover, yet, on top of that, to boot; plus, again, over and above.

tool *See centre pages for lists of* **Hammers Knives Saws Tools**
▸ **noun 1** *a set of garden tools* **implement**, instrument, utensil, device, apparatus, gadget, appliance, machine, contrivance, contraption, mechanism, aid; *informal* gimmick, gizmo; (**tools**) hardware, equipment, gear, kit, tackle, paraphernalia.
2 *the beautiful Estella is Miss Havisham's tool* **dupe**, puppet, pawn, minion, lackey, flunkey, instrument, henchman, creature, cat's paw; *informal* stooge, sucker, poodle.
▸ **verb 1** *the book's spine was of red leather, tooled in gold* **ornament**, embellish, decorate, work, shape, cut, chase, dress, fashion.
2 (*informal*) *they tooled around town in their souped up cars* **drive**, bowl, ride, motor, travel, *informal* spin.

tooth *See centre pages for lists of* **Tooth Parts Tooth Types**
▸ **noun 1** *he clenched his teeth | a huge creature with massive teeth* **fang**, denticulation; tusk; *Zoology* denticle; (**teeth**) dentition; *informal* gnasher; *rare* tush.
2 *repairs were made to the gearing, including the replacement of several hundred cog teeth* **prong**, point, tine, cog, ratchet, sprocket.

WORD LINKS
relating to teeth **dental**
related prefixes **dent- (e.g. *dentine*), odont- (e.g. *ondontalgia*)**
related suffix **-odon (e.g. *mastodon*)**
study of teeth **odontology**

toothsome ▸ **adjective** *a toothsome delicacy* **tasty**, delicious, luscious, mouth-watering, delectable, succulent, palatable; tempting, appetizing, inviting; *informal* scrumptious, yummy, scrummy, finger-licking, delish, yum-yum; *Brit. informal* moreish.

top ▸ **noun 1** *we walked along the top of the cliff* **summit**, peak, pinnacle, crest, crown, brow, brink, ridge, head, highest point/part, tip, apex, vertex, acme, apogee.
OPPOSITES bottom, base.
2 *Mike tapped the top of the table with his knuckles* **upper part**, upper surface, upper layer.
3 *some growers clip off the carrots' green tops in the field* **leaves**, shoots, stem, stalk.
OPPOSITE root.
4 *she couldn't screw the top of the coffee jar on straight* **lid**, cap, cover, stopper, cork, bung, plug.
5 *United increased their lead at the top of the table* **high point**, height, peak, pinnacle, zenith, acme, culmination, climax, crowning point, prime, meridian; success.
OPPOSITES low point; failure.
6 *she was screaming at the top of her voice* **highest level**, utmost extent.
▫ **over the top** (*informal*) *her reaction had been a bit over the top* **excessive**, immoderate, inordinate, extreme, over the limit, exaggerated, extravagant, overblown, too much, unreasonable, needless, disproportionate, undue, unwarranted, uncalled for, unnecessary, going too far; *informal* a bit much, OTT.
OPPOSITES moderate, restrained.
▸ **adjective 1** *her office is on the top floor* **highest**, topmost, uppermost, upmost, upper, furthest up, loftiest.
OPPOSITES bottom, lowest.
2 *some of the world's top scientists attended the conference* **foremost**, leading, principal, pre-eminent, greatest, finest, worthiest, highest, elite; *informal* top-notch.
3 *the top management of the organization* **chief**, principal, main, leading, highest, high, high-ranking, ruling, commanding; most powerful, most important, prominent, eminent, notable, illustrious.
4 *a top Paris hotel* **prime**, excellent, superb, superior, choice, select, elite, quality, top-quality, top-grade, first-rate, first-class, top-class, high-grade, grade A, best, finest, premier, choicest, superlative, unsurpassed, unexcelled, unparalleled, peerless, second to none; *informal* A1, top-notch, ace, crack.
OPPOSITES inferior, mediocre.
5 *they are travelling at top speed* **maximum**, maximal, greatest, topmost, utmost.
OPPOSITES minimum, lowest.
▸ **verb 1** *sales are expected to top £1.3 billion* **exceed**, surpass, go beyond, transcend, better, best, beat, defeat, excel, outstrip, outdo, outshine, eclipse, surmount, improve on, go one better than, cap, trump, trounce.

T

2 *their debut CD is currently topping the charts* **lead**, head, be first in, be at the top of.
3 *they topped a hill and began the run down the other side* **reach the top of**, crest, climb, scale, ascend, mount, conquer.
4 *chocolate sponge topped with white chocolate mousse* **cover**, cap, crown, coat, overspread, finish, garnish.

□ **top something up** *he topped up his glass* **fill**, refill, refresh, freshen, replenish, recharge, resupply; supplement, add to, augment.
OPPOSITES empty, finish.

topcoat *See centre pages for list of* **Coats, Cloaks, and Jackets**
▶ noun **overcoat**, coat, greatcoat.

topic ▶ noun *he brought the conversation round to the topic of food and drink* **subject**, subject matter, theme, issue, matter, point, talking point, question, concern, argument, discussion, thesis, text, concept, field, area, keynote, leitmotif.

CHOOSE THE RIGHT WORD

topic, subject, theme

See SUBJECT.

topical ▶ adjective *a forum for the discussion of topical issues* **current**, up to date, up to the minute, contemporary, recent; newsworthy, in the news; **relevant**, pressing, important, vital, timely, popular; *informal* trendy.
OPPOSITES out of date, outdated.

topmost ▶ adjective **1** *the topmost branches of the tree* **highest**, top, uppermost, upmost, upper, furthest up, loftiest.
2 *the topmost authority on the subject* **foremost**, **leading**, principal, pre-eminent, greatest, top, finest, worthiest, highest, elite; **chief**, main, highest-ranking, ruling, commanding, powerful, important, prominent, eminent, notable, illustrious; *informal* top-notch.

top-notch ▶ adjective (*informal*) *a pub that serves top-notch beer* **first-rate**, first-class, top-grade, top-level; **excellent**, superb, splendid, fine, outstanding, great, marvellous, brilliant, superlative, sterling, prime, very good, choice, select, superior; *informal* A1, ace, crack, top-drawer, tip-top, super, out of this world, wicked, mega, crucial; *Brit. informal* brill, wizard; *Brit. informal, dated* top-hole, topping.

topple ▶ verb **1** *he banged the table, causing some of the bottles to topple over* **fall**, tumble, overturn, overbalance, tip, keel, drop, pitch, plunge, capsize, collapse, founder, plummet, dive, lose one's balance, go head over heels.
2 *protesters toppled a huge statue* **knock over**, knock down, upset, push over, tip over, upend, capsize; fell, tear down, flatten, level.
3 *a plot to topple the government* **overthrow**, oust, depose, unseat, overturn, bring down, overcome, bring low, defeat, get rid of, dislodge, eject, supplant, dethrone, defenestrate.

topsy-turvy ▶ adverb & adjective **1** *a topsy-turvy flag* **upside down**, wrong side up, head over heels, inverted, reversed, upset, backwards, vice versa.
OPPOSITE right way up.
2 *my emotions are all topsy-turvy* **in disorder**, disordered, disorderly, in confusion, confused, mixed up, in a muddle, muddled, in a jumble, jumbled, in chaos, chaotic, disorganized, messy, untidy, in disarray, in a mess, awry, askew, upside down, upset, disrupted, at sixes and sevens; *informal* higgledy-piggledy, every which way.
OPPOSITES ordered, neat.

torch ▶ noun **1** *he clicked on the torch and a weak beam shone forth* **lamp**, light, flashlight, beacon; *rare* illuminant, flambeau.
2 *he held a wolf at bay using a flaming torch* **firebrand**, brand; lantern, candle, taper; *historical* link, cresset.
▶ verb (*informal*) *one of the shacks had been torched* **burn**, set fire to, set on fire, set light to, set alight, incinerate, ignite, kindle, put/set a match to, light, start, touch off; reduce to ashes, destroy by fire.

T

torment ▶ noun (stress on the first syllable) **1** *a voice screamed in torment* **agony**, suffering, torture, pain, anguish, misery, distress, affliction, trauma, wretchedness, woe; hell, purgatory; *rare* excruciation.
OPPOSITES pleasure, joy.
2 *the solitary nights she spent were a torment* **ordeal**, affliction, scourge, curse, plague, bane, thorn in someone's side/flesh, cross to bear; calamity, sorrow, tribulation, vexation, persecution, trouble, pest, irritation, irritant, annoyance, worry, nuisance, misfortune, bother, discomfort, soreness, harassment; *informal* pain in the neck.
▶ verb (stress on the second syllable) **1** *she was tormented by shame* **torture**, afflict, harrow, plague, distress, agonize, cause agony to, cause suffering to, cause pain to, inflict anguish on; excruciate, crucify, rack, pain; mortify, worry, trouble; abuse, maltreat, mistreat, molest.
2 *Maggie began to torment the two younger boys* **tease**, taunt, victimize, bully, bait, chaff, harass, rib, scorn; irritate, vex, annoy, pester, badger, harry, hector, plague, be a nuisance to, bother, trouble, bedevil, be a pest to, nag, persecute, worry, nettle, chivvy, irk; *informal* needle, rag, hassle, aggravate.
OPPOSITES encourage, support.

torn ▶ adjective **1** *a torn shirt* **ripped**, split, slit, cut, lacerated, rent, separated, severed, cracked, destroyed, ruined, in disrepair; ragged, tattered, in tatters, holey, frayed, shabby, threadbare, in rags, in ribbons; *informal* tatty.
2 *she was torn between joy and despair* **divided**, split, wavering, vacillating, irresolute, dithering, uncertain, unsure, undecided, in two minds.
OPPOSITES certain, decided.

tornado ▶ noun **whirlwind**, windstorm, cyclone, typhoon, tropical storm/cyclone, tempest, dust devil, storm, hurricane, gale, squall; *N. Amer. informal* twister.

torpid ▶ adjective *we lay torpid in the heat* **lethargic**, sluggish, inert, inactive, slow, slow-moving, lifeless, dull, listless, languid, lazy, idle, indolent, shiftless, slothful, heavy, stagnant, somnolent, sleepy, tired, fatigued, languorous, apathetic, passive, supine, comatose, narcotic.
OPPOSITES energetic, active, lively.

torpor ▶ noun *he spent most of the journey in a state of torpor* **lethargy**, torpidity, sluggishness, inertia, inertness, inactivity, inaction, slowness, lifelessness, dullness, heaviness, listlessness, languor, languidness, stagnation, laziness, idleness, indolence, shiftlessness, sloth, slothfulness, apathy, accidie, passivity, weariness, tiredness, lassitude, fatigue, sleepiness, drowsiness, enervation, somnolence, narcosis.
OPPOSITES vigour, energy, animation.

torrent ▶ noun **1** *they were swept down the hillside in a torrent of water* **flood**, deluge, inundation, spate, cascade, rush, stream, current, gushing, flow, overflow, tide, fountain.
OPPOSITES trickle, drop.
2 *the rain fell in torrents* **downpour**, deluge, rainstorm, rain, shower.
3 *he directed a torrent of abuse at me* **outburst**, stream, volley, outpouring, hail, onslaught, avalanche, flow, barrage, battery, tide, spate, effusion, inundation.

torrential ▶ adjective *torrential rain caused the game to be stopped* **copious**, severe, heavy, rapid, relentless, violent; soaking, teeming.

torrid ▶ adjective **1** *a torrid summer* **hot**, sweltering, sultry, scorching, boiling, parching, sizzling, roasting, blazing, burning, blistering, tropical, stifling, suffocating, oppressive; **dry**, arid, barren, parched, waterless, desert.
OPPOSITES cold, cool, wet.
2 *a torrid affair* **passionate**, impassioned, ardent, intense, inflamed, fervent, fervid, lustful, amorous, erotic, sexy; *informal* steamy, sizzling, hot.
OPPOSITES passionless, unemotional.

tortuous ▶ adjective **1** *the road follows a tortuous route* **twisting**, winding, curving, curvy, bending, sinuous, undulating, coiling, looping, meandering, serpentine, snaking, snaky, zigzag, convoluted, spiralling, twisty, circuitous, rambling, wandering, indirect, deviating, devious, labyrinthine, mazy; *rare* anfractuous, flexuous.
OPPOSITE straight.
2 *a tortuous argument* **convoluted**, roundabout, circuitous, indirect, unstraightforward, involved, complicated, complex, confusing, lengthy, overlong, verbose, difficult to follow.
OPPOSITE straightforward.

tortuous or torturous?

Tortuous and **torturous** have different meanings. *Tortuous* means 'full of twists and turns', as in *a tortuous route*, while *torturous* means 'involving or causing torture', as in *a torturous five days of fitness training*—although something which is *tortuous* in the word's extended sense 'excessively lengthy and complex' may also be *torturous* (*a tortuous piece of bureaucratese*). This overlap has led to *tortuous* being sometimes used where *torturous* would be correct, as in *he would at last draw in a tortuous gasp of air*.

torture *See centre pages for lists of* **Torture Instruments** **Punishments**
▶ noun **1** *the torture of political prisoners* **infliction of pain**, abuse, torment; **ill-treatment**, maltreatment, harsh treatment, punishment, persecution.
2 *the torture of losing a loved one* **torment**, agony, suffering, pain; **anguish**, misery, distress, heartbreak, affliction, trauma, wretchedness, woe; hell, purgatory; *rare* excruciation.
OPPOSITE pleasure.
▶ verb **1** *the security forces routinely tortured suspects* **inflict pain on**, inflict suffering on; **torment**, ill-treat, abuse, mistreat, maltreat, molest, scourge, wound, put someone on the rack, persecute, punish; *informal* work over, give someone the works.
OPPOSITES relieve, comfort.
2 *he was tortured by grief* **torment**, **afflict**, harrow, plague, distress, agonize, cause agony to, cause suffering to, inflict anguish on; crucify, rack, pain, mortify; worry, trouble, beset.

toss ▶ verb **1** *he tossed his tools into the boot* **throw**, hurl, cast, fling, sling, pitch, shy, lob, propel, launch, project, send, dash, bowl; *informal* heave, chuck, bung.

2 *he tossed a coin and it landed heads up* **flip**, flick, spin, twist.
3 *I tossed and turned all night* **flail**, thrash about, roll, tumble; jerk, twitch, wriggle, writhe, squirm.
4 *the ship tossed about, shaken furiously* **lurch**, reel, list, keel, veer, labour, flounder, plunge, rock, roll, sway, undulate, pitch, heave, wallow, make heavy weather; Nautical pitchpole.
5 *toss the salad ingredients together gently* **shake**, stir, turn, churn, mix, combine.
6 *Paula pursed her lips and tossed her head* **throw back**, jerk, jolt.
□ **toss something off** *Roger tossed off a full glass of wine* **drink (up/down)**, quaff, swallow, gulp (down), drain, put away, guzzle, sup, sip, finish off; informal down, swill, swig, slug, sink, kill, polish off, knock back; Brit. informal, bevvy; N. Amer. informal scarf (down/up), snarf (down/up); rare ingurgitate, bib.
▶ **noun** *Louise gave a small toss of her head* **jerk**, jolt, throw; cast, fling, hurl, heave, delivery, lob.

tot[1] ▶ **noun 1** *the tot looks just like her mum* **baby**, babe, infant, toddler, newborn, tiny tot, child, little one, mite; Scottish bairn, wean; informal sprog, young 'un; N. Amer. informal rug rat; technical neonate.
OPPOSITE adult.
2 *a tot of rum* **dram**, small measure, drink, nip, slug, drop, draught, swallow, swig; informal shot, finger, snifter; rare libation.

tot[2] ▶ **verb 1** *he picked up the account book and totted up some figures* **add**, total, sum, count, calculate, compute, reckon, enumerate, tally, work something out, figure something out, take stock of something, quantify; dated cast something up.
2 *we've totted up 89 victories* **accumulate**, gather, build up, amass, accrue, stockpile, acquire; mount up.

total ▶ **adjective 1** *the total number of casualties | the total cost of the funeral* **entire**, complete, whole, full, comprehensive, combined, aggregate, gross, overall, composite, integral.
2 *they drove home in total silence | a total stranger* **complete**, **utter**, absolute, thorough, perfect, downright, out-and-out, outright, thoroughgoing, all-out, sheer, positive, prize, rank, pure, dyed-in-the-wool, deep-dyed, real, consummate, veritable, unmitigated, unqualified, unadulterated, unalloyed, unconditional, unequivocal, full, unlimited, limitless, infinite, ultimate, through and through, in-depth; unbroken, undivided, uninterrupted; Brit. informal right, proper; archaic arrant.
OPPOSITE partial.
▶ **noun** *lorries and merchandise worth a total of £160,000 were stolen* **sum**, sum total, grand total, aggregate; whole, entirety, totality, summation, result.
▶ **verb 1** *the prize money totalled £33,050* **add up to**, amount to, mount up to, come to, run to, make, correspond to, equal, work out as, number; Brit. tot up to.
2 *my father totalled up his score* **add**, sum, count, reckon, tot, compute, work out, take stock of.
3 (informal) *he almost totalled the car* **wreck**, crash, smash, destroy, damage beyond repair, demolish; Brit. **write off**; Brit. informal prang.

totalitarian ▶ **adjective** *a totalitarian state* **authoritarian**, autocratic, autarchic, dictatorial, tyrannical, oppressive, repressive, one-party, monocratic, absolute, absolutist, undemocratic, illiberal, despotic, fascist, fascistic, Nazi, neo-Nazi, Stalinist; dystopian.
OPPOSITES democratic, liberal.
▶ **noun** **authoritarian**, autocrat, dictator, tyrant, absolutist, despot, fascist, Nazi, neo-Nazi, Stalinist.
OPPOSITES democrat, liberal.

totality ▶ **noun 1** *the unifying spiritual whole is by definition difficult to grasp in its totality* **entirety**, entireness, wholeness, fullness, completeness, inclusiveness, unity.
2 *the conference didn't succeed in the totality of its aims* **aggregate**, whole, total, sum, sum total, entirety, beginning and end, alpha and omega, be-all and end-all; all, everything.

totally ▶ **adverb** *she was totally deaf* **completely**, absolutely, entirely, wholly, fully, thoroughly, utterly, quite, altogether, one hundred per cent; downright, unqualifiedly, in all respects, unconditionally, perfectly, unrestrictedly, consummately, undisputedly, unmitigatedly, wholeheartedly, radically, stark, just, to the hilt, all the way, to the maximum extent; informal clean, plumb, dead, bang.
OPPOSITES partly, partially, somewhat.

totter ▶ **verb 1** *she tottered off on her four-inch heels* **teeter**, walk unsteadily, stagger, wobble, stumble, dodder, shuffle, shamble, falter, reel, toddle, hobble, sway, roll, lurch.
2 *the foundations began to heave and totter* **shake**, sway, tremble, quiver, teeter, shudder, judder, rock, quake, reel, lurch; vibrate, oscillate.
3 *the Habsburg Empire was tottering* **be unstable**, be unsteady, be shaky, be insecure, be precarious, be on the point of collapse, falter; informal wobble.

touch ▶ **verb 1** *his shoes were touching the end of the bed* **be in contact (with)**, come into contact (with), come together (with), meet, join, connect, converge (with), be contiguous (with), border (on), be (up) against, link up (with), adjoin, abut, neighbour.
2 *he reached out and touched her cheek* **press lightly**, tap, pat, nudge, prod, poke; feel, stroke, rub, rub (up) against, brush, brush (up) against, graze; fondle, caress, pet, tickle, toy with, play about with, fiddle with, finger, thumb, handle; put one's hand on, lay a hand on, lay a finger on.
3 *in June the government touched its lowest point of popularity* **reach**, attain, arrive at, come to, make; get up to, rise to, soar to; get down to, sink to, plummet to, dive to; informal hit.
4 *nobody can touch him when he's on form* **compare with**, be on a par with, equal, match, be a match for, be in the same class as, be in the same league as, be on an equal footing with, parallel, rival, come near, get near, approach, come up to, come/get close to, measure up to/against; better, beat; informal hold a candle to.
5 *you're not supposed to touch my typewriter* **handle**, hold, pick up, move; **meddle with**, play (about/around) with, toy with, fiddle with, interfere with, tamper with, disturb, harm, lay a hand on, lay a finger on; **use**, employ, make use of, put to use, have access to, access, avail oneself of, get (at), take advantage of.
6 *normally he wouldn't touch a job as small as this* **be associated with**, concern oneself with, involve oneself in/with, get involved with/in, have something to do with, have dealings with, deal with, handle, be a party to; informal touch something with a bargepole.
7 *he wouldn't touch his food* **taste**, consume, eat, drink, take, partake of.
OPPOSITE refrain from.
8 *Germany was comparatively little touched by the Renaissance* **affect**, have an effect on, concern, involve, have a bearing on, be relevant to, be pertinent to.
9 *Lisa felt touched by the girl's unexpected kindness* **affect**, move, stir, arouse, make/leave an impression on, impress, have an impact on, have an effect on; influence, impassion; upset, disturb, make sad, arouse sympathy, melt, soften; informal get (to).
10 (informal) *do you think you can touch him for some more money?* **ask**, approach; beg, borrow from.
□ **touch down** *his plane touched down at Nice airport* **land**, alight, come in to land, come down, come to earth, come to rest, put down, make a landing, arrive.
OPPOSITE take off.
□ **touch something off 1** *he touched off two of the bombs* **detonate**, set off, trigger, explode, spark (off).
2 *the plan touched off a major political storm* **initiate**, set off, start, begin, set in motion, instigate, ignite, trigger (off), stir up, provoke, foment, cause, give rise to, lead to, generate, actuate, launch.
□ **touch on/upon 1** *many television programmes have touched on the subject of mental handicap* **refer to**, mention, give a mention to, comment on, remark on, bring up, speak of, talk about, write about, deal with, raise, broach, cover, allude to, make an allusion to, hint at, skim over.
2 *a self-confident manner touching on the arrogant* **come close to**, verge on, border on, incline to, approach, resemble, be tantamount to, be more or less, be not far from/off.
□ **touch someone up** (Brit. informal) *he was sacked after one of his pupils accused him of touching her up* **fondle**, molest, feel up; informal grope, paw, maul, goose; N. Amer. informal cop a feel.
□ **touch something up 1** *the flagstaffs were being touched up with gold paint* **repaint**, patch up, retouch, renovate, refurbish, spruce up, restore, revive, renew, revamp, brush up, rehabilitate, overhaul, recondition, refresh, rejuvenate; enhance, beautify; informal do something up, give something a facelift, titivate.
2 *touch up your CV and improve your interview skills* **improve**, enhance, gloss, dress up, embellish, embroider; finish off, round off, perfect; update, upgrade; bring up to date, modernize, revamp, revise, redo, polish up, rewrite, edit.
□ **touch wood** *I haven't been caught yet, touch wood!* **hope for the best**; knock on wood, cross one's fingers, keep one's fingers crossed.
▶ **noun 1** *communicating by touch is the most primitive mode* **feeling**, feel, sense of touch, contact, tactile sense, tactility; texture.
2 *I gave her a touch on the shoulder* **press**, tap, pat, nudge, prod, poke, push, glance, flick; stroke, brush, graze; pressure.
3 *she has a lovely touch on the putting greens* **skill**, skilfulness, expertise, dexterity, deftness, virtuosity, adroitness, adeptness, ability, talent, flair, facility, proficiency; **knack**, technique, approach, style, manner, execution, method; feel, craftsmanship, workmanship, artistry, performance.
4 *she replied with a touch of bravado* **small amount**, **trace**, bit, suggestion, suspicion, hint, scintilla, tinge, tincture, whiff, whisper, overtone, undertone, nuance, murmur, colouring, breath, vein; dash, taste, spot, drop, dab, pinch, speck, smack, smattering, sprinkling, splash, soupçon.
5 *there were flowers in a vase on the dressing table—a nice touch* **detail**, feature, fine point, nicety, addition, accessory; (**touches**) minutiae.
6 *visitors put the severity of the house down to the lack of a woman's touch* **influence**, effect, hand, handling; direction, management, technique, method.

7 *they finished training a few months apart and lost touch | over the next few days I was* **in touch** *with Eliot by letter and by phone* **contact**, communication, correspondence, connection, association; having dealings with, up to date with, abreast of, up with, informed about.

WORD LINKS
relating to touch **tactile, haptic**

touch-and-go ▶ **adjective** *it was touch-and-go whether he would be fit enough to play* **uncertain**, unsure, unclear, dubious, tight, delicate; sticky, tricky, precarious, risky, in jeopardy, in danger, hazardous, dangerous, critical, unsafe, treacherous, suspenseful, cliffhanging, on thin ice, hanging by a thread; *informal* hairy; *Brit. informal* dodgy.
OPPOSITE certain.

touched ▶ **adjective 1** *the plumber was so touched by their plight that he waived his fee* **affected**, **softened**, moved, stirred, swayed, aroused, impressed, influenced, warmed, impassioned, upset, disturbed, distressed.
OPPOSITES unmoved, unimpressed.
2 (*informal*) *you have to be a little touched to do what I do* **mad**, insane, unbalanced, unhinged, deranged, demented, crazed, out of one's mind, off one's head, eccentric, distracted, simple, mad as a hatter, mad as a March hare, away with the fairies; *Latin* non compos mentis; *informal* daft, barmy, batty, dotty, nuts, nutty, doolally, screwy, loco, soft in the head, off one's rocker, round the bend/twist, with a screw loose, gaga, not all there, as daft as a brush.
OPPOSITES sane, well adjusted.

touchiness ▶ **noun** *the visitors' touchiness about defeat* **sensitivity**, oversensitivity, hypersensitivity; **irritability**, tetchiness, testiness, crotchetiness, irascibility, peevishness, querulousness, bad-temperedness, short-temperedness, hot-temperedness, quick-temperedness, snappiness, captiousness, prickliness, edginess, crossness, surliness, crustiness, curmudgeonliness, cantankerousness, petulance, waspishness, pettishness, quarrelsomeness, spleen, grumpiness, fractiousness, tension; *informal* grouchiness, crankiness, rattiness, stickiness.

touching ▶ **adjective** *her devotion to him was very touching | at her death Hardy wrote a touching poem entitled 'The Lodging House'* **moving**, affecting, stirring, warming, heart-warming, impressive; **poignant**, upsetting, saddening, pitiful, piteous, pathetic, plaintive, heartbreaking, heart-rending, tear-jerking, tragic, disturbing, evocative; emotive, emotional, tender, sentimental.
OPPOSITE hard-headed.

CHOOSE THE RIGHT WORD
touching, moving, affecting
See MOVING.

touchstone ▶ **noun** *pupil behaviour is a touchstone of the quality of the school system* **criterion**, standard, yardstick, benchmark, barometer, litmus test, indicator, indication; **measure**, point of reference, norm, gauge, reference, test, guide, guideline, exemplar, model, pattern.

touchy ▶ **adjective 1** *she's very touchy about her past | anxiety was making her touchy* **sensitive**, oversensitive, hypersensitive, easily offended, thin-skinned; **irritable**, tetchy, testy, crotchety, irascible, peevish, querulous, bad-tempered, short-tempered, hot-tempered, quick-tempered, temperamental, snappy, captious, crabbed, prickly, edgy, cross, surly, crusty, curmudgeonly, cantankerous, petulant, waspish, pettish, quarrelsome, splenetic, grumpy, fractious, highly strung, tense; *informal* grouchy, cranky, ratty.
OPPOSITES calm, affable, good-humoured.
2 *a touchy subject* **delicate**, sensitive, tricky, ticklish, thorny, knotty, embarrassing, uncomfortable, uneasy, precarious, chancy, risky, uncertain, contentious, controversial, awkward, difficult; *informal* sticky.

tough ▶ **adjective 1** *they had tough leather gloves* **durable**, strong, resilient, resistant, sturdy, rugged, firm, solid, substantial, sound, stout, indestructible, unbreakable, hard, rigid, stiff, inflexible, toughened; **hard-wearing**, long-lasting, heavy-duty, well built, made to last.
OPPOSITES soft, fragile, flimsy.
2 *the hastily prepared steak was tough* **chewy**, leathery, gristly, stringy, fibrous, sinewy, cartilaginous.
OPPOSITE tender.
3 *he must have been a tough little lad to have survived it all* **resilient**, strong, hardy, gritty, determined, resolute, dogged, stalwart; rugged, fit, robust, powerful, red-blooded, doughty; hardened, cynical, hardbitten; *informal* hard, (as) tough as old boots.
OPPOSITES weak; sentimental.
4 *he conceded the need for tough sentencing | the police will be told to get tough on car theft* **strict**, stern, severe, hard, harsh, firm, hard-hitting, adamant, inflexible, unyielding, unbending, uncompromising, unsentimental, unsympathetic; **merciless**, ruthless, callous, hard-hearted, uncaring, cold, cool, stony, stony-hearted, flinty; *informal* hard-nosed, hard-boiled.
OPPOSITES soft, light.
5 *a tough area of London* **rough**, rowdy, unruly, disorderly, violent, wild, lawless, lawbreaking, criminal; vicious, callous, hardened.
6 *my father had a tough job underground* **arduous**, onerous, difficult, demanding, hard, heavy, taxing, burdensome, tiring, exhausting, punishing, wearying, fatiguing, laborious, strenuous, exacting, troublesome, formidable, stressful, Herculean; *rare* toilsome, exigent.
OPPOSITE easy.
7 *their book raises tough questions for American policy-makers* **difficult**, hard, knotty, thorny, baffling, tricky, ticklish, prickly, perplexing, puzzling, mystifying, troublesome, bothersome, irksome, intractable.
OPPOSITE easy.
8 *the tough way of life of a fisherman* **harsh**, hard, austere, rigorous, rugged, spartan, bleak, grim, straitened, forbidding, cruel, savage, hostile, unfriendly, dark, dire, rough, taxing, exacting, disagreeable, unpleasant, awful.
OPPOSITE easy.
9 (*informal*) *they had tough luck when a shot bounced off the crossbar* **unfortunate**, unlucky, hard, unpleasant, regrettable, distressing; *informal* too bad.
OPPOSITES good, lucky.
▶ **noun** *a gang of toughs* **ruffian**, rowdy, thug, hoodlum, hooligan, brute, bully, bully boy, rough, gangster, desperado; *informal* hard man, roughneck, yob, yobbo, heavy, bruiser, tough guy, toughie, gorilla, yahoo; *N. Amer. informal* hood.

toughen ▶ **verb 1** *this process tightens and toughens the wood fibres* **strengthen**, fortify, reinforce, harden, stiffen, consolidate, temper, season, rigidify, thicken, coarsen; *technical* indurate, anneal, cement.
OPPOSITE soften.
2 *measures to toughen prison discipline* **make stricter**, make more severe, toughen up, stiffen, tighten; *informal* beef up.
3 *it is surprising how the army toughens the lads* **harden**, fortify, strengthen, give strength to, steel, harshen, make resilient; make unfeeling, brutalize, make callous, case-harden, inure.

tour ▶ **noun 1** *he went on a grand tour of Europe* **excursion**, journey, expedition, trip, jaunt, outing, day trip, junket, voyage, trek, safari; *rare* peregrination.
2 *a tour of a car factory* **visit**, inspection, guided tour, walk round, survey, walkabout, ramble.
3 *they lost all four matches on the tour* **circuit**, ambit; round, course, beat, leg, lap.
4 *his* **tour of duty** *in Ulster was ending* **stint**, stretch, spell, shift, turn, assignment, duty, period of service, period of enlistment.
▶ **verb 1** *this hotel is well placed for touring Somerset* **travel round**, travel through, journey through, go on a trip through, go on an excursion in, explore, voyage around, trek around, sightsee in, holiday in, cruise, range over, roam in, rove through, wander through, globetrot; *informal* do.
2 *you'll have to tour the client's factory and see how the product is made* **visit**, go round, go around, walk round, drive round, see, explore, inspect, review, survey, scrutinize, reconnoitre.

tourist ▶ **noun** *in the summer London is full of tourists* **holidaymaker**, traveller, sightseer, visitor, excursionist, backpacker, globetrotter, day tripper, tripper; explorer, pilgrim, voyager, journeyer; *N. Amer.* vacationer, vacationist, out-of-towner; *Brit. informal* grockle, emmet.
OPPOSITE local.

tournament ▶ **noun 1** *a golf tournament* **competition**, contest, championship, series, meeting, meet, event, match, trial, bout, fixture.
2 *a knight preparing for a tournament* **joust**, jousting, tourney, tilt; lists.

tousled ▶ **adjective** *she ran a hand through her tousled hair* **untidy**, messy, unkempt, disordered, disarranged, messed up, rumpled, dishevelled, bedraggled; uncombed, ungroomed, ruffled, tangled, matted, windblown, wild; *informal* mussed up.
OPPOSITES neat, tidy.

tout ▶ **verb 1** *he's touting his autobiography* **peddle**, sell, hawk, offer for sale, market, vend; **promote**, talk up, push, flaunt, advertise, publicize, puff, give a puff to; *informal* flog, hype, plug.
2 *minicab drivers were* **touting for** *business* **solicit**, seek, drum up; ask, petition, appeal, canvas, beg.
3 *he's being touted as the next Scotland manager* **commend**, endorse, praise, recommend, support, urge, push, speak of, talk of; *Brit.* tip.
▶ **noun ticket tout**, illegal salesman; *N. Amer. informal* scalper.

tow ▶ **verb** *a garage man called to tow the car away* **pull**, draw, drag, haul, tug, trail, lug, heave, trawl, hoist, transport; *informal* yank.
▶ **noun** *a tow to the garage costs from £95 to £155* **tug**, towing, haul, pull, drawing, drag, trailing, trawl.
□ **in tow** *they arrived with several young children in tow* **accompanying**, following, in attendance, in convoy, by one's side, in one's charge, under one's protection.

towards ▶ **preposition 1** *Henry strode towards her | he was heading towards Manhattan* **in the direction of**, to, toward, so as to approach, so as to near; on the way to, on the road to, en route for, in the vicinity of.
OPPOSITE away from.
2 *they're working towards a drug-free future* **with the aim of**, in order to

T

obtain, in order to achieve, so as to achieve, for.
OPPOSITE away from.
3 *towards evening dark clouds gathered* **just before**, shortly before, near, nearing, around, approaching, close to, coming to, getting on for, not quite.
4 *it is impossible to be indifferent towards her* **with regard to**, as regards, regarding, in/with regard to, in/with respect to, respecting, in relation to, concerning, about, in connection with, apropos.
5 *they offered to contribute £2,000 towards a fund to restore the church's organ* **as a contribution to**, for, as a help to, to help, to assist, supporting, promoting, assisting.

tower *See centre pages for list of* **Towers**
▶ **noun 1** *a church tower* **steeple**, spire; column, pillar, obelisk.
2 *much of the land was acquired by later monarchs to increase the tower's defences* **fortress**, fort, citadel, stronghold, fortification, keep, castle, garrison, bastion, donjon.
▶ **verb 1** *he towered above her | the wall towered, impossibly high* **soar**, rise, loom, ascend, mount, rear, reach high, stand high; overshadow, overlook, overhang, hang over, dominate.
2 *tourism towers over all other features of the urban economy* **surpass**, excel, outshine, outclass, outstrip, overshadow, cap, top, transcend, trump, dominate, eclipse, dwarf, be head and shoulders above, put something in the shade, put something to shame; upstage, beat, better; *informal* be a cut above, run rings/circles around, leave something standing; *archaic* outrival, outvie.

towering ▶ **adjective 1** *a towering skyscraper* **high**, tall, lofty, elevated, soaring, sky-high, sky-scraping, steep, mountainous, imposing, multi-storey; giant, gigantic, enormous, huge, colossal, vast, immense, massive, hulking, monstrous, mammoth, monumental, titanic, Brobdingnagian; *informal* whopping, ginormous.
OPPOSITES low, short.
2 *a towering rock idol* **outstanding**, pre-eminent, leading, foremost, finest, chief, excellent, distinguished, prominent, eminent, important, major, star, top, topmost, surpassing, superior, supreme, exceptional, great, incomparable, unrivalled, unsurpassed, peerless, matchless, unequalled, famous, renowned, celebrated, illustrious, extraordinary.
OPPOSITES undistinguished, inferior.
3 *he was in a towering rage* **extreme**, fierce, terrible, intense, overpowering, mighty, violent, fiery, unrestrained, vehement, passionate, ardent, immoderate, intemperate, inordinate, frenzied, fanatical, zealous, frantic, deep.
OPPOSITES minor, half-hearted.

town ▶ **noun** *a small market town* **urban area**, conurbation, municipality, borough, township, settlement; city, metropolis, megalopolis; *American Indian* pueblo; *Scottish* burgh.
OPPOSITES country, countryside.

WORD LINKS
relating to a town **municipal, urban**

toxic ▶ **adjective** *they were killed by smoke and toxic gases* **poisonous**, venomous, virulent, noxious, dangerous, destructive, harmful, unsafe, malignant, injurious, pestilential, pernicious; fatal, deadly, lethal, mortal, death-dealing; *archaic* baneful.
OPPOSITES non-toxic, harmless, safe.

toy *See centre pages for list of* **Toys**
▶ **noun 1** *a cuddly toy* **plaything**, game.
2 *an executive toy* **trinket**, bauble, knick-knack, ornament, gewgaw, trifle, gimcrack, bagatelle, triviality; *N. Amer.* kickshaw; *informal* whatnot; *Brit. informal* doodah.
▶ **adjective 1** *a toy car* **model**, miniature, imitation, make-believe, fake, simulation, artificial.
OPPOSITES real, authentic.
2 *a toy poodle* **miniature**, small, tiny, diminutive, dwarf, midget, pygmy.
OPPOSITES full-size, big.
▶ **verb**
□ **toy with 1** *I was toying with the idea of writing a book* **think idly about**, play with, flirt with, trifle with, entertain the possibility of, consider, have thoughts about, argue the pros and cons of; *informal* kick around/about.
2 *he had been toying with her that day on the river* **flirt with**, dally with, sport with, play with, amuse oneself with, trifle with, fool with.
3 *she could only toy with her food* **fidget with**, play (about/around) with, fiddle (about/around) with, fool about/around with, tinker with, finger, twiddle (with); nibble, pick at, gnaw (at), peck at, pick over, eat listlessly, eat like a bird; *informal* mess about/around with.

trace ▶ **verb 1** *Police hope to trace the owner of the jewellery* **track down**, find, discover, detect, unearth, uncover, turn up, hunt down, dig up, ferret out, run to ground; follow, pursue, trail, shadow, stalk, dog.
2 *we've traced the call* **find the source of**, find the origins of, find the roots of, follow to its source, source.
3 *trace a map of the world on to a large piece of paper* **copy**, reproduce, go over, draw over, draw the lines of; **draw**, draw up, sketch, draft, outline, rough out, mark out, delineate, map, chart, record, indicate, show, depict.
▶ **noun 1** *in the east wall is the trace of a pointed arch | no trace had been found of the missing plane* **vestige**, sign, mark, indication, suggestion, evidence, clue; **remains**, remnant, relic, survival; ghost, echo, memory.
2 *she spoke good English with only a trace of an accent* **bit**, spot, speck, touch, hint, suggestion, suspicion, nuance, intimation; trifle, drop, dash, tinge, tincture, streak, shred, crumb, fragment, shadow, whiff, breath, jot, iota; *informal* smidgen, tad.
3 *there was enough dust on the floor to have preserved traces of feet* **trail**, track, spoor, marks, tracks, prints, imprints, footprints, footmarks, footsteps.

track ▶ **noun 1** *she pedalled her bicycle up the gravel track to the south porch* **path**, pathway, footpath, lane, trail, route, way, course.
2 *he broke into a run along the track* **course**, racecourse; running track, racetrack, speedway, velodrome, piste; *Brit.* circuit.
3 (usually **tracks**) *he followed the tracks of a car* **traces**, marks, impressions, prints, imprints; footprints, footmarks, footsteps, trail, spoor; scent; wake, slipstream.
4 *Orkney lies on the track of the Atlantic winds* **course**, path, line, orbit, route, way, trajectory, flight path.
5 *commuters had to leave trains and walk along the tracks* **rail**, line; railway line, tramlines; metal; *N. Amer.* railroad.
6 *the title track of their forthcoming album* **song**, recording, number, piece.
□ **keep track of** *an online diary which allows you to keep track of your appointments* **monitor**, follow, keep up with, record, keep a record of; supervise, oversee, watch, keep an eye on; keep in touch with, keep up to date with.
OPPOSITE lose track of.
□ **lose track of** *he would quite often lose track of the time at work* **forget about**, forget, be unaware of, lose/cease contact with; lose sight of.
OPPOSITE keep track of.
□ **on track** *we're well on track to surpass expectations* **on course**, on target, on schedule, on time.
▶ **verb** *he tracked a bear for 40 km* **follow**, trail, trace, pursue, shadow, stalk, dog, spoor, hunt (down), chase, hound, course, keep an eye on, keep in sight; *informal* tail, keep tabs on, keep a tab on.
□ **track someone/something down** *it took seventeen years to track down the wreck of the ship* **discover**, **detect**, find (out), hunt down, hunt out, unearth, uncover, disinter, turn up, dig up, seek out, ferret out, root out, nose out, bring to light, expose, recover, capture, catch, smell out, sniff out, run to earth, run to ground, run down; *informal* suss out.

tract[1] ▶ **noun** *the lords owned large tracts of land* **area**, region, expanse, span, sweep, stretch, extent, belt, swathe, zone, plot, patch, parcel, portion, section, sector, quarter; territory, estate, acreage, allotment.

tract[2] ▶ **noun** *a great political tract* **treatise**, essay, article, paper, monograph, disquisition, dissertation, thesis, exposition, study, piece of writing, lecture, homily, sermon, work; **pamphlet**, booklet, leaflet, brochure.

tractable ▶ **adjective** *children are no longer as tractable as they used to be* **controllable**, manageable, malleable, governable, yielding, amenable, complaisant, compliant; adjustable; **docile**, submissive, obedient, tame, meek, easily handled, biddable, persuadable, persuasible, accommodating, trusting, gullible, dutiful, willing, unassertive, passive, deferential, humble, obsequious, servile, sycophantic.
OPPOSITES obstinate, defiant, recalcitrant.

traction ▶ **noun** *the shoes have studs for extra traction* **grip**, friction, adhesion, purchase, resistance; pull, haulage, propulsion, drag.

trade ▶ **noun 1** *the illicit trade in stolen cattle* **commerce**, buying and selling, dealing, traffic, trafficking, business, marketing, merchandising, bargaining; dealings, transactions, negotiations, proceedings.
2 *he left school to learn the glazier's trade* **craft**, occupation, job, career, profession, business, pursuit, living, livelihood, line, line of work, line of business, vocation, calling, walk of life, province, field; work, employment; *French* métier.
3 *we'll do a trade—I'll give you Foster if you get me some information* **swap**, exchange, switch, barter, interchange, substitution, replacement, trade-off; *archaic* truck.
▶ **verb 1** *he made his fortune trading in beaver pelts* **deal**, traffic; buy and sell, market, peddle, merchandise, barter; *informal* hawk, tout, flog, run.
2 *the business is trading at a loss* **do business**, deal, run, operate.
3 *I traded the old machine for a newer model* **swap**, exchange, switch, barter, substitute, replace; *archaic* truck.
□ **trade on** *he trades on his friendship with powerful people* **exploit**, take advantage of, capitalize on, profit from, use, make use of; milk, abuse, misuse; *informal* cash in on.

WORD LINKS
relating to trade **mercantile**

trademark ▶ **noun 1** *there was a trademark on the back of his jacket* **logo**, emblem, sign, stamp, symbol, device, badge, crest, insignia, seal, coat of arms, shield, motif, hallmark, mark, figure, monogram, logotype, colophon; trade name, brand name, proprietary name.
2 *long hair was the trademark of the hippy* **characteristic**, trait, quality,

attribute, feature, peculiarity, idiosyncrasy, hallmark, quirk, speciality, sign, telltale sign, penchant, proclivity.

trader ▶ noun *a market trader* **dealer**, merchant, buyer, seller, salesman, saleswoman, buyer and seller, marketeer, merchandiser, broker, agent; businessman, businesswoman, business person, distributor, vendor, purveyor, supplier, trafficker; shopkeeper, retailer, wholesaler; *Brit.* stockist; *informal* runner, pusher; *dated* pedlar, hawker.

tradesman, tradeswoman ▶ noun **1** *tradesmen standing nonchalantly outside their stores* **shopkeeper**, retailer, vendor, merchant, dealer, trader, supplier, stockist; salesman, saleswoman, salesperson, tradesperson, wholesaler; *N. Amer.* storekeeper; *historical* chandler, shopman, roundsman.
2 *the installation should be carried out by a qualified tradesman* **craftsman**, workman, skilled worker, artisan, employee, tradesperson, mechanic.

tradition ▶ noun **1** *the Chancellor is, by tradition, allowed to bring alcohol into the House on Budget day* **historical convention**, unwritten law, oral history, heritage; lore, folklore, old wives' tales.
2 *the hunt maintains a centuries-old tradition* **custom**, **practice**, convention, ritual, ceremony, observance, wont, routine, way, rule, usage, habit; institution, principle, belief; *formal* praxis.
3 *a poem in the tradition of Horace's 'Ars Poetica'* **style**, movement, method.

traditional ▶ adjective **1** *Paula always hankered after a traditional white wedding | the traditional nuclear family* **conventional**, customary, established, long-established, accepted, orthodox, standard, regular, normal, conservative; common, run-of-the-mill, habitual, set, fixed, routine, usual, accustomed; old-fashioned, staid, unadventurous, conformist, stereotyped, clichéd, undistinguished, wonted; old, time-honoured, proven, tried and tested, historic, classical, classic, old-world, folk, familial, ancestral; ritual, ritualistic, ceremonial.
OPPOSITES novel, unconventional, modern.
2 *traditional beliefs* **handed-down**, folk, historical, unwritten, oral.

traduce ▶ verb *it was regarded as respectable political tactics to traduce him on any grounds* **defame**, slander, speak ill of, speak evil of, gossip about, misrepresent, malign, vilify, calumniate, denigrate, disparage, slur, decry, sully, impugn, smear, besmirch, dishonour, back-bite, revile, run down, blacken the name of, cast aspersions on; *informal* do a hatchet job on, slag (off), rubbish, knock, drag someone's name through the mud; *N. Amer. informal* bad-mouth, dump on; *rare* asperse.

CHOOSE THE RIGHT WORD

traduce, malign, slander, libel, defame
See MALIGN.

traducer ▶ noun **defamer**, slanderer, calumniator, gossip, vilifier, disparager, denigrator, deprecator, abuser, smearer, detractor; *informal* mud-slinger, knocker; *rare* asperser.

traffic ▶ noun **1** *the bridge is not open to traffic* **vehicles**, cars, lorries, trucks.
2 *they might be stuck in traffic* **congestion**, traffic jam, jam, tailback, hold-up, bottleneck, gridlock, queue, stoppage, obstruction; *informal* snarl-up.
3 *he owned teams of horses for goods traffic* **transport**, transportation, movement of goods/people, freight, shipping, conveyancing.
4 *the illegal traffic in stolen art* **trade**, trading, trafficking, dealing, commerce, business, peddling, buying and selling; smuggling, bootlegging; market, black market; dealings, transactions, negotiations, proceedings.
5 (*archaic*) *he has little traffic with his neighbours* **contact**, communication, intercourse, dealings, relations.
▶ verb *he confessed to* ***trafficking in*** *gold and ivory* **trade**, deal, do business, peddle, bargain; buy and sell, market, barter; smuggle, bootleg; *informal* hawk, tout, flog, push, run.

T

tragedy ▶ noun **1** *the tragedy of her daughter's suicide | an age of tragedy and conflict* **disaster**, calamity, catastrophe, cataclysm, devastation, misfortune, misadventure, mishap, reverse, vicissitude, setback, trial, tribulation, affliction, blight, injury, adversity, sad event, serious accident; shock, blow; pain, sorrow, misery, distress, agony, unhappiness, sadness, disappointment; *informal* bummer.
OPPOSITES fortune, joy.
2 *Shakespeare's tragedies* **tragic drama**, drama, play; *literary* buskin.
OPPOSITE comedy.

WORD LINKS
Muse of tragedy **Melpomene**

tragic ▶ adjective **1** *a boy died after a tragic accident* **disastrous**, calamitous, catastrophic, cataclysmic, devastating, terrible, dreadful, appalling, horrendous, dire, ruinous, gruesome, awful, miserable, wretched, unfortunate; fatal, deadly, mortal, lethal.
OPPOSITES fortunate, lucky.
2 *they were a tragic family* **sad**, unhappy, pathetic, moving, distressing, painful, sorrowful, heart-rending, agonizing, stirring, disturbing, pitiful, piteous; melancholy, doleful, mournful, dejected, despondent, anguished, desolate, dismal, gloomy.
OPPOSITES happy, joyful.
3 *a tragic waste of talent* **dreadful**, terrible, awful, deplorable, lamentable, regrettable, abject, miserable, wretched, grievous, galling, vexatious.

trail ▶ noun **1** *he left a trail of clues* **series**, stream, string, line, chain, row, succession, train.
2 *wolves on the trail of their prey* **track**, spoor, path, scent; traces, marks, signs, prints, imprints, impressions, footprints, footmarks, footsteps.
3 *the plane was leaving an impressive vapour trail* **wake**, tail, stream, slipstream.
4 *the torrential rain left a trail of devastation* **train**, chain, series, sequence, aftermath.
5 *a trail of ants* **line**, queue, row, train, file, rank, column, procession, string, chain, array, group, following, entourage, convoy.
6 *country parks with nature trails* **path**, beaten path, pathway, way, footpath, track, course, road, route.
▶ verb **1** *my hands were trailing in the water* **drag**, sweep, be drawn, draw, stream, dangle, hang (down), tow, droop; *archaic* depend.
2 *the roses grew wild, their stems trailing over the banks* **creep**, crawl, slide, slink, slither.
3 *Sharpe suspected that they were trailing him* **follow**, pursue, track, trace, shadow, stalk, dog, hound, spoor, hunt (down), course, keep an eye on, keep in sight, run to earth, run to ground, run down; *informal* tail, keep tabs on, keep a tab on.
4 *the defending champions were trailing 10–5 at half time* **lose**, be down, be behind, lag behind, fall behind, drop behind.
5 *Mark baulked at the idea of trailing around the shops all day | a maid* ***trailed behind*** *them* **trudge**, plod, drag oneself, wander, amble, meander, drift; dawdle, straggle, loiter, linger, lag; fall behind, take one's time, not keep up, bring up the rear; *informal* tag along behind.
6 *he let his voice* ***trail off*** **fade**, dwindle, diminish, lessen, wane, ebb, subside, weaken, peter out, melt away, fizzle out, taper off, tail off, grow faint, grow dim, evaporate, disappear, vanish, die, come to nothing, come to a halt, come to an end, run out.
7 *the BBC trailed the series as unsuitable for young people* **advertise**, publicize, announce, proclaim; **preview**, show excerpts of, call attention to; *informal* hype.

train *See centre pages for list of* **Trains and Rolling Stock**
▶ verb **1** *the scheme involved workers training their colleagues* **instruct**, teach, coach, tutor, give lessons to, school, educate, edify, prime, drill, demonstrate something to, make something clear to; put someone through their paces; inculcate, indoctrinate, condition.
2 *she is now training to be a hairdresser* **study**, learn, prepare, be taught, take instruction, qualify.
3 *with the Olympics in mind, athletes are training hard* **exercise**, do exercises, work out, get into shape, practise, prepare.
4 *the race is to include three horses that are trained in Dubai* **coach**, drill, exercise, prepare, practise, ground, rehearse, make ready, make fit.
5 *she trained the gun on his chest* **aim**, point, direct, level, line something up, turn something on, fix something on, sight, position, focus; take aim, zero in on.
▶ noun **1** *he caught a train from Paddington to Reading* locomotive, railway train; *baby talk* choo-choo.
2 *a minister and his train of attendants* **retinue**, entourage, cortège, following, staff, household, court, suite; attendants, retainers, followers, bodyguards.
3 *a train of elephants dragging logs* **procession**, line, file, column, convoy, cavalcade, caravan, queue, rank, string, succession, progression, array.
4 *this set in motion a bizarre train of events* **chain**, string, series, sequence, succession, set, progression, course, cycle, line, row, order, trail, concatenation.
5 *the bride wore a cream silk dress with a train* **tail**, appendage.

trainer ▶ noun **1** *a fitness trainer* **instructor**, coach, teacher, mentor, adviser, counsellor, guide, guru, manager, handler, tutor, educator.
2 (*Brit.*) *a decent pair of trainers* **training shoe**, running shoe, sports shoe, tennis shoe, plimsoll; football boot; *N. Amer.* sneaker.

training ▶ noun **1** *he got training in word-processing techniques* **instruction**, teaching, coaching, tuition, tutoring, tutelage, schooling, education, drilling, priming, preparation, grounding, guidance, indoctrination, inculcation; lessons.
2 *he was overweight when he went back into training* **exercise**, exercises, physical exercises, working out, bodybuilding; drill, practice, preparation.

traipse ▶ verb *I haven't the time to go traipsing around art galleries* **trudge**, trek, tramp, trail, hike, plod, shuffle, slouch, drag oneself, drag one's feet, clump, slog, wade, footslog.

trait ▶ noun *she had an unfortunate trait of bending the truth to suit her* **characteristic**, attribute, feature, quality, essential quality, property, distinction, idiosyncrasy, peculiarity, quirk, foible, singularity, oddity, eccentricity, abnormality, mark, trademark, hallmark, earmark; mannerism, way, trick, habit, custom, tendency; *literary* lineament.

traitor ▶ noun *he was tried in a military court as a traitor* **betrayer**, back-stabber, double-crosser, double-dealer, renegade, Judas, quisling, fifth

columnist, viper; turncoat, defector, apostate, deserter; collaborator, fraternizer, colluder, informer, double agent; *informal* snake in the grass, two-timer, rat, scab; *rare* traditor, tergiversator, renegado.
OPPOSITES loyalist, patriot.

traitorous ▶ adjective *an agent who had ties with a traitorous party* **treacherous**, disloyal, treasonous, back-stabbing; double-crossing, double-dealing, faithless, unfaithful, perfidious, two-faced, false-hearted, duplicitous, deceitful, false, untrue, untrustworthy, unreliable, undependable, fickle; *informal* two-timing.
OPPOSITES loyal, faithful, patriotic.

trajectory ▶ noun *aerodynamic forces change the trajectory of the ball* **course**, route, path, track, line, orbit, flight, flight path, ambit, direction, bearing, orientation, way, tack, approach.

trammel (*literary*) ▶ noun *he made progress towards an ideal which the trammels of tradition never allowed him to attain* **restraint**, constraint, curb, check, impediment, obstacle, barrier, handicap, bar, block, hindrance, encumbrance, disadvantage, drawback, snag, stumbling block; (**trammels**) shackles, fetters, bonds.
OPPOSITES help, assistance.
▶ verb *the narrow skirt trammelled her steps* **restrict**, restrain, constrain, hamper, confine, curb, check, hinder, handicap, obstruct, impede, interfere with, forestall, thwart, frustrate; hold back, retard, slow down, cramp, clog, straiten, hem in; hamstring, bridle, encumber, enmesh, ensnare; *informal* stymie; *Brit. informal* throw a spanner in the works of; *N. Amer. informal* throw a monkey wrench in the works of.
OPPOSITES help, assist.

tramp[1] ▶ verb **1** *men were tramping through the shrubbery* **trudge**, plod, stamp, trample, lumber, clump, clomp, stump, stomp, stumble, pad, march, thunder; *informal* traipse, galumph.
2 *he spent ten days tramping through the jungle* **trek**, trudge, slog, footslog, plod, drag oneself, walk, ramble, hike, march, roam, range, rove, backpack; *informal* traipse, hoof it, leg it, take Shanks's pony; *Brit. informal* yomp.
3 *this is one of the few wines still tramped by foot* **trample**, tread on, step on, stamp on; squash, crush, flatten, pulp.
▶ noun **1** *she heard the regular tramp of the sentry's boots* **footstep**, step, footfall, tread, stamp, stomp, stomping.
2 *Theodora returned from a tramp round Norwich* **trek**, trudge, slog, hike, march, walk, constitutional, ramble, roam, wander; *informal* traipse; *Brit. informal* yomp.

tramp[2] ▶ noun **1** *Herbert's eccentricity was to dress as a tramp* **vagrant**, vagabond, homeless person, derelict, down-and-out; itinerant, traveller, drifter, wanderer, person of no fixed address, beachcomber; ne'er do well, good for nothing; outcast, pariah; beggar, mendicant; *N. Amer.* hobo, bum; *Austral./NZ* bagman, sundowner, swagman; *informal* crusty, bag lady; *Brit. informal* dosser; *Austral./NZ informal* derro.
2 (*N. Amer. informal*) *he knew she was a tramp, available for any man with enough money* **slut**, promiscuous woman, prostitute, whore; *informal* tart, floozie, slag, scrubber, slapper; *dated* wanton, scarlet woman, loose woman, fallen woman, hussy, trollop, strumpet, slattern.

trample ▶ verb **1** *a fence was erected to prevent people **trampling on** the flowers* **tread**, tramp, stamp, walk over; squash, crush, flatten, compress, press (down), compact, pound, tamp down, mangle, pulp, mash, pulverize.
2 *we do nothing but **trample over** their feelings* **treat with contempt**, ride roughshod over, disregard, set at naught, show no consideration for, treat inconsiderately, treat disrespectfully, take for granted, encroach on, infringe, abuse, do violence to.

trance ▶ noun **daze**, stupor, haze, hypnotic state, half-conscious state, dream, daydream, reverie, brown study, suspended animation; *Scottish* dwam.

tranquil ▶ adjective **1** *a wonderfully tranquil village* **peaceful**, restful, reposeful, calm, quiet, still, serene, placid, relaxing, soothing, undisturbed, idyllic, halcyon, mild, pleasant.
OPPOSITES disturbed, busy.
2 *Martha smiled, perfectly tranquil* **calm**, placid, composed, relaxed, at peace, cool, {cool, calm, and collected}, cool-headed, serene, even-tempered, self-possessed, controlled, unexcitable, unflappable, unruffled, unperturbed, imperturbable, undisturbed, unagitated, dispassionate, stoical, sober, unemotional, untroubled, pacific; *informal* together, laid-back.
OPPOSITE excitable.

> **CHOOSE THE RIGHT WORD**
>
> **tranquil, serene, calm, placid, peaceful**
>
> *See* CALM.

tranquillity ▶ noun **1** *the peace and tranquillity of the Norfolk countryside* **peace**, peacefulness, restfulness, repose, reposefulness, calm, calmness, quiet, quietness, quietude, silence, hush, noiselessness, stillness, serenity, sedateness, placidity, mildness.
OPPOSITES commotion, busyness.
2 *the crash had jolted her out of her tranquillity* **calm**, calmness, placidity, composure, coolness, cool-headedness, serenity, contentment, content, even-temperedness, self-possession, control, equanimity, unexcitability, unflappability, imperturbability, restraint, self-restraint, stoicism, sobriety, untroubledness; *informal* togetherness; *rare* ataraxy, ataraxia.
OPPOSITE excitability.

tranquillize ▶ verb *as a last resort you may need to tranquillize the horse* **sedate**, calm (down), soothe, quiet, quieten (down), pacify, settle someone's/something's nerves, mollify, lull, relax; stupefy, anaesthetize, narcotize, knock out, drug; administer a sedative/tranquillizer to; *informal* dope, zonk.
OPPOSITES agitate, disturb, ruffle.

tranquillizer ▶ noun **sedative**, calmative, depressant, opiate, neuroleptic, sleeping pill, soporific, drug, narcotic; barbiturate, temazepam, diazepam, chlordiazepoxide, chlorpromazine, meprobamate, benzodiazepine, thioridazine, prochlorperazine; *informal* downer, trank, sleeper; *trademark* Valium, Librium; *dated* bromide.
OPPOSITE stimulant.

transact ▶ verb *those who transact business in London must know what the rules are* **negotiate**, **conduct**, carry out, do, perform, execute, enact, manage, handle, organize, take care of, prosecute, work out, thrash out, hammer out, see to, administer, operate; settle, conclude, finish, clinch, discharge, accomplish, reach an agreement on, agree on, come to terms about, reach terms on; *informal* sort out.

transaction ▶ noun **1** *property transactions* **deal**, business, agreement, undertaking, affair, arrangement, bargain, negotiation, treaty, contract, pact, compact, bond, settlement; (**transactions**) proceedings.
2 (**transactions**) *the transactions of the Jewish Historical Society* **proceedings**, affairs, concerns, dealings, matters, activities; **records**, report, publication, journal, minutes, annals, log, account, chronicle; *informal* doings, goings-on.
3 *the transaction of government business* **negotiation**, **conduct**, conducting, carrying out, performance, execution, enactment, management, handling, organization, prosecution, working out, thrashing out, hammering out, administration, operation; settling, conclusion, clinching, discharge, accomplishment, agreement, settlement.

transcend ▶ verb **1** *there were differences of opinion transcending Party lines* **go beyond**, rise above, cut across.
2 *his latest bout of bad behaviour transcended even his own worst excesses* **surpass**, excel, exceed, beat, trump, top, cap, outdo, outstrip, leave behind, outrival, outvie, outrank, outshine, eclipse, overstep, overshadow, throw into the shade, upstage.

transcendence, transcendency ▶ noun *this novel's theme is the transcendence of human love over the coercions of church and state* **superiority**, supremacy, predominance, pre-eminence, ascendancy; incomparability, matchlessness, peerlessness; excellence, greatness, magnificence, sublimity, importance; *rare* paramountcy.

transcendent ▶ adjective **1** *a transcendent god* **supernatural**, preternatural, transcendental, other-worldly, superhuman, mystical, mystic, spiritual, divine, heavenly, exalted, sublime, ethereal, numinous, transmundane, ineffable.
OPPOSITE mundane.
2 *a transcendent genius* **superior**, supreme, consummate, predominant, pre-eminent, ascendant, paramount, superlative, unique, unsurpassed, incomparable, unrivalled, unequalled, unparalleled, matchless, peerless, second to none; excellent, excelling, great, magnificent.
OPPOSITES average, mediocre.

transcendental ▶ adjective. *See* TRANSCENDENT *sense* 1.

transcribe ▶ verb **1** *the following passage is transcribed from a tape recording of spontaneous speech* **write out**, copy out, write/copy in full, put in writing, set down, take down, type out, print out, put on paper, commit to paper, reproduce.
2 *the court was adjourned so that they could transcribe their notes* **transliterate**, interpret, translate, render, convert, write up, rewrite; *Law* engross.

transcript ▶ noun *a newspaper printed a transcript of the tapes* **written version**, written copy, copy, printed version, transliteration, reproduction, record, text, script, note, summary, log, documentation.

transfer ▶ verb (stress on the second syllable) **1** *the plants should be transferred into a tank* **move**, convey, shift, remove, take, carry, fetch, lift, bring, bear, conduct, send, pass on, transport, relay, change, relocate, resettle, transplant, uproot.
2 *we will transfer full planning responsibility to local authorities* **hand over**, pass on, make over, turn over, sign over, transmit, convey, consign, commit, devolve, assign, cede, surrender, relinquish, delegate, entrust, grant, give, refer; divert, channel, redirect.
OPPOSITE retain.
▶ noun (stress on the first syllable) **1** *he got a free transfer to a Spanish team* **movement**, **move**, moving, shifting, shift, handover, relocation,

repositioning, transplant, redirection, conveyance, transferral, transference, removal, change, changeover, switch, conversion.
2 *she signed the transfer in her maiden name* **conveyance**, transfer document; papers, deeds, documentation.

transfigure ▸ verb *the glow of the sunrise transfigured the whole landscape* **transform**, change, alter, convert, metamorphose, vary, modify, transmute, mutate; rearrange, reshape, remodel, redo, reconstruct, recast, rebuild, reorganize, renew, revolutionize; *humorous* transmogrify.

transfix ▸ verb **1** *he sat transfixed by the film's sheer beauty* **mesmerize**, hypnotize, spellbind, bewitch, captivate, entrance, enthral, fascinate, engross, enrapture, stun, stupefy, astound, grip, root someone to the spot, stop someone dead, stop someone in their tracks; paralyse, petrify, immobilize, freeze, rivet; *rare* gorgonize.
2 *a picture of a nail transfixing a splayed hand* **impale**, stab, spear, pierce, spike, skewer, stick, gore, pin, bayonet, harpoon, lance, run through, puncture, perforate; *rare* transpierce.

transform ▸ verb *the city has been transformed into a magnet for foreign investment | this development will transform the site* **change**, alter, modify, convert, metamorphose, transfigure, transmute, mutate; remodel, reshape, remould, redo, reconstruct, rebuild, recast, reorganize, rearrange, reorder, reshuffle, restyle, rejig, rework, renew, revamp, renovate, overhaul, remake; revolutionize, stir up, turn upside down; *humorous* transmogrify.
OPPOSITES preserve, keep the same.

transformation ▸ noun *the food-manufacturing industry underwent a transformation* **change**, alteration, modification, variation, conversion, revision, amendment, metamorphosis, transfiguration, evolution, mutation, sea change; remodelling, reshaping, remoulding, redoing, reconstruction, rebuilding, recasting, reorganization, rearrangement, reordering, reshuffling, restyling, rejigging, reworking, renewal, renewing, revamping, renovation, overhaul, remaking; revolutionizing, revolution, transmutation; *humorous* transmogrification.
OPPOSITES preservation, conservation.

transgress ▸ verb **1** *they must control the impulses which lead them to transgress* **misbehave**, behave badly, break the law, err, lapse, commit an offence, fall from grace, stray from the straight and narrow, sin, degenerate, do wrong, go astray; *informal* slip up, be out of order; *archaic* trespass.
2 *few of us will go through life without transgressing some rule of public law* **disobey**, defy, infringe, breach, contravene, violate, break, flout, infract, commit a breach of.
OPPOSITE obey.

transgression ▸ noun **1** *they were granted full amnesty for their transgressions* **offence**, crime, sin, wrong, wrongdoing, misdemeanour, felony, misdeed, lawbreaking, vice, evil-doing, indiscretion, peccadillo, mischief, mischievousness, wickedness, misbehaviour, bad behaviour; error, lapse, fault; *archaic* trespass.
2 *Adam's transgression of God's law* **infringement**, breach, contravention, violation, defiance, infraction, disobedience, breaking, flouting, non-observance, overstepping, exceeding.
OPPOSITE obedience.

transgressor ▸ noun *a transgressor against human rights* **offender**, wrongdoer, culprit, lawbreaker, criminal, delinquent, villain, felon, reprobate, outlaw, malefactor, guilty party; sinner, trespasser, evil-doer; *Law* malfeasant, misfeasor; *informal* crook; *archaic* miscreant.

transience ▸ noun *the transience of life on earth* **temporariness**, transitoriness, impermanence, brevity, briefness, shortness, ephemerality, short-livedness, momentariness, mutability, instability, volatility; *literary* evanescence; *rare* caducity, fugitiveness.
OPPOSITE permanence.

transient ▸ adjective *a transient post-war baby boom* **transitory**, temporary, short-lived, short-term, ephemeral, impermanent, brief, short, momentary; fleeting, flying, evanescent, passing, fugitive, fading, mutable, unstable, volatile, here today and gone tomorrow, fly-by-night; *rare* fugacious.
OPPOSITES permanent, perpetual, constant.

transit ▸ noun *an agreement on the free transit of goods between states* **movement**; **transport**, transportation, conveyance, shipment, haulage, freightage, carriage; moving, travel, travelling, journeying, passage, passing, transfer, crossing, progress.
□ **in transit** *a painting was damaged in transit* **en route**, on the journey, during transport, on the way, on the road, on the move, along/on the road, in motion; *informal* on the go.

transition ▸ noun *the transition from school to work* **change**, move, passage, transformation, conversion, adaptation, adjustment, alteration, changeover, metamorphosis; shift, switch, jump, leap, progression, progress, gradation, development, evolution; transfiguration, flux, mutation, transmutation, vicissitude.

transitional ▸ adjective **1** *we will need assistance in the transitional period* **intermediate**, middle, midway, intervening, interposed; fluid, unsettled; changing, developmental, evolutionary.

> **CHOOSE THE RIGHT WORD**
>
> **transient, transitory, ephemeral, fleeting**
>
> None of these words is much used in everyday speech and writing: they are all quite literary, and their shared meaning is 'impermanent' or 'lasting only a short time'.
>
> - The basic meaning of **transient** is mainly applied to short-lived phenomena (*a transient upturn in Germany's fortunes*) and often in technical language (*a transient rise in gastric acid output*). The sense of impermanence can derive from the fact that people or animals described as *transient* only stay or work in a place for a short time (*agency workers and their close equivalents form a very transient population | a large proportion of our birds are transient*).
> - **Transitory** is very similar but less used in technical contexts (*this transitory life | the report to his school mentioned some transitory emotional difficulties the child was having*) and almost never in relation to the movement of people or animals.
> - **Ephemeral** implies that something is not only short-lived but also inconsequential or of limited value (*ephemeral material like leaflets, posters, postcards, etc.*). However, it can be used as a neutral scientific or technical term (*melting coastal snow supports an ephemeral algal flora*).
> - **Fleeting** conveys the greatest degree of impermanence and often a note of regret that the phenomenon does not last longer (*she only caught a fleeting glimpse of him all day | Carol was paying a fleeting visit to Paris*).

OPPOSITES initial, final.
2 *the transitional government* **interim**, temporary, provisional, pro tem, stopgap, short-term, fill-in, make-do, acting, conditional, caretaker, working, contingent, makeshift.
OPPOSITE permanent.

transitory ▸ adjective *a transitory fashion* **temporary**, transient, brief, short, short-lived, short-term, impermanent, ephemeral, evanescent, momentary, fleeting, flying, passing, fugitive, flitting, fading, mutable, unstable, volatile, here today and gone tomorrow, fly-by-night; *rare* fugacious.
OPPOSITES permanent, perpetual, lasting.

> **CHOOSE THE RIGHT WORD**
>
> **transitory, transient, ephemeral, fleeting**
>
> See TRANSIENT.

translate ▸ verb **1** *the German original had been translated into English* **interpret**, render, gloss, put, express, convert, change, construe, transcribe, transliterate.
2 *be prepared to translate the jargon of your profession into normal English* **render**, paraphrase, reword, rephrase, recast, convert, decipher, decode, gloss, explain, unravel, reveal, elucidate, expound, clarify, spell out.
3 *without some form of supervisory body, their good intentions will not be translated into reality* **change**, convert, transform, alter, turn, metamorphose, transmute, transfigure, render; *humorous* transmogrify.
4 *my husband and I, recently translated from California to the North-east, were given similar advice* **relocate**, transfer, move, remove, shift, convey, transport, transplant.

translation ▸ noun **1** *a translation of the 'Odyssey'* **rendering**, rendition, gloss, conversion, construing, transcription, transliteration, metaphrase.
2 *a modern translation of Hamlet's 'to be, or not to be' speech* **rendition**, adaptation, version, rendering, paraphrase, paraphrasing, rewording, rephrase, rephrasing, recasting, conversion, deciphering, decoding, gloss, crib, simplification, explanation, elucidation, clarification.
3 *the translation of these policies into practice will vary according to local circumstances* **change**, conversion, transformation, alteration, adaptation, turning, metamorphosis, transmutation, transfiguration, rendering; *humorous* transmogrification.
4 *the translation of the Archbishop's remains from London to Canterbury* **relocation**, transfer, transferral, move, moving, movement, removal, shift, conveyance, conveying, transport, transportation.

translator ▸ noun *she worked as a translator at the United Nations* **interpreter**, transcriber, transliterator, paraphraser, decipherer; **linguist**, polyglot; *technical* exegete, glossator, glossarist; *rare* dragoman.

translucent ▸ adjective *a mantle of translucent ice* **semi-transparent**, pellucid, diaphanous, colourless, glassy, glass-like, gossamer, clear, crystalline, see-through, limpid, transparent; *rare* transpicuous, translucid.
OPPOSITE opaque.

transmission ▸ noun **1** *the transmission of the HIV virus | teaching practice aims at transmission of knowledge and culture* **transference**, transferral, passing on, communication, conveyance, imparting, channelling,

carrying, relaying, dispatch, mediation; dissemination, spreading, circulation, diffusion, emanation, scattering, radiation.
2 *after the transmission of the film she received instant celebrity status* **broadcasting**, relaying, sending out, putting on (the) air, airing, televising, radioing, telecasting, showing, publication, emission.
3 *a live transmission* **broadcast**, programme, show, presentation, feature, telecast.

transmit ▸ verb **1** *modems are used for transmitting data between computers* **transfer**, pass on, hand on, communicate, convey, impart, channel, carry, bear, relay, dispatch, mediate; disseminate, spread, circulate, diffuse, radiate.
OPPOSITE receive.
2 *this programme will be transmitted on Sunday* **broadcast**, relay, send out, put on (the) air, air, televise, radio, telecast, show, publish, emit, wire, beam, pipe.

transmute ▸ verb *these books were transmuted into workable scripts* **change**, alter, adapt, modify, transform, transfigure, convert, metamorphose, mutate, reconstruct, remake, recast, reorganize, translate; *humorous* transmogrify.

transparency ▸ noun **1** *the transparency of the dew on a rose* **translucency**, lucidity, pellucidity, limpidness, limpidity, glassiness, liquidity, clearness, clarity; *rare* transpicuousness.
OPPOSITES opacity, cloudiness.
2 *the transparency of classical writing* **clarity**, clearness, lucidity, straightforwardness, plainness, obviousness, explicitness, unambiguity, unambiguousness; *rare* transpicuousness.
OPPOSITES obscurity, ambiguity.
3 *the transparency of their predatory motives* **blatantness**, flagrancy, obviousness, patentness, manifestness, barefacedness, shamelessness, brazenness, boldness, unmistakableness, clearness, clarity, plainness, visibility, distinctness, apparentness, perceptibility, discernibility, palpability.
OPPOSITE obscurity.
4 *the report said that the country's economic management lacked transparency* **frankness**, openness, candidness, honesty, directness, forthrightness, unreservedness, plain-spokenness, straightness, straightforwardness, ingenuousness, innocence, guilelessness, simplicity.
OPPOSITES cunning, secrecy.
5 *a colour transparency of the Grand Canyon* photograph, slide, photo, picture, snap, image, portrait, print, plate, film, exposure, still.

transparent ▸ adjective **1** *a transparent plastic film* **see-through**, clear, translucent, pellucid, crystal clear, crystalline, limpid, glassy, glass-like, liquid; unclouded, uncloudy; *rare* transpicuous.
OPPOSITES opaque, cloudy.
2 *a transparent dress* **filmy**, gauzy, fine, sheer, light, lightweight, thin, flimsy, see-through, diaphanous, chiffony, gossamer, delicate.
OPPOSITES thick, coarse.
3 *the symbolism of this myth is transparent* **obvious**, explicit, unambiguous, unequivocal, clear, lucid, straightforward, plain, (as) plain as the nose on your face, apparent, unmistakable, manifest, conspicuous, patent, indisputable, self-evident; *rare* transpicuous.
OPPOSITES obscure, ambiguous.
4 *transparent lies* **blatant**, flagrant, obvious, patent, manifest, undisguised, unconcealed, barefaced, glaring, shameless, brazen, bold, unmistakable, clear, plain, visible, noticeable, recognizable, distinct, evident, apparent, perceptible, discernible, palpable; *archaic* arrant.
5 *parliament should render government transparent* **frank**, open, candid, honest, direct, forthright, unreserved, plain-spoken, straight, straightforward, ingenuous, innocent, guileless, simple, artless; accountable; *informal* upfront.
OPPOSITES cunning, secretive.

transpire ▸ verb **1** *it transpired that Mr. Washington had been in London throughout the period of the robberies* **become known**, become apparent, be revealed, be disclosed, come to light, emerge, come out, get out, be discovered, be uncovered, materialize, leak out, turn out, be made public.
2 *the visitors explained where they had come from and what had transpired there* **happen**, occur, take place, come about, come to pass, crop up, turn up, arise, chance, ensue, befall, be realized, take shape; pan out, end up.

transplant ▸ verb **1** *the Second Empire style was copied and transplanted to other European capitals* **transfer**, transport, move, remove, shift, convey, displace, relocate, reposition, resettle, take, carry, fetch, bring.
2 *lift and transplant bulbs when they are becoming overcrowded* **replant**, repot, relocate; uproot.
3 *the heart valves will be transplanted into local patients* **graft**, transfer, implant.

transport *See centre pages for lists of* **Aircraft** **Cars** **Carriages and Carts** **Sailing Ships and Boats** **Ships and Boats** **Trains and Rolling Stock** **Vehicles**
▸ verb (stress on the second syllable) **1** *the concrete blocks have been transported by lorry* **convey**, carry, take, transfer, move, shift, bring, fetch, send, deliver, bear, conduct, haul, lug, cart, run, ship, ferry.
2 *he was convicted of theft and transported* **banish**, exile, deport, drive away, expatriate, extradite.
3 *she was completely transported by the excitement of her passion* **thrill**, delight, ravish, carry away, enrapture, entrance, enchant, enthral, electrify, captivate, bewitch, fascinate, spellbind, charm, overjoy, elate; *informal* send.
▸ noun (stress on the first syllable) **1** *this service is used mainly by the elderly who have no access to alternative forms of transport* **conveyance**, transportation, transfer, transference, transmission, movement; vehicle, car, carriage, carrier.
2 *protect the camera in case it is dropped during transport* **transit**, transportation, conveyance, traffic, carriage, freight, freightage, shipment, shipping, haulage, delivery, distribution, carrying.
3 *the mother, in a transport of grief, clung to her husband* **frenzy**, fit, rhapsody; intense feeling, strong emotion, passion, fervour, vehemence.
4 (**transports**) *the transports of passion* **rapture**, **ecstasy**, elation, exaltation, exhilaration, euphoria, bliss, seventh heaven, heaven, paradise, high; *informal* cloud nine.

transpose ▸ verb **1** *a pair of pictures in which the colours of the flowers and foliage are transposed* **interchange**, exchange, switch, swap (round), transfer, reverse, invert, rearrange, reorder, turn about/around, change (round), move (around), substitute, trade, alter, convert.
2 *it had been shown that science fiction could be transposed into popular television entertainment* **shift**, relocate, reposition, transplant, move, displace.

transverse ▸ adjective *a transverse bar* **crosswise**, crossways, cross, diagonal, horizontal, oblique, athwart; *technical* transversal.

trap *See centre pages for list of* **Traps**
▸ noun **1** *it is quite possible that the question was set as a trap* **trick**, stratagem, ploy, ruse, wile, deception, artifice, subterfuge, device, trickery; *informal* set-up; *archaic* toils.
2 *he was fairly certain now that he was walking into a trap, and wished he'd come armed* **ambush**, lure, decoy, bait; *dated* ambuscade.
3 *she wrote about what a trap her marriage was* **snare**, net; cage, prison; encumbrance, burden, problem.
4 (*informal*) *shut your trap!* **mouth**, jaws, lips, maw; *informal* chops, kisser, yap; *Brit. informal* **gob**, cakehole, mush; *N. Amer. informal* puss, bazoo.
▸ verb **1** *police trapped the two men, who admitted blackmail* **snare**, entrap, ensnare, enmesh, lay a trap for; **capture**, catch, bag, land, hook, corner, waylay, ambush; seize, take, lay hold of, run to earth/ground; *archaic* ambuscade.
2 *a rat trapped in a barn* **confine**, **catch**, cut off, corner, pin down, drive into a corner, pen, hem in, close in, shut in, hedge in, imprison, hold captive.
3 *he trapped his finger in a spring-loaded hinge* **get stuck**, catch, get caught.
4 *the politicians had trapped him into a game played by their rules* **trick**, dupe, deceive, cheat, lure, inveigle, beguile, fool, hoodwink, seduce, cajole, wheedle, gull; catch out, trip up, outwit, outsmart; *archaic* cozen.

trappings ▸ plural noun *some of the appeal of monarchy lay in its ritual and spectacular trappings* **accessories**, trimmings, frills, accompaniments, extras, ornaments, ornamentation, adornment, decoration; regalia, paraphernalia, apparatus, finery, frippery, livery, fittings, accoutrements; appurtenances, appointments, equipage, equipment, gear, effects, things, panoply; baggage, impedimenta; *informal* bells and whistles, stuff, bits and pieces, bits and bobs; *archaic* trumpery.

trash ▸ noun **1** (*N. Amer.*) *the subway entrance was blocked with trash* **rubbish**, waste, waste material, refuse, litter, garbage, debris, junk, dross, detritus, sweepings, dregs, remains; *vulgar slang* crap.
2 *politicians should think and inquire before they speak trash* **nonsense**, drivel, pap, gibberish, balderdash, bunkum, humbug, rubbish, moonshine; *informal* bull, poppycock, gobbledegook, hot air, twaddle, rot, tommyrot, bunk, tripe, bilge, piffle, bosh, tosh, hooey; *N. Amer. informal* garbage, flapdoodle, blathers, wack, bushwa, applesauce; *vulgar slang* crap, bullshit; *Austral./NZ vulgar slang* bulldust.
OPPOSITES logic, good sense.
3 *get home, you convict trash!* **rabble**, scum, vermin, dregs, good-for-nothings, lowest of the low, underclass, the dregs, untouchables, the hoi polloi; *French* canaille; *informal* riff-raff.
▸ verb **1** (*N. Amer. informal*) *they trashed their guitars and threw them into the audience* **wreck**, ruin, damage, destroy; deface, mar, spoil, vandalize; *informal* total.
2 *his directorial debut had been trashed by the critics* **criticize**, **lambaste**, censure, attack, insult, abuse, give a bad press to, condemn, flay, savage; *informal* pan, knock, take to pieces, take/pull apart, crucify, hammer, slam, bash, roast, maul, throw brickbats at; *Brit. informal* slate, rubbish, slag off; *N. Amer.* bad-mouth, pummel.

trauma ▸ noun **1** *the trauma of divorce* **shock**, upheaval, distress, stress, strain, pain, anguish, suffering, upset, agony, misery, sorrow, grief, heartache, heartbreak, torture; disturbance, disorder, jolt, ordeal, trial, tribulation, trouble, worry, anxiety, burden, adversity, hardship, nightmare.
2 *the gallstone can be extracted without unnecessary trauma to the liver* **injury**, damage, hurt, wound, wounding, sore, bruise, cut, laceration, lesion, abrasion, contusion.
OPPOSITE healing.

traumatic ▸ adjective **1** *they had had traumatic experiences in the war*

disturbing, shocking, distressing, disquieting, upsetting, damaging, scarring, injurious, harmful, hurtful, painful, agonizing, awful, chilling, alarming, devastating, harrowing, excruciating, horrifying, terrifying; (*informal*) mind-blowing.
OPPOSITES soothing, calming.
2 *bankruptcy looked possible after the traumatic first year* **stressful**, demanding, trying, taxing, terrible, bad, unpleasant, disagreeable, irksome, troublesome, vexatious.
OPPOSITES successful, pleasing.

travail (*literary*) ▶ **noun 1** *the travails of austerity in the late 1940s* **ordeal**, trial, tribulation; trials and tribulations, trouble, hardship, privation, stress; **drudgery**, toil, slog, effort, exertion, labour, work, endeavour; sweat, striving, struggle, industry.
2 (*archaic*) *a woman in travail* **childbirth**, labour, birth, birthing, confinement, delivery, nativity; labour pains, contractions, labour pangs, labour throes; *technical* parturition; *archaic* accouchement, lying-in, childbed.

travel ▶ **verb 1** *people seeking an exit visa to travel abroad* **journey**, **tour**, take a trip, go on a trip, voyage, go on an expedition, go on an excursion, go sightseeing, globetrot, backpack; roam, rove, range, wend one's way, cruise, hike, trek, tramp, ride, roll; cross, traverse, cover, make one's way over, circumnavigate, go round, move round; move, go, proceed; *informal* gallivant, knock about/around; *rare* peregrinate.
2 *light travels faster than sound* **move**, proceed, progress, advance; be transmitted, carry.
3 (*informal*) *that lorry's travelling!* **go fast**, go rapidly, drive fast, speed, race, go at breakneck speed, hurry, hurtle, hasten, hotfoot it, whip (along), whizz, go like (greased) lightning; *informal* go hell for leather, go like a bat out of hell, tear up the miles, steam, belt, tear, zip, get cracking, get a move on, burn rubber; *Brit. informal* bomb, put one's foot down.
▶ **noun** *he amassed great wealth during his travels* **journeys**, expeditions, trips, tours, excursions, voyages, treks, safaris, odysseys, pilgrimages, jaunts; journeying, travelling, touring, sightseeing, voyaging, cruising, sailing, backpacking, globetrotting, jet-setting, exploration, trekking, wandering, roving, roaming; *informal* gallivanting; *rare* peregrinations.
WORD LINKS
fear of travel **hodophobia**

traveller ▶ **noun 1** *thousands of air travellers were left stranded* **passenger**, **tourist**, tripper, tourer, journeyer, voyager, excursionist, holidaymaker, sightseer, visitor, globetrotter, jet-setter; backpacker, pilgrim, gadabout; rover, wanderer, explorer, discoverer, scout, surveyor, reconnoitrer, prospector; commuter, fare payer, fare; *N. Amer.* vacationer, vacationist; *informal* gallivanter.
2 *a travellers' site* **gypsy**, Romany, tzigane, didicoi; New Age traveller, New Ager; **nomad**, migrant, wanderer, wayfarer, itinerant, drifter; **tramp**, vagrant, transient, vagabond, tinker; (**travellers**) travelling people, travelling folk.

travelling ▶ **adjective 1** *a survey of the travelling population* **nomadic**, itinerant, peripatetic, migratory, migrating, wandering, roaming, roving, wayfaring, rambling, touring, drifting, floating, unsettled, restless, on the move, on the go, on the wing; displaced, homeless; gypsy, Romany, tzigane, didicoi; globetrotting, jet-setting; *archaic* errant.
OPPOSITE fixed, settled.
2 *a travelling circus* **itinerant**, peripatetic, moving, mobile.
3 *a little travelling clock* **portable**, mobile, transportable, movable, transferable, easily carried, easy to carry, conveyable, travel, lightweight, compact, handy, convenient, manageable; *rare* portative.
OPPOSITE full-sized.

traverse ▶ **verb 1** *he traversed the deserts of Persia and Baluchistan* **travel over**/**across**, cross, journey over/across, make one's way across, pass over, go across, negotiate; cover; ply; wander, roam, range.
2 *a ditch traversed by a small wooden bridge* **extend across**, lie across, stretch across, go across, cross, cut across; bridge, span.

travesty ▶ **noun** *he dismissed the proceedings as a travesty of justice* **misrepresentation**, distortion, perversion, corruption, poor imitation, poor substitute, mockery, parody, caricature; farce, charade, pantomime, sham; apology for, excuse for.
▶ **verb** *he felt that Michael had betrayed the family by travestying them in his plays* **misrepresent**, parody, caricature, burlesque, mock, make a mockery of, ridicule, make fun of; distort, pervert.

treacherous ▶ **adjective 1** *two treacherous Scottish lords betrayed Wallace's whereabouts* **traitorous**, disloyal, perfidious, faithless, unfaithful, duplicitous, false-hearted, deceitful, false, untrue, back-stabbing, double-crossing, double-dealing, two-faced, untrustworthy, unreliable, undependable, fickle; apostate, renegade, subversive, seditious, rebellious, mutinous, breakaway; treasonable, treasonous; *informal* two-timing; *rare* Janus-faced, Punic.
OPPOSITES loyal, faithful.
2 *treacherous driving conditions* **dangerous**, hazardous, perilous, unsafe, precarious, risky, deceptive, unreliable, undependable, unstable; icy, ice-covered, slippery, glassy; *informal* dicey, hairy, slippy; *N. Amer. informal* gnarly.
OPPOSITES safe, reliable.

treachery ▶ **noun** *the damning evidence of her treachery* **betrayal**, disloyalty, perfidy, perfidiousness, faithlessness, unfaithfulness, infidelity, bad faith, breach of trust, duplicity, deceit, deceitfulness, deception, false-heartedness, falseness, stab in the back, back-stabbing, double-dealing, untrustworthiness; treason; *informal* two-timing; *rare* Punic faith.
OPPOSITES loyalty, faithfulness.

tread ▶ **verb 1** *he trod purposefully down the hall* **walk**, step, stride, pace, go; march, tramp, plod, stomp, trudge.
2 *the snow had been trodden down by the horses* **crush**, flatten, press down, squash; **trample on**, tramp on, step on, stamp on, stomp on.
▶ **noun** *she heard Bryony's heavy tread upstairs* **step**, footstep, footfall, tramp.

treason ▶ **noun treachery**, lese-majesty; disloyalty, betrayal, faithlessness, perfidy, perfidiousness, duplicity, infidelity; sedition, subversion, mutiny, rebellion; high treason; *rare* Punic faith.
OPPOSITES allegiance, loyalty.

treasonable ▶ **adjective** *there was no evidence of treasonable activity* **traitorous**, treacherous, perfidious, treasonous, disloyal, faithless, duplicitous; seditious, subversive, mutinous, rebellious.
OPPOSITE loyal.

treasure ▶ **noun 1** *a casket of treasure* **riches**, valuables, jewels, gems, gold, silver, precious metals, money, cash; wealth, fortune; *Brit.* treasure trove.
2 *art treasures* **valuable object**, valuable, work of art, objet of virtu, masterpiece.
3 (*informal*) *she's been a real treasure—I don't know what I would have done without her* **paragon**, gem, angel, nonpareil; find, prize; *informal* star, one of a kind, one in a million, something else, the tops.
4 (*informal*) *he was no longer her treasure but a naughty child too old to be smacked* **darling**, angel, apple of one's eye, pride and joy.
▶ **verb** *I treasure the photographs I took of Jack* **cherish**, hold dear, place great value on, prize, set great store by, value greatly, esteem; **adore**, dote on, love dearly, be devoted to, idolize, worship, think very highly of, appreciate greatly; preserve, keep safe.

treasury ▶ **noun 1** *she transferred billions from the national treasury to her personal bank account* **exchequer**, purse; bank, coffers; revenues, finances, funds, money, resources; *archaic* fisc.
2 *the area is a treasury of early fossils* **rich source**, repository, storehouse, store, treasure house, treasure trove; fund, mine, bank.
3 *a treasury of stories* **anthology**, collection, miscellany, compilation, compendium; *archaic* garland.

treat ▶ **verb 1** *Charlotte treated him very badly* **behave towards**, act towards, conduct oneself towards, use, serve; deal with, handle, manage.
2 *police are treating the fires as arson* **regard**, consider, view, look on; put down as.
3 *chapter 8 treats topics such as the educational disadvantages of women* **deal with**, be about, cover, be concerned with, concern itself with, discuss, write/speak/talk about, go into, explore, investigate, tackle, handle; touch on, refer to; consider, study, review, analyse, critique.
4 *Lisa is being treated at Addenbrooke's Hospital* **attend to**, tend, minister to, nurse, give treatment to; prescribe medicine for, medicate, dose; *informal* doctor.
5 *the plants may prove useful in treating cancer* **cure**, heal, remedy, make better.
6 *the wood can be treated with chemical preservative* **prime**, prepare, process, cover.
7 *he* **treated** *her* **to** *a slap-up lunch* **buy**, take out for, stand, give; pay for, pay/foot the bill for; entertain, wine and dine.
8 *delegates were* **treated to** *authentic Indonesian dance performances* **regale with**, entertain with/by, fête with, amuse with/by, divert with/by.
9 (*formal*) *propagandists claimed that he was treating with the enemy* **negotiate**, discuss terms, have talks, consult, parley, talk, confer; make a bargain, bargain.
▶ **noun 1** *a birthday treat* **celebration**, entertainment, amusement, diversion; surprise; party, excursion, outing.
2 *I bought you some chocolate biscuits as a treat* **present**, gift; titbit, delicacy, little something, luxury, indulgence, extravagance; *informal* goodie.
3 *it was a real treat to see them* **pleasure**, source of pleasure, delight, thrill, joy.
4 *'my treat,' he insisted, reaching for the bill* one's turn to pay; *informal* shout.

treatise ▶ **noun** *his treatise on medical ethics* **disquisition**, essay, paper, work, piece of writing, exposition, discourse, dissertation, thesis, monograph, study, critique; tract, pamphlet; *rare* tractate, institutes.

treatment *See centre pages for lists of* **Therapies** *and branches of* **Medicine**
▶ **noun 1** *she accepted his* **treatment** *of her as if it was no more than she deserved* **behaviour towards**, conduct towards, action towards, usage of, use of; handling of, management of; dealings with; reception.
2 *she's responding well to treatment* **therapy**, surgery, medical care/attention,

care, ministrations, nursing; therapeutics; (course of) medication, (course of) drugs, medicaments; cure, remedy.
3 *her treatment of the topic* **presentation**, discussion, coverage, handling, investigation, exploration, consideration, study, analysis, critique.

treaty ▶ noun *the two countries signed a peace treaty* **agreement**, settlement, pact, deal, entente, concordat, accord, concord, protocol, compact, convention, contract, covenant, bargain, pledge; armistice, truce; alliance.

tree *See centre pages for list of* **Trees and Shrubs**
▶ noun sapling; conifer, evergreen; bush, shrub.

WORD LINKS

relating to trees	**arboreal**
related prefix	**dendro-** (e.g. *dendrochronology*)
study of trees	**dendrology**
farming of trees	**forestry, agroforestry, arboriculture, silviculture**

trek ▶ noun *a three-day trek across the desert* **journey**, trip, expedition, safari, odyssey; hike, march, slog, footslog, tramp, trudge, walk; long haul; *Brit. informal* yomp, trog.
▶ verb *he's trekked across some of the most inhospitable terrain in the world* **hike**, tramp, march, slog, footslog, trudge, traipse, walk; travel, journey; *Brit. informal* yomp, trog.

trellis ▶ noun **lattice**, framework, open framework, espalier; network, mesh, tracery; grille, grid, grating; latticework, trelliswork; *technical* reticulation.

tremble ▶ verb **1** *Joe's face was pale and his hands were trembling* **shake**, shake like a leaf, quiver, twitch, palpitate; quaver, waver; *rare* tremor, quave.
2 *the entire building trembled* **shake**, shudder, judder, wobble, rock, vibrate, move, sway, totter, teeter.
3 *she trembled at the thought of what he had in store for her* **be afraid**, be fearful, be filled with fear, be frightened, be apprehensive, worry, be anxious, be in a state of anxiety, shake in one's shoes; quail, shrink from, blench from, blanch from; *informal* be in a blue funk, be all of a tremble, be all of a quiver.
▶ noun *the slight tremble in her hands* **tremor**, shake, shakiness, trembling, quiver, twitch, twitchiness.
OPPOSITE steadiness.

CHOOSE THE RIGHT WORD

tremble, shake, shiver, quiver, quake

See SHAKE.

tremendous ▶ adjective **1** *tremendous sums of money* **very great**, huge, enormous, immense, colossal, massive, prodigious, stupendous, monumental, mammoth, vast, gigantic, giant, mighty, epic, monstrous, titanic, towering, king-sized, king-size, gargantuan, Herculean, Brobdingnagian; substantial; *informal* whopping, whopping great, thumping, thumping great, astronomical, astronomic, mega, monster, humongous, jumbo, hulking, bumper; *Brit. informal* whacking, whacking great, ginormous.
OPPOSITES tiny, small, slight.
2 *a tremendous explosion* **very loud**, deafening, ear-splitting, ear-piercing, booming, thundering, thunderous, roaring, resounding, crashing.
OPPOSITE soft.
3 (*informal*) *I've seen him play and he's tremendous* **excellent**, **wonderful**, marvellous, magnificent, superb, splendid, glorious, sublime, lovely, delightful, first-class, first-rate, outstanding; consummate, perfect; *informal* super, great, smashing, amazing, fantastic, terrific, phenomenal, sensational, incredible, heavenly, gorgeous, dreamy, grand, fabulous, fab, fabby, fantabulous, awesome, magic, ace, crack, cool, mean, bad, wicked, mega, crucial, mind-blowing, far out, A1, sound, out of this world, marvy, spanking; *Brit. informal* brilliant, brill; *N. Amer. informal* peachy, dandy, jim-dandy, neat, badass, boss, radical, rad, boffo, bully, bitching, bodacious, crackerjack; *Austral./NZ informal* beaut, bonzer; *S. African informal* kif, lank; *black English* dope, def, phat; *informal, dated* groovy, divine; *Brit. informal, dated* capital, champion, wizard, corking, ripping, cracking, spiffing, top-hole, topping, beezer; *N. Amer. informal, dated* swell, keen; *vulgar slang* shit-hot; *archaic* goodly.
OPPOSITES bad, poor.

tremor ▶ noun **1** *she tried to still the sudden tremor of her hands* **trembling**, shaking, shakiness, tremble, shake, quivering, quiver, twitching, twitch, convulsion, vibration, juddering, judder; quavering, quaver; tic.
OPPOSITE steadiness.
2 *a tremor of fear ran through her* **frisson**, shiver, spasm, thrill, tingle, stab, dart, shaft; wave, surge, rush, ripple.
3 *the epicentre of the tremor was 65 miles north of LA* **earthquake**, earth tremor, shock, foreshock, aftershock; *informal* quake, shake; *N. Amer. informal* tremblor.

WORD LINKS

relating to tremors	**seismic**

tremulous ▶ adjective **1** *'where?' she asked, in a tremulous voice* **shaky**, trembling, shaking, unsteady, quavering, wavering, quivering, quivery, quaking; nervous, weak; *informal* trembly, all of a tremble.
OPPOSITE steady.
2 *a tremulous smile* **timid**, diffident, shy, hesitant, uncertain, timorous, unconfident, fearful, frightened, scared; nervous, anxious, apprehensive.
OPPOSITE confident.

trench ▶ noun **ditch**, channel, trough, excavation, pit, furrow, rut, conduit, cut, drain, waterway, watercourse; earthwork, entrenchment, moat; *technical* fosse; *historical* sap.

trenchant ▶ adjective *he made trenchant criticisms of her style of leadership* **incisive**, cutting, pointed, piercing, penetrating, sharp, keen, acute, razor-sharp, razor-edged, rapier-like; vigorous, forceful, strong, telling, emphatic, forthright, blunt; biting, stinging, mordant, pungent, scathing, caustic, acid, tart, acerbic, astringent, sarcastic; devastating, savage, fierce, searing, blistering, withering; *N. Amer.* acerb; *rare* mordacious, acidulous.
OPPOSITES woolly, vague.

trend ▶ noun **1** *an upward trend in unemployment* **tendency**, movement, drift, swing, shift, course, current, run, direction, inclination, leaning; bias, bent.
2 *the latest trend in dance music* **fashion**, vogue, style, mode, craze, mania, rage; *informal* fad, thing.
▶ verb *interest rates are trending up in Japan* **move**, go, tend, head, drift, gravitate, swing, shift, turn, incline, lean, veer.

trendy ▶ adjective (*informal*) *trendy clothes* **fashionable**, in fashion, in vogue, stylish, modish, chic, designer, up to date, up to the minute, latest, contemporary, popular, all the rage; trendsetting; *French* à la mode, le dernier cri; *informal* cool, funky, in, the in thing, hot, big, with it, hip, happening, now, smart, sharp, groovy, mod, swinging, snazzy, natty, nifty; *N. Amer. informal* kicky, tony, fly; *Brit. informal, dated* all the go, swagger.
OPPOSITE unfashionable.

trepidation ▶ noun *he sat in the waiting room, full of trepidation* **fear**, **apprehension**, dread, fearfulness, apprehensiveness, agitation, anxiety, worry, nervousness, tension, misgivings, unease, uneasiness, foreboding, disquiet, disquietude, perturbation, discomposure, dismay, consternation, alarm, panic, trembling, jumpiness; *Brit.* nerviness; *informal* butterflies, jitteriness, the jitters, a cold sweat, a blue funk, the heebie-jeebies, the willies, the shakes, the yips, the jim-jams, collywobbles, cold feet; *Brit. informal* the (screaming) abdabs/habdabs; *Austral. rhyming slang* Joe Blakes.
OPPOSITES calm, equanimity, composure.

trespass ▶ verb **1** *there is no excuse for* **trespassing on** *railway property* **enter without permission**, intrude on, encroach on, invade, infringe, impinge on; *archaic* entrench on.
2 *I must not* **trespass on** *your good nature* **take advantage of**, impose on, make use of, play on, exploit, abuse, make unfair claims on.
3 (*archaic*) *he would be the last among us to trespass* **sin**, commit a sin, commit an offence, transgress, do wrong, err, go astray, fall from grace, stray from the straight and narrow, go down the primrose path.
4 (*archaic*) *he found it increasingly hard to forgive those who* **trespassed against** *him* **wrong**, do wrong to, cause harm to; offend, distress.
▶ noun **1** *clearly, he is guilty of trespass* **unlawful entry**, intrusion, encroachment, invasion, infringement, impingement.
2 (*archaic*) *he asked forgiveness for his trespasses* **sin**, wrong, wrongdoing, transgression, crime, offence, misdeed, misdemeanour, error, lapse, fall from grace; *rare* malefaction.

trespasser ▶ noun **1** *a high stone wall discouraged would-be trespassers* **intruder**, interloper, unwelcome visitor, encroacher.
2 (*archaic*) *trespassers asking for forgiveness* **sinner**, transgressor, wrongdoer, evil-doer, offender, criminal, malefactor.

tresses ▶ plural noun *her long blonde tresses* **hair**, head of hair, mane, mop of hair, shock of hair; locks, curls, ringlets.

trial ▶ noun **1** *the trial is expected to last several weeks* **court case**, case, lawsuit, suit, hearing, inquiry, tribunal, litigation, judicial proceedings, legal proceedings, proceedings, legal action; court martial; appeal, retrial.
2 *the drug is still undergoing clinical trials* **test**, try-out, experiment, pilot study; examination, check, assessment, evaluation, appraisal; trial/test period, trial/test run, probation, testing, dummy run; audition, screen test; *informal* dry run; *technical* assay.
3 *Eleanor could be a bit of a trial at times* **nuisance**, pest, bother, irritant, source of irritation/annoyance, worry, problem, inconvenience, vexation, plague, source of aggravation, thorn in one's flesh, the bane of one's life, one's cross to bear; bore; *informal* pain, pain in the neck, pain in the backside, headache, drag, pill, nightmare; *Scottish informal* skelf; *N. Amer. informal* pain in the butt, nudnik, burr under/in someone's saddle; *Brit. informal, dated* blister; *vulgar slang* pain in the arse.
4 *a long account of her trials and tribulations* **trouble**, worry, anxiety, burden, affliction, ordeal, tribulation, adversity, hardship, tragedy, trauma, reverse, setback, difficulty, problem, misfortune, bad luck, stroke of bad luck, ill fortune, mishap, misadventure; suffering, distress, misery, wretchedness, unhappiness, sadness, woe, grief, pain; *informal* hassle; *archaic* travails.

▶ adjective *a three-month trial period* **test**, experimental, pilot, exploratory, probationary, provisional.
▶ verb *the electronic cash card has been trialled by several banks* **test**, try out, carry out trials on, put to the test, put through its paces, experiment with; pilot; *technical* assay.

triangle ▶ noun. *See centre pages for list of* **Triangles**

triangular ▶ adjective **three-sided**, three-cornered, triangle-shaped; *technical* trilateral; *rare* trigonal, trigonous, trigonic.

tribe ▶ noun **1** *the nomadic tribes of the Sahara* **ethnic group**, people, race, nation; family, dynasty, house; clan, sept; *technical* gens; *archaic* folk.
2 *a tribe of children trailed after her* **group**, crowd, gang, company, body, band, host, bevy, party, pack, army, herd, flock, drove, horde, mob; *informal* bunch, crew, gaggle, posse, load.

tribulation ▶ noun *despite his tribulations he maintained a zest for life* **trouble**, worry, anxiety, burden, cross to bear, affliction, ordeal, trial, adversity, hardship, tragedy, trauma, reverse, setback, blow, difficulty, problem, misfortune, bad luck, stroke of bad luck, ill fortune, mishap, misadventure; suffering, distress, misery, wretchedness, unhappiness, sadness, heartache, woe, grief, pain, anguish, agony; *informal* hassle; *archaic* travails.

tribunal ▶ noun **1** *a rent tribunal* **arbitration board/panel**, board, panel, committee; industrial tribunal.
2 *an international war crimes tribunal* **court**, court of justice, court of law, law court, bar; court of inquiry; *N. Amer.* forum.

tributary ▶ noun *a tributary of the Mississippi* **headwater**, branch, feeder, side stream; *N. Amer. & Austral./NZ* creek; *technical* influent; *rare* confluent.

tribute ▶ noun **1** *tributes flooded in from friends and colleagues* **accolade**, praise, commendation, acclaim, acclamation, salute, testimonial, paean, eulogy, panegyric, encomium, homage; celebration, exaltation, extolment, glorification; congratulations, compliments, plaudits; gift, present, offering; *informal* bouquet; *rare* laudation.
OPPOSITES criticism, condemnation.
2 *it is a* **tribute to** *his determination that he ever played again* **testimony to**, indication of, manifestation of, evidence of, proof of, attestation of.
3 *the Vikings demanded tributes in silver* **payment**, contribution, dues, levy, tax, duty, impost, tariff, charge; offering, gift; ransom.
□ **pay tribute to** *Mr Turnbull paid tribute to all the staff at the Airedale hospital* **praise**, sing the praises of, speak highly of, express admiration of, commend, acclaim, take one's hat off to, applaud, salute, honour, show appreciation of, appreciate, recognize, acknowledge, give recognition to, show gratitude to, be grateful for, pay homage to, extol; *rare* laud.

trice ▶ noun
□ **in a trice** *he should be here in a trice* **in a moment**, in a minute, in a second, shortly, any minute, any minute now, in a short time, (very) soon, in an instant, in the twinkling of an eye, in a flash, in (less than) no time, in no time at all, before you know it, before long; **very quickly**, swiftly, without delay, at once, straight away, right away, directly; *N. Amer.* momentarily; *informal* in a jiffy, in two shakes, in two shakes of a lamb's tail, before you can say Jack Robinson, in the blink of an eye, in a blink, in the wink of an eye, in a wink, before you can say knife; *Brit. informal* in a tick, in two ticks, in a mo; *N. Amer. informal* in a snap.

trick ▶ noun **1** *he's capable of any mean trick* **stratagem**, ploy, ruse, scheme, device, move, manoeuvre, contrivance, machination, expedient, artifice, wile, dodge; deceit, deception, trickery, subterfuge, chicanery, sharp practice; swindle, hoax, fraud, confidence trick; *informal* con, con trick, set-up, game, scam, sting, gyp, flimflam; *Brit. informal* wheeze; *N. Amer. informal* bunco, grift; *Austral. informal* lurk, rort; *S. African informal* schlenter; *Brit. informal, dated* flanker; *archaic* shift, fetch, rig.
2 *I think he's playing a trick on us* **practical joke**, joke, prank, jape, stunt, antic, caper; *informal* leg-pull, spoof, put-on; *Brit. informal* cod; *N. Amer. informal* dido; *Austral. informal* goak; *archaic* cutup, quiz; *Scottish archaic* cantrip.
3 *he entertained the children with conjuring tricks* **feat**, stunt; (**tricks**) **sleight of hand**, legerdemain, prestidigitation; magic.
4 *it was probably* **a trick of the light** **illusion**, optical illusion, deception, figment of the imagination; mirage.
5 *Arthur taught her the tricks of the trade* **technique**, knack, art, skill; secret; *informal* know-how.
6 *he sat biting his fingernails, a trick of his when he was excited or angry* **mannerism**, habit, practice, quirk, idiosyncrasy, peculiarity, foible, eccentricity, way, characteristic, trait.
□ **do the trick** (*informal*) *a glass of whisky did the trick—I slept like a log* **be effective**, work, solve the problem, take care of the problem, achieve the desired result, fill/fit the bill; *N. Amer.* turn the trick; *informal* do the necessary.
▶ verb *many people have been tricked by villains with false identity cards* **deceive**, delude, hoodwink, mislead, take in, dupe, fool, double-cross, cheat, defraud, swindle, outwit, outmanoeuvre, catch out, gull, hoax, bamboozle, beguile; entrap; *informal* con, bilk, diddle, rook, put one over on, pull a fast one on, pull the wool over someone's eyes, take for a ride, lead up the garden path, spoof, shaft, do, have, gyp, flimflam; *N. Amer. informal* sucker, snooker, goldbrick, give someone a bum steer; *Austral. informal* pull a swifty on; *archaic* cozen, chicane, sell; *rare* illude.
□ **trick someone/something out** *he was tricked out in wide silk trousers, a red sash, and a necklace of silver dollars* **dress (up)**, array, attire, rig out, garb, get up; **adorn**, decorate, deck (out), embellish, ornament, festoon; *literary* bedeck, accoutre, apparel, bedizen, caparison, trap out, furbelow.

trickery ▶ noun *she looked at me coldly as if suspecting some kind of trickery* **deception**, deceit, dishonesty, cheating, duplicity, double-dealing, legerdemain, sleight of hand, guile, intrigue, deviousness, cunning, craft, craftiness, artfulness, slyness, subterfuge, skulduggery, chicanery, wiles, fraud, fraudulence, swindling, sophistry, sharp practice, underhandedness; dissimulation, pretence; *informal* monkey business, funny business, hanky-panky, jiggery-pokery, kidology, shenanigans, flimflam; *Irish informal* codology; *archaic* management.
OPPOSITES honesty, candour.

trickle ▶ verb *blood was trickling from two deep cuts in his bottom lip* **drip**, dribble, drizzle, flow, run, spill; ooze, leak, seep, exude, percolate.
OPPOSITES pour, gush, stream.
▶ noun *trickles of water ran down inside his collar* **dribble**, drip, thin stream, rivulet, runnel.

trickster ▶ noun **swindler**, cheat, fraud, fraudster, defrauder, confidence man; charlatan, mountebank, quack, impostor, sham; rogue, villain, scoundrel; deceiver, deluder, dissembler, hoodwinker, hoaxer; joker, practical joker; *informal* con man, con artist, sharp, phoney, flimflam man, flimflammer; *Brit. informal* twister; *N. Amer. informal* grifter, bunco artist, gold brick, chiseller; *Austral. informal* illywhacker, magsman, shicer; *S. African informal* schlenter; *rare* tregetour.

tricky ▶ adjective **1** *a tricky situation* **difficult**, awkward, problematic, delicate, ticklish, sensitive, touchy, risky, uncertain, precarious, touch-and-go; thorny, knotty, involved, complex, complicated, convoluted; vexed; embarrassing; *informal* sticky, dicey, hairy; *N. Amer. informal* gnarly.
OPPOSITES straightforward, uncomplicated.
2 *a tricky and unscrupulous politician* **cunning**, crafty, wily, artful, guileful, devious, scheming, sly, slippery, slick, deceitful, deceptive, duplicitous, dishonest, disingenuous, Machiavellian; *N. Amer.* snide; *informal* foxy, shifty; *Brit. informal* fly, dodgy; *S. African informal* slim; *Austral./NZ informal* shonky; *rare* subtle, carny.
OPPOSITE honest.

tried ▶ adjective *a* **tried-and-trusted** *method for solving the problem* **reliable**, dependable, trustworthy, trusted, certain, sure, true; **proven**, proved, tested, tried out, tried and tested, put to the test, established, fail-safe, time-honoured, classic; reputable.
OPPOSITES experimental, novel.

trifle ▶ noun **1** *we needn't bother the headmaster over such trifles* **unimportant thing/matter**, trivial thing/matter, triviality, thing/matter of no consequence, thing/matter of no importance, bagatelle, inessential, nothing; technicality; (**trifles**) trivia, minutiae.
2 *a horse he had bought for a trifle and sold for an incredible sum* **very small amount**, next to nothing, hardly anything; pittance; *informal* peanuts, piddling amount; *N. Amer. informal* chump change.
OPPOSITE small fortune.
3 *he went into town to buy a few trifles for Christmas* **bauble**, trinket, knick-knack, gimcrack, gewgaw, toy; *informal* whatnot; *Brit. informal* doodah.
□ **a trifle** *he looked a trifle apprehensive* **a little**, a bit, somewhat, a touch, a spot, a mite, a whit; *informal* a tad.
OPPOSITES very, extremely.
▶ verb
□ **trifle with** *I loathe men who trifle with women's affections* **treat in a cavalier fashion**, treat lightly, treat frivolously, treat casually, play ducks and drakes with; dally with, play with, amuse oneself with, toy with, flirt with, play fast and loose with; *informal* mess about/around; *archaic* sport with, wanton with, palter with.

trifling ▶ adjective *a trifling matter | trifling sums were awarded in damages* **trivial**, unimportant, insignificant, inconsequential, petty, minor, of little/no account, of little/no consequence, not worth mentioning, not worth bothering about, light, footling, fiddling, pettifogging, incidental; frivolous, silly, idle, superficial; **small**, tiny, inconsiderable, nominal, negligible, nugatory, minute, minuscule; paltry, derisory, pitiful, pathetic, miserable; *informal* piffling, piddling, measly, mingy; *Brit. informal* poxy; *N. Amer. informal* picayune, nickel-and-dime, small-bore, dinky; *rare* exiguous.
OPPOSITES important, serious; considerable.

trigger ▶ verb **1** *the incident triggered an acrimonious debate* **precipitate**, prompt, trigger off, set off, spark (off), touch off, stimulate, provoke, stir up, fan the flames of; cause, give rise to, lead to, set in motion, occasion, be the cause of, bring about, generate, engender, begin, start, initiate; *literary* enkindle.
2 *burglars triggered the alarm* **activate**, set off, set going, trip.

trill ▶ verb *a skylark was trilling overhead* **warble**, sing, chirp, chirrup, tweet, twitter, cheep, peep.

trim ▶ verb **1** *his straggly hair had been washed and trimmed* **cut**, barber, crop,

T

bob, shorten, clip, snip, shear; prune, pollard; mow; neaten, shape, tidy up, even up.
2 *trim off the lower leaves using a sharp knife* **cut off**, remove, take off, chop off, lop off, shave off, hack off, nip off.
3 *production and labour costs need to be trimmed* **reduce**, decrease, make reductions in, cut down, cut back on, make cutbacks in, scale down, prune, slim down, pare down, dock, retrench on.
4 *the story was severely trimmed for the film version* **shorten**, abridge, condense, abbreviate, telescope, truncate, curtail.
5 *a pair of black leather gloves trimmed with fake fur* **decorate**, adorn, ornament, embellish; edge, pipe, border, hem, fringe; *literary* bedizen.
▶ **noun 1** *white curtains with a blue trim* **decoration**, trimming, ornamentation, adornment, embellishment; **border**, edging, piping, purfling, rickrack, hem, fringe, frill.
2 *an unruly mop in desperate need of a trim* **haircut**, cut, barbering, clip, snip; pruning; tidy-up.
□ **in trim** *she keeps herself in trim with regular visits to the health club* **fit**, fighting fit, as fit as a fiddle, in good health, in good condition, in fine fettle; **slim**, in shape.
▶ **adjective 1** *a cropped, fitted jacket looks trim with a long-line skirt* **smart**, stylish, chic, spruce, dapper, elegant, crisp; *informal* natty, sharp; *N. Amer. informal* spiffy; *archaic* trig.
2 *a trim little villa* **neat**, **tidy**, neat and tidy, as neat as a new pin, orderly, in (good) order, well kept, well looked-after, well maintained, shipshape (and Bristol fashion), in apple-pie order, immaculate, spick and span, uncluttered, straight, spruce; *archaic* tricksy.
OPPOSITES untidy, messy, scruffy.
3 *men find her trim figure and vivacious personality very appealing* **slim**, slender, lean, clean-limbed, sleek, willowy, lissom, sylphlike, svelte, snake-hipped; streamlined.
OPPOSITE fat.

trimming ▶ **noun 1** *a black party dress with lace trimming* **decoration**, trim, ornamentation, adornment, passementerie, embroidery, frou-frou; border, edging, piping, purfling, rickrack, fringes, fringing, frills; *rare* falbalas, passement, fimbriations.
2 (**trimmings**) *roast turkey with all the trimmings* **accompaniments**, extras, frills, accessories, accoutrements, trappings, paraphernalia; garnishing, garnish.
3 (**trimmings**) *hedge trimmings* **cuttings**, clippings, parings, shavings, ends; *rare* brash.

trinket ▶ **noun knick-knack**, bauble, ornament, piece of bric-a-brac, bibelot, curio, trifle, toy, novelty, gimcrack, gewgaw; *French* objet; *informal* whatnot, dingle-dangle; *Brit. informal* doodah; *N. Amer. informal* tchotchke, tsatske; *archaic* folderol, furbelow, whim-wham, kickshaw, bijou, gaud.

trio ▶ **noun threesome**, three, triumvirate, triad, troika, triplex, trinity, trilogy, triptych, triplets; *rare* triunity, triune, triplicity.

trip ▶ **verb 1** *Owen tripped on the loose stones* **stumble**, lose one's footing, catch one's foot, slip, lose one's balance, stagger, totter, slide, fall, fall down, tumble, topple, take a spill; *dated* measure one's length.
2 *taxpayers often* **trip up** *by not declaring taxable income* **make a mistake**, miscalculate, make a blunder, blunder, go wrong, get something wrong, make an error, err; *informal* slip up, screw up, make a boo-boo; *Brit. informal* boob, drop a clanger; *N. Amer. informal* goof up.
3 *the question was intended to* **trip up** *the prime minister* **catch out**, trap, trick, outwit, outsmart; put someone off their stride, throw off balance, disconcert, unsettle, discountenance, discomfit; *informal* throw, wrong-foot; *Brit. informal* catch on the hop.
4 *they tripped up the terrace steps* **run lightly**, skip, dance, prance, waltz, bound, spring, hop, gambol, caper, frisk, scamper.
OPPOSITE trudge.
5 *Hoffman tripped the alarm* **set off**, activate, trigger; turn on, switch on, flip, throw.
6 *when tripping through the Yukon, take time to explore our museums* **travel**, take a trip, go on a trip/excursion/journey, journey, tour, trek, hike, cruise; *rare* peregrinate.
▶ **noun 1** *a four-day trip to Paris* **excursion**, outing, jaunt; **holiday**, visit, tour, journey, expedition, voyage; drive, run, day out; pilgrimage; *informal* junket, spin, hop; *Scottish informal* hurl; *rare* peregrination.
2 *trips and falls cause nearly half of all such accidents* **stumble**, slip, misstep, false step; fall, tumble, spill.
3 *an occasional trip in the performance* **mistake**, error, blunder, gaffe, slip, slip of the tongue/pen, lapse, oversight, indiscretion; *French* faux pas; *Latin* lapsus linguae, lapsus calami; *informal* slip-up, boo-boo, boner, howler; *Brit. informal* boob, clanger; *N. Amer. informal* goof, blooper, bloop.

tripe ▶ **noun** (*informal*) *you do talk tripe sometimes.* See NONSENSE *sense* 1.

triple ▶ **adjective 1** *a triple alliance* **three-way**, tripartite; threefold.
2 *they paid him triple the going rate* **three times**, three times as much as, treble.
▶ **noun trio**, threesome, triumvirate, triad, troika; three.
▶ **verb** *the party more than tripled its share of the vote* **treble**, increase by three.

tripper ▶ **noun** (*Brit. informal*) *hordes of trippers flocked into Blackpool* **tourist**, holidaymaker, sightseer, day tripper, visitor, traveller, excursionist; *N. Amer.* vacationer, vacationist, out-of-towner; *Brit. informal* grockle, emmet.

trite ▶ **adjective** *the observation struck me as both trite and irrelevant* **hackneyed**, banal, clichéd, platitudinous, vapid, commonplace, ordinary, common, stock, conventional, stereotyped, predictable; **stale**, overused, overworked, overdone, worn out, time-worn, tired, threadbare, hoary, hack, unimaginative, unoriginal, uninspired, dull, pedestrian, run-of-the-mill, routine, humdrum; *informal* old hat, corny, played out; *N. Amer. informal* cornball, dime-store; *rare* truistic, bromidic.
OPPOSITES original, fresh, imaginative.

> **CHOOSE THE RIGHT WORD**
>
> **trite, hackneyed, stale**
>
> All these words suggest a lack of originality, generally springing from laziness on the part of a speaker or writer.
>
> - A **trite** remark is intrinsically banal or shallow (*trite stuff about decadence in Tinseltown*). While it is not likely to contain anything that someone could disagree with, it is an easy option, which may cause offence in contexts where one should have made a greater effort (*trite answers for grieving people*).
> - A **hackneyed** theme or idea has been overused, often because it is an easy trigger for emotion (*hackneyed dramatic devices | the hackneyed image of the poor benighted savage*). There is a sense that a hackneyed phrase, idea, or image is used mindlessly, even to the point of dishonesty: it may well still have some emotional impact, but this may not be justified by the context in which it is used.
> - **Stale** expressions and ideas were once telling or valid but have been repeated so often that they have lost their force (*the jokes are a bit stale*).

triumph ▶ **noun 1** *a garden built to celebrate Napoleon's many triumphs* **victory**, win, conquest, success; achievement; ascendancy, mastery.
OPPOSITE defeat.
2 *his eyes shone with triumph* **jubilation**, exultation, elation, rejoicing, delight, joy, joyfulness, happiness, glee, pride, satisfaction.
OPPOSITE disappointment.
3 *it was a triumph of Victorian engineering* **tour de force**, masterpiece, supreme example, coup, marvellous feat, feather in one's cap, wonder, sensation, master stroke; *French* coup de maître; *informal* hit, knockout.
OPPOSITE failure.
▶ **verb 1** *he triumphed in the British Grand Prix* **win**, succeed, be successful, come first, be the victor, be victorious, gain a victory, carry the day, carry all before one, prevail, take the honours/prize/crown, come out on top.
OPPOSITES lose, fail.
2 *they had no chance of* **triumphing over** *the Nationalists* **defeat**, beat, conquer, trounce, vanquish, best, worst, overcome, overpower, overwhelm, get the better of, gain ascendancy over, gain mastery of; bring someone to their knees, prevail against, subdue, subjugate; *informal* lick.
OPPOSITE be defeated by.
3 *'You can't touch me,' she triumphed* **crow**, gloat, swagger, brag, boast; **exult**, rejoice, celebrate, revel, glory; *rare* jubilate.

triumphant ▶ **adjective 1** *the triumphant British team* **victorious**, successful, winning, prize-winning, conquering; undefeated, unbeaten, unvanquished.
OPPOSITES unsuccessful, defeated, losing.
2 *she looked up, a triumphant expression on her face* **jubilant**, exultant, elated, rejoicing, joyful, joyous, delighted, gleeful, proud, cock-a-hoop; gloating, boastful, swaggering.
OPPOSITES despondent, disappointed.

> **triumphant, triumphal, or triumphalist?**
>
> A **triumphant** army might march under a **triumphal** arch, possibly uttering *triumphant* cheers. *Triumphant* means 'having won a battle' or 'feeling or expressing elation at victory' (*Simon couldn't suppress a triumphant smile*). *Triumphal*, on the other hand, means 'made or performed to celebrate a victory' (*an imperial triumphal procession*). While these two words are generally neutral, **triumphalist** conveys disapproval of brash and offensive celebration of victory (*they do not want to offend people by appearing triumphalist*).

trivia ▶ **plural noun** *domestic trivia* **(petty) details**, minutiae, niceties, technicalities, trivialities, trifles, irrelevancies, non-essentials.
OPPOSITES essentials, nitty-gritty.

trivial ▶ **adjective 1** *your problems are trivial in comparison with Peter's* **unimportant**, insignificant, inconsequential, minor, of no/little account, of no/little consequence, of no/little importance, not worth bothering about, not worth mentioning; incidental, inessential, non-essential, petty, trifling, fiddling, pettifogging, footling, small, slight, little, inconsiderable, negligible, paltry, nugatory; meaningless, pointless,

T

worthless, idle; flimsy, insubstantial; *informal* piddling, piffling, penny-ante; *Brit. informal* twopenny-halfpenny; *N. Amer. informal* nickel-and-dime, small-bore; *N. Amer. vulgar slang* chickenshit.
OPPOSITES important, significant, life-and-death.
2 *I think I used to be quite a trivial person* **frivolous**, superficial, shallow, unthinking, empty-headed, feather-brained, lightweight, foolish, silly.
OPPOSITES serious, profound.

triviality ▶ noun **1** *the triviality of the subject matter* **unimportance**, insignificance, frivolousness, inconsequence, inconsequentiality, pettiness, slightness, paltriness, negligibility; meaninglessness, pointlessness, worthlessness, flimsiness, insubstantiality.
OPPOSITES importance, profundity.
2 *he need not concern himself with such trivialities* **minor detail**, petty detail, mere detail, matter/thing of no importance, matter/thing of no consequence, trifle, non-essential, inessential, nothing; technicality, incidental; (**trivialities**) trivia, minutiae.
OPPOSITE essential.

trivialize ▶ verb *the problem was either trivialized or ignored by teachers* **treat as unimportant**, minimize, play down, underplay, make light of, treat lightly, make little of, think little of, laugh off, dismiss, underestimate, undervalue, devalue, belittle, deprecate, scoff at; *informal* pooh-pooh; *archaic* hold cheap; *rare* misprize, derogate, minify.
OPPOSITE make a big thing of.

troop ▶ noun **1** *a troop of tourists* **group**, party, band, gang, bevy, body, company, troupe, assemblage, gathering, crowd, throng, horde, pack, drove, flock, swarm, stream, multitude, host, army, cohort; mob; corps, contingent, squad, detachment, unit, detail, patrol; *informal* bunch, gaggle, crew, posse, load.
2 (**troops**) *British troops were stationed here during the war* **soldiers**, armed forces, service men, men, service women; the services, the army, the military, soldiery.
▶ verb **1** *the children trooped behind him* **walk**, march, file, straggle; flock, crowd, throng, stream, swarm, surge, spill.
2 *Caroline trooped wearily home from work* **trudge**, plod, traipse, trail, drag oneself, tramp; *N. Amer. informal* schlep.

trophy ▶ noun **1** *a swimming trophy* **cup**, medal; **prize**, award; laurels, bays, palm.
2 *tusks from the male are highly coveted as trophies* **souvenir**, memento, keepsake, reminder, record, relic; spoils, booty.

tropical ▶ adjective *the tropical weather was debilitating* **very hot**, sweltering, baking hot, torrid; **humid**, sultry, steamy, sticky, oppressive, stifling, suffocating, heavy; *informal* boiling.
OPPOSITES cold, arctic.

trot ▶ verb *Doyle trotted across the patio and into the house* **run**, jog, jogtrot, dogtrot, lope; scamper, scuttle, scurry, bustle.
□ **trot something out** (*informal*) *he trotted out the official Downing Street line* **recite**, repeat, reiterate, restate, regurgitate, churn out; come out with, produce.
▶ noun
□ **on the trot** (*Brit. informal*) *they lost seven matches on the trot* **in succession**, one after the other, in a row, consecutively, successively, in sequence, one behind the other; running, straight.

troubadour ▶ noun (*historical*) **minstrel**, singer, balladeer, poet; *historical* jongleur, trouvère, trouveur, Minnesinger; *rare* joculator.

trouble ▶ noun **1** *it's the least you can do after all the trouble you've caused* **problems**, difficulty, bother, inconvenience, worry, anxiety, distress, concern, disquiet, unease, irritation, vexation, annoyance, stress, agitation, harassment, unpleasantness; *informal* hassle.
2 *she ought not to be spilling out her troubles to you* **problem**, misfortune, difficulty, trial, tribulation, trauma, adversity, hardship, burden, distress, pain, suffering, affliction, torment, woe, grief, unhappiness, sadness, heartache, misery; *archaic* travails.
3 *he's gone to a lot of trouble to help you* **bother**, inconvenience, fuss, effort, exertion, work, labour; pains, care, attention, thought; *informal* hassle.
4 *I wouldn't want to be a trouble to her* **nuisance**, bother, inconvenience, irritation, irritant, problem, trial, pest, cause of annoyance, source of difficulty, thorn in someone's flesh/side; *informal* headache, pain in the neck, pain, pain in the backside, drag, bore; *N. Amer. informal* pain in the butt, burr in/under someone's saddle, nudnik; *Brit. vulgar slang* pain in the arse.
5 *you're too gullible, that's your trouble* **shortcoming**, **weakness**, weak point, failing, fault, imperfection, defect, blemish; **problem**, difficulty.
6 *he had a history of heart trouble* **disease**, illness, sickness, ailment, complaint, problem; **disorder**, disability.
7 *the crash was apparently due to engine trouble* **malfunction**, dysfunction, failure, breakdown, fault.
8 *there was crowd trouble before the match* **disturbance**, disorder, unrest, bother, fighting, scuffling, conflict, tumult, commotion, turbulence, uproar, ructions, fracas, rumpus, brouhaha, furore, breach of the peace; *Law, dated* affray; *informal* to-do, hoo-ha, hullabaloo; *Brit. informal* kerfuffle.
OPPOSITES order, peace.
□ **in trouble** *by 1995, the firm was in trouble* **in difficulty**, in difficulties, having problems, in a mess, in a bad way, in a predicament, in dire/desperate straits, heading for disaster, heading for the rocks, with one's back against the wall; *informal* in shtook, in a tight corner/spot, in a fix, in a hole, in hot water, up the creek (without a paddle), in a jam, in a pickle, in the soup, screwed, up against it; *Brit. informal* up a gum tree; *vulgar slang* in the shit, in deep shit, up shit creek.
▶ verb **1** *this matter had been troubling her for some time* **worry**, bother, cause concern to, concern, disturb, upset, make anxious, make uncomfortable, make uneasy, agitate, distress, grieve, alarm, perturb, annoy, irritate, vex, irk, torment, plague, nag, niggle, gnaw at, prey on someone's mind, weigh/lie heavy on someone's mind, oppress, weigh down, burden, afflict; perplex, puzzle; *informal* bug.
2 *lately he has been troubled by bouts of ill health* **be afflicted with/by**, be bedevilled by, be beset with/by, be dogged by, be incapacitated with, be racked with, be cursed with; suffer from; *informal* be a martyr to; *archaic* ail with.
3 *there is nothing you need trouble about* **be anxious**, be distressed, be concerned, concern oneself, worry, upset oneself, fret, agonize.
4 *don't trouble to see me out* **bother**, take the trouble/time, go to the trouble, make the effort, exert oneself, go out of one's way.
5 *I'm sorry to trouble you* **inconvenience**, cause inconvenience to, bother, impose on, create difficulties for, disturb, put out, disoblige; *informal* hassle; *rare* discommode, incommode.

troubled ▶ adjective **1** *Joanna looked troubled* **anxious**, worried, concerned, perturbed, disturbed, bothered, ill at ease, uneasy, unsettled; **distressed**, upset, dismayed, disconcerted, discomposed, agitated, apprehensive.
OPPOSITES unworried, unperturbed, carefree.
2 *we live in troubled times* **difficult**, problematic, full of problems, beset by problems, unsettled, hard, tough, stressful, dark.

troublemaker ▶ noun **mischief-maker**, rabble-rouser, firebrand, agitator, ringleader, incendiary, inciter, instigator; demagogue; scandalmonger, gossipmonger, meddler; *French* agent provocateur; *informal* stirrer; *rare* stormy petrel.
OPPOSITE peacemaker.

troublesome ▶ adjective **1** *a troublesome problem* **annoying**, irritating, exasperating, maddening, infuriating, irksome, vexatious, vexing, inconvenient, bothersome, tiresome, worrying, worrisome, disturbing, upsetting, distressing, perturbing, niggling, nagging; difficult, awkward, problematic, demanding, taxing, tricky, thorny; *informal* aggravating, pestiferous, plaguy, pestilential, pestilent; *N. Amer. informal* pesky.
OPPOSITES simple, straightforward.
2 *troublesome adolescents* **disruptive**, uncooperative, rebellious, unmanageable, unruly, troublemaking, obstreperous, badly behaved, disobedient, naughty, refractory, recalcitrant, difficult, awkward, trying; *informal* the limit.
OPPOSITES cooperative, obedient.

trough ▶ noun **1** *a large feeding trough* **manger**, feeding container, feedbox, feeder, fodder rack, crib.
2 *a thirty-yard trough* **channel**, conduit, trench, ditch, gully, drain, culvert, cut, flume, gutter, furrow, groove, depression.

trounce ▶ verb **1** *Wigan trounced Halifax 32–8* **defeat utterly**, beat hollow, win a resounding victory over, annihilate, drub, rout, give someone a drubbing, crush, overwhelm, bring someone to their knees; *informal* hammer, clobber, thrash, paste, give someone a pasting, whip, pound, pulverize, massacre, crucify, demolish, destroy, wipe the floor with, take to the cleaners, make mincemeat of, murder, flatten, turn inside out, run rings around; *Brit. informal* stuff, marmalize; *N. Amer. informal* shellac, blow out, cream, skunk.
2 *he should be soundly trounced* **thrash**, beat, whip, flog, lash, birch, cane, leather, spank, chastise, lambaste; *informal* belt, wallop, give a hiding to, tan the hide of.

troupe ▶ noun **group**, company, band, ensemble, set; cast.

trousers *See centre pages for list of* **Trousers**
▶ plural noun slacks; *N. Amer.* pants; *Brit. informal* trews, strides, kecks; *Austral. informal* daks; *Austral. & S. African informal* rammies; *dated* reach-me-downs, unmentionables.

truancy ▶ noun **absenteeism**, non-attendance, absence, playing truant, truanting; *Brit. informal* skiving, bunking off, wagging; *N. Amer. informal* playing hookey, goofing off, ditching; *Austral./NZ informal* playing the wag.
OPPOSITE attendance.

truant ▶ noun **absentee**, non-attender; *Brit. informal* skiver; *Austral./NZ informal* wag.
□ **play truant** *it's bad news when youngsters play truant from school* **stay away from school**, not go to school, be absent, truant; *Brit. informal* skive (off), bunk off; *Irish informal* mitch (off); *N. Amer. informal* play hookey, goof off, ditch; *Austral./NZ informal* play the wag; *rare* bag it, hook Jack, mooch, play the hop, hop the wag.
▶ verb *teachers reported on whether pupils had truanted See* PLAY TRUANT.

truce ▶ noun *the rebels agreed to a truce* **ceasefire**, armistice, suspension of hostilities, cessation of hostilities, peace; break, respite, lull, moratorium; treaty, peace treaty; *informal* let-up.

OPPOSITES fighting, hostilities.

truck[1] ▶ noun *a succession of heavy trucks rumbled down the street* **lorry**, articulated lorry, heavy goods vehicle, juggernaut; van, pickup, pickup truck; dumper, dumper truck, tipper, tipper truck; *Brit.* HGV; *N. English* bogie; *S. African* bakkie; *dated* pantechnicon.

truck[2] ▶ noun *members of the agency were advised to have no truck with him* **dealings**, association, contact, communication, connection, relations, intercourse; business, trade, transactions, traffic.

truckle ▶ verb *an ambitious and dauntless woman who* **truckled to** *no man* **kowtow**, submit, defer, yield, bend the knee, bow and scrape, make up, be obsequious, pander, toady, prostrate oneself, grovel; fawn on, dance attendance on, curry favour with, ingratiate oneself with, abase oneself before; *informal* suck up, crawl, lick someone's boots; *N. Amer. informal* brown-nose; *Austral./NZ informal* smoodge; *vulgar slang* kiss/lick someone's arse.
OPPOSITES defy, stand up to.

truculent ▶ adjective *'what do you want?' he demanded, sounding truculent* **defiant**, aggressive, antagonistic, belligerent, pugnacious, bellicose, combative, confrontational, ready for a fight, hostile, obstreperous, argumentative, quarrelsome, contentious, uncooperative; bad-tempered, ill-tempered, sullen, surly, cross, ill-natured, rude, discourteous, unpleasant; *informal* feisty, spoiling for a fight; *Brit. informal* stroppy, bolshie; *N. Amer. informal* scrappy.
OPPOSITES cooperative, friendly, amiable.

trudge ▶ verb *he trudged wearily through the snow* **plod**, tramp, drag oneself, walk heavily, walk slowly, plough, slog, footslog, toil, trek, clump, clomp, lumber; *informal* traipse, galumph; *Brit. informal* yomp, trog.
OPPOSITES skip, trip.

true ▶ adjective **1** *it may seem hard to believe, but I can assure you it's true* **accurate**, correct, verifiable, faithful, literal, veracious; in accordance with reality, what actually/really happened, the case, so; unelaborated, unvarnished; *informal* as true as I'm sitting/standing here.
OPPOSITES untrue, false, fallacious.
2 *people are still willing to pay for true craftsmanship* **genuine**, authentic, real, actual, proper, veritable; *Latin* bona fide; *informal* honest-to-goodness, kosher, pukka, legit, the real McCoy, regular; *Austral./NZ informal* dinkum.
OPPOSITES bogus, phoney.
3 *the true owner of the goods* **rightful**, legitimate, legal, lawful, authorized, recognized, valid; *Latin* bona fide; *Law* de jure.
OPPOSITE de facto.
4 *the necessity for true repentance* **sincere**, genuine, real, unfeigned, unpretended, unaffected, heartfelt, from the heart.
OPPOSITES insincere, feigned.
5 *she was always a true friend to me* **loyal**, faithful, true-hearted, devoted, dedicated, staunch, true-blue, constant, unswerving, unwavering; trustworthy, trusty, reliable, dependable, firm, steady, dutiful, supportive.
OPPOSITES disloyal, faithless.
6 *a true reflection of life in the 50s* **accurate**, true to life, faithful, telling it like it is, as it really happened, fact-based, realistic, close, lifelike, convincing; correct, unerring, exact, precise, perfect; on target, on the mark; *French* vérité; *Brit. informal* spot on; *N. Amer. informal* on the money; *rare* verisimilar, veristic.
OPPOSITE inaccurate.
▶ adverb (*literary*) **1** *I swear I will speak true* **truthfully**, honestly, sincerely, candidly, frankly, truly, veraciously.
2 *the weapon flew true as an arrow* **accurately**, unerringly, unswervingly, without deviating.
□ **come true** *seven years later, his dream came true* **be fulfilled**, be realized, become a reality, happen, occur, take place; *literary* come to pass.

> **CHOOSE THE RIGHT WORD**
> **true, faithful, loyal, constant**
> *See* FAITHFUL.

true-blue ▶ adjective *true-blue supporters of the club* **staunch**, loyal, faithful, stalwart, committed, card-carrying, confirmed, dyed-in-the-wool, devoted, dedicated, firm, steadfast, dependable, reliable, trusty, steady, constant, unswerving, unwavering, unfaltering; *informal* deep-dyed.
OPPOSITE half-hearted.

truism ▶ noun **platitude**, commonplace, cliché, hackneyed/trite/banal/overworked saying, stock phrase, banality, old chestnut, bromide; maxim, axiom, saw.

truly ▶ adverb **1** *tell me truly what you want to do* **truthfully**, honestly, frankly, candidly, openly, to someone's face, without dissembling, laying one's cards on the table; *informal* with no punches pulled.
2 *I'm truly grateful to them all* **sincerely**, genuinely, really, indeed, from the bottom of one's heart, heartily, profoundly, veritably; **very**, extremely, awfully, dreadfully, frightfully, exceptionally, exceedingly, immensely, uncommonly, incredibly, most, positively; *Scottish* unco; *N. Amer.* quite; *informal* terribly, terrifically, tremendously, fearfully, desperately, seriously, majorly, hugely, fantastically, madly; *Brit. informal* jolly, ever so, dead, well, fair, right; *N. Amer. informal* real, mighty, awful, plumb, powerful, way, bitching; *S. African informal* lekker; *archaic* exceeding, sore.
3 *a truly dreadful song* **really**, absolutely, simply, utterly, totally, perfectly, thoroughly, positively, completely.
4 *this is truly a miracle* **without (a) doubt**, unquestionably, undoubtedly, certainly, surely, definitely, beyond doubt/question, indubitably, undeniably, beyond the shadow of a doubt; in truth, really, in reality, actually, in fact; *archaic* forsooth, in sooth, verily.
5 *the streaming system does not truly reflect children's ability* **accurately**, correctly, exactly, precisely, faithfully, closely, unerringly.
6 (*archaic*) *they served their prince truly* **loyally**, faithfully, devotedly, with devotion, with dedication, staunchly, constantly, unswervingly; reliably, steadily, dutifully.

trump ▶ verb *by wearing the simplest of dresses and no jewellery, she had trumped them all* **outshine**, outclass, upstage, put in the shade, eclipse, surpass, outdo, outperform; beat, do/be better than, better, top, cap; *informal* be a cut above, be head and shoulders above, leave standing, walk away from; *Brit. informal* knock spots off; *archaic* outrival, outvie.
□ **trump something up** *since her arrest, they've trumped up charges against her* **invent**, make up, fabricate, concoct, contrive, manufacture, devise, hatch; fake, falsify; *informal* cook up.

trumped-up ▶ adjective *the men were arrested on trumped-up charges of espionage* **bogus**, spurious, specious, false, fabricated, invented, manufactured, made-up, fake, faked, not genuine, factitious, contrived; unfounded, unsubstantiated, unproven, without foundation, groundless, baseless; *informal* phoney, cooked up.
OPPOSITES true, genuine, bona fide.

trumpery (*archaic*) ▶ noun *tables piled with all sorts of trumpery* **trinkets**, baubles, cheap finery, knick-knacks, ornaments, bibelots, gewgaws, gimcracks.
▶ adjective *trumpery jewellery* **showy**, gaudy, garish, vulgar, tasteless; **worthless**, valueless, cheap, tawdry, shoddy, meretricious, Brummagem; *informal* flashy, flash, trashy, tacky, rubbishy.

trumpet ▶ noun *See centre pages for list of* **Brass Instruments**
□ **blow one's own trumpet** *he refused to blow his own trumpet and blushingly declined to speak* **boast**, brag, sing one's own praises, show off, swank, congratulate oneself; *N. Amer. informal* blow/toot one's own horn; *Austral./NZ informal* skite; *archaic* vaunt, rodomontade, gasconade.
▶ verb **1** *'come on!' he trumpeted* **shout**, bellow, roar, yell, cry out, call out; *informal* holler.
2 *the team of British researchers trumpeted a major medical breakthrough* **proclaim**, announce, declare, broadcast, promulgate, noise abroad, shout from the rooftops, blazon.

truncate ▶ verb *the programme may need to be truncated or adapted* **shorten**, cut, cut short, curtail, dock, prune, trim, lop, abbreviate, telescope; reduce, diminish, decrease.
OPPOSITES lengthen, extend.

> **CHOOSE THE RIGHT WORD**
> **truncate, shorten, abbreviate, abridge, curtail**
> *See* SHORTEN.

truncheon ▶ noun (*Brit.*) **club**, baton, cudgel, bludgeon; stick, staff; *N. Amer.* billy, billy club, blackjack, nightstick; *Brit. informal* life preserver, cosh.

trunk ▶ noun **1** *the trunk of a cedar tree* **main stem**, bole, stock.
2 *his powerful trunk* **torso**, body.
3 *an elephant's trunk* **proboscis**, nose, snout.
4 *the papers had been stored in an enormous tin trunk* **chest**, box, storage box, crate, coffer; suitcase, case, portmanteau; *S. African* kist.
5 (*N. Amer.*) *the trunk of his car* luggage compartment; *Brit.* **boot**.

truss ▶ noun **1** *the bridge is supported by three steel trusses* **support**, buttress, joist, brace, prop, strut, stay, stanchion, shore, pier.
2 *a hernia truss* **surgical appliance**, support, pad.
▶ verb *they* **trussed** *us* **up** *with ropes and chains* **tie up**, bind, chain up; pinion, fetter, tether, secure, fasten.

trust ▶ noun **1** *a relationship built on mutual trust and respect* **confidence**, belief, faith, freedom from suspicion/doubt, sureness, certainty, certitude, assurance, conviction, credence, reliance.
OPPOSITES distrust, mistrust, scepticism.
2 *a position of trust* **responsibility**, duty, obligation.
3 *the money is to be held in trust for his son* **safe keeping**, keeping, protection, charge, care, custody; trusteeship, guardianship.
▶ verb **1** *I should never have trusted her* **have faith in**, put/place one's trust in, have (every) confidence in, believe in, pin one's hopes/faith on; **rely on**, depend on, bank on, count on, be sure of, be convinced by, swear by; confide in.
OPPOSITES distrust, mistrust, doubt.
2 *I trust we shall meet again* **hope**, expect, think likely, dare say, imagine, believe, assume, presume, suppose, take it; *informal* guess.

T

3 *can I trust you with my car?* **entrust**, put in the hands of, allow to look after/use.
4 *they don't like to trust their money to anyone outside the family* **consign**, commit, give, hand over, turn over, assign, commend.

WORD LINKS
relating to trust **fiduciary**

trustee ▶ noun **administrator**, agent; custodian, keeper, steward, depositary; executor, executrix; *Law* fiduciary, feoffee.

trustful ▶ adjective *she looked up at him with trustful eyes.* See TRUSTING.

trusting ▶ adjective *she was no longer as trusting as she had once been* **trustful**, unsuspicious, unquestioning, unsuspecting, unguarded, unwary; naive, innocent, childlike, ingenuous, wide-eyed, credulous, gullible, easily taken in, easily deceived.
OPPOSITES distrustful, suspicious, cynical.

trustworthy ▶ adjective *the staff are trustworthy and hard-working* **reliable**, dependable, honest, full of integrity, worthy of trust, honourable, upright, principled, true, truthful, as good as one's word, ethical, virtuous, incorruptible, unimpeachable, above suspicion; responsible, sensible, level-headed; loyal, faithful, true-blue, staunch, steadfast, trusty, constant, unswerving, unwavering; tried and trusted, tried and true, safe, secure, sound, guaranteed, unfailing, foolproof, never-failing, reputable; *informal* on the level, sure-fire; *N. Amer. informal* straight-up.
OPPOSITES untrustworthy, unreliable, shifty.

trusty ▶ adjective *her trusty servant* **reliable**, dependable, trustworthy, never-failing, unfailing, tried and true, tried and trusted, trusted; loyal, faithful, true, honest, staunch, steadfast, constant, unswerving, unwavering.
OPPOSITE unreliable.

truth ▶ noun **1** *he doubted the truth of her last statement* **veracity**, truthfulness, verity, sincerity, candour, honesty, genuineness; gospel, gospel truth; accuracy, correctness, rightness, validity, factualness, factuality, authenticity.
OPPOSITES dishonesty, falsity.
2 *it's the truth, I swear it* **the fact of the matter**, what actually/really happened, the case, so; gospel, gospel truth, God's truth, the honest truth.
OPPOSITE lies.
3 *truth is stranger than fiction* **fact(s)**, reality, real life, actuality.
OPPOSITE fiction.
4 *scientific truths* **fact**, verity, certainty, certitude; law, principle.
OPPOSITES lie, falsehood, old wives' tale.
□ **in truth** *in truth, she was more than a little unhappy* **in fact**, in actual fact, in point of fact, as a matter of fact, in reality, really, actually, to tell the truth, if truth be told; *archaic* in sooth.

truthful ▶ adjective **1** *I want a truthful answer* **honest**, sincere, trustworthy, genuine, meaning what one says; candid, frank, open, forthright, straight, plain-spoken; *informal* upfront, on the level; *N. Amer. informal* on the up and up; *archaic* round, free-spoken.
OPPOSITES untruthful, deceptive, deceitful.
2 *a comprehensive and truthful account* **true**, accurate, correct, true to life, factual, in accordance with the facts, right, exact, faithful, reliable, veracious, verifiable; unvarnished, unembellished, unelaborated; *rare* veridical.
OPPOSITES inaccurate, untrue.

truthfulness ▶ noun **honesty**, veracity, sincerity, lack of deceit, trustworthiness, genuineness, candour, candidness, frankness, openness, forthrightness; truth.

try ▶ verb **1** *we've got to try to help him* **attempt**, endeavour, make an effort, exert oneself, seek, strive, struggle, do one's best, do one's utmost, do all one can; undertake, aim, set out, take it on oneself; try one's hand at; *informal* have a go/shot/crack/stab/bash, give it one's best shot, bend/lean over backwards, bust a gut, do one's damnedest, pull out all the stops, go all out, go for broke, knock oneself out, break one's neck, move heaven and earth; *Austral./NZ informal* give it a burl, give it a fly; *formal* essay; *archaic* assay.
2 *why don't you try it and see what you think?* **test**, try out, check out, put to the test, experiment with; sample, taste, have a taste of; inspect, investigate, examine, appraise, evaluate, assess; *informal* try something on for size, give something a whirl.
3 *Mary tried everyone's patience to the limit* **tax**, make severe demands on, strain, put a strain on, test, stretch, sap, drain, exhaust, wear out, tire out, weary.
4 *the case is to be tried by a jury in the Crown Court* **adjudicate**, consider, hear, pass judgement on, adjudge, examine.
□ **try one's hand**. See HAND.
□ **try something out** *the scheme has been tried out in 20 local authorities* **test**, trial, experiment with, pilot; put to the test, put through its paces, put into practice; assess, evaluate.
▶ noun *I decided to have one last try* **attempt**, go, effort, endeavour, bid; *informal* shot, crack, stab, bash, whack; *formal* essay.

trying ▶ adjective **1** *it had been a particularly trying day* **stressful**, difficult, taxing, demanding, tough, hard, heavy; pressured, testing, frustrating, fraught, traumatic, arduous, gruelling; tiring, fatiguing, exhausting, wearing; *informal* hellish, a bitch of a, a stinker of a.
OPPOSITES easy, painless.
2 *Steve was turning out to be very trying* **annoying**, irritating, exasperating, maddening, infuriating; **tiresome**, irksome, troublesome, bothersome, vexatious; *informal* aggravating.
OPPOSITE accommodating.

tub ▶ noun **1** *a large wooden tub* **container**; butt, barrel, cask, drum, keg; *rare* kid.
2 *a tub of yogurt* **pot**, carton.
3 (*N. Amer.*) *a soak in the tub* **bath**, bathtub; hot tub.

tubby ▶ adjective (*informal*) *a tubby little man with a balding head* **chubby**, **plump**, stout, roly-poly, dumpy, chunky, broad in the beam, portly, rotund; buxom, well upholstered, well covered, well padded, of ample proportions, ample, round, rounded, well rounded; fat, overweight, fleshy, paunchy, pot-bellied, bulky, corpulent; *informal* pudgy, beefy, porky, blubbery, poddy; *Brit. informal* podgy, fubsy; *N. Amer. informal* zaftig, corn-fed, lard-assed; *rare* pursy, abdominous.
OPPOSITES thin, slender, skinny.

tubular ▶ adjective *a long tubular structure* **tube-shaped**, tubiform, pipe-like; *rare* tubulous, tubulate, tubate, vasiform.

tuck ▶ verb **1** *he tucked his shirt into his trousers* **push**, ease, insert, slip; thrust, stuff, stick, cram; *informal* pop.
OPPOSITES take out, pull out.
2 *the dress was pinned and tucked all over* **pleat**, gather, fold, ruffle.
3 *he tucked the knife behind his seat* **hide**, conceal, secrete; store, stow; *informal* stash.
□ **tuck someone in/up** *he carried her back to bed and tucked her in* **make snug**, make comfortable, settle in, cover up; put to bed.
□ **tuck in/into** (*informal*) *I tucked into the bacon and scrambled eggs* **eat heartily**, devour, consume, gobble up, wolf down; *informal* get stuck into, dig in/into, dispose of, polish off, get outside of, put away, pack away, scoff (down), shovel down, get one's laughing gear round; *Brit. informal* shift, gollop; *N. Amer. informal* scarf (down/up), snarf (down/up), inhale; *rare* ingurgitate.
▶ noun **1** *a dress with tucks along the bodice* **pleat**, gather, fold, ruffle.
2 (*Brit. informal*) *they squabbled and pinched each other's tuck* **food**; *informal* eats, grub, nosh, chow, feed; *Brit. informal* scoff; *N. Amer. informal* chuck; *archaic* vittles, victuals, viands.

tuft ▶ noun *spiky tufts of grass | a tuft of hair* **clump**, bunch, knot, cluster, tussock, tuffet; lock, wisp; crest, topknot; tassel; *technical* floccule, flocculus, floccus, byssus, coma, pappus, scopa; *rare* panache.

tug ▶ verb **1** *Benjamin tugged at her sleeve* **pull**, pluck; tweak, twitch, jerk, wrench, wrest; grab, clutch, catch hold of; *informal* yank.
2 *she tugged him towards the door* **drag**, pull, draw, haul, heave, tow, trail; *informal* lug.
▶ noun *the ropes still held but one good tug would do it* **pull**, jerk, wrench, heave; *informal* yank.

tuition ▶ noun *private tuition in French* **teaching**, instruction, coaching, tutoring, lessons, tutorials, education, schooling, tutelage; training, drill, preparation; direction, guidance.

tumble ▶ verb **1** *he staggered a step or two and tumbled over* **fall (over)**, fall down, topple over, lose one's footing, lose one's balance, keel over, pitch over, take a spill, collapse, fall headlong, fall head over heels, fall end over end; trip, trip up, stumble; *informal* come a cropper; *dated* measure one's length; *archaic* grabble.
2 *journalists tumbled from the room, jabbering excitedly* **hurry**, rush, scramble, pile; scurry, scuttle; jump, spring, bound.
3 *a narrow brook tumbled over the rocks* **cascade**, fall, stream, flow, pour, spill.
4 *oil prices tumbled* **fall steeply/sharply**, plummet, plunge, dive, nosedive, take a dive, drop rapidly, slump, slide, fall, decrease, decline; *informal* crash, go into a tailspin.
OPPOSITES rise, soar.
5 *her face was devoid of make-up, and her hair was tumbled* **tousle**, dishevel, ruffle, rumple, make untidy, disarrange, disorder, mess up; *N. Amer. informal* muss (up).
6 (*informal*) *I finally tumbled to what was happening* **realize**, understand, grasp, comprehend, take in, apprehend, perceive, see, recognize; see the light; *informal* latch on to, cotton on to, catch on to, get, get wise to, get one's head around, figure out, get a fix on, get the message, get the picture; *Brit. informal* twig, suss; *N. Amer. informal* savvy.
▶ noun **1** *I took a tumble in the nettles* **fall**, trip, spill; *informal* nosedive, header, cropper.
2 *a tumble in share prices* **drop**, fall, plunge, dive, nosedive, slump, decline, collapse; *informal* crash.
OPPOSITE rise.
3 *a tumble of bed linen* **jumble**, mess, clutter, confusion; chaos, disorder, disarray.

tumbledown ▶ adjective *a small tumbledown cottage* **dilapidated**,

T

ramshackle, crumbling, falling to pieces, disintegrating, decaying, decrepit, broken-down, neglected, run down, in disrepair, uncared-for, badly maintained; ruined, in ruins, derelict, gone to rack and ruin, ruinous; rickety, shaky; *N. Amer. informal* shacky.
OPPOSITES well kept, well maintained.

tumbler ▶ noun **glass**, drinking glass, beaker; goblet, wine glass; *N. Amer.* highball glass; *archaic* stoup; *rare* rummer.

tumid (*rare*) ▶ adjective **1** *her tumid belly* **swollen**, distended, tumescent, engorged, tumefied, enlarged, bloated, bulging, protuberant, bulbous; puffy, puffed up; *rare* oedematose, oedematous, dropsical, turgescent, ventricose.
OPPOSITE shrunken.
2 *tumid oratory* **bombastic**, pompous, turgid, overblown, inflated, high-flown, affected, pretentious, grandiose, florid, flowery, ornate, magniloquent, grandiloquent, rhetorical, oratorical, orotund; laboured, strained, stilted; *informal* highfalutin, purple, windy; *rare* euphuistic, fustian, sesquipedalian, Ossianic.
OPPOSITE simple.

tummy ▶ noun (*informal*) **stomach**, abdomen, belly, gut, middle; *informal* tum, breadbasket, insides; *Austral. informal* bingy.

tumour ▶ noun **cancerous growth**, malignant growth, cancer, malignancy; lump, growth, swelling; *technical* carcinoma, sarcoma, melanoma, lymphoma, myeloma, neoplasm, metastasis, neurofibroma, teratoma, fibroadenoma, meningioma.

WORD LINKS

related prefix	**onco-** (e.g. *oncogenic*)
related suffix	**-oma** (e.g. *sarcoma*)
branch of medicine concerning tumours	**oncology**
removal of breast tumour	**lumpectomy**

tumult ▶ noun **1** *she added her own voice to the tumult* **din**, loud noise, racket, uproar, commotion, ruckus, rumpus, hubbub, pandemonium, babel, bedlam, brouhaha, fracas, furore, melee, frenzy, ado; shouting, yelling, clamour, clangour; *Scottish & N. English* stramash; *informal* hullabaloo; *Brit. informal* row; *Law, dated* affray.
OPPOSITE silence.
2 *years of political tumult* **turmoil**, confusion, disorder, disarray, disturbance, unrest, chaos, turbulence, mayhem, havoc, upheaval, upset, ferment, agitation, trouble; storms, tempests, maelstroms, convulsions.
OPPOSITES peace, tranquillity.

tumultuous ▶ adjective **1** *he left the stage to tumultuous applause* **loud**, deafening, thunderous, thundering, ear-shattering, ear-splitting, ear-piercing, uproarious, noisy, clamorous, vociferous.
OPPOSITE soft.
2 *their tumultuous relationship* **tempestuous**, stormy, turbulent, in turmoil, passionate, intense, explosive, violent, volatile, full of upheavals, full of ups and downs, roller-coaster, exciting; hectic, chaotic, confused.
OPPOSITES peaceful, uneventful.
3 *a tumultuous crowd* **disorderly**, unruly, rowdy, uncontrolled, out of control, unrestrained, turbulent, boisterous, excited, agitated, restless, in turmoil, wild, riotous, hysterical, frenzied; *Brit. informal* rumbustious.
OPPOSITE orderly.

tune ▶ noun *she left the theatre humming a cheerful tune* **melody**, air, strain; song, number, jingle, ditty; theme, motif.
▶ verb **1** *the band were still tuning their guitars* **adjust (to the correct pitch)**, tune up.
2 *like many marine organisms, they have a body clock tuned to the rhythm of the tides* **attune**, adapt, adjust, fine-tune; regulate, modulate, calibrate.
□ **change one's tune** *by the following week, she had changed her tune* **change one's mind**, think differently, express a different view/opinion, sing a different song/tune, shift one's ground, do a U-turn, march to the beat of a different drum, have a change of heart; *Brit.* do an about-turn.
□ **in tune** *their message was in tune with the prevailing intellectual climate* **in accord**, in keeping, in accordance, in agreement, in harmony, harmonious, in step, in line, in sympathy.
□ **out of tune** *he was out of tune with conventional belief* **in disagreement**, at odds, at variance, out of step, not in harmony, at outs, out of kilter.

tuneful ▶ adjective *a remarkable musical full of tuneful songs* **melodious**, melodic, musical, mellifluous, sweet-sounding, pleasant-sounding, dulcet, euphonious, harmonious, lyrical, lilting; mellow, smooth, sweet, pleasant, agreeable, easy-listening; catchy, rhythmical; *informal* easy on the ear, foot-tapping, poppy; *rare* canorous, euphonic, mellifluent.
OPPOSITES discordant, tuneless.

tuneless ▶ adjective *tuneless whistling emanated from the kitchen* **discordant**, unmelodious, unmelodic, unmusical, dissonant, harsh, cacophonous; *rare* horrisonant.
OPPOSITES melodious, tuneful.

tunnel ▶ noun *a two-mile tunnel under the Pennine Hills* **underground passage**, subterranean passage; underpass, subway, hole, burrow; shaft, gallery; *historical* mine, sap.
▶ verb *he tunnelled under the fence* **dig**, dig one's way, burrow; excavate, mine, bore, drill.

turbid ▶ adjective *the turbid waters of the river* **murky**, muddy, thick; opaque, cloudy, clouded; *N. Amer.* riled, roily, roiled; *rare* feculent.
OPPOSITE clear.

turbulence ▶ noun **1** *a time of political turbulence* **turmoil**, instability, conflict, upheaval, tumult, troubles, unrest, ferment, disorder, disruption, disturbance, chaos, confusion; *German* Sturm und Drang.
OPPOSITES peace, calmness.
2 *the plane hit some turbulence* **rough air currents**, irregular atmospheric motion, uneven air movement.
3 *the turbulence of the seas* **roughness**, storminess, tempestuousness, heaviness, violence, wildness, choppiness, agitation.
OPPOSITE calmness.

turbulent ▶ adjective **1** *the country's turbulent past* **tempestuous**, stormy, unstable, unsettled, tumultuous, explosive, in turmoil, full of upheavals, full of conflict, full of ups and downs, roller-coaster, chaotic, full of confusion; violent, wild, anarchic, lawless.
OPPOSITE peaceful.
2 *turbulent seas* **rough**, stormy, tempestuous, storm-tossed, heavy, violent, wild, angry, raging, boiling, seething, foaming, choppy, bumpy, agitated; squally, blustery; *N. Amer.* roily; *literary* weltering; *rare* boisterous.
OPPOSITES calm, quiet, glassy.

turf ▶ noun **1** *they walked across the springy turf* **grass**, lawn, sod; *literary* sward, greensward.
2 (**the turf**) *they are both devotees of the turf* **horse racing**, racing, the racing world; racecourses, racetracks.
3 *the vice president was keen to protect his own turf* **area/sphere of influence**, area/sphere of activity, territory, domain, province, preserve; stamping ground, home ground; *informal* bailiwick; *Brit. informal* patch, manor.
▶ verb *the front and rear lawns have been turfed* **grass over**, lay grass on.
□ **turf someone/something out** (*Brit. informal*) *he was turfed out of office after 15 years* **throw out**, remove, eject, expel, turn out, fling out, force out, drive out, evict, dislodge, oust; dismiss, discharge; *informal* chuck out, kick out, send packing, boot out, give someone the boot, give someone their marching orders, throw someone out on their ear, show someone the door, sack, fire, give someone the push, give someone the (old) heave-ho; *N. Amer. informal* give someone the bum's rush.

turgid ▶ adjective **1** *his turgid prose* **bombastic**, pompous, overblown, inflated, high-flown, affected, pretentious, grandiose, florid, flowery, ornate, magniloquent, grandiloquent, rhetorical, oratorical, orotund; stodgy, ponderous, laboured, strained, stilted; *informal* highfalutin, purple, windy; *rare* tumid, euphuistic, fustian, sesquipedalian, Ossianic.
OPPOSITES simple, plain.
2 *a turgid and fast-moving river* **swollen**, congested; in spate, in flood.

turmoil ▶ noun *a time of great political turmoil* **confusion**, upheaval(s), turbulence, tumult, disorder, commotion, disturbance, agitation, ferment, unrest, trouble, disruption, upset, convulsions, chaos, mayhem, pandemonium, bedlam, uproar; uncertainty; *German* Sturm und Drang; *N. Amer. informal* tohubohu; *archaic* moil, coil.
OPPOSITES calm, peace.
□ **in turmoil** *as he spoke, his mind was in turmoil* **in confusion**, in a whirl, at sixes and sevens; reeling, spinning, disorientated; *informal* all over the place, not knowing whether one is coming or going.

turn ▶ verb **1** *the wheels were still turning* **go round**, revolve, rotate, spin, go round and round, go round in circles, roll, circle, wheel, whirl, twirl, gyrate, swivel, spiral, pivot.
2 *I turned and headed back the way I had come* **change direction**, turn round, change course, make a U-turn, reverse direction; swing round, wheel round, turn about.
3 *the BMW turned the corner and vanished from sight* **go round**, pass round, sweep round, round; negotiate, take.
4 *a narrow path that turned alternately to right and left* **bend**, curve, wind, twist, loop, meander, snake, zigzag.
5 *he* **turned** *his pistol* **on** *Laidlaw* **aim at**, point at, level at, direct at, train at, focus on.
6 *Wright turned his ankle in the first minute of the game* **sprain**, twist, rick, wrench; hurt, injure.
7 *their dream honeymoon* **turned into** *a nightmare* **become**, develop into, prove to be, turn out to be; change into, be transformed into, metamorphose into.
8 *Emmeline turned pale* **become**, go, grow, get, come to be.
9 *he turned the house into three flats* **convert**, change, transform, make; adapt, modify, rebuild, reconstruct, refashion, remake, make over, restyle.
10 *I've just turned forty* **reach (the age of)**, get to (the age of), become, pass; *informal* hit.
11 *the milk had turned* **go/become sour**, go off, sour, curdle, become rancid, go bad, spoil, taint.
12 *in 1959, he* **turned to** *politics* **take up**, become/get involved with, involve oneself in, begin to participate in, go in for, enter, become interested in, start doing, undertake.
OPPOSITES give up, drop.

T

13 *we can now turn to another aspect of the problem* **move on to**, go on to, begin to consider, turn one's attention to, attend to, address/apply oneself to; pick up, take up, refer to.
14 *she turned a clumsy somersault* **perform**, execute, do, carry out.
15 *wooden objects turned on a lathe* **fashion**, make, shape, mould, cast, form.
□ **turn against someone** *people had turned against him* **become hostile to**, take a dislike to, become unsympathetic to, become disenchanted with, become disillusioned with.
OPPOSITES take someone's part, stand up for.
□ **turn someone against someone else** *Helen turned him against his father* **make hostile to**, set against, cause to dislike, cause to be unfriendly towards, prejudice against, influence against; alienate from, drive a wedge between, estrange from.
OPPOSITE reconcile.
□ **turn someone away** *reporters were turned away from the college* **refuse admittance to**, send away; reject, rebuff, repel, cold-shoulder; *informal* send packing, give someone the brush-off.
OPPOSITE admit.
□ **turn back** *they turned back before reaching the church* **retrace one's steps**, go back, return; retreat.
OPPOSITES continue, carry on.
□ **turn someone/something back** *demonstrators attempted to storm the naval base, but were turned back by police* **repulse**, drive back, fight back, force back, beat back, beat off, put to flight, repel.
□ **turn someone/something down 1** *his novel was turned down by publisher after publisher* **reject**, spurn, rebuff, refuse, decline, say no to; *informal* give the thumbs down to, give the red light to; *Brit. informal* knock back.
OPPOSITE accept.
2 *Pete turned the sound down* **reduce**, lower, decrease, lessen; muffle, mute.
OPPOSITE turn up.
□ **turn in** (*informal*) *I think I'll turn in* **go to bed**, retire, call it a day, go to sleep; *informal* hit the hay, hit the sack; *Brit. informal* go up the stairs to Bedfordshire.
□ **turn someone in** *she turned her husband in to the police* **hand over**, turn over; **betray**, inform on, denounce, sell out, stab someone in the back; *informal* split on, blow the whistle on, rat on, peach on, squeal on, squeak on; *Brit. informal* grass on, sneak on, shop; *N. Amer. informal* rat out, drop a/the dime on, finger; *Austral./NZ informal* dob on, pimp on, pool, shelf, put someone's pot on; *rare* delate.
□ **turn something in 1** *the documents must be turned in at a licensing office* **hand in/over**, give in, submit, tender, proffer, offer; deliver; return, give back, surrender, give up.
2 *he turned in a score of 199 not out* **achieve**, attain, reach, make; notch up, chalk up, rack up, register, record.
□ **turn off** *they turned off the main road* **leave**, branch off; take a side road, take another road; *informal* make/take a left/right; *N. Amer. informal* hang a left/right.
OPPOSITE join.
□ **turn someone off** (*informal*) *most people were turned off by the extreme sentimentality of the film* **put off**, leave someone cold, repel, disgust, revolt, nauseate, sicken, offend; disenchant, alienate; bore; *N. Amer. informal* gross out.
OPPOSITES attract, arouse.
□ **turn something off** *she turned the light off and lay back on the bed* **switch off**, turn out, put off, shut off, power down, flick off, extinguish, deactivate, trip; unplug, disconnect; *informal* kill, cut.
OPPOSITE turn on.
□ **turn on** *the decision turned on a principle of civil law* **depend on**, rest on, hang on, hinge on, be contingent on, be decided by; concern, revolve round, relate to.
□ **turn someone on** (*informal*) **arouse**, sexually arouse, excite, stimulate, make someone feel sexually excited, make someone feel sexy, titillate; please, attract; *informal* give someone a thrill, get someone going, float someone's boat, do it for someone, light someone's fire, tickle someone's fancy.
OPPOSITE leave someone cold.
□ **turn something on** *she turned on the TV* **switch on**, put on, power up, flick on; plug in; start up, boot up, activate, cause to operate.
OPPOSITE turn off.
□ **turn on someone** *he turned on her with cold savagery* **attack**, set on, fall on, launch an attack on, let fly at, lash out at, hit out at; weigh into, round on, lose one's temper with; *informal* lay into, tear into, lace into, sail into, pitch into, let someone have it, get stuck into, wade into, bite someone's head off, jump down someone's throat; *Brit. informal* have a go at; *N. Amer. informal* light into.
□ **turn out 1** *a huge crowd turned out to cheer the home team* **come**, go, be present, attend, put in an appearance, appear, turn up, arrive; assemble, gather; *informal* show up.
2 *it turned out that she had been two-timing him* **transpire**, prove to be the case, emerge, come to light, become known, become apparent, be revealed, be disclosed.
3 *things didn't quite turn out as I'd intended* **happen**, occur, come about; develop, evolve; work out, come out, end up, result; *informal* pan out; *rare* eventuate.
□ **turn someone out** *her father turned her out of the house* **throw out**, put out, eject, evict; expel, oust, drive out, force out, drum out; deport, banish; *informal* kick out, chuck out, send packing, boot out, show someone the door, give someone their marching orders, throw someone out on their ear; *Brit. informal* turf out.
□ **turn something out 1** *he turned out the light* **switch off**, turn off, put off, shut off, flick off; extinguish; unplug, disconnect.
OPPOSITE turn on.
2 *the firm turns out a million meters a year* **produce**, make, manufacture, fabricate, assemble, put together, process, bring out, put out, churn out.
3 *she had taken it into her head to turn out the kitchen cupboards* **clear out**, clean out, empty (out).
□ **turn over** *the little dinghy turned over on the lake* **overturn**, upturn, capsize, keel over, turn turtle, roll over, be upended.
□ **turn something over 1** *I quickly turned over the first few pages* **flip over**, flick over/through, leaf through.
2 *she turned the proposal over in her mind* **think about**, think over, consider, weigh up, ponder, contemplate, reflect on, chew over, mull over, muse on, ruminate on, give thought to; *archaic* pore on.
3 *he turned over the retail side of the business to his brother* **transfer**, hand over, pass on, give, consign, assign, commit.
□ **turn over a new leaf**. See LEAF.
□ **turn someone's stomach** *the sight of all that blood turned her stomach* **nauseate**, cause to feel sick, cause to feel nauseous, sicken, make sick, make someone's gorge rise, make someone's stomach rise; *informal* make someone want to throw up.
□ **turn tail**. See TAIL.
□ **turn to someone/something 1** *they turned to the social services* **seek help from**, have recourse to, approach, apply to, look to, appeal to.
2 *he turned to drink* **take to**, resort to, have recourse to.
OPPOSITES give up, abstain from.
□ **turn up 1** *all the missing documents had turned up* **be found**, be discovered, be located, come to light; reappear.
OPPOSITES disappear, go missing.
2 *a couple of policemen turned up* **arrive**, put in an appearance, make an appearance, appear, be present, present oneself, turn out; *informal* show up, show, show one's face.
OPPOSITE stay away.
3 *wait and see—something better will turn up* **present itself**, occur, happen, crop up.
□ **turn something up 1** *she turned up the volume* **increase**, raise, amplify, make louder, intensify.
OPPOSITE turn down.
2 *they turned up quite a bit of information about his early life* **discover**, uncover, unearth, bring to light, find, hit on, dig up, ferret out, root out, expose.
3 *I had turned up the hem of my skirt* **take up**, raise; shorten.
OPPOSITE let down.
▶ **noun 1** *a turn of the wheel* **rotation**, revolution, spin, circle, whirl, twirl, gyration, swivel.
2 *the vehicle slowed and made a turn to the left* **change of direction**, change of course, turning, veer, divergence.
3 *they negotiated the sharp turn at the end of the narrow street* **bend**, corner, dog-leg, twist, zigzag; *Brit.* hairpin bend.
4 *slow down, we're approaching the turn* **turning**, junction, crossroads; *N. Amer.* turnout.
5 *you'll get your turn in a minute* **opportunity**, chance, say; stint, spell, time; try, attempt; *informal* **go**, shot, stab, crack.
6 *a highly entertaining comic turn* **act**, routine, performance, number, piece; show.
7 *why don't you take a turn around the garden?* **stroll**, walk, saunter, amble, wander, airing, promenade; drive, ride, outing, excursion, jaunt; *informal* mosey, tootle, spin; *Brit. informal* pootle; *dated* constitutional; *rare* perambulation.
8 *you gave me quite a turn!* **shock**, start, surprise, jolt; fright, scare.
9 *she had done me some good turns over the previous few months* **service**, deed, act, action; (**a good turn**) **favour**, act of kindness, kindness; (**a bad turn**) **disservice**, wrong, harm, injury.
□ **at every turn** *her name seemed to come up at every turn* **repeatedly**, recurrently, all the time, always, continually, constantly, on every occasion, again and again, over and over again.
□ **in turn** *let's consider these three points in turn* **one after the other**, one by one, one at a time, in succession, successively, sequentially, in order; *Latin* seriatim.
□ **take a turn for the better** *his fortunes took a turn for the better in 1988* **improve**, get better, pick up, look up, perk up, rally, turn a/the corner; recover, revive.
□ **take a turn for the worse** *Anglo-French relations had taken a turn for the worse* **deteriorate**, get/grow worse, worsen, decline, retrogress; *informal* go downhill.
□ **to a turn** *beefburgers done to a turn* **perfectly**, just right, exactly right, to

perfection; *informal* to a T.

□ **turn of events** *she was utterly unprepared for this turn of events* **development**, incident, occurrence, happening, circumstance, phenomenon.

□ **turn of mind** *those of us of a less scientific turn of mind* **bent**, disposition, inclination, tendency, propensity, bias, way of thinking; aptitude, talent, gift, flair.

□ **turn of phrase** *it's not exactly a turn of phrase that trips off the tongue* **expression**, idiom, choice of words; word, phrase, term, locution.

turncoat ▶ noun **traitor**, renegade, defector, deserter, betrayer, Judas; fifth columnist, quisling; *informal* rat; *rare* tergiversator, renegate, renegado.

turning ▶ noun *take the first turning on the left* **turn-off**, turn, side road, exit; *N. Amer.* turnout.

turning point ▶ noun *it was a turning point in Jack's life* **watershed**, critical moment, decisive moment, crossroads, crisis, climacteric, moment of truth; landmark.

turnout ▶ noun **1** *his recent lecture attracted a good turnout* **attendance**, number of people present, audience, house; **crowd**, gathering, throng, assembly, assemblage, congregation; *Sport* gate; *Austral. informal* muster.
2 *his turnout was exceedingly elegant* **outfit**, clothes, clothing, dress, garb, attire, ensemble, suit; uniform; *informal* get-up, gear, togs; *Brit. informal* clobber, kit, rig-out; *formal* apparel; *literary* array, raiment, habit.

turnover ▶ noun **1** *a company with an annual turnover of £2.25 million* **(gross) revenue**, income, yield; volume of business, business; sales.
2 *a high turnover of staff* **rate of replacement**, coming and going, change, movement.
3 *cash-and-carry outlets rely on a rapid turnover of stock* **throughput**, rate of buying and selling, movement.

turpitude ▶ noun *acts of moral turpitude* **wickedness**, **immorality**, depravity, corruption, corruptness, vice, degeneracy, evil, baseness, iniquity, sinfulness, vileness; *rare* nefariousness, flagitiousness.
OPPOSITES virtue, honour.

tussle ▶ noun **1** *in the ensuing tussle his glasses were smashed* **scuffle**, fight, struggle, skirmish, brawl, scrimmage, scramble, scrum, fisticuffs, wrestling match, rough and tumble, free-for-all, fracas, fray, rumpus, melee, disturbance; *Irish, N. Amer., & Austral.* donnybrook; *Law, dated* affray; *informal* scrap, dust-up, punch-up, set-to, shindy, shindig, run-in, spat, ruck, ruckus; *Brit. informal* ding-dong, bust-up, bit of argy-bargy; *Scottish informal* rammy, swedge; *N. Amer. informal* rough house; *Austral./NZ informal* stoush; *archaic* broil, miff.
2 *an acrimonious tussle between the two departments* **argument**, quarrel, squabble, contretemps, disagreement, contention, clash, war of words; *Brit. informal* row.
▶ verb *demonstrators tussled with police* **scuffle**, fight, struggle, exchange blows, come to blows, brawl, grapple, wrestle, clash, scrimmage; *informal* scrap, have a dust-up, have a punch-up, have a set-to; *N. Amer. informal* rough-house.

tutor ▶ noun *my history tutor* **teacher**, instructor, educator, educationalist, educationist; academic, lecturer, don; coach, trainer; guide, mentor, guru, counsellor; *Scottish* dominie; *Indian* pandit; *informal* teach; *archaic* doctor; *rare* pedagogue, preceptor.
▶ verb *he was tutored at home by his father* **teach**, instruct, give lessons to, educate, school, coach, train, drill, direct, guide, groom.

tutorial ▶ noun **lesson**, class, seminar, period of instruction, period of teaching; *informal* tute.

TV *See centre pages for list of* **Television Components**
▶ noun **television**; television set; *informal* small screen; *Brit. informal* telly, the box, the goggle-box; *N. Amer. informal* the tube, the boob tube, the idiot box.

twaddle ▶ noun (*informal*) *what a load of absolute twaddle* **nonsense**, rubbish, balderdash, gibberish, claptrap, blather, blether; *informal* rot, tripe, hogwash, baloney, drivel, bilge, bosh, bull, bunk, guff, eyewash, piffle, poppycock, phooey, hooey, malarkey, dribble; *Brit. informal* cobblers, codswallop, cock, stuff and nonsense, tosh, cack; *Scottish & N. English informal* havers; *Irish informal* codology; *N. Amer. informal* garbage, flapdoodle, blathers, wack, bushwa, applesauce; *informal, dated* bunkum, tommyrot, cod, gammon, toffee; *vulgar slang* shit, bullshit, horseshit, crap, bollocks, balls; *Austral./NZ vulgar slang* bulldust.
OPPOSITE sense.

tweak ▶ verb **1** *he tweaked the boy's ear* **pull sharply**, **twist**, tug, pinch, nip, twitch, squeeze, jerk.
2 (*informal*) *the programme can be tweaked to suit your needs* **adjust**, make adjustments to, modify, alter, make alterations to, change, adapt; refine, improve, make improvements to.
▶ noun **1** *Robin gave her hair a friendly tweak* **sharp pull**, **twist**, tug, pinch, nip, twitch, squeeze, jerk.
2 (*informal*) *a few minor tweaks were required* **adjustment**, modification, alteration, change, adaptation; refinement, improvement.

twee ▶ adjective (*Brit.*) **1** *a town full of twee little shops* **quaint**, sweet, bijou, dainty, pretty, pretty-pretty; *informal* cute, cutesy.
2 *the lyrics are stomach-churningly twee in places* **sentimental**, over-sentimental, mawkish, affected, precious; *Brit. informal* soppy.

twelve ▶ cardinal number **dozen**, zodiac; *Music* dodecuplet; *rare* duodecad.

WORD LINKS
related prefix **dodeca-** (e.g. ***dodecahedron***)
relating to twelve **duodecimal, duodenary**
twelve-sided figure **dodecagon**

twenty ▶ cardinal number **score**.

WORD LINKS
related prefixes **icos-** (e.g. ***icosahedron***); *Chemistry* **eicos-** (e.g. ***eicosanoic***)
relating to twenty **vigesimal**

twiddle ▶ verb *she twiddled the dials on the radio* **turn**, twist, swivel, twirl, adjust, move, jiggle; **fiddle with**, play with, toy with, fidget with.

□ **twiddle one's thumbs** *we've been sitting here twiddling our thumbs all afternoon* **have nothing to do**, kick one's heels, do nothing, be idle, be unoccupied, sit around, kill time, waste time; *informal* hang around/round; *Brit. informal* hang about.

twig[1] ▶ noun *she plucked some leafy twigs from the bushes* **small branch**, shoot, offshoot, stem, scion; **sprig**, spray; stick; withy, withe; *rare* branchlet, ramulus.

twig[2] ▶ verb (*Brit. informal*) *she finally twigged what I was driving at* **realize**, **understand**, grasp, comprehend, take in, fathom, apprehend, perceive, see, recognize; see the light; *informal* latch on to, cotton on to, catch on to, tumble to, get, get wise to, get one's head around, wrap one's mind around, figure out, get a fix on, get the message, get the picture; *Brit. informal* suss; *N. Amer. informal* savvy.

twilight ▶ noun **1** *we reached the village by twilight* **dusk**, early evening, evening, close of day; sunset, sundown, nightfall; *literary* eventide, the gloaming; *rare* owl light, crepuscule, crepuscle, evenfall.
OPPOSITES dawn, daybreak.
2 *it was scarcely visible in the evening twilight* **half-light**, semi-darkness, dimness, gloom.
3 *he was approaching the twilight of his career* **decline**, waning, downturn, ebb; autumn, final years, closing years, last years.
OPPOSITES peak, height.
▶ adjective *a twilight world* **shadowy**, dark, twilit, shady, dim, gloomy, obscure; *literary* darkling, darksome, crepuscular.

WORD LINKS
relating to twilight **crepuscular**

twin ▶ noun **1** *his wife discovered she was expecting twins* (**twins**) identical twins, non-identical twins, fraternal twins; monozygotic/monozygous twins, dizygotic/dizygous twins; Siamese twins.
2 *he led the way into a sitting room that was the twin of her own* **exact likeness**, mirror image, double, duplicate, carbon copy, replica, (living) image, lookalike, clone; **counterpart**, match, pair, fellow, mate, partner; *German* Doppelgänger; *informal* **spitting image**, spit and image, ringer, dead ringer.
▶ adjective **1** *the twin blocks of the stadium* **matching**, identical, matched, paired.
2 *the need to balance the twin aims of conservation and recreation* **closely related**, closely linked, closely connected; corresponding, parallel, complementary; equivalent.
3 *the twin blows of the party's electoral losses and its split over partition* **twofold**, double, dual.
▶ verb *the company twinned its core business of brewing with that of distilling* **combine**, join, link, couple, pair, yoke, match.

twine ▶ noun *a ball of twine* **string**, cord, strong thread, yarn.
▶ verb **1** *she twined her arms around his neck* **wind**, entwine; wrap, lace, wreathe.
2 *convolvulus had twined around the stems of the espaliers* **entwine itself**, coil, loop, twist, spiral, curl, snake.
3 *a spray of jasmine was twined in her hair* **weave**, interweave, interlace, intertwine, plait, braid, twist.

twinge ▶ noun **1** *she's complaining of twinges in her stomach* **pain**, sharp pain, shooting pain, stab of pain, spasm, ache, throb; cramp, stitch; *archaic* throe.
2 *Kate felt a twinge of guilt* **pang**, prick, dart; qualm, scruple, misgiving.

twinkle ▶ verb **1** *the lights of the city twinkled below me* **glitter**, sparkle, shine, glimmer, shimmer, glint, gleam, scintillate, glisten, flicker, flash, wink, blink; *literary* glister; *rare* coruscate, fulgurate, effulge.
2 *his sandalled feet twinkled over the ground* **run lightly**, dart, dance, skip, flit, glide.
▶ noun *the distant twinkle of the lights* **glitter**, sparkle, twinkling, glimmer, shimmer, glint, gleam, flicker, dazzle, flash, wink, blink; *rare* scintillation, coruscation, fulguration.

twinkling ▶ adjective *the twinkling lights of the harbour* **glittering**, sparkling, glimmering, glinting, gleaming, glistening, flickering, winking; bright, shining, brilliant; *rare* coruscating, scintillating, scintillant, refulgent, effulgent, fulgent, nitid, luculent.
▶ noun

□ **in a twinkling** *I'll be back in a twinkling* **(very) soon**, in a second, in a minute, in a moment, in a trice, in a flash, in an instant, in the

T

twinkling of an eye, in (less than) no time, in no time at all, before you know it, before long, shortly, in a very short time, any second (now), any minute (now); *N. Amer.* momentarily; *informal* in a jiffy, in two shakes (of a lamb's tail), before you can say Jack Robinson, in a sec, in the blink of an eye, in a blink, in the wink of an eye, in a wink, before you can say knife; *Brit. informal* in a tick, in two ticks, in a mo, sharpish; *N. Amer. informal* in a snap; *dated* directly.

twirl ▶ verb **1** *Katy twirled in front of the mirror | she twirled her parasol* **spin (round)**, pirouette, whirl, turn (round), wheel, gyrate, pivot, swivel; twist, revolve, rotate; *Scottish* birl.
2 *absent-mindedly, Sybil twirled a strand of hair round her fingers* **wind**, twist, coil, curl, wrap.
▶ noun *she did a quick twirl in the middle of the room* **pirouette**, spin, whirl, turn; twist, rotation, revolution, gyration; *Scottish* birl.

twist ▶ verb **1** *the force of the impact had twisted the chassis* **crumple**, crush, buckle, mangle, warp, bend out of shape, misshape, deform, distort; *N. Amer. informal* pretzel.
OPPOSITE straighten.
2 *her face twisted with rage* **contort**, screw up, quirk.
3 *Ma was anxiously twisting a handkerchief* **wring**, squeeze, knead.
4 *Marco twisted round in his seat to look at her* **turn (round)**, swivel (round), skew (round), spin (round), pivot, rotate, revolve.
5 *she twisted out of his grasp* **wriggle**, writhe, squirm, worm, wiggle.
6 *he landed awkwardly and twisted his ankle* **sprain**, wrench, turn, rick, crick.
7 *you are deliberately twisting my words* **distort**, misrepresent, change, alter, pervert, falsify, warp, skew, put the wrong slant on, misinterpret, misconstrue, misstate, misquote, quote/take out of context, misreport; garble.
8 *he reached for the radio and twisted the knob* **twiddle**, adjust, turn, rotate, swivel.
9 *she twisted a lock of hair around her finger* **wind**, twirl, coil, curl, wrap.
10 *cables made up of several wires twisted together* **intertwine**, twine, entwine, interlace, weave, plait, interweave, braid, wreathe, coil, wind; *literary* pleach.
11 *the road twisted and turned through the hills* **wind**, bend, curve, turn, meander, weave, zigzag, swerve, loop, corkscrew, snake, worm.
□ **twist someone's arm** (*informal*) *don't let him twist your arm if you really don't want to go* **pressurize**, coerce, bulldoze, force, railroad; persuade; talk someone into something; *informal* lean on, put the screws on.
▶ noun **1** *the twist of a dial* **turn**, twirl, spin, rotation, roll.
2 *the strange twist of his mouth betrayed an inner fury* **contortion**, contorted/distorted shape.
3 *a slight personality twist which could cause her problems* **quirk**, idiosyncrasy, foible, eccentricity, peculiarity, oddity, kink; **aberration**, fault, flaw, imperfection, defect, failing, weakness; deviation, perversion.
4 (*dated*) *a twist of tobacco* **wad**, quid, plug, chew; *Brit.* screw; *N. Amer. informal* chaw; *rare* cud, cake, pigtail.
5 *long twists of black hair* **ringlet**, curl, corkscrew, coil; lock, hank.
6 *the twists and turns of the mountain road* **bend**, curve, turn, zigzag, loop, kink, dog-leg; *Brit.* hairpin bend.
7 *the twists and turns of the plot* **convolution**, complication, complexity, intricacy; surprise, revelation.
8 *Loretta was still trying to take in this curious twist of fate* **development**, turn of events, incident, happening, occurrence; turnabout.
9 *a new twist on an old theme* **interpretation**, slant, outlook, angle, approach, treatment; alteration, variation.

twisted ▶ adjective **1** *a tangle of twisted metal* **crumpled**, bent out of shape, crushed, buckled, warped, misshapen, distorted, deformed; *N. Amer. informal* pretzeled.
2 *a twisted smile* **crooked**, wry, lopsided; contorted.
3 *his twisted mind* **perverted**, warped, deviant, depraved, corrupt, abnormal, unhealthy, aberrant, distorted, corrupted, debauched, debased, degenerate, sadistic, evil, wicked; *informal* sick, kinky, pervy, sicko.

twisty ▶ adjective *a twisty road* **winding**, windy, twisting, turning, full of twists and turns, bending, bendy, zigzag, zigzagging, meandering, curving, sinuous, snaking, snaky, tortuous; *rare* anfractuous, flexuous, meandrous, serpentiform.
OPPOSITE straight.

twit ▶ noun (*Brit. informal*) *she must think I'm a real twit. See* FOOL.

twitch ▶ verb **1** *his body twitched and then lay still* **jerk**, move spasmodically/convulsively, spasm, convulse, flutter, quiver, tremble, shiver, quaver, shudder.
2 *he twitched the note out of Ellie's hand* **snatch**, pluck, pull, tug, tweak; *informal* yank.
▶ noun **1** *an involuntary twitch of her lips* **spasm**, convulsive movement, convulsion, jerk, flutter, quiver, tremor, shiver, shudder; tic.
2 *he gave a twitch at his moustache* **pull**, tug, tweak; *informal* yank.
3 *he felt a twitch of annoyance* **twinge**, dart, stab, prick; pang.

twitter ▶ verb **1** *sparrows twittered under the eaves* **chirp**, chirrup, cheep, tweet, peep, chitter, chatter, trill, warble, sing.
2 *oh, for heaven's sake stop twittering about Fabio* **prattle**, babble, chatter, prate, gabble, jabber, go on, run on, rattle on/away, yap, jibber-jabber, patter, blather, blether, blither, maunder, ramble, drivel; *informal* yak, yackety-yak, yabber, yatter; *Brit. informal* witter, rabbit, chunter, natter, waffle; *Scottish & Irish informal* slabber; *Austral./NZ informal* mag; *archaic* twaddle, clack, twattle.
▶ noun **1** *a bird's faint twitter* **chirp**, chirping, chirrup, chirruping, cheep, cheeping, tweet, tweeting, peep, peeping, chitter, chittering, trill, trilling, warble, warbling; song, cry, call.
2 *her non-stop twitter* **prattle**, chatter, babble, talk, prating, gabble, jabber, blather, blether, rambling; *informal* yackety-yak, yabbering, yatter; *Brit. informal* wittering, nattering, chuntering; *archaic* clack, twattle.
3 (*informal*) *why are you in such a twitter?* **panic**, frenzy, fluster, flutter, flurry, pother; *informal* tizz/tizzy, tiz-woz, state, sweat, stew, flap, dither; *N. Amer. informal* twit.

two ▶ cardinal number **pair**, duo, duet, dyad, duplet, tandem; *archaic* twain.

WORD LINKS

related prefixes	**bi-** (e.g. ***bicycle***), **di-** (e.g. ***diode, dihedral***), **duo-** (e.g. ***duologue, duopoly***)
relating to two	**binary, dual, dyadic**
occurring twice a year	**biannual**
occurring every two years	**biennial**
two-hundredth anniversary	**bicentenary**

two-faced ▶ adjective *she's nothing but a two-faced liar* **deceitful, insincere**, double-dealing, hypocritical, back-stabbing, false, untrustworthy, duplicitous, deceiving, dissembling, dishonest; disloyal, treacherous, perfidious, faithless; lying, untruthful, mendacious; *rare* Janus-faced.
OPPOSITES sincere, honest.

twosome ▶ noun **couple**, pair, duo.

tycoon ▶ noun *a newspaper tycoon* **magnate**, mogul, big businessman, baron, merchant prince, captain of industry, industrialist, financier, top executive, chief, lord, magnifico, nabob, grandee; entrepreneur; millionaire, billionaire, multimillionaire; *informal* big shot, big gun, top dog, Big Daddy, Big Chief, bigwig, honcho, zillionaire; *Brit. informal* supremo; *N. Amer. informal* big wheel, kahuna, top banana, big enchilada; *derogatory* fat cat.

type *See centre pages for list of* **Typefaces**
▶ noun **1** *this type of heather grows better in a drier habitat | a curate of the old-fashioned type* **kind**, sort, variety, class, category, classification, group, set, bracket, genre, genus, species, family, order, breed, race, strain; style, description, designation, condition, quality, nature, manner, design, shape, form, pattern, rank; brand, make, model, line, mark, generation, vintage; stamp, ilk, kidney, cast, grain, mould; *N. Amer.* stripe.
2 (*informal*) *two sporty types in tracksuits* **person**, individual, character, sort; *Brit. informal* bod.
3 *she characterized his witty sayings as the type of modern wisdom* **epitome**, quintessence, essence, perfect example, archetype, model, pattern, paradigm, exemplar, embodiment, personification, avatar; prototype.
4 *extracts from the report are set in italic type* **print**, typeface, face, characters, lettering, letters; font; *Brit.* fount.

typeface ▶ noun. *See centre pages for list of* **Typefaces**

typhoon ▶ noun **cyclone**, tropical storm, storm, tornado, hurricane, windstorm, whirlwind; *N. Amer. informal* twister.

typical ▶ adjective **1** *a typical example of 1930s art deco* **representative**, classic, quintessential, archetypal, model, prototypical, stereotypical; distinctive, distinguishing, particular.
OPPOSITES atypical, unusual, abnormal.
2 *the 30th of June had been a fairly typical day* **normal**, average, ordinary, standard, regular, routine, run-of-the-mill, stock, orthodox, conventional, predictable, unsurprising, unremarkable, unexceptional; *informal* bog-standard.
OPPOSITES exceptional, unusual, atypical.
3 *it's typical of him to forget to tell me* **characteristic**, in character, in keeping, to be expected, usual, normal, par for the course, predictable, true to form, true to type; customary, habitual; proverbial; *informal* … all over.
OPPOSITES uncharacteristic, out of keeping.

CHOOSE THE RIGHT WORD

typical, characteristic, distinctive
See CHARACTERISTIC.

typify ▶ verb **1** *he typified a new breed of civil servant* **epitomize**, exemplify, be representative of, represent, be characteristic of, characterize; personify, embody, be the embodiment of, be the incarnation of; *rare* instantiate, incarnate.
2 *the sun typified the Greeks, and the moon the Persians* **symbolize**, be

T

symbolic of, represent, stand for, be emblematic of; *rare* emblematize.

tyrannical ▶ adjective *a tyrannical government* **dictatorial**, despotic, autocratic, oppressive, repressive, fascistic, tyrannous, absolute, totalitarian, arbitrary, undemocratic, illiberal; authoritarian, domineering, dominating, overbearing, high-handed, imperious, bullying, harsh, strict, iron-handed, iron-fisted, severe, cruel, brutal, ruthless, unjust; *rare* Neronian.
OPPOSITES democratic, liberal, easy-going.

CHOOSE THE RIGHT WORD

tyrannical, autocratic, despotic
See AUTOCRATIC.

tyrannize ▶ verb *she tyrannized her daughter-in-law* **domineer over**, dominate, order about/around, dictate to, browbeat, intimidate, bully, ride roughshod over, lord it over, keep someone under one's thumb; persecute, victimize, torment; oppress, rule with a rod of iron, rule with an iron hand, rule despotically, suppress, repress, crush, subjugate, hold down, keep down, grind down, trample underfoot, enslave, bring someone to their knees, treat harshly, treat brutally; *informal* push around.

tyranny ▶ noun **despotism**, absolutism, absolute power, autocracy, dictatorship, undemocratic rule, reign of terror, totalitarianism, Fascism; oppression, suppression, repression, subjugation, enslavement; authoritarianism, high-handedness, imperiousness, bullying, harshness, strictness, severity, cruelty, brutality, ruthlessness, injustice, unjustness.
OPPOSITES democracy, liberality.

tyrant ▶ noun **1** *an evil tyrant who has imprisoned all who oppose his regime* **dictator**, despot, autocrat, absolute ruler, authoritarian, oppressor.
2 *her boss is an absolute tyrant* **slave-driver**, martinet, hard taskmaster, scourge; bully.

WORD LINKS
killing of a tyrant **tyrannicide**

tyro ▶ noun *he first entered parliament in 1977 as a 34-year-old political tyro* **novice**, **beginner**, learner, inexperienced person, neophyte, newcomer, new member, new recruit, raw recruit, new boy/girl, initiate, fledgling; apprentice, trainee, probationer, student, pupil; *N. Amer.* tenderfoot; *informal* rookie, new kid, newie, newbie; *N. Amer. informal* greenhorn, punk.
OPPOSITES expert, veteran.

T

ubiquitous ▶ adjective *tracking stray dogs may soon be easier thanks to the ubiquitous microchip* **omnipresent**, ever-present, present everywhere, everywhere, all-over, all over the place, pervasive, all-pervasive, universal, worldwide, global; rife, prevalent, predominant, very common, popular, extensive, wide-ranging, far-reaching, inescapable.
OPPOSITES rare, scarce.

UFO ▶ noun flying saucer, foo fighter.

WORD LINKS
study of UFOs **ufology**

ugly ▶ adjective **1** *an old man with a horribly ugly face* **unattractive**, ill-favoured, hideous, plain, plain-featured, plain-looking, unlovely, unprepossessing, unsightly, displeasing, disagreeable; horrible, frightful, awful, ghastly, gruesome, grisly, unpleasant, foul, nasty, grim, vile, shocking, disgusting, revolting, repellent, repugnant, grotesque, monstrous, reptilian, misshapen, deformed, disfigured; N. Amer. homely; informal not much to look at, short on looks, as plain as a pikestaff, as ugly as sin; Brit. informal no oil painting.
OPPOSITES beautiful, attractive.
2 *a huge fight ensued and things got pretty ugly* **unpleasant**, nasty, alarming, disagreeable, tense, charged, serious, grave, dangerous, perilous, threatening, menacing, hostile, ominous, sinister; archaic direful; rare minacious.
OPPOSITES pleasant, calm, peaceable.
3 *an ugly rumour* **horrible**, unpleasant, disagreeable, despicable, reprehensible, nasty, horrid, appalling, objectionable, offensive, obnoxious, foul, vile, base, dishonourable, dishonest, rotten, vicious, spiteful, malevolent, evil, wicked.

ulcer ▶ noun *most leg ulcers will heal spontaneously* **sore**, ulceration, open sore, abscess, boil, carbuncle, pustule, blister, cyst, gumboil, wen; N. Amer. canker sore; technical aphtha, chancre, furuncle, vesication, noma; archaic gathering, fester, impostume.

ulcerous ▶ adjective *the parasites created ulcerous sores* **suppurative**, ulcerative, festering, cankerous, cankered; technical aphthous, furunculous; archaic ulcerate.

ulterior ▶ adjective *I helped your mother for my own ulterior motives* **secondary**, underlying, undisclosed, undivulged, unexpressed, unapparent, under wraps, unrevealed, concealed, hidden, covert, secret, personal, private, selfish.
OPPOSITES primary; overt.

ultimate ▶ adjective **1** *the decline and ultimate collapse of the Empire* **eventual**, last, final, concluding, conclusive, terminal, end, endmost, furthest; resulting, ensuing, consequent, subsequent.
OPPOSITE immediate.
2 *ultimate truths about human civilization* **fundamental**, basic, primary, prime, elementary, elemental, absolute, actual, definitive, central, key, crucial, vital, essential, pivotal.
OPPOSITE peripheral.
3 *the ultimate gift for cat lovers* **best**, ideal, greatest, supreme, paramount, superlative, highest, unsurpassed, unrivalled, topmost, utmost, optimum, quintessential; rare apogean.
OPPOSITE worst.
▶ noun *a studio apartment offering the ultimate in luxury living* **utmost**, optimum, last word, very limit, height, epitome, peak, pinnacle, acme, apex, apogee, zenith, culmination, perfection, nonpareil, extreme, extremity; French crème de la crème, dernier cri, beau idéal; Latin ne plus ultra; informal the best thing since sliced bread, the bee's knees, the cat's pyjamas/whiskers; archaic nonsuch.

ultimately ▶ adverb **1** *the cost will ultimately fall on the local authorities* **eventually**, in the end, in the long run, at length, finally, sooner or later, in time, in the fullness of time, after some time, in the final analysis, when all is said and done, one day, some day, sometime, at last, at long last; informal when push comes to shove; Brit. informal at the end of the day.
OPPOSITE immediately.
2 *he gave two ultimately contradictory reasons* **fundamentally**, basically, primarily, essentially, at heart, deep down.

ultra- ▶ combining form *an ultra-conservative politician* **extremely**, exceedingly, excessively, immensely, especially, exceptionally, unusually, extraordinarily, remarkably, uncommonly, extra; N. English right; Scottish unco; informal mega, mucho, seriously, majorly, oh-so; Brit. informal jolly, dead, ever so, well, fair; N. Amer. informal real, mighty, awful, plumb, powerful, way; S. African informal lekker; informal, dated devilish, frightfully; archaic exceeding.
▶ noun (**ultra**) *there is a new school of ultras in the animal rights movement* **extremist**, radical, fanatic, zealot, diehard, revolutionary, rebel, militant, subversive.

ultra-modern ▶ adjective *this computer is a high-performance ultra-modern machine* **futuristic**, ahead of its/one's time, avant-garde, modernistic, advanced, progressive, forward-looking, up to the minute; informal way-out; rare neoteric.
OPPOSITES outdated, old-fashioned.

umbrage ▶ noun
□ **take umbrage** *she took umbrage at his remarks* **take offence**, be offended, take exception, bridle, take something personally, be aggrieved, be affronted, take something amiss, be upset, be annoyed, be angry, be indignant, get one's hackles up, be put out, be insulted, be hurt, be wounded, be piqued, be resentful, be disgruntled, get/go into a huff, get huffy; informal be miffed, have one's nose put out of joint, be riled; Brit. informal get the hump.

umbrella ▶ noun **1** *they huddled under the umbrella* parasol, sunshade; Brit. informal brolly; N. Amer. informal bumbershoots; Brit. informal, dated gamp.
2 *television surveys are conducted under the umbrella of two national bodies* **aegis**, auspices, patronage, championship, protection, safe keeping, protectorship, guardianship, support, guidance, charge, responsibility, care, cover, backing, agency.

umpire ▶ noun *the crowd were clamouring for the umpire to reverse the decision* **referee**, linesman, adjudicator, arbitrator, arbiter, judge, moderator, overseer, supervisor; informal ref; N. Amer. informal ump.
▶ verb *he umpired boat races on the River Wear* **referee**, adjudicate, arbitrate, judge, moderate, oversee, supervise; Cricket stand; informal ref.

umpteen ▶ adjective (informal) *she'd phoned the apartment umpteen times* **countless**, numerous, innumerable, very many, ever so many, untold; informal lots of, loads of, masses of, heaps of, stacks of, piles of, bags of, oodles of, tons of, hundreds of, thousands of; literary myriad, divers.
OPPOSITE few.

unabashed ▶ adjective *she watched the meeting with unabashed interest* **unashamed**, shameless, unembarrassed, brazen, audacious, barefaced, blatant, flagrant, bold, bold as brass, confident, immodest, unblushing, unrepentant, undaunted, unconcerned, undismayed, unshrinking, unflinching, fearless; informal cocky, brass-necked.
OPPOSITES abashed, ashamed, sheepish.

unable ▶ adjective *he was unable to account for the error* **not able**, powerless, impotent, not up/equal to, at a loss, inadequate, ineffectual, incompetent, unfit, unfitted, unqualified; incapable of; literary impuissant.
OPPOSITES able, capable.

unabridged ▶ adjective *each story is unabridged and wholly authentic* **complete**, entire, whole, intact, full-length, uncut, unshortened, unreduced, uncondensed, unexpurgated.

OPPOSITE abridged.

unacceptable ▶ adjective *four boys have been suspended for unacceptable behaviour* **intolerable**, insufferable, unsatisfactory, impermissible, inadmissible, inappropriate, unsuitable, undesirable, unreasonable, objectionable, insupportable; offensive, obnoxious, disagreeable, disgraceful, deplorable, terrible, distasteful, displeasing, improper, unseemly, beyond the pale, bad, poor; *informal* not on, a bit much, out of order, out, not quite the done thing, too much; *Brit. informal* a bit thick, a bit off, off, not cricket; *Austral./NZ informal* over the fence; *rare* exceptionable, condemnable.
OPPOSITES acceptable, satisfactory.

unaccompanied ▶ adjective *our parents would not let us go out unaccompanied in the evenings* **alone**, on one's own, all alone, by oneself, solo, lone, solitary, single, single-handed; **unescorted**, without an escort, unattended, unchaperoned, partnerless, companionless; *Latin* solus; *informal* by one's lonesome; *Brit. informal* on one's tod, on one's lonesome, on one's jack, on one's Jack Jones; *Austral./NZ informal* on one's pat, on one's Pat Malone.
OPPOSITE accompanied.

unaccomplished ▶ adjective **1** *the unaccomplished works of Nature's hand* **uncompleted**, incomplete, unfinished, undone, half-done, unperformed, unexecuted, undeveloped, unfulfilled, neglected.
OPPOSITES accomplished, complete.
2 *he was an unaccomplished poet* **inexpert**, unskilful, unskilled, without finesse, incompetent, incapable, talentless, amateur, amateurish, unqualified, untrained, dilettante, maladroit, blundering; *rare* dilettantish.
OPPOSITES accomplished, expert, skilful.

unaccountable ▶ adjective **1** *for some unaccountable reason, the horses drawing the cart stopped short* **inexplicable**, unexplainable, insoluble, unsolvable, incomprehensible, beyond comprehension, beyond understanding, unfathomable, impenetrable, puzzling, perplexing, baffling, bewildering, mystifying, mysterious, arcane, inscrutable, peculiar, unusual, curious, strange, freak, freakish, unparalleled, queer, odd, bizarre, extraordinary, astonishing, obscure, abstruse, enigmatic; *informal* weird, fluky, freaky, spooky; *Brit. informal* rum; *N. Amer. informal* off the wall; *archaic* wildering.
2 *the Council is literally unaccountable to anyone* **not responsible**, unanswerable, not answerable, not liable; free, clear, exempt, immune; out of control, unsupervised.
OPPOSITES accountable, liable.

unaccustomed ▶ adjective **1** *she was unaccustomed to being told what to do* **unused**, not used, new, fresh, a stranger; unpractised in, unfamiliar with, inexperienced in, unversed in, unconversant with, unacquainted with; *archaic* strange.
OPPOSITE accustomed.
2 *he showed unaccustomed emotion as he spoke* **unusual**, unfamiliar, uncommon, unwonted, new, exceptional, out of the ordinary, extraordinary, special, remarkable, singular, rare, surprising, strange, abnormal, atypical, out of the way, curious, peculiar.
OPPOSITES habitual, usual.

unacquainted ▶ adjective *I regret that I am unacquainted with the place* **unfamiliar with**, unaccustomed to, unused to; **new to**, fresh to, a stranger to; inexperienced in, ignorant of, uninformed about, unschooled in, untutored in, unenlightened about, unconversant with; *informal* in the dark about; *archaic* strange to; *rare* nescient of.
OPPOSITES acquainted, familiar.

unadorned ▶ adjective *they preferred sparse and unadorned church interiors* **unembellished**, unornamented, undecorated, unelaborate, unvarnished, unfurnished, unpatterned, uncluttered, unostentatious, unfussy, no-nonsense, without frills, plain, penny plain, simple, basic, modest, restrained, straightforward; bare, bald, austere, stark, severe, spartan, ascetic, clinical, clean; *informal* no-frills.
OPPOSITES ornate, fancy.

unadventurous ▶ adjective *he led a leisurely, unadventurous life* **cautious**, careful, prudent, chary, circumspect, wary, hesitant, tentative, timid; conservative, conventional, traditional, unenterprising, unexciting, unimaginative, uncreative, restrained, limited, boring, strait-laced, stuffy, narrow-minded; *informal* cagey, square, straight, stick-in-the-mud, uptight.
OPPOSITES adventurous, enterprising, imaginative.

unaffected ▶ adjective **1** *the government's position is unaffected by the cabinet reshuffle* **unchanged**, unaltered, uninfluenced; untouched, unmoved, unimpressed, unstirred; unresponsive to; proof against, impervious to, immune to, not liable to, not subject to.
OPPOSITES changed, influenced, affected.
2 *his manner was natural and unaffected* **unassuming**, unpretentious, down-to-earth, without airs, natural, spontaneous, easy, uninhibited, open, artless, guileless, ingenuous, naive, childlike, innocent, unsophisticated, unworldly, plain, simple.
OPPOSITES pretentious, affected.
3 *she was welcomed with unaffected warmth into the family home* **genuine**, real, sincere, unfeigned, unpretended, unforced, uncontrived, unstilted, honest, earnest, wholehearted, heartfelt, true, bona fide, candid, frank, open, profound; *informal* upfront; *rare* full-hearted.
OPPOSITES false, feigned.

CHOOSE THE RIGHT WORD

unaffected, sincere, genuine, unfeigned
See SINCERE.

unafraid ▶ adjective *these companies are unafraid of risks* **undaunted by**, unabashed by, unalarmed by; **fearless**, brave, courageous, plucky, intrepid, stout-hearted, lionhearted, bold, daring, confident, stout, audacious, doughty, mettlesome, unflinching, unshrinking, unblenching; *informal* game, gutsy, spunky, ballsy.
OPPOSITES afraid, cowardly, timid.

unanimity ▶ noun *we have achieved a degree of unanimity* **agreement**, accord, harmony, concord, unity, union, solidarity, unison, consensus, like-mindedness, assent; uniformity, consistency, congruence, concertedness.
OPPOSITES disagreement, division.

unanimous ▶ adjective **1** *doctors were unanimous about the effects of lead emission on health* **united**, in complete agreement, in complete accord, of one mind, like-minded, of the same mind, in harmony, at one, with one voice, concordant, undivided; *rare* consentient.
OPPOSITES divided, at odds.
2 *a unanimous vote of confidence* **uniform**, consistent, solid, united, concerted, congruent, undivided.

unanimously ▶ adverb *a committee of MPs has unanimously agreed to back his bill* **without opposition**, **with one accord**, with one mind, to a man, as one, one and all, each and every one, bar none, without exception; in complete agreement, unitedly, concertedly.

unanswerable ▶ adjective **1** *an unanswerable case for investment* **irrefutable**, inarguable, unarguable, indisputable, undeniable, incontestable, incontrovertible; conclusive, absolute, positive; *rare* irrefragable.
OPPOSITES weak, flawed.
2 *it was no use pondering on unanswerable questions* **insoluble**, unsolvable, insolvable, unresolvable, unexplainable, inexplicable, unascertainable.
OPPOSITE obvious.

unanswered ▶ adjective *there were a number of unanswered questions* **unresolved**, undecided, to be decided, unsettled, undetermined, pending, open, open to debate, open to question, up in the air, in doubt, doubtful, disputed; ignored, neglected.

unappetizing ▶ adjective *an unappetizing leg of chicken in breadcrumbs* **unpalatable**, uninviting, unappealing, unpleasant, off-putting, disagreeable, distasteful, unsavoury, insipid, tasteless, flavourless, unattractive, uninteresting, dull; inedible, uneatable, revolting, nauseating, foul, nasty, detestable, loathsome, abhorrent; *informal* yucky, sick-making, gross.
OPPOSITES appetizing, tempting.

unapproachable ▶ adjective **1** *unapproachable islands* **inaccessible**, out of reach, beyond reach, unreachable, remote, out of the way, isolated, far-flung, off the map, in the middle of nowhere, in the hinterlands; *informal* off the beaten track, in the back of beyond, in the sticks, unget-at-able; *N. Amer. informal* jerkwater, in the tall timbers; *Austral./NZ informal* Barcoo, beyond the black stump.
OPPOSITE accessible.
2 *her boss appeared fierce and unapproachable* **aloof**, distant, remote, detached, reserved, withdrawn, uncommunicative, guarded, undemonstrative, unresponsive, unforthcoming, unfriendly, unsympathetic, unsociable, cool, cold, icy, chilly, frosty, frigid, stiff, formal, dispassionate; *informal* stand-offish, offish, off.
OPPOSITES approachable, friendly.

unarmed ▶ adjective *troops fired into a crowd of unarmed civilians* **defenceless**, without arms, without weapons, weaponless, open to attack, wide open, open; **unprotected**, undefended, unguarded, unshielded, vulnerable, exposed, assailable; weak, helpless; *rare* pregnable.
OPPOSITES armed, protected.

unassailable ▶ adjective **1** *the world's most unassailable fortress* **impregnable**, invulnerable, impenetrable, inviolable, invincible, unconquerable, unattackable; secure, safe, safe and sound, well defended, well fortified; strong, stout, indestructible.
OPPOSITES assailable; defenceless.
2 *his logic was unassailable* **indisputable**, undeniable, unquestionable, incontestable, incontrovertible, irrefutable, indubitable, watertight, sound, conclusive, absolute, positive, proven, beyond dispute, beyond question, beyond doubt, beyond a shadow of a doubt, certain, sure, manifest, patent, obvious.

unassertive ▶ adjective *she seemed unassertive and lacking confidence*

passive, retiring, submissive, unassuming, self-effacing, modest, humble, meek, unconfident, unforthcoming, diffident, shy, timid, timorous, shrinking, hesitant, insecure, unsure; *informal* mousy.
OPPOSITES assertive, bold.

unassuming ▶ adjective *a quiet unassuming man* **modest**, self-effacing, humble, meek, mild, retiring, demure, restrained, reserved, withdrawn, reticent, diffident, shy, bashful, timid, timorous, shrinking, unconfident, insecure, unassertive; unobtrusive, unostentatious, unpretentious, unaffected, natural, genuine, simple, artless, ingenuous.
OPPOSITES bold, boastful, pretentious.

unattached ▶ adjective **1** *they were both unattached and deeply attracted to one another* **unmarried**, **single**, unwed, unwedded; unengaged, unbetrothed; wifeless, husbandless, spouseless, partnerless, without a partner/husband/wife; with no ties, uncommitted, free, available, footloose and fancy free, not going out with anyone, on one's own, by oneself, unescorted, lone, on the shelf, unloved; separated, divorced, widowed; *archaic* sole.
OPPOSITES attached, married, engaged, spoken for.
2 *most of the runners were local people* **unattached to** *any organization* **unaffiliated**, unallied, uncommitted; unassociated with, independent of; autonomous, non-aligned, self-governing, self-ruling, non-partisan, neutral, separate, unconnected, individual, distinct, detached.
OPPOSITE attached.

unattended ▶ adjective **1** *his cries went quite unattended* **ignored**, disregarded, neglected, passed over, forgotten, forsaken, abandoned, left.
2 *an unattended vehicle* **unguarded**, unwatched, by itself, alone, left alone, on its own, solitary, solo.
3 *she had to walk unattended to the drawing room* **unaccompanied**, unescorted, without an escort, partnerless, companionless, unchaperoned, alone, all alone, lone, on one's own, by oneself, solo; *Latin* solus; *informal* by one's lonesome; *Brit. informal* on one's tod, on one's lonesome, on one's jack, on one's Jack Jones; *Austral./NZ* on one's pat, on one's Pat Malone.
OPPOSITES attended, accompanied.

unattractive ▶ adjective *an unattractive little town* **plain**, **ugly**, plain-looking, ugly-looking, plain-featured, ill-favoured, unappealing, unsightly, unlovely, unprepossessing, displeasing; hideous, monstrous, grotesque, deformed, disfigured; *N. Amer.* homely; *informal* not much to look at, short on looks, as plain as a pikestaff, as ugly as sin; *Brit. informal* no oil painting; *Austral./NZ informal* drack.
OPPOSITES attractive, beautiful.

unauthorized ▶ adjective *they issued a ban on all unauthorized rallies* **unofficial**, unsanctioned, uncertified, unaccredited, unlicensed, unwarranted, unapproved; disallowed, prohibited, banned, barred, forbidden, outlawed, illegal, illegitimate, illicit, interdicted, proscribed; *informal* wildcat.
OPPOSITES authorized, official, lawful.

unavailing ▶ adjective *persistent calls for justice were unavailing* **ineffective**, ineffectual, inefficacious, vain, in vain, futile, useless, unsuccessful, non-successful, nugatory, failed, fruitless, unproductive, profitless, unprofitable, pointless, to no avail, to no purpose, to no effect, abortive, inadequate; *archaic* for nought, bootless; *rare* Sisyphean.
OPPOSITES effective, successful.

unavoidable ▶ adjective *workers have been told that redundancies are unavoidable* **inescapable**, inevitable, bound/sure to happen, inexorable, assured, certain, for sure, sure, fated, predestined, predetermined, preordained, ineluctable, necessary, compulsory, required, obligatory, mandatory, prescribed, out of one's hands; *rare* ineludible.

unaware ▶ adjective *the President was unaware of what was going on* **ignorant**, unknowing, unconscious, heedless, unmindful, oblivious, unsuspecting, uninformed, unenlightened, unwitting, innocent, inattentive, unobservant, unperceptive, unresponsive, blind, deaf, insensible, insensitive; *informal* in the dark; *rare* incognizant, nescient.
OPPOSITES aware, conscious.

U

unawares ▶ adverb **1** *a party of brigands caught them unawares* **by surprise**, unexpectedly, without warning, suddenly, abruptly, unprepared, off-guard, cold; red-handed, in the act, in flagrante delicto; *informal* with one's trousers/pants down, napping, in flagrante; *Brit. informal* on the hop.
OPPOSITE prepared.
2 *a shoal of young roach approached the pike unawares* **unknowingly**, unwittingly, unconsciously, without noticing, in all innocence; unintentionally, inadvertently, accidentally, by accident, by mistake, mistakenly.
OPPOSITES knowingly; deliberately.

unbalanced ▶ adjective **1** *he was considered unbalanced and dangerous* **unstable**, of unsound mind, mentally ill, deranged, demented, crazed, troubled, disturbed, unhinged, insane, mad, mad as a hatter, mad as a March hare, raving mad, out of one's mind, not in one's right mind, neurotic, psychotic; *Latin* non compos mentis; *informal* crazy, loopy, loony, mixed up, nuts, nutty, nutty as a fruitcake, bananas, cracked, crackpot, daft, dippy, screwy, with a screw loose, batty, dotty, cuckoo, bonkers, potty, mental, screwed up, not all there, off one's head, out of one's head, out to lunch, a bit lacking, round the bend, round the twist, away with the fairies; *Brit. informal* barmy, crackers, barking, barking mad, off one's trolley, off one's rocker, daft as a brush, not the full shilling; *N. Amer. informal* nutsy, nutso, squirrelly, wacko, buggy; *dated* touched.
OPPOSITES balanced, stable, sane.
2 *a most unbalanced article on a fundamental topic* **biased**, prejudiced, skewed, one-sided, lopsided, partisan, factional, partial, inequitable, unjust, unfair, uneven, unequal; *French* parti pris.
OPPOSITES balanced, unbiased, fair.

unbearable ▶ adjective *the frustration is almost unbearable* **intolerable**, insufferable, unsupportable, insupportable, unendurable, beyond endurance, unacceptable, unmanageable, impossible, more than flesh and blood can stand, too much to bear, past bearing, not to be borne, overpowering; *informal* too much, enough to try the patience of Job, enough to try the patience of a saint.
OPPOSITES bearable, tolerable.

unbeatable ▶ adjective *she has been in unbeatable form since her World Championship triumph* **invincible**, unstoppable, unassailable, indomitable, unconquerable, invulnerable, unsurpassable, unsurpassed, matchless, unmatched, peerless; excellent, supreme, outstanding.
OPPOSITES poor, weak.

unbeaten ▶ adjective *Edinburgh are the only unbeaten team in the division | an unbeaten record* **undefeated**, unconquered, unbowed, unvanquished, unsubdued, unsurpassed, unequalled, unrivalled, unbroken; triumphant, victorious, supreme, matchless, second to none.
OPPOSITES beaten, defeated.

unbecoming ▶ adjective **1** *a stout lady in an unbecoming striped sundress* **unflattering**, unattractive, unsightly, plain, ugly, ugly-looking, hideous; unsuitable, unsuited, ill-suited.
OPPOSITES becoming, flattering.
2 *they condemned him for conduct* **unbecoming** *to the Senate* **inappropriate**, unfitting, unbefitting, unsuitable, unsuited, ill-suited, inapt, out of keeping, untoward, incorrect, unacceptable; **unworthy of**; improper, lacking in propriety, indecorous, unseemly, unladylike, ungentlemanly, unmannerly, undignified, indelicate, indecent, tasteless.
OPPOSITES becoming, proper, appropriate.

unbelief ▶ noun *a symptom of unbelief was an inability to pray* **atheism**, non-belief, agnosticism, heresy, apostasy, irreligion, heathenism, godlessness, nihilism, lack of faith; scepticism, cynicism, disbelief, incredulity, suspicion, distrust, mistrust, doubt, non-conviction, dubiety.
OPPOSITES belief, faith.

unbelievable ▶ adjective *your audacity is simply unbelievable* **incredible**, beyond belief, difficult to believe, scarcely credible, inconceivable, unthinkable, unimaginable; unconvincing, far-fetched, implausible, improbable, impossible; *informal* hard to swallow, mind-boggling, mind-blowing.
OPPOSITES believable, credible.

unbeliever ▶ noun *a Holy War against the unbelievers* **infidel**, heretic, heathen, non-believer, atheist, agnostic, pagan, nihilist, apostate, freethinker, dissenter, nonconformist; disbeliever, sceptic, cynic, doubter, doubting Thomas, questioner, scoffer; *archaic* paynim; *rare* nullifidian.
OPPOSITE believer.

unbelieving ▶ adjective *they were to preach to the unbelieving people* **faithless**, non-believing, agnostic, atheistic, heathen, pagan, infidel, irreligious, unenlightened; disbelieving, doubting, doubtful, sceptical, cynical, unconvinced, incredulous.
OPPOSITE believing.

unbend ▶ verb **1** *I had trouble unbending my cramped knees* **straighten**, straighten out, extend, flex, uncurl, flatten.
OPPOSITE bend.
2 *you could be fun too, you know, if you'd only unbend a little* **relax**, become less formal, become informal, unwind, de-stress, loosen up, let oneself go; *informal* let one's hair down, let up, let it all hang out, hang loose, come down from one's high horse.
OPPOSITE tense up.

unbending ▶ adjective **1** *the giraffe moves towards me on unbending legs* **stiff**, rigid, inflexible, unpliable, inelastic, unmalleable; straight, undeviating, linear, unswerving, uncurving, as straight as an arrow.
OPPOSITE flexible.
2 *an unbending and somewhat formal man* **aloof**, formal, stiff, reserved, remote, distant, forbidding, stand-offish, strait-laced, conventional, stuffy, cool, unfeeling, unemotional, unfriendly, austere; *informal* uptight.
OPPOSITES relaxed, informal.
3 *the unbending attitudes of the authorities* **uncompromising**, inflexible, unyielding, unfaltering, unwavering, hard-line, tough, harsh, strict, stern, severe, firm, resolute, determined, unrelenting, relentless, inexorable, intransigent, immovable.

unbiased ▶ adjective *unbiased professional advice* **impartial**, unprejudiced, non-partisan, neutral, objective, outside, disinterested, without fear or

favour, dispassionate, detached, unswayed, even-handed, open-minded, equitable, fair, fair-minded, just; *informal* on the level, with no axe to grind, sitting on the fence.
OPPOSITES biased, partisan, prejudiced.

unbidden ▶ adjective **1** *often the unbidden guest proves the best company* **uninvited**, unasked, unrequested, unsolicited; unwanted, unwelcome.
2 *unbidden excitement grew deep inside her* **spontaneous**, unprompted, voluntary, unforced, uncompelled, unplanned, unpremeditated, spur-of-the-moment; *informal* off-the-cuff.

unbind ▶ verb *unbind her at once* **untie**, unchain, unfetter, unshackle, unmanacle, unyoke, unfasten, untether, unknot, unlace, undo, loosen, unloose, disentangle; **release**, emancipate, free, set free/loose, liberate, discharge.
OPPOSITES bind, confine.

unblemished ▶ adjective *he had an unblemished record as a law-abiding citizen* **impeccable**, flawless, faultless, without fault, without blemish, perfect, pure, pure as the driven snow, lily-white, whiter than white, clean, spotless, stainless, unsullied, unspoilt, undefiled, untouched, untarnished, uncontaminated, unpolluted, incorrupt, beyond/above reproach, guiltless, sinless, innocent, unimpeachable, blameless; exemplary, ideal, model; *informal* squeaky clean, A1.
OPPOSITES flawed, corrupt.

unborn ▶ adjective **1** *German measles can damage your unborn child* **embryonic**, fetal, expected, awaited; *Latin* in utero.
2 *the unborn generations which shall follow us on this earth* **future**, to come, coming, forthcoming, subsequent; *formal* hereafter.

unbounded ▶ adjective *I retained my unbounded enthusiasm for work* **unlimited**, boundless, limitless, without limit, illimitable; unrestrained, unrestricted, unconditional, unconstrained, uncontrolled, unchecked, unbridled; untold, vast, immense; immeasurable, measureless, inestimable; endless, unending, never-ending, interminable, everlasting, infinite, inexhaustible, unflagging; absolute, total, full, utter; *informal* with no holds barred.
OPPOSITES limited, restricted.

unbreakable ▶ adjective *a new type of unbreakable plastic bottle* **shatterproof**, non-breakable, indestructible, imperishable, resistant, durable, everlasting, long-lasting, made to last; toughened, sturdy, stout, hard-wearing, heavy-duty; *literary* adamantine; *rare* infrangible.
OPPOSITES fragile, flimsy.

unbridled ▶ adjective *she strikes the ball with an unbridled enthusiasm* **unrestrained**, unconstrained, uncontrolled, uninhibited, unrestricted, unchecked, uncurbed, rampant, runaway, irrepressible, unstoppable, uncontainable, unquenchable, excessive, wild, intemperate, immoderate, wanton, self-indulgent.
OPPOSITES restrained, controlled.

unbroken ▶ adjective **1** *there were no doors or windows left unbroken* **undamaged**, unimpaired, unharmed, unscathed, unspoilt, untouched, sound, intact, in one piece, whole, complete, entire, perfect.
OPPOSITE broken.
2 *an unbroken horse* **untamed**, unsubdued, wild, undomesticated, feral.
OPPOSITE broken.
3 *an unbroken chain of glorious victories* **uninterrupted**, continuous, ceaseless, unceasing, endless, incessant, constant, unremitting, perpetual, non-stop, without stopping, never-ending, ongoing.
OPPOSITE intermittent.
4 *his record of 10.2 seconds is still unbroken* **unbeaten**, undefeated, unsurpassed, unrivalled, supreme, unmatched, matchless, second to none.
OPPOSITES broken, beaten.

unburden ▶ verb *he would have liked to* **unburden himself** *to somebody* **open one's heart**, confess, tell all, tell one's all, unbosom oneself; confide in; *informal* come clean, spill all.
OPPOSITES keep it all in, bottle it all up.

uncalled for ▶ adjective *I'm ignoring that uncalled-for remark* **gratuitous**, unnecessary, needless, unneeded, inessential; undeserved, unmerited, unwarranted, unjustified, unreasonable, unfair, inappropriate, pointless; unsought, unasked, unsolicited, unrequested, unprompted, unprovoked, undesired, unwanted, unwelcome.

uncanny ▶ adjective **1** *all the clocks had stopped and the silence was uncanny* **eerie**, unnatural, preternatural, supernatural, unearthly, other-worldly, unreal, ghostly, mysterious, strange, abnormal, odd, curious, queer, weird, bizarre, freakish; *Scottish* eldritch; *informal* creepy, spooky, freaky; *Brit. informal* rum; *N. Amer. informal* bizarro.
OPPOSITES ordinary, normal.
2 *there was an uncanny resemblance between the two pictures* **striking**, remarkable, extraordinary, out of the ordinary, out of the way, unusual, exceptional, astounding, astonishing, incredible, conspicuous, noteworthy, notable, considerable, distinctive, arresting.
OPPOSITES unremarkable, run-of-the-mill.

unceasing ▶ adjective *the unceasing efforts of the staff* **incessant**, ceaseless, unending, endless, never-ending, interminable, non-stop, constant, continuous, continual, uninterrupted, unabated, unabating, unremitting, relentless, unrelenting, unrelieved, sustained, persistent, lasting, eternal, perpetual; unfaltering, unflagging, untiring, unwearied, unwavering, unswerving, undeviating, persevering, dogged, tireless, indefatigable.
OPPOSITES intermittent, occasional; half-hearted.

unceremonious ▶ adjective **1** *he waved them to an unceremonious halt* **abrupt**, sudden, hasty, hurried, summary, perfunctory, undignified, rude, impolite, uncivil, discourteous, unmannerly, offhand, dismissive; *informal* off.
OPPOSITE polite.
2 *an affable, unceremonious man* **informal**, not formal, casual, relaxed; **easy-going**, easy, familiar, natural, unreserved, open, free, loose; *informal* laid-back, free and easy.
OPPOSITE formal.

uncertain ▶ adjective **1** *the environmental effects of the project are uncertain* **unknown**, undetermined, unsettled, unresolved, unsure, pending, in the balance, in limbo, up in the air, debatable, open to question, in doubt; unpredictable, unforeseeable, incalculable, speculative; unreliable, untrustworthy, undependable, risky, chancy; *informal* dicey, hairy, iffy; *Brit. informal* dodgy.
OPPOSITES certain, settled; predictable.
2 *the uncertain weather meant that passengers needed to pack a pullover or two* **changeable**, variable, varying, irregular, fitful, unpredictable, unreliable, unsettled, unstable, erratic, fluctuating; *rare* changeful, fluctuant.
3 *Edward was a little uncertain about the decision* **unsure**, doubtful, dubious, undecided, unresolved, indecisive, irresolute, hesitant, wavering, vacillating, oscillating, equivocating, vague, hazy, unclear, ambivalent, in two minds, on the horns of a dilemma, torn; *informal* iffy, blowing hot and cold, on the fence.
OPPOSITES certain, sure.
4 *I gave her an uncertain smile* **hesitant**, hesitating, tentative, halting, faltering, unsure, unconfident, diffident, doubtful.
OPPOSITE confident.

uncertainty ▶ noun **1** *the uncertainty of the future* **unpredictability**, unreliability, riskiness, chanciness, precariousness, unsureness; changeability, changeableness, variability, inconstancy, fitfulness, fickleness.
OPPOSITES certainty, predictability.
2 *uncertainty about the future is always bad for morale* **unsureness**, lack of certainty, indecision, irresolution, hesitancy, doubt, doubtfulness, wavering, vacillation, equivocation, vagueness, ambivalence, lack of conviction, disquiet, disquietude, wariness, chariness, scepticism; queries, questions; *rare* dubiety, incertitude.
OPPOSITE certainty.
3 *she pushed the anxious uncertainties out of her mind* **doubt**, qualm, misgiving, apprehension, quandary, dilemma, reservation, niggle, scruple, second thought, query, question, question mark, suspicion.
4 *there was uncertainty in his voice* **hesitancy**, tentativeness, unsureness, lack of confidence, diffidence, doubtfulness, doubt.
OPPOSITE confidence.

unchangeable ▶ adjective *many people think of personality characteristics as virtually unchangeable* **unalterable**, immutable, invariable, unvarying, invariant, changeless, firm, fixed, hard and fast, cast-iron, set in stone, set, decided, established, permanent, deep-rooted, enduring, abiding, lasting, indestructible, ineradicable, irreversible, unfading, constant, perpetual, eternal, lifelong; *rare* incommutable, perdurable.
OPPOSITES variable, changeable.

unchanging ▶ adjective *the unchanging passivity of her face enraged him* **consistent**, constant, regular, even, uniform, unvarying, predictable, stable, steady, fixed, permanent, perpetual, eternal; sustained, lasting, persistent, uninterrupted, continuous, continual, ceaseless, incessant, unceasing, never-ending, non-stop, interminable, unabating, unabated, unrelieved, unremitting, relentless.
OPPOSITES varying, changeable, inconsistent.

uncharitable ▶ adjective *I regretted all the uncharitable things I had thought or said* **unkind**, inconsiderate, thoughtless, insensitive, heedless, selfish, self-centred, mean, mean-spirited, unfriendly, unpleasant; **unsympathetic**, uncaring, lacking compassion, ungenerous, ungracious, unfeeling; unforgiving, merciless, ruthless, harsh, severe, stern, hard, hard-hearted, censorious, uncompromising, inflexible, unfair.
OPPOSITE charitable.

uncharted ▶ adjective *we ran Borneo's uncharted rapids in canoes* **unexplored**, untravelled, undiscovered, unresearched, unplumbed, unfamiliar, unknown, strange; **unmapped**, unsurveyed.

uncivil ▶ adjective *he'd been short and uncivil with her* **impolite**, rude, insulting, discourteous, disrespectful, unmannerly, bad-mannered, ill-mannered, impertinent, impudent, ill-bred, ungallant, unchivalrous, ungracious, brusque, tart, sharp, short, curt, offhand, gruff, surly, sullen, churlish, uncouth, ungentlemanly, unladylike, boorish, oafish, loutish, rough, coarse, vulgar; *informal* off, offish, fresh, flip.
OPPOSITES civil, polite.

uncivilized ▶ adjective *the human boy is an uncivilized creature* **uncouth**, coarse, rough, boorish, vulgar, philistine, uneducated, uncultured, uncultivated, benighted, unsophisticated, unrefined, unpolished, ill-bred, ill-mannered, thuggish, loutish; **barbaric**, barbarian, barbarous, primitive, savage, wild, brutish, Neanderthal, in a state of nature; *informal* yobbish, slobbish; *archaic* rude.
OPPOSITE civilized.

unclean ▶ adjective **1** *they were charged with carrying on a food business in unclean premises* **dirty**, filthy, grubby, grimy, mucky, fouled, foul, impure, adulterated, tainted, tarnished, stained, soiled, begrimed, smeared, unwashed; dusty, sooty, muddy, scummy; polluted, contaminated, infected, insanitary, unhygienic, unhealthy, germ-ridden, germy, disease-ridden, septic; *informal* yucky, cruddy, icky; *Brit. informal* manky, grotty, gungy; *Austral./NZ informal* scungy; *archaic* uncleanly; *literary* besmirched; *rare* feculent.
OPPOSITE clean.
2 *sex was considered to be naughty or unclean* **sinful**, immoral, bad, wicked, evil, corrupt, impure, sullied, unwholesome, sordid, disgusting, debased, degenerate, depraved, licentious, lewd, unchaste, lustful; *archaic* uncleanly.
OPPOSITE pure.
3 *pork is an unclean meat for Muslims* impure; forbidden.
OPPOSITES halal, kosher.

unclear ▶ adjective *it was unclear how much fluid had leaked out* **uncertain**, unsure, unsettled, up in the air, debatable, open to question, in doubt, doubtful, unpredictable, unforeseeable, incalculable, speculative; **ambiguous**, inexact, imprecise, inexplicit, ill-defined, equivocal, indefinite, vague, abstruse, puzzling, perplexing, mysterious, arcane, cryptic, obscure, confused, confusing, hazy, misty, foggy, fogged, clouded, lacking definition, nebulous; *informal* iffy, dicey; *Brit. informal* dodgy.
OPPOSITES clear, evident, certain.

unclothed ▶ adjective *she felt awkwardly unclothed in her skimpy bikini* **naked**, bare, nude, in the nude, stark naked, with nothing on, undressed, disrobed, uncovered, in a state of nature, unclad, undraped, exposed; *French* au naturel; *informal* without a stitch on, in one's birthday suit, in the raw, in the altogether, in the buff, as naked as the day one was born, in the nuddy, mother naked; *Brit. informal* starkers; *Scottish informal* in the scud, scuddy; *N. Amer. informal* bare-assed, buck naked; *Austral./NZ informal* bollocky; *Brit. vulgar slang* bollock-naked.
OPPOSITES clothed, dressed.

uncomfortable ▶ adjective **1** *a high-backed uncomfortable chair* **painful**, not comfortable, intolerable, unbearable, disagreeable, excruciating, agonizing, confining, cramped, Spartan.
OPPOSITE comfortable.
2 *I have always felt rather uncomfortable in her presence* **uneasy**, awkward, ill at ease, nervous, tense, edgy, restless, self-conscious, embarrassed, discomfited, disturbed, troubled, upset, worried, anxious, apprehensive; *informal* rattled, fazed, discombobulated, twitchy; *N. Amer. informal* antsy; *rare* unquiet.
OPPOSITES relaxed, comfortable.
3 *an uncomfortable silence* **awkward**, uneasy, unpleasant, disagreeable, distressing, painful, disturbing, embarrassing, embarrassed, tense, strained, charged, worrisome, fraught; *informal* sticky.
OPPOSITES comfortable, pleasant.

uncommitted ▶ adjective **1** *ministers were scrambling to woo uncommitted delegates* **floating**, undecided, non-aligned, non-partisan, unaffiliated, neutral, impartial, independent, undeclared, uncertain, vacillating; *informal* sitting on the fence.
OPPOSITES committed, aligned.
2 *a book about the uncommitted male* **unmarried**, **unattached**, unwed, unwedded, wifeless, husbandless, partnerless, unengaged, unbetrothed, unpledged, unpromised, free, footloose and fancy free, available, single, lone, not going out with anyone.
OPPOSITES committed, attached, married.

uncommon ▶ adjective **1** *it is a handsome and relatively uncommon plant* **unusual**, abnormal, rare, atypical, uncustomary, unconventional, unexpected, unfamiliar, strange, odd, curious, out of the ordinary, extraordinary, out of the way, outlandish, offbeat, irregular, deviant, novel, singular, peculiar, queer, bizarre, freakish, quirky, alien; *informal* weird, oddball, way out, freaky, something else; *N. Amer. informal* off the wall.
OPPOSITE common.
2 *attempted abductions of children are uncommon* **rare**, scarce, few and far between, thin on the ground, exceptional, abnormal, isolated, occasional, infrequent, irregular, sporadic; *Brit.* out of the common; *dated* seldom.
OPPOSITE common.
3 *she displays an uncommon capacity for hard work* **remarkable**, extraordinary, exceptional, singular, particular, marked, outstanding, notable, noteworthy, distinctive, striking, significant, especial, special, signal, superior, unique, unparalleled, unprecedented, prodigious; *informal* mind-boggling, mind-blowing.
OPPOSITES ordinary, run-of-the-mill.

uncommonly ▶ adverb *he is an uncommonly good talker* **unusually**, remarkably, extraordinarily, extra, exceptionally, outstandingly, singularly, particularly, especially, strikingly, markedly, decidedly, notably, eminently, signally, uniquely, extremely, very, inordinately, incredibly, amazingly, awfully, terribly; *N. English* right; *informal* seriously, majorly, ultra; *Brit. informal* jolly, dead, well; *N. Amer. informal* powerful; *dated* devilishly, frightfully.

uncommunicative ▶ adjective *he had always been quiet and uncommunicative* **taciturn**, reserved, shy, retiring, diffident, reticent, laconic, tongue-tied, at a loss for words, mute, quiet, unforthcoming, unconversational, untalkative, silent, tight-lipped, close-mouthed, guarded, secretive, secret, unresponsive, close, private, distant, remote, aloof, withdrawn, stand-offish, unsociable, antisocial, unfriendly, clamlike, playing one's cards close to one's chest; *informal* mum; *archaic* mumchance, retired.
OPPOSITES communicative, talkative, open.

uncomplicated ▶ adjective *an uncomplicated computer interface that is truly easy to use* **simple**, not difficult, straightforward, clear, accessible, direct, undemanding, unexacting, unchallenging, unsophisticated, trouble-free, painless, effortless, easy, facile, elementary, idiot-proof, plain sailing, a five-finger exercise, nothing; *informal* easy-peasy, as easy as pie, as easy as falling off a log, as easy as ABC, a piece of cake, child's play, kids' stuff, a cinch, no sweat, a doddle, a breeze, a pushover, money for old rope, money for jam; *N. Amer. informal* duck soup, a snap; *Austral./NZ informal* a bludge; *S. African informal* a piece of old tackle; *Brit. vulgar slang* a piece of piss; *dated* a snip.
OPPOSITES complicated, difficult, demanding.

uncompromising ▶ adjective *her uncompromising attitude led to clashes with the governor* **inflexible**, unbending, unyielding, unshakeable, unwavering, resolute, unpersuadable, unmalleable, rigid, stiff, hard-line, hard and fast, tough, immovable, intractable, firm, determined, iron-willed, dogged, obstinate, stubborn, not giving an inch, diehard, adamant, obdurate, tenacious, pertinacious, relentless, implacable, inexorable, intransigent, headstrong, pig-headed, bull-headed, single-minded, stiff-necked; *Brit. informal* bloody-minded; *rare* indurate.
OPPOSITES flexible, compliant.

unconcern ▶ noun *I affected a supreme unconcern* **indifference**, apathy, lack of concern, lack of interest, uninterestedness, nonchalance, equanimity, insouciance, lack of involvement, passivity, dispassionateness, dispassion, detachment, aloofness, remoteness, reserve.
OPPOSITES concern, commitment.

unconcerned ▶ adjective **1** *readers think that the author is unconcerned with their responses to the text* **indifferent about**, unmoved by, apathetic about, uninterested in, incurious about, uninvolved in/with, dispassionate about, deaf to, heedless of, unmindful of, bored by; cool, remote, aloof, detached, lukewarm, unenthusiastic.
OPPOSITES concerned, interested, attentive.
2 *Stanley shrugged and tried to look unconcerned* **untroubled**, unworried, unperturbed, unruffled, unanxious, insouciant, nonchalant, blasé, carefree, blithe, casual, without a care in the world, serene, relaxed, at ease, devil-may-care, happy-go-lucky, {cool, calm, and collected}; *informal* laid-back, unflappable; *rare* poco-curante.
OPPOSITES concerned, anxious.

unconditional ▶ adjective *he could count on the unconditional support of the president* **unquestioning**, unqualified, unreserved, unlimited, unrestricted, wholesale, wholehearted; complete, total, entire, full, outright, absolute, downright, out-and-out, utter, all-out, thoroughgoing, unequivocal, positive, express, indubitable, categorical.
OPPOSITE conditional.

unconnected ▶ adjective **1** *the earth wire was left unconnected* **detached**, disconnected, unjoined, separate, loose; dangling, hanging, trailing.
OPPOSITE connected.
2 *a series of unconnected tasks* **unrelated**, unassociated, dissociated, separate, independent, distinct, different, disparate, individual, detached, discrete.
OPPOSITE related.
3 *there is a tendency to drift off into unconnected chains of thought* **disjointed**, incoherent, disconnected, rambling, wandering, diffuse, ununified, disorderly, disordered, haphazard, disorganized, garbled, mixed up, muddled, jumbled, scrambled, meaningless, uncoordinated, aimless.
OPPOSITE coherent.

unconscionable ▶ adjective **1** *the unconscionable use of humans as test animals* **unethical**, amoral, immoral, unprincipled, indefensible, wrong; unscrupulous, unfair, underhand, dishonourable, dishonest, corrupt, depraved; *informal* shady.
OPPOSITES ethical, acceptable.
2 *we have had to wait an unconscionable time* **excessive**, unwarranted, uncalled for, unreasonable, unfair, inordinate, disproportionate, immoderate, extreme, undue, outrageous, preposterous, monstrous, inexcusable, unnecessary, needless; *informal* over the top, OTT.
OPPOSITES acceptable, moderate, reasonable.

unconscious ▶ adjective **1** *to make sure he stayed unconscious she hit him twice over the head* **knocked out**, insensible, senseless, insentient, insensate, passed out, comatose, in a coma, inert; stunned, dazed, stupefied, torpid, befuddled, benumbed, numb; collapsed, keeled over, motionless, immobile, prostrate; *informal* **out cold**, out for the count, blacked out, KO'd, kayoed, out like a light, laid out, flaked out, out, dead to the world; *Brit. informal* spark out; *rare* soporose, soporous.
OPPOSITE conscious.
2 *she concealed herself in the nettles, unconscious of the pain* **heedless**, unheeding, unmindful, disregardful, disregarding, taking no notice; oblivious to, insensible to, blind to, deaf to, impervious to, unaffected by, unconcerned by, indifferent to, detached from, removed from; **unaware**, ignorant, in ignorance, unknowing, unsuspecting, unenlightened; *informal* in the dark; *rare* incognizant, nescient.
OPPOSITES conscious, aware.
3 *an unconscious desire for recognition* **unintentional**, unintended, accidental, unthinking, unwitting, inadvertent, unpremeditated, unplanned; **uncalculating**, chance; **natural**, innate, inherent, unlearned, instinctive, automatic, mechanical, reflex, involuntary, knee-jerk, uncontrolled, spontaneous, subliminal, subconscious, latent, suppressed, sleeping, deep; *informal* gut, bottled up.
OPPOSITES intentional, voluntary; forced.
▶ noun *Oedipal fantasies were supposed to be raging in the unconscious* **subconscious mind**, subconscious, unconscious mind, psyche, ego, superego, id, inner self, innermost self, self, inner man/woman.
OPPOSITE conscious mind.

unconsciousness ▶ noun *someone gave me a crack across the head and I slipped into unconsciousness* **insensibility**, senselessness, stupefaction, oblivion, unawareness, blankness, lack of sensation, lack of feeling; blackout, coma, stupor, torpor, trance, sopor, collapse.
OPPOSITE consciousness.

uncontrollable ▶ adjective **1** *the crowds were fast becoming uncontrollable* **unmanageable**, out of control, ungovernable, wild, unruly, disorderly, recalcitrant, refractory, obstreperous, turbulent, intractable, incorrigible, disobedient, delinquent, insubordinate, defiant, non-compliant, undisciplined; *Brit. informal* stroppy, bolshie; *archaic* contumacious.
OPPOSITES under control, obedient, compliant.
2 *his dad flew into an uncontrollable rage* **ungovernable**, irresistible, irrepressible, unstoppable, unquenchable, uncontainable; wild, violent, forceful, frantic, frenzied, furious, raging, raving, mad, crazed, hysterical, maniacal, manic; *informal* crazy, hyper; *rare* fervid, perfervid, passional.
OPPOSITE controllable.

uncontrolled ▶ adjective *she was horrified by her uncontrolled outburst | the uncontrolled dumping of toxic waste* **unrestrained**, unconstrained, unrestricted, unchecked, unbridled, uncurbed, unlimited, unfettered, untrammelled, uninhibited, unconfined, unimpeded, unhampered, unbounded, unsuppressed, undisciplined, out of control, out of hand, rampant, wild, runaway, incontinent, immoderate, intemperate.
OPPOSITES controlled, restrained.

unconventional ▶ adjective *contemporary art employs unconventional techniques and materials* **unusual**, irregular, unorthodox, unfamiliar, uncommon, uncustomary, unwonted, rare, out of the ordinary, atypical, singular, distinctive, individual, individualistic, alternative, different; new, fresh, novel, newfangled, innovative, groundbreaking, experimental, pioneering, original, unprecedented, unheard of; **eccentric**, idiosyncratic, maverick, quirky, odd, strange, bizarre, weird, outlandish, freakish, funny, quaint, queer, curious, abnormal, anomalous, aberrant, extraordinary, offbeat, radical, esoteric, nonconformist, bohemian; *French* outré, avant-garde; *N. Amer.* left-field; *informal* freaky, way out, far out, oddball, wacky, cranky, kinky, screwy, off the wall, something else, madcap, zany, hippy; *Brit. informal* rum; *N. Amer. informal* kooky, wacko, bizarro.
OPPOSITES conventional, orthodox, ordinary.

> **CHOOSE THE RIGHT WORD**
>
> **unconventional, eccentric, idiosyncratic, quirky**
> See ECCENTRIC.

unconvincing ▶ adjective *he had a plausible though highly unconvincing story* **improbable**, unlikely, implausible; incredible, scarcely credible, unbelievable, difficult to believe, beyond belief, questionable, dubious, doubtful; strained, laboured, ponderous, forced, far-fetched, remote, unrealistic, fanciful, fantastic, strange; feeble, weak, unsound, thin, transparent, poor, lame, trifling, shallow, inadequate, unsatisfactory, ineffectual, half-baked, pathetic; *informal* hard to swallow/take.
OPPOSITES convincing, cogent, persuasive.

uncooperative ▶ adjective *the authorities were inclined to be uncooperative* **unhelpful**, awkward, disobliging, unaccommodating, unamenable, unreasonable, unwilling, recalcitrant, perverse, contrary, stubborn, wilful, stiff-necked, unyielding, unbending, inflexible, unadaptable, immovable, obstructive, difficult, obstreperous, troublesome, tiresome, disobedient; *Scottish* thrawn; *N. Amer.* rock-ribbed; *Brit. informal* bolshie, bloody-minded, stroppy, sticky.
OPPOSITES cooperative, obliging.

uncoordinated ▶ adjective *as he ran, his uncoordinated limbs flung out in all directions* **clumsy**, **awkward**, blundering, bumbling, lumbering, shambling; flat-footed, heavy-footed, heavy-handed, graceless; **gawky**, gangling, ungainly, ungraceful, inelegant, clownish, cumbersome, bovine, ponderous; inept, unhandy, unskilful, inexpert, maladroit, bungling; *informal* butterfingered, cack-handed, ham-fisted, ham-handed, clodhopping, like a bull in a china shop; *Brit. informal* all thumbs, all fingers and thumbs; *N. Amer. informal* klutzy; *archaic* lubberly.
OPPOSITES well coordinated, adroit, dexterous.

uncouth ▶ adjective *the porters shouted to each other in uncouth tones* **uncivilized**, uncultured, uncultivated, unrefined, unpolished, unsophisticated, common, low, plebeian, philistine, rough, coarse, provincial, rustic, crude, gross, loutish, hooligan, boorish, oafish; Neanderthal, barbarian, barbarous, barbaric, bearish, primitive, savage; churlish, uncivil, rude, impolite, discourteous, disrespectful, unmannerly, bad-mannered, ill-mannered, ill-bred, indecorous, ungallant, ungentlemanly, unladylike, vulgar, crass, indelicate, offensive; *N. Amer.* backwoods, hillbilly, hick; *informal* yobbish, slobbish, clodhopping.
OPPOSITES refined, cultivated; polite.

uncover ▶ verb **1** *she uncovered the cheese sandwiches* **lay bare**, bare, expose, expose to view, leave unprotected, reveal, display, put on display, put on show, exhibit; **unwrap**, unveil, strip, denude.
OPPOSITES cover, conceal, clothe.
2 *police claim to have uncovered a money-laundering operation* **detect**, discover, come across, stumble on/across, chance on, hit on, encounter, find, find out, turn up, unearth, dig up, dredge up, root out, hunt out, nose out, ferret out, grub out, disinter, extricate; **expose**, bring to light, bring into the open, unmask, unveil, reveal, lay bare, make known, make public, divulge, disclose, betray, give away, smoke out; *informal* blow the whistle on, pull the plug on, spill the beans on, let the cat out of the bag, nail; *rare* uncloak.
OPPOSITES conceal, hide, cover up.

unctuous ▶ adjective *she sees through his unctuous manners | an unctuous smile* **sycophantic**, ingratiating, obsequious, fawning, servile, self-abasing, grovelling, subservient, wheedling, cajoling, crawling, cringing, Uriah Heepish, humble, toadying, hypocritical, insincere, flattering, adulatory, honey-tongued, silver-tongued, gushing, effusive, suave, urbane, glib, smooth, smooth-tongued, smooth-spoken, smooth-talking, slick, slippery, saccharine; **oily**, oleaginous, greasy; cloying, nauseating, sickening; *informal* smarmy, slimy, bootlicking, forelock-tugging, phoney, sucky, soapy; *N. Amer. informal* brown-nosing, apple-polishing; *Brit. vulgar slang* arse-licking, bum-sucking; *N. Amer. vulgar slang* ass-kissing, kiss-ass; *rare* saponaceous, pinguid.
OPPOSITES blunt, no-nonsense.

undaunted ▶ adjective *despite the tempest the crews were undaunted* **unafraid**, undismayed, unalarmed, unflinching, unshrinking, unabashed, unfaltering, unflagging, fearless, dauntless, intrepid, bold, valiant, brave, stout-hearted, lionhearted, courageous, heroic, gallant, doughty, plucky, game, mettlesome, gritty, steely, indomitable, resolute, determined, confident, audacious, daring, daredevil; *informal* gutsy, spunky, ballsy, feisty, cocky.
OPPOSITES afraid, fearful.

undecided ▶ adjective **1** *her father's fate was still undecided* **unresolved**, yet to be decided, uncertain, unsure, unclear, unsettled, indefinite; **undetermined**, indeterminate, unknown, unestablished, unascertained, pending, outstanding, in the balance, up in the air, debatable, arguable, disputable, moot, problematic, controversial, open to question, open to doubt, open, doubtful, dubious, borderline, ambiguous, vague; *informal* iffy, on the back burner, on ice; *Brit. informal* dodgy.
OPPOSITES decided, sealed.
2 *they remained undecided as to the precise role for the EC* **unsure**, uncertain, doubtful, dubious, unresolved, indecisive, irresolute, hesitant, tentative, wavering, vacillating, oscillating, equivocating, dithering, uncommitted, floating, shilly-shallying, wobbling, vague, hazy, unclear, ambivalent, in two minds, torn, split; in a quandary, in a dilemma, on the horns of a dilemma, in doubt; *informal* iffy, blowing hot and cold, on the fence.
OPPOSITE certain.

undefined ▶ adjective **1** *the contract leaves some matters undefined* **unspecified**, unexplained, non-specific, unspecific, indeterminate, undetermined, unfixed, unsettled; unclear, woolly, imprecise, inexact, indefinite, vague.
OPPOSITES specific, definite.
2 *the lights gave a gentle, warm glow with undefined shapes and shadows* **indistinct**, indefinite, formless, indistinguishable, barely perceptible, vague, hazy, misty, shadowy, nebulous, dim, obscure, blurred, blurry, bleary, out of focus.
OPPOSITES distinct, clear.

undemonstrative ▶ adjective *my grandmother was an undemonstrative woman* **unemotional**, unaffectionate, impassive, dispassionate; self-

contained, restrained, reserved, unresponsive, unmoved, unloving, unfriendly, unfeeling, passionless, wooden, uncommunicative, unforthcoming, sober, stiff, reticent, guarded, secretive, close, taciturn, aloof, distant, detached, remote, withdrawn; cool, cold, cold-blooded, chilly, frosty, frigid, glacial; *informal* stand-offish, offish.
OPPOSITES demonstrative, gushing.

undeniable ▶ adjective *the force of his theory is undeniable* **indisputable**, indubitable, unquestionable, beyond doubt, beyond question, beyond a shadow of a doubt, inarguable, undebatable, incontrovertible, incontestable, irrefutable, unassailable; **certain**, sure, definite, positive, conclusive, watertight, proven, clear, clear-cut, straightforward, plain, as plain as a pikestaff, transparent, obvious, unmistakable, evident, self-evident, manifest, staring one in the face, patent, marked, pronounced, express, emphatic, categorical, unequivocal, compelling; *rare* irrefragable, apodictic.
OPPOSITES debatable, questionable.

under ▶ preposition **1** *they found the baby under a bush* **beneath**, below, underneath, at the foot/bottom of.
OPPOSITES above, over.
2 *the present rent is just under £1200* **less than**, lower than, smaller than, not so much as, not as much as, below.
OPPOSITES more than, over.
3 *all branch managers are under the retail director* **subordinate to**, junior to, inferior to, secondary to, subservient to, reporting to, answerable to, responsible to, subject to; controlled by, at the mercy of, under the heel of.
OPPOSITES above, over.
4 *forty holiday homes are under construction* **undergoing**, in the process of, receiving.
5 *half of the town was under water* **flooded by**, immersed in, submerged by, sunk in, engulfed by, inundated by, drowned by.
OPPOSITE above.
6 *the finances of the council are under pressure* **subject to**, liable to, bound by, controlled by, constrained by, under the control of, at the mercy of.
▶ adverb *coughing and spluttering she went under* **down**, downward, lower, below, underneath, beneath; underwater, to the bottom.

underclothes ▶ plural noun **underwear**, undergarments, underclothing, lingerie, underlinen, underthings; *informal* undies, frillies, unmentionables; *Brit. informal* smalls.

undercover ▶ adjective *they were arrested after a three-year undercover investigation* **covert**, secret, clandestine, private, confidential, conspiratorial, underground, surreptitious, furtive, cloak-and-dagger, hole-and-corner, hugger-mugger, back-alley, backstair, stealthy, closet; intelligence; hidden, concealed, masked, veiled, shrouded; *informal* hush-hush, sneaky.
OPPOSITES open, overt.

undercurrent ▶ noun **1** *beware the dangerous undercurrents in the cove* **undertow**, underflow, underswell, underdrift, understream, undertide, underrun; *Nautical* underset; *rare* underwork.
2 *she sensed the undercurrent of despair in what he was saying* **undertone**, overtone, suggestion, connotation, implication, intimation, hint, nuance, trace, suspicion, whisper, murmur, touch, tinge; feeling, atmosphere, aura, tenor, echo, flavour, colouring, vein; vibrations; *informal* vibes; *rare* subcurrent.

undercut ▶ verb **1** *English cloth manufacturers were able to undercut their continental rivals* **charge less than**, charge a lower price than, undersell, underbid.
2 *the company denied that his authority was being undercut* **undermine**, weaken, impair, damage, sap, threaten, subvert, sabotage, ruin, disrupt, undo, destabilize, demolish, wreck, destroy, chip away.

underdog ▶ noun *he particularly relished a political battle when he was the underdog* **weaker party**, victim, prey; loser, scapegoat; *informal* little fellow, little guy, fall guy, stooge.

underestimate ▶ verb **1** *official statistics tend to underestimate the actual volume of economic activity that occurs* **set too low**, underrate; miscalculate, misjudge, judge incorrectly, estimate wrongly, calculate wrongly, be wrong about, misconstrue, misread; err, be wide of the mark.
OPPOSITES overestimate, exaggerate.
2 *his political opponents managed to underestimate his capabilities* **underrate**, rate too low, undervalue, set little/no store by, not do justice to, do an injustice to, be wrong about, sell short, play down, understate; minimize, de-emphasize, underemphasize, diminish, downgrade, deflate, reduce, lessen, brush aside, gloss over, trivialize; hold cheap, shrug off, belittle; *rare* misprize, minify.
OPPOSITES overestimate, overrate, exaggerate.

undergo ▶ verb *she had to undergo a ferocious and lengthy cross-examination* **go through**, **experience**, engage in, undertake, live through, face, encounter, submit to, be subjected to, come in for, receive, sustain, endure, brave, bear, tolerate, stand, withstand, put up with, weather, support, brook, suffer, cope with; *Scottish* thole; *Brit. informal* wear.

underground ▶ adjective **1** *they drove up the ramp from the underground car park* **subterranean**, subterrestrial, below ground, buried, sunken, lower-level, basement; *rare* hypogean.
OPPOSITES surface; overhead.
2 *the underground organizations are designed to spread populist propaganda* **clandestine**, secret, surreptitious, covert, undercover, private, confidential, closet, hole-and-corner, cloak-and-dagger, hugger-mugger, back-alley, backstair, stealthy, conspiratorial, concealed, hidden, shrouded; sneaky, sly, underhand, shifty, furtive; resistance, subversive, guerrilla, mercenary, revolutionary, rebellious, dissident, insurgent, insurrectionary, renegade, mutinous; *informal* hush-hush.
3 *the New York underground art scene* **alternative**, radical, revolutionary, unconventional, unorthodox, avant-garde, experimental, innovative, groundbreaking, pioneering, novel; subversive.
▶ adverb **1** *the insects spend years underground as larvae* **below ground**, below the surface, under the earth, in the earth.
2 *the group went underground and issued calls for national resistance* **into hiding**, into secrecy, into seclusion, undercover, behind closed doors, out of sight.
▶ noun **1** *he took the underground back to his studio apartment* **underground railway**, metro; *N. Amer.* subway; *Brit. informal* tube.
2 *the information had been furnished by the French underground* **resistance movement**, resistance, illegal opposition; partisans, guerrillas, freedom fighters; (*in France, historical*) Maquis.

undergrowth ▶ noun *she groped her way through the thick undergrowth* **shrubbery**, vegetation, greenery, ground cover, underwood, copsewood, brushwood, brush, scrub, underscrub, cover, covert, thicket, copse, coppice, wood, jungle; bushes, plants, weeds, brambles; *N. Amer.* underbrush, underbush, shin-tangle; *SE English* frith; *archaic* rone; *rare* herbage, verdure.

underhand ▶ adjective *he was accused of employing underhand tactics* **deceitful**, underhanded, dishonest, dishonourable, disreputable, unethical, unprincipled, immoral, unscrupulous, fraudulent, cheating, dubious, dirty, unfair, treacherous, duplicitous, double-dealing, below the belt, two-timing, two-faced, unsporting, unsportsmanlike; devious, calculating, artful, crafty, cunning, conniving, scheming, designing, sly, wily, guileful, tricky; criminal, illegal, unlawful, nefarious; **secret**, secretive, clandestine, surreptitious, sneaky, sneaking, furtive, covert, veiled, shrouded, cloak-and-dagger, hugger-mugger, hole-and-corner, hidden, back-alley, backstairs, under the table, conspiratorial; *N. Amer.* snide, snidey; *informal* crooked, shady, bent, low-down, murky, fishy; *Brit. informal* dodgy; *Austral./NZ informal* shonky; *S. African informal* slim.
OPPOSITES honest, fair, above board.

underline ▶ verb **1** *she underlined the important words* **underscore**, mark, pick out, emphasize, highlight; italicize.
2 *the programme will underline the health benefits of white meat* **emphasize**, give emphasis to, stress, put/lay stress on, highlight, accentuate, accent, call/draw attention to, focus (attention) on, zero in on, spotlight, throw into relief, give prominence to, bring to the fore, foreground, bring home, point up, play up, make a feature of; *informal* rub in.
OPPOSITES play down, minimize.

underling ▶ noun *he dishes out orders to his underlings* **subordinate**, inferior, deputy, junior, assistant, adjutant, aide, minion, lackey, flunkey, menial, retainer, vassal, subject, serf, hireling, servant, henchman, myrmidon, right-hand man/woman, girl/man Friday, factotum, stooge; follower, camp follower, hanger-on, disciple; *informal* sidekick, dogsbody, skivvy; *N. Amer. informal* gofer, peon; *archaic* scullion, servitor.
OPPOSITES boss, leader.

underlying ▶ adjective **1** *he took issue with the underlying aims of the research* **fundamental**, basic, basal, primary, prime, first, cardinal, central, principal, chief, key, elementary, elemental, rudimentary, root, intrinsic, essential.
OPPOSITE subordinate.
2 *she spoke airily despite an underlying feeling of irritation* **latent**, lurking, repressed, suppressed, unrevealed, undisclosed, unexpressed, undivulged, concealed, hidden, veiled, masked, shrouded, under wraps.
OPPOSITE overt.

undermine ▶ verb **1** *the integrity of government statistics is being undermined* **subvert**, sabotage, threaten, weaken, compromise, diminish, reduce, impair, mar, spoil, ruin, impede, hinder, damage, hurt, injure, cripple, disable, enfeeble, sap, shake; whittle away, eat away; *informal* foul up, botch, put the kibosh on, drag through the mud; *Brit. informal* throw a spanner in the works of, queer the pitch of; *N. Amer. informal* throw a monkey wrench in the works of.
OPPOSITES enhance, improve, strengthen.
2 *we had no other way to break in but by undermining the building* **tunnel under**, dig under, burrow under, excavate, sap.
3 *the damp had so undermined the structure that the wall fell down* **erode**, wear away, eat away at, chip away, undercut.
OPPOSITES shore up, support.

underprivileged ▶ adjective *the charity arranges holidays for underprivileged children* **needy**, **deprived**, in need, in want, in distress, disadvantaged, needful, poor, destitute, in reduced circumstances, in straitened

U

circumstances, impoverished, poverty-stricken, penurious, indigent, as poor as a church mouse, unable to keep the wolf from the door; *Brit.* on the breadline, without two pennies/brass farthings to rub together; *informal* on one's uppers, on one's beam-ends; *rare* pauperized, beggared, necessitous.
OPPOSITES privileged, wealthy, well off.

underrate ▸ verb *most of us have a tendency to underrate our own skills* **undervalue**, underestimate, set little store by, rate too low, not do justice to, do an injustice to, be wrong about, sell short, play down, understate, minimize, de-emphasize, underemphasize, diminish, downgrade, reduce, lessen, brush aside, gloss over, trivialize; *rare* misprize, minify.
OPPOSITES overrate, exaggerate.

undersized ▸ adjective *a skinny, undersized 15-year-old* **underdeveloped**, **stunted**, small, short, little, tiny, petite, small-boned, slight, compact, minuscule, miniature, mini, diminutive, dwarf, dwarfish, elfin, pygmy, bantam, homuncular, Lilliputian, runtish, puny; *Scottish* wee; *informal* pint-sized, half-pint, pocket-sized, knee-high to a grasshopper, baby, teeny, teeny-weeny, teensy-weensy, itsy-bitsy.
OPPOSITES enormous, overgrown.

understand ▸ verb **1** *he couldn't understand anything we said to him* **comprehend**, apprehend, grasp, see, take in, perceive, discern, make out, puzzle out, recognize, keep up with, master, get to know, follow, fathom, get to the bottom of, penetrate, divine, interpret, unravel, decipher, see the light about, envisage; *informal* get the hang of, get the drift of, catch on to, latch on to, tumble to, crack, make head or tail of, figure out, dig, get, get one's head around, wrap one's mind around, see daylight, get the picture, get the message; *Brit. informal* twig, suss out, suss; *N. Amer. informal* savvy; *rare* cognize.
OPPOSITES misunderstand, misinterpret.
2 *Suzanne understood how hard her husband had worked* **appreciate**, recognize, realize, acknowledge, know, be aware of, be conscious of, be cognizant of, accept; commiserate with, feel compassionate towards, sympathize with, empathize with; *informal* take on board, be wise to.
OPPOSITE ignore.
3 *I understand that you wish to take legal action* **believe**, be led to believe, be given to understand, think, conclude, come to the conclusion, deduce, infer, draw the inference, assume, surmise, fancy; gather, take it, hear, hear tell, be informed, notice, see, learn, discover.

understandable ▸ adjective **1** *he made me rewrite the book to make it understandable to non-scientists* **comprehensible**, easy to understand, intelligible, penetrable, fathomable, graspable, lucid, coherent, clear, crystal clear, explicit, unambiguous, transparent, plain, straightforward, digestible, user-friendly; perspicuous.
OPPOSITES incomprehensible, unfathomable.
2 *parents have a wholly understandable desire for their children to be happy* **unsurprising**, expected, to be expected, predictable, foreseeable, inevitable; **reasonable**, acceptable, logical, rational, normal, natural, par for the course, explicable, explainable, conceivable, imaginable, thinkable, plausible, tenable; justifiable, justified, admissible, allowable, accountable, defensible, excusable, pardonable, forgivable; *informal* on the cards.
OPPOSITES surprising, mysterious.

understanding ▸ noun **1** *the aim of the examination is to test basic understanding of the written language* **comprehension**, apprehension, grasp, grip, mastery, perception, discernment, appreciation, interpretation, cognizance, ken, conception, digestion, assimilation, absorption; knowledge, awareness, consciousness; insight into, familiarity with, acquaintance with; skill in, expertise in, proficiency in; *informal* know-how.
OPPOSITES ignorance; misunderstanding.
2 *a young man of brilliant understanding and great eloquence* **intellect**, intelligence, mind, brainpower, capability, insight, judgement, sense, reason, reasoning; intuition, shrewdness, sharpness, quickness, acumen, sagacity, perspicacity, wisdom, wit; thought, mentality; brains, powers of reasoning/intuition; *French* savoir faire; *informal* grey matter, nous, savvy, know-how.
3 *it was my understanding that because of the war there would be no ceremonies* **belief**, perception, view, notion, idea, conclusion, conviction, feeling, opinion, intuition, impression, assumption, supposition, postulation, way of thinking, point of view; suspicion, sneaking suspicion, hunch, funny feeling.
4 *he always treated me with great kindness and understanding* **compassion**, sympathy, pity, empathy, feeling, concern, considerateness, consideration, tenderness, tender-heartedness, kindness, kind-heartedness, sensitivity, insight, fellow feeling, brotherly love, neighbourliness, decency, humanity, humanitarianism, humaneness, charity, goodwill, mercy, mercifulness, gentleness, tolerance, lenience, leniency, warmth, warm-heartedness, affection, love.
OPPOSITES ignorance, indifference.
5 *we had a tacit understanding that we would keep it secret* **agreement**, gentleman's agreement, arrangement, deal, bargain, settlement, pledge, promise, pact, compact, contract, concord, treaty, covenant, bond.

▸ adjective *he's a very good and understanding friend* **compassionate**, sympathetic, sensitive, considerate, tender, kind, kindly, kind-hearted, thoughtful, tolerant, patient, forbearing, lenient, merciful, forgiving, humane, human, good-natured, approachable, supportive, reassuring; tactful, diplomatic, perceptive, subtle, prudent.

understate ▸ verb *we have been guilty of understating the size of the problem* **play down**, downplay, make light of, underrate, rate too low, not do justice to, do an injustice to, underplay, de-emphasize, underemphasize, trivialize, minimize, diminish, downgrade, reduce, lessen, brush aside, gloss over, shrug off; *informal* soft-pedal, sell short; *rare* misprize, minify.
OPPOSITES overstate, exaggerate, emphasize.

understatement ▸ noun *to say I am delighted is an understatement* | *he spoke with a delightful degree of understatement* **minimization**, trivialization, euphemism; understatedness, restraint, reserve, underplaying, underemphasis; subtlety, delicacy; *technical* litotes, meiosis.
OPPOSITES overstatement, exaggeration.

understudy ▸ noun *he muffed his lines and was often replaced by an understudy* **stand-in**, substitute, replacement, reserve, fill-in, locum, proxy, backup, relief, standby, supply, surrogate, stopgap, second, alternative, ancillary; *Latin* locum tenens; *informal* sub; *N. Amer. informal* pinch-hitter.
▸ verb *the director allowed him to understudy the leading actor* be ready to stand in for, learn someone's part (as well as one's own).

undertake ▸ verb *the team were asked to undertake a further project* **tackle**, take on, take on oneself, take up, accept, shoulder, handle, assume, manage, deal with, take responsibility for, be responsible for; engage in, become involved in, take part in, participate in, devote oneself to, concentrate on, address oneself to, turn one's hand to, go about, set about, approach, get down to, get to grips with; launch into, enter on, begin, start, embark on, venture on; attempt, try, endeavour; *informal* get cracking on, have a crack/go/shot/stab at, give something a whirl; *formal* commence, essay.
OPPOSITES neglect, forgo.

undertaker ▸ noun *the undertaker brought the coffin to our house* **funeral director**; *N. Amer.* **mortician**; *archaic* upholder, blackmaster, cold cook, death-hunter; *rare* thanatologist.

undertaking ▸ noun **1** *why did you get involved in such a risky undertaking?* **enterprise**, venture, project, campaign, scheme, plan, operation, endeavour, effort, task, assignment, charge, activity, pursuit, exploit, job, business, affair, procedure, proceeding, process, transaction; mission, quest, exploration, expedition.
2 *all students shall sign an undertaking to comply with the regulations of the university* **pledge**, agreement, promise, oath, covenant, vow, word, word of honour, solemn word, bond, commitment, guarantee, assurance, warrant, contract, compact.

undertone ▸ noun **1** *he said something in an undertone to the woman at his side* **low voice**, murmur, whisper, mutter; low tones, hushed tones.
OPPOSITE shout.
2 *she was deeply affected by the story's dark undertones* **undercurrent**, hint, overtone, suggestion; **connotation**, nuance, intimation, inkling, insinuation, implication, trace, suspicion, tinge, touch, vein, breath, whiff, whisper, glimmer, atmosphere, aura, tenor, flavour, colouring, shade, smack; *rare* subcurrent.

undervalue ▸ verb *the enthusiasm and initiative of youth was often undervalued by the older generation* **underrate**, set little store by, rate too low, think too little of, underestimate, not do justice to, do an injustice to, play down, understate, underemphasize, de-emphasize, diminish, minimize, downgrade, reduce, lessen, brush aside, gloss over, shrug off, trivialize; belittle, hold cheap; *informal* sell short; *rare* misprize, minify.
OPPOSITE overrate.

underwater ▸ adjective *there are some underwater caves nearby* **undersea**, submarine, sub-aquatic, subaqueous; **submerged**, immersed, sunken.

underwear ▸ noun. *See centre pages for list of* **Underwear**

underworld ▸ noun **1** *vagrants were forced into the violent underworld of Southwark* **criminal world**, world of crime, organized crime; criminals, gangsters; *informal* gangland, mob, mobsters.
2 *Osiris, the god of the underworld* **the netherworld**, the land/abode of the dead, the infernal regions, the nether regions, hell, the abyss; the abode of the damned, eternal damnation, eternal punishment, perdition; *Biblical* Gehenna, Tophet, Abaddon; *Judaism* Sheol; *Greek Mythology* Hades, Tartarus, Acheron; *Roman Mythology* Avernus; *Scandinavian Mythology* Niflheim; *Brit.* the other place; *literary* the pit, the shades; *archaic* the lower world.
OPPOSITES heaven, paradise.

WORD LINKS
relating to the underworld **Plutonic**

underwrite ▸ verb **1** *the London-based company which underwrote the deal has crashed* **sponsor**, support, back, insure, indemnify, provide security for, take the risk for, subsidize, contribute to, pay for, provide capital for, finance, fund; **sanction**, agree to, approve, confirm, ratify, validate, authenticate, certify, seal, guarantee, warrant, accredit; *informal* foot the bill for, pick up the tab for; *N. Amer. informal* bankroll.

U

2 *(archaic) a letter signed by his Lordship and underwritten by myself* **sign**, countersign, subscribe, inscribe, initial, autograph, witness, endorse; put one's mark on; *Law* set one's hand to; *archaic* style, side-sign; *rare* chirographate.

undesirable ▶ **adjective 1** *a mix of medicines may result in undesirable side effects* **unpleasant**, disagreeable, nasty, unacceptable, unwelcome, unwanted, unwished-for, unenviable, unappealing; unfortunate, infelicitous.
OPPOSITES desirable, pleasant, preferable.
2 *William had been involved with some very undesirable people* **unpleasant**, disagreeable, distasteful, displeasing, unacceptable, off-putting, obnoxious; **nasty**, disgusting, awful, terrible, dreadful, frightful, repulsive, repellent, repugnant, revolting, abhorrent, loathsome, hateful, detestable, reprehensible, deplorable, appalling, insufferable, intolerable, despicable, contemptible, beyond the pale, odious, vile, obscene, foul, unsavoury, unpalatable, sickening, nauseating, nauseous, noxious; *informal* ghastly, horrible, horrid; *Brit. informal* beastly; *archaic* disgustful, loathly; *rare* exceptionable, rebarbative.
OPPOSITES pleasant, agreeable, acceptable.

undignified ▶ **adjective** *there was an undignified scramble for seats on the train* **unseemly**, demeaning, unbecoming, ungentlemanly, unladylike, unworthy, unfitting, unbefitting, degrading, debasing, cheapening, belittling, lowering, shaming, shameful, humiliating, mortifying, dishonourable, ignominious, discreditable, ignoble, inglorious, unceremonious, scandalous, disgraceful, indecent, untoward, unsuitable, abject, sorry, low, base, wretched; *informal* infra dig.
OPPOSITES dignified, seemly.

undisciplined ▶ **adjective 1** *the school said that his kid was lazy and undisciplined* **unruly**, disorderly, disobedient, badly behaved, obstreperous, recalcitrant, refractory, intractable, wilful, wayward, delinquent, perverse, naughty, contrary, rebellious, mutinous, insubordinate, disruptive, turbulent, errant, out of hand, out of control; uncontrolled, uncontrollable, unrestrained, ungovernable, wild, capricious, unsteady, untrained, unschooled; *Brit. informal* stroppy, bolshie; *archaic* contumacious.
OPPOSITES disciplined, well behaved.
2 *nobody knew how undisciplined she had been with her money* **disorganized**, unorganized, erratic, unsystematic, unmethodical, disorderly, chaotic, random, irregular, haphazard, in disarray, confused, muddled, jumbled; lax, slapdash, slipshod, sloppy; *informal* all over the place; *Brit. informal* shambolic, all over the shop; *N. Amer. informal* all over the map, all over the lot.
OPPOSITES orderly, organized.

undisguised ▶ **adjective** *he regarded her with undisguised affection* **obvious**, evident, patent, manifest, transparent, open, overt, unconcealed, unhidden, unrestrained, unmistakable, undeniable, plain, plain to see, as plain as a pikestaff, straightforward, frank, clear, clear-cut, as clear as day, explicit, naked, palpable, visible, recognizable, observable, writ large; blatant, barefaced, flagrant, glaring, bold, bald, stark, pointed, out-and-out, brazen, shameless, audacious; *informal* as plain as the nose on one's face, standing/sticking out like a sore thumb, standing/sticking out a mile, right under one's nose.
OPPOSITES disguised, hidden, imperceptible.

undisputed ▶ **adjective** *his military pre-eminence was undisputed* **undoubted**, uncontested, unchallenged, unquestioned, not in question, unquestionable, indubitable, not in doubt, incontrovertible, incontestable, unequivocal, undeniable, irrefutable, unmistakable, sure, certain, clear, clear-cut, manifest, decided, definite, confirmed, absolute, accepted, acknowledged, recognized, positive.
OPPOSITES disputed, doubtful.

undistinguished ▶ **adjective** *he had an undistinguished career as a lecturer in mathematics* **run-of-the-mill**, ordinary, middle-of-the-road, average, common, commonplace, everyday, workaday, quotidian, pedestrian, suburban, mundane, mediocre, humdrum, prosaic, lacklustre, unexceptional, indifferent, forgettable, unmemorable, uninspired, unimpressive, unexciting, unspectacular, uneventful, unremarkable, inconsequential, unnoticeable, inconspicuous, characterless, featureless, nondescript, plain, simple, fair, not bad, passable, all right, middling, moderate; hackneyed, trite, jejune; *N. Amer.* garden-variety; *informal* nothing special, no big deal, no great shakes, nothing to write home about, nothing to get excited about, not so hot, not up to much, not much cop, OK, okay, so-so, bog standard, (plain) vanilla, fair-to-middling, a dime a dozen; *Brit. informal* common or garden; *N. Amer. informal* ornery, bush-league; *Austral./NZ informal* half-pie.
OPPOSITES distinguished, remarkable, extraordinary.

undivided ▶ **adjective** *they need the undivided attention of a sympathetic listener* **complete**, full, total, whole, entire, out-and-out, absolute, unqualified, unadulterated, unalloyed, unreserved, unmitigated, unshared, unbroken, solid, consistent, thorough, concentrated, exclusive, dedicated, wholehearted, sincere, consummate; undistracted, focused, engrossed, absorbed, attentive, committed.
OPPOSITES divided, distracted.

undo ▶ **verb 1** *Gerald undid another button of his waistcoat* **unfasten**, unbutton, unhook, untie, unlace; unbind, unfetter, unshackle, unmanacle, unbridle, unlock, unbolt, uncouple, unhitch, unlink, loosen, loose, disentangle, disentwine, extricate, release, detach, free, set free, liberate, open, unseal, unwrap, let out; disconnect, disjoin, disengage, disunite, separate.
OPPOSITES fasten, do up.
2 *the British government has just refused to undo a decision by the law lords* **revoke**, overrule, overturn, repeal, rescind, reverse, retract, take back, rule against, disallow, veto, countermand, cancel, annul, nullify, render null and void, invalidate, render invalid, negate, abrogate, disestablish, make ineffective, set aside, do away with, wipe out, bring to an end; *Law* avoid, vacate; *archaic* recall; *rare* disannul.
OPPOSITE ratify.
3 *the action of one individual can undo much of the good work done by others* **ruin**, undermine, put an end to, put at risk, subvert, overturn, topple, scupper, scotch, sabotage, spoil, mess up, make a mess of, quash, squelch, crush, harm, cripple, impair, mar, destroy, devastate, play havoc with, wreck, smash, shatter, annihilate, eradicate, obliterate, defeat; cancel out, neutralize, render ineffective; thwart, upset, foil, frustrate, hamper, hinder, obstruct; *informal* botch, blow, put the kibosh on, foul up, muck up, louse up, blow a hole in, do for; *Brit. informal* cock up, throw a spanner in the works of; *N. Amer. informal* rain on someone's parade, throw a monkey wrench in the works of; *vulgar slang* bugger up, fuck up, balls up; *archaic* bring to naught.
OPPOSITES further, enhance, help.

undoing ▶ **noun 1** *she was constantly plotting the king's undoing* **downfall**, defeat, conquest, vanquishing, toppling, deposition, ousting, unseating, overthrow, ruin, ruination, destruction, annihilation, elimination, end, collapse, failure, loss of power, debasement; nemesis, Waterloo; *rare* labefaction.
OPPOSITES betterment, preferment.
2 *their complacency was to be their undoing* **fatal flaw**, Achilles heel, weakness, weak point/spot, (soft) underbelly, failing, blight, misfortune, affliction, trouble, curse.
OPPOSITE making.

undone ▶ **adjective 1** *some improvement work was to be left undone due to the cost* **unfinished**, incomplete, half-done; not started, not done, unaccomplished, unperformed, unexecuted, unfulfilled, unconcluded, unattended to, omitted, neglected, passed over, disregarded, ignored, left, remaining, outstanding, deferred, pending, on ice, awaiting attention, (up) in the air; *informal* on the back burner.
OPPOSITES finished, complete.
2 *she had lost her one advantage and would be utterly undone* **done for**, finished, ruined, destroyed, doomed, lost, defeated, beaten, foiled, frustrated, thwarted; *informal* washed up.
OPPOSITES successful, established.

undoubted ▶ **adjective** *there has been an undoubted improvement in VDU design* **undisputed**, uncontested, unchallenged, unquestioned, not in question, unquestionable, indubitable, not in doubt, incontrovertible, irrefutable, incontestable, unequivocal, sure, certain, obvious, evident, unmistakable, transparent, manifest, patent; **definite**, confirmed, accepted, acknowledged, recognized, positive, clear-cut.
OPPOSITES doubtful, possible.

undoubtedly ▶ **adverb** *they are undoubtedly guilty* **doubtless**, indubitably, doubtlessly, no doubt, without (a) doubt, beyond (a) doubt, beyond the shadow of a doubt; unquestionably, beyond question, indisputably, undeniably, incontrovertibly, irrefutably; unequivocally, clearly, plainly, obviously, patently, positively, absolutely, certainly, with certainty; decidedly, definitely, surely, assuredly, of course, indeed.
OPPOSITE possibly.

undress ▶ **verb 1** *he undressed and got into bed* **take one's clothes off**, strip, strip naked, disrobe, remove one's clothes, doff one's clothes, shed one's clothes, uncover oneself; *informal* peel off; *dated* divest oneself of one's clothes.
2 *she undressed the little boy* **take someone's clothes off**, strip, unclothe, disrobe; *dated* divest someone of their clothes; *literary* disarray.
▶ **noun** *she was wandering about her bedroom in a state of undress* **nudity**, nakedness, bareness; *French* déshabillé; *informal* one's birthday suit.

undressed ▶ **adjective 1** *he was undressed and ready for bed* **naked**, nude, stark naked, bare, unclothed, unclad, stripped, denuded, disrobed, undraped, with nothing on, exposed; *French* au naturel; *informal* in one's birthday suit, without a stitch on, in the raw, in the altogether, in the buff, in the nuddy, mother naked; *Brit. informal* starkers; *N. Amer. informal* bare-assed, buck naked; *Brit. vulgar slang* bollock-naked.
OPPOSITES dressed, clothed.
2 *a rough undressed stone slab* **untreated**, unprocessed, unprepared, unfinished, raw, rough, natural.

undue ▶ **adjective** *make sure that you can afford the repayments without putting undue strain on your finances* **excessive**, extreme, immoderate, intemperate, disproportionate, inordinate; fulsome, superfluous, too much, too great; uncalled for, unneeded, unnecessary, non-essential, not required, needless; unwarranted, unjustified, unreasonable;

inappropriate, unmerited, unsuitable, unseemly, unbecoming, improper, ill-advised.
OPPOSITES due, appropriate, proper.

undulate ▶ verb *the land undulates between 200 and 250 feet above sea level | dark shapes undulated through the jungle* **rise and fall**, surge, wave, billow, roll, swell, ripple, heave, flow, wind, swing, whirl, wobble, oscillate.

unduly ▶ adverb *that may seem an unduly harsh judgement* **excessively**, immoderately, intemperately, disproportionately, out of all proportion, inordinately; superfluously, too, overly, overmuch; unnecessarily, needlessly; unwarrantedly, unjustifiably, unreasonably; inappropriately, unsuitably, improperly, ill-advisedly.
OPPOSITES duly, appropriately.

undying ▶ adjective *his undying devotion to the club* **abiding**, lasting, enduring, permanent, continuing, constant, perennial, infinite; unceasing, perpetual, ceaseless, incessant, unending, never-ending, unfading; immortal, eternal, deathless, never-dying; indestructible, imperishable, inextinguishable; undiminished, undestroyed; *rare* sempiternal.
OPPOSITES transient, ephemeral; mortal.

unearth ▶ verb **1** *workmen unearthed an ancient artillery shell* **dig up**, excavate, exhume, disinter, bring to the surface, mine, quarry, pull out, root out, scoop out, disentomb, unbury.
OPPOSITE bury.
2 *some recent research has unearthed an interesting fact* **discover**, uncover, find, come across, hit on, strike on, encounter, track down, bring to light, reveal, expose, elicit, turn up, dredge up, ferret out, hunt out, fish out, nose out, sniff out, smell out, take the wraps off.
OPPOSITE cover up.

unearthly ▶ adjective **1** *there was an unearthly chill in that ghastly chamber* **other-worldly**, not of this world, supernatural, preternatural, extraterrestrial, alien; ghostly, spectral, phantom, mysterious, haunted, chilling, spine-chilling, hair-raising, blood-curdling; uncanny, eerie, macabre, strange, weird, unnatural, bizarre; *Scottish* eldritch; *informal* spooky, creepy, scary; *rare* phantasmal, phantasmic.
OPPOSITES normal, mundane.
2 (*informal*) *they rise at some unearthly hour for the long drive* **unreasonable**, preposterous, abnormal, extraordinary, absurd, ridiculous, horrendous, outrageous, unheard of, out of the ordinary; *informal* ungodly, unholy, God-awful.
OPPOSITE reasonable.

uneasy ▶ adjective **1** *the doctor made him feel uneasy* **worried**, anxious, ill at ease, troubled, disturbed, agitated, nervous, tense, overwrought, keyed up, on edge, edgy, apprehensive, restive, restless, fidgety, discomposed, discomfited, perturbed, alarmed, fearful, fraught, upset; uncomfortable, self-conscious, embarrassed, unsettled; *informal* jittery, nervy.
OPPOSITES calm, at ease.
2 *he had an uneasy feeling that it was going to cause trouble* **worrying**, disturbing, troubling, agitating, alarming, dismaying, perturbing, disquieting, unsettling, disconcerting, upsetting.
3 *this victory ensured an uneasy peace for nearly three years* **tense**, awkward, strained, constrained, forced, fraught, precarious, unstable, insecure.
OPPOSITE stable.

uneconomic ▶ adjective *it was uneconomic for landlords to maintain rent-controlled housing* **unprofitable**, uncommercial, unremunerative, non-viable; loss-making, non-paying, non-profit-making, worthless; wasteful, inefficient, unfrugal, improvident, squandering.
OPPOSITES economic, profitable.

uneducated ▶ adjective *the workforce remains largely uneducated and unskilled* **untaught**, unschooled, ill-educated, untutored, untrained, unread, unscholarly, illiterate, unlettered, ignorant, ill-informed, uninformed, lowbrow; uncouth, unsophisticated, uncultivated, uncultured, unaccomplished, unenlightened, philistine, benighted, backward, vulgar, simple; *archaic* rude.
OPPOSITES educated, learned.

unemotional ▶ adjective *professionals should remain detached and unemotional* **reserved**, controlled, undemonstrative, restrained, self-controlled, impersonal, clinical, passionless, emotionless, cold, frigid, cool, calm, composed, collected, {cool, calm, and collected}, cool-headed, level-headed, hard-headed, businesslike, rational, sober, unsentimental, unfeeling, unresponsive, unexcitable, unmoved, unagitated, unruffled, serene, impassive, tranquil, indifferent, apathetic, phlegmatic, stoical, equable, detached, distant, remote, aloof, disinterested, unconcerned.
OPPOSITES emotional, expressive.

unemployed ▶ adjective *he lost his job in February and is still unemployed* **jobless**, out of work, out of a job, not working, between jobs, workless, unwaged, unoccupied, idle; redundant, laid off, sacked, dismissed; on benefit; *Brit.* signing on; *N. Amer.* on welfare, collecting unemployment; *Brit. informal* on the dole, 'resting'; *Austral./NZ informal* on the wallaby track.
OPPOSITES employed, in work.

unending ▶ adjective *she toiled at unending tasks* **endless**, never-ending, without end; **interminable**, perpetual, eternal, infinite, undying, ceaseless, incessant, unceasing, non-stop, uninterrupted, continuous, continual, constant, persistent, unbroken, abiding, unabating, unremitting, unrelenting, relentless, limitless, boundless.
OPPOSITES finite, intermittent.

unendurable ▶ adjective *the heat of the stoves made the kitchen almost unendurable* **intolerable**, unbearable, unacceptable, insufferable, insupportable, not to be borne, more than flesh and blood can stand; oppressive, overwhelming, overpowering, impossible; *informal* too much.
OPPOSITES endurable, bearable.

unenthusiastic ▶ adjective *he was unenthusiastic about the proposal* **indifferent**, apathetic, uninvolved, passive, phlegmatic, half-hearted, lukewarm, tepid, casual, cool, listless, lacklustre, languid, lethargic, offhand, emotionless, cursory, perfunctory, unmoved; *informal* unenthused; *rare* Laodicean.
OPPOSITES enthusiastic, keen.

unenviable ▶ adjective *he had the unenviable task of trying to reconcile their disparate interests* **disagreeable**, unpleasant, undesirable, difficult, nasty, horrible, painful, thankless; unwanted, uncoveted, unwished-for.
OPPOSITES enviable, desirable.

unequal ▶ adjective **1** *they are unequal in length* **different**, differing, dissimilar, unlike, unalike, unidentical, disparate, not uniform, unmatched, not matching; uneven, unbalanced, asymmetrical, unsymmetrical, lopsided, irregular, random, fluctuating, varying, variable.
OPPOSITES equal, identical.
2 *the unequal distribution of wealth* **unfair**, unjust, random, disproportionate, inequitable, biased, prejudiced.
OPPOSITE fair.
3 *the interlopers soon gave up the unequal contest* **one-sided**, uneven, unfair, unjust, inequitable, ill-matched, unbalanced, lopsided.
OPPOSITES equal, fair, evenly balanced, neck and neck.
4 *she suddenly felt **unequal to** the task she had set herself* **inadequate for**, insufficient for, incapable of, unqualified for, unsuited to, unfitted for, incompetent at, not up to, found wanting in; *informal* not cut out for.
OPPOSITES equal, competent.

unequalled ▶ adjective *an unequalled record of five World Cup victories* **unbeaten**, unmatched, matchless, unrivalled, without equal, unsurpassed, unparalleled, without parallel, peerless, incomparable, beyond compare, inimitable, second to none, record, best ever, nonpareil, unique; *French* par excellence.

unequivocal ▶ adjective *the report's advice was unequivocal* **unambiguous**, unmistakable, indisputable, incontrovertible, indubitable, undeniable; clear, clear-cut, crystal clear, plain, well defined, explicit, specific, unqualified, unreserved, categorical, outright, downright, direct, straightforward, blunt, outspoken, candid, point-blank, straight from the shoulder, black and white, positive, certain, decisive, emphatic, absolute, manifest, distinct.
OPPOSITES equivocal, ambiguous, vague.

unerring ▶ adjective *with unerring accuracy he hit the gold* **unfailing**, infallible, unswerving, perfect, flawless, faultless, error-free, impeccable, unimpeachable, sure, true, inevitable, assured, certain, uncanny, deadly, scrupulous, meticulous; *informal* sure fire, spot on, dead.
OPPOSITES fallible, imperfect.

unethical ▶ adjective *it is unethical to produce and market a drug which would harm the patient* **immoral**, amoral, unprincipled, unscrupulous, dishonourable, wrong, dishonest, deceitful, disreputable, unconscionable, fraudulent, dirty, unfair, underhand, devious, slippery, bad, wicked, evil, sinful, iniquitous, corrupt, depraved, villainous; unprofessional, improper, unseemly, unworthy, negligent; *informal* shady, crooked, not cricket; *Brit. informal* dodgy.
OPPOSITES ethical, acceptable.

uneven ▶ adjective **1** *they stumbled over the uneven ground* **bumpy**, rough, lumpy, stony, rocky, potholed, holey, rutted, rutty, pitted, jagged, cragged, craggy, dented, indented, knobby.
OPPOSITES even, flat, smooth.
2 *her uneven yellow teeth* **irregular**, unequal, differing, dissimilar, unlike, unalike, unidentical, unbalanced, lopsided, awry, askew, crooked, asymmetrical, unsymmetrical, disproportionate, not matching.
OPPOSITES even, regular.
3 *an uneven double album* **inconsistent**, variable, varying, changeable, fluctuating, intermittent, wavering, irregular, erratic, patchy, bitty.
OPPOSITE consistent.
4 *an uneven contest | the uneven distribution of land* **one-sided**, unequal, unfair, unjust, inequitable, ill-matched, unbalanced, lopsided; biased, prejudiced, skewed.
OPPOSITES equal, fair.
5 *an uneven number* **odd**, not divisible by two.
OPPOSITE even.

uneventful ▶ adjective *a place where dull people live uneventful lives* **unexciting**, uninteresting, monotonous, unchanging, boring, dull,

tedious, slow, flat, humdrum, routine, bland, insipid, unvaried, ordinary, run-of-the-mill, pedestrian, commonplace, everyday, mundane, predictable, unexceptional, unremarkable, uninspiring, unmemorable.
OPPOSITES eventful, exciting.

unexceptional ▶ adjective *an adequate but unexceptional hotel* **ordinary**, average, typical, common, everyday, run-of-the-mill, middle-of-the-road, stock, mediocre, so-so, pedestrian, unremarkable, undistinguished, indifferent, unimpressive; adequate, acceptable, tolerable, decent, unpretentious; *informal* OK, nothing special, nothing to write home about, no great shakes, not much cop, fair-to-middling, bog standard.
OPPOSITES exceptional, noteworthy.

unexceptional or unexceptionable?

The clear distinction in meaning between *exceptionable* ('open to objection') and *exceptional* ('out of the ordinary; very good') has become blurred in the negative forms **unexceptionable** and **unexceptional**. Strictly speaking, *unexceptionable* means 'not open to objection', as in *this view is unexceptionable in itself*, while *unexceptional* means 'not outstanding', as in *the hotel was adequate but unexceptional*. However, *unexceptionable* is often used in contexts where it could equally well mean 'ordinary', as in *the food was bland and unexceptionable*.

unexpected ▶ adjective *he received an unexpected invitation from Professor Dobson* **unforeseen**, unanticipated, unpredicted, not bargained for, unlooked for, unhoped for, out of the blue, without warning, without notice; chance, fortuitous, unplanned, serendipitous, adventitious; sudden, abrupt, surprising, startling, astonishing, uncommon, abnormal, extraordinary.
OPPOSITES expected, predictable.

unexpressive ▶ adjective *his big brown eyes were dull and unexpressive* **emotionless**, expressionless, inexpressive, blank, vacant, impassive, inscrutable, deadpan.
OPPOSITE expressive.

unfailing ▶ adjective *he was remembered for his modesty and his unfailing good humour* **constant**, reliable, dependable, steadfast, steady, sure; endless, undying, unfading, inexhaustible, boundless, ceaseless, never-failing, infallible.
OPPOSITES ephemeral; unreliable.

unfair ▶ adjective **1** *an unfair trial* **unjust**, inequitable, prejudiced, biased, discriminatory; preferential, one-sided, unequal, uneven, unbalanced, non-objective, partisan, partial, intolerant, bigoted, coloured, distorted, warped, loaded, weighted, slanted.
OPPOSITES fair, just.
2 *his comments were excessive and unfair* **undeserved**, unmerited, uncalled for, unreasonable, unjustified, unjustifiable, unwarrantable, out of proportion, disproportionate, excessive, extreme, immoderate; *informal* a bit much; *Brit. informal* off, a bit thick.
OPPOSITES fair, justified.
3 *unfair play* **unsporting**, foul, unsportsmanlike, dirty, below the belt, illegal, illegitimate, illicit, underhand, unscrupulous, dishonourable; *informal* crooked, low-down.
OPPOSITES fair, sporting.
4 *I'm being unfair, prattling on like this when you need your rest* **inconsiderate**, thoughtless, insensitive, selfish, mean, unkind, unreasonable, uncharitable, unfeeling, callous.

unfaithful ▶ adjective **1** *she found out that her husband had been unfaithful* **adulterous**, faithless, fickle, untrue, inconstant, flighty; *informal* cheating, two-timing.
OPPOSITE faithful.
2 *you have proved to be an unfaithful member of this community* **disloyal**, treacherous, traitorous, untrustworthy, unreliable, undependable, false, false-hearted, faithless, perfidious, insincere, two-faced, back-stabbing, double-crossing, double-dealing, deceitful; *archaic* recreant.
OPPOSITE loyal.

unfaltering ▶ adjective *he moved with an unfaltering step* **steady**, resolute, resolved, firm, steadfast, fixed, decided, unswerving, unfluctuating, unhesitating, unwavering, unvacillating, untiring, tireless, unflagging, indefatigable, persistent, unyielding, relentless, unremitting, unrelenting, sustained, inexorable, unshakeable.
OPPOSITES faltering, unsteady.

unfamiliar ▶ adjective **1** *a part of the city unfamiliar to him* **unknown**, new, strange, queer, foreign, alien, unheard of, beyond someone's ken.
OPPOSITE familiar.
2 *the unfamiliar sound of a Scottish dance band* **unusual**, uncommon, unconventional, novel, different, exotic, alternative, unorthodox, odd, peculiar, curious, atypical, uncharacteristic, unwonted, abnormal, anomalous, aberrant, out of the ordinary.
OPPOSITE common.
3 *the aim is to encourage investors* **unfamiliar with** *the stock market to trade more freely* **unacquainted with**, unused to, unaccustomed to, unconversant with, unpractised in, inexperienced in, unskilled in, unversed in, uninformed about, unenlightened about, ignorant of, uninitiated in, new to, fresh to, strange to, a stranger to, unaware of; *informal* in the dark about; *rare* nescient of.
OPPOSITE conversant.

unfashionable ▶ adjective *unfashionable clothes* **out of fashion**, out of date, outdated, old-fashioned, outmoded, out of style, dated, behind the times, last year's, yesterday's, unpopular, unstylish, superseded, archaic, obsolete, antiquated; bygone, old-fangled, crusty, olde worlde, prehistoric, antediluvian; *French* passé, démodé; *informal* old hat, out, square, out of the ark.
OPPOSITE fashionable.

unfasten ▶ verb *Ron unfastened his seat belt* **undo**, open, detach, disconnect, remove, untie, unbutton, unzip, loose, loosen, free, separate, disengage, disjoin, uncouple, unwrap, unbind, unhook, unlace, unhitch, untether, unlock, unbolt.
OPPOSITES fasten, do something up, lock.

unfathomable ▶ adjective **1** *the dark unfathomable eyes of a stranger* **inscrutable**, incomprehensible, enigmatic, incalculable, indecipherable, obscure, esoteric, abstruse, puzzling, cryptic, mysterious, mystifying, baffling, deep, profound, secretive.
OPPOSITES comprehensible, penetrable.
2 *a pool of dark, unfathomable water* **deep**, immeasurable, fathomless, unfathomed, unplumbed, unplumbable, bottomless, unsounded, profound.
OPPOSITE shallow.

unfavourable ▶ adjective **1** *his poor turnout received unfavourable comment* **adverse**, critical, hostile, inimical, unfriendly, antagonistic, unsympathetic, negative; opposing, ill-disposed, contrary, discouraging, disapproving, uncomplimentary, unflattering, damaging, injurious, poor, low, bad, antipathetic.
OPPOSITES favourable, positive.
2 *the unfavourable economic climate* **disadvantageous**, adverse, inauspicious, unpropitious, unfortunate, unlucky, unhappy, detrimental, bad, gloomy; unsuitable, inappropriate, inconvenient, inopportune, inapt.
OPPOSITES favourable, advantageous.

unfeeling ▶ adjective *my mother is a cold, unfeeling, and unresponsive woman* **uncaring**, unsympathetic, unemotional, unfriendly, uncharitable; hard-hearted, stony-hearted, with a heart of stone, heartless, hard, harsh, austere, cold, cold-blooded, cold-hearted, callous, cruel, severe, pitiless, ruthless, unforgiving, unpitying, inhumane, brutal, sadistic, inhuman; *informal* hard-boiled, hard-nosed, thick-skinned.
OPPOSITES sympathetic, compassionate.

unfeigned ▶ adjective *he looked at his wife with unfeigned admiration* **sincere**, genuine, real, true, honest, authentic, unaffected, unpretended, unforced, uncontrived, artless, candid, frank, bona fide, earnest, heartfelt, wholehearted, deep, from the heart; *informal* pukka, upfront, on the level; *rare* full-hearted.
OPPOSITES insincere, feigned, pretended.

CHOOSE THE RIGHT WORD

unfeigned, sincere, genuine, unaffected
See SINCERE.

unfettered ▶ adjective *the choice between a planned economy and an unfettered market* **unrestrained**, unrestricted, unconstrained, free, unbridled, untrammelled, unchecked, unconfined, unimpeded, unhampered, uncontrolled, unbound, untied, unchained, unshackled, loose.
OPPOSITES restricted, fettered.

unfinished ▶ adjective **1** *an unfinished essay* **incomplete**, uncompleted, truncated, aborted; partial, undone, half-done, unexecuted, undeveloped, deferred, put off, abandoned; imperfect, unaccomplished, immature, defective, deficient, lacking, wanting, unpolished, unrefined, sketchy, fragmentary, patchy, rough, crude.
OPPOSITES finished, complete.
2 *the door can be supplied unfinished for you to paint yourself* **unpainted**, unvarnished, undressed, untreated, unprocessed, unprepared, raw, rough, natural.
OPPOSITES finished, painted.

unfit ▶ adjective **1** *the video has been deemed* **unfit** *for broadcast* | *a medical board found him* **unfit** *for duty* **unsuitable for**, unsuited to, inappropriate to, ill-suited to, ill-adapted to, unequipped for, inadequate for, unprepared for, unfitted for, not designed for, ineligible for, unworthy of; **incapable of**, incompetent at, unable to do something, not up to, not equal to, not good enough for; unqualified for, untrained for; improper, unbecoming; *informal* not cut out for, not up to scratch.
OPPOSITES fit, suitable, capable.

U

2 *unfit and overweight children* **unhealthy**, out of condition, out of shape, in poor condition, in poor shape, flabby, debilitated, weak, infirm, decrepit.
OPPOSITE fit.

unflagging ▶ adjective *an unflagging commitment to the ideals of peace* **tireless**, persistent, dogged, tenacious, determined, resolute, staunch, single-minded, unremitting, unrelenting, unswerving, unfaltering, unfailing, unending, zealous.
OPPOSITES flagging, inconstant.

unflappable ▶ adjective (*informal*) *I prided myself on being unflappable even in the most chaotic circumstances* **imperturbable**, unexcitable, cool, calm, collected, {cool, calm, and collected}, controlled, self-controlled, self-possessed, cool-headed, level-headed, relaxed, insouciant, serene, stoical, phlegmatic, unmoved; *informal* laid-back, together.
OPPOSITE excitable.

unflattering ▶ adjective **1** *an unflattering review of his new book* **unfavourable**, uncomplimentary, harsh, unsympathetic, critical, attacking, hostile, disapproving, scathing, biting; blunt, candid, honest, stark, realistic, straightforward, outspoken, straight from the shoulder; *informal* warts and all.
OPPOSITES flattering, complimentary.
2 *I wore an unflattering dress* **unattractive**, unbecoming, unsightly, ugly, ugly-looking, plain, hideous; ill-fitting, unsuitable, unsuited, ill-suited.
OPPOSITES flattering, becoming.

unflinching ▶ adjective *they stood together in unflinching determination to win* **resolute**, determined, single-minded, dogged, decided, resolved, firm, persistent, persevering, committed, unshrinking, unshakeable, steady, unwavering, unblinking, immoveable, unflagging, unswerving, unfaltering, untiring, undaunted, fearless, courageous, stalwart.
OPPOSITES unsteady, wavering.

unfold ▶ verb **1** *Ma unfolded the evening paper* **open out**, spread out, stretch out, flatten, straighten out, unfurl, unroll, unravel, uncoil, unwind, extend.
OPPOSITE fold up.
2 *as she unfolded her tale Joanna's face fell* **narrate**, relate, recount, tell, reveal, make known, disclose, divulge, present, communicate, report, recite, portray, elaborate, spell out, give an account of, set forth, set out.
3 *I watched the events unfold* **develop**, evolve, happen, take place, occur, transpire, unroll, emerge, grow, progress, mature, work out, untangle, bear fruit, blossom.

unforeseen ▶ adjective *due to unforeseen circumstances* **unpredicted**, unexpected, unanticipated, unplanned, accidental, unlooked for, unsought, not bargained for, unthought of; sudden, abrupt, surprising, startling, astonishing, abnormal, out of the blue.
OPPOSITES expected, predictable.

unforgettable ▶ adjective *a visit to Morocco is a truly unforgettable experience* **memorable**, indelible, not/never to be forgotten, fixed in the mind, haunting, catchy, persistent; striking, impressive, distinctive, significant, special, outstanding, spectacular, extraordinary, exceptional, remarkable, arresting, singular, signal.
OPPOSITES forgettable, unexceptional.

unforgivable ▶ adjective *he had committed the unforgivable sin—he had informed on his friends* **inexcusable**, unpardonable, unjustifiable, indefensible, reprehensible, outrageous, deplorable, insupportable, despicable, contemptible, disgraceful, shameful; inexpiable, irremissible, unwarrantable, condemnable; mortal, deadly.
OPPOSITES forgivable, unserious; venial.

unfortunate ▶ adjective **1** *today, many unfortunate people have too much enforced leisure* **unlucky**, hapless, out of luck, down on one's luck, luckless, wretched, miserable, forlorn, unhappy, poor, pitiful; ill-starred, ill-fated, ill-omened, star-crossed, jinxed, cursed, doomed.
OPPOSITES fortunate, lucky.
2 *it was a very unfortunate chain of circumstances* **adverse**, disadvantageous, unadvantageous, unfavourable, unlucky, untoward, unwelcome; untimely, unpromising, inauspicious, unpropitious, hostile, tough, hard, inimical, harmful, detrimental, injurious, ruinous, disastrous, calamitous, dire, miserable, distressing, grievous, black, lamentable, tragic, terrible, awful, wretched.
OPPOSITES fortunate, auspicious.
3 *an unfortunate remark* **regrettable**, inappropriate, unsuitable, inapt, infelicitous, tactless, untoward, injudicious.
OPPOSITES tactful, appropriate.

unfortunately ▶ adverb *unfortunately, when my husband mentioned this to his mother all hell broke loose* **unluckily**, sadly, regrettably, unhappily, woefully, lamentably, alas, sad to say, sad to relate; *informal* worse luck.
OPPOSITE luckily.

unfounded ▶ adjective *the article was a piece of unfounded speculation* **groundless**, baseless, unsubstantiated, unproven, unsupported, uncorroborated, untested, unconfirmed, unverified, unattested, unjustified, unwarranted, foundationless, ill-founded, without basis, without foundation, not backed up by evidence; speculative, conjectural, idle, vain, unsound, unreliable, questionable, misinformed, misguided, spurious, specious, fallacious, erroneous, fabricated, untrue, trumped-up.
OPPOSITES well founded, proven, substantiated.

CHOOSE THE RIGHT WORD

unfortunate, unlucky, ill-starred, hapless

These words all express a recognition that something undesirable and probably undeserved has happened to someone, with some degree of sympathy for them. All but *hapless* can describe the event, as well as the person to whom it happens.

- **Unfortunate** is used to acknowledge the unpleasantness of a situation (*the unfortunate Cunningham was sacked | we are just glad the whole unfortunate episode has had a happy ending*). *Unfortunate* can also be used of a regrettable event or situation, often euphemistically ascribing blame (*the Judge was severely reprimanded for a number of unfortunate remarks made by him*).
- Describing someone as **unlucky** lays some emphasis on the element of chance involved in their misfortune (*John and Alison were one of the unlucky couples to have their wedding cancelled | a series of unlucky breakdowns curtailed his career*). *Unlucky* is often used of people who are unsuccessful despite their best efforts (*Cooper was unlucky, coming 11th*).
- **Ill-starred** is seldom found outside self-consciously literary writing and is the only one of these four words to retain any significant sense of fate, with which the stars are often associated; it means 'doomed from the outset' (*Scott's ill-starred Polar expedition | none of my ill-starred relations has ever died by the gun*).
- The pity expressed for a **hapless** person is sometimes tinged with amusement or exasperation. It is strongly hinted that they have contributed to their own misfortune through incompetence or weakness (*a powerful cross which the hapless Robinson diverted into his own net | some documents were lost by hapless temps*). The similarity in sound of 'hopeless' and 'helpless' may have played a part in the development of this implication. Often, the victim's inability to improve their plight is emphasized (*the hapless victims of some depraved international conspiracy*).

unfriendly ▶ adjective **1** *she directed an unfriendly look at Harold* **hostile**, disagreeable, misanthropic, antagonistic, aggressive; ill-natured, unpleasant, surly, sour, inimical, unamicable, uncongenial; inhospitable, unneighbourly, unwelcoming, unkind, unsympathetic, unaffable; unsociable, unsocial, antisocial; aloof, cold, cool, chilly, frigid, frosty, distant, stand-offish, unapproachable, withdrawn, reserved, unforthcoming, uncommunicative, impersonal, haughty, supercilious, disdainful, indifferent; stiff, stern, severe; ungracious, obnoxious, menacing, nasty; quarrelsome; rude, discourteous, uncivil, impolite, unmannerly, cross; *informal* starchy; *rare* Olympian.
OPPOSITES friendly, amiable.
2 *Mesopotamia was discovered to be unfriendly terrain for military manoeuvres* **unfavourable**, disadvantageous, unpropitious, inauspicious, hostile, inimical, uncongenial, negative, alien, damaging, destructive.
OPPOSITES friendly, favourable.

ungainly ▶ adjective *an uncouth man with an ungainly walk* **awkward**, **clumsy**, ungraceful, graceless, inelegant, gawky, gangling, maladroit, gauche, inept, blundering, bungling, bumbling, lumbering, uncoordinated; inexpert, unskilful, unhandy, oafish, hulking, bovine, like a bull in a china shop; *informal* cack-handed, ham-fisted, ham-handed, butterfingered, all thumbs; *archaic* lubberly.
OPPOSITES graceful, elegant.

ungodly ▶ adjective **1** *blasphemy, whoredom, drunkenness, and other ungodly behaviour* **unholy**, godless, irreligious, impious, blasphemous, sacrilegious, profane, heathen, pagan, atheistic, irreverent; immoral, corrupt, depraved, sinful, wicked, evil, iniquitous, devilish, fiendish, demonic, diabolical, satanic, infernal.
OPPOSITES godly, holy.
2 (*informal*) *he wasn't expecting her at this ungodly hour* **unreasonable**, preposterous, abnormal, extraordinary, absurd, ridiculous, horrendous, outrageous, unheard of; unsocial, antisocial; *informal* unholy, unearthly, God-awful.
OPPOSITE reasonable.

ungovernable ▶ adjective *the country had become ungovernable* **uncontrollable**, unmanageable, anarchic, chaotic, intractable; unruly, disorderly, rebellious, riotous, wild, mutinous, obstreperous, recalcitrant, refractory, undisciplined, disobedient; without law and order.
OPPOSITES orderly, tractable.

ungracious ▶ adjective *it was ungracious not to thank them* **rude**, impolite, uncivil, discourteous, ill-mannered, bad-mannered, unmannerly, uncouth, disrespectful, ungallant, insolent, impertinent, impudent, churlish, boorish, gauche, cavalier, offhand, unladylike, ungentlemanly, blunt, gruff, curt, terse, sharp, short, surly, unfriendly, hostile, unkind,

inconsiderate, insensitive.
OPPOSITES gracious, polite.

ungrateful ▶ adjective *she's so rude and ungrateful for everything we do* **unappreciative**, unthankful, thankless, ungracious.
OPPOSITES grateful, thankful.

unguarded ▶ adjective **1** *an unguarded frontier* **undefended**, unprotected, defenceless, unfortified, unshielded, unarmed; vulnerable, insecure, assailable, open to attack, wide open, exposed, in danger, endangered; unpatrolled, unattended, unwatched; *rare* pregnable.
OPPOSITES guarded, secure.
2 *an unguarded remark* **careless**, ill-advised, ill-considered, incautious, thoughtless, unthinking, rash, foolhardy, foolish, indiscreet, imprudent, injudicious, ill-judged, ill-thought-out, unthought-out, unwise; undiplomatic, misguided, hasty, spur-of-the-moment, hare-brained, inadvertent, insensitive; *rare* temerarious.
3 *in an unguarded moment, Iris had let drop that she was receiving no fee to run the course* **unwary**, inattentive, unobservant, off guard, unmindful, unwatchful, unheeding, heedless, distracted, absent-minded.

unhappiness ▶ noun *I've seen too much unhappiness caused by broken marriages* **sadness**, sorrow, dejection, depression, misery, cheerlessness, downheartedness, despondency, despair, desolation, wretchedness, malaise, glumness, gloom, gloominess, dolefulness; regret, melancholy, low spirits, mournfulness, woe, broken-heartedness, heartache, distress, chagrin, grief, pain, agony, mortification; *informal* the blues, down; *rare* disconsolateness, disconsolation.

unhappy ▶ adjective **1** *an unhappy childhood | she looked tired and unhappy* **sad**, miserable, sorrowful, dejected, despondent, disconsolate, morose, regretful, broken-hearted, heartbroken, down, downcast, dispirited, downhearted, heavy-hearted, crestfallen, depressed, melancholy, blue, gloomy, glum, mournful, despairing, doleful, forlorn, woebegone, woeful, tearful, long-faced, joyless, cheerless, out of sorts; *informal* down in the mouth, down in the dumps, fed up, grumpy; *rare* lachrymose.
OPPOSITES happy, cheerful.
2 *in the unhappy event of litigation* **unfortunate**, unlucky, luckless, hapless, ill-starred, ill-fated, star-crossed, ill-omened, doomed, blighted, wretched, miserable; disadvantageous, adverse; *informal* jinxed.
3 *if you are* **unhappy with** *a new hairstyle, complain to your hairdresser while you are still in the salon* **dissatisfied**, displeased, discontented, disappointed, disgruntled; disapproving of.
4 *indeed, 'disorganized capitalism' seems an unhappy term for conveying what they are dealing with* **inappropriate**, unsuitable, inapt, unfortunate; regrettable, ill-chosen, tactless, ill-advised, injudicious; awkward, clumsy.

unharmed ▶ adjective **1** *negotiators persuaded the man to release his hostage unharmed* **uninjured**, unhurt, unscathed, safe, safe and sound, alive and well, all right, fine, in one piece, without a scratch; *informal* OK.
OPPOSITES harmed, injured.
2 *the saint's tomb was a grey and time-worn block unharmed by the Reformation* **undamaged**, unbroken, unmarred, unspoilt, unsullied, unmarked, unmutilated; sound, intact, perfect, unimpaired, unblemished, unflawed, pristine.
OPPOSITES harmed, damaged.

unhealthy ▶ adjective **1** *she was leading a very unhealthy lifestyle* **harmful**, detrimental, destructive, injurious, damaging, deleterious, ruinous, malign, noxious, poisonous, insalubrious, baleful; risky, dangerous, perilous.
2 *he had a bony face and an unhealthy pallor* **ill-looking**, ill, unwell, in poor health, ailing, sick, sickly, poorly, indisposed, unsound, unfit, weak, feeble, frail, delicate, debilitated, infirm, valetudinarian, washed out, run down, peaky, out of condition/shape, in poor condition/shape.
3 *he had an unhealthy obsession with drugs* **unwholesome**, undesirable, morbid, macabre, ghoulish, twisted, warped, depraved, abnormal, unnatural; *informal* sick.

unheard of ▶ adjective **1** *in those days it was unheard of for a girl to leave her family and become independent* **unprecedented**, exceptional, extraordinary, out of the ordinary, uncommon, unusual, unparalleled, unrivalled, unmatched, unequalled, singular, unique; unthought of, undreamt of, unbelievable, inconceivable, unimagined, unimaginable, unthinkable, implausible, shocking, outrageous; *rare* unexampled.
OPPOSITE common.
2 *we were to play a game unheard of in the UK* **unknown**, unfamiliar, new, little known, undiscovered, obscure, nameless, unsung, unheralded, groundbreaking.
OPPOSITES famous, well known.

unheeded ▶ adjective *my protest went unheeded* **disregarded**, ignored, neglected, overlooked, unobserved, unnoted, unrecognized, disobeyed, unnoticed, passed over, spurned.
OPPOSITES heeded, noted.

unhinged ▶ adjective *Lydia was unhinged with the shock of bereavement* **deranged**, demented, unbalanced, out of one's mind, crazed, mad, insane; lunatic, manic, maniac, berserk, disturbed, distracted, confused; *informal* crazy, mental, potty, bonkers, bats, batty, loopy, bananas, touched, out to lunch, off one's head, off one's rocker.
OPPOSITES sane, stable.

unholy ▶ adjective **1** *a grin of unholy amusement spread across his face* **ungodly**, godless, irreligious, impious, blasphemous, sacrilegious, profane, heathen, pagan, atheistic, irreverent; **wicked**, evil, iniquitous, immoral, corrupt, depraved, sinful, devilish, fiendish, demonic, diabolical, satanic, infernal.
OPPOSITES righteous, holy.
2 *she'd had an unholy row with Mama* **shocking**, dreadful, outrageous, appalling, terrible, horrifying, horrendous, horrific, frightful; *informal* ungodly.
OPPOSITE mild.
3 *an unholy alliance between the Fascists and Communists* **unnatural**, discordant, incompatible, unusual, improbable; hellish, made in hell.

unhoped for ▶ adjective *he had given her an unhoped-for opportunity to go on in a big part* **unexpected**, unanticipated, unforeseen, unpredicted, unlooked-for, unplanned, not bargained for, without warning, without notice; **undreamed of**, out of the blue, beyond one's wildest dreams, like a dream come true; startling, astonishing, surprising, unbelievable.
OPPOSITES expected; unwanted.

unhurried ▶ adjective *he began opening the drawers of his desk in an unhurried way* **leisurely**, unhasty, leisured, easy, easy-going, relaxed, unrushed, slow, slow-moving, slow-going, slow and steady; deliberate, careful, cautious, sedate, measured, calm; gradual, lingering, loitering.
OPPOSITES hurried, hasty.

unhygienic ▶ adjective *animals are kept in cramped and often unhygienic conditions* **insanitary**, unsanitary, dirty, filthy, unclean, impure, contaminated, unhealthy, deleterious, detrimental, harmful, unwholesome, germ-ridden, germy, disease-ridden, infested, insalubrious, noxious, polluted, foul, septic.
OPPOSITES hygienic, sanitary.

unidentified ▶ adjective *he had been followed by unidentified armed men* **unknown**, unnamed, anonymous, incognito, nameless; obscure, unfamiliar, strange, mysterious, unspecified, unmarked, undesignated, unclassified; *rare* innominate.
OPPOSITES identified, known.

unification ▶ noun *the costs of German unification* **union**, merger, fusion, fusing, amalgamation, integration, coalition, junction, combination, consolidation, confederation, federation; synthesis, joining, marrying, marriage; *Greek* enosis.

uniform ▶ adjective **1** *a uniform temperature of between 18 and 21 degrees* **constant**, consistent, steady, invariable, unvarying, unfluctuating, unvaried, unchanging, unwavering, undeviating, stable, static, sustained, regular, fixed, even, equal, equable, monotonous.
OPPOSITES changeable, variable.
2 *cut the vegetables into pieces of uniform size* **identical**, matching, similar, equal; **same**, alike, like, selfsame, homogeneous, consistent, corresponding, equivalent.
OPPOSITES varied, different.
▶ noun *a soldier in uniform* **costume**, livery, regalia, habit, suit, dress, garb, attire, ensemble, outfit; regimentals, colours, garments, trappings; *informal* get-up, rig, gear, togs; *formal* apparel; *literary* raiment; *archaic* vestments.

uniformity ▶ noun **1** *Philip moved to establish greater uniformity in urban law* **constancy**, consistency, conformity, steadiness, invariability, invariableness, stability, regularity, evenness, lack of variation, lack of change, equality, equability.
OPPOSITES variation, changeableness.
2 *there seems to be no uniformity in the size of clothes in shops* **sameness**, likeness, resemblance, alikeness, identicalness, similarity, equality, equalness, homogeneity, homogeneousness, consistency, equivalence, comparability, compatibility, correspondence, agreement, concord, accord, interchangeability, parallelism, symmetry.
OPPOSITES variety, difference.
3 *there was a dull uniformity about the place* **monotony**, tedium, tediousness, lack of variety, dullness, drabness, dreariness, colourlessness, flatness, featurelessness, sameness, humdrumness; *Brit. informal* sameyness.
OPPOSITES diversity, variety.

unify ▶ verb *he unified the confederacy into a powerful entity* **unite**, bring together, join (together), merge, fuse, amalgamate, coalesce, combine, blend, mix, bind, link up, consolidate, integrate, marry, synthesize, federate, weld together.
OPPOSITES separate, split, disunite.

unimaginable ▶ adjective *unimaginable riches* **unthinkable**, inconceivable, incredible, unbelievable, unheard of, unthought of, unspeakable, unutterable, untold, ineffable, implausible, improbable, unlikely, impossible, undreamed of, beyond one's wildest dreams, beyond the realm of reason; astounding, amazing, astonishing, fantastic, fabulous, breathtaking, overwhelming, staggering; *informal* mind-boggling, mind-blowing.

unimaginative ▶ adjective *the production was plodding and unimaginative*

U

uninspired, uninventive, unoriginal, uncreative, unartistic, commonplace, pedestrian, mundane, matter-of-fact, ordinary, usual, routine, humdrum, prosaic, workaday, run of the mill, (plain) vanilla; stale, hackneyed, trite, derived, derivative, conventional, unadventurous, dull, banal, monotonous, lifeless, lacklustre, sterile, uninspiring, spiritless, vapid, insipid, bland, dry, barren, flat, stodgy; *informal* common or garden.
OPPOSITES imaginative, creative, original.

unimpeachable ▶ adjective *this was information that I got from an unimpeachable source* **trustworthy**, reliable, dependable, unquestionable, unassailable, unchallengeable, above suspicion, beyond suspicion; perfect, faultless, blameless, impeccable, irreproachable, unblemished.
OPPOSITES dubious, unreliable.

unimpeded ▶ adjective *he had an unimpeded view of them* **unrestricted**, unconstrained, unhindered, unblocked, unhampered, free, open, clear, unchecked, uninhibited, untrammelled, unlimited.
OPPOSITES impeded, obstructed.

unimportant ▶ adjective *the details are unimportant at this stage* **insignificant**, inconsequential, trivial, minor, slight, trifling, of little/no importance, of little/no consequence, of no account, of no moment, non-essential, immaterial, irrelevant, peripheral, extraneous, not worth mentioning, not worth speaking of, petty, paltry, insubstantial, light, inconsiderable, superficial, inferior, worthless, nugatory, pointless, frivolous; *informal* small-time, piddling, small-fry, no great shakes; *Brit. informal* twopenny-halfpenny, tinpot; *N. Amer. informal* dinky, picayune.
OPPOSITE important.

uninhabited ▶ adjective **1** *much of this land was uninhabited* **unpopulated**, unpeopled, unsettled, unfrequented, unoccupied; barren, desert, desolate, lonely, deserted, depopulated, bare, wild.
2 *an uninhabited hut* **vacant**, empty, unoccupied, untenanted, tenantless, unfilled, to let, free; abandoned, deserted, forsaken.

uninhibited ▶ adjective **1** *the uninhibited dancing of the local people* **unrestrained**, unrepressed, abandoned, wild, impetuous, carefree, reckless; unrestricted, unconstrained, uncontrolled, uncurbed, unchecked, unbridled, intemperate, boisterous, wanton.
OPPOSITES inhibited, controlled.
2 *I'm a pretty uninhibited sort of person* **unreserved**, unrepressed, liberated, unconstrained, unselfconscious, free and easy, relaxed, informal, open, outgoing, extrovert, candid, outspoken, frank, forthright, spontaneous, instinctive, shameless; *informal* upfront.
OPPOSITES inhibited, reserved, repressed.

uninspired ▶ adjective *an album full of uninspired love songs* **unimaginative**, uninventive, pedestrian, mundane, unoriginal, prosaic, commonplace, ordinary, routine, second-rate, undistinguished, unexceptional, indifferent, humdrum, matter-of-fact, run of the mill, workaday, everyday, quotidian, (plain) vanilla; **spiritless**, colourless, passionless, anaemic, stale, hackneyed, trite, derived, derivative, conventional, unadventurous, dull, banal, monotonous, lifeless, lacklustre, sterile, uninspiring, vapid, insipid, bland, dry, barren, flat, stodgy; *informal* common or garden.
OPPOSITE inspired.

uninspiring ▶ adjective *they remained a weak and uninspiring political force* **boring**, dull, dreary, drab, unexciting, unstimulating; dry, insipid, colourless, grey, bland, anaemic, watery, tame, flat, lifeless, lacklustre, tedious, vapid, humdrum, run of the mill, unromantic, jejune, dull as ditchwater, as dry as dust.
OPPOSITES inspiring, exciting.

unintelligent ▶ adjective *he treated me like an erring and somewhat unintelligent son* **stupid**, ignorant, dense, brainless, mindless, foolish, dull-witted, witless, slow, dunce-like, simple-minded, empty-headed, vacuous, vapid, half-witted, idiotic, moronic, imbecilic, imbecile, obtuse; *informal* thick, thick as two short planks, dim, dumb, dopey, dozy, cretinous, birdbrained, pea-brained, wooden-headed, fat-headed.
OPPOSITE intelligent.

unintelligible ▶ adjective **1** *jargon words usually sound ugly and unintelligible to outsiders* **incomprehensible**, indiscernible, meaningless, unfathomable, obscure, cryptic, inscrutable, enigmatic, mumbled, indistinct, unclear, slurred, inarticulate, incoherent, confused, garbled, scrambled, muddled, jumbled, senseless; *informal* all Greek to me.
2 *unintelligible graffiti* **illegible**, indecipherable, unreadable, hard to read, scrawled, scribbled, crabbed.

unintentional ▶ adjective *I assure you, the insult was unintentional* **unintended**, accidental, inadvertent, involuntary, unwitting, unthinking, unmeant, unplanned, unpremeditated, unexpected, unforeseen, fortuitous, chance, coincidental, serendipitous, unconscious, subconscious.
OPPOSITES intentional, deliberate.

uninterested ▶ adjective *Derek was uninterested in politics* **indifferent to**, unconcerned about, uninvolved in/with, incurious about, apathetic towards, bored by, unmoved by, unresponsive to, blasé about, nonchalant about, offhand about, lukewarm about, unenthusiastic about, phlegmatic about; impassive, dispassionate; aloof from, detached from, distant from.
OPPOSITE interested.

uninterested or disinterested?
See DISINTERESTED.

uninteresting ▶ adjective *an uninteresting book about genealogy* **unexciting**, boring, dull, tiresome, wearisome, tedious, dreary, tiring, flat, lifeless, monotonous, humdrum, uneventful, slow, unvaried, repetitious, commonplace, colourless, bland, insipid, banal, dry, pedestrian, prosaic, hackneyed, trite, clichéd, stale; *informal* samey, mind-numbing.
OPPOSITES interesting, exciting.

uninterrupted ▶ adjective *ten hours of uninterrupted sleep* **unbroken**, continuous, continual, undisturbed, steady, constant, sustained, consecutive, successive, in succession, non-stop, without stopping, unceasing, incessant, untroubled, smooth, peaceful; running, solid, straight.
OPPOSITES interrupted, intermittent.

uninvited ▶ adjective **1** *an uninvited guest* **unasked**, unbidden, unwelcome, unwanted, unexpected.
OPPOSITE invited.
2 *uninvited suggestions* **unsolicited**, unrequested, unwanted, not required, unprompted, unsought.
OPPOSITE solicited.

uninviting ▶ adjective *the bed looked cold and uninviting* **unappealing**, untempting, undesirable, unattractive, unappetizing; bleak, cheerless, joyless, dreary, dismal, depressing, grim, comfortless, inhospitable; unpleasant, disagreeable, distasteful, objectionable, offensive, unpalatable, sickening, nauseating, foul; repellent, revolting, repugnant; *informal* off-putting.
OPPOSITES inviting, tempting.

union ▶ noun **1** *the gardens are an example of the union of art and nature* **unification**, uniting, joining, merging, merger, fusion, fusing, amalgamating, amalgamation, junction, coalition, combining, combination, consolidation, conjunction, confederation, federation, integration, synthesis, blend, blending, mixture, mingling, commingling.
OPPOSITES separation, parting.
2 *the crowd moved in union to the beat* **unity**, accord, unison, unanimity, harmony, concord, agreement, concurrence, undividedness.
3 *his daughter's union with the prince* **marriage**, wedding, partnership, pairing, alliance, match, compact, affiliation; **coupling**, intercourse, mating; *formal* coition, coitus, copulation.
OPPOSITES divorce, annulment.
4 *all employees should have the right to be represented by a union* **association**, trade union, alliance, league, guild; coalition, consortium, combine, syndicate, confederation, federation, confederacy, partnership, fraternity, brotherhood, sorority, society, club, group, organization.

unique ▶ adjective **1** *each archaeological site is unique* **distinctive**, individual, special, especial, idiosyncratic, quirky, eccentric, isolated; **single**, sole, lone, unrepeated, unrepeatable, solitary, exclusive, only, one and only, in a class by itself; rare, uncommon, unusual, peculiar, novel, strange, odd; *Latin* sui generis; *informal* one-off.
OPPOSITES common, ordinary.
2 *a unique insight into the history of this beautiful region* **remarkable**, special, singular, noteworthy, notable, signal, outstanding, extraordinary; **unequalled**, without equal, unparalleled, unmatched, matchless, peerless, nonpareil, unsurpassed, unexcelled, incomparable, beyond compare, superior, inimitable, second to none; *rare* unexampled.
OPPOSITE unremarkable.
3 *the two species are* **unique to** *the island* **peculiar**, specific, particular, found only in; characteristic of, typical of.

U

unison ▶ noun
□ **in unison 1** *they lifted their arms in unison* **simultaneously**, at (one and) the same time, (all) at once, at the same moment, (all) together, as one, in concert, in chorus.
2 *both ministers have spoken in complete unison on this* **in agreement**, in accord, in rapport, in harmony, in unity, in concord, in concert, unanimously, in sympathy, in cooperation, as one, identically; in partnership, shoulder to shoulder, side by side, arm in arm, hand in hand.

unit *See centre pages for lists of* **Units** **Currency Units**
▶ noun **1** *the family is the fundamental unit of British society* **component**, part, section, element, constituent, subdivision, portion, segment, module, item, member, ingredient, factor, feature, piece, fragment; entity, whole, discrete item.
2 *the farthing was still a useful unit of currency* **quantity**, measure, measurement, denomination, value.

3 *a guerrilla unit* **detachment**, contingent, outfit, section, division, company, squadron, corps, regiment, brigade, platoon, battalion, force, garrison, legion, formation, crew, squad, detail; cell, faction.

unite ▶ verb 1 *the fight against communism seemed to unite the nation* **unify**, join, link, connect, combine, amalgamate, fuse, integrate, weld, bond, stick together, bring together, knit together; glue, cement, coalesce.
OPPOSITES divide, separate.
2 *environmentalists and union activists united to demand changes* **join together**, join forces, combine, associate, band together, club together, ally, cooperate, collaborate, work together, act together, pull together, get together, team up, go into partnership, work side by side, pool resources; *informal* gang up.
OPPOSITE split.
3 *in his designs he sought to unite comfort with elegance* **merge**, mix, blend, mingle, combine, synthesize, commix, admix, intermix, commingle, homogenize.

united ▶ adjective 1 *a united Germany* **unified**, integrated, consolidated, amalgamated, joined, merged, banded together; federal, federated, confederate.
OPPOSITES divided, separated.
2 *the parties must decide on a united response to the proposals* **common**, shared, joint, combined, corporate, mutual, communal, allied, cooperative, collective, collaborative, aggregate, undivided, solid, consistent, concerted, pooled, cross-party.
OPPOSITE different.
3 *they were united in their views* **in agreement**, agreed, in unison, of the same opinion, of the same mind, of like mind, like-minded, at one, as one, in accord, in concord, unanimous, in sympathy, in rapport, in harmony, in unity, shoulder to shoulder.
OPPOSITES disagreeing, differing.

United States of America ▶ noun **the States**, the land of the free, God's own country; *informal* the US of A; *literary* Columbia.

unity ▶ noun 1 *some officials saw European unity as the solution* **union**, unification, integration, amalgamation; coalition, federation, confederation.
OPPOSITES division, disunity.
2 *their leaders called for unity between opposing factions* **harmony**, accord, concord, concurrence, cooperation, collaboration, agreement, unanimity, consensus, assent, concert, togetherness, solidarity, like-mindedness, peace, synthesis.
OPPOSITES discord, strife.
3 *they believed in the organic unity of the whole universe* **oneness**, singleness, wholeness, entity, integrity, undividedness, cohesion, coherence, congruity, congruence, uniformity, homogeneity, identity, sameness.
OPPOSITE disunity.

universal ▶ adjective *the universal features of language* **general**, **ubiquitous**, comprehensive, common, omnipresent, all-embracing, all-inclusive, all-round, across the board; global, worldwide, international, widespread, blanket, sweeping, rampant, catholic, inescapable, pervading, pervasive, permeating.
OPPOSITES particular, restricted, local.

universally ▶ adverb *it was universally accepted that no man married merely for love* **invariably**, always, without exception, in all instances, in all cases, in every case, in every instance; **everywhere**, worldwide, globally, internationally; broadly, widely, commonly, generally.

universe ▶ noun 1 *the laws of the physical universe* **cosmos**, macrocosm, totality, whole world, Creation, (outer) space, the heavens, the firmament; infinity, all existence.
2 *the ROM chip clearly belongs to the universe of hardware* **province**, world, sphere, preserve, domain, circle, milieu, territory, quarter.

WORD LINKS
relating to the universe **cosmic**
study of the universe **cosmology, astronomy, cosmogony**

U

university ▶ noun **college**, academy, educational establishment/institution, institute, varsity; *N. Amer.* school; *historical* polytechnic.

unjust ▶ adjective 1 *several groups have attacked the report as unjust* **biased**, prejudiced, unfair, inequitable, discriminatory, partisan, preferential, weighted, partial, one-sided, influenced, slanted, bigoted.
OPPOSITES just, fair, balanced.
2 *an unjust law* **wrongful**, wrong, unfair, undue, undeserved, unmerited, unwarranted, uncalled for, unreasonable, gratuitous, unjustifiable, indefensible, groundless, inappropriate.
OPPOSITES just, fair, reasonable.

unjustifiable ▶ adjective 1 *an unjustifiable extravagance* **indefensible**, inexcusable, unforgivable, unpardonable; uncalled for, unprovoked, without justification, without cause, without reason, unreasonable; regrettable, unacceptable, unworthy, remiss, blameworthy, culpable, unwarrantable; excessive, immoderate, unconscionable, outrageous.
OPPOSITES justifiable, reasonable.
2 *an unjustifiable slur on his character* **groundless**, unfounded, without foundation, foundationless, baseless, without basis, unsupported, unsubstantiated, unconfirmed, uncorroborated, invalid, untenable, weak, shaky, flawed, defective.
OPPOSITES justifiable, true.

unkempt ▶ adjective *a rough-looking youth with long unkempt hair* **untidy**, messy, scruffy, disordered, dishevelled, disarranged, rumpled, windblown, ungroomed, bedraggled, in a mess, messed up, shabby, slovenly, shaggy; tousled, uncombed, knotted, matted; *informal* sloppy, tatty, the worse for wear; *Brit. informal* grotty; *N. Amer. informal* mussed up.
OPPOSITES tidy, neat.

unkind ▶ adjective 1 *everyone was being rude and unkind to him* **uncharitable**, unpleasant, disagreeable, nasty, mean, mean-spirited, cruel, vicious, spiteful, malicious, malevolent, harsh, callous, pitiless, ruthless, unsympathetic, unfeeling, compassionless, uncaring, snide, shabby, hurtful, wounding, upsetting, ill-natured, hard-hearted, heartless, cold-hearted, merciless, brutal, savage, inhuman; unfriendly, unamiable, uncivil, inconsiderate, insensitive, ungenerous, inhospitable, unkindly, hostile; *informal* beastly, bitchy, catty.
OPPOSITE kind.
2 *we were unlucky to have such unkind weather* **inclement**, harsh, intemperate, rough, severe, bitter, filthy.
OPPOSITE fine.

unkindness ▶ noun *she had had enough of her father's unkindness* **nastiness**, unpleasantness, disagreeableness, cruelty, spite, malice, meanness, mean-spiritedness, viciousness, malevolence, uncharitableness; harshness, callousness, pitilessness, ruthlessness, unfeelingness, compassionlessness, shabbiness, hard-heartedness, heartlessness, cold-heartedness, mercilessness, brutality, savagery, savageness, inhumanity; unfriendliness, inconsiderateness, insensitivity, ungenerousness, inhospitality, unkindliness, hostility; *informal* beastliness, bitchiness, cattiness.
OPPOSITE kindness.

unknown ▶ adjective 1 *the ultimate outcome of their dispute was unknown* **undisclosed**, unrevealed, undivulged, untold, unspecified, secret, mysterious, dark, hidden, concealed; **undetermined**, undecided, unresolved, unfixed, unestablished, unsettled, unsure; pending, unascertained, undefined, indefinite, inconclusive, in the balance, in limbo, up in the air.
OPPOSITES known, decided.
2 *all his instincts were warning him of the dangers in the unknown country ahead* **unexplored**, uncharted, unmapped, untravelled, undiscovered, virgin; remote, exotic, outlandish.
OPPOSITES familiar, well travelled.
3 *he was murdered by a person or persons unknown* **unidentified**, unnamed, nameless, anonymous, undesignated, incognito, mysterious; *rare* innominate.
OPPOSITES identified, named.
4 *firearms were unknown to the Indians at the time of the conquest* **unfamiliar**, unheard of, unprecedented, new, novel, strange, exotic.
OPPOSITE familiar.
5 *unknown artists of the avant-garde* **obscure**, unheard of, little known, unsung, minor, insignificant, unimportant, undistinguished, unrenowned, inconsequential, lowly, unhonoured, forgotten.
OPPOSITES famous, celebrated.

unlawful ▶ adjective *unlawful imports of recreational drugs* **illegal**, illicit, lawbreaking, illegitimate, against the law; **criminal**, felonious, indictable, actionable, delinquent, culpable; prohibited, banned, outlawed, proscribed, forbidden, unauthorized, unsanctioned, unwarranted, unlicensed, contraband, black-market, under the counter/table; villainous, corrupt, dishonest, fraudulent, nefarious; *German* verboten; *informal* crooked, shady, bent; *archaic* miscreant.
OPPOSITES lawful, legal.

CHOOSE THE RIGHT WORD
unlawful, illegal, illicit
See ILLEGAL.

unleash ▶ verb *we unleashed the dog* **let loose**, release, free, set free, loose, unloose, unbridle, untie, untether, unchain, unbind, unshackle, unmanacle; discharge, let go of, let fly.
OPPOSITE restrain.

unlettered ▶ adjective *the unwashed, unlettered people who worked in the foundry* **illiterate**, **uneducated**, poorly educated, untaught, unschooled, untutored, untrained, uninstructed, unlearned, unread, uninformed, ignorant, unenlightened, unsophisticated, uncultivated, uncultured, philistine, benighted, vulgar, simple; *rare* nescient.
OPPOSITES lettered, educated.

unlike ▶ preposition 1 *England was totally unlike Jamaica* **different from**, unalike, dissimilar to, not like, not similar to, not resembling, far from, far apart from, distant from.
OPPOSITES like, similar to.

2 *unlike Linda, Chrissy was a bit of a radical* **in contrast to/with**, differently from, in contradistinction to, as opposed to, not like, not typical of, uncharacteristic of.
OPPOSITES like, similarly to.
▶ adjective *a meeting of unlike minds* **dissimilar**, unalike, disparate, contrastive, contrasting, contrasted, contrary, antithetical, different, distinct, non-identical, diverse, heterogeneous, divergent, distinguishable, incompatible, inconsistent, opposed, at variance, varying, variant, at odds, clashing, conflicting, discrepant, ill-matched, incongruous; *informal* like chalk and cheese.
OPPOSITES like, identical.

unlikely ▶ adjective **1** *it is unlikely that the band will play here again this year* **improbable**, not likely, doubtful, dubious, unexpected, beyond belief, implausible.
OPPOSITES likely, certain.
2 *they laughed at themselves for believing such an unlikely story* **implausible**, improbable, questionable, unconvincing, remote, far-fetched, strained, laboured, unrealistic, incredible, unbelievable, inconceivable, unimaginable, fantastic, fabulous, fanciful, ridiculous, absurd, preposterous; *informal* tall, cock and bull, hard to swallow/take.
OPPOSITES likely, believable.

unlimited ▶ adjective **1** *the land has unlimited supplies of water* **inexhaustible**, limitless, illimitable, boundless, unbounded, immense, vast, great, extensive, immeasurable, incalculable, untold, unfailing, everlasting, infinite, endless, never-ending, bottomless, measureless, inestimable.
OPPOSITES limited, finite.
2 *the ticket gives unlimited travel on city buses for as little as £5* **unrestricted**, unconstrained, uncontrolled, unrestrained, unchecked, unhindered, unhampered, unimpeded, unfettered, untrammelled, unbridled, uncurbed.
OPPOSITES limited, restricted.
3 *the unit will be given unlimited power to curb all environmentally destructive activities* **total**, unqualified, unconditional, unrestricted, absolute, full, utter, ultimate, supreme, sovereign, omnipotent.
OPPOSITE limited.

unload ▶ verb **1** *we unloaded the van* **unpack**, empty, unburden, disburden; *rare* unlade.
OPPOSITE load.
2 *they began to unload the cases from the lorry* **remove**, offload, discharge, jettison, drop, deliver, deposit, set down, leave, put off, tip out, pour out.
OPPOSITE load.
3 *the state will unload its 25 per cent stake in a few weeks* **sell**, **discard**, jettison, offload, eject, get rid of, dispose of, pass off, throw out/away, clear out, scrap, destroy; palm something off on someone, foist something on someone, fob something off on someone; *informal* dump, lose, junk, get shot/shut of, see the back of.
OPPOSITES buy, acquire.

unlock ▶ verb *I unlocked the door and led the way in* **unbolt**, unlatch, unbar, undo, unfasten, unpick, unseal, unclose, open, free, throw open/wide.
OPPOSITE lock.

unlooked-for ▶ adjective *the unlooked-for publicity made his work more saleable* **unexpected**, unforeseen, unanticipated, not bargained for, unhoped-for, unsought, undreamed of, unpredicted; unintentional, unintended, inadvertent, unplanned, unpremeditated, unwitting, fortuitous, chance, coincidental, serendipitous, random, fluky; sudden, abrupt, surprise, surprising, without warning, without notice, startling, astonishing, out of the blue.
OPPOSITES deliberate, planned.

unloved ▶ adjective *Melanie felt lonely and unloved* **uncared-for**, unwanted, friendless, unbeloved, uncherished, unvalued; unpopular, disliked, hated, detested, loathed; forsaken, rejected, unwelcome, jilted, shunned, spurned, neglected, outcast, abandoned.
OPPOSITES loved, popular.

unlucky ▶ adjective **1** *he was unlucky not to score* **unfortunate**, luckless, out of luck, down on one's luck, hapless, ill-fated, ill-starred, star-crossed, blighted, unhappy, unsuccessful, wretched, miserable, poor, pitiful; accident-prone.
OPPOSITES lucky, fortunate.
2 *three can be an unlucky number* **unfavourable**, unpromising, inauspicious, unpropitious, ominous, doomed, jinxed, damned, cursed, ill-fated, ill-omened, bringing bad luck, adverse, disadvantageous, unfortunate, detrimental, deleterious, ruinous.
OPPOSITES lucky, favourable.

CHOOSE THE RIGHT WORD

unlucky, unfortunate, ill-starred, hapless

See UNFORTUNATE.

unmanageable ▶ adjective **1** *the huge Victorian house was unmanageable and uneconomic* **troublesome**, demanding, awkward, inconvenient; cumbersome, bulky, unmanoeuvrable, unwieldy, incommodious.
OPPOSITE manageable.
2 *his behaviour was becoming unmanageable at home* **uncontrollable**, ungovernable, irrepressible, unruly, disorderly, rowdy, out of hand, wild, boisterous, difficult, disruptive, ill-disciplined, undisciplined, refractory, recalcitrant, intractable, impossible, obstreperous, fractious, wayward, incorrigible; *informal* stroppy; *archaic* contumacious.
OPPOSITES manageable, controllable.

unmanly ▶ adjective *he was on the verge of tears, but did not wish to appear unmanly* **effeminate**, effete, unmasculine; womanish, girlish, feminine; **weak**, soft, timid, timorous, fearful, cowardly, lily-livered, limp-wristed, spineless, craven, milksoppish, pusillanimous, chicken-hearted, weak-kneed; *informal* sissy, wimpish, wimpy, pansy-like.
OPPOSITES manly, virile.

unmannerly ▶ adjective *a rough, unmannerly soldier* **rude**, impolite, uncivil, discourteous, bad-mannered, ill-mannered, mannerless, disrespectful, impertinent, impudent, insolent, badly behaved, abusive, blunt; uncouth, ungallant, ungracious, graceless, ungentlemanly, unladylike, unchivalrous, boorish, oafish, loutish, ill-bred, low-bred, coarse, rough, vulgar.
OPPOSITES mannerly, polite.

unmarried ▶ adjective *an unmarried woman* **unwed**, unwedded, single, spouseless, partnerless, husbandless, wifeless; spinster, bachelor; celibate, chaste, maiden, virgin; unattached, available, eligible, free, {young, free, and single}, footloose and fancy free; separated, divorced, widowed; left on the shelf.
OPPOSITE married.

unmatched ▶ adjective **1** *he had a talent for publicity unmatched by any other politician of this century* **unequalled**, unrivalled, unparalleled, unbeaten, unsurpassed.
2 *they have captured all the subtleties of Beethoven with unmatched clarity, depth, and balance* **peerless**, matchless, without equal, without parallel, incomparable, beyond compare, inimitable, superlative, extraordinary, supreme, top, paramount, outstanding, second to none, in a class of its own, consummate, record, best ever, nonpareil, unique, singular, rare, perfect; *French* par excellence.

unmentionable ▶ adjective *sex was the unmentionable subject* **taboo**, censored, forbidden, banned, interdicted, proscribed, prohibited, not to be spoken of, ineffable, unspeakable, unutterable, unprintable, indescribable, out of bounds, beyond the pale, off limits, that dare not speak its name, disapproved of, frowned on; offensive, embarrassing, shocking, indecent, indecorous, rude, immodest, impolite; scandalous, disgraceful, appalling, shameful, obscene, filthy; *informal* no go.

unmerciful ▶ adjective *he gave me an unmerciful thrashing* **ruthless**, **cruel**, harsh, merciless, pitiless, unpitying, remorseless, cold-blooded, hard-hearted, hard, callous, brutal, brutish, severe, rigorous, draconian, unrelenting, unforgiving, unsparing, barbarous, savage, inhumane, inhuman, stony, heartless, cut-throat, unsympathetic, unfeeling, illiberal, uncharitable, inflexible, intolerant, rigid, stern, strict, punishing, sadistic.
OPPOSITE merciful.

unmistakable ▶ adjective *there was the unmistakable odour of whisky on his breath* **distinctive**, distinct, telltale, well defined; indisputable, indubitable, undoubted, beyond a doubt, unquestionable, beyond question, undeniable; **plain**, clear, clear-cut, sure, definite, obvious, evident, self-evident, manifest, apparent, patent, unambiguous, unequivocal, categorical, palpable, conspicuous, noticeable, pronounced, striking, glaring, blatant, obtrusive, as plain as the nose on your face, as plain as daylight.
OPPOSITES unclear, uncertain.

unmitigated ▶ adjective *the raid was an unmitigated disaster* **absolute**, unqualified, unconditional, categorical, complete, total, thoroughgoing, downright, outright, utter, out-and-out, unadulterated, unalloyed, undiluted, unmixed, untempered, unmoderated, unmodified, unabated, undiminished, unmollified, unsoftened, unredeemed, unambiguous, unequivocal, veritable, perfect, consummate, pure, sheer, rank, in every way, positive, real, deep-dyed; *archaic* arrant.
OPPOSITE partial.

unmoved ▶ adjective **1** *he was totally unmoved by her outburst* **unaffected**, untouched, unstirred, unimpressed, unperturbed, unruffled, untroubled, undismayed, unworried; aloof, cool, cold, stolid, stony, stony-hearted, hard-hearted, dry-eyed; unconcerned, uncaring, indifferent, uninterested, unflappable, apathetic; impassive, unfeeling, unemotional, unresponsive, stoical, phlegmatic, equable; impervious (to), oblivious (to), heedless (of), immune (to), unmindful (of), proof against, deaf to.
2 *the American negotiator remained unmoved on the crucial issues* **steadfast**, firm, unshaken, staunch, unwavering, unswerving, undeviating, uninfluenced, determined, resolute, decided, resolved, inflexible, unbending, implacable, adamant.

unnatural ▶ adjective **1** *the life of a battery hen is completely unnatural* **abnormal**, unusual, uncommon, extraordinary, strange, freakish, freak,

queer, odd, peculiar, weird, unorthodox, exceptional, irregular, atypical, untypical, non-typical, anomalous, divergent, aberrant, bizarre, preternatural.
OPPOSITES natural, normal.
2 *the tractor passed in a flash of unnatural colour* **artificial**, man-made, synthetic, manufactured, fabricated, fake, false, faux, simulated, not found/existing in nature.
OPPOSITES natural, genuine.
3 *he was beheaded for unnatural vice* **perverted**, warped, twisted, deviant, depraved, degenerate, bestial, unhealthy, immoral, abnormal, decadent; *informal* kinky, pervy, sick, sicko; *rare* deviative.
4 *her voice sounded unnatural* **affected**, artificial, stilted, self-conscious, contrived, forced, laboured, studied, strained, stiff, wooden; assumed, feigned, false, bogus, fake, insincere, pretended, unspontaneous, theatrical, stagy, mannered, pretentious; *informal* put on, phoney.
5 *they condemned her as an unnatural woman* **uncaring**, unconcerned, unfeeling, inhuman, soulless, heartless, cold, cold-blooded, hard, hard-hearted, callous, cruel, brutal, merciless, pitiless, remorseless, inhumane, evil, wicked, monstrous.
OPPOSITE caring.

unnecessary ▶ **adjective** *many people feel that holiday insurance is unnecessary for travel in Britain* **unneeded**, needless, inessential, non-essential, not required, uncalled for, gratuitous, useless, unmerited, unwarranted, unwanted, undesired, dispensable, avoidable, peripheral, cosmetic, unimportant, trivial, incidental, optional, extraneous, expendable, disposable, redundant, pointless, purposeless, to no purpose, to no avail; wasted, wasteful, wanton; superfluous, excess, excessive, too much, disproportionate, surplus (to requirements); *French* de trop; *rare* supererogatory.
OPPOSITES necessary, essential, useful.

unnerve ▶ **verb** *the bleakness of his gaze unnerved her* **demoralize**, discourage, dishearten, dispirit, deject, daunt, cow, alarm, frighten, unman, dismay, distress, disconcert, discompose, perturb, upset, discomfit, take aback, unsettle, disquiet, jolt, startle, fluster, agitate, shake, ruffle, throw, throw off balance, put someone off their stroke, cause someone to lose their composure, confound, panic, stupefy, stun; *informal* rattle, faze, put into a flap, throw into a tizz, discombobulate, shake up; *Brit. informal* put the wind up.
OPPOSITES encourage, hearten.

unobtrusive ▶ **adjective 1** *she was unobtrusive and shy* **self-effacing**, retiring, unassuming, modest, demure, quiet, meek, humble; shy, bashful, unconfident, timid, timorous, shrinking, diffident, insecure, reserved, withdrawn, introvert, introverted, reticent, unforthcoming, unpresuming, unpretentious, unaggressive, unassertive, mousy, low-profile.
OPPOSITES bold, extrovert.
2 *our staff offer efficient, unobtrusive service* **inconspicuous**, unnoticeable, restrained, subdued, quiet, low-key, discreet, circumspect, understated, muted, subtle, played down, toned down, unostentatious, unshowy, relaxed, downbeat, out of sight, in the background.
OPPOSITES obtrusive, conspicuous.

unoccupied ▶ **adjective 1** *an unoccupied house* **vacant**, empty, uninhabited, untenanted, tenantless, vacated, unused; free, untaken, available, to let.
OPPOSITES occupied, inhabited.
2 *an unoccupied territory* **uninhabited**, unpopulated, unpeopled, unsettled, unfrequented; deserted, evacuated, depopulated, abandoned, forsaken; desolate, bare, barren, wild, godforsaken.
OPPOSITES occupied, populated.
3 *at weekends the young people were unoccupied* **at leisure**, idle, free, inactive, not at work, not busy, not tied up, unengaged, with time on one's hands, with time to spare, at a loose end; **unemployed**, jobless, out of work, without work, workless.
OPPOSITES occupied, busy, employed.

unofficial ▶ **adjective 1** *unofficial figures put the death toll at over 300* **unauthenticated**, unconfirmed, uncorroborated, unsubstantiated, unratified; undocumented, off the record; unauthorized, unsanctioned, uncertified.
OPPOSITES official, confirmed.
2 *he took it on himself to act as chairman of an unofficial committee* **informal**, casual; unauthorized, unsanctioned, unaccredited; wildcat.
OPPOSITES official, formal.

unorthodox ▶ **adjective 1** *Hobson's unorthodox views denied him an academic career* **unconventional**, unusual, uncommon, unwonted, out of the ordinary, radical, revolutionary, nonconformist, irregular, offbeat, avant-garde, original, new, novel, fresh, eccentric, exotic, Bohemian, alternative, idiosyncratic, abnormal, extreme, divergent, aberrant, anomalous, bizarre, outlandish, perverse; *informal* off the wall, oddball, way out, cranky, zany; *rare* heteroclite.
OPPOSITES orthodox, conventional.
2 *unorthodox religious views* **heterodox**, uncanonical, heretical, nonconformist, dissenting, dissentient, renegade.
OPPOSITE orthodox.

unpaid ▶ **adjective 1** *a string of unpaid bills* **unsettled**, outstanding, unresolved, unattended to, due, overdue, owing, owed, receivable, to be paid, payable, undischarged, in arrears, in the red; *N. Amer.* delinquent, past due.
OPPOSITES paid, settled.
2 *unpaid charity work* **voluntary**, volunteer, honorary, unrewarded, unremunerative, unsalaried, gratuitous, free; *Law* pro bono (publico).
OPPOSITES paid, professional.

unpalatable ▶ **adjective 1** *scraps of unpalatable food* **unappetizing**, uninviting, unappealing, unsavoury, off-putting, inedible, uneatable; bitter, sour, rancid; disgusting, revolting, nauseating, sickening, horrible, tasteless, flavourless, bland, insipid; *informal* yucky, sick-making, gross.
OPPOSITES palatable, tasty.
2 *he had been bold enough to speak the unpalatable truth* **disagreeable**, unpleasant, displeasing, unattractive, regrettable, unwelcome, upsetting, distressing, lamentable, repugnant, nasty, horrible, dreadful, hateful, distasteful, offensive, objectionable, obnoxious, repulsive, repellent, vile, foul.
OPPOSITE palatable.

unparalleled ▶ **adjective** *an unparalleled opportunity to change society* **exceptional**, unique, singular, rare, unprecedented, without parallel, without equal, unequalled; matchless, unmatched, peerless, unrivalled, unsurpassed, unsurpassable, unexcelled, superlative, incomparable, beyond compare, nonpareil, inimitable, second to none, in a league of its own, supreme; unheard of, unusual, aberrant, freak; *French* hors concours; *rare* unexampled.
OPPOSITES ordinary, unexceptional.

unperturbed ▶ **adjective** *Daniel was unperturbed by the outburst* **untroubled**, undisturbed, unworried, unconcerned, unmoved, unflustered, unruffled, unshaken, undismayed; calm, composed, cool, collected, controlled, unemotional, serene, tranquil, self-possessed, self-assured, poised, level-headed, at ease, placid, {cool, calm, and collected}, unflappable, unflinching, as cool as a cucumber; unfazed, laid-back, together.
OPPOSITES perturbed, anxious.

unpleasant ▶ **adjective 1** *a very unpleasant situation* **disagreeable**, irksome, troublesome, annoying, irritating, vexatious, displeasing, uncomfortable, distressing, nasty, horrible, appalling, terrible, awful, dreadful, hateful, detestable, miserable, abominable, execrable, odious, invidious, objectionable, offensive, obnoxious, repugnant, repulsive, repellent, revolting, disgusting, distasteful, nauseating, unsavoury, unpalatable, ugly.
OPPOSITES pleasant, agreeable.
2 *he was the most unpleasant man I knew* **unlikable**, unlovable, unattractive, disagreeable; unfriendly, inconsiderate, rude, impolite, obnoxious, nasty, spiteful, cruel, malicious, mean, mean-spirited, vicious, poisonous, venomous, vindictive, malign; frightful, ghastly, insufferable, unbearable, annoying, irritating; churlish, ill-natured, ill-humoured, ill-tempered, cross, bad-tempered.
OPPOSITES pleasant, likeable.
3 *an unpleasant burnt sugar taste* **unappetizing**, unpalatable, unsavoury, uninviting, unappealing, off-putting, inedible, uneatable, bitter, sour, rancid; disgusting, repugnant, revolting, nauseating, sickening, offensive, foul, rotten, vile.
OPPOSITES pleasant, palatable.

unpolished ▶ **adjective 1** *the floor was of pale unpolished wood* **unvarnished**, unlacquered, unfinished, unprocessed, untreated, unworked, plain, raw, unrefined, natural, coarse, rough; stripped.
OPPOSITES polished, varnished.
2 *you must not mind his unpolished ways* **unsophisticated**, unrefined, uncouth, uncultured, uncultivated, coarse, inelegant, crude, crass, raw, rough, rough and ready, awkward, clumsy, gauche, graceless, tactless, insensitive, vulgar, philistine, uneducated; provincial, parochial, rustic.
OPPOSITES polished, sophisticated.
3 *it was an unpolished performance lacking spark* **slipshod**, rough, crude, untidy, uneven, incoherent, defective, deficient, scrappy, sketchy, bitty.
OPPOSITE polished.

unpopular ▶ **adjective** *he was unpopular at school* **disliked**, friendless, unliked, unloved, unbefriended, uncherished, hated, detested, despised, loathed; unwanted, unwelcome, avoided, ignored, rejected, shunned, spurned, unsought after, out in the cold, cold-shouldered, out of favour, not in the swim, in bad odour; *Brit.* sent to Coventry.
OPPOSITES popular, liked.

unprecedented ▶ **adjective** *an era of warfare on an unprecedented scale* **unparalleled**, unequalled, unmatched, unrivalled, without parallel, without equal; extraordinary, uncommon, out of the ordinary, unusual, outstanding, striking, exceptional, prodigious, abnormal, singular, remarkable, unique, anomalous, atypical, untypical, freakish; unheard of, unknown, novel, original, new, groundbreaking, revolutionary, pioneering; *informal* one of a kind; *rare* unexampled.
OPPOSITES normal, common.

unpredictable ▸ adjective **1** *the unpredictable results of the first-past-the-post system* **unforeseeable**, undivinable, incalculable, uncertain, unsure, doubtful, dubious, in the balance, up in the air, random, arbitrary; *informal* iffy, hit and miss.
OPPOSITE predictable.
2 *the men in here are unpredictable, violent, and dangerous* **erratic**, moody, volatile, unstable, fickle, capricious, whimsical, temperamental, mercurial, changeable, variable, inconstant, undependable, unreliable, unmanageable, impulsive.
OPPOSITES predictable, reliable.

unprejudiced ▸ adjective **1** *science must start with unprejudiced observation* **objective**, impartial, unbiased, fair, neutral, even-handed, non-partisan, detached, uninvolved, disinterested.
OPPOSITES prejudiced, partisan.
2 *we need unprejudiced support for lesbians and gay men* **unbiased**, non-discriminatory, tolerant, liberal, broad-minded, open-minded, unbigoted, just, freethinking, progressive, enlightened.
OPPOSITES prejudiced, intolerant.

unpremeditated ▸ adjective *her unpremeditated reply* **unplanned**, spontaneous, unprepared, unarranged, uncontrolled, unintentional, unintended, extempore, extemporary, extemporized, extemporaneous, impromptu, ad lib; spur-of-the-moment, on-the-spot, improvised, improvisatory, unrehearsed, unscripted, unstudied, uncontrived, casual; impulsive, hasty, unthinking, natural, involuntary, automatic; *Latin* ad libitum; *informal* off-the-cuff.
OPPOSITES premeditated, planned.

unprepared ▸ adjective **1** *four out of ten companies were unprepared for the new VAT regime* **not ready**, unready, off (one's) guard, surprised, taken aback, unsuspecting; unrehearsed, unwatchful, unqualified, ineligible, unfit, incompetent, incapable, ill-equipped, unequipped, not equal/up to; *informal* caught napping, caught on the hop.
OPPOSITES prepared, ready.
2 *the Whigs showed themselves unprepared to support the reforms* **unwilling**, disinclined, averse, loath, reluctant, indisposed, resistant, opposed.
OPPOSITES prepared, willing.

unpretentious ▸ adjective **1** *in spite of his fame he was thoroughly unpretentious* **unaffected**, modest, unassuming, without airs, natural, straightforward, open, honest, sincere, frank, ingenuous, artless, guileless, honest-to-goodness.
OPPOSITE pretentious.
2 *a friendly and unpretentious hotel* **simple**, plain, modest, ordinary, humble, unostentatious, unshowy, restrained, unfussy, unimposing, homely, unsophisticated, unspoilt.
OPPOSITES pretentious, showy.

unprincipled ▸ adjective *he is an unprincipled opportunist* **immoral**, unethical, unscrupulous, amoral, dishonourable, reprobate, dishonest, unprofessional, deceitful, devious, corrupt, corrupted, dissolute, underhand, crooked, bad, wicked, evil, villainous, roguish, shameless, sinful, ignoble, base, low, degenerate, sordid; *archaic* dastardly.
OPPOSITES principled, ethical.

unproductive ▸ adjective **1** *acidic, unproductive soil* **sterile**, barren, infertile, uncultivatable, unfruitful, poor, lifeless, lean, arid.
OPPOSITES productive, fruitful.
2 *a costly and unproductive bureaucracy* **fruitless**, futile, vain, idle, useless, worthless, valueless, pointless, ineffective, ineffectual, to no effect, impotent, inefficacious, unprofitable, unremunerative, unrewarding; *rare* otiose.
OPPOSITES productive, efficient.

unprofessional ▸ adjective **1** *she was reprimanded for unprofessional conduct* **improper**, unethical, unprincipled, unscrupulous, dishonourable, disreputable, unseemly, unbecoming, unbefitting, indecorous, unworthy, lax, negligent; *informal* shady, crooked, not cricket; *Brit. informal* dodgy.
2 *he accused the detectives of being unprofessional and incompetent* **amateurish**, amateur, unskilled, unskilful, inexpert, untrained, unqualified, inexperienced, unpractised, incompetent, sloppy, careless, slapdash, slipshod, shoddy, bungling, bumbling, blundering, second-rate, clumsy, crude, inefficient; *informal* cack-handed, cowboy.

unpromising ▸ adjective *they were not deterred by this unpromising start* **inauspicious**, unfavourable, adverse, disadvantageous, unpropitious, uninviting, discouraging, disheartening, gloomy, bleak, black, portentous, foreboding, hopeless, ominous, creepy, baleful, doomed, jinxed, damned, cursed, ill-fated, ill-omened.
OPPOSITES promising, auspicious.

unqualified ▸ adjective **1** *no company would permit an unqualified accountant to audit its books* **uncertificated**, unlicensed, unchartered, untrained, inexperienced.
OPPOSITE qualified.
2 *we cannot leave children in the hands of those unqualified to look after them* **unsuitable**, unfit, ineligible, incompetent, unable, inadequate, incapable, unequipped, ill-equipped, unprepared, unfitted, inapt, not equal/up to, not cut out, insufficient.
OPPOSITES fit, qualified.
3 *the chairman gave the manager his unqualified support* **unconditional**, unreserved, unlimited, without reservations, categorical, unequivocal, unambiguous, unrestricted, wholehearted, positive, unmitigated, unadulterated, undiluted, unalloyed, unvarnished, unstinting; complete, absolute, downright, entire, undivided, solid, thorough, thoroughgoing, total, utter, outright, out-and-out; *archaic* arrant.
OPPOSITES limited, qualified.

unquestionable ▸ adjective *the sincerity of his beliefs is unquestionable* **indubitable**, undoubted, beyond question, beyond doubt, indisputable, undeniable, irrefutable, incontestable, incontrovertible, unimpeachable, unambiguous, unequivocal, unassailable; certain, sure, definite, positive, dependable, conclusive, self-evident, evident, manifest, obvious, apparent, patent, proven, settled, decided; *rare* undoubtable.

unravel ▸ verb **1** *he cut the rope and started to unravel its strands* **untangle**, disentangle, straighten out, separate out, unsnarl, unknot, unwind, untwist, undo, untie, unkink, unjumble.
OPPOSITES entangle, tangle.
2 *detectives are still trying to unravel the mystery surrounding the death of a wealthy farmer* **solve**, resolve, work out, clear up, puzzle out, find an answer to, get to the bottom of, explain, elucidate, fathom, decipher, decode, crack, penetrate, untangle, unfold, settle, reveal, clarify, sort out, make head or tail of; *informal* figure out, suss (out).
OPPOSITE complicate.
3 *a society that does not shelter its young is a society starting to unravel* **fall apart**, come apart (at the seams), fail, collapse, go wrong.
OPPOSITE succeed.

unreadable ▸ adjective **1** *an almost unreadable photocopy* **illegible**, hard to read, indecipherable, unintelligible; faint, faded, pale, indistinct, obscure, scrawled, scribbled, hieroglyphic, squiggly, crabbed; *informal* clear as mud.
OPPOSITES clear, legible.
2 *the heavy, unreadable novels which so often win prizes* **dull**, tedious, boring, uninteresting, dry, (as) dry as dust, wearisome, difficult, heavy-going, heavy, turgid, incoherent, inarticulate, incomprehensible.
OPPOSITES readable, accessible.
3 *Nathan's expression was unreadable* **inscrutable**, enigmatic, impenetrable, cryptic, impossible to interpret, mysterious, puzzling, deadpan; *informal* poker-faced.
OPPOSITE transparent.

unreal ▸ adjective *the unreal world of art* **imaginary**, imagined, fictitious, pretend, make-believe, made-up, dreamed-up, non-existent, mock, false, invented, illusory, mythical, fanciful, fancied, fantastic, fabulous, legendary, chimerical, fairy-tale, phantasmagoric; hypothetical, theoretical, ideal; *informal* phoney.
OPPOSITE real.

unrealistic ▸ adjective **1** *it is unrealistic to expect a government minister to know all about administration* **impractical**, impracticable, unworkable, unfeasible, non-viable; unreasonable, irrational, illogical, senseless, silly, improbable, impossible, foolish, fanciful, wild, absurd, delusory, quixotic; idealistic, Utopian, far-fetched, perfectionist, unworldly, romantic, starry-eyed, visionary; *informal* half baked, crazy, potty.
OPPOSITES realistic, pragmatic.
2 *manga comics are deliberately stylized and unrealistic* **unlifelike**, non-realistic, unreal-looking, non-naturalistic, unnatural, non-representational, unrepresentative, abstract.
OPPOSITES realistic, lifelike.

unreasonable ▸ adjective **1** *an unreasonable old woman* **uncooperative**, obstructive, unhelpful, disobliging, unaccommodating, troublesome, awkward, contrary, difficult, tiresome, annoying, vexatious; **obstinate**, obdurate, wilful, headstrong, pig-headed, bull-headed, intractable, intransigent, inflexible, mulish; **irrational**, illogical, opinionated, biased, prejudiced, intolerant, blinkered.
2 *the bill placed unreasonable demands on industry* **unacceptable**, preposterous, outrageous, ludicrous, absurd, senseless, nonsensical, irrational, illogical; excessive, immoderate, extreme, disproportionate, undue, inordinate, exorbitant, extortionate, extravagant, intolerable, unconscionable; unnecessary, unjustified, unwarranted, uncalled for; *informal* over the top, OTT, steep.

unrecognizable ▸ adjective *with his moustache and beard he is practically unrecognizable* **unidentifiable**, unknowable; disguised, incognito; changed, altered.
OPPOSITE recognizable.

unrefined ▸ adjective **1** *unrefined clay* **unprocessed**, untreated, unpurified, crude, raw, natural, plain, coarse, rough, unworked, unprepared, unmilled, unfinished.
OPPOSITES refined, processed.
2 *the miners were hard, unrefined men* **uncultured**, uncultivated, uncivilized, philistine, uneducated, unsophisticated, unpolished, indelicate, inelegant, ungraceful; boorish, oafish, loutish, barbarian, coarse, vulgar, rude, uncouth, crude, ill-bred, ill-mannered, crass, raw, rough, rough and ready; provincial, parochial, rustic.
OPPOSITES refined, cultured; effete.

unrelated ▸ adjective **1** *two men had been arrested in unrelated incidents* **separate**, unconnected, independent, unattached, unassociated, unlinked, unallied, distinct, discrete, individual, uncoupled; unlike, varying, variant, disparate.
OPPOSITES related, similar.
2 *I chose London for another reason, unrelated to my work* **irrelevant**, immaterial, inapplicable, unconcerned, inapt, foreign, alien, extraneous, extrinsic, peripheral, off the subject, beside/off the point, wide of the mark, not pertinent, not germane; *informal* neither here nor there.
OPPOSITE relevant.

unrelenting ▸ adjective **1** *a vicious, unrelenting guerrilla war* **continual**, constant, continuous, relentless, unremitting, unabating, unrelieved, sustained, incessant, unceasing, ceaseless, steady, unbroken, non-stop, endless, unending, persistent, perpetual.
OPPOSITES intermittent, spasmodic.
2 *he was an unrelenting opponent of the Jacobite cause* **implacable**, inflexible, uncompromising, unyielding, unbending, inexorable, relentless, resolute, determined, unstoppable, dogged, tireless, unflagging, unshakeable, unswerving, unwavering, assiduous, sedulous; intransigent, merciless, pitiless, unforgiving, unsparing, ruthless, cruel, rigid, rigorous, hard, strict, harsh, stern, adamant, steely, tough.

unreliable ▸ adjective **1** *an unreliable group of volunteers* **undependable**, untrustworthy, irresponsible, reckless, fickle, capricious, irregular, erratic, unpredictable, inconstant, mutable, faithless, untrue, flighty, slippery.
OPPOSITES reliable, steadfast.
2 *unemployment can be an unreliable indicator of the tightness of labour markets* **questionable**, open to question, open to doubt, doubtful, dubious, suspect, unsound, tenuous, flimsy, weak, unsubstantial, implausible, unconvincing, unsupported, unsubstantiated, fallible, shaky, rocky; risky, chancy, disreputable, specious, defective; inaccurate, vague, untrue, incorrect, wide of the mark, off-target, wrong; *informal* iffy, dicey; *Brit. informal* dodgy.
OPPOSITES reliable, accurate.

unremitting ▸ adjective *their lives were little more than unremitting toil* **relentless**, unrelenting, continual, constant, continuous, unabating, unrelieved, sustained, incessant, unceasing, ceaseless, steady, unbroken, non-stop, endless, unending, persistent, perpetual, interminable, unyielding, inexorable, unsparing, without respite; hard, harsh, stern.
OPPOSITES intermittent, spasmodic.

unrepentant ▸ adjective *an unrepentant sinner* **impenitent**, unrepenting, uncontrite, remorseless, unremorseful, shameless, unashamed, unblushing, unapologetic, unregenerate, obdurate, unabashed; incorrigible, incurable, confirmed, inveterate, irredeemable, unreformable, brazen, hardened, callous, abandoned, conscienceless.
OPPOSITES repentant, regretful.

unreserved ▸ adjective **1** *the Prime Minister has had the unreserved support of the Opposition* **unconditional**, unqualified, without reservations, unlimited, unrestricted, categorical, unequivocal, unambiguous, positive, unadulterated, undiluted, unalloyed, unvarnished, unstinting; absolute, complete, thorough, thoroughgoing, through and through, wholehearted, total, utter, outright, out-and-out, downright, entire, undivided, solid, sheer, deep-dyed, perfect, consummate; *archaic* arrant.
OPPOSITES qualified, tentative.
2 *an unreserved young man* **uninhibited**, liberated, extrovert, outgoing, unrestrained, expressive, open, affable, talkative, effusive, demonstrative, unconstrained, unselfconscious, bold, communicative, expansive, ebullient, exuberant, gushing, outspoken, frank, candid, warm.
OPPOSITES reserved, reticent.
3 *unreserved seats* **unbooked**, unhired, unallocated, unchartered, unoccupied, untaken, free, empty, vacant, spare.
OPPOSITES reserved, booked.

unresolved ▸ adjective *the judge said that some questions remained unresolved* **undecided**, to be decided, unsettled, undetermined, uncertain, open, arguable, debatable, unsolved, unanswered, pending, open to debate, open to question, doubtful, in doubt, borderline, moot, up in the air, indefinite, inconclusive, unconfirmed, confused, problematic, vexed, ambiguous, equivocal, vague, in (a state of) limbo, in a state of uncertainty, ongoing, incomplete; *informal* iffy.
OPPOSITES resolved, decided.

unrest ▸ noun *the government was clearly fearful of social unrest* **disruption**, disturbance, agitation, upset, trouble, turmoil, tumult, disorder, chaos, anarchy, turbulence, uproar; **discord**, dissension, dissent, strife, protest, sedition, rebellion, uprising, rioting; **dissatisfaction**, discontent, discontentment, disaffection, unease, anxiety, anguish, disquiet; *informal* ructions.
OPPOSITES calm, peace.

unrestrained ▸ adjective *this was a period of unrestrained corruption* **uncontrolled**, unconstrained, unrestricted, unchecked, unbridled, unlimited, unfettered, unshackled, untrammelled, uninhibited, unconfined, unimpeded, unhampered, unbounded, boundless, unsuppressed, undisciplined, uncontrollable, out of control, out of hand; outrageous, rampant, reckless, wild, wanton, free, runaway, irrepressible, unstoppable, uncontainable, unquenchable, immoderate, intemperate, inordinate.
OPPOSITES restrained, restricted.

unrestricted ▸ adjective *open drives provide unrestricted access to the rear of the property* **unlimited**, open, free, clear, unhindered, unimpeded, unhampered, unchecked, unopposed, unbridled, unrestrained, unconstrained, unblocked, untrammelled, unbounded, unconfined, uncurbed, unconditional, unqualified, absolute, total; *informal* free for all, with no holds barred.
OPPOSITES restricted, limited.

unripe ▸ adjective *unripe fruit* **immature**, unready, not ripe, undeveloped, unfinished, incomplete, half-grown, unmellowed, green, sour.
OPPOSITES ripe, mature.

unrivalled ▸ adjective *an unrivalled collection of rare coins* **unequalled**, without equal, unparalleled, without parallel, matchless, unmatched, peerless, without peer, unsurpassed, unbeaten, unexcelled, incomparable, beyond compare, inimitable; superlative, extraordinary, supreme, top, paramount, outstanding, singular, unique, rare, perfect, second to none, in a class of its own, consummate, record, best ever, nonpareil; *French* par excellence.
OPPOSITE average.

unruffled ▸ adjective **1** *Julius replied in an unruffled tone* **calm**, composed, undisturbed, unagitated, unmoved, controlled, self-controlled, self-possessed, untroubled, undismayed, unperturbed, at ease, tranquil, relaxed, serene, cool, {cool, calm, and collected}, cool-headed, unshaken, unbothered, unexcitable, unemotional, equanimous, unflappable, imperturbable, equable, stoical, urbane; *informal* together, unfazed.
OPPOSITES frantic, nervous.
2 *an unruffled sea* **tranquil**, calm, smooth, still, flat, even, motionless, placid, waveless, pacific, undisturbed, unagitated, unbroken, like a millpond.
OPPOSITES choppy, stormy.

unruly ▸ adjective *she was scolding some unruly children* **disorderly**, rowdy, wild, unmanageable, uncontrollable, disobedient, disruptive, undisciplined, troublemaking, rebellious, mutinous, anarchic, chaotic, lawless, insubordinate, defiant, wayward, wilful, headstrong, irrepressible, unrestrained, obstreperous, difficult, intractable, out of hand, refractory, recalcitrant; boisterous, lively, loud, noisy, rollicking, romping, rumbustious, reckless, heedless; *archaic* contumacious.
OPPOSITES disciplined, obedient.

unsafe ▸ adjective **1** *the building was becoming unsafe | many women feel that it is unsafe to go out alone* **dangerous**, risky, perilous, hazardous, precarious, life-threatening, high-risk, treacherous, insecure, unsound, vulnerable, exposed, defenceless; destructive, harmful, injurious, malignant, toxic; threatening, menacing; *informal* hairy, chancy; *Brit. informal* dodgy.
OPPOSITES safe, harmless, secure.
2 *the verdict was unsafe* **unreliable**, insecure, unsound, questionable, open to question, doubtful, open to doubt, dubious, uncertain, suspect, shaky, flimsy, weak, unconvincing, unsupported, unsubstantiated, fallible; *informal* iffy, dodgy, dicey.
OPPOSITES safe, reliable.

unsaid ▸ adjective *you've made me say things much better left unsaid* **unspoken**, unuttered, unstated, unmentioned, untold, unarticulated, unexpressed, unvoiced, unpronounced, untalked-of, suppressed, unrevealed, undeclared, unavowed; **tacit**, implicit, understood, not spelt out, taken for granted, taken as read, inferred, implied, hinted, suggested, insinuated, left to the/someone's imagination.
OPPOSITES said, spoken; explicit.

unsanitary ▸ adjective *the houses themselves are overcrowded and unsanitary* **unhygienic**, insanitary, dirty, filthy, unclean, impure, contaminated, unhealthy, unwholesome, germ-ridden, germy, disease-ridden, infested; insalubrious, noxious, polluted, foul, septic, harmful.
OPPOSITES sanitary, hygienic, clean.

unsatisfactory ▸ adjective *this was a most unsatisfactory outcome* **disappointing**, dissatisfying, undesirable, disagreeable, displeasing, deplorable; inadequate, unacceptable, unworthy, poor, bad, substandard, weak, mediocre, lacking, not good enough, defective, deficient, insufficient, faulty, imperfect, inferior; terrible, intolerable, insufferable; impermissible, inadmissible, inappropriate, unsuitable; *informal* lousy, sad, leaving a lot to be desired, no great shakes, not much cop, not up to par, not up to scratch.
OPPOSITES satisfactory, good.

unsavoury ▸ adjective **1** *the scanty, unsavoury portions of food doled out to them* **unpalatable**, unappetizing, unpleasant, distasteful, disagreeable, uninviting, unappealing, unattractive; inedible, uneatable, disgusting, loathsome, repugnant, revolting, nauseating, sickening, foul, nasty, vile; insipid, tasteless, bland, flavourless, dull, uninteresting; *informal* yucky, sick-making, gross; *literary* noisome.
OPPOSITES tasty, appetizing.
2 *the unsavoury characters lurking about* **disreputable**, unpleasant,

U

disagreeable, nasty, mean, rough, seedy, sleazy, seamy, unwholesome, objectionable, offensive, obnoxious, repellent, repulsive, immoral; degenerate, dishonourable, dishonest, unprincipled, unscrupulous, villainous, notorious, suspicious, suspect, dubious, base, low, rascally, despicable, coarse, gross, vulgar, boorish, churlish, rude, uncouth; informal shady, crooked, funny, iffy; Brit. informal dodgy; literary noisome.
OPPOSITE reputable.

unscathed ▶ adjective *his wife and son were fortunate to escape unscathed* **unharmed**, unhurt, uninjured, undamaged, in one piece, intact, safe, safe and sound, unmarked, untouched, unscarred, unscratched, secure, well, as (good as) new; informal like new; rare scatheless.
OPPOSITES harmed, injured.

unscrupulous ▶ adjective *a crackdown on unscrupulous landlords* **unprincipled**, unethical, immoral, amoral, conscienceless, untrustworthy, shameless, reprobate, exploitative, corrupt, corrupted, dishonest, fraudulent, cheating, dishonourable, deceitful, devious, underhand, guileful, cunning, furtive, sly, wrongdoing, unsavoury, disreputable, improper, bad, evil, wicked, villainous, roguish, sinful, ignoble, degenerate, venal; informal crooked, shady, shifty, slippery; Brit. informal dodgy; archaic dastardly.
OPPOSITES ethical, honest.

unseat ▶ verb **1** *the favourite unseated his rider at the start* **dislodge**, throw, dismount, spill, upset, unhorse.
2 *an attempt to unseat the party leader* **depose**, oust, remove from office, topple, overthrow, bring down, dislodge, discharge, dethrone, displace, supplant, usurp, overturn, dismiss, eject, evict; informal drum out.

unseemly ▶ adjective *an unseemly squabble* **indecorous**, improper, inappropriate, unbecoming, unfitting, unbefitting, unsuitable, unworthy, undignified, unrefined, indiscreet, indelicate, ungentlemanly, unladylike, impolite; ill-advised, out of place/keeping, tasteless, in poor/bad taste, disreputable, coarse, crass, shameful.
OPPOSITES seemly, decorous.

unseen ▶ adjective *an unseen sniper* **hidden**, concealed, obscured, camouflaged, unrevealed, out of sight, invisible, not visible, imperceptible, undetectable, unnoticeable, unnoticed, unobserved, covered, masked, shrouded, veiled.
OPPOSITES seen, spotted.

unselfish ▶ adjective *he always acted from unselfish motives* **altruistic**, disinterested, selfless, self-denying, self-forgetting, self-sacrificing; generous, philanthropic, public-spirited, humanitarian, humane, charitable, compassionate, benevolent, caring, kind, considerate, open-handed, magnanimous, liberal, unsparing, ungrudging, unstinting, decent, noble.
OPPOSITES selfish, greedy.

unsettle ▶ verb *all this talk of death was unsettling him* **discompose**, unnerve, upset, disturb, disquiet, make anxious, make uneasy, perturb, discomfit, disconcert, alarm, confuse, nonplus, bewilder, confound, perplex; daunt, dismay, trouble, bother, agitate, fluster, ruffle, jolt, shake (up), throw, put off, take aback, unbalance, destabilize, throw off balance, put someone off their stroke, pull the rug (out) from under; informal rattle, faze, psych out.

unsettled ▶ adjective **1** *an unsettled, unsatisfied life* **aimless**, directionless, purposeless, without purpose, without a goal; rootless, moving, wandering, nomadic, travelling, transient.
OPPOSITES settled, purposeful.
2 *I was an unsettled child* **restless**, restive, fidgety, anxious, worried, troubled, fretful; disquieted, flustered, agitated, ruffled, uneasy, disconcerted, discomposed, unnerved, ill at ease, uncomfortable, edgy, on edge, tense, nervous, apprehensive, alarmed, concerned, dismayed, disturbed, turbulent, perturbed, shaken, upset, bothered, distressed; informal thrown, rattled, fazed, twitchy, shaky, wired.
OPPOSITES settled, composed.
3 *more unsettled weather is forecast* **changeable**, changing, variable, varying, inconstant, inconsistent, ever-changing, erratic, unstable, unsteady, shifting, fluid, undependable, unreliable, uncertain, unpredictable, mercurial, quicksilver, kaleidoscopic, chameleon-like; rare protean.
OPPOSITES settled, unchanging, predictable.
4 *the question remains unsettled* **undecided**, to be decided, unresolved, undetermined, uncertain, open, arguable, debatable, disputed, unanswered, open to debate, doubtful, in doubt, moot, up in the air, in (a state of) limbo, in a state of uncertainty, indefinite, inconclusive, unconfirmed, unsolved, ongoing, pending; confused, problematic, vexed, ambiguous, equivocal, vague, borderline; informal iffy.
OPPOSITE settled.
5 *they charge interest on debts that remain unsettled after 30 days* **unpaid**, payable, outstanding, owing, owed, to be paid, due, overdue, undischarged, in arrears, in the red, receivable; N. Amer. delinquent, past due.
OPPOSITES settled, paid.
6 *unsettled or thinly populated areas* **uninhabited**, unpopulated, unpeopled, unoccupied, unfrequented; empty, vacant, abandoned, deserted, depopulated, forsaken, desolate, lonely.
OPPOSITES settled, populated.

unshakeable ▶ adjective *they both have an unshakeable confidence in the rightness of their own opinions* **steadfast**, resolute, staunch, firm, constant, decided, determined, fixed, ingrained, unswerving, unwavering, unvacillating, unfaltering, unflinching; unyielding, inflexible, dogged, obstinate, persistent, unassailable, immovable, irremovable, indelible, iron, adamant, deep-dyed, indefatigable, tireless, unflagging, unremitting, unrelenting, relentless.
OPPOSITES weak, half-hearted.

unsightly ▶ adjective *an unsightly concrete church* **ugly**, unattractive, unprepossessing, unlovely, ill-favoured, disagreeable, displeasing, awful-looking, frightful-looking, hideous, horrible, repulsive, revolting, repellent, disgusting, offensive, grotesque, monstrous, gruesome, ghastly.
OPPOSITES beautiful, attractive.

unskilful ▶ adjective *the furniture had been repaired by an unskilful hand* **inexpert**, incompetent, inept, unskilled, clumsy, awkward, maladroit, unhandy, amateur, amateurish, unprofessional, inexperienced, untrained, unpractised, crude, rude, unsophisticated, gauche, fumbling, bungling, blundering, botching; informal ham-fisted, ham-handed, cack-handed, cowboy, not up to scratch.
OPPOSITE skilful.

unskilled ▶ adjective *unskilled manual workers* **untrained**, unqualified, untaught, unschooled; manual, blue-collar, labouring, menial; inexpert, inexperienced, unpractised, unequipped, unversed, unaccomplished, uneducated, amateur, amateurish, unprofessional.
OPPOSITE skilled.

unsociable ▶ adjective *he was grumpy and unsociable* **unfriendly**, unamiable, unaffable, uncongenial, unneighbourly, inhospitable, hostile, unapproachable, reclusive, introverted, solitary, private, misanthropic, uncommunicative, unforthcoming, reticent, reserved, withdrawn, aloof, distant, remote, detached, stand-offish, unsocial, antisocial, taciturn, silent, quiet, sulky, mopey, mopish, uncivil, rude, cold, cool, chilly, frigid, haughty, suspicious, distrustful, scowling, glowering.
OPPOSITES sociable, friendly.

unsociable, unsocial, or antisocial?
There is some overlap in the use of the adjectives **unsociable**, **unsocial**, and **antisocial**, but they have distinct core meanings. *Unsociable* means 'not enjoying the company of others', as in *Terry was grumpy and unsociable*. *Antisocial* means 'contrary to the laws and customs of a society', as in *aggressive and antisocial behaviour*. *Unsocial* is usually restricted to the sense '(of hours) falling outside the normal working day', as in *employees were expected to work unsocial hours*.

unsolicited ▶ adjective *he did not take easily to unsolicited advice* **uninvited**, unsought, unasked for, unrequested, undemanded, uncalled for, not required, unprompted, unbidden, unwelcome, gratuitous, volunteered, voluntary, spontaneous.
OPPOSITES requested, invited.

unsophisticated ▶ adjective **1** *she seemed terribly unsophisticated* **unworldly**, naive, simple, innocent, ignorant, green, immature, callow, inexperienced, childlike, artless, guileless, ingenuous, down-to-earth, natural, unaffected, unassuming, unpretentious, modest, without airs; unrefined, unpolished, gauche, provincial, parochial, rustic.
OPPOSITES sophisticated, worldly.
2 *unsophisticated computer software* **simple**, **crude**, unrefined, basic, rudimentary, primitive, rough and ready, rough-hewn, make-do, cobbled together, undeveloped, homespun; straightforward, uncomplicated, uninvolved, unspecialized; dated rude.
OPPOSITES sophisticated, complex.

unsound ▶ adjective **1** *the tower is structurally unsound* **rickety**, flimsy, shaky, wobbly, unstable, tottery, defective, disintegrating, crumbling, decaying, broken, broken-down, damaged, rotten, ramshackle, insubstantial, jerry-built, unsafe, unreliable, dangerous.
OPPOSITES sound, strong.
2 *this submission appears to us unsound on several grounds* **untenable**, flawed, defective, faulty, ill-founded, flimsy, weak, shaky, unreliable, questionable, dubious, tenuous, suspect, illogical, irrational, unfounded, ungrounded, unsubstantiated, unsupported, specious, hollow, spurious, false, fallacious, fallible, erroneous, wrong, sophistic, casuistic; informal iffy; Brit. informal dodgy.
OPPOSITES sound, strong.
3 *of unsound mind* **disordered**, diseased, deranged, disturbed, troubled, demented, unstable, unbalanced, unhinged, insane, crazed, distracted; informal touched.
OPPOSITE sane.

unsparing ▶ adjective **1** *an unsparing analysis of the way the two parties collude to stay in power* **merciless**, pitiless, unpitying, ruthless, relentless,

remorseless, unmerciful, unforgiving, implacable, uncompromising; stern, strict, severe, stringent, harsh, tough, rigorous, exacting, demanding, inflexible, draconian; Austral./NZ informal solid.
OPPOSITES merciful, gentle, mild.
2 *she had won her mother's unsparing approval* **ungrudging**, unstinting, willingly given, free, free-handed, ready, beneficent, benevolent, big-hearted, kind-hearted, kind, unselfish; **lavish**, liberal, generous, magnanimous, open-handed, munificent, bountiful; profuse, abundant; literary bounteous, plenteous.
OPPOSITES grudging, mean.

unspeakable ▶ adjective **1** *the book is a treasure trove of unspeakable delights* **indescribable**, beyond words, beyond description, inexpressible, unutterable, indefinable, beggaring description, ineffable, unimaginable, inconceivable, unthinkable, unheard of, marvellous, wonderful.
2 *an unspeakable crime* **dreadful**, awful, appalling, horrific, horrifying, horrible, terrible, horrendous, atrocious, insufferable, abominable, abhorrent, repellent, repulsive, repugnant, revolting, sickening, frightful, fearful, shocking, hideous, ghastly, grim, dire, hateful, odious, loathsome, gruesome, monstrous, outrageous, heinous, deplorable, despicable, contemptible, execrable, vile, indescribable, indescribably bad/wicked/evil; rare egregious.
OPPOSITE commendable.

unspecified ▶ adjective *he proposed to resign at an unspecified date* **unnamed**, unstated, unidentified, unquantified, undesignated, undefined, unfixed, undecided, undetermined, uncertain, uncounted; nameless, anonymous, mystery, mysterious, incognito, unknown; indefinite, indeterminate, vague, obscure, arbitrary, such-and-such a ..., some, any; informal this, nth, x number of ...; rare innominate.
OPPOSITES specified, fixed, known.

unspectacular ▶ adjective *he had a steady, unspectacular career* **unremarkable**, unexceptional, undistinguished, uneventful, unmemorable, inconspicuous; **ordinary**, average, normal, commonplace, nothing out of the ordinary; **mediocre**, middling, run-of-the-mill, workaday, indifferent, amateur, amateurish, dull, boring, plodding.
OPPOSITES spectacular, remarkable.

unspoilt ▶ adjective **1** *unspoilt countryside* **unimpaired**, preserved, intact, as good as new/before, perfect, spotless, pristine, immaculate, virgin, unblemished, unharmed, unbroken, unflawed, undamaged, unmutilated, untouched, unmarked, untainted, unaffected, unchanged.
OPPOSITES spoilt, devastated, overdeveloped.
2 *a noble and unspoilt man* **innocent**, wholesome, natural, simple, artless, unaffected, pure, uncorrupted, unsullied, undefiled, unblemished, untarnished, stainless, spotless, impeccable.
OPPOSITES spoilt, corrupt.

unspoken ▶ adjective *there was an unspoken contract between them* **unstated**, unexpressed, unuttered, unsaid, unmentioned, unvoiced, unarticulated, undeclared, unavowed, not spelt out, mute, silent, wordless, voiceless; **tacit**, implicit, implied, understood, taken for granted, taken as read, inferred, hinted (at), suggested, insinuated.
OPPOSITES stated, explicit.

> CHOOSE THE RIGHT WORD
>
> **unspoken, implicit, unspoken**
> See IMPLICIT.

unstable ▶ adjective **1** *icebergs are notoriously unstable and may flip over* **unsteady**, rocky, wobbly, wobbling, rickety, shaky, tottery, tottering, teetering, doddery, unsafe, unbalanced, unreliable, insecure, not secure, unfastened, unsecured, movable, precarious; Irish bockety.
OPPOSITES stable, steady.
2 *the country suffered from unstable coffee prices* **changeable**, volatile, variable, unsettled, fluctuating, inconstant, inconsistent, irregular, fitful, unpredictable, unreliable, fickle, capricious, mercurial, erratic, uncertain, wavering.
OPPOSITES stable, firm.
3 *he was mentally unstable* **unbalanced**, of unsound mind, mentally ill, deranged, demented, crazed, distracted, troubled, disturbed, unhinged, insane, mad, mad as a hatter, mad as a March hare, raving mad, lunatic, out of one's mind/head, not in one's right mind, neurotic, psychotic; Latin non compos mentis; informal crazy, loopy, loony, mixed up, nuts, nutty, nutty as a fruitcake, bananas, cracked, crackpot, daft, dippy, screwy, bats, batty, dotty, cuckoo, bonkers, potty, mental, screwed up, not all there, off one's head, out to lunch, a bit lacking, round the bend/twist, away with the fairies; Brit. informal barmy, crackers, barking, barking mad, off one's trolley/rocker, daft as a brush, not the full shilling; N. Amer. informal nutsy, nutso, squirrelly, wacko, buggy; dated touched.
OPPOSITES stable, balanced.

unsteady ▶ adjective **1** *she was unsteady on her feet* **unstable**, rocky, wobbly, wobbling, rickety, shaky, shaking, tottery, tottering, teetering, unsafe, unbalanced, unreliable, insecure, not secure, unfastened, unsecured, movable, precarious; dizzy, light-headed, faint, weak-kneed, weak at the knees, groggy, punch-drunk; feeble, faltering, doddery, doddering; tentative, nervous, timid, hesitant; informal trembly, all of a quiver, teetery, (with legs) like jelly; rare vertiginous.
OPPOSITES steady, stable.
2 *the baby poured tea in an unsteady stream on to the pink carpet* **irregular**, uneven, varying, variable, erratic, jerky, unreliable, volatile, spasmodic, sporadic, changeable, changing, fluctuating, wavering, vacillating, inconstant, intermittent, fitful, desultory, occasional, unsystematic; flickering, flashing, trembling; technical aperiodic.

unstinted ▶ adjective *Gina gave him the unstinted praise he deserved* **lavish**, liberal, generous, magnanimous, open-handed, munificent, bountiful; **ungrudging**, unsparing, willingly given, ready, beneficent, benevolent, kind, unselfish; profuse, abundant, ample; literary bounteous, plenteous.

unstinting ▶ adjective *her unstinting charity work* **ungrudging**, unsparing, willingly given, free, free-handed, ready, beneficent, benevolent, big-hearted, kind-hearted, kind, unselfish; lavish, liberal, generous, magnanimous, open-handed, munificent, bountiful; profuse, abundant, ample; literary bounteous, plenteous.

unstudied ▶ adjective *he always does it with unstudied grace | she writes a seemingly unstudied prose* **natural**, unlaboured, easy, unaffected, unforced, uncontrived, unmannered, unstilted, unpretentious, without airs, artless, guileless, informal, casual, nonchalant, spontaneous, impromptu, ad lib; unrehearsed, improvised, unscripted, unpremeditated, extempore, extemporized; Latin ad libitum; rare extemporary, extemporaneous.
OPPOSITES studied, stilted, prepared.

unsubstantiated ▶ adjective *there were unsubstantiated allegations of serious misbehaviour* **unconfirmed**, unsupported, uncorroborated, not backed up by evidence, unverified, unattested, unproven, not validated, untested; unfounded, ill-founded, groundless, baseless, without basis, without foundation, unjustified, unwarranted, unjustifiable, unreasonable; speculative, conjectural, assumed, presumed; questionable, open to question, disputable, debatable; unreliable, untrustworthy, dubious, doubtful, tenuous, spurious, suspect, flimsy, weak, nebulous, unsound, undependable; informal iffy; Brit. informal dodgy; rare unestablished, suppositious, suppositive.
OPPOSITES well founded, undeniable.

unsuccessful ▶ adjective **1** *an unsuccessful attempt* **failed**, without success, abortive, misfired; vain, in vain, futile, useless, pointless, worthless, nugatory; ineffective, ineffectual, inefficacious, unavailing, fruitless, profitless, unproductive; thwarted, baulked, frustrated, foiled; archaic bootless.
OPPOSITE successful.
2 *an unsuccessful business venture | an unsuccessful candidate* **unprofitable**, unprosperous, loss-making; **failed**, losing, beaten; unlucky, luckless, out of luck, unfortunate, ill-starred, fated, ill-fated, ill-omened.
OPPOSITES profitable; winning.

unsuitable ▶ adjective **1** *they had been sold an unsuitable product* **inappropriate**, unsuited, ill-suited, inapt, inapposite, unfitting, unbefitting, undue, incompatible, out of place, out of keeping, out of character, incongruous; unacceptable, ineligible, not good enough.
OPPOSITE suitable.
2 *unsuitable reading matter for a young lady* **unbecoming**, unseemly, indecorous, improper.
OPPOSITE becoming.
3 *her comment came at an unsuitable moment* **inopportune**, unseasonable, infelicitous, malapropos; badly chosen.
OPPOSITE opportune.

unsullied ▶ adjective *he came with an unsullied reputation* **spotless**, untarnished, unblemished, untainted, impeccable, undamaged, unspoilt, unimpaired, undefiled, stainless, intact, perfect, pristine, immaculate, virgin, unharmed, unbroken, unflawed, unmutilated, untouched, unmarked, unaffected.
OPPOSITES sullied, tarnished.

unsung ▶ adjective *one of the finest unsung heroes of the last war* **unacknowledged**, uncelebrated, unacclaimed, unapplauded, unpraised, unhailed, unlauded, unhonoured, unrenowned, untrumpeted, unbemoaned; **neglected**, disregarded, unrecognized, overlooked, forgotten; unknown, anonymous, nameless, unnamed, obscure, unmissed.
OPPOSITES famous, celebrated.

unsure ▶ adjective **1** *she felt very unsure* **unconfident**, not confident, lacking confidence, lacking self-confidence, not self-assured, lacking assurance, unassertive; **insecure**, hesitant, diffident, timid, timorous, anxious, apprehensive, fearful.
OPPOSITES confident, assertive.
2 *Sally was unsure whether to be pleased* **undecided**, irresolute, dithering, equivocating, in two minds, in a dilemma, in a quandary, ambivalent, vague.
OPPOSITE decided.
3 *some teachers are unsure about the proposed strike* **dubious**, doubtful,

U

sceptical, distrustful, suspicious, mistrustful, uncertain, unconvinced; *informal* iffy.
OPPOSITES happy, convinced.
4 *the date is unsure* **not fixed**, not settled, undecided, indeterminate, uncertain, unknown.
OPPOSITE fixed.

unsurpassed ▶ adjective *Beethoven's nine unsurpassed masterpieces* **unmatched**, unrivalled, unparalleled, unequalled, matchless, peerless, without peer, without equal, in a class of its own, all-time best, inimitable, incomparable, beyond compare, beyond comparison, second to none, unsurpassable, surpassing, nonpareil; unique, consummate, perfect, rare, exquisite, transcendent, superlative, supreme, outstanding, pre-eminent, top, towering, leading, foremost, premier, the best; *rare* unexampled; *French* hors concours; (**be unsurpassed**) stand alone.
OPPOSITES inferior; eclipsed.

unsurprising ▶ adjective *his failure to win the leadership of the party was unsurprising* **predictable**, foreseeable, (only) to be expected, what one would expect, not unexpected, predicted, foreseen, forecast, anticipated, awaited; probable, likely, par for the course, normal; logical, understandable, plausible, obvious; *informal* inevitable, on the cards.
OPPOSITES surprising, unpredictable.

unsuspecting ▶ adjective *this is a very nasty trick to play on the unsuspecting public* **unsuspicious**, unwary, unaware, unconscious, off guard, ignorant, unknowing, unwitting, oblivious, heedless, unmindful; **trusting**, trustful; gullible, credulous, ingenuous, naive, innocent, dupable, easily deceived, easily taken in, exploitable; *rare* incognizant, nescient.
OPPOSITES suspicious, knowing, wary.

unswerving ▶ adjective *she has always demanded unswerving loyalty* **unwavering**, unfaltering, unhesitating, unflinching, steadfast, unshakeable, undaunted, staunch, firm, resolute, stalwart, dedicated, committed, constant, single-minded, earnest; stubborn, tenacious, bulldog, strong-minded, strong-willed, dogged, indefatigable, unyielding, unbending, immovable, unrelenting; spirited, brave, bold, courageous, plucky, stout, stout-hearted, mettlesome, indomitable, strenuous, vigorous, gritty, stiff; *N. Amer.* rock-ribbed.
OPPOSITES half-hearted, ambiguous, unreliable.

unsympathetic ▶ adjective **1** *benefit claimants often encounter unsympathetic staff* **uncaring**, unconcerned, unfeeling, insensitive, unkind, compassionless, uncharitable, unpitying, pitiless, uncommiserating, indifferent, unresponsive, apathetic, unmoved, untouched, heartless, cold, hard-hearted, stony-hearted, hard, harsh, callous, cruel, inhuman.
OPPOSITES sympathetic, caring.
2 *the new Assembly was quite* **unsympathetic** *to these views* **opposed to**, against, (dead) set against, antagonistic towards, inimical to, anti, ill-disposed towards, disapproving of.
OPPOSITES sympathetic, in agreement with.
3 *he is a totally unsympathetic character* **unlikeable**, disagreeable, unpleasant, objectionable, obnoxious, unsavoury, unattractive; unsociable, uncongenial, unfriendly, inhospitable, unneighbourly, unapproachable, aloof, cool, cold, distant; **nasty**, ill-natured, cross, bad-tempered.
OPPOSITE likeable.

unsystematic ▶ adjective *the burial mound was excavated in an unsystematic way* **unmethodical**, uncoordinated, undirected, disorganized, unarranged, unplanned, unpremeditated, indiscriminate; random, inconsistent, desultory, patchy, fragmentary, sketchy, sporadic, spasmodic, fitful, inconstant, intermittent, irregular, erratic, stray, spot, casual, occasional, haphazard; chaotic, non-linear, entropic, fractal.
OPPOSITES systematic, well planned.

untamed ▶ adjective *the untamed wildlife which proliferates in the region* **wild**, savage, feral, natural, free, uncontrollable; **undomesticated**, unbroken, not broken in, untrained, unused to humans; *rare* brutish, bestial.
OPPOSITES tame, domesticated.

untangle ▶ verb **1** *I untangled the fishing tackle* **disentangle**, unravel, unsnarl, unjumble, straighten out, sort out, untwist, untwine, untie, unknot, undo.
OPPOSITES tangle, jumble.
2 *I started to try and untangle the mystery* **solve**, find the/an answer to, answer, find a/the solution to, resolve, work out, puzzle out, fathom, understand, find the key to, find the answer to, decipher, clear up, make easier to understand, make simpler, make plainer, clarify, make more comprehensible, make more intelligible, remove the complexities from, straighten out, sort out, get to the bottom of, make head or tail of, unravel, disentangle, unfold, piece together, simplify, explain, expound, elucidate, illuminate; *informal* figure out, suss out, crack.
OPPOSITES complicate, confuse, cloud.

untarnished ▶ adjective *the reputation of the school was untarnished* **unsullied**, unblemished, untainted, impeccable, undamaged, unspoilt, unimpaired, undefiled, spotless, stainless, intact, perfect, pristine, immaculate, virgin, unharmed, unbroken, unflawed, untouched, unmarked, unaffected.
OPPOSITE tarnished.

untenable ▶ adjective *the Government's position is untenable* **indefensible**, undefendable, unarguable, insupportable, refutable, unsustainable, unjustified, unwarranted, unjustifiable, inadmissible, unsound, ill-founded, flimsy, weak, shaky, flawed, defective, faulty, implausible, specious, groundless, unfounded, baseless, invalid, absurd, illogical, irrational, preposterous, senseless, unacceptable.
OPPOSITES tenable, defensible.

unthinkable ▶ adjective **1** *Beethoven is unthinkable without the tradition of western music* **unimaginable**, inconceivable, unbelievable, incredible, beyond belief, highly unlikely, unheard of, implausible, illogical, impossible, beyond the bounds of possibility.
OPPOSITES likely, imaginable, plausible.
2 *to me a lentil soup is unthinkable without lemon and olive oil* **highly undesirable**, not to be considered, unconscionable, out of the question, absurd, unreasonable, preposterous, ludicrous, outrageous, shocking; *informal* not on.
OPPOSITE desirable.

unthinking ▶ adjective **1** *Dorothea was often an unthinking woman* **thoughtless**, inconsiderate, uncaring, heedless, unmindful, regardless, insensitive, injudicious, blundering, uncharitable, unkind; tactless, undiplomatic, indiscreet, careless, selfish, impolite, rude.
OPPOSITES thoughtful, careful.
2 *don't encourage the unthinking sprinkling of salt over food* **absent-minded**, heedless, thoughtless, unmindful, careless, injudicious, ill-advised, ill-considered, imprudent, unwise, foolish, silly, stupid, reckless, rash, precipitate, negligent, neglectful, remiss; involuntary, inadvertent, unintentional, unintended, mechanical, automatic, reflex, spontaneous, instinctive, impulsive, intuitive, unpremeditated, unconscious.
OPPOSITES intentional, planned.

untidy ▶ adjective **1** *Fran smoothed her untidy hair* **scruffy**, tousled, dishevelled, unkempt, messy, disordered, disarranged, messed up, rumpled, bedraggled, uncombed, ungroomed, straggly, ruffled, tangled, matted, windblown, wild; frowzy, dirty, sleazy, seedy, slovenly, slatternly, sloppy; *informal* ratty, mussed up, slobbish, slobby; *N. Amer. informal* raggedy, schlumpy, raunchy; *archaic* draggle-tailed.
OPPOSITES tidy, neat.
2 *the place was dreadfully untidy* **disordered**, messy, in a mess, disorderly, disorganized, in disorder, in confusion, confused, cluttered, in a clutter, mixed up, in a muddle, muddled, in a jumble, jumbled, in chaos, chaotic, haywire, topsy-turvy, in disarray, awry, askew, upside down, upset, disrupted, at sixes and sevens; *informal* higgledy-piggledy, every which way; *Brit. informal* shambolic, like a dog's dinner/breakfast.
OPPOSITES tidy, orderly.

untie ▶ verb *she knelt to untie her laces | he hung over the bank and untied the boat* **undo**, unknot, unbind, unfasten, unwrap, unlace, untether, unfetter, unhitch, unmoor, **loose**, detach, free, set free, release, let go, set adrift, cast off.
OPPOSITE tie up.

until ▶ preposition & conjunction **1** *I was working away until midnight | young trees should be staked until they are well established* **till**, up to, up till, up until, as late as, up to the time of/that, until such time as, pending; *N. Amer.* through.
OPPOSITES beyond, after.
2 *this did not happen until 1998* **before**, prior to, previous to, up to, up until, till, up till, earlier than, in advance of, ante-, pre-.
OPPOSITE after.

untimely ▶ adjective **1** *I would like to explain the untimely interruption you heard a few minutes ago* **ill-timed**, badly timed, mistimed; inopportune, inappropriate, unseasonable; inconvenient, awkward, unwelcome, unfavourable, unfortunate, infelicitous, inapt, unsuitable; *rare* malapropos.
OPPOSITES timely, opportune.
2 *his untimely death* **premature**, early, too early, too soon, before time, unseasonable.
OPPOSITE expected.

untiring ▶ adjective *an untiring advocate of political and economic reform* **vigorous**, energetic, industrious, determined, resolute, enthusiastic, keen, zealous, forceful, strong, Herculean, spirited, dynamic, intense, dogged, tenacious, persistent, persevering, constant, incessant, unceasing, steady, stout, staunch, pertinacious; **tireless**, unwearied, unflagging, unfailing, unfaltering, unwavering, indefatigable, unshakeable, unrelenting, unremitting, unswerving.
OPPOSITES lazy, half-hearted.

untold ▶ adjective **1** *thieves caused untold damage* **boundless**, measureless, limitless, without limit, unlimited, unbounded, immense, vast, great, endless, unending, never-ending, without end, inexhaustible, infinite, interminable, unceasing, everlasting, immeasurable, incalculable.
OPPOSITE limited.
2 *untold billions have been poured into research* **countless**, innumerable, unlimited, endless, limitless, numberless, an infinite number of, an

incalculable number of, more than one can count, too many to be counted, without number, uncountable, uncounted; numerous, many, multiple, manifold, legion; informal more ... than one can shake a stick at; literary multitudinous, myriad; rare unnumbered, unnumberable, innumerous, unsummed.
3 *a £300,000 docudrama will reveal the untold story that led to his acquittal* **unreported**, unrecounted, unrelated, unrevealed, undisclosed, undivulged, unpublished, secret, suppressed, unnarrated, unmentioned, unstated, unspoken.

untouched ▶ adjective **1** *the food sat on their plates untouched* **uneaten**, unconsumed, undrunk; left over, surplus, unwanted.
2 *one of the few untouched areas left on this fast developing island* **unspoilt**, unmarked, unblemished, untarnished, unsullied, undefiled, undamaged, unharmed, unscathed, unmarred, unpolluted; **pristine**, intact, natural, immaculate, in perfect condition, perfect, spotless, flawless, clean, fresh, virgin, pure; unaffected, unchanged, unaltered, uninfluenced.
OPPOSITES developed, built-up, industrialized.

untoward ▶ adjective *Tom had noticed nothing untoward* **unexpected**, unanticipated, unforeseen, unpredictable, unpredicted; surprising, unusual; inopportune, untimely, unseasonable, ill-timed, badly timed, mistimed; inconvenient, awkward, unwelcome, unfavourable, adverse, unfortunate, infelicitous; inappropriate, unsuitable, inapt; rare malapropos.
OPPOSITES expected, timely, appropriate.

untrained ▶ adjective *the system can be utilized quickly by untrained users* **unskilled**, untaught, non-technical, unschooled, untutored, unpractised, inexperienced, unequipped, unversed, uninformed, unacquainted; unqualified, unlicensed, uncertificated, unchartered; incompetent, incapable, inexpert, ignorant, green, raw; amateur, non-professional, lay, dilettante.
OPPOSITES trained, professional.

untried ▶ adjective *he chose two untried actors for leading roles | dealers used their clients as guinea pigs for their untried techniques* **untested**, unestablished, new; **experimental**, exploratory, unattempted, prototype, trial, test, pilot; speculative, conjectural, unproven, unsubstantiated.
OPPOSITES established, well tried.

untroubled ▶ adjective *a man untroubled by a guilty conscience* **unworried**, unperturbed, unconcerned, unruffled, undisturbed, undismayed, unbothered, unagitated, unflustered; unanxious, insouciant, nonchalant, blasé, carefree, blithe, casual, without a care in the world; serene, composed, relaxed, peaceful, tranquil, at ease, devil-may-care, happy-go-lucky, {cool, calm, and collected}; trouble-free, unbroken, uninterrupted; informal laid-back, unflappable.
OPPOSITES troubled, anxious.

untrue ▶ adjective **1** *these suggestions are totally untrue* **false**, untruthful, fabricated, made up, invented, concocted, trumped up; erroneous, in error, wrong, incorrect, inaccurate, inexact; flawed, specious, fallacious, unsound, unfounded, misguided, distorted, out, misleading; fictitious, fabulous, mythical, mythological; humorous economical with the truth.
OPPOSITES true, correct.
2 *he was untrue to himself* **unfaithful**, disloyal, faithless, false, false-hearted, treacherous, traitorous, perfidious, deceitful, deceiving, untrustworthy, duplicitous, double-dealing, insincere, unreliable, undependable, inconstant; adulterous; informal two-timing.
OPPOSITES true, faithful.

untrustworthy ▶ adjective *the clubs are vulnerable to untrustworthy treasurers* **dishonest**, deceitful, not to be trusted, double-dealing, treacherous, traitorous, two-faced, unfaithful, duplicitous, dishonourable, unprincipled, unscrupulous, corrupt, shady, shifty, underhand; **unreliable**, undependable, capricious, fickle, slippery; informal iffy; Brit. informal dodgy; Austral./NZ informal shonky; rare Janus-faced.
OPPOSITES trustworthy, reliable.

untruth ▶ noun **1** *her account of what had happened was a patent untruth* **lie**, falsehood, fib, fabrication, deception, made-up story, trumped-up story, invention, fiction, piece of fiction, falsification, falsity, cock and bull story, barefaced lie; (little) white lie, half-truth, exaggeration, prevarication, departure from the truth; yarn, story, red herring, rumour, fable, myth, flight of fancy, figment of the imagination; pretence, pretext, sham, ruse, wile, stratagem; (**untruths**) misinformation, disinformation, trickery, perjury, dissimulation, gossip, propaganda; informal tall story, tall tale, fairy story, fairy tale, whopper; Brit. informal porky, pork pie, porky pie; humorous terminological inexactitude, economy with the truth; vulgar slang bullshit; Austral./NZ vulgar slang bulldust.
2 *he was livid at the total untruth of the story* **falsity**, falsehood, falseness, untruthfulness, fallaciousness, fiction, fictitiousness, inaccuracy, hollowness; **mendacity**, fabrication, dishonesty, deceit, deceitfulness, deception, duplicity, disingenuousness, hypocrisy, fraud, fraudulence; informal kidology; rare unveracity.

untruthful ▶ adjective **1** *the answers may be untruthful* **false**, untrue, fabricated, made up, invented, concocted, trumped up; erroneous, in error, wrong, incorrect, inaccurate, inexact; flawed, specious, fallacious, unsound, unfounded, misguided, distorted, out, misleading; fictitious, fabulous, mythical, mythological; humorous economical with the truth.
2 *an untruthful person* **lying**, mendacious, perfidious, dishonest, deceitful, deceiving, deceptive, duplicitous, dissimulating, dissembling, false, double-dealing, two-faced, guileful, underhand, sneaky, disingenuous; informal crooked, bent, tricky; archaic hollow-hearted.
OPPOSITES honest, truthful.

untutored ▶ adjective *such articles will make little sense to an untutored reader* **uneducated**, untaught, unschooled, ill-educated, untrained; illiterate, unlettered, ignorant, ill-informed, uninformed, lowbrow; uncouth, unsophisticated, uncultivated, uncultured, unaccomplished, unenlightened, philistine, benighted, backward, vulgar, simple; archaic rude.
OPPOSITES tutored, educated.

untwine ▶ verb *Robyn untwined her fingers* **untwist**, disentwine, disentangle, unravel, unsnarl, unwind, unroll, uncoil, unreel, undo, spread out, unfurl, open (out), lay out, straighten (out), unkink; Nautical unlay.
OPPOSITE twine.

untwist ▶ verb *he untwisted the wire and straightened it out* **untwine**, disentwine, disentangle, unravel, unsnarl, unwind, unroll, uncoil, unreel, undo, spread out, unfurl, open (out), lay out, straighten (out), unkink; Nautical unlay.
OPPOSITE twist.

unused ▶ adjective **1** *the new operating theatre will stand unused until next April | a charitable organization collects unused food* **unutilized**, not made use of, unemployed, unexploited, not in service, non-functioning; **left over**, remaining, uneaten, unconsumed, untouched, unneeded, not required, still available, surplus to requirements, to spare, superfluous, surplus, extra; **pristine**, immaculate, as new, unspoilt, spotless, flawless, clean, fresh, blank, new, virgin, pure, untouched, unopened, unmarked, unblemished, untarnished, unsullied, undefiled, unworn; informal going begging.
OPPOSITES used, in use.
2 *he was unused to such directness* **unaccustomed**, not used, new, fresh, a stranger; unfamiliar with, unconversant with, unacquainted with; unpractised in, inexperienced in, unversed in; archaic strange.
OPPOSITES used, accustomed.

unusual ▶ adjective **1** *the unusual sight of a golden eagle flying over Regents Park* **uncommon**, abnormal, atypical, unexpected, surprising, unfamiliar, unwonted, different; strange, odd, curious, out of the ordinary, extraordinary, out of the way, unorthodox, uncustomary, unconventional, outlandish, offbeat, deviant, novel, singular, peculiar, queer, bizarre, freakish, quirky, alien; **rare**, scarce, few and far between, thin on the ground, exceptional, isolated, occasional, infrequent, irregular, sporadic; Brit. out of the common; informal weird, oddball, way out, freaky, something else; N. Amer. informal off the wall; dated seldom.
OPPOSITES common, everyday.
2 *a man of unusual talent* **remarkable**, extraordinary, exceptional, singular, particular, marked, outstanding, notable, noteworthy, distinctive, striking, significant, especial, special, signal, superior, unique, unparalleled, unprecedented, prodigious; informal mind-boggling, mind-blowing.
OPPOSITE unremarkable.

unutterable ▶ adjective **1** *an existence of unutterable boredom* **indescribable**, beyond words, beyond description, inexpressible, unspeakable, undefinable, beggaring description, inconceivable, unthinkable, unheard of; **extreme**, intense, great, overwhelming; **dreadful**, awful, appalling, horrible, terrible, insufferable.
2 *unutterable joy suffused her whole being* **marvellous**, wonderful, superb, splendid, ineffable, unimaginable, profound, deep, ecstatic.
OPPOSITE mild.

unvarnished ▶ adjective **1** *the unvarnished wood panelling* **bare**, plain, unpainted, unlacquered, unpolished, unfinished, untreated, raw, natural, matt; stripped.
OPPOSITE varnished.
2 *the programme gives an unvarnished account of the proceedings of the House* **straightforward**, plain, simple, stark, naked, bald; truthful, realistic, true to life; candid, honest, frank, outspoken, forthright, plain-spoken, direct, blunt, downright, brutal, harsh, straight from the shoulder, explicit, unequivocal, unambiguous, unexaggerated, unadorned, undisguised, unveiled, unqualified; informal upfront, warts and all.
OPPOSITE qualified.

unveil ▶ verb *the club has unveiled plans for a new 1600-seat stand* **reveal**, present, disclose, divulge, make known, make public, air, communicate, publish, broadcast; display, show, exhibit, demonstrate, put on show, put on display, put on view, expose to view, parade, flaunt; release, bring out, launch, introduce.

unwanted ▶ adjective **1** *the Council said the plan was an unwanted development* **unwelcome**, undesirable, undesired, unpopular, unfortunate, unlucky, unfavourable, untoward, too bad; unpleasant, disagreeable,

displeasing, unpalatable, distasteful, objectionable, offensive, upsetting, disappointing, distressing; regrettable, deplorable, lamentable, reprehensible, blameworthy, ill-advised; unacceptable, intolerable, awful, terrible, wretched, sad, dire, disastrous, appalling; ignominious, pitiful, disgraceful, shameful.
OPPOSITES wanted, welcome, desirable.
2 *a Darlington couple are collecting tins of unwanted pet food for an animal rescue centre* **unused**, left over, surplus, superfluous, redundant; uneaten, unconsumed, untouched.
3 *any unwanted guest soon found himself bundled out* **uninvited**, intruding, gatecrashing, unbidden, unasked, unrequested, unsolicited.
OPPOSITE invited.
4 *many ageing people feel unwanted* **friendless**, unloved, uncared-for, uncherished, unpopular, forsaken, rejected, shunned, disliked; superfluous, useless, unnecessary; *French* de trop.
OPPOSITE loved.

unwarranted ▶ adjective **1** *they feel the criticism is unwarranted* **unjustified**, unjustifiable, indefensible, inexcusable, unforgivable, unpardonable, uncalled for, gratuitous, unnecessary, undue, unreasonable, unjust, groundless, inappropriate, unsuitable, unseemly, unbecoming, improper, ill-advised, excessive, immoderate, disproportionate, inordinate.
OPPOSITE justified.
2 *random drug testing of employees is an unwarranted invasion of privacy* **unauthorized**, unsanctioned, unapproved, uncertified, unaccredited, unlicensed; illegal, unlawful, illicit, illegitimate, criminal, punishable, felonious, actionable, prohibited.
OPPOSITES permitted, legal.

unwary ▶ adjective *accidents can happen to the unwary traveller* **incautious**, careless, thoughtless, unthinking, heedless, inattentive, unwatchful, unobservant, off-guard, off one's guard, absent-minded; *informal* napping; *Brit. informal* dozy.

unwavering ▶ adjective *she fixed him with an unwavering stare* **steady**, fixed, resolute, resolved, firm, steadfast, decided, unswerving, unfluctuating, unhesitating, unfaltering, unvacillating, untiring, tireless, unflagging, indefatigable, persistent, unyielding, relentless, unremitting, unrelenting, sustained, inexorable, unshakeable.
OPPOSITES wavering, unsteady.

unwelcome ▶ adjective **1** *I did not mean to make you feel unwelcome* **unwanted**, uninvited, unbidden, unasked, unrequested, unsolicited; *French* de trop.
OPPOSITE welcome.
2 *even a small increase in unemployment is unwelcome* **undesirable**, undesired, unpopular, unfortunate, unlucky, too bad; disappointing, upsetting, distressing, unpleasant, disagreeable, displeasing, unpalatable, distasteful; **regrettable**, deplorable, lamentable, reprehensible, blameworthy, ill-advised.
OPPOSITES welcome, desirable.

unwell ▶ adjective *he had been unwell for some time* **ill**, sick, poorly, indisposed, ailing, not (very) well, not oneself, not in good shape, in a bad way, out of sorts, not up to par, under/below par, peaky, liverish, queasy, nauseous; *Brit.* off, off colour; *informal* under the weather, not up to snuff, funny, peculiar, crummy, lousy, rough; *Brit. informal* ropy, grotty; *Scottish informal* wabbit; *Austral./NZ informal* crook; *dated* queer, seedy.
OPPOSITES well, in good health.

unwholesome ▶ adjective **1** *the unwholesome smoke-filled air* **unhealthy**, noxious, poisonous; unnourishing, innutritious; **insalubrious**, unhygienic, insanitary; harmful, injurious, detrimental, destructive, damaging, deleterious, ruinous, malign, baleful.
OPPOSITES wholesome, healthy, beneficial.
2 *the application allows parents to limit children's access to unwholesome Web pages* **improper**, immoral, indecent, corrupting, depraving, salacious, subversive, exploitative.
OPPOSITES proper, seemly.

unwieldy ▶ adjective *he dragged his big unwieldy sword out of its scabbard* **cumbersome**, unmanageable, unhandy, unmanoeuvrable; awkward, difficult, clumsy, ungainly; massive, heavy, hefty, bulky, weighty, ponderous; *informal* hulking, clunky.
OPPOSITES manageable, dainty.

unwilling ▶ adjective **1** *unwilling conscripts* **reluctant**, unenthusiastic, hesitant, afraid, resistant, grudging, involuntary, forced, enforced.
OPPOSITES willing, keen.
2 *he was unwilling to take on that responsibility* **disinclined**, reluctant, averse, loath, indisposed, not in the mood, slow, not about; (**be unwilling to do something**) not have the heart to, baulk at, jib at, demur at, shy away from, flinch from, recoil from, shrink from, mind, have qualms about, have scruples about, have misgivings about, have reservations about, stick at, think twice about, waver about, vacillate about, drag one's feet/heels over, can't be bothered doing something; *informal* be cagey about, boggle at; *archaic* sweer, disrelish something.
OPPOSITES willing, keen.

unwillingness ▶ adjective *he deplored the Government's unwillingness to provide adequate funds* **disinclination**, **reluctance**, slowness, lack of enthusiasm; hesitation, hesitance, hesitancy, diffidence, coyness, timidity, timorousness, trepidation, backwardness (in coming forward); aversion to, dislike for, distaste for; demurral, wavering, vacillation, foot-dragging; resistance to, objection to, opposition to; doubts, second thoughts, scruples, qualms, pangs of conscience, misgivings; *archaic* disrelish; *rare* indisposedness, nolence, nolition, sweerness.

unwind ▶ verb **1** *Ella unwound the long woollen scarf from her neck* **unroll**, uncoil, unreel, undo, unravel, untwine, untwist, disentangle, spread out, unfurl, open (out), lay out, straighten (out), unkink.
2 *it's a good place to unwind after work* **relax**, loosen up, ease up/off, let up, slow down, de-stress, unbend, rest, repose; laze, idle, loaf, do nothing, sit back, stand down, lounge, loll, slump, flop, put one's feet up, take it easy, luxuriate, take time off, slack off, be at leisure, take one's leisure, take one's ease, enjoy oneself, amuse oneself, play, entertain oneself; *informal* wind down, let it all hang out, let one's hair down, unbutton, veg out; *N. Amer. informal* hang loose, stay loose, chill out, kick back.

unwise ▶ adjective *it would have been unwise to argue* **injudicious**, ill-advised, imprudent; **foolish**, silly, ill-considered, ill-judged, inadvisable, impolitic, incautious, indiscreet, short-sighted, misguided, foolhardy, wrong-headed, irresponsible, rash, hasty, overhasty, reckless, thoughtless.
OPPOSITES wise, sensible.

> **CHOOSE THE RIGHT WORD**
>
> **unwise, imprudent, injudicious, ill-advised**
>
> These terms are all used to criticize a person or their behaviour as foolish; they generally suggest that the person should have been capable of taking a more sensible decision, if they had been prepared to think more carefully.
>
> - **Unwise** is typically used with an impersonal *it* and followed by an infinitive (*it would be unwise to try and fight*). Besides indicating foolishness, it may be applied to an intellectual judgement that is merely not justified (*it would be unwise to see the Jacobite unrest as typical of public opinion at the time*).
> - **Imprudent** emphasizes a person's failure to think of the future, and it is often used in financial contexts (*it would be imprudent to leave her winter coat behind | the banks made hundreds of imprudent loans in the 1970s*).
> - **Injudicious** is a relatively formal word. It is typically used of an action, rather than the person performing it, and not followed by an infinitive (*he will probably pay dearly for his injudicious comments*).
> - **Ill-advised** is typically used to describe an action and implies that others could have warned the perpetrator of the consequences of their folly (*the strike was ill-advised and would play into the hands of the management | you would be ill-advised to go on your own*).

unwitting ▶ adjective **1** *an unwitting accomplice* **unknowing**, unconscious, unsuspecting, oblivious, unaware, innocent; unmindful, uninformed, ignorant, unenlightened; *informal* in the dark; *rare* incognizant, nescient.
OPPOSITES witting, knowing.
2 *an unwitting mistake* **unintentional**, unintended, inadvertent, involuntary, unmeant, unthinking, unplanned, unpremeditated, unconscious, accidental, chance.
OPPOSITES deliberate, conscious.

unwonted ▶ adjective *they came running with unwonted energy* **unusual**, uncommon, unaccustomed, uncustomary, unfamiliar, unprecedented, atypical, untypical, abnormal, strange, peculiar, curious, out of the way, irregular, anomalous, exceptional, extraordinary, special, remarkable, singular, rare, surprising.
OPPOSITES usual, customary, habitual.

unworldly ▶ adjective **1** *the transformation from gauche, unworldly girl to dignified lady* **naive**, simple, inexperienced, innocent, green, raw, callow, immature, uninitiated, natural, unaffected, unsophisticated, gullible, born yesterday, ingenuous, artless, guileless, childlike, trusting, credulous, idealistic.
2 *the region has a stark, unworldly beauty* **unearthly**, other-worldly, extraterrestrial, ethereal, ghostly, spectral, phantom, preternatural, supernatural, paranormal, mystical, transcendent, numinous; *rare* extramundane.
3 *a completely unworldly religious order* **non-materialistic**, non-material, immaterial; spiritual, spiritualistic, religious.

unworthy ▶ adjective **1** *he was unworthy of trust* **undeserving**, not worthy, not good enough for, ineligible for, unqualified for, unfit for.
OPPOSITES worthy, deserving.
2 *he despised such unworthy behaviour* **unbecoming**, unsuitable, inappropriate, unbefitting, unfitting, unseemly, improper, incongruous; inconsistent, incompatible, out of keeping, out of character, out of place;

degrading, discreditable, shameful, dishonourable, despicable, ignoble, contemptible, reprehensible, inexcusable, unforgivable.
OPPOSITES worthy, becoming.

unwritten ▸ adjective *there are unwritten rules about what is acceptable dress* **tacit**, implicit, unvoiced, silent, implied, taken for granted, accepted, recognized, understood, unrecorded; traditional, customary, conventional, folk, handed down; oral, verbal, spoken, vocal, word-of-mouth, by mouth, by word of mouth; Latin viva voce.
OPPOSITE written.

unyielding ▸ adjective **1** *a basket made from unyielding spikes of cane* **stiff**, inflexible, unpliable, non-flexible, unbending, inelastic, firm, hard, solid, tough, tight, taut, compact, compacted, compressed, dense; rare impliable, unmalleable, renitent.
2 *an unyielding policy on inflation* **resolute**, inflexible, uncompromising, unbending, unshakeable, unwavering; unpersuadable, uncooperative, immovable, intractable, intransigent, rigid, stiff, hard-line, hard and fast, tough, firm, determined, iron-willed, dogged, obstinate, stubborn, not giving an inch, diehard, adamant, obdurate, tenacious, pertinacious, relentless, implacable, inexorable, single-minded, stiff-necked; Brit. informal bloody-minded; rare indurate, renitent, unmalleable.

up-and-coming ▸ adjective *up-and-coming young players* **promising**, budding, rising, coming, on the up and up, in the making, with potential, likely to succeed; talented, gifted, able, apt.
OPPOSITE on the way out.

upbeat ▸ adjective (informal) *the share price rose 13p after an upbeat presentation to brokers* **optimistic**, **cheerful**, cheery, positive, confident, hopeful, sanguine, bullish, buoyant, bright; disposed to look on the bright side, inclined to look through rose-coloured spectacles, idealistic, always expecting the best, full of hope, Pollyannaish, Panglossian; informal chirpy; archaic of good cheer.
OPPOSITES pessimistic, negative, cynical.

upbraid ▸ verb *she had upbraided him firmly for his deception* **reprimand**, rebuke, reproach, scold, admonish, reprove, remonstrate with, chastise, chide, berate, take to task, pull up, castigate, lambaste, read someone the Riot Act, give someone a piece of one's mind, haul over the coals, criticize, censure; informal tell off, give someone a talking-to, give someone a telling-off, dress down, give someone a dressing-down, give someone an earful, give someone a roasting, give someone a rocket, give someone a rollicking, rap, rap someone over the knuckles, slap someone's wrist, let someone have it, bawl out, give someone hell, come down on, blow up, pitch into, lay into, lace into, give someone a caning, blast, rag, keelhaul; Brit. informal tick off, have a go at, carpet, give someone a mouthful, tear someone off a strip, give someone what for, wig, give someone a wigging, row, give someone a row; N. Amer. informal chew out, ream out; Austral. informal monster; Brit. vulgar slang bollock, give someone a bollocking; N. Amer. vulgar slang chew someone's ass, ream someone's ass; dated call down, rate, give someone a rating, trim; rare reprehend, objurgate.
OPPOSITE congratulate.

upbringing ▸ noun *her upbringing had not prepared her for that* **bringing up**, rearing, raising, breeding, care, upkeep, cultivation, fostering, tending; **nurture**, training, teaching, education; childhood, early life, family history, background; nature, character; (in ancient Greece) paideia.

update ▸ verb **1** *security measures are continually updated* **modernize**, bring up to date, bring into the twenty-first century, renovate, refurbish, recondition, overhaul, re-equip, improve, better, upgrade, streamline, rationalize, reform, revise, correct, amend; N. Amer. bring up to code.
2 *I'm going to update the Colonel on today's developments* **brief**, bring up to date, inform, fill in, advise, notify, apprise, report to, give details to, explain the situation to, give information to, give someone the latest information, refresh, explain the circumstances to, describe the state of affairs to; keep someone informed, keep someone posted, keep someone briefed, keep someone in the picture, keep someone up to date; informal clue in, give a sitrep to, bring up to speed, keep someone up to speed.

upgrade ▸ verb **1** *there are also plans to upgrade the rail system* **improve**, better, make better, ameliorate, reform, enhance, add to, customize, touch up; rehabilitate, refurbish, recondition, modernize, update, bring up to date, renovate, redecorate, revamp, restore, remodel, redo, brighten up, spruce up; N. Amer. bring up to code; informal do up, fix up.
OPPOSITE degrade.
2 *some primary school teachers were upgraded to teach in secondary schools* **promote**, give a higher rank to, place in a higher rank, give promotion to, give a higher position to, elevate, advance, move up, raise, lift, boost, improve the position/status of, aggrandize, exalt; informal kick upstairs; archaic prefer.
OPPOSITES downgrade, demote.

upheaval ▸ noun *the upheaval caused by wartime evacuation* **disruption**, upset, disturbance, trouble, turbulence; disorder, disorganization, confusion, turmoil, pandemonium, bedlam, furore, uproar, disarray, chaos, mayhem, cataclysm; revolution, violent change, sudden change.
OPPOSITES stability, tranquillity.

uphill ▸ adjective **1** *an uphill path* **upward**, rising, ascending, climbing, mounting; rare acclivitous, upsloping.
OPPOSITE downhill.
2 *an uphill job* **arduous**, difficult, hard, tough, taxing, demanding, exacting, stiff, formidable, heavy, exhausting, tiring, wearying, wearisome, fatiguing, laborious, gruelling, back-breaking, murderous, punishing, burdensome, onerous, Herculean; informal no picnic, killing; Brit. informal knackering; archaic toilsome.
OPPOSITE easy.

uphold ▸ verb **1** *the court upheld his claim for damages* **confirm**, endorse, sustain, validate, ratify, verify, vindicate, justify, approve; support, give one's support to, be supportive of, back, back up, give one's backing to, stand by, champion, defend, come to the defence of, stick up for.
OPPOSITES overturn, oppose.
2 *they've a tradition to uphold* **maintain**, sustain, continue, preserve, protect, keep, hold to, keep alive, keep going, strengthen, nurture.
OPPOSITE abandon.

upkeep ▸ noun **1** *we will be responsible for the upkeep of the access road* **maintenance**, repair(s), service, servicing, care, aftercare, preservation, conservation, running.
2 *Casey paid a monthly sum for the child's upkeep* **subsistence**, care, upbringing, support, keep, maintenance, sustenance, welfare.

uplift ▸ verb *this is the kind of music that uplifts him* **boost**, raise, buoy up, elevate, edify, inspire, lift, give a lift to, cheer up, perk up, enliven, brighten up, lighten, ginger up, gladden, encourage, stimulate, arouse, revive, restore; informal buck up.

uplifted ▸ adjective *his uplifted hand shot to his face* **raised**, elevated, hoisted, upraised, upthrust, reared, hitched up, held high, erect, proud; rare upheaved, upreared.
OPPOSITE lowered.

uplifting ▸ adjective *it's a sweet, uplifting story about an English girl at a mission in India* **inspiring**, stirring, moving, touching, affecting, warming, cheering, cheerful, gladdening, encouraging; emotional, profound, fervent, heartfelt, sincere, passionate; meaningful, significant, eloquent, expressive; sad, soulful, mournful, doleful.

upper ▸ adjective **1** *he made his way to the upper floor* **higher**, further-up, loftier; overlying, superior; top.
OPPOSITE lower.
2 *the upper echelons of the party* **senior**, superior, higher-level, higher-ranking, highest-ranking, top, chief, more/most important, elevated, eminent.
OPPOSITES junior, inferior.
□ **the upper hand** *I decided to gain the upper hand by launching a surprise attack* **an advantage**, a commanding position, an/the edge, the whip hand, a lead, a head start, ascendancy, superiority, supremacy, sway, control, predominance, power, mastery, dominance, command; rare prepotence, prepotency, paramountcy, prepollency.

upper-class ▸ adjective *she was born into an upper-class family* **aristocratic**, noble, noble-born, of noble birth, patrician, titled, blue-blooded, high-born, well born, elite, upper-crust, landowning, landed, born with a silver spoon in one's mouth; high-class, select, exclusive; Brit. county, upmarket; informal top-drawer, top-people's, {huntin', shootin', and fishin'}, classy, posh, snobby; archaic gentle, of gentle birth.

uppermost ▸ adjective **1** *she gazed at the uppermost branches* **highest**, furthest up, loftiest, top, topmost, most elevated.
2 *their own problems remained uppermost in their minds* **predominant**, most important, of greatest importance, to the fore, foremost, top, dominant, preponderant, principal, leading, greatest, chief, main, paramount, major.

uppish ▸ adjective (informal) *she sensed that her accent made her sound uppish* **arrogant**, bumptious, self-assertive, bullish, overweening, presumptuous, pushy, throwing one's weight about, overconfident, conceited, affected, snobbish, cocksure, cocky, brash, smug, haughty, supercilious, disdainful, lofty, patronizing, self-important, high-handed, cavalier, imperious, domineering, dictatorial, overbearing, lordly, peremptory, pompous, officious, blustering, boastful, opinionated, bold, forward, insolent; informal hoity-toity, high and mighty, stuck-up, toffee-nosed; N. Amer. informal chesty; vulgar slang pissy; rare pushful, hubristic.

upright ▸ adjective **1** *check that the posts are upright* **vertical**, perpendicular, plumb, straight (up), straight up and down, bolt upright, erect, on end, standing up, rearing, rampant; on one's feet.
OPPOSITE horizontal.
2 *an upright member of the community* **honest**, **honourable**, upstanding, respectable, reputable, high-minded, law-abiding, right-minded, worthy, moral, ethical, righteous, decent, good, virtuous, principled, high-principled, of principle, proper, correct, just, noble, incorruptible, conscientious.
OPPOSITES dishonourable, crooked.

▶ noun *he peered between the uprights of the gate* **column**, standard, stanchion, post, pole.

uprightness ▶ noun *there is a general lack of uprightness in these postmodern times* **rectitude**, decency, integrity, principle, honesty, honour, honourableness, upstandingness, respectability, high-mindedness, right-mindedness, worthiness, morality, righteousness, goodness, virtue, moral virtue, ethics, principles, correctness, probity, trustworthiness, truthfulness, good character, scrupulousness, nobility, conscientiousness, incorruptibility, fairness, equity, justice.

uprising ▶ noun *the uprising was put down by the action of the police and the army* **rebellion**, revolt, insurrection, mutiny, revolution, insurgence, insurgency, rising, rioting, riot; civil disobedience, civil disorder, unrest, anarchy, fighting in the streets; coup; French coup d'état, jacquerie; German putsch.

uproar ▶ noun **1** *the headmistress found the class in uproar | Joseph's voice rose above the uproar* **turmoil**, disorder, confusion, chaos, commotion, disturbance, tumult, turbulence, mayhem, pandemonium, havoc, bedlam, all hell broken loose; **noise**, din, clamour, hubbub, racket, row, clangour; babble, shouting, yelling, babel; W. Indian bangarang; informal hullabaloo, rumpus.
OPPOSITE calm.
2 *there was an uproar when he was dismissed* **outcry**, furore, outrage, howl of protest, protest, protestation, complaint, objection; clamour, fuss, commotion, hue and cry, row, ruckus, brouhaha; opposition, dissent, vociferation, indignation; informal hullabaloo, rumpus, ballyhoo, stink, ruction.
OPPOSITE acquiescence.

uproarious ▶ adjective **1** *an uproarious party* **disorderly**, tumultuous, riotous, unruly, wild, unrestrained, rip-roaring, rollicking, boisterous, roisterous; noisy, loud, rowdy, rackety, clamorous; Brit. informal rumbustious; N. Amer. informal rambunctious; archaic robustious.
OPPOSITES quiet, tame.
2 *they were laughing as if at some uproarious joke* **hilarious**, extremely amusing, very funny, comic, riotous, screamingly/hysterically funny, too funny for words, side-splitting, rib-tickling, comical, absurd, ridiculous; informal priceless, a scream, a hoot; dated killing, killingly funny.
OPPOSITES solemn; unfunny.

uproot ▶ verb **1** *don't pick or uproot wild flowers* **pull up**, root out, take out, rip out/up, tear up by the roots, grub out/up; rare deracinate.
OPPOSITE plant.
2 *a revolution is necessary to uproot the social order* **eradicate**, get rid of, eliminate, root out, weed out, remove, destroy, put an end to, do away with, wipe out, stamp out, extirpate, abolish, extinguish.
OPPOSITE establish.

upset ▶ verb (stress on the second syllable) **1** *the accusation upset her* **distress**, trouble, perturb, disturb, discompose, unsettle, disconcert, discountenance, dismay, disquiet, worry, bother, inconvenience, agitate, fluster, throw, ruffle, unnerve, shake, frighten, alarm, anger, annoy, irritate, vex, irk, fret, pester, harass, torment, plague, hurt, grieve; informal hassle.
OPPOSITE put at ease.
2 *he upset a tureen of soup* **knock over**, overturn, upend, tip over, push over, topple (over), capsize, turn topsy-turvy; spill, slop, slosh; archaic overset.
OPPOSITE right.
3 *the dam will upset the ecological balance* **disrupt**, interfere with, disturb, throw out, turn topsy-turvy, disorder, unsettle, confuse, throw into confusion, throw into chaos, throw into disorder, disorganize, disarrange, mix up, jumble, mess up, wreck, ruin.
OPPOSITE maintain.
4 *his side were upset 2-1 by Sheffield United* **defeat**, beat, conquer, vanquish, rout, overthrow, overcome, triumph over, be victorious over, get the better of, worst, thrash, trounce, topple.
▶ noun **1** (stress on the first syllable) *a legal dispute will cause worry and upset* **distress**, trouble, perturbation, disturbance, discomposure, dismay, disquiet, worry, bother, inconvenience, agitation, fluster, alarm, fright, anger, annoyance, irritation, vexation, harassment, torment, hurt, grief.
OPPOSITES calm, ease.
2 *they nearly pulled off one of motor sport's biggest upsets* **unexpected result**; **major defeat**, rout, trouncing, thrashing, drubbing, toppling; **surprise victory**, coup, tour de force, feat, master stroke; informal hammering.
OPPOSITE walkover.
3 *a stomach upset* **disorder**, complaint, ailment, illness, sickness, disease, malady, affliction, indisposition, infirmity; informal lurgy, bug; Austral. informal wog.
▶ adjective **1** *I was upset by Sheila's illness* **distressed**, troubled, perturbed, disturbed, discomposed, unsettled, disconcerted, discountenanced, dismayed, disquieted, worried, bothered, inconvenienced, anxious, agitated, flustered, ruffled, unnerved, shaken, frightened, alarmed, angered, annoyed, irritated, vexed, irked, fretted, hurt, saddened, grieved; informal cut up, choked; Brit. informal gutted.
OPPOSITES unperturbed, calm about.
2 *an upset stomach* **disordered**, disturbed, unsettled, queasy, bad, poorly, ill, sick; informal gippy, holiday.
OPPOSITE settled.

upshot ▶ noun *the upshot of this conflict of interests was a compromise* **result**, consequence, outcome, out-turn, sequel, effect, reaction, repercussion, reverberations, ramification, end, end result, conclusion, termination, culmination, denouement, corollary, concomitant, aftermath, fruit(s), product, produce, by-product; Medicine sequelae; informal pay-off; dated issue; archaic success.
OPPOSITES cause, origin.

upside down ▶ adjective **1** *the mangled remains of a vehicle were found hanging upside down in a tree* **upturned**, upended, bottom up, wrong side up, head over heels, inverted, reversed, overturned, capsized, upset, flipped.
OPPOSITES upright, the right way up.
2 *they left the flat upside down | my world was thrown upside down* **in/into disarray**, in/into disorder, jumbled up, in/into a jumble, in/into a muddle, untidy, disorganized, chaotic, all over the place, in/into chaos, in/into confusion, topsy-turvy, at sixes and sevens; informal messed up, higgledy-piggledy.
OPPOSITE tidy.

□ **turn something upside down** *the burglars have turned our house upside down* **throw into disarray**, throw into disorder, make disorderly, disorder, untidy, make untidy, disorganize, disturb, jumble, mix up, muddle, upset, turn something topsy-turvy; informal mess up; N. Amer. informal muss up.
OPPOSITE tidy.

upstanding ▶ adjective **1** *an upstanding member of the community* **honest**, **honourable**, upright, respectable, reputable, high minded, law-abiding, right-minded, worthy, moral, ethical, righteous, decent, good, virtuous, principled, high-principled, of principle, proper, correct, just, noble, incorruptible, conscientious.
OPPOSITES dishonourable, crooked.
2 *a strong breeze caught the upstanding feathered plumes* **upright**, erect, vertical, plumb, upended, on end, rearing, straight (up and down), perpendicular; on one's feet, standing, in a standing position; Heraldry rampant.
OPPOSITES flat, lying down, seated.

upstart ▶ noun *these upstarts, they don't know their place* **parvenu(e)**, arriviste, nouveau riche, vulgarian; status seeker, social climber; (**upstarts**) the new rich, new money; informal would-be, wannabe.

up to date ▶ adjective **1** *the Unit is trying to raise £40,000 to buy an up-to-date scanner* **modern**, contemporary, the latest, up to the minute, recent, new, the newest, newfangled, new-fashioned, ultra-modern, fresh, current, prevalent, prevailing, present-day; **fashionable**, in fashion, in vogue, voguish, trendsetting; French à la mode; informal bang up to date, in the swim, all the rage, trendy, with it, mod, cool, now, in, hip, big.
OPPOSITES out of date, old-fashioned.
2 *the monthly bulletin keeps staff **up to date on** topical issues* **informed about**, conversant with, au fait with, up to speed on, in touch with, up with, au courant with, familiar with, knowledgeable about, acquainted with, aware of.

upturn ▶ noun **1** *there was a general upturn in beer consumption* **increase**, rise, jump, leap, surge, upswing, upsurge, boost, acceleration, escalation, soaring, step up.
OPPOSITE fall.
2 *an upturn in the economy* **improvement**, recovery, revival, rally, pickup, comeback, resurgence, renewal, reinvigoration, upswing, advancement, betterment, a turn for the better.
OPPOSITES slump, downturn.

upward ▶ adjective *an upward trend in nickel prices* **rising**, ascending, climbing, mounting; skyward, heavenward; uphill; rare acclivitous, upsloping.
OPPOSITE downward.
▶ adverb. See UPWARDS.

upwards ▶ adverb *the taxi went on ever upwards | she peered upwards at the sky* **up**, upward, uphill, towards a higher level, to the top; skywards, heavenwards.
OPPOSITE downward.

□ **upward(s) of** *it will cost upwards of a million dollars* **more than**, above, over, in excess of, exceeding, beyond, greater than.
OPPOSITE less than.

urban ▶ adjective *crime rates are significantly higher in urban areas* **built-up**, town, city, inner-city, densely populated, townified, citified, metropolitan, suburban, non-rural; municipal, civic, borough; informal towny, townish; rare oppidan.
OPPOSITE rural.

urbane ▶ adjective *the urbane and scholarly former information minister* **suave**, sophisticated, debonair, worldly, elegant, cultivated, cultured, civilized, well bred, worldly-wise; **glib**, smooth, slick, polished, refined, poised,

U

self-possessed, dignified; **courteous**, polite, civil, well mannered, gentlemanly, gallant, courtly, charming, affable, tactful, diplomatic; *informal* cool; *dated* mannerly.
OPPOSITES uncouth, unsophisticated, boorish.

CHOOSE THE RIGHT WORD

urbane, glib, slick, smooth
See GLIB.

urbanity ▶ **noun** *she could see him growing quite testy beneath that polished urbanity of his* **suaveness**, sophistication, worldliness, elegance, cultivation, culture, civilization, breeding, smoothness, polish, refinement, poise, self-possession, dignity; courtesy, politeness, civility, mannerliness, manners, gentlemanliness, gallantry, courtliness, graciousness, charm, affability, tact, diplomacy; *informal* cool.

urchin ▶ **noun** *he was surrounded by a dozen urchins imploring him to be generous* **mischievous child**, imp, monkey, Puck, rascal, rogue, minx, mischief-maker, prankster, tearaway; ragamuffin, guttersnipe, waif, stray; *informal* scamp, scallywag, brat, whippersnapper, horror, varmint, scarecrow; *Brit. informal* perisher, pickle, tinker; *N. Amer. informal* hellion; *dated* jackanapes, rip, gamin, gamine; *historical* mudlark; *archaic* scapegrace, street Arab, wastrel, tatterdemalion.

urge ▶ **verb 1** *she urged him to buy a boat* **encourage**, try to persuade, enjoin, adjure, admonish, press, prompt, prod, goad, egg on, spur, push, pressure, put pressure on, use pressure on, pressurize, lean on; dragoon, constrain; entreat, exhort, implore, call on, appeal, beg, beseech, plead, nag; *informal* psych up, put the heat on, put the screws on, twist someone's arm, railroad into, bulldoze into.
OPPOSITE discourage.
2 *she urged her horse down the rutted lane* **impel**, spur (on), force, drive, coerce, goad.
3 *I urge caution in interpreting these results* **advise**, counsel, advocate, recommend, suggest; support, endorse, back, champion.
▶ **noun** *I also have this urge to travel* **desire**, wish, need, impulse, compulsion, longing, yearning, hankering, craving, appetite, hunger, thirst, lust, fancy; *informal* yen, itch.

urgency ▶ **noun 1** *the discovery of the ozone hole gave urgency to the issue of CFCs* **importance**, top priority, imperativeness, weight, weightiness, gravity, necessity, exigency, seriousness, momentousness, cruciality, extremity, hurry, haste.
2 *Emilia heard the urgency in his voice* **insistence**, persistence, determination, resolution, tenacity, obstinacy, doggedness; importunateness, clamour, clamorousness, earnestness, pleading, begging.

urgent ▶ **adjective 1** *an urgent need for better storage* **acute**, grave, pressing, dire, desperate, critical, crucial, sore, serious, intense, crying, burning, compelling, drastic, extreme; life-and-death, great, very great, terrible; *archaic or humorous* parlous.
OPPOSITE trivial.
2 *she needs urgent treatment* **emergency**, high-priority, top-priority, important, vital, crucial; hurried, rushed, hasty, fast, quick, rapid, swift; *N. Amer. informal* hurry-up.
OPPOSITES non-urgent, elective.
3 *'In here!' came an urgent whisper* **insistent**, persistent, determined, resolute, tenacious, obstinate, dogged, pressing, unrelenting; importunate, demanding, earnest, entreating, pleading, begging, clamorous; repeated, unremitting, continuous, incessant; *rare* exigent.
OPPOSITE casual.

urinate ▶ **verb** **pass water**, go to the loo, go to the toilet, go to the lavatory, relieve oneself; wet one's bed/pants, wet oneself; cock/lift its leg; *informal* go, do it, spend a penny, have/take a leak, shake hands with an old friend, answer the call of nature, pee, pee oneself, pee one's pants, piddle, have a piddle, widdle, have a widdle, tinkle, have a tinkle; *Brit. informal* wee, have a wee, wee-wee, have a Jimmy (Riddle), have a slash, have a wazz; *N. Amer. informal* whizz, take a whizz; *vulgar slang* piss, have a piss; *technical* micturate.

usable ▶ **adjective 1** *his family owned about one sixth of the usable land in the country* **available for use**, utilizable, disposable, at someone's disposal, ready for use, fit for use; working, in working order, functioning, functional, serviceable, workable, operational, operative, running, up and running; viable, feasible, practicable.
2 *a usable waterway* **negotiable**, passable, navigable.
OPPOSITE unusable.

usage ▶ **noun 1** *the increased usage of private cars | significant increases in energy usage* **utilization**, use, employment, consumption, operation, manipulation, running, handling.
2 *the intricacies of English usage* **phraseology**, phrasing, diction, parlance, idiom, choice of words, terminology; way of speaking/writing, manner of speaking/writing, style (of speaking/writing), mode of speaking/writing, mode of expression; *French* façon de parler; *technical* idiolect, sociolect.
3 *the dictates and usages of polite society* **custom**, practice, habit, tradition, convention, routine, rule, rite, ritual, observance, ordinance, ceremony, ceremonial; way, procedure, method, mode, form, formality, wont; *formal* praxis; (**usages**) *Latin* mores; *French* moeurs.

use ▶ **verb 1** *she used her key to open the front door* **utilize**, make use of, avail oneself of, employ, work, operate, wield, ply, apply, manoeuvre, manipulate, put to use, put into service, find a use for, resort to.
2 *the court will use its discretion in making an order* **exercise**, employ, apply, exert, bring into play, practise, implement, draw on.
3 *use your troops well and they will not let you down* **manage**, handle, treat, behave towards, act towards, conduct oneself towards, deal with.
4 *he may be innocent, but his sort use people like us* **take advantage of**, exploit, make use of, manipulate, take liberties with, capitalize on, profit from, trade on, milk, impose on, abuse, misuse, mistreat, maltreat, treat lightly, trifle with, play with; *informal* cash in on, bleed, walk all over, play someone for a sucker.
5 *I'm afraid I've* **used up** *all the eggs* **consume**, get through, go through, exhaust, deplete, expend, spend, waste, fritter away, squander, dissipate.
▶ **noun 1** *they renounced the use of such weapons* **utilization**, application, usage, employment, operation, manipulation, manoeuvring.
2 *his use of other people for his own ends* **exploitation**, manipulation; abuse, misuse, mistreatment, maltreatment.
3 *what is the use of that?* **usefulness**, advantage, benefit, service, utility, help, good, gain, avail, profit, value, worth, point, object, motive, aim, goal, purpose, sense, reason.
4 *composers do not seem to have found much use for the device* **need**, necessity, call, demand, occasion, purpose, reason, cause, grounds, justification, requirement, excuse.

used ▶ **adjective** *a used car* **second-hand**, old, nearly new, worn, pre-owned, handed-down, cast-off; *informal* hand-me-down, reach-me-down.
OPPOSITES unused, new.
□ **used to** *I'm used to hard work* **accustomed to**, not new to, no stranger to; practised in, familiar with, at home with, in the habit of, experienced in, versed in, conversant with, acquainted with; given to, prone to, wont to; habituated to, addicted to.
OPPOSITES unused, unaccustomed.

useful ▶ **adjective 1** *it is such a useful box* **functional**, practical, handy, neat, convenient, utilitarian, utility, helpful, applicable, serviceable, of use, of service; *informal* nifty.
OPPOSITE useless.
2 *they found watching the court proceedings a useful experience* **beneficial**, advantageous, helpful, worthwhile, profitable, gainful, rewarding, productive, constructive, effective, efficacious, valuable, fruitful, of help, of assistance.
OPPOSITE disadvantageous.
3 *they had some very useful players* **competent**, capable, able, expert, skilful, skilled, proficient, practised, experienced, effective, handy.
OPPOSITE incompetent.

usefulness ▶ **noun** *faults that affect the book's usefulness* **functionality**, practicality, serviceability, fitness, adequacy, handiness, neatness, convenience, utility, use, effectiveness, efficacy; value, worth, merit, success; benefits, advantages, helpfulness, good, avail, help, assistance; *informal* niftiness.
OPPOSITES uselessness, disadvantage.

useless ▶ **adjective 1** *it was useless to try | a piece of useless knowledge* **futile**, pointless, purposeless, impractical, vain, in vain, to no purpose, to no avail, unavailing, bootless, nugatory, hopeless, unusable, ineffectual, inefficacious, impotent, fruitless, unprofitable, profitless, unproductive, unachievable, Sisyphean; unworkable, broken, kaput, unserviceable; *informal* junky; *rare* inutile.
OPPOSITES useful, beneficial.
2 (*informal*) *he was useless at his job* **incompetent**, ineffective, worthless, ineffectual, incapable, inept, inadequate, hopeless, weak, bad, no good; *informal* bum, a dead loss.
OPPOSITES competent, effective.

usher ▶ **verb** *he ushered him to a window seat* **escort**, accompany, help, assist, take, show, see, lead, show someone the way, lead the way, conduct, guide, steer, pilot, shepherd, convoy.
□ **usher in** *the railways ushered in an era of cheap mass travel* **herald**, mark the start of, signal, announce, give notice of, ring in, show in, set the scene for, pave the way for, clear the way for, open the way for, smooth the path of; portend, foreshadow; start, begin, initiate, introduce, open the door to, allow to happen, inaugurate, get going, get off the ground, set in motion, get under way, kick off, launch, cause; precede, antecede.
▶ **noun** (fem. **usherette**) **attendant**, escort, guide; doorkeeper, commissionaire, aide, lackey, flunkey.

usual ▶ **adjective** *his usual route to work* **habitual**, customary, accustomed, wonted, normal, routine, regular, constant, standard, typical, established, recognized, set, fixed, settled, stock, conventional, traditional, orthodox, accepted, expected, predictable, familiar, average, general, ordinary, everyday, daily, quotidian.
OPPOSITES unusual, strange, exceptional.

usually ▶ adverb *he usually arrived home about one o'clock* **normally**, generally, habitually, customarily, standardly, routinely, regularly, typically, ordinarily, commonly, conventionally, traditionally, historically; as a rule, as a general rule, in general, in the general run of things, by and large, more often than not, almost always, in the main, mainly, mostly, for the most part, most of the time, on the whole.
OPPOSITE exceptionally.

usurer ▶ noun **extortionate moneylender**, Shylock; *Irish* gombeen man; *informal* loan shark.

usurp ▶ verb **1** *Richard usurped the throne* **seize**, take over, expropriate, take possession of, take, appropriate, steal, wrest, arrogate, commandeer, annex, assume, lay claim to.
2 *the Hanoverian dynasty had usurped the Stuarts* **oust**, overthrow, remove, topple, unseat, depose, dethrone, eject, dispel; succeed, come after, step into the shoes of, supplant, replace; *informal* fill someone's boots, crowd out; *archaic* deprive.

usury ▶ noun **extortionate moneylending**, shylocking; *informal* loan-sharking.

utensil ▶ noun *kitchen utensils* **implement**, tool, instrument, device, apparatus, gadget, appliance, machine, contrivance, contraption, mechanism, aid; *informal* gimmick, gizmo; (**utensils**) hardware, equipment, gear, kit, tackle, paraphernalia, things, bits.

utilitarian ▶ adjective *coal-burning fires have been replaced with utilitarian heaters and radiators* **practical**, functional, serviceable, useful, sensible, effective, efficient, (suited) to the purpose, pragmatic, realistic, utility, working, workaday, handy, neat, ordinary, down-to-earth; plain, unadorned, undecorative, unpretentious, unsentimental, soulless; hard-wearing, durable, lasting, long-lasting, tough, strong, robust, wear-resistant.
OPPOSITE decorative.

utility ▶ noun *a study that looks at the utility of using sled dogs rather than snowmobiles* **usefulness**, use, advantage, benefit, value, help, helpfulness, profitability, convenience, practicality, effectiveness, efficacy, avail, service, serviceableness, advantageousness; **feasibility**, viability, workability, practicability, possibility; *informal* mileage.

utilize ▶ verb *concrete had long been utilized as a bonding and covering material* **make use of**, put to use, use, employ, avail oneself of, have recourse to, resort to, look to, bring into service, press into service, take advantage of, exploit, milk, tap, turn to account, bring into play, bring into effective action, deploy.

utmost ▶ adjective **1** *a matter of the utmost importance* **greatest**, maximum, greatest possible, highest, most, most extreme, greatest amount of, uttermost; maximal, extreme, supreme, paramount, superlative, enormous, major.
OPPOSITES least possible, very little.
2 *the utmost tip of Shetland* **furthest**, farthest, furthermost, farthermost, furthest/farthest away, extreme, very, uttermost, outermost, aftermost, endmost, ultimate, final, last, terminal, remotest; *rare* outmost.
OPPOSITE nearest.
▶ noun *we will do our utmost to help you* **best**, uttermost, hardest, maximum, greatest possible extent.
OPPOSITE least.

Utopia ▶ noun *it may be your idea of Utopia, but it's not mine* **ideal place**, paradise, heaven, heaven on earth, Eden, Garden of Eden, Shangri-La, Elysium, the Elysian Fields, Happy Valley, seventh heaven, idyll, nirvana, bliss; *literary* Arcadia, Arcady, Erewhon.
OPPOSITE hell on earth.

Utopian ▶ adjective **1** *a Utopian community of farmers and skilled craftsmen* **unworldly**, non-materialistic, non-material, immaterial; progressive, reforming, socialist; ideal, paradisal, heavenly, idyllic, blissful, divine, sublime, Elysian, perfect; *literary* Arcadian, Erewhonian; *rare* Edenic, paradisiacal, paradisaical, paradisical.
OPPOSITES materialistic, real-life.
2 *a Utopian vision of gender equality* **idealistic**, visionary, perfectionist, romantic, idealized, fairy-tale, quixotic, starry-eyed, fanciful, unrealistic, impracticable.
OPPOSITES realistic, practicable, down-to-earth.

utter[1] ▶ adjective *Charlotte stared at her in utter amazement* **complete**, total, absolute, thorough, perfect, downright, out-and-out, outright, thoroughgoing, all-out, sheer, positive, prize, rank, pure, dyed-in-the-wool, deep-dyed, real, veritable, consummate, categorical, unmitigated, unqualified, unadulterated, unalloyed, unconditional, unequivocal, full, unlimited, limitless, infinite, ultimate; *Brit. informal* right, proper; *archaic* arrant.
OPPOSITE partial.

utter[2] ▶ verb **1** *he uttered an exasperated snort* **emit**, let out, give, produce, give vent to, issue, come out with, breathe.
2 *Alan uttered an impatient curse* **voice**, express, put into words, speak, say, deliver, sound, mouth, breathe, articulate, pronounce, enunciate, verbalize, vocalize, state, declare.

utterance ▶ noun **1** *the victory was soured by the jingoistic utterances of the commentators* **remark**, comment, word, expression, statement, observation, declaration, pronouncement; reflection, thought, opinion.
2 *there was a gasp at this public utterance of the forbidden word* **voicing**, saying, speaking, expression, delivery, sounding, mouthing, breathing, articulation, enunciation, verbalization, vocalization.

utterly ▶ adverb *he looked utterly ridiculous* **completely**, totally, absolutely, entirely, wholly, fully, thoroughly, quite, altogether, one hundred per cent, downright, outright, unqualifiedly, in all respects, unconditionally, perfectly, implicitly, unrestrictedly, really, veritably, categorically, consummately, undisputedly, unmitigatedly, wholeheartedly, radically, stark, just, to the hilt, to the core, all the way, to the maximum extent, extremely, infinitely, unlimitedly, limitlessly, ultimately; *informal* clean, plumb, dead, bang.
OPPOSITES partly, partially, somewhat.

uttermost ▶ adjective **1** *he changed from one character to another with the uttermost rapidity* **greatest**, maximum, greatest possible, highest, most, most extreme, greatest amount of; maximal, extreme, supreme, paramount, superlative, enormous, major.
OPPOSITES least possible, very little.
2 *New Zealand's uttermost southern extremity* **furthest**, farthest, furthermost, farthermost, furthest/farthest away, extreme, very, utmost, outermost, aftermost, endmost, ultimate, final, last, terminal, remotest; *rare* outmost.
OPPOSITE nearest.
▶ noun **1** *I will do my uttermost against him* **best**, utmost, hardest.
OPPOSITE least.
2 *a desire to use every instant to the uttermost* **utmost**, maximum, greatest possible extent.

U-turn ▶ noun **1** *he did an angry U-turn then roared up the drive* one-eighty; *Brit.* about-turn; *N. Amer.* about-face; *informal* U-ey.
2 *a complete U-turn in economic policy* **reversal**, reversal of policy, volte-face, about-face, sea change, shift, change of heart, change of mind, turnaround, turnround, turnabout, backtracking, retraction, eating one's words, change of plan; *informal* one-eighty; *Brit.* about-turn.

vacancy ▸ noun **1** *there are vacancies for computer technicians* **opening**, position, vacant position, situation, situation vacant, post, job, opportunity, job opportunity, placement, place, niche, slot; *informal* berth.
2 *every seaside guest house had a 'No Vacancies' sign hanging in the window* **unoccupied room**, room; (**vacancies**) accommodation available.
3 *Cathy stared into vacancy, seeing nothing* **empty space**, emptiness, vacuity, nothingness, void, vacantness, nullity, oblivion; *rare* voidness.
4 *impartiality is nothing more than a vacancy of mind* **empty-headedness**, lack of thought, lack of intelligence, brainlessness, denseness, thickness, vacuousness, vacuity, inaneness, inanity, stupidity.
OPPOSITE intelligence.

vacant ▸ adjective **1** *a vacant house* **empty**, unoccupied, unfilled, free, available, not in use, unused, unengaged, uninhabited, untenanted, tenantless, to let, for sale, on the market, abandoned, deserted; *informal* up for grabs.
OPPOSITES full, occupied, open.
2 *an oddly vacant look had come over her features* **blank**, expressionless, deadpan, inscrutable, inexpressive, poker-faced, emotionless, impassive, absent, absent-minded, uninterested, vacuous, empty, glassy, stony, wooden, motionless, lifeless, inanimate.
OPPOSITES expressive, meaningful.
3 *he continued to look vacant* **empty-headed**, unintelligent, without thought, brainless, dense, dull-witted, thick, vacuous, inane, stupid; *informal* brain-dead.
OPPOSITES thinking, intelligent.

vacate ▸ verb **1** *guests are requested to vacate their rooms by 12 noon* **leave**, get out of, move out of, evacuate, quit, go away from, depart from, exit from, withdraw from, pull out of; abandon, desert, relinquish; *archaic* forsake.
OPPOSITES occupy, inhabit.
2 *he will be vacating his post next year* **resign from**, leave, stand down from, give up, bow out of, relinquish, depart from, walk out on, retire from, abdicate; *informal* quit, chuck, pack in.
OPPOSITE take up.

vacation ▸ noun **1** *he is on vacation* **holiday**, holidays, trip, tour, break, mini-break, stopover; day off, recess, adjournment, furlough, rest, respite, leave of absence; leave, time off; *informal* hols, vac; *formal* sojourn.
OPPOSITES work; term.
2 *he insisted on the squatters' vacation of the occupied land* **quitting**, evacuation, abandonment, desertion, relinquishment, leaving; departure from, exit from, withdrawal from.
OPPOSITE occupation.
▸ verb (*N. Amer.*) *I was vacationing in Europe with my family* **holiday**, take a holiday, be on holiday, take a break, travel, tour, stay, visit, stop over; *formal* sojourn.

> **CHOOSE THE RIGHT WORD**
>
> **vacation, holiday, break**
>
> *See* HOLIDAY.

vacillate ▸ verb *I had for a time vacillated between teaching and journalism* **dither**, be indecisive, be irresolute, be undecided, be uncertain, be unsure, be doubtful, waver, teeter, temporize, hesitate, oscillate, fluctuate, keep changing one's mind; *Brit.* haver, hum and haw; *Scottish* swither; *informal* dilly-dally, shilly-shally, blow hot and cold.

vacillating ▸ adjective *he became the target for accusations of vacillating leadership* **irresolute**, hesitant, tentative, dithering, wavering, teetering, fluctuating, ambivalent, divided, doubtful, unsure, uncertain, in two minds, undecided, indefinite, unresolved, undetermined; *informal* dilly-dallying, shilly-shallying, iffy, blowing hot and cold.
OPPOSITE resolute.

vacillation ▸ noun *a decision is always easier to defend than vacillation* **dithering**, indecision, indecisiveness, irresoluteness, uncertainty, unsureness, doubt, wavering, teetering, temporization, hesitation, oscillation, fluctuation, inconstancy; *Brit.* havering, humming and hawing; *Scottish* swither; *informal* dilly-dallying, shilly-shallying, blowing hot and cold.

vacuity ▸ noun **1** *she looked northwards into the vast vacuity which had spawned the Mongol hordes* **empty space**, emptiness, vacancy, nothingness, void, nullity, oblivion; *rare* voidness.
2 *the book's principal defect remains the vacuity of its protagonist* **empty-headedness**, lack of thought, lack of intelligence, brainlessness, denseness, thickness, vacuousness, vacancy, inaneness, inanity, stupidity.
OPPOSITES intelligence, depth.

vacuous ▸ adjective **1** *he had a vacuous expression on his face* **blank**, vacant, expressionless, deadpan, inscrutable, inexpressive, poker-faced, emotionless, impassive, absent, absent-minded, uninterested, empty, glassy, stony, wooden, motionless, lifeless, inanimate.
OPPOSITES expressive, meaningful.
2 *an elite clique of vacuous High School beauties* **empty-headed**, unintelligent, without thought, brainless, dense, dull-witted, thick, vacant, inane, stupid; *informal* brain-dead.
OPPOSITES thinking, intelligent.

vacuum ▸ noun **1** *the experiment has to be conducted in a vacuum* **empty space**, emptiness, void, nothingness, vacuity, vacancy; *rare* voidness, nihility.
2 *the death of Chairman Mao led to a brief power vacuum* **gap**, space, absence, lack, deficiency, blank, lacuna.
OPPOSITE continuity.
3 *if you just clear your bits off the floor I can get round with the vacuum* **vacuum cleaner**; *Brit. informal* vac; *trademark* Hoover.
▸ verb *the carpets must be vacuumed* **vacuum-clean**; *Brit.* hoover.

vagabond ▸ noun *the police had hauled him up as a vagabond* **itinerant**, wanderer, nomad, wayfarer, traveller, gypsy, rover, tramp, vagrant, drifter, transient, migrant, homeless person, derelict, beachcomber, down-and-out, beggar, person of no fixed address/abode, knight of the road, bird of passage, rolling stone; *N. Amer.* hobo; *Austral.* bagman, knockabout, overlander, sundowner, whaler; *informal* bag lady; *N. Amer. informal* bum, bindlestiff; *S. African informal* outie; *Austral./NZ informal* derro.
▸ adjective *a vagabond poacher* **itinerant**, wandering, nomadic, travelling, ambulatory, mobile, on the move, journeying, roving, roaming, vagrant, transient, floating, migrant, migrating, migratory; refugee, displaced, homeless, rootless; drifting, unsettled, footloose; of no fixed address/abode; *archaic* errant.

vagary ▸ noun *the vagaries of the weather* **quirk**, idiosyncrasy, peculiarity, oddity, eccentricity, unpredictability, fluctuation, foible, whim, whimsy, notion, conceit, caprice, fancy, kink, crotchet; *informal* hang-up, thing; *rare* megrim, singularity.

vagina ▸ noun vulva; *children's word* front bottom; *black slang* punani; *vulgar slang* cunt, pussy, twat, snatch, honeypot, muff, tail; *Brit. vulgar slang* fanny, quim, minge; *N. Amer. vulgar slang* box, beaver, jelly roll; *W. Indian vulgar slang* pum-pum.

vagrancy ▸ noun *sleeping in parks constituted vagrancy* **homelessness**, drifting, roving, roaming, wandering, travelling, itinerancy, migrancy, nomadism, vagabondism.

vagrant ▸ noun *the old car was a welcome shelter for the occasional vagrant* **tramp**, drifter, down-and-out, derelict, beggar, itinerant, wanderer, nomad, wayfarer, traveller, gypsy, rover, vagabond, transient, migrant, homeless person, beachcomber, person of no fixed address/abode, knight of the road, bird of passage, rolling stone; *N. Amer.* hobo; *Austral.* bagman, knockabout, overlander, sundowner, whaler; *informal* bag lady; *N. Amer.*

informal bum, bindlestiff; *S. African informal* outie; *Austral./NZ informal* derro.
▶ **adjective** *the Council provides facilities for vagrant alcoholics* **homeless**, drifting, transient, roving, roaming, floating, unsettled, footloose, itinerant, wandering, nomadic, travelling, ambulatory, mobile, on the move, journeying, rambling, touring, vagabond, migrant, migrating, migratory, rootless; of no fixed address/abode; *archaic* errant.

vague ▶ **adjective 1** *they could just make out the vague shape of a ship in the mist* **indistinct**, indefinite, indeterminate, unclear; **hazy**, cloudy, fuzzy, misty, lacking definition, blurred, blurry, out of focus, murky, foggy, faint, shadowy, dim, obscure, nebulous, shapeless, formless, unformed, amorphous; *rare* nebulose.
OPPOSITES clear, precise.
2 *a vague description* **imprecise**, inexact, rough, approximate, inexplicit, non-specific, loose, ill-defined, generalized, ambiguous, equivocal, hazy, woolly; **sketchy**, incomplete, inadequate, imperfect; superficial, cursory, perfunctory.
3 *I'm a little vague about the details* **unclear**, hazy, uncertain, unsure, undecided; **puzzled**, baffled, mystified, bemused, bewildered, confused, nonplussed; indecisive, irresolute, hesitant, tentative, wavering, vacillating; *informal* iffy.
OPPOSITES clear, certain.
4 *they had only vague plans* **uncertain**, undecided, yet to be decided, unsure, unclear, unsettled, indefinite, indeterminate, unknown, unestablished, unconfirmed, unresolved, unascertained, pending, outstanding, in the balance, up in the air, speculative.
OPPOSITE firm.
5 *she was so vague in everyday life* **absent-minded**, forgetful, with a mind like a sieve, disorganized, unsystematic, unreliable, undependable; dreamy, inattentive, abstracted, with one's head in the clouds, scatterbrained, feather-brained, feather-headed, birdbrained, empty-headed, erratic, giddy; *informal* scatty, dizzy, dippy, not with it.
OPPOSITES organized, together.

> **CHOOSE THE RIGHT WORD**
>
> **vague, hazy, indistinct**
>
> These words all describe something that is hard to define or understand precisely.
>
> - A **vague** idea or statement is too imprecise to have a single definite interpretation (*the allusion to 'properly conducted' sports and games is vague*). A person described as *vague* does not think or communicate in a focused or precise way (*he had been very vague about his activities*).
> - **Hazy** is used in connection with memory or understanding (*I have only hazy memories of that event | he has only a hazy idea of how librarians organize book selection*). It can also be used of a person lacking recollection or understanding (*we English tend to be a trifle hazy about the finer detail of Spanish art*).
> - **Indistinct** is used of opinions or ideas that cannot be identified and understood because they are not clearly defined or delimited (*this whole paragraph is very weak and indistinct | we have a very indistinct line between the unavoidable problems of ageing and those which may be reducible*).

vaguely ▶ **adverb 1** *she looks vaguely familiar* **slightly**, a little, a bit, somewhat, rather, moderately, to some degree, to a certain extent, in a way, to a slight extent, faintly, obscurely, dimly; marginally, a shade; *informal* sort of, kind of, kinda, through a glass darkly.
OPPOSITE very.
2 *he fired his rifle vaguely in our direction* **roughly**, more or less, approximately, nearly, just about, practically, virtually, as near as dammit, for all practical purposes, to all intents and purposes; *S. African* plus-minus; *informal* pretty much.
OPPOSITE exactly.
3 *he just smiles vaguely* **absent-mindedly**, abstractedly, inattentively, with one's head in the clouds, vacantly, vacuously, giddily, forgetfully; *informal* scattily, dizzily, dippily.

vagueness ▶ **noun 1** *she used the vagueness and flexibility of the constitution to her own ends* **impreciseness**, inexactness, lack of precision, ambiguity, woolliness, looseness, unclearness, obscurity, indistinctness, generality, indefiniteness, indeterminateness, haziness, cloudiness, fuzziness, mistiness, lack of definition.
OPPOSITE precision.
2 *the scene had the swirling vagueness of a painting by Turner* **fuzziness**, blurriness, indeterminateness, indefiniteness, lack of focus, lack of definition, obscurity, haziness, cloudiness, mistiness, murkiness, fogginess, faintness, shadowiness, dimness, nebulosity, nebulousness, shapelessness, formlessness, amorphousness.
OPPOSITE sharpness.
3 *an amiable eccentric whose vagueness probably results from constant imbibing* **absent-mindedness**, forgetfulness, disorganization, dreaminess, inattention, abstraction, wool-gathering, empty-headedness, giddiness, confusion, befuddlement.
OPPOSITE sharpness.

vain ▶ **adjective 1** *he was vain about his looks* **conceited**, narcissistic, self-loving, in love with oneself, self-admiring, self-regarding, wrapped up in oneself, self-absorbed, self-obsessed, self-centred, egotistic, egotistical, egoistic, egocentric, egomaniac; proud, haughty, arrogant, boastful, swaggering, imperious, overweening, cocky, affected; *literary* vainglorious; *rare* peacockish; (**be vain**) have an excessively high opinion of oneself, think too highly of oneself, think a lot of oneself; *informal* think one is the cat's whiskers/pyjamas, think one is God's gift (to women).
OPPOSITE modest.
2 *a vain attempt to tidy up the room* **futile**, useless, pointless, worthless, nugatory, to no purpose, in vain; **ineffective**, ineffectual, inefficacious, impotent, powerless, unavailing, to no avail, fruitless, profitless, unproductive; unsuccessful, failed, without success, abortive, misfired; thwarted, baulked, frustrated, foiled; *archaic* bootless.
OPPOSITES successful, productive.
□ **in vain 1** *they waited in vain for a response* **unsuccessfully**, vainly, without success, to no avail, to no purpose, ineffectually, with no result, fruitlessly, profitlessly, unproductively.
OPPOSITE successfully.
2 *his efforts were in vain* **futile**, useless, pointless, to no purpose, worthless, nugatory; **ineffective**, ineffectual, inefficacious, impotent, powerless, unavailing, to no avail, fruitless, profitless, unproductive; unsuccessful, without success, abortive; thwarted, baulked, frustrated, foiled; *archaic* bootless.
OPPOSITES successful, productive.

> **CHOOSE THE RIGHT WORD**
>
> **vain, futile, fruitless, pointless**
>
> *See* FUTILE.

valediction ▶ **noun** *he left her without a valediction* **farewell**, goodbye, adieu, leave-taking, parting, send-off; *Latin* vale.
OPPOSITES salutation, welcome.

valedictory ▶ **adjective** *a valedictory message from the retiring ambassador* **farewell**, goodbye, leaving, parting, departing, going away, last, final.
OPPOSITES welcome, salutatory.

valet ▶ **noun manservant**, man, personal attendant, gentleman's gentleman, Jeeves; *French* valet de chambre; *Brit. dated* batman.

valetudinarian ▶ **noun** *an elderly valetudinarian in search of medical advice* **hypochondriac**, neurotic, invalid, valetudinary; *French* malade imaginaire; *archaic* melancholico.
▶ **adjective** *the valetudinarian English* **hypochondriac**, self-obsessed, neurotic, obsessed with one's health; sickly, ailing, poorly, in poor health, weak, feeble, frail, delicate, debilitated, invalid, bedridden, infirm, washed out, run down, valetudinary; *archaic* splenetic; *rare* hipped, hippish.

valiant ▶ **adjective** *a valiant warrior | a valiant attempt* **brave**, fearless, courageous, valorous, plucky, intrepid, heroic, stout-hearted, lionhearted, manly, manful, bold, daring, audacious, gallant, confident, spirited, stout, undaunted, dauntless, doughty, mettlesome, unalarmed, unflinching, unshrinking, unblenching, unabashed, undismayed; **determined**, stalwart, staunch, indomitable, resolute, steadfast, firm, unyielding, unbending, unfaltering, unswerving, unwavering, stubborn, dogged; *N. Amer.* rock-ribbed; *informal* game, gutsy, spunky, ballsy.
OPPOSITES cowardly, irresolute.

> **CHOOSE THE RIGHT WORD**
>
> **valid, sound, cogent**
>
> - When applied to reasoning, **valid** indicates that something has the power to convince: a *valid argument* contains no errors of logic, and a *valid conclusion* follows logically from the argument in its favour. *Valid* can also refer to things that are legally binding or acceptable (*a valid passport is essential when you travel abroad*).
> - **Sound** can have the sense 'solid' or 'dependable'. An argument or position that is *sound* is secure against objections because it is based on good evidence and accurate reasoning (*scientifically sound papers*).
> - **Cogent** denotes arguments that are clear, logical, and likely to influence the opinions of others (*it was Williams who marshalled the evidence, and he did so in cogent terms | an impassioned and cogent plea for judicial reform*).

valid ▶ **adjective 1** *a valid criticism* **well founded**, sound, well grounded, reasonable, rational, logical, justifiable, defensible, defendable, supportable, sustainable, maintainable, workable, arguable, able to hold water, plausible, telling, viable, bona fide; cogent, effective, powerful, convincing, credible, believable, substantial, forceful, strong, weighty, authoritative, reliable; *rare* vindicable.

2 *only one valid nomination was received* **correct**, authentic, legally acceptable, proper, bona fide, genuine, official, signed and sealed; lawful, legal, licit, legitimate, legally binding, binding, contractual; in force, in effect, effective.
OPPOSITES invalid, illegal, void.

validate ▶ verb **1** *clinical trials now exist to validate this claim* **prove**, give proof of, show to be true, give substance to; **uphold**, support, back up, bear out, justify, vindicate, substantiate, corroborate, verify, demonstrate, authenticate, confirm, endorse, give credence to, lend weight to; vouch for, attest to, testify to, stand by, bear witness to.
OPPOSITES invalidate, disprove.
2 *the board refused to validate the aircraft's US certificate of airworthiness* **ratify**, endorse, confirm, approve, agree to, accept, consent to, assent to, affirm, authorize, make valid, sanction, formalize, recognize, legalize, legitimize, warrant, license, certify; sign, countersign, put one's name to, set one's seal to.
OPPOSITES invalidate, reject, revoke.

validity ▶ noun **1** *it is time to examine the validity of this argument* **soundness**, reasonableness, rationality, logic, justifiability, defensibility, sustainability, plausibility, viability, bona fides, effectiveness, cogency, power, credibility, believability, force, strength, weight, foundation, substance, substantiality, authority, reliability.
OPPOSITE invalidity.
2 *the judges have recognized the validity of the contract* **legal acceptability**, authenticity, correctness, bona fides, genuineness; lawfulness, legality, legitimacy, binding nature, contractual nature; force, effect, effectiveness.

valley ▶ noun **dale**, vale; hollow, depression, hole, basin, gully, gorge, pass, ravine, canyon, rift, gap; *Brit.* combe, slade, dene; *N. English* clough; *Scottish* glen, strath; *Indian* nullah; *S. African* kloof; *Spanish* vega; (*in Arabic-speaking countries*) wadi; *literary* dell, dingle.

valour ▶ noun *the medals are awarded for acts of valour* **bravery**, courage, fearlessness, courageousness, braveness, intrepidity, intrepidness, pluck, pluckiness, nerve, backbone, spine, heroism, stout-heartedness, manliness, manfulness, audacity, boldness, gallantry, daring, spirit, fortitude, mettle, dauntlessness, doughtiness, hardihood; *informal* guts, spunk; *Brit. informal* bottle, ballsiness; *N. Amer. informal* cojones, sand, moxie; *vulgar slang* balls.
OPPOSITE cowardice.

valuable ▶ adjective **1** *a valuable watch* **precious**, **costly**, high-priced, high-cost, expensive, dear, worth its weight in gold, worth a king's ransom, priceless, beyond price, without price, of incalculable value/worth, of inestimable value/worth, of immeasurable value/worth, invaluable, irreplaceable, inestimable; prized, cherished, valued, treasured.
OPPOSITES cheap, worthless.
2 *a valuable contribution* **useful**, helpful, of use, of help, of assistance, practical, beneficial, invaluable, productive, constructive, effective, handy, advantageous, worthwhile, profitable, rewarding, gainful, fruitful, worthy, important.
OPPOSITE useless.

valuables ▶ plural noun *valuables may be left in the hotel safe* **precious items**, costly articles, prized possessions, personal effects, treasures.

valuation ▶ noun *you should obtain an insurance valuation on the painting* **price**, value, evaluation, costing, quotation, estimate.

value ▶ noun **1** *houses exceeding £250,000 in value* **price**, **cost**, worth; market price, selling price, asking price, monetary value, face value.
2 *the value of adequate preparation cannot be understated* **merit**, worth, usefulness, use, utility, practicality, advantage, desirability, benefit, gain, profit, good, service, help, helpfulness, assistance, effectiveness, efficacy, avail, importance, significance, point, sense; *informal* mileage.
3 (**values**) *society's values are passed on to us as children* **principles**, moral principles, ethics, moral code, morals, moral values, standards, moral standards, code of behaviour, rules of conduct, standards of behaviour.
▶ verb **1** *his estate was valued at £45,000* **evaluate**, assess, estimate, appraise, assay, rate, price, put/set a price on, cost (out).
2 *teachers must value the child's contribution* **appreciate**, rate (highly), esteem, hold in high esteem, hold in high regard, hold dear, have a high opinion of, think highly of, think much of, set (great) store by, attach importance to, respect, admire, prize, cherish, treasure.

valued ▶ adjective *a valued friend* **cherished**, treasured, dear, prized, favourite, precious, worth its/one's weight in gold; special, appreciated, esteemed, respected, highly regarded, well thought of.

valueless ▶ adjective **1** *the watercolours turned out to be valueless* **worthless**, of no (financial) value, of little/negligible value, trifling; **inferior**, substandard, second-rate, third-rate, poor-quality, low-quality, low-grade, cheap, shoddy, trashy, rubbishy, tawdry, gimcrack, twopenny-halfpenny, Brummagem; (**be valueless**) would fetch nothing.
2 *their efforts were valueless* **pointless**, useless, to no purpose, (of) no use, unprofitable, profitless, futile, vain, in vain, to no avail, to no effect, fruitless, senseless, unproductive, purposeless, idle, worthless, ineffective, unavailing, nugatory, unrewarding, thankless; *archaic* bootless.

vamp[1] ▶ verb (*informal*) *a newly vamped museum* **refurbish**, renovate, modernize, redecorate, revamp, make over, restore, recondition, rehabilitate, overhaul, repair, redevelop, rebuild, reconstruct, remodel; update, bring up to date, improve; upgrade; refit, re-equip, refurnish; *N. Amer.* bring something up to code; *informal* do up, fix up, give something a facelift, tart up, vamp up, patch up; *N. Amer. informal* rehab.

vamp[2] (*N. Amer. informal*) ▶ noun *she portrayed man-devouring vamps in a succession of films* **seductress**, temptress, siren, femme fatale, enchantress, Delilah, Circe, Lorelei, Mata Hari; **flirt**, coquette, tease, Lolita; *informal* tart, mantrap.
▶ verb *will you promise you won't vamp him?* **seduce**, tempt, lure, beguile, entice; **flirt with**, make up to, make eyes at, lead on, toy with, trifle with, philander with; *informal* pull, chat up.

van[1] ▶ noun. *See centre pages for list of* **Vehicles**

van[2] ▶ noun *he was in the van of the movement. See* VANGUARD.

vanguard ▶ noun *women are often in the vanguard of linguistic change* **forefront**, van, advance guard, avant-garde, spearhead, front, front line, front rank, fore, lead, leading position, cutting edge, driving force; leaders, founders, founding fathers, pioneers, architects, creators, instigators, trailblazers, pathfinders, avant-gardists, trendsetters, innovators, groundbreakers.
OPPOSITES rear; followers.

vanish ▶ verb **1** *she caught Archie trying to vanish upstairs* **disappear**, vanish into thin air, be lost to sight/view, be/become invisible, evaporate, dissipate, disperse, fade, fade away, melt away, evanesce, recede from view, withdraw, depart, leave, go away.
OPPOSITES appear, materialize.
2 *all hope of freedom vanished* **come to an end**, end, cease to exist/be, pass away, pass, die out, be no more, become extinct/obsolete, evaporate; **dwindle**, fizzle out, peter out, wear off, become/grow less, become/grow smaller, decrease, lessen, diminish, shrink, contract, fade, wane.
OPPOSITES materialize; last.

vanity ▶ noun **1** *she had none of the vanity so often associated with beautiful women* **conceit**, conceitedness, self-conceit, narcissism, self-love, self-admiration, self-regard, self-absorption, self-obsession, self-centredness, egotism, egoism, egocentrism, egomania; pride, haughtiness, arrogance, boastfulness, swagger, imperiousness, cockiness, pretension, affectation, airs, show, ostentation; *literary* vainglory, braggadocio.
OPPOSITE modesty.
2 *the vanity of all desires of the will* **futility**, uselessness, pointlessness, worthlessness, purposelessness, idleness, fruitlessness, profitlessness.

vanquish ▶ verb *after five weeks, government troops vanquished the rebels* **conquer**, defeat (utterly), beat (hollow), trounce, annihilate, triumph over, win a resounding victory over, be victorious over, best, get the better of, worst, bring someone to their knees, overcome, overwhelm, subdue, subjugate, put down, quell, quash, crush, repress, rout; *informal* lick, hammer, clobber, thrash, paste, pound, pulverize, crucify, demolish, destroy, drub, give someone a drubbing, cane, wipe the floor with, walk all over, give someone a hiding, take to the cleaners, blow someone out of the water, make mincemeat of, murder, massacre, slaughter, flatten, turn inside out, tank; *Brit. informal* stuff; *N. Amer. informal* blow out, cream, shellac, skunk, slam.

vapid ▶ adjective *tuneful but vapid musical comedies* **insipid**, uninspired, colourless, uninteresting, feeble, flat, dead, dull, boring, tedious, tired, unexciting, uninspiring, unimaginative, lifeless, zestless, spiritless, sterile, anaemic, tame, bloodless, jejune, vacuous, bland, stale, trite, pallid, wishy-washy, watery, tasteless, milk-and-water, flavourless.
OPPOSITES lively, colourful, exciting.

vapour ▶ noun **haze**, mist, spray, steam, water vapour, condensation, smoke, fumes, exhalation, fog, smog, murk, cloud, cloudiness, drizzle, dampness, humidity, mistiness, Scotch mist.

variable ▶ adjective *the wind was variable in direction and strength* **changeable**, changing, varying, shifting, fluctuating, irregular, wavering, vacillating, inconstant, inconsistent, fluid, floating, unsteady, uneven, unstable, unsettled, movable, mutable, protean, chameleonic, unfixed, fitful, capricious, temperamental, fickle, kaleidoscopic, volatile, unpredictable, undependable, unreliable; *informal* up and down, blowing hot and cold; *rare* changeful, variational.
OPPOSITES constant, uniform.

variance ▶ noun *data indicate no variance in church attendance between blue- and white-collar workers* **difference**, variation, discrepancy, dissimilarity, disagreement, conflict, divergence, deviation, contrast, distinction, contradiction, imbalance, incongruity.
□ **at variance 1** *his recollections were at variance with documentary evidence* **inconsistent**, at odds, not in keeping, out of keeping, out of line, out of step, in opposition, conflicting, clashing, disagreeing, in disagreement, differing, contrary, incompatible, contradictory, irreconcilable, incongruous, discrepant.
2 *science and religion do not need to be at variance* **conflicting**, in conflict, contrasting, incompatible, irreconcilable, antithetical, contradictory, clashing, contrary, different, differing, divergent, dissimilar, disagreeing,

in disagreement, at odds, at cross purposes, at loggerheads, opposed, opposing, opposite, in opposition, poles apart, polar, at outs; *N. Amer.* on the outs; *rare* oppugnant.

variant ▶ noun *there are a number of variants of the same idea* **variation**, form, alternative, alternative form, other form, different form, derived form, development, adaptation, alteration, modification, revision, revised version, transformation, permutation, transfiguration, metamorphosis, mutant, deviant, rogue, aberration.
OPPOSITES standard form; identical form.
▶ adjective *a variant spelling* **alternative**, other, different, divergent, disparate, derived, adapted, modified, revised, altered, mutant, deviant, rogue, aberrant.
OPPOSITES standard; identical.

variation ▶ noun **1** *regional variations in farming practice* **difference**, dissimilarity, disparity, inequality, contrast, discrepancy, imbalance, dissimilitude, differential, distinction.
OPPOSITE constant.
2 *opening times are likely to be subject to variation* **change**, alteration, modification, varying, variety, variability, diversification.
OPPOSITES uniformity, standardization.
3 *there was very little variation from an understood pattern* **deviation**, variance, divergence, departure, fluctuation, tolerance.
4 *he was wearing a variation of court dress* **variant**, form, alternative, alternative form, other form, different form, derived form, development, adaptation, alteration, modification, revision, revised version.
OPPOSITE standard form.

varied ▶ adjective *a varied selection* **diverse**, assorted, diversified, differing, miscellaneous, mixed, motley, sundry, jumbled, haphazard, heterogeneous, manifold, wide-ranging, disparate, variegated, multifarious.
OPPOSITE uniform.

variegated ▶ adjective *evergreen shrubs with variegated foliage* **multicoloured**, particoloured, varicoloured, multicolour, many-coloured, many-hued, polychromatic, colourful, prismatic, rainbow-like, rainbow, kaleidoscopic, psychedelic, jazzy, harlequin, motley; **mottled**, marbled, striated, streaked, speckled, flecked, patchy, blotchy, blotched, dappled; *informal* splotchy, splodgy; *technical* poikilo-; *rare* marled, jaspé.
OPPOSITES plain, monochrome.

variety ▶ noun **1** *his mother introduced more variety into his diet* **diversity**, variation, diversification, multifariousness, heterogeneity, variegation, many-sidedness, change, difference.
OPPOSITE uniformity.
2 *there was a variety of wildfowl* **assortment**, miscellany, range, array, collection, selection, line-up, mixture, medley, mixed bag, mix, diversity, multiplicity, motley, motley collection, pot-pourri; *rare* omnium gatherum.
3 *fifty varieties of fresh and frozen pasta* **sort**, kind, type, class, category, classification, style, description, status, quality, nature, manner, design, shape, form, pattern, group, set, bracket, genre, species, rank, genus, family, order, breed, race, strain, generation, vintage, make, model, brand, stamp, ilk, kidney, cast, grain, mould; *N. Amer.* stripe.

various ▶ adjective **1** *there are various kinds of evidence for this* **diverse**, different, differing, varied, varying, a variety of, dissimilar, disparate, assorted, mixed, sundry, miscellaneous, variegated, heterogeneous; *literary* divers.
2 *he needed somewhere to store the various artefacts he had collected* **numerous**, many, several, copious, abundant, profuse, countless, innumerable, large number of, multiplicity of.

varnish ▶ noun *several coats of varnish* **lacquer**, lac, shellac, japan, enamel, glaze, polish, oil, resin, wax.
▶ verb *we stripped the floor and varnished it* **lacquer**, shellac, japan, enamel, glaze, polish, oil, resin, wax.

vary ▶ verb **1** *estimates of the development cost vary greatly* **differ**, be different, be unlike, be dissimilar.
OPPOSITE agree.
2 *rates vary from £50 to £90 per hour* **range**, extend, stretch, reach, cover, go, run, pass.
3 *rates of interest vary over time* **fluctuate**, rise and fall, go up and down, change, alter, shift, swing, waver, oscillate, see-saw, yo-yo.
OPPOSITE be static.
4 *the diaphragm is used for varying the aperture of the lens* **modify**, change, alter, adjust, make adjustments to, regulate, control, set.
5 *he tried to vary his diet* **diversify**, variegate, bring variety to, assort, mix, enlarge, expand, widen, broaden, increase, proliferate, extend; reorder; *rare* permutate.
6 *the routine never varied* **change**, alter, deviate, diverge, depart, differ, fluctuate, move on.

vassal ▶ noun (*historical*) **villein**, liege, liegeman, man, bondsman, vavasour, serf, helot, slave, thrall, subject.
OPPOSITES freeman; lord.

vast ▶ adjective *a vast plain full of orchards* **huge**, extensive, expansive, broad, wide, boundless, immeasurable, limitless, infinite, enormous, gigantic, very big, very large, great, giant, massive, colossal, mammoth, immense, tremendous, mighty, stupendous, monumental, epic, prodigious, mountainous, monstrous, titanic, towering, elephantine, king-sized, king-size, gargantuan, Herculean, Brobdingnagian; substantial, hefty, bulky, weighty, heavy, gross; *informal* mega, monster, whopping, whopping great, thumping, thumping great, humongous, jumbo, hulking, bumper, astronomical, astronomic; *Brit. informal* whacking, whacking great, ginormous.
OPPOSITE tiny.

vat ▶ noun **tub**, tank, cistern, bin, drum, canister, basin, steeper, boiler; vessel, receptacle, container, holder, storage chamber, repository, reservoir; barrel, butt, cask, keg, tun; *rare* kid, kier, keeve.

vault[1] *See centre pages for list of* **Vaulting Types**
▶ noun **1** *the vault was supported on eight massive stone piers* **arched roof**, arched ceiling, dome, arch.
2 *the vault under the church* **cellar**, basement, underground chamber, crypt, undercroft, catacomb, cavern; burial chamber, tomb, sepulchre.
3 *valuables stored in the vault* **strongroom**, safe deposit, safety deposit, safe, repository, depository, treasury.

vault[2] ▶ verb *he vaulted over the gate | I vaulted the fence* **jump (over)**, leap (over), skip (over), leapfrog (over), spring over, bound over, sail over, hurdle, clear, pole-vault.
▶ noun *the barman was quickly back with a practised vault of the bar* **jump**, leap, spring, bound, skip, hurdle, clearance, leapfrog, pole vault.

vaulted ▶ adjective *a high vaulted ceiling* **arched**, curved, rounded, bowed, domed, humped; *literary* embowed.

vaunt ▶ verb (usually **vaunted**) *the much vaunted health-care system* **boast about**, brag about, make much of, crow about, gloat over, give oneself airs about, exult in, parade, flaunt, show off, flourish; **acclaim**, esteem, revere, extol, celebrate; *informal* show off about, flash; *rare* laud.

veer ▶ verb *the car veered to the left and crashed into the van* **swerve**, career, skew, swing, sheer, weave, wheel; change direction, change course, go off course, deviate, be deflected, diverge; turn (aside), branch off, curve, twist, bend, curl, incline, swivel, zigzag; *Sailing* tack; *rare* divagate.

vegetable ▶ noun. *See centre pages for list of* **Vegetables**

vegetate ▶ verb *it is important not to let him vegetate in front of the television* **do nothing**, idle, be inactive, languish, laze (around/about), lounge (around/about), loll (around/about), loaf (around/about), slouch (around/about); go to seed, degenerate, moulder, stagnate; *informal* hang around/round, veg out; *Brit. informal* hang about, mooch about/around, slummock; *N. Amer. informal* bum around, bat around/about, lollygag.

vegetation *See centre pages for lists of* **Plant Types** **Plant Parts** **Flowering Plants and Shrubs** **Fruit** **Fungi, Mushrooms, and Toadstools** **Grasses, Sedges, and Rushes** **Nuts** **Poisonous Plants and Fungi** **Trees and Shrubs** **Vegetables**
▶ noun **plants**, plant life, flora; greenery, foliage; *rare* herbage, verdure.
WORD LINKS
substance used to kill vegetation **herbicide**

vehemence ▶ noun *the vehemence of her answer surprised both of them* **passion**, force, forcefulness, ardour, fervour, spirit, spiritedness, urgency, strength, forcibleness, emphasis, vigour, intensity, violence, earnestness, eagerness, keenness, enthusiasm, zeal, zealousness, fanaticism; vociferousness, outspokenness, forthrightness, insistence.
OPPOSITES mildness, apathy.

vehement ▶ adjective *parents are vehement in their support for the school* **passionate**, forceful, ardent, impassioned, heated, spirited, urgent, fervent, fervid, strong, forcible, powerful, emphatic, vigorous, animated, intense, violent, fierce, earnest, eager, keen, enthusiastic, zealous, fanatical; loud, noisy, clamorous, vocal, vociferous, outspoken, strident, forthright, insistent.
OPPOSITES mild, apathetic.

vehicle *See centre pages for lists of* **Cars** **Carriages and Carts** **Trains and Rolling Stock** **Vehicles**
▶ noun **1** *they were hit by a stolen vehicle* **automobile**, motor vehicle, motorized vehicle, means of transport, conveyance, machine; *informal* wheels, heap, crate, jalopy; *N. Amer. informal* auto.
2 *education was a vehicle for the cultural assimilation of colonized peoples* **channel**, medium, means, means of expression, agency, agent, instrument, mechanism, organ, apparatus, structure, machine, machinery; force, catalyst; route, avenue, course, technique, method.
WORD LINKS
relating to vehicles **automotive**

veil ▶ noun **1** *her face was hidden behind a black veil* **face covering**, veiling; (*in Spanish-speaking countries*) mantilla; (*in Muslim & Hindu societies*) yashmak, purdah.
2 *a thin veil of high cloud made the sun hazy* **covering**, cover, screen, shield, curtain, layer, film, mantle, cloak, mask, blanket, shroud, canopy, cloud, blur, haze, mist, pall.
▶ verb *the peak was often veiled in mist* **envelop**, surround, swathe, enfold,

cover, cover up, conceal, hide, secrete, camouflage, disguise, mask, screen, shield, cloak, blanket, shroud, enwrap, canopy, overlay; obscure, shade, shadow, eclipse, cloud, blot out, block out, blank out, obliterate, overshadow; *literary* enshroud, mantle, bedim, benight, becloud, befog; *rare* obnubilate.
OPPOSITES unveil, expose, uncover.

veiled ▶ adjective *they backed up their demands with veiled threats* **covert**, surreptitious, hidden, concealed, disguised, camouflaged, masked, suppressed, underlying, unrevealed, implied, indirect, hinted at; ill-defined, indistinct, vague, obscure, unclear.
OPPOSITES overt, blatant.

vein *See centre pages for list of* **Veins and Arteries**
▶ noun **1** *the mineral veins in the rock vary in thickness* **layer**, lode, seam, stratum, stratification, bed, deposit, accumulation.
2 *the floor was made of cold, white marble with grey veins* **streak**, marking, mark, line, stripe, strip, band, thread, fleck, dash, flash, swathe, strand; *technical* stria, striation, lane.
3 *drinking produced a vein of brilliance in him* **streak**, strain, trait, element, dash, dab, smattering, sprinkling, trace, hint, sign, suggestion, suspicion, indication, nuance.
4 *he closes the article in a somewhat humorous vein* **mood**, humour, temper, temperament, disposition, frame of mind, state of mind, attitude, inclination, tendency, tenor, tone, key, spirit, character, stamp, feel, feeling, flavour, quality, atmosphere; manner, way, style.

WORD LINKS
relating to veins **vascular, venous**
relating to blood vessels **angio- (e.g. *angioplasty*)**
incision into a vein **phlebotomy**

velocity ▶ noun *light always travels at the same constant velocity* **speed**, pace, rate, tempo, momentum, impetus; swiftness, swift/fast pace, fastness, quickness, speediness, rapidity, briskness, expeditiousness, expedition, dispatch; acceleration; *informal* clip, fair old rate, fair lick, steam, nippiness; *literary* fleetness, celerity.

venal ▶ adjective *the law courts are venal and can take decades to decide a case* **corrupt**, corruptible, bribable, open to bribery, purchasable, buyable, grafting; dishonest, fraudulent, dishonourable, untrustworthy, unscrupulous, unprincipled; mercenary, avaricious, grasping, rapacious; *informal* bent, crooked, warped, shady; *rare* simoniacal, simoniac.
OPPOSITES honourable, honest.

venal or venial?
See VENIAL.

vendetta ▶ noun *he was the victim of a political vendetta* **feud**, blood feud, quarrel, argument, falling-out, wrangle, clash, altercation, dispute, fight, war; bad blood, bitterness, enmity, rivalry, conflict, discord, strife; *informal* tiff, scrap, spat, ruction, bust-up.

vendor ▶ noun *the ice-cream vendors were doing a brisk trade* **seller**, salesperson, salesman, saleswoman, dealer, trader, tradesman, retailer, shopkeeper, shopman, shop girl, shop boy, sales assistant, assistant, wholesaler, merchant, trafficker, purveyor, supplier, stockist, marketer, marketeer, sales representative, door-to-door salesman, travelling salesman, commercial traveller; tout, barrow boy; broker, agent, representative, negotiator; *N. Amer.* sales clerk, clerk, storekeeper; *informal* counter-jumper, rep, knight of the road, runner, pusher; *dated* chandler, pedlar, hawker; *rare* huckster, crier, colporteur.

veneer ▶ noun **1** *the boxes are made from American cherry wood with maple veneer* **surface**, **lamination**, overlay, facing, covering, coat, finish, finishing coat, layer, decorative/protective layer, cladding, exterior; patina, varnish, polish, glaze, film, membrane, skin, sheet.
2 *a rigid veneer of courtesy hid her mounting fury* **facade**, front, false front, show, outward display, appearance, false appearance, outward appearance, impression, image, semblance, posture, pose, guise, disguise, mask, masquerade, pretence, charade, illusion, gloss, camouflage, false colours, smokescreen, cover, cloak; *archaic* snivel.

venerable ▶ adjective *he was a venerable and most pious king* **respected**, venerated, revered, reverenced, worshipped, honoured, esteemed, hallowed, august, distinguished, acclaimed, celebrated, lionized; renowned, illustrious, glorious, legendary, famed, eminent, pre-eminent, great, elevated, prominent, notable, noted; respectable, reputable, decent, honourable, worthy, exemplary.
OPPOSITES disreputable, dishonourable.

venerate ▶ verb *the Hindus venerate oxen* **revere**, reverence, respect, worship, adulate, hallow, deify, idolize, hold sacred, exalt, honour, esteem, look up to, think highly of, pay homage to, pay tribute to; adore, praise, extol, aggrandize, lionize, hold in awe, stand in awe of, marvel at, value; *informal* put on a pedestal; *rare* magnify, laud.
OPPOSITE despise.

veneration ▶ noun *in parts of India the snake is an object of veneration* **reverence**, respect, worship, adoration, homage, exaltation, adulation, glorification, extolment, idolization, devotion; honour, esteem, regard, high regard, praise; respectfulness, worshipfulness, obeisance, submission, deference, awe; *rare* laudation, magnification.
OPPOSITE disrespect.

vengeance ▶ noun *he demanded vengeance for the murder of his father* **revenge**, avengement, retribution, retributive justice, retaliation, requital, reprisal; counterstroke, comeback, nemesis, satisfaction, an eye for an eye (and a tooth for a tooth), tit for tat, measure for measure, blow for blow; *Latin* quid pro quo, lex talionis; *informal* comeuppance, a taste of one's own medicine; *rare* ultion, a Roland for an Oliver.
□ **with a vengeance** *she set to work with a vengeance* **vigorously**, strenuously, energetically, with a will, with might and main, with all the stops out, for all one is worth, to the utmost, to the greatest extreme, to the full, to the limit, all out, flat out, at full tilt; powerfully, strongly, forcefully, violently, vehemently, furiously, wildly, madly; *informal* hammer and tongs, like crazy, like mad; *Brit. informal* like billy-o.

vengeful ▶ adjective *he was such a vengeful man that he had wanted his attacker dead* **vindictive**, revengeful, out for revenge, avenging, unforgiving, resentful, grudge-bearing, bitter, acrimonious; *literary* malefic, maleficent.
OPPOSITES forgiving, benevolent.

venial ▶ adjective *he had compounded a number of venial failings with the mortal sin of adultery* **pardonable**, forgivable, excusable, condonable, tolerable, permissible, allowable, understandable, justifiable; slight, minor, unimportant, insignificant, trivial, trifling, not serious, all right, within accepted bounds.
OPPOSITES unforgivable, unpardonable, mortal.

venial or venal?
There is only one letter's difference in the spelling of these words; but it marks the difference between a word used to excuse a minor transgression and one denoting something far worse. **Venial** is a Christian theological term for a sin that is less serious than a mortal sin; more loosely, it denotes faults or offences that are regarded as slight and pardonable (*smoking cigarettes became a venial sin in suburban high schools*). **Venal**, on the other hand, means 'susceptible to bribery' (*drug traffickers flourish where policemen are venal or lazy*).

venom ▶ noun **1** *vipers kill their victims by injecting them with venom* **poison**, toxin; *archaic* bane; *rare* toxicant.
2 *the venom in his voice was shocking* **rancour**, **malevolence**, vitriol, spite, spitefulness, vindictiveness, malice, maliciousness, malignity, malignancy, viciousness, nastiness, ill will, ill feeling, animosity, animus, acrimony, acrimoniousness, bitterness, embitterment, embitteredness, sourness, resentment, grudgingness, virulence, antagonism, hostility, bad blood, bile, spleen, gall, enmity, hate, hatred, dislike, antipathy, aversion; *informal* bitchiness, cattiness; *rare* maleficence, causticity, mordacity.
OPPOSITES love, goodwill.

venomous ▶ adjective **1** *black mambas are among the most venomous snakes in the world* **poisonous**, toxic, noxious, dangerous, harmful; **deadly**, lethal, death-dealing, life-threatening, fatal, mortal, terminal, killing; *literary* deathly, nocuous, mephitic; *archaic* baneful.
OPPOSITES harmless, innocuous.
2 *the porter threw a venomous look at Ralf* **vicious**, spiteful; **rancorous**, **malevolent**, vitriolic, vindictive, malicious, malignant, malign, poisonous, baleful, bitter, acrimonious, resentful, grudging, virulent, pernicious, antagonistic, hostile, hate-filled, menacing, nasty, evil, evil-intentioned, unfriendly, cruel, unkind, unpleasant; acerbic, sharp, acid, tart, caustic, astringent, cutting, biting, razor-edged, waspish, wounding, barbed; *informal* bitchy, catty; *literary* malefic, maleficent.
OPPOSITES friendly, benevolent, kind.

vent ▶ noun *inside the tent are two funnel-shaped air vents* **outlet**, **inlet**, opening, aperture, vent hole, hole, gap, orifice, space, cavity, cleft, slit, pore, port; duct, flue, shaft, channel, well, passage, air passage, airway, blowhole, breather.
▶ verb *the crowd vented their fury by pelting him with rotten eggs* **let out**, give vent to, give free rein to, release, pour out, emit, discharge; reveal, bring into the open, come out with, express, give expression to, air, communicate, utter, voice, give voice to, verbalize, articulate, broadcast, make public, proclaim, assert, ventilate, find an outlet for.

ventilate ▶ verb **1** *the conservatory will become stiflingly hot if not properly ventilated* **aerate**, air, oxygenate, air-condition, fan, freshen, refresh, cool.
2 *the workers ventilated their discontent* **express**, give expression to, air, give an airing to, bring into the open, raise, register, lodge, bring up, come out with, reveal, assert, declare, communicate, utter, voice, give voice to, put into words, verbalize, talk about, discuss, debate, talk over.

venture ▶ noun *their fortune was wiped out by an unsuccessful business venture* **enterprise**, undertaking, project, scheme, pursuit, operation, endeavour, campaign, activity, act, deed, move, measure, task, exploit, mission, adventure, trial; speculation, plunge, gamble, leap in the dark,

experiment, crusade; *formal* essay.
▶ **verb 1** *some villagers rarely ventured beyond their nearest market town* **travel**, journey, go, move, proceed, progress, set out, set forth, rove; wander, stray, drift, migrate.
2 *he ventured the opinion that Peter was dangerously insane* **put forward**, volunteer, advance, submit, proffer, offer, air, bring up, suggest, propound, posit, propose, moot, ventilate, table, broach, lodge, introduce, put up, present; conjecture, speculate, postulate; *formal* opine, essay.
3 *I ventured to ask her to come and dine with me* **dare**, make so bold as, be so bold as, presume, have the temerity, have the effrontery, have the audacity, have the nerve, be brave enough, have the courage, go so far as; take the liberty of; *informal* stick one's neck out, go out on a limb; *N. Amer. informal* take a flyer.

veracious ▶ **adjective** *the manuscripts contain veracious accounts of the event* **true**, accurate, veritable, correct, errorless, unerring, exact, precise, factual, literal, realistic, authentic, faithful, close, strict, just, unelaborated, unvarnished; truthful, honest, sincere, frank, candid, honourable, reputable, trustworthy, trusty, reliable, dependable, scrupulous, upright, upstanding, ethical, moral, righteous, virtuous, decent, good; *informal* on the nail, spot on, as true as I'm sitting/standing here.
OPPOSITES untrue; dishonest.

veracity ▶ **noun** *they expressed doubts about the veracity of the story* **truthfulness**, truth, accuracy, accurateness, correctness, exactness, precision, preciseness, realism, authenticity, faithfulness, fidelity; reputability, honesty, sincerity, trustworthiness, reliability, dependability, scrupulousness, ethics, morality, righteousness, virtuousness, decency, goodness, probity.
OPPOSITE falsity.

verbal ▶ **adjective** *he was given a verbal assurance that his application would be approved* **oral**, spoken, said, uttered, articulated, expressed, stated, verbalized, vocal, unwritten, by mouth, word-of-mouth; *Latin* viva voce.
OPPOSITES non-verbal, unspoken; written.
▶ **noun** (*Brit. informal*) *I'd go out on the pitch and get a load of verbal from the crowd* **abuse**, stream/torrent of abuse, teasing, hectoring, jeering, barracking, cursing, scolding, upbraiding, rebuke, reproval, castigation, revilement, vilification, vituperation, defamation, slander, flak; insults, curses, aspersions; *informal* mud-slinging, bad-mouthing, tongue-lashing, a lashing, a roasting, a caning; *Brit. informal* stick, slagging off, slating, a rollicking, a wigging, a rocket; *Brit. vulgar slang* a bollocking.
OPPOSITE praise.

verbatim ▶ **adverb** *their stories were taped and then transcribed verbatim* **word for word**, letter for letter, line for line, to the letter, literally, exactly, precisely, in every detail, closely, faithfully, religiously, rigorously, punctiliously, with strict attention to detail, strictly; *rare* literatim.
OPPOSITES loosely, imprecisely.
▶ **adjective** *a verbatim record of the proceedings* **word for word**, letter for letter, line for line, literal, exact, direct, precise, close, faithful, undeviating, strict; unadulterated, unabridged, unvarnished, unembellished.
OPPOSITES loose, imprecise.

verbiage ▶ **noun** *there is plenty of irrelevant verbiage but no real information* **verbosity**, verboseness, padding, wordiness, prolixity, prolixness, superfluity, redundancy, long-windedness, lengthiness, protractedness, discursiveness, expansiveness, digressiveness, convolution, circumlocution, circuitousness, rambling, wandering, meandering; *Brit. informal* waffle, waffling, wittering, flannel; *rare* logorrhoea.

verbose ▶ **adjective** *verbose articles from amateur authors* **wordy**, loquacious, garrulous, talkative, voluble, orotund, expansive, babbling, blathering, prattling, prating, jabbering, gushing, effusive; long-winded, lengthy, protracted, prolix, periphrastic, circumlocutory, circuitous, tautological, repetitious, redundant, tortuous, indirect, convoluted; diffuse, discursive, digressive, rambling, wandering, meandering; *informal* mouthy, gabby, windy, gassy, with the gift of the gab, having kissed the Blarney stone, yakking, big-mouthed; *Brit. informal* wittering; *rare* multiloquent, multiloquous, ambagious, logorrhoeic, pleonastic.
OPPOSITES succinct, laconic.

verbosity ▶ **noun** *the dialogue is a reasonable compromise between clarity and verbosity* **wordiness**, verboseness, loquacity, garrulity, talkativeness, volubility, expansiveness, babbling, blathering, waffling, prattling, prating, jabbering, gushing, long-windedness, lengthiness, protractedness, verbiage, prolixity, periphrasis, tautology, circumlocution, convolution, redundancy; diffuseness, discursiveness, digressiveness; *informal* the gift of the gab, big mouth, mouthiness, gassiness, gabbiness, windiness, blah-blah, gobbledegook; *Brit. informal* wittering; *rare* orotundity, logorrhoea, multiloquence, pleonasm, perissology.
OPPOSITES brevity, taciturnity.

verdant ▶ **adjective** *the verdant forests of southern Vermont* **green**, leafy, grassy, grass-covered; **lush**, rich, flourishing, thriving, teeming, prolific, rampant, overgrown, dense, thick, jungle-like; *informal* jungly; *rare* verdurous, viridescent, virid, graminaceous, gramineous.

verdict ▶ **noun** *the coroner recorded a verdict of death by misadventure* **judgement**, adjudication, adjudgement, decision, finding, ruling, resolution, pronouncement, decree, order, settlement, result, conclusion, opinion, prognosis, conviction, assumption, presumption; sentence, punishment; *N. Amer.* resolve; *Law* determination.

verge ▶ **noun 1** *park your car on the road verge* **edge**, border, margin, side, brink, rim, lip, limit, boundary, outskirts, perimeter, periphery, borderline, frontier; end, extremity, termination; fringes, bounds, limits, confines; *literary* bourn, marge, skirt.
OPPOSITES centre, middle.
2 *Spain was on the verge of a major economic crisis* **brink**, threshold, edge, point, dawn; starting point, start.
OPPOSITE middle.
▶ **verb** *she showed a degree of caution that* **verged on** *the obsessive* **tend towards**, incline to, incline towards, border on, approach, near, come near, be close/near to, touch on, be tantamount to, be more or less, be not far from, approximate to, resemble, be similar to.

verification ▶ **noun** *the banking software has an array of functions including signature verification* **confirmation**, substantiation, corroboration, attestation, affirmation, validation, authentication, endorsement, accreditation, ratification, establishment, certification; evidence, proof, support, witness, testament, documentation.

verify ▶ **verb** *reports of the massacre could not be verified* **substantiate**, confirm, prove, show to be true, corroborate, back up, support, uphold, evidence, establish, demonstrate, demonstrate the truth of, show, show beyond doubt, attest to, testify to, validate, authenticate, endorse, certify, accredit, ratify, warrant, vouch for, bear out, bear witness to, give credence to, give force to, give/lend weight to, justify, vindicate; make sure, make certain, check; *informal* pin down; *Brit. informal* suss out.
OPPOSITE refute.

vernacular ▶ **noun** *he wrote in the vernacular and adopted a non-academic style accessible to the public* **everyday language**, spoken language, colloquial speech, native speech, conversational language, common parlance, non-standard language, jargon, -speak, cant, slang, idiom, argot, patois, dialect; regional language, local tongue, regionalism, localism, provincialism; *informal* lingo, local lingo, patter; *rare* idiolect.
OPPOSITES formal language; Latin.

versatile ▶ **adjective** *he was versatile enough to play on either wing* **adaptable**, flexible, all-round, multifaceted, multitalented, many-sided, resourceful, protean; adjustable, variable, convertible, alterable, modifiable, multi-purpose, all-purpose, handy; *rare* polytropic, flexile.
OPPOSITES inflexible, limited.

verse *See centre pages for lists of* **Poems** **Verse Forms** **Verse Metres**
▶ **noun 1** *she provides written commentary in prose and verse* **poetry**, versification, metrical composition, rhythmical composition, rhyme, rhyming, balladry, doggerel; poems, lyrics, rhymes; *literary* poesy, Parnassus.
OPPOSITE prose.
2 *he sent me a verse he'd composed especially to mark my anniversary* **poem**, piece of poetry, lyric, sonnet, ode, limerick, rhyme, composition, metrical composition, piece of doggerel; ditty, song, jingle, lay, ballad; *rare* tenson, verselet.
3 *a poem with sixty verses* **stanza**, strophe, stave, canto; couplet, distich, triplet, tercet, tetrastich; part, section, portion.

version ▶ **noun 1** *the court accepted the policeman's version of events* **report**, statement, description, record, account, story, tale, history, chronicle, narrative, narration, rendition, rendering, interpretation, explanation, construction, construal, analysis, understanding, reading, impression, side, view; *informal* take (on).
2 *he published a German version of his book* **edition**, **translation**, adaptation, rendering, interpretation, variant, variation, form, copy, reproduction, impression, issue, release, instalment, revision.
3 *they have replaced coal-burning fires with gas versions* **sort**, kind, type, variety, genre, class, category, style, form, brand, make, model, design.

vertebra ▶ **noun.** *See centre pages for list of* **Vertebrae**

vertex ▶ **noun** *a line was drawn from the vertex of the figure to the middle of the base* **apex**, peak, tip, top, summit, pinnacle, crest, brow, crown, height, highest point; *technical* acme, zenith, apogee.

vertical ▶ **adjective** *in this exercise the legs are raised to an almost vertical position | the manhole lid conceals a vertical shaft* **upright**, erect, perpendicular, plumb, straight (up and down), on end, standing, upstanding, bolt upright, upended; sheer, steep, sharp, precipitous, bluff, vertiginous; *Heraldry* rampant; *rare* acclivitous, declivitous, scarped.
OPPOSITES horizontal, flat.

vertigo ▶ **noun** *she kept well away from the edge and steeled herself against a spasm of vertigo* **dizziness**, giddiness, light-headedness, loss of balance, loss of equilibrium, spinning/swimming of the head; fear of heights, acrophobia; *Scottish* mirligoes; *informal* wooziness; *technical* sturdy; *rare* turnsick, vertiginousness.

verve ▶ **noun** *I played most sports with schoolboy verve* **enthusiasm**, vigour, energy, pep, dynamism, go, elan, vitality, vivacity, buoyancy, liveliness, animation, sprightliness, zest, sparkle, effervescence, fizz, spirit, spiritedness, ebullience, life, dash, brio, fervour, gusto, eagerness, keenness, passion, zeal, relish, feeling, ardour, fire, fieriness, drive, forcefulness, force, strength, determination, motivation, push, vehemence, fanaticism; *informal* zing, zip, vim, punch, get-up-and-go, pizzazz, oomph, feistiness.

CHOOSE THE RIGHT WORD

verve, zest, gusto
See ZEST.

very ▶ adverb *I'm not very brave | read each question very carefully* **extremely**, exceedingly, exceptionally, especially, tremendously, immensely, vastly, hugely; extraordinarily, extra, excessively, overly, over, abundantly, inordinately, singularly, significantly, distinctly, outstandingly, uncommonly, unusually, decidedly, particularly, eminently, supremely, highly, remarkably, really, truly, mightily, thoroughly; all that, to a great extent, most, so, too; *Scottish* unco; *French* très; *N. English* right; *informal* terrifically, awfully, terribly, devilishly, madly, majorly, seriously, desperately, mega, ultra, oh-so, too-too, stinking, mucho, damn, damned, too ... for words; *informal, dated* devilish, hellish, frightfully; *Brit. informal* ever so, well, bloody, dead, dirty, jolly, fair; *N. Amer. informal* real, mighty, powerful, awful, plumb, darned, way, bitching; *S. African informal* lekker; *archaic* exceeding, sore.
OPPOSITES slightly, sort of, not particularly.
▶ adjective **1** *that is the very thing I was thinking of myself* **exact**, actual, precise, particular, specific, distinct.
2 *this boy's a gold mine—he's the very thing I need* **ideal**, perfect, appropriate, suitable, apt, fitting, fit, right, just right, made to order, tailor-made; *Brit. informal* spot on, just the job.
3 *the very word 'modern' was exciting to them* **mere**, simple, pure, pure and simple, plain, basic; sheer, utter.

vessel *See centre pages for lists of* **Drinking Vessels** **Sailing Ships and Boats** **Ships and Boats** **Veins and Arteries**
▶ noun **1** *the lifeboat was called to the aid of a fishing vessel* **boat**, sailing boat, ship, yacht, craft, watercraft; *literary* barque, keel.
2 *pour the decoction into a heatproof vessel* **container**, receptacle, repository, holder, carrier; basin, bowl, dish, pan, pot, can, tin, jar, jug, pitcher, carafe, flask, decanter; urn, tub, bin, tank, drum, canister, butt, vat, cask, barrel; box, case, chest, casket; *archaic* reservatory.
3 *he burst a blood vessel during a fit of coughing* **duct**, tube, channel, passage, pipe; artery, vein; *technical* vas, trachea.

vest ▶ verb *the executive power of the state is vested in the Governor* **entrust to**, invest in, bestow on, confer on, grant to, give to; endow, lodge, lay, place; put in the hands of.

vestibule ▶ noun *we sat in a high vestibule between the street and the courtyard* **entrance hall**, hall, hallway, entrance, porch, portico, foyer, reception area, lobby, anteroom, antechamber, outer room, waiting room.

vestige ▶ noun **1** *vestiges of England's Tudor past were still evident* **remnant**, remainder, fragment, relic, echo, indication, sign, trace, mark, print, imprint, impression, legacy, reminder, memento, souvenir, token, trophy; remains, leftovers, leavings, evidence, residue; *archaic* memorandum, memory, remembrancer.
2 *she showed no vestige of emotion* **trace**, scrap, touch, tinge, hint, suggestion, suspicion, soupçon, inkling, whisper, scintilla, whit, spark, glimmer, flicker, atom, speck, bit, ounce, drop, dash, jot, iota, shred, crumb, morsel, fragment, grain, spot, mite, modicum; *informal* smidgen, smidge, tad; *Irish informal* stim; *archaic* scantling, scruple.

vestigial ▶ adjective **1** *vestigial limbs enabled the fish to crawl on to the land* **rudimentary**, undeveloped, incomplete, embryonic, immature; non-functional; *technical* abortive, primitive, obsolete.
OPPOSITE well developed.
2 *he feels a vestigial flicker of anger from last night* **remaining**, surviving, residual, leftover, lingering; persisting, abiding, lasting, enduring.

vestment ▶ noun. *See centre pages for list of clerical* **Vestments**

vet ▶ verb *they try to vet all the publications they sell* **screen**, assess, evaluate, appraise, weigh up, examine, look over, review, consider, scrutinize, study, inspect; **investigate**, **censor**, check, check out, check up on; probe, research, look into, delve into, dig into, search into; *informal* give something a/the once-over, size up.
▶ noun *I took the cat to the vet* **animal doctor**, veterinary surgeon, VS, horse doctor; *N. Amer.* **veterinarian**, doctor; *dated* veterinary.

veteran ▶ noun *an army veteran* **retired soldier**; **old hand**, old-timer, old stager; past master, doyen, authority, master, grandmaster, master hand, expert, virtuoso, maestro; *informal* pro, ace, hotshot, old warhorse.
OPPOSITES novice, apprentice, recruit.
▶ adjective *a veteran diplomat specializing in US affairs* **long-serving**, seasoned, mature, old, established; hardened; adept, master, expert, consummate, well versed, well trained, practised, experienced, worldly-wise, qualified, proficient, professional; *informal* battle-scarred, crack, ace, mean.

veto ▶ noun *the Soviet Union had no power of veto* **rejection**, vetoing, dismissal, denial, declination, turndown; **prohibition**, prohibiting, proscription, preclusion, restriction, suppression, stoppage; embargo, ban, boycott, bar, interdict; *informal* thumbs down, red light, knock-back.
OPPOSITES approval, OK.
▶ verb *the president carried out his threat to veto the bill* **reject**, turn down, throw out, dismiss, say 'no' to, rule against, overrule, rule out, quash; **prohibit**, forbid, interdict, proscribe, disallow, outlaw, embargo, place an embargo on, ban, bar, block, preclude, put a stop to, put an end to, stop, nullify, declare null and void; *informal* kill, squash, put the kibosh on, give the thumbs down to, give the red light to.
OPPOSITES approve, authorize.

vex ▶ verb *Alice was vexed by his remarks* **annoy**, irritate, infuriate, anger, incense, inflame, enrage, irk, chagrin, exasperate, madden, pique, provoke, nettle, disturb, upset, perturb, discompose, put out; try, try someone's patience, get on someone's nerves, bother, trouble, worry, agitate, harass, harry, fuss, fluster, ruffle, hound; rankle with, nag, torment, pain, distress, tease, frustrate, chafe, grate, fret, gall, outrage, displease, offend, disgust, dissatisfy, disquiet; *Brit.* rub up the wrong way; *N. English* mither; *informal* peeve, aggravate, miff, bug, bite, eat, hassle, rile, get to, hack off, make someone's blood boil, make someone see red, get someone's goat, get someone's hackles up, make someone's hackles rise, get someone's back up, get someone's dander up, drive up the wall, drive bananas, needle, be a thorn in someone's side/flesh, be a pain in the neck, ruffle someone's feathers, get in someone's hair, get up someone's nose, get under someone's skin, give someone a hard time; *Brit. informal* nark, get on someone's wick, give someone the hump, wind up, get across; *N. Amer. informal* tick off, ride, rankle, gravel; *vulgar slang* piss off, get on someone's tits.
OPPOSITES mollify, appease.

CHOOSE THE RIGHT WORD

vex, annoy, irritate, aggravate, peeve
See ANNOY.

vexation ▶ noun *Erica stamped her foot in vexation* **annoyance**, irritation, irritability, exasperation, anger, rage, fury, temper, bad temper, hot temper, wrath, spleen, chagrin, pique, crossness, indignation, displeasure, discontent, dissatisfaction, disgruntlement, ill humour, peevishness, petulance, testiness, tetchiness, gall, resentment, umbrage; perturbation, discomposure, worry, agitation, harassment; *informal* needling, aggravation, being rubbed up the wrong way, crabbiness; *Brit. informal* stroppiness; *literary* ire, choler.

vexatious ▶ adjective *he had been left in a very vexatious position* **annoying**, vexing, irritating, irksome, displeasing, infuriating, maddening, exasperating, provoking, galling, rankling, grating, jarring, harassing, harrying, bothersome, tiresome, troublesome, niggling; upsetting, perturbing, worrying, worrisome, trying, taxing, distressing, traumatic, unsettling, unpleasant; difficult, awkward, problematic, inconvenient, lamentable, deplorable; *informal* aggravating.

vexed ▶ adjective **1** *a vexed expression crossed Louise's face* **annoyed**, irritated, angry, irate, furious, incensed, inflamed, enraged, infuriated, maddened, fuming, wrathful, choleric, exasperated, piqued, irked, nettled, ill-humoured, hot-tempered, testy, cross, in a bad mood, in a temper, in high dudgeon, huffy, in a huff, put out, fed up, disgruntled, displeased, dissatisfied, frustrated, resentful; upset, perturbed, fretted, bothered, troubled, worried, agitated, harassed, harried, flustered, distressed; *informal* aggravated, peeved, miffed, miffy, mad, riled, hacked off, peed off, hot under the collar, foaming at the mouth; *Brit. informal* browned off, cheesed off, brassed off, narked, eggy; *N. Amer. informal* teed off, ticked off, sore, steamed; *W. Indian informal* vex; *vulgar slang* pissed off; *N. Amer. vulgar slang* pissed; *literary* ireful; *archaic* snuffy, wrath.
OPPOSITES calm, content.
2 *the vexed issue of immigration* **disputed**, in dispute, contested, in contention, contentious, debated, debatable, open to debate, open to question, questionable, at issue, open to doubt, controversial, moot, unresolved, unsettled, up in the air, undecided, yet to be decided, undetermined, unconcluded, ongoing; problematic, problematical, taxing, knotty, thorny, ticklish, delicate; *informal* sticky, dicey, hairy, iffy; *Brit. informal* dodgy.
OPPOSITES undisputed, resolved.

viable ▶ adjective *the committee came forward with the only viable solution* **workable**, feasible, practicable, practical, applicable, usable, manageable, operable, operational, possible, within the bounds/realms of possibility, within reach, within reason, likely, achievable, attainable, accomplishable, realizable, reasonable, sensible, realistic, logical, useful, of use, serviceable, suitable, expedient, effective, valid, tenable; sound, well advised, well thought out, well grounded, judicious, level-headed, wise; *informal* doable.

OPPOSITE impracticable.

vibrant ▶ **adjective** **1** *they listened to vibrant tunes in the open air* **resonant**, sonorous, throbbing, pulsating, reverberating, reverberant, resounding, ringing, echoing, carrying, booming, blaring, thunderous, strident; rich, full, full-bodied, strong, fruity, lively; *rare* canorous.
OPPOSITES soft, mellow.
2 *she was a vibrant and passionate woman* **spirited**, lively, full of life, full of spirit, high-spirited, energetic, sprightly, vigorous, vital, full of vim and vigour, animated, sparkling, effervescent, vivacious, dynamic, flamboyant, electrifying, dazzling, stimulating, exciting, dashing, passionate, fiery, determined; *informal* peppy, zippy, full of beans, feisty, spunky, have-a-go, ballsy; *rare* coruscating.
OPPOSITES spiritless, listless, dull.
3 *in spring the flower fields burst into vibrant colour* **vivid**, striking, intense, brilliant, bright, strong, rich, deep, warm, full; psychedelic, flamboyant, luminous; *informal* jazzy.
OPPOSITES pale, washed out.
4 *she was vibrant with excitement* **quivering**, trembling, shaking, shaky, shivering, shivery, shuddering, shuddery, quavering, quavery, quaking; *informal* trembly.

vibrate ▶ **verb** **1** *the ground beneath their feet began to vibrate* **quiver**, shake, tremble, quaver, waver, shiver, shudder, judder, jiggle, wobble; rock, undulate, move, heave, convulse, jerk, jolt, jar; **oscillate**, vacillate, swing, sway, move to and fro, swing back and forth, swing backwards and forwards, wave, agitate, waggle, wag; *N. Amer.* wigwag.
2 *a low rumbling sound began to vibrate through the car* **throb**, reverberate, pulsate, pulse, palpitate, resonate, resound, ring, echo, re-echo, boom, thunder, thump, pound, beat, drum, thud, thrum, hammer; ripple, murmur, hum, drone; *rare* quop.

vibration ▶ **noun** **1** *the slightest vibration of the water's surface is detected by the beetle* **quiver**, quivering, shake, shaking, shaking movement, quaver, quavering, quake, quaking, tremble, trembling, tremor, judder, shiver, shivering, shudder, shuddering; oscillation, vacillation.
2 *the room shakes with the vibration of rock rhythms* **reverberation**, resonance, throbbing, throb, vibrating, pulsation, pulsing, rumbling, rumble, beating, beat, drumming, drum, thumping, thump, thrumming, thrum, pounding, pound, palpitating, palpitation; hum, humming, murmur, murmuring, drone, droning, buzz, buzzing.

vicar *See centre pages for list of* **Priests**
▶ **noun** *as vicar of a large parish he had many and constant duties* **minister**, rector, priest, parson, minister of religion, clergyman, clergywoman, cleric, churchman, churchwoman, ecclesiastic, pastor, father, man/woman of the cloth, man/woman of god, curate, chaplain, curé, presbyter, preacher, lay preacher, evangelist, divine; *Scottish* kirkman; *N. Amer.* dominie, *informal* reverend, padre, Holy Joe, sky pilot; *Austral. informal* josser.

vicarious ▶ **adjective** *my friend was going to Italy and I was in a fever of vicarious excitement* **indirect**, second-hand, secondary, derivative, derived, at one remove, surrogate, substitute, substituted, by proxy; empathetic, empathic.

vice ▶ **noun** **1** *people may be driven to vice by cruel social circumstances* **immorality**, wrongdoing, wrong, wickedness, badness, evil-doing, evil, iniquity, villainy, venality, impurity, corruption, corruptness, misconduct; sin, sinfulness, ungodliness, godlessness, unholiness, unrighteousness, profanity; **depravity**, degeneracy, turpitude, sordidity, perversion, pervertedness, dissolution, dissipation, debauchery, decadence, lasciviousness, lewdness, lechery, lecherousness, degradation; crime, transgression, offence, immoral act, evil act, act of wickedness, fall from grace; *archaic* trespass; *rare* peccability, peccancy.
OPPOSITES virtue, righteousness.
2 *smoking is my only vice* **shortcoming**, failing, flaw, fault, defect, weakness, weak point, deficiency, limitation, imperfection, blemish, foible, fallibility, frailty, infirmity.
OPPOSITES virtue, strong point.

vice versa ▶ **adverb** *dancers can teach actors a lot and vice versa* **conversely**, inversely, the other way round, contrariwise, oppositely, in reverse, reciprocally.

vicinity ▶ **noun** **1** *many famous writers made their homes in the vicinity* **surrounding district**, surrounding area, neighbourhood, locality, locale, local area, area, district, region, quarter, sector, territory, domain, place, zone; environs, surroundings, surrounds, precincts, purlieus; *informal* this neck of the woods; *technical* locus; *rare* vicinage.
2 *the forest's vicinity to the dockyards made it a vital source of timber* **nearness**, closeness, proximity, propinquity, adjacency, juxtaposition; accessibility, handiness; *rare* contiguity, contiguousness, vicinage.
□ **in the vicinity** *his fortune is in the vicinity of three million pounds* **around**, about, nearly, approaching, just about, just over, just under, roughly, something like, more or less; in the region of, in the neighbourhood of, near to, close to, close on; *Brit.* getting on for; *Latin* circa; *N. Amer. informal* in the ballpark of.

vicious ▶ **adjective** **1** *there was a vicious killer at large* **brutal**, ferocious, savage, violent, dangerous, ruthless, remorseless, merciless, heartless, callous, cruel, harsh, cold-blooded, inhuman, fierce, barbarous, barbaric, brutish, bestial, bloodthirsty, bloody, fiendish, sadistic, monstrous, villainous, murderous, homicidal, heinous, atrocious, diabolical, terrible, dreadful, awful, grim; *Brit. informal* beastly; *archaic* fell, sanguinary.
OPPOSITE gentle.
2 *the MP was the victim of a vicious hate campaign* **malicious**, malevolent, malignant, malign, spiteful, vindictive, venomous, poisonous, baleful, virulent, pernicious, backbiting, rancorous, caustic, mean, cruel, bitter, acrimonious, hostile, hate-filled, menacing, nasty, unpleasant, evil; defamatory, slanderous; *informal* bitchy, catty; *literary* malefic, maleficent.
OPPOSITES kindly, benevolent.

vicissitude ▶ **noun** *he maintains his sunny disposition despite life's vicissitudes* **change**, alteration, alternation, transformation, metamorphosis, transmutation, mutation, modification, transition, development, shift, switch, turn; **reversal**, reverse, downturn; inconstancy, instability, uncertainty, unpredictability, chanciness, fickleness, variability, changeability, fluctuation, vacillation; ups and downs.

victim ▶ **noun** **1** *a victim of violent crime* **sufferer**, injured party, casualty, injured person, wounded person; dead person, fatality, loss; loser.
OPPOSITES attacker, assailant.
2 *they intended me to be the victim of a confidence trick* **dupe**, easy target, easy prey, fair game, sitting target, everybody's fool, stooge, gull, fool, Aunt Sally; **target**, prey, quarry, object, subject, recipient, focus; *informal* sitting duck, sucker, fall guy, pushover, soft touch, easy touch, chump, muggins, charlie; *N. Amer. informal* patsy, pigeon, sap, schlemiel, mark; *Austral./NZ informal* dill.
3 *he offered himself as a sacrificial victim* **sacrifice**, offering, burnt offering, scapegoat.
□ **fall victim to** *the girls had fallen victim to a flu epidemic* **fall ill with**, be stricken with, become infected with, catch, develop, contract, pick up; succumb to, be overcome by, be overwhelmed by; *informal* come/go down with.
OPPOSITE resist.

victimize ▶ **verb** *he was victimized by cruel practical jokers* **exploit**, prey on, take advantage of, swindle, dupe, cheat, trick, hoodwink, double-cross, defraud; **persecute**, pick on, push around, lean on, bully, abuse, discriminate against, ill-treat, mistreat, maltreat, harass, hound, torment, terrorize, torture, punish unfairly; *informal* get at, have it in for, have a down on, be down on, give someone a hard time, hassle, needle, get on someone's back, make things hot for someone, take for a ride, con, diddle, rip off, fleece.

victor ▶ **verb** *a disastrous civil war from which no victor can emerge* **winner**, champion, conqueror, vanquisher, conquering hero, hero; prizewinner, medallist, cup winner, prizeman; *Spanish* conquistador; *Latin* victor ludorum; *informal* champ, top dog, number one.
OPPOSITES loser, vanquished.

victorious ▶ **adjective** *the victorious British team brought the trophy back from Paris* **triumphant**, conquering, vanquishing, winning, champion, successful, top, first, second to none; prizewinning, cup-winning; undefeated, unbeaten, unconquered, unvanquished, unsubdued.
OPPOSITES unsuccessful, defeated.

victory ▶ **noun** *they had won a tremendous victory* **success**, triumph, conquest, win, successful outcome, positive result, favourable result, landslide, achievement, coup; conquering, beating, overpowering, vanquishment, crushing, mastery, superiority, supremacy, pre-eminence, the upper hand; *informal* walkover, thrashing, trouncing.
OPPOSITE defeat.

victuals ▶ **plural noun** (*archaic*) *visitors were offered fine victuals* **food**, food and drink, fare, cooking, cuisine, sustenance, nutriment, nourishment, nutrition; bread, daily bread; **foodstuffs**, refreshments, eatables, edibles, food supplies, provisions, rations, stores, staples; *Scottish* vivers; *informal* eats, grub, nosh, chow, scoff, tuck, nibbles; *N. English informal* scran; *N. Amer. informal* chuck; *archaic* viands, commons, meat; *rare* comestibles, provender, aliment, commissariat, pabulum, viaticum.

vie ▶ **verb** *restaurants vied with each other to attract custom* **compete**, contend, contest, struggle, fight, battle, cross swords, lock horns, jockey, jostle, grapple, wrestle; war, wage war, feud.

view ▶ **noun** **1** *the view from her top-floor flat never failed to please her* **outlook**, prospect, panorama, vista, scene, aspect, perspective, spectacle, sight; scenery, landscape, seascape, riverscape, cityscape, townscape, snowscape; *archaic* lookout.
2 *not all adolescents agree with this view* **opinion**, point of view, viewpoint, belief, judgement, reckoning, way of thinking, thinking, thought, notion, idea, conviction, persuasion, attitude, feeling, sentiment, impression, concept, conception, hypothesis, theory, thesis, estimate, estimation, conclusion, verdict; statement, observation, remark, point; angle, slant, stance, posture, standpoint, approach.
3 *as one walks down the lane, the parish church comes into view* **sight**, perspective, field of vision, range of vision, vision, visibility, eyeshot.
□ **in view of** *in view of its location, no removal of the tumour was attempted*

considering, taking into consideration, bearing in mind, keeping in mind, mindful of, taking into account, on account of, taking note of, in the light of, owing to, because of, as a result of.

▫ **on view** *over one hundred of Van Gogh's paintings are on view in Amsterdam* **on display**, on exhibition, on show; displayed, showing.

▶ **verb 1** *they viewed the passing landscape from their carriages* **look at**, gaze at, stare at, peer at, eye, observe, ogle, contemplate, regard, scan, survey, watch; look over, see over, be shown over, examine, inspect, scrutinize; catch sight of, glimpse, lay eyes on, spy, spot; *N. Amer.* check something out; *informal* get a load of, gawp at, rubberneck at, give something a/the once-over, have a look-see at, have/take a gander at, have a squint at, clap eyes on; *Brit. informal*, have/take a dekko at, have/take a butcher's at, take a shufti at, clock; *N. Amer. informal* eyeball; *literary* espy, behold, descry. **2** *the law was often viewed as a last resort* **consider**, regard, look on, see, perceive, judge, adjudge, estimate, deem, reckon, think of, treat.

viewer ▶ **noun** *the new television series has been a smash hit with viewers* **watcher**, television watcher, spectator, onlooker, observer, non-participant; witness, eyewitness, looker-on; (**viewers**) audience, crowd; *informal* couch potato; *literary* beholder.

viewpoint ▶ **noun** *you seem to have adopted a very cynical viewpoint* **way of thinking**, point of view, view, frame of reference, outlook, perspective, angle, slant, standpoint, position, posture, stance, stand, attitude, opinion, belief, judgement, interpretation, thought, school of thought, mind, line, policy; ideas, thoughts, sentiments, feelings.

vigilance ▶ **noun** *his security duties demand long hours of vigilance* **watchfulness**, careful observation, surveillance, attentiveness, attention, alertness, guardedness, carefulness, care, caution, cautiousness, wariness, chariness, circumspection, prudence, heedfulness, heed, mindfulness. OPPOSITE inattentiveness.

vigilant ▶ **adjective** *there had been a rash of petty thefts and we were warned to be vigilant* **watchful**, on the lookout, observant, sharp-eyed, keen-eyed, gimlet-eyed, eagle-eyed, hawk-eyed, with eyes like a hawk, with one's eyes open, keeping one's eyes peeled/skinned, attentive, paying attention, alert, on the alert, on one's toes, on the qui vive; awake, wide awake, unsleeping, on one's guard, on guard, concentrating, careful, cautious, wary, chary, circumspect, prudent, heedful, mindful; prepared, ready; *informal* beady-eyed, not missing a trick, on the ball, keeping a weather eye on things, leery; *rare* regardful, Argus-eyed. OPPOSITES negligent, inattentive.

vigorous ▶ **adjective 1** *the child was strong and vigorous* **robust**, healthy, in good health, hale and hearty, strong, strong as an ox/horse/lion, sturdy, fine, fit, in good condition, in tip-top condition, in good shape, in good trim, in good kilter; hardy, tough, athletic, strapping, able-bodied; bouncing, thriving, flourishing, blooming; **energetic**, lively, active, spry, sprightly, perky, playful, jaunty, vivacious, animated, spirited, high-spirited, dynamic, vibrant, full of life, vital, sparkling, effervescent, zestful, buoyant, tireless, indefatigable; *informal* go-getting, zippy, peppy, bouncy, upbeat, full of vim, full of beans, raring to go, bright-eyed and bushy-tailed, in the pink, fit as a fiddle; *N. English informal* wick; *N. Amer. informal* chipper. OPPOSITES frail, weak.
2 *a vigorous defence of government policy* **strenuous**, powerful, potent, forceful, forcible, spirited, mettlesome, determined, resolute, aggressive, eager, keen, active, enthusiastic, zealous, ardent, fervent, vehement, intense, intensive, passionate, fiery, wild, unrestrained, uncontrolled, unbridled; tough, blunt, hard-hitting, pulling no punches; *informal* all-out, punchy, in-your-face. OPPOSITES weak, feeble.

vigorously ▶ **adverb** *she pedalled vigorously down the farm track* **strenuously**, with great vigour, strongly, powerfully, potently, forcefully, with force, forcibly, energetically, aggressively, heartily, eagerly, with eagerness, enthusiastically, with enthusiasm, with great effort, with all one's might, with might and main, with a will, for dear life, for all one is worth, to the best of one's abilities, as best one can, all out, with a vengeance, fiercely, intensely, hard, as hard as possible, as hard as one can, with all the stops out, like the devil, like the deuce, at full tilt; *informal* like mad, like crazy, like nobody's business, like it's going out of style, like billy-o, hammer and tongs, going great guns.

vigour ▶ **noun** *they ran with great vigour* **robustness**, healthiness, good health, hardiness, strength, stamina, sturdiness, fitness, good shape, good trim, good condition, fine fettle, toughness, ruggedness, muscle, power; bloom, radiance, sap; **energy**, activity, liveliness, life, spryness, sprightliness, vitality, vivacity, vivaciousness, verve, animation, spiritedness, spirit, enthusiasm, fire, fieriness, fervour, ardour, zeal, passion, might, forcefulness, determination, intensity, dynamism, sparkle, effervescence, zest, dash, snap, spark, gusto, pep, bounce, exuberance, drive, push, elan; *informal* zip, zing, oomph, vim, go, get-up-and-go, punch; *Brit. informal* welly; *literary* thew, thewiness. OPPOSITES weakness, listlessness, lethargy.

vile ▶ **adjective** *a vile smell | he shouldn't be allowed to get away with such vile behaviour* **foul**, nasty, unpleasant, bad, disagreeable, horrid, horrible, dreadful, abominable, atrocious, offensive, obnoxious, odious, unsavoury, repulsive, off-putting, repellent, revolting, repugnant, disgusting, distasteful, loathsome, hateful, nauseating, sickening; base, low, mean, wretched, disgraceful, appalling, shocking, ugly, vulgar, sorry, shabby, shameful, dishonourable, execrable, heinous, abhorrent, deplorable, monstrous, wicked, evil, dark, dirty, vicious, iniquitous, sinful, corrupt, sordid, depraved, perverted, debased, reprobate, degenerate, debauched, dissolute, contemptible, despicable, reprehensible, diabolical, diabolic, devilish, fiendish, hellish, damnable; *informal* yucky, sick-making, gut-churning, icky, gross, God-awful, low-down, rotten, sick; *Brit. informal* beastly; *N. Amer. informal* lousy, vomitous; *vulgar slang* shitty; *literary* noisome; *archaic* scurvy, disgustful, loathly; *rare* egregious, flagitious. OPPOSITE pleasant.

vilification ▶ **noun** *he was singled out for vilification in a sermon* **condemnation**, criticism, censure, castigation, denunciation, vituperation, abuse, flak, defamation, denigration, disparagement, obloquy, opprobrium, derogation, slander, revilement, reviling, calumny, calumniation, execration, excoriation, lambasting, upbraiding, a bad press, character assassination, attack, invective, libel, insults, aspersions; *informal* mud-slinging, bad-mouthing, tongue-lashing; *Brit. informal* stick, verbal, slagging off; *archaic* contumely; *rare* animadversion, objurgation. OPPOSITE praise.

vilify ▶ **verb** *the media vilified several of the election candidates* **disparage**, denigrate, defame, run down, revile, berate, belittle, abuse, insult, slight, attack, speak ill of, speak evil of, pour scorn on, cast aspersions on, criticize, censure, condemn, decry, denounce, pillory, lambaste; fulminate against, rail against, inveigh against, malign, slander, libel, conduct a smear campaign against, spread lies about, blacken the name/reputation of, sully the reputation of, give someone a bad name, bring someone into disrepute, discredit, stigmatize, traduce, calumniate, impugn; *N. Amer.* slur; *informal* do down, do a hatchet job on, take to pieces, pull apart, throw mud at, drag through the mud, slate, have a go at, hit out at, jump on, lay into, tear into, knock, slam, pan, bash, hammer, roast, skewer, bad-mouth, throw brickbats at; *Brit. informal* rubbish, slag off; *N. Amer. informal* pummel, dump on; *Austral./NZ informal* bag, monster; *archaic* contemn; *rare* derogate, vituperate, asperse, vilipend. OPPOSITES commend, lionize.

villain ▶ **noun** *an evil villain bent on destroying and dominating the world* **criminal**, lawbreaker, outlaw, offender, felon, convict, jailbird, malefactor, wrongdoer; transgressor, sinner; gangster, gunman, bandit, brigand, desperado, thief, robber, mugger, swindler, fraudster, racketeer, terrorist, pirate; **rogue**, scoundrel, wretch, heel, reprobate, charlatan, evil-doer, ruffian, hoodlum, hooligan, thug, delinquent, ne'er-do-well, good-for-nothing; *informal* **crook**, con, crim, baddy, shark, rat, snake, snake in the grass, dog, hound, louse, swine, scumbag, wrong 'un; *Brit. informal, dated* rotter, bounder, bad egg, stinker; *Law* malfeasant, misfeasor, infractor; *dated* cad, knave, rake; *archaic* miscreant, blackguard.

villainous ▶ **adjective** *Captain Mason led the villainous attack on the sleeping village* **wicked**, evil, iniquitous, sinful, nefarious, vile, foul, monstrous, shocking, outrageous, atrocious, abominable, reprehensible, hateful, detestable, despicable, odious, contemptible, horrible, heinous, execrable, diabolical, diabolic, fiendish, vicious, murderous, barbarous, black, dark, rotten; criminal, illicit, unlawful, illegal, illegitimate, lawless, felonious, indictable, transgressing, wrong, immoral, corrupt, degenerate, reprobate, sordid, depraved, dissolute, bad, base, dishonourable, dishonest, unscrupulous, unprincipled, underhand, roguish; *informal* crooked, bent, warped, low-down, stinking, dirty, shady, rascally, scoundrelly; *Brit. informal* beastly, not cricket; *Law* malfeasant; *archaic* dastardly; *rare* egregious, flagitious. OPPOSITES good, virtuous.

villainy ▶ **noun** *the potential to degenerate into villainy lies within even a nobleman* **wickedness**, badness, evil, evil-doing, sin, sinfulness, iniquity, vileness, baseness, wrong, wrongdoing, dishonesty, double-dealing, unscrupulousness, roguery, rascality, delinquency, disgrace, viciousness, degeneracy, depravity, dissolution, dissipation, immorality, turpitude, devilry, devilishness, heinousness; **crime**, vice, criminality, lawlessness, lawbreaking, corruption, venality; offence, misdeed, misconduct, transgression; *informal* crookedness, shadiness; *Law* malfeasance; *archaic* knavery, deviltry.

vindicate ▶ **verb 1** *he maintained his innocence throughout the trial and has been fully vindicated by the jury* **acquit**, clear, absolve, free from blame, declare innocent, exonerate, exculpate, discharge, liberate, free, deliver, redeem; *informal* let off, let off the hook. OPPOSITES convict, blame, incriminate.
2 *I felt I had fully vindicated my request* **justify**, warrant, substantiate, establish, demonstrate, ratify, authenticate, verify, confirm, corroborate, prove, defend, offer grounds for, support, back, evidence, bear out, bear witness to, endorse, give credence to, lend weight to; *rare* extenuate. OPPOSITE disprove.

vindictive ▶ **adjective** *he never destroyed a person simply on the say-so of vindictive enemies* **vengeful**, out for revenge, revengeful, avenging, unforgiving, grudge-bearing, resentful, ill-disposed, implacable, unrelenting, acrimonious, bitter; **spiteful**, mean, mean-spirited,

rancorous, venomous, poisonous, malicious, malevolent, malignant, malign, evil, evil-intentioned, nasty, cruel, unkind, ill-natured, baleful; *informal* catty, bitchy; *literary* malefic, maleficent.
OPPOSITE forgiving.

vintage ▶ noun **1** *1986 was a classic vintage for the Cabernet Sauvignon grape* year.
2 *he never lost a vintage through frost* **grape harvest**, grape gathering, grape crop, harvest, crop, yield, year's growth.
3 *the hotel was furnished with some choice pieces of Louis XV vintage* **period**, era, epoch, time, origin; genre, style, kind, sort, type, cast, stamp, school, ilk.
▶ adjective **1** *vintage French wine* **high-quality**, quality, prime, choice, select, superior, best.
2 *a vintage Sherlock Holmes adventure | vintage motor vehicles* **classic**, ageless, timeless, enduring; old, antique, veteran, heritage, historic, old-world, age-old.
3 *his reaction to her letter was vintage Francis* **characteristic**, typical, most typical, supreme, absolute, at his/her/its best.

violate ▶ verb **1** *the directive violates fundamental human rights* **contravene**, breach, commit a breach of, infringe, infract, break, transgress, overstep, not comply with, disobey, defy, flout, fly in the face of, rebel against; disregard, ignore, pay no heed to, take no notice of; *archaic* set at naught.
OPPOSITE comply with.
2 *her daughter's tomb had been violated* **desecrate**, profane, treat sacrilegiously, treat with disrespect, blaspheme, defile, degrade, debase; damage, vandalize, deface, destroy; *N. Amer. informal* trash.
OPPOSITE respect.
3 *she did not like having her personal space violated* **invade**, intrude on, encroach on, impinge on, trespass on, obtrude on, break into, interfere with, disturb, disrupt, upset, shatter.
4 *he drugged her and then violated her* **rape**, indecently assault, sexually assault, assault, force oneself on, force, sexually abuse, abuse, molest, interfere with, seduce; *informal* pop someone's cherry, bed; *euphemistic* have one's (evil) way with, take advantage of; *dated* ravish, deflower, defile, dishonour, ruin, take away someone's innocence.

violation ▶ noun **1** *a flagrant violation of human rights* **contravention**, breach, infringement, infraction, breaking, transgression, non-observance, lack of compliance with, disobeying, disobedience, defiance, defying, flouting, flying in the face of, rebelling against; neglect, ignoring, paying no heed to, taking no notice of.
2 *the wiretaps were a severe violation of the victims' private lives* **invasion**, interruption, breach, infraction; trespass, intrusion, encroachment, disruption, disturbance, upset.
3 *his daughter was threatened with violation* **rape**, sexual assault, indecent assault, sexual abuse, abuse, molestation, molesting, interference, interfering, seduction, seducing; *informal* bedding; *dated* ravishing, ravishment, deflowering, defloration, defilement, dishonour, ruin, ruination.

violence ▶ noun **1** *there had been widespread fears of police violence* **brutality**, brute force, roughness, ferocity, fierceness, savagery, cruelty, sadism, barbarity, barbarousness, brutishness, murderousness, bloodthirstiness, ruthlessness, inhumanity, heartlessness, pitilessness, mercilessness; strong-arm tactics; *rare* ferity.
OPPOSITES gentleness, kindness.
2 *the violence of the blow* **forcefulness**, force, full force, power, powerfulness, strength, might, savagery, ferocity, brutality, destructiveness.
OPPOSITE weakness.
3 *the violence of his passion* **intensity**, severity, strength, force, great force, vehemence, powerfulness, power, potency, ferocity, forcefulness, wildness, frenziedness, fury, storminess, tempestuousness, turbulence; lack of control, lack of restraint, passionateness; *rare* fervency, ardency.
OPPOSITE mildness.

violent ▶ adjective **1** *I was married to a violent alcoholic* **brutal**, vicious, savage, harsh, rough, aggressive, bullying, threatening, terrorizing, fierce, wild, intemperate, hot-headed, hot-tempered, bloodthirsty, ferocious, berserk, frenzied; in a frenzy, out of control, barbarous, barbaric, thuggish, cut-throat, homicidal, murderous, maniacal, rabid, inhuman, heartless, callous, ruthless, merciless, pitiless, cruel.
OPPOSITE gentle.
2 *she killed him with one violent blow* **powerful**, forceful, hard, sharp, smart, strong, vigorous, mighty, hefty, harsh, thunderous, savage, ferocious, fierce, brutal, vicious, destructive, damaging, painful; lethal, deadly, fatal, mortal, death-dealing.
OPPOSITE weak.
3 *a rush of violent jealousy swept through her* **intense**, extreme, strong, powerful, forceful, great, vehement, wild, frenzied, raging, riotous, rampaging, rampant, out of control, stormy, tempestuous, turbulent, tumultuous, intemperate, uncontrolled, unrestrained, uncurbed, unchecked, unbridled, unfettered, uncontrollable, unmanageable, ungovernable, inordinate, excessive, consuming, passionate, overwhelming, immoderate.
OPPOSITE mild.

VIP ▶ noun *even the most humble visitors are treated like VIPs* **celebrity**, famous person, very important person, personality, name, big name, famous name, household name, star, superstar, leading light, mogul, giant, great, master, king, guru; **dignitary**, luminary, worthy, grandee, lion, public figure, pillar of society, notable, notability, personage, panjandrum; *informal* heavyweight, celeb, somebody, someone, bigwig, biggie, big shot, big noise, big gun, big cheese, big chief, nob, lady muck, lord muck, top brass, honcho, head honcho, top dog, supremo, megastar, heavy, fat cat; *N. Amer. informal* big wheel, big kahuna, kahuna, top banana, big enchilada, macher, high muckamuck, high muckety-muck.
OPPOSITES nobody, nonentity.

virago ▶ noun **harridan**, shrew, dragon, termagant, vixen; fishwife, witch, hellcat, she-devil, tartar, martinet, spitfire, hag, gorgon, fury, ogress, harpy, nag, trout; *informal* battleaxe, old bag, old bat, cow, old cow, bitch; *archaic* scold; *rare* Xanthippe.

virgin ▶ noun *she wished to remain a virgin* **maiden**, unmarried girl, maid, vestal virgin, chaste woman, celibate; *Latin* virgo intacta; *literary* vestal.
▶ adjective **1** *extensive tracts of virgin forest* **untouched**, unspoilt, untainted, untarnished, unadulterated, pure, immaculate, pristine, flawless; **unmarked**, unblemished, spotless, stainless, unsullied, unpolluted, undefiled, unaffected, unchanged, intact, inviolate, preserved; unused, in mint condition, perfect, in perfect condition; unexplored, uncharted, unmapped.
2 *virgin teenage girls* **chaste**, virginal, celibate, abstinent, self-restrained, self-denying; unmarried, unwed, maiden, maidenly; **pure**, pure as the driven snow, virtuous, uncorrupted, incorrupt, undefiled, unblemished, unsullied, innocent, sinless, moral, decent, demure; *literary* vestal.

virginal ▶ adjective *the vampire sucks the blood from a virginal girl. See* VIRGIN *sense 2.*

virginity ▶ noun *I managed to graduate from high school with my virginity intact* **chastity**, **maidenhood**, chasteness, virtue, honour, purity, pureness; innocence, decency, virtuousness, respectability, dignity, modesty; lack of sin, sinlessness, spotlessness; celibacy, abstinence, self-restraint, self-denial; *informal* cherry; *Theology* immaculateness.

virile ▶ adjective *she liked to read about strong, virile heroes* **manly**, masculine, male, all-male; gallant, chivalrous, swashbuckling, valiant, valorous, courageous, brave, intrepid, fearless, stout-hearted, lionhearted, bold, heroic, daring; strong, tough, vigorous, robust, powerfully built, well made, well built, muscular, muscly, brawny, rugged, strapping, sturdy, hefty, husky, burly, solid, substantial; red-blooded, sexually potent, fertile, fecund; *informal* macho, laddish, butch, beefy, hunky, studly.
OPPOSITES unmanly, effeminate, weak.

virility ▶ noun *there was a virility about him that showed in his every movement* **manliness**, masculinity, maleness, manfulness, manhood, machismo, gallantry, chivalry, valour, valiance, fearlessness, bravery, intrepidity, stout-heartedness, lionheartedness, boldness, daring, heroism, mettle, spirit; strength, vigour, toughness, robustness, powerful build, muscularity, muscle, brawniness, sturdiness, ruggedness, heftiness, huskiness; red-bloodedness, sexual potency, potency, sexuality, fertility, fecundity; *informal* laddishness, hunkiness, beefiness.

virtual ▶ adjective *we drove to the cottage in virtual silence* **effective**, in effect, near, near enough, essential, practical, for all practical purposes, to all intents and purposes, in all but name, indirect, implied, implicit, unacknowledged, tacit.

virtually ▶ adverb *the huge building was virtually empty* **in effect**, effectively, all but, more or less, practically, almost, nearly, close to, approaching, not far from, nearing, verging on, bordering on, well nigh, nigh on, just about, as good as, essentially, in essence, in practical terms, for all practical purposes, to all intents and purposes, in all but name, as near as dammit; roughly, approximately, not quite; *S. African* plus-minus; *informal* pretty much, pretty nearly, pretty well.

virtue *See centre pages for lists of* **Virtues** **Sins**
▶ noun **1** *the simple virtue and integrity of peasant life* **goodness**, virtuousness, righteousness, morality, ethicalness, uprightness, upstandingness, integrity, dignity, rectitude, honesty, honourableness, honourability, honour, incorruptibility, probity, propriety, decency, respectability, nobility, nobility of soul/spirit, nobleness, worthiness, worth, good, trustworthiness, meritoriousness, irreproachableness, blamelessness, purity, pureness, lack of corruption, merit; principles, high principles, ethics.
OPPOSITES vice, iniquity.
2 *promptness was not one of his virtues* **good point**, good quality, strong point, strong suit, long suit, asset, forte, attribute, advantage, benefit, strength, talent; *informal* plus.
OPPOSITE failing.
3 (*dated*) *she lost her wealth and her virtue in the great city* **virginity**, honour, maidenhood, maidenhead, chastity, chasteness, purity, pureness, lack of sin, sinlessness, spotlessness, wholesomeness, innocence, decency, virtuousness, respectability, dignity, modesty; celibacy, abstinence, self-

restraint, self-denial; *informal* cherry; *Theology* immaculateness; *rare* continence.
OPPOSITE promiscuity.
4 *I can see no virtue in such an arrangement* **merit**, advantage, benefit, usefulness, efficacy, efficaciousness, power, potency, force, strength.
OPPOSITE disadvantage.
□ **by virtue of** *they hold the posts by virtue of family connections* **because of**, on account of, by reason of, by dint of, by means of, by way of, via, through, as a result of, as a consequence of, on the strength of, owing to, thanks to, due to, based on; with the help of, with the aid of, with the assistance of.

virtuosity ▸ noun *the singer has to display extreme virtuosity* **skill**, skilfulness, mastery, expertise, expertness, prowess, proficiency, ability, aptitude, adroitness, dexterity, deftness, excellence, brilliance, talent, genius, artistry, technique, art, creativity, flair, finish, polish, panache, finesse, wizardry, calibre, quality, professionalism; craftsmanship, handiness, workmanship, musicianship; *French* éclat; *informal* know-how.
OPPOSITE lack of skill.

virtuoso ▸ noun *the piano player is clearly a virtuoso of the first order* **genius**, expert, master, master hand, artist, maestro, prodigy, marvel, adept, past master, specialist, skilled person, professional, doyen, authority, veteran; star, champion; *German* wunderkind; *informal* hotshot, wizard, wiz, whizz, whizz-kid, buff, pro, ace, something else, something to shout about, something to write home about; *Brit. informal* dab hand; *N. Amer. informal* maven, crackerjack; *rare* proficient.
OPPOSITES beginner, amateur, duffer.
▸ adjective *a virtuoso violinist* **skilful**, expert, accomplished, masterly, master, consummate, proficient, talented, gifted, adept, adroit, dexterous, deft, able, good, competent, capable, efficient, experienced, professional, polished, well versed, smart, clever, artful, impressive, outstanding, exceptional, exceptionally good, magnificent, supreme, first-rate, first-class, fine, brilliant, excellent, dazzling, bravura; *informal* superb, out of this world, mean, ace, crack, A1; *vulgar slang* shit-hot.
OPPOSITES inexpert, incompetent.

virtuous ▸ adjective **1** *they were entirely virtuous in their endeavours* **righteous**, good, moral, morally correct, ethical, upright, upstanding, high-minded, right-minded, right-thinking, principled, exemplary, clean, law-abiding, lawful, irreproachable, blameless, guiltless, unimpeachable, just, honest, honourable, unbribable, incorruptible; scrupulous, reputable, decent, respectable, noble, lofty, elevated, worthy, trustworthy, meritorious, praiseworthy, commendable, admirable, laudable; pure, pure as the driven snow, whiter than white, sinless, saintly, saintlike, godly, angelic; *Christianity* immaculate, impeccable; *informal* squeaky clean.
OPPOSITES bad, sinful.
2 *his virtuous sister had been threatened with seduction* **virginal**, virgin, chaste, maidenly, vestal, celibate, abstinent; **pure**, pure as the driven snow, sinless, free from sin, flawless, spotless, undefiled, untainted, unsullied, uncorrupted, intact, innocent, demure, modest, decent, seemly, decorous, wholesome.
OPPOSITES promiscuous, sinful.

virulent ▸ adjective **1** *some plant varieties can withstand being sprayed by the most virulent herbicides* **poisonous**, toxic, venomous, noxious, deadly, lethal, fatal, mortal, terminal, death-dealing, life-threatening, dangerous, harmful, injurious, pernicious, damaging, destructive, unsafe; contaminating, polluting; *literary* deathly, nocuous, mephitic; *archaic* baneful.
OPPOSITES non-toxic, harmless, safe.
2 *a virulent epidemic of cholera swept through London* **highly infectious**, highly infective, highly contagious, infectious, infective, contagious, rapidly spreading, communicable, transmittable, transmissible, spreading, malignant, uncontrollable, pernicious, pestilential; severe, extreme, violent, dangerous, harmful, lethal, life-threatening; *informal* catching; *literary* pestiferous.
OPPOSITE non-contagious.
3 *a virulent attack on contemporary morals* **vitriolic**, malicious, malevolent, malignant, malign, evil-intentioned, resentful, hostile, spiteful, venomous, vicious, vindictive, bitter, rancorous, acrimonious, mordant, astringent, incisive, cutting, biting, scathing, caustic, stinging, blistering, searing, withering, abusive, mean, nasty, aggressive, savage, harsh, devastating; *informal* bitchy, catty; *literary* malefic, maleficent.
OPPOSITES amicable, benevolent.

virus ▸ noun. *See centre pages for list of* **Viruses**

WORD LINKS
study of viruses **virology**

viscous ▸ adjective *pools of viscous liquid had started to spread across the floor* **sticky**, gummy, glue-like, gluey, adhesive, tacky, adhering, adherent, sticking, clinging, treacly, syrupy; **glutinous**, gelatinous, thick, viscid, pasty, mucous, mucoid, mucilaginous, jelly-like, slimy; *informal* gooey, gunky, gloopy, cloggy, icky; *N. Amer. informal* gloppy; *rare* viscoid.
OPPOSITE watery.

visible ▸ adjective *light from the fires was visible for many miles | he made a visible effort to control himself* **perceptible**, perceivable, seeable, observable, noticeable, easily seen, detectable, discernible, recognizable, in view, in sight, on view, on display; evident, self-evident, in evidence, apparent, manifest, transparent, plain, plain to see, clear, clear-cut, conspicuous, obvious, patent, palpable, tangible, unmistakable, unconcealed, undisguised, distinct, distinguishable, prominent, salient, striking, arresting, blatant, glaring, writ large; *informal* as plain as the nose on your face, as plain as a pikestaff, sticking out like a sore thumb, standing out a mile, right under one's nose, staring someone in the face, written all over someone; *archaic* sensible.
OPPOSITES invisible, hidden.

vision ▸ noun **1** *her vision was blurred by tears* **eyesight**, sight, power of sight, faculty of sight, ability to see, power of seeing, powers of observation, observation, perception, visual perception; eyes; field of vision, view, perspective.
2 *he gazes into the fire seeing visions of the ancestral pilgrims* **apparition**, spectre, phantom, hallucination, ghost, wraith, shadow, manifestation, chimera, illusion, mirage, image; *Scottish & Irish* bodach; *W. Indian* duppy; *informal* spook; *literary* phantasm, shade, revenant, wight, visitant; *rare* eidolon, manes.
3 *they have visions of a more hopeful future* **dream**, daydream, reverie, mental picture, conceptualization; plans, hopes; fantasy, fancy, flight of fancy, fanciful notion, pipe dream, delusion, figment of the imagination, prospect.
4 *his conference speech was a little lacking in vision* **imagination**, creativity, creative power, inventiveness, innovation, inspiration, intuition, perceptiveness, perception, breadth of view, foresight, insight, far-sightedness, prescience, discernment, awareness, penetration, shrewdness, sharpness, cleverness.
5 *Melissa was a vision in pale lilac* **beautiful sight**, vision of loveliness, feast for the eyes, pleasure to behold, delight, dream, beauty, spectacle, picture, joy, marvel, sensation; *informal* sight for sore eyes, eyeful, stunner, cracker, smasher, knockout, looker, good-looker, bobby-dazzler, peach, honey.

WORD LINKS
relating to vision **visual, optical**
measurement of field of vision **perimetry**

visionary ▸ adjective **1** *a visionary leader* **inspired**, imaginative, creative, inventive, insightful, ingenious, enterprising, innovative, perceptive, intuitive, far-sighted, prescient, discerning, penetrating, sharp, shrewd, wise, clever, talented, gifted, resourceful; idealistic, idealized, utopian, romantic, quixotic, impractical, unrealistic, unworkable, unfeasible, out of touch with reality, fairy-tale, fanciful, dreamy, ivory-towered, theoretical, hypothetical; *informal* starry-eyed, head-in-the-clouds.
2 (*archaic*) *a visionary image of the four horsemen of the Apocalypse* **imaginary**, imagined, unreal, fanciful, fancied, fantastic, illusory, illusive, delusory, dreamy, dreamlike, shadowy, figmental, hallucinatory, phantasmagoric, phantasmagorical, spectral, ghostly, ghostlike, wraithlike, incorporeal, insubstantial, impalpable, chimerical, vaporous; *rare* phantasmal, phantasmic.
▸ noun **1** *a contemporary visionary pictured him in hell* **seer**, mystic, oracle, prophet, prophetess, soothsayer, sibyl, augur, diviner, prognosticator, clairvoyant, psychic, crystal-gazer; dreamer; *Scottish* spaeman, spaewife; *rare* oracler, vaticinator.
2 *he was too much of a visionary to run a business effectively* **dreamer**, daydreamer, idealist, romantic, romanticist, fantasist, theorist, utopian.

visit ▸ verb **1** *I was away visiting a dear uncle of mine* **call on**, call in on, pay a call on, pay a visit to, pay someone a call, pay someone a visit, go to see, come to see, look in on; stay with, spend time with, be the guest of, holiday with; stop by, drop by, pay a call, pay a visit, come to stay; *N. Amer.* visit with, go see; *informal* pop in on, drop in on, blow in on, drop round to see, look up.
2 *Alex was visiting America on a hectic tour* **stay in**, stop over in, spend time in, holiday in; tour, drive round, go round, explore; see, view, inspect, survey, examine; *N. Amer.* vacation in.
3 *the citizens were visited with repeated epidemics of a strange disease* **afflict**, attack, assail, trouble, harrow, torment, torture; descend on; *archaic* smite.
▸ noun **1** *after reading the play she paid a visit to the poet* **social call**, call.
2 *a school visit to the Ashmolean Museum* **trip to**, tour of, look around/round; stopover, stop-off, stay, stop; holiday, break; *N. Amer.* vacation, sojourn.

visitation ▸ noun **1** *the bishop conducted a busy schedule of pastoral visitations* **official visit**, visit, inspection, tour of inspection, survey, review, scrutiny, examination.
2 *the blinding light had signified a visitation from God* **apparition**, appearance, manifestation, materialization, emergence, vision.
3 *Jehovah was considered as punishing sinners by providential visitations* **affliction**, scourge, bane, curse, ordeal, plague, pestilence, blight, disaster, tragedy, calamity, catastrophe, cataclysm; punishment, retribution, penalty, vengeance.
OPPOSITE blessing.

visitor ▶ noun **1** *I am expecting a visitor* **guest**, caller; company; archaic visitant.
2 *the monument attracts visitors from all over the world* **tourist**, traveller, holidaymaker, day tripper, tripper, sightseer, globetrotter, jet-setter, backpacker, voyager, tourer, explorer, pilgrim; foreigner, outsider, stranger, alien; N. Amer. vacationer, vacationist, out-of-towner; Brit. informal emmet, grockle; rare excursionist.

vista ▶ noun *there's a marvellous vista from the hotel balcony* **view**, prospect, panorama, aspect, perspective, spectacle, sight; scenery, landscape, seascape, riverscape, townscape, cityscape, snowscape; archaic outlook.

visual ▶ adjective **1** *the child has visual defects* **optical**, seeing, optic, ocular, eye; vision, sight.
2 *many cheap car alarms have no visual indication that they are in operation* **visible**, perceptible, perceivable, seeable, to be seen, discernible.

visualize ▶ verb *it is not easy to visualize the future* **envisage**, envision, conjure up, conjure up an image/picture of, picture in the mind's eye, picture, call to mind, see, imagine, evoke, fancy, dream about, dream up, fantasize about, conceptualize, conceive of, think about, contemplate; foresee, predict, forecast, anticipate.

vital ▶ adjective **1** *it is vital that action is taken to protect jobs* **essential**, indispensable, crucial, key, necessary, needed, required, requisite, important, all-important, of the utmost importance, of great consequence, of the essence, critical, life-and-death, imperative, mandatory, urgent, pressing, burning, compelling, acute, paramount, pre-eminent, high-priority, significant, consequential; informal earth-shattering, world-shaking.
OPPOSITES unimportant, peripheral, secondary.
2 *a layer of fat protects the vital organs* **life-preserving**, life-sustaining, basic, fundamental, essential, necessary; major, main, chief, key, prime.
OPPOSITES minor, dispensable.
3 *the new president appeared young and vital* **lively**, energetic, active, sprightly, spry, animated, spirited, high-spirited, vivacious, exuberant, bouncy, enthusiastic, vibrant, zestful, sparkling, dynamic, vigorous, full of vim and vigour, forceful, fiery, lusty, hale and hearty, in fine fettle; informal go-getting, zippy, peppy, feisty, spunky, raring to go, full of beans, bright-eyed and bushy-tailed; N. Amer. chipper.
OPPOSITE listless.

vitality ▶ noun *everything about Nicola shone with vitality* **liveliness**, life, energy, animation, spirit, spiritedness, high-spiritedness, vivacity, exuberance, buoyancy, bounce, vibrancy, verve, vim, pep, brio, zest, zestfulness, sparkle, spark, effervescence, dynamism, passion, fire, vigour, forcefulness, ardour, zeal, relish, gusto, push, drive, punch, elan; informal zip, zing, fizz, get-up-and-go, oomph, pizzazz, feistiness.

vitamin ▶ noun. *See centre pages for list of* **Vitamins**

vitriolic ▶ adjective *he launched a vitriolic attack on the government* **acrimonious**, rancorous, bitter, caustic, mordant, acerbic, astringent, acid, acrid, trenchant, virulent, spiteful, crabbed, savage, venomous, poisonous, malicious, malignant, malign, pernicious, splenetic; nasty, mean, cruel, unkind, harsh, ill-natured, evil-intentioned, vindictive, scathing, searing, biting, barbed, wounding, stinging, tart, sharp, rapier-like, razor-edged, cutting, withering, sarcastic, sardonic, irascible; informal bitchy, catty, slashing; literary malefic, maleficent; rare acidulous, mordacious, squint-eyed.
OPPOSITES pleasant, kind.

vituperate ▶ verb *he **vituperated against** all presidents with equal gusto* **revile**, rail against, inveigh against, fulminate against, attack, upbraid, berate, harangue, lambaste, reprimand, castigate, chastise, rebuke, scold, chide, censure, condemn, damn, denounce, find fault with, run down, take to task, vilify, denigrate, calumniate, insult, abuse, curse, slander, smear; informal slate, slam, knock, hammer, carpet, roast, skewer, crucify, read someone the Riot Act, lay into, tear a strip off, bawl out, give someone a dressing-down, tell off, bad-mouth; Brit. informal rubbish, slag off; archaic contemn; rare asperse, excoriate, vilipend.
OPPOSITE praise.

vituperation ▶ noun *they were unprepared for the hate and vituperation which descended on them* **revilement**, invective, condemnation, castigation, chastisement, opprobrium, rebuke, scolding, criticism, flak, disapprobation, fault-finding; blame, reprimand, upbraiding, admonition; abuse, insults, curses, tongue-lashing, harangue, vilification, denunciation, obloquy, denouncement, denigration, disparagement, slander, slandering, libel, defamation, calumny, calumniation, evil-speaking, backbiting, malice, spite, spitefulness, vitriol, venom; slurs, aspersions, fulminations; informal slamming, knocking, bashing, mud-slinging, cattiness, bitchiness, bitching, bad-mouthing; Brit. informal rubbishing, slagging off, slating, stick, verbal; archaic contumely; rare objurgation, animadversion, derogation.
OPPOSITE praise.

vivacious ▶ adjective *she was a pretty and vivacious brunette* **lively**, animated, full of life, spirited, high-spirited, effervescent, bubbling, bubbly, ebullient, buoyant, sparkling, scintillating, light-hearted, carefree, happy-go-lucky, jaunty, merry, happy, jolly, joyful, full of fun, full of the joys of spring, cheery, cheerful, perky, sunny, airy, breezy, bright, enthusiastic, irrepressible, vibrant, vivid, vital, zestful, energetic, dynamic, vigorous, full of vim and vigour, lusty; informal bright-eyed and bushy-tailed, bright and breezy, peppy, zingy, zippy, bouncy, upbeat, chirpy, full of beans, chipper; N. Amer. informal peart; dated gay.
OPPOSITES dull, listless.

vivacity ▶ noun *she had none of her mother's vivacity* **liveliness**, animation, effervescence, ebullience, sparkle, scintillation, spirit, spiritedness, high-spiritedness, high spirits, sprightliness, jauntiness, light-heartedness, gaiety, merriment, jollity, happiness, cheerfulness, perkiness, breeziness, brightness, enthusiasm, irrepressibility, vibrancy, vividness, vitality, life, verve, zeal, gusto, relish, zest, energy, dynamism, spark, fire, fieriness, vigour, vim, brio, dash; French joie de vivre, elan, éclat; informal pep, zing, zip, bounce, chirpiness, go, get-up-and-go, oomph, pizzazz.
OPPOSITE listlessness.

vivid ▶ adjective **1** *a vivid blue Mediterranean sea* **bright**, bright-coloured, colourful, deep-coloured, brilliant, glowing, radiant, vibrant, strong, bold, deep, intense, rich, warm, flaming, flamboyant, glaring, eye-catching; informal jazzy.
OPPOSITES dull, washed out.
2 *Dickens provides us with a vivid account of nineteenth-century urban poverty* **graphic**, evocative, realistic, true to life, lifelike, faithful, authentic, clear, crystal clear, detailed, lucid, striking, arresting, impressive, colourful, highly coloured, rich, dramatic, picturesque, lively, stimulating, interesting, fascinating, scintillating; memorable, unforgettable, powerful, stirring, affecting, emotive, moving, haunting.
OPPOSITES vague; boring.
3 *she had a deep voice and a strikingly vivid personality* **dynamic**, flamboyant, striking, strong, powerful, fiery, lively, animated, spirited, vibrant, vital, vigorous, energetic, vivacious, zestful.

vixen ▶ noun **1** female fox.
2 *Margaret proved to be a fiery little vixen* **virago**, harridan, shrew, dragon, termagant, cat, witch, hellcat, she-devil, tartar, martinet, spitfire, hag, gorgon, fury, ogress, harpy, nag; informal bitch; archaic scold; rare Xanthippe.

viz. ▶ adverb *article one sets out its purpose, viz. to ensure the continuation of farming* **namely**, that is to say, that is, to wit, to be specific, specifically, in other words, to put it another way; such as, as, like, for instance, for example; Latin videlicet, scilicet, sc., id est.

vocabulary ▶ noun **1** *they are intelligent people with an extensive vocabulary* **lexicon**, word stock, lexis.
2 *we listed the acceptable terms in a vocabulary* **wordbook**, dictionary, word list, wordfinder, glossary, lexicon, concordance, thesaurus.

vocal ▶ adjective **1** *Neanderthal man could produce a reasonable range of vocal sounds* **vocalized**, voiced, spoken, said, uttered, expressed, articulated, oral, by mouth.
2 *he is a vocal critic of the government* **vociferous**, outspoken, forthright, plain-spoken, blunt, frank, direct, candid, open, uninhibited; vehement, vigorous, emphatic, insistent, forceful, keen, zealous, enthusiastic; clamorous, strident, loud, noisy; archaic free-spoken.
OPPOSITES taciturn, reticent.

vocation ▶ noun *his vocation as a clergyman was not eclipsed by his scientific career* **calling**, life's work, mission, purpose, function, position, niche; **profession**, occupation, career, job, work, employment, pursuit, trade, craft, business, line, line of work, speciality, specialty, province, sphere, walk of life; French métier; informal line of country, game, thing, bag, racket.

vociferous ▶ adjective *a vociferous champion of equal rights* **vehement**, outspoken, vocal, forthright, plain-spoken, frank, candid, open, uninhibited, direct, earnest, eager, enthusiastic, vigorous, insistent, emphatic, demanding; clamorous, strident, loud, loud-mouthed, raucous, noisy, rowdy.
OPPOSITES silent, quiet.

vogue ▶ noun *utility furniture is now enjoying a new vogue* **fashion**, mode, style, trend, taste, fad, fancy, passing fancy, craze, rage, enthusiasm, passion, infatuation, obsession, mania, fascination; fashionableness, modishness, popularity, currency, prevalence, favour; French dernier cri; informal thing, trendiness, coolness, snazziness.

□ **in vogue** *crochet garments were in vogue* **fashionable**, in fashion, voguish, stylish, in style, modish, up to date, up to the minute, modern, ultra-modern, current, prevalent, popular, in favour, in demand, desired, sought-after, all the rage, trendsetting, chic, smart; the latest thing, the big thing, the last word; French à la mode, le dernier cri; informal trendy, hip, cool, big, happening, now, in, with it, ritzy, flash, snazzy, natty, nifty, swinging, bang up to date; N. Amer. informal tony, kicky.
OPPOSITES unfashionable, out of date.

voice *See centre pages for lists of* **Voices** **Singers**
▶ noun **1** *there was great dismay when the starlet lost her voice* **power of speech**; powers of articulation.
2 *he gave voice to the anger and frustration of urban youth* **expression**, utterance, verbalization, vocalization, airing.

3 *the government promised to listen to the voice of the people* **opinion**, view, comment, feeling, wish, desire, vote, input; one's say; *informal* one's twopence worth, one's twopenn'orth.
4 *the body could be a powerful voice for conservation* **mouthpiece**, forum, organ, agency, agent, representative, spokesperson, spokesman, spokeswoman, intermediary, medium, vehicle, instrument, channel, means of expression.
▶ **verb** *party leaders voiced their total opposition to terrorism* **express**, give expression to, vocalize, give voice to, put in words, give utterance to, communicate, declare, state, set forth, bring into the open, make public, assert, divulge, reveal, proclaim, announce, raise, table, air, ventilate, vent, give vent to, pour out, mention, talk of, point out, go into; utter, say, speak, articulate, enunciate, pronounce, mouth; *informal* come out with.

void ▶ **noun** *the black void of space* **gap**, empty space, space, blank space, blank, vacuum, lacuna, hole, cavity, chasm, abyss, gulf, pit, hiatus; emptiness, nothingness, blankness, vacancy, vacuity, oblivion, nullity; *rare* voidness, nihility.
▶ **verb 1** *the contract was voided* **invalidate**, render invalid, annul, nullify; negate, disallow, quash, cancel, countermand, repeal, revoke, rescind, retract, withdraw, reverse, abrogate, undo, abolish, obliterate, terminate, repudiate; *Law* avoid, vacate.
OPPOSITES validate, ratify.
2 *the patients had difficulty in voiding their bladders* **evacuate**, empty, empty out, drain, clear, unload, unburden, purge.
OPPOSITE fill.
3 *the bacteria are present in the kidneys of the rat and are voided in the urine* **eject**, expel, emit, discharge, pass, excrete, egest, let out, send out, release, exude, eliminate; *rare* disembogue.
OPPOSITE take in.
▶ **adjective 1** *the cathedral has vast void spaces* **empty**, emptied, vacant, without contents, containing nothing, blank, bare, clear, free, unfilled, unoccupied, uninhabited, desolate, barren.
OPPOSITE full.
2 *a populous country suddenly left void of man or beast* **devoid of**, empty of, vacant of, bare of, destitute of, bereft of, denuded of, deficient in, free from; lacking, wanting, without.
OPPOSITE occupied.
3 *the election had been declared void* **invalid**, null and void, null, nullified, cancelled, revoked, rescinded, abolished, inoperative, ineffective, not binding, not in force, non-viable, useless, worthless, nugatory; lapsed, expired, out of date, terminated, discontinued, unrenewed.
OPPOSITE valid.

volatile ▶ **adjective 1** *her sister was headstrong and volatile* **unpredictable, changeable**, variable, inconstant, inconsistent, uncertain, erratic, irregular, unstable, turbulent, unsteady, unsettled, unreliable, undependable, changing, ever-changing, varying, shifting, fluctuating, fluid, mutable, protean, fitful, wavering, full of ups and downs; mercurial, capricious, whimsical, fickle, flighty, giddy, impulsive, wayward, temperamental, highly strung, excitable, emotional, overemotional, fiery, moody, choleric, stormy, tempestuous, volcanic; *informal* blowing hot and cold; *technical* labile; *rare* fluctuant, changeful.
OPPOSITES stable, constant.
2 *the atmosphere in the capital seems far too volatile for any talk of elections* **tense**, strained, fraught, uneasy, uncomfortable, charged, explosive, eruptive, inflammatory, turbulent, in turmoil, full of upheavals; *informal* hairy, nail-biting, white-knuckle; *Brit. informal* dodgy.
OPPOSITES stable, calm.
3 *a plume of pollution caused by a volatile organic compound* **evaporative**, vaporous, vaporescent; explosive, eruptive, inflammable; unstable; *technical* labile.

volition ▶ **noun**
□ **of one's own volition** *they chose to leave early of their own volition* **of one's own free will**, of one's own accord, of one's own choice, of one's own choosing, by choice, by preference, by one's own preference; voluntarily, willingly, readily, freely, intentionally, consciously, deliberately, on purpose, purposely, spontaneously, without being asked, without hesitation, without reluctance; gladly, with pleasure, with good grace, eagerly, enthusiastically.
OPPOSITE reluctantly.

volley ▶ **noun** *he fired off a volley of shots from his semi-automatic rifle* **barrage**, cannonade, battery, blast, bombardment, broadside, salvo, fusillade; storm, hail, shower, cascade, rain, stream, deluge, torrent, avalanche, blitz; wall/curtain/barrier of fire.

volubility ▶ **noun** *he is a figure of magnetic charm and great volubility* **talkativeness**, loquaciousness, loquacity, garrulousness, garrulity, verboseness, long-windedness, wordiness, chattiness, effusiveness, profuseness, communicativeness, expansiveness, openness, lack of reserve; articulacy, articulateness, eloquence, fluency, glibness; *informal* mouthiness, gabbiness, windiness, gassiness, big mouth, gift of the gab; *Brit. informal* wittering; *rare* logorrhoea, multiloquence.
OPPOSITE taciturnity.

voluble ▶ **adjective** *Mrs Maddox was as voluble as her husband was silent* **talkative**, loquacious, garrulous, verbose, long-winded, wordy, chatty, chattery, gossipy, chattering, babbling, blathering, prattling, jabbering, effusive, gushing, forthcoming, conversational, communicative, expansive, open, unreserved; articulate, eloquent, fluent, glib, silver-tongued; *informal* mouthy, gabby, gassy, windy, yakking, big-mouthed, with the gift of the gab, having kissed the Blarney Stone; *Brit. informal* wittering, able to talk the hind legs off a donkey; *rare* multiloquent, multiloquous.
OPPOSITES taciturn, uncommunicative, mute.

volume ▶ **noun 1** *this volume could stand in pride of place in any library* **book**, publication, tome, hardback, paperback, softback, work, opus, title, treatise, manual, almanac, compendium.
2 *a large glass syringe of known volume is weighed with and without the gas* **capacity**, cubic measure, size, magnitude, largeness, bigness, mass, bulk, extent, extensiveness; dimensions, proportions, measurements.
3 *a huge volume of water is released from the dam* **quantity**, amount, proportion, portion, measure, mass, bulk; level, degree.
4 *she leaned forward to turn the volume down* **loudness**, sound, amplification.

voluminous ▶ **adjective** *he folded his arms into the voluminous sleeves of his robe* **capacious**, commodious, roomy, spacious, ample, full, big, large, sizeable, immense, vast, generous; billowing, baggy, loose-fitting; *rare* spacey.
OPPOSITES tiny; tight-fitting.

voluntarily ▶ **adverb** *they signed a paper agreeing to leave the country voluntarily* **of one's own free will**, of one's own accord, of one's own volition, of one's own choice, of one's own choosing, by choice, by preference; willingly, readily, freely, intentionally, deliberately, on purpose, purposely, spontaneously, without being asked, without being forced, without hesitation, without reluctance; gladly, with pleasure, with good grace, eagerly, enthusiastically.
OPPOSITE under duress.

voluntary ▶ **adjective 1** *attendance at lectures is voluntary* **optional**, discretionary, at one's discretion, elective, non-compulsory, non-mandatory, not required, open, open to choice, volitional, up to the individual; *Law* permissive; *rare* discretional.
OPPOSITES compulsory, obligatory.
2 *she spent some time doing voluntary work* **unpaid**, unsalaried, without pay, without payment, free of charge, without charge, for nothing, for free; honorary, volunteer, unrewarded; *Law* pro bono (publico).
OPPOSITE paid.

volunteer ▶ **verb 1** *I volunteered my services as a school governor* **offer**, tender, proffer, present, put forward, put up, venture.
OPPOSITES refuse, withdraw.
2 *he volunteered as an ambulance driver on the Italian front* **offer one's services**, present oneself, step forward, come forward, make oneself available.
OPPOSITE be conscripted.
▶ **noun** *during the investigation, each volunteer was studied three times* **subject**, participant, case, client, patient; *informal* guinea pig.

voluptuous ▶ **adjective 1** *a voluptuous girl with black hair* **curvaceous**, shapely, opulent, full-figured, well formed, well proportioned, Junoesque, ample, Rubensesque, buxom, full-bosomed, lush, luscious; seductive, alluring, sultry, sensuous, sexually attractive; *informal* curvy, busty, sexy, slinky, beddable; *archaic* well turned, gainly, comely.
OPPOSITES scrawny, plain.
2 *the voluptuous charms of a luscious pudding* **hedonistic**, sybaritic, epicurean, pleasure-loving, pleasure-seeking, self-indulgent, indulgent; lotus-eating, decadent, intemperate, immoderate, dissipated, dissolute, abandoned; sensual, carnal, licentious, lascivious, salacious.
OPPOSITE ascetic.

vomit ▶ **verb 1** *he desperately wanted to vomit* **be sick**, spew, spew up, fetch up; heave, retch, reach, gag; *N. Amer.* get sick; *informal* throw up, puke, chunder, chuck up, hurl, pray to the porcelain god, do the technicolor yawn, keck, ralph; *Brit. informal* honk, shoot the cat; *Scottish informal* boke; *N. Amer. informal* barf, spit up, upchuck, blow chunks, toss one's cookies; *Austral./NZ informal* go for the big spit, play the whale, yodel, perk; *archaic* regorge, purge, brake, cascade; *rare* egurgitate.
2 *I vomited my breakfast all over the car* **regurgitate**, bring up, spew up, heave up, cough up; *Medicine* reject, lose; *informal* chuck up, throw up, puke; *Brit. informal* sick up; *N. Amer. informal* spit up; *archaic* regorge, void.
3 *the printer is vomiting folds of perforated paper* **eject**, issue, emit, expel, send forth, discharge, disgorge, spout, throw out, cast out, spew out, belch; *rare* disembogue, eruct.
▶ **noun** *the front of his jacket was stained with vomit* **sick**; *technical* vomitus, ejecta; *informal* chunder, puke, spew, pavement pizza, technicolor yawn, liquid laugh; *N. Amer. informal* barf, upchuck; *archaic* purge, parbreak.

WORD LINKS
fear of vomiting **emetophobia**

voracious ▶ **adjective** *boxer dogs have voracious appetites* **insatiable**, unquenchable, unappeasable, prodigious, uncontrollable, uncontrolled, omnivorous, compulsive, gluttonous, greedy, rapacious; enthusiastic, eager, keen, avid, desirous, craving, hungry, ravenous, ravening, wolfish; *informal* piggish, hoggish, swinish, gutsy; *Brit. informal* gannet-like; *rare* insatiate, edacious, esurient.

vortex ▶ **noun** *a whirling vortex of buff-coloured smoke* **whirlwind, whirlpool**, gyre, maelstrom, eddy, swirl, swirling, countercurrent, counterflow; *literary* Charybdis.

vote ▶ **noun 1** *she was elected in a rigged vote* **ballot**, poll, election, referendum, plebiscite, public vote, general election, local election, popular vote, straw poll, show of hands; voting, polling.
2 *in 1918 women over thirty got the vote in Britain* **suffrage**, franchise, enfranchisement, right to vote, voting rights; voice, say, option, choice.
OPPOSITE disenfranchisement.
▶ **verb 1** *only 28 per cent of the electorate voted in the referendum* **go to the polls**, cast one's vote, mark one's ballot paper.
2 *I vote we have one more game* **suggest**, propose, recommend, advocate, move, table, submit.
□ **vote someone in** *he was voted in as honorary secretary* **elect**, return, put in power, select, choose, pick, adopt, appoint, designate, opt for, plump for, decide on, settle on, fix on.
□ **vote someone out** *he persuaded delegates to vote out the prime minister* **depose**, oust, push out, turn out, remove from office, remove from power, unseat, dethrone, displace, dismiss, discharge, dislodge, eject, cashier; *informal* boot out, kick out, drum out, give someone the boot; *Brit. informal* turf out; *dated* out.

WORD LINKS
study of elections and voting **psephology**

vouch ▶ **verb**
□ **vouch for** *I can vouch for the veracity of his story* **attest to**, confirm, affirm, verify, swear to, testify to, bear witness to, bear out, back up, support, corroborate, substantiate, prove, uphold, show the truth of, give substance to, give credence to, second, endorse, certify, warrant, validate, give assurance of; answer for, be responsible for, be liable for, go/stand bail for; *informal* stick up for, throw one's weight behind.

voucher ▶ **noun** *a free travel voucher* **coupon**, token, ticket, document, certificate, licence, permit, carnet, pass, paper, card, form, deed; chit, slip, stub, docket; *Brit. informal* chitty; *N. Amer. informal* ducat, comp.

vouchsafe ▶ **verb 1** *he gave thanks to God for the grace which had been vouchsafed to him* **grant**, give, accord, award, offer, hand; confer on, bestow on, yield to, cede to, favour with.
OPPOSITES withhold, refuse.
2 *you'd never vouchsafed that titbit of information before* **disclose**, reveal, divulge, impart, pass on, tell, let out, let slip, give away, bring into the open, make public, make known, broadcast, air, circulate; *informal* blab, spill, come clean about; *Brit. informal* cough, blow the gaff on.
OPPOSITES withhold, conceal.
3 *if he would vouchsafe to talk with them he might hear some unexpected revelations* **deign**, condescend, stoop, unbend, sink, lower oneself, humble oneself, demean oneself; *informal* come down from one's high horse.

vow ▶ **noun** *the monks had taken a vow of silence* **oath**, pledge, promise, bond, covenant, commitment, avowal, profession, sworn statement, affirmation, attestation, assurance, word, word of honour, guarantee; *archaic* troth; *rare* asseveration, averment.
▶ **verb** *I vowed to do better* **swear**, swear/state under oath, swear on the Bible, take an oath, pledge, promise, affirm, avow, undertake, give an undertaking, engage, commit, commit oneself, make a commitment, give one's word, give one's word of honour, give an assurance, guarantee; *Law* depose, make a deposition, bind oneself; *archaic* plight, asseverate.

WORD LINKS
relating to a vow **votive**

voyage ▶ **noun** *the voyage lasted some eighteen days* **journey**, trip, expedition, excursion, tour, hike, trek, tramp, safari, pilgrimage, quest, crusade, odyssey; crossing, cruise, sail, sailing, passage, flight, drive; travels, globetrotting, journeying, wandering; *rare* peregrination, itineration.
▶ **verb** *he voyaged through Venezuela and Peru* **travel**, journey, take a trip, go on a trip, go on an expedition, go on an excursion, tour, globetrot; sail, steam, cruise, fly, drive; *informal* gallivant, do, knock about/around; *rare* peregrinate, itinerate.

vulgar ▶ **adjective 1** *a vulgar seaside postcard | vulgar verbal abuse* **rude**, indecent, indelicate, offensive, distasteful, obnoxious, risqué, suggestive, racy, earthy, off colour, colourful, coarse, crude, ribald, Rabelaisian, bawdy, obscene, lewd, salacious, licentious, vile, depraved, sordid, smutty, dirty, filthy, pornographic, X-rated, scatological; profane, foul, foul-mouthed, blasphemous, abusive, scurrilous; *informal* sleazy, porno, porn, raunchy, naughty, blue, steamy, spicy, locker-room; *Brit. informal* fruity, saucy, near the knuckle, close to the bone; *N. Amer. informal* gamy; *euphemistic* adult; *rare* concupiscent.
OPPOSITES decent, wholesome, inoffensive.
2 *the decor showed that one could be lavish without being vulgar* **tasteless**, gross, crass, unrefined, tawdry, ostentatious, flamboyant, over-elaborate, overdone, showy, flashy, gaudy, garish, brassy, kitsch, tinselly, flaunting, glaring, brash, loud, harsh; *informal* flash, tacky, over the top, OTT, glitzy, swanky.
OPPOSITES tasteful, restrained.
3 *it was considered vulgar for a woman to whistle* **impolite**, ill-mannered, unmannerly, indecorous, unseemly, ill-bred, boorish, low, low-minded, gross, uncouth, crude, rough; uncultured, uncultivated, unsophisticated, unrefined; illiterate, uneducated, philistine; common, ordinary, low-born, plebeian; *informal* yobbish, loutish, plebby, ignorant; *archaic* baseborn.
OPPOSITES genteel, decorous.

vulgarity ▶ **noun 1** *he avoided vulgarity and innuendo* **rudeness**, crudity, indecency, indelicacy, offensiveness, suggestiveness, bawdiness, ribaldry, obscenity, lewdness, salaciousness, licentiousness, depravity, sordidness, smuttiness, dirtiness, filthiness, smut, dirt, filth, pornography; profanity, blasphemy, swearing, bad language, strong language, foulness, abusiveness, scurrilousness; *informal* raunchiness, raunch, sleaziness, sleaze, porn, blueness; *Brit. informal* fruitiness, sauciness; *rare* concupiscence, bawdry, salacity.
OPPOSITE decency.
2 *she thought the quantities of gilt were evidence of shocking vulgarity* **tastelessness**, bad taste, grossness, crassness, lack of refinement, tawdriness, flamboyance, flamboyancy, ostentation, excess, gaudiness, garishness, showiness, flashiness, brassiness, tinsel, kitsch, loudness, harshness; *informal* tackiness, swankiness, swank, glitziness.
OPPOSITES tastefulness, restraint.
3 *her mother was free from any trace of vulgarity* **impoliteness**, ill manners, bad manners, impropriety, grossness, indecorousness, uncouthness, crudeness, coarseness, roughness; commonness, lowness, unsophisticatedness, lack of refinement, lack of sophistication; *informal* ignorance.
OPPOSITES gentility, decorum.

vulnerable ▶ **adjective 1** *they evacuated children from the most vulnerable cities* **in danger**, in peril, in jeopardy, at risk, endangered, unsafe, unprotected, ill-protected, unguarded; open to attack, attackable, assailable, exposed, wide open; undefended, unshielded, unfortified, unarmed, without arms, without weapons, defenceless, easily hurt/wounded/damaged, powerless, helpless; *rare* pregnable, impuissant, resistless.
OPPOSITES well protected, invulnerable, resilient.
2 *he is extremely sensible and less **vulnerable to** criticism than most* **exposed to**, open to, wide open to, liable to, prone to, prey to, susceptible to, subject to, not above, in danger of, at risk of, at the mercy of, an easy target for, easily affected by; in the firing line; *rare* susceptive of.
OPPOSITES immune to, above.

wacky ▸ adjective (*informal*) *a wacky movie spoof* **zany**, madcap, offbeat, quirky, outlandish, eccentric, idiosyncratic, surreal, ridiculous, nonsensical, crazy, absurd, insane, far out, fantastic, bizarre, peculiar, weird, odd, strange, cranky, freakish; **funny**, amusing, comic, clownish; *informal* loopy, loony, mad, dotty, nutty, nuts, freaky, batty, potty, goofy, bonkers, crackpot, screwy, screwball, oddball, way-out, off-centre, off the wall, dippy, cuckoo, kinky; *Brit. informal* barmy, daft; *N. Amer. informal* kooky, wacko; bizarro.
OPPOSITES conventional; sensible.

wad ▸ noun **1** *a wad of cotton wool | a wad of sealing wax* **lump**, mass, chunk, hunk, wedge, ball, clump, block, pat, brick, cube, bar, cake, slab, nugget, plug, pad, knob, gobbet, glob, dollop, cluster, nub; bit, piece, portion, segment; *Brit. informal* wodge, gob.
2 *Mike pulled out a wad of hundred-dollar bills* **bundle**, roll, bankroll, pile, stack, sheaf, pocketful, load.
3 *a huge wad of tobacco* **quid**, twist, plug, chew; *N. Amer. informal* chaw; *rare* pigtail, cud, cake.
▸ verb *the teddy bear had huge empty eye sockets wadded with cotton* **stuff**, pad, fill, pack, line; wrap, cover, encase, cushion, protect.

wadding ▸ noun **stuffing**, filling, filler, packing, padding, lining, cushioning, quilting; reinforcement, buffer, protection, guard.

waddle ▸ verb *he waddled forward to greet her* **toddle**, dodder, wobble, totter, shamble; sway, rock, lurch, limp, shuffle, stumble, reel, stagger; duckwalk, walk like a duck; *informal* waggle.

wade ▸ verb **1** *five or six men were wading in the icy water* **paddle**, wallow, dabble, slop, squelch, trudge, plod; *informal* splosh.
2 *Tony* ***waded across*** *the stream* **ford**, cross, traverse, walk across, make one's way across.
3 *they could just click it up on screen, rather than having to* ***wade through*** *some hefty document* **work one's way**, plough, plod, trawl, proceed with difficulty, labour, toil away at, plug away at; peruse, study; browse, leaf, flick, skim, look, thumb; *informal* slog.
□ **wade in** (*informal*) *police with truncheons waded in* **move in**, set to, set to work, pitch in, buckle down, go to it, put one's shoulder to the wheel; *informal* plunge in, dive in, get stuck in, get cracking.
□ **wade into someone** (*informal*) *I waded into those skinheads* **attack**, set upon, assault, launch oneself at, weigh into, fly at, let fly at, turn on, round on, lash out at, hit out at, fall on, jump on/at, lunge at, charge, rush, storm; *informal* lay into, light into, tear into, lace into, pitch into, beat up; *Brit. informal* have a go at.
□ **wade into something** (*informal*) *Flynn would gladly wade into the attack* **get involved in**, intervene in, get to work on, set to work on, tackle.

waffle (*Brit. informal*) ▸ verb *they were waffling on about the baby* **prattle**, chatter, babble, ramble, jabber, gibber, gabble, gab, burble, flannel, run on, mutter, mumble, prate, drivel, bleat, cackle; *Brit.* hum and haw; *informal* blather; *Brit. informal* rabbit, witter, natter.
▸ noun *my panic reduced the interview to waffle* **prattle**, jabbering, verbiage, drivel, meaningless talk, nonsense, twaddle, gibberish, stuff and nonsense, bunkum, mumbo-jumbo, padding, flannel, verbosity, prolixity; *informal* hot air, poppycock, tripe, bosh, bunk, blah, hogwash, eyewash, gobbledegook, rot, tommyrot, guff; *Brit. informal* wittering; *rare* logorrhoea.

waft ▸ verb **1** *spicy smells wafted through the air* **drift**, float, glide, whirl, travel, be carried, be borne, be conveyed, be transported.
2 *a breeze wafted the smell of barbecued lamb kebabs towards us* **convey**, transport, transmit, carry, bear; blow, puff.

wag[1] ▸ verb **1** *the dog's tail began to wag frantically* **swing**, sway, shake, move to and fro, swish, switch, quiver, twitch, flutter, waver, whip; oscillate, vibrate, undulate.
2 *he shouted and wagged his finger* **shake**, wave, waggle, wiggle, wobble, flourish, brandish, raise.
▸ noun **1** *Flossie managed a feeble wag of her tail* **swing**, sway, shake, swish, switch, quiver, twitch, flutter, waver, whip, oscillation, vibration, undulation.
2 *a wag of the finger* **waggle**, wiggle, wobble, wave, shake, flourish, brandish.

wag[2] ▸ noun (*dated*) *he's a bit of a wag* **joker**, jester, wit, humorist, comic, comedian, comedienne, funny man, funny woman, wisecracker, punner, jokester; prankster, clown, fool, buffoon; *informal* card, laugh; *informal, dated* caution.

wage ▸ noun **1** (usually **wages**) *the wages of farm workers are determined by the local labour market | a fair wage* **pay**, payment, remuneration, salary, emolument, stipend, fee, allowance, honorarium; income, revenue; yield, profit, gain, reward; compensation, recompense, reimbursement; (**wages**) earnings, takings, proceeds.
2 (**wages**) *the wages of sin is death* **reward**, recompense, requital, retribution; returns, deserts.
▸ verb *the government continued to wage war on the guerrillas* **engage in**, carry on, conduct, execute, pursue, undertake, prosecute, practise, proceed with, devote oneself to, go on with.

wager ▸ noun **bet**, gamble, speculation, venture, game of chance; stake, pledge, hazard, ante; *Brit. informal* flutter.
▸ verb *I'll wager that there will be no trace of them | I'll wager a pound or two on the home team* **bet**, gamble, lay a wager, place/make/lay a bet, lay odds, put money on; stake, pledge, risk, venture, hazard, chance, speculate; *informal* punt; *Brit. informal* put one's shirt on.

waggish ▸ adjective (*dated*) *a waggish riposte* **playful**, roguish, impish, mischievous, puckish, joking, jokey, jesting, jocular, jolly, merry, in fun, in jest, facetious, witty, amusing, entertaining, funny, droll, comic, comical; tongue-in-cheek, light-hearted, high-spirited, frivolous, bantering, flippant, flip, glib, whimsical, teasing, arch; *archaic* frolicsome, sportive; *rare* jocose.

waggle ▸ verb (*informal*) *Jonathan waggled his finger at Rex* **wag**, shake, wiggle, wobble, wave, quiver, jerk, twitch, flutter, jiggle, joggle, bobble, brandish, flourish, flail about.

waif ▸ noun **ragamuffin**, street urchin, guttersnipe; abandoned infant, foundling, orphan, stray, outcast; *archaic* gamin, mudlark.

wail ▸ noun *I heard a wail of anguish* **howl**, bawl, yowl, keening; cry, cry of grief, cry of pain, lament, lamentation, sob, moan, groan; shriek, scream, yelp, bellow, roar, caterwaul; whine, complaint, whimper; *rare* ululation.
▸ verb *the children immediately began to wail* **howl**, weep, cry, sob, moan, groan, keen, lament, yowl, blubber, snivel, whimper, whine, squall, bawl, shriek, scream, yelp, caterwaul, waul; complain, grumble, carp, sorrow, beat one's breast; *Scottish* greet; *rare* ululate.

wait ▸ verb **1** *they waited in the airport for two hours* **stay**, remain, rest, linger, loiter, dally, stop, stay put; *informal* stick around, kick around/about; *dated* tarry; *archaic* bide.
OPPOSITE leave.
2 *she had to wait until her passport came through* **stand by**, hold back, be patient, bide one's time, hang fire, mark time, kill time, waste time, cool one's heels, kick one's heels, twiddle one's thumbs; pause, stop, cease, halt, discontinue, rest; *informal* hold on, hang around, sit tight, hold one's horses, sweat it out; *Brit. informal* hang about.
3 *they were* ***waiting for*** *the kettle to boil* **await**, look/watch out; **anticipate**, expect, be ready, be in readiness; long for, hope for, count the days until.
4 *it will have to wait until we've got some money* **be postponed**, be delayed, be put off, be held back, be deferred; *informal* be put on the back burner, be put on ice.
5 (*informal*) *we've waited dinner for forty minutes* **delay**, postpone, put off, hold off, hold back, defer.
□ **wait on** *the men ate in silence, waited on by the two girls* **serve**, attend to, tend, cater for/to, act as a waitress/waiter to; accommodate, minister to, take care of, look after, see to, succour, pander to.

□ **wait up** *I'll be back late—don't wait up for me* **stay awake**, stay up, keep vigil.
▶ **noun** *we resigned ourselves to a long wait* **delay**, hold-up, period of waiting, interval, interlude, intermission, pause, break, stay, cessation, suspension, detention, check, stoppage, halt, interruption, lull, respite, recess, postponement, discontinuation, moratorium, hiatus, gap, lapse, rest, entr'acte.

waiter, waitress ▶ **noun** *the waitress came to take their order* **server**, stewardess, steward, attendant; head waitress/waiter, hostess, host; wine steward, wine waiter; butler, servant, page, flunkey; *N. Amer.* waitperson, carhop; *French* garçon, maître d'hôtel, sommelier (des vins).

waive ▶ **verb 1** *an individual can waive his right to a hearing* **relinquish**, renounce, give up, abandon, reject, surrender, yield, cede, do without, dispense with, set/put aside, abdicate, abjure, sacrifice, refuse, turn down, spurn, sign away.
OPPOSITES claim; pursue.
2 *the manager waived the rules and let us in* **disregard**, ignore, overlook, set aside, forgo, drop, omit, cast aside, brush aside.
OPPOSITES uphold; follow.

waiver ▶ **noun** *a waiver of one's rights* **renunciation**, surrender, repudiation, rejection, relinquishment, abdication, disavowal, refusal, disaffirmation, dispensation, abandonment, deferral; disclaimer; *rare* abjuration.

wake[1] ▶ **verb 1** *if Gran wakes she'll want a glass of water | at 4.30 a.m. Mark* **woke up** **awake**, awaken, waken (up), rouse, stir, come to, come around; get up, get out of bed, bestir oneself, get going, come alive, show signs of life; *literary* arise.
OPPOSITES sleep; fall asleep.
2 *she opened the door before waking her husband | he* **woke** *her* **up** *with a cup of tea* **waken**, rouse, arouse, bring to, bring around; *Brit. informal* knock up.
3 *a clip round the ear might wake him up a bit* **stir up**, activate, stimulate, spur, prod, galvanize, enliven, give a lift/boost to, ginger up, buoy up, refresh, invigorate, revitalize, inspire; *informal* perk up, pep up.
4 *they finally* **woke up to** *what we have been saying* **realize**, become aware of, become conscious of, become mindful of, become heedful of, become alert to.
5 *the name woke a forgotten and embarrassing memory* **evoke**, call up, conjure up, rouse, stir, revive, awaken, refresh, renew, resuscitate, revivify, rekindle, reignite, rejuvenate, stimulate.
▶ **noun** *a mourner at a wake* **vigil**, death-watch, watch; funeral.

wake[2] ▶ **noun 1** *a flotilla of rafts followed in the wake of the cruiser* **backwash**, wash, slipstream, turbulence; trail, path, track.
2 *share prices tumbled* **in the wake of** *the interest-rate rise* **aftermath**; as a result of, as a consequence of, on account of, because of, owing to, after, subsequent to, following, behind.

wakeful ▶ **adjective 1** *he had been wakeful all night* **unsleeping**, awake, restless, restive, tossing and turning, without sleep, wide awake, insomniac; *archaic* watchful.
OPPOSITES sleeping, asleep.
2 *I was suddenly wakeful* **alert**, on the alert, vigilant, on the lookout, on one's guard, on one's toes, on the qui vive, watchful, observant, attentive, sharp, heedful, wary.
OPPOSITE inattentive.

waken ▶ **verb**. *See* WAKE[1].

Wales ▶ **noun** *Welsh* Cymru; *Brit.* the Principality; *Latin* Cambria; *informal* the Land of Song.

walk ▶ **verb 1** *the two men walked along the road deep in conversation* **stroll**, saunter, amble, wend one's way, trudge, plod, hike, tramp, trek, march, stride, troop, patrol, step out, wander, ramble, tread, prowl, footslog, promenade, roam, traipse; stretch one's legs, go for a walk, take the air; advance, proceed, move, go, make one's way; *informal* mosey, pootle; *Brit. informal* yomp; *rare* perambulate.
2 *he walked the five miles into town* **go by/on foot**, travel on foot, foot it, be a pedestrian; *informal* go by/on Shanks's pony, hoof it.
3 *she thanked him for walking her home* **accompany**, escort, guide, show, see, convoy, conduct, usher, marshal, lead, take, attend, chaperone, steer, herd, shepherd.
□ **walk all over someone** (*informal*) **1** *be a bit firmer with the kids or they'll walk all over you* **take advantage of**, impose on, exploit, make use of, use, abuse, misuse, manipulate, take liberties with, trifle with, play with; *informal* walk over, take for a ride, put one over on, play for a sucker, run rings around.
2 *Kelburne looked as though they were going to walk all over the home team* **trounce**, beat hollow, defeat utterly, rout, annihilate, triumph over, win a resounding victory over, be victorious over, crush, overwhelm, best, get the better of, worst, bring someone to their knees; *informal* thrash, lick, hammer, clobber, paste, pound, pulverize, crucify, demolish, destroy, drub, give someone a drubbing, cane, wipe the floor with, give someone a hiding, take to the cleaners, blow someone out of the water, make mincemeat of, murder, massacre, slaughter, flatten, turn inside out, tank; *Brit. informal* stuff, marmalize; *N. Amer. informal* blow out, cream, shellac, skunk, slam.
□ **walk off/away with 1** (*informal*) *someone's walked off with my car keys* **steal**, thieve, make/run off with, carry off, help oneself to, rob, pilfer, purloin, pocket, snatch, take, appropriate, abstract; *informal* filch, swipe, nab, snaffle, blag, 'borrow', 'liberate', rip something off; *Brit. informal* pinch, nick, half-inch, whip, knock off, trouser.
2 *he walked off with four awards* **win easily**, win hands down, achieve, attain, earn, gain, receive, obtain, acquire, secure, collect, pick up, come away with, net; *informal* bag.
□ **walk out 1** *he had walked out in a temper* **leave suddenly**, make a sudden departure, get up and go, storm off/out, flounce out, push off, depart, leave, get out, absent oneself, take wing; *informal* take off.
2 *teachers are ready to walk out in a protest over class sizes* **go on strike**, call a strike, strike, withdraw one's labour, stop work, take industrial action; protest, mutiny, revolt; *Brit. informal* down tools.
□ **walk out on** *he walked out on his pregnant girlfriend* **desert**, abandon, leave, leave in the lurch, betray, run away from, throw over, jilt, run out on, rat on; *informal* chuck, dump, ditch, leave someone holding the baby; *archaic* forsake.
▶ **noun 1** *country walks* **stroll**, saunter, amble, promenade; **ramble**, hike, tramp, march; constitutional, turn, airing, excursion, outing, breather.
2 *he admired her elegant walk* **gait**, manner of walking, pace, step, stride, tread, carriage, bearing.
3 *street lamps illuminated the riverside walk* **pathway**, path, footpath, track, lane, alley, alleyway, walkway, promenade, footway, pavement, trail, trackway, ride, towpath; road, avenue, drive.
4 *the first job is to sort the post into different walks* **route**, beat, round, run, circuit.
□ **walk of life** *people from all walks of life* **class**, status, rank, caste, station, sphere, arena, area, domain, realm; line of work, line, profession, career, vocation, calling, job, occupation, employment, business, trade, craft, pursuit, work, province, field; *French* métier.

walker ▶ **noun** **hiker**, rambler, wayfarer, traveller, roamer, rover, footslogger; pedestrian, person on foot, foot traveller, stroller.

walkout ▶ **noun** **strike**, industrial action, stoppage, withdrawal of labour, go-slow, protest; revolt, mutiny, rebellion.

walkover ▶ **noun** *away games are never a walkover* **easy victory**, runaway victory, rout, landslide, triumph, gift; *informal* piece of cake, kid's stuff, child's play, doddle, pushover, cinch, breeze, sitter, picnic, like taking candy from a baby, thrashing, whitewash; *N. Amer. informal* shoo-in, cake walk, duck soup; *dated* snip; *Brit. vulgar slang* piece of piss.
OPPOSITE struggle.

wall ▶ **noun 1** *solid brick walls* **barrier**, partition, room divider, enclosure, screen, panel, separator; palisade; dam, dyke.
2 *an ancient city wall* **fortification**, rampart, barricade, parapet, bulwark, stockade, bailey, breastwork.
3 *we will work to break down the walls that stop world trade* **obstacle**, barrier, barricade, fence; impediment, hindrance, block, check.
□ **go to the wall** (*informal*) *thousands of businesses are expected to go to the wall this year* **fail**, collapse, go bankrupt, become insolvent, go into receivership, go into liquidation, crash, fold (up), go under, founder, be ruined, cave in; *informal* go broke, go bust, go bump, go belly up, come a cropper, flop.
□ **off the wall** (*N. Amer. informal*) *an off-the-wall cable television programme* **eccentric**, zany, far out, freakish, quirky, idiosyncratic, unconventional, unorthodox, weird, outlandish, offbeat, bizarre, strange, unfamiliar; *French* outré; *informal* way-out, wacky, freaky, kooky, screwy, kinky, oddball, cranky; *N. Amer. informal* in left field.
OPPOSITE conventional.
▶ **verb 1** *the tenements* **walled in** *the space completely* **enclose**, bound, encircle, confine, hem, circumscribe, close, shut, fence; separate, partition.
2 *one doorway had been* **walled up** **block**, seal, close, brick up.

WORD LINKS
relating to a wall **mural**

wallet ▶ **noun** *he pulled out a wallet and took a photograph from it* **notecase**, purse, pouch, pochette; *N. Amer.* billfold, pocketbook.

wallop ▶ **verb** (*informal*) *Grandma walloped him with her stick. See* THUMP.

wallow ▶ **verb 1** *a pond in which water buffalo wallowed* **loll about/around**, lie about/around, tumble about/around, splash about/around; slosh, wade, paddle, slop, squelch, welter; *informal* splosh.
2 *a ship wallowing in stormy seas* **roll**, lurch, toss (about), plunge, reel, sway, rock, flounder, keel, list; labour, make heavy weather.
3 *she seems to* **wallow in** *her self-pity* **luxuriate**, bask, take pleasure, take satisfaction, indulge (oneself), delight, revel, glory; give oneself up to, take to; enjoy, like, love, relish, savour, rejoice in, exult in; *informal* get a kick/buzz out of, get a kick/buzz from; *N. Amer. informal* get a bang from, get a charge out of.
OPPOSITE eschew.

wan ▶ **adjective 1** *she looked so wan and frail* **pale**, pallid, ashen, white, white as a sheet, grey; anaemic, jaundiced, colourless, bloodless, waxen,

chalky, milky, pasty, pasty-faced, whey-faced, peaky, sickly, tired-looking, washed out, sallow, drained, drawn, sapped, ghostly, deathly, deathlike, bleached; *rare* etiolated.
OPPOSITES flushed, ruddy.
2 *the wan light of the moon* **dim**, faint, weak, feeble, pale, watery, wishy-washy.
OPPOSITE bright.

wand ▶ **noun** *a magic wand* **baton**, stick, staff, pole, bar, dowel, rod, stake; club, truncheon, mace, sceptre; twig, cane, birch, switch, sprig, withe, withy; *Greek & Roman Mythology* caduceus.

wander ▶ **verb 1** *you can spend the afternoon wandering around the estate* **stroll**, amble, saunter, walk, dawdle, potter, ramble, maunder, meander; **roam**, rove, range, knock about/around, drift, coast, gallivant, gad about, prowl, mill about/around/round; trek, trudge, stretch one's legs; *Scottish & Irish* stravaig; *informal* traipse, mosey, tootle; *Brit. informal* mooch; *rare* peregrinate.
2 *he had wandered away from his mates | we are wandering from the point* **stray**, depart, diverge, veer, swerve, deviate, digress, vary, drift, get separated, get sidetracked, go wool-gathering; *rare* divagate.
3 *the child wandered off when we weren't looking* **get lost**, lose one's way, go off course, lose one's bearings, go astray, go off at a tangent.
4 *the narrow road wanders along the foreshore* **meander**, wind, twist, turn, curve, zigzag, bend, snake, worm.
5 *he was wandering now, his voice had dropped as he struggled to keep his thread* **be incoherent**, ramble, babble, talk nonsense, rave, be delirious.
▶ **noun stroll**, amble, saunter, walk, roam, meander, dawdle, potter, ramble; gallivant, prowl, drift, maunder, promenade, constitutional; turn, breather, airing, trek, trudge; *informal* traipse, mosey, tootle; *Brit. informal* mooch; *rare* perambulation, peregrination.

CHOOSE THE RIGHT WORD

wander, roam, rove, range, stray

These words all denote walking or moving in some way that is not a direct line. Some imply more energy and purpose than others.

- **Wandering** denotes movement that is not purposefully directed towards a particular goal. This lack of purpose may result from indecision or lack of energy, or may simply indicate that someone is not in a hurry (*she wandered aimlessly about the living room | wandering around looking at different displays*).
- Those who **roam** move around with little forward planning but generally show more energy than the wanderer (*packs of savage dogs roamed the streets | dark lanes where gangs roamed*).
- **Rove** is a rather old-fashioned word meaning 'travel constantly without a fixed long-term destination' (*he had roved the district in search of cinematic distraction*) but is now most commonly used as *roving*, which conveys quite a strong sense of purpose (*a roving busload of activists who went all over Europe*). *Roving* often means 'employed to work in many different places' (*communication with a roving agent was always fraught with difficulties*).
- **Range** is a less common word, indicating movement that is free from restrictions or constraints and is usually over a wide area but is nevertheless purposeful (*railway entrepreneurs ranged the globe in search of trade | they ranged over the Pacific in outriggers*).
- **Stray** denotes movement away from where one should be (*if you stray off the route it's almost impossible to get back | for an instant her tired mind strayed*), or into a wrong or inappropriate place (*the military arrested anyone who strayed into the exclusion zone*).

wanderer ▶ **noun** *a wanderer in the wilderness* **traveller**, rambler, hiker, wayfarer, migrant, globetrotter, roamer, rover; itinerant, rolling stone; nomad, gypsy, Romany; tramp, drifter, tinker, vagabond, vagrant; homeless person, displaced person, person of no fixed address/abode; *informal* dosser, bag lady; *N. Amer. informal* hobo, bum; *dated* bird of passage.

wandering ▶ **adjective** *a wandering minstrel* **travelling**, rambling, roaming, roving, journeying, drifting, itinerant, floating, wayfaring, voyaging, touring; peripatetic, unsettled, rootless, restless, on the move, on the go, on the wing; nomadic, gypsy, Romany; vagabond, vagrant, migrant, migratory, migrating, transient, homeless, displaced; *archaic* errant.

wane ▶ **verb 1** *the moon is waning* **pass full moon**, decrease, diminish, dwindle.
OPPOSITE wax.
2 *support for the strike was waning* **decrease**, decline, diminish, dwindle, shrink, contract, taper off, tail off, subside, slacken, droop, sink, ebb, dim, fade (away), grow faint, lessen, dissolve, peter out, wind down, fall off, attenuate, be on the way out, abate, fail, recede, slump, flag, atrophy, become weak, weaken, give in, give way, melt away, deteriorate, crumble, wither, disintegrate, degenerate, evaporate, collapse, go downhill, draw to a close, vanish, die out; *rare* evanesce, remit.
OPPOSITES increase, grow.
▶ **noun**
□ **on the wane** *the popularity of these films may be on the wane* **declining**, on the decline, decreasing, diminishing, dwindling, shrinking, contracting, tapering off, tailing off, subsiding, slackening, drooping, sinking, ebbing, dimming, fading away, growing faint, lessening, dissolving, petering out, winding down, falling off, attenuating, on the way out, abating, failing, receding, slumping, in a slump, in remission, flagging, atrophying, weakening, giving way, melting away, deteriorating, in a state of deterioration, crumbling, withering, disintegrating, degenerating, evaporating, collapsing, drawing to a close, vanishing, dying out, obsolescent, moribund; *informal* on one's last legs; *rare* evanescing.
OPPOSITES increasing, growing.

wangle ▶ **verb** (*informal*) *I think we should be able to wangle it so that you can start tomorrow | I wangled an invitation to her flat* **contrive**, manipulate, manoeuvre, engineer, devise, orchestrate, fix, arrange, direct, conduct, handle, work, pull off, scheme, plot; acquire, attain, achieve, bring about, net, win, grab, hook; *informal* fiddle, finagle, swing.

want ▶ **verb 1** *do you want more coffee? | he wants a place in the squad* **desire**, wish for, hope for, fancy, have a fancy for, take a fancy to, have an inclination for, care for, like, set one's heart on; long for, yearn for, pine for, sigh for, crave, hanker after, hunger for, thirst for, lust after, cry out for, be desperate for, itch for, covet, need, be bent on; *informal* have a yen for, be dying for.
2 (*informal*) *his toaster wants repairing* **need**, be/stand in need of, require, demand, cry out for.
3 (*informal*) *you want to be more careful* **should**, ought, need, must.
4 (*archaic*) *he has invented a new species of poetry which wants a name* **lack**, be lacking, be without, have need of, be devoid of, be bereft of, be/fall short of, be deficient in, have insufficient.
OPPOSITES have, possess.
▶ **noun 1** *millions perished for want of a safe haven | his want of vigilance* **lack**, absence, non-existence, unavailability; dearth, deficiency, inadequacy, insufficiency, paucity, shortage, shortfall, shortness, scarcity, scarceness, scantiness, undersupply, deficit; *rare* exiguity.
OPPOSITES abundance; presence.
2 (*archaic*) *a time of want* **need**, neediness, austerity, privation, deprivation, poverty, impoverishment, impecuniousness, impecuniosity, pennilessness, pauperism, penury, destitution, famine, drought, indigence.
OPPOSITES wealth, plenty.
3 *she had faith that all her wants would be taken care of* **wish**, desire, demand, longing, yearning, fancy, craving, hankering; **need**, requirement, necessity, essential, requisite; *informal* yen.

wanting ▶ **adjective 1** *when they came under siege the defences were found wanting* **deficient**, inadequate, lacking, insufficient, imperfect, not up to standard/par, not good enough, disappointing, unsatisfying, unacceptable, not acceptable, not up to expectations, leaving much to be desired, flawed, faulty, defective, impaired, unsound, substandard, inferior, second-rate, poor, shabby, shoddy, patchy, sketchy, limited, restricted, incomplete, unfinished, unpolished, unrefined; *Brit. informal* not much cop.
OPPOSITES sufficient, acceptable.
2 *the kneecap is wanting in amphibians and reptiles* **absent**, missing, lacking, not there, not present, non-existent, not to be found, unavailable, short.
OPPOSITE present.
3 *millions were left wanting for food | we will not be wanting in confidence* **without**, lacking, devoid of, bereft of, bankrupt of, destitute of, empty of, deprived of, free from/of, in need of; deficient in, low on, short on; *informal* minus, sans.

wanton ▶ **adjective 1** *wanton destruction* **deliberate**, wilful, malicious, malevolent, spiteful, vicious, wicked, evil, cruel; **unprovoked**, unmotivated, motiveless, arbitrary, groundless, unjustifiable, unjustified, needless, unnecessary, uncalled for, gratuitous, senseless, pointless, purposeless, aimless, useless, meaningless, empty, vacuous.
OPPOSITE justifiable.
2 *a wanton seductress* **promiscuous**, immoral, loose, immodest, indecent, shameless, unblushing, unchaste, unvirtuous, fast, of easy virtue, impure, abandoned, lustful, lecherous, lascivious, salacious, lubricious, libidinous, licentious, libertine, profligate, dissolute, dissipated, debauched, degenerate, reprobate, corrupt, sinful, whorish, disreputable.
OPPOSITES chaste, moral.
3 (*literary*) *the interlacings of every wanton vine* **wild**, unrestrained, uncontrolled, undisciplined, unmanageable; immoderate, lavish, extravagant, abundant, profuse, luxuriant, luxurious.
4 (*literary*) *a wanton fawn* **capricious**, playful, frisky, jolly, fun-loving, lively, full of life, high-spirited, spirited, careless, heedless, impulsive, impetuous, rash, reckless, abandoned, audacious, cavalier, devil-may-care, happy-go-lucky; *archaic* frolicsome, sportive.
OPPOSITE serious.

war ▶ **noun 1** *the Napoleonic wars | the outbreak of war* **conflict**, warfare, combat, fighting, struggle, armed conflict, action, military action, bloodshed, contest, tussle; battle, skirmish, fight, clash, confrontation,

engagement, affray, encounter, collision, offensive, attack, blitz, siege; campaign, crusade, feud, vendetta; strife, hostility, enmity, antagonism, discord, disunity, animus, ill will, bad blood; hostilities; *Islam* jihad.
OPPOSITES peace; truce, ceasefire; harmony.
2 *the war against drugs* **campaign**, crusade, battle, fight, struggle, movement, drive, mission.
▶ **verb** *rival Emperors* ***warred against*** *each other* **fight**, battle, combat, wage war, make war, be at war, be in conflict, conduct a war, do battle, join battle, take the field, take up arms; feud, quarrel, struggle, strive, contend, grapple, wrangle, tilt, cross swords, lock horns, come to blows; attack, engage, clash with, encounter, take on, set to, skirmish with, grapple with; *informal* be at each other's throats, fight like cat and dog.
OPPOSITE make peace.

WORD LINKS
relating to war **belligerent, martial**

warble ▶ **verb** *larks warbled in the blue sky* **trill**, sing, chirp, chirrup, chirr, cheep, twitter, tweet, whistle, chatter, squeak, pipe, peep.
▶ **noun** *a solitary warble pierces the air* **trill**, trilling, song, birdsong, cry, warbling, chirp, chirping, chirrup, chirruping, chirr, chirring, cheep, cheeping, twitter, twittering, tweet, tweeting, whistle, whistling, chatter, chattering, squeak, squeaking, pipe, piping, peep, peeping, call, calling.

war cry ▶ **noun battle cry**, war whoop, rallying call.

ward ▶ **noun 1** *the men's surgical ward* **room**, compartment, department, unit, area.
2 *the second most marginal ward in Westminster* **district**, constituency, division, quarter, zone, parish, community, department, canton.
3 *for the last three years the boy has been my ward* **dependant**, charge, protégé, pupil, trainee, apprentice; minor.
OPPOSITE guardian.
▶ **verb** *the last of the accident victims was warded* **admit to hospital**, admit, take in, let in, accept, receive, give entry to.
OPPOSITE discharge.
□ **ward someone off** *Kelly held out a hand to ward him off* **fend off**, drive back, keep off, stave off, repel, repulse, beat back, rout, put to flight, chase away; *informal* send packing.
□ **ward something off 1** *Candy held up her hands as though warding off a blow* **parry**, avert, deflect, block, turn aside, defend oneself against, guard against, evade, avoid, dodge.
2 *garlands of turmeric and garlic are worn to ward off evil spirits* **avert**, **rebuff**, rebut, keep at bay, keep at arm's length, fend off, stave off, oppose, resist, prevent, hinder, obstruct, impede, foil, frustrate, thwart, check, baulk, stop, head off.

warden ▶ **noun 1** *a group of self-contained flats with a resident warden* **superintendent**, supervisor, steward, overseer, caretaker, janitor, porter, custodian, watchman, concierge, doorman.
2 *the chief game warden* **ranger**, custodian, keeper, guardian, protector, preserver, curator.
3 *handcuffed to a warden, he was led to his cell* **prison officer**, guard, jailer, (prison) warder, (prison) wardress, keeper, sentry, captor; *informal* screw.
4 (*Brit.*) *the Warden of All Souls College* **principal**, head, governor, master, mistress, rector, provost, president, chief, director, chancellor, vice-chancellor; *N. Amer. informal* prexy, prex.

warder, **wardress** ▶ **noun prison officer**, guard, jailer, (prison) warden, keeper; sentry, captor; *informal* screw; *archaic* turnkey.

wardrobe ▶ **noun 1** *she left the doors of the wardrobe open* **clothes cupboard**, cupboard, cabinet, locker, storage room; *N. Amer.* closet.
2 *her wardrobe is extensive, with an outfit to match every mood* **collection of clothes**; clothes, garments, attire, outfits, wear; trousseau.

warehouse ▶ **noun** *a furniture warehouse* **storeroom**, storehouse, store, depot, depository, repository, stockroom; magazine; granary, silo; (*in India & Malaysia*) godown; *informal* lock-up; *archaic* garner.

wares ▶ **plural noun merchandise**, goods, products, produce, stock, commodities, items/articles for sale, lines, range; *rare* vendibles.

warfare ▶ **noun** *the reality of modern warfare* **fighting**, war, combat, conflict, armed conflict, struggle, military action, hostilities; bloodshed, battles, skirmishes, campaigning, passage of/at arms; strife, hostility, enmity, antagonism, discord.
OPPOSITES peace; harmony.

warily ▶ **adverb 1** *he walked towards it, treading warily to avoid the puddles* **carefully**, with care, cautiously, gingerly, circumspectly, charily, guardedly, on one's guard, on the alert, on the lookout, on the qui vive, attentively, heedfully, watchfully, vigilantly, observantly, alertly, cannily; hesitantly, timidly, timorously.
OPPOSITE recklessly.
2 *the little boy eyed her warily* **suspiciously**, distrustfully, mistrustfully, charily, cautiously, uneasily; *informal* cagily.
OPPOSITE trustingly.

wariness ▶ **noun 1** *the issue should be treated with a degree of wariness* **caution**, carefulness, care, circumspection, prudence, guardedness, alertness, attention, heed, heedfulness, watchfulness, vigilance, observance, awareness, mindfulness, canniness; hesitance, hesitancy, hesitation, timidness, timidity, timorousness.
OPPOSITE recklessness.
2 *they have the same wariness of strangers as everyone else* **suspicion**, distrust, mistrust, caution, unease, scepticism, doubt, chariness; *informal* caginess.
OPPOSITE trust.

warlike ▶ **adjective** *a warlike ruler* **aggressive**, belligerent, warmongering, warring, bellicose, pugnacious, combative, bloodthirsty, hawkish, gung-ho, jingoistic, sabre-rattling; hostile, threatening, inimical, violent, quarrelsome; militaristic, militant, martial, soldierly; *archaic* sanguinary.
OPPOSITE peaceable.

warlock ▶ **noun sorcerer**, wizard, male witch, (black) magician, diviner, occultist, enchanter, necromancer, spell-caster, thaumaturge; *Irish* pishogue; *literary* magus, mage.

warm ▶ **adjective 1** *Patsy was in the big, warm kitchen* **hot**, warming; cosy, snug, comfortable, homely, mellow; *informal* comfy, toasty.
OPPOSITES cold, cool.
2 *the first really warm day of spring* **balmy**, summery, sultry, hot, mild, temperate, pleasant, agreeable; sunny, bright, fine.
OPPOSITES cold, chilly.
3 *a tumbler of warm water* **heated**, tepid, lukewarm; *French* chambré.
OPPOSITES cold, chilled.
4 *she dressed in jeans and a warm sweater* **thick**, chunky, thermal, winter, woolly.
OPPOSITES light, summery.
5 *he gave her a warm smile | a warm welcome* **friendly**, comradely, affable, amiable, genial, cordial, kindly, kind, pleasant, sympathetic, affectionate, warm-hearted, good-natured, loving, tender, fond; welcoming, hospitable, liberal; caring, benevolent, benign, fatherly, motherly, paternal, maternal, comforting, charitable, solicitous; sincere, genuine, earnest, wholehearted, heartfelt, enthusiastic, eager, hearty.
OPPOSITES unfriendly, hostile, cold.
6 (*informal*) *they haven't found it yet, but they're getting warm* **close**, near, about to make a discovery, on the brink of making a discovery; *informal* hot.
OPPOSITES cold; distant.
▶ **verb** *she sat by the fire, warming her hands and feet | can you* ***warm*** *the soup* ***up*** *for me?* **heat (up)**, make/become warm, make/become hot, raise the temperature of, increase in temperature, thaw (out), melt; reheat, cook; *N. Amer.* warm over; *informal* hot (up), zap.
OPPOSITES cool, chill.
□ **warm to/towards 1** *everyone immediately warmed to him* **like**, **take to**, get on (well) with, feel a fondness for, feel attracted to, feel well disposed towards, hit it off with, be on good terms with, feel sympathetic to.
OPPOSITE dislike.
2 *he couldn't warm to the notion* **become enthusiastic about**, become supportive of, become excited about/over, become animated over/about.
□ **warm up** *if you don't warm up first you can easily pull a muscle* **limber up**, loosen up, stretch, work out, exercise, get into condition, get into shape, practise, prepare, get ready; rehearse.
□ **warm someone/something up** *on stage, Miles was warming up the crowd* **enliven**, liven (up), stimulate, animate, rouse, put some life into, stir (up), move, excite, cheer up; *informal* get going.
OPPOSITE calm down.

warm-blooded ▶ **adjective 1** *birds, like mammals, are warm-blooded technical* **homeothermic**, homeothermal.
OPPOSITES cold-blooded, poikilothermic.
2 *a warm-blooded young Latin lady* **passionate**, ardent, red-blooded, hot-blooded, fervid, impetuous, emotional, intense, lively, spirited, fiery, tempestuous, hot, sultry, torrid.
OPPOSITES cool, reserved.

warmed-up ▶ **adjective 1** *a warmed-up pasty* **reheated**, heated up; *N. Amer.* warmed-over.
OPPOSITE fresh.
2 *the proposal is a mishmash of warmed-up ideas* **unoriginal**, derivative, imitative, uninventive, copied, plagiarized, plagiaristic, second-hand, rehashed; trite, hackneyed, stale, tired, worn out, flat, stock, banal, uninspired; *informal* old hat.
OPPOSITES original, innovative.

warm-hearted ▶ **adjective** *they are perhaps the most generous, warm-hearted people in the universe* **kind**, warm, kind-hearted, kindly, soft-hearted, good-hearted, big-hearted, tender-hearted, tender, loving, caring, feeling, unselfish, selfless, benevolent, humane, good-natured, affectionate; gentle, mild, indulgent, friendly, open, sympathetic, understanding, compassionate, charitable, generous, magnanimous.
OPPOSITES unkind, unfriendly.

warmonger ▶ **noun** *a trigger-happy warmonger* **militarist**, hawk, jingoist, sabre-rattler, aggressor, provoker, belligerent.
OPPOSITE pacifist.

warmth ▶ **noun 1** *the warmth of the fire* **heat**, warmness, hotness; cosiness, snugness, comfort, homeliness, mellowness.
OPPOSITES cool, chill.
2 *she was surprised by the warmth of his smile | the warmth of their welcome* **friendliness**, affability, amiability, geniality, cordiality, kindliness,

kindness, sympathy, understanding, affection, warm-heartedness, good-naturedness, love, tenderness, fondness; welcomingness, hospitality, liberality; care, benevolence, benignity, charity, charitableness; wholeheartedness, enthusiasm, eagerness, heartiness, ardour, vehemence, passion, intensity, fervour, zeal, zest, effusiveness, spiritedness.
OPPOSITES hostility, half-heartedness.

warn ▶ verb **1** *David had warned her that it would be late when he returned* **notify**, alert, apprise, give notice, inform, tell, let someone know, make someone aware, give a warning to, give fair warning to, forewarn, put someone on notice/guard, remind; raise/sound the alarm; *informal* tip off, put wise.
2 *police are warning museums and galleries to take extra precautions* **advise**, exhort, urge, counsel, caution; put on the alert, put someone on guard.

warning ▶ noun **1** *the earthquake came without warning* **notice**, advance notice, a word of warning, forewarning, alert; hint, signal, sign, alarm bells; *informal* a tip-off.
2 *cigarette packets are required to carry a health warning* **caution**, piece of advice, notification, information; exhortation, injunction, a (warning) shot across the bows; advice, counselling; *informal* a word to the wise.
3 *a warning of things to come* **omen**, premonition, foreboding, prophecy, prediction, forecast, token, portent, augury, signal, sign, threat; *literary* foretoken.
4 *he was considering locking Lenny up as a warning to other young drivers* **example**, deterrent, lesson, caution, exemplar, message, moral.
5 *a further complaint may lead to a written warning* **admonition**, caution, remonstrance, injunction, reprimand, censure, caveat; *informal* dressing-down, talking-to, ticking-off, telling-off; *Brit. informal* carpeting.

warp ▶ verb **1** *timber which is too dry will warp and lose its strength* **buckle**, twist, bend, distort, deform, misshape, malform, curve, make/become crooked/curved, flex, bow, arch, contort, gnarl, kink, wrinkle.
OPPOSITES straighten; keep shape.
2 *a fanatic who warped the mind of her only child* **corrupt**, twist, pervert, deprave, bend, skew.

warrant ▶ noun **1** *a judge has now issued a warrant for his arrest* **authorization**, written order, licence, permit, official document; writ, order, summons, subpoena; mandate, decree, fiat, edict; papers.
2 *a travel warrant* **voucher**, chit, slip, paper, ticket, coupon, pass.
3 *the legislation gives no warrant for this assumption* **justification**, grounds, cause, rationale, basis, assurance; authority, licence, authorization, sanction, vindication.
▶ verb **1** *the charges warranted a severe sentence* **justify**, vindicate, call for, sanction, validate, be a justification/reason for; permit, authorize, entitle, empower; uphold, condone, endorse, deserve, excuse, be a defence of, explain away, account for, offer grounds for, legitimize; support, consent to, license, approve of; merit, qualify for, rate, be worthy of, be worth, be entitled to, be deserving of.
2 *the authors warrant that their texts do not infringe any copyright* **guarantee**, affirm, swear, promise, vow, pledge, give an undertaking, undertake, state, assert, declare, aver, proclaim, pronounce, profess, attest; vouch, testify, bear witness; support, endorse, underwrite, back up, stand by.

warrantable ▶ adjective *his interference was scarcely warrantable* **justifiable**, vindicable, excusable, explainable, explicable, reasonable, supportable.

warranty ▶ noun *a three-year warranty* **guarantee**, assurance, promise, commitment, covenant, undertaking, agreement.

warring ▶ adjective *envoys for peace are trying to bring the warring factions together* **opposing**, conflicting, clashing, at war, contending, fighting, battling, quarrelling; pugnacious, quarrelsome, aggressive, belligerent, militant, martial, warlike, warmongering; competing, hostile, rival, at loggerheads, at daggers drawn; *informal* at each other's throats.

warrior *See centre pages for list of* **Soldiers**
▶ noun *fearsome warriors* **fighter**, soldier, fighting man, serviceman, combatant; brave.

wart ▶ noun *she had a wart on her cheek* **growth**, lump, swelling, protuberance, carbuncle, boil, blister, verruca, corn, tumour, excrescence; *rare* tumescence.

wary ▶ adjective **1** *as a soldier, he was trained to be wary* **cautious**, careful, circumspect, on one's guard, chary, alert, on the alert, on the lookout, on the qui vive, prudent; attentive, heedful, watchful, vigilant, observant; *informal* wide awake, on one's toes, cagey.
OPPOSITES unwary, inattentive.
2 *we are wary of strangers in the city these days* **suspicious**, chary, careful, distrustful, mistrustful, sceptical, doubtful, dubious; guarded, on one's guard; *informal* leery.
OPPOSITES unwary, trustful.

wash ▶ verb **1** *he reached for the soap and began to wash* **clean oneself**, have a wash, wash oneself; bathe, bath, shower, have a bath/shower, take a bath/shower, soak, douche, freshen up; *formal or humorous* perform one's ablutions; *dated* make one's toilet.
2 *Melissa slipped indoors to wash her face and hands* **clean**, cleanse, sponge, scrub, wipe, scour; *literary* lave.
OPPOSITES dirty, soil.
3 *I washed and waxed the floor* **clean**, cleanse, sponge, scrub, mop, hose down, squeegee, sluice (down), swill (down), douse, swab (down), flush, disinfect.
OPPOSITES dirty, soil.
4 *she washed off the dried blood* **remove by washing**, sponge off, scrub off, wipe off, rinse off, remove, flush out/away, expunge, eradicate.
5 *a few women were washing clothes beside the shore* **launder**, clean, rinse (out); dry-clean; *literary* lave.
6 *I must shower and wash my hair* **shampoo**, lather, clean.
7 *gentle waves were washing against the hull* **splash**, lap, splosh, dash, break, beat, strike, sweep, move, surge, ripple, roll, flow; *literary* plash, lave.
8 *wreckage was washed up on the coast of Alaska* **sweep**, carry, convey, transport, move, deliver, deposit, drive.
9 *a wave of guilt washed over her* **affect**, rush over/through, thrill through, race over, surge through, course through, flood over, flow over, sweep over, flutter through.
10 *the stonework was washed with water-based paint* **paint**, colour, apply paint to, tint, highlight, shade, dye, stain, distemper; coat, cover.
11 *copper washed with silver* **plate**, cover, coat, overlay, laminate, veneer, glaze, gild, silver.
12 (*informal*) *people will see that this budget is merely an election bribe and it won't wash* **be accepted**, be acceptable, be plausible, be convincing, hold up, hold water, stand up, bear scrutiny, stand the test of time, be believable/credible, pass muster, prove true, make sense; *informal* stick.
□ **wash something away** *about two acres of land has been washed away* **erode**, abrade, wear away, corrode, eat away, eat into, denude, grind down, undermine.
□ **wash one's hands of** *I'm going to wash my hands of the whole business* **disown**, disclaim, renounce, reject, abjure, forswear, disavow, have nothing to do with, have done with, be finished/through with, give up on, turn one's back on, cast aside, end relations with, abandon; *Law* disaffirm.
□ **wash up** *I cook for him, but he usually washes up* **wash the dishes**, wash the crockery, do the dishes, do the washing-up.
□ **wash something up** *he washed up the dishes* **clean**, rinse, do, scrub, scour.
▶ noun **1** *her hair needs a wash | he had a quick wash and shave* **clean**, cleaning, cleansing; shower, douche, dip, bath, soak; *formal or humorous* ablutions; *rare* lavation.
2 *that shirt should really go in the wash straight away* **laundry**, washing; dirty washing, dirty clothes, soiled linen; *Brit. dated* bagwash.
3 *an antiseptic skin wash* **lotion**, salve, application, preparation, rinse, liquid, liniment, embrocation, emulsion.
4 *his jet ski ploughed into the wash of a motor boat* **backwash**, backflow, wake, trail, train, path; churning, disturbance.
5 *the wash of the waves on the pebbled beach* **surge**, flow, swell, welling, sweep, undulation, rise and fall, ebb and flow, roll, splash.
6 *water was applied to thin out the crayon into a wash* **paint**, stain, varnish, coat, layer, film, overlay.

washed out ▶ adjective **1** *a washed-out denim jacket* **faded**, blanched, bleached, lightened, decolorized; stonewashed.
OPPOSITE bold.
2 *wooden shutters of washed-out blue and green* **pale**, light, flat, drab, grey, muted, lacklustre, lustreless, watery.
OPPOSITE vivid.
3 *a woman with a worn, washed-out face* **wan**, pallid, pale, white, grey, pasty, pasty-faced, anaemic, colourless, bloodless, drawn, haggard, blanched, drained, pinched, peaky, peakish, ashen, ashen-faced, chalky, chalk-white, waxy, waxen, sickly, sallow, whey-faced, ghostly, deathlike, deathly pale, as white as a sheet, looking as if one has seen a ghost; *rare* lymphatic.
OPPOSITES ruddy, flushed.
4 *he was looking washed out after his exams* **exhausted**, tired (out), worn out, weary, fatigued, spent, drained, enfeebled, enervated, run down; *informal* all in, done in, dead on one's feet, dead, dog-tired, played out, knocked out, bushed, fagged (out), beat, zonked, like death warmed up; *Brit. informal* knackered, whacked; *N. Amer. informal* pooped, tuckered out; *rare* etiolated.
OPPOSITES energetic, perky.

washout ▶ noun (*informal*) *I was a bit of a washout at school | the last dance was a total washout financially speaking* **failure**, disappointment, let-down, loser, non-achiever, ne'er-do-well; fiasco, setback, blow, misfortune, disaster, catastrophe, mess, debacle, damp squib; *informal* flop, dud, non-starter, no-hoper, lead balloon; *N. Amer.* clinker.
OPPOSITES success, triumph.

waspish ▶ adjective *she sounded waspish and impatient* **irritable**, touchy, testy, irascible, cross, snappish, cantankerous, splenetic, short-tempered, ill-tempered, bad-tempered, foul-tempered, moody, crabbed, crotchety, grumpy, huffy, ratty, petulant, peevish, querulous, angry, sharp; *informal* grouchy; *N. English informal* mardy.

waste ▶ **verb 1** *he doesn't like to waste money on bus fares* **squander**, fritter away, misspend, misuse, spend recklessly, throw away, lavish, be wasteful with, dissipate, spend like water, throw around like confetti; go through, run through, exhaust, drain, deplete, burn up, use up, consume; *informal* blow, splurge.
OPPOSITE conserve.
2 *junkies wasting away in the streets* **grow weak**, wither, atrophy, become emaciated, shrivel up, shrink, decay; decline, wilt, fade, flag, deteriorate, degenerate, rot, moulder, languish, be abandoned, be neglected, be forgotten, be disregarded.
OPPOSITES flourish, thrive.
3 *the disease had wasted his legs* **emaciate, atrophy**, wither, debilitate, shrivel, shrink, weaken, enfeeble, sap the strength of.
4 (*archaic*) *without him your country would have been wasted by the English* **destroy**, devastate, wipe out, demolish, wreak havoc on, pillage, plunder, rob, sack, ravage, annihilate, raid, ransack, loot, ruin, leave in ruins, wreck, level, flatten, gut, maraud, harry; *literary* despoil; *rare* depredate, spoliate, forage.
5 (*N. Amer. informal*) *I saw them waste the guy I worked for* **murder**, kill, do away with, assassinate, liquidate, do to death, eliminate, terminate, dispatch, finish off, put to death, execute; slaughter, butcher, massacre, wipe out, destroy, annihilate, eradicate, exterminate, extirpate, decimate, mow down, shoot down, cut down, cut to pieces; *informal* bump off, polish off, do in, knock off, top, take out, croak, stiff; *N. Amer. informal* ice, off, rub out, whack, smoke; *literary* slay.
▶ **adjective 1** *I collected two bags containing waste material* **unwanted**, excess, superfluous, left over, scrap, extra, unused, useless, worthless; unproductive, unusable, unprofitable.
OPPOSITE useful.
2 *she took a short cut across waste ground* **uncultivated**, barren, desert, unproductive, infertile, unfruitful, arid, bare; desolate, solitary, lonely, empty, void, uninhabited, unpopulated; wild.
OPPOSITE cultivated.
▶ **noun 1** *what a waste of money* **squandering**, dissipation, frittering away, misspending, misuse, misapplication, misemployment, abuse; prodigality, extravagance, wastefulness, lavishness, unthriftiness.
2 *household waste* **rubbish**, refuse, litter, debris, dross, junk, detritus, scrap; dregs, leavings, remains, scraps, offscourings; sewage, effluent, effluvium; *N. Amer.* garbage, trash.
3 (usually **wastes**) *the frozen wastes of the South Pole* **desert**, wasteland, wilderness, barrenness, emptiness, vastness, wilds.
□ **lay waste**. *See* LAY[1].

wasted ▶ **adjective 1** *it was a wasted effort* **squandered**, misspent, misdirected, misused, dissipated, frittered away; pointless, useless, unnecessary, needless, not needed; *informal* blown, splurged.
2 *a wasted opportunity* **missed**, lost, past, forfeited, neglected, squandered, bungled, gone, gone by the board; *informal* down the drain.
3 *I'm wasted in this job* **underemployed**, underused, too good for; abandoned, neglected, forgotten, disregarded, languishing.
4 *his skinny wasted legs* **emaciated, atrophied**, withered, shrivelled, weak, weakened, frail, shrunken, skeletal, rickety, scrawny, cadaverous, wilted, faded, flagging, deteriorating, degenerative; gaunt, haggard, wizened, undernourished, starved, half-starved.
5 (*informal*) *everybody at the party was pretty wasted* **drunk**, drunken, blind drunk, dead drunk; **intoxicated**, inebriated, inebriate, stupefied, dazed, befuddled, bewildered; *informal* smashed, blotto, bombed, blasted, hammered, blitzed, stoned, high, wired, paralytic, wrecked, zonked, under the table, out of it, plastered, sloshed, stewed, pickled, tanked up; *Brit. informal* legless.
OPPOSITE sober.

wasteful ▶ **adjective** *wasteful use of energy in the home* **prodigal**, profligate, uneconomical, extravagant, lavish, excessive, careless, imprudent, improvident, reckless; thriftless, spendthrift, squandering; needless, useless, not needed, squandered.
OPPOSITES thrifty, frugal.

wasteland ▶ **noun** *he turned the land into a desolate wasteland* **wilderness**, desert, waste, barren land, dust bowl; wilds, badlands.

waster ▶ **noun** (*informal*) *all her friends are drunks or wasters* **idler**, loafer, good-for-nothing, drone, ne'er-do-well, do-nothing, slob, lounger, shirker, sluggard, laggard, slugabed; *informal* loser, skiver, slacker, lazybones; *N. Amer. informal* bum, gold brick; *literary* wastrel.

wastrel ▶ **noun** (*literary*) **1** *her money was gambled away by her wastrel of a husband* **spendthrift**, prodigal, profligate, squanderer; *informal* big spender.
2 *he was mixing with thieves and wastrels when he ought to have been studying* **idler**, loafer, good-for-nothing, drone, ne'er-do-well, do-nothing, layabout, slob, lounger, shirker, sluggard, laggard, slugabed; *informal* waster, loser, slacker, lazybones; *Brit. informal* skiver.

watch *See centre pages for list of* **Clocks and Watches**
▶ **verb 1** *Philippa continued to watch him as he spoke* **observe**, view, look at, eye, gaze at, stare at, gape at, peer at; contemplate, survey, feast one's eyes on, watch like a hawk, keep a weather eye on; inspect, scrutinize, scan, examine, study, take in, take stock of, glance at; see, notice, spot, glimpse, spy, catch sight of, lay one's eyes on, perceive, witness; ogle, leer at, make eyes at; pay attention to, regard, attend, take note of, mark; *informal* check out, get a load of, recce, eyeball, not take one's eyes off; *Brit. informal* take a dekko at, take a butcher's at; *literary* behold.
OPPOSITES ignore, disregard.
2 *he was being watched by plain-clothes police* **spy on**, keep watch on, keep an eye on, keep in sight, keep track of, track, monitor, survey, follow, keep under observation, keep under surveillance; *informal* keep tabs on, keep a beady eye on, stake out; *rare* surveil.
3 *we need to find a trustworthy person to watch the kids* **look after**, mind, take care of, care for, supervise, superintend, tend, attend to, minister to, foster, nurse, guard, safeguard, protect; *informal* keep an eye on.
OPPOSITE neglect.
4 *they came to a large set of steel doors, watched over by a single guard | two men stayed to watch the boat* **guard**, stand guard over, keep guard on, protect, shield, preserve, defend, safeguard, screen, shelter; cover, patrol, police, picket, keep a lookout at.
5 *most women watch their diet during pregnancy | watch what you say to him* **be careful about/of**, exercise care/caution/restraint about; be aware of, pay attention to, consider, take into account/consideration, bear in mind, keep in mind; mind, attend to, pay heed to.
□ **watch out/it/yourself** *'Watch out' he yelled | watch it, Bob, or you'll go over the edge* **be careful**, be watchful, beware, be on the watch, be wary, be cautious, be on your guard, mind out, look out, pay attention, take heed/care, have a care, be on the alert/lookout, keep a sharp lookout, be vigilant, be on the qui vive; *informal* keep an eye open/out, keep one's eyes peeled/skinned.
□ **watch (out) for** *he made idle banter as they watched for the van* **look out for**, wait for, await, stand by for, hold back for; anticipate, expect; *informal* keep an eye open for.
▶ **noun 1** *Harvey looked at his watch and said 'Time to get ready'* **timepiece**, chronometer, small clock, timer; wristwatch, pocket watch, fob watch, digital watch, stopwatch.
2 *we kept watch on the yacht* **guard**, vigil, lookout, an eye; observance, observation, surveillance, vigilance, view, notice.
3 *Ratagan took the first watch while the rest slept* **shift**, stint, spell, stretch, turn.

watchdog ▶ **noun 1** *they use watchdogs and armed guards to ward off trespassers* **guard dog**, house dog.
2 *the department acts as a watchdog over life assurance companies | a consumer watchdog* **ombudsman**, monitor, scrutineer, inspector, observer, supervisor; custodian, guardian, guard, protector.

watcher ▶ **noun onlooker**, spectator, observer, viewer, looker-on, witness, eyewitness, fly on the wall, sightseer; bystander, passer-by, non-participant; spy; *informal* rubberneck; *literary* beholder.

watchful ▶ **adjective** *her mother kept a watchful eye on her* **observant**, alert, vigilant, attentive, perceptive; awake, wakeful, aware, heedful, sharp; sharp-eyed, keen-eyed, eagle-eyed, hawk-eyed, gimlet-eyed, with one's eyes open; on the lookout, on the qui vive, wary, cautious, careful, suspicious, circumspect, chary; *informal* with one's eyes skinned/peeled.
OPPOSITES inattentive, careless.

watchman ▶ **noun 1** *a night watchman* **security guard**, security man, guard, custodian, doorman; caretaker, janitor, superintendent, warden, steward, curator.
2 (*archaic*) *as the raiding party drew near, a watchman sounded the alarm* **sentry**, guard, patrolman, policeman, lookout, sentinel, scout, watch, picket; *historical* vedette.

watchword ▶ **noun 1** *efficiency in all things was the watchword* **guiding principle, slogan**, motto, maxim, axiom, mantra, truism, catchword, catchphrase, catchline, sound bite, byword, battle/rallying cry, formula, refrain, saying; *informal* buzzword.
2 (*archaic*) *if our sentinels challenge you, the watchword is 'God and our country'* **password**, sign, signal, word, magic word, shibboleth; open sesame; *archaic* countersign.

water ▶ **noun 1** *a glass of water* drinking water, tap water, mineral water, bottled water, distilled water; rainwater, seawater, brine, spa water, spring water; *Latin* aqua; *technical* H_2O; *rare* Adam's ale.
2 *he had a house down by the water* **sea**, ocean; **lake**, loch, pond, pool, reservoir; **river**.
OPPOSITE land.
□ **hold water** *there are times when this theory just does not hold water* **be tenable**, ring true, bear examination/scrutiny, survive investigation, make sense, work out, stand up, hold up, be convincing, be plausible, be verifiable, be provable, be sound.
OPPOSITE fall down.
▶ **verb 1** *he told me to water the plants* **sprinkle**, moisten, dampen, wet, spray, splash; soak, douse, souse, drench, saturate, flood, waterlog; hose (down), water down; *archaic* sodden.
OPPOSITES dry out, parch.
2 *Ralph's eyes were watering | my mouth watered as I looked at the strawberries* **moisten**, exude water, become wet, leak; cry, weep; salivate.
3 *he was accused of watering the claret. See* WATER SOMETHING DOWN *sense* 1.

□ **water something down 1** *staff at the club had watered down the drinks* **dilute**, add water to, water, thin (out), make thin/thinner, weaken, make weak/weaker; adulterate, doctor, taint, mix; *informal* cut.
2 *in the end the proposals were considerably watered down* **moderate**, temper, qualify, mitigate, mute, mellow, tone down, soften; subdue, curb, tame, calm, bridle; understate, underemphasize, play down, soft-pedal, downplay.
OPPOSITES enhance, strengthen.

WORD LINKS
relating to water **aqueous**
related prefixes **aqua- (e.g. *aquaculture*), hydro- (e.g. *hydroelectric*)**
fear of water **hydrophobia**

waterfall ▶ noun **cascade**, cataract, shower, torrent, outpouring, white water, chute; falls, rapids; *N. English* force; *Scottish archaic* linn.

waterproof ▶ adjective *a warm waterproof jacket* **watertight**, water-repellent, water-resistant, weatherproof; damp-proof; impermeable, impervious; coated, proofed, rubberized, waxed.
OPPOSITE leaky.
▶ noun (*Brit.*) *she put on boots and a waterproof* **raincoat**, anorak, mackintosh, sou'wester, oilskin, cagoule, cape; *Brit. informal* mac.

watertight ▶ adjective **1** *a watertight container* **waterproof**, water-repellent, water-resistant, weatherproof; damp-proof; **impermeable**, impervious, sealed, hermetically sealed, coated, proofed, rubberized.
OPPOSITE leaky.
2 *Sam had arranged a watertight alibi* **indisputable**, unquestionable, incontrovertible, undeniable, irrefutable, unassailable, impregnable, beyond dispute, beyond question, beyond doubt, indubitable; foolproof, sound, flawless, airtight, conclusive, perfect, without loopholes.
OPPOSITE flawed.

watery ▶ adjective **1** *the patient's nose may be streaming with a watery discharge* **liquid**, fluid, liquefied; *technical* aqueous, hydrous.
OPPOSITE solid.
2 *a watery meadow* **wet**, damp, moist, sodden, soggy, squelchy, soft; saturated, waterlogged; marshy, boggy, swampy, fenny, miry, muddy, oozy.
OPPOSITE dry.
3 *a bowl of watery porridge* **thin**, runny, weak, sloppy, dilute, diluted, watered down, thinned down, adulterated; tasteless, flavourless, insipid, bland; *informal* wishy-washy.
OPPOSITES thick, concentrated.
4 *the light was watery and grey* **pale**, wan, thin, faint, weak, feeble, washed out, anaemic, colourless, insipid; *informal* wishy-washy.
OPPOSITE bright.
5 *she dabbed at a watery eye* **tearful**, teary, weeping, weepy, moist, rheumy, dewy-eyed; *formal* lachrymose.
OPPOSITE dry.

wave *See centre pages for list of* **Radiation Types**
▶ verb **1** *Farrell waved a hand dismissively | the linesman waved his flag furiously* **move to and fro**, move up and down, wag, waggle; swing, shake, swish, sweep, swipe, brandish, flourish, flaunt, wield, flick, flutter.
2 *the grass waved in the morning breeze* **ripple**, flutter, undulate, stir, flap, sway, swing, waft, shake, quiver, oscillate, move; blow.
3 *the waiter was waving to them to sit closer* **gesture**, gesticulate, signal, sign, beckon, indicate, motion, nod, bid.
4 *her thick dark hair fell in a waving mass to her shoulders* **curl**, kink, coil, undulate; crimp, frizz, frizzle.
□ **wave something aside** *he waved aside her protest* **dismiss**, reject, set/put/brush aside, shrug off, disregard, ignore, spurn, rebuff, discount, repudiate, put out of one's mind, play down, treat with contempt; *informal* pooh-pooh, pour cold water on.
□ **wave something down** *he waved down a taxi and drove off* **flag down**, hail, signal to stop, stop, signal, summon, call, shout to, accost.
▶ noun **1** *Whitlock gave him a friendly wave as he drove past* **gesture**, gesticulation, hand movement; signal, sign, motion, indication.
2 *he loves surfing the big waves* **breaker**, billow, roller, comber, ripple, white horse, white cap; (**waves**) swell, surf, froth; *Austral./NZ* bombora; *informal* boomer; *N. Amer. informal* kahuna.
3 *the wave of emigration to Israel* **flow**, rush, surge, flood, stream, swell, tide, deluge, torrent, spate, billow.
4 *Lee felt a wave of self-pity | a crime wave* **surge**, rush, ripple, spasm, thrill, frisson, shiver, tingle, stab, dart; upsurge, welling up, outbreak, rash; feeling.
5 *he had dark hair that sprang in thick waves from his forehead* **curl**, kink, corkscrew, crimp, twist, twirl, ringlet, frizz, coil, loop, undulation.
6 *electromagnetic waves | light waves* ripple, vibration, oscillation, undulation.
□ **make waves** (*informal*) *plenty of backbenchers continue to make waves* **cause trouble**, be disruptive, be troublesome, cause a disturbance; make an impression, be noticed.

waver ▶ verb **1** *the candlelight in the room wavered in a warm draught* **flicker**, quiver, tremble, twinkle, glimmer, wink, blink.
2 *his voice wavered with a hint of uncertainty* **become unsteady**, falter, wobble, tremble, hesitate.
3 *he had wavered between the Church of Ireland and Catholicism* **be undecided**, be irresolute, be indecisive, hesitate, dither, equivocate, vacillate, fluctuate, see-saw, yo-yo; think twice, change one's mind, get cold feet, dally, stall; *Brit.* haver, hum and haw; *informal* dilly-dally, shilly-shally, pussyfoot around, blow hot and cold, sit on the fence; *rare* tergiversate.

wavy ▶ adjective *the leaf has a wavy edge* **curling**, curly, curvy, curving, curved, undulating, meandering, winding, squiggly, rippled, crinkly, kinked, zigzag.
OPPOSITE straight.

wax ▶ verb **1** *the moon is waxing* **approach full moon**, get bigger, increase in size, enlarge.
OPPOSITE wane.
2 (*literary*) *price sensitivity is waxing and brand loyalty waning* **increase**, grow, develop, rise, expand, swell, enlarge, magnify, extend, escalate, deepen, intensify, widen, broaden, spread, mushroom, snowball.
OPPOSITES decrease, wane.
3 *Jimmy seldom waxed enthusiastic about anything* **become**, grow, get, come to be, turn.
□ **wax lyrical** *he waxed lyrical about how he would spend his earnings* **become enthusiastic**, enthuse, rave, gush, get carried away.

waxen ▶ adjective *the waxen pallor of a corpse* **pallid**, pale, pasty, wan, ashen, colourless, anaemic, bloodless, washed out, ashy, chalky, chalk-white, white, grey, whitish, waxy, blanched, drained, ghastly, sickly, sallow, as white as a sheet/ghost, deathly pale; milky, creamy, cream, ivory, milk-white, alabaster.
OPPOSITE ruddy.

way ▶ noun **1** *a way of reducing environmental damage* **method**, course of action, process, procedure, technique, system; plan, strategy, scheme; means, mechanism, routine, manner, approach, route, road; *Latin* modus operandi.
2 *she kissed him in her brisk way* **manner**, style, fashion, mode, method.
3 *I've learned my lesson and changed my ways* **practice**, wont, habit, custom, characteristic, policy, procedure, convention, fashion, use, routine, rule; trait, attribute, mannerism, peculiarity, idiosyncrasy, oddity; **conduct**, behaviour, manner, style, nature, personality, temperament, disposition, character; *Latin* modus operandi, modus vivendi; *formal* praxis.
4 *he tried to remember which way led home* **road**, roadway, street, thoroughfare, track, path, pathway, lane, avenue, drive, channel; **route**, course, direction.
5 *I'll go out the back way* **door**, doorway, gate, exit, entrance, entry, portal; route.
6 *the mill stands a short way downstream* **distance**, length, stretch, journey, extent; space, interval, span, gap, separation.
7 *April seems a long way away* **period of time**, time, stretch, term, span, duration.
8 *she swerved to miss a car coming the other way* **direction**, bearing, course, orientation, line, run, tack.
9 (*informal*) *what do they call a missel thrush down your way?* **locality**, neighbourhood, area, district, locale, quarter, community, region, zone, part; *informal* neck of the woods, parts; *Brit. informal* manor; *N. Amer. informal* hood, nabe.
10 *in some ways, he may be better off in Birmingham* **aspect**, regard, facet, respect; sense, feature, detail, point, particular, characteristic, question, connection.
11 *I hear that the country is in a bad way* **state**, condition, situation, circumstances, position; predicament, plight; *informal* shape.
□ **by the way** *oh, by the way Katie, you had a call* **incidentally**, by the by, in passing, en passant.
□ **give way 1** *the government finally gave way and passed the bill* **yield**, back down, make concessions, surrender, concede/admit defeat, give up/in, submit, succumb, raise/show the white flag; acquiesce, agree, concur, approve, assent; *informal* throw in the towel/sponge, cave in.
2 *he crashed into the door and it gave way* **collapse**, give, fall to pieces, come apart, crumple, crumble, cave in, fall in, disintegrate, go to pieces.
3 *she never gave way to anger* **succumb**, yield, give in, submit, surrender, fall victim; be overcome by, be overwhelmed by, be conquered by.
4 *grief gave way to a feeling of guilt* **be replaced by**, be succeeded by, be followed by, be superseded by, be supplanted by, be ousted by.
□ **make way**. *See* MAKE.
□ **on the/one's way** *the doctor's on his way* **coming**, imminent, forthcoming, approaching, impending, close, near, on us; proceeding, journeying, travelling, en route, in transit.

wayfarer ▶ noun **traveller**, journeyer, nomad, migrant, gypsy, vagabond, vagrant, itinerant, drifter; **walker**, hiker, rambler, wanderer, roamer, rover, backpacker, footslogger.

wayfaring ▶ adjective *a wayfaring man* **travelling**, journeying, walking, hiking, rambling, touring; wandering, roaming, roving, drifting, nomadic, itinerant, peripatetic, migratory, migrating, floating, on the move/go/wing.

waylay ▶ verb **1** *we were on our way to Winchester when we were waylaid and*

robbed **ambush**, hold up, attack, assail, rob; lie in wait for, lay a trap for, trap, entrap; *informal* mug, stick up.
2 *a series of people waylaid her to chat before she was out of the room* **accost**, detain, intercept, take aside, stop and talk to, pounce on, swoop down on, importune; *informal* buttonhole.

way-out ▶ adjective (*informal*) *a way-out ideology* **unconventional**, offbeat, outlandish, eccentric, quirky, aberrant, unusual, crazy, absurd, bizarre, mad, strange, weird, freakish, peculiar, odd, uncommon, avant-garde; *informal* far out, oddball, wacky, screwy, nutty, batty; *Brit. informal* rum; *N. Amer. informal* bizarro, off the wall.
OPPOSITES normal, ordinary.

wayward ▶ adjective *a wayward child | wayward behaviour* **wilful**, self-willed, headstrong, stubborn, obstinate, obdurate, perverse, contrary, rebellious, defiant, uncooperative, refractory, recalcitrant, unruly, wild, ungovernable, unmanageable, unpredictable, capricious, whimsical, fickle, inconstant, changeable, erratic, intractable, difficult, impossible, intolerable, unbearable, fractious, disobedient, insubordinate, undisciplined; *archaic* contumacious.
OPPOSITES well behaved, docile.

weak ▶ adjective **1** *many of the refugees in the camp are too weak to move* **frail**, feeble, puny, fragile, delicate, weakly; infirm, sick, sickly, shaky, debilitated, incapacitated, ailing, indisposed, decrepit, enervated, tired, fatigued, exhausted, spent, worn out; *informal* weedy.
OPPOSITE strong.
2 *bats have very weak eyes* **inadequate**, poor, feeble; defective, faulty, flawed, deficient, imperfect, substandard, lacking, wanting.
OPPOSITES strong, powerful, keen.
3 *she made some weak excuse to break the appointment* **unconvincing**, untenable, tenuous, implausible, unsatisfactory, slight, poor, inadequate, thin, transparent; unsound, feeble, flimsy, lame, hollow; *informal* pathetic.
OPPOSITE convincing.
4 *I was too weak to be a rebel* **irresolute**, **spineless**, craven, cowardly, pusillanimous, timorous, timid, indecisive, ineffectual, useless, inept, effete, meek, tame, powerless, ineffective, impotent, namby-pamby, soft, lily-livered, faint-hearted; *informal* yellow, weak-kneed, gutless, yellow-bellied, chicken-hearted, chicken.
OPPOSITES strong, resolute.
5 *he had only a weak light to work by* **dim**, pale, wan, faint, dull, feeble, muted.
OPPOSITES strong, bright.
6 *'You did this to her,' he said in a weak voice | a weak signal* **indistinct**, muffled, stifled, muted, hushed, faint, low, scarcely audible.
OPPOSITES strong, loud.
7 *they drank weak coffee* **watery**, diluted, dilute, watered down, thinned down, thin, adulterated, tasteless, flavourless, bland, insipid, mild, under-strength; *informal* wishy-washy.
OPPOSITES strong, powerful.
8 *a weak smile* **unenthusiastic**, feeble, half-hearted, limp, lame.

weaken ▶ verb **1** *the virus has weakened him terribly* **enfeeble**, debilitate, incapacitate, sap one's strength, enervate, tire, exhaust, wear out; wither, erode, diminish, destroy; paralyse, cripple, disable.
OPPOSITE strengthen.
2 *she tried to weaken the impact of what she'd just said* **reduce**, decrease, diminish, lessen, moderate, temper, sap, dilute, water down, thin, blunt, mitigate, deplete, soften (up).
OPPOSITES increase, boost.
3 *our morale weakened* **abate**, lessen, decrease, dwindle, diminish, ease up, let up, trail off, wane, ebb, subside, peter out, melt away, fizzle out, taper off, tail off, grow dim, grow faint; decline, deteriorate, degenerate, shrivel, wilt, tire, languish, falter.
OPPOSITES strengthen, intensify.
4 *the move weakened her authority* **impair**, undermine, compromise; invalidate, refute, rebut, negate, discredit.
OPPOSITES strengthen, bolster.
5 *when she wept and begged him not to turn her out he weakened* **relent**, give in, acquiesce, yield, give way, accede, succumb, come round; consent, assent, agree; soften, bend, ease up, ease off.
OPPOSITE stand firm.

weakling ▶ noun *a nine-stone weakling* **milksop**, namby-pamby, weak person, coward, pushover, mouse; *informal* wimp, weed, sissy, drip, wet, ninny, mummy's boy, pansy, softie, doormat, runt, chicken, yellow-belly, fraidy-cat, scaredy-cat; *N. Amer. informal* wuss, pussy; *archaic* poltroon.
OPPOSITES strongman, hero.

weak-minded ▶ adjective *he is just a weak-minded fool* **irresolute**, weak-willed, weak, impressionable, spineless, indecisive, unassertive, persuadable, persuasible, submissive, compliant, pusillanimous; foolish, simple, feeble-minded, witless, mindless, brainless, stupid, idiotic.
OPPOSITES strong-willed; intelligent.

weakness ▶ noun **1** *his illness resulted in weakness for the rest of his life* **frailty**, feebleness, enfeeblement, puniness, fragility, delicateness, delicacy, weakliness; infirmity, sickness, sickliness, shakiness, debility, incapacity, indisposition, decrepitude, enervation, fatigue, exhaustion, tiredness; *informal* weediness.
OPPOSITES strength, vigour.
2 *he has worked on his weaknesses and his form has improved* **fault**, flaw, defect, deficiency, weak point/spot, failing, foible, shortcoming, imperfection, blemish, Achilles heel, chink in one's armour.
OPPOSITES strength, forte.
3 *he had a weakness for champagne* **fondness**, liking, love, passion, partiality, preference, penchant, soft spot, bent, predisposition, predilection, leaning, inclination, proneness, proclivity, disposition, taste, eye; relish, zeal, enthusiasm, appetite.
OPPOSITE dislike.
4 *the President's public changes of mind led to accusations of indecision and weakness* **spinelessness**, **timidity**, cravenness, cowardliness, pusillanimity, timorousness, indecisiveness, indecision, irresolution, ineffectuality, uselessness, ineptness, ineptitude, effeteness, meekness, tameness, powerlessness, ineffectiveness, impotence, faint-heartedness; *informal* chicken-heartedness.
OPPOSITES strength, resolve.
5 *the symptoms include weakness of the eyes* **inadequacy**, defectiveness, faultiness, deficiency, imperfection.
OPPOSITES strength, power.
6 *the weakness of this argument was soon shown up* **unconvincingness**, untenability, tenuousness, implausibility, unsatisfactoriness, slightness, poverty, inadequacy, thinness, transparency; unsoundness, flimsiness, lameness, hollowness.
OPPOSITE strength.
7 *the weakness of the sound | the weakness of the street lamps* **indistinctness**, muffledness, mutedness, faintness, lowness, low intensity; **dimness**, paleness, wanness, dullness, feebleness.
OPPOSITE strength.

WORD LINKS
fear of weakness **asthenophobia**

weak-willed ▶ adjective *I was too weak-willed to give up* **irresolute**, **spineless**, weak, weak-minded, impressionable, indecisive, doubtful, unassertive, persuadable, persuasible, submissive, compliant, pusillanimous, weak-kneed; *informal* wimpish, chicken.
OPPOSITES strong-willed, resolute.

weal ▶ noun *blood dripped from a weal on his shoulders* **welt**, wound, lesion, swelling; scar, cicatrix, mark, blemish, discoloration, pockmark.

wealth ▶ noun **1** *a gentleman of wealth and distinction* **affluence**, prosperity, opulence, riches, means, substance, luxury, well-being, plenty; Mammon; money, cash, lucre, capital, principal, treasure, fortune, finance; assets, possessions, resources, effects, goods, funds, valuables; property, stock, reserves, securities, holdings, belongings, chattels; ill-gotten gains; *informal* wherewithal, dough, bread; *archaic* pelf.
OPPOSITES poverty, privation.
2 *the coastline has a wealth of bird life | a wealth of information* **abundance**, profusion, plethora, mine, store, treasury, copiousness, plenitude, amplitude, bounty, cornucopia; *informal* lot, load, heap, mass, pile, mountain, ocean, sea, stack, ton; *Brit. informal* shedload; *Austral./NZ informal* swag; *vulgar slang* shitload.
OPPOSITES dearth, lack.

wealthy ▶ adjective *he enjoyed the company of wealthy people* **rich**, affluent, moneyed, well off, with deep pockets, well-to-do, prosperous, comfortable, opulent, propertied, of means, of substance, in clover, plutocratic; *N. Amer.* silk-stocking; *informal* well heeled, rolling in it/money, in the money, made of money, filthy rich, stinking rich, loaded, flush, on easy street, quids in, worth a packet/bundle; *Austral./NZ informal* financial; *informal, dated* oofy.
OPPOSITES poor, impoverished.

weapon ▶ noun. *See centre pages for lists of* **Bombs and Mines** **Bullets and Shot** **Guns** **Knives and Daggers** **Projectiles and Projectile Weapons** **Weapons (Personal)**

wear ▶ verb **1** *he was wearing a dark green suit* **be dressed in**, be clothed in, have on, sport; dress in, clothe oneself in, put on, don.
2 *Barbara wore a sweet smile* **have (on one's face)**, present, show, display, exhibit, bear; give, put on, assume, form one's face into, make one's face into, compose one's face into, rearrange one's face into, ease one's face into, smooth one's face into, draw one's face into, twist one's face into, tug one's face into, pull one's face into, pinch one's face into, crease one's face into, crack one's face into, screw (up) one's face into.
3 *the bricks have been* **worn down** *by centuries of knife-sharpening | the waterproofing coating soon starts to* **wear away** **erode**, abrade, scour, scratch, scrape, rasp, rub away, rub down, grind away, fret, waste away, wash away, crumble (away), wear down; corrode, eat away (at), gnaw away (at), dissolve, bite into.
4 *the tyres are wearing well* **last**, endure, hold up, survive, bear up, keep going, carry on, prove durable, stand/withstand/resist wear, stand up to wear, do; *informal* hang in there.
5 (*Brit. informal*) *I've asked him to keep the bar open an hour later, but he won't wear it* **allow**, permit, authorize, sanction, condone, indulge, agree to, accede to, approve of; endure, put up with, bear, take, stand, support,

submit to, undergo; **accept**, swallow, tolerate, brook, countenance, admit of; *Scottish* thole; *informal* stick, hack, abide, stomach; *Brit. informal* be doing with; *archaic* suffer.

□ **wear something down** *she protested, but he wore down her resistance* **gradually overcome**, slowly reduce/diminish/lessen, drain, erode, wear away, exhaust, undermine, chip away at.

□ **wear off** *the novelty soon wore off* **fade**, dwindle, diminish, lessen, decrease, wane, ebb, subside, weaken, lose intensity, lose strength, peter out, melt away, fizzle out, pall, taper off, tail off, grow faint, grow dim, evaporate, disappear, vanish, die, come to nothing, come to a halt, come to an end, run out; lose its effectiveness/effect.

□ **wear on** *as the afternoon wore on he began to look unhappy* **pass**, elapse, proceed, progress, advance, move on, run its course, go by/past/on, roll by/past/on, march on, glide by/past, slide by/past, slip by/away/past, fly by/past, steal by/past, tick by/past.

□ **wear out** *a cheap bed will wear out faster than a quality one* **deteriorate**, become worn, show signs of wear, come to the end of its life, become useless, wear thin, fray, become threadbare, go into holes, go through, wear through.

□ **wear something out** *he wore out six pairs of walking boots* **use up**, consume, go through, wear holes in, make threadbare, make worn.

□ **wear someone out** *eventually her exertions wore her out* **fatigue**, tire out, overtire, weary, exhaust, drain, sap, wash out, tax, overtax, enervate, debilitate, enfeeble, jade, incapacitate, devitalize, prostrate; *informal* whack, bush, shatter, frazzle, wear to a frazzle, poop, take it out of, fag out, do in; *Brit. informal* knacker.

▶ **noun 1** *you won't get much wear out of something so cheap* **use**, wearing, service, employment, utility, value; *informal* mileage.
2 *the band were dressed in evening wear* **clothes**, dress, clothing, attire, garb, finery, garments, outfits, wardrobe; *Brit.* kit, strip; *informal* get-up, gear, togs, clobber; *formal* apparel; *literary* array, raiment, habiliments.
3 *choose a varnish which will withstand wear* **damage**, wear and tear, battering, friction, erosion, attrition, corrosion, abrasion, deterioration, degeneration; *informal* a few knocks; *rare* detrition.

weariness ▶ **noun** *stumbling with weariness, she forced herself on* **tiredness**, fatigue, exhaustion, prostration, overtiredness, collapse; jet lag; sleepiness, drowsiness, somnolence, doziness; **lethargy**, lassitude, languor, languidness, debility, enervation, listlessness, sluggishness, lifelessness, torpor, inertia.

wearing ▶ **adjective** *it had been a rather wearing day* **tiring**, exhausting, wearying, fatiguing, enervating, draining, sapping, stressful, weary, crushing; demanding, exacting, taxing, trying, challenging, burdensome, arduous, gruelling, punishing, grinding, onerous, difficult, hard, tough, heavy, laborious, back-breaking, crippling, strenuous, rigorous, uphill.
OPPOSITES refreshing, relaxing.

wearisome ▶ **adjective** *I can't think of anything more wearisome than traipsing round a factory all day* **tiring**, exhausting, wearying, fatiguing, enervating, draining, sapping, stressful, wearing, crushing; demanding, exacting, taxing, trying, challenging, burdensome, arduous, gruelling, punishing, grinding, onerous, difficult, hard, tough, heavy, laborious, back-breaking, crippling, strenuous, rigorous, uphill; tiresome, irksome, weary, boring, dull, tedious, monotonous, humdrum, prosaic, unexciting, uninteresting.
OPPOSITES refreshing; interesting, enjoyable.

weary ▶ **adjective 1** *he arrived home weary after cycling several miles* **tired**, tired out, worn out, exhausted, fatigued, overtired, sleepy, drowsy, wearied, sapped, dog-tired, spent, drained, jet-lagged, played out, debilitated, prostrate, enervated, jaded, low; *informal* all in, done (in/up), dead, dead beat, dead tired, dead on one's feet, asleep on one's feet, ready to drop, fagged out, burnt out, bushed, worn to a frazzle, shattered; *Brit. informal* knackered, whacked; *N. Amer. informal* pooped, tuckered out.
OPPOSITES energetic, fresh.
2 *she was weary of their constant arguments* **tired of**, fed up with, bored with/by, sick of, sick and tired of, jaded with/by, surfeited with/by, satiated by, glutted with/by; (**be weary of**) have had enough of; *informal* have had a basinful of, have had it up to here with, have had something up to here.
OPPOSITE enthusiastic.
3 *the weary journey began* **tiring**, exhausting, wearying, fatiguing, enervating, draining, sapping, stressful, wearing, trying, crushing; demanding, exacting, taxing, challenging, burdensome, arduous, gruelling, punishing, grinding, onerous, difficult, hard, tough, heavy, laborious, back-breaking, crippling, strenuous, rigorous, uphill.
OPPOSITES refreshing, enjoyable.

▶ **verb 1** *she was wearied by her persistent cough* **tire**, tire out, fatigue, wear out, overtire, exhaust, drain, sap, wash out, tax, overtax, enervate, debilitate, enfeeble, jade, incapacitate, devitalize, prostrate; *informal* whack, bush, shatter, frazzle, wear to a frazzle, poop, take it out of, fag out, do in, knock out; *Brit. informal* knacker.
OPPOSITE refresh.
2 *this must be stated again at the risk of wearying the reader* **bore**, tire, make fed up; irk, irritate, exhaust someone's patience, annoy, exasperate, get on someone's nerves; *informal* get to.
OPPOSITE interest.
3 *her friend had also wearied of the struggle* **tire of**, become/get weary of, become/get tired of, become/get fed up with, become/get fed to death with, become/get bored with/by, become/get satiated with, become/get jaded with, become/get sick of, become/get sick to death of, sicken of; have had enough of, have had a surfeit of, have had a glut of; *informal* become/get bored of, have had something up to here.

wearying ▶ **adjective** *it will be a long and wearying discussion* **tiring**, exhausting, wearing, trying, fatiguing, enervating, draining, sapping, stressful, weary, crushing; demanding, exacting, taxing, challenging, burdensome, arduous, gruelling, punishing, grinding, onerous, difficult, hard, tough, heavy, laborious, back-breaking, crippling, strenuous, rigorous, uphill; tiresome, irksome, wearisome, boring, dull, tedious, monotonous, humdrum, prosaic, unexciting, uninteresting.
OPPOSITE refreshing.

weasel *See centre pages for list of* **Weasels and Similar Animals**
▶ **noun** *he was a double-crossing weasel* **scoundrel**, wretch, rogue; *informal* swine, bastard, creep, louse, rat, toad, snake, snake in the grass, serpent, viper, skunk, dog, cur, scumbag, heel, bad lot, nasty piece of work; *Brit. informal* rotter, hound, bounder; *N. Amer. informal* rat fink; *Irish informal* sleeveen; *Austral. informal* dingo; *vulgar slang* shit, sod, son of a bitch, s.o.b.; *dated* cad; *archaic* blackguard, dastard, knave, varlet.

WORD LINKS
relating to weasels **musteline**

weather *See centre pages for lists of* **Climatic Zones** **Cloud Formations** **Weather Phenomena** **Winds**
▶ **noun** *what's the weather like?* **meteorological conditions**, atmospheric conditions, meteorology, climate; temperature, humidity, cloud cover, wind speed, atmospheric pressure; elements; **forecast**, outlook; *informal* met, met report.

□ **under the weather** *I feel a bit under the weather—I haven't eaten all day* **ill**, unwell, indisposed, ailing, poorly, not (very) well, not oneself, not in good shape, out of sorts, not up to par, under/below par, peaky, liverish; sick, queasy, nauseous; *Brit.* off colour; *informal* not up to snuff, funny, peculiar, crummy, lousy, rough; *Brit. informal* ropy, grotty; *Scottish informal* wabbit; *Austral./NZ informal* crook; *dated* queer, seedy.

▶ **verb** *most member companies weathered the recession* **survive**, come/get through, ride out, live through, pull through, come through (unscathed), outlast, outlive; **withstand**, stand up to, bear up against, stand, endure, rise above, surmount, overcome, resist; *informal* stick out.

weathered ▶ **adjective** *a weathered stone urn | his weathered face* **weather-beaten**, eroded, worn, disintegrating, crumbling; bleached, discoloured, tanned, bronzed; lined, creased, wrinkled, wizened, shrivelled, gnarled.

weave[1] ▶ **verb 1** *grass and twigs were woven into their uniforms to break up their silhouettes* **entwine**, lace, work, twist, knit, interlace, intertwine, interwork, intertwist, interknit, twist together, criss-cross, braid, twine, plait.
2 *he weaves colourful, cinematic plots* **invent**, make up, fabricate, put together, construct, create, contrive, spin; tell, recount, relate, narrate, unfold.

weave[2] ▶ **verb** *he had to weave his way through the crowds* **thread (one's way)**, wind (one's way), work (one's way), dodge, move in and out, swerve, zigzag, criss-cross.

web ▶ **noun 1** *a spider's web | a fine-spun cotton web* **mesh**, netting, net, lattice; latticework, lacework, interlacing, webbing; tissue, gauze, gossamer, chiffon; fabric, material, textile, fibre.
2 *a web of friendships* **network**, nexus, tangle, knot, complex, mass, conglomeration, set, series, chain, maze, snare, trap.

wed ▶ **verb 1** *they are old enough to wed* **marry**, get/be married, be wed, become husband and wife, become man and wife, plight/pledge one's troth; *informal* tie the knot, walk down the aisle, take the plunge, get spliced, get hitched, get yoked, say 'I do'; *archaic* become espoused.
OPPOSITES divorce, separate.
2 *he's planning to wed his long-term girlfriend* **get/be married to**, marry, be wed to, take as one's wife/husband, lead to the altar; *informal* get hitched to, get spliced to, tie the knot with, make an honest woman of; *archaic* espouse, wive.
OPPOSITES divorce; jilt.
3 *she wedded the old and new forms of spirituality* **unite**, unify, join, link, connect, combine, amalgamate, fuse, integrate, weld, bond, stick together, bring together, knit together, glue, cement, coalesce, merge.

wedded ▶ **adjective 1** *wedded bliss* **married**, matrimonial, marital, conjugal, connubial, nuptial, marriage, wedding; *Law* spousal; *literary* hymeneal, epithalamic.
2 *the company became wedded to the project* **dedicated to**, devoted to, attached to, fixated on, obsessive about, fanatical about, single-minded about, addicted to, hell-bent on; (**be wedded to**) stick to, refuse to give up.

wedding ▶ noun **marriage**, marriage ceremony, wedding ceremony, nuptial ceremony, marriage service, wedding service, marriage rites, wedding rites, nuptials, union; *archaic* espousal(s).

WORD LINKS
relating to a wedding **nuptial**

wedge ▶ noun **1** *the door was secured by a wedge* **tapered block**, chock, door stop.
2 *a wedge of cheese* **triangle**, tapered piece, segment, slice, section; **chunk**, lump, slab, hunk, block; *Brit. informal* wodge.
▶ verb *she wedged her holdall between two bags* **squeeze**, cram, jam, crush, pack, thrust, ram, force, push, stow; *informal* stuff, shove, bung.

wedlock ▶ noun **marriage**, matrimony, holy matrimony, married state, union, conjugal bond.

wee ▶ adjective (*Scottish*) *a wee boy | it was all just a wee misunderstanding* **little**, small, tiny, minute, miniature, small-scale, compact, mini, undersized, diminutive, dwarf, midget, Lilliputian, infinitesimal, microscopic, minuscule, bijou, toy; **trivial**, trifling, negligible, insignificant, unimportant, minor, of no account, of no consequence, of no importance, not worth bothering about, not worth mentioning, inconsequential, minimal, inappreciable, imperceptible, nugatory, petty; *informal* teeny, teeny-weeny, teensy, teensy-weensy, itsy-bitsy, half-pint, dinky, piddling, piffling; *Brit. informal* titchy; *N. Amer. informal* little-bitty, vest-pocket.
OPPOSITES big; major.

weed ▶ verb
□ **weed something/someone out** *a good agency will weed out those unsuitable candidates* **isolate**, separate out, set apart, put to one side, divide, segregate, sort out, sift out, winnow out, filter out, sieve; eliminate, get rid of, remove, dispense with, shed; *informal* dump, lose.

weedy ▶ adjective (*informal*) *a weedy little man* **puny**, feeble, weak, frail, delicate, underdeveloped, thin, undersized, slight, slightly built, skinny, scrawny, a slip of a ...; *informal* pint-sized.
OPPOSITE burly.

weekly ▶ adjective *he was paying off his debt in weekly instalments* **once a week**, seven-day; lasting a week; *rare* hebdomadal, hebdomadary.
▶ adverb *the directors meet weekly* **once a week**, every week, each week, on a weekly basis; by the week, per week, a week; *rare* hebdomadally.

weep ▶ verb *I've seen the toughest soldiers break down and weep* **cry**, shed tears, sob, snivel, whimper, whine, mewl, bawl, lament, grieve, mourn, keen, wail; *Scottish* greet; *informal* boohoo, blub, blubber; *literary* pule.
OPPOSITES laugh, rejoice.
▶ noun *you sit and have a weep* **cry**, sob, snivel, whimper, mewl, bawl, lament; flood of tears; *informal* blub, blubber; *Brit. informal* grizzle; *literary* pule.

WORD LINKS
relating to weeping **lachrymal**
given to weeping **lachrymose**

weepy ▶ adjective *she was weepy when her husband was first admitted to hospital* **tearful**, in tears, crying, weeping, sobbing, wailing, snivelling, whimpering; close to tears, on the verge of tears, with tears in one's eyes; emotional, upset, distressed, sad, unhappy; *Scottish* greeting; *informal* teary, blubbing, blubbering; *rare* lachrymose, larmoyant.

weigh ▶ verb **1** *the vendor at our market weighs the vegetables carefully* **measure the weight of**, measure how heavy someone/something is, put someone/something on the scales.
2 *he weighed 118 kg* tip/turn the scales at, come to.
3 *the destructive family situation* **weighed** *heavily* **on** *him* **oppress**, lie heavy on, press down on, burden, be a burden on/to, weigh down, cast down, hang over, gnaw at, prey on, prey on someone's mind; **trouble**, worry, beset, bother, disturb, upset, get someone down, depress, distress, grieve, haunt, nag, torment, afflict, perturb; plague, obsess, take over, take control of.
4 *the consequences of the move would need to be very carefully weighed | he has to* **weigh up** *the possibility of a conviction* **consider**, contemplate, think about, give thought to, entertain the idea of, deliberate about, turn over in one's mind, mull over, chew over, reflect on, ruminate about, muse on; **assess**, appraise, analyse, investigate, inquire into, look into, make inquiries into, examine, scrutinize, research, review, explore, probe, study, survey, inspect, take stock of; *N. Amer.* think on.
OPPOSITES ignore, take on trust.
5 *they need to* **weigh** *benefit* **against** *risk* **balance**; compare with, evaluate, juxtapose with, place side by side (with), contrast with.
6 *the opinions of chief fire officers will obviously* **weigh with** *the Government* **influence**, have influence with, be influential to, carry weight with, count with, tell with, matter to, be important to, be significant to, mean something to, make an impression on, get to, register with.
□ **weigh someone down 1** *my waders and fishing gear weighed me down* **burden**, weight, saddle, charge; overload, overburden, overwhelm, encumber, hamper, handicap, tax, strain; *literary* trammel.
2 *the awful silence of the terrible prison weighed me down* **oppress**, **depress**, lie heavy on, weigh on, press down on, burden, be a burden on/to, cast down, hang over, gnaw at, prey on, prey on someone's mind; **trouble**, worry, beset, bother, disturb, upset, get someone down, distress, grieve, haunt, nag, torment, afflict, perturb; plague, obsess, take over, take control of.

weight ▶ noun **1** *she misjudged the weight of the book* **heaviness**, mass, load, burden, pressure, force; poundage, tonnage; *informal* avoirdupois.
2 *a recommendation by the committee will carry great weight* **influence**, force, leverage, sway, muscle, teeth, importance, significance, consequence, value, substance, power, authority, prestige; *informal* clout, beef, pull.
3 *that will take a weight off his mind* **burden**, load, onus, millstone, millstone round one's neck, albatross, cross to bear, encumbrance; oppression, trouble, worry, strain; obligation, responsibility, liability.
4 *the weight of the evidence is against him* **preponderance**, majority, bulk, mass, greater quantity/number, larger part/number, best/better part, main part, most, almost all, more than half, (main) body, lion's share, predominance, generality.

WORD LINKS
measurement of weight **gravimetry**

weighty ▶ adjective **1** *a weighty tome of rules and regulations* **heavy**, massive, thick, bulky, hefty, cumbersome, clumsy, ponderous, overweight.
OPPOSITE light.
2 *a weighty subject* **important**, of great import/importance, significant, of significance, momentous, of moment, consequential, of consequence, far-reaching, key, major, vital, critical, crucial, life-and-death, high-priority, decisive, serious, grave, solemn; no joke, no laughing matter.
OPPOSITES unimportant, trivial.
3 *it is a rather weighty responsibility to shoulder* **burdensome**, onerous, heavy, oppressive, stressful, taxing, troublesome, worrisome, vexatious.
4 *weighty arguments* **compelling**, cogent, strong, forceful, powerful, potent, convincing, plausible, effective, efficacious, effectual, sound, valid, well founded, telling; impressive, persuasive, influential, authoritative.
OPPOSITE weak.

weird ▶ adjective **1** *they have experienced all sorts of weird events* **uncanny**, eerie, unnatural, preternatural, supernatural, unearthly, other-worldly, unreal, ghostly, mysterious, mystifying, strange, abnormal, unusual; *Scottish* eldritch; *informal* creepy, spooky, freaky; *Brit. informal* rum.
OPPOSITES normal, ordinary.
2 *some people have a weird sense of humour* **bizarre**, offbeat, quirky, outlandish, eccentric, unconventional, unorthodox, idiosyncratic, surreal, crazy, absurd, grotesque, peculiar, odd, curious, strange, queer, cranky, freakish, insane, zany, madcap, off-centre, far out, alternative; *French* outré; *informal* wacky, freaky, way-out, rum; *N. Amer. informal* wacko, off the wall, in left field, bizarro.
OPPOSITE conventional.

weirdo ▶ noun (*informal*) *he's a real weirdo* **eccentric**, oddity, unorthodox person, individualist, individual, nonconformist, free spirit, bohemian, maverick, deviant, pervert, misfit, dropout; *informal* oddball, odd/queer fish, freak, character, weirdie, crackpot, loony, nut, nutter, nutcase, head case, sicko, perv; *Brit. informal* one-off, odd bod; *N. Amer. informal* wacko, wack, screwball, kook; *informal, dated* case, card.

welcome ▶ noun *the festival starts at 6.30 p.m. with a welcome from the vicar* **greeting**, salutation, hail, welcoming, reception, warm reception, favourable reception, acceptance, hospitality, red carpet; *Scottish & Irish* fáilte.
OPPOSITES farewell; rebuff.
▶ verb **1** *hotels should welcome guests in their own language* **greet**, say hello to, salute, bid someone welcome, play host/hostess to, show hospitality to, receive, meet, embrace, receive with open arms, roll out the red carpet for, fête; usher in.
OPPOSITES shun, spurn.
2 *we welcomed the bank's decision to cut its rates* **express pleasure/satisfaction at**, be pleased by, be glad about, take pleasure in, approve of, appreciate, accept, embrace; *informal* give the thumbs up to.
OPPOSITES reject, disapprove of.
▶ adjective **1** *I'm pleased to see you, lad—you're welcome* **gladly received**, wanted, appreciated, popular, desirable, acceptable, accepted.
OPPOSITE unwelcome.
2 *that is very welcome news* **pleasing**, agreeable, encouraging, gratifying, heartening, promising, refreshing, favourable, propitious, cheering, much needed, pleasant, to one's liking, to one's taste.
OPPOSITES unpleasant, disappointing.

weld ▶ verb *they simply welded sheets of metal together* **fuse**, unite, bond, connect, stick, join, link, attach, bind, seal, amalgamate, knit, splice, meld, melt, blend, solder, cement, glue, gum, paste.
OPPOSITE separate.

welfare ▶ noun **1** *local authorities have a duty to promote the welfare of children* **well-being**, health, good health, happiness, comfort, security, safety, protection, prosperity, profit, good, success, fortune, good fortune, advantage, interest, prosperousness, successfulness.
OPPOSITE hardship.
2 *youngsters cannot claim welfare* **social security**, benefit, state benefit, benefit payment, public assistance; allowance, pension, credit, support;

sick pay, sickness benefit, unemployment benefit/pay.

well[1] ▶ adverb **1** *I am sure you will behave well* **satisfactorily**, in a satisfactory manner/way, nicely, correctly, rightly, properly, fittingly, suitably, aptly, appropriately.
OPPOSITE badly.
2 *they get on well together* **harmoniously**, agreeably, pleasantly, nicely, happily, politely, amicably, amiably, affably, genially, peaceably; *informal* famously.
OPPOSITE badly.
3 *he plays the piano well* **skilfully**, with skill, ably, competently, proficiently, adeptly, adroitly, deftly, dexterously, effectively, expertly, with expertise, admirably, excellently, consummately, professionally.
OPPOSITE poorly.
4 *treating employees well makes good business sense* **decently**, **fairly**, civilly, politely, genially, kindly, in a kind/kindly way, generously, hospitably; respectably, honestly.
OPPOSITE harshly.
5 *mix the ingredients well* **thoroughly**, completely, efficiently, rigorously, effectively, conscientiously, industriously, carefully.
6 *I know her quite well* **intimately**, thoroughly, fully, deeply, profoundly, personally.
7 *the company has obviously studied the car market well* **carefully**, closely, attentively, rigorously, in depth, exhaustively, from top to bottom, minutely, in detail, meticulously, scrupulously, assiduously, conscientiously, painstakingly, methodically, completely, comprehensively, fully, to the fullest extent, intensively, extensively.
OPPOSITES casually, negligently.
8 *they all speak well of him* **admiringly**, highly, approvingly, favourably, appreciatively, warmly, enthusiastically, glowingly, with admiration, with praise, with approbation.
OPPOSITE scornfully.
9 *she hopes to make enough money to live well* **comfortably**, in comfort, in (the lap of) luxury, in ease, splendidly, prosperously, without hardship.
10 *you may well be right* **quite possibly**, conceivably, quite likely, probably; undoubtedly, certainly, unquestionably; justifiably, reasonably.
11 *he is well over forty* **considerably**, very much, greatly, to a great/marked extent/degree, a great deal, markedly, decidedly, substantially, easily, comfortably, materially, significantly, signally; *informal* seriously.
OPPOSITES barely, little.
12 *she could well afford it* **easily**, comfortably, readily, with ease, without difficulty, effortlessly.
OPPOSITE barely.
□ **as well** *ducks eat waterweed and tadpoles as well* **too**, also, in addition, additionally, into the bargain, besides, furthermore, moreover, to boot.
□ **as well as** *we sell books as well as newspapers* **together with**, in addition to, along with, besides, plus, and, coupled with, with, over and above, on top of, over and beyond, not to mention, to say nothing of, let alone.
▶ adjective **1** *it would be some time before she was completely well* **healthy**, in good health, all right, fine, fit, fighting fit, as fit as a fiddle, as fit as a flea, robust, strong, vigorous, blooming, thriving, bursting with health, in rude health, hale, hale and hearty, hearty, in good shape, in excellent shape, in good condition, in tip-top condition, in good trim, in fine fettle, sound, sound in body and limb; *informal* in the pink, up to snuff.
OPPOSITE poorly.
2 *all is not well in further education* **satisfactory**, all right, fine, in order, as it should be, acceptable; *informal* OK, fine and dandy, hunky-dory; *N. Amer. & Austral./NZ informal* jake; *Brit. informal, dated* tickety-boo.
OPPOSITE unsatisfactory.
3 *it would be well to know just what this suggestion entails* **advisable**, sensible, prudent, politic, commonsensical, wise, canny, judicious, shrewd, expedient, provident, recommended, advantageous, beneficial, profitable, gainful, desirable; a good idea.
OPPOSITE inadvisable.

well[2] ▶ noun **1** spring, waterhole, borehole, bore, shaft, hole.
2 *it is not a priest's function to be a bottomless well of uncritical forgiveness* **source**, **supply**, wellspring, fount, fountainhead, reservoir, mine, fund, bank, repository, storehouse, treasury.
▶ verb *tears were beginning to well from her eyes* **flow**, stream, run, rush, gush, course, roll, cascade, flood, surge, rise, spurt, spout, squirt, jet; ooze, seep, trickle; burst, issue, discharge; spill, overflow, brim over; *rare* disembogue.

well advised ▶ adjective *you would be well advised to take your time* **wise**, prudent, sensible, advised.
OPPOSITE unwise.

well balanced ▶ adjective **1** *stick to a diet that is well balanced* **mixed**, varied; sensible, balanced; healthy.
OPPOSITES unbalanced; unhealthy.
2 *they created a well-balanced Palladian house* **graceful**, elegant; harmonious, balanced, well proportioned, proportional, in proportion, well arranged; regular, even; symmetrical.
OPPOSITES uneven, out of proportion.
3 *a well-balanced young woman* **sensible**, well adjusted, reasonable, rational, level-headed, sound, practical, discerning, logical, able to think clearly, lucid, clear-headed, coherent; steady, stable, responsible, equable, self-controlled, even-tempered, sober, down-to-earth, matter-of-fact, with both one's feet on the ground, in one's right mind, in possession of all one's faculties, mentally sound, of sound mind, sane, normal, right in the head; *Latin* compos mentis; *informal* all there.
OPPOSITE silly.

well behaved ▶ adjective *well-behaved children* **well mannered**, polite, civil, courteous, respectful, deferential, obedient, gentlemanly, chivalrous, gallant, ladylike, genteel, cultivated, gracious, obliging, considerate, thoughtful, urbane, civilized, well spoken, formal, proper, decorous, refined, polished, well brought up; **orderly**, law-abiding, disciplined, peaceful, peaceable, non-violent, tranquil, docile, controlled, restrained, cooperative, compliant; *dated* mannerly; *archaic* well conducted, ruly.
OPPOSITES naughty; rude; disorderly.

well-being ▶ noun *the nurse's prime concern is the well-being of the patient* **welfare**, health, good health, happiness, comfort, security, safety, protection, prosperity, profit, good, success, fortune, good fortune, advantage, interest, prosperousness, successfulness.

well bred ▶ adjective *she is too well bred to say anything* **well brought up**, **well mannered**, well behaved, polite, civil, courteous, respectful, deferential; ladylike, gentlemanly, chivalrous, gallant, genteel, cultivated, gracious, obliging, considerate, thoughtful, urbane, formal, proper, refined, polished; *dated* mannerly.
OPPOSITES rude, discourteous, ill-bred.

well built ▶ adjective *he was about six feet tall and well built* **sturdy**, sturdily built, strapping, brawny, burly, hefty, broad-shouldered, muscular, muscly, well muscled, strong, robust, rugged, lusty, Herculean; *informal* hunky, beefy, husky, hulking; *dated* stalwart; *literary* thewy, stark.
OPPOSITES puny, slight.

well dressed ▶ adjective *he was always well dressed, regardless of the time of day* **smart**, fashionable, stylish, well turned out, besuited, fashionably dressed, chic, modish, elegant, neat, spruce, trim, dapper, debonair; *French* soigné(e); *informal* snazzy, natty, snappy, sharp, nifty, cool, with it; *N. Amer. informal* sassy, spiffy, fly, kicky; *dated* as if one had just stepped out of a bandbox; *archaic* trig.
OPPOSITE scruffy.

well founded ▶ adjective *they have a well-founded fear of persecution if they are deported* **justifiable**, justified, warranted, legitimate, defensible, supportable, sustainable, tenable, well grounded, valid, admissible, allowable, understandable, excusable, warrantable, acceptable, reasonable, logical, sensible, sound, just, bona fide, genuine, plausible, credible, believable.
OPPOSITES unjustified, groundless.

well groomed ▶ adjective *she always appeared well groomed at her golf club* **neat**, **smart**, well turned out, well dressed, neatly dressed, besuited, trim, dapper, elegant, chic, with not a hair out of place; *French* soigné(e); *informal* natty, snazzy; *N. Amer. informal* spiffy; *dated* as if one had just stepped out of a bandbox; *archaic* trig.
OPPOSITES untidy, unkempt.

well heeled ▶ adjective (*informal*) *a group of well-heeled tourists* **wealthy**, rich, well off, affluent, moneyed, with deep pockets, well-to-do, prosperous, opulent, substantial, comfortable, propertied; of means, of substance; *informal* rolling in money, rolling in it, in the money, loaded, stinking rich, filthy rich, flush, made of money, quids in, worth a packet, worth a bundle, on easy street; *informal, dated* oofy.
OPPOSITE poor.

well known ▶ adjective **1** *their behaviour conforms to fairly well-known principles* **familiar**, widely known, popular, common, usual, everyday, customary, conventional, established.
OPPOSITES unknown, abstruse.
2 *Wyatt was a member of a well-known family of architects* **famous**, noted, notable, famed, prominent, renowned; distinguished, leading, eminent, illustrious, great, celebrated, acclaimed, esteemed, august, recognized, pre-eminent, important, of high standing, of distinction, of repute, considerable.
OPPOSITES obscure, unimportant; unsung.

> **CHOOSE THE RIGHT WORD**
> **well known, famous, celebrated, renowned**
> *See* FAMOUS.

well mannered ▶ adjective *they were well mannered and eager to please* **polite**, courteous, well behaved, civil, gentlemanly, ladylike, genteel, decorous, respectful, refined, polished, civilized, cultivated, gracious, chivalrous, urbane, well bred, well brought up; *dated* mannerly.
OPPOSITE rude.

well-nigh ▶ adverb *policing the coastline all the time was well-nigh impossible* **almost**, nearly, just about, about, more or less, practically, virtually, all but, as good as, next to, close to, near, nigh on, to all intents and purposes, approaching, bordering on, verging on, nearing; roughly, approximately; not quite; *informal* pretty nearly, pretty much, pretty well.

well off ▶ adjective **1** *See* WELL-TO-DO.
2 *the Basque shepherds were just as well off with their little woodstoves* **fortunate**, lucky, comfortable, well placed, in a fortunate position, in a privileged position, thriving, successful, flourishing; *informal* sitting pretty.
OPPOSITE unfortunate.
3 *central Greece is not* **well off** *for harbours* **well supplied with**, well stocked with, well furnished with, well equipped with; (**be well off for**) have plenty of, have enough of.
OPPOSITE badly off.

well read ▶ adjective *he was very* **well read** *in this field* **knowledgeable (about)**, well informed (about), well versed in, widely read; erudite, scholarly, literate, educated, cultured, literary, bookish, studious; *dated* lettered.
OPPOSITE ignorant.

well spoken ▶ adjective **articulate**, nicely spoken, speaking correctly, with a nice/standard accent; refined, polite, elegant; *Brit. informal* posh, posh-sounding, with a posh accent.

well thought of ▶ adjective *Joe was well thought of by his employers* **esteemed**, highly thought of, highly regarded, (well) respected, looked up to, acclaimed, admired, honoured, revered, venerated, with a good reputation, reputable, of good repute, of high standing; *archaic* of good report.
OPPOSITE disdained.

well-to-do ▶ adjective **wealthy**, rich, affluent, moneyed, with deep pockets, well off, prosperous, opulent, substantial, comfortable, propertied; of means, of substance; *informal* rolling in money, rolling in it, in the money, loaded, stinking rich, filthy rich, well heeled, flush, made of money, quids in, worth a packet, worth a bundle, on easy street; *informal, dated* oofy.

well worn ▶ adjective **1** *a well-worn leather armchair* **shabby**, scruffy, battered, worn, old, thin, threadbare, worn out, holey, moth-eaten, mangy, ragged, frayed, tattered, falling apart at the seams, in shreds, in tatters, falling to pieces, decrepit, having seen better days; *informal* tatty, ratty, the worse for wear; *N. Amer. informal* raggedy, raggedy-ass; *Austral. informal* warby; *rare* out at elbows.
OPPOSITE pristine.
2 *a well worn argument* **stale**, hackneyed, clichéd, stock, trite, banal, worn out, time-worn, threadbare, hoary, tired, overused, obsolete, antiquated, old; *informal* played out, clapped out, old hat.
OPPOSITE novel.

welter ▶ noun *a welter of confused sounds* **confusion**, jumble, tangle, clutter, mess, hotchpotch, mishmash, flurry, rush, mass.

wend ▶ verb *they* **wended** *their way across the city* **meander**, make one's way, wind one's way, find one's way, pick one's way; wander, potter, amble, stroll, saunter, drift, roam, breeze, float, cruise, swan, waltz, traipse, trog; go, proceed, travel, move, pass, walk, journey; perambulate; *informal* mosey, toddle, truck, bat.

west ▶ noun (**the West**) **the Occident**.
OPPOSITE the East.
▶ adjective *the Scottish west coast | a west wind* **western**, westerly, westwardly, occidental.
OPPOSITE east.
▶ adverb *the Great Black cockatoo never ventures further west than New Guinea and northern Queensland* **to the west**, westward, westwards, westwardly.
OPPOSITE east.

wet ▶ adjective **1** *he draped his wet clothes in front of the stove | their feet sank into the wet ground* **damp**, dampened, moist, moistened; **soaked**, drenched, saturated, wet through, sopping/dripping/wringing wet, sopping, dripping, soggy; waterlogged, squelchy, marshy, boggy, swampy, miry.
OPPOSITE dry.
2 *it was cold and wet that day* **rainy**, raining, pouring, teeming, showery, drizzly, drizzling; damp, humid, dank, misty.
OPPOSITES dry, fine.
3 *the paint is still wet* **sticky**, not set, not hardened, not hard, tacky; fresh.
OPPOSITES dry, set, hard.
4 *a wet mortar mix* **aqueous**, watery, sloppy.
OPPOSITE dry.
5 (*Brit. informal*) *they thought the cadets were a bit wet* **feeble**, **silly**, weak, foolish, inept, ineffective, ineffectual, effete, soft, namby-pamby, timid, timorous, spiritless, cowardly, spineless; *informal* sissy, sissified, pathetic, drippy, wimpish, wimpy, weedy, daft, chicken, yellow-bellied.
OPPOSITES strong; brave.
▶ verb *wet the clothes before ironing them* **dampen**, damp, moisten, humidify; sprinkle, spray, splash; **soak**, saturate, waterlog, flood, deluge, douse, souse, drench; hose down, water, irrigate; *technical* ret; *Scottish & N. English* drouk; *archaic* sop.
OPPOSITE dry.
▶ noun **1** *I could feel the wet of his tears* **wetness**, damp, dampness, moisture, moistness; clamminess, sogginess; wateriness, water, liquid.
2 *the race was held in the wet* **rain**, rains, drizzle, wet/rainy/showery/damp weather, precipitation, spray, dew, damp.
3 (*Brit. informal*) *come on, don't be such a wet* **namby-pamby**, weakling, milksop, Milquetoast, baby; coward, mouse; *informal* wimp, weed, drip, mummy's boy, mollycoddle, sissy, softie, jellyfish, chicken, yellow-belly, fraidy-cat, scaredy-cat; *Brit. informal* big girl's blouse, jessie; *N. Amer. informal* candy-ass, cupcake, pantywaist, pussy; *Austral./NZ informal* sook; *archaic* poltroon.

wetness ▶ noun **moisture**, moistness, dampness, damp; condensation, steam, vapour, humidity, mugginess, clamminess, dankness, sogginess; wateriness, wet, water, liquid.
OPPOSITE dryness.

whack (*informal*) ▶ verb *his attacker whacked him on the head* **hit**, beat, strike, punch, knock, rap, smack, slap, thump, thwack, crack, cudgel, thrash, bang, drub, welt, cuff, buffet, pummel, box someone's ears; *informal* bash, clobber, clout, clip, wallop, belt, tan, biff, bop, lay into, pitch into, lace into, let someone have it, knock into the middle of next week, sock, lam, whomp; *Brit. informal* stick one on, slosh; *N. Amer. informal* boff, bust, slug, light into, whale; *Austral./NZ informal* dong, quilt; *literary* smite, swinge.
▶ noun **1** *one of his mates got a whack with a stick* **blow**, hit, punch, thump, thwack, crack, smack, slap, bang, welt, cuff, box; *informal* bash, clobber, clout, clip, wallop, belt, biff, bop, sock, lam, whomp; *Brit. informal* slosh; *N. Amer. informal* boff, bust, slug, whale; *Austral./NZ informal* dong; *dated* buffet.
2 (*Brit. informal*) *everyone will get their whack* **share**, quota, portion, slice, part, allocation, ration, allowance, allotment, amount, quantity, bit, piece, percentage, proportion, section, segment, division, fraction, measure, due; *informal* cut, piece/slice of the cake, piece of the action, rake-off; *Brit. informal* divvy; *rare* apportionment, quantum, moiety.

whacking ▶ adjective (*Brit. informal*) *we weren't prepared to pay a whacking salary* **huge**, massive, enormous, gigantic, very big, very large, great, giant, colossal, mammoth, vast, immense, tremendous, mighty, stupendous, monumental, epic, prodigious, mountainous, monstrous, titanic, towering, elephantine, king-sized, king-size, gargantuan, Herculean, Brobdingnagian, substantial, extensive, hefty, bulky, weighty, heavy, gross; *informal* mega, monster, whopping, whopping great, thumping, thumping great, humongous, jumbo, hulking, bumper, astronomical, astronomic; *Brit. informal* whacking great, ginormous.

whale *See centre pages for list of* **Whales and Dolphins**
▶ noun **cetacean**, leviathan.

WORD LINKS

male	**bull**
female	**cow**
young	**calf**
collective noun	**school, pod**

wharf ▶ noun **quay**, pier, dock, berth, landing stage, landing place, landing, jetty; harbour, dockyard, yard, marina; waterfront.

whatsit ▶ noun (*informal*) **thing**, so-and-so, whatever it is, whatever it is called; *informal* whatnot, what-d'you-call-it, what's-its-name, whatchamacallit, thingummy, thingy, thingamabob, thingamajig, oojamaflip, oojah, gizmo; *Brit. informal* gubbins, doings, doodah, doobry; *N. Amer. informal* doodad, doohickey, doojigger, dingus, hootenanny.

wheedle ▶ verb *she had wheedled us into employing her brother* **coax**, cajole, inveigle, lure, induce, blarney, entice, charm, tempt, beguile, flatter, persuade, influence, sway, win someone over, bring someone round, prod, talk, convince, make, get, press, prevail on, get round, argue, reason, urge, pressure, pressurize, bring pressure to bear on, coerce; *informal* sweet-talk, soft-soap, twist someone's arm, smooth-talk, butter someone up.

wheel ▶ noun **1** *a wagon wheel* **disc**, hoop, ring, circle.
2 *a right wheel* **turn**, rotation, pivot, swivel, gyration.
□ **at the wheel/behind the wheel** *he was* **at the wheel** *of his Mercedes* **driving**, steering, in the driving seat, in the driver's seat, in charge of.
▶ verb **1** *she wheeled the trolley into the kitchen* **push**, trundle, roll.
2 *a flock of doves rose up into the air, wheeled round, and flew off* **turn**, turn round, go round, rotate, revolve, circle, orbit.

wheeze ▶ verb *the illness often leaves her wheezing* **breathe audibly/noisily**, gasp, whistle, hiss, rasp, croak, pant, cough.
▶ noun **1** *she still had a slight wheeze* **constricted breathing**, gasp, whistle, hiss, rasp, croak, pant, cough.
2 (*Brit. informal*) *a brilliant wheeze dreamed up by the fashion industry* **scheme**, plan, idea, tactic, move, stratagem, ploy, gambit, device, manoeuvre, contrivance, expedient; trick, dodge, subterfuge, game, wile, ruse, joke, prank, stunt; *archaic* shift.

whereabouts ▶ noun *his whereabouts remain secret* **location**, position, site, place, situation, locality, spot, point, placement, locale, neighbourhood, vicinity; home, address; bearings, orientation; *technical* locus.

wherewithal ▶ noun *she had the wherewithal to buy anything which took her fancy* **money**, ready money, cash, capital, finance(s), resources, funds, reserves; **means**, ability, capability; *informal* dough, bread, loot, the ready, readies, shekels, moolah, the necessary, wad, boodle, dibs, gelt, ducats, rhino, gravy, scratch, stuff, oof; *Brit. informal* dosh, brass, lolly, spondulicks, wonga, ackers; *N. Amer. informal* dinero, greenbacks, simoleons, bucks, jack, mazuma; *Austral./NZ informal* Oscar; *informal, dated* splosh, green, tin; *Brit. dated* l.s.d.; *N. Amer. informal, dated* kale, rocks, shinplasters; *archaic* pelf.

whet ▶ verb **1** *he whetted his knife on a stone* **sharpen**, hone, put an edge on, strop, grind, file; *rare* edge, acuminate.
OPPOSITE blunt.
2 *is that enough to whet your appetite?* **stimulate**, excite, arouse, rouse, kindle, trigger, spark, quicken, waken, stir, inspire, animate, fan, fuel, fire, activate, incite, titillate, tempt, galvanize, prompt, strengthen, intensify.
OPPOSITES dull, spoil.

whiff ▶ noun **1** *I caught a whiff of peachy perfume* **faint smell**, brief smell, trace, sniff, scent, odour, aroma.
2 (*Brit. informal*) *there's a terrible whiff in here* **stench**, stink, foul smell, reek, fetidness, effluvium, miasma; *Brit. informal* pong, niff, hum; *Brit. rhyming slang* pen and ink; *Scottish informal* guff; *N. Amer. informal* funk; *rare* fetor, malodour, mephitis, noisomeness.
3 *there was the faintest whiff of irony in his letter* **trace**, hint, note, suggestion, impression, suspicion, soupçon, touch, nuance, intimation, trifle, drop, dash, tinge, tincture, streak, vein, shred, crumb, shadow, breath, whisper, air, savour, flavour, element, overtone, scintilla, jot, bit, spot, speck, iota; *informal* smidgen, tad.
4 *whiffs of smoke emerged from the boiler* **puff**, gust, blast, rush, flurry, gale, breath, draught, waft.

while ▶ noun *we chatted for a while* **time**, spell, stretch, stint, span, season, interval, period, period of time, length of time, duration, run, phase, stage, term; *Brit. informal* patch.
▶ verb *tennis and quoits helped to* **while away** *the time during the voyage* **pass**, spend, occupy, use up, kill, beguile.

whim ▶ noun **1** *she bought it on a whim* **impulse**, urge, notion, fancy, whimsy, foible, idea, caprice, conceit, vagary, kink, megrim, crotchet, craze, fad, passion, inclination, bent; *archaic* freak, maggot, humour, whim-wham.
2 *success depends upon something as arbitrary as human whim* **capriciousness**, whimsy, caprice, volatility, fickleness, idiosyncrasy, eccentricity, unpredictability.

whimper ▶ verb *he fell to his knees, whimpering in pain* **whine**, cry, sniffle, snivel, sob, moan, bleat, mewl, wail, groan; *informal* grizzle.
▶ noun *she gave a whimper of protest* **whine**, cry, sniffle, snivel, sob, moan, bleat, mewl, wail, groan; *informal* grizzle.

whimsical ▶ adjective **1** *a whimsical sense of humour* **fanciful**, playful, mischievous, waggish, quaint, fantastic, unusual, curious, droll; eccentric, quirky, offbeat, idiosyncratic, unconventional, outlandish, peculiar, queer, bizarre, weird, odd, freakish; *informal* dotty, freaky.
2 *the whimsical arbitrariness of autocracy* **volatile**, capricious, temperamental, impulsive, excitable, fickle, changeable, unpredictable, variable, erratic, quicksilver, mercurial, mutable, inconstant, inconsistent, unstable, unsteady, fluctuating, ever-changing, protean, kaleidoscopic, fluid, wavering, vacillating, wayward; *technical* labile.

whine ▶ noun **1** *the dog gave a small whine* **whimper**, wail, cry, mewl, groan, moan, howl, yowl.
2 *the whine of an electric motor* **hum**, drone, singing, note.
3 *a constant whine about the quality of public services* **complaint**, complaining, grouse, grousing, moan, moaning, moans and groans, grouch, grouching, grumble, whining, carping, muttering, murmur, murmuring, whispering; *informal* gripe, griping, whinge, whingeing, bellyache, bitch, beef, beefing; *N. English informal* mithering.
▶ verb **1** *a child was whining* **wail**, whimper, cry, sob, mewl, groan, moan, howl, yowl.
2 *the lift began to whine* **hum**, drone, sing.
3 *he's always whining about the state of the country* **complain**, grouse, grouch, grumble, moan, carp, mutter, murmur, whisper; *informal* gripe, bellyache, bitch, beef, whinge; *N. English informal* mither.

whinge (*informal*) ▶ verb *I am not going to whinge about the weather* **complain**, grouse, grouch, grumble, whine, moan, carp, mutter, murmur, whisper; *informal* gripe, bellyache, bitch, beef; *N. English informal* mither.

▶ noun *his sorry tale is one long whinge about his own suffering* **complaint**, grouse, moan, grouch, grumble, whine, carp, mutter, murmur, whisper; *informal* gripe, bellyache, bitch, beef; *N. English informal* mither.

whip ▶ noun *he would use a whip on anyone trespassing on his property* **lash**, scourge, thong, strap, belt; crop, switch, birch, cane; *historical* cat-o'-nine-tails, cat, knout.
▶ verb **1** *Lewis whipped the boy twenty times* **flog**, scourge, flagellate, lash, birch, switch, tan, strap, belt, cane, thrash, beat, leather, tan/whip someone's hide, give someone a hiding, beat the living daylights out of.
2 *whip the cream until it forms soft peaks* **whisk**, beat, mix, stir.
3 *the radio host whipped his listeners into a frenzy* **rouse**, stir up, excite, galvanize, electrify, stimulate, inspire, move, fire up, fire the enthusiasm of, fire the imagination of, get someone going, inflame, agitate, goad, provoke; incite, egg on, spur on; *N. Amer.* light a fire under; *rare* inspirit.
4 (*informal*) *Cleveland whipped Los Angeles 28–16 in the third game of last season.* See **TROUNCE** sense 1.
5 (*informal*) *he whipped round the corner.* See **DASH** sense 1.
6 (*informal*) *he* **whipped out** *a revolver* **pull**, whisk, snatch, pluck, tug, jerk, remove, take; produce; *informal* yank.
7 (*Brit. informal*) *they whipped the cones from a building site.* See **STEAL** sense 1.
□ **whip something up** *we tried hard to whip up interest in the products* **stimulate**, **rouse**, arouse, stir up, work up, wake, waken, awaken, quicken, inspire, call forth, call/bring into being, draw forth, bring out, excite, evoke, whet, stir, provoke, spur, fire, inflame, trigger, prompt, induce, encourage, actuate, activate, touch off, spark off, set off, set going, incite, promote, engender, generate; *literary* enkindle.

whippersnapper ▶ noun (*Brit. informal*) **young upstart**; *informal* pipsqueak, squirt, stripling, brat, minx, slip of a ...; *Brit. informal* squit; *N. Amer. informal* snip; *dated* puppy, pup; *archaic* malapert.
OPPOSITE old hand.

whipping ▶ noun *whipping was to be abolished as a punishment* **lashing**, flogging, scourging, flagellation, switching, birching, strapping, belting, caning, thrashing, tanning, hiding, beating, leathering; the lash, the scourge, the birch, the switch, the cane.

whirl ▶ verb **1** *leaves whirled in eddies of wind* **rotate**, turn, turn round, go round, revolve, circle, wheel, orbit, pivot, swivel, gyrate, spin, roll, twirl, pirouette; *Scottish* birl.
2 *Sybil stood waving as they whirled past* **hurry**, speed, race, run, sprint, dash, bolt, dart, rush, hasten, hurtle, career, streak, shoot, whizz, zoom, go like lightning, go hell for leather, spank along, bowl along, rattle along, whoosh, buzz, swoop, flash, blast, charge, stampede, gallop, sweep, hare, fly, wing, scurry, scud, scutter, scramble; *informal* belt, pelt, tear, hotfoot it, leg it, zap, zip, whip, scoot, go like a bat out of hell; *Brit. informal* bomb, bucket, shift, go like the clappers; *Scottish informal* wheech; *N. Amer. informal* clip, boogie, hightail, barrel; *N. Amer. vulgar slang* drag/tear/haul ass; *literary* fleet; *archaic* post, hie.
3 *his mind was whirling* **spin**, reel, go round, be in a whirl, swim, be/feel giddy, be/feel dizzy.
▶ noun **1** *he was gone in a whirl of dust* **swirl**, flurry, eddy.
2 *all part of the mad social whirl* **hurly-burly**, hectic activity, bustle, rush, flurry, to-do, fuss, panic, turmoil; *archaic* hurry scurry.
3 *her life was a whirl of parties* **succession**, series, sequence, progression, string, chain, cycle, round, merry-go-round.
4 *Laura's mind was in a whirl* **spin**, daze, stupor, muddle, jumble; confusion; *informal* dither.
5 *the only way to find out was to give it a whirl* **try**, try-out, test; *informal* go, shot, bash, stab.

whirlpool ▶ noun **1** *there was a whirlpool which appeared without warning and sucked ships down* **eddy**, vortex, maelstrom, swirl, whirl; *N. Amer. informal* suckhole; *literary* Charybdis.
2 *we also have a sauna, Turkish bath, whirlpool, and solarium* **spa bath**, hot tub; *trademark* jacuzzi.

whirlwind ▶ noun **1** *the building was hit by a hellish whirlwind* **tornado**, hurricane, typhoon, cyclone, tropical storm, tropical cyclone, vortex; dust devil, waterspout; *N. Amer. informal* twister; *Austral./NZ informal* willy-willy.
2 *a hectic whirlwind of activity* **bedlam**, madhouse, mayhem, maelstrom, babel, chaos, pandemonium, uproar, turmoil, turbulence, swirl, tumult, hurly-burly, commotion, disorder, jumble, disarray, confusion, seething mass, welter; *informal* all hell broken loose; *N. Amer.* three-ring circus.
▶ adjective *a whirlwind romance* **rapid**, lightning, overnight, instant, headlong, impulsive, breakneck, whistle-stop, fast-track, accelerated, meteoric, sudden, swift, fast, quick, speedy; *informal* quickie.

whisk ▶ verb **1** *the cable car will whisk you to the top of the mountain* **speed**, hurry, rush, catapult; sweep, hurtle, shoot.
2 *she did not have the audacity to simply whisk the cloth away* **pull**, snatch, pluck, tug, jerk, take; remove; *informal* whip, yank.
3 *they just recognized him before he whisked out of sight* **dash**, rush, tear, dart, hasten, hurry, scurry, scuttle, scamper, sprint, race, run, hare, bolt, bound, fly, gallop, career, charge, pound, shoot, hurtle, speed, streak, whizz, zoom, sweep, go like lightning, go hell for leather, go like the wind, flash, double; *informal* pelt, scoot, hotfoot it, leg it, belt, zip, whip, go like a bat out of hell; *Brit. informal* go like the clappers, bomb, bucket; *Scottish informal* wheech; *N. Amer. informal* boogie, hightail it, barrel, get the lead out; *informal, dated* cut along; *archaic* post, hie.
4 *horses whisk their tails for various purposes* **flick**, twitch, wave, brandish.
5 *whisk the yolks with half the sugar* **whip**, beat, stir/mix vigorously.
▶ noun **1** *the horse gave a whisk of its tail* **flick**, twitch, wave, sweep, swipe.
2 *combine the eggs and milk with a whisk* **beater**, mixer, blender, swizzle stick.

whisky *See centre pages for list of* **Whiskies**
▶ noun the water of life; *Irish & Scottish* usquebaugh; *Scottish* usque, screigh; *informal* screech; *N. Amer. informal* red-eye.

whisper ▶ verb **1** *Alison was whispering in his ear* **murmur**, mutter,

mumble, speak/say softly, speak/say in muted tones, speak/say in hushed tones, speak/say sotto voce; breathe, purr, say under one's breath.
OPPOSITE shout.
2 (*literary*) *the wind and the mist whispered in the grass* **rustle**, murmur, sigh, moan, sough, whoosh, whirr, swish, blow, breathe; *rare* susurrate.
OPPOSITES howl, roar.
3 (*literary*) *the water whispered and rippled* **babble**, burble, purl, lap; *literary* plash.
OPPOSITES roar, thunder.
▶ **noun 1** *she spoke in a whisper* **murmur**, mutter, mumble, low voice, hushed tone, undertone.
OPPOSITE shout.
2 (*literary*) *the hot desert wind died to a whisper* **rustle**, murmur, sigh, moan, sough, whoosh, whirr, swish; *rare* susurration.
OPPOSITES howl, roar.
3 (*literary*) *the whisper of falling water* **babble**, burble, purl, lap; *literary* plash.
OPPOSITES roar, thunder.
4 *I heard a whisper that he's been selling coins lately* **rumour**, story, report, speculation, insinuation, suggestion, hint; (**whispers**) gossip, hearsay, word, scandal, tittle-tattle, idle talk; *French* on dit, bavardage; *German* Kaffeeklatsch; *W. Indian* labrish, shu-shu; *informal* buzz; *Brit. informal* goss; *N. Amer. informal* scuttlebutt; *Austral./NZ informal* furphy; *S. African informal* skinder; *rare* bruit.
5 *he didn't even show a whisper of interest* **trace**, scrap, touch, tinge, hint, suggestion, suspicion, soupçon, whiff, inkling, scintilla, whit, spark, glimmer, flicker, atom, speck, bit, ounce, drop, dash, jot, iota, shred, crumb, morsel, fragment, vestige, grain, spot, mite, modicum; *informal* smidgen, smidge, tad; *Irish informal* stim; *archaic* scantling, scruple.

whit ▶ **noun** *his death wouldn't have made a whit of difference* **scrap**, bit, tiny amount, speck, iota, particle, ounce, jot, atom, crumb, shred, morsel, trifle, fragment, grain, drop, touch, trace, shadow, suggestion, whisper, suspicion, scintilla, spot, mite, tittle, jot or tittle, modicum; *Irish* stim; *informal* smidgen, smidge; *archaic* scantling, scruple.

white ▶ **adjective 1** *a clean white bandage* **colourless**, unpigmented, undyed, bleached, natural; snowy, milky, chalky, snow-white, snowy-white, milk-white, milky-white, chalk-white, chalky-white, ivory; pale, clear, transparent.
OPPOSITE black.
2 *her face was white with fear* **pale**, pallid, wan, ashen, white as a ghost/sheet, grey, anaemic, jaundiced, colourless, bloodless, waxen, chalky, chalk-white, milky, pasty, pasty-faced, whey-faced, peaky, sickly, tired-looking, washed out, sallow, drained, drawn, sapped, ghostly, deathly, deathlike, bleached; *rare* etiolated.
OPPOSITES healthy; ruddy; tanned.
3 *he had a mane of white hair* **snowy**, snowy-white, grey, silver, silvery, hoary, grizzled; albino.
4 *the early white settlers of Australia* **Caucasian**, European, non-black.
5 *a whiter than white, no-sleaze government* **virtuous**, moral, ethical, good, righteous, angelic, saintly, pious, honourable, reputable, wholesome, clean, honest, upright, upstanding, exemplary, beyond/above reproach, irreproachable, innocent; decent, worthy, noble; blameless, guiltless, sinless, stainless, spotless, immaculate, impeccable, unsullied, unblemished, unspoilt, unaffected, uncorrupted, untainted, undefiled; *informal* squeaky clean.
OPPOSITE immoral.

WORD LINKS
related prefixes **leuc-** (e.g. ***leucocyte***), **leuk-** (e.g. ***leukaemia***)

white-collar ▶ **adjective** *white-collar workers* **non-manual**, office, clerical, professional, executive, salaried; *technical* ABC1.

whiten ▶ **verb** *snow whitened the mountain tops* | *her knuckles whitened* **make/become white**, make/become pale, bleach, blanch, lighten, fade, wash out, be washed out, etiolate; *Brit. Military* blanco; *archaic* white.
OPPOSITES blacken, darken, colour.

whitewash ▶ **noun** *the report was dismissed as a whitewash* **cover-up**, -gate, camouflage, disguise, mask, concealment, suppression, deception, false front, facade, veneer, pretext.
OPPOSITE exposé.
▶ **verb** *I just want to make sure they don't whitewash what happened* **cover up**, sweep under the carpet, hush up, suppress, draw/pull a veil over, conceal, camouflage, keep secret, keep dark, cloak, screen, veil, obscure; gloss over, deal rapidly with, downplay, make light of, soft-pedal, minimize, de-emphasize, treat as unimportant.
OPPOSITE expose.

whittle ▶ **verb 1** *he sat whittling a piece of wood with a knife* **pare**, shave, peel, cut, hew, trim, carve, shape, model.
2 *the powers of the papacy were gradually* ***whittled away*** **erode**, wear away, eat away, consume, use up, reduce, diminish, undermine, weaken, threaten, sabotage, subvert, compromise, destroy, impair, mar, spoil, ruin, impede, hinder, damage, hurt, injure, cripple, disable, enfeeble, emasculate, sap, shake, break, crush.
OPPOSITE increase.
3 *the ten teams in contention have been* ***whittled down*** *to six* **reduce**, cut down, cut back, cut, prune, trim, slim down, pare down, shrink, make cutbacks in, lessen, decrease, diminish, make reductions in, scale down.
OPPOSITE augment.

whole ▶ **adjective 1** *they refused to publish the whole report* **entire**, complete, full, total; unabridged, full-length, uncut, uncondensed, unexpurgated, unreduced, undivided.
OPPOSITES partial, incomplete.
2 *they discovered a whole marble mantelpiece* **intact**, in one piece, sound, unbroken; unimpaired, undamaged, unharmed, unhurt, untouched, uninjured, unscathed, unmutilated, inviolate, flawless, faultless, unmarked, unspoilt, perfect, mint, pristine.
OPPOSITES in pieces, broken.
▶ **noun 1** *the two movements had been fused into a single whole* **entity**, unit, body, piece, discrete item, ensemble, combination, package, conglomeration, object; totality, entirety, unity.
2 *it may take* ***the whole*** *of the year* **all**, every part, everything, the lot, the sum, the sum total, the aggregate.
□ **on the whole** *on the whole they lived peaceably* **overall**, all in all, all things considered, altogether, taking everything into consideration/account, on balance, on average, for the most part, mostly, mainly, in the main, chiefly, principally, predominantly, largely, in general, generally, generally speaking, as a rule, as a general rule, in the general run of things, by and large, to a large extent, to a great degree, basically, substantially, effectively, virtually, to all intents and purposes; **normally**, usually, more often than not, almost always, most of the time, habitually, customarily, regularly, typically, ordinarily, commonly.

WORD LINKS
related prefix **holo-** (e.g. ***holocaust, Holocene***)

wholehearted ▶ **adjective** *you have my wholehearted support* **committed**, positive, emphatic, devoted, dedicated, enthusiastic, unshakeable, unflinching, unswerving, constant, staunch, loyal, stalwart; **unqualified**, unreserved, unlimited, without reservations, unconditional, categorical, unequivocal, unambiguous, unrestricted, unmitigated, unadulterated, undiluted, unalloyed, unstinting; complete, full, total, absolute, undivided, entire, solid, thorough, thoroughgoing, utter, outright, out-and-out.
OPPOSITES half-hearted, qualified, partial.

wholesale ▶ **adverb** *images were removed from churches wholesale* **extensively**, on a large scale, comprehensively, thoroughly; **indiscriminately**, undiscriminatingly, without exception, across the board.
OPPOSITES partially, selectively.
▶ **adjective** *the wholesale destruction of a city* **extensive**, widespread, large-scale, wide-ranging, far-reaching, comprehensive, all-inclusive, total, outright, thorough, sweeping, blanket, broad, mass; indiscriminate.
OPPOSITES partial, selective.

wholesome ▶ **adjective 1** *wholesome food* **healthy**, health-giving, healthful, good, good for one, beneficial, sustaining, strengthening, nutritious, nourishing, full of nourishment, full of nutrients, nutritive, unrefined; natural, uncontaminated, organic, additive-free; *rare* nutrimental, nutrient, alimentary, alible.
2 *good wholesome fun* **moral**, ethical, good, nice, clean, virtuous, pure, innocent, chaste; uplifting, edifying, improving, non-erotic, non-violent, righteous, upright, upstanding, high-minded, right-minded, proper, correct, honourable, honest, just, noble, respectable, decent, simple; *informal* squeaky clean.

wholly ▶ **adverb 1** *the budget measures were wholly inadequate* **completely**, totally, absolutely, entirely, fully, thoroughly, utterly, quite, perfectly, altogether, downright, without qualification, without reservation, unreservedly, in every respect, in all respects, unconditionally, unconstrainedly, unrestrictedly, consummately, undisputedly, unmitigatedly, wholeheartedly, radically, stark, just, to the hilt, all the way, to the maximum extent; *informal* one hundred per cent.
2 *they still rely wholly on you* **exclusively**, only, solely, purely, simply, merely, alone, to the exclusion of everything/everyone else.

whoop ▶ **noun** *whoops of delight* **shout**, cry, call, yell, roar, scream, shriek, screech, hoot, hoop, cheer, hurrah; *informal* holler; *archaic* huzza.
▶ **verb** *he whooped for joy* **shout**, cry, call, yell, roar, scream, shriek, screech, hoot, hoop, cheer, hurrah; *informal* holler; *archaic* huzza.

whopper ▶ **noun** (*informal*) **1** *the largest salmon ever caught was a 64-pound whopper* **monster**, brute, beast, giant, colossus, mountain, behemoth, leviathan, mammoth, monstrosity; *informal* jumbo.
2 *Joseph's story is turning out to be a whopper* **lie**, untruth, falsehood, fib, fabrication, deception, made-up story, trumped-up story, invention, piece of fiction, fiction, falsification, falsity, fairy story/tale, cock and bull story, barefaced lie; (little) white lie, half-truth, exaggeration, prevarication, departure from the truth; yarn, story, red herring, rumour, fable, myth, flight of fancy, figment of the imagination; pretence, pretext, sham, ruse, wile, trickery, stratagem; *informal* tall story, tall tale; *Brit. rhyming slang* pork pie, porky, porky pie; *humorous* terminological inexactitude.

whopping ▶ adjective (*informal*) *they made a whopping £74 million loss* **huge**, massive, enormous, gigantic, very big, very large, great, giant, colossal, mammoth, vast, immense, tremendous, mighty, stupendous, monumental, epic, prodigious, mountainous, monstrous, titanic, towering, elephantine, king-sized, king-size, gargantuan, Herculean, Brobdingnagian, substantial, extensive, hefty, bulky, weighty, heavy, gross; *informal* mega, monster, whopping great, thumping, thumping great, humongous, jumbo, hulking, bumper, astronomical, astronomic; *Brit. informal* whacking, whacking great, ginormous.

whore ▶ noun **prostitute**, promiscuous woman, slut, sex worker, call girl, white slave; *French* fille de joie, demi-mondaine, grande horizontale; *Spanish* puta; *informal* tart, pro, moll, brass nail, tom, woman on the game, working girl, member of the oldest profession, tramp, floozie, scrubber, slapper; *Brit. informal* slag; *N. Amer. informal* hooker, hustler, roundheel; *black English, informal* ho; *euphemistic* model, escort, masseuse; *dated* streetwalker, woman of the streets, lady/woman of the night, scarlet woman, fallen woman, woman of easy virtue, cocotte, wanton, loose woman; *archaic* courtesan, strumpet, harlot, trollop, woman of ill repute, lady of pleasure, Cyprian, doxy, drab, quean, trull, wench.
▶ verb **1** *she spent her life whoring* **work as a prostitute**, prostitute oneself, sell one's body, sell oneself, walk the streets, be on the streets, solicit, work in the sex industry; *informal* be on the game, tom, practise the oldest profession.
2 *the pilots whored and drank like madmen* **use prostitutes**; *archaic* wench.

whorehouse ▶ noun (*informal*) **brothel**, bordello, house of ill repute; *Law* disorderly house; *informal* cathouse, drum; *Brit. informal* knocking shop; *N. Amer. informal* creepjoint; *Austral./NZ informal* crib; *euphemistic* massage parlour; *archaic* bawdy house, house of ill fame, bagnio, stew.

whorl ▶ noun *elegant whorls of wrought iron* **loop**, coil, hoop, ring, turn, curl, twirl, twist, spiral, helix, lap, tier, lock, convolution.

wicked ▶ adjective **1** *a wicked man | a wicked deed* **evil**, sinful, immoral, wrong, morally wrong, wrongful, bad, iniquitous, corrupt, black-hearted, ungodly, unholy, irreligious, unrighteous, sacrilegious, profane, blasphemous, impious, base, mean, vile; irreverent, villainous, nefarious, erring, fallen, impure, sullied, tainted, foul, monstrous, shocking, outrageous, atrocious, abominable, reprehensible, hateful, detestable, despicable, odious, contemptible, horrible, heinous, execrable, godless, diabolical, diabolic, fiendish, vicious, murderous, barbarous, black, dark, rotten; criminal, illicit, unlawful, illegal, illegitimate, lawless, felonious, indictable; perverted, reprobate, sordid, depraved, degenerate, dissolute, dishonourable, dishonest, unscrupulous, unprincipled, underhand, roguish; *informal* crooked, warped, low-down, stinking, dirty, shady, rascally, scoundrelly; *Brit. informal* beastly, bent, not cricket; *Law* malfeasant; *archaic* dastardly; *rare* peccable, egregious, flagitious.
OPPOSITE virtuous.
2 *the wind outside was wicked* **disagreeable**, unpleasant, foul, fierce, bad, nasty, irksome, troublesome, annoying, irritating, vexatious, displeasing, uncomfortable, distressing, hateful, detestable, miserable, abominable, execrable, odious, invidious, objectionable.
OPPOSITE agreeable.
3 *a wicked sense of humour* **mischievous**, playful, naughty, impish, roguish, arch, rascally, rakish, puckish, waggish, devilish, tricksy, cheeky, raffish, teasing.
4 (*informal*) *Sophie makes wicked cakes* **excellent**, superb, superlative, first-rate, first-class, superior, outstanding, remarkable, dazzling, marvellous, magnificent, wonderful, splendid, admirable, noteworthy, impressive, fine, exquisite, exceptional, glorious, sublime, peerless, perfect, of the first water; *informal* great, fantastic, fabulous, terrific, awesome, heavenly, ace, smashing, A1, tip-top, top-notch, neat, mega, cool, banging, cracking, crucial; *Brit. informal* brilliant, brill; *informal, dated* divine.
OPPOSITE lousy.

wickedness ▶ noun *they had been punished for their wickedness* **evil-doing**, evil, evilness, sin, sinfulness, iniquity, iniquitousness, vileness, foulness, baseness, badness, wrong, wrongdoing, dishonesty, double-dealing, unscrupulousness, roguery, villainy, rascality, delinquency, viciousness, degeneracy, depravity, dissolution, dissipation, immorality, vice, perversion, pervertedness, corruption, corruptness, turpitude, devilry, devilishness, fiendishness; ungodliness, godlessness, unholiness, irreligiousness, sacrilegiousness, profanity, blasphemy, impiety, impiousness, irreverence, impurity, heinousness; *informal* crookedness, shadiness; *Law* malfeasance; *archaic* knavery, deviltry; *rare* peccability, peccancy.

wide ▶ adjective **1** *a wide river | a wide road* **broad**, extensive, spacious, open, vast, spread out, outspread.
OPPOSITE narrow.
2 *their mouths were wide with shock* **fully open**, gaping, agape, wide open, yawning.
OPPOSITE closed.
3 *a wide range of opinion* **comprehensive**, ample, broad, extensive, large, large-scale, vast, immense, far-ranging, wide-ranging, expansive, sweeping, encyclopedic, exhaustive, general, all-inclusive, all-embracing, universal, catholic, compendious.
OPPOSITES restricted, limited.
4 *wide trousers* **baggy**, loose, capacious, roomy, ample, full, generous, generously cut, commodious, voluminous, oversize; slack, sloppy, shapeless, sack-like, ill-fitting, ballooning, billowing, floppy.
OPPOSITE tight.
5 *his shot was wide* **off target**, off the mark, wide of the mark/target, inaccurate, off course, astray, nowhere near, out; *informal* off beam.
OPPOSITES on target, accurate.
▶ adverb **1** *he opened his eyes wide* **fully**, to the fullest/furthest extent, as far/much as possible, all the way, completely.
OPPOSITE partly.
2 *he shot wide* **off target**, wide of the mark/target, off course, inaccurately, astray; *informal* off beam.
OPPOSITE accurately.

wide awake ▶ adjective **fully awake**, conscious, open-eyed, not asleep, sleepless, unsleeping, insomniac; *archaic* watchful.
OPPOSITES asleep; tired.

wide-eyed ▶ adjective **1** *the whole class was wide-eyed, glued to the television* **staring in amazement**, goggle-eyed; agape, open-mouthed, tongue-tied, at a loss for words, speechless, dumbfounded, dumbstruck; surprised, amazed, astonished, astounded, stunned, staggered, thunderstruck, aghast, stupefied, dazed, taken aback, shocked, in shock, nonplussed; *informal* flabbergasted, bowled over; *Brit. informal* gobsmacked.
2 *locals with tales to tell latch on to the wide-eyed visitor* **innocent**, naive, impressionable, ingenuous, childlike, credulous, trusting, over-trusting, trustful, unsuspicious, unquestioning, unsuspecting, unguarded, unwary, simple, unsophisticated, inexperienced, raw, green, green as grass, jejune, gullible, easily taken in, easily deceived; *informal* wet behind the ears, born yesterday.
OPPOSITES knowing, sophisticated.

widen ▶ verb **1** *a proposal to widen the motorway | his grin widened* **broaden**, make/become wider, open up, open out, spread, expand, extend, enlarge, stretch; fatten, distend, dilate.
OPPOSITE narrow.
2 *the Party must widen its support* **increase**, augment, add to, develop, boost, swell, supplement, amplify, enlarge, make larger/bigger/greater.
OPPOSITES restrict, limit.

wide open ▶ adjective **1** *his eyes were wide open* **fully open**, open wide, gaping, agape, yawning, cavernous.
OPPOSITE shut.
2 *the championship race is wide open* **unpredictable**, **uncertain**, unsure, indeterminate, undetermined, unsettled, unforeseeable, in the balance, up in the air; *informal* anyone's guess.
OPPOSITE settled.
3 *they were* **wide open to** *fighter attacks* **vulnerable**, exposed; unprotected, unguarded, defenceless, undefended, at risk, in danger, endangered; *rare* pregnable.
OPPOSITE well protected.

widespread ▶ adjective *there is widespread concern about the outcome* **general**, extensive, universal, common, global, worldwide, international, omnipresent, ubiquitous, wholesale, all-embracing, all-inclusive, all-round, across the board, far-reaching, predominant, prevalent, rife, broad, blanket, sweeping, rampant, catholic, inescapable, pervading, pervasive, permeating, epidemic; *rare* preponderate.
OPPOSITES local; limited.

width ▶ noun **1** *the width of the river* **wideness**, breadth, broadness, thickness, spread, span, diameter, girth; *technical* calibre, gauge; *Nautical* beam.
OPPOSITE length.
2 *candidates under the age of 30 are unlikely to have the width of experience required* **range**, breadth, compass, scope, span, scale, sweep, extent, extensiveness, vastness, immensity, immenseness, expansiveness, comprehensiveness, compendiousness; *rare* catholicity.
OPPOSITE narrowness.

wield ▶ verb **1** *one of our assailants was wielding a sword* **brandish**, flourish, wave, twirl, display, flaunt, hold aloft, show off, swing, shake; use, put to use, employ, handle, ply, manipulate, operate.
2 *he had wielded power since the coup in 1972* **exercise**, exert, be possessed of, have, have at one's disposal, hold, maintain, command, control, manage, be in charge of.

wife ▶ noun **spouse**, partner, mate, consort, woman, bride; *informal* old lady, wifey, one's better half, the missus, the little woman; *Brit. informal* one's other half, her indoors, (old) dutch; *Brit. rhyming slang* trouble and strife; *dated* lady, memsahib; *archaic* helpmate, helpmeet.

WORD LINKS
relating to a wife **uxorial**
killing of one's wife **uxoricide**

wiggle ▶ verb *she wiggled her toes* **jiggle**, wriggle, twitch, flutter, shimmy, joggle, wag, wobble, shake, twist, squirm, writhe, wave, quiver, jerk, bobble; *informal* waggle.

wild ▶ adjective **1** *wild animals* **untamed**, undomesticated, feral; unbroken; fierce, ferocious, savage.
OPPOSITE tame.
2 *wild flowers* **uncultivated**, natural; native, indigenous; *technical* agrestal.
OPPOSITES cultivated, hothouse.
3 *a wild tribe* **primitive**, uncivilized, uncultured, uncultivated, uneducated, ignorant; savage, barbarous, barbaric, brutish, ferocious, fierce; *Indian* jungli; *archaic* rude.
OPPOSITE civilized.
4 *a tract of wild hill country* **uninhabited**, unpopulated, uncultivated, unfarmed, unmanaged, virgin; **rugged**, rough, inhospitable, desolate, empty, deserted, trackless, waste, barren.
5 *a wild night* | *the wild sea* **stormy**, squally, tempestuous, turbulent, blustery, windy, howling, raging, roaring, furious, violent; angry, dirty, foul, nasty, inclement; rough, storm-tossed, choppy, boiling; *rare* boisterous.
OPPOSITE calm.
6 *her wild black hair* **dishevelled**, tousled, tangled, windswept; windblown, untidy, messy, disordered, disarranged; uncombed, unkempt; *N. Amer.* mussed up.
OPPOSITES tidy, sleek.
7 *he had a reputation for wild behaviour* **uncontrolled**, unrestrained, out of control, undisciplined, unconstrained, uncurbed, unbridled, unchecked, chaotic; uninhibited, extrovert, unconventional; wayward, self-willed, ungovernable, unmanageable, unruly, rowdy, disorderly, riotous, lawless; *rare* corybantic.
OPPOSITE self-disciplined.
8 *the crowd was wild with excitement* **very excited**, jumping up and down, on fire, delirious, in a frenzy, frantic; uproarious, tumultuous, passionate, vehement, eager, unrestrained, untrammelled.
OPPOSITE calm.
9 (*informal*) *I was wild with jealousy* **distraught**, frantic, beside oneself, not knowing what to do with oneself, frenzied, in a frenzy, hysterical, crazed, deranged, berserk; *informal* mad, crazy.
10 (*informal*) *Hank's going to be wild when he finds out* **furious**, very angry, infuriated, incensed, enraged, beside oneself, irate, fuming, in a rage, raging, seething, maddened, exasperated; *informal* livid, mad, hopping mad, seeing red, hot under the collar, up in arms, foaming at the mouth, on the warpath, steamed up, fit to be tied; *Brit. informal* spare.
OPPOSITE pleased.
11 (*informal*) *his family weren't exactly wild about me* **very keen on**, very enthusiastic about, passionate about, enamoured of, infatuated with, smitten with; *informal* crazy about, mad about, nutty/nuts about, potty about, gone on.
OPPOSITES unenthusiastic, indifferent.
12 *Bill's wild schemes* **madcap**, ridiculous, ludicrous, foolish, stupid, lunatic, foolhardy, idiotic, absurd, silly, asinine, unwise, ill-advised, ill-considered, ill-conceived, illogical, senseless, nonsensical; impractical, impracticable, unpractical, unworkable, imprudent, reckless, preposterous, outrageous; extravagant, fantastical, fantastic, fanciful; *informal* crazy, crackpot, crackbrained, cock-eyed; *Brit. informal* daft.
OPPOSITES sensible, practical.
13 *a wild guess* **random**, arbitrary, hit-or-miss, haphazard, uninformed; *informal* shot-in-the-dark.
OPPOSITE considered.
□ **run wild 1** *the vegetable garden had been allowed to run wild* **grow unchecked**, grow profusely, run riot, spread like wildfire, ramble, straggle.
2 *children in the city are running wild* **run free**, **run amok**, run riot, get out of control, cut loose, be undisciplined, go on the rampage; *Austral.* go bush; *informal* raise hell; *N. Amer. informal* go postal.

wilderness ▶ noun **1** *the Siberian wilderness of Kamchatka* **wilds**, wastes, uninhabited region, inhospitable region, uncultivated region, badlands; jungle; desert; *S. African* bundu.
2 *a litter-strewn north London wilderness* **wasteland**, neglected area, abandoned area, no-man's-land.
3 *a wilderness of boxes, suitcases, and trunks* **jumble**, muddle, clutter, confusion.

wildlife ▶ noun **(wild) animals**, fauna; flora and fauna.

wilds ▶ plural noun *he spent a year in the wilds of Canada* **remote areas**, wilderness; backwoods, hinterlands; *N. Amer.* backcountry, backland; *Austral./NZ* outback, bush, backblocks, booay; *S. African* backveld, platteland; *N. Amer. informal* boondocks, boonies, tall timbers; *Austral./NZ informal* Woop Woop, beyond the black stump.

wiles ▶ plural noun *feminine wiles* **tricks**, ruses, ploys, schemes, dodges, manoeuvres, gambits, subterfuges, cunning stratagems, artifices, devices, contrivances; guile, artfulness, art, cunning, craftiness.

wilful ▶ adjective **1** *the wilful destruction of property* **deliberate**, intentional, intended, done on purpose, premeditated, planned, calculated, purposeful, conscious, knowing; voluntary, volitional.
OPPOSITES accidental, unintentional.
2 *a spoiled and wilful child* **headstrong**, self-willed, strong-willed, with a will of one's own, determined to have one's own way; **obstinate**, stubborn, as stubborn as a mule, mulish, pig-headed, bull-headed, refractory, recalcitrant, uncooperative, intractable, obstreperous, contrary, perverse, wayward, defiant, disobedient, ungovernable, unmanageable, rebellious, mutinous, insubordinate; *Scottish* thrawn; *informal* cussed; *Brit. informal* bloody-minded, bolshie; *N. Amer. informal* balky; *archaic* froward, contumacious; *rare* contrarious, renitent, pervicacious.
OPPOSITES biddable, amenable.

> **CHOOSE THE RIGHT WORD**
> **wilful, obstinate, stubborn, headstrong**
> *See* OBSTINATE.

will[1] ▶ verb *accidents will happen* **have a tendency to**, are bound to, have a habit of, do.

will[2] ▶ noun **1** *she has the will to succeed* | *a stupendous effort of will* **determination**, firmness of purpose, fixity of purpose, will power, strength of character, resolution, resolve, resoluteness, purposefulness, single-mindedness, drive, commitment, dedication, doggedness, tenacity, tenaciousness, staying power, backbone, spine; self-control, self-restraint, self-discipline, self-mastery; volition; *German* Sitzfleisch; *informal* stickability; *N. Amer. informal* stick-to-it-iveness; *rare* perseveration.
2 *Jane had not wanted them to stay against their will* | *the political will of the electorate* **desire**, wish, preference, inclination, mind, disposition; intention, intent.
3 *they believed it to be God's will* **wish**, desire, decision, choice, intention; decree, ordinance, command, dictate.
4 *freedom of the will* **volition**, choice, option, decision, discretion, prerogative.
5 *his late father's will* **testament**, last will and testament, last wishes; bequest(s).
□ **at will** *he seemed to think he could walk in and out of my life at will* **as one pleases**, as one wishes, as one thinks fit, to suit oneself, at one's pleasure, at one's inclination/discretion, at whim.
▶ verb **1** *do what you will—it makes no difference to me* **want**, wish, desire, please, see/think fit, think best, like, feel like; choose, prefer.
2 *God willed it* **decree**, order, ordain, command, direct; intend, wish, want.
3 *she willed the money to her husband* **bequeath**, leave, give, hand down, hand on, pass on, settle on, make over, transfer, gift; *Law* devise.

willing ▶ adjective **1** *I'm perfectly willing to give it a try* | *a crowd of willing helpers* **ready**, **prepared**, disposed, inclined, nothing loath, of a mind, so minded, minded, in the mood; happy, glad, pleased; eager, keen, enthusiastic; consenting, agreeable, amenable, accommodating, obliging, compliant, acquiescent; *informal* game.
OPPOSITES unwilling, reluctant, disinclined.
2 *there was no lack of willing help* **readily given**, gladly given, willingly given, promptly given, ungrudging.
OPPOSITE grudging.

willingly ▶ adverb *Joe had gone with her willingly* | *those who willingly gave their time to help us* **voluntarily**, of one's own free will, of one's own accord, of one's own volition, by choice; readily, without hesitation, without reluctance, ungrudgingly, cheerfully, happily, gladly, with pleasure, with good grace, eagerly, enthusiastically; freely, spontaneously, unforced; *informal* at the drop of a hat, like a shot.
OPPOSITES reluctantly, unwillingly.

willingness ▶ noun *many people have expressed a willingness to help* **readiness**, preparedness, disposition, inclination, will, wish, desire; eagerness, keenness, enthusiasm.
OPPOSITES reluctance, unwillingness.

willowy ▶ adjective *a willowy blonde* **tall**, **slim**, slender, lean, svelte, lissom, sylphlike, snake-hipped, rangy, long-limbed, clean-limbed, graceful, lithe, loose-limbed; *informal* slinky; *rare* gracile, attenuate.
OPPOSITES short, fat.

will power ▶ noun *it took every ounce of will power she possessed not to give in* **determination**, strength of will, strength of character, firmness of purpose, fixity of purpose, resolution, resolve, resoluteness, purposefulness, single-mindedness, drive, commitment, dedication, doggedness, tenacity, tenaciousness, staying power, backbone, spine; self-control, self-restraint, self-discipline, self-mastery; *German* Sitzfleisch; *informal* stickability; *N. Amer. informal* stick-to-it-iveness; *rare* perseveration.

willy-nilly ▶ adverb **1** *cars and trucks were parked willy-nilly* **haphazardly**, at random, randomly, without planning, without method.
2 *it is becoming painfully obvious that we are, willy-nilly, in a totally new situation* **whether one likes it or not**, of necessity, necessarily; one way or the other; *Latin* nolens volens; *informal* like it or not, like it or lump it; *formal* perforce.

wilt ▶ verb **1** *the roses had begun to wilt* **droop**, sag, become limp, become flaccid, flop; wither, shrivel (up).
OPPOSITES thrive, flourish.
2 *people were wilting in the heat* **languish**, flag, lose energy, become listless, feel weak/faint; droop, sag.
OPPOSITE perk up.
3 *Shelley's happy mood wilted* **diminish**, dwindle, lessen, grow less, fade, ebb, wane, weaken; evaporate, melt away, disappear.

wily ▶ adjective *a wily old rascal* **shrewd**, clever, sharp, sharp-witted, astute, canny, smart; **crafty**, cunning, artful, sly, scheming, calculating, guileful, disingenuous, devious, Machiavellian; deceitful, deceptive, dishonest, cheating, double-dealing; *informal* tricky, foxy; *Brit. informal* fly; *Scottish & N. English informal* pawky; *N. Amer. informal* heads-up; *S. African informal* slim; *archaic* subtle; *rare* vulpine, carny.
OPPOSITES naive, guileless.

wimp ▶ noun (*informal*) **coward**, namby-pamby, milksop, Milquetoast, mouse, weakling; *informal* drip, sissy, weed, doormat, wuss, pansy, jellyfish, crybaby, scaredy-cat, chicken; *Brit. informal* wet, mummy's boy, big girl's blouse, jessie, chinless wonder, cream puff, yellow-belly; *N. Amer. informal* candy-ass, cupcake, pantywaist, nebbish, pussy; *Austral./NZ informal* sook; *S. African informal* moffie; *archaic* poltroon.

win ▶ verb **1** *Steve has won the Isle of Man race three times* **come first in**, finish first in, be victorious in, triumph in, take first prize in, achieve success in, be successful in, prevail in; *informal* wrap up.
OPPOSITE lose.
2 *she was determined to win* **come first**, finish first, be the winner, be victorious, be the victor, carry/win the day, carry all before one, defeat/overcome the opposition, take the honours/crown, gain the palm, come out ahead, come out on top, succeed, triumph, prevail, achieve mastery; sweep the board, make a clean sweep; *informal* win out, clean up.
OPPOSITES lose, be beaten.
3 *he won a £20,000 cash prize* **secure**, gain, achieve, attain, earn, obtain, acquire, procure, get, collect, pick up, walk away/off with, come away with, carry off; receive; *informal* land, net, bag, bank, pot, scoop.
4 *Ilona seems to have won his heart* **captivate**, steal, gain.
□ **win someone round/over** *Daisy made heroic efforts to win him round* **persuade**, talk round, bring round, convince, induce, sway, prevail on.
▶ noun *a 3–0 win over Birmingham* **victory**, triumph, conquest, success.
OPPOSITE defeat.

wince ▶ verb *he winced as she dabbed disinfectant on the cut* **grimace**, pull a face; **flinch**, blench, start, draw back, shrink away, recoil, cringe, squirm.
▶ noun *a wince of pain* **grimace**; flinch, start.

wind[1] (rhymes with 'tinned') *See centre pages for lists of* **Winds** **Wind Instruments** **Brass Instruments**
▶ noun **1** *the slender pine trees were swaying in the wind* **breeze**; air current, current of air; gale, hurricane; draught; *informal* blow; *literary* zephyr.
2 *he waited while Jez got his wind back* **breath**; *informal* puff.
3 *you do talk a lot of wind* **nonsense**, balderdash, gibberish, claptrap, blarney, blather, blether; *informal* hogwash, baloney, tripe, drivel, bilge, bosh, bull, bunk, rot, hot air, eyewash, piffle, poppycock, phooey, hooey, malarkey, twaddle, guff; boastful talk, bombast, bluster, fanfaronade; *Brit. informal* codswallop, cobblers, stuff and nonsense, tosh, taradiddle, cock, cack; *Scottish & N. English informal* havers; *Irish informal* codology; *N. Amer. informal* garbage, flapdoodle, blathers, wack, bushwa; *informal, dated* bunkum, tommyrot; *literary* rodomontade, braggadocio; *vulgar slang* shit, crap, bullshit, bollocks, balls; *Austral./NZ vulgar slang* bulldust.
4 **flatulence**, flatus, gas; *technical* borborygmus.
5 *a concerto for piano, violin, and wind* **wind instruments**.
□ **get wind of** (*informal*) *White House officials got wind of the plan* **hear about/of**, learn of, find out about, become aware of, be made aware of, be told about, be informed of, hear tell of, have brought to one's notice; *informal* hear something on the grapevine.
□ **in the wind** *there is trouble in the wind* **on the way**, coming, about to happen, in the offing, in the air, close at hand, on the horizon, approaching, imminent, impending, looming, brewing, afoot; likely, probable; *informal* on the cards.
□ **put the wind up someone** (*Brit. informal*) *stop playing silly buggers—you're putting the wind up me* **scare**, frighten, make afraid, make nervous, throw into a panic, panic, alarm, unnerve; *informal* give someone the heebie-jeebies; *N. Amer. informal* spook.
OPPOSITE reassure.

W

WORD LINKS

relating to the wind	**aeolian**
related prefix	**anemo- (e.g. *anemotropic*)**
instrument for measuring wind speed	**anemometer**

wind[2] (rhymes with 'mind') ▶ verb **1** *the road winds up through the mountainside to the village* **twist and turn**, twist, turn, bend, curve, loop, zigzag, weave, snake, meander, ramble; swerve, veer.
2 *he wound a towel around his midriff | he wound a lock of her hair round his fingers* **wrap**, furl, fold; entwine, lace, wreathe.
3 *Anne wound the wool into a ball* **coil**, roll, twist, twine; reel.
□ **wind down 1** (*informal*) *he needed to wind down after the spiralling tensions of the day* **relax**, unwind, calm down, cool down/off, ease up/off, take it easy, rest, put one's feet up; *informal* de-stress, let it all hang out, unbutton; *N. Amer. informal* hang loose, stay loose, chill out, chill, kick back.
2 *the campaign was winding down* **draw to a close**, come to an end, tail off, taper off, diminish, lessen, dwindle, decline; **slacken off**, slack off, slow down.
OPPOSITE escalate.
□ **wind something down** *a decision was taken to wind down the property development business* **bring to a close/end**, wind up, run down, close down, phase out; *N. Amer.* close out.
OPPOSITE expand.
□ **wind up** (*informal*) *it's no wonder he wound up in hospital* **end up**, finish up, find oneself, land up, land oneself; *informal* fetch up.
□ **wind someone up 1** (*Brit. informal*) *I knew Katie was just winding me up* **tease**, make fun of, chaff; annoy, vex; *informal* take the mickey out of, send up, rib, josh, kid, have on, pull someone's leg, rag; *N. Amer. informal* goof on, rag on, put on, pull someone's chain, razz, fun, shuck; *Austral./NZ informal* poke mullock at, poke borak at, sling off at; *Brit. vulgar slang* take the piss out of; *dated* make sport of, twit.
2 *Alan was getting hot under the collar—David seemed to be winding him up on purpose* **annoy**, anger, irritate, exasperate, get/put someone's back up, nettle, pique, get on someone's nerves, ruffle someone's feathers; provoke, goad, work up, make tense; *informal* aggravate, rile, niggle, get in someone's hair, get to, bug, miff, peeve, get under someone's skin, get up someone's nose, hack off; *Brit. informal* rub up the wrong way, nark, get across; *N. Amer. informal* ride; *vulgar slang* piss off.
□ **wind something up 1** *Richard wound up the meeting just before noon* **conclude**, bring to an end/close, end, terminate, finish; tie up, tie up the loose ends of; *informal* wrap up.
OPPOSITES open, begin.
2 *the company has since been wound up* **close (down)**, dissolve, liquidate, put into liquidation.

winded ▶ adjective *he lay there for a moment, winded* **out of breath**, breathless, gasping for breath, panting, puffing, huffing and puffing, puffing and blowing; *informal* puffed out, out of puff.

windfall ▶ noun *a £43,000 windfall* **bonanza**, jackpot, pennies from heaven, unexpected gain; piece/stroke of good luck, godsend, manna from heaven.

winding ▶ noun *the windings of the stream* **twist**, turn, turning, bend, loop, curve, zigzag, convolution, meander, meandering; oxbow; *rare* anfractuosity, flexuosity.
▶ adjective *the winding country roads* **twisting and turning**, full of twists and turns, meandering, windy, twisty, bending, curving, looping, zigzag, zigzagging, serpentine, sinuous, snaking, snaky, tortuous, convoluted; circuitous, roundabout, indirect; *rare* anfractuous, flexuous, meandrous, serpentiform.
OPPOSITE straight.

window *See centre pages for list of* **Windows**
▶ noun casement, opening, aperture.

windpipe ▶ noun **trachea**, pharynx; throat; *archaic* weasand.

WORD LINKS

relating to the windpipe **tracheal**

windswept ▶ adjective **1** *the windswept moors* **exposed**, unprotected, bleak, bare, desolate; windy, blowy.
OPPOSITE sheltered.
2 *his windswept hair* **dishevelled**, tousled, unkempt, windblown, untidy, messy, disordered, disarranged; *N. Amer.* mussed up.
OPPOSITES tidy, sleek.

windy ▶ adjective **1** *a windy day* **breezy**, blowy, fresh, blustery, gusty; wild, stormy, squally, tempestuous, turbulent; *rare* boisterous, blusterous.
OPPOSITES still, windless.
2 *the cold windy hills* **windswept**, exposed, unprotected, open to the elements, bare, bleak.
OPPOSITE sheltered.
3 (*informal*) *a series of windy speeches* **verbose**, long-winded, wordy, prolix, lengthy, overlong, prolonged, protracted, long-drawn-out, tedious; talkative, garrulous, voluble, loquacious; rambling, meandering, repetitious, tautological, periphrastic, circumlocutory, tortuous; *rare* pleonastic.
OPPOSITES concise, succinct.
4 (*Brit. informal*) *she felt a bit windy about his visit* **nervous**, **anxious**, worried, apprehensive, on edge, edgy, tense, stressed, fretful, uneasy, jumpy, with one's stomach in knots; frightened, scared, afraid, fearful; *informal* with butterflies in one's stomach, jittery, twitchy, trepidatious, in a state, uptight, in a stew, in a dither, all of a dither, in a sweat, in a flap, in a tizz/tizzy, all of a lather, het up, in a twitter; *Brit. informal* strung up, all of a doodah; *N. Amer. informal* spooky, squirrelly, in a twit; *Austral./NZ informal* toey; *dated* overstrung.
OPPOSITES calm, unperturbed.

wine *See centre pages for lists of* **Wines** **Sherries**
▶ noun *French* vin de table, vin ordinaire, vin du pays; *informal* plonk, vino, the grape.

WORD LINKS
relating to wine **vinous**
related prefix **oeno- (e.g. *oenophile*)**
wine production **viniculture**
study of wine **oenology**

wing ▶ noun **1** *a bird's wings* organ of flight; *literary* pinion, van; *rare* pennon.
2 *the east wing of the house* **part**, section, side; annexe, extension; *N. Amer.* ell.
3 *the radical wing of the party* **faction**, camp, caucus, arm, side, branch, group, grouping, section, set, clique, coterie, cabal; fringe movement; lobby.
▶ verb **1** *a solitary seagull **winged its way** over the sea* **fly**, glide, soar; take wing.
2 *there was a high-pitched whistle as the bomb winged along its trajectory* **hurtle**, speed, shoot, whizz, zoom, streak, sweep, fly, race; sail.
3 *she was shot at and winged by border guards* **wound**, graze, hit, clip.
□ **wing it** (*informal*) *there were no guidelines—I just had to wing it* **improvise**, play it by ear, extemporize, ad lib; *informal* busk it.

WORD LINKS
related prefix **ptero- (e.g. *pterosaur*)**

wink ▶ verb **1** *he winked an eye at his companion* **blink**, flutter, bat; *technical* nictate, nictitate.
2 *the diamond on her finger winked in the moonlight* **sparkle**, twinkle, flash, flicker, glitter, gleam, shimmer, shine; blink; *rare* scintillate.
□ **wink at** *the authorities winked at their illegal trade* **turn a blind eye to**, close/shut one's eyes to, ignore, overlook, disregard, pretend not to notice; look the other way; connive at, condone, tolerate.
▶ noun *he noticed a wink of light in the west* **glimmer**, glimmering, gleam, glint, flash, flicker, twinkle, sparkle; blink.
□ **in the wink of an eye** (*informal*) **very soon/quickly**, in a second, in a minute, in a moment, in a trice, in a flash, in an instant, in the twinkling of an eye, in (less than) no time, in no time at all, before you know it, in a very short time; *N. Amer.* momentarily; *informal* in a jiffy, in two shakes (of a lamb's tail), before you can say Jack Robinson, in a sec, in the blink of an eye, in a blink, before you can say knife; *Brit. informal* in a tick, in two ticks, in a mo; *N. Amer. informal* in a snap.

winkle ▶ verb
□ **winkle something/someone out 1** *Ewan managed to winkle the details out of him* **worm out**, prise out, dig out, extract with difficulty, draw out.
2 *there were huge profits to be made from winkling out sitting tenants* **force out**, dislodge, displace, remove, evict, uproot.

winner ▶ noun **victor**, champion, conqueror, vanquisher, defeater, conquering hero, hero; gold medallist, cup winner, prizewinner, prizeman; *Spanish* conquistador; *Latin* victor ludorum; *informal* champ, top dog, number one.
OPPOSITE loser.

winning ▶ adjective **1** *the winning team* **victorious**, successful, triumphant, vanquishing, conquering; first, top, top-scoring; unbeaten, undefeated, unvanquished.
OPPOSITE losing.
2 *a winning smile* **engaging**, charming, appealing, endearing, sweet, cute, winsome, attractive, pretty, prepossessing, fetching, lovely, adorable, lovable, delightful, disarming, captivating, enchanting, beguiling, persuasive, irresistible; *dated* taking.
OPPOSITES off-putting, unattractive.

winnings ▶ plural noun *Sanchez collected his winnings* **prize money**, money won, gains; prize(s), booty, spoils; proceeds, profits, takings; *Sport* purse.
OPPOSITE losses.

winnow ▶ verb **1** *the dust and chaff is winnowed from the grain* **separate**, divide, sort out; remove, get rid of.
2 *it's difficult to **winnow out** the truth* **separate out**, sift out, filter out, isolate, sort out, find, identify, ferret out; separate the wheat from the chaff.

winsome ▶ adjective *his winsome daughter | a winsome smile* **appealing**, engaging, charming, winning, attractive, pretty, sweet, cute, endearing, darling, dear, lovable, adorable, lovely, delightful, enchanting, captivating, fetching; *dated* taking.

winter ▶ noun

WORD LINKS
relating to winter **hibernal**

wintry ▶ adjective **1** *wintry weather* **bleak**, **cold**, chilly, frosty, freezing, icy, snowy, icy-cold, arctic, glacial, frigid, bitter, biting, piercing, sharp, raw; *informal* nippy; *Brit. informal* parky; *literary* chill; *rare* hyperborean, hibernal, hiemal, brumal.
OPPOSITES summery, balmy, hot.
2 *his wintry smile* **unfriendly**, cool, chilly, cold, frosty, frigid, glacial, bleak, distant, remote.
OPPOSITES friendly, warm.

wipe ▶ verb **1** *Beth wiped the kitchen table with a damp cloth* **rub**, **clean**, mop, sponge, swab; dry, polish; *Scottish & N. English* dight.
2 *he **wiped** the marks **off** the window* **rub off**, clean off, sponge off, polish off; remove, get rid of, dispose of, take off, erase, efface.
3 *they **wiped up** the mess* **clean up**, clear up, mop up, sponge up; remove, get rid of.
4 *she wiped the unpleasant memory from her mind* **obliterate**, expunge, erase, blot out, remove, remove all traces of, blank out.
□ **wipe someone/something out** *soldiers wiped out an entire village in Lampung province* **destroy**, annihilate, eradicate, eliminate, extirpate; slaughter, massacre, kill, kill off, exterminate; demolish, raze to the ground, level; *informal* wipe off the face of the earth, wipe off the map, take out, liquidate, zap; *N. Amer. informal* waste; *literary* slay.
▶ noun *Bert gave the table a final wipe* **rub**, clean, mop, sponge, swab, polish.

wire ▶ noun **cable**, lead, flex.

wiry ▶ adjective **1** *a small, wiry man* **sinewy**, strong, tough, athletic; **lean**, spare, thin, stringy, skinny; *literary* thewy.
OPPOSITES frail; flabby.
2 *his wiry black hair* **coarse**, rough, stiff, tough, strong; curly, wavy.
OPPOSITES straight, smooth.

wisdom ▶ noun **1** *a number of senior politicians questioned the wisdom of the decision* **sagacity**, sageness, intelligence, understanding, insight, perception, perceptiveness, percipience, penetration, perspicuity, acuity, discernment, sense, good sense, common sense, shrewdness, astuteness, acumen, smartness, judiciousness, judgement, foresight, clear-sightedness, prudence, circumspection; logic, rationale, rationality, soundness, saneness, advisability; *informal* sharpness; *N. Amer. informal* savvy, smarts; *rare* sapience, arguteness.
OPPOSITES stupidity, folly.
2 *the wisdom of the East* **knowledge**, learning, erudition, scholarship, philosophy; lore.

wise ▶ adjective *a wise old man | a wise decision* **sage**, sagacious, intelligent, clever, learned, with/showing great knowledge, knowledgeable, informed, enlightened; astute, shrewd, acute, sharp, sharp-witted, canny, knowing, sensible, prudent, discerning, judicious, penetrating, perceptive, full of insight, insightful, clear-sighted, percipient, perspicacious, perspicuous, owlish; well advised, well thought out, well judged, politic, expedient, strategic, tactical, far-sighted; rational, logical, sound, sane; *informal* smart; *Brit. informal* fly; *dated* long-headed; *rare* sapient, argute.
OPPOSITES stupid, silly, foolish.
□ **put someone wise** (*informal*) *I suppose Lucy put you wise* **tell**, inform, notify, apprise, make aware, put in the picture, fill in, break the news to; warn, forewarn, alert; *informal* clue in/up, tip off, tip someone the wink.
□ **wise to** (*informal*) *Alpine climbers have been wise to these techniques for years* **aware of**, familiar with, acquainted with, cognizant of.

wisecrack ▶ noun (*informal*) **joke**, **witticism**, quip, witty remark, flash of wit, jest, rejoinder, sally; pun; barb, gibe; *French* bon mot; *informal* crack, gag, funny, one-liner, comeback.

wish ▶ verb **1** *I have never **wished for** power* **desire**, want, hope for, long for, yearn for, crave, hunger for, thirst for, lust after, covet, sigh for, pine for, dream of; aspire to, set one's heart on, have as one's goal/aim, seek, be bent on; *informal* fancy, hanker after, have a yen for, itch for; *archaic* be desirous of; *rare* desiderate.
2 *if you wish to leave a message, please speak after the tone | they can do as they wish* **want**, desire, have an inclination, feel/be inclined, feel like, care; choose, please, think fit.
3 *I wish you to send them a message* **want**, desire, require.
4 *I wished him farewell* **bid**.
▶ noun **1** *he had never expressed a wish to own a Mercedes* **desire**, longing, hope, yearning, inclination, urge, whim, craving, hunger, thirst, lust; aspiration, aim, ambition, dream; *informal* fancy, hankering, yen, itch.
2 *she was unwilling to go against her parents' wishes* **request**, requirement, bidding, instruction, direction, demand, order, command; want, desire; will; *literary* behest.

WORD LINKS
relating to a wish **precatorial**

wishy-washy ▶ adjective **1** *I feel like an idiot for being so wishy-washy* **feeble**, ineffectual, weak, vapid, milk-and-water, effete, spineless, limp, limp-wristed, namby-pamby, half-hearted, spiritless, irresolute, indecisive; *informal* wet, pathetic, weak-kneed; *Brit. informal* half-arsed.
OPPOSITES strong, firm, decisive.
2 *wishy-washy soup* **watery**, weak, watered down, thin; tasteless, flavourless, insipid.
OPPOSITES thick; flavoursome.
3 *a wishy-washy colour* **pale**, insipid; pallid, wan, sickly.

wisp ▶ noun *a stray wisp of hair* **strand**, tendril, lock; piece, scrap, shred, thread.

wispy ▶ adjective *her wispy blonde hair* **thin**, fine, feathery, flyaway, straggly.

wistful ▶ adjective *his wistful expression* **regretful**, **nostalgic**, yearning, longing; plaintive, rueful, melancholy, sad, mournful, forlorn, disconsolate, woebegone, doleful; pensive, reflective, contemplative, meditative, dreamy, daydreaming, in a reverie.

> CHOOSE THE RIGHT WORD
>
> **wistful, plaintive, pensive**
>
> ■ A **wistful** person feels or shows a sad longing for something lost or unattainable. The word suggests a gentle sadness; the loss or impossibility is accepted but still regretted (*he gave a wistful smile for what might have been*).
>
> ■ **Plaintive** is used typically of music or cries that express or seem to express grief, often beautifully (*a plaintive song of lost love | the strangely sad and beautiful cry of the muezzin, whose plaintive voice drifted across the old city*).
>
> ■ **Pensive** people or things are not necessarily sad: they are quiet and solemn because they are engaged in or involve deep thought (*she is pensive and slightly sulky when she considers the future | Ashley took a pensive drink of coffee*).

wit ▶ noun **1** (also **wits**) *Eleanor was possessed of a great deal of native wit | he needed all his wits to figure out the way back* **intelligence**, shrewdness, astuteness, cleverness, canniness, acuteness, acuity, sharpness, sharp-wittedness, sense, good sense, common sense, wisdom, sagacity, judgement, understanding, acumen, discernment, perception, insight, percipience, perspicacity; brains, mind; *informal* nous, gumption, horse sense; *Brit. informal* common; *N. Amer. informal* savvy, smarts.
OPPOSITE stupidity.
2 *I wanted to bowl him over with my sparkling wit* **wittiness**, humour, funniness, facetiousness, drollery, waggishness; **repartee**, badinage, banter, wordplay, raillery, jokes, witticisms, quips, puns.
OPPOSITE humourlessness.
3 *she's such a wit* **wag**, comedian, humorist, funny person, comic, joker, jokester; *French* farceur; *informal* character; *informal, dated* card, caution; *rare* punster.

witch ▶ noun **1** **sorceress**, enchantress, occultist, necromancer, Wiccan; *archaic* beldam; *rare* hex, pythoness.
2 (*informal*) *she's a right old witch* **hag**, crone, harpy, harridan, termagant, she-devil; *informal* battleaxe, old bag; *archaic* scold.

witchcraft ▶ noun **sorcery**, black magic, the black arts, the occult, occultism, wizardry, witching, necromancy, voodooism, voodoo, hoodoo, wonder-working, divination; Wicca, white magic, natural magic; *NZ* makutu; *rare* thaumaturgy, theurgy, the old religion, witchery, demonry, diablerie, sortilege.

witch doctor ▶ noun **medicine man**, shaman, healer; *Austral.* boyla; (*in southern Africa*) sangoma; (*in Hawaii*) kahuna; (*in Greenland*) angekok.

with ▶ preposition *she's gone out with her boyfriend* **accompanied by**, in the company of, escorted by.

withdraw ▶ verb **1** *he withdrew a roll of banknotes from his pocket | Ruth withdrew her hand from his* **remove**, extract, draw out, pull out, take out; take back, pull back, take away.
OPPOSITE insert.
2 *the ban on advertising was withdrawn* **abolish**, **cancel**, lift, raise, set aside, discontinue, end, stop, terminate, remove, reverse, revoke, rescind, repeal, countermand, annul, void.
OPPOSITES introduce, bring in.
3 *she withdrew all her money from the bank* **take out**, draw out.
OPPOSITE deposit.
4 *she later withdrew the allegation* **retract**, take back, unsay, go back on, recall, recant, disavow, disclaim, abjure, repudiate, renounce; back down, climb down, backtrack, back-pedal, do a U-turn, eat one's words; *Brit.* do an about-turn.
OPPOSITE put forward.
5 *government troops withdrew from the city* **leave**, pull out of, move out of, evacuate, quit, retire from, retreat from, pull back from; disengage from.
OPPOSITE enter.
6 *at the last minute, his co-partner withdrew from the project* **pull out of**, back out of, beg off, bow out of, scratch from; get cold feet; *N. Amer. informal* crap out; *Austral./NZ informal* pike on; *archaic* recede from.
7 *they withdrew to their rooms* **go**, retire, retreat, take oneself, leave, depart, absent oneself, adjourn, decamp, beat a retreat; shut oneself away; *formal* repair, remove; *literary* betake oneself; *rare* abstract oneself.
8 *Mrs Reynolds withdrew into the shadows* **draw back**, retreat, shrink back.

withdrawal ▶ noun **1** *the withdrawal of state subsidies* **removal**, taking away; abolition, cancellation, discontinuation, ending, stopping, termination, elimination.
OPPOSITE introduction.
2 *the withdrawal of the troops* **departure**, pull-out, exit, exodus, evacuation, retirement, retreat, disengagement.

withdrawn ▶ adjective *over the last few months he had become very withdrawn* **introverted**, inward-looking, unsociable, socially inhibited; **uncommunicative**, unforthcoming, taciturn, silent, quiet, reticent, reserved, retiring, distant, remote, private, reclusive; shy, timid, diffident, shrinking, timorous; stand-offish, aloof.
OPPOSITES outgoing, extrovert, sociable.

wither ▶ verb **1** *the flowers had withered in the hot summer sun* **wilt**, become limp, droop, fade; **shrivel (up)**, dry up; die, perish; *technical* become marcescent.
OPPOSITES thrive, flourish.
2 *the muscles in his leg had withered* **waste (away)**, become shrunken, shrivel (up), atrophy, decay.
OPPOSITE strengthen.
3 *her confidence* ***withered away*** **diminish**, dwindle, shrink, lessen, fade, ebb (away), wane, weaken, languish; evaporate, melt away, disappear.
OPPOSITE grow.

withering ▶ adjective *a withering look | withering remarks* **scornful**, contemptuous, full of contempt, mocking, sneering; scathing, stinging, searing, blistering, biting, devastating; supercilious, disdainful, superior, dismissive; humiliating, mortifying.
OPPOSITES encouraging, admiring.

withhold ▶ verb **1** *the council withheld payments to some contractors | he deliberately withheld the information* **refuse to give**, hold back, keep back, stop; retain, keep hold of, hold on to; fail to disclose, hide, conceal, keep secret; *informal* sit on, keep under one's hat.
2 *Elizabeth could no longer withhold her tears* **suppress**, repress, hold back, keep back, fight back, choke back, swallow, control, keep in check, check, restrain, contain, curb.

within ▶ preposition **1** *within the walls of the prison* **inside**, in, within the bounds/confines of, enclosed by, surrounded by.
OPPOSITE outside.
2 *within the speed limit* **inside**, inside the range/limits of, within the bounds of.
OPPOSITE outside.
3 *within a few hours* **in less than**, in under, in no more than, after only.

with it ▶ adjective (*informal*) See **FASHIONABLE**.

without ▶ preposition **1** *thousands were left homeless and without food* **lacking**, in need of, wanting for, needing, requiring, short of; deprived of, destitute of.
OPPOSITE with.
2 *I don't want to go without you* **unaccompanied by**, unescorted by; in the absence of.
OPPOSITE with.

withstand ▶ verb *the company was able to withstand the rigours of the recession* **resist**, hold out against, stand firm against, stand/hold one's ground against, bear up against, hold the line against, persevere in the face of, stand up to, fight, combat, grapple with, oppose, face, confront, defy, brave; weather, survive, live through, ride out, endure, take, cope with, stand, tolerate, bear, put up with; *informal* go the distance against.
OPPOSITES give in, surrender, yield.

witless ▶ adjective **1** *a witless youth* **foolish**, **stupid**, unintelligent, idiotic, brainless, mindless, imbecilic, imbecile; fatuous, inane, immature, childish, puerile, half-baked, empty-headed, half-witted, slow-witted, weak-minded, doltish; *informal* crazy, dotty, scatty, loopy, brain-dead, cretinous, thick, thickheaded, birdbrained, pea-brained, pinheaded, dopey, dim, dim-witted, dippy, blockheaded, boneheaded, lamebrained, chuckleheaded, dunderheaded, wooden-headed, muttonheaded, damfool; *Brit. informal* daft, divvy; *Scottish & N. English informal* glaikit; *N. Amer. informal* dumb-ass, chowderheaded; *S. African informal* dof; *W. Indian informal* dotish.
2 *I was bored witless* **out of one's mind**, to death, to tears, silly, stupid, sick.

witness ▶ noun **1** *several witnesses claimed that Slater started the fight* **observer**, onlooker, looker-on, eyewitness, spectator, viewer, watcher; bystander, passer-by.
2 *a key witness at the trial* person giving evidence, testifier; *Law* deponent.
3 *a bottle of whisky was the only witness of his low mood* **evidence**, indication, proof, testimony.
□ **bear/stand/give witness** *the surviving letters* ***bear witness to*** *the extent of his involvement* **attest to**, be evidence/proof of, testify to, confirm, evidence, prove, corroborate, verify, substantiate, bear out; show, demonstrate, establish, be a monument to, indicate, reveal, bespeak.
OPPOSITE belie.
▶ verb **1** *police are anxious to hear from anyone who witnessed the incident* **see**, observe, watch, look on at, be a witness to, view, note, notice, spot; be present at, attend; *literary* behold.
2 *it is important to ensure that a will is correctly witnessed* **countersign**, sign, endorse, validate; certificate, document; *N. Amer.* notarize.
3 *his writings witness to an inner toughness* **attest to**, be evidence/proof of, testify to, bear witness to, confirm, evidence, prove, verify, corroborate, substantiate, bear out; show, demonstrate, establish, be a monument to, indicate, reveal; *literary* bespeak.

witter ▶ verb (*Brit. informal*) *she smiled and nodded as he wittered on* **prattle**, babble, chatter, prate, gabble, jabber, go on, run on, rattle on/away, yap, jibber-jabber, patter, blather, blether, blither, maunder, ramble, drivel; *informal* yak, yackety-yak, yabber, yatter; *Brit. informal* rabbit, chunter, natter, waffle; *Scottish & Irish informal* slabber; *Austral./NZ informal* mag; *archaic* twaddle, clack, twattle.

witticism ▶ noun **joke**, quip, witty remark, flash of wit, jest, pun, play on words, double entendre, sally, riposte, pleasantry; epigram; (**witticisms**) repartee, banter, badinage; *French* bon mot; *informal* one-liner, gag, funny, crack, wisecrack, comeback; *rare* paronomasia, equivoque, Atticism.

witty ▶ adjective *his witty conversation* **humorous**, amusing, droll, funny, comic, comical; sparkling, scintillating, lively, entertaining; **clever**, quick-witted, sharp-witted, piquant, original, ingenious; jocular, facetious, waggish; epigrammatic.
OPPOSITES boring, dull.

> CHOOSE THE RIGHT WORD
>
> **witty, humorous, funny, comical**
>
> *See* HUMOROUS.

wizard ▶ noun **1** *the wizard had cast a spell over them* **sorcerer**, warlock, male witch, magus, (black) magician, necromancer, occultist, enchanter; *Irish* pishogue; *archaic* mage; *rare* thaumaturge, thaumaturgist.
2 *a financial wizard* **genius**, expert, master, adept, virtuoso, maestro, past master, marvel, prodigy; star; *German* wunderkind; *informal* hotshot, demon, wiz, whizz, whizz-kid, buff, old hand, pro, ace, something else, something to shout about, something to write home about; *Brit. informal* dab hand; *N. Amer. informal* maven, crackerjack; *rare* proficient.
OPPOSITES beginner, amateur; duffer.

wizened ▶ adjective *his wizened face* **wrinkled**, lined, creased, shrivelled (up), withered, weather-beaten, thin, shrunken, gnarled, dried up, worn, wasted; *literary* sear.

wobble ▶ verb **1** *the table wobbled and milk spilled over the edge of her bowl* **rock**, move unsteadily, jiggle, sway, see-saw, teeter; shake, vibrate.
2 *he got up and wobbled across to the door* **teeter**, totter, stagger, walk unsteadily, lurch.
3 *her voice wobbled and she felt close to tears* **tremble**, shake, quiver, quaver, waver; *rare* quave.
4 *for a few days the prime minister wobbled* **waver**, **hesitate**, vacillate, dither, shilly-shally, be undecided, be uncertain, be indecisive, be unable to make up one's mind, keep changing one's mind, yo-yo; *Scottish* swither; *informal* blow hot and cold.
▶ noun **1** *Mimi stood up with a slight wobble* **unsteady movement**, totter, teeter, sway; rocking, swaying, shaking.
2 *the operatic wobble in her voice* **tremor**, quiver, quaver, shaking, trembling; *technical* vibrato.

wobbly ▶ adjective **1** *a wobbly table* **unsteady**, unstable, shaky, rocky, rickety; flimsy, frail, spindly, unsafe, precarious, insecure; uneven, unbalanced; *informal* teetery; *Brit. informal* wonky, dicky.
OPPOSITES stable, steady.
2 *her legs were still a bit wobbly* **shaky**, trembling, shaking, tremulous, quivering, quivery, doddery, unsteady; *informal* trembly.
3 *I must sit down—I feel so wobbly* **faint**, **dizzy**, light-headed, giddy; weak, weak-kneed, weak at the knees, quivery, unsteady, groggy, muzzy; *informal* trembly, all of a tremble, all of a quiver, like jelly, with rubbery legs, woozy; *rare* vertiginous.

woe ▶ noun **1** *she launched into another tale of woe* **misery**, sorrow, distress, wretchedness, sadness, unhappiness, heartache, heartbreak, despondency, desolation, despair, dejection, depression, gloom, melancholy; **adversity**, misfortune, disaster, affliction, suffering, hardship, pain, agony, grief, anguish, torment; *literary* dolour.
OPPOSITES happiness, joy.
2 *the company's recent financial woes* **trouble**, difficulty, problem, trial, tribulation, burden, cross to bear, misfortune, stroke of bad luck, setback, reverse, blow, misadventure, mishap, vicissitude, failure, accident, disaster, tragedy, catastrophe, calamity, adversity, affliction.

woebegone ▶ adjective *her woebegone expression* **sad**, unhappy, miserable, dejected, disconsolate, forlorn, crestfallen, sorry for oneself, hangdog, abject, downcast, glum, gloomy, doleful, downhearted, despondent, melancholy, sorrowful, mournful, woeful, lugubrious, long-faced, depressed, despairing, desolate, wretched; tearful; *informal* down in the mouth, down in the dumps, blue; *literary* dolorous; *archaic* chap-fallen.
OPPOSITES cheerful, happy.

woeful ▶ adjective **1** *her face was woeful* **sad**, unhappy, miserable, woebegone, doleful, forlorn, crestfallen, glum, gloomy, dejected, downcast, disconsolate, downhearted, despondent, depressed, despairing, dismal, melancholy, broken-hearted, heartbroken, inconsolable, grief-stricken; *informal* blue, down in the mouth, down in the dumps.
OPPOSITES happy, cheerful.
2 *a woeful tale of broken romance* **tragic**, sad, saddening, unhappy, sorrowful, miserable, cheerless, wretched, sorry, pitiful, pathetic, pitiable, gloomy, grievous, traumatic, upsetting, depressing, distressing, heartbreaking, heart-rending, tear-jerking, agonizing, harrowing; *rare* distressful.
OPPOSITES uplifting, cheerful.
3 *the team's woeful midweek performance* **dreadful**, very bad, awful, terrible, frightful, atrocious, disgraceful, deplorable, shameful, hopeless, lamentable, laughable, substandard, poor, inadequate, inferior, unsatisfactory; *informal* rotten, appalling, crummy, pathetic, pitiful, useless, lousy, shocking, abysmal, dire, the pits; *Brit. informal* duff, chronic, rubbish, pants, a load of pants, poxy; *N. Amer. vulgar slang* chickenshit.
OPPOSITE excellent.

wolf *See centre pages for list of* **Dogs** *(wild dogs)*
▶ noun (*informal*) *he's a bit of a wolf* **womanizer**, Casanova, Romeo, Don Juan, Lothario, flirt, ladies' man, playboy, philanderer, seducer, rake, roué, libertine, debauchee; *informal* skirt-chaser, ladykiller, goat; *informal, dated* gay dog.
▶ verb *he wolfed down his breakfast* **devour greedily**, gobble (up), guzzle, gulp down, bolt, cram down, gorge oneself with; *informal* pack away, demolish, shovel down, stuff one's face with, stuff oneself with, pig oneself on, pig out on, sink, scoff (down), put away, get outside of; *Brit. informal* gollop, shift; *N. Amer. informal* scarf (down/up), snarf (down/up), inhale; *rare* ingurgitate.
OPPOSITES nibble, pick at.

WORD LINKS

male	**dog**
female	**bitch**
young	**cub**
relating to wolves	**lupine**
collective noun	**pack**

wolfish ▶ adjective *he gave her a wolfish grin* **lascivious**, lecherous, lustful, leering; **predatory**, greedy, rapacious.

woman ▶ noun **1** *a car drew up and two women got out* **lady**, girl, member of the fair/gentle sex, female; matron, dowager; *Scottish & N. English* lass, lassie; *Irish* colleen; *informal* chick, girlie, filly, biddy; *Brit. informal* bird, bint, popsy; *Scottish & N. English informal* besom, wifie; *N. Amer. informal* dame, broad, gal, jane; *Austral./NZ informal* sheila; *black English* bitch, sister; *Brit. informal, dated* Judy; *N. Amer. informal, dated* frail; *derogatory* piece, bit, mare, baggage; *literary* maid, maiden, damsel, demoiselle; *archaic or humorous* wench; *archaic* gentlewoman, petticoat.
2 *apparently he's found himself a new woman* **girlfriend**, girl, sweetheart, partner, significant other, inamorata, fiancée; wife, spouse, helpmate, helpmeet, consort; lover, mistress, paramour; *informal* bird, fancy woman, old lady, missus, missis, better half, other half, POSSLQ (person of the opposite sex sharing living quarters), queen; *Brit. informal* Dutch, her indoors; *Irish informal* mot; *N. Amer. informal* squeeze, patootie; *Austral. informal* dona; *Indian informal* bibi; *Brit. rhyming slang* trouble and strife; *dated* lady friend, lady love, young lady, lady, lady wife; *archaic* leman, doxy, concubine.
3 *her daily woman was due to arrive any minute* **cleaning woman**, cleaner, domestic help, domestic, maid; *Brit. dated* charwoman, char; *Brit. informal* daily, Mrs Mop.

WORD LINKS

relating to women	**female, feminine**
related prefixes	**gyn(o)- (e.g. *gynocentric*), gynaeco-**
branch of medicine concerning women	**gynaecology**
fear of women	**gynophobia**
hatred of women	**misogyny**
rule by women	**gynaecocracy, gynarchy**

> CHOOSE THE RIGHT WORD
>
> **woman, girl, lady**
>
> - **Woman** is the most commonly neutral word for an adult female person, but can be insulting when used to address a woman directly (*don't be daft, woman!*) or when referring to a man's girlfriend or wife (*he wondered whether Billy had his woman with him*).
> - **Girl** is considered by some women to be patronizing when used by a man to describe a grown woman, especially in a role that could equally be taken by a man (*the girl in the ticket office*). On the other hand, it can be used acceptably by other women, in certain phrases (*a girls' night out*), or of a man's girlfriend (*you're my girl now, aren't you?*).
> - **Lady** used to be the standard polite word but is now slightly formal or dated, as in *the lady at the travel agency* or when used of a man's wife (*the Colonel and his lady*). It can be complimentary, meaning a courteous, decorous, or genteel woman (*his wife was a real lady, with such nice manners*).

womanhood ▶ noun **1** *she was on the brink of womanhood* **adulthood**, maturity; *rare* muliebrity.

2 *Mary was considered to be an ideal of womanhood* **womanliness**, femininity, feminineness, womanly/feminine qualities.
3 *the Western media stereotype of Soviet womanhood* **women**, womenfolk; womankind, womenkind, woman; the female sex.

womanish ▶ adjective *his high womanish voice* **effeminate**, effete, unmanly, unmasculine, girlish, namby-pamby; *informal* sissy, girly, camp, limp-wristed; *rare* epicene, emasculate.
OPPOSITES manly, macho.

womanizer ▶ noun **philanderer**, Casanova, Don Juan, Romeo, Lothario, flirt, ladies' man, playboy, seducer, rake, roué, libertine, debauchee, lecher; *informal* skirt-chaser, ladykiller, wolf, goat, lech; *informal, dated* gay dog.

womankind ▶ noun **women**, the female sex, womenkind, womanhood, womenfolk, woman.

womanly ▶ adjective **1** *her womanly virtues* **feminine**, female; *archaic* feminal.
OPPOSITE masculine.
2 *the womanly curves of her hips and thighs* **voluptuous**, curvaceous, shapely, ample, opulent, full-figured, well formed, well proportioned, Junoesque, Rubensesque, buxom, full-bosomed, lush, luscious; *informal* curvy, busty.
OPPOSITE boyish.

womb ▶ noun
WORD LINKS
related prefix **hyster(o)-**
surgical removal of womb **hysterectomy**

wonder ▶ noun **1** *the sight left her speechless with wonder* **awe**, admiration, wonderment, fascination; surprise, astonishment, amazement.
2 *the wonders of nature* **marvel**, miracle, phenomenon, wonderful thing, sensation, sight, spectacle, beauty; curiosity, rarity, nonpareil.
▶ verb **1** *I began to wonder what was going through her mind* **ponder**, ask oneself, think about, meditate on, reflect on, deliberate about, muse on, speculate about, conjecture; puzzle about, be curious about, be inquisitive about; *informal* cudgel one's brains about.
2 *I wonder you were so patient with him* **be surprised**, express surprise, find it surprising, be astonished/amazed.
3 *people stood by and wondered at such bravery* **marvel**, be amazed, be filled with amazement, be filled with admiration, be astonished, be surprised, be awed, stand in awe, be full of wonder, be lost for words, not believe one's eyes/ears, not know what to say, be dumbfounded, gape, goggle, gawk; *informal* be flabbergasted, boggle.

wonderful ▶ adjective *I've had a wonderful evening* **marvellous**, magnificent, superb, glorious, sublime, lovely, delightful, first-class, first-rate; *informal* super, great, smashing, amazing, fantastic, terrific, tremendous, sensational, incredible, heavenly, gorgeous, dreamy, grand, fabulous, fab, fabby, fantabulous, awesome, magic, ace, cool, mean, bad, wicked, mega, crucial, mind-blowing, far out, A1, sound, out of this world, marvy, spanking; *Brit. informal* brilliant, brill; *N. Amer. informal* peachy, dandy, jim-dandy, neat, badass, boss, radical, rad, boffo, bully, bitching, bodacious; *Austral./NZ informal* beaut, bonzer; *S. African informal* kif, lank; *black English* dope, def, phat; *informal, dated* groovy, divine; *Brit. informal, dated* capital, champion, wizard, corking, cracking, ripping, spiffing, top-hole, topping, beezer; *N. Amer. informal, dated* swell, keen; *literary* wondrous; *archaic* goodly.
OPPOSITES awful, dreadful.

wonky ▶ adjective (*Brit. informal*) **1** *a wonky nose* **crooked**, off-centre, lopsided, askew, skew; *Brit. informal* skew-whiff.
OPPOSITE straight.
2 *wonky stools* **wobbly**, unsteady, unstable, shaky, rocky; *Irish* bockety.
OPPOSITE stable.

wont ▶ adjective *he was wont to arise at 5.30 every morning* **accustomed**, used, given, inclined; in the habit of.
▶ noun *Paul, as was his wont, was driving far too fast* **custom**, habit, way, practice, convention, routine, use, rule.

wonted ▶ adjective *McTeague had relapsed into his wonted stolidity* **customary**, habitual, usual, accustomed, familiar, normal, conventional, traditional; routine, regular, common, frequent, daily.

woo ▶ verb **1** *Richard wooed Joan with single-minded persistence* **court**, pay court to, pursue, chase, chase after, run after; *dated* romance, seek the hand of, press one's suit with, set one's cap at, make love to; *archaic* spark.
2 *the party wooed voters with promises of electoral reform* **seek the support of**, seek the favour of, try to win, try to attract, try to cultivate, chase, pursue, try to ingratiate oneself with, curry favour with.
3 *an attempt to woo Green out of his semi-retirement* **entice**, tempt, coax, persuade, wheedle; *informal* sweet-talk, smooth-talk.

wood *See centre pages for list of* **Forests**
▶ noun **1** *a table made of dark polished wood* **timber**, planks, planking; *N. Amer.* lumber.
2 *Bob fetched wood and lit a fire* **firewood**, kindling, logs; fuel.
3 *a short walk through the pine woods* **forest**, woodland, trees; copse, thicket, coppice, grove, brake; plantation; *Brit.* spinney; *archaic* holt, greenwood; *rare* boscage.
WORD LINKS
relating to wood **ligneous**
farming of wood **agroforestry, arboriculture, forestry, silviculture**

wooded ▶ adjective *a wooded valley* **forested**, afforested, tree-covered, woody; *literary* sylvan, bosky, tree-clad; *rare* timbered.

wooden ▶ adjective **1** *the heavy wooden door* **made of wood**, wood, timber, woody; ligneous; *rare* treen.
2 *wooden acting* **stilted**, stiff, unnatural, clumsy, awkward, graceless, inelegant, ungainly, leaden; dry, flat, stodgy, lifeless, lacking vitality, passionless, unimpassioned, spiritless, soulless.
OPPOSITES lively, flowing.
3 *her eyes were hard and her face wooden* **expressionless**, impassive, poker-faced, devoid of emotion, emotionless, blank, empty, vacant, unresponsive.

woodland ▶ noun *1000 acres of natural woodland* **woods**, wood, forest, trees; *archaic* greenwood; *rare* boscage.

woodwind ▶ noun. *See centre pages for list of* **Wind Instruments**

woodwork ▶ noun **carpentry**, joinery.

wool *See centre pages for list of* **Fabrics and Fibres**
▶ noun *tufts of sheep's wool* **fleece**, hair, coat; *rare* floccus.
□ **pull the wool over someone's eyes** (*informal*) **deceive**, fool, trick, take in, hoodwink, dupe, delude; *informal* lead up the garden path, pull a fast one on, put one over on, bamboozle, con.
WORD LINKS
relating to wool **lanate**

wool-gathering ▶ noun **daydreaming**, dreaming, building castles in the air, building castles in Spain, reverie, musing, abstraction, preoccupation, brown study, distraction, inattention; absent-mindedness, forgetfulness.
OPPOSITES concentration, attentiveness.

woolly ▶ adjective **1** *a woolly hat* **woollen**, made of wool, wool, fleecy.
2 *a sheep's woolly coat* **fleecy**, shaggy, hairy, fluffy; wool-bearing; *rare* flocculent, laniferous, lanigerous.
3 *woolly grey-green foliage* **downy**; *technical* floccose, lanate.
4 *woolly generalizations about economic growth* **vague**, ill-defined, hazy, unclear, unfocused, fuzzy, blurry, foggy, nebulous, imprecise, inexact, indefinite; **confused**, muddled, muddle-headed, disorganized.
OPPOSITE clear.

woozy ▶ adjective (*informal*) *I still felt woozy from all the pills* **light-headed**, dizzy, giddy, faint; unsteady, groggy, wobbly, weak; muzzy, dazed, confused; *informal* dopey, not with it; *rare* vertiginous.
OPPOSITE clear-headed.

word ▶ noun **1** *the Italian word for 'ham'* **term**, name, expression, designation, locution; turn of phrase, idiom; *formal* appellation; *rare* vocable.
2 (usually **words**) *his grandfather's words had been meant kindly* **remark**, comment, statement, utterance, observation, pronouncement, declaration.
3 (**words**) *I've only got three weeks to learn the words* **script**, text; **lyrics**, libretto.
4 *everything will be taken care of—I give you my word* **promise**, word of honour, assurance, guarantee, undertaking; pledge, vow, oath, bond; *archaic* troth, parole.
5 *I want a word with you in private* **talk**, conversation, chat, tête-à-tête, heart-to-heart, one-on-one, one-to-one, head-to-head; discussion, consultation, exchange of views, colloquy; *informal* confab, powwow; *formal* confabulation.
6 *apparently there's no word from the hospital yet* **news**, information, communication, intelligence, notice; message, report, communiqué, dispatch, bulletin, account; data, facts; *informal* info, the gen, the low-down; *N. Amer. informal* the dope, the poop; *literary* tidings; *archaic* advices.
7 *word has it he's turned over a new leaf* **rumour**, hearsay, talk, gossip; *informal* the grapevine, the word on the street; *N. Amer. informal* the scuttlebutt.
8 *I'm waiting for the word from the Department of Justice* **instruction**, order, command; signal, prompt, cue, tip-off; *informal* go-ahead, thumbs up, green light; *N. Amer. informal* high sign.
9 *he was a strict disciplinarian whose word was law* **command**, order, decree, edict, mandate; bidding, will.
10 *our word now must be success* **motto**, slogan, watchword, password, catchword; buzz word.
□ **have words** *it's obvious the two of you have had words* **quarrel**, argue, disagree, row, squabble, bicker, fight, wrangle, dispute, feud, have a row, cross swords, lock horns, clash, be at each other's throats; *informal* fall out, have a tiff, have a spat; *Brit. informal* have a barney; *archaic* altercate.
□ **in a word** *the answer, in a word, is yes* **to put it briefly**, to be brief, briefly,

in short, in a nutshell, succinctly, concisely, to come to the point, to cut a long story short, not to mince words, not to beat about the bush, not to put too fine a point on it; to sum up, to summarize, in sum, in summary.

□ **word for word 1** *reporters took down the speeches word for word* **verbatim**, line for line, letter for letter, to the letter; exactly, precisely, faithfully; *rare* literatim.
2 *a word-for-word translation* **verbatim**, literal, exact, direct, precise, accurate, faithful, strict, undeviating; unadulterated, unabridged, unvarnished, unembellished.
OPPOSITE loose.

▶ **verb** *the question had been carefully worded* **phrase**, express, put, couch, frame, set forth, formulate, style; say, utter, state.

WORD LINKS
relating to words **verbal, lexical**
study of words **lexicology**

wording ▶ **noun** *the wording of the question was ambiguous* **phrasing**, phraseology, choice of words, words, language, mode of expression, expression, terminology, diction.

wordplay ▶ **noun** **punning**, puns, double entendres, play on words; wit, witticisms, repartee; *rare* paronomasia.

wordy ▶ **adjective** *a wordy speech* **long-winded**, **verbose**, prolix, full of verbiage, lengthy, protracted, long-drawn-out, diffuse, discursive, rambling, digressive, maundering, circumlocutory, periphrastic, repetitious, tautological, tortuous; loquacious, garrulous, voluble; *informal* windy; *Brit. informal* waffly; *rare* pleonastic, logorrhoeic, ambagious.
OPPOSITES concise, succinct.

work ▶ **noun 1** *he was tired after a day's work in the fields* **labour**, toil, exertion, effort, slog, drudgery, the sweat of one's brow; industry; service; *informal* grind, sweat, donkey work, spadework, elbow grease; *Brit. informal* graft, fag; *Austral./NZ informal* yakka; *archaic* travail, moil.
OPPOSITES leisure, rest.
2 *I'm still looking for work | his work takes him to France, Spain, and Germany* **employment**, a job, a post, a position, a situation, a means of earning one's living; occupation, profession, career, business, trade, line; vocation, calling; *archaic* employ.
3 *haven't you got any work to do?* **tasks**, jobs, duties, assignments, commissions, projects; chores.
4 *one of the best works of modern English literature* **composition**, piece, creation, achievement, accomplishment; work of art, opus, oeuvre.
5 *the shooting was the work of a radical left-wing group* **handiwork**, doing, act, deed, feat, performance.
6 (**works**) *a lifetime spent doing good works* **deeds**, acts, actions.
7 (**works**) *the complete works of Shakespeare* **writings**, oeuvre, canon, output.
8 (**works**) *the site of a former car works* **factory**, plant, manufacturing complex, mill, foundry, yard, industrial unit; workshop, shop.
9 (**works**) *the works of a clock* **mechanism**, machinery, workings, working parts, parts, movement, action; *informal* innards, insides.
10 (**the works**) (*informal*) *for only $60 you can get the works* **everything**, the full treatment; *informal* everything but the kitchen sink, the lot, the whole shooting match, the whole (kit and) caboodle, the whole shebang, the whole nine yards; *Brit. informal* the full monty; *N. Amer. informal* the whole ball of wax.

▶ **verb 1** *staff worked late into the night to make the necessary repairs* **toil**, labour, exert oneself, slave (away), plod away; work one's fingers to the bone, work like a Trojan/dog, work day and night, keep at it, keep one's nose to the grindstone; *informal* slog (away), beaver away, plug away, peg away, put one's back into something, work one's guts out, work one's socks off, knock oneself out, sweat blood, kill oneself; *Brit. informal* graft, fag; *Austral./NZ informal* bullock; *Brit. vulgar slang* work one's balls/arse off; *N. Amer. vulgar slang* work one's ass/butt off; *archaic* drudge, travail, moil.
OPPOSITES rest, play.
2 *Taylor has worked in education for 17 years* **be employed**, have a job, earn one's living, hold down a job, do business, follow/ply one's trade.
3 *many farmers had given up working the land* **cultivate**, farm, till, plough.
4 *Dino's car was now working perfectly* **function**, go, run, operate, perform; be in working order; *informal* behave.
5 *she showed me how to work the ice-cream machine* **operate**, use, handle, control, manipulate, manoeuvre, drive, run, direct; ply, wield.
6 *their desperate ploy had worked* **succeed**, be successful, work out, turn out well, go as planned, have the desired result, get results; be effective, take effect, be efficacious; *informal* come off, pay off, do the trick, do the business; *N. Amer. informal* turn the trick.
OPPOSITE fail.
7 *with a dash of blusher you can work miracles* **bring about**, accomplish, achieve, produce, do, perform, carry out, implement, execute, create, engender, contrive, effect.
8 (*informal*) *the chairman was prepared to work it for Philip if he was interested* **arrange**, manipulate, manoeuvre, contrive; pull strings; *N. Amer.* pull wires; *informal* fix, swing, wangle, fiddle.
9 *he worked the crowd into a frenzy* **stir (up)**, excite, drive, move, spur, rouse, fire, galvanize; whip up, inflame, incite, agitate.
10 *work the mixture into a paste* **knead**, squeeze, form, shape, fashion, mould, model; mix, stir, blend.
11 *he worked the blade into the padlock* **manoeuvre**, manipulate, negotiate, guide, edge.
12 *Bella's mouth worked furiously for a few seconds* **twitch**, quiver, twist, move spasmodically, convulse.
13 *John had worked his way through the crowd* **manoeuvre**, make, thread, wind, weave.

□ **work on someone** *leave him to me—I'll work on him* **persuade**, **manipulate**, influence, sway, put pressure on, lean on; coax, cajole, wheedle, soften up; *informal* twist someone's arm, put the squeeze on.

□ **work out 1** *the bill works out at £50* **amount to**, add up to, come to, total; *Brit.* tot up to.
2 *I'm glad my idea worked out* **succeed**, be successful, work, turn out well, go as planned, get results, be effective; *informal* come off, pay off, do the trick, do the business.
OPPOSITE fail.
3 *things didn't quite work out the way she had planned* **end up**, turn out, go, come out, develop, evolve, result; happen, occur; *informal* pan out.
4 *Bob keeps in shape by working out at the local gym* **exercise**, do exercises, train.

□ **work something out 1** *work out how much you can afford to spend* **calculate**, compute, reckon up, determine.
2 *I'm still trying to work out what she meant* **understand**, comprehend, puzzle out, sort out, reason out, make sense of, think out, think through, get to the bottom of, make head or tail of, solve, find an answer/solution to, unravel, untangle, decipher, decode, find the key to, piece together; *informal* figure out, crack; *Brit. informal* suss out.
3 *they worked out a plan of action* **devise**, formulate, draw up, put together, develop, prepare, construct, arrange, organize, plan, think up, contrive, concoct; hammer out, thrash out, reach an agreement on, negotiate.

□ **work something up** *he couldn't seem to work up any enthusiasm* **stimulate**, rouse, raise, arouse, awaken, excite, build up, whet; develop, produce.

WORD LINKS
fear of work **ergophobia**

CHOOSE THE RIGHT WORD

work, labour, toil

- **Work** is the general term for things that one has to do in order to earn a living or to achieve a particular aim (*she did clerical work before she married | work on landscaping the disused railway line was started in 1980*). When applied to the actual doing of these things, *work* implies that effort is involved (*thank you for your hard work on the project*). As a verb, the word means simply to carry out any kind of such activity (*a man was working in the garden*).
- **Labour** typically denotes physical work, especially when this is hard and exhausting (*manual labour | exhausted by labour in the fields*). To *labour* is to work hard (*they laboured from dawn to dusk*) or to have difficulty in doing something in spite of working hard (*the media group is currently labouring to reduce its debt mountain*).
- **Toil**, as a noun or a verb, refers to exhausting, tedious, and seemingly unending hard work (*most of the poet's life was spent in toil on the farm | the clerks sat toiling into the night over some urgent piece of business*). To *toil* in a stated direction means to struggle to move somewhere (*she toiled up the path with her packages*).

workable ▶ **adjective** *a workable solution to the problem* **practicable**, **feasible**, viable, possible, within the bounds/realms of possibility, achievable, accomplishable; realistic, reasonable, sensible, practical; *informal* doable.
OPPOSITES unworkable, impracticable, impossible.

workaday ▶ **adjective** *workaday prose | her workaday life* **ordinary**, average, run-of-the-mill, middle-of-the-road, mainstream, conventional, unremarkable, unexceptional, unpretentious, plain, simple, undistinguished, nondescript, characterless, colourless, commonplace, humdrum, mundane, unmemorable, unspectacular, pedestrian, prosaic; routine, everyday, day-to-day, quotidian; *N. Amer.* garden-variety; *informal* bog-standard, vanilla, plain vanilla, nothing to write home about, a dime a dozen; *Brit. informal* common or garden, two a penny; *N. Amer. informal* ornery.
OPPOSITES extraordinary, exceptional.

worker *See centre pages for list of* **Agricultural Workers**
▶ **noun 1** *an unofficial strike by 500 workers at the factory* **employee**, member of staff, working man, working woman, workman, labourer, hand, operative, operator; blue-collar worker, white-collar worker; proletarian; artisan, journeyman, craftsman, craftswoman; wage-earner, breadwinner; *archaic* mechanical.
2 (*informal*) *I got a reputation for being a worker* **hard worker**, toiler, workhorse, Stakhanovite; *informal* busy bee, eager beaver, workaholic; *N. Amer. informal* wheel horse, wonk.

workforce ▶ noun **employees**, staff, personnel, human resources; **workers**, labour force, manpower; *humorous* liveware.

working ▶ adjective **1** *childcare for working mothers* **employed**, in work, in a job, waged, in gainful employment.
OPPOSITES unemployed, out of work.
2 *the mill still has a working waterwheel* **functioning**, operating, going, running, active; in working order, operational, functional, able to function, usable, serviceable; *informal* up and running.
OPPOSITES broken, faulty.
3 *a working knowledge of contract law* **sufficient**, adequate, good enough, viable; useful, effective.
▶ noun **1** *the working of a carburettor* **functioning**, operation, running, action, performance.
2 (**workings**) *the workings of a pocket watch* **mechanism**, machinery, working/moving parts, movement, action, works; *informal* innards, insides.

workman ▶ noun **worker**, manual worker, labourer, hand, operative, operator; employee; journeyman, artisan; *Indian* maistry.

workmanlike ▶ adjective *the team put up a good, workmanlike performance* **efficient**, competent, satisfactory; professional, proficient, skilled, skilful, adept, masterly.
OPPOSITE amateurish.

workmanship ▶ noun **craftsmanship**, artistry, craft, art, artisanship, handiwork, work; **skill**, skilfulness, technique, expertise.

workout ▶ noun **exercise session**, keep-fit session, physical training session, drill; warm-up, limbering up; exercises, aerobics, isometrics, gymnastics, callisthenics; *informal, dated* daily dozen.

workshop *See centre pages for list of* **Factories and Workshops**
▶ noun **1** *a car repair workshop* **factory**, works, plant; shop, industrial unit; garage.
2 *the craftsmen worked in a freezing cold workshop* **workroom**, studio, atelier.
3 *a workshop on 'Combating Job Stress'* **study group**, discussion group, seminar, class.

world ▶ noun **1** *he travelled the world with the army* **earth**, globe, planet, sphere.
2 *he was convinced of the possibility of life on other worlds* **planet**, satellite, moon, star, heavenly body, orb.
3 *the academic world | the world of work is not where all her life ambitions lie* **sphere**, society, circle, arena, milieu, province, domain, territory, orbit, preserve, realm, field, discipline, area, department, sector, section, group, division.
4 (**the world**) *she would show the world that she was no weak-kneed lady of leisure* **everyone**, everybody, each and every one, people, mankind, humankind, humanity, people everywhere, the whole world, the world at large, the public, the general public, the population, the populace, all and sundry, every mother's son, {every Tom, Dick, and Harry}, every man jack.
5 *there's a world of difference between the two men* **huge amount**, vast amount, enormous amount, good deal, great deal, abundance, wealth, profusion, mountain, immensity; many, much, plenty, reams; *informal* heap, pile, lot, load, stack, ton, masses; *Brit. informal* shedload, lashings; *Austral./NZ informal* swag.
OPPOSITE very little.
6 *she renounced the world and became a nun* **society**, high society; secular interests, temporal concerns, earthly concerns; human existence.
□ **on top of the world** (*informal*) See OVERJOYED.
□ **out of this world** (*informal*) *her breakfasts are out of this world.* See WONDERFUL.

WORD LINKS
relating to the whole world **mondial**

worldly ▶ adjective **1** *his youth was being wasted on worldly and dissolute pursuits* **earthly**, terrestrial, temporal, mundane, mortal, human, non-spiritual, unspiritual, material, materialistic, physical, tangible, carnal, fleshly, bodily, corporeal, gross, sensual, base, sordid, vile, profane; secular, lay, non-church, non-religious; *rare* sublunary, terrene, laic.
OPPOSITE spiritual.
2 *a charming worldly man* **sophisticated**, experienced, worldly-wise, knowledgeable, knowing, aware, enlightened, shrewd, astute, perceptive, mature, seasoned, cosmopolitan, urbane, cultivated, cultured, unprovincial; *informal* having been around.
OPPOSITES naive, unsophisticated.

worldly-wise ▶ adjective *Lisa was sufficiently worldly-wise to understand the situation* **sophisticated**, **experienced**, worldly, knowledgeable, knowing, aware, enlightened, shrewd, astute, perceptive, mature, seasoned, cosmopolitan, urbane, cultivated, cultured, unprovincial; *informal* having been around.
OPPOSITES naive, unsophisticated.

worldwide ▶ adjective *a worldwide effort to stop the spread of AIDS* **global**, international, intercontinental, world, universal, planetary, pandemic; general, common, ubiquitous, extensive, widespread, far-reaching, wide-ranging, all-embracing, across the board.
OPPOSITES local, restricted.

worm ▶ noun. *See centre pages for list of* **Worms**

WORD LINKS

related prefix	**vermi-**
worm-shaped	**vermiform**
worm-eating	**vermivorous**
substance used to kill worms	**vermicide**
fear of worms	**helminthophobia**

worn ▶ adjective **1** *his hat was old and worn* **shabby**, well worn, worn out, worn to shreds, threadbare, tattered, in tatters, in ribbons, in rags, in holes, holey, falling to pieces, falling apart at the seams, ragged, frayed, patched, moth-eaten, faded, seedy, shoddy, sorry, scruffy, dilapidated, crumbling, broken-down, run down, tumbledown, decrepit, deteriorated, on its last legs, having seen better days, time-worn; *informal* tatty, ratty, the worse for wear, clapped out; *Brit. informal* grotty; *N. Amer. informal* raggedy, raggedy-ass; *Austral./NZ informal* warby; *literary* rent.
OPPOSITES new, smart.
2 *her face looked tired and worn* **strained**, drawn, drained, worn out, fatigued, tired, tired out, exhausted, weary, wearied, wan, sapped, spent, careworn, haggard, hollow-cheeked, hollow-eyed, gaunt, pinched, pale, peaky, pasty-faced, washed out, ashen, blanched; *informal* worn to a frazzle, all in, done in, dog-tired, dead on one's feet, dead beat, fit to drop, played out, fagged out, shattered, bushed; *Brit. informal* knackered, whacked; *N. Amer. informal* pooped, tuckered out.
OPPOSITES fresh, energetic.

worn out ▶ adjective **1** *he wore old jeans and a worn-out shirt* **shabby**, well worn, worn, worn to shreds, threadbare, tattered, in tatters, in ribbons, in rags, in holes, holey, falling to pieces, falling apart at the seams, ragged, frayed, patched, moth-eaten, faded, seedy, shoddy, sorry, scruffy, dilapidated, crumbling, broken-down, run down, tumbledown, decrepit, deteriorated, on its last legs, having seen better days, time-worn; *informal* tatty, ratty, the worse for wear, clapped out; *Brit. informal* grotty; *N. Amer. informal* raggedy, raggedy-ass; *Austral./NZ informal* warby; *literary* rent.
OPPOSITES new, smart.
2 *they were slogging away and looked pretty well worn out* **exhausted**, fatigued, tired, tired out, weary, wearied, strained, drained, worn, drawn, wan, sapped, spent, careworn, haggard, hollow-cheeked, hollow-eyed, gaunt, pinched, pale, peaky, pasty-faced, washed out, ashen, blanched; *informal* worn to a frazzle, all in, done in, dog-tired, dead on one's feet, dead beat, fit to drop, played out, fagged out, shattered, bushed; *Brit. informal* knackered, whacked, jiggered; *N. Amer. informal* pooped, tuckered out; *rare* fordone.
OPPOSITES fresh, energetic.
3 *they portrayed the opposition as the party of worn-out ideas* **obsolete**, antiquated, old, well worn, stale, time-worn, hackneyed, banal, trite, overused, overworked, stereotyped, clichéd, unoriginal, unimaginative, commonplace, common, pedestrian, prosaic, run-of-the-mill, stock, conventional; *informal* played out, corny, old hat.
OPPOSITE fresh.

worried ▶ adjective *they kept their fingers crossed but they weren't too worried* **anxious**, disturbed, perturbed, troubled, bothered, distressed, concerned, upset, distraught, worried sick, disquieted, uneasy, ill at ease, fretful, fretting, agitated, in a state of agitation, nervous, edgy, on edge, like a cat on a hot tin roof, tense, overwrought, worked up, keyed up, strung out, jumpy, with one's stomach in knots, stressed, under stress; distracted, apprehensive, fearful, afraid, frightened, scared, with one's heart in one's mouth, quaking, trembling, shaking in one's shoes, in a cold sweat; *informal* uptight, a bundle of nerves, on tenterhooks, with butterflies in one's stomach, hassled, jittery, twitchy, in a state, wired, in a stew, in a dither, all of a dither, in a flap, in a sweat, in a tizz/tizzy, all of a lather, het up, in a twitter, rattled; *Brit. informal* strung up, windy, having kittens; *N. Amer. informal* antsy, spooky, spooked, squirrelly, in a twit; *Austral./NZ informal* toey; *Brit. vulgar slang* shitting bricks, bricking oneself; *dated* overstrung, unquiet.
OPPOSITES carefree, calm, unconcerned.

worrisome ▶ adjective *the most worrisome of all environmental threats* **worrying**, daunting, alarming, perturbing, trying, taxing, vexatious, niggling, bothersome, troublesome, unsettling, harassing, harrying, harrowing, nerve-racking, distressing, dismaying, disquieting, upsetting, traumatic, unpleasant, awkward, difficult, tricky, thorny, problematic, grave; *informal* scary, hairy, sticky, prickly, anxious-making.

worry ▶ verb **1** *she worries about his blood pressure* **fret**, be worried, be concerned, be anxious, agonize, brood, dwell on, panic, get in a panic, lose sleep, get worked up, get in a fluster, get overwrought, be on tenterhooks; *informal* have butterflies in one's stomach, get stressed, get in a flap, get in a state, get in a tizz/tizzy, get in a sweat, sweat, get steamed up, get in a lather, stew, torture oneself, torment oneself; *Brit. informal* be in a blue funk.
2 *I can see that something is worrying you* **trouble**, bother, cause anxiety, make anxious, disturb, distress, upset, concern, disquiet, discompose, fret, agitate, unsettle, perturb, frighten, alarm, scare, fluster, flurry, stress, strain, tax, harass, torment, plague, bedevil, besiege, irk, vex; prey on one's mind, weigh heavily on one's mind, weigh down, oppress,

burden, be a great weight on, lie heavy on, gnaw at; *informal* hassle, give someone a hard time, throw, faze, rattle, bug, get to, do someone's head in, discombobulate; *N. Amer. informal* mess with someone's head.
3 *a dog was worrying his sheep* **attack**, savage, maul, mutilate, mangle, go for, tear at, tear to pieces, claw, bite, gnaw at, lacerate, shake, pull at; molest, torment, persecute.
▶ **noun 1** *I'm beside myself with worry* **anxiety**, disturbance, perturbation, trouble, bother, distress, concern, care, upset, uneasiness, unease, disquiet, disquietude, disconcertment, fretfulness, restlessness, nervousness, nerves, agitation, edginess, tension, tenseness, stress, strain; apprehension, fear, fearfulness, dread, foreboding, trepidation, misgiving, angst; *informal* butterflies (in the stomach), the willies, the heebie-jeebies, the shakes, the jumps, jitteriness, twitchiness.
2 *the rats are a worry because they can contaminate food* **problem**, cause for concern; nuisance, pest, plague, trial, tribulation, trouble, irritation, irritant, vexation, bane, bugbear, thorn in one's flesh/side, burden, cross, cross to bear; *informal* pain, pain in the neck, headache, hassle, stress.

worrying ▶ **adjective** *their financial situation was very worrying* **alarming**, worrisome, daunting, perturbing, trying, taxing, vexatious, niggling, bothersome, troublesome, unsettling, harassing, harrying, harrowing, nerve-racking; distressing, dismaying, disquieting, upsetting, traumatic, unpleasant, awkward, difficult, tricky, thorny, problematic, grave; *informal* scary, hairy, sticky, prickly, anxious-making.

worsen ▶ **verb 1** *insomnia can considerably worsen a patient's distress* **aggravate**, **exacerbate**, make worse, compound, add to, intensify, increase, magnify, heighten, inflame, augment; *informal* add fuel to the fire/flames, put salt on the wound.
OPPOSITES improve, ameliorate.
2 *the economic recession continued to worsen* **deteriorate**, degenerate, decline, get/grow/become worse, take a turn for the worse, weaken; sink, slip, slide, slump, fall off, ebb, wane, lapse, regress, retrogress; *informal* go downhill, go to pot, go to the dogs, go down the toilet, go down the tubes, hit the skids, nosedive, take a nosedive.
OPPOSITES improve, recover.

worship *See centre pages for list of* **Places of Worship**
▶ **noun 1** *the new Church rejected the worship of saints and relics* **reverence**, revering, worshipping, veneration, venerating, adoration, adoring, -olatry, devotion, praise, thanksgiving, praising, praying to, glorification, glorifying, glory, exaltation, exalting, extolment, extolling, homage, respect, honour, honouring, esteem; *Roman Catholic Church* dulia, latria; *rare* laudation, magnification.
2 *morning worship* **service**, church service, religious rite, religious act, prayer, prayer meeting, praise, devotion, religious observance; matins, morning prayer, vespers, evening prayer, evensong.
3 *he contemplated the pin-up with worship* **admiration**, adulation, idolization, deification, lionization, hero-worship.
▶ **verb** *they do not worship pagan gods | the ladies worshipped their brother* **revere**, reverence, venerate, pay homage to, honour, adore, praise, pray to, bow down before, glorify, exalt, extol; **be devoted to**, dote on, love, hold dear, cherish, treasure, admire, esteem, adulate, idolize, deify, hero-worship, lionize, have a high regard for, hold in high regard, hold in esteem, hold in awe, look up to; *informal* be wild about, put on a pedestal; *archaic* magnify; *rare* laud.
OPPOSITES loathe, despise.

worst ▶ **verb** *they were worsted by a large and desperate band of armed malefactors* **defeat**, beat, best, get the better of, gain the advantage over, prevail over, triumph over, gain a victory over, trounce, rout, thrash, drub, vanquish, conquer, master, overcome, overwhelm, overpower, overthrow, crush, subdue, subjugate; outdo, outclass, outstrip, surpass, outwit, outsmart, score points off, make a fool of, humiliate; *informal* lick, clobber, whip, hammer, beat hollow, slaughter, murder, kill, wipe out, do in, crucify, demolish, wipe the floor with, take to the cleaners, walk all over, run rings around, make mincemeat of, blow out of the water, give someone a hiding, get one up on, get one over on; *Brit. informal* stuff; *N. Amer. informal* shellac, blow out, cream, skunk, slam.

worth ▶ **noun 1** *a buyer may require independent evidence of the rug's worth* **value**, financial value, monetary value, price, asking price, selling price, cost; valuation, quotation, estimate, assessment.
2 *the intrinsic worth of education* **benefit**, advantage, use, value, virtue, usefulness, utility, service, gain, profit, avail, validity, help, assistance, aid; desirability, attractiveness, allure, appeal; significance, point, sense; *informal* mileage, percentage; *archaic* behoof.
3 *club members have a sense of belonging and personal worth* **worthiness**, merit, meritoriousness, credit, value, excellence, calibre, quality, stature, eminence, greatness, consequence, importance, significance, distinction, superiority; gifts, talents, strengths, endowments.

worthless ▶ **adjective 1** *the icon turns out to be worthless* **valueless**, of little/no value, of little/no worth, without value, of little/no financial value; rubbishy, trashy, paltry, (of) poor quality, (of) low quality, inferior, second-rate, third-rate, low-grade, cheap, cheap and nasty, shoddy, tawdry, gimcrack; *informal* crummy; *Brit. informal* two a penny, ten a penny, twopenny-halfpenny; *N. Amer. informal* nickel-and-dime.
OPPOSITES valuable, precious.
2 *your conclusions are utterly worthless* **useless**, no use, of no benefit, to no avail, futile, ineffective, ineffectual, fruitless, unproductive, unavailing, pointless, nugatory, valueless, inadequate, deficient, defective, inferior, unsatisfactory, meaningless, senseless, insubstantial, empty, hollow, silly, banal, trifling, petty, inconsequential, lame, paltry, pathetic, piddling; *informal* a dead loss; *archaic* bootless; *rare* unfructuous.
OPPOSITE useful.
3 *he was destroyed by his loyalty to his worthless son* **good-for-nothing**, ne'er-do-well, useless, despicable, contemptible, base, low, vile, abject, debased, degraded, ignominious, mean, corrupt, villainous, depraved, degenerate, wretched, miserable, sorry, shiftless, feckless, incompetent; *informal* no-good, no-account, lousy.

worthwhile ▶ **adjective** *everyone felt that the campaign had been worthwhile | a worthwhile job* **valuable**, of value, worth it, worth the effort, useful, of use, usable, of service, beneficial, rewarding, advantageous, positive, helpful, of help, of assistance, purposeful, profitable, gainful, fruitful, productive, constructive, effective, efficacious, effectual, justifiable, significant, important, substantial, meaningful, worthy; excellent, exemplary, good.
OPPOSITES worthless, useless.

worthy ▶ **adjective** *Samuel was a worthy and responsible citizen | a worthy cause* **virtuous**, good, moral, ethical, principled, high-principled, high-minded, right-thinking, noble, upright, upstanding, righteous, solid, decent, law-abiding, honest, honourable, respectable, respected, venerable, reputable, trustworthy, trusty, trusted, reliable, dependable, conscientious, irreproachable, blameless, unimpeachable, exemplary, admirable, praiseworthy, laudable, commendable, estimable, deserving, meritorious, creditable, sterling; *informal* squeaky clean; *archaic* of good report; *rare* applaudable.
OPPOSITES disreputable, unworthy.
□ **be worthy of** *he believes everyone has ideas that are worthy of attention* **deserve**, be deserving of, merit, warrant, rate, justify, earn, be entitled to, have a right to, have a claim to/on, be qualified for, qualify for.
OPPOSITES be unworthy of, be undeserving of.
▶ **noun** *the candidate gained the support of some significant local worthies* **dignitary**, notable, notability, celebrity, personage, famous person, important person, person of note, luminary, public figure, official, pillar of society, grandee, panjandrum, leading light, name, big name, somebody, someone; *informal* VIP, top brass, Mr Big, big Daddy, big shot, bigwig, big cheese, big fish, big gun, big noise, celeb, biggie, heavy, hotshot; *Brit. informal* Lady Muck, Lord Muck, nob; *N. Amer. informal* big wheel, kahuna, big kahuna, macher, high muckamuck, high muckety-muck.
OPPOSITE nobody.

would-be ▶ **adjective** *would-be actors* **aspiring**, budding, promising, prospective, potential, striving, hopeful, optimistic, keen, eager, ambitious, enterprising, wishful, longing; *informal* wannabe.

wound ▶ **noun 1** *he had a large wound in his chest* **injury**, **lesion**, cut, gash, laceration, tear, rent, puncture, slash; sore, graze, scratch, scrape, abrasion; bruise, contusion; *Medicine* trauma, traumatism.
2 *the wounds inflicted by the media will take a long time to heal* **insult**, blow, slight, offence, affront; hurt, harm, damage, injury, pain, pang, ache, distress, grief, trauma, anguish, torment, torture.
▶ **verb 1** *he was critically wounded in the battle and nearly died | they were wounded by shrapnel* **injure**, hurt, damage, harm, maim, mutilate, disable, incapacitate, cripple, scar; lacerate, cut, cut to ribbons, graze, scratch, gash, tear, tear apart, hack, rip, puncture, pierce, stab, slash; *informal* zap, plug, blast.
OPPOSITE heal.
2 *she could see that her words had wounded him* **hurt**, hurt the feelings of, scar, damage, harm, injure, insult, slight, offend, give offence to, affront, distress, disturb, upset, make miserable, trouble, discomfort; grieve, sadden, mortify, anguish, pain, sting, cut to the quick, shock, traumatize, cause suffering to, torment, torture, crucify, tear to pieces, gnaw at.
OPPOSITE boost.

wraith ▶ **noun** **ghost**, spectre, spirit, phantom, apparition, manifestation, vision, shadow, presence, poltergeist, supernatural being; *Scottish & Irish* bodach; *W. Indian* duppy; *informal* spook; *literary* shade, visitant, revenant, phantasm, wight; *rare* eidolon, manes, lemures.

wrangle ▶ **noun** *a demeaning wrangle over a small amount of money* **argument**, **dispute**, disagreement, quarrel, row, fight, squabble, difference of opinion, altercation, angry exchange, war of words, shouting match, tiff; tussle, brouhaha, fracas, rumpus, brawl, clash, scuffle, battle, war, feud; controversy, uproar; *Irish, N. Amer., & Austral.* donnybrook; *informal* falling-out, set-to, run-in, shindig, shindy, dust-up, punch-up, scrap, spat, free-for-all, argy-bargy, ruckus, fisticuffs, ruction; *Brit. informal* barney, bunfight, ding-dong, bust-up, ruck, slanging match; *Scottish informal* rammy; *N. Amer. informal* rhubarb; *archaic* broil, miff.
OPPOSITE agreement.
▶ **verb** *negotiators had wrangled over details of the agreement* **argue**, quarrel, row, have a row, bicker, squabble, have words, debate, disagree, have a disagreement, have an altercation, be at odds, bandy words; contend,

fight, have a fight, war, battle, feud, clash, grapple, brawl, spar, wrestle, tilt, come to blows, cross swords, lock horns, be at each other's throats, be at loggerheads; *informal* fall out, scrap, go at it hammer and tongs, fight like cat and dog; *rare* altercate, chop logic; *Scottish archaic* threap.
OPPOSITE agree.

CHOOSE THE RIGHT WORD

wrangle, quarrel, argue, dispute, bicker
See QUARREL.

wrap ▶ **verb 1** *Flora got out of the bath and wrapped herself in a towel* **swathe**, bundle up, swaddle, sheathe, muffle, cloak, enfold, envelop, encase, enclose, cover, fold, wind; *literary* lap.
2 *I wrapped the vase carefully in newspaper | he* ***wrapped*** *the book* ***up*** *as a present for her* **parcel up**, parcel, package, pack, pack up, bundle, bundle up, do up, tie up, gift-wrap.
□ **wrap up 1** *wrap up well before you go into that garden* **dress warmly**, wear warm clothes, put on more clothes, muffle up.
2 (*Brit. informal*) *tell that child to wrap up* **be quiet**, quieten down, be silent, fall silent, stop talking, hold one's tongue, keep one's lips sealed; *informal* shut up, shut one's mouth, shut one's face, shut one's trap, button one's lip, put a sock in it, pipe down, belt up, cut the cackle, give it a rest; *Brit. informal* shut one's gob, wrap it up; *N. Amer. informal* save it.
□ **wrap something up** *it was time to wrap up the conference* **conclude**, finish, end, bring to an end, bring to a close, bring to a conclusion, round off, terminate, stop, cease, finalize, complete, settle, tie up, put the finishing touches to; *informal* wind up, sew up, polish off.
▶ **noun** *he put a wrap round her shoulders* **shawl**, stole, cloak, cape, mantle, scarf; *S. American* poncho, serape; *rare* pelisse, pelerine, mantlet.

wrapper ▶ **noun 1** *a sweet wrapper* **cover**, wrapping, covering, packaging, paper; jacket, dust jacket, binding, sheath, sheathing.
2 (*N. Amer.*) *she was lying down in her cotton wrapper* **housecoat**, bathrobe, dressing gown, robe, negligee, kimono; *French* peignoir, robe de chambre.

wrath ▶ **noun** *he hadn't the nerve to face his mother's wrath* **anger**, rage, fury, annoyance, indignation, outrage, pique, spleen, chagrin, vexation, exasperation, dudgeon, high dudgeon, hot temper, bad temper, bad mood, ill humour, irritation, irritability, crossness, displeasure, discontentment, disgruntlement, irascibility, cantankerousness, peevishness, querulousness, crabbiness, testiness, tetchiness, snappishness; *literary* ire, choler.
OPPOSITES happiness, good humour.

wrathful ▶ **adjective** *all at once he grew wrathful, his face purpling* **angry**, irate, raging, enraged, incensed, infuriated, furious, choleric, fuming, ranting, raving, seething, frenzied, in a frenzy, beside oneself, indignant, outraged, vexed, in high dudgeon, exasperated, in a temper, irritated, provoked, piqued, cross, displeased; bad-tempered, hot-tempered, ill-humoured, irascible; *informal* mad, wild, livid, boiling, spare, aerated, hot under the collar, on the warpath, up in arms, with all guns blazing, foaming at the mouth, seeing red, steamed up, fit to be tied; *N. Amer. informal* sore; *literary* ireful.
OPPOSITES calm, good-humoured.

wreak ▶ **verb** *these policies would wreak havoc on the British economy* **inflict**, create, cause, result in, effect, engender, bring about, perpetrate, unleash, vent, bestow, deal out, mete out, serve out, administer, carry out, deliver, apply, lay on, impose, exact; *rare* effectuate.

wreath ▶ **noun** *a delicate wreath of roses* **garland**, chaplet, circlet, coronet, crown, diadem, festoon, lei, swathe, fillet; ring, loop, circle.

wreathe ▶ **verb 1** *the pulpit had been wreathed in holly | their faces were wreathed in ecstatic smiles* **festoon**, garland, drape, cover, envelop, array, bedeck, deck, decorate, ornament, adorn.
2 *blue smoke wreathed upwards* **spiral**, coil, loop, gyrate, wind, curl, twist, twist and turn, corkscrew, snake, curve, meander, zigzag.

wreck ▶ **noun 1** *heavy seas prevented salvage teams from landing on the wreck* **shipwreck**, sunken ship, sunken vessel, derelict, hulk; shell, skeleton, hull, frame.
2 *the wreck of a stolen car* **wreckage**, debris, detritus, remainder; ruins, remains, remnants, fragments, pieces, relics.
3 *his voyage ended in the wreck of his ship off Greece* **destruction**, **sinking**, wrecking; devastation, ruination, ruin, demolition, smashing, shattering, disintegration.

▶ **verb 1** *she knew who had wrecked her car* **demolish**, **crash**, smash, smash up, ruin, damage, damage beyond repair, destroy, break up, dismantle, vandalize, deface, desecrate, sabotage, leave in ruins; *informal* write off; *Brit. informal* prang; *N. Amer. informal* trash, total.
2 *he was drowned when his ship was wrecked* **shipwreck**, sink, capsize, run aground, break up.
3 *the crisis had wrecked his plans for the week* **ruin**, spoil, disrupt, undo, mar, play havoc with, make a mess of, put an end to, end, bring to an end, put a stop to, prevent, frustrate, blight, crush, quell, quash, dash, destroy, scotch, shatter, devastate, demolish, sabotage; *informal* mess up, screw up, louse up, foul up, make a hash of, do in, put paid to, put the lid on, put the kibosh on, stymie, queer, nix, banjax, blow a hole in; *Brit. informal* scupper, dish, throw a spanner in the works of; *N. Amer. informal* throw a monkey wrench in the works of; *Austral. informal* euchre, cruel; *archaic* bring to naught.
OPPOSITE facilitate.

wreckage ▶ **noun** *the wreckage of a crashed aircraft* **wreck**, debris, detritus, remainder; hulk, shell, skeleton, hull, frame; ruins, remains, remnants, relics, fragments, pieces.

wrench ▶ **noun 1** *she felt a terrific wrench on her shoulders as he tried to haul her back* **tug**, pull, jerk, jolt, wrest, heave, twist; *informal* **yank**.
2 *hold the piston with a wrench and unscrew the washer Brit.* **spanner**, adjustable spanner; *N. Amer.* monkey wrench.
3 *he had no injury other than a wrench in his arm* **sprain**, twist, strain, rick, crick, dislocation.
4 *leaving Africa was an immense wrench* **painful parting**, distressing separation, traumatic event; pain, ache, pang, trauma.
▶ **verb 1** *he wrenched the gun from her hand* **tug**, pull, jerk, wrest, heave, twist, tear, rip, pluck, grab, seize, snatch, force, take by force, remove by force, prise, peel; *N. Amer.* pry; *informal* **yank**.
2 *Ruth had slipped and wrenched her ankle* **sprain**, twist, turn, strain, rick, crick, pull, dislocate, put out of joint; damage, injure, hurt.

wrest ▶ **verb** *he tried to wrest the broom from Angela's grasp* **wrench**, snatch, seize, grab, take by force, remove by force, force, prise, peel, pluck, tear, rip, heave, twist, tug, pull, jerk, dislodge; *N. Amer.* pry; *informal* yank.

wrestle ▶ **verb** *the two men wrestled each other in deadly silence | she wrestled with her conscience* **grapple**, **fight**, struggle, wrangle, contend, vie, battle, combat; scuffle, tussle, jostle, brawl, clash; get to grips, come to grips; *informal* scrap.

wretch ▶ **noun 1** *the unfortunate wretches were driven to kill themselves* **poor creature**, poor soul, poor thing, miserable creature, sad case, unfortunate, poor unfortunate; *informal* poor devil, poor beggar, poor bastard, poor bunny; *Brit. vulgar slang* sod, bugger.
2 *I wouldn't trust the old wretch an inch* **scoundrel**, villain, ruffian, rogue, rascal, reprobate, criminal, delinquent, good-for-nothing, cad; *informal* heel, creep, jerk, louse, rat, swine, pig, skunk, dog, hound, weasel, toad, snake, snake in the grass, lowlife, scumbag, bad egg, stinker, bad lot, nasty piece of work; *Scottish informal* scrote; *Irish informal* sleeveen, spalpeen; *N. Amer. informal* rat fink, varmint; *informal, dated* rotter, bounder, blighter; *vulgar slang* shit, bugger, bastard, son of a bitch, s.o.b.; *archaic* blackguard, miscreant, knave, dastard, varlet, wastrel, rapscallion, whoreson.

wretched ▶ **adjective 1** *I felt so wretched because I thought I might never see you again* **miserable**, unhappy, sad, broken-hearted, heartbroken, grief-stricken, grieving, sorrowful, sorrowing, mourning, anguished, distressed, desolate, devastated, despairing, inconsolable, disconsolate, downcast, down, downhearted, dejected, crestfallen, cheerless, depressed, melancholy, morose, gloomy, glum, mournful, doleful, dismal, forlorn, woeful, woebegone, abject, low-spirited, long-faced; *informal* blue, down in the mouth, down in the dumps, choked, cut up; *Brit. informal* gutted; *literary* dolorous; *archaic* chap-fallen.
OPPOSITE cheerful.
2 *I feel wretched* **ill**, unwell, poorly, sick, sickly, ailing, below par; *Brit.* off colour; *informal* under the weather, out of sorts.
OPPOSITE well.
3 *their living conditions are particularly wretched* **harsh**, hard, grim, stark, difficult; poor, poverty-stricken, run down, down at heel, impoverished; pitiful, piteous, pathetic, tragic, miserable, bleak, cheerless, hopeless, sorry, sordid, shabby, seedy, dilapidated, shoddy, godforsaken; *informal* scummy, crummy; *Brit. informal* grotty.
OPPOSITES comfortable, luxurious.
4 *the wretched dweller in the shanty town doesn't choose to live there* **unfortunate**, unlucky, luckless, down on one's luck, ill-starred, star-crossed, damned, blighted, hapless, poor, pitiable, distressed, downtrodden, oppressed, powerless, helpless.
OPPOSITE fortunate.
5 *he's a wretched coward* **despicable**, contemptible, beyond contempt, reprehensible, base, low, vile, mean, scurvy, abominable, loathsome, hateful, detestable, odious, disreputable, depraved, debased, infamous, villainous, ignoble, shameful, shabby, worthless; *informal* dirty, filthy, dirty rotten, rotten, low-down, no-good, lousy; *Brit. informal* beastly.
OPPOSITES worthy, admirable.
6 *they had several days of wretched weather* **terrible**, awful, dire, dreadful, atrocious, unspeakable, dismal, bad, poor, lamentable, deplorable, unsatisfactory, substandard, low-quality, inferior; *informal* yucky, God-awful; *Brit. informal* beastly, pants, a load of pants.
OPPOSITE excellent.
7 *I keep telling you, I don't want the wretched money informal* **damn**, damned, blasted, blessed, flaming, precious, confounded, rotten; *Brit. informal* flipping, blinking, blooming, bloody, bleeding, effing, naffing, chuffing; *N. Amer. informal* goddam; *Austral./NZ informal* plurry; *Brit. informal, dated* bally, ruddy, deuced; *vulgar slang* fucking, frigging; *Brit. vulgar slang* sodding; *Irish vulgar slang* fecking.

wriggle ▶ **verb 1** *she tried to hug him but he fought and wriggled* **squirm**, writhe, wiggle, jiggle, jerk, thresh, flounder, flail, twitch, turn, twist, twist and turn, zigzag; snake, worm, slither, slink, crawl, creep.
2 *he tried to* **wriggle out of** *his responsibilities* **avoid**, **shirk**, dodge, evade, elude, sidestep, circumvent, eschew; hide from, escape from, extricate oneself from, steer clear of; *informal* duck; *archaic* bilk.
OPPOSITE face up to.
▶ **noun squirm**, jiggle, wiggle, jerk, twist, turn.

wring ▶ **verb 1** *she showed me how to* **wring out** *the clothes* **twist**, squeeze, screw, scrunch, knead, press, mangle; dry, squeeze dry, screw the water out of.
2 *a few concessions were wrung from the government* **extract**, elicit, force, coerce, exact, extort, wrest, wrench, screw, squeeze, milk; *informal* bleed.
3 *the expression she saw in his eyes wrung her heart* **rend**, tear at, harrow, pierce, stab, wound, lacerate, rack; **distress**, pain, hurt, torment, torture.

wrinkle ▶ **noun 1** *there were fine wrinkles about her mouth | she smoothed out the wrinkles in his coat* **crease**, fold, pucker, gather, furrow, ridge, line, corrugation, groove, crinkle, crumple, rumple; *informal* crow's feet.
2 (*informal*) *learning the wrinkles from someone more experienced saves time* **guideline**, hint, tip, pointer, clue, cue, suggestion, piece of advice, word of advice; (**wrinkles**) **inside information**, guidance, advice, help, counsel.
▶ **verb** *overexposed skin will age and wrinkle prematurely | his coat sleeve wrinkled up* **crease**, pucker, gather, furrow, line, cover with lines, corrugate, crinkle, crimp, crumple, rumple, ruck up, scrunch up; *Brit. rare* ruckle.

wrinkled ▶ **adjective** *an elderly man with a deeply wrinkled face* **creased**, wrinkly, lined, covered with lines, crinkled, crinkly, furrowed, grooved, ridged, crumpled, puckered, shrivelled, wizened; weather-beaten, time-worn, worn, leathery.
OPPOSITE smooth.

writ ▶ **noun** *they were served with a High Court writ* **summons**, subpoena, warrant, arraignment, indictment, court order, process, decree; *N. Amer.* citation; *Latin* subpoena ad testificandum.

write ▶ **verb 1** *he wrote her name in the school jotter | Oliver* **wrote down** *the address for me* **put in writing**, write down, put down, put in black and white, commit to paper, jot down, note, note down, make a note of, set down, take down, mark down, record, register, log, list, make a list of, inscribe, sign, scribble, scrawl, pencil.
2 *I'll go and write a poem* **compose**, draft, create, invent, think up, draw up, formulate, compile, put together, pen, dash off, produce.
3 *he had her address and was going to write* **correspond**, write a letter, communicate, get in touch, keep in touch, keep in contact; *informal* drop someone a line, drop someone a note.
□ **write someone/something off 1** *they have had to write off loans and lose their investments* **forget about**, disregard, give up on, give up for lost, cancel, annul, nullify, wipe out, cross out, score out.
2 *he drove off the road and wrote off his new car* **wreck**, damage beyond repair, smash, smash up, crash, destroy, demolish, ruin; *Brit. informal* prang; *N. Amer. informal* total.
3 *who would write off a player of his stature?* **disregard**, regard as finished, consider unimportant, dismiss, ignore.

writer *See centre pages for list of types of* **Writer**
▶ **noun author**, wordsmith, man/woman of letters, penman, creative writer; *informal* scribbler, scribe, pen-pusher, hack, potboiler.

writhe ▶ **verb** *she writhed about on the floor in agony* **squirm**, wriggle, thrash, flounder, flail, toss, toss and turn, twitch, twist, twist and turn, roll, jiggle, wiggle, jerk, jolt.

writing *See centre pages for list of* **Writing Implements**
▶ **noun 1** *his writing is much larger than mine* **handwriting**, hand, script, penmanship, pen, print, printing, longhand, calligraphy, chirography; letters; *informal* scribble, scrawl, fist.
2 (**writings**) *she has had published various writings on comparative education* **compositions**, works, oeuvre, opus, books, volumes, publications, titles, tomes; papers, articles, essays.
□ **the writing on the wall omen**, ill omen, bad omen, portent, sign, indication, presage, warning, forewarning, foreshadowing, forecast, harbinger, augury, threat, menace, signal, hint, straw in the wind; *literary* foretoken.

WORD LINKS

relating to writing	**scriptorial**
study of handwriting	**graphology**
study of ancient writing systems	**palaeography**
fear of writing	**graphophobia**

wrong ▶ **adjective 1** *there were no right or wrong answers | in my opinion the judge was wrong* **incorrect**, **mistaken**, in error, erroneous, inaccurate, not accurate, inexact, not exact, imprecise, invalid, untrue, false, fallacious, wide of the mark, off target; misleading, illogical, unsound, unfounded, without foundation, faulty, flawed; *informal* off beam, bogus, phoney, out, way out, full of holes, dicey, iffy; *Brit. informal* dodgy; *archaic* abroad.
OPPOSITES right, correct, spot on.
2 *he knew at once that he had said the wrong thing* **inappropriate**, unsuitable, inapt, inapposite, undesirable; ill-advised, ill-considered, ill-judged, impolitic, injudicious, infelicitous, unacceptable, beyond the pale, unwarranted, unfitting, out of keeping, improper, unseemly, unbecoming, indecorous, lacking in propriety; *informal* out of order.
OPPOSITE appropriate.
3 *driving while drunk is wrong* **illegal**, unlawful, illicit, indictable, lawless, lawbreaking, criminal, delinquent, felonious, dishonest, dishonourable, corrupt; **unethical**, immoral, morally wrong, bad, wicked, base, evil, sinful, foul, despicable, iniquitous, nefarious, blameworthy, condemnable, culpable; *informal* crooked, shady; *Brit. informal* bent, not cricket.
OPPOSITES legal; ethical.
4 *there is no sign of anything wrong with your heart* **amiss**, awry, out of order, not right, faulty, defective, unsatisfactory, incorrect, inappropriate.
5 *lay the curtain out flat with the wrong side uppermost* **reverse**, inside, opposite, inverse.
▶ **adverb** *the government might do its sums wrong* **incorrectly**, wrongly, inaccurately, erroneously, mistakenly; inexactly, imprecisely, falsely.
□ **get someone/something wrong** *don't get me wrong, motorways aren't always a bad thing* **misunderstand**, misinterpret, misapprehend, misconstrue, misconceive, mistake, misread, take amiss; get the wrong idea, receive a false impression, be under a delusion, be at cross purposes; *informal* be barking up the wrong tree, get the wrong end of the stick.
□ **go wrong 1** *there's no need to beat yourself up if you go wrong* **make a mistake**, make an error, err, make a blunder, blunder, go astray, miscalculate, be incorrect, be wide of the mark, trip up; *informal* slip up, screw up, make a boo-boo, make a bloomer; *Brit. informal* boob, drop a clanger.
2 *their plans to poison him went wrong* **go awry**, go amiss, go adrift, go off course, fail, not succeed, be unsuccessful, go badly, be ruined, fall through, fall flat, fall apart, come apart at the seams, break down, come to nothing, flounder, collapse, meet with disaster, backfire, rebound, boomerang, misfire, miscarry, abort; *informal* come to grief, flop, come a cropper, go haywire, bite the dust, go up in smoke.
3 *the new television sets will contain fewer components to go wrong* **break down**, malfunction, fail, stop working, stop functioning, cease to function, crash, give out, go out of control, develop a fault, act up, be defective; *informal* be on the blink, conk out, go kaput, go phut, go haywire, bite the dust, have had it; *Brit. informal* play up, pack up.
4 *young people who go wrong* **go astray**, err, do wrong, commit a crime, commit a sin, fall into a life of crime, get into bad ways, stray from the straight and narrow, fall from grace; *informal* go to the dogs.
▶ **noun 1** *they knew the difference between right and wrong* **immorality**, **badness**, sin, sinfulness, wickedness, evil, vice, depravity, vileness, iniquity; unlawfulness, crime, corruption, villainy, dishonesty, injustice, wrongdoing, misconduct, transgression; *informal* crookedness.
OPPOSITES right, virtue, honour.
2 *no one is entitled to profit from his own wrong | the fellow had really done him a wrong* **misdeed**, bad deed, bad act/action, offence, injury, crime, unlawful act, illegal act, violation, infringement, infraction, transgression, peccadillo, sin; **injustice**, unfairness, unjust act, grievance, outrage, atrocity; *Law* malfeasance, tort; *archaic* trespass, *rare* malefaction.
□ **in the wrong 1** *he was ashamed to admit that he was in the wrong* **mistaken**, **in error**, erring, errant, off course, off target, wide of the mark; *informal* off beam.
OPPOSITE right.
2 *the law considers you to be in the wrong* **to blame**, blameworthy, at fault, condemnable, censurable, reproachable, reprehensible, responsible, culpable, answerable, guilty; *archaic* peccant.
OPPOSITE blameless.
▶ **verb** *when you have wronged someone admit it and apologize* **malign**, misrepresent, do a disservice to, do an injustice to, dishonour, impugn, vilify, defame, slander, libel, denigrate, insult; **mistreat**, do wrong to, abuse, maltreat, ill-treat, ill-use, harm, hurt, injure, do injury to, offend against, oppress; *informal* bad mouth, kick in the teeth, do the dirty on.

wrongdoer ▶ **noun offender**, lawbreaker, criminal, felon, convict, jailbird, delinquent, villain, culprit, guilty party, evil-doer, sinner, transgressor, malefactor, reprobate, rogue, scoundrel, rascal, outlaw; *informal* crook, con, crim, wrong 'un, baddy, bad guy, bad egg; *Law* malfeasant, misfeasor, infractor; *archaic* miscreant, trespasser.
OPPOSITE law-abiding citizen.

wrongdoing ▶ **noun** *good journalism can expose wrongdoing | he had admitted his wrongdoings* **crime**, lawbreaking, lawlessness, criminality, misconduct, malpractice, corruption, unethical behaviour, immorality, sin, sinfulness, wickedness, badness, evil, vice, iniquity, villainy, delinquency, misbehaviour, mischief, naughtiness; offence, felony, criminal act, wrong, misdeed, misdemeanour, fault, error, lapse, peccadillo, transgression, immoral act, evil act; *Law* malfeasance, tort; *archaic* trespass; *rare* maleficence, malefaction, malversation.

wrongful ▶ **adjective** *she's suing the police for wrongful arrest* **unjustified**, unwarranted, unjust, unfair, undue, undeserved, uncalled for, unreasonable, unnecessary, groundless, indefensible, inappropriate,

improper, unlawful, illegal, illegitimate, illicit.
OPPOSITES rightful, fair.

wrongly ▶ adverb *the two women were wrongly accused of kidnapping* **incorrectly**, mistakenly, by mistake, erroneously, in error, falsely, fallaciously, inaccurately, imprecisely, inappropriately.
OPPOSITES rightly, correctly.

wrought up ▶ adjective *it was easy to see that she was wrought up over something* **agitated**, in a state of agitation, tense, stressed, overwrought, nervous, in a state of nerves, on edge, edgy, keyed up, strung out, jumpy, nervy, on tenterhooks, ruffled, flustered, flurried, perturbed, disquieted, fretful, fearful, frightened, scared, with one's heart in one's mouth, with one's stomach in knots, like a cat on a hot tin roof, shaking in one's shoes, on pins and needles, in a cold sweat; *informal* with butterflies in one's stomach, jittery, twitchy, in a state, in a stew, in a sweat, in a flap, in a twitter, in a dither, all of a dither, all of a lather, het up, wired, uptight; *Brit. informal* strung up, windy, having kittens; *N. Amer. informal* spooky, squirrelly, in a twit.

wry ▶ adjective **1** *his wry humour made her laugh* **ironic**, sardonic, satirical, mocking, scoffing, sneering, derisive, scornful, sarcastic, double-edged, dry, droll, witty, humorous; *Brit. informal* sarky.
2 *he sipped his cold coffee and made a wry face* **disgusted**, displeased, discontented, offended, unimpressed, annoyed, irritated, irked, vexed, piqued, nettled, put out, disgruntled; *informal* peeved, narked, hacked off; *Brit. informal* cheesed off; *N. Amer. informal* sore, ticked off, teed off; *vulgar slang* pissed off.
3 (*archaic*) *she was a poor creature and had a wry neck* **twisted**, crooked, contorted, distorted, deformed, misshapen, warped, out of shape, bent, lopsided, askew; *Scottish* thrawn.

xenophobia ▶ noun *there must be no room for xenophobia in today's Europe* **racism**, racialism, racial hatred, ethnocentrism, ethnocentricity; nationalism, jingoism, isolationism; prejudice, intolerance, bigotry, bias; (*in S. Africa, historical*) apartheid; *rare* xenophoby.
OPPOSITE xenomania.

xenophobic ▶ adjective *an unadventurous and xenophobic nation* **racist**, racialist, ethnocentric, ethnocentrist; nationalist, nationalistic, jingoistic, jingo, isolationist; prejudiced, intolerant, bigoted, parochial, insular.
OPPOSITE xenomaniac.

xerox ▶ verb *he xeroxed the printout and faxed it to his agent* **photocopy**, copy, duplicate, replicate, make a replica of, make a facsimile of, reproduce, photostat, mimeograph, mimeo, print, run off; *trademark* make a Xerox of.

▶ noun (**Xerox**) (*trademark*) *in case you haven't read the article I enclose a Xerox* **photocopy**, copy, carbon copy, duplicate, replica, reproduction, reprint, facsimile, mimeograph, mimeo; transcript; *trademark* photostat; *informal* dupe.

Xmas ▶ noun (*informal*) *an Xmas panto* **Christmas**, Christmastime, Christmastide, festive season; Nativity; *Indian* Burra Din; *Brit. informal* Chrimbo, Crimbo, Chrissie, Chrissy; *literary* Yuletide, Yule, Noel.

X-ray ▶ noun *an X-ray of her left knee* **radiogram**, radiograph, X-ray image; *technical* roentgenogram; *Medicine* angiogram, lymphangiogram, mammogram, pyelogram, cholangiogram.

WORD LINKS

making images using X-rays	**radiography**
study of X-rays	**radiology**

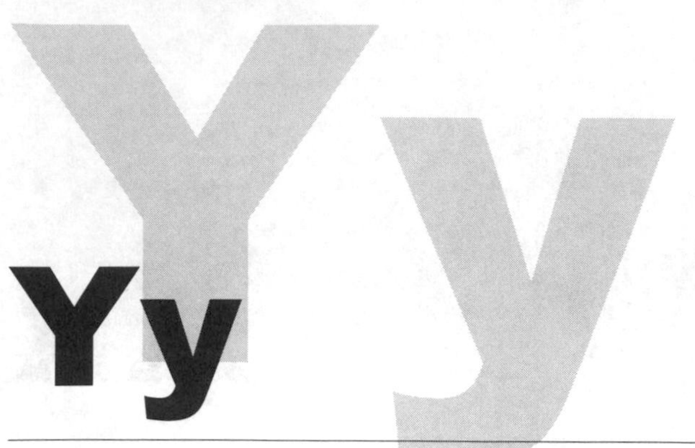

yahoo ▶ noun *you're no yahoo; you're too smart* **barbarian**, philistine, vulgarian, savage, brute, beast, boor, oaf, ruffian, thug, lout, hoodlum, hooligan, vandal, rowdy, bully boy, brawler; *informal* clod, clodhopper, tough, toughie, roughneck, bruiser, hard man; *Brit. informal* yobbo, yob, bovver boy, lager lout, oik, ape, gorilla, bear, lump; *N. Amer. informal* lummox.

yak, yack ▶ verb *she was yakking about her passion for antiques* **prattle**, blather, blether, blither, babble (on), gabble, prate, drivel, rattle on/away, ramble, maunder, go on, run on, talk at length, talk incessantly, talk a lot, chatter, yap, gossip; *Brit.* talk nineteen to the dozen; *Scottish & Irish* slabber on; *informal* jabber, blabber, yatter, jaw, gab, gas, chit-chat, yackety-yak; *Brit. informal* rabbit, witter, waffle, natter, chunter, talk the hind legs off a donkey; *N. Amer. informal* run off at the mouth; *Austral./NZ informal* mag; *archaic* twaddle, twattle, claver, clack.

yank (*informal*) ▶ verb *Gilbert yanked open the door to the office* **jerk**, pull, tug, wrench, heave, haul, drag, tweak, twitch, pluck, snatch, seize, rip, tear, whisk, jolt, force; *informal* whip.
▶ noun *she gave his hat a sharp yank* **jerk**, pull, tug, jolt, wrench, heave, tweak, twitch.

yap ▶ verb **1** *the dogs yapped about his heels* **yelp**, bark, woof, bay.
2 *the presenter was **yapping away** on the television* **chatter**, prattle, prate, gibber, babble, blather, blether, blither, gabble, gossip, rattle, ramble, maunder; go on, run on, talk at length, talk incessantly, talk a lot; *Brit.* talk nineteen to the dozen; *Scottish & Irish* slabber on; *informal* jabber, blabber, yatter, jaw, gab, gas, chit-chat, yackety-yak; *Brit. informal* rabbit, witter, waffle, natter, chunter, talk the hind legs off a donkey; *N. Amer. informal* run off at the mouth; *Austral./NZ informal* mag; *archaic* twaddle, twattle, claver, clack.
▶ noun **1** *her dog greeted her with excited yaps* **yelp**, bark, woof.
2 (*N. Amer. informal*) *will you kindly keep your yap shut for a minute?* See MOUTH.

yard ▶ noun **1** *they kicked a football about the yard* **backyard**, garden; courtyard, court, quadrangle, enclosure, cloister, close; *informal* quad.
2 *we took over the management of a boatbuilding yard* **workshop**, works, factory, garage, plant, foundry, mill, industrial unit; shipyard; *archaic* manufactory.

yardstick ▶ noun *they ought to appraise their investments against a more realistic yardstick* **standard**, measure, gauge, scale, guide, guideline, indicator, test, touchstone, barometer, specification, criterion, norm, average, benchmark, point of reference, model, pattern, rule, principle, paradigm, convention, ideal.

yarn ▶ noun **1** *you need to use a fine yarn* **thread**, cotton, wool, fibre, filament, strand; ply; cord, twine, string, line.
2 *he told a rather tedious yarn about two Italian peasants* **story**, tale, anecdote, fable, parable, traveller's tale, fairy story, rigmarole, saga, sketch, narrative, reminiscence, account, report, history; *informal* tall tale, tall story, cock and bull story, shaggy-dog story, spiel.

yawning ▶ adjective *there was a yawning hole where the door had been wrenched off* **gaping**, wide open, wide, cavernous, deep; large, huge, great, big; *rare* chasmal.

year ▶ noun *he become Head of Campaigns for one year* **twelve-month period**, twelve-month session; calendar year, tax year, financial year, fiscal year, FY; *literary* sun, summer, winter; *archaic* twelvemonth.
□ **year in, year out** *we pay the same fixed sum year in, year out* **repeatedly**, again and again, time and (time) again, time after time, over and over (again), {week in, week out}, {day in, day out}, recurrently, continuously, continually, constantly, habitually, regularly, without a break, persistently, unfailingly, always.
OPPOSITE occasionally.

WORD LINKS
occurring once a year or lasting a year **annual**

yearly ▶ adjective *a yearly payment of £5* **annual**, once a year, every year, each year.
▶ adverb *the guide is published yearly* **annually**, once a year, by the year, per annum, every year, each year.

yearn ▶ verb *she yearned to be with him* **long**, pine, crave, desire, want, want badly, wish, have/feel a longing, covet, lust, pant, hunger, thirst, ache, be aching, itch, be itching; hanker after, dream of, fancy, have one's heart set on, be bent on, eat one's heart out over; *informal* have a yen, yen, be dying; *archaic* be athirst for, be desirous; *rare* suspire for.

CHOOSE THE RIGHT WORD

yearn, long, pine, hanker

- To **yearn** for something is to desire it intensely, even though it is difficult or impossible to obtain; recognition of this means that the desire tends to be mixed with sorrow or melancholy (*she yearned for her missing father | his ambition was always yearning after the impossible | I yearned to live a semi-bohemian lifestyle*).
- To **long** is also to feel a deep desire (*she'd longed to hear him whisper that he loved her*), but it may also be used more trivially to say that one very much wants something, especially food or drink, that one is quite likely to get soon (*I'm longing for a cup of tea*).
- To **pine** is to long for someone or something that one has lost (*even though he had a new girlfriend she still pined for him*), and is often used of animals who lose their owners. When used without *for*, it means to decline mentally or physically as a result of such longing (*she was the Major's gundog and had pined badly when her master died*).
- **Hanker** is a less formal word than *yearn* and, compared with *long*, implies a vaguer, more wistful, or more forlorn desire (*it may be that you hanker after some lost love | she had always hankered for a job in uniform | I've been hankering to play country music again*).

yearning ▶ noun *they sometimes feel a yearning for the mountains and the sea* **longing**, pining, craving, desire, want, wish, hankering, urge, need, hunger, hungering, thirst, appetite, greed, lust, ache, burning, fancy, inclination, eagerness, fervour; *informal* yen, itch; *rare* cacoethes.

yell ▶ noun *the creature gave an unearthly yell* **cry**, yelp, call, shout, howl, yowl, wail, scream, shriek, screech, squawk, squeal; bay, roar, bawl, yawp, whoop, caterwaul; *informal* holler.
OPPOSITES whisper, murmur.
▶ verb *he yelled in agony* **cry out**, call out, call at the top of one's voice, yelp, shout, howl, yowl, wail, scream, shriek, screech, squawk, squeal; bay, roar, bawl, yawp, whoop, caterwaul; *informal* holler; *rare* ululate.
OPPOSITES whisper, murmur.

yellow ▶ adjective **1** *bright yellow flowers | the man with the yellow hair* yellowish, yellowy, lemon, lemony, amber, gold, golden; blonde, light brown, fair, flaxen.
2 (*informal*) *he'd better get back there quick and prove he's not yellow* **cowardly**, lily-livered, faint-hearted, chicken-hearted, pigeon-hearted, craven, spiritless, spineless, timid, timorous, fearful, trembling, quaking, shrinking, cowering, afraid of one's own shadow, pusillanimous, weak, feeble, soft; *informal* **chicken**, weak-kneed, gutless, yellow-bellied, wimpish, wimpy, sissy, sissified; *Brit. informal* wet; *N. Amer. informal* candy-assed; *N. Amer. vulgar slang* chickenshit; *archaic* poltroon, recreant, poor-spirited.
OPPOSITES brave, courageous.

yelp ▶ verb *he yelped in pain | the red setter yelped and skittered across the floor* **squeal**, squawk, screech, shriek, scream, howl, yowl, wail, yell, cry out, call out, shout, bawl, yawp; yap, bark, woof, bay; *informal* holler.
▶ noun *she gave an involuntary yelp | her dog gave a loud, happy yelp* **squeal**, squawk, screech, shriek, scream, howl, yowl, wail, yell, cry, call, shout,

bawl, yawl, whoop; yap, bark, woof, bay; *informal* holler.

yen ▶ noun (*informal*) *he had a yen for foreign travel* **hankering**, yearning, longing, craving, urge, desire, want, wish, hunger, thirst, lust, appetite, greed, ache, burning, eagerness, fervour; fancy, inclination; *informal* itch.

yes ▶ adverb *yes, I'll come to your party* **all right**, alright, very well, of course, by all means, sure, certainly, absolutely, indeed, affirmative, in the affirmative, agreed, roger; *Scottish, N. English, & archaic* aye; *Nautical* aye aye; *informal* yeah, yah, yep, yup, uh-huh, okay, OK, okey-dokey, okey-doke; *Brit. informal* righto, righty-ho; *N. Amer. informal* surely; *Indian informal* acha; *archaic or formal* yea.
OPPOSITE no.

yes-man ▶ noun (*informal*) *a Hollywood yes-man* **sycophant**, toady, lackey, flunkey, minion, stooge, kowtower, truckler, groveller, crawler, creep, fawner, flatterer, lickspittle, Uriah Heep, puppet, cat's paw, instrument, pawn, underling, hanger-on, camp follower, doormat, spaniel; *informal* bootlicker; *Brit. informal* poodle, dogsbody; *N. Amer. informal* suck-up; *Indian informal* chamcha; *Brit. vulgar slang* arse-licker, bum-sucker; *N. Amer. vulgar slang* brown-nose, ass-kisser, suckhole; *archaic* toad-eater.

yet ▶ adverb **1** *he has not made up his mind yet* **so far**, thus far, as yet, still, even now, up till now, up to now, until now, up to the present time.
2 *don't celebrate just yet* **now**, right now, at this time, at this moment in time; already, so soon.
3 *he was doing nothing, yet he appeared purposeful* **nevertheless**, nonetheless, even so, but, however, still, notwithstanding, despite that, in spite of that, for all that, all the same, just the same, at the same time, be that as it may; though, although; *archaic* natheless.
4 *he supplied yet more unsolicited advice* **even**, still, further, in addition, additionally, besides, into the bargain, to boot.

yield ▶ verb **1** *too many projects yield poor returns* **produce**, bear, give, supply, provide, afford, return, bring in, pull in, haul in, gather in, fetch, earn, net, realize, generate, furnish, bestow, pay out, contribute; *informal* rake in.
2 *she yielded her seat to the doctor* **relinquish**, surrender, part with, deliver up, hand over, turn over, give over; make over, bequeath, remit, cede, leave, sacrifice.
OPPOSITE retain.
3 *the younger child was forced to yield* **surrender**, capitulate, submit, relent, admit defeat, accept defeat, concede defeat, back down, climb down, quit, give in, give up the struggle, lay down one's arms, raise/show the white flag, knuckle under; be overcome, be overwhelmed, be conquered, be beaten, fall victim; *informal* throw in the towel, throw in the sponge, cave in.
4 *he yielded to the plea of his dying godson* **accede to**, submit to, bow down to, defer to, comply with, conform to, agree to, consent to, go along with, be guided by, heed, note, pay attention to; grant, permit, allow, sanction, warrant.
OPPOSITES resist, defy.
5 *the floorboards yielded underfoot* **bend**, give, flex, be flexible, be pliant.
▶ noun *risky investments usually have higher yields* **profit**, gain, return, reward, revenue, dividend, proceeds, receipts, earnings, takings; product, production, produce, output, crop, harvest; *N. Amer.* take; *informal* pickings; *Brit. informal* bunce.

yob, yobbo ▶ noun (*Brit. informal*) *yobs showered the police with broken bottles.* *See* HOOLIGAN.

yoke ▶ noun **1** *the horses were loosened from the yoke* **harness**, collar, coupling, tackle, tack, equipage.
2 *these countries were struggling under the yoke of imperialism* **tyranny**, oppression, domination, hegemony, enslavement, slavery, servitude, subjugation, subjection, bondage, serfdom, vassalage; bonds, chains, fetters, shackles; *literary* thrall, thraldom.
3 *the yoke of marriage* **bond**, tie, link.
▶ verb **1** *I yoke my oxen to the plough* **harness**, hitch, hitch up, couple, tether, fasten, attach, join, join up, team.
OPPOSITE unhitch.
2 *Mariana is yoked in an arranged marriage to her cousin* **unite**, join, link, connect, bond, tie, bind.

yokel ▶ noun *the yokels drank cider and pronounced it 'zyder'* **bumpkin**, country bumpkin, country cousin, rustic, countryman, countrywoman, country dweller, son/daughter of the soil, peasant, provincial, oaf, lout, boor, barbarian; *French* paysan; *Spanish* campesino; *Italian* contadino, contadina, paisano; *Russian* muzhik, kulak; *Egyptian* fellah; *Indian* ryot; *informal* clod, clodhopper, yahoo, yob, yobbo; *Irish informal* culchie, bogman; *N. Amer. informal* hayseed, hillbilly, hick, rube, schlub; *Austral. informal* bushy; *archaic* carl, churl, hind, kern; *rare* bucolic.

young *See centre pages for list of* **Young Animals**
▶ adjective **1** *I hate to see a young man throwing his life away* **youthful**, juvenile, junior, adolescent, teenage, teenaged; immature, childlike, babyish, boyish, girlish; in the springtime of life, in one's salad days; *informal* teen.
OPPOSITES old, elderly; mature.
2 *a very agreeable young wine* **new**, recent, fresh, immature, undeveloped, developing, in the making, in its infancy.
OPPOSITE mature.
▶ noun **1** *female flycatchers usually raise five or six young* **offspring**, progeny, family, children, issue, little ones, youngsters, babies; sons, daughters, heirs, descendants, successors, scions; *informal* kids, kiddies, nippers, tots, tinies; *Brit. informal* sprogs; *N. Amer. informal* rug rats; *Austral./NZ informal* ankle-biters; *literary* babes, the fruit of one's loins; *rare* progeniture.
2 (**the young**) **young people**, youths, children, boys and girls, youngsters, young ones, the younger generation, the next generation, juveniles, minors, schoolboys, schoolgirls, whippersnappers, striplings; *informal* kids, kiddies, young 'uns, lads, lasses.

youngster ▶ noun *a new magazine for youngsters* **young person**, young adult, young man/woman, youth, juvenile, teenager, adolescent, junior, stripling, whippersnapper, young one, little one, child; lad, boy, schoolboy, lass, girl, schoolgirl; *Scottish & N. English* bairn, wean; *derogatory* brat, chit; *informal* kid, kiddie, kiddiewink, shaver, nipper, young 'un, teen; *Brit. informal* sprog; *N. Amer. informal* rug rat; *Austral./NZ informal* ankle-biter; *Law* minor.

yourself, yourselves ▶ pronoun
□ **by yourself/yourselves.** *See* BY ONESELF *at* BY.

youth ▶ noun **1** *he had been a keen sportsman in his youth* **early years**, early life, young days, teens, teenage years, adolescence, young adulthood, boyhood, girlhood, childhood; immaturity; prime, heyday, day, hour, time, springtime, salad days, bloom, peak, pinnacle, height; *Law* minority; *rare* juvenility, juvenescence.
OPPOSITES adulthood, old age.
2 *she had kept her youth and beauty* **youthfulness**, youngness, freshness, bloom.
OPPOSITE maturity.
3 *the problem of unemployment among local youths* **young man**, boy, lad, youngster, juvenile, teenager, adolescent, junior, minor, young one; stripling, whippersnapper, fledgling; *Scottish & N. English* bairn; *informal* kid, shaver, teen, teeny-bopper.
OPPOSITE old man.
4 *the youth of the nation are looking for a hero* **young people**, young, younger generation, rising generation, next generation; *informal* kids.
OPPOSITE elderly.

youthful ▶ adjective *the party had a youthful new leader* **young-looking**, spry, sprightly, vigorous, active; young, juvenile, boyish, girlish, childlike; fresh-faced, in the springtime of life, in one's salad days.
OPPOSITES old, elderly, doddering.

zany ▶ adjective *the film has a zany plot and some peculiar characters* **eccentric**, bizarre, weird, peculiar, odd, quirky, avant-garde, unconventional, strange, outlandish, ridiculous, ludicrous; mad, insane, crazy, absurd, comic, comical, clownish, farcical, madcap, silly, light-hearted, funny, amusing, diverting, waggish, hilarious; *informal* wacky, screwy, nutty, nuts, crackpot, cracked, oddball, cranky, kinky, off the wall, way out, dippy, cuckoo; *Brit. informal* daft; *N. Amer. informal* kooky, wacko, in left field; *Austral./NZ informal, dated* dilly.
OPPOSITES conventional, sensible, serious.

zap ▶ verb (*informal*) **1** *the monster gets zapped by a flying saucer.* See KILL, DESTROY.
2 *racing cars zapped past on the track below.* See SPEED.

zeal ▶ noun *his zeal for football* **passion**, zealousness, committedness, ardour, love, fervour, fire, avidity, fondness, devotion, devotedness, enthusiasm, eagerness, keenness, appetite, taste, relish, gusto; vigour, energy, verve, zest; *rare* fervency, ardency.
OPPOSITES apathy, indifference.

zealot ▶ noun *reforming zealots destroyed a vast collection of papers* **fanatic**, enthusiast, extremist, radical, Young Turk, diehard, activist, militant; bigot, dogmatist, sectarian, partisan; *informal* fiend, maniac, ultra, nut.
OPPOSITE moderate.

zealotry ▶ noun *religious zealotry could lead to communal tension* **fanaticism**, zeal, zealousness, extremism, radicalism, militancy, dogmatism, bigotry, single-mindedness; vehemence, forcefulness.
OPPOSITE apathy.

zealous ▶ adjective *he is a zealous worker* **fervent**, ardent, fervid, fiery, passionate, impassioned, devout, devoted; **committed**, dedicated, enthusiastic, eager, keen, avid, sincere, wholehearted, hearty, earnest, vigorous, energetic, zestful, purposeful, forceful, intense, fierce, single-minded; *informal* go-ahead, pushy; *rare* perfervid.
OPPOSITES apathetic, indifferent.

zenith ▶ noun *the king was at the zenith of his power* **highest point**, high point, crowning point, height, top, acme, peak, pinnacle, apex, apogee, vertex, tip, crown, crest, summit, climax, culmination, maximum, optimum, prime, meridian, flower; *informal* high noon.
OPPOSITES nadir, bottom.

zero ▶ noun **1** *the sum's wrong—you've left off a zero* **nought**, nothing, cipher, nil, 0; *Computing* null character; *archaic* naught.
2 *the allowable dolphin kill will be gradually reduced each year to zero* **nothing**, nil, nothing at all, not a single thing, not anything, none; *N. English* nowt; *informal* zilch, nix, sweet Fanny Adams, sweet FA, not a dicky bird; *Brit. informal* damn all, not a sausage; *N. Amer. informal* zip, zippo, nada, diddly-squat, a goose egg, bupkis; *Brit. vulgar slang* bugger all, fuck all, sod all; *archaic* naught, nought.
3 *his energy levels were at zero* **rock bottom**, the bottom, the lowest point, the all-time low, as low as one can get, low-water mark, the depths, the nadir; *informal* the pits.
▶ verb *zero the counter at the end point of the tape* **return to nought**, return to zero, adjust to zero point.
□ **zero in on** *different scientists chose to zero in on different diseases* **focus on**, focus attention on, centre on, concentrate on, home in on, fix on, pinpoint, give prominence to, highlight, spotlight, underline, emphasize; *informal* zoom in on.

zero hour ▶ noun *as zero hour approached, thirty ships swung into position* **the appointed time**, the appointed hour, the crucial moment, the vital moment, the critical moment, the moment of truth, the point/moment of decision, the Rubicon, the critical point, the crux; *informal* the crunch.

zest ▶ noun **1** *she had a great zest for life* **enthusiasm**, **gusto**, relish, zestfulness, appetite, eagerness, keenness, avidity, zeal, fervour, ardour, passion, love, enjoyment, joy, delight, excitement; verve, vigour, liveliness, sparkle, fizz, effervescence, fire, animation, vitality, dynamism, energy, buoyancy, brio, bounce, pep, spirit, spiritedness, exuberance, high spirits, high-spiritedness; *informal* zing, zip, oomph, vim, pizzazz, get-up-and-go.
OPPOSITES apathy, indifference; distaste.
2 *the slice of lemon in a gin and tonic is there to add zest* **piquancy**, tang, sharpness, tartness, flavour, flavouring, savour, taste, tastiness, pungency, spice, spiciness, relish, bite; interest, an edge, effect, potency; *informal* kick, punch, zing, oomph.
OPPOSITE blandness.
3 *add the finely grated zest of an orange* **rind**, peel, skin, covering, outer layer; *technical* epicarp, pericarp, exocarp.

CHOOSE THE RIGHT WORD

zest, gusto, verve

- **Zest** originally denoted the grated outer rind of a lemon, orange, or lime; hence it has also come to refer to a quality of excitement or piquancy (*I try to beat previous records in order to give zest to an otherwise monotonous job*). It also describes the eager enthusiasm inspired by such a quality (*the grass court season has given him renewed zest, and he is playing the best tennis of his career | she had a zest for life and boundless energy*).
- To do something with **gusto** is to do it with obvious enthusiasm, enjoyment, and energy (*the crowd sang the anthem with gusto | I was attacking a delicious crême brûlée with great gusto*).
- **Verve** also denotes energy and liveliness, but additionally suggests stylishness and expertise (*performances of undeniable verve and grace | he drove with assurance and verve*).

zigzag ▶ adjective *I steered a zigzag course between the trees* **meandering**, zigzagging, snaking, snaky, winding, wiggly, squiggly, crooked, tacking, twisting, twisty, full of twists and turns, curving, curvy, wavy, deviating, undulating, sinuous, serpentine, tortuous, irregular; *technical* sinuate, ogee; *rare* anfractuous, flexuous, meandrous, serpentiform.
OPPOSITE straight.
▶ verb *a narrow path zigzagged steeply down from the house* **meander**, snake, twist, twist and turn, tack, wind, weave, wander, wiggle, squiggle, undulate.

zing ▶ noun (*informal*) **1** *he had a real zing in his sprightly voice* **enthusiasm**, zest, zestfulness, appetite, relish, gusto, eagerness, keenness, avidity, zeal, fervour, ardour, passion, love, enjoyment, joy, delight, pleasure, excitement; **vigour**, verve, liveliness, sparkle, fizz, effervescence, fire, animation, vitality, dynamism, energy, buoyancy, brio, bounce, pep, spirit, spiritedness, exuberance, high spirits, high-spiritedness; *informal* zip, oomph, vim, pizzazz, get-up-and-go.
2 *sprinkle Cajun seasoning on chops to give them zing* **piquancy**, pungency, spice, spiciness, saltiness, pepperiness, flavour, flavouring, savour, taste, tastiness, relish, bite, tang, zest, sharpness, tartness; interest, edge, effect, potency; *informal* kick, punch, oomph.

zip (*informal*) ▶ noun *we were full of vim and zip.* See ZING.
▶ verb *house martins zipped back and forth over the lake.* See SPEED.

zone ▶ noun *the immediate vicinity of a radar mast is a dangerous zone* **area**, sector, section, belt, region, territory, tract, stretch, expanse, district, quarter, precinct, locality, neighbourhood, province, land.

zoom ▶ verb (*informal*) *a motorbike zoomed across their path.* See SPEED.